Presented to:

By:

On:

Old Testament Chronology

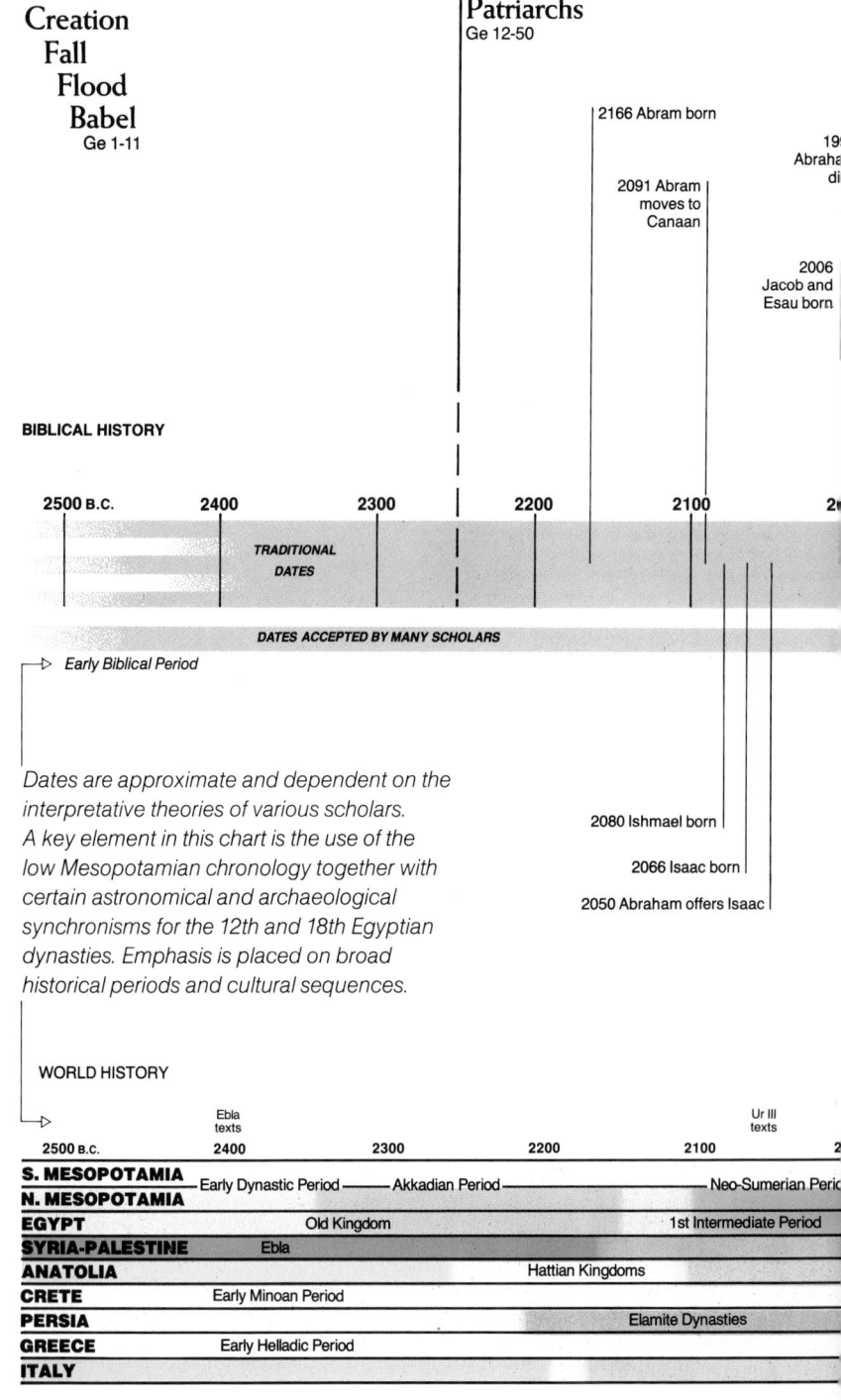

Creation
Fall
Flood
Babel
Ge 1-11

Patriarchs
Ge 12-50

2166 Abram born

191
Abraha
di

2091 Abram
moves to
Canaan

2006
Jacob and
Esau born

BIBLICAL HISTORY

2500 B.C.	2400	2300	2200	2100	2

*TRADITIONAL
DATES*

DATES ACCEPTED BY MANY SCHOLARS

▷ *Early Biblical Period*

*Dates are approximate and dependent on the
interpretative theories of various scholars.
A key element in this chart is the use of the
low Mesopotamian chronology together with
certain astronomical and archaeological
synchronisms for the 12th and 18th Egyptian
dynasties. Emphasis is placed on broad
historical periods and cultural sequences.*

2080 Ishmael born
2066 Isaac born
2050 Abraham offers Isaac

WORLD HISTORY

▷

	Ebla texts			Ur III texts	
2500 B.C.	2400	2300	2200	2100	2

S. MESOPOTAMIA	Early Dynastic Period —— Akkadian Period ——			—— Neo-Sumerian Peric	
N. MESOPOTAMIA					
EGYPT	Old Kingdom			1st Intermediate Period	
SYRIA-PALESTINE	Ebla				
ANATOLIA			Hattian Kingdoms		
CRETE	Early Minoan Period				
PERSIA				Elamite Dynasties	
GREECE	Early Helladic Period				
ITALY					

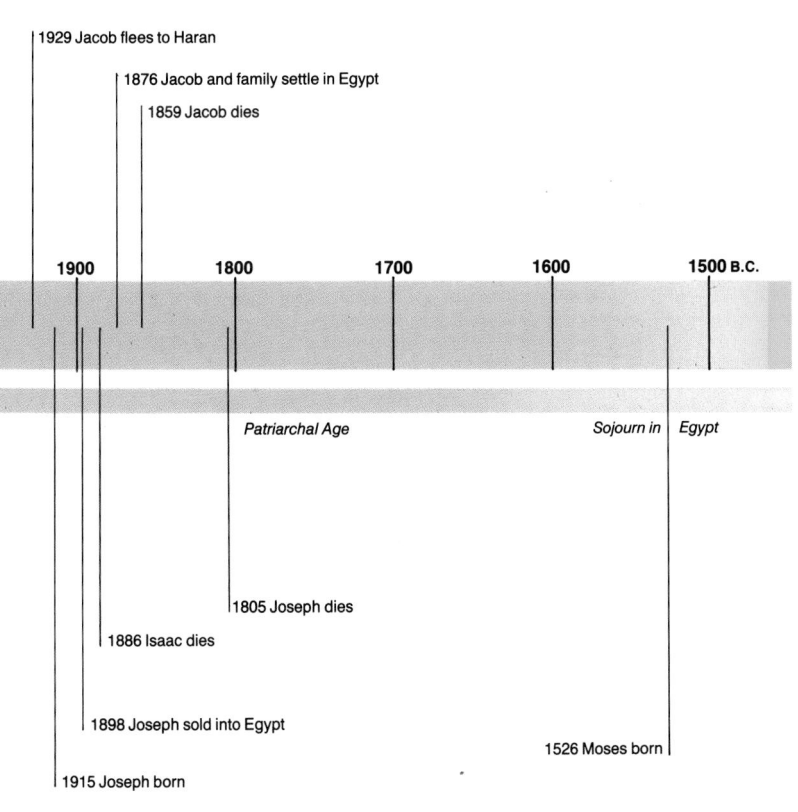

1929 Jacob flees to Haran

1876 Jacob and family settle in Egypt

1859 Jacob dies

| 1900 | 1800 | 1700 | 1600 | 1500 B.C. |

Patriarchal Age

Sojourn in Egypt

1805 Joseph dies

1886 Isaac dies

1898 Joseph sold into Egypt

1526 Moses born

1915 Joseph born

Cappadocian texts		Mari texts	Hammurapi texts		
1900	**1800**		**1700**	**1600**	**1500** B.C.
Isin-Larsa Period			Old Babylonian Period		
Middle Kingdom			2nd Intermediate (Hyksos) Period		New Kingdom
norite Period			Hyksos Period		Late Canaanite Per.
					Hittite Old Kingdom
	Middle Minoan Period				
Middle Helladic Period					

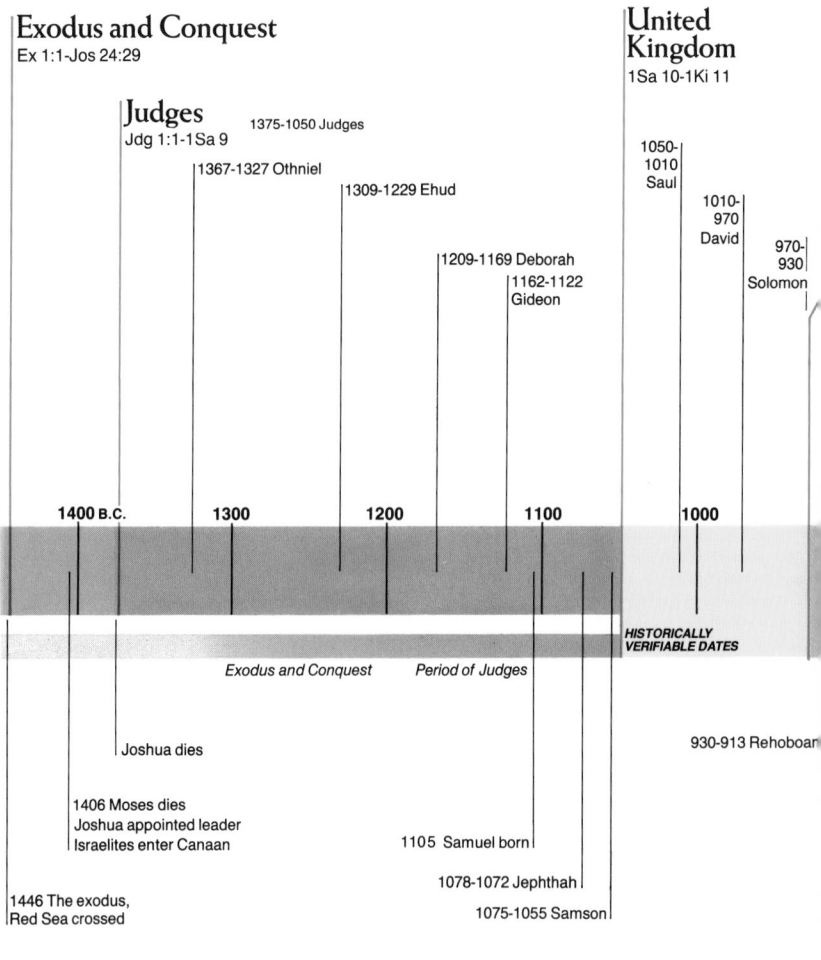

Exodus and Conquest
Ex 1:1-Jos 24:29

United Kingdom
1Sa 10-1Ki 11

Judges
Jdg 1:1-1Sa 9

1375-1050 Judges

1367-1327 Othniel

1309-1229 Ehud

1209-1169 Deborah

1162-1122 Gideon

1050-1010 Saul

1010-970 David

970-930 Solomon

1400 B.C.   1300   1200   1100   1000

HISTORICALLY VERIFIABLE DATES

Exodus and Conquest   Period of Judges

Joshua dies

930-913 Rehoboar

1406 Moses dies
Joshua appointed leader
Israelites enter Canaan

1105 Samuel born

1078-1072 Jephthah

1446 The exodus,
Red Sea crossed

1075-1055 Samson

	Nuzi texts	Ugaritic texts					
		Amarna texts		Merneptah inscription	Medinet Habu inscriptions		Shish inscript
	1400 B.C.	1300	1200	1100	1000		
S. MESOPOTAMIA		Kassite Period					
N. MESOPOTAMIA	← Mitannian Kingdom		Middle Assyrian Period				
EGYPT		New Kingdom					
SYRIA-PALESTINE	Late Canaanite Period		Sea Peoples			Phoenici	
ANATOLIA	Hittite Empire		Phrygian Period				
CRETE	Late Minoan Period					Dorian Sta	
PERSIA							
GREECE	Late Helladic (Mycenean) Period			Dorian States			
ITALY							

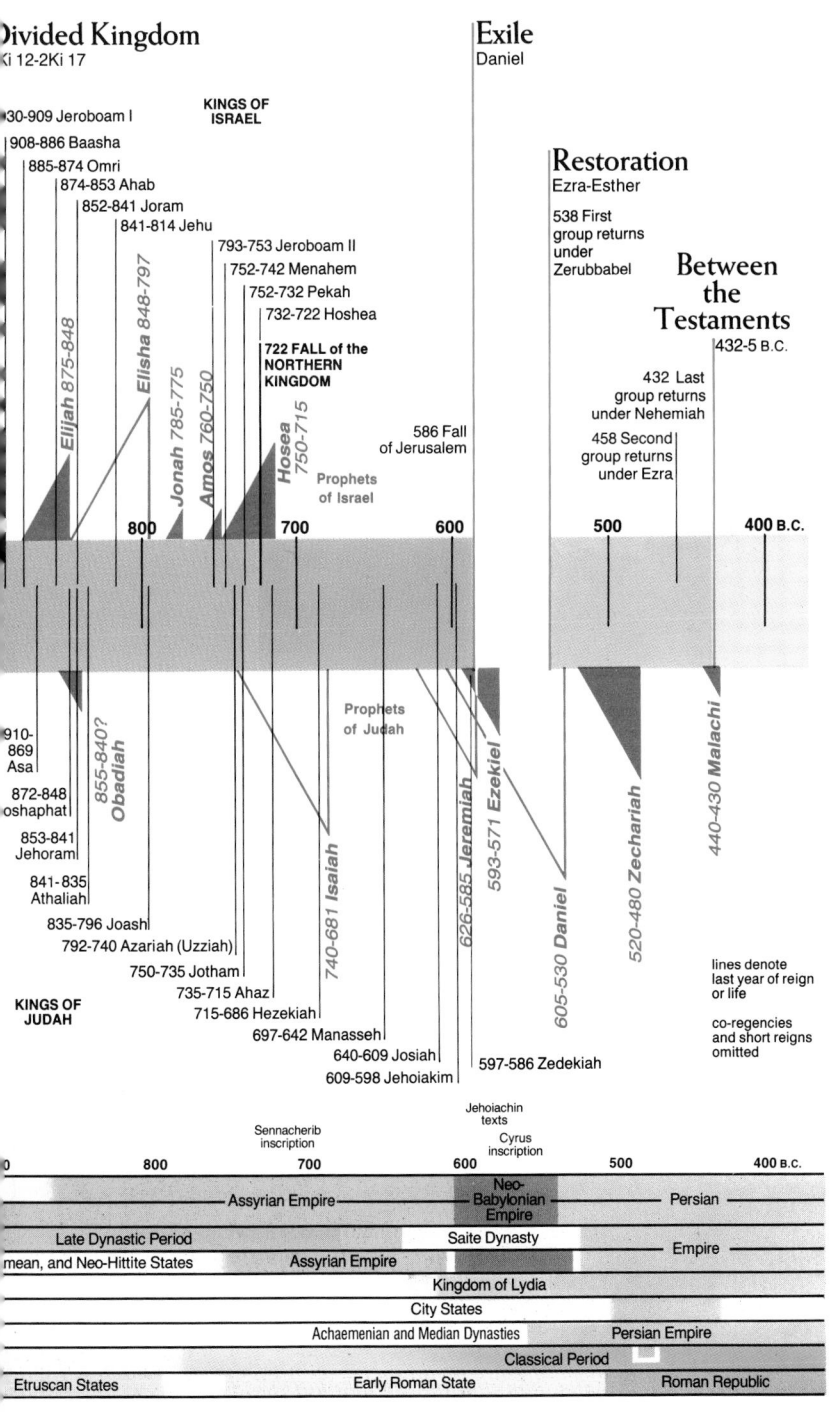

Divided Kingdom
1Ki 12-2Ki 17

Exile
Daniel

KINGS OF ISRAEL

930-909 Jeroboam I
908-886 Baasha
885-874 Omri
874-853 Ahab
852-841 Joram
841-814 Jehu
793-753 Jeroboam II
752-742 Menahem
752-732 Pekah
732-722 Hoshea

722 FALL of the NORTHERN KINGDOM

586 Fall of Jerusalem

Prophets of Israel

Restoration
Ezra-Esther

538 First group returns under Zerubbabel

Between the Testaments
432-5 B.C.

432 Last group returns under Nehemiah

458 Second group returns under Ezra

Elijah 875-848

Elisha 848-797

Jonah 785-775

Amos 760-750

Hosea 750-715

800 700 600 500 400 B.C.

910-869 Asa

Obadiah 855-840?

872-848 Jehoshaphat
853-841 Jehoram
841-835 Athaliah
835-796 Joash
792-740 Azariah (Uzziah)
750-735 Jotham
735-715 Ahaz
715-686 Hezekiah
697-642 Manasseh
640-609 Josiah
609-598 Jehoiakim

Prophets of Judah

KINGS OF JUDAH

740-681 Isaiah

626-585 Jeremiah

593-571 Ezekiel

605-530 Daniel

520-480 Zechariah

440-430 Malachi

597-586 Zedekiah

lines denote last year of reign or life

co-regencies and short reigns omitted

Jehoiachin texts

Sennacherib inscription

Cyrus inscription

0 800 700 600 500 400 B.C.

| | Assyrian Empire | Neo-Babylonian Empire | Persian |

| Late Dynastic Period | | Saite Dynasty | |
| ...mean, and Neo-Hittite States | Assyrian Empire | | Empire |

Kingdom of Lydia

City States

Achaemenian and Median Dynasties | Persian Empire

Classical Period

Etruscan States | Early Roman State | Roman Republic

Christ's Ministr
(Mt 2-28; Mk; Lk 3-24; J

30 Christ crucifie
The ascensio

29 Christ at Feast of Tabernacles
Christ at Feast of Dedication

Christ's Early Life
(Mt 1-2; Lk 1-2)

6/5 B.C.
Christ born

28/29 John the
Baptist dies

27/28 John the Baptist
imprisoned

A.D. 7/8
Christ in
temple at
age 12

26 Christ
baptized

26 Christ
begins ministry

26 John
the Baptist
begins ministry

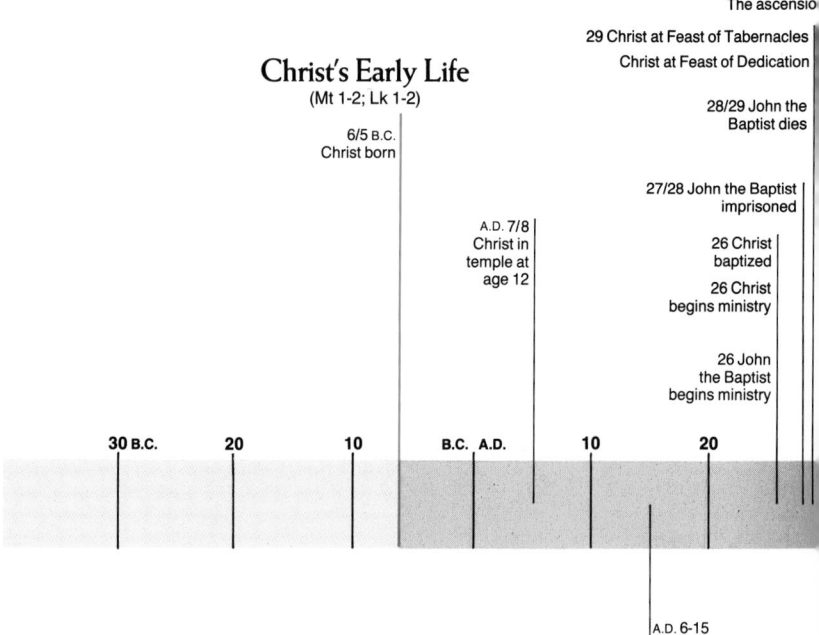

| 30 B.C. | 20 | 10 | B.C. A.D. | 10 | 20 |

A.D. 6-15
Annas I

37-4 B.C.
Herod the Great

4 B.C. Herod
the Great dies

A.D. 6
Roman procurators
begin rule

A.D. 26-36
Pontius Pilate

RULERS IN PALESTINE

| 30 B.C. | 20 | 10 | B.C. A.D. | 10 | 20 |

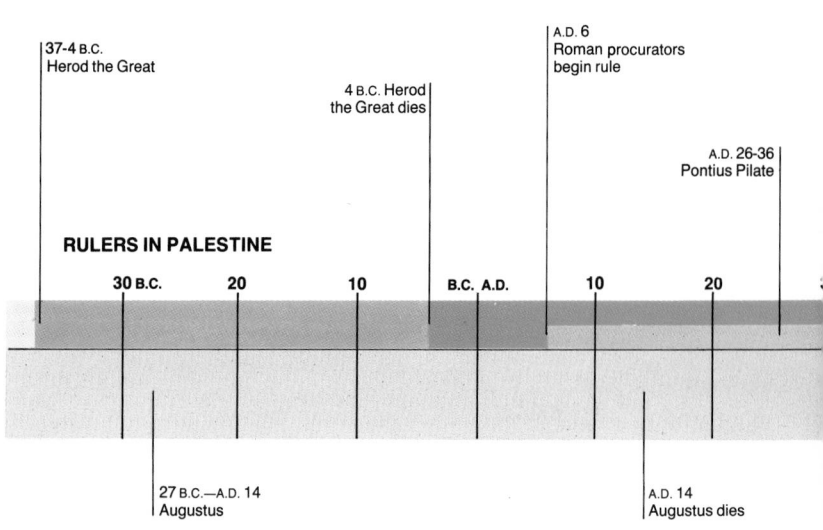

27 B.C.—A.D. 14
Augustus

A.D. 14
Augustus dies

ROMAN EMPERORS

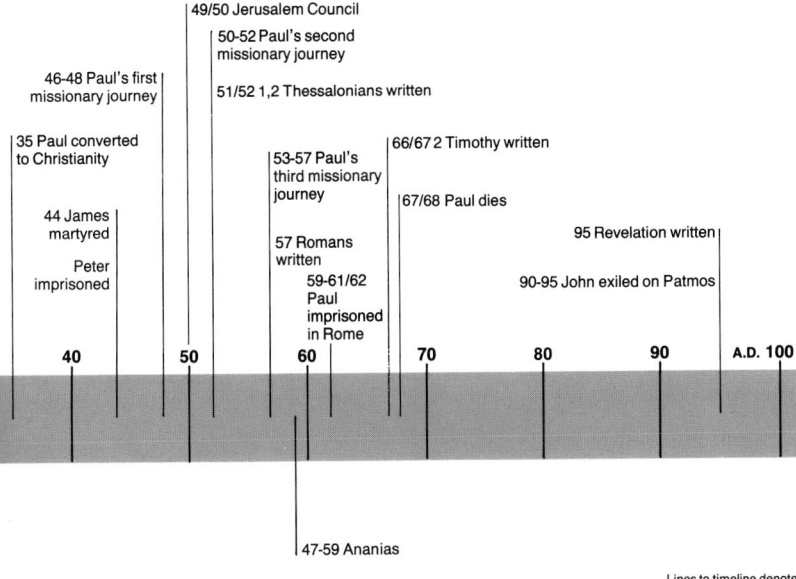

e Early Church
(Acts-Revelation)

entecost

46-48 Paul's first
missionary journey

49/50 Jerusalem Council

50-52 Paul's second
missionary journey

51/52 1,2 Thessalonians written

35 Paul converted
to Christianity

66/67 2 Timothy written

53-57 Paul's
third missionary
journey

67/68 Paul dies

44 James
martyred

57 Romans
written

95 Revelation written

Peter
imprisoned

59-61/62
Paul
imprisoned
in Rome

90-95 John exiled on Patmos

40   50   60   70   80   90   A.D. 100

47-59 Ananias

Lines to timeline denote
end of journey or reign

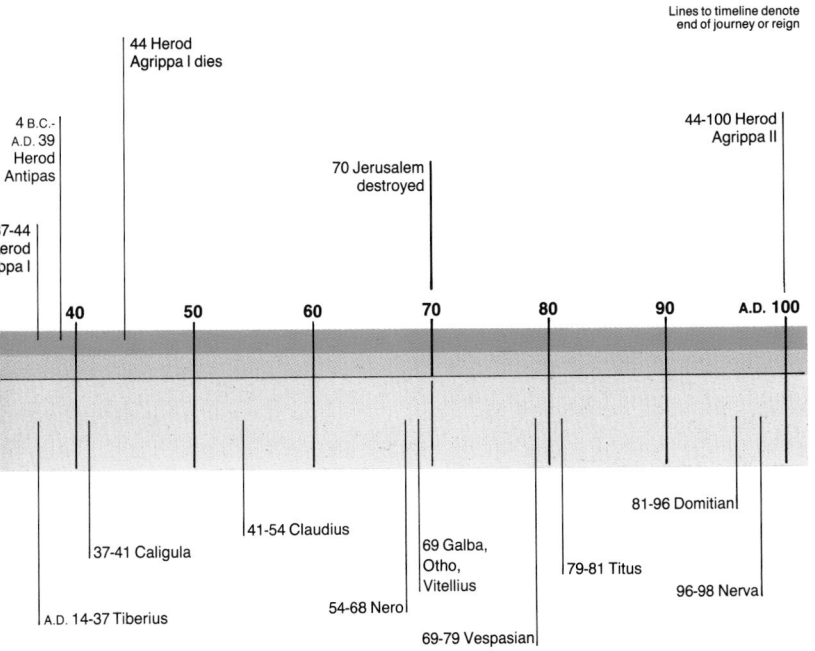

44 Herod
Agrippa I dies

4 B.C.-
A.D. 39
Herod
Antipas

44-100 Herod
Agrippa II

70 Jerusalem
destroyed

7-44
erod
ppa I

40   50   60   70   80   90   A.D. 100

81-96 Domitian

41-54 Claudius

37-41 Caligula

69 Galba,
Otho,
Vitellius

79-81 Titus

96-98 Nerva

A.D. 14-37 Tiberius

54-68 Nero

69-79 Vespasian

Family Record

BIRTHS

NAME	DATE	NAME	DATE

DEATHS

NAME	DATE	NAME	DATE

MARRIAGES

NAME	PLACE	DATE

SPECIAL EVENTS

EVENT	PLACE	DATE

The NIV Study Bible

New International Version

General Editor
KENNETH BARKER

Associate Editors
DONALD BURDICK
JOHN STEK
WALTER WESSEL
RONALD YOUNGBLOOD

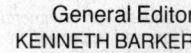

ZONDERVAN
PUBLISHING HOUSE
GRAND RAPIDS, MICHIGAN 49506, U.S.A.

You will be pleased to know that a portion of the purchase price of your new NIV Bible has been
provided to International Bible Society to help spread the gospel of Jesus Christ around the world!

Tribute to Edwin H. Palmer

Edwin H. Palmer, who had served so capably as Executive Secretary of the NIV Committee on Bible Translation and as coordinator of all translation work on the NIV, was appointed General Editor of *The NIV Study Bible* by Zondervan Bible Publishers in 1979. On September 16, 1980, he departed this life to "be with Christ, which is better by far" (Philippians 1:23). Before his death, however, he had laid most of the plans for the Study Bible, had recruited the majority of the contributors, and had done some editorial work on the first manuscripts submitted. We gratefully acknowledge his significant contributions to the earliest stages of this project.

Table of Contents

TABLE OF CONTENTS

Contents: Maps

Contents: Charts

Preface

The New International Version is a completely new translation of the Holy Bible made by over a hundred scholars working directly from the best available Hebrew, Aramaic and Greek texts. It had its beginning in 1965 when, after several years of exploratory study by committees from the Christian Reformed Church and the National Association of Evangelicals, a group of scholars met at Palos Heights, Illinois, and concurred in the need for a new translation of the Bible in contemporary English. This group, though not made up of official church representatives, was transdenominational. Its conclusion was endorsed by a large number of leaders from many denominations who met in Chicago in 1966.

Responsibility for the new version was delegated by the Palos Heights group to a self-governing body of fifteen, the Committee on Bible Translation, composed for the most part of biblical scholars from colleges, universities and seminaries. In 1967 the New York Bible Society (now the International Bible Society) generously undertook the financial sponsorship of the project—a sponsorship that made it possible to enlist the help of many distinguished scholars. The fact that participants from the United States, Great Britain, Canada, Australia and New Zealand worked together gave the project its international scope. That they were from many denominations—including Anglican, Assemblies of God, Baptist, Brethren, Christian Reformed, Church of Christ, Evangelical Free, Lutheran, Mennonite, Methodist, Nazarene, Presbyterian, Wesleyan and other churches—helped to safeguard the translation from sectarian bias.

How it was made helps to give the New International Version its distinctiveness. The translation of each book was assigned to a team of scholars. Next, one of the Intermediate Editorial Committees revised the initial translation, with constant reference to the Hebrew, Aramaic or Greek. Their work then went to one of the General Editorial Committees, which checked it in detail and made another thorough revision. This revision in turn was carefully reviewed by the Committee on Bible Translation, which made further changes and then released the final version for publication. In this way the entire Bible underwent three revisions, during each of which the translation was examined for its faithfulness to the original languages and for its English style.

All this involved many thousands of hours of research and discussion regarding the meaning of the texts and the precise way of putting them into English. It may well be that no other translation has been made by a more thorough process of review and revision from committee to committee than this one.

From the beginning of the project, the Committee on Bible Translation held to certain goals for the New International Version: that it would be an accurate translation and one that would have clarity and literary quality and so prove suitable for public and private reading, teaching, preaching, memorizing and liturgical use. The Committee also sought to preserve some measure of continuity with the long tradition of translating the Scriptures into English.

In working toward these goals, the translators were united in their commitment to the authority and infallibility of the Bible as God's Word in written form. They believe that it contains the divine answer to the deepest needs of humanity, that it sheds unique light on our path in a dark world, and that it sets forth the way to our eternal well-being.

The first concern of the translators has been the accuracy of the translation and its fidelity to the thought of the biblical writers. They have weighed the significance of the lexical and grammatical details of the Hebrew, Aramaic and Greek texts. At the same time, they have striven for more than a word-for-word translation. Because thought patterns and syntax differ from language to language, faithful communication of the meaning of the writers of the Bible demands frequent modifications in sentence structure and constant regard for the contextual meanings of words.

A sensitive feeling for style does not always accompany scholarship. Accordingly the Committee on Bible Translation submitted the developing version to a number of stylistic consultants. Two of them read every book of both Old and New Testaments twice—once before and once after the last major revision—and made invaluable suggestions. Samples of the translation were tested for clarity and ease of reading by various kinds of people—young and old, highly educated and less well educated, ministers and laymen.

Concern for clear and natural English—that the New International Version should be idiomatic but

not idiosyncratic, contemporary but not dated—motivated the translators and consultants. At the same time, they tried to reflect the differing styles of the biblical writers. In view of the international use of English, the translators sought to avoid obvious Americanisms on the one hand and obvious Anglicisms on the other. A British edition reflects the comparatively few differences of significant idiom and of spelling.

As for the traditional pronouns "thou," "thee" and "thine" in reference to the Deity, the translators judged that to use these archaisms (along with the old verb forms such as "doest," "wouldest" and "hadst") would violate accuracy in translation. Neither Hebrew, Aramaic nor Greek uses special pronouns for the persons of the Godhead. A present-day translation is not enhanced by forms that in the time of the King James Version were used in everyday speech, whether referring to God or man.

For the Old Testament the standard Hebrew text, the Masoretic Text as published in the latest editions of *Biblia Hebraica,* was used throughout. The Dead Sea Scrolls contain material bearing on an earlier stage of the Hebrew text. They were consulted, as were the Samaritan Pentateuch and the ancient scribal traditions relating to textual changes. Sometimes a variant Hebrew reading in the margin of the Masoretic Text was followed instead of the text itself. Such instances, being variants within the Masoretic tradition, are not specified by footnotes. In rare cases, words in the consonantal text were divided differently from the way they appear in the Masoretic Text. Footnotes indicate this. The translators also consulted the more important early versions—the Septuagint; Aquila, Symmachus and Theodotion; the Vulgate; the Syriac Peshitta; the Targums; and for the Psalms the *Juxta Hebraica* of Jerome. Readings from these versions were occasionally followed where the Masoretic Text seemed doubtful and where accepted principles of textual criticism showed that one or more of these textual witnesses appeared to provide the correct reading. Such instances are footnoted. Sometimes vowel letters and vowel signs did not, in the judgment of the translators, represent the correct vowels for the original consonantal text. Accordingly some words were read with a different set of vowels. These instances are usually not indicated by footnotes.

The Greek text used in translating the New Testament was an eclectic one. No other piece of ancient literature has such an abundance of manuscript witnesses as does the New Testament. Where existing manuscripts differ, the translators made their choice of readings according to accepted principles of New Testament textual criticism. Footnotes call attention to places where there was uncertainty about what the original text was. The best current printed texts of the Greek New Testament were used.

There is a sense in which the work of translation is never wholly finished. This applies to all great literature and uniquely so to the Bible. In 1973 the New Testament in the New International Version was published. Since then, suggestions for corrections and revisions have been received from various sources. The Committee on Bible Translation carefully considered the suggestions and adopted a number of them. These were incorporated in the first printing of the entire Bible in 1978. Additional revisions were made by the Committee on Bible Translation in 1983 and appear in printings after that date.

As in other ancient documents, the precise meaning of the biblical texts is sometimes uncertain. This is more often the case with the Hebrew and Aramaic texts than with the Greek text. Although archaeological and linguistic discoveries in this century aid in understanding difficult passages, some uncertainties remain. The more significant of these have been called to the reader's attention in the footnotes.

In regard to the divine name *YHWH,* commonly referred to as the *Tetragrammaton,* the translators adopted the device used in most English versions of rendering that name as "Lord" in capital letters to distinguish it from *Adonai,* another Hebrew word rendered "Lord," for which small letters are used. Wherever the two names stand together in the Old Testament as a compound name of God, they are rendered "Sovereign Lord."

Because for most readers today the phrases "the Lord of hosts" and "God of hosts" have little meaning, this version renders them "the Lord Almighty" and "God Almighty." These renderings convey the sense of the Hebrew, namely, "he who is sovereign over all the 'hosts' (powers) in heaven and on earth, especially over the 'hosts' (armies) of Israel." For readers unacquainted with Hebrew this does not make clear the distinction between *Sabaoth* ("hosts" or "Almighty") and *Shaddai* (which can also be translated "Almighty"), but the latter occurs infrequently and is always footnoted. When *Adonai* and *YHWH Sabaoth* occur together, they are rendered "the Lord, the Lord Almighty."

As for other proper nouns, the familiar spellings of the King James Version are generally retained.

Introduction

About the Study Bible

The New International Version of the Bible is unsurpassed in accuracy, clarity and literary grace. The commitments that led to the completion of this version later guided several of its translators to spearhead publication of *The NIV Study Bible*. Their purpose was unchanged: to communicate the word of God to the hearts of people.

Like the NIV itself, *The NIV Study Bible* is the work of a transdenominational team of Biblical scholars. All confess the authority of the Bible as God's infallible word to humanity. They have sought to clarify understanding of, develop appreciation for, and provide insight into that word.

But why a study Bible when the NIV text itself is so clearly written? Surely there is no substitute for the reading of the text itself; nothing people write *about* God's word can be on a level with the word itself. Further, it is the Holy Spirit alone—not fallible human beings—who can open the human mind to the divine message.

However, the Spirit also uses people to explain God's word to others. It was the Spirit who led Philip to the Ethiopian eunuch's chariot, where he asked, "Do you understand what you are reading?" (Ac 8:31). "How can I," the Ethiopian replied, "unless someone explains it to me?" Philip then showed him how an Old Testament passage in Isaiah related to the good news of Jesus.

This interrelationship of the Scriptures—so essential to understanding the complete Biblical message—is a major theme of the Study Bible notes.

Doctrinally, the Study Bible reflects traditional evangelical theology. Where editors were aware of significant differences of opinion on key passages or doctrines, they tried to follow an evenhanded approach by indicating those differences (e.g., see note on Rev 20:2). In finding solutions to problems mentioned in the book introductions, they went only as far as evidence (Biblical and non-Biblical) could carry them.

The result is a study Bible that can be used profitably by all Christians who want to be serious Bible students.

Features of the NIV Study Bible

The NIV Study Bible features the text of the New International Version, study notes keyed to and listed with Bible verses, introductions and outlines to books of the Bible, text notes, a cross-reference system (100,000 entries), parallel passages, a concordance (over 35,000 references), charts, maps, essays and comprehensive indexes.

The text of the NIV, which is divided into paragraphs as well as verses, is organized into sections with headings.

Study Notes

The outstanding feature of this Study Bible is its nearly 20,000 study notes located on the same pages as the verses and passages they explain.

The study notes provide new information to supplement that found in the NIV text notes. Among other things, they

1. explain important words and concepts (see note on Lev 11:44 about "holiness");
2. interpret "difficult verses" (see notes on Mal 1:3 and Lk 14:26 for the concept of "hating" your parents);
3. draw parallels between specific people and events (see note on Ex 32:30 for the parallels between Moses and Christ as mediators);
4. describe historical and textual contexts of passages (see note on 1Co 8:1 for the practice of eating meat sacrificed to idols); and
5. demonstrate how one passage sheds light on another (see note on Ps 26:8 for how the presence of God's glory marked his presence in the tabernacle, in the temple, and finally in Jesus Christ himself).

Some elements of style should be noted:

1. Study notes on a *passage* precede notes on individual verses within that passage.
2. When a book of the Bible is referred to within a note on that book, the book name is not repeated. For example, a reference to 2 Timothy 2:18 within the notes on 2 Timothy is written 2:18, not 2Ti 2:18.

3. In lists of references within a note, references from the book under discussion are placed first. The rest appear in Biblical order.

Introductions to Books

Each introduction to each book of the Bible is different. Introductions vary in length and reflect both the nature of the material itself and the strengths and interests of contributing editors.

An introduction frequently reports on a book's title, author, and date of writing. It details the book's background and purpose, explores themes and theological significance, and points out special problems and distinctive literary features. Where appropriate, such as in Paul's letters to the churches, it describes the original recipients of a book and the city in which they lived.

A complete outline of the book's content is provided in each introduction (except for the introduction to Psalms). For Genesis, two outlines—a literary and a thematic—are given. Pairs of books that were originally one literary work, such as 1 and 2 Samuel, 1 and 2 Kings, and 1 and 2 Chronicles, are outlined together.

Text Notes

NIV text notes are indicated by raised, bold-faced letters following the words or phrases they explain. They examine such things as alternate translations, meanings of Hebrew and Greek terms, Old Testament quotations, and variant readings in ancient Biblical manuscripts. Text notes appear at the bottom of the right-hand column, preceded by their bold letters and verse numbers.

Cross-Reference System

The cross-reference system, developed over many years by June Gunden, John R. Kohlenberger III (OT) and Donald H. Madvig (NT), can be used to explore concepts, as well as specific words. For example, one can either study "angels as protectors" (see Mt 18:10) or focus on the word "angel" (see Jn 20:12).

The NIV cross-reference system resembles a series of interlocking chains with many links. The head, or organizing, link in each concept chain is indicated by the letter "S" (short for "See"). The appearance of a head link in a list of references usually signals another list of references that will cover a slightly different aspect of the concept or word being studied. The various chains in the cross-reference system—which is virtually inexhaustible—continually intersect and diverge.

Cross references are indicated by raised light-italic letters. When a single word is addressed by both text notes and cross references, the bold NIV text-note letter comes first. The cross references normally appear in the center column and, when necessary, continue at the bottom of the right-hand column preceding the NIV text notes.

The lists of references are in Biblical order with one exception: If reference is made to a verse within the same chapter, that verse (indicated by "ver") is listed first. If an Old Testament verse is quoted in the New Testament, the New Testament reference is marked with an asterisk (*).

Genesis 1:1 provides a good example of the resources of the cross-reference system.

The Beginning

1 In the beginning^a God created^b the heavens^c and the earth.^d 2Now the earth was^a formless^e and empty,^f darkness was over the surface of the deep,^g and the Spirit of God^h was hoveringⁱ over the waters.

3And God said,^j "Let there be light," and there was light.^k 4God saw that the light was good,^l and he separated the light from the darkness.^m 5God calledⁿ the light "day," and the darkness he called "night."^o And there was evening, and there was morning^p—the first day.

1:1 ^aPs 102:25; Pr 8:23; Isa 40:21; 41:4, 26; Jn 1:1-2 *ver 21,27; Ge 2:3 *ver 6; Ne 9:6; Job 9:8; 37:18; Ps 96:5; 104:2; 115:15; 121:2; 136:5; Isa 40:22; 42:5; 51:13; Jer 10:12; 51:15 *Ge 14:19; 2Ki 19:15; Ne 9:6; Job 38:4; Ps 90:2; 136:6; 146:6; Isa 37:16; 40:28; 42:5; 44:24; 45:12,18; Jer 27:5; 32:17; Ac 14:15; 17:24; Eph 3:9; Col 1:16; Heb 3:4; 11:3; Rev 4:11; 10:6 1:2 *Isa 23:1;

The four lists of references all relate to creation, but each takes a different perspective. Note a takes up the time of creation: "in the beginning." Note b lists three other occurrences of the word "created" in Genesis 1-2. Note c focuses on "the heavens" as God's creation. Because note d is attached to the end of the verse as well as to the word "earth," it deals with the word "earth," with the phrase "the heavens and the earth" and with creation itself (the whole verse).

Parallel Passages

When two or more passages of Scripture are nearly identical or deal with the same event, this

"parallel" is noted at the sectional headings for those passages. Such passages are especially common in Matthew, Mark, Luke and John, and in Samuel, Kings and Chronicles.

Identical or nearly identical passages are noted with *"pp."* Similar passages—those not dealing with the same event—are noted with *"Ref."*

To conserve space and avoid repetition, when a parallel passage is noted at a sectional heading, no further parallels are listed in the cross-reference system. It was compiled and edited by John R. Kohlenberger III and Edward W. Goodrick.

Concordance

The concordance is the largest ever bound together with an English Bible. By looking up key words, you can find verses for which you remember a word or two but not their location. For example, to find the verse that states that the word of God is "sharper than any double-edged sword," you could look in the concordance under either "sharper," "double-edged," or "sword."

Maps

The Study Bible includes 57 maps: 13 full color and 44 black and white. The 13 full-color maps at the end of this Bible cover nearly 4,000 years of history, from the patriarchs to Christianity in the world today.

Strategically placed throughout the text are almost four dozen black-and-white maps specially designed for the Study Bible. The Contents contains a complete list of the topics covered.

The cities of Damascus, Rome, Corinth, Ephesus and Philippi have been reconstructed as they might have been in New Testament times. These recreations allow Bible students to visualize the places through which Paul traveled on his missionary journeys.

Charts

Complementing the study notes are 35 charts, diagrams and drawings designed specifically for the Study Bible. Two full-color time lines, located in the front of this Bible, pinpoint significant dates in the Old and New Testaments. Other charts, carefully placed within the text, give detailed information about ancient non-Biblical texts, about Old Testament covenants, sacrifices, and feast days, about Jewish sects, and about major archaeological finds relating to the New Testament.

Essays

Four brief essays give additional information on specific sections of the Bible: the Minor Prophets, the Synoptic Gospels, the Pastoral Letters, and the General Letters.

A fifth essay details the history, literature and social developments of the 400 years between the Old and New Testaments.

Subject and Map Indexes

The subject index pinpoints other references to persons, places, events and topics mentioned in the Study Bible notes.

Two map indexes help in locating place-names on a map.

Acknowledgments

My greatest debt of gratitude is owed to God for giving me the privilege of serving as General Editor of *The NIV Study Bible*. Special thanks go to the four Associate Editors: Donald W. Burdick, John H. Stek, Walter W. Wessel, and Ronald Youngblood. Without their help, it would have been impossible to complete this project in a little over five years.

In addition, grateful acknowledgment is given to all those listed on the Contributors page. Obviously the editors and contributors have profited immensely from the labors of others. We feel deeply indebted to all the commentaries and other sources we have used in our work.

I should also thank the following individuals for rendering help in various ways (though I fear that I have inadvertently omitted a few names): Caroline Blauwkamp, David R. Douglass, Stanley N. Gundry, N. David Hill, Betty Hockenberry, Charles E. Hummel, Alan F. Johnson, Janet Johnston Murphy, Donald H. Madvig, Frances Steenwyk, and Edward Viening.

Nehemiah 8:7-8, 12 says:

> The Levites . . . instructed the people in the Law while the people were standing there. They read from the Book of the Law of God, making it clear and giving the meaning so that the people could understand what was being read. . . . Then all the people went away . . . to celebrate with great joy, because they now understood the words that had been made known to them.

My associates and I will feel amply rewarded if those who use this Study Bible have an experience similar to that of God's people in Nehemiah's time.

Kenneth L. Barker
General Editor

Contributors

General Editor: Kenneth L. Barker
Associate Editors: Donald W. Burdick
                            John H. Stek
                            Walter W. Wessel
                            Ronald Youngblood

The individuals named below contributed and/or reviewed material for *The NIV Study Bible*. However, since the General Editor and the Associate Editors extensively edited the notes on most books, they alone are responsible for their final form and content.

The chief contributors of original material to the Study Bible are listed first. Where the Associate Editors and General Editor contributed an unusually large number of notes on certain books, their names are also listed.

Genesis	Ronald Youngblood	Micah	Allan A. MacRae;
Exodus	Ronald Youngblood;		Thomas E. McComiskey
	Walter C. Kaiser, Jr.	Nahum	G. Herbert Livingston;
Leviticus	R. Laird Harris;		Kenneth L. Barker
	Ronald Youngblood	Habakkuk	Roland K. Harrison;
Numbers	Ronald B. Allen;		William C. Williams
	Kenneth L. Barker	Zephaniah	Roland K. Harrison
Deuteronomy	Earl S. Kalland;	Haggai	Herbert Wolf
	Kenneth L. Barker	Zechariah	Kenneth L. Barker;
Joshua	Arthur Lewis		Larry L. Walker
Judges	John J. Davis;	Malachi	Herbert Wolf;
	Herbert Wolf		John H. Stek
Ruth	Marvin R. Wilson;	Matthew	Ralph Earle
	John H. Stek	Mark	Walter W. Wessel;
1,2 Samuel	J. Robert Vannoy		William L. Lane
1,2 Kings	J. Robert Vannoy	Luke	Lewis Foster
1,2 Chronicles	Raymond Dillard	John	Leon Morris
Ezra	Edwin Yamauchi;	Acts	Lewis Foster
	Ronald Youngblood	Romans	Walter W. Wessel
Nehemiah	Edwin Yamauchi;	1 Corinthians	W. Harold Mare
	Ronald Youngblood	2 Corinthians	Philip E. Hughes
Esther	Raymond Dillard;	Galatians	Robert Mounce
	Edwin Yamauchi	Ephesians	Walter L. Liefeld
Job	Elmer B. Smick;	Philippians	Richard B. Gaffin, Jr.
	Ronald Youngblood	Colossians	Gerald F. Hawthorne;
Psalms	John H. Stek		Wilber B. Wallis
Proverbs	Herbert Wolf	1,2 Thessalonians	Leon Morris
Ecclesiastes	Derek Kidner	1,2 Timothy	Walter W. Wessel;
Song of Songs	John H. Stek		George W. Knight, III
Isaiah	Herbert Wolf;	Titus	D. Edmond Hiebert
	John H. Stek	Philemon	John Werner
Jeremiah	Ronald Youngblood	Hebrews	Philip E. Hughes;
Lamentations	Ronald Youngblood		Donald W. Burdick
Ezekiel	Mark Hillmer	James	Donald W. Burdick
Daniel	Gleason L. Archer, Jr.;	1,2 Peter	Donald W. Burdick;
	Ronald Youngblood		John H. Skilton
Hosea	Jack P. Lewis	1,2,3 John	Donald W. Burdick
Joel	Jack P. Lewis	Jude	Donald W. Burdick;
Amos	Alan R. Millard;		John H. Skilton
	John H. Stek	Revelation	Robert Mounce
Obadiah	John M. Zinkand	"The Time between	David O'Brien
Jonah	Marvin R. Wilson;	the Testaments"	
	John H. Stek	(essay)	

Managing Editor: Doris Wynbeek Rikkers
Copy Editor and Stylist: June Gunden
Artist: Hugh O. Claycombe
Art Consultant: James E. Jennings

Abbreviations

Transliterations

A simplified system has been used for transliterating words from ancient Biblical languages into English. The only transliterations calling for comment are these:

Transliteration	Pronunciation
'	Glottal stop
ḥ	Similar to the "ch" in the German word *Buch*
ṭ	Similar to the "t" in the verb "tear"
'	Similar to the glottal stop
ṣ	Similar to the "ts" in "hits"
ś	Similar to the "s" in "sing"

THE OLD TESTAMENT

GENESIS

Title

The first phrase in the Hebrew text of 1:1 is *bereshith* ("in [the] beginning"), which is also the Hebrew title of the book (books in ancient times customarily were named after their first word or two). The English title, Genesis, is Greek in origin and comes from the word *geneseos,* which appears in the Greek translation (Septuagint) of 2:4; 5:1. Depending on its context, the word can mean "birth," "genealogy," or "history of origin." In both its Hebrew and Greek forms, then, the title of Genesis appropriately describes its contents, since it is primarily a book of beginnings.

Background

Chs. 1-38 reflect a great deal of what we know from other sources about ancient Mesopotamian life and culture. Creation, genealogies, destructive floods, geography and mapmaking, construction techniques, migrations of peoples, sale and purchase of land, legal customs and procedures, sheep-herding and cattle-raising—all these subjects and many others were matters of vital concern to the peoples of Mesopotamia during this time. They were also of interest to the individuals, families and tribes of whom we read in the first 38 chapters of Genesis. The author appears to locate Eden, man's first home, in or near Mesopotamia; the tower of Babel was built there; Abram was born there; Isaac took a wife from there; and Jacob lived there for 20 years. Although these patriarchs settled in Palestine, their original homeland was Mesopotamia.

The closest ancient literary parallels to Ge 1-38 also come from Mesopotamia. *Enuma elish,* the story of the god Marduk's rise to supremacy in the Babylonian pantheon, is similar in some respects (though thoroughly mythical and polytheistic) to the Ge 1 creation account. Some of the features of certain king lists from Sumer bear striking resemblance to the genealogy in Ge 5. The 11th tablet of the *Gilgamesh* epic is quite similar in outline to the flood narrative in Ge 6-8. Several of the major events of Ge 1-8 are narrated in the same order as similar events in the *Atrahasis* epic. In fact, the latter features the same basic motif of creation-rebellion-flood as the Biblical account. Clay tablets found recently at the ancient (c. 2500-2300 B.C.) site of Ebla (modern Tell Mardikh) in northern Syria may also contain some intriguing parallels (see chart on "Ancient Texts Relating to the OT," p. 5).

Two other important sets of documents demonstrate the reflection of Mesopotamia in the first 38 chapters of Genesis. From the Mari letters (see chart on p. 5), dating from the patriarchal period, we learn that the names of the patriarchs (including especially Abram, Jacob and Job) were typical of that time. The letters also clearly illustrate the freedom of travel that was possible between various parts of the Amorite world in which the patriarchs lived. The Nuzi tablets (see chart on p. 5), though a few centuries later than the patriarchal period, shed light on patriarchal customs, which tended to survive virtually intact for many centuries. The inheritance right of an adopted household member or slave (see 15:1-4), the obligation of a barren wife to furnish her husband with sons through a servant girl (see 16:2-4), strictures against expelling such a servant girl and her son (see 21:10-11), the authority of oral statements in ancient Near Eastern law, such as the deathbed bequest (see 27:1-4,22-23,33)—these and other legal customs, social contracts and provisions are graphically illustrated in Mesopotamian documents.

As Ge 1-38 is Mesopotamian in character and background, so chs. 39-50 reflect Egyptian influence—though in not quite so direct a way. Examples of such influence are: Egyptian grape cultivation (40:9-11), the riverside scene (ch. 41), Egypt as Canaan's breadbasket (ch. 42), Canaan as the source of numerous products for Egyptian consumption (ch. 43), Egyptian religious and social customs (the end of chs. 43; 46), Egyptian administrative procedures (ch. 47), Egyptian funerary practices (ch. 50) and several Egyptian words and names used throughout these chapters. The closest specific literary parallel from Egypt is the *Tale of Two Brothers,* which bears some resemblance to the story of Joseph

and Potiphar's wife (ch. 39). Egyptian autobiographical narratives (such as the *Story of Sinuhe* and the *Report of Wenamun*) and certain historical legends offer more general literary parallels.

Author and Date of Writing

Historically, Jews and Christians alike have held that Moses was the author/compiler of the first five books of the OT. These books, known also as the Pentateuch (meaning "five-volumed book"), were referred to in Jewish tradition as the five fifths of the law (of Moses). The Bible itself suggests Mosaic authorship of Genesis, since Ac 15:1 refers to circumcision as "the custom taught by Moses," an allusion to Ge 17. However, a certain amount of later editorial updating does appear to be indicated (see, e.g., notes on 14:14; 36:31; 47:11).

The historical period during which Moses lived seems to be fixed with a fair degree of accuracy by 1 Kings. We are told that "the fourth year of Solomon's reign over Israel" was the same as "the four hundred and eightieth year after the Israelites had come out of Egypt" (1Ki 6:1). Since the former was c. 966 B.C., the latter—and thus the date of the exodus—was c. 1446 (assuming that the 480 in 1Ki 6:1 is to be taken literally; see Introduction.to Judges: Background). The 40-year period of Israel's wanderings in the desert, which lasted from c. 1446 to c. 1406, would have been the most likely time for Moses to write the bulk of what is today known as the Pentateuch.

During the last two centuries some scholars have claimed to find in the Pentateuch four underlying sources. The presumed documents, allegedly dating from the tenth to the fifth centuries B.C., are called *J* (for Jahweh/Yahweh, the personal OT name for God), *E* (for Elohim, a generic name for God), *D* (for Deuteronomic) and *P* (for Priestly). Each of these documents is claimed to have its own characteristics and its own theology, which often contradicts that of the other documents. The Pentateuch is thus depicted as a patchwork of stories, poems and laws. However, this view is not supported by conclusive evidence, and intensive archaeological and literary research has undercut many of the arguments used to challenge Mosaic authorship.

Theme and Message

Genesis speaks of beginnings—of the heavens and the earth, of light and darkness, of seas and skies, of land and vegetation, of sun and moon and stars, of sea and air and land animals, of human beings (made in God's own image, the climax of his creative activity), of sin and redemption, of blessing and cursing, of society and civilization, of marriage and family, of art and craft and industry. The list could go on and on. A key word in Genesis is "account," which also serves to divide the book into its ten major parts (see Literary Features and Literary Outline) and which includes such concepts as birth, genealogy and history.

The book of Genesis is foundational to the understanding of the rest of the Bible. Its message is rich and complex, and listing its main elements gives a succinct outline of the Biblical message as a whole. It is supremely a book of relationships, highlighting those between God and nature, God and man, and man and man. It is thoroughly monotheistic, taking for granted that there is only one God worthy of the name and opposing the ideas that there are many gods (polytheism), that there is no god at all (atheism) or that everything is divine (pantheism). It clearly teaches that the one true God is sovereign over all that exists (i.e., his entire creation), and that by divine election he often exercises his unlimited freedom to overturn human customs, traditions and plans. It introduces us to the way in which God initiates and makes covenants with his chosen people, pledging his love and faithfulness to them and calling them to promise theirs to him. It establishes sacrifice as the substitution of life for life (ch. 22). It gives us the first hint of God's provision for redemption from the forces of evil (compare 3:15 with Ro 16:17-20) and contains the oldest and most profound definition of faith (15:6). More than half of Heb 11—the NT roll of the faithful—refers to characters in Genesis.

Literary Features

The message of a book is often enhanced by its literary structure and characteristics. Genesis is divided into ten main sections, each beginning with the word "account" (see 2:4; 5:1; 6:9; 10:1; 11:10; 11:27; 25:12; 25:19; 36:1—repeated for emphasis at 36:9—and 37:2). The first five sections can be grouped together and, along with the introduction to the book as a whole (1:1-2:3), can be appropriately called "primeval history" (1:1-11:26), sketching the period from Adam to Abraham. The last five sections constitute a much longer (but equally unified) account, and relate the story of God's dealings with Abraham, Isaac, Jacob and Joseph and their families—a section often called "patriarchal history" (11:27-50:26). This section is in turn composed of three narrative cycles (Abraham-Isaac,

11:27-25:11; Isaac-Jacob, 25:19-35:29; 37:1; Jacob-Joseph, 37:2-50:26), interspersed by the genealogies of Ishmael (25:12-18) and Esau (ch. 36).

The narrative frequently concentrates on the life of a later son in preference to the firstborn: Seth over Cain, Shem over Japheth (but see NIV text note on 10:21), Isaac over Ishmael, Jacob over Esau, Judah and Joseph over their brothers, and Ephraim over Manasseh. Such emphasis on divinely chosen men and their families is perhaps the most obvious literary and theological characteristic of the book of Genesis as a whole. It strikingly underscores the fact that the people of God are not the product of natural human developments, but are the result of God's sovereign and gracious intrusion into human history. He brings out of the fallen human race a new humanity consecrated to himself, called and destined to be the people of his kingdom and the channel of his blessing to the whole earth.

Numbers with symbolic significance figure prominently in Genesis. The number ten, in addition to being the number of sections into which Genesis is divided, is also the number of names appearing in the genealogies of chs. 5 and 11 (see note on 5:5). The number seven also occurs frequently. The Hebrew text of 1:1 consists of exactly seven words and that of 1:2 of exactly 14 (twice seven). There are seven days of creation, seven names in the genealogy of ch. 4 (see note on 4:17-18; see also 4:15,24; 5:31), various sevens in the flood story, 70 descendants of Noah's sons (ch. 10), a sevenfold promise to Abram (12:2-3), seven years of abundance and then seven of famine in Egypt (ch. 41), and 70 descendants of Jacob (ch. 46). Other significant numbers, such as 12 and 40, are used with similar frequency.

The book of Genesis is basically prose narrative, punctuated here and there by brief poems (the longest is the so-called Blessing of Jacob in 49:2-27). Much of the prose has a lyrical quality and uses the full range of figures of speech and other devices that characterize the world's finest epic literature. Vertical and horizontal parallelism between the two sets of three days in the creation account (see note on 1:11); the ebb and flow of sin and judgment in ch. 3 (the serpent and woman and man sin successively; then God questions them in reverse order; then he judges them in the original order); the powerful monotony of "and then he died" at the end of paragraphs in ch. 5; the climactic hinge effect of the phrase "But God remembered Noah" (8:1) at the midpoint of the flood story; the hourglass structure of the account of the tower of Babel in 11:1-9 (narrative in vv. 1-2,8-9; discourse in vv. 3-4,6-7; v. 5 acting as transition); the macabre pun in 40:19 (see 40:13); the alternation between brief accounts about firstborn sons and lengthy accounts about younger sons—these and numerous other literary devices add interest to the narrative and provide interpretive signals to which the reader should pay close attention.

It is no coincidence that many of the subjects and themes of the first three chapters of Genesis are reflected in the last three chapters of Revelation. We can only marvel at the superintending influence of the Lord himself, who assures us that "all Scripture is God-breathed" (2Ti 3:16) and that the people who wrote it "spoke from God as they were carried along by the Holy Spirit" (2Pe 1:21).

Outlines

Literary Outline:

I. Introduction (1:1-2:3)
II. Body (2:4-50:26)
   A. "The account of the heavens and the earth" (2:4-4:26)
   B. "The written account of Adam's line" (5:1-6:8)
   C. "The account of Noah" (6:9-9:29)
   D. "The account of Shem, Ham and Japheth" (10:1-11:9)
   E. "The account of Shem" (11:10-26)
   F. "The account of Terah" (11:27-25:11)
   G. "The account of Abraham's son Ishmael" (25:12-18)
   H. "The account of Abraham's son Isaac" (25:19-35:29)
   I. "The account of Esau" (36:1-37:1)
   J. "The account of Jacob" (37:2-50:26)

Thematic Outline:

I. Primeval History (1:1-11:26)
   A. Creation (1:1-2:3)
      1. Introduction (1:1-2)

Ancient Texts Relating to the Old Testament

Major representative examples of ancient Near Eastern non-Biblical documents that provide parallels to or shed light on various OT passages.

AMARNA LETTERS
Canaanite Akkadian—*14th century B.C.*
Hundreds of letters, written primarily by Canaanite scribes, illuminate social, political and religious relationships between Canaan and Egypt during the reigns of Amunhotep III and Akhenaten.

AMENEMOPE'S WISDOM
Egyptian—*early 1st millennium B.C.*
Thirty chapters of wisdom instruction are similar to Pr 22:17-24:22 and provide the closest external parallels to OT wisdom literature.

ATRAHASIS EPIC
Akkadian—*early 2nd millennium B.C.*
A cosmological epic depicts creation and early human history, including the flood (cf. Ge 1-9).

BABYLONIAN THEODICY
Akkadian—*early 1st millennium B.C.*
A sufferer and his friend dialogue with each other (cf. Job).

CYRUS CYLINDER
Akkadian—*6th century B.C.*
King Cyrus of Persia records the conquest of Babylon (cf. Da 5:30; 6:28) and boasts of his generous policies toward his new subjects and their gods.

DEAD SEA SCROLLS
Hebrew, Aramaic, Greek—*3rd century B.C. to 1st century A.D.*
Several hundred scrolls and fragments include the oldest copies of OT books and passages.

EBLA TABLETS
Sumerian, Eblaite—*mid-3rd millennium B.C.*
Thousands of commercial, legal, literary and epistolary texts describe the cultural vitality and political power of a pre-patriarchal civilization in northern Syria.

ELEPHANTINE PAPYRI
Aramaic—*late 5th century B.C.*
Contracts and letters document life among Jews who fled to southern Egypt after Jerusalem was destroyed in 586 B.C.

ENUMA ELISH
Akkadian—*early 2nd millennium B.C.*
Marduk, the Babylonian god of cosmic order, is elevated to the supreme position in the pantheon. The 7-tablet epic contains an account of creation (cf. Ge 1-2).

GEZER CALENDAR
Hebrew—*10th century B.C.*
A schoolboy from west-central Israel describes the seasons, crops and farming activity of the agricultural year.

GILGAMESH EPIC
Akkadian—*early 2nd millennium B.C.*
Gilgamesh, ruler of Uruk, experiences numerous adventures, including a meeting with Utnapishtim, the only survivor of a great deluge (cf. Ge 6-9).

HAMMURAPI'S CODE
Akkadian—*18th century B.C.*
Together with similar law codes that preceded and followed it, the Code of Hammurapi exhibits close parallels to numerous passages in the Mosaic legislation of the OT.

HYMN TO THE ATEN
Egyptian—*14th century B.C.*
The poem praises the beneficence and universality of the sun in language somewhat similar to that used in Ps 104.

ISHTAR'S DESCENT
Akkadian—*1st millennium B.C.*
The goddess Ishtar temporarily descends to the netherworld, which is pictured in terms reminiscent of OT descriptions of Sheol.

JEHOIACHIN'S RATION DOCKETS
Akkadian—*early 6th century B.C.*
Brief texts from the reign of Nebuchadnezzar II refer to rations allotted to Judah's exiled king Jehoiachin and his sons (cf. 2Ki 25:27-30).

KING LISTS
Sumerian—*late 3rd millennium B.C.*
The reigns of Sumerian kings before the flood are described as lasting for thousands of years, reminding us of the longevity of the pre-flood patriarchs in Ge 5.

LACHISH LETTERS
Hebrew—*early 6th century B.C.*
Inscriptions on pottery fragments vividly portray the desperate days preceding the Babylonian siege of Jerusalem in 588-586 B.C. (cf. Jer 34:7).

LAMENTATION OVER THE DESTRUCTION OF UR
Sumerian—*early 2nd millennium B.C.*
The poem mourns the destruction of the city of Ur at the hands of the Elamites (cf. the OT book of Lamentations).

LUDLUL BEL NEMEQI
Akkadian—*late 2nd millennium B.C.*
A suffering Babylonian nobleman describes his distress in terms faintly reminiscent of the experiences of Job.

MARI TABLETS
Akkadian—*18th century B.C.*
Letters and administrative texts provide detailed information regarding customs, language and personal names that reflect the culture of the OT patriarchs.

MERNEPTAH STELE
Egyptian—*13th century B.C.*
Pharaoh Merneptah figuratively describes his victory over various peoples in western Asia, including "Israel."

MESHA STELE (MOABITE STONE)
Moabite—*9th century B.C.*
Mesha, king of Moab (see 2Ki 3:4), rebels against a successor of Israel's king Omri.

MURASHU TABLETS
Akkadian—*5th century B.C.*
Commercial documents describe financial transactions engaged in by Murashu and Sons, a Babylonian firm that did business with Jews and other exiles.

MURSILIS'S TREATY WITH DUPPI-TESSUB
Hittite—*mid-2nd millennium B.C.*
King Mursilis imposes a suzerainty treaty on King Duppi-Tessub. The literary outline of this and other Hittite treaties is strikingly paralleled in OT covenants established by God with his people.

NABONIDUS CHRONICLE
Akkadian—*mid-6th century B.C.*
The account describes the absence of King Nabonidus from Babylon. His son Belshazzar is therefore the regent in charge of the kingdom (cf. Da 5:29-30).

NEBUCHADNEZZAR CHRONICLE
Akkadian—*early 6th century B.C.*
A chronicle from the reign of Nebuchadnezzar II includes the Babylonian account of the siege of Jerusalem in 597 B.C. (see 2Ki 24:10-17).

NUZI TABLETS
Akkadian—*mid-2nd millennium B.C.*
Adoption, birthright-sale and other legal documents graphically illustrate OT patriarchal customs current centuries earlier.

PESSIMISTIC DIALOGUE
Akkadian—*early 1st millennium B.C.*
A master and his servant discuss the pros and cons of various activities (cf. Ecc 2).

RAS SHAMRA TABLETS
Ugaritic—*15th century B.C.*
Canaanite deities and rulers experience adventures in epics that enrich our understanding of Canaanite mythology and religion and of OT poetry.

SARGON LEGEND
Akkadian—*1st millennium B.C.*
Sargon I (the Great), ruler of Akkad in the late 3rd millennium B.C., claims to have been rescued as an infant from a reed basket found floating in a river (cf. Ex 2).

SARGON'S DISPLAY INSCRIPTION
Akkadian—*8th century B.C.*
Sargon II takes credit for the conquest of Samaria in 722/721 B.C. and states that he captured and exiled 27,290 Israelites.

SENNACHERIB'S PRISM
Akkadian—*early 7th century B.C.*
Sennacherib vividly describes his siege of Jerusalem in 701 B.C., making Hezekiah a prisoner in his own royal city (but cf. 2Ki 19:35-37).

SEVEN LEAN YEARS TRADITION
Egyptian—*2nd century B.C.*
Egypt experiences 7 years of low Niles and famine, which, by a contractual agreement between Pharaoh Djoser (28th century B.C.) and a god, will be followed by prosperity (cf. Ge 41).

SHALMANESER'S BLACK OBELISK
Akkadian—*9th century B.C.*
Israel's king Jehu (or his servant) presents tribute to Assyria's king Shalmaneser III. Additional Assyrian and Babylonian texts refer to other kings of Israel and Judah.

SHISHAK'S GEOGRAPHICAL LIST
Egyptian—*10th century B.C.*
Pharaoh Shishak lists the cities that he captured or made tributary during his campaign in Judah and Israel (cf. 1Ki 14:25-26).

SILOAM INSCRIPTION
Hebrew—*late 8th century B.C.*
A Judahite workman describes the construction of an underground conduit to guarantee Jerusalem's water supply during Hezekiah's reign (cf. 2Ki 20:20; 2Ch 32:30).

SINUHE'S STORY
Egyptian—*20th-19th centuries B.C.*
An Egyptian official of the 12th dynasty goes into voluntary exile in Syria and Canaan during the OT patriarchal period.

TALE OF TWO BROTHERS
Egyptian—*13th century B.C.*
A young man rejects the amorous advances of his older brother's wife (cf. Ge 39).

WENAMUN'S JOURNEY
Egyptian—*11th century B.C.*
An official of the Temple of Amun at Thebes in Egypt is sent to Byblos in Canaan to buy lumber for the ceremonial barge of his god.

The Beginning

1 In the beginning[a] God created[b] the heavens[c] and the earth.[d] ²Now the earth was[a] formless[e] and empty,[f] darkness was over the surface of the deep,[g] and the Spirit of God[h] was hovering[i] over the waters.

³And God said,[j] "Let there be light," and there was light.[k] ⁴God saw that the light was good,[l] and he separated the light from the darkness.[m] ⁵God called[n] the light "day," and the darkness he called "night."[o] And there was evening, and there was morning[p]—the first day.

⁶And God said,[q] "Let there be an expanse[r] between the waters[s] to separate water from water." ⁷So God made the expanse and separated the water under the expanse from the water above it.[t] And it was so.[u]

⁸God called[v] the expanse "sky."[w] And there was evening, and there was morning[x]—the second day.

⁹And God said, "Let the water under the sky be gathered to one place,[y] and let dry ground[z] appear." And it was so.[a] ¹⁰God called[b] the dry ground "land," and the gathered waters[c] he called "seas."[d] And God saw that it was good.[e]

¹¹Then God said, "Let the land

1:1 [a]Ps 102:25; Pr 8:23; Isa 40:21; 41:4, 26; Jn 1:1-2 [b]ver 21,27; Ge 2:3 [c]ver 6; Ne 9:6; Job 9:8; 37:18; Ps 96:5; 104:2; 115:15; 121:2; 136:5; Isa 40:22; 42:5; 51:13; Jer 10:12; 51:15 [d]Ge 14:19; 2Ki 19:15; Ne 9:6; Job 38:4; Ps 90:2; 136:6; 146:6; Isa 37:16; 40:28; 42:5; 44:24; 45:12,18; Jer 27:5; 32:17; Ac 14:15; 17:24; Eph 3:9; Col 1:16; Heb 3:4; 11:3; Rev 4:11; 10:6 **1:2** [e]Isa 23:1; 24:10; 27:10; 32:14; 34:11 [f]Isa 45:18; Jer 4:23 [g]Ge 8:2; Job 7:12; 26:8; 38:9; Ps 36:6; 42:7; 104:6; 107:24; Pr 30:4 [h]Ge 2:7;

Job 33:4; Ps 104:30; Isa 32:15 [i]Dt 32:11; Isa 31:5 **1:3** [j]ver 6; Ps 33:6,9; 148:5; Heb 11:3 [k]2Co 4:6*; 1Jn 1:5-7 **1:4** [l]ver 10,12,18,21,25,31; Ps 104:31; 119:68; Jer 31:35 [m]ver 14; Ex 10:21-23; Job 26:10; 38:19; Ps 18:28; 104:20; 105:28; Isa 42:16; 45:7 **1:5** [n]ver 8,10; Ge 2:19,23 [o]Ps 74:16 [p]ver 8, 13,19,23,31 **1:6** [q]S ver 3 [r]S ver 1; Isa 44:24; 2Pe 3:5 [s]ver 9; Ps 24:2; 136:6 **1:7** [t]Ge 7:11; Job 26:10; 38:8-11,16; Ps 68:33; 148:4; Pr 8:28 [u]ver 9,11,15,24 **1:8** [v]S ver 5 [w]Job 9:8; 37:18; Ps 19:1; 104:2; Isa 40:22; 44:24; 45:12; Jer 10:12; Zec 12:1 [x]S ver 5 **1:9** [y]Job 38:8-11; Ps 33:7; 104:6-9; Pr 8:29; Jer 5:22; 2Pe 3:5 [z]Ps 95:5; Jnh 1:9; Hag 2:6 [a]S ver 7 **1:10** [b]S ver 5 [c]Ps 33:7 [d]Job 38:8; Ps 90:2; 95:5 [e]S ver 4

[a]2 Or possibly *became*

1:1 A summary statement introducing the six days of creative activity. The truth of this majestic verse was joyfully affirmed by poet (Ps 102:25) and prophet (Isa 40:21). *In the beginning God.* The Bible always assumes, and never argues, God's existence. Although everything else had a beginning, God has always been (Ps 90:2). *In the beginning.* Jn 1:1–10, which stresses the work of Christ in creation, opens with the same phrase. *God created.* The Hebrew noun *Elohim* is plural but the verb is singular, a normal usage in the OT when reference is to the one true God. This use of the plural expresses intensification rather than number and has been called the plural of majesty, or of potentiality. In the OT the Hebrew verb for "create" is used only of divine, never of human, activity. *the heavens and the earth.* "All things" (Isa 44:24). That God created everything is also taught in Ecc 1:5; Jer 10:16; Jn 1:3; Col 1:16; Heb 1:2. The positive, life-oriented teaching of v. 1 is beautifully summarized in Isa 45:18.

1:2 *earth.* The focus of this account. *formless and empty.* The phrase, which appears elsewhere only in Jer 4:23, gives structure to the rest of the chapter (see note on v. 11). God's "separating" and "gathering" on days 1–3 gave form, and his "making" and "filling" on days 4–6 removed the emptiness. *darkness . . . the waters.* Completes the picture of a world awaiting God's light-giving, order-making and life-creating word. *and.* Or "but." The awesome (and, for ancient man, fearful) picture of the original state of the visible creation is relieved by the majestic announcement that the mighty Spirit of God hovers over creation. The announcement anticipates God's creative words that follow. *Spirit of God.* He was active in creation, and his creative power continues today (see Job 33:4; Ps 104:30). *hovering over.* Like a bird that provides for and protects its young (see Dt 32:11; Isa 31:5). The imagery may also suggest the winged sun disk, which throughout the ancient Near East was a symbol of divine majesty.

1:3 *God said.* Merely by speaking, God brought all things into being (Ps 33:6,9; 148:5; Heb 11:3). *Let there be light.* God's first creative word called forth light in the midst of the primeval darkness. Light is necessary for making God's creative works visible and life possible. In the OT it is also symbolic of life and blessing (see 2Sa 22:29; Job 3:20; 30:26; 33:30; Ps 49:19; 56:13; 97:11; 112:4; Isa 53:11; 58:8,10; 59:9; 60:1,3). Paul uses this word to illustrate

God's re-creating work in sin-darkened hearts (2Co 4:6).

1:4 Everything God created is good (see vv. 10,12,18,21, 25); in fact, the conclusion declares it to be "very good" (v. 31). The creation, as fashioned and ordered by God, had no lingering traces of disorder and no dark and threatening forces arrayed against God or man. Even darkness and the deep were given benevolent functions in a world fashioned to bless and sustain life (see Ps 104:19–26; 127:2).

1:5 *called.* See vv. 8,10. In ancient times, to name something or someone implied having dominion or ownership (see 17:5,15; 41:45; 2Ki 23:34; 24:17; Da 1:7). Both day and night belong to the Lord (Ps 74:16). *first day.* Some say that the creation days were 24-hour days, others that they were indefinite periods.

1:6 *expanse.* The atmosphere, or "sky" (v. 8), as seen from the earth. "Hard as a mirror" (Job 37:18) and "like a canopy" (Isa 40:22) are among the many pictorial phrases used to describe it.

1:7 *And it was so.* The only possible outcome, whether stated (vv. 9,11,15,24,30) or implied, to God's "Let there be."

1:9 *one place.* A picturesque way of referring to the "seas" (v. 10) that surround the dry ground on all sides and into which the waters of the lakes and rivers flow. The earth was "formed out of water" (2Pe 3:5) and "founded . . . upon the seas" (Ps 24:2), and the waters are not to cross the boundaries set for them (Ps 104:7–9; Jer 5:22).

1:11 *God said.* This phrase is used twice on the third day (vv. 9,11) and three times (vv. 24,26,29) on the sixth day. These two days are climactic, as the following structure of ch. 1 reveals (see note on v. 2 regarding "formless and empty"):

Days of forming	Days of filling
1. "light" (v. 3)	4. "lights" (v. 14)
2. "water under the expanse . . . water above it" (v. 7)	5. "every living and moving thing with which the water teems . . . every winged bird" (v. 21)
3a. "dry ground" (v. 9)	6a₁. "livestock, creatures that move along the ground, and wild animals" (v. 24)
	a₂. "man" (v. 26)
b. "vegetation" (v. 11)	b. "every green plant for food" (v. 30)

produce vegetation:*f* seed-bearing plants and trees on the land that bear fruit with seed in it, according to their various kinds.*g*" And it was so.*h* 12The land produced vegetation: plants bearing seed according to their kinds*i* and trees bearing fruit with seed in it according to their kinds. And God saw that it was good.*j* 13And there was evening, and there was morning*k*—the third day.

14And God said, "Let there be lights*l* in the expanse of the sky to separate the day from the night,*m* and let them serve as signs*n* to mark seasons*o* and days and years,*p* 15and let them be lights in the expanse of the sky to give light on the earth." And it was so.*q* 16God made two great lights—the greater light*r* to govern*s* the day and the lesser light to govern*t* the night.*u* He also made the stars.*v* 17God set them in the expanse of the sky to give light on the earth, 18to govern the day and the night,*w* and to separate light from darkness. And God saw that it was good.*x* 19And there was evening, and there was morning*y*—the fourth day.

20And God said, "Let the water teem with living creatures,*z* and let birds fly above the earth across the expanse of the sky."*a* 21So God created*b* the great creatures of the sea*c* and every

living and moving thing with which the water teems,*d* according to their kinds, and every winged bird according to its kind.*e* And God saw that it was good.*f* 22God blessed them and said, "Be fruitful and increase in number and fill the water in the seas, and let the birds increase on the earth."*g* 23And there was evening, and there was morning*h*—the fifth day.

24And God said, "Let the land produce living creatures*i* according to their kinds:*j* livestock, creatures that move along the ground, and wild animals, each according to its kind." And it was so.*k* 25God made the wild animals*l* according to their kinds, the livestock according to their kinds, and all the creatures that move along the ground according to their kinds.*m* And God saw that it was good.*n*

26Then God said, "Let us*o* make man*p* in our image,*q* in our likeness,*r* and let them rule*s* over the fish of the sea and the birds of the air,*t* over the livestock, over all the earth,*b* and over all the creatures that move along the ground."

1:11 *f* Ps 65:9-13; 104:14 *g* ver 12, 21,24,25; Ge 2:5; 6:20; 7:14; Lev 11:14,19,22; Dt 14:13,18; 1Co 15:38 *h* S ver 7
1:12 *i* S ver 11 /S ver 4
1:13 *k* S ver 5
1:14 *l* Ps 74:16; 136:7 *m* S ver 4 *n* Jer 10:2 *o* Ps 104:19 *p* Ge 8:22; Jer 31:35-36; 33:20,25
1:15 *q* S ver 7
1:16 *r* Dt 17:3; Job 31:26; Jer 43:13; Eze 8:16 *s* Ps 136:8 *t* Ps 136:9 *u* Job 38:33; Ps 74:16; 104:19; Jer 31:35; Jas 1:17 *v* Dt 4:19; Job 9:9; 38:7, 31-32; Ps 8:3; 33:6; Ecc 12:2; Isa 40:26; Jer 8:2; Am 5:8
1:18 *w* Jer 33:20, 25 *x* S ver 4
1:19 *y* S ver 5
1:20 *z* Ps 146:6 *a* Ge 2:19
1:21 *b* S ver 1 *c* Job 3:8; 7:12; Ps 74:13; 148:7; Isa 27:1; Eze 32:2

d Ps 104:25-26 *e* S ver 11 /S ver 4
1:22 *g* ver 28; Ge 8:17; 9:1,7, 19; 47:27; Lev 26:9; Eze 36:11
1:23 *h* S ver 5
1:24 *i* Ge 2:19 /S ver 11 *k* S ver 7
1:25 *l* Ge 7:21-22; Jer 27:5 *m* S ver

---

11 *n* S ver 4 **1:26** *o* Ge 3:5,22; 11:7; Ps 100:3; Isa 6:8 *p* Isa 45:18 *q* ver 27; Ge 5:3; 9:6; Ps 8:5; 82:6; 89:6; 1Co 11:7; 2Co 4:4; Col 1:15; 3:10; Jas 3:9 *r* Ac 17:28-29 *s* Ge 9:2; Ps 8:6-8 *t* Ps 8:8

b 26 Hebrew; Syriac *all the wild animals*

Both the horizontal and vertical relationships between the days demonstrate the literary beauty of the chapter and stress the orderliness and symmetry of God's creative activity. *kinds.* See vv. 12,21,24–25. Both creation and reproduction are orderly.

1:14 *serve as signs.* In the ways mentioned here, not in any astrological or other such sense.

1:16 *two great lights.* The words "sun" and "moon" seem to be avoided deliberately here, since both were used as proper names for the pagan deities associated with these heavenly bodies. They are light-givers to be appreciated, not powers to be feared, because the one true God made them (see Isa 40:26). Perhaps because of the emphasis on the greater light and lesser light, the stars seem to be mentioned almost as an afterthought. But Ps 136:9 indicates that the stars help the moon "govern the night." *to govern.* The great Creator-King assigns subordinate regulating roles to certain of his creatures (see vv. 26,28).

1:17–18 The three main functions of the heavenly bodies.

1:21 *creatures of the sea.* The Hebrew word underlying this phrase was used in Canaanite mythology to name a dreaded sea monster. He is often referred to figuratively in OT poetry as one of God's most powerful opponents. He is pictured as national (Babylon, Jer 51:34; Egypt, Isa 51:9; Eze 29:3; 32:2) or cosmic (Job 7:12; Ps 74:13; Isa 27:1, though some take the latter as a reference to Egypt). In Genesis, however, the creatures of the sea are portrayed not

as enemies to be feared but as part of God's good creation to be appreciated. *winged bird.* The term denotes anything that flies, including insects (see Dt 14:19–20).

1:22 *Be fruitful and increase in number.* God's benediction on living things that inhabit the water and that fly in the air. By his blessing they flourish and fill both realms with life (see note on v. 28). God's rule over his created realm promotes and blesses life.

1:26 *us . . . our . . . our.* God speaks as the Creator-King, announcing his crowning work to the members of his heavenly court (see 3:22; 11:7; Isa 6:8; see also 1Ki 22:19–23; Job 15:8; Jer 23:18). *image . . . likeness.* No distinction should be made between "image" and "likeness," which are synonyms in both the OT (5:1; 9:6) and the NT (1Co 11:7; Col 3:10; Jas 3:9). Since man is made in God's image, every human being is worthy of honor and respect; he is neither to be murdered (9:6) nor cursed (Jas 3:9). "Image" includes such characteristics as "righteousness and holiness" (Eph 4:24) and "knowledge" (Col 3:10). Believers are to be "conformed to the likeness" of Christ (Ro 8:29) and will someday be "like him" (1Jn 3:2). *rule.* Man is the climax of God's creative activity, and God has "crowned him with glory and honor" and "made him ruler" over the rest of his creation (Ps 8:5–8). Since man was created in the image of the divine King, delegated sovereignty (kingship) was bestowed on him. (For redeemed man's ultimate kingship see notes on Heb 2:5–9.)

27So God created[u] man[v] in his own
image,[w]
in the image of God[x] he created
him;
male and female[y] he created them.[z]

28God blessed them and said to
them,[a] "Be fruitful and increase in
number;[b] fill the earth[c] and subdue
it. Rule over[d] the fish of the sea and
the birds of the air and over every
living creature that moves on the
ground.[e]"

29Then God said, "I give you every
seed-bearing plant on the face of the
whole earth and every tree that has
fruit with seed in it. They will be
yours for food.[f] 30And to all the
beasts of the earth and all the birds
of the air and all the creatures that
move on the ground—everything
that has the breath of life[g] in it—I
give every green plant for food.[h]"
And it was so.

31God saw all that he had made,[i]
and it was very good.[j] And there
was evening, and there was morning[k]—the sixth day.

2 Thus the heavens and the earth
were completed in all their vast
array.[l]

2By the seventh day[m] God had finished
the work he had been doing; so on
the seventh day he rested[c] from all
his work.[n] 3And God blessed the
seventh day and made it holy,[o] because on it he rested[p] from all the
work of creating[q] that he had done.

Adam and Eve

4This is the account[r] of the heavens and
the earth when they were created.[s]

When the LORD God made the earth
and the heavens— 5and no shrub of the
field had yet appeared on the earth[d] and
no plant of the field had yet sprung up,[t]
for the LORD God had not sent rain on the
earth[d][u] and there was no man to work
the ground, 6but streams[e] came up from
the earth and watered the whole surface of
the ground— 7the LORD God formed[v] the

1:27 uS ver 1
vGe 2:7;
Ps 103:14;
119:73, wS ver 26
xGe 5:1, yGe 5:2;
Mt 19:4*;
Mk 10:6*;
Gal 3:28, zDt 4:32
1:28 aGe 33:5;
Jos 24:3;
Ps 113:9; 127:3,5
bS Ge 17:6, cS ver
22; Ge 6:1;
Ac 17:26, dver 26;
Ps 115:16
ePs 8:6-8
1:29 fGe 9:3;
Dt 12:15;
Ps 104:14;
1Ti 4:3
1:30 gGe 2:7;
7:22, hJob 38:41;
Ps 78:25; 104:14,
27; 111:5;
136:25; 145:15;
147:9
1:31 iPs 104:24;
136:5; Pr 3:19;
Jer 10:12, jS ver 4;
1Ti 4:4, kS ver 5

2:1 lDt 4:19;
17:3; 2Ki 17:16;
21:3; Ps 104:2;
Isa 44:24; 45:12;
48:13; 51:13
2:2 mDt 5:14
nver 2-3;
Ex 20:11; 31:17;
34:21; Jn 5:17;
Heb 4:4*
2:3 oEx 16:23;
20:10; 23:12;
31:15; 35:2;
Lev 23:3;
Ne 9:14;
Isa 58:13;

Jer 17:22 pPs 95:11; Heb 4:1-11 qS Ge 1:1 2:4 rGe 5:1; 6:9;
10:1; 11:10,27; 25:12,19; 36:1,9; 37:2 sGe 1:1; Job 38:8-11
2:5 tS Ge 1:11 uJob 38:28; Ps 65:9-10; Jer 10:13 2:7
vIsa 29:16; 43:1,21; 44:2

c2 Or ceased; also in verse 3   d5 Or land; also in
verse 6   e6 Or mist

1:27 This highly significant verse is the first occurrence of
poetry in the OT (which is about 40 percent poetry). created.
The word is used here three times to describe the central
divine act of the sixth day (see note on v. 1). male and
female. Alike they bear the image of God, and together they
share in the divine benediction that follows.
1:28 God blessed them . . . fill . . . subdue . . . Rule. Man
goes forth under this divine benediction—flourishing, filling
the earth with his kind, and exercising dominion over the
other earthly creatures (see v. 26; 2:15; Ps 8:6-8). Human
culture, accordingly, is not anti-God (though fallen man
often has turned his efforts into proud rebellion against God).
Rather, it is the expression of man's bearing the image of his
Creator and sharing, as God's servant, in God's kingly rule.
As God's representative in the creaturely realm, he is steward of God's creatures. He is not to exploit, waste or despoil
them, but to care for them and use them in the service of God
and man.
1:29-30 People and animals seem to be portrayed as
originally vegetarian (see 9:3).
1:31 very good. See note on v. 4. the sixth day. Perhaps to
stress the finality and importance of this day, in the Hebrew
text the definite article is first used here in regard to the
creation days.
2:2 finished . . . rested. God rested on the seventh day, not
because he was weary, but because nothing formless or
empty remained (see NIV text note). His creative work was
completed—and it was totally effective, absolutely perfect,
"very good" (1:31). It did not have to be repeated, repaired
or revised, and the Creator rested to commemorate it.
2:3 God blessed the seventh day and made it holy . . .
rested. Although the word "Sabbath" is not used here, the
Hebrew verb translated "rested" (see v. 2) is the origin of the
noun "Sabbath." Ex 20:11 quotes the first half of v. 3, but
substitutes "Sabbath" for "seventh," clearly equating the

two. The first record of obligatory Sabbath observance is of
Israel on her way from Egypt to Sinai (Ex 16), and according
to Ne 9:13-14 the Sabbath was not an official covenant
obligation until the giving of the law at Mount Sinai.
2:4 account. The word occurs ten times in Genesis—at the
beginning of each main section (see Introduction: Literary
Features). the heavens and the earth. See note on 1:1. The
phrase "the account of the heavens and the earth" introduces the record of what happened to God's creation. The
blight of sin and rebellion brought a threefold curse that
darkens the story of Adam and Eve in God's good and
beautiful garden: (1) on Satan (3:14); (2) on the ground,
because of man (3:17); and (3) on Cain (4:11). 1:1–2:3 is a
general account of creation, while 2:4–4:26 focuses on the
beginning of human history. LORD God. "LORD" (Hebrew
YHWH, "Yahweh") is the personal and covenant name of
God (see note on Ex 3:15), emphasizing his role as Israel's
Redeemer and covenant Lord (see note on Ex 6:6), while
"God" (Hebrew Elohim) is a general term. Both names occur
thousands of times in the OT, and often, as here, they appear
together—clearly indicating that they refer to the same one
and only God.
2:7 formed. The Hebrew for this verb commonly referred
to the work of a potter (see Isa 45:9; Jer 18:6), who fashions
vessels from clay (see Job 33:6). "Make" (1:26), "create"
(1:27) and "form" are used to describe God's creation of
both man and animals (v. 19; 1:21,25). breath of life. Humans and animals alike have the breath of life in them (see
1:30; Job 33:4). man became a living being. The Hebrew
phrase here translated "living being" is translated "living
creatures" in 1:20,24. The words of 2:7 therefore imply that
people, at least physically, have affinity with the animals. The
great difference is that man is made "in the image of God"
(1:27) and has an absolutely unique relation both to God as
his servant and to the other creatures as their divinely ap-

man[f][w] from the dust[x] of the ground[y] and breathed into his nostrils the breath[z] of life,[a] and the man became a living being.[b]

[8]Now the LORD God had planted a garden in the east, in Eden;[c] and there he put the man he had formed. [9]And the LORD God made all kinds of trees grow out of the ground—trees[d] that were pleasing to the eye and good for food. In the middle of the garden were the tree of life[e] and the tree of the knowledge of good and evil.[f]

[10]A river[g] watering the garden flowed from Eden;[h] from there it was separated into four headwaters. [11]The name of the first is the Pishon; it winds through the entire land of Havilah,[i] where there is gold. [12](The gold of that land is good; aromatic resin[g][j] and onyx are also there.) [13]The name of the second river is the Gihon; it winds through the entire land of Cush.[h] [14]The name of the third river is the Tigris;[k] it runs along the east side of Asshur. And the fourth river is the Euphrates.[l]

[15]The LORD God took the man and put him in the Garden of Eden[m] to work it and take care of it. [16]And the LORD God commanded the man, "You are free to eat from any tree in the garden;[n] [17]but you must not eat from the tree of the knowledge of good and evil,[o] for when you eat of it you will surely die."[p]

[18]The LORD God said, "It is not good for the man to be alone. I will make a helper suitable for him."[q]

[19]Now the LORD God had formed out of the ground all the beasts of the field[r] and all the birds of the air.[s] He brought them to the man to see what he would name them; and whatever the man called[t] each living creature,[u] that was its name. [20]So the man gave names to all the livestock, the birds of the air and all the beasts of the field.

But for Adam[i] no suitable helper[v] was found. [21]So the LORD God caused the man to fall into a deep sleep;[w] and while he was sleeping, he took one of the man's ribs[j] and closed up the place with flesh. [22]Then the LORD God made a woman from the rib[k][x] he had taken out of the man, and he brought her to the man.

[23]The man said,

"This is now bone of my bones
    and flesh of my flesh;[y]
she shall be called[z] 'woman,[l] '
    for she was taken out of man.[a]"

[24]For this reason a man will leave his fa-

Reference column:

2:7 wS Ge 1:27;
xGe 3:19; 18:27;
Job 4:19; 10:9;
17:16; 34:15;
Ps 90:3; Ecc 3:20;
12:7 yGe 3:23;
4:2; Ps 103:14;
Jer 18:6;
1Co 15:47
zS Ge 1:2;
Job 27:3; Isa 2:22
aS Ge 1:30;
Isa 42:5;
Ac 17:25
bJob 12:10; 32:8;
33:4; 34:14;
Ps 104:29;
Isa 57:16;
Eze 37:5;
1Co 15:45*
2:8 cver 10,15;
Ge 3:23,24; 4:16;
13:10; Isa 51:3;
Eze 28:13; 31:9,
16; 36:35;
Joel 2:3
2:9 dEze 31:8
eGe 3:22,24;
Pr 3:18; 11:30;
S Rev 2:7
fEze 47:12
2:10 gNu 24:6;
Ps 46:4; Eze 47:5
hS ver 8
2:11 iGe 10:7;
25:18
2:12 jNu 11:7
2:14 kGe 41:1;
Da 10:4
lGe 15:18; 31:21;
Ex 23:31;
Nu 22:5; Dt 1:7;
11:24; Jos 1:4;
2Sa 8:3; 1Ki 4:21;
2Ki 23:29; 24:7;
1Ch 5:9; 18:3;
2Ch 35:20;
Jer 13:4; 46:2;
51:63; S Rev 9:14
2:15 mS ver 8
2:16 nGe 3:1-2
2:17 oGe 3:11,17
pGe 3:1,3; 5:5;
9:29; Dt 30:15,
19; Jer 42:16;
Eze 3:18;

S Ro 5:12; S 6:23 2:18 qPr 31:11; 1Co 11:9; 1Ti 2:13 2:19 rPs 8:7 sS Ge 1:20 tS Ge 1:5 uGe 1:24 2:20 vGe 3:20; 4:1 2:21 wGe 15:12; 1Sa 26:12; Job 33:15 2:22 x1Co 11:8,9,12; 1Ti 2:13 2:23 yGe 29:14; Eph 5:28-30 zS Ge 1:5 a1Co 11:8

f7 The Hebrew for man (adam) sounds like and may be related to the Hebrew for ground (adamah); it is also the name Adam (see Gen. 2:20).   g12 Or good; pearls   h13 Possibly southeast Mesopotamia   i20 Or the man   j21 Or took part of the man's side   k22 Or part   l23 The Hebrew for woman sounds like the Hebrew for man.

Study notes:

pointed steward (Ps 8:5–8).

2:8 *in the east.* From the standpoint of the author of Genesis. The garden was perhaps near where the Tigris and Euphrates rivers (see v. 14) meet, in what is today southern Iraq. *Eden.* A name synonymous with "paradise" and related to either (1) a Hebrew word meaning "bliss" or "delight" or (2) a Mesopotamian word meaning "a plain." Perhaps the author subtly suggests both.

2:9 *tree of life.* Signifying and giving life, without death, to those who eat its fruit (see 3:22; Rev 2:7; 22:2,14). *tree of the knowledge of good and evil.* Signifying and giving knowledge of good and evil, leading ultimately to death, to those who eat its fruit (v. 17; 3:3). "Knowledge of good and evil" refers to moral knowledge or ethical discernment (see Dt 1:39; Isa 7:15–16). Adam and Eve possessed both life and moral discernment as they came from the hand of God. Their access to the fruit of the tree of life showed that God's will and intention for them was life. Ancient pagans believed that the gods intended for man always to be mortal. In eating the fruit of the tree of the knowledge of good and evil, Adam and Eve sought a creaturely source of discernment in order to be morally independent of God.

2:11 *Pishon.* Location unknown. The Hebrew word may be a common noun meaning "gusher." *Havilah.* Location unknown; perhaps mentioned again in 10:29. It is probably to be distinguished from the Havilah of 10:7, which was in Egypt.

2:13 *Gihon.* Location unknown. The Hebrew word may be

a common noun meaning "spurter." Both the Pishon and the Gihon may have been streams in Lower Mesopotamia near the Persian Gulf. The names were those current when Moses wrote.

2:14 *Asshur.* An ancient capital city of Assyria ("Assyria" and "Asshur" are related words). *Euphrates.* Often called simply "the River" (1Ki 4:21,24) because of its size and importance.

2:15 *work . . . take care.* See note on 1:28. Man is now charged to govern the earth responsibly under God's sovereignty.

2:16 *any tree.* Including the tree of life (v. 9).

2:17 *surely die.* Despite the serpent's denial (3:4), disobeying God ultimately results in death.

2:18–25 The only full account of the creation of woman in ancient Near Eastern literature.

2:18 *not good . . . to be alone.* Without female companionship and a partner in reproduction, the man could not fully realize his humanity.

2:19 *name them.* His first act of dominion over the creatures around him (see note on 1:5).

2:24 *leave his father and mother.* Instead of remaining under the protective custody of his parents a man leaves them and, with his wife, establishes a new family unit. *united . . . one flesh.* The divine intention for husband and wife was monogamy. Together they were to form an inseparable union, of which "one flesh" is both a sign and an expression.

ther and mother and be united[b] to his wife, and they will become one flesh.[c]

25The man and his wife were both naked,[d] and they felt no shame.

The Fall of Man

3 Now the serpent[e] was more crafty than any of the wild animals the LORD God had made. He said to the woman, "Did God really say, 'You must not eat from any tree in the garden'?[f]"

2The woman said to the serpent, "We may eat fruit from the trees in the garden,[g] 3but God did say, 'You must not eat fruit from the tree that is in the middle of the garden, and you must not touch it, or you will die.'"[h]

4"You will not surely die," the serpent said to the woman.[i] 5"For God knows that when you eat of it your eyes will be opened, and you will be like God,[j] knowing good and evil."

6When the woman saw that the fruit of the tree was good for food and pleasing to the eye, and also desirable[k] for gaining wisdom, she took some and ate it. She also gave some to her husband,[l] who was with her, and he ate it.[m] 7Then the eyes of both of them were opened, and they realized they were naked;[n] so they sewed fig leaves together and made coverings for themselves.[o]

8Then the man and his wife heard the sound of the LORD God as he was walk-ing[p] in the garden in the cool of the day, and they hid[q] from the LORD God among the trees of the garden. 9But the LORD God called to the man, "Where are you?"[r]

10He answered, "I heard you in the garden, and I was afraid[s] because I was naked;[t] so I hid."

11And he said, "Who told you that you were naked?[u] Have you eaten from the tree that I commanded you not to eat from?[v]"

12The man said, "The woman you put here with me[w]—she gave me some fruit from the tree, and I ate it."

13Then the LORD God said to the woman, "What is this you have done?"

The woman said, "The serpent deceived me,[x] and I ate."

14So the LORD God said to the serpent, "Because you have done this,

"Cursed[y] are you above all the
     livestock
and all the wild animals!
You will crawl on your belly
     and you will eat dust[z]
     all the days of your life.
15And I will put enmity
     between you and the woman,
     and between your offspring[m][a] and
       hers;[b]

2:24 [b]Mal 2:15 [c]Mt 19:5*; Mk 10:7-8*; 1Co 6:16*; Eph 5:31* **2:25** [d]Ge 3:7, 10-11; Isa 47:3; La 1:8 **3:1** [e]Job 1:7; 2:2; 2Co 11:3; Rev 12:9; 20:2 [f]S Ge 2:17 **3:2** [g]Ge 2:16 **3:3** [h]S Ge 2:17 **3:4** [i]S Jn 8:44; 2Co 11:3 **3:5** [j]S Ge 1:26; 14:18,19; Ps 7:8; Isa 14:14; Eze 28:2 **3:6** [k]Jas 1:14-15; 1Jn 2:16 [l]Nu 30:7-8; Jer 44:15,19,24 [m]2Co 11:3; 1Ti 2:14 **3:7** [n]Ge 2:25 [o]ver 21 **3:8** [p]Lev 26:12; Dt 23:14 [q]Job 13:16; 23:7; 31:33; 34:22,23; Ps 5:5; 139:7-12; Isa 29:15; Jer 16:17; 23:24; 49:10; Rev 6:15-16 **3:9** [r]Ge 4:9; 16:8; 18:9; 1Ki 19:9,13 **3:10** [s]Ex 19:16; 20:18; Dt 5:5; 1Sa 12:18 [t]Ge 2:25 **3:11** [u]Ge 2:25 [v]S Ge 2:17 **3:12** [w]Ge 2:22 **3:13** [x]Ro 7:11; 2Co 11:3; 1Ti 2:14 **3:14** [y]Dt 28:15-20 [z]Ps 72:9; Isa 49:23; 65:25; Mic 7:17 **3:15** [a]Jn 8:44; Ac 13:10; 1Jn 3:8 [b]Ge 16:11; Jdg 13:5; Isa 7:14; 8:3; 9:6; Mt 1:23; Lk 1:31; Gal 4:4; Rev 12:17

[m]15 Or seed

2:25 *naked . . . no shame.* Freedom from shame, signifying moral innocence, would soon be lost as a result of sin (see 3:7).
3:1 *serpent.* The great deceiver clothed himself as a serpent, one of God's good creatures. He insinuated a falsehood and portrayed rebellion as clever, but essentially innocent, self-interest. Therefore "the devil, or Satan," is later referred to as "that ancient serpent" (Rev 12:9; 20:2). *crafty.* The Hebrew words for "crafty" and "naked" are almost identical. Though naked, the man and his wife felt no shame (2:25). The craftiness of the serpent led them to sin, and they then became ashamed of their nakedness (see v. 7). *Did God really say . . . ?* The question and the response changed the course of human history. By causing the woman to doubt God's word, Satan brought evil into the world. Here the deceiver undertook to alienate man from God. In Job 1-2 he, as the accuser, acted to alienate God from man (see also Zec 3:1).
3:3 *and you must not touch it.* The woman adds to God's word, distorting his directive and demonstrating that the serpent's subtle challenge was working its poison.
3:4 *You will not surely die.* The blatant denial of a specific divine pronouncement (see 2:17).
3:5 *God knows.* Satan accuses God of having unworthy motives. In Job 1:9-11; 2:4-5 he accuses the righteous man of the same. *your eyes will be opened, and you will be like God.* The statement is only half true. Their eyes were opened, to be sure (see v. 7), but the result was quite different from what the serpent had promised. *knowing good*

and evil. See note on 2:9.
3:6 *good for food . . . pleasing to the eye . . . desirable for gaining wisdom.* Three aspects of temptation. Cf. 1Jn 2:16; Lk 4:3,5,9.
3:7 *they realized they were naked.* No longer innocent like children, they had a new awareness of themselves and of each other in their nakedness and shame. *they . . . made coverings.* Their own feeble and futile attempt to hide their shame, which only God could cover (see note on v. 21).
3:8 *the garden.* Once a place of joy and fellowship with God, it became a place of fear and of hiding from God.
3:9 *Where are you?* A rhetorical question (see 4:9).
3:12 *The woman you put here . . . gave me.* The man blames God and the woman—anyone but himself—for his sin.
3:13 *The serpent deceived me.* The woman blames the serpent rather than herself.
3:14 *Cursed.* The serpent, the woman and the man were all judged, but only the serpent and the ground were cursed—the latter because of Adam (v. 17). *dust.* The symbol of death itself (v. 19) would be the serpent's food.
3:15 *he will crush your head, and you will strike his heel.* The antagonism between people and snakes is used to symbolize the outcome of the titanic struggle between God and the evil one, a struggle played out in the hearts and history of mankind. The offspring of the woman would eventually crush the serpent's head, a promise fulfilled in Christ's victory over Satan—a victory in which all believers will share (see Ro 16:20).

he will crush[n] your head,[c]
and you will strike his heel."

[16]To the woman he said,

"I will greatly increase your pains in
    childbearing;
with pain you will give birth to
    children.[d]
Your desire will be for your husband,
    and he will rule over you.[e]"

[17]To Adam he said, "Because you listened to your wife and ate from the tree
about which I commanded you, 'You must
not eat of it,'[f]

"Cursed[g] is the ground[h] because of
    you;
through painful toil[i] you will eat of it
    all the days of your life.[j]
[18]It will produce thorns and thistles[k] for
    you,
    and you will eat the plants of the
    field.[l]
[19]By the sweat of your brow[m]
    you will eat your food[n]
until you return to the ground,
    since from it you were taken;
for dust you are
    and to dust you will return."[o]

[20]Adam[o] named his wife Eve,[p][p] because she would become the mother of all
the living.
[21]The LORD God made garments of skin
for Adam and his wife and clothed them.[q]

---

[22]And the LORD God said, "The man has
now become like one of us,[r] knowing
good and evil. He must not be allowed to
reach out his hand and take also from the
tree of life[s] and eat, and live forever." [23]So
the LORD God banished him from the Garden of Eden[t] to work the ground[u] from
which he had been taken. [24]After he drove
the man out, he placed on the east side[q] of
the Garden of Eden[v] cherubim[w] and a
flaming sword[x] flashing back and forth to
guard the way to the tree of life.[y]

Cain and Abel

4 Adam[o] lay with his wife[z] Eve,[a] and
    she became pregnant and gave birth to
Cain.[r][b] She said, "With the help of the
LORD I have brought forth[s] a man." [2]Later
she gave birth to his brother Abel.[c]

Now Abel kept flocks, and Cain worked
the soil.[d] [3]In the course of time Cain
brought some of the fruits of the soil as an
offering[e] to the LORD.[f] [4]But Abel brought
fat portions[g] from some of the firstborn of
his flock.[h] The LORD looked with favor on
Abel and his offering,[i] [5]but on Cain and
his offering he did not look with favor. So

Cross references (center column)

3:15 cRo 16:20;
    Heb 2:14
3:16 dPs 48:5-6;
    Isa 13:8; 21:3;
    26:17; Jer 4:31;
    6:24; Mic 4:9;
    1Ti 2:15
    e1Co 11:3;
    S Eph 5:22
3:17 fS Ge 2:17
    gGe 5:29;
    Nu 35:33;
    Ps 106:39;
    Isa 24:5; Jer 3:1;
    Ro 8:20-22
    hGe 6:13; 8:21;
    Isa 54:9
    iGe 29:32; 31:42;
    Ex 3:7; Ps 66:11;
    127:2; Ecc 1:13
    jGe 47:9; Job 5:7;
    7:1; 14:1;
    Ecc 2:23;
    Jer 20:18
3:18 kJob 31:40;
    Isa 5:6; Heb 6:8
    lPs 104:14
3:19 mPs 104:23
    nGe 14:18;
    Dt 8:3,9; 23:4;
    Ru 1:6; 2:14;
    2Th 3:10
    oS Ge 2:7;
    S Job 7:21;
    S Ps 146:4;
    1Co 15:47;
    Heb 9:27
3:20 pS Ge 2:20;
    2Co 11:3;
    1Ti 2:13
3:21 qS ver 7

3:22 rS Ge 1:26
    sS Ge 2:9;
    S Rev 2:7
3:23 tS Ge 2:8
    uS Ge 2:7
3:24 vS Ge 2:8
    wEx 25:18-22;
    1Sa 4:4; 2Sa 6:2;
    22:11; 1Ki 6:27;
    2Ch 5:8;
    Ps 18:10; 80:1;
    99:1; Isa 37:16;

Eze 10:1; 28:16 xJob 40:19; Ps 104:4; Isa 27:1 yS Ge 2:9 **4:1**
zver 17,25 aS Ge 2:20 bHeb 11:4; 1Jn 3:12; Jude 1:11 **4:2**
cMt 23:35; Lk 11:51; Heb 11:4; 12:24 dS Ge 2:7 **4:3**
eLev 2:1-2; Isa 43:23; Jer 41:5 fNu 18:12 **4:4** gLev 3:16;
2Ch 29:35 hEx 13:2,12; Dt 15:19 iHeb 11:4

[n]15 Or *strike*   [o]20,1 Or *The man*   [p]20 *Eve*
probably means *living.*   [q]24 Or *placed in front*
[r]1 *Cain* sounds like the Hebrew for *brought forth* or
acquired.   [s]1 Or *have acquired*

Study notes (bottom section)

3:16 *pains in childbearing.* Her judgment fell on what was
most uniquely hers as a woman and as a "suitable helper"
(2:20) for her husband. Similarly, the man's "painful toil" (v.
17) was a judgment on him as worker of the soil. Some
believe that the Hebrew root underlying "pains," "pain" and
"painful toil" should here be understood in the sense of
burdensome labor (see Pr 5:10, "toil"; 14:23, "hard
work"). *give birth to children.* As a sign of grace in the midst
of judgment, the human race would continue. *desire . . .
rule.* Her sexual attraction for the man, and his headship over
her, will become intimate aspects of her life in which she
experiences trouble and anguish rather than unalloyed joy
and blessing.
3:17-19 *you will eat.* Though he would have to work hard
and long (judgment), the man would be able to produce food
that would sustain life (grace).
3:19 *return to the ground . . . to dust you will return.*
Man's labor would not be able to stave off death. The origin
of his body (see 2:7) and the source of his food (see v. 17)
became a symbol of his eventual death.
3:21 *clothed them.* God graciously provided Adam and
Eve with more effective clothing (cf. v. 7) to cover their
shame (cf. v. 10).
3:22 *us.* See note on 1:26. *knowing good and evil.* In a
terribly perverted way, Satan's prediction (v. 5) came true.
live forever. Sin, which always results in death (Ro 6:23; Jas
1:14-15), cuts the sinner off from God's gift of eternal
life.
3:23 *banished him from the Garden . . . to work the*

ground. Before he sinned, man had worked in a beautiful
and pleasant garden (2:15). Now he would have to work
hard ground cursed with thorns and thistles (v. 18).
3:24 *cherubim.* Similar to the statues of winged, human-
headed bulls or lions that stood guard at the entrances to
palaces and temples in ancient Mesopotamia (see note on Ex
25:18). *to guard.* The sword of God's judgment stood between fallen man and God's garden. The reason is given in v.
22. Only through God's redemption in Christ does man have
access again to the tree of life (see Rev 2:7; 22:2,14,19).
4:1 *With the help of the LORD.* Eve acknowledged that God
is the ultimate source of life (see Ac 17:25).
4:2 *Abel.* The name means "breath" or "temporary" or
"meaningless" (the translation of the same basic Hebrew
word that is in Ecc 1:2; 12:8) and hints at the shortness of
Abel's life.
4:3-4 *Cain brought some of the fruits . . . But Abel
brought fat portions from some of the firstborn of his flock.*
The contrast is not between an offering of plant life and an
offering of animal life, but between a careless, thoughtless
offering and a choice, generous offering (cf. Lev 3:16). Motivation and heart attitude are all-important, and God looked
with favor on Abel and his offering because of Abel's faith
(Heb 11:4). *firstborn.* Indicative of the recognition that all
the productivity of the flock is from the Lord and all of it
belongs to him.
4:5 *angry.* God did not look with favor on Cain and his
offering, and Cain (whose motivation and attitude were bad
from the outset) reacted predictably.

Cain was very angry, and his face was
downcast.
6 Then the LORD said to Cain, "Why are
you angry?[j] Why is your face downcast?
7 If you do what is right, will you not be
accepted? But if you do not do what is
right, sin is crouching at your door;[k] it
desires to have you, but you must master
it.[l]"
8 Now Cain said to his brother Abel,
"Let's go out to the field."[t] And while
they were in the field, Cain attacked his
brother Abel and killed him.[m]
9 Then the LORD said to Cain, "Where is
your brother Abel?"[n]

"I don't know,[o]" he replied. "Am I my
brother's keeper?"
10 The LORD said, "What have you done?
Listen! Your brother's blood cries out to
me from the ground.[p] 11 Now you are under a curse[q] and driven from the ground,
which opened its mouth to receive your
brother's blood from your hand. 12 When
you work the ground, it will no longer
yield its crops for you.[r] You will be a restless wanderer[s] on the earth.[t]"
13 Cain said to the LORD, "My punishment is more than I can bear. 14 Today you
are driving me from the land, and I will be
hidden from your presence;[u] I will be a
restless wanderer on the earth,[v] and whoever finds me will kill me."[w]
15 But the LORD said to him, "Not so[u]; if
anyone kills Cain[x], he will suffer vengeance[y] seven times over.[z]" Then the
LORD put a mark on Cain so that no one
who found him would kill him. 16 So Cain
went out from the LORD's presence[a] and
lived in the land of Nod,[v] east of Eden.[b]
17 Cain lay with his wife,[c] and she
became pregnant and gave birth to Enoch.
Cain was then building a city,[d] and he
named it after his son[e] Enoch. 18 To Enoch
was born Irad, and Irad was the father of
Mehujael, and Mehujael was the father of
Methushael, and Methushael was the father of Lamech.
19 Lamech married[f] two women,[g] one
named Adah and the other Zillah. 20 Adah

4:6 [j]Jnh 4:4 **4:7** [k]Ge 44:16; Nu 32:23; Isa 59:12 [l]Job 11:15; 22:27; Ps 27:3; 46:2; S Ro 6:16 **4:8** [m]Mt 23:35; Lk 11:51; 1Jn 3:12; Jude 1:11 **4:9** [n]S Ge 3:9 [o]S Jn 8:44 **4:10** [p]Ge 9:5; 37:20,26; Ex 21:12; Nu 35:33; Dt 21:7,9; 2Sa 4:11; Job 16:18; 24:2; 31:38; Ps 9:12; 106:38; Heb 12:24; Rev 6:9-10 **4:11** [q]Dt 11:28; 2Ki 2:24 **4:12** [r]Dt 28:15-24 [s]Ps 37:25; 59:15; 109:10 [t]ver 14 **4:14** [u]2Ki 17:18; Ps 51:11; 139:7-12; Jer 7:15; 52:3 [v]ver 12; Dt 28:64-67 [w]Ge 9:6; Ex 21:12,14; Lev 24:17; Nu 35:19,21,27, 33; 1Ki 2:32; 2Ki 11:16

4:15 [x]Eze 9:4,6 [y]Ex 21:20 [z]ver 24; Lev 26:21; Ps 79:12 **4:16** [a]Jude 1:11 [b]S Ge 2:8 **4:17** [c]S ver 1 [d]Ps 55:9 [e]Ps 49:11 **4:19** [f]Ge 6:2 [g]Ge 29:28; Dt 21:15; Ru 4:11; 1Sa 1:2

[t] *8* Samaritan Pentateuch, Septuagint, Vulgate and Syriac; Masoretic Text does not have *"Let's go out to the field."*
[u] *15* Septuagint, Vulgate and Syriac; Hebrew *Very well*
[v] *16* *Nod* means *wandering* (see verses 12 and 14).

4:7 *sin is crouching at your door.* The Hebrew word for "crouching" is the same as an ancient Babylonian word referring to an evil demon crouching at the door of a building to threaten the people inside. Sin may thus be pictured here as just such a demon, waiting to pounce on Cain—it desires to have him. He may already have been plotting his brother's murder. *it desires to have you.* In Hebrew, the same expression as that for "Your desire will be for [your husband]" in 3:16 (see also SS 7:10).

4:8 *attacked his brother . . . and killed him.* The first murder was especially monstrous because it was committed with deliberate deceit ("Let's go out to the field"), against a brother (see vv. 9–11; 1Jn 3:12) and against a good man (Mt 23:35; Heb 11:4)—a striking illustration of the awful consequences of the fall.

4:9 *Where . . . ?* A rhetorical question (see 3:9). *I don't know.* An outright lie. *Am I my brother's keeper?* A statement of callous indifference—all too common through the whole course of human history.

4:10 *Your brother's blood cries out.* Abel, in one sense a prophet (Lk 11:50–51), "still speaks, even though he is dead" (Heb 11:4), for his spilled blood continues to cry out to God against all those who do violence to their human brothers. But the blood of Christ "speaks a better word" (Heb 12:24).

4:11 *curse.* The ground had been cursed because of human sin (3:17), and now Cain himself is cursed. Formerly he had worked the ground, and it had produced life for him (vv. 2–3). Now the ground, soaked with his brother's blood, would symbolize death and would no longer yield for him its produce (v. 12).

4:12 *wanderer.* Estranged from his fellowman and finding even the ground inhospitable, he became a wanderer in the land of wandering (see NIV text note on v. 16).

4:13 *My punishment is more than I can bear.* Confronted with his crime and its resulting curse, Cain responded not with remorse but with self-pity. His sin was virtually uninterrupted: impiety (v. 3), anger (v. 5), jealousy, deception and murder (v. 8), falsehood (v. 9) and self-seeking (v. 13). The final result was alienation from God himself (vv. 14,16).

4:14–15 *whoever . . . anyone . . . no one.* These words seem to imply the presence of substantial numbers of people outside Cain's immediate family, but perhaps they only anticipate the future rapid growth of the race.

4:15 *mark.* A warning sign to protect him from an avenger. For the time being, the life of the murderer is spared (but see 6:7; 9:6). For a possible parallel see Eze 9:4.

4:16 *Nod.* Location unknown. See NIV text note.

4:17–18 *Cain . . . Enoch . . . Irad . . . Mehujael . . . Methushael . . . Lamech.* Together with that of Adam, these names add up to a total of seven, a number often signifying completeness (see v. 15). Each of the six names listed here is paralleled by a similar or identical name in the genealogy of Seth in ch. 5 as follows: Kenan (5:12), Enoch (5:21), Jared (5:18), Mahalalel (5:15), Methuselah (5:25), Lamech (5:28). The similarity between the two sets of names is striking and may suggest the selective nature of such genealogies (see note on 5:5). See also Introduction to 1 Chronicles: Genealogies.

4:17 *city.* The Hebrew for this word can refer to any permanent settlement, however small. Cain tried to redeem himself from his wandering state by the activity of his own hands—in the land of wandering he builds a city.

4:19 *married two women.* Polygamy entered history. Haughty Lamech, the seventh from Adam in the line of Cain, perhaps sought to attain the benefits of God's primeval blessing (see 1:28 and note) by his own device—multiplying his wives. Monogamy, however, was the original divine intention (see 2:23–24).

4:20–22 *Jabal . . . Jubal . . . Tubal-Cain.* Lamech's three sons had similar names, each derived from a Hebrew verb meaning "to bring, carry, lead," and emphasizing activity. Tubal-Cain's name was especially appropriate, since "Cain" means "metalsmith."

gave birth to Jabal; he was the father of those who live in tents and raise livestock. [21]His brother's name was Jubal; he was the father of all who play the harp[h] and flute.[i] [22]Zillah also had a son, Tubal-Cain, who forged[j] all kinds of tools out of[w] bronze and iron. Tubal-Cain's sister was Naamah.

[23]Lamech said to his wives,

"Adah and Zillah, listen to me;
  wives of Lamech, hear my words.
I have killed[x][k] a man for wounding
  me,
  a young man for injuring me.
[24]If Cain is avenged[l] seven times,[m]
  then Lamech seventy-seven times.[n]"

[25]Adam lay with his wife[o] again, and she gave birth to a son and named him Seth,[y][p] saying, "God has granted me another child in place of Abel, since Cain killed him."[q] [26]Seth also had a son, and he named him Enosh.[r]

At that time men began to call on[z] the name of the LORD.[s]

From Adam to Noah

5 This is the written account[t] of Adam's line.[u]

When God created man, he made him in the likeness of God.[v] [2]He created them[w] male and female[x] and blessed them. And when they were created, he called them "man.[a]"

[3]When Adam had lived 130 years, he had a son in his own likeness, in his own image;[y] and he named him Seth.[z] [4]After

Seth was born, Adam lived 800 years and had other sons and daughters. [5]Altogether, Adam lived 930 years, and then he died.[a]

[6]When Seth had lived 105 years, he became the father[b] of Enosh.[b] [7]And after he became the father of Enosh, Seth lived 807 years and had other sons and daughters. [8]Altogether, Seth lived 912 years, and then he died.

[9]When Enosh had lived 90 years, he became the father of Kenan.[c] [10]And after he became the father of Kenan, Enosh lived 815 years and had other sons and daughters. [11]Altogether, Enosh lived 905 years, and then he died.

[12]When Kenan had lived 70 years, he became the father of Mahalalel.[d] [13]And after he became the father of Mahalalel, Kenan lived 840 years and had other sons and daughters. [14]Altogether, Kenan lived 910 years, and then he died.

[15]When Mahalalel had lived 65 years, he became the father of Jared.[e] [16]And after he became the father of Jared, Mahalalel lived 830 years and had other sons and daughters. [17]Altogether, Mahalalel lived 895 years, and then he died.

[18]When Jared had lived 162 years, he became the father of Enoch.[f] [19]And after he became the father of Enoch, Jared lived 800 years and had other sons and daugh-

---

4:21 [h]Ge 31:27; Ex 15:20; 1Sa 16:16; 1Ch 25:3; Ps 33:2; 43:4; [i]Isa 16:11; Da 3:5 [j]Job 21:12; 30:31; Ps 150:4 **4:22** [k]Ex 35:35; 1Sa 13:19; 2Ki 24:14 **4:23** [k]Ge 9:5-6; Ex 20:13; 21:12; 23:7; Lev 19:18; 24:17; Dt 27:24; 32:35 **4:24** [l]Dt 32:35; 2Ki 9:7; Ps 18:47; 94:1; Isa 35:4; Jer 51:56; Na 1:2 [m]S ver 15 [n]Mt 18:22 **4:25** [o]ver 1 [p]Ge 5:3; 1Ch 1:1 [q]ver 8 **4:26** [r]Ge 5:6; 1Ch 1:1; Lk 3:38 [s]Ge 12:8; 13:4; 21:33; 22:9; 26:25; 33:20; 35:1; Ex 17:15; 1Ki 18:24; Ps 116:17; Joel 2:32; Zep 3:9; S Ac 2:21 **5:1** [t]S Ge 2:4 [u]1Ch 1:1 [v]S Ge 1:27; Col 3:10 **5:2** [w]Ge 1:28 [x]S Ge 1:27; Mt 19:4; Mk 10:6; Gal 3:28 **5:3** [y]S Ge 1:26; 1Co 15:49 [z]S Ge 4:25; Lk 3:38 **5:5** [a]S Ge 2:17; Heb 9:27 **5:6** [b]S Ge 4:26; Lk 3:38 **5:9** [c]1Ch 1:2; Lk 3:37 **5:12** [d]1Ch 1:2; Lk 3:37

5:15 [e]1Ch 1:2; Lk 3:37 **5:18** [f]1Ch 1:3; Lk 3:37; Jude 1:14

[w]22 Or *who instructed all who work in* [x]23 Or *I will kill* [y]25 *Seth* probably means *granted.* [z]26 Or *to proclaim* [a]2 Hebrew *adam* [b]6 *Father* may mean *ancestor,* also in verses 7-26.

4:22 *tools.* For agriculture and construction, but they were also weapons.

4:23 *killed a man for wounding me.* Violent and wanton destruction of human life by one who proclaimed his complete independence from God by taking vengeance with his own hands (see Dt 32:35). Lamech proudly claimed to be master of his own destiny, thinking that he and his sons, by their own achievements, would redeem themselves from the curse on the line of Cain. This titanic claim climaxes the catalog of sins that began with Cain's prideful selfishness at the beginning of the chapter.

4:24 *seventy-seven times.* Lamech's vicious announcement of personal revenge found its counterpoint in Jesus' response to Peter's question about forgiveness in Mt 18:21-22.

4:25 *again . . . another child.* Abel was dead, and Cain was alienated; so Adam and Eve were granted a third son to carry on the family line.

4:26 *Enosh.* The name, like "Adam" (see NIV text note on 2:7), means "man." *began to call on the name of the LORD.* Lamech's proud self-reliance, so characteristic of the line of Cain, is contrasted with dependence on God found in the line of Seth.

5:1 *account.* See note on 2:4. *likeness.* See note on 1:26.

5:2 *male and female.* See note on 1:27. *blessed them.* See

1:28 and note. *called them.* See note on 1:5. *man.* Often refers to both sexes (mankind) in the early chapters of Genesis (see, e.g., 3:22-24).

5:3 *his own likeness . . . his own image.* See note on 1:26. As God created man in his own perfect image, so now sinful Adam has a son in his own imperfect image.

5:5 *930 years.* See notes on v. 27; 6:3. Whether the large numbers describing human longevity in the early chapters of Genesis are literal or have a conventional literary function—or both—is uncertain. Some believe that several of the numbers have symbolic significance, such as Enoch's 365 (v. 23) years (365 being the number of days in a year, thus a full life) and Lamech's 777 (v. 31) years (777 being an expansion and multiple of seven, the number of completeness; cf. the "seventy-seven times" of Lamech's namesake in 4:24). The fact that there are exactly ten names in the Ge 5 list (as in the genealogy of 11:10-26) makes it likely that it includes gaps, the lengths of which may be summarized in the large numbers. Other ancient genealogies outside the Bible exhibit similarly large figures. For example, three kings in a Sumerian list (which also contains exactly ten names) are said to have reigned 72,000 years each—obviously exaggerated time spans. *and then he died.* Repeated as a sad refrain throughout the chapter, the only exception being Enoch (see note on v. 24). The phrase is a stark reminder of God's judgment on sin resulting from Adam's fall.

ters. ²⁰Altogether, Jared lived 962 years, and then he died.

²¹When Enoch had lived 65 years, he became the father of Methuselah.ᵍ ²²And after he became the father of Methuselah, Enoch walked with Godʰ 300 years and had other sons and daughters. ²³Altogether, Enoch lived 365 years. ²⁴Enoch walked with God;ⁱ then he was no more, because God took him away.ʲ

²⁵When Methuselah had lived 187 years, he became the father of Lamech.ᵏ ²⁶And after he became the father of Lamech, Methuselah lived 782 years and had other sons and daughters. ²⁷Altogether, Methuselah lived 969 years, and then he died.

²⁸When Lamech had lived 182 years, he had a son. ²⁹He named him Noahᶜˡ and said, "He will comfort us in the labor and painful toil of our hands caused by the ground the Lᴏʀᴅ has cursed.ᵐ" ³⁰After Noah was born, Lamech lived 595 years and had other sons and daughters. ³¹Altogether, Lamech lived 777 years, and then he died.

³²After Noah was 500 years old,ⁿ he became the father of Shem,ᵒ Ham and Japheth.ᵖ

The Flood

6 When men began to increase in number on the earthᑫ and daughters were born to them, ²the sons of Godʳ saw that the daughters of menˢ were beautiful,ᵗ and they marriedᵘ any of them they chose. ³Then the Lᴏʀᴅ said, "My Spiritᵛ will not contend withᵈ man forever,ʷ for he is mortal^e;ˣ his days will be a hundred and twenty years."

⁴The Nephilimʸ were on the earth in those days—and also afterward—when the sons of God went to the daughters of menᶻ and had children by them. They were the heroes of old, men of renown.ᵃ

⁵The Lᴏʀᴅ saw how great man's wickedness on the earth had become,ᵇ and that every inclination of the thoughts of his heart was only evil all the time.ᶜ ⁶The Lᴏʀᴅ was grievedᵈ that he had made man on the earth, and his heart was filled with pain. ⁷So the Lᴏʀᴅ said, "I will wipe mankind, whom I have created, from the face of the earthᵉ—men and animals, and creatures that move along the ground, and

---

Cross references (center column):

5:21 g1Ch 1:3; Lk 3:37
5:22 hver 24; Ge 6:9; 17:1; 24:40; 48:15; 2Ki 20:3; Ps 116:9; Mic 6:8; Mal 2:6
5:24 iS ver 22 j2Ki 2:1,11; Ps 49:15; 73:24; 89:48; Heb 11:5
5:25 k1Ch 1:3; Lk 3:36
5:29 l1Ch 1:3; Lk 3:36 mS Ge 3:17; Ro 8:20
5:32 nGe 7:6,11; 8:13 oLk 3:36 pGe 6:10; 9:18; 10:1; 1Ch 1:4; Isa 65:20
6:1 qS Ge 1:28
6:2 rJob 1:6 fn; 2:1 fn sver 4 tDt 21:11 uS Ge 4:19
6:3 vJob 34:14; Gal 5:16-17 wIsa 57:16; 1Pe 3:20 xJob 10:9; Ps 78:39; 103:14; Isa 40:6
6:4 yNu 13:33 zver 2 aGe 11:4
6:5 bGe 38:7; Job 34:26; Jer 1:16; 44:5; Eze 3:19 cGe 8:21; Ps 14:1-3
6:6 dEx 32:14; 1Sa 15:11,35; 2Sa 24:16;

1Ch 21:15; Isa 63:10; Jer 18:7-10; Eph 4:30 6:7 eEze 33:28; Zep 1:2,18

c29 *Noah* sounds like the Hebrew for *comfort.*   d3 Or *My spirit will not remain in*   e3 Or *corrupt*

5:22 *walked with God.* The phrase replaces the word "lived" in the other paragraphs of the chapter and reminds us that there is a difference between walking with God and merely living.

5:24 *then he was no more, because God took him away.* The phrase replaces "and then he died" in the other paragraphs of the chapter. Like Elijah, who was "taken" (2Ki 2:10) to heaven, Enoch was taken away (cf. Ps 49:15; 73:24) to the presence of God without experiencing death (Heb 11:5). Lamech, the seventh from Adam in the genealogy of Cain, was evil personified. But "Enoch, the seventh from Adam" (Jude 14) in the genealogy of Seth, "was commended as one who pleased God" (Heb 11:5).

5:27 *969 years.* Only Noah and his family survived the flood. If the figures concerning life spans are literal, Methuselah died in the year of the flood (the figures in vv. 25,28 and 7:6 add up to exactly 969).

6:1 *increase in number.* See note on 1:22.

6:2 *sons of God saw . . . daughters of men . . . and they married.* See v. 4. The phrase "sons of God" here has been interpreted to refer either to angels or to human beings. In such places as Job 1:6; 2:1 it refers to angels, and perhaps also in Ps 29:1 (where it is translated "mighty ones"). Some interpreters also appeal to Jude 6–7 (as well as to Jewish literature) in referring the phrase here to angels.

Others, however, maintain that intermarriage and cohabitation between angels and human beings, though commonly mentioned in ancient mythologies, are surely excluded by the very nature of the created order (ch. 1; Mk 12:25). Elsewhere, expressions equivalent to "sons of God" often refer to human beings, though in contexts quite different from the present one (see Dt 14:1; 32:5; Ps 73:15; Isa 43:6; Hos 1:10; 11:1; Lk 3:38; 1Jn 3:1–2,10). "Sons of God" (vv. 2,4) possibly refers to godly men, and "daughters of men" to sinful women (significantly, they are not called "daughters of

God"), probably from the wicked line of Cain. If so, the context suggests that vv. 1–2 describe the intermarriage of the Sethites ("sons of God") of ch. 5 with the Cainites ("daughters of men") of ch. 4, indicating a breakdown in the separation of the two groups.

Another plausible suggestion is that the "sons of God" refers to royal figures (kings were closely associated with gods in the ancient Near East) who proudly perpetuated and aggravated the corrupt life-style of Lamech son of Cain (virtually a royal figure) and established for themselves royal harems.

6:3 Two key phrases in the Hebrew of this verse are obscure: the one rendered "contend with" (see NIV text note) and the one rendered "for he is mortal." The verse seems to announce that the period of grace between God's declaration of judgment and its arrival would be 120 years (cf. 1Pe 3:20). But if the NIV text note reading is accepted, the verse announces that man's life span would henceforth be limited to 120 years (but see 11:10–26).

6:4 *Nephilim.* People of great size and strength (see Nu 13:31–33). The Hebrew word means "fallen ones." In men's eyes they were "the heroes of old, men of renown," but in God's eyes they were sinners ("fallen ones") ripe for judgment.

6:5 One of the Bible's most vivid descriptions of total depravity. And because man's nature remained unchanged, things were no better after the flood (8:21).

6:6 *The Lᴏʀᴅ was grieved . . . his heart was filled with pain.* Man's sin is God's sorrow (see Eph 4:30).

6:7 *I will wipe mankind . . . from the face of the earth.* The period of grace (see v. 3 and note) was coming to an end. *animals . . . creatures . . . birds.* Though morally innocent, the animal world, as creatures under man's corrupted rule, shared in his judgment.

birds of the air—for I am grieved that I have made them. *f* " ⁸But Noah*g* found favor in the eyes of the LORD. *h*

⁹This is the account *i* of Noah.

Noah was a righteous man, blameless *j* among the people of his time, *k* and he walked with God. *l* ¹⁰Noah had three sons: Shem, *m* Ham and Japheth. *n*

¹¹Now the earth was corrupt *o* in God's sight and was full of violence. *p* ¹²God saw how corrupt *q* the earth had become, for all the people on earth had corrupted their ways. *r* ¹³So God said to Noah, "I am going to put an end to all people, for the earth is filled with violence because of them. I am surely going to destroy *s* both them and the earth. *t* ¹⁴So make yourself an ark of cypress *f* wood; *u* make rooms in it and coat it with pitch *v* inside and out. ¹⁵This is how you are to build it: The ark is to be 450 feet long, 75 feet wide and 45 feet high. *g* ¹⁶Make a roof for it and finish *h* the ark to within 18 inches *i* of the top. Put a door in the side of the ark and make lower, middle and upper decks. ¹⁷I am going to bring floodwaters *w* on the earth to destroy all life under the heavens, every creature that has the breath of life in it. Everything on earth will perish. *x* ¹⁸But I

will establish my covenant with you, *y* and you will enter the ark *z*—you and your sons and your wife and your sons' wives with you. ¹⁹You are to bring into the ark two of all living creatures, male and female, to keep them alive with you. *a* ²⁰Two *b* of every kind of bird, of every kind of animal and of every kind *c* of creature that moves along the ground will come to you to be kept alive. *d* ²¹You are to take every kind of food that is to be eaten and store it away as food for you and for them."

²²Noah did everything just as God commanded him. *e*

7 The LORD then said to Noah, "Go into the ark, you and your whole family, *f* because I have found you righteous *g* in this generation. ²Take with you seven *j* of

Cross references column:

6:7 *f* ver 17; Ge 7:4,21;
6:8 *g* Eze 14:14 *h* Ge 19:19; 39:4; Ex 33:12,13,17; 34:9; Nu 11:15; Ru 2:2; Lk 1:30; Ac 7:46
6:9 *i* S Ge 2:4 /Ge 17:1; Dt 18:13; 2Sa 22:24; Job 1:1; 4:6; 9:21; 12:4; 31:6; Ps 15:2; 18:23; 19:13; 37:37; Pr 2:7 *k* Ge 7:1; Ps 37:39; Jer 15:1; Eze 14:14,20; Da 10:11; S Lk 1:6; Heb 11:7; 2Pe 2:5 *l* S Ge 5:22
6:10 *m* Lk 3:36 *n* S Ge 5:32
6:11 *o* Dt 31:29; Jdg 2:19 *p* Ps 7:9; 73:6; Eze 7:23; 8:17; 28:16; Mal 2:16
6:12 *q* Ex 32:7; Dt 4:16; 9:12,24 *r* Ps 14:1-3
6:13 *s* Dt 28:63; 2Ki 8:19; Ezr 9:14; Jer 44:11 *t* ver 17; Ge 7:4,21-23; Job 34:15; Isa 5:6; 24:1-3; Jer 44:27; Eze 7:2-3
6:14 *u* Heb 11:7; 1Pe 3:20 *v* Ex 2:3
6:17 *w* Ps 29:10 *x* S ver 7,S 13;

2Pe 2:5 6:18 *y* Ge 9:9-16; 17:7; 19:12; Ex 6:4; 34:10,27; Dt 29:13,14-15; Ps 25:10; 74:20; 106:45; Isa 55:3; Jer 32:40; Eze 16:60; Hag 2:5; 1Pe 3:20 *z* Ge 7:1,7,13 6:19 *a* Ge 7:15 6:20 *b* Ge 7:15 *c* S Ge 1:11 *d* Ge 7:3 6:22 *e* Ge 7:5, 9,16; Ex 7:6; 39:43; 40:16,19,21,23,25,27,29,32 7:1 *f* S Ge 6:18; Mt 24:38; Lk 17:26-27; Heb 11:7; 1Pe 3:20; 2Pe 2:5 *g* S Ge 6:9; Eze 14:14

f 14 The meaning of the Hebrew for this word is uncertain.   *g* 15 Hebrew *300 cubits long, 50 cubits wide and 30 cubits high* (about 140 meters long, 23 meters wide and 13.5 meters high)   *h* 16 Or *Make an opening for light by finishing*   *i* 16 Hebrew *a cubit* (about 0.5 meter)   *j* 2 Or *seven pairs*; also in verse 3

6:8–9 *found favor . . . righteous . . . blameless . . . walked with God.* See note on 5:22. Noah's godly life was a powerful contrast to the wicked lives of his contemporaries (see v. 5 and note; see also v. 12). This description of Noah does not imply sinless perfection.

6:9 *account.* See note on 2:4. *righteous.* See note on Ps 1:5.

6:14 *ark.* The Hebrew for this word is used elsewhere only in reference to the basket that saved the baby Moses (Ex 2:3,5). *coat it with pitch.* Moses' mother made his basket watertight in the same way (see Ex 2:3).

6:16 *roof.* Perhaps overhanging, to keep the rain from coming in. *within 18 inches of the top.* Noah's ark probably had a series of small windows (see 8:6) encircling the entire vessel 18 inches from the top to admit light and air.

6:17 *floodwaters on the earth to destroy all life under the heavens.* Some believe that the deluge was worldwide, partly because of the apparently universal terms of the text—both here and elsewhere (vv. 7,12–13; 7:4,19, 21–23; 8:21; 9:11,15). Others argue that nothing in the narrative of chs. 6–9 prevents the flood from being understood as regional—destroying everything in its wake, but of relatively limited scope and universal only from the standpoint of Moses' geographic knowledge. "Earth," e.g., may be defined in the more restricted sense of "land" (see 2:5). "All life under the heavens" may mean all life within the range of Noah's perception. (See the universal language used to describe the drought and famine in the time of Joseph—41:54,57; see also note on 41:57.) Since the purpose of the floodwaters was to destroy sinful mankind (see v. 13), and since the writer possibly had in mind only the inhabitants of the ancient Near East, this flood may not have had to be worldwide to destroy them. The apostle Peter, however, seems to assume that the flood and its devastation were

universal and total, except for Noah and his family (2Pe 3:6; but see note there).

6:18 *covenant.* See note on 9:9. Noah would understand the full implications of God's covenant with him only after the floodwaters had dried up (see 9:8–17). *enter the ark.* The story of Noah's salvation from the flood illustrates God's redemption of his children (see Heb 11:7; 2Pe 2:5) and typifies baptism (see 1Pe 3:20–21). *your sons and your wife and your sons' wives with you.* God extends his loving concern to the whole family of righteous Noah—a consistent pattern in God's dealings with his people, underscoring the moral and responsible relationship of parents to their children (see 17:7–27; 18:19; Dt 30:19; Ps 78:1–7; 102:28; 103:17–18; 112:1–2; Ac 2:38–39; 16:31; 1Co 7:14).

6:19 *two of all living creatures . . . to keep them alive.* Most animals were doomed to die in the flood (see note on v. 7), but at least one pair of each kind was preserved to restock the earth after the waters subsided.

6:20 *kind.* See note on 1:11.

6:22 *did everything just as God commanded.* The account stresses Noah's obedience (see 7:5,9,16).

7:1 *Go into the ark.* The beginning of God's final word to Noah before the flood. God's first word to Noah after the flood begins similarly: "Come out of the ark" (8:16). *righteous.* See note on 6:8–9. As a "preacher of righteousness" (2Pe 2:5), Noah warned his contemporaries of coming judgment and testified to the vitality of his own faith (see Heb 11:7).

7:2 *seven of every kind of clean animal . . . two of every kind of unclean animal.* The ceremonially unclean animals would only have to reproduce themselves after the flood, but ceremonially clean animals would be needed also for the burnt offerings that Noah would sacrifice (see 8:20) and for food (see 9:3).

every kind of clean[h] animal, a male and its mate, and two of every kind of unclean animal, a male and its mate, [3]and also seven of every kind of bird, male and female, to keep their various kinds alive[i] throughout the earth. [4]Seven days from now I will send rain[j] on the earth[k] for forty days[l] and forty nights,[m] and I will wipe from the face of the earth every living creature I have made.[n]"

[5]And Noah did all that the LORD commanded him.[o]

[6]Noah was six hundred years old[p] when the floodwaters came on the earth. [7]And Noah and his sons and his wife and his sons' wives entered the ark[q] to escape the waters of the flood. [8]Pairs of clean and unclean[r] animals, of birds and of all creatures that move along the ground, [9]male and female, came to Noah and entered the ark, as God had commanded Noah.[s] [10]And after the seven days[t] the floodwaters came on the earth.

[11]In the six hundredth year of Noah's life,[u] on the seventeenth day of the second month[v]—on that day all the springs of the great deep[w] burst forth, and the floodgates of the heavens[x] were opened. [12]And rain fell on the earth forty days and forty nights.[y]

[13]On that very day Noah and his sons,[z] Shem, Ham and Japheth, together with his wife and the wives of his three sons, entered the ark.[a] [14]They had with them every wild animal according to its kind, all livestock according to their kinds, every creature that moves along the ground according to its kind and every bird according to its kind,[b] everything with wings. [15]Pairs of all creatures that have the breath of life in them came to Noah and entered the ark.[c] [16]The animals going in were male and female of every living thing, as God had commanded Noah.[d] Then the LORD shut him in.

[17]For forty days[e] the flood kept coming on the earth, and as the waters increased they lifted the ark high above the earth. [18]The waters rose and increased greatly on the earth, and the ark floated on the surface of the water. [19]They rose greatly on the earth, and all the high mountains under the entire heavens were covered.[f] [20]The waters rose and covered the mountains to a depth of more than twenty feet.[k,l,g] [21]Every living thing that moved on the earth perished—birds, livestock, wild animals, all the creatures that swarm over the earth, and all mankind.[h] [22]Everything on dry land that had the breath of life[i] in its nostrils died. [23]Every living thing on the face of the earth was wiped out; men and animals and the creatures that move along the ground and the birds of the air were wiped from the earth.[j] Only Noah was left, and those with him in the ark.[k]

[24]The waters flooded the earth for a hundred and fifty days.[l]

8 But God remembered[m] Noah and all the wild animals and the livestock that were with him in the ark, and he sent a wind over the earth,[n] and the waters receded. [2]Now the springs of the deep and the floodgates of the heavens[o] had been closed, and the rain[p] had stopped falling from the sky. [3]The water receded steadily from the earth. At the end of the hundred

7:2 [h]ver 8; Ge 8:20; Lev 10:10; 11:1-47; Dt 14:3-20; Eze 44:23; Hag 2:12; Ac 10:14-15 **7:3** [i]Ge 6:20 **7:4** [j]Ge 8:2 [k]1Ki 13:34; Jer 28:16 [l]Nu 13:25; Dt 9:9; 1Sa 17:16; 1Ki 19:8 [m]ver 12, 17; Ex 24:18; 32:1; 34:28; Dt 9:9,11,18,25; 10:10; Job 37:6, 13; Mt 4:2 [n]S Ge 6:7,13 **7:5** [o]S Ge 6:22 **7:6** [p]S Ge 5:32 **7:7** [q]S Ge 6:18 **7:8** [r]S ver 2 **7:9** [s]S Ge 6:22 **7:10** [t]S ver 4 **7:11** [u]S Ge 5:32 [v]Ge 8:4,14 [w]S Ge 1:7; Job 28:11; Ps 36:6; 42:7; Pr 8:24; Isa 51:10; Eze 26:19 [x]Ge 8:2; 2Ki 7:2; Ps 78:23; Isa 24:18; Mal 3:10 **7:12** [y]S ver 4; S 1Sa 12:17; S Job 28:26 **7:13** [z]Ge 8:16; 1Pe 3:20; 2Pe 2:5 [a]S Ge 6:18 **7:14** [b]S Ge 1:11 **7:15** [c]ver 8-9; Ge 6:19 **7:16** [d]S Ge 6:22 **7:17** [e]S ver 4 **7:19** [f]Ps 104:6 **7:20** [g]Ge 8:4-5, 2Pe 3:6 **7:21** [h]S Ge 6:7, 13; 2Pe 3:6 **7:22** [i]S Ge 1:30 **7:23** [j]Job 14:19; 21:18; 22:11,16; Ps 90:5; Isa 28:2; Mt 24:39; Lk 17:27; 1Pe 3:20; 2Pe 2:5 [k]Heb 11:7 **7:24** [l]Ge 8:3; Job 12:15

8:1 [m]Ge 9:15; 19:29; 21:1; 30:22; Ex 2:24; Nu 10:9; Ru 4:13; 1Sa 1:11,19; 2Ki 20:3; 1Ch 16:15; Ne 1:8; 5:19; 13:14,22,31; Job 14:13; Ps 105:42; 106:4; Lk 1:54,72 [n]Ex 14:21; Jos 2:10; 3:16; Job 12:15; Ps 66:6; Isa 11:15; 44:27; Na 1:4 **8:2** [o]S Ge 7:11 [p]S Ge 7:4

[k]20 Hebrew *fifteen cubits* (about 6.9 meters) [l]20 Or *rose more than twenty feet, and the mountains were covered*

7:4 *forty days and forty nights.* A length of time often characterizing a critical period in redemptive history (see v. 12; Dt 9:11; Mt 4:1–11).

7:7 *entered the ark to escape the waters.* Noah and his family were saved, but life as usual continued for everyone else until it was too late (see Mt 24:37–39).

7:13 *Noah and his sons . . . together with his wife and the wives of his three sons.* "Only a few people, eight in all" (1Pe 3:20; see 2Pe 2:5), survived the flood.

7:14 *every wild animal . . . all livestock . . . every creature that moves along the ground . . . every bird.* Four of the five categories of animate life mentioned in 1:21–25. The fifth category—sea creatures—could remain alive outside the ark.

7:16 *God had commanded Noah . . . the LORD shut him in.* "God" gave the command, but in his role as redeeming "LORD" (see notes on 2:4; Ex 6:6) he closed the door of the ark behind Noah and his family. Neither divine name is mentioned in the rest of ch. 7, as the full fury of the flood was unleashed on sinful mankind.

7:20 *covered the mountains to a depth of more than twenty feet.* The ark was 45 feet high (6:15), so the water was deep enough to keep it from running aground.

7:22 *breath of life.* God's gift at creation (see 1:30; 2:7) was taken away because of sin.

8:1 So far the flood narrative has been an account of judgment; from this point on it is a story of redemption. *God remembered Noah.* Though he had not been mentioned since 7:16 or heard from for 150 days (see 7:24), God had not forgotten Noah and his family. To "remember" in the Bible is not merely to recall to mind; it is to express concern for someone, to act with loving care for him. When God remembers his people, he does so "with favor" (Ne 5:19; 13:31). *wind.* The Hebrew word translated "Spirit" in 1:2 is here rendered "wind," and introduces a series of parallels between the events of chs. 8–9 and those of ch. 1 in their literary order: Compare 8:2 with 1:7; 8:5 with 1:9; 8:7 with 1:20; 8:17 with 1:25; 9:1 with 1:28a; 9:2 with 1:28b; 9:3 with 1:30. Ch. 1 describes the original beginning, while chs. 8–9 describe a new beginning after the flood.

and fifty days ^{q} the water had gone down, ^{4}and on the seventeenth day of the seventh month ^{r} the ark came to rest on the mountains ^{s} of Ararat. ^{t} ^{5}The waters continued to recede until the tenth month, and on the first day of the tenth month the tops of the mountains became visible.

^{6}After forty days ^{u} Noah opened the window he had made in the ark ^{7}and sent out a raven, ^{v} and it kept flying back and forth until the water had dried up from the earth. ^{w} ^{8}Then he sent out a dove ^{x} to see if the water had receded from the surface of the ground. ^{9}But the dove could find no place to set its feet because there was water over all the surface of the earth; so it returned to Noah in the ark. He reached out his hand and took the dove and brought it back to himself in the ark. ^{10}He waited seven more days and again sent out the dove from the ark. ^{11}When the dove returned to him in the evening, there in its beak was a freshly plucked olive leaf! Then Noah knew that the water had receded from the earth. ^{y} ^{12}He waited seven more days and sent the dove out again, but this time it did not return to him.

^{13}By the first day of the first month of Noah's six hundred and first year, ^{z} the water had dried up from the earth. Noah then removed the covering from the ark and saw that the surface of the ground was dry. ^{14}By the twenty-seventh day of the second month ^{a} the earth was completely dry.

^{15}Then God said to Noah, ^{16}"Come out of the ark, you and your wife and your sons and their wives. ^{b} ^{17}Bring out every kind of living creature that is with you—the birds, the animals, and all the creatures that move along the ground—so they can multiply on the earth and be fruitful and increase in number upon it." ^{c}

^{18}So Noah came out, together with his sons and his wife and his sons' wives. ^{d} ^{19}All the animals and all the creatures that move along the ground and all the birds—everything that moves on the earth—came out of the ark, one kind after another.

^{20}Then Noah built an altar to the LORD ^{e} and, taking some of all the clean animals and clean ^{f} birds, he sacrificed burnt offerings ^{g} on it. ^{21}The LORD smelled the pleasing aroma ^{h} and said in his heart: "Never again will I curse the ground ^{i} because of man, even though ^{m} every inclination of his heart is evil from childhood. ^{j} And never again will I destroy ^{k} all living creatures, ^{l} as I have done.

^{22}"As long as the earth endures,
    seedtime and harvest, ^{m}
    cold and heat,
    summer and winter, ^{n}
    day and night
    will never cease." ^{o}

God's Covenant With Noah

9 Then God blessed Noah and his sons, saying to them, "Be fruitful and in-

8:3 ^{q}S Ge 7:24
8:4 ^{r}S Ge 7:11
^{s}Ge 7:20
^{t}2Ki 19:37;
Jer 51:27
8:6 ^{u}Ge 7:12
8:7 ^{v}Lev 11:15;
Dt 14:14;
1Ki 17:4,6;
Job 38:41;
Ps 147:9;
Pr 30:17;
Isa 34:11;
Lk 12:24 ^{w}ver 11
8:8 ^{x}Job 30:31;
Ps 55:6; 74:19;
SS 2:12,14;
Isa 38:14; 59:11;
60:8; Jer 48:28;
Eze 7:16;
Hos 7:11; 11:11;
10:16; Jn 1:32
8:11 ^{y}ver 7
8:13 ^{z}S Ge 5:32
8:14 ^{a}S Ge 7:11

8:16 ^{b}S Ge 7:13
8:17 ^{c}S Ge 1:22
8:18 ^{d}1Pe 3:20;
2Pe 2:5
8:20 ^{e}Ge 12:7-8;
13:18; 22:9;
26:25; 33:20;
35:7; Ex 17:15;
24:4 ^{f}S Ge 7:8
^{g}Ge 22:2,13;
Ex 10:25; 20:24;
40:29; Lev 1:3;
4:29; 6:8-13;
Nu 6:11;
Jdg 6:26; 11:31;
1Sa 20:29;
Job 1:5; 42:8
8:21 ^{h}Ex 29:18,
25; Lev 1:9,13;
2:9; 4:31;
Nu 15:3,7;
2Co 2:15
^{i}S Ge 3:17
^{j}Ge 6:5; Ps 51:5;
Jer 17:9;
Mt 15:19;
Ro 1:21
^{k}Jer 44:11
^{l}Ge 9:11,15;
Isa 54:9
8:22 ^{m}Jos 3:15;
Ps 67:6; Jer 5:24

^{n}Ps 74:17; Zec 14:8 ^{o}S Ge 1:14

m21 Or man, for

8:4 *mountains.* The word is plural and refers to a range of mountains. *Ararat.* The name is related to Assyrian Urartu, which became an extensive and mountainous kingdom (see Jer 51:27; see also Isa 37:38), including much of the territory north of Mesopotamia and east of modern Turkey. The ark's landfall was probably in southern Urartu.

8:6 *window.* See note on 6:16.

8:11 *the dove returned . . . in its beak was a freshly plucked olive leaf.* Olives do not grow at high elevations, and the fresh leaf was a sign to Noah that the water had receded from the earth. The modern symbol of peace represented by a dove carrying an olive branch in its beak has its origin in this story.

8:13 *first day of the first month of Noah's six hundred and first year.* The date formula signals mankind's new beginning after the flood.

8:14 *twenty-seventh day of the second month.* More than a year after the flood began (see 7:11).

8:16 *Come out of the ark.* See note on 7:1.

8:17 *multiply . . . be fruitful . . . increase in number.* See 1:22 and note. The animals and birds could now repopulate their former habitats.

8:20 *LORD.* Since worship is a very personal matter, it is to God as "the LORD" (see note on 2:4) that Noah brought his sacrifice (see 4:4). *burnt offerings.* See Lev 1:4.

8:21 *smelled the pleasing aroma.* A figurative way of saying that the Lord takes delight in his children's worship of him (see Eph 5:2; Php 4:18). *curse the ground.* Although the Hebrew here has a different word for "curse," the reference appears to be to the curse of 3:17. It may be that the Lord here pledged never to add curse upon curse as he had in regard to Cain (4:12). *even though every inclination of his heart is evil.* For almost identical phraseology see 6:5. Because of man's extreme wickedness, God had destroyed him (6:7) by means of a flood (6:17). Although righteous Noah and his family had been saved, he and his offspring were descendants of Adam and carried in their hearts the inheritance of sin. God graciously promises never again to deal with sin by sending such a devastating deluge (see 9:11,15). Human history is held open for God's dealing with sin in a new and redemptive way—the way that was prepared for by God's action at Babel (see notes on 11:6,8) and that begins to unfold with the call of Abram (12:1). *from childhood.* The phrase replaces "all the time" in 6:5 and emphasizes the truth that sin infects a person's life from his conception and birth (Ps 51:5; 58:3).

8:22 Times and seasons, created by God in the beginning (see 1:14), will never cease till the end of history.

9:1–7 At this new beginning, God renewed his original benediction (1:28) and his provision for man's food (cf. v. 3; 1:29–30). But because sin had brought violence into man's world and because God now appointed meat as a part of

crease in number and fill the earth. *p* ²The fear and dread of you will fall upon all the beasts of the earth and all the birds of the air, upon every creature that moves along the ground, and upon all the fish of the sea; they are given into your hands. *q* ³Everything that lives and moves will be food for you. *r* Just as I gave you the green plants, I now give you everything. *s*

⁴"But you must not eat meat that has its lifeblood still in it. *t* ⁵And for your lifeblood I will surely demand an accounting. *u* I will demand an accounting from every animal. *v* And from each man, too, I will demand an accounting for the life of his fellow man. *w*

⁶"Whoever sheds the blood of man,
　　by man shall his blood be shed; *x*
for in the image of God *y*
　　has God made man.

⁷As for you, be fruitful and increase in number; multiply on the earth and increase upon it." *z*

⁸Then God said to Noah and to his sons with him: ⁹"I now establish my covenant with you *a* and with your descendants after you ¹⁰and with every living creature that was with you—the birds, the livestock and all the wild animals, all those that came out of the ark with you—every living creature on earth. ¹¹I establish my covenant *b* with you: *c* Never again will all life be cut

off by the waters of a flood; never again will there be a flood to destroy the earth. *d*"

¹²And God said, "This is the sign of the covenant *e* I am making between me and you and every living creature with you, a covenant for all generations to come: *f* ¹³I have set my rainbow *g* in the clouds, and it will be the sign of the covenant between me and the earth. ¹⁴Whenever I bring clouds over the earth and the rainbow *h* appears in the clouds, ¹⁵I will remember my covenant *i* between me and you and all living creatures of every kind. Never again will the waters become a flood to destroy all life. *j* ¹⁶Whenever the rainbow *k* appears in the clouds, I will see it and remember the everlasting covenant *l* between God and all living creatures of every kind on the earth."

¹⁷So God said to Noah, "This is the sign of the covenant *m* I have established between me and all life on the earth."

The Sons of Noah

¹⁸The sons of Noah who came out of the ark were Shem, Ham and Japheth. *n* (Ham was the father of Canaan.) *o* ¹⁹These were the three sons of Noah, *p* and from them came the people who were scattered over the earth. *q*

9:1 *p*S Ge 1:22
9:2 *q*S Ge 1:26
9:3 *r*S Ge 1:29
　*s*S Ac 10:15;
　Col 2:16
9:4 *t*Lev 3:17;
　7:26; 17:10-14;
　19:26; Dt 12:16,
　23-25; 15:23;
　1Sa 14:33;
　Eze 33:25;
　Ac 15:20,29
9:5 *u*Ge 42:22;
　50:15; 1Ki 2:32;
　2Ch 24:22;
　Ps 9:12
　*v*Ex 21:28-32
　*w*S Ge 4:10
9:6 *x*S Ge 4:14;
　S Jdg 9:24;
　S Mt 26:52
　*y*S Ge 1:26
9:7 *z*S Ge 1:22
9:9 *a*ver 11;
　S Ge 6:18
9:11 *b*ver 16;
　Isa 24:5; 33:8;
　Hos 6:7 *c*S ver 9
　*d*S Ge 8:21
9:12 *e*ver 17;
　Ge 17:11
　*f*Ge 17:12;
　Ex 12:14;
　Lev 3:17; 6:18;
　17:7; Nu 10:8
9:13 *g*ver 14;
　Eze 1:28;
　Rev 4:3; 10:1
9:14 *h*S ver 13
9:15 *i*S Ge 8:1;
　Ex 2:24; 6:5;
　34:10; Lev 26:42,
　45; Dt 7:9;
　Ps 89:34; 103:18;
　105:8; 106:45;
　Eze 16:60
　*j*S Ge 8:21
9:16 *k*ver 13
　*l*S ver 11;
　Ge 17:7,13,19;
　2Sa 7:13; 23:5;
　Ps 105:9-10;
　Isa 9:7; 54:10;
　55:3; 59:21;
　61:8;

Jer 31:31-34; 32:40; 33:21; Eze 16:60; 37:26; S Heb 13:20
9:17 *m*S ver 12 *n*S Ge 5:32; Lk 3:36 *o*ver 25-27;
Ge 10:6,15 9:19 *p*Ge 5:32 *q*S Ge 1:22; 10:32; 11:4,8,9

man's food (v. 3), further divine provisions and stipulations are added (vv. 4–6). Yet God's benediction dominates and encloses the whole (see v. 7).

9:2 *they are given into your hands.* God reaffirmed that mankind would rule over all creation, including the animals (see note on 1:26).

9:3 *Everything that lives and moves will be food.* Meat would now supplement mankind's diet.

9:4 *you must not eat meat that has its lifeblood.* Lev 17:14 stresses the intimate relationship between blood and life by twice declaring that "the life of every creature is its blood." Life is the precious and mysterious gift of God, and man is not to seek to preserve it or increase the life-force within him by eating "life" that is "in the blood" (Lev 17:11)—as many pagan peoples throughout history have thought they could do.

9:5 *for your lifeblood . . . I will demand an accounting from every animal.* God himself is the great defender of human life (see 4:9–12), which is precious to him because man was created in his image (v. 6) and because man is the earthly representative and focal point of God's kingdom. In the theocracy (kingdom of God) established at Sinai, a domestic animal that had taken human life was to be stoned to death (Ex 21:28–32).

9:6 *Whoever sheds the blood of man, by man shall his blood be shed.* In the later theocracy, those guilty of premeditated murder were to be executed (see Ex 21:12–14; Nu 35:16–32; see also Ro 13:3–4; 1Pe 2:13–14). *for in the image of God has God made man.* See

1:26 and note. In killing a human being, a murderer demonstrates his contempt for God as well as for his fellow-man.

9:9 *I now establish my covenant.* God sovereignly promised in this covenant to Noah, to Noah's descendants and to all other living things (as a kind of gracious reward to righteous Noah, the new father of the human race—see 6:18) never again to destroy man and the earth until his purposes for his creation are fully realized ("as long as the earth endures," 8:22). For similar commitments by God see his covenants with Abram (15:18–20), Phinehas (Nu 25:10–13) and David (2Sa 7). See chart on "Major Covenants in the OT," p. 19.

9:11 *Never again will all life be cut off by the waters of a flood.* A summary of the provisions of the Lord's covenant with Noah—an eternal covenant, as seen in such words and phrases as "never again" (vv. 11,15), "for all generations to come" (v. 12) and "everlasting" (v. 16).

9:12 *sign.* A covenant sign was a visible seal and reminder of covenant commitments. Circumcision would become the sign of the covenant with Abraham (see 17:11), and the Sabbath would be the sign of the covenant with Israel at Sinai (see Ex 31:16–17).

9:13 *rainbow.* Rain and the rainbow doubtless existed long before the time of Noah's flood, but after the flood the rainbow took on new meaning as the sign of the Noahic covenant.

9:19 *scattered.* Thus anticipating the table of nations (see note on 11:8).

Major Covenants in the Old Testament

COVENANTS	REFERENCE	TYPE	PARTICIPANT	DESCRIPTION
Noahic	Ge 9:8-17	Royal Grant	Made with "righteous" (6:9) Noah (and his descendants and every living thing on earth—all life that is subject to man's jurisdiction)	An unconditional divine promise never to destroy all earthly life with some natural catastrophe; the covenant "sign" being the rainbow in the storm cloud
Abrahamic A	Ge 15:9-21	Royal (land) Grant	Made with "righteous" (his faith was "credited to him as righteousness," v. 6) Abram (and his descendants, v. 16)	An unconditional divine promise to fulfill the grant of the land; a self-maledictory oath symbolically enacted it (v. 17)
Abrahamic B	Ge 17	Suzerain-vassal	Made with Abraham as patriarchal head of his household	A conditional divine pledge to be Abraham's God and the God of his descendants (cf. "As for me," v. 4; "As for you," v. 9); the condition: total consecration to the Lord as symbolized by circumcision
Sinaitic	Ex 19-24	Suzerain-vassal	Made with Israel as the descendants of Abraham, Isaac and Jacob and as the people the Lord has redeemed from bondage to an earthly power	A conditional divine pledge to be Israel's God (as her Protector and the Guarantor of her blessed destiny); the condition: Israel's total consecration to the Lord as his people (his kingdom) who live by his rule and serve his purposes in history
Phinehas	Nu 25:10-13	Royal Grant	Made with the zealous priest Phinehas	An unconditional divine promise to maintain the family of Phinehas in a "lasting priesthood" (implicitly a pledge to Israel to provide her forever with a faithful priesthood)
Davidic	2Sa 7:5-16	Royal Grant	Made with faithful King David after his devotion to God as Israel's king and the Lord's anointed vassal had come to special expression (v. 2)	An unconditional divine promise to establish and maintain the Davidic dynasty on the throne of Israel (implicitly a pledge to Israel) to provide her forever with a godly king like David and through that dynasty to do for her what he had done through David—bring her into rest in the promised land (1Ki 4:20-21; 5:3-4).
New	Jer 31:31-34	Royal Grant	Promised to rebellious Israel as she is about to be expelled from the promised land in actualization of the most severe covenant curse (Lev 26:27-39; Dt 28:36-37, 45-68)	An unconditional divine promise to unfaithful Israel to forgive her sins and establish his relationship with her on a new basis by writing his law "on their hearts"—a covenant of pure grace

Major Types of Royal Covenants/Treaties in the Ancient Near East

Royal Grant (unconditional)
A king's grant (of land or some other benefit) to a loyal servant for faithful or exceptional service. The grant was normally perpetual and unconditional, but the servant's heirs benefited from it only as they continued their father's loyalty and service. (Cf. 1Sa 8:14; 22:7; 27:6; Est 8:1.)

Parity
A covenant between equals, binding them to mutual friendship or at least to mutual respect for each other's spheres and interests. Participants called each other "brothers." (Cf. Ge 21:27; 26:31; 31:44-54; 1Ki 5:12; 15:19; 20:32-34; Am 1:9.)

Suzerain-vassal (conditional)
A covenant regulating the relationship between a great king and one of his subject kings. The great king claimed absolute right of sovereignty, demanded total loyalty and service (the vassal must "love" his suzerain) and pledged protection of the subject's realm and dynasty, conditional on the vassal's faithfulness and loyalty to him. The vassal pledged absolute loyalty to his suzerain—whatever service his suzerain demanded—and exclusive reliance on the suzerain's protection. Participants called each other "lord" and "servant" or "father" and "son." (Cf. Jos 9:6,8; Eze 17:13-18; Hos 12:1.)

Commitments made in these covenants were accompanied by self-maledictory oaths (made orally, ceremonially or both). The gods were called upon to witness the covenants and implement the curses of the oaths if the covenants were violated.

20Noah, a man of the soil, proceeded[n] to plant a vineyard. 21When he drank some of its wine,[r] he became drunk and lay uncovered inside his tent. 22Ham, the father of Canaan, saw his father's nakedness[s] and told his two brothers outside. 23But Shem and Japheth took a garment and laid it across their shoulders; then they walked in backward and covered their father's nakedness. Their faces were turned the other way so that they would not see their father's nakedness.

24When Noah awoke from his wine and found out what his youngest son had done to him, 25he said,

"Cursed[t] be Canaan![u]
     The lowest of slaves
     will he be to his brothers.[v]"

26He also said,

"Blessed be the LORD, the God of
     Shem![w]
May Canaan be the slave[x] of Shem.[o]
27May God extend the territory of
     Japheth;[p][y]
may Japheth live in the tents of
     Shem,[z]
and may Canaan be his[q] slave."

28After the flood Noah lived 350 years. 29Altogether, Noah lived 950 years, and then he died.[a]

The Table of Nations

10 This is the account[b] of Shem, Ham and Japheth,[c] Noah's sons,[d] who themselves had sons after the flood.

The Japhethites

10:2–5pp — 1Ch 1:5–7

2The sons[r] of Japheth:
     Gomer,[e] Magog,[f] Madai, Javan,[g]
     Tubal,[h] Meshech[i] and Tiras.
3The sons of Gomer:
     Ashkenaz,[j] Riphath and Togarmah.[k]
4The sons of Javan:
     Elishah,[l] Tarshish,[m] the Kittim[n] and the Rodanim.[s] 5(From these the maritime peoples spread out into their territories by their clans

Cross-references (center column)

9:21 [r]Ge 19:35
9:22 [s]Hab 2:15
9:25 [t]Ge 27:12
     [u]ver 18; Ex 20:5;
     Ps 79:8;
     Isa 14:21;
     Jer 31:29; 32:18
     [v]Ge 25:23;
     27:29,37,40;
     37:10; 49:8;
     Nu 24:18;
     Jos 9:23
9:26 [w]Ge 14:20;
     Ex 18:10; Ps 7:17
     [x]1Ki 9:21
9:27 [y]Ge 10:2-5
     [z]Eph 2:13-14;
     3:6
9:29 [a]S Ge 2:17
10:1 [b]S Ge 2:4
     [c]S Ge 5:32 [d]ver
     32; 1Ch 1:4
10:2 [e]Eze 38:6
     [f]Eze 38:2; 39:6;
     Rev 20:8
     [g]Eze 27:19
     [h]Isa 66:19;
     Eze 27:13; 32:26
     [i]Eze 39:1
10:3 [j]Jer 51:27
     [k]Eze 27:14; 38:6
10:4 [l]Eze 27:7
     [m]Ps 48:7; 72:10;
     Isa 2:16; 23:1,6,
     10,14; 60:9;
     66:19; Jer 10:9;
     Eze 27:12,25;
     38:13; Jnh 1:3
     [n]Nu 24:24;
     Isa 23:12;
     Jer 2:10;
     Eze 27:6;
     Da 11:30

[n]20 Or *soil, was the first*   [o]26 Or *be his slave*
[p]27 *Japheth* sounds like the Hebrew for *extend.*
[q]27 Or *their*   [r]2 *Sons* may mean *descendants* or *successors* or *nations*; also in verses 3, 4, 6, 7, 20-23, 29 and 31.   [s]4 Some manuscripts of the Masoretic Text and Samaritan Pentateuch (see also Septuagint and 1 Chron. 1:7); most manuscripts of the Masoretic Text *Dodanim*

9:20 *man of the soil.* Noah, like his father Lamech (see 5:29), was a farmer.
9:21 *When he drank some of its wine, he became drunk.* The first reference to wine connects it with drunkenness. *uncovered inside his tent.* Excessive use of wine led, among other things, to immodest behavior (see 19:30–35).
9:22 *father of Canaan.* Mentioned here because Ham, in acting as he did, showed himself to be the true father of Canaan (i.e., of the Canaanites; see note on 15:16). *told his two brothers.* He broadcast, rather than covered, his father's immodesty.
9:23 *faces were turned . . . so that they would not see.* They wanted to avoid further disgrace to their father.
9:24 *from his wine.* From the drunkenness caused by the wine.
9:25 *Cursed be Canaan!* Some maintain that Ham's son (see vv. 18,22) was to be punished because of his father's sin (see Ex 20:5), but Ex 20 restricts such punishment to "those who hate me." It is probably better to hold that Canaan and his descendants were to be punished because they were going to be even worse than Ham (Lev 18:2–3,6–30). *lowest of slaves.* Joshua's subjection of the Gibeonites (Jos 9:27) is one of the fulfillments (see also Jos 16:10; Jdg 1:28,30, 33,35; 1Ki 9:20–21). Noah's prophecy cannot be used to justify the enslavement of blacks, since those cursed here were Canaanites, who were Caucasian.
9:26 *Blessed be the LORD.* The Lord (instead of Shem) is blessed (praised) because he is the source of Shem's blessing. He is also the "God of Shem" (and his descendants, the Semites—which included the Israelites) in a special sense.
9:27 *live in the tents of Shem.* Share in the blessings bestowed on Shem.
9:29 *and then he died.* See note on 5:5. As the tenth and last member of the genealogy of Seth (5:3–32), Noah had an obituary that ends like those of his worthy ancestors.
10:1 *account.* See note on 2:4. The links affirmed here

may not all be based on strictly physical descent, but may include geographical, historical and linguistic associations (see note on v. 5 and NIV text notes on vv. 2,8; 11:10). See also Introduction to 1 Chronicles: Genealogies.
10:2 *Japheth.* As the least involved in the Biblical narrative and perhaps also as the oldest of Noah's sons (see v. 21 and NIV text note), his descendants or successors are listed first. The genealogy of Shem, the chosen line, appears last in the chapter (see vv. 21–31; see also 11:10–26). The 14 nations that came from Japheth plus the 30 from Ham and the 26 from Shem add up to 70 (the multiple of 10 and 7, both numbers signifying completeness; see note on 5:5), perhaps in anticipation of the 70 members of Jacob's family in Egypt (see 46:27; Ex 1:5; cf. Dt 32:8). The Japhethites lived generally north and west of Palestine in Eurasia. *Gomer.* The people of Gomer (the later Cimmerians) and related nations (see v. 3) lived near the Black Sea. *Magog.* Possibly the father of a Scythian people who inhabited the Caucasus and adjacent regions southeast of the Black Sea. *Madai.* The later Medes. *Javan.* Ionia (southern Greece) and perhaps western Asia Minor. *Tubal, Meshech.* Not related to Tobolsk and Moscow in modern Russia. Together with Magog they are mentioned in later Assyrian inscriptions. See also Eze 38:2. Probably Tubal was in Pontus, and Meshech was in the Moschian Mountains. Their movement was from eastern Asia Minor north to the Black Sea. *Tiras.* Possibly the Thrace of later times.
10:3 *Ashkenaz.* The later Scythians. All three names in this verse refer to peoples located in the upper Euphrates region.
10:4 *Elishah.* Either Alashia (an ancient name for Cyprus) or a reference to Sicily and southern Italy. *Tarshish.* Probably southern Spain. *the Kittim.* A people living on Cyprus. *Rodanim.* A people whose name is perhaps reflected in Rhodes (a Greek isle).
10:5 See vv. 20,31. *territories . . . clans . . . nations . . . language.* Geographic, ethnic, political and linguistic terms,

within their nations, each with its own language.) [o]

The Hamites

10:6–20pp — 1Ch 1:8–16

[6]The sons of Ham:

Cush, [p] Mizraim, [t] Put [q] and Canaan. [r]

[7]The sons of Cush:

Seba, [s] Havilah, [t] Sabtah, Raamah [u] and Sabteca.

The sons of Raamah:

Sheba [v] and Dedan. [w]

[8]Cush was the father [u] of Nimrod, [x] who grew to be a mighty warrior on the earth. [9]He was a mighty [y] hunter [z] before the LORD; that is why it is said, "Like Nimrod, a mighty hunter before the LORD." [10]The first centers of his kingdom were Babylon, [a] Erech, [b] Akkad and Calneh, [c] in [v] Shinar. [w] [d] [11]From that land he went to Assyria, [e] where he built Nineveh, [f] Rehoboth Ir, [x] Calah [12]and Resen, which is between Nineveh and Calah; that is the great city.

[13]Mizraim was the father of

the Ludites, Anamites, Lehabites, Naphtuhites, [14]Pathrusites, Casluhites (from whom the Philistines [g] came) and Caphtorites. [h]

[15]Canaan [i] was the father of

Cross-references column

10:5 [o]Ge 9:27
10:6 [p]2Ki 19:9; 2Ch 12:3; 16:8; Isa 11:11; 18:1; 20:3; 43:3; Jer 46:9; Eze 30:4,9; 38:5; Na 3:9; Zep 2:12; 3:10 [q]Eze 27:10; 38:5 [r]S Ge 9:18
10:7 [s]Isa 43:3 [t]S Ge 2:11 [u]Eze 27:22 [v]Ge 25:3; 1Ki 10:1; 2Ch 9:1; Job 1:15; 6:19; 16:11; Ps 72:10, 15; Isa 60:6; Jer 6:20; Eze 27:22; 38:13; Joel 3:8 [w]1Ch 1:32; Isa 21:13; Jer 25:23-24; 49:8; Eze 27:15, 20; 38:13
10:8 [x]Mic 5:6
10:9 [y]2Ch 14:9; 16:8; Isa 18:2 [z]Ge 25:27; 27:3
10:10 [a]Ge 11:9; 2Ch 36:17;
Isa 13:1; 47:1; Jer 21:2; 25:12; 50:1 [b]Ezr 4:9 [c]Isa 10:9; Am 6:2 [d]Ge 11:2; 14:1; Zec 5:11 10:11 [e]Ps 83:8; Mic 5:6 [f]2Ki 19:36; Isa 37:37; Jnh 1:2; 3:2,3; 4:11; Na 1:1; Zep 2:13 10:14 [g]Ge 21:32,34; 26:1,8; Jos 13:2; Jdg 3:3; Isa 14:31; Jer 47:1,4; Am 9:7 [h]Dt 2:23; 1Ch 1:12 10:15 [i]S Ge 9:18

[t]6 That is, Egypt; also in verse 13   [u]8 Father may mean ancestor or predecessor or founder; also in verses 13, 15, 24 and 26.   [v]10 Or Erech and Akkad—all of them in   [w]10 That is, Babylonia   [x]11 Or Nineveh with its city squares

Study notes (lower two columns)

respectively. These several criteria were used to differentiate the various groups of people.

10:6 *Ham.* The Hamites were located in southwestern Asia and northeast Africa. *Cush.* The upper Nile region, south of Egypt. *Mizraim.* Means "two Egypts," a reference to Upper and Lower Egypt. *Put.* Either Libya (see note on v. 13) or the land the ancient Egyptians called Punt (modern Somalia). *Canaan.* The name means "land of purple" (as does Phoenicia, the Greek name for the same general region)—so called because Canaan was a major producer and exporter of purple dye, highly prized by royalty. The territory was much later called Palestine after the Philistines (see v. 14).

10:7 *sons of Cush.* The seven Cushite nations here mentioned were all in Arabia. Sheba and Dedan (or their namesakes) reappear as two of Abraham's grandsons (see 25:3). Together with Raamah they are mentioned in Eze 27:20–22.

10:8 *Cush.* Probably not the same as that in vv. 6–7.

Located in Mesopotamia, its name may be related to that of the later Kassites. *Nimrod.* Possibly the Hebrew name of Sargon I, an early ruler of Akkad (see v. 10).

10:10 *Erech.* The Hebrew name for Uruk (modern Warka), one of the important cities in ancient Mesopotamia.

10:12 *great city.* Possibly a reference to Calah (or even Resen), but most likely to Nineveh (see Jnh 1:2; 3:2; 4:11), either alone or including the surrounding urban areas.

10:13 *Ludites.* Perhaps the Lydians in Asia Minor (see note on v. 22). *Anamites.* Located in north Africa, west of Egypt, near Cyrene. *Lehabites.* Perhaps the Libyan desert tribes (see note on v. 6). *Naphtuhites.* People of Lower Egypt.

10:14 *Pathrusites.* The inhabitants of Upper Egypt (see note on v. 6). *Caphtorites.* Crete, known as Caphtor in ancient times, was for a while the homeland of various Philistine groups (see Jer 47:4; Am 9:7). The Philistines themselves were a vigorous Indo-European maritime people who invaded Egypt early in the 12th century B.C. After being

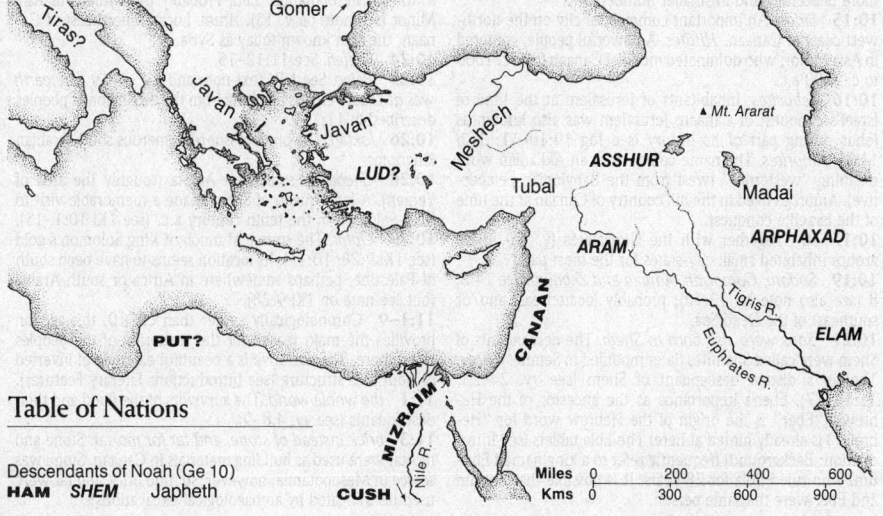

Tiras?

Gomer

Javan

Javan

Meshech

▲ Mt. Ararat

LUD?

Tubal

ASSHUR

Madai

ARAM

ARPHAXAD

Tigris R.

Euphrates R.

ELAM

PUT?

CANAAN

Nile R.

MIZRAIM

CUSH

Table of Nations

Descendants of Noah (Ge 10)
HAM *SHEM* Japheth

Miles   0   200   400   600
Kms   0   300   600   900

Sidon[j] his firstborn,[y][k] and of the
Hittites,[l] 16Jebusites,[m] Amorites,[n]
Girgashites,[o] 17Hivites,[p] Arkites,
Sinites, 18Arvadites,[q] Zemarites
and Hamathites.[r]

Later the Canaanite[s] clans scattered
19and the borders of Canaan[t] reached
from Sidon[u] toward Gerar[v] as far as
Gaza,[w] and then toward Sodom, Gomorrah, Admah and Zeboiim,[x] as far as Lasha.
20These are the sons of Ham by their
clans and languages, in their territories and
nations.

The Semites

10:21–31pp — Ge 11:10–27; 1Ch 1:17–27

21Sons were also born to Shem, whose
older brother was[z] Japheth; Shem was the
ancestor of all the sons of Eber.[y]

22The sons of Shem:
Elam,[z] Asshur,[a] Arphaxad,[b] Lud
and Aram.[c]
23The sons of Aram:
Uz,[d] Hul, Gether and Meshech.[a]
24Arphaxad was the father of[b] Shelah,
and Shelah the father of Eber.[e]
25Two sons were born to Eber:
One was named Peleg,[c] because
in his time the earth was divided;
his brother was named Joktan.
26Joktan was the father of
Almodad, Sheleph, Hazarmaveth,
Jerah, 27Hadoram, Uzal,[f] Diklah,
28Obal, Abimael, Sheba,[g]
29Ophir,[h] Havilah and Jobab. All
these were sons of Joktan.

30The region where they lived stretched
from Mesha toward Sephar, in the eastern
hill country.

31These are the sons of Shem by their
clans and languages, in their territories and
nations.

32These are the clans of Noah's sons,[i]
according to their lines of descent, within
their nations. From these the nations
spread out over the earth[j] after the flood.

The Tower of Babel

11 Now the whole world had one language[k] and a common speech. 2As
men moved eastward,[d] they found a plain
in Shinar[e][l] and settled there.
3They said to each other, "Come, let's

10:15 [j]ver 19; Jos 11:8; Jdg 10:6; Isa 23:2, 4; Jer 25:22; 27:3; 47:4; Eze 28:21; 32:30; Joel 3:4; Zec 9:2 [k]Ex 4:22; Nu 1:20; 3:2; 18:15; 26:5; 33:4 [l]Ge 15:20; 23:3, 20; 25:10; 26:34; 27:46; 49:32; Nu 13:29; Jos 1:4; 1Sa 26:6; Eze 16:3 **10:16** [m]Jdg 19:10; 1Ch 11:4; Ezr 9:1 [n]Ex 3:8; Nu 13:29; 21:13; 32:39; Dt 1:4; Jos 2:10; 2Ch 8:7 [o]Ge 15:18-21; Dt 7:1 **10:17** [p]Ge 34:2; 36:2; Ex 3:8; Dt 7:1; Jdg 3:3 **10:18** [q]Eze 27:8 [r]1Ch 18:3 [s]Ge 12:6; 13:7; 50:11; Ex 13:11; Nu 13:29; 14:25; 21:3; 33:40; Dt 1:7; Jdg 1:1 **10:19** [t]Ge 11:31; 12:1; 13:12; 17:8; 24:3; 26:34; 27:46; 28:1,6,8; 31:18; 35:6; 37:1; Lev 25:38 [u]S ver 15; Ge 49:13; Jos 19:28; Jdg 1:31; 18:28; 2Sa 24:6 [v]2Ch 14:13 [w]Dt 2:23; Jos 10:41; 11:22; 15:47; Jdg 1:18; 6:4; 16:1,21; 1Sa 6:17; Jer 25:20; 47:1; Am 1:6; Zep 2:4 [x]Ge 14:2; Dt 29:23 **10:21** [y]ver 24; Nu 24:24 **10:22** [z]Ge 14:1; Isa 11:11; 21:2; Jer 25:25; 49:34; Eze 32:24; Da 8:2 [a]Nu 24:22,24; Eze 27:23 [b]Lk 3:36 [c]Jdg 3:10; 1Ki 11:25; 19:15; 20:34; 22:31; 2Ki 5:1; 8:7 **10:23** [d]Ge 22:21; Job 1:1; Jer 25:20; La 4:21 **10:24** [e]S ver 21; Lk 3:35 **10:27** [f]Eze 27:19 **10:28** [g]1Ki 10:1; Job 6:19; Ps 72:10,15; Isa 60:6; Eze 27:22 **10:29** [h]1Ki 9:28; 10:11; 1Ch 29:4; Job 22:24; 28:16; Ps 45:9; Isa 13:12 **10:32** [i]S ver 1 [j]S Ge 9:19 **11:1** [k]ver 6 **11:2** [l]S Ge 10:10

[y] *15* Or *of the Sidonians, the foremost* [z] *21* Or *Shem, the older brother of* [a] *23* See Septuagint and 1 Chron. 1:17; Hebrew *Mash* [b] *24* Hebrew; Septuagint *father of Cainan, and Cainan was the father of* [c] *25 Peleg* means *division.* [d] *2* Or *from the east*; or *in the east* [e] *2* That is, Babylonia

driven out, they migrated in large numbers to southwest Canaan, later extending their influence over most of the land. The Philistines of the patriarchal period (see 21:32,34; 26:1,8,14–15,18) no doubt had earlier settled in Canaan more peacefully and in smaller numbers.

10:15 *Sidon.* An important commercial city on the northwest coast of Canaan. *Hittites.* A powerful people, centered in Asia Minor, who dominated much of Canaan from c. 1800 to c. 1200 B.C.

10:16 *Jebusites.* Inhabitants of Jerusalem at the time of Israel's conquest of Canaan. Jerusalem was also known as Jebus during part of its history (see Jdg 19:10–11; 1Ch 11:4). *Amorites.* The name comes from an Akkadian word meaning "westerner" (west from the Babylonian perspective). Amorites lived in the hill country of Canaan at the time of the Israelite conquest.

10:17–18 Together with the Girgashites (v. 16), these groups inhabited small city-states for the most part.

10:19 *Sodom, Gomorrah, Admah and Zeboiim.* See 14:2, 8 (see also note on 13:10); probably located east and/or southeast of the Dead Sea.

10:21 *Sons were also born to Shem.* The descendants of Shem were called Shemites (later modified to Semites). *Eber.* Though a distant descendant of Shem (see vv. 24–25; 11:14–17), Eber's importance as the ancestor of the Hebrews ("Eber" is the origin of the Hebrew word for "Hebrew") is already hinted at here. The Ebla tablets (see Introduction: Background) frequently refer to a king named Ebrium, who ruled Ebla for 28 years. It is possible that Ebrium and Eber were the same person.

10:22 *Elam.* The Elamites lived east of Mesopotamia. *Asshur.* An early name for Assyria (see note on 2:14) in northern Mesopotamia. *Arphaxad.* See also 11:10–13; perhaps a compound form of the Hebrew word for Chaldea, in southern Mesopotamia. *Lud.* Probably the Lydians of Asia Minor (see note on v. 13). *Aram.* Located northeast of Canaan, the area known today as Syria.

10:24 *Shelah.* See 11:12–15.

10:25 *Peleg.* See NIV text note and 11:16–19. *the earth was divided.* Perhaps resulting from the dispersion of peoples described in 11:1–9.

10:26 *Joktan.* The predecessor of numerous south Arabian kingdoms.

10:28 *Sheba.* In southwest Arabia (roughly the area of Yemen). A later queen of Sheba made a memorable visit to King Solomon in the tenth century B.C. (see 1Ki 10:1–13).

10:29 *Ophir.* The source of much of King Solomon's gold (see 1Ki 9:28; 10:11). Its location seems to have been south of Palestine, perhaps somewhere in Africa or south Arabia (but see note on 1Ki 9:28).

11:1–9 Chronologically earlier than ch. 10, this section provides the main reason for the scattering of the peoples listed there. The narrative is a beautiful example of inverted or hourglass structure (see Introduction: Literary Features).

11:1 *the whole world.* The survivors of the flood and their descendants (see vv. 4,8–9).

11:3 *brick instead of stone, and tar for mortar.* Stone and mortar were used as building materials in Canaan. Stone was scarce in Mesopotamia, however, so mud brick and tar were used (as indicated by archaeological excavations).

make bricks ^{m} and bake them thoroughly."
They used brick instead of stone, ^{n} and
tar ^{o} for mortar. 4Then they said, "Come,
let us build ourselves a city, with a tower
that reaches to the heavens, ^{p} so that we
may make a name ^{q} for ourselves and not
be scattered ^{r} over the face of the whole
earth." ^{s}

5But the Lord came down ^{t} to see the
city and the tower that the men were
building. 6The Lord said, "If as one people
speaking the same language ^{u} they have
begun to do this, then nothing they plan to
do will be impossible for them. 7Come, let
us ^{v} go down ^{w} and confuse their language
so they will not understand each other." ^{x}

8So the Lord scattered them from there
over all the earth, ^{y} and they stopped
building the city. 9That is why it was called
Babel ^{z}—because there the Lord confused the language ^{a} of the whole world. ^{b}
From there the Lord scattered ^{c} them over
the face of the whole earth.

From Shem to Abram

11:10–27pp — Ge 10:21–31; 1Ch 1:17–27

10This is the account ^{d} of Shem.

Two years after the flood, when Shem
was 100 years old, he became the father ^{g}
of Arphaxad. ^{e} 11And after he became the
father of Arphaxad, Shem lived 500 years
and had other sons and daughters.

12When Arphaxad had lived 35 years,
he became the father of Shelah. ^{f} 13And
after he became the father of Shelah, Arphaxad lived 403 years and had other sons
and daughters. ^{h}

14When Shelah had lived 30 years, he
became the father of Eber. ^{g} 15And after he
became the father of Eber, Shelah lived
403 years and had other sons and daughters.

16When Eber had lived 34 years, he
became the father of Peleg. ^{h} 17And after
he became the father of Peleg, Eber lived
430 years and had other sons and daughters.

18When Peleg had lived 30 years, he
became the father of Reu. ^{i} 19And after he
became the father of Reu, Peleg lived 209
years and had other sons and daughters.

20When Reu had lived 32 years, he
became the father of Serug. ^{j} 21And after
he became the father of Serug, Reu lived
207 years and had other sons and daughters.

22When Serug had lived 30 years, he
became the father of Nahor. ^{k} 23And after
he became the father of Nahor, Serug lived
200 years and had other sons and daughters.

24When Nahor had lived 29 years, he
became the father of Terah. ^{l} 25And after
he became the father of Terah, Nahor lived
119 years and had other sons and daughters.

26After Terah had lived 70 years, he

f9 That is, Babylon; *Babel* sounds like the Hebrew for
confused. g10 *Father* may mean *ancestor*; also in
verses 11-25. h12,13 Hebrew; Septuagint (see also
Luke 3:35, 36 and note at Gen. 10:24) *35 years, he
became the father of Cainan. 13And after he became the
father of Cainan, Arphaxad lived 430 years and had other
sons and daughters, and then he died. When Cainan had
lived 130 years, he became the father of Shelah. And
after he became the father of Shelah, Cainan lived 330
years and had other sons and daughters*

Cross references

11:3 ^{m}Ex 1:14; 5:7; Jer 43:9 ^{n}Isa 9:10; Am 5:11 ^{o}Ge 14:10
11:4 ^{p}Dt 1:28; 6:10; 9:1; Job 20:6; Jer 51:53 ^{q}Ge 6:4 ^{r}Dt 30:3; 1Ki 22:17; Est 3:8; Ps 44:11; Jer 31:10; 40:15; Eze 6:8; Joel 3:2 ^{s}S Ge 9:19; Dt 4:27
11:5 ^{t}ver 7; Ge 18:21; Ex 3:8; 19:11,18,20; Ps 18:9; 144:5 ^{u}S ver 1
11:7 ^{v}S Ge 1:26 ^{w}S ver 5 ^{x}Ge 42:23; Dt 28:49; Isa 28:11; 33:19; Jer 5:15; 1Co 14:2,11
11:8 ^{y}S Ge 9:19; Dt 32:8; S Lk 1:51
11:9 ^{z}S Ge 10:10 ^{a}Ps 55:9 ^{b}Ac 2:5-11 ^{c}Isa 2:10,21; 13:14; 24:1
11:10 ^{d}S Ge 2:4 ^{e}Lk 3:36
11:12 ^{f}Lk 3:35
11:14 ^{g}Lk 3:35
11:16 ^{h}Lk 3:35
11:18 ^{i}Lk 3:35
11:20 ^{j}Lk 3:35
11:22 ^{k}Lk 3:34
11:24 ^{l}Lk 3:34

Notes

11:4 *us . . . ourselves . . . we . . . ourselves.* The people's
plans were egotistical and proud. *tower.* The typical Mesopotamian temple-tower, known as a ziggurat, was square at the
base and had sloping, stepped sides that led upward to a
small shrine at the top. *reaches to the heavens.* A similar
ziggurat may be described in 28:12. Other Mesopotamian
ziggurats were given names demonstrating that they, too,
were meant to serve as staircases from earth to heaven: "The
House of the Link between Heaven and Earth" (at Larsa),
"The House of the Seven Guides of Heaven and Earth" (at
Borsippa), "The House of the Foundation-Platform of
Heaven and Earth" (at Babylon), "The House of the Mountain of the Universe" (at Asshur). *name.* In the OT, "name"
also refers to reputation, fame or renown. (The Nephilim
were "men of renown [lit. 'name']," 6:4.) At Babel (see note
on v. 9) rebellious man undertook a united and godless effort
to establish for himself, by a titanic human enterprise, a
world renown by which he would dominate God's creation
(cf. 10:8–12; 2Sa 18:18). *scattered.* See note on v. 8.
11:6 *If . . . then.* If the whole human race remained united
in the proud attempt to take its destiny into its own hands
and, by its man-centered efforts, to seize the reins of history,
there would be no limit to its unrestrained rebellion against
God. The kingdom of man would displace and exclude the
kingdom of God.

11:7 *let us.* See notes on 1:1,26. God's "Come, let us"
from above counters proud man's "Come, let us" (v. 4) from
below. *not understand each other.* Without a common language, joint effort became impossible (see v. 8).
11:8 *scattered.* See v. 4; 9:19. God dispersed the people
because of their rebellious pride. Even the greatest of human
powers cannot defy God and long survive.
11:9 *Babel.* See NIV text note and 10:10. The word is of
Akkadian origin and means "gateway to a god" (Jacob's
stairway was similarly called "gate of heaven"; see 28:17).
confused. The Hebrew word used here (*balal*) sounds like
"Babel," the Hebrew word for Babylon and the origin of the
English word "babel."
11:10–26 A ten-name genealogy, like that of Seth (see
5:3–31; see also note on 5:5). Unlike the Sethite genealogy,
however, the genealogy of Shem does not give total figures
for the ages of the men at death and does not end each
paragraph with "and then he died." It covers the centuries
between Shem and Abram as briefly as possible.
11:10 *account.* See note on 2:4.
11:26 *Terah . . . became the father of Abram, Nahor and
Haran.* As in the case of Shem, Ham and Japheth, the names
of the three sons may not be in chronological order by age
(see 9:24; see also 10:21 and NIV text note). Haran died
while his father was still alive (see v. 28).

became the father of Abram, [m] Nahor [n] and Haran. [o]

27This is the account [p] of Terah.

Terah became the father of Abram, Nahor [q] and Haran. And Haran became the father of Lot. [r] 28While his father Terah was still alive, Haran died in Ur of the Chaldeans, [s] in the land of his birth. 29Abram and Nahor [t] both married. The name of Abram's wife was Sarai, [u] and the name of Nahor's wife was Milcah; [v] she was the daughter of Haran, the father of both Milcah and Iscah. 30Now Sarai was barren; she had no children. [w]

31Terah took his son Abram, his grandson Lot [x] son of Haran, and his daughter-in-law [y] Sarai, the wife of his son Abram, and together they set out from Ur of the Chaldeans [z] to go to Canaan. [a] But when they came to Haran, [b] they settled there. 32Terah [c] lived 205 years, and he died in Haran.

The Call of Abram

12 The LORD had said to Abram, "Leave your country, your people and your father's household [d] and go to the land [e] I will show you. [f]

2"I will make you into a great nation [g] and I will bless you; [h]

I will make your name great,
    and you will be a blessing. [i]
3I will bless those who bless you,
    and whoever curses you I will
        curse; [j]
and all peoples on earth
    will be blessed through you. [k]"

4So Abram left, as the LORD had told him; and Lot [l] went with him. Abram was seventy-five years old [m] when he set out from Haran. [n] 5He took his wife Sarai, [o] his nephew Lot, all the possessions they had accumulated [p] and the people [q] they had acquired in Haran, and they set out for the land of Canaan, [r] and they arrived there. 6Abram traveled through the land [s] as far as the site of the great tree of Moreh [t] at Shechem. [u] At that time the Canaanites [v] were in the land. 7The LORD ap-

11:26 mLk 3:34
nJos 24:2
11:27 o2Ki 19:12;
Isa 37:12;
Eze 27:23
11:27 pS Ge 2:4
qver 29;
Ge 31:53 rver 31;
Ge 12:4; 13:1,5,
8,12; 14:12;
19:1; Lk 17:28;
2Pe 2:7
11:28 sver 31;
Ge 15:7; Ne 9:7;
Job 1:17; 16:11;
Eze 23:23; Ac 7:4
11:29 tS ver 27,
31; Ge 22:20,23;
24:10,15,24;
29:5 uGe 12:5,
11; 16:1; 17:15
vGe 22:20
11:30 wGe 16:1;
18:11; 25:21;
29:31; 30:1,22;
Jdg 13:2; 1Sa 1:5;
Ps 113:9; Lk 1:7,
36
11:31 xS ver 27
yGe 38:11;
Lev 18:15; 20:12;
Ru 1:6,22; 2:20;
4:15; 1Sa 4:19;
1Ch 2:4;
Eze 22:11;
Mic 7:6 zS ver
28; Ac 7:4
aS Ge 10:19
bS ver 29;
Ge 12:4; 27:43;
28:5,10; 29:4;
2Ki 19:12;
Eze 27:23
11:32 cJos 24:2
12:1 dGe 20:13;
24:4,27,40
eS Ge 10:19
fGe 15:7; 26:2;
Jos 24:3; Ac 7:3*;
Heb 11:8

12:2 gGe 13:16; 15:5; 17:2,4; 18:18; 22:17; 26:4; 28:3,14;
32:12; 35:11; 41:49; 46:3; 47:27; 48:4,16,19; Ex 1:7; 5:5;
32:13; Dt 1:10; 10:22; 13:17; 26:5; Jos 11:4; 24:3;
2Sa 17:11; 1Ki 3:8; 4:20; 1Ch 27:23; 2Ch 1:9; Ne 9:23;
Ps 107:38; Isa 6:13; 10:22; 48:19; 51:2; 54:3; 60:22;
Jer 33:22; Mic 4:7 hGe 24:1,35; 25:11; 26:3; 28:4;
Ex 20:24; Nu 22:12; 23:8,20; 24:9; Ps 67:6; 115:12;
Isa 44:3; 61:9; 65:23; Mal 3:12 iGe 22:18; Isa 19:24;
Jer 4:2; Hag 2:19; Zec 8:13 12:3 jGe 27:29; Ex 23:22;
Nu 24:9; Dt 30:7 kGe 15:5; 18:18; 22:18; 26:4; 28:4,14;
Dt 9:5; Ps 72:17; Isa 19:25; Ac 3:25; Gal 3:8* 12:4
lS Ge 11:29 mGe 16:3,16; 17:1,17,24; 21:5 nS Ge 11:31
12:5 oS Ge 11:29 pver 16; Ge 13:2,6; 31:18; 46:6
qGe 14:14; 15:3; 17:23; Ecc 2:7 rGe 11:31; 16:3; Heb 11:8
12:6 sHeb 11:9 tGe 35:4; Dt 11:30; Jos 24:26; Jdg 7:1; 9:6
uGe 33:18; 37:12; Jos 17:7; 20:7; 24:1; Jdg 8:31; 21:19;
1Ki 12:1; Ps 60:6; 108:7 vS Ge 10:18

11:27 account. See note on 2:4.

11:28 Ur of the Chaldeans. Possibly in northern Mesopotamia, but more likely the site on the Euphrates in southern Iraq excavated by Leonard Woolley between 1922 and 1934. Ruins and artifacts from Ur reveal a civilization and culture that reached high levels before Abram's time. King Ur-Nammu, who may have been Abram's contemporary, is famous for his law code.

11:30 Sarai was barren. The sterility of Abram's wife (see 15:2–3; 17:17) emphasized the fact that God's people would not come by natural generation from the post-Babel peoples. God was bringing a new humanity into being, of whom Abram was father (17:5), just as Adam and Noah were fathers of the fallen human race.

11:31 they came to Haran. In Hebrew the name of the town is spelled differently from that of Abram's brother (v. 26). The moon-god was worshiped at both Ur and Haran, and since Terah was an idolater (see Jos 24:2) he probably felt at home in either place. Haran was a flourishing caravan city in the 19th century B.C. In the 18th century it was ruled by Amorites (see note on 10:16).

12:1 had said. God had spoken to Abram "while he was still in Mesopotamia, before he lived in Haran" (Ac 7:2). Leave . . . show you. Abram must leave the settled world of the post-Babel nations and begin a pilgrimage with God to a better world of God's making (see 24:7).

12:2–3 God's promise to Abram has a sevenfold structure: (1) "I will make you into a great nation," (2) "I will bless you," (3) "I will make your name great," (4) "you will be a blessing," (5) "I will bless those who bless you," (6) "whoever curses you I will curse," and (7) "all peoples on earth will be blessed through you." God's original blessing on all

mankind (1:28) would be restored and fulfilled through Abram and his offspring. In various ways and degrees, these promises were reaffirmed to Abram (v. 7; 15:5–21; 17:4–8; 18:18–19; 22:17–18), to Isaac (26:2–4), to Jacob (28:13–15; 35:11–12; 46:3) and to Moses (Ex 3:6–8; 6:2–8). The seventh promise is quoted in Ac 3:25 with reference to Peter's Jewish listeners (see Ac 3:12)—Abram's physical descendants—and in Gal 3:8 with reference to Paul's Gentile listeners—Abram's spiritual descendants.

12:4 Abram left, as the LORD had told him. See Heb 11:8. Prompt obedience grounded in faith characterized this patriarch throughout his life (see 17:23; 21:14; 22:3). Lot went with him. See 13:1,5. Lot at first was little more than Abram's ward. seventy-five years old. Although advanced in age at the time of his call, Abram would live for another full century (see 25:7; see also note on 5:5).

12:5 people they had acquired. Wealthy people in that ancient world always had servants to help them with their flocks and herds (see 15:3; 24:2). Not all servants were slaves; many were voluntarily employed.

12:6 site of the great tree of Moreh. See perhaps 35:4; Jdg 9:6,37. A famous sanctuary was located at Shechem in central Canaan, and a large tree was often a conspicuous feature at such holy places. But Abram worshiped the Lord there, not the local deity.

12:7 The LORD appeared. The Lord frequently appeared visibly to Abram and to others, but not in all his glory (see Ex 33:18–20; Jn 1:18). an altar. The first of several that Abram built at places where he had memorable spiritual experiences (see v. 8; 13:18; 22:9). He acknowledged that the land of Canaan belonged to the Lord in a special way (see Ex 20:24; Jos 22:19).

peared to Abram[w] and said, "To your off-spring[i] I will give this land.[x]"[y] So he built an altar there to the LORD,[z] who had appeared to him.

[8]From there he went on toward the hills east of Bethel[a] and pitched his tent,[b] with Bethel on the west and Ai[c] on the east. There he built an altar to the LORD and called on the name of the LORD.[d] [9]Then Abram set out and continued toward the Negev.[e]

Abram in Egypt

12:10–20Ref — Ge 20:1–18; 26:1–11

[10]Now there was a famine in the land,[f] and Abram went down to Egypt to live there for a while because the famine was severe.[g] [11]As he was about to enter Egypt, he said to his wife Sarai,[h] "I know what a beautiful woman[i] you are. [12]When the Egyptians see you, they will say, 'This is his wife.' Then they will kill me but will let you live. [13]Say you are my sister,[j] so that I will be treated well for your sake and my life will be spared because of you."

[14]When Abram came to Egypt, the Egyptians saw that she was a very beautiful woman.[k] [15]And when Pharaoh's officials saw her, they praised her to Pharaoh, and she was taken into his palace. [16]He treated Abram well for her sake, and Abram acquired sheep and cattle, male and female donkeys, menservants and maidservants, and camels.[l]

[17]But the LORD inflicted[m] serious diseases on Pharaoh and his household[n] because of Abram's wife Sarai. [18]So Pharaoh summoned Abram. "What have you done to me?"[o] he said. "Why didn't you tell me she was your wife?[p] [19]Why did you say,

'She is my sister,'[q] so that I took her to be my wife? Now then, here is your wife. Take her and go!" [20]Then Pharaoh gave orders about Abram to his men, and they sent him on his way, with his wife and everything he had.

Abram and Lot Separate

13 So Abram went up from Egypt[r] to the Negev,[s] with his wife and everything he had, and Lot[t] went with him. [2]Abram had become very wealthy[u] in livestock[v] and in silver and gold.

[3]From the Negev[w] he went from place to place until he came to Bethel,[x] to the place between Bethel and Ai[y] where his tent had been earlier [4]and where he had first built an altar.[z] There Abram called on the name of the LORD.[a]

[5]Now Lot,[b] who was moving about with Abram, also had flocks and herds and tents. [6]But the land could not support them while they stayed together, for their possessions were so great that they were not able to stay together.[c] [7]And quarreling[d] arose between Abram's herdsmen and the herdsmen of Lot. The Canaanites[e] and Perizzites[f] were also living in the land[g] at that time.

[8]So Abram said to Lot,[h] "Let's not have any quarreling between you and me,[i] or between your herdsmen and mine, for we

---

Cross references (center column):

12:7 [w]Ge 17:1; 18:1; 26:2; 35:1; [x]Ex 6:3; Ac 7:2 [x]Ex 3:8; Nu 10:29; Dt 30:5; Heb 11:8 [y]Ge 13:15,17; 15:18; 17:8; 23:18; 24:7; 26:3-4; 28:13; 35:12; 48:4; 50:24; Ex 6:4,8; 13:5,11; 32:13; 33:1; Nu 11:12; Dt 1:8; 2:31; 9:5; 11:9; 34:4; 2Ki 25:21; 1Ch 16:16; 2Ch 20:7; Ps 105:9-11; Jer 25:5; Eze 47:14; Ac 7:5; Ro 4:13; Gal 3:16* [z]S Ge 8:20; 13:4 **12:8** [a]Ge 13:3; 28:11,19; 35:1,8, 15; Jos 7:2; 8:9; 1Sa 7:16; 1Ki 12:29; Hos 12:4; Am 3:14; 4:4 [b]Ge 26:25; 33:19; Heb 11:9 [c]Jos 7:2; 12:9; Ezr 2:28; Ne 7:32; Jer 49:3 [d]S Ge 4:26; S 8:20 **12:9** [e]Ge 13:1,3; 20:1; 24:62; Nu 13:17; 33:40; Dt 34:3; Jos 10:40 **12:10** [f]Ge 41:27, 57; 42:5; 43:1; 47:4,13; Ru 1:1; 2Sa 21:1; 2Ki 8:1; Ps 105:19 [g]Ge 41:30,54,56; 47:20; Ps 105:16 **12:11** [h]S Ge 11:29 [i]ver 14; Ge 24:16; 26:7; 29:17; 39:6 **12:13** [j]Ge 20:2; 26:7 **12:14** [k]S ver 11 **12:16** [l]S ver 5; Ge 24:35; 26:14; 30:43; 32:5; 34:23; 47:17; Job 1:3; 31:25

12:17 [m]2Ki 15:5; Job 30:11; Isa 53:4,10 [n]1Ch 16:21; Ps 105:14 **12:18** [o]Ge 20:9; 26:10; 29:25; 31:26; 44:15 [p]Isa 43:27; 51:2; Eze 16:3 **12:19** [q]Ge 20:5; 26:9 **13:1** [r]Ge 45:25 [s]S Ge 12:9 [t]S Ge 11:27 **13:2** [u]S Ge 12:5; 26:13; Pr 10:22 [v]Ge 32:15; Job 1:3; 42:12 **13:3** [w]S Ge 12:9 [x]S Ge 12:8 [y]Jos 7:2 **13:4** [z]S Ge 12:7 [a]S Ge 4:26 **13:5** [b]S Ge 11:27 **13:6** [c]S Ge 12:5; 33:9; 36:7 **13:7** [d]Ge 26:20, 21; Nu 20:3 [e]S Ge 10:18 [f]Ge 15:20; 34:30; Ex 3:8; Jdg 1:4 [g]Ge 12:6; 34:30 **13:8** [h]S Ge 1:27 [i]Pr 15:18; 20:3

[i] Or *seed*

12:8 *Bethel.* Just north of Jerusalem, it was an important town in the religious history of God's ancient people (see, e.g., 28:10–22; 35:1–8; 1Ki 12:26–29). Only Jerusalem is mentioned more often in the OT.
12:9 *Negev.* The dry wasteland stretching southward from Beersheba. The same Hebrew word is translated "south" in 13:14.
12:10 *went down to Egypt ... because the famine was severe.* Egypt's food supply was usually plentiful because the Nile's water supply was normally dependable.
12:11 *beautiful.* See v. 14. She was 65 at the time (see v. 4; 17:17). The Genesis Apocryphon (one of the Dead Sea Scrolls) praises Sarai's beauty. Abram's experience in this episode foreshadows Israel's later experience in Egypt, as the author of Genesis, writing after the exodus, was very much aware. Abram was truly the "father" of Israel.
12:13 *Say you are my sister.* If Pharaoh were to add Sarai to his harem while knowing that she was Abram's wife, he would have to kill Abram first.
12:15 *Pharaoh.* See note on Ex 1:11.
12:16 Livestock was an important measure of wealth in ancient times (see 13:2). *menservants and maidservants.*

See note on v. 5. *camels.* Although camels were not widely used until much later (see, e.g., Jdg 6:5), archaeology has confirmed their occasional domestication as early as the patriarchal period.
12:19 *Why did you say, 'She is my sister' ... ?* Egyptian ethics emphasized the importance of absolute truthfulness, and Abram was put in the uncomfortable position of being exposed as a liar.
12:20 *Pharaoh gave orders.* See Ex 12:31–32.
13:2 *had become very wealthy.* Abram left Egypt with greater wealth than he had before—even as Israel would later leave Egypt laden with wealth from the Egyptians (Ex 3:22; 12:36).
13:4 *Abram called on the name of the LORD.* As he had done earlier at the same place (see 12:8).
13:6 *the land could not support them.* Livestock made up the greater part of their possessions, and the region around Bethel and Ai did not have enough water or pasture for such large flocks and herds (see v. 10; 26:17–22,32; 36:7).
13:7 *Perizzites.* May refer to rural inhabitants in contrast to city dwellers.
13:8 *brothers.* Relatives (as often in the Bible).

are brothers.[i] 9Is not the whole land before you? Let's part company. If you go to the left, I'll go to the right; if you go to the right, I'll go to the left."[k]

10Lot looked up and saw that the whole plain[l] of the Jordan[m] was well watered, like the garden of the LORD,[n] like the land of Egypt,[o] toward Zoar.[p] (This was before the LORD destroyed Sodom[q] and Gomorrah.)[r] 11So Lot chose for himself the whole plain of the Jordan and set out toward the east. The two men parted company: 12Abram lived in the land of Canaan,[s] while Lot[t] lived among the cities of the plain[u] and pitched his tents near Sodom.[v] 13Now the men of Sodom[w] were wicked and were sinning greatly against the LORD.[x]

14The LORD said to Abram after Lot had parted from him, "Lift up your eyes from where you are and look north and south, east and west.[y] 15All the land that you see I will give to you and your offspring[j] forever.[z] 16I will make your offspring like the dust of the earth, so that if anyone could count the dust, then your offspring could be counted.[a] 17Go, walk through the length and breadth of the land,[b] for I am giving it to you."[c]

18So Abram moved his tents and went to live near the great trees of Mamre[d] at Hebron,[e] where he built an altar to the LORD.[f]

Abram Rescues Lot

14 At this time Amraphel king of Shinar,[k][g] Arioch king of Ellasar, Ked-

orlaomer[h] king of Elam[i] and Tidal king of Goiim 2went to war against Bera king of Sodom, Birsha king of Gomorrah, Shinab king of Admah, Shemeber king of Zeboiim,[j] and the king of Bela (that is, Zoar).[k] 3All these latter kings joined forces in the Valley of Siddim[l] (the Salt Sea[1] [m]). 4For twelve years they had been subject to Kedorlaomer,[n] but in the thirteenth year they rebelled.

5In the fourteenth year, Kedorlaomer[o] and the kings allied with him went out and defeated the Rephaites[p] in Ashteroth Karnaim, the Zuzites in Ham, the Emites[q] in Shaveh Kiriathaim[o]and the Horites[r] in the hill country of Seir,[s] as far as El Paran[t] near the desert. 7Then they turned back and went to En Mishpat (that is, Kadesh),[u] and they conquered the whole territory of the Amalekites,[v] as well as the Amorites[w] who were living in Hazazon Tamar.[x]

8Then the king of Sodom, the king of Gomorrah,[y] the king of Admah, the king of Zeboiim[z] and the king of Bela (that is,

13:8 /Ge 19:9; Ex 2:14;
9 Nu 16:13; Ps 133:1
13:9 kGe 20:15; 34:10; 47:6; Jer 40:4
13:10 /1Ki 7:46; 2Ch 4:17; mNu 13:29; 33:48; nGe 2:8-10; Isa 51:3; Eze 31:8-9 oGe 46:7 pGe 14:2; 19:22, 30; Dt 34:3; Isa 15:5; Jer 48:34 qDt 29:23; Job 39:6; Ps 107:34; Jer 4:26 rGe 14:8; 19:17-29
13:12 sS Ge 10:19 tS Ge 11:27 uS ver 10; Ge 19:17,25,29 vGe 14:12
13:13 wGe 19:4; Isa 1:10; 3:9 xGe 18:20; 19:5; 20:6; 39:9; Nu 32:23; 1Sa 12:23; 2Sa 12:13; Ps 51:4; Eze 16:49-50; 2Pe 2:8
13:14 yGe 28:14; 32:12; 48:16; Dt 3:27; 13:17; Isa 54:3
13:15 zS Ge 12:7; Gal 3:16*
13:16 aS Ge 12:2; 16:10; 17:20; 21:13,18; 25:16; Nu 23:10
13:17 bver 15; Nu 13:17-25 cS Ge 12:7; 15:7
13:18 dGe 14:13, 24; 18:1; 23:17, 19; 25:9; 49:30; 50:13 eGe 23:2;

35:27; 37:14; Nu 13:22; Jos 10:3,36; Jdg 1:10; 1Sa 30:31; 2Sa 2:1,3,11; 1Ch 11:1 /S Ge 8:20 **14:1** gS Ge 10:10 hver 4, 9,17 iS Ge 10:22 **14:2** /S Ge 10:19 kS Ge 13:10 **14:3** lver 8, 10 mNu 34:3,12; Dt 3:17; Jos 3:16; 12:3; 15:2,5; 18:19 **14:4** nver 1 **14:5** oGe 15:20; Dt 2:11,20; 3:11, 13; Jos 12:4; 13:12; 17:15; 1Ch 20:4 qDt 2:10 **14:6** rGe 36:20; Dt 2:12,22 sGe 32:3; 33:14,16; 36:8; Dt 1:2; 2:1,5,22; Jos 11:17; 24:4; 1Ch 4:42; Isa 34:5; Eze 25:8; 35:2; Am 1:6 tGe 21:21; Nu 10:12; 12:16; 13:3,26; Hab 3:3 **14:7** uGe 16:14; 20:1; Nu 13:26; 20:1; 32:8; Dt 1:2; Jos 10:41; Jdg 11:16; Ps 29:8 vEx 17:8; Nu 13:29; 14:25; 24:20; Dt 25:17; Jdg 3:13; 6:3; 10:12; 12:15; 1Sa 14:48; 15:2; 28:18; 2Sa 1:1; 1Ch 4:43; Ps 83:7 wNu 13:29; Dt 1:4; Jos 2:10; 13:4 x2Ch 20:2; Eze 48:28 **14:8** yS Ge 13:10 zDt 29:23; Hos 11:8

i15 Or seed; also in verse 16   *k1 That is, Babylonia;* also in verse 9   *l3 That is, the Dead Sea*

13:9 Abram, always generous, gave his young nephew the opportunity to choose the land he wanted. He himself would not obtain wealth except by the Lord's blessing (see 14:22–24).

13:10 *plain.* The Hebrew for this word picturesquely describes this section of the Jordan Valley as oval in shape. *like the land of Egypt.* Because of its abundant and dependable water supply (see note on 12:10), Egypt came the closest to matching Eden's ideal conditions (see 2:10). *the LORD destroyed Sodom and Gomorrah.* See especially 18:16–19:29. The names of Sodom and Gomorrah became proverbial for vile wickedness and for divine judgment on sin. Archaeology has confirmed that, prior to this catastrophe, the now dry area east and southeast of the Dead Sea (see note on 10:19) had ample water and was well populated.

13:12 *Lot . . . pitched his tents near Sodom.* Since the men of Sodom were known to be wicked (see v. 13), Lot was flirting with temptation by choosing to live near them. Contrast the actions of Abram (v. 18).

13:14 *Lift up your eyes . . . and look.* See Dt 34:1–4. Lot and Abram are a study in contrasts. The former looked selfishly and coveted (v. 10); the latter looked as God commanded and was blessed.

13:16 *like the dust of the earth.* A simile (common in the ancient Near East) for the large number of Abram's offspring (see 28:14; 2Ch 1:9; see also Nu 23:10). Similar phrases

are: "as numerous as the stars in the sky" and "as the sand on the seashore" (22:17).

13:17 *walk through . . . the land.* Either to inspect it or to exercise authority over it, demonstrating the promised ownership.

13:18 *great trees.* See note on 12:6. *Mamre.* A town named after one of Abram's allies (see 14:13). *Hebron.* Kiriath Arba (see note on 23:2). *altar.* See note on 12:7.

14:1 *Amraphel king of Shinar.* Not the great Babylonian king Hammurapi, as once thought. *Elam.* See note on 10:22. *Goiim.* The Hebrew word means "Gentile nations" and may be a common noun here (as in Isa 9:1).

14:3 *Salt Sea.* The Dead Sea, whose water contains a 25 percent concentration of chloride and bromide salts, making it the densest large body of water on earth.

14:6 *Horites.* Formerly thought to be cave dwellers (the Hebrew word *ḥor* means "cave"), they are now known to have been the Hurrians, a non-Semitic people widely dispersed throughout the ancient Near East.

14:7 *En Mishpat.* Another name for Kadesh, it means "spring of judgment/justice." It is called Meribah Kadesh, "quarreling/litigation at Kadesh," in Dt 32:51 (see Nu 27:14). *Kadesh.* Located in the southwest Negev (see note on 12:9), it was later called Kadesh Barnea (see Nu 32:8). *Amalekites.* A tribal people living in the Negev and in the Sinai peninsula. *Amorites.* See note on 10:16.

Zoar)[a] marched out and drew up their battle lines in the Valley of Siddim[b] [9]against Kedorlaomer[c] king of Elam,[d] Tidal king of Goiim, Amraphel king of Shinar and Arioch king of Ellasar—four kings against five. [10]Now the Valley of Siddim[e] was full of tar[f] pits, and when the kings of Sodom and Gomorrah[g] fled, some of the men fell into them and the rest fled to the hills.[h] [11]The four kings seized all the goods[i] of Sodom and Gomorrah and all their food; then they went away. [12]They also carried off Abram's nephew Lot[j] and his possessions, since he was living in Sodom.

[13]One who had escaped came and reported this to Abram the Hebrew.[k] Now Abram was living near the great trees of Mamre[l] the Amorite, a brother[m] of Eshcol[m] and Aner, all of whom were allied with Abram. [14]When Abram heard that his relative[n] had been taken captive, he called out the 318 trained[o] men born in his household[p] and went in pursuit as far as Dan.[q] [15]During the night Abram divided his men[r] to attack them and he routed them, pursuing them as far as Hobah, north of Damascus.[s] [16]He recovered[t] all the goods[u] and brought back his relative Lot and his possessions, together with the women and the other people.

[17]After Abram returned from defeating

Kedorlaomer[v] and the kings allied with him, the king of Sodom[w] came out to meet him in the Valley of Shaveh (that is, the King's Valley).[x]

[18]Then Melchizedek[y] king of Salem[n] [z] brought out bread[a] and wine.[b] He was priest of God Most High,[c] [19]and he blessed Abram,[d] saying,

"Blessed be Abram by God Most High,[e]
     Creator[o] of heaven and earth.[f]
[20]And blessed be[p] God Most High,[g]
     who delivered your enemies into
        your hand."

Then Abram gave him a tenth of everything.[h]

[21]The king of Sodom[i] said to Abram, "Give me the people and keep the goods[j] for yourself."

[22]But Abram said to the king of Sodom,[k] "I have raised my hand[l] to the LORD, God Most High,[m] Creator of heaven and earth,[n] and have taken an oath [23]that I will accept nothing belonging to you,[o]

Cross-references (center column):

14:8 [a]S Ge 13:10
[b]S ver 3
14:9 [c]S ver 1
[d]S Ge 10:22
14:10 [e]S ver 3
[f]Ge 11:3 [g]ver 17,
21 [h]Ge 19:17,30;
Jos 2:16; Ps 11:1
14:11 [i]ver 16,21
14:12
[j]S Ge 11:27
14:13 [k]Ge 37:28;
39:14,17; 40:15;
41:12; 43:32;
Ex 3:18; 1Sa 4:6;
14:11
[l]S Ge 13:18
[m]Nu 13:23; 32:9;
Dt 1:24
14:14 [n]ver 12
[o]Dt 4:9; Pr 22:6
[p]S Ge 12:5
[q]Dt 34:1;
1Ki 15:20
14:15 [r]Jdg 7:16
[s]Ge 15:2;
2Sa 8:5;
1Ki 20:34;
2Ki 16:9; Isa 7:8;
8:4; 10:9; 17:1;
Jer 49:23,27;
Eze 27:18;
Am 1:3-5
14:16 [t]1Sa 30:8,
18 [u]S ver 11
14:17 [v]S ver 1
[w]S ver 10
[x]2Sa 18:18
14:18 [y]Ps 110:4;
Heb 5:6; 7:17,21
[z]Ps 76:2; Heb 7:2
[a]S Ge 3:19
[b]Jdg 9:13; 19:19;
Est 1:10;
Ps 104:15;
Pr 31:6;
Ecc 10:19; SS 1:2
[c]ver 22; Ps 7:8,
17; Da 7:27

14:19 [d]Heb 7:6 [e]ver 18 [f]ver 22; S Ge 1:1; 24:3; Jos 2:11;
Ps 148:5; Mt 11:25 14:20 [g]S Ge 9:26; S 24:27 [h]Ge 28:22;
Dt 14:22; 26:12; Lk 18:12; Heb 7:4 14:21 [i]S ver 10 /S ver
11 14:22 [k]S ver 10 [l]Ex 6:8; Nu 14:30; Dt 32:40; Ne 9:15;
Eze 20:5; Da 12:7; Rev 10:5-6 [m]S ver 18 [n]S ver 19 14:23
[o]1Sa 15:3,19; 2Ki 5:16; Est 8:11; 9:10,15

[m]13 Or a relative; or an ally   [n]18 That is, Jerusalem
[o]19 Or Possessor; also in verse 22   [p]20 Or And
praise be to

14:10 *tar pits.* Lumps of asphalt are often seen even today floating in the southern end of the Dead Sea. *hills.* The Dead Sea, the lowest body of water on earth (about 1,300 feet below sea level), is flanked by hills on both sides.
14:12 *Lot . . . was living in Sodom.* He moved into the town and was living among its wicked people (see 2Pe 2:8). Though Lot was "righteous," he was now in danger of imitating the "filthy lives of lawless men" (2Pe 2:7).
14:13 *Hebrew.* Abram, the father of the Hebrew people, is the first Biblical character to be called a Hebrew (see "Eber" in note on 10:21). Usually an ethnic term in the Bible, it was normally used by non-Israelites in a disparaging sense (see, e.g., 39:17). Outside the Bible, people known as the Habiru/Apiru (a word probably related to Hebrew) are referred to as a propertyless, dependent, immigrant (foreign) social class rather than as a specific ethnic group. Negative descriptions of them are given in the Amarna letters (clay tablets found in Egypt). *Mamre.* A town was named after him (see 13:18 and note).
14:14 *318 trained men born in his household.* A clear indication of Abram's great wealth. The Hebrew for "trained men" is found only here in the Bible. A related word used elsewhere in very ancient texts means "armed retainers." *Dan.* This well-known city in the north was not given the name "Dan" until the days of the judges (see Jdg 18:29). The designation here is thus an editorial updating subsequent to Moses' time.
14:17 *King's Valley.* Near Jerusalem, probably to the east (see 2Sa 18:18).
14:18 *Melchizedek king of Salem . . . priest.* See Heb 7:1. In ancient times, particularly in non-Israelite circles, kingly and priestly duties were often performed by the same indi-

vidual. "Melchizedek" means "My king is righteousness" or "king of righteousness" (see Heb 7:2). "Salem" is a shortened form of "Jerusalem" (see Ps 76:2) and is related to the Hebrew word for "peace" (see Heb 7:2). The name of Adoni-Zedek, another king of Jerusalem (see Jos 10:1), is very similar to that of Melchizedek and means "My lord is righteousness" or "lord of righteousness." *bread and wine.* An ordinary meal (see Jdg 19:19), in no way related to the NT ordinance of communion. Melchizedek offered the food and drink as a show of friendship and hospitality.
14:19 *God Most High, Creator of heaven and earth.* The titles "most high," "lord of heaven" and "creator of earth" were frequently applied to the chief Canaanite deity in ancient times. Terminology and location (Jerusalem was in central Canaan) thus indicate that Melchizedek was probably a Canaanite king-priest. But Abram, by identifying Melchizedek's "God Most High" with "the LORD" (see v. 22), bore testimony to the one true God, whom Melchizedek had come to know.
14:20 *Abram gave him a tenth of everything.* Although Melchizedek's view of God was no doubt deficient, and perhaps even corrupted, Abram's response to his blessing seems to indicate that he recognized that Melchizedek served the same God as he (see v. 18). So Abram took the occasion to offer him a tithe of his spoils for God Most High. A tenth was the king's share (see 1Sa 8:15,17). Melchizedek is later spoken of as a type or prefiguration of Jesus, our "great high priest" (Heb 4:14), whose priesthood is therefore "in the order of Melchizedek, not in the order of Aaron" (Heb 7:11; see Ps 110:4).
14:22 *I have raised my hand.* A standard oath-taking practice in ancient times (see Dt 32:40; Rev 10:5-6).

not even a thread or the thong of a sandal, so that you will never be able to say, 'I made Abram rich.' 24I will accept nothing but what my men have eaten and the share that belongs to the men who went with me—to Aner, Eshcol and Mamre.p Let them have their share."

God's Covenant With Abram

15 After this, the word of the LORD came to Abram q in a vision: r

"Do not be afraid, s Abram.
I am your shield, q t
your very great reward. r u"

2But Abram said, "O Sovereign LORD, v what can you give me since I remain childless w and the one who will inherit s my estate is Eliezer of Damascus? x" 3And Abram said, "You have given me no children; so a servant y in my household z will be my heir."

4Then the word of the LORD came to him: "This man will not be your heir, but a son coming from your own body will be your heir. a" 5He took him outside and said, "Look up at the heavens and count the stars b—if indeed you can count them." Then he said to him, "So shall your offspring be." c

6Abram believed the LORD, and he credited it to him as righteousness. d

7He also said to him, "I am the LORD, who brought you out e of Ur of the Chaldeans f to give you this land to take possession of it." g

8But Abram said, "O Sovereign LORD, h how can I know i that I will gain possession of it?" i

9So the LORD said to him, "Bring me a heifer, k a goat and a ram, each three years old, l along with a dove and a young pigeon. m"

10Abram brought all these to him, cut them in two and arranged the halves opposite each other; n the birds, however, he did not cut in half. o 11Then birds of prey came down on the carcasses, p but Abram drove them away.

12As the sun was setting, Abram fell into a deep sleep, q and a thick and dreadful darkness came over him. 13Then the LORD said to him, "Know for certain that your descendants will be strangers in a country not their own, and they will be enslaved r and mistreated four hundred years. s 14But I will punish the nation they serve as slaves, and afterward they will come out t with great possessions. u 15You, however, will go to your fathers v in peace and be buried at a good old age. w 16In the fourth

Cross references (center column)

14:24
p Ge 13:18
15:1 q 1Sa 15:10;
2Sa 7:4; 1Ki 6:11;
12:22; Jer 1:13;
Eze 3:16; Da 10:1
r Ge 46:2;
Nu 12:6; 24:4;
Ru 1:20;
Job 33:15
s Ge 21:17;
26:24; 46:3;
Ex 14:13; 20:20;
2Ki 6:16;
2Ch 20:15,17;
Ps 27:1; Isa 7:4;
41:10,13-14;
43:1,5; Jer 1:8;
Hag 2:5
t Dt 33:29;
2Sa 22:3,31;
Ps 3:3; 5:12;
18:2; 28:7;
33:20; 84:11;
119:114; 144:2;
Pr 2:7; 30:5
u Ps 18:20; 37:25;
58:11; Isa 3:10
15:2 v ver 8;
Isa 49:22;
Jer 44:26;
Eze 5:11; 16:48
w Ac 7:5
x Ge 14:15
15:3 y Ge 24:2,34
z Ge 12:5
15:4 a Gal 4:28
15:5 b Job 11:8;
35:5; Ps 8:3;
147:4; Jer 33:22
c Ge 12:2;
S Jer 30:19;
Ro 4:18*;
Heb 11:12
15:6 d Ps 106:31;
Ro 4:3*,20-24*;
Gal 3:6*;
Jas 2:23*
15:7 e Ge 12:1;
Ex 20:2; Ac 7:3;
Heb 11:8
f S Ge 11:28;
Ac 7:4
g Ge 13:17;
17:8; 28:4;
35:12; 48:4;
Ex 6:8; Dt 9:5

15:8 h S ver 2 i Lk 1:18 j Dt 12:20; 19:8 15:9 k Nu 19:2;
Dt 21:3; Hos 4:16; Am 4:1 l 1Sa 1:24 m Lev 1:14; 5:7,11;
12:8 15:10 n ver 17; Jer 34:18 o Lev 1:17; 5:8 15:11
p Dt 28:26; Jer 7:33 15:12 q S Ge 2:21 15:13 r Ex 1:11; 3:7;
5:6,10-14,18; 6:5; Dt 5:15; Job 3:18 s ver 16; Ex 12:40;
Nu 20:15; Ac 7:6,17; Gal 3:17 15:14 t Ge 50:24; Ex 3:8;
6:6-8; 12:25; Nu 10:29; Jos 1:2; Ac 7:7* u Ex 12:32-38
15:15 v Ge 47:30; 49:29; Dt 31:16; 2Sa 7:12; 1Ki 1:21;
Ps 49:19 w Ge 25:8; 35:29; Ex 23:26; Dt 34:7; Jos 14:11;
Jdg 8:32; 1Ch 29:28; Job 5:26; 21:23; 42:17; Ps 91:16;
Pr 3:16; 9:11; Isa 65:20

q j Or sovereign   r l Or shield; l your reward will be very great   s 2 The meaning of the Hebrew for this phrase is uncertain.

14:23 *I will accept nothing belonging to you.* Cf. 2Ki 5:16. Abram refused to let himself become obligated to anyone but the Lord. Had he done so, this Canaanite king might later have claimed the right of kingship over Abram.

15:1 *I am your shield.* Whether "shield" or "sovereign" is meant (see NIV text note), the reference is to the Lord as Abram's King. As elsewhere, "shield" stands for king (e.g., Dt 33:29; 2Sa 22:3; Ps 7:10; 84:9). *your very great reward.* Though Abram was quite rich (13:2), God himself was Abram's greatest treasure (cf. Dt 10:9).

15:2 *Eliezer of Damascus.* A servant probably acquired by Abram on his journey southward from Haran (see 12:5). He may also be the unnamed "chief servant" of 24:2.

15:3–4 Ancient documents uncovered at Nuzi (see chart on "Ancient Texts Relating to the OT," p. 5) near Kirkuk on a branch of the Tigris River, as well as at other places, demonstrate that a childless man could adopt one of his own male servants to be heir and guardian of his estate. Abram apparently contemplated doing this with Eliezer, or perhaps had already done so.

15:5 *count the stars—if indeed you can.* See 22:17. More than 8,000 stars are clearly visible in the darkness of a Near Eastern night. *So shall your offspring be.* The promise was initially fulfilled in Egypt (see Ex 1; see also Dt 1:10; Heb 11:12). Ultimately, all who belong to Christ are Abram's offspring (see Gal 3:29).

15:6 Abram is the "father of all who believe" (Ro 4:11),

and this verse is the first specific reference to faith in God's promises. It also teaches that God graciously responds to a man's faith by crediting righteousness to him (see Heb 11:7).

15:7 *I am the LORD, who brought you out.* Ancient royal covenants often began with (1) the self-identification of the king and (2) a brief historical prologue, as here (see Ex 20:2).

15:8 *how can I know . . . ?* Cf. Lk 1:18. Abram believed God's promise of a son, but he asked for a guarantee of the promise of the land.

15:9 *three years old.* The prime age for most sacrificial animals (see 1Sa 1:24).

15:10 *the birds . . . he did not cut in half.* Perhaps because they were too small (see Lev 1:17).

15:13 *a country not their own.* Egypt (see 46:3–4). *four hundred years.* A round number. According to Ex 12:40 Israel spent 430 years in Egypt.

15:15 The fulfillment is recorded in 25:8.

15:16 *In the fourth generation.* That is, after 400 years (see v. 13). A "generation" was the age of a man when his first son (from the legal standpoint) was born—in Abram's case, 100 years (see 21:5). *the sin of the Amorites has not yet reached its full measure.* Just how sinful many Canaanite religious practices were is now known from archaeological artifacts and from their own epic literature, discovered at Ras Shamra (ancient Ugarit) on the north Syrian coast beginning in 1929 (see chart on "Ancient Texts Relating to the OT," p. 5). Their "worship" was polytheistic and included child

generation[x] your descendants will come back here,[y] for the sin of the Amorites[z] has not yet reached its full measure."

[17]When the sun had set and darkness had fallen, a smoking firepot with a blazing torch[a] appeared and passed between the pieces.[b] [18]On that day the LORD made a covenant with Abram[c] and said, "To your descendants I give this land,[d] from the river[t] of Egypt[e] to the great river, the Euphrates[f]— [19]the land of the Kenites,[g] Kenizzites, Kadmonites, [20]Hittites,[h] Perizzites,[i] Rephaites,[j] [21]Amorites, Canaanites, Girgashites and Jebusites."[k]

Hagar and Ishmael

16 Now Sarai,[l] Abram's wife, had borne him no children.[m] But she had an Egyptian maidservant[n] named Hagar;[o] [2]so she said to Abram, "The LORD has kept me from having children.[p] Go, sleep with my maidservant; perhaps I can build a family through her."[q]

Abram agreed to what Sarai said. [3]So after Abram had been living in Canaan[r] ten years,[s] Sarai his wife took her Egyptian maidservant Hagar and gave her to her husband to be his wife. [4]He slept with Hagar,[t] and she conceived.

When she knew she was pregnant, she began to despise her mistress.[u] [5]Then Sarai said to Abram, "You are responsible for the wrong I am suffering. I put my servant in your arms, and now that she knows she is pregnant, she despises me. May the LORD judge between you and me."[v]

[6]"Your servant is in your hands,[w]" Abram said. "Do with her whatever you think best." Then Sarai mistreated[x] Hagar; so she fled from her.

[7]The angel of the LORD[y] found Hagar near a spring[z] in the desert; it was the spring that is beside the road to Shur.[a] [8]And he said, "Hagar,[b] servant of Sarai, where have you come from, and where are you going?"[c]

"I'm running away from my mistress Sarai," she answered.

[9]Then the angel of the LORD told her, "Go back to your mistress and submit to her." [10]The angel added, "I will so increase your descendants that they will be too numerous to count."[d]

Center column cross-references:

15:16 [x]S ver 13; Ex 12:40
[y]Ge 28:15; 46:4; 48:21; 50:24; Ex 3:8,17
[z]Lev 18:28; Jos 13:4; Jdg 10:11; 1Ki 21:26; 2Ki 16:3; 21:11; Eze 16:3
15:17 [a]Jdg 7:16, 20; 15:4,5 [b]S ver 10
15:18 [c]Ge 17:2, 4,7; Ex 6:4; 34:10,27; 1Ch 16:16; Ps 105:9 [d]S Ge 12:7 [e]Nu 34:5; Jos 15:4,47; 1Ki 8:65; 2Ki 24:7; 2Ch 7:8; Isa 27:12; Jer 37:5; 46:2; La 4:17; Eze 30:22; 47:19 [f]S Ge 2:14
15:19 [g]Nu 24:21; Jdg 1:16; 4:11, 17; 5:24; 1Sa 15:6; 27:10; 30:29; 1Ch 2:55
15:20 [h]S Ge 10:15; S Dt 7:1 [i]S Ge 13:7 [j]S Ge 14:5
15:21 [k]S Ge 10:16; Jos 3:10; 24:11; Ne 9:8
16:1 [l]S Ge 11:29 [m]S Ge 11:30; Lk 1:7,36; Gal 4:24-25 [n]Ge 24:61; 29:24,29; 31:33;

46:18 [o]ver 3-4,8,15; Ge 21:14; 25:12 **16:2** [p]Ge 29:31; 30:2 [q]Ge 19:32; 30:3-4,9-10 **16:3** [r]S Ge 12:5 [s]S Ge 12:4 **16:4** [t]S ver 1 [u]Ge 30:1; 1Sa 1:6 **16:5** [v]Ge 31:53; Ex 5:21; Jdg 11:27; 1Sa 24:12,15; 26:10,23; Ps 50:6; 75:7 **16:6** [w]Jos 9:25 [x]Ge 31:50 **16:7** [y]ver 11; Ge 21:17; 22:11,15; 24:7,40; 31:11; 48:16; Ex 3:2; 14:19; 23:20,23; 32:34; 33:2; Nu 22:22; Jdg 2:1; 6:11; 13:3; 2Sa 24:16; 1Ki 19:5; 2Ki 1:3; 19:35; Ps 34:7; Zec 1:11; S Ac 5:19 [z]ver 14; Ge 21:19 [a]Ge 20:1; 25:18; Ex 15:22; 1Sa 15:7; 27:8 **16:8** [b]S ver 1 [c]S Ge 3:9 **16:10** [d]S Ge 13:16

[t]18 Or *Wadi*

---

sacrifice, idolatry, religious prostitution and divination (cf. Dt 18:9–12). God was patient in judgment, even with the wicked Canaanites.

15:17 *a smoking firepot with a blazing torch.* Symbolizing the presence of God (see Ex 3:2; 14:24; 19:18; 1Ki 18:38; Ac 2:3–4). *passed between the pieces.* Of the slaughtered animals (v. 10). In ancient times the parties solemnized a covenant by walking down an aisle flanked by the pieces of slaughtered animals (see Jer 34:18–19). The practice signified a self-maledictory oath: "May it be so done to me if I do not keep my oath and pledge." Having credited Abram's faith as righteousness, God now graciously ministered to his need for assurance concerning the land. He granted Abram a promissory covenant, as he had to Noah (see 9:9 and note; see also chart on "Major Covenants in the OT," p. 19).

15:18 *made a covenant.* Lit. "cut a covenant," referring to the slaughtering of the animals (the same Hebrew verb is translated "made" and "cut" in Jer 34:18). *I give this land.* The Lord initially fulfilled this covenant through Joshua (see Jos 1:2–9; 21:43; see also 1Ki 4:20–21). *river of Egypt.* Probably the modern Wadi el-Arish in northeastern Sinai.

15:19–21 A similar list of ten peoples is found in 10:15–18 (see notes there). The number ten signifies completeness.

16:1 *no children.* See note on 11:30. *Egyptian.* Perhaps Hagar was acquired while Abram and Sarai were in Egypt (see 12:10–20).

16:2 *The LORD has kept me from having children.* Some time had passed since the revelation of 15:4 (see 16:3), and Sarai impatiently implied that God was not keeping his promise. *Go, sleep with my maidservant.* An ancient custom, illustrated in Old Assyrian marriage contracts, the Code of Hammurapi and the Nuzi tablets (see note on 15:3–4), to ensure the birth of a male heir. Sarai would herself solve the problem of her barrenness.

16:3 *ten years.* Abram was now 85 years old (see 12:4; 16:16).

16:4 *despise her mistress.* Peninnah acted similarly toward Hannah (see 1Sa 1:6).

16:5 *May the LORD judge between you and me.* An expression of hostility or suspicion (see 31:53; see also 31:49).

16:7 *The angel of the LORD.* Since the angel of the Lord speaks for God in the first person (v. 10) and Hagar is said to name "the LORD who spoke to her: 'You are the God who sees me' " (v. 13), the angel appears to be both distinguished from the Lord (in that he is called "messenger"—the Hebrew for "angel" means "messenger") and identified with him. Similar distinction and identification can be found in 19:1,21; 31:11,13; Ex 3:2,4; Jdg 2:1–5; 6:11–12,14; 13:3,6,8–11,13,15–17,20–23; Zec 3:1–6; 12:8. Traditional Christian interpretation has held that this "angel" was a preincarnate manifestation of Christ as God's Messenger-Servant. It may be, however, that, as the Lord's personal messenger who represented him and bore his credentials, the angel could speak on behalf of (and so be identified with) the One who sent him (see especially 19:21; cf. 18:2,22; 19:2). Whether this "angel" was the second person of the Trinity remains therefore uncertain. *Shur.* Located east of Egypt (see 25:18; 1Sa 15:7).

16:8 *I'm running away from my mistress.* Not yet knowing exactly where she was going, Hagar answered only the first of the angel's questions.

16:10 A promise reaffirmed in 17:20 and fulfilled in 25:13–16.

11The angel of the Lord[e] also said to her:

"You are now with child
 and you will have a son.[f]
You shall name him[g] Ishmael,[u] [h]
 for the Lord has heard of your
   misery.[i]
12He will be a wild donkey[j] of a man;
 his hand will be against everyone
 and everyone's hand against him,
 and he will live in hostility
   toward[v] all his brothers.[k]"

13She gave this name to the Lord who spoke to her: "You are the God who sees me,[l]" for she said, "I have now seen[w] the One who sees me."[m] 14That is why the well[n] was called Beer Lahai Roi[x]; [o] it is still there, between Kadesh[p] and Bered.

15So Hagar[q] bore Abram a son,[r] and Abram gave the name Ishmael[s] to the son she had borne. 16Abram was eighty-six years old[t] when Hagar bore him Ishmael.

The Covenant of Circumcision

17 When Abram was ninety-nine years old,[u] the Lord appeared to him[v] and said, "I am God Almighty[y]; [w] walk before me and be blameless.[x] 2I will confirm my covenant between me and you[y] and will greatly increase your numbers."[z]

3Abram fell facedown,[a] and God said to him, 4"As for me, this is my covenant with you:[b] You will be the father of many nations.[c] 5No longer will you be called Abram[z]; your name will be Abraham,[a] [d] for I have made you a father of many nations.[e] 6I will make you very fruitful;[f] I will make nations of you, and kings will come from you.[g] 7I will establish my covenant[h] as an everlasting covenant[j][k] between me and you and your descendants after you for the generations to come, to be your God[l] and the God of your descendants after you.[m] 8The whole land of Canaan,[n] where you are now an alien,[o] I will give as an everlasting possession to

16:11 eS ver 7; S Ac 5:19 /S Ge 3:15 gGe 12:2-3; 18:19; Ne 9:7; Isa 44:1; Am 3:2; Mt 1:21; Lk 1:13, 31 hGe 17:19; 21:3; 37:25,28; 39:1; Jdg 8:24 iGe 29:32; 31:42; Ex 2:24; 3:7,9; 4:31; Nu 20:16; Dt 26:7; 1Sa 9:16 16:12 jJob 6:5; 11:12; 24:5; 39:5; Ps 104:11; Jer 2:24; Hos 8:9 kGe 25:18 16:13 lPs 139:1-12 mGe 32:30; 33:10; Ex 24:10; 33:20,23; Nu 12:8; Jdg 6:22; 13:22; Isa 6:5 16:14 nS ver 7 oGe 24:62; 25:11 pS Ge 14:7 16:15 qS ver 1 rGe 21:9; Gal 4:22 sGe 17:18; 25:12; 28:9 16:16 tS Ge 12:4 17:1 uS Ge 12:4 vS Ge 12:7 wGe 28:3; 35:11; 43:14; 48:3; 49:25; Ex 6:3; Ru 1:20; Job 5:17; 6:4,14; 22:21; 33:19; 36:16; Isa 13:6; Joel 1:15; Mic 6:9 xS Ge 5:22; 20:5; Dt 18:13; 1Ki 3:6; 9:4; Job 1:1; Ps 15:2; 18:23; 78:72;

101:2 17:2 yS Ge 15:18; S 22:16-18 zS Ge 12:2 17:3 aver 17; Ge 18:2; 19:1; 33:3; Ex 18:7; Nu 14:5; Jos 5:14; 7:6; Jdg 13:20; Eze 1:28; 3:23 17:4 bS Ge 15:18 cver 16; S Ge 12:2; 25:23 17:5 dver 15; Ge 32:28; 35:10; 37:3,13; 43:6; 46:2; 1Ki 18:31; 2Ki 17:34; 1Ch 1:34; Ne 9:7; Isa 48:1; S Jn 1:42 eRo 4:17* 17:6 fGe 1:28; 22:17; 26:22; 28:3; 35:11; 41:52; 47:27; 48:4; 49:22; Lev 26:9; Dt 7:13 gver 16,19; Ge 18:10; 21:1; 36:31; Isa 51:2; Mt 1:6 17:7 hS Ge 15:18; Lev 26:9,15 iS Ge 6:18 /S Heb 13:20 kS Ge 9:16 lEx 6:7; 20:2; 29:45,46; Lev 11:44-45; 18:2; 22:33; 25:38; 26:12,45; Nu 15:41; Dt 4:20; 7:6,21; 29:13; 2Sa 7:24; Jer 14:9; Rev 21:7 mRo 9:8; Gal 3:16 17:8 nS Ge 10:19 oGe 23:4; 28:4; 35:27; 37:1; Ex 6:4; 1Ch 29:15

u11 Ishmael means God hears.   v12 Or live to the east / of   w13 Or seen the back of   x14 Beer Lahai Roi means well of the Living One who sees me.   y1 Hebrew El-Shaddai   z5 Abram means exalted father.   a5 Abraham means father of many.

16:11 Ishmael. See NIV text note and 17:20.
16:12 wild donkey. Away from human settlements, Ishmael would roam the desert like a wild donkey (see Job 24:5; Hos 8:9). hostility. The hostility between Sarai and Hagar (see vv. 4-6) was passed on to their descendants (see 25:18).
16:13 I have now seen the One who sees me. See NIV text note and cf. Ex 33:23. To see God's face was believed to bring death (see 32:30; Ex 33:20).
16:14 Beer Lahai Roi. See NIV text note. Another possible translation that fits the context equally well is: "well of the one who sees me and who lives." Kadesh. See note on 14:7.
17:1 ninety-nine years old. Thirteen years had passed since Ishmael's birth (see 16:16; 17:24-25). appeared. See note on 12:7. I am. See note on 15:7. God Almighty. The Hebrew (El-Shaddai) perhaps means "God, the Mountain One," either highlighting the invincible power of God or referring to the mountains as God's symbolic home (see Ps 121:1). It was the special name by which God revealed himself to the patriarchs (see Ex 6:3). Shaddai occurs 31 times in the book of Job and 17 times in the rest of the Bible. walk before me and be blameless. Perhaps equivalent to "walk with me and be blameless" (see notes on 5:22; 6:8-9). After Abram's and Sarai's attempt to obtain the promised offspring by using a surrogate mother, God appeared to Abram. The Lord made it clear that, if Abram was to receive God's promised and covenanted benefits, he must be God's faithful and obedient servant. His faith must be accompanied by the "obedience that comes from faith" (Ro 1:5; see ch. 22).
17:2 my covenant. See 12:2-3; 13:14-16; 15:4-5. The

covenant is God's. God calls it "my covenant" nine times in vv. 2-21, and he initiates (see 15:18), confirms (v. 2) and establishes (v. 7) it. numbers. See 13:16 and note. Earlier God had covenanted to keep his promise concerning the land (ch. 15); here he broadens his covenant to include the promised offspring. See chart on "Major Covenants in the OT," p. 19.
17:5 Abram ... Abraham. See NIV text notes. The first name means "Exalted Father," probably in reference to God (i.e., "[God is] Exalted Father"); the second means "father of many," in reference to Abraham. your name will be. By giving Abram a new name (see Ne 9:7) God marked him in a special way as his servant (see notes on 1:5; 2:19).
17:6 nations ... kings. This promise came also to Sarah (v. 16) and was renewed to Jacob (35:11; see 48:19). It referred to the proliferation of Abraham's offspring, who, like the descendants of Noah (see ch. 10), would someday become many nations and spread over the earth. Ultimately it finds fulfillment in such passages as Ro 4:16-18; 15:8-12; Gal 3:29; Rev 7:9; 21:24.
17:7 everlasting. From God's standpoint (see vv. 13,19), but capable of being broken from man's standpoint (see v. 14; cf. Isa 24:5; Jer 31:32). to be your God. The heart of God's covenant promise, repeated over and over in the OT (see, e.g., v. 8; Jer 24:7; 31:33; Eze 34:30-31; Hos 2:23; Zec 8:8). This is God's pledge to be the protector of his people and the One who provides for their well-being and guarantees their future blessing (see 15:1).
17:8 land. See 12:7; 15:18; Ac 7:5. everlasting possession. The land, though an everlasting possession given by God, could be temporarily lost because of disobedience (see Dt 28:62-63; 30:1-10).

31   GENESIS 17:26

you and your descendants after you; *p* and I will be their God. *q* "

⁹Then God said to Abraham, "As for you, you must keep my covenant, *r* you and your descendants after you for the generations to come. *s* ¹⁰This is my covenant with you and your descendants after you, the covenant you are to keep: Every male among you shall be circumcised. *t* ¹¹You are to undergo circumcision, *u* and it will be the sign of the covenant *v* between me and you. ¹²For the generations to come *w* every male among you who is eight days old must be circumcised, *x* including those born in your household or bought with money from a foreigner—those who are not your offspring. ¹³Whether born in your household or bought with your money, they must be circumcised. *y* My covenant in your flesh is to be an everlasting covenant. *z* ¹⁴Any uncircumcised male, who has not been circumcised *a* in the flesh, will be cut off from his people; *b* he has broken my covenant. *c* "

¹⁵God also said to Abraham, "As for Sarai *d* your wife, you are no longer to call her Sarai; her name will be Sarah. *e* ¹⁶I will bless her and will surely give you a son by her. *f* I will bless her so that she will be the mother of nations; *g* kings of peoples will come from her."

¹⁷Abraham fell facedown; *h* he laughed *i* and said to himself, "Will a son be born to a man a hundred years old? *j* Will Sarah bear a child at the age of ninety?" *k* ¹⁸And Abraham said to God, "If only Ishmael *l* might live under your blessing!" *m*

¹⁹Then God said, "Yes, but your wife Sarah will bear you a son, *n* and you will call him Isaac. *b o* I will establish my covenant with him *p* as an everlasting covenant *q* for his descendants after him. ²⁰And as for Ishmael, I have heard you: I will surely bless him; I will make him fruitful and will greatly increase his numbers. *r* He will be the father of twelve rulers, *s* and I will make him into a great nation. *t* ²¹But my covenant *u* I will establish with Isaac, whom Sarah will bear to you *v* by this time next year." *w* ²²When he had finished speaking with Abraham, God went up from him. *x*

²³On that very day Abraham took his son Ishmael and all those born in his household *y* or bought with his money, every male in his household, and circumcised them, as God told him. *z* ²⁴Abraham was ninety-nine years old *a* when he was circumcised, *b* ²⁵and his son Ishmael *c* was thirteen; ²⁶Abraham and his son Ishmael

17:8 *p* S Ge 12:7; S 15:7 *q* S ver 7; Jer 31:1
17:9 *r* Ge 22:18; Ex 19:5; Dt 5:2 *s* Ge 18:19
17:10 *t* ver 23; Ge 21:4; Lev 12:3; Jos 5:2, 5,7; Jn 7:22; Ac 7:8; Ro 4:11
17:11 *u* Ex 12:48; Dt 10:16 *v* S Ge 9:12; Ro 4:11
17:12 *w* S Ge 9:12 *x* Ge 21:4; Lev 12:3; Jos 5:2; S Lk 1:59
17:13 *y* Ex 12:44, 48 *z* S Ge 9:16
17:14 *a* ver 23 *b* Ex 4:24-26; 12:15,19; 30:33; Lev 7:20,25; 17:4; 18:29; 19:8; 20:17; Nu 9:13; 15:30; 19:13; Dt 17:12; Jos 5:2-8; Job 38:15; Ps 37:28 *c* Eze 44:7
17:15 *d* S Ge 11:29 *e* S ver 5
17:16 *f* S ver 6; S Isa 29:22 *g* S ver 4; Ge 24:60; Gal 4:31
17:17 *h* S ver 3 *i* Ge 18:12; 21:6
17:18 *l* S Ge 16:15

m Ge 21:11 *n* S ver 6,21; Ge 18:14; 21:2; 1Sa 1:20 *o* S Ge 16:11; Mt 1:21; Lk 1:13,31 *p* Ge 26:3; 50:24; Ex 13:11; Dt 1:8 *q* S Ge 9:16; S Gal 3:16 17:20 *r* S Ge 13:16 *s* Ge 25:12-16 *t* Ge 25:18; 48:19 17:21 *u* Ex 34:10 *v* S ver 6 *w* Ge 18:10,14 17:22 *x* Ge 18:33; 35:13; Nu 12:9 17:23 *y* S Ge 12:4 *z* S ver 10,S 14 17:24 *a* S Ge 12:4 *b* Ro 4:11 17:25 *c* Ge 16:16

b 19 Isaac means *he laughs.*

17:9 *As for you.* Balances the "As for me" of v. 4. Having reviewed his covenanted commitment to Abraham (see 15:8–21), and having broadened it to include the promise of offspring, God now called upon Abraham to make a covenanted commitment to him—to "walk before me and be blameless" (v. 1). *keep my covenant.* Participation in the blessings of the Abrahamic covenant was conditioned on obedience (see 18:19; 22:18; 26:4–5).
17:10 *circumcised.* Circumcision was God's appointed "sign of the covenant" (v. 11), which signified Abraham's covenanted commitment to the Lord—that the Lord alone would be his God, whom he would trust and serve. It symbolized a self-maledictory oath (analogous to the oath to which God had submitted himself; see note on 15:17): "If I am not loyal in faith and obedience to the Lord, may the sword of the Lord cut off me and my offspring (see v. 14) as I have cut off my foreskin." Thus Abraham was to place himself under the rule of the Lord as his King, consecrating himself, his offspring and all he possessed to the service of the Lord. For circumcision as signifying consecration to the Lord see Ex 6:12 (NIV text note); Lev 19:23 (NIV text note); 26:41; Dt 10:16; 30:6; Jer 4:4; 6:10 (NIV text note); 9:25–26; Eze 44:7,9. Other nations also practiced circumcision (see Jer 9:25–26; Eze 32:18–19), but not for the covenant reasons that Israel did.
17:11 *sign of the covenant.* See notes on 9:12; 15:17. As the covenant sign, circumcision also (see note on v. 10) marked Abraham as the one to whom God had made covenant commitment (15:7–21) in response to Abraham's faith, which he "credited . . . to him as righteousness"

(15:6). Paul comments on this aspect of the covenant sign in Ro 4:11.
17:12 *eight days old.* See 21:4 and Ac 7:8 (Isaac); Lk 1:59 (John the Baptist); 2:21 (Jesus); Php 3:5 (Paul). Abraham was 99 years old when the newly initiated rite of circumcision was performed on him (see v. 24). The Arabs, who consider themselves descendants of Ishmael, are circumcised at the age of 13 (see v. 25). For them, as for other peoples, it serves as a rite of transition from childhood to manhood, thus into full participation in the community.
17:14 *cut off from his people.* Removed from the covenant people by divine judgment (see note on v. 10).
17:15 *Sarai . . . Sarah.* Both names evidently mean "princess." The renaming stressed that she was to be the mother of nations and kings (see v. 16) and thus to serve the Lord's purpose (see note on v. 5).
17:16 *son.* Fulfilled in Isaac (see 21:2–3).
17:17 *laughed.* In temporary disbelief (see 18:12; cf. Ro 4:19–21). The verb is a pun on the name "Isaac," which means "he laughs" (see NIV text notes on v. 19 and 21:3; see also 18:12–15; 21:6).
17:20 *numbers.* See note on 13:16. *father of twelve rulers.* Fulfilled in 25:16.
17:21 Paul cites the choice of Isaac (and not Ishmael) as one proof of God's sovereign right to choose to save by grace alone (see Ro 9:6–13). *by this time next year.* See 21:2.
17:22 *God went up from him.* A solemn conclusion to the conversation.
17:23 *On that very day.* Abraham was characterized by prompt obedience (see note on 12:4).

were both circumcised on that same day.
²⁷And every male in Abraham's household *d*, including those born in his household or bought from a foreigner, was circumcised with him.

The Three Visitors

18 The LORD appeared to Abraham *e* near the great trees of Mamre *f* while he was sitting at the entrance to his tent *g* in the heat of the day. ²Abraham looked up *h* and saw three men *i* standing nearby. When he saw them, he hurried from the entrance of his tent to meet them and bowed low to the ground. *j*

³He said, "If I have found favor in your eyes, *k* my lord, *c* do not pass your servant *l* by. ⁴Let a little water be brought, and then you may all wash your feet *m* and rest under this tree. ⁵Let me get you something to eat, *n* so you can be refreshed and then go on your way—now that you have come to your servant."

"Very well," they answered, "do as you say."

⁶So Abraham hurried into the tent to Sarah. "Quick," he said, "get three seahs *d* of fine flour and knead it and bake some bread." *o*

⁷Then he ran to the herd and selected a choice, tender calf *p* and gave it to a servant, who hurried to prepare it. ⁸He then brought some curds *q* and milk *r* and the calf that had been prepared, and set these before them. *s* While they ate, he stood near them under a tree.

⁹"Where is your wife Sarah?" *t* they asked him.

"There, in the tent, *u*" he said.

¹⁰Then the LORD *e* said, "I will surely return to you about this time next year, *v* and Sarah your wife will have a son." *w*

Now Sarah was listening at the entrance to the tent, which was behind him. ¹¹Abraham and Sarah were already old and well advanced in years, *x* and Sarah was past the age of childbearing. *y* ¹²So Sarah laughed *z* to herself as she thought, "After I am worn out and my master *f a* is old, will I now have this pleasure?"

¹³Then the LORD said to Abraham, "Why did Sarah laugh and say, 'Will I really have a child, now that I am old?' *b* ¹⁴Is anything too hard for the LORD? *c* I will return to you at the appointed time next year *d* and Sarah will have a son." *e*

¹⁵Sarah was afraid, so she lied and said, "I did not laugh."

But he said, "Yes, you did laugh."

Abraham Pleads for Sodom

¹⁶When the men *f* got up to leave, they looked down toward Sodom, and Abraham walked along with them to see them on their way. ¹⁷Then the LORD said, "Shall I hide from Abraham *g* what I am about to do? *h* ¹⁸Abraham will surely become a great and powerful nation, *i* and all nations on earth will be blessed through him. *i* ¹⁹For I have chosen him *j*, so that he will direct

---

Cross references (center column):

17:27 *d*Ge 14:14
18:1 *e*S Ge 12:7;
Ac 7:2
*f*S Ge 13:18
*g*Ge 19:1; 23:10,
18; 34:20,24;
Ru 4:1; Ps 69:12;
Heb 11:9
18:2 *h*Ge 24:63
*i*ver 16,22;
Ge 19:1,10;
32:24; Jos 5:13;
Jdg 13:6-11;
Hos 12:3-4;
Heb 13:2
*j*S Ge 17:3;
S 43:28
18:3 *k*Ge 19:19;
39:4; Ru 2:2,10,
13; 1Sa 1:18;
Est 2:15 *l*Ge 32:4,
18,20; 33:5
18:4 *m*Ge 19:2;
24:32; 43:24;
Jdg 19:21;
2Sa 11:8;
S Lk 7:44
18:5 *n*Jdg 13:15;
19:5
18:6 *o*Ge 19:3;
2Sa 13:8
18:7 *p*1Sa 28:24;
Lk 15:23
18:8 *q*Isa 7:15,22
*r*Jdg 4:19; 5:25
*s*Jdg 6:19
18:9 *t*S Ge 3:9

*u*Ge 24:67;
Heb 11:9
18:10
*v*S Ge 17:21;
21:2; 2Ki 4:16
*w*S Ge 17:6;
Ro 9:9*
18:11
*x*S Ge 17:17;
Lk 1:18
*y*S Ge 11:30;
Ro 4:19;
Heb 11:11-12
18:12
*z*S Ge 17:17
*a*1Pe 3:6
18:13
*b*S Ge 17:17
18:14 *c*Job 42:2;
Isa 40:29; 50:2;
51:9; Jer 32:17,
27; S Mt 19:26;

Ro 4:21 *d*S ver 10 *e*S Ge 17:19; Ro 9:9*; Gal 4:23 18:16
*f*S ver 2 18:17 *g*Am 3:7 *h*Ge 19:24; Job 1:16; Ps 107:34
18:18 *i*S Ge 12:2; Gal 3:8* 18:19 *j*Ge 17:9

*c*3 Or *O Lord*   *d*6 That is, probably about 20 quarts
(about 22 liters)   *e*10 Hebrew *Then he*   *f*12 Or
husband

18:1 *appeared.* See note on 12:7. *great trees.* See note on 12:6. *Mamre.* See note on 13:18. *the heat of the day.* Early afternoon.
18:2 *three men.* At least two of the "men" were angels (see 19:1; see also note on 16:7). The third may have been the Lord himself (see vv. 1,13,17,20,26,33; see especially v. 22). *hurried.* The story in vv. 2–8 illustrates Near Eastern hospitality in several ways: 1. Abraham gave prompt attention to the needs of his guests (vv. 2,6–7). 2. He bowed low to the ground (v. 2). 3. He politely addressed one of his guests as "my lord" and called himself "your servant" (vv. 3,5), a common way of speaking when addressing a superior (see, e.g., 19:2,18–19). 4. He acted as if it would be a favor to him if they allowed him to serve them (vv. 3–5). 5. He asked that water be brought to wash their feet (see v. 4), an act of courtesy to refresh a traveler in a hot, dusty climate (see 19:2; 24:32; 43:24). 6. He prepared a lavish meal for them (vv. 5–8; a similar lavish offering was presented to a divine messenger in Jdg 6:18–19; 13:15–16). 7. He stood nearby (v. 8), assuming the posture of a servant (see v. 22), to meet their every wish. Heb 13:2 is probably a reference to vv. 2–8 and 19:1–3.
18:6 *bread.* A plural word referring to round, thin loaves.
18:10 See 17:21. Paul quotes this promise of Isaac's birth (see v. 14) in Ro 9:9 and relates it to Abraham's spiritual

offspring (see Ro 9:7–8).
18:12 *laughed.* In disbelief, as also Abraham had at first (see note on 17:17).
18:14 *Is anything too hard for the LORD?* The answer is no, for Sarah as well as for her descendants Mary and Elizabeth (see Lk 1:34–37). Nothing within God's will, including creation (see Jer 32:17) and redemption (see Mt 19:25–26), is impossible for him.
18:16 *Sodom.* See notes on 10:19; 13:10.
18:17 Abraham was God's friend (see v. 19; 2Ch 20:7; Jas 2:23; see also Isa 41:8, but see note there). And because he was now God's covenant friend (see Job 29:4), God convened his heavenly council (see note on 1:26) at Abraham's tent. There he announced his purpose for Abraham (v. 10) and for the wicked of the plain (vv. 20–21)—redemption and judgment. He thus even gave Abraham opportunity to speak in his court and to intercede for the righteous in Sodom and Gomorrah. Abraham was later called a prophet (20:7). Here, in Abraham, is exemplified the great privilege of God's covenant people throughout the ages: God has revealed his purposes to them and allows their voice to be heard (in intercession) in the court of heaven.
18:18 *a great and powerful nation . . . blessed through him.* See note on 12:2–3.
18:19 *chosen.* Lit. "known" (as in Am 3:2).

his children[k] and his household after him to keep the way of the LORD[l] by doing what is right and just,[m] so that the LORD will bring about for Abraham what he has promised him."[n]

20Then the LORD said, "The outcry against Sodom[o] and Gomorrah is so great[p] and their sin so grievous[q] 21that I will go down[r] and see if what they have done is as bad as the outcry that has reached me. If not, I will know."

22The men[s] turned away and went toward Sodom,[t] but Abraham remained standing before the LORD.[8][u] 23Then Abraham approached him and said: "Will you sweep away the righteous with the wicked?[v] 24What if there are fifty righteous people in the city? Will you really sweep it away and not spare[h] the place for the sake of the fifty righteous people in it?[w] 25Far be it from you to do such a thing[x]—to kill the righteous with the wicked, treating the righteous[y] and the wicked alike.[z] Far be it from you! Will not the Judge[1a] of all the earth do right?"[b]

26The LORD said, "If I find fifty righteous people in the city of Sodom, I will spare the whole place for their sake.[c]"

27Then Abraham spoke up again: "Now that I have been so bold as to speak to the Lord, though I am nothing but dust and ashes,[d] 28what if the number of the righteous is five less than fifty? Will you destroy the whole city because of five people?"

"If I find forty-five there," he said, "I will not destroy it."

29Once again he spoke to him, "What if only forty are found there?"

He said, "For the sake of forty, I will not do it."

30Then he said, "May the Lord not be angry,[e] but let me speak. What if only thirty can be found there?"

He answered, "I will not do it if I find thirty there."

31Abraham said, "Now that I have been so bold as to speak to the Lord, what if only twenty can be found there?"

He said, "For the sake of twenty, I will not destroy it."

32Then he said, "May the Lord not be angry, but let me speak just once more.[f] What if only ten can be found there?"

He answered, "For the sake of ten,[g] I will not destroy it."

33When the LORD had finished speaking[h] with Abraham, he left,[i] and Abraham returned home.[j]

Sodom and Gomorrah Destroyed

19 The two angels[k] arrived at Sodom[l] in the evening, and Lot[m] was sitting in the gateway of the city.[n] When he saw them, he got up to meet them and bowed down with his face to the ground.[o] 2"My lords," he said, "please turn aside to your servant's house. You can wash your feet[p] and spend the night and then go on your way early in the morning."

"No," they answered, "we will spend the night in the square."[q]

3But he insisted[r] so strongly that they did go with him and entered his house.[s]

18:19 [k]Dt 4:9-10; 6:7 [l]Jos 24:15; Eph 6:4 [m]Ge 22:12,18; 26:5; 2Sa 8:15; Ps 17:2; 99:4; Jer 23:5 [n]S Ge 16:11; S Isa 14:1
18:20 [o]Isa 1:10; Jer 23:14; Eze 16:46 [p]Ge 19:13 [q]S Ge 13:13
18:21 [r]S Ge 11:5
18:22 [s]S ver 2 [t]Ge 19:1 [u]Ge 19:27
18:23 [v]Ex 23:7; Lev 4:3,22,27; Nu 16:22; Dt 27:25; 2Sa 24:17; Ps 11:4-7; 94:21; Eze 18:4; 2Pe 2:9
18:24 [w]ver 26; Jer 5:1
18:25 [x]Ge 44:7, 17; Dt 32:4; Job 8:3-7; 34:10 [y]Isa 5:20; Am 5:15; Mal 2:17; 3:18 [z]Dt 1:16-17 [a]Jdg 11:27; Job 9:15; Ps 7:11; 94:2; Heb 12:23 [b]Ge 20:4; Dt 32:4; 2Ch 19:7; Ezr 9:15; Ne 9:33; Job 8:3, 20; 34:10; 36:23; Ps 58:11; 75:7; 94:2; 119:137; Isa 3:10-11; Eze 18:25; Da 4:37; 9:14; Mal 2:17; Ro 3:6
18:26 [c]S ver 24
18:27 [d]S Ge 2:7; S Job 2:8
18:30 [e]ver 32; Ge 44:18; Ex 32:22
18:32 [f]S ver 30; Jdg 6:39 [g]Jer 5:1
18:33 [h]Ex 31:18 [i]S Ge 17:22 [j]Ge 31:55
19:1 [k]S Ge 18:2; Heb 13:2

[l]Ge 18:22 [m]S Ge 11:27 [n]S Ge 18:1 [o]S Ge 17:3; 48:12; Ru 2:10; 1Sa 25:23; 2Sa 14:33; 2Ki 2:15 19:2 [p]S Ge 18:4; Lk 7:44 [q]Jdg 19:15,20 19:3 [r]Ge 33:11 [s]Job 31:32

822 Masoretic Text; an ancient Hebrew scribal tradition *but the LORD remained standing before Abraham* **h**24 *Or forgive*; also in verse 26 **i**25 *Or Ruler*

18:20 *outcry.* A cry of righteous indignation (cf. the blood of Abel, 4:10) that became one of the reasons for the destruction of the cities (see 19:13). See notes on 10:19; 13:10. *sin so grievous.* The sin of Sodom (and probably of Gomorrah as well) was already proverbial (see 13:13) and remained so for centuries (see Eze 16:49–50).
18:21 *I will go down.* The result would be judgment (as in 11:5–9), but God also comes down to redeem (as in Ex 3:8). *see.* Not a denial of God's infinite knowledge but a figurative way of stating that he does not act out of ignorance or on the basis of mere complaints.
18:22 *Abraham remained standing before the LORD.* The text and NIV text note both illustrate the mutual accessibility that existed between God and his servant.
18:23 The second time Abraham intervened for his relatives and for Sodom (see 14:14–16).
18:25 *Judge of all the earth.* Abraham based his plea on the justice and authority (see NIV text note) of God, confident that God would do what was right (see Dt 32:4).
18:27 *Lord.* Abraham used the title "Lord," not the intimate name "LORD," throughout his prayer. He was appealing to God as "Judge of all the earth." *dust and ashes.* In

contrast to God's exalted position, Abraham described himself as insignificant (see Job 30:19; 42:6).
18:32 *just once more.* Abraham's questioning in vv. 23–32 did not arise from a spirit of haggling but of compassion for his relatives and of wanting to know God's ways. *ten.* Perhaps Abraham stopped at ten because he had been counting while praying: Lot, his wife, possibly two sons (see 19:12), at least two married daughters and their husbands (see 19:14 and NIV text note), and two unmarried daughters (see 19:8).
18:33 *home.* To Mamre (see v. 1). The next morning Abraham went back to see what God had done (see 19:27).
19:1–3 See note on 18:2.
19:1 *The two angels.* See notes on 16:7; 18:2. *Lot was sitting in the gateway of the city.* Lot had probably become a member of Sodom's ruling council, since a city gateway served as the administrative and judicial center where legal matters were discussed and prosecuted (see Ru 4:1–12).
19:2 *square.* A large open space near the main city gateway (see 2Ch 32:6) where public gatherings were held. Important cities like Jerusalem could have two or more squares (see Ne 8:16).

He prepared a meal for them, baking bread without yeast,[t] and they ate.[u] 4Before they had gone to bed, all the men from every part of the city of Sodom[v]—both young and old—surrounded the house. 5They called to Lot, "Where are the men who came to you tonight? Bring them out to us so that we can have sex with them."[w]

6Lot went outside to meet them[x] and shut the door behind him 7and said, "No, my friends. Don't do this wicked thing. 8Look, I have two daughters who have never slept with a man. Let me bring them out to you, and you can do what you like with them. But don't do anything to these men, for they have come under the protection of my roof."[y]

9"Get out of our way," they replied. And they said, "This fellow came here as an alien,[z] and now he wants to play the judge![a] We'll treat you worse than them." They kept bringing pressure on Lot and moved forward to break down the door.

10But the men[b] inside reached out and pulled Lot back into the house and shut the door. 11Then they struck the men who were at the door of the house, young and old, with blindness[c] so that they could not find the door.

12The two men said to Lot, "Do you have anyone else here—sons-in-law, sons or daughters, or anyone else in the city who belongs to you?[d] Get them out of here, 13because we[e] are going to destroy this place. The outcry to the LORD against its people is so great[f] that he has sent us to destroy it."[g]

14So Lot went out and spoke to his sons-in-law, who were pledged to marry[j] his daughters. He said, "Hurry and get out of this place, because the LORD is about to destroy the city![h]" But his sons-in-law thought he was joking.[i]

15With the coming of dawn, the angels urged Lot, saying, "Hurry! Take your wife and your two daughters who are here, or you will be swept away[j] when the city is punished.[k]"

16When he hesitated, the men grasped his hand and the hands of his wife and of his two daughters[l] and led them safely out of the city, for the LORD was merciful to them.[m] 17As soon as they had brought them out, one of them said, "Flee for your lives![n] Don't look back,[o] and don't stop anywhere in the plain![p] Flee to the mountains[q] or you will be swept away!"

18But Lot said to them, "No, my lords,[k] please! 19Your[l] servant has found favor in your[l] eyes,[r] and you[l] have shown great kindness[s] to me in sparing my life. But I can't flee to the mountains;[t] this disaster will overtake me, and I'll die. 20Look, here is a town near enough to run to, and it is small. Let me flee to it—it is very small, isn't it? Then my life will be spared."

21He said to him, "Very well, I will grant this request[u] too; I will not overthrow the town you speak of. 22But flee there quickly, because I cannot do anything until you reach it." (That is why the town was called Zoar.[m][v])

23By the time Lot reached Zoar,[w] the sun had risen over the land. 24Then the LORD rained down burning sulfur[x] on Sodom and Gomorrah[y]—from the LORD out of the heavens.[z] 25Thus he overthrew those cities[a] and the entire plain,[b] including all those living in the cities—and also the vegetation in the land.[c] 26But Lot's wife looked back,[d] and she became a pillar of salt.[e]

19:3 [t]Ex 12:39
[u]S Ge 18:6
19:4 [v]S Ge 13:13
19:5
[w]S Ge 13:13;
Lev 18:22;
Dt 23:18;
Jdg 19:22;
Ro 1:24-27
19:6 [x]Jdg 19:23
19:8 [y]Jdg 19:24;
2Pe 2:7-8
19:9 [z]Ge 23:4
[a]S Ge 13:8;
Ac 7:27
19:10 [b]S Ge 18:2
19:11
[c]Dt 28:28-29;
2Ki 6:18;
Ac 13:11
19:12 [d]S Ge 6:18
19:13 [e]Ex 12:29;
2Sa 24:16;
2Ki 19:35;
1Ch 21:12;
2Ch 32:21
[f]Ge 18:20
[g]1Ch 21:15;
Ps 78:49;
Jer 21:12; 25:18;
44:22; 51:45
19:14
[h]Nu 16:21;
Rev 18:4
[i]Ex 9:21;
1Ki 13:18;
Jer 5:12; 43:2;
Lk 17:28

19:15 [j]Nu 16:26;
Job 21:18;
Ps 58:9; 73:19;
90:5 [k]Rev 18:4
19:16 [l]2Pe 2:7
[m]Ex 34:6;
Ps 33:18-19
19:17 [n]1Ki 19:3;
Jer 48:6 [o]ver 26
[p]S Ge 13:12
[q]S ver 19;
S Ge 14:10;
Mt 24:16
19:19 [r]S Ge 6:8;
S 18:3 [s]Ge 24:12;
39:21; 40:14;
47:29; Ru 1:8;
2:20; 3:10 [t]S ver
17,30
19:21
[u]1Sa 25:35;
2Sa 14:8;
Job 42:9
19:22
[v]S Ge 13:10
19:23
[w]S Ge 13:10
19:24
[x]Job 18:15;
Ps 11:6;
Isa 30:33; 34:9;
Eze 38:22
[y]Dt 29:23;

Isa 1:9; 13:19; Jer 49:18; 50:40; Am 4:11 [z]S Ge 18:17;
S Lev 10:2; S Mt 10:15; Lk 17:29 19:25 [a]S ver 24;
Eze 26:16; Zep 3:8; Hag 2:22 [b]S Ge 13:12 [c]Ps 107:34;
Isa 1:10; Jer 20:16; 23:14; La 4:6; Eze 16:48 19:26 [d]S ver
17 [e]Lk 17:32

j14 Or were married to   k18 Or No, Lord; or No, my
lord   l19 The Hebrew is singular.   m22 Zoar means
small.

19:3 *bread without yeast.* So that it could be baked quickly (see 18:6; Ex 12:39).

19:4–9 See Jdg 19:22-25.

19:5 *have sex with them.* Homosexuality was so characteristic of the men of Sodom (see Jude 7) that it is still often called sodomy.

19:8 *under the protection of my roof.* Ancient hospitality obliged a host to protect his guests in every situation.

19:9 *This fellow came here as an alien, and now he wants to play the judge.* Centuries later, Moses was also considered an outsider and accused of setting himself up as a judge (see Ex 2:14; Ac 7:27).

19:13 *we are going to destroy this place.* Sodom's wickedness had made it ripe for destruction (see Isa 3:9; Jer 23:14; La 4:6; Zep 2:8–9; 2Pe 2:6; Jude 7).

19:14 *his sons-in-law thought he was joking.* Lot apparently had lost his power of moral persuasion even among his family members.

19:16 *hesitated.* Perhaps because of reluctance to leave his material possessions. *his hand and the hands of his wife and of his two daughters.* The ten righteous people required to save Sodom (see 18:32) had now been reduced to four. *the LORD was merciful to them.* Deliverance is due to divine mercy, not to human righteousness (cf. Tit 3:5).

19:24 *rained down burning sulfur.* Perhaps from a violent earthquake spewing up asphalt, such as is still found in this region.

19:26 *Lot's wife looked back, and she became a pillar of salt.* Her disobedient hesitation (see v. 17) became proverbial in later generations (see Lk 17:32). Even today, grotesque salt formations near the southern end of the Dead Sea are reminders of her folly.

27Early the next morning Abraham got up and returned to the place where he had stood before the LORD.[f] 28He looked down toward Sodom and Gomorrah, toward all the land of the plain, and he saw dense smoke rising from the land, like smoke from a furnace.[g]

29So when God destroyed the cities of the plain,[h] he remembered[i] Abraham, and he brought Lot out of the catastrophe[j] that overthrew the cities where Lot had lived.[k]

Lot and His Daughters

30Lot and his two daughters left Zoar[l] and settled in the mountains,[m] for he was afraid to stay in Zoar. He and his two daughters lived in a cave. 31One day the older daughter said to the younger, "Our father is old, and there is no man around here to lie with us, as is the custom all over the earth. 32Let's get our father to drink wine and then lie with him and preserve our family line[n] through our father."[o]

33That night they got their father to drink wine, and the older daughter went in and lay with him. He was not aware of it when she lay down or when she got up.[p]

34The next day the older daughter said to the younger, "Last night I lay with my father. Let's get him to drink wine again tonight, and you go in and lie with him so we can preserve our family line through our father."[q] 35So they got their father to drink wine[r] that night also, and the younger daughter went and lay with him. Again he was not aware of it when she lay down or when she got up.[s]

36So both of Lot's daughters became pregnant by their father.[t] 37The older daughter had a son, and she named him Moab**[n]**;[u] he is the father of the Moabites[v] of today. 38The younger daughter also had a son, and she named him Ben-Ammi**[o]**; he is the father of the Ammonites[w] of today.

19:27 [f]Ge 18:22 **19:28** [g]Ge 15:17; Ex 19:18; Rev 9:2; 18:9 **19:29** [h]S Ge 13:12 [i]S Ge 8:1 [j]2Pe 2:7 [k]Ge 14:12; Eze 14:16 **19:30** [l]ver 22; S Ge 13:10 [m]S ver 19; S Ge 14:10 **19:32** [n]S Ge 16:2 [o]ver 34,36; Ge 38:18 **19:33** [p]ver 35 **19:34** [q]S ver 32 **19:35** [r]Ge 9:21 [s]ver 33 **19:36** [t]S ver 32 **19:37** [u]Ge 36:35; Ex 15:15; Nu 25:1; Isa 15:1; 25:10; Jer 25:21; 48:1; Eze 25:8; Zep 2:9 [v]Nu 22:4; 24:17; Dt 2:9; Jdg 3:28; Ru 1:4,22; 1Sa 14:47; 22:3-4; 2Sa 8:2; 2Ki 1:1; 3:4; Ezr 9:1; Ps 108:9; Jer 48:1 **19:38** [w]Nu 21:24; Dt 2:19; 23:3; Jos 12:2; Jdg 3:13; 10:6,7; 1Sa 11:1-11; 14:47; 1Ch 19:1; 2Ch 20:23; 26:8; 27:5; Ne 2:19; 4:3; Jer 25:21; 40:14; 49:1; Eze 21:28; 25:2; Am 1:13

20:1 [x]Ge 18:1 [y]S Ge 12:9 [z]S Ge 14:7 [a]S Ge 16:7 [b]Ge 26:3 [c]Ge 26:1,6,17 **20:2** [d]S Ge 12:13 [e]ver 14; Ge 21:22; 26:1 [f]S Ge 12:15 **20:3** [g]Nu 22:9,20 [h]Ge 28:12; 31:10,24; 37:5,9; 40:5; 41:1; Nu 12:6; Dt 13:1; Job 33:15; Da 2:1; 4:5 [i]Ex 10:7; 12:33; Ps 105:38 [j]ver 7; Ge 26:11; 1Ch 16:21; Ps 105:14 **20:4** [k]S Ge 18:25 **20:5** [l]S Ge 12:19 [m]S Ge 17:1 [n]Ps 7:8; 25:21; 26:6; 41:12

Abraham and Abimelech

20:1-18Ref — Ge 12:10-20; 26:1-11

20 Now Abraham moved on from there[x] into the region of the Negev[y] and lived between Kadesh[z] and Shur.[a] For a while[b] he stayed in Gerar,[c] 2and there Abraham said of his wife Sarah, "She is my sister."[d] Then Abimelech[e] king of Gerar sent for Sarah and took her.[f]

3But God came to Abimelech[g] in a dream[h] one night and said to him, "You are as good as dead[i] because of the woman you have taken; she is a married woman."[j]

4Now Abimelech had not gone near her, so he said, "Lord, will you destroy an innocent nation?[k] 5Did he not say to me, 'She is my sister,'[l] and didn't she also say, 'He is my brother'? I have done this with a clear conscience[m] and clean hands."[n]

6Then God said to him in the dream, "Yes, I know you did this with a clear conscience, and so I have kept[o] you from sinning against me.[p] That is why I did not let you touch her. 7Now return the man's wife, for he is a prophet,[q] and he will pray for you[r] and you will live. But if you do not return her, you may be sure that you and all yours will die."[s]

8Early the next morning Abimelech summoned all his officials, and when he told them all that had happened, they were very much afraid. 9Then Abimelech called Abraham in and said, "What have you done to us? How have I wronged you that you have brought such great guilt upon me and my kingdom? You have done things to me that should not be done."[t] 10And Abimelech asked Abraham, "What was your reason for doing this?"

20:6 [o]1Sa 25:26,34 [p]S Ge 13:13; Ps 41:4; 51:4 **20:7** [q]Dt 18:18; 34:10; 2Ki 3:11; 5:3; 1Ch 16:22; Ps 105:15 [r]ver 17; Ex 8:8; Nu 11:2; 12:13; 1Sa 7:5; 1Ki 13:6; Job 42:8; Jer 18:20; 37:3; 42:2 [s]S ver 3; S Ps 9:5 **20:9** [t]S Ge 12:18; 34:7

[n]37 *Moab* sounds like the Hebrew for *from father.*
[o]38 *Ben-Ammi* means *son of my people.*

19:29 *God . . . remembered Abraham.* See note on 8:1. *he brought Lot out of the catastrophe.* Lot's deliverance was the main concern of Abraham's prayer (18:23–32), which God now answered.

19:33 *they got their father to drink wine, and the older daughter went in and lay with him.* Though Lot's role was somewhat passive, he bore the basic responsibility for the drunkenness and incest that eventually resulted in his two daughters' becoming pregnant by him (see v. 36).

19:36–38 The sons born to Lot's daughters were the ancestors of the Moabites and Ammonites (see Dt 2:9,19), two nations that were to become bitter enemies of Abraham's descendants (see, e.g., 1Sa 14:47; 2Ch 20:1).

20:1 *between Kadesh and Shur.* See notes on 14:7; 16:7. *Gerar.* Located at the edge of Philistine territory, about halfway between Gaza on the Mediterranean coast and Beersheba in the northern Negev.

20:2 *Abimelech.* Probably the father or grandfather of the later king who bore the same name (see 26:1).

20:3 *dream.* Once again God intervened to spare the mother of the promised offspring. Dreams were a frequent mode of revelation in the OT (see 28:12; 31:10–11; 37:5–9; 40:5; 41:1; Nu 12:6; Jdg 7:13; 1Ki 3:5; Da 2:3; 4:5; 7:1).

20:7 *prophet.* See note on 18:17. Abraham was the first man to bear this title (see Ps 105:15).

11Abraham replied, "I said to myself,
'There is surely no fear of God[u] in this
place, and they will kill me because of my
wife.'[v] 12Besides, she really is my sister,[w]
the daughter of my father though not of
my mother; and she became my wife.
13And when God had me wander[x] from
my father's household,[y] I said to her, 'This
is how you can show your love to me:
Everywhere we go, say of me, "He is my
brother." ' "
14Then Abimelech[z] brought sheep and
cattle and male and female slaves and gave
them to Abraham,[a] and he returned Sarah
his wife to him. 15And Abimelech said,
"My land is before you; live wherever you
like."[b]
16To Sarah he said, "I am giving your
brother a thousand shekels[p] of silver. This
is to cover the offense against you before
all who are with you; you are completely
vindicated."
17Then Abraham prayed to God,[c] and
God healed Abimelech, his wife and his
slave girls so they could have children
again, 18for the LORD had closed up every
womb in Abimelech's household because
of Abraham's wife Sarah.[d]

The Birth of Isaac

21 Now the LORD was gracious to Sarah[e] as he had said, and the LORD
did for Sarah what he had promised.[f]
2Sarah became pregnant and bore a son[g]
to Abraham in his old age,[h] at the very
time God had promised him.[i] 3Abraham
gave the name Isaac[q][j] to the son Sarah
bore him. 4When his son Isaac was eight
days old, Abraham circumcised him,[k] as
God commanded him. 5Abraham was a
hundred years old[l] when his son Isaac
was born to him.
6Sarah said, "God has brought me
laughter,[m] and everyone who hears about
this will laugh with me." 7And she added,
"Who would have said to Abraham that
Sarah would nurse children? Yet I have
borne him a son in his old age."[n]

Hagar and Ishmael Sent Away

8The child grew and was weaned,[o] and
on the day Isaac was weaned Abraham
held a great feast. 9But Sarah saw that the
son whom Hagar the Egyptian had borne
to Abraham[p] was mocking,[q] 10and she
said to Abraham, "Get rid of that slave
woman[r] and her son, for that slave
woman's son will never share in the inheritance with my son Isaac."[s]
11The matter distressed Abraham greatly
because it concerned his son.[t] 12But God
said to him, "Do not be so distressed about
the boy and your maidservant. Listen to
whatever Sarah tells you, because it is
through Isaac that your offspring[r] will be
reckoned.[u] 13I will make the son of the
maidservant into a nation[v] also, because
he is your offspring."
14Early the next morning Abraham took
some food and a skin of water and gave
them to Hagar.[w] He set them on her
shoulders and then sent her off with the

20:11 [u]Ge 42:18; Ne 5:15; Job 31:23; Ps 36:1; Pr 16:6 [v]S Ge 12:12; 31:31
20:12 [w]S Ge 12:13
20:13 [x]Dt 26:5; 1Ch 16:20; Isa 30:28; 63:17 [y]S Ge 12:1
20:14 [z]S ver 2 [a]S Ge 12:16
20:15 [b]S Ge 13:9; S 45:18
20:17 [c]S ver 7; Job 42:9
20:18 [d]Ge 12:17
21:1 [e]1Sa 2:21 [f]S Ge 8:1; S 17:6, 21; 18:14; Gal 4:23; Heb 11:11
21:2 [g]S Ge 17:19; S 30:6 [h]Gal 4:22; Heb 11:11 [i]S Ge 18:10
21:3 [j]S Ge 16:11; S 17:19; Jos 24:3
21:4 [k]S Ge 17:10,12; Ac 7:8
21:5 [l]S Ge 12:4; Heb 6:15
21:6 [m]Ge 17:17; Job 8:21; Ps 126:2; Isa 12:6; 35:2; 44:23; 52:9; 54:1
21:7 [n]S Ge 17:17
21:8 [o]1Sa 1:23
21:9 [p]S Ge 16:15 [q]Ge 39:14; Gal 4:29
21:10 [r]Ge 39:17 [s]Ge 25:6; Gal 4:30*
21:11 [t]Ge 17:18
21:12 [u]Mt 1:2; Ro 9:7*; Heb 11:18*
21:13 [v]S Ge 13:16
21:14 [w]S Ge 16:1

[p] *16* That is, about 25 pounds (about 11.5 kilograms)
[q] *3* *Isaac* means *he laughs.*
[r] *12* Or *seed*

20:11 *fear of God.* A conventional phrase equivalent to "true religion." "Fear" in this phrase has the sense of reverential trust in God that includes commitment to his revealed will (word).
20:12 *she really is my sister, the daughter of my father though not of my mother.* Abraham's half-truth was a sinful deception, not a legitimate explanation.
20:14–16 Abimelech's generosity was a strong contrast to Abraham's fearfulness and deception.
20:16 *shekels.* Though not in the Hebrew, the word is correctly supplied here as the most common unit of weight in ancient times. Originally the shekel was only a weight, not a coin, since coinage was not invented till the seventh century B.C.
21:1 *was gracious to Sarah as he had said.* See 17:16. *did for Sarah what he had promised.* See Gal 4:22–23,28.
21:3 *Isaac.* See note on 17:17.
21:4 See notes on 17:10,12.
21:5 Abraham, in fulfillment of the promise made to him (see 17:16), miraculously became a father at the age of 100 years (see 17:17).
21:6 *laughter . . . laugh.* See note on 17:17.
21:8 *weaned.* At age two or three, as was customary in the ancient Near East.
21:9 *the son whom Hagar the Egyptian had borne.* Ishmael, who was in his late teens at this time (see 16:15–16). *mocking.* Or "at play." In either case, Sarah saw Ishmael as a potential threat to Isaac's inheritance (v. 10).
21:10 *Get rid of that slave woman and her son.* See Gal 4:21–31. Driving them out would have had the effect of disinheriting Ishmael.
21:11 *The matter distressed Abraham.* Both love and legal custom played a part in Abraham's anguish. He knew that the customs of his day, illustrated later in the Nuzi tablets (see chart on "Ancient Texts Relating to the OT," p. 5), prohibited the arbitrary expulsion of a servant girl's son (whose legal status was relatively weak in any case).
21:12 *Listen to whatever Sarah tells you.* God overruled in this matter (as he had done earlier; see 15:4), promising Abraham that both Isaac and Ishmael would have numerous descendants. *it is through Isaac that your offspring will be reckoned.* See Ro 9:6–8 and Heb 11:17–19 for broader spiritual applications of this statement.
21:14 *Early the next morning.* Though Abraham would now be separated from Ishmael for the first time, he responded to God's command with prompt obedience (see note on 12:4). *Beersheba.* See note on v. 31.

boy. She went on her way and wandered
in the desert of Beersheba.[x]
15 When the water in the skin was gone,
she put the boy under one of the bushes.
16 Then she went off and sat down nearby,
about a bowshot away, for she thought, "I
cannot watch the boy die." And as she sat
there nearby, she[s] began to sob.[y]
17 God heard the boy crying,[z] and the
angel of God[a] called to Hagar from
heaven[b] and said to her, "What is the
matter, Hagar? Do not be afraid;[c] God has
heard the boy crying as he lies there. 18 Lift
the boy up and take him by the hand, for I
will make him into a great nation.[d]"
19 Then God opened her eyes[e] and she
saw a well of water.[f] So she went and
filled the skin with water and gave the boy
a drink.
20 God was with the boy[g] as he grew up.
He lived in the desert and became an archer.
21 While he was living in the Desert of
Paran,[h] his mother got a wife for him[i]
from Egypt.

The Treaty at Beersheba

22 At that time Abimelech[j] and Phicol
the commander of his forces[k] said to Abraham,
"God is with you in everything you
do.[l] 23 Now swear[m] to me here before
God that you will not deal falsely with me
or my children or my descendants.[n] Show
to me and the country where you are living
as an alien the same kindness I have
shown to you."[o]
24 Abraham said, "I swear it."
25 Then Abraham complained to Abimelech
about a well of water that Abimelech's
servants had seized.[p] 26 But Abimelech
said, "I don't know who has done
this. You did not tell me, and I heard about
it only today."
27 So Abraham brought sheep and cattle
and gave them to Abimelech, and the two
men made a treaty.[q] 28 Abraham set apart
seven ewe lambs from the flock, 29 and
Abimelech asked Abraham, "What is the
meaning of these seven ewe lambs you
have set apart by themselves?"
30 He replied, "Accept these seven lambs
from my hand as a witness[r] that I dug this
well.[s]"
31 So that place was called Beersheba,[t][t]
because the two men swore an oath[u]
there.
32 After the treaty[v] had been made at
Beersheba,[w] Abimelech and Phicol the
commander of his forces[x] returned to the
land of the Philistines.[y] 33 Abraham
planted a tamarisk tree[z] in Beersheba, and
there he called upon the name of the
LORD,[a] the Eternal God.[b] 34 And Abraham
stayed in the land of the Philistines[c] for a
long time.

Abraham Tested

22 Some time later God tested[d] Abraham.
He said to him, "Abraham!"
"Here I am,"[e] he replied.
2 Then God said, "Take your son,[f] your
only son, Isaac, whom you love, and go to

21:14 [x]ver 31, 32; Ge 22:19; 26:33; 28:10; 46:1,5; Jos 15:28; 19:2; Jdg 20:1; 1Sa 3:20; 1Ch 4:28; Ne 11:27 **21:16** [y]Jer 6:26; Am 8:10; Zec 12:10 **21:17** [z]Ex 3:7; Nu 20:16; Dt 26:7; Ps 6:8 [a]S Ge 16:7 [b]Ge 22:11,15 [c]S Ge 15:1 **21:18** [d]S Ge 17:20 **21:19** [e]Nu 22:31 [f]S Ge 16:7 **21:20** [g]Ge 26:3, 24; 28:15; 39:2, 21,23; Lk 1:66 **21:21** [h]S Ge 14:6 [i]Ge 24:4,38; 28:2; 34:4,8; Jdg 14:2 **21:22** [j]S Ge 20:2 [k]ver 32; Ge 26:26 [l]ver 23; Ge 26:28; 28:15; 31:3,5,42; 39:2, 3; 1Sa 3:19; 16:18; 2Ch 1:1; Ps 46:7; Isa 7:14; 8:8,10; 41:10; 43:5 **21:23** [m]ver 31; Ge 25:33; 26:31; 31:53; Jos 2:12; 1Ki 2:8 [n]1Sa 24:21 [o]S ver 22; Jos 2:12 **21:25** [p]Ge 26:15, 18,20-22 **21:27** [q]ver 31, 32; Ge 26:28,31; 31:44,53 **21:30** [r]Ge 31:44, 47,48,50,52; Jos 22:27,28,34; 24:27; Isa 19:20; Mal 2:14 [s]ver 25; Ge 26:25,32 **21:31** [t]S ver 14 [u]S ver 23,S 27 **21:32** [v]S ver 27 [w]S ver 14 [x]S ver 22 [y]S Ge 10:14 **21:33** [z]1Sa 22:6; 31:13 [a]S Ge 4:26

[b]Ex 15:18; Dt 32:40; 33:27; Job 36:26; Ps 10:16; 45:6; 90:2; 93:2; 102:24; 103:19; 146:10; Isa 40:28; Jer 10:10; Hab 1:12; 3:6; Heb 13:8 **21:34** [c]S Ge 10:14 **22:1** [d]Ex 15:25; 16:4; 20:20; Dt 8:2,16; 13:3; Jdg 2:22; 3:1; 2Ch 32:31; Ps 66:10; Heb 11:17; Jas 1:12-13 [e]ver 11; Ge 31:11; 46:2; 1Sa 3:4,6,8; Isa 6:8 **22:2** [f]ver 12,16; Jn 3:16; Heb 11:17; 1Jn 4:9

[s]16 Hebrew; Septuagint *the child* [t]31 *Beersheba* can mean *well of seven* or *well of the oath.*

21:15 *one of the bushes.* See note on v. 33.
21:17 *God heard . . . God has heard.* A pun on the name "Ishmael" (see NIV text note on 16:11; see also 17:20).
21:21 *Desert of Paran.* Located in north central Sinai. *his mother got a wife for him from Egypt.* Parents often arranged their children's marriages (see ch. 24).
21:22 *Abimelech.* See 20:2 and note. *Phicol.* Either a family name or an official title, since it reappears over 60 years later (25:26) in a similar context (26:26).
21:23 *swear to me . . . before God . . . Show to me . . . kindness.* Phrases commonly used when making covenants or treaties (see vv. 27,32). "Kindness" as used here refers to acts of friendship (cf. v. 27; 20:14). Such covenants always involved oaths.
21:27 *sheep and cattle.* Probably to be used in the treaty ceremony (see 15:10).
21:31 *Beersheba, because the two men swore an oath there.* See NIV text note. For a similar pun on the name see 26:33. Beersheba, an important town in the northern Negev, marked the southernmost boundary of the Israelite monarchy in later times (see, e.g., 2Sa 17:11). An ancient well there is still pointed out as "Abraham's well" (see v. 25), but its authenticity is not certain.
21:32 *Philistines.* See note on 10:14.
21:33 *tamarisk.* A shrub or small tree that thrives in arid regions. Its leafy branches provide welcome shade, and it is probably the unidentified bush under which Hagar put Ishmael in v. 15. *Eternal God.* The Hebrew is *El Olam,* a phrase unique to this passage. It is one of a series of names that include *El,* "God," as an element (see 14:19 and note; 17:1 and note; 33:20; 35:7).
22:1 *Some time later.* Isaac had grown into adolescence or young manhood, as implied also by 21:34 ("a long time"). *tested.* Not "tempted," for God does not tempt (Jas 1:13). Satan tempts us (see 1Co 7:5) in order to make us fall; God tests us in order to confirm our faith (Ex 20:20) or prove our commitment (Dt 8:2). See note on Mt 4:1. *Here I am.* Abraham answered with the response of a servant, as did Moses and Samuel when God called them by name (see Ex 3:4; 1Sa 3:4,6,8).
22:2 *your son, your only son, Isaac, whom you love.* In the Hebrew text "Isaac" follows the clause "whom you love," in order to heighten the effect: "your son, your only son, whom you love—Isaac." Isaac was the "only son" of the promise (21:12). *region of Moriah.* The author of Chronicles identifies the area as the temple mount in Jerusalem (2Ch 3:1).

the region of Moriah.[g] Sacrifice him there
as a burnt offering[h] on one of the mountains I will tell you about.[i]"

3Early the next morning[j] Abraham got
up and saddled his donkey. He took with
him two of his servants and his son Isaac.
When he had cut enough wood for the
burnt offering, he set out for the place God
had told him about. 4On the third day
Abraham looked up and saw the place in
the distance. 5He said to his servants, "Stay
here with the donkey while I and the boy
go over there. We will worship and then
we will come back to you.[k]"

6Abraham took the wood for the burnt
offering and placed it on his son Isaac,[l]
and he himself carried the fire and the
knife.[m] As the two of them went on together, 7Isaac spoke up and said to his father Abraham, "Father?"

"Yes, my son?" Abraham replied.

"The fire and wood are here," Isaac
said, "but where is the lamb[n] for the burnt
offering?"

8Abraham answered, "God himself will
provide[o] the lamb[p] for the burnt offering,
my son." And the two of them went on
together.

9When they reached the place God had
told him about,[q] Abraham built an altar[r]
there and arranged the wood[s] on it. He
bound his son Isaac and laid him on the
altar,[t] on top of the wood. 10Then he
reached out his hand and took the knife[u]
to slay his son.[v] 11But the angel of the
LORD[w] called out to him from heaven,[x]
"Abraham! Abraham!"[y]

"Here I am,"[z] he replied.

12"Do not lay a hand on the boy," he
said. "Do not do anything to him. Now I
know that you fear God,[a] because you
have not withheld from me your son, your
only son.[b]"

13Abraham looked up and there in a
thicket he saw a ram[u] caught by its
horns.[c] He went over and took the ram
and sacrificed it as a burnt offering instead
of his son.[d] 14So Abraham called[e] that
place The LORD[f] Will Provide. And to this
day it is said, "On the mountain of the
LORD it will be provided.[g]"

15The angel of the LORD[h] called to
Abraham from heaven[i] a second time
16and said, "I swear by myself,[j] declares
the LORD, that because you have done this
and have not withheld your son, your only
son,[k] 17I will surely bless you[l] and make
your descendants[m] as numerous as the
stars in the sky[n] and as the sand on the
seashore.[o] Your descendants will take
possession of the cities of their enemies,[p]
18and through your offspring[v] all nations

22:2 [g]2Ch 3:1 [h]S Ge 8:20 [i]ver 9 **22:3** [j]Jos 8:10 **22:5** [k]Ex 24:14 **22:6** [l]Jn 19:17 [m]ver 10; Jdg 19:29 **22:7** [n]Ex 29:38-42; Lev 1:10; Rev 13:8 **22:8** [o]ver 14 [p]ver 13; S Jn 1:29 **22:9** [q]ver 2 [r]S Ge 4:26; S 8:20 [s]Lev 1:7; 1Ki 18:33 [t]Heb 11:17-19; Jas 2:21 **22:10** [u]S ver 6 [v]ver 3; S Ge 18:19 **22:11** [w]S Ge 16:7 [x]S Ge 21:17 [y]Ge 46:2 [z]S ver 1 **22:12** [a]S Ge 18:19; 42:18; Ex 18:21; 1Sa 15:22; Job 1:1; 37:24; Pr 8:13; Jas 2:21-22 [b]S ver 2; Jn 3:16; 1Jn 4:9 **22:13** [c]S ver 8 [d]S Ge 8:20; Ro 8:32 **22:14** [e]Ex 17:15; Jdg 6:24 [f]Isa 30:29 [g]ver 8 **22:15** [h]S Ge 16:7 [i]S Ge 21:17 **22:16** [j]Ex 13:11; 32:13; 33:1; Isa 45:23; 62:8; Jer 22:5; 44:26; 49:13; 51:14; Am 6:8; Lk 1:73; Heb 6:13 [k]S ver 2 **22:17** [l]S Ge 12:2 [m]Heb 6:14* [n]S Ge 15:5; Ex 32:13; Dt 7:7; 28:62 [o]S Ge 12:2; S 26:24; Hos 1:10; Ro 9:27; Heb 11:12 [p]Ge 24:60; Est 9:2

[u]*13* Many manuscripts of the Masoretic Text, Samaritan Pentateuch, Septuagint and Syriac; most manuscripts of the Masoretic Text *a ram behind* ⌊*him*⌋ [v]*18* Or *seed*

Today "Mount Moriah" is occupied by the Dome of the Rock, an impressive Muslim structure erected in A.D. 691. A large outcropping of rock inside the building is still pointed to as the traditional site of the intended sacrifice of Isaac. *Sacrifice him.* Abraham had committed himself by covenant to be obedient to the Lord and had consecrated his son Isaac to the Lord by circumcision. The Lord put his servant's faith and loyalty to the supreme test, thereby instructing Abraham, Isaac and their descendants as to the kind of total consecration the Lord's covenant requires. The test also foreshadowed the perfect consecration in sacrifice that another offspring of Abraham would undergo (see note on v. 16) in order to wholly consecrate Abraham and his spiritual descendants to God and to fulfill the covenant promises.

22:3 *Early the next morning.* Prompt obedience, even under such trying circumstances, characterized Abraham's response to God (see note on 12:4).

22:4 *third day.* Three days would be necessary for the journey from Beersheba (see v. 19) to Jerusalem.

22:5 *boy.* See v. 12. The Hebrew for this word has a wide range of meaning, from an infant (see Ex 2:6) to a young man of military age (see 1Ch 12:28). *we will come back to you.* Abraham, the man of faith and "the father of all who believe" (Ro 4:11), "reasoned that God could raise the dead" (Heb 11:19) if that were necessary to fulfill his promise.

22:8 *God himself will provide the lamb.* The immediate fulfillment of Abraham's trusting response was the ram of v. 13, but its ultimate fulfillment is the Lamb of God (Jn 1:29, 36).

22:9 *laid him on the altar, on top of the wood.* Isaac is here a type (prefiguration) of Christ (see note on v. 16).

22:11 *angel of the LORD.* See note on 16:7. *Abraham! Abraham!* The repetition of the name indicates urgency (see 46:2; Ex 3:4; 1Sa 3:10; Ac 9:4). *Here I am.* See note on v. 1.

22:12 *fear God.* See note on 20:11. *you have not withheld from me your son, your only son.* See v. 16. Abraham's "faith was made complete by what he did" (Jas 2:21–22).

22:13 *instead of.* Substitutionary sacrifice of one life for another is here mentioned for the first time. As the ram died in Isaac's place, so also Jesus gave his life as a ransom "for" (lit. "instead of") many (Mk 10:45).

22:14 *mountain of the LORD.* During the Israelite monarchy the phrase referred to the temple mount in Jerusalem (see Ps 24:3; Isa 2:3; 30:29; Zec 8:3).

22:16 *I swear by myself.* There is no greater name in which the Lord can take an oath (see Heb 6:13). *you . . . have not withheld your son, your only son.* Abraham's devotion is paralleled by God's love to us in Christ as reflected in Jn 3:16 and Ro 8:32, which may allude to this verse.

22:17 *descendants as numerous as the stars in the sky.* See 13:16; 15:5 and notes. *sand on the seashore.* Fulfilled, at least in part, during Solomon's reign (see 1Ki 4:20). *cities.* Lit. "gates." Taking possession of the gate of a city was tantamount to occupying the city itself (see 24:60).

22:18 *all nations on earth will be blessed.* See note on 12:2–3. *because you have obeyed me.* See note on 17:9.

on earth will be blessed,*q* because you have obeyed me."*r*

¹⁹Then Abraham returned to his servants, and they set off together for Beersheba.*s* And Abraham stayed in Beersheba.

Nahor's Sons

²⁰Some time later Abraham was told, "Milcah is also a mother; she has borne sons to your brother Nahor:*t* ²¹Uz*u* the firstborn, Buz*v* his brother, Kemuel (the father of Aram), ²²Kesed, Hazo, Pildash, Jidlaph and Bethuel.*w*" ²³Bethuel became the father of Rebekah.*x* Milcah bore these eight sons to Abraham's brother Nahor.*y* ²⁴His concubine,*z* whose name was Reumah, also had sons: Tebah, Gaham, Tahash and Maacah.

The Death of Sarah

23 Sarah lived to be a hundred and twenty-seven years old. ²She died at Kiriath Arba*a* (that is, Hebron)*b* in the land of Canaan, and Abraham went to mourn for Sarah and to weep over her.*c*

³Then Abraham rose from beside his dead wife and spoke to the Hittites.*w d* He said, ⁴"I am an alien and a stranger*e* among you. Sell me some property for a burial site here so I can bury my dead.*f*"

⁵The Hittites replied to Abraham, ⁶"Sir, listen to us. You are a mighty prince*g* among us. Bury your dead in the choicest of our tombs. None of us will refuse you his tomb for burying your dead."

⁷Then Abraham rose and bowed down before the people of the land, the Hittites. ⁸He said to them, "If you are willing to let me bury my dead, then listen to me and intercede with Ephron son of Zohar*h* on my behalf ⁹so he will sell me the cave of Machpelah,*i* which belongs to him and is at the end of his field. Ask him to sell it to me for the full price as a burial site among you."

¹⁰Ephron the Hittite was sitting among his people and he replied to Abraham in the hearing of all the Hittites*j* who had come to the gate*k* of his city. ¹¹"No, my lord," he said. "Listen to me; I give*x l* you the field, and I give*x* you the cave that is in it. I give*x* it to you in the presence of my people. Bury your dead."

¹²Again Abraham bowed down before the people of the land ¹³and he said to Ephron in their hearing, "Listen to me, if you will. I will pay the price of the field. Accept it from me so I can bury my dead there."

¹⁴Ephron answered Abraham, ¹⁵"Listen to me, my lord; the land is worth four hundred shekels*y* of silver,*m* but what is that between me and you? Bury your dead."

¹⁶Abraham agreed to Ephron's terms and weighed out for him the price he had named in the hearing of the Hittites: four

Cross references (center column)

22:18
q S Ge 12:2,3;
Ac 3:25*;
Gal 3:8* *r* S ver
10; Ge 17:2,9;
Ps 105:9
22:19 *s* Ge 21:14;
26:23; 28:10
22:20
t S Ge 11:29
22:21
u S Ge 10:23
v Job 32:2;
Jer 25:23
22:22
w Ge 24:15,47;
25:20
22:23 *x* Ge 24:15
y S Ge 11:29
22:24 *z* Ge 25:6;
35:22; 36:12;
Jdg 8:31; 2Sa 3:7;
1Ki 2:22; 11:3;
1Ch 1:32; SS 6:8
23:2 *a* Jos 14:15;
15:13; 20:7;
21:11
b S Ge 13:18
c Ge 24:67
23:3 *d* S Ge 10:15
23:4 *e* S Ge 17:8;
19:9; Ex 2:22;
Lev 25:23;
Ps 39:12; 105:12;
119:19;
Heb 11:9,13
f Ge 49:30;
Ac 7:16
23:6
g Ge 14:14-16;
24:35

23:8 *h* Ge 25:9
23:9 *i* ver 17,19;
Ge 25:9; 47:30;
49:30; 50:13
23:10 *j* ver 18
k S Ge 18:1;
Dt 22:15; 25:7;
Jos 20:4; Ru 4:11;
2Sa 15:2;
2Ki 15:35;
Ps 127:5;
Pr 31:23;
Jer 26:10; 36:10
23:11 *l* 2Sa 24:23

23:15 *m* Eze 45:12

w 3 Or *the sons of Heth*; also in verses 5, 7, 10, 16, 18
and 20   *x* 11 Or *sell*   *y* 15 That is, about 10 pounds
(about 4.5 kilograms)

22:23–24 Abraham's brother Nahor (see 11:26) became the father of eight sons by his wife and four by his concubine. They would later become the ancestors of 12 Aramean (see v. 21) tribes, just as Abraham's grandson Jacob would become the ancestor of the 12 tribes of Israel (see 49:28).
23:2 *Kiriath Arba.* Means "the town of Arba" (Arba was the most prominent member of a tribe living in the Hebron area [see Jos 14:15]). It can also mean "the town of four," referring to the place where Anak (see Jos 15:13–14; 21:11) and his three sons lived (see Jdg 1:10,20). *went.* Either from Beersheba to Hebron or into where Sarah's body was lying.
23:3 *Hittites.* See note on 10:15. They were apparently in control of the Hebron area at this time.
23:4 *an alien and a stranger.* The phrase was used often by the patriarchs and their descendants in reference to themselves (see 1Ch 29:15; Ps 39:12; see also Heb 11:13). On this earth Abraham "lived in tents" (Heb 11:9), the most temporary of dwellings. But he looked forward to the more permanent home promised him, which the author of Hebrews calls "the city with foundations, whose architect and builder is God" (Heb 11:10).
23:6 *You are a mighty prince.* Probably intended as words of flattery.
23:9 *cave of Machpelah.* Though inaccessible today, the tombs of several patriarchs and their wives—Abraham and Sarah, Isaac and Rebekah, Jacob and Leah (see v. 19; 25:8–10; 49:30–31; 50:12–13)—are, according to tradi-

tion, located in a large cave deep beneath the Mosque of Abraham, a Muslim shrine in Hebron. *end of his field.* Because buying the entire field would have made Abraham responsible for certain additional financial and social obligations, he wanted to buy only a small part of it. Hittite laws stipulated that when a landowner sold only part of his property to someone else, the original and principal landowner had to continue paying all dues on the land. But if the landowner disposed of an entire tract, the new owner had to pay the dues.
23:10 *in the hearing of all the Hittites who had come to the gate.* The main gateway of a city was usually the place where legal matters were transacted and attested (see v. 18; see also note on 19:1).
23:11 *my lord.* Perhaps intended to flatter Abraham (see v. 15). *give.* See NIV text note.
23:15 *four hundred shekels of silver, but what is that between me and you?* See note on 20:16. Despite Ephron's pretense of generosity, 400 shekels of silver was an exorbitant price for a field (see, e.g., Jer 32:9). Ephron was taking advantage of Abraham during a time of grief and bereavement. He knew that Abraham had to deal quickly in order to have a place to bury Sarah, so he insisted that Abraham buy the entire lot and assume responsibility for the dues as well.
23:16 *weight current among the merchants.* Subject to more variation and therefore greater dishonesty than the later royal standard (see 2Sa 14:26), which was carefully

hundred shekels of silver, [n] according to the weight current among the merchants. [o]

[17]So Ephron's field in Machpelah [p] near Mamre [q]—both the field and the cave in it, and all the trees within the borders of the field—was deeded [18]to Abraham as his property [r] in the presence of all the Hittites [s] who had come to the gate [t] of the city. [19]Afterward Abraham buried his wife Sarah in the cave in the field of Machpelah [u] near Mamre (which is at Hebron [v]) in the land of Canaan. [w] [20]So the field and the cave in it were deeded [x] to Abraham by the Hittites as a burial site. [y]

Isaac and Rebekah

24 Abraham was now old and well advanced in years, [z] and the LORD had blessed [a] him in every way. [b] [2]He said to the chief [z] servant [c] in his household, the one in charge of all that he had, [d] "Put your hand under my thigh. [e] [3]I want you to swear [f] by the LORD, the God of heaven [g] and the God of earth, [h] that you will not get a wife for my son [i] from the daughters of the Canaanites, [j] among whom I am living, [k] [4]but will go to my country and my own relatives [l] and get a wife for my son Isaac. [m]"

[5]The servant asked him, "What if the woman is unwilling to come back with me to this land? [n] Shall I then take your son back to the country you came from? [o]"

[6]"Make sure that you do not take my son back there," [p] Abraham said. [7]"The LORD, the God of heaven, [q] who brought me out of my father's household and my native land [r] and who spoke to me and promised me on oath, saying, 'To your off-

spring [a] [s] I will give this land' [t]—he will send his angel before you [u] so that you can get a wife for my son from there. [8]If the woman is unwilling to come back with you, then you will be released from this oath [v] of mine. Only do not take my son back there." [w] [9]So the servant put his hand under the thigh [x] of his master [y] Abraham and swore an oath to him concerning this matter.

[10]Then the servant took ten of his master's camels [z] and left, taking with him all kinds of good things [a] from his master. He set out for Aram Naharaim [b] [b] and made his way to the town of Nahor. [c] [11]He had the camels kneel down near the well [d] outside the town; it was toward evening, the time the women go out to draw water. [e]

[12]Then he prayed, "O LORD, God of my master Abraham, [f] give me success [g] today, and show kindness [h] to my master Abraham. [13]See, I am standing beside this spring, and the daughters of the townspeople are coming out to draw water. [i] [14]May it be that when I say to a girl, 'Please let down your jar that I may have a drink,' and she says, 'Drink, [j] and I'll water your camels too' [k]—let her be the one you have chosen for your servant Isaac. [l] By this I will know [m] that you have shown kindness to my master."

[15]Before he had finished praying, [n] Re-

Cross references (center column)

23:16 [n]2Sa 24:24; Jer 32:9; Zec 11:12 [o]2Sa 14:26
23:17 [p]S ver 9 [q]S Ge 13:18
23:18 [r]S Ge 12:7 [s]ver 10 [t]S Ge 18:1
23:19 [u]S ver 9 [v]S Ge 13:18; Jos 14:13; 1Ch 29:27 [w]Ge 49:31
23:20 [x]Jer 32:10 [y]S Ge 10:15; 35:29; 47:30; 49:30; 50:5,13
24:1 [z]S Ge 17:17; Jos 23:1 [a]Ge 12:2; Gal 3:9 [b]ver 35
24:2 [c]S Ge 15:3 [d]Ge 39:4-6 [e]ver 9; Ge 47:29
24:3 [f]Ge 47:31; 50:25 [g]ver 7 [h]S Ge 14:19; S Nu 20:14 [i]Dt 7:3; 2Co 6:14-17 [j]S Ge 10:15-19 [k]ver 37
24:4 [l]S Ge 12:1; Jdg 14:3 [m]S ver 29; S Ge 21:21
24:5 [n]ver 39 [o]Heb 11:15
24:6 [p]ver 8
24:7 [q]ver 3 [r]Ge 12:1
[s]Ro 4:13; Gal 3:16* [t]S Ge 12:7 [u]S Ge 16:7
24:8 [v]ver 41; Jos 2:12,17,20; 9:20 [w]S ver 6
24:9 [x]S ver 2 [y]Ge 32:4; 33:8
24:10 [z]ver 19; 1Ki 10:2; 1Ch 12:40; Isa 30:6 [a]ver 22, 30,47,53; Ge 43:11; 45:23 [b]Nu 23:7; Dt 23:4; Jdg 3:8 [c]S Ge 11:29
24:11 [d]Ex 2:15 [e]ver 13; Ge 29:2,9-10; Ex 2:16; 1Sa 9:11; Jn 4:7 24:12 [f]ver 27,42,48; Ge 26:24; 28:13; 31:42,53; 32:9; 43:23; 46:3; Ex 3:6,15,16; 4:5; 1Ki 18:36; Ps 75:9; 94:7 [g]ver 21,40,51,56; Ge 27:20; Ne 1:11 [h]S Ge 19:19; Jos 2:12; Job 10:12 24:13 [i]S ver 11,43; Ge 29:8 24:14 [j]ver 18,46 [k]ver 19 [l]ver 44 [m]Jos 2:12; Jdg 6:17,37; 1Sa 14:10; 1Ki 13:3; Ps 86:17; Isa 38:7; Jer 44:29 24:15 [n]ver 45

[z]2 Or oldest   [a]7 Or seed   [b]10 That is, Northwest Mesopotamia

---

regulated and more precise.

23:17 *the field and the cave in it, and all the trees.* In order to be free of all obligations relating to the field in which the cave of Machpelah was located, Ephron had held out for the sale of the entire field and its contents (see note on v. 9).

23:19 *buried his wife . . . in the land of Canaan.* In that culture, people had a strong desire to be buried "with their fathers" (see note on 25:8) in their native land. By purchasing a burial place in Canaan, Abraham indicated his unswerving commitment to the Lord's promise. Canaan was his new homeland.

24:2 *chief servant in his household.* Probably Eliezer of Damascus (see note on 15:2). *Put your hand under my thigh.* Near the organ of procreation, probably because this oath was related to the continuation of Abraham's line through Isaac (see 47:29).

24:3 *the LORD, the God of heaven and the God of earth.* See v. 7. For a similar majestic title used by Abraham in an oath see 14:22.

24:4 *my country.* Mesopotamia (see note on v. 10). *get a wife for my son.* See note on 21:21.

24:7 *To your offspring I will give this land.* Repeats the

promise of 12:7. *his angel.* See note on 16:7.

24:10 *camels.* See note on 12:16. *Aram Naharaim.* See NIV text note; lit. "Aram of the two rivers"—the Euphrates and the Tigris. Aram (see note on 10:22) Naharaim was the northern part of the area called later by the Greeks "Mesopotamia"—lit. "between the rivers." *town of Nahor.* Perhaps named after Abraham's brother (see v. 15; 11:26). It is mentioned in clay tablets excavated by the French beginning in 1933 at the ancient city of Mari on the Euphrates (see chart on "Ancient Texts Relating to the OT," p. 5). Nahor was located in the Haran (see note on 11:31) district and was ruled by an Amorite prince in the 18th century B.C.

24:11 *toward evening, the time the women go out to draw water.* The coolest time of day.

24:14 *By this I will know.* Like his master Abraham, the servant asked God for a sign to validate his errand (see note on 15:8). *kindness.* See v. 27; probably a reference to God's covenant with Abraham, which had promised numerous descendants through Isaac (see 17:19; 21:12).

24:15 *Before he had finished praying.* God had already begun to answer. *Rebekah . . . was the daughter of Bethuel son of . . . the wife of Abraham's brother.* Isaac would thus be marrying his father's grandniece (see v. 48).

bekah[o] came out with her jar on her shoulder. She was the daughter of Bethuel[p] son of Milcah,[q] who was the wife of Abraham's brother Nahor.[r] 16The girl was very beautiful,[s] a virgin;[t] no man had ever lain with her. She went down to the spring, filled her jar and came up again.

17The servant hurried to meet her and said, "Please give me a little water from your jar."[u]

18"Drink,[v] my lord," she said, and quickly lowered the jar to her hands and gave him a drink.

19After she had given him a drink, she said, "I'll draw water for your camels[w] too,[x] until they have finished drinking." 20So she quickly emptied her jar into the trough, ran back to the well to draw more water, and drew enough for all his camels.[y] 21Without saying a word, the man watched her closely to learn whether or not the LORD had made his journey successful.[z]

22When the camels had finished drinking, the man took out a gold nose ring[a] weighing a beka[c] and two gold bracelets[b] weighing ten shekels.[d] 23Then he asked, "Whose daughter are you?[c] Please tell me, is there room in your father's house for us to spend the night?[d]"

24She answered him, "I am the daughter of Bethuel, the son that Milcah bore to Nahor.[e]" 25And she added, "We have plenty of straw and fodder,[f] as well as room for you to spend the night."

26Then the man bowed down and worshiped the LORD,[g] 27saying, "Praise be to the LORD,[h] the God of my master Abraham,[i] who has not abandoned his kindness and faithfulness[j] to my master. As for me, the LORD has led me on the journey[k] to the house of my master's relatives."[l]

28The girl ran and told her mother's household about these things.[m] 29Now Rebekah had a brother named Laban,[n] and he hurried out to the man at the spring. 30As soon as he had seen the nose ring, and the bracelets on his sister's arms,[o] and had heard Rebekah tell what the man said to her, he went out to the man and found him standing by the camels near the spring. 31"Come, you who are blessed by the LORD,"[p] he said. "Why are you stand-

ing out here? I have prepared the house and a place for the camels."

32So the man went to the house, and the camels were unloaded. Straw and fodder[q] were brought for the camels, and water for him and his men to wash their feet.[r] 33Then food was set before him, but he said, "I will not eat until I have told you what I have to say."

"Then tell us," Laban said.

34So he said, "I am Abraham's servant.[s] 35The LORD has blessed[t] my master abundantly,[u] and he has become wealthy.[v] He has given him sheep and cattle, silver and gold, menservants and maidservants, and camels and donkeys.[w] 36My master's wife Sarah has borne him a son in her[e] old age,[x] and he has given him everything he owns.[y] 37And my master made me swear an oath,[z] and said, 'You must not get a wife for my son from the daughters of the Canaanites, in whose land I live,[a] 38but go to my father's family and to my own clan, and get a wife for my son.'[b]

39"Then I asked my master, 'What if the woman will not come back with me?'[c]

40"He replied, 'The LORD, before whom I have walked,[d] will send his angel with you[e] and make your journey a success,[f] so that you can get a wife for my son from my own clan and from my father's family.[g] 41Then, when you go to my clan, you will be released from my oath even if they refuse to give her to you—you will be released from my oath.'[h]

42"When I came to the spring today, I said, 'O LORD, God of my master Abraham, if you will, please grant success[i] to the journey on which I have come. 43See, I am standing beside this spring;[j] if a maiden[k] comes out to draw water and I say to her, "Please let me drink a little water from your jar,"[l] 44and if she says to me, "Drink, and I'll draw water for your camels too," let her be the one the LORD has chosen for my master's son.'[m]

45"Before I finished praying in my heart,[n] Rebekah came out, with her jar on her shoulder.[o] She went down to the spring and drew water, and I said to her, 'Please give me a drink.'[p]

46"She quickly lowered her jar from her

24:15
oS Ge 22:23
pS Ge 22:22
qS Ge 11:29
rS Ge 11:29
24:16
sS Ge 12:11
tDt 22:15-21
24:17 uver 45;
1Ki 17:10; Jn 4:7
24:18 vS ver 14
24:19 wS ver 10
xver 14
24:20 yver 46
24:21 zS ver 12
24:22 aver 47;
Ge 41:42;
Isa 3:21;
Eze 16:11-12
bS ver 10
24:23 cver 47
dJdg 19:15; 20:4
24:24 ever 29,
47; S Ge 11:29
24:25 fver 32;
Jdg 19:19
24:26 gver 48,
52; Ex 4:31;
12:27;
1Ch 29:20;
2Ch 20:18
24:27
hGe 14:20;
Ex 18:10;
Ru 4:14;
1Sa 25:32;
2Sa 18:28;
1Ki 1:48; 8:56;
Ps 28:6; 41:13;
68:19; 106:48;
Lk 1:68 iS ver 12
jver 49;
Ge 32:10; 47:29;
Jos 2:14; Ps 98:3
kver 21 lS ver 12;
48; S Ge 12:1
24:28 mGe 29:12
24:29 nver 4;
Ge 25:20; 27:43;
28:2,5; 29:5,12,
13
24:30 oS ver 10;
Eze 23:42
24:31
pGe 26:29;
Ps 115:15

24:32 qS ver 25
rS Ge 18:4
24:34 sS Ge 15:3
24:35 tS Ge 12:2
uver 1 vS Ge 23:6
wS Ge 12:16
24:36
xS Ge 17:17
yGe 25:5; 26:14
24:37 zGe 50:5,
25 aver 3
24:38
bS Ge 21:21
24:39 cS ver 5
24:40 dS Ge 5:22
eS Ge 16:7 fS ver
12 gS Ge 12:1
24:41 hS ver 8
24:42 iS ver 12
24:43 jS ver 13
kPr 30:19;
Isa 7:14 lS ver 14
24:44 mver 14
24:45 n1Sa 1:13
over 15 pS ver
17; Jn 4:7

c22 That is, about 1/5 ounce (about 5.5 grams)
d22 That is, about 4 ounces (about 110 grams)
e36 Or his

24:22 *beka.* Half a shekel (see Ex 38:26); see note on 20:16.
24:32–33 See note on 18:2.
24:34–49 The servant explained his mission to Rebekah's family. His speech, which summarizes the narrative of the earlier part of the chapter, is an excellent example of the ancient storyteller's art, which was designed to fix the details of a story in the hearer's memory.
24:40 *before whom I have walked.* See notes on 5:22; 6:8–9; 17:1.

shoulder and said, 'Drink, and I'll water your camels too.' *q* So I drank, and she watered the camels also. *r*

⁴⁷"I asked her, 'Whose daughter are you?' *s*

"She said, 'The daughter of Bethuel *t* son of Nahor, whom Milcah bore to him.' *u*

"Then I put the ring in her nose *v* and the bracelets on her arms, *w* ⁴⁸and I bowed down and worshiped the LORD. *x* I praised the LORD, the God of my master Abraham, *y* who had led me on the right road to get the granddaughter of my master's brother for his son. *z* ⁴⁹Now if you will show kindness and faithfulness *a* to my master, tell me; and if not, tell me, so I may know which way to turn."

⁵⁰Laban and Bethuel *b* answered, "This is from the LORD; *c* we can say nothing to you one way or the other. *d* ⁵¹Here is Rebekah; take her and go, and let her become the wife of your master's son, as the LORD has directed. *e* "

⁵²When Abraham's servant heard what they said, he bowed down to the ground before the LORD. *f* ⁵³Then the servant brought out gold and silver jewelry and articles of clothing *g* and gave them to Rebekah; he also gave costly gifts *h* to her brother and to her mother. ⁵⁴Then he and the men who were with him ate and drank and spent the night there.

When they got up the next morning, he said, "Send me on my way *i* to my master."

⁵⁵But her brother and her mother replied, "Let the girl remain with us ten days or so; *j* then you *t* may go."

⁵⁶But he said to them, "Do not detain me, now that the LORD has granted success *k* to my journey. Send me on my way *l* so I may go to my master."

⁵⁷Then they said, "Let's call the girl and ask her about it." *m* ⁵⁸So they called Rebekah and asked her, "Will you go with this man?"

"I will go," *n* she said.

⁵⁹So they sent their sister Rebekah on

her way, *o* along with her nurse *p* and Abraham's servant and his men. ⁶⁰And they blessed *q* Rebekah and said to her,

"Our sister, may you increase
    to thousands upon thousands; *r*
may your offspring possess
    the gates of their enemies." *s*

⁶¹Then Rebekah and her maids *t* got ready and mounted their camels and went back with the man. So the servant took Rebekah and left.

⁶²Now Isaac had come from Beer Lahai Roi, *u* for he was living in the Negev. *v* ⁶³He went out to the field one evening to meditate, *g w* and as he looked up, *x* he saw camels approaching. ⁶⁴Rebekah also looked up and saw Isaac. She got down from her camel *y* ⁶⁵and asked the servant, "Who is that man in the field coming to meet us?"

"He is my master," the servant answered. So she took her veil *z* and covered herself.

⁶⁶Then the servant told Isaac all he had done. ⁶⁷Isaac brought her into the tent *a* of his mother Sarah, *b* and he married Rebekah. *c* So she became his wife, and he loved her; *d* and Isaac was comforted after his mother's death. *e*

The Death of Abraham

25:1–4pp — 1Ch 1:32–33

25 Abraham took *h* another wife, whose name was Keturah. ²She bore him Zimran, *f* Jokshan, Medan, Midian, *g* Ishbak and Shuah. *h* ³Jokshan was the father of Sheba *i* and Dedan; *j* the descendants of Dedan were the Asshurites, the Letushites and the Leummites. ⁴The sons of Midian were Ephah, *k* Epher, Hanoch, Abida and Eldaah. All these were descendants of Keturah.

⁵Abraham left everything he owned to Isaac. *l* ⁶But while he was still living, he gave gifts to the sons of his concubines *m*

25:4 *k* Isa 60:6   25:5 *l* S Ge 24:36   25:6 *m* S Ge 22:24

t 55 Or *she*   *g* 63 The meaning of the Hebrew for this word is uncertain.   *h* 1 Or *had taken*

Cross references (center column)

24:46 *q* ver 18-19
r ver 20
24:47 *s* ver 23
t S Ge 22:22
u S ver 24 *v* S ver 22 *w* S ver 10;
Isa 3:19;
Eze 16:11-12
24:48 *x* S ver 26 *y* S ver 12 *z* S ver 27
24:49 *a* S ver 27
24:50 *b* Ge 22:22
c Ps 118:23
d Ge 31:7,24,29, 42; 48:16
24:51 *e* S ver 12
24:52 *f* S ver 26
24:53 *g* Ge 45:22; Ex 3:22; 12:35; 2Ki 5:5 *h* S ver 10 Ge 30:25
24:54 *i* ver 56,59; Ge 30:25
24:55 *j* Jdg 19:4
24:56 *k* S ver 12 *l* S ver 54
24:57 *m* Jdg 19:3
24:58 *n* Ru 1:16

24:59 *o* S ver 54
p Ge 35:8
24:60 *q* Ge 27:4, 19; 28:1; 31:55; 48:9,15,20; Jos 22:6
r S Ge 17:16
s Ge 22:17;
Ps 127:5;
Pr 27:11
24:61 *t* S Ge 16:1; 30:3; 46:25
24:62 *u* S Ge 16:14 *v* S Ge 12:9
24:63 *w* Jos 1:8; Ps 1:2; 77:12; 119:15,27,48,97, 148; 143:5; 145:5 *x* Ge 18:2
24:64 *y* Ge 31:17, 34; 1Sa 30:17
24:65 *z* Ge 38:14; SS 1:7; 4:1,3; 6:7; Isa 47:2
24:67 *a* Ge 31:33 *b* S Ge 18:9
c Ge 25:20; 49:31
d Ge 29:18,20; 34:3; Jdg 16:4
e Ge 23:1-2
25:2 *f* Jer 25:25
g Ge 36:35; 37:28,36;
Ex 2:15; Nu 22:4; 25:6,18; 31:2; Jos 13:21;
Jdg 6:1,3; 7:1; 8:1,22,24; 9:17; 1Ki 11:18;
Ps 83:9; Isa 9:4; 10:26; 60:6;
Hab 3:7
h Job 2:11; 8:1
25:3 *i* S Ge 10:7 *j* S Ge 10:7

24:53 The rich gifts bestowed on Rebekah and her family indicated the wealth of the household into which she was being asked to marry—far from her loved ones and homeland.

24:60 See 22:17 and note.

24:62 *Beer Lahai Roi.* See note on 16:14.

24:65 *she took her veil and covered herself.* Apparently a sign that she was unmarried (cf. 38:14,19).

24:67 *tent.* Often used as a bridal chamber (see Ps 19:4–5).

25:1 *took another wife.* Or "married another woman"—his "concubine" (1Ch 1:32). *took.* Or "had tak-

en" (see NIV text note), since Abraham would have been 140 years old at this time if the order is chronological.

25:5 *left everything he owned to Isaac.* The law of primogeniture provided that at least a double share of the father's property be given to the firstborn son when the father died (Dt 21:15–17). Parallels to this practice come from Nuzi, from Larsa in the Old Babylonian period and from Assyria in the Middle Assyrian period. Isaac was Abraham's firstborn son according to law.

25:6 *gifts.* These doubtless represented the inheritance left to Abraham's other sons. *concubines.* Polygamy was practiced even by godly men in ancient times, though it was not

and sent them away from his son Isaac[n] to the land of the east.[o]

[7]Altogether, Abraham lived a hundred and seventy-five years.[p] [8]Then Abraham breathed his last and died at a good old age,[q] an old man and full of years; and he was gathered to his people.[r] [9]His sons Isaac and Ishmael buried him[s] in the cave of Machpelah[t] near Mamre,[u] in the field of Ephron[v] son of Zohar the Hittite,[w] [10]the field Abraham had bought from the Hittites.[i][x] There Abraham was buried with his wife Sarah. [11]After Abraham's death, God blessed his son Isaac,[y] who then lived near Beer Lahai Roi.[z]

Ishmael's Sons

25:12–16pp — 1Ch 1:29–31

[12]This is the account[a] of Abraham's son Ishmael, whom Sarah's maidservant, Hagar[b] the Egyptian, bore to Abraham.[c]

[13]These are the names of the sons of Ishmael, listed in the order of their birth: Nebaioth[d] the firstborn of Ishmael, Kedar,[e] Adbeel, Mibsam, [14]Mishma, Dumah,[f] Massa, [15]Hadad, Tema,[g] Jetur,[h] Naphish and Kedemah. [16]These were the sons of Ishmael, and these are the names of the twelve tribal rulers[i] according to their settlements and camps.[j] [17]Altogether, Ishmael lived a hundred and thirty-seven years. He breathed his last and died, and he was gathered to his people.[k] [18]His descendants[l] settled in the area from Havilah to Shur,[m] near the border of Egypt, as you go toward Asshur. And they lived in hostility toward[j] all their brothers.[n]

Jacob and Esau

[19]This is the account[o] of Abraham's son Isaac.

Abraham became the father of Isaac, [20]and Isaac was forty years old[p] when he married Rebekah[q] daughter of Bethuel[r] the Aramean from Paddan Aram[k][s] and sister of Laban[t] the Aramean.[u]

[21]Isaac prayed to the LORD on behalf of his wife, because she was barren.[v] The LORD answered his prayer,[w] and his wife Rebekah became pregnant. [22]The babies jostled each other within her, and she said, "Why is this happening to me?" So she went to inquire of the LORD.[x]

[23]The LORD said to her,

"Two nations[y] are in your womb,
    and two peoples from within you will
        be separated;
one people will be stronger than the
        other,
    and the older will serve the
        younger.[z] "

[24]When the time came for her to give birth,[a] there were twin boys in her womb.[b] [25]The first to come out was red,[c] and his whole body was like a hairy garment;[d] so they named him Esau.[l][e] [26]After this, his brother came out,[f] with his

---

25:6 [n]S Ge 21:10; [o]Ge 29:1; Jdg 6:3,33; 1Ki 4:30; Job 1:3; Eze 25:4
25:7 [p]ver 26; Ge 12:4; 35:28; 47:9,28; 50:22, 26; Job 42:16
25:8 [q]S Ge 15:15 [r]ver 17; Ge 35:29; 49:29, 33; Nu 20:24; 31:2; Dt 31:14; 32:50; 34:5
25:9 [s]Ge 35:29; 47:30; 49:31 [t]S Ge 23:9 [u]S Ge 13:18 [v]Ge 23:8 [w]Ge 49:29; 50:13
25:10 [x]S Ge 10:15
25:11 [y]S Ge 12:2 [z]S Ge 16:14
25:12 [a]S Ge 2:4 [b]S Ge 16:1 [c]S Ge 17:20; 21:18
25:13 [d]Ge 28:9; 36:3 [e]Ps 120:5; SS 1:5; Isa 21:16; 42:11; 60:7; Jer 2:10; 49:28; Eze 27:21
25:14 [f]Jos 15:52; Isa 21:11; Ob 1:1
25:15 [g]Job 6:19; Isa 21:14; Jer 25:23 [h]1Ch 5:19
25:16 [i]Ge 17:20 [j]S Ge 13:16; Ps 83:6
25:17 [k]S ver 8
25:18 [l]S Ge 17:20; 21:18 [m]S Ge 16:7 [n]Ge 16:12

25:19 [o]S Ge 2:4
25:20 [p]ver 26; Ge 26:34; 35:28 [q]S Ge 24:67 [r]S Ge 22:22 [s]Ge 28:2,5,6; 30:20; 31:18; 33:18; 35:9,26; 46:15; 48:7 [t]S Ge 24:29 [u]Ge 31:20,24; Dt 26:5

25:21 [v]S Ge 11:30 [w]Ge 30:17,22; 1Sa 1:17,23; 1Ch 5:20; 2Ch 33:13; Ezr 8:23; Ps 127:3 25:22 [x]Ex 18:15; 28:30; 33:7; Lev 24:12; Nu 9:6-8; 27:5,21; Dt 17:9; Jdg 18:5; 1Sa 9:9; 10:22; 14:36; 22:10; 1Ki 22:8; 2Ki 3:11; 22:13; Isa 30:2; Jer 21:2; 37:7,17; Eze 14:7; 20:1,3 25:23 [y]S Ge 17:4 [z]S Ge 9:25; 48:14,19; Ro 9:11-12* 25:24 [a]Lk 1:57; 2:6 [b]Ge 38:27 25:25 [c]1Sa 16:12 [d]Ge 27:11 [e]Ge 27:1,15 25:26 [f]Ge 38:29

[i]10 Or *the sons of Heth*   [j]18 Or *lived to the east of*   [k]20 That is, Northwest Mesopotamia   [l]25 *Esau* may mean *hairy*; he was also called Edom, which means *red.*

---

the original divine intention (see note on 4:19).
25:7 *a hundred and seventy-five years.* Abraham lived for a full century after "he set out from Haran" (12:4).
25:8 *died at a good old age.* As God had promised (see 15:15). *an old man and full of years.* A phrase used also of the patriarch Job (see Job 42:17). *was gathered to his people.* Joined his ancestors and/or deceased relatives in death (see 2Ki 22:20; 2Ch 34:28).
25:9 *Isaac and Ishmael.* Isaac, legally the firstborn (see note on v. 5), is listed first.
25:11 *Beer Lahai Roi.* See note on 16:14.
25:12 *account.* See note on 2:4.
25:13 *names of the sons of Ishmael.* Many are Arab names, giving credence to the Arab tradition that Ishmael is their ancestor.
25:16 *twelve tribal rulers.* Twelve major tribes descended from Abraham's son Ishmael (as predicted in 17:20)—as was also true of Abraham's brother Nahor (see note on 22:23–24).
25:18 *in hostility toward.* See note on 16:12; or possibly "to the east of " (see NIV text notes here and on 16:12; see also 25:6).
25:19 *account.* See note on 2:4.

25:20 *Paddan Aram.* See NIV text note; means "plain of Aram," another name for Aram Naharaim (see note on 24:10).
25:22 *jostled each other.* The struggle between Jacob and Esau began in the womb (see also v. 26). *went.* Perhaps to a nearby place of worship.
25:23 *the older will serve the younger.* The ancient law of primogeniture (see note on v. 5) provided that, under ordinary circumstances, the younger of two sons would be subservient to the older. God's election of the younger son highlights the fact that God's people are the product not of natural or worldly development but of his sovereign intervention in the affairs of men (see note on 11:30). Part of this verse is quoted in Ro 9:10–12 as an example of God's sovereign right to do "whatever pleases him" (Ps 115:3)—not in an arbitrary way (see Ro 9:14), but according to his own perfect will.
25:24–26 For another unusual birth of twin boys see 38:27–30.
25:25 *red.* A pun on Edom, one of Esau's other names (see v. 30 and NIV text note).
25:26 *his hand grasping Esau's heel.* Hostility between the Israelites (Jacob's descendants) and Edomites (Esau's de-

hand grasping Esau's heel;*g* so he was named Jacob.*m h* Isaac was sixty years old*i* when Rebekah gave birth to them.

27The boys grew up, and Esau became a skillful hunter,*j* a man of the open country,*k* while Jacob was a quiet man, staying among the tents. 28Isaac, who had a taste for wild game,*l* loved Esau, but Rebekah loved Jacob.*m*

29Once when Jacob was cooking some stew,*n* Esau came in from the open country,*o* famished. 30He said to Jacob, "Quick, let me have some of that red stew!*p* I'm famished!" (That is why he was also called Edom.*n*)*q*

31Jacob replied, "First sell me your birthright.*r* "

32"Look, I am about to die," Esau said. "What good is the birthright to me?"

33But Jacob said, "Swear*s* to me first." So he swore an oath to him, selling his birthright*t* to Jacob.

34Then Jacob gave Esau some bread and some lentil stew.*u* He ate and drank, and then got up and left.

So Esau despised his birthright.

Isaac and Abimelech

26:1–11Ref — Ge 12:10–20; 20:1–18

26 Now there was a famine in the land*v*—besides the earlier famine of Abraham's time—and Isaac went to Abimelech king of the Philistines*w* in Gerar.*x* 2The LORD appeared*y* to Isaac and said, "Do not go down to Egypt;*z* live in the land where I tell you to live.*a* 3Stay in

this land for a while,*b* and I will be with you*c* and will bless you.*d* For to you and your descendants I will give all these lands*e* and will confirm the oath I swore to your father Abraham.*f* 4I will make your descendants*g* as numerous as the stars in the sky*h* and will give them all these lands,*i* and through your offspring*o* all nations on earth will be blessed,*j* 5because Abraham obeyed me*k* and kept my requirements, my commands, my decrees*l* and my laws.*m* " 6So Isaac stayed in Gerar.*n*

7When the men of that place asked him about his wife, he said, "She is my sister,*o* " because he was afraid to say, "She is my wife." He thought, "The men of this place might kill me on account of Rebekah, because she is beautiful."

8When Isaac had been there a long time, Abimelech king of the Philistines*p* looked down from a window and saw Isaac caressing his wife Rebekah. 9So Abimelech summoned Isaac and said, "She is really your wife! Why did you say, 'She is my sister'? *q* "

Isaac answered him, "Because I thought I might lose my life on account of her."

10Then Abimelech said, "What is this you have done to us?*r* One of the men

Cross references (center column)

25:26 *g*Hos 12:3
*h*Ge 27:36;
32:27; Dt 23:7;
Jos 24:4; Ob 1:10,
12 /S ver 7,S 20
25:27 /S Ge 10:9
*k*ver 29; Ge 27:3,
5
25:28 /Ge 27:3,4,
9,14,19
*m*Ge 27:6; 37:3
25:29
*n*2Ki 4:38-40
*o*S ver 27
25:30 *p*ver 34
*q*Ge 32:3; 36:1,8,
8-9,19; Nu 20:14;
Dt 23:7;
Ps 137:7;
Jer 25:21; 40:11;
49:7
25:31
*r*Dt 21:16-17;
1Ch 5:1-2
25:33
*s*S Ge 21:23;
S 47:31
*t*Ge 27:36;
Heb 12:16
25:34 *u*ver 30
26:1
*v*S Ge 12:10;
S Dt 32:24
*w*S Ge 10:14;
Jdg 10:6
*x*S Ge 20:1
26:2 *y*S Ge 12:7
*z*Ge 46:3
*a*S Ge 12:1
26:3 *b*Ge 20:1
*c*S Ge 21:20;
27:45; 31:3,5;
32:9; 35:3;
48:21; Ex 3:12;
33:14-16;
Nu 23:21;
Dt 31:23; Jos 1:5;
Isa 43:2; Jer 1:8,
19; Hag 1:13 *d*ver
12; S Ge 12:2
*e*S Ge 12:7;
Ac 7:5
*f*S Ge 17:19
26:4 *g*ver 24;
Ge 48:4
*h*S Ge 12:2;

S Nu 10:36 /S Ge 12:7 /S Ge 12:3; Ac 3:25*; Gal 3:8 26:5 *k*S Ge 18:19 /Ps 119:80,112; Eze 18:21 *m*Lev 18:4,5,26; 19:19,37; 20:8,22; 25:18; 26:3; Nu 15:40; Dt 4:40; 6:2; 11:1; 1Ki 2:3 26:6 *n*S Ge 20:1 26:7 *o*S Ge 12:13 26:8 *p*S Ge 10:14 26:9 *q*S Ge 12:19 26:10 *r*S Ge 12:18

m 26 Jacob means *he grasps the heel* (figuratively, *he deceives*).   *n 30 Edom* means *red.*   *o 4* Or *seed*

Footnotes (bottom)

scendants) became the rule rather than the exception (see, e.g., Nu 20:14–21; Ob 9–10). *Jacob.* See NIV text note. The name became proverbial for the unsavory quality of deceptiveness (see NIV text note on Jer 9:4).

25:31 *sell me your birthright.* In ancient times the birthright included the inheritance rights of the firstborn (see Heb 12:16; see also note on v. 5). Jacob was ever the schemer, seeking by any means to gain advantage over others. But it was by God's appointment and care, not Jacob's wits, that he came into the blessing.

25:33 *Swear to me first.* A verbal oath was all that was required to make the transaction legal.

25:34 *lentil.* A small pea-like annual plant, the pods of which turn reddish-brown when boiled. It grows well even in bad soil and has provided an important source of nourishment in the Near East since ancient times (see 2Sa 17:28; 23:11; Eze 4:9). *Esau despised his birthright.* In so doing, he proved himself to be "godless" (Heb 12:16), since at the heart of the birthright were the covenant promises that Isaac had inherited from Abraham.

26:1–33 The events of some of these verses (e.g. vv. 1–11) occurred before the birth of Esau and Jacob. Verses 1–33 are placed here to highlight the fact that the birthright and blessing Jacob struggled to obtain from his father (see 25:22, 31–33; 27:5–29) involved the covenant inheritance of Abraham that Isaac had received.

26:1 *the earlier famine of Abraham's time.* See 12:10.

Abimelech. Probably the son or grandson of the earlier king who bore the same name (see 20:2). *Philistines.* See note on 10:14. *Gerar.* See note on 20:1.

26:2 *appeared.* See note on 12:7.

26:3 *I will be with you.* God's promise to be a sustainer and protector of his people is repeated often (see, e.g., v. 24; 28:15; 31:3; Jos 1:5; Isa 41:10; Jer 1:8,19; Mt 28:20; Ac 18:10; see also Ge 17:7 and note). *the oath I swore to your father Abraham.* See 22:16–18.

26:4 *descendants as numerous as the stars in the sky.* See 13:16; 15:5 and notes. *through your offspring all nations on earth will be blessed.* See note on 12:2–3.

26:5 *because Abraham obeyed me.* See note on 17:9. *requirements . . . commands . . . decrees . . . laws.* Legal language describing various aspects of the divine regulations that God's people were expected to keep (see Lev 26:14–15,46; Dt 11:1). Addressing Israel after the covenant at Sinai, the author of Genesis used language that strictly applied only to that covenant. But he emphasized to Israel that their father Abraham had been obedient to God's will in his time and that they must follow his example if they were to receive the covenant promises.

26:7 *because she is beautiful.* See 12:11,14.

26:8 *caressing.* The word in Hebrew (a form of the verb translated "laugh" in 17:17; 18:12–13,15; 21:6 and "mock" in 21:9) is yet another pun on Isaac's name.

might well have slept with your wife, and you would have brought guilt upon us."

[11]So Abimelech gave orders to all the people: "Anyone who molests[s] this man or his wife shall surely be put to death."[t]

[12]Isaac planted crops in that land and the same year reaped a hundredfold,[u] because the LORD blessed him.[v] [13]The man became rich, and his wealth continued to grow until he became very wealthy.[w] [14]He had so many flocks and herds and servants[x] that the Philistines envied him.[y] [15]So all the wells[z] that his father's servants had dug in the time of his father Abraham, the Philistines stopped up,[a] filling them with earth.

[16]Then Abimelech said to Isaac, "Move away from us;[b] you have become too powerful for us.[c]"

[17]So Isaac moved away from there and encamped in the Valley of Gerar[d] and settled there. [18]Isaac reopened the wells[e] that had been dug in the time of his father Abraham, which the Philistines had stopped up after Abraham died, and he gave them the same names his father had given them.

[19]Isaac's servants dug in the valley and discovered a well of fresh water there. [20]But the herdsmen of Gerar quarreled[f] with Isaac's herdsmen and said, "The water is ours!"[g] So he named the well Esek,[p] because they disputed with him. [21]Then they dug another well, but they quarreled[h] over that one also; so he named it Sitnah.[q] [22]He moved on from there and dug another well, and no one quarreled over it. He named it Rehoboth,[r][i] saying, "Now the LORD has given us room[j] and we will flourish[k] in the land."

[23]From there he went up to Beersheba.[l] [24]That night the LORD appeared to him and said, "I am the God of your father Abra-

ham.[m] Do not be afraid,[n] for I am with you;[o] I will bless you and will increase the number of your descendants[p] for the sake of my servant Abraham."[q]

[25]Isaac built an altar[r] there and called on the name of the LORD.[s] There he pitched his tent, and there his servants dug a well.[t]

[26]Meanwhile, Abimelech had come to him from Gerar, with Ahuzzath his personal adviser and Phicol the commander of his forces.[u] [27]Isaac asked them, "Why have you come to me, since you were hostile to me and sent me away?[v]"

[28]They answered, "We saw clearly that the LORD was with you;[w] so we said, 'There ought to be a sworn agreement between us'—between us and you. Let us make a treaty[x] with you [29]that you will do us no harm,[y] just as we did not molest you but always treated you well and sent you away in peace. And now you are blessed by the LORD."[z]

[30]Isaac then made a feast[a] for them, and they ate and drank. [31]Early the next morning the men swore an oath[b] to each other. Then Isaac sent them on their way, and they left him in peace.

[32]That day Isaac's servants came and told him about the well[c] they had dug. They said, "We've found water!" [33]He called it Shibah,[s] and to this day the name of the town has been Beersheba.[t] [d]

[34]When Esau was forty years old,[e] he married Judith daughter of Beeri the Hittite, and also Basemath daughter of Elon the Hittite.[f] [35]They were a source of grief to Isaac and Rebekah.[g]

26:11 s1Sa 24:6; 26:9; Ps 105:15
tS Ge 20:3
26:12 uMt 13:8
vS ver 3
26:13 wS Ge 13:2; S Dt 8:18
26:14 xS Ge 12:16; S 24:36; 32:23
yGe 37:11
26:15 zS Ge 21:30
aS Ge 21:25
26:16 bver 27; Jdg 11:7 cEx 1:9; Ps 105:24-25
26:17 dS Ge 20:1
26:18 eS Ge 21:30
26:20 fS Ge 13:7 gGe 21:25
26:21 hS Ge 13:7
26:22 iGe 36:37 jPs 18:19;
Isa 33:20; 54:2; Am 9:11
kS Ge 17:6
26:23 lS Ge 22:19

26:24 mS Ge 24:12 nS Ge 15:1;
S Jos 8:1
oS Ge 21:20 pS ver 4 qver 4;
Ge 17:7; S 22:17; 28:14; 30:27;
39:5; Dt 13:17
26:25 rS Ge 8:20 sS Ge 4:26;
S Ac 2:21
tS Ge 21:30
26:26 uS Ge 21:22
26:27 vS ver 16
26:28 wS Ge 21:22 xS Ge 21:27;
Jos 9:6
26:29 yGe 31:29, 52 zS Ge 24:31
26:30 aGe 31:54;
Ex 18:12; 24:11; 1Sa 20:27
26:31 bS Ge 21:23,27
26:32 cS Ge 21:30
26:33 dS Ge 21:14
26:34 eS Ge 25:20 fS Ge 10:15;
28:9; 36:2;
Jos 3:10;
1Sa 26:6;
1Ki 10:29

26:35 gGe 27:46; 28:8; Job 7:16

p20 *Esek* means *dispute.* q21 *Sitnah* means *opposition.* r22 *Rehoboth* means *room.* s33 *Shibah* can mean *oath* or *seven.* t33 *Beersheba* can mean *well of the oath* or *well of seven.*

26:16 *you have become too powerful for us.* An indication that the covenant promises were being fulfilled. Already in the days of the patriarchs, the presence of God's people in the land was seen as a threat by the peoples of the world. As the world's people pursued their own godless living, God's people aroused their hostility. A similar complaint was voiced by an Egyptian pharaoh hundreds of years later (Ex 1:9).

26:20 *The water is ours!* In those arid regions, disputes over water rights and pasturelands were common (see 13:6–11; 21:25; 36:7).

26:25 *built an altar.* See note on 12:7. *called on the name of the LORD.* See 4:26 and note.

26:26 *Phicol.* See note on 21:22.

26:30 *made a feast.* Covenants were often concluded with a shared meal, signifying the bond of friendship (see 31:54; Ex 24:11).

26:33 *the name of the town has been Beersheba.* See note on 21:31.

26:34 *When Esau was forty years old, he married.* As had his father Isaac (see 25:20). Forty years was roughly equivalent to a generation in later times (see Nu 32:13). *Judith . . . Basemath.* In addition to these two wives, Esau also married Mahalath, "sister of Nebaioth and daughter of Ishmael" (28:9). The Esau genealogy of ch. 36 also mentions three wives, but they are identified as "Adah daughter of Elon the Hittite," "Oholibamah daughter of Anah . . . the Hivite" and "Basemath daughter of Ishmael and sister of Nebaioth" (36:2–3). Possibly the lists may have suffered in transmission, or perhaps alternate names or nicknames are used. It may also be that Esau married more than three wives.

26:35 *They were a source of grief.* Isaac and Rebekah were determined not to allow Jacob to make the same mistake of marrying Hittite or Canaanite women (see 27:46–28:2).

Jacob Gets Isaac's Blessing

27 When Isaac was old and his eyes were so weak that he could no longer see,[h] he called for Esau his older son[i] and said to him, "My son."

"Here I am," he answered.

[2]Isaac said, "I am now an old man and don't know the day of my death.[j] [3]Now then, get your weapons—your quiver and bow—and go out to the open country[k] to hunt some wild game for me. [4]Prepare me the kind of tasty food I like[l] and bring it to me to eat, so that I may give you my blessing[m] before I die." [n]

[5]Now Rebekah was listening as Isaac spoke to his son Esau. When Esau left for the open country[o] to hunt game and bring it back, [6]Rebekah said to her son Jacob,[p] "Look, I overheard your father say to your brother Esau, [7]'Bring me some game and prepare me some tasty food to eat, so that I may give you my blessing in the presence of the LORD before I die.'[q] [8]Now, my son, listen carefully and do what I tell you:[r] [9]Go out to the flock and bring me two choice young goats,[s] so I can prepare some tasty food for your father, just the way he likes it.[t] [10]Then take it to your father to eat, so that he may give you his blessing[u] before he dies."

[11]Jacob said to Rebekah his mother, "But my brother Esau is a hairy man,[v] and I'm a man with smooth skin. [12]What if my father touches me?[w] I would appear to be tricking him and would bring down a curse[x] on myself rather than a blessing."

[13]His mother said to him, "My son, let the curse fall on me.[y] Just do what I say;[z] go and get them for me."

[14]So he went and got them and brought them to his mother, and she prepared some tasty food, just the way his father liked it.[a] [15]Then Rebekah took the best clothes[b] of Esau her older son,[c] which she had in the house, and put them on her younger son Jacob. [16]She also covered his hands and the smooth part of his neck with the goatskins.[d] [17]Then she handed to her son Jacob the tasty food and the bread she had made.

[18]He went to his father and said, "My father."

"Yes, my son," he answered. "Who is it?"[e]

[19]Jacob said to his father, "I am Esau your firstborn.[f] I have done as you told me. Please sit up and eat some of my game[g] so that you may give me your blessing."[h]

[20]Isaac asked his son, "How did you find it so quickly, my son?"

"The LORD your God gave me success,[i]" he replied.

[21]Then Isaac said to Jacob, "Come near so I can touch you,[j] my son, to know whether you really are my son Esau or not."

[22]Jacob went close to his father Isaac,[k] who touched[l] him and said, "The voice is the voice of Jacob, but the hands are the hands of Esau." [23]He did not recognize him, for his hands were hairy like those of his brother Esau;[m] so he blessed him. [24]"Are you really my son Esau?" he asked.

"I am," he replied.

[25]Then he said, "My son, bring me some of your game to eat, so that I may give you my blessing."[n]

Jacob brought it to him and he ate; and he brought some wine and he drank. [26]Then his father Isaac said to him, "Come here, my son, and kiss me."

[27]So he went to him and kissed[o] him.[p] When Isaac caught the smell of his clothes,[q] he blessed him and said,

"Ah, the smell of my son
   is like the smell of a field
   that the LORD has blessed.[r]
[28]May God give you of heaven's dew[s]
   and of earth's richness[t] —

Cross references

27:1 [h]Ge 48:10; Dt 34:7; 1Sa 3:2 [i]S Ge 25:25
27:2 [j]Ge 47:29; 1Ki 2:1
27:3 [k]S Ge 25:27
27:4 [l]S Ge 25:28 [m]ver 10,25,31; S Ge 24:60; 49:28; Dt 33:1; Heb 11:20 [n]ver 7
27:5 [o]S Ge 25:27
27:6 [p]S Ge 25:28
27:7 [q]ver 4
27:8 [r]ver 13,43
27:9 [s]1Sa 16:20 [t]S Ge 25:28
27:10 [u]S ver 4
27:11 [v]Ge 25:25
27:12 [w]ver 22 [x]S Ge 9:25
27:13 [y]Mt 27:25 [z]S ver 8
27:14 [a]S Ge 25:28
27:15 [b]ver 27; SS 4:11 [c]S Ge 25:25
27:16 [d]ver 22-23
27:18 [e]ver 32
27:19 [f]ver 32 [g]S Ge 25:28 [h]S ver 4
27:20 [i]S Ge 24:12
27:21 [j]ver 12
27:22 [k]Ge 45:4 [l]ver 12
27:23 [m]ver 16
27:25 [n]S ver 4
27:27 [o]Ge 31:28, 55; 33:4; 48:10; Ex 4:27; 18:7; Ru 1:9; 1Sa 20:41; 2Sa 14:33; 19:39 [p]Heb 11:20 [q]S ver 15 [r]Ps 65:9-13
27:28 [s]Dt 33:13; 2Sa 1:21; Job 18:16; 29:19; Pr 3:20; Isa 26:19; Hos 14:5; Hag 1:10; Zec 8:12 [t]ver 39; Ge 49:25; Lev 26:20; Dt 33:13

27:1 *eyes were so weak that he could no longer see.* In ancient times, blindness and near blindness were common among elderly people (see 48:10; 1Sa 4:15). *Here I am.* See note on 22:1.

27:4 *the kind of tasty food I like.* Rebekah and Jacob took advantage of Isaac's love for a certain kind of food (see vv. 9,14). *give you my blessing before I die.* Oral statements, including deathbed bequests (see 49:28–33), had legal force in ancient Near Eastern law. *blessing.* See note on v. 36.

27:5 *listening.* Eavesdropping.

27:6 *Rebekah.* Throughout the Jacob story the author develops a wordplay on "birthright" (*bekorah*) and "blessing" (*berakah*), both of which Jacob seeks to obtain; and Rebekah (*ribqah*) does her best to further the cause of her favorite son. *said to her son Jacob.* The parental favoritism mentioned in 25:28 is about to bear its poisonous fruit.

27:8 *my son, . . . do what I tell you.* Rebekah proves to be just as deceitful as Jacob, whose very name signifies deceit (see NIV text notes on v. 36; 25:26).

27:13 *let the curse fall on me.* Cf. the similar self-imprecation in Mt 27:25.

27:20 *your God.* Consistent with Jacob's language elsewhere (31:5,42; 32:9). Not until his safe return from Haran did he speak of the Lord as his own God (cf. 28:20–22; 33:18–20).

27:24 *Are you really my son Esau?* To the very end of the charade, Isaac remained suspicious.

27:27 *kissed him.* In his attempt to obtain the covenant blessing, Jacob the father of Israel betrayed with a kiss. Jesus the great Son of Israel, who ultimately obtained the blessing for Israel, was betrayed with a kiss (Mt 26:48–49; Lk 22:48).

an abundance of grain[u] and new
wine.[v]
[29]May nations serve you
and peoples bow down to you.[w]
Be lord over your brothers,
and may the sons of your mother
bow down to you.[x]
May those who curse you be cursed
and those who bless you be
blessed.[y] "

[30]After Isaac finished blessing him and
Jacob had scarcely left his father's presence, his brother Esau came in from hunting. [31]He too prepared some tasty food and
brought it to his father. Then he said to
him, "My father, sit up and eat some of my
game, so that you may give me your
blessing."[z]

[32]His father Isaac asked him, "Who are
you?"[a]

"I am your son," he answered, "your
firstborn, Esau.[b]"

[33]Isaac trembled violently and said,
"Who was it, then, that hunted game and
brought it to me?[c] I ate it just before you
came and I blessed him—and indeed he
will be blessed![d]"

[34]When Esau heard his father's words,
he burst out with a loud and bitter cry[e]
and said to his father, "Bless[f] me—me
too, my father!"

[35]But he said, "Your brother came deceitfully[g] and took your blessing."[h]

[36]Esau said, "Isn't he rightly named
Jacob[u]?[i] He has deceived[j] me these two
times: He took my birthright,[k] and now
he's taken my blessing!"[l] Then he asked,
"Haven't you reserved any blessing for
me?"

[37]Isaac answered Esau, "I have made
him lord over you and have made all his
relatives his servants, and I have sustained
him with grain and new wine.[m] So what
can I possibly do for you, my son?"

[38]Esau said to his father, "Do you have

only one blessing, my father? Bless me too,
my father!" Then Esau wept aloud.[n]

[39]His father Isaac answered him,[o]

"Your dwelling will be
away from the earth's richness,
away from the dew[p] of heaven
above.[q]
[40]You will live by the sword
and you will serve[r] your brother.[s]
But when you grow restless,
you will throw his yoke
from off your neck.[t] "

Jacob Flees to Laban

[41]Esau held a grudge[u] against Jacob[v]
because of the blessing his father had given
him. He said to himself, "The days of
mourning[w] for my father are near; then I
will kill[x] my brother Jacob."[y]

[42]When Rebekah was told what her older son Esau[z] had said, she sent for her
younger son Jacob and said to him, "Your
brother Esau is consoling himself with the
thought of killing you.[a] [43]Now then, my
son, do what I say:[b] Flee at once to my
brother Laban[c] in Haran.[d] [44]Stay with
him for a while[e] until your brother's fury
subsides. [45]When your brother is no longer
angry with you and forgets what you did to
him,[f] I'll send word for you to come back
from there.[g] Why should I lose both of
you in one day?"

[46]Then Rebekah said to Isaac, "I'm dis-
gusted with living because of these Hittite[h] women. If Jacob takes a wife from
among the women of this land,[i] from Hittite women like these, my life will not be
worth living."[j]

28

So Isaac called for Jacob and
blessed[v][k] him and commanded
him: "Do not marry a Canaanite woman.[l]

27:28 [u]Ps 65:9; 72:16 vver 37; Nu 18:12; Dt 7:13; 33:28; 2Ki 18:32; Ps 4:7; Isa 36:17; Jer 31:12; 40:10
27:29 [w]2Sa 8:14; Ps 68:31; 72:11; Isa 19:21,23; 27:13; 45:14,23; 49:7,23; 60:12, 14; 66:23; Jer 12:17; Da 2:44; Zec 14:17-18 [x]S Ge 9:25; [y]S 25:23; S 37:7 yver 33; Ge 12:3
27:31 [z]S ver 4
27:32 [a]ver 18 [b]ver 19
27:33 [c]ver 35 [d]S ver 29
27:34 [e]Heb 12:17 [f]Ex 12:32
27:35 [g]Jer 9:4; 12:6 [h]ver 19,45
27:36 [i]S Ge 25:26 [j]Ge 29:25; 31:20, 26; 34:13; 1Sa 28:12 [k]S Ge 25:33 [l]Heb 12:16-17
27:37 [m]S ver 28; Dt 16:13; Ezr 6:9; Isa 16:10; Jer 40:12
27:38 [n]Ge 29:11; Nu 14:1; Jdg 2:4; 21:2; Ru 1:9; 1Sa 11:4; 30:4; Heb 12:17
27:39 [o]Heb 11:20 [p]ver 28 [q]Ge 36:6
27:40 [r]2Sa 8:14 [s]S Ge 9:25 [t]2Ki 8:20-22
27:41 [u]Ge 37:4; 49:23; 50:15; 1Sa 17:28 [v]Ge 31:17; 32:11; Hos 10:14 [w]Ge 50:4,10; Nu 20:29 [x]ver 42 [y]Ob 1:10
27:42 [z]Ge 32:3, 11; 33:4 [a]ver 41
27:43 [b]S ver 8 [c]S Ge 24:29 [d]S Ge 11:31
27:44 [e]Ge 31:38, 41
27:45 [f]S ver 35 [g]S Ge 26:3
27:46 [h]S Ge 10:15

28:1 [i]S Ge 10:15-19 [j]S Ge 26:35; S Job 7:7 28:1 [k]S Ge 24:60 [l]Ge 24:3

[u]36 Jacob means he grasps the heel (figuratively, he deceives).   [v]1 Or greeted

27:29 *Be lord over your brothers.* Isaac was unwittingly blessing Jacob and thus fulfilling God's promise to Rebekah in 25:23.
27:33 *indeed he will be blessed.* The ancient world be-lieved that blessings and curses had a kind of magical power to accomplish what they pronounced. But Isaac, as heir and steward of God's covenant blessing, acknowledged that he had solemnly transmitted that heritage to Jacob by way of a legally binding bequest (see note on v. 4).
27:34 *loud and bitter cry.* Esau's tears "could bring about no change of mind" (Heb 12:17).
27:36 *Isn't he rightly named Jacob?* See NIV text notes here and on 25:26. *He took my birthright, and now he's taken my blessing!* The Hebrew for "birthright" is *bekorah*, and for "blessing" it is *berakah* (see note on v. 6). Though

Esau tried to separate birthright from blessing, the former led inevitably to the latter, since both involved the inheritance of the firstborn (see Heb 12:16–17).
27:39 *away from the earth's richness, away from the dew of heaven.* Cf. v. 28. Isaac's secondary blessing of Esau could be only a parody of his primary blessing of Jacob.
27:40 See 25:23 and notes on 25:22,26.
27:43 *do what I say.* Bad advice earlier (see vv. 8,13), but sensible counsel this time.
27:44 *for a while.* Twenty years, as it turned out (see 31:38,41).
27:45 *both of you.* Either Jacob and Isaac or Jacob and Esau, who would become a target for blood revenge if he killed Jacob (cf. 2Sa 14:6–7).
27:46 See note on 26:35.

2Go at once to Paddan Aram,[w][m] to the
house of your mother's father Bethuel.[n]
Take a wife for yourself there, from among
the daughters of Laban, your mother's
brother.[o] 3May God Almighty[x][p] bless[q]
you and make you fruitful[r] and increase
your numbers[s] until you become a community of peoples. 4May he give you and
your descendants the blessing given to
Abraham,[t] so that you may take possession of the land[u] where you now live as an
alien,[v] the land God gave to Abraham."
5Then Isaac sent Jacob on his way,[w] and
he went to Paddan Aram,[x] to Laban son of
Bethuel the Aramean,[y] the brother of Rebekah,[z] who was the mother of Jacob and
Esau.

6Now Esau learned that Isaac had
blessed Jacob and had sent him to Paddan
Aram to take a wife from there, and that
when he blessed him he commanded him,
"Do not marry a Canaanite woman,"[a]
7and that Jacob had obeyed his father and
mother and had gone to Paddan Aram.
8Esau then realized how displeasing the
Canaanite women[b] were to his father
Isaac;[c] 9so he went to Ishmael[d] and married Mahalath, the sister of Nebaioth[e] and
daughter of Ishmael son of Abraham, in
addition to the wives he already had.[f]

Jacob's Dream at Bethel

10Jacob left Beersheba[g] and set out for
Haran.[h] 11When he reached a certain
place,[i] he stopped for the night because
the sun had set. Taking one of the stones
there, he put it under his head[j] and lay
down to sleep. 12He had a dream[k] in
which he saw a stairway[y] resting on the
earth, with its top reaching to heaven, and
the angels of God were ascending and descending on it.[l] 13There above it[z] stood
the LORD,[m] and he said: "I am the LORD,
the God of your father Abraham and the
God of Isaac.[n] I will give you and your
descendants the land[o] on which you are
lying.[p] 14Your descendants will be like the
dust of the earth, and you[q] will spread out
to the west and to the east, to the north
and to the south.[r] All peoples on earth
will be blessed through you and your offspring.[s] 15I am with you[t] and will watch
over you[u][v] wherever you go,[w] and I will
bring you back to this land.[x] I will not
leave you[y] until I have done what I have
promised you.[z]"[a]

16When Jacob awoke from his sleep,[b]
he thought, "Surely the LORD is in this
place, and I was not aware of it." 17He was
afraid and said, "How awesome is this
place![c] This is none other than the house
of God;[d] this is the gate of heaven."

18Early the next morning Jacob took the
stone he had placed under his head[e] and
set it up as a pillar[f] and poured oil on top
of it.[g] 19He called that place Bethel,[a][h]
though the city used to be called Luz.[i]

20Then Jacob made a vow,[j] saying, "If
God will be with me and will watch over
me[k] on this journey I am taking and will
give me food to eat and clothes to wear[l]
21so that I return safely[m] to my father's

28:2 [m]S Ge 25:20 [n]S Ge 25:20 [o]S Ge 21:21; S 24:29 **28:3** [p]S Ge 17:1 [q]Ge 48:16; Nu 6:24; Ru 2:4; Ps 129:8; 134:3; Jer 31:23 [r]S Ge 17:6 [s]S Ge 12:2 **28:4** [t]S Ge 12:2,3 [u]S Ge 15:7 [v]S Ge 17:8 **28:5** [w]S Ge 11:31 [x]Hos 12:12 [y]S Ge 25:20 [z]S Ge 24:29 **28:6** [a]S ver 1 **28:8** [b]S Ge 10:15-19 [c]S Ge 26:35 **28:9** [d]S Ge 16:15 [e]S Ge 25:13 [f]S Ge 26:34 **28:10** [g]S Ge 21:14 [h]S Ge 11:31 **28:11** [i]S Ge 12:8 [j]ver 18 **28:12** [k]S Ge 20:3; 37:19 [l]Jn 1:51 **28:13** [m]S Ge 12:7; 35:7,9; 48:3 [n]S Ge 24:12; 48:16; 49:25; 50:17 [o]S Ge 12:7 [p]Ge 46:4; 48:21 **28:14** [q]Ge 26:4 [r]S Ge 12:2; S 13:14; S 26:24 [s]S Ge 12:3; Ac 3:25; Gal 3:8 **28:15** [t]S Ge 21:20 [u]Ps 121:5,7-8 [v]ver 20 [w]ver 22; Ge 35:3 [x]ver 21; S Ge 15:16; 30:25; 31:30 [y]Dt 31:6,8; Jos 1:5; Ne 4:14; Ps 9:10 [z]Lev 26:42 [a]Ps 105:10 **28:16** [b]1Ki 3:15; Jer 31:26 **28:17** [c]Ex 3:5; 19:21; Jos 5:15; Ps 68:24,35 [d]ver 22; Ge 32:2; 1Ch 22:1; 2Ch 3:1 **28:18** [e]ver 11 [f]ver 22; Ge 31:13,45,51; 35:14; Ex 24:4; Jos 24:26,27; Isa 19:19 [g]Lev 8:11; Jos 4:9 **28:19** [h]S Ge 12:8 [i]Ge 35:6; 48:3; Jos 16:2; 18:13; Jdg 1:23,26 **28:20** [j]Ge 31:13; Lev 7:16; 22:18; 23:38; 27:2,9; Nu 6:2; 15:3; Dt 12:6; Jdg 11:30; 1Sa 1:21; 2Sa 15:8 [k]S ver 15 [l]1Ti 6:8 **28:21** [m]Jdg 11:31

[w] *2* That is, Northwest Mesopotamia; also in verses 5, 6 and 7 [x] *3* Hebrew *El-Shaddai* [y] *12* Or *ladder* [z] *13* Or *There beside him* [a] *19* *Bethel* means *house of God.*

28:2 *Paddan Aram.* Means "plain of Aram," another name for Aram Naharaim (see note on 24:10). *Take a wife for yourself there.* See 24:3–4.
28:3 *God Almighty.* See note on 17:1.
28:4 *the blessing given to Abraham.* For Paul's application of this phrase to Christian believers see Gal 3:14.
28:5 See map of "Jacob's Journeys," p. 53.
28:9 *in addition to the wives he already had.* See 26:34 and note.
28:11 *one of the stones . . . under his head.* In ancient times headrests (e.g., in Egypt) were often quite hard, sometimes being made of metal. People were used to sleeping on the ground.
28:12 *stairway.* Not a ladder with rungs, it was more likely a stairway such as mounted the sloping side of a ziggurat (see note on 11:4). *angels of God were ascending and descending on it.* A sign that the Lord offered to be Jacob's God. Jesus told a disciple that he would "see heaven open, and the angels of God ascending and descending on the Son of Man" (Jn 1:51). Jesus himself is the bridge between heaven and earth (see Jn 14:6), the only "mediator between God and men" (1Ti 2:5).
28:13 *above it stood the LORD.* Mesopotamian ziggurats were topped with a small shrine where worshipers prayed to their gods.
28:14 *like the dust of the earth.* See note on 13:16. *All peoples on earth will be blessed through you.* Repeats the blessing of 12:3.
28:15 *I am with you.* See note on 26:3. *I will not leave you.* Unlike the gods of pagan religions, in which the gods were merely local deities who gave protection only within their own territories, the one true God assured Jacob that he would always be with him wherever he went.
28:17 *house of God . . . gate of heaven.* Phrases that related Jacob's stairway to the Mesopotamian ziggurats (see notes on 11:4,9).
28:18 *pillar.* A memorial of worship or of communion between man and God, common in ancient times. *poured oil on top of it.* To consecrate it (see Ex 30:25–29).
28:21 *return safely.* Partially fulfilled in 33:18. *the LORD will be my God.* For the first time Jacob considered (conditionally: "If . . .") acknowledging the God of Abraham and Isaac (see v. 13; 27:20) as his own. His full acknowledgment came only after his safe return from Haran (see 33:20 and

house,[n] then the LORD[b] will be my God[o] [22]and[c] this stone that I have set up as a pillar[p] will be God's house,[q] and of all that you give me I will give you a tenth.[r] "

Jacob Arrives in Paddan Aram

29 Then Jacob continued on his journey and came to the land of the eastern peoples.[s] [2]There he saw a well in the field, with three flocks of sheep lying near it because the flocks were watered from that well.[t] The stone[u] over the mouth of the well was large. [3]When all the flocks were gathered there, the shepherds would roll the stone[v] away from the well's mouth and water the sheep.[w] Then they would return the stone to its place over the mouth of the well.

[4]Jacob asked the shepherds, "My brothers, where are you from?"[x]

"We're from Haran,"[y] they replied.

[5]He said to them, "Do you know Laban, Nahor's grandson?"[z]

"Yes, we know him," they answered.

[6]Then Jacob asked them, "Is he well?"

"Yes, he is," they said, "and here comes his daughter Rachel[a] with the sheep.[b]"

[7]"Look," he said, "the sun is still high; it is not time for the flocks to be gathered. Water the sheep and take them back to pasture."

[8]"We can't," they replied, "until all the flocks are gathered and the stone[c] has been rolled away from the mouth of the well. Then we will water[d] the sheep."

[9]While he was still talking with them, Rachel came with her father's sheep,[e] for she was a shepherdess. [10]When Jacob saw Rachel[f] daughter of Laban, his mother's brother, and Laban's sheep, he went over and rolled the stone[g] away from the mouth of the well and watered[h] his uncle's sheep.[i] [11]Then Jacob kissed[j] Rachel and began to weep aloud.[k] [12]He had told Rachel that he was a relative[l] of her father

and a son of Rebekah.[m] So she ran and told her father.[n]

[13]As soon as Laban[o] heard the news about Jacob, his sister's son, he hurried to meet him. He embraced him[p] and kissed him and brought him to his home, and there Jacob told him all these things. [14]Then Laban said to him, "You are my own flesh and blood."[q]

Jacob Marries Leah and Rachel

After Jacob had stayed with him for a whole month, [15]Laban said to him, "Just because you are a relative[r] of mine, should you work for me for nothing? Tell me what your wages[s] should be."

[16]Now Laban had two daughters; the name of the older was Leah,[t] and the name of the younger was Rachel.[u] [17]Leah had weak[d] eyes, but Rachel[v] was lovely in form, and beautiful.[w] [18]Jacob was in love with Rachel[x] and said, "I'll work for you seven years in return for your younger daughter Rachel."[y]

[19]Laban said, "It's better that I give her to you than to some other man. Stay here with me." [20]So Jacob served seven years to get Rachel,[z] but they seemed like only a few days to him because of his love for her.[a]

[21]Then Jacob said to Laban, "Give me my wife. My time is completed, and I want to lie with her.[b]"

[22]So Laban brought together all the people of the place and gave a feast.[c] [23]But when evening came, he took his daughter Leah[d] and gave her to Jacob, and Jacob lay with her. [24]And Laban gave his servant girl Zilpah[e] to his daughter as her maidservant.[f]

[25]When morning came, there was Leah!

Cross references (center column):

28:21 [n]S ver 15
　[o]Ex 15:2;
　Dt 26:17;
　Jos 24:18;
　Ps 48:14; 118:28
28:22 [p]S ver 18;
　1Sa 7:12 [q]S ver
　17 [r]S Ge 14:20;
　S Nu 18:21;
　Lk 18:12
29:1 [s]S Ge 25:6
29:2 [t]S Ge 24:11
　[u]ver 3,8,10
29:3 [v]S ver 2
　[w]ver 8
29:4 [x]Ge 42:7;
　Jdg 19:17
　[y]S Ge 11:31
29:5 [z]S Ge 11:29
29:6
　[a]Ge 30:22-24;
　35:16; 46:19,22
　[b]Ex 2:16
29:8 [c]S ver 2
　[d]S Ge 24:13
29:9 [e]Ex 2:16
29:10 [f]ver 16
　[g]S ver 2
　[h]S Ge 24:11 [i]ver
　3; Ex 2:17
29:11 [j]ver 13
　[k]Ge 33:4; 42:24;
　43:30; 45:2,
　14-15; 46:29;
　50:1,17; Ru 1:9
29:12 [l]ver 15

[m]S Ge 24:29
[n]Ge 24:28
29:13
　[o]S Ge 24:29
　[p]Ge 33:4;
　45:14-15,14;
　48:10; Ex 4:27;
　18:7; Lk 15:20
29:14 [q]Ge 2:23;
　37:27; Jdg 9:2;
　2Sa 5:1;
　19:12-13; 20:1;
　Ne 5:5; Isa 58:7
29:15 [r]ver 12
　[s]Ge 30:28,32;
　31:7,41
29:16 [t]ver 17,23,
　28,30; Ge 30:9;
　35:23; 47:30;
　49:31; Ru 4:11
　[u]ver 9-10
29:17 [v]S ver 16
　[w]S Ge 12:11
29:18
　[x]S Ge 24:67 [y]ver
　20,27,30;
　Ge 30:26;
　Hos 12:12
29:20 [z]S ver 18;
　Ge 31:15 [a]SS 8:7;
　Hos 12:12
29:21 [b]Jdg 15:1
29:22
　[c]Jdg 14:10;
　Isa 25:6; Jn 2:1-2

29:23 [d]S ver 16 29:24 [e]Ge 30:9 [f]S Ge 16:1

[b]20,21 Or *Since God … father's house, the LORD*
[c]21,22 Or *house, and the LORD will be my God,* 22*then*
[d]17 Or *delicate*

Study notes (bottom):

note).
28:22 *this stone … will be God's house.* In the sense that it would memorialize Jacob's meeting with God at Bethel (see NIV text note on v. 19). *of all that you give me I will give you a tenth.* A way of acknowledging the Lord as his God and King (see note on 14:20).
29:5 *Laban, Nahor's grandson.* See 24:15,29. The Hebrew word here for "grandson" is lit. "son," which can refer to any male descendant (see NIV text note on 10:2).
29:9 *shepherdess.* The task of caring for sheep and goats in the Middle East was shared by men and women.
29:10 *rolled the stone away.* A feat of unusual strength for one man, because the stone was large (see v. 2).
29:11 *weep aloud.* For joy.
29:14 *flesh and blood.* The English equivalent of a Hebrew phrase that means lit. "bone and flesh" and that stresses

blood kinship (see, e.g., 2:23).
29:16 *Leah … Rachel.* The names mean "cow" and "ewe" respectively, appropriate in a herdsman's family.
29:21 *my wife.* If Jacob had said "Rachel," Laban would have had no excuse for giving him Leah.
29:22 *feast.* A wedding feast was usually seven days long (see vv. 27–28; Jdg 14:10,12).
29:23 *when evening came … Jacob lay with her.* The darkness, or perhaps a veil (see 24:65), may have concealed Leah's identity.
29:24 See v. 29; a wedding custom documented in Old Babylonian marriage contracts.
29:25 *you deceived me.* Jacob, the deceiver in name (see NIV text notes on 25:26; 27:36) as well as in behavior (see 27:36), had himself been deceived. The one who had tried everything to obtain the benefits of the firstborn had now,

So Jacob said to Laban, "What is this you have done to me? *g* I served you for Rachel, didn't I? Why have you deceived me? *h*"

26Laban replied, "It is not our custom here to give the younger daughter in marriage before the older one. *i* 27Finish this daughter's bridal week; *j* then we will give you the younger one also, in return for another seven years of work. *k*"

28And Jacob did so. He finished the week with Leah, and then Laban gave him his daughter Rachel to be his wife. *l* 29Laban gave his servant girl Bilhah *m* to his daughter Rachel as her maidservant. *n* 30Jacob lay with Rachel also, and he loved Rachel more than Leah. *o* And he worked for Laban another seven years. *p*

Jacob's Children

31When the LORD saw that Leah was not loved, *q* he opened her womb, *r* but Rachel was barren. 32Leah became pregnant and gave birth to a son. *s* She named him Reuben, *et* for she said, "It is because the LORD has seen my misery. *u* Surely my husband will love me now."

33She conceived again, and when she gave birth to a son she said, "Because the LORD heard that I am not loved, *v* he gave me this one too." So she named him Simeon. *f w*

34Again she conceived, and when she gave birth to a son she said, "Now at last my husband will become attached to me, *x* because I have borne him three sons." So he was named Levi. *g y*

35She conceived again, and when she gave birth to a son she said, "This time I will praise the LORD." So she named him Judah. *h z* Then she stopped having children. *a*

30 When Rachel saw that she was not bearing Jacob any children, *b* she became jealous of her sister. *c* So she said to Jacob, "Give me children, or I'll die!"

2Jacob became angry with her and said, "Am I in the place of God, *d* who has kept you from having children?" *e*

3Then she said, "Here is Bilhah, *f* my maidservant. *g* Sleep with her so that she can bear children for me and that through her I too can build a family." *h*

4So she gave him her servant Bilhah as a wife. *i* Jacob slept with her, *j* 5and she became pregnant and bore him a son. 6Then Rachel said, "God has vindicated me; *k* he has listened to my plea and given me a son." *l* Because of this she named him Dan. *i m*

7Rachel's servant Bilhah *n* conceived again and bore Jacob a second son. 8Then Rachel said, "I have had a great struggle with my sister, and I have won." *o* So she named him Naphtali. *j p*

9When Leah *q* saw that she had stopped having children, *r* she took her maidservant Zilpah *s* and gave her to Jacob as a wife. *t* 10Leah's servant Zilpah *u* bore Jacob a son. 11Then Leah said, "What good fortune!" *k* So she named him Gad. *l v*

12Leah's servant Zilpah bore Jacob a second son. 13Then Leah said, "How happy I am! The women will call me *w* happy." *x* So she named him Asher. *m y*

14During wheat harvest, *z* Reuben went out into the fields and found some man-

---

29:25 *g* S Ge 12:18; *h* S Ge 27:36 **29:26** *i* Jdg 15:2; 1Sa 14:49; 18:17, 20; 2Sa 6:23 **29:27** *j* Jdg 14:12 *k* S ver 18; Ge 31:41 **29:28** *l* S ver 16; S Ge 4:19 **29:29** *m* Ge 30:3; 35:22; 49:4; Dt 22:30; 1Ch 5:1 *n* S Ge 16:1 **29:30** *o* S ver 16 *p* S ver 20 **29:31** *q* ver 33; Dt 21:15-17 *r* S Ge 11:30; S 16:2; Ru 4:13; 1Sa 1:19; Ps 127:3 **29:32** *s* Ge 30:23; Ru 4:13; 1Sa 1:20 *t* Ge 37:21; 46:8; 48:5,14; 49:3; Ex 6:14; Nu 1:5, 20; 26:5; Dt 33:6; Jos 4:12; 1Ch 5:1,3 *u* S Ge 16:11 **29:33** *v* S ver 31 *w* Ge 34:25; 46:10; 48:5; 49:5; Ex 6:15; Nu 1:6,22; 34:20; 1Ch 4:24; Eze 48:24 **29:34** *x* Ge 30:20; 1Sa 1:2-4 *y* Ge 34:25; 46:11; 49:5-7; Ex 2:1; 6:16,19; Nu 1:47; 3:17-20; 26:57; Dt 33:8; 1Ch 6:1, 16; 23:6-24, 13-14 **29:35** *z* Ge 35:23; 37:26; 38:1; 43:8; 44:14,18; 46:12; 49:8; 1Ch 2:3; 4:1; Isa 48:1; Mt 1:2-3 *a* Ge 30:9 **30:1** *b* S Ge 11:30; Isa 49:21; 54:1 *c* S Ge 16:4; Lev 18:18

30:2 *d* Ge 50:19; Dt 32:35; 2Ki 5:7 *e* S Ge 16:2 **30:3** *f* ver 7; S Ge 29:29 *g* S Ge 24:61 *h* Ge 16:2 **30:4** *i* ver 9,18 *j* Ge 16:3-4

30:6 *k* Ps 35:24; 43:1 *l* ver 23; Ge 21:2; Ru 4:13; 1Sa 1:20 *m* Ge 46:23; 49:16-17; Nu 26:42-43; Jos 19:40-48; Jdg 13:2; 18:2; Jer 4:15; 8:16; Eze 48:1 **30:7** *n* S ver 3 **30:8** *o* Ge 32:28; Hos 12:3-4 *p* Ge 35:25; 46:24; 49:21; Nu 1:42; 26:48; Dt 33:23; Jdg 4:6; 5:18; 1Ch 7:13 **30:9** *q* S Ge 29:16 *r* Ge 29:35 *s* Ge 29:24 *t* S ver 4 **30:10** *u* Ge 46:18 **30:11** *v* Ge 35:26; 46:16; 49:19; Ex 1:4; Nu 1:24; 26:15; Jos 4:12; 1Ch 5:11; 12:8; Jer 49:1 **30:13** *w* Ps 127:3 *x* Ru 4:14; Ps 127:4-5; Lk 1:48 *y* Ge 35:26; 46:17; 49:20; Nu 1:40; 26:47; Dt 33:24; Jos 19:24-31; 1Ch 7:30-31 **30:14** *z* Ex 34:22; Jdg 15:1; Ru 2:23; 1Sa 6:13; 12:17

e 32 Reuben sounds like the Hebrew for *he has seen my misery;* the name means *see, a son.* *f 33* Simeon probably means *one who hears.* *g 34* Levi sounds like and may be derived from the Hebrew for *attached.* *h 35* Judah sounds like and may be derived from the Hebrew for *praise.* *i 6 Dan* here means *he has vindicated.* *j 8 Naphtali* means *my struggle.* *k 11* Or *"A troop is coming!"* *l 11 Gad* can mean *good fortune* or *a troop.* *m 13* Asher means *happy.*

---

against his will, received the firstborn (vv. 16,26).

29:28 *then Laban gave him his daughter Rachel.* Before Jacob worked another seven years (see v. 30).

29:30 *Jacob . . . loved Rachel more than Leah.* Not only because Rachel had been his choice from the beginning but also, no doubt, because Laban had tricked Jacob into marrying Leah.

29:31–35 Leah, though unloved, nevertheless became the mother of Jacob's first four sons, including Levi (ancestor of the Aaronic priestly line) and Judah (ancestor of David and his royal line, and ultimately of Jesus).

29:32 *named him Reuben . . . because the LORD has seen my misery.* Ishmael had received his name in similar circumstances (see 16:11).

30:1 *she became jealous of her sister.* As Jacob was of his

older brother. *Give me children, or I'll die!* Tragically prophetic words (see 35:16–19).

30:2 *Am I in the place of God . . . ?* Jacob was forever trying to secure the blessing by his own efforts. Here he has to acknowledge that the blessing of offspring could come only from God (see 31:7–13 for the blessing of flocks). Joseph later echoed these words (see 50:19).

30:3 *Sleep with her.* See v. 9; see also 16:2 and note. *for me.* Lit. "on my knees," apparently an expression symbolic of adoption (see 48:10–16) and meaning "as though my own" (see 50:23 and NIV text note).

30:4 *as a wife.* As a concubine (see 35:22).

30:5–12 Jacob's fifth, sixth, seventh and eighth sons were born to him through his maidservant concubines.

30:14 *give me some of your son's mandrakes.* The man-

drake plants,[a] which he brought to his mother Leah. Rachel said to Leah, "Please give me some of your son's mandrakes."

[15]But she said to her, "Wasn't it enough[b] that you took away my husband? Will you take my son's mandrakes too?"

"Very well," Rachel said, "he can sleep with you tonight in return for your son's mandrakes."[c]

[16]So when Jacob came in from the fields that evening, Leah went out to meet him. "You must sleep with me," she said. "I have hired you with my son's mandrakes."[d] So he slept with her that night.

[17]God listened to Leah,[e] and she became pregnant and bore Jacob a fifth son. [18]Then Leah said, "God has rewarded me for giving my maidservant to my husband."[f] So she named him Issachar.[n][g]

[19]Leah conceived again and bore Jacob a sixth son. [20]Then Leah said, "God has presented me with a precious gift. This time my husband will treat me with honor,[h] because I have borne him six sons." So she named him Zebulun.[o][i]

[21]Some time later she gave birth to a daughter and named her Dinah.[j]

[22]Then God remembered Rachel;[k] he listened to her[l] and opened her womb. [m] [23]She became pregnant and gave birth to a son[n] and said, "God has taken away my disgrace."[o] [24]She named him Joseph,[p][p] and said, "May the LORD add to me another son."[q]

Jacob's Flocks Increase

[25]After Rachel gave birth to Joseph, Jacob said to Laban, "Send me on my way[r] so I can go back to my own homeland.[s] [26]Give me my wives and children, for whom I have served you,[t] and I will be on my way. You know how much work I've done for you."

[27]But Laban said to him, "If I have found favor in your eyes,[u] please stay. I

have learned by divination[v] that[q] the LORD has blessed me because of you."[w] [28]He added, "Name your wages,[x] and I will pay them."

[29]Jacob said to him, "You know how I have worked for you[y] and how your livestock has fared under my care.[z] [30]The little you had before I came has increased greatly, and the LORD has blessed you wherever I have been.[a] But now, when may I do something for my own household?[b]"

[31]"What shall I give you?" he asked.

"Don't give me anything," Jacob replied. "But if you will do this one thing for me, I will go on tending your flocks and watching over them: [32]Let me go through all your flocks today and remove from them every speckled or spotted sheep, every dark-colored lamb and every spotted or speckled goat.[c] They will be my wages.[d] [33]And my honesty will testify for me in the future, whenever you check on the wages you have paid me. Any goat in my possession that is not speckled or spotted, or any lamb that is not dark-colored,[e] will be considered stolen.[f]"

[34]"Agreed," said Laban. "Let it be as you have said." [35]That same day he removed all the male goats that were streaked or spotted, and all the speckled or spotted female goats (all that had white on them) and all the dark-colored lambs,[g] and he placed them in the care of his sons.[h] [36]Then he put a three-day journey[i] between himself and Jacob, while Jacob continued to tend the rest of Laban's flocks.

[37]Jacob, however, took fresh-cut

30:14 aver 15, 16; SS 7:13
30:15 bNu 16:9, 13; Isa 7:13; Eze 34:18 cGe 38:16; Eze 16:33; Hos 9:1
30:16 dS ver 14
30:17 eS Ge 25:21
30:18 fS ver 4 gGe 46:13; 49:14; Nu 1:8,28, 29; 26:25; Dt 27:12; 33:18; Jos 17:10; 19:17; 21:6,28; Jdg 5:15; 10:1; 1Ch 7:1
30:20 hS Ge 29:34; 1Pe 3:7 iGe 35:23; 46:14; 49:13; Nu 1:30; 26:27; 34:25; Dt 33:18; Jdg 5:18
30:21 jGe 34:1; 46:15
30:22 kS Ge 8:1 lS Ge 25:21 mS Ge 11:30
30:23 nS ver 6; S Ge 29:32 oIsa 4:1; 25:8; 45:17; 54:4; Lk 1:25
30:24 pS Ge 29:6; 32:22; 33:2,7; 35:24; 37:2; 39:1; 49:22-26; Dt 33:13 qGe 35:17; 1Sa 4:20
30:25 rS Ge 24:54 sS Ge 28:15
30:26 tS Ge 29:18
30:27 uGe 33:10; 50:4; Est 2:15
vGe 44:5,15; Lev 19:26; Nu 22:7; 23:23; 24:1; Jos 13:22; 2Ki 17:17; Jer 27:9 wver 30; S Ge 26:24; 31:38; Dt 28:11; 2Sa 6:11
30:28 xS Ge 29:15
30:29 yGe 31:6 zGe 31:38-40
30:30 aS ver 27 b1Ti 5:8
30:32 cver 33,35, 39,40; Ge 31:8,

12 dS Ge 29:15 30:33 eS ver 32 fGe 31:39 30:35 gS ver 32 hGe 31:1 30:36 iGe 31:22; Ex 3:18; 5:3; 8:27

n18 Issachar sounds like the Hebrew for reward.
o20 Zebulun probably means honor. p24 Joseph means may he add. q27 Or possibly have become rich and

---

drake has fleshy, forked roots that resemble the lower part of a human body and were therefore superstitiously thought to induce pregnancy when eaten (see SS 7:13). Rachel, like Jacob (vv. 37–43), tried to obtain what she wanted by magical means.
30:16 hired. The Hebrew for this word is a pun on the name Issachar (see NIV text note on v. 18).
30:17–20 Jacob's ninth and tenth sons were born through Leah, who was thus the mother of half of Jacob's 12 sons (see note on 29:31–35).
30:20 presented . . . gift. The Hebrew terms for these words are puns on the name Zebulun (see NIV text note).
30:21 Dinah. See ch. 34.
30:22 God remembered Rachel. See note on 8:1.
30:23 disgrace. Barrenness was considered to be shameful, a mark of divine disfavor (see 16:2; 30:2).

30:24 May the LORD add to me another son. The fulfillment of Rachel's wish would bring about her death (see 35:16–19).
30:27 divination. The attempt to discover hidden knowledge through mechanical means (see 44:5), the interpretation of omens (see Eze 21:21) or the aid of supernatural powers (see Ac 16:16). It was strictly forbidden to Israel (Lev 19:26; Dt 18:10,14) because it reflected a pagan concept of the world controlled by evil forces, and therefore obviously not under the sovereign rule of the Lord. the LORD has blessed me because of you. Cf. 21:22; 26:28–29. The offspring of Abraham were a source of blessing (see 12:2).
30:35 he removed. Secretly and without telling Jacob.
30:37 poplar . . . white. The Hebrew terms for these words are puns on the name Laban. As Jacob had gotten the best of Esau (whose other name, Edom, means "red"; see note on

branches from poplar, almond[j] and plane trees[k] and made white stripes on them by peeling the bark and exposing the white inner wood of the branches.[l] ³⁸Then he placed the peeled branches[m] in all the watering troughs,[n] so that they would be directly in front of the flocks when they came to drink. When the flocks were in heat[o] and came to drink, ³⁹they mated in front of the branches.[p] And they bore young that were streaked or speckled or spotted.[q] ⁴⁰Jacob set apart the young of the flock by themselves, but made the rest face the streaked and dark-colored animals[r] that belonged to Laban. Thus he made separate flocks for himself and did not put them with Laban's animals. ⁴¹Whenever the stronger females were in heat,[s] Jacob would place the branches in the troughs in front of the animals so they would mate near the branches,[t] ⁴²but if the animals were weak, he would not place them there. So the weak animals went to Laban and the strong ones to Jacob.[u] ⁴³In this way the man grew exceedingly prosperous and came to own large flocks, and maidservants and menservants, and camels and donkeys.[v]

Jacob Flees From Laban

31 Jacob heard that Laban's sons[w] were saying, "Jacob has taken everything our father owned and has gained all this wealth from what belonged to our father."[x] ²And Jacob noticed that Laban's attitude toward him was not what it had been.[y]

³Then the LORD said to Jacob, "Go back[z] to the land of your fathers and to your relatives, and I will be with you."[a]

⁴So Jacob sent word to Rachel and Leah to come out to the fields where his flocks were. ⁵He said to them, "I see that your father[b]'s attitude toward me is not what it was before,[c] but the God of my father has

been with me.[d] ⁶You know that I've worked for your father with all my strength,[e] ⁷yet your father has cheated[f] me by changing my wages[g] ten times.[h] However, God has not allowed him to harm me.[i] ⁸If he said, 'The speckled ones will be your wages,' then all the flocks gave birth to speckled young; and if he said, 'The streaked ones will be your wages,'[j] then all the flocks bore streaked young. ⁹So God has taken away your father's livestock[k] and has given them to me.[l]

¹⁰"In breeding season I once had a dream[m] in which I looked up and saw that the male goats mating with the flock were streaked, speckled or spotted. ¹¹The angel of God[n] said to me in the dream,[o] 'Jacob.' I answered, 'Here I am.'[p] ¹²And he said, 'Look up and see that all the male goats mating with the flock are streaked, speckled or spotted,[q] for I have seen all that Laban has been doing to you.[r] ¹³I am the God of Bethel,[s] where you anointed a pillar[t] and where you made a vow[u] to me. Now leave this land at once and go back to your native land.[v] '"

¹⁴Then Rachel and Leah replied, "Do we still have any share[w] in the inheritance of our father's estate? ¹⁵Does he not regard us as foreigners?[x] Not only has he sold us, but he has used up what was paid for us.[y] ¹⁶Surely all the wealth that God took away from our father belongs to us and our children.[z] So do whatever God has told you."

¹⁷Then Jacob put his children and his wives[a] on camels,[b] ¹⁸and he drove all his livestock ahead of him, along with all the goods he had accumulated[c] in Paddan Aram,[r][d] to go to his father Isaac[e] in the land of Canaan.[f]

¹⁹When Laban had gone to shear his sheep,[g] Rachel stole her father's house-

30:37	*j*Jer 1:11
	*k*Eze 31:8 *l*ver 38,41
30:38	*m*S ver 37 *n*Ex 2:16 *o*ver 41; Jer 2:24
30:39	*p*ver 41 *q*S ver 32
30:40	*r*S ver 32
30:41	*s*S ver 38 *t*S ver 37
30:42	*u*Ge 31:1, 9,16,43
30:43	*v*S Ge 12:16
31:1	*w*Ge 30:35 *x*S Ge 30:42
31:2	*y*ver 5
31:3	*z*ver 13; Ge 32:9; Dt 30:3; Isa 10:21; 35:10; Jer 30:3; 42:12 *a*S Ge 21:22; S 26:3
31:5	*b*ver 29,42, 53; Ge 43:23; Da 2:23 *c*ver 2
31:6	*d*S Ge 21:22; S 26:3 *e*Ge 30:29
31:7	*f*S Ge 29:25 *g*S Ge 29:15 *h*ver 41; Nu 14:22; Job 19:3 *i*ver 52; S Ge 24:50
31:8	*j*S Ge 30:32
31:9	*k*Job 39:2; Eze 31:6
31:10	*l*S Ge 30:42
31:11	*m*S Ge 20:3 *n*S Ge 16:7 *o*S Ge 20:3 *p*S Ge 22:1; S Ex 3:4
31:12	*q*S Ge 30:32 *r*Ex 3:7
31:13	*s*Ge 28:10-22 *t*S Ge 28:18 *u*S Ge 28:20 *v*S ver 3
31:14	*w*2Sa 20:1; 1Ki 12:16
31:15	*x*Dt 15:3; 23:20; Ru 2:10; 2Sa 15:19; 1Ki 8:41; Ob 1:11 *y*S Ge 29:20
31:16	*z*S Ge 30:42
31:17	*a*S Ge 27:41 *b*S Ge 24:63-64
31:18	*c*S Ge 12:5 *d*S Ge 25:20 *e*S Ge 35:27 *f*S Ge 10:19

31:19 *g*Ge 38:12,13; 1Sa 25:2,4,7; 2Sa 13:23

r18 That is, Northwest Mesopotamia

25:25) by means of red stew (25:30), so he now tries to get the best of Laban (whose name means "white") by means of white branches. In effect, Jacob was using Laban's own tactic (deception) against him.

30:39 The scheme worked—but only because of God's intervention (see Jacob's own admission in 31:9), not because of Jacob's superstition.

30:43 *the man grew exceedingly prosperous.* Over a period of six years (see 31:41). While in Haran Jacob obtained both family and wealth.

31:3 *Go back to the land of your fathers.* Every sign Jacob was getting—from his wives (see vv. 14–16), from Laban (see v. 2), from Laban's sons (see v. 1) and now from God himself—told him that it was time to return to Canaan. *I will be with you.* See note on 26:3.

31:4 *Rachel and Leah.* At long last (see v. 14) Rachel, the

younger, has been given precedence over Leah—but she will soon become a deceiver like her husband Jacob (see vv. 31,35).

31:7 *ten times.* See v. 41. "Ten" here probably signifies completeness. In effect, Jacob accused Laban of cheating him at every turn.

31:9 See note on 30:39.

31:11 *angel of God.* See note on 16:7. *Here I am.* See note on 22:1.

31:13 *Bethel, where you anointed a pillar.* See note on 28:18.

31:18 *Paddan Aram.* Means "plain of Aram," another name for Aram Naharaim (see note on 24:10). See map of "Jacob's Journeys," p. 53.

31:19 *household gods.* Small portable idols, which Rachel probably stole because she thought they would bring her

hold gods.[h] [20]Moreover, Jacob deceived[i] Laban the Aramean[j] by not telling him he was running away.[k] [21]So he fled[l] with all he had, and crossing the River,[s][m] he headed for the hill country of Gilead.[n]

Laban Pursues Jacob

[22]On the third day[o] Laban was told that Jacob had fled.[p] [23]Taking his relatives[r] with him[r], he pursued Jacob for seven days and caught up with him in the hill country of Gilead.[s] [24]Then God came to Laban the Aramean[t] in a dream at night and said to him,[u] "Be careful not to say anything to Jacob, either good or bad."[v]

[25]Jacob had pitched his tent in the hill country of Gilead[w] when Laban overtook him, and Laban and his relatives camped there too. [26]Then Laban said to Jacob, "What have you done?[x] You've deceived

me,[y] and you've carried off my daughters like captives in war.[z] [27]Why did you run off secretly and deceive me? Why didn't you tell me,[a] so I could send you away with joy and singing to the music of tambourines[b] and harps?[c] [28]You didn't even let me kiss my grandchildren and my daughters good-by.[d] You have done a foolish thing. [29]I have the power to harm you;[e] but last night the God of your father[f] said to me, 'Be careful not to say anything to Jacob, either good or bad.'[g] [30]Now you have gone off because you

31:19 [h]ver 30, 32,34-35;
Ge 35:2;
Jos 24:14;
Jdg 17:5; 18:14, 17,24,30;
1Sa 7:3; 19:13;
2Ki 23:24;
Hos 3:4
31:20 [i]S Ge 27:36 [j]S Ge 25:20 [k]ver 27
31:21 [l]ver 22; Ex 2:15; 14:5; 1Ki 18:46; 19:3; Jer 26:21 [m]S Ge 2:14 [n]ver 23,25; Ge 37:25; Nu 26:30; 32:1; Dt 3:10; Jos 12:2; Jer 22:6
31:22 [o]S Ge 30:36 [p]S ver 21
31:23 [q]ver 37 [r]Ex 14:9 [s]S ver 21
31:24 [t]S Ge 25:20 [u]S Ge 20:3 [v]S Ge 24:50

31:25 [w]S ver 21 **31:26** [x]S Ge 12:18 [y]S Ge 27:36 [z]Ge 34:29; 1Sa 30:2-3 **31:27** [a]ver 20 [b]Ex 15:20; Jdg 11:34; 1Sa 10:5; 2Sa 6:5; Ps 68:25; Isa 24:8; Jer 31:4 [c]S Ge 4:21 **31:28** [d]S Ge 27:27; Ru 1:14; Ac 20:37 **31:29** [e]S ver 7; S Ge 26:29 [f]S ver 5 [g]S Ge 24:50

[s]*21* That is, the Euphrates

protection and blessing. Or perhaps she wanted to have something tangible to worship on the long journey ahead, a practice referred to much later in the writings of Josephus, a first-century Jewish historian. In any case, Rachel was not yet free of her pagan background (see 35:2; Jos 24:2).
31:21 *So he fled.* As he had fled earlier from Esau

(27:42-43). Jacob's devious dealings produced only hostility from which he had to flee. *Gilead.* A fertile region southeast of the Sea of Galilee.
31:26 *deceived.* Jacob's character, reflected in his name (see NIV text notes on 25:26; 27:36), is emphasized in the narrative again and again.

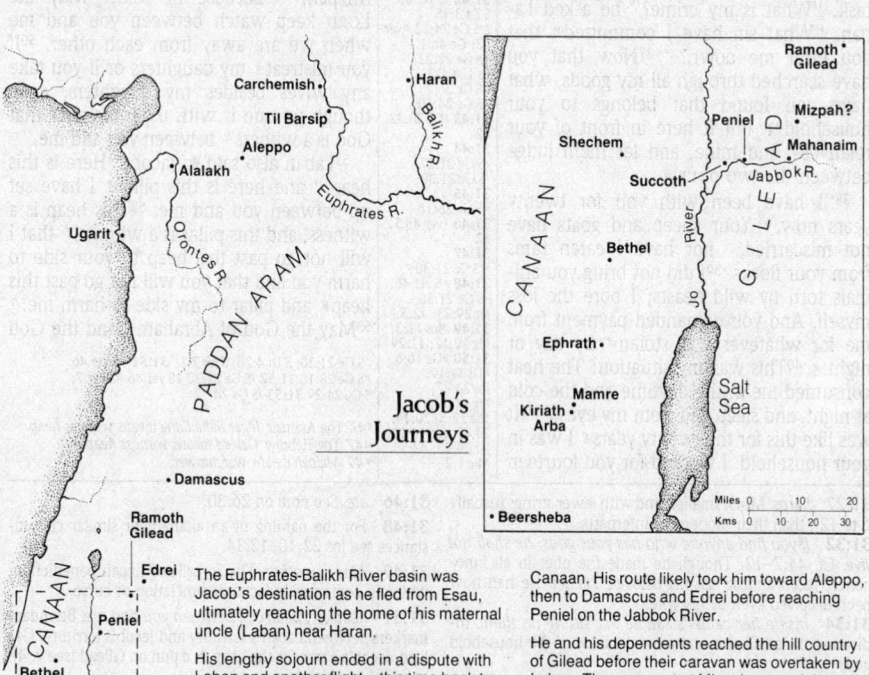

Jacob's Journeys

The Euphrates-Balikh River basin was Jacob's destination as he fled from Esau, ultimately reaching the home of his maternal uncle (Laban) near Haran.

His lengthy sojourn ended in a dispute with Laban and another flight—this time back to

Canaan. His route likely took him toward Aleppo, then to Damascus and Edrei before reaching Peniel on the Jabbok River.

He and his dependents reached the hill country of Gilead before their caravan was overtaken by Laban. The covenant at Mizpah was celebrated on one of the hills later used as a border station between Aramean and Israelite territories.

Jacob tarried at Succoth, entered Canaan and proceeded to Shechem, where he erected an altar to the Lord.

longed to return to your father's house.ʰ But why did you steal¹ my gods?ʲ"

³¹Jacob answered Laban, "I was afraid, because I thought you would take your daughters away from me by force.ᵏ ³²But if you find anyone who has your gods, he shall not live.ˡ In the presence of our relatives, see for yourself whether there is anything of yours here with me; and if so, take it." Now Jacob did not know that Rachel had stolen the gods.ᵐ

³³So Laban went into Jacob's tent and into Leah's tentⁿ and into the tent of the two maidservants,ᵒ but he found nothing.ᵖ After he came out of Leah's tent, he entered Rachel's tent. ³⁴Now Rachel had taken the household godsᵠ and put them inside her camel's saddleʳ and was sitting on them. Laban searchedˢ through everything in the tent but found nothing.

³⁵Rachel said to her father, "Don't be angry, my lord, that I cannot stand up in your presence;ᵗ I'm having my period.ᵘ" So he searched but could not find the household gods.ᵛ

³⁶Jacob was angry and took Laban to task. "What is my crime?" he asked Laban. "What sin have I committedʷ that you hunt me down?ˣ ³⁷Now that you have searched through all my goods, what have you found that belongs to your household?ʸ Put it here in front of your relativesᶻ and mine, and let them judge between the two of us.ᵃ

³⁸"I have been with you for twenty years now.ᵇ Your sheep and goats have not miscarried,ᶜ nor have I eaten rams from your flocks. ³⁹I did not bring you animals torn by wild beasts; I bore the loss myself. And you demanded payment from me for whatever was stolenᵈ by day or night.ᵉ ⁴⁰This was my situation: The heat consumed me in the daytime and the cold at night, and sleep fled from my eyes.ᶠ ⁴¹It was like this for the twenty yearsᵍ I was in your household. I worked for you fourteen

years for your two daughtersʰ and six years for your flocks,ⁱ and you changed my wagesʲ ten times.ᵏ ⁴²If the God of my father,ˡ the God of Abrahamᵐ and the Fear of Isaac,ⁿ had not been with me,ᵒ you would surely have sent me away empty-handed. But God has seen my hardship and the toil of my hands,ᵖ and last night he rebuked you.ᵠ"

⁴³Laban answered Jacob, "The women are my daughters, the children are my children, and the flocks are my flocks.ʳ All you see is mine. Yet what can I do today about these daughters of mine, or about the children they have borne? ⁴⁴Come now, let's make a covenant,ˢ you and I, and let it serve as a witness between us."ᵗ

⁴⁵So Jacob took a stone and set it up as a pillar.ᵘ ⁴⁶He said to his relatives, "Gather some stones." So they took stones and piled them in a heap,ᵛ and they ate there by the heap. ⁴⁷Laban called it Jegar Sahadutha,ᵗ and Jacob called it Galeed.ᵘ ʷ

⁴⁸Laban said, "This heapˣ is a witness between you and me today."ʸ That is why it was called Galeed. ⁴⁹It was also called Mizpah,ᵛ ᶻ because he said, "May the LORD keep watch between you and me when we are away from each other. ⁵⁰If you mistreatᵃ my daughters or if you take any wives besides my daughters, even though no one is with us, remember that God is a witnessᵇ between you and me."ᶜ

⁵¹Laban also said to Jacob, "Here is this heap,ᵈ and here is this pillarᵉ I have set up between you and me. ⁵²This heap is a witness, and this pillar is a witness,ᶠ that I will not go past this heap to your side to harm you and that you will not go past this heapᵍ and pillar to my side to harm me.ʰ ⁵³May the God of Abrahamⁱ and the God

31:30
ʰS Ge 28:15;
Job 29:2 ¹Ge 44:8
/S ver 19
31:31
ᵏS Ge 20:11
31:32 ˡGe 44:9
ᵐS ver 19
31:33 ⁿGe 24:67
ᵒS Ge 16:1 ᵖver 37
31:34 ᵠS ver 19
ʳS Ge 24:63-64
ˢver 37; Ge 44:12
31:35 ᵗEx 20:12;
Lev 19:3,32;
Dt 21:18; 27:16;
Jer 35:18
ᵘLev 15:19-23
ᵛver 19
31:36 ʷ1Sa 19:5;
20:32
ˣ1Sa 23:23;
24:11
31:37 ʸver 33
ᶻver 23 ᵃDt 1:16;
16:18
31:38
ᵇS Ge 27:44
ᶜS Ge 30:27
31:39 ᵈGe 30:33
ᵉEx 22:13
31:40 ᶠPs 132:4;
2Co 11:27
31:41
ᵍS Ge 27:44

ʰGe 29:30
ⁱS Ge 30:32
ʲS Ge 29:15
ᵏS ver 7
31:42 ˡS ver 5;
S Ex 3:15
ᵐS Ge 24:12 ⁿver
53; Ge 46:1
ᵒS Ge 21:22;
Ps 124:1-2
ᵖS Ge 3:17
ᵠS Ge 24:50
31:43 ʳGe 30:32,
42
31:44
ˢS Ge 21:27
ᵗS Ge 21:30
31:45
ᵘS Ge 28:18
31:46 ᵛver 48,51,
52
31:47
ʷS Ge 21:30
31:48 ˣS ver 46
ʸS Ge 21:30;
Jer 29:23; 42:5
31:49 ᶻJos 15:3;
Jdg 10:17; 11:29
31:50 ᵃGe 16:6
ᵇDt 31:19;
Jos 24:27;
Jdg 11:10;
1Sa 12:5; 20:14,
23,42; Job 16:19;
Jer 29:23; 42:5;
Mic 1:2

ᶜS Ge 21:30; S Dt 4:26; S Jer 7:11 **31:51** ᵈS ver 46
ᵉS Ge 28:18 **31:52** ᶠS Ge 21:30 ᵍS ver 46 ʰS ver 7;
S Ge 26:29 **31:53** ⁱS Ge 24:12

ᵗ47 The Aramaic *Jegar Sahadutha* means *witness heap.*
ᵘ47 The Hebrew *Galeed* means *witness heap.*
ᵛ49 *Mizpah* means *watchtower.*

31:27 *harps.* Much smaller, and with fewer strings (usually 6 to 12), than their modern counterparts.
31:32 *if you find anyone who has your gods, he shall not live.* Cf. 44:7-12. Though he made the offer in all innocence, Jacob almost lost his beloved Rachel. He had now been deceived even by his wife.
31:34 *inside her camel's saddle . . . sitting on them.* Indicating the small size and powerlessness of the household gods.
31:35 *I'm having my period.* In later times, anything a menstruating woman sat on was considered ritually unclean (Lev 15:20). Rachel, too, had become a deceiver.
31:42 *Fear.* Here a surrogate for God. Or perhaps the Hebrew for this word means "Kinsman," stressing the intimacy of God's relationship to the patriarch.

31:46 *ate.* See note on 26:30.
31:48 For the naming of an altar under similar circumstances see Jos 22:10-12,34.
31:49 *May . . . other.* The so-called Mizpah benediction, which in context is in fact a denunciation or curse.
31:51 *heap . . . pillar . . . between you and me.* Boundary markers between Laban's territory and Jacob's territory. Galeed, Jacob's name for the heap, is a pun on Gilead (see v. 47 and NIV text note).
31:53 *God of their father.* Or possibly "gods of their father [i.e., Terah]," reflecting Laban's polytheistic background (see Jos 24:2). *Fear of his father Isaac.* See note on v. 42. Jacob had met the "God of Isaac" (28:13) at Bethel 20 years earlier.

of Nahor,[i] the God of their father, judge between us." [k]

So Jacob took an oath[l] in the name of the Fear of his father Isaac. [m] 54He offered a sacrifice[n] there in the hill country and invited his relatives to a meal.[o] After they had eaten, they spent the night there.

55Early the next morning Laban kissed his grandchildren and his daughters[p] and blessed[q] them. Then he left and returned home.[r]

Jacob Prepares to Meet Esau

32 Jacob also went on his way, and the angels of God[s] met him. 2When Jacob saw them, he said, "This is the camp of God!"[t] So he named that place Mahanaim.[w u]

3Jacob sent messengers[v] ahead of him to his brother Esau[w] in the land of Seir,[x] the country of Edom.[y] 4He instructed them: "This is what you are to say to my master[z] Esau: 'Your servant[a] Jacob says, I have been staying with Laban[b] and have remained there till now. 5I have cattle and donkeys, sheep and goats, menservants and maidservants.[c] Now I am sending this message to my lord,[d] that I may find favor in your eyes.[e]'"

6When the messengers returned to Jacob, they said, "We went to your brother Esau, and now he is coming to meet you, and four hundred men are with him."[f]

7In great fear[g] and distress[h] Jacob divided the people who were with him into two groups,[x i] and the flocks and herds and camels as well. 8He thought, "If Esau comes and attacks one group,[y] the group[y] that is left may escape."

9Then Jacob prayed, "O God of my father Abraham,[j] God of my father Isaac,[k]

O LORD, who said to me, 'Go back to your country and your relatives, and I will make you prosper,'[l] 10I am unworthy of all the kindness and faithfulness[m] you have shown your servant. I had only my staff[n] when I crossed this Jordan, but now I have become two groups.[o] 11Save me, I pray, from the hand of my brother Esau, for I am afraid[p] he will come and attack me,[q] and also the mothers with their children.[r] 12But you have said, 'I will surely make you prosper and will make your descendants like the sand[s] of the sea, which cannot be counted.'[t]"

13He spent the night there, and from what he had with him he selected a gift[u] for his brother Esau: 14two hundred female goats and twenty male goats, two hundred ewes and twenty rams,[v] 15thirty female camels with their young, forty cows and ten bulls, and twenty female donkeys and ten male donkeys.[w] 16He put them in the care of his servants, each herd by itself, and said to his servants, "Go ahead of me, and keep some space between the herds."[x]

17He instructed the one in the lead: "When my brother Esau meets you and asks, 'To whom do you belong, and where are you going, and who owns all these animals in front of you?' 18then you are to say, 'They belong to your servant[y] Jacob. They are a gift[z] sent to my lord Esau, and he is coming behind us.'"

19He also instructed the second, the third and all the others who followed the

31:53
/S Ge 11:27
*k*S Ge 16:5
/S Ge 21:23,27
*m*S ver 42
31:54 *n*Ge 46:1; Ex 24:5; Lev 3:1
*o*S Ge 26:30
31:55 *p*S ver 28; Ru 1:9
*q*S Ge 24:60; S Ex 39:43
*r*Ge 18:33
32:1 *s*S Ge 16:11; 2Ki 6:16-17; 1Ch 21:15; Ps 34:7; 35:5; 91:11; Da 6:22
32:2 *t*S Ge 28:17 *u*Jos 15:26,30; 21:38; 2Sa 2:8, 29; 17:24; 19:32; 1Ki 2:8; 4:14; 1Ch 6:80
32:3 *v*Nu 21:21; Jdg 11:17 *w*S Ge 27:41-42 *x*S Ge 14:6; S Nu 24:18 *y*S Ge 25:30; S 36:16
32:4 *z*S Ge 24:9 *a*S Ge 18:3 *b*Ge 31:41
32:5 *c*S Ge 12:16 *d*S Ge 24:9 *e*Ge 33:8,10,15; 34:11; 47:25,29; 50:4; Ru 2:13
32:6 *f*Ge 33:1
32:7 *g*ver 11 *h*Ge 35:3; Ps 4:1; 77:2; 107:6 *i*ver 10; Ge 33:1
32:9 *j*S Ge 24:12 *k*S Ge 28:13

/S Ge 26:3; 31:13
32:10 *m*S Ge 24:27 *n*Ge 38:18; 47:31; Nu 17:2 *o*S ver 7
32:11 *p*S ver 7 *q*Ge 43:18; Ps 59:2 *r*S Ge 27:41
32:12 *s*S Ge 22:17; 1Ki 4:20,29 *t*S Ge 12:2; S 13:14; Hos 1:10; Ro 9:27

32:13 *u*ver 13-15,18,20,21; Ge 33:10; 43:11,15,25,26; 1Sa 16:20; Pr 18:16; 21:14 **32:14** *v*Nu 7:88 **32:15** *w*S Ge 13:2; 42:26; 45:23 **32:16** *x*Ge 33:8 **32:18** *y*S Ge 18:3 *z*S ver 13

*w*2 *Mahanaim* means *two camps.* *x*7 Or *camps;* also in verse 10 *y*8 Or *camp*

31:54 *sacrifice . . . meal.* Two important aspects of the covenant-making (see v. 44) process (see Ex 24:5–8,11). *relatives.* Those with whom he had now entered into a covenant. The common meal indicated mutual acceptance (see note on 26:30).
31:55 *blessed.* Or "said farewell to" (see NIV text note on 47:10; see also 31:28).
32:1 *angels of God met him.* Jacob had just left the region of the hostile Laban and is about to enter the region of the hostile Esau. He was met by the angels of God, whom he had seen at Bethel when he was fleeing from Esau to go to Laban (28:12). Thus God was with Jacob, as he had promised (see 28:15; 31:3; see also note on 26:3).
32:2 *Mahanaim.* Located in Gilead (see note on 31:21) east of the Jordan and north of the Jabbok (see note on v. 22). Two camps (see NIV text note) had just met in hostility and separated in peace. Two camps were again about to meet (in hostility, Jacob thought) and separate in peace. But Jacob called this crucial place "two camps" after seeing the angelic encampment, suggesting that he saw God's encampment as a divine assurance. God's host had come to escort him safely

to Canaan (see 33:12,15). Yet he also feared meeting with Esau, so he divided his household into two camps (see vv. 7,10 and NIV text note on v. 7), still trying to protect himself by his own devices.
32:3 *Seir . . . Edom.* Far to the south of Jacob's ultimate destination, but he assumed that Esau would come seeking revenge as soon as he heard that Jacob was on his way back.
32:4 *Your servant.* A phrase suggesting both courtesy and humility.
32:6 *four hundred.* A round number for a sizable unit of fighting men (see 1Sa 22:2; 25:13; 30:10).
32:9 *Jacob prayed.* His first recorded prayer since leaving Bethel.
32:11 *mothers with their children.* Jacob was afraid that Esau's wrath would extend to Jacob's family as well.
32:12 *your descendants like the sand of the sea.* A reference to God's promise in 28:14 (see 22:17 and note).
32:13 *gift.* Probably a wordplay: Out of his "two camps" (Hebrew *mahanayim,* v. 2; see vv. 7–8,10) Jacob selects a "gift" (*minhah*) for his brother.

can settle among us; *c* the land is open to you. *d* Live in it, trade *i* in it, *e* and acquire property in it. *f* "

¹¹Then Shechem said to Dinah's father and brothers, "Let me find favor in your eyes, *g* and I will give you whatever you ask. ¹²Make the price for the bride *h* and the gift I am to bring as great as you like, and I'll pay whatever you ask me. Only give me the girl as my wife."

¹³Because their sister Dinah had been defiled, *i* Jacob's sons replied deceitfully *j* as they spoke to Shechem and his father Hamor. ¹⁴They said to them, "We can't do such a thing; we can't give our sister to a man who is not circumcised. *k* That would be a disgrace to us. ¹⁵We will give our consent to you on one condition *l* only: that you become like us by circumcising all your males. *m* ¹⁶Then we will give you our daughters and take your daughters for ourselves. *n* We'll settle among you and become one people with you. *o* ¹⁷But if you will not agree to be circumcised, we'll take our sister *j* and go."

¹⁸Their proposal seemed good to Hamor and his son Shechem. ¹⁹The young man, who was the most honored *p* of all his father's household, lost no time in doing what they said, because he was delighted with Jacob's daughter. *q* ²⁰So Hamor and his son Shechem went to the gate of their city *r* to speak to their fellow townsmen. ²¹"These men are friendly toward us," they said. "Let them live in our land and trade in it; *s* the land has plenty of room for them. We can marry their daughters and they can marry ours. *t* ²²But the men will consent to live with us as one people only on the condition that our males be circumcised, *u* as they themselves are. ²³Won't their livestock, their property and all their other animals become ours? *v* So let us give our consent to them, and they will settle among us. *w* "

²⁴All the men who went out of the city gate *x* agreed with Hamor and his son She-

chem, and every male in the city was circumcised.

²⁵Three days later, while all of them were still in pain, *y* two of Jacob's sons, Simeon *z* and Levi, *a* Dinah's brothers, took their swords *b* and attacked the unsuspecting city, *c* killing every male. *d* ²⁶They put Hamor and his son Shechem to the sword *e* and took Dinah *f* from Shechem's house and left. ²⁷The sons of Jacob came upon the dead bodies and looted the city *g* where *k* their sister had been defiled. *h* ²⁸They seized their flocks and herds and donkeys *i* and everything else of theirs in the city and out in the fields. *j* ²⁹They carried off all their wealth and all their women and children, *k* taking as plunder *l* everything in the houses. *m*

³⁰Then Jacob said to Simeon and Levi, "You have brought trouble *n* on me by making me a stench *o* to the Canaanites and Perizzites, the people living in this land. *p* We are few in number, *q* and if they join forces against me and attack me, I and my household will be destroyed."

³¹But they replied, "Should he have treated our sister like a prostitute? *r* "

Jacob Returns to Bethel

35 Then God said to Jacob, "Go up to Bethel *s* and settle there, and build an altar *t* there to God, *u* who appeared to you *v* when you were fleeing from your brother Esau." *w*

²So Jacob said to his household *x* and to all who were with him, "Get rid of the foreign gods *y* you have with you, and purify yourselves and change your clothes. *z* ³Then come, let us go up to Bethel, where I will build an altar to God, *a* who answered me in the day of my distress *b* and who has been with me wherever I have gone. *c* " ⁴So they gave

Center reference column

34:10 *c* ver 23; Ge 46:34; 47:6, 27 *d* S Ge 13:9 *e* Ge 42:34 *f* S Ge 33:19
34:11 *g* S Ge 32:5
34:12 *h* Ex 22:16; Dt 22:29; 1Sa 18:25
34:13 *i* S ver 5 *j* S Ge 27:36
34:14 *k* Ge 17:14; Jdg 14:3; 1Sa 31:4; Isa 52:1
34:15 *l* 1Sa 11:2 *m* ver 22; Ex 12:48
34:16 *n* S ver 9 *o* S Ge 33:19
34:19 *p* Ge 49:3; 1Ch 11:21 *q* ver 3
34:20 *r* S Ge 18:1
34:21 *s* S Ge 33:19 *t* S ver 9
34:22 *u* S ver 15
34:23 *v* ver 28; S Ge 12:16 *w* S ver 10
34:24 *x* S Ge 18:1

34:25 *y* Jos 5:8 *z* S Ge 29:33 *a* S Ge 29:34 *b* Ge 49:5; Mal 2:16 *c* Jdg 18:7,10,27; Eze 38:11 *d* Ge 49:7
34:26 *e* S ver 7; Ge 48:22 *f* ver 3
34:27 *g* 2Ki 21:14 *h* S ver 5
34:28 *i* Ge 43:18 *j* S ver 23
34:29 *k* S Ge 31:26 *l* Nu 14:3; 31:9, 53; Dt 2:35; Jos 7:21 *m* 2Ki 8:12; Isa 13:16; La 5:11; Am 1:13; Zec 14:2
34:30 *n* Ge 43:6; Ex 5:23; Nu 11:11 *o* Ex 5:21; 6:9; 1Sa 13:4; 27:12; 2Sa 10:6; 1Ch 19:6 *p* S Ge 13:7 *q* Ge 35:26; 46:27; Ex 1:5; Dt 10:22; 26:5; 1Ch 16:19; Ps 105:12
34:31 *r* ver 2
35:1 *s* S Ge 12:8 *t* S Ge 4:26; 8:20 *u* ver 3 *v* ver 7; Ge 27:43
35:2 *x* Ge 18:19; Jos 24:15

y S Ge 31:19; S Jos 24:14 *z* Ex 19:10,14; Nu 8:7,21; 19:19
35:3 *a* ver 1 *b* S Ge 32:7; S Jdg 2:15 *c* S Ge 26:3

i 10 Or *move about freely;* also in verse 21
j 17 Hebrew *daughter*   *k* 27 Or *because*

34:12 *the price for the bride and the gift I am to bring.* For a specific example of this marriage custom see 24:53.
34:13 *Jacob's sons replied deceitfully.* Like father, like son (see 27:24; see also note on 25:26).
34:15 Using a sacred ceremony for a sinful purpose (see vv. 24–25).
34:20 *gate of their city.* See notes on 19:1; 23:10.
34:23 The greed of the men of Shechem led to their destruction.
34:24 The Canaanites were even willing to submit to Israel's covenant rite in order to attain their purposes.
34:25 *Simeon and Levi.* Because they slaughtered the men of Shechem, their own descendants would be scattered far and wide (see note on 49:7). *Dinah's brothers.* All three

were children of Leah (29:33–34; 30:21). *killing every male.* Shechem's crime, serious as it was, hardly warranted such brutal and extensive retaliation (see vv. 27–29).
34:30 *Perizzites.* See note on 13:7.
35:1 *God . . . appeared to you when you were fleeing.* See v.7; 28:13.
35:2 *foreign gods you have with you.* See note on 31:19 (see also Jos 24:23).
35:3 *God . . . who has been with me.* See 28:15; see also note on 26:3.
35:4 *rings.* Worn as amulets or charms; a pagan religious custom (cf. Hos 2:13). *the oak at Shechem.* Obviously a well-known tree, perhaps the "great tree" mentioned in 12:6 (see Jos 24:26).

Jacob all the foreign gods they had and the rings in their ears,[d] and Jacob buried them under the oak[e] at Shechem.[f] [5]Then they set out, and the terror of God[g] fell upon the towns all around them so that no one pursued them.[h]

[6]Jacob and all the people with him came to Luz[i] (that is, Bethel) in the land of Canaan.[j] [7]There he built an altar,[k] and he called the place El Bethel,[l] because it was there that God revealed himself to him[m] when he was fleeing from his brother.[n]

[8]Now Deborah, Rebekah's nurse,[o] died and was buried under the oak[p] below Bethel.[q] So it was named Allon Bacuth.[m]

[9]After Jacob returned from Paddan Aram,[n][r] God appeared to him again and blessed him.[s] [10]God said to him, "Your name is Jacob,[o] but you will no longer be called Jacob; your name will be Israel.[p]"[t] So he named him Israel.

[11]And God said to him, "I am God Almighty[q];[u] be fruitful and increase in number.[v] A nation[w] and a community of nations will come from you, and kings will come from your body.[x] [12]The land I gave to Abraham and Isaac I also give to you, and I will give this land to your descendants after you.[y]"[z] [13]Then God went up from him[a] at the place where he had talked with him.

[14]Jacob set up a stone pillar[b] at the place where God had talked with him, and he poured out a drink offering[c] on it; he also poured oil on it.[d] [15]Jacob called the place where God had talked with him Bethel.[r] [e]

The Deaths of Rachel and Isaac
35:23–26pp — 1Ch 2:1–2

[16]Then they moved on from Bethel. While they were still some distance from Ephrath,[f] Rachel[g] began to give birth and had great difficulty. [17]And as she was having great difficulty in childbirth, the midwife[h] said to her, "Don't be afraid, for you have another son."[i] [18]As she breathed her last—for she was dying—she named her son Ben-Oni.[s][j] But his father named him Benjamin.[t] [k]

[19]So Rachel died and was buried on the way to Ephrath[l] (that is, Bethlehem[m]). [20]Over her tomb Jacob set up a pillar, and to this day[n] that pillar marks Rachel's tomb.[o]

[21]Israel moved on again and pitched his tent beyond Migdal Eder.[p] [22]While Israel was living in that region, Reuben went in and slept with his father's concubine[q] Bilhah,[r] and Israel heard of it.

Jacob had twelve sons:

[23]The sons of Leah:[s]

Reuben the firstborn[t] of Jacob,

35:4
[d]S Ge 24:22;
Ex 32:3; 35:22;
Jdg 8:24; Pr 25:12
[e]ver 8 /S Ge 12:6
35:5 [g]Ex 15:16;
23:27; Dt 2:25;
Jos 2:9; 1Sa 7:10;
13:7; 14:15;
2Ch 14:14;
17:10; 20:29;
Ps 9:20
[i]Isa 19:17;
Zec 14:13
[h]Ps 105:14
35:6 /S Ge 28:19
/S Ge 10:19
35:7 [k]S Ge 8:20
/Ge 28:19
[m]S Ge 28:13
[n]S ver 1
35:8 [o]Ge 24:59
[p]ver 4
[q]S Ge 12:8;
1Sa 10:3
35:9 [r]S Ge 25:20
[s]S Ge 28:13;
S 32:29
35:10 [t]S Ge 17:5
35:11 [u]S Ge 17:1
[v]S Ge 12:2
[w]S Ge 12:2
[x]S Ge 17:6
35:12
[y]S Ge 28:13
[z]S Ge 12:7;
S 15:7
35:13
[a]S Ge 17:22
35:14
[b]S Ge 28:22
[c]Ex 29:40;
Lev 23:13;
Nu 6:15,17; 15:5;
28:7,14;
2Sa 23:16;
2Ch 29:35
[d]S Ge 28:18
35:15 [e]S Ge 12:8

35:16 [f]ver 19;
Ge 48:7; Ru 1:2;
4:11; 1Sa 17:12;
Mic 5:2
[g]S Ge 29:6
35:17
[h]Ge 38:28;
Ex 1:15
[i]S Ge 30:24
35:18 /1Sa 4:21;
14:3 [k]ver 24;

Ge 42:4; 43:16,29; 45:12,14; 49:27; Nu 1:36; Dt 33:12
35:19 /S ver 16 [m]Ge 48:7; Jos 19:15; Jdg 12:8; 17:7; 19:1,
18; Ru 1:1,19; 1Sa 17:12; Mic 5:2 **35:20** [n]Jos 4:9; 7:26;
8:28; 10:27; 18:24 [o]S Ge 28:18; Jos 15:21 **35:22**
[q]S Ge 22:24 [r]S Ge 29:29; S 34:5; S Lev 18:8 **35:23**
[s]S Ge 29:16 [t]Ge 43:33; 46:8

[17] *El Bethel* means *God of Bethel.* [m]8 *Allon Bacuth*
means *oak of weeping.* [n]9 That is, Northwest
Mesopotamia; also in verse 26 [o]10 *Jacob* means *he
grasps the heel* (figuratively, *he deceives*). [p]10 *Israel*
means *he struggles with God.* [q]11 Hebrew
El-Shaddai [r]15 *Bethel* means *house of God.*
[s]18 *Ben-Oni* means *son of my trouble.* [t]18 *Benjamin*
means *son of my right hand.*

35:5 *the terror of God.* God protected his servant.
35:7 *built an altar.* See note on 12:7.
35:8 *Deborah, Rebekah's nurse, died.* After long years of
faithful service (see 24:59). *the oak.* Again probably a well-
known tree (see note on v. 4), perhaps the "great tree"
mentioned in 1Sa 10:3. *below.* Either "lower than" or "to
the south of."
35:9 *Jacob returned.* See map of "Jacob's Journeys," p. 53.
Paddan Aram. Means "plain of Aram," another name for
Aram Naharaim (see note on 24:10).
35:10 *Jacob ... Israel.* The previous assignment of an
additional name (see 32:28) is here confirmed. For similar
examples compare 21:31 with 26:33, and 28:19 with
35:15.
35:11–12 This event climaxes the Isaac-Jacob cycle (see
Introduction: Literary Features). Now that Jacob was at last
back at Bethel, where God had begun his direct relationship
with him, God confirmed to this chosen son of Isaac the
covenant promises made to Abraham (17:1–8; see 28:3).
His words echo his original benediction pronounced on man
in the beginning (1:28) and renewed after the flood (9:1,7).
God's blessing on mankind would be fulfilled in and through
Jacob and his offspring. See also 47:27; Ex 1:7.
35:13 See note on 17:22.

35:14 See 28:18 and note. *drink offering.* A liquid poured
out as a sacrifice to a deity.
35:15 See 28:19; see also note on v. 10.
35:16 *Ephrath.* The older name for Bethlehem (see v. 19)
in Judah (see Ru 1:2; Mic 5:2).
35:17 *another son.* An echo of Rachel's own plea at the
time of Joseph's birth (see 30:24).
35:18 *Benjamin.* See NIV text note. The name can also
mean "son of the south"—in distinction from the other sons,
who were born in the north. One set of Hebrew terms for
indicating direction was based on facing east, so south was
on the right.
35:19 *Rachel died.* In childbirth (see note on 30:1).
35:20 *Rachel's tomb.* See 1Sa 10:2. The traditional,
though not authentic, site is near Bethlehem.
35:21 *Migdal Eder.* Means "tower of the flock," doubtless
referring to a watchtower built to discourage thieves from
stealing sheep and other animals (see, e.g., 2Ch 26:10). The
same Hebrew phrase is used figuratively in Mic 4:8, where
"flock" refers to the people of Judah (see Mic 4:6–7).
35:22 Reuben's act was an arrogant and premature claim
to the rights of the firstborn—here the right to inherit his
father's concubine. For this he would lose his legal status as
firstborn (see 49:3–4; 1Ch 5:1; see also note on 37:21).

Simeon, Levi, Judah, *u* Issachar and Zebulun. *v*

24The sons of Rachel:
Joseph *w* and Benjamin. *x*

25The sons of Rachel's maidservant Bilhah: *y*
Dan and Naphtali. *z*

26The sons of Leah's maidservant Zilpah: *a*
Gad *b* and Asher. *c*

These were the sons of Jacob, *d* who were born to him in Paddan Aram. *e*

27Jacob came home to his father Isaac *f* in Mamre, *g* near Kiriath Arba *h* (that is, Hebron), *i* where Abraham and Isaac had stayed. *j* 28Isaac lived a hundred and eighty years. *k* 29Then he breathed his last and died and was gathered to his people, *l* old and full of years. *m* And his sons Esau and Jacob buried him. *n*

Esau's Descendants

36:10–14pp — 1Ch 1:35–37
36:20–28pp — 1Ch 1:38–42

36 This is the account *o* of Esau (that is, Edom). *p*

2Esau took his wives from the women of Canaan: *q* Adah daughter of Elon the Hittite, *r* and Oholibamah *s* daughter of Anah *t* and granddaughter of Zibeon the Hivite *u* — 3also Basemath *v* daughter of Ishmael and sister of Nebaioth. *w*

4Adah bore Eliphaz to Esau, Basemath bore Reuel, *x* 5and Oholibamah bore Jeush, Jalam and Korah. *y* These were the sons of Esau, who were born to him in Canaan.

6Esau took his wives and sons and daughters and all the members of his household, as well as his livestock and all his other animals and all the goods he had acquired in Canaan, *z* and moved to a land some distance from his brother Jacob. *a* 7Their possessions

were too great for them to remain together; the land where they were staying could not support them both because of their livestock. *b* 8So Esau *c* (that is, Edom) *d* settled in the hill country of Seir. *e*

9This is the account *f* of Esau the father of the Edomites *g* in the hill country of Seir.

10These are the names of Esau's sons:
Eliphaz, the son of Esau's wife Adah, and Reuel, the son of Esau's wife Basemath. *h*

11The sons of Eliphaz: *i*
Teman, *j* Omar, Zepho, Gatam and Kenaz. *k*

12Esau's son Eliphaz also had a concubine *l* named Timna, who bore him Amalek. *m* These were grandsons of Esau's wife Adah. *n*

13The sons of Reuel:
Nahath, Zerah, Shammah and Mizzah. These were grandsons of Esau's wife Basemath. *o*

14The sons of Esau's wife Oholibamah *p* daughter of Anah and granddaughter of Zibeon, whom she bore to Esau:
Jeush, Jalam and Korah. *q*

15These were the chiefs *r* among Esau's descendants:

The sons of Eliphaz the firstborn of Esau:
Chiefs Teman, *s* Omar, Zepho, Kenaz, *t* 16Korah, *u* Gatam and Amalek. These were the chiefs descended from Eliphaz *u* in Edom; *v* they were grandsons of Adah. *w*

17The sons of Esau's son Reuel: *x*
Chiefs Nahath, Zerah, Shammah and Mizzah. These were the chiefs

Cross references

35:23 *u* S Ge 29:35; *v* S Ge 30:20
35:24 *w* S Ge 30:24; *x* ver 18
35:25 *y* Ge 37:2; *z* S Ge 30:8
35:26 *a* Ge 37:2; *b* S Ge 30:11; *c* S Ge 30:13; *d* S Ge 34:30; 46:8; Ex 1:1-4; *e* S Ge 25:20
35:27 *f* Ge 31:18; *g* S Ge 13:18; *h* Ge 23:2; Jos 15:54; Jdg 1:10; Ne 11:25; *i* S Ge 13:18; *j* S Ge 17:8
35:28 *k* S Ge 25:7,20
35:29 *l* S Ge 25:8; *m* S Ge 15:15; *n* S Ge 23:20; S 25:9
36:1 *o* S Ge 2:4; *p* S Ge 25:30
36:2 *q* Ge 28:8-9; *r* Ge 26:34; *s* ver 14,18; *t* ver 25; 1Ch 1:40; *u* ver 24; S Ge 10:17; 1Ch 1:40
36:3 *v* ver 4,10,13,17; *w* S Ge 25:13
36:4 *x* S ver 3; 1Ch 1:35
36:5 *y* ver 14,18; 1Ch 1:35
36:6 *z* Ge 12:5; *a* Ge 27:39
36:7 *b* S Ge 13:6
36:8 *c* Dt 2:4; *d* S Ge 25:30; *e* S Ge 14:6
36:9 *f* S Ge 2:4; *g* ver 1,43
36:10 *h* S ver 3
36:11 *i* ver 15-16; 1Ch 1:45; Job 2:11; 4:1; *j* Jer 49:7,20; Eze 25:13; Am 1:12; Ob 1:9; Hab 3:3 *k* ver 15
36:12 *l* S Ge 22:24; *m* Ex 17:8,16; Nu 24:20; Dt 25:17,19; 1Sa 15:2; 27:8 *n* ver 16
36:13 *o* S ver 3
36:14 *p* S ver 2; *q* S ver 5
36:15 *r* ver 19,40; Ex 15:15; *s* Job 2:11; Jer 49:7; Eze 25:13; Am 1:12; Hab 3:3 *t* S ver 11 36:16 *u* S ver 11 *v* Ge 32:3; Ex 15:15; Nu 20:14; 33:37 *w* ver 12
36:17 *x* 1Ch 1:37

u 16 Masoretic Text; Samaritan Pentateuch (see also Gen. 36:11 and 1 Chron. 1:36) does not have *Korah*.

Notes

35:26 *sons of Jacob . . . born to him in Paddan Aram.* Obviously a summary statement since Benjamin was born in Canaan (see vv. 16–18).

35:27 *Mamre, near Kiriath Arba (that is, Hebron).* See notes on 13:18; 23:2.

35:29 See note on 25:8. *buried him.* In the family tomb, the cave of Machpelah (49:30–31).

36:1 *account.* See note on 2:4. Though repeated in v. 9, the word does not mark the start of a new main section there since the information in vv. 9–43 is merely an expansion of that in vv. 1–8. *Esau (that is, Edom).* See 25:30 and NIV text note. Reddish rock formations, primarily sandstone, are conspicuous in the territory of the Edomites, located south and southeast of the Dead Sea.

36:2–3 See note on 26:34.

36:7 See 13:6; see also 26:20 and note.

36:8 *Seir.* Another name for Edom. The word itself is related to the Hebrew word meaning "hair," a possible meaning also for the name "Esau" (see NIV text note on 25:25). Esau's clan must have driven away the original Horite (see v. 20) inhabitants of Seir (see 14:6 and note). The descendants of Seir are listed in vv. 20–28.

36:10–14 The same list of Esau's descendants (see 1Ch 1:35–37) is repeated in vv. 15–19 as a list of tribal chieftains.

36:11 *Eliphaz: Teman.* One of Job's friends was named Eliphaz the Temanite (Job 2:11), and Job himself was from the land of Uz (Job 1:1). Thus Job probably lived in Edom (see vv. 28,34).

36:12 *Amalek.* See note on 14:7.

descended from Reuel in Edom; they were grandsons of Esau's wife Basemath. [y]

[18] The sons of Esau's wife Oholibamah: [z]

Chiefs Jeush, Jalam and Korah. [a] These were the chiefs descended from Esau's wife Oholibamah daughter of Anah.

[19] These were the sons of Esau [b] (that is, Edom), [c] and these were their chiefs. [d]

[20] These were the sons of Seir the Horite, [e] who were living in the region:

Lotan, Shobal, Zibeon, Anah, [f] [21] Dishon, Ezer and Dishan. These sons of Seir in Edom were Horite chiefs. [g]

[22] The sons of Lotan:

Hori and Homam. [v] Timna was Lotan's sister.

[23] The sons of Shobal:

Alvan, Manahath, Ebal, Shepho and Onam.

[24] The sons of Zibeon: [h]

Aiah and Anah. This is the Anah who discovered the hot springs [w][i] in the desert while he was grazing the donkeys [j] of his father Zibeon.

[25] The children of Anah: [k]

Dishon and Oholibamah [l] daughter of Anah.

[26] The sons of Dishon [x]:

Hemdan, Eshban, Ithran and Keran.

[27] The sons of Ezer:

Bilhan, Zaavan and Akan.

[28] The sons of Dishan:

Uz and Aran.

[29] These were the Horite chiefs:

Lotan, Shobal, Zibeon, Anah, [m] [30] Dishon, Ezer and Dishan. These were the Horite chiefs, [n] according to their divisions, in the land of Seir.

The Rulers of Edom

36:31–43pp — 1Ch 1:43–54

[31] These were the kings who reigned in Edom before any Israelite king [o] reigned [y]: [32] Bela son of Beor became king of

Edom. His city was named Dinhabah.

[33] When Bela died, Jobab son of Zerah from Bozrah [p] succeeded him as king.

[34] When Jobab died, Husham from the land of the Temanites [q] succeeded him as king.

[35] When Husham died, Hadad son of Bedad, who defeated Midian [r] in the country of Moab, [s] succeeded him as king. His city was named Avith.

[36] When Hadad died, Samlah from Masrekah succeeded him as king.

[37] When Samlah died, Shaul from Rehoboth [t] on the river [z] succeeded him as king.

[38] When Shaul died, Baal-Hanan son of Acbor succeeded him as king.

[39] When Baal-Hanan son of Acbor died, Hadad [a] succeeded him as king. His city was named Pau, and his wife's name was Mehetabel daughter of Matred, the daughter of Me-Zahab.

[40] These were the chiefs [u] descended from Esau, by name, according to their clans and regions:

Timna, Alvah, Jetheth, [41] Oholibamah, Elah, Pinon, [42] Kenaz, Teman, Mibzar, [43] Magdiel and Iram. These were the chiefs of Edom, according to their settlements in the land they occupied.

This was Esau the father of the Edomites. [v]

Joseph's Dreams

37 Jacob lived in the land where his father had stayed, [w] the land of Canaan. [x]

[2] This is the account [y] of Jacob.

36:17 [y] S ver 3
36:18 [z] S ver 2
[a] ver 5
36:19 [b] 1Ch 1:35
[c] S Ge 25:30
[d] S ver 15
36:20 [e] S Ge 14:6
[f] ver 29
36:21 [g] ver 30
36:24 [h] S ver 2
[i] Jos 15:19
[j] Job 1:14
36:25 [k] S ver 2
[l] S ver 2
36:29 [m] ver 20
36:30 [n] ver 21
36:31 [o] S Ge 17:6

36:33 [p] Isa 34:6;
63:1; Jer 49:13,
22
36:34 [q] Jer 49:7;
Eze 25:13; Ob 1:9
36:35 [r] S Ge 25:2
[s] S Ge 19:37;
Dt 1:5; Jdg 3:30;
Ru 1:1,6
36:37 [t] Ge 26:22
36:40 [u] S ver 15
36:43 [v] S ver 9
37:1 [w] S Ge 17:8
[x] S Ge 10:19
37:2 [y] S Ge 2:4

[v] 22 Hebrew *Hemam,* a variant of *Homam* (see 1 Chron. 1:39)   [w] 24 Vulgate; Syriac *discovered water;* the meaning of the Hebrew for this word is uncertain.   [x] 26 Hebrew *Dishan,* a variant of *Dishon*   [y] 31 Or *before an Israelite king reigned over them*   [z] 37 Possibly the Euphrates   [a] 39 Many manuscripts of the Masoretic Text, Samaritan Pentateuch and Syriac (see also 1 Chron. 1:50); most manuscripts of the Masoretic Text *Hadar*

36:20–28 *See note on v. 8.* The same list of Seir's descendants (see 1Ch 1:38–42) is repeated in abbreviated form in vv. 29–30 as a list of tribal chieftains.

36:24 *This is the Anah who . . . Zibeon.* To distinguish him from the other Anah mentioned in vv. 2,14,18. The two Anahs appear earlier in v. 25.

36:31 *before any Israelite king reigned.* Presupposes the later Israelite monarchy and is therefore an editorial updating subsequent to Moses' time (see note on 14:14).

36:43 *This . . . Edomites.* A summary statement for the whole chapter (just as v. 1 is a title for the whole chapter).

37:1 *Canaan.* Jacob made the promised land his homeland and was later buried there (49:29–30; 50:13). His son Joseph also insisted on being buried in Canaan, which he recognized as the land the Lord had promised to Israel (50:24–25). The Jacob-Joseph cycle (see Introduction: Literary Features) begins and ends with references to the land of promise.

Joseph,[z] a young man of seventeen,[a] was tending the flocks[b] with his brothers, the sons of Bilhah[c] and the sons of Zilpah,[d] his father's wives, and he brought their father a bad report[e] about them.

[3]Now Israel[f] loved Joseph more than any of his other sons,[g] because he had been born to him in his old age;[h] and he made a richly ornamented[b] robe[i] for him.[j] [4]When his brothers saw that their father loved him more than any of them, they hated him[k] and could not speak a kind word to him.

[5]Joseph had a dream,[l] and when he told it to his brothers,[m] they hated him all the more.[n] [6]He said to them, "Listen to this dream I had: [7]We were binding sheaves[o] of grain out in the field when suddenly my sheaf rose and stood upright, while your sheaves gathered around mine and bowed down to it."[p]

[8]His brothers said to him, "Do you intend to reign over us? Will you actually rule us?"[q] And they hated him all the more[r] because of his dream and what he had said.

[9]Then he had another dream,[s] and he told it to his brothers. "Listen," he said, "I had another dream, and this time the sun and moon and eleven stars[t] were bowing down to me."[u]

[10]When he told his father as well as his brothers,[v] his father rebuked[w] him and said, "What is this dream you had? Will your mother and I and your brothers actually come and bow down to the ground before you?"[x] [11]His brothers were jealous of him,[y] but his father kept the matter in mind.[z]

Joseph Sold by His Brothers

[12]Now his brothers had gone to graze their father's flocks near Shechem,[a] [13]and Israel[b] said to Joseph, "As you know, your brothers are grazing the flocks near Shechem.[c] Come, I am going to send you to them."

"Very well," he replied.

[14]So he said to him, "Go and see if all is well with your brothers[d] and with the flocks, and bring word back to me." Then he sent him off from the Valley of Hebron.[e]

When Joseph arrived at Shechem, [15]a man found him wandering around in the fields and asked him, "What are you looking for?"

[16]He replied, "I'm looking for my brothers. Can you tell me where they are grazing their flocks?"

[17]"They have moved on from here," the man answered. "I heard them say, 'Let's go to Dothan.'[f] "

So Joseph went after his brothers and found them near Dothan. [18]But they saw him in the distance, and before he reached them, they plotted to kill him.[g]

[19]"Here comes that dreamer![h]" they said to each other. [20]"Come now, let's kill him and throw him into one of these cisterns[i] and say that a ferocious animal[j] devoured him.[k] Then we'll see what comes of his dreams."[l]

[21]When Reuben[m] heard this, he tried to

Cross references (center column):

37:2 [z]S Ge 30:24
[a]Ge 41:46;
2Sa 5:4
[b]Ge 46:32;
1Sa 16:11; 17:15;
Ps 78:71;
Am 7:15
[c]Ge 35:25
[d]Ge 35:26
[e]1Sa 2:24
37:3 [f]S Ge 17:5
[g]S Ge 25:28
[h]Ge 43:27; 44:20
[i]Ver 23,31,32;
2Sa 13:18-19
[j]Ge 43:34; 45:22;
1Sa 1:4-5; Est 2:9
37:4 [k]S ver 24;
S Ge 27:41;
Ac 7:9
37:5 [l]S Ge 20:3;
S 28:12 [m]ver 10
[n]ver 8
37:7 [o]Ru 2:7,15
[p]ver 9,10;
Ge 27:29; 42:6,9;
43:26,28; 44:14;
50:18; 2Sa 1:2;
9:6
37:8 [q]Ge 41:44;
42:10; 44:16,18;
48:22; 49:26;
Dt 33:16 [r]ver 5
37:9 [s]S ver 7;
Ge 28:12
[t]Rev 12:1
[u]Dt 4:19; 17:3
37:10 [v]ver 5
[w]Ru 2:16; Ps 9:5;
68:30; 106:9;
119:21;
Isa 17:13; 54:9;
Zec 3:2 [x]S ver 7;
S Ge 9:25; S 33:3
37:11 [y]Ge 26:14;
Ac 7:9 [z]Lk 2:19,
51
37:12 [a]S Ge 12:6
37:13 [b]S Ge 17:5
[c]Ge 33:19
37:14 [d]1Sa 17:18
[e]S Ge 13:18
37:17 [f]2Ki 6:13
37:18 [g]1Sa 19:1;
2Ch 24:21;
Ps 31:13,20;
37:12,32;
S Mt 12:14;
Mk 14:1;
Ac 23:12
37:19
[h]S Ge 28:12

37:20 [i]ver 22; Jer 38:6,9 [j]ver 33; Lev 26:6,22; Dt 32:24;
2Ki 17:25; Eze 34:25 [k]ver 31-33; S Ge 4:10 [l]Ge 50:20 37:21
[m]S Ge 29:32

[b]3 The meaning of the Hebrew for *richly ornamented* is uncertain; also in verses 23 and 32.

37:2 *account.* See note on 2:4. The word here introduces the tenth and final main section of Genesis. *Joseph.* The author immediately introduces Joseph, on whom the last cycle of the patriarchal narrative centers. In his generation, he, more than any other, represented Israel—as a people who struggled with God and with men and overcame (see note on 32:28) and as a source of blessing to the nations (see 12:2–3). It is, moreover, through the life of Joseph that the covenant family in Canaan becomes an emerging nation in Egypt, thus setting the stage for the exodus. The story of God's dealings with the patriarchs foreshadows the subsequent Biblical account of God's purpose with Israel. It begins with the election and calling out of Abram from the post-Babel nations and ends with Israel in Egypt (in the person of Joseph) preserving the life of the nations (see 41:57; 50:20). So God would deliver Israel out of the nations (the exodus), eventually to send them on a mission of life to the nations (cf. Mt 28:18–20; Ac 1:8). *a bad report about them.* Doubtless about all his brothers (as the later context indicates), not just the sons of his father's concubines.
37:3 *richly ornamented robe.* A mark of Jacob's favoritism, "the kind of garment the virgin daughters of the king wore" (2Sa 13:18).

37:5 *dream.* See note on 20:3.
37:7 *bowed down.* Joseph's dream would later come true (42:6; 43:26; 44:14).
37:8 *Will you actually rule us?* Joseph would later become the "prince among his brothers" (Dt 33:16) and receive "the rights of the firstborn" (1Ch 5:2), at least the double portion of the inheritance (see note on 25:5), since his father adopted his two sons (48:5).
37:10 *your mother.* Jacob possibly refers to Leah, since Rachel has already died (see 35:19). *bow down . . . before you.* An unsettling echo of a hope expressed earlier to Jacob by his father Isaac (see 27:29).
37:11 *kept the matter in mind.* A hint that Jacob later recalled Joseph's dreams when events brought about their fulfillment. Cf. Mary's equally sensitive response to events during Jesus' boyhood days (Lk 2:19,51).
37:12 *Shechem.* See note on 33:18.
37:17 *Dothan.* Located about 13 miles north of Shechem, Dothan was already an ancient city by this time.
37:19 *dreamer.* The Hebrew for this word means "master of dreams" or "dream expert" and is here used with obvious sarcasm.
37:21 *Reuben . . . tried to rescue him.* As Jacob's firstborn,

rescue him from their hands. "Let's not take his life," he said. *n* 22"Don't shed any blood. Throw him into this cistern *o* here in the desert, but don't lay a hand on him." Reuben said this to rescue him from them and take him back to his father. *p*

23So when Joseph came to his brothers, they stripped him of his robe—the richly ornamented robe *q* he was wearing— 24and they took him and threw him into the cistern. *r* Now the cistern was empty; there was no water in it.

25As they sat down to eat their meal, they looked up and saw a caravan of Ishmaelites *s* coming from Gilead. *t* Their camels were loaded with spices, balm *u* and myrrh, *v* and they were on their way to take them down to Egypt. *w*

26Judah *x* said to his brothers, "What will we gain if we kill our brother and cover up his blood? *y* 27Come, let's sell him to the Ishmaelites and not lay our hands on him; after all, he is our brother, *z* our own flesh and blood. *a*" His brothers agreed.

28So when the Midianite *b* merchants came by, his brothers pulled Joseph up out of the cistern *c* and sold *d* him for twenty shekels *c* of silver *e* to the Ishmaelites, *f* who took him to Egypt. *g*

29When Reuben returned to the cistern and saw that Joseph was not there, he tore his clothes. *h* 30He went back to his brothers and said, "The boy isn't there! Where can I turn now?" *i*

31Then they got Joseph's robe, *j* slaughtered a goat and dipped the robe in the blood. *k* 32They took the ornamented robe *l* back to their father and said, "We found this. Examine it to see whether it is your son's robe."

33He recognized it and said, "It is my son's robe! Some ferocious animal *m* has devoured him. Joseph has surely been torn to pieces." *n*

34Then Jacob tore his clothes, *o* put on sackcloth *p* and mourned for his son many days. *q* 35All his sons and daughters came to comfort him, *r* but he refused to be comforted. *s* "No," he said, "in mourning will I go down to the grave *d* *t* to my son. *u*" So his father wept for him.

36Meanwhile, the Midianites *e* *v* sold Joseph *w* in Egypt to Potiphar, one of Pharaoh's officials, the captain of the guard. *x*

Judah and Tamar

38 At that time, Judah *y* left his brothers and went down to stay with a man of Adullam *z* named Hirah. *a* 2There

37:21 *n*Ge 42:22
37:22 *o*S ver 20
*p*ver 29-30
37:23 *q*ver 3
37:24 *r*S ver 4;
Ge 49:23;
Jer 38:6; 41:7;
Eze 22:27
37:25
*s*S Ge 16:11
*t*S Ge 31:21;
S SS 4:1
*u*Jer 8:22; 22:6;
46:11 *v*Ge 43:11;
Ex 30:23;
Ps 45:8; Pr 7:17;
SS 1:13; Mt 2:11
*w*ver 28;
Ge 105:17
37:26
*x*S Ge 29:35
*y*S Ge 4:10
37:27 *z*Ge 42:21
*a*S Ge 29:14
37:28 *b*S Ge 25:2
*c*Jer 38:13
*d*Ex 21:16
*e*Lev 27:5;
Mt 26:15
*f*S Ge 16:11 *g*ver
36; Ge 39:1;
45:4-5;
Ps 105:17;
Jer 12:6; Ac 7:9
37:29 *h*ver 34;
Ge 44:13;
2Sa 1:11;
2Ki 2:12; 5:7;
11:14; 22:11;
Job 1:20; 2:12;
Isa 36:22; 37:1;
Jer 36:24; 41:5;
Joel 2:13
37:30 *i*ver 22

37:31 *j*S ver 3
*k*Rev 19:13
37:32 *l*S ver 3
37:33 *m*S ver 20
*n*Ge 42:13,38;
44:20,28
37:34 *o*S ver 29
*p*2Sa 3:31;

1Ki 20:31; 21:27; 2Ki 6:30; 19:1,2; Job 16:15; Ps 69:11;
Isa 3:24; 15:3; 22:12; 32:11; 37:1; Jer 48:37; 49:3;
Joel 1:13 *q*Ge 50:3,10,11; Nu 20:29; Dt 34:8 37:35
*r*Job 2:11; 15:11; 16:5; 42:11 *s*2Sa 12:17; Ps 77:2; Jer 31:15
*t*Ge 42:38; 44:22,29,31 *u*2Sa 12:23 37:36 *v*S Ge 25:2 *w*S ver
28 *x*Ge 39:1; 40:3; 41:10,12; 1Sa 22:14 38:1 *y*S Ge 29:35
*z*Jos 12:15; 15:35; 1Sa 22:1; 2Sa 23:13; 2Ch 11:7 *a*ver 12,20

*c*28 That is, about 8 ounces (about 0.2 kilogram)
*d*35 Hebrew *Sheol*   *e*36 Samaritan Pentateuch,
Septuagint, Vulgate and Syriac (see also verse 28);
Masoretic Text *Medanites*

he felt responsible for Joseph. He would later remind his brothers of this day (42:22). Initially Reuben's attempts to influence events seemed successful (30:14–17). But after his arrogant incest with Bilhah (see 35:22 and note) his efforts were always ineffective (see 42:37–38)—demonstrating his loss of the status of firstborn (see 49:3–4). Effective leadership passed to Judah (see vv. 26–27; 43:3–5,8–10; 44:14–34; 46:28; 49:8–12).

37:23–24 Similarly, in Egypt Joseph (though innocent of any wrongdoing) would be stripped of his position of privilege and thrown into prison—also as a result of domestic intrigue (ch. 39). His cloak also would be torn from him and shown to Potiphar, but he would be rescued (41:14).

37:25 *Ishmaelites.* Also called Midianites (v. 28; see Jdg 8:22,24,26) and Medanites (see NIV text note on v. 36). These various tribal groups were interrelated, since Midian and Medan, like Ishmael, were also sons of Abraham (25:2). *Gilead.* See note on 31:21. *balm.* An oil or gum, with healing properties (see Jer 51:8), exuded by the fruit or stems of one or more kinds of small trees. The balm of Gilead was especially effective (see Jer 8:22; 46:11). *myrrh.* Probably to be identified with labdanum, an aromatic gum (see Ps 45:8; Pr 7:17; SS 3:6; 5:13) exuded from the leaves of the cistus rose. Its oil was used in beauty treatments (see Est 2:12), and it was sometimes mixed with wine and drunk to relieve pain (see Mk 15:23). As a gift fit for a king, myrrh was brought to Jesus after his birth (Mt 2:11) and applied to his body after his death (Jn 19:39–40).

37:28 *twenty shekels of silver.* In later times, this amount

was the value of a male of Joseph's age who had been dedicated to the Lord (see Lev 27:5).

37:31–33 Again a slaughtered goat figures prominently in an act of deception (see 27:5–13).

37:34 *tore his clothes.* See v. 29. *put on sackcloth.* Wearing coarse and uncomfortable sackcloth instead of ordinary clothes was a sign of mourning.

37:35 *daughters.* The term can include daughters-in-law (e.g., a daughter-in-law of Jacob is mentioned in 38:2). *grave.* According to some, the Hebrew word *Sheol* (see NIV text note) can also refer in a more general way to the realm of the dead, the netherworld, where, it was thought, departed spirits live (for a description of *Sheol* see, e.g., Job 3:13–19).

37:36 *sold.* "As a slave" (Ps 105:17). The peoples of the Arabian Desert were long involved in international slave trade (cf. Am 1:6,9). *guard.* The Hebrew for this word can mean "executioners" (the captain of which was in charge of the royal prisoners; see 40:4), or it can mean "butchers" (the captain of whom was the chief cook in the royal court; cf. 1Sa 9:23–24).

38:1–30 The unsavory events of this chapter illustrate the danger that Israel as God's separated people faced if they remained among the Canaanites (see 15:16 and note). In Egypt the Israelites were kept separate because the Egyptians despised them (43:32; 46:34). While there, God's people were able to develop into a nation without losing their identity. Judah's actions contrasted with those of Joseph (ch. 39)—demonstrating the moral superiority of Joseph, to

Judah met the daughter of a Canaanite man named Shua.[b] He married her and lay with her; [3]she became pregnant and gave birth to a son, who was named Er.[c] [4]She conceived again and gave birth to a son and named him Onan.[d] [5]She gave birth to still another son and named him Shelah.[e] It was at Kezib that she gave birth to him.

[6]Judah got a wife for Er, his firstborn, and her name was Tamar.[f] [7]But Er, Judah's firstborn, was wicked in the LORD's sight;[g] so the LORD put him to death.[h]

[8]Then Judah said to Onan, "Lie with your brother's wife and fulfill your duty to her as a brother-in-law to produce offspring for your brother."[i] [9]But Onan knew that the offspring would not be his; so whenever he lay with his brother's wife, he spilled his semen on the ground to keep from producing offspring for his brother. [10]What he did was wicked in the LORD's sight; so he put him to death also.[j]

[11]Judah then said to his daughter-in-law[k] Tamar,[l] "Live as a widow in your father's house[m] until my son Shelah[n] grows up."[o] For he thought, "He may die too, just like his brothers." So Tamar went to live in her father's house.

[12]After a long time Judah's wife, the daughter of Shua,[p] died. When Judah had recovered from his grief, he went up to Timnah,[q] to the men who were shearing his sheep,[r] and his friend Hirah the Adullamite[s] went with him.

[13]When Tamar[t] was told, "Your father-in-law is on his way to Timnah to shear his sheep,"[u] [14]she took off her widow's

clothes,[v] covered herself with a veil[w] to disguise herself, and then sat down[x] at the entrance to Enaim, which is on the road to Timnah.[y] For she saw that, though Shelah[z] had now grown up, she had not been given to him as his wife.

[15]When Judah saw her, he thought she was a prostitute,[a] for she had covered her face. [16]Not realizing[b] that she was his daughter-in-law,[c] he went over to her by the roadside and said, "Come now, let me sleep with you."[d]

"And what will you give me to sleep with you?"[e] she asked.

[17]"I'll send you a young goat[f] from my flock," he said.

"Will you give me something as a pledge[g] until you send it?" she asked.

[18]He said, "What pledge should I give you?"

"Your seal[h] and its cord, and the staff[i] in your hand," she answered. So he gave them to her and slept with her, and she became pregnant by him.[j] [19]After she left, she took off her veil and put on her widow's clothes[k] again.

[20]Meanwhile Judah sent the young goat by his friend the Adullamite[l] in order to get his pledge[m] back from the woman, but he did not find her. [21]He asked the men who lived there, "Where is the shrine prostitute[n] who was beside the road at Enaim?"

"There hasn't been any shrine prostitute here," they said.

[22]So he went back to Judah and said, "I didn't find her. Besides, the men who lived

38:2 [b]ver 12; 1Ch 2:3
38:3 [c]ver 6; Ge 46:12; Nu 26:19
38:4 [d]ver 8,9; Ge 46:12; Nu 26:19
38:5 [e]Nu 26:20; 1Ch 2:3; 4:21
38:6 [f]ver 11,13
38:7 [g]S Ge 6:5
[h]ver 10; Ge 46:12; Lev 10:1-2; 1Ch 2:3
38:8 [i]Dt 25:5-6; Ru 4:5; Mt 22:24-28
38:10 [j]S ver 7; Dt 25:7-10
38:11 [k]S Ge 11:31
[l]S ver 6 [m]Ru 1:8 [n]ver 14,26 [o]Ru 1:13
38:12 [p]S ver 2 [q]ver 13; Jos 15:10,57; 19:43; Jdg 14:1, 2; 2Ch 28:18 [r]S Ge 31:19 [s]S ver 1
38:13 [t]S ver 6 [u]S Ge 31:19
38:14 [v]ver 19 [w]S Ge 24:65 [x]Jer 3:2 [y]S ver 12 [z]S ver 11
38:15 [a]Jdg 11:1; 16:1
38:16 [b]Ge 42:23 [c]Lev 18:15; 20:12; Ru 1:6 [d]Ge 39:7,12; 2Sa 13:11 [e]S Ge 30:15
38:17 [f]Jdg 15:1 [g]ver 20
38:18 [h]ver 25; 1Ki 21:8; Est 3:12; 8:8; SS 8:6; Isa 49:16; Jer 22:24; Hag 2:23; 2Co 1:22; Eph 1:13 [i]S Ge 32:10; [j]S Ex 4:2 [k]S Ge 19:32
38:19 [k]ver 14
38:20 [l]S ver 1 [m]ver 17 **38:21** [n]S Ge 19:5; Lev 19:29; Dt 22:21; 23:17; 2Ki 23:7; Hos 4:14

whom leadership in Israel fell in his generation (see 37:5–9).
38:1 *left his brothers.* Joseph was separated from his brothers by force, but Judah voluntarily separated himself to seek his fortune among the Canaanites. *Adullam.* A town southwest of Jerusalem (see 2Ch 11:5,7).
38:3–4 *Er . . . Onan.* The names also appear as designations of tribes in Mesopotamian documents of this time.
38:5 *Kezib.* Probably the same as Aczib (Jos 15:44), three miles west of Adullam. The "men of Cozeba" (another form of the same word) were descendants of Shelah son of Judah (see 1Ch 4:21–22). The Hebrew root of the name means "deception" (see Mic 1:14 and NIV text note), a theme running throughout the story of Jacob and his sons.
38:6 *Judah got a wife for Er.* See note on 21:21.
38:8 A concise description of the custom known as "levirate marriage" (Latin *levir* means "brother-in-law"). Details of the practice are given in Dt 25:5–6, where it is laid down as a legal obligation within Israel (cf. Mt 22:24). The custom is illustrated in Ru 4:5, though there it is extended to the nearest living relative ("kinsman-redeemer," Ru 3:12), since neither Boaz nor the nearer kinsman was a brother-in-law.
38:9 *knew that the offspring would not be his.* Similarly, Ruth's nearest kinsman was fearful that if he married Ruth he

would endanger his own estate (Ru 4:5–6). *spilled his semen on the ground.* A means of birth control sometimes called "onanism" (after Onan).
38:10 *What he did.* His refusal to perform his levirate duty.
38:11 *he thought, "He may die too, just like his brothers."* Thus Judah had no intention of giving Shelah to Tamar (see v. 14).
38:12 *Timnah.* Exact location unknown, but somewhere in the hill country of Judah (see Jos 15:48,57).
38:14 *sat down . . . the road.* Prostitutes (see v. 15) customarily stationed themselves by the roadside (Jer 3:2). *Enaim.* Means "two springs"; probably the same as Enam in the western foothills of Judah (see Jos 15:33–34).
38:18 *seal and its cord.* Probably a small cylinder seal of the type used to sign clay documents by rolling them over the clay. The owner wore it around his neck on a cord threaded through a hole drilled lengthwise through it.
38:21 *shrine prostitute.* The Hebrew here differs from that used for "prostitute" in v. 15. Judah's friend perhaps deliberately used the more acceptable term, since ritual prostitutes enjoyed a higher social status in Canaan than did ordinary prostitutes.

there said, 'There hasn't been any shrine prostitute here.' "

23Then Judah said, "Let her keep what she has,o or we will become a laughing-stock.p After all, I did send her this young goat, but you didn't find her."

24About three months later Judah was told, "Your daughter-in-law Tamar is guilty of prostitution, and as a result she is now pregnant."

Judah said, "Bring her out and have her burned to death!"q

25As she was being brought out, she sent a message to her father-in-law. "I am pregnant by the man who owns these," she said. And she added, "See if you recognize whose seal and cord and staff these are."r

26Judah recognized them and said, "She is more righteous than I,s since I wouldn't give her to my son Shelah.t" And he did not sleep with her again.

27When the time came for her to give birth, there were twin boys in her womb.u 28As she was giving birth, one of them put out his hand; so the midwifev took a scarlet thread and tied it on his wristw and said, "This one came out first." 29But when he drew back his hand, his brother came out,x and she said, "So this is how you have broken out!" And he was named Perez.fy 30Then his brother, who had the scarlet thread on his wrist,z came out and he was given the name Zerah.g a

Joseph and Potiphar's Wife

39 Now Josephb had been taken down to Egypt. Potiphar, an Egyptian who was one of Pharaoh's officials, the captain of the guard,c bought him from the Ishmaelites who had taken him there.d

2The Lord was with Josephe and he prospered, and he lived in the house of his Egyptian master. 3When his master saw that the Lord was with himf and that the Lord gave him success in everything he did,g 4Joseph found favor in his eyesh and became his attendant. Potiphar put him in charge of his household,i and he entrusted to his care everything he owned.j 5From the time he put him in charge of his household and of all that he owned, the Lord blessed the householdk of the Egyptian because of Joseph.l The blessing of the Lord was on everything Potiphar had, both in the house and in the field.m 6So he left in Joseph's care everything he had;n with Joseph in charge, he did not concern himself with anything except the food he ate.

Now Joseph was well-built and handsome,o 7and after a while his master's wife took notice of Joseph and said, "Come to bed with me!"p

8But he refused.q "With me in charge," he told her, "my master does not concern himself with anything in the house; everything he owns he has entrusted to my care.r 9No one is greater in this house than I am.s My master has withheld nothing from me except you, because you are his wife. How then could I do such a wicked thing and sin against God?"t

38:23 over 18
pEx 32:25;
Job 12:4;
Jer 20:7; La 3:14
38:24
qLev 20:10,14;
21:9; Dt 22:21,
22; Jos 7:25;
Jdg 15:6;
1Sa 31:12;
Job 31:11,28;
Eze 16:38
38:25 rS ver 18
38:26 sS a 24:17
tS ver 11
38:27 uGe 25:24
38:28
vS Ge 35:17 wver 30
38:29 xGe 25:26
yGe 46:12;
Nu 26:20,21;
Ru 4:12,18;
2Sa 5:20; 6:8;
Isa 28:21; Mt 1:3
38:30 zver 28
aGe 46:12;
1Ch 2:4;
Ne 11:24
39:1 bS Ge 30:24

cS Ge 37:36
dS Ge 37:25
39:2
eS Ge 21:20,22;
Jos 1:5; 6:27;
Jdg 1:19;
1Sa 18:14; Ac 7:9
39:3 fS Ge 21:22
gver 23;
1Sa 18:14;
2Ki 18:7;
2Ch 20:20;
Ps 1:3; 128:2;
Isa 33:6
39:4 hS Ge 6:8;
S 18:3 iGe 47:6;
1Ki 11:28;
Pr 22:29 jver 8,
22; Ge 40:4;
42:37
39:5 k2Sa 6:11
lS Ge 26:24
mDt 28:3;
Ps 128:4
39:6 nGe 24:2
oS Ge 12:11;
Ex 2:2; 1Sa 9:2;
16:12; 17:42;
Est 2:7; Da 1:4

39:7 pS Ge 38:16; Pr 7:15-18 39:8 qPr 6:23-24 rS ver 4
39:9 sGe 41:33,40 tS Ge 13:13; S Nu 22:34

f29 Perez means breaking out.   g30 Zerah can mean scarlet or brightness.

38:24 have her burned to death. In later times, burning was the legal penalty for prostitution (see Lev 21:9).
38:27–30 For a similarly unusual birth of twin boys see 25:24–26.
38:29 Perez. Became the head of the leading clan in Judah and the ancestor of David (see Ru 4:18–22) and ultimately of Christ (see Mt 1:1–6).
39:1 See 37:36. taken down to Egypt. Joseph's experiences in Egypt, as well as those of his youth in Canaan (see note on 37:23–24), are similar to Israel's national experiences in Egypt. Initially, because of God's blessing, Joseph attains a position of honor (in Potiphar's house); he is then unjustly thrown into prison, his only crime being his attractiveness and moral integrity; and finally he is raised up among the Egyptians as the one who, because God is with him, holds their lives in his hands. Similarly Israel was first received with honor in Egypt (because of Joseph); then she was subjected to cruel bondage, her only crime being God's evident blessings upon her; and finally God raised her up in the eyes of the Egyptians (through the ministry of Moses) as they came fearfully to recognize that these people and their God did indeed hold their lives in their hands. The author of Genesis knew the events of the exodus and shows how the history of God and the patriarchs moved forward to and foreshadowed that event (see also 15:13–16; 48:21–22; 50:24–25). Ishmaelites. See note on 37:25.
39:2–6 See vv. 20–23. Though Joseph's situation changed drastically, God's relationship to him remained the same.
39:2 The Lord was with Joseph. See note on 26:3. This fact, mentioned several times here (vv. 3,21,23), is stressed also by Stephen (Ac 7:9).
39:5 the Lord blessed the household of the Egyptian because of Joseph. The offspring of Abraham are becoming a blessing to the nations (see 12:2–3; 30:27).
39:6 left in Joseph's care everything he had. Joseph had full responsibility for the welfare of Potiphar's house, as later he would have full responsibility in prison (vv. 22–23) and later still in all Egypt (41:41). Always this Israelite came to hold the welfare of his "world" in his hands—but always by the blessing and overruling of God, never by his own wits, as his father Jacob had so long attempted. In the role that he played in Israel's history and in the manner in which he lived it, Joseph was a true representative of Israel.
39:7 took notice of. Looked with desire at. The phrase is used in the same sense in Akkadian in Section 25 of the Code of Hammurapi.
39:9 sin against God. All sin is against God, first and foremost (see Ps 51:4).

10And though she spoke to Joseph day after day, he refused[u] to go to bed with her or even be with her.

11One day he went into the house to attend to his duties,[v] and none of the household servants[w] was inside. 12She caught him by his cloak[x] and said, "Come to bed with me!"[y] But he left his cloak in her hand and ran out of the house.[z]

13When she saw that he had left his cloak in her hand and had run out of the house, 14she called her household servants.[a] "Look," she said to them, "this Hebrew[b] has been brought to us to make sport of us![c] He came in here to sleep with me, but I screamed.[d] 15When he heard me scream for help, he left his cloak beside me and ran out of the house."[e]

16She kept his cloak beside her until his master came home. 17Then she told him this story:[f] "That Hebrew[g] slave[h] you brought us came to me to make sport of me. 18But as soon as I screamed for help, he left his cloak beside me and ran out of the house."

19When his master heard the story his wife told him, saying, "This is how your slave treated me," he burned with anger.[i] 20Joseph's master took him and put him in prison,[j] the place where the king's prisoners were confined.

But while Joseph was there in the prison, 21the LORD was with him;[k] he showed him kindness[l] and granted him favor in the eyes of the prison warden.[m] 22So the warden put Joseph in charge of all those held in the prison, and he was made responsible for all that was done there.[n] 23The warden paid no attention to anything under Joseph's[o] care, because the LORD was with Joseph and gave him success in whatever he did.[p]

The Cupbearer and the Baker

40 Some time later, the cupbearer[q] and the baker[r] of the king of Egypt offended their master, the king of Egypt. 2Pharaoh was angry[s] with his two officials,[t] the chief cupbearer and the chief baker, 3and put them in custody in the house of the captain of the guard,[u] in the same prison where Joseph was confined. 4The captain of the guard[v] assigned them to Joseph,[w] and he attended them.

After they had been in custody[x] for some time, 5each of the two men—the cupbearer and the baker of the king of Egypt, who were being held in prison—had a dream[y] the same night, and each dream had a meaning of its own.[z]

6When Joseph came to them the next morning, he saw that they were dejected. 7So he asked Pharaoh's officials who were in custody[a] with him in his master's house, "Why are your faces so sad today?"[b]

8"We both had dreams," they answered, "but there is no one to interpret them."[c]

Then Joseph said to them, "Do not interpretations belong to God?[d] Tell me your dreams."

9So the chief cupbearer[e] told Joseph his dream. He said to him, "In my dream I saw a vine in front of me, 10and on the vine were three branches. As soon as it budded, it blossomed,[f] and its clusters ripened into grapes. 11Pharaoh's cup was in my hand, and I took the grapes, squeezed them into Pharaoh's cup and put the cup in his hand."

12"This is what it means,[g]" Joseph said to him. "The three branches are three days.[h] 13Within three days[i] Pharaoh will lift up your head[j] and restore you to your position, and you will put Pharaoh's cup in his hand, just as you used to do when you were his cupbearer.[k] 14But when all goes

---

Cross-reference column:

39:10 [u]Est 3:4
39:11 [v]Ex 18:20; Dt 1:18 [w]ver 14
39:12 [x]2Sa 13:11; Pr 7:13 [y]S Ge 38:16 [z]ver 15; Pr 5:8; 2Ti 2:22
39:14 [a]ver 11 [b]S Ge 14:13 [c]S Ge 21:9 [d]Dt 22:24,27
39:15 [e]S ver 12
39:17 [f]Ex 20:16; 23:1,7; Dt 5:20; Ps 101:5 [g]S Ge 14:13 [h]Ge 21:10
39:19 [i]S Ge 34:7; S Est 1:12
39:20 [j]Ge 40:3; 41:10; Ps 105:18
39:21 [k]S Ge 21:20 [l]S Ge 19:19 [m]Ex 3:21; 11:3; 12:36; Est 2:9; Ps 106:46;
Pr 16:7; Da 1:9
39:22 [n]S ver 4
39:23 [o]S Ge 21:20; S Nu 14:43 [p]S ver 3

40:1 [q]ver 9,13, 21; Ne 1:11 [r]ver 16,20
40:2 [s]Pr 16:14, 15; 19:12 [t]Ge 41:10; Est 2:21
40:3 [u]S Ge 37:36; S 39:20
40:4 [v]S Ge 37:36 [w]S Ge 39:4 [x]ver 7; Ge 42:17
40:5 [y]S Ge 20:3 [z]Ge 41:11
40:7 [a]S ver 4 [b]Ne 2:2
40:8 [c]Ge 41:8,15 [d]Ge 41:16,25,28, 32; Dt 29:29; Da 2:22,28,47
40:9 [e]S ver 1
40:10 [f]Isa 27:6; 35:1-2; Hos 14:7
40:12 [g]ver 16; Ge 41:12,15,25; Da 2:36; 4:19 [h]ver 18
40:13 [i]ver 19,20; Jos 1:11; 3:2; Ezr 8:32; Ne 2:11 [j]ver 19 [k]S ver 1

39:10 *though she spoke to Joseph day after day, he refused.* Samson twice succumbed under similar pressure (Jdg 14:17; 16:16–17).

39:14 *this Hebrew.* See v. 17; see also note on 14:13.

39:20–23 See note on vv. 2–6.

39:20 *the place where the king's prisoners were confined.* Though understandably angry (see v. 19), Potiphar put Joseph in the "house of the captain of the guard" (40:3)—certainly not the worst prison available.

40:2 *chief cupbearer.* Would be the divinely appointed agent for introducing Joseph to Pharaoh (see 41:9–14).

40:5 *each dream had a meaning.* Throughout the ancient Near East it was believed that dreams had specific meanings and that proper interpretation of them could help the dreamer predict his future (see note on 20:3). God was beginning

to prepare the way for Joseph's rise in Egypt.

40:8 *interpretations belong to God.* Only God can interpret dreams properly and accurately (see 41:16,25,28; Da 2:28). *Tell me.* Joseph presents himself as God's agent through whom God will make known the revelation contained in their dreams—Israel is God's prophetic people through whom God's revelation comes to the nations (see 18:17 and note; 41:16,28,32).

40:13 *lift up your head and restore you to your position.* See Ps 3:3; 27:6. For this meaning of the idiom "lift up one's head" see 2Ki 25:27 and Jer 52:31, where the Hebrew for "released" in the context of freeing a prisoner means lit. "lifted up the head of."

40:14 *when all goes well with you, remember me.* Unfortunately, the cupbearer "forgot him" (v. 23) until two full years later (see 41:1,9–13).

well with you, remember me[l] and show me kindness;[m] mention me to Pharaoh[n] and get me out of this prison. [15]For I was forcibly carried off from the land of the Hebrews,[o] and even here I have done nothing to deserve being put in a dungeon."[p]

[16]When the chief baker[q] saw that Joseph had given a favorable interpretation,[r] he said to Joseph, "I too had a dream: On my head were three baskets[s] of bread.[h] [17]In the top basket were all kinds of baked goods for Pharaoh, but the birds were eating them out of the basket on my head."

[18]"This is what it means," Joseph said. "The three baskets are three days.[t] [19]Within three days[u] Pharaoh will lift off your head[v] and hang you on a tree.[i] [w] And the birds will eat away your flesh."[x]

[20]Now the third day[y] was Pharaoh's birthday,[z] and he gave a feast for all his officials.[a] He lifted up the heads of the chief cupbearer and the chief baker[b] in the presence of his officials: [21]He restored the chief cupbearer[c] to his position,[d] so that he once again put the cup into Pharaoh's hand,[e] [22]but he hanged[j] the chief baker,[f] just as Joseph had said to them in his interpretation.[g]

[23]The chief cupbearer, however, did not remember Joseph; he forgot him.[h]

Pharaoh's Dreams

41 When two full years had passed, Pharaoh had a dream:[i] He was standing by the Nile,[j] [2]when out of the river there came up seven cows, sleek and fat,[k] and they grazed among the reeds.[l] [3]After them, seven other cows, ugly and gaunt, came up out of the Nile and stood beside those on the riverbank. [4]And the cows that were ugly and gaunt ate up the seven sleek, fat cows. Then Pharaoh woke up.[m]

[5]He fell asleep again and had a second dream: Seven heads of grain,[n] healthy and good, were growing on a single stalk. [6]Af-

ter them, seven other heads of grain sprouted—thin and scorched by the east wind.[o] [7]The thin heads of grain swallowed up the seven healthy, full heads. Then Pharaoh woke up;[p] it had been a dream.

[8]In the morning his mind was troubled,[q] so he sent for all the magicians[r] and wise men of Egypt. Pharaoh told them his dreams, but no one could interpret them for him.[s]

[9]Then the chief cupbearer said to Pharaoh, "Today I am reminded of my shortcomings.[t] [10]Pharaoh was once angry with his servants,[u] and he imprisoned me and the chief baker in the house of the captain of the guard.[v] [11]Each of us had a dream the same night, and each dream had a meaning of its own.[w] [12]Now a young Hebrew[x] was there with us, a servant of the captain of the guard.[y] We told him our dreams, and he interpreted them for us, giving each man the interpretation of his dream.[z] [13]And things turned out exactly as he interpreted them to us: I was restored to my position, and the other man was hanged.[i] [a]"

[14]So Pharaoh sent for Joseph, and he was quickly brought from the dungeon.[b] When he had shaved[c] and changed his clothes,[i] he came before Pharaoh.

[15]Pharaoh said to Joseph, "I had a dream, and no one can interpret it.[e] But I have heard it said of you that when you hear a dream you can interpret it."[f]

[16]"I cannot do it," Joseph replied to Pharaoh, "but God will give Pharaoh the answer he desires."[g]

[17]Then Pharaoh said to Joseph, "In my dream I was standing on the bank of the Nile,[h] [18]when out of the river there came up seven cows, fat and sleek, and they

Cross references (center column)

40:14 [l]1Sa 25:31; Lk 23:42 [m]S Ge 19:19; 1Sa 20:14,42; 2Sa 9:1; 1Ki 2:7 [n]ver 23; Ge 41:9; Ecc 9:15
40:15 [o]S Ge 14:13 [p]Ge 39:20; Job 13:27
40:16 [q]S ver 1 [r]S ver 12 [s]Am 8:1-2
40:18 [t]ver 12
40:19 [u]ver 13 [v]S ver 13 [w]ver 22; Dt 21:22-23; Est 2:23; 7:10 [x]Dt 28:26; 1Sa 17:44; 2Sa 21:10; 1Ki 14:11; 16:4; 21:24; Eze 39:4
40:20 [y]S ver 13 [z]Mt 14:6-10 [a]Est 2:18; Mk 6:21 [b]S ver 1
40:21 [c]S ver 1 [d]2Ki 25:27; Jer 52:31 [e]ver 13
40:22 [f]S ver 19 [g]Ge 41:13; Ps 105:19
40:23 [h]S ver 14; S Ecc 1:11
41:1 [i]S Ge 20:3 [j]ver 17; S Ge 2:14; Ex 1:22; 2:5; 7:15
41:2 [k]ver 26; Jer 5:28 [i]ver 18; Ex 2:3; Job 40:21; Isa 19:6
41:4 [m]ver 7
41:5 [n]Jos 13:3; 2Ki 4:42; 1Ch 13:5; Isa 23:3; Jer 2:18
41:6 [o]Ex 10:13; 14:21; Job 6:26; 11:2; 15:2; Ps 11:6; 48:7; Isa 11:15; 17:8; Jer 4:11; 18:17; Eze 19:12; 27:26; Hos 12:1; 13:15; Jnh 4:8
41:7 [p]ver 4
41:8 [q]Job 7:14; Da 2:1,3; 4:5,19 [r]Ex 7:11,22; Da 1:20; 2:2,27; 4:7; 5:7 [s]ver 24; S Ge 40:8; Da 4:18
41:10 [u]S Ge 40:2 [v]S Ge 37:36; S 39:20
41:11 [w]Ge 40:5 41:12 [x]S Ge 14:13; 39:17 [y]S Ge 37:36; 40:4 [z]S Ge 40:12 41:13 [i]S Ge 40:22 41:14 [b]Ps 105:20 [c]Isa 18:2,7 [d]S Ge 35:2; 45:22; Ru 3:3; 2Sa 12:20 41:15 [e]S Ge 40:8 [f]S Ge 40:12; Da 4:18; 5:16 41:16 [g]S Ge 40:8
41:17 [h]S ver 1

Footnotes (center/bottom)

[h]16 Or three wicker baskets   [i]19 Or and impale you on a pole   [j]22,13 Or impaled

---

40:15 *dungeon.* Probably hyperbole to reflect Joseph's despair (see note on 39:20). Since the same Hebrew word is translated "cistern" in 37:24, the author Genesis has established a link with Joseph's earlier experience at the hands of his brothers.

40:19 *lift off your head.* A grisly pun based on the same idiom used in v. 13.

40:20 *Pharaoh's birthday.* Centuries later, the birthday of Herod the tetrarch would become the occasion for another beheading (see Mt 14:6-10).

41:2 *out of the river there came up seven cows.* Cattle often submerged themselves up to their necks in the Nile to escape sun and insects.

41:6 *scorched by the east wind.* The Palestinian sirocco

(in Egypt the khamsin), which blows in from the desert (see Hos 13:15) in late spring and early fall, often withers vegetation (see Isa 40:7; Eze 17:10).

41:8 *his mind was troubled.* See 40:6-7. *magicians.* Probably priests who claimed to possess occult knowledge. *no one could interpret them.* See Da 2:10-11.

41:13 *things turned out exactly as he interpreted them.* Because his words were from the Lord (see Ps 105:19).

41:14 *Pharaoh sent for Joseph.* Effecting his permanent release from prison (see Ps 105:20). *shaved.* Egyptians were normally smooth-shaven, while Palestinians wore beards (see 2Sa 10:5; Jer 41:5).

41:16 *I cannot do it ... but God will give Pharaoh the answer.* See 40:8; Da 2:27-28,30; 2Co 3:5.

grazed among the reeds. [i] 19After them, seven other cows came up—scrawny and very ugly and lean. I had never seen such ugly cows in all the land of Egypt. 20The lean, ugly cows ate up the seven fat cows that came up first. 21But even after they ate them, no one could tell that they had done so; they looked just as ugly as before. Then I woke up.

22"In my dreams I also saw seven heads of grain, full and good, growing on a single stalk. 23After them, seven other heads sprouted—withered and thin and scorched by the east wind. 24The thin heads of grain swallowed up the seven good heads. I told this to the magicians, but none could explain it to me. [j] "

25Then Joseph said to Pharaoh, "The dreams of Pharaoh are one and the same. [k] God has revealed to Pharaoh what he is about to do. [l] 26The seven good cows [m] are seven years, and the seven good heads of grain are seven years; it is one and the same dream. 27The seven lean, ugly cows that came up afterward are seven years, and so are the seven worthless heads of grain scorched by the east wind: They are seven years of famine. [n]

28"It is just as I said to Pharaoh: God has shown Pharaoh what he is about to do. [o] 29Seven years of great abundance [p] are coming throughout the land of Egypt, 30but seven years of famine [q] will follow them. Then all the abundance in Egypt will be forgotten, and the famine will ravage the land. [r] 31The abundance in the land will not be remembered, because the famine that follows it will be so severe. 32The reason the dream was given to Pharaoh in two forms is that the matter has been firmly decided [s] by God, and God will do it soon. [t]

33"And now let Pharaoh look for a discerning and wise man [u] and put him in

charge of the land of Egypt. [v] 34Let Pharaoh appoint commissioners [w] over the land to take a fifth [x] of the harvest of Egypt during the seven years of abundance. [y] 35They should collect all the food of these good years that are coming and store up the grain under the authority of Pharaoh, to be kept in the cities for food. [z] 36This food should be held in reserve for the country, to be used during the seven years of famine that will come upon Egypt, [a] so that the country may not be ruined by the famine."

37The plan seemed good to Pharaoh and to all his officials. [b] 38So Pharaoh asked them, "Can we find anyone like this man, one in whom is the spirit of God [k]?" [c]

39Then Pharaoh said to Joseph, "Since God has made all this known to you, [d] there is no one so discerning and wise as you. [e] 40You shall be in charge of my palace, [f] and all my people are to submit to your orders. [g] Only with respect to the throne will I be greater than you. [h]"

Joseph in Charge of Egypt

41So Pharaoh said to Joseph, "I hereby put you in charge of the whole land of Egypt." [i] 42Then Pharaoh took his signet ring [j] from his finger and put it on Joseph's finger. He dressed him in robes [k] of fine linen [l] and put a gold chain around his neck. [m] 43He had him ride in a chariot [n] as his second-in-command, [1o] and men shouted before him, "Make way [m]!" [p] Thus he put him in charge of the whole land of Egypt. [q]

44Then Pharaoh said to Joseph, "I am Pharaoh, but without your word no one will lift hand or foot in all Egypt." [r] 45Phar-

---

41:18 [i]S ver 2
41:24 [j]S ver 8
41:25
[k]S Ge 40:12
[l]S Ge 40:8;
Isa 46:11;
Da 2:45
41:26 [m]S ver 2
41:27
[n]S Ge 12:10
41:28 [o]S Ge 40:8
41:29 [p]ver 47
41:30 [q]ver 54;
Ge 45:6,11;
47:13; Ps 105:16
[r]ver 56;
S Ge 12:10
41:32 [s]Da 2:5
[t]S Ge 40:8
41:33 [u]ver 39

[v]S Ge 39:9
41:34 [w]Est 2:3
[x]Ge 47:24,26;
1Sa 8:15 [y]ver 48;
Ge 47:14
41:35 [z]ver 48
41:36 [a]ver 56;
Ge 42:6; 47:14
41:37 [b]Ge 45:16;
Est 2:4; Isa 19:11
41:38
[c]Nu 27:18;
Dt 34:9; Da 2:11;
4:8,8,9,18; 5:11,
14
41:39 [d]Da 2:11;
5:11 [e]ver 33
41:40 [f]1Ki 4:6;
2Ki 15:5;
Isa 22:15; 36:3
[g]S Ge 39:9;
Ps 105:21-22;
Ac 7:10 [h]Est 10:3
41:41 [i]ver 43,55;
Ge 42:6; 45:8,13,
26; Est 8:2;
Jer 40:7; Da 6:3
41:42
[j]S Ge 24:22;
Est 3:10; 8:2,8
[k]1Sa 17:38; 18:4;
1Ki 19:19;
Est 6:8,11;
Da 5:29; Zec 3:4
[l]Ex 25:4;
Est 8:15; Da 5:29
[m]Ps 73:6; SS 4:9;
Isa 3:18;
Eze 16:11;
Da 5:7,16,29
41:43
[n]Ge 46:29; 50:9;
Isa 2:7; 22:18
[o]Est 10:3
[p]Est 6:9 [q]S ver 41
41:44
[r]S Ge 37:8; Est
10:2; Ps 105:22

---

[k]38 Or *of the gods*   [l]43 Or *in the chariot of his second-in-command;* or *in his second chariot*
[m]43 Or *Bow down*

41:27 *seven years of famine.* See Ac 7:11. Long famines were rare in Egypt because of the regularity of the annual overflow of the Nile, but not uncommon elsewhere (see 2Ki 8:1). According to the NT, the great famine in the time of Elijah lasted three and a half years (Jas 5:17), thus half of seven years; it had been cut short by Elijah's intercession (1Ki 18:42; Jas 5:18).
41:32 Repetition of a divine revelation was often used for emphasis (see 37:5-9; Am 7:1-6,7-9; 8:1-3).
41:38 *in whom is the spirit of God.* See NIV text note. The word "spirit" should probably not be capitalized in such passages, since reference to the Holy Spirit would be out of character in statements by pagan rulers.
41:40 *You shall be in charge.* Pharaoh took Joseph's advice (see v. 33) and decided that Joseph himself should be "ruler over Egypt" (Ac 7:10; see also Ps 105:21). *all my people are to submit to your orders.* More lit. "at your command all my people are to kiss (you)"—i.e., kiss your hands or feet in an

act of homage and submission (see Ps 2:12 and note).
41:42 Three symbols of transfer and/or sharing of royal authority, referred to also in Est 3:10 (signet ring); Est 6:11 (robe); and Da 5:7,16,29 (gold chain).
41:43 *second-in-command.* The position was probably that of vizier, the highest executive office below that of the king himself. *Make way!* See NIV text note. The Hebrew here may be an Egyptian imperative of a Semitic loanword, meaning "Bow the knee!"
41:45 *gave Joseph the name Zaphenath-Paneah.* As a part of assigning Joseph an official position within his royal administration (see note on 1:5). Pharaoh presumed to use this marvelously endowed servant of the Lord for his own royal purposes—as a later Pharaoh would attempt to use divinely blessed Israel for the enrichment of Egypt (Ex 1). He did not recognize that Joseph served a Higher Power, whose kingdom and redemptive purposes are being advanced. (The meaning of Joseph's Egyptian name is uncertain.) *Asenath.*

aoh gave Joseph ^{s} the name Zaphenath-Paneah and gave him Asenath daughter of Potiphera, priest ^{t} of On,$^{n\,u}$ to be his wife. ^{v} And Joseph went throughout the land of Egypt.

^{46}Joseph was thirty years old ^{w} when he entered the service ^{x} of Pharaoh king of Egypt. And Joseph went out from Pharaoh's presence and traveled throughout Egypt. ^{47}During the seven years of abundance ^{y} the land produced plentifully. ^{48}Joseph collected all the food produced in those seven years of abundance in Egypt and stored it in the cities. ^{z} In each city he put the food grown in the fields surrounding it. ^{49}Joseph stored up huge quantities of grain, like the sand of the sea; ^{a} it was so much that he stopped keeping records because it was beyond measure.

^{50}Before the years of famine came, two sons were born to Joseph by Asenath daughter of Potiphera, priest of On. ^{b} ^{51}Joseph named his firstborn ^{c} Manasseh $^{o\,d}$ and said, "It is because God has made me forget all my trouble and all my father's household." ^{52}The second son he named Ephraim $^{p\,e}$ and said, "It is because God has made me fruitful ^{f} in the land of my suffering."

^{53}The seven years of abundance in Egypt came to an end, ^{54}and the seven years of famine ^{g} began, ^{h} just as Joseph had said. There was famine in all the other lands, but in the whole land of Egypt there was food. ^{55}When all Egypt began to feel the famine, ^{i} the people cried to Pharaoh for food. Then Pharaoh told all the Egyptians, "Go to Joseph and do what he tells you." ^{j} ^{56}When the famine had spread over the whole country, Joseph opened the store-

houses and sold grain to the Egyptians, ^{k} for the famine ^{l} was severe throughout Egypt. ^{m} ^{57}And all the countries came to Egypt to buy grain from Joseph, ^{n} because the famine was severe in all the world. ^{o}

Joseph's Brothers Go to Egypt

42 When Jacob learned that there was grain in Egypt, ^{p} he said to his sons, "Why do you just keep looking at each other?" ^{2}He continued, "I have heard that there is grain in Egypt. Go down there and buy some for us, ^{q} so that we may live and not die." ^{r}

^{3}Then ten of Joseph's brothers went down to buy grain ^{s} from Egypt. ^{4}But Jacob did not send Benjamin, ^{t} Joseph's brother, with the others, because he was afraid that harm might come to him. ^{u} ^{5}So Israel's sons were among those who went to buy grain, ^{v} for the famine was in the land of Canaan ^{w} also. ^{x}

^{6}Now Joseph was the governor of the land, ^{y} the one who sold grain to all its people. ^{z} So when Joseph's brothers arrived, they bowed down to him with their faces to the ground. ^{a} ^{7}As soon as Joseph saw his brothers, he recognized them, but he pretended to be a stranger and spoke harshly to them. ^{b} "Where do you come from?" ^{c} he asked.

"From the land of Canaan," they replied, "to buy food."

^{8}Although Joseph recognized his brothers, they did not recognize him. ^{d} ^{9}Then he

---

41:45 ^{s}Est 2:7
^{t}Ex 2:16
^{u}Eze 30:17 vver 50; Ge 46:20,27
41:46
wS Ge 37:2
x1Sa 8:11; 16:21; Pr 22:29; Da 1:19
41:47 yver 29
41:48 zS ver 34
41:49 aS Ge 12:2
41:50 bS ver 45
41:51 cGe 48:14, 18,20; 49:3
dGe 46:20; 48:1; 50:23; Nu 1:34; Dt 33:17; Jos 4:12; 17:1; 1Ch 7:14
41:52 eGe 46:20; 48:1,5; 50:23; Nu 1:32; 26:28; Dt 33:17; Jos 14:4; Jdg 5:14; 1Ch 7:20; 2Ch 30:1; Ps 60:7; Jer 7:15; Ob 1:19
fS Ge 17:6
41:54
gS Ge 12:10
hAc 7:11
41:55 iDt 32:24; 2Ch 20:9; Isa 51:19; Jer 5:12; 27:8; 42:16; 44:27
/S ver 41; Jn 2:5
41:56 kS ver 36
lS Ge 12:10
mS ver 30
41:57 nGe 42:5; 47:15
oS Ge 12:10
42:1 pAc 7:12
42:2 qGe 43:2,4; 44:25 rver 19,33; Ge 43:8; 47:19; Ps 33:18-19
42:3 sver 10; Ge 43:20
42:4 tS Ge 35:18 uver 38
42:5 vS Ge 41:57 wver 13,29; Ge 31:18; 45:17 xS Ge 12:10; S Dt 32:24; Ac 7:11
42:6
yS Ge 41:41; S Ne 5:14

zS Ge 41:36 aS Ge 33:3 **42:7** bver 30 cS Ge 29:4 **42:8** dGe 37:2

n45 That is, Heliopolis; also in verse 50
o51 Manasseh sounds like and may be derived from the Hebrew for forget. p52 Ephraim sounds like the Hebrew for twice fruitful.

The name is Egyptian and probably means "She belongs to (the goddess) Neith." Potiphera. Not the same person as "Potiphar" (37:36; 39:1); the name (also Egyptian) means "he whom (the sun-god) Ra has given." On. Located ten miles northeast of modern Cairo, it was called Heliopolis ("city of the sun") by the Greeks and was an important center for the worship of Ra, who had a temple there. Potiphera therefore bore an appropriate name.

41:46 thirty years old. In just 13 years (see 37:2), Joseph had become second-in-command (v. 43) in Egypt.

41:49 like the sand of the sea. A simile also for the large number of offspring promised to Abraham and Jacob (see 22:17; 32:12).

41:52 Ephraim. The meaning of the name (see NIV text note) reflects the fact that God gave Joseph "two" (see v. 50) sons.

41:57 all the world. The known world from the writer's perspective (the Middle East). This description of the famine in the time of Joseph echoes the author's description of the flood in the time of Noah. God saved only Noah and his family from the flood, so that Noah became the new (after Adam) father of the race. With the call of Abram out of the

post-flood and post-Babel nations, God once more singled out one man, now to be the father of his special people. God promised that, through this man and his descendants, "all peoples on earth will be blessed" (12:3). The author highlights the fact that in this new crisis hope rested with one of these descendants.

42:2–3 Stephen refers to this incident (Ac 7:12).

42:4 did not send Benjamin, Joseph's brother. Their mother Rachel had died (35:19), and Jacob thought Joseph also was dead (37:33). Jacob did not want to lose Benjamin, the remaining son of his beloved Rachel.

42:5 famine was in the land of Canaan also. As in the time of Abram (see 12:10 and note).

42:6 bowed down. In fulfillment of Joseph's dreams (see 37:7,9).

42:8 Joseph recognized his brothers. Although at least 20 years had passed since he had last seen them (see 37:2; 41:46,53–54), they had been adults at the time and their appearance had not changed much. they did not recognize him. Joseph, a teenager at the time of his enslavement, was now an adult in an unexpected position of authority, wearing Egyptian clothes and speaking to his brothers through an

remembered his dreams[e] about them and said to them, "You are spies![f] You have come to see where our land is unprotected."[g]

[10]"No, my lord,[h]" they answered. "Your servants have come to buy food.[i] [11]We are all the sons of one man. Your servants[j] are honest men,[k] not spies.[l]"

[12]"No!" he said to them. "You have come to see where our land is unprotected."[m]

[13]But they replied, "Your servants[n] were twelve brothers, the sons of one man, who lives in the land of Canaan.[o] The youngest is now with our father, and one is no more."[p]

[14]Joseph said to them, "It is just as I told you: You are spies![q] [15]And this is how you will be tested: As surely as Pharaoh lives,[r] you will not leave this place unless your youngest brother comes here.[s] [16]Send one of your number to get your brother;[t] the rest of you will be kept in prison,[u] so that your words may be tested to see if you are telling the truth.[v] If you are not, then as surely as Pharaoh lives, you are spies![w]" [17]And he put them all in custody[x] for three days.

[18]On the third day, Joseph said to them, "Do this and you will live, for I fear God:[y] [19]If you are honest men,[z] let one of your brothers stay here in prison,[a] while the rest of you go and take grain back for your starving households.[b] [20]But you must bring your youngest brother to me,[c] so that your words may be verified and that you may not die." This they proceeded to do.

[21]They said to one another, "Surely we are being punished because of our brother.[d] We saw how distressed he was when he pleaded with us for his life, but we would not listen; that's why this distress[e] has come upon us."

[22]Reuben replied, "Didn't I tell you not to sin against the boy?[f] But you wouldn't listen! Now we must give an accounting[g] for his blood."[h] [23]They did not realize[i] that Joseph could understand them,[j] since he was using an interpreter.

[24]He turned away from them and began to weep,[k] but then turned back and spoke to them again. He had Simeon taken from them and bound before their eyes.[l]

[25]Joseph gave orders to fill their bags with grain,[m] to put each man's silver back in his sack,[n] and to give them provisions[o] for their journey.[p] After this was done for them, [26]they loaded their grain on their donkeys[q] and left.

[27]At the place where they stopped for the night one of them opened his sack to get feed for his donkey,[r] and he saw his silver in the mouth of his sack.[s] [28]"My silver has been returned," he said to his brothers. "Here it is in my sack."

Their hearts sank[t] and they turned to each other trembling[u] and said, "What is this that God has done to us?"[v]

[29]When they came to their father Jacob in the land of Canaan,[w] they told him all that had happened to them.[x] They said, [30]"The man who is lord over the land spoke harshly to us[y] and treated us as though we were spying on the land.[z] [31]But we said to him, 'We are honest men; we are not spies.[a] [32]We were twelve brothers, sons of one father. One is no more, and the youngest is now with our father in Canaan.'[b]

[33]"Then the man who is lord over the land said to us, 'This is how I will know whether you are honest men: Leave one of your brothers here with me, and take food for your starving households and go.[c] [34]But bring your youngest brother to me so I will know that you are not spies but honest men.[d] Then I will give your brother back to you,[e] and you can trade[q] in the land.[f]'"

[35]As they were emptying their sacks, there in each man's sack was his pouch of silver![g] When they and their father saw the money pouches, they were frightened.[h] [36]Their father Jacob said to them, "You have deprived me of my children. Joseph is no more and Simeon is no more,[i] and now you want to take Benjamin.[j] Everything is against me![k]"

42:9 eS Ge 37:7
fver 14,16,30;
Dt 1:22; Jos 2:1;
6:22 gver 12
42:10 hS Ge 37:8
iS ver 3
42:11 jver 13;
Ge 44:7,9,16,19,
21,31; 46:34;
47:3 kver 15,16,
19,20,34 lver 31
42:12 mver 9
42:13 nS ver 11
oS ver 5;
Ge 46:31; 47:1
pver 24,32,36;
S Ge 37:33; 43:7,
29,33; 44:8;
Jer 31:15
42:14 qS ver 9
42:15 rISa 17:55
sS ver 11;
Ge 43:3,5,7;
44:21,23
42:16 tver 15
uver 19 vS ver 11
wS ver 9
42:17 xS Ge 40:4
42:18
yS Ge 20:11;
S 22:12;
Lev 19:14; 25:43;
2Sa 23:3
42:19 zS ver 11
aver 16 bS ver 2
42:20 cS ver 15
42:21
dGe 37:26-28
eGe 45:5
42:22
fGe 37:21-22
gS Ge 9:5
hGe 45:24
42:23 iGe 38:16
jS Ge 11:7

42:24
kS Ge 29:11
lS ver 13;
Ge 43:14,23
42:25 mGe 43:2
nver 27,35;
Ge 43:12,18,21;
44:1,8 over 40:5
pGe 45:21,23
42:26
qS Ge 32:15;
44:13; 45:17;
1Sa 25:18;
Isa 30:6
42:27 rJdg 19:19;
Job 39:9; Isa 1:3
sS ver 25
42:28 tJos 2:11;
5:1; 7:5
uMk 5:33
vGe 43:23
42:29 wS ver 5
xGe 44:24
42:30 yver 7
zS ver 9
42:31 aver 11
42:32 bS ver 13
42:33 cS ver 2
42:34 dS ver 11
eS ver 24
fGe 34:10
42:35 gS ver 25
hGe 43:18
42:36 iS ver 13
jS ver 24

kJob 3:25; Pr 10:24; Ro 8:31

q34 Or move about freely

interpreter (see v. 23). He was, moreover, shaven in the Egyptian manner (see note on 41:14).
42:10 my lord ... Your servants. Unwittingly, Joseph's brothers again fulfilled his dreams and their own scornful fears (see 37:8).
42:15 As surely as Pharaoh lives. The most solemn oaths were pronounced in the name of the reigning monarch (as here) or of the speaker's deities (Ps 16:4; Am 8:14) or of the Lord himself (Jdg 8:19; 1Sa 14:39,45; 19:6).

42:21 how distressed he was ... distress has come upon us. The brothers realized they were beginning to reap what they had sown (see Gal 6:7).
42:22 See 37:21-22 and note on 37:21.
42:24 He had Simeon taken. Jacob's second son (see 29:32-33) is imprisoned instead of the firstborn Reuben, perhaps because the latter had saved Joseph's life years earlier (37:21-22).

[37]Then Reuben said to his father, "You may put both of my sons to death if I do not bring him back to you. Entrust him to my care,[l] and I will bring him back." [m] [38]But Jacob said, "My son will not go down there with you; his brother is dead [n] and he is the only one left. If harm comes to him [o] on the journey you are taking, you will bring my gray head down to the grave [r p] in sorrow. [q]"

The Second Journey to Egypt

43 Now the famine was still severe in the land. [r] [2]So when they had eaten all the grain they had brought from Egypt, [s] their father said to them, "Go back and buy us a little more food." [t]

[3]But Judah [u] said to him, "The man warned us solemnly, 'You will not see my face again unless your brother is with you.' [v] [4]If you will send our brother along with us, we will go down and buy food for you. [w] [5]But if you will not send him, we will not go down, because the man said to us, 'You will not see my face again unless your brother is with you. [x]'"

[6]Israel [y] asked, "Why did you bring this trouble [z] on me by telling the man you had another brother?"

[7]They replied, "The man questioned us closely about ourselves and our family. 'Is your father still living?' [a] he asked us. 'Do you have another brother?' [b] We simply answered his questions. How were we to know he would say, 'Bring your brother down here'?" [c]

[8]Then Judah [d] said to Israel [e] his father, "Send the boy along with me and we will go at once, so that we and you and our children may live and not die. [f] [9]I myself will guarantee his safety; you can hold me personally responsible for him. [g] If I do not bring him back to you and set him here before you, I will bear the blame [h] before you all my life. [i] [10]As it is, if we had not delayed, [j] we could have gone and returned twice."

[11]Then their father Israel [k] said to them, "If it must be, then do this: Put some of the best products [l] of the land in your bags and take them down to the man as a gift [m]—a little balm [n] and a little honey, some spices [o] and myrrh, [p] some pistachio nuts and almonds. [12]Take double the amount [q] of silver with you, for you must return the silver that was put back into the mouths of your sacks. [r] Perhaps it was a mistake. [13]Take your brother also and go back to the man at once. [s] [14]And may God Almighty [s t] grant you mercy [u] before the man so that he will let your other brother and Benjamin come back with you. [v] As for me, if I am bereaved, I am bereaved." [w]

[15]So the men took the gifts and double the amount of silver, [x] and Benjamin also. They hurried [y] down to Egypt and presented themselves [z] to Joseph. [16]When Joseph saw Benjamin [a] with them, he said to the steward of his house, [b] "Take these men to my house, slaughter an animal and prepare dinner; [c] they are to eat with me at noon."

[17]The man did as Joseph told him and took the men to Joseph's house. [d] [18]Now the men were frightened [e] when they were taken to his house. [f] They thought, "We were brought here because of the silver that was put back into our sacks [g] the first time. He wants to attack us [h] and overpower us and seize us as slaves [i] and take our donkeys. [j]"

[19]So they went up to Joseph's steward [k] and spoke to him at the entrance to the house. [20]"Please, sir," they said, "we came down here the first time to buy food. [l] [21]But at the place where we stopped for the night we opened our sacks and each of us found his silver—the exact weight—in the mouth of his sack. So we have brought it back with us. [m] [22]We have also brought additional silver with us to buy food. We don't know who put our silver in our sacks."

[23]"It's all right," he said. "Don't be

Cross references (center column)

42:37 [l]S Ge 39:4
[m]Ge 43:9; 44:32
42:38
[n]S Ge 37:33 [o]ver 4 [p]S Ge 37:35
[q]Ge 44:29,34; 48:7
43:1 [r]S Ge 12:10
43:2 [s]Ge 42:25
[t]S Ge 42:2
43:3 [u]ver 8; Ge 44:14,18; 46:28
[v]S Ge 42:15
43:4 [w]S Ge 42:2
43:5
[x]S Ge 42:15; 44:26; 2Sa 3:13
43:6 [y]ver 8,11; S Ge 17:5
[z]S Ge 34:30
43:7 [a]ver 27; Ge 45:3
[b]S Ge 42:13; 44:19
[c]S Ge 42:15
43:8 [d]S ver 3; S Ge 29:35 [e]S ver 6 [f]S Ge 42:2; Ps 33:18-19
43:9 [g]1Sa 23:20 [h]Ge 44:10,17
[i]S Ge 42:37; Phm 1:18-19
43:10 [j]Ge 45:9
43:11 [k]S ver 6

[l]S Ge 24:10
[m]S Ge 32:13
[n]S Ge 37:25; Eze 27:17
[o]Ex 30:23; 1Ki 10:2; Eze 27:22
[p]S Ge 37:25
43:12 [q]ver 15; Ex 22:4,7; Pr 6:31
[r]S Ge 42:25
43:13 [s]ver 3
43:14 [t]S Ge 17:1
[u]Dt 13:17; Ps 25:6
[v]S Ge 42:24
[w]2Sa 18:33; Est 4:16
43:15 [x]ver 12
[y]Ge 45:9,13
[z]Ge 47:2,7; Mt 2:11
43:16
[a]S Ge 35:18 [b]ver 17,24,26; Ge 44:1,4,12; 2Sa 19:17; Isa 22:15 [c]ver 31; Lk 15:23
43:17 [d]S ver 16
43:18 [e]Ge 42:35 [f]Ge 44:14 [g]S Ge 42:25 [h]S Ge 32:11 [i]Ge 44:9,16,33; 50:18 [j]Ge 34:28
43:19 [k]ver 16
43:20 [l]S Ge 42:3

43:21 [m]S ver 15; S Ge 42:25

[r]38 Hebrew Sheol   [s]14 Hebrew El-Shaddai

Study notes (bottom)

42:37 both of my sons. Reuben's generous offer as security for Benjamin's safety (see note on 37:21).
43:3 Judah said. From this point on, Judah became the spokesman for his brothers (see vv. 8–10; 44:14–34; 46:28). His tribe would become preeminent among the 12 (see 49:8–10), and he would be an ancestor of Jesus (see Mt 1:2,17; Lk 3:23,33).
43:9 Judah offered himself as security for Benjamin's safety—an even more generous gesture than that of Reuben (see 42:37 and note).
43:11 take them . . . as a gift. A customary practice when approaching one's superior, whether political (see 1Sa

16:20), military (see 1Sa 17:18) or religious (see 2Ki 5:15). balm . . . myrrh. See 37:25 and note. honey. Either that produced by bees, or an inferior substitute made by boiling grape or date juice down to a thick syrup. pistachio nuts. Mentioned only here in the Bible; the fruit of a small, broad-crowned tree that is native to Asia Minor, Syria and Palestine but not to Egypt.
43:14 God Almighty. See note on 17:1. if I am bereaved, I am bereaved. Cf. Esther's similar phrase of resignation in Est 4:16.
43:21 The brothers' statement to Joseph's steward compressed the details (see 42:27,35).

afraid. Your God, the God of your father,[n] has given you treasure in your sacks;[o] I received your silver." Then he brought Simeon out to them.[p]

24The steward took the men into Joseph's house,[q] gave them water to wash their feet[r] and provided fodder for their donkeys. 25They prepared their gifts[s] for Joseph's arrival at noon,[t] because they had heard that they were to eat there.

26When Joseph came home,[u] they presented to him the gifts[v] they had brought into the house, and they bowed down before him to the ground.[w] 27He asked them how they were, and then he said, "How is your aged father[x] you told me about? Is he still living?"[y]

28They replied, "Your servant our father[z] is still alive and well." And they bowed low[a] to pay him honor.[b]

29As he looked about and saw his brother Benjamin, his own mother's son,[c] he asked, "Is this your youngest brother, the one you told me about?"[d] And he said, "God be gracious to you,[e] my son." 30Deeply moved[f] at the sight of his brother, Joseph hurried out and looked for a place to weep. He went into his private room and wept[g] there.

31After he had washed his face, he came out and, controlling himself,[h] said, "Serve the food."[i]

32They served him by himself, the brothers by themselves, and the Egyptians who ate with him by themselves, because Egyptians could not eat with Hebrews,[j] for that is detestable to Egyptians.[k] 33The men had been seated before him in the order of their ages, from the firstborn[l] to the youngest;[m] and they looked at each other in astonishment. 34When portions were served to them from Joseph's table, Benjamin's portion was five times as much as anyone else's.[n] So they feasted[o] and drank freely with him.

A Silver Cup in a Sack

44 Now Joseph gave these instructions to the steward of his house:[p] "Fill the men's sacks with as much food as they can carry, and put each man's silver in the mouth of his sack.[q] 2Then put my cup,[r] the silver one,[s] in the mouth of the youngest one's sack, along with the silver for his grain." And he did as Joseph said.

3As morning dawned, the men were sent on their way with their donkeys.[t] 4They had not gone far from the city when Joseph said to his steward,[u] "Go after those men at once, and when you catch up with them, say to them, 'Why have you repaid good with evil?[v] 5Isn't this the cup[w] my master drinks from and also uses for divination?[x] This is a wicked thing you have done.'"

6When he caught up with them, he repeated these words to them. 7But they said to him, "Why does my lord say such things? Far be it from your servants[y] to do anything like that![z] 8We even brought back to you from the land of Canaan[a] the silver[b] we found inside the mouths of our sacks.[c] So why would we steal[d] silver or gold from your master's house? 9If any of your servants[e] is found to have it, he will die;[f] and the rest of us will become my lord's slaves.[g]"

10"Very well, then," he said, "let it be as you say. Whoever is found to have it[h] will become my slave;[i] the rest of you will be free from blame."[j]

11Each of them quickly lowered his sack to the ground and opened it. 12Then the steward[k] proceeded to search,[l] beginning with the oldest and ending with the youngest.[m] And the cup was found in Benjamin's sack.[n] 13At this, they tore their clothes.[o] Then they all loaded their donkeys[p] and returned to the city.

Cross references (center column)

43:23
[n]S Ge 24:12;
S 31:5; Ex 3:6
[o]Ge 42:28
[p]S Ge 42:24
43:24 [q]S ver 16
[r]S Ge 18:4
43:25
[s]S Ge 32:13 [t]ver 16
43:26 [u]S ver 16
[v]S Ge 32:13;
Mt 2:11
[w]S Ge 33:3
43:27 [x]S Ge 37:3
[y]S ver 7
43:28 [z]Ge 44:24, 27,30 [a]Ge 18:2;
Ex 18:7
[b]S Ge 37:7
43:29
[c]S Ge 35:18
[d]S Ge 42:13
[e]Nu 6:25;
Ps 67:1; 119:58;
Isa 30:18-19;
33:2
43:30 [f]Jn 11:33,
38 [g]S Ge 29:11
43:31 [h]Ge 45:1;
Isa 30:18; 42:14;
63:15; 64:12
[i]S ver 16
43:32
[j]S Ge 14:13;
Gal 2:12
[k]Ge 46:34;
Ex 8:26
43:33
[l]S Ge 35:23
[m]S Ge 42:13;
44:12
43:34
[n]S Ge 37:3;
S 2Ki 25:30
[o]Lk 15:23
44:1 [p]S Ge 43:16
[q]S Ge 42:25
44:2 [r]ver 5,10,
12,16 [s]ver 8
44:3 [t]Jdg 19:9
44:4 [u]S Ge 43:16
[v]Ps 35:12; 38:20;
109:5; Pr 17:13;
Jer 18:20
44:5 [w]S ver 2
[x]S Ge 30:27;
Dt 18:10-14
44:7 [y]S Ge 42:11
[z]S Ge 18:25
44:8 [a]S Ge 42:13
[b]ver 2
[c]S Ge 42:25;
S 43:15
[d]Ge 31:30
44:9 [e]S Ge 42:11
[f]Ge 31:32 [g]S ver 10; S Ge 43:18
44:10 [h]S ver 2
[i]ver 9,17,33
[j]S Ge 43:9

44:12 [k]S Ge 43:16 [l]S Ge 31:34 [m]S Ge 43:33 [n]ver 2 44:13 [o]S Ge 37:29 [p]S Ge 42:26

43:23 *Your God ... has given you treasure.* The steward spoke better than he knew.
43:24 See note on 18:2.
43:26 *bowed down.* Additional fulfillment of Joseph's dreams (37:7,9; see also 42:6; 43:28).
43:29 *Benjamin, his own mother's son.* Joseph's special relationship to Benjamin is clear. *God be gracious to you.* Later blessings and benedictions would echo these words (see Nu 6:25; Ps 67:1).
43:30 *Joseph ... wept.* Both emotional and sensitive, he wept often (see 42:24; 45:2,14–15; 46:29).
43:32 *Egyptians could not eat with Hebrews.* The taboo was probably based on ritual or religious reasons (see Ex 8:26), unlike the Egyptian refusal to associate with shepherds (see 46:34), which was probably based on social custom.

43:34 *Benjamin's portion was five times as much.* Again reflecting his special status with Joseph (see note on v. 29; see also 45:22).
44:4 *the city.* Identity unknown, though Memphis (about 13 miles south of modern Cairo) and Zoan (in the eastern delta region) have been suggested.
44:5 *divination.* See v. 15; see also note on 30:27.
44:9 *If any of your servants is found to have it, he will die.* Years earlier, Jacob had given Laban a similar rash response (see 31:32 and note).
44:10 The steward softened the penalty contained in the brothers' proposal.
44:12 *beginning with the oldest and ending with the youngest.* For a similar building up of suspense see 31:33.
44:13 *tore their clothes.* A sign of distress and grief (see 37:29).

¹⁴Joseph was still in the house^q when Judah^r and his brothers came in, and they threw themselves to the ground before him. ^s ¹⁵Joseph said to them, "What is this you have done?^t Don't you know that a man like me can find things out by divination?^u"

¹⁶"What can we say to my lord?^v" Judah^w replied. "What can we say? How can we prove our innocence?^x God has uncovered your servants'^y guilt. We are now my lord's slaves^z—we ourselves and the one who was found to have the cup. ^a"

¹⁷But Joseph said, "Far be it from me to do such a thing!^b Only the man who was found to have the cup will become my slave. ^c The rest of you, go back to your father in peace." ^d

¹⁸Then Judah^e went up to him and said: "Please, my lord,^f let your servant speak a word to my lord. Do not be angry^g with your servant, though you are equal to Pharaoh himself. ¹⁹My lord asked his servants,^h 'Do you have a father or a brother?'ⁱ ²⁰And we answered, 'We have an aged father, and there is a young son born to him in his old age.^j His brother is dead,^k and he is the only one of his mother's sons left, and his father loves him.'^l

²¹"Then you said to your servants,^m 'Bring him down to me so I can see him for myself.'ⁿ ²²And we said to my lord,^o 'The boy cannot leave his father; if he leaves him, his father will die.'^p ²³But you told your servants, 'Unless your youngest brother comes down with you, you will not see my face again.'^q ²⁴When we went back to your servant my father,^r we told him what my lord^s had said. ^t

²⁵"Then our father said, 'Go back and buy a little more food.'^u ²⁶But we said, 'We cannot go down. Only if our youngest brother is with us will we go. We cannot see the man's face unless our youngest brother is with us.'^v

²⁷"Your servant my father^w said to us,

'You know that my wife bore me two sons. ^x ²⁸One of them went away from me, and I said, "He has surely been torn to pieces."^y And I have not seen him since. ^z ²⁹If you take this one from me too and harm comes to him, you will bring my gray head down to the grave^{†a} in misery.'^b

³⁰"So now, if the boy is not with us when I go back to your servant my father^c and if my father, whose life is closely bound up with the boy's life,^d ³¹sees that the boy isn't there, he will die. ^e Your servants^f will bring the gray head of our father down to the grave^g in sorrow. ³²Your servant guaranteed the boy's safety to my father. I said, 'If I do not bring him back to you, I will bear the blame before you, my father, all my life!'^h

³³"Now then, please let your servant remain here as my lord's slaveⁱ in place of the boy,^j and let the boy return with his brothers. ³⁴How can I go back to my father if the boy is not with me? No! Do not let me see the misery^k that would come upon my father." ^l

Joseph Makes Himself Known

45 Then Joseph could no longer control himself^m before all his attendants, and he cried out, "Have everyone leave my presence!" ⁿ So there was no one with Joseph when he made himself known to his brothers. ²And he wept^o so loudly that the Egyptians heard him, and Pharaoh's household heard about it. ^p

³Joseph said to his brothers, "I am Joseph! Is my father still living?"^q But his brothers were not able to answer him,^r because they were terrified at his presence. ^s

⁴Then Joseph said to his brothers, "Come close to me." ^t When they had done so, he said, "I am your brother Joseph, the one you sold into Egypt!^u ⁵And

---

44:14 ^qGe 43:18
^rver 16;
S Ge 29:35;
S 43:3 ^sS Ge 33:3
44:15
^tS Ge 12:18
^uS Ge 30:27
44:16 ^vver 22,
24; S Ge 37:8
^wS ver 14
^xPs 26:6; 73:13
^yS Ge 42:11
^zS Ge 43:18
^aS ver 2
44:17
^bS Ge 18:25
^cS ver 10
^dS Ge 43:9
44:18
^eS Ge 29:35
^fS ver 16
^gS Ge 18:30
44:19
^hS Ge 42:11
ⁱS Ge 43:7
44:20 ^jS Ge 37:3
^kS Ge 37:33
^lS Ge 42:13
44:21
^mS Ge 42:11
ⁿS Ge 42:15
44:22 ^oS ver 16
^pS Ge 37:35
44:23
^qS Ge 42:15;
43:5
44:24
^rS Ge 43:28
^sS ver 16
^tGe 42:29
44:25 ^uS Ge 42:2
44:26 ^vS Ge 43:5
44:27
^wS Ge 43:28
44:28
^xGe 46:19
^yS Ge 37:33
^zGe 45:26,28;
46:30; 48:11
44:29
^aS Ge 37:35
^bS Ge 42:38
44:30
^cS Ge 43:28
^d1Sa 18:1;
2Sa 1:26
44:31 ^eS ver 22
^fS Ge 42:11
^gS Ge 37:35
44:32
^hS Ge 42:37
44:33 ⁱS ver 10;
S Ge 43:18
^jJn 15:13
44:34
^kS Ge 42:38
^lEst 8:6
45:1
^mS Ge 43:31
ⁿ2Sa 13:9
45:2 ^oS Ge 29:11
^pver 16; Ac 7:13
45:3 ^qS Ge 43:7
^rver 15

^sGe 44:20; Job 21:6; 23:15; Mt 17:6; Mk 6:49-50 **45:4**
^tGe 27:21-22 ^uGe 37:28

[†]29 Hebrew *Sheol*; also in verse 31

44:14 *threw themselves to the ground before him.* Further fulfillment of Joseph's dreams in 37:7,9 (see 42:6; 43:26, 28).

44:16 *God has uncovered your servants' guilt.* Like Joseph's steward (see note on 43:23), Judah spoke better than he knew—or perhaps his words had a double meaning (see 42:21).

44:18 *Judah . . . said.* See note on 43:3. *lord . . . servant.* See note on 42:10. *you are equal to Pharaoh.* Words more flattering than true (see 41:40,43).

44:30 *whose life is closely bound up with the boy's life.* The Hebrew underlying this clause is later used of Jonathan's becoming "one in spirit with David" (1Sa 18:1).

44:33 *in place of the boy.* Judah's willingness to be a

substitute for Benjamin helped make amends for his role in selling Joseph (see 37:26-27).

44:34 *Do not let me see the misery.* Judah remembers an earlier scene (37:34-35).

45:2 *wept.* See vv. 14-15; see also 43:30 and note.

45:3 *brothers . . . were terrified.* Either because they thought they were seeing a ghost or because they were afraid of what Joseph would do to them.

45:4 *I am your brother Joseph.* See v. 3; Ac 7:13. This time Joseph emphasized his relationship to them. *you sold.* See note on 37:28.

45:5 *God sent me.* See vv. 7-9; Ac 7:9. God had a purpose to work through the brothers' thoughtless and cruel act (see Ac 2:23; 4:28).

now, do not be distressed[v] and do not be angry with yourselves for selling me here,[w] because it was to save lives that God sent me ahead of you.[x] [6]For two years now there has been famine[y] in the land, and for the next five years there will not be plowing and reaping. [7]But God sent me ahead of you to preserve for you a remnant[z] on earth and to save your lives by a great deliverance.[u][a]

[8]"So then, it was not you who sent me here, but God.[b] He made me father[c] to Pharaoh, lord of his entire household and ruler of all Egypt.[d] [9]Now hurry[e] back to my father and say to him, 'This is what your son Joseph says: God has made me lord of all Egypt. Come down to me; don't delay.[f] [10]You shall live in the region of Goshen[g] and be near me—you, your children and grandchildren, your flocks and herds, and all you have.[h] [11]I will provide for you there,[i] because five years of famine[j] are still to come. Otherwise you and your household and all who belong to you will become destitute.'[k]

[12]"You can see for yourselves, and so can my brother Benjamin,[l] that it is really I who am speaking to you.[m] [13]Tell my father about all the honor accorded me in Egypt[n] and about everything you have seen. And bring my father down here quickly.[o]"

[14]Then he threw his arms around his brother Benjamin and wept, and Benjamin[p] embraced him,[q] weeping. [15]And he kissed[r] all his brothers and wept over them.[s] Afterward his brothers talked with him.[t]

[16]When the news reached Pharaoh's palace that Joseph's brothers had come,[u] Pharaoh and all his officials[v] were pleased.[w] [17]Pharaoh said to Joseph, "Tell your brothers, 'Do this: Load your animals[x] and return to the land of Canaan,[y] [18]and bring your father and your families back to me. I will give you the best of the land of Egypt[z] and you can enjoy the fat of the land.'[a]

[19]"You are also directed to tell them, 'Do this: Take some carts[b] from Egypt for your children and your wives, and get your father and come. [20]Never mind about your belongings,[c] because the best of all Egypt[d] will be yours.'"

[21]So the sons of Israel did this. Joseph gave them carts,[e] as Pharaoh had commanded, and he also gave them provisions for their journey.[f] [22]To each of them he gave new clothing,[g] but to Benjamin he gave three hundred shekels[v] of silver and five sets of clothes.[h] [23]And this is what he sent to his father: ten donkeys[i] loaded with the best things[j] of Egypt, and ten female donkeys loaded with grain and bread and other provisions for his journey.[k] [24]Then he sent his brothers away, and as they were leaving he said to them, "Don't quarrel on the way!"[l]

[25]So they went up out of Egypt[m] and came to their father Jacob in the land of Canaan.[n] [26]They told him, "Joseph is still alive! In fact, he is ruler of all Egypt."[o] Jacob was stunned; he did not believe them.[p] [27]But when they told him everything Joseph had said to them, and when he saw the carts[q] Joseph had sent to carry him back, the spirit of their father Jacob revived. [28]And Israel said, "I'm convinced![r] My son Joseph is still alive. I will go and see him before I die."[s]

Jacob Goes to Egypt

46 So Israel[t] set out with all that was his, and when he reached Beer-

45:5 [v]Ge 42:21 [w]Ge 42:22 [x]ver 7-8; Ge 50:20; Job 10:12; Ps 105:17
45:6 [y]S Ge 41:30
45:7 [z]2Ki 19:4, 30,31; Ezr 9:8, 13; Isa 1:9; 10:20,21; 11:11, 16; 46:3; Jer 6:9; 42:2; 50:20; Mic 4:7; 5:7; Zep 2:7 [a]S ver 5; Ge 49:18; Ex 15:2; 1Sa 14:45; 2Ki 13:5; Est 4:14; Isa 25:9; Mic 7:7
45:8 [b]ver 5 [c]Jdg 17:10; 2Ki 6:21; 13:14 [d]S Ge 41:41
45:9 [e]S Ge 43:15 [f]Ge 43:10; Ac 7:14
45:10 [g]Ge 46:28, 34; 47:1,11,27; 50:8; Ex 8:22; 9:26; 10:24 [h]Ge 46:6-7
45:11 [i]Ge 47:12; 50:21 [j]S Ge 41:30 [k]Ps 102:17
45:12 [l]S Ge 35:18 [m]Mk 6:50
45:13 [n]S Ge 41:41 [o]S Ge 43:15; Ac 7:14
45:14 [p]S Ge 35:18 [q]S Ge 29:13
45:15 [r]S Ge 29:11; Lk 15:20 [s]S Ge 29:11,13; S 46:4 [t]ver 3
45:16 [u]S ver 2; Ac 7:13 [v]Ge 50:7 [w]S Ge 41:37
45:17 [x]S Ge 42:26 [y]S Ge 42:5
45:18 [z]ver 20; Ge 20:15; 46:34; 47:6,11,27; Jer 40:4 [a]Ezr 9:12; Ps 37:19; Isa 1:19
45:19 [b]ver 21, 27; Ge 46:5; Nu 7:3-8
45:20 [c]Ge 46:6, 32 [d]S ver 18
45:21 [e]S ver 19 [f]S Ge 42:25
45:22 [g]S Ge 24:53

[h]S Ge 37:3; S 41:14; Jdg 14:12,13; 2Ki 5:22 45:23 [i]S Ge 42:26 [j]S Ge 24:10 [k]S Ge 42:25 45:24 [l]Ge 42:21-22 45:25 [m]Ge 13:1 [n]Ge 42:29 45:26 [o]S Ge 41:41 [p]S Ge 44:28; 1Ki 10:7 45:27 [q]S ver 19 45:28 [r]Lk 16:31 [s]S Ge 44:28 46:1 [t]ver 5

[u]7 Or save you as a great band of survivors   [v]22 That is, about 7 1/2 pounds (about 3.5 kilograms)

45:6 Joseph was now 39 years old (see 41:46,53).
45:7 a remnant. Although none had been lost, they had escaped a great threat to them all; so Joseph called them a remnant in the confidence that they would live to produce a great people.
45:8 father. A title of honor given to viziers (see note on 41:43) and other high officials (in the Apocrypha see 1 Maccabees 11:32). All three titles of Joseph in this verse were originally Egyptian.
45:9 hurry back . . . don't delay. Joseph is anxious to see Jacob as soon as possible (see v. 13).
45:10 Goshen. A region in the eastern part of the Nile delta, it was very fertile (see v. 18) and remains so today.
45:12 I . . . am speaking. Not through an interpreter as before (see 42:23).

45:14 wept. See 43:30 and note.
45:15 his brothers talked with him. In intimate fellowship and friendship, rather than hostility or fear, for the first time in over 20 years (see 37:2 and note on 45:6).
45:18 you can enjoy the fat of the land. An echo of Isaac's blessing on Jacob (see 27:28).
45:22 to Benjamin he gave . . . five sets of clothes. See note on 43:34. shekels. See note on 20:16.
45:24 Don't quarrel. Joseph wanted nothing to delay their return (see note on v. 9), and he wanted them to avoid mutual accusation and recrimination concerning the past.
46:1 set out. Probably from the family estate at Hebron (see 35:27). when he reached Beersheba, he offered sacrifices. Abraham and Isaac had also worshiped the Lord there (see 21:33; 26:23–25).

sheba,[u] he offered sacrifices[v] to the God of his father Isaac.[w]

[2]And God spoke to Israel[x] in a vision at night[y] and said, "Jacob! Jacob!"

"Here I am,"[z] he replied.

[3]"I am God, the God of your father,"[a] he said. "Do not be afraid[b] to go down to Egypt,[c] for I will make you into a great nation[d] there.[e] [4]I will go down to Egypt with you, and I will surely bring you back again.[f] And Joseph's own hand will close your eyes.[g]"

[5]Then Jacob left Beersheba,[h] and Israel's[i] sons took their father Jacob and their children and their wives in the carts[j] that Pharaoh had sent to transport him. [6]They also took with them their livestock and the possessions[k] they had acquired[l] in Canaan, and Jacob and all his offspring went to Egypt.[m] [7]He took with him to Egypt[n] his sons and grandsons and his daughters and granddaughters—all his offspring.[o]

[8]These are the names of the sons of Israel[p] (Jacob and his descendants) who went to Egypt:

Reuben the firstborn[q] of Jacob.
[9]The sons of Reuben:[r]
Hanoch, Pallu,[s] Hezron and Carmi.[t]
[10]The sons of Simeon:[u]
Jemuel,[v] Jamin, Ohad, Jakin, Zohar[w] and Shaul the son of a Canaanite woman.
[11]The sons of Levi:[x]
Gershon,[y] Kohath[z] and Merari.[a]
[12]The sons of Judah:[b]
Er,[c] Onan,[d] Shelah, Perez[e] and Zerah[f] (but Er and Onan had died in the land of Canaan).[g]
The sons of Perez:[h]
Hezron and Hamul.[i]
[13]The sons of Issachar:[j]
Tola, Puah,[w][k] Jashub[x][l] and Shimron.
[14]The sons of Zebulun:[m]

Sered, Elon and Jahleel.

[15]These were the sons Leah bore to Jacob in Paddan Aram,[y][n] besides his daughter Dinah.[o] These sons and daughters of his were thirty-three in all.

[16]The sons of Gad:[p]
Zephon,[z][q] Haggi, Shuni, Ezbon, Eri, Arodi and Areli.
[17]The sons of Asher:[r]
Imnah, Ishvah, Ishvi and Beriah.
Their sister was Serah.
The sons of Beriah:
Heber and Malkiel.

[18]These were the children born to Jacob by Zilpah,[s] whom Laban had given to his daughter Leah[t]—sixteen in all.

[19]The sons of Jacob's wife Rachel:[u]
Joseph and Benjamin.[v] [20]In Egypt, Manasseh[w] and Ephraim[x] were born to Joseph[y] by Asenath daughter of Potiphera, priest of On.[a][z]

[21]The sons of Benjamin:[a]
Bela, Beker, Ashbel, Gera, Naaman, Ehi, Rosh, Muppim, Huppim and Ard.[b]

[22]These were the sons of Rachel[c] who were born to Jacob—fourteen in all.

[23]The son of Dan:[d]
Hushim.[e]
[24]The sons of Naphtali:[f]
Jahziel, Guni, Jezer and Shillem.
[25]These were the sons born to Jacob by Bilhah,[g] whom Laban had given to his daughter Rachel[h]—seven in all.

Cross references (center column):

46:1 [u]S Ge 21:14
[v]S Ge 31:54
[w]S Ge 31:42
46:2 [x]S Ge 17:5
[y]S Ge 15:1
[z]S Ge 22:1
46:3 [a]S Ge 28:13
[b]S Ge 15:1
[c]Ge 26:2
[d]S Ge 12:2
[e]Ex 1:7
46:4 [f]S Ge 15:16; S 28:13 [g]ver 29; Ge 45:14-15; 50:1
46:5 [h]S Ge 21:14 [i]ver 1 / S Ge 45:19
46:6 [k]S Ge 45:20 [l]S Ge 12:5
[m]Nu 20:15; Dt 26:5; Jos 24:4; 1Sa 12:8; Ps 105:23; Isa 52:4; Ac 7:15
46:7 [n]Ge 13:10 over 6; Ge 45:10
46:8 [p]S Ge 35:26; Ex 1:1; Nu 26:4 [q]S Ge 29:32
46:9 [r]Ex 6:14; Nu 1:20; 26:7; 1Ch 5:3 [s]Nu 26:5; 1Ch 5:3 [t]Nu 26:6
46:10 [u]S Ge 29:33; Nu 26:14 [v]Ex 6:15; Nu 26:12 [w]Nu 26:13
46:11 [x]S Ge 29:34; S Nu 3:17 [y]Ex 6:16; Nu 3:21; 4:38 [z]Ex 6:16; Nu 3:27; 1Ch 23:12 [a]Ex 6:19; Nu 3:20,33; 4:29; 26:57; 1Ch 6:19
46:12 [b]S Ge 29:35 [c]S Ge 38:3 [d]S Ge 38:4 [e]S Ge 38:29 [f]S Ge 38:30 [g]S Ge 38:7; Nu 26:19 [h]1Ch 2:5; Mt 1:3 [i]Nu 26:21
46:13 [j]S Ge 30:18 [k]Nu 26:23; Jdg 10:1; 1Ch 7:1 [l]Nu 26:24
46:14 [m]S Ge 30:20
46:15 [n]S Ge 25:20; 29:31-35 [o]S Ge 30:21
46:16 [p]S Ge 30:11; S Nu 1:25 [q]Nu 26:15 **46:17** [r]S Ge 30:13
46:18 [s]Ge 30:10 [t]S Ge 16:1 **46:19** [u]Ge 29:6 [v]Ge 44:27
46:20 [w]S Ge 41:51 [x]S Ge 41:52 [y]Nu 26:28-37 [z]S Ge 41:45
46:21 [a]Nu 26:38-41; 1Ch 7:6-12; 8:1 [b]Nu 26:40; 1Ch 8:3
46:22 [c]S Ge 29:6 **46:23** [d]S Ge 30:6 [e]Nu 26:42 **46:24**
[f]S Ge 30:8 **46:25** [g]Ge 30:8 [h]S Ge 24:61

[w]13 Samaritan Pentateuch and Syriac (see also 1 Chron. 7:1); Masoretic Text *Puvah*   [x]13 Samaritan Pentateuch and some Septuagint manuscripts (see also Num. 26:24 and 1 Chron. 7:1); Masoretic Text *Iob*   [y]15 That is, Northwest Mesopotamia   [z]16 Samaritan Pentateuch and Septuagint (see also Num. 26:15); Masoretic Text *Ziphion*   [a]20 That is, Heliopolis

---

46:2 *God spoke to Israel in a vision at night. Jacob! Jacob!* See note on 22:11. *Here I am.* See note on 22:1.

46:3-4 As Israel and his family were about to leave Canaan, God reaffirmed his covenant promises.

46:3 *I am . . . the God of your father . . . Do not be afraid.* A verbatim repetition of God's statement to Isaac in 26:24. *I will make you into a great nation.* The Lord reaffirmed one aspect of his promise to Abraham (see 12:2). *there.* See Ex 1:7.

46:4 *I will go down to Egypt with you.* God would be with Jacob as he went south to Egypt just as he was with him when he went north to Haran, and would again bring him back as he had done before (see 28:15; see also 15:16; 48:21).

46:8 *These are the names of the sons of Israel . . . who went to Egypt.* Repeated verbatim in Ex 1:1 (see note there), where it introduces the background for the story of the exodus (predicted here in v. 4).

46:15 *Paddan Aram.* See note on 25:20. *thirty-three in all.* There are 34 names in vv. 8-15. To bring the number to 33 the name Ohad in v. 10 should probably be removed, since it does not appear in the parallel lists in Nu 26:12-13; 1Ch 4:24. The Hebrew form of "Ohad" looks very much like that of the nearby "Zohar" (see Ex 6:15), and a later scribe probably added Ohad to the text accidentally.

46:20 See note on 41:45.

26All those who went to Egypt with Jacob—those who were his direct descendants, not counting his sons' wives—numbered sixty-six persons.[i] 27With the two sons[b] who had been born to Joseph in Egypt,[j] the members of Jacob's family, which went to Egypt, were seventy[c] in all.[k]

28Now Jacob sent Judah[l] ahead of him to Joseph to get directions to Goshen.[m] When they arrived in the region of Goshen, 29Joseph had his chariot[n] made ready and went to Goshen to meet his father Israel.[o] As soon as Joseph appeared before him, he threw his arms around his father[p] and wept[p] for a long time.[q]

30Israel[r] said to Joseph, "Now I am ready to die, since I have seen for myself that you are still alive."[s]

31Then Joseph said to his brothers and to his father's household, "I will go up and speak to Pharaoh and will say to him, 'My brothers and my father's household, who were living in the land of Canaan,[t] have come to me.[u] 32The men are shepherds;[v] they tend livestock,[w] and they have brought along their flocks and herds and everything they own.'[x] 33When Pharaoh calls you in and asks, 'What is your occupation?'[y] 34you should answer, 'Your servants[z] have tended livestock from our boyhood on, just as our fathers did.'[a] Then you will be allowed to settle[b] in the region of Goshen,[c] for all shepherds are detestable to the Egyptians.[d]"

47 Joseph went and told Pharaoh, "My father and brothers, with their flocks and herds and everything they own, have come from the land of Canaan[e] and are now in Goshen."[f] 2He chose five of his brothers and presented them[g] before Pharaoh.

3Pharaoh asked the brothers, "What is your occupation?"[h]

"Your servants[i] are shepherds,[j]" they replied to Pharaoh, "just as our fathers were." 4They also said to him, "We have come to live here awhile,[k] because the famine is severe in Canaan[l] and your servants' flocks have no pasture.[m] So now, please let your servants settle in Goshen."[n]

5Pharaoh said to Joseph, "Your father and your brothers have come to you, 6and the land of Egypt is before you; settle[o] your father and your brothers in the best part of the land.[p] Let them live in Goshen. And if you know of any among them with special ability,[q] put them in charge of my own livestock.[r]"

7Then Joseph brought his father Jacob in and presented him[s] before Pharaoh. After Jacob blessed[e] Pharaoh,[t] 8Pharaoh asked him, "How old are you?"

9And Jacob said to Pharaoh, "The years of my pilgrimage are a hundred and thirty.[u] My years have been few and difficult,[v] and they do not equal the years of the pilgrimage of my fathers.[w]" 10Then Jacob blessed[f] Pharaoh[x] and went out from his presence.

11So Joseph settled his father and his brothers in Egypt and gave them property in the best part of the land,[y] the district of Rameses,[z] as Pharaoh directed. 12Joseph also provided his father and his brothers and all his father's household with food, according to the number of their children.[a]

Joseph and the Famine

13There was no food, however, in the whole region because the famine was

---

Cross references (center column):

46:26 [i] ver 5-7; Ex 1:5; Dt 10:22
46:27 [j] S Ge 41:45 [k] S Ge 34:30;
Ac 7:14
46:28 [l] S Ge 43:3
46:29 [m] S Ge 45:10
[n] S Ge 41:43 [o] ver 1,30; S Ge 32:28; 47:29,31
[p] S Ge 29:11
[q] S ver 4; Lk 15:20
46:30 [r] S ver 29
[s] S Ge 44:28
46:31 [t] S Ge 42:13
[u] S Ge 45:10
46:32 [v] Ge 47:3 [w] S Ge 37:2
[x] S Ge 45:20
46:33 [y] Ge 47:3
46:34 [z] S Ge 42:11
[a] Ge 47:3 [b] S Ge 34:10 [c] S Ge 45:10 [d] S Ge 43:32
47:1 [e] S Ge 42:13 [f] S Ge 46:31
47:2 [g] S Ge 43:15
47:3 [h] Ge 46:33

[i] S Ge 42:11 [j] Ge 46:32
47:4 [k] Ru 1:1 [l] S Ge 12:10 [m] 1Ki 18:5; Jer 14:5-6; Joel 1:18 [n] Ge 46:34
47:6 [o] S Ge 34:10 [p] S Ge 13:9; S 45:18 [q] Ex 18:21,25; Dt 1:13,15; 2Ch 19:5; Ps 15:2 [r] S Ge 39:4
47:7 [s] S Ge 43:15 [t] ver 10; 2Sa 14:22; 19:39; 1Ki 8:66
47:9 [u] S Ge 25:7 [v] S Ge 3:17; Ps 39:4; 89:47 [w] Job 8:9; Ps 39:12
47:10 [x] S ver 7
47:11 [y] S Ge 45:10,18 [z] Ex 1:11; 12:37; Nu 33:3,5
47:12 [a] S Ge 45:11

Footnotes (center column):

[b] 27 Hebrew; Septuagint the nine children
[c] 27 Hebrew (see also Exodus 1:5 and footnote); Septuagint (see also Acts 7:14) seventy-five
[d] 29 Hebrew around him   [e] 7 Or greeted   [f] 10 Or said farewell to

---

46:26 All those who went to Egypt with Jacob . . . numbered sixty-six persons. The total of 33 (see v. 15 and note), 16 (v. 18), 14 (v. 22) and 7 (see v. 25) is 70 (v. 27). To arrive at 66 we must subtract Er and Onan, who "had died in the land of Canaan" (v. 12), and Manasseh and Ephraim (v. 20), who "had been born . . . in Egypt" (v. 27).

46:27 seventy. See NIV text note; see also Dt 10:22. Seventy is the ideal and complete number (see Introduction: Literary Features; see also notes on 5:5; 10:2) of Jacob's descendants who would have been in Egypt if Er and Onan had not died earlier (see 38:7–10). For the number 75 in Ac 7:14 see note there.

46:28 Jacob sent Judah ahead. See note on 43:3.

46:29 wept. See 43:30 and note.

46:34 shepherds are detestable to the Egyptians. See note on 43:32.

47:9 pilgrimage. Jacob referred to the itinerant nature of

patriarchal life in general and of his own in particular as he hopefully awaited the fulfillment of the promise of a land (see also Dt 26:5). they do not equal the years of . . . my fathers. Abraham lived to the age of 175 (25:7), Isaac to 180 (35:28).

47:11 best part of the land. See note on 45:10. district of Rameses. The city of Rameses is mentioned in Ex 1:11; 12:37; Nu 33:3,5. The name doubtless refers to the great Egyptian pharaoh Rameses II, who reigned centuries later (the designation here involves an editorial updating). In addition to being known as Goshen (see v. 27), the "district of Rameses" was called the "region of Zoan" in Ps 78:12,43 (see note on Ge 44:4).

47:13 the famine was severe. After the people used up all their money to buy grain (see vv. 14–15), they traded their livestock (vv. 16–17), then their land (v. 20), then themselves (v. 21).

severe; both Egypt and Canaan wasted away because of the famine. [b] [14]Joseph collected all the money that was to be found in Egypt and Canaan in payment for the grain they were buying, [c] and he brought it to Pharaoh's palace. [d] [15]When the money of the people of Egypt and Canaan was gone, [e] all Egypt came to Joseph [f] and said, "Give us food. Why should we die before your eyes? [g] Our money is used up."

[16]"Then bring your livestock, [h]" said Joseph. "I will sell you food in exchange for your livestock, since your money is gone. [i]" [17]So they brought their livestock to Joseph, and he gave them food in exchange for their horses, [j] their sheep and goats, their cattle and donkeys. [k] And he brought them through that year with food in exchange for all their livestock.

[18]When that year was over, they came to him the following year and said, "We cannot hide from our lord the fact that since our money is gone [l] and our livestock belongs to you, [m] there is nothing left for our lord except our bodies and our land. [19]Why should we perish before your eyes [n]—we and our land as well? Buy us and our land in exchange for food, [o] and we with our land will be in bondage to Pharaoh. [p] Give us seed so that we may live and not die, [q] and that the land may not become desolate."

[20]So Joseph bought all the land in Egypt for Pharaoh. The Egyptians, one and all, sold their fields, because the famine was too severe [r] for them. The land became Pharaoh's, [21]and Joseph reduced the people to servitude, [g] [s] from one end of Egypt to the other. [22]However, he did not buy the land of the priests, [t] because they received a regular allotment from Pharaoh and had food enough from the allotment [u] Pharaoh gave them. That is why they did not sell their land.

[23]Joseph said to the people, "Now that I have bought you and your land today for Pharaoh, here is seed [v] for you so you can plant the ground. [w] [24]But when the crop comes in, give a fifth [x] of it to Pharaoh. The other four-fifths you may keep as seed

for the fields and as food for yourselves and your households and your children."

[25]"You have saved our lives," they said. "May we find favor in the eyes of our lord; [y] we will be in bondage to Pharaoh." [z]

[26]So Joseph established it as a law concerning land in Egypt—still in force today—that a fifth [a] of the produce belongs to Pharaoh. It was only the land of the priests that did not become Pharaoh's. [b]

[27]Now the Israelites settled in Egypt in the region of Goshen. [c] They acquired property there [d] and were fruitful and increased greatly in number. [e]

[28]Jacob lived in Egypt [f] seventeen years, and the years of his life were a hundred and forty-seven. [g] [29]When the time drew near for Israel [h] to die, [i] he called for his son Joseph and said to him, "If I have found favor in your eyes, [j] put your hand under my thigh [k] and promise that you will show me kindness [l] and faithfulness. [m] Do not bury me in Egypt, [30]but when I rest with my fathers, [n] carry me out of Egypt and bury me where they are buried." [o]

"I will do as you say," he said.

[31]"Swear to me," [p] he said. Then Joseph swore to him, [q] and Israel [r] worshiped as he leaned on the top of his staff. [h] [s]

Manasseh and Ephraim

48 Some time later Joseph was told, "Your father is ill." So he took his two sons Manasseh and Ephraim [t] along with him. [2]When Jacob was told, "Your son Joseph has come to you," Israel [u] rallied his strength and sat up on the bed.

[3]Jacob said to Joseph, "God Almighty [i] [v] appeared to me at Luz [w] in the land of Canaan, and there he blessed me [x] [4]and said to me, 'I am going to make you fruitful and will increase your numbers. [y] I will make you a community of peoples, and I will give this land [z] as an everlasting possession to your descendants after you.' [a]

[5]"Now then, your two sons born to you

47:13
[b] S Ge 12:10; S 41:30
47:14
[c] S Ge 41:36
[d] S Ge 41:34; Ex 7:23; 8:24; Jer 43:9
47:15
[e] ver 16,18
[f] S Ge 41:57 [ever] 19; Ex 16:3
47:16
[h] ver 18,19
[i] ver 15
47:17
[j] Ex 14:9
[k] S Ge 12:16
47:18
[l] S ver 15
[m] S ver 16
47:19
[n] S ver 15
[o] S ver 16 [p] ver 21,25 [q] S Ge 42:2
47:20
[r] S Ge 12:10
47:21
[s] S ver 19
47:22
[t] ver 26
[u] Dt 14:28-29
47:23
[v] Isa 55:10; 61:11 [w] Ne 5:3
47:24
[x] S Ge 41:34
47:25
[y] S Ge 32:5
[z] S ver 19
47:26
[a] S Ge 41:34
[b] ver 22
47:27
[c] S Ge 45:10,18
[d] S Ge 33:19
[e] S Ge 1:22; S 12:2; S 17:6
47:28
[f] Ps 105:23
[g] S Ge 25:7
47:29
[h] S Ge 46:29
[i] S Ge 27:2
[j] S Ge 32:5
[k] S Ge 24:2
[l] S Ge 19:19
[m] S Ge 24:27; Jdg 1:24; 2Sa 2:6
47:30
[n] S Ge 15:15
[o] S Ge 23:20; S 25:9; S 29:16; 50:25; Ex 13:19; Jos 24:32; Ac 7:15-16
47:31
[p] Ge 21:23; Jos 2:20; Jdg 15:12; 1Sa 24:21; 30:15 [q] S Ge 24:3 [r] S Ge 46:29 [s] S Ge 32:10; Heb 11:21 [fn] 1Ki 1:47
48:1 [t] S Ge 41:52; Heb 11:21
48:2 [u] ver 8,9,11, 14,20
48:3 [v] S Ge 17:1 [w] S Ge 28:19 [x] S Ge 28:13; S 32:29
48:4 [y] S Ge 12:2; S 17:6
[z] S Ge 12:7; S 28:13
[a] S Ge 15:7

47:21 The NIV text note reading would mean that the Egyptians were to move temporarily into the cities until seed could be distributed to them for planting (see v. 23).

47:26 *a fifth of the produce belongs to Pharaoh.* The same was true "during the seven years of abundance" (41:34)—but now all the land on which the produce grew belonged to Pharaoh as well.

47:27 *the Israelites . . . were fruitful and increased greatly in number.* See 35:11-12; 46:3 and notes.

47:29 *put your hand under my thigh.* See 24:2 and note.

In both cases, ties of family kinship are being stressed.

47:30 *rest with my fathers.* See note on 25:8. *bury me where they are buried.* In the cave of Machpelah (see 50:12-13).

47:31 *worshiped as he leaned on the top of his staff.* Quoted in Heb 11:21. Compare 48:2 with the NIV text note reading here.

48:3 *God Almighty.* See note on 17:1. *Luz.* The older name for Bethel (see 28:19).

48:5 *your two sons . . . will be reckoned as mine.* Jacob

in Egypt[b] before I came to you here will be reckoned as mine; Ephraim and Manasseh will be mine,[c] just as Reuben[d] and Simeon[e] are mine. [6]Any children born to you after them will be yours; in the territory they inherit they will be reckoned under the names of their brothers. [7]As I was returning from Paddan,[f] to my sorrow[g] Rachel died in the land of Canaan while we were still on the way, a little distance from Ephrath. So I buried her there beside the road to Ephrath" (that is, Bethlehem).[h]

[8]When Israel[i] saw the sons of Joseph,[j] he asked, "Who are these?"

[9]"They are the sons God has given me here," [k] Joseph said to his father.

Then Israel said, "Bring them to me so I may bless[l] them."

[10]Now Israel's eyes were failing because of old age, and he could hardly see. [m] So Joseph brought his sons close to him, and his father kissed them[n] and embraced them.[o]

[11]Israel[p] said to Joseph, "I never expected to see your face again,[q] and now God has allowed me to see your children too."[r]

[12]Then Joseph removed them from Israel's knees[s] and bowed down with his face to the ground.[t] [13]And Joseph took both of them, Ephraim on his right toward Israel's left hand and Manasseh on his left toward Israel's right hand,[u] and brought them close to him. [14]But Israel[v] reached

out his right hand and put it on Ephraim's head,[w] though he was the younger,[x] and crossing his arms, he put his left hand on Manasseh's head, even though Manasseh was the firstborn.[y]

[15]Then he blessed[z] Joseph and said,

"May the God before whom my fathers
    Abraham and Isaac walked,[a]
the God who has been my shepherd[b]
    all my life to this day,
[16]the Angel[c] who has delivered me from
    all harm[d]
    —may he bless[e] these boys.[f]
May they be called by my name
    and the names of my fathers
    Abraham and Isaac,[g]
and may they increase greatly
    upon the earth."[h]

[17]When Joseph saw his father placing his right hand[i] on Ephraim's head[j] he was displeased; so he took hold of his father's hand to move it from Ephraim's head to Manasseh's head. [18]Joseph said to him, "No, my father, this one is the firstborn; put your right hand on his head."[k]

[19]But his father refused and said, "I know, my son, I know. He too will become a people, and he too will become great.[l] Nevertheless, his younger brother will be greater than he,[m] and his descendants will become a group of nations.[n]"

48:5 [b]S Ge 41:50-52 [c]1Ch 5:1 [d]S Ge 29:32 [e]S Ge 29:33
48:7 [f]S Ge 25:20 [g]S Ge 42:38 [h]Ge 35:19; Ru 1:2; 1Sa 16:4
48:8 [i]S ver 2 /ver 10
48:9 [k]S Ge 33:5 [l]S Ge 24:60
48:10 [m]S Ge 27:1 [n]S Ge 27:27 [o]S Ge 29:13
48:11 [p]S ver 2 [q]S Ge 44:28 [r]Ge 50:23; Job 42:16; Ps 103:17; 128:6
48:12 [s]Ge 50:23; Job 3:12 [t]S Ge 19:1; S 33:3; 37:10
48:13 [u]Ps 16:8; 73:23; 110:1; Mt 25:33
48:14 [v]S ver 2 [w]ver 17,18 [x]S Ge 25:23 [y]S Ge 29:32; S 41:51
48:15 [z]S Ge 24:60 [a]S Ge 5:22 [b]Ge 49:24; 2Sa 5:2; Ps 23:1; 80:1; Isa 40:11; Jer 23:4
48:16 [c]S Ge 16:7 [d]S Ge 24:50; 2Sa 4:9; Ps 71:4; Jer 15:21; Da 3:17 [e]S Ge 28:3 [f]1Ch 5:1; Eze 47:13; Heb 11:21 [g]S Ge 28:13 [h]S Ge 12:2; S 13:14
48:17 [i]ver 13 [j]S ver 14
48:18 [k]S ver 14 **48:19** [l]S Ge 17:20 [m]S Ge 25:23 [n]S Ge 12:2

[j]7 That is, Northwest Mesopotamia

---

would adopt them as his own. *Ephraim and Manasseh.* See v. 1 for the expected order, since Manasseh was Joseph's firstborn (see 41:51). Jacob mentions Ephraim first because he intends to give him the primary blessing and thus "put Ephraim ahead of Manasseh" (v. 20). *mine, just as Reuben and Simeon are mine.* Joseph's first two sons would enjoy equal status with Jacob's first two sons (35:23) and in fact would eventually supersede them. Because of an earlier sinful act (see 35:22 and note), Reuben would lose his birthright to Jacob's favorite son, Joseph (see 49:3–4; 1Ch 5:2), and thus to Joseph's sons (see 1Ch 5:1).

48:6 *children born to you after them will be yours.* They would take the place of Ephraim and Manasseh, whom Jacob had adopted. *in the territory they inherit they will be reckoned under the names of their brothers.* They would perpetuate the names of Ephraim and Manasseh for purposes of inheritance (for a similar provision see 38:8 and note; Dt 25:5–6). Joseph's territory would thus be divided between Ephraim and Manasseh, but Levi (Jacob's third son; see 35:23) would receive "no share of the land" (Jos 14:4). The total number of tribal allotments would therefore remain the same.

48:7 *Paddan.* That is, Paddan Aram, meaning "plain of Aram," another name for Aram Naharaim (see note on 24:10). *Rachel died.* See 35:16–19. Adopted by Joseph's father, Ephraim and Manasseh in effect took the place of other sons whom Joseph's mother, Rachel, might have borne had she not died. *Ephrath.* See note on 35:16.

48:8 *Israel . . . asked, "Who are these?"* Either because he had never met them or because, being old, he could not see them clearly.

48:10 *because of old age . . . he could hardly see.* See note on 27:1. *kissed them and embraced them.* While they were on Jacob's knees (see v. 12), probably symbolizing adoption (see note on 30:3).

48:13–20 See note on Ac 6:6.

48:13 *Manasseh . . . toward Israel's right hand.* Joseph wanted Jacob to bless Manasseh, Joseph's firstborn, by placing his right hand on Manasseh's head.

48:15 *blessed.* As his father Isaac had blessed him (27:27–29). *Joseph.* Used here collectively for Ephraim and Manasseh (see NIV text note on v. 21). *before whom . . . Abraham and Isaac . . . walked.* See notes on 5:22; 17:1. *shepherd.* An intimate royal metaphor for God (see Ps 23:1), used in Genesis only here and in Jacob's later blessing of Joseph (49:24).

48:16 *Angel.* See note on 16:7. The angel—God himself—had earlier blessed Jacob (see 32:29; see also note on 32:24).

48:19 *his younger brother will be greater than he.* See note on 25:23. During the divided monarchy (930–722 B.C.), Ephraim's descendants were the most powerful tribe in the north. "Ephraim" was often used to refer to the northern kingdom as a whole (see, e.g., Isa 7:2,5,8–9; Hos 9:13; 12:1,8).

 ²⁰He blessed⁰ them that day ᵖ and said,

"In your ᵏ name will Israel ᑫ pronounce
this blessing: ʳ
'May God make you like Ephraim ˢ
and Manasseh. ᵗ '"

So he put Ephraim ahead of Manasseh.
²¹Then Israel said to Joseph, "I am about
to die, but God will be with you ᵘ and
take you ¹ back to the land of your ¹ fathers. ᵛ ²²And to you, as one who is over
your brothers, ʷ I give the ridge of land ᵐ x I
took from the Amorites with my sword ʸ
and my bow."

Jacob Blesses His Sons

49:1–28Ref — Dt 33:1–29

49 Then Jacob called for his sons and
said: "Gather around so I can tell
you what will happen to you in days to
come. ᶻ

²"Assemble ᵃ and listen, sons of Jacob;
listen to your father Israel. ᵇ

³"Reuben, you are my firstborn, ᶜ
my might, the first sign of my
strength, ᵈ
excelling in honor, ᵉ excelling in
power.
⁴Turbulent as the waters, ᶠ you will no
longer excel,
for you went up onto your father's
bed,
onto my couch and defiled it. ᵍ

⁵"Simeon ʰ and Levi ⁱ are brothers—

their swords ⁿ are weapons of
violence. ʲ
⁶Let me not enter their council,
let me not join their assembly, ᵏ
for they have killed men in their anger ˡ
and hamstrung ᵐ oxen as they
pleased.
⁷Cursed be their anger, so fierce,
and their fury, ⁿ so cruel! ⁰
I will scatter them in Jacob
and disperse them in Israel. ᵖ

⁸"Judah, ⁰ ᑫ your brothers will praise
you;
your hand will be on the neck ʳ of
your enemies;
your father's sons will bow down to
you. ˢ
⁹You are a lion's cub, ᵘ O Judah; ᵛ
you return from the prey, ʷ my son.
Like a lion he crouches and lies down,
like a lioness—who dares to rouse
him?
¹⁰The scepter will not depart from
Judah, ˣ
nor the ruler's staff from between his
feet,

48:20 ⁰S Ge 24:60; ᵖHeb 11:21; ᑫS ver 2; ʳLev 9:22; Nu 6:23; Dt 10:8; 21:5 ˢNu 2:18; Jer 31:9 ᵗS Ge 41:51; Nu 2:20; 10:23; Ru 4:11 48:21 ᵘS Ge 26:3 ᵛS Ge 15:16; S 28:13; Dt 30:3; Ps 126:1; Jer 29:14; Eze 34:13 48:22 ʷS Ge 37:8 ˣJos 34:32; Jn 4:5 ʸS Ge 34:26 49:1 ᶻNu 24:14; Dt 31:29; Jer 23:20; Da 2:28,45 49:2 ᵃJos 24:1 ᵇver 16,28; Ps 34:11 49:3 ᶜS Ge 29:32; S 41:51 ᵈDt 21:17; Ps 78:51; 105:36 ᵉS Ge 34:19 49:4 ᶠIsa 57:20; Jer 49:23 ᵍS Ge 29:29; S 34:5 49:5 ʰS Ge 29:33 ⁱGe 29:34 ʲS Ge 34:25; S Pr 4:17 49:6 ᵏPs 1:1; Pr 1:15; Eph 5:11 ˡS Ge 34:26 ᵐJos 11:6,9; 2Sa 8:4; 1Ch 18:4 49:7 ⁿGe 34:7 ⁰Ge 34:25 ᵖJos 19:1,9; 21:1-42 49:8 ᑫS Ge 29:35 ʳDt 28:48 ˢS Ge 9:25; 1Ch 5:2

49:9 ᵗNu 24:9; Ps 7:2; 10:9; Eze 19:5; Mic 5:8 ᵘEze 19:2 ᵛRev 5:5 ʷver 27; Nu 23:24; Job 38:39; Ps 17:12; 22:13; 104:21 49:10 ˣNu 24:17,19; Jdg 1:1-2; 20:18; 1Ch 5:2; 28:4; Ps 60:7; 108:8

ᵏ20 The Hebrew is singular. ˡ21 The Hebrew is plural. ᵐ22 Or *And to you I give one portion more than to your brothers—the portion* ⁿ5 The meaning of the Hebrew for this word is uncertain. ⁰8 *Judah* sounds like and may be derived from the Hebrew for *praise.*

48:20 *he put Ephraim ahead of Manasseh.* Jacob, the younger son who struggled with Esau for the birthright and blessing and who preferred the younger sister (Rachel) above the older (Leah), now advanced Joseph's younger son ahead of the older.

48:21 *Joseph.* See note on v. 15. *I am about to die.* Years later, Joseph spoke these words to his brothers (50:24).

48:22 *ridge of land.* The Hebrew for this phrase is identical with the place-name Shechem, where Joseph was later buried in a plot of ground inherited by his descendants (see Jos 24:32; see also 33:19; Jn 4:5). *I took from the Amorites.* Possibly referring to the event of 34:25–29.

49:2–27 Often called the "Blessing of Jacob," this is the longest poem in Genesis. Its various blessings were intended not only for Jacob's 12 sons but also for the tribes that descended from them (see v. 28). For other poetic blessings in Genesis see 9:26–27; 14:19–20; 27:27–29; 27:39–40; 48:15–16; 48:20.

49:4 *Turbulent.* Reuben's descendants were characterized by indecision (see Jdg 5:15–16). *You will no longer excel, for you went up onto your father's bed.* See 35:22 and note; see also notes on 37:21; 48:5.

49:5 *Simeon and Levi are brothers.* They shared the traits of violence, anger and cruelty (see vv. 6–7).

49:7 *I will scatter them.* Fulfilled when Simeon's descendants were absorbed into the territory of Judah (see Jos 19:1, 9) and when Levi's descendants were dispersed throughout

the land, living in 48 towns and the surrounding pasture-lands (see note on 48:6; see also Nu 35:2,7; Jos 14:4; 21:41).

49:8 Cf. 27:29,40; 37:7,9. *Judah, your brothers . . . will bow down to you.* See note on 43:3. As those who would become the leading tribes of southern and northern Israel respectively, Judah and Joseph were given the longest (vv. 8–12 and vv. 22–26) of Jacob's blessings. Judah was the fourth of Leah's sons and also the fourth son born to Jacob (29:35), but Reuben, Simeon and Levi had forfeited their right of leadership. So Jacob assigns leadership to Judah (a son of Leah) but a double portion to Joseph (a son of Rachel). See also 1Ch 5:2.

49:9 *You are a lion's cub.* A symbol of sovereignty, strength and courage. Judah (or Israel) is often pictured as a lion in later times (see Eze 19:1–7; Mic 5:8; and especially Nu 24:9). Judah's greatest descendant, Jesus Christ (see note on 43:3), is himself called "the Lion of the tribe of Judah" (Rev 5:5).

49:10 Though difficult to translate (see NIV text note), the verse has been traditionally understood as Messianic. It was initially fulfilled in David, and ultimately in Christ. *scepter.* See Nu 24:17 and note. *until he comes to whom it belongs.* Repeated almost verbatim in Eze 21:27 in a section where Zedekiah, the last king of Judah, is told to "remove the crown" (Eze 21:26) from his head because dominion over Jerusalem will ultimately be given to the one "to whom it rightfully belongs."

until he comes to whom it belongs[p][y]
and the obedience of the nations is
his.[z]

[11]He will tether his donkey[a] to a vine,
his colt to the choicest branch;[b]
he will wash his garments in wine,
his robes in the blood of grapes.[c]

[12]His eyes will be darker than wine,
his teeth whiter than milk.[q][d]

[13]"Zebulun[e] will live by the seashore
and become a haven for ships;
his border will extend toward
Sidon.[f]

[14]"Issachar[g] is a rawboned[r] donkey
lying down between two
saddlebags.[s][h]

[15]When he sees how good is his resting
place
and how pleasant is his land,[i]
he will bend his shoulder to the
burden[j]
and submit to forced labor.[k]

[16]"Dan[t][l] will provide justice for his
people
as one of the tribes of Israel.[m]

[17]Dan[n] will be a serpent by the roadside,
a viper along the path,[o]
that bites the horse's heels[p]
so that its rider tumbles backward.

[18]"I look for your deliverance,[q]
O LORD.[r]

[19]"Gad[u][s] will be attacked by a band of
raiders,
but he will attack them at their
heels.[t]

[20]"Asher's[u] food will be rich;[v]

he will provide delicacies fit for a
king.[w]

[21]"Naphtali[x] is a doe set free
that bears beautiful fawns.[v][y]

[22]"Joseph[z] is a fruitful vine,[a]
a fruitful vine near a spring,
whose branches[b] climb over a wall.[w]

[23]With bitterness archers attacked him;[c]
they shot at him with hostility.[d]

[24]But his bow remained steady,[e]
his strong arms[f] stayed[x] limber,
because of the hand of the Mighty One
of Jacob,[g]
because of the Shepherd,[h] the Rock
of Israel,[i]

[25]because of your father's God,[j] who
helps[k] you,
because of the Almighty,[y][l] who
blesses you
with blessings of the heavens above,
blessings of the deep that lies
below,[m]
blessings of the breast[n] and womb.[o]

[26]Your father's blessings are greater
than the blessings of the ancient
mountains,

49:10 [y]Eze 21:27
[z]Ps 2:9; 72:8-11;
98:3; 110:2;
Isa 2:4; 26:18;
42:1,4; 45:22;
48:20; 49:6; 51:5
49:11 [a]Jdg 5:10;
10:4; Zec 9:9
[b]Dt 8:8;
2Ki 18:32
[c]Dt 32:14;
Isa 63:2
49:12 [d]SS 5:12
49:13
[e]S Ge 30:20
[f]S Ge 10:19
49:14
[g]S Ge 30:18
[h]Jdg 5:16;
Ps 68:13
49:15
[i]Jos 19:17-23
[j]Eze 29:18
[k]1Ki 4:6; 5:13;
9:21; Isa 14:2;
31:8
49:16 [l]Ge 30:6
[m]S ver 2
49:17 [n]Jdg 18:27
[o]Jer 8:17; Am 9:3
[p]ver 19
49:18
[q]S Ge 45:7;
Ps 40:1-3
[r]Ps 119:166,174
49:19
[s]S Ge 30:11 [t]ver
17
49:20
[u]S Ge 30:13
[v]Isa 25:6

[w]Job 29:6
49:21 [x]S Ge 30:8
[y]Job 39:1
49:22 [z]Ge 30:24
[a]S Ge 17:6;
Ps 128:3;
Eze 19:10
[b]Ps 80:10
49:23 [c]1Ch 10:3
[d]S Ge 27:41;
S 37:24
49:24 [e]Job 29:20
[f]Ps 18:34;
Isa 63:12
[g]Ps 132:2,5;
Isa 1:24; 10:34;
49:26; 60:16
[h]S Ge 48:15
[i]Dt 32:4,15,18,
31; 1Sa 2:2;
2Sa 22:32;

Ps 18:2,31; 19:14; 78:35; 89:26; 144:1; Isa 17:10; 26:4;
30:29; 44:8; Hab 1:12 **49:25** [j]S Ge 28:13 [k]Ex 18:4; Ps 27:9
[l]S Ge 17:1 [m]S Ge 27:28 [n]Isa 66:11 [o]Dt 7:13; 28:4;
Ps 107:38; Pr 10:22

[p]10 Or until Shiloh comes; or until he comes to whom
tribute belongs   [q]12 Or will be dull from wine, / his
teeth white from milk   [r]14 Or strong   [s]14 Or
campfires   [t]16 Dan here means he provides justice.
[u]19 Gad can mean attack and band of raiders.
[v]21 Or free; / he utters beautiful words   [w]22 Or
Joseph is a wild colt, / a wild colt near a spring, / a wild
donkey on a terraced hill   [x]23,24 Or archers will
attack . . . will shoot . . . will remain . . . will stay
[y]25 Hebrew Shaddai

49:11 Judah's descendants would someday enjoy a settled and prosperous life.

49:13 Though landlocked by the tribes of Asher and Manasseh, the descendants of Zebulun were close enough to the Mediterranean (within ten miles) to "feast on the abundance of the seas" (Dt 33:19).

49:17 *Dan will be a serpent.* The treachery of a group of Danites in later times is described in Jdg 18:27. *that bites the horse's heels.* Samson, from the tribe of Dan, would single-handedly hold the Philistines at bay (Jdg 14–16).

49:18 Jacob pauses midway through his series of blessings to utter a brief prayer for God's help.

49:19 *Gad will be attacked.* Located east of the Jordan (see Jos 13:24–27), the descendants of Gad were vulnerable to raids by the Moabites to the south, as the Mesha (see 2Ki 3:4) Stele (a Moabite inscription dating from the late ninth century B.C.) illustrates (see chart on "Ancient Texts Relating to the OT," p. 5).

49:20 *Asher's food will be rich.* Fertile farmlands near the Mediterranean (see Jos 19:24–30) would ensure the prosperity of Asher's descendants.

49:21 *Naphtali is a doe set free.* Perhaps a reference to an independent spirit fostered in the descendants of Naphtali by

their somewhat isolated location in the hill country north of the Sea of Galilee (see Jos 19:32–38).

49:22 *fruitful . . . fruitful.* A pun on the name Ephraim (see NIV text note on 41:52), who Jacob predicted would be greater than Joseph's firstborn son Manasseh (48:19–20). *branches climb over a wall.* Ephraim's descendants tended to expand their territory (see Jos 17:14–18).

49:24 *his bow remained steady.* The warlike Ephraimites (see Jdg 8:1; 12:1) would often prove victorious in battle (see Jos 17:18). *Mighty One of Jacob.* Stresses the activity of God in saving and redeeming his people (see Isa 49:26). *Shepherd.* See note on 48:15. *Rock of Israel.* Israel's sure defense (see Dt 32:4,15,18,30–31)—a figure often used also in Psalms and Isaiah.

49:25 *Almighty.* See note on 17:1. *blessings of the heavens . . . of the deep.* The fertility of the soil watered by rains from above and springs and streams from below. *of the breast and womb.* The fertility of man and animals. For the later prosperity of Ephraim's descendants see Hos 12:8.

49:26 *Joseph . . . the prince among his brothers.* See note on v. 8. Ephraim would gain supremacy, especially over the northern tribes (see Jos 16:9; Isa 7:1–2; Hos 13:1).

than[z] the bounty of the age-old
hills. [p]
Let all these rest on the head of
Joseph, [q]
on the brow of the prince among[a]
his brothers. [r]

27"Benjamin[s] is a ravenous wolf; [t]
in the morning he devours the prey, [u]
in the evening he divides the
plunder." [v]

28All these are the twelve tribes of Israel, [w] and this is what their father said to
them when he blessed them, giving each
the blessing[x] appropriate to him.

The Death of Jacob

29Then he gave them these instructions: [y] "I am about to be gathered to my
people. [z] Bury me with my fathers[a] in the
cave in the field of Ephron the Hittite, [b]
30the cave in the field of Machpelah, [c] near
Mamre[d] in Canaan, which Abraham
bought as a burial place[e] from Ephron the
Hittite, along with the field. [f] 31There
Abraham[g] and his wife Sarah[h] were buried, there Isaac and his wife Rebekah[i]
were buried, and there I buried Leah. [j]

32The field and the cave in it were bought
from the Hittites. [b] [k]"

33When Jacob had finished giving instructions to his sons, he drew his feet up
into the bed, breathed his last and was
gathered to his people. [l]

50 Joseph threw himself upon his father and wept over him and kissed
him. [m] 2Then Joseph directed the physicians in his service to embalm his father
Israel. So the physicians embalmed him, [n]
3taking a full forty days, for that was the
time required for embalming. And the
Egyptians mourned for him seventy days. [o]

4When the days of mourning[p] had
passed, Joseph said to Pharaoh's court, [q]
"If I have found favor in your eyes, [r] speak
to Pharaoh for me. Tell him, 5'My father
made me swear an oath[s] and said, "I am
about to die; [t] bury me in the tomb I dug
for myself[u] in the land of Canaan." [v] Now
let me go up and bury my father; [w] then I
will return.' "

49:26 pHab 3:6
q1Ch 5:1;
Eze 47:13
rS Ge 37:8
49:27 sGe 35:18;
Jdg 20:12-13
tHab 1:8; Zep 3:3
uS ver 9
vNu 31:11;
Dt 2:35; Jos 7:21;
8:2; 22:8;
Jdg 8:24
49:28 wS ver 2
xS Ge 27:4
49:29 yGe 50:16
zS Ge 25:8
aS Ge 15:15;
50:25; 2Sa 2:32;
19:37 bS Ge 25:9
49:30 cS Ge 23:9
dS Ge 13:18
eS Ge 23:4
fS Ge 23:20
49:31 gGe 25:9
hGe 23:19
iS Ge 24:67
jS Ge 23:20;
S 29:16

49:32
kS Ge 10:15
49:33 lS Ge 25:8;
Ac 7:15
50:1
mS Ge 29:11;
S 46:4
50:2 nver 26;
2Ch 16:14;
Mt 26:12;
Mk 16:1;
Jn 19:39-40
50:3
oS Ge 37:34;
S Dt 1:3

50:4 pS Ge 27:41 qver 7 rS Ge 30:27; S 32:5 50:5
sS Ge 24:37 tver 24 u2Sa 18:18; 2Ch 16:14; Isa 22:16;
Mt 27:60 vGe 47:31 wMt 8:21

z26 Or of my progenitors, / as great as a26 Or the
one separated from b32 Or the sons of Heth

49:27 *Benjamin is a ravenous wolf.* See the exploits of
Ehud (Jdg 3:12–30) and Saul and Jonathan (1Sa 11–15). See
Jdg 19–21 for examples of the savagery that characterized
one group of Benjamin's descendants.
49:28 *twelve tribes of Israel.* See note on vv. 2–27.
49:29 *Bury me with my fathers.* See note on 25:8. Jacob
does not forget that the land of his fathers is his God-appoint-
ed homeland (see note on 23:19).
49:33 *was gathered to his people.* See note on 25:8.
50:1 *wept.* See note on 43:30.

50:2 *physicians embalmed him.* Professional embalmers
could have been hired for the purpose, but Joseph perhaps
wanted to avoid involvement with the pagan religious
ceremonies accompanying their services.
50:3 *forty days . . . seventy days.* The two periods probably
overlapped.
50:5 *My father made me swear an oath.* See 47:29–31.
dug. Or "bought," as the Hebrew for this verb is translated in
Hos 3:2 (see also Dt 2:6). *go up.* To Hebron, which has a
higher elevation than Goshen.

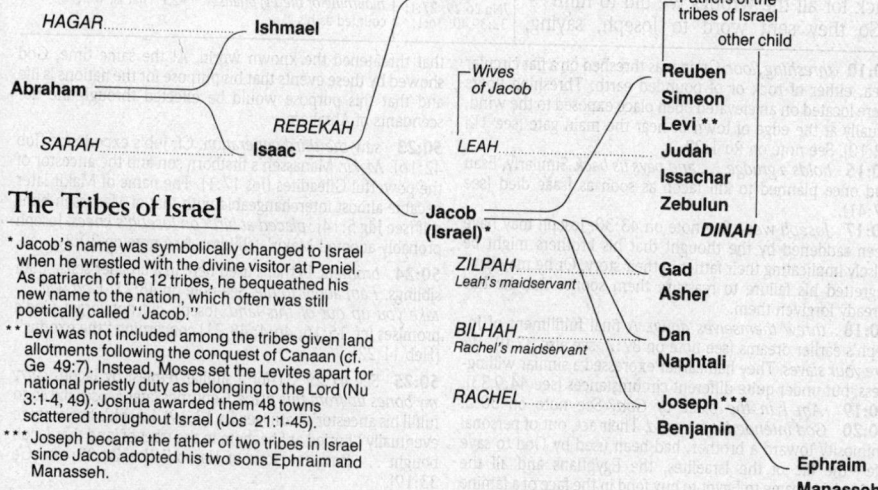

Wives of Abraham

HAGAR .... Ishmael

Abraham

Esau

*Wives
of Jacob*

Reuben
Simeon
Levi **
Judah
Issachar
Zebulun

*Fathers of the
tribes of Israel*

other child

REBEKAH

SARAH .... Isaac

LEAH .... Jacob
(Israel)*

DINAH

The Tribes of Israel

* Jacob's name was symbolically changed to Israel
when he wrestled with the divine visitor at Peniel.
As patriarch of the 12 tribes, he bequeathed his
new name to the nation, which often was still
poetically called "Jacob."

** Levi was not included among the tribes given land
allotments following the conquest of Canaan (cf.
Ge 49:7). Instead, Moses set the Levites apart for
national priestly duty as belonging to the Lord (Nu
3:1-4, 49). Joshua awarded them 48 towns
scattered throughout Israel (Jos 21:1-45).

*** Joseph became the father of two tribes in Israel
since Jacob adopted his two sons Ephraim and
Manasseh.

ZILPAH .... Gad
Leah's maidservant Asher

BILHAH .... Dan
Rachel's maidservant Naphtali

RACHEL .... Joseph***
Benjamin

Ephraim
Manasseh

⁶Pharaoh said, "Go up and bury your father, as he made you swear to do."

⁷So Joseph went up to bury his father. All Pharaoh's officials[x] accompanied him—the dignitaries of his court[y] and all the dignitaries of Egypt— ⁸besides all the members of Joseph's household and his brothers and those belonging to his father's household.[z] Only their children and their flocks and herds were left in Goshen.[a] ⁹Chariots[b] and horsemen[c] also went up with him. It was a very large company.

¹⁰When they reached the threshing floor[c] of Atad, near the Jordan, they lamented loudly and bitterly; [d] and there Joseph observed a seven-day period[e] of mourning[f] for his father.[g] ¹¹When the Canaanites[h] who lived there saw the mourning at the threshing floor of Atad, they said, "The Egyptians are holding a solemn ceremony of mourning."[i] That is why that place near the Jordan is called Abel Mizraim.[d]

¹²So Jacob's sons did as he had commanded them:[j] ¹³They carried him to the land of Canaan and buried him in the cave in the field of Machpelah,[k] near Mamre,[l] which Abraham had bought as a burial place from Ephron the Hittite,[m] along with the field.[n] ¹⁴After burying his father, Joseph returned to Egypt, together with his brothers and all the others who had gone with him to bury his father.[o]

Joseph Reassures His Brothers

¹⁵When Joseph's brothers saw that their father was dead, they said, "What if Joseph holds a grudge[p] against us and pays us back for all the wrongs we did to him?"[q] ¹⁶So they sent word to Joseph, saying,

"Your father left these instructions[r] before he died: ¹⁷'This is what you are to say to Joseph: I ask you to forgive your brothers the sins[s] and the wrongs they committed in treating you so badly.'[t] Now please forgive the sins of the servants of the God of your father.[u]" When their message came to him, Joseph wept.[v]

¹⁸His brothers then came and threw themselves down before him.[w] "We are your slaves,"[x] they said.

¹⁹But Joseph said to them, "Don't be afraid. Am I in the place of God?[y] ²⁰You intended to harm me,[z] but God intended[a] it for good[b] to accomplish what is now being done, the saving of many lives.[c] ²¹So then, don't be afraid. I will provide for you and your children.[d]" And he reassured them and spoke kindly[e] to them.

The Death of Joseph

²²Joseph stayed in Egypt, along with all his father's family. He lived a hundred and ten years[f] ²³and saw the third generation[g] of Ephraim's[h] children.[i] Also the children of Makir[j] son of Manasseh[k] were placed at birth on Joseph's knees.[e] [l]

²⁴Then Joseph said to his brothers, "I am about to die.[m] But God will surely come to your aid[n] and take you up out of this land to the land[o] he promised on oath to Abraham,[p] Isaac[q] and Jacob."[r] ²⁵And Joseph made the sons of Israel swear an oath[s] and said, "God will surely come to

50:7 ×Ge 45:16
yver 4
50:8 zver 14
ªS Ge 45:10
50:9 bS Ge 41:43
50:10
cNu 15:20;
Ru 3:2;
2Sa 24:18;
1Ki 22:10
d2Sa 1:17; 3:33;
2Ch 35:25;
Eze 32:16; Ac 8:2
e1Sa 31:13;
Job 2:13;
Eze 3:15
fS Ge 27:41;
S Lev 10:6
gS Ge 37:34
50:11
hS Ge 10:18
iS Ge 37:34
50:12 jGe 49:29
50:13 kS Ge 23:9
lS Ge 13:18
mS Ge 25:9
nS Ge 23:20
50:14 over 8
50:15
pS Ge 27:41 qver 17; S Ge 9:5;
37:28; Zep 3:11;
1Pe 3:9

50:16 rGe 49:29
50:17 sS Mt 6:14
tS ver 15
uS Ge 28:13
vS Ge 29:11
50:18
wS Ge 37:7
×S Ge 43:18
50:19
yS Ge 30:2;
S Ex 32:34;
Ro 12:19;
Heb 10:30
50:20 zGe 37:20
ªIsa 10:7;
Mic 4:11-12
bRo 8:28
cS Ge 45:5;
Est 4:14
50:21
dS Ge 45:11
eS Ge 34:3;
Eph 4:32
50:22 fS Ge 25:7;
Jos 24:29
50:23 gJob 42:16
hS Ge 41:52
iS Ge 48:11
jNu 26:29; 27:1;
32:39,40; 36:1;

Dt 3:15; Jos 13:31; 17:1; Jdg 5:14 kS Ge 41:51 lS Ge 48:12
50:24 mver 5 nRu 1:20; Ps 35:2; 106:4; Isa 38:14
oS Ge 15:14 pS Ge 13:17 qS Ge 17:19 rS Ge 12:7; S 15:16
50:25 sS Ge 24:37

c9 Or charioteers   d11 Abel Mizraim means
mourning of the Egyptians.   e23 That is, were
counted as his

50:10 *threshing floor.* Grain was threshed on a flat circular area, either of rock or of pounded earth. Threshing floors were located on an elevated open place exposed to the wind, usually at the edge of town or near the main gate (see 1Ki 22:10). See note on Ru 1:22.

50:15 *holds a grudge . . . and pays us back.* Similarly, Esau had once planned to kill Jacob as soon as Isaac died (see 27:41).

50:17 *Joseph wept.* See note on 43:30. Joseph may have been saddened by the thought that his brothers might be falsely implicating their father in their story. Or he may have regretted his failure to reassure them sooner that he had already forgiven them.

50:18 *threw themselves down.* A final fulfillment of Joseph's earlier dreams (see note on 37:7; see also 37:9). *We are your slaves.* They had earlier expressed a similar willingness, but under quite different circumstances (see 44:9,33).

50:19 *Am I in the place of God?* See note on 30:2.

50:20 *God intended it for good.* Their act, out of personal animosity toward a brother, had been used by God to save life—the life of the Israelites, the Egyptians and all the nations that came to Egypt to buy food in the face of a famine

that threatened the known world. At the same time, God showed by these events that his purpose for the nations is life and that this purpose would be effected through the descendants of Abraham.

50:23 *saw the third generation.* Cf. Job's experience (Job 42:16). *Makir.* Manasseh's firstborn son and the ancestor of the powerful Gileadites (Jos 17:1). The name of Makir later became almost interchangeable with that of Manasseh himself (see Jdg 5:14). *placed at birth on Joseph's knees.* Joseph probably adopted Makir's children (see note on 30:3).

50:24 *brothers.* Perhaps used here in a broader sense than siblings. *I am about to die.* See note on 48:21. *God will . . . take you up out of this land.* Joseph did not forget God's promises (cf. 15:16; 46:4; 48:21) concerning "the exodus" (Heb 11:22).

50:25 See 47:29-31 for a similar request by Jacob. *carry my bones up from this place.* Centuries later Moses did so to fulfill his ancestor's oath (see Ex 13:19). Joseph's bones were eventually "buried at Shechem in the tract of land that Jacob bought . . . from the sons of Hamor" (Jos 24:32; see Ge 33:19).

your aid, and then you must carry my bones[t] up from this place."[u] [26]So Joseph died[v] at the age of a hun-

dred and ten.[w] And after they embalmed him,[x] he was placed in a coffin in Egypt.

50:25 tS Ge 49:29 uS Ge 47:29-30; Heb 11:22

50:26 vEx 1:6 wS Ge 25:7 xS ver 2

50:26 *Joseph died at the age of a hundred and ten.* See v. 22. Ancient Egyptian records indicate that 110 years was considered to be the ideal life span; to the Egyptians this would have signified divine blessing upon Joseph.

EXODUS

Title

"Exodus" is a Latin word derived from Greek *Exodos,* the name given to the book by those who translated it into Greek. The word means "exit," "departure" (see Lk 9:31; Heb 11:22). The name was retained by the Latin Vulgate, by the Jewish author Philo (a contemporary of Christ) and by the Syriac version. In Hebrew the book is named after its first two words, *we'elleh shemoth* ("These are the names of"). The same phrase occurs in Ge 46:8, where it likewise introduces a list of the names of those Israelites "who went to Egypt with Jacob" (1:1). Thus Exodus was not intended to exist separately, but was thought of as a continuation of a narrative that began in Genesis and was completed in Leviticus, Numbers and Deuteronomy. The first five books of the Bible are together known as the Pentateuch (see Introduction to Genesis: Author and Date of Writing).

Author and Date of Writing

Several statements in Exodus indicate that Moses wrote certain sections of the book (see 17:14; 24:4; 34:27). In addition, Jos 8:31 refers to the command of Ex 20:25 as having been "written in the Book of the Law of Moses." The NT also claims Mosaic authorship for various passages in Exodus (see, e.g., Mk 7:10; 12:26 and NIV text notes; see also Lk 2:22-23). Taken together, these references strongly suggest that Moses was largely responsible for writing the book of Exodus—a traditional view not convincingly challenged by the commonly held notion that the Pentateuch as a whole contains four underlying sources (see Introduction to Genesis: Author and Date of Writing).

Chronology

According to 1Ki 6:1, the exodus took place 480 years before "the fourth year of Solomon's reign over Israel." Since that year was c. 966 B.C., it has been traditionally held that the exodus occurred c. 1446. The "three hundred years" of Jdg 11:26 fits comfortably within this time span (see Introduction to Judges: Background). In addition, although Egyptian chronology relating to the 18th dynasty remains somewhat uncertain, recent research tends to support the traditional view that two of this dynasty's pharaohs, Thutmose III and his son Amunhotep II, were the pharaohs of the oppression and the exodus respectively (see notes on 2:15,23; 3:10).

On the other hand, the appearance of the name Rameses in 1:11 has led many to the conclusion that the 19th-dynasty pharaoh Seti I and his son Rameses II were the pharaohs of the oppression and the exodus respectively. Furthermore, archaeological evidence of the destruction of numerous Canaanite cities in the 13th century B.C. has been interpreted as proof that Joshua's troops invaded the promised land in that century. These and similar lines of argument lead to a date for the exodus of c. 1290 (see Introduction to Joshua: Historical Setting).

The identity of the cities' attackers, however, cannot be positively ascertained. The raids may have been initiated by later Israelite armies, or by Philistines or other outsiders. In addition, the archaeological evidence itself has become increasingly ambiguous, and recent evaluations have tended to redate some of it to the 18th dynasty. Also, the name Rameses in 1:11 could very well be the result of an editorial updating by someone who lived centuries after Moses—a procedure that probably accounts for the appearance of the same word in Ge 47:11 (see note there).

In short, there are no compelling reasons to modify in any substantial way the traditional 1446 B.C. date for the exodus of the Israelites from Egyptian bondage.

The Route of the Exodus

At least three routes of escape from Pithom and Rameses (1:11) have been proposed: (1) a northern route through the land of the Philistines (but see 13:17); (2) a middle route leading eastward across

Sinai to Beersheba; and (3) a southern route along the west coast of Sinai to the southeastern extremities of the peninsula. The southern route seems most likely, since several of the sites in Israel's desert itinerary have been tentatively identified along it. See map No. 3 at the end of the Study Bible. The exact place where Israel crossed the "Red Sea" is uncertain, however (see notes on 13:18; 14:2).

Themes and Theology

Exodus lays a foundational theology in which God reveals his name, his attributes, his redemption, his law and how he is to be worshiped. It also reports the appointment and work of the first covenant mediator (Moses), describes the beginnings of the priesthood, defines the role of the prophet and relates how the ancient covenant relationship between God and his people came under a new administration (the Sinai covenant).

Profound insights into the nature of God are found in chs. 3; 6; 33-34. The focus of these texts is on the fact and importance of his presence (as signified by his name Yahweh and by his glory). But emphasis is also placed on his attributes of justice, truthfulness, mercy, faithfulness and holiness. Thus to know God's "name" is to know him and to know his character (see 3:13-15; 6:3).

God is also the Lord of history, for there is no one like him: "majestic in holiness, awesome in glory, working wonders" (15:11). Neither the affliction of Israel nor the plagues in Egypt were outside his control. Pharaoh, the Egyptians and all Israel saw the power of God.

It is reassuring to know that God remembers and is concerned about his people (see 2:24). What he had promised centuries earlier to Abraham, Isaac and Jacob he now begins to bring to fruition as Israel is freed from Egyptian bondage and sets out for the land of promise. The covenant at Sinai is but another step in God's fulfillment of his promise to the patriarchs (3:15-17; 6:2-8; 19:3-8).

The theology of salvation is likewise one of the strong emphases of the book. The verb "redeem" is used, e.g., in 6:6; 15:13. But the heart of redemption theology is best seen in the Passover narrative of ch. 12 and the sealing of the covenant in ch. 24. The apostle Paul viewed the death of the Passover lamb as fulfilled in Christ (1Co 5:7). Indeed, John the Baptist called Jesus the "Lamb of God, who takes away the sin of the world" (Jn 1:29).

The foundation of Biblical ethics and morality is laid out first in the gracious character of God as revealed in the exodus itself and then in the Ten Commandments (20:1-17) and the ordinances of the Book of the Covenant (20:22-23:33), which taught Israel how to apply in a practical way the principles of the commandments.

The book concludes with an elaborate discussion of the theology of worship. Though costly in time, effort and monetary value, the tabernacle, in meaning and function, points to the chief end of man: "to glorify God and to enjoy him forever" (Westminster Shorter Catechism). By means of the tabernacle, the omnipotent, unchanging and transcendent God of the universe came to "dwell" or "tabernacle" with his people, thereby revealing his gracious nearness as well. God is not only mighty in Israel's behalf; he is also present in her midst.

However, these theological elements do not merely sit side by side in the Exodus narrative. They receive their fullest and richest significance from the fact that they are embedded in the account of God's raising up his servant Moses (1) to liberate his people from Egyptian bondage, (2) to inaugurate his earthly kingdom among them by bringing them into a special national covenant with him, and (3) to erect within Israel God's royal tent. And this account of redemption from bondage leading to consecration in covenant and the pitching of God's royal tent in the earth, all through the ministry of a chosen mediator, discloses God's purpose in history—the purpose he would fulfill through Israel, and ultimately through Jesus Christ the supreme Mediator.

Outline

I. Divine Redemption (chs. 1-18)
   A. Fulfilled Multiplication (ch. 1)
      1. The promised increase (1:1-7)
      2. The first pogrom (1:8-14)
      3. The second pogrom (1:15-21)
      4. The third pogrom (1:22)
   B. Preparations for Deliverance (2:1-4:26)
      1. Preparing a leader (2:1-10)
      2. Extending the time of preparation (2:11-22)
      3. Preparing the people (2:23-25)

The Israelites Oppressed

1 These are the names of the sons of Israel[a] who went to Egypt with Jacob, each with his family: [2]Reuben, Simeon, Levi and Judah; [3]Issachar, Zebulun and Benjamin; [4]Dan and Naphtali; Gad and Asher.[b] [5]The descendants of Jacob numbered seventy[a] in all;[c] Joseph was already in Egypt.

[6]Now Joseph and all his brothers and all that generation died,[d] [7]but the Israelites were fruitful and multiplied greatly and became exceedingly numerous,[e] so that the land was filled with them.

[8]Then a new king, who did not know about Joseph, came to power in Egypt.[f] [9]"Look," he said to his people, "the Israelites have become much too numerous[g] for us.[h] [10]Come, we must deal shrewdly[i] with them or they will become even more numerous and, if war breaks out, will join our enemies, fight against us and leave the country."[j]

[11]So they put slave masters[k] over them to oppress them with forced labor,[l] and they built Pithom and Rameses[m] as store cities[n] for Pharaoh. [12]But the more they were oppressed, the more they multiplied and spread; so the Egyptians came to dread the Israelites [13]and worked them ruthlessly.[o] [14]They made their lives bitter with hard labor[p] in brick[q] and mortar and with all kinds of work in the fields; in all their hard labor the Egyptians used them ruthlessly.[r]

[15]The king of Egypt said to the Hebrew midwives,[s] whose names were Shiphrah and Puah, [16]"When you help the Hebrew women in childbirth and observe them on the delivery stool, if it is a boy, kill him; but if it is a girl, let her live."[t] [17]The midwives, however, feared[u] God and did not do what the king of Egypt had told them to do; [v] they let the boys live. [18]Then the king of Egypt summoned the midwives and asked them, "Why have you done this? Why have you let the boys live?"

[19]The midwives answered Pharaoh, "Hebrew women are not like Egyptian women; they are vigorous and give birth before the midwives arrive."[w]

[20]So God was kind to the midwives[x] and the people increased and became even more numerous. [21]And because the midwives feared[y] God, he gave them families[z] of their own.

[22]Then Pharaoh gave this order to all his people: "Every boy that is born[b] you must throw into the Nile,[a] but let every girl live."[b]

The Birth of Moses

2 Now a man of the house of Levi[c] married a Levite woman,[d] [2]and she

---

1:1 [a]S Ge 46:8
1:4 [b]Ge 35:22-26; Nu 1:20-43
1:5 [c]S Ge 46:26
1:6 [d]Ge 50:26; Ac 7:15
1:7 [e]ver 9; S Ge 12:2; Dt 7:13; Eze 16:7
1:8 [f]Jer 43:11; 46:2
1:9 [g]S ver 7
[h]S Ge 26:16
1:10 [i]Ge 15:13; Ex 3:7; 18:11; Ps 64:2; 71:10; 83:3; Isa 53:3
[j]Ps 105:24-25; Ac 7:17-19
1:11 [k]Ex 3:7; 5:10,13,14
[l]S Ge 15:13; Ex 2:11; 5:4; 6:6-7; Jos 9:27; 1Ki 9:21; 1Ch 22:2; Isa 60:10
[m]S Ge 47:11
[n]1Ki 9:19; 2Ch 8:4
1:13 [o]ver 14; Ge 15:13-14; Ex 5:21; 16:3; Lev 25:43,46,53; Dt 4:20; 26:6; 1Ki 8:51; Ps 129:1; Isa 30:6; 48:10; Jer 11:4
1:14 [p]Dt 26:6; Ezr 9:9; Isa 14:3
[q]S Ge 11:3
[r]Ex 2:23; 3:9; Nu 20:15; 1Sa 10:18; 2Ki 13:4; Ps 66:11; 81:6; Ac 7:19
1:15 [s]S Ge 35:17
1:16 [t]ver 22
1:17 [u]ver 21; Pr 16:6
[v]1Sa 22:17; Da 3:16-18; Ac 4:18-20; 5:29
1:19 [w]Lev 19:11; Jos 2:4-6; 1Sa 19:14; 2Sa 17:20 1:20
[x]Pr 11:18; 22:8; Ecc 8:12; Isa 3:10; Heb 6:10 1:21 [y]S ver 17
[z]1Sa 2:35; 2Sa 7:11,27-29; 1Ki 11:38; 14:10 1:22
[a]S Ge 41:1 [b]ver 16; Ac 7:19 2:1 [c]S Ge 29:34 [d]ver 2; Ex 6:20; Nu 26:59

[a]5 Masoretic Text (see also Gen. 46:27); Dead Sea Scrolls and Septuagint (see also Acts 7:14 and note at Gen. 46:27) seventy-five [b]22 Masoretic Text; Samaritan Pentateuch, Septuagint and Targums born to the Hebrews

---

1:1–5 These verses clearly indicate that Exodus was written as a continuation of Genesis. The Israelites lived in Egypt 430 years (see 12:40).
1:1 *These are the names of.* The same expression appears in Ge 46:8 at the head of a list of Jacob's descendants. *Israel . . . Jacob.* Jacob had earlier been given the additional name Israel (see Ge 32:28; 35:10 and notes).
1:2–4 The sons of Leah (Reuben through Zebulun) and Rachel (Benjamin; Joseph is not mentioned because the list includes only those "who went to Egypt with Jacob," v. 1) are listed in the order of their seniority and before the sons of Rachel's and Leah's maidservants: Bilhah had Dan and Naphtali, Zilpah had Gad and Asher (see Ge 35:23–26).
1:5 *seventy.* See note on Ge 46:27.
1:6–7 From the death of Joseph to the rise of a new king (v. 8) was more than 200 years.
1:7 See Ac 7:17. God's promised blessing of fruitfulness and increase had been given to Adam (Ge 1:28), Noah (Ge 8:17; 9:1,7), Abraham (Ge 17:2,6; 22:17), Isaac (Ge 26:4) and Jacob (Ge 28:14; 35:11; 48:4). God continued to fulfill his promise during the 430-year sojourn in Egypt. *the land was filled with them.* The Hebrew used here echoes the blessing of Adam (Ge 1:28)—God's initial blessing of mankind was being fulfilled in Israel. The Israelites who left Egypt are said to number about 600,000 men, "besides women and children" (12:37). *land.* Goshen (see note on Ge 45:10).

1:8 See Ac 7:18. *new king.* Probably Ahmose, the founder of the 18th dynasty, who expelled the Hyksos (foreign—predominantly Semitic—rulers of Egypt).
1:11 *slave masters.* The same official Egyptian designation appears on a wall painting in the Theban tomb of Rekhmire during the reign of the 18th-dynasty pharaoh Thutmose III (see Introduction: Chronology). *Rameses.* See note on Ge 47:11. *Pharaoh.* The word, which is Egyptian in origin and means "great house," is a royal title rather than a personal name.
1:14 *made their lives bitter.* A fact commemorated in the Passover meal, which was eaten "with bitter herbs" (12:8). *all kinds of work in the fields.* Including pumping the waters of the Nile into the fields to irrigate them (see Dt 11:10).
1:15 *Hebrew.* See note on Ge 14:13. *Shiphrah and Puah.* Semitic, not Egyptian, names. Since the Israelites were so numerous, there were probably other midwives under Shiphrah and Puah.
1:16 *delivery stool.* The Hebrew term means lit. "two stones"; a woman sat on them while giving birth.
1:17 See Ac 5:29 for a parallel in the early church. *feared God.* See note on Ge 20:11.
2:1 *a man . . . a Levite woman.* Perhaps Amram and Jochebed (but see note on 6:20).
2:2 *a fine child.* Moses was "no ordinary child" (Ac 7:20; Heb 11:23), "fair in the sight of God" (see NIV text note on Ac 7:20). The account of Moses' remarkable deliverance in

became pregnant and gave birth to a son. When she saw that he was a fine[e] child, she hid him for three months.[f] 3But when she could hide him no longer, she got a papyrus[g] basket for him and coated it with tar and pitch.[h] Then she placed the child in it and put it among the reeds[i] along the bank of the Nile. 4His sister[j] stood at a distance to see what would happen to him.

5Then Pharaoh's daughter went down to the Nile to bathe, and her attendants were walking along the river bank.[k] She saw the basket among the reeds and sent her slave girl to get it. 6She opened it and saw the baby. He was crying, and she felt sorry for him. "This is one of the Hebrew babies," she said.

7Then his sister asked Pharaoh's daughter, "Shall I go and get one of the Hebrew women to nurse the baby for you?"

8"Yes, go," she answered. And the girl went and got the baby's mother. 9Pharaoh's daughter said to her, "Take this baby and nurse him for me, and I will pay you." So the woman took the baby and nursed him. 10When the child grew older, she took him to Pharaoh's daughter and he became her son. She named[l] him Moses,[c] saying, "I drew[m] him out of the water."

Moses Flees to Midian

11One day, after Moses had grown up, he went out to where his own people[n] were and watched them at their hard labor.[o] He saw an Egyptian beating a Hebrew, one of his own people. 12Glancing this way and that and seeing no one, he killed the Egyptian and hid him in the sand. 13The next day he went out and saw two Hebrews fighting. He asked the one in the wrong, "Why are you hitting your fellow Hebrew?"[p]

14The man said, "Who made you ruler and judge over us?[q] Are you thinking of killing me as you killed the Egyptian?" Then Moses was afraid and thought, "What I did must have become known."

15When Pharaoh heard of this, he tried to kill[r] Moses, but Moses fled[s] from Pharaoh and went to live in Midian,[t] where he sat down by a well. 16Now a priest of Midian[u] had seven daughters, and they came to draw water[v] and fill the troughs[w] to water their father's flock. 17Some shepherds came along and drove them away, but Moses got up and came to their rescue[x] and watered their flock.[y]

18When the girls returned to Reuel[z] their father, he asked them, "Why have you returned so early today?"

19They answered, "An Egyptian rescued us from the shepherds. He even drew water for us and watered the flock."

20"And where is he?" he asked his daughters. "Why did you leave him? Invite him to have something to eat."[a]

21Moses agreed to stay with the man, who gave his daughter Zipporah[b] to Moses in marriage. 22Zipporah gave birth to a son, and Moses named him Gershom,[d][c] saying, "I have become an alien[d] in a foreign land."

23During that long period,[e] the king of

2:2 eS Ge 39:6; fHeb 11:23
2:3 gIsa 18:2
hGe 6:14
iS Ge 41:2; S Job 8:11; Ac 7:21
2:4 jEx 15:20
2:5 kEx 7:15; 8:20
2:10 lS Ge 1:20
mS Ge 22:17
2:11 nAc 7:23; Heb 11:24-26
oS Ex 1:11

2:13 pAc 7:26
2:14 qS Ge 13:8; Ac 7:27*
2:15 rEx 4:19
sS Ge 31:21
tHeb 11:27
2:16 uEx 3:1; 18:1 vS Ge 24:11
wS Ge 30:38
2:17 xS 1Sa 30:8; Ps 31:2
yS Ge 29:10
2:18 zEx 3:1; 4:18; 18:1,5,12; Nu 10:29
2:20 aGe 18:2-5
2:21 bEx 4:25; 18:2; Nu 12:1
2:22 cJdg 18:30
dS Ge 23:4; Heb 11:13
2:23 eAc 7:30

c10 Moses sounds like the Hebrew for *draw out.*
d22 Gershom sounds like the Hebrew for *an alien there.*

infancy foreshadows the deliverance from Egypt that God would later effect through him.
2:3 *papyrus basket.* Each of the two Hebrew words lying behind this phrase is of Egyptian origin. The word for "basket" is used only here and of Noah's ark (see note on Ge 6:14). Moses' basket was a miniature version of the large, seaworthy "papyrus boats" mentioned in Isa 18:2. *reeds.* A word of Egyptian derivation, reflected in the proper name "Red Sea" (see NIV text note on 10:19).
2:4 *his sister.* Miriam (see 15:20).
2:5 *Pharaoh's daughter.* Perhaps the famous 18th-dynasty princess who later became Queen Hatshepsut. *attendants.* They stayed on the river bank to bathe the princess.
2:10 See Ac 7:21–22. *he became her son.* Throughout this early part of Exodus, all the pharaoh's efforts to suppress Israel were thwarted by women: the midwives (1:17), the Israelite mothers (1:19), Moses' mother and sister (vv. 3–4, 7–9), the pharaoh's daughter (here). The pharaoh's impotence to destroy the people of God is thus ironically exposed. *Moses.* The name, of Egyptian origin, means "is born" and forms the second element in such pharaonic names as Ahmose (see note on 1:8), Thutmose and Rameses (see note on 1:11). *drew him out.* A Hebrew wordplay on the name Moses (see NIV text note), emphasizing his providential rescue from the Nile. Thus Moses' name may also have

served as a reminder of the great act of deliverance God worked through him at the "Red Sea" (see 13:17–14:31).
2:11–15 See Ac 7:23–29; Heb 11:24–27.
2:11 *Moses had grown up.* He was now 40 years old (see Ac 7:23).
2:14 *Who made you ruler and judge . . . ?* Unwittingly, the speaker made a prediction that would be fulfilled 40 years later (see Ac 7:27,30,35). The Hebrew word for "judge" could also refer to a deliverer, as in the book of Judges (see Ac 7:35); it was often a synonym for "ruler" in the OT (see Ge 18:25 and note) as well as in ancient Canaanite usage. *Moses was afraid.* See note on Heb 11:27.
2:15 *Pharaoh.* Probably Thutmose III (see Introduction: Chronology). *Midian.* Named after one of Abraham's younger sons (see Ge 25:2; see also note on Ge 37:25). Midian was located in southeastern Sinai and west central Arabia, flanking the eastern arm of the Red Sea (Gulf of Aqaba) on either side. Dry and desolate, it formed a stark contrast to Moses' former home in the royal court. He lived in Midian 40 years (see Ac 7:29–30).
2:16 *priest of Midian.* Reuel (see v. 18), which means "friend of God." His other name, Jethro (see 3:1), may be a title meaning "his excellency."
2:23 *During that long period.* Thutmose III (see note on v. 15) enjoyed a long reign.

Egypt died.*f* The Israelites groaned in their slavery*g* and cried out, and their cry*h* for help because of their slavery went up to God. 24God heard their groaning and he remembered*i* his covenant*j* with Abraham, with Isaac and with Jacob. 25So God looked on the Israelites and was concerned*k* about them.

Moses and the Burning Bush

3 Now Moses was tending the flock of Jethro*l* his father-in-law, the priest of Midian,*m* and he led the flock to the far side of the desert and came to Horeb,*n* the mountain*o* of God. 2There the angel of the LORD*p* appeared to him in flames of fire*q* from within a bush.*r* Moses saw that though the bush was on fire it did not burn up. 3So Moses thought, "I will go over and see this strange sight—why the bush does not burn up."

4When the LORD saw that he had gone over to look, God called*s* to him from within the bush,*t* "Moses! Moses!"

And Moses said, "Here I am."*u*

5"Do not come any closer," *v* God said. "Take off your sandals, for the place where you are standing is holy ground."*w* 6Then he said, "I am the God of your father, the God of Abraham, the God of Isaac and the God of Jacob."*x* At this, Moses hid*y* his face, because he was afraid to look at God.*z*

7The LORD said, "I have indeed seen*a* the misery*b* of my people in Egypt. I have heard them crying out because of their slave drivers, and I am concerned*c* about their suffering. *d* 8So I have come down*e* to rescue them from the hand of the Egyptians and to bring them up out of that land into a good and spacious land,*f* a land flowing with milk and honey*g*—the home of the Canaanites, Hittites, Amorites, Perizzites, Hivites*h* and Jebusites. *i* 9And now the cry of the Israelites has reached me, and I have seen the way the Egyptians are oppressing*j* them. 10So now, go. I am sending*k* you to Pharaoh to bring my people the Israelites out of Egypt.*l*

11But Moses said to God, "Who am I,*m* that I should go to Pharaoh and bring the Israelites out of Egypt?"

12And God said, "I will be with you. *n* And this will be the sign*o* to you that it is I who have sent you: When you have brought the people out of Egypt, you*e* will worship God on this mountain. *p* "

13Moses said to God, "Suppose I go to the Israelites and say to them, 'The God of your fathers has sent me to you,' and they

Center reference column

2:23 *f*Ex 4:19
*g*S Ex 1:14 *h*ver 24; Ex 3:7,9; 6:5; Nu 20:15-16; Dt 26:7; Jdg 2:18; 1Sa 12:8; Ps 5:2; 18:6; 39:12; 81:7; 102:1; Jas 5:4
2:24 *i*S Ge 8:1 */*S Ge 9:15; 15:15; 17:4; 22:16-18; 26:3; 28:13-15; Ex 32:13; 2Ki 13:23; Ps 105:10,42; Jer 14:21
2:25 *k*Ex 3:7; 4:31; Lk 1:25
3:1 *l*S Ex 2:18; Jdg 1:16 *m*S Ex 2:16 *n*ver 12; Ex 17:6; 19:1-11,5; 33:6; Dt 1:2,6; 4:10; 5:2; 29:1; 1Ki 19:8; Mal 4:4 *o*Ex 4:27; 18:5; 24:13; Dt 4:11,15
3:2 *p*S Ge 16:7; S Ex 12:23; S Ac 5:19 *q*Ex 19:18; 1Ki 19:12 *r*ver 4; Ex 2:2-6; Dt 33:16; Mk 12:26; Lk 20:37; Ac 7:30
3:4 *s*Ex 19:3; Lev 1:1 *t*Ex 4:5 *u*Ge 31:11; 1Sa 3:4; Isa 6:8
3:5 *v*Jer 30:21 *w*S Ge 28:17; Ac 7:33*
3:6 *x*S Ge 24:12; S Ex 4:5; Mt 22:32*; Mk 12:26*; Lk 20:37*; Ac 3:13; 7:32* *y*1Ki 19:13 *z*Ex 24:11; 33:20; Jdg 13:22; Job 13:11; 23:16; 30:15; Isa 6:5

3:7 *a*1Sa 9:16 *b*ver 16; S Ge 16:11; 1Sa 1:11; Ne 9:9; Ps 106:44 *c*S Ex 2:25; Ac 7:34* *d*S Ex 1:10 3:8 *e*S Ge 11:5; Ac 7:34* *f*S Ge 12:7; S 15:14 *g*ver 17; Ex 13:5; 33:3; Lev 20:24; Nu 13:27; Dt 1:25; 6:3; 8:7-9; 11:9; 26:9; 27:3; Jos 5:6; Jer 11:5; 32:22; Eze 20:6 *h*Jos 11:3; Jdg 3:3; 2Sa 24:7 *i*S Ge 15:18-21; Ezr 9:1 3:9 *j*S Ex 1:14; S Nu 10:9 3:10 *k*Ex 4:12; Jos 24:5; 1Sa 12:8; Ps 105:26; Ac 7:34* *l*Ex 6:13,26; 12:41,51; 20:2; Dt 4:20; 1Sa 12:6; 1Ki 8:16; Mic 6:4 3:11 *m*Ex 4:10; 6:12,30; Jdg 6:15; 1Sa 9:21; 15:17; 18:18; 2Sa 7:18; 2Ch 2:6; Isa 6:5; Jer 1:6 3:12 *n*S Ge 26:3; S Ex 14:22; Ro 8:31 *o*Nu 26:10; Jos 2:12; Jdg 6:17; Ps 86:17; Isa 7:14; 8:18; 20:3; Jer 44:29 *p*S ver 1; Ac 7:7

e 12 The Hebrew is plural.

Study notes

2:24 *covenant with Abraham.* See Ge 15:17–18; 17:7 and notes. *with Isaac.* See Ge 17:19; 26:24. *with Jacob.* See Ge 35:11–12.
3:1 Like David (2Sa 7:8), Moses was called from tending the flock to be the shepherd of God's people. *Jethro.* See note on 2:16. *Horeb.* Means "desert," "desolation"; either (1) an alternate name for Mount Sinai or (2) another high mountain in the same vicinity in the southeast region of the Sinai peninsula. Tradition identifies Mount Horeb with Ras es-Safsaf ("willow peak"), 6,500 feet high, and Mount Sinai with Jebel Musa ("mountain of Moses"), 7,400 feet high, but both identifications are uncertain.
3:2 *angel of the LORD.* Used interchangeably with "the LORD" and "God" in v. 4 (see note on Ge 16:7). *appeared to him in flames of fire.* God's revelation of himself and his will was often accompanied by fire (see 13:21; 19:18; 1Ki 18:24,38).
3:4 Every true prophet was called by God (see, e.g., 1Sa 3:4; Isa 6:8; Jer 1:4–5; Eze 2:1–8; Hos 1:2; Am 7:15; Jnh 1:1–2; see also note on 7:1–2). *Moses, Moses! . . . Here I am.* See notes on Ge 22:1,11.
3:5 *Take off your sandals.* A practice still followed by Muslims before entering a mosque. *holy.* The ground was not holy by nature but was made so by the divine presence (see, e.g., Ge 2:3). Holiness involves being consecrated to the Lord's service and thus being separated from the commonplace.

3:6 See 2:24 and note. *afraid to look at God.* See notes on Ge 16:13; 32:30. Later, as the Lord's servant, Moses would meet with God on Mount Sinai (19:3) and even ask to see God's glory (33:18).
3:8 *I have come down to rescue.* God may also come down to judge (see Ge 11:5–9; 18:21). *land flowing with milk and honey.* The traditional and proverbial description of the hill country of Canaan—in its original pastoral state (see note on Isa 7:15). *Canaanites . . . Jebusites.* See notes on Ge 10:6, 15–16; 13:7. The list of the Canaanite nations ranges from two names (see Ge 13:7) to five (see Nu 13:29) to six (as here; see also Jdg 3:5) to ten (see Ge 15:19–21) to twelve (see Ge 10:15–18). The classic description includes seven names (see, e.g., Dt 7:1), seven being the number of completeness (see note on Ge 4:17–18).
3:10 *Pharaoh.* Probably Amunhotep II (see Introduction: Chronology).
3:11 Moses' first expression of reluctance (see v. 13; 4:1, 10,13).
3:12 *I will be with you.* See note on Ge 26:3. The Hebrew word translated "I will be" is the same as the one translated "I AM" in v. 14. *sign.* A visible proof or guarantee that what God had promised he would surely fulfill (see notes on 4:8; Ge 15:8).
3:13 Moses' second expression of reluctance. *What is his name?* God had not yet identified himself to Moses by name (see v. 6; cf. Ge 17:1).

ask me, 'What is his name?' *q* Then what shall I tell them?''

[14]God said to Moses, "I AM WHO I AM. *f* This is what you are to say to the Israelites: 'I AM *r* has sent me to you.' ''

[15]God also said to Moses, "Say to the Israelites, 'The LORD, *g* the God of your fathers *s*—the God of Abraham, the God of Isaac and the God of Jacob *t*—has sent me to you.' This is my name *u* forever, the name by which I am to be remembered from generation to generation. *v*

[16]"Go, assemble the elders *w* of Israel and say to them, 'The LORD, the God of your fathers—the God of Abraham, Isaac and Jacob *x*— appeared to me and said: I have watched over you and have seen *y* what has been done to you in Egypt. [17]And I have promised to bring you up out of your misery in Egypt *z* into the land of the Canaanites, Hittites, Amorites, Perizzites, Hivites and Jebusites—a land flowing with milk and honey.' *a*

[18]"The elders of Israel will listen *b* to you. Then you and the elders are to go to the king of Egypt and say to him, 'The LORD, the God of the Hebrews, *c* has met *d* with us. Let us take a three-day journey *e* into the desert to offer sacrifices *f* to the LORD our God.' [19]But I know that the king of Egypt will not let you go unless a mighty hand *g* compels him. [20]So I will stretch out my hand *h* and strike the Egyptians with all the wonders *i* that I will perform among them. After that, he will let you go. *j*

[21]"And I will make the Egyptians favorably disposed *k* toward this people, so that when you leave you will not go empty-handed. *l* [22]Every woman is to ask her

neighbor and any woman living in her house for articles of silver *m* and gold *n* and for clothing, which you will put on your sons and daughters. And so you will plunder *o* the Egyptians.'' *p*

Signs for Moses

4 Moses answered, "What if they do not believe me or listen *q* to me and say, 'The LORD did not appear to you'?''

[2]Then the LORD said to him, "What is that in your hand?"

"A staff," *r* he replied.

[3]The LORD said, "Throw it on the ground."

Moses threw it on the ground and it became a snake, *s* and he ran from it. [4]Then the LORD said to him, "Reach out your hand and take it by the tail." So Moses reached out and took hold of the snake and it turned back into a staff in his hand. [5]"This," said the LORD, "is so that they may believe *t* that the LORD, the God of their fathers—the God of Abraham, the God of Isaac and the God of Jacob—has appeared to you."

[6]Then the LORD said, "Put your hand inside your cloak." So Moses put his hand

---

3:13 *q*S Ge 32:29
3:14 *r*Ex 6:2-3;
Jn 8:58;
Heb 13:8;
Rev 1:8; 4:8
3:15 *s*Ge 31:42;
Da 2:23
*t*S Ge 24:12
*u*Ex 6:3,7; 15:3;
23:21; 34:5-7;
Lev 24:11;
Dt 28:58;
Ps 30:4; 83:18;
96:2; 97:12;
135:13; 145:21;
Isa 42:8;
Jer 16:21; 33:2;
Hos 12:5
*v*Ps 45:17; 72:17;
102:12
3:16 *w*Ex 4:29;
17:5; Lev 4:15;
Nu 11:16; 16:25;
Dt 5:23; 19:12;
Jdg 8:14; Ru 4:2;
Pr 31:23;
Eze 8:11
*x*S Ge 24:12
*y*Ex 4:31;
2Ki 19:16;
2Ch 6:20;
Ps 33:18; 66:7
3:17
*z*S Ge 15:16;
46:4; Ex 6:6
*a*S ver 8
3:18 *b*Ex 4:1,8,
31; 6:12,30
*c*S Ge 14:13
*d*Nu 23:4,16
*e*S Ge 30:36
*f*Ex 4:23; 5:1,3;
6:11; 7:16; 8:20,
27; 9:13; 10:9,26
3:19 *g*Ex 4:21;
6:6; 7:3; 10:1;
11:9; Dt 4:34;
2Ch 6:32
3:20 *h*Ex 6:1,6;
7:4-5; 9:15;
13:3,9,14,16;
15:6,12; Dt 4:34,
37; 5:15; 7:8;
26:8; 2Ki 17:36;
2Ch 6:32;
Ps 118:15-16;
136:12;
Isa 41:10; 63:12;
Jer 21:5; 51:25;
Da 9:15 *i*Ex 4:21;
7:3; 11:9,10;
15:11; 34:10;
Nu 14:11;
Dt 3:24; 4:34;

6:22; Ne 9:10; Ps 71:19; 72:18; 77:14; 78:43; 86:10;
105:27; 106:22; 135:9; 136:4; Jer 32:20; Mic 7:15; Ac 7:36
*j*Ex 11:1; 12:31-33 3:21 *k*S Ge 39:21 *l*Ex 11:2; 2Ch 30:9;
Ne 1:11; Ps 105:37; 106:46; Jer 42:12 3:22 *m*Job 27:16-17
*n*Ex 11:2; 12:35; Ezr 1:4,6; 7:16; Ps 105:37 *o*S Ge 15:14;
Eze 39:10 *p*Eze 29:10 4:1 *q*S Ex 3:18 4:2 *r*ver 17,20;
20:8; Jos 8:18; Jdg 6:21; 1Sa 14:27; 2Ki 4:29 4:3
*s*Ex 7:8-12,15 4:5 *t*ver 31; S Ex 3:6; 14:31; 19:9

f14 Or *I WILL BE WHAT I WILL BE*   *g15* The Hebrew for
LORD sounds like and may be derived from the Hebrew for
I AM in verse 14.

3:14 *I AM WHO I AM.* The name by which God wished to be known and worshiped in Israel—the name that expressed his character as the dependable and faithful God who desires the full trust of his people (see v. 12, where "I will be" is completed by "with you"; see also 34:5–7). *I AM.* The shortened form of the name is perhaps found also in Ps 50:21 (see NIV text note there). Jesus applied the phrase to himself; in so doing he claimed to be God and risked being stoned for blasphemy (see Jn 8:58–59).

3:15 *The LORD.* The Hebrew for this name is *Yahweh* (often incorrectly spelled "Jehovah"; see note on Dt 28:58). It means "He is" or "He will be" and is the third-person form of the verb translated "I will be" in v. 12 and "I AM" in v. 14. When God speaks of himself he says, "I AM," and when we speak of him we say, "He is."

3:16 *elders.* The Hebrew for this word means lit. "bearded ones," perhaps reflecting the age, wisdom, experience and influence necessary for a man expected to function as an elder. As heads of local families and tribes, "elders" had a recognized position also among the Babylonians, Hittites, Egyptians (see Ge 50:7), Moabites and Midianites (see Nu 22:7). Their duties included judicial arbitration and sentenc-

ing (see Dt 22:13–19) as well as military leadership (see Jos 8:10) and counsel (see 1Sa 4:3).

3:18 *Hebrews.* See note on Ge 14:13. *three-day journey.* Probably a conventional expression for a short trip rather than a journey of exactly three days. *desert.* God had met with Moses there (see vv. 1–2) and would meet with him there again (see v. 12).

3:20 *wonders.* A prediction of the plagues that God would send against Egypt (see 7:14–12:30).

3:21–22 See 11:2–3; 12:35–36.

3:21 *when you leave you will not go empty-handed.* God had promised Abraham that after Israel had served for 400 years they would "come out with great possessions" (Ge 15:14; see Ps 105:37). Israel herself was to live by the same principle of providing gifts to a released slave (see Dt 15:12–15).

4:1 Moses' third expression of reluctance (in spite of God's assurance in 3:18).

4:2 *staff.* Probably a shepherd's crook.

4:3 *snake.* See 7:9–10 and note. Throughout much of Egypt's history the pharaoh wore a cobra made of metal on the front of his headdress as a symbol of his sovereignty.

into his cloak, and when he took it out, it was leprous,[h] like snow.[u]

7"Now put it back into your cloak," he said. So Moses put his hand back into his cloak, and when he took it out, it was restored,[v] like the rest of his flesh.

8Then the LORD said, "If they do not believe[w] you or pay attention to the first miraculous sign,[x] they may believe the second. 9But if they do not believe these two signs or listen to you, take some water from the Nile and pour it on the dry ground. The water you take from the river will become blood[y] on the ground."

10Moses said to the LORD, "O Lord, I have never been eloquent, neither in the past nor since you have spoken to your servant. I am slow of speech and tongue."[z]

11The LORD said to him, "Who gave man his mouth? Who makes him deaf or mute?[a] Who gives him sight or makes him blind?[b] Is it not I, the LORD? 12Now go;[c] I will help you speak and will teach you what to say."[d]

13But Moses said, "O Lord, please send someone else to do it."[e]

14Then the LORD's anger burned[f] against Moses and he said, "What about your brother, Aaron the Levite? I know he can speak well. He is already on his way to meet[g] you, and his heart will be glad when he sees you. 15You shall speak to him and put words in his mouth;[h] I will help both of you speak and will teach you what to do. 16He will speak to the people for you, and it will be as if he were your mouth[i] and as if you were God to him.[j]

17But take this staff[k] in your hand[l] so you can perform miraculous signs[m] with it."

Moses Returns to Egypt

18Then Moses went back to Jethro his father-in-law and said to him, "Let me go back to my own people in Egypt to see if any of them are still alive."

Jethro said, "Go, and I wish you well."

19Now the LORD had said to Moses in Midian, "Go back to Egypt, for all the men who wanted to kill[n] you are dead.[o]" 20Moses took his wife and sons,[p] put them on a donkey and started back to Egypt. And he took the staff[q] of God in his hand.

21The LORD said to Moses, "When you return to Egypt, see that you perform before Pharaoh all the wonders[r] I have given you the power to do. But I will harden his heart[s] so that he will not let the people go.[t] 22Then say to Pharaoh, 'This is what the LORD says: Israel is my firstborn son,[u] 23and I told you, "Let my son go,[v] so he may worship[w] me." But you refused to let him go; so I will kill your firstborn son.' "[x]

24At a lodging place on the way, the LORD met Moses,[i] and was about to kill[y] him. 25But Zipporah[z] took a flint knife, cut off her son's foreskin[a] and touched

---

Cross references (center column):

4:6 uLev 13:2,11; Nu 12:10; Dt 24:9; 2Ki 5:1, 27; 2Ch 26:21
4:7 v2Ki 5:14; Mt 8:3; Lk 17:12-14
4:8 wS Ex 3:18 xver 30; Jdg 6:17; 1Ki 13:3; Isa 7:14; Jer 44:29
4:9 yEx 7:17-21
4:10 zS Ex 3:11 aLk 1:20,64 bPs 94:9; 146:8; Mt 11:5; Jn 10:21
4:12 cS Ex 3:10 dver 15-16; Nu 23:5; Dt 18:15,18; Isa 50:4; 51:16; Jer 1:9; Mt 10:19-20; Mk 13:11; S Lk 12:12
4:13 eJnh 1:1-3
4:14 fNu 11:1, 10,33; 12:9; 16:15; 22:22; 24:10; 32:13; Dt 7:25; Jos 7:1; Job 17:8 gver 27; 1Sa 10:2-5
4:15 hver 30; Nu 23:5,12,16; Dt 18:18; Jos 1:8; Isa 51:16; 59:21; Jer 1:9; 31:33
4:16 iEx 7:1-2; Jer 15:19; 36:6 jNu 33:1; Ps 77:20; 105:26; Mic 6:4

4:17 kS ver 2 lver 20; Ex 17:9 mEx 7-9:21; 8:5, 16; 9:22; 10:12-15,21-23; 14:15-18,26; Nu 14:11; Dt 4:34; Ps 74:9; 78:43; 105:27
4:19 nEx 2:15 oEx 2:23; Mt 2:20
4:20 pEx 2:22; 18:3; Ac 7:29 qS ver 2

4:21 rS Ex 3:19,20 sEx 7:3,13; 8:15; 9:12,35; 10:1,20,27; 11:10; 14:4,8; Dt 2:30; Jos 11:20; 1Sa 6:6; Ps 105:25; Isa 6:10; 63:17; Jn 12:40; Ro 9:18 tEx 8:32; 9:17 4:22 uDt 10:15; Dt 32:6; Isa 9:6; 63:16; 64:8; Jer 3:19; 31:9; Hos 11:1; Mal 2:10; Ro 9:4; 2Co 6:18 4:23 vEx 5:1; 7:16 wS Ex 3:18 xGe 49:3; Ex 11:5; 12:12,29; Nu 8:17; 33:4; Ps 78:51; 105:36; 135:8; 136:10 4:24 yNu 22:22 4:25 zS Ex 2:21 aGe 17:14; Jos 5:2,3

h6 The Hebrew word was used for various diseases affecting the skin—not necessarily leprosy.   i24 Or Moses' son; Hebrew him

---

4:8 *miraculous sign.* A supernatural event or phenomenon designed to demonstrate authority, provide assurance (see Jos 2:12–13), bear testimony (see Isa 19:19–20), give warning (see Nu 17:10) or encourage faith. See note on 3:12.
4:10 Moses' fourth expression of reluctance. *I am slow of speech and tongue.* Not in the sense of a speech impediment (see Ac 7:22). He complained, instead, of not being eloquent or quick-witted enough to respond to the pharaoh (see 6:12). Cf. the description of Paul in 2Co 10:10.
4:13 Moses' fifth and final expression of reluctance.
4:14 *the LORD's anger burned against Moses.* Although the Lord is "slow to anger" (34:6), he does not withhold his anger or punishment from his disobedient children forever (see 34:7). *Levite.* Under Aaron's leadership Israel's priesthood would come from the tribe of Levi.
4:15–16 See note on 7:1–2.
4:19 *all the men . . . are dead.* Including Thutmose III (see 2:15,23; see also Introduction: Chronology).
4:20 *sons.* Gershom (see 2:22) and Eliezer. The latter, though unmentioned by name until 18:4, had already been born.
4:21 *wonders.* See note on 3:20. *I will harden his heart.* Nine times in Exodus the hardening of the pharaoh's heart is ascribed to God (here; 7:3; 9:12; 10:1,20,27; 11:10; 14:4, 8; see Ro 9:17–18 and notes); another nine times the phar-

aoh is said to have hardened his own heart (7:13–14,22; 8:15,19,32; 9:7,34–35). The pharaoh alone was the agent of the hardening in each of the first five plagues. Not until the sixth plague did God confirm the pharaoh's willful action (see 9:12), as he had told Moses he would do (see similarly Ro 1:24–28).
4:22 *firstborn son.* A figure of speech indicating Israel's special relationship with God (see Jer 31:9; Hos 11:1). *son.* Used collectively of the Israelites also in Hos 11:1.
4:23 *kill your firstborn son.* Anticipates the tenth plague (see 11:5; 12:12).
4:24 *lodging place.* Perhaps near water, where travelers could spend the night. *The LORD . . . was about to kill him.* Evidently because Moses had failed to circumcise his son (see Ge 17:9–14).
4:25 *Zipporah . . . cut off her son's foreskin.* Sensing that divine displeasure had threatened Moses' life, she quickly performed the circumcision on their young son. *flint knife.* Continued to be used for circumcision long after metal was introduced, probably because flint knives were sharper than the metal instruments available and thus more efficient for the surgical procedure (see Jos 5:2 and note). *feet.* Probably a euphemism for "genitals," as in Dt 28:57 ("womb," lit. "feet").

Moses', feet with it.[j] "Surely you are a bridegroom of blood to me," she said. [26]So the LORD let him alone. (At that time she said "bridegroom of blood," referring to circumcision.)

[27]The LORD said to Aaron, "Go into the desert to meet Moses." So he met Moses at the mountain[b] of God and kissed[c] him. [28]Then Moses told Aaron everything the LORD had sent him to say,[d] and also about all the miraculous signs he had commanded him to perform.

[29]Moses and Aaron brought together all the elders[e] of the Israelites, [30]and Aaron told them everything the LORD had said to Moses. He also performed the signs[f] before the people, [31]and they believed.[g] And when they heard that the LORD was concerned[h] about them and had seen their misery,[i] they bowed down and worshiped.[j]

Bricks Without Straw

5 Afterward Moses and Aaron went to Pharaoh and said, "This is what the LORD, the God of Israel, says: 'Let my people go,[k] so that they may hold a festival[l] to me in the desert.'"

[2]Pharaoh said, "Who is the LORD,[m] that I should obey him and let Israel go? I do not know the LORD and I will not let Israel go."[n]

[3]Then they said, "The God of the Hebrews has met with us. Now let us take a three-day journey[o] into the desert to offer sacrifices to the LORD our God, or he may strike us with plagues[p] or with the sword."

[4]But the king of Egypt said, "Moses and Aaron, why are you taking the people away from their labor?[q] Get back to your work!" [5]Then Pharaoh said, "Look, the people of the land are now numerous,[r] and you are stopping them from working."

[6]That same day Pharaoh gave this order to the slave drivers[s] and foremen in charge of the people: [7]"You are no longer to supply the people with straw for making bricks;[t] let them go and gather their own straw. [8]But require them to make the same number of bricks as before; don't reduce the quota.[u] They are lazy;[v] that is why they are crying out, 'Let us go and sacrifice to our God.'[w] [9]Make the work harder for the men so that they keep working and pay no attention to lies."

[10]Then the slave drivers[x] and the foremen went out and said to the people, "This is what Pharaoh says: 'I will not give you any more straw. [11]Go and get your own straw wherever you can find it, but your work will not be reduced[y] at all.'" [12]So the people scattered all over Egypt to gather stubble to use for straw. [13]The slave drivers kept pressing them, saying, "Complete the work required of you for each day, just as when you had straw." [14]The Israelite foremen appointed by Pharaoh's slave drivers were beaten[z] and were asked, "Why didn't you meet your quota of bricks yesterday or today, as before?"

[15]Then the Israelite foremen went and appealed to Pharaoh: "Why have you treated your servants this way? [16]Your servants are given no straw, yet we are told, 'Make bricks!' Your servants are being beaten, but the fault is with your own people."

[17]Pharaoh said, "Lazy, that's what you are—lazy![a] That is why you keep saying, 'Let us go and sacrifice to the LORD.' [18]Now get to work.[b] You will not be given any straw, yet you must produce your full quota of bricks."

[19]The Israelite foremen realized they were in trouble when they were told, "You are not to reduce the number of bricks required of you for each day." [20]When they left Pharaoh, they found Moses and Aaron waiting to meet them, [21]and they said, "May the LORD look upon you and judge[c] you! You have made us a stench[d] to Pharaoh and his officials and have put a sword[e] in their hand to kill us."[f]

God Promises Deliverance

[22]Moses returned to the LORD and said, "O Lord, why have you brought trouble

Cross references (center column)

4:27 [b]S Ex 3:1; [c]S Ge 27:27; S 29:13
4:28 [d]ver 16
4:29 [e]S Ex 3:16
4:30 [f]S ver 8
4:31 [g]S Ex 3:18; [h]S Ex 2:25
[i]S Ge 16:11; [j]S Ge 24:26
5:1 [k]S Ex 4:23; [l]S Ex 3:18
5:2 [m]Jdg 2:10; Job 21:15; Mal 3:14; [n]Ex 3:19
5:3 [o]S Ge 30:36; [p]Lev 26:25; Nu 14:12; Dt 28:21; 2Sa 24:13
5:4 [q]S Ex 1:11; 6:6-7
5:5 [r]S Ge 12:2
5:6 [s]S Ge 15:13
5:7 [t]S Ge 11:3
5:8 [u]ver 14,18; [v]ver 17; [w]Ex 10:11
5:10 [x]ver 13; Ex 1:11
5:11 [y]ver 19
5:14 [z]ver 16; Isa 10:24
5:17 [a]ver 8
5:18 [b]S Ge 15:13
5:21 [c]S Ge 16:5; [d]S Ge 34:30; [e]Ex 16:3; Nu 14:3; 20:3; [f]S Ex 1:13; S 14:11

j25 Or *and drew near* Moses', *feet*

4:26 *bridegroom of blood.* Circumcision may have been repulsive to Zipporah—though it was practiced for various reasons among many peoples of the ancient Near East.

4:30 *Aaron told them everything the LORD had said to Moses.* See note on 7:1–2.

5:1 *Pharaoh.* See note on 3:10.

5:3 See 3:18 and note. The reason for sacrificing where the Egyptians could not see them is given in 8:26 (see note on Ge 43:32).

5:6 *slave drivers.* Probably the same as the Egyptian "slave masters" in 1:11 (see note there). *foremen.* Israelite supervisors whose method of appointment and whose functions are indicated in vv. 14–16.

5:7 *straw.* Chopped and mixed with the clay as binder to make the bricks stronger.

5:9 *lies.* The pharaoh labels all hopes of a quick release for Israel as presumptuous and false.

5:21 *May the LORD look upon you and judge you!* See Ge 16:5; 31:49 and notes.

upon this people?[g] Is this why you sent me? 23Ever since I went to Pharaoh to speak in your name, he has brought trouble upon this people, and you have not rescued[h] your people at all."

6 Then the LORD said to Moses, "Now you will see what I will do to Pharaoh: Because of my mighty hand[i] he will let them go;[j] because of my mighty hand he will drive them out of his country."[k]

2God also said to Moses, "I am the LORD.[l] 3I appeared to Abraham, to Isaac and to Jacob as God Almighty,[k][m] but by my name[n] the LORD[l][o] I did not make myself known to them.[m] 4I also established my covenant[p] with them to give them the land[q] of Canaan, where they lived as aliens.[r] 5Moreover, I have heard the groaning[s] of the Israelites, whom the Egyptians are enslaving, and I have remembered my covenant.[t]

6"Therefore, say to the Israelites: 'I am the LORD, and I will bring you out from under the yoke of the Egyptians.[u] I will free you from being slaves to them, and I will redeem[v] you with an outstretched arm[w] and with mighty acts of judgment.[x] 7I will take you as my own people, and I will be your God.[y] Then you will know[z] that I am the LORD your God, who brought you out from under the yoke of the Egyptians. 8And I will bring you to the land[a] I swore[b] with uplifted hand[c] to give to Abraham, to Isaac and to Jacob.[d] I will give it to you as a possession. I am the LORD.' "[e]

9Moses reported this to the Israelites, but they did not listen to him because of their discouragement and cruel bondage.[f]

10Then the LORD said to Moses, 11"Go, tell[g] Pharaoh king of Egypt to let the Israelites go out of his country."[h]

12But Moses said to the LORD, "If the Israelites will not listen[i] to me, why would Pharaoh listen to me, since I speak with faltering lips[n]?"[j]

Family Record of Moses and Aaron

13Now the LORD spoke to Moses and Aaron about the Israelites and Pharaoh king of Egypt, and he commanded them to bring the Israelites out of Egypt.[k]

14These were the heads of their families[o]:[l]

The sons of Reuben[m] the firstborn son of Israel were Hanoch and Pallu, Hezron and Carmi. These were the clans of Reuben.

15The sons of Simeon[n] were Jemuel, Jamin, Ohad, Jakin, Zohar and Shaul the son of a Canaanite woman. These were the clans of Simeon.

16These were the names of the sons of Levi[o] according to their records: Gershon,[p] Kohath and Merari.[q] Levi lived 137 years.

5:22 [g]Nu 11:11; Dt 1:12; Jos 7:7 **5:23** [h]Jer 4:10; 20:7; Eze 14:9 **6:1** [i]S Ex 3:20; S Dt 5:15 [j]S Ex 3:20 [k]Ex 11:1; 12:31, 33,39 **6:2** [l]ver 6,7,8,29; Ex 3:14,15; 7:5, 17; 8:22; 10:2; 12:12; 14:4,18; 16:12; Lev 11:44; 18:21; 20:7; Isa 25:3; 41:20; 43:11; 49:23; 60:16; Eze 13:9; 25:17; 36:38; 37:6,13; Joel 2:27 **6:3** [m]S Ge 17:1 [n]S Ex 3:15; 2Sa 7:26; Ps 48:10; 61:5; 68:4; 83:18; 99:3; Isa 52:6 [o]Ex 3:14; Jn 8:58 **6:4** [p]S Ge 6:18; S 15:18 [q]S Ge 12:7; Ac 7:5; Ro 4:13; Gal 3:16; Heb 11:8-10 [r]S Ge 17:8 **6:5** [s]S Ex 2:23; Ac 7:34 [t]S Ge 9:15 **6:6** [u]ver 7; Ex 3:8; 12:17,51; 16:1,6; 18:1; 19:1; 20:2; 29:46; Lev 22:33; 26:13; Dt 6:12; Ps 81:10; 136:11; Jer 2:6; Hos 13:4; Am 2:10; Mic 6:4 [v]Ex 15:13; Dt 7:8; 9:26; 1Ch 17:21; Job 19:25; Ps 19:14; 34:22; 74:2; 77:15; 107:2; Isa 29:22; 35:9; 43:1; 44:23; 48:20; Jer 15:21; 31:11; 50:34 [w]S Ex 3:19,20; S Jer 32:21; Ac 13:17 [x]Ex 3:20; Ps 9:16; 105:27

6:7 [y]S Ge 17:7; S Ex 34:9; Eze 11:19-20; Ro 9:4 [z]S ver 2; 1Ki 20:13,28; Isa 43:10; 48:7; Eze 39:6; Joel 3:17 **6:8** [a]S Ge 12:7; Ex 3:8 [b]Jer 11:5; Eze 20:6 [c]S Ge 14:22; Rev 10:5-6 [d]Ps 136:21-22 [e]Lev 18:21 **6:9** [f]S Ge 34:30; Ex 2:23 **6:11** [g]ver 29 [h]S Ex 3:18 **6:12** [i]S Ex 3:18 [j]Ex 4:10 **6:13** [k]S Ex 3:10 **6:14** [l]Ex 13:3; Nu 1:1; 26:4 [m]S Ge 29:32 **6:15** [n]S Ge 29:33 **6:16** [o]S Ge 29:34 [p]S Ge 46:11 [q]Nu 3:17; Jos 21:7; 1Ch 6:1,16

[k]*3* Hebrew *El-Shaddai* [l]*3* See note at Exodus 3:15. [m]*3* Or *Almighty, and by my name the LORD did I not let myself be known to them?* [n]*12* Hebrew *I am uncircumcised of lips*; also in verse 30 [o]*14* The Hebrew for *families* here and in verse 25 refers to units larger than clans.

6:1 *Now.* Without further delay, God will act.
6:2 *I am the LORD.* Appears four times in this passage: (1) to introduce the message; (2) to confirm God's promise of redemption (v. 6) based on the evidence of vv. 2–5; (3) to underscore God's intention to adopt Israel (v. 7); (4) to confirm his promise of the land and to conclude the message (v. 8).
6:3 *God Almighty.* See note on Ge 17:1. *by my name the LORD I did not make myself known to them.* See notes on 3:14–15. This does not necessarily mean that the patriarchs were totally ignorant of the name Yahweh ("the LORD"), but it indicates that they did not understand its full implications as the name of the One who would redeem his people (see notes on v. 6; Ge 2:4). That fact could be comprehended only by the Israelites who were to experience the exodus, and by their descendants. *make myself known.* This experiential sense of the verb "to know" is intended also in its repeated use throughout the account of the plagues (see v. 7; 7:17; 8:10,22; 9:14,29; 10:2; 11:7) and in connection with the exodus itself (see 14:4,18; 16:6,8,12; 18:11).
6:5 *remembered.* See note on Ge 8:1.
6:6 *I will bring you out . . . will free you . . . will redeem you.* The verbs stress the true significance of the name Yahweh—"the LORD"—who is the Redeemer of his people (see note on v. 3). *mighty acts of judgment.* See 7:4. The Lord's acts include redemption (for Israel) and judgment (against Egypt).
6:7–8 *brought you out from . . . will bring you to.* Redemption means not only release from slavery and suffering but also deliverance to freedom and joy.
6:7 *I will take you as my own people, and I will be your God.* Words that anticipate the covenant at Mount Sinai (see 19:5–6; see also Jer 31:33).
6:8 See Ge 22:15–17. *swore with uplifted hand.* See note on Ge 14:22.
6:12 *I speak with faltering lips.* See note on 4:10.
6:13 *Moses and Aaron.* The genealogy contained in vv. 14–25 gives details concerning the background of Moses and Aaron. Only the first three of Jacob's 12 sons (Reuben, Simeon and Levi) are listed since Moses and Aaron were from the third tribe.
6:16 *Merari.* The name is of Egyptian origin, as are those of Putiel and Phinehas (see v. 25) and of Moses himself (see note on 2:10). *Levi lived 137 years.* See vv. 18,20. In the OT, attention is usually called to a person's life span only when it exceeds 100 years.

17The sons of Gershon, by clans, were Libni and Shimei.[r]

18The sons of Kohath[s] were Amram, Izhar, Hebron and Uzziel.[t] Kohath lived 133 years.

19The sons of Merari were Mahli and Mushi.[u]

These were the clans of Levi according to their records.

20Amram[v] married his father's sister Jochebed, who bore him Aaron and Moses.[w] Amram lived 137 years.

21The sons of Izhar[x] were Korah, Nepheg and Zicri.

22The sons of Uzziel were Mishael, Elzaphan[y] and Sithri.

23Aaron married Elisheba, daughter of Amminadab[z] and sister of Nahshon,[a] and she bore him Nadab and Abihu,[b] Eleazar[c] and Ithamar.[d]

24The sons of Korah[e] were Assir, Elkanah and Abiasaph. These were the Korahite clans.

25Eleazar son of Aaron married one of the daughters of Putiel, and she bore him Phinehas.[f]

These were the heads of the Levite families, clan by clan.

26It was this same Aaron and Moses to whom the LORD said, "Bring the Israelites out of Egypt[g] by their divisions."[h] 27They were the ones who spoke to Pharaoh[i] king of Egypt about bringing the Israelites out of Egypt. It was the same Moses and Aaron.[j]

Aaron to Speak for Moses

28Now when the LORD spoke to Moses in Egypt, 29he said to him, "I am the LORD.[k] Tell Pharaoh king of Egypt everything I tell you."

30But Moses said to the LORD, "Since I speak with faltering lips,[l] why would Pharaoh listen to me?"

7 Then the LORD said to Moses, "See, I have made you like God[m] to Pharaoh, and your brother Aaron will be your prophet.[n] 2You are to say everything I command you, and your brother Aaron is to tell Pharaoh to let the Israelites go out of his country. 3But I will harden Pharaoh's heart,[o] and though I multiply my miraculous signs and wonders[p] in Egypt, 4he will not listen[q] to you. Then I will lay my hand on Egypt and with mighty acts of judgment[r] I will bring out my divisions,[s] my people the Israelites. 5And the Egyptians will know that I am the LORD[t] when I stretch out my hand[u] against Egypt and bring the Israelites out of it."

6Moses and Aaron did just as the LORD commanded[v] them. 7Moses was eighty years old[w] and Aaron eighty-three when they spoke to Pharaoh.

Aaron's Staff Becomes a Snake

8The LORD said to Moses and Aaron, 9"When Pharaoh says to you, 'Perform a miracle,'[x] then say to Aaron, 'Take your staff and throw it down before Pharaoh,' and it will become a snake."[y]

10So Moses and Aaron went to Pharaoh and did just as the LORD commanded. Aaron threw his staff down in front of Pharaoh and his officials, and it became a snake. 11Pharaoh then summoned wise men and sorcerers,[z] and the Egyptian magicians[a] also did the same things by their secret arts:[b] 12Each one threw down

6:17 rNu 3:18; 1Ch 6:17
6:18 sNu 3:27; 1Ch 23:12 tNu 3:19; 1Ch 6:2,18
6:19 uNu 3:20, 33; 1Ch 6:19; 23:21
6:20 v1Ch 23:13 wEx 2:1-2; Nu 26:59
6:21 x1Ch 6:38
6:22 yLev 10:4; Nu 3:30; 1Ch 15:8; 2Ch 29:13
6:23 zRu 4:19, 20; 1Ch 2:10 aNu 1:7; 2:3; Mt 1:4 bEx 24:1; 28:1; Lev 10:1 cLev 10:6; Nu 3:2,32; 16:37, 39; Dt 10:6; Jos 14:1 dEx 28:1; Lev 10:12,16; Nu 3:2; 4:28; 26:60; 1Ch 6:3; 24:1
6:24 ever 21; Nu 16:1; 1Ch 6:22,37
6:25 fNu 25:7, 11; 31:6; Jos 24:33; Ps 106:30
6:26 gEx 3:10 hEx 7:4; 12:17, 41,51
6:27 iEx 5:1 jNu 3:1; Ps 77:20
6:29 kS ver 2

6:30 lS Ex 3:11
7:1 mS Ex 4:16 nEx 4:15; Ac 14:12
7:3 oS Ex 4:21; Ro 9:18 pS Ex 3:20; S 10:1; Ac 7:36
7:4 qver 13,16, 22; Ex 8:15,19; 9:12; 11:9 rS Ex 3:20; Ac 7:36 sS Ex 6:26
7:5 tS Ex 6:2 uEx 3:20; Ps 138:7; Eze 6:14; 25:13
7:6 vver 2,10,20; Ge 6:22
7:7 wDt 31:2; 34:7; Ac 7:23,30

7:9 xDt 6:22; 2Ki 19:29; Ps 78:43; 86:17; 105:27; 135:9; Isa 7:11; 37:30; 38:7-8; 55:13; S Jn 2:11 yEx 4:2-5 7:11 zEx 22:18; Dt 18:10; 1Sa 6:2; 2Ki 21:6; Isa 2:6; 47:12; Jer 27:9; Mal 3:5 aS Ge 41:8; 2Ti 3:8 bver 22; Ex 8:7,18; S Mt 24:24

6:20 Amram . . . Aaron and Moses. There is some reason to believe that Amram and Jochebed were not the immediate parents but the ancestors of Aaron and Moses. Kohath, Amram's father (see v. 18), was born before Jacob's (Israel's) descent into Egypt (see Ge 46:11), where the Israelites then stayed 430 years (see 12:40–41). Since Moses was 80 years old at the time of the exodus (see 7:7), he must have been born at least 350 years after Kohath, who consequently could not have been Moses' grandfather (see v. 18). Therefore Amram must not have been Moses' father, and the Hebrew verb for "bore" must have the same meaning it sometimes has in Ge 10 (see NIV text note on Ge 10:8, where it is translated "was the father of"). Jochebed. The name appears to mean "The LORD is glory." If so, it shows that the name Yahweh (here abbreviated as Jo-) was known before Moses was born (see note on v. 3). Aaron and Moses. Aaron, as the firstborn (see 7:7), is listed first in the official genealogy.

6:30 faltering lips. See v. 12 and note on 4:10.

7:1–2 As God transmits his word through his prophets to

his people, so Moses will transmit God's message through Aaron to the pharaoh. The prophet's task was to speak God's word on God's behalf. He was God's "mouth" (4:15–16).

7:3 harden. See note on 4:21. miraculous signs. See notes on 3:12; 4:8.

7:4 mighty acts of judgment. See note on 6:6.

7:7 Moses was eighty years old. See notes on 2:11,15.

7:9–10 snake. The Hebrew for this word is different from that used in 4:3 (see Ps 74:13, "monster"). A related word (also translated "monster") is used in Eze 29:3 as a designation for Egypt and her king.

7:11 wise men and . . . magicians. See note on Ge 41:8. According to tradition, two of the magicians who opposed Moses were named Jannes and Jambres (see 2Ti 3:8; the first is also mentioned in the pre-Christian Dead Sea Scrolls). did the same things by their secret arts. Either through sleight of hand or by means of demonic power.

7:12 Aaron's staff swallowed up their staffs. Demonstrating God's mastery over the pharaoh and the gods of Egypt.

his staff and it became a snake. But Aaron's staff swallowed up their staffs. [13]Yet Pharaoh's heart[c] became hard and he would not listen[d] to them, just as the LORD had said.

The Plague of Blood

[14]Then the LORD said to Moses, "Pharaoh's heart is unyielding;[e] he refuses to let the people go. [15]Go to Pharaoh in the morning as he goes out to the water.[f] Wait on the bank of the Nile[g] to meet him, and take in your hand the staff that was changed into a snake. [16]Then say to him, 'The LORD, the God of the Hebrews, has sent me to say to you: Let my people go, so that they may worship[h] me in the desert. But until now you have not listened.[i] [17]This is what the LORD says: By this you will know that I am the LORD:[j] With the staff that is in my hand I will strike the water of the Nile, and it will be changed into blood.[k] [18]The fish in the Nile will die, and the river will stink;[l] the Egyptians will not be able to drink its water.' "[m]

[19]The LORD said to Moses, "Tell Aaron, 'Take your staff[n] and stretch out your hand[o] over the waters of Egypt—over the streams and canals, over the ponds and all the reservoirs'—and they will turn to blood. Blood will be everywhere in Egypt, even in the wooden buckets and stone jars."

[20]Moses and Aaron did just as the LORD had commanded.[p] He raised his staff in the presence of Pharaoh and his officials and struck the water of the Nile,[q] and all the water was changed into blood.[r] [21]The fish in the Nile died, and the river smelled so bad that the Egyptians could not drink its water. Blood was everywhere in Egypt.

[22]But the Egyptian magicians[s] did the same things by their secret arts,[t] and Pharaoh's heart[u] became hard; he would not listen to Moses and Aaron, just as the LORD had said. [23]Instead, he turned and went into his palace, and did not take even this to heart. [24]And all the Egyptians dug along the Nile to get drinking water[v], because they could not drink the water of the river.

The Plague of Frogs

[25]Seven days passed after the LORD struck the Nile. [1]Then the LORD said to Moses, "Go to Pharaoh and say to him, 'This is what the LORD says: Let my people go, so that they may worship[w] me. [2]If you refuse to let them go, I will plague your whole country with frogs.[x] [3]The Nile will teem with frogs. They will come up into your palace and your bedroom and onto your bed, into the houses of your officials and on your people,[y] and into your ovens and kneading troughs.[z] [4]The frogs will go up on you and your people and all your officials.' "

[5]Then the LORD said to Moses, "Tell Aaron, 'Stretch out your hand with your staff[a] over the streams and canals and ponds, and make frogs[b] come up on the land of Egypt.' "

[6]So Aaron stretched out his hand over the waters of Egypt, and the frogs[c] came up and covered the land. [7]But the magicians did the same things by their secret arts;[d] they also made frogs come up on the land of Egypt.

[8]Pharaoh summoned Moses and Aaron and said, "Pray[e] to the LORD to take the frogs away from me and my people, and I will let your people go to offer sacrifices[f] to the LORD."

Cross references (center column):

7:13 [c]S Ex 4:21
[d]S ver 4
7:14 [e]ver 22;
Ex 8:15,32; 9:7;
10:1,20,27
7:15 [f]Ex 8:20
[g]S Ge 41:1
7:16 [h]S Ex 3:18
[i]S ver 4
7:17 [j]S Ex 6:2;
14:25 [k]ver 19-21;
Ex 4:9; Rev 11:6;
16:4
7:18 [l]Isa 19:6
[m]ver 21,24;
Ps 78:44
7:19 [n]S Ex 4:2
[o]Ex 14:21;
2Ki 5:11
7:20 [p]S ver 6
[q]Ex 17:5
[r]Ps 78:44;
105:29; 114:3;
Hab 3:8

7:22 [s]S Ge 41:8
[t]S ver 11;
S Mt 24:24 [u]ver
13,S 14; Ex 8:19;
Ps 105:28
7:24 [v]S ver 18
8:1 [w]Ex 3:12;
4:23; 5:1; 9:1
8:2 [x]Ps 78:45;
105:30;
Rev 16:13
8:3 [y]Ex 12:34
[z]Ex 12:34
8:5 [a]S Ex 4:2;
7:9-20; 9:23;
10:13,21-22;
14:27 [b]S Ex 4:17
8:6 [c]Ps 78:45;
105:30
8:7 [d]S Ex 7:11;
S Mt 24:24
8:8 [e]ver 28;
Ex 9:28; 10:17;
Nu 21:7;
1Sa 12:19;
1Ki 13:6;
Jer 42:2; Ac 8:24
[f]ver 25; Ex 10:8,
24; 12:31

7:13 *heart became hard.* See note on 4:21.
7:14—10:29 The first nine plagues can be divided into three groups of three plagues each—7:14–8:19; 8:20–9:12; 9:13–10:29—with the first plague in each group (the first, the fourth and the seventh) introduced by a warning delivered to the pharaoh in the morning as he went out to the Nile (see v. 15; 8:20; 9:13).
7:17 *my.* Moses'. *the water of the Nile . . . will be changed into blood.* See Ps 78:44; 105:29. The first nine plagues may have been a series of miraculous intensifications of natural events taking place in less than a year, and coming at God's bidding and timing. If so, the first plague resulted from the flooding of the Nile in late summer and early fall as large quantities of red sediment were washed down from Ethiopia, causing the water to become as red as blood (see the similar incident in 2Ki 3:22).
7:19 *your staff.* Aaron was acting on Moses' behalf (see v. 17). *in the wooden buckets and stone jars.* Lit. "in/on the wooden things and in/on the stone things." Some think that, since the Egyptians believed that their gods inhabited idols

and images made of wood, clay and stone (see Dt 29:16–17), the plague may have been intended as a rebuke to their religion (see 12:12).
7:20 *Nile.* Egypt's dependence on the life-sustaining waters of the Nile led to its deification as the god Hopi, for whom hymns of adoration were composed. See note on v. 19.
7:24 *dug along the Nile to get drinking water.* Filtered through sandy soil near the river bank, the polluted water would become safe for drinking.
7:25 *Seven days passed.* The plagues did not follow each other in rapid succession.
8:2 *I will plague your whole country with frogs.* The frog (or toad) was deified in the goddess Heqt, who assisted women in childbirth.
8:3 *come up.* The frogs abandoned the Nile and swarmed over the land, perhaps because the unusually high concentration of bacteria-laden algae had by now proved fatal to most of the fish, thus polluting the river.

9Moses said to Pharaoh, "I leave to you the honor of setting the time g for me to pray for you and your officials and your people that you and your houses may be rid of the frogs, except for those that remain in the Nile."

10"Tomorrow," Pharaoh said.

Moses replied, "It will be as you say, so that you may know there is no one like the LORD our God. h 11The frogs will leave you and your houses, your officials and your people; they will remain only in the Nile."

12After Moses and Aaron left Pharaoh, Moses cried out to the LORD about the frogs he had brought on Pharaoh. 13And the LORD did what Moses asked. i The frogs died in the houses, in the courtyards and in the fields. 14They were piled into heaps, and the land reeked of them. 15But when Pharaoh saw that there was relief, j he hardened his heart k and would not listen to Moses and Aaron, just as the LORD had said.

The Plague of Gnats

16Then the LORD said to Moses, "Tell Aaron, 'Stretch out your staff l and strike the dust of the ground,' and throughout the land of Egypt the dust will become gnats." 17They did this, and when Aaron stretched out his hand with the staff and struck the dust of the ground, gnats m came upon men and animals. All the dust throughout the land of Egypt became gnats. 18But when the magicians n tried to produce gnats by their secret arts, o they could not. And the gnats were on men and animals.

19The magicians said to Pharaoh, "This is the finger p of God." But Pharaoh's heart q was hard and he would not listen, r just as the LORD had said.

The Plague of Flies

20Then the LORD said to Moses, "Get up early in the morning s and confront Pharaoh as he goes to the water and say to him, 'This is what the LORD says: Let my people go, so that they may worship t me. 21If you do not let my people go, I will send swarms of flies on you and your officials, on your people and into your houses. The houses of the Egyptians will be full of flies, and even the ground where they are.

22" 'But on that day I will deal differently with the land of Goshen, u where my people live; v no swarms of flies will be there, so that you will know w that I, the LORD, am in this land. 23I will make a distinction p between my people and your people. x This miraculous sign will occur tomorrow.' "

24And the LORD did this. Dense swarms of flies poured into Pharaoh's palace and into the houses of his officials, and throughout Egypt the land was ruined by the flies. y

25Then Pharaoh summoned z Moses and Aaron and said, "Go, sacrifice to your God here in the land."

26But Moses said, "That would not be right. The sacrifices we offer the LORD our God would be detestable to the Egyptians. a And if we offer sacrifices that are detestable in their eyes, will they not stone us? 27We must take a three-day journey b into the desert to offer sacrifices c to the LORD our God, as he commands us."

28Pharaoh said, "I will let you go to offer sacrifices to the LORD your God in the desert, but you must not go very far. Now pray d for me."

29Moses answered, "As soon as I leave you, I will pray to the LORD, and tomorrow the flies will leave Pharaoh and his officials and his people. Only be sure that Pharaoh does not act deceitfully e again by not letting the people go to offer sacrifices to the LORD."

30Then Moses left Pharaoh and prayed to the LORD, f 31and the LORD did what Moses asked: The flies left Pharaoh and his officials and his people; not a fly remained. 32But this time also Pharaoh hardened his

Cross references (center column)

8:9 gEx 9:5
8:10 hEx 9:14; 15:11; Dt 3:24; 4:35; 33:26; 2Sa 7:22; 1Ki 8:23; 1Ch 17:20; 2Ch 6:14; Ps 71:19; 86:8; 89:6; 113:5; Isa 40:18; 42:8; 46:9; Jer 10:6; 49:19; Mic 7:18
8:13 iJas 5:16-18
8:15 jEcc 8:11 kS Ex 7:14
8:16 lS Ex 4:2
8:17 mPs 105:31
8:18 nEx 9:11; Da 5:8 oS Ex 7:11
8:19 pEx 7:5; 10:7; 12:33; 31:18; 1Sa 6:9; Ne 9:6; Ps 8:3; 33:6; Lk 11:20 qS Ex 7:22 rS Ex 7:4
8:20 sEx 7:15; 9:13

lS Ex 3:18
8:22 uS Ge 45:10 vEx 9:4,6,26; 10:23; 11:7; 12:13; 11:7; Dt 4:20; 7:6; 14:2; 26:18; 1Ki 8:36; Job 36:11; Ps 33:12; 135:4; Mal 3:17 wEx 7:5; 9:29
8:23 xEx 9:4,6; 10:23; 11:7; 12:13,23,27
8:24 yPs 78:45; 105:31
8:25 zver 8; Ex 9:27; 10:16; 12:31
8:26 aS Ge 43:32
8:27 bS Ge 30:36 cS Ex 3:18
8:28 dS ver 8; S Jer 37:3; Ac 8:24
8:29 ever 15; Ex 9:30; 10:11; Isa 26:10
8:30 fver 12; Ex 9:33; 10:18

p23 Septuagint and Vulgate; Hebrew will put a deliverance

8:13 *the LORD did what Moses asked.* For similar occurrences see v. 31; 1Sa 12:18; 1Ki 18:42–45; Am 7:1–6. *The frogs died.* Probably because they had been infected by the bacteria (*Bacillus anthracis*) in the Nile algae (see note on v. 3).

8:16 *dust will become gnats.* The word "dust" is perhaps a reference to the enormous number (see, e.g., Ge 13:16) of the gnats, bred in the flooded fields of Egypt in late autumn.

8:19 *finger of God.* A concise and colorful figure of speech referring to God's miraculous power (see 31:18; Ps 8:3). Jesus drove out demons "by the finger of God" (Lk 11:20). Cf. the similar use of the phrase "hand of the LORD" in 9:3.

8:21 *I will send swarms of flies.* Probably *Stomoxys calci-* *trans*, which would have multiplied rapidly as the receding Nile left breeding places in its wake. Full-grown, such flies infest houses and stables and bite men and animals.

8:22 *I will deal differently.* See 33:16. God makes a "distinction" (v. 23) between Moses' people and the pharaoh's people in this plague as well as in the fifth (see 9:4,6), the seventh (see 9:26), the ninth (see 10:23) and the tenth (see 11:7)—and probably also the sixth and eighth (see 9:11; 10:6)—demonstrating that the Lord can preserve his own people while judging Egypt. *Goshen.* See note on Ge 45:10.

8:26 *detestable to the Egyptians.* See Ge 46:34; see also Ge 43:32 and note.

8:31 *the LORD did what Moses asked.* See note on v. 13.

heart[g] and would not let the people go.

The Plague on Livestock

9 Then the LORD said to Moses, "Go to Pharaoh and say to him, 'This is what the LORD, the God of the Hebrews, says: "Let my people go, so that they may worship[h] me." [2]If you refuse to let them go and continue to hold them back, [3]the hand[i] of the LORD will bring a terrible plague[j] on your livestock in the field—on your horses and donkeys and camels and on your cattle and sheep and goats. [4]But the LORD will make a distinction between the livestock of Israel and that of Egypt,[k] so that no animal belonging to the Israelites will die.' "

[5]The LORD set a time and said, "Tomorrow the LORD will do this in the land." [6]And the next day the LORD did it: All the livestock[l] of the Egyptians died,[m] but not one animal belonging to the Israelites died. [7]Pharaoh sent men to investigate and found that not even one of the animals of the Israelites had died. Yet his heart[n] was unyielding and he would not let the people go.[o]

The Plague of Boils

[8]Then the LORD said to Moses and Aaron, "Take handfuls of soot from a furnace and have Moses toss it into the air in the presence of Pharaoh. [9]It will become fine dust over the whole land of Egypt, and festering boils[p] will break out on men and animals throughout the land."

[10]So they took soot from a furnace and stood before Pharaoh. Moses tossed it into the air, and festering boils broke out on men and animals. [11]The magicians[q] could not stand before Moses because of the boils that were on them and on all the

Egyptians. [12]But the LORD hardened Pharaoh's heart[r] and he would not listen[s] to Moses and Aaron, just as the LORD had said to Moses.

The Plague of Hail

[13]Then the LORD said to Moses, "Get up early in the morning, confront Pharaoh and say to him, 'This is what the LORD, the God of the Hebrews, says: Let my people go, so that they may worship[t] me, [14]or this time I will send the full force of my plagues against you and against your officials and your people, so you may know[u] that there is no one like[v] me in all the earth. [15]For by now I could have stretched out my hand and struck you and your people[w] with a plague that would have wiped you off the earth. [16]But I have raised you up[q] for this very purpose,[x] that I might show you my power[y] and that my name might be proclaimed in all the earth. [17]You still set yourself against my people and will not let them go. [18]Therefore, at this time tomorrow I will send the worst hailstorm[z] that has ever fallen on Egypt, from the day it was founded till now.[a] [19]Give an order now to bring your livestock and everything you have in the field to a place of shelter, because the hail will fall on every man and animal that has not been brought in and is still out in the field, and they will die.' "

[20]Those officials of Pharaoh who feared[b] the word of the LORD hurried to bring their slaves and their livestock inside. [21]But those who ignored[c] the word of the LORD left their slaves and livestock in the field.

[22]Then the LORD said to Moses, "Stretch

8:32 [g]S Ex 7:14
9:1 [h]S Ex 8:1
9:3 [i]Ex 7:4;
1Sa 5:6;
Job 13:21;
Ps 32:4; 39:10;
Ac 13:11
[j]Lev 26:25;
Ps 78:50;
Am 4:10
9:4 [k]ver 26;
S Ex 8:23
9:6 [l]ver 19-21;
Ex 11:5; 12:29
[m]Ps 78:48-50
9:7 [n]S Ex 7:22
[o]Ex 7:14; 8:32
9:9 [p]Lev 13:18,
19; Dt 28:27,35;
2Ki 20:7; Job 2:7;
Isa 38:21;
Rev 16:2
9:11 [q]S Ex 8:18

9:12 [r]S Ex 4:21
[s]S Ex 7:4
9:13 [t]S Ex 3:18
9:14 [u]S Ex 8:10
[v]Ex 15:11;
1Sa 2:2;
2Sa 7:22;
1Ki 8:23;
1Ch 17:20;
Ps 35:10; 71:19;
86:8; 89:6;
Isa 46:9; Jer 10:6;
Mic 7:18
9:15 [w]Ex 3:20
9:16 [x]Pr 16:4
[y]Ex 14:4,17,31;
Ps 20:6; 25:11;
68:28; 71:18;
106:8; 109:21;
Ro 9:17*
9:18 [z]ver 23;
Jos 10:11;
Ps 78:47-48;
105:32; 148:8;
Isa 30:30;
Eze 38:22;
Hag 2:17 [a]ver 24;
Ex 10:6
9:20 [b]Pr 13:13
9:21
[c]S Ge 19:14;
Eze 33:4-5

[q]16 Or *have spared you*

9:3 *hand of the LORD.* See note on 8:19. *terrible plague on your livestock.* The flies of the fourth plague (see note on 8:21) probably carried the anthrax bacteria (see note on 8:13) that would now infect the animals, which had been brought into the fields again as the floodwaters subsided. The Egyptians worshiped many animals and animal-headed deities, including the bull-gods Apis and Mnevis, the cow-god Hathor and the ram-god Khnum. Thus Egyptian religion is again rebuked and ridiculed (see note on 7:19).
9:4 *distinction.* See note on 8:22.
9:5 *Tomorrow.* To give those Egyptians who feared God time to bring their livestock in from the fields and out of danger (see also v. 20).
9:6 *All the livestock of the Egyptians died.* That is, all that were left out in the fields. Protected livestock remained alive (see vv. 19-21).
9:8 *Take... soot... toss it into the air.* Perhaps symbolizing either the widespread extent of the plague of boils or their black coloration. *furnace.* Possibly a kiln for firing bricks, the symbol of Israel's bondage (see 1:14; 5:7-19).

The same word is used in Ge 19:28 as a simile for the destruction of Sodom and Gomorrah.
9:9 *boils.* Probably skin anthrax (a variety of the plague that struck the livestock in vv. 1-7), a black, burning abscess that develops into a pustule. *men and animals.* The plague on the livestock now extended to other animals as well as to the people of Egypt.
9:11 *magicians could not stand.* The "boils of Egypt" (Dt 28:27) seriously affected the knees and legs (see Dt 28:35).
9:12 *the LORD hardened Pharaoh's heart.* See note on 4:21.
9:16 Paul quotes this verse as an outstanding illustration of the sovereignty of God (see Ro 9:17).
9:18 *I will send... hailstorm.* The flooding of the Nile (the probable occasion of the first six plagues) came to an end late in the fall. The hailstorm is thus in the proper chronological position, taking place in January or February when the flax and barley were in flower but the wheat and spelt had not yet germinated (see vv. 31-32).
9:19-21 See note on v. 6.

out your hand toward the sky so that hail will fall all over Egypt—on men and animals and on everything growing in the fields of Egypt." 23When Moses stretched out his staff toward the sky, the LORD sent thunder*d* and hail,*e* and lightning flashed down to the ground. So the LORD rained hail on the land of Egypt; 24hail fell and lightning flashed back and forth. It was the worst storm in all the land of Egypt since it had become a nation.*f* 25Throughout Egypt hail struck everything in the fields—both men and animals; it beat down everything growing in the fields and stripped every tree.*g* 26The only place it did not hail was the land of Goshen,*h* where the Israelites were.*i*

27Then Pharaoh summoned Moses and Aaron. "This time I have sinned,"*j* he said to them. "The LORD is in the right,*k* and I and my people are in the wrong. 28Pray*l* to the LORD, for we have had enough thunder and hail. I will let you go;*m* you don't have to stay any longer."

29Moses replied, "When I have gone out of the city, I will spread out my hands*n* in prayer to the LORD. The thunder will stop and there will be no more hail, so you may know that the earth*o* is the LORD's. 30But I know that you and your officials still do not fear*p* the LORD God."

31(The flax and barley*q* were destroyed, since the barley had headed and the flax was in bloom. 32The wheat and spelt,*r* however, were not destroyed, because they ripen later.)

33Then Moses left Pharaoh and went out of the city. He spread out his hands toward the LORD; the thunder and hail stopped, and the rain no longer poured down on the land. 34When Pharaoh saw that the rain and hail and thunder had stopped, he sinned again: He and his officials hardened their hearts. 35So Pharaoh's heart*s* was hard and he would not let the Israelites go, just as the LORD had said through Moses.

The Plague of Locusts

10 Then the LORD said to Moses, "Go to Pharaoh, for I have hardened his heart*t* and the hearts of his officials so that I may perform these miraculous signs*u* of mine among them 2that you may tell your children*v* and grandchildren how I dealt harshly*w* with the Egyptians and how I performed my signs among them, and that you may know that I am the LORD."*x*

3So Moses and Aaron went to Pharaoh and said to him, "This is what the LORD, the God of the Hebrews, says: 'How long will you refuse to humble*y* yourself before me? Let my people go, so that they may worship me. 4If you refuse*z* to let them go, I will bring locusts*a* into your country tomorrow. 5They will cover the face of the ground so that it cannot be seen. They will devour what little you have left*b* after the hail, including every tree that is growing in your fields. *c* 6They will fill your houses*d* and those of all your officials and all the Egyptians—something neither your fathers nor your forefathers have ever seen from the day they settled in this land till now.'"*e* Then Moses turned and left Pharaoh.

7Pharaoh's officials said to him, "How long will this man be a snare*f* to us? Let the people go, so that they may worship the LORD their God. Do you not yet realize that Egypt is ruined?"*g*

8Then Moses and Aaron were brought back to Pharaoh. "Go, worship*h* the LORD your God," he said. "But just who will be going?"

9Moses answered, "We will go with our young and old, with our sons and daughters, and with our flocks and herds, because we are to celebrate a festival*i* to the LORD."

9:23 *d*Ex 20:18; 1Sa 7:10; 12:17; Ps 18:13; 29:3; 68:33; 77:17; 104:7 *e*S ver 18; Rev 8:7; 16:21 9:24 *f*S ver 18 9:25 *g*Ps 105:32-33; Eze 13:13 9:26 *h*S ver 4; Isa 32:18-20 *i*Ex 10:23; 11:7; 12:13; Am 4:7 9:27 *j*ver 34; Ex 10:16; Nu 14:40; Dt 1:41; Jos 7:11; Jdg 10:10; 1Sa 15:24; 24:17; 26:21 *k*Ps 11:7; 116:5; 119:137; 129:4; 145:17; Jer 12:1; La 1:18 9:28 *l*S Ex 8:8; Ac 8:24 *m*S Ex 8:8 9:29 *n*ver 33; 1Ki 8:22,38; Job 11:13; Ps 77:2; 88:9; 143:6; Isa 1:15 *o*Ex 19:5; Job 41:11; Ps 24:1; 50:12; 1Co 10:26 9:30 *p*S Ex 8:29 9:31 *q*Dt 8:8; Ru 1:22; 2:23; 2Sa 14:30; 17:28; Isa 28:25; Eze 4:9; Joel 1:11 9:32 *r*Isa 28:25 9:35 *s*S Ex 4:21

10:1 *t*S Ex 4:21 *u*S Ex 3:19; S 7:3; Jos 24:17; Ne 9:10; Ps 74:9; 105:26-36 10:2 *v*Ex 12:26-27; 13:8,14; Dt 4:9; 6:20; 32:7; Jos 4:6; Ps 44:1; 71:18; 78:4,5; Joel 1:3 *w*1Sa 6:6 *x*S Ex 6:2 10:3 *y*1Ki 21:29; 2Ki 22:19; 2Ch 7:14; 12:7; 33:23; 34:27; Job 42:6; Isa 58:3; Da 5:22; Jas 4:10; 1Pe 5:6 10:4 *z*Ex 8:2; 9:2 *a*Dt 28:38; Ps 105:34; Pr 30:27; Joel 1:4; Rev 9:3 10:5 *b*Ex 9:32; Joel 1:4 *c*ver 15

10:6 *d*Joel 2:9 *e*S Ex 9:18 10:7 *f*Ex 23:33; 34:12; Dt 7:16; 12:30; 20:18; Jos 23:7-13,13; Jdg 2:3; 8:27; 16:5; 1Sa 18:21; Ps 106:36; Ecc 7:26 *g*S Ge 20:3; S Ex 8:19 10:8 *h*S Ex 8:8 10:9 *i*S Ex 3:18

9:27 *This time I have sinned.* For the first time the pharaoh acknowledges his sinfulness and perceives its devastating results.

9:29 *spread out my hands.* See 1Ki 8:22,38,54; 2Ch 6:12–13,29; Ezr 9:5; Ps 44:20; 88:9; 143:6; Isa 1:15; 1Ti 2:8. Statues of men praying with hands upraised have been found by archaeologists at several ancient sites in the Middle East.

9:30 *LORD God.* See note on Ge 2:4.

9:31–32 See note on v. 18.

9:32 *spelt.* Grains of spelt, a member of the grass family allied to wheat, have been found in ancient Egyptian tombs. Although inferior to wheat, it grows well in poorer and drier soil.

10:2 *tell your children.* The memory of God's redemptive acts is to be kept alive by reciting them to our descendants (see 12:26–27; 13:8,14–15; Dt 4:9; Ps 77:11–20; 78:4–6,43–53; 105:26–38; 106:7–12; 114:1–3; 135: 8–9; 136:10–15).

10:4 *I will bring locusts.* In March or April the prevailing east winds (see v. 13) would bring in hordes of migratory locusts at their immature and most voracious stage. As also today, locust plagues were greatly feared in ancient times and became a powerful symbol of divine judgment (see Joel 1:4–7; 2:1–11; Am 7:1–3).

10:7 *How long . . . ?* The pharaoh's officials ironically echo the phrase used by Moses in v. 3. *Egypt is ruined.* Human rebellion and disobedience always bring death and destruction in their wake.

10Pharaoh said, "The LORD be with
you—if I let you go, along with your
women and children! Clearly you are bent
on evil.[r] 11No! Have only the men go; and
worship the LORD, since that's what you
have been asking for." Then Moses and
Aaron were driven out of Pharaoh's presence.

12And the LORD said to Moses, "Stretch
out your hand[j] over Egypt so that locusts
will swarm over the land and devour
everything growing in the fields, everything left by the hail."

13So Moses stretched out his staff[k] over
Egypt, and the LORD made an east wind
blow across the land all that day and all
that night. By morning the wind had
brought the locusts;[l] 14they invaded all
Egypt and settled down in every area of
the country in great numbers. Never before had there been such a plague of locusts,[m] nor will there ever be again.
15They covered all the ground until it was
black. They devoured[n] all that was left after the hail—everything growing in the
fields and the fruit on the trees. Nothing
green remained on tree or plant in all the
land of Egypt.

16Pharaoh quickly summoned[o] Moses
and Aaron and said, "I have sinned[p]
against the LORD your God and against
you. 17Now forgive[q] my sin once more
and pray[r] to the LORD your God to take
this deadly plague away from me."

18Moses then left Pharaoh and prayed to
the LORD.[s] 19And the LORD changed the
wind to a very strong west wind, which
caught up the locusts and carried them
into the Red Sea.[s] Not a locust was left
anywhere in Egypt. 20But the LORD hardened Pharaoh's heart,[t] and he would not
let the Israelites go.

The Plague of Darkness

21Then the LORD said to Moses, "Stretch
out your hand toward the sky so that darkness[u] will spread over Egypt—darkness
that can be felt." 22So Moses stretched out
his hand toward the sky, and total darkness[v] covered all Egypt for three days.
23No one could see anyone else or leave
his place for three days. Yet all the Israelites had light in the places where they
lived.[w]

24Then Pharaoh summoned Moses and
said, "Go,[x] worship the LORD. Even your
women and children[y] may go with you;
only leave your flocks and herds behind."[z]

25But Moses said, "You must allow us to
have sacrifices and burnt offerings[a] to
present to the LORD our God. 26Our livestock too must go with us; not a hoof is to
be left behind. We have to use some of
them in worshiping the LORD our God, and
until we get there we will not know what
we are to use to worship the LORD."

27But the LORD hardened Pharaoh's
heart,[b] and he was not willing to let them
go. 28Pharaoh said to Moses, "Get out of
my sight! Make sure you do not appear
before me again! The day you see my face
you will die."

29"Just as you say," Moses replied, "I
will never appear[c] before you again."

The Plague on the Firstborn

11 Now the LORD had said to Moses,
"I will bring one more plague on
Pharaoh and on Egypt. After that, he will
let you go[d] from here, and when he does,
he will drive you out completely.[e] 2Tell
the people that men and women alike are
to ask their neighbors for articles of silver
and gold."[f] 3(The LORD made the Egyptians favorably disposed[g] toward the
people, and Moses himself was highly regarded[h] in Egypt by Pharaoh's officials and
by the people.)

4So Moses said, "This is what the LORD
says: 'About midnight[i] I will go throughout Egypt.[j] 5Every firstborn[k] son in Egypt
will die, from the firstborn son of Pharaoh,

10:12 [j]Ex 7:19
10:13 [k]ver 21-22; Ex 4:17; 8:5,17; 9:23; 14:15-16,26-27; 17:5; Nu 20:8 [l]ver 4; 1Ki 8:37; Ps 78:46; 105:34; Am 4:9; Na 3:16
10:14 [m]Dt 28:38; Ps 78:46; Isa 33:4; Joel 1:4; 2:1-11,25; Am 4:9
10:15 [n]Dt 28:38; Ps 105:34-35; Joel 1:4; Am 7:2; Mal 3:11
10:16 [o]S Ex 8:25 [p]S Ex 9:27
10:17 [q]1Sa 15:25 [r]S Ex 8:8
10:18 [s]S Ex 8:30
10:20 [t]S Ex 4:21
10:21 [u]Dt 28:29
10:22 [v]Ps 105:28; Isa 13:10; 45:7; 50:3; Rev 16:10
10:23 [w]S Ex 8:22; Am 4:7
10:24 [x]S Ex 8:8 [y]ver 8-10 [z]S Ge 45:10
10:25 [a]S Ge 8:20; S Ex 18:12
10:27 [b]S Ex 4:21
10:29 [c]Ex 11:8; Heb 11:27
11:1 [d]S Ex 3:20 [e]S Ex 6:1
11:2 [f]S Ex 3:21, 22
11:3 [g]S Ge 39:21 [h]Dt 34:11; 2Sa 7:9; 8:13; 22:44; 23:1; Est 9:4; Ps 89:27
11:4 [i]Ex 12:29; Job 34:20 [j]Ex 12:23; Ps 81:5
11:5 [k]S Ex 4:23

[r] *10* Or *Be careful, trouble is in store for you!*
[s] *19* Hebrew *Yam Suph;* that is, Sea of Reeds

10:11 *Have only the men go.* From the pharaoh's standpoint, (1) the women and children should remain behind as hostages, and (2) it was typically only the men who participated fully in worship.
10:13 *east wind.* See note on v. 4.
10:19 *the LORD changed the wind.* The forces of nature are compelled to obey his sovereign will (see 14:21; Mt 8:23–27). *Red Sea.* See NIV text note.
10:21 *darkness will spread over Egypt.* Like the third and sixth plagues, this ninth plague was unannounced to Pharaoh. It was possibly caused by the arrival of an unusually severe khamsin, the blinding sandstorm that blows in from the desert each year in the early spring. The darkness was an insult to the sun-god Ra (or Re), one of the chief deities of Egypt.
10:28 Pharaoh declares that he will never again grant Moses an audience. *The day you see my face.* During a plague of darkness, these words are somewhat ironic.
11:1 *and when he does.* The Hebrew for this phrase can also be read "as one sends away [a bride]"—i.e., laden with gifts (see Ge 24:53).
11:2–3 See 12:35–36.
11:4 *Moses said.* Continuing the speech of 10:29.
11:5 *Every firstborn son in Egypt will die.* See Ps 78:51; 105:36; 135:8; 136:10. This is the ultimate disaster, since all the plans and dreams of a father were bound up in his firstborn son, who received a double share of the family estate when the father died (see Dt 21:17 and note). More-

who sits on the throne, to the firstborn son of the slave girl, who is at her hand mill, *l* and all the firstborn of the cattle as well. [6]There will be loud wailing *m* throughout Egypt—worse than there has ever been or ever will be again. [7]But among the Israelites not a dog will bark at any man or animal.' Then you will know that the LORD makes a distinction *n* between Egypt and Israel. [8]All these officials of yours will come to me, bowing down before me and saying, 'Go, *o* you and all the people who follow you!' After that I will leave." *p* Then Moses, hot with anger, left Pharaoh.

[9]The LORD had said to Moses, "Pharaoh will refuse to listen *q* to you—so that my wonders *r* may be multiplied in Egypt." [10]Moses and Aaron performed all these wonders before Pharaoh, but the LORD hardened Pharaoh's heart, *s* and he would not let the Israelites go out of his country.

The Passover

12:14–20pp — Lev 23:4–8; Nu 28:16–25; Dt 16:1–8

12 The LORD said to Moses and Aaron in Egypt, [2]"This month is to be for you the first month, *t* the first month of your year. [3]Tell the whole community of Israel that on the tenth day of this month each man is to take a lamb *t u* for his family, one for each household. *v* [4]If any household is too small for a whole lamb, they must share one with their nearest neighbor, having taken into account the number of people there are. You are to determine the amount of lamb needed in accordance with what each person will

eat. [5]The animals you choose must be year-old males without defect, *w* and you may take them from the sheep or the goats. [6]Take care of them until the fourteenth day of the month, *x* when all the people of the community of Israel must slaughter them at twilight. *y* [7]Then they are to take some of the blood *z* and put it on the sides and tops of the doorframes of the houses where they eat the lambs. [8]That same night *a* they are to eat the meat roasted *b* over the fire, along with bitter herbs, *c* and bread made without yeast. *d* [9]Do not eat the meat raw or cooked in water, but roast it over the fire—head, legs and inner parts. *e* [10]Do not leave any of it till morning; *f* if some is left till morning, you must burn it. [11]This is how you are to eat it: with your cloak tucked into your belt, your sandals on your feet and your staff in your hand. Eat it in haste; *g* it is the LORD's Passover. *h*

[12]"On that same night I will pass through *i* Egypt and strike down *j* every firstborn *k*—both men and animals—and I will bring judgment on all the gods *l* of Egypt. I am the LORD. *m* [13]The blood will be a sign for you on the houses where you are; and when I see the blood, I will pass over *n* you. No destructive plague will touch you when I strike Egypt. *o*

11:5 *l*Isa 47:2
11:6 *m*Ex 12:30; Pr 21:13; Am 5:17
11:7 *n*S Ex 8:22
11:8 *o*Ex 12:31-33; *p*Heb 11:27
11:9 *q*S Ex 7:4; *r*S Ex 3:20
11:10 *s*S Ex 4:21; Ro 2:5
12:2 *t*ver 18; Ex 13:4; 23:15; 34:18; 40:2; Dt 16:1
12:3 *u*Mk 14:12; 1Co 5:7 *v*ver 21
12:5 *w*Ex 29:1; Lev 1:3; 3:1; 4:3; 22:18-21; 23:12; Nu 6:14; 15:8; 28:3; Dt 15:21; 17:1; Heb 9:14; 1Pe 1:19
12:6 *x*ver 19; Lev 23:5; Nu 9:1-3,5,11; Jos 5:10; 2Ch 30:2 *y*Ex 16:12; Dt 16:4,6
12:7 *z*ver 13,23; Eze 9:6
12:8 *a*ver 10; Ex 16:19; 23:18; 34:25; Lev 7:15; Nu 9:12 *b*Dt 16:7; 2Ch 35:13 *c*Nu 9:11 *d*ver 19-20; Ex 13:3; Dt 16:3-4; 1Co 5:8
12:9 *e*Ex 29:13, 17,22; Lev 3:3
12:10 *f*S ver 8; Ex 13:7; 29:34; Lev 22:30; Dt 16:4
12:11 *g*ver 33; Dt 16:3; Isa 48:20; 52:12 *h*ver 13,21,27,43; Lev 23:5; Nu 9:2, 4; 28:16; Dt 16:1; Jos 5:10;

2Ki 23:21,23; 2Ch 30:1; Ezr 6:19; Isa 31:5; Eze 45:21 **12:12** *i*Am 5:17 *j*Isa 10:33; 31:8; 37:36 *k*ver 29; S Ex 4:23; 13:15 *l*Ex 15:11; 18:11; Nu 33:4; 2Ch 2:5; Ps 95:3; 97:9; 135:5; Isa 19:1; Jer 43:12; 44:8 *m*S Ex 6:2 **12:13** *n*S ver 11,23; Heb 11:28 *o*S Ex 8:23

*t3 The Hebrew word can mean lamb or kid; also in verse 4.

---

over, judgment on the firstborn represented judgment on the entire community. *slave girl, who is at her hand mill.* The lowliest of occupations (see Isa 47:2).
11:7 *distinction.* See note on 8:22.
12:2 *This month is . . . the first month.* The inauguration of the religious calendar in Israel (see chart on "Hebrew Calendar," p. 102). In the ancient Near East, new year festivals normally coincided with the new season of life in nature. The designation of this month as Israel's religious New Year reminded Israel that her life as the people of God was grounded in God's redemptive act in the exodus. The Canaanite name for this month was Abib (see 13:4; 23:15; 34:18; Dt 16:1), which means "young head of grain." Later the Babylonian name Nisan was used (see Ne 2:1; Est 3:7). Israel's agricultural calendar began in the fall (see note on 23:16), and during the monarchy it dominated the nation's civil calendar. Both calendars (civil and religious) existed side by side until after the exile. Judaism today uses only the calendar that begins in the fall.
12:3 *community of Israel.* The Israelites gathered in assembly.
12:5 *animals . . . without defect.* See Lev 22:18–25. Similarly, Jesus was like "a lamb without blemish or defect" (1Pe 1:19).
12:6 *at twilight.* Lit. "between the two evenings," an idiom meaning either (1) between the decline of the sun and

sunset, or (2) between sunset and nightfall—which has given rise to disputes about when the Sabbath and other holy days begin.
12:7 *blood.* Symbolizes a sacrifice offered as a substitute, one life laid down for another (see Lev 17:11). Thus Israel escapes the judgment about to fall on Egypt only through the mediation of a sacrifice (see Heb 9:22; 1Jn 1:7).
12:8 *bitter herbs.* Endive, chicory and other bitter-tasting plants are indigenous to Egypt. Eating them would recall the bitter years of servitude there (see 1:14). *bread made without yeast.* Reflecting the haste with which the people left Egypt (see vv. 11,39; Dt 16:3).
12:9 *roast it . . . head, legs and inner parts.* The method wandering shepherds used to cook meat.
12:11 *Passover.* Explained in vv. 13,23,27 to mean that the Lord would "pass over" and not destroy the occupants of houses that were under the sign of the blood.
12:12 *judgment on all the gods of Egypt.* Some had already been judged (see notes on 7:19; 8:2; 9:3; 10:21), and now all would be: (1) They would be shown to be powerless to deliver from the impending slaughter, and (2) many animals sacred to the gods would be killed.
12:13 *sign.* Just as the plagues were miraculous signs of judgment on Pharaoh and his people (see 8:23), so the Lord's "passing over" the Israelites who placed themselves under the sign of blood was a pledge of God's mercy.

14"This is a day you are to commemorate;[p] for the generations to come you shall celebrate it as a festival to the LORD—a lasting ordinance.[q] 15For seven days you are to eat bread made without yeast.[r] On the first day remove the yeast from your houses, for whoever eats anything with yeast in it from the first day through the seventh must be cut off[s] from Israel. 16On the first day hold a sacred assembly, and another one on the seventh day. Do no work[t] at all on these days, except to prepare food for everyone to eat—that is all you may do.

17"Celebrate the Feast of Unleavened Bread,[u] because it was on this very day that I brought your divisions out of Egypt.[v] Celebrate this day as a lasting ordinance for the generations to come.[w] 18In the first month[x] you are to eat bread made without yeast, from the evening of the fourteenth day until the evening of the twenty-first day. 19For seven days no yeast is to be found in your houses. And whoever eats anything with yeast in it must be cut off[y] from the community of Israel, whether he is an alien[z] or native-born. 20Eat nothing made with yeast. Wherever you live,[a] you must eat unleavened bread."[b]

21Then Moses summoned all the elders of Israel and said to them, "Go at once and select the animals for your families and slaughter the Passover[c] lamb. 22Take a bunch of hyssop,[d] dip it into the blood in the basin and put some of the blood[e] on the top and on both sides of the doorframe. Not one of you shall go out the door of his

Cross references

12:14 [p]Ex 13:9; 23:14; 32:5 [q]ver 17,24; Ex 13:5, 10; 27:21; Lev 3:17; 10:9; 16:29; 17:7; 23:14; 24:3; Nu 18:23
12:15 [r]Ex 13:6-7; 23:15; 34:18; Lev 23:6; Nu 28:17; Dt 16:3; 1Co 5:7 [s]Ge 17:14
12:16 [t]Nu 29:35
12:17 [u]Ex 23:15; 34:18; Dt 16:16; 2Ch 8:13; 30:21; Ezr 6:22; Mt 26:17; Lk 22:1; Ac 12:3 [v]ver 41; S Ex 6:6, 26; 13:3; [w]Lev 3:17
12:18 [x]S ver 2
12:19 [y]S Ge 17:14 [z]Nu 9:14; 15:14; 35:15; Dt 1:16;
Jos 8:33 12:20 [a]Lev 3:17; Nu 35:29; Eze 6:6 [b]Ex 13:6
12:21 [c]S ver 11; Mk 14:12-16 12:22 [d]Lev 14:4,6; Nu 19:18; Ps 51:7 [e]Heb 11:28

12:14 *celebrate it as ... a lasting ordinance.* Frequent references to Passover observance occur in the rest of Scripture (see Nu 9:1–5; Jos 5:10; 2Ki 23:21–23; 2Ch 30:1–27; 35:1–19; Ezr 6:19–22; Lk 2:41–43; Jn 2:13,23; 6:4; 11:55–12:1). The ordinance is still kept by practicing Jews today.

12:15 *remove the yeast from your houses.* Yeast later was often used as a symbol of sin, such as "hypocrisy" (Lk 12:1) or "malice and wickedness" (1Co 5:8). Before celebrating Passover, the observant Jew today conducts a systematic (often symbolic) search of his house to remove every crumb of leavened bread that might be there (see v. 19). *cut off from*

Hebrew calendar and selected events

NUMBER of MONTH			HEBREW NAME	MODERN EQUIVALENT
1	Sacred sequence begins	7	Abib; Nisan	MARCH—APRIL
2		8	Ziv (Iyyar)*	APRIL—MAY
3		9	Sivan	MAY—JUNE
4		10	(Tammuz)*	JUNE—JULY
5		11	(Ab)*	JULY—AUGUST
6		12	Elul	AUGUST—SEPTEMBER
7		1 Civil sequence	Ethanim (Tishri)*	SEPTEMBER—OCTOBER
8		2	Bul (Marcheshvan)*	OCTOBER—NOVEMBER
9		3	Kislev	NOVEMBER—DECEMBER
10		4	Tebeth	DECEMBER—JANUARY
11		5	Shebat	JANUARY—FEBRUARY
12		6	Adar	FEBRUARY—MARCH
			(Adar Sheni)* Second Adar	This intercalary month was added about every three years so the lunar calendar would correspond to the solar year.

* Names in parentheses are not in the Bible

house until morning. 23When the LORD goes through the land to strike/ down the Egyptians, he will see the blood$g$ on the top and sides of the doorframe and will pass over$h$ that doorway, and he will not permit the destroyer$i$ to enter your houses and strike you down.

24"Obey these instructions as a lasting ordinance$j$ for you and your descendants. 25When you enter the land$k$ that the LORD will give you as he promised, observe this ceremony. 26And when your children$l$ ask you, 'What does this ceremony mean to you?' 27then tell them, 'It is the Passover$m$ sacrifice to the LORD, who passed over the houses of the Israelites in Egypt and spared our homes when he struck down the Egyptians.'"n Then the people bowed down and worshiped.o 28The Israelites did

just what the LORD commanded$p$ Moses and Aaron.

29At midnight$q$ the LORDr struck down all the firstborn$s$ in Egypt, from the first-born of Pharaoh, who sat on the throne, to the firstborn of the prisoner, who was in the dungeon, and the firstborn of all the livestock$t$ as well. 30Pharaoh and all his officials and all the Egyptians got up during the night, and there was loud wailing$u$ in Egypt, for there was not a house without someone dead.

The Exodus

31During the night Pharaoh summoned Moses and Aaron and said, "Up! Leave my people, you and the Israelites! Go, worship$v$ the LORD as you have requested. 32Take your flocks and herds,w as you have said, and go. And also bless$x$ me."

Cross references (center column):
12:23 /Isa 19:22
gS ver 7; Rev 7:3
hS ver 13
/S Ge 16:7;
Isa 37:36;
Jer 6:26; 48:8;
1Co 10:10;
Heb 11:28
12:24 /S ver 14
12:25
kS Ge 15:14;
Ex 3:17
12:26 /Ex 10:2
12:27 mS ver 11
nS Ex 8:23
oS Ge 24:26

12:28 $p$ver 50
12:29 qS Ex 11:4
rS Ge 19:13
sS Ex 4:23
/S Ex 9:6
12:30 uS Ex 11:6
12:31 vS Ex 8:8
12:32 wEx 10:9,
26 xGe 27:34

Notes:
Israel. Removed from the covenant people by execution (see, e.g., 31:14; Lev 20:2–3) or banishment. See also Ge 17:14 and note.
12:17 Feast of Unleavened Bread. Began with the Pass-over meal and continued for seven days (see vv. 18–19; see also Mk 14:12).

12:21 Passover lamb. Jesus is "our Passover lamb" (1Co 5:7), sacrificed "once for all" (Heb 7:27) for us.
12:22 hyssop. Here probably refers to an aromatic plant (Origanum maru) of the mint family with a straight stalk (see Jn 19:29) and white flowers. The hairy surface of its leaves and branches held liquids well and made it suitable as a

BIBLICAL REFERENCES	AGRICULTURE	FEASTS
Ex 12:2; 13:4; 23:15; 34:18; Dt 16:1; Ne 2:1; Est 3:7	Spring (later) rains; barley and flax harvest begins	Passover; Unleavened Bread; Firstfruits
1 Ki 6:1, 37	Barley harvest; dry season begins	
Est 8:9	Wheat harvest	Pentecost (Weeks)
	Tending vines	
	Ripening of grapes, figs and olives	
Ne 6:15	Processing grapes, figs and olives	
1 Ki 8:2	Autumn (early) rains begin; plowing	Trumpets; Atonement; Tabernacles (Booths)
1 Ki 6:38	Sowing of wheat and barley	
Ne 1:1; Zec 7:1	Winter rains begin (snow in some areas)	Hanukkah ("Dedication")
Est 2:16		
Zec 1:7		
Ezr 6:15; Est 3:7,13; 8:12; 9:1,15,17,19,21	Almond trees bloom; citrus fruit harvest	Purim

33The Egyptians urged the people to hurry[y] and leave[z] the country. "For otherwise," they said, "we will all die!"[a] 34So the people took their dough before the yeast was added, and carried it on their shoulders in kneading troughs[b] wrapped in clothing. 35The Israelites did as Moses instructed and asked the Egyptians for articles of silver and gold[c] and for clothing.[d] 36The LORD had made the Egyptians favorably disposed[e] toward the people, and they gave them what they asked for; so they plundered[f] the Egyptians.

37The Israelites journeyed from Rameses[g] to Succoth.[h] There were about six hundred thousand men[i] on foot, besides women and children. 38Many other people[j] went up with them, as well as large droves of livestock, both flocks and herds. 39With the dough they had brought from Egypt, they baked cakes of unleavened bread. The dough was without yeast because they had been driven out[k] of Egypt and did not have time to prepare food for themselves.

40Now the length of time the Israelite people lived in Egypt[u] was 430 years.[l] 41At the end of the 430 years, to the very day, all the LORD's divisions[m] left Egypt.[n] 42Because the LORD kept vigil that night to bring them out of Egypt, on this night all the Israelites are to keep vigil to honor the LORD for the generations to come.[o]

Passover Restrictions

43The LORD said to Moses and Aaron, "These are the regulations for the Passover:[p]

"No foreigner[q] is to eat of it. 44Any slave you have bought may eat of it after you have circumcised[r] him, 45but a temporary resident and a hired worker[s] may not eat of it.

46"It must be eaten inside one house; take none of the meat outside the house. Do not break any of the bones.[t] 47The whole community of Israel must celebrate it.

48"An alien living among you who wants to celebrate the LORD's Passover must have all the males in his household circumcised; then he may take part like one born in the land.[u] No uncircumcised[v] male may eat of it. 49The same law applies to the native-born and to the alien[w] living among you."

50All the Israelites did just what the LORD had commanded[x] Moses and Aaron. 51And on that very day the LORD brought the Israelites out of Egypt[y] by their divisions.[z]

Consecration of the Firstborn

13 The LORD said to Moses, 2"Consecrate to me every firstborn male.[a] The first offspring of every womb among the Israelites belongs to me, whether man or animal."

3Then Moses said to the people, "Commemorate this day, the day you came out

Cross references

12:33 [y]S ver 11; [z]S Ex 6:1; 1Sa 6:6
[a]S Ge 20:3; S Ex 8:19
12:34 [b]Ex 8:3
12:35 [c]S Ex 3:22; [d]S Ge 24:53
12:36 [e]S Ge 39:21; [f]S Ex 3:22
12:37 [g]S Ge 47:11; [h]Ex 13:20; Nu 33:3-5; [i]Ge 12:2; Ex 38:26; Nu 1:46; 2:32; 11:13,21; 26:51
12:38 [j]Nu 11:4; Jos 8:35
12:39 [k]Ex 3:20; 11:1
12:40 [l]S Ge 15:13; Ac 7:6; Gal 3:17
12:41 [m]S Ex 6:26; [n]S Ex 3:10
12:42 [o]Ex 13:10; Lev 3:17; Nu 9:3; Dt 16:1,6
12:43 [p]S ver 11

[q]ver 48; Nu 9:14; 15:14; 2Ch 6:32-33; Isa 14:1; 56:3,6; 60:10
12:44 [r]S Ge 17:12-13
12:45 [s]Lev 22:10
12:46 [t]Nu 9:12; Ps 22:14; 34:20; 51:8; Pr 17:22; Jn 19:36*
12:48 [u]ver 49; Lev 19:18,34; 24:22; Nu 9:14; 10:32 [v]Eze 44:7
12:49 [w]Lev 24:22; Nu 15:15-16,29; Dt 1:16
12:50 [x]ver 28
12:51 [y]S Ex 3:10; S 6:6 [z]S Ex 6:26
13:2 [a]ver 12,13, 15; Ex 22:29; 34:20; Lev 27:26; Nu 3:13; 8:17;

18:15; Dt 15:19; Ne 10:36; Lk 2:23*

[u]40 Masoretic Text; Samaritan Pentateuch and Septuagint *Egypt and Canaan*

Footnotes / Study notes

sprinkling device for use in purification rituals (see Lev 14:4,6,49,51–52; Nu 19:6,18; Heb 9:19; see also Ps 51:7). *dip it into the blood.* Today at Passover meals a sprig of parsley or other plant is dipped in salt water to symbolize the lowly diet and tears of the Israelites during their time of slavery.

12:23 *pass over.* See note on v. 11. *the destroyer.* In Ps 78:49 the agent of God's wrath against the Egyptians is described as "a band of destroying angels." God often used angels to bring destructive plagues (see 2Sa 24:15–16; 2Ki 19:35; see also 1Co 10:10, a reference to Nu 16:41–49).

12:26 *your children ask you, 'What does this ceremony mean to you?'* See 13:14. The Passover was to be observed as a memorial feast commemorating Israel's redemption and appropriating it anew. As observed today, it includes the asking of similar questions by the youngest child present.

12:27 *Passover sacrifice.* See note on v. 21. *passed over.* See note on v. 11.

12:29 *prisoner, who was in the dungeon.* The lowliest of situations (see note on 11:5).

12:31 *Pharaoh summoned Moses.* Though he had sworn never again to grant Moses an audience (see 10:28 and note), Pharaoh now summons Moses (and Aaron) into his presence.

12:35–36 See 3:21–22; 11:2–3.

12:37 *journeyed from Rameses.* See 1:11; see also note on Ge 47:11. The Israelite departure took place "the day after the Passover" (Nu 33:3). *Succoth.* Probably modern Tell el-Maskhutah in the Wadi Tumeilat, west of the Bitter Lakes. *about six hundred thousand men.* A round number for 603,550 (see note on 38:26).

12:38 *many other people.* Possibly including such Egyptians as those mentioned in 9:20.

12:41 *430 years, to the very day.* See note on Ac 7:6.

12:46 *Do not break any of the bones.* See Nu 9:12; Ps 34:20; quoted in Jn 19:36 in reference to Jesus.

12:48 *No uncircumcised male may eat of it.* Only those consecrated to the Lord in covenant commitment could partake of Passover; only for them could it have its full meaning (see Ge 17:9–14). Concerning participants in the Lord's Supper see 1Co 11:28.

13:2 *Consecrate to me every firstborn male.* God had adopted Israel as his firstborn (see 4:22) and had delivered every firstborn among the Israelites, whether man or animal, from the tenth plague (see 12:12–13). All the firstborn in Israel were therefore his. Jesus, Mary's firstborn son (see Lk 2:7), was presented to the Lord in accordance with this law (see Lk 2:22–23).

of Egypt,[b] out of the land of slavery, because the LORD brought you out of it with a mighty hand.[c] Eat nothing containing yeast.[d] [4]Today, in the month of Abib,[e] you are leaving. [5]When the LORD brings you into the land of the Canaanites,[f] Hittites, Amorites, Hivites and Jebusites[g]—the land he swore to your forefathers to give you, a land flowing with milk and honey[h]—you are to observe this ceremony[i] in this month: [6]For seven days eat bread made without yeast and on the seventh day hold a festival[j] to the LORD. [7]Eat unleavened bread during those seven days; nothing with yeast in it is to be seen among you, nor shall any yeast be seen anywhere within your borders. [8]On that day tell your son,[k] 'I do this because of what the LORD did for me when I came out of Egypt.' [9]This observance will be for you like a sign on your hand[l] and a reminder on your forehead[m] that the law of the LORD is to be on your lips. For the LORD brought you out of Egypt with his mighty hand.[n] [10]You must keep this ordinance[o] at the appointed time[p] year after year.

[11]"After the LORD brings you into the land of the Canaanites[q] and gives it to you, as he promised on oath[r] to you and your forefathers,[s] [12]you are to give over to the LORD the first offspring of every womb. All the firstborn males of your livestock belong to the LORD.[t] [13]Redeem with a lamb every firstborn donkey,[u] but if you do not redeem it, break its neck.[v] Redeem[w] every firstborn among your sons.[x]

[14]"In days to come, when your son[y] asks you, 'What does this mean?' say to him, 'With a mighty hand the LORD brought us out of Egypt, out of the land of slavery.[z] [15]When Pharaoh stubbornly

refused to let us go, the LORD killed every firstborn in Egypt, both man and animal. This is why I sacrifice to the LORD the first male offspring of every womb and redeem each of my firstborn sons.'[a] [16]And it will be like a sign on your hand and a symbol on your forehead[b] that the LORD brought us out of Egypt with his mighty hand."

Crossing the Sea

[17]When Pharaoh let the people go, God did not lead them on the road through the Philistine country, though that was shorter. For God said, "If they face war, they might change their minds and return to Egypt."[c] [18]So God led[d] the people around by the desert road toward the Red Sea.[v] The Israelites went up out of Egypt armed for battle.[e]

[19]Moses took the bones of Joseph[f] with him because Joseph had made the sons of Israel swear an oath. He had said, "God will surely come to your aid, and then you must carry my bones up with you from this place."[w][g] [20]After leaving Succoth[h] they camped at Etham on the edge of the desert.[i] [21]By day the LORD went ahead[j] of them in a pillar of cloud[k] to guide them on their way and by night in a pillar of fire to give them light, so that they could travel by day or night. [22]Neither the pillar of cloud by day nor the pillar of fire by night left[l] its place in front of the people.

14 Then the LORD said to Moses, [2]"Tell the Israelites to turn back and encamp near Pi Hahiroth, between

---

13:3 [b]ver 14; Ex 7:4; Lev 26:13; Nu 1:1; 9:1; 22:5; 26:4; Dt 4:45; 5:6; Ps 81:10; 114:1 [c]S Ex 3:20 [d]S Ex 12:8 **13:4** [e]S Ex 12:2 **13:5** [f]ver 11 [g]S Ex 3:8 [h]S Ex 3:8 [i]Ex 12:25-26 **13:6** [j]S Ex 12:15-20 **13:8** [k]S Ex 10:2; Ps 78:5-6 **13:9** [l]Isa 44:5 [m]ver 16; Dt 6:8; 11:18; Pr 3:3; Mt 23:5 [n]S Ex 3:20 **13:10** [o]S Ex 12:14 [p]Ps 75:2; 102:13 **13:11** [q]S ver 5 [r]S Ge 22:16; Dt 1:8 [s]S Ge 12:7; S 17:19; Ps 105:42-45 **13:12** [t]S Ge 4:4; Lev 27:26; Nu 3:13; 18:15, 17; Lk 2:23* **13:13** [u]ver 15; Lev 27:11 [v]Ex 34:20; Isa 66:3 [w]Nu 3:46-47 [x]Nu 18:15 **13:14** [y]S Ex 10:2 [z]Ex 20:2; Dt 7:8; 28:68 **13:15** [a]S ver 2 **13:16** [b]S ver 9 **13:17** [c]Ex 14:11; Nu 14:1-4; Dt 17:16; Hos 11:5 **13:18** [d]Ex 15:22; Ps 136:16; Eze 20:10 [e]Jos 1:14; 4:13 **13:19** [f]Jos 24:32; Ac 7:16; Heb 11:22 [g]Ge 47:29-30 **13:20** [h]S Ex 12:37 [i]Nu 33:6 **13:21** [j]Ex 32:1; 33:14; Dt 2:7; 31:8; Jdg 4:14; 5:4; Ps 68:7; 77:20; Jer 2:2; Hab 3:13 [k]Ex 14:19,24; 24:16; 33:9-10; 34:5; 40:38; Nu 9:16; 12:5; 14:14; Dt 1:33; Ne 9:12,19; Ps 78:14; 99:7; 105:39; Isa 4:5; 1Co 10:1 **13:22** [l]Ne 9:19

[v]18 Hebrew *Yam Suph*; that is, Sea of Reeds   [w]19 See Gen. 50:25.

13:5 See note on 3:8.
13:9 *like a sign on your hand and a reminder on your forehead.* A figure of speech (see v. 16; Dt 6:8; 11:18; see also Pr 3:3; 6:21; 7:3; SS 8:6). A literal reading of this verse has led to the practice of writing the texts of vv. 1–10, vv. 11–16, Dt 6:4–9 and Dt 11:13–21 on separate strips of parchment and placing them in two small leather boxes, which the observant Jew straps on his forehead and left arm before his morning prayers. The boxes are called "phylacteries" (Mt 23:5). This practice seems to have originated after the exile to Babylon.
13:13 *Redeem.* See 6:6. The verb means "obtain release by means of payment." *every firstborn donkey.* The economic importance of pack animals allowed for their redemption through sacrificing a lamb. *every firstborn among your sons.* Humans were to be consecrated to the Lord by their life, not by their death (see Ge 22:12; Nu 3:39–51; cf. Ro 12:1).
13:14 See note on 12:26.
13:16 See note on v. 9.

13:17 *road through the Philistine country.* Although the most direct route from Goshen to Canaan, it was heavily guarded by a string of Egyptian fortresses.
13:18 *desert road.* Leading south along the west coast of the Sinai peninsula. *Red Sea.* See NIV text note. Various locations of the crossing have been proposed along the line of the modern Suez Canal and including the northern end of the Gulf of Suez (see map No. 2 at the end of the Study Bible; but see also note on 14:2). *armed for battle.* Probably only with spears, bows and slings.
13:19 See notes on Ge 50:24–26.
13:20 *Succoth.* See note on 12:37. *Etham.* Location unknown.
13:21 *pillar of cloud . . . pillar of fire.* The visible symbol of God's presence among his people (see 14:24; see also note on 3:2). The Lord often spoke to them from the pillar (see Nu 12:5–6; Dt 31:15–16; Ps 99:6–7).
14:2 *turn back.* Northward, in the general direction from which they had come. *Pi Hahiroth.* Located "east of Baal Zephon" (Nu 33:7). *Migdol.* Location unknown. The name

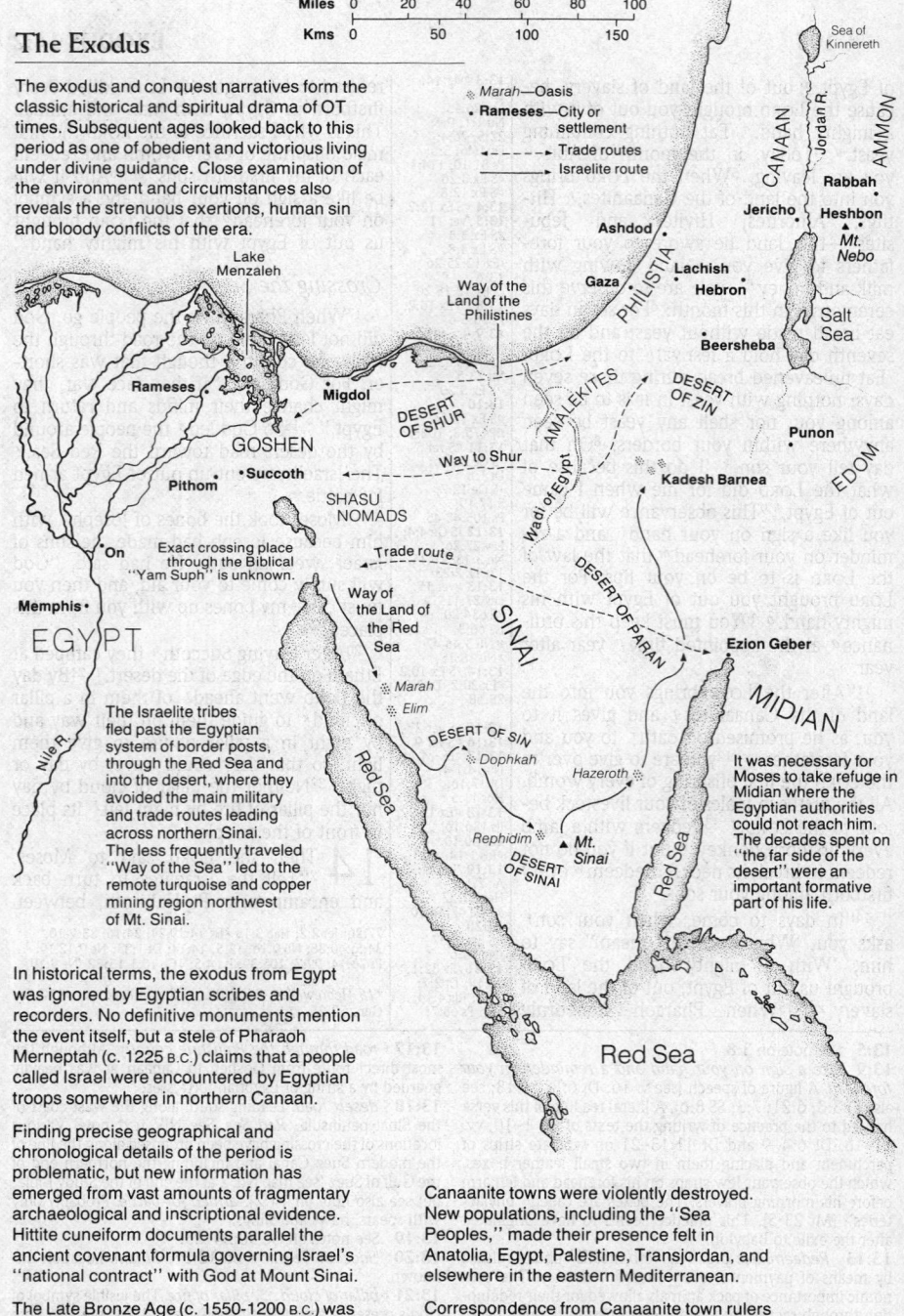

The Exodus

The exodus and conquest narratives form the classic historical and spiritual drama of OT times. Subsequent ages looked back to this period as one of obedient and victorious living under divine guidance. Close examination of the environment and circumstances also reveals the strenuous exertions, human sin and bloody conflicts of the era.

Miles 0   20   40   60   80   100
Kms 0   50   100   150

Marah—Oasis
Rameses—City or settlement
- - - ► Trade routes
———► Israelite route

Sea of Kinnereth

CANAAN   AMMON

Jordan R.

Rabbah

Jericho   Heshbon

Mt. Nebo

Ashdod

Lachish

Gaza   Hebron

PHILISTIA

Salt Sea

Beersheba

Lake Menzaleh

Way of the Land of the Philistines

DESERT OF ZIN

AMALEKITES

Punon

EDOM

Rameses   Migdol

GOSHEN

DESERT OF SHUR

Way to Shur

Wadi of Egypt

Kadesh Barnea

Pithom   Succoth

SHASU NOMADS

On

Exact crossing place through the Biblical "Yam Suph" is unknown.

Trade route

DESERT OF PARAN

Way of the Land of the Red Sea

SINAI

Ezion Geber

Memphis

EGYPT

Nile R.

The Israelite tribes fled past the Egyptian system of border posts, through the Red Sea and into the desert, where they avoided the main military and trade routes leading across northern Sinai. The less frequently traveled "Way of the Sea" led to the remote turquoise and copper mining region northwest of Mt. Sinai.

Marah
Elim

Red Sea

DESERT OF SIN

Dophkah

Hazeroth

MIDIAN

Red Sea

It was necessary for Moses to take refuge in Midian where the Egyptian authorities could not reach him. The decades spent on "the far side of the desert" were an important formative part of his life.

Rephidim   Mt. Sinai

DESERT OF SINAI

In historical terms, the exodus from Egypt was ignored by Egyptian scribes and recorders. No definitive monuments mention the event itself, but a stele of Pharaoh Merneptah (c. 1225 B.C.) claims that a people called Israel were encountered by Egyptian troops somewhere in northern Canaan.

Red Sea

Finding precise geographical and chronological details of the period is problematic, but new information has emerged from vast amounts of fragmentary archaeological and inscriptional evidence. Hittite cuneiform documents parallel the ancient covenant formula governing Israel's "national contract" with God at Mount Sinai.

The Late Bronze Age (c. 1550-1200 B.C.) was a time of major social migrations. Egyptian control over the Semites in the eastern Nile delta was harsh, with a system of brickmaking quotas imposed on the labor force, often the landless, low-class "Apiru." Numerous Canaanite towns were violently destroyed. New populations, including the "Sea Peoples," made their presence felt in Anatolia, Egypt, Palestine, Transjordan, and elsewhere in the eastern Mediterranean.

Correspondence from Canaanite town rulers to the Egyptian court in the time of Akhenaten (c. 1375 B.C.) reveals a weak structure of alliances, with an intermittent Egyptian military presence and an ominous fear of people called "Habiru" ("Apiru").

Migdol[m] and the sea. They are to encamp by the sea, directly opposite Baal Zephon.[n] [3]Pharaoh will think, 'The Israelites are wandering around the land in confusion, hemmed in by the desert.' [4]And I will harden Pharaoh's heart,[o] and he will pursue them.[p] But I will gain glory[q] for myself through Pharaoh and all his army, and the Egyptians will know that I am the LORD."[r] So the Israelites did this.

[5]When the king of Egypt was told that the people had fled,[s] Pharaoh and his officials changed their minds[t] about them and said, "What have we done? We have let the Israelites go and have lost their services!" [6]So he had his chariot made ready and took his army with him. [7]He took six hundred of the best chariots,[u] along with all the other chariots of Egypt, with officers over all of them. [8]The LORD hardened the heart[v] of Pharaoh king of Egypt, so that he pursued the Israelites, who were marching out boldly.[w] [9]The Egyptians—all Pharaoh's horses[x] and chariots, horsemen[x] and troops[y]—pursued the Israelites and overtook[z] them as they camped by the sea near Pi Hahiroth, opposite Baal Zephon.[a]

[10]As Pharaoh approached, the Israelites looked up, and there were the Egyptians, marching after them. They were terrified and cried[b] out to the LORD. [11]They said to Moses, "Was it because there were no graves in Egypt that you brought us to the desert to die?[c] What have you done to us by bringing us out of Egypt? [12]Didn't we say to you in Egypt, 'Leave us alone; let us serve the Egyptians'? It would have been better for us to serve the Egyptians than to die in the desert!"[d]

[13]Moses answered the people, "Do not be afraid.[e] Stand firm and you will see[f] the deliverance the LORD will bring you today. The Egyptians you see today you will never see[g] again. [14]The LORD will fight[h] for you; you need only to be still."[i]

[15]Then the LORD said to Moses, "Why are you crying out to me?[j] Tell the Israelites to move on. [16]Raise your staff[k] and stretch out your hand over the sea to divide the water[l] so that the Israelites can go through the sea on dry ground. [17]I will harden the hearts[m] of the Egyptians so that they will go in after them.[n] And I will gain glory through Pharaoh and all his army, through his chariots and his horsemen. [18]The Egyptians will know that I am the LORD[o] when I gain glory through Pharaoh, his chariots and his horsemen."

[19]Then the angel of God,[p] who had been traveling in front of Israel's army, withdrew and went behind them. The pillar of cloud[q] also moved from in front and stood behind[r] them, [20]coming between the armies of Egypt and Israel. Throughout the night the cloud brought darkness[s] to the one side and light to the other side; so neither went near the other all night long.

[21]Then Moses stretched out his hand[t] over the sea,[u] and all that night the LORD drove the sea back with a strong east wind[v] and turned it into dry land.[w] The waters were divided,[x] [22]and the Israelites went through the sea[y] on dry ground,[z] with a wall[a] of water on their right and on their left.

[23]The Egyptians pursued them, and all Pharaoh's horses and chariots and horsemen[b] followed them into the sea. [24]During the last watch of the night the LORD

14:2 [m]Nu 33:7; Jer 44:1; Eze 29:10 [n]ver 9
14:4 [o]S Ex 4:21 [p]ver 8,17,23; Ps 71:11 [q]S Ex 9:16; Ro 9:17,22-23 [r]S Ex 6:2; Eze 32:15
14:5 [s]S Ge 31:21 [t]Ps 105:25
14:7 [u]Ex 15:4
14:8 [v]S Ex 11:10 [w]Nu 33:3; Ac 13:17
14:9 [x]Ge 47:17 [y]ver 6-7,25; Jos 24:6; Isa 43:17 [z]Ex 15:9 [a]ver 2
14:10 [b]Ex 15:25; Jos 24:7; Ne 9:9; Ps 5:2; 34:17; 50:15; 107:6,28
14:11 [c]S Ex 5:21; 16:3; 17:3; Nu 11:1; 14:22; 20:4; 21:5; Dt 9:7
14:12 [d]S Ex 5:21; 15:24; 17:2; Ps 106:7-8
14:13 [e]S Ge 15:1 [f]1Sa 12:16; 2Ch 20:17 [g]ver 30

14:14 [h]ver 25; Ex 15:3; Dt 1:30; 3:22; 20:4; Jos 10:14; 23:3, 10; 2Sa 5:24; 2Ch 20:29; Ne 4:20; Ps 24:8; 35:1; Isa 42:13; Jer 41:12 [i]1Sa 12:16; Ps 37:7; 46:10; 116:7; Isa 28:12; 30:15; Zec 2:13
14:15 [j]Jos 7:10
14:16 [k]S Ex 4:2 [l]ver 27; Isa 10:26
14:17 [m]Ex 4:21 [n]S ver 4
14:18 [o]S Ex 6:2; Eze 32:15
14:19 [p]S Ge 16:7; Isa 63:9 [q]S Ex 13:21; 1Co 10:1 [r]Isa 26:7; 42:16; 49:10; 52:12; 58:8
14:20 [s]Jos 24:7

14:21 [t]S Ex 7:19 [u]S Ex 4:2; Job 26:12; Isa 14:27; 23:11; 51:15; Jer 31:35; Ac 7:36 [v]S Ge 41:6; Ex 15:8; 2Sa 22:16; 1Ki 19:11; Job 38:1; 40:6; Jer 23:19; Na 1:3 [w]S ver 22; S Ge 8:1 [x]2Ki 2:8; Ps 74:13; 78:13; 114:5; 136:13; Isa 63:12
14:22 [y]ver 16; Nu 33:8; Jos 24:6; Isa 43:16; 63:11; 1Co 10:1 [z]ver 21,29; S Ge 3:12; 15:19; Dt 31:6-8; Jos 3:16, 17; x22; Ne 9:11; Ps 66:6; 77:19; 106:9; Isa 11:15; 41:10; 43:5; 44:27; 50:2; 51:10; 63:13; Jer 46:28; Na 1:4; Heb 11:29 [a]Ex 15:8; Jos 3:13; Ps 78:13 14:23 [b]ver 7

[x]9 Or charioteers; also in verses 17, 18, 23, 26 and 28

---

means "watchtower." sea. The sea that the NIV, in accordance with established tradition, calls the Red Sea—in Hebrew Yam Suph, i.e., Sea of Reeds (see 13:18 and NIV text note). Reference can hardly be to the northern end of the Gulf of Suez since reeds do not grow in salt water. Moreover, an Egyptian papyrus locates Baal Zephon in the vicinity of Tahpanhes (see note on Jer 2:16), a site near Lake Menzaleh about 20 miles east of Rameses. The crossing of the "Red Sea" thus probably occurred at the southern end of Lake Menzaleh (see map of "The Exodus," p. 106; but see note on 13:18). Baal Zephon. Means "Baal of the north" or "Baal of North (Mountain)"—also the name of a Canaanite god.
14:4 know that I am the LORD. See note on 6:3.
14:7 officers. The Hebrew for the singular of this word means "third man," perhaps referring to his place in a chariot crew.
14:14 The LORD will fight for you. A necessary reminder that although Israel was "armed for battle" (13:18) and

"marching out boldly" (v. 8), the victory would be won by God alone.
14:19 angel of God. See note on Ge 16:7; here associated with the cloud (see 13:21).
14:20 coming between the armies of Egypt and Israel. The pillar of cloud (signifying the Lord's presence) protected Israel (see Ps 105:39).
14:21 strong east wind. See 10:13. In 15:8 the poet praises the Lord and calls the wind the "blast of your nostrils," affirming (as here) that the miracle occurred in accordance with God's timing and under his direction (see 15:10).
14:22 through the sea on dry ground. In later times, psalmists and prophets reminded Israel of what God had done for them (see Ps 66:6; 106:9; 136:13–14; Isa 51:10; 63:11–13). wall of water. See v. 29. The waters were "piled up" (15:8) on both sides.
14:24 last watch of the night. Often the time for surprise attack (see Jos 10:9; 1Sa 11:11). the LORD looked down. See

looked down from the pillar of fire and cloud[c] at the Egyptian army and threw it into confusion.[d] 25He made the wheels of their chariots come off[y] so that they had difficulty driving. And the Egyptians said, "Let's get away from the Israelites! The LORD is fighting[e] for them against Egypt."[f]

26Then the LORD said to Moses, "Stretch out your hand over the sea so that the waters may flow back over the Egyptians and their chariots and horsemen." 27Moses stretched out his hand over the sea, and at daybreak the sea went back to its place.[g] The Egyptians were fleeing toward[z] it, and the LORD swept them into the sea.[h] 28The water flowed back and covered the chariots and horsemen—the entire army of Pharaoh that had followed the Israelites into the sea.[i] Not one of them survived.[j]

29But the Israelites went through the sea on dry ground,[k] with a wall[l] of water on their right and on their left. 30That day the LORD saved[m] Israel from the hands of the Egyptians, and Israel saw the Egyptians lying dead on the shore. 31And when the Israelites saw the great power[n] the LORD displayed against the Egyptians, the people feared[o] the LORD and put their trust[p] in him and in Moses his servant.

The Song of Moses and Miriam

15 Then Moses and the Israelites sang this song[q] to the LORD:

"I will sing[r] to the LORD,
  for he is highly exalted.
The horse and its rider[s]
  he has hurled into the sea.[t]
2The LORD is my strength[u] and my song;
  he has become my salvation.[v]
He is my God,[w] and I will praise him,
  my father's God, and I will exalt[x]
  him.

3The LORD is a warrior;[y]
  the LORD is his name.[z]
4Pharaoh's chariots and his army[a]
  he has hurled into the sea.
The best of Pharaoh's officers
  are drowned in the Red Sea.[a]
5The deep waters[b] have covered them;
  they sank to the depths like a stone.[c]

6"Your right hand,[d] O LORD,
  was majestic in power.
Your right hand,[e] O LORD,
  shattered[f] the enemy.
7In the greatness of your majesty[g]
  you threw down those who opposed
  you.
You unleashed your burning anger;[h]
  it consumed[i] them like stubble.
8By the blast of your nostrils[j]
  the waters piled up.[k]
The surging waters stood firm like a
  wall;[l]
the deep waters congealed in the
  heart of the sea.[m]

9"The enemy boasted,
  'I will pursue,[n] I will overtake them.
I will divide the spoils;[o]
  I will gorge myself on them.
I will draw my sword
  and my hand will destroy them.'
10But you blew with your breath,[p]

14:24 cS Ex 13:21; 1Co 10:1 dEx 23:27; Jos 10:10; 1Sa 5:9; 7:10; 14:15; 2Sa 5:24; 2Ki 7:6; 19:7 14:25 eS ver 14 fS ver 9; Dt 32:31; 1Sa 2:2; 4:8 14:27 gJos 4:18 hver 28; Ex 15:1, 21; Dt 1:40; 2:1; 11:4; Ps 78:53; 106:11; 136:15; Heb 11:29 14:28 iver 23; Ex 15:19; Jos 24:7 jS ver 27; Ex 15:5; Jdg 4:16; Ne 9:11 14:29 kver 21, S 22; Jos 24:11; 2Ki 2:8; Ps 74:15 lPs 78:13 14:30 mver 29; 1Sa 14:23; 1Ch 11:14; Ps 44:7; 106:8, 10,21; Isa 43:3; 50:2; 51:9-10; 60:16; 63:8,11 14:31 nS Ex 9:16; Ps 147:5 oEx 20:18; Dt 31:13; Jos 4:24; 1Sa 12:18; Ps 76:7; 112:1 pS Ex 4:5; Ps 22:4; 40:3; 106:12; Jn 2:11; 11:45 15:1 qNu 21:17; Jdg 5:1; 2Sa 22:1; 1Ch 16:9; Job 36:24; Ps 59:16; 105:2; Rev 15:3 rJdg 5:3; Ps 13:6; 21:13; 27:6; 61:8; 104:33; 106:12; Isa 12:5,6; 42:10-11,10; 44:23 sDt 11:4; Ps 76:6; Jer 51:21 tS Ex 14:27 15:2 uPs 18:1; 59:17 vS Ge 45:7; Ex 14:13; Ps 18:2,46; 25:5; 27:1; 62:2; 118:14; Isa 12:2; 33:2; Jnh 2:9; Hab 3:18 wS Ge 28:21

xDt 10:21; 2Sa 22:47; Ps 22:3; 30:1; 34:3; 35:27; 99:5; 103:19; 107:32; 108:5; 109:1; 118:28; 145:11; 148:14; Isa 24:15; 25:1; Jer 17:14; Da 4:37 15:3 yS Ex 14:14; Rev 19:11 zS Ex 3:15 15:4 aEx 14:6-7; Jer 51:21 15:5 bS Ex 14:28 cver 10; Ne 9:11 15:6 dPs 16:11; 17:7; 21:8; 63:8; 74:11; 77:10; 89:13; 98:1; 118:15; 138:7 eS Ex 3:20; S Job 40:14 fNu 24:8; 1Sa 2:10; Ps 2:9 15:7 gDt 33:26; Ps 150:2 hPs 2:5; 78:49-50; Jer 12:13; 25:38 iEx 24:17; Dt 4:24; 9:3; Ps 18:8; 59:13; Heb 12:29 15:8 jS Ex 14:21; Ps 18:15 kJos 3:13; Ps 78:13; Isa 43:16 lS Ex 14:22 mPs 46:2 15:9 nEx 14:5-9; Dt 28:45; Ps 7:5; La 1:3 oJdg 5:30; Isa 9:3; 53:12; Lk 11:22 15:10 pJob 4:9; 15:30; Isa 11:4; 30:33; 40:7

y25 Or He jammed the wheels of their chariots (see Samaritan Pentateuch, Septuagint and Syriac)   z27 Or from   a4 Hebrew Yam Suph; that is, Sea of Reeds; also in verse 22

note on 13:21.
14:25 *The Lord is fighting for them.* See note on v. 14.
14:27 *The Lord swept them into the sea.* As he had done with the locusts of the eighth plague (see 10:19).
14:28 *Not one of them survived.* The Lord's victory over the pharaoh's army was complete.
14:31 *feared the Lord.* See note on Ge 20:11. *put their trust in him and in Moses.* Faith in God's mighty power and confidence in Moses' leadership. *his servant.* Here refers to one who has the status of a high official in the Lord's kingly administration (see Nu 12:8; Dt 34:5). See also the same title applied to Joshua (Jos 24:29), Samuel (1Sa 3:10), David (2Sa 3:18) and Elijah (2Ki 9:36).
15:1–18 A hymn celebrating God's spectacular victory over the pharaoh and his army. The focus of the song is God himself (see v. 11); the divine name Yahweh ("the Lord") appears ten times. Similes—"like a stone" (v. 5), "like a wall" (v. 8) and "like lead" (v. 10)—mark the conclusion of

three of the five stanzas. The first four stanzas (vv. 1–5, 6–8, 9–10, 11–12) retell the story of the "deliverance" (14:13) at the Red Sea, and the final stanza (vv. 13–18) anticipates the future approach to and conquest of Canaan.
15:1 *Moses and the Israelites sang.* As though one person, the whole community praises God. *I will sing.* A common way to begin a hymn of praise (see Jdg 5:3; Ps 89:1; 101:1; 108:1).
15:2 The first half of the verse is quoted verbatim in Ps 118:14 (see Isa 12:2).
15:3 *The Lord is a warrior.* See note on 14:14. God is often pictured as a king leading his people into battle (see, e.g., Dt 1:30; Jdg 4:14; 2Sa 5:24; 2Ch 20:17–18).
15:4 *officers.* See note on 14:7.
15:5 *sank . . . like a stone.* Babylon is similarly described in Jer 51:63–64.
15:8 See note on 14:22. *blast of your nostrils.* See note on 14:21; see also Ps 18:15.

and the sea covered them.
They sank like lead
  in the mighty waters. *q*

11"Who among the gods is like you, *r*
  O LORD?
Who is like you—
  majestic in holiness, *s*
awesome in glory, *t*
  working wonders? *u*
12You stretched out *v* your right hand
  and the earth swallowed them. *w*

13"In your unfailing love you will lead *x*
  the people you have redeemed. *y*
In your strength you will guide them
  to your holy dwelling. *z*
14The nations will hear and tremble; *a*
  anguish *b* will grip the people of
    Philistia. *c*
15The chiefs *d* of Edom *e* will be terrified,
  the leaders of Moab will be seized
    with trembling, *f*
the people *b* of Canaan will melt *g* away;
16 terror *h* and dread will fall upon
    them.
By the power of your arm
  they will be as still as a stone *i* —
until your people pass by, O LORD,
  until the people you bought *c j* pass
    by. *k*
17You will bring *l* them in and plant *m*
  them
on the mountain *n* of your
  inheritance—
the place, O LORD, you made for your
  dwelling, *o*
the sanctuary, *p* O Lord, your hands
  established.

18The LORD will reign
  for ever and ever." *q*

19When Pharaoh's horses, chariots and
horsemen *d* went into the sea, *r* the LORD
brought the waters of the sea back over
them, but the Israelites walked through
the sea on dry ground. *s* 20Then Miriam *t*
the prophetess, *u* Aaron's sister, took a
tambourine in her hand, and all the
women followed her, with tambourines *v*
and dancing. *w* 21Miriam sang *x* to them:

"Sing to the LORD,
  for he is highly exalted.
The horse and its rider *y*
  he has hurled into the sea." *z*

The Waters of Marah and Elim

22Then Moses led Israel from the Red
Sea and they went into the Desert *a* of
Shur. *b* For three days they traveled in the
desert without finding water. *c* 23When
they came to Marah, they could not drink
its water because it was bitter. (That is
why the place is called Marah. *e d*) 24So the
people grumbled *e* against Moses, saying,
"What are we to drink?" *f*

15:10 *q*ver 5;
Ne 9:11; Ps 29:3;
32:6; 77:19
15:11 *r*S Ex 8:10;
Ps 77:13;
S Isa 46:5
*s*Lev 19:2;
1Sa 2:2;
1Ch 16:29;
Ps 99:3; 110:3;
Isa 6:3; Rev 4:8
*t*S Ex 14:4;
Ps 4:2; 8:1; 26:8;
Isa 35:2; 40:5
*u*S Ex 3:20
15:12 *v*S Ex 7:5
*w*Nu 16:32;
26:10; Dt 11:6;
Ps 106:17
15:13 *x*Ne 9:12;
Ps 77:20
*y*S Ex 6:6;
Job 33:28;
Ps 71:23; 106:10;
Isa 1:27; 41:14;
43:14; 44:22-24;
51:10; 63:9;
Tit 2:14 *z*ver 17;
Ps 68:16; 76:2;
78:54
15:14 *a*ver 16;
Ex 23:27;
Dt 2:25; Jos 2:9;
5:1; 9:24;
1Sa 4:7; Est 8:17;
Ps 48:6; 96:9;
99:1; 114:7;
Eze 38:20
*b*Isa 13:8
*c*Ps 83:7
15:15
*d*S Ge 36:15
*e*Dt 2:4 /Nu 22:3;
Ps 114:7 *g*Jos 2:9,
24
15:16 *h*S ver 14;
S Ge 35:5
*i*1Sa 25:37
/Ps 74:2; 2Pe 2:1
*k*Dt 2:4
15:17 /Ex 23:20;
32:34; 33:12
*m*2Sa 7:10;
Ps 44:2; 80:8,15;
Isa 5:2; 60:21;
Jer 2:21; 11:17;
24:6; Am 9:15
*n*Dt 33:19;
Ps 2:6; 3:4; 15:1;
78:54,68; 133:3;

15:18 Da 9:16; Joel 2:1; Ob 1:16; Zep 3:11 *o*S ver 13; Ps 132:13-14
*p*Ps 78:69; 114:2 **15:18** *q*S Ge 21:33; Ps 9:7; 29:10; 55:19;
66:7; 80:1; 102:12; 145:13; La 5:19 **15:19** *r*S Ex 14:28
*s*S Ex 14:22 **15:20** *t*ver 21; Nu 12:1; 20:1; 26:59;
1Ch 4:17; 6:3 *u*Jdg 4:4; 2Ki 22:14; 2Ch 34:22; Ne 6:14;
Isa 8:3; Eze 13:17; 1Sa 18:6; Ps 81:2; Isa 30:32
*w*S Ge 4:21; Jdg 11:34; 21:21; 1Sa 18:6; 2Sa 6:5,14,16;
Ps 30:11; 149:3; 150:4; SS 6:13; Jer 31:4,13 **15:21**
*x*1Sa 18:7 *y*Am 2:15; Hag 2:22 *z*S Ex 14:27 **15:22** *a*Ps 78:52
*b*S Ge 16:7 *c*Ex 17:1,3; Nu 20:2,5; 33:14; Ps 107:5 **15:23**
*d*Nu 33:8; Ru 1:20 **15:24** *e*S Ex 14:12; 16:2; 17:3; Nu 14:2;
Jos 9:18; Ps 78:18,42; 106:13,25; Eze 16:43 /Mt 6:31

*b*15 Or *rulers*   *c*16 Or *created*   *d*19 Or *charioteers*
*e*23 *Marah* means *bitter.*

15:10 *you blew with your breath.* See note on 14:21.
15:11 *Who is like you . . . ?* See Ps 35:10; 71:19; 89:6;
113:5; Mic 7:18. The Lord, who tolerates no rivals, has
defeated all the gods of Egypt and their worshipers.
15:12 *earth.* Perhaps refers to Sheol or the grave (see Ps
63:9; 71:20), the "realm of death below" (Dt 32:22), since
it was the sea that swallowed the Egyptians.
15:13 *people you have redeemed.* See note on 6:6. *your
holy dwelling.* Perhaps a reference to the house of worship at
Shiloh (see Jer 7:12), and ultimately the temple on Mount
Zion (see Ps 76:2), the "place" God would "choose" (Dt
12:14,18,26; 14:25; 16:7,15–16; 17:8,10; 18:6; 31:11)
to put "his Name" (Dt 12:5,11,21; 14:23–24; 16:2,6,11;
26:2). But the phrase may refer to the promised land, which
is called "your dwelling" and "the sanctuary . . . your hands
established" in v. 17.
15:14–15 *Philistia . . . Edom . . . Moab . . . Canaan.* The
order is roughly that along the route Israel would follow from
Mount Sinai to the promised land.
15:15 *chiefs.* The term used earlier of the Edomite rulers
(see Ge 36:15–19,21,29–30,40,43).
15:16 *dread will fall upon them.* See note on 1Ch 14:17.
bought. See NIV text note; see also Dt 32:6 and NIV text
note. In Ps 74:2 the meaning "bought" or "purchased" is
found in context with "redeemed" (see note on 13:13).

15:17 *inheritance.* The promised land (see 1Sa 26:19; Ps
79:1).
15:20 *prophetess.* See Nu 12:1–2 for a statement by
Miriam concerning her prophetic gift (see note on 7:1–2).
Other prophetesses in the Bible were Deborah (Jdg 4:4),
Isaiah's wife (Isa 8:3, but see note there), Huldah (2Ki
22:14), Noadiah (Ne 6:14), Anna (Lk 2:36) and Philip's
daughters (Ac 21:9). *women followed her, with tambourines and dancing.* Such celebration was common after victory in battle (see 1Sa 18:6; 2Sa 1:20).
15:21 Miriam repeats the first four lines of the victory
hymn (see v. 1), changing only the form of the first verb.
15:22 *Desert of Shur.* Located east of Egypt (see Ge 25:18;
1Sa 15:7) in the northwestern part of the Sinai peninsula. In
Nu 33:8 it is called the "Desert of Etham." Shur and Etham
both mean "fortress wall" (Shur in Hebrew, Etham in Egyptian).
15:23 *Marah.* Probably modern Ain Hawarah, inland from
the Gulf of Suez and 50 miles south of its northern end.
15:24 *grumbled.* During their desert wanderings, the Israelites grumbled against Moses and Aaron whenever they
faced a crisis (see 16:2; 17:3; Nu 14:2; 16:11,41). In reality,
however, they were grumbling "against the LORD" (16:8).
Paul warns us not to follow their example (see 1Co 10:
10).

²⁵Then Moses cried out[g] to the LORD, and the LORD showed him a piece of wood. He threw[h] it into the water, and the water became sweet.

There the LORD made a decree and a law for them, and there he tested[i] them. ²⁶He said, "If you listen carefully to the voice of the LORD your God and do what is right in his eyes, if you pay attention to his commands and keep[j] all his decrees,[k] I will not bring on you any of the diseases[l] I brought on the Egyptians, for I am the LORD, who heals[m] you."

²⁷Then they came to Elim, where there were twelve springs and seventy palm trees, and they camped[n] there near the water.

Manna and Quail

16 The whole Israelite community set out from Elim and came to the Desert of Sin,[o] which is between Elim and Sinai, on the fifteenth day of the second month after they had come out of Egypt.[p] ²In the desert the whole community grumbled[q] against Moses and Aaron. ³The Israelites said to them, "If only we had died by the LORD's hand in Egypt![r] There we sat around pots of meat and ate all the food[s] we wanted, but you have brought us out into this desert to starve this entire assembly to death."[t]

⁴Then the LORD said to Moses, "I will rain down bread from heaven[u] for you. The people are to go out each day and gather enough for that day. In this way I will test[v] them and see whether they will follow my instructions. ⁵On the sixth day they are to prepare what they bring in, and that is to be twice[w] as much as they gather on the other days."

⁶So Moses and Aaron said to all the Isra-

elites, "In the evening you will know that it was the LORD who brought you out of Egypt,[x] ⁷and in the morning you will see the glory[y] of the LORD, because he has heard your grumbling[z] against him. Who are we, that you should grumble against us?" ⁸Moses also said, "You will know that it was the LORD when he gives you meat to eat in the evening and all the bread you want in the morning, because he has heard your grumbling[b] against him. Who are we? You are not grumbling against us, but against the LORD."[c]

⁹Then Moses told Aaron, "Say to the entire Israelite community, 'Come before the LORD, for he has heard your grumbling.' "

¹⁰While Aaron was speaking to the whole Israelite community, they looked toward the desert, and there was the glory[d] of the LORD appearing in the cloud.[e]

¹¹The LORD said to Moses, ¹²"I have heard the grumbling[f] of the Israelites. Tell them, 'At twilight you will eat meat, and in the morning you will be filled with bread. Then you will know that I am the LORD your God.' "[g]

¹³That evening quail[h] came and covered the camp, and in the morning there was a layer of dew[i] around the camp. ¹⁴When the dew was gone, thin flakes like frost[j] on the ground appeared on the desert floor. ¹⁵When the Israelites saw it, they said to each other, "What is it?" For they did not know[k] what it was.

Moses said to them, "It is the bread[l] the LORD has given you to eat. ¹⁶This is

Cross references (center column)

15:25
gS Ex 14:10
h2Ki 2:21; 4:41; 6:6 /S Ge 22:1; Jdg 3:4; Job 23:10; Ps 81:7; Isa 48:10
15:26 /Ex 23:22; Dt 11:13; 15:5; 28:1; Jer 11:6
kEx 19:5-6; 20:2-17; Dt 7:12
lDt 7:15; 28:27, 58-60; 32:39; 1Sa 5:6; Ps 30:2; 41:3-4; 103:3
mEx 23:25-26; 2Ki 20:5; Ps 25:11; 103:3; 107:20; Jer 30:17; Hos 11:3
15:27 nNu 33:9
16:1 oEx 17:1; Nu 33:11,12
pS Ex 6:6; 12:1-2
16:2
qS Ex 15:24; 1Co 10:10
16:3 rEx 17:3; Nu 14:2; 20:3
sNu 11:4,34; Dt 12:20; Ps 78:18; 106:14; Jer 44:17
16:4 uver 14-15; Dt 8:3; Ne 9:15; Ps 78:24; 105:40; S Jn 6:31*
vS Ge 22:1
16:5 wver 22; Lev 25:21
16:6 xS Ex 6:6
16:7 yver 10; Ex 24:16; 29:43; 33:18,22; 40:34; Lev 9:6; Nu 16:19,42; Dt 5:24; 1Ki 8:11; Ps 63:2; Isa 6:3; 35:2; 40:5; 44:23; 60:1; 66:18; Eze 1:28; 10:4; 43:5; Hab 2:14; Hag 2:7; Jn 11:40
zver 12; Nu 11:1, 18; 14:2,27,28; 17:5
16:8 bver 7
cNu 23:21; Dt 33:5; Jdg 8:23; 1Sa 8:7; 12:12; S Mt 10:40;
dNu 16:11
Ro 13:2; 1Th 4:8 16:10 dS ver 7; Jn 11:4 eEx 13:21; 40:34-35; 1Ki 8:10; 2Ch 7:1; Eze 10:4 16:12 fS ver 7
gS Ex 6:2; S 20:2 16:13 hNu 11:31; Ps 78:27-28; 105:40; 106:15 /Nu 11:9 16:14 /ver 31; Nu 11:7-9; Dt 8:3,16; Ps 105:40 16:15 kDt 8:16 /S ver 4; Ne 9:20; S Jn 6:31

15:25 *He threw it into the water, and the water became sweet.* For a similar occurrence see 2Ki 2:19–22. *a decree and a law.* Technical terms presumably referring to what follows in v. 26. *tested.* See note on Ge 22:1. God tested Israel also in connection with his provision of manna (see 16:4; Dt 8:2–3) and the giving of the Ten Commandments (see 20:20).

15:27 *Elim.* Seven miles south of Ain Hawarah (see note on v. 23) in the well-watered valley of Gharandel. *palm trees.* Elim means "large trees."

16:1 *from Elim . . . to the Desert of Sin.* See Nu 33:10–11. The Desert of Sin was in southwestern Sinai ("Sin" is probably derived from "Sinai") in the region today called Debbet er-Ramleh. *fifteenth day of the second month.* Exactly one month had passed since Israel's exodus from Egypt (see 12:2,6,29,31).

16:2 *grumbled.* See note on 15:24.

16:3 *meat.* Nu 11:5 lists additional items of food from Egypt that the Israelites craved.

16:4 *bread from heaven.* Jesus called himself "the true

bread from heaven" (Jn 6:32), "the bread of God" (Jn 6:33), "the bread of life" (Jn 6:35,48), "the living bread that came down from heaven" (Jn 6:51)—all in the spiritual sense (Jn 6:63). For a similar application see Dt 8:3 and Jesus' quotation of it in Mt 4:4. *go out each day and gather enough for that day.* Probably the background for Jesus' model petition in Mt 6:11; Lk 11:3. *test.* See notes on 15:25; Ge 22:1.

16:5 *sixth day . . . twice as much as they gather on the other days.* To provide for "the seventh day, the Sabbath" (v. 26), "a day of rest" (v. 23). See v. 29.

16:6 *know.* See note on 6:3.

16:8 *meat . . . in the evening and bread . . . in the morning.* See vv. 13–14.

16:10 *glory of the LORD appearing in the cloud.* See 24:15–17; see also note on 13:21.

16:12 *twilight.* See note on 12:6.

16:13 *quail came.* For a similar incident see Nu 11:31–33.

16:14 *thin flakes like frost.* See note on Nu 11:7.

16:15 *What is it?* See v. 31 and NIV text note.

what the LORD has commanded: 'Each one is to gather as much as he needs. Take an omer[f][m] for each person you have in your tent.' "

[17]The Israelites did as they were told; some gathered much, some little. [18]And when they measured it by the omer, he who gathered much did not have too much, and he who gathered little did not have too little.[n] Each one gathered as much as he needed.

[19]Then Moses said to them, "No one is to keep any of it until morning."[o]

[20]However, some of them paid no attention to Moses; they kept part of it until morning, but it was full of maggots and began to smell.[p] So Moses was angry[q] with them.

[21]Each morning everyone gathered as much as he needed, and when the sun grew hot, it melted away. [22]On the sixth day, they gathered twice[r] as much—two omers[g] for each person—and the leaders of the community[s] came and reported this to Moses. [23]He said to them, "This is what the LORD commanded: 'Tomorrow is to be a day of rest, a holy Sabbath[t] to the LORD. So bake what you want to bake and boil what you want to boil. Save whatever is left and keep it until morning.' "

[24]So they saved it until morning, as Moses commanded, and it did not stink or get maggots in it. [25]"Eat it today," Moses said, "because today is a Sabbath to the LORD. You will not find any of it on the ground today. [26]Six days you are to gather it, but on the seventh day, the Sabbath,[u] there will not be any."

[27]Nevertheless, some of the people went out on the seventh day to gather it, but they found none. [28]Then the LORD said to Moses, "How long will you[h] refuse to keep my commands[v] and my instructions? [29]Bear in mind that the LORD has given you the Sabbath; that is why on the sixth day he gives you bread for two days.

Everyone is to stay where he is on the seventh day; no one is to go out." [30]So the people rested on the seventh day.

[31]The people of Israel called the bread manna.[i][w] It was white like coriander seed and tasted like wafers made with honey. [32]Moses said, "This is what the LORD has commanded: 'Take an omer of manna and keep it for the generations to come, so they can see the bread I gave you to eat in the desert when I brought you out of Egypt.' "

[33]So Moses said to Aaron, "Take a jar and put an omer of manna[x] in it. Then place it before the LORD to be kept for the generations to come."

[34]As the LORD commanded Moses, Aaron put the manna in front of the Testimony,[y] that it might be kept. [35]The Israelites ate manna[z] forty years,[a] until they came to a land that was settled; they ate manna until they reached the border of Canaan.[b]

[36](An omer[c] is one tenth of an ephah.)[d]

Water From the Rock

17 The whole Israelite community set out from the Desert of Sin,[e] traveling from place to place as the LORD commanded. They camped at Rephidim,[f] but there was no water[g] for the people to drink. [2]So they quarreled with Moses and said, "Give us water[h] to drink."[i]

Moses replied, "Why do you quarrel with me? Why do you put the LORD to the test?"[j]

[3]But the people were thirsty[k] for water there, and they grumbled[l] against Moses. They said, "Why did you bring us up out of Egypt to make us and our children and livestock die[m] of thirst?"

[4]Then Moses cried out to the LORD,

16:16 [m]ver 32,36
16:18 [n]2Co 8:15*
16:19 [o]ver 23; Ex 12:10
16:20 [p]ver 24
[q]Ex 32:19
16:22 [r]ver 5
[s]Ex 34:31
16:23 [t]S Ge 2:3; S Ex 20:8; Dt 5:13-14
16:26 [u]ver 23
16:28 [v]Jos 9:14; Ps 78:10; 106:13; 107:11; 119:1; Jer 32:23

16:31 [w]S ver 14
16:33 [x]Heb 9:4; Rev 2:17
16:34 [y]Ex 25:16, 21,22; 27:21; 31:18; 40:20; Lev 16:13; Nu 1:50; 7:89; 10:11; 17:4,10; Dt 10:2; 1Ki 8:9; 2Ch 5:10
16:35 [z]Jn 6:31, 49 [a]Nu 14:33; 33:38; Dt 1:3; 2:7; 8:2-4; Jos 5:6; Jdg 3:11; Ne 9:21; Ps 95:10; Am 5:25
[b]Jos 5:12
16:36 [c]S ver 16
[d]Lev 5:11; 6:20; Nu 5:15; 15:4; 28:5
17:1 [e]S Ex 16:1
[f]ver 8; Ex 19:2; Nu 33:15
[g]Nu 20:5; 21:5; 33:14
17:2 [h]Nu 20:2; 33:14; Ps 107:5
[i]S Ex 14:12
[j]Dt 6:16; Ps 78:18,41; 106:14; Mt 4:7; 1Co 10:9
17:3 [k]S Ex 15:22
[l]S Ex 15:24
[m]S Ex 14:11

[f]16 That is, probably about 2 quarts (about 2 liters); also in verses 18, 32, 33 and 36   [g]22 That is, probably about 4 quarts (about 4.5 liters)   [h]28 The Hebrew is plural.   [i]31 *Manna* means *What is it?* (see verse 15).

16:18 See 2Co 8:15, where Paul quotes the heart of the verse as an illustration of Christians who share with each other what they possess.
16:23 *Sabbath.* The first occurrence of the word itself, though the principle of the seventh day as a day of rest and holiness is set forth in the account of creation (see note on Ge 2:3).
16:29 See note on v. 5.
16:31 *manna.* See note on Nu 11:7.
16:33 *jar.* Said in Heb 9:4 to be made of gold.
16:34 *Testimony.* Anticipates the later description of the tablets containing the Ten Commandments as the "two tablets of the Testimony" (31:18; 32:15; 34:29), which gave their name to the "ark of the Testimony" (25:22; 26:33) in which they were placed (see 25:16,21) along with

the jar of manna (see Heb 9:4; see also Rev 2:17 and note).
16:35 *ate manna forty years . . . until they reached . . . Canaan.* The manna stopped at the time the Israelites celebrated their first Passover in Canaan (see Jos 5:10-12).
17:1 *traveling from place to place.* For a list of specific sites see Nu 33:12-14. *Rephidim.* Probably either the Wadi Refayid or the Wadi Feiran, both near Jebel Musa (see note on 3:1) in southern Sinai.
17:2 *put the LORD to the test.* Israel fails the Lord's testing of her (see 16:4) by putting the Lord to the test.
17:3 *grumbled.* See note on 15:24.
17:4 *these people.* The same note of distance and alienation ("these people" instead of "my people") in such situations is found often in the prophets (see, e.g., Isa 6:9; Hag 1:2).

"What am I to do with these people? They are almost ready to stone[n] me."

[5]The LORD answered Moses, "Walk on ahead of the people. Take with you some of the elders of Israel and take in your hand the staff[o] with which you struck the Nile,[p] and go. [6]I will stand there before you by the rock at Horeb.[q] Strike[r] the rock, and water[s] will come out of it for the people to drink." So Moses did this in the sight of the elders of Israel. [7]And he called the place Massah[j][t] and Meribah[k][u] because the Israelites quarreled and because they tested the LORD saying, "Is the LORD among us or not?"

The Amalekites Defeated

[8]The Amalekites[v] came and attacked the Israelites at Rephidim.[w] [9]Moses said to Joshua,[x] "Choose some of our men and go out to fight the Amalekites. Tomorrow I will stand on top of the hill with the staff[y] of God in my hands."

[10]So Joshua fought the Amalekites as Moses had ordered, and Moses, Aaron and Hur[z] went to the top of the hill. [11]As long as Moses held up his hands, the Israelites were winning,[a] but whenever he lowered his hands, the Amalekites were winning. [12]When Moses' hands grew tired, they took a stone and put it under him and he sat on it. Aaron and Hur held his hands up—one on one side, one on the other—so that his hands remained steady

till sunset.[b] [13]So Joshua overcame the Amalekite[c] army with the sword.

[14]Then the LORD said to Moses, "Write[d] this on a scroll as something to be remembered and make sure that Joshua hears it, because I will completely blot out[e] the memory of Amalek[f] from under heaven."

[15]Moses built an altar[g] and called[h] it The LORD is my Banner. [16]He said, "For hands were lifted up to the throne of the LORD. The[l] LORD will be at war against the Amalekites[i] from generation to generation."[j]

Jethro Visits Moses

18 Now Jethro,[k] the priest of Midian[l] and father-in-law of Moses, heard of everything God had done for Moses and for his people Israel, and how the LORD had brought Israel out of Egypt.[m]

[2]After Moses had sent away his wife Zipporah,[n] his father-in-law Jethro received her [3]and her two sons.[o] One son was named Gershom,[m] for Moses said, "I have become an alien in a foreign land";[p] [4]and the other was named Eliezer,[n][q] for

17:4 [n]Nu 14:10; 1Sa 30:6; S Jn 8:59
17:5 [o]S Ex 4:2; S 10:12-13 [p]Ex 7:20
17:6 [o]S Ex 3:1 [r]Nu 20:8 [s]Nu 20:11; Dt 8:15; Jdg 15:19; 2Ki 3:20; Ne 9:15; Ps 74:15; 78:15-16; 105:41; 107:35; 114:8; Isa 30:25; 35:6; 43:19; 48:21; 1Co 10:4
17:7 [t]Dt 6:16; 9:22; 33:8; Ps 95:8 [u]Nu 20:13,24; 27:14; Ps 81:7; 106:32
17:8 [v]S Ge 36:12 [w]S ver 1
17:9 [x]Ex 24:13; 32:17; 33:11; Nu 11:28; 27:22; Dt 1:38; Jos 1:1; Ac 7:45 [y]S Ex 4:17
17:10 [z]ver 10-12; Ex 24:14; 31:2
17:11 [a]Jas 5:16
17:12 [b]Jos 8:26
17:13 [c]ver 8
17:14 [d]Ex 24:4; 34:27; Nu 33:2; Dt 31:9; Job 19:23; Isa 30:8; Jer 36:2; 45:1; 51:60 [e]Ex 32:33; Dt 29:20; Job 18:17; Ps 9:5; 34:16; 109:15; Eze 18:4 [f]ver 13; S Ge 36:12; Nu 24:7; Jdg 3:13; 1Sa 30:17-18; Ps 83:7
17:15 [g]S Ge 8:20 [h]S Ge 22:14 17:16 [i]Nu 24:7; 1Ch 4:43; Est 3:1; 8:3; 9:24 [j]Est 9:5 18:1 [k]S Ex 2:18 [l]S Ex 2:16 [m]S Ex 6:6 18:2 [n]S Ex 2:21 18:3 [o]S Ex 4:20; Ac 7:29 [p]Ex 2:22 18:4 [q]1Ch 23:15

[j]7 Massah means testing.   [k]7 Meribah means quarreling.   [l]16 Or "Because a hand was against the throne of the LORD, the   [m]3 Gershom sounds like the Hebrew for an alien there.   [n]4 Eliezer means my God is helper.

17:6 I will stand there . . . by the rock. Paul may have had this incident in mind when he spoke of Christ as "the spiritual rock that accompanied" Israel (see 1Co 10:4; see also Heb 11:24–26). Horeb. See note on 3:1. Strike the rock, and water will come out. The event was later celebrated by Israel's hymn writers and prophets (see Ps 78:15–16,20; 105:41; 114:8; Isa 48:21).
17:7 Massah and Meribah. Heb 3:7–8,15 (quoting Ps 95:7–8) gives the meaning "testing" for Massah and "rebellion" for Meribah. Another Meribah, where a similar incident occurred near Kadesh Barnea (see note on Ge 14:7), is referred to in Nu 20:13,24; 27:14; Dt 32:51; 33:8; Ps 81:7; 106:32; Eze 47:19; 48:28.
17:8 Amalekites. See note on Ge 14:7.
17:9 Joshua. The name given by Moses to Hoshea son of Nun (see Nu 13:16). "Hoshea" means "salvation," while "Joshua" means "The LORD saves." The Greek form of the name Joshua is the same as that of the name Jesus, for the meaning of which see NIV text note on Mt 1:21. Joshua was from the tribe of Ephraim (Nu 13:8), one of the most powerful of the 12 tribes (see notes on Ge 48:6,19). fight the Amalekites. Joshua's military prowess uniquely suited him to be the conqueror of Canaan 40 years later, while his faith in God and loyalty to Moses suited him to be Moses' "aide" (24:13; 33:11) and successor (see Dt 1:38; 3:28; 31:14; 34:9; Jos 1:5).
17:10 Hur. Perhaps the same Hur who was the son of Caleb and the grandfather of Bezalel (see 1Ch 2:19–20), one

of the builders of the tabernacle (see 31:2–5).
17:11 held up his hands. A symbol of appeal to God for help and enablement (see note on 9:29; see also 9:22; 10:12; 14:16).
17:14 Write. See 24:4; 34:27–28; Nu 33:2; Dt 28:58; 29:20,21,27; 30:10; 31:9,19,22,24; see also Introduction: Author and Date of Writing. scroll. A long strip of leather or papyrus on which scribes wrote in columns (see Jer 36:23) with pen (see Isa 8:1) and ink (see Jer 36:18), sometimes on both sides (see Eze 2:10; Rev 5:1). After being rolled up, a scroll was often sealed (see Isa 29:11; Da 12:4; Rev 5:1–2, 5,9) to protect its contents. Scrolls were of various sizes (see Isa 8:1; Rev 10:2,9–10). Certain Egyptian examples reached lengths of over 100 feet; Biblical scrolls, however, rarely exceeded 30 feet in length, as in the case of a book like Isaiah (see Lk 4:17). Reading the contents of a scroll involved the awkward procedure of unrolling it with one hand while rolling it up with the other (see Isa 34:4; Eze 2:10; Lk 4:17,20; Rev 6:14). Shortly after the time of Christ the scroll gave way to the book form still used today.
17:15 my Banner. Recalling Moses' petition with upraised hands (see vv. 11–12,16) and testifying to the power of God displayed in defense of his people.
18:1 Jethro the priest of Midian. See note on 2:16.
18:2 sent away his wife. Apparently Moses sent Zipporah to her father with the news that the Lord had blessed his mission (see v. 1) and that he was in the vicinity of Mount Sinai with Israel.

he said, "My father's God was my helper;[r] he saved me from the sword of Pharaoh."

[5]Jethro, Moses' father-in-law, together
with Moses' sons and wife, came to him in
the desert, where he was camped near the
mountain[s] of God. [6]Jethro had sent word
to him, "I, your father-in-law Jethro, am
coming to you with your wife and her two
sons."

[7]So Moses went out to meet his father-
in-law and bowed down[t] and kissed[u]
him. They greeted each other and then
went into the tent. [8]Moses told his father-
in-law about everything the LORD had
done to Pharaoh and the Egyptians for Israel's sake and about all the hardships[v]
they had met along the way and how the
LORD had saved[w] them.

[9]Jethro was delighted to hear about all
the good things[x] the LORD had done for
Israel in rescuing them from the hand of
the Egyptians. [10]He said, "Praise be to the
LORD,[y] who rescued you from the hand of
the Egyptians and of Pharaoh, and who
rescued the people from the hand of the
Egyptians. [11]Now I know that the LORD is
greater than all other gods,[z] for he did this
to those who had treated Israel arrogantly."[a] [12]Then Jethro, Moses' father-in-
law,[b] brought a burnt offering[c] and other
sacrifices[d] to God, and Aaron came with
all the elders of Israel to eat bread[e] with
Moses' father-in-law in the presence[f] of
God.

[13]The next day Moses took his seat to
serve as judge for the people, and they
stood around him from morning till evening. [14]When his father-in-law saw all that
Moses was doing for the people, he said,
"What is this you are doing for the people?
Why do you alone sit as judge, while all
these people stand around you from morning till evening?"

[15]Moses answered him, "Because the
people come to me to seek God's will.[g]
[16]Whenever they have a dispute,[h] it is
brought to me, and I decide between the

parties and inform them of God's decrees
and laws."[i]

[17]Moses' father-in-law replied, "What
you are doing is not good. [18]You and these
people who come to you will only wear
yourselves out. The work is too heavy for
you; you cannot handle it alone.[j] [19]Listen
now to me and I will give you some advice, and may God be with you.[k] You
must be the people's representative before
God and bring their disputes[l] to him.
[20]Teach them the decrees and laws,[m] and
show them the way to live[n] and the duties
they are to perform.[o] [21]But select capable
men[p] from all the people—men who
fear[q] God, trustworthy men who hate dishonest gain[r]—and appoint them as officials[s] over thousands, hundreds, fifties
and tens. [22]Have them serve as judges for
the people at all times, but have them
bring every difficult case[t] to you; the simple cases they can decide themselves. That
will make your load lighter, because they
will share[u] it with you. [23]If you do this and
God so commands, you will be able to
stand the strain, and all these people will
go home satisfied."

[24]Moses listened to his father-in-law and
did everything he said. [25]He chose capable
men from all Israel and made them leaders[v] of the people, officials over thousands,
hundreds, fifties and tens.[w] [26]They served
as judges[x] for the people at all times. The
difficult cases[y] they brought to Moses, but
the simple ones they decided themselves.[z]

[27]Then Moses sent his father-in-law on
his way, and Jethro returned to his own
country.[a]

At Mount Sinai

19 In the third month after the Israelites left Egypt[b]—on the very
day—they came to the Desert of Sinai.[c]
[2]After they set out from Rephidim,[d] they
entered the Desert of Sinai, and Israel
camped there in the desert in front of the
mountain.[e]

18:4
[r]S Ge 49:25;
S Dt 33:29
18:5 [s]S Ex 3:1
18:7 [t]S Ge 17:3;
S 43:28
[u]S Ge 29:13
18:8 [v]Nu 20:14;
Ne 9:32
[w]Ex 15:6,16;
Ps 81:7
18:9 [x]Jos 21:45;
1Ki 8:66;
Ne 9:25;
Ps 145:7; Isa 63:7
18:10
[y]S Ge 9:26;
S 24:27
18:11
[z]S Ex 12:12;
S 1Ch 16:25
[a]S Ex 1:10;
S Lk 1:51
18:12 [b]S Ex 3:1
[c]Ex 10:25;
20:24; Lev 1:2-9
[d]Ge 31:54;
Ex 24:5
[e]S Ge 26:30
[f]Dt 12:7
18:15 [g]S ver 19;
S Ge 25:22
18:16 [h]Ex 24:14

[i]ver 15;
Lev 24:12;
Nu 15:34;
Dt 1:17;
2Ch 19:7;
Pr 24:23; Mal 2:9
18:18 [j]Nu 11:11,
14,17; Dt 1:9,12
18:19 [k]Ex 3:12
[l]ver 15; Nu 27:5
18:20 [m]Dt 4:1,5;
5:1; Ps 119:12,
26,68 [n]Ps 143:8
[o]S Ge 39:11
18:21
[p]S Ge 47:6;
Ac 6:3
[q]S Ge 22:12
[r]Ex 23:8;
Dt 16:19;
1Sa 12:3; Ps 15:5;
Pr 17:23; 28:8;
Ecc 7:7;
Eze 18:8; 22:12
[s]Nu 1:16; 7:2;
10:4; Dt 16:18;
Ezr 7:25
18:22
[t]Lev 24:11;
Dt 1:17-18
[u]Nu 11:17;
Dt 1:9
18:25 [v]Nu 1:16;
7:2; 11:16;
Dt 16:18
[w]Dt 1:13-15
18:26 [x]Dt 16:18;
2Ch 19:5;
Ezr 7:25 [y]Dt 1:17
[z]ver 22
18:27
[a]Nu 10:29-30
19:1 [b]S Ex 6:6
[c]Nu 1:1; 3:14;
33:15

19:2 [d]S Ex 17:1 [e]S ver 17; S Ex 3:1; Dt 5:2-4

18:5 *mountain of God.* See 3:1 and note.
18:11 *Now I know that the LORD is greater than all other
gods.* See the similar confession of Naaman in 2Ki 5:15.
18:12 *brought.* The verb means "provided" an animal for
sacrifice (see, e.g., 25:2; Lev 12:8), not "officiated at" a
sacrifice. *eat bread with.* A token of friendship (contrast the
battle with the Amalekites, 17:8–16). Such a meal often
climaxed the establishment of a treaty (see Ge 31:54; Ex
24:11).
18:15 *seek God's will.* Inquire of God, usually by going to
a place of worship (see Ge 25:22 and note; Nu 27:21) or to

a prophet (see 1Sa 9:9; 1Ki 22:8).
18:16 *God's decrees and laws.* The process of compiling
and systematizing the body of divine law that would govern
the newly formed nation of Israel may have already begun
(see 15:25–26 and note on Ge 26:5).
18:21 *men who fear God.* See note on Ge 20:11.
19:2 *Desert of Sinai.* Located in the southeast region of the
peninsula (see note on 3:1). The narrator locates there the
events recorded in the rest of Exodus, all of Leviticus, and Nu
1:1–10:10.

3 Then Moses went up to God,[f] and the
LORD called[g] to him from the mountain
and said, "This is what you are to say to
the house of Jacob and what you are to tell
the people of Israel: 4 'You yourselves have
seen what I did to Egypt,[h] and how I carried you on eagles' wings[i] and brought
you to myself.[j] 5 Now if you obey me fully[k] and keep my covenant,[l] then out of
all nations you will be my treasured
possession.[m] Although the whole earth[n] is
mine, 6 you[o] will be for me a kingdom of
priests[o] and a holy nation.'[p] These are the
words you are to speak to the Israelites."
7 So Moses went back and summoned
the elders[q] of the people and set before
them all the words the LORD had commanded him to speak.[r] 8 The people all responded together, "We will do everything
the LORD has said."[s] So Moses brought
their answer back to the LORD.
9 The LORD said to Moses, "I am going to
come to you in a dense cloud,[t] so that the
people will hear me speaking[u] with you
and will always put their trust[v] in you."
Then Moses told the LORD what the people
had said.
10 And the LORD said to Moses, "Go to
the people and consecrate[w] them today
and tomorrow. Have them wash their
clothes[x] 11 and be ready by the third day,[y]
because on that day the LORD will come
down[z] on Mount Sinai[a] in the sight of all
the people. 12 Put limits[b] for the people
around the mountain and tell them, 'Be
careful that you do not go up the mountain
or touch the foot of it. Whoever touches
the mountain shall surely be put to death.
13 He shall surely be stoned[c] or shot with
arrows; not a hand is to be laid on him.
Whether man or animal, he shall not be
permitted to live.' Only when the ram's
horn[d] sounds a long blast may they go up
to the mountain."[e]
14 After Moses had gone down the
mountain to the people, he consecrated
them, and they washed their clothes.[f]
15 Then he said to the people, "Prepare
yourselves for the third day. Abstain[g] from
sexual relations."
16 On the morning of the third day there
was thunder[h] and lightning, with a thick
cloud[i] over the mountain, and a very loud
trumpet blast.[j] Everyone in the camp
trembled.[k] 17 Then Moses led the people
out of the camp to meet with God, and
they stood at the foot of the mountain.[l]
18 Mount Sinai was covered with smoke,[m]
because the LORD descended on it in fire.[n]
The smoke billowed up from it like smoke
from a furnace,[o] the whole mountain[p]
trembled[p] violently, 19 and the sound of
the trumpet grew louder and louder. Then
Moses spoke and the voice[q] of God answered[r] him.[q]
20 The LORD descended to the top of
Mount Sinai[s] and called Moses to the top
of the mountain. So Moses went up 21 and

19:3 [f]Ex 20:21 [g]S Ex 3:4; S 25:22; Ac 7:38 **19:4** [h]Dt 29:2; Jos 24:7 [i]Dt 32:11; Ps 103:5; Isa 40:31; Jer 4:13; 48:40; Rev 12:14 [j]Dt 33:12; Isa 31:5; Eze 16:6 **19:5** [k]Ex 15:26; Dt 6:3; Ps 78:10; Jer 7:23 [l]S Ge 17:9; S Ex 3:1 [m]S Ex 8:22; S 34:9; S Dt 8:1; S Tit 2:14 [n]S Ex 9:29; 1Co 10:26 **19:6** [o]Isa 61:6; 66:21; S 1Pe 2:5 [p]Ge 18:19; Lev 11:44-45; Dt 4:37; 7:6; 26:19; 28:9; 29:13; 33:3; Isa 4:3; 62:12; Jer 2:3; Am 3:2 **19:7** [q]Ex 18:12; Lev 4:15; 9:1; Nu 16:25 [r]Ex 4:30; 1Sa 8:10 **19:8** [s]Ex 24:3,7; Dt 5:27; 26:17 **19:9** [t]ver 16; Ex 20:21; 24:15-16; 33:9; 34:5; Dt 4:11; 2Sa 22:10,12; 2Ch 6:1; Ps 18:11; 97:2; 99:7; Mt 17:5 [u]Dt 4:12,36; Jn 12:29-30 [v]S Ex 4:5 **19:10** [w]ver 14, 22; Lev 11:44; Nu 11:18; 1Sa 16:5; Joel 2:16; Heb 10:22 [x]S Ge 35:2; Rev 22:14 **19:11** [y]ver 16 [z]S Ge 11:5 [a]ver 3,20; S Ex 3:1; 24:16; 31:18; 34:2,4,29,32; Lev 7:38; 26:46; 27:34; Nu 3:1; Dt 10:5; Ne 9:13; Gal 4:24-25 **19:12** [b]ver 23 **19:13** [c]Heb 12:20* [d]Jos 6:4; 1Ch 15:28; Ps 81:3; 98:6 [e]ver 21; Ex 34:3 **19:14** [f]S Ge 35:2 **19:15** [g]1Sa 21:4; 1Co 7:5 **19:16** [h]1Sa 2:10; Isa 29:6 [i]S ver 9 [j]Heb 12:18-19; Rev 4:1 [k]S Ge 3:10; 1Sa 13:7; 14:15; 28:5; Ps 99:1; Heb 12:21 **19:17** [l]S ver 2; Dt 4:11 **19:18** [m]Ex 20:18; Ps 104:32; Isa 6:4; Rev 15:8 [n]S Ex 3:2; 24:17; Lev 9:24; Dt 4:11,24,33, 36; 5:4; 9:3; 1Ki 18:24,38; 1Ch 21:26; 2Ch 7:1; Ps 18:8; Heb 12:18 [o]S Ge 19:28; Rev 9:2 [p]Jdg 5:5; 2Sa 22:8; Ps 18:7; 68:8; Isa 2:19; 5:25; 41:15; 64:1; Jer 4:24; 10:10; Mic 1:4; Na 1:5; Hab 3:6,10; Hag 2:6 **19:19** [q]S ver 9; Dt 4:33; Ne 9:13 [r]Ps 81:7 **19:20** [s]S ver 11

[o] *5,6* Or *possession, for the whole earth is mine.* [6] *You*
[p] *18* Most Hebrew manuscripts; a few Hebrew manuscripts and Septuagint *all the people*
[q] *19* Or *and God answered him with thunder*

19:3 *Jacob . . . Israel.* See note on 1:1.
19:4 *I carried you on eagles' wings.* The description best fits the female golden eagle.
19:5 *if . . . then.* The covenant between God and Israel at Mount Sinai is the outgrowth and extension of the Lord's covenant with Abraham and his descendants 600 years earlier (see chart on "Major Covenants in the OT," p. 19). Participation in the divine blessings is conditioned on obedience added to faith (see note on Ge 17:9). *my covenant.* See note on Ge 9:9. *out of all nations . . . my treasured possession.* The equivalent phrases used of Christians in 1Pe 2:9 are "chosen people" and "people belonging to God" (see Dt 7:6; 14:2; 26:18; Ps 135:4; Mal 3:17). *the whole earth is mine.* God is the Creator and Possessor of the earth and everything in it (see Ge 14:19,22; Ps 24:1–2).
19:6 *kingdom of priests.* Israel was to constitute the Lord's kingdom (the people who acknowledged him as their King) and, like priests, was to be wholly consecrated to his service (see Isa 61:6; cf. 1Pe 2:5; Rev 1:6; 5:10; 20:6). *holy nation.* See 1Pe 2:9. God's people, both individually and collectively, are to be "set apart" (see note on 3:5) to do his will (see Dt 7:6; 14:2,21; 26:19; Isa 62:12).
19:8 *We will do everything the LORD has said.* The people promised to obey the terms of the covenant (see 24:3,7; Dt 5:27).
19:9 *dense cloud.* See 13:21 and note. *the people will hear me speaking.* See Dt 4:33. *put their trust in you.* See 14:31 and note.
19:10–11 Outward preparation to meet God symbolizes the inward consecration God requires of his people.
19:12–13 The whole mountain becomes holy because of God's presence (see 3:5 and note). Israel must keep herself from the mountain even as she is to keep herself from the tabernacle (see Nu 3:10).
19:15 *Abstain from sexual relations.* Not because sex is sinful but because it may leave the participants ceremonially unclean (see Lev 15:18; see also 1Sa 21:4–5).
19:16 *thunder . . . lightning . . . trumpet blast.* God's appearance is often accompanied by an impressive display of meteorological sights and sounds (see, e.g., 1Sa 7:10; 12:18; Job 38:1; 40:6; Ps 18:13–14). *thick cloud.* See 13:21 and note.
19:18 *fire . . . smoke from a furnace.* See Ge 15:17 and note.

the LORD said to him, "Go down and warn the people so they do not force their way through to see[t] the LORD and many of them perish.[u] 22Even the priests, who approach[v] the LORD, must consecrate[w] themselves, or the LORD will break out against them."[x]

23Moses said to the LORD, "The people cannot come up Mount Sinai,[y] because you yourself warned us, 'Put limits[z] around the mountain and set it apart as holy.'"

24The LORD replied, "Go down and bring Aaron[a] up with you. But the priests and the people must not force their way through to come up to the LORD, or he will break out against them."[b]

25So Moses went down to the people and told them.

The Ten Commandments

20:1–17pp — Dt 5:6–21

20 And God spoke[c] all these words:[d]

2"I am the LORD your God,[e] who brought you out[f] of Egypt,[g] out of the land of slavery.[h]

3"You shall have no other gods before[r] me.[i]

4"You shall not make for yourself an idol[j] in the form of anything in heaven above or on the earth beneath or in the waters below. 5You shall not bow down to them or worship[k] them; for I, the LORD your God, am a jealous God,[l] punishing the children for the sin of the fathers[m] to the third and fourth generation[n] of those who hate me, 6but showing love to a thousand[o] generations, of those who love me and keep my commandments.

7"You shall not misuse the name of the LORD your God, for the LORD

Cross references (center column)

19:21 [t]Ex 24:10-11; Nu 4:20; 1Sa 6:19 [u]S ver 13
19:22 [v]Lev 10:3 [w]1Sa 16:5; 2Ch 29:5; Joel 2:16 [x]ver 24; 2Sa 6:7
19:23 [y]ver 11 [z]ver 12
19:24 [a]Ex 24:1,9 [b]ver 22
20:1 [c]Dt 10:4 [d]Ne 9:13; Ps 119:9; 147:19; Mal 4:4
20:2 [e]S Ge 17:7; Ex 16:12; Lev 19:2; 20:7; Isa 43:3; Eze 20:19
20:3 [f]ver 23; Ex 34:14; Dt 6:14; 13:10; 2Ki 17:35; Ps 44:20; 81:9; Jer 1:16; 7:6,9; 11:13; 19:4; 25:6; 35:15
20:4 [g]ver 5,23; Ex 32:8; 34:17; Lev 19:4; 26:1; Dt 4:15-19,23; 27:15; 2Sa 7:22;

1Ki 14:9; 2Ki 17:12; Isa 40:19; 42:8; 44:9 20:5 [k]Ex 23:13, 24; Jos 23:7; Jdg 6:10; 2Ki 17:35; Isa 44:15,17,19; 46:6 [l]Ex 34:14; Dt 4:24; Jos 24:19; Na 1:2 [m]S Ge 9:25; S Lev 26:39 [n]Ex 34:7; Nu 14:18; Jer 32:18 20:6 [o]Ex 34:7; Nu 14:18; Dt 7:9; Jer 32:18; Lk 1:50; Ro 11:28

[r]3 Or besides

19:22 *priests.* See also v. 24. Before the Aaronic priesthood was established (see 28:1), priestly functions were performed either by the elders (see note on 3:16; see also 3:18; 12:21; 18:12) or by designated younger men (see 24:5). But perhaps the verse anticipates the regulations for the Aaronic priests who will be appointed. *who approach the LORD.* To officiate at sacrifices (see 40:32; Lev 21:23).

20:1–17 See Dt 5:6–21; see also Mt 5:21,27; 19:17–19; Mk 10:19; Lk 18:20; Ro 13:9; Eph 6:2–3.

20:1 *words.* A technical term for "(covenant) stipulations" in the ancient Near East (e.g., among the Hittites; see also 24:3,8; 34:28). The basic code in Israel's divine law is found in vv. 2–17, elsewhere called the "Ten Commandments" (34:28; Dt 4:13; 10:4), the Hebrew words for which mean lit. "Ten Words." "Decalogue," a term of Greek origin often used as a synonym for the Ten Commandments, also means lit. "Ten Words."

20:2 *I am the LORD your God, who brought you out.* The Decalogue reflects the structure of the contemporary royal treaties (see note on Ge 15:7). On the basis of (1) a preamble, in which the great king identified himself ("I am the LORD your God"), and (2) a historical prologue, in which he sketched his previous gracious acts toward the subject king or people ("who brought you out . . ."), he then set forth (3) the treaty (covenant) stipulations (see Dt 5:1–3,7–21) to be obeyed (in this case, ten in number: vv. 3–17). Use of this ancient royal treaty pattern shows that the Lord is here formally acknowledged as Israel's King and that Israel is his subject people. As his subjects, his covenant people are to render complete submission, allegiance and obedience to him out of gratitude for his mercies, reverence for his sovereignty, and trust in his continuing care. See chart on "Major Covenants in the OT," p. 19.

20:3 *before.* The Hebrew for this word is translated "in hostility toward" in Ge 16:12; that sense may be intended here. In any event, no deity, real or imagined, is to rival the one true God in Israel's heart and life.

20:4 *idol in the form of anything.* Because God has no visible form, any idol intended to resemble him would be a sinful misrepresentation of him (see Dt 4:12,15–18). Since other gods are not to be worshiped (see v. 5), making idols of them would be equally sinful (see Dt 4:19,23–28).

20:5 *jealous God.* God will not put up with rivalry or unfaithfulness. Usually his "jealousy" concerns Israel and assumes the covenant relationship (analogous to marriage) and the Lord's exclusive right to possess Israel and to claim her love and allegiance. Actually, jealousy is part of the vocabulary of love. The "jealousy" of God (1) demands exclusive devotion to himself (see v. 14; Dt 4:24; 32:16, 21; Jos 24:19; Ps 78:58; 1Co 10:22; Jas 4:5 and NIV text note), (2) delivers to judgment all who oppose him (see Dt 29:20; 1Ki 14:22; Ps 79:5; Isa 42:13; 59:17; Eze 5:13; 16:38; 23:25; 36:5; Na 1:2; Zep 1:18; 3:8) and (3) vindicates his people (see 2Ki 19:31; Isa 9:7; 26:11; Eze 39:25; Joel 2:18; Zec 1:14; 8:2). In some of these passages the meaning is closer to "zeal" (the same Hebrew word may be translated either way, depending on context). *to the third and fourth generation of those who hate me.* Those Israelites who blatantly violate God's covenant and thus show that they reject the Lord as their King will bring down judgment on themselves and their households (see, e.g., Nu 16:31–34; Jos 7:24 and note)—households were usually extended to "three or four" generations. See note on Ps 109:12. *hate.* In covenant contexts the terms "hate" and "love" (v. 6) were conventionally used to indicate rejection of or loyalty to the covenant Lord.

20:6 *a thousand generations, of those.* See 1Ch 16:15; Ps 105:8. *love me and keep my commandments.* See Jn 14:15; 1Jn 5:3. In the treaty language of the ancient Near East the "love" owed to the great king was a conventional term for total allegiance and implicit trust expressing itself in obedient service.

20:7 *misuse the name of the LORD.* By profaning God's name—e.g., by swearing falsely by it (see Lev 19:12; see also Jer 7:9 and NIV text note), as on the witness stand in court. Jesus elaborates on oath-taking in Mt 5:33–37.

will not hold anyone guiltless who misuses his name. *p*

8"Remember the Sabbath *q* day by keeping it holy. 9Six days you shall labor and do all your work, *r* 10but the seventh day is a Sabbath *s* to the LORD your God. On it you shall not do any work, neither you, nor your son or daughter, nor your manservant or maidservant, nor your animals, nor the alien within your gates. 11For in six days the LORD made the heavens and the earth, *t* the sea, and all that is in them, but he rested *u* on the seventh day. *v* Therefore the LORD blessed the Sabbath day and made it holy.

12"Honor your father and your mother, *w* so that you may live long *x* in the land *y* the LORD your God is giving you.

13"You shall not murder. *z*

14"You shall not commit adultery. *a*

15"You shall not steal. *b*

16"You shall not give false testimony *c* against your neighbor. *d*

17"You shall not covet *e* your neighbor's house. You shall not covet your neighbor's wife, or his manservant or maidservant, his ox or donkey, or anything that belongs to your neighbor."

18When the people saw the thunder and lightning and heard the trumpet *f* and saw the mountain in smoke, *g* they trembled with fear. *h* They stayed at a distance 19and said to Moses, "Speak to us yourself and we will listen. But do not have God speak *i* to us or we will die." *j*

20Moses said to the people, "Do not be afraid. *k* God has come to test *l* you, so that the fear *m* of God will be with you to keep you from sinning." *n*

21The people remained at a distance, while Moses approached the thick darkness *o* where God was.

Idols and Altars

22Then the LORD said to Moses, "Tell the Israelites this: 'You have seen for yourselves that I have spoken to you from heaven: *p* 23Do not make any gods to be

Cross references

20:7 *p*Ex 22:28; Lev 18:21; 19:12; 22:2; 24:11,16; Dt 6:13; 10:20; Job 2:5,9; Ps 63:11; Isa 8:21; Eze 20:39; 39:7; S Mt 5:33
20:8 *q*S Ex 16:23; 31:13-16; 35:3; Lev 19:3,30; 26:2; Isa 56:2; Jer 17:21-27; Eze 22:8
20:9 *r*Ex 23:12; 31:13-17; 34:21; 35:2-3; Lev 23:3; Lk 13:14
20:10 *s*S Ge 2:3; Ex 31:14; Lev 23:38; Nu 28:9; Isa 56:2; Eze 20:12,20
20:11 *t*Ge 1:3-2:1 *u*S Ge 2:2 *v*Ex 31:17; Heb 4:4
20:12 *w*S Ge 31:35; S Dt 5:16; Mt 15:4*; 19:19*; Mk 7:10*; 10:19*; Lk 18:20*; Eph 6:2 *x*Dt 6:2; Eph 6:3 *y*Dt 11:9; 25:15; Jer 35:7
20:13 *z*S Ge 4:23; Mt 5:21*; 19:18*; Mk 10:19*; Lk 18:20*; Ro 13:9*; Jas 2:11*
20:14 *a*Lev 18:20; 20:10; Nu 5:12,

13,29; Pr 6:29,32; Mt 5:27*; 19:18*; Mk 10:19*; Lk 18:20*; Ro 13:9*; Jas 2:11* 20:15 *b*Lev 19:11,13; Eze 18:7; Mt 19:18*; Mk 10:19*; Lk 18:20*; Ro 13:9* 20:16 *c*Lev 19:11; Jer 9:3,5 *d*Ex 23:1,7; Lev 19:18; Ps 50:20; 101:5; 119:29; Mt 19:18*; Mk 10:19; Lk 3:14*; 18:20* 20:17 *e*Lk 12:15; Ro 7:7*; 13:9*; Eph 5:3; Heb 13:5 20:18 *f*Ex 19:16-19; Dt 4:36; Isa 58:1; Jer 6:17; Eze 33:3; Heb 12:18-19; Rev 1:10 *g*S Ex 19:18 *h*S Ge 3:10; S Ex 14:31; S 19:16 20:19 *i*Job 37:4,5; 40:9; Ps 29:3-4 *j*Dt 5:5,23-27; 18:16; Gal 3:19 20:20 *k*S Ge 15:1 *l*S Ge 22:1 *m*Dt 4:10; 6:2, 24; 10:12; Ps 111:10; 128:1; Pr 1:7; Ecc 12:13; Isa 8:13 *n*Job 1:8; 2:3; 28:28; Pr 3:7; 8:13; 14:16; 16:6 20:21 *o*S Ex 19:9; Dt 5:22; Ps 18:9; 68:4; 97:2; Isa 19:1 20:22 *p*Dt 5:24,26; Ne 9:13

20:8 See Ge 2:3. *Sabbath.* See note on 16:23. *holy.* See note on 3:5.

20:9 *Six days.* The question of a shorter "work week" in a modern industrialized culture is not in view.

20:10 *On it you shall not do any work.* Two reasons (one here and one in Deuteronomy) are given: (1) Having completed his work of creation God "rested on the seventh day" (v. 11), and the Israelites are to observe the same pattern in their service of God in the creation; (2) the Israelites must cease all labor so that their servants can also participate in the Sabbath-rest—just as God had delivered his people from the burden of slavery in Egypt (see Dt 5:14–15). The Sabbath thus became a "sign" of the covenant between God and Israel at Mount Sinai (see 31:12–17; see also note on Ge 9:12).

20:12 *Honor.* (1) Prize highly (see Pr 4:8), (2) care for (see Ps 91:15), (3) show respect for (see Lev 19:3; 20:9), and (4) obey (see Dt 21:18–21; cf. Eph 6:1). *so that you may live long.* "The first commandment with a promise" (Eph 6:2). See also note on Dt 6:2.

20:13 See Mt 5:21–26. *murder.* The Hebrew for this verb usually refers to a premeditated and deliberate act.

20:14 See Mt 5:27–30. *adultery.* A sin "against God" (Ge 39:9) as well as against the marriage partner.

20:17 *covet.* Desire something with evil motivation (see Mt 15:19). To break God's commandments inwardly is equivalent to breaking them outwardly (see Mt 5:21–30).

20:18–21 Concludes the account of the giving of the Decalogue. The order of the narrative appears to be different from the order of events, since v. 18 is most likely a continua-

tion of 19:25. On this reading, the proclamation of the Decalogue took place after Moses approached God (v. 21). Biblical writers often did not follow chronological sequence in their narratives for various literary reasons. The purpose of chronological displacement here may have been either (1) to keep the Decalogue distinct from the "Book of the Covenant" (24:7) that follows (20:22–23:19), or (2) to conclude the account with the formal institution of Moses' office as covenant mediator—or both.

20:19 See Heb 12:19–20. Israel requests a mediator to stand between them and God, a role fulfilled by Moses and subsequently by priests, prophets and kings—and ultimately by Jesus Christ.

20:20 *Do not be afraid.* Do not think that God's display of his majesty is intended simply to fill you with abject fear. He has come to enter into covenant with you as your heavenly King. *test.* See note on Ge 22:1. *fear of God.* See note on Ge 20:11.

20:22–23:19 The stipulations of the "Book of the Covenant" (24:7), consisting largely of expansions on and expositions of the Ten Commandments. See chart on "Major Social Concerns in the Covenant," p. 271.

20:22–26 Initial stipulations governing Israel's basic relationship with God (cf. v. 3).

20:22 *heaven.* God's dwelling place. Even on "top of Mount Sinai" (19:20) God spoke from heaven.

20:23 See vv. 3–4. The contrast between the one true God "in heaven," who "does whatever pleases him" (Ps 115:3), and idols of silver or gold, who can do nothing at all (see Ps 115:4–7; see also Ps 135:5–6,15–17), is striking indeed.

alongside me;^{q} do not make for yourselves gods of silver or gods of gold. ^{r}

24 " 'Make an altar^s of earth for me and sacrifice on it your burnt offerings^t and fellowship offerings,^{s} your sheep and goats and your cattle. Wherever I cause my name^u to be honored, I will come to you and bless^v you. ^{25}If you make an altar of stones for me, do not build it with dressed stones, for you will defile it if you use a tool^w on it. ^{26}And do not go up to my altar on steps, lest your nakedness^x be exposed on it.'

21

"These are the laws^y you are to set before them:

Hebrew Servants

21:2–6pp — Dt 15:12–18
21:2–11Ref — Lev 25:39–55

^{2}"If you buy a Hebrew servant,^{z} he is to serve you for six years. But in the seventh year, he shall go free,^{a} without paying anything. ^{3}If he comes alone, he is to go free alone; but if he has a wife when he comes, she is to go with him. ^{4}If his master gives him a wife and she bears him sons or daughters, the woman and her children shall belong to her master, and only the man shall go free.

^{5}"But if the servant declares, 'I love my master and my wife and children and do not want to go free,'^{b} ^{6}then his master must take him before the judges.^{tc} He shall take him to the door or the doorpost and pierce^d his ear with an awl. Then he will be his servant for life. ^{e}

^{7}"If a man sells his daughter as a ser-

vant, she is not to go free as menservants do. ^{8}If she does not please the master who has selected her for himself,^{u} he must let her be redeemed. He has no right to sell her to foreigners, because he has broken faith with her. ^{9}If he selects her for his son, he must grant her the rights of a daughter. ^{10}If he marries another woman, he must not deprive the first one of her food, clothing and marital rights.^{f} ^{11}If he does not provide her with these three things, she is to go free, without any payment of money.

Personal Injuries

^{12}"Anyone who strikes a man and kills him shall surely be put to death. ^{g} ^{13}However, if he does not do it intentionally, but God lets it happen, he is to flee to a place^h I will designate. ^{14}But if a man schemes and kills another man deliberately,^{i} take him away from my altar and put him to death.^{j}

^{15}"Anyone who attacks^v his father or his mother must be put to death.

^{16}"Anyone who kidnaps another and either sells^k him or still has him when he is caught must be put to death. ^{l}

^{17}"Anyone who curses his father or mother must be put to death. ^{m}

^{18}"If men quarrel and one hits the other with a stone or with his fist^w and he does not die but is confined to bed, ^{19}the one who struck the blow will not be held re-

---

Cross-references (center column):

20:23 ^{q}S ver 3
^{r}Ex 22:20; 32:4,
8,31; 34:17;
Dt 29:17-18;
Ne 9:18
20:24 ^{s}Ex 27:1;
40:29; Nu 16:38;
Dt 27:5; Jos 8:30;
2Ki 16:14;
2Ch 4:1; Ezr 3:2;
Eze 43:13
^{t}S Ge 8:20;
S Ex 18:12
^{u}Dt 12:5; 16:6,
11; 26:2; 1Ki 9:3;
2Ki 21:4,7;
2Ch 6:6; 12:13;
Ezr 6:12
^{v}S Ge 12:2; 22:17
20:25 ^{w}Jos 8:31;
1Ki 6:7
20:26 ^{x}Eze 43:17
21:1 ^{y}Ex 24:3;
34:32; Dt 4:14;
6:1
21:2 ^{z}Ex 22:3
^{a}ver 7; Jer 34:8,
14
21:5 ^{b}Dt 15:16
21:6 ^{c}Ex 22:8-9;
Dt 17:9; 19:17;
25:1 ^{d}Ps 40:6
^{e}Job 39:9; 41:4

21:10 ^{f}1Co 7:3-5
21:12 ^{g}ver 15,
17; S Ge 4:14,23;
Ex 31:15;
Lev 20:9,10;
24:16; 27:29;
Nu 1:51; 35:16,
30-31; Dt 13:5;
19:11; 22:22;
27:16; Job 31:11;
Pr 20:20;
S Mt 26:52
21:13
^{h}Nu 35:10-34;
Dt 4:42; 19:2-13;
Jos 20:9
21:14 ^{i}Ge 4:8;
Nu 35:20;
2Sa 3:27; 20:10;
Heb 10:26
^{j}Dt 19:11-12;
1Ki 2:28-34
21:16 ^{k}Ge 37:28
^{l}Ex 22:4; Dt 24:7
21:17 ^{m}S ver 12;
S Dt 5:16;

Mt 15:4*; Mk 7:10*

^{s}24 Traditionally *peace offerings* ^{t}6 Or *before God* ^{u}8 Or *master so that he does not choose her* ^{v}15 Or *kills* ^{w}18 Or *with a tool*

20:24 *altar of earth.* Such an altar, with dimensions the same as those of the altar in the tabernacle (see 27:1), has been found in the excavated ruins of a small Iron Age (10th, or possibly 11th, century B.C.) Israelite temple at Arad in southern Palestine. *burnt offerings.* See note on Lev 1:3. *fellowship offerings.* See note on Ex 3:1. *Wherever.* Not the later central sanctuary at Jerusalem, but numerous temporary places of worship (see, e.g., Jos 8:30-31; Jdg 6:24; 21:4; 1Sa 7:17; 14:35; 2Sa 24:25; 1Ki 18:30).
20:25 *do not build it with dressed stones.* Many ancient altars of undressed stones (from various periods) have been found in Palestine. *defile it if you use a tool on it.* For reasons not now clear, but perhaps related to pagan practices.
20:26 *steps.* The oldest stepped altar known in Palestine is at Megiddo and dates between 3000 and 2500 B.C. *nakedness be exposed.* Men who ascended to such altars would expose their nakedness in the presence of God. Although Aaron and his descendants served at stepped altars (see Lev 9:22; Eze 43:17), they were instructed to wear linen undergarments (see 28:42-43; Lev 6:10; 16:3-4; Eze 44:17-18).
21:2-11 See Jer 34:8-22.
21:2 *Hebrew.* See note on Ge 14:13. *in the seventh year, he shall go free.* The Lord's servants are not to be anyone's perpetual slaves (see 20:10 and note).

21:6 *the judges.* See 22:8-9,28 and NIV text notes. *pierce his ear with an awl.* See Dt 15:17. Submission to this rite symbolized willing service (see Ps 40:6-8 and note on Ps 40:6).
21:12-15 See 20:13 and note; see also Nu 35:16-34; Dt 19:1-13; 21:1-9; 24:7; 27:24-25; Jos 20:1-9.
21:12 See Ge 9:6 and note.
21:13 *does not do it intentionally.* Related terms and expressions are "accidentally" (Nu 35:11), "without hostility" (Nu 35:22), "was not his enemy" (Nu 35:23), "did not intend to harm him" (Nu 35:23) and "without malice aforethought" (Dt 19:4). Premeditated murder is thus distinguished from accidental manslaughter. *God lets it happen.* The event is beyond human control—in modern legal terminology, an "act of God." *place.* A city of refuge (see Nu 35:6-32; Dt 19:1-13; Jos 20:1-9; 21:13,21,27,32, 38).
21:14 *away from my altar.* Or "even from my altar." The horns of the altar were a final refuge for those subject to judicial action (see 1Ki 1:50-51; 2:28; Am 3:14 and notes)
21:15 See 20:12.
21:16 See 20:15.
21:19 *walks around outside with his staff.* Is convalescing in a satisfactory way. *the loss of his time.* Lit. "his sitting," i.e., his enforced idleness.

sponsible if the other gets up and walks around outside with his staff; however, he must pay the injured man for the loss of his time and see that he is completely healed.

20"If a man beats his male or female slave with a rod and the slave dies as a direct result, he must be punished, 21but he is not to be punished if the slave gets up after a day or two, since the slave is his property. n

22"If men who are fighting hit a pregnant woman and she gives birth prematurelyx but there is no serious injury, the offender must be fined whatever the woman's husband demandso and the court allows. 23But if there is serious injury, you are to take life for life,p 24eye for eye, tooth for tooth,q hand for hand, foot for foot, 25burn for burn, wound for wound, bruise for bruise.

26"If a man hits a manservant or maidservant in the eye and destroys it, he must let the servant go free to compensate for the eye. 27And if he knocks out the tooth of a manservant or maidservant, he must let the servant go free to compensate for the tooth.

28"If a bull gores a man or a woman to death, the bull must be stoned to death,r and its meat must not be eaten. But the owner of the bull will not be held responsible. 29If, however, the bull has had the habit of goring and the owner has been warned but has not kept it penned ups and it kills a man or woman, the bull must be stoned and the owner also must be put to death. 30However, if payment is demanded of him, he may redeem his life by paying whatever is demanded. t 31This law also applies if the bull gores a son or daughter. 32If the bull gores a male or female slave, the owner must pay thirty shekelsv u of silver to the master of the slave, and the bull must be stoned.

33"If a man uncovers a pitv or digs one

and fails to cover it and an ox or a donkey falls into it, 34the owner of the pit must pay for the loss; he must pay its owner, and the dead animal will be his.

35"If a man's bull injures the bull of another and it dies, they are to sell the live one and divide both the money and the dead animal equally. 36However, if it was known that the bull had the habit of goring, yet the owner did not keep it penned up,w the owner must pay, animal for animal, and the dead animal will be his.

Protection of Property

22 "If a man steals an ox or a sheep and slaughters it or sells it, he must pay backx five head of cattle for the ox and four sheep for the sheep.

2"If a thief is caught breaking iny and is struck so that he dies, the defender is not guilty of bloodshed;z 3but if it happensz after sunrise, he is guilty of bloodshed.

"A thief must certainly make restitution,a but if he has nothing, he must be soldb to pay for his theft.

4"If the stolen animal is found alive in his possessionc—whether ox or donkey or sheep—he must pay back double. d

5"If a man grazes his livestock in a field or vineyard and lets them stray and they graze in another man's field, he must make restitutione from the best of his own field or vineyard.

6"If a fire breaks out and spreads into thornbushes so that it burns shocksf of grain or standing grain or the whole field, the one who started the fire must make restitution.g

7"If a man gives his neighbor silver or goods for safekeepingh and they are stolen from the neighbor's house, the thief, if he is caught, must pay back double. i 8But if the thief is not found, the owner of the

Cross references (center column)

21:21
nLev 25:44-46
21:22 over 30
21:23
pLev 24:19;
Dt 19:21
21:24 qS ver 23;
Mt 5:38*
21:28 rver 32;
Ge 9:5
21:29 sver 36
21:30 tver 22
21:32
uGe 37:28;
Zec 11:12-13;
Mt 26:15; 27:3,9
21:33 vLk 14:5

21:36 wver 29
22:1 xLev 6:1-7;
2Sa 12:6; Pr 6:31;
S Lk 19:8
22:2 yJob 24:16;
Jer 2:34; Hos 7:1;
Mt 6:19-20;
24:43 zNu 35:27
22:3 aver 1
bSa Ex 21:2;
S Mt 18:25
22:4 cISa 12:5
dS Ge 43:12
22:5 ever 1
22:6 fJdg 15:5
gver 1
22:7 hver 10;
Lev 6:2
iS Ge 43:12

x22 Or she has a miscarriage   y32 That is, about 12
ounces (about 0.3 kilogram)   z3 Or if he strikes him

Footnotes (bottom)

21:20–21 Benefit of doubt was granted to the slaveholder where no homicidal intentions could be proved.

21:23–25 See Dt 19:21. The so-called law of retaliation, as its contexts show, was meant to limit the punishment to fit the crime. By invoking the law of love, Jesus corrected the popular misunderstanding of the law of retaliation (see Mt 5:38–42).

21:23 serious injury. Either to mother or to child.

21:26–27 Humane applications of the law of retaliation.

21:28–32 The law of the goring bull.

21:28 the bull must be stoned to death. By killing someone, the bull becomes accountable for that person's life (see Ge 9:6).

21:30 if payment is demanded. If the victim's family is willing to accept a ransom payment instead of demanding the death penalty. he may redeem his life by paying. The pay-

ment (lit. "ransom," as in Nu 35:31) is not to compensate the victim's family but to save the negligent man's life.

21:32 thirty shekels of silver. Apparently the standard price for a slave. It was also the amount Judas was willing to accept as his price for betraying Jesus (see Mt 26:14–15; see also Zec 11:12–13). shekels. See note on Ge 20:16.

21:33–36 Laws concerning injuries to animals.

22:1–15 Laws concerning property rights (see 20:15).

22:2 An act of self-defense in darkness does not produce bloodguilt.

22:3 Killing an intruder in broad daylight is not justifiable.

22:5 from the best. Restitution should always err on the side of quality and generosity.

22:6 thornbushes. Often used as hedges (see Mic 7:4) bordering cultivated areas.

house must appear before the judges[a][i] to determine whether he has laid his hands on the other man's property. [9]In all cases of illegal possession of an ox, a donkey, a sheep, a garment, or any other lost property about which somebody says, 'This is mine,' both parties are to bring their cases before the judges.[k] The one whom the judges declare[b] guilty must pay back double to his neighbor.

[10]"If a man gives a donkey, an ox, a sheep or any other animal to his neighbor for safekeeping[l] and it dies or is injured or is taken away while no one is looking, [11]the issue between them will be settled by the taking of an oath[m] before the LORD that the neighbor did not lay hands on the other person's property. The owner is to accept this, and no restitution is required. [12]But if the animal was stolen from the neighbor, he must make restitution[n] to the owner. [13]If it was torn to pieces by a wild animal, he shall bring in the remains as evidence and he will not be required to pay for the torn animal.[o]

[14]"If a man borrows an animal from his neighbor and it is injured or dies while the owner is not present, he must make restitution.[p] [15]But if the owner is with the animal, the borrower will not have to pay. If the animal was hired, the money paid for the hire covers the loss.[q]

Social Responsibility

[16]"If a man seduces a virgin[r] who is not pledged to be married and sleeps with her, he must pay the bride-price,[s] and she shall be his wife. [17]If her father absolutely refuses to give her to him, he must still pay the bride-price for virgins.

[18]"Do not allow a sorceress[t] to live.

[19]"Anyone who has sexual relations with an animal[u] must be put to death.

[20]"Whoever sacrifices to any god[v] other than the LORD must be destroyed.[c][w]

[21]"Do not mistreat an alien[x] or oppress him, for you were aliens[y] in Egypt.

[22]"Do not take advantage of a widow or an orphan.[z] [23]If you do and they cry out[a] to me, I will certainly hear their cry.[b] [24]My anger will be aroused, and I will kill you with the sword; your wives will become widows and your children fatherless.[c]

[25]"If you lend money to one of my people among you who is needy, do not be like a moneylender; charge him no interest.[d][d] [26]If you take your neighbor's cloak as a pledge,[e] return it to him by sunset, [27]because his cloak is the only covering he has for his body. What else will he sleep in?[f] When he cries out to me, I will hear, for I am compassionate.[g]

[28]"Do not blaspheme God[e][h] or curse[i] the ruler of your people.[j]

[29]"Do not hold back offerings[k] from your granaries or your vats.[f]

"You must give me the firstborn of your sons.[l] [30]Do the same with your cattle and

22:8 /S Ex 21:6
22:9 kver 8;
Dt 25:1
22:10 /S ver 7
22:11 mLev 6:3;
1Ki 8:31;
2Ch 6:22;
Heb 6:16
22:12 nver 1
22:13 oGe 31:39
22:14 pver 1
22:15
qLev 19:13;
Job 17:5
22:16 rDt 22:28
sS Ge 34:12
22:18 tS Ex 7:11;
Lev 19:26,31;
20:27; Dt 18:11;
1Sa 28:3;
2Ch 33:6;
Isa 57:3

22:19
uLev 18:23;
20:15; Dt 27:21
22:20
vS Ex 20:23;
34:15; Lev 17:7;
Nu 25:2;
Dt 32:17;
Ps 106:37
wLev 27:29;
Dt 13:5; 17:2-5;
18:20; 1Ki 18:40;
19:1; 2Ki 10:25;
23:20; 2Ch 15:13
22:21 xEx 23:9;
Lev 19:33; 24:22;
Nu 15:14;
Dt 1:16; 24:17;
Eze 22:29
yDt 10:19; 27:19;
Zec 7:10; Mal 3:5
22:22 zver 26;
Dt 10:18; 24:6,
10,12,17;
Job 22:6,9; 24:3,
21; Ps 68:5;
146:9; Pr 23:10;
Isa 1:17; Jer 7:5,
6; 21:12; 22:3;
Eze 18:5-9,12;
Zec 7:9-10;
Mal 3:5; Jas 1:27
22:23 aLk 18:7
bDt 10:18; 15:9;
24:15; Job 34:28;
35:9; Ps 10:14,
17; 12:5; 18:6;
34:15; Jas 5:4
22:24 cPs 109:9;
La 5:3
22:25
dLev 25:35-37;

Dt 15:7-11; 23:20; Ne 5:7,10; Ps 15:5; Eze 18:8 **22:26** eS ver 22; Pr 20:16; Eze 33:15; Am 2:8 **22:27** fDt 24:13,17; Job 22:6; 24:7; 29:11; 31:19-20; Eze 18:12,16 gEx 34:6; Dt 4:31; 2Ch 30:9; Ne 9:17; Ps 99:8; 103:8; 116:5; 145:8; Joel 2:13; Jnh 4:2 **22:28** hS Ex 20:7 i2Sa 16:5,9; 19:21; 1Ki 21:10; 2Ki 2:23; Ps 102:8 /Ecc 10:20; Ac 23:5* **22:29** kEx 23:15,16,19; 34:20,26; Lev 19:24; 23:10; Nu 18:13; 28:26; Dt 14:4; 26:2,10; 1Sa 6:3; Ne 10:35; Pr 3:9; Mal 3:10 /S Ex 13:2; Nu 8:16-17; Lk 2:23

a8 Or before God; also in verse 9　　b9 Or whom God declares　　c20 The Hebrew term refers to the irrevocable giving over of things or persons to the LORD, often by totally destroying them.　　d25 Or excessive interest　　e28 Or Do not revile the judges　　f29 The meaning of the Hebrew for this phrase is uncertain.

22:11 See 20:7 and note. *an oath before the LORD*. The judges were God's representatives in court cases (see 21:6; 22:8–9,28 and NIV text notes).

22:12–13 Similar laws apparently existed as early as the patriarchal period (see Ge 31:39).

22:16–31 General laws related to social obligations.

22:16 *bride-price*. A gift, usually substantial, given by the prospective groom to the bride's family as payment for her (see Ge 24:53). The custom is still followed today in parts of the Middle East.

22:18 See Dt 18:10,14; 1Sa 28:9; Isa 47:12–14.

22:19 Ancient myths and epics describe acts of bestiality performed by pagan gods and demigods in Babylon and Canaan.

22:20 See 20:3–5. The total destruction (see NIV text note) of the idolatrous Canaanites was later commanded by the Lord (see Nu 21:2; Dt 2:34; 3:6; 7:2; 13:15; 20:17; Jos 2:10; 6:17,21; 8:25; 10:1,28,35,37,39–40; 11:11–12, 20–21; Jdg 1:17).

22:21–27 That the poor, the widow, the orphan, the alien—in fact, all defenseless people—are objects of God's special concern and providential care is clear from the writings of Moses (see 21:26–27; 23:6–12; Lev 19:9–10; Dt 14:29; 16:11,14; 24:19–21; 26:12–13), the psalmists (see Ps 10:14,17–18; 68:5; 82:3; 146:9) and the prophets (see Isa 1:23; 10:2; Jer 7:6; 22:3; Zec 7:10; Mal 3:5) as well as from the teachings of Jesus (see, e.g., Mt 25:34–45).

22:25–27 Laws dealing with interest on loans (see Lev 25:35–37; Dt 15:7–11; 23:19–20; see also Ne 5:7–12; Job 24:9; Pr 28:8; Eze 18:13; 22:12). Interest for profit was not to be charged at the expense of the poor. Generosity in such matters was extended even further by Jesus (see Lk 6:34–35).

22:26–27 If all that a man had to offer as his pledge for a loan was his cloak, he was among the poorest of the poor (see Am 2:8 and note).

22:28 *Do not . . . curse the ruler of your people*. A ruler was God's representative; quoted by a penitent Paul after he had unwittingly insulted the high priest (see Ac 23:4–5).

22:29 *give me the firstborn*. See notes on 4:22; 13:2,13; see also 13:15.

22:30 *Do the same with your cattle and your sheep*. See

your sheep. *m* Let them stay with their mothers for seven days, but give them to me on the eighth day. *n*

31"You are to be my holy people. *o* So do not eat the meat of an animal torn by wild beasts; *p* throw it to the dogs.

Laws of Justice and Mercy

23 "Do not spread false reports. *q* Do not help a wicked man by being a malicious witness. *r*

2"Do not follow the crowd in doing wrong. When you give testimony in a lawsuit, do not pervert justice *s* by siding with the crowd, *t* 3and do not show favoritism *u* to a poor man in his lawsuit.

4"If you come across your enemy's *v* ox or donkey wandering off, be sure to take it back to him. *w* 5If you see the donkey *x* of someone who hates you fallen down under its load, do not leave it there; be sure you help him with it.

6"Do not deny justice *y* to your poor people in their lawsuits. 7Have nothing to do with a false charge *z* and do not put an innocent *a* or honest person to death, *b* for I will not acquit the guilty. *c*

8"Do not accept a bribe, *d* for a bribe blinds those who see and twists the words of the righteous.

9"Do not oppress an alien; *e* you yourselves know how it feels to be aliens, because you were aliens in Egypt.

Sabbath Laws

10"For six years you are to sow your fields and harvest the crops, 11but during the seventh year let the land lie unplowed and unused. *f* Then the poor among your

people may get food from it, and the wild animals may eat what they leave. Do the same with your vineyard and your olive grove.

12"Six days do your work, *g* but on the seventh day do not work, so that your ox and your donkey may rest and the slave born in your household, and the alien as well, may be refreshed. *h*

13"Be careful *i* to do everything I have said to you. Do not invoke the names of other gods; *j* do not let them be heard on your lips. *k*

The Three Annual Festivals

14"Three times *l* a year you are to celebrate a festival to me.

15"Celebrate the Feast of Unleavened Bread; *m* for seven days eat bread made without yeast, as I commanded you. Do this at the appointed time in the month of Abib, *n* for in that month you came out of Egypt.

"No one is to appear before me empty-handed. *o*

16"Celebrate the Feast of Harvest *p* with the firstfruits *q* of the crops you sow in your field.

"Celebrate the Feast of Ingathering *r* at the end of the year, when you gather in your crops from the field. *s*

17"Three times *t* a year all the men are to appear before the Sovereign LORD.

22:30	*m*Ex 34:19; Dt 15:19 *n*Ge 17:12; Lev 12:3; 22:27
22:31	*o*Ex 19:6; Lev 19:2; 22:31; Ezr 9:2 *p*Lev 7:24; 17:15; 22:8; Dt 14:21; Eze 4:14; 44:31
23:1	*q*Ge 39:17; Mt 19:18; Lk 3:14 *r*S Ex 20:16; Dt 5:20; 19:16-21; Ps 27:12; 35:11; Pr 19:5; Ac 6:11
23:2	*s*ver 3,6,9; Lev 19:15,33; Dt 1:17; 16:19; 24:17; 27:19; 1Sa 8:3 *t*Job 31:34
23:3	*u*Dt 1:17
23:4	*v*Ro 12:20 *w*Lev 6:3; 19:11; Dt 22:1-3
23:5	*x*Dt 22:4
23:6	*y*S ver 2; Dt 23:16; Pr 22:22
23:7	*z*S Ex 20:16; S Eph 4:25 *a*Mt 27:4 *b*S Ge 18:23 *c*Ex 34:7; Dt 19:18; 25:1
23:8	*d*S Ex 18:21; Lev 19:15; Dt 10:17; 27:25; Job 15:34; 36:18; Ps 26:10; Pr 6:35; 15:27; 17:8; Isa 1:23; 5:23; Mic 3:1; 7:3
23:9	*e*S ver 2; S Ex 22:21; Lev 19:33-34; Eze 22:7
23:11	*f*Lev 25:1-7; Ne 10:31
23:12	*g*S Ex 20:9; Lk 13:14 *h*Ge 2:2-3

23:13 *l*Dt 4:9,23; 1Ti 4:16 *j*ver 32; Dt 12:3; Jos 23:7; Ps 16:4; Zec 13:2 *k*Dt 18:20; Jos 23:7; Ps 16:4; Hos 2:17 23:14 *l*ver 17; S Ex 12:14; 34:23,24; Dt 16:16; 1Ki 9:25; 2Ch 8:13; Eze 46:9 23:15 *m*S Ex 12:17; Mt 26:17; Lk 22:1; Ac 12:3 *n*S Ex 12:2 *o*S Ex 22:29 23:16 *p*Lev 23:15-21; Nu 28:26; Dt 16:9; 2Ch 8:13 *q*S Ex 22:29; S 34:22 *r*Ex 34:22; Lev 23:34,42; Dt 16:16; 31:10; Ezr 3:4; Ne 8:14; Zec 14:16 *s*Lev 23:39; Dt 16:13; Jer 40:10 23:17 *t*S ver 14

---

notes on 13:2; 13:13; see also 13:12,15. *give them to me on the eighth day.* The same principle applied in a different way to firstborn sons as well (see note on Ge 17:12).
22:31 Since God's people were "a kingdom of priests" (see 19:6 and note), they were to obey a law later specified for members of the Aaronic priesthood (see Lev 22:8) as well.
23:1–9 Most of the regulations in this section pertain to 20:16.
23:1 See Lev 19:16; Dt 22:13–19; 1Ki 21:10–13.
23:4–5 Those hostile to you are to be shown the same consideration as others (see Dt 22:1–4; Pr 25:21). Jesus teaches that this means "Love your enemies" (Mt 5:44).
23:7 1Ki 21:10–13 is a vivid illustration of violation of this law.
23:8 See Dt 16:19. Samuel exemplifies faithful stewardship in this regard (see 1Sa 12:3), while his sons do not (see 1Sa 8:3).
23:10–13 Extensions of the principles taught in 20:8–11; Dt 5:12–15.
23:14–19 See 34:18–26; Lev 23:4–44; Nu 28:16–29:40; Dt 16:1–17.
23:15 *Feast of Unleavened Bread.* Celebrated from the

15th through the 21st days of the first month (usually about mid-March to mid-April; see note on 12:2) at the beginning of the barley harvest; it commemorated the exodus.
23:16 *Feast of Harvest.* Also called the "Feast of Weeks" (34:22) because it was held seven weeks after the Feast of Unleavened Bread. It was celebrated on the sixth day of the third month (usually about mid-May to mid-June) during the wheat harvest. In later Judaism it came to commemorate the giving of the law on Mount Sinai, though there is no evidence of this significance in the OT. In NT times it was called "(the day of) Pentecost" (Ac 2:1; 20:16; 1Co 16:8), which means "50" (see Lev 23:16). *Feast of Ingathering.* Also called the "Feast of Tabernacles" (Lev 23:34) or "Booths" because the Israelites lived in temporary shelters when God brought them out of Egypt (see Lev 23:43). It was celebrated from the 15th through the 22nd days of the seventh month (usually about mid-September to mid-October) when the produce of the orchards and vines had been harvested; it commemorated the desert wanderings after the exodus. *end of the year.* End of the agricultural year, which began in the fall (see note on 12:2).
23:17 *all the men.* Normally accompanied by their families (see, e.g., 1Sa 1).

[18]"Do not offer the blood of a sacrifice to me along with anything containing yeast.[u]

"The fat of my festival offerings must not be kept until morning.[v]

[19]"Bring the best of the firstfruits[w] of your soil to the house of the LORD your God.

"Do not cook a young goat in its mother's milk.[x]

God's Angel to Prepare the Way

[20]"See, I am sending an angel[y] ahead of you to guard you along the way and to bring you to the place I have prepared.[z] [21]Pay attention to him and listen[a] to what he says. Do not rebel against him; he will not forgive[b] your rebellion,[c] since my Name[d] is in him. [22]If you listen carefully to what he says and do[e] all that I say, I will be an enemy[f] to your enemies and will oppose those who oppose you. [23]My angel will go ahead of you and bring you into the land of the Amorites, Hittites, Perizzites, Canaanites, Hivites and Jebusites,[g] and I will wipe them out. [24]Do not bow down before their gods or worship[h] them or follow their practices.[i] You must demolish[j] them and break their sacred stones[k] to pieces. [25]Worship the LORD your God,[l] and his blessing[m] will be on your food and water. I will take away sickness[n] from among you, [26]and none will miscarry or be barren[o] in your land. I will give you a full life span.[p]

[27]"I will send my terror[q] ahead of you and throw into confusion[r] every nation you encounter. I will make all your enemies turn their backs and run.[s] [28]I will

send the hornet[t] ahead of you to drive the Hivites, Canaanites and Hittites[u] out of your way. [29]But I will not drive them out in a single year, because the land would become desolate and the wild animals[v] too numerous for you. [30]Little by little I will drive them out before you, until you have increased enough to take possession[w] of the land.

[31]"I will establish your borders from the Red Sea[g] to the Sea of the Philistines,[h] and from the desert to the River.[i][x] I will hand over to you the people who live in the land and you will drive them out[y] before you. [32]Do not make a covenant[z] with them or with their gods. [33]Do not let them live in your land, or they will cause you to sin against me, because the worship of their gods will certainly be a snare[a] to you."

The Covenant Confirmed

24 Then he said to Moses, "Come up to the LORD, you and Aaron,[b] Nadab and Abihu,[c] and seventy of the elders[d] of Israel. You are to worship at a distance, [2]but Moses alone is to approach[e] the LORD; the others must not come near. And the people may not come up with him."

23:18 [u]Ex 34:25; Lev 2:11 [v]S Ex 12:8
23:19 [w]S Ex 22:29; S 34:22; S Nu 18:12 [x]Ex 34:26; Dt 14:21
23:20 [y]S Ge 16:7 [z]Ex 15:17
23:21 [a]Dt 18:19; Jer 13:15 [b]Dt 29:20; 2Ki 24:4; La 1:17 [c]Nu 17:10; Dt 9:7; 31:27; Jos 24:19; Ps 25:7; 78:8,40, 56; 106:33; 107:11; 1Jn 5:16 [d]S Ex 3:15
23:22 [e]S Ex 15:26 [f]S Ge 12:3; Isa 41:11; Jer 30:20
23:23 [g]Nu 13:29; 21:21; Jos 3:10; 24:8,11; Ezr 9:1; Ps 135:11
23:24 [h]S Ex 20:5 [i]Lev 18:3; 20:23; Dt 9:4; 12:30-31; Jer 10:2 [j]Ex 34:13; Nu 33:52; Dt 7:5; 12:3; Jdg 2:2; 2Ki 18:4; 23:14 [k]Lev 26:1; Dt 16:22; 1Ki 14:23; 2Ki 3:2; 10:26; 17:10; 2Ch 14:3; Isa 27:9
23:25 [l]Mt 4:10 [m]Lev 26:3-13; 28:1-14 [n]S Ex 15:26
23:26 [o]Lev 26:3-4; Dt 7:14; 28:4; Mal 3:11 [p]S Ge 15:15; Dt 4:1,40; 32:47; Ps 90:10
23:27 [q]S Ge 35:5; S Ex 15:14; S Ex 14:24; Dt 7:23
[s]2Sa 22:41; Ps 18:40; 21:12 **23:28** [t]Dt 7:20; Jos 24:12 [u]Ex 33:2; 34:11,24; Nu 13:29; Dt 4:38; 11:23; 18:12; Jos 3:10; 24:11; Ps 78:55 **23:29** [v]Dt 7:22 **23:30** [w]Jos 23:5 **23:31** [x]S Ge 2:14; Dt 34:2; Ezr 4:20 [y]Dt 7:24; 9:3; Jos 21:44; 24:12,18; Ps 80:8 **23:32** [z]S Ge 26:28; Ex 34:12; Dt 7:2; Jos 9:7; Jdg 2:2; 1Sa 11:1; 1Ki 15:19; 20:34; Eze 17:13 **23:33** [a]S Ex 10:7 **24:1** [b]S Ex 19:24 [c]S Ex 6:23 [d]ver 9; Nu 11:16 **24:2** [e]Nu 12:6-8

[g]31 Hebrew *Yam Suph*; that is, Sea of Reeds [h]31 That is, the Mediterranean [i]31 That is, the Euphrates

23:18 *not . . . with anything containing yeast.* See note on 12:15. *not be kept until morning.* See 12:9–10.

23:19 *firstfruits.* Representative of the whole harvest. The offering of firstfruits was an acknowledgment that the harvest was from the Lord and belonged wholly to him. *Do not cook a young goat in its mother's milk.* Perhaps a protest against a Canaanite pagan ritual (see v. 33; 34:15).

23:20 *angel.* See 14:19; see also note on Ge 16:7. *place I have prepared.* Canaan (cf. the similar statement of Jesus in Jn 14:2–3).

23:21 *Name.* Representing God's presence.

23:22 *If.* See note on 19:5.

23:23 See 3:8 and note.

23:28 *hornet.* The meaning of the Hebrew for this word is uncertain. The Septuagint (the Greek translation of the OT) renders it "wasp," but the translators may have been guessing. In any event, the Lord promises to send some agent to disable or frighten the peoples of Canaan so that they will not be able to resist Israel's invasion. But probably the word involves concrete imagery and the focus of the statement is on the effects—therefore we are not to look for some historical agent to which the word metaphorically refers (cf. Isa

7:18).

23:30 *Little by little.* See Jdg 1.

23:31 See Ge 15:18; 1Ki 4:21. *Red Sea.* The (south)eastern border (here the modern Gulf of Aqaba; see note on 1Ki 9:26). *Sea of the Philistines.* The western border (see NIV text note). *the desert.* The southern border (northeastern Sinai; see note on Ge 15:18). *the River.* The northern border (see NIV text note).

23:33 *snare.* A symbol of destruction (see 10:7; Job 18:9; Ps 18:5; Pr 13:14; 21:6; Isa 24:17–18).

24:1 *Come up.* The action, temporarily interrupted for the Book of the Covenant (20:22–23:33), is resumed from 20:21. Moses and his associates would ascend the mountain after the events of vv. 3–8. *Nadab and Abihu.* Aaron's two oldest sons. Nadab would have succeeded Aaron as high priest, but he and his brother died because they offered unauthorized fire before the Lord (see Lev 10:1–2; Nu 3:4). *seventy . . . elders.* Cf. Nu 11:16; perhaps representing Jacob's 70 descendants (see 1:5; Ge 46:27 and note). *elders.* See note on 3:16. *at a distance.* See 20:21.

24:2 *Moses alone.* The mediator between God and the people of Israel. Jesus, the second Moses (see Heb 3:1–6), is the "mediator of a new covenant" (Heb 12:24).

3When Moses went and told the people all the LORD's words and laws,[f] they responded with one voice, "Everything the LORD has said we will do."[g] 4Moses then wrote[h] down everything the LORD had said.

He got up early the next morning and built an altar[i] at the foot of the mountain and set up twelve stone pillars[j] representing the twelve tribes of Israel. 5Then he sent young Israelite men, and they offered burnt offerings[k] and sacrificed young bulls as fellowship offerings[i][l] to the LORD. 6Moses[m] took half of the blood[n] and put it in bowls, and the other half he sprinkled[o] on the altar. 7Then he took the Book of the Covenant[p] and read it to the people. They responded, "We will do everything the LORD has said; we will obey."[q]

8Moses then took the blood, sprinkled it on the people[r] and said, "This is the blood of the covenant[s] that the LORD has made with you in accordance with all these words."

9Moses and Aaron, Nadab and Abihu, and the seventy elders[t] of Israel went up 10and saw[u] the God of Israel. Under his feet was something like a pavement made of sapphire,[k][v] clear as the sky[w] itself. 11But God did not raise his hand against these leaders of the Israelites; they saw[x] God, and they ate and drank.[y]

12The LORD said to Moses, "Come up to me on the mountain and stay here, and I will give you the tablets of stone,[z] with the law and commands I have written for their instruction."

13Then Moses set out with Joshua[a] his aide, and Moses went up on the mountain[b] of God. 14He said to the elders, "Wait here for us until we come back to you. Aaron and Hur[c] are with you, and anyone involved in a dispute[d] can go to them."

15When Moses went up on the mountain, the cloud[e] covered it, 16and the glory[f] of the LORD settled on Mount Sinai.[g] For six days the cloud covered the mountain, and on the seventh day the LORD called to Moses from within the cloud.[h] 17To the Israelites the glory of the LORD looked like a consuming fire[i] on top of the mountain. 18Then Moses entered the cloud as he went on up the mountain. And he stayed on the mountain forty[j] days and forty nights.[k]

Offerings for the Tabernacle

25:1–7pp — Ex 35:4–9

25 The LORD said to Moses, 2"Tell the Israelites to bring me an offering. You are to receive the offering for me from each man whose heart prompts[l] him to give. 3These are the offerings you are to receive from them: gold, silver and bronze; 4blue, purple and scarlet yarn[m] and fine linen; goat hair; 5ram skins dyed

24:3 [f]S Ex 21:1; Gal 3:19 [g]S Ex 19:8; Jos 24:24 **24:4** [h]S Ex 17:14 [i]S Ge 8:20 [j]S Ge 28:18; S Dt 27:2 **24:5** [k]Lev 1:3 [l]S Ge 31:54 **24:6** [m]Ex 14:15; 32:31; Ps 99:6 [n]Heb 9:18 [o]Lev 1:11; 3:2,8, 13; 5:9; Mt 26:28 **24:7** [p]2Ki 23:2, 21; Heb 9:19 [q]Ex 19:8; Jer 40:3; 42:6,21; 43:2 **24:8** [r]Heb 9:19; 1Pe 1:2 [s]Lev 26:3; Dt 5:2-3; Jos 24:25; 2Ki 11:17; Jer 11:4,8; 31:32; 34:13; Zec 9:11; S Mt 26:28; S Lk 22:20; Heb 9:20* **24:9** [t]S ver 1 **24:10** [u]S Ge 16:13; Nu 12:6; Isa 6:1; Eze 1:1; 8:3; 40:2; S Jn 1:18 [v]Job 28:16; Isa 54:11; Eze 1:26; 10:1 [w]Rev 4:3 **24:11** [x]S ver 10; S Ex 3:6; S 19:21 [y]Eze 44:3; Mt 26:29 **24:12** [z]Ex 31:18; 32:15-16; 34:1, 28,29; Dt 4:13; 5:22; 8:3; 9:9,10, 11; 10:4; 2Co 3:3 **24:13** [a]S Ex 17:9 [b]S Ex 3:1 **24:14** [c]S Ex 17:10 [d]Ex 18:16 **24:15** [e]S Ex 19:9; Mt 17:5 **24:16** [f]S Ex 16:7; Lev 9:23; Nu 14:10; 1Sa 4:21,22; Eze 8:4; 11:22 [g]S Ex 19:11 [h]Ps 99:7 **24:17** [i]S Ex 15:7; S 19:18; Heb 12:18,29 **24:18** [j]1Ki 19:8 [k]S Ge 7:4; Mt 4:2 **25:2** [l]Ex 35:21,22,26,27,29; 36:2; 2Ki 12:4; 1Ch 29:5,7,9; 2Ch 24:10; 29:31; Ezr 2:68; Ne 7:70-72; 2Co 8:11-12; 9:7 **25:4** [m]Ex 28:4-8

i5 Traditionally *peace offerings* k10 Or *lapis lazuli*

24:3 *words.* Probably refers to the Ten Commandments (see 20:1 and note). *laws.* Probably refers to the stipulations of the Book of the Covenant (21:1–23:19). *we will do.* See v. 7; see also 19:8 and note.
24:4 *Moses . . . wrote.* See note on 17:14; see also Introduction: Author and Date of Writing. *twelve stone pillars representing.* See Jos 4:5,20; 1Ki 18:31.
24:5 *young Israelite men . . . offered.* See note on 19:22.
24:6 *half of the blood . . . the other half.* The division of the blood points to the twofold aspect of the "blood of the covenant" (v. 8): The blood on the altar symbolizes God's forgiveness and his acceptance of the offering; the blood on the people points to an oath that binds them in obedience (see vv. 3,7).
24:7 *Book of the Covenant.* Strictly speaking, 20:22–23:19 (see note there)—but here implying also the stipulations of 20:2–17; 23:20–33. *We will do . . . we will obey.* See v. 3; see also 19:8 and note.
24:8 *then.* Only after the people agreed to obey the Lord could they participate in his covenant with them. *blood of the covenant.* See Mk 14:24 and note.
24:9 *went up.* See v. 1 and note.
24:10 *saw . . . God.* But not in the fullness of his glory (see 33:20; see also notes on 3:6; Ge 16:13; Nu 12:8; Eze 1:28). *sapphire.* See NIV text note. *sky.* Symbolized by the blue color of the "sapphire" (see Eze 1:26).
24:11 *raise his hand against.* See 9:15. *leaders.* Lit. "corners," "corner supports"; used in the sense of "leaders" only here. Cf. Gal 2:9. *ate and drank.* A covenant meal (cf. Ge 26:30; 31:54), celebrating the sealing of the covenant described in vv. 3–8. It foreshadows the Lord's Supper, which celebrates the new covenant sealed by Christ's death (see 1Co 11:25–26).
24:12 *Come up.* See note on v. 1. *tablets of stone.* See note on 31:18. *their.* The people's. *instruction.* As instruction from the covenant Lord, the laws were divine directives.
24:13 *Joshua his aide.* See note on 17:9.
24:14 *Hur.* See note on 17:10.
24:17 *glory of the LORD.* See 16:10.
24:18 *stayed on the mountain.* Moses did not come down until he had received instructions concerning the tabernacle and its furnishings (see 32:15). *forty days and forty nights.* Jesus, the second Moses (see note on v. 2), fasted for the same length of time (see Mt 4:2).
25:2 *offering.* Here refers to a voluntary contribution.
25:4 *blue, purple and scarlet.* Royal colors. *blue, purple.* Dyes derived from various shellfish (primarily the *murex*) that swarm in the waters of the northeast Mediterranean. So important for the local economy was the dyeing industry that the promised land was known as Canaan (which means "land of purple"), later called Phoenicia (also meaning "land of purple") by the Greeks. *scarlet.* Derived from the eggs and

red and hides of sea cows[l]; [n] acacia wood; [o] [6]olive oil [p] for the light; spices for the anointing oil and for the fragrant incense; [q] [7]and onyx stones and other gems to be mounted on the ephod [r] and breastpiece. [s]

[8]"Then have them make a sanctuary [t] for me, and I will dwell [u] among them. [9]Make this tabernacle and all its furnishings exactly like the pattern [v] I will show you.

The Ark

25:10–20pp – Ex 37:1–9

[10]"Have them make a chest [w] of acacia wood—two and a half cubits long, a cubit and a half wide, and a cubit and a half high. [m] [11]Overlay [x] it with pure gold, both inside and out, and make a gold molding around it. [12]Cast four gold rings for it and fasten them to its four feet, with two rings [y] on one side and two rings on the other. [13]Then make poles of acacia wood and overlay them with gold. [z] [14]Insert the poles [a] into the rings on the sides of the chest to carry it. [15]The poles are to remain in the rings of this ark; they are not to be

removed. [b] [16]Then put in the ark the Testimony, [c] which I will give you.

[17]"Make an atonement cover [n] [d] of pure gold—two and a half cubits long and a cubit and a half wide. [o] [18]And make two cherubim [e] out of hammered gold at the ends of the cover. [19]Make one cherub on one end and the second cherub on the other; make the cherubim of one piece with the cover, at the two ends. [20]The cherubim [f] are to have their wings spread upward, overshadowing [g] the cover with them. The cherubim are to face each other, looking toward the cover. [21]Place the cover on top of the ark [h] and put in the ark the Testimony, [i] which I will give you. [22]There, above the cover between the two

---

25:5 [n]Nu 4:6,10
[o]Dt 10:3
25:6 [p]Ex 27:20; 30:22-32; 35:28; 39:37; Nu 4:16
[q]Ex 30:1,7,35; 31:11; 35:28; Lev 16:12; Nu 4:16; 7:14; 2Ch 13:11
25:7 [r]Ex 28:4, 6-14; 29:5; Jdg 8:27; Hos 3:4
[s]Lev 8:8
25:8 [t]Ex 36:1-5; Lev 4:6; 10:4,7; 21:12,23; Nu 3:28; Heb 9:1-2
[u]Ex 29:45; Lev 26:11-12; Nu 5:3; Dt 12:11; 1Ki 6:13; Zec 2:10; 2Co 6:16
25:9 [v]ver 40; Ex 26:30; 27:8; 31:11; 39:32,42, 43; Nu 8:4; 1Ch 28:11,19; Ac 7:44; Heb 8:5
25:10 [w]Dt 10:1-5; 1Ki 6:19; Heb 9:4
25:11 [x]ver 24; Ex 30:3
25:12 [y]ver 26; Ex 30:4
25:13 [z]ver 28; Ex 27:6; 30:5; 37:28
25:14 [a]Ex 27:7; 40:20; 1Ch 15:15

25:15 [b]1Ki 8:8 25:16 [c]S Ex 16:34; Heb 9:4 25:17 [d]ver 21; Lev 16:13; Ro 3:25 25:18 [e]Ex 26:1,31; 36:35; 1Ki 6:23,27; 8:6; 2Ch 3:10-13; Heb 9:5 25:20 [f]S Ge 3:24 [g]Ex 37:9; 1Ki 8:7; 1Ch 28:18; Heb 9:5 25:21 [h]ver 10-15; Ex 26:34; 40:20; Dt 10:5 [i]S Ex 16:34; Heb 9:4

[l]5 That is, dugongs   [m]10 That is, about 3 3/4 feet (about 1.1 meters) long and 2 1/4 feet (about 0.7 meter) wide and high   [n]17 Traditionally *a mercy seat*   [o]17 That is, about 3 3/4 feet (about 1.1 meters) long and 2 1/4 feet (about 0.7 meter) wide

---

carcasses of the worm *Coccus ilicis,* which attaches itself to the leaves of the holly plant. *fine linen.* A very high quality cloth (often used by Egyptian royalty) made from thread spun from the fibers of flax straw. The Hebrew for this term derives ultimately from Egyptian. Excellent examples of unusually white, tightly woven linen have been found in ancient Egyptian tombs. Some are so finely woven that they cannot be distinguished from silk without the use of a magnifying glass. *goat hair.* From long-haired goats. A coarse, black (cf. SS 1:5; 6:5) material, it was often used to weave cloth for tents.

25:5 *ram skins dyed red.* After all the wool had been removed from the skins. The final product was similar to present-day morocco leather. *sea cows.* Native to the Red Sea. *acacia.* The wood is darker and harder than oak and is avoided by wood-eating insects. It is common in the Sinai peninsula.

25:6 *spices.* Those used in the anointing oil are identified in 30:23–24 as myrrh (balsam sap), cinnamon (bark of the cinnamon tree, a species of laurel), cane (pith from the root of a reed plant) and cassia (made from dried flowers of the cinnamon tree). Those used in the fragrant incense are identified in 30:34 as gum resin (a powder taken from the middle of hardened drops of myrrh—rare and very valuable), onycha (made from mollusk shells) and galbanum (a rubbery resin taken from the roots of a flowering plant that thrives in Syria and Persia).

25:7 *other gems.* See 28:17–20.

25:8 *sanctuary.* Lit. "holy place," "place set apart." See note on 3:5.

25:9 *tabernacle.* Lit. "dwelling place." The word is rarely used of human dwellings; it almost always signifies the place where God dwells among his people (see v. 8; 29:45–46; Lev 26:11; Eze 37:27; cf. Jn 1:14; Rev 21:3). *pattern.* See note on v. 40.

25:10 *chest.* See v. 14. Such was its form and function. The Hebrew for this word is translated by the more traditional term "ark" throughout the rest of Exodus (see note on Dt

10:1–3); it is different from that used to refer to Noah's ark and to the reed basket in which the infant Moses was placed (see note on 2:3). Of all the tabernacle furnishings, the ark is mentioned first probably because it symbolized the throne of the Lord (see 1Sa 4:4; 2Sa 6:2), the great King, who chose to dwell among his people (see note on v. 9).

25:11 *pure gold.* Uncontaminated by silver or other impurities.

25:12 *rings.* Lit. "houses," "housings," into which poles were inserted to carry the ark (see v. 14).

25:16 *Testimony.* The two tablets on which were inscribed the Ten Commandments as the basic stipulations of the Sinai covenant (see 20:1–17; 31:18). The Hebrew word for "Testimony" is related to a Babylonian word meaning "covenant stipulations." See also notes on v. 22; 16:34.

25:17 *atonement.* Reconciliation, the divine act of grace whereby God draws to himself and makes "at one" with him those who were once alienated from him. In the OT, the shed blood of sacrificial offerings effected atonement (see Lev 17:11 and note); in the NT, the blood of Jesus, shed once for all time, does the same (see Ro 3:25; 1Jn 2:2). *atonement cover.* See NIV text note; see also Lev 16:2 and note. That God's symbolic throne was capped with an atonement cover signified his great mercy toward his people—only such a God can be revered (see Ps 130:3–4).

25:18 *cherubim.* Probably similar to the carvings of winged sphinxes that adorned the armrests of royal thrones (see note on v. 10) in many parts of the ancient Near East (see also note on Ge 3:24). In the OT the cherubim were symbolic attendants that marked the place of the Lord's "enthronement" in his earthly kingdom (see 1Sa 4:4; 2Sa 6:2; 2Ki 19:15; Ps 99:1). From the cover of the ark (God's symbolic throne) the Lord gave directions to Moses (see v. 22; Nu 7:89). Later the ark's presence in the temple at Jerusalem would designate it as God's earthly royal city (see Ps 9:11; 18:10 and notes).

25:22 *ark of the Testimony.* Called this because it contained the Testimony (see note on v. 16). The phrase "ark of the Testimony" is a synonym of the more familiar phrase

cherubim[j] that are over the ark of the Testimony, I will meet[k] with you and give you all my commands for the Israelites.[l]

The Table

25:23–29pp — Ex 37:10–16

23"Make a table[m] of acacia wood—two cubits long, a cubit wide and a cubit and a half high.[p] 24Overlay it with pure gold and make a gold molding around it. 25Also make around it a rim a handbreadth[q] wide and put a gold molding on the rim. 26Make four gold rings for the table and fasten them to the four corners, where the four legs are. 27The rings are to be close to the rim to hold the poles used in carrying the table. 28Make the poles of acacia wood, overlay them with gold[n] and carry the table with them. 29And make its plates and dishes of pure gold, as well as its pitchers

and bowls for the pouring out of offerings.[o] 30Put the bread of the Presence[p] on this table to be before me at all times.

The Lampstand

25:31–39pp — Ex 37:17–24

31"Make a lampstand[q] of pure gold and hammer it out, base and shaft; its flower-like cups, buds and blossoms shall be of one piece with it. 32Six branches are to extend from the sides of the lampstand—three on one side and three on the other. 33Three cups shaped like almond flowers with buds and blossoms are to be on one branch, three on the next branch,

---

25:22 /Nu 7:89; 1Sa 4:4; 2Sa 6:2; 22:11; 2Ki 19:15; 1Ch 13:6; 28:18; Ps 18:10; 80:1; 99:1; Isa 37:16
*k*S Ex 19:3; 29:42; 30:6,36; Lev 1:1; 16:2; Nu 17:4 /Jer 3:16
25:23 *m*ver 30; Ex 26:35; 40:4, 22; Lev 24:6; Nu 3:31; 1Ki 7:48; 1Ch 28:16; 2Ch 4:8,19; Eze 41:22; 44:16; Heb 9:2
25:28 *n*S ver 13

25:29 *o*Nu 4:7
25:30 *p*Ex 35:13; 39:36; 40:4,23; Lev 24:5-9; Nu 4:7; 1Sa 21:4-6; 1Ki 7:48; 1Ch 23:29
25:31 *q*Ex 26:35; 31:8; 35:14; 39:37; 40:4,24;

Lev 24:4; Nu 3:31; 1Ki 7:49; 2Ch 4:7; Zec 4:2; Heb 9:2; Rev 1:12

p*23* That is, about 3 feet (about 0.9 meter) long and 1 1/2 feet (about 0.5 meter) wide and 2 1/4 feet (about 0.7 meter) high   **q***25* That is, about 3 inches (about 8 centimeters)

"ark of the covenant" (see, e.g., Nu 10:33). *I will meet with you.* See note on 27:21.
25:23 *table.* The table taken from the second (Zerubbabel's) temple by Antiochus Epiphanes is depicted on the Arch of Titus among the items the Romans took back to Rome after conquering Jerusalem in A.D. 70.

25:26 *rings.* See note on v. 12.
25:30 *bread of the Presence.* Traditionally "showbread." In this phrase, "Presence" refers to the presence of God himself (as in 33:14–15; Isa 63:9). The bread (twelve loaves, one for each tribe) represented a perpetual bread offering to the Lord by which Israel declared that she conse-

---

The Tabernacle

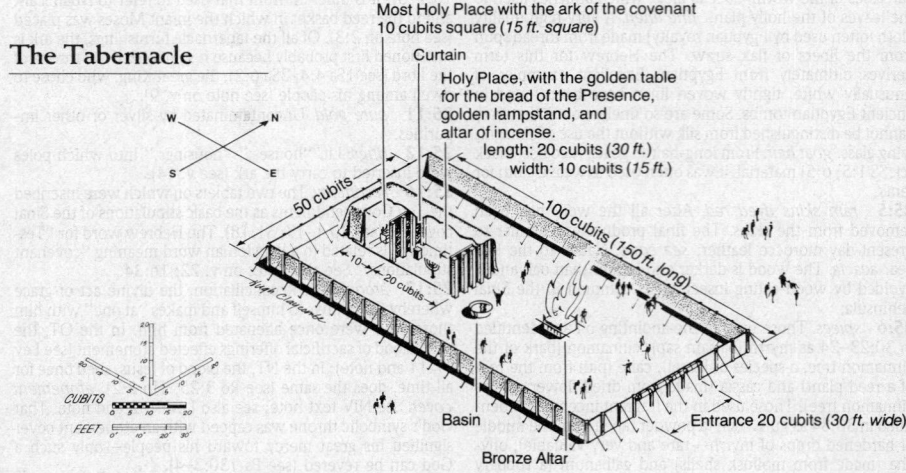

Most Holy Place with the ark of the covenant
10 cubits square (*15 ft. square*)

Curtain

Holy Place, with the golden table
for the bread of the Presence,
golden lampstand, and
altar of incense.
length: 20 cubits (*30 ft.*)
width: 10 cubits (*15 ft.*)

50 cubits

100 cubits (*150 ft. long*)

CUBITS
FEET

Basin

Bronze Altar

Entrance 20 cubits (*30 ft. wide*)

The new religious observances taught by Moses in the desert centered on rituals connected with the tabernacle, and amplified Israel's sense of separateness, purity and oneness under the Lordship of Yahweh.

A few desert shrines have been found in Sinai, notably at Serabit el-Khadem and at Timnah in the Negev, and show marked Egyptian influence.

Specific cultural antecedents to portable shrines carried on poles and covered with thin sheets of gold can be found in

ancient Egypt as early as the Old Kingdom (2800-2250 B.C.), but were especially prominent in the 18th and 19th dynasties (1570-1180). The best examples come from the fabulous tomb of Tutankhamun, c. 1350.

Comparisons of construction details in the text of Ex 25-40 with the frames, shrines, poles, sheathing, draped fabric covers, gilt rosettes, and winged protective figures from the shrine of Tutankhamun are instructive. The period, the Late Bronze Age, is equivalent in all dating systems to the era of Moses and the exodus. © Hugh Claycombe 1981

and the same for all six branches extending from the lampstand. 34And on the lampstand there are to be four cups shaped like almond flowers with buds and blossoms. 35One bud shall be under the first pair of branches extending from the lampstand, a second bud under the second pair, and a third bud under the third pair—six branches in all. 36The buds and branches shall all be of one piece with the lampstand, hammered out of pure gold. r

37"Then make its seven lamps s and set them up on it so that they light the space in front of it. 38Its wick trimmers and trays t are to be of pure gold. 39A talent r of pure gold is to be used for the lampstand and all these accessories. 40See that you make them according to the pattern u shown you on the mountain.

The Tabernacle

26:1–37pp — Ex 36:8–38

26 "Make the tabernacle v with ten curtains of finely twisted linen and blue, purple and scarlet yarn, with cherubim w worked into them by a skilled craftsman. 2All the curtains are to be the same size x—twenty-eight cubits long and four cubits wide. s 3Join five of the curtains together, and do the same with the other five. 4Make loops of blue material along the edge of the end curtain in one set, and do the same with the end curtain in the other set. 5Make fifty loops on one curtain and fifty loops on the end curtain of the other set, with the loops opposite each other. 6Then make fifty gold clasps and use

them to fasten the curtains together so that the tabernacle is a unit. y

7"Make curtains of goat hair for the tent over the tabernacle—eleven altogether. 8All eleven curtains are to be the same size z—thirty cubits long and four cubits wide. t 9Join five of the curtains together into one set and the other six into another set. Fold the sixth curtain double at the front of the tent. 10Make fifty loops along the edge of the end curtain in one set and also along the edge of the end curtain in the other set. 11Then make fifty bronze clasps and put them in the loops to fasten the tent together as a unit. a 12As for the additional length of the tent curtains, the half curtain that is left over is to hang down at the rear of the tabernacle. 13The tent curtains will be a cubit u longer on both sides; what is left will hang over the sides of the tabernacle so as to cover it. 14Make for the tent a covering b of ram skins dyed red, and over that a covering of hides of sea cows. v c

15"Make upright frames of acacia wood for the tabernacle. 16Each frame is to be ten cubits long and a cubit and a half wide, w 17with two projections set parallel to each other. Make all the frames of the tabernacle in this way. 18Make twenty frames for the south side of the tabernacle 19and make forty silver bases d to go under

25:36 rver 18; Nu 8:4
25:37 sEx 27:21; 30:8; Lev 24:3-4; Nu 8:2; 1Sa 3:3; 2Ch 13:11
25:38 tS ver 37; Nu 4:9
25:40 uS ver 9; Ac 7:44; Heb 8:5*
26:1 vEx 29:42; 40:2; Lev 8:10; Nu 1:50; Jos 22:19,29; 2Sa 7:2; 1Ki 1:39; Ac 7:44; Heb 8:2, 5; 13:10; S Rev 21:3 wS Ex 25:18
26:2 xver 8

26:6 yver 11
26:8 zver 2
26:11 aver 6
26:14 bNu 3:25 cNu 4:25
26:19 dver 21, 25,32; Ex 38:27

r39 That is, about 75 pounds (about 34 kilograms)
s2 That is, about 42 feet (about 12.5 meters) long and 6 feet (about 1.8 meters) wide   t8 That is, about 45 feet (about 13.5 meters) long and 6 feet (about 1.8 meters) wide   u13 That is, about 1 1/2 feet (about 0.5 meter)
v14 That is, dugongs   w16 That is, about 15 feet (about 4.5 meters) long and 2 1/4 feet (about 0.7 meter) wide

crated to God the fruits of her labors, and by which she at the same time acknowledged that all such fruit had been hers only by God's blessing. See Lev 24:5–9.
25:31 *flowerlike cups, buds and blossoms.* The design is patterned after an almond tree (see v. 33), the first of the trees in the Near East to blossom in spring. The cups of the lampstand resemble either the calyx (outer covering of the flower) or the almond nut.
25:37 *seven.* Signifying completeness. *lamps.* The ancient lamp was a small clay saucer with part of its rim pinched together to form a spout from which protruded the top of a wick fed by oil contained in the saucer. (Examples of seven-spouted lamps come from the time of Moses.) The ruins of Beth Shan and Megiddo have yielded examples of a metal pedestal topped by a ledge designed to carry a lamp. The classic representation of the shape of the tabernacle lampstand comes from the time of Herod the Great and may be seen on the Arch of Titus in Rome. The lamps were to burn all night in the tabernacle, tended by the priests. Oil for the lamps was to be supplied by the people; the light from the lamps represented the glory of the Lord reflected in the consecrated lives of the Israelites—Israel's glory answering to God's glory in the tabernacle (29:43). See 27:20–21.
25:40 Quoted in Heb 8:5 in order to contrast the "shad-

ow" (the trappings of the old covenant) with the reality (the Christ of the new covenant). See also Heb 10:1.
26:1 *tabernacle.* See note on 25:9. Its basic structure was to be 15 feet wide by 45 feet long by 15 feet high. Over an inner lining of embroidered linen (vv. 1–6), it was to have a covering woven of goat hair (vv. 7–13) and two additional coverings of leather, one made from ram skins dyed red and one from the hides of sea cows (v. 14). Internally, the ceiling was probably flat, but whether the leather coverings had a ridge line with sloping sides (like a tent) is not known. Symbolically the tabernacle represented God's royal tent. *finely twisted linen and blue, purple and scarlet yarn.* See note on 25:4. *cherubim.* Signifying a royal chamber (see 25:18 and note).
26:7 *goat hair.* See note on 25:4.
26:14 *ram skins dyed red . . . sea cows.* See note on 25:5.
26:17 *projections.* Lit. "hands"; probably the two tenons at the bottom of each frame that were inserted into its two bases (see v. 19).
26:19 *forty silver bases.* These plus the 40 in v. 21, the 16 in v. 25 and the 4 in v. 32 make up a grand total of 100, the number of talents of silver obtained from the Israelite community to be used to cast the bases (see 38:27).

them—two bases for each frame, one under each projection. 20For the other side, the north side of the tabernacle, make twenty frames 21and forty silver bases *e*—two under each frame. 22Make six frames for the far end, that is, the west end of the tabernacle, 23and make two frames for the corners at the far end. 24At these two corners they must be double from the bottom all the way to the top, and fitted into a single ring; both shall be like that. 25So there will be eight frames and sixteen silver bases—two under each frame.

26"Also make crossbars of acacia wood: five for the frames on one side of the tabernacle, 27five for those on the other side, and five for the frames on the west, at the far end of the tabernacle. 28The center crossbar is to extend from end to end at

the middle of the frames. 29Overlay the frames with gold and make gold rings to hold the crossbars. Also overlay the crossbars with gold.

30"Set up the tabernacle*f* according to the plan *g* shown you on the mountain.

31"Make a curtain *h* of blue, purple and scarlet yarn and finely twisted linen, with cherubim *i* worked into it by a skilled craftsman. 32Hang it with gold hooks on four posts of acacia wood overlaid with gold and standing on four silver bases.*j* 33Hang the curtain from the clasps and place the ark of the Testimony behind the curtain.*k* The curtain will separate the Holy Place from the Most Holy Place.*l* 34Put the atonement cover *m* on the ark of the Testimony in the Most Holy Place. 35Place the table *n* outside the curtain on the north side of the tabernacle and put

26:21 *e*S ver 19

26:30 *f*Ex 40:2; Nu 9:15
*g*S Ex 25:9
26:31 *h*Nu 4:5; 2Ch 3:14; Lk 23:45; Heb 9:3
*i*S Ex 25:18
26:32 *j*S ver 19
26:33 *k*Ex 27:21; 35:12; 40:3,21; Lev 16:2; Nu 3:31; 4:5; 2Ch 3:14
*l*Lev 16:2,16; 1Ki 6:16; 7:50; 8:6; 2Ch 3:8; 5:7; Eze 41:4; Heb 9:2-3
26:34 *m*Ex 25:21; 30:6; 37:6; Lev 16:2; Heb 9:5
26:35 *n*S Ex 25:23; Heb 9:2

26:23 *corners.* Or "angles," perhaps referring to mitered joints at the corners.
26:26 *crossbars.* To strengthen the frames on the north, south and west sides of the courtyard.
26:29 *rings.* Lit. "houses," "housings" (see note on 25:12).

26:30 *plan.* See note on 25:40.
26:31–35 A curtain was to divide the tabernacle into two rooms, the Holy Place and the Most Holy Place, with the former twice as large as the latter. The Most Holy Place probably formed a perfect cube, 15 feet by 15 feet by 15 feet. Enclosed with linen curtains embroidered with cherubim

Tabernacle Furnishings

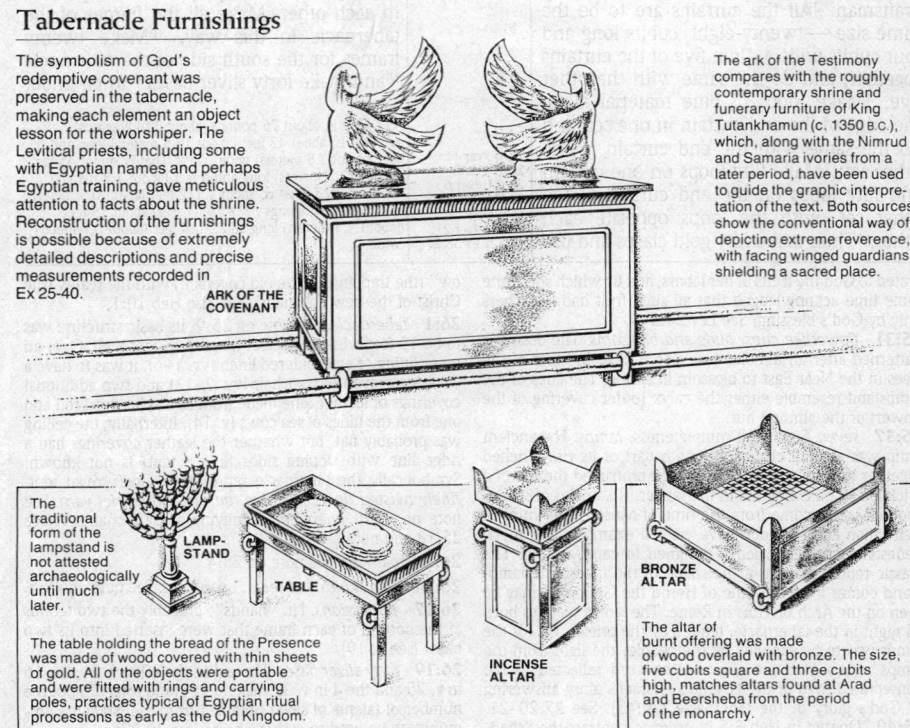

The symbolism of God's redemptive covenant was preserved in the tabernacle, making each element an object lesson for the worshiper. The Levitical priests, including some with Egyptian names and perhaps Egyptian training, gave meticulous attention to facts about the shrine. Reconstruction of the furnishings is possible because of extremely detailed descriptions and precise measurements recorded in Ex 25-40. **ARK OF THE COVENANT**

The ark of the Testimony compares with the roughly contemporary shrine and funerary furniture of King Tutankhamun (c. 1350 B.C.), which, along with the Nimrud and Samaria ivories from a later period, have been used to guide the graphic interpretation of the text. Both sources show the conventional way of depicting extreme reverence, with facing winged guardians shielding a sacred place.

The traditional form of the lampstand is not attested archaeologically until much later. **LAMP-STAND**

TABLE

The table holding the bread of the Presence was made of wood covered with thin sheets of gold. All of the objects were portable and were fitted with rings and carrying poles, practices typical of Egyptian ritual processions as early as the Old Kingdom.

INCENSE ALTAR

BRONZE ALTAR

The altar of burnt offering was made of wood overlaid with bronze. The size, five cubits square and three cubits high, matches altars found at Arad and Beersheba from the period of the monarchy.

the lampstand[o] opposite it on the south side.

36"For the entrance to the tent make a curtain[p] of blue, purple and scarlet yarn and finely twisted linen—the work of an embroiderer.[q] 37Make gold hooks for this curtain and five posts of acacia wood overlaid with gold. And cast five bronze bases for them.

The Altar of Burnt Offering

27:1–8pp — Ex 38:1–7

27 "Build an altar[r] of acacia wood, three cubits[x] high; it is to be square, five cubits long and five cubits wide.[y] 2Make a horn[s] at each of the four corners, so that the horns and the altar are of one piece, and overlay the altar with bronze. 3Make all its utensils of bronze—its pots to remove the ashes, and its shovels, sprinkling bowls,[t] meat forks and firepans.[u] 4Make a grating for it, a bronze network, and make a bronze ring at each of the four corners of the network. 5Put it under the ledge of the altar so that it is halfway up the altar. 6Make poles of acacia wood for the altar and overlay them with bronze.[v] 7The poles are to be inserted into the rings so they will be on two sides of the altar when it is carried.[w] 8Make the altar hollow, out of boards. It is to be made just as you were shown[x] on the mountain.

The Courtyard

27:9–19pp — Ex 38:9–20

9"Make a courtyard[y] for the tabernacle. The south side shall be a hundred cubits[z] long and is to have curtains of finely twisted linen, 10with twenty posts and twenty bronze bases and with silver hooks and bands on the posts. 11The north side shall also be a hundred cubits long and is to have curtains, with twenty posts and twenty bronze bases and with silver hooks and bands on the posts.

12"The west end of the courtyard shall be fifty cubits[a] wide and have curtains, with ten posts and ten bases. 13On the east end, toward the sunrise, the courtyard shall also be fifty cubits wide. 14Curtains fifteen cubits[b] long are to be on one side of the entrance, with three posts and three bases, 15and curtains fifteen cubits long are to be on the other side, with three posts and three bases.

16"For the entrance to the courtyard, provide a curtain[z] twenty cubits[c] long, of blue, purple and scarlet yarn and finely twisted linen—the work of an embroiderer[a]—with four posts and four bases. 17All the posts around the courtyard are to have silver bands and hooks, and bronze

Cross references

26:35 oS Ex 25:31
26:36 pEx 35:15; 40:5,28
qPs 45:14;
Eze 16:10; 26:16; 27:7
27:1 rS Ex 20:24; S 40:6; S 1Ki 8:64
27:2 sEx 29:12; 30:2; 37:25;
Lev 4:7; 1Ki 1:50; 2:28; Ps 118:27;
Jer 17:1;
Eze 43:15;
Am 3:14;
Zec 9:15
27:3 tNu 7:13; 1Ki 7:40,45; 2Ki 12:13
uNu 4:14; 1Ch 28:17; Jer 52:18
27:6 vS Ex 25:13
27:7 wEx 25:14, 28
27:8 xS Ex 25:9

27:9 yEx 35:17; 40:8,33;
Lev 6:16,26;
Eze 40:14; 42:1
27:16 zEx 40:33
aEx 36:37

x 1 That is, about 4 1/2 feet (about 1.3 meters)
y 1 That is, about 7 1/2 feet (about 2.3 meters) long and wide   z 9 That is, about 150 feet (about 46 meters); also in verse 11   a 12 That is, about 75 feet (about 23 meters); also in verse 13   b 14 That is, about 22 1/2 feet (about 6.9 meters); also in verse 15   c 16 That is, about 30 feet (about 9 meters)

and containing only the ark of the Testimony, it represented God's throne room. The Holy Place represented his royal guest chamber where his people symbolically came before him in the bread of the Presence (see note on 25:30), the light from the lampstand (see note on 25:37) and the incense from the altar of incense (see note on 30:1).
26:31 *curtain.* To separate the Holy Place from the Most Holy Place (see v. 33). It was called the "shielding curtain" (39:34; 40:21; Nu 4:5) because it shielded the ark (see 27:21; see also notes on 16:34; 25:22). At the moment when Christ died, the curtain of Herod's temple was torn, thereby giving the believer direct access to the presence of God (see Mk 15:38; Heb 6:19–20; 10:19–22). *cherubim.* See v. 1 and note. The curtain at the entrance to the Holy Place did not have cherubim (see v. 36).
26:37 *bronze.* Inside the tabernacle, gold was the metal of choice; outside—beginning with the bases of the outer curtain (see v. 36)—the metal of choice was bronze. The furnishings close to the place of God's dwelling were made of, or overlaid with, gold; those farther away (see 27:2–6; 30:18) were made of, or overlaid with, bronze. The bases that supported the frames of the tabernacle and the four posts holding the dividing curtain were of silver (see vv. 19,21, 25,32).
27:1 *altar.* The altar of burnt offering (see Lev 4:7,10,18). *acacia wood.* See note on 25:5.
27:2 *horns.* Projections of the four corner posts. They were symbols of help and refuge (see 1Ki 1:50; 2:28; Ps 18:2).

They also symbolized the atoning power of the altar: Some of the blood was put on the horns of the altar before the rest was poured out at the base (see 29:12; Lev 4:7,18,25,30, 34; 8:15; 9:9; 16:18).
27:3 *pots to remove the ashes.* From the grating (see v. 4). *shovels.* To haul the ashes away. *sprinkling bowls.* To catch the blood of the animals slain beside the altar and to sprinkle it at the base. *meat forks.* Three-pronged forks for arranging the sacrifice or removing the priests' portion from the container in which it was being boiled (see 1Sa 2:13–14). *firepans.* Probably for carrying fire from the altar of burnt offering to the altar of incense inside the Holy Place (see Lev 10:1; 16:12–13).
27:4 *grating.* Placed midway between the top and bottom of the boxlike structure. Since the intense heat of the fire built inside the upper half of the altar would have eventually destroyed it, perhaps the hollow altar (see v. 8) was designed to be filled with earth when it was in use. *ring.* See note on 25:12.
27:12–13 *west end . . . east end.* The courtyard is described as having two equal parts. The Most Holy Place probably occupied the central position in the western half, the altar of burnt offering the central position in the eastern half.
27:13–14 *toward the sunrise . . . the entrance.* The entrance to the tabernacle courtyard faced east, as did that of Solomon's temple (see Eze 8:16) and of Herod's temple.

bases. [18]The courtyard shall be a hundred cubits long and fifty cubits wide,[d] with curtains of finely twisted linen five cubits[e] high, and with bronze bases. [19]All the other articles used in the service of the tabernacle, whatever their function, including all the tent pegs for it and those for the courtyard, are to be of bronze.

Oil for the Lampstand

27:20–21pp — Lev 24:1–3

[20]"Command the Israelites to bring you clear oil[b] of pressed olives for the light so that the lamps may be kept burning. [21]In the Tent of Meeting,[c] outside the curtain that is in front of the Testimony,[d] Aaron and his sons are to keep the lamps[e] burning before the LORD from evening till morning. This is to be a lasting ordinance[f] among the Israelites for the generations to come.

The Priestly Garments

28 "Have Aaron[g] your brother brought to you from among the Israelites, along with his sons Nadab and Abihu,[h] Eleazar and Ithamar,[i] so they may serve me as priests.[j] [2]Make sacred garments[k] for your brother Aaron, to give him dignity and honor.[l] [3]Tell all the skilled men[m] to whom I have given wisdom[n] in such matters that they are to make garments for Aaron, for his consecration, so he may serve me as priest. [4]These are the garments they are to make: a breastpiece,[o] an ephod,[p] a robe,[q] a woven tunic,[r] a turban[s] and a sash. They are to make these sacred garments for your brother Aaron and his sons, so they may serve me as priests. [5]Have them use gold, and blue, purple and scarlet yarn, and fine linen.[t]

Cross references (center column)

27:20 *b*S Ex 25:6
27:21 *c*Ex 28:43; 29:42; 30:36; 33:7; Lev 1:1; 6:26; 8:3,31; Nu 1:1; 31:54; Jos 18:1; 1Ki 1:39
*d*S Ex 16:34
*e*S Ex 25:37
*f*Ex 29:9; 30:21; Lev 3:17; 16:34; 17:7; Nu 18:23; 19:21; 1Sa 30:25
28:1 *g*Lev 8:30; Ps 99:6; Heb 5:4
*h*S Ex 6:23; 24:9
*i*S Ex 6:23
*j*Lev 8:2; 21:1; Nu 18:1-7; Dt 18:5; 1Sa 2:28; Heb 5:1
28:2 *k*Lev 29:5, 29; 31:10; 35:19; 39:1; Lev 8:7-9, 30; 16:32;
*l*Nu 20:26-28 *l*ver 40
28:3 *m*Ex 31:6; 35:10,25,35; 36:1 *n*Ex 31:3; Dt 34:9; Isa 11:2; 1Co 12:8; S Eph 1:17
28:4 *o*ver 15-30 *p*S Ex 25:7 *q*ver 31-35 *r*ver 39; Lev 10:5 *s*ver 37
28:5 *t*Ex 25:4

28:6 *u*S Ex 25:7
28:8 *v*Ex 29:5
28:9 *w*SS 8:6; Isa 49:16; Hag 2:23
28:12 *x*Dt 33:12; Job 31:36 *y*ver 29; Ex 30:16; Nu 10:10; 31:54; Jos 4:7; Zec 6:14
28:15 *z*S Ex 25:7
28:17 *a*Eze 28:13; Rev 21:19-20

The Ephod

28:6–14pp — Ex 39:2–7

[6]"Make the ephod[u] of gold, and of blue, purple and scarlet yarn, and of finely twisted linen—the work of a skilled craftsman. [7]It is to have two shoulder pieces attached to two of its corners, so it can be fastened. [8]Its skillfully woven waistband[v] is to be like it—of one piece with the ephod and made with gold, and with blue, purple and scarlet yarn, and with finely twisted linen.

[9]"Take two onyx stones and engrave[w] on them the names of the sons of Israel [10]in the order of their birth—six names on one stone and the remaining six on the other. [11]Engrave the names of the sons of Israel on the two stones the way a gem cutter engraves a seal. Then mount the stones in gold filigree settings [12]and fasten them on the shoulder pieces of the ephod as memorial stones for the sons of Israel. Aaron is to bear the names on his shoulders[x] as a memorial[y] before the LORD. [13]Make gold filigree settings [14]and two braided chains of pure gold, like a rope, and attach the chains to the settings.

The Breastpiece

28:15–28pp — Ex 39:8–21

[15]"Fashion a breastpiece[z] for making decisions—the work of a skilled craftsman. Make it like the ephod: of gold, and of blue, purple and scarlet yarn, and of finely twisted linen. [16]It is to be square—a span[f] long and a span wide—and folded double. [17]Then mount four rows of precious stones[a] on it. In the first row there shall be a ruby, a topaz and a beryl; [18]in the second row a turquoise, a sapphire[g] and an em-

d18 That is, about 150 feet (about 46 meters) long and 75 feet (about 23 meters) wide   e18 That is, about 7 1/2 feet (about 2.3 meters)   f16 That is, about 9 inches (about 22 centimeters)   g18 Or lapis lazuli

---

27:18 *five cubits.* See NIV text note; high enough to block the view of people standing outside the courtyard, thus protecting the sanctity and privacy of the worship taking place inside.
27:20 *clear oil of pressed olives.* Unripe olives were crushed in a mortar. The pulpy mass was then placed in a cloth basket through the bottom of which the oil dripped, producing a clear fuel that burned with little or no smoke.
27:21 *Tent of Meeting.* The tabernacle; it was not a place where God's people met for collective worship but one where God himself met—by appointment, not by accident—with his people (see 29:42–43). *curtain that is in front of the Testimony.* See note on 26:31. *lamps burning . . . from evening till morning.* The lamps were lit in the evening (see 30:8) and apparently extinguished in the morning (1Sa 3:3).
28:1 *Nadab and Abihu.* See note on 24:1. *serve me as priests.* In order "to offer gifts and sacrifices for sins" and "to

deal gently with those who are ignorant and are going astray" (Heb 5:1–2). Another important function of the priests was to read the law of Moses to the people and remind them of their covenant obligations (see Dt 31:9–13; Ne 8:2–3).
28:2 *to give him dignity and honor.* The garments were to exalt the office and functions of lesser priests (see v. 40) as well as of the high priest.
28:6 *ephod.* A sleeveless vestment worn by the high priest. Sometimes the word refers to an otherwise unidentified object of worship (see, e.g., Jdg 8:27; 18:17; Hos 3:4).
28:8 *waistband.* Apparently to hold the front and the back of the ephod to the priest's body.
28:12 *Aaron is to bear the names on his shoulders.* To symbolize the fact that the high priest represents all Israel when he ministers in the tabernacle.
28:15 *for making decisions.* By means of the Urim and Thummim (see note on v. 30).

erald; [19]in the third row a jacinth, an agate and an amethyst; [20]in the fourth row a chrysolite, [b] an onyx and a jasper. [h] Mount them in gold filigree settings. [21]There are to be twelve stones, one for each of the names of the sons of Israel, [c] each engraved like a seal with the name of one of the twelve tribes. [d]

[22]"For the breastpiece make braided chains of pure gold, like a rope. [23]Make two gold rings for it and fasten them to two corners of the breastpiece. [24]Fasten the two gold chains to the rings at the corners of the breastpiece, [25]and the other ends of the chains to the two settings, attaching them to the shoulder pieces of the ephod at the front. [26]Make two gold rings and attach them to the other two corners of the breastpiece on the inside edge next to the ephod. [27]Make two more gold rings and attach them to the bottom of the shoulder pieces on the front of the ephod, close to the seam just above the waistband of the ephod. [28]The rings of the breastpiece are to be tied to the rings of the ephod with blue cord, connecting it to the waistband, so that the breastpiece will not swing out from the ephod.

[29]"Whenever Aaron enters the Holy Place, [e] he will bear the names of the sons of Israel over his heart on the breastpiece of decision as a continuing memorial before the LORD. [30]Also put the Urim and the Thummim[f] in the breastpiece, so they may be over Aaron's heart whenever he enters the presence of the LORD. Thus Aaron will always bear the means of making decisions for the Israelites over his heart before the LORD.

Other Priestly Garments

28:31–43pp — Ex 39:22–31

[31]"Make the robe of the ephod entirely of blue cloth, [32]with an opening for the head in its center. There shall be a woven edge like a collar[i] around this opening, so that it will not tear. [33]Make pomegran-

ates[g] of blue, purple and scarlet yarn around the hem of the robe, with gold bells between them. [34]The gold bells and the pomegranates are to alternate around the hem of the robe. [35]Aaron must wear it when he ministers. The sound of the bells will be heard when he enters the Holy Place before the LORD and when he comes out, so that he will not die.

[36]"Make a plate[h] of pure gold and engrave on it as on a seal: HOLY TO THE LORD.[i] [37]Fasten a blue cord to it to attach it to the turban; it is to be on the front of the turban. [38]It will be on Aaron's forehead, and he will bear the guilt[j] involved in the sacred gifts the Israelites consecrate, whatever their gifts may be. It will be on Aaron's forehead continually so that they will be acceptable[k] to the LORD.

[39]"Weave the tunic[l] of fine linen and make the turban[m] of fine linen. The sash is to be the work of an embroiderer. [40]Make tunics, sashes and headbands for Aaron's sons, [n] to give them dignity and honor. [o] [41]After you put these clothes[p] on your brother Aaron and his sons, anoint[q] and ordain them. Consecrate them so they may serve me as priests. [r]

[42]"Make linen undergarments[s] as a covering for the body, reaching from the waist to the thigh. [43]Aaron and his sons must wear them whenever they enter the Tent of Meeting[t] or approach the altar to minister in the Holy Place, [u] so that they will not incur guilt and die. [v]

"This is to be a lasting ordinance[w] for Aaron and his descendants.

Consecration of the Priests

29:1–37pp — Lev 8:1–36

29 "This is what you are to do to consecrate[x] them, so they may serve me as priests: Take a young bull and two rams without defect.[y] [2]And from fine

Cross references

28:20 [b]Eze 1:16; 10:9; Da 10:6
28:21 [c]Jos 4:8
[d]Rev 21:12
28:29 [e]ver 43
28:30 [f]Lev 8:8; Nu 27:21; Dt 33:8; 1Sa 28:6; Ezr 2:63; Ne 7:65

28:33 [g]Nu 13:23; 1Sa 14:2; 1Ki 7:18; SS 4:3; Jer 52:22; Joel 1:12; Hag 2:19
28:36 [h]ver 37; Ex 29:6; Lev 8:9 [i]Zec 14:20
28:38 [j]Lev 5:1; 10:17; 16:22; 22:9,16; Nu 18:1; Isa 53:5,6,11; Eze 4:4-6; Heb 9:28; 1Pe 2:24 [k]S Ge 32:20; Lev 22:20,27; 23:11; Isa 56:7
28:39 [l]ver 4 [m]Ex 29:6; Lev 16:4; Eze 24:17,23; 44:18
28:40 [n]ver 4; Ex 29:8-9; 39:41; 40:14; Lev 8:13 [o]ver 2
28:41 [p]Ex 40:13 [q]Ex 29:7; Lev 6:20; 10:7; 21:12; Nu 35:25 [r]Ex 29:7-9; 30:30; 40:15; Lev 4:3; 6:22; 8:1-36; Nu 3:3; Heb 7:28
28:42 [s]Lev 6:10; 16:4,23; Eze 44:18
28:43 [t]S Ex 27:21 [u]ver 29 [v]Ex 30:20,21; Lev 16:13; 22:9; Nu 1:51; 4:15,20; 18:22 [w]S Ex 27:21
29:1 [x]ver 21,44; Lev 20:7; Jos 3:5; 1Ch 15:12 [y]Eze 43:23

[h]20 The precise identification of some of these precious stones is uncertain. [i]32 The meaning of the Hebrew for this word is uncertain.

28:29 *Aaron . . . will bear the names . . . over his heart.* Thus the nation was doubly represented before the Lord (see v. 12 and note).

28:30 *the Urim and the Thummim.* The Hebrew for this phrase probably means "the curses and the perfections." The Hebrew word *Urim* begins with the first letter of the Hebrew alphabet (*aleph*) and *Thummim* begins with the last letter (*taw*). They were sacred lots and were often used in times of crisis to determine the will of God (see Nu 27:21). It has been suggested that if Urim ("curses") dominated when the lots were cast the answer was "no," but if Thummim ("perfections") dominated it was "yes." In any event, their "every decision" was "from the LORD" (Pr 16:33).

28:31 *robe.* Worn under the ephod.

28:35 According to Jewish tradition, one end of a length of rope was tied to the high priest's ankle and the other end remained outside the tabernacle. If the bells on his robe stopped tinkling while he was in the Holy Place, the assumption that he had died could be tested by pulling gently on the rope.

28:38 *bear the guilt.* Symbolically.

28:39 *tunic.* Worn under the robe.

28:40 *to give them dignity and honor.* See note on v. 2.

28:42–43 See note on 20:26.

28:43 *Tent of Meeting.* See note on 27:21.

29:1 *consecrate them.* See note on 19:10–11. *without defect.* See note on 12:5.

wheat flour, without yeast, make bread, and cakes mixed with oil, and wafers spread with oil. [z] [3]Put them in a basket and present them in it—along with the bull and the two rams. [a] [4]Then bring Aaron and his sons to the entrance to the Tent of Meeting and wash them with water. [b] [5]Take the garments [c] and dress Aaron with the tunic, the robe of the ephod, the ephod itself and the breastpiece. Fasten the ephod on him by its skillfully woven waistband. [d] [6]Put the turban [e] on his head and attach the sacred diadem [f] to the turban. [7]Take the anointing oil [g] and anoint him by pouring it on his head. [8]Bring his sons and dress them in tunics [h] [9]and put headbands on them. Then tie sashes on Aaron and his sons. [i] [i] The priesthood is theirs by a lasting ordinance. [j] In this way you shall ordain Aaron and his sons.

[10]"Bring the bull to the front of the Tent of Meeting, and Aaron and his sons shall lay their hands on its head. [k] [11]Slaughter it in the LORD's presence [l] at the entrance to the Tent of Meeting. [12]Take some of the bull's blood and put it on the horns [m] of the altar with your finger, and pour out the rest of it at the base of the altar. [n] [13]Then take all the fat [o] on the inner parts, [p] the covering of the liver, and both kidneys with the fat on them, and burn them on the altar. [14]But burn the bull's flesh and its hide and its offal [q] outside the camp. [r] It is a sin offering.

[15]"Take one of the rams, [s] and Aaron and his sons shall lay their hands on its head. [t] [16]Slaughter it and take the blood and sprinkle it against the altar on all sides. [17]Cut the ram into pieces and wash [u] the inner parts and the legs, putting them with the head and the other pieces. [18]Then burn the entire ram on the altar. It is a burnt offering to the LORD, a pleasing aroma, [v] an offering made to the LORD by fire.

[19]"Take the other ram, [w] and Aaron and his sons shall lay their hands on its head. [x] [20]Slaughter it, take some of its blood and put it on the lobes of the right ears of

Aaron and his sons, on the thumbs of their right hands, and on the big toes of their right feet. [y] Then sprinkle blood against the altar on all sides. [z] [21]And take some of the blood [a] on the altar and some of the anointing oil [b] and sprinkle it on Aaron and his garments and on his sons and their garments. Then he and his sons and their garments will be consecrated. [c]

[22]"Take from this ram the fat, [d] the fat tail, the fat around the inner parts, the covering of the liver, both kidneys with the fat around them, and the right thigh. (This is the ram for the ordination.) [23]From the basket of bread made without yeast, which is before the LORD, take a loaf, and a cake made with oil, and a wafer. [24]Put all these in the hands of Aaron and his sons and wave them before the LORD as a wave offering. [e] [25]Then take them from their hands and burn them on the altar along with the burnt offering for a pleasing aroma to the LORD, an offering made to the LORD by fire. [f] [26]After you take the breast of the ram for Aaron's ordination, wave it before the LORD as a wave offering, and it will be your share. [g]

[27]"Consecrate those parts of the ordination ram that belong to Aaron and his sons: [h] the breast that was waved and the thigh that was presented. [28]This is always to be the regular share from the Israelites for Aaron and his sons. It is the contribution the Israelites are to make to the LORD from their fellowship offerings. [k] [i]

[29]"Aaron's sacred garments [j] will belong to his descendants so that they can be anointed and ordained in them. [k] [30]The son [l] who succeeds him as priest and comes to the Tent of Meeting to minister in the Holy Place is to wear them seven days.

[31]"Take the ram [m] for the ordination and

Cross references (center column):

29:2 [z]ver 23; Lev 2:1,4; 6:19-23; Nu 6:15
29:3 [a]ver 15,19
29:4 [b]Ex 40:12; Lev 14:8; 16:4; Heb 10:22
29:5 [c]S Ex 28:2 [d]Ex 28:8
29:6 [e]Ex 28:39; Isa 3:23; Zec 3:5 [f]S Ex 28:36
29:7 [g]ver 21; S Ex 28:41; 30:25,30,31; 37:29; 40:9; Lev 21:10; 1Sa 10:1; 1Ki 1:39; Ps 89:20; 133:2; 141:5
29:8 [h]S Ex 28:4; Lev 16:4
29:9 [i]Ex 28:40 /S Ex 27:21; 40:15; Nu 3:10; 18:7; 25:13; Dt 18:5; Jdg 17:5; 1Sa 2:30; 1Ki 12:31
29:10 [k]ver 19; Lev 1:4; 4:15; 16:21; Nu 8:12
29:11 [l]Lev 1:5, 11; 4:24; 6:16, 25; 14:13
29:12 [m]S Ex 27:2 [n]Lev 4:7; 9:9
29:13 [o]ver 22; Lev 1:8; 3:3,5,9; 4:10; 6:12; 7:3,5, 31; 9:10; Nu 18:17; 1Sa 2:15; 1Ki 8:64; 2Ch 7:7; 29:35; 35:14; Isa 43:24; Eze 44:15 [p]S Ex 12:9
29:14 [q]Na 3:6; Mal 2:3 [r]Lev 4:12,21; 16:27; Nu 19:3-5; Heb 13:11
29:15 [s]S ver 3 [t]ver 10; Lev 3:2; 2Ch 29:23
29:17 [u]Lev 1:9, 13
29:18 [v]S Ge 8:21; 2Co 2:15
29:19 [w]S ver 3 [x]S ver 10
29:20 [y]Lev 14:14,25 [z]ver 16; Lev 1:5, 11; 3:2
29:21 [a]Heb 9:22 [b]S ver 7 [c]S ver 1
29:22 [d]S ver 13
29:24 [e]Lev 7:30; 9:21; 10:15; 14:12; 23:11,20; Nu 6:20; 8:11,13,

15 29:25 [f]ver 18 29:26 [g]Lev 7:31-34 29:27 [h]Ex 22:29; Lev 7:31,34; Nu 18:11,12; Dt 18:3 29:28 [i]ver 22-27; Lev 7:30,34; 10:15 29:29 [j]S Ex 28:2; S Lev 16:4 [k]Nu 20:28 29:30 [l]Lev 6:22; Nu 3:3; 20:28 29:31 [m]Lev 7:37; 2Ch 13:9

[i]9 Hebrew; Septuagint *on them*   [k]28 Traditionally *peace offerings*

29:4 *Tent of Meeting.* See note on 27:21. *wash them with water.* Symbolizing the removal of ceremonial uncleanness (cf. Heb 10:22) and thus signifying the purity that must characterize them.

29:7 *anoint him.* Symbolizing spiritual enduement for serving God (see Isa 61:1).

29:10 *Bring the bull.* As a sin offering (see v. 14) to atone for the past sins of Aaron and his sons (see Lev 4:3). *lay their hands on its head.* As a symbol of (1) the animal's becoming their substitute and (2) transferring their sins to the sin-bearer (see Lev 16:20–22 and note).

29:12 *horns of the altar.* See note on 27:2.

29:13 *fat.* The most select parts of the bull (see Lev 3:3–5, 16) were burned on the altar as a sacrifice to the Lord.

29:14 *flesh . . . hide . . . offal.* Thought of as bearing sin, and thus burned outside the camp (see Heb 13:11–13).

29:18 *burn the entire ram.* Symbolizing total dedication.

29:20 *right ears.* Symbolizing sensitivity to God and his word. *right hands . . . right feet.* Symbolizing a life of service to others on God's behalf.

29:24 *wave offering.* See note on Lev 7:30–32.

29:28 *regular share . . . for Aaron and his sons.* Parts of certain sacrificial animals were set aside as food for the priests and their families (see Lev 10:14).

cook the meat in a sacred place.[n] [32]At the entrance to the Tent of Meeting, Aaron and his sons are to eat the meat of the ram and the bread[o] that is in the basket. [33]They are to eat these offerings by which atonement was made for their ordination and consecration. But no one else may eat[p] them, because they are sacred. [34]And if any of the meat of the ordination ram or any bread is left over till morning,[q] burn it up. It must not be eaten, because it is sacred.

[35]"Do for Aaron and his sons everything I have commanded you, taking seven days to ordain them. [36]Sacrifice a bull each day[r] as a sin offering to make atonement[s]. Purify the altar by making atonement for it, and anoint it to consecrate[t] it. [37]For seven days make atonement for the altar and consecrate it. Then the altar will be most holy, and whatever touches it will be holy.[u]

[38]"This is what you are to offer on the altar regularly each day:[v] two lambs a year old. [39]Offer one in the morning and the other at twilight.[w] [40]With the first lamb offer a tenth of an ephah[l] of fine flour mixed with a quarter of a hin[m] of oil[x] from pressed olives, and a quarter of a hin of wine as a drink offering.[y] [41]Sacrifice the other lamb at twilight[z] with the same grain offering[a] and its drink offering as in the morning—a pleasing aroma, an offering made to the LORD by fire.

[42]"For the generations to come[b] this burnt offering is to be made regularly[c] at the entrance to the Tent of Meeting[d] before the LORD. There I will meet you and speak to you; [e] [43]there also I will meet with the Israelites, and the place will be consecrated by my glory.[f]

[44]"So I will consecrate the Tent of Meeting and the altar and will consecrate Aaron and his sons to serve me as priests.[g] [45]Then I will dwell[h] among the Israelites and be their God. [i] [46]They will know that I am the LORD their God, who brought them out of Egypt[j] so that I might dwell among them. I am the LORD their God.[k]

The Altar of Incense

30:1–5pp — Ex 37:25–28

30 "Make an altar[l] of acacia wood for burning incense.[m] [2]It is to be square, a cubit long and a cubit wide, and two cubits high[n]—its horns[n] of one piece with it. [3]Overlay the top and all the sides and the horns with pure gold, and make a gold molding around it.[o] [4]Make two gold rings[p] for the altar below the molding—two on opposite sides—to hold the poles used to carry it. [5]Make the poles of acacia wood and overlay them with gold.[q] [6]Put the altar in front of the curtain that is before the ark of the Testimony—before the atonement cover[r] that is over the Testimony—where I will meet with you.

[7]"Aaron must burn fragrant incense[s] on the altar every morning when he tends the lamps. [8]He must burn incense again when he lights the lamps at twilight so incense will burn regularly before the LORD for the generations to come.[t] [9]Do not offer on this altar any other incense[u] or any burnt offering or grain offering, and do not pour a drink offering on it. [10]Once a year[v] Aaron shall make atonement[w] on its horns. This annual atonement must be made with the blood of the atoning sin offering[x] for the generations to come.[y] It is most holy to the LORD."

Atonement Money

[11]Then the LORD said to Moses, [12]"When you take a census[z] of the Israelites to count them, each one must pay the LORD a ransom[a] for his life at the time he

Cross references (center column)

29:31
[n]Lev 10:14;
Nu 19:9;
Eze 42:13
29:32 [o]Mt 12:4
29:33
[p]Lev 22:10,13
29:34
[q]S Ex 12:10
29:36
[r]Heb 10:11 [s]ver
33,37; Ex 30:10;
Lev 1:4; 4:20;
16:16; Nu 6:11;
8:12,19; 16:46;
25:13; 2Ch 29:24
[t]Ex 40:10;
Nu 7:10
29:37
[u]Ex 30:28-29;
40:10; Eze 43:25;
Mt 23:19
29:38 [v]Lev 23:2;
Nu 28:3-8;
1Ch 16:40;
2Ch 8:13;
Eze 46:13-15;
Da 12:11
29:39 [w]Nu 28:4,
8; 1Ki 18:36;
2Ch 13:11;
Ezr 3:3; Ps 141:2;
Da 9:21
29:40 [x]Ex 30:24;
Nu 15:4; 28:5
[y]S Ge 35:14;
Lev 23:37;
2Ki 16:13
29:41
[z]1Ki 18:29,36;
2Ki 3:20; 16:15;
Ezr 9:4,5;
Ps 141:2; Da 9:21
[a]Lev 2:1; 5:13;
10:12; Nu 4:16;
6:17; 1Ki 8:64;
Isa 43:23
29:42 [b]Ex 30:8,
10,21,31; 31:13
[c]Eze 46:15
[d]S Ex 26:1;
S 27:21 [e]ver 43;
Ex 25:22; 33:9,
11; Nu 7:89
29:43 [f]Ex 33:18;
40:34; Lev 9:6;
1Ki 8:11;
2Ch 5:14; 7:2;
Ps 26:8; 85:9;
Eze 1:28; 43:5;
Hag 1:8; 2:7
29:44 [g]S ver 1
29:45
[h]S Ex 25:8;
Nu 35:34;
Jn 14:17;
S Ro 8:10
[i]S Ge 17:7;
2Co 6:16
29:46 [j]S Ex 6:6;
19:4-6; Dt 5:6;
Ps 114:1; Hag 2:5
[k]S Ge 17:7

30:1 [l]Ex 40:5,26;
Nu 4:11;
1Ki 6:20;

Eze 41:22 [m]S Ex 25:6; 37:29; Lk 1:11; Heb 9:4; Rev 8:3
30:2 [n]S Ex 27:2; Rev 9:13 30:3 [o]S Ex 25:11 30:4
[p]S Ex 25:12 30:5 [q]S Ex 25:13 30:6 [r]Ex 25:22; S 26:34 30:7
[s]S Ex 25:6; 40:27; Nu 3:10; Dt 33:10; 1Sa 2:28; 1Ch 6:49;
2Ch 2:4; 26:18; 29:7 30:8 [t]S Ex 25:37; S 29:42 30:9
[u]Lev 10:1; Nu 16:7,40 30:10 [v]Lev 16:2 [w]Lev 9:7; 16:18-19,
30; 23:27,28; 25:9 [x]Ex 29:14; Lev 4:3; 6:25; 7:7; 8:2,14;
Nu 6:11 [y]S Ex 29:42 30:12 [z]Ex 38:25; Nu 1:2,49; 4:2,29;
14:29; 26:2; 31:26; 2Sa 24:1; 2Ki 12:4 [a]Ex 38:26;
Nu 31:50; S Mt 20:28

[l]40 That is, probably about 2 quarts (about 2 liters)
[m]40 That is, probably about 1 quart (about 1 liter)
[n]2 That is, about 1 1/2 feet (about 0.5 meter) long and wide and about 3 feet (about 0.9 meter) high

---

29:31 *sacred place.* Probably the tabernacle courtyard.
29:38–39 Institution of the daily morning and evening offerings—sometimes observed even during days of apostasy (see 2Ki 16:15).
29:42–43 *I will meet.* See note on 27:21.
29:43 *my glory.* Symbolic of God's presence over the ark of the covenant (see note on 25:10; see also 40:34–35; 1Ki 8:10–13).
29:45–46 *dwell among.* See note on 25:9.
29:45 *I will . . . be their God.* Commonly denotes the essence of the divine promise pledged in his covenant with his people (see note on 6:7).

29:46 *I am the LORD . . . who brought them out.* See note on 20:2.
30:1 *incense.* Its fragrant smoke symbolized the prayers of God's people (see Ps 141:2; Lk 1:10; Rev 5:8; 8:3–4).
30:3 *gold.* See note on 26:37.
30:4 *rings.* See note on 25:12.
30:6 *curtain that is before the ark of the Testimony.* See notes on 25:16,22; 26:31.
30:10 *annual atonement.* See Lev 16:34.
30:12 *take a census.* Perhaps such censuses were taken on various occasions (and at stated intervals) to enter the Israelites into an official roll for public duties in the Lord's service

is counted. Then no plague[b] will come on them when you number them. 13Each one who crosses over to those already counted is to give a half shekel,[o] according to the sanctuary shekel,[c] which weighs twenty gerahs. This half shekel is an offering to the LORD. 14All who cross over, those twenty years old or more,[d] are to give an offering to the LORD. 15The rich are not to give more than a half shekel and the poor are not to give less[e] when you make the offering to the LORD to atone for your lives. 16Receive the atonement[f] money from the Israelites and use it for the service of the Tent of Meeting.[g] It will be a memorial[h] for the Israelites before the LORD, making atonement for your lives."

Basin for Washing

17Then the LORD said to Moses, 18"Make a bronze basin,[i] with its bronze stand, for washing. Place it between the Tent of Meeting and the altar, and put water in it. 19Aaron and his sons are to wash their hands and feet[j] with water[k] from it. 20Whenever they enter the Tent of Meeting, they shall wash with water so that they will not die.[l] Also, when they approach the altar to minister by presenting an offering made to the LORD by fire, 21they shall wash their hands and feet so that they will not die. This is to be a lasting ordinance[m] for Aaron and his descendants for the generations to come."[n]

Anointing Oil

22Then the LORD said to Moses, 23"Take the following fine spices:[o] 500 shekels[p] of liquid myrrh,[p] half as much (that is, 250 shekels) of fragrant cinnamon,[q] 250 shekels of fragrant cane,[r] 24500 shekels[s] of cassia[t]—all according to the sanctuary shekel—and a hin[q] of olive oil. 25Make these into a sacred anointing oil, a fragrant blend, the work of a perfumer.[u] It will be the sacred anointing oil.[v] 26Then use it to anoint[w] the Tent of Meeting, the ark of the Testimony, 27the table and all its articles, the lampstand and its accessories, the altar of incense, 28the altar of burnt offering and all its utensils, and the basin with its stand.

29You shall consecrate them[x] so they will be most holy, and whatever touches them will be holy.[y]

30"Anoint Aaron and his sons and consecrate[z] them so they may serve me as priests.[a] 31Say to the Israelites, 'This is to be my sacred anointing oil[b] for the generations to come.[c] 32Do not pour it on men's bodies and do not make any oil with the same formula. It is sacred, and you are to consider it sacred.[d] 33Whoever makes perfume like it and whoever puts it on anyone other than a priest must be cut off[e] from his people.'"

Incense

34Then the LORD said to Moses, "Take fragrant spices[f]—gum resin, onycha and galbanum—and pure frankincense, all in equal amounts, 35and make a fragrant blend of incense,[g] the work of a perfumer.[h] It is to be salted and pure and sacred. 36Grind some of it to powder and place it in front of the Testimony in the Tent of Meeting, where I will meet[i] with you. It shall be most holy[j] to you. 37Do not make any incense with this formula for yourselves; consider it holy[k] to the LORD. 38Whoever makes any like it to enjoy its fragrance must be cut off[l] from his people."

Bezalel and Oholiab

31:2–6pp — Ex 35:30–35

31 Then the LORD said to Moses, 2"See, I have chosen Bezalel[m] son of Uri, the son of Hur,[n] of the tribe of Judah, 3and I have filled him with the Spirit of God, with skill, ability and knowledge[o] in all kinds of crafts[p]— 4to make artistic designs for work in gold, silver and bronze, 5to cut and set stones, to work in wood, and to engage in all kinds of craftsmanship. 6Moreover, I have appointed Oholiab[q] son of Ahisamach, of the tribe of

30:12
bNu 14:12;
Dt 28:58-61;
2Sa 24:13;
1Ki 8:37
30:13 cver 24;
Ex 38:24,26;
Lev 5:15; 27:3,
25; Nu 3:47;
7:13; 18:16;
Eze 4:10; 45:12;
Mt 17:24
30:14 dEx 38:26;
Nu 1:3,18; 14:29;
26:2; 32:11;
2Ch 25:5
30:15 ePr 22:2;
Eph 6:9
30:16 fver 12
gEze 38:25-28;
2Ch 24:5
hNu 31:54
30:18 iEx 31:9;
35:16; 38:8;
39:39; 40:7,30;
1Ki 7:38; 2Ch 4:6
30:19
jEx 40:31-32;
Jn 13:10
kEx 29:4; 40:12;
Lev 8:6; Ps 26:6;
Heb 10:22
30:20
lS Ex 28:43
30:21
mS Ex 27:21
nEx 29:42
30:23
oS Ge 43:11
pS Ge 37:25
qPr 7:17; SS 4:14
rSS 4:14;
Isa 43:24;
Jer 6:20
30:24 sS ver 13
tPs 45:8;
Eze 27:19
30:25 uver 35;
Ex 37:29;
1Ch 9:30
vS Ex 29:7;
S 1Sa 9:16
30:26 wEx 40:9;
Lev 8:10; Nu 7:1

30:29
xLev 8:10-11
yEx 29:37;
Lev 6:18,27;
Mt 23:17
30:30 zEx 29:7;
Lev 8:2,12,30;
10:7; 16:32;
21:10,12;
1Ch 15:12;
Ps 133:2
aS Ex 28:41
30:31 bS Ex 29:7
cS Ex 29:42
30:32 dver 25,37
30:33 ever 38;
S Ge 17:14
30:34 fSS 3:6
30:35 gS Ex 25:6
hS ver 25
30:36
iS Ex 25:22 jver
32; Ex 29:37;
Lev 2:3
30:37 kS ver 32

30:38 lS ver 33 31:2 mEx 36:1,2; 37:1; 38:22; 1Ch 2:20;
2Ch 1:5 nS Ex 17:10 31:3 oS Ex 28:3 p1Ki 7:14; 1Co 12:4
31:6 qEx 36:1,2; 38:23

o13 That is, about 1/5 ounce (about 6 grams); also in
verse 15   p23 That is, about 12 1/2 pounds (about 6
kilograms)   q24 That is, probably about 4 quarts (about
4 liters)

(see Nu 1:2; 26:2). *pay . . . a ransom for his life.* An extension of the principle stated in 13:13,15 (see note on 13:13).
30:14 *twenty years old or more.* Of military age (see Nu 1:3).
30:16 *Tent of Meeting.* See note on 27:21.
30:18 *basin.* Made from bronze mirrors contributed by Israelite women (see 38:8). *washing.* See note on 29:4.
30:23–24 *myrrh . . . cinnamon . . . cane . . . cassia.* See note on 25:6.

30:33 *cut off from his people.* See note on 12:15.
30:34 *gum resin, onycha and galbanum.* See note on 25:6. *frankincense.* A resin from the bark of *Boswellia carteri,* which grows in southern Arabia.
31:2 *Bezalel.* Means "in the shadow/protection of God." *Hur.* See note on 17:10.
31:3 *filled him with the Spirit of God.* Ability to work as a skilled craftsman was a spiritual gift, equipping a person for special service to God.

Dan, [r] to help him. Also I have given skill to all the craftsmen [s] to make everything I have commanded you: [7]the Tent of Meeting, [t] the ark of the Testimony [u] with the atonement cover [v] on it, and all the other furnishings of the tent— [8]the table [w] and its articles, the pure gold lampstand [x] and all its accessories, the altar of incense, [y] [9]the altar of burnt offering [z] and all its utensils, the basin [a] with its stand— [10]and also the woven garments [b], both the sacred garments for Aaron the priest and the garments for his sons when they serve as priests, [11]and the anointing oil [c] and fragrant incense [d] for the Holy Place. They are to make them just as I commanded [e] you."

The Sabbath

[12]Then the LORD said to Moses, [13]"Say to the Israelites, 'You must observe my Sabbaths. [f] This will be a sign [g] between me and you for the generations to come, [h] so you may know that I am the LORD, who makes you holy. [r] [i]

[14]" 'Observe the Sabbath, because it is holy to you. Anyone who desecrates it must be put to death; [j] whoever does any work on that day must be cut off from his people. [15]For six days, work [k] is to be done, but the seventh day is a Sabbath of rest, [l] holy to the LORD. Whoever does any work on the Sabbath day must be put to death. [16]The Israelites are to observe the Sabbath, [m] celebrating it for the generations to come as a lasting covenant. [17]It will be a sign [n] between me and the Israelites for-

ever, for in six days the LORD made the heavens and the earth, and on the seventh day he abstained from work and rested. [o] ' " [p]

[18]When the LORD finished speaking to Moses on Mount Sinai, [q] he gave him the two tablets of the Testimony, the tablets of stone [r] inscribed by the finger of God. [s]

The Golden Calf

32 When the people saw that Moses was so long in coming down from the mountain, [t] they gathered around Aaron and said, "Come, make us gods [s] who will go before [u] us. As for this fellow Moses who brought us up out of Egypt, we don't know what has happened to him." [v]

[2]Aaron answered them, "Take off the gold earrings [w] that your wives, your sons and your daughters are wearing, and bring them to me." [3]So all the people took off their earrings and brought them to Aaron. [4]He took what they handed him and made it into an idol [x] cast in the shape of a calf, [y] fashioning it with a tool. Then they said, "These are your gods, [t] [z] O Israel, who brought you up out of Egypt." [a]

[5]When Aaron saw this, he built an altar in front of the calf and announced, "Tomorrow there will be a festival [b] to the LORD." [6]So the next day the people rose

---

Cross references (center column):

31:6 [r]1Ki 7:14; 2Ch 2:14
[s]S Ex 28:3
31:7 [t]Ex 36:8-38
[u]Ex 37:1-5
[v]Ex 37:6; 40:20
31:8 [w]Ex 37:10-16
[x]Ex 37:17-24; Lev 24:4
[y]Ex 37:25-28
31:9 [z]Ex 38:3; Nu 4:14
[a]S Ex 30:18
31:10 [b]S Ex 28:2
31:11 [c]Ex 30:22-32; 37:29 [d]S Ex 25:6
[e]S Ex 25:9
31:13 [f]S Ex 20:8
[g]ver 17; Isa 56:4; Eze 20:12,20
[h]S Ex 29:42
[i]Lev 11:44; 20:8; 21:8; Eze 37:28
31:14 [j]Ex 35:2; Nu 15:32-36
31:15 [k]S Ex 20:8, 9-11; 35:2;
Lev 16:29; 23:3; Nu 29:7 [l]S Ge 2:3
31:16 [m]S Ex 20:8
31:17 [n]S ver 13

[o]S Ge 2:2-3
[p]S Ge 2:2;
S Ex 20:9;
Isa 56:2; 58:13; 66:23;
Jer 17:21-22; Eze 20:12,20
31:18 [q]S Ex 19:11
[r]S Ex 24:12;
2Co 3:3; Heb 9:4
[s]Ex 32:15-16; 34:1,28; Dt 4:13; 9:10
32:1 [t]S Ge 7:4; Dt 9:9-12
[u]S Ex 13:21 [v]ver 23; Ac 7:40*
32:2 [w]Jdg 8:24-27
32:4 [x]S Ex 20:23; Jdg 17:3-4; Isa 30:22 [y]ver 8, 24,35; Dt 9:16;

Ne 9:18; Ps 106:19; Ac 7:41 [z]Ex 20:23; Isa 42:17
[a]1Ki 12:28; 14:9; 2Ki 10:29; 17:16; 2Ch 13:8; Hos 8:6;
10:5 32:5 [b]Lev 23:2,37; 2Ki 10:20; Joel 2:15

[r]13 Or who sanctifies you; or who sets you apart as holy [s]1 Or a god; also in verses 23 and 31 [t]4 Or This is your god; also in verse 8

31:6 *Oholiab.* Means "The (divine) father is my tent/tabernacle." The names of Bezalel (see note on v. 2) and Oholiab were appropriate for the chief craftsmen working on the tabernacle.

31:7 *Tent of Meeting.* See note on 27:21.

31:13 *observe my Sabbaths.* Instructions for building the tabernacle and making the priestly garments are concluded by impressing on the Israelites the importance and necessity of keeping the Sabbath even while carrying out this special task.

31:14 *cut off from his people.* See note on 12:15.

31:16–17 *covenant . . . sign.* In her rhythm of work and rest in the service of God, Israel is to emulate God's pattern in creation as an ever-renewed sign of her covenant with God (see note on Ge 9:12).

31:18 *two tablets.* In keeping with ancient Near Eastern practice, these were duplicates of the covenant document, not two sections of the Ten Commandments. One copy belonged to each party of the covenant. Since Israel's copy was to be laid up in the presence of her God (according to custom), both covenant tablets (God's and Israel's) were placed in the ark (see 25:21). *Testimony.* See notes on 16:34; 25:16. *inscribed by the finger of God.* Because it was God's covenant (see 19:5-6), and the stipulations of the covenant (20:1-17) were his.

32:1 *so long.* Forty days and forty nights (see 24:18 and

note). *they.* Probably the tribe and clan leaders. *gods.* See NIV text note. *Moses who brought us up out of Egypt.* A rebellious contrast to the gracious statement of Israel's covenant Lord (see 20:2 and note; 29:46).

32:2 *gold earrings.* Probably part of the plunder brought from Eygpt (see 3:21–22; 11:2–3; 12:35–36).

32:4 *cast in the shape of a calf.* Either gold plating over a carved wooden calf (it was later burned, v. 20) or crudely cast in solid gold and then further shaped with a tool, later to be melted down in the fire. The calf was probably similar to representations of the Egyptian bull-god Apis (see note on Jer 46:15). Its manufacture was a flagrant violation of the second commandment (20:4-5). *they.* The leaders among the people (see note on v. 1). *These are your gods . . . up out of Egypt.* A parody of 20:2 (see note on v. 1). Centuries later, King Jeroboam would quote these words when he set up two golden calves in the northern kingdom of Israel (see 1Ki 12:28–29).

32:5 *altar in front of the calf . . . festival to the LORD.* Apparently Aaron recognized the idolatrous consequences of his deed and acted quickly to keep the people from turning completely away from the Lord.

32:6 *they sat down . . . indulge in revelry.* A pagan symbol evoked pagan religious practices. Paul quotes this sentence as a vivid example of Israel's tendency toward idolatry (see 1Co 10:7). The Hebrew verb translated "indulge in revelry"

early and sacrificed burnt offerings and presented fellowship offerings.[u][c] Afterward they sat down to eat and drink[d] and got up to indulge in revelry.[e]

[7]Then the LORD said to Moses, "Go down, because your people, whom you brought up out of Egypt,[f] have become corrupt.[g] [8]They have been quick to turn away[h] from what I commanded them and have made themselves an idol[i] cast in the shape of a calf.[j] They have bowed down to it and sacrificed[k] to it and have said, 'These are your gods, O Israel, who brought you up out of Egypt.'[l]

[9]"I have seen these people," the LORD said to Moses, "and they are a stiff-necked[m] people. [10]Now leave me alone[n] so that my anger may burn against them and that I may destroy[o] them. Then I will make you into a great nation."[p]

[11]But Moses sought the favor[q] of the LORD his God. "O LORD," he said, "why should your anger burn against your people, whom you brought out of Egypt with great power and a mighty hand?[r] [12]Why should the Egyptians say, 'It was with evil intent that he brought them out, to kill them in the mountains and to wipe them off the face of the earth'?[s] Turn from your fierce anger; relent and do not bring disaster[t] on your people. [13]Remember[u] your servants Abraham, Isaac and Israel, to whom you swore by your own self:[v] 'I will make your descendants as numerous as the stars[w] in the sky and I will give your descendants all this land[x] I promised them, and it will be their inheritance forever.'" [14]Then the LORD relented[y] and did not bring on his people the disaster he had threatened.

[15]Moses turned and went down the mountain with the two tablets of the Testimony[z] in his hands.[a] They were in-

scribed[b] on both sides, front and back. [16]The tablets were the work of God; the writing was the writing of God, engraved on the tablets.[c]

[17]When Joshua[d] heard the noise of the people shouting, he said to Moses, "There is the sound of war in the camp."

[18]Moses replied:

"It is not the sound of victory,
    it is not the sound of defeat;
    it is the sound of singing that I hear."

[19]When Moses approached the camp and saw the calf[e] and the dancing,[f] his anger burned[g] and he threw the tablets out of his hands, breaking them to pieces[h] at the foot of the mountain. [20]And he took the calf they had made and burned[i] it in the fire; then he ground it to powder,[j] scattered it on the water[k] and made the Israelites drink it.

[21]He said to Aaron, "What did these people do to you, that you led them into such great sin?"

[22]"Do not be angry,[l] my lord," Aaron answered. "You know how prone these people are to evil.[m] [23]They said to me, 'Make us gods who will go before us. As for this fellow Moses who brought us up out of Egypt, we don't know what has happened to him.'[n] [24]So I told them, 'Whoever has any gold jewelry, take it off.' Then they gave me the gold, and I threw it into the fire, and out came this calf!"[o]

[25]Moses saw that the people were run-

32:6 [c]Ex 20:24; 34:15; Lev 3:1; 4:10; 6:12; 9:4; 22:21; Nu 6:14; 25:2; Dt 27:7; Jdg 20:26; Eze 43:27; Ac 7:41; [d]Jdg 19:4; Ru 3:3; 1Sa 1:9; 2Sa 11:11; 1Ki 13:23; 18:42; Ne 8:12; Job 1:4; Ecc 5:18; 8:15; Jer 16:8 [e]ver 17-19; 1Co 10:7*
32:7 [f]ver 4,11; Ex 33:1 [g]S Ge 6:11-12; Eze 20:8
32:8 [h]Jer 7:26; 16:12; Mal 2:8; 3:7 [i]S Ex 20:4 /S ver 4 [k]Ex 22:20 [l]1Ki 12:28; Eze 23:8
32:9 [m]Ex 33:3,5; 34:9; Dt 9:6,13; 10:16; 31:27; Jdg 2:19; 2Ki 17:14; 2Ch 30:8; 36:13; Ne 9:16; Ps 78:8; Pr 29:1; Isa 46:12; 48:4; Jer 7:26; Eze 2:4; Hos 4:16; Ac 7:51
32:10 [n]Isa 2:25; Jer 7:16; 11:14; 14:11 [o]Ex 22:24; 33:3,5; Nu 16:21, 45; Dt 9:14,19; Ps 106:23; Jer 14:12; Eze 20:13 [p]Nu 14:12; Dt 9:14
32:11 [q]Dt 9:18; 2Sa 21:1; 2Ch 15:2; Ps 9:10; 34:4; 106:23; Isa 9:13; Jer 15:1 [r]ver 13; Dt 9:26; 1Sa 7:9; Ne 1:10; Ps 136:12
32:12 [s]Nu 14:13-16; Dt 9:28 [t]ver 14; Ex 33:13
32:13 [u]S Ex 2:24; 33:13 [v]S Ge 22:16; Heb 6:13 [w]Ge 15:5; 22:17 [x]S Ge 12:7

32:14 [y]Dt 9:19; 1Sa 15:11; 2Sa 24:16; 1Ki 21:29; 1Ch 21:15; Ps 106:45; Jer 18:8; 26:3,19; Am 7:3,6; Jnh 3:10 **32:15** [z]Ex 31:18; Heb 9:4 [a]S Ex 19:18; 34:4,29; Dt 9:15 [b]2Co 3:3 **32:16** [c]S Ex 24:12 [d]S Ex 17:9 **32:19** [e]Dt 9:16 /ver 6; 1Co 10:7 [g]Ezr 9:3; Ps 119:53,158 [h]Ex 34:1; Dt 9:17 **32:20** [i]Dt 7:25; 12:3; Jos 7:1; 2Ki 23:6; 1Ch 14:12 /2Ch 34:7; Mic 1:7 [k]Dt 9:21 **32:22** [l]S Ge 18:30 [m]Dt 9:24; 28:20; 2Ki 21:15; Ezr 9:13; Ne 9:28; Jer 4:4; 44:3; Eze 6:9 **32:23** [n]S ver 1; Ac 7:40 **32:24** [o]S ver 4

---

[u]6 Traditionally *peace offerings*

---

often has sexual connotations (see, e.g., "caressing," Ge 26:8). Immoral orgies frequently accompanied pagan worship in ancient times.
32:7,9 *your people . . . these people.* By not calling Israel "my people" (as, e.g., in 3:10), God indicates that he is disowning them for breaking his covenant with them.
32:7 *corrupt.* And, therefore, ripe for destruction (see v. 10; Ge 6:11-13).
32:9 *stiff-necked.* Like unresponsive oxen or horses (see Jer 27:11-12; see also note on Ne 3:5).
32:10 *I will make you into a great nation.* After Israel—Abraham's descendants—has been destroyed, God will transfer to Moses the pledge originally given to Abraham (see Ge 12:2).
32:11 *your people.* Using God's own words (see v. 7 and note), Moses appeals to God's special relationship to Israel, then to God's need to vindicate his name in the eyes of the Egyptians (see v. 12), and finally to the great patriarchal promises (see v. 13).

32:13 *Israel.* Jacob (see 33:1; see also Ge 32:28).
32:14 *the LORD relented.* See note on Jer 18:7-10; see also 2Sa 24:16; Ps 106:45; Am 7:1-6; Jas 5:16.
32:15 *went down the mountain.* See note on 24:18. *two tablets.* See note on 31:18. *Testimony.* See notes on 16:34; 25:16. *inscribed on both sides.* Tablets were often thus inscribed in ancient times.
32:16 *work of God . . . writing of God.* See 31:18.
32:17 *Joshua.* Perhaps he had accompanied Moses part of the way up the mountain (see 24:13).
32:19 *breaking them to pieces.* Thus testifying against Israel that they had broken the covenant.
32:20 *burned it . . . ground it to powder.* King Jeroboam's altar (see note on v. 4) at Bethel received the same treatment (see 2Ki 23:15).
32:22-24 In his desperation, Aaron blamed the people (see notes on Ge 3:12-13).
32:24 *out came this calf.* Aaron could hardly have thought that Moses would believe such an incredible story.

ning wild and that Aaron had let them get out of control and so become a laughingstock[p] to their enemies. 26So he stood at the entrance to the camp and said, "Whoever is for the LORD, come to me." And all the Levites rallied to him.

27Then he said to them, "This is what the LORD, the God of Israel, says: 'Each man strap a sword to his side. Go back and forth through the camp from one end to the other, each killing his brother and friend and neighbor.' "[q] 28The Levites did as Moses commanded, and that day about three thousand of the people died. 29Then Moses said, "You have been set apart to the LORD today, for you were against your own sons and brothers, and he has blessed you this day."

30The next day Moses said to the people, "You have committed a great sin.[r] But now I will go up to the LORD; perhaps I can make atonement[s] for your sin."

31So Moses went back to the LORD and said, "Oh, what a great sin these people have committed![t] They have made themselves gods of gold.[u] 32But now, please forgive their sin[v]—but if not, then blot me[w] out of the book[x] you have written."

33The LORD replied to Moses, "Whoever has sinned against me I will blot out[y] of my book. 34Now go, lead[z] the people to the place[a] I spoke of, and my angel[b] will go before you. However, when the time comes for me to punish,[c] I will punish them for their sin."

35And the LORD struck the people with a plague because of what they did with the calf[d] Aaron had made.

33 Then the LORD said to Moses, "Leave this place, you and the people you brought up out of Egypt, and go up to the land I promised on oath[e] to Abraham, Isaac and Jacob, saying, 'I will give it to your descendants.'[f] 2I will send an angel[g] before you and drive out the Canaanites, Amorites, Hittites, Perizzites, Hivites and Jebusites.[h] 3Go up to the land flowing with milk and honey.[i] But I will not go with you, because you are a stiff-necked[j] people and I might destroy[k] you on the way."

4When the people heard these distressing words, they began to mourn[l] and no one put on any ornaments. 5For the LORD had said to Moses, "Tell the Israelites, 'You are a stiff-necked people.[m] If I were to go with you even for a moment, I might destroy[n] you. Now take off your ornaments and I will decide what to do with you.' " 6So the Israelites stripped off their ornaments at Mount Horeb.[o]

The Tent of Meeting

7Now Moses used to take a tent and pitch it outside the camp some distance away, calling it the "tent of meeting."[p] Anyone inquiring[q] of the LORD would go to the tent of meeting outside the camp. 8And whenever Moses went out to the tent, all the people rose and stood at the entrances to their tents,[r] watching Moses

---

Cross references (center column):

32:25
pS Ge 38:23
32:27 qNu 25:3, 5; Dt 33:9;
Eze 9:5
32:30
rISa 12:20;
Ps 25:11; 85:2
sLev 1:4; 4:20, 26; 5:6,10,13; 6:7
32:31 tEx 34:9;
Dt 9:18
uS Ex 20:23
32:32 vNu 14:19
wRo 9:3
xPs 69:28;
Eze 13:9;
Da 7:10; 12:1;
Mal 3:16;
S Lk 10:20
32:33
yS Ex 17:14;
S Job 21:20;
Rev 3:5
32:34
zS Ex 15:17
aEx 3:17
bS Ex 14:19
cS Ge 50:19;
Dt 32:35;
Ps 89:32; 94:23; 99:8; 109:20;
Isa 27:1; Jer 5:9; 11:22; 23:2; 44:13,29;
Hos 12:2;
Ro 2:5-6
32:35 dS ver 4
33:1
eS Ex 13:11;
S Nu 14:23;
Heb 6:13
fS Ge 12:7
33:2 gS Ex 14:19
hS Ex 3:28
33:3 iS Ex 3:8
jEx 32:9; Ac 7:51
kS Ex 32:10
33:4 lNu 14:39;
Ezr 9:3; Est 4:1;
Ps 119:53
33:5 mS Ex 32:9
nS Ex 32:10
33:6 oS Ex 3:1
33:7 pS Ex 27:21
qS Ge 25:22;
S 1Ki 22:5

33:8 rver 10; Nu 16:27

Footnotes / Study notes (bottom):

32:25 *were running wild . . . get out of control.* The same Hebrew root underlies both phrases and is found also in Pr 29:18 ("cast off restraint"). Anarchy reigns among people who refuse to obey and worship the Lord.
32:26 *Whoever is for the LORD, come to me.* See Jos 24:15; 1Ki 18:21; Mt 6:24. *all.* A generalization since Dt 33:9 implies that some of the Levites were also slain. *Levites.* The descendants of Levi (Ge 29:34) may have originally been regarded as priests (Dt 18:6-8). But at some stage they became subordinate to the priests who were descendants of Aaron, the brother of Moses (38:21; Nu 3:9-10; 1 Ch 16:4-6,37-42).
32:27 *killing his brother and friend and neighbor.* See Mt 10:37; Lk 14:26.
32:28 *The Levites did as Moses commanded.* Their zeal for the Lord is later matched by Aaron's grandson Phinehas, resulting in a perpetual covenant of the priesthood (see Nu 25:7-13).
32:29 *You have been set apart to the LORD today.* Because of their zeal for the Lord the Levites were set apart to be caretakers of the tabernacle and aides to the priests (see Nu 1:47-53; 3:5-9,12,41,45; 4:2-3).
32:30 *make atonement for your sin.* By making urgent intercession before God, as the mediator God had appointed between himself and Israel. No sacrifice that Israel or Moses might bring could atone for this sin. But Moses so identified

himself with Israel that he made his own death the condition for God's destruction of the nation (see v. 32). Jesus Christ, the great Mediator, offered himself on the cross to make atonement for his people.
32:32 *book you have written.* See notes on Ps 9:5; 51:1; 69:28.
32:33 *Whoever has sinned . . . I will blot out.* Moses' gracious offer is refused, because the person who sins is responsible for his own sin (see Dt 24:16; Eze 18:4 and note).
32:34 *Now go, lead the people.* Thus Moses received assurance that the Lord will continue his covenant with wayward Israel and fulfill his promise concerning the land. *the place I spoke of.* Canaan (see 33:1).
33:2 *Canaanites . . . Jebusites.* See note on 3:8.
33:3 *land flowing with milk and honey.* See note on 3:8. *I will not go with you.* The Lord's presence, earlier assured to his people (see 23:21 and note), is now temporarily withdrawn because of sin. *stiff-necked.* See note on 32:9.
33:6 *stripped off their ornaments.* As a sign of mourning (see Eze 26:16-17).
33:7 *tent of meeting outside the camp.* Not the tabernacle (contrast 27:21), which occupied a central location within the Israelite camp, but a temporary structure where the people could inquire of the Lord until the more durable tabernacle was completed.

until he entered the tent. ⁹As Moses went into the tent, the pillar of cloud*s* would come down and stay at the entrance, while the Lord spoke*t* with Moses. ¹⁰Whenever the people saw the pillar of cloud standing at the entrance to the tent, they all stood and worshiped, each at the entrance to his tent.*u* ¹¹The Lord would speak to Moses face to face,*v* as a man speaks with his friend. Then Moses would return to the camp, but his young aide Joshua*w* son of Nun did not leave the tent.

Moses and the Glory of the Lord

¹²Moses said to the Lord, "You have been telling me, 'Lead these people,'*x* but you have not let me know whom you will send with me. You have said, 'I know you by name*y* and you have found favor*z* with me.' ¹³If you are pleased with me, teach me your ways*a* so I may know you and continue to find favor with you. Remember that this nation is your people."*b*

¹⁴The Lord replied, "My Presence*c* will go with you, and I will give you rest."*d*

¹⁵Then Moses said to him, "If your Presence*e* does not go with us, do not send us up from here. ¹⁶How will anyone know that you are pleased with me and with your people unless you go with us?*f* What else will distinguish me and your people from all the other people on the face of the earth?"*g*

¹⁷And the Lord said to Moses, "I will do the very thing you have asked,*h* because I am pleased with you and I know you by name."*i*

¹⁸Then Moses said, "Now show me your glory."*j*

¹⁹And the Lord said, "I will cause all my goodness to pass*k* in front of you, and I will proclaim my name,*l* the Lord, in your presence. I will have mercy on whom I will have mercy, and I will have compassion on whom I will have compassion.*m* ²⁰But," he said, "you cannot see my face, for no one may see*n* me and live."

²¹Then the Lord said, "There is a place near me where you may stand on a rock. ²²When my glory passes by, I will put you in a cleft in the rock*o* and cover you with my hand*p* until I have passed by. ²³Then I will remove my hand and you will see my back; but my face must not be seen."

The New Stone Tablets

34 The Lord said to Moses, "Chisel out two stone tablets like the first ones,*q* and I will write on them the words that were on the first tablets,*r* which you broke.*s* ²Be ready in the morning, and then come up on Mount Sinai.*t* Present yourself to me there on top of the mountain. ³No one is to come with you or be seen anywhere on the mountain;*u* not even the flocks and herds may graze in front of the mountain."

⁴So Moses chiseled*v* out two stone tablets like the first ones and went up Mount Sinai early in the morning, as the Lord had commanded him; and he carried the two stone tablets in his hands.*w* ⁵Then the Lord came down in the cloud*x* and stood there with him and proclaimed his name, the Lord.*y* ⁶And he passed in front of Moses, proclaiming, "The Lord, the Lord, the compassionate*z* and gracious God,

33:9 *s*Ex 13:21; S 19:9; Dt 31:15; 1Co 10:1 *t*S Ex 29:42; 31:18; Ps 99:7 **33:10** *u*S ver 8 **33:11** *v*Nu 12:8; Dt 5:4; 34:10 *w*S Ex 17:9 **33:12** *x*Ex 3:10; S 15:17 *y*ver 17; Isa 43:1; 45:3; 49:1; Jn 10:14-15; 2Ti 2:19 *z*S Ge 6:8 **33:13** *a*Ps 25:4; 27:11; 51:13; 86:11; 103:7; 143:8 *b*Ex 3:7; Dt 9:26,29; Ps 77:15 **33:14** *c*S Ex 13:21; Dt 4:37; Isa 63:9; Hag 1:13; 2:4 *d*Dt 12:9,10; 25:19; Jos 1:13; 11:23; 21:44; 22:4; 23:1; 1Ki 8:56; Isa 63:14; Jer 31:2; Mt 11:28; Heb 4:1-11 **33:15** *e*ver 3; Ex 34:9; 2Ki 13:23; 17:18; 23:27; 24:20; Ps 51:11; 80:3,7, 19; Jer 7:15; 52:3 **33:16** *f*Ex 34:5; 40:34,35; Nu 9:15; 14:14 *g*Ex 23:9; Lev 20:24,26; Nu 23:9; Dt 4:7, 32,34; 32:9; 33:28 **33:17** *h*Ex 34:28; Dt 9:18,25; 10:10; Jas 5:16 *i*S Ge 6:8 **33:18** *j*S Ex 16:7; Jn 1:14; 12:41; 1Ti 6:16; Rev 15:8 **33:19** *k*1Ki 19:11

*l*Ex 6:3; 34:5-7 *m*Ro 9:15* **33:20** *n*S Ge 16:13; S Ex 3:6; S Dt 5:26;

S Jn 1:18 **33:22** *o*Ge 49:24; 1Ki 19:9; Ps 27:5; 31:20; 62:7; 91:1; Isa 2:21; Jer 4:29 *p*Ps 91:4; Isa 49:2; 51:16 **34:1** *q*S Ex 24:12 *r*Dt 10:2,4 *s*S Ex 32:19 **34:2** *t*S Ex 19:11 **34:3** *u*S Ex 19:13 **34:4** *v*Dt 10:3 *w*S Ex 32:15 **34:5** *x*S Ex 13:21; S 19:9 *y*Ex 6:3; 33:19 **34:6** *z*S Ex 22:27; S Nu 14:20; S Ps 86:15

33:9 *pillar of cloud would come down.* Symbolizing God's communication with Moses "as a man speaks with his friend" (v. 11). Later, a similar descent crowned the completion of the tabernacle (see 40:33–34; see also note on 13:21).

33:11 *The Lord would speak to Moses face to face.* As the OT mediator, Moses was unique among the prophets. *Joshua . . . did not leave the tent.* Probably his task was to guard the tent against intrusion by others.

33:12 *you have not let me know whom you will send with me.* See note on v. 3. Moses objects that a mere angel is no substitute for God's own presence. *I know you by name.* I have chosen you for my special purpose.

33:13 *teach me your ways.* A prayer that is answered in 34:6–7.

33:14 *My Presence will go with you.* The Lord's gracious response to Moses' concern (see note on v. 12).

33:17 *because I am pleased with you.* How much more does God hear the prayers of his Son Jesus Christ (see Mt 17:5; Heb 3:1–6)!

33:18 See v. 22. In a sense, Moses' prayer was finally

answered on the Mount of Transfiguration (Lk 9:30–32), where he shared a vision—however brief—of the Lord's glory with Elijah and three of Jesus' disciples.

33:19 *goodness.* God's nature and character. *name.* A further symbol of God's nature, character and person (see Ps 20:1; Jn 1:12; 17:6 and NIV text note). Here his name implies his mercy (grace) and his compassion (as it does also in 34:6).

33:20 See note on Ge 16:13; see also Jn 1:18; 6:46; 1Ti 1:17; 1Jn 4:12.

33:21–23 God speaks of himself in human language. See 34:5–7 for the fulfillment of his promise.

34:1 *two stone tablets . . . I will write on them.* See note on 31:18. *words.* See note on 20:1.

34:5 *name.* See note on 33:19.

34:6–7 See 33:19 and note. The Lord's proclamation of the meaning and implications of his name in these verses became a classic exposition that was frequently recalled elsewhere in the OT (see Nu 14:18; Ne 9:17; Ps 86:15; 103:8; 145:8; Joel 2:13; Jnh 4:2). See also notes on 3:14–15; 6:2–3.

slow to anger,[a] abounding in love[b] and faithfulness,[c] [7]maintaining love to thousands,[d] and forgiving wickedness, rebellion and sin.[e] Yet he does not leave the guilty unpunished;[f] he punishes the children and their children for the sin of the fathers to the third and fourth generation."[g]

[8]Moses bowed to the ground at once and worshiped. [9]"O Lord, if I have found favor[h] in your eyes," he said, "then let the Lord go with us.[i] Although this is a stiffnecked[j] people, forgive our wickedness and our sin,[k] and take us as your inheritance."[l]

[10]Then the LORD said: "I am making a covenant[m] with you. Before all your people I will do wonders[n] never before done in any nation in all the world.[o] The people you live among will see how awesome is the work that I, the LORD, will do for you. [11]Obey what I command[p] you to-day. I will drive out before you the Amorites, Canaanites, Hittites, Perizzites, Hivites and Jebusites.[q] [12]Be careful not to make a treaty[r] with those who live in the land where you are going, or they will be a snare[s] among you. [13]Break down their altars, smash their sacred stones and cut down their Asherah poles.[v][t] [14]Do not worship any other god,[u] for the LORD, whose name[v] is Jealous, is a jealous God.[w]

[15]"Be careful not to make a treaty[x] with those who live in the land; for when they prostitute[y] themselves to their gods and sacrifice to them, they will invite you and you will eat their sacrifices.[z] [16]And when you choose some of their daughters as wives[a] for your sons and those daughters prostitute themselves to their gods,[b] they will lead your sons to do the same.

[17]"Do not make cast idols.[c]

[18]"Celebrate the Feast of Unleavened Bread.[d] For seven days eat bread made without yeast,[e] as I commanded you. Do this at the appointed time in the month of Abib,[f] for in that month you came out of Egypt.

[19]"The first offspring[g] of every womb belongs to me, including all the firstborn males of your livestock, whether from herd or flock. [20]Redeem the firstborn donkey with a lamb, but if you do not redeem it, break its neck.[h] Redeem all your firstborn sons.[i]

"No one is to appear before me empty-handed.[j]

[21]"Six days you shall labor, but on the seventh day you shall rest;[k] even during the plowing season and harvest[l] you must rest.

[22]"Celebrate the Feast of Weeks with the firstfruits[m] of the wheat harvest, and the Feast of Ingathering[n] at the turn of the year.[w] [23]Three times[o] a year all your men are to appear before the Sovereign LORD, the God of Israel. [24]I will drive out nations[p] before you and enlarge your territory,[q] and no one will covet your land when you go up three times each year to appear before the LORD your God.

[25]"Do not offer the blood of a sacrifice to me along with anything containing yeast,[r] and do not let any of the sacrifice from the Passover Feast remain until morning.[s]

[26]"Bring the best of the firstfruits[t] of your soil to the house of the LORD your God.

"Do not cook a young goat in its mother's milk."[u]

34:6 [a]Nu 14:18; Ps 78:38; Jer 15:15; Ro 2:4 [b]S Ge 19:16 [c]Ps 61:7; 108:4; 115:1; 138:2; 143:1; La 3:23; Jas 5:11
34:7 [d]S Ex 20:6; Dt 5:10 [e]1Ki 8:30; Ps 86:5; 103:3; 130:4,8; Isa 43:25; Da 9:9; 1Jn 1:9 [f]Ex 23:7; Jos 24:19; Job 7:20-21; 9:28; 10:14; Mic 6:1-16; Na 1:3 [g]S Ex 20:5
34:9 [h]Ex 33:13; Nu 11:15 [i]S Ex 33:15 [j]Ex 32:9 [k]Nu 14:19; 1Ki 8:30; 2Ch 6:21; Ps 19:12; 25:11; Jer 33:8; Hos 14:2 [l]S Ex 6:7; 19:5; Dt 4:20; 7:6; 9:26,29; 14:2; 26:18; 32:9; 1Sa 10:1; 2Sa 14:16; 1Ki 8:51,53; Ps 28:9; 33:12; 74:2; 79:1; 94:14; 106:5,40; Isa 19:25; 63:17; Jer 10:16; 51:19; Mic 7:18; Zec 2:12
34:10 [m]S Ge 6:18; [n]S 9:15; S 15:18; Dt 5:2-3 [n]S Ex 3:20 [o]S Ex 33:16
34:11 [p]Dt 6:25; Jos 11:15 [q]S Ex 23:28
34:12 [r]Jdg 2:2 [s]S Ex 10:7
34:13 [t]S Ex 23:24; Nu 33:52; Dt 7:5; 12:3; Jdg 6:26; 1Ki 15:13; 2Ch 15:16; 17:6; 34:3-4; Mic 5:14
34:14 [u]S Ex 20:3 [v]Isa 9:6 [w]S Ex 20:5
34:15 [x]ver 12; Dt 23:6; Ezr 9:12 [y]Ex 22:20; 32:8; Dt 31:16; Jdg 2:17; 2Ki 17:8; 1Ch 5:25; 2Ch 11:15; Am 2:4
[z]S Ex 32:6; 1Co 8:4 **34:16** [a]Dt 7:3; 17:17; Jos 23:12; Jdg 3:6; 14:3; 1Ki 11:1,2; 16:31; Ezr 9:2; 10:3; Ne 10:30; 13:25,26 [b]Dt 7:4; 12:31; 20:18; 1Ki 11:4; 2Ki 21:3-15; Ps 106:34-41; Mal 2:11 **34:17** [c]S Ex 20:4 **34:18** [d]S Ex 12:17; Mt 26:17; Lk 22:1; Ac 12:3 [e]S Ex 12:15 [f]S Ex 12:2 **34:19** [g]Ex 13:2 **34:20** [h]S Ex 13:13 [i]S Ex 13:2 [j]S Ex 22:29; Dt 16:16; Eze 46:9 **34:21** [k]Ge 2:2-3 [l]Ne 13:15; Isa 56:2; 58:13 **34:22** [m]ver 26; Ex 23:19; Lev 2:12,14; [n]S Ex 23:16 **34:23** [o]S Ex 23:14 **34:24** [p]S Ex 23:28 [q]Dt 12:20; 19:8; Job 12:23 **34:25** [r]S Ex 23:18 [s]S Ex 12:8 **34:26** [t]S Ex 22:29; S Nu 18:12 [u]S Ex 23:19

[v]13 That is, symbols of the goddess Asherah
[w]22 That is, in the fall

34:7 *thousands.* Or "a thousand generations" (see 20:6). *wickedness, rebellion and sin.* See Isa 59:12 and note. **34:10** *making a covenant.* Renewing the covenant he had earlier made (chs. 19–24). Verses 10–26, many of which are quoted almost verbatim from previous sections of Exodus (compare especially vv. 18–26 with 23:14–19), are sometimes referred to as the Ritual Decalogue since they can be convincingly divided into ten sections (see, e.g., the NIV paragraphing of vv. 15–26). **34:12** *not to make a treaty with those who live in the land.* Israel is not to make a treaty of peace with any of the people of Canaan to let them live in the land. *treaty.* The Hebrew for this word is the same as that for "covenant" in v. 10 (see also v. 15). **34:13** *Asherah poles.* Asherah was the name of the consort

(wife) of El, the chief Canaanite god. Wooden poles, perhaps carved in her image, were often set up in her honor and placed near other pagan objects of worship (see, e.g., Jdg 6:25).

34:14 *whose name is Jealous.* See note on 20:5.

34:15 *prostitute themselves.* See Jdg 2:17 and note. *eat their sacrifices.* Partaking of food sacrificed to a pagan deity invites compromise (cf. 1Co 8; 10:18–21).

34:17 *Do not make cast idols.* As Aaron had done when he made the golden calf (see 32:4).

34:18–26 See notes on 23:14–19.

34:21 *even during the plowing season and harvest you must rest.* Just as they were also to rest while building the tabernacle (see notes on 31:13,16–17).

27Then the LORD said to Moses,
"Write[v] down these words, for in accordance with these words I have made a covenant[w] with you and with Israel." 28Moses
was there with the LORD forty days and
forty nights[x] without eating bread or
drinking water.[y] And he wrote on the tablets[z] the words of the covenant—the Ten
Commandments.[a]

The Radiant Face of Moses

29When Moses came down from Mount
Sinai[b] with the two tablets of the Testimony in his hands,[c] he was not aware that
his face was radiant[d] because he had
spoken with the LORD. 30When Aaron and
all the Israelites saw Moses, his face was
radiant, and they were afraid to come near
him. 31But Moses called to them; so Aaron
and all the leaders of the community[e]
came back to him, and he spoke to them.
32Afterward all the Israelites came near
him, and he gave them all the commands[f]
the LORD had given him on Mount Sinai.
33When Moses finished speaking to
them, he put a veil[g] over his face. 34But
whenever he entered the LORD's presence
to speak with him, he removed the veil
until he came out. And when he came out
and told the Israelites what he had been
commanded, 35they saw that his face was
radiant.[h] Then Moses would put the veil
back over his face until he went in to speak
with the LORD.

Sabbath Regulations

35 Moses assembled the whole Israelite community and said to them,
"These are the things the LORD has commanded[i] you to do: 2For six days, work is
to be done, but the seventh day shall be
your holy day, a Sabbath[j] of rest to the
LORD. Whoever does any work on it must
be put to death.[k] 3Do not light a fire in any
of your dwellings on the Sabbath day.[l]"

Materials for the Tabernacle

35:4–9pp — Ex 25:1–7
35:10–19pp — Ex 39:32–41

4Moses said to the whole Israelite community, "This is what the LORD has commanded: 5From what you have, take an
offering for the LORD. Everyone who is
willing is to bring to the LORD an offering
of gold, silver and bronze; 6blue, purple
and scarlet yarn and fine linen; goat hair;
7ram skins dyed red and hides of sea
cows[x]; acacia wood; 8olive oil[m] for the
light; spices for the anointing oil and for
the fragrant incense; 9and onyx stones and
other gems to be mounted on the ephod
and breastpiece.

10"All who are skilled among you are to
come and make everything the LORD has
commanded:[n] 11the tabernacle[o] with its
tent and its covering, clasps, frames, crossbars, posts and bases; 12the ark[p] with its
poles and the atonement cover and the
curtain[q] that shields it; 13the table[r] with
its poles and all its articles and the bread of
the Presence; 14the lampstand[s] that is for
light with its accessories, lamps and oil for
the light; 15the altar[t] of incense with its
poles, the anointing oil[u] and the fragrant
incense;[v] the curtain for the doorway at
the entrance to the tabernacle;[w] 16the altar[x] of burnt offering with its bronze grating, its poles and all its utensils; the bronze
basin[y] with its stand; 17the curtains of the
courtyard with its posts and bases, and the
curtain for the entrance to the courtyard;[z]
18the tent pegs[a] for the tabernacle and for
the courtyard, and their ropes; 19the woven garments worn for ministering in the
sanctuary—both the sacred garments[b] for
Aaron the priest and the garments for his
sons when they serve as priests."

[x] *7* That is, dugongs; also in verse 23

34:27 [v]S Ex 17:14 [w]S Ge 6:18; S 15:18
34:28 [x]S Ge 7:4; Mt 4:2; Lk 4:2 [y]Dt 9:9,18; Ezr 10:6 [z]ver 1; Ex 31:18 [a]Dt 4:13; 10:4
34:29 [b]S Ex 19:11 [c]S Ex 32:15 [d]ver 35; Ps 34:5; Isa 60:5; Mt 17:2; 2Co 3:7,13
34:31 [e]Ex 16:22
34:32 [f]S Ex 21:1; 35:1,4
34:33 [g]2Co 3:13
34:35 [h]S ver 29
35:1 [i]S Ex 34:32
35:2 [j]S Ge 2:3; Ex 34:21; Dt 5:13-14 [k]S Ex 31:14
35:3 [l]Ex 16:23
35:8 [m]S Ex 25:6
35:10 [n]Ex 31:6; 39:43
35:11 [o]Ex 26:1-37; 36:8-38
35:12 [p]Ex 25:10-22; 37:1-9 [q]S Ex 26:33
35:13 [r]Ex 25:23-30; 37:10-16
35:14 [s]S Ex 25:31
35:15 [t]Ex 30:1-6; 37:25-28 [u]Ex 30:25 [v]Ex 30:34-38 [w]S Ex 26:36
35:16 [x]Ex 27:1-8; 38:1-7 [y]S Ex 30:18
35:17 [z]S Ex 27:9; 38:9-20
35:18 [a]Ex 27:19; 38:20
35:19 [b]S Ex 28:2

34:27 *Write down these words.* As he had earlier written down similar words (see 24:4).
34:28 *he wrote.* Here the Lord, rather than Moses, is probably the subject (see v. 1). *the words of the covenant—the Ten Commandments.* The two phrases are synonymous (see note on 20:1).
34:29 *Testimony.* See notes on 16:34; 25:16. *was radiant.* He who had asked to see God's glory (33:18) now, quite unawares, reflects the divine glory. The Hebrew for "was radiant" is related to the Hebrew noun for "horn." The meaning of the phrase was therefore misunderstood by the Vulgate (the Latin translation), and thus European medieval art often showed horns sprouting from Moses' head.
34:33 *he put a veil over his face.* So that the Israelites would not see the fading away of the radiance but would continue to honor Moses as the one who represented God. For a NT reflection on Moses' action see 2Co 3:7–18 and notes.
35:1–3 Just as the Israelites had been reminded of the importance of Sabbath observance immediately after the instructions for building the tabernacle and making the priestly garments (see note on 31:13), so now—just before the fulfilling of those instructions—the people are given the same reminder.
35:4–39:43 For the most part repeated from chs. 25–28; 30:1–5; 31:1–11 (see notes on those passages), sometimes verbatim, but with the verbs primarily in the past rather than the future tense and with the topics arranged in a different order. Such repetition was a common feature of ancient Near Eastern literature and was intended to fix the details of a narrative in the reader's mind (see note on Ge 24:34–49).
35:5 *Everyone who is willing.* The voluntary motivation behind the offering of materials and services for the tabernacle is stressed (see vv. 21–22,26,29; 36:2–3).

²⁰Then the whole Israelite community withdrew from Moses' presence, ²¹and everyone who was willing and whose heart moved him came and brought an offering to the LORD for the work on the Tent of Meeting, for all its service, and for the sacred garments. ²²All who were willing, men and women alike, came and brought gold jewelry of all kinds: brooches, earrings, rings and ornaments. They all presented their gold as a wave offering to the LORD. ²³Everyone who had blue, purple or scarlet yarn c or fine linen, or goat hair, ram skins dyed red or hides of sea cows brought them. ²⁴Those presenting an offering of silver or bronze brought it as an offering to the LORD, and everyone who had acacia wood for any part of the work brought it. ²⁵Every skilled woman d spun with her hands and brought what she had spun—blue, purple or scarlet yarn or fine linen. ²⁶And all the women who were willing and had the skill spun the goat hair. ²⁷The leaders e brought onyx stones and other gems f to be mounted on the ephod and breastpiece. ²⁸They also brought spices and olive oil for the light and for the anointing oil and for the fragrant incense. g ²⁹All the Israelite men and women who were willing h brought to the LORD freewill offerings i for all the work the LORD through Moses had commanded them to do.

Bezalel and Oholiab

35:30–35pp — Ex 31:2–6

³⁰Then Moses said to the Israelites, "See, the LORD has chosen Bezalel son of Uri, the son of Hur, of the tribe of Judah, ³¹and he has filled him with the Spirit of God, with skill, ability and knowledge in all kinds of crafts j— ³²to make artistic designs for work in gold, silver and bronze, ³³to cut and set stones, to work in wood and to engage in all kinds of artistic craftsmanship. ³⁴And he has given both him and Oholiab k son of Ahisamach, of the tribe of Dan, the ability to teach l others. ³⁵He has filled them with skill to do all kinds of work m as craftsmen, designers, embroiderers in blue, purple and scarlet yarn and fine linen, and weavers—all of them master craftsmen and designers. ¹So **36** Bezalel, Oholiab and every skilled person n to whom the LORD has given skill and ability to know how to carry out all the work of constructing the sanctuary o

35:23 cEx 39:1
35:25 dS Ex 28:3
35:27 eS Ex 25:2;
1Ch 29:6
fS Ex 25:2;
1Ch 29:8
35:28 gS Ex 25:6
35:29 hS Ex 25:2
iver 4-9;
Ex 25:1-7; 36:3;
2Ki 12:4
35:31 jver 35;
2Ch 2:7,14
35:34 kS Ex 31:6
l2Ch 2:14
35:35 mver 31
36:1 nS Ex 28:3
oEx 25:8

36:2 pS Ex 31:2
qS Ex 31:6
rS Ex 25:2
36:3 sS Ex 35:29
36:5 t2Ch 24:14;
31:10; 2Co 8:2-3
36:7 u1Ki 7:47
36:13 vver 18

are to do the work just as the Lord has commanded."

²Then Moses summoned Bezalel p and Oholiab q and every skilled person to whom the LORD had given ability and who was willing r to come and do the work. ³They received from Moses all the offerings s the Israelites had brought to carry out the work of constructing the sanctuary. And the people continued to bring freewill offerings morning after morning. ⁴So all the skilled craftsmen who were doing all the work on the sanctuary left their work ⁵and said to Moses, "The people are bringing more than enough t for doing the work the LORD commanded to be done."

⁶Then Moses gave an order and they sent this word throughout the camp: "No man or woman is to make anything else as an offering for the sanctuary." And so the people were restrained from bringing more, ⁷because what they already had was more u than enough to do all the work.

The Tabernacle

36:8–38pp — Ex 26:1–37

⁸All the skilled men among the workmen made the tabernacle with ten curtains of finely twisted linen and blue, purple and scarlet yarn, with cherubim worked into them by a skilled craftsman. ⁹All the curtains were the same size—twenty-eight cubits long and four cubits wide. y ¹⁰They joined five of the curtains together and did the same with the other five. ¹¹Then they made loops of blue material along the edge of the end curtain in one set, and the same was done with the end curtain in the other set. ¹²They also made fifty loops on one curtain and fifty loops on the end curtain of the other set, with the loops opposite each other. ¹³Then they made fifty gold clasps and used them to fasten the two sets of curtains together so that the tabernacle was a unit. v ¹⁴They made curtains of goat hair for the tent over the tabernacle—eleven altogether. ¹⁵All eleven curtains were the same size—thirty cubits long and four cubits wide. z ¹⁶They joined five of the curtains into one set and the other six into another

y 9 That is, about 42 feet (about 12.5 meters) long and 6 feet (about 1.8 meters) wide   z 15 That is, about 45 feet (about 13.5 meters) long and 6 feet (about 1.8 meters) wide

---

35:21 *Tent of Meeting.* See note on 27:21.   **36:1–38** See note on 35:4–39:43.

set. [17]Then they made fifty loops along the edge of the end curtain in one set and also along the edge of the end curtain in the other set. [18]They made fifty bronze clasps to fasten the tent together as a unit.[w] [19]Then they made for the tent a covering of ram skins dyed red, and over that a covering of hides of sea cows.[a]

[20]They made upright frames of acacia wood for the tabernacle. [21]Each frame was ten cubits long and a cubit and a half wide,[b] [22]with two projections set parallel to each other. They made all the frames of the tabernacle in this way. [23]They made twenty frames for the south side of the tabernacle [24]and made forty silver bases to go under them—two bases for each frame, one under each projection. [25]For the other side, the north side of the tabernacle, they made twenty frames [26]and forty silver bases—two under each frame. [27]They made six frames for the far end, that is, the west end of the tabernacle, [28]and two frames were made for the corners of the tabernacle at the far end. [29]At these two corners the frames were double from the bottom all the way to the top and fitted into a single ring; both were made alike. [30]So there were eight frames and sixteen silver bases—two under each frame.

[31]They also made crossbars of acacia wood: five for the frames on one side of the tabernacle, [32]five for those on the other side, and five for the frames on the west, at the far end of the tabernacle. [33]They made the center crossbar so that it extended from end to end at the middle of the frames. [34]They overlaid the frames with gold and made gold rings to hold the crossbars. They also overlaid the crossbars with gold.

[35]They made the curtain[x] of blue, purple and scarlet yarn and finely twisted linen, with cherubim worked into it by a skilled craftsman. [36]They made four posts of acacia wood for it and overlaid them with gold. They made gold hooks for them and cast their four silver bases. [37]For the entrance to the tent they made a curtain of blue, purple and scarlet yarn and finely twisted linen—the work of an embroiderer;[y] [38]and they made five posts with hooks for them. They overlaid the tops of the posts and their bands with gold and made their five bases of bronze.

36:18 [w]ver 13
36:35 [x]Ex 39:38;
Mt 27:51;
Lk 23:45; Heb 9:3
36:37 [y]Ex 27:16

The Ark

37:1–9pp — Ex 25:10–20

37 Bezalel[z] made the ark[a] of acacia wood—two and a half cubits long, a cubit and a half wide, and a cubit and a half high.[c] [2]He overlaid it with pure gold,[b] both inside and out, and made a gold molding around it. [3]He cast four gold rings for it and fastened them to its four feet, with two rings on one side and two rings on the other. [4]Then he made poles of acacia wood and overlaid them with gold. [5]And he inserted the poles into the rings on the sides of the ark to carry it.

[6]He made the atonement cover[c] of pure gold—two and a half cubits long and a cubit and a half wide.[d] [7]Then he made two cherubim[d] out of hammered gold at the ends of the cover. [8]He made one cherub on one end and the second cherub on the other; at the two ends he made them of one piece with the cover. [9]The cherubim had their wings spread upward, overshadowing[e] the cover with them. The cherubim faced each other, looking toward the cover.[f]

The Table

37:10–16pp — Ex 25:23–29

[10]They[e] made the table[g] of acacia wood—two cubits long, a cubit wide, and a cubit and a half high.[f] [11]Then they overlaid it with pure gold[h] and made a gold molding around it. [12]They also made around it a rim a handbreadth[g] wide and put a gold molding on the rim. [13]They cast four gold rings for the table and fastened them to the four corners, where the four legs were. [14]The rings[i] were put close to the rim to hold the poles used in carrying the table. [15]The poles for carrying the table were made of acacia wood and were overlaid with gold. [16]And they made from pure gold the articles for the table—its plates and dishes and bowls and its pitchers for the pouring out of drink offerings.

[a]*19* That is, dugongs   [b]*21* That is, about 15 feet (about 4.5 meters) long and 2 1/4 feet (about 0.7 meter) wide   [c]*1* That is, about 3 3/4 feet (about 1.1 meters) long and 2 1/4 feet (about 0.7 meter) wide and high   [d]*6* That is, about 3 3/4 feet (about 1.1 meters) long and 2 1/4 feet (about 0.7 meter) wide   [e]*10* Or *He*; also in verses 11-29   [f]*10* That is, about 3 feet (about 0.9 meter) long, 1 1/2 feet (about 0.5 meter) wide, and 2 1/4 feet (about 0.7 meter) high   [g]*12* That is, about 3 inches (about 8 centimeters)

37:1 [z]S Ex 31:2
[a]Ex 30:6; 39:35;
Dt 10:3
37:2 [b]ver 11,26
37:6 [c]S Ex 26:34;
S 31:7; Heb 9:5
37:7 [d]Eze 41:18
37:9 [e]Heb 9:5
/Dt 10:3
37:10 [g]Heb 9:2
37:11 [h]S ver 2
37:14 [i]ver 27

37:1–29 See note on 35:4–39:43.
37:1 *Bezalel made the ark.* The chief craftsman (see 31:2–3) was given the honor of making the most sacred object (see 25:10 and note) among the furnishings for the tabernacle.

The Lampstand

37:17–24pp — Ex 25:31–39

[17]They made the lampstand[j] of pure gold and hammered it out, base and shaft; its flowerlike cups, buds and blossoms were of one piece with it. [18]Six branches extended from the sides of the lampstand—three on one side and three on the other. [19]Three cups shaped like almond flowers with buds and blossoms were on one branch, three on the next branch and the same for all six branches extending from the lampstand. [20]And on the lampstand were four cups shaped like almond flowers with buds and blossoms. [21]One bud was under the first pair of branches extending from the lampstand, a second bud under the second pair, and a third bud under the third pair—six branches in all. [22]The buds and the branches were all of one piece with the lampstand, hammered out of pure gold.[k]

[23]They made its seven lamps,[l] as well as its wick trimmers and trays, of pure gold. [24]They made the lampstand and all its accessories from one talent[h] of pure gold.

The Altar of Incense

37:25–28pp — Ex 30:1–5

[25]They made the altar of incense[m] out of acacia wood. It was square, a cubit long and a cubit wide, and two cubits high[l]—its horns[n] of one piece with it. [26]They overlaid the top and all the sides and the horns with pure gold, and made a gold molding around it. [27]They made two gold rings[o] below the molding—two on opposite sides—to hold the poles used to carry it. [28]They made the poles of acacia wood and overlaid them with gold.[p]

[29]They also made the sacred anointing oil[q] and the pure, fragrant incense[r] —the work of a perfumer.

The Altar of Burnt Offering

38:1–7pp — Ex 27:1–8

38 They[j] built the altar of burnt offering of acacia wood, three cubits[k] high; it was square, five cubits long and five cubits wide.[l] [2]They made a horn at each of the four corners, so that the horns and the altar were of one piece, and they overlaid the altar with bronze.[s] [3]They made all its utensils[t] of bronze—its pots, shovels, sprinkling bowls, meat forks and

firepans. [4]They made a grating for the altar, a bronze network, to be under its ledge, halfway up the altar. [5]They cast bronze rings to hold the poles for the four corners of the bronze grating. [6]They made the poles of acacia wood and overlaid them with bronze. [7]They inserted the poles into the rings so they would be on the sides of the altar for carrying it. They made it hollow, out of boards.

Basin for Washing

[8]They made the bronze basin[u] and its bronze stand from the mirrors of the women[v] who served at the entrance to the Tent of Meeting.

The Courtyard

38:9–20pp — Ex 27:9–19

[9]Next they made the courtyard. The south side was a hundred cubits[m] long and had curtains of finely twisted linen, [10]with twenty posts and twenty bronze bases, and with silver hooks and bands on the posts. [11]The north side was also a hundred cubits long and had twenty posts and twenty bronze bases, with silver hooks and bands on the posts.

[12]The west end was fifty cubits[n] wide and had curtains, with ten posts and ten bases, with silver hooks and bands on the posts. [13]The east end, toward the sunrise, was also fifty cubits wide. [14]Curtains fifteen cubits[o] long were on one side of the entrance, with three posts and three bases, [15]and curtains fifteen cubits long were on the other side of the entrance to the courtyard, with three posts and three bases. [16]All the curtains around the courtyard were of finely twisted linen. [17]The bases for the posts were bronze. The hooks and bands on the posts were silver, and their tops were overlaid with silver; so all the posts of the courtyard had silver bands.

[18]The curtain for the entrance to the courtyard was of blue, purple and scarlet yarn and finely twisted linen—the work of an embroiderer. It was twenty cubits[p] long and, like the curtains of the courtyard,

37:17 /Heb 9:2; Rev 1:12
37:22 kver 17; Nu 8:4
37:23 /Ex 40:4, 25
37:25 mEx 30:34-36; Lk 1:11; Heb 9:4; Rev 8:3
nS Ex 27:2; Rev 9:13
37:27 over 14
37:28 pS Ex 25:13
37:29 qS Ex 31:11
rEx 30:1,25; 39:38
38:2 sS 2Ch 1:5
38:3 tS Ex 31:9
38:8 uS Ex 30:18; vDt 23:17; 1Sa 2:22; 1Ki 14:24

h24 That is, about 75 pounds (about 34 kilograms) i25 That is, about 1 1/2 feet (about 0.5 meter) long and wide, and about 3 feet (about 0.9 meter) high j1 Or He; also in verses 2-9 k1 That is, about 4 1/2 feet (about 1.3 meters) l1 That is, about 7 1/2 feet (about 2.3 meters) long and wide m9 That is, about 150 feet (about 46 meters) n12 That is, about 75 feet (about 23 meters) o14 That is, about 22 1/2 feet (about 6.9 meters) p18 That is, about 30 feet (about 9 meters)

38:1–31 See note on 35:4–39:43.
38:8 *bronze . . . mirrors.* Mirrored glass was unknown in ancient times, but highly polished bronze gave adequate reflection. *Tent of Meeting.* See note on 27:21.

five cubits[q] high, [19]with four posts and four bronze bases. Their hooks and bands were silver, and their tops were overlaid with silver. [20]All the tent pegs[w] of the tabernacle and of the surrounding courtyard were bronze.

The Materials Used

[21]These are the amounts of the materials used for the tabernacle, the tabernacle of the Testimony,[x] which were recorded at Moses' command by the Levites under the direction of Ithamar[y] son of Aaron, the priest. [22](Bezalel[z] son of Uri, the son of Hur, of the tribe of Judah, made everything the LORD commanded Moses; [23]with him was Oholiab[a] son of Ahisamach, of the tribe of Dan—a craftsman and designer, and an embroiderer in blue, purple and scarlet yarn and fine linen.) [24]The total amount of the gold from the wave offering used for all the work on the sanctuary[b] was 29 talents and 730 shekels,[r] according to the sanctuary shekel. [c]

[25]The silver obtained from those of the community who were counted in the census[d] was 100 talents and 1,775 shekels,[s] according to the sanctuary shekel— [26]one beka per person,[e] that is, half a shekel,[t] according to the sanctuary shekel,[f] from everyone who had crossed over to those counted, twenty years old or more,[g] a total of 603,550 men.[h] [27]The 100 talents[u] of silver were used to cast the bases[i] for the sanctuary and for the curtain—100 bases from the 100 talents, one talent for each base. [28]They used the 1,775 shekels[v] to make the hooks for the posts, to overlay the tops of the posts, and to make their bands.

[29]The bronze from the wave offering was 70 talents and 2,400 shekels. [w] [30]They used it to make the bases for the entrance to the Tent of Meeting, the bronze altar with its bronze grating and all its utensils, [31]the bases for the surrounding courtyard and those for its entrance and all the tent pegs for the tabernacle and those for the surrounding courtyard.

The Priestly Garments

39 From the blue, purple and scarlet yarn[j] they made woven garments for ministering in the sanctuary. [k] They

38:20
wS Ex 35:18
38:21 xNu 1:50,
53; 8:24; 9:15;
10:11; 17:7;
1Ch 23:32;
2Ch 24:6;
Ac 7:44; Rev 15:5
yNu 4:28,33
38:22 zS Ex 31:2
38:23 aS Ex 31:6
38:24
bS Ex 30:16
cS Ex 30:13
38:25
dS Ex 30:12
eS Ex 30:12
fS Ex 30:13
gS Ex 30:14
hS Ex 12:37
38:27
iS Ex 26:19
39:1 /Ex 35:23
kEx 35:19

/ver 41; Ex 28:2
39:7 mLev 24:7;
Jos 4:7
39:8 nLev 8:8

also made sacred garments[l] for Aaron, as the LORD commanded Moses.

The Ephod

39:2–7pp — Ex 28:6–14

[2]They[x] made the ephod of gold, and of blue, purple and scarlet yarn, and of finely twisted linen. [3]They hammered out thin sheets of gold and cut strands to be worked into the blue, purple and scarlet yarn and fine linen—the work of a skilled craftsman. [4]They made shoulder pieces for the ephod, which were attached to two of its corners, so it could be fastened. [5]Its skillfully woven waistband was like it—of one piece with the ephod and made with gold, and with blue, purple and scarlet yarn, and with finely twisted linen, as the LORD commanded Moses.

[6]They mounted the onyx stones in gold filigree settings and engraved them like a seal with the names of the sons of Israel. [7]Then they fastened them on the shoulder pieces of the ephod as memorial[m] stones for the sons of Israel, as the LORD commanded Moses.

The Breastpiece

39:8–21pp — Ex 28:15–28

[8]They fashioned the breastpiece[n]—the work of a skilled craftsman. They made it like the ephod: of gold, and of blue, purple and scarlet yarn, and of finely twisted linen. [9]It was square—a span[y] long and a span wide—and folded double. [10]Then they mounted four rows of precious stones on it. In the first row there was a ruby, a topaz and a beryl; [11]in the second row a turquoise, a sapphire[z] and an emerald; [12]in the third row a jacinth, an agate and an amethyst; [13]in the fourth row a chrysolite, an onyx and a jasper.[a] They were mounted in gold filigree settings. [14]There

q18 That is, about 7 1/2 feet (about 2.3 meters)
r24 The weight of the gold was a little over one ton (about 1 metric ton).   s25 The weight of the silver was a little over 3 3/4 tons (about 3.4 metric tons).
t26 That is, about 1/5 ounce (about 5.5 grams)
u27 That is, about 3 3/4 tons (about 3.4 metric tons)
v28 That is, about 45 pounds (about 20 kilograms)
w29 The weight of the bronze was about 2 1/2 tons (about 2.4 metric tons).   x2 Or He; also in verses 7, 8 and 22   y9 That is, about 9 inches (about 22 centimeters)   z11 Or lapis lazuli   a13 The precise identification of some of these precious stones is uncertain.

38:25 *100 talents and 1,775 shekels.* Since there are 3,000 shekels in a talent, 100 talents equals 300,000 shekels, which, when added to the 1,775 shekels, gives a grand total of 301,775—half a shekel for each of the 603,550 men of military age (v. 26).
38:26 *603,550 men.* The number is doubtless to be under-

stood literally, since the figures in the tribal census (see Nu 1:21–43; 2:4–31) total 603,550 (see Nu 1:46 and note). See Introduction to Numbers: Special Problem.
38:27 *one talent for each base.* See note on 26:19.
39:1–43 See note on 35:4–39:43.

were twelve stones, one for each of the names of the sons of Israel, each engraved like a seal with the name of one of the twelve tribes. [o]

[15]For the breastpiece they made braided chains of pure gold, like a rope. [16]They made two gold filigree settings and two gold rings, and fastened the rings to two of the corners of the breastpiece. [17]They fastened the two gold chains to the rings at the corners of the breastpiece, [18]and the other ends of the chains to the two settings, attaching them to the shoulder pieces of the ephod at the front. [19]They made two gold rings and attached them to the other two corners of the breastpiece on the inside edge next to the ephod. [20]Then they made two more gold rings and attached them to the bottom of the shoulder pieces on the front of the ephod, close to the seam just above the waistband of the ephod. [21]They tied the rings of the breastpiece to the rings of the ephod with blue cord, connecting it to the waistband so that the breastpiece would not swing out from the ephod—as the LORD commanded Moses.

Other Priestly Garments

39:22–31pp — Ex 28:31–43

[22]They made the robe of the ephod entirely of blue cloth—the work of a weaver— [23]with an opening in the center of the robe like the opening of a collar, [b] and a band around this opening, so that it would not tear. [24]They made pomegranates of blue, purple and scarlet yarn and finely twisted linen around the hem of the robe. [25]And they made bells of pure gold and attached them around the hem between the pomegranates. [26]The bells and pomegranates alternated around the hem of the robe to be worn for ministering, as the LORD commanded Moses.

[27]For Aaron and his sons, they made tunics of fine linen [p]—the work of a weaver— [28]and the turban [q] of fine linen, the linen headbands and the undergarments of finely twisted linen. [29]The sash was of finely twisted linen and blue, purple and scarlet yarn—the work of an embroiderer—as the LORD commanded Moses.

[30]They made the plate, the sacred diadem, out of pure gold and engraved on it,

like an inscription on a seal: HOLY TO THE LORD. [r] [31]Then they fastened a blue cord to it to attach it to the turban, [s] as the LORD commanded Moses.

Moses Inspects the Tabernacle

39:32–41pp — Ex 35:10–19

[32]So all the work on the tabernacle, the Tent of Meeting, was completed. The Israelites did everything just as the LORD commanded Moses. [t] [33]Then they brought the tabernacle [u] to Moses: the tent and all its furnishings, its clasps, frames, crossbars, posts and bases; [34]the covering of ram skins dyed red, the covering of hides of sea cows [c] and the shielding curtain; [35]the ark of the Testimony [v] with its poles and the atonement cover; [36]the table [w] with all its articles and the bread of the Presence; [x] [37]the pure gold lampstand [y] with its row of lamps and all its accessories, [z] and the oil [a] for the light; [38]the gold altar, [b] the anointing oil, [c] the fragrant incense, [d] and the curtain [e] for the entrance to the tent; [39]the bronze altar [f] with its bronze grating, its poles and all its utensils; the basin [g] with its stand; [40]the curtains of the courtyard with its posts and bases, and the curtain for the entrance to the courtyard; [h] the ropes and tent pegs for the courtyard; all the furnishings for the tabernacle, the Tent of Meeting; [41]and the woven garments [i] worn for ministering in the sanctuary, both the sacred garments for Aaron the priest and the garments for his sons when serving as priests.

[42]The Israelites had done all the work just as the LORD had commanded Moses. [j] [43]Moses inspected the work and saw that they had done it just as the LORD had commanded. [k] So Moses blessed [l] them.

Setting Up the Tabernacle

40 Then the LORD said to Moses: [2]"Set up [m] the tabernacle, the Tent of Meeting, [n] on the first day of the first month. [o] [3]Place the ark [p] of the Testimony in it and shield the ark with the curtain. [4]Bring in the table [q] and set out what belongs on it. [r] Then bring in the lampstand [s] and set up its lamps. [5]Place the gold altar [t]

39:14
[o]Rev 21:12
39:27 [p]Lev 6:10; 8:2
39:28 [q]ver 31; S Ex 28:4; Lev 8:9; Isa 61:10

39:30 [r]Isa 23:18; Zec 14:20
39:31 [s]S ver 28
39:32 [t]S Ex 25:9
39:33
[u]Ex 25:8-40; 36:8-38
39:35 [v]S Ex 37:1
39:36
[w]Ex 25:23-30; 37:10-16
[x]S Ex 25:30
39:37
[y]S Ex 25:31
[z]Ex 25:31-39
[a]S Ex 25:6
39:38
[b]Ex 30:1-10; 37:25-28
[c]Ex 30:22-32; 37:29
[d]Ex 30:34-38; S 37:29
[e]S Ex 36:35
39:39
[f]Ex 27:1-8; 38:1-7
[g]S Ex 30:18
39:40
[h]Ex 27:9-19; 38:9-20
39:41 [i]S ver 1
39:42 [j]S Ex 25:9
39:43
[k]S Ex 25:9; S 35:10
[l]Ge 31:55; Lev 9:22,23; Nu 6:23-27; Dt 21:5; 26:15; 2Sa 6:18; 1Ki 8:14,55; 1Ch 16:2; 2Ch 30:27
40:2 [m]S Ex 26:30
[n]ver 34,35; Lev 1:1; 3:2; 6:26; 9:23; 16:16; Nu 1:1; 7:89; 11:16; 17:4; 20:6; Jos 18:1; 19:51; Jer 7:12 [o]ver 17; S Ex 12:2; Nu 9:1
40:3 [p]S Ex 26:33
40:4 [q]S Ex 25:23
[r]S Ex 25:30
[s]S Ex 25:31
40:5 [t]S Ex 30:1

[b]23 The meaning of the Hebrew for this word is uncertain.   [c]34 That is, dugongs

---

39:30 *sacred diadem.* An official designation (not found in 28:36–37) for the plate of the turban.
39:32 *all the work . . . was completed.* Reminiscent of the concluding words of the creation narrative (see Ge 2:1–3).
39:43 *Moses blessed them.* For the faithfulness with which the Israelites had donated their gifts, time and talents

in building the tabernacle and all its furnishings —faithfulness in service brings divine benediction.
40:2 *first day of the first month.* The tabernacle was set up almost a year after the institution of the Passover (see v. 17; 12:2,6).

of incense in front of the ark of the Testimony and put the curtain at the entrance to the tabernacle.

6"Place the altar[u] of burnt offering in front of the entrance to the tabernacle, the Tent of Meeting; 7place the basin[v] between the Tent of Meeting and the altar and put water in it. 8Set up the courtyard[w] around it and put the curtain at the entrance to the courtyard.

9"Take the anointing oil and anoint[x] the tabernacle and everything in it; consecrate it and all its furnishings,[y] and it will be holy. 10Then anoint the altar of burnt offering and all its utensils; consecrate[z] the altar, and it will be most holy. 11Anoint the basin and its stand and consecrate them.

12"Bring Aaron and his sons to the entrance to the Tent of Meeting[a] and wash them with water.[b] 13Then dress Aaron in the sacred garments,[c] anoint him and consecrate[d] him so he may serve me as priest. 14Bring his sons and dress them in tunics.[e] 15Anoint them just as you anointed their father, so they may serve me as priests. Their anointing will be to a priesthood that will continue for all generations to come.[f]" 16Moses did everything just as the Lord commanded[g] him.

17So the tabernacle[h] was set up on the first day of the first month[i] in the second year. 18When Moses[j] set up the tabernacle, he put the bases in place, erected the frames,[k] inserted the crossbars and set up the posts. 19Then he spread the tent over the tabernacle and put the covering[l] over the tent, as the Lord commanded[m] him.

20He took the Testimony[n] and placed it in the ark,[o] attached the poles to the ark and put the atonement cover[p] over it. 21Then he brought the ark into the tabernacle and hung the shielding curtain[q] and shielded the ark of the Testimony, as the Lord commanded[r] him.

22Moses placed the table[s] in the Tent of Meeting on the north side of the tabernacle outside the curtain 23and set out the

bread[t] on it before the Lord, as the Lord commanded[u] him.

24He placed the lampstand[v] in the Tent of Meeting opposite the table on the south side of the tabernacle 25and set up the lamps[w] before the Lord, as the Lord commanded[x] him.

26Moses placed the gold altar[y] in the Tent of Meeting in front of the curtain 27and burned fragrant incense on it, as the Lord commanded[z] him. 28Then he put up the curtain[a] at the entrance to the tabernacle.

29He set the altar[b] of burnt offering near the entrance to the tabernacle, the Tent of Meeting, and offered on it burnt offerings and grain offerings,[c] as the Lord commanded[d] him.

30He placed the basin[e] between the Tent of Meeting and the altar and put water in it for washing, 31and Moses and Aaron and his sons used it to wash[f] their hands and feet. 32They washed whenever they entered the Tent of Meeting or approached the altar,[g] as the Lord commanded[h] Moses.

33Then Moses set up the courtyard[i] around the tabernacle and altar and put up the curtain[j] at the entrance to the courtyard. And so Moses finished the work.

The Glory of the Lord

34Then the cloud[k] covered the Tent of Meeting, and the glory[l] of the Lord filled the tabernacle. 35Moses could not enter the Tent of Meeting because the cloud had settled upon it, and the glory[m] of the Lord filled the tabernacle.[n]

36In all the travels of the Israelites, whenever the cloud lifted from above the tabernacle, they would set out;[o] 37but if the cloud did not lift, they did not set out—until the day it lifted. 38So the cloud[p] of the Lord was over the tabernacle by day, and fire was in the cloud by night, in the sight of all the house of Israel during all their travels.

40:6 uS Ex 27:1; 2Ki 16:14; 2Ch 4:1
40:7 vEx 30:18
40:8 wS Ex 27:9
40:9 xS Ex 30:26 yNu 7:1
40:10 zS Ex 29:36
40:12 aNu 8:9 bS Ex 29:4; S 30:19
40:13 cS Ex 28:41 dLev 8:12
40:14 eS Ex 28:40; Lev 10:5
40:15 fS Ex 29:9
40:16 gS Ge 6:22
40:17 hNu 7:1 iS ver 2
40:18 j2Ch 1:3 kEx 36:20-34
40:19 lEx 36:19 mS Ge 6:22
40:20 nS Ex 16:34; Heb 9:4
40:21 oS Ex 25:21 pEx 25:17-22; S 26:34; S 31:7 qS Ex 26:33 rS Ge 6:22
40:22 sS Ex 25:23
40:23 tS Ex 25:30; Lev 24:5-8 uS Ge 6:22
40:24 vS Ex 25:31
40:25 wS Ex 37:23 xS Ge 6:22
40:26 yS Ex 30:1
40:27 zS Ge 6:22
40:28 aS Ex 26:36
40:29 bS Ex 20:24 cEx 29:38-42 dS Ge 6:22
40:30 eS ver 7; S Ex 30:18
40:31 fEx 30:19-21
40:32 gEx 30:20 hS Ge 6:22
40:33 iS Ex 27:9; 38:9-20 jEx 27:16
40:34 kEx 19:16; Lev 16:2; Nu 9:15-23; 1Ki 8:12; 2Ch 5:13; Isa 6:4; Eze 10:4 lS Ex 16:7; Jn 1:14; 12:41; Rev 15:8
40:35 mS Ex 16:10 n1Ki 8:11; 2Ch 5:13-14; 7:2
40:36 oNu 9:17-23; 10:13 40:38 pS Ex 13:21; 1Co 10:1

40:16 *Moses did . . . just as the Lord commanded.* Moses' obedience to God's command is a key theme of the final chapter of Exodus (see vv. 19,21,23,25,27,29,32). It was the people who provided all the resources and made all the components, but it was the Lord's servant Moses who was authorized to erect the tabernacle and prepare it for the Lord's entry.
40:33 *Moses finished the work.* See note on 39:32.
40:34 With the glory of the Lord entering the tabernacle,

the great series of events that began with the birth of Moses and his rescue from the Nile, foreshadowing the deliverance of Israel from Egypt, comes to a grand climax. From now on, the Israelites march through the desert, and through history, with the Lord tenting among them and leading them to the land of fulfilled promises.
40:38 See note on 13:21. *house of Israel.* The nation, viewed as an extended family household.

LEVITICUS

Author and Date

See note on 1:1 and Introduction to Genesis: Author and Date of Writing.

Title

Leviticus receives its name from the Septuagint (the Greek translation of the OT) and means "relating to the Levites." Its Hebrew title, *wayyiqra'*, is the first word in the Hebrew text of the book and means "And he [i.e., the Lord] called." Although Leviticus does not deal only with the special duties of the Levites, it is so named because it concerns mainly the service of worship at the tabernacle, which was conducted by the priests who were the sons of Aaron, assisted by many from the rest of the tribe of Levi. Exodus gave the directions for building the tabernacle, and now Leviticus gives the laws and regulations for worship there including instructions on ceremonial cleanness, moral laws, holy days, the sabbath year and the Year of Jubilee. These laws were given, at least for the most part, during the year that Israel camped at Mount Sinai, when God directed Moses in organizing Israel's worship, government and military forces. The book of Numbers continues the history with preparations for moving on from Sinai to Canaan.

Themes

The key thought of Leviticus is holiness (see note on 11:44)—the holiness of God and man (man must revere God in "holiness"). In Leviticus spiritual holiness is symbolized by physical perfection. Therefore the book demands perfect animals for its many sacrifices (chs. 1-7) and requires priests without deformity (chs. 8-10). A woman's hemorrhaging after giving birth (ch. 12); sores, burns or baldness (chs. 13-14); a man's bodily discharge (15:1-18); specific activities during a woman's monthly period (15:19-33)—all may be signs of blemish (a lack of perfection) and may symbolize man's spiritual defects, which break his spiritual wholeness. The person with visible skin disease must be banished from the camp, the place of God's special presence, just as Adam and Eve were banished from the Garden of Eden. Such a person can return to the camp (and therefore to God's presence) when he is pronounced whole again by the examining priests. Before he can reenter the camp, however, he has to offer the prescribed, perfect sacrifices (symbolizing the perfect, whole sacrifice of Christ).

After the covenant at Sinai, Israel was the earthly representation of God's kingdom (the theocracy), and, as her King, the Lord established his administration over all of Israel's life. Her religious, communal and personal life was so regulated as to establish her as God's holy people and to instruct her in holiness. Special attention was given to Israel's religious ritual. The sacrifices were to be offered at an approved sanctuary, which would symbolize both God's holiness and his compassion. They were to be controlled by the priests, who by care and instruction would preserve them in purity and carefully teach their meaning to the people. Each particular sacrifice was to have meaning for the people of Israel but would also have spiritual and symbolic import.

For more information on the meaning of sacrifice in general see the solemn ritual of the Day of Atonement (ch. 16). For the meaning of the blood of the offering see 17:11; Ge 9:4. For the emphasis on substitution see 16:21.

Some suppose that the OT sacrifices were remains of old agricultural offerings—a human desire to offer part of one's possessions as a love gift to the deity. But the OT sacrifices were specifically prescribed by God and received their meaning from the Lord's covenant relationship with Israel—whatever their superficial resemblances to pagan sacrifices. They indeed include the idea of a gift, but this is accompanied by such other values as dedication, communion, propitiation (appeasing God's judicial wrath against sin) and restitution. The various offerings have differing functions, the primary ones being atonement (see note on Ex 25:17) and worship.

Outline

The subjects treated in Leviticus, as in any book of laws and regulations, cover several categories:

The Burnt Offering

1 The LORD called to Moses[a] and spoke to him from the Tent of Meeting.[b] He said, [2]"Speak to the Israelites and say to them: 'When any of you brings an offering to the LORD,[c] bring as your offering an animal from either the herd or the flock.[d]

[3] "'If the offering is a burnt offering[e] from the herd,[f] he is to offer a male without defect.[g] He must present it at the entrance to the Tent[h] of Meeting so that it[a] will be acceptable[i] to the LORD. [4]He is to lay his hand on the head[j] of the burnt offering,[k] and it will be accepted[l] on his behalf to make atonement[m] for him. [5]He is to slaughter[n] the young bull[o] before the LORD, and then Aaron's sons[p] the priests shall bring the blood and sprinkle it against the altar on all sides[q] at the entrance to the Tent of Meeting. [6]He is to skin[r] the burnt offering and cut it into pieces.[s] [7]The sons of Aaron the priest are to put fire on the altar and arrange wood[t] on the fire. [8]Then Aaron's sons the priests shall arrange the pieces, including the head and the fat,[u] on the burning wood[v] that is on the altar. [9]He is to wash the inner parts and the legs with water,[w] and the priest is

to burn all of it[x] on the altar.[y] It is a burnt offering,[z] an offering made by fire,[a] an aroma pleasing to the LORD.[b]

[10] "'If the offering is a burnt offering from the flock, from either the sheep[c] or the goats,[d] he is to offer a male without defect. [11]He is to slaughter it at the north side of the altar[e] before the LORD, and Aaron's sons the priests shall sprinkle its blood against the altar on all sides.[f] [12]He is to cut it into pieces, and the priest shall arrange them, including the head and the fat,[g] on the burning wood that is on the altar. [13]He is to wash the inner parts and the legs with water,[h] and the priest is to bring all of it and burn it[i] on the altar.[j] It is a burnt offering,[k] an offering made by fire, an aroma pleasing to the LORD.

[14] "'If the offering to the LORD is a burnt offering of birds, he is to offer a dove or a young pigeon.[l] [15]The priest shall bring it to the altar, wring off the head[m] and burn

1:1 [a]S Ex 3:4; S 25:22
[b]S Ex 27:21; S 40:2
1:2 [c]Lev 7:16,38; 22:21; 23:38; 27:9
[d]Lev 22:18-19; Nu 15:3
1:3 [e]S Ge 8:20 [f]ver 10; Lev 22:27; Ezr 8:35; Mal 1:8
[g]S ver 5; S Ex 12:5; S Lev 22:19,20; Heb 9:14; 1Pe 1:19
[h]Lev 6:25; 17:9; Nu 6:16; Dt 12:5-6,11
[i]Isa 58:5
1:4 [j]S Ex 29:10, 15 [k]ver 3; Lev 4:29; 6:25; Eze 45:15
[l]S Ge 32:20
[m]S Ex 29:36; S 32:30
1:5 [n]Ex 29:11; Lev 3:2,8 [o]S ver 3; Ex 29:1; Nu 15:8; Dt 18:3; Ps 50:9; 69:31
[p]Lev 8:2; 10:6; 21:1 [q]S Ex 29:20; Heb 12:24; 1Pe 1:2
1:6 [r]Lev 7:8 [s]Ex 29:17
1:7 [t]ver 17; S Ge 22:9; Lev 3:5; 6:12
1:8 [u]ver 12; S Ex 29:13;

Lev 8:20 [v]Lev 9:13 1:9 [w]S Ex 29:17 [x]Lev 6:22 [y]ver 13; Ex 29:18; Lev 9:14 [z]ver 3 [a]Lev 23:8,25,36; Nu 28:6,19 [b]ver 13; Ge 8:21; Lev 2:2; 3:5,16; 17:6; Nu 18:17; 28:11-13; Eph 5:2 1:10 [c]S Ge 22:7 [d]S ver 3; Lev 12:5; Lev 3:12; 4:23, 28; 5:6; Nu 15:11 1:11 [e]S Ex 29:11 [f]S Ex 29:20 1:12 [g]S ver 8 1:13 [h]S Ex 29:17 [i]Lev 6:22 [j]S ver 9 [k]Dt 12:27 1:14 [l]S Ge 15:9; Lk 2:24 1:15 [m]Lev 5:8

[a]3 Or he

1:1 Emphasizes that the contents of Leviticus were given to Moses by God at Mount Sinai. Cf. also the concluding verse (27:34). In more than 50 places it is said that the Lord spoke to Moses. Modern criticism has attributed practically the whole book to priestly legislation written during or after the exile. But this is without objective evidence, is against the repeated claim of the book to be Mosaic, is against the traditional Jewish view, and runs counter to other OT and NT witness (Ro 10:5). Many items in Leviticus are now seen to be best explained in terms of a second-millennium B.C. date, which is also the most likely time for Moses to have written the Pentateuch (see Introduction to Genesis: Author and Date of Writing). There is no convincing reason not to take at face value the many references to Moses and his work. *Tent of Meeting.* The tabernacle, where God met with Israel (see note on Ex 27:21).
1:2 *brings an offering.* The Hebrew word for "offering" used here comes from the word translated "brings." An "offering" is something that someone "brings" to God as a gift (most offerings were voluntary, such as the burnt offering). *Corban* is the word for "offering" and is used in Mk 7:11, where Mark also translates it "gift" (see note there).
1:3 *burnt offering.* See further priestly regulations in 6:8-13 (see also chart on "OT Sacrifices," p. 150). A burnt offering was offered every morning and evening for all Israel (Ex 29:39-42). Double burnt offerings were brought on the Sabbath (Nu 28:9-10) and extra ones on feast days (Nu 28-29). In addition, anyone could offer special burnt offerings to express devotion to the Lord. *male.* The burnt offering had to be a male animal because of its greater value, and also perhaps because it was thought to better represent vigor and fertility. It was usually a young sheep or goat (for the average individual), but bulls (for the wealthy) and doves or pigeons (for the poor) were also specified. *without defect.* The animal had to be unblemished (cf. Mal 1:8). As in all offerings, the offerer was to lay his hand on the head of the animal to

express identification between himself and the animal (16:21), whose death would then be accepted in "atonement" (v. 4). The blood was sprinkled on the sides of the great altar (located outside the tabernacle—later the temple—in the eastern half of the courtyard), where the fire of sacrifice was never to go out (6:13). The whole sacrifice was to be burned up (v. 9), including the head, legs, fat and inner organs. It is therefore sometimes called a holocaust offering (holo means "whole," and caust means "burnt"). When a bull was offered, however, the officiating priest could keep its hide (7:8). The burnt offering may have been the usual sacrifice offered by the patriarchs. It was the most comprehensive in its meaning. Its Hebrew name means "going up," perhaps symbolizing worship and prayer as its aroma ascended to the Lord (v. 17). The completeness of its burning also speaks of dedication on the part of the worshiper. *entrance to the Tent of Meeting.* Where the altar of burnt offering was (see Ex 40:29). *acceptable to the LORD.* See Ro 12:1; Php 4:18.
1:4 *lay his hand on.* See notes on v. 3; Ex 29:10. *atonement.* See notes on 16:20-22; 17:11.
1:5 Only after the offerer killed the animal (symbolizing substitution of a perfect animal sacrifice for a sinful human life) did the priestly work begin. *blood.* See notes on 17:11; Heb 9:18. *sprinkle it against the altar.* See Ex 24:6; Heb 9:19-21.
1:6 *skin.* The whole animal was burned except the hide, which was given to the priest (7:8).
1:9,13,17 *aroma pleasing to the LORD.* The OT sacrifices foreshadowed Christ, who was a "fragrant offering" (Eph 5:2; cf. Php 4:18).
1:11 *north side.* See diagram of "The Tabernacle," p. 124.
1:14 *birds.* Three categories of sacrifices are mentioned: (1) herds (vv. 3-9), (2) flocks (vv. 10-13) and (3) birds (vv. 14-17). Sacrifices of birds were allowed for the poor (see 5:7; 12:8; Lk 2:24).

it on the altar; its blood shall be drained out on the side of the altar. *n* [16] He is to remove the crop with its contents[b] and throw it to the east side of the altar, where the ashes[o] are. [17] He shall tear it open by the wings, not severing it completely,[p] and then the priest shall burn it on the wood[q] that is on the fire on the altar. It is a burnt offering, an offering made by fire, an aroma pleasing to the LORD.

The Grain Offering

2 " 'When someone brings a grain offering[r] to the LORD, his offering is to be of fine flour.[s] He is to pour oil[t] on it,[u] put incense on it[v] [2] and take it to Aaron's sons the priests. The priest shall take a handful of the fine flour[w] and oil, together with all the incense,[x] and burn this as a memorial portion[y] on the altar, an offering made by fire,[z] an aroma pleasing to the LORD.[a] [3] The rest of the grain offering belongs to Aaron and his sons;[b] it is a most holy[c] part of the offerings made to the LORD by fire.

[4] " 'If you bring a grain offering baked in an oven,[d] it is to consist of fine flour: cakes made without yeast and mixed with oil, or[e] wafers[f] made without yeast and spread with oil.[f] [5] If your grain offering is prepared on a griddle,[g] it is to be made of fine flour mixed with oil, and without yeast. [6] Crumble it and pour oil on it; it is a grain offering. [7] If your grain offering is cooked in a pan,[h] it is to be made of fine flour and oil. [8] Bring the grain offering

made of these things to the LORD; present it to the priest, who shall take it to the altar. [9] He shall take out the memorial portion[i] from the grain offering and burn it on the altar as an offering made by fire, an aroma pleasing to the LORD.[j] [10] The rest of the grain offering belongs to Aaron and his sons;[k] it is a most holy part of the offerings made to the LORD by fire.[l]

[11] " 'Every grain offering you bring to the LORD must be made without yeast,[m] for you are not to burn any yeast or honey in an offering made to the LORD by fire. [12] You may bring them to the LORD as an offering of the firstfruits,[n] but they are not to be offered on the altar as a pleasing aroma. [13] Season all your grain offerings with salt.[o] Do not leave the salt of the covenant[p] of your God out of your grain offerings; add salt to all your offerings.

[14] " 'If you bring a grain offering of first-fruits[q] to the LORD, offer crushed heads of new grain roasted in the fire. [15] Put oil and incense[r] on it; it is a grain offering. [16] The priest shall burn the memorial portion[s] of the crushed grain and the oil, together with all the incense,[t] as an offering made to the LORD by fire.[u]

The Fellowship Offering

3 " 'If someone's offering is a fellowship offering,[d,v] and he offers an animal

---

Cross-references (center column):

1:15 *n*Lev 5:9
1:16 *o*Lev 4:12; 6:10; Nu 4:13
1:17 *p*S Ge 15:10 *q*S ver 7
2:1 *r*S Ex 29:41; Lev 6:14-18 *s*Ex 29:2,40; Lev 5:11 *t*Nu 15:4; 28:5 *u*S Ex 29:2; Lev 7:12 *v*ver 2, 15,16; Lev 24:7; Ne 13:9; Isa 43:23
2:2 *w*Lev 5:11 *x*Lev 6:15; Isa 1:13; 65:3; 66:3 *y*ver 9,16; Lev 5:12; 6:15; 24:7; Nu 5:26; 18:8; Ps 16:5; 73:26; Isa 53:12 *z*ver 16 *a*S Lev 1:9
2:3 *b*ver 10; Lev 6:16; 10:12, 13 *c*S Ex 30:36
2:4 *d*Lev 7:9; 26:26 *e*Lev 7:12; 8:26 /S Ex 29:2
2:5 *g*Lev 6:21; 7:9; Eze 4:3
2:7 *h*Lev 7:9

2:9 *i*S ver 2 /S Ge 8:21
2:10 *k*ver 3 /Ezr 2:63
2:11 *m*S Ex 23:18; Lev 6:16
2:12 *n*S Ex 34:22
2:13 *o*Mk 9:49 *p*Nu 18:19; 2Ch 13:5; Eze 43:24
2:14 *q*S Ex 34:22; Nu 15:20; Dt 16:13; 26:2; Ru 3:2
2:15 *r*S ver 1
2:16 *s*S ver 2 *t*S ver 1 *u*Nu 4:16; Jer 14:12

3:1 *v*S ver 6; S Ex 32:6; Lev 7:11-34; S 17:5

b 16 Or *crop and the feathers*; the meaning of the Hebrew for this word is uncertain. *c* 4 Or *and* *d* 1 Traditionally *peace offering*; also in verses 3, 6 and 9

1:17 *not severing it completely.* See note on Ge 15:10.
2:1 *grain offering.* See further priestly regulations in 6:14–23; 7:9–10. It was made of grain or fine flour. If baked or cooked, it consisted of cakes or wafers made in a pan or oven or on a griddle. It was the only bloodless offering, but it was to accompany the burnt offering (see Nu 28:3–6), sin offering (see Nu 6:14–15) and fellowship offering (see 9:4; Nu 6:17). The amounts of grain offering ingredients specified to accompany a bull, ram or lamb sacrificed as a burnt offering are given in Nu 28:12–13. A representative handful of flour was to be burned on the altar with the accompanying offerings, and the balance was to be baked without yeast and eaten by the priests in their holy meals (6:14–17). The flour that was burned on the altar was mixed with olive oil for shortening, salted for taste and accompanied by incense, but it was to have no yeast or honey—neither of which was allowed on the altar (vv. 11–13). The cooked product was similar to pie crust. The worshiper was not to eat any of the grain offering, and the priests were not to eat any of their own grain offerings, which were to be totally burned (6:22–23). The Hebrew word for grain offering can mean "present" or "gift" and is often used in that way (see Ge 43:11). The sacred gifts expressed devotion to God (see v. 2). *fine flour.* Grain that was milled and sifted. *oil.* Olive oil is often mentioned in connection with grain and new wine as fresh products of the harvest (see Dt 7:13). Used extensively in cooking, it was a suitable part of the worshiper's gift.

incense. Frankincense was the chief ingredient (see Ex 30:34–35).
2:3 *most holy part.* For this reason, the priests were to eat it in the sanctuary area proper and not feed their families with it (6:16–18).
2:4 *without yeast.* See notes on Ex 12:8,15.
2:5 *griddle.* A clay pan that rested on a stone heated by a fire. Later, iron pans were sometimes used.
2:11 *honey.* It was forbidden on the altar perhaps because of its use in brewing beer (as an aid to fermentation), though some suggest that it was because of its use in Canaanite cultic practice.
2:12 *firstfruits.* See 23:10–11; Ex 23:16,19; Nu 15:18–20; Dt 18:4–5; 26:1–11.
2:13 *salt of the covenant.* In ancient times salt was often costly and a valuable part of the diet. Perhaps this is why it was used as a covenant sign and was required for sacrifices.
3:1 *fellowship offering.* See further priestly regulations in 7:11–21,28–34. Two basic ideas are included in this offering: peace and fellowship. The traditional translation is "peace offering," a name that comes from the Hebrew word for the offering, which in turn is related to the Hebrew word *shalom,* meaning "peace" or "wholeness." Thus the offering perhaps symbolized peace between God and man as well as the inward peace that resulted. The fellowship offering was the only sacrifice of which the offerer might eat a part. Fellowship was involved because the offerer, on the basis of

from the herd, whether male or female, he is to present before the LORD an animal without defect. *w* 2He is to lay his hand on the head *x* of his offering and slaughter it *y* at the entrance to the Tent of Meeting. *z* Then Aaron's sons the priests shall sprinkle *a* the blood against the altar *b* on all sides. *c* 3From the fellowship offering he is to bring a sacrifice made to the LORD by fire: all the fat *d* that covers the inner parts *e* or is connected to them, 4both kidneys *f* with the fat on them near the loins, and the covering of the liver, which he will remove with the kidneys. 5Then Aaron's sons *g* are to burn it on the altar *h* on top of the burnt offering *i* that is on the burning wood, *j* as an offering made by fire, an aroma pleasing to the LORD. *k*

6" 'If he offers an animal from the flock as a fellowship offering *l* to the LORD, he is to offer a male or female without defect. 7If he offers a lamb, *m* he is to present it before the LORD. *n* 8He is to lay his hand on the head of his offering and slaughter it *o* in front of the Tent of Meeting. Then Aaron's sons shall sprinkle its blood against the altar on all sides. 9From the fellowship offering he is to bring a sacrifice *p* made to the LORD by fire: its fat, the entire fat tail cut off close to the backbone, all the fat that covers the inner parts or is connected to them, 10both kidneys with the fat on them near the loins, and the covering of the liver, which he will remove with the kidneys. 11The priest shall burn them on the altar *q* as food, *r* an offering made to the LORD by fire. *s*

12" 'If his offering is a goat, *t* he is to present it before the LORD. 13He is to lay his hand on its head and slaughter it in front of the Tent of Meeting. Then Aaron's sons shall sprinkle *u* its blood against the altar on all sides. *v* 14From what he offers he is to make this offering to the LORD by fire: all the fat that covers the inner parts or is connected to them, 15both kidneys with the fat on them near the loins, and the covering of the liver, which he will remove with the kidneys. *w* 16The priest shall burn them on the altar *x* as food, *y* an offering made by fire, a pleasing aroma. *z* All the fat *a* is the LORD's. *b*

17" 'This is a lasting ordinance *c* for the generations to come, *d* wherever you live: *e* You must not eat any fat or any blood. *f* ' "

The Sin Offering

4 The LORD said to Moses, 2"Say to the Israelites: 'When anyone sins unintentionally *g* and does what is forbidden in any of the LORD's commands *h*—

3" 'If the anointed priest *i* sins, *j* bringing guilt on the people, he must bring to the LORD a young bull *k* without defect *l* as a sin offering *m* for the sin he has committed. *n* 4He is to present the bull at the entrance to the Tent of Meeting before the LORD. *o* He is to lay his hand on its head

Cross references

3:1 *w*S Ex 12:5
3:2 *x*S Ex 29:15; Nu 8:10
*y*S Lev 1:5
*z*S Ex 40:2
*a*S Ex 24:6
*b*Lev 17:6;
Nu 18:17
*c*S Ex 29:20
3:3 *d*S Ex 29:13
*e*S Ex 12:9
3:4 *f*ver 10;
Ex 29:13; Lev 4:9
3:5 *g*Lev 7:29-34
*h*ver 11,16
*i*Ex 29:13,38-42;
/S Lev 1:7
*k*S Lev 1:9
3:6 *l*S ver 1;
Nu 15:3,8
3:7 *m*Lev 17:3;
Nu 15:5; 28:5,7,8
*n*Lev 17:8-9;
1Ki 8:62
3:8 *o*S Lev 1:5
3:9 *p*Isa 34:6;
Jer 46:10;
Eze 39:19;
Zep 1:7
3:11 *q*S ver 5
*r*ver 16; Lev 21:6,
17; Nu 28:2
*s*Lev 9:18
3:12 *t*S Lev 1:10;
S 4:3
3:13 *u*S Lev 24:6
*v*Lev 1:5
3:15 *w*Lev 7:4
3:16 *x*S ver 5;
Lev 7:31 *y*S ver
11 *z*S Lev 1:9
*a*S Ge 4:4
*b*1Sa 2:16
3:17
*c*S Ex 12:14;
S 27:21
*d*S Ge 9:12
*e*S Ex 12:20
*f*Ge 9:4;
Lev 7:25-26;
17:10-16;
Dt 12:16;
Ac 15:20
4:2 *g*ver 13,27;
Lev 5:15-18;
22:14;

Nu 15:24-29; 35:11-15; Jos 20:3,9; Heb 9:7 *h*ver 22;
Nu 15:22 4:3 *i*S Ex 28:41 /S Ge 18:23 *k*ver 14; Lev 3:12;
8:14; 10:16; 16:3,5; Nu 15:27; Ps 66:15; Eze 43:19,23
/S Ex 12:5 *m*S ver 24; S Ex 30:10; Lev 5:6-13; 9:2-22;
Heb 9:13-14 *n*ver 32 4:4 *o*ver 15,24; Lev 1:3; Nu 8:12

---

the sacrifice, had fellowship with God and with the priest, who also ate part of the offering (7:14–15,31–34). This sacrifice—along with others—was offered by the thousands during the three annual festivals in Israel (see Ex 23:14–17; Nu 29:39) because multitudes of people came to the temple to worship and share in a communal meal. During the monarchy, the animals offered by the people were usually supplemented by large numbers given by the king. At the dedication of the temple, Solomon offered 20,000 cattle and 120,-000 sheep and goats as fellowship offerings over a period of 14 days (1Ki 8:63–65).
3:2 *lay his hand on.* See notes on 1:3; Ex 29:10.
3:5 *on top of the burnt offering.* The burnt offerings for the nation as a whole were offered every morning and evening, and the fellowship offerings were offered on top of them.
3:9 *fat tail.* A breed of sheep still much used in the Middle East has a tail heavy with fat.
3:11,16 *on the altar as food.* Israelite sacrifices were not "food for the gods" (as in other ancient cultures; see Eze 16:20; cf. Ps 50:9–13) but were sometimes called "food" metaphorically (21:6,8,17,21; 22:25) in the sense that they were gifts to God and that he received them with delight.
3:17 *not eat any fat or any blood.* See note on 17:11.
4:2 *unintentionally.* See 5:15; contrast Nu 15:30–31. Four classes of people involved in committing unintentional sins are listed: (1) "the anointed priest" (vv. 3–12), (2) the

"whole Israelite community" (vv. 13–21), (3) a "leader" (vv. 22–26) and (4) a "member of the community" (vv. 27–35). Heb 9:7 speaks of sins "committed in ignorance" in referring to the Day of Atonement.
4:3 *anointed priest.* The high priest (see 6:20,22). *sins.* All high priests sinned except the high priest Jesus Christ (Heb 5:1–3; 7:26–28). *on the people.* The relationship of the priests to the people was so intimate in Israel (as a nation consecrated to God) that the people became guilty when the priest sinned. *must.* Although the burnt, grain and fellowship offerings (chs. 1–3) were voluntary, the sin offering was compulsory (see vv. 14,23,28). *without defect.* A defective sacrifice could not be a substitute for a defective people. The final perfect sacrifice for the sins of God's people was the crucified Christ, who was without any moral defect (Heb 9:13–14; 1Pe 1:19). *sin offering.* See further priestly regulations in 6:24–29; Nu 15:22–29. As soon as an "anointed priest" (or a person from one of the other classes of people) became aware of unintentional sin, he was to bring his sin offering to the Lord. On the other hand, should the priest (or others) remain unaware of unintentional sin, this lack was atoned for on the Day of Atonement.
4:4 Three principles of atonement are found in this verse: (1) substitution ("present the bull"), (2) identification ("lay his hand on its head") and (3) the death of the substitute ("slaughter it").

NAME	OT REFERENCES	ELEMENTS	PURPOSE
BURNT OFFERING	Lev 1; 6:8-13; 8:18-21; 16:24	Bull, ram or male bird (dove or young pigeon for poor); wholly consumed; no defect	Voluntary act of worship; atonement for unintentional sin in general; expression of devotion, commitment and complete surrender to God
GRAIN OFFERING	Lev 2; 6:14-23	Grain, fine flour, olive oil, incense, baked bread (cakes or wafers), salt; no yeast or honey; accompanied burnt offering and fellowship offering (along with drink offering)	Voluntary act of worship; recognition of God's goodness and provisions; devotion to God
FELLOWSHIP OFFERING	Lev 3; 7:11-34	Any animal without defect from herd or flock; variety of breads	Voluntary act of worship; thanksgiving and fellowship (it included a communal meal)
SIN OFFERING	Lev 4:1-5:13; 6:24-30; 8:14-17; 16:3-22	1. Young bull: for high priest and congregation 2. Male goat: for leader 3. Female goat or lamb: for common person 4. Dove or pigeon: for the poor 5. Tenth of an ephah of fine flour: for the very poor	Mandatory atonement for specific unintentional sin; confession of sin; forgiveness of sin; cleansing from defilement
GUILT OFFERING	Lev 5:14-6:7; 7:1-6	Ram or lamb	Mandatory atonement for unintentional sin requiring restitution; cleansing from defilement; make restitution; pay 20% fine

When more than one kind of offering was presented (as in Nu 6:16, 17), the procedure was usually as follows: (1) sin offering or guilt offering, (2) burnt offering, (3) fellowship offering and grain offering (along with a drink offering). This sequence furnishes part of the spiritual significance of the sacrificial system. First, sin had to be dealt with (sin offering or guilt offering). Second, the worshiper committed himself completely to God (burnt offering and grain offering). Third, fellowship or communion between the Lord, the priest and the worshiper (fellowship offering) was established. To state it another way, there were sacrifices of expiation (sin offerings and guilt offerings), consecration (burnt offerings and grain offerings) and communion (fellowship offerings—these included vow offerings, thank offerings and freewill offerings).

and slaughter it before the LORD. [5]Then the anointed priest shall take some of the bull's blood[p] and carry it into the Tent of Meeting. [6]He is to dip his finger into the blood and sprinkle[q] some of it seven times before the LORD,[r] in front of the curtain of the sanctuary.[s] [7]The priest shall then put some of the blood on the horns[t] of the altar of fragrant incense that is before the LORD in the Tent of Meeting. The rest of the bull's blood he shall pour out at the base of the altar[u] of burnt offering[v] at the entrance to the Tent of Meeting. [8]He shall remove all the fat[w] from the bull of the sin offering—the fat that covers the inner parts or is connected to them, [9]both kidneys with the fat on them near the loins, and the covering of the liver, which he will remove with the kidneys[x]— [10]just as the fat is removed from the ox[e][y] sacrificed as a fellowship offering.[f][z] Then the priest shall burn them on the altar of burnt offering.[a] [11]But the hide of the bull and all its flesh, as well as the head and legs, the inner parts and offal[b]— [12]that is, all the rest of the bull—he must take outside the camp[c] to a place ceremonially clean,[d] where the ashes[e] are thrown, and burn it[f] in a wood fire on the ash heap.[g]

[13]" 'If the whole Israelite community sins unintentionally[h] and does what is forbidden in any of the LORD's commands, even though the community is unaware of the matter, they are guilty. [14]When they become aware of the sin they committed,

the assembly must bring a young bull[i] as a sin offering[j] and present it before the Tent of Meeting. [15]The elders[k] of the community are to lay their hands[l] on the bull's head[m] before the LORD, and the bull shall be slaughtered before the LORD.[n] [16]Then the anointed priest is to take some of the bull's blood[o] into the Tent of Meeting. [17]He shall dip his finger into the blood and sprinkle[p] it before the LORD[q] seven times in front of the curtain. [18]He is to put some of the blood[r] on the horns of the altar that is before the LORD[s] in the Tent of Meeting. The rest of the blood he shall pour out at the base of the altar[t] of burnt offering at the entrance to the Tent of Meeting. [19]He shall remove all the fat[u] from it and burn it on the altar,[v] [20]and do with this bull just as he did with the bull for the sin offering. In this way the priest will make atonement[w] for them, and they will be forgiven.[x] [21]Then he shall take the bull outside the camp[y] and burn it as he burned the first bull. This is the sin offering for the community.[z]

[22]" 'When a leader[a] sins unintentionally[b] and does what is forbidden in any of the commands of the LORD his God, he is guilty. [23]When he is made aware of the sin he committed, he must bring as his offering a male goat[c] without defect. [24]He is to

---

4:5 [p]ver 16;
Lev 16:14
4:6 [q]Ex 24:8 [r]ver
17; Lev 16:14,19
[s]S Ex 25:8
4:7 [t]S Ex 27:2
[u]ver 34;
S Ex 29:12;
Lev 8:15 [v]ver 18,
30; Lev 5:9; 9:9;
16:18
4:8 [w]ver 19
4:9 [x]S Lev 3:4
4:10 [y]Lev 9:4
[z]S Ex 32:6
[a]S Ex 29:13
4:11 [b]Ex 29:14;
Lev 8:17; 9:11;
Nu 19:5
4:12
[c]S Ex 29:14;
Lev 8:17; 9:11;
Heb 13:11
[d]Lev 6:11; 10:14;
Nu 19:9
[e]S Lev 1:16
[f]Lev 6:30
[g]Lev 16:3
4:13 [h]S ver 2

4:14 [i]S ver 3
[j]Nu 15:24
4:15 [k]S Ex 3:16;
S 19:7
[l]2Ch 29:23
[m]S Ex 29:10;
Lev 8:14,22;
Nu 8:10 [n]S ver 4
4:16 [o]S ver 5
4:17 [p]Nu 19:4,
18 [q]S ver 6
4:18 [r]Lev 8:15;
17:6; 2Ch 29:22
[s]ver 7; Lev 6:30;
10:18 [t]Lev 5:9
4:19 [u]ver 8 [v]ver
26
4:20
[w]S Ex 29:36;
S 32:30;
S Ro 3:25;
Heb 10:10-12
[x]ver 26,31,35;
Nu 15:25
4:21 [y]S ver 12
[z]Lev 16:5,15;

2Ch 29:21 4:22 [a]Nu 31:13 [b]ver 2 4:23 [c]S ver 3; S Lev 1:10

[e] 10 The Hebrew word can include both male and female.
[f] 10 Traditionally *peace offering*; also in verses 26, 31 and 35

4:5 *blood.* See note on 17:11. There were two types of sin offerings. The first (vv. 3–21) and more important involved sprinkling the blood in the tabernacle in front of the inner curtain or, in the case of the solemn Day of Atonement (ch. 16), on and in front of the atonement cover (traditionally "mercy seat") itself. This type of sin offering was not eaten. The fat, kidneys and covering of the liver were burned on the great altar, but all the rest was burned outside the camp (v. 12). Heb 13:11–13 clearly draws the parallel to our sin offering, Jesus, who suffered outside the city gate. This type of sin offering was offered by and for a priest or by the elders for the whole community. In general, the animal to be sacrificed was a young bull, but on the Day of Atonement the sin offering was to be a goat (16:9).

The second type of sin offering (4:22–5:13) was for a leader of the nation or a private individual. Some of the blood was applied to the horns of the great altar, the rest poured out at its base. The fat, etc., was burned on the altar, but the rest of the offering was given to the priest and his male relatives as food to be eaten in a holy place (6:29–30; see 10:16–20). The sin offering brought by a private person was to be a female goat or lamb. If the person was poor, he could bring a dove or young pigeon (5:7–8; 12:6,8; cf. Lk 2:24), or even about two quarts of flour (5:11). The offering included confession (5:5) and the symbolic transfer of guilt by laying hands on the sacrifice (v. 29; 16:21). Then the priest who offered the sacrifice made atonement for the sin, and the Lord promised forgiveness (5:13). By bringing such a sin

offering, a faithful Israelite under conviction of sin sought restoration of fellowship with God.
4:6 *finger.* The right forefinger (see 14:16). *seven.* The number was symbolic of perfection and completeness (see note on Ge 5:5). *curtain.* The great curtain that separated the Holy Place from the Most Holy Place (Ex 26:33).
4:7 *horns.* The four horns of the altar (see Ex 30:1–3) were symbols of the atoning power of the sin offering (Ex 30:10).
4:8–10 See 3:3–5.
4:12 *outside the camp.* See note on 13:45–46. So also Jesus was crucified outside Jerusalem (Heb 13:11–13; see 9:11; 16:26–28; Nu 19:3; Eze 43:21). *ceremonially clean.* The distinction between clean and unclean was a matter of ritual or religious purity, not a concern for physical cleanliness (see chs. 11–15 for examples; see also Mk 7:1–4). *burn.* Since the sins of the offerer were symbolically transferred to the sacrificial bull, the bull had to be entirely destroyed and not thrown on the ash pile of 1:16.
4:15 *elders.* See note on Ex 3:16.
4:18 *altar.* Of incense (see v. 7).
4:20 *sin offering.* The offering of the priest who had sinned (v. 3). *will be forgiven.* In 4:20–6:7 this is a key phrase, occurring nine times and referring to forgiveness by God.
4:23 *male goat.* Less valuable animals were sacrificed for those with lesser standing in the community or of lesser economic means. Thus a bull was required for the high priest (v. 3) and the whole community (v. 14), but a male goat for a civic leader (v. 23) and a female goat (v. 28) or lamb (v. 32)

lay his hand on the goat's head and slaughter it at the place where the burnt offering is slaughtered before the LORD. [d] It is a sin offering. [e] 25Then the priest shall take some of the blood of the sin offering with his finger and put it on the horns of the altar [f] of burnt offering and pour out the rest of the blood at the base of the altar. [g] 26He shall burn all the fat on the altar as he burned the fat of the fellowship offering. In this way the priest will make atonement [h] for the man's sin, and he will be forgiven. [i]

27" 'If a member of the community sins unintentionally [j] and does what is forbidden in any of the LORD's commands, he is guilty. 28When he is made aware of the sin he committed, he must bring as his offering [k] for the sin he committed a female goat [l] without defect. 29He is to lay his hand on the head [m] of the sin offering [n] and slaughter it at the place of the burnt offering. [o] 30Then the priest is to take some of the blood with his finger and put it on the horns of the altar of burnt offering [p] and pour out the rest of the blood at the base of the altar. 31He shall remove all the fat, just as the fat is removed from the fellowship offering, and the priest shall burn it on the altar [q] as an aroma pleasing to the LORD. [r] In this way the priest will make atonement [s] for him, and he will be forgiven. [t]

32" 'If he brings a lamb [u] as his sin offering, he is to bring a female without defect. [v] 33He is to lay his hand on its head and slaughter it [w] for a sin offering [x] at the place where the burnt offering is slaughtered. [y] 34Then the priest shall take some of the blood of the sin offering with his finger and put it on the horns of the altar of burnt offering and pour out the rest of the blood at the base of the altar. [z] 35He shall remove all the fat, just as the fat is removed from the lamb of the fellowship offering, and the priest shall burn it on the altar [a] on top of the offerings made to the LORD by fire. In this way the priest will make atonement for him for the sin he has committed, and he will be forgiven.

5　" 'If a person sins because he does not speak up when he hears a public charge to testify [b] regarding something he has seen or learned about, he will be held responsible. [c]

2" 'Or if a person touches anything ceremonially unclean—whether the carcasses of unclean wild animals or of unclean livestock or of unclean creatures that move along the ground [d]—even though he is unaware of it, he has become unclean [e] and is guilty.

3" 'Or if he touches human uncleanness [f]—anything that would make him unclean [g]—even though he is unaware of it, when he learns of it he will be guilty.

4" 'Or if a person thoughtlessly takes an oath [h] to do anything, whether good or evil [i]—in any matter one might carelessly swear about—even though he is unaware of it, in any case when he learns of it he will be guilty.

5" 'When anyone is guilty in any of these ways, he must confess [j] in what way he has sinned 6and, as a penalty for the sin he has committed, he must bring to the LORD a female lamb or goat [k] from the flock as a sin offering; [l] and the priest shall make atonement [m] for him for his sin.

7" 'If he cannot afford [n] a lamb, [o] he is to bring two doves or two young pigeons [p] to the LORD as a penalty for his sin—one for a sin offering and the other for a burnt offering. 8He is to bring them to the priest, who shall first offer the one for the sin offering. He is to wring its head from its neck, [q] not severing it completely, [r] 9and is to sprinkle [s] some of the blood of the sin offering against the side of the altar; [t] the rest of the blood must be drained out at the base of the altar. [u] It is a sin offering. 10The priest shall then offer the other as a burnt offering in the prescribed way [v] and make atonement [w] for him for the sin he has committed, and he will be forgiven. [x]

11" 'If, however, he cannot afford [y] two doves or two young pigeons, [z] he is to bring as an offering for his sin a tenth of an

---

4:24 [d]S ver 4
[e]S ver 3; Lev 6:25
4:25 [f]Lev 16:18;
Eze 43:20,22
[g]Lev 9:9
4:26 [h]S Ex 32:30
[i]Lev 5:10; 12:8
4:27 [j]S ver 2
4:28 [k]Lev 5:6;
Eze 40:39; 44:27
[l]S ver 3;
S Lev 1:10
4:29 [m]ver 4,24
[n]S Lev 1:4
[o]S Ge 8:20
4:30 [p]S ver 7
4:31 [q]ver 35
[r]S Ge 8:21
[s]Lev 1:4 [t]S ver 20
4:32 [u]Ex 29:38;
Lev 9:3; 14:10
[v]Lev 1:3
4:33 [w]Lev 1:5
[x]Lev 1:4 [y]ver 29
4:34 [z]S ver 7
4:35 [a]ver 31

5:1 [b]Pr 29:24;
Mt 26:63 [c]ver
17; S Ex 28:38;
Lev 7:18; 17:16;
19:8; 20:17;
24:15; Nu 5:31;
9:13; 15:31;
19:20; 30:15
5:2 [d]Lev 11:11,
24-40; Dt 14:8;
Isa 52:11 [e]ver 3;
Lev 7:21; 11:8,
24; 13:45;
Nu 19:22;
Job 15:16;
Ps 51:5; Isa 6:5;
64:6; Eze 36:17;
Hag 2:13
5:3 [f]Nu 19:11-16
[g]Lev 7:20; 11:25;
14:19; 21:1;
Nu 5:2; 9:6;
19:7; Eze 44:25
5:4 [h]Nu 30:6,8
[i]Isa 41:23
5:5 [j]Lev 16:21;
26:40; Nu 5:7;
Jos 7:19;
1Ki 8:47;
Pr 28:13
5:6 [k]S Lev 1:10;
S 4:3 [l]S Lev 4:28
[m]S Ex 32:30
5:7 [n]ver 11;
Lev 12:8; 14:21;
27:8 [o]Lev 12:8;
14:22,30
[p]S Ge 15:9;
Nu 6:10
5:8 [q]Lev 1:15
[r]Lev 1:17
5:9 [s]S Ex 24:6
[t]Lev 1:15
[u]S Lev 4:7
5:10
[v]Lev 1:14-17;
1Ch 15:13
[w]S Ex 32:30
[x]S Lev 4:26
5:11 [y]S ver 7
[z]S Ge 15:9

---

for an ordinary Israelite. If an offerer was too poor, then doves and pigeons were sufficient (5:7) or even a handful of fine flour (5:11–12).

4:25 *priest.* The priest who officiated for the civil authority or the lay person (see vv. 30,34).

4:28 *female goat.* See note on v. 23.

4:29 *lay his hand on.* See notes on 1:3; Ex 29:10.

4:30 *horns.* See note on v. 7.

4:32 *lamb . . . female.* See note on v. 23.

4:35 *fat . . . of the fellowship offering.* See 3:3–5.

5:1–4 Four examples of the unintentional sins (see 4:2–3,

13,22,27) the sin offering covers.

5:2 *ceremonially unclean.* See note on 4:12.

5:3 *human uncleanness.* See chs. 11–15.

5:5 *confess.* The offerer had to acknowledge his sin to God in order to receive forgiveness.

5:7 *two doves . . . pigeons.* See note on 4:23.

5:11 *fine flour.* See note on 4:23. Although no blood was used with a flour offering, it was offered "on top of the offerings made to the LORD by fire" (v. 12). Heb 9:22 may refer to such a situation.

ephah[g][a] of fine flour[b] for a sin offering. He must not put oil or incense on it, because it is a sin offering. [12]He is to bring it to the priest, who shall take a handful of it as a memorial portion[c] and burn it on the altar[d] on top of the offerings made to the LORD by fire. It is a sin offering. [13]In this way the priest will make atonement[e] for him for any of these sins he has committed, and he will be forgiven. The rest of the offering will belong to the priest,[f] as in the case of the grain offering.[g] ' "

The Guilt Offering

[14]The LORD said to Moses: [15]"When a person commits a violation and sins unintentionally[h] in regard to any of the LORD's holy things, he is to bring to the LORD as a penalty[i] a ram[j] from the flock, one without defect and of the proper value in silver, according to the sanctuary shekel.[h][k] It is a guilt offering.[l] [16]He must make restitution[m] for what he has failed to do in regard to the holy things, add a fifth of the value[n] to that and give it all to the priest, who will make atonement for him with the ram as a guilt offering, and he will be forgiven.

[17]"If a person sins and does what is forbidden in any of the LORD's commands, even though he does not know it,[o] he is guilty and will be held responsible.[p] [18]He is to bring to the priest as a guilt offering[q] a ram from the flock, one without defect and of the proper value. In this way the priest will make atonement for him for the wrong he has committed unintentionally, and he will be forgiven.[r] [19]It is a guilt offering; he has been guilty of[i] wrongdoing before the LORD."[s]

6 The LORD said to Moses: [2]"If anyone sins and is unfaithful to the LORD[t] by deceiving his neighbor[u] about something entrusted to him or left in his care[v] or stolen, or if he cheats[w] him, [3]or if he finds lost property and lies about it,[x] or if he swears falsely,[y] or if he commits any such sin that people may do— [4]when he thus sins and becomes guilty, he must return[z] what he has stolen or taken by extortion,

or what was entrusted to him, or the lost property he found, [5]or whatever it was he swore falsely about. He must make restitution[a] in full, add a fifth of the value to it and give it all to the owner on the day he presents his guilt offering. [b] [6]And as a penalty he must bring to the priest, that is, to the LORD, his guilt offering,[c] a ram from the flock, one without defect and of the proper value. [d] [7]In this way the priest will make atonement[e] for him before the LORD, and he will be forgiven for any of these things he did that made him guilty."

The Burnt Offering

[8]The LORD said to Moses: [9]"Give Aaron and his sons this command: 'These are the regulations for the burnt offering[f]: The burnt offering is to remain on the altar hearth throughout the night, till morning, and the fire must be kept burning on the altar.[g] [10]The priest shall then put on his linen clothes,[h] with linen undergarments next to his body,[i] and shall remove the ashes[j] of the burnt offering that the fire has consumed on the altar and place them beside the altar. [11]Then he is to take off these clothes and put on others, and carry the ashes outside the camp to a place that is ceremonially clean.[k] [12]The fire on the altar must be kept burning; it must not go out. Every morning the priest is to add firewood[l] and arrange the burnt offering on the fire and burn the fat[m] of the fellowship offerings[j][n] on it. [13]The fire must be kept burning on the altar continuously; it must not go out.

The Grain Offering

[14]" 'These are the regulations for the grain offering:[o] Aaron's sons are to bring it before the LORD, in front of the altar. [15]The priest is to take a handful of fine flour and oil, together with all the incense[p] on the grain offering,[q] and burn the memorial

---

Cross references (center column):

5:11 [a]S Ex 16:36
[b]S Lev 2:1
5:12 [c]S Lev 2:2
[d]Lev 2:9
5:13 [e]S Ex 32:30
[f]Lev 2:3
[g]S Ex 29:41
5:15 [h]S Lev 4:2
[i]Lev 22:14
[j]S Ex 29:3;
Lev 6:6; Nu 5:8;
6:14; 15:6; 28:11
[k]S Ex 30:13 [i]ver
16,18; Lev 6:5,6;
7:1,6-10,7;
14:12-17; 19:21,
22; Nu 6:12;
18:9; 1Sa 6:3;
Ezr 10:19;
Isa 53:10
5:16 [m]Lev 6:4
[n]ver 15;
Lev 27:13;
Nu 5:7
5:17 [o]ver 15
[p]S ver 1
5:18 [q]Lev 6:6;
14:12 [r]S ver 15
5:19 [s]2Ki 12:16
6:2 [t]Nu 5:6;
Ps 73:27; Ac 5:4;
Col 3:9
[u]Lev 19:11;
Jer 9:4,5
[v]S Ex 22:7
[w]S Ge 31:7
6:3 [x]S Ex 23:4
[y]S Ex 22:11
6:4 [z]Lev 5:16;
Eze 33:15;
S Lk 19:8

6:5 [a]Nu 5:7
[b]S Lev 5:15
6:6 [c]S Lev 5:15
[d]Nu 5:8
6:7 [e]S Ex 32:30
6:9 [f]Lev 7:37
[g]ver 12
6:10 [h]S Ex 39:27
[i]Ex 28:39-42,43;
39:28 /S Lev 1:16
6:11 [k]S Lev 4:12
6:12 [l]S Lev 1:7
[m]S Ex 29:13
[n]S Ex 32:6
6:14 [o]S Lev 2:1;
Nu 6:15; 15:4;
28:13
6:15 [p]S Lev 2:1
[q]Lev 2:9

---

[g]11 That is, probably about 2 quarts (about 2 liters)
[h]15 That is, about 2/5 ounce (about 11.5 grams)
[i]19 Or has made full expiation for his
[j]12 Traditionally peace offerings

5:15 guilt offering. See further priestly regulations in 7:1-6 (see also Isa 53:10). Traditionally called the "trespass offering," it was very similar to the sin offering (cf. 7:7), and the Hebrew words for the two were apparently sometimes interchanged. The major difference between the guilt and sin offerings was that the guilt offering was brought in cases where restitution for the sin was possible and therefore required (v. 16). Thus in cases of theft and cheating (6:2-5) the stolen property had to be returned along with 20 percent indemnity. By contrast, the sin offering was prescribed in cases of sin where no restitution was possible. The animal sacrificed as a guilt offering was always a ram.

6:3 lost property. See Dt 22:1-3.
6:6 to the priest, that is, to the LORD. Sacrifices were brought to the Lord, but priests were his authorized representatives.
6:8—7:36 Further regulations concerning the sacrifices, dealing mainly with the portions to be eaten by the priests or, in the case of the fellowship offering, by the one offering the sacrifice.
6:9 burnt offering. See ch. 1; Nu 15:1-16 and notes.
6:13 The perpetual fire on the altar represented uninterrupted offering and appeal to God on behalf of Israel.
6:14 grain offering. See ch. 2 and notes.

portion[r] on the altar as an aroma pleasing to the LORD. [16]Aaron and his sons[s] shall eat the rest[t] of it, but it is to be eaten without yeast[u] in a holy place;[v] they are to eat it in the courtyard[w] of the Tent of Meeting.[x] [17]It must not be baked with yeast; I have given it as their share[y] of the offerings made to me by fire.[z] Like the sin offering and the guilt offering, it is most holy.[a] [18]Any male descendant of Aaron may eat it.[b] It is his regular share[c] of the offerings made to the LORD by fire for the generations to come.[d] Whatever touches them will become holy.[k] [e]' "

[19]The LORD also said to Moses, [20]"This is the offering Aaron and his sons are to bring to the LORD on the day he[l] is anointed:[f] a tenth of an ephah[m] [g] of fine flour[h] as a regular grain offering,[i] half of it in the morning and half in the evening. [21]Prepare it with oil on a griddle;[j] bring it well-mixed and present the grain offering broken[n] in pieces as an aroma pleasing to the LORD. [22]The son who is to succeed him as anointed priest[k] shall prepare it. It is the LORD's regular share and is to be burned completely.[l] [23]Every grain offering of a priest shall be burned completely; it must not be eaten."

The Sin Offering

[24]The LORD said to Moses, [25]"Say to Aaron and his sons: 'These are the regulations for the sin offering:[m] The sin offering is to be slaughtered before the LORD[n] in the place[o] the burnt offering is slaughtered; it is most holy. [26]The priest who offers it shall eat it; it is to be eaten in a holy place,[p] in the courtyard[q] of the Tent of Meeting.[r] [27]Whatever touches any of the flesh will become holy,[s] and if any of the blood is spattered on a garment, you must wash it in a holy place. [28]The clay pot[t] the meat is cooked in must be broken; but if it is cooked in a bronze pot, the pot is to be scoured and rinsed with water. [29]Any male in a priest's family may eat it;[u] it is most holy.[v] [30]But any sin offering whose blood is brought into the Tent of Meeting to make atonement[w] in the Holy

Place[x] must not be eaten; it must be burned.[y]

The Guilt Offering

7 " 'These are the regulations for the guilt offering,[z] which is most holy: [2]The guilt offering is to be slaughtered in the place where the burnt offering is slaughtered, and its blood is to be sprinkled against the altar on all sides. [3]All its fat[a] shall be offered: the fat tail and the fat that covers the inner parts, [4]both kidneys with the fat on them near the loins, and the covering of the liver, which is to be removed with the kidneys.[b] [5]The priest shall burn them on the altar[c] as an offering made to the LORD by fire. It is a guilt offering. [6]Any male in a priest's family may eat it,[d] but it must be eaten in a holy place; it is most holy.[e]

[7]" 'The same law applies to both the sin offering[f] and the guilt offering:[g] They belong to the priest[h] who makes atonement with them.[i] [8]The priest who offers a burnt offering for anyone may keep its hide[j] for himself. [9]Every grain offering baked in an oven[k] or cooked in a pan[l] or on a griddle[m] belongs to the priest who offers it, [10]and every grain offering, whether mixed with oil or dry, belongs equally to all the sons of Aaron.

The Fellowship Offering

[11]" 'These are the regulations for the fellowship offering[o] a person may present to the LORD:

[12]" 'If he offers it as an expression of thankfulness, then along with this thank offering[n] he is to offer cakes[o] of bread made without yeast[p] and mixed with oil, wafers[q] made without yeast and spread with oil,[r] and cakes of fine flour well-kneaded and mixed with oil. [13]Along with his fellowship offering of thanksgiving[s] he is to present an offering with cakes of

Cross references (center column)

6:15 [r]S Lev 2:2
6:16 [s]S Lev 2:3
[r]Eze 44:29
[u]S Lev 2:11 [v]ver 26; S Ex 29:11; Lev 10:13; 16:24; 24:9; Nu 18:10
[w]S Ex 27:9
[x]Ex 29:31; Lev 8:31
6:17 [y]Nu 5:9
[z]Ex 29:28; Lev 7:7; 10:16-18
[a]ver 29; Ex 40:10; Lev 10:12; 21:22; 24:9; Nu 18:9,10
6:18 [b]ver 29; Lev 2:3; 7:6; Nu 18:9-10
[c]Nu 5:9
[d]S Ge 9:12
[e]S Ex 30:29
6:20 [f]S Ex 28:41
[g]S Ex 16:36
[h]Nu 5:15; 28:5
[i]Ex 29:2; Lev 23:13; Nu 4:16
6:21 [j]Lev 2:5
6:22
[k]S Ex 28:41; S 29:30 [l]S Lev 1:9
6:25
[m]S Ex 30:10; S Lev 4:24
[n]S Lev 1:3
[o]S Ex 29:11
6:26 [p]S ver 16
[q]S Ex 27:9
[r]S Ex 27:21; S 40:2
6:27 [s]S Ex 29:37; Lev 10:10; Eze 44:19; 46:20; Hag 2:12
6:28 [t]Lev 11:33; 15:12; Nu 19:15
6:29 [u]S ver 18
[v]S ver 17; Eze 42:13
6:30 [w]Eze 45:15

[x]S Lev 4:18
[y]Lev 4:12
7:1 [z]S Lev 5:15; Eze 40:39
7:3 [a]S Ex 29:13
7:4 [b]Lev 3:15
7:5 [c]S Ex 29:13
7:6 [d]S Lev 6:18
[e]Eze 42:13
7:7 [f]S Ex 30:10
[g]S Lev 5:15 [h]ver 6; Lev 2:3; 6:17, 26; 14:13; 2Ki 12:16; 1Co 9:13; 10:18
[i]Nu 5:8
7:8 [j]Lev 1:6
7:9 [k]S Lev 2:4
[l]Lev 2:7
[m]S Lev 2:5
7:12 [n]ver 13,15; Lev 22:29; Ps 50:14; 54:6; 107:22; 116:17; Jer 33:11
[o]Jer 44:19
[p]Nu 6:19

[q]S Lev 2:4 [r]S Lev 2:1 7:13 [s]S ver 12; S Ex 34:22

[k]18 Or *Whoever touches them must be holy*; similarly in verse 27   [l]20 Or *each*   [m]20 That is, probably about 2 quarts (about 2 liters)   [n]21 The meaning of the Hebrew for this word is uncertain.   [o]11 Traditionally *peace offering*; also in verses 13-37

6:25 *sin offering.* See 4:1-5:13 and notes.
6:28 *clay.* Ordinary kitchen utensils and domestic ware were made of clay, usually fired in a kiln and often painted or burnished.
7:2 *guilt offering.* See 5:14-6:7 and notes. *place.* On the north side of the altar of burnt offering in front of the tabernacle (1:11).
7:3 *fat tail.* See note on 3:9.
7:7-10 See Nu 18:8-20; 1Co 9:13.
7:11-36 This section supplements ch. 3, adding regula-

tions about (1) three types of fellowship offerings (thank, vv. 12-15; vow, v. 16; freewill, v. 16), (2) prohibition of eating fat and blood (vv. 22-27) and (3) the priests' share (vv. 28-36).
7:12-15 Thank offerings were given in gratitude for deliverance from sickness (Ps 116:17), trouble (Ps 107:22) or death (Ps 56:12), or for a blessing received.
7:13 *with yeast.* This regulation was not against the prohibition of 2:11 or Ex 23:18 since the offering here was not burned on the altar.

bread made with yeast.[t] [14]He is to bring one of each kind as an offering, a contribution to the LORD; it belongs to the priest who sprinkles the blood of the fellowship offerings. [15]The meat of his fellowship offering of thanksgiving must be eaten on the day it is offered; he must leave none of it till morning.[u]

[16]" 'If, however, his offering is the result of a vow[v] or is a freewill offering,[w] the sacrifice shall be eaten on the day he offers it, but anything left over may be eaten on the next day.[x] [17]Any meat of the sacrifice left over till the third day must be burned up.[y] [18]If any meat of the fellowship offering[z] is eaten on the third day, it will not be accepted.[a] It will not be credited[b] to the one who offered it, for it is impure; the person who eats any of it will be held responsible.[c]

[19]" 'Meat that touches anything ceremonially unclean must not be eaten; it must be burned up. As for other meat, anyone ceremonially clean may eat it. [20]But if anyone who is unclean[d] eats any meat of the fellowship offering belonging to the LORD, that person must be cut off from his people.[e] [21]If anyone touches something unclean[f]—whether human uncleanness or an unclean animal or any unclean, detestable thing—and then eats any of the meat of the fellowship offering belonging to the LORD, that person must be cut off from his people.' "

Eating Fat and Blood Forbidden

[22]The LORD said to Moses, [23]"Say to the Israelites: 'Do not eat any of the fat of cattle, sheep or goats.[g] [24]The fat of an animal found dead or torn by wild animals[h] may be used for any other purpose, but you must not eat it. [25]Anyone who eats the fat

of an animal from which an offering by fire may be[p] made to the LORD must be cut off from his people. [26]And wherever you live, you must not eat the blood[i] of any bird or animal. [27]If anyone eats blood,[j] that person must be cut off from his people.' "

The Priests' Share

[28]The LORD said to Moses, [29]"Say to the Israelites: 'Anyone who brings a fellowship offering to the LORD is to bring part of it as his sacrifice to the LORD. [30]With his own hands he is to bring the offering made to the LORD by fire; he is to bring the fat, together with the breast, and wave the breast before the LORD as a wave offering.[k] [31]The priest shall burn the fat on the altar,[l] but the breast belongs to Aaron and his sons.[m] [32]You are to give the right thigh of your fellowship offerings to the priest as a contribution.[n] [33]The son of Aaron who offers the blood and the fat of the fellowship offering shall have the right thigh as his share. [34]From the fellowship offerings of the Israelites, I have taken the breast that is waved and the thigh[o] that is presented and have given them to Aaron the priest and his sons[p] as their regular share from the Israelites.' "

[35]This is the portion of the offerings made to the LORD by fire that were allotted to Aaron and his sons on the day they were presented to serve the LORD as priests. [36]On the day they were anointed,[q] the LORD commanded that the Israelites give this to them as their regular share for their generations to come.

[37]These, then, are the regulations for the burnt offering,[r] the grain offering,[s] the sin offering, the guilt offering, the ordination

Cross references (center column)

7:13 [r]Lev 23:17; Am 4:5
7:15 [u]S Ex 12:10
7:16
[v]S Ge 28:20;
S Lev 1:2;
Dt 23:21-23
[w]Ex 35:29;
Lev 22:18,21;
23:38; Nu 15:3;
29:39; Dt 12:6;
Ps 54:6;
Eze 46:12
[x]Lev 19:5-8
7:17 [y]Ex 12:10;
Lev 19:6
7:18 [z]2Ch 33:16
[a]Lev 19:7
[b]Nu 18:27
[c]S Lev 5:1
7:20 [d]S Lev 5:3
[e]S Ge 17:14;
Lev 22:3-7
7:21 [f]S Lev 5:2
7:23 [g]Lev 17:3;
Dt 14:4
7:24 [h]S Ex 22:31

7:26 [i]S Ge 9:4
7:27 [j]S Ge 9:4
7:30 [k]S Ex 29:24
7:31 [l]S Ex 29:13
[m]S Ex 29:27;
Lev 10:14,15;
Nu 5:9; 6:20;
18:18
7:34 [o]Ex 29:22;
Lev 10:15;
Nu 6:20;
1Sa 9:24
[p]S Ex 29:27
7:36 [q]Lev 8:12, 30
7:37 [r]Lev 6:9
[s]Lev 6:14

[p]25 Or fire is

7:15–18 See 19:5–8. All meat had to be eaten promptly (in the case of the thank offering on the same day, and in the case of the vow and freewill offerings within two days). One reason may have been that in Canaan meat spoiled quickly and thus became ceremonially impure (v. 18) because it was not then perfect (1:3; see 21:16–23). The prohibition applied also to the Passover (Ex 12:10).

7:16 vow. See 22:18–23. A vow was a solemn promise to offer a gift to God in response to a divine deliverance or blessing. Such vows often accompanied prayers for deliverance or blessing (see note on Ps 7:17). freewill offering. See 22:18–23.

7:19 ceremonially unclean. See note on 4:12.

7:20 cut off from his people. Removed from the covenant people through direct divine judgment (Ge 17:14), or (as here and in vv. 21,25,27; 17:4,9–10,14; 18:29; 19:8; 20:3,5–6,17–18; 23:29) through execution (see, e.g., 20:2–3; Ex 31:14), or possibly sometimes through banishment.

7:21 detestable. The penalty for doing things that were

abominable in the Lord's eyes was severe (see note on v. 20; see also 18:29; 20:13).

7:22–27 See note on 17:11.

7:23 fat. The prohibition of fat for food was as strict as that of blood, but the reason was different. The fat of the fellowship offerings was the Lord's and was to be burned on the altar. There was no explicit prohibition of eating the fat of hunted animals like the gazelle or deer, but probably that was included (see 3:17; Dt 12:15–22).

7:26 not eat the blood. See note on 17:11; see also 3:17; 19:26; Ge 9:4–6; Dt 12:16,23–25; 15:23; 1Sa 14:32–34; Eze 33:25.

7:28–36 See 10:12–15; Nu 18:8–20; Dt 18:1–5.

7:30–32 breast . . . right thigh. The breast and right thigh given to the priest were first presented to the Lord with gestures described as waving the breast and presenting the thigh (v. 34). See also 8:25–29; 9:21; 10:14–15; Ex 29:26–27; Nu 6:20; 18:11,18.

7:37–38 A summary of chs. 1–7.

7:37 ordination offering. See 8:14–36; Ex 29:1–35.

offering[t] and the fellowship offering, [38]which the LORD gave Moses[u] on Mount Sinai[v] on the day he commanded the Israelites to bring their offerings to the LORD,[w] in the Desert of Sinai.

The Ordination of Aaron and His Sons

8:1-36pp — Ex 29:1-37

8 The LORD said to Moses, [2]"Bring Aaron and his sons,[x] their garments,[y] the anointing oil,[z] the bull for the sin offering,[a] the two rams[b] and the basket containing bread made without yeast,[c] [3]and gather the entire assembly[d] at the entrance to the Tent of Meeting." [4]Moses did as the LORD commanded him, and the assembly gathered at the entrance to the Tent of Meeting.

[5]Moses said to the assembly, "This is what the LORD has commanded to be done.[e]" [6]Then Moses brought Aaron and his sons forward and washed them with water.[f] [7]He put the tunic on Aaron, tied the sash around him, clothed him with the robe and put the ephod on him. He also tied the ephod to him by its skillfully woven waistband; so it was fastened on him.[g] [8]He placed the breastpiece[h] on him and put the Urim and Thummim[i] in the breastpiece. [9]Then he placed the turban[j] on Aaron's head and set the gold plate, the sacred diadem,[k] on the front of it, as the LORD commanded Moses.[l]

[10]Then Moses took the anointing oil[m] and anointed[n] the tabernacle[o] and everything in it, and so consecrated them. [11]He sprinkled some of the oil on the altar seven times, anointing the altar and all its utensils and the basin with its stand, to consecrate them.[p] [12]He poured some of the anointing oil on Aaron's head and anointed[q] him to consecrate him.[r] [13]Then he brought Aaron's sons[s] forward, put tunics[t] on them, tied sashes around them and put headbands on them, as the LORD commanded Moses.[u]

[14]He then presented the bull[v] for the sin offering,[w] and Aaron and his sons laid their hands on its head.[x] [15]Moses slaughtered the bull and took some of the blood,[y] and with his finger he put it on all the horns of the altar[z] to purify the altar.[a] He poured out the rest of the blood at the base of the altar. So he consecrated it to make atonement for it.[b] [16]Moses also took all the fat around the inner parts, the covering of the liver, and both kidneys and their fat, and burned it on the altar. [17]But the bull with its hide and its flesh and its offal[c] he burned up outside the camp,[d] as the LORD commanded Moses.

[18]He then presented the ram[e] for the burnt offering, and Aaron and his sons laid their hands on its head. [19]Then Moses slaughtered the ram and sprinkled the blood against the altar on all sides. [20]He cut the ram into pieces and burned the head, the pieces and the fat.[f] [21]He washed the inner parts and the legs with water and burned the whole ram on the altar as a burnt offering, a pleasing aroma, an offering made to the LORD by fire, as the LORD commanded Moses.

[22]He then presented the other ram, the ram for the ordination,[g] and Aaron and his sons laid their hands on its head.[h] [23]Moses slaughtered the ram and took some of its blood and put it on the lobe of Aaron's right ear, on the thumb of his right hand and on the big toe of his right foot.[i] [24]Moses also brought Aaron's sons forward and put some of the blood on the lobes of their right ears, on the thumbs of their right hands and on the big toes of their right feet. Then he sprinkled blood against the altar on all sides.[j] [25]He took the fat,[k] the fat tail, all the fat around the inner parts, the covering of the liver, both kidneys and their fat and the right thigh. [26]Then from the basket of bread made without yeast, which was before the LORD, he took a cake of bread, and one made with oil, and a wafer;[l] he put these on the fat portions and on the right thigh. [27]He put all these in the hands of Aaron and his sons and waved them before the LORD[m] as

---

7:37 [t]S Ex 29:31
7:38 [u]Lev 26:46; Nu 36:13; Dt 4:5; 29:1 [v]S Ex 19:11 [w]S Lev 1:2
8:2 [x]S Ex 28:1; S Lev 1:5 [y]Ex 28:2,4,43; S 39:27 [z]Ex 30:23-25,30 [a]S Ex 30:10 [b]ver 18,22 [c]Ex 29:2-3
8:3 [d]Nu 8:9
8:5 [e]Ex 29:1
8:6 [f]S Ex 29:4; S 30:19;
8:7 [g]Ex 28:4
8:8 [h]S Ex 25:7 [i]S Ex 28:30
8:9 [j]S Ex 39:28 [k]S Ex 28:36 [l]S Ex 28:2; Lev 21:10
8:10 [m]ver 2 [n]S Ex 30:26 [o]S Ex 26:1
8:11 [p]S Ex 30:29
8:12 [q]S Lev 7:36 [r]S Ex 30:30
8:13 [s]S Ex 28:40 [t]S Ex 28:4,39; 39:27 [u]Lev 21:10
8:14 [v]S Lev 4:3

[w]S Ex 30:10 [x]S Lev 4:15
8:15 [y]S Lev 4:18 [z]S Lev 4:7 [a]Heb 9:22 [b]Eze 43:20
8:17 [c]S Lev 4:11 [d]S Lev 4:12
8:18 [e]S ver 2
8:20 [f]S Lev 1:8
8:22 [g]S ver 2 [h]S Lev 4:15
8:23 [i]Lev 14:14, 25
8:24 [/]Heb 9:18-22
8:25 [k]Lev 3:3-5
8:26 [l]S Lev 2:4
8:27 [m]Nu 5:25

8:2 *their garments.* See Ex 39:1-31; 40:12-16. The garments that the high priest was to wear when he ministered are detailed in Ex 28:4-43 (see notes there). *anointing oil.* See note on Ex 25:6. The oil was used to anoint the tabernacle, sacred objects and consecrated priests (vv. 10-12,30). It was later used to anoint leaders and kings (1Sa 10:1; 16:13). See also note on Ex 29:7.
8:6 *washed them with water.* In the bronze basin (see v. 11) in the courtyard of the tabernacle (see Ex 30:17-21).
8:7 *ephod.* See note on Ex 28:6.
8:8 *Urim and Thummim.* See notes on Ex 28:30; 1Sa 2:28.

8:9 *sacred diadem.* See note on Ex 39:30.
8:11 *seven times.* See note on 4:6.
8:12 *oil on Aaron's head.* See Ps 133.
8:14 *sin offering.* See 4:3-11 and notes. The consecration service included a sin offering for atonement, a burnt offering for worship (v. 18) and a "ram for ordination" (v. 22), whose blood was applied to the high priest on his right ear, thumb and toe (v. 23). After this was done, Aaron offered sacrifices for the people (9:15-21). Then he blessed the people in his capacity as priest, and the Lord accepted his ministry with the sign of miraculous fire (9:23-24). *laid their hands on.* See notes on 1:3; Ex 29:15.

a wave offering. 28Then Moses took them from their hands and burned them on the altar on top of the burnt offering as an ordination offering, a pleasing aroma, an offering made to the LORD by fire. 29He also took the breast—Moses' share of the ordination ram *n*—and waved it before the LORD as a wave offering, as the LORD commanded Moses.

30Then Moses *o* took some of the anointing oil and some of the blood from the altar and sprinkled them on Aaron and his garments *p* and on his sons and their garments. So he consecrated *q* Aaron and his garments and his sons and their garments.

31Moses then said to Aaron and his sons, "Cook the meat at the entrance to the Tent of Meeting *r* and eat it there with the bread from the basket of ordination offerings, as I commanded, saying, *q* 'Aaron and his sons are to eat it.' 32Then burn up the rest of the meat and the bread. 33Do not leave the entrance to the Tent of Meeting for seven days, until the days of your ordination are completed, for your ordination will last seven days. *s* 34What has been done today was commanded by the LORD *t* to make atonement for you. 35You must stay at the entrance to the Tent of Meeting day and night for seven days and do what the LORD requires, *u* so you will not die; for that is what I have been commanded." 36So Aaron and his sons did everything the LORD commanded through Moses.

The Priests Begin Their Ministry

9 On the eighth day *v* Moses summoned Aaron and his sons and the elders *w* of Israel. 2He said to Aaron, "Take a bull calf for your sin offering and a ram for your burnt offering, both without defect, and present them before the LORD. 3Then say to the Israelites: 'Take a male goat *x* for a sin offering, *y* a calf *z* and a lamb *a*—both a year old and without defect—for a burnt offering, 4and an ox *r b* and a ram for a fellowship offering *s c* to sacrifice before the LORD, together with a grain offering mixed with oil. For today the LORD will appear to you. *d* '"

5They took the things Moses commanded to the front of the Tent of Meeting, and the entire assembly came near and

stood before the LORD. 6Then Moses said, "This is what the LORD has commanded you to do, so that the glory of the LORD *e* may appear to you."

7Moses said to Aaron, "Come to the altar and sacrifice your sin offering and your burnt offering and make atonement for yourself and the people; *f* sacrifice the offering that is for the people and make atonement for them, as the LORD has commanded. *g* "

8So Aaron came to the altar and slaughtered the calf as a sin offering *h* for himself. 9His sons brought the blood to him, *i* and he dipped his finger into the blood and put it on the horns of the altar; the rest of the blood he poured out at the base of the altar. *j k* 10On the altar he burned the fat, the kidneys and the covering of the liver from the sin offering, as the LORD commanded Moses; 11the flesh and the hide *l* he burned up outside the camp. *m*

12Then he slaughtered the burnt offering. *n* His sons handed him the blood, *o* and he sprinkled it against the altar on all sides. 13They handed him the burnt offering piece by piece, including the head, and he burned them on the altar. *p* 14He washed the inner parts and the legs and burned them on top of the burnt offering on the altar. *q*

15Aaron then brought the offering that was for the people. *r* He took the goat for the people's sin offering and slaughtered it and offered it for a sin offering as he did with the first one.

16He brought the burnt offering and offered it in the prescribed way. *s* 17He also brought the grain offering, took a handful of it and burned it on the altar in addition to the morning's burnt offering. *t*

18He slaughtered the ox and the ram as the fellowship offering for the people. *u* His sons handed him the blood, and he sprinkled it against the altar on all sides. 19But the fat portions of the ox and the ram—the fat tail, the layer of fat, the kidneys and the covering of the liver— 20these they laid on the breasts, and then Aaron burned the fat on the altar. 21Aaron waved the breasts

8:29
*n*Lev 7:31-34
8:30 *o*S Ex 28:1
*p*S Ex 28:2
*q*S Lev 7:36
8:31 *r*S Lev 6:16
8:33 *s*Lev 14:8;
15:13,28;
Nu 19:11;
Eze 43:25
8:34 *t*Heb 7:16
8:35 *u*Lev 18:30;
22:9; Nu 3:7;
9:19; Dt 11:1;
1Ki 2:3;
Eze 48:11;
Zec 3:7
9:1 *v*Eze 43:27
*w*S Lev 4:15
9:3 *x*S Lev 4:3
*y*ver 15;
Lev 10:16 *z*ver 8
*a*S Lev 4:32
9:4 *b*Lev 4:10
*c*S Ex 32:6
*d*Ex 29:43

9:6 *e*S Ex 16:7
9:7 *f*Lev 16:6
*g*S Ex 30:10;
Heb 5:1,3; 7:27
9:8 *h*Lev 4:1-12;
10:19
9:9 *i*ver 12,18
*j*S Ex 29:12
*k*Eze 43:20
9:11 *l*S Lev 4:11
*m*S Lev 4:12
9:12 *n*Lev 10:19
*o*S ver 9
9:13 *p*S Lev 1:8
9:14 *q*S Lev 1:9
9:15
*r*Lev 4:27-31
9:16 *s*Lev 1:1-13
9:17 *t*Lev 3:5
9:18 *u*Lev 3:1-11

q31 Or *I was commanded:*   *r4* The Hebrew word can include both male and female; also in verses 18 and 19.   *s4* Traditionally *peace offering;* also in verses 18 and 22

8:28 *on top of the burnt offering.* See note on 3:5.
8:31 *saying, 'Aaron and his sons are to eat it.'* Quoted from Ex 29:32.
9:1 *eighth day.* After the seven days of ordination (8:33).
9:2 *sin offering.* See notes on 4:3,5. *burnt offering.* See note on 1:3.

9:4 *fellowship offering.* See note on 3:1. *grain offering.* See note on 2:1. *LORD will appear.* See vv. 6,23; see also note on Ge 12:7.
9:17 *morning's burnt offering.* See Ex 29:38–42.
9:21 *wave offering.* See note on 7:30–32.

and the right thigh before the LORD as a wave offering, [v] as Moses commanded.

[22] Then Aaron lifted his hands toward the people and blessed them. [w] And having sacrificed the sin offering, the burnt offering and the fellowship offering, he stepped down.

[23] Moses and Aaron then went into the Tent of Meeting. [x] When they came out, they blessed the people; and the glory of the LORD [y] appeared to all the people. [24] Fire [z] came out from the presence of the LORD and consumed the burnt offering and the fat portions on the altar. And when all the people saw it, they shouted for joy and fell facedown. [a]

The Death of Nadab and Abihu

10 Aaron's sons Nadab and Abihu [b] took their censers, [c] put fire in them [d] and added incense; [e] and they offered unauthorized fire before the LORD, [f] contrary to his command. [g] [2] So fire came out [h] from the presence of the LORD and consumed them, [i] and they died before the LORD. [j] [3] Moses then said to Aaron, "This is what the LORD spoke of when he said:

" 'Among those who approach me [k]
I will show myself holy; [l]
in the sight of all the people
I will be honored. [m] ' "

Aaron remained silent.

[4] Moses summoned Mishael and Elzaphan, [n] sons of Aaron's uncle Uzziel, [o] and said to them, "Come here; carry your cousins outside the camp, [p] away from the front of the sanctuary. [q]" [5] So they came and carried them, still in their tunics, [r] outside the camp, as Moses ordered.

[6] Then Moses said to Aaron and his sons Eleazar and Ithamar, [s] "Do not let your hair become unkempt, [t] [t] and do not tear your clothes, [u] or you will die and the LORD will be angry with the whole com-

munity. [v] But your relatives, all the house of Israel, may mourn [w] for those the LORD has destroyed by fire. [7] Do not leave the entrance to the Tent of Meeting [x] or you will die, because the LORD's anointing oil [y] is on you." So they did as Moses said.

[8] Then the LORD said to Aaron, [9] "You and your sons are not to drink wine [z] or other fermented drink [a] whenever you go into the Tent of Meeting, or you will die. This is a lasting ordinance [b] for the generations to come. [10] You must distinguish between the holy and the common, between the unclean and the clean, [c] [11] and you must teach [d] the Israelites all the decrees the LORD has given them through Moses. [e]"

[12] Moses said to Aaron and his remaining sons, Eleazar and Ithamar, "Take the grain offering [f] left over from the offerings made to the LORD by fire and eat it prepared without yeast beside the altar, [g] for it is most holy. [13] Eat it in a holy place, [h] because it is your share and your sons' share of the offerings made to the LORD by fire; for so I have been commanded. [i] [14] But you and your sons and your daughters may eat the breast [j] that was waved and the thigh that was presented. Eat them in a ceremonially clean place; [k] they have been given to you and your children as your share of the Israelites' fellowship offerings. [u] [15] The thigh [l] that was presented and the breast that was waved must be brought with the fat portions of the offerings made by fire, to be waved before the LORD as a wave offering. [m] This will be the regular share for you

Cross references (center column)

9:21 [v] S Ex 29:24, 26
9:22 [w] S Ge 48:20; S Ex 39:43; Lk 24:50
9:23 [x] S Ex 40:2 [y] S Ex 24:16
9:24 [z] S Ex 19:18; Jdg 6:21; 13:20 [a] 1Ki 18:39
10:1 [b] Ex 6:23; 24:1; 28:1; Nu 3:2-4; 26:61; 1Ch 6:3 [c] Nu 16:46; 1Ki 7:50; 2Ki 25:15; 2Ch 4:22; Jer 52:19; Eze 8:11 [d] Lev 16:12; Nu 16:7,18; Isa 6:6 [e] S Ex 30:9 [f] ver 2; Lev 16:1 [g] Ex 30:9
10:2 [h] Ps 106:18 [i] Nu 11:1; 16:35; Ps 2:12; 50:3; Isa 29:6 [j] S Ge 19:24; S 38:7; Nu 16:35; 1Ch 24:2; Job 1:16
10:3 [k] Ex 19:22 [l] Ex 30:29; Lev 21:6; 22:32; Nu 16:5; 20:13; Isa 5:16; Eze 28:22; 38:16 [m] Ex 14:4; Isa 44:23; 49:3; 55:5; 60:21
10:4 [n] S Ex 6:22 [o] Ex 6:18 [p] Ac 5:6, 9,10 [q] S Ex 25:8
10:5 [r] S Lev 8:13
10:6 [s] S Ex 6:23 [t] Lev 13:45; 21:10; Nu 5:18 [u] Jer 41:5; S Mk 14:63

[v] Nu 1:53; 16:22; Jos 7:1; 22:18 [w] Ge 50:3,10; Nu 20:29; 1Sa 25:1
10:7 [x] S Ex 25:8 [y] S Ex 28:41
10:9 [z] Ge 9:21; Ex 29:40; Lev 23:13; Nu 15:5; Dt 28:39; Isa 5:22; 28:1; 29:9; 56:12; Jer 35:6; Hos 4:11; Hab 2:15-16 [a] Nu 6:3; 28:7; Dt 14:26; 29:6;

Jdg 13:4; Pr 20:1; 23:29-35; 31:4-7; Isa 28:7; Eze 44:21; Mic 2:11; Lk 1:15; S Eph 5:18; 1Ti 3:3; Tit 1:7 [b] S Ex 12:14
10:10 [c] S Ge 7:2; S Lev 6:27; 14:57; 20:25; Eze 22:26 10:11 [d] 2Ch 15:3; 17:7; Ezr 7:25; Ne 8:7; Mal 2:7 [e] Dt 17:10,11; 24:8; 25:1; 33:10; Pr 4:27; Hag 2:11; Mal 2:7 10:12 [f] S Ex 29:41 [g] Lev 6:14-18 10:13 [h] S Lev 6:16 [i] Eze 42:13
10:14 [j] Nu 5:9 [k] S Ex 29:31; S Lev 4:12 10:15 [l] S Lev 7:34 [m] S Ex 29:28

[t] 6 Or Do not uncover your heads   [u] 14 Traditionally peace offerings

---

9:22 blessed. The Aaronic benediction, a threefold blessing, is given in Nu 6:23–26. Cf. the threefold apostolic benediction in 2Co 13:14.

9:23 glory of the LORD. See v. 6; cf. the display of the Lord's glory at the erection of the tabernacle (Ex 40:34–35); cf. also God's acceptance of sacrifices at the dedication of Solomon's temple (2Ch 7:1).

9:24 Fire came out from the presence of the LORD. See 10:2; 1Ki 18:38.

10:1 censers. Ceremonial vessels containing hot coals and used for burning incense (see 16:12–13; 2Ch 26:19; Rev 8:3–4).

10:2 died before the LORD. Aaron's older sons are mentioned also in Ex 6:23; 24:1,9; 28:1; Nu 3:2–4; 26:60–61; 1Ch 6:3; 24:1–2. They are regularly remembered as having

died before the Lord and as having had no sons. Their death was tragic and at first seems harsh, but no more so than that of Ananias and Sapphira (Ac 5:1–11). In both cases a new era was being inaugurated (cf. also the judgment on Achan, Jos 7, and on Uzzah, 2Sa 6:1–7). The new community had to be made aware that it existed for God, not vice versa.

10:6 tear your clothes. See 21:10; see also note on Ge 44:13.

10:7 Do not leave. To join the mourners (see 21:11–12).

10:10 between the holy and the common. The distinction between what was holy (sacred) and what was common (profane) was carefully maintained (see Eze 22:26; 42:20; 44:23; 48:14–15).

10:12–15 See 7:28–36; Nu 18:8–20; Dt 18:1–5.

and your children, as the LORD has commanded."

[16]When Moses inquired about the goat of the sin offering[n] and found that it had been burned up, he was angry with Eleazar and Ithamar, Aaron's remaining sons, and asked, [17]"Why didn't you eat the sin offering[o] in the sanctuary area? It is most holy; it was given to you to take away the guilt[p] of the community by making atonement for them before the LORD. [18]Since its blood was not taken into the Holy Place,[q] you should have eaten the goat in the sanctuary area, as I commanded.[r]"

[19]Aaron replied to Moses, "Today they sacrificed their sin offering and their burnt offering[s] before the LORD, but such things as this have happened to me. Would the LORD have been pleased if I had eaten the sin offering today?" [20]When Moses heard this, he was satisfied.

Clean and Unclean Food

11:1–23pp — Dt 14:3–20

11 The LORD said to Moses and Aaron, [2]"Say to the Israelites: 'Of all the animals that live on land, these are the ones you may eat:[t] [3]You may eat any animal that has a split hoof completely divided and that chews the cud.

[4]"'There are some that only chew the cud or only have a split hoof, but you must not eat them.[u] The camel, though it chews the cud, does not have a split hoof; it is ceremonially unclean for you. [5]The coney,[v] though it chews the cud, does not have a split hoof; it is unclean for you. [6]The rabbit, though it chews the cud, does not have a split hoof; it is unclean for you. [7]And the pig,[v] though it has a split hoof completely divided, does not chew the cud; it is unclean for you. [8]You must not eat their meat or touch their carcasses; they are unclean for you.[w]

[9]"'Of all the creatures living in the water of the seas and the streams, you may eat any that have fins and scales. [10]But all creatures in the seas or streams that do not have fins and scales—whether among all the swarming things or among all the other living creatures in the water—you are to detest.[x] [11]And since you are to detest them, you must not eat their meat and you must detest their carcasses.[y] [12]Anything living in the water that does not have fins and scales is to be detestable to you.[z]

[13]"'These are the birds you are to detest and not eat because they are detestable: the eagle, the vulture, the black vulture, [14]the red kite, any kind[a] of black kite, [15]any kind of raven,[b] [16]the horned owl, the screech owl, the gull, any kind of hawk, [17]the little owl, the cormorant, the great owl, [18]the white owl,[c] the desert owl, the osprey, [19]the stork,[d] any kind[e] of heron, the hoopoe and the bat.[w][f]

[20]"'All flying insects that walk on all fours are to be detestable to you.[g] [21]There are, however, some winged creatures that walk on all fours that you may eat: those that have jointed legs for hopping on the ground. [22]Of these you may eat any kind of locust,[h] katydid, cricket or grasshopper. [23]But all other winged creatures that have four legs you are to detest.

[24]"'You will make yourselves unclean by these;[i] whoever touches their carcasses will be unclean till evening.[j] [25]Whoever picks up one of their carcasses must wash his clothes,[k] and he will be unclean till evening.[l]

[26]"'Every animal that has a split hoof not completely divided or that does not chew the cud is unclean for you; whoever touches the carcass of any of them will be unclean. [27]Of all the animals that walk on

---

Cross references (center column):

10:16 [n]S Lev 9:3
10:17
[o]Lev 6:24-30; Eze 42:13
[p]S Ex 28:38
10:18
[q]S Lev 4:18; 6:26
[r]S Lev 6:17
10:19 [s]Lev 9:12
11:2
[t]Ac 10:12-14
11:4 [u]Ac 10:14
11:7 [v]Isa 65:4; 66:3,17
11:8 [w]S Lev 5:2; Heb 9:10

11:10 [x]ver 12
11:11 [y]S Lev 5:2
11:12 [z]ver 10
11:14 [a]S Ge 1:11
11:15 [b]S Ge 8:7
11:18 [c]Isa 13:21; 14:23; 34:11,13; Zep 2:14
11:19 [d]Zec 5:9
[e]S Ge 1:11
[f]Isa 2:20
11:20 [g]Ac 10:14
11:22 [h]Mt 3:4; Mk 1:6
11:24 [i]S Lev 5:2
[j]ver 27-40; Lev 13:3; 14:46; 15:5; 22:6; Nu 19:7,19
11:25 [k]ver 28; S Ex 19:10; Lev 13:6; 14:8, 47; 15:5; 16:26; Nu 8:7; 19:7
[l]Lev 13:34; Nu 19:8; 31:24

---

[v]*5* That is, the hyrax or rock badger   [w]*19* The precise identification of some of the birds, insects and animals in this chapter is uncertain.

10:18 *Since its blood was not taken into the Holy Place, you should have eaten.* There were two types of sin offerings: (1) those in which the blood was sprinkled within the tabernacle, and (2) those in which it was sprinkled only on the great altar. Portions of the second type normally should have been eaten (see note on 4:5). But Moses was satisfied when he learned that Aaron had acted sincerely and not in negligence or rebellion (vv. 19–20).

10:19 *such things as this have happened to me.* Perhaps referring to the death of his two oldest sons (v. 2), for which he mourned by fasting. Or possibly something had occurred that made him ceremonially unclean.

11:2 *the ones you may eat.* Ch. 11 is closely paralleled in Dt 14:3–21 but is more extensive. The animals acceptable for human consumption were those that chewed the cud and had a split hoof (v. 3). Of marine life, only creatures with fins and scales were permissible (v. 9). Birds and insects are also

covered in the instructions (vv. 13–23). The distinction between clean and unclean food was as old as the time of Noah (Ge 7:2). The main reason for the laws concerning clean and unclean food is the same as for other laws concerning the clean and unclean—to preserve the sanctity of Israel as God's holy people (see v. 44). Some hold that certain animal life was considered unclean for health considerations, but it is difficult to substantiate this idea. Uncleanness typified sin and defilement. For the uncleanness of disease and bodily discharges see chs. 13–15.

11:6 *rabbit.* Does not technically chew the cud with regurgitation. The apparent chewing movements of the rabbit caused it to be classified popularly with cud chewers.

11:20 *all fours.* Although insects have six legs, perhaps people in ancient times did not count as ordinary legs the two large hind legs used for jumping.

all fours, those that walk on their paws are unclean for you; whoever touches their carcasses will be unclean till evening. 28Anyone who picks up their carcasses must wash his clothes, and he will be unclean till evening. *m* They are unclean for you.

29" 'Of the animals that move about on the ground, these are unclean for you: *n* the weasel, the rat, *o* any kind of great lizard, 30the gecko, the monitor lizard, the wall lizard, the skink and the chameleon. 31Of all those that move along the ground, these are unclean for you. Whoever touches them when they are dead will be unclean till evening. 32When one of them dies and falls on something, that article, whatever its use, will be unclean, whether it is made of wood, cloth, hide or sackcloth. *p* Put it in water; it will be unclean till evening, and then it will be clean. 33If one of them falls into a clay pot, everything in it will be unclean, and you must break the pot. *q* 34Any food that could be eaten but has water on it from such a pot is unclean, and any liquid that could be drunk from it is unclean. 35Anything that one of their carcasses falls on becomes unclean; an oven or cooking pot must be broken up. They are unclean, and you are to regard them as unclean. 36A spring, however, or a cistern for collecting water remains clean, but anyone who touches one of these carcasses is unclean. 37If a carcass falls on any seeds that are to be planted, they remain clean. 38But if water has been put on the seed and a carcass falls on it, it is unclean for you.

39" 'If an animal that you are allowed to eat dies, *r* anyone who touches the carcass *s* will be unclean till evening. 40Anyone who eats some of the carcass *t* must wash his clothes, and he will be unclean till evening. *u* Anyone who picks up the carcass must wash his clothes, and he will be unclean till evening.

41" 'Every creature that moves about on

the ground is detestable; it is not to be eaten. 42You are not to eat any creature that moves about on the ground, whether it moves on its belly or walks on all fours or on many feet; it is detestable. 43Do not defile yourselves by any of these creatures. *v* Do not make yourselves unclean by means of them or be made unclean by them. 44I am the LORD your God; *w* consecrate yourselves *x* and be holy, *y* because I am holy. *z* Do not make yourselves unclean by any creature that moves about on the ground. *a* 45I am the LORD who brought you up out of Egypt *b* to be your God; *c* therefore be holy, because I am holy. *d*

46" 'These are the regulations concerning animals, birds, every living thing that moves in the water and every creature that moves about on the ground. 47You must distinguish between the unclean and the clean, between living creatures that may be eaten and those that may not be eaten. *e* '"

Purification After Childbirth

12 The LORD said to Moses, 2"Say to the Israelites: 'A woman who becomes pregnant and gives birth to a son will be ceremonially unclean for seven days, just as she is unclean during her monthly period. *f* 3On the eighth day *g* the boy is to be circumcised. *h* 4Then the woman must wait thirty-three days to be purified from her bleeding. She must not touch anything sacred or go to the sanctuary until the days of her purification are over. 5If she gives birth to a daughter, for two weeks the woman will be unclean, as during her period. Then she must wait sixty-six days to be purified from her bleeding.

6" 'When the days of her purification for a son or daughter are over, *i* she is to bring to the priest at the entrance to the Tent of Meeting a year-old lamb *j* for a burnt offering and a young pigeon or a dove for a sin

11:28 *m*Heb 9:10
11:29 *n*ver 41
*o*Isa 66:17
11:32
*p*Lev 15:12;
Nu 19:18; 31:20
11:33
*q*S Lev 6:28
11:39
*r*Lev 17:15; 22:8;
Dt 14:21;
Eze 4:14; 44:31
*s*ver 40;
Lev 22:4;
Nu 19:11
11:40 *t*S ver 39
*u*ver 25;
Lev 14:8; 17:15;
22:8; Eze 44:31;
Heb 9:10

11:43 *v*ver 44;
Lev 20:25; 22:5
11:44 *w*S Ex 6:2,
7; 20:2; Isa 43:3;
51:15; Eze 20:5
*x*S Ex 19:10;
Lev 20:7;
Nu 15:40;
Jos 3:5; 7:13;
1Ch 15:12;
2Ch 29:5; 35:6
*y*S Ex 22:31;
S Dt 14:2
*z*S Ex 31:13;
Lev 19:2; 20:7;
Jos 24:19;
1Sa 2:2; Job 6:10;
Ps 99:3; Eph 1:4;
1Th 4:7;
1Pe 1:15,16*
*a*S ver 43
11:45
*b*Lev 25:38,55
*c*S Ge 17:7
*d*S Ex 19:6;
1Pe 1:16*
11:47 *e*Lev 10:10
12:2 *f*Lev 15:19;
18:19; Isa 64:6;
Eze 18:6; 22:10;
36:17
12:3 *g*S Ex 22:30
*h*S Ge 17:10;
S Lk 1:59
12:6 *i*Lk 2:22
*j*Ex 29:38;
Lev 23:12;
Nu 6:12,14; 7:15

11:36 *cistern for collecting water.* The use of waterproof plaster for lining cisterns dug in the ground was an important factor in helping the Israelites to settle the dry areas of Canaan after the conquest (cf. 2Ch 26:10).
11:41 *ground.* Verses 29–30 identify the animals that move about (or swarm) on the ground.
11:44 *be holy, because I am holy.* Holiness is the key theme of Leviticus, ringing like a refrain in various forms throughout the book (e.g., v. 45; 19:2; 20:7,26; 21:8,15; 22:9,16,32). The word "holy" appears more often in Leviticus than in any other book of the Bible. Israel was to be totally consecrated to God. Her holiness was to be expressed in every aspect of her life, to the extent that all of life had a certain ceremonial quality. Because of who God is and what

he has done (v. 45), his people must dedicate themselves fully to him (cf. Mt 5:48). See Ro 12:1.
11:45 *brought ... out of Egypt.* A refrain found 8 more times in Leviticus (19:36; 22:33; 23:43; 25:38,42,55; 26:13,45) and nearly 60 times in 18 other books of the OT.
11:46–47 A summary of ch. 11.
12:2 *unclean.* The uncleanness came from the bleeding (vv. 4–5,7), not from the birth. It is not clear why the period of uncleanness after the birth of a baby boy (40 days) was half the period for a girl (80 days). *monthly period.* See 15:19–24.
12:3 See notes on Ge 17:10,12.
12:6 *burnt offering.* See note on 1:3. *sin offering.* See notes on 4:3,5.

offering. *k* 7He shall offer them before the LORD to make atonement for her, and then she will be ceremonially clean from her flow of blood.

" 'These are the regulations for the woman who gives birth to a boy or a girl. 8If she cannot afford a lamb, she is to bring two doves or two young pigeons, *l* one for a burnt offering and the other for a sin offering. *m* In this way the priest will make atonement for her, and she will be clean. *n* ' "

Regulations About Infectious Skin Diseases

13 The LORD said to Moses and Aaron, 2"When anyone has a swelling *o* or a rash or a bright spot *p* on his skin that may become an infectious skin disease, *x q* he must be brought to Aaron the priest *r* or to one of his sons *y* who is a priest. 3The priest is to examine the sore on his skin, and if the hair in the sore has turned white and the sore appears to be more than skin deep, *z* it is an infectious skin disease. When the priest examines him, he shall pronounce him ceremonially unclean. *s* 4If the spot *t* on his skin is white but does not appear to be more than skin deep and the hair in it has not turned white, the priest is to put the infected person in isolation for seven days. *u* 5On the seventh day *v* the priest is to examine him, *w* and if he sees that the sore is unchanged and has not spread in the skin, he is to keep him in isolation another seven days. 6On the seventh day the priest is to examine him again, and if the sore has faded and has not spread in the skin, the priest shall pronounce him clean; *x* it is only a rash. The man must wash his clothes, *y* and he will be clean. *z* 7But if the rash does spread in his skin after he has shown himself to the priest to be pronounced clean, he must appear before the priest again. *a* 8The priest is to examine him, and if the rash has spread in the skin, he shall pronounce him unclean; it is an infectious disease.

9"When anyone has an infectious skin

disease, he must be brought to the priest. 10The priest is to examine him, and if there is a white swelling in the skin that has turned the hair white and if there is raw flesh in the swelling, 11it is a chronic skin disease *b* and the priest shall pronounce him unclean. He is not to put him in isolation, because he is already unclean.

12"If the disease breaks out all over his skin and, so far as the priest can see, it covers all the skin of the infected person from head to foot, 13the priest is to examine him, and if the disease has covered his whole body, he shall pronounce that person clean. Since it has all turned white, he is clean. 14But whenever raw flesh appears on him, he will be unclean. 15When the priest sees the raw flesh, he shall pronounce him unclean. The raw flesh is unclean; he has an infectious disease. *c* 16Should the raw flesh change and turn white, he must go to the priest. 17The priest is to examine him, and if the sores have turned white, the priest shall pronounce the infected person clean; *d* then he will be clean.

18"When someone has a boil *e* on his skin and it heals, 19and in the place where the boil was, a white swelling or reddish-white *f* spot *g* appears, he must present himself to the priest. 20The priest is to examine it, and if it appears to be more than skin deep and the hair in it has turned white, the priest shall pronounce him unclean. It is an infectious skin disease *h* that has broken out where the boil was. 21But if, when the priest examines it, there is no white hair in it and it is not more than skin deep and has faded, then the priest is to put him in isolation for seven days. 22If it is spreading in the skin, the priest shall pronounce him unclean; it is infectious. 23But if the spot is unchanged and has not spread, it is only a scar from the boil, and the priest shall pronounce him clean. *i*

12:6 *k*Lev 5:7
12:8 *l*S Ge 15:9;
Lev 14:22
*m*Lev 5:7;
Lk 2:22-24*
*n*S Lev 4:26
13:2 *o*ver 10,19,
28,43 *p*ver 4,38,
39; Lev 14:56
*q*ver 3,9,15;
S Ex 4:6;
Lev 14:3,32;
Nu 5:2; Dt 24:8
*r*Dt 24:8
13:3 *s*ver 8,11,
20,30; Lev 21:1;
Nu 9:6
13:4 *t*S ver 2
*u*ver 5,23,26,33,
46; Lev 14:38;
Nu 12:14,15;
Dt 24:9
13:5 *v*Lev 14:9
*w*ver 27,32,34,51
13:6 *x*ver 13,17,
23,28,34; Mt 8:3;
Lk 5:12-14
*y*S Lev 11:25
*z*Lev 11:25; 14:8,
9,20,48; 15:8;
Nu 8:7
13:7 *a*Lk 5:14

13:11 *b*S Ex 4:6;
S Lev 14:8;
S Nu 12:10;
Mt 8:2
13:15 *c*S ver 2
13:17 *d*S ver 6
13:18 *e*S Ex 9:9
13:19 *f*ver 24,42;
Lev 14:37 *g*S ver 2
13:20 *h*ver 2
13:23 *i*S ver 6

---

*x*2 Traditionally *leprosy;* the Hebrew word was used for various diseases affecting the skin—not necessarily leprosy; also elsewhere in this chapter.   *y*2 Or *descendants*   *z*3 Or *be lower than the rest of the skin;* also elsewhere in this chapter

---

12:8 See 1:14–17 and note on 1:14; see also 5:7–10; 14:21–22; and especially Lk 2:24 (Mary's offering for Jesus).

13:1–46 This section deals with preliminary symptoms of skin diseases (vv. 1–8) and then with the symptoms of (1) raw flesh (vv. 9–17), (2) boils (vv. 18–23), (3) burns (vv. 24–28), (4) sores on the head or chin (vv. 29–37), (5) white spots (vv. 38–39) and (6) skin diseases on the head that cause baldness (vv. 40–44).

13:2 *infectious skin disease.* Occurs often in chs. 13–14; see also 22:4; Nu 5:2. Since it is unlikely that ancient people would have understood the concept of infectiousness, this

rendering is questionable; the Hebrew should perhaps be translated simply "skin disease." Such diseases show visible defects that could function aptly as a symbol for defilement—as could mildew (cf. vv. 47–59). *disease.* See NIV text note; see also 22:4–8; Nu 5:2–4; Dt 24:8–9. The symptoms described, and the fact that they may rapidly change (vv. 6,26–27,32–37), show that the disease was not true leprosy (Hansen's disease). They apply also to a number of other diseases, as well as to rather harmless skin eruptions. The Hebrew word translated "infectious skin disease" can also mean "mildew" (v. 47; 14:34; and especially 14:57).

24"When someone has a burn on his skin and a reddish-white or white spot appears in the raw flesh of the burn, 25the priest is to examine the spot, and if the hair in it has turned white, and it appears to be more than skin deep, it is an infectious disease that has broken out in the burn. The priest shall pronounce him unclean; it is an infectious skin disease.*j* 26But if the priest examines it and there is no white hair in the spot and if it is not more than skin deep and has faded, then the priest is to put him in isolation for seven days.*k* 27On the seventh day the priest is to examine him,*l* and if it is spreading in the skin, the priest shall pronounce him unclean; it is an infectious skin disease. 28If, however, the spot is unchanged and has not spread in the skin but has faded, it is a swelling from the burn, and the priest shall pronounce him clean; it is only a scar from the burn.*m*

29"If a man or woman has a sore on the head*n* or on the chin, 30the priest is to examine the sore, and if it appears to be more than skin deep and the hair in it is yellow and thin, the priest shall pronounce that person unclean; it is an itch, an infectious disease of the head or chin. 31But if, when the priest examines this kind of sore, it does not seem to be more than skin deep and there is no black hair in it, then the priest is to put the infected person in isolation for seven days.*o* 32On the seventh day the priest is to examine the sore,*p* and if the itch has not spread and there is no yellow hair in it and it does not appear to be more than skin deep, 33he must be shaved except for the diseased area, and the priest is to keep him in isolation another seven days. 34On the seventh day the priest is to examine the itch,*q* and if it has not spread in the skin and appears to be no more than skin deep, the priest shall pronounce him clean. He must wash his clothes, and he will be clean.*r* 35But if the itch does spread in the skin after he is pronounced clean, 36the priest is to examine him, and if the itch has spread in the skin, the priest does not need to look for yellow hair; the person is unclean.*s* 37If, however, in his judgment it is unchanged and black hair has grown in it, the itch is

healed. He is clean, and the priest shall pronounce him clean.

38"When a man or woman has white spots on the skin, 39the priest is to examine them, and if the spots are dull white, it is a harmless rash that has broken out on the skin; that person is clean.

40"When a man has lost his hair and is bald,*t* he is clean. 41If he has lost his hair from the front of his scalp and has a bald forehead, he is clean. 42But if he has a reddish-white sore on his bald head or forehead, it is an infectious disease breaking out on his head or forehead. 43The priest is to examine him, and if the swollen sore on his head or forehead is reddish-white like an infectious skin disease, 44the man is diseased and is unclean. The priest shall pronounce him unclean because of the sore on his head.

45"The person with such an infectious disease must wear torn clothes,*u* let his hair be unkempt,*a* cover the lower part of his face*v* and cry out, 'Unclean! Unclean!'*w* 46As long as he has the infection he remains unclean. He must live alone; he must live outside the camp.*x*

Regulations About Mildew

47"If any clothing is contaminated with mildew—any woolen or linen clothing, 48any woven or knitted material of linen or wool, any leather or anything made of leather— 49and if the contamination in the clothing, or leather, or woven or knitted material, or any leather article, is greenish or reddish, it is a spreading mildew and must be shown to the priest.*y* 50The priest is to examine the mildew*z* and isolate the affected article for seven days. 51On the seventh day he is to examine it,*a* and if the mildew has spread in the clothing, or the woven or knitted material, or the leather, whatever its use, it is a destructive mildew; the article is unclean.*b* 52He must burn up the clothing, or the woven or knitted material of wool or linen, or any leather article that has the contamination in it, because the mildew is destructive; the article must be burned up.*c*

53"But if, when the priest examines it,

13:25 *j*ver 11
13:26 *k*S ver 4
13:27 *l*S ver 5
13:28 *m*S ver 2
13:29 *n*ver 43,44
13:31 *o*ver 4
13:32 *p*S ver 5
13:34 *q*S ver 5
*r*S Lev 11:25
13:36 *s*ver 30

13:40 *t*Lev 21:5;
2Ki 2:23;
Isa 3:24; 15:2;
22:12; Eze 27:31;
29:18; Am 8:10;
Mic 1:16
13:45
*u*S Lev 10:6
*v*Eze 24:17,22;
Mic 3:7
*w*S Lev 5:2;
La 4:15; Lk 17:12
13:46 *x*Nu 5:1-4;
12:14; 2Ki 7:3;
15:5
13:49 *y*Mk 1:44
13:50 *z*Eze 44:23
13:51 *a*S ver 5
*b*Lev 14:44
13:52 *c*ver 55,57   *a*45 Or *clothes, uncover his head*

13:45—46 The ceremonially unclean were excluded from the camp (the area around the tabernacle and courtyard), where the Israelites lived in tents. Later, no unclean person was allowed in the temple area, where he could mingle with others. Not only was God present in the tabernacle in a special way, but also in the camp (Nu 5:3; Dt 23:14). Therefore unclean people were not to be in the camp (see Nu 5:1–4; 12:14–15, Miriam; 31:19–24; see also Lev 10:4–5;

Nu 15:35–36; 2Ki 7:3–4; 2Ch 26:21, Uzziah). As a result of their separation from God, the unclean were to exhibit their grief by tearing their clothes, by having unkempt hair and by partially covering their faces (v. 45).
13:47 *mildew.* During Israel's rainy season (October through March), this is a problem along the coast and by the Sea of Galilee, where it is very humid.

the mildew has not spread in the clothing, or the woven or knitted material, or the leather article, [54]he shall order that the contaminated article be washed. Then he is to isolate it for another seven days. [55]After the affected article has been washed, the priest is to examine it, and if the mildew has not changed its appearance, even though it has not spread, it is unclean. Burn it with fire, whether the mildew has affected one side or the other. [56]If, when the priest examines it, the mildew has faded after the article has been washed, he is to tear the contaminated part out of the clothing, or the leather, or the woven or knitted material. [57]But if it reappears in the clothing, or in the woven or knitted material, or in the leather article, it is spreading, and whatever has the mildew must be burned with fire. [58]The clothing, or the woven or knitted material, or any leather article that has been washed and is rid of the mildew, must be washed again, and it will be clean."

[59]These are the regulations concerning contamination by mildew in woolen or linen clothing, woven or knitted material, or any leather article, for pronouncing them clean or unclean.

Cleansing From Infectious Skin Diseases

14 The LORD said to Moses, [2]"These are the regulations for the diseased person at the time of his ceremonial cleansing, when he is brought to the priest: [d] [3]The priest is to go outside the camp and examine him. [e] If the person has been healed of his infectious skin disease, [b,f] [4]the priest shall order that two live clean birds and some cedar wood, scarlet yarn and hyssop [g] be brought for the one to be cleansed. [h] [5]Then the priest shall order that one of the birds be killed over fresh water in a clay pot. [i] [6]He is then to take the live bird and dip it, together with the cedar wood, the scarlet yarn and the hyssop, into the blood of the bird that was

killed over the fresh water. [j] [7]Seven times [k] he shall sprinkle [l] the one to be cleansed of the infectious disease and pronounce him clean. Then he is to release the live bird in the open fields. [m]

[8]"The person to be cleansed must wash his clothes, [n] shave off all his hair and bathe with water; [o] then he will be ceremonially clean. [p] After this he may come into the camp, [q] but he must stay outside his tent for seven days. [9]On the seventh day [r] he must shave off all his hair; [s] he must shave his head, his beard, his eyebrows and the rest of his hair. He must wash his clothes and bathe himself with water, and he will be clean. [t]

[10]"On the eighth day [u] he must bring two male lambs and one ewe lamb [v] a year old, each without defect, along with three-tenths of an ephah [c,w] of fine flour mixed with oil for a grain offering, [x] and one log [d] of oil. [y] [11]The priest who pronounces him clean shall present [z] both the one to be cleansed and his offerings before the LORD at the entrance to the Tent of Meeting. [a]

[12]"Then the priest is to take one of the male lambs and offer it as a guilt offering, [b] along with the log of oil; he shall wave them before the LORD as a wave offering. [c] [13]He is to slaughter the lamb in the holy place [d] where the sin offering and the burnt offering are slaughtered. Like the sin offering, the guilt offering belongs to the priest; [e] it is most holy. [14]The priest is to take some of the blood of the guilt offering and put it on the lobe of the right ear of the one to be cleansed, on the thumb of his right hand and on the big toe of his right foot. [f] [15]The priest shall then take some of the log of oil, pour it in the palm of his own left hand, [g] [16]dip his right forefinger into the oil in his palm, and with his finger sprinkle some of it before the LORD seven

Cross references (center column)

14:2 [d]Lev 13:57; Dt 24:8; Mt 8:2-4; Mk 1:40-44; Lk 5:12-14; 17:14
14:3 [e]Lev 13:46 / S Lev 13:2
14:4 [g]S Ex 12:22 [h]ver 6,49,51,52; Nu 19:6; Ps 51:7
14:5 [i]ver 50

14:6 [j]S ver 4
14:7 [k]ver 51 [l]2Ki 5:10,14; Isa 52:15; Eze 36:25 [m]ver 53
14:8 [n]S Lev 11:25 [o]ver 9; S Ex 29:4; Lev 15:5; 17:15; 22:6; Nu 19:7,8 [p]ver 20
[q]S Lev 13:11; Nu 5:2,3; 12:14, 15; 19:20; 31:24; 2Ch 26:21
14:9 [r]S Lev 13:5 [s]Nu 6:9; Dt 21:12 [t]S Lev 13:6
14:10 [u]Nu 6:10; Mt 8:4; Mk 1:44; Lk 5:14 [v]S Lev 4:32 [w]Nu 15:9; 28:20 [x]Lev 2:1 [y]ver 12, 15,21,24
14:11 [z]Nu 6:16 [a]Nu 6:10
14:12 [b]S Lev 5:18 [c]S Ex 29:24
14:13 [d]S Ex 29:11 [e]Lev 6:24-30; S 7:7
14:14 [f]S Ex 29:20
14:15 [g]ver 26

[b,3] Traditionally *leprosy*; the Hebrew word was used for various diseases affecting the skin—not necessarily leprosy; also elsewhere in this chapter.   [c,10] That is, probably about 6 quarts (about 6.5 liters)   [d,10] That is, probably about 2/3 pint (about 0.3 liter); also in verses 12, 15, 21 and 24

13:54 *washed.* See vv. 34,55–56,58. The treatment of disorders commonly included washing.
13:59 A summary of ch. 13.
14:1–32 The ritual after the skin disease had been cured had three parts: (1) ritual for the first week (outside the camp, vv. 1–7), (2) ritual for the second week (inside the camp, vv. 8–20) and (3) special permission for the poor (vv. 21–32).
14:4 *hyssop.* A plant used in ceremonial cleansing (see note on Ex 12:22).
14:5 *killed.* Diseases and disorders were a symbol of sin and rendered a person or object ceremonially unclean. The prescribed cleansing included sacrifice as well as washing

(see note on 13:54).
14:6 *cedar . . . yarn . . . hyssop.* Also used for cleansing in vv. 51–52; Nu 19:6.
14:7,16,51 *seven times.* See note on 4:6.
14:7 *clean.* Perhaps the yarn and cedar stick were used as well as the hyssop plant to sprinkle the blood for cleansing (see Ps 51:7). Further sacrifices are specified in vv. 10–31. *release the live bird.* Cf. 16:22; see note on 16:5.
14:8 The Levites were similarly cleansed (see Nu 8:7).
14:10 *grain offering.* See note on 2:1.
14:12 *guilt offering.* See 5:14–6:7 and note on 5:15. *wave offering.* See note on 7:30–32.
14:14 See note on 8:14.

times. *h* ¹⁷The priest is to put some of the oil remaining in his palm on the lobe of the right ear of the one to be cleansed, on the thumb of his right hand and on the big toe of his right foot, on top of the blood of the guilt offering. *i* ¹⁸The rest of the oil in his palm the priest shall put on the head of the one to be cleansed *j* and make atonement for him before the LORD.

¹⁹"Then the priest is to sacrifice the sin offering and make atonement for the one to be cleansed from his uncleanness. *k* After that, the priest shall slaughter the burnt offering ²⁰and offer it on the altar, together with the grain offering, and make atonement for him, *l* and he will be clean. *m*

²¹"If, however, he is poor *n* and cannot afford these, *o* he must take one male lamb as a guilt offering to be waved to make atonement for him, together with a tenth of an ephah *e* of fine flour mixed with oil for a grain offering, a log of oil, ²²and two doves or two young pigeons, *p* which he can afford, one for a sin offering and the other for a burnt offering. *q*

²³"On the eighth day he must bring them for his cleansing to the priest at the entrance to the Tent of Meeting, *r* before the LORD. *s* ²⁴The priest is to take the lamb for the guilt offering, *t* together with the log of oil, *u* and wave them before the LORD as a wave offering. *v* ²⁵He shall slaughter the lamb for the guilt offering and take some of its blood and put it on the lobe of the right ear of the one to be cleansed, on the thumb of his right hand and on the big toe of his right foot. *w* ²⁶The priest is to pour some of the oil into the palm of his own left hand, *x* ²⁷and with his right forefinger sprinkle some of the oil from his palm seven times before the LORD. ²⁸Some of the oil in his palm he is to put on the same places he put the blood of the guilt offering—on the lobe of the right ear of the one to be cleansed, on the thumb of his right hand and on the big toe of his right foot. ²⁹The rest of the oil in his palm the priest shall put on the head of the one to be cleansed, to make atonement for him before the LORD. *y* ³⁰Then he shall sacrifice the doves or the young pigeons, which the person can afford, *z* ³¹one *f* as a sin offering and the other as a burnt offering, *a* together with the grain offering. In

this way the priest will make atonement before the LORD on behalf of the one to be cleansed. *b* "

³²These are the regulations for anyone who has an infectious skin disease *c* and who cannot afford the regular offerings *d* for his cleansing.

Cleansing From Mildew

³³The LORD said to Moses and Aaron, ³⁴"When you enter the land of Canaan, *e* which I am giving you as your possession, *f* and I put a spreading mildew in a house in that land, ³⁵the owner of the house must go and tell the priest, 'I have seen something that looks like mildew in my house.' ³⁶The priest is to order the house to be emptied before he goes in to examine the mildew, so that nothing in the house will be pronounced unclean. After this the priest is to go in and inspect the house. ³⁷He is to examine the mildew on the walls, and if it has greenish or reddish *g* depressions that appear to be deeper than the surface of the wall, ³⁸the priest shall go out the doorway of the house and close it up for seven days. *h* ³⁹On the seventh day *i* the priest shall return to inspect the house. If the mildew has spread on the walls, ⁴⁰he is to order that the contaminated stones be torn out and thrown into an unclean place outside the town. *j* ⁴¹He must have all the inside walls of the house scraped and the material that is scraped off dumped into an unclean place outside the town. ⁴²Then they are to take other stones to replace these and take new clay and plaster the house.

⁴³"If the mildew reappears in the house after the stones have been torn out and the house scraped and plastered, ⁴⁴the priest is to go and examine it and, if the mildew has spread in the house, it is a destructive mildew; the house is unclean. *k* ⁴⁵It must be torn down—its stones, timbers and all the plaster—and taken out of the town to an unclean place.

⁴⁶"Anyone who goes into the house while it is closed up will be unclean till evening. *l* ⁴⁷Anyone who sleeps or eats in the house must wash his clothes. *m*

⁴⁸"But if the priest comes to examine it

Cross references (center column)

14:16 *h*ver 27
14:17 *i*ver 28
14:18 *j*ver 31;
Lev 15:15
14:19 *k*ver 31;
S Lev 5:3; 15:15
14:20 *l*Lev 15:30
*m*ver 8
14:21 *n*S Lev 5:7
*o*ver 22,32
14:22 *p*S Lev 5:7
*q*Lev 15:30
14:23
*r*Lev 15:14,29
*s*S ver 10,11
14:24 *t*Nu 6:14
*u*S ver 10 *v*ver 12
14:25
*w*S Ex 29:20
14:26 *x*ver 15
14:29 *y*ver 18
14:30 *z*S Lev 5:7
14:31 *a*ver 22;
Lev 5:7; 15:15,30

*b*S ver 18,S 19
14:32
*c*S Lev 13:2
*d*S ver 21
14:34 *e*Ge 12:5;
Ex 6:4; Nu 13:2
*f*Ge 17:8; 48:4;
Nu 27:12; 32:22;
Dt 3:27; 7:1;
32:49
14:37
*g*S Lev 13:19
14:38
*h*S Lev 13:4
14:39 *i*Lev 13:5
14:40 *j*ver 45
14:44 *k*Lev 13:51
14:46
*l*S Lev 11:24
14:47
*m*S Lev 11:25

*e*21 That is, probably about 2 quarts (about 2 liters)
*f*31 Septuagint and Syriac; Hebrew *31*such as the person can afford, one

---

14:19 *sin offering.* See 4:1–5:13 and notes on 4:3,5. *burnt offering.* See note on 1:3.

14:20 *grain offering.* See note on 2:1.

14:33–53 There are many similarities between this section and the previous one, particularly in the manner of restoration.

14:45 *torn down.* A house desecrated by mildew, mold or fungus would be a defiled place to live in, so drastic measures had to be taken.

and the mildew has not spread after the house has been plastered, he shall pronounce the house clean, [n] because the mildew is gone. [49]To purify the house he is to take two birds and some cedar wood, scarlet yarn and hyssop. [o] [50]He shall kill one of the birds over fresh water in a clay pot. [p] [51]Then he is to take the cedar wood, the hyssop, [q] the scarlet yarn and the live bird, dip them into the blood of the dead bird and the fresh water, and sprinkle the house seven times. [r] [52]He shall purify the house with the bird's blood, the fresh water, the live bird, the cedar wood, the hyssop and the scarlet yarn. [53]Then he is to release the live bird in the open fields [s] outside the town. In this way he will make atonement for the house, and it will be clean. [t] "

[54]These are the regulations for any infectious skin disease, [u] for an itch, [55]for mildew [v] in clothing or in a house, [56]and for a swelling, a rash or a bright spot, [w] [57]to determine when something is clean or unclean.

These are the regulations for infectious skin diseases and mildew. [x]

Discharges Causing Uncleanness

15 The LORD said to Moses and Aaron, [2]"Speak to the Israelites and say to them: 'When any man has a bodily discharge, [y] the discharge is unclean. [3]Whether it continues flowing from his body or is blocked, it will make him unclean. This is how his discharge will bring about uncleanness:

[4]"'Any bed the man with a discharge lies on will be unclean, and anything he sits on will be unclean. [5]Anyone who touches his bed must wash his clothes [z] and bathe with water, [a] and he will be unclean till evening. [b] [6]Whoever sits on anything that the man with a discharge sat on must wash his clothes and bathe with water, and he will be unclean till evening.

[7]"'Whoever touches the man [c] who has a discharge [d] must wash his clothes and bathe with water, and he will be unclean till evening.

[8]"'If the man with the discharge spits [e] on someone who is clean, that person must wash his clothes and bathe with water, and he will be unclean till evening.

[9]"'Everything the man sits on when riding will be unclean, [10]and whoever touches any of the things that were under him will be unclean till evening; whoever picks up those things [f] must wash his clothes and bathe with water, and he will be unclean till evening.

[11]"'Anyone the man with a discharge touches without rinsing his hands with water must wash his clothes and bathe with water, and he will be unclean till evening.

[12]"'A clay pot [g] that the man touches must be broken, and any wooden article [h] is to be rinsed with water.

[13]"'When a man is cleansed from his discharge, he is to count off seven days [i] for his ceremonial cleansing; he must wash his clothes and bathe himself with fresh water, and he will be clean. [j] [14]On the eighth day he must take two doves or two young pigeons [k] and come before the LORD to the entrance to the Tent of Meeting and give them to the priest. [15]The priest is to sacrifice them, the one for a sin offering [l] and the other for a burnt offering. [m] In this way he will make atonement before the LORD for the man because of his discharge. [n]

[16]"'When a man has an emission of semen, [o] he must bathe his whole body with water, and he will be unclean till evening. [p] [17]Any clothing or leather that has semen on it must be washed with water, and it will be unclean till evening. [18]When a man lies with a woman and there is an emission of semen, [q] both must bathe with water, and they will be unclean till evening.

[19]"'When a woman has her regular flow of blood, the impurity of her monthly period [r] will last seven days, and anyone who touches her will be unclean till evening.

[20]"'Anything she lies on during her period will be unclean, and anything she sits

14:48
nS Lev 13:6
14:49 oIKi 4:33
14:50 pver 5
14:51 qver 6;
Ps 51:7 rS ver 4,7
14:53 sS ver 7
tver 20
14:54 uLev 13:2
14:55
vLev 13:47-52
14:56 wLev 13:2
14:57
xS Lev 10:10
15:2 yver 16,32;
Lev 22:4; Nu 5:2;
2Sa 3:29; Mt 9:20
15:5
zS Lev 11:25
aLev 14:8
bS Lev 11:24
15:7 cver 19;
Lev 22:5 dver 16;
Lev 22:4

15:8 eNu 12:14
15:10 fNu 19:10
15:12
gS Lev 6:28
hS Lev 11:32
15:13 iS Lev 8:33
jver 5
15:14 kLev 14:22
15:15 lLev 5:7
mLev 14:31
nS Lev 14:18,19
15:16 oS ver 2;
Dt 23:10 pver 5;
Dt 23:11
15:18 qIsa 21:4
15:19 rS ver 24

15:1–33 The chapter deals with (1) male uncleanness caused by bodily discharge (vv. 2–15) or emission of semen (vv. 16–18); (2) female uncleanness caused by her monthly period (vv. 19–24) or lengthy hemorrhaging (vv. 25–30); (3) summary (vv. 31–33).
15:2 *bodily discharge*. Probably either diarrhea or urethral discharge (various kinds of infections). The contamination of anything under the man (v. 10), whether he sat (vv. 4,6,9) or lay (v. 4) on it, indicates that the bodily discharge had to do with the buttocks or genitals.

15:4 *bed*. Something like a mat (cf. 2Sa 11:13).
15:13 *cleansed*. God brought about the healing; the priest could only ascertain that a person was already healed.
15:16 *semen*. Normal sexual activity and a woman's menstruation required no sacrifices but only washing and a minimal period of uncleanness.
15:19 *seven days*. See 12:2. This regulation is the background of 2Sa 11:4 (Bathsheba).
15:20 See note on Ge 31:35.

on will be unclean. 21Whoever touches her bed must wash his clothes and bathe with water, and he will be unclean till evening.s 22Whoever touches anything she sits on must wash his clothes and bathe with water, and he will be unclean till evening. 23Whether it is the bed or anything she was sitting on, when anyone touches it, he will be unclean till evening.

24" 'If a man lies with her and her monthly flowt touches him, he will be unclean for seven days; any bed he lies on will be unclean.

25" 'When a woman has a discharge of blood for many days at a time other than her monthly periodu or has a discharge that continues beyond her period, she will be unclean as long as she has the discharge, just as in the days of her period. 26Any bed she lies on while her discharge continues will be unclean, as is her bed during her monthly period, and anything she sits on will be unclean, as during her period. 27Whoever touches them will be unclean; he must wash his clothes and bathe with water, and he will be unclean till evening.

28" 'When she is cleansed from her discharge, she must count off seven days, and after that she will be ceremonially clean. 29On the eighth day she must take two doves or two young pigeonsv and bring them to the priest at the entrance to the

Tent of Meeting. 30The priest is to sacrifice one for a sin offering and the other for a burnt offering. In this way he will make atonement for her before the LORD for the uncleanness of her discharge.w

31" 'You must keep the Israelites separate from things that make them unclean, so they will not die in their uncleanness for defiling my dwelling place,gx which is among them.' "

32These are the regulations for a man with a discharge, for anyone made unclean by an emission of semen,y 33for a woman in her monthly period, for a man or a woman with a discharge, and for a man who lies with a woman who is ceremonially unclean.z

The Day of Atonement

16:2–34pp — Lev 23:26–32; Nu 29:7–11

16 The LORD spoke to Moses after the death of the two sons of Aaron who died when they approached the LORD.a 2The LORD said to Moses: "Tell your brother Aaron not to come whenever he choosesb into the Most Holy Placec behind the curtaind in front of the atonement covere on the ark, or else he will die, because I appearf in the cloudg over the atonement cover.

3"This is how Aaron is to enter the sanc-

g31 Or *my tabernacle*

Cross references (center column)

15:21 sver 27
15:24 tver 19; Lev 12:2; 18:19; 20:18; Eze 18:6
15:25 uMt 9:20; Mk 5:25; Lk 8:43
15:29 vLev 14:22

15:30 wLev 5:10; 14:20,31; 18:19; 2Sa 11:4; Mk 5:25; Lk 8:43
15:31 xLev 20:3; Nu 5:3; 19:13,20; 2Sa 15:25; 2Ki 21:7; Ps 33:14; 74:7; 76:2; Eze 5:11; 23:38
15:32 yS ver 2
15:33 zver 19,24, 25
16:1 aS Lev 10:1
16:2 bEx 30:10; Heb 9:7
cS Ex 26:33; Heb 9:25; 10:19
dS Ex 26:33; Heb 6:19
eS Ex 26:34
fS Ex 25:22
gS Ex 40:34;
S 2Sa 22:10

15:24 A case of the woman's period beginning during intercourse. This is different from 18:19 and 20:18. *flow.* During her period a woman was protected from sexual activity. No offering was required for uncleanness contracted by a man in this way, but the uncleanness lasted seven days.
15:25 *discharge of blood for many days.* As, e.g., the woman in Mt 9:20. *beyond her period.* An unnatural discharge, possibly caused by disease, was treated like a sickness and required an offering upon recovery (vv. 28–30; see vv. 14–15).
15:31 Addressed to the priests, thus emphasizing the importance of the regulations. Since God dwelt in the tabernacle, any unholiness, symbolized by the discharges of ch. 15, could result in death if the people came into his presence. Sin separates all people from a holy God and results in their death, unless atonement is made (see the next chapter).
16:1–34 See 23:26–32; 25:9; Ex 30:10; Nu 29:7–11; Heb 9:7. The order of ritual for the Day of Atonement was as follows: 1. The high priest went to the basin in the courtyard, removed his regular garments, washed himself (v. 4) and went into the Holy Place to put on the special garments for the Day of Atonement (v. 4). 2. He went out to sacrifice a bull at the altar of burnt offering as a sin offering for himself and the other priests (v. 11). 3. He went into the Most Holy Place with some of the bull's blood, with incense and with coals from the altar of burnt offering (vv. 12–13). The incense was placed on the burning coals, and the smoke of the incense hid the ark from view. 4. He sprinkled some of the bull's blood on and in front of the cover of the ark (v. 14). 5. He went outside the tabernacle and cast lots for two goats to see which was to be sacrificed and which was to be the

scapegoat (vv. 7–8). 6. At the altar of burnt offering the high priest killed the goat for the sin offering for the people, and for a second time he went into the Most Holy Place, this time to sprinkle the goat's blood in front of and on the atonement cover (vv. 5,9,15–16a). 7. He returned to the Holy Place (called "Tent of Meeting" in v. 16) and sprinkled the goat's blood there (v. 16b). 8. He went outside to the altar of burnt offering and sprinkled it (v. 18) with the blood of the bull (for himself, v. 11) and of the goat (for the people, v. 15). 9. While in the courtyard, he laid both hands on the second goat, thus symbolizing the transfer of Israel's sin, and sent it out into the desert (vv. 20–22). 10. The man who took the goat away, after he accomplished his task, washed himself and his clothes outside the camp (v. 26) before rejoining the people. 11. The high priest entered the Holy Place to remove his special garments (v. 23). 12. He went out to the basin to wash and put on his regular priestly clothes (v. 24). 13. As a final sacrifice he went out to the great altar and offered a ram (v. 3) as a burnt offering for himself, and another ram (v. 5) for the people (v. 24). 14. The conclusion of the entire day was the removal of the sacrifices for the sin offerings to a place outside the camp, where they were burned, and there the man who performed this ritual bathed and washed his clothes (vv. 27–28) before rejoining the people.
16:1 *sons of Aaron who died.* See 10:1–3.
16:2 *atonement cover.* See Ex 25:17 and note. Blood sprinkled on the lid of the ark made atonement for Israel on the Day of Atonement (vv. 15–17). In the Septuagint (the Greek translation of the OT) the word for "atonement cover" is the same one used of Christ and translated "sacrifice of atonement" in Ro 3:25 (see NIV text note there).

tuary area: *h* with a young bull *i* for a sin offering and a ram for a burnt offering. *j* ⁴He is to put on the sacred linen tunic, *k* with linen undergarments next to his body; he is to tie the linen sash around him and put on the linen turban. *l* These are sacred garments; *m* so he must bathe himself with water *n* before he puts them on. *o* ⁵From the Israelite community *p* he is to take two male goats *q* for a sin offering and a ram for a burnt offering.

⁶"Aaron is to offer the bull for his own sin offering to make atonement for himself and his household. *r* ⁷Then he is to take the two goats and present them before the LORD at the entrance to the Tent of Meeting. ⁸He is to cast lots *s* for the two goats—one lot for the LORD and the other for the scapegoat. *h* *t* ⁹Aaron shall bring the goat whose lot falls to the LORD and sacrifice it for a sin offering. ¹⁰But the goat chosen by lot as the scapegoat shall be presented alive before the LORD to be used for making atonement *u* by sending it into the desert as a scapegoat.

¹¹"Aaron shall bring the bull for his own sin offering to make atonement for himself and his household, *v* and he is to slaughter the bull for his own sin offering. ¹²He is to take a censer full of burning coals *w* from the altar before the LORD and two handfuls of finely ground fragrant incense *x* and take them behind the curtain. ¹³He is to put the incense on the fire before the LORD, and the smoke of the incense will conceal the atonement cover *y* above the Testimony, so that he will not die. *z* ¹⁴He is to take some of the bull's blood *a* and with his finger sprinkle it on the front of the atonement cover; then he shall sprinkle some of it with his finger seven times before the atonement cover. *b*

¹⁵"He shall then slaughter the goat for the sin offering for the people *c* and take its blood behind the curtain *d* and do with it

as he did with the bull's blood: He shall sprinkle *e* it on the atonement cover and in front of it. ¹⁶In this way he will make atonement *f* for the Most Holy Place *g* because of the uncleanness and rebellion of the Israelites, whatever their sins have been. He is to do the same for the Tent of Meeting, *h* which is among them in the midst of their uncleanness. ¹⁷No one is to be in the Tent of Meeting from the time Aaron goes in to make atonement in the Most Holy Place until he comes out, having made atonement for himself, his household and the whole community of Israel.

¹⁸"Then he shall come out to the altar *i* that is before the LORD and make atonement for it. He shall take some of the bull's blood and some of the goat's blood and put it on all the horns of the altar. *j* ¹⁹He shall sprinkle some of the blood on it with his finger seven times to cleanse it and to consecrate it from the uncleanness of the Israelites. *k*

²⁰"When Aaron has finished making atonement for the Most Holy Place, the Tent of Meeting and the altar, he shall bring forward the live goat. *l* ²¹He is to lay both hands on the head of the live goat *m* and confess *n* over it all the wickedness and rebellion of the Israelites—all their sins—and put them on the goat's head. He shall send the goat away into the desert in the care of a man appointed for the task. ²²The goat will carry on itself all their sins *o* to a solitary place; and the man shall release it in the desert.

²³"Then Aaron is to go into the Tent of Meeting and take off the linen garments *p* he put on before he entered the Most Holy Place, and he is to leave them there. *q* ²⁴He shall bathe himself with water in a holy

---

16:3 *h* ver 6; Lev 4:1-12; Heb 9:24,25
16:4 *i* S Lev 4:3 *j* ver 5 *k* S Lev 8:13 *l* S Ex 28:39 *m* ver 32; S Ex 28:42; 29:29,30; Lev 21:10; Nu 20:26,28 *n* S Ex 29:4; Heb 10:22 *o* Eze 9:2; 44:17-18
16:5 *p* S Lev 4:13-21 *q* ver 20; S Lev 4:3; 2Ch 29:23; Ps 50:9
16:6 *r* Lev 9:7; Heb 7:27; 9:7,12
16:8 *s* Nu 26:55, 56; 33:54; 34:13; Jos 14:2; 18:6; Jdg 20:9; Ne 10:34; Est 3:7; 9:24; Ps 22:18; Pr 16:33 *t* ver 10, 26
16:10 *u* Isa 53:4-10; S Ro 3:25
16:11 *v* S ver 6, 24,33
16:12 *w* S Lev 10:1; Rev 8:5 *x* S Ex 25:6; 30:34-38
16:13 *y* S Ex 25:17 *z* S Ex 28:43
16:14 *a* S Lev 4:5; Heb 9:7,13,25 *b* S Lev 4:6
16:15 *c* S Lev 4:13-21; Heb 7:27; 9:7,12; 13:11 *d* Heb 9:3
16:16 *e* S Lev 4:17; Nu 19:19; Isa 52:15; Eze 36:25
16:18 *f* S Ex 29:36; S Ro 3:25 *g* S Ex 26:33; Heb 9:25 *h* Ex 29:4; S 40:2
16:18 *i* S Lev 4:7 *j* S Lev 4:25
16:19 *k* Eze 43:20
16:20 *l* S ver 5
16:21 *m* S Ex 29:10 *n* S Lev 5:5
16:22 *o* S Ex 28:38; Isa 53:12

16:23 *p* S Ex 28:42 *q* Eze 42:14

h 8 That is, the goat of removal; Hebrew *azazel*; also in verses 10 and 26

16:3 *sanctuary area.* The Most Holy Place (see v. 2). *bull.* For Aaron's cleansing (vv. 6,11). Before Aaron could minister in the Most Holy Place for the nation, he himself had to be cleansed (Heb 5:1–3); not so Christ, who is our high priest and Aaron's antitype (Heb 7:26–28).
16:5 *two male goats for a sin offering.* One was the usual sin offering (see notes on 4:3,5) and the other a scapegoat. No single offering could fully typify the atonement of Christ. The one goat was killed, its blood sprinkled in the Most Holy Place and its body burned outside the camp (vv. 15,27), symbolizing the payment of the price of Christ's atonement. The other goat, sent away alive and bearing the sins of the nation (v. 21), symbolized the removal of sin and its guilt. *ram.* For the sins of the people; the one in v. 3 was for the sins of the high priest. Both were sacrificed at the end of the ceremony (v. 24).

16:6–10 An outline of vv. 11–22.
16:11 *make atonement for himself.* See note on v. 3.
16:13 The smoke of the incense covered the ark so that the high priest would not see the glorious presence of God (v. 2) and thus die.
16:14 See Ro 3:25. *seven times.* See note on 4:6.
16:16 *Tent of Meeting.* Here and in vv. 17,20,33 the term means the Holy Place.
16:20–22 A summary description of substitutionary atonement. The sin of the worshipers was confessed and symbolically transferred to the sacrificial animal, on which hands were laid (see notes on 1:3; Ex 29:10; see also Lev 1:4; 3:8; 4:4).
16:24 *holy place.* Cf. 6:26. *burnt offering . . . burnt offering.* The two rams mentioned in vv. 3,5.

place[r] and put on his regular garments.[s] Then he shall come out and sacrifice the burnt offering for himself and the burnt offering for the people,[t] to make atonement for himself and for the people.[u] 25He shall also burn the fat of the sin offering on the altar.

26"The man who releases the goat as a scapegoat[v] must wash his clothes[w] and bathe himself with water;[x] afterward he may come into the camp. 27The bull and the goat for the sin offerings, whose blood was brought into the Most Holy Place to make atonement, must be taken outside the camp;[y] their hides, flesh and offal are to be burned up. 28The man who burns them must wash his clothes and bathe himself with water; afterward he may come into the camp.[z]

29"This is to be a lasting ordinance[a] for you: On the tenth day of the seventh month[b] you must deny yourselves[i][c] and not do any work[d]—whether native-born[e] or an alien living among you— 30because on this day atonement will be made[f] for you, to cleanse you. Then, before the LORD, you will be clean from all your sins.[g] 31It is a sabbath of rest, and you must deny yourselves;[h] it is a lasting ordinance.[i] 32The priest who is anointed and ordained[j] to succeed his father as high priest is to make atonement. He is to put on the sacred linen garments[k] 33and make atonement for the Most Holy Place, for the Tent of Meeting and the altar, for the priests and all the people of the community.[l]

34"This is to be a lasting ordinance[m] for you: Atonement is to be made once a year[n] for all the sins of the Israelites."

And it was done, as the LORD commanded Moses.

Eating Blood Forbidden

17 The LORD said to Moses, 2"Speak to Aaron and his sons[o] and to all the Israelites and say to them: 'This is what the LORD has commanded: 3Any Israelite who sacrifices an ox,[i] a lamb[p] or a goat[q] in the camp or outside of it 4instead of bringing it to the entrance to the Tent of Meeting[r] to present it as an offering to the LORD in front of the tabernacle of the LORD[s]—that man shall be considered guilty of bloodshed; he has shed blood and must be cut off from his people.[t] 5This is so the Israelites will bring to the LORD the sacrifices they are now making in the open fields. They must bring them to the priest, that is, to the LORD, at the entrance to the Tent of Meeting and sacrifice them as fellowship offerings.[k][u] 6The priest is to sprinkle the blood against the altar[v] of the LORD[w] at the entrance to the Tent of Meeting and burn the fat as an aroma pleasing to the LORD.[x] 7They must no longer offer any of their sacrifices to the goat idols[l][y] to whom they prostitute themselves.[z] This is to be a lasting ordinance[a] for them and for the generations to come.'[b]

8"Say to them: 'Any Israelite or any alien living among them who offers a burnt offering or sacrifice 9and does not bring it to the entrance to the Tent[c] of Meeting[d] to sacrifice it to the LORD[e]—that man must be cut off from his people.

10"' 'Any Israelite or any alien living among them who eats any blood—I will set my face against that person who eats blood[f] and will cut him off from his people. 11For the life of a creature is in the

i29 Or *must fast; also in verse 31*   i3 The Hebrew word can include both male and female.
k5 Traditionally *peace offerings*   l7 Or *demons*

16:24 rS Lev 6:16;
sver 3-5 tLev 1:3
uS ver 11
16:26 vS ver 8
wS Lev 11:25
xLev 14:8
16:27
yS Ex 29:14
16:28 zNu 19:8, 10
16:29
aS Ex 12:14
bLev 25:9 cver 31; Lev 23:27,32; Nu 29:7; Isa 58:3
dS Ex 31:15; S Lev 23:28
eEx 12:19
16:30
fS Ex 30:10
gPs 51:2; Jer 33:8; Eze 36:33; Zec 13:1; Eph 5:26
16:31 hEzr 8:21; Isa 58:3,5; Da 10:12
iAc 27:9
16:32
jS Ex 30:30 kS ver 4; S Ex 28:2
16:33 lS ver 11, 16-18; Eze 45:18
16:34
mS Ex 27:21
nHeb 9:7,25

17:2 oLev 10:6, 12
17:3 pS Lev 3:7
qS Lev 7:23
17:4 rver 9;
sKi 8:4; 2Ch 1:3
sDt 12:5-21
17:5 uS Lev 3:1; Eze 43:27
tS Ge 17:14
17:6 vS Lev 4:18
wS Lev 3:2
xS Lev 1:9
17:7 yS Ex 22:20
zS Ex 34:15; Jer 3:6,9; Eze 23:3; 1Co 10:20
aS Ex 12:14
bS Ge 9:12
17:9 cS Lev 1:3
dS ver 4
eS Lev 3:7
17:10 fS Ge 9:4

16:25 *fat of the sin offering.* See 4:8–10.
16:27 *outside the camp.* See note on 4:12.
16:29,31 *deny yourselves.* See NIV text note; more lit. "humble (or afflict) yourselves." The expression came to be used of fasting (Ps 35:13). The Day of Atonement was the only regular fast day stipulated in the OT (see 23:27,29,32 and NIV text note), though tradition later added other fast days to the Jewish calendar (see Zec 7:5; 8:19).
16:29 *seventh month.* Tishri, the seventh month, begins with the Feast of Trumpets (see note on 23:24). The Day of Atonement follows on the 10th day, and on the 15th day the Feast of Tabernacles begins (see 23:23–36).
16:30 *clean from all your sins.* On the Day of Atonement the repentant Israelite was assured of sins forgiven.
16:34 *once a year.* Heb 9:11–10:14 repeatedly points out this contrast with Christ's "once for all" sacrifice.
17:4 *tabernacle of the LORD.* The people, with few exceptions (e.g., Dt 12:15,20–21), were directed to sacrifice only at the central sanctuary (Dt 12:5–6). Sennacherib's representative referred to Hezekiah's requiring worship only in

Jerusalem (2Ki 18:22). One reason for such a regulation was to keep the Israelites from becoming corrupted by the Canaanites' pagan worship. *cut off from his people.* See note on 7:20.
17:5 *to the priest, that is, to the LORD.* See note on 6:6.
17:7 *prostitute themselves.* See 20:5–6; see also Jdg 2:17 and note.
17:11 *the life of a creature is in the blood.* See note on Ge 9:4. The blood shed in the sacrifices was sacred. It epitomized the life of the sacrificial victim. Since life was sacred, blood (a symbol of life) had to be treated with respect (see 9:5–6). Eating blood was therefore strictly forbidden (see 7:26–27; Dt 12:16,23–25; 15:23; 1Sa 14:32–34). *blood ... makes atonement.* Practically every sacrifice included the sprinkling or smearing of blood on the altar or within the tabernacle (v. 6; 1:5; 3:2; 4:6,25; 7:2), thus teaching that atonement involves the substitution of life for life. The blood of the OT sacrifice pointed forward to the blood of the Lamb of God, who obtained for his people "eternal redemption" (Heb 9:12). "Without the shedding of blood there is no

blood, *g* and I have given it to you to make atonement for yourselves on the altar; it is the blood that makes atonement for one's life. *h* 12Therefore I say to the Israelites, "None of you may eat blood, nor may an alien living among you eat blood."

13" 'Any Israelite or any alien living among you who hunts any animal or bird that may be eaten must drain out the blood and cover it with earth, *i* 14because the life of every creature is its blood. That is why I have said to the Israelites, "You must not eat the blood of any creature, because the life of every creature is its blood; anyone who eats it must be cut off." *j*

15" 'Anyone, whether native-born or alien, who eats anything *k* found dead or torn by wild animals *l* must wash his clothes and bathe with water, *m* and he will be ceremonially unclean till evening; *n* then he will be clean. 16But if he does not wash his clothes and bathe himself, he will be held responsible. *o* ' "

Unlawful Sexual Relations

18 The LORD said to Moses, 2"Speak to the Israelites and say to them: 'I am the LORD your God. *p* 3You must not do as they do in Egypt, where you used to live, and you must not do as they do in the land of Canaan, where I am bringing you. Do not follow their practices. *q* 4You must obey my laws *r* and be careful to follow my decrees. *s* I am the LORD your God. *t* 5Keep my decrees and laws, *u* for the man who obeys them will live by them. *v* I am the LORD.

6" 'No one is to approach any close rela-

17:11 *g*ver 14
*h*Heb 9:22
17:13 *i*Lev 7:26; Eze 24:7; 33:25; Ac 15:20
17:14 *j*S Ge 9:4
17:15 *k*S Lev 7:24
*l*S Ex 22:31
*m*S Lev 14:8
*n*S Lev 11:40
17:16 *o*S Lev 5:1
18:2 *p*S Ge 17:7
18:3 *q*ver 24-30; S Ex 23:24; Dt 18:9; 2Ki 16:3; 17:8; 1Ch 5:25
18:4 *r*S Ge 26:5
*s*Dt 4:1; 1Ki 11:11; Jer 44:10,23; Eze 11:12 *t*ver 2
18:5 *u*S Ge 26:5
*v*Dt 4:1; Ne 9:29; Isa 55:3; Eze 18:9; 20:11; Am 5:4-6; Mt 19:17; S Ro 10:5*; Gal 3:12*

18:7 *w*ver 8; Lev 20:11; Dt 27:20
*x*Eze 22:10
18:8 *y*1Co 5:1
*z*Ge 35:22; Lev 20:11; Dt 22:30; 27:20
18:9 *a*ver 11; Lev 20:17; Dt 27:22
*b*Lev 20:17; Dt 27:22; 2Sa 13:13; Eze 22:11
18:12 *c*ver 13; Lev 20:19
18:13 *d*S ver 12, 14; Lev 20:20
18:14 *e*S ver 13
18:15 *f*S Ge 11:31; S 38:16 *g*Eze 22:11
18:16 *h*Lev 20:21; Mt 14:4; Mk 6:18

18:17 *i*Lev 20:14; Dt 27:23

---

tive to have sexual relations. I am the LORD.

7" 'Do not dishonor your father *w* by having sexual relations with your mother. *x* She is your mother; do not have relations with her.

8" 'Do not have sexual relations with your father's wife; *y* that would dishonor your father. *z*

9" 'Do not have sexual relations with your sister, *a* either your father's daughter or your mother's daughter, whether she was born in the same home or elsewhere. *b*

10" 'Do not have sexual relations with your son's daughter or your daughter's daughter; that would dishonor you.

11" 'Do not have sexual relations with the daughter of your father's wife, born to your father; she is your sister.

12" 'Do not have sexual relations with your father's sister; *c* she is your father's close relative.

13" 'Do not have sexual relations with your mother's sister, *d* because she is your mother's close relative.

14" 'Do not dishonor your father's brother by approaching his wife to have sexual relations; she is your aunt. *e*

15" 'Do not have sexual relations with your daughter-in-law. *f* She is your son's wife; do not have relations with her. *g*

16" 'Do not have sexual relations with your brother's wife; *h* that would dishonor your brother.

17" 'Do not have sexual relations with both a woman and her daughter. *i* Do not

---

forgiveness" (Heb 9:22).

17:15 *found dead or torn.* Such animals would not have had the blood drained from them and therefore would be forbidden.

18:1–20:27 Here God's people are given instructions concerning interpersonal relations and a morality reflecting God's holiness. Israel was thereby prepared for a life different from the Canaanites, whose life-style was deplorably immoral. Ch. 18 contains prohibitions in the moral sphere, ch. 19 expands the Ten Commandments to detail correct morality, and ch. 20 assesses the penalties for violating God's standard of morality. See chart on "Major Social Concerns in the Covenant," p. 271.

18:2 In chs. 18–26 The phrase "I am the LORD" occurs 42 times. The Lord's name (i.e., his revealed character as Yahweh, "the LORD") is the authority that stands behind his instructions. See note on Ex 3:15.

18:3 Six times in this chapter Israel is warned not to follow the example of pagans (here, two times; see also vv. 24, 26–27,30).

18:5 *live.* With God's full blessing. The law was the way of life for the redeemed (see Eze 20:11,13,21), not a way of salvation for the lost (see Ro 10:5; Gal 3:12).

18:6 A summary of the laws against incest (vv. 7–18).

Penalties for incestuous relations are given in ch. 20.

18:7 This prohibition applied also after the father's death. If the father was still living, the act was adulterous and therefore forbidden.

18:8 *your father's wife.* Other than your mother—assuming there is more than one wife.

18:11 *sister.* There would be many half-sisters in a polygamous society. Tamar claimed that an exception to this prohibition could be made (2Sa 13:12–13; but see note there).

18:14 *your aunt.* See 20:20. If the father's brother was alive, the act would be adulterous. If he was dead, one could rationalize such a marriage because the aunt was not a blood relative—but it was forbidden.

18:15 Cf. the account of Judah and Tamar (Ge 38:18).

18:16 *your brother's wife.* The law also applied to a time after divorce or the brother's death. To marry one's brother's widow was not immoral but might damage the brother's inheritance. The levirate law of Dt 25:5–6 offered an exception that preserved the dead brother's inheritance and continued his line.

18:17 *daughter.* Stepdaughter (granddaughter-in-law is also covered in the verse). The law applied even after the mother's death.

have sexual relations with either her son's daughter or her daughter's daughter; they are her close relatives. That is wickedness.

18“ 'Do not take your wife's sister^j as a rival wife and have sexual relations with her while your wife is living.

19“ 'Do not approach a woman to have sexual relations during the uncleanness^k of her monthly period.^{l}

20“ 'Do not have sexual relations with your neighbor's wife^m and defile yourself with her.

21“ 'Do not give any of your children^n to be sacrificed^m to Molech,^{o} for you must not profane the name of your God.^{p} I am the LORD.^{q}

22“ 'Do not lie with a man as one lies with a woman;^{r} that is detestable.^{s}

23“ 'Do not have sexual relations with an animal and defile yourself with it. A woman must not present herself to an animal to nave sexual relations with it; that is a perversion.^{t}

24“ 'Do not defile yourselves in any of these ways, because this is how the nations that I am going to drive out before you^u became defiled.^{v} 25Even the land was defiled;^{w} so I punished it for its sin,^{x} and the land vomited out its inhabitants.^{y} 26But you must keep my decrees and my laws.^{z} The native-born and the aliens living among you must not do any of these detestable things, 27for all these things were done by the people who lived in the land before you, and the land became defiled. 28And if you defile the land,^{a} it will vomit you out^b as it vomited out the nations that were before you.

29“ 'Everyone who does any of these detestable things—such persons must be cut off from their people. 30Keep my requirements^c and do not follow any of the detestable customs that were practiced before you came and do not defile yourselves with them. I am the LORD your God.^{d} ' ”

Various Laws

19 The LORD said to Moses, 2“Speak to the entire assembly of Israel^e

and say to them: 'Be holy because I, the LORD your God,^{f} am holy.^{g}

3“ 'Each of you must respect his mother and father,^{h} and you must observe my Sabbaths.^{i} I am the LORD your God.^{j}

4“ 'Do not turn to idols or make gods of cast metal for yourselves.^{k} I am the LORD your God.^{l}

5“ 'When you sacrifice a fellowship offering^n to the LORD, sacrifice it in such a way that it will be accepted on your behalf. 6It shall be eaten on the day you sacrifice it or on the next day; anything left over until the third day must be burned up.^{m} 7If any of it is eaten on the third day, it is impure and will not be accepted.^{n} 8Whoever eats it will be held responsible^o because he has desecrated what is holy^p to the LORD; that person must be cut off from his people.^{q}

9“ 'When you reap the harvest of your land, do not reap to the very edges^r of your field or gather the gleanings of your harvest.^{s} 10Do not go over your vineyard a second time^t or pick up the grapes that have fallen.^{u} Leave them for the poor and the alien.^{v} I am the LORD your God.

11“ 'Do not steal.^{w}

“ 'Do not lie.^{x}

“ 'Do not deceive one another.^{y}

12“ 'Do not swear falsely^z by my name^a and so profane^b the name of your God. I am the LORD.

13“ 'Do not defraud your neighbor^c or rob^d him.^{e}

“ 'Do not hold back the wages of a hired man^f overnight.^{g}

14“ 'Do not curse the deaf or put a stumbling block in front of the blind,^{h} but fear your God.^{i} I am the LORD.

Cross references (center column)

18:18 ^{j}S Ge 30:1
18:19 ^{k}S Lev 15:25-30
^{l}S Lev 15:24
18:20 ^{m}S Ex 20:14; Mt 5:27,28; 1Co 6:9; Heb 13:4
18:21 ^{n}Dt 12:31; 18:10; 2Ki 16:3; 17:17; 21:6; 23:10; 2Ch 28:1-4; 33:6; Ps 106:37,38; Isa 57:5; Jer 7:30,31; 19:5; 32:35; Eze 16:20; Mic 6:7
^{o}Lev 20:2-5; Dt 9:4; 1Ki 11:5, 7,33; Isa 57:9; Jer 32:35; 49:1; Zep 1:5
^{p}Lev 19:12; 21:6; Isa 48:11; Eze 22:26; 36:20; Am 2:7; Mal 1:12
^{q}S Ex 6:2
18:22 ^{r}Lev 20:13; Dt 23:18; Ro 1:27; 1Co 6:9
^{s}S Ge 19:5
18:23 ^{t}Ex 22:19; Lev 20:15; Dt 27:21
18:24 ^{u}ver 3,27, 30; Lev 20:23
^{v}Dt 9:4; 18:12
18:25 ^{w}Nu 35:34; Dt 21:23
^{x}Lev 20:23; Dt 9:5; 12:31; 18:12 ^{y}ver 28; Lev 20:22; Job 20:15; Jer 51:34
18:26 ^{z}S Ge 26:5
18:28 ^{a}Lev 20:22; Ezr 9:11; La 1:17
^{b}S ver 25
18:30 ^{c}S Lev 8:35 ^{d}ver 2
19:2 ^{e}Nu 14:5; Ps 68:26

^{f}S Ex 20:2
^{g}S Ex 15:11; 1Pe 1:16*; S Lev 11:44; S 20:26
19:3 ^{h}Ex 20:12
^{i}S Ex 20:8
^{j}Lev 11:44
19:4 ^{k}S Ex 20:4; Jdg 17:3; Ps 96:5; 115:4-7; 135:15
^{l}Lev 11:44
19:6 ^{m}Lev 7:16-17
19:7 ^{n}Lev 7:18
19:8 ^{o}S Lev 5:1
^{p}Lev 22:2,15,16;

Nu 18:32 ^{q}S Ge 17:14 19:9 ^{r}Ru 2:2,3,7,16,17 ^{s}Lev 23:10, 22; Dt 24:19-22; Job 24:10 19:10 ^{t}Dt 24:20 ^{u}ver 9 ^{v}Dt 24:19,21 19:11 ^{w}Ex 20:15; S 23:4; Lk 3:14 ^{x}S Lev 20:16; S Eph 4:25 ^{y}S Lev 6:2 19:12 ^{z}Jer 5:2; 7:9; Mal 3:5 ^{a}Ex 3:13; 20:7; Dt 18:19; Pr 18:10; Isa 42:8; Jer 44:16,26; S Mt 5:33 ^{b}Jer 34:16 19:13 ^{c}Lev 25:14,17 ^{d}S Ex 20:15 ^{e}S Ex 22:15,25-27 ^{f}Job 7:2; 24:12; 31:39; Isa 16:14; Mal 3:5 ^{g}Dt 24:15; Jer 22:13; Mt 20:8; 1Ti 5:18; Jas 5:4 19:14 ^{h}S Ex 4:11; Lev 21:18; Dt 27:18 ^{i}ver 32; Lev 25:17,36

^{m}21 Or to be passed through the fire
^{n}5 Traditionally peace offering

18:18 Cf. the account of Jacob with Leah and Rachel (Ge 29:23-30).
18:19 See Eze 18:6; 22:10.
18:21 Molech. The god of the Ammonites (see 20:2-5; 1Ki 11:5 and note). The detestable practice of sacrificing children to Molech was common in Phoenicia and other surrounding countries. Cf. 1Ki 3:26-27. King Manasseh evidently sacrificed his sons to Molech (2Ch 33:6; see 2Ki 23:10). Jer 32:35 protests the practice.
18:22 lie with a man. See 20:13, where the penalty for homosexual acts is death.
18:29 detestable. See note on 7:21. cut off from their

people. See note on 7:20.
19:1 See note on 18:1–20:27.
19:2 Be holy. See note on 11:44.
19:3–4 See v. 30; Ex 20:4–6,8–11. See also chart on "Major Social Concerns in the Covenant," p. 271.
19:5 fellowship offering. See note on 3:1.
19:6 third day. See note on 7:15–18.
19:8 cut off from his people. See note on 7:20.
19:9–10 See 23:22; see also Dt 24:19–21. Ru 2 gives an example of the application of the law of gleaning.
19:11–12 See Ex 20:7,15–16.
19:13 wages of a hired man. See Dt 24:14–15; Mt 20:8.

15"'Do not pervert justice;[j] do not show partiality[k] to the poor or favoritism to the great,[l] but judge your neighbor fairly.[m]

16"'Do not go about spreading slander[n] among your people.

"'Do not do anything that endangers your neighbor's life.[o] I am the LORD.

17"'Do not hate your brother in your heart.[p] Rebuke your neighbor frankly[q] so you will not share in his guilt.

18"'Do not seek revenge[r] or bear a grudge[s] against one of your people,[t] but love your neighbor[u] as yourself.[v] I am the LORD.

19"'Keep my decrees.[w]

"'Do not mate different kinds of animals.

"'Do not plant your field with two kinds of seed.[x]

"'Do not wear clothing woven of two kinds of material.[y]

20"'If a man sleeps with a woman who is a slave girl promised to another man[z] but who has not been ransomed or given her freedom, there must be due punishment. Yet they are not to be put to death, because she had not been freed. 21The man, however, must bring a ram to the entrance to the Tent of Meeting for a guilt offering to the LORD.[a] 22With the ram of the guilt offering the priest is to make atonement for him before the LORD for the sin he has committed, and his sin will be forgiven.[b]

23"'When you enter the land and plant any kind of fruit tree, regard its fruit as forbidden.[o] For three years you are to consider it forbidden[o]; it must not be eaten. 24In the fourth year all its fruit will be holy,[c] an offering of praise to the LORD. 25But in the fifth year you may eat its fruit. In this way your harvest will be increased. I am the LORD your God.

26"'Do not eat any meat with the blood still in it.[d]

"'Do not practice divination[e] or sorcery.[f]

27"'Do not cut the hair at the sides of your head or clip off the edges of your beard.[g]

28"'Do not cut[h] your bodies for the dead or put tattoo marks on yourselves. I am the LORD.

29"'Do not degrade your daughter by making her a prostitute,[i] or the land will turn to prostitution and be filled with wickedness.[j]

30"'Observe my Sabbaths[k] and have reverence for my sanctuary. I am the LORD.[l]

31"'Do not turn to mediums[m] or seek out spiritists,[n] for you will be defiled by them. I am the LORD your God.

32"'Rise in the presence of the aged, show respect[o] for the elderly[p] and revere your God.[q] I am the LORD.[r]

33"'When an alien lives with you in your land, do not mistreat him. 34The alien living with you must be treated as one of your native-born.[s] Love him as yourself,[t] for you were aliens[u] in Egypt.[v] I am the LORD your God.

35"'Do not use dishonest standards when measuring length, weight or quantity.[w] 36Use honest scales[x] and honest weights, an honest ephah[p][y] and an honest hin.[q][z] I am the LORD your God, who brought you out of Egypt.[a]

37"'Keep all my decrees[b] and all my laws[c] and follow them. I am the LORD.'"

Punishments for Sin

20 The LORD said to Moses, 2"Say to the Israelites: 'Any Israelite or any

19:15 /S Ex 23:2
[k]Dt 24:17;
Job 13:8,10;
32:21; Pr 28:21
/Job 34:19
[m]S Ex 23:8;
Pr 24:23;
Mal 2:9; Jas 2:1-4
19:16 [n]Ps 15:3;
31:13; 41:6;
101:5; Jer 6:28;
9:4; Eze 22:9
[o]Ex 23:7;
Dt 10:17; 27:25;
Ps 15:5;
Eze 22:12
19:17 [p]S 1Jn 2:9
[q]S Mt 18:15
19:18
[r]S Ge 4:23;
Ro 12:19;
Heb 10:30
[s]Ps 103:9
[t]S Ex 12:48
[u]S Ex 20:16 [x]ver
34; S Mt 5:43*;
19:16*; 22:39*;
Mk 12:31*;
Lk 10:27*;
Jn 13:34;
Ro 13:9*;
Gal 5:14*;
Jas 2:8*
19:19
[w]S Ge 26:5
[x]Dt 22:9
[y]Dt 22:11
19:20
[z]Dt 22:23-27
19:21
[a]S Lev 5:15
19:22
[b]S Lev 5:15
19:24
[c]S Ex 22:29
19:26 [d]S Ge 9:4

[e]S Ge 30:27;
S Isa 44:25
/S Ex 22:18;
2Ki 17:17
19:27 [g]Lev 21:5;
Dt 14:1;
2Sa 10:4-5;
Jer 41:5; 48:37;
Eze 5:1-5
19:28 [h]Lev 21:5;
Dt 14:1;
1Ki 18:28;
Jer 16:6; 41:5;
47:5
19:29 /Lev 21:9;
Dt 23:18
/Ge 34:7;
Lev 21:9
19:30 [k]S Ex 20:8
/Lev 26:2
19:31
[m]S Ex 22:18;
1Sa 28:7-20;
1Ch 10:13
[n]Lev 20:6;
2Ki 21:6; 23:24;
Isa 8:19; 19:3;
29:4; 47:12; 65:4

19:32 [o]1Ki 12:8 [p]Job 32:4; Pr 23:22; La 5:12; 1Ti 5:1 [q]S ver 14; Job 29:8 [r]Lev 11:44; 25:17 **19:34** [s]S Ex 12:48 [t]S ver 18 [u]S Ex 22:21 [v]Ex 23:9; Dt 10:19; 23:7; Ps 146:9 **19:35** [w]Dt 25:13-16 **19:36** [x]Job 31:6; Pr 11:1; Hos 12:7; Mic 6:11 [y]Jdg 6:19; Ru 2:17; 1Sa 1:24; 17:17; Eze 45:10 [z]Dt 25:13-15; Pr 20:10; Eze 45:11 [a]S Ex 12:17 **19:37** [b]2Ki 17:37; 2Ch 7:17; Ps 119:5; Eze 18:9 [c]S Ge 26:5

[o]23 Hebrew *uncircumcised*   [p]36 An ephah was a dry measure.   [q]36 A hin was a liquid measure.

19:17 *Do not hate your brother.* See 1Jn 2:9,11; 3:15; 4:20.

19:18 *love your neighbor as yourself.* Quoted by Christ (Mt 22:39; Mk 12:31; Lk 10:27), Paul (Ro 13:9; Gal 5:14) and James (2:8). The stricter Pharisees (school of Shammai) added to this command what they thought it implied: "Hate your enemy" (Mt 5:43). Jesus' reaction, "Love your enemies," was in line with true OT teaching (see vv. 17,34) and was more in agreement with the middle-of-the-road Pharisees. Rabbi Nahmanides caught their sentiments: "One should place no limitations upon the love for the neighbor, but instead a person should love to do an abundance of good for his fellow being as he does for himself." "Neighbor" does not merely mean one who lives nearby, but anyone with whom one comes in contact.

19:21—22 *guilt offering.* See 5:14—6:7 and note on 5:15.

19:26 *meat with the blood.* See note on 17:11. *sorcery.* See v. 31; Ex 22:18; Dt 18:14; 1Sa 28:9; Isa 47:12—14.

19:27 *Do not cut the hair at the sides of your head.* A prohibition still followed by orthodox Jews.

19:28 There was to be no disfiguring of the body, after the manner of the pagans (see note on 21:5).

19:34 *you were aliens in Egypt.* See Dt 5:15.

19:35 *dishonest standards.* In a culture with no bureau of weights and measures, cheating in business transactions by falsification of standards was common (see Dt 25:13—16; Pr 11:1; 16:11; 20:10,23). The prophets also condemned such sin (Am 8:5; Mic 6:10—11).

alien living in Israel who gives[r] any of his children to Molech must be put to death.[d] The people of the community are to stone him.[e] 3I will set my face against that man and I will cut him off from his people;[f] for by giving his children to Molech, he has defiled[g] my sanctuary[h] and profaned my holy name.[i] 4If the people of the community close their eyes when that man gives one of his children to Molech and they fail to put him to death,[j] 5I will set my face against that man and his family and will cut off from their people both him and all who follow him in prostituting themselves to Molech.

6" 'I will set my face against the person who turns to mediums and spiritists to prostitute himself by following them, and I will cut him off from his people.[k]

7" 'Consecrate yourselves[l] and be holy,[m] because I am the LORD your God.[n] 8Keep my decrees[o] and follow them. I am the LORD, who makes you holy.[s] [p]

9" 'If anyone curses his father[q] or mother,[r] he must be put to death.[s] He has cursed his father or his mother, and his blood will be on his own head.[t]

10" 'If a man commits adultery with another man's wife[u]—with the wife of his neighbor—both the adulterer and the adulteress must be put to death.[v]

11" 'If a man sleeps with his father's wife, he has dishonored his father.[w] Both the man and the woman must be put to death; their blood will be on their own heads.[x]

12" 'If a man sleeps with his daughter-in-law,[y] both of them must be put to death. What they have done is a perversion; their blood will be on their own heads.

13" 'If a man lies with a man as one lies with a woman, both of them have done what is detestable.[z] They must be put to death; their blood will be on their own heads.

14" 'If a man marries both a woman and

her mother,[a] it is wicked. Both he and they must be burned in the fire,[b] so that no wickedness will be among you.[c]

15" 'If a man has sexual relations with an animal,[d] he must be put to death,[e] and you must kill the animal.

16" 'If a woman approaches an animal to have sexual relations with it, kill both the woman and the animal. They must be put to death; their blood will be on their own heads.

17" 'If a man marries his sister,[f] the daughter of either his father or his mother, and they have sexual relations, it is a disgrace. They must be cut off before the eyes[g] of their people. He has dishonored his sister and will be held responsible.[h]

18" 'If a man lies with a woman during her monthly period[i] and has sexual relations with her, he has exposed the source of her flow, and she has also uncovered it. Both of them must be cut off from their people.[j]

19" 'Do not have sexual relations with the sister of either your mother or your father,[k] for that would dishonor a close relative; both of you would be held responsible.

20" 'If a man sleeps with his aunt,[l] he has dishonored his uncle. They will be held responsible; they will die childless.[m]

21" 'If a man marries his brother's wife,[n] it is an act of impurity; he has dishonored his brother. They will be childless.[o]

22" 'Keep all my decrees and laws[p] and follow them, so that the land[q] where I am bringing you to live may not vomit you out. 23You must not live according to the customs of the nations[r] I am going to drive out before you.[s] Because they did all these things, I abhorred them.[t] 24But I

20:2 [d]ver 10; Ge 26:11; Ex 19:12 [e]ver 27; Lev 24:14; Nu 15:35,36; Dt 21:21; Jos 7:25
20:3 [f]ver 5,6; Lev 23:30 [g]Ps 74:7; 79:1; Jer 7:30; Eze 5:11 [h]S Lev 15:31 [i]S Lev 18:21
20:4 [j]Dt 17:2-5
20:6 [k]S ver 3; S Lev 19:31
20:7 [l]S Lev 11:44 [m]S Ex 29:1; 31:13; Lev 11:45; Eph 1:4; 1Pe 1:16* [n]S Ex 6:2; S 20:2
20:8 [o]S Ge 26:5 [p]S Ex 31:13; Eze 20:12
20:9 [q]Ex 20:12; Mal 1:6; 2:10 [r]S Ex 20:12; Dt 27:16; Eze 22:7 [s]Ex 21:17; Dt 21:20-21; Mt 15:4*; Mk 7:10* [t]ver 11; Dt 22:30; Jos 2:19; 2Sa 1:16; 3:29; 1Ki 2:37; Eze 18:13; 33:4,5
20:10 [u]Ex 20:14; Dt 5:18; 22:22; Jn 8:5 [v]S Ge 38:24; S Ex 21:12
20:11 [w]S Lev 18:7 [x]S ver 9; S Lev 18:8
20:12 [y]S Ge 11:31; S 38:16
20:13 [z]Lev 18:22
20:14 [a]S Lev 18:17 [b]Lev 21:9; Nu 16:39; Jdg 14:15; 15:6 [c]S Lev 18:8; Dt 27:23
20:15 [d]S Ex 22:19 [e]ver 10
20:17 [f]S Lev 18:9 [g]S Ge 17:14 [h]S Lev 5:1
20:18 [i]S Lev 15:24 [j]Eze 18:6
20:19 [k]S Lev 18:12
20:20 [l]S Lev 18:13 [m]ver 21; Ge 15:2
20:21 [n]S Lev 18:16; Mt 14:4; Mk 6:18 [o]S ver 20 20:22 [p]S Ge 26:5 [q]S Lev 18:25-28 20:23 [r]S Lev 18:3 [s]S Lev 18:24 [t]S Lev 18:25

[2] Or sacrifices; also in verses 3 and 4   [s]8 Or who sanctifies you; or who sets you apart as holy

---

20:1–27 In ch. 20 many of the same sins listed in ch. 18 are mentioned again, but this time usually with the death penalty specified. Israel's God is a jealous God and tolerates no rivals (see note on Ex 20:5). He requires exclusive allegiance (see Ex 20:3). See note on 18:1–20:27.
20:2–5 *Molech.* See note on 18:21.
20:3 *cut off from his people.* See note on 7:20.
20:5 *prostituting themselves.* See v. 6; 17:7; see also note on Ex 34:15.
20:6 *mediums and spiritists.* Consulting a medium was no less a sin than being one (v. 27). See Dt 18:10–11. Only God was to be consulted—through either the priest or a prophet.
20:7 *be holy.* See note on 11:44.

20:8 *who makes . . . holy.* This phrase and the expression, "I am the LORD (your God)," are characteristic of chs. 18–26.
20:9 Cf. the penalty of a profligate son in Dt 21:20–21.
20:10 See 18:20.
20:12 See 18:15.
20:13 *detestable.* See note on 7:21.
20:15–16 See 18:23.
20:18 See 18:19.
20:20 See 18:14.
20:21 See 18:16 and note.
20:24 *land flowing with milk and honey.* A common phrase in Exodus, Numbers and Deuteronomy (see Ex 3:8 and note; see also Jos 5:6; Jer 11:5; 32:22; Eze 20:6,15).

said to you, "You will possess their land; I will give it to you as an inheritance, a land flowing with milk and honey." *u* I am the LORD your God, who has set you apart from the nations. *v*

25" 'You must therefore make a distinction between clean and unclean animals and between unclean and clean birds. *w* Do not defile yourselves by any animal or bird or anything that moves along the ground—those which I have set apart as unclean for you. 26You are to be holy to me *tx* because I, the LORD, am holy, *y* and I have set you apart from the nations *z* to be my own.

27" 'A man or woman who is a medium *a* or spiritist among you must be put to death. *b* You are to stone them; *c* their blood will be on their own heads.' "

Rules for Priests

21 The LORD said to Moses, "Speak to the priests, the sons of Aaron, *d* and say to them: 'A priest must not make himself ceremonially unclean *e* for any of his people who die, *f* 2except for a close relative, such as his mother or father, *g* his son or daughter, his brother, 3or an unmarried sister who is dependent on him since she has no husband—for her he may make himself unclean. *h* 4He must not make himself unclean for people related to him by marriage, *u* and so defile himself.

5" 'Priests must not shave *i* their heads or shave off the edges of their beards *j* or cut their bodies. *k* 6They must be holy to their God *l* and must not profane the name of their God. *m* Because they present the offerings made to the LORD by fire, *n* the food of their God, *o* they are to be holy. *p*

7" 'They must not marry women defiled by prostitution or divorced from their husbands, *q* because priests are holy to their God. *r* 8Regard them as holy, *s* because they offer up the food of your God. *t* Consider them holy, because I the LORD am holy—I who make you holy. *v u*

9" 'If a priest's daughter defiles herself by becoming a prostitute, she disgraces her father; she must be burned in the fire. *v*

10" 'The high priest, the one among his brothers who has had the anointing oil poured on his head *w* and who has been ordained to wear the priestly garments, *x* must not let his hair become unkempt *w* or tear his clothes. *y* 11He must not enter a place where there is a dead body. *z* He must not make himself unclean, *a* even for his father or mother, *b* 12nor leave the sanctuary *c* of his God or desecrate it, because he has been dedicated by the anointing oil *d* of his God. I am the LORD.

13" 'The woman he marries must be a virgin. *e* 14He must not marry a widow, a divorced woman, or a woman defiled by prostitution, but only a virgin from his own people, 15so he will not defile his offspring among his people. I am the LORD, who makes him holy. *x* ' "

16The LORD said to Moses, 17"Say to Aaron: 'For the generations to come none of your descendants who has a defect *f* may come near to offer the food of his God. *g* 18No man who has any defect *h* may come near: no man who is blind *i* or lame, *j* disfigured or deformed; 19no man with a crippled foot or hand, 20or who is hunchbacked or dwarfed, or who has any eye defect, or who has festering or running sores or damaged testicles. *k* 21No descendant of Aaron the priest who has any defect *l* is to come near to present the offerings made to the LORD by fire. *m* He has a defect; he must not come near to offer the food of his God. *n* 22He may eat the most holy food of his God, *o* as well as the holy food; 23yet because of his defect, *p* he must not go near the curtain or approach the altar, and so desecrate my sanctuary. *q* I am the LORD, who makes them holy. *v r* ' "

24So Moses told this to Aaron and his sons and to all the Israelites.

20:24 *u*S Ex 3:8; Nu 14:8; 16:14
*v*S Ex 33:16
20:25
*w*Lev 10:10; Dt 14:3-21; Ac 10:14
20:26 *x*Dt 14:2
*y*ver 8; Lev 19:2; Jos 24:19; 2Ki 19:22; Ps 99:3
*z*S Ex 33:16
20:27
*a*S Ex 22:18
*b*S Lev 19:31
*c*S ver 2; S Lev 24:14
21:1 *d*S Ex 28:1; S Lev 1:5
*e*S Lev 5:3; S 13:3
*f*ver 11; Nu 5:2; 6:6; 19:11; 31:19
21:2 *g*ver 11
21:3 *h*Nu 6:6
21:5
*i*S Lev 13:40; Jer 7:29; 16:6 /Eze 5:1; 44:20
*k*S Lev 19:28
21:6 *l*ver 8; Ezr 8:28
*m*Lev 18:21
*n*S Lev 3:11 *o*ver 17,22; Lev 22:25
*p*S Ex 19:22; S Lev 10:3
21:7 *q*ver 13,14
*r*Eze 44:22
21:8 *s*ver 6
*t*Lev 3:11
*u*S Ex 31:13

21:9
*v*S Ge 38:24; S Lev 19:29
21:10 *w*S Ex 29:7
*x*S Lev 8:7-9,13; S 16:4
*y*S Lev 10:6
21:11 *z*Nu 5:2; 6:6; 9:6; 19:11, 13,14; 31:19
*a*Lev 19:28 *b*ver 2
21:12 *c*S Ex 25:8
*d*S Ex 28:41
21:13 *e*Eze 44:22
21:17 *f*ver 18,21, 23 *g*S ver 6
21:18
*h*Lev 22:19-25 *i*S Lev 19:14 /2Sa 4:4; 9:3; 19:26
21:20
*k*Lev 22:24; Dt 23:1; Isa 56:3
21:21 *l*S ver 17
*m*S Lev 3:11
*n*Lev 22:19
21:22 *o*1Co 9:13
21:23 *p*S ver 17
*q*S Ex 25:8
*r*Lev 20:8

*t*26 Or *be my holy ones*   *u*4 Or *unclean as a leader among his people*   *v*8 Or *who sanctify you; or who set you apart as holy*   *w*10 Or *not uncover his head*   *x*15 Or *who sanctifies him; or who sets him apart as holy*   *y*23 Or *who sanctifies them; or who sets them apart as holy*

20:25 See ch. 11 and notes.
20:27 See note on v. 6.
21:1—22:33 Directions for the priests' conduct, especially about separation from ceremonial uncleanness.
21:1 *for any . . . who die.* Touching a corpse (Nu 19:11) or entering the home of a person who had died (Nu 19:14) made one unclean. A priest was only to contract such uncleanness at the death of a close relative (vv. 2–3), and the regulations for the high priest denied him even this (vv. 11–12).
21:5 *cut their bodies.* See 19:27–28. Such lacerations and disfigurement were common among pagans as signs of

mourning and to secure the attention of their deity (see 1Ki 18:28). Israelite faith had a much less grotesque view of death (see, e.g., vv. 1–4; Ge 5:24; 2Sa 12:23; Heb 11:19).
21:8 *I . . . am holy.* See note on 11:44.
21:9 See Ge 38:24 and note.
21:11—12 See note on v. 1.
21:17 *defect.* Like the sacrifices that had to be without defect, the priests were to typify Christ's perfection (Heb 9:13–14).
21:23 *curtain.* Between the Holy Place and the Most Holy Place (see Ex 26:33).

22 The LORD said to Moses, [2]"Tell Aaron and his sons to treat with respect the sacred offerings[s] the Israelites consecrate to me, so they will not profane my holy name.[t] I am the LORD.[u]

[3]"Say to them: 'For the generations to come, if any of your descendants is ceremonially unclean and yet comes near the sacred offerings that the Israelites consecrate to the LORD,[v] that person must be cut off from my presence.[w] I am the LORD.

[4]"If a descendant of Aaron has an infectious skin disease[z] or a bodily discharge,[x] he may not eat the sacred offerings until he is cleansed. He will also be unclean if he touches something defiled by a corpse[y] or by anyone who has an emission of semen, [5]or if he touches any crawling thing[z] that makes him unclean, or any person[a] who makes him unclean, whatever the uncleanness may be. [6]The one who touches any such thing will be unclean[b] till evening.[c] He must not eat any of the sacred offerings unless he has bathed himself with water.[d] [7]When the sun goes down, he will be clean, and after that he may eat the sacred offerings, for they are his food.[e] [8]He must not eat anything found dead[f] or torn by wild animals,[g] and so become unclean[h] through it. I am the LORD.[i]

[9]"The priests are to keep my requirements[j] so that they do not become guilty[k] and die[l] for treating them with contempt. I am the LORD, who makes them holy.[a] [m]

[10]"No one outside a priest's family may eat the sacred offering, nor may the guest of a priest or his hired worker eat it.[n] [11]But if a priest buys a slave with money, or if a slave is born in his household, that slave may eat his food.[o] [12]If a priest's daughter marries anyone other than a priest, she may not eat any of the sacred contributions. [13]But if a priest's daughter becomes a widow or is divorced, yet has no children, and she returns to live in her father's house as in her youth, she may eat of her father's food. No unauthorized person, however, may eat any of it.

[14]"If anyone eats a sacred offering by mistake,[p] he must make restitution to the priest for the offering and add a fifth of the value[q] to it. [15]The priests must not desecrate the sacred offerings[r] the Israelites present to the LORD[s] [16]by allowing them to eat[t] the sacred offerings and so bring upon them guilt[u] requiring payment.[v] I am the LORD, who makes them holy.[w]"

Unacceptable Sacrifices

[17]The LORD said to Moses, [18]"Speak to Aaron and his sons and to all the Israelites and say to them: 'If any of you—either an Israelite or an alien living in Israel[x]—presents a gift[y] for a burnt offering to the LORD, either to fulfill a vow[z] or as a freewill offering,[a] [19]you must present a male without defect[b] from the cattle, sheep or goats in order that it may be accepted on your behalf.[c] [20]Do not bring anything with a defect,[d] because it will not be accepted on your behalf.[e] [21]When anyone brings from the herd or flock[f] a fellowship offering[b][g] to the LORD to fulfill a special vow or as a freewill offering,[h] it must be without defect or blemish[i] to be acceptable.[j] [22]Do not offer to the LORD the blind, the injured or the maimed, or anything with warts or festering or running sores. Do not place any of these on the altar as an offering made to the LORD by fire. [23]You may, however, present as a freewill offering an ox[c] or a sheep that is deformed or stunted, but it will not be accepted in fulfillment of a vow. [24]You must not offer to the LORD an animal whose testicles are bruised, crushed, torn or cut.[k] You must not do this in your own land, [25]and you must not accept such animals from the hand of a foreigner and offer them as the food of your God.[l] They will not be accepted on your behalf, because they are deformed and have defects.[m]'"

[26]The LORD said to Moses, [27]"When a

Cross references (center column):

22:2 [s]S Lev 19:8; [t]S Ex 20:7; S Mt 5:33; [u]Eze 44:8
22:3 [v]Ezr 8:28; [w]Lev 7:20,21; Nu 19:13
22:4 [x]Lev 15:2-15; [y]Lev 11:24-28,39
22:5 [z]Lev 11:24-28,43; [a]S Lev 15:7
22:6 [b]Hag 2:13; [c]S Lev 11:24; [d]S Lev 14:8
22:7 [e]Nu 18:11
22:8 [f]S Lev 11:39; [g]S Ex 22:31; [h]S Lev 11:40; [i]Lev 11:44
22:9 [j]S Lev 8:35; [k]S Ex 28:38 /[ver 16; S Ex 28:43; [m]Lev 20:8
22:10 [n]ver 13; Ex 12:45; 29:33
22:11 [o]Ge 17:13; Ex 12:44

22:14 [p]S Lev 4:2; [q]Lev 5:15
22:15 [r]S Lev 19:8; [s]Nu 18:32
22:16 [t]Nu 18:11; [u]S Ex 28:38; [v]ver 9; [w]Lev 20:8
22:18 [x]Nu 15:16; 19:10; Jos 8:33; [y]S Lev 1:2; [z]ver 21; S Ge 28:20; Nu 15:8; Ps 22:25; 76:11; 116:18; [a]S Lev 7:16
22:19 [b]S Lev 1:3; 21:18-21; Nu 28:11; Dt 15:21; [c]S Lev 1:2
22:20 [d]S Lev 1:3; Dt 15:21; 17:1; Eze 43:23; 45:18; 46:6; Mal 1:8; Heb 9:14; 1Pe 1:19; [e]S Ex 28:38
22:21 [f]S Lev 1:2; [g]S Ex 32:6; S Lev 3:6; [h]S Lev 7:16; [i]S Ex 12:5; Mal 1:14 /Am 4:5
22:24 [k]S Lev 21:20
22:25 [l]S Lev 21:6; [m]S Lev 1:3; S 3:1; Nu 19:2

---

[z]4 Traditionally *leprosy*; the Hebrew word was used for various diseases affecting the skin—not necessarily leprosy.   [a]9 Or *who sanctifies them*; or *who sets them apart as holy*; also in verse 16   [b]21 Traditionally *peace offering*   [c]23 The Hebrew word can include both male and female.

22:3 *cut off from my presence.* Excluded from the worshiping community.
22:4 See 13:1–46 and note on 13:45–46; 15:1–18 and notes; 21:11.
22:5 See 11:29–31.
22:8 See 17:15 and note.
22:9 *die for treating them with contempt.* The laws of cleanness were the same for priests and people, but the penalties were far more severe for the priests, who had greater responsibility. Cf. Nadab and Abihu (10:1–3) and the

faithless priests of Malachi's day (Mal 1:6–2:9). *holy.* See note on 11:44.
22:14 *make restitution . . . add a fifth.* Cf. 5:16.
22:16 *holy.* See note on 11:44.
22:18 *burnt offering.* See note on 1:3.
22:20–22 See Mal 1:8.
22:21 *fellowship offering.* See note on 3:1.
22:24 *bruised, crushed, torn or cut.* Castrated animals were not acceptable offerings.

calf, a lamb or a goat[n] is born, it is to remain with its mother for seven days.[o] From the eighth day[p] on, it will be acceptable[q] as an offering made to the LORD by fire. [28]Do not slaughter a cow or a sheep and its young on the same day.[r]

[29]"When you sacrifice a thank offering[s] to the LORD, sacrifice it in such a way that it will be accepted on your behalf. [30]It must be eaten that same day; leave none of it till morning.[t] I am the LORD.[u]

[31]"Keep[v] my commands and follow them.[w] I am the LORD. [32]Do not profane my holy name.[x] I must be acknowledged as holy by the Israelites.[y] I am the LORD, who makes[d] you holy[e][z] [33]and who brought you out of Egypt[a] to be your God.[b] I am the LORD."

23

The LORD said to Moses, [2]"Speak to the Israelites and say to them: 'These are my appointed feasts,[c] the appointed feasts of the LORD, which you are to proclaim as sacred assemblies.[d]

The Sabbath

[3]"'There are six days when you may work,[e] but the seventh day is a Sabbath of rest,[f] a day of sacred assembly. You are not to do any work;[g] wherever you live, it is a Sabbath to the LORD.

The Passover and Unleavened Bread

23:4–8pp — Ex 12:14–20; Nu 28:16–25; Dt 16:1–8

[4]"'These are the LORD's appointed feasts, the sacred assemblies you are to proclaim at their appointed times:[h] [5]The LORD's Passover[i] begins at twilight on the fourteenth day of the first month.[j] [6]On the fifteenth day of that month the LORD's Feast of Unleavened Bread[k] begins; for seven days[l] you must eat bread made without yeast. [7]On the first day hold a sacred assembly[m] and do no regular work. [8]For seven days present an offering made

to the LORD by fire.[n] And on the seventh day hold a sacred assembly and do no regular work.' "

Firstfruits

[9]The LORD said to Moses, [10]"Speak to the Israelites and say to them: 'When you enter the land I am going to give you[o] and you reap its harvest,[p] bring to the priest a sheaf[q] of the first grain you harvest.[r] [11]He is to wave the sheaf before the LORD[s] so it will be accepted[t] on your behalf; the priest is to wave it on the day after the Sabbath. [12]On the day you wave the sheaf, you must sacrifice as a burnt offering to the LORD a lamb a year old[u] without defect,[v] [13]together with its grain offering[w] of two-tenths of an ephah[f][x] of fine flour mixed with oil—an offering made to the LORD by fire, a pleasing aroma—and its drink offering[y] of a quarter of a hin[g] of wine.[z] [14]You must not eat any bread, or roasted or new grain,[a] until the very day you bring this offering to your God.[b] This is to be a lasting ordinance for the generations to come,[c] wherever you live.[d]

Feast of Weeks

23:15–22pp — Nu 28:26–31; Dt 16:9–12

[15]"'From the day after the Sabbath, the day you brought the sheaf of the wave offering, count off seven full weeks. [16]Count off fifty days up to the day after the seventh Sabbath,[e] and then present an offering of new grain to the LORD. [17]From wherever you live, bring two loaves made of two-tenths of an ephah[f] of fine flour, baked with yeast, as a wave offering of firstfruits[g] to the LORD. [18]Present with this bread seven male lambs, each a year old and without defect, one young bull and two rams. They will be a burnt offering to the

---

Cross references (center column):

22:27 [n]S Lev 1:3
[o]S Ex 22:30
[p]S Ex 22:30
[q]S Ex 28:38
22:28 [r]Dt 22:6,7
22:29
[s]S Lev 7:12
22:30 [t]Lev 7:15
[u]Lev 11:44
22:31 [v]Dt 4:2, 40; Ps 105:45
[w]S Ex 22:31
22:32 [x]Lev 18:21
[y]S Lev 10:3
[z]Lev 20:8
22:33 [a]S Ex 6:6
[b]S Ge 17:7
23:2 [c]ver 4,37, 44; Nu 29:39; Eze 44:24; Col 2:16 [d]ver 2, 27
23:3 [e]Ex 20:9 [f]S Ex 20:10; Heb 4:9,10 [g]ver 7,21,35; Nu 28:26
23:4 [h]Na 1:15
23:5 [i]S Ex 12:11
[j]S Ex 12:6
23:6 [k]S Ex 12:17
[l]S Ex 12:19
23:7 [m]ver 3,8

23:8 [n]S Lev 1:9
23:10 [o]Nu 15:2, 18 [p]S Lev 19:9
[q]S Lev 19:9
[r]S Ex 22:29;
S 34:22; Ro 11:16
23:11
[s]S Ex 29:24
[t]S Ex 28:38
23:12
[u]S Lev 12:6
[v]S Ex 12:5
23:13
[w]Lev 2:14-16;
S 6:20 [x]ver 17;
Lev 24:5;
Nu 15:6; 28:9
[y]S Ge 35:14
[z]S Lev 10:9
23:14 [a]Jos 5:11;
Ru 2:14;
1Sa 17:17; 25:18;
2Sa 17:28
[b]Ex 34:26
[c]Lev 3:17;
Nu 10:8; 15:21
[d]Jer 2:3
23:16 [e]Ac 2:1;
20:16
23:17 [f]S ver 13
[g]S Ex 34:22

Text notes (small print):

[d]32 Or *made*   [e]32 Or *who sanctifies you*; or *who sets you apart as holy*   [f]13 That is, probably about 4 quarts (about 4.5 liters); also in verse 17   [g]13 That is, probably about 1 quart (about 1 liter)

Study notes (bottom):

22:28 Perhaps the prohibition was humanitarian (see v. 27), or possibly it was practical: The mother was to be saved to build up the flock (see Dt 22:6–7). Or it may have been a *law to avoid an otherwise unknown pagan custom* (see note on Ex 23:19).

22:30 *that same day.* The rule applied also to the Passover (Ex 34:25); however, the fellowship offering could be saved and eaten on the following day (7:16).

23:2 *appointed feasts.* See Ex 23:14–17 and notes; 34:18–25; Nu 28–29; Dt 16:1–17. The parallel in Numbers (the fullest and closest to Leviticus) specifies in great detail the offerings to be made at each feast. See chart on "OT Feasts and Other Sacred Days," p. 176.

23:3 *Sabbath.* See notes on Ex 16:23; 20:9–10. The Sabbath is associated with the annual feasts also in Ex 23:12. Two additional lambs were to be sacrificed as a burnt offering

every weekly Sabbath (Nu 28:9–10).

23:5 *Passover.* See notes on Ex 12:11,14,21. *first month.* See note on Ex 12:2. The Israelites had three systems of referring to months. In one, the months were simply numbered (as here and in v. 24). In another, the Canaanite names were used (Abib, Bul, etc.), of which only four are known. In the third system, the Babylonian names (Nisan, Adar, Tishri, Kislev, etc.) were used—in the exilic and postexilic books only—and are still used today. See chart on "Hebrew Calendar," p. 102.

23:6 *Feast of Unleavened Bread.* See note on Ex 23:15. During the Feast the first sheaf of the barley harvest was brought (see vv. 10–11).

23:15 *seven full weeks.* See note on Ex 23:16.

23:16 *fifty days.* The NT name for the Feast of Weeks was Pentecost (see Ac 2:1; 20:16; 1Co 16:8), meaning "fifty."

LORD, together with their grain offerings and drink offerings *h*—an offering made by fire, an aroma pleasing to the LORD. ¹⁹Then sacrifice one male goat for a sin offering and two lambs, each a year old, for a fellowship offering. *h* ²⁰The priest is to wave the two lambs before the LORD as a wave offering, *i* together with the bread of the firstfruits. They are a sacred offering to the LORD for the priest. ²¹On that same day you are to proclaim a sacred assembly *j* and do no regular work. *k* This is to be a lasting ordinance for the generations to come, wherever you live.

²²" 'When you reap the harvest *l* of your land, do not reap to the very edges of your field or gather the gleanings of your harvest. *m* Leave them for the poor and the alien. *n* I am the LORD your God.' "

Feast of Trumpets

23:23–25pp — Nu 29:1–6

²³The LORD said to Moses, ²⁴"Say to the Israelites: 'On the first day of the seventh month you are to have a day of rest, a sacred assembly *o* commemorated with trumpet blasts. *p* ²⁵Do no regular work, *q* but present an offering made to the LORD by fire. *r* ' "

Day of Atonement

23:26–32pp — Lev 16:2–34; Nu 29:7–11

²⁶The LORD said to Moses, ²⁷"The tenth day of this seventh month *s* is the Day of Atonement. *t* Hold a sacred assembly *u* and deny yourselves, *i* and present an offering made to the LORD by fire. ²⁸Do no work *v* on that day, because it is the Day of Atone-

Cross references (center column):

23:18 *h*ver 13; Ex 29:41; 30:9; 37:16; Jer 19:13; 44:18
23:20 *i*S Ex 29:24
23:21 *j*S ver 2; Ex 32:5 *k*S ver 3
23:22 *l*S Lev 19:9 *m*S Lev 19:10; Dt 24:19-21; Ru 2:15 *n*Ru 2:2

23:24 *o*ver 27, 36; Ezr 3:1 *p*Lev 25:9; Nu 10:9,10; 29:1; 31:6; 2Ki 11:14; 2Ch 13:12; Ps 98:6
23:25 *q*ver 21 *r*S Lev 1:9
23:27 *s*S Lev 16:29 *t*S Ex 30:10 *u*S ver 2,S 24
23:28 *v*ver 31

*h*19 Traditionally *peace offering*   *i*27 Or *and fast;* also in verses 29 and 32

23:22 See note on 19:9–10.
23:24 *first day of the seventh month.* Today known as the Jewish New Year (*Rosh Hashanah,* "the beginning of the year"), but not so called in the Bible (the Hebrew expression is only used in Eze 40:1 in a date formula). *trumpet blasts.* Trumpets were blown on the first of every month (Ps 81:3).

With no calendars available, the trumpets sounding across the land were an important signal of the beginning of the new season, the end of the agricultural year. See note on 16:29; see also chart on "Hebrew Calendar," p. 102.
23:27 *Day of Atonement.* For details see notes on 16:1–34. Aaron was to enter the Most Holy Place only once

---

Old Testament Feasts AND OTHER SACRED DAYS

NAME	OT REFERENCES	OT TIME	MODERN EQUIVALENT
Sabbath	Ex 20:8–11; 31:12–17; Lev 23:3; Dt 5:12–15	7th day	Same
Sabbath Year	Ex 23:10–11; Lev 25:1–7	7th year	Same
Year of Jubilee	Lev 25:8–55; 27:17–24; Nu 36:4	50th year	Same
Passover	Ex 12:1–14; Lev 23:5; Nu 9:1–14; 28:16; Dt 16:1–3a, 4b–7	1st month (Abib) 14	Mar.-Apr.
Unleavened Bread	Ex 12:15–20; 13:3–10; 23:15; 34:18; Lev 23:6–8; Nu 28:17–25; Dt 16:3b, 4a, 8	1st month (Abib) 15-21	Mar.-Apr.
Firstfruits	Lev 23:9–14	1st month (Abib) 16	Mar.-Apr.
Weeks (Pentecost) (Harvest)	Ex 23:16a; 34:22a; Lev 23:15–21; Nu 28:26–31; Dt 16:9–12	3rd month (Sivan) 6	May-June
Trumpets (Later: Rosh Hashanah—New Year's Day)	Lev 23:23–25; Nu 29:1–6	7th month (Tishri) 1	Sept.-Oct.
Day of Atonement (Yom Kippur)	Lev 16; 23:26–32; Nu 29:7–11	7th month (Tishri) 10	Sept.-Oct.
Tabernacles (Booths) (Ingathering)	Ex 23:16b; 34:22b; Lev 23:33–36a, 39–43; Nu 29:12–34; Dt 16:13–15; Zec 14:16–19	7th month (Tishri) 15-21	Sept.-Oct.
Sacred Assembly	Lev 23:36b; Nu 29:35–38	7th month (Tishri) 22	Sept.-Oct.
Purim	Est 9:18–32	12th month (Adar) 14,15	Feb.-Mar.

On Kislev 25 (mid-December) Hanukkah, the feast of dedication or festival of lights, commemorated the purification of the temple and altar in the Maccabean period (165/4 B.C.). This feast is mentioned in Jn 10:22.

ment, when atonement is made for you before the LORD your God. ²⁹Anyone who does not deny himself on that day must be cut off from his people.ʷ ³⁰I will destroy from among his peopleˣ anyone who does any work on that day. ³¹You shall do no work at all. This is to be a lasting ordinanceʸ for the generations to come, wherever you live. ³²It is a sabbath of restᶻ for you, and you must deny yourselves. From the evening of the ninth day of the month until the following evening you are to observe your sabbath."ᵃ

Feast of Tabernacles

23:33–43pp — Nu 29:12–39; Dt 16:13–17

³³The LORD said to Moses, ³⁴"Say to the Israelites: 'On the fifteenth day of the seventhᵇ month the LORD's Feast of Tabernaclesᶜ begins, and it lasts for seven days.

³⁵The first day is a sacred assembly;ᵈ do no regular work.ᵉ ³⁶For seven days present offerings made to the LORD by fire, and on the eighth day hold a sacred assemblyᶠ and present an offering made to the LORD by fire.ᵍ It is the closing assembly; do no regular work.

³⁷("These are the LORD's appointed feasts, which you are to proclaim as sacred assemblies for bringing offerings made to the LORD by fire—the burnt offerings and grain offerings, sacrifices and drink offeringsʰ required for each day. ³⁸These offeringsⁱ are in addition to those for the LORD's Sabbathsʲ andʲ in addition to your gifts and whatever you have vowed and all the freewill offeringsᵏ you give to the LORD.)

Cross references (center column):

23:29 ʷGe 17:14; Lev 7:20; Nu 5:2
23:30 ˣS Lev 20:3
23:31 ʸLev 3:17
23:32 ᶻS Lev 16:31
ᵃNe 13:19
23:34 ᵇ1 Ki 8:2; Hag 2:1
ᶜS Ex 23:16; Jn 7:2

23:35 ᵈver 2
ᵉver 3
23:36 ᶠS ver 24; 1 Ki 8:2; 2 Ch 7:9; Ne 8:18; Jn 7:37
ᵍS Lev 1:9
23:37 ʰver 13
23:38 ⁱS Lev 1:2
ʲS Ex 20:10; 2 Ch 2:4; Eze 45:17
ᵏS Lev 7:16

i38 Or *These feasts are in addition to the LORD's Sabbaths, and these offerings are*

---

a year (16:29–34) on the day called by modern Jews *Yom Kippur.* The Biblical name, however, is the plural *Yom Hakkippurim* (as in this verse), derived from the Hebrew words *yom* ("day") and *kipper* ("to atone"). The day was typological, foreshadowing the work of Christ, our high priest (see Heb 9:7; 13:11–12). *deny yourselves.* See note on 16:29,

31.
23:29 *cut off from his people.* See note on 7:20.
23:34 *Feast of Tabernacles.* See notes on Ex 23:16; Jn 7:37–39. Tabernacles was the last of the three annual pilgrimage festivals (Ex 23:14–17; Dt 16:16).

DESCRIPTION	PURPOSE	NT REFERENCES
		Mt 12:1–14; 28:1; Lk 4:16; Jn 5:9; Ac 13:42; Col 2:16; Heb 4:1–11
Day of rest; no work	Rest for people and animals	
Year of rest; fallow fields	Rest for land	
Canceled debts; liberation of slaves and indentured servants; land returned to original family owners	Help for poor; stabilize society	
Slaying and eating a lamb, together with bitter herbs and bread made without yeast, in every household	Remember Israel's deliverance from Egypt	Mt 26:17; Mk 14:12–26; Jn 2:13; 11:55; 1Co 5:7; Heb 11:28
Eating bread made without yeast; holding several assemblies; making designated offerings	Remember how the Lord brought the Israelites out of Egypt in haste	Mk 14:1,12; Ac 12:3; 1 Co 5:6–8
Presenting a sheaf of the first of the barley harvest as a wave offering; making a burnt offering and a grain offering	Recognize the Lord's bounty in the land	Ro 8:23; 1 Co 15:20–23
A festival of joy; mandatory and voluntary offerings, including the firstfruits of the wheat harvest	Show joy and thankfulness for the Lord's blessing of harvest	Ac 2:1–4; 20:16; 1Co 16:8
An assembly on a day of rest commemorated with trumpet blasts and sacrifices	Present Israel before the Lord for his favor	
A day of rest, fasting and sacrifices of atonement for priests and people and atonement for the tabernacle and altar	Cleanse priests and people from their sins and purify the Holy Place	Ro 3:24–26; Heb 9:7; 10:3, 19–22
A week of celebration for the harvest; living in booths and offering sacrifices	Memorialize the journey from Egypt to Canaan; give thanks for the productivity of Canaan	Jn 7:2,37
A day of convocation, rest and offering sacrifices	Commemorate the closing of the cycle of feasts	
A day of joy and feasting and giving presents	Remind the Israelites of their national deliverance in the time of Esther	

In addition, new moons were often special feast days (Nu 10:10; 1 Ch 23:31; Ezr 3:5; Ne 10:33; Ps 81:3; Isa 1:13–14; 66:23; Hos 5:7; Am 8:5; Col 2:16).

39" 'So beginning with the fifteenth day of the seventh month, after you have gathered the crops of the land, celebrate the festival[l] to the LORD for seven days; [m] the first day is a day of rest, and the eighth day also is a day of rest. [40]On the first day you are to take choice fruit from the trees, and palm fronds, leafy branches[n] and poplars,[o] and rejoice[p] before the LORD your God for seven days. [41]Celebrate this as a festival to the LORD for seven days each year. This is to be a lasting ordinance for the generations to come; celebrate it in the seventh month. [42]Live in booths[q] for seven days: All native-born Israelites are to live in booths [43]so your descendants will know[r] that I had the Israelites live in booths when I brought them out of Egypt. I am the LORD your God.' "

[44]So Moses announced to the Israelites the appointed feasts of the LORD.

Oil and Bread Set Before the LORD
24:1–3pp — Ex 27:20–21

24 The LORD said to Moses, [2]"Command the Israelites to bring you clear oil of pressed olives for the light so that the lamps may be kept burning continually. [3]Outside the curtain of the Testimony in the Tent of Meeting, Aaron is to tend the lamps before the LORD from evening till morning, continually. This is to be a lasting ordinance[s] for the generations to come. [4]The lamps on the pure gold lampstand[t] before the LORD must be tended continually.

[5]"Take fine flour and bake twelve loaves of bread, [u] using two-tenths of an ephah[k][v] for each loaf. [6]Set them in two rows, six in each row, on the table of pure gold[w] before the LORD. [7]Along each row put some pure incense[x] as a memorial portion[y] to represent the bread and to be an offering

made to the LORD by fire. [8]This bread is to be set out before the LORD regularly,[z] Sabbath after Sabbath,[a] on behalf of the Israelites, as a lasting covenant. [9]It belongs to Aaron and his sons,[b] who are to eat it in a holy place,[c] because it is a most holy[d] part of their regular share of the offerings made to the LORD by fire."

A Blasphemer Stoned

[10]Now the son of an Israelite mother and an Egyptian father went out among the Israelites, and a fight broke out in the camp between him and an Israelite. [11]The son of the Israelite woman blasphemed the Name[e] with a curse;[f] so they brought him to Moses.[g] (His mother's name was Shelomith, the daughter of Dibri the Danite.)[h] [12]They put him in custody until the will of the LORD should be made clear to them.[i]

[13]Then the LORD said to Moses: [14]"Take the blasphemer outside the camp. All those who heard him are to lay their hands on his head, and the entire assembly is to stone him.[j] [15]Say to the Israelites: 'If anyone curses his God,[k] he will be held responsible;[l] [16]anyone who blasphemes[m] the name of the LORD must be put to death.[n] The entire assembly must stone him. Whether an alien or native-born, when he blasphemes the Name, he must be put to death.

[17]" 'If anyone takes the life of a human being, he must be put to death.[o] [18]Anyone who takes the life of someone's animal must make restitution[p]—life for life. [19]If anyone injures his neighbor, whatever he has done must be done to him: [20]fracture for fracture, eye for eye, tooth for tooth.[q] As he has injured the other, so he is to be

Cross references (center column)

23:39 [l]Isa 62:9
[m]S Ex 23:16
23:40 [n]Ps 118:27
[o]Ne 8:14-17;
Ps 137:2; Isa 44:4
[p]Dt 12:7; 14:26;
28:47; Ne 8:10;
Ps 9:2; 66:6;
105:43; Joel 2:26
23:42
[q]S Ex 23:16
23:43 [r]Ps 78:5
24:3 [s]S Ex 12:14
24:4 [t]S Ex 25:31
24:5
[u]S Ex 25:30;
Heb 9:2
[v]S Lev 23:13
24:6
[w]Ex 25:23-30;
Nu 4:7
24:7 [x]S Lev 2:1
[y]S Lev 2:2

24:8 [z]Ex 25:30;
Nu 4:7;
1Ch 9:32;
2Ch 2:4 [a]Mt 12:5
24:9 [b]Mt 12:4;
Mk 2:26; Lk 6:4
[c]S Lev 6:16
[d]S Lev 6:17
24:11 [e]S Ex 3:15
[f]S Ex 20:7;
S 2Ki 6:33;
S Job 1:11
[g]S Ex 18:22
[h]Ex 31:2;
Nu 1:4; 7:2;
10:15; 13:2;
17:2; Jos 7:18;
1Ki 7:14
24:12
[i]S Ex 18:16
24:14 [j]ver 23;
S Lev 20:2;
Dt 13:9; 17:5,7;
Ac 7:58
24:15
[k]S Ex 22:28
[l]S Lev 5:1
24:16
[m]S Ex 22:28
[n]S Ex 21:12;
1Ki 21:10,13;
Mt 26:66;
Mk 14:64;
Jn 10:33; 19:7;
Ac 7:58
24:17 [o]ver 21;
Ge 9:6;
S Ex 21:12;
Dt 27:24
24:18 [p]ver 21
24:20
[q]S Ex 21:24;
Mt 5:38*

[k]5 That is, probably about 4 quarts (about 4.5 liters)

23:42 *booths.* The Hebrew for this word is *Sukkot* and is also translated "Tabernacles" (as in v. 34), giving the feast its name. Even today, orthodox Jews construct small booths (see Ne 8:13–17) to remind them of the booths they lived in when God brought them out of Egypt at the time of the exodus (v. 43).

24:2–4 See Ex 27:20–21.

24:3 *Testimony.* See note on Ex 16:34. *tend the lamps.* So that they would burn all night. *continually.* Every night without interruption, but not throughout the day. See 1Sa 3:3 and note.

24:5 *two-tenths of an ephah.* See NIV text note. Either the loaves were quite large or a smaller unit of measurement is intended (the Hebrew word *ephah* is not expressed).

24:7 *pure incense.* Not used as a condiment for the bread, but burned either in piles on the table or in small receptacles alongside the rows of bread.

24:8 *This bread.* Often called the "bread of the Presence" (see Ex 25:30 and note). It represented a gift from the 12

tribes and signified the fact that God sustained his people. It was eaten by the priests (24:9).

24:9 See 1Sa 21:4–6.

24:10 *Egyptian father.* An alien. The laws, at least in the judicial sphere, applied equally to both the alien and the native-born Israelite (v. 22; see Ex 12:49).

24:11 *blasphemed.* See Ex 20:7 and note.

24:17,21 See Ge 9:6 and note.

24:20 *eye for eye, tooth for tooth.* See note on Ex 21:23–25. This represents a statement of principle: The penalty is to fit the crime, not exceed it. An actual eye or tooth was not to be required, nor is there evidence that such a penalty was ever exacted. A similar law of retaliation is found in the Code of Hammurapi, which also seems not to have been literally applied. Christ, like the middle-of-the-road Pharisees (school of Hillel), objected to an extremist use of this judicial principle to excuse private vengeance, such as by the strict Pharisees (school of Shammai); see Mt 5:38–42.

injured. [21]Whoever kills an animal must make restitution,[r] but whoever kills a man must be put to death.[s] [22]You are to have the same law for the alien[t] and the native-born.[u] I am the LORD your God.' "

[23]Then Moses spoke to the Israelites, and they took the blasphemer outside the camp and stoned him.[v] The Israelites did as the LORD commanded Moses.

The Sabbath Year

25 The LORD said to Moses on Mount Sinai,[w] [2]"Speak to the Israelites and say to them: 'When you enter the land I am going to give you, the land itself must observe a sabbath to the LORD. [3]For six years sow your fields, and for six years prune your vineyards and gather their crops.[x] [4]But in the seventh year the land is to have a sabbath of rest,[y] a sabbath to the LORD. Do not sow your fields or prune your vineyards.[z] [5]Do not reap what grows of itself[a] or harvest the grapes[b] of your untended vines.[c] The land is to have a year of rest. [6]Whatever the land yields during the sabbath year[d] will be food for you—for yourself, your manservant and maidservant, and the hired worker and temporary resident who live among you, [7]as well as for your livestock and the wild animals[e] in your land. Whatever the land produces may be eaten.

The Year of Jubilee

25:8–38Ref — Dt 15:1–11
25:39–55Ref — Ex 21:2–11; Dt 15:12–18

[8]"Count off seven sabbaths of years—seven times seven years—so that the seven sabbaths of years amount to a period of forty-nine years. [9]Then have the trumpet[f] sounded everywhere on the tenth day of the seventh month;[g] on the Day of Atonement[h] sound the trumpet throughout your land. [10]Consecrate the fiftieth year and proclaim liberty[i] through-

out the land to all its inhabitants. It shall be a jubilee[j] for you; each one of you is to return to his family property[k] and each to his own clan. [11]The fiftieth year shall be a jubilee[l] for you; do not sow and do not reap what grows of itself or harvest the untended vines. [m] [12]For it is a jubilee and is to be holy for you; eat only what is taken directly from the fields.

[13]'In this Year of Jubilee[n] everyone is to return to his own property.

[14]'If you sell land to one of your countrymen or buy any from him, do not take advantage of each other.[o] [15]You are to buy from your countryman on the basis of the number of years[p] since the Jubilee. And he is to sell to you on the basis of the number of years left for harvesting crops. [16]When the years are many, you are to increase the price, and when the years are few, you are to decrease the price,[q] because what he is really selling you is the number of crops. [17]Do not take advantage of each other,[r] but fear your God.[s] I am the LORD your God.[t]

[18]'Follow my decrees and be careful to obey my laws,[u] and you will live safely in the land.[v] [19]Then the land will yield its fruit,[w] and you will eat your fill and live there in safety.[x] [20]You may ask, "What will we eat in the seventh year[y] if we do not plant or harvest our crops?" [21]I will send you such a blessing[z] in the sixth year that the land will yield enough for three years.[a] [22]While you plant during the eighth year, you will eat from the old crop and will continue to eat from it until the harvest of the ninth year comes in.[b]

[23]'The land[c] must not be sold permanently, because the land is mine[d] and you are but aliens[e] and my tenants.

24:21 [r]S ver 18
[s]S ver 17
24:22
[t]S Ex 12:49;
S 22:21;
Eze 47:22
[u]Nu 9:14
24:23 [v]S ver 14
25:1 [w]Ex 19:11
25:3 [x]Ex 23:10
25:4 [y]ver 5,6,20;
Lev 26:35;
2Ch 36:21
[z]Isa 36:16; 37:30
25:5 [a]2Ki 19:29
[b]Ge 40:10;
Nu 6:3; 13:20;
Dt 23:24;
Ne 13:15; Isa 5:2
[c]ver 4,11
25:6 [d]S ver 4
25:7 [e]Ex 23:11
25:9 [f]Lev 23:24;
Nu 10:8; Jos 6:4;
Jdg 3:27; 7:16;
1Sa 13:3;
Isa 27:13;
Zec 9:14
[g]S Lev 16:29
[h]S Ex 30:10
25:10 [i]Isa 61:1;
Jer 34:8,15,17;
S Lk 4:19
[j]ver 11,28,50;
Lev 27:17,21;
Nu 36:4;
Eze 46:17 [k]ver 27
25:11 [l]S ver 10
[m]S ver 5
25:13 [n]ver 10
25:14
[o]S Lev 19:13;
1Sa 12:3,4;
1Co 6:8
25:15 [p]ver 27;
Lev 27:18,23
25:16 [q]ver 27,
51,52
25:17
[r]S Lev 19:13;
Job 31:16;
Pr 22:22; Jer 7:5,
6; 21:12; 22:3,
15; Zec 7:9-10;
1Th 4:6
[s]S Lev 19:14
[t]S Lev 19:32
25:18 [u]S Ge 26:5
[v]ver 19; Lev 26:4,
5; Dt 12:10;
33:28; Job 5:22;
Ps 4:8; Jer 23:6;
30:10; 32:37;
33:16; Eze 28:26;
34:25; 38:14
25:19 [w]Lev 26:4;
Dt 11:14; 28:12;
Isa 55:10 [x]S ver
18
25:20 [y]S ver 4 25:21 [z]Dt 28:8,12; Ps 133:3; 134:3; 147:13;
Eze 44:30; Hag 2:19; Mal 3:10 [a]S Ex 16:5 25:22 [b]Lev 26:10
25:23 [c]Nu 36:7; 1Ki 21:3; Eze 46:18 [d]Ex 19:5 [e]S Ge 23:4;
S Heb 11:13

24:22 See note on v. 10.
25:4 *land is to have a sabbath.* See Ex 23:10–11. The Israelites did not practice crop rotation, but the fallow year (when the crops were not planted) served somewhat the same purpose. And just as the land was to have a sabbath year, so the servitude of a Hebrew slave was limited to six years, apparently whether or not the year he was freed was a sabbath year (see Ex 21:2 and note). Dt 15:1–11 specifies that debts were also to be canceled in the sabbath year. The care for the poor in the laws of Israel (see Ex 23:11) is noteworthy. See 23:7,35; Dt 31:10; Ne 10:31.
25:9 *Day of Atonement.* See notes on 16:1–34; see also 23:27.
25:10 *fiftieth year.* Possibly a fallow year in addition to the seventh sabbath year, or perhaps the same as the 49th year (counting the first and last years). Jewish sources from the period between the Testaments favor the latter interpreta-

tion. *proclaim liberty . . . inhabitants.* See vv. 39–43,47–55. The Liberty Bell in Philadelphia is so named because this statement was written on it. Cf. Isa 61:1–2; Lk 4:16–21. *jubilee.* The Hebrew for this word is the same as and may be related to one of the Hebrew words for "[ram's] horn," "trumpet" (see, e.g., Ex 19:13), though in v. 9 a different Hebrew word for "trumpet" is used. Trumpets were blown at the close of the Day of Atonement to inaugurate the Year of Jubilee. Cf. 23:24.

25:13 *return to his own property.* See v. 10. The Lord prohibited the accumulation of property to the detriment of the poor. "The land is mine," said the Lord (v. 23). God's people are only tenants (see 1Ch 29:15; Heb 11:13).

25:15 *number of years left for harvesting.* In a way, the sale of land in Israel was a lease until the Year of Jubilee (see 27:18,23).

²⁴Throughout the country that you hold as a possession, you must provide for the redemption/ of the land.

²⁵" 'If one of your countrymen becomes poor and sells some of his property, his nearest relative⁸ is to come and redeem ʰ what his countryman has sold. ²⁶If, however, a man has no one to redeem it for him but he himself prospers ⁱ and acquires sufficient means to redeem it, ²⁷he is to determine the value for the years ʲ since he sold it and refund the balance to the man to whom he sold it; he can then go back to his own property. ᵏ ²⁸But if he does not acquire the means to repay him, what he sold will remain in the possession of the buyer until the Year of Jubilee. It will be returned ˡ in the Jubilee, and he can then go back to his property. ᵐ

²⁹" 'If a man sells a house in a walled city, he retains the right of redemption a full year after its sale. During that time he may redeem it. ³⁰If it is not redeemed before a full year has passed, the house in the walled city shall belong permanently to the buyer and his descendants. It is not to be returned in the Jubilee. ³¹But houses in villages without walls around them are to be considered as open country. They can be redeemed, and they are to be returned in the Jubilee.

³²" 'The Levites always have the right to redeem their houses in the Levitical towns, ⁿ which they possess. ³³So the property of the Levites is redeemable—that is, a house sold in any town they hold—and is to be returned in the Jubilee, because the houses in the towns of the Levites are their property among the Israelites. ³⁴But the pastureland belonging to their towns must not be sold; it is their permanent possession. ᵒ

³⁵" 'If one of your countrymen becomes poor ᵖ and is unable to support himself among you, help him ᑫ as you would an alien or a temporary resident, so he can continue to live among you. ³⁶Do not take interest ʳ of any kind¹ from him, but fear your God, ˢ so that your countryman may continue to live among you. ³⁷You must not lend him money at interest ᵗ or sell him food at a profit. ³⁸I am the LORD your God, who brought you out of Egypt to give

25:24 /ver 29,48;
Ru 4:7; Jer 32:8
25:25 ᵍver 48;
Ru 2:20; Jer 32:7
ʰLev 27:13,19,
31; Ru 4:4
25:26 ⁱver 49
25:27 /S ver 15
ᵏver 10
25:28 /Lev 27:24
ᵐS ver 10
25:32
ⁿNu 35:1-8;
Jos 21:2
25:34
ᵒNu 35:2-5;
Eze 48:14
25:35 ᵖDt 24:14,
15 ᑫDt 15:8;
Ps 37:21,26;
Pr 21:26; Lk 6:35
25:36
ʳS Ex 22:25;
Jer 15:10
ˢS Lev 19:32
25:37
ᵗS Ex 22:25

25:38
ᵘS Ge 10:19
ᵛS Ge 17:7
25:39 ʷ1Ki 5:13;
9:22; Jer 34:14
25:40 ˣver 53
25:41 ʸver 28
ᶻJer 34:8
25:42 ᵃver 38
25:43
ᵇS Ex 1:13;
Eze 34:4; Col 4:1
ᶜS Ge 42:18
25:47 ᵈNe 5:5;
Job 24:9
25:48 ᵉS ver 24
/S ver 25
25:49 ᵍver 26
25:50 ʰS ver 10
/Job 7:1; 14:6;
Isa 16:14; 21:16
25:52 /S ver 16
25:53 ᵏCol 4:1

you the land of Canaan ᵘ and to be your God. ᵛ

³⁹" 'If one of your countrymen becomes poor among you and sells himself to you, do not make him work as a slave. ʷ ⁴⁰He is to be treated as a hired worker ˣ or a temporary resident among you; he is to work for you until the Year of Jubilee. ⁴¹Then he and his children are to be released, and he will go back to his own clan and to the property ʸ of his forefathers. ᶻ ⁴²Because the Israelites are my servants, whom I brought out of Egypt, ᵃ they must not be sold as slaves. ⁴³Do not rule over them ruthlessly, ᵇ but fear your God. ᶜ

⁴⁴" 'Your male and female slaves are to come from the nations around you; from them you may buy slaves. ⁴⁵You may also buy some of the temporary residents living among you and members of their clans born in your country, and they will become your property. ⁴⁶You can will them to your children as inherited property and can make them slaves for life, but you must not rule over your fellow Israelites ruthlessly.

⁴⁷" 'If an alien or a temporary resident among you becomes rich and one of your countrymen becomes poor and sells himself ᵈ to the alien living among you or to a member of the alien's clan, ⁴⁸he retains the right of redemption ᵉ after he has sold himself. One of his relatives/ may redeem him: ⁴⁹An uncle or a cousin or any blood relative in his clan may redeem him. Or if he prospers, ᵍ he may redeem himself. ⁵⁰He and his buyer are to count the time from the year he sold himself up to the Year of Jubilee. ʰ The price for his release is to be based on the rate paid to a hired man ⁱ for that number of years. ⁵¹If many years remain, he must pay for his redemption a larger share of the price paid for him. ⁵²If only a few years remain until the Year of Jubilee, he is to compute that and pay for his redemption accordingly./ ⁵³He is to be treated as a man hired from year to year; you must see to it that his owner does not rule over him ruthlessly. ᵏ

⁵⁴" 'Even if he is not redeemed in any of these ways, he and his children are to be released in the Year of Jubilee, ⁵⁵for the

¹36 Or take excessive interest; similarly in verse 37

25:24 redemption of the land. That is, the right to repurchase the land by (or for) the original family.
25:25 nearest relative is to come and redeem. See Jer 32:6–15. This is apparently what the nearest relative was to do for Naomi and Ruth (Ru 4:1–4), but he was also obligated to marry the widow and support the family (see Dt 25:5–10). Only Boaz was willing to do both (Ru 4:9–10).
25:33 towns of the Levites. See Nu 35:1–8; Jos 21:1–42.
25:36 interest. The main idea (see NIV text note) is not necessarily to forbid all interest, but to assist the poor. The law did not forbid lending so much as it encouraged giving.
25:55 servants. Covenant terminology, similar to "vas-

Israelites belong to me as servants. They are my servants, whom I brought out of Egypt. *l* I am the LORD your God. *m*

Reward for Obedience

26 " 'Do not make idols *n* or set up an image *o* or a sacred stone *p* for yourselves, and do not place a carved stone *q* in your land to bow down before it. I am the LORD your God.

2" 'Observe my Sabbaths *r* and have reverence for my sanctuary. *s* I am the LORD.

3" 'If you follow my decrees and are careful to obey *t* my commands, 4I will send you rain *u* in its season, *v* and the ground will yield its crops and the trees of the field their fruit. *w* 5Your threshing will continue until grape harvest and the grape harvest will continue until planting, and you will eat all the food you want *x* and live in safety in your land. *y*

6" 'I will grant peace in the land, *z* and you will lie down *a* and no one will make you afraid. *b* I will remove savage beasts *c* from the land, and the sword will not pass through your country. 7You will pursue your enemies, *d* and they will fall by the sword before you. 8Five *e* of you will chase a hundred, and a hundred of you will chase ten thousand, and your enemies will fall by the sword before you. *f*

9" 'I will look on you with favor and make you fruitful and increase your numbers, *g* and I will keep my covenant *h* with you. 10You will still be eating last year's harvest when you will have to move it out to make room for the new. *i* 11I will put my dwelling place *m/* among you, and I will not abhor you. *k* 12I will walk *l* among you and be your God, *m* and you will be my people. *n* 13I am the LORD your God, *o* who brought you out of Egypt *p* so that you would no longer be slaves to the Egyptians; I broke the bars of your yoke *q* and enabled you to walk with heads held high.

Punishment for Disobedience

14" 'But if you will not listen to me and

carry out all these commands, *r* 15and if you reject my decrees and abhor my laws *s* and fail to carry out all my commands and so violate my covenant, *t* 16then I will do this to you: I will bring upon you sudden terror, wasting diseases and fever *u* that will destroy your sight and drain away your life. *v* You will plant seed in vain, because your enemies will eat it. *w* 17I will set my face *x* against you so that you will be defeated *y* by your enemies; *z* those who hate you will rule over you, *a* and you will flee even when no one is pursuing you. *b*

18" 'If after all this you will not listen to me, *c* I will punish *d* you for your sins seven times over. *e* 19I will break down your stubborn pride *f* and make the sky above you like iron and the ground beneath you like bronze. *g* 20Your strength will be spent in vain, *h* because your soil will not yield its crops, nor will the trees of the land yield their fruit. *i*

21" 'If you remain hostile *j* toward me and refuse to listen to me, I will multiply your afflictions seven times over, *k* as your sins deserve. 22I will send wild animals *l* against you, and they will rob you of your children, destroy your cattle and make you so few *m* in number that your roads will be deserted. *n*

23" 'If in spite of these things you do not accept my correction *o* but continue to be hostile toward me, 24I myself will be hostile *p* toward you and will afflict you for your sins seven times over. 25And I will bring the sword *q* upon you to avenge *r* the breaking of the covenant. When you with-

25:55 /S Lev 11:45
m Lev 11:44
26:1 *n* S Ex 20:4
o Ps 97:7;
Isa 48:5;
Jer 44:19;
Hab 2:18
p S Ex 23:24
q Nu 33:52
26:2 *r* S Ex 20:8
s Lev 19:30
26:3 *t* S Ge 26:5;
S Ex 24:8;
Dt 6:17; 7:12;
11:13,22; 28:1,9
26:4 *u* Dt 11:14;
28:12; Ps 68:9;
Jer 5:24; Hos 6:3;
Joel 2:23;
Zec 10:1
v Job 5:10;
Ps 65:9; 104:13;
147:8; Jer 5:24
w S Ex 23:26;
S Lev 25:19;
S Job 14:9;
Ps 67:6
26:5 *x* Dt 6:11;
11:15;
Eze 36:29-30;
Joel 2:19,26
y S Lev 25:18
26:6 *z* Ps 29:11;
37:11; 85:8;
147:14; Isa 26:3;
54:13; 60:18;
Hag 2:9 *a* Ps 3:5;
4:8; Pr 3:24
b Job 11:18,19;
Isa 17:2;
Jer 30:10;
Mic 4:4; Zep 3:13
c S ver 22;
S Ge 37:20
26:7 *d* Ps 18:37;
44:5
26:8 *e* Isa 30:17
/Dt 28:7; 32:30;
Jos 23:10;
Jdg 15:15;
1Ch 5:21
26:9 *g* S Ge 1:22;
S 17:6; Ne 9:23
h S Ge 17:7
26:10 *i* Lev 25:22
26:11 /Ex 25:8;
Ps 74:7; 76:2;
Eze 37:27 *k* ver
15,43,44;
Dt 31:6;
1Sa 12:22;
1Ki 6:13;
2Ki 17:15
26:12 /S Ge 3:8
m S Ge 17:7
n Ex 6:7; Jer 7:23;
11:4; 24:7;
30:22; 31:1;
Zec 13:9;
2Co 6:16*
26:13 *o* Lev 11:44
p S Ex 6:6; S 13:3
q Isa 10:27;
Jer 2:20; 27:2;
28:10; 30:8;
Eze 30:18; 34:27;
Hos 11:4

26:14 *r* Dt 28:15-68; Mal 2:2 **26:15** *s* S ver 11 *t* S Ge 17:7
26:16 *u* Dt 28:22,35; Ps 78:33 *v* ver 39; 1Sa 2:33; Ps 107:17;
Eze 4:17; 24:23; 33:10 *w* Jdg 6:3; Job 31:8 **26:17**
x Lev 17:10; Eze 15:7 *y* Dt 28:48; Jos 7:12; Jdg 2:15;
1Ki 8:33; 2Ch 6:24 *z* Jos 7:4; Jer 19:7; 21:7 *a* Ps 106:41 *b* ver
36,37; Dt 28:7,25; Ps 53:5; Pr 28:1; Isa 30:17 **26:18** *c* ver 14
d Ps 99:8; Jer 21:14; Am 3:14 *e* ver 21 **26:19** /Ps 10:4; 73:6;
Isa 16:6; 25:11; 28:1-3; Jer 13:9; 48:29; Eze 24:21; Am 6:8;
Zep 3:11 *g* Dt 28:23; Job 38:38 **26:20** *h* Dt 28:38; Ps 127:1;
Isa 17:11; 49:4; Jer 12:13; Mic 6:15; Hag 1:6 **26:21** /ver
28:24 **26:21** /ver 41 *k* ver 18; S Ge 4:15 **26:22** /S Ge 37:20
m Dt 28:62; Jer 42:2 *n* Jer 5:6; 14:16; 15:3; 16:4; Eze 14:15
26:23 *o* Jer 2:30; 5:3; 7:28; 17:23; 32:33; Zep 3:2 **26:24**
p 2Sa 22:27 **26:25** *q* Jer 5:17; 15:3; 47:6; Eze 11:8; 14:17;
21:4; 33:2 *r* Jer 50:28; 51:6,11

m 11 Or *my tabernacle*

sals." Slavery, however demeaning, is not brutal where the masters truly recognize themselves as God's servants. Cf. Paul's exhortation to both slaves and masters (Eph 6:5–9; Col 3:22–4:1).

26:1 *Do not make idols.* This verse probably does not forbid making statues, but it does forbid worshiping God in any material form (see Ex 20:4 and note). "God is spirit" (Jn 4:24; see Dt 4:15–19).

26:3 *obey my commands.* Obedience is the key to blessing (see Gal 6:7–10; Jas 1:22–25). Compare the blessings promised in vv. 3–13 with those in Dt 28:1–14.

26:9 *fruitful and increase.* See note on Ge 1:22; contrast Lev 26:22.

26:12 *your God ... my people.* Covenantal terms later made famous by Hosea (1:9–10; 2:23). See Jer 31:33; Eze 36:28; Heb 8:10.

26:14 *if you will not listen.* The list of curses for covenant disobedience (see vv. 14–39) is usually much longer than that of blessings for obedience (as in vv. 3–13; see Dt 28:15–29:28; cf. Dt 28:1–14).

26:17 See v. 36 and the allusion to this statement in Pr 28:1.

draw into your cities, I will send a plague[s] among you, and you will be given into enemy hands. [26]When I cut off your supply of bread,[t] ten women will be able to bake your bread in one oven, and they will dole out the bread by weight. You will eat, but you will not be satisfied.

[27]" 'If in spite of this you still do not listen to me[u] but continue to be hostile toward me, [28]then in my anger[v] I will be hostile[w] toward you, and I myself will punish you for your sins seven times over.[x] [29]You will eat[y] the flesh of your sons and the flesh of your daughters.[z] [30]I will destroy your high places,[a] cut down your incense altars[b] and pile your dead bodies on the lifeless forms of your idols,[c] and I will abhor[d] you. [31]I will turn your cities into ruins[e] and lay waste[f] your sanctuaries,[g] and I will take no delight in the pleasing aroma of your offerings.[h] [32]I will lay waste the land,[i] so that your enemies who live there will be appalled.[j] [33]I will scatter[k] you among the nations[l] and will draw out my sword[m] and pursue you. Your land will be laid waste,[n] and your cities will lie in ruins.[o] [34]Then the land will enjoy its sabbath years all the time that it lies desolate[p] and you are in the country of your enemies; [q] then the land will rest and enjoy its sabbaths. [35]All the time that it lies desolate, the land will have the rest[r] it did not have during the sabbaths you lived in it.

[36]" 'As for those of you who are left, I will make their hearts so fearful in the lands of their enemies that the sound of a windblown leaf[s] will put them to flight.[t] They will run as though fleeing from the sword, and they will fall, even though no one is pursuing them.[u] [37]They will stumble over one another[v] as though fleeing from the sword, even though no one is pursuing you. So you will not be able to stand before your enemies.[w] [38]You will perish[x] among the nations; the land of your enemies will devour you.[y] [39]Those of you who are left will waste away in the lands of their enemies because of their sins; also because of their fathers'[z] sins they will waste away.[a]

[40]" 'But if they will confess[b] their sins[c]

and the sins of their fathers[d]—their treachery against me and their hostility toward me, [41]which made me hostile[e] toward them so that I sent them into the land of their enemies—then when their uncircumcised hearts[f] are humbled[g] and they pay[h] for their sin, [42]I will remember my covenant with Jacob[i] and my covenant with Isaac[j] and my covenant with Abraham,[k] and I will remember the land. [43]For the land will be deserted[l] by them and will enjoy its sabbaths while it lies desolate without them. They will pay for their sins because they rejected[m] my laws and abhorred my decrees.[n] [44]Yet in spite of this, when they are in the land of their enemies,[o] I will not reject them or abhor[p] them so as to destroy them completely,[q] breaking my covenant[r] with them. I am the Lord their God. [45]But for their sake I will remember[s] the covenant with their ancestors whom I brought out of Egypt[t] in the sight of the nations to be their God. I am the Lord.' "

[46]These are the decrees, the laws and the regulations that the Lord established on Mount Sinai[u] between himself and the Israelites through Moses.[v]

Redeeming What Is the Lord's

27 The Lord said to Moses, [2]"Speak to the Israelites and say to them: 'If anyone makes a special vow[w] to dedicate persons to the Lord by giving equivalent values, [3]set the value of a male between the ages of twenty and sixty at fifty shekels[n] of silver, according to the sanctu-

Cross references (center column)

26:25 sS Ex 5:3; S 9:3; Nu 16:46; 1Ki 8:37; Hab 3:5
26:26 tI Ki 8:37; 18:2; 2Ki 4:38; 6:25; 8:1; 25:3; Ps 105:16; Isa 3:1; 9:20; Jer 37:21; 52:6; Eze 4:16,17; 5:16; 14:13; Hos 4:10; Mic 6:14
26:27 uver 14
26:28 vDt 32:19; Jdg 2:14; Ps 78:59; 106:40 wDt 7:10; Job 34:11; Isa 59:18; 65:6-7; 66:6; Jer 17:10; 25:29; Joel 3:4 xver 18
26:29 y2Ki 6:29; Jer 19:9; La 4:10; Eze 5:10 zDt 28:53
26:30 aDt 12:2; 1Sa 9:12; 10:5; 1Ki 3:2,4; 12:31; 13:2,32; 2Ki 17:29; 23:20; 2Ch 34:3; Ps 78:58; Eze 6:3; 16:16; Am 7:9 b2Ch 34:4; Isa 17:8; 27:9; Eze 6:6 cIsa 21:9; Jer 50:2; Eze 6:13 dPs 106:40; Am 6:8
26:31 eNe 1:3; Isa 1:7; 3:8,26; 6:11; 24:12; 61:4; Jer 4:7; 9:11; 25:11; 34:22; 44:2,6,22; Eze 36:33; Mic 2:4; 3:12; Zep 2:5; 3:6 f2Ki 22:19 gPs 74:3-7; Isa 63:18; 64:11; La 2:7; Eze 24:21; Am 7:9 hAm 5:21,22; 8:10
26:32 iIsa 5:6; Jer 9:11; 12:11; 25:11; 26:9; 33:10; 34:22; 44:22 j1Ki 9:8; 2Ch 29:8; Isa 52:14; Jer 18:16; 19:8; 48:39; Eze 5:14; 26:16; 27:35; 28:19
26:33 kJer 40:15; 50:17; Eze 34:6; Joel 3:2 lDt 4:27; 28:64; Ne 1:8; Ps 44:11; 106:27; Jer 4:11; 9:16; 13:24; 31:10; Eze 5:10; 12:15; 17:21; 20:23; 22:15; Zec 7:14 mJer 42:16; Am 9:4 nIsa 49:19;

Jer 7:34 over 31; 1Sa 15:22; Job 36:11; Jer 40:3 26:34 pIsa 1:7; Jer 7:34; 25:11; 44:6; Eze 33:29 qver 43; 2Ch 36:21 26:35 rS Lev 25:4 26:36 sJob 13:25 t2Ki 25:5; Ps 58:7; La 1:3,6; 4:19; Eze 21:7 uS ver 17 26:37 vJer 6:21; 13:16; 46:16; Eze 3:20; Na 3:3 wJos 7:12 26:38 xJob 4:9; 36:12; Ps 1:6; Isa 1:28; Jer 16:4; 44:27 yDt 4:26 26:39 zEx 20:5; Isa 14:21 aS ver 16; Isa 24:16 26:40 bS Lev 5:5 cPs 32:5; 38:18 dNe 9:2; Ps 106:6; Jer 3:12-15; 14:20; Hos 5:15; Lk 15:18; 1Jn 1:9 26:41 eS ver 21 fDt 10:16; 30:6; Jer 4:4; 9:25,26; Eze 44:7,9; Ac 7:51 g2Ch 7:14; 12:6; Eze 20:43 hIsa 6:7; 33:24; 40:2; 53:5,6,11 26:42 iGe 28:15; 35:11-12 jS Ge 26:5 kS Ex 2:24 26:43 lPs 69:25; Isa 6:11; 32:14; 62:4; Jer 2:15; 44:2; La 1:1; Eze 36:4 mNu 11:20; 14:31; 1Sa 8:7; Ps 106:24 nS ver 11; Eze 20:13 26:44 oS ver 33; 2Ki 17:20; 25:11; 2Ch 6:36; 36:20 pS ver 11; Ro 11:2 qDt 4:31; Jer 4:27; 5:10; 30:11 rJdg 2:1; Jer 31:37; 33:26; 51:5 26:45 sDt 4:31 tEx 6:8; Lev 25:38 26:46 uS Ex 19:11 vS Lev 7:38; 27:34 27:2 wS Ge 28:20

n3 That is, about 1 1/4 pounds (about 0.6 kilogram); also in verse 16

26:41 uncircumcised hearts. See note on Ge 17:10.
26:44 not reject them. See Jer 31:37; 33:25-26; Ro 11:1-29.
26:46 A summary statement concerning chs. 1-26.
27:1-34 This final chapter concerns things promised to the Lord in kind—servants, animals, houses or lands. But provisions were made to give money instead of the item, in which case usually the adding of a fifth of its value was

required. Such vows were expressions of special thanksgiving (cf. Hannah, 1Sa 1:28) and were given over and above the expected sacrifices.
27:2 to dedicate persons. Possibly to give slaves to the service of the temple, but more likely to offer oneself or a member of one's family. Since only Levites were acceptable for most work of this kind, other people gave the monetary equivalent—but see 1Sa 1:11.

ary shekel[o]; [x] [4]and if it is a female, set her value at thirty shekels.[p] [5]If it is a person between the ages of five and twenty, set the value of a male at twenty shekels[q] [y] and of a female at ten shekels.[r] [6]If it is a person between one month and five years, set the value of a male at five shekels[s] [z] of silver and that of a female at three shekels[t] of silver. [7]If it is a person sixty years old or more, set the value of a male at fifteen shekels[u] and of a female at ten shekels. [8]If anyone making the vow is too poor to pay[a] the specified amount, he is to present the person to the priest, who will set the value[b] for him according to what the man making the vow can afford.

[9]" 'If what he vowed is an animal that is acceptable as an offering to the LORD,[c] such an animal given to the LORD becomes holy.[d] [10]He must not exchange it or substitute a good one for a bad one, or a bad one for a good one;[e] if he should substitute one animal for another, both it and the substitute become holy. [11]If what he vowed is a ceremonially unclean animal[f]—one that is not acceptable as an offering to the LORD—the animal must be presented to the priest, [12]who will judge its quality as good or bad. Whatever value the priest then sets, that is what it will be. [13]If the owner wishes to redeem[g] the animal, he must add a fifth to its value.[h]

[14]" 'If a man dedicates his house as something holy to the LORD, the priest will judge its quality as good or bad. Whatever value the priest then sets, so it will remain. [15]If the man who dedicates his house redeems it,[i] he must add a fifth to its value, and the house will again become his.

[16]" 'If a man dedicates to the LORD part of his family land, its value is to be set according to the amount of seed required for it—fifty shekels of silver to a homer[v] of barley seed. [17]If he dedicates his field during the Year of Jubilee, the value that has been set remains. [18]But if he dedicates his field after the Jubilee,[j] the priest will determine the value according to the number of years that remain[k] until the next Year of

Jubilee, and its set value will be reduced. [19]If the man who dedicates the field wishes to redeem it,[l] he must add a fifth to its value, and the field will again become his. [20]If, however, he does not redeem the field, or if he has sold it to someone else, it can never be redeemed. [21]When the field is released in the Jubilee,[m] it will become holy,[n] like a field devoted to the LORD;[o] it will become the property of the priests.[w]

[22]" 'If a man dedicates to the LORD a field he has bought, which is not part of his family land, [23]the priest will determine its value up to the Year of Jubilee,[p] and the man must pay its value on that day as something holy to the LORD. [24]In the Year of Jubilee the field will revert to the person from whom he bought it,[q] the one whose land it was. [25]Every value is to be set according to the sanctuary shekel,[r] twenty gerahs[s] to the shekel.

[26]" 'No one, however, may dedicate the firstborn of an animal, since the firstborn already belongs to the LORD;[t] whether an ox[x] or a sheep, it is the LORD's. [27]If it is one of the unclean animals,[u] he may buy it back at its set value, adding a fifth of the value to it. If he does not redeem it, it is to be sold at its set value.

[28]" 'But nothing that a man owns and devotes[y] [v] to the LORD—whether man or animal or family land—may be sold or redeemed; everything so devoted is most holy[w] to the LORD.

[29]" 'No person devoted to destruction[z] may be ransomed; he must be put to death.[x]

27:3 [x]S Ex 30:13
27:5 [y]S Ge 37:28
27:6 [z]Nu 3:47; 18:16
27:8 [a]S Lev 5:11 [b]ver 12,14
27:9 [c]S Ge 28:20; S Lev 1:2 [d]ver 21, 26,28; Ex 40:9; Nu 6:20; 18:17; Dt 15:19
27:10 [e]ver 33
27:11 [f]ver 27; S Ex 13:13; Nu 18:15
27:13 [g]S Lev 25:25 [h]S Lev 5:16
27:15 [i]ver 13,20
27:18 [j]Lev 25:10 [k]Lev 25:15

27:19 [l]S Lev 25:25
27:21 [m]S Lev 25:10 [n]S ver 9 [o]ver 28; Nu 18:14; Eze 44:29
27:23 [p]S Lev 25:15
27:24 [q]Lev 25:28
27:25 [r]S Ex 30:13 [s]Nu 3:47; Eze 45:12
27:26 [t]S Ex 13:12
27:27 [u]S ver 11
27:28 [v]Nu 18:14; Jos 6:17-19 [w]S ver 9
27:29 [x]Dt 7:26

[o]3 That is, about 2/5 ounce (about 11.5 grams); also in verse 25   [p]4 That is, about 12 ounces (about 0.3 kilogram)   [q]5 That is, about 8 ounces (about 0.2 kilogram)   [r]5 That is, about 4 ounces (about 110 grams); also in verse 7   [s]6 That is, about 2 ounces (about 55 grams)   [t]6 That is, about 1 1/4 ounces (about 35 grams)   [u]7 That is, about 6 ounces (about 170 grams)   [v]16 That is, probably about 6 bushels (about 220 liters)   [w]21 Or priest   [x]26 The Hebrew word can include both male and female.   [y]28 The Hebrew term refers to the irrevocable giving over of things or persons to the LORD.   [z]29 The Hebrew term refers to the irrevocable giving over of things or persons to the LORD, often by totally destroying them.

27:9 *becomes holy.* An animal given for a sacrifice could not be exchanged for another (v. 10). The people of Malachi's day chose the poorest animals after having vowed to offer good ones (Mal 1:13–14). If an unclean animal was given, it could be redeemed with the 20 percent penalty (vv. 11–13).
27:28 *devotes to the LORD.* See NIV text note. Devoting something was far more serious than dedicating it to sacred use. The devoted thing became totally the Lord's. Achan's sin was the greater because he stole what had been devoted to the Lord (Jos 7:11). Persons devoted to destruction were

usually the captives in the wars of Canaan (cf. 1Sa 15:3,18).
27:29 Saul sinned in this regard when he did not totally destroy the Amalekites (1Sa 15).
27:30 *tithe.* A tenth (see Nu 18:21–29; Dt 12:6–18; 14:22–29; 26:12). From these passages it appears that Israel actually had three tithes: (1) the general tithe (here), paid to the Levites (Nu 18:21), who in turn had to give a tenth of that to the priests (Nu 18:26); (2) the tithe associated with the sacred meal involving offerer and Levite (Dt 14:22–27); (3) the tithe paid every three years to the poor (Dt 14:28–29).

30 " 'A tithe^y of everything from the land, whether grain from the soil or fruit from the trees, belongs to the LORD; it is holy^z to the LORD. 31If a man redeems^a any of his tithe, he must add a fifth of the value^b to it. 32The entire tithe of the herd and flock—every tenth animal that passes under the shepherd's rod^c—will be holy to the LORD. 33He must not pick out the good from the bad or make any substitution.^d If he does make a substitution, both the animal and its substitute become holy and cannot be redeemed.^e ' "

34These are the commands the LORD gave Moses on Mount Sinai^f for the Israelites.^g

---

27:30
^y Nu 18:26;
Dt 12:6,17;
14:22,28;
2Ch 31:6;
Ne 10:37; 12:44;
13:5; Mal 3:8;
^z Dt 7:6; Ezr 9:2;
Isa 6:13
27:31
^a S Lev 25:25
^b Lev 5:16
27:32 ^c Ps 89:32;
Jer 33:13;
Eze 20:37

27:33 ^d ver 10 ^e Nu 18:21 **27:34** ^f S Ex 19:11 ^g S Lev 7:38;
Ac 7:38

27:34 *the LORD gave Moses.* See 1:1; 7:37–38; 25:1; 26:46. This is strong testimony for the Mosaic authorship and divine origin of the book.

NUMBERS

Title

The English name of the book comes from the Septuagint (the Greek translation of the OT) and is based on the census lists found in chs. 1; 26. The Hebrew title of the book (*bemidbar*, "in the desert") is more descriptive of its contents. Numbers presents an account of the 38-year period of Israel's wandering in the desert following the establishment of the covenant of Sinai (compare 1:1 with Dt 1:1).

Author and Date

The book has traditionally been ascribed to Moses. This conclusion is based on (1) statements concerning Moses' writing activity (e.g., 33:1-2; Ex 17:14; 24:4; 34:27) and (2) the assumption that the first five books of the Bible, the Pentateuch, are a unit and come from one author. See Introduction to Genesis: Author and Date of Writing.

It is not necessary, however, to claim that Numbers came from Moses' hand complete and in final form. Portions of the book were probably added by scribes or editors from later periods of Israel's history. For example, the protestation of the humility of Moses (12:3) would hardly be convincing if it came from his own mouth. But it seems reasonable to assume that Moses wrote the essential content of the book.

Contents

Numbers relates the story of Israel's journey from Mount Sinai to the plains of Moab on the border of Canaan. Much of its legislation for people and priests is similar to that in Exodus, Leviticus and Deuteronomy. The book tells of the murmuring and rebellion of God's people and of their subsequent judgment. Those whom God had redeemed from slavery in Egypt and with whom he had made a covenant at Mount Sinai responded not with faith, gratitude and obedience but with unbelief, ingratitude and repeated acts of rebellion, which came to extreme expression in their refusal to undertake the conquest of Canaan (ch. 14). The community of the redeemed forfeited their part in the promised land. They were condemned to live out their lives in the desert; only their children would enjoy the fulfillment of the promise that had originally been theirs (cf. Heb 3:7-4:11).

Theological Teaching

In telling the story of Israel's desert wanderings, Numbers offers much that is theologically significant. During the first year after Israel's deliverance from Egypt, she entered into covenant with the Lord at Sinai to be the people of his kingdom, among whom he pitched his royal tent (the tabernacle)—this is the story of Exodus. As the account of Numbers begins, the Lord organizes Israel into a military camp. Leaving Sinai, she marches forth as his conquering army, with the Lord at her head, to establish his kingdom in the promised land in the midst of the nations. The book graphically portrays Israel's identity as the Lord's redeemed covenant people and her vocation as the servant people of God, charged with establishing his kingdom on earth. God's purpose in history is implicitly disclosed: to invade the arena of fallen humanity and effect the redemption of his creation—the mission in which his people are also to be totally engaged.

Numbers also presents the chastening wrath of God against his disobedient people. Because of her rebellion (and especially her refusal to undertake the conquest of Canaan), Israel was in breach of covenant. The fourth book of the Pentateuch presents a sobering reality: The God who had entered into covenant with Abraham (Ge 15; 17), who had delivered his people from bondage in the exodus (Ex 14-15), who had brought Israel into covenant with himself as his "treasured possession" (Ex 19; see especially Ex 19:5) and who had revealed his holiness and the gracious means of approaching him

(Lev 1-7) was also a God of wrath. His wrath extended to his errant children as well as to the enemy nations of Egypt and Canaan.

Even Moses, the great prophet and servant of the Lord, was not exempt from God's wrath when he disobeyed God. Ch. 20, which records his error, begins with the notice of Miriam's death (20:1) and concludes with the record of Aaron's death (20:22-29). Here is the passing of the old guard. Those whom God has used to establish the nation are dying before the nation has come into its own.

The questions arise: Is God finished with the nation as a whole (cf. Ro 11:1)? Are his promises a thing of the past? In one of the most remarkable sections of the Bible—the account of Balaam, the pagan diviner (chs. 22-24)—the reply is given. The Lord, working in a providential and direct way, proclaims his continued faithfulness to his purpose for his people despite their unfaithfulness to him.

Balaam is Moab's answer to Moses, the man of God. He is an internationally known prophet who shares the pagan belief that the God of Israel is like any other deity who might be manipulated by acts of magic or sorcery. But from the early part of the narrative, when Balaam first encounters the one true God in visions, and in the narrative of the journey on the donkey (ch. 22), he begins to learn that dealing with the true God is fundamentally different from anything he has ever known. When he attempts to curse Israel at the instigation of Balak king of Moab, Balaam finds his mouth unable to express the curse he desires to pronounce. Instead, from his lips come blessings on Israel and curses on her enemies (chs. 23-24).

In his seven prophetic oracles, Balaam proclaims God's great blessing for his people (see 23:20). Though the immediate enjoyment of this blessing will always depend on the faithfulness of his people, the ultimate realization of God's blessing is sure—because of the character of God (see 23:19). Thus Numbers reaffirms the ongoing purposes of God. Despite his judgment on his rebellious people, God is still determined to bring Israel into the land of promise. His blessing to her rests in his sovereign will.

The teaching of the book has lasting significance for Israel and for the church (cf. Ro 15:4; 1Co 10:6,11). God does display his wrath even against his errant people, but his grace is renewed as surely as is the dawn and his redemptive purpose will not be thwarted.

Special Problem

The large numbers of men conscripted into Israel's army puzzle modern scholars (see, e.g., the figures in 1:46; 26:51). These numbers of men mustered for warfare demand a total population in excess of 2,000,000. Such numbers seem to be exceedingly large for the times, for the locale, for the desert wanderings, and in comparison with the inhabitants of Canaan. See note on 3:43.

Various possibilities have been suggested to solve this problem. Some have thought that the numbers may have been corrupted in transmission. The present text, however, does not betray textual difficulties with the numbers.

Others have felt that the Hebrew word for "thousand" might have a different meaning here from its usual numerical connotation. In some passages, for example, the word is a technical term for a company of men that may or may not equal 1,000 (e.g., Jos 22:14, "family division"; 1Sa 23:23, "clans"). Further, some have postulated that this Hebrew word means "chief" (as in Ge 36:15). In this way the figure 53,400 (26:47) would mean "53 chiefs plus 400 men." Such a procedure would yield a greatly reduced total, but it would also be at variance with the fact that the Hebrew text adds the "thousands" in the same way it adds the "hundreds" for a large total. Also, this would make the proportion of chiefs to fighting men top-heavy (59 chiefs for 300 men in Simeon).

Another option is to read the Hebrew word for "thousand" with a dual meaning of "chief" and "1,000," with the chiefs numbering one less than the stated figure. For example, the 46,500 of Reuben (1:20) is read as 45 chiefs and 1,500 fighting men, the 59,300 of Simeon (1:23) is read as 58 chiefs and 1,300 fighting men, etc. But in this case, as in the former, the totals of 1:46 and 2:32 must then be regarded as errors of understanding (perhaps by later scribes).

Still another approach is to regard the numbers as symbolic figures rather than as strictly mathematical. The numerical value of the Hebrew letters in the expression *bene yisra'el* ("the Israelite community," 1:2) equals 603 (the number of the thousands of the fighting men, 1:46); the remaining 550 (plus 1 for Moses) might come from the numerical equivalent of the Hebrew letters in the expression "all the men . . . who are able to serve in the army" (1:3). This symbolic use of numbers (called "gematria") is not unknown in the Bible (see Rev 13:18), but it is not likely in Numbers, where there are no literary clues pointing in that direction.

While the problem of the large numbers has not been satisfactorily solved, the Bible does point to

a remarkable increase of Jacob's descendants during the four centuries of their sojourn in Egypt (see Ex 1:7-12). With all their difficulties, these numbers also point to the great role of providence and miracles in God's dealings with his people during their life in the desert (see note on 1:46).

Structure and Outline

The book has three major divisions, based on Israel's geographical locations. Each of the three divisions has two parts, as the following breakdown demonstrates: (1) Israel at Sinai, preparing to depart for the land of promise (1:1-10:10), followed by the journey from Sinai to Kadesh (10:11-12:16); (2) Israel at Kadesh, delayed as a result of rebellion (13:1-20:13), followed by the journey from Kadesh to the plains of Moab (20:14-22:1); (3) Israel on the plains of Moab, anticipating the conquest of the land of promise (22:2-32:42), followed by appendixes dealing with various matters (chs. 33-36).

I. Israel at Sinai, Preparing to Depart for the Promised Land (1:1-10:10)
   A. The Commands for the Census of the People (chs. 1-4)
      1. The numbers of men from each tribe mustered for war (ch. 1)
      2. The placement of the tribes around the tabernacle and their order for march (ch. 2)
      3. The placement of the Levites around the tabernacle, and the numbers of the Levites and the firstborn of Israel (ch. 3)
      4. The numbers of the Levites in their tabernacle service for the Lord (ch. 4)
   B. The Commands for Purity of the People (5:1-10:10)
      1. The test for purity in the law of jealousy (ch. 5)
      2. The Nazirite vow and the Aaronic benediction (ch. 6)
      3. The offerings of the 12 leaders at the dedication of the tabernacle (ch. 7)
      4. The setting up of the lamps and the separation of the Levites (ch. 8)
      5. The observance of the Passover (9:1-14)
      6. The covering cloud and the silver trumpets (9:15-10:10)
II. The Journey from Sinai to Kadesh (10:11-12:16)
   A. The Beginning of the Journey (10:11-36)
   B. The Beginning of the Sorrows: Fire and Quail (ch. 11)
   C. The Opposition of Miriam and Aaron (ch. 12)
III. Israel at Kadesh, the Delay Resulting from Rebellion (13:1-20:13)
   A. The 12 Spies and Their Mixed Report of the Good Land (ch. 13)
   B. The People's Rebellion against God's Commission, and Their Defeat (ch. 14)
   C. A Collection of Laws on Offerings, the Sabbath and Tassels on Garments (ch. 15)
   D. The Rebellion of Korah and His Allies (ch. 16)
   E. The Budding of Aaron's Staff: A Sign for Rebels (ch. 17)
   F. Concerning Priests, Their Duties and Their Support (ch. 18)
   G. The Red Heifer and the Cleansing Water (ch. 19)
   H. The Sin of Moses (20:1-13)
IV. The Journey from Kadesh to the Plains of Moab (20:14-22:1)
   A. The Resistance of Edom (20:14-21)
   B. The Death of Aaron (20:22-29)
   C. The Destruction of Arad (21:1-3)
   D. The Bronze Snake (21:4-9)
   E. The Song of the Well (21:10-20)
   F. The Defeat of Sihon and Og (21:21-30)
   G. Israel Enters Moab (21:31-22:1)
V. Israel on the Plains of Moab, in Anticipation of Taking the Promised Land (22:2-32:42)
   A. Balak of Moab Hires Balaam to Curse Israel (22:2-41)
   B. Balaam Blesses Israel in Seven Oracles (chs. 23-24)
   C. The Baal of Peor and Israel's Apostasy (ch. 25)
   D. The Second Census (ch. 26)
   E. Instructions for the New Generation (chs. 27-30)
      1. The inheritance for women (27:1-11)
      2. The successor to Moses (27:12-23)
      3. Commands regarding offerings (28:1-15)
      4. Commands regarding festivals (28:16-29:40)

The Census

1 The LORD spoke to Moses in the Tent of Meeting[a] in the Desert of Sinai[b] on the first day of the second month[c] of the second year after the Israelites came out of Egypt.[d] He said: [2]"Take a census[e] of the whole Israelite community by their clans and families,[f] listing every man by name,[g] one by one. [3]You and Aaron[h] are to number by their divisions all the men in Israel twenty years old or more[i] who are able to serve in the army.[j] [4]One man from each tribe,[k] each the head of his family,[l] is to help you. [m] [5]These are the names[n] of the men who are to assist you:

from Reuben,[o] Elizur son of Shedeur;[p]
[6]from Simeon,[q] Shelumiel son of Zurishaddai;[r]
[7]from Judah,[s] Nahshon son of Amminadab;[t]
[8]from Issachar,[u] Nethanel son of Zuar;[v]
[9]from Zebulun,[w] Eliab son of Helon;[x]
[10]from the sons of Joseph:
from Ephraim,[y] Elishama son of Ammihud;[z]
from Manasseh,[a] Gamaliel son of Pedahzur;[b]
[11]from Benjamin,[c] Abidan son of Gideoni;[d]
[12]from Dan,[e] Ahiezer son of Ammishaddai;[f]
[13]from Asher,[g] Pagiel son of Ocran;[h]
[14]from Gad,[i] Eliasaph son of Deuel;[j]
[15]from Naphtali,[k] Ahira son of Enan.[l] "

[16]These were the men appointed from the community, the leaders[m] of their ancestral tribes. [n] They were the heads of the clans of Israel.[o]

[17]Moses and Aaron took these men whose names had been given, [18]and they called the whole community together on the first day of the second month.[p] The people indicated their ancestry[q] by their clans and families,[r] and the men twenty years old or more[s] were listed by name, one by one, [19]as the LORD commanded Moses. And so he counted[t] them in the Desert of Sinai:

[20]From the descendants of Reuben[u] the firstborn son[v] of Israel:
All the men twenty years old or more who were able to serve in the army were listed by name, one by one, according to the records of their clans and families. [21]The number from the tribe of Reuben[w] was 46,500.

[22]From the descendants of Simeon:[x]
All the men twenty years old or more who were able to serve in the army were counted and listed by name, one by one, according to the records of their clans and families. [23]The number from the tribe of Simeon was 59,300.[y]

Cross references

1:1 [a]S Ex 27:21; S 40:2 [b]S Ex 19:1 [c]ver 18 [d]S Ex 6:14 **1:2** [e]Ex 30:11-16 [f]ver 18 [g]Nu 3:40 **1:3** [h]Ex 4:14; Nu 17:3 [i]S Ex 30:14 /ver 20; Nu 26:2; Jos 5:4; 1Ch 5:18 **1:4** [k]S Lev 24:11; S Jos 7:1 [l]ver 16; Nu 7:2; 30:1; 31:26 [m]Ex 18:21; Nu 34:18; Dt 1:15; Jos 22:14 **1:5** [n]Nu 17:2 [o]S Ge 29:32; Rev 7:5 [p]Nu 2:10; 7:30; 10:18 **1:6** [q]ver 22; Nu 25:14 [r]Nu 2:12; 7:36, 41; 10:19 **1:7** [s]ver 26; S Ge 29:35; Ps 78:68 [t]Ex 6:23; Nu 7:12; Ru 4:20; 1Ch 2:10; Mt 1:4; Lk 3:32 **1:8** [u]S Ge 30:18; Nu 10:15 [v]Nu 2:5; 7:18 **1:9** [w]ver 30; Nu 10:16 [x]Nu 2:7; 7:24 **1:10** [y]ver 32 [z]Nu 2:18; 7:48, 53; 10:22 [a]ver 34; Nu 10:23 [b]Nu 2:20; 7:54 **1:11** [c]Nu 10:24 [d]Nu 2:22; 7:60; Ps 68:27 **1:12** [e]ver 38 /Nu 2:25; 7:66; 10:25 **1:13** [g]ver 40; Nu 10:26 [h]Nu 2:27; 7:72 **1:14** [i]ver 24; Nu 10:20 /Nu 2:14; 7:42 **1:15** [k]ver 42; Nu 10:27 [l]Nu 2:29; 7:78 **1:16** [m]S Ex 18:25 [n]Nu 32:28 [o]S ver 4 **1:18** [p]ver 1 [q]Ezr 2:59; Heb 7:3 [r]ver 2 [s]S Ex 30:14 **1:19** [t]Ex 30:12; Nu 26:63; 31:49 **1:20** [u]S Ge 29:32; S 46:9; Rev 7:5 [v]S Ge 10:15 **1:21** [w]Nu 26:7 **1:22** [x]S Ge 29:33; Rev 7:7 **1:23** [y]Nu 26:14

Study notes

1:1 The LORD spoke to Moses. One of the most pervasive emphases in Numbers is the fact that the Lord spoke to Moses and through Moses to Israel. From the opening words to the closing words (36:13), this is stated over 150 times and in more than 20 ways. The Lord's use of Moses as his prophet is described in 12:6–8. One of the Hebrew names for the book is wayedabber ("And he [the LORD] spoke"), from the first word in the Hebrew text. Tent of Meeting. The tabernacle. Desert of Sinai. The more common Hebrew name for Numbers is bemidbar ("in the desert"), the fifth word in the Hebrew text. The events of Numbers cover a period of 38 years and nine or ten months, i.e., the period of Israel's desert wanderings. first day . . . second month . . . second year. Thirteen months after the exodus, Numbers begins. Israel had spent the previous year in the region of Mount Sinai receiving the law and erecting the tabernacle. Now she was to be mustered as a military force for an orderly march. Dating events from the exodus (for another example see 1Ki 6:1) is similar to the Christian practice of dating years in reference to the incarnation of Christ (B.C. and A.D.). The exodus was God's great act of deliverance of his people from bondage.
1:2 Take. The Hebrew for this word is plural, indicating that Moses and Aaron were to complete this task together (see v. 3, "You and Aaron"), but the primary responsibility lay with Moses. census. Its main purpose was to form a military roster, not a social, political or taxing document.
1:3 able to serve in the army. Refers to the principal military purpose of the census. The phrase occurs 14 times in ch. 1 and again in 26:2.
1:4 One man from each tribe. By having a representative from each tribe assist Moses and Aaron, the count would be regarded as legitimate by all.
1:5–16 The names of these men occur again in chs. 2; 7; 10. Most contain within them a reference to the name of God. Levi is not represented in the list (see vv. 47–53).
1:19 And so he counted them in the Desert of Sinai. A summary statement; vv. 20–43 provide the details.
1:20–43 For each tribe there are two verses in repetitive formulaic structure, giving: (1) the name of the tribe, (2) the specifics of those numbered, (3) the name of the tribe again and (4) the total count for that tribe. The numbers for each tribe are rounded off to the hundred (but Gad to the 50, v. 25). The same numbers are given for each tribe in ch. 2, where there are four triads of tribes. A peculiarity in the numbers that leads some to believe that they are symbolic is that the hundreds are grouped between 200 and 700. Also, various speculations have arisen regarding the meaning of the Hebrew word for "thousand" (see Introduction: Special Problem). In this chapter, the word has been used to mean 1,000 in order for the totals to be achieved.

24From the descendants of Gad: z
  All the men twenty years old or
  more who were able to serve in
  the army were listed by name, according to the records of their
  clans and families. 25The number
  from the tribe of Gad a was 45,-
  650.

26From the descendants of Judah: b
  All the men twenty years old or
  more who were able to serve in
  the army were listed by name, according to the records of their
  clans and families. 27The number
  from the tribe of Judah c was 74,-
  600.

28From the descendants of Issachar: d
  All the men twenty years old or
  more who were able to serve in
  the army were listed by name, according to the records of their
  clans and families. 29The number
  from the tribe of Issachar e was
  54,400. f

30From the descendants of Zebulun: g
  All the men twenty years old or
  more who were able to serve in
  the army were listed by name, according to the records of their
  clans and families. 31The number
  from the tribe of Zebulun was 57,-
  400. h

32From the sons of Joseph: i
From the descendants of Ephraim: j
  All the men twenty years old or
  more who were able to serve in
  the army were listed by name, according to the records of their
  clans and families. 33The number
  from the tribe of Ephraim k was
  40,500.

34From the descendants of Manasseh: l
  All the men twenty years old or
  more who were able to serve in
  the army were listed by name, ac-

cording to the records of their
clans and families. 35The number
from the tribe of Manasseh was
32,200.

36From the descendants of Benjamin: m
  All the men twenty years old or
  more who were able to serve in
  the army were listed by name, according to the records of their
  clans and families. 37The number
  from the tribe of Benjamin n was
  35,400.

38From the descendants of Dan: o
  All the men twenty years old or
  more who were able to serve in
  the army were listed by name, according to the records of their
  clans and families. 39The number
  from the tribe of Dan was 62,-
  700. p

40From the descendants of Asher: q
  All the men twenty years old or
  more who were able to serve in
  the army were listed by name, according to the records of their
  clans and families. 41The number
  from the tribe of Asher r was 41,-
  500.

42From the descendants of Naphtali: s
  All the men twenty years old or
  more who were able to serve in
  the army were listed by name, according to the records of their
  clans and families. 43The number
  from the tribe of Naphtali t was
  53,400. u

44These were the men counted by
Moses and Aaron v and the twelve leaders
of Israel, each one representing his family.
45All the Israelites twenty years old or
more w who were able to serve in Israel's
army were counted according to their
families. x 46The total number was 603,-
550. y
  47The families of the tribe of Levi, z

1:24
zS Ge 30:11;
S Jos 13:24-28;
Rev 7:5
1:25 aGe 46:16;
Nu 26:18;
1Ch 5:11
1:26 bS ver 7;
Mt 1:2; Rev 7:5
1:27 cNu 26:22
1:28
dS Ge 30:18;
Rev 7:7
1:29 eS Ge 30:18
fNu 26:25
1:30
gS Ge 30:20;
Rev 7:8
1:31 hNu 26:27
1:32 iGe 49:26
jS Ge 41:52
1:33 kNu 26:37;
1Ch 7:20
1:34 lS Ge 41:51;
Rev 7:6

1:36
mS Ge 35:18;
2Ch 17:17;
Jer 32:44;
Ob 1:19; Rev 7:8
1:37 nNu 26:41
1:38 oGe 30:6;
Dt 33:22
1:39 pNu 26:43
1:40
qS Ge 30:13;
Nu 26:44;
Rev 7:6
1:41 rNu 26:47
1:42 sS Ge 30:8;
Rev 7:6
1:43 tNu 26:50
uS Ex 1:1-4
1:44 vNu 26:64
1:45 wver 3;
Nu 14:29
xNu 2:32
1:46 yS Ex 12:37;
2Sa 24:9
1:47
zS Nu 3:17-20

1:32–35 Because the descendants of Levi were excluded from the census (see note on v. 47), the descendants of Joseph are listed according to the families of his two sons, Ephraim (vv. 32–33) and Manasseh (vv. 34–35). In this way the traditional tribal number of 12 is maintained, and Joseph is given the "double portion" of the ranking heir (cf. Ge 49:22–26; Dt 33:13–17; 2Ki 2:9).

1:46 *603,550.* Except for Joshua and Caleb, all these died in the desert. The mathematics of these numbers is accurate and complex. It is complex in that the totals are reached in two ways: (1) a linear listing of 12 units (vv. 20–43), with the total given (v. 46); (2) four sets of triads, each with a subtotal, and then the grand total (2:3–32). These figures are also consistent with those in Ex 12:37; 38:26. This large

number of men conscripted for the army suggests a population for the entire community in excess of 2,000,000 (see Introduction: Special Problem). Ex 1:7 describes the remarkable growth of the Hebrew people in Egypt during the 400-year sojourn. They had become so numerous that they were regarded as a grave threat to the security of Egypt (Ex 1:9–10,20). Israel's amazing growth from the 70 who entered Egypt (Ex 1:5) was an evidence of God's great blessing and his faithfulness to his covenant with Abraham (Ge 12:2; 15:5; 17:4–6; 22:17).

1:47 Because of their special tasks, the Levites were excluded from this military count. They too had to perform service to the Lord, but they were to be engaged in the ceremonies and maintenance of the tabernacle (see note on

however, were not counted[a] along with the others. [48]The LORD had said to Moses: [49]"You must not count the tribe of Levi or include them in the census of the other Israelites. [50]Instead, appoint the Levites to be in charge of the tabernacle[b] of the Testimony[c]—over all its furnishings[d] and everything belonging to it. They are to carry the tabernacle and all its furnishings; they are to take care of it and encamp around it. [51]Whenever the tabernacle[e] is to move,[f] the Levites are to take it down, and whenever the tabernacle is to be set up, the Levites shall do it.[g] Anyone else who goes near it shall be put to death.[h] [52]The Israelites are to set up their tents by divisions, each man in his own camp under his own standard.[i] [53]The Levites, however, are to set up their tents around the tabernacle[j] of the Testimony so that wrath will not fall[k] on the Israelite community. The Levites are to be responsible for the care of the tabernacle of the Testimony.[l] "

[54]The Israelites did all this just as the LORD commanded Moses.

The Arrangement of the Tribal Camps

2 The LORD said to Moses and Aaron: [2]"The Israelites are to camp around the Tent of Meeting some distance from it,

each man under his standard[m] with the banners of his family."

[3]On the east, toward the sunrise, the divisions of the camp of Judah are to encamp under their standard. The leader of the people of Judah is Nahshon son of Amminadab.[n] [4]His division numbers 74,600.

[5]The tribe of Issachar[o] will camp next to them. The leader of the people of Issachar is Nethanel son of Zuar.[p] [6]His division numbers 54,400.

[7]The tribe of Zebulun will be next. The leader of the people of Zebulun is Eliab son of Helon.[q] [8]His division numbers 57,400.

[9]All the men assigned to the camp of Judah, according to their divisions, number 186,400. They will set out first.[r]

[10]On the south[s] will be the divisions of the camp of Reuben under their standard. The leader of the people of Reuben is Elizur son of Shedeur.[t] [11]His division numbers 46,500.

[12]The tribe of Simeon[u] will camp next to them. The leader of the people of Simeon is Shelumiel son of Zurishaddai.[v] [13]His division numbers 59,300.

[14]The tribe of Gad[w] will be next.

1:47 [a]Nu 4:3,49
1:50 [b]Ex 25:9; [c]S 26:1 [c]S Ex 16:34; Ac 7:44; Rev 15:5 [d]Nu 3:31
1:51 [e]S Ex 26:1 [f]Nu 4:5 [g]Nu 3:38; 4:15 [h]S Ex 21:12
1:52 [i]Nu 10:14; Ps 20:5; SS 2:4; 6:4
1:53 [j]Nu 2:10; 3:23,29,38 [k]Lev 10:6; Nu 16:46; 18:5; Dt 9:22 [l]S Ex 38:21; Nu 18:2-4

2:2 [m]Ps 74:4; Isa 31:9; Jer 4:21
2:3 [n]S Ex 6:23
2:5 [o]Nu 10:15 [p]S Nu 1:8
2:7 [q]Nu 1:9; 10:16
2:9 [r]Nu 10:14; Jdg 1:1
2:10 [s]S Nu 1:53 [t]Nu 1:5
2:12 [u]Nu 10:19 [v]S Nu 1:6
2:14 [w]Nu 10:20

---

vv. 32–35).

1:50 *Testimony.* The Ten Commandments written on stone tablets (see Ex 31:18; 32:15; 34:29), which were placed in the ark (Ex 25:16,21; 40:20), leading to the phrase the "ark of the Testimony" (Ex 25:22; 26:33,34).

1:51 *Anyone else.* The Hebrew for this phrase is often translated "stranger," "alien" or "foreigner" (e.g., Isa 1:7; Hos 7:9). Thus a non-Levite Israelite was considered an alien to the religious duties of the tabernacle (see Ex 29:33; 30:33; Lev 22:12). *death.* See 3:10,38; 18:7; cf. 16:31–33; 1Sa 6:19.

1:53 *their tents around the tabernacle.* See 3:21–38. *wrath.* The Levites formed a protective hedge against trespassing by the non-Levites to keep them from experiencing divine wrath.

1:54 *as the LORD commanded Moses.* In view of Israel's great disobedience in the later chapters of Numbers, these words of initial compliance have a special poignancy.

2:1–34 This chapter is symmetrically structured:
  Summary command (vv. 1-2)
  Details of execution (vv. 3-33):
    Eastern camp (vv. 3-9)
    Southern camp (vv. 10-16)
    Tent and Levites (v. 17)
    Western camp (vv. 18-24)
    Northern camp (vv. 25-31)
      Summary totals (vv. 32-33)
  Summary conclusion (v. 34)
In ch. 1 the nation is mustered, and the genealogical relationships are clarified. In ch. 2 the nation is put in structural order, and the line of march and place of

encampment are established. The numbers of ch. 1 are given in a new pattern, and the same leaders are named here again. **2:2** *some distance from it.* See 1:52–53. *each man.* Each was to know his exact position within the camp. *standard . . . banners.* Each tribe had its banner, and each triad of tribes had its standard. Jewish tradition suggests that the tribal banners corresponded in color to the 12 stones in the breastpiece of the high priest (Ex 28:15–21). Tradition also holds that the standard of the triad led by Judah had the figure of a lion, that of Reuben the figure of a man, that of Ephraim the figure of an ox and that of Dan the figure of an eagle (see the four living creatures described by Eze 1:10; cf. Rev 4:7). But these traditions are not otherwise substantiated. See diagram of "Encampment of the Tribes of Israel," p. 192.

2:3–7 *Judah . . . Issachar . . . Zebulun.* The fourth, fifth and sixth sons of Jacob and Leah. It is somewhat surprising to have these three tribes first in the order of march, since Reuben is regularly noted as Jacob's firstborn son (1:20). However, because of the failure of the older brothers (Reuben, Simeon and Levi; see Ge 49:3–7), Judah is granted pride of place among his brothers (Ge 49:8). Judah produced the royal line from which the Messiah came (Ge 49:10; Ru 4:18–21; Mt 1:1–16).

2:10–12 *Reuben . . . Simeon.* The first and second sons of Jacob and Leah.

2:14 *Gad.* The first son of Jacob and Zilpah (Leah's maidservant). Levi, Leah's third son, is not included with the divisions of the congregation. *Deuel.* See NIV text note. The Hebrew letters for *d* and *r* were easily confused by scribes (copyists) because of their similarity in form (see note on Ge

The leader of the people of Gad is Eliasaph son of Deuel. [a][x] 15His division numbers 45,650.

16All the men assigned to the camp of Reuben,[y] according to their divisions, number 151,450. They will set out second.

17Then the Tent of Meeting and the camp of the Levites[z] will set out in the middle of the camps. They will set out in the same order as they encamp, each in his own place under his standard.

18On the west[a] will be the divisions of the camp of Ephraim[b] under their standard. The leader of the people of Ephraim is Elishama son of Ammihud.[c] 19His division numbers 40,500.

20The tribe of Manasseh[d] will be next to them. The leader of the people of Manasseh is Gamaliel son of Pedahzur.[e] 21His division numbers 32,200.

22The tribe of Benjamin[f] will be next. The leader of the people of Benjamin is Abidan son of Gideoni.[g] 23His division numbers 35,400.

24All the men assigned to the camp

of Ephraim,[h] according to their divisions, number 108,100. They will set out third.[i]

25On the north[j] will be the divisions of the camp of Dan, under their standard.[k] The leader of the people of Dan is Ahiezer son of Ammishaddai.[l] 26His division numbers 62,700.

27The tribe of Asher will camp next to them. The leader of the people of Asher is Pagiel son of Ocran.[m] 28His division numbers 41,500.

29The tribe of Naphtali[n] will be next. The leader of the people of Naphtali is Ahira son of Enan.[o] 30His division numbers 53,400.

31All the men assigned to the camp of Dan number 157,600. They will set out last,[p] under their standards.

32These are the Israelites, counted according to their families.[q] All those in the camps, by their divisions, number 603,550.[r] 33The Levites, however, were not counted[s] along with

2:14 [x]Nu 1:14; 10:20
2:16 [y]Nu 10:18
2:17 [z]Nu 1:50; 10:21
2:18 [a]S Nu 1:53
[b]S Ge 48:20; Jer 31:18-20
[c]Nu 1:10
2:20 [d]S Ge 48:20
[e]S Nu 1:10
2:22 [f]Nu 10:24
[g]S Nu 1:11

2:24 [h]Nu 10:22
[i]Ps 80:2
2:25 [j]S Nu 1:53
[k]Nu 10:25
[l]S Nu 1:12
2:27 [m]Nu 1:13; 10:26
2:29 [n]Nu 10:27
[o]Nu 1:15; 10:27
2:31 [p]Nu 10:25; Jos 6:9
2:32 [q]Nu 1:45
[r]S Ex 12:37
2:33 [s]Nu 1:47; 26:57-62

[a]14 Many manuscripts of the Masoretic Text, Samaritan Pentateuch and Vulgate (see also Num. 1:14); most manuscripts of the Masoretic Text *Reuel*

10:4).
2:17 *Tent of Meeting.* Representing God's presence in the heart of the camp (see 1:1 and note). *Levites.* In the line of march, the Judah and Reuben triads would lead the community, then would come the tabernacle with the attendant protective hedge of Levites (see note on 1:53), and last would come the Ephraim and Dan triads.
2:18–22 The Rachel tribes (Joseph and Benjamin) were on the west. Joseph's two sons Manasseh and Ephraim received

a special blessing from their grandfather Jacob, but the younger son, Ephraim, was given precedence over Manasseh (Ge 48:5–20). Here, true to Jacob's words, Ephraim is ahead of Manasseh. Last comes Benjamin, the last son born to Jacob.
2:25 *Dan.* The first son of Bilhah, Rachel's maidservant.
2:27 *Asher.* The second son of Zilpah, Leah's maidservant.
2:29 *Naphtali.* The second son of Bilhah.
2:32 *603,550.* See 1:46 and note.
2:33 *Levites.* See notes on 1:47,53.

Encampment of the
Tribes of Israel NU 2:1-31   NU 10:11-33

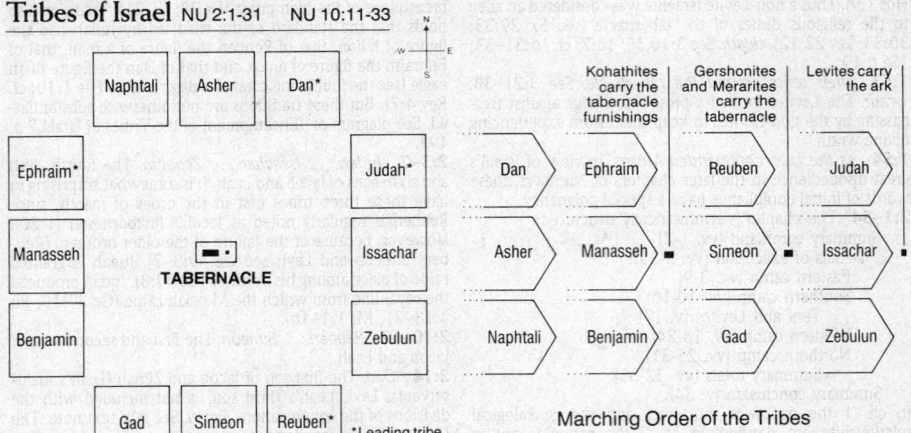

* Leading tribe of the group

Marching Order of the Tribes

the other Israelites, as the LORD commanded Moses.

[34]So the Israelites did everything the LORD commanded Moses; that is the way they encamped under their standards, and that is the way they set out, each with his clan and family.

The Levites

3 This is the account of the family of Aaron and Moses[t] at the time the LORD talked with Moses on Mount Sinai. [u]

[2]The names of the sons of Aaron were Nadab the firstborn[v] and Abihu, Eleazar and Ithamar. [w] [3]Those were the names of Aaron's sons, the anointed priests,[x] who were ordained to serve as priests. [4]Nadab and Abihu, however, fell dead before the LORD[y] when they made an offering with unauthorized fire before him in the Desert of Sinai. [z] They had no sons; so only Eleazar and Ithamar[a] served as priests during the lifetime of their father Aaron. [b]

[5]The LORD said to Moses, [6]"Bring the tribe of Levi[c] and present them to Aaron the priest to assist him. [d] [7]They are to perform duties for him and for the whole community[e] at the Tent of Meeting by doing the work[f] of the tabernacle. [8]They are to take care of all the furnishings of the Tent of Meeting, fulfilling the obligations

of the Israelites by doing the work of the tabernacle. [9]Give the Levites to Aaron and his sons;[g] they are the Israelites who are to be given wholly to him. [b] [10]Appoint Aaron[h] and his sons to serve as priests; [i] anyone else who approaches the sanctuary must be put to death."[j]

[11]The LORD also said to Moses, [12]"I have taken the Levites[k] from among the Israelites in place of the first male offspring[l] of every Israelite woman. The Levites are mine, [m] [13]for all the firstborn are mine. [n] When I struck down all the firstborn in Egypt, I set apart for myself every firstborn in Israel, whether man or animal. They are to be mine. I am the LORD."[o]

[14]The LORD said to Moses in the Desert of Sinai, [p] [15]"Count[q] the Levites by their families and clans. Count every male a month old or more."[r] [16]So Moses counted them, as he was commanded by the word of the LORD.

[17]These were the names of the sons of Levi: [s]

Gershon, [t] Kohath[u] and Merari. [v]

[18]These were the names of the Gershonite clans:

Libni and Shimei. [w]

[19]The Kohathite clans:

Cross-references column:

3:1 [t]S Ex 6:27
[u]S Ex 19:11
3:2 [v]Nu 1:20
[w]S Ex 6:23
3:3 [x]S Ex 28:41;
S 29:30
3:4 [y]S Lev 10:2
[z]S Lev 10:1
[a]Lev 10:6,12;
Nu 4:28
[b]1Ch 24:1
3:6 [c]Dt 10:8;
31:9; 1Ch 15:2
[d]Nu 8:6-22;
18:1-7;
2Ch 29:11
3:7 [e]Nu 1:53;
8:19 [f]S Lev 8:35

3:9 [g]ver 12,45;
Nu 8:19; 18:6
3:10 [h]S Ex 30:7
[i]S Ex 29:9
[j]Nu 1:51
3:12 [k]Ne 13:29;
Mal 2:4 [l]ver 41;
Nu 8:16,18
[m]S ver 9;
Ex 13:2; Nu 8:14;
16:9
3:13 [n]S Ex 13:12
[o]Lev 11:44
3:14 [p]S Ex 19:1
3:15 [q]ver 39;
S Nu 1:19 [r]ver
22; Nu 18:16;
26:62
3:17
[s]S Ge 29:34;
S 46:11; Nu 1:47;
1Ch 15:4; 23:6;
2Ch 29:12
[t]Jos 21:6
[u]Jos 21:4
[v]S Ex 6:16
3:18 [w]Ex 6:17

[b]9 Most manuscripts of the Masoretic Text; some manuscripts of the Masoretic Text, Samaritan Pentateuch and Septuagint (see also Num. 8:16) to me

---

2:34 *did everything the* LORD *commanded Moses.* As in 1:54, these words of absolute compliance contrast with Israel's later folly. *under their standards . . . each with his clan and family.* A major accomplishment for a people so numerous, so recently enslaved and more recently a mob in disarray. It may have been the orderliness of this encampment that led Balaam to say: "How beautiful are your tents, O Jacob, your dwelling places, O Israel!" (24:5).

3:1 *Aaron and Moses.* At first glance, the names seem out of order, but the emphasis is correct: It is the family of Aaron that is about to be described (see v. 2).

3:3 *anointed priests.* Ex 28:41 records God's command to Moses to anoint his brother Aaron and his sons as priests of the Lord (see Ex 30:30; Lev 8:30). By this solemn act they were consecrated in a special way to the Lord. Kings (1Sa 16:13) were also anointed with oil for special service to God. Physical objects could be anointed as well (see Ge 28:18; Ex 29:36). The Hebrew term for "anointed" (*mashiah*) later became the specific term for the Messiah (Christ); see NIV text note on Mt 1:17. *ordained.* The Hebrew for this word means lit. "fill the hand of" (see Ex 32:29). By this act there was an investing of authority, a consecration and a setting apart.

3:4 *Nadab and Abihu.* See Lev 10:1–3 and notes. *unauthorized fire.* Or "strange fire." This seems to be a deliberately obscure expression, as though the narrator finds the very concept distasteful. They were using fire that the Lord had not commanded (see Lev 10:1). Proximity to God's holiness requires righteousness and obedience from his priests. For all time, the deaths of Aaron's newly consecrated sons serve to warn God's ministers of the awesome seriousness of their tasks (cf. 1Sa 2:12–17,22–25,27–36; 3:11–14; 4:1–11).

For similar divine judgments at the beginning of new stages in salvation history see Jos 7; 2Sa 6:7; Ac 5:1–11.

3:5–10 These commands are not followed by a report of obedience as were the commands in chs. 1–2, but further details are given in ch. 8. Clear distinctions are made here between the priestly house (the sons of Aaron) and the Levites. The latter were to be aides to the priests, and served not only Aaron but the whole nation in the process (see vv. 7–8).

3:9 *to him.* See NIV text note. It appears that the issue here is service to Aaron (and through him to the Lord); in 8:16 the service is to the Lord.

3:10 *anyone else.* Lit. "stranger"—anyone lacking authorization. Service at the tabernacle may be performed only at the express appointment of the Lord. The words of v. 10 follow the paragraph telling of the death of Aaron's sons. They were authorized persons, but used unauthorized means. If the sons of Aaron were put to death at the commencement of their duties, how dare an unauthorized person even think to trespass? See v. 38; 18:7.

3:12–13 See note on Ex 13:2. *mine.* Repeated for emphasis.

3:12 *in place of.* An example of the practice of substitution (see Ge 22:13 and note; Mt 20:28).

3:15 *a month old or more.* The counting of the Levites corresponds to that of the other tribes in chs. 1–2, except that all males from the age of one month, rather than from 20 years, were to be counted. The Levites were not being mustered for war, but for special service in the sacred precincts of the Lord.

3:16 *as he was commanded.* The obedience of Moses to the Lord's command is explicit and total.

Amram, Izhar, Hebron and Uzziel. *x*

20The Merarite clans: *y*

Mahli and Mushi. *z*

These were the Levite clans, according to their families.

21To Gershon *a* belonged the clans of the Libnites and Shimeites; *b* these were the Gershonite clans. 22The number of all the males a month old or more who were counted was 7,500. 23The Gershonite clans were to camp on the west, behind the tabernacle. *c* 24The leader of the families of the Gershonites was Eliasaph son of Lael. 25At the Tent of Meeting the Gershonites were responsible for the care of the tabernacle *d* and tent, its coverings, *e* the curtain at the entrance *f* to the Tent of Meeting, *g* 26the curtains of the courtyard *h*, the curtain at the entrance to the courtyard surrounding the tabernacle and altar, *i* and the ropes *j*—and everything *k* related to their use.

27To Kohath *l* belonged the clans of the Amramites, Izharites, Hebronites and Uzzielites; *m* these were the Kohathite *n* clans. 28The number of all the males a month old or more *o* was 8,600. *c* The Kohathites were responsible *p* for the care of the sanctuary. *q* 29The Kohathite clans were to camp on the south side *r* of the tabernacle. 30The leader of the families of the Kohathite clans was Elizaphan *s* son of Uzziel. 31They were responsible for the care of the ark, *t* the table, *u* the lampstand, *v* the altars, *w* the articles *x* of the sanctuary used in ministering, the curtain, *y* and everything related to their use. *z* 32The chief leader of the Levites was Eleazar *a* son of

Aaron, the priest. He was appointed over those who were responsible *b* for the care of the sanctuary. *c*

33To Merari belonged the clans of the Mahlites and the Mushites; *d* these were the Merarite clans. *e* 34The number of all the males a month old or more *f* who were counted was 6,200. 35The leader of the families of the Merarite clans was Zuriel son of Abihail; they were to camp on the north side of the tabernacle. *g* 36The Merarites were appointed *h* to take care of the frames of the tabernacle, *i* its crossbars, *j* posts, *k* bases, all its equipment, and everything related to their use, *l* 37as well as the posts of the surrounding courtyard *m* with their bases, tent pegs *n* and ropes.

38Moses and Aaron and his sons were to camp to the east *o* of the tabernacle, toward the sunrise, in front of the Tent of Meeting. *p* They were responsible for the care of the sanctuary *q* on behalf of the Israelites. Anyone else who approached the sanctuary was to be put to death. *r*

39The total number of Levites counted *s* at the LORD's command by Moses and Aaron according to their clans, including every male a month old or more, was 22,000. *t*

40The LORD said to Moses, "Count all the firstborn Israelite males who are a month old or more *u* and make a list of their names. *v* 41Take the Levites for me in place of all the firstborn of the Israelites, *w* and the livestock of the Levites in place of

---

Cross references (center column):

3:19 *x* S Ex 6:18
3:20 *y* S Ge 46:11
z S Ex 6:19
3:21 *a* S Ge 46:11
b Ex 6:17
3:23 *c* S Nu 2:18
Nu 7:1 *d* Ex 26:14
f Ex 26:36;
Nu 4:25 *g* Ex 40:2
3:26 *h* Ex 27:9
i ver 31 *j* Ex 35:18
k Nu 4:26
3:27 *l* S Ge 46:11;
S Ex 6:18
m Ex 6:18;
1Ch 26:23
n Nu 4:15,37
3:28 *o* ver 15
p Nu 4:4,15
q S Ex 25:8;
30:13;
2Ch 30:19;
Ps 15:1; 20:2;
Eze 44:27
3:29 *r* S Nu 1:53
3:30 *s* S Ex 6:22
3:31
t S Ex 25:10-22;
Dt 10:1-8;
2Ch 5:2; Jer 3:16
u S Ex 25:23
v S Ex 25:31;
1Ch 28:15;
Jer 52:19 *w* ver 26
x Nu 1:50
y S Ex 26:33;
Nu 4:5 *z* Nu 4:15;
18:3
3:32 *a* S Ex 6:23

b ver 28
c Nu 4:19; 18:3
3:33 *d* S Ex 6:19
e S Ge 46:11
3:34 *f* ver 15
3:35 *g* S Nu 2:25
3:36 *h* Nu 4:32
i Ex 26:15-25;
35:20-29
j Ex 26:26-29
k Ex 36:36
l Nu 18:3
3:37
m Ex 27:10-17
n Ex 27:19
3:38 *o* Nu 2:3
p S Nu 1:53;
1Ch 9:27; 23:32
q ver 7; Nu 18:5
r ver 10; Nu 1:51
3:39 *s* S ver 15
t Nu 26:62
3:40 *u* ver 15
v Nu 1:2

3:41 *w* ver 12

c 28 Hebrew; some Septuagint manuscripts *8,300*

3:21–38 The words of 1:53, "their tents around the tabernacle of the Testimony," are detailed by the four paragraphs in this section: (1) Gershon to the west (vv. 21–26); (2) Kohath to the south (vv. 27–32); (3) Merari to the north (vv. 33–37); (4) Moses and Aaron and sons to the east (v. 38). The other tribes began with the most favored: (1) Judah on the east (2:3); (2) Reuben on the south (2:10); (3) Ephraim on the west (2:18); (4) Dan on the north (2:25). The Levitical clans lead up to the most favored. The leaders of the Levitical houses correspond to the leaders of the other tribes (see note on 1:5–16). As do the names of the other tribal leaders, these names include a form of God's name.
3:24 *Eliasaph.* Means "(My) God has added." *Lael.* Means "belonging to God."
3:25–26 There were three curtains or covering screens for the tabernacle: (1) at the gate of the courtyard (v. 26; 4:26); (2) at the entrance to the Tent (vv. 25,31; 4:25); (3) between the Most Holy Place and the Holy Place (4:5).
3:27 *Amramites.* Aaron was an Amramite (see Ex 6:20); thus he and Moses were from the family of Kohath. To the Kohathites was given the care of the most holy things (see

4:4–18).
3:28 *8,600.* The total number of Levites given in v. 39 is 22,000—300 less than the totals of 7,500 Gershonites (v. 22), 8,600 Kohathites (here) and 6,200 Merarites (v. 34). Many believe that a copyist may have made a mistake here, and that the correct number is 8,300 (see NIV text note).
3:30 *Elizaphan.* Means "(My) God has protected." *Uzziel.* Means "My strength is God."
3:35 *Zuriel.* Means "My Rock is God." *Abihail.* Means "My (divine) Father is power."
3:38 *toward the sunrise.* The most honored location, but Moses and Aaron were placed there for a representative ministry (on behalf of the Israelites). *Anyone else . . . was to be put to death.* Service in the tabernacle was an act of mercy, a means for the people to come before God. Yet it was marked by strict discipline—it had to be done in God's way. The sovereignty of God was evident in his limitations on the means to approach him (see v. 10; 1:51; 18:7).
3:41 *I am the LORD.* What is being commanded conforms to God's character as Yahweh ("the LORD"; see note on Ex 3:14).

all the firstborn of the livestock of the Israelites. I am the LORD."[x]

[x] Lev 11:44
[43] Ver 15 [z] ver 39

[45] [a] S ver 9
[b] Lev 11:44
[46] [c] Ex 13:13; Nu 18:15
[47] [d] S Lev 27:6 [e] S Ex 30:13 [f] S Lev 27:25
[48] [g] ver 51 [h] ver 50

[49] [i] ver 48
[50] [j] ver 41,45 [k] S ver 46-48
[4:2] [l] S Ex 30:12
[4:3] [m] S Nu 1:47 [n] ver 23; Nu 8:25; 1Ch 23:3,24,27; Ezr 3:8
[4:4] [o] S Nu 3:28 [p] Nu 7:9 [q] ver 19
[4:5] [r] Nu 1:51 [s] S Ex 26:31,33 [t] 1Ch 23:26
[4:6] [u] S Ex 25:5 [v] S Ex 25:13-15; 1Ki 8:7; 2Ch 5:8
[4:7] [w] S Lev 24:6

42So Moses counted all the firstborn of the Israelites, as the LORD commanded him. 43The total number of firstborn males a month old or more,[y] listed by name, was 22,273.[z]

44The LORD also said to Moses, 45"Take the Levites in place of all the firstborn of Israel, and the livestock of the Levites in place of their livestock. The Levites are to be mine.[a] I am the LORD.[b] 46To redeem[c] the 273 firstborn Israelites who exceed the number of the Levites, 47collect five shekels[d] [d] for each one, according to the sanctuary shekel,[e] which weighs twenty gerahs.[f] 48Give the money for the redemption[g] of the additional Israelites to Aaron and his sons."[h]

49So Moses collected the redemption money[i] from those who exceeded the number redeemed by the Levites. 50From the firstborn of the Israelites[j] he collected silver weighing 1,365 shekels,[e] [k] according to the sanctuary shekel. 51Moses gave the redemption money to Aaron and his sons, as he was commanded by the word of the LORD.

The Kohathites

4 The LORD said to Moses and Aaron: 2"Take a census[l] of the Kohathite branch of the Levites by their clans and families. 3Count[m] all the men from thirty to fifty years of age[n] who come to serve in the work in the Tent of Meeting.

4"This is the work[o] of the Kohathites[p] in the Tent of Meeting: the care of the most holy things.[q] 5When the camp is to move,[r] Aaron and his sons are to go in and take down the shielding curtain[s] and cover the ark of the Testimony with it.[t] 6Then they are to cover this with hides of sea cows,[f] [u] spread a cloth of solid blue over that and put the poles[v] in place.

7"Over the table of the Presence[w] they

[x] Ex 39:36; Jer 52:19
[y] S Ex 25:30
[4:8] [z] Ex 26:26-28
[4:9] [a] S Ex 25:38
[4:10] [b] ver 12
[4:11] [c] S Ex 30:1 [d] Ex 30:4
[4:12] [e] Nu 3:31 [f] ver 10
[4:13] [g] S Lev 1:16 [h] Ex 27:1-8; Nu 3:31
[4:14] [i] S Ex 31:9 [j] S Ex 27:3 [k] 1Ch 28:17; 2Ch 4:16 [l] 2Ch 4:11 [m] Ex 27:3; Nu 7:84; 2Ch 4:8; Jer 52:18 [n] Ex 27:6
[4:15] [o] ver 5 [p] S Nu 3:27 [q] Nu 7:9 [r] ver 4 [s] S Ex 28:43 [t] Nu 1:51; 2Sa 6:6,7
[4:16] [u] Lev 10:6; Nu 3:32 [v] S Ex 25:6 [w] S Ex 25:6

are to spread a blue cloth and put on it the plates, dishes and bowls, and the jars for drink offerings;[x] the bread that is continually there[y] is to remain on it. 8Over these they are to spread a scarlet cloth, cover that with hides of sea cows and put its poles[z] in place.

9"They are to take a blue cloth and cover the lampstand that is for light, together with its lamps, its wick trimmers and trays,[a] and all its jars for the oil used to supply it. 10Then they are to wrap it and all its accessories in a covering of hides of sea cows and put it on a carrying frame.[b]

11"Over the gold altar[c] they are to spread a blue cloth and cover that with hides of sea cows and put its poles[d] in place.

12"They are to take all the articles[e] used for ministering in the sanctuary, wrap them in a blue cloth, cover that with hides of sea cows and put them on a carrying frame.[f]

13"They are to remove the ashes[g] from the bronze altar[h] and spread a purple cloth over it. 14Then they are to place on it all the utensils[i] used for ministering at the altar, including the firepans,[j] meat forks,[k] shovels[l] and sprinkling bowls.[m] Over it they are to spread a covering of hides of sea cows and put its poles[n] in place.

15"After Aaron and his sons have finished covering the holy furnishings and all the holy articles, and when the camp is ready to move,[o] the Kohathites[p] are to come to do the carrying.[q] But they must not touch the holy things[r] or they will die.[s] [t] The Kohathites are to carry those things that are in the Tent of Meeting.

16"Eleazar[u] son of Aaron, the priest, is to have charge of the oil for the light,[v] the fragrant incense,[w] the regular grain offer-

[d] 47 That is, about 2 ounces (about 55 grams)
[e] 50 That is, about 35 pounds (about 15.5 kilograms)
[f] 6 That is, dugongs; also in verses 8, 10, 11, 12, 14 and 25

3:43 *22,273.* Seems too small for a population in excess of 2,000,000, and is used as an argument for attempting to find a means of reducing the total number of the people (calculations based on this number suggest a total population of about 250,000). Some suggest that the 22,273 firstborn of Israel were those born since the exodus, all the firstborn at the time of the exodus having already been set apart for the Lord at the first Passover (see Ex 12:22–23). This, however, creates a new problem since nowhere is that allegedly distinct group assigned any special service of the Lord. See Introduction: Special Problem.
4:3 *thirty to fifty years.* Ch. 3 listed all males over the age of one month (3:15). Ch. 4 lists those Levites who were of age to serve in the tabernacle. Of the 22,000 Levite males (3:39), 8,580 were of age for service (v. 48). From 8:24 we learn

that the beginning age for service was 25; perhaps the first 5 years were something of an apprenticeship.

4:4 *most holy things.* Despite the fact that the primary care of these holy things was given to the Kohathites, they were forbidden to touch them (v. 15) or even to look at them (v. 20), on pain of death. All the work of the Kohathites was to be strictly supervised by Aaron and his sons, and only the priests were able to touch and look at the unveiled holy things.

4:6 *sea cows.* See NIV text note.

4:16 *Eleazar . . . the priest, is to have charge.* The high priest could draw near to the most holy things on behalf of the people. If he had not been able to do so, there could have been no worship by the community.

ing[x] and the anointing oil. He is to be in charge of the entire tabernacle and everything in it, including its holy furnishings and articles."

[17]The LORD said to Moses and Aaron, [18]"See that the Kohathite tribal clans are not cut off from the Levites. [19]So that they may live and not die when they come near the most holy things,[y] do this for them: Aaron and his sons[z] are to go into the sanctuary and assign to each man his work and what he is to carry.[a] [20]But the Kohathites must not go in to look[b] at the holy things, even for a moment, or they will die."

The Gershonites

[21]The LORD said to Moses, [22]"Take a census also of the Gershonites by their families and clans. [23]Count all the men from thirty to fifty years of age[c] who come to serve in the work at the Tent of Meeting.

[24]"This is the service of the Gershonite clans as they work and carry burdens: [25]They are to carry the curtains of the tabernacle, [d] the Tent of Meeting,[e] its covering[f] and the outer covering of hides of sea cows, the curtains for the entrance to the Tent of Meeting, [26]the curtains of the courtyard surrounding the tabernacle and altar,[g] the curtain for the entrance,[h] the ropes and all the equipment[i] used in its service. The Gershonites are to do all that needs to be done with these things. [27]All their service, whether carrying or doing other work, is to be done under the direction of Aaron and his sons.[j] You shall assign to them as their responsibility[k] all they are to carry. [28]This is the service of the Gershonite clans[l] at the Tent of Meeting. Their duties are to be under the direction of Ithamar[m] son of Aaron, the priest.

The Merarites

[29]"Count[n] the Merarites by their clans and families.[o] [30]Count all the men from thirty to fifty years of age who come to serve in the work at the Tent of Meeting. [31]This is their duty as they perform service at the Tent of Meeting: to carry the frames of the tabernacle, its crossbars, posts and bases,[p] [32]as well as the posts of the sur-

rounding courtyard with their bases, tent pegs, ropes,[q] all their equipment and everything related to their use. Assign to each man the specific things he is to carry. [33]This is the service of the Merarite clans as they work at the Tent of Meeting under the direction of Ithamar[r] son of Aaron, the priest."

The Numbering of the Levite Clans

[34]Moses, Aaron and the leaders of the community counted the Kohathites[s] by their clans and families. [35]All the men from thirty to fifty years of age[t] who came to serve in the work in the Tent of Meeting, [36]counted by clans, were 2,750. [37]This was the total of all those in the Kohathite clans[u] who served in the Tent of Meeting. Moses and Aaron counted them according to the LORD's command through Moses.

[38]The Gershonites[v] were counted by their clans and families. [39]All the men from thirty to fifty years of age who came to serve in the work at the Tent of Meeting, [40]counted by their clans and families, were 2,630. [41]This was the total of those in the Gershonite clans who served at the Tent of Meeting. Moses and Aaron counted them according to the LORD's command.

[42]The Merarites were counted by their clans and families. [43]All the men from thirty to fifty years of age[w] who came to serve in the work at the Tent of Meeting, [44]counted by their clans, were 3,200. [45]This was the total of those in the Merarite clans.[x] Moses and Aaron counted them according to the LORD's command through Moses.

[46]So Moses, Aaron and the leaders of Israel counted[y] all the Levites by their clans and families. [47]All the men from thirty to fifty years of age[z] who came to do the work of serving and carrying the Tent of Meeting [48]numbered 8,580.[a] [49]At the LORD's command through Moses, each was assigned his work and told what to carry.

Thus they were counted,[b] as the LORD commanded Moses.

The Purity of the Camp

5 The LORD said to Moses, [2]"Command the Israelites to send away from the

4:16
[x]S Ex 29:41;
Lev 6:14-23
4:19 [y]S ver 15
[z]ver 27
[a]S Nu 3:32
4:20 [b]S Ex 19:21
4:23 [c]S ver 3
4:25
[d]Ex 27:10-18
[e]Nu 3:25
[f]Ex 26:14
4:26 [g]Ex 27:9
[h]Ex 27:16
[i]Nu 3:26
4:27 [j]ver 19
[k]Nu 3:25,26
4:28 [l]Nu 7:7
[m]S Ex 6:23
4:29 [n]S Ex 30:12
[o]S Ge 46:11
4:31 [p]Nu 3:36

4:32 [q]Nu 3:37
4:33 [r]S Ex 38:21
4:34 [s]ver 2
4:35 [t]ver 3
4:37 [u]S Nu 3:27
4:38 [v]S Ge 46:11
4:43 [w]ver 3
4:45 [x]ver 29
4:46 [y]Nu 1:19
4:47 [z]ver 3
4:48 [a]Nu 3:39
4:49 [b]S Nu 1:47

5:2 *infectious skin disease.* See NIV text note; see also note on Lev 13:2; cf. Lk 5:12–16; 17:11–19. *discharge of any kind.* See note on Lev 15:2. Such discharges were primarily from the sexual organs and were chronic in nature (cf. Lk 8:43–48). The people who suffered from them became living object lessons to the whole camp on the necessity for all people to be "clean" in their approach to

God. *unclean.* Ceremonially unfit to be with the community, and a possible contaminant to the tabernacle and the pure worship of the Lord. Aspects of uncleanness were not left in the abstract or theoretical; the focus was on tangible issues, such as clearly evident skin diseases and discharges. *dead body.* The ultimate tangible sign of uncleanness. Processes of decay and disease in dead flesh were evident to all. Physical

camp anyone who has an infectious skin disease[g][c] or a discharge[d] of any kind, or who is ceremonially unclean[e] because of a dead body.[f] 3Send away male and female alike; send them outside the camp so they will not defile their camp, where I dwell among them.[g] 4The Israelites did this; they sent them outside the camp. They did just as the LORD had instructed Moses.

Restitution for Wrongs

5The LORD said to Moses, 6"Say to the Israelites: 'When a man or woman wrongs another in any way[h] and so is unfaithful[h] to the LORD, that person is guilty[i] 7and must confess[j] the sin he has committed. He must make full restitution[k] for his wrong, add one fifth to it and give it all to the person he has wronged. 8But if that person has no close relative to whom restitution can be made for the wrong, the restitution belongs to the LORD and must be given to the priest, along with the ram[l] with which atonement is made for him.[m] 9All the sacred contributions the Israelites bring to a priest will belong to him.[n] 10Each man's sacred gifts are his own, but what he gives to the priest will belong to the priest.[o] '"

The Test for an Unfaithful Wife

11Then the LORD said to Moses, 12"Speak to the Israelites and say to them:

'If a man's wife goes astray[p] and is unfaithful to him 13by sleeping with another man,[q] and this is hidden from her husband and her impurity is undetected (since there is no witness against her and she has not been caught in the act), 14and if feelings of jealousy[r] come over her husband and he suspects his wife and she is impure—or if he is jealous and suspects her even though she is not impure— 15then he is to take his wife to the priest. He must also take an offering of a tenth of an ephah[i][s] of barley flour[t] on her behalf. He must not pour oil on it or put incense on it, because it is a grain offering for jealousy,[u] a reminder[v] offering to draw attention to guilt.

16"'The priest shall bring her and have her stand before the LORD. 17Then he shall take some holy water in a clay jar and put some dust from the tabernacle floor into the water. 18After the priest has had the woman stand before the LORD, he shall loosen her hair[w] and place in her hands the reminder offering, the grain offering for jealousy,[x] while he himself holds the bitter water that brings a curse.[y] 19Then the priest shall put the woman under oath and

Cross references

5:2 [c]S Lev 13:2; [d]S Lev 15:2; Mt 9:20 [e]Lev 13:3; Nu 9:6-10 [f]S Lev 21:11
5:3 [g]S Ex 29:45; Lev 26:12; 2Co 6:16
5:6 [h]S Lev 6:2 [i]Lev 5:14-6:7
5:7 [j]S Lev 5:5; S Lk 19:8 [k]S Lev 5:16
5:8 [l]S Lev 5:15 [m]Lev 6:6,7
5:9 [n]Lev 6:17
5:10 [o]Lev 7:29-34

5:12 [p]ver 19-21; S Ex 20:14
5:13 [q]S Ex 20:14
5:14 [r]ver 30; Pr 6:34; 27:4; SS 8:6
5:15 [s]S Ex 16:36 [t]S Lev 6:20 [u]ver 18,25 [v]Eze 21:23; 29:16
5:18 [w]S Lev 10:6; 1Co 11:6 [x]ver 15 [y]ver 19

---

[g]2 Traditionally *leprosy*; the Hebrew word was used for various diseases affecting the skin—not necessarily leprosy. [h]6 Or *woman commits any wrong common to mankind* [i]15 That is, probably about 2 quarts (about 2 liters)

---

contact with a corpse was a sure mark of uncleanness; normal contacts with the living would have to be curtailed until proper cleansing had been made. See note on 6:6 for application to the Nazirite vow. Jesus reached out to the dead as well as to the living; his raising of Jairus's daughter began with holding her limp hand (Lk 8:54).

5:3 *male and female alike.* The concept of clean versus unclean cuts across sexual lines. The essential issue was the presence of the Lord in the camp; there can be no uncleanness where he dwells. In the new Jerusalem (Rev 21:2–3) the dwelling of God with man will be uncompromised by any form of uncleanness (Rev 21:27).

5:5–10 The connection of these verses (on personal wrongs) with the first paragraph (on ritual uncleanness) may be that of moving from the outward, visible defects to the inward, more secret faults that mar the purity of the community. Those with evident marks of uncleanness are to be expelled for the duration of their malady. But more insidious are those people who have overtly sinned against others in the community, and who think that they may continue to function as though there was no wrong.

5:11–31 Again, the connection with the preceding two paragraphs seems to be a movement from the more open, obvious sins to the more personal, hidden ones. Issues of purity begin with physical marks (vv. 1–4), are expanded to interpersonal relationships (vv. 5–10), and then intrude into the most intimate of relationships—the purity of a man and woman in their marriage bed. A test for marital fidelity is far more difficult to prove than a test for a skin disorder; hence, the larger part of the chapter is given to this most sensitive of issues.

5:14 *feelings of jealousy.* These may have been provoked on the basis of good cause, and the issue must be faced. The concern is not just for the bruised feelings of the husband but is ultimately based on the reality of God's dwelling among his people (v. 3). Yet the chapter is designed to prevent unfounded charges of unfaithfulness. This text was not to be used by a capricious, petty or malevolent husband to badger an innocent woman. *impure.* The subject of the chapter is consistent; the purity of the camp where God dwells (v. 3) is the burden of the passage.

5:15–28 The actions presented here seem severe and harsh. But the consequences would have been worse for a woman charged with adultery by an angry husband if there was no provision for her guilt or innocence to be demonstrated. That she was taken to the priest (v. 15) is finally an act of mercy. The gravity of the ritual for a suspected unfaithful wife shows that the law regards marital infidelity most seriously. This was not just a concern of a jealous husband. The entire community was affected by this breach of faith; hence, the judgment was in the context of the community.

5:18 *loosen her hair.* A sign of openness; for the guilty, an expectation of judgment and mourning. *bitter water that brings a curse.* Or "curse-bringing water of bitterness." It is not just that the water was bitter tasting but that the water had the potential of bringing with it a bitter curse. The Lord's role in the proceedings (vv. 16,21,25) is emphasized repeatedly to show that this potion was neither simply a tool of magic nor merely a psychological device to determine stress. The verdict with respect to the woman was precipitated by her physiological and psychological responses to the bitter water, but the judgment was from the Lord.

say to her, "If no other man has slept with you and you have not gone astray[z] and become impure while married to your husband, may this bitter water that brings a curse[a] not harm you. 20But if you have gone astray[b] while married to your husband and you have defiled yourself by sleeping with a man other than your husband"— 21here the priest is to put the woman under this curse of the oath[c]—"may the LORD cause your people to curse and denounce you when he causes your thigh to waste away and your abdomen to swell.[j] 22May this water[d] that brings a curse[e] enter your body so that your abdomen swells and your thigh wastes away.[k]"

"'Then the woman is to say, "Amen. So be it.[f]"'

23"'The priest is to write these curses on a scroll[g] and then wash them off into the bitter water. 24He shall have the woman drink the bitter water that brings a curse, and this water will enter her and cause bitter suffering. 25The priest is to take from her hands the grain offering for jealousy, wave it before the LORD[h] and bring it to the altar. 26The priest is then to take a handful of the grain offering as a memorial offering[i] and burn it on the altar; after that, he is to have the woman drink the water. 27If she has defiled herself and been unfaithful to her husband, then when she is made to drink the water that brings a curse, it will go into her and cause bitter suffering; her abdomen will swell and her thigh waste away,[l] and she will become accursed[j] among her people. 28If, however, the woman has not defiled herself and is free from impurity, she will be cleared of guilt and will be able to have children.

29"'This, then, is the law of jealousy

when a woman goes astray[k] and defiles herself while married to her husband, 30or when feelings of jealousy[l] come over a man because he suspects his wife. The priest is to have her stand before the LORD and is to apply this entire law to her. 31The husband will be innocent of any wrongdoing, but the woman will bear the consequences[m] of her sin.'"

The Nazirite

6 The LORD said to Moses, 2"Speak to the Israelites and say to them: 'If a man or woman wants to make a special vow[n], a vow of separation[o] to the LORD as a Nazirite,[p] 3he must abstain from wine[q] and other fermented drink and must not drink vinegar[r] made from wine or from other fermented drink. He must not drink grape juice or eat grapes[s] or raisins. 4As long as he is a Nazirite, he must not eat anything that comes from the grapevine, not even the seeds or skins.

5"'During the entire period of his vow of separation no razor[t] may be used on his head.[u] He must be holy until the period of his separation to the LORD is over; he must let the hair of his head grow long. 6Throughout the period of his separation to the LORD he must not go near a dead body.[v] 7Even if his own father or mother or brother or sister dies, he must not make himself ceremonially unclean[w] on account of them, because the symbol of his separation to God is on his head. 8Throughout the period of his separation he is consecrated to the LORD.

9"'If someone dies suddenly in his presence, thus defiling the hair he has dedicat-

Cross references

5:19 zver 12,29; aver 18
5:20 bver 12
5:21 cJos 6:26; 1Sa 14:24; Ne 10:29
5:22 dPs 109:18; ever 18 /Dt 27:15
5:23 gJer 45:1
5:25 hLev 8:27
5:26 iS Lev 2:2
5:27 /Isa 43:28; 65:15; Jer 26:6; 29:18; 42:18; 44:12,22; Zec 8:13

5:29 kS ver 19
5:30 lS ver 14
5:31 mS Lev 5:1
6:2 nver 5; S Ge 28:20; Ac 21:23 over 6 pJdg 13:5; 16:17
6:3 qS Lev 10:9; S Lk 1:15 rRu 2:14; Ps 69:21; Pr 10:26 sS Lev 25:5
6:5 tPs 52:2; 57:4; 59:7; Isa 7:20; Eze 5:1 u1Sa 1:11
6:6 vS Lev 21:1-3; Nu 9:11-22
6:7 wNu 9:6

[j]21 Or causes you to have a miscarrying womb and barrenness [k]22 Or body and cause you to be barren and have a miscarrying womb [l]27 Or suffering; she will have barrenness and a miscarrying womb

---

5:21 your thigh to waste away and your abdomen to swell. See NIV text note. The figurative language here (and in vv. 22,27) speaks of the loss of the capacity for childbearing (and, if pregnant, the miscarriage of the child). This is demonstrated by the determination of the fate of a woman wrongly charged (v. 28). For a woman in the ancient Near East to be denied the ability to bear children was a personal loss of inestimable proportions. Since it was in the bearing of children that a woman's worth was realized in the ancient world, this was a grievous punishment indeed.

6:2 man or woman. See ch. 30 for the differences between the vows of men and women. vow . . . Nazirite. Involved separation or consecration for a specific period of special devotion to God—on occasion even for life. Attention is usually given to the prohibitions for the Nazirite; more important to the Lord is the positive separation (see v. 8). This was not just a vow of personal self-discipline; it was an act of total devotion to the Lord.

6:4 anything that comes from the grapevine. Not only was

the fermented beverage forbidden, but even the seed and skin of the grape. During the period of a Nazirite's vow, three areas of his (or her) life were governed: (1) diet, (2) appearance and (3) associations. Every Israelite was regulated in these areas, but for the Nazirite each regulation was heightened. An analogy may be the practice of some Christians to forgo certain (good) foods during the period of Lent to enhance spiritual devotion to Christ in the special period of remembering his sufferings.

6:5 no razor. See Jdg 13:5. The unusually long hair of a Nazirite would become a physical mark of his (or her) vow of special devotion to the Lord. Cf. Lev 21:5.

6:6 dead body. See note on 5:2. For the Nazirite, the prohibition of contact with dead bodies extended even to the deceased within his (or her) own family (v. 7; contrast Lev 21:1-3).

6:9–12 The provisions of the Nazirite vow concerned areas where he (or she) was able to make conscious decisions. This section deals with the unexpected and the un-

ed,[x] he must shave his head on the day of
his cleansing[y]—the seventh day. 10 Then
on the eighth day[z] he must bring two
doves or two young pigeons[a] to the priest
at the entrance to the Tent of Meeting.[b]
11 The priest is to offer one as a sin offering[c] and the other as a burnt offering[d] to
make atonement[e] for him because he
sinned by being in the presence of the dead
body. That same day he is to consecrate his
head. 12 He must dedicate himself to the
LORD for the period of his separation and
must bring a year-old male lamb[f] as a guilt
offering.[g] The previous days do not count,
because he became defiled during his separation.

13 " 'Now this is the law for the Nazirite
when the period of his separation is over.[h]
He is to be brought to the entrance to the
Tent of Meeting.[i] 14 There he is to present
his offerings to the LORD: a year-old male
lamb without defect[j] for a burnt offering,
a year-old ewe lamb without defect for a
sin offering,[k] a ram[l] without defect for a
fellowship offering,[m][m] 15 together with
their grain offerings[n] and drink offerings,[o]
and a basket of bread made without
yeast—cakes made of fine flour mixed
with oil, and wafers spread with oil.[p]

16 " 'The priest is to present them[q] before the LORD[r] and make the sin offering
and the burnt offering.[s] 17 He is to present
the basket of unleavened bread and is to
sacrifice the ram as a fellowship offering[t]
to the LORD, together with its grain offering[u] and drink offering.[v]

18 " 'Then at the entrance to the Tent of
Meeting, the Nazirite must shave off the
hair that he dedicated.[w] He is to take the
hair and put it in the fire that is under the
sacrifice of the fellowship offering.

19 " 'After the Nazirite has shaved off the
hair of his dedication, the priest is to place
in his hands a boiled shoulder of the ram,
and a cake and a wafer from the basket,
both made without yeast.[x] 20 The priest
shall then wave them before the LORD as a
wave offering;[y] they are holy[z] and belong
to the priest, together with the breast that
was waved and the thigh that was
presented.[a] After that, the Nazirite may
drink wine.[b]

21 " 'This is the law of the Nazirite[c] who
vows his offering to the LORD in accordance with his separation, in addition to
whatever else he can afford. He must fulfill
the vow[d] he has made, according to the
law of the Nazirite.' "

The Priestly Blessing

22 The LORD said to Moses, 23 "Tell Aaron
and his sons, 'This is how you are to bless[e]
the Israelites. Say to them:

24 " ' "The LORD bless you[f]
and keep you;[g]
25 the LORD make his face shine upon
you[h]
and be gracious to you;[i]
26 the LORD turn his face[j] toward you
and give you peace.[k]" '

27 "So they will put my name[l] on the
Israelites, and I will bless them."

Offerings at the Dedication of the Tabernacle

7 When Moses finished setting up the
tabernacle,[m] he anointed[n] it and consecrated it and all its furnishings.[o] He also
anointed and consecrated the altar and all
its utensils.[p] 2 Then the leaders of Israel,[q]
the heads of families who were the tribal
leaders in charge of those who were counted,[r] made offerings. 3 They brought as
their gifts before the LORD six covered
carts[s] and twelve oxen—an ox from each
leader and a cart from every two. These
they presented before the tabernacle.

[m] *14* Traditionally *peace offering*; also in verses 17 and 18

6:9 [x]ver 18 [y]S Lev 14:9 **6:10** [z]S Lev 14:10 [a]S Lev 5:7 [b]Lev 14:11 **6:11** [c]S Ex 30:10 [d]S Ge 8:20 [e]S Ex 29:36 **6:12** [f]S Lev 12:6 [g]S Lev 5:15 **6:13** [h]Ac 21:26 [i]Lev 14:11 **6:14** [j]S Ex 12:5 [k]ver 11; Lev 4:3; 14:10 [l]S Lev 5:15 [m]Lev 3:1 **6:15** [n]Lev 2:1; S 6:14 [o]S Ge 35:14 [p]S Ex 29:2 **6:16** [q]Lev 1:3 [r]ver 10 [s]ver 11 **6:17** [t]Lev 3:1 [u]S Ex 29:41 [v]Lev 23:13 **6:18** [w]ver 9; Ac 21:24
6:19 [x]Lev 7:12 **6:20** [y]Lev 7:30 [z]S Lev 27:9 [a]S Lev 7:34 [b]Ecc 9:7 **6:21** [c]ver 13 [d]ver 2 **6:23** [e]Dt 21:5; 1Ch 23:13 **6:24** [f]S Ge 28:3; Dt 28:3-6; Ps 28:9; 128:5 [g]1Sa 2:9; Ps 17:8 **6:25** [h]Job 29:24; Ps 4:6; 31:16; 80:3; 119:135 [i]Ge 43:29; Ps 25:16; 86:16; 119:29 **6:26** [j]Ps 4:6; 44:3 [k]Ps 4:8; 29:11; 37:11,37; 127:2; Isa 14:7; Jer 33:6; Jn 14:27 **6:27** [l]Dt 28:10; 2Sa 7:23; 2Ch 7:14; Ne 9:10; Jer 25:29; Eze 36:23 **7:1** [m]Ex 40:17 [n]S Ex 30:26 [o]S Ex 40:9 [p]ver 84,88; Ex 40:10; 2Ch 7:9 **7:2** [q]Nu 1:5-16 [r]Nu 1:19 **7:3** [s]Ge 45:19; 1Sa 6:7-14; 1Ch 13:7

planned events of daily living.

6:13–20 The offerings of the Nazirite at the completion of the period of the vow were extensive, expensive and expressive of the spirit of total commitment to the Lord during this time of special devotion. In addition to these several offerings the Nazirite burned his (or her) hair (the sign of the vow).

6:21 *This is the law of the Nazirite.* Summary statements such as this not only end a section, but also solemnize its contents.

6:24–26 The Aaronic benediction. The threefold repetition of the divine name Yahweh ("the LORD") is for emphasis and gives force to the expression in v. 27: "So they will put my name on the Israelites." Each verse conveys two elements of benediction, and the verses are progressively longer (in the Hebrew text, the first verse has three words, the second has five and the third has seven).

6:25 *make his face shine upon you.* In acceptance and favor.

6:26 *peace.* The Hebrew for this word is *shalom,* here seen in its most expressive fullness—not the absence of war, but a positive state of rightness and well-being. Such peace comes only from the Lord.

7:1–89 See Ex 40, which describes the setting up of the tabernacle and ends with the report of the cloud covering and the presence of the Lord filling the tabernacle. With much repetition of language, this chapter (the longest in the Pentateuch) records the magnificent (and identical) gifts to the Lord for tabernacle service from the leaders of the 12 tribes. The fact that the record of these gifts follows the text of the Aaronic benediction (6:24–26) seems fitting: In response to God's promise to bless his people, they bring gifts to him in 12 sequential days of celebrative pageantry.

⁴The LORD said to Moses, ⁵"Accept these from them, that they may be used in the work at the Tent of Meeting. Give them to the Levites as each man's work requires."

⁶So Moses took the carts and oxen and gave them to the Levites. ⁷He gave two carts and four oxen to the Gershonites,ᵗ as their work required, ⁸and he gave four carts and eight oxen to the Merarites,ᵘ as their work required. They were all under the direction of Ithamar son of Aaron, the priest. ⁹But Moses did not give any to the Kohathites,ᵛ because they were to carry on their shouldersʷ the holy things, for which they were responsible.

¹⁰When the altar was anointed,ˣ the leaders brought their offerings for its dedicationʸ and presented them before the altar. ¹¹For the LORD had said to Moses, "Each day one leader is to bring his offering for the dedication of the altar."

¹²The one who brought his offering on the first day was Nahshonᶻ son of Amminadab of the tribe of Judah.

¹³His offering was one silver plate weighing a hundred and thirty shekels,ⁿ and one silver sprinkling bowlᵃ weighing seventy shekels,ᵒ ᵇ both according to the sanctuary shekel,ᶜ each filled with fine flour mixed with oil as a grain offering;ᵈ ¹⁴one gold dishᵉ weighing ten shekels,ᵖᶠ filled with incense;ᵍ ¹⁵one young bull,ʰ one ram and one male lamb a year old, for a burnt offering;ⁱ ¹⁶one male goat for a sin offering;ʲ ¹⁷and two oxen, five rams, five goats and five male lambs a year old, to be sacrificed as a fellowship offering.ᑫᵏ This was the offering of Nahshon son of Amminadab.ˡ

¹⁸On the second day Nathanel son of Zuar,ᵐ the leader of Issachar, brought his offering.

¹⁹The offering he brought was one silver plate weighing a hundred and thirty shekels, and one silver sprinkling bowl weighing seventy shekels, both according to the sanctuary shekel, each filled with fine flour mixed with oil as a grain offering; ²⁰one gold dishⁿ weighing ten shekels, filled with incense; ²¹one

young bull, one ram and one male lamb a year old, for a burnt offering; ²²one male goat for a sin offering; ²³and two oxen, five rams, five goats and five male lambs a year old, to be sacrificed as a fellowship offering. This was the offering of Nethanel son of Zuar.

²⁴On the third day, Eliab son of Helon,ᵒ the leader of the people of Zebulun, brought his offering.

²⁵His offering was one silver plate weighing a hundred and thirty shekels, and one silver sprinkling bowl weighing seventy shekels, both according to the sanctuary shekel, each filled with fine flour mixed with oil as a grain offering; ²⁶one gold dish weighing ten shekels, filled with incense; ²⁷one young bull, one ram and one male lamb a year old, for a burnt offering; ²⁸one male goat for a sin offering; ²⁹and two oxen, five rams, five male goats and five male lambs a year old, to be sacrificed as a fellowship offering. This was the offering of Eliab son of Helon.

³⁰On the fourth day Elizur son of Shedeur,ᵖ the leader of the people of Reuben, brought his offering.

³¹His offering was one silver plate weighing a hundred and thirty shekels, and one silver sprinkling bowl weighing seventy shekels, both according to the sanctuary shekel, each filled with fine flour mixed with oil as a grain offering; ³²one gold dish weighing ten shekels, filled with incense; ³³one young bull, one ram and one male lamb a year old, for a burnt offering; ³⁴one male goat for a sin offering; ³⁵and two oxen, five rams, five male goats and five male lambs a year old, to be sacrificed as a fellowship offering. This was the offering of Elizur son of Shedeur.

³⁶On the fifth day Shelumiel son of Zuri-

Cross references (center column):

7:7 ᵗNu 4:24-26, 28
7:8 ᵘNu 4:31-33
7:9 ᵛNu 4:4
ʷNu 4:15
7:10 ˣver 1; S Ex 29:36
ʸ2Ch 7:9
7:12 ᶻS Nu 1:7
7:13 ᵃS Ex 27:3
ᵇver 85
ᶜS Ex 30:13; Lev 27:3-7
ᵈLev 2:1; Nu 6:15; 15:4
7:14 ᵉver 20; 1Ki 7:50; 2Ki 25:14; 2Ch 4:22; 24:14
ᶠver 86
ᵍS Ex 25:6
7:15 ʰEx 24:5; 29:3; Nu 28:11
ⁱLev 1:3
7:16 ʲLev 4:3
7:17 ᵏLev 3:1
ˡNu 1:7
7:18 ᵐS Nu 1:8
7:20 ⁿS ver 14

7:24 ᵒS Nu 1:9
7:30 ᵖS Nu 1:5

ⁿ13 That is, about 3 1/4 pounds (about 1.5 kilograms); also elsewhere in this chapter　ᵒ13 That is, about 1 3/4 pounds (about 0.8 kilogram); also elsewhere in this chapter　ᵖ14 That is, about 4 ounces (about 110 grams); also elsewhere in this chapter　ᑫ17 Traditionally *peace offering*; also elsewhere in this chapter

---

7:12–78 The leaders of the 12 tribes have already been named in 1:5–15; 2:3–32. The order of the presentation of their offerings to the Lord is the same as the order of march: first, the triad of tribes camped east of the tabernacle (Judah, Issachar and Zebulun: 2:3–9; 7:12,18,24); second, the triad camped to the south (Reuben, Simeon and Gad: 2:10–16; 7:30,36,42); third, the triad to the west (Ephraim, Manasseh and Benjamin: 2:18–24; 7:48,54,60); finally, those to the north (Dan, Asher and Naphtali: 2:25–31; 7:66,72,78). See diagram of "Encampment of the Tribes of Israel," p. 192.

shaddai, *q* the leader of the people of Simeon, brought his offering.

7:36 *q*S Nu 1:6
7:42 *r*S Nu 1:14
7:48 *s*S Nu 1:10
7:53 *t*S Nu 1:10

37His offering was one silver plate weighing a hundred and thirty shekels, and one silver sprinkling bowl weighing seventy shekels, both according to the sanctuary shekel, each filled with fine flour mixed with oil as a grain offering; 38one gold dish weighing ten shekels, filled with incense; 39one young bull, one ram and one male lamb a year old, for a burnt offering; 40one male goat for a sin offering; 41and two oxen, five rams, five male goats and five male lambs a year old, to be sacrificed as a fellowship offering. This was the offering of Shelumiel son of Zurishaddai.

42On the sixth day Eliasaph son of Deuel, *r* the leader of the people of Gad, brought his offering.

43His offering was one silver plate weighing a hundred and thirty shekels, and one silver sprinkling bowl weighing seventy shekels, both according to the sanctuary shekel, each filled with fine flour mixed with oil as a grain offering; 44one gold dish weighing ten shekels, filled with incense; 45one young bull, one ram and one male lamb a year old, for a burnt offering; 46one male goat for a sin offering; 47and two oxen, five rams, five male goats and five male lambs a year old, to be sacrificed as a fellowship offering. This was the offering of Eliasaph son of Deuel.

48On the seventh day Elishama son of Ammihud, *s* the leader of the people of Ephraim, brought his offering.

49His offering was one silver plate weighing a hundred and thirty shekels, and one silver sprinkling bowl weighing seventy shekels, both according to the sanctuary shekel, each filled with fine flour mixed with oil as a grain offering; 50one gold dish weighing ten shekels, filled with incense; 51one young bull, one ram and one male lamb a year old, for a burnt offering; 52one male goat for a sin offering; 53and two oxen, five rams, five male goats and five male lambs a year old, to be sacrificed as a fellowship offering. This was the offering of Elishama son of Ammihud. *t*

54On the eighth day Gamaliel son of

Pedahzur, *u* the leader of the people of Manasseh, brought his offering.

55His offering was one silver plate weighing a hundred and thirty shekels, and one silver sprinkling bowl weighing seventy shekels, both according to the sanctuary shekel, each filled with fine flour mixed with oil as a grain offering; 56one gold dish weighing ten shekels, filled with incense; 57one young bull, one ram and one male lamb a year old, for a burnt offering; 58one male goat for a sin offering; 59and two oxen, five rams, five male goats and five male lambs a year old, to be sacrificed as a fellowship offering. This was the offering of Gamaliel son of Pedahzur.

60On the ninth day Abidan son of Gideoni, *v* the leader of the people of Benjamin, brought his offering.

61His offering was one silver plate weighing a hundred and thirty shekels, and one silver sprinkling bowl weighing seventy shekels, both according to the sanctuary shekel, each filled with fine flour mixed with oil as a grain offering; 62one gold dish weighing ten shekels, filled with incense; 63one young bull, one ram and one male lamb a year old, for a burnt offering; 64one male goat for a sin offering; 65and two oxen, five rams, five male goats and five male lambs a year old, to be sacrificed as a fellowship offering. This was the offering of Abidan son of Gideoni.

66On the tenth day Ahiezer son of Ammishaddai, *w* the leader of the people of Dan, brought his offering.

67His offering was one silver plate weighing a hundred and thirty shekels, and one silver sprinkling bowl weighing seventy shekels, both according to the sanctuary shekel, each filled with fine flour mixed with oil as a grain offering; 68one gold dish weighing ten shekels, filled with incense; 69one young bull, one ram and one male lamb a year old, for a burnt offering; 70one male goat for a sin offering; 71and two oxen, five rams, five male goats and five male lambs a year old, to be sacrificed as a fellowship offering. This was the offering of Ahiezer son of Ammishaddai.

7:54 *u*S Nu 1:10
7:60 *v*S Nu 1:11
7:66 *w*S Nu 1:12

72On the eleventh day Pagiel son of

Ocran,[x] the leader of the people of Asher, brought his offering.

73His offering was one silver plate weighing a hundred and thirty shekels, and one silver sprinkling bowl weighing seventy shekels, both according to the sanctuary shekel, each filled with fine flour mixed with oil as a grain offering; 74one gold dish weighing ten shekels, filled with incense; 75one young bull, one ram and one male lamb a year old, for a burnt offering; 76one male goat for a sin offering; 77and two oxen, five rams, five male goats and five male lambs a year old, to be sacrificed as a fellowship offering. This was the offering of Pagiel son of Ocran.

78On the twelfth day Ahira son of Enan,[y] the leader of the people of Naphtali, brought his offering.

79His offering was one silver plate weighing a hundred and thirty shekels, and one silver sprinkling bowl weighing seventy shekels, both according to the sanctuary shekel, each filled with fine flour mixed with oil as a grain offering; 80one gold dish weighing ten shekels, filled with incense; 81one young bull, one ram and one male lamb a year old, for a burnt offering; 82one male goat for a sin offering; 83and two oxen, five rams, five male goats and five male lambs a year old, to be sacrificed as a fellowship offering. This was the offering of Ahira son of Enan.

84These were the offerings of the Israelite leaders for the dedication of the altar when it was anointed:[z] twelve silver plates, twelve silver sprinkling bowls[a] and twelve gold dishes.[b] 85Each silver plate weighed a hundred and thirty shekels, and each sprinkling bowl seventy shekels. Altogether, the silver dishes weighed two thousand four hundred shekels,[r] according to the sanctuary shekel.[c] 86The twelve gold dishes filled with incense weighed ten shekels each, according to the sanctuary shekel.[d] Altogether, the gold dishes weighed a hundred and twenty shekels.[s] 87The total number of animals for the burnt offering[e] came to twelve young bulls, twelve rams and twelve male lambs a year old, together with their grain offering.[f] Twelve male goats were used for the sin offering.[g] 88The total number of animals for the sacrifice of the fellowship offering[h] came to twenty-four oxen, sixty rams, sixty male goats and sixty male lambs[i] a year old. These were the offerings for the dedication of the altar after it was anointed.[j]

89When Moses entered the Tent of Meeting[k] to speak with the LORD,[l] he heard the voice speaking to him from between the two cherubim above the atonement cover[m] on the ark of the Testimony.[n] And he spoke with him.

Setting Up the Lamps

8 The LORD said to Moses, 2"Speak to Aaron and say to him, 'When you set up the seven lamps, they are to light the area in front of the lampstand.[o]' "

3Aaron did so; he set up the lamps so that they faced forward on the lampstand, just as the LORD commanded Moses. 4This is how the lampstand was made: It was made of hammered gold[p]—from its base to its blossoms. The lampstand was made exactly like the pattern[q] the LORD had shown Moses.

The Setting Apart of the Levites

5The LORD said to Moses: 6"Take the Levites from among the other Israelites and make them ceremonially clean.[r] 7To purify them, do this: Sprinkle the water of cleansing[s] on them; then have them shave their whole bodies[t] and wash their clothes,[u] and so purify themselves.[v] 8Have them take a young bull with its grain offering of fine flour mixed with oil;[w] then you are to take a second young bull for a sin offering.[x] 9Bring the Levites to the front of the Tent of Meeting[y] and assemble the whole Israelite community.[z] 10You are to bring the Levites before the LORD,

7:72 [x]S Nu 1:13 **7:78** [y]S Nu 1:15 **7:84** [z]ver 1,10 [a]S Nu 4:14 [b]ver 14 **7:85** [c]ver 13 **7:86** [d]ver 13 **7:87** [e]ver 15 [f]ver 13 [g]ver 16 **7:88** [h]ver 17 [i]Ge 32:14 [j]S ver 1,10 **7:89** [k]S Ex 40:2 [l]S Ex 29:42 [m]S Ex 16:34; Ps 80:1; 99:1 [n]Nu 3:31 **8:2** [o]Ex 25:37 **8:4** [p]S Ex 25:36 [q]S Ex 25:9 **8:6** [r]Lev 22:2; Isa 1:16; 52:11 **8:7** [s]Nu 19:9,17; 31:23 [t]S Lev 14:9; Nu 6:9; Dt 21:12 [u]S Ge 35:2; Lev 14:8 [v]S Ge 35:2 **8:8** [w]Lev 2:1; Nu 15:8-10 [x]Lev 4:3 **8:9** [y]Ex 40:12 [z]Lev 8:3

[r]*85* That is, about 60 pounds (about 28 kilograms)
[s]*86* That is, about 3 pounds (about 1.4 kilograms)

7:84–88 The totals of the 12 sets of gifts.
7:89 The climax: Communion is established between the Lord and his prophet. The people have an advocate with God.
8:2 *area in front of the lampstand.* The Holy Place in the tabernacle (see Ex 25:37; 26:33; 27:21).
8:5–26 Describes the cleansing of the Levites and may be compared with the account of the ordination of Aaron and his sons to the priesthood (Lev 8). The Levites are helpers to the priests, and the language describing their consecration is somewhat different from that of the priests. The priests were made holy, the Levites clean; the priests were anointed and washed, the Levites sprinkled; the priests were given new garments, the Levites washed theirs; blood was applied to the priests, it was waved over the Levites.
8:7 *shave their whole bodies.* Symbolic of the completeness of their cleansing, as in the case of the ritual cleansing of one cured of skin disease (Lev 14:8).

and the Israelites are to lay their hands on them. [a] [11] Aaron is to present the Levites before the LORD as a wave offering [b] from the Israelites, so that they may be ready to do the work of the LORD.

[12] "After the Levites lay their hands on the heads of the bulls, [c] use the one for a sin offering [d] to the LORD and the other for a burnt offering, [e] to make atonement [f] for the Levites. [13] Have the Levites stand in front of Aaron and his sons and then present them as a wave offering [g] to the LORD. [14] In this way you are to set the Levites apart from the other Israelites, and the Levites will be mine. [h]

[15] "After you have purified the Levites and presented them as a wave offering, [i] they are to come to do their work at the Tent of Meeting. [j] [16] They are the Israelites who are to be given wholly to me. I have taken them as my own in place of the first-born, [k] the first male offspring [l] from every Israelite woman. [17] Every firstborn male in Israel, whether man or animal, [m] is mine. When I struck down all the firstborn in Egypt, I set them apart for myself. [n] [o] [18] And I have taken the Levites in place of all the firstborn sons in Israel. [p] [19] Of all the Israelites, I have given the Levites as gifts to Aaron and his sons [q] to do the work at the Tent of Meeting on behalf of the Israelites [r] and to make atonement for them [s] so that no plague will strike the Israelites when they go near the sanctuary."

[20] Moses, Aaron and the whole Israelite community did with the Levites just as the LORD commanded Moses. [21] The Levites purified themselves and washed their clothes. [t] Then Aaron presented them as a

wave offering before the LORD and made atonement [u] for them to purify them. [v] [22] After that, the Levites came to do their work [w] at the Tent of Meeting under the supervision of Aaron and his sons. They did with the Levites just as the LORD commanded Moses.

[23] The LORD said to Moses, [24] "This applies to the Levites: Men twenty-five years old or more [x] shall come to take part in the work at the Tent of Meeting, [y] [25] but at the age of fifty, [z] they must retire from their regular service and work no longer. [26] They may assist their brothers in performing their duties at the Tent of Meeting, but they themselves must not do the work. [a] This, then, is how you are to assign the responsibilities of the Levites."

The Passover

9 The LORD spoke to Moses in the Desert of Sinai in the first month [b] of the second year after they came out of Egypt. [c] He said, [2] "Have the Israelites celebrate the Passover [d] at the appointed time. [e] [3] Celebrate it at the appointed time, at twilight on the fourteenth day of this month, [f] in accordance with all its rules and regulations. [g] "

[4] So Moses told the Israelites to celebrate the Passover, [h] [5] and they did so in the Desert of Sinai [i] at twilight on the fourteenth day of the first month. [j] The Israelites did everything just as the LORD commanded Moses. [k]

[6] But some of them could not celebrate the Passover on that day because they were ceremonially unclean [l] on account of a dead body. [m] So they came to Moses and

Cross references (center column)

8:10 [a] S Lev 3:2; Ac 6:6
8:11 [b] S Ex 29:24
8:12 [c] S Ex 29:10 [d] Lev 4:3; Nu 6:11 [e] Lev 1:3 [f] S Ex 29:36
8:13 [g] S Ex 29:24
8:14 [h] S Nu 3:12
8:15 [i] S Ex 29:24 [j] Ex 40:2
8:16 [k] Nu 1:20 [l] S Nu 3:12
8:17 [m] S Ex 4:23 [n] S Ex 22:29 [o] S Ex 13:2
8:18 [p] S Nu 3:12
8:19 [q] S Nu 3:9 [r] S Nu 3:7 [s] Nu 16:46
8:21 [t] ver 7; S Ge 35:2

[u] Nu 16:47 [v] ver 12
8:22 [w] ver 11
8:24 [x] 1Ch 23:3 [y] S Ex 38:21
8:25 [z] S Nu 4:3
8:26 [a] ver 11
9:1 [b] S Ex 40:2 [c] Nu 1:1
9:2 [d] S Ex 12:11 [e] ver 7
9:3 [f] S Ex 12:6,42 [g] Ex 12:2-11, 43-49; Lev 23:5-8; Dt 16:1-8
9:4 [h] ver 2; S Ex 12:11
9:5 [i] ver 1 [j] S Ex 12:6 [k] ver 3
9:6 [l] S Lev 5:3; S 13:3 [m] S Lev 21:11

8:10 *Israelites are to lay their hands on them.* The Levites were substitutes for the nation; by laying hands on them, the other people of the nation were acknowledging this substitutionary act (see vv. 16-18).

8:16 *to me.* See note on 3:9.

8:19 *I have given the Levites as gifts to Aaron and his sons.* The Levites were given to the Lord for his exclusive use (see v. 14). Now the Lord gives his Levites to the priests as their aides for the work of ministry in the tabernacle worship. *so that no plague will strike the Israelites.* The Levites were a protective hedge for the community against trespassing in the sacred precincts of the tabernacle (see note on 1:53).

8:20 *as the LORD commanded Moses.* See vv. 4,22; 1:54; 2:34; 3:16,51; 4:49; 5:4; 9:5,23. The implicit obedience of Moses and the Israelites to God's commands in the areas of ritual and regimen stands in sharp contrast to the people's complaints against the Lord's loving character and to their breaches of faith that begin in ch. 11.

8:24 *twenty-five years old.* See note on 4:3. The age at which the Levites entered service was reduced to 20 by David (see 1Ch 23:24,27), as the circumstances of their work had greatly changed by the time of the monarchy (see 1Ch 23:26). It is difficult to imagine a change in circum-

stances between 4:3 and this verse, however. Therefore the rabbinical suggestion that these two verses indicate a five-year period of apprenticeship seems reasonable.

8:26 *They may assist.* After a Levite had reached the mandatory retirement age of 50 (see v. 25), he was still free to assist his younger co-workers (perhaps at festivals), but he was no longer to do the difficult work he had done in his prime.

9:1-14 This unit is in four parts: (1) the command to keep the Passover (vv. 1-5); (2) the question concerning those ceremonially clean (vv. 6-8); (3) the response of the Lord—giving permission for legitimate delay, but judgment for willful neglect (vv. 9-13); (4) the rights of the alien at Passover (v. 14). The first Passover was held in Egypt (see Ex 12). The second is here at Sinai a year later. Because of Israel's rebellion and God's judgment on her (ch. 14), Israel would not celebrate the Passover again until she entered the promised land (see Jos 5:10).

9:1 *first month of the second year.* The events of this chapter preceded the beginning of the census in ch. 1 (see 1:1).

9:3 *twilight.* Traditional Jewish practice regards this period as the end of one day and the beginning of the next.

Aaron[n] that same day [7]and said to Moses, "We have become unclean because of a dead body, but why should we be kept from presenting the LORD's offering with the other Israelites at the appointed time?[o]"

[8]Moses answered them, "Wait until I find out what the LORD commands concerning you."[p]

[9]Then the LORD said to Moses, [10]"Tell the Israelites: 'When any of you or your descendants are unclean because of a dead body[q] or are away on a journey, they may still celebrate[r] the LORD's Passover. [11]They are to celebrate it on the fourteenth day of the second month[s] at twilight. They are to eat the lamb, together with unleavened bread and bitter herbs.[t] [12]They must not leave any of it till morning[u] or break any of its bones.[v] When they celebrate the Passover, they must follow all the regulations.[w] [13]But if a man who is ceremonially clean and not on a journey fails to celebrate the Passover, that person must be cut off from his people[x] because he did not present the LORD's offering at the appointed time. That man will bear the consequences of his sin.

[14]" 'An alien[y] living among you who wants to celebrate the LORD's Passover must do so in accordance with its rules and regulations. You must have the same regulations for the alien and the native-born.' "

The Cloud Above the Tabernacle

[15]On the day the tabernacle, the Tent of the Testimony,[z] was set up,[a] the cloud[b] covered it. From evening till morning the cloud above the tabernacle looked like fire.[c] [16]That is how it continued to be; the

cloud covered it, and at night it looked like fire.[d] [17]Whenever the cloud lifted from above the Tent, the Israelites set out;[e] wherever the cloud settled, the Israelites encamped.[f] [18]At the LORD's command the Israelites set out, and at his command they encamped. As long as the cloud stayed over the tabernacle, they remained[g] in camp. [19]When the cloud remained over the tabernacle a long time, the Israelites obeyed the LORD's order[h] and did not set out.[i] [20]Sometimes the cloud was over the tabernacle only a few days; at the LORD's command they would encamp, and then at his command they would set out. [21]Sometimes the cloud stayed only from evening till morning, and when it lifted in the morning, they set out. Whether by day or by night, whenever the cloud lifted, they set out. [22]Whether the cloud stayed over the tabernacle for two days or a month or a year, the Israelites would remain in camp and not set out; but when it lifted, they would set out. [23]At the LORD's command they encamped, and at the LORD's command they set out. They obeyed the LORD's order, in accordance with his command through Moses.

The Silver Trumpets

10 The LORD said to Moses: [2]"Make two trumpets[j] of hammered silver, and use them for calling the community[k] together and for having the camps set out.[l] [3]When both are sounded, the whole community is to assemble before you at the entrance to the Tent of Meeting. [4]If only one is sounded, the leaders[m]—the heads of the clans of Israel—are to assemble before you. [5]When a trumpet blast is

---

Cross references (center column):

9:6 [n]Ex 18:15; Nu 27:2
9:7 [o]ver 2
9:8 [p]Ex 18:15; Lev 24:12; Nu 15:34; 27:5, 21; Ps 85:8
9:10 [q]ver 6
[r]2Ch 30:2
9:11 [s]S Ex 12:6
[t]Ex 12:8
9:12 [u]S Ex 12:8
[v]S Ex 12:46; Jn 19:36* [w]ver 3
9:13 [x]S Ge 17:14
9:14 [y]S Ex 12:19, 43
9:15 [z]S Ex 38:21
[a]S Ex 26:30
[b]S Ex 33:16
[c]Ex 13:21

9:16 [d]S Ex 40:38
9:17 [e]ver 21
[f]1Co 10:1
9:18 [g]Ex 40:37
9:19 [h]S Lev 8:35
[i]Ex 40:37
10:2 [j]ver 8,9; Nu 31:6; Ne 12:35; Ps 47:5; 98:6; 150:3 [k]Ne 4:18; Jer 4:5,19; 6:1; Hos 5:8; 8:1; Joel 2:1,15; Am 3:6 [l]Nu 33:3
10:4 [m]S Ex 18:21

9:7 *why should we be kept from presenting the LORD's offering . . . ?*Those with ceremonial uncleanness had a keen desire to worship the Lord "in spirit and in truth" (Jn 4:24).
9:10 *they may still celebrate.* God's gracious provision for these people was an alternative day one month later (v. 11) so that they would not be excluded totally from the Passover celebration. The Lord thus demonstrates the reality of the distance that uncleanness brings between a believer and his (or her) participation in the worship of the community, but he also provides a merciful alternative.
9:12 *not . . . break any of its bones.* When Jesus ("our Passover lamb," 1Co 5:7; cf. Jn 1:29) was crucified, it was reported that none of his bones was broken, in fulfillment of Scripture (Jn 19:36). See also Ex 12:46; Ps 34:20.
9:13 *fails to celebrate . . . cut off.* The NT also issues grave warnings concerning the abuse or misuse of the celebration of the Lord's Supper (1Co 11:28–30). See note on Ex 12:15.
9:14 *alien.* Must first be circumcised before participating in the Passover celebration (Ex 12:48).
9:15 *cloud covered it.* See notes on Ex 13:21; 40:34. The cloud was the visible symbol of the Lord's presence hovering above the tabernacle. That this was no ordinary cloud is

attested not only by its spontaneous appearance at the completion of the setting up of the tabernacle, but also by the fact that at night it had the appearance of fire. The Lord also directed the movements of his people by means of the cloud (vv. 17–18).
9:18 *At the LORD's command.* The lifting and settling of the cloud are identified with the Lord's command.
9:23 *obeyed the LORD's order.* The repetitious nature of vv. 15–23 enhances the expectation of continued complete obedience to the Lord's direction of Israel's movements through the desert. The role of Moses is mentioned for balance: Moses was the Lord's agent, who interpreted the movement of the cloud as signaling the movement of the people. The tragedy of their subsequent disobedience (ch. 11) is heightened by this paragraph on their obedience.
10:2 *trumpets.* Long, straight, slender metal tubes with flared ends. They were blown for order and discipline.
10:3 *sounded.* Not only for assembling but also for marching (vv. 5–6), battle (v. 9) and festivals (v. 10). Since different signals were used (v. 7), a guild of priestly musicians was developed (v. 8). See Jos 6:4 for the use of seven trumpets of rams' horns (Hebrew *shophar*) in the battle of Jericho.

sounded, the tribes camping on the east are to set out.[n] [6]At the sounding of a second blast, the camps on the south are to set out.[o] The blast will be the signal for setting out. [7]To gather the assembly, blow the trumpets,[p] but not with the same signal.[q]

[8]"The sons of Aaron, the priests, are to blow the trumpets. This is to be a lasting ordinance for you and the generations to come.[r] [9]When you go into battle in your own land against an enemy who is oppressing you,[s] sound a blast on the trumpets.[t] Then you will be remembered[u] by the LORD your God and rescued from your enemies.[v] [10]Also at your times of rejoicing—your appointed feasts and New Moon festivals[w]—you are to sound the trumpets[x] over your burnt offerings[y] and fellowship offerings,[t][z] and they will be a memorial for you before your God. I am the LORD your God.[a]"

The Israelites Leave Sinai

[11]On the twentieth day of the second month of the second year,[b] the cloud lifted[c] from above the tabernacle of the Testimony.[d] [12]Then the Israelites set out from the Desert of Sinai and traveled from place to place until the cloud came to rest in the Desert of Paran.[e] [13]They set out, this first time, at the LORD's command through Moses.[f]

[14]The divisions of the camp of Judah went first, under their standard.[g] Nahshon son of Amminadab[h] was in command. [15]Nethanel son of Zuar was over the division of the tribe[i] of Issachar,[j] [16]and Eliab son of Helon[k] was over the division of the tribe of Zebulun.[l] [17]Then the tabernacle was taken down, and the Gershonites and Merarites, who carried it, set out.[m]

[18]The divisions of the camp of Reuben[n] went next, under their standard.[o] Elizur

son of Shedeur[p] was in command. [19]Shelumiel son of Zurishaddai was over the division of the tribe of Simeon,[q] [20]and Eliasaph son of Deuel was over the division of the tribe of Gad.[r] [21]Then the Kohathites[s] set out, carrying the holy things.[t] The tabernacle was to be set up before they arrived.[u]

[22]The divisions of the camp of Ephraim[v] went next, under their standard. Elishama son of Ammihud[w] was in command. [23]Gamaliel son of Pedahzur was over the division of the tribe of Manasseh,[x] [24]and Abidan son of Gideoni was over the division of the tribe of Benjamin.[y]

[25]Finally, as the rear guard[z] for all the units, the divisions of the camp of Dan set out, under their standard. Ahiezer son of Ammishaddai[a] was in command. [26]Pagiel son of Ocran was over the division of the tribe of Asher,[b] [27]and Ahira son of Enan was over the division of the tribe of Naphtali.[c] [28]This was the order of march for the Israelite divisions as they set out.

[29]Now Moses said to Hobab[d] son of Reuel[e] the Midianite, Moses' father-in-law,[f] "We are setting out for the place about which the LORD said, 'I will give it to you.'[g] Come with us and we will treat you well, for the LORD has promised good things to Israel."

[30]He answered, "No, I will not go;[h] I am going back to my own land and my own people.[i]"

[31]But Moses said, "Please do not leave us. You know where we should camp in the desert, and you can be our eyes.[j] [32]If you come with us, we will share with you[k] whatever good things the LORD gives us.[l]"

10:5 [h]ver 14
10:6 [o]ver 18
10:7 [p]Jer 4:5; 6:1; Eze 33:3; Joel 2:1
[q]1Co 14:8
10:8 [r]S Ge 9:12; Nu 15:14; 35:29
10:9 [s]Ex 3:9; Jdg 2:18; 6:9; 1Sa 10:18; 2Ki 13:4; Ps 106:42
[t]S Lev 23:24
[u]S Ge 8:1
[v]2Ch 13:12; Ps 106:4
10:10 [w]Nu 28:11; 1Sa 20:5,24; 2Ki 4:23; 2Ch 8:13; Ps 81:3; Isa 1:13; Eze 45:17; 46:6; Am 8:5
[x]S Lev 23:24
[y]Lev 1:3
[z]Lev 3:1; Nu 6:14
[a]Lev 11:44
10:11 [b]Ex 40:17
[c]Nu 9:17
[d]S Ex 38:21
10:12 [e]S Ge 14:6; Dt 1:1; 33:2
10:13 [f]Dt 1:6
10:14 [g]S Nu 1:52; S 2:3-9 [h]Nu 1:7
10:15 [i]S Lev 24:11
[j]S Nu 1:8
10:16 [k]S Nu 2:7
[l]S Nu 1:9
10:17 [m]ver 21; Nu 4:21-32
10:18 [n]Nu 2:16
[o]Nu 2:10-16

[p]S Nu 1:5
10:19 [q]Nu 1:6
10:20 [r]S Nu 1:14
10:21 [s]S Nu 2:17
[t]Nu 4:20 [u]S ver 17
10:22 [v]Nu 2:24
[w]S Nu 1:10
10:23 [x]S Nu 1:10
10:24 [y]Nu 1:11
10:25 [z]S Nu 2:31
[a]S Nu 1:12
10:26 [b]S Nu 1:13
10:27 [c]S Nu 1:15
10:29 [d]Jdg 4:11
[e]S Ex 2:18
[f]S Ex 3:1
[g]S Ge 12:7; S 15:14

10:30 [h]Mt 21:29 [i]S Ex 18:27 10:31 [j]Job 29:15 10:32 [k]S Ex 12:48; Dt 10:18 [l]Ps 22:27-31; 67:5-7

[t]10 Traditionally *peace offerings*

10:10 *at your . . . appointed feasts . . . sound the trumpets.* As an introit to prepare the people for communion with God. Later, David expanded the instruments to include the full orchestra in the worship of the Lord (see, e.g., 1Ch 25), but he maintained the playing of the silver trumpets regularly before the ark of the covenant (1Ch 16:6).

10:11–28 The structure of this section is: (1) v. 11, time frame; (2) vv. 12–13, introductory summary of setting out; (3) vv. 14–17, setting out of the tribes led by Judah (see 2:3–9); (4) vv. 18–21, setting out of the tribes led by Reuben (see 2:10–16); (5) vv. 22–24, setting out of the tribes led by Ephraim (see 2:18–24); (6) vv. 25–27, setting out of the tribes led by Dan (see 2:25–31); (7) v. 28, concluding summary of the line of march.

10:11 *twentieth day of the second month.* After 11 months in the region of Mount Sinai, the people set out for the promised land, led by the cloud. This verse begins the second great section of the book of Numbers (10:11–22:1).

Israel leaves on a journey that in a few months should have led to the conquest of Canaan.

10:14–27 The names of the leaders of the 12 tribes are given for the fourth time in the book (see 1:5–15; 2:3–31; 7:12–83). The order of the line of march is essentially the same as that in ch. 2. The new details are that the Gershonites and Merarites, who carry the tabernacle, follow the triad of the Judah tribes (v. 17), and the Kohathites, who carry the holy things, follow the triad of the Reuben tribes (v. 21) (see diagram of "Encampment of the Tribes of Israel," p. 192).

10:14 *standard.* As in 2:3,10,18,25, each of the four triads of tribes had a standard or banner for rallying and organization.

10:29 *Hobab son of Reuel.* Thus Hobab was Moses' brother-in-law. *Reuel.* Jethro (see Ex 2:18; 3:1).

10:31 *be our eyes.* Jdg 1:16 indicates that Hobab acceded to Moses' request.

³³So they set out ^m from the mountain of the LORD and traveled for three days. The ark of the covenant of the LORD ⁿ went before them during those three days to find them a place to rest. ^o ³⁴The cloud of the LORD was over them by day when they set out from the camp. ^p

³⁵Whenever the ark set out, Moses said,

"Rise up, ^q O LORD!
    May your enemies be scattered; ^r
    may your foes flee before you. ^s " ^t

³⁶Whenever it came to rest, he said,

"Return, ^u O LORD,
    to the countless thousands of
    Israel. ^v "

Fire From the LORD

11 Now the people complained ^w about their hardships in the hearing of the LORD, ^x and when he heard them his anger was aroused. ^y Then fire from the LORD burned among them ^z and consumed ^a some of the outskirts of the camp. ²When the people cried out to Moses, he prayed ^b to the LORD ^c and the fire died down. ³So that place was called Tabe-

rah, ^u ^d because fire from the LORD had burned among them. ^e

Quail From the LORD

⁴The rabble with them began to crave other food, ^f and again the Israelites started wailing ^g and said, "If only we had meat to eat! ⁵We remember the fish we ate in Egypt at no cost—also the cucumbers, melons, leeks, onions and garlic. ^h ⁶But now we have lost our appetite; we never see anything but this manna! ⁱ "

⁷The manna was like coriander seed ^j and looked like resin. ^k ⁸The people went around gathering it, ^l and then ground it in a handmill or crushed it in a mortar. They cooked it in a pot or made it into cakes. And it tasted like something made with olive oil. ⁹When the dew ^m settled on the camp at night, the manna also came down.

¹⁰Moses heard the people of every family wailing, ⁿ each at the entrance to his tent. The LORD became exceedingly angry, and Moses was troubled. ¹¹He asked the

10:33 ^mver 12; Dt 1:33 ⁿDt 10:8; 31:9; Jos 3:3; Jdg 20:27; 2Sa 15:24 ^oJer 31:2
10:34 ^pNu 9:15-23
10:35 ^q2Ch 6:41; Ps 17:13; 44:26; 94:2; 132:8 ^rJdg 5:31; 1Sa 2:1; Ps 68:1; 92:9 ^sDt 5:9; 7:10; 32:41; Ps 68:2; Isa 17:12-14 ^tIsa 59:18
10:36 ^uIsa 52:8; 63:17 ^vGe 15:5; 26:4; Dt 1:10; 10:22; Ne 9:23
11:1 ^wS Ex 14:11; S 16:7; La 3:39 ^xNu 12:2; Dt 1:34 ^yS Ex 4:14 ^zS Lev 10:2 ^aNu 21:28; Ps 78:63; Isa 26:11
11:2 ^bDt 9:19; 1Sa 2:25; 12:23; Ps 106:23 ^cS Ge 20:7; Nu 21:7; Dt 9:20; Jnh 2:1

11:3 ^dDt 9:22 ^eNu 16:35; Job 1:16; Isa 10:17

11:4 ^fS Ex 16:3 ^gver 18 11:5 ^hS Ex 16:3; Nu 21:5 11:6 ⁱEx 16:14 11:7 ^jS Ex 16:31 ^kGe 2:12 11:8 ^lEx 16:16 11:9 ^mEx 16:13 11:10 ⁿver 4

^u3 *Taberah* means *burning.*

10:33 *three days.* Because of the huge numbers of people in the tribes of Israel, and because this was their first organized march, it is not likely that this first journey covered much territory.
10:35–36 Reinforces the portrayal of Israel as the Lord's army on the march, with the Lord in the vanguard.
10:35 Later used in the opening words of a psalm celebrating God's triumphal march from Sinai to Jerusalem (see Ps 68:1).
11:1 *people complained.* The first ten chapters of Numbers repeatedly emphasize the complete obedience of Moses and the people to the dictates of the Lord. But only three days into their march, the people reverted to disloyal complaints. They had expressed the same complaints a year earlier only three days after their deliverance at the waters of the "Red Sea" (Ex 15:22–27) and subsequently had complained about manna (Ex 16) and a lack of water (Ex 17:1–7). *fire from the LORD.* By God's mercy, this purging fire was limited to the outskirts of the camp. The phrase sometimes refers to fire ignited by lightning (as probably in 1Ki 18:38).
11:3 *Taberah.* See NIV text note.
11:4 *rabble.* An apt term for the non-Israelite mixed group of people who followed the Israelites out of Egypt, pointing to a recurring source of complaints and trouble in the camp. Those who did not know the Lord and his mercies incited those who did know him to rebel against him. *If only we had meat to eat!* As in Ex 16, the people began to complain about their diet, forgetting what God had done for them (see Ps 106:14). Certainly meat was not their common fare when they were slaves in Egypt. Now that they were in a new type of distress, the people romanticized the past and minimized its discomforts.
11:5 *fish . . . cucumbers . . . garlic.* Suggestive of the varieties of foods available in Egypt, in contrast to the diet of manna in the desert.
11:7 *manna.* Several naturalistic explanations for the man-

na have been given. For example, some equate it with the sticky and often granular honeydew that is excreted in Sinai in early June by various scale insects and that solidifies rapidly through evaporation. But no naturally occurring substance fits all the data of the text, and several factors suggest that manna was in fact the Lord's unique provision for his people in the desert: 1. The meaning of the Hebrew word for "manna" suggests that it was something unknown by the people at the time (see Ex 16:31 and NIV text note). 2. The appearance and taste of the manna (see Ex 16:31) suggest that it is not something experienced by other peoples in other times. 3. The daily abundance of the manna and its regular periodic surge and slump (double amounts on the sixth day but none on the seventh day, Ex 16:22,27) hardly fit a natural phenomenon. 4. Its availability in ample supply for the entire desert experience, no matter where the people were (Ex 16:35), argues against a natural substance. 5. The keeping of a sample of the manna in the ark for future generations (Ex 16:33–34) suggests that it was a unique food.
11:10 *The LORD became exceedingly angry.* The rejection of his gracious gift of heavenly food (called "bread from heaven" in Ex 16:4) angered the Lord. God had said that the reception of the manna by the people would be a significant test of their obedience (Ex 16:4). In view of the good things he was to give them (10:32), the people were expected to receive each day's supply of manna as a gracious gift of a merciful God, and a promise of abundance to come. In spurning the manna, the people had spurned the Lord. They had failed the test of faith. *Moses was troubled.* The people's reaction to God's provision of manna was troubling to Moses as well. Instead of asking the Lord to understand the substance of their complaint, Moses asked him why he was given such an ungrateful people to lead.
11:11–15 A prayer of distress and complaint, filled with urgency, irony and passion.

Lord, "Why have you brought this trouble[o] on your servant? What have I done to displease you that you put the burden of all these people on me?[p] 12Did I conceive all these people? Did I give them birth? Why do you tell me to carry them in my arms, as a nurse carries an infant,[q] to the land you promised on oath[r] to their forefathers?[s] 13Where can I get meat for all these people?[t] They keep wailing to me, 'Give us meat to eat!' 14I cannot carry all these people by myself; the burden is too heavy for me.[u] 15If this is how you are going to treat me, put me to death[v] right now[w]—if I have found favor in your eyes—and do not let me face my own ruin."

16The Lord said to Moses: "Bring me seventy of Israel's elders[x] who are known to you as leaders and officials among the people.[y] Have them come to the Tent of Meeting,[z] that they may stand there with you. 17I will come down and speak with you[a] there, and I will take of the Spirit that is on you and put the Spirit on them.[b] They will help you carry the burden of the people so that you will not have to carry it alone.[c]

18"Tell the people: 'Consecrate yourselves[d] in preparation for tomorrow, when you will eat meat. The Lord heard you when you wailed,[e] "If only we had meat to eat! We were better off in Egypt!"[f] Now the Lord will give you meat,[g] and you will eat it. 19You will not eat it for just one day, or two days, or five, ten or twenty days, 20but for a whole month—until it comes out of your nostrils and you loathe it[h]—because you have rejected the Lord,[i] who is among you, and have

wailed before him, saying, "Why did we ever leave Egypt?" ' "[j]

21But Moses said, "Here I am among six hundred thousand men[k] on foot, and you say, 'I will give them meat to eat for a whole month!' 22Would they have enough if flocks and herds were slaughtered for them? Would they have enough if all the fish in the sea were caught for them?"[l]

23The Lord answered Moses, "Is the Lord's arm too short?[m] You will now see whether or not what I say will come true for you.[n]"

24So Moses went out and told the people what the Lord had said. He brought together seventy of their elders and had them stand around the Tent. 25Then the Lord came down in the cloud[o] and spoke with him,[p] and he took of the Spirit[q] that was on him and put the Spirit on the seventy elders.[r] When the Spirit rested on them, they prophesied,[s] but they did not do so again.[v]

26However, two men, whose names were Eldad and Medad, had remained in the camp. They were listed among the elders, but did not go out to the Tent. Yet the Spirit also rested on them,[t] and they prophesied in the camp. 27A young man ran and told Moses, "Eldad and Medad are prophesying in the camp."

28Joshua son of Nun,[u] who had been Moses' aide[v] since youth, spoke up and said, "Moses, my lord, stop them!"[w]

29But Moses replied, "Are you jealous for my sake? I wish that all the Lord's

---

11:11
o Ge 34:30
p S Ex 5:22;
S 18:18
11:12 q Isa 40:11;
49:23; 66:11,12
r Nu 14:16
s S Ge 12:7;
Ex 13:5
11:13
t S Ex 12:37;
Jn 6:5-9
11:14
u S Ex 18:18
11:15 v Ex 32:32
w 1Ki 19:4;
Job 6:9; 7:15-16;
9:21; 10:1;
Isa 38:12; Jnh 4:3
11:16 x S Ex 3:16
y S Ex 18:25
z S Ex 40:2
11:17 a Ex 19:20
b ver 25,29;
1Sa 10:6; 2Ki 2:9,
15; 3:12;
Isa 32:15; 40:5;
63:11; Joel 2:28;
Hag 2:5
c S Ex 18:18;
Jer 19:1
11:18
d S Ex 19:10
e S Ex 16:7 f ver 5;
Ac 7:39 g Ps 78:20
11:20 h Ps 78:29;
106:14,15
i S Lev 26:43;
Jos 24:27;
Jdg 8:23;
1Sa 10:19;
Job 31:28;
Isa 59:13;
Hos 13:11

/ver 33;
Job 20:13,23
11:21
k S Ex 12:37
11:22 l Mt 15:33
11:23 m Isa 50:2;
59:1 n Nu 23:19;
1Sa 15:29;
Eze 12:25; 24:14
11:25
o S Ex 19:9;
Nu 12:5 p ver 17
q ver 29;
1Sa 10:6; 19:23
r S Ac 2:17 s ver
26; Nu 24:2;
Jdg 3:10;
1Sa 10:10; 19:20;
2Ch 15:1

11:26 t S ver 25; 1Ch 12:18; Rev 1:10 **11:28** u Ex 17:9;
Nu 13:8; 26:65; Jos 14:10 v Ex 33:11; Jos 1:1 w Mk 9:38-40

v 25 Or *prophesied and continued to do so*

11:12 *Did I conceive all these people?* The implication is that the Lord conceived the people of Israel, that he was their nurse and that their promises were his. Moses asks that he be relieved of his mediatorial office, for "the burden is too heavy for me" (v. 14; cf. Elijah, 1Ki 19). Even death, Moses asserts (v. 15), would be preferable to facing the continuing complaints of the people.
11:16–34 The Lord's response to the great distress of his prophet was twofold—mercy and curse: 1. There was mercy to Moses in that his responsibility was now to be shared by 70 leaders (vv. 16–17). 2. There was a curse on the people that was analogous to their complaint: They asked for meat and would now become sick with meat (vv. 18–34).
11:18 *you will eat meat.* Their distress at the lack of variety in the daily manna had led the people to challenge the Lord's goodness. They had wailed for meat. Now they were going to get their fill of meat, so much that it would make them physically ill (v. 20).
11:20 *you have rejected the Lord.* The principal issue was not meat at all, but a failure to demonstrate proper gratitude to the Lord, who was in their midst and who was their

constant source of good.
11:21 *six hundred thousand men on foot.* The numbers are consistent: A marching force of this size suggests a total population of over 2,000,000 (see note on 1:46). Moses' distress at providing meat for this immense number of people (v. 22) is nearly comical—the task is impossible.
11:23 *Is the Lord's arm too short?* The human impossibility is an occasion for demonstrating the Lord's power.
11:25 *they prophesied.* Probably means that they gave ecstatic expression to an intense religious experience (see 1Sa 10:5–6; 18:10; 19:20–24; 1Ki 18:29). *but they did not do so again.* It seems that the temporary gift of prophecy to the elders was primarily to establish their credentials as Spirit-empowered leaders.
11:29 *Are you jealous for my sake?* Here the true spirit of Moses is demonstrated. Rather than being threatened by the public demonstration of the gifts of the Spirit by Eldad and Medad, Moses desired that all God's people might have the full gifts of the Spirit (cf. Php 1:15–18). This verse is a fitting introduction to the inexcusable challenge to Moses' leadership in ch. 12.

people were prophets[x] and that the LORD would put his Spirit[y] on them!"[z] [30]Then Moses and the elders of Israel returned to the camp.

[31]Now a wind went out from the LORD and drove quail[a] in from the sea. It brought them[w] down all around the camp to about three feet[x] above the ground, as far as a day's walk in any direction. [32]All that day and night and all the next day the people went out and gathered quail. No one gathered less than ten homers.[y] Then they spread them out all around the camp. [33]But while the meat was still between their teeth[b] and before it could be consumed, the anger[c] of the LORD burned against the people, and he struck them with a severe plague.[d] [34]Therefore the place was named Kibroth Hattaavah,[z] [e] because there they buried the people who had craved other food.

[35]From Kibroth Hattaavah the people traveled to Hazeroth[f] and stayed there.

Miriam and Aaron Oppose Moses

12 Miriam[g] and Aaron began to talk against Moses because of his Cushite wife,[h] for he had married a Cushite. [2]"Has the LORD spoken only through Moses?" they asked. "Hasn't he also spoken through us?"[i] And the LORD heard this.[j]

[3](Now Moses was a very humble man,[k] more humble than anyone else on the face of the earth.)

[4]At once the LORD said to Moses, Aaron

and Miriam, "Come out to the Tent of Meeting, all three of you." So the three of them came out. [5]Then the LORD came down in a pillar of cloud;[l] he stood at the entrance to the Tent and summoned Aaron and Miriam. When both of them stepped forward, [6]he said, "Listen to my words:

"When a prophet of the LORD is among you,
    I reveal[m] myself to him in visions,[n]
    I speak to him in dreams.[o]
[7]But this is not true of my servant Moses;[p]
    he is faithful in all my house.[q]
[8]With him I speak face to face,
    clearly and not in riddles;[r]
    he sees the form of the LORD.[s]
Why then were you not afraid
    to speak against my servant Moses?"[t]

[9]The anger of the LORD burned against them,[u] and he left them.[v]

[10]When the cloud lifted from above the Tent,[w] there stood Miriam—leprous,[a] like snow.[x] Aaron turned toward her and saw that she had leprosy;[y] [11]and he said to Moses, "Please, my lord, do not hold against us the sin we have so foolishly committed.[z] [12]Do not let her be like a

Center cross-reference column

11:29 [x]1Sa 10:5; 19:20; 2Ch 24:19; Jer 7:25; 44:4; 1Co 14:5 [y]S ver 17 [z]Nu 27:18
11:31 [a]S Ex 16:13; Ps 78:26-28
11:33 [b]Ps 78:30 [c]Nu 14:18; Dt 9:7; Jdg 2:12; 2Ki 22:17; Ps 106:29; Jer 44:3; Eze 8:17 [d]S ver 18-20; Ps 106:15; Isa 10:16
11:34 [e]Nu 33:16; Dt 9:22
11:35 [f]Nu 33:17
12:1 [g]S Ex 15:20 [h]S Ex 2:21
12:2 [i]Nu 16:3 [j]S Nu 11:1
12:3 [k]Mt 11:29
12:5 [l]S Ex 13:21; S Nu 11:25
12:6 [m]1Sa 3:7,21 [n]S Ge 15:1 [o]S Ge 20:3; S Mt 27:19; Heb 1:1
12:7 [p]Dt 34:5; Jos 1:1-2,1; Ps 105:26 [q]Heb 3:2,5
12:8 [r]Jdg 14:12; 1Ki 10:1; Ps 49:4; Pr 1:6; Da 5:12 [s]Ex 20:4; Job 19:26; Ps 17:15; 140:13; Isa 6:1 [t]Ex 24:2
12:9 [u]S Ex 4:14 [v]S Ge 17:22
12:10 [w]Ex 40:2 [x]S Ex 4:6; Dt 24:9 [y]S Lev 13:11; 2Ki 5:1,27; 2Ch 16:12; 21:12-15; 26:19
12:11 [z]Sa 19:19; 24:10

24:10

w[31] Or *They flew*   x[31] Hebrew *two cubits* (about 1 meter)   y[32] That is, probably about 60 bushels (about 2.2 kiloliters)   z[34] *Kibroth Hattaavah* means *graves of craving.*   a[10] The Hebrew word was used for various diseases affecting the skin—not necessarily leprosy.

11:31–32 Cf. the great provision of Jesus in the feeding of the 5,000 (Jn 6:5–13) and the 4,000 (Mt 15:29–39). In those cases the feeding was a demonstration of God's grace; in this instance it was a demonstration of God's wrath.
11:34 *Kibroth Hattaavah.* See NIV text note. These graves marked the death camp of those who had turned against the food of the Lord's mercy.
12:1 *his Cushite wife.* Cush was the first son of Ham, the father of the southernmost peoples known to the Hebrews (Ge 10:6–7), living in the southern Nile valley. Moses' wife Zipporah may be referred to here (see Ex 2:15–22); if so, the term "Cushite" is used in contempt of her Midianite ancestry. It is more likely, however, that the reference is to a new wife taken by Moses, perhaps after the death of his first wife. The attack on the woman was a pretext; its focus was the prophetic gift of Moses and his special relationship with the Lord (v. 2).
12:2 *Hasn't he also spoken through us?* Of course he had. Mic 6:4 speaks of Moses, Aaron and Miriam as God's gracious provision for Israel. The prophetic gifting of the 70 elders (11:24–30) seems to have been the immediate provocation for the attack of Miriam and Aaron on their brother.
12:3 Perhaps a later addition to the text, alerting the reader to the great unfairness of the charge of arrogance against Moses.
12:4 *At once.* The abruptness of the Lord's response instilled terror (see Job 22:10; Isa 47:11; Jer 4:20).

12:5 *came down.* Often used of divine manifestations. In 11:25 the Lord came down in grace; here and in Ge 11:5 he came down in judgment. In a sense every theophany (appearance of God) is a picture and promise of the grand theophany, the incarnation of Jesus, both in grace and in judgment.
12:6–8 The poetic cast of these words adds a sense of solemnity to them. The point of the poem is clear: All true prophetic vision is from the Lord, but in the case of Moses his position and faithfulness enhance his special relationship with the Lord.
12:7 *my servant.* See notes on Ex 14:31; Ps 18 title; Isa 41:8–9; 42:1. *my house.* The household of God's people Israel.
12:8 *clearly and not in riddles.* God's revelation does not come with equal clarity to his servants. There may be oracles of the Lord that a prophet might not fully understand at the time; to him they may be riddles and mysteries (cf. 1Pe 1:10–11). But to Moses, God spoke with special clarity, as though face to face (see also Dt 34:10).
12:10 *leprous.* See NIV text note. Miriam, the principal offender against her brother Moses, has become an outcast, as she now suffers from a skin disease that would exclude her from the community of Israel (see 5:1–4).
12:11 *Please, my lord.* Aaron's repentance for the sin of presumption is touching, both in its intensity and in his concern for his (and Moses') sister.

stillborn infant coming from its mother's
womb with its flesh half eaten away."
13So Moses cried out to the LORD, "O
God, please heal her![a]"
14The LORD replied to Moses, "If her father had spit in her face,[b] would she not
have been in disgrace for seven days? Confine her outside the camp[c] for seven days;
after that she can be brought back." 15So
Miriam was confined outside the camp[d]
for seven days,[e] and the people did not
move on till she was brought back.
16After that, the people left Hazeroth[f]
and encamped in the Desert of Paran.[g]

Exploring Canaan

13 The LORD said to Moses, 2"Send
some men to explore[h] the land of
Canaan,[i] which I am giving to the Israelites.[j] From each ancestral tribe[k] send one
of its leaders."
3So at the LORD's command Moses sent
them out from the Desert of Paran. All of
them were leaders of the Israelites.[l]
4These are their names:

from the tribe of Reuben, Shammua son of Zaccur;
5from the tribe of Simeon, Shaphat son of Hori;
6from the tribe of Judah, Caleb son of Jephunneh;[m]
7from the tribe of Issachar, Igal son of Joseph;
8from the tribe of Ephraim, Hoshea son of Nun;[n]
9from the tribe of Benjamin, Palti son of Raphu;
10from the tribe of Zebulun, Gaddiel son of Sodi;
11from the tribe of Manasseh (a tribe of Joseph), Gaddi son of Susi;
12from the tribe of Dan, Ammiel son of Gemalli;
13from the tribe of Asher, Sethur son of Michael;
14from the tribe of Naphtali, Nahbi son of Vophsi;
15from the tribe of Gad, Geuel son of Maki.

16These are the names of the men Moses
sent to explore[o] the land. (Moses gave Hoshea son of Nun[p] the name Joshua.)[q]
17When Moses sent them to explore Canaan,[r] he said, "Go up through the
Negev[s] and on into the hill country.[t]
18See what the land is like and whether
the people who live there are strong or
weak, few or many. 19What kind of land
do they live in? Is it good or bad? What
kind of towns do they live in? Are they
unwalled or fortified? 20How is the soil? Is
it fertile or poor? Are there trees on it or
not? Do your best to bring back some of
the fruit of the land.[u]" (It was the season
for the first ripe grapes.)[v]
21So they went up and explored the land
from the Desert of Zin[w] as far as Rehob,[x]
toward Lebo[b] Hamath.[y] 22They went up
through the Negev and came to Hebron,[z]
where Ahiman, Sheshai and Talmai,[a] the
descendants of Anak,[b] lived. (Hebron had
been built seven years before Zoan in

12:13 [a]Ex 15:26; Ps 6:2; 147:3; Isa 1:6; 30:26; 53:5; Jer 17:14; Hos 6:1
12:14 [b]Dt 25:9; Job 17:6; 30:9-10; Isa 50:6 [c]S Lev 13:46
12:15 [d]S Lev 14:8 [e]S Lev 13:4
12:16 [f]Nu 11:35 [g]Ge 21:21; Nu 10:12; 15:32
13:2 [h]ver 16; Dt 1:22 [i]S Lev 14:34 [j]Jos 1:3 [k]S Lev 24:11
13:3 [l]Nu 1:16
13:6 [m]ver 30; Nu 14:6,24; 34:19; Dt 1:36; Jdg 1:12-15
13:8 [n]S Nu 11:28
13:16 [o]S ver 2 [p]ver 8 [q]Dt 32:44
13:17 [r]ver 2; Jos 14:7 [s]S Ge 12:9 [t]Dt 1:7; Jos 9:1; Jdg 1:9
13:20 [u]Dt 1:25 [v]S Lev 25:5
13:21 [w]Nu 20:1; 27:14; 33:36; Dt 32:51; Jos 15:1 [x]Jos 19:28; Jdg 1:31; 18:28; 2Sa 10:6; 1Ch 6:75 [y]Nu 34:8; Jos 13:5; Jdg 3:3; 1Ki 8:65; 2Ki 14:25; 1Ch 13:5; 2Ch 7:8; Jer 52:9; Eze 47:16,20; Am 6:14
13:22 [z]S Ge 13:18; S 23:19 [a]Jos 15:14; Jdg 1:10 [b]ver 28; Dt 2:10; 9:2; Jos 11:21; 15:13; Jdg 1:20

[b]21 Or *toward the entrance to*

12:14 *disgrace for seven days.* An act of public rebuke (see Dt 25:9) demands a period of public shame. A period of seven days was a standard time for uncleanness occasioned by being in contact with a dead body (see 19:11,14,16).
12:16 *Desert of Paran.* The southernmost region of the promised land. The people's opportunity to conquer the land was soon to come.
13:2 *Send some men to explore the land of Canaan.* The use of spies was a common practice in the ancient Near East (see note on Jos 2:1–24). From Dt 1:22–23 it appears that this directive of the Lord was in response to the people's request. Thus the very sending of the spies was an expression of God's grace.
13:4–15 The names listed here are different from those in chs. 1–2; 7; 10. Presumably the tribal leaders in the four earlier lists were older men. The task for the spies called for men who were younger and more robust, but no less respected by their peers.
13:16 *Moses gave Hoshea son of Nun the name Joshua.* A parenthetical statement anticipating the later prominence of Joshua. The reader is alerted to the significance of this name in the list of the spies; here is a man of destiny. Hoshea means "salvation"; Joshua means "The LORD saves" (see NIV text note on Mt 1:21).
13:17–20 Moses' instruction to the 12 spies was comprehensive; a thorough report of the land and its produce and the peoples and their towns was required in their reconnaissance mission.
13:21 *explored the land.* The journey of the spies began in the southernmost extremity of the land (the Desert of Zin) and took them to the northernmost point (Rehob, near Lebo Hamath; see 34:8). This journey of about 250 miles each way took them 40 days (v. 25), perhaps a round number.
13:22 *Hebron.* The first city the spies came to in Canaan. The parenthetical comment about the city's being built seven years before Zoan in Egypt may have been prompted by their amazement at the size and fortifications of the city that was so closely associated with the lives of their ancestors four centuries before this time (see Ge 13:14–18; 14:13; 23:2; 25:9; 35:27–29; 50:13). In the stories of the ancestors of their people, Hebron had not been a great city, but a dwelling and trading place for shepherds and herdsmen. *descendants of Anak.* Three notable Anak descendants are mentioned as living at Hebron. The Anakites were men of great stature; their physical size brought fear to the people (see vv. 32–33). In a later day of faith, Caleb was to drive them from their city (Jos 15:14; Jdg 1:10).

Egypt.)^c ²³When they reached the Valley of Eshcol,^{c d} they cut off a branch bearing a single cluster of grapes. Two of them carried it on a pole between them, along with some pomegranates^e and figs.^f ²⁴That place was called the Valley of Eshcol because of the cluster of grapes the Israelites cut off there. ²⁵At the end of forty days^g they returned from exploring the land.^h

Report on the Exploration

²⁶They came back to Moses and Aaron and the whole Israelite community at Kadeshⁱ in the Desert of Paran.^j There they reported to them^k and to the whole assembly and showed them the fruit of the land.^l ²⁷They gave Moses this account: "We went into the land to which you sent us, and it does flow with milk and honey!^m Here is its fruit.ⁿ ²⁸But the people who live there are powerful, and the cities are fortified and very large.^o We even saw descendants of Anak^p there.^q ²⁹The Amalekites^r live in the Negev; the Hittites,^s Jebusites^t and Amorites^u live in the hill country;^v and the Canaanites^w live near the sea and along the Jordan.^x"

³⁰Then Caleb^y silenced the people before Moses and said, "We should go up and take possession of the land, for we can certainly do it."

³¹But the men who had gone up with him said, "We can't attack those people; they are stronger than we are."^z ³²And they spread among the Israelites a bad report^a about the land they had explored. They said, "The land we explored devours^b those living in it. All the people we saw there are of great size.^c ³³We saw the Nephilim^d there (the descendants of Anak^e come from the Nephilim). We seemed like grasshoppers^f in our own eyes, and we looked the same to them."

The People Rebel

14 That night all the people of the community raised their voices and wept aloud.^g ²All the Israelites grumbled^h against Moses and Aaron, and the whole assembly said to them, "If only we had died in Egypt!ⁱ Or in this desert!^j ³Why is the LORD bringing us to this land only to let us fall by the sword?^k Our wives and children^l will be taken as plunder.^m Wouldn't it be better for us to go back to Egypt?ⁿ" ⁴And they said to each other, "We should choose a leader and go back to Egypt.^o"

⁵Then Moses and Aaron fell facedown^p in front of the whole Israelite assembly^q gathered there. ⁶Joshua son of Nun^r and Caleb son of Jephunneh, who were among those who had explored the land, tore their clothes^s ⁷and said to the entire Israelite assembly, "The land we passed through and explored is exceedingly good.^t ⁸If the LORD is pleased with us,^u he will lead us into that land, a land flowing with milk and honey,^v and will give it to us.^w ⁹Only do not rebel^x against the LORD. And do not be afraid^y of the people of the land,^z because we will swallow them up. Their protection is gone, but the LORD is with^a us.^b Do not be afraid of them."^c

¹⁰But the whole assembly talked about stoning^d them. Then the glory of the LORD^e appeared at the Tent of Meeting to all the Israelites. ¹¹The LORD said to Moses,

Cross references (center column)

13:22 ^cPs 78:12, 43; Isa 19:11,13; 30:4; Eze 30:14
13:23 ^dS Ge 14:13 ^eS Ex 28:33 ^fGe 3:7; Nu 20:5; Dt 8:8;
2Ki 18:31; Ne 13:15
13:25 ^gS Ge 7:4 ^hNu 14:34
13:26 ⁱS Ge 14:7 ^jS Ge 14:6 ^kNu 32:8 ^lDt 1:25
13:27 ^mS Ex 3:8 ⁿDt 1:25; Jer 2:7
13:28 ^oDt 1:28; 9:1,2 ^pS ver 22 ^qJos 14:12
13:29 ^rS Ge 14:7 ^sS Ge 10:15; Dt 7:1; 20:17;
1Ki 9:20; 10:29; 2Ki 7:6 ^tS Ex 3:8 ^uS Ge 10:16 ^vver 17 ^wS Ge 10:18 ^xS Ge 13:10; Nu 22:1; 32:5; Dt 1:1; Jos 1:2; Jdg 3:28; Ps 42:6
13:30 ^yS ver 6
13:31 ^zDt 9:1; Jos 14:8
13:32 ^aNu 14:36, 37 ^bEze 36:13,14 ^cDt 1:28; Am 2:9
13:33 ^dGe 6:4 ^ever 28; Dt 1:28; Jos 11:22; 14:12 ^fEcc 12:5; Isa 40:22

14:1 ^gS Ge 27:38; Ex 33:4; Nu 25:6; Dt 1:45; Jdg 20:23,26; 2Sa 3:32; Job 31:29
14:2 ^hS Ex 15:24; Heb 3:16 ⁱS Ex 16:3 ^jS Nu 11:1; 16:13; 20:4; 21:5
14:3 ^kS Ex 5:21 ^lver 31 ^mS Ge 34:29; Dt 1:39; Ps 109:11; Isa 33:4; Eze 7:21; 25:7; 26:5 ⁿAc 7:39
14:4 ^oNe 9:17
14:5 ^pS Lev 9:24; Nu 16:4,22,45; 20:6; Jos 5:14;

2Sa 14:4; 1Ch 21:16; Eze 1:28 ^qS Lev 19:2 14:6 ^rNu 11:28 ^sS Ge 37:29,34; Jdg 11:35; 2Sa 13:31; 2Ki 19:1; Ezr 9:3; Est 4:1; S Mk 14:63 14:7 ^tNu 13:27; Dt 1:25 14:8 ^uDt 7:8; 10:15; Ps 18:19; 22:8; 37:23; 41:11; 56:9; 147:11; Pr 11:20; Isa 62:4; Mal 2:17 ^vNu 13:27 ^wDt 1:21 14:9 ^xDt 1:26; 9:7,23,24 ^yGe 26:24; 2Ch 32:7; Ps 118:6; Jer 41:18; 42:11 ^zDt 1:21; 7:18; 20:1 ^aHag 2:4 ^bS Ge 21:22; Dt 1:30; 2Ch 13:12; Jer 15:20; 46:28; Hag 1:13 ^cver 24 14:10 ^dS Ex 17:4 ^eS Ex 24:16

^c23 *Eshcol* means *cluster*, also in verse 24.

Study notes (bottom)

13:23 *Valley of Eshcol.* See NIV text note. This valley is near Hebron; presumably the spies cut the cluster of grapes on their return journey. The size of the grape cluster should have indicated the goodness of the land God was giving them.

13:26–29 The first part of the spies' report was truthful, but the goodness of the land was offset in their fearful eyes by the powerful peoples who lived there.

13:30 *Caleb silenced the people.* Only Caleb and Hoshea (Joshua) gave a report prompted by faith in God.

13:32 *bad report about the land.* The promised land was a good land, a gracious gift from God. By speaking bad things about it, the faithless spies were speaking evil of the Lord (cf. 10:29).

13:33 Their words became exaggerations and distortions. The Anakites were now said to be Nephilim (see note on Ge 6:4). The reference to the Nephilim seems deliberately intended to evoke fear. The exaggeration of the faithless led to

their final folly: "We seemed like grasshoppers."

14:1 *all the people . . . wept.* The frightening words of the faithless spies led to mourning by the entire community and to their great rebellion against the Lord. They forgot all the miracles the Lord had done for them. They despised his mercies, and they spurned his might. In their ingratitude they preferred death (v. 2).

14:3 *children.* The most reprehensible charge against God's grace was that concerning their children. Only their children would survive (see vv. 31–33).

14:9 *the LORD is with us.* There are no walls, no fortifications, no factors of size or bearing, and certainly no gods that can withstand the onslaught of God's people when the Lord is with them.

14:10 *the glory of the LORD appeared.* The theophany (manifestation of God) must have been staggering in its sudden and intense display of his majesty and wrath.

14:11 *treat me with contempt.* By refusing to believe in

"How long will these people treat me with contempt?[f] How long will they refuse to believe in me,[g] in spite of all the miraculous signs[h] I have performed among them? [12]I will strike them down with a plague[i] and destroy them, but I will make you into a nation[j] greater and stronger than they."[k]

[13]Moses said to the LORD, "Then the Egyptians will hear about it! By your power you brought these people up from among them.[l] [14]And they will tell the inhabitants of this land about it. They have already heard[m] that you, O LORD, are with these people[n] and that you, O LORD, have been seen face to face,[o] that your cloud stays over them,[p] and that you go before them in a pillar of cloud by day and a pillar of fire by night.[q] [15]If you put these people to death all at one time, the nations who have heard this report about you will say, [16]'The LORD was not able to bring these people into the land he promised them on oath;[r] so he slaughtered them in the desert.'[s]

[17]"Now may the Lord's strength be displayed, just as you have declared: [18]'The LORD is slow to anger, abounding in love and forgiving sin and rebellion.[t] Yet he does not leave the guilty unpunished; he punishes the children for the sin of the fathers to the third and fourth generation.'[u] [19]In accordance with your great love, forgive[v] the sin of these people,[w] just as you have pardoned them from the time they left Egypt until now."[x]

[20]The LORD replied, "I have forgiven them,[y] as you asked. [21]Nevertheless, as surely as I live[z] and as surely as the glory of the LORD[a] fills the whole earth,[b] [22]not one of the men who saw my glory and the miraculous signs[c] I performed in Egypt and in the desert but who disobeyed me

and tested me ten times[d]— [23]not one of them will ever see the land I promised on oath[e] to their forefathers. No one who has treated me with contempt[f] will ever see it.[g] [24]But because my servant Caleb[h] has a different spirit and follows me wholeheartedly,[i] I will bring him into the land he went to, and his descendants will inherit it.[j] [25]Since the Amalekites[k] and Canaanites[l] are living in the valleys, turn[m] back tomorrow and set out toward the desert along the route to the Red Sea.[d] [n]"

[26]The LORD said to Moses and Aaron: [27]"How long will this wicked community grumble against me? I have heard the complaints of these grumbling Israelites.[o] [28]So tell them, 'As surely as I live,[p] declares the LORD, I will do to you[q] the very things I heard you say: [29]In this desert your bodies will fall'—every one of you twenty years old or more[s] who was counted in the census[t] and who has grumbled against me. [30]Not one of you will enter the land[u] I swore with uplifted hand[v] to make your home, except Caleb son of Jephunneh[w] and Joshua son of Nun.[x] [31]As for your children that you said would be taken as plunder, I will bring them in to enjoy the land you have rejected.[y] [32]But you—your bodies will fall[z] in this desert. [33]Your children will be shepherds here for forty years,[a] suffering for your unfaithfulness, until the last of your bodies lies in the desert. [34]For forty years[b]—one year for each of the forty days you explored the

Cross references (center column):

14:11 [f]Ex 23:21; Nu 15:31; 16:30; 1Sa 2:17; Eze 31:14; Mal 1:13 [g]Dt 1:32; Ps 78:22; 106:24; Jn 3:15 [h]S Ex 3:20; S 4:17; S 10:1
14:12 [i]S Ex 5:3; S 30:12 [j]S Ex 32:10 [k]Dt 9:14; 29:20; 32:26; Ps 109:13
14:13 [l]Ex 32:11-14; Ps 106:23
14:14 [m]Ex 15:14 [n]Nu 5:3; 16:3; Jos 2:9 [o]Dt 5:4; 34:10 [p]S Ex 33:16 [q]S Ex 13:21
14:16 [r]Nu 11:12 [s]Ex 32:12; Jos 7:7
14:18 [t]S Ex 20:6; 34:6; Ps 145:8; Jnh 4:2; Jas 5:11 [u]Ex 20:5
14:19 [v]S Ex 34:9; 1Ki 8:34; Ps 85:2; 103:3 [w]Ps 106:45 [x]Ps 78:38
14:20 [y]Ex 34:6; Ps 99:8; 106:23; Mic 7:18-20
14:21 [z]ver 28; Dt 32:40; Jdg 8:19; Ru 3:13; 1Sa 14:39; 19:6; Isa 49:18; Jer 4:2; Eze 5:11; Zep 2:9 [a]Lev 9:6 [b]Ps 72:19; Isa 6:3; 40:5; Hab 2:14
14:22 [c]ver 11

[d]S Ex 14:11; 17:7; 32:1; Ps 81:7; 1Co 10:5
14:23 [e]ver 16; S Ex 33:1; Dt 1:34; Ps 95:11; 106:26 [f]ver 11 [g]Heb 3:18
14:24 [h]Nu 13:6 [i]ver 6-9; Dt 1:36; Jos 14:8,14 [j]Nu 26:65; 32:12; Ps 25:13; 37:9,11

14:25 [k]S Ge 14:7 [l]S Ge 10:18 [m]Dt 1:40 [n]Ex 23:31; Nu 21:4; 1Ki 9:26 14:27 [o]Ex 16:12; Dt 1:34,35 14:28 [p]S ver 21 [q]Nu 33:56 14:29 [r]ver 23,30,32; Nu 26:65; 32:13; 1Co 10:5; Heb 3:17; Jude 1:5 [s]S Nu 1:45 [t]S Ex 30:12 14:30 [u]S ver 29 [v]Ex 6:8; Dt 32:40; Ne 9:15; Ps 106:26; Eze 20:5; 36:7 [w]Nu 13:6 [x]Nu 11:28 14:31 [y]S Lev 26:43 14:32 [z]S ver 29,35 14:33 [a]ver 34; S Ex 16:35; Ac 13:18; Heb 3:9 14:34 [b]S ver 33

[d]25 Hebrew *Yam Suph*; that is, Sea of Reeds

Footnotes (bottom):

the Lord's power, especially in view of all the wonders they had experienced, the people of Israel were holding him in contempt.
14:12 *I will make you into a nation.* For the second time since the exodus, God speaks of starting over with Moses in creating a people faithful to himself (see Ex 32:10).
14:13 *the Egyptians will hear about it!* Moses desires to protect the Lord's reputation. The enemies of God's people will charge the Lord with inability to complete his deliverance and will be contemptuous of his power.
14:17–19 Moses now moves from the Lord's reputation to his character, presenting a composite quotation of his own words of loyal love for and faithful discipline of his people (see Ex 20:6; 34:6–7).
14:22 *ten times.* Perhaps to be enumerated as follows: (1) Ex 14:10–12; (2) Ex 15:22–24; (3) Ex 16:1–3; (4) Ex 16:19–20; (5) Ex 16:27–30; (6) Ex 17:1–4; (7) Ex 32:1–35; (8) Nu 11:1–3; (9) 11:4–34; (10) 14:3. But "ten times" may also be a way of saying "many times."

14:24 *my servant Caleb has a different spirit.* Caleb seems to be singled out; perhaps the words of vv. 7–9 were his, and he was joined in them by Joshua. Caleb's ultimate vindication came 45 years later (see note on 13:22; see also Jos 14:10).
14:28 *I will do to you the very things I heard you say.* The people of Israel brought upon themselves their punishment. They had said that they would rather die in the desert (v. 2) than be led into Canaan to die by the sword. All those 20 years old or more, who were counted in the census, were to die in the desert (v. 29). The only exceptions would be Joshua and Caleb (v. 30). Only their children would survive (v. 31)—the children that the people said God would allow to die in the desert (v. 3).
14:34 The 40 days of the travels of the spies became the numerical pattern for their suffering: one year for one day—for 40 years they would recount their misjudgment, and for 40 years the people 20 years old or more would be dying, so that only the young generation might enter the

land c—you will suffer for your sins and know what it is like to have me against you.' 35I, the LORD, have spoken, and I will surely do these things d to this whole wicked community, which has banded together against me. They will meet their end in this desert; here they will die. e"

36So the men whom Moses had sent f to explore the land, who returned and made the whole community grumble g against him by spreading a bad report h about it— 37these men responsible for spreading the bad report i about the land were struck down and died of a plague j before the LORD. 38Of the men who went to explore the land, k only Joshua son of Nun and Caleb son of Jephunneh survived. l

39When Moses reported this m to all the Israelites, they mourned n bitterly. 40Early the next morning they went up toward the high hill country. o "We have sinned p," they said. "We will go up to the place the LORD promised."

41But Moses said, "Why are you disobeying the LORD's command? This will not succeed! q 42Do not go up, because the LORD is not with you. You will be defeated by your enemies, r 43for the Amalekites s and Canaanites t will face you there. Because you have turned away from the LORD, he will not be with you u and you will fall by the sword."

44Nevertheless, in their presumption they went up v toward the high hill country, though neither Moses nor the ark of the LORD's covenant moved from the camp. w 45Then the Amalekites and Canaanites x who lived in that hill country y came down and attacked them and beat them down all the way to Hormah. z

Supplementary Offerings

15 The LORD said to Moses, 2"Speak to the Israelites and say to them:

'After you enter the land I am giving you a as a home 3and you present to the LORD offerings made by fire, from the herd or the flock, b as an aroma pleasing to the LORD c—whether burnt offerings d or sacrifices, for special vows or freewill offerings e or festival offerings f— 4then the one who brings his offering shall present to the LORD a grain offering g of a tenth of an ephah e of fine flour h mixed with a quarter of a hin f of oil. 5With each lamb i for the burnt offering or the sacrifice, prepare a quarter of a hin of wine j as a drink offering. k

6"'With a ram l prepare a grain offering m of two-tenths of an ephah g n of fine flour mixed with a third of a hin h of oil, o 7and a third of a hin of wine p as a drink offering. q Offer it as an aroma pleasing to the LORD. r

8"'When you prepare a young bull s as a burnt offering or sacrifice, for a special vow t or a fellowship offering i u to the LORD, 9bring with the bull a grain offering v of three-tenths of an ephah j w of fine flour mixed with half a hin k of oil. 10Also bring half a hin of wine x as a drink offering. y It will be an offering made by fire, an aroma pleasing to the LORD. z 11Each bull or ram, each lamb or young goat, is to be prepared in this manner. 12Do this for each one, for as many as you prepare. a

13"'Everyone who is native-born b must do these things in this way when he brings an offering made by fire as an aroma pleasing to the LORD. c 14For the generations to

14:34 cNu 13:25
14:35 dNu 23:19
eS ver 32
14:36
fNu 13:4-16 gver 2 hS Nu 13:32
14:37
iS Nu 13:32;
1Co 10:10;
Heb 3:17
jNu 16:49; 25:9;
26:1; 31:16;
Dt 4:3
14:38 kver 30;
Nu 13:4-16 lver 24; Jos 14:6
14:39 mver 28-35 nS Ex 33:4
14:40 over 45;
Nu 13:17
pS Ex 9:27
14:41
q2Ch 24:20
14:42 rDt 1:42
14:43 sJdg 3:13
tver 45; Nu 13:29
uS Ge 39:23;
Dt 31:8; Jos 6:27;
Jdg 1:19; 6:16;
1Sa 3:19; 18:14;
2Ch 1:1
14:44 vDt 1:43
wNu 31:6
14:45 xS ver 43
yS ver 40
zNu 21:3;
Dt 1:44;
Jos 12:14; 15:30;
19:4; Jdg 1:17;
1Sa 30:30;
1Ch 4:30

15:2
aS Lev 23:10
15:3 bS Lev 1:2
cver 24; S Lev 1:9
dLev 1:3;
Nu 28:13
eS Lev 7:16;
S Ezr 1:4
fLev 23:1-44
15:4 gS Lev 6:14
hS Ex 16:36
15:5 iS Lev 3:7
jS Lev 10:9
kS Ge 35:14
15:6 lS Lev 5:15
mNu 28:12;
29:14
nS Lev 23:13
oEze 46:14
15:7 pver 5
qLev 23:13;
Nu 28:14; 29:18
rS Lev 1:9
15:8 sS Ex 12:5;
S Lev 1:5
tS Lev 22:18
uS Lev 3:6
15:9 vLev 2:1
wS Lev 14:10

15:10 xNu 28:14 yLev 23:13 zLev 1:9 15:12 aEzr 7:17
15:13 bS Lev 16:29 cLev 1:9

e4 That is, probably about 2 quarts (about 2 liters)
f4 That is, probably about 1 quart (about 1 liter); also in verse 5   g6 That is, probably about 4 quarts (about 4.5 liters)   h6 That is, probably about 1 1/4 quarts (about 1.2 liters); also in verse 7   i8 Traditionally peace offering   j9 That is, probably about 6 quarts (about 6.5 liters)   k9 That is, probably about 2 quarts (about 2 liters); also in verse 10

---

land. Significantly, Israel's refusal to carry out the Lord's commission to conquer his land is the climactic act of rebellion for which God condemns Israel to die in the desert.
14:37 these men responsible for spreading the bad report . . . were struck down. The judgment on the ten evil spies was immediate; the generation that they influenced would live out their lives in the desert.
14:40 We will go up. Now, too late, the people determine to go up to the land they had refused. Such a course of action was doomed to failure. Not only was the Lord not with them; he was against them (v. 41). Their subsequent defeat (v. 45) was another judgment the rebellious people brought down upon their own heads.
15:1–41 This chapter is divided into three units, each introduced by the phrase, "The Lord said to Moses" (vv. 1,17,37). The people were under terrible judgment because they had disobeyed the specific commands of the Lord and

had despised his character.
15:2 After you enter the land. The juxtaposition of this clause with the sad ending of ch. 14 is dramatic. The sins of the people were manifold; they would be judged. The grace and mercy of the Lord are magnified as he points to the ultimate realization of his ancient promise to Abraham (Ge 12:7), as well as to his continuing promise to the nation that they would indeed enter the land.
15:3–12 Grain and wine offerings were to accompany the offerings by fire; the grain was to be mixed with oil. The offerings increased in amounts with the increase of size of the sacrificial animal (vv. 6–12). These passages are the first to indicate that wine offerings must accompany all burnt and fellowship offerings.
15:14 alien. As in the case of the celebration of the Passover (see note on 9:14), the alien had the same regulations as the native-born Israelite. The commonwealth of Israel would

come, *d* whenever an alien *e* or anyone else living among you presents an offering *f* made by fire *g* as an aroma pleasing to the LORD, he must do exactly as you do. 15The community is to have the same rules for you and for the alien living among you; this is a lasting ordinance for the generations to come. *h* You and the alien shall be the same before the LORD: 16The same laws and regulations will apply both to you and to the alien living among you. *i* ' "

17The LORD said to Moses, 18"Speak to the Israelites and say to them: 'When you enter the land to which I am taking you *j* 19and you eat the food of the land, *k* present a portion as an offering to the LORD. *l* 20Present a cake from the first of your ground meal *m* and present it as an offering from the threshing floor. *n o* 21Throughout the generations to come *p* you are to give this offering to the LORD from the first of your ground meal. *q*

Offerings for Unintentional Sins

22" 'Now if you unintentionally fail to keep any of these commands the LORD gave Moses *r*— 23any of the LORD's commands to you through him, from the day the LORD gave them and continuing through the generations to come *s*— 24and if this is done unintentionally *t* without the community being aware of it, *u* then the whole community is to offer a young bull for a burnt offering *v* as an aroma pleasing to the LORD, *w* along with its prescribed grain offering *x* and drink offering, *y* and a male goat for a sin offering. *z* 25The priest is to make atonement for the whole Israelite community, and they will be forgiven, *a* for it was not intentional *b* and they have brought to the LORD for their wrong an offering made by fire *c* and a sin offering. *d* 26The whole Israelite community and the aliens living among them will be forgiven,

because all the people were involved in the unintentional wrong. *e*

27" 'But if just one person sins unintentionally, *f* he must bring a year-old female goat for a sin offering. *g* 28The priest is to make atonement *h* before the LORD for the one who erred by sinning unintentionally, and when atonement has been made for him, he will be forgiven. *i* 29One and the same law applies to everyone who sins unintentionally, whether he is a native-born Israelite or an alien. *j*

30" 'But anyone who sins defiantly, *k* whether native-born or alien, *l* blasphemes the LORD, *m* and that person must be cut off from his people. *n* 31Because he has despised *o* the LORD's word and broken his commands, *p* that person must surely be cut off; his guilt remains on him. *q* ' "

The Sabbath-Breaker Put to Death

32While the Israelites were in the desert, *r* a man was found gathering wood on the Sabbath day. *s* 33Those who found him gathering wood brought him to Moses and Aaron and the whole assembly, 34and they kept him in custody, because it was not clear what should be done to him. *t* 35Then the LORD said to Moses, "The man must die. *u* The whole assembly must stone him outside the camp. *v*" 36So the assembly took him outside the camp and stoned him *w* to death, *x* as the LORD commanded Moses. *y*

Tassels on Garments

37The LORD said to Moses, 38"Speak to the Israelites and say to them: 'Throughout the generations to come *z* you are to make tassels on the corners of your garments, *a* with a blue cord on each tassel. 39You will have these tassels to look at and so you

Center column cross-references

15:14 *d* Lev 3:17; Nu 10:8
e S Ex 12:19,43; S 22:21
f S Lev 22:18 *g* ver 25
15:15 *h* ver 14,21
15:16 *i* Ex 12:49; S Lev 22:18; Nu 9:14
15:18 *j* S Lev 23:10
15:19 *k* Jos 5:11, 12 *l* Nu 18:8
15:20 *m* S Lev 23:14 *n* S Lev 2:14; S Nu 18:27 *o* S Ge 50:10
15:21 *p* S Lev 23:14 *q* Eze 44:30; Ro 11:16
15:22 *r* S Lev 4:2
15:23 *s* ver 21
15:24 *t* ver 25,26 *u* S Lev 5:15 *v* Lev 4:14 *w* S ver 3 *x* Lev 2:1 *y* Lev 23:13; Nu 6:15 *z* Lev 4:3
15:25 *a* Lev 4:20; S Ro 3:25 *b* ver 22,S 24 *c* ver 14 *d* Lev 4:3
15:26 *e* S ver 24
15:27 *f* Lev 4:27 *g* Lev 4:3; Nu 6:14
15:28 *h* Nu 8:12; 28:22 *i* Lev 4:20
15:29 *j* S Ex 12:49
15:30 *k* Nu 14:40-44; Dt 1:43; 17:13; Ps 19:13 *l* ver 14 *m* 2Ki 19:6,20; Isa 37:6,23; Eze 20:27 *n* S Ge 17:14; S Job 31:22
15:31 *o* S Nu 14:11 *p* 1Sa 15:23,26; 2Sa 11:27; 12:9; Ps 119:126; Pr 13:13 *q* S Lev 5:1; Eze 18:20
15:32 *r* S Nu 12:16 *s* Ex 31:14,15; 35:2,3
15:34 *t* Nu 9:8
15:35 *u* Ex 31:14, 15 *v* S Lev 20:2; Lk 4:29; Ac 7:58
15:36 *w* S Lev 20:2

x S Ex 31:14 *y* Jer 17:21 **15:38** *z* Lev 3:17; Nu 10:8 *a* Dt 22:12; Mt 23:5

---

always be open to proselytes. Indeed, the charter of Israel's faith embraces all peoples of the earth (Ge 12:3).

15:20 *Present a cake from the first.* This law also looks forward to the time when the Israelites would be in the land. The first of the threshed grain was to be made into a cake and presented to the Lord. This concept of the firstfruits is a symbol that all blessing is from the Lord and all produce belongs to him.

15:22 *unintentionally fail.* Sins may be unintentional, but they still need to be dealt with (see note on Lev 4:2). Such unintentional sins may be committed by the people as a whole (vv. 22–26) or by an individual (vv. 27–29).

15:30 *defiantly.* Lit. "with a high hand." Unlike unintentional sins, for which there are provisions of God's mercy, one who sets his hand defiantly to despise the word of God and to blaspheme his name must be punished. This was the experience of the nation in ch. 14, and it is described in the

case of an individual here in vv. 32–36. *cut off from his people.* See note on Ex 12:15.

15:32 *gathering wood on the Sabbath day.* The penalty for breaking the Sabbath was death (v. 36; Ex 31:15; 35:2). As in the case of the willful blasphemer (Lev 24:10–16), the Sabbath-breaker was guilty of high-handed rebellion (see note on v. 30) and was judged with death. By the time of Christ, Sabbath-keeping had become distorted to the point that its regulations were regarded as more important than the needs of people. Jesus confronted the Pharisees on this issue on several occasions (see, e.g., Mt 12:1–14). From their point of view, these regulations (vv. 32–36) gave them reasons to seek his death (Mt 12:14).

15:38 *tassels on the corners of your garments.* As one would walk along, the tassels would swirl about at the edge of his garment (cf. v. 39), serving as excellent memory prods to obey God's commands (cf. Dt 6:4–9).

will remember[b] all the commands of the LORD, that you may obey them and not prostitute yourselves[c] by going after the lusts of your own hearts[d] and eyes. [40]Then you will remember to obey all my commands[e] and will be consecrated to your God.[f] [41]I am the LORD your God, who brought you out of Egypt to be your God.[g] I am the LORD your God.[h]' "

Korah, Dathan and Abiram

16 Korah[i] son of Izhar, the son of Kohath, the son of Levi, and certain Reubenites—Dathan and Abiram[j], sons of Eliab,[k] and On son of Peleth—became insolent[l] [2]and rose up against Moses.[l] With them were 250 Israelite men, well-known community leaders who had been appointed members of the council.[m] [3]They came as a group to oppose Moses and Aaron[n] and said to them, "You have gone too far! The whole community is holy,[o] every one of them, and the LORD is with them.[p] Why then do you set yourselves above the LORD's assembly?"[q]

[4]When Moses heard this, he fell facedown.[r] [5]Then he said to Korah and all his followers: "In the morning the LORD will show who belongs to him and who is holy,[s] and he will have that person come near him.[t] The man he chooses[u] he will cause to come near him. [6]You, Korah, and all your followers[v] are to do this: Take censers[w] [7]and tomorrow put fire[x] and incense[y] in them before the LORD. The man the LORD chooses[z] will be the one who is holy.[a] You Levites have gone too far!"

[8]Moses also said to Korah, "Now listen, you Levites! [9]Isn't it enough[b] for you that the God of Israel has separated you from the rest of the Israelite community and brought you near himself to do the work at the LORD's tabernacle and to stand before the community and minister to them?[c]

[10]He has brought you and all your fellow Levites near himself, but now you are trying to get the priesthood too.[d] [11]It is against the LORD that you and all your followers have banded together. Who is Aaron that you should grumble[e] against him?[f] "

[12]Then Moses summoned Dathan and Abiram,[g] the sons of Eliab. But they said, "We will not come![h] [13]Isn't it enough that you have brought us up out of a land flowing with milk and honey[i] to kill us in the desert?[j] And now you also want to lord it over us?[k] [14]Moreover, you haven't brought us into a land flowing with milk and honey[l] or given us an inheritance of fields and vineyards.[m] Will you gouge out the eyes of[m] these men?[n] No, we will not come![o]"

[15]Then Moses became very angry[p] and said to the LORD, "Do not accept their offering. I have not taken so much as a donkey[q] from them, nor have I wronged any of them."

[16]Moses said to Korah, "You and all your followers are to appear before the LORD tomorrow—you and they and Aaron.[r] [17]Each man is to take his censer and put incense in it—250 censers in all—and present it before the LORD. You and Aaron are to present your censers also.[s]" [18]So each man took his censer,[t] put fire and incense in it, and stood with Moses and Aaron at the entrance to the Tent of Meeting. [19]When Korah had gathered all his followers in opposition to them[u] at the entrance to the Tent of Meeting, the glory of the LORD[v] appeared

---

Cross references (center column):

15:39 [b]Dt 4:23; 6:12; Ps 73:27 [c]S Lev 17:7; Jdg 2:17; Ps 106:39; [e]Jer 3:2; Hos 4:12 [d]Ps 78:37; Jer 7:24; Eze 20:16 **15:40** [e]S Ge 26:5; Dt 11:13; Ps 103:18; 119:56 [f]S Lev 11:44; Ro 12:1; Col 1:22; 1Pe 1:15 **15:41** [g]S Ge 17:7 [h]S Ex 20:2 **16:1** [i]S Ex 6:24; Jude 1:11 [j]ver 24; Ps 106:17 [k]Nu 26:8; Dt 11:6 **16:2** [l]Nu 27:3 [m]Nu 1:16; 26:9 **16:3** [n]ver 7; Ps 106:16 [o]Ex 19:6 [p]S Nu 14:14 [q]Nu 12:2 **16:4** [r]Nu 14:5 **16:5** [s]S Lev 10:3; 2Ti 2:19* [t]Jer 30:21 [u]Nu 17:5; Ps 65:4; 105:26; Jer 50:44 **16:6** [v]ver 7,16 [w]S Lev 10:1; Rev 8:3 **16:7** [x]S Lev 10:1 [y]S Ex 30:9 [z]S ver 6 [a]ver 5 **16:9** [b]S Ge 30:15 [c]Nu 3:6; Dt 10:8; 17:12; 21:5; 1Sa 2:11; Ps 134:1; Eze 44:11 **16:10** [d]Nu 3:10; 18:7; Jdg 17:5,12 **16:11** [e]ver 41; 1Co 10:10 [f]S Ex 16:7 **16:12** [g]S ver 1,27 [h]ver 14 **16:13** [i]Nu 13:27 [j]Nu 14:2 [k]S Ge 13:8; Ac 7:27,35 **16:14** [l]S Lev 20:24 [m]Ex 22:5; 23:11; Nu 20:5; 1Ki 4:21; Ne 13:15; Ps 105:33; Jer 5:17; Hos 2:12; Joel 2:22; Hag 2:19; Zec 3:10 [n]Jdg 16:21; 1Sa 11:2; Jer 39:7 [o]ver 12 **16:15** [p]S Ex 4:14 [q]1Sa 12:3 **16:16** [r]S ver 6 **16:17** [s]Eze 8:11 **16:18** [t]Lev 10:1 **16:19** [u]ver 42; Nu 20:2 [v]S Ex 16:7; Nu 14:10; 20:6

[l]1 Or Peleth—took men [m]14 Or you make slaves of; or you deceive

---

15:41 *I am the LORD your God, who brought you out.* The demands that God made upon his people were grounded in his act of redemption (see Ex 20:2 and note).

16:1–7 Earlier, Miriam and Aaron had led a rebellion against the leadership of Moses (ch. 12). Now Korah and his allies attack the leadership of Moses and Aaron. Korah was descended from Levi through Kohath. As a Kohathite, he had high duties in the service of the Lord at the tabernacle (see 4:1–20), but he desired more. His passion was to assume the role of priest, and he used deception to advance his claim. Korah was joined by the Reubenites, Dathan, Abiram and On, and about 250 other leaders of Israel who had their own complaints. Their charge was that Moses had "gone too far" (v. 3) in taking the role of spiritual leadership of the people; "the whole community is holy" (v. 7). To this abusive charge Moses retorts, "You Levites have gone too far!" (v. 7), and sets up a trial by fire.

16:12 *Dathan and Abiram.* Their charge against Moses

was that he had not led them into the land of promise. They claimed that Moses had in fact led the people "out of a land flowing with milk and honey" (v. 13). By this strange alchemy, in their minds the land of Egypt has been transformed from prison to paradise.

16:15 *nor have I wronged any of them.* Moses' humanity is seen in his plea of innocence.

16:18–21 The trial was to be by fire: Which men would the Lord accept as his priests in the holy tabernacle? The 250 men allied with Korah came with arrogance to withstand Moses and Aaron at the entrance to the Tent of Meeting. The revelation of the Lord's glory was sure and sudden (v. 19), with words of impending doom for the rebellious people (v. 21). The punishment was fittingly ironic. Those 250 men who dared to present themselves as priests before the Lord with fire in their censers were themselves put to death by fire (perhaps lightning) from the Lord (see v. 35).

to the entire assembly. [20]The LORD said to Moses and Aaron, [21]"Separate yourselves[w] from this assembly so I can put an end to them at once."[x]

[22]But Moses and Aaron fell facedown[y] and cried out, "O God, God of the spirits of all mankind,[z] will you be angry with the entire assembly[a] when only one man sins?"[b]

[23]Then the LORD said to Moses, [24]"Say to the assembly, 'Move away from the tents of Korah, Dathan and Abiram.'"

[25]Moses got up and went to Dathan and Abiram, and the elders of Israel[c] followed him. [26]He warned the assembly, "Move back from the tents of these wicked men![d] Do not touch anything belonging to them, or you will be swept away[e] because of all their sins.[f]" [27]So they moved away from the tents of Korah, Dathan and Abiram.[g] Dathan and Abiram had come out and were standing with their wives, children[h] and little ones at the entrances to their tents.[i]

[28]Then Moses said, "This is how you will know[j] that the LORD has sent me[k] to do all these things and that it was not my idea: [29]If these men die a natural death and experience only what usually happens to men, then the LORD has not sent me.[l] [30]But if the LORD brings about something totally new, and the earth opens its mouth[m] and swallows them, with everything that belongs to them, and they go down alive into the grave,[n][n] then you will know that these men have treated the LORD with contempt.[o]"

[31]As soon as he finished saying all this, the ground under them split apart[p] [32]and the earth opened its mouth and swallowed them,[q] with their households and all Korah's men and all their possessions. [33]They went down alive into the grave,[r] with everything they owned; the earth closed over them, and they perished and were gone from the community. [34]At their cries, all the Israelites around them fled,

shouting, "The earth is going to swallow us too!"

[35]And fire came out from the LORD[s] and consumed[t] the 250 men who were offering the incense.

[36]The LORD said to Moses, [37]"Tell Eleazar[u] son of Aaron, the priest, to take the censers[v] out of the smoldering remains and scatter the coals some distance away, for the censers are holy— [38]the censers of the men who sinned at the cost of their lives.[w] Hammer the censers into sheets to overlay the altar,[x] for they were presented before the LORD and have become holy. Let them be a sign[y] to the Israelites."

[39]So Eleazar the priest[z] collected the bronze censers brought by those who had been burned up,[a] and he had them hammered out to overlay the altar, [40]as the LORD directed him through Moses. This was to remind the Israelites that no one except a descendant of Aaron should come to burn incense[b] before the LORD,[c] or he would become like Korah and his followers.[d]

[41]The next day the whole Israelite community grumbled against Moses and Aaron. "You have killed the LORD's people," they said.

[42]But when the assembly gathered in opposition[e] to Moses and Aaron and turned toward the Tent of Meeting, suddenly the cloud covered it and the glory of the LORD[f] appeared. [43]Then Moses and Aaron went to the front of the Tent of Meeting, [44]and the LORD said to Moses, [45]"Get away from this assembly so I can put an end[g] to them at once." And they fell facedown.

[46]Then Moses said to Aaron, "Take your censer[h] and put incense in it, along with fire from the altar, and hurry to the assembly[i] to make atonement[j] for them. Wrath has come out from the LORD;[k] the

---

Cross references (center column):

16:21 [w]ver 24
[x]S Ge 19:14;
S Ex 32:10
16:22 [y]S Nu 14:5
[z]Nu 27:16;
Job 12:10; 27:8;
33:4; 34:14;
Jer 32:27;
Eze 18:4;
Heb 12:9
[a]S Lev 10:6
[b]S Ge 18:23;
S Job 21:20
16:25 [c]S Ex 19:7
16:26 [d]Isa 52:11
[e]S Ge 19:15
[f]Jer 51:6
16:27 [g]S ver 12
[h]ver 32; Jos 7:24;
[i]S Ex 33:8
16:28 [j]1Ki 18:36
[k]Ex 3:12;
Jn 5:36; 6:38
16:29 [l]Nu 24:13;
Job 31:2;
Ecc 3:19
16:30 [m]Ps 141:7;
Isa 5:14 [n]ver 33;
S Ge 37:35;
1Sa 2:6; Job 5:26;
21:13; Ps 9:17;
16:10; 55:15;
Isa 14:11; 38:18
[o]S Nu 14:11;
S Eze 26:20
16:31
[p]Isa 64:1-2;
Eze 47:1-12;
Mic 1:3-4;
Zec 14:4
16:32
[q]S Ex 15:12
16:33 [r]S ver 30;
S Ecc 9:10

16:35
[s]S Nu 11:1-3;
26:10; Rev 11:5
[t]S Lev 10:2
16:37 [u]S Ex 6:23
[v]ver 6
16:38 [w]Lev 10:1;
[x]S Ex 20:24;
38:1-7
[y]Nu 26:10;
Dt 28:46;
Jer 44:29;
Eze 14:8; 2Pe 2:6
16:39
[z]2Ch 26:18
[a]S Lev 20:14
16:40
[b]S Ex 30:1;
2Ki 12:3;
Isa 1:13; 66:3;
Jer 41:5; 44:3
[c]S Ex 30:9;
2Ch 26:18
[d]S Nu 3:10
16:42 [e]S ver 19
[f]Ex 16:7;
Nu 14:10
16:45
[g]S Ex 32:10

16:46 [h]S Lev 10:1 [i]Lev 10:6 [j]S Ex 29:36 [k]S Nu 1:53

[n]30 Hebrew *Sheol*; also in verse 33

16:22 Here the magnanimity of Moses and Aaron is seen.
16:24 *Move away.* God's judgment was going to be severe, but he did not want to lash out against bystanders. It appears that Korah himself had left the 250 false priests and was standing with Dathan and Abiram to continue their opposition to Moses.
16:30 *something totally new.* Moses wished to assure the people that the imminent judgment was the direct work of the Lord and not a chance event that might be interpreted differently. The opening of the earth to swallow the rebels was a sure sign of the wrath of God and the vindication of Moses and Aaron.
16:32 *swallowed them, with their households.* The sons of

Korah did not die (26:11); apparently they did not join their father in his rash plan. The households of the other rebels died with them.
16:37 *take the censers.* The true priests took the censers of the 250 deceased impostors from their charred remains and hammered them into bronze sheets for the altar as a memorial of the folly of a self-proclaimed priest (v. 40).
16:41 *the whole Israelite community grumbled.* Again the community attacked Moses, unfairly charging him with the death of the Lord's people. Except for the intervention of Moses and Aaron (see vv. 4,22), the entire nation might have been destroyed because of their continued rebellion (see v. 45).

plague[l] has started." [47]So Aaron did as Moses said, and ran into the midst of the assembly. The plague had already started among the people,[m] but Aaron offered the incense and made atonement for them. [48]He stood between the living and the dead, and the plague stopped.[n] [49]But 14,700 people died from the plague, in addition to those who had died because of Korah.[o] [50]Then Aaron returned to Moses at the entrance to the Tent of Meeting, for the plague had stopped.

The Budding of Aaron's Staff

17 The LORD said to Moses, [2]"Speak to the Israelites and get twelve staffs[p] from them, one from the leader of each of their ancestral tribes.[q] Write the name of each man on his staff. [3]On the staff of Levi write Aaron's name,[r] for there must be one staff for the head of each ancestral tribe. [4]Place them in the Tent of Meeting[s] in front of the Testimony,[t] where I meet with you.[u] [5]The staff belonging to the man I choose[v] will sprout,[w] and I will rid myself of this constant grumbling[x] against you by the Israelites."

[6]So Moses spoke to the Israelites, and their leaders gave him twelve staffs, one for the leader of each of their ancestral tribes, and Aaron's staff was among them. [7]Moses placed the staffs before the LORD in the Tent of the Testimony.[y]

[8]The next day Moses entered the Tent of the Testimony[z] and saw that Aaron's staff,[a] which represented the house of Levi, had not only sprouted but had budded, blossomed and produced almonds.[b]

[9]Then Moses brought out all the staffs[c] from the LORD's presence to all the Israelites. They looked at them, and each man took his own staff.

[10]The LORD said to Moses, "Put back Aaron's staff[d] in front of the Testimony, to be kept as a sign to the rebellious.[e] This will put an end to their grumbling against me, so that they will not die." [11]Moses did just as the LORD commanded him.

[12]The Israelites said to Moses, "We will die! We are lost, we are all lost![f] [13]Anyone who even comes near the tabernacle of the LORD will die.[g] Are we all going to die?"

Duties of Priests and Levites

18 The LORD said to Aaron, "You, your sons and your father's family are to bear the responsibility for offenses against the sanctuary,[h] and you and your sons alone are to bear the responsibility for offenses against the priesthood. [2]Bring your fellow Levites from your ancestral tribe to join you and assist you when you and your sons minister[i] before the Tent of the Testimony. [3]They are to be responsible to you[j] and are to perform all the duties of the Tent,[k] but they must not go near the furnishings of the sanctuary or the altar, or both they and you will die.[l] [4]They are to join you and be responsible for the care of the Tent of Meeting—all the work at the Tent—and no one else may come near where you are.[m]

[5]"You are to be responsible for the care of the sanctuary and the altar,[n] so that wrath will not fall on the Israelites again. [6]I myself have selected your fellow Levites

---

Cross references (center column):

16:46 /S Lev 26:25; Nu 8:19; Ps 106:29
16:47
16:48 nNu 25:6-8; Ps 106:30
16:49 over 32
17:2 pS Ge 32:10; S Ex 4:2 qNu 1:4
17:3 rS Nu 1:3
17:4 sS Ex 40:2 tver 7; S Ex 16:34 uEx 25:22
17:5 vS Nu 16:5 wver 8 xS Ex 16:7
17:7 yS Ex 38:21
17:8 zver 7; Nu 1:50 aver 2,10 bEze 17:24; Heb 9:4

17:9 cver 2
17:10 dS ver 8 eS Ex 23:21; Dt 9:24; Ps 66:7; 68:18; Pr 24:21
17:12 fJdg 13:22; Isa 6:5; 15:1
17:13 gNu 1:51
18:1 hS Ex 28:38
18:2 iNu 3:10
18:3 jS Nu 3:32 kNu 1:51 lver 7
18:4 mS Nu 3:38
18:5 nver 3; Lev 6:12

mNu 25:6-8

16:49 *14,700 people died.* The number makes sense only if the community is as large as the census lists of ch. 2 suggest.

17:1–13 This story follows the account of the divine judgment of Korah (16:1–35) and the narrative of the symbolic use given to the censers of the rebels and its aftermath (16:36–50). Ch. 17 is thus the third in a series of accounts vindicating the Aaronic priesthood against all opposition. The selection of 12 staffs, one from each tribe, was a symbolic act whereby the divine choice of Aaron would be indicated again.

17:3 *On the staff of Levi write Aaron's name.* The test needed to be unequivocal because of the wide support given to Korah's rebellion. The 250 who had joined with Korah were from many, perhaps all, of the tribes.

17:4 *in front of the Testimony.* In front of the ark, with the Ten Commandments, thus probably in the Holy Place, near the altar of incense.

17:8 *had not only sprouted but had budded, blossomed and produced almonds.* God exceeded the demands of the test so that there might be no uncertainty as to who had acted or what he intended by his action.

17:10 *in front of the Testimony.* Aaron's rod joined the stone tablets of the law of Moses (see note on Ex 25:16) and the jar of manna (Ex 16:33–34) within or near the ark of the

covenant (see Heb 9:4). These holy symbols were ever before the Lord as memorials of his special deeds in behalf of his people. Moreover, should anyone of a later age dare to question the unique and holy place of the Aaronic priests in the Lord's service, this symbolic memorial of God's choice of Aaron would stand in opposition to his audacity. It is difficult to overestimate the importance of the role of Aaron and his sons in the worship of Israel (see note on 18:1–7).

17:12 *We will die!* At last the people realized the sin of their arrogance in challenging Aaron's role. The appropriate ways of approaching the Lord are detailed in chs. 18–19.

18:1–7 Aaron and his family, chosen by the Lord to be the true priests of holy worship, faced a burdensome task. The lament of the people in 17:12–13 was real; grievous sins against the holy meeting place of the Lord and his people would be judged by death. The Lord's mercy in providing a legitimate priesthood was actually an aspect of his grace (cf. Ps 99:6–8), because it was the people's only hope for deliverance from judgment.

18:2 *Bring your fellow Levites.* The Aaronic priests were to be assisted by the others in the tribe of Levi, but the assistants were not to go beyond their serving role. If they did so, not only would they die, but so would the priests who were responsible (v. 3).

from among the Israelites as a gift to you, [o] dedicated to the LORD to do the work at the Tent of Meeting. [p] [7]But only you and your sons may serve as priests in connection with everything at the altar and inside the curtain. [q] I am giving you the service of the priesthood as a gift. [r] Anyone else who comes near the sanctuary must be put to death. [s] ”

Offerings for Priests and Levites

[8]Then the LORD said to Aaron, "I myself have put you in charge of the offerings presented to me; all the holy offerings the Israelites give me I give to you and your sons as your portion [t] and regular share. [u] [9]You are to have the part of the most holy offerings [v] that is kept from the fire. From all the gifts they bring me as most holy offerings, whether grain [w] or sin [x] or guilt offerings, [y] that part belongs to you and your sons. [10]Eat it as something most holy; every male shall eat it. [z] You must regard it as holy. [a]

[11]"This also is yours: whatever is set aside from the gifts of all the wave offerings [b] of the Israelites. I give this to you and your sons and daughters as your regular share. [c] Everyone in your household who is ceremonially clean [d] may eat it.

[12]"I give you all the finest olive oil and all the finest new wine and grain [e] they give the LORD [f] as the firstfruits of their harvest. [g] [13]All the land's firstfruits that they bring to the LORD will be yours. [h] Everyone in your household who is ceremonially clean may eat it. [i]

[14]"Everything in Israel that is devoted [o] to the LORD [j] is yours. [15]The first offspring of every womb, both man and animal, that is offered to the LORD is yours. [k] But you must redeem [l] every firstborn [m] son and every firstborn male of unclean animals. [n] [16]When they are a month old, [o] you must redeem them at the redemption price set

at five shekels [p] [p] of silver, according to the sanctuary shekel, [q] which weighs twenty gerahs. [r]

[17]"But you must not redeem the firstborn of an ox, a sheep or a goat; they are holy. [s] Sprinkle their blood [t] on the altar and burn their fat [u] as an offering made by fire, an aroma pleasing to the LORD. [v] [18]Their meat is to be yours, just as the breast of the wave offering [w] and the right thigh are yours. [x] [19]Whatever is set aside from the holy [y] offerings the Israelites present to the LORD I give to you and your sons and daughters as your regular share. It is an everlasting covenant of salt [z] before the LORD for both you and your offspring."

[20]The LORD said to Aaron, "You will have no inheritance in their land, nor will you have any share among them; [a] I am your share and your inheritance [b] among the Israelites.

[21]"I give to the Levites all the tithes [c] in Israel as their inheritance [d] in return for the work they do while serving at the Tent of Meeting. [e] [22]From now on the Israelites must not go near the Tent of Meeting, or they will bear the consequences of their sin and will die. [f] [23]It is the Levites who are to do the work at the Tent of Meeting and bear the responsibility for offenses against it. This is a lasting ordinance [g] for the generations to come. [h] They will receive no inheritance [i] among the Israelites. [j] [24]Instead, I give to the Levites as their inheritance the tithes that the Israelites present as an offering to the LORD. [k] That is why I said concerning them: 'They will have no inheritance among the Israelites.' "

[25]The LORD said to Moses, [26]"Speak to

18:6 [o]S Nu 3:9
[p]Nu 3:8
18:7 [q]Heb 9:3,6
[r]ver 20; Ex 29:9;
40:13; Heb 5:4
[s]ver 3; Nu 3:10
18:8 [t]S Lev 2:2
[u]Lev 6:16; 7:6,
31-34,36;
Dt 18:1;
2Ch 31:4
18:9 [v]S Lev 6:17
[w]Lev 2:1
[x]Lev 6:25
[y]S Lev 5:15
18:10
[z]S Lev 6:16
[a]Lev 6:17,18
18:11 [b]Ex 29:26;
Lev 7:30;
Nu 6:20
[c]Lev 7:31-34
[d]Lev 13:3;
22:1-16
18:12 [e]Dt 7:13;
11:14; 12:17;
28:51; 2Ki 18:32;
2Ch 31:5;
Ne 10:37;
Jer 31:12;
Eze 23:41;
Hos 2:8;
Joel 1:10;
Hag 1:11
[f]S Ge 4:3
[g]Ex 23:19;
34:26; Ne 10:35
18:13
[h]S Ex 29:27 [i]ver 11
18:14
[j]S Lev 27:21;
Jos 6:17-19
18:15 [k]Ex 13:2
[l]S Nu 3:46
[m]S Ge 10:15
[n]S Ex 13:13
18:16 [o]S Nu 3:15

[p]S Lev 27:6
[q]S Ex 30:13
[r]Nu 3:47
18:17
[s]S Lev 27:9
[t]S Lev 3:2
[u]S Ex 29:13
[v]S Lev 1:9
18:18 [w]Lev 7:30
[x]ver 11
18:19 [y]2Ki 12:4
[z]S Lev 2:13
18:20
[a]Nu 26:62;
Dt 12:12 [b]ver 24;
Dt 10:9; 14:27;
18:1-2; Jos 13:33;
Eze 44:28
18:21 [c]ver 24;
S Ge 28:22;
Nu 31:28;
Dt 14:22;
Ne 10:37; 13:5;

Mal 3:8 [d]Lev 27:30-33; Heb 7:5 [e]Nu 1:53 **18:22** [f]S Ex 28:43
18:23 [g]S Ex 12:14; S 27:21 [h]Nu 10:8 [i]ver 20; Nu 26:62;
Dt 10:9 [j]Eze 44:10 **18:24** [k]Lev 27:30; Dt 26:12

[o]14 The Hebrew term refers to the irrevocable giving over of things or persons to the LORD.   [p]16 That is, about 2 ounces (about 55 grams)

18:7 the service of the priesthood as a gift. Of all men, the priests were privileged to approach the Holy Place and minister before the Lord. The priesthood was a gift of God's grace to both priests and people.

18:8 your portion and regular share. The priests were to be supported in their work of ministry (see Lev 6:14–7:36). Since the Levites as a whole and the priests in particular had no part in the land that God was going to give them, it was necessary that the means for their provision be spelled out fully. They were not to have a part in the land; their share was the Lord himself (v. 20).

18:11 your sons and daughters. Provision was made not only for the priests, but for their families as well. Only family members who were ceremonially unclean were forbidden to eat the gifts and offerings of the people (see v. 13). Provisions for cleansing were stated in Lev 22:4–8.

18:12 finest olive oil . . . finest new wine and grain. Since the best items of produce were to be given to the Lord, these became the special foods of the priests and their families. The NT writers similarly argue that those who minister the word of God in the present period should also be paid suitably for their work (see, e.g., 1Co 9:3–10 and notes).

18:19 everlasting covenant of salt. A permanent provision for the priests. The phrase "covenant of salt" (see 2Ch 13:5) remains obscure. In Lev 2:13 the salt that must accompany grain offerings is called the "salt of the covenant." According to Eze 43:24, salt is also to be sprinkled on burnt offerings, and Ex 30:35 specifies salt as one of the ingredients in the special incense compounded for the sanctuary. A "covenant of salt" is perhaps an allusion to the salt used in the sacrificial meal that commonly accompanied the making of a covenant (see Ge 31:54; Ex 24:5–11; Ps 50:5).

the Levites and say to them: 'When you receive from the Israelites the tithe I give you[l] as your inheritance, you must present a tenth of that tithe as the LORD's offering.[m] 27Your offering will be reckoned[n] to you as grain from the threshing floor[o] or juice from the winepress.[p] 28In this way you also will present an offering to the LORD from all the tithes[q] you receive from the Israelites. From these tithes you must give the LORD's portion to Aaron the priest. 29You must present as the LORD's portion the best and holiest part of everything given to you.'

30"Say to the Levites: 'When you present the best part, it will be reckoned to you as the product of the threshing floor or the winepress.[r] 31You and your households may eat the rest of it anywhere, for it is your wages for your work at the Tent of Meeting.[s] 32By presenting the best part[t] of it you will not be guilty in this matter;[u] then you will not defile the holy offerings[v] of the Israelites, and you will not die.' "

The Water of Cleansing

19 The LORD said to Moses and Aaron: 2"This is a requirement of the law that the LORD has commanded: Tell the Israelites to bring you a red heifer[w] without defect or blemish[x] and that has never been under a yoke.[y] 3Give it to Eleazar[z] the priest; it is to be taken outside the camp[a] and slaughtered in his presence. 4Then Eleazar the priest is to take some of its blood on his finger and sprinkle[b] it seven times toward the front of the Tent of Meeting. 5While he watches, the heifer is to be burned—its hide, flesh, blood and offal.[c] 6The priest is to take some cedar wood, hyssop[d] and scarlet wool[e] and throw them onto the burning

heifer. 7After that, the priest must wash his clothes and bathe himself with water.[f] He may then come into the camp, but he will be ceremonially unclean till evening. 8The man who burns it must also wash his clothes and bathe with water, and he too will be unclean till evening.

9"A man who is clean shall gather up the ashes of the heifer[g] and put them in a ceremonially clean place[h] outside the camp. They shall be kept by the Israelite community for use in the water of cleansing;[i] it is for purification from sin.[j] 10The man who gathers up[k] the ashes of the heifer must also wash his clothes, and he too will be unclean till evening.[l] This will be a lasting ordinance[m] both for the Israelites and for the aliens living among them.[n]

11"Whoever touches the dead body[o] of anyone will be unclean for seven days.[p] 12He must purify himself with the water on the third day and on the seventh day;[q] then he will be clean. But if he does not purify himself on the third and seventh days, he will not be clean.[r] 13Whoever touches the dead body[s] of anyone and fails to purify himself defiles the LORD's tabernacle.[t] That person must be cut off from Israel.[u] Because the water of cleansing has not been sprinkled on him, he is unclean;[v] his uncleanness remains on him.

14"This is the law that applies when a person dies in a tent: Anyone who enters the tent and anyone who is in it will be unclean for seven days, 15and every open container[w] without a lid fastened on it will be unclean.

16"Anyone out in the open who touches someone who has been killed with a sword or someone who has died a natural death,[x] or anyone who touches a human

---

18:26 [l]ver 21
[m]ver 28;
Ne 10:38
18:27 [n]Lev 7:18
[o]Ge 50:10;
Dt 15:14;
Jdg 6:37; Ru 3:3,
6,14; 1Sa 23:1
[p]ver 12,30
18:28 [q]Mal 3:8
18:30 [r]S ver 27
18:31 [s]ver 23
18:32 [t]Lev 22:15
[u]ver 29
[v]S Lev 19:8
19:2 [w]S Ge 15:9;
Heb 9:13
[x]S Lev 22:19-25
[y]Dt 21:3; 1Sa 6:7
19:3 [z]Nu 3:4
[a]S Ex 29:14
19:4 [b]S Lev 4:17
19:5 [c]S Lev 29:14
19:6 [d]ver 18;
Ps 51:7
[e]S Lev 14:4

19:7
[f]S Lev 11:25;
S 14:8
19:9 [g]Heb 9:13
[h]S Ex 29:31;
S Lev 4:12 [i]ver
13; Nu 8:7
[j]S Ge 35:2
19:10 [k]Lev 15:10
[l]Lev 14:46
[m]Lev 3:17
[n]S Lev 22:18
19:11
[o]S Lev 21:1
[p]S Lev 8:33;
Nu 31:19
19:12 [q]ver 19;
Nu 31:19 [r]ver 20;
2Ch 26:21
19:13
[s]S Lev 21:11
[t]S Lev 15:31;
2Ch 36:14;
Ps 79:1
[u]Lev 7:20; 22:3
[v]ver 22; Hag 2:13
19:15
[w]S Lev 6:28
19:16 [x]Nu 31:19

18:26–32 Although the Levites were the recipients of the tithe given to the Lord, they were not themselves exempt from worshiping God by tithing. They in turn were to give a tenth of their income to Aaron (v. 28) and were to be sure that the best part was given as the Lord's portion (v. 29). By obedient compliance the Levites would escape judicial death (v. 32).

19:2 *red heifer.* The qualifying words, "without defect or blemish," are familiar in contexts of sacrificial worship in the OT. But this is not a sacrificial animal. It is a cow, not an ox; it is to be slaughtered, not sacrificed; and it is to be killed outside the camp, not at the holy altar. The ashes of the red heifer (v. 9) are the primary focus of this act, for they will be used in the ritual of the water of cleansing. The burning of the animal with its blood and offal (v. 5) is unprecedented in the OT. The normal pattern for the sacrifice of the burnt offering is given in Lev 1:3–9. In every respect the killing of the red heifer is distinct: A female animal was taken outside the camp to be killed; the priest had to be present, but he did

not identify himself with it; and a bit of the heifer's blood was sprinkled from the priest's finger toward the tabernacle seven times, but the rest of the animal was to be burned in its entirety, without the draining of its blood or the cleansing of its offal.

19:6 *cedar wood, hyssop and scarlet wool.* Associated with the cleansing properties of the ashes of the red heifer.

19:12 *purify himself with the water.* The ashes from the red heifer were kept outside the camp and would be mixed as needed with water to provide a means of cleansing after contact with dead bodies.

19:13 *defiles the LORD's tabernacle.* Willful neglect of the provision for cleansing brought not only judgment on the person, but also a pollution of the tabernacle itself. *cut off from Israel.* See note on Ex 12:15.

19:14 *anyone who is in it.* There would be many occasions in which a person would become unclean, not because of deliberate contact with a dead body, but just by being in the proximity of one who died.

bone[y] or a grave,[z] will be unclean for seven days.[a]

17"For the unclean person, put some ashes[b] from the burned purification offering into a jar and pour fresh water[c] over them. 18Then a man who is ceremonially clean is to take some hyssop,[d] dip it in the water and sprinkle[e] the tent and all the furnishings and the people who were there. He must also sprinkle anyone who has touched a human bone or a grave[f] or someone who has been killed or someone who has died a natural death. 19The man who is clean is to sprinkle[g] the unclean person on the third and seventh days, and on the seventh day he is to purify him.[h] The person being cleansed must wash his clothes[i] and bathe with water, and that evening he will be clean. 20But if a person who is unclean does not purify himself, he must be cut off from the community, because he has defiled[j] the sanctuary of the Lord.[k] The water of cleansing has not been sprinkled on him, and he is unclean.[l] 21This is a lasting ordinance[m] for them.

"The man who sprinkles the water of cleansing must also wash his clothes, and anyone who touches the water of cleansing will be unclean till evening. 22Anything that an unclean[n] person touches becomes unclean, and anyone who touches it becomes unclean till evening."

Water From the Rock

20 In the first month the whole Israelite community arrived at the Desert of Zin,[o] and they stayed at Ka-

desh.[p] There Miriam[q] died and was buried.

2Now there was no water[r] for the community,[s] and the people gathered in opposition[t] to Moses and Aaron. 3They quarreled[u] with Moses and said, "If only we had died when our brothers fell dead[v] before the Lord![w] 4Why did you bring the Lord's community into this desert,[x] that we and our livestock should die here?[y] 5Why did you bring us up out of Egypt to this terrible place? It has no grain or figs, grapevines or pomegranates.[z] And there is no water to drink![a]"

6Moses and Aaron went from the assembly to the entrance to the Tent of Meeting[b] and fell facedown,[c] and the glory of the Lord[d] appeared to them. 7The Lord said to Moses, 8"Take the staff,[e] and you and your brother Aaron gather the assembly together. Speak to that rock before their eyes and it will pour out its water.[f] You will bring water out of the rock for the community so they and their livestock can drink."

9So Moses took the staff[g] from the Lord's presence,[h] just as he commanded him. 10He and Aaron gathered the assembly together[i] in front of the rock and Moses said to them, "Listen, you rebels, must we bring you water out of this rock?"[j] 11Then Moses raised his arm and struck the rock twice with his staff. Water[k] gushed out, and the community and their livestock drank.

12But the Lord said to Moses and

19:16 y1Ki 13:2; 2Ki 23:14; Eze 6:5
z2Ki 23:6; Mt 23:27
aS Lev 5:3
19:17 bver 9
cS Nu 8:7
19:18 dS ver 6; S Ex 12:22
eS Lev 4:17 fver 16
19:19 gS Lev 16:14-15 hNu 31:19; Eze 36:25; Heb 10:22 iS Ge 35:2
19:20 jPs 74:7 kS Lev 15:31 lS ver 12; S Lev 14:8
19:21 mS Ex 27:21 nS Lev 5:2; 15:4-12
20:1 oNu 13:21
pver 14; Nu 13:26; 33:36; Dt 1:46; Jdg 11:17; Ps 29:8
qS Ex 15:20
20:2 rS Ex 15:22 sEx 17:1 tS Nu 16:19
20:3 uver 13; S Ge 13:7; Ex 17:2; 21:18 vS Ex 5:21 wS Nu 14:2; 16:31-35
20:4 xS Nu 14:2 yS Ex 14:11; Nu 14:3; 16:13
20:5 zNu 13:23; 16:14 aS Ex 17:1
20:6 bS Ex 40:2 cNu 14:5 dS Nu 16:19
20:8 eS Ex 4:2; S 10:12-13 fEx 17:6; Isa 41:18; 43:20; Jer 31:9
20:9 gNu 17:2 hNu 17:10
20:10 iver 8 jPs 106:32,33
20:11 kS Ex 17:6; S Isa 33:21

19:18 *hyssop, dip it in the water and sprinkle.* Here the method of the cleansing ritual is explained. A ceremonially clean person had to sprinkle the ceremonially unclean person or thing. The cleansing power of the blood of Christ is specifically contrasted ("much more"; Heb 9:13–14) with the cleansing effectiveness of the water of the ashes of the red heifer. *cut off from his people.* See note on Lev 7:20.

20:1–29 This chapter begins with the death of Miriam (v. 1), concludes with the death of Aaron (v. 28), includes the record of the conflict with Edom (vv. 14–21) and centers on the tragic sin of Moses (vv. 11–12). Such was the sad beginning of Israel's last year in the desert.

20:1 *first month.* The year is not given, but a comparison of vv. 22–29 with 33:38 leads to the conclusion that this chapter begins in the 40th year after the exodus (see notes on 1:1; 9:1). Most of the people 20 years old or more at the time of the rebellion at Kadesh (chs. 13–14) would already have died. *at Kadesh.* The larger part of the desert wandering is left without record. The people may have gone through a cycle of roving travels, seeking the water sources and the sparse vegetation, supported primarily by manna. But their circuits would bring them back to the central camp at Kadesh, the scene of their great rebellion (chs. 13–14). They have now come full circle; the land of promise lies before them again.

20:2 *no water.* Forty years earlier, the Lord had instructed Moses to take the staff he had used to strike the Nile (Ex 7:17) and to strike the rock at Horeb to initiate a flow of water (Ex 17:1–7). Now, 40 years later, at the place of Israel's worst acts of rebellion, the scene was recurring. The children of the rebellious nation now desire to die with their parents; the complaints about the bread from heaven were repeated by the sons.

20:8 *Speak to that rock.* Moses was told to take his staff, through which God had performed wonders in Egypt and in the desert all these years, but this time he was merely to speak to the rock and it would pour out its water for the people. Cf. Ps 114:8.

20:10 *Listen, you rebels.* At once the accumulated anger, exasperation and frustration of 40 years came to expression (see Ps 106:33).

20:11 *struck the rock twice with his staff.* In his rage Moses disobeyed the Lord's instruction to speak to the rock (v. 8). Moses' rash action brought a stern rebuke from the Lord (v. 12). The nature of Moses' offense is not clearly stated in this text, but these factors appear to be involved: 1. Moses' action was a lack of trust in God (v. 12), as though he believed that a word alone would not suffice. 2. God's holiness was offended by Moses' rash action (v. 12), for he had not shown proper deference to God's presence.

Aaron, "Because you did not trust in me enough to honor me as holy *l* in the sight of the Israelites, you will not bring this community into the land I give them." *m*

13These were the waters of Meribah, ¶ *n* where the Israelites quarreled *o* with the LORD and where he showed himself holy among them. *p*

Edom Denies Israel Passage

14Moses sent messengers from Kadesh *q* to the king of Edom, *r* saying:

"This is what your brother Israel says: You know *s* about all the hardships *t* that have come upon us. 15Our forefathers went down into Egypt, *u* and we lived there many years. *v* The Egyptians mistreated *w* us and our fathers, 16but when we cried out to the LORD, he heard our cry *x* and sent an angel *y* and brought us out of Egypt. *z*

"Now we are here at Kadesh, a town on the edge of your territory. *a* 17Please let us pass through your country. We will not go through any field or vineyard, or drink water from any well. We will travel along the king's highway and not turn to the right or to the left until we have passed through your territory. *b*"

18But Edom *c* answered:

"You may not pass through here; if you try, we will march out and attack you with the sword. *d*"

19The Israelites replied:

"We will go along the main road, and if we or our livestock *e* drink any of your water, we will pay for it. *f* We

only want to pass through on foot—nothing else."

20Again they answered:

"You may not pass through. *g*"

Then Edom *h* came out against them with a large and powerful army. 21Since Edom refused to let them go through their territory, *i* Israel turned away from them. *j*

The Death of Aaron

22The whole Israelite community set out from Kadesh *k* and came to Mount Hor. *l* 23At Mount Hor, near the border of Edom, *m* the LORD said to Moses and Aaron, 24"Aaron will be gathered to his people. *n* He will not enter the land I give the Israelites, because both of you rebelled against my command *o* at the waters of Meribah. *p* 25Get Aaron and his son Eleazar and take them up Mount Hor. *q* 26Remove Aaron's garments *r* and put them on his son Eleazar, for Aaron will be gathered to his people; *s* he will die there."

27Moses did as the LORD commanded: They went up Mount Hor *t* in the sight of the whole community. 28Moses removed Aaron's garments and put them on his son Eleazar. *u* And Aaron died there *v* on top of the mountain. Then Moses and Eleazar came down from the mountain, 29and when the whole community learned that Aaron had died, *w* the entire house of Israel mourned for him *x* thirty days.

Arad Destroyed

21 When the Canaanite king of Arad, *y* who lived in the Negev, *z*

Cross references (center column)

20:12 *l*Nu 27:14; Dt 32:51;
Isa 5:16; 8:13
*m*ver 24; Dt 1:37; 3:27
20:13 *n*S Ex 17:7
*o*S ver 3
*p*S Lev 10:3
20:14 *q*S ver 1
*r*S ver 16;
S Ge 25:30;
S 36:16 *s*Ge 24:3;
Dt 4:39; Jos 2:11;
9:9 *t*S Ex 18:8
20:15 *u*S Ge 46:6
*v*S Ge 15:13
*w*S Ex 1:14
20:16
*x*S Ge 16:11;
S 21:17;
S Ex 2:23
*y*Ex 14:19
*z*Ex 12:42;
Dt 26:8 *a*ver 14, 23; Nu 33:37
20:17 *b*ver 20;
Nu 21:22;
Dt 2:27;
Jdg 11:17
20:18 *c*ver 14
*d*Nu 21:23
20:19 *e*Ex 12:38
*f*Dt 2:6,28

20:20 *g*S ver 17, 18 *h*ver 14
20:21 *i*Nu 21:23
/Nu 21:4; Dt 2:8;
Jdg 11:18
20:22 *k*Dt 1:46
*l*Nu 33:37; 34:7;
Dt 32:50
20:23 *m*S ver 16
20:24 *n*S Ge 25:8
*o*S ver 10
*p*S Ex 17:7
20:25 *q*Nu 33:38
20:26
*r*Ex 28:1-4;
40:13; S Lev 16:4
*s*ver 24;
Nu 27:13; 31:2
20:27 *t*Nu 33:38
20:28
*u*S Ex 29:29 *v*ver 26; Nu 33:38;
Dt 10:6; 32:50
20:29 *w*Dt 32:50
*x*S Ge 27:41;
S Lev 10:6;
S Dt 34:8
21:1 *y*Nu 33:40;
Jos 12:14
*z*S Ge 12:9;

Nu 13:17; Dt 1:7; Jdg 1:9,16

¶*13 Meribah* means *quarreling.*

20:12 *you will not bring this community into the land.* The end result of Moses' action is sure: Neither Aaron nor Moses would enter the land of promise. Of their contemporaries only Joshua and Caleb would survive to enter the land. The inclusion of Aaron demonstrates his partnership with his brother in the breach against God's holiness.

20:13 *Meribah.* See NIV text note. The same name was used 40 years earlier at the first occasion of bringing water from the rock (Ex 17:7, where it is also called Massah, "testing"). Ps 95:8 laments the rebellion at Meribah and Massah.

20:14–21 Moses' attempt to pass through the territory of Edom by peaceful negotiation and payment for services rendered is met by arrogant rebuff.

20:14 *your brother Israel.* The people of Edom were descended from Esau, the brother of Jacob (see Ge 36:1).

20:17 *king's highway.* The major north-south trade route in Transjordan, extending from Arabia to Damascus.

20:20 *large and powerful army.* The show of force by Edom caused Israel to turn away so as not to risk conflict with this brother nation. Israel was forbidden by the Lord to

take even a foothold in Edom (see Dt 2:4–6).

20:22 *Mount Hor.* Other than its proximity to the border of Edom (v. 23), nothing is known for certain about its location.

20:24 *gathered to his people.* A euphemism for death (see, e.g., Ge 25:8,17; 35:29). *both of you.* Aaron had joined Moses in rebellion against God (v. 12); his impending death was a precursor of Moses' death as well (see Dt 34).

20:25 *Aaron and his son Eleazar.* There was no doubt about Aaron's successor, just as there was no doubt about Moses' successor (see Dt 34).

20:26–28 While Aaron was still alive, his garments were to be placed on his son; only then did he die.

20:29 *mourned for him.* His death (and that of Moses) marked the passing of a generation. The old generation was now nearly gone; in 40 years there had been almost a complete turnover of the people 20 years old or more.

21:1–3 The first battle of the new community against the Canaanites was provoked by the king of Arad, perhaps as he was raiding them. The result was a complete victory for the Israelites—a new day for them, since they had been defeated by the Amalekites and Canaanites a generation before

heard that Israel was coming along the road to Atharim, he attacked the Israelites and captured some of them. ²Then Israel made this vow[a] to the LORD: "If you will deliver these people into our hands, we will totally destroy[r][b] their cities." ³The LORD listened to Israel's plea and gave the Canaanites[c] over to them. They completely destroyed them[d] and their towns; so the place was named Hormah.[s][e]

The Bronze Snake

⁴They traveled from Mount Hor[f] along the route to the Red Sea,[t][g] to go around Edom.[h] But the people grew impatient on the way;[i] ⁵they spoke against God[j] and against Moses, and said, "Why have you brought us up out of Egypt[k] to die in the desert?[l] There is no bread! There is no water![m] And we detest this miserable food!"[n]

⁶Then the LORD sent venomous snakes[o] among them; they bit the people and many Israelites died.[p] ⁷The people came to Moses[q] and said, "We sinned[r] when we spoke against the LORD and against you. Pray that the LORD[s] will take the snakes away from us." So Moses prayed[t] for the people.

⁸The LORD said to Moses, "Make a snake and put it up on a pole;[u] anyone who is bitten can look at it and live." ⁹So Moses made a bronze snake[v] and put it up on a pole. Then when anyone was bitten by a snake and looked at the bronze snake, he lived.[w]

The Journey to Moab

¹⁰The Israelites moved on and camped at Oboth.[x] ¹¹Then they set out from

Oboth and camped in Iye Abarim, in the desert that faces Moab[y] toward the sunrise. ¹²From there they moved on and camped in the Zered Valley.[z] ¹³They set out from there and camped alongside the Arnon[a], which is in the desert extending into Amorite territory. The Arnon is the border of Moab, between Moab and the Amorites.[b] ¹⁴That is why the Book of the Wars[c] of the LORD says:

"... Waheb in Suphah[u] and the
        ravines,
    the Arnon ¹⁵and[v] the slopes of the
        ravines
that lead to the site of Ar[d]
    and lie along the border of Moab."

¹⁶From there they continued on to Beer,[e] the well where the LORD said to Moses, "Gather the people together and I will give them water."

¹⁷Then Israel sang this song:[f]

"Spring up, O well!
    Sing about it,
¹⁸about the well that the princes dug,
    that the nobles of the people sank—
    the nobles with scepters and staffs."

Then they went from the desert to Mattanah, ¹⁹from Mattanah to Nahaliel, from Nahaliel to Bamoth, ²⁰and from Bamoth to the valley in Moab where the top of Pisgah[g] overlooks the wasteland.

21:2 aLev 7:16
bver 3; Ex 22:20;
Dt 2:34; Jos 2:10;
8:26; Jer 25:9;
50:21
21:3 cS Ge 10:18
dS ver 2
eS Nu 14:45
21:4 fNu 20:22
gNu 14:25;
Dt 2:1; 11:4
hS Nu 20:21
iDt 2:8; Jdg 11:18
21:5 jPs 78:19
kNu 11:20
lS Ex 14:11;
Nu 14:2,3
mNu 20:5
nS Nu 11:5
21:6 over 7;
Dt 8:15; 32:33;
Job 20:14;
Ps 58:4; 140:3;
Jer 8:17
p1Co 10:9
21:7 qPs 78:34;
Hos 5:15
rEx 8:8; 1Sa 7:8;
Jer 27:18; 37:3;
Ac 8:24
tS Nu 11:2
21:8 uJn 3:14
21:9 v2Ki 18:4
wJn 3:14-15
21:10 xNu 33:43
21:11
yS Ge 36:35;
Nu 33:44;
Dt 34:8; Jer 40:11

21:12 zDt 2:13,
14
21:13
aNu 22:36;
Dt 2:24; Jos 12:1;
Jdg 11:13,18;
2Ki 10:33;
Isa 16:2;
Jer 48:20
bS Ge 10:16
21:14
c1Sa 17:47;
18:17; 25:28
21:15 dver 28;
Dt 2:9,18;
Isa 15:1
21:16 eNu 25:1;
33:49; Jdg 9:21;
Isa 15:8
21:17 fS Ex 15:1
21:20
gNu 23:14;
Dt 3:17,27; 34:1;
Jos 12:3; 13:20

r2 The Hebrew term refers to the irrevocable giving over of things or persons to the LORD, often by totally destroying them; also in verse 3.   s3 Hormah means destruction.   t4 Hebrew Yam Suph; that is, Sea of Reeds   u14 The meaning of the Hebrew for this phrase is uncertain.   v14,15 Or "I have been given from Suphah and the ravines of the Arnon ¹⁵to

---

(14:41–45).
21:2 totally destroy. See NIV text note.
21:3 Hormah. See NIV text note; the association with Israel's earlier defeat is made certain by the use of this place-name (see 14:45).
21:4 With Moses' determination not to engage Edom in battle (see note on 20:20), the people became impatient with him and with the direction the Lord was taking them. Flushed with victory, they were confident in themselves. They forgot that their victory over Arad was granted by the Lord in response to their solemn pledge (v. 2); now they were ready to rebel again.
21:5 we detest this miserable food! The people's impatience (v. 4) led them to blaspheme God, to reject his servant Moses and to despise the bread from heaven. This is the most bitter of their several attacks on the manna (see note on 11:7). Just as Moses' attack on the rock was more than it appeared to be (see note on 20:11), so the people's contempt for the heavenly bread was more serious than one might think. Rejecting the heavenly manna was tantamount to

spurning God's grace (cf. Jn 6:32–35,48–51,58).
21:8–9 In response to the people's confession of sin (v. 7), God directed Moses to make an image of a snake and put it on a pole, so that anyone who had been bitten could look at it and live. See the typological use of this incident in Jn 3:14–15.
21:10–13 The people skirt Edom and make their way to the Arnon, the wadi that serves as the border between Moab and the region of the Amorites and that flows west into the midpoint of the Dead Sea.
21:14 Book of the Wars of the LORD. Mentioned only here in the OT. This is not in existence today; it was presumably an ancient collection of songs of war in praise of God (see note on 10:3 for music in war). Cf. the "Book of Jashar" (Jos 10:13; 2Sa 1:18).
21:16 I will give them water. The quest for water had been a constant problem during the desert experience (see ch. 20; Ex 17).
21:17–18 The "song of the well" may also come from the Book of the Wars of the Lord (v. 14).

Defeat of Sihon and Og

[21]Israel sent messengers[h] to say to Sihon[i] king of the Amorites:[j]

[22]"Let us pass through your country. We will not turn aside into any field or vineyard, or drink water from any well. We will travel along the king's highway until we have passed through your territory.[k]"

[23]But Sihon would not let Israel pass through his territory.[l] He mustered his entire army and marched out into the desert against Israel. When he reached Jahaz,[m] he fought with Israel.[n] [24]Israel, however, put him to the sword[o] and took over his land[p] from the Arnon to the Jabbok,[q] but only as far as the Ammonites,[r] because their border was fortified. [25]Israel captured all the cities of the Amorites[s] and occupied them,[t] including Heshbon[u] and all its surrounding settlements. [26]Heshbon was the city of Sihon[v] king of the Amorites,[w] who had fought against the former king of Moab[x] and had taken from him all his land as far as the Arnon.[y]

[27]That is why the poets say:

"Come to Heshbon and let it be rebuilt;
let Sihon's city be restored.

[28]"Fire went out from Heshbon,
a blaze from the city of Sihon.[z]
It consumed[a] Ar[b] of Moab,
the citizens of Arnon's heights.[c]
[29]Woe to you, O Moab![d]
You are destroyed, O people of
Chemosh![e]
He has given up his sons as fugitives[f]
and his daughters as captives[g]
to Sihon king of the Amorites.

[30]"But we have overthrown them;
Heshbon is destroyed all the way to
Dibon.[h]
We have demolished them as far as
Nophah,

which extends to Medeba.[i]"

[31]So Israel settled in the land of the Amorites.[j]

[32]After Moses had sent spies[k] to Jazer,[l] the Israelites captured its surrounding settlements and drove out the Amorites who were there. [33]Then they turned and went up along the road toward Bashan,[m, n] and Og king of Bashan and his whole army marched out to meet them in battle at Edrei.[o]

[34]The LORD said to Moses, "Do not be afraid of him, for I have handed him over to you, with his whole army and his land. Do to him what you did to Sihon king of the Amorites, who reigned in Heshbon.[p]"

[35]So they struck him down, together with his sons and his whole army, leaving them no survivors.[q] And they took possession of his land.[r]

Balak Summons Balaam

22 Then the Israelites traveled to the plains of Moab[s] and camped along the Jordan[t] across from Jericho.[w, u]

[2]Now Balak son of Zippor[v] saw all that Israel had done to the Amorites, [3]and Moab was terrified because there were so many people. Indeed, Moab was filled with dread[w] because of the Israelites.

[4]The Moabites[x] said to the elders of Midian,[y] "This horde is going to lick up everything[z] around us, as an ox licks up the grass of the field.[a]"

21:21 *h*S Ge 32:3
*i*Nu 32:33;
Dt 1:4; Jos 2:10;
12:2,4; 13:10;
Jdg 11:19-21;
1Ki 4:19;
Ne 9:22;
Ps 135:11;
136:19; Jer 48:45
*j*S Ex 23:23
21:22
*k*S Nu 20:17
21:23 *l*Nu 20:21
*m*Dt 2:32;
Jos 13:18; 21:36;
Jdg 11:20;
Isa 15:4;
Jer 48:21,34
*n*Nu 20:18
21:24 *o*Dt 2:33;
3:3; 29:7;
Ps 135:10-11;
Am 2:9 *p*ver 35;
Dt 3:4
*q*S Ge 32:22;
Nu 32:33;
Jdg 11:13,22
*r*S Ge 19:38;
Dt 2:37;
Jos 13:10
21:25
*s*Nu 13:29;
Jdg 10:11;
Am 2:10
*t*Jdg 11:26 *u*ver
30; Nu 32:3;
Dt 1:4; 29:7;
Jos 9:10; 12:2;
Isa 15:4; 16:8;
Jer 48:2,34
21:26 *v*ver 21;
Dt 29:7;
Ps 135:11
*w*Nu 13:29 *x*ver
11 *y*ver 13
21:28 *z*Jer 48:45
*a*S Nu 11:1 *b*S ver
15 *c*Nu 22:41;
Dt 12:2;
Jos 13:17;
Isa 15:2; Jer 19:5
21:29
*d*Nu 24:17;
2Sa 8:2;
1Ch 18:2;
Ps 60:8;
Isa 25:10;
*e*Jdg 10:6; 11:24;
Ru 1:15;
1Ki 11:7,33;
2Ki 23:13;
Jer 48:7,46
*f*Isa 15:5
*g*Isa 16:2
21:30 *h*Nu 32:3;
Jos 13:9,17;
Ne 11:25;
Isa 15:2;
Jer 48:18,22

*i*Jos 13:16;

1Ch 19:7 21:31 *j*Nu 13:29 21:32 *k*Jos 2:1; 6:22; 7:2;
Jdg 18:2; 2Sa 10:3; 1Ch 19:3 *l*Nu 32:1,3,35; Jos 13:25;
2Sa 24:5; 1Ch 6:81; Isa 16:8; Jer 48:32 21:33 *m*Nu 32:33;
Dt 3:3; 31:4; Jos 2:10; 12:4; 13:30; 1Ki 4:19; Ne 9:22;
Ps 135:11; 136:20 *n*Dt 3:4; 32:14; Jos 9:10; 1Ki 4:13
*o*Dt 1:4; 3:1,10; Jos 12:4; 13:12,31; 19:37 21:34 *p*Dt 3:2
21:35 *q*Jos 9:10 *r*S ver 24 22:1 *s*S Nu 21:11 *t*S Nu 13:29;
S Jos 2:7 *u*Nu 31:12; 33:48; Dt 32:49; Jos 2:1 22:2
*v*Nu 23:1-3; Jos 24:9; Jdg 11:25; Mic 6:5; Rev 2:14 22:3
*w*S Ex 15:15 22:4 *x*S Ge 19:37 *y*S Ge 25:2 *z*Nu 32:17,18,29
*a*Job 5:25; Ps 72:16

w *l* Hebrew *Jordan of Jericho*; possibly an ancient name
for the Jordan River

21:21–26 As with Edom (20:14–19), Israel requested freedom to pass through the land of the Amorites. When Sihon, their king, tried to meet Israel with a show of force, he suffered an overwhelming defeat. The land of the Amorites was in Transjordan, extending from the Arnon River (at the midpoint of the Dead Sea) to the Jabbok River (v. 24), which flows into the Jordan some 24 miles north of the Dead Sea. **21:27–30** This third ancient poem in ch. 21 was an Amorite taunt song about their earlier victory over Moab (v. 29). Perhaps the "song of Heshbon" was also preserved in the Book of the Wars of the Lord (v. 14). **21:33** *Bashan.* The region northeast of the Sea of Galilee. **21:35** *struck him down.* By defeating Og, Israel now controlled Transjordan from Moab to the heights of Bashan in the vicinity of Mount Hermon. The victory over Sihon and Og became a subject of song (Ps 135:11; 136:19–20), and is

a regular part of the commemoration of the works of the Lord in the Passover celebration.

22:1 *plains of Moab.* Israel now marched back to their staging area east of the Jordan and just north of the Dead Sea. From this point they would launch their attack on Canaan, beginning with the ancient city of Jericho. Moab did not trust Israel's intentions, however. Moab's fear leads to a remarkable interval in the story of Israel: the account of Balak and Balaam (chs. 22–24).

22:3 *Moab was terrified.* Balak king of Moab did not know that Israel had no plans against him.

22:4 *said to the elders of Midian.* Balak made an alliance with the Midianites to oppose Israel (see v. 7). *as an ox licks up the grass of the field.* A proverbial simile particularly fitting for a pastoral people.

So Balak son of Zippor, who was king of Moab at that time, [5]sent messengers to summon Balaam son of Beor, [b] who was at Pethor, near the River, [x][c] in his native land. Balak said:

"A people has come out of Egypt; [d] they cover the face of the land and have settled next to me. [6]Now come and put a curse [e] on these people, because they are too powerful for me. Perhaps then I will be able to defeat them and drive them out of the country. [f] For I know that those you bless are blessed, and those you curse are cursed."

[7]The elders of Moab and Midian left, taking with them the fee for divination. [g] When they came to Balaam, they told him what Balak had said.

[8]"Spend the night here," Balaam said to them, "and I will bring you back the answer the LORD gives me. [h]" So the Moabite princes stayed with him.

[9]God came to Balaam [i] and asked, [j] "Who are these men with you?"

[10]Balaam said to God, "Balak son of Zippor, king of Moab, sent me this message: [11]'A people that has come out of Egypt covers the face of the land. Now come and put a curse on them for me. Perhaps then I will be able to fight them and drive them away.' "

[12]But God said to Balaam, "Do not go with them. You must not put a curse on those people, because they are blessed. [k]"

[13]The next morning Balaam got up and said to Balak's princes, "Go back to your own country, for the LORD has refused to let me go with you."

[14]So the Moabite princes returned to Balak and said, "Balaam refused to come with us."

[15]Then Balak sent other princes, more numerous and more distinguished than the first. [16]They came to Balaam and said:

"This is what Balak son of Zippor says: Do not let anything keep you from coming to me, [17]because I will reward you handsomely [l] and do whatever you say. Come and put a curse [m] on these people for me."

[18]But Balaam answered them, "Even if Balak gave me his palace filled with silver and gold, I could not do anything great or small to go beyond the command of the LORD my God. [n] [19]Now stay here tonight as the others did, and I will find out what else the LORD will tell me. [o]"

[20]That night God came to Balaam [p] and said, "Since these men have come to summon you, go with them, but do only what I tell you." [q]

Balaam's Donkey

[21]Balaam got up in the morning, saddled his donkey and went with the princes of Moab. [22]But God was very angry [r] when he went, and the angel of the LORD [s] stood in the road to oppose him. Balaam was riding on his donkey, and his two servants were with him. [23]When the donkey saw the angel of the LORD standing in the road with a drawn sword [t] in his hand, she turned off the road into a field. Balaam beat her [u] to get her back on the road. [24]Then the angel of the LORD stood in a narrow path between two vineyards, with walls on both sides. [25]When the donkey saw the angel of the LORD, she pressed

Cross references

22:5 [b]ver 7; Nu 24:25; 31:8, 16; Dt 23:4; Jos 13:22; Ne 13:2; Mic 6:5; S 2Pe 2:15 [c]S Ge 2:14 [d]S Ex 13:3
22:6 [e]ver 12,17; Nu 23:7,11,13; 24:9,10 [f]ver 11
22:7 [g]S Ge 30:27
22:8 [h]ver 19
22:9 [i]S Ge 20:3 [j]ver 20; Nu 23:5; 24:4,16
22:12 [k]S Ge 12:2
22:17 [l]ver 37; Nu 24:11 [m]S ver 6
22:18 [n]ver 38; Nu 23:12,26; 24:13; 1Ki 22:14; 2Ch 18:13; Jer 42:4
22:19 [o]ver 8
22:20 [p]S Ge 20:3 [q]ver 35,38; Nu 23:5,12,16, 26; 24:13; 2Ch 18:13
22:22 [r]S Ex 4:14 [s]S Ge 16:7; Jdg 13:3,6,13
22:23 [t]Jos 5:13 [u]ver 25,27

[x]5 That is, the Euphrates

22:5 *summon Balaam son of Beor.* Since Balak believed that there was no military way to withstand Israel, he sought to oppose them through pagan divination (vv. 6–7), sending for a diviner with an international reputation. (One of Balaam's non-Biblical prophecies is preserved in an Aramaic text from Deir Alla in the Jordan Valley dating to c. 700 B.C.)
22:8 *the answer the LORD gives me.* The language here and in v. 18 ("the LORD my God") has led some to believe that Balaam was a believer in Yahweh ("the LORD"), God of Israel. Based on the subsequent narrative, however, it seems best to take Balaam's words as claiming to be the spokesman for any god. Balaam is universally condemned in Scripture for moral, ethical and religious faults (see 31:7–8,15–16; Dt 23:3–6; Jos 13:22; 24:9–10; Ne 13:1–3; Mic 6:5; 2Pe 2:15–16; Jude 11; Rev 2:14).
22:9 *God came to Balaam.* The author shows his aversion to the pagan prophet Balaam by using "God" instead of "the LORD" (Yahweh), as Balaam does (e.g., in v. 8). By this subtle device, the narrator distances himself from Balaam's outrageous claims. That God spoke to Balaam is not to be denied,

but Balaam did not yet realize that the God of Israel was unlike the supposed deities that he usually schemed against.
22:12 *they are blessed.* Israel was under the Lord's blessing promised to Abraham (see note on Ge 12:2–3).
22:20 *go with them.* There appears to be a contradiction between the permission God grants Balaam here and the prohibition he had given earlier (v. 12), and then the anger the Lord displayed against Balaam on his journey (v. 22). The difficulty is best understood as lying in the contrary character of Balaam. God had forbidden him to go to curse Israel. He then allowed Balaam to go, but only if he would follow the Lord's direction. But Balaam's real intentions were known to the Lord, and so with severe displeasure he confronted the pagan prophet.
22:23 *the donkey saw the angel of the LORD.* The internationally known seer is blind to spiritual reality, but his proverbially dumb beast is able to see the angel of the Lord on the path. As a pagan prophet, Balaam was a specialist in animal divination, but his animal saw what he was blind to observe.

close to the wall, crushing Balaam's foot against it. So he beat her again.

²⁶Then the angel of the LORD moved on ahead and stood in a narrow place where there was no room to turn, either to the right or to the left. ²⁷When the donkey saw the angel of the LORD, she lay down under Balaam, and he was angry ᵛ and beat her with his staff. ²⁸Then the LORD opened the donkey's mouth, ʷ and she said to Balaam, "What have I done to you to make you beat me these three times? ˣ "

²⁹Balaam answered the donkey, "You have made a fool of me! If I had a sword in my hand, I would kill you right now. ʸ "

³⁰The donkey said to Balaam, "Am I not your own donkey, which you have always ridden, to this day? Have I been in the habit of doing this to you?"

"No," he said.

³¹Then the LORD opened Balaam's eyes, ᶻ and he saw the angel of the LORD standing in the road with his sword drawn. So he bowed low and fell facedown.

³²The angel of the LORD asked him, "Why have you beaten your donkey these three times? I have come here to oppose you because your path is a reckless one before me. ᵛ ³³The donkey saw me and turned away from me these three times. If she had not turned away, I would certainly have killed you by now, ᵃ but I would have spared her."

³⁴Balaam said to the angel of the LORD, "I have sinned. ᵇ I did not realize you were standing in the road to oppose me. Now if you are displeased, I will go back."

³⁵The angel of the LORD said to Balaam, "Go with the men, but speak only what I tell you." So Balaam went with the princes of Balak.

³⁶When Balak ᶜ heard that Balaam was coming, he went out to meet him at the

22:27 ᵛNu 11:1;
Jas 1:19
22:28 ʷ2Pe 2:16
ˣver 32
22:29 ʸver 33;
Dt 25:4;
Pr 12:10;
27:23-27;
Mt 15:19
22:31 ᶻGe 21:19
22:33 ᵃS ver 29
22:34 ᵇGe 39:9;
Nu 14:40;
1Sa 15:24,30;
2Sa 12:13; 24:10;
Job 33:27;
Ps 51:4
22:36 ᶜver 2

ᵈS Nu 21:13
22:38 ᵉNu 23:5,
16,26
22:40 ᶠNu 23:1,
14,29; Eze 45:23
22:41
ᵍS Nu 21:28
ʰNu 23:13
23:1 ⁱS Nu 22:40
23:2 ʲver 14,30
23:3 ᵏver 15
23:4 ˡver 16
23:5 ᵐS Ex 4:12;
Isa 59:21
ⁿS Ex 4:15
ᵒS Nu 22:20
23:6 ᵖver 17
23:7 ᵠNu 22:5;
Jos 24:9 ʳver 18;
Nu 24:3,21;
2Sa 23:1 ˢ2Ki 5:1

Moabite town on the Arnon ᵈ border, at the edge of his territory. ³⁷Balak said to Balaam, "Did I not send you an urgent summons? Why didn't you come to me? Am I really not able to reward you?"

³⁸"Well, I have come to you now," Balaam replied. "But can I say just anything? I must speak only what God puts in my mouth." ᵉ

³⁹Then Balaam went with Balak to Kiriath Huzoth. ⁴⁰Balak sacrificed cattle and sheep, ᶠ and gave some to Balaam and the princes who were with him. ⁴¹The next morning Balak took Balaam up to Bamoth Baal, ᵍ and from there he saw part of the people. ʰ

Balaam's First Oracle

23 Balaam said, "Build me seven altars here, and prepare seven bulls and seven rams ⁱ for me." ²Balak did as Balaam said, and the two of them offered a bull and a ram on each altar. ʲ

³Then Balaam said to Balak, "Stay here beside your offering while I go aside. Perhaps the LORD will come to meet with me. ᵏ Whatever he reveals to me I will tell you." Then he went off to a barren height.

⁴God met with him, ˡ and Balaam said, "I have prepared seven altars, and on each altar I have offered a bull and a ram."

⁵The LORD put a message in Balaam's mouth ᵐ ⁿ and said, "Go back to Balak and give him this message." ᵒ

⁶So he went back to him and found him standing beside his offering, with all the princes of Moab. ᵖ ⁷Then Balaam ᵠ uttered his oracle: ʳ

"Balak brought me from Aram, ˢ

ᵛ32 The meaning of the Hebrew for this clause is uncertain.

22:29 *If I had a sword.* A ridiculous picture of the hapless Balaam. A sword was nearby (see vv. 23,31–33), but its victim was not going to be the donkey.

22:31 *Then the LORD opened Balaam's eyes.* The language follows the same structure as the opening words of v. 28. In some ways, the opening of the eyes of the pagan prophet to see the reality of the angel was the greater miracle.

22:35 *speak only what I tell you.* The one great gain was that Balaam was now more aware of the seriousness of the task before him; he would not be able to change the word the Lord would give him (see 23:12,20,26).

22:37 *Did I not send you an urgent summons?* The comic element of the story is seen not only in the hapless Balaam but also in the frustrated Balak (see 23:11,25; 24:10).

22:40 *Balak sacrificed cattle and sheep.* Not sacrifices to the Lord. The pieces given to Balaam would have included the livers, for, as a pagan diviner, Balaam was a specialist in liver divination. Balaam subsequently gave up his acts of sorcery as the power of the Lord's word came upon him

(24:1).

23:1 *seven altars . . . seven bulls and seven rams.* These sacrifices were prepared as a part of Balaam's pagan actions. The number seven (signifying completeness) was held in high regard among Semitic peoples in general; the many animals would provide abundant liver and organ materials for the diviner from the east.

23:2 *Balak did as Balaam said.* Balaam is in charge; Balak is now his subordinate.

23:7–24:24 There are seven poetic oracles here: The first four are longer, have introductory narrative bridges and are written in exquisite poetry (23:7–10; 23:18–24; 24:3–9; 24:15–19). The last three are brief, are much more difficult to understand, and follow one another in a staccato pattern (24:20,21,22,23–24).

23:7 *oracle.* Hebrew *mashal,* usually translated "proverb," but here "oracle" is appropriate. By this word the distinctive nature of Balaam's prophecies is established; none of the prophecies of Israel's true prophets is described by this term.

the king of Moab from the eastern
        mountains. *t*
'Come,' he said, 'curse Jacob for me;
        come, denounce Israel.' *u*
[8]How can I curse
        those whom God has not cursed? *v*
How can I denounce
        those whom the LORD has not
                denounced? *w*
[9]From the rocky peaks I see them,
        from the heights I view them. *x*
I see a people who live apart
        and do not consider themselves one
                of the nations. *y*
[10]Who can count the dust of Jacob *z*
        or number the fourth part of Israel?
Let me die the death of the righteous, *a*
        and may my end be like theirs! *b* ”

[11]Balak said to Balaam, "What have you
done to me? I brought you to curse my
enemies, *c* but you have done nothing but
bless them!" *d*

[12]He answered, "Must I not speak what
the LORD puts in my mouth?" *e*

Balaam's Second Oracle

[13]Then Balak said to him, "Come with
me to another place *f* where you can see
them; you will see only a part but not all of
them. *g* And from there, curse them for
me." *h* [14]So he took him to the field of
Zophim on the top of Pisgah, *i* and there
he built seven altars and offered a bull and
a ram on each altar. *j*

[15]Balaam said to Balak, "Stay here beside your offering while I meet with him
over there."

[16]The LORD met with Balaam and put a
message in his mouth *k* and said, "Go back
to Balak and give him this message."

[17]So he went to him and found him
standing beside his offering, with the
princes of Moab. *l* Balak asked him,
"What did the LORD say?"

[18]Then he uttered his oracle: *m*

"Arise, Balak, and listen;
        hear me, son of Zippor. *n*
[19]God is not a man, *o* that he should lie, *p*
        nor a son of man, that he should
                change his mind. *q*
Does he speak and then not act?
        Does he promise *r* and not fulfill?
[20]I have received a command to bless; *s*
        he has blessed, *t* and I cannot change
                it. *u*

[21]"No misfortune is seen in Jacob, *v*
        no misery observed in Israel. *z w*
The LORD their God is with them; *x*
        the shout of the King *y* is among
                them.
[22]God brought them out of Egypt; *z*
        they have the strength of a wild ox. *a*
[23]There is no sorcery against Jacob,
        no divination *b* against Israel.
It will now be said of Jacob
        and of Israel, 'See what God has
                done!'
[24]The people rise like a lioness; *c*
        they rouse themselves like a lion *d*
that does not rest till he devours his
                prey
        and drinks the blood *e* of his
                victims."

[25]Then Balak said to Balaam, "Neither
curse them at all nor bless them at all!"

[26]Balaam answered, "Did I not tell you I
must do whatever the LORD says?" *f*

Balaam's Third Oracle

[27]Then Balak said to Balaam, "Come, let
me take you to another place. *g* Perhaps it
will please God to let you curse them for
me *h* from there." [28]And Balak took Balaam to the top of Peor, *i* overlooking the
wasteland.

23:7 *t*S Ge 24:10
*u*S Nu 22:6;
Ne 13:2
23:8 *v*Nu 22:12
*w*ver 20;
Isa 43:13
23:9 *x*Nu 22:41
*y*S Ex 33:16;
S Dt 32:8
23:10
*z*S Ge 13:16
*a*Ps 16:3; 116:15;
Isa 57:1
*b*Ps 37:37
23:11 *c*S Nu 22:6
*d*Nu 24:10;
Jos 24:10;
Ne 13:2
23:12
*e*S Nu 22:18,20
23:13 *f*ver 27
*g*Nu 22:41
*h*S Nu 22:6
23:14
*i*S Nu 21:20;
27:12 /S ver 2
23:16
*k*S Ex 4:15;
S Nu 22:38
23:17 *l*ver 6
23:18 *m*S ver 7

*n*Nu 22:2
23:19 *o*Job 9:32;
Isa 55:9; Hos 11:9
*p*S Nu 11:23
*q*1Sa 15:29;
Job 12:13; 36:5;
Ps 33:11; 89:34;
102:27; 110:4;
Jer 4:28; 7:16;
Mal 3:6; Tit 1:2;
Heb 6:18; 7:21;
Jas 1:17
*r*2Sa 7:25;
Ps 119:38
23:20 *s*ver 5,16;
Nu 24:1
*t*Ge 22:17;
Nu 22:12 *u*S ver
8; S Job 9:12
23:21 *v*Ps 32:2,5;
85:2; Ro 4:7-8
*w*Isa 33:24; 40:2;
Jer 50:20
*x*S Ge 26:3;
Ex 29:45,46;
Dt 4:7;
Ps 34:17-18;
145:18; Zec 2:10
*y*Dt 32:15; 33:5;
Ps 89:15-18;
Isa 44:2
23:22 *z*Nu 24:8;
Jos 2:10; 9:9
*a*Dt 33:17;
Job 39:9;
Ps 22:21; 29:6;
92:10; Isa 34:7
23:23 *b*ver 3;
S Ge 30:27;
Nu 24:1

23:24 *c*Nu 24:9; Eze 19:2; Na 2:11 *d*S Ge 49:9 *e*Isa 49:26
23:26 *f*S Nu 22:18,20 **23:27** *g*ver 13 *h*Nu 24:10 **23:28**
*i*Nu 25:3,18; 31:16; Dt 3:29; 4:3; Jos 22:17; Ps 106:28;
Hos 9:10

*z*21 Or *He has not looked on Jacob's offenses / or on
the wrongs found in Israel.*

23:8 *How can I curse those whom God has not cursed?*
That which Balaam had been hired to do he was unable to
do. God kept him from pronouncing a curse on his people,
who were unlike the nations of the world (v. 9).
23:10 *Let me die the death of the righteous.* A wish not
granted (see 31:8,16). *may my end be like theirs!* He who
had come to curse desired to share in Israel's blessing.
23:13 *a part but not all.* Balak attempted to reduce Israel's
power by selecting a point where their immense numbers
would be obscured. Unfortunately for Balak, the oracle that
followed (vv. 18–24) exceeded the first in its blessing on
Israel.
23:19 *God is not a man, that he should lie.* These sublime
words describe the immutability of the Lord and the integrity
of his word. Balaam is a foil for God—constantly shifting,

prevaricating, equivocating, changing—a prime example of
the distinction between God and man.
23:21 *the shout of the King is among them.* That the first
explicit declaration of the Lord's kingship in the Pentateuch
was made by Balaam is a suitable improbability. Because God
is King (Sovereign), he was able to use Balaam for his own
ends—to bless his people in a new and wonderful manner.
23:22 *wild ox.* Or "aurochs" or "oryx," a traditional image
of power in the ancient Near East (see also 24:8).
23:23 *no sorcery against Jacob.* Balaam speaks from his
frightful experience. He had no means in his bag of tricks to
withstand God's blessing of Israel.
23:24 *like a lioness.* Israel was about to arise and devour its
foes, like a lioness on the hunt (see 24:9; Ge 49:9).

²⁹Balaam said, "Build me seven altars here, and prepare seven bulls and seven rams for me." ³⁰Balak did as Balaam had said, and offered a bull and a ram on each altar.^j

24 Now when Balaam saw that it pleased the LORD to bless Israel,^k he did not resort to sorcery^l as at other times, but turned his face toward the desert.^m ²When Balaam looked out and saw Israel encamped tribe by tribe, the Spirit of God came upon himⁿ ³and he uttered his oracle:

"The oracle of Balaam son of Beor,
    the oracle of one whose eye sees
        clearly,^o
⁴the oracle of one who hears the words
        of God,^p
    who sees a vision from the
        Almighty,^{a q}
    who falls prostrate, and whose eyes
        are opened:

⁵"How beautiful are your tents,^r
        O Jacob,
    your dwelling places, O Israel!

⁶"Like valleys they spread out,
    like gardens beside a river,^s
like aloes^t planted by the LORD,
    like cedars beside the waters.^u
⁷Water will flow from their buckets;
    their seed will have abundant water.

"Their king will be greater than Agag;^v
    their kingdom will be exalted.^w

⁸"God brought them out of Egypt;
    they have the strength of a wild ox.
They devour hostile nations
    and break their bones in pieces;^x
    with their arrows they pierce them.^y
⁹Like a lion they crouch and lie down,

like a lioness^z—who dares to rouse
        them?

"May those who bless you be blessed^a
    and those who curse you be
        cursed!"^b

¹⁰Then Balak's anger burned^c against Balaam. He struck his hands together^d and said to him, "I summoned you to curse my enemies,^e but you have blessed them^f these three times.^g ¹¹Now leave at once and go home!^h I said I would reward you handsomely,ⁱ but the LORD has kept you from being rewarded."

¹²Balaam answered Balak, "Did I not tell the messengers you sent me,^j ¹³'Even if Balak gave me his palace filled with silver and gold, I could not do anything of my own accord, good or bad, to go beyond the command of the LORD^k—and I must say only what the LORD says'? ^l ¹⁴Now I am going back to my people, but come, let me warn you of what this people will do to your people in days to come." ^m

Balaam's Fourth Oracle

¹⁵Then he uttered his oracle:

"The oracle of Balaam son of Beor,
    the oracle of one whose eye sees
        clearly,
¹⁶the oracle of one who hears the wordsⁿ
        of God,
    who has knowledge from the Most
        High,^o
    who sees a vision from the Almighty,
    who falls prostrate, and whose eyes
        are opened:

¹⁷"I see him, but not now;
    I behold him, but not near.^p

23:30 /S ver 2
24:1 ^kS Nu 23:20
/S Nu 23:23
^mNu 23:28
24:2
ⁿS Nu 11:25,26
24:3 over 15
24:4 ^pS Nu 22:9
^qS Ge 15:1
24:5 ^rJer 4:20;
30:18; Mal 2:12
^tPs 45:8; SS 4:14
24:6 ^sS Ge 2:10
^uJob 29:19;
Ps 1:3; 104:16;
Eze 31:5
24:7
^vS Ex 17:8-16,14
^wDt 28:1;
2Sa 5:12;
1Ch 14:2;
Ps 89:27;
145:11-13
24:8 ^xS Ex 15:6;
Jer 50:17
^y2Sa 18:14;
Ps 45:5

24:9 ^zS Nu 23:24
^aS Ge 12:2
^bS Ge 12:3
24:10 ^cS Ex 4:14
^dJob 27:23;
34:37; La 2:15;
Eze 21:14; 22:13;
25:6 ^eS Nu 22:6
/S Nu 23:11;
S Dt 23:5 ^gver
3-9; Nu 23:7-10,
18-24
24:11 ^hver 14,25
/S Nu 22:17
24:12 /Nu 22:18
24:13
^kS Nu 22:18
/S Nu 22:20
24:14
^mS Ge 49:1;
Nu 31:8,16;
Mic 6:5
24:16 ⁿS Nu 22:9
^oGe 14:18;
Isa 14:14
24:17 ^pRev 1:7

a4 Hebrew *Shaddai*; also in verse 16

24:1 *sorcery as at other times.* Balaam's magic and sorcery are identified here (see notes on 22:40; 23:1).

24:2 *the Spirit of God came upon him.* Not to be confused with the filling of the Spirit (Ac 2:1-4), or with the anointing of the Spirit (Isa 61:1). This unexpected language prepares the reader for the heightened revelation that is about to come from the unwitting messenger.

24:3-4 The extensive introduction of this oracle describes Balaam's experience in the Lord's presence. Now Balaam's eyes were opened (see note on 22:31).

24:6-7 Balaam speaks here in general, but luxuriant, terms of the blessings that will come to the Israelites as they settle in their new land. The lushness of their blessing from the Lord is reminiscent of Eden.

24:7 *greater than Agag.* Possibly a specific future prophecy concerning the opponent of King Saul (1Sa 15:32-33)—setting the stage for the even more remarkable words of the fourth oracle (vv. 15-19). But it may be that Agag was a common name among Amalekite kings and that the allusion here is to the Amalekites who attacked Israel when she came out of Egypt (see Ex 17:8-13) and again when she first

approached Canaan (see 14:45).

24:8 *God brought them out of Egypt.* These central words about Israel's salvation are recited by one who was a hostile outsider (see note on 25:1).

24:9 *May those who bless you be blessed . . . cursed!* The theology of blessing and cursing in the promises made to Abraham (Ge 12:2-3) is now a part of this oracle of blessing. Perhaps here Balaam was reasserting his desire to be a part of Israel's blessing (see note on 23:10).

24:11 *the LORD has kept you from being rewarded.* In his disgust with Balaam's failure to curse Israel, Balak now dismisses him without pay—the ultimate insult to his greed (see 2Pe 2:15).

24:14 *in days to come.* The distant (Messianic) future is usually indicated by this expression (see, e.g., Jer 48:47 and note).

24:15-16 As in the third oracle (see vv. 3-4), the introduction to the fourth oracle is lengthy, helping to prepare the reader for the startling words of the prophecy.

24:17 *star . . . scepter.* Perhaps fulfilled initially in David, but ultimately in the coming Messianic ruler. Israel's future

A star will come out of Jacob; [q]
  a scepter will rise out of Israel. [r]
He will crush the foreheads of Moab, [s]
  the skulls[b] [t] of[c] all the sons of
  Sheth. [d]
[18]Edom [u] will be conquered;
  Seir, [v] his enemy, will be
  conquered, [w]
  but Israel [x] will grow strong.
[19]A ruler will come out of Jacob [y]
  and destroy the survivors of the city."

Balaam's Final Oracles

[20]Then Balaam saw Amalek [z] and uttered his oracle:

"Amalek was first among the nations,
  but he will come to ruin at last." [a]

[21]Then he saw the Kenites [b] and uttered his oracle:

"Your dwelling place is secure, [c]
  your nest is set in a rock;
[22]yet you Kenites will be destroyed
  when Asshur [d] takes you captive."

[23]Then he uttered his oracle:

"Ah, who can live when God does
    this? [e]
[24]   Ships will come from the shores of
    Kittim; [e]
they will subdue Asshur [f] and Eber, [g]
  but they too will come to ruin. [h]"

[25]Then Balaam [i] got up and returned home and Balak went his own way.

Moab Seduces Israel

25 While Israel was staying in Shittim, [j] the men began to indulge in

sexual immorality [k] with Moabite [l] women, [m] [2]who invited them to the sacrifices [n] to their gods. [o] The people ate and bowed down before these gods. [3]So Israel joined in worshiping [p] the Baal of Peor. [q] And the LORD's anger burned against them.

[4]The LORD said to Moses, "Take all the leaders [r] of these people, kill them and expose [s] them in broad daylight before the LORD, [t] so that the LORD's fierce anger [u] may turn away from Israel."

[5]So Moses said to Israel's judges, "Each of you must put to death [v] those of your men who have joined in worshiping Baal of Peor." [w]

[6]Then an Israelite man brought to his family a Midianite [x] woman right before the eyes of Moses and the whole assembly of Israel while they were weeping [y] at the entrance to the Tent of Meeting. [7]When Phinehas [z] son of Eleazar, the son of Aaron, the priest, saw this, he left the assembly, took a spear [a] in his hand [8]and followed the Israelite into the tent. He drove the spear through both of them—through the Israelite and into the woman's body. Then the plague against the Israelites was stopped; [b] [9]but those

---

Center column cross-references:

24:17 [q]Mt 2:2
[r]S Ge 49:10
[s]S Ge 19:37;
S Nu 21:29;
S Dt 23:6;
Isa 15:1-16:14
[t]Jer 48:45
24:18 [u]2Sa 8:12;
1Ch 18:11;
Ps 60:8;
Isa 11:14;
Am 9:12
[v]S Ge 14:6;
Dt 1:44; Jos 12:7;
15:10; Jdg 5:4
[w]Ob 1:2
[x]S Ge 9:25
24:19
[y]S Ge 49:10;
Mic 5:2
24:20
[z]S Ge 14:7;
S Ex 17:14
[a]Dt 25:19;
1Sa 15:20;
30:17-20;
2Sa 8:12;
1Ch 18:11
24:21
[b]S Ge 15:19
[c]Ps 37:27;
Pr 1:33;
Isa 32:18;
Eze 34:27
24:22
[d]S Ge 10:22
24:24 [e]S Ge 10:4
[f]ver 22
[g]S Ge 10:21 [h]ver
20
24:25 [i]S Nu 22:5
25:1
[j]S Nu 21:16;
Jos 2:1; Isa 66:11;
Joel 3:18; Mic 6:5

[k]Jer 5:7; 7:9;
9:2; 1Co 10:8;
Rev 2:14
[l]S Ge 19:37
[m]Nu 31:16
25:2 [n]S Ex 32:6
[o]Ex 20:5;
Dt 32:38;
1Co 10:20
25:3 [p]Dt 4:19;
Jdg 2:19; 1Ki 9:9;
Jer 1:16; 44:3
[q]S Nu 23:28
25:4 [r]Nu 7:2;
13:3 [s]2Sa 21:6
[t]Dt 4:3
[u]Ex 32:12;

Dt 13:17; Jos 7:26; 2Ki 23:26; 2Ch 28:11; 29:10; 30:8;
Ezr 10:14; Jer 44:3 **25:5** [v]S Ex 32:27 [w]Hos 9:10 **25:6**
[x]S Ge 25:2 [y]S Nu 14:1; Jdg 2:4; Ru 1:9; 1Sa 11:4; 2Sa 15:30;
Jdg 20:28 [a]Jdg 5:8; 1Sa 13:19,22; 1Ki 18:28; Ps 35:3; 46:9;
Joel 3:10; Mic 4:3 **25:8** [b]Ps 106:30

Footnotes:

[b]17 Samaritan Pentateuch (see also Jer. 48:45); the meaning of the word in the Masoretic Text is uncertain.
[c]17 Or possibly Moab, / batter   [d]17 Or all the noisy boasters   [e]23 Masoretic Text; with a different word division of the Hebrew A people will gather from the north.

Study notes (bottom):

Deliverer will be like a star (cf. Rev 22:16) and scepter in his royalty and will bring victory over the enemies of his people (see v. 19). *Sheth.* Possibly the early inhabitants of Moab known as the Shutu people in ancient Egyptian documents. **24:20** *Amalek was first.* The first to attack Israel and oppose the Lord's purpose with his people (see Ex 17:8-13). **24:21** *Kenites.* The name suggests a tribe of metal workers. In other passages the Kenites are allied with Israel (see, e.g., Jdg 1:16; 4:11; 1Sa 15:6). Since Moses' father-in-law was a Kenite but also associated with Midian (see Ex 2:16), it may be that Balaam's reference is to Midianites (see 22:4,7). *nest.* Hebrew *qen,* a wordplay on the word for Kenites (Hebrew *qeni*). **24:22** *Asshur.* Assyria. **24:24** *Kittim.* Probably ancient Kition in Cyprus. *they will subdue Asshur and Eber, but . . . ruin.* One nation will rise and supplant another, only to face its own doom. By contrast, there is the implied ongoing blessing on Israel, and their sure promise of a future deliverer who will have the final victory (vv. 17-19). **25:1-18** It is not until 31:8,16 that we learn that the principal instigator of Israel's apostasy was Balaam (see notes on 22:5,8). Failing to destroy Israel by pronouncing curses

on her, Balaam seduced Israel by the Canaanite fertility rites of Baal. **25:1** *Shittim.* Another name for the region of Israel's staging for the conquest of Canaan; it was across the Jordan River opposite the ancient city of Jericho (see Jos 2:1). *indulge in sexual immorality.* Israel's engagement in the fertility rites of Baal involved not only the evil of sexual immorality; it was also a breach of covenant with the Lord, a worship of the gods of the land (vv. 2-3) and a foretaste of the people's ruin in the unfolding of their history. **25:4** *kill them and expose them in broad daylight.* The special display of the corpses would warn survivors of the consequences of sin. **25:6** *brought to his family a Midianite woman.* The contempt for the holy things and the word of the Lord shown by Zimri (v. 14) and his lover Cozbi (v. 15) is unimaginable. **25:9** *24,000.* The number of those who died because of the flagrant actions of the people in their worship of Baal exceeded even those who died in the rebellion of Korah and his allies (14,700; see 16:49). Again, the large number of those who died fits well with the immense number of the people stated in the first census (1:46) and the second (26:51).

who died in the plague[c] numbered 24,-000.[d]

[10]The LORD said to Moses, [11]"Phinehas son of Eleazar, the son of Aaron, the priest, has turned my anger away from the Israelites; [e] for he was as zealous as I am for my honor[f] among them, so that in my zeal I did not put an end to them. [12]Therefore tell him I am making my covenant of peace[g] with him. [13]He and his descendants will have a covenant of a lasting priesthood, [h] because he was zealous[i] for the honor[j] of his God and made atonement[k] for the Israelites." [l]

[14]The name of the Israelite who was killed with the Midianite woman[m] was Zimri son of Salu, the leader of a Simeonite family. [n] [15]And the name of the Midianite woman who was put to death was Cozbi[o] daughter of Zur, a tribal chief of a Midianite family.[p]

[16]The LORD said to Moses, [q] [17]"Treat the Midianites[r] as enemies[s] and kill them, [t] [18]because they treated you as enemies when they deceived you in the affair of Peor[u] and their sister Cozbi, the daughter of a Midianite leader, the woman who was killed when the plague came as a result of Peor."

The Second Census

26 After the plague[v] the LORD said to Moses and Eleazar son of Aaron, the priest, [2]"Take a census[w] of the whole Israelite community by families—all those twenty years old or more who are able to serve in the army[x] of Israel." [3]So on the plains of Moab[y] by the Jordan across from Jericho, [f][z] Moses and Eleazar the priest

spoke with them and said, [4]"Take a census of the men twenty years old or more, as the LORD commanded Moses."

These were the Israelites who came out of Egypt: [a]

[5]The descendants of Reuben, [b] the first-born son of Israel, were:

through Hanoch, [c] the Hanochite clan;

through Pallu, [d] the Palluite clan;

[6]through Hezron, [e] the Hezronite clan;

through Carmi, [f] the Carmite clan.

[7]These were the clans of Reuben; those numbered were 43,730.

[8]The son of Pallu was Eliab, [9]and the sons of Eliab[g] were Nemuel, Dathan and Abiram. The same Dathan and Abiram were the community[h] officials who rebelled against Moses and Aaron and were among Korah's followers when they rebelled against the LORD. [i] [10]The earth opened its mouth and swallowed them[j] along with Korah, whose followers died when the fire devoured the 250 men. [k] And they served as a warning sign. [l] [11]The line of Korah, [m] however, did not die out. [n]

[12]The descendants of Simeon by their clans were:

through Nemuel, [o] the Nemuelite clan;

through Jamin, [p] the Jaminite clan;

through Jakin, the Jakinite clan;

[13]through Zerah, [q] the Zerahite clan;

Cross references (center column)

25:9
[c]S Nu 14:37;
1Co 10:8
[d]Nu 31:16
25:11 [e]Ps 106:30
[f]Ex 20:5;
Dt 32:16,21;
Ps 78:58
25:12 [g]Isa 11:9;
54:10; Eze 34:25;
37:26; Mal 2:4,5
25:13 [h]S Ex 29:9
[i]1Ki 19:10;
2Ki 10:16 [j]ver 11
[k]S Ex 29:36;
S Ro 3:25
[l]Ps 106:31;
Jer 33:18
25:14 [m]ver 6
[n]S Nu 1:6
25:15 [o]ver 18
[p]Nu 31:8;
Jos 13:21;
Hab 3:7
25:16 [q]Nu 31:7
25:17 [r]Nu 31:1-3
[s]Ex 23:22;
Jdg 2:16-18;
Ne 9:27; Ps 8:2;
21:8; 74:23
[t]Dt 21:1;
1Sa 17:9,35;
2Ki 9:27; 10:25
25:18
[u]S Nu 23:28
26:1
[v]S Nu 14:37;
25:8
26:2
[w]Ex 30:11-16
[x]S Nu 1:3
26:3 [y]ver 63;
Nu 33:48;
Jos 13:32
[z]Nu 22:1

26:4 [a]S Ex 6:14;
S 13:3
26:5 [b]Nu 1:20
[c]S Ge 46:9
[d]1Ch 5:3
26:6 [e]1Ch 5:3
[f]Ge 46:9
26:9 [g]Nu 16:1
[h]Nu 1:16
[i]S Nu 16:2
26:10
[j]S Ex 15:12
[k]S Nu 16:35
[l]S Ex 3:12;
S Nu 16:38
26:11 [m]Ex 6:24
[n]Nu 16:33;

Dt 5:9; 24:16; 2Ki 14:6; 2Ch 25:4; Eze 18:20 26:12
[o]S Ge 46:10 [p]1Ch 4:24 26:13 [q]S Ge 46:10

[f] 3 Hebrew *Jordan of Jericho*; possibly an ancient name for the Jordan River; also in verse 63

25:11 *He was as zealous as I am for my honor.* Cf. Ex 20:4–6. The zeal of Phinehas for the Lord's honor became the occasion for the Lord's covenanting with him and his descendants as God's true priests (see note on Ge 9:9). This son of Eleazar contrasts with the casual wickedness of his uncles, Nadab and Abihu (see Lev 10:1–3 and notes).

25:17 *Treat the Midianites as enemies.* Because of their active participation in the seduction of the Israelites. Midianites had been in league with Balak from the beginning of the confrontation (see 22:4,7) and became the objects of a holy war (31:1–24).

26:1–51 The first census of those who were mustered for the war of conquest had been taken over 38 years earlier. That first generation of men 20 years old or more had nearly all died. It was now time for the new generation to be numbered and mustered for the campaign that awaited them. The aged Moses was joined in the task this time by his nephew Eleazar; Aaron was dead (see 20:28). In this second census the prominent clans of each tribe are listed. The numbers of most of the tribes increase. Reuben is one of the tribes that shows a decline. It is possible that the slight reduction of the families of Reuben was brought about by the judgment on their members during the rebellion of Korah

and his Reubenite allies (see note on v. 9). In the intervening years the family of Reuben had nearly caught up with its former numbers (see note on v. 14). Note the comparison of the numbers of each tribe from the first census to the second:

Tribe	First Census	Second Census
Reuben	46,500	43,730
Simeon	59,300	22,200
Gad	45,650	40,500
Judah	74,600	76,500
Issachar	54,400	64,300
Zebulun	57,400	60,500
Ephraim	40,500	32,500
Manasseh	32,200	52,700
Benjamin	35,400	45,600
Dan	62,700	64,400
Asher	41,500	53,400
Naphtali	53,400	45,400
Total	603,550	601,730

26:9 *Dathan and Abiram.* The listing of Reuben's families becomes an occasion to remind the reader of the part that certain of their number had in Korah's rebellion (see 16:1; cf. Jude 11).

through Shaul, the Shaulite clan. [14]These were the clans of Simeon;[r] there were 22,200 men.[s]

[15]The descendants of Gad by their clans were:

through Zephon,[t] the Zephonite clan;
through Haggi, the Haggite clan;
through Shuni, the Shunite clan;
[16]through Ozni, the Oznite clan;
through Eri, the Erite clan;
[17]through Arodi,[g] the Arodite clan;
through Areli, the Arelite clan.

[18]These were the clans of Gad;[u] those numbered were 40,500.

[19]Er[v] and Onan[w] were sons of Judah, but they died[x] in Canaan. [20]The descendants of Judah by their clans were:

through Shelah,[y] the Shelanite clan;
through Perez,[z] the Perezite clan;
through Zerah, the Zerahite clan.[a]
[21]The descendants of Perez[b] were:
through Hezron,[c] the Hezronite clan;
through Hamul, the Hamulite clan.

[22]These were the clans of Judah;[d] those numbered were 76,500.

[23]The descendants of Issachar by their clans were:

through Tola,[e] the Tolaite clan;
through Puah, the Puite[h] clan;
[24]through Jashub,[f] the Jashubite clan;
through Shimron, the Shimronite clan.

[25]These were the clans of Issachar;[g] those numbered were 64,300.

[26]The descendants of Zebulun[h] by their clans were:

through Sered, the Seredite clan;
through Elon, the Elonite clan;
through Jahleel, the Jahleelite clan.

[27]These were the clans of Zebulun;[i] those numbered were 60,500.

[28]The descendants of Joseph[j] by their clans through Manasseh and Ephraim[k] were:

[29]The descendants of Manasseh:[l]
through Makir,[m] the Makirite clan

(Makir was the father of Gilead[n]);
through Gilead, the Gileadite clan.

[30]These were the descendants of Gilead:[o]

through Iezer,[p] the Iezerite clan;
through Helek, the Helekite clan;
[31]through Asriel, the Asrielite clan;
through Shechem, the Shechemite clan;
[32]through Shemida, the Shemidaite clan;
through Hepher, the Hepherite clan.

[33](Zelophehad[q] son of Hepher had no sons;[r] he had only daughters, whose names were Mahlah, Noah, Hoglah, Milcah and Tirzah.)[s]

[34]These were the clans of Manasseh; those numbered were 52,700.[t]

[35]These were the descendants of Ephraim[u] by their clans:

through Shuthelah, the Shuthelahite clan;
through Beker, the Bekerite clan;
through Tahan, the Tahanite clan.
[36]These were the descendants of Shuthelah:
through Eran, the Eranite clan.

[37]These were the clans of Ephraim;[v] those numbered were 32,500.

These were the descendants of Joseph by their clans.

[38]The descendants of Benjamin[w] by their clans were:

through Bela, the Belaite clan;
through Ashbel, the Ashbelite clan;
through Ahiram, the Ahiramite clan;
[39]through Shupham,[i] the Shuphamite clan;
through Hupham, the Huphamite clan.

[40]The descendants of Bela through Ard[x] and Naaman were:

26:14 [r]S Ge 46:10; [s]Nu 1:23
26:15 [t]Ge 46:16
26:18 [u]S Ge 30:11; S Nu 1:25; S Jos 13:24-28
26:19 [v]S Ge 38:3; [w]S Ge 38:4; [x]Ge 38:7
26:20 [y]S Ge 38:5; [z]S Ge 38:29; [a]Jos 7:17
26:21 [b]S Ge 38:29; [c]Ru 4:19; 1Ch 2:9
26:22 [d]Nu 1:27
26:23 [e]S Ge 46:13
26:24 [f]Ge 46:13
26:25 [g]S Ge 30:18
26:26 [h]Nu 1:30
26:27 [i]S Ge 30:20
26:28 [j]Nu 1:32; 36:1 [k]S Ge 41:52
26:29 [l]Nu 1:34; [m]S Ge 50:23

26:30 [n]Jdg 11:1 [o]Nu 27:1; 36:1; 1Ch 7:14, 17 [p]Jos 17:2; Jdg 6:11; 8:2
26:33 [q]Nu 27:1; 36:2; Jos 17:3; 1Ch 7:15 [r]Nu 27:3 [s]Nu 36:11
26:34 [t]Nu 1:35
26:35 [u]Nu 1:32
26:37 [v]S Nu 1:33
26:38 [w]Ge 46:21; Nu 1:36; 1Ch 8:40
26:40 [x]S Ge 46:21

[g]17 Samaritan Pentateuch and Syriac (see also Gen. 46:16); Masoretic Text *Arod*   [h]23 Samaritan Pentateuch, Septuagint, Vulgate and Syriac (see also 1 Chron. 7:1); Masoretic Text *through Puvah, the Punite*   [i]39 A few manuscripts of the Masoretic Text, Samaritan Pentateuch, Vulgate and Syriac (see also Septuagint); most manuscripts of the Masoretic Text *Shephupham*

26:14 *22,200.* The greatest loss was in the tribe of Simeon (down from 59,300). Zimri was from the house of Simeon (25:14). Perhaps most of the 24,000 who died in the plague of that time were from Simeon. The judgment was so recent that the tribe had not had time to recover, as had the tribe of Reuben (see note on vv. 1–51).

26:19 *Er and Onan.* The names of the evil sons of Judah had not been forgotten, but they had no heritage (see Ge 38:1–10).

26:20 *Perez.* The line of David and Jesus would be traced through him (Ru 4:18–22; Mt 1:1–3).

26:29,35 *Manasseh . . . Ephraim.* The order of the tribes is the same as in ch. 1, except for the inversion of Ephraim and Manasseh.

26:33 *Zelophehad . . . daughters.* See 27:1–11; 36.

26:34 *52,700.* The greatest gain was in the tribe of Manasseh (up from 32,200). The reason for this increase is not known.

through Ard,[j] the Ardite clan;
through Naaman, the Naamite clan.

[41]These were the clans of Benjamin;[y] those numbered were 45,600.

[42]These were the descendants of Dan[z] by their clans:[a]

through Shuham,[b] the Shuhamite clan.

These were the clans of Dan: [43]All of them were Shuhamite clans; and those numbered were 64,400.

[44]The descendants of Asher[c] by their clans were:

through Imnah, the Imnite clan;
through Ishvi, the Ishvite clan;
through Beriah, the Beriite clan;
[45]and through the descendants of Beriah:
through Heber, the Heberite clan;
through Malkiel, the Malkielite clan.

[46](Asher had a daughter named Serah.)

[47]These were the clans of Asher;[d] those numbered were 53,400.

[48]The descendants of Naphtali[e] by their clans were:

through Jahzeel, the Jahzeelite clan;
through Guni, the Gunite clan;
[49]through Jezer, the Jezerite clan;
through Shillem, the Shillemite clan.

[50]These were the clans of Naphtali;[f] those numbered were 45,400.[g]

[51]The total number of the men of Israel was 601,730.[h]

[52]The LORD said to Moses, [53]"The land is to be allotted to them as an inheritance based on the number of names.[i] [54]To a larger group give a larger inheritance, and to a smaller group a smaller one; each is to receive its inheritance according to the number[j] of those listed.[k] [55]Be sure that the land is distributed by lot.[l] What each group inherits will be according to the names for its ancestral tribe. [56]Each inheritance is to be distributed by lot among the larger and smaller groups."

[57]These were the Levites[m] who were counted by their clans:

through Gershon, the Gershonite clan;
through Kohath, the Kohathite clan;
through Merari, the Merarite clan.

[58]These also were Levite clans:

the Libnite clan,
the Hebronite clan,
the Mahlite clan,
the Mushite clan,
the Korahite clan.

(Kohath was the forefather of Amram;[n] [59]the name of Amram's wife was Jochebed,[o] a descendant of Levi, who was born to the Levites[k] in Egypt. To Amram she bore Aaron, Moses[p] and their sister[q] Miriam.[r] [60]Aaron was the father of Nadab and Abihu, Eleazar and Ithamar.[s] [61]But Nadab and Abihu[t] died when they made an offering before the LORD with unauthorized fire.)[u]

[62]All the male Levites a month old or more numbered 23,000.[v] They were not counted[w] along with the other Israelites because they received no inheritance[x] among them.[y]

[63]These are the ones counted[z] by Moses and Eleazar the priest when they counted the Israelites on the plains of Moab[a] by the Jordan across from Jericho.[b] [64]Not one of them was among those counted[c] by Moses and Aaron[d] the priest when they counted the Israelites in the Desert of Sinai. [65]For the LORD had told those Israelites they would surely die in the desert,[e] and not one of them was left except Caleb[f] son of Jephunneh and Joshua son of Nun.[g]

Zelophehad's Daughters

27:1–11pp — Nu 36:1–12

27 The daughters of Zelophehad[h] son of Hepher,[i] the son of Gilead,[j] the son of Makir,[k] the son of Manasseh,

---

Cross references (center column):

26:41 [y]Nu 1:37
26:42 [z]Nu 1:38
[a]Jdg 18:19
[b]Ge 46:23
26:44 [c]S Nu 1:40
26:47 [d]Nu 1:41
26:48 [e]S Ge 30:8
26:50 [f]Nu 1:43
[g]Nu 1:42
26:51 [h]S Ex 12:37
26:53 [i]ver 55;
Jos 11:23; 14:1;
Eze 45:8
26:54 [j]Nu 33:54
[k]Nu 35:8
26:55 [l]S Lev 16:8

26:57 [m]S Ge 46:11
26:58 [n]Ex 6:20
26:59 [o]S Ex 2:1
[p]S Ex 6:20
[q]S Ex 2:4
[r]S Ex 15:20
26:60 [s]Ex 6:23
26:61 [t]S Lev 10:1-2
[u]Nu 3:4
26:62 [v]Nu 3:39
[w]Nu 1:47
[x]S Nu 18:23
[y]S Nu 2:33
26:63 [z]S Nu 1:19
[a]S ver 3 [b]Nu 22:1
26:64 [c]S Nu 14:29
[d]Nu 1:44
26:65 [e]Nu 14:28;
1Co 10:5
[f]Nu 13:6
[g]S Nu 11:28
27:1 [h]S Nu 26:33
[i]Jos 17:2,3
[j]S Nu 26:30
[k]S Ge 50:23;
1Ch 2:21

[j]40 Samaritan Pentateuch and Vulgate (see also Septuagint); Masoretic Text does not have *through Ard.*
[k]59 Or *Jochebed, a daughter of Levi, who was born to Levi*

26:46 *daughter named Serah.* The listing of this solitary daughter is striking.

26:51 *601,730.* Despite all that the people had been through during the years of desert experience, their total number was nearly the same as that of those who were first numbered. This remarkable fact is to be regarded as the blessing of the Lord, in fulfillment of his many promises to give numerical strength to the people descended from Abraham through Jacob (see note on Ge 12:2–3). This grand total and its parts are in accord with the general pattern of the numbers in the book (see note on 1:46).

26:53 *allotted ... based on the number.* Larger tribes would receive larger shares, but decisions of place would be made by lot (v. 65).

26:57 *Levites.* As in the first census (ch. 3), the Levites were counted separately.

27:1–11 The daughters of a man who had no son (see 26:33) were concerned about their rights of inheritance and the preservation of their father's name in the land (v. 4). Their action in approaching Moses, Eleazar and the leaders

belonged to the clans of Manasseh son of Joseph. The names of the daughters were Mahlah, Noah, Hoglah, Milcah and Tirzah. They approached [2]the entrance to the Tent of Meeting[l] and stood before Moses,[m] Eleazar the priest, the leaders[n] and the whole assembly, and said, [3]"Our father died in the desert.[o] He was not among Korah's followers, who banded together against the LORD,[p] but he died for his own sin and left no sons.[q] [4]Why should our father's name disappear from his clan because he had no son? Give us property among our father's relatives."

[5]So Moses brought their case[r] before the LORD[s] [6]and the LORD said to him, [7]"What Zelophehad's daughters are saying is right. You must certainly give them property as an inheritance[t] among their father's relatives and turn their father's inheritance over to them.[u]

[8]"Say to the Israelites, 'If a man dies and leaves no son, turn his inheritance over to his daughter. [9]If he has no daughter, give his inheritance to his brothers. [10]If he has no brothers, give his inheritance to his father's brothers. [11]If his father had no brothers, give his inheritance to the nearest relative in his clan, that he may possess it. This is to be a legal requirement[v] for the Israelites, as the LORD commanded Moses.'"

Joshua to Succeed Moses

[12]Then the LORD said to Moses, "Go up this mountain[w] in the Abarim range[x] and see the land[y] I have given the Israelites.[z] [13]After you have seen it, you too will be gathered to your people,[a] as your brother Aaron[b] was, [14]for when the community rebelled at the waters in the Desert of Zin,[c] both of you disobeyed my command

27:2 /Ex 40:2,17;
mS Nu 9:6
nNu 1:16; 31:13;
32:2; 36:1
27:3 oNu 26:65
pNu 16:2
qNu 26:33
27:5 rS Ge 25:22;
SEx 18:19
sS Nu 9:8
27:7 tJob 42:15
uver 8; Jos 17:4
27:11 vNu 35:29
27:12 wNu 23:14
xNu 33:47;
Jer 22:20
yDt 3:23-27;
32:48-52
zS Lev 14:34
27:13 aNu 20:12; 31:2;
Dt 4:22; 31:14;
32:50; 1Ki 2:1
bNu 20:28
27:14 cS Nu 20:1,2-5

dS Nu 20:12
eS Ex 17:7
27:16 fS Nu 16:22;
SJob 21:20
27:17 g1Ki 22:17;
2Ch 18:16;
Eze 34:5;
Zec 10:2;
SMt 9:36
27:18 hS Ge 41:38;
Nu 11:25-29 iver 23; Dt 34:9;
Ac 6:6
27:19 jver 23;
Dt 3:28; 31:14,23;
kDt 31:7
27:20 lJos 1:16,17
27:21 mS Ge 25:22;
Jos 9:14;
Ps 106:13;
Isa 8:19;
Hag 1:13;
Mal 2:7; 3:1
nS Ex 28:30
27:23 oS ver 19
28:2 pLev 23:1-44
qS Lev 3:11
rLev 1:9

to honor me as holy[d] before their eyes." (These were the waters of Meribah[e] Kadesh, in the Desert of Zin.)

[15]Moses said to the LORD, [16]"May the LORD, the God of the spirits of all mankind,[f] appoint a man over this community [17]to go out and come in before them, one who will lead them out and bring them in, so the LORD's people will not be like sheep without a shepherd."[g]

[18]So the LORD said to Moses, "Take Joshua son of Nun, a man in whom is the spirit,[1][h] and lay your hand on him.[i] [19]Have him stand before Eleazar the priest and the entire assembly and commission him[j] in their presence.[k] [20]Give him some of your authority so the whole Israelite community will obey him.[l] [21]He is to stand before Eleazar the priest, who will obtain decisions for him by inquiring[m] of the Urim[n] before the LORD. At his command he and the entire community of the Israelites will go out, and at his command they will come in."

[22]Moses did as the LORD commanded him. He took Joshua and had him stand before Eleazar the priest and the whole assembly. [23]Then he laid his hands on him and commissioned him,[o] as the LORD instructed through Moses.

Daily Offerings

28 The LORD said to Moses, [2]"Give this command to the Israelites and say to them: 'See that you present to me at the appointed time[p] the food[q] for my offerings made by fire, as an aroma pleasing to me.'[r] [3]Say to them: 'This is the offering made by fire that you are to present to the LORD: two lambs a year old without de-

1*18* Or *Spirit*

---

of the nation was unprecedented, an act of courage and conviction.
27:3 *he died for his own sin.* A particular case from among those who died in the desert (see 26:64–65). These pious women had a sound understanding of the nature of the desert experience and a just claim for their family.
27:5 *Moses brought their case before the LORD.* This verse indicates how case law might have operated in Israel. The general laws would be proclaimed. Then legitimate exceptions or special considerations would come to the elders, and perhaps to Moses himself. He then would await a decision from the Lord. In this case, the Lord gave a favorable decision for these women. Ch. 36 provides an appendix to this account.
27:12–23 The juxtaposition of the story of Zelophehad's daughters' request for an inheritance in the land (vv. 1–11) and the Lord's words to Moses about his own exclusion from the land (vv. 12–14) is touching. Provisions are made for exceptions and irregularities in the inheritance laws, but there is no provision for Moses. His sin at the waters of

Meribah at Kadesh (20:1–13) was always before him.
27:16 *appoint a man.* Moses' reaction to this reassertion of his restriction is a prayer for his successor.
27:18 *Take Joshua.* As Moses and Aaron needed to determine the true successor of Aaron before his death (20:22–29), so the true successor of Moses also needed to be established. Joshua and Caleb were the two heroes in the darkest hour of Israel's apostasy (chs. 13–14). It was fitting that the Lord selected one of them (cf. Ex 17:9–14; 24:13; 32:17; 33:11).
27:20 *Give him some of your authority.* The transition from Moses' leadership to that of any successor would be difficult. The change would be smoother by a gradual shift of power while Moses was still alive.
28:1–29:40 These chapters attest to the all-pervasiveness of sacrifice in the life of the people and to the enormity of the work of the priests. Perhaps the reason for these passages at this time is to give continuity to the impending transition from the leadership of Moses to that of Joshua (27:12–23).
28:1–8 See Ex 29:38–41; Lev 1–7 and notes.

fect,[s] as a regular burnt offering each day.[t] 4Prepare one lamb in the morning and the other at twilight,[u] 5together with a grain offering[v] of a tenth of an ephah[m] of fine flour[w] mixed with a quarter of a hin[n] of oil[x] from pressed olives. 6This is the regular burnt offering[y] instituted at Mount Sinai[z] as a pleasing aroma, an offering made to the LORD by fire.[a] 7The accompanying drink offering[b] is to be a quarter of a hin of fermented drink[c] with each lamb. Pour out the drink offering to the LORD at the sanctuary.[d] 8Prepare the second lamb at twilight,[e] along with the same kind of grain offering and drink offering that you prepare in the morning.[f] This is an offering made by fire, an aroma pleasing to the LORD.[g]

Sabbath Offerings

9" 'On the Sabbath[h] day, make an offering of two lambs a year old without defect,[i] together with its drink offering and a grain offering of two-tenths of an ephah[o] of fine flour mixed with oil.[k] 10This is the burnt offering for every Sabbath,[l] in addition to the regular burnt offering[m] and its drink offering.

Monthly Offerings

11" 'On the first of every month,[n] present to the LORD a burnt offering of two young bulls,[o] one ram[p] and seven male lambs a year old, all without defect.[q] 12With each bull there is to be a grain offering[r] of three-tenths of an ephah[p][s] of fine flour mixed with oil; with the ram, a grain offering of two-tenths[t] of an ephah of fine flour mixed with oil; 13and with each lamb, a grain offering[u] of a tenth[v] of an ephah of fine flour mixed with oil. This is for a burnt offering,[w] a pleasing aroma, an offering made to the LORD[x] by fire. 14With each bull there is to be a drink offering[y] of half a hin[q] of wine; with the ram, a third of a hin[r]; and with each lamb, a quarter of a hin. This is the monthly burnt offering to be made at each new moon[z] during the year. 15Besides the regular burnt offering[a] with its drink offering, one male goat[b] is to be presented to the LORD as a sin offering.[c]

28:3 sS Ex 12:5
tEx 29:38;
Am 4:4
28:4 uS Ex 29:39
28:5 vNu 29:6
wLev 6:20
xS Lev 2:1
28:6 yLev 1:3
zEx 19:3
aS Lev 1:9
28:7 bNu 6:15
cS Lev 10:9;
S 23:13
dS Lev 3:7;
Nu 3:28
28:8 eS Ex 29:39
fS Lev 3:7 gver 2;
Lev 1:9
28:9
hS Ex 20:10;
Mt 12:5 iver 3
jS Lev 23:13 kver 5
28:10
lS Lev 23:38 mver 3
28:11
nS Nu 10:10
oS Nu 7:15
pS Nu 5:15
qLev 1:3
28:12
rS Nu 15:6;
S 29:3 sNu 15:9
tver 20
28:13
uS Lev 6:14 vver 21 wS Nu 15:3
xLev 1:9
28:14 yS Nu 15:7
zver 11; 2Ch 2:4;
Ezr 3:5
28:15 aver 3,23, 24 bver 30
cLev 4:3;
Nu 29:16,19

28:16
dS Ex 12:11;
2Ch 30:13; 35:1
28:17
eS Ex 12:19
fS Ex 12:15
28:18
gS Ex 12:16
28:19 hS Lev 1:9
iver 11
28:20
jS Lev 14:10 kver 12
28:21 lver 13
28:22 mLev 4:3;
Ro 8:3
nS Nu 15:28
28:24 oLev 1:9
28:26
pS Ex 34:22
qS Ex 23:16 rver 18
28:27 sver 19
28:28 tver 12
28:29 uver 13
28:30 vver 15

The Passover

28:16–25pp — Ex 12:14–20; Lev 23:4–8; Dt 16:1–8

16" 'On the fourteenth day of the first month the LORD's Passover[d] is to be held. 17On the fifteenth day of this month there is to be a festival; for seven days[e] eat bread made without yeast.[f] 18On the first day hold a sacred assembly and do no regular work.[g] 19Present to the LORD an offering made by fire,[h] a burnt offering of two young bulls, one ram and seven male lambs a year old, all without defect.[i] 20With each bull prepare a grain offering of three-tenths of an ephah[j] of fine flour mixed with oil; with the ram, two-tenths;[k] 21and with each of the seven lambs, one-tenth.[l] 22Include one male goat as a sin offering[m] to make atonement for you.[n] 23Prepare these in addition to the regular morning burnt offering. 24In this way prepare the food for the offering made by fire every day for seven days as an aroma pleasing to the LORD;[o] it is to be prepared in addition to the regular burnt offering and its drink offering. 25On the seventh day hold a sacred assembly and do no regular work.

Feast of Weeks

28:26–31pp — Lev 23:15–22; Dt 16:9–12

26" 'On the day of firstfruits,[p] when you present to the LORD an offering of new grain during the Feast of Weeks,[q] hold a sacred assembly and do no regular work.[r] 27Present a burnt offering of two young bulls, one ram and seven male lambs a year old as an aroma pleasing to the LORD.[s] 28With each bull there is to be a grain offering of three-tenths of an ephah of fine flour mixed with oil; with the ram, two-tenths;[t] 29and with each of the seven lambs, one-tenth.[u] 30Include one male goat[v] to make atonement for you. 31Prepare these together with their drink offerings, in addition to the regular burnt offer-

m5 That is, probably about 2 quarts (about 2 liters); also in verses 13, 21 and 29   n5 That is, probably about 1 quart (about 1 liter); also in verses 7 and 14   o9 That is, probably about 4 quarts (about 4.5 liters); also in verses 12, 20 and 28   p12 That is, probably about 6 quarts (about 6.5 liters); also in verses 20 and 28   q14 That is, probably about 2 quarts (about 2 liters)   r14 That is, probably about 1 1/4 quarts (about 1.2 liters)

28:9–10 The Sabbath offerings were in addition to the daily offerings.
28:11–15 The sacrifices at the beginning of the month were of great significance. These were times for celebration and blowing of trumpets in worship (see 10:10).
28:16–25 The priests are instructed as to the proper preparation for the Passover in the first month of the year. Passover

is also associated with the Feast of Unleavened Bread (see Ex 12:15; Lev 23:4–8). The number 7 (and 14, its multiple) reappears frequently in the paragraph.
28:26–31 The Feast of Weeks came 50 days after the Feast of Unleavened Bread (see Lev 23:9–22); from this number the term "Pentecost" (meaning "fifty") was used in the NT (Ac 2:1).

ing[w] and its grain offering. Be sure the animals are without defect.

Feast of Trumpets
29:1–6pp — Lev 23:23–25

29 " 'On the first day of the seventh month hold a sacred assembly and do no regular work.[x] It is a day for you to sound the trumpets. [2]As an aroma pleasing to the LORD,[y] prepare a burnt offering[z] of one young bull, one ram and seven male lambs a year old,[a] all without defect.[b] [3]With the bull prepare a grain offering[c] of three-tenths of an ephah[s] of fine flour mixed with oil; with the ram, two-tenths[t]; [4]and with each of the seven lambs, one-tenth.[u][d] [5]Include one male goat[e] as a sin offering to make atonement for you. [6]These are in addition to the monthly[f] and daily burnt offerings[g] with their grain offerings[h] and drink offerings[i] as specified. They are offerings made to the LORD by fire—a pleasing aroma.[j]

Day of Atonement
29:7–11pp — Lev 16:2–34; 23:26–32

[7]" 'On the tenth day of this seventh month hold a sacred assembly. You must deny yourselves[v][k] and do no work.[l] [8]Present as an aroma pleasing to the LORD a burnt offering of one young bull, one ram and seven male lambs a year old, all without defect.[m] [9]With the bull prepare a grain offering[n] of three-tenths of an ephah of fine flour mixed with oil; with the ram, two-tenths;[o] [10]and with each of the seven lambs, one-tenth.[p] [11]Include one male goat[q] as a sin offering, in addition to the sin offering for atonement and the regular burnt offering[r] with its grain offering, and their drink offerings.[s]

Feast of Tabernacles
29:12–39pp — Lev 23:33–43; Dt 16:13–17

[12]" 'On the fifteenth day of the seventh[t] month,[u] hold a sacred assembly and do no regular work. Celebrate a festival to the LORD for seven days. [13]Present an offering made by fire as an aroma pleasing to the LORD,[v] a burnt offering of thirteen young bulls, two rams and fourteen male lambs a year old, all without defect.[w] [14]With each of the thirteen bulls prepare a

grain offering[x] of three-tenths of an ephah of fine flour mixed with oil; with each of the two rams, two-tenths; [15]and with each of the fourteen lambs, one-tenth.[y] [16]Include one male goat as a sin offering,[z] in addition to the regular burnt offering with its grain offering and drink offering.[a]

[17]" 'On the second day[b] prepare twelve young bulls, two rams and fourteen male lambs a year old, all without defect.[c] [18]With the bulls, rams and lambs, prepare their grain offerings[d] and drink offerings[e] according to the number specified.[f] [19]Include one male goat as a sin offering,[g] in addition to the regular burnt offering[h] with its grain offering, and their drink offerings.[i]

[20]" 'On the third day prepare eleven bulls, two rams and fourteen male lambs a year old, all without defect.[j] [21]With the bulls, rams and lambs, prepare their grain offerings and drink offerings according to the number specified.[k] [22]Include one male goat as a sin offering, in addition to the regular burnt offering with its grain offering and drink offering.

[23]" 'On the fourth day prepare ten bulls, two rams and fourteen male lambs a year old, all without defect. [24]With the bulls, rams and lambs, prepare their grain offerings and drink offerings according to the number specified. [25]Include one male goat as a sin offering, in addition to the regular burnt offering with its grain offering and drink offering.

[26]" 'On the fifth day prepare nine bulls, two rams and fourteen male lambs a year old, all without defect. [27]With the bulls, rams and lambs, prepare their grain offerings and drink offerings according to the number specified. [28]Include one male goat as a sin offering, in addition to the regular burnt offering with its grain offering and drink offering.

[29]" 'On the sixth day prepare eight bulls, two rams and fourteen male lambs a year old, all without defect. [30]With the bulls, rams and lambs, prepare their grain

Cross references (center column)

28:31 [w]ver 3,19
29:1 [x]Nu 28:18
29:2 [y]Nu 28:2
[z]Lev 1:9;
Nu 28:11 [a]ver 36
[b]Lev 1:3;
Nu 28:3
29:3 [c]ver 14;
Nu 28:12
29:4 [d]Nu 28:13
29:5 [e]Nu 28:15
29:6 [f]Nu 28:11
[g]Nu 28:3
[h]Nu 28:5
[i]Nu 28:7
[j]Lev 1:9; Nu 28:2
29:7 [k]Ac 27:9
[l]S Ex 31:15
29:8 [m]ver 2
29:9 [n]S ver 3,18
[o]Nu 28:12
29:10 [p]Nu 28:13
29:11 [q]ver 5;
Nu 28:15
[r]S Lev 16:3 [s]S ver 6
29:12 [t]1Ki 8:2; 12:32
[u]S Lev 23:24
29:13 [v]ver 2;
Nu 28:2
[w]Nu 28:3

29:14 [x]S ver 3;
S Nu 15:6
29:15 [y]ver 4;
Nu 28:13
29:16 [z]ver 5;
S Nu 28:15 [a]ver 6
29:17 [b]Lev 23:36
[c]ver 2; Nu 28:3
29:18 [d]S ver 9
[e]Nu 28:7
[f]Nu 15:4-12
29:19
[g]S Nu 28:15
[h]Nu 28:3 [i]ver 6
29:20 [j]S ver 17
29:21 [k]S ver 18

[s]3 That is, probably about 6 quarts (about 6.5 liters); also in verses 9 and 14   [t]3 That is, probably about 4 quarts (about 4.5 liters); also in verses 9 and 14   [u]4 That is, probably about 2 quarts (about 2 liters); also in verses 10 and 15   [v]7 Or *must fast*

29:1–6 The Feast of Trumpets came at the beginning of the seventh month, a busy month for the worship of the Lord in holy festivals (see Lev 23:23–25; see also chart on "OT Feasts and Other Sacred Days," p. 176). Later in Jewish tradition this feast commemorated the New Year, *Rosh Hashanah*. The trumpet used was the *shophar,* the ram's horn.
29:7–11 The Feast of Trumpets leads into the Day of Atonement, a time of confession, contrition and celebration (see Lev 16; 23:26–32).
29:12–34 In the seventh month the Feast of Trumpets took place on the first day, the Day of Atonement occurred on the tenth day, and the Feast of Tabernacles began on the 15th day and lasted for seven days (see Lev 23:33–44). Each day of the Feast of Tabernacles had its own order for sacrifice.

offerings and drink offerings according to the number specified. [31]Include one male goat as a sin offering, in addition to the regular burnt offering with its grain offering and drink offering.

[32]"On the seventh day prepare seven bulls, two rams and fourteen male lambs a year old, all without defect. [33]With the bulls, rams and lambs, prepare their grain offerings and drink offerings according to the number specified. [34]Include one male goat as a sin offering, in addition to the regular burnt offering with its grain offering and drink offering.

[35]" 'On the eighth day hold an assembly[l] and do no regular work. [36]Present an offering made by fire as an aroma pleasing to the Lord, [m] a burnt offering of one bull, one ram and seven male lambs a year old, [n] all without defect. [37]With the bull, the ram and the lambs, prepare their grain offerings and drink offerings according to the number specified. [38]Include one male goat as a sin offering, in addition to the regular burnt offering with its grain offering and drink offering.

[39]" 'In addition to what you vow[o] and your freewill offerings,[p] prepare these for the Lord at your appointed feasts:[q] your burnt offerings,[r] grain offerings, drink offerings and fellowship offerings.[w][s] '"

[40]Moses told the Israelites all that the Lord commanded him.

Vows

30 Moses said to the heads of the tribes of Israel:[t] "This is what the Lord commands: [2]When a man makes a vow to the Lord or takes an oath to obligate himself by a pledge, he must not break his word but must do everything he said.[u]

[3]"When a young woman still living in her father's house makes a vow to the Lord or obligates herself by a pledge [4]and her father hears about her vow or pledge but says nothing to her, then all her vows and every pledge by which she obligated

herself will stand.[v] [5]But if her father forbids her[w] when he hears about it, none of her vows or the pledges by which she obligated herself will stand; the Lord will release her because her father has forbidden her.

[6]"If she marries after she makes a vow[x] or after her lips utter a rash promise by which she obligates herself [7]and her husband hears about it but says nothing to her, then her vows or the pledges by which she obligated herself will stand. [8]But if her husband[y] forbids her when he hears about it, he nullifies the vow that obligates her or the rash promise by which she obligates herself, and the Lord will release her.[z]

[9]"Any vow or obligation taken by a widow or divorced woman will be binding on her.

[10]"If a woman living with her husband makes a vow or obligates herself by a pledge under oath [11]and her husband hears about it but says nothing to her and does not forbid her, then all her vows or the pledges by which she obligated herself will stand. [12]But if her husband nullifies them when he hears about them, then none of the vows or pledges that came from her lips will stand.[a] Her husband has nullified them, and the Lord will release her. [13]Her husband may confirm or nullify any vow she makes or any sworn pledge to deny herself. [14]But if her husband says nothing to her about it from day to day, then he confirms all her vows or the pledges binding on her. He confirms them by saying nothing to her when he hears about them. [15]If, however, he nullifies them[b] some time after he hears about them, then he is responsible for her guilt."

[16]These are the regulations the Lord gave Moses concerning relationships between a man and his wife, and between a father and his young daughter still living in his house.

Cross references

29:35
l S Lev 23:36
29:36 *m* Lev 1:9
n ver 2
29:39 *o* Nu 6:2
p S Lev 7:16
q S Lev 23:2
r Lev 1:3;
1Ch 23:31;
2Ch 31:3
s Lev 3:1
30:1 *t* S Nu 1:4
30:2
u Dt 23:21-23;
Jdg 11:35;
Job 22:27;
Ps 22:25; 50:14;
61:5,8; 76:11;
116:14; Pr 20:25;
Ecc 5:4,5;
Isa 19:21;
Jnh 1:16; 2:9

30:4 *v* ver 7
30:5 *w* ver 8,12,15
30:6 *x* S Lev 5:4
30:8 *y* S Ge 3:6
z ver 5
30:12 *a* Eph 5:22;
Col 3:18
30:15 *b* S ver 5

w 39 Traditionally *peace offerings*

29:40 *Moses told the Israelites.* The recapitulation of these festivals was a necessary part of the transfer of power from Moses to Joshua.

30:1–16 The principal OT passage on vows (see Dt 23:21–23). A vow is not to be made rashly (cf. Ecc 5:1–7), and a vow to the Lord must be kept.

30:3–5 The vow of an unmarried woman still under her father's protection might be nullified by her father. This and the following law were probably designed for the protection of the woman, who in ancient Near Eastern society was subject to strong societal pressures, some of which would leave her without defense.

30:6–8 The vow of a married woman might be nullified by her husband.

30:9 *widow or divorced woman.* She is her own agent in the taking of vows.

30:10–15 Further examples of the complications that come in the taking of vows within the husband-wife relationship. Such complications may have come up much as in the case of Zelophehad's daughters (27:1–11). One case after another presented itself, resulting in this final codification. Presumably, in the centuries leading up to the NT, the legal decisions on vows became even more complex. The words of Jesus that one is to avoid complications connected with oaths (Mt 5:33–37) are liberating.

Vengeance on the Midianites

31 The LORD said to Moses, 2"Take vengeance on the Midianites[c] for the Israelites. After that, you will be gathered to your people.[d]"

3So Moses said to the people, "Arm some of your men to go to war against the Midianites and to carry out the LORD's vengeance[e] on them. 4Send into battle a thousand men from each of the tribes of Israel." 5So twelve thousand men armed for battle,[f] a thousand from each tribe, were supplied from the clans of Israel. 6Moses sent them into battle,[g] a thousand from each tribe, along with Phinehas[h] son of Eleazar, the priest, who took with him articles from the sanctuary[i] and the trumpets[j] for signaling.

7They fought against Midian, as the LORD commanded Moses,[k] and killed every man.[l] 8Among their victims were Evi, Rekem, Zur, Hur and Reba[m]—the five kings of Midian.[n] They also killed Balaam son of Beor[o] with the sword.[p] 9The Israelites captured the Midianite women[q] and children and took all the Midianite herds, flocks and goods as plunder.[r] 10They burned[s] all the towns where the Midianites had settled, as well as all their camps.[t] 11They took all the plunder and spoils, including the people and animals,[u] 12and brought the captives, spoils[v] and plunder to Moses and Eleazar the priest and the Israelite assembly[w] at their camp on the plains of Moab, by the Jordan across from Jericho.[x] [x]

13Moses, Eleazar the priest and all the leaders of the community went to meet them outside the camp. 14Moses was angry with the officers of the army[y]—the commanders of thousands and commanders

hundreds—who returned from the battle.

15"Have you allowed all the women to live?" he asked them. 16"They were the ones who followed Balaam's advice[z] and were the means of turning the Israelites away from the LORD in what happened at Peor,[a] so that a plague[b] struck the LORD's people. 17Now kill all the boys. And kill every woman who has slept with a man,[c] 18but save for yourselves every girl who has never slept with a man.

19"All of you who have killed anyone or touched anyone who was killed[d] must stay outside the camp seven days.[e] On the third and seventh days you must purify yourselves[f] and your captives. 20Purify every garment[g] as well as everything made of leather, goat hair or wood.[h]"

21Then Eleazar the priest said to the soldiers who had gone into battle,[i] "This is the requirement of the law that the LORD gave Moses: 22Gold, silver, bronze, iron,[j] tin, lead 23and anything else that can withstand fire must be put through the fire,[k] and then it will be clean. But it must also be purified with the water of cleansing.[l] And whatever cannot withstand fire must be put through that water. 24On the seventh day wash your clothes and you will be clean.[m] Then you may come into the camp.[n]"

Dividing the Spoils

25The LORD said to Moses, 26"You and Eleazar the priest and the family heads[o] of the community are to count all the people[p] and animals that were captured.[q] 27Divide[r] the spoils between the soldiers

---

31:2 [c]S Ge 25:2 [d]S Nu 20:26
31:3 [e]Jdg 11:36; 1Sa 24:12; 2Sa 4:8; 22:48; Ps 94:1; 149:7; Isa 34:8; Jer 11:20; 46:10; Eze 25:17
31:5 [f]ver 6,21
31:6 [g]S ver 5 [h]S Ex 6:25 [i]Nu 14:44 [j]S Nu 10:2
31:7 [k]Nu 25:16 [l]Dt 20:13; Jdg 21:11; 1Ki 11:15,16
31:8 [m]Jos 13:21 [n]S Nu 25:15 [o]S Nu 22:5; S 24:14 [p]Jos 13:22
31:9 [q]ver 15 [r]S Ge 34:29
31:10 [s]Jos 6:24; 8:28; 11:11; Jdg 18:27 [t]Ge 25:16; 1Ch 6:54; Ps 69:25; Eze 25:4
31:11 [u]ver 26; Dt 20:14; 2Ch 28:8
31:12 [v]ver 32, 53; Ge 49:27; Ex 15:9 [w]S Nu 27:2 [x]Nu 22:1
31:14 [y]ver 48; Ex 18:21; Dt 1:15; 2Sa 18:1
31:16 [z]S Nu 22:5; S 24:14; S 2Pe 2:15 [a]S Nu 23:28; 25:1-9 [b]S Nu 14:37
31:17 [c]Dt 7:2; 20:16-18; Jdg 21:11
31:19 [d]Nu 19:16 [e]S Lev 21:1 [f]Nu 19:12
31:20 [g]Nu 19:19 [h]S Lev 11:32
31:21 [i]S ver 5
31:22 [j]Jos 6:19; 22:8
31:23 [k]S 1Co 3:13
31:24 [l]S Nu 8:7 [m]S Lev 11:25

[n]S Lev 14:8 31:26 [o]S Nu 1:4 [p]S Nu 1:19 [q]S ver 11,12 31:27 [r]Jos 22:8; 1Sa 25:13; 30:24

[x]12 Hebrew *Jordan of Jericho*; possibly an ancient name for the Jordan River

---

31:1–24 The Lord declares a holy war (see Introduction to Joshua: The Conquest and the Ethical Question of War) against the Midianites as one of Moses' last actions before the end of his life. Moses was not motivated by petty jealousy; rather, the war was "the LORD's vengeance" (v. 3) for the Midianites' part in seducing the Israelites to engage in sexual immorality and to worship the Baal of Peor. (See 25:16–18, where the specific mention of Cozbi, a Midianite woman, heightens the anger expressed in ch. 31.)
31:1 *gathered to your people.* A euphemism for death (see, e.g., Ge 25:8,17; 35:29).
31:4 *a thousand men from each of the tribes of Israel.* The burden of the holy war had to be shared equally among the tribes.
31:6 *Phinehas.* His zeal for the Lord's honor led him to execute Zimri and Cozbi (25:8). Now he leads in the sacred aspects of the battle to demonstrate that this is a holy war. *trumpets.* See note on 10:3.
31:7 *as the LORD commanded Moses.* The battle was the Lord's.

31:8 *They also killed Balaam.* Ch. 25 lacks the name of the principal instigator of the seduction of the Israelite men to the depraved worship of Baal. But here he is found among the dead. What Balaam had been unable to accomplish through acts of magic or sorcery (chs. 22–24) he was almost able to achieve by his advice to the Midianites (v. 16).
31:9–18 While the troops killed the men of Midian, they spared the women and children as plunder. Moses commanded that only the virgin women (who were thus innocent of the indecencies at Peor) could be spared; the guilty women and the boys (who might endanger the inheritance rights of Israelite men) were to be put to death (vv. 15–17).
31:19–24 Since this was holy war, both people (vv. 19–20) and things (vv. 21–24) had to be cleansed (cf. 19:11–13).
31:26–35 Another aspect of holy war was the fair distribution of the spoils of war, both among those who fought in the battle and among those who stayed with the community, with appropriate shares to be given to the Lord, whose battle it was (v. 28).

who took part in the battle and the rest of the community. 28From the soldiers who fought in the battle, set apart as tribute for the LORD[s] one out of every five hundred, whether persons, cattle, donkeys, sheep or goats. 29Take this tribute from their half share and give it to Eleazar the priest as the LORD's part. 30From the Israelites' half, select one out of every fifty, whether persons, cattle, donkeys, sheep, goats or other animals. Give them to the Levites, who are responsible for the care of the LORD's tabernacle.[t]" 31So Moses and Eleazar the priest did as the LORD commanded Moses.

32The plunder remaining from the spoils[u] that the soldiers took was 675,000 sheep, 33372,000 cattle, 3461,000 donkeys 35and 32,000 women who had never slept with a man.

36The half share of those who fought in the battle was:

337,500 sheep, 37of which the tribute for the LORD[v] was 675;

3836,000 cattle, of which the tribute for the LORD was 72;

3930,500 donkeys, of which the tribute for the LORD was 61;

4016,000 people, of which the tribute for the LORD was 32.

41Moses gave the tribute to Eleazar the priest as the LORD's part,[w] as the LORD commanded Moses.[x]

42The half belonging to the Israelites, which Moses set apart from that of the fighting men— 43the community's half—was 337,500 sheep, 4436,000 cattle, 4530,500 donkeys 46and 16,000 people. 47From the Israelites' half, Moses selected one out of every fifty persons and animals, as the LORD commanded him, and gave them to the Levites, who were responsible for the care of the LORD's tabernacle.

48Then the officers[y] who were over the units of the army—the commanders of thousands and commanders of hundreds—went to Moses 49and said to him, "Your servants have counted[z] the soldiers under our command, and not one is missing.[a] 50So we have brought as an offering to the LORD the gold articles each of us acquired—armlets, bracelets, signet rings, earrings and necklaces—to make atonement for ourselves[b] before the LORD."

51Moses and Eleazar the priest accepted from them the gold—all the crafted articles. 52All the gold from the commanders of thousands and commanders of hundreds that Moses and Eleazar presented as a gift to the LORD weighed 16,750 shekels.[y] 53Each soldier had taken plunder[c] for himself. 54Moses and Eleazar the priest accepted the gold from the commanders of thousands and commanders of hundreds and brought it into the Tent of Meeting[d] as a memorial[e] for the Israelites before the LORD.

The Transjordan Tribes

32 The Reubenites and Gadites, who had very large herds and flocks,[f] saw that the lands of Jazer[g] and Gilead[h] were suitable for livestock. [i] 2So they came to Moses and Eleazar the priest and to the leaders of the community,[j] and said, 3"Ataroth,[k] Dibon,[l] Jazer,[m] Nimrah,[n] Heshbon,[o] Elealeh,[p] Sebam,[q] Nebo[r] and Beon[s]— 4the land the LORD subdued[t] before the people of Israel—are suitable for livestock,[u] and your servants have livestock. 5If we have found favor in your eyes," they said, "let this land be given to your servants as our possession. Do not make us cross the Jordan.[v]"

6Moses said to the Gadites and Reubenites, "Shall your countrymen go to war while you sit here? 7Why do you discourage the Israelites from going over into the land the LORD has given them?[w] 8This is what your fathers did when I sent them from Kadesh Barnea to look over the land.[x] 9After they went up to the Valley of Eshcol[y] and viewed the land, they discouraged the Israelites from entering the land the LORD had given them. 10The LORD's anger was aroused[z] that day and he swore this oath:[a] 11'Because they have not followed me wholeheartedly, not one of the men twenty years old or more[b] who came up out of Egypt[c] will see the land I promised on oath[d] to Abraham, Isaac and Jacob[e]— 12not one except Caleb son of Jephunneh the Kenizzite and Joshua son of Nun, for they followed the LORD wholeheartedly.'[f] 13The LORD's anger burned against Israel[g] and he made them wander

---

31:28 [s]ver 37-41;
S Nu 18:21
31:30 [t]Nu 3:7; 18:3
31:32 [u]S ver 12
31:37 [v]ver 38-41
31:41 [w]Nu 5:9; 18:8 [x]ver 21,28
31:48 [y]S ver 14
31:49 [z]S Nu 1:19
[a]Jer 23:4
31:50 [b]S Ex 30:16

31:53 [c]S Ge 34:29; Dt 20:14
31:54 [d]S Ex 27:21; 40:2 [e]S Ex 28:12
32:1 [f]ver 24,36; Jdg 5:16 [g]S Nu 21:32 [h]S Ge 31:21 [i]Ex 12:38
32:2 [j]Lev 4:22; Nu 27:2
32:3 [k]ver 34; Jos 16:2,7; 18:13 [l]ver 34; S Nu 21:30 [m]ver 36; 1 [n]ver 36; Jos 13:27 [o]Nu 21:25 [p]ver 37; Isa 15:4; 16:9; Jer 48:34 [q]Jos 13:19; Isa 16:8,9; Jer 48:32 [r]Nu 33:47; Dt 32:49; 34:1; 1Ch 5:8 [s]ver 38; Jos 13:17; Eze 25:9
32:4 [t]Nu 21:34 [u]Ex 12:38
32:5 [v]S Nu 13:29
32:7 [w]Nu 13:27-14:4
32:8 [x]Nu 13:3, 26; Dt 1:19-25
32:9 [y]Nu 13:23; Dt 1:24
32:10 [z]Nu 11:1 [a]S Nu 14:20-23
32:11 [b]S Ex 30:14 [c]Nu 1:1 [d]S Nu 14:23 [e]Nu 14:28-30
32:12 [f]Nu 14:24, 30; Ps 63:8
32:13 [g]S Ex 4:14

[y]52 That is, about 420 pounds (about 190 kilograms)

32:1 *Reubenites and Gadites.* The abundance of fertile grazing land in Transjordan prompted the leaders of these two tribes to request that they be allowed to settle there and not cross the Jordan. This area too was a gift of God won by conquest.
32:8 *This is what your fathers did.* Moses' fear was that the failure of these two tribes to stay with the whole community in conquering Canaan would be the beginning of a general revolt against entering the land. It would be the failure of Kadesh (chs. 13–14) all over again. Moreover, the conquest of Canaan was a commission to all Israel.

in the desert forty years, until the whole generation of those who had done evil in his sight was gone. [h]

14"And here you are, a brood of sinners, standing in the place of your fathers and making the LORD even more angry with Israel. [i] 15If you turn away from following him, he will again leave all this people in the desert, and you will be the cause of their destruction. [j] "

16Then they came up to him and said, "We would like to build pens [k] here for our livestock [l] and cities for our women and children. 17But we are ready to arm ourselves and go ahead of the Israelites [m] until we have brought them to their place. [n] Meanwhile our women and children will live in fortified cities, for protection from the inhabitants of the land. 18We will not return to our homes until every Israelite has received his inheritance. [o] 19We will not receive any inheritance with them on the other side of the Jordan, because our inheritance [p] has come to us on the east side of the Jordan." [q]

20Then Moses said to them, "If you will do this—if you will arm yourselves before the LORD for battle, [r] 21and if all of you will go armed over the Jordan before the LORD until he has driven his enemies out before him [s]— 22then when the land is subdued before the LORD, you may return [t] and be free from your obligation to the LORD and to Israel. And this land will be your possession [u] before the LORD. [v]

23"But if you fail to do this, you will be sinning against the LORD; and you may be sure that your sin will find you out. [w] 24Build cities for your women and children, and pens for your flocks, [x] but do what you have promised. [y] "

25The Gadites and Reubenites said to Moses, "We your servants will do as our lord commands. [z] 26Our children and wives, our flocks and herds will remain here in the cities of Gilead. [a] 27But your servants, every man armed for battle, will cross over to fight [b] before the LORD, just as our lord says."

28Then Moses gave orders about them [c] to Eleazar the priest and Joshua son of Nun [d] and to the family heads of the Israel-

ite tribes. [e] 29He said to them, "If the Gadites and Reubenites, every man armed for battle, cross over the Jordan with you before the LORD, then when the land is subdued before you, [f] give them the land of Gilead as their possession. [g] 30But if they do not cross over [h] with you armed, they must accept their possession with you in Canaan. [i] "

31The Gadites and Reubenites answered, "Your servants will do what the LORD has said. [j] 32We will cross over before the LORD into Canaan armed, [k] but the property we inherit will be on this side of the Jordan. [l] "

33Then Moses gave to the Gadites, [m] the Reubenites and the half-tribe of Manasseh [n] son of Joseph the kingdom of Sihon king of the Amorites [o] and the kingdom of Og king of Bashan [p]—the whole land with its cities and the territory around them. [q]

34The Gadites built up Dibon, Ataroth, Aroer, [r] 35Atroth Shophan, Jazer, [s] Jogbehah, [t] 36Beth Nimrah [u] and Beth Haran as fortified cities, and built pens for their flocks. [v] 37And the Reubenites rebuilt Heshbon, [w] Elealeh [x] and Kiriathaim, [y] 38as well as Nebo [z] and Baal Meon (these names were changed) and Sibmah. [a] They gave names to the cities they rebuilt.

39The descendants of Makir [b] son of Manasseh went to Gilead, [c] captured it and drove out the Amorites [d] who were there. 40So Moses gave Gilead to the Makirites, [e] the descendants of Manasseh, and they settled there. 41Jair, [f] a descendant of Manasseh, captured their settlements and called them Havvoth Jair. [z][g] 42And Nobah captured Kenath [h] and its surrounding settlements and called it Nobah [i] after himself. [j]

Stages in Israel's Journey

33 Here are the stages in the journey [k] of the Israelites when they came out of Egypt [l] by divisions under the lead-

Cross References

32:13
[h] Nu 14:28-35;
26:64,65
32:14 [i] S ver 10;
Dt 1:34; Ps 78:59
32:15
[j] Dt 30:17-18;
2Ch 7:20
32:16 [k] ver 24,
36; 1Sa 24:3;
Ps 50:9; 78:70
[l] Ex 12:38;
Dt 3:19
32:17 [m] Dt 3:18;
Jos 4:12,13
[n] S Nu 22:4;
Dt 3:20
32:18
[o] Jos 22:1-4
32:19 [p] ver 22,29
[q] Nu 21:33;
Jos 12:1; 22:7
32:20 [r] ver 17
32:21 [s] ver 17
32:22 [t] Jos 22:4
[u] S Lev 14:34
[v] Dt 3:18-20
32:23 [w] S Ge 4:7;
S Isa 3:9
32:24 [x] S ver 1,16
[y] Nu 30:2
32:25 [z] ver 29;
Jos 1:16,18; 22:2
32:26 [a] ver 16,
24; Jos 1:14;
12:2; 22:9;
2Sa 2:9; 1Ch 5:9
32:27 [b] ver 17,21
32:28 [c] ver 29;
Dt 3:18-20;
Jos 1:13
[d] Nu 11:28
32:29 [e] Nu 1:16
[f] S Nu 22:4
[g] S ver 19
32:30 [h] ver 23
[i] ver 29,32
32:31 [j] ver 29
32:32 [k] ver 17
[l] S ver 30; Jos 12:6
32:33
[m] Jos 13:24-28;
1Sa 13:7
[n] Jos 1:12
[o] Nu 21:21;
Dt 2:26 [p] S ver
19; S Jos 12:5
[q] S Nu 21:24;
34:14; Dt 2:36;
Jos 12:6
32:34 [r] Dt 2:36;
3:12; 4:48;
Jos 12:2; 13:9;
Jdg 11:26;
1Sa 30:28;
1Ch 5:8;
Jer 48:19
32:35 [s] ver 3
[t] Jdg 8:11
32:36 [u] S ver 3
[v] S ver 1
32:37 [w] Nu 21:25
[x] S ver 3
[y] Jos 13:19;
1Ch 6:76;
Jer 48:1,23;
Eze 25:9
32:38 [z] S ver 3;
Isa 15:2; Jer 48:1,
22 [a] S ver 3
32:39
[b] S Ge 50:23

[c] Nu 26:29; Dt 2:36 [d] S Ge 10:16 32:40 [e] S Ge 50:23; Dt 3:15
32:41 [f] 1Ki 4:13 [g] Dt 3:14; Jdg 10:4; 1Ch 2:23
32:42 [h] 1Ch 2:23 [i] Jdg 8:11 [j] Isa 15:12; 2Sa 18:18; Ps 49:11;
Isa 22:16; 56:5 33:1 [k] Ex 17:1; 40:36 [l] Nu 1:1

[z] 41 Or them the settlements of Jair

32:17 *we are ready to arm ourselves.* The leaders of Reuben and Gad sought to assure Moses that they did not wish to shirk their duty in helping to conquer the land. They would join their brothers in battle but wished to leave their families and livestock behind in the territory of their choosing.
32:23 *your sin will find you out.* The bargain was struck, but not without strong warnings if they failed to live up to

their word.
32:33 *and the half-tribe of Manasseh.* It appears that after the requirements for Transjordan settlement were established with the tribes of Reuben and Gad, half the tribe of Manasseh joined with them.
33:1—49 The numerous places (significantly 40 in number between Rameses and the plains of Moab) in Israel's desert experience are listed. Unfortunately, most of the sites were

ership of Moses and Aaron. *m* 2At the LORD's command Moses recorded *n* the stages in their journey *o*. This is their journey by stages:

3The Israelites set out *p* from Rameses *q* on the fifteenth day of the first month, the day after the Passover. *r* They marched out boldly *s* in full view of all the Egyptians, 4who were burying all their firstborn, *t* whom the LORD had struck down among them; for the LORD had brought judgment *u* on their gods. *v*

5The Israelites left Rameses and camped at Succoth. *w*

6They left Succoth and camped at Etham, on the edge of the desert. *x*

7They left Etham, turned back to Pi Hahiroth, to the east of Baal Zephon, *y* and camped near Migdol. *z*

8They left Pi Hahiroth *a a* and passed through the sea *b* into the desert, and when they had traveled for three days in the Desert of Etham, they camped at Marah. *c*

9They left Marah and went to Elim, where there were twelve springs and seventy palm trees, and they camped *d* there.

10They left Elim *e* and camped by the Red Sea. *b*

11They left the Red Sea and camped in the Desert of Sin. *f*

12They left the Desert of Sin and camped at Dophkah.

13They left Dophkah and camped at Alush.

14They left Alush and camped at Rephidim, where there was no water for the people to drink. *g*

15They left Rephidim *h* and camped in the Desert of Sinai. *i*

16They left the Desert of Sinai and camped at Kibroth Hattaavah. *j*

17They left Kibroth Hattaavah and camped at Hazeroth. *k*

18They left Hazeroth and camped at Rithmah.

19They left Rithmah and camped at Rimmon Perez.

20They left Rimmon Perez and camped at Libnah. *l*

21They left Libnah and camped at Rissah.

22They left Rissah and camped at Kehelathah.

23They left Kehelathah and camped at Mount Shepher.

24They left Mount Shepher and camped at Haradah.

25They left Haradah and camped at Makheloth.

26They left Makheloth and camped at Tahath.

27They left Tahath and camped at Terah.

28They left Terah and camped at Mithcah.

29They left Mithcah and camped at Hashmonah.

30They left Hashmonah and camped at Moseroth. *m*

31They left Moseroth and camped at Bene Jaakan. *n*

32They left Bene Jaakan and camped at Hor Haggidgad.

33They left Hor Haggidgad and camped at Jotbathah. *o*

34They left Jotbathah and camped at Abronah.

35They left Abronah and camped at Ezion Geber. *p*

36They left Ezion Geber and camped at Kadesh, in the Desert of Zin. *q*

37They left Kadesh and camped at Mount Hor, *r* on the border of Edom. *s* 38At the LORD's command Aaron the priest went up Mount Hor, where he died *t* on the first day of the fifth month of the fortieth year *u* after the Israelites came out of Egypt. *v* 39Aaron was a hundred and twenty-three years old when he died on Mount Hor.

40The Canaanite king *w* of Arad, *x* who lived in the Negev *y* of Canaan,

33:1 *m*S Ex 4:16; 6:26
33:2 *n*S Ex 17:14
*o*S ver 1
33:3 *p*Nu 10:2
*q*S Ge 47:11
*r*Jos 5:10
*s*S Ex 14:8
33:4 *t*S Ex 4:23
*u*2Ch 24:24; Jer 15:3; Eze 14:21
*v*S Ex 12:12
33:5 *w*Ex 12:37
33:6 *x*Ex 13:20
33:7 *y*Ex 14:9
*z*S Ex 14:2
33:8 *a*Ex 14:2
*b*S Ex 14:22
*c*S Ex 15:23
33:9 *d*Ex 15:27
33:10 *e*Ex 16:1
33:11 *f*S Ex 16:1
33:14
*g*S Ex 15:22; S 17:2
33:15 *h*S Ex 17:1
*i*S Ex 19:1
33:16
*j*S Nu 11:34
33:17 *k*Nu 11:35

33:20 *l*Jos 10:29; 12:15; 15:42; 21:13; 2Ki 8:22; 19:8; 23:31; 1Ch 6:57; 2Ch 21:10; Isa 37:8; Jer 52:1
33:30 *m*Dt 10:6
33:31 *n*Dt 10:6
33:33 *o*Dt 10:7
33:35 *p*Dt 2:8; 1Ki 9:26; 22:48
33:36
*q*S Nu 13:21
33:37
*r*S Nu 20:22
*s*S Ge 36:16; S Nu 20:16
33:38
*t*S Nu 27:13
*u*S Ex 16:35
*v*Nu 20:25-28
33:40
*w*S Ge 10:18
*x*S Nu 21:1
*y*S Ge 12:9

a 8 Many manuscripts of the Masoretic Text, Samaritan Pentateuch and Vulgate; most manuscripts of the Masoretic Text *left from before Hahiroth*   *b 10* Hebrew *Yam Suph*; that is, Sea of Reeds; also in verse 11

---

desert encampments, not cities with lasting archaeological records; so they are difficult to locate. Many of the places (e.g., in vv. 19–29) are not recorded elsewhere in Exodus and Numbers. Some of the places mentioned elsewhere (e.g., Taberah, 11:2; see 21:19) are missing here. The data warrant these conclusions: 1. Moses recorded the list at the Lord's command (v. 2). 2. The list should be taken seriously, as an accurate recapitulation of the stages of the journey, despite difficulty in locating many of the sites. 3. The numerical factor of 40 sites between Rameses and the plains of

Moab suggests some styling of the list, which helps to account for the sites not included. 4. As in the case of genealogies in the Pentateuch, some factors of ancient significance may not be clear to us today. 5. Ultimately the record is a recital of the Lord's blessing on his people for the extended period of their desert experience. Although certainly not without geographical importance, the listing of the stages of Israel's experience in the desert is fundamentally a religious document, a litany of the Lord's deliverance of his people.

heard that the Israelites were coming.
⁴¹They left Mount Hor and camped at Zalmonah.
⁴²They left Zalmonah and camped at Punon.
⁴³They left Punon and camped at Oboth. ᶻ
⁴⁴They left Oboth and camped at Iye Abarim, on the border of Moab. ᵃ
⁴⁵They left Iyimᶜ and camped at Dibon Gad.
⁴⁶They left Dibon Gad and camped at Almon Diblathaim.
⁴⁷They left Almon Diblathaim and camped in the mountains of Abarim, ᵇ near Nebo. ᶜ
⁴⁸They left the mountains of Abarim ᵈ and camped on the plains of Moab ᵉ by the Jordan ᶠ across from Jericho. ᵈᵍ ⁴⁹There on the plains of Moab they camped along the Jordan from Beth Jeshimoth ʰ to Abel Shittim. ⁱ

⁵⁰On the plains of Moab by the Jordan across from Jericho ʲ the Lord said to Moses, ⁵¹"Speak to the Israelites and say to them: 'When you cross the Jordan into Canaan, ᵏ ⁵²drive out all the inhabitants of the land before you. Destroy all their carved images and their cast idols, and demolish all their high places. ˡ ⁵³Take possession of the land and settle in it, for I have given you the land to possess. ᵐ ⁵⁴Distribute the land by lot, ⁿ according to your clans. ᵒ To a larger group give a larger inheritance, and to a smaller group a smaller one. ᵖ Whatever falls to them by lot will be theirs. Distribute it according to your ancestral tribes. ᵠ

⁵⁵"'But if you do not drive out the inhabitants of the land, those you allow to remain will become barbs in your eyes and thorns ʳ in your sides. They will give you trouble in the land where you will live. ⁵⁶And then I will do to you what I plan to do to them. ˢ '"

Boundaries of Canaan

34 The Lord said to Moses, ²"Command the Israelites and say to them: 'When you enter Canaan, ᵗ the land

that will be allotted to you as an inheritance ᵘ will have these boundaries: ᵛ

³"'Your southern side will include some of the Desert of Zin ʷ along the border of Edom. On the east, your southern boundary will start from the end of the Salt Sea, ᵉˣ ⁴cross south of Scorpion ᶠ Pass, ʸ continue on to Zin and go south of Kadesh Barnea. ᶻ Then it will go to Hazar Addar and over to Azmon, ᵃ ⁵where it will turn, join the Wadi of Egypt ᵇ and end at the Sea. ᵍ

⁶"'Your western boundary will be the coast of the Great Sea. ᶜ This will be your boundary on the west. ᵈ

⁷"'For your northern boundary, ᵉ run a line from the Great Sea to Mount Hor ᶠ ⁸and from Mount Hor to Lebo ʰ Hamath. ᵍ Then the boundary will go to Zedad, ⁹continue to Ziphron and end at Hazar Enan. This will be your boundary on the north.

¹⁰"'For your eastern boundary, ʰ run a line from Hazar Enan to Shepham. ¹¹The boundary will go down from Shepham to Riblah ⁱ on the east side of Ain ʲ and continue along the slopes east of the Sea of Kinnereth. ⁱᵏ ¹²Then the boundary will go down along the Jordan and end at the Salt Sea.

"'This will be your land, with its boundaries on every side.'"

¹³Moses commanded the Israelites: "Assign this land by lot ˡ as an inheritance. ᵐ The Lord has ordered that it be given to the nine and a half tribes, ¹⁴because the families of the tribe of Reuben, the tribe of Gad and the half-tribe of Manasseh have received their inheritance. ⁿ ¹⁵These two and a half tribes have received their inheritance on the east side of the Jordan of Jericho, ʲ toward the sunrise."

¹⁶The Lord said to Moses, ¹⁷"These are the names of the men who are to assign the land for you as an inheritance: Eleazar

---

33:43 ᶻNu 21:10
33:44 ᵃS Nu 21:11
33:47 ᵇNu 27:12
         ᶜNu 32:3
33:48 ᵈNu 27:12
         ᵉS Nu 26:3
         ᶠS Ge 13:10
         ᵍNu 22:1;
         Jos 12:9
33:49 ʰJos 12:3;
         13:20; Eze 25:9
         ⁱS Nu 21:16
33:50 ʲver 48
33:51 ᵏNu 34:2;
         Jos 3:17
33:52 ˡS Lev 26:1;
         Ps 106:34-36
33:53 ᵐDt 11:31;
         17:14; Jos 1:11;
         21:43
33:54 ⁿS Lev 16:8;
         Nu 36:2
         ᵒNu 26:54
         ᵖNu 35:8
         ᵠJos 18:10
33:55 ʳJos 23:13;
         Jdg 2:3;
         Ps 106:36;
         Isa 55:13;
         Eze 2:6; 28:24;
         Mic 7:4;
         2Co 12:7
33:56 ˢNu 14:28
34:2 ᵗS Nu 33:51

ᵘGe 17:8;
Dt 1:7-8;
Jos 23:4;
Ps 78:54-55;
105:11
ᵛEze 47:15
34:3 ʷNu 13:21;
Jos 15:1-3
ˣS Ge 14:3
34:4 ʸJos 15:3;
Jdg 1:36
ᶻNu 32:8
ᵃJos 15:4
34:5 ᵇGe 15:18
34:6 ᶜJos 1:4;
9:1; 15:12,47;
23:4; Eze 47:10,
15; 48:28
ᵈEze 47:19-20
34:7
ᵉEze 47:15-17
ᶠS Nu 20:22
34:8 ᵍNu 13:21;
Jos 13:5
34:10 ʰJos 15:5
34:11
ⁱ2Ki 23:33; 25:6,
21; Jer 39:5;
52:9,27
ʲJos 12:3; 21:16;
1Ch 4:32
ᵏDt 3:17;
Jos 11:2; 13:27
34:13
ˡS Lev 16:8;
Jos 18:10;
Mic 2:5
ᵐJos 13:6;
14:1-5; Isa 49:8;
65:9; Eze 45:1
34:14
ⁿNu 32:19;
Dt 33:21;
Jos 14:3

ᶜ45 That is, Iye Abarim   ᵈ48 Hebrew *Jordan of Jericho*; possibly an ancient name for the Jordan River; also in verse 50   ᵉ3 That is, the Dead Sea; also in verse 12   ᶠ4 Hebrew *Akrabbim*   ᵍ5 That is, the Mediterranean; also in verses 6 and 7   ʰ8 Or *to the entrance to*   ⁱ11 That is, Galilee   ʲ15 *Jordan of Jericho* was possibly an ancient name for the Jordan River

---

33:52 *drive out all the inhabitants of the land . . . Destroy all their . . . idols.* What Israel had accomplished in the war against the Midianites (ch. 31) was now to be extended to all the inhabitants of Canaan. Particularly important was the command to destroy all symbols of the pagan religious system of the Canaanites.
34:3–12 The listing of the four boundaries is not only for information, but also to display again the dimensions of

God's great gift to his people.
34:13–15 The new realities that the settlement of Reuben, Gad and the half-tribe of Manasseh in Transjordan brought about (see ch. 32).
34:16–29 The listing of the new tribal leaders recalls the listing of the leaders of the first generation (1:5–16). This time the promise will be realized; these new leaders will assist Eleazar and Joshua in actually allotting the land.

the priest and Joshua[o] son of Nun. [18]And appoint one leader from each tribe to help[p] assign the land.[q] [19]These are their names:[r]

Caleb[s] son of Jephunneh,
　　from the tribe of Judah;[t]
[20]Shemuel son of Ammihud,
　　from the tribe of Simeon;[u]
[21]Elidad son of Kislon,
　　from the tribe of Benjamin;[v]
[22]Bukki son of Jogli,
　　the leader from the tribe of Dan;
[23]Hanniel son of Ephod,
　　the leader from the tribe of Manasseh[w] son of Joseph;
[24]Kemuel son of Shiphtan,
　　the leader from the tribe of Ephraim[x] son of Joseph;
[25]Elizaphan son of Parnach,
　　the leader from the tribe of Zebulun;[y]
[26]Paltiel son of Azzan,
　　the leader from the tribe of Issachar;
[27]Ahihud son of Shelomi,
　　the leader from the tribe of Asher;[z]
[28]Pedahel son of Ammihud,
　　the leader from the tribe of Naphtali."

[29]These are the men the LORD commanded to assign the inheritance to the Israelites in the land of Canaan.[a]

Towns for the Levites

35 On the plains of Moab by the Jordan across from Jericho,[k][b] the LORD said to Moses, [2]"Command the Israelites to give the Levites towns to live in[c] from the inheritance the Israelites will possess. And give them pasturelands[d] around the towns. [3]Then they will have towns to live in and pasturelands for their cattle, flocks and all their other livestock.[e]

[4]"The pasturelands around the towns that you give the Levites will extend out fifteen hundred feet[1] from the town wall. [5]Outside the town, measure three thousand feet[m][f] on the east side, three thousand on the south side, three thousand on the west and three thousand on the north,

with the town in the center. They will have this area as pastureland for the towns.[g]

Cities of Refuge

35:6–34Ref — Dt 4:41–43; 19:1–14; Jos 20:1–9

[6]"Six of the towns you give the Levites will be cities of refuge, to which a person who has killed someone may flee.[h] In addition, give them forty-two other towns. [7]In all you must give the Levites forty-eight towns, together with their pasturelands. [8]The towns you give the Levites from the land the Israelites possess are to be given in proportion to the inheritance of each tribe: Take many towns from a tribe that has many, but few from one that has few."[i]

[9]Then the LORD said to Moses: [10]"Speak to the Israelites and say to them: 'When you cross the Jordan into Canaan,[j] [11]select some towns to be your cities of refuge, to which a person who has killed someone[k] accidentally[l] may flee. [12]They will be places of refuge from the avenger,[m] so that a person accused of murder[n] may not die before he stands trial before the assembly.[o] [13]These six towns you give will be your cities of refuge.[p] [14]Give three on this side of the Jordan and three in Canaan as cities of refuge. [15]These six towns will be a place of refuge for Israelites, aliens and any other people living among them, so that anyone who has killed another accidentally can flee there.

[16]" 'If a man strikes someone with an iron object so that he dies, he is a murderer; the murderer shall be put to death.[q] [17]Or if anyone has a stone in his hand that could kill, and he strikes someone so that he dies, he is a murderer; the murderer shall be put to death. [18]Or if anyone has a wooden object in his hand that could kill, and he hits someone so that he dies, he is a murderer; the murderer shall be put to death. [19]The avenger of blood[r] shall put the murderer to death; when he meets him, he shall put him to death.[s] [20]If any-

Cross references (center column)
34:17 [o]Nu 11:28; Dt 1:38
34:18 [p]S Nu 1:4 [q]Jos 14:1
34:19 [r]ver 29 [s]S Nu 26:65 [t]Ge 29:35; Dt 33:7; Ps 60:7
34:20 [u]S Ge 29:33
34:21 [v]Ge 49:27; Jdg 5:14; Ps 68:27
34:23 [w]Nu 1:34
34:24 [x]Nu 1:32
34:25 [y]S Ge 30:20
34:27 [z]Nu 1:40
34:29 [a]ver 19
35:1 [b]Nu 22:1
35:2 [c]Lev 25:32-34; Jos 14:3,4 [d]Jos 21:1-42
35:3 [e]Dt 18:6; Jos 14:4; 21:2
35:5 [f]Jos 3:4

[g]Lev 25:34; 2Ch 11:14; 13:9; 23:2; 31:19
35:6 [h]ver 11; Jos 21:13
35:8 [i]Nu 26:54; 33:54
35:10 [j]Nu 33:51; Dt 9:1; Jos 1:2,11
35:11 [k]ver 22-25 [l]S Ex 21:13
35:12 [m]ver 19; Dt 19:6; Jos 20:3; 2Sa 14:11 [n]ver 26,27,28 [o]ver 24, 25
35:13 [p]ver 6,14
35:16 [q]S Ex 21:12
35:19 [r]S ver 12 [s]ver 21

k[1] Hebrew *Jordan of Jericho*; possibly an ancient name for the Jordan River
l[4] Hebrew *a thousand cubits* (about 450 meters)
m[5] Hebrew *two thousand cubits* (about 900 meters)

35:1–5 Since the Levites would not receive an allotment with the other tribes in the land (1:47–53), they would need towns in which to live and to raise their families and care for their livestock. The Levites were to be spread throughout the land, not in an isolated encampment. Jos 21 presents the fulfillment of this command.
35:6–15 Six Levitical cities were to be stationed strategi-

cally in the land—three in Transjordan and three in Canaan proper—as cities of refuge, where a person guilty of unintentional manslaughter might escape blood revenge. Jos 20 describes the sites that were chosen.
35:16–21 Various descriptions of the taking of life are presented that would indicate willful murder.

one with malice aforethought shoves an-other or throws something at him inten-tionally *t* so that he dies ²¹or if in hostility he hits him with his fist so that he dies, that person shall be put to death; *u* he is a murderer. The avenger of blood *v* shall put the murderer to death when he meets him.

²²" 'But if without hostility someone suddenly shoves another or throws some-thing at him unintentionally *w* ²³or, with-out seeing him, drops a stone on him that could kill him, and he dies, then since he was not his enemy and he did not intend to harm him, ²⁴the assembly *x* must judge between him and the avenger of blood ac-cording to these regulations. ²⁵The assem-bly must protect the one accused of mur-der from the avenger of blood and send him back to the city of refuge to which he fled. He must stay there until the death of the high priest, *y* who was anointed *z* with the holy oil. *a*

²⁶" 'But if the accused ever goes outside the limits of the city of refuge to which he has fled ²⁷and the avenger of blood finds him outside the city, the avenger of blood may kill the accused without being guilty

35:20
t S Ex 21:14
35:21 *u* Ex 21:14
v ver 19
35:22
w S Ex 21:13
35:24 *x* S ver 12
35:25 *y* ver 32
z S Ex 28:41
a S Ex 29:7

35:29 *b* Nu 27:11
c Nu 10:8
d S Ex 12:20
35:30 *e* Dt 17:6;
19:15;
S Mt 18:16;
Jn 7:51
35:31 *f* Ex 21:30;
Job 6:22; Ps 49:8;
Pr 13:8
35:33 *g* S Ge 4:10
35:34
h Lev 18:24,25
i S Ex 29:45

of murder. ²⁸The accused must stay in his city of refuge until the death of the high priest; only after the death of the high priest may he return to his own proper-ty.

²⁹" 'These are to be legal requirements *b* for you throughout the generations to come, *c* wherever you live. *d*

³⁰" 'Anyone who kills a person is to be put to death as a murderer only on the testimony of witnesses. But no one is to be put to death on the testimony of only one witness. *e*

³¹" 'Do not accept a ransom *f* for the life of a murderer, who deserves to die. He must surely be put to death.

³²" 'Do not accept a ransom for anyone who has fled to a city of refuge and so allow him to go back and live on his own land before the death of the high priest.

³³" 'Do not pollute the land where you are. Bloodshed pollutes the land, *g* and atonement cannot be made for the land on which blood has been shed, except by the blood of the one who shed it. ³⁴Do not defile the land *h* where you live and where I dwell, *i* for I, the LORD, dwell among the Israelites.' "

35:22 *without hostility.* The cities of refuge were to be established for the person who had committed an act of involuntary manslaughter.
35:24 *according to these regulations.* Any gracious provi-sion is subject to abuse. For this reason the case of the involuntary slayer had to be determined by the judges. Fur-ther, the accused man had to stay in the city of refuge until the death of the high priest (when there would be a general amnesty). If the accused left the city of refuge, he would become fair game again for the avenger of blood.

35:25–28 See note on Jos 20:6.
35:30 *witnesses.* To avoid the possibility of an innocent party being accused and sentenced to death on insufficient evidence.
35:32 Not even an involuntary slayer could leave the city of refuge on the payment of a ransom.
35:33 *Bloodshed pollutes the land.* The crime of murder is not only an offense against the sanctity of life; it is in fact a pollutant to the Lord's sacred land.

Cities of Refuge

The idea of providing cities of refuge (Jos 20:1-9) for capital offenses is rooted in the tension between customary tribal law (retaliation or revenge, in which the blood relative is obligated to execute vengeance) and civil law (carried out less personally by an assembly according to a standard code of justice).

Blood feuds are usually associated with nomadic groups; legal procedures, with villages and towns. Israel, a society in the process of sedentarization, found it necessary to adopt an intermediate step regulating manslaughter, so that an innocent person would not be killed before standing trial. Absolution was possible only by being cleared by his hometown assembly, and by the eventual death of the high priest, which freed the offender from ritual pollution.

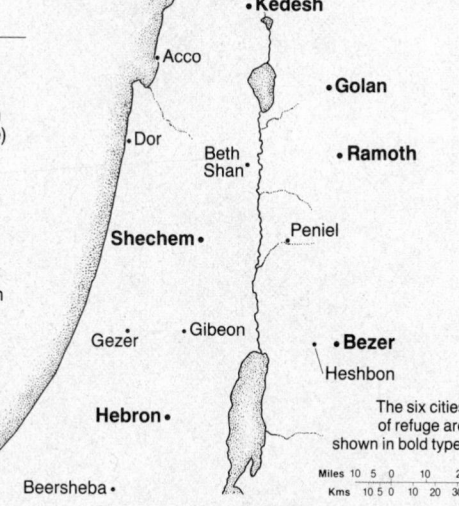

• **Kedesh**

• Acco

• **Golan**

• Dor

Beth Shan •

• **Ramoth**

Shechem •

• Peniel

Gezer

• Gibeon

• • **Bezer**

Heshbon

Hebron •

The six cities of refuge are shown in bold type.

Miles 10 5 0   10   20
Kms 10 5 0   10   20   30

Beersheba •

Inheritance of Zelophehad's Daughters

36:1–12pp — Nu 27:1–11

36 The family heads of the clan of Gilead*ʲ* son of Makir,*ᵏ* the son of Manasseh, who were from the clans of the descendants of Joseph,*ˡ* came and spoke before Moses and the leaders,*ᵐ* the heads of the Israelite families. ²They said, "When the LORD commanded my lord to give the land as an inheritance to the Israelites by lot,*ⁿ* he ordered you to give the inheritance of our brother Zelophehad*ᵒ* to his daughters. ³Now suppose they marry men from other Israelite tribes; then their inheritance will be taken from our ancestral inheritance and added to that of the tribe they marry into. And so part of the inheritance allotted to us will be taken away. ⁴When the Year of Jubilee*ᵖ* for the Israelites comes, their inheritance will be added to that of the tribe into which they marry, and their property will be taken from the tribal inheritance of our forefathers."

⁵Then at the LORD's command Moses gave this order to the Israelites: "What the tribe of the descendants of Joseph is saying is right. ⁶This is what the LORD commands

for Zelophehad's daughters: They may marry anyone they please as long as they marry within the tribal clan of their father. ⁷No inheritance*�q* in Israel is to pass from tribe to tribe, for every Israelite shall keep the tribal land inherited from his forefathers. ⁸Every daughter who inherits land in any Israelite tribe must marry someone in her father's tribal clan,*ʳ* so that every Israelite will possess the inheritance of his fathers. ⁹No inheritance may pass from tribe to tribe, for each Israelite tribe is to keep the land it inherits."

¹⁰So Zelophehad's daughters did as the LORD commanded Moses. ¹¹Zelophehad's daughters—Mahlah, Tirzah, Hoglah, Milcah and Noah*ˢ*—married their cousins on their father's side. ¹²They married within the clans of the descendants of Manasseh son of Joseph, and their inheritance remained in their father's clan and tribe.*ᵗ*

¹³These are the commands and regulations the LORD gave through Moses*ᵘ* to the Israelites on the plains of Moab by the Jordan across from Jericho.*ⁿ ᵛ*

36:1 *ʲ*S Nu 26:30
*ᵏ*S Ge 50:23
*ˡ*S Nu 26:28
*ᵐ*S Nu 27:2
36:2 *ⁿ*S Nu 33:54
*ᵒ*S Nu 26:33
36:4
*ᵖ*S Lev 25:10
36:7
*q*S Lev 25:23
36:8 *ʳ*1Ch 23:22
36:11 *ˢ*Nu 26:33
36:12 *ᵗ*1Ch 7:15
36:13
*ᵘ*S Lev 7:38;
S 27:34 *ᵛ*Nu 22:1

ⁿ13 Hebrew *Jordan of Jericho*; possibly an ancient name for the Jordan River

---

36:1–13 Presents an interesting further development of the account of Zelophehad's daughters (see 27:1–11). Since the Lord had instructed Moses that the women might inherit their father's land, new questions arose: What will happen to the family lands if these daughters marry among other tribes? Will not the original intention of the first provision be frustrated? Such questions led to the decision that marriage is to be kept within one's own tribe, so that the family allotments

will not "pass from tribe to tribe" (v. 9).
36:10 *Zelophehad's daughters did as the LORD commanded.* The book of Numbers, which so often presents the rebellion of God's people against his grace and in defiance of his will, ends on a happy note. These noble women, who were concerned for their father's name and their own place in the land, obeyed the Lord.

DEUTERONOMY

Title

The word "Deuteronomy" (meaning "repetition of the law"), as the name of the last book of the Pentateuch, arose from a mistranslation in the Greek Septuagint and the Latin Vulgate of a phrase in Dt 17:18, which in Hebrew means "copy of this law." The error is not serious, however, since Deuteronomy is, in a certain sense, a "repetition of the law" (see Structure and Outline). The Hebrew name of the book is *'elleh haddebarim* ("These are the words") or, more simply, *debarim* ("words"; see 1:1).

Author

The book itself testifies that, for the most part, Moses wrote it (1:5; 31:9,22,24), and other OT books agree (1Ki 2:3; 8:53; 2Ki 14:6; 18:12)—though, of course, the preamble (1:1-5) and the report of Moses' death (ch. 34) were written by someone else. Jesus also bears testimony to Mosaic authorship (Mt 19:7-8; Mk 10:3-5; Jn 5:46-47), and so do other NT writers (Ac 3:22-23; 7:37-38; Ro 10:19). Moreover, Jesus quotes Deuteronomy as authoritative (Mt 4:4,7,10). In the NT there are almost 100 quotations of and allusions to Deuteronomy. Tradition uniformly testifies to the Mosaic authorship of the book (see, e.g., Mk 12:19). See Introduction to Genesis: Author and Date of Writing.

Date

The book is probably to be dated c. 1406 B.C. (see Introduction to Genesis: Author and Date of Writing).

Historical Setting

Deuteronomy locates Moses and the Israelites in the territory of Moab in the area where the Jordan flows into the Dead Sea (1:5). As his final act at this important time of transferring leadership to Joshua, Moses delivered his farewell addresses to prepare the people for their entrance into Canaan. These addresses were actually a covenant renewal (see Structure and Outline). In them, Moses emphasized the laws that were especially needed at such a time, and he presented them in a way appropriate to the situation. In contrast to the matter-of-fact narratives of Leviticus and Numbers, the book of Deuteronomy comes to us from Moses' heart in a warm, personal, sermonic form of expression.

Theological Teaching

The love relationship of the Lord to his people and that of the people to the Lord as their sovereign God pervade the whole book. Deuteronomy's spiritual emphasis and its call to total commitment to the Lord in worship and obedience inspired references to its message throughout the rest of Scripture.

Structure and Outline

Deuteronomy's literary structure supports its historical setting. By its interpretive, repetitious, reminiscent and somewhat irregular style it shows that it is a series of more or less extemporaneous addresses, sometimes describing events in nonchronological order (see, e.g., 10:3). But it also bears in its structure clear reflections of the suzerain-vassal treaties (see chart on "Major Covenants in the OT," p. 19) of the preceding and then-current Near Eastern states, a structure that lends itself to the Biblical emphasis on the covenant between the Lord and his people. In this sense Deuteronomy is a covenant renewal document, as the following outline shows:

I. The Preamble (1:1-5)
II. The Historical Prologue (1:6-4:43)
III. The Stipulations of the Covenant (4:44-26:19)

The Command to Leave Horeb

1 These are the words Moses spoke to all Israel in the desert east of the Jordan^a—that is, in the Arabah^b—opposite Suph, between Paran^c and Tophel, Laban, Hazeroth and Dizahab. ²(It takes eleven days to go from Horeb^d to Kadesh Barnea^e by the Mount Seir^f road.)^g

³In the fortieth year,^h on the first day of the eleventh month,ⁱ Moses proclaimed^j to the Israelites all that the LORD had commanded him concerning them. ⁴This was after he had defeated Sihon^k king of the Amorites,^l who reigned in Heshbon,^m and at Edrei had defeated Ogⁿ king of Bashan, who reigned in Ashtaroth.^o

⁵East of the Jordan in the territory of Moab,^p Moses began to expound this law, saying:

⁶The LORD our God said to us^q at Horeb,^r "You have stayed long enough^s at this mountain. ⁷Break camp and advance into the hill country of the Amorites;^t go to all the neighboring peoples in the Arabah,^u in the mountains, in the western foothills, in the Negev^v and along the coast, to the land of the Canaanites^w and to Lebanon,^x as far as the great river, the Euphrates.^y ⁸See, I have given you this land^{z, a} Go in and take possession of the land that the LORD swore^b he would give to your fathers—to Abraham, Isaac and Jacob—and to their descendants after them."

The Appointment of Leaders

⁹At that time I said to you, "You are too heavy a burden^c for me to carry alone.^d

¹⁰The LORD your God has increased^e your numbers^f so that today you are as many^g as the stars in the sky.^h ¹¹May the LORD, the God of your fathers, increaseⁱ you a thousand times and bless you as he has promised!^j ¹²But how can I bear your problems and your burdens and your disputes all by myself?^k ¹³Choose some wise, understanding and respected men^l from each of your tribes, and I will set them over you."

¹⁴You answered me, "What you propose to do is good."

¹⁵So I took^m the leading men of your tribes,ⁿ wise and respected men,^o and appointed them to have authority over you—as commanders^p of thousands, of hundreds, of fifties and of tens and as tribal officials.^q ¹⁶And I charged your judges at that time: Hear the disputes between your brothers and judge^r fairly,^s whether the case is between brother Israelites or between one of them and an alien.^t ¹⁷Do not show partiality^u in judging; hear both small and great alike. Do not be afraid of any man,^v for judgment belongs to God. Bring me any case too hard for you, and I will hear it.^w ¹⁸And at that time I told you everything you were to do.^x

Spies Sent Out

¹⁹Then, as the LORD our God commanded us, we set out from Horeb and went toward the hill country of the Amo-

---

1:1 ^aS Nu 13:29; Dt 4:46 ^bver 7; Dt 2:8; 3:17; Jos 3:16; 8:14; 11:2; Eze 47:8 ^cS Nu 10:12
1:2 ^dS Ex 3:1 ^eS Ge 14:7; Dt 2:14; 9:23; Jos 15:3 ^fS Nu 24:18 ^gver 19
1:3 ^hNu 14:33; 32:13; Dt 8:2; Heb 3:7-9 ⁱGe 50:3; Dt 34:8; Jos 4:19 ^jDt 4:1-2
1:4 ^kNu 21:21-26 ^lS Ge 10:16; S 14:7 ^mS Nu 21:25 ⁿNu 21:33-35; Dt 3:10 ^oJos 9:10; 12:4; 1Ch 11:44
1:5 ^pS Nu 21:11
1:6 ^qNu 10:13 ^rS Ex 3:1 ^sDt 2:3
1:7 ^tver 19; Dt 2:24; 7:1; Jos 10:5 ^uS ver 1 ^vS Nu 21:1; Jos 11:16; 12:8; 2Sa 24:7 ^wS Ge 10:18 ^xDt 11:24 ^yS Ge 2:14
1:8 ^zS Nu 23:13 ^aS Nu 34:2 ^bS Ex 13:11; S Nu 14:23; Heb 6:13-14
1:9 ^cS Nu 11:14; Ps 38:4 ^dS Ex 18:18
1:10 ^ever 11; Eze 16:7 ^fS Dt 7:13 ^gS Ge 15:5; Isa 51:2; 60:22; Eze 33:24 ^hS Ge 22:17; S Nu 10:36
1:11 ⁱS ver 10 ^jver 8; Ex 32:13; 2Sa 24:3; 1Ch 21:3
1:12 ^kS Ex 5:22; S 18:18
1:13 ^lS Ge 47:6 **1:15** ^mEx 18:25 ⁿEx 5:14; Nu 11:16; Jos 1:10; 3:2 ^oS Ge 47:6 ^pNu 31:14; 1Sa 8:12; 22:7; 1Ki 14:27 ^qS Nu 1:4 **1:16** ^r1Ki 3:9; Ps 72:1; Pr 2:9 ^sS Ge 31:37; Jn 7:24 ^tS Ex 12:19,49; S 22:21 **1:17** ^uS Ex 18:16; S Lev 19:15; Ac 10:34; Jas 2:1 ^vPr 29:25 ^wEx 18:26 **1:18** ^xS Ge 39:11

1:1–5 The preamble gives the historical setting for the entire book.

1:1 *Moses spoke.* Almost all of Deuteronomy is made up of speeches by Moses during the final months of his life, just before the Israelites crossed the Jordan to enter Canaan. *Arabah.* Includes the valley of the Jordan (from the Sea of Galilee to the southern end of the Dead Sea) and the valley extending down to the Gulf of Aqaba. *Suph . . . Paran . . . Tophel, Laban, Hazeroth and Dizahab.* Places along the route from Sinai to the territory of Moab.

1:2 *Horeb.* The usual name for Mount Sinai in Deuteronomy (the only exception is in 33:2). *Kadesh Barnea.* See note on Ge 14:7. *Seir.* See note on Ge 36:8.

1:3 *fortieth year.* After leaving Egypt. The Lord had condemned Israel to 40 years of wandering in Sinai as punishment for not entering Canaan as he had commanded them to do at Kadesh (Nu 14:33–34). The 40 years included the time spent at Sinai and on the journey to Kadesh as well as the next 38 years (see 2:14). See 8:2–5; 29:5–6; Nu 14:29–35; 32:13; Heb 3:7–19. *eleventh month.* January-February.

1:5 *this law.* The Ten Commandments and other laws given at Mount Sinai and recorded in Ex 20–24, Leviticus and Numbers. In Deuteronomy the laws are summarized and interpreted, and adjusted to the new, specific situation

Israel would face in Canaan. Thus Deuteronomy is, in essence, a covenant renewal (and updating) document.

1:7 See Jos 1:4. The land is described by its various geographical areas (see map No. 2 at the end of the Study Bible). *Arabah.* See note on v. 1; here the Jordan Valley and the Dead Sea area. *mountains.* The midsection running north and south. *western foothills.* Sloping toward the Mediterranean. *Negev.* See note on Ge 12:9. *coast.* The Mediterranean coastal strip. The "land of the Canaanites" and "Lebanon, as far as . . . the Euphrates" make up the northern sector. The "hill country of the Amorites" is, in general, the central and southern mountains. This description of the land agrees with that in the promise (see v. 8) to Abraham in Ge 15:18–21, a promise later limited to Isaac's descendants (Ge 26:2–4) and still later to the descendants of Jacob (Ge 35:11–12).

1:9–18 Cf. 16:18–20; Ex 18:13–26.

1:10 *The Lord your God.* This title occurs almost 300 times in Deuteronomy in addition to the many times that "Lord" is used alone or in other combinations. *as the stars in the sky.* See 10:22; 28:62; Ge 13:16 and note; 15:5 and note; 22:17; 26:4; Ex 32:13.

1:19–46 See Nu 13–14.

rites y through all that vast and dreadful desert z that you have seen, and so we reached Kadesh Barnea. a 20Then I said to you, "You have reached the hill country of the Amorites, which the LORD our God is giving us. 21See, the LORD your God has given you the land. Go up and take possession b of it as the LORD, the God of your fathers, told you. Do not be afraid; c do not be discouraged." d

22Then all of you came to me and said, "Let us send men ahead to spy e out the land f for us and bring back a report about the route we are to take and the towns we will come to."

23The idea seemed good to me; so I selected g twelve of you, one man from each tribe. 24They left and went up into the hill country, and came to the Valley of Eshcol h and explored it. 25Taking with them some of the fruit of the land, they brought it down to us and reported, i "It is a good land j that the LORD our God is giving us." k

Rebellion Against the LORD

26But you were unwilling to go up; l you rebelled m against the command of the LORD your God. 27You grumbled n in your tents and said, "The LORD hates us; so he brought us out of Egypt to deliver us into the hands of the Amorites to destroy us. 28Where can we go? Our brothers have made us lose heart. They say, 'The people are stronger and taller o than we are; the cities are large, with walls up to the sky. We even saw the Anakites p there.' "

29Then I said to you, "Do not be terrified; do not be afraid q of them. r 30The LORD your God, who is going before you, will fight s for you, as he did for you in Egypt, before your very eyes, 31and in the desert. There you saw how the LORD your God carried t you, as a father carries his

son, all the way you went until you reached this place." u

32In spite of this, v you did not trust w in the LORD your God, 33who went ahead of you on your journey, in fire by night and in a cloud by day, x to search y out places for you to camp and to show you the way you should go.

34When the LORD heard z what you said, he was angry a and solemnly swore: b 35"Not a man of this evil generation shall see the good land c I swore to give your forefathers, 36except Caleb d son of Jephunneh. He will see it, and I will give him and his descendants the land he set his feet on, because he followed the LORD wholeheartedly. e "

37Because of you the LORD became angry f with me also and said, "You shall not enter g it, either. 38But your assistant, Joshua h son of Nun, will enter it. Encourage i him, because he will lead j Israel to inherit k it. 39And the little ones that you said would be taken captive, l your children who do not yet know m good from bad—they will enter the land. I will give it to them and they will take possession of it. 40But as for you, turn around and set out toward the desert along the route to the Red Sea. a n"

41Then you replied, "We have sinned against the LORD. We will go up and fight, as the LORD our God commanded us." So every one of you put on his weapons, thinking it easy to go up into the hill country.

42But the LORD said to me, "Tell them, 'Do not go up and fight, because I will not be with you. You will be defeated by your enemies.' " o

43So I told you, but you would not lis-

Cross references (center column)

1:19 y S ver 7
z Dt 2:7; 8:15;
32:10; Ps 136:16;
Jer 2:2,6;
Hos 13:5 a ver 2;
Nu 13:26
1:21 b Dt 9:23
c S Nu 14:9;
Jos 1:6,9,18;
2Sa 10:12;
Ps 27:14
d Dt 7:18; Jos 8:1;
10:8
1:22 e Nu 13:1-3
f S Ge 42:9
1:23 g Nu 13:1-3
1:24
h Nu 13:21-25;
S 32:9
1:25 i S Nu 13:27
j S Nu 14:7
k Jos 1:2
1:26 l Nu 14:1-4
m S Nu 14:9
1:27 n Dt 9:28;
Ps 106:25
1:28 o S Nu 13:32
p S Nu 13:33;
Dt 9:1-3
1:29 q Dt 3:22;
20:3; Ne 4:14
r Dt 7:18; 20:1;
31:6
1:30 s S Ex 14:14
1:31 t Ex 19:4;
Dt 32:10-12;
Ps 28:9;
Isa 46:3-4; 63:9;
Hos 11:3;
Ac 13:18

u Jer 31:32
1:32 v S Nu 14:11
w Dt 9:23;
Ps 78:22; 106:24;
Zep 3:2;
Heb 3:19;
Jude 1:5
1:33 x Ex 13:21;
Nu 9:15-23;
Ne 9:12; Ps 78:14
y S Nu 10:33
1:34 z S Nu 11:1
a S Nu 32:14
b S Nu 14:23,
28-30; Eze 20:15;
Heb 3:11
1:35 c S Nu 14:29
1:36 d S Nu 13:6
e S Nu 14:24
1:37 f Ps 106:32
g S Nu 27:13
1:38 h S Nu 11:28
i Dt 31:7 /Dt 3:28
k Jos 11:23;
Ps 78:55; 136:21
1:39 l S Nu 14:3
m Isa 7:15-16

1:40 n S Ex 14:27; Jdg 11:16 1:42 o S Nu 14:41-43

a 40 Hebrew Yam Suph; that is, Sea of Reeds

1:21 *as the LORD . . . told you.* The promise of the land (see note on v. 7) was reaffirmed to Moses at the burning bush (v. 8; Ex 3:8,17). Now the Israelites are told to enter the land and conquer it. *Do not be afraid . . . discouraged.* See 31:8; Jos 1:9; 8:1; 10:25.
1:23 *twelve.* They are named in Nu 13:4–15.
1:24 *Eshcol.* See NIV text note on Nu 13:23.
1:26 *you rebelled.* Although they themselves had not rebelled, the people were being addressed as a nation united with the earlier rebellious generation (see 5:2; cf. 29:1).
1:27 *grumbled.* See note on Ex 15:24. *The LORD hates us.* The people's statement is ironic indeed in the light of Deuteronomy's major theme (see Introduction: Theological Teaching).
1:28 *Anakites.* Earlier inhabitants of Canaan, described as giants (see 2:10,21; 9:2; Nu 13:32).
1:30 *as he did for you in Egypt.* See Ex 14:1–15:19.
1:31 *God carried you.* See notes on Isa 41:10,13; 43:1–2;

cf. Isa 40:11; Jer 31:10; Eze 34:11–16.
1:33 *in fire by night and in a cloud by day.* The presence of the Lord was in the cloud over the tabernacle to guide the Israelites through their desert journeys (see Ex 13:21 and note; 40:34–38).
1:36 *Caleb.* See Nu 13:30–14:38; Jos 14:6–15.
1:37 *Because of you.* See 3:26; 4:21. God was angry with Moses when in a wrong spirit he struck the rock at Meribah to get water (Nu 20:9–13; 27:12–14). And since it was the Israelites who had incited him to sin, God was angry with them too. This event (v. 37) occurred almost 40 years after that of the preceding verses (vv. 34–36), but Moses, interested in telling of the Israelites' sin and his own, brings the two events together.
1:39 *do not yet know good from bad.* See notes on Ge 2:9; Isa 7:15.
1:41 *you.* See note on v. 26.
1:43 *You rebelled against the LORD's command.* The same

ten. You rebelled against the LORD's command and in your arrogance you marched up into the hill country. [44]The Amorites who lived in those hills came out against you; they chased you like a swarm of bees[p] and beat you down from Seir[q] all the way to Hormah.[r] [45]You came back and wept before the LORD,[s] but he paid no attention[t] to your weeping and turned a deaf ear[u] to you. [46]And so you stayed in Kadesh[v] many days—all the time you spent there.

Wanderings in the Desert

2 Then we turned back and set out toward the desert along the route to the Red Sea,[b] [w] as the LORD had directed me. For a long time we made our way around the hill country of Seir.[x]

[2]Then the LORD said to me, [3]"You have made your way around this hill country long enough;[y] now turn north. [4]Give the people these orders:[z] 'You are about to pass through the territory of your brothers the descendants of Esau,[a] who live in Seir.[b] They will be afraid[c] of you, but be very careful. [5]Do not provoke them to war, for I will not give you any of their land, not even enough to put your foot on. I have given Esau the hill country of Seir as his own.[d] [6]You are to pay them in silver for the food you eat and the water you drink.' "

[7]The LORD your God has blessed you in all the work of your hands. He has watched[e] over your journey through this vast desert.[f] These forty years[g] the LORD your God has been with you, and you have not lacked anything.[h]

[8]So we went on past our brothers the descendants of Esau, who live in Seir. We turned from[i] the Arabah[j] road, which comes up from Elath and Ezion Geber,[k]

and traveled along the desert road of Moab.[l]

[9]Then the LORD said to me, "Do not harass the Moabites or provoke them to war, for I will not give you any part of their land. I have given Ar[m] to the descendants of Lot[n] as a possession."

[10](The Emites[o] used to live there—a people strong and numerous, and as tall as the Anakites.[p] [11]Like the Anakites, they too were considered Rephaites,[q] but the Moabites called them Emites. [12]Horites[r] used to live in Seir, but the descendants of Esau drove them out. They destroyed the Horites from before them and settled in their place, just as Israel did[s] in the land the LORD gave them as their possession.)

[13]And the LORD said, "Now get up and cross the Zered Valley.[t]" So we crossed the valley.

[14]Thirty-eight years[u] passed from the time we left Kadesh Barnea[v] until we crossed the Zered Valley. By then, that entire generation[w] of fighting men had perished from the camp, as the LORD had sworn to them.[x] [15]The LORD's hand was against them until he had completely eliminated[y] them from the camp.

[16]Now when the last of these fighting men among the people had died, [17]the LORD said to me, [18]"Today you are to pass by the region of Moab at Ar.[z] [19]When you come to the Ammonites,[a] do not harass them or provoke them to war,[b] for I will not give you possession of any land belonging to the Ammonites. I have given it as a possession to the descendants of Lot.[c]"

[20](That too was considered a land of the Rephaites,[d] who used to live there; but the Ammonites called them Zamzummites. [21]They were a people strong and numer-

Cross references (center column)

1:44 [p]Ps 118:12
[q]S Nu 24:18
[r]S Nu 14:45
1:45 [s]S Nu 14:1
[t]Job 27:9; 35:13;
Ps 18:41; 66:18;
Pr 1:28; Isa 1:15;
Jer 14:12; La 3:8;
Mic 3:4; S Jn 9:31
[u]Ps 28:1; 39:12;
Pr 28:9
1:46 [v]S Nu 20:1
2:1 [w]S Ex 14:27;
S Nu 21:4
[x]S Nu 24:18
2:3 [y]Dt 1:6
2:4 [z]Nu 20:14-21
[a]Ge 36:8 [b]ver 1
[c]Ex 15:16
2:5 [d]Jos 24:4
2:7 [e]Dt 8:2-4
[f]S Ex 13:21;
Dt 1:19 [g]ver
14; S Nu 14:33;
32:13; Jos 5:6
[h]Ne 9:21;
Am 2:10
2:8 [i]S Nu 20:21
[j]S Dt 1:1
[k]Nu 33:35;
1Ki 9:26

[i]S Nu 21:4
2:9 [m]S Nu 21:15
[n]Ge 19:38;
Ps 83:8
2:10 [o]Ge 14:5
[p]S Nu 13:22,33
2:11 [q]S Ge 14:5
2:12 [r]S Ge 14:6
[s]Nu 21:25,35
2:13 [t]S Nu 21:12
2:14 [u]S ver 7
[v]S Dt 1:2
[w]Nu 14:29-35
[x]Dt 1:34-35;
Jos 5:6
2:15 [y]Ps 106:26;
Jude 1:5
2:18 [z]S Nu 21:15
2:19 [a]S Ge 19:38
[b]2Ch 20:10
[c]S ver 9
2:20 [d]S Ge 14:5

[b]1 Hebrew Yam Suph; that is, Sea of Reeds

---

charge as in v. 26. First the people rebelled against the Lord's command to go into the land, then against his command not to enter the land. After their first rebellion the Lord would not go with them. His presence was essential, and Israel needed to learn that lesson.

1:44 *bees.* See note on Ex 23:28.

1:45 *before the LORD.* At the tabernacle.

2:1–3:11 See Nu 20:14–21:35.

2:1 *Red Sea.* Here probably the Gulf of Aqaba (see note on 1Ki 9:26). *hill country of Seir.* The mountainous area south of the Dead Sea.

2:5 *I will not give you any of their land.* See vv. 9,19. The Lord told Moses to bypass Edom, Moab and Ammon because of their blood relationship to Israel. The Israelites were to take over only those lands east of the Jordan that were in the hands of the Amorites (see v. 24; 3:2). *I have given.* See vv. 9,19. The Lord had given the descendants of Esau (Edomites) and Lot (Moabites and Ammonites) their lands, just as he was giving the Israelites the territories of Transjordan and

Canaan.

2:8 *Elath and Ezion Geber.* At the head of the Gulf of Aqaba. The "Arabah road" ran from the head of the gulf northward and to the east of Moab.

2:9 *Ar.* Location unknown.

2:10 *Emites.* Possibly meaning "terrors." *Anakites.* See note on 1:28.

2:11 *Rephaites.* Ancient people of large stature.

2:12 *Horites.* See note on Ge 14:6. *the land the LORD gave them.* Either (1) the Transjordan regions (see 2:24–3:20), (2) Canaan itself or (3) Transjordan and Canaan. If either (2) or (3) is intended, editorial updating is involved (see note on Ge 14:14).

2:13 *Zered.* The main stream (intermittent) that flows into the southern end of the Dead Sea from the east (see map No. 4 at the end of the Study Bible).

2:14 *Thirty-eight years.* See note on 1:3.

2:20 *Zamzummites.* Possibly meaning "murmurers," and perhaps to be identified with the Zuzites of Ge 14:5.

ous, and as tall as the Anakites. *e* The LORD destroyed them from before the Ammonites, who drove them out and settled in their place. 22The LORD had done the same for the descendants of Esau, who lived in Seir,*f* when he destroyed the Horites from before them. They drove them out and have lived in their place to this day. 23And as for the Avvites*g* who lived in villages as far as Gaza,*h* the Caphtorites*i* coming out from Caphtor*c* *j* destroyed them and settled in their place.)

Defeat of Sihon King of Heshbon

24"Set out now and cross the Arnon Gorge.*k* See, I have given into your hand Sihon the Amorite,*l* king of Heshbon, and his country. Begin to take possession of it and engage*m* him in battle. 25This very day I will begin to put the terror*n* and fear*o* of you on all the nations under heaven. They will hear reports of you and will tremble*p* and be in anguish because of you."

26From the desert of Kedemoth*q* I sent messengers to Sihon*r* king of Heshbon offering peace*s* and saying, 27"Let us pass through your country. We will stay on the main road; we will not turn aside to the right or to the left.*t* 28Sell us food to eat*u* and water to drink for their price in silver. Only let us pass through on foot*v*— 29as the descendants of Esau, who live in Seir, and the Moabites, who live in Ar, did for us—until we cross the Jordan into the land the LORD our God is giving us." 30But Sihon king of Heshbon refused to let us pass through. For the LORD*w* your God had made his spirit stubborn*x* and his heart obstinate*y* in order to give him into your hands,*z* as he has now done.

31The LORD said to me, "See, I have begun to deliver Sihon and his country over to you. Now begin to conquer and possess his land."*a*

32When Sihon and all his army came out

to meet us in battle*b* at Jahaz, 33the LORD our God delivered*c* him over to us and we struck him down,*d* together with his sons and his whole army. 34At that time we took all his towns and completely destroyed*d* *e* them—men, women and children. We left no survivors. 35But the livestock*f* and the plunder*g* from the towns we had captured we carried off for ourselves. 36From Aroer*h* on the rim of the Arnon Gorge, and from the town in the gorge, even as far as Gilead,*i* not one town was too strong for us. The LORD our God gave*j* us all of them. 37But in accordance with the command of the LORD our God,*k* you did not encroach on any of the land of the Ammonites,*l* neither the land along the course of the Jabbok*m* nor that around the towns in the hills.

Defeat of Og King of Bashan

3 Next we turned and went up along the road toward Bashan, and Og king of Bashan*n* with his whole army marched out to meet us in battle at Edrei.*o* 2The LORD said to me, "Do not be afraid*p* of him, for I have handed him over to you with his whole army and his land. Do to him what you did to Sihon king of the Amorites, who reigned in Heshbon."

3So the LORD our God also gave into our hands Og king of Bashan and all his army. We struck them down,*q* leaving no survivors.*r* 4At that time we took all his cities.*s* There was not one of the sixty cities that we did not take from them—the whole region of Argob, Og's kingdom*t* in Bashan.*u* 5All these cities were fortified with high walls and with gates and bars, and there were also a great many unwalled villages. 6We completely destroyed*d* them, as we had done with Sihon king of Heshbon,

---

*2:21 e*ver 10
*2:22 f*S Ge 14:6
*2:23 g*Jos 13:3;
18:23; 2Ki 17:31
*h*S Ge 10:19
*i*S Ge 10:14
/Jer 47:4; Am 9:7
2:24
*k*Nu 21:13-14;
Jdg 11:13,18
*l*S Dt 1:7 *m*Dt 3:6
*2:25 n*S Ge 35:5;
Dt 11:25 *o*Jos 2:9,
11; 1Ch 14:17;
2Ch 14:14;
17:10; 20:29;
Isa 2:19; 13:13;
19:16
*p*Ex 15:14-16
*2:26 q*Jos 13:18;
1Ch 6:79 *r*Dt 1:4;
Jdg 11:21-22
*s*Dt 20:10;
Jdg 21:13;
2Sa 20:19
2:27
*t*Nu 21:21-22
*2:28 u*Dt 23:4
*v*S Nu 20:19
*2:30 w*Jdg 14:4;
1Ki 12:15
*x*S Ex 4:21;
Ro 9:18
*y*S Ex 14:17
*z*La 3:65
*2:31 a*S Ge 12:7

*2:32 b*S Nu 21:23
*2:33 c*Ex 23:31;
Dt 7:2; 31:5
*d*S Nu 21:24
*2:34 e*S Nu 21:2;
Dt 3:6; 7:2;
Ps 106:34
*2:35 f*Dt 3:7
*g*S Ge 34:29;
S 49:27
*2:36 h*S Nu 32:34
*i*S Nu 32:39
/Ps 44:3
*2:37 k*ver 18-19
*l*S Nu 21:24
*m*S Ge 32:22
*3:1 n*S Nu 32:19
*o*S Nu 21:33
*3:2 p*Jos 10:8;
2Ki 19:6; Isa 7:4
*3:3 q*S Nu 21:24
*r*Nu 21:35
*3:4 s*S Nu 21:24
*t*ver 13
*u*S Nu 21:33

*c*23 That is, Crete   *d*34,6 The Hebrew term refers to the irrevocable giving over of things or persons to the LORD, often by totally destroying them.

2:23 *Avvites.* Pre-Philistine people otherwise unknown (Jos 13:3). *Caphtorites.* See note on Ge 10:14.
2:24 *Arnon.* See note on Nu 21:10–13.
2:26 *Kedemoth.* Means "eastern regions."
2:30 *his spirit stubborn and his heart obstinate.* In the OT, actions are often attributed to God without the mention of mediate or contributing situations or persons. Sihon by his own conscious will refused Israel passage, but it was God who would give Sihon's land to Israel (see note on Ex 4:21).
2:32 *Jahaz.* See note on Isa 15:4.
2:34 *completely destroyed.* See NIV text note. The Hebrew for this expression usually denotes the destruction of everyone and everything that could be destroyed. Objects like gold, silver and bronze, not subject to destruction, were put in a secure place as God's possession. Destruction of people and things made them useless to the conquerors but

put them in the hands of God. So the word is sometimes translated "destroyed" and sometimes "devoted" (see, e.g., Jos 6:17). The practice was sometimes limited, as when God assigned captured livestock and other plunder to his people as recompense for service in his army (see v. 35; 3:7; Jos 8:2).
2:36 *Aroer.* See note on Isa 17:2. *Gilead.* See note on Ge 31:21.
2:37 *Jabbok.* See note on Ge 32:22.
3:3 *gave into our hands Og.* As in 2:26–37.
3:4 *sixty cities.* The cities were large and walled (1Ki 4:13), implying a heavily populated territory (see v. 5). *region of Argob.* An otherwise unidentified area in Bashan (see vv. 13–14; 1Ki 4:13).
3:6–7 See note on 2:34.

destroying[e][v] every city—men, women and children. [7]But all the livestock[w] and the plunder from their cities we carried off for ourselves.

[8]So at that time we took from these two kings of the Amorites[x] the territory east of the Jordan, from the Arnon Gorge as far as Mount Hermon.[y] [9](Hermon is called Sirion[z] by the Sidonians; the Amorites call it Senir.)[a] [10]We took all the towns on the plateau, and all Gilead, and all Bashan as far as Salecah[b] and Edrei, towns of Og's kingdom in Bashan. [11](Only Og king of Bashan was left of the remnant of the Rephaites.[c] His bed[f] was made of iron and was more than thirteen feet long and six feet wide.[g] It is still in Rabbah[d] of the Ammonites.)

Division of the Land

[12]Of the land that we took over at that time, I gave the Reubenites and the Gadites the territory north of Aroer[e] by the Arnon Gorge, including half the hill country of Gilead, together with its towns. [13]The rest of Gilead and also all of Bashan, the kingdom of Og, I gave to the half tribe of Manasseh.[f] (The whole region of Argob in Bashan used to be known as a land of the Rephaites.[g] [14]Jair,[h] a descendant of Manasseh, took the whole region of Argob as far as the border of the Geshurites and the Maacathites;[i] it was named[j] after him, so that to this day Bashan is called Havvoth Jair.[h]) [15]And I gave Gilead to Makir.[k] [16]But to the Reubenites and the Gadites I gave the territory extending from Gilead down to the Arnon Gorge (the middle of the gorge being the border) and out to the Jabbok River,[l] which is the border of the Ammonites. [17]Its western border was the Jordan in the Arabah,[m] from Kin-

nereth[n] to the Sea of the Arabah[o] (the Salt Sea[i][p]), below the slopes of Pisgah.

[18]I commanded you at that time: "The LORD your God has given[q] you this land to take possession of it. But all your able-bodied men, armed for battle, must cross over ahead of your brother Israelites.[r] [19]However, your wives,[s] your children and your livestock[t] (I know you have much livestock) may stay in the towns I have given you, [20]until the LORD gives rest to your brothers as he has to you, and they too have taken over the land that the LORD your God is giving them, across the Jordan. After that, each of you may go back to the possession I have given you."

Moses Forbidden to Cross the Jordan

[21]At that time I commanded Joshua: "You have seen with your own eyes all that the LORD your God has done to these two kings. The LORD will do the same to all the kingdoms over there where you are going. [22]Do not be afraid[u] of them;[v] the LORD your God himself will fight[w] for you."

[23]At that time I pleaded[x] with the LORD: [24]"O Sovereign LORD, you have begun to show to your servant your greatness[y] and your strong hand. For what god[z] is there in heaven or on earth who can do the deeds and mighty works[a] you do?[b] [25]Let me go over and see the good land[c] beyond the Jordan—that fine hill country and Lebanon.[d]"

[26]But because of you the LORD was angry[e] with me and would not listen to me. "That is enough," the LORD said. "Do not

3:6 vDt 2:24
3:7 wDt 2:35
3:8 xNu 32:33; Jos 13:8-12
yDt 4:48; Jos 11:3,17; 12:1; 13:5; Jdg 3:3; 1Ch 5:23;
Ps 42:6; 89:12; 133:3; SS 4:8
3:9 zPs 29:6
a1Ch 5:23; SS 4:8; Eze 27:5
3:10 bJos 12:5; 1Ch 5:11
3:11 cGe 14:5
dJos 13:25; 15:60; 2Sa 11:1; 12:26; 17:27; 1Ch 20:1; Jer 49:2; Eze 21:20; 25:5; Am 1:14
3:12 eDt 2:36
3:13 fDt 29:8
gGe 14:5
3:14 hS Nu 32:41
iJos 12:5; 13:11, 13; 2Sa 10:6; 23:34; 2Ki 25:23; 1Ch 4:19; Jer 40:8
jJos 19:47; Ps 49:11
3:15 kS Ge 50:23; Nu 32:39-40
3:16 lS Nu 21:24
3:17 m2Sa 2:29; 4:7; Eze 47:8

nS Nu 34:11
oS Dt 1:1
pS Ge 14:3
3:18 qJos 1:13
rS Nu 32:17
3:19 sJos 1:14
tS Nu 32:16
3:22 uS Dt 1:29
vDt 7:18; 20:1; 31:6; 2Ch 32:8; Ps 23:4; Isa 41:10
wS Ex 14:14
3:23 xDt 1:37; 31:2; 32:52; 34:4
3:24 yDt 5:24; 11:2; 32:3
zS Ex 8:10
aPs 71:16; 106:2; 145:12; 150:2
b2Sa 7:22
3:25 cDt 4:22
dDt 1:7; Jos 1:4; 9:1; 11:17; 12:7; 13:5; Jdg 3:3; 9:15; 1Ki 4:33
3:26 ever 27; Dt 1:37; 31:2

e6 The Hebrew term refers to the irrevocable giving over of things or persons to the LORD, often by totally destroying them. f11 Or *sarcophagus* g11 Hebrew *nine cubits long and four cubits wide* (about 4 meters long and 1.8 meters wide) h14 Or *called the settlements of Jair* i17 That is, the Dead Sea

---

3:8 *Mount Hermon.* Snowcapped throughout the year and rising to a height of over 9,200 feet, it is one of the most prominent and beautiful mountains in Lebanon.
3:9 *Sirion.* This name for Mount Hermon is found also in a Canaanite document contemporary with Moses. *Senir.* This name for Mount Hermon is also found in Assyrian sources.
3:10 *Salecah.* A city marking the eastern boundary of Bashan (see Jos 13:11).
3:11 *bed . . . of iron.* Sarcophagi (stone coffins) of basalt have been found in Bashan, and the Hebrew for "bed" (see NIV text note) may reflect this. If an actual bed, it was probably made of wood but with certain iron fixtures, as were the "iron chariots" (see note on Jos 17:16). *Rabbah of the Ammonites.* Called Philadelphia in NT times, Rabbah was the capital of ancient Ammon (Am 1:13–14). Today its name is Amman, the capital of the kingdom of Jordan.
3:12–20 See Nu 32; 34:13–15.
3:14 *Jair . . . Havvoth Jair.* See NIV text note; see also note on Jdg 10:3. *the Geshurites and the Maacathites.* Two

comparatively small kingdoms, Geshur was east of the Sea of Galilee and Maacah was east of the Waters of Merom (see note on Jos 11:5) and north of Geshur.
3:15 *Makir.* See note on Ge 50:23.
3:17 *Kinnereth.* See note on Mk 1:16. *Pisgah.* On the edge of the high plateau overlooking the Dead Sea from the east.
3:20 *rest.* A peaceful situation—free from external threat and oppression, and untroubled within by conflict, famine or plague (see 12:9–10; 25:19; see also notes on Jos 1:13; 1Ki 5:4; Heb 4:1–11).
3:22 *God himself.* The conquest narratives emphasize the truth that without the Lord's help Israel's victory would be impossible. The Lord's power, not Israel's unaided strength, achieved victory. Moses bolstered Israel's resolve and faith by this assurance (see 1:30; 2:21–22,31; 20:4).
3:23–25 Moses' final plea to be allowed to enter the land (see 1:37 and note; 31:2).
3:26 *because of you.* See note on 1:37.

speak to me anymore about this matter. ²⁷Go up to the top of Pisgah[f] and look west and north and south and east.[g] Look at the land with your own eyes, since you are not going to cross[h] this Jordan.[i] ²⁸But commission[j] Joshua, and encourage[k] and strengthen him, for he will lead this people across[l] and will cause them to inherit the land that you will see." ²⁹So we stayed in the valley near Beth Peor.[m]

Obedience Commanded

4 Hear now, O Israel, the decrees[n] and laws I am about to teach[o] you. Follow them so that you may live[p] and may go in and take possession of the land that the LORD, the God of your fathers, is giving you. ²Do not add[q] to what I command you and do not subtract[r] from it, but keep the commands[t] of the LORD your God that I give you.

³You saw with your own eyes what the LORD did at Baal Peor.[u] The LORD your God destroyed from among you everyone who followed the Baal of Peor, ⁴but all of you who held fast to the LORD your God are still alive today.

⁵See, I have taught[v] you decrees and laws[w] as the LORD my God commanded[x] me, so that you may follow them in the land you are entering[y] to take possession of it. ⁶Observe[z] them carefully, for this will show your wisdom[a] and understanding to the nations, who will hear about all these decrees and say, "Surely this great nation is a wise and understanding people."[b] ⁷What other nation is so great[c] as to have their gods near[d] them the way the LORD our God is near us whenever we pray to him? ⁸And what other nation is so great as to have such righteous decrees and laws[e] as this body of laws I am setting before you today?

⁹Only be careful,[f] and watch yourselves closely so that you do not forget the things your eyes have seen or let them slip from your heart as long as you live. Teach[g] them to your children[h] and to their children after them. ¹⁰Remember the day you stood before the LORD your God at Horeb,[i] when he said to me, "Assemble the people before me to hear my words so that they may learn[j] to revere[k] me as long as they live in the land[l] and may teach[m] them to their children." ¹¹You came near and stood at the foot of the mountain[n] while it blazed with fire[o] to the very heavens, with black clouds and deep darkness.[p] ¹²Then the LORD spoke[q] to you out of the fire. You heard the sound of words but saw no form;[r] there was only a voice.[s] ¹³He declared to you his covenant,[t] the Ten Commandments,[u] which he commanded you to follow and then wrote them on two stone tablets. ¹⁴And the LORD directed me at that time to teach you the decrees and laws[v] you are to follow in the land that you are crossing the Jordan to possess.

Idolatry Forbidden

¹⁵You saw no form[w] of any kind the day the LORD spoke to you at Horeb[x] out of the fire. Therefore watch yourselves very carefully,[y] ¹⁶so that you do not become corrupt[z] and make for yourselves an idol,[a] an image of any shape, whether formed like a man or a woman, ¹⁷or like any animal on earth or any bird that flies in the air,[b] ¹⁸or like any creature that moves

Cross references (center column)

3:27 /S Nu 21:20
gS Ge 13:14
hS ver 26;
S Nu 20:12;
Dt 32:52
iS Nu 27:12
3:28
/Nu 27:18-23
kDt 31:7
/Dt 1:38; 31:3,23
3:29
mS Nu 23:28;
Dt 4:46; 34:6;
Jos 13:20
4:1 nS Lev 18:4
oDt 1:3
pS Lev 18:5;
Dt 30:15-20;
S Ro 10:5
4:2 qDt 12:32;
Jos 1:7; Pr 30:6;
Rev 22:18-19
rJer 26:2
sS Lev 22:31
tDt 10:12-13;
Ecc 12:13
4:3 uNu 25:1-9;
Ps 106:28
4:5 vPs 71:17;
119:102;
Jer 32:33
wS Ex 18:20
xS Lev 27:34
yEzr 9:11
4:6 zDt 29:9;
1Ki 2:3
aDt 30:19-20;
32:46-47;
Ps 19:7; 119:98;
Pr 1:7; 2Ti 3:15
bJob 11:1; 28:28;
Ps 111:10; Pr 2:5;
3:7; 9:10;
Ecc 12:13;
Eze 5:5
4:7 cver 32-34;
2Sa 7:23
dS Nu 23:21;
S Ps 46:1;
Ac 17:27
4:8 ePs 89:14;
97:2; 119:7,62,
144,160,172;
Ro 3:2
4:9 /S Ex 23:13
gS Ge 14:14;
18:19;
Dt 6:20-25;
Eph 6:4
hS Ex 10:2
4:10 iS Ex 3:1
/Dt 14:23; 17:19;
31:12-13;
Ps 2:11; 111:10;
147:11; Isa 8:13;
Jer 32:40
kS Ex 20:20
lDt 12:1 mver 9 4:11 nS Ex 3:1; S 19:17 oS Ex 19:18
pS Ex 19:9; Ps 18:11; 97:2 4:12 qEx 20:22; Dt 5:4,22;
S Mt 3:17; Heb 12:19 rJn 5:37 sS Ex 19:9 4:13 tDt 9:9;
Ro 9:4 uS Ex 24:12 4:14 vS Ex 21:1 4:15 wIsa 40:18;
41:22-24 xS Ex 3:1 yJos 23:11; Mal 2:15 4:16
zS Ge 6:11-12; Dt 9:12; 31:29; 32:5; Jdg 2:19 aEx 20:4-5;
Ro 1:23 4:17 bRo 1:23

3:27 *Go up to the top of Pisgah.* Moses did so after he had expounded the law to the Israelites to prepare them for life in the promised land (see 32:48-52; 34:1-6). *Pisgah.* See note on v. 17. *look west and north and south and east.* Like Abraham (see Ge 13:14), Moses would inherit the promised land only through his descendants (see 34:1-4).
3:28 *commission Joshua.* See 31:7-8.
3:29 *Beth Peor.* Means "house/sanctuary of Peor." Very likely, reference is to the cult place where the Baal of Peor was worshiped (see Nu 23:28; 25:3,5).
4:1 *Hear ... O Israel.* God's call to his people to hear and obey is a frequent theme in Deuteronomy (see, e.g., 5:1; 6:3-4; 9:1; 20:3) and elsewhere in the OT. See also note on 6:4-9.
4:2 *Do not add ... do not subtract.* The revelation the Lord gives is sufficient. All of it must be obeyed, and anything that adulterates or contradicts it cannot be tolerated (see 12:32; Pr 30:6; Gal 3:15; Rev 22:18-19).
4:4 *held fast.* See note on 10:20.

4:7 *near us whenever we pray.* The Israelites always had access to the Lord in prayer. His presence was symbolized by the tabernacle in the center of the camp, and by the pillar of cloud over the tabernacle (see Ex 40:34-38; Nu 23:21).
4:9 *Teach them to your children.* See v. 10; 11:19; cf. Ex 12:26-27.
4:10-14 See Ex 19-24.
4:10 *Remember.* The divine call to Israel to remember the Lord's past redemptive acts—especially how he delivered them from slavery in Egypt—is a common theme in Deuteronomy (5:15; 7:18; 8:2,18; 9:7,27; 11:2; 15:15; 16:3,12; 24:9,18,22; 25:17) and is summarized in 32:7: "Remember the days of old."
4:12 *no form.* See v. 15; see also note on Ex 20:4. "God is spirit" (Jn 4:24; cf. Isa 31:3).
4:13 *his covenant, the Ten Commandments.* See notes on Ex 20:1; 34:28. *two stone tablets.* See note on Ex 31:18.
4:15-18 See note on Ex 20:4.

along the ground or any fish in the waters below. [19]And when you look up to the sky and see the sun,[c] the moon and the stars[d]—all the heavenly array[e]—do not be enticed[f] into bowing down to them and worshiping[g] things the LORD your God has apportioned to all the nations under heaven. [20]But as for you, the LORD took you and brought you out of the iron-smelting furnace,[h] out of Egypt,[i] to be the people of his inheritance,[j] as you now are.

[21]The LORD was angry with me[k] because of you, and he solemnly swore that I would not cross the Jordan and enter the good land the LORD your God is giving you as your inheritance. [22]I will die in this land;[l] I will not cross the Jordan; but you are about to cross over and take possession of that good land. [m] [23]Be careful not to forget the covenant[n] of the LORD your God that he made with you; do not make for yourselves an idol[o] in the form of anything the LORD your God has forbidden. [24]For the LORD your God is a consuming fire,[p] a jealous God. [q]

[25]After you have had children and grandchildren and have lived in the land a long time—if you then become corrupt[r] and make any kind of idol,[s] doing evil[t] in the eyes of the LORD your God and provoking him to anger, [26]I call heaven and earth as witnesses[u] against you[v] this day that you will quickly perish[w] from the land that you are crossing the Jordan to possess. You will not live there long but will certainly be destroyed. [27]The LORD will scatter[x] you among the peoples, and only a few of you will survive[y] among the nations to which the LORD will drive you. [28]There you will worship man-made gods[z] of wood and stone,[a] which cannot see or hear or eat or smell. [b] [29]But if from there you seek[c] the LORD your God, you will find him if you look for him with all your heart[d] and with all your soul. [e] [30]When you are in distress[f]

and all these things have happened to you, then in later days[g] you will return[h] to the LORD your God and obey him. [31]For the LORD your God is a merciful[i] God; he will not abandon[j] or destroy[k] you or forget[l] the covenant with your forefathers, which he confirmed to them by oath.

The LORD Is God

[32]Ask[m] now about the former days, long before your time, from the day God created man on the earth; [n] ask from one end of the heavens to the other. [o] Has anything so great[p] as this ever happened, or has anything like it ever been heard of? [33]Has any other people heard the voice of God[j] speaking out of fire, as you have, and lived? [q] [34]Has any god ever tried to take for himself one nation out of another nation,[r] by testings,[s] by miraculous signs[t] and wonders, [u] by war, by a mighty hand and an outstretched arm, [v] or by great and awesome deeds, [w] like all the things the LORD your God did for you in Egypt before your very eyes?

[35]You were shown these things so that you might know that the LORD is God; besides him there is no other. [x] [36]From heaven he made you hear his voice[y] to discipline[z] you. On earth he showed you his great fire, and you heard his words from out of the fire. [37]Because he loved[a] your forefathers and chose their descendants after them, he brought you out of

---

4:19 [c]Dt 17:3; 2Ki 23:11; Job 31:26; Jer 8:2; 43:13; Eze 8:16 [d]Ge 1:16 [e]S Ge 2:1; S 37:9; Ro 1:25 [f]Dt 13:5 [g]S Nu 25:3 4:20 [h]S Ex 1:13 [i]S Ex 3:10 [j]S Ge 17:7; S Ex 8:22; S 34:9; Tit 2:14 4:21 [k]Nu 20:12; Dt 1:37 4:22 [l]Nu 27:13-14 [m]Dt 3:25 4:23 [n]ver 9 [o]S Ex 20:4 4:24 [p]S Ex 15:7; S 19:18; Heb 12:29 [q]S Ex 20:5 4:25 [r]ver 16 [s]ver 23 [t]1Ki 11:6; 15:20; 16:25,30; 2Ki 17:2,17; 21:2 4:26 [u]Ge 31:50; Pr 14:5 [v]Dt 30:18-19; 31:28; 32:1; Ps 50:4; Isa 1:2; Mic 6:2 [w]Dt 6:15; 7:4 4:27 [x]S Lev 26:33; Dt 28:36,64; 29:28; 1Ki 8:46; 2Ki 17:6; Ps 44:11; 106:27; Jer 3:8; Mic 1:16 [y]Isa 17:6; 21:17; Ob 1:5 4:28 [z]Dt 13:2; 28:36,64; Jer 16:19; Jer 5:19; 16:13; Ac 19:26 [a]Dt 29:17 [b]Ps 115:4-8; 135:15-18; Isa 8:19; 26:14; 44:17-20; Rev 9:20 4:29 [c]1Sa 13:12; 2Ki 13:4; 2Ch 7:14; 15:4; 33:12; Ps 78:34; 119:58; Isa 45:19,22; 55:6; Jer 26:19; Da 9:13; Hos 3:5; Am 5:4 [d]1Sa 7:3; 1Ki 8:48; Jer 29:13 [e]Dt 6:5; 30:1-3,10 4:30 [f]Lev 26:41; Dt 31:17,21;

Ps 4:1; 18:6; 46:1; 59:16; 107:6 [g]Dt 31:29; Jer 23:20; Hos 3:5; Heb 1:2 [h]Dt 30:2; 1Ki 8:48; Ne 1:9; Jer 3:1,12,22; 4:1; 18:11; Joel 2:12 4:31 [i]Ex 34:6; Ne 9:31; Ps 111:4 [j]Dt 31:6,8; Jos 1:5; 1Ki 8:57; 1Ch 28:9,20; Ps 9:10; 27:9; 71:9; Isa 42:16; Heb 13:5 [k]S Lev 26:44 [l]Lev 26:45 4:32 [m]Dt 32:7 [n]S Ge 1:27; Isa 45:12 [o]Dt 28:64; 30:1; Jer 9:16; Mt 24:31 [p]ver 7; 2Sa 7:23 4:33 [q]Ex 20:22; Dt 5:24-26 4:34 [r]Ex 14:30 [s]Isa 7:12 [t]S Ex 4:17 [u]Dt 7:19; 26:8; 29:3; 1Ch 16:12; Ps 9:1; 40:5; Jer 32:20 [v]S Ex 3:20; Dt 5:15; 6:21; 15:15 [w]Ex 15:11; Dt 34:12; Ps 45:4; 65:5 4:35 [x]ver 39; Ex 8:10; Dt 7:9; 32:4,12; 1Sa 2:2; 1Ki 8:60; 2Ki 19:19; Isa 43:10; Mk 12:32 4:36 [y]S Ex 19:19; Heb 12:25 [z]Dt 8:5 4:37 [a]Dt 7:8; 10:15; 23:5; 33:3; Ps 44:3; Jer 31:3; Hos 11:1; Mal 1:2; 2:11

[j]33 Or of a god

4:19 *do not be enticed.* As kings of Judah would be later (2Ki 23:5).
4:20 *iron-smelting furnace.* Suggests that the period in Egypt was a time of affliction, testing and refinement for the Israelites (see 1Ki 8:51; Jer 11:4; see also Isa 48:10).
4:21 *because of you.* See note on 1:37.
4:24 *consuming fire.* See 9:3; see also note on Ex 24:17. *jealous God.* See 5:9; 6:15; see also note on Ex 20:5.
4:25 *After you . . . have lived in the land.* The pattern of Israel's rebellion, resulting in expulsion from the land, and then their repentance, leading to restoration to the land, is prominent in Deuteronomy (see, e.g., the blessing and curse formulas in chs. 27–28).
4:26 *heaven and earth as witnesses.* See notes on 30:19; Ps 50:1; Isa 1:2.
4:27 *will scatter you.* See note on 28:64.

4:29 *with all your heart and . . . soul.* Indicates total involvement and commitment. The phrase is applied not only to how the Lord's people should seek him, but also to how they should fear (revere) him, live in obedience to him, love and serve him (6:5; 10:12; 11:13; 13:3; 30:6), and, after forsaking them, renew their allegiance and commitment (26:16; 30:2,10).
4:31 *covenant . . . confirmed . . . by oath.* See notes on Ge 21:23; 22:16; Heb 6:13,18. In ancient times, parties to a covenant were expected to confirm their intentions by means of a self-maledictory oath (see note on Ge 15:17).
4:35 *so that you might know.* See v. 10. *besides him there is no other.* See v. 39; 5:7; 6:4 and note; 32:39. Moses' belief in one God was total and uncompromising (see note on Ge 1:1).
4:37 *he loved.* The first reference in Deuteronomy to God's

Egypt by his Presence and his great strength,[b] [38]to drive out before you nations greater and stronger than you and to bring you into their land to give it to you for your inheritance,[c] as it is today.

[39]Acknowledge[d] and take to heart this day that the LORD is God in heaven above and on the earth below. There is no other.[e] [40]Keep[f] his decrees and commands,[g] which I am giving you today, so that it may go well[h] with you and your children after you and that you may live long[i] in the land the LORD your God gives you for all time.

Cities of Refuge

4:41–43Ref — Nu 35:6–34; Dt 19:1–14; Jos 20:1–9

[41]Then Moses set aside three cities east of the Jordan, [42]to which anyone who had killed a person could flee if he had unintentionally[j] killed his neighbor without malice aforethought. He could flee into one of these cities and save his life. [43]The cities were these: Bezer in the desert plateau, for the Reubenites; Ramoth[k] in Gilead, for the Gadites; and Golan in Bashan, for the Manassites.

Introduction to the Law

[44]This is the law Moses set before the Israelites. [45]These are the stipulations, decrees and laws Moses gave them when they came out of Egypt [46]and were in the valley near Beth Peor east of the Jordan, in the land of Sihon[l] king of the Amorites, who reigned in Heshbon and was defeated by Moses and the Israelites as they came out of Egypt. [47]They took possession of his land and the land of Og king of Bashan, the two Amorite kings east of the Jordan. [48]This land extended from Aroer[m] on the rim of the Arnon Gorge to Mount Siyon[k] [n] (that is, Hermon[o]), [49]and included all the Arabah east of the Jordan, as far as the Sea of the Arabah,[l] below the slopes of Pisgah.

The Ten Commandments

5:6–21pp — Ex 20:1–17

5 Moses summoned all Israel and said: Hear, O Israel, the decrees and laws[p] I declare in your hearing today. Learn them and be sure to follow them. [2]The LORD our God made a covenant[q] with us at Horeb.[r] [3]It was not with our fathers that the LORD made this covenant, but with us,[s] with all of us who are alive here today.[t] [4]The LORD spoke[u] to you face to face[v] out of the fire[w] on the mountain. [5](At that time I stood between[x] the LORD and you to declare to you the word of the LORD, because you were afraid[y] of the fire and did not go up the mountain.) And he said:

> [6]"I am the LORD your God, who brought you out of Egypt,[z] out of the land of slavery.[a]
>
> [7]"You shall have no other gods before[m] me.
>
> [8]"You shall not make for yourself an idol in the form of anything in heaven above or on the earth beneath or in the waters below.[b] [9]You shall not bow down to them or worship them; for I, the LORD your God, am a jealous God, punishing the children for the sin of the fathers[c] to the third and fourth generation of those who hate me,[d] [10]but showing love to a thousand[e] generations, of those who love me and keep my commandments.[f]
>
> [11]"You shall not misuse the name[g] of the LORD your God, for the LORD will not hold anyone guiltless who misuses his name.[h]
>
> [12]"Observe the Sabbath day by keeping

Cross references (center column)

4:37 [b]S Ex 3:20; S 33:14
4:38 [c]Nu 34:14-15; Dt 7:1; 9:5
4:39 [d]Ex 8:10 [e]S ver 35; Ex 15:11
4:40 [f]S Lev 22:31 [g]ver 1; S Ge 26:5; Dt 5:29; 11:1; Ps 105:45; Isa 48:18 [h]Dt 5:16; 12:25; Isa 3:10 [i]S Ex 23:26; Eph 6:2-3
4:42 [j]S Ex 21:13
4:43 [k]Jos 21:38; 1Ki 22:3; 2Ki 8:28; 9:14
4:46 [l]Nu 21:26
4:48 [m]Dt 2:36 [n]Dt 3:9 [o]S Dt 3:8

5:1 [p]S Ex 18:20
5:2 [q]Ex 19:5; Jer 11:2; Heb 9:15; 10:15-17 [r]S Ge 17:9; S Ex 3:1
5:3 [s]Dt 11:2-7 [t]Nu 26:63-65; Heb 8:9
5:4 [u]S Dt 4:12 [v]S Nu 14:14 [w]S Ex 19:18
5:5 [x]Gal 3:19 [y]S Ge 3:10; Heb 12:18-21
5:6 [z]S Ex 13:3; S 29:46 [a]Lev 26:1;
5:8 [b]Lev 26:1; Dt 4:15-18; Ps 78:58; 97:7
5:9 [c]S Nu 26:11 [d]Ex 34:7; S Nu 10:35; 14:18
5:10 [e]S Ex 34:7 [f]Nu 14:18; Dt 7:9; Ne 1:5; Jer 32:18; Da 9:4
5:11 [g]Ps 139:20 [h]Lev 19:12; Dt 10:20; Mt 5:33-37

[k]48 Hebrew; Syriac (see also Deut. 3:9) Sirion   l49 That is, the Dead Sea   m7 Or besides

Footnotes (bottom)

love for his people (see Introduction: Theological Teaching). See note on 7:8; see also 5:10; 7:9,13; 10:15; 23:5. The corollary truth is that his people should love him (see note on 6:5).
4:39 See v. 35 and note.
4:41–43 See 19:1–13; Nu 35:9–28; Jos 20.
4:43 *Bezer.* About 20 miles east of the northeast corner of the Dead Sea.
5:1 *Hear, O Israel.* See note on 4:1.
5:2 *covenant with us at Horeb.* See note on Ex 19:5. God's covenant with Israel, given at Mount Horeb (Sinai) and now being confirmed, bound Israel to the Lord as their absolute Sovereign, and to his laws and regulations as their way of life. Adherence to the covenant would bring to Israel the blessings of the Lord, while breaking the covenant would bring against them the punishments described as "curses" (see,

e.g., 28:15–20). Jer 31:31–34 predicted the establishing of a new covenant, which made the Sinaitic covenant obsolete (see Heb 7:22; see also Heb 8:6–13; 10:15–18 and notes). See chart on "Major Covenants in the OT," p. 19.
5:3 *not with our fathers . . . but with us.* The covenant was made with those who were present at Sinai, but since they were representatives of the nation, it was made with all succeeding generations as well.
5:5 See vv. 23–26; Ex 20:18–21.
5:6–21 The Ten Commandments are both the basis and the heart of Israel's relationship with the Lord. It is almost impossible to exaggerate their effect on subsequent history. They constitute the basis of moral principles throughout the Western world, and they summarize what the one true God expects of his people in terms of faith, worship and conduct (see notes on Ex 20:3–17).

it holy,[i] as the LORD your God has commanded you. [13]Six days you shall labor and do all your work, [14]but the seventh day[j] is a Sabbath to the LORD your God. On it you shall not do any work, neither you, nor your son or daughter, nor your manservant or maidservant,[k] nor your ox, your donkey or any of your animals, nor the alien within your gates, so that your manservant and maidservant may rest, as you do.[l] [15]Remember that you were slaves[m] in Egypt and that the LORD your God brought you out of there with a mighty hand[n] and an outstretched arm.[o] Therefore the LORD your God has commanded you to observe the Sabbath day.

[16]"Honor your father[p] and your mother,[q] as the LORD your God has commanded you, so that you may live long[r] and that it may go well with you in the land the LORD your God is giving you.

[17]"You shall not murder.[s]

[18]"You shall not commit adultery.[t]

[19]"You shall not steal.[u]

[20]"You shall not give false testimony against your neighbor.[v]

[21]"You shall not covet your neighbor's wife. You shall not set your desire on your neighbor's house or land, his manservant or maidservant, his ox or donkey, or anything that belongs to your neighbor."[w]

[22]These are the commandments the LORD proclaimed in a loud voice to your whole assembly there on the mountain from out of the fire, the cloud and the deep darkness;[x] and he added nothing more. Then he wrote them on two stone tablets[y] and gave them to me.

[23]When you heard the voice out of the darkness, while the mountain was ablaze with fire, all the leading men of your tribes

and your elders[z] came to me. [24]And you said, "The LORD our God has shown us[a] his glory and his majesty,[b] and we have heard his voice from the fire. Today we have seen that a man can live even if God speaks with him.[c] [25]But now, why should we die? This great fire will consume us, and we will die if we hear the voice of the LORD our God any longer.[d] [26]For what mortal man has ever heard the voice of the living God speaking out of fire, as we have, and survived?[e] [27]Go near and listen to all that the LORD our God says.[f] Then tell us whatever the LORD our God tells us. We will listen and obey."[g]

[28]The LORD heard you when you spoke to me and the LORD said to me, "I have heard what this people said to you. Everything they said was good.[h] [29]Oh, that their hearts would be inclined to fear me[i] and keep all my commands[j] always, so that it might go well with them and their children forever![k]

[30]"Go, tell them to return to their tents. [31]But you stay here[l] with me so that I may give you all the commands, decrees and laws you are to teach them to follow in the land I am giving them to possess."

[32]So be careful to do what the LORD your God has commanded you;[m] do not turn aside to the right or to the left.[n] [33]Walk in all the way that the LORD your God has commanded you,[o] so that you may live and prosper and prolong your days[p] in the land that you will possess.

Love the LORD Your God

6 These are the commands, decrees and laws the LORD your God directed me to teach you to observe in the land that you are crossing the Jordan to possess, [2]so that you, your children and their children after them may fear[q] the LORD your God as long as you live[r] by keeping all his decrees and commands[s] that I give you, and so that you may enjoy long life.[t] [3]Hear, O

5:12 [i]Ex 16:23-30; 31:13-17; Mk 2:27-28
5:14 [j]S Ge 2:2; Mt 12:2; Mk 2:27; Heb 4:4 [k]Job 31:13; Jer 34:9-11 [l]Jer 17:21,24
5:15 [m]S Ge 15:13 [n]Ex 6:1; Ps 108:6; Jer 32:21 [o]S Dt 4:34
5:16 [p]Mal 1:6 [q]Ex 21:17; Lev 19:3; Eze 22:7; Mt 15:4*; 19:19*; Mk 7:10*;10:19*; Lk 18:20*; Eph 6:2-3* [r]S Dt 4:40; 11:9; Pr 3:1-2
5:17 [s]Ge 9:6; Lev 24:17; Ecc 3:3; Jer 40:15; 41:3; Mt 5:21-22*; 19:19*; Mk 10:19*; Lk 18:20*; Ro 13:9*; Jas 2:11*
5:18 [t]Lev 20:10; Mt 5:27-30; 19:18*; Mk 10:19*; Lk 18:20*; Ro 13:9*; Jas 2:11*
5:19 [u]Lev 19:11; Mt 19:19*; Mk 10:19*; Lk 18:20*; Ro 13:9*
5:20 [v]S Ex 23:1; Mt 19:18*; Mk 10:19*; Lk 18:20*
5:21 [w]Ro 7:7*; 13:9*
5:22 [x]S Ex 20:21 [y]S Ex 24:12
5:23 [z]S Ex 3:16
5:24 [a]Dt 4:34; 8:5; 11:2; Isa 53:4 [b]S Dt 3:24 [c]Ex 19:19
5:25 [d]Ex 20:18-19; Dt 18:16; Heb 12:19
5:26 [e]S Ex 33:20; Dt 4:33; Jdg 6:22-23; 13:22; Isa 6:5
5:27 [f]S Ex 19:8 [g]S Ex 24:7
5:28 [h]Dt 18:17
5:29 [i]Ps 81:8,13 [j]Jos 22:5; Ps 78:7 [k]ver 33; S Dt 4:1,

40; 12:25; 22:7 5:31 [l]Ex 24:12 5:32 [m]S Dt 4:29; 10:12 [n]Dt 17:11,20; 28:14; Jos 1:7; 1Ki 15:5; 2Ki 22:2; Pr 4:27 5:33 [o]Isa 3:10; Jer 7:23; 38:20; S Lk 1:6 [p]S ver 29 6:2 [q]S Ex 20:20; 1Sa 12:24 [r]Dt 4:9 [s]S Ge 26:5 [t]S Ex 20:12

5:12 *as the LORD your God has commanded you.* Missing from the parallel verse in Exodus (20:8), this clause reminds the people of the divine origin of the Ten Commandments 40 years earlier (see vv. 15–16).
5:14 *so that your manservant and maidservant may rest.* See note on Ex 20:10; see also v. 15.
5:15 *Remember.* See note on 4:10.
5:16–21 The NT quotes often from this section of the Ten Commandments.
5:20 See 19:18–19.
5:22 *commandments.* Lit. "words" (see note on Ex 20:1).

two stone tablets. See note on Ex 31:18.
5:25 *we will die.* See notes on Ge 16:13; 32:30.
5:27 *We will listen and obey.* See note on Ex 19:8.
6:2 *fear the LORD.* See note on Ge 20:11. *enjoy long life.* See 4:40; 5:16,33. By obeying the Lord and keeping his decrees, individual Israelites would enjoy long life in the land, and the people as a whole would enjoy a long national existence in the land.
6:3–4 *Hear, O Israel.* See note on 4:1.
6:3 *land flowing with milk and honey.* See note on Ex 3:8. The phrase is used 14 times from Exodus through

Israel, and be careful to obey[u] so that it may go well with you and that you may increase greatly[v] in a land flowing with milk and honey,[w] just as the LORD, the God of your fathers, promised[x] you.

[4]Hear, O Israel: The LORD our God, the LORD is one.[n][y] [5]Love[z] the LORD your God with all your heart[a] and with all your soul and with all your strength.[b] [6]These commandments that I give you today are to be upon your hearts.[c] [7]Impress them on your children. Talk about them when you sit at home and when you walk along the road, when you lie down and when you get up.[d] [8]Tie them as symbols on your hands and bind them on your foreheads.[e] [9]Write them on the doorframes of your houses and on your gates.[f]

[10]When the LORD your God brings you into the land he swore to your fathers, to Abraham, Isaac and Jacob, to give you—a land with large, flourishing cities you did not build,[g] [11]houses filled with all kinds of good things you did not provide, wells you did not dig,[h] and vineyards and olive groves you did not plant—then when you eat and are satisfied,[i] [12]be careful that you do not forget[j] the LORD, who brought you out of Egypt, out of the land of slavery.

[13]Fear the LORD[k] your God, serve him only[l] and take your oaths[m] in his name.[n] [14]Do not follow other gods, the gods of the peoples around you; [15]for the LORD your God[o], who is among you, is a jealous God and his anger will burn against you, and he will destroy you from the face of the land. [16]Do not test the LORD your God[p] as you did at Massah. [17]Be sure to keep[q] the commands of the LORD your God and the stipulations and decrees he has given you.[r] [18]Do what is right and good in the

LORD's sight,[s] so that it may go well[t] with you and you may go in and take over the good land that the LORD promised on oath to your forefathers, [19]thrusting out all your enemies[u] before you, as the LORD said.

[20]In the future, when your son asks you,[v] "What is the meaning of the stipulations, decrees and laws the LORD our God has commanded you?" [21]tell him: "We were slaves of Pharaoh in Egypt, but the LORD brought us out of Egypt with a mighty hand.[w] [22]Before our eyes the LORD sent miraculous signs and wonders—great and terrible—upon Egypt and Pharaoh and his whole household. [23]But he brought us out from there to bring us in and give us the land that he promised on oath to our forefathers. [24]The LORD commanded us to obey all these decrees and to fear the LORD our God,[x] so that we might always prosper and be kept alive, as is the case today.[y] [25]And if we are careful to obey all this law[z] before the LORD our God, as he has commanded us, that will be our righteousness.[a]"

Driving Out the Nations

7 When the LORD your God brings you into the land you are entering to possess[b] and drives out before you many nations[c]—the Hittites,[d] Girgashites,[e] Amorites,[f] Canaanites, Perizzites,[g] Hivites[h] and Jebusites,[i] seven nations larger and

6:3 [u]S Ex 19:5; [v]Ge 15:5; Dt 5:33; [w]S Ex 3:8; Dt 32:13-14; [x]Ex 13:5
6:4 [y]Dt 4:35,39; Ne 9:6; Ps 86:10; Isa 44:6; Zec 14:9; Mk 12:29*; Jn 10:30; 1Co 8:4; Eph 4:6; Jas 2:19
6:5 [z]Dt 11:1,22; Mt 22:37*; Mk 12:30*; Lk 10:27*; [a]1Sa 12:24; [b]Dt 4:29; 10:12; Jos 22:5
6:6 [c]ver 8; Dt 11:18; 30:14; 32:46; Ps 26:2; 37:31; 40:8; 119:11; Pr 3:3; Isa 51:7; Jer 17:1; 31:33; Eze 40:4
6:7 [d]Dt 4:9; 11:19; Pr 22:6; Eph 6:4
6:8 [e]S ver 6; S Ex 13:9; Mt 23:5
6:9 [f]Dt 11:20
6:10 [g]S Ge 11:4; Dt 12:29; 19:1; Jos 24:13; Ps 105:44
6:11 [h]Jer 2:13; [i]S Lev 26:5; Dt 8:10; 14:29; 31:20
6:12 [j]Dt 4:9,23; 2Ki 17:38; Ps 44:17; 78:7; 103:2
6:13 [k]Ps 33:8; 34:9; [l]Dt 13:4; 1Sa 7:3; Jer 44:10; Mt 4:10*; Lk 4:4; 4:8*; [m]1Sa 20:3; [n]S Ex 20:7; S Mt 5:33
6:15 [o]Dt 4:24; 5:9
6:16 [p]S Ex 17:2; Mt 4:7*; Lk 4:12*
6:17 [q]S Lev 26:3; [r]Dt 11:22; Ps 119:4,56,100, 134,168

6:18 [s]2Ki 18:6; Isa 36:7; 38:3; [t]Dt 4:40; [u]Ex 23:27; Jos 21:44; Ps 78:53; 107:2; 136:24 6:20 [v]S Ex 10:2 6:21 [w]S Dt 4:34 6:24 [x]Dt 10:12; 30:6; Ps 86:11; Jer 32:39 [y]Ps 27:12; 41:2; S Ro 10:5 6:25 [z]Ps 103:18; 119:34,55 [a]Dt 24:13; S Ro 9:31 7:1 [b]S Lev 14:34; S Dt 4:38 [c]Dt 20:16-18; 31:3 [d]Ge 15:20 [e]S Ge 10:16 [f]S Dt 1:7 [g]Ge 13:7 [h]S Ge 10:17 [i]Jos 3:10

[n]4 Or The LORD our God is one LORD; or The LORD is our God, the LORD is one; or The LORD is our God, the LORD alone

Deuteronomy and 5 times elsewhere in the OT (see especially 32:13–14).

6:4–9 Known as the *Shema,* Hebrew for "Hear." It has become the Jewish confession of faith, recited daily by the pious (see Mt 22:37–38; Mk 12:29–30; Lk 10:27).

6:4 *the LORD is one.* A divinely revealed insight, especially important in view of the multiplicity of Baals and other gods of Canaan and elsewhere (see, e.g., Jdg 2:11–13).

6:5 *Love the LORD.* Love for God and neighbor (see Lev 19:18) is built on the love that the Lord has for his people (1Jn 4:19–21) and on his identification with them. Such love is to be total, involving one's whole being (see notes on 4:29; Jos 22:5).

6:6 *commandments . . . upon your hearts.* A feature that would especially characterize the "new covenant" (see Jer 31:33).

6:8–9 Many Jews take these verses literally and tie phylacteries (see note on Mt 23:5) to their foreheads and left arms. They also attach mezuzot (small wooden or metal containers in which passages of Scripture are placed) to the doorframes of their houses. But a figurative interpretation is

supported by 11:18–20; Ex 13:9,16. See note on Ex 13:9.

6:10–12 Because the emphasis in Scripture is always on what God does and not on what his people achieve, they are never to forget what he has done for them.

6:13 Quoted in part by Jesus in response to Satan's temptation (Mt 4:10; Lk 4:8). Jesus quoted from Deuteronomy in response to the devil's other two temptations as well (see notes on v. 16; 8:3).

6:15 *jealous God.* See note on Ex 20:5.

6:16 Quoted in part by Jesus in Mt 4:7; Lk 4:12 (see also note on v. 13). *as you did at Massah.* See 9:22; 33:8; see also note on Ex 17:7.

6:20 See Ex 12:26 and note.

6:23 *brought us out . . . to bring us in.* See note on Ex 6:7–8.

6:25 *righteousness.* Probably here refers to a true, personal relationship with the covenant Lord that manifests itself in the daily lives of God's people (see 24:13).

7:1 *Hittites . . . Jebusites.* See 20:17; see also notes on Ge 10:6,15–18; 13:7. *seven nations.* See note on Ex 3:8.

stronger than you— [2]and when the LORD your God has delivered[j] them over to you and you have defeated them, then you must destroy[k] them totally.[o][l] Make no treaty[m] with them, and show them no mercy.[n] [3]Do not intermarry with them.[o] Do not give your daughters to their sons or take their daughters for your sons, [4]for they will turn your sons away from following me to serve other gods,[p] and the LORD's anger will burn against you and will quickly destroy[q] you. [5]This is what you are to do to them: Break down their altars, smash their sacred stones, cut down their Asherah poles[p][r] and burn their idols in the fire.[s] [6]For you are a people holy[t] to the LORD your God.[u] The LORD your God has chosen[v] you out of all the peoples on the face of the earth to be his people, his treasured possession.[w]

[7]The LORD did not set his affection on you and choose you because you were more numerous[x] than other peoples, for you were the fewest[y] of all peoples.[z] [8]But it was because the LORD loved[a] you and kept the oath he swore[b] to your forefathers that he brought you out with a mighty hand[c] and redeemed[d] you from the land of slavery,[e] from the power of Pharaoh king of Egypt. [9]Know therefore that the LORD your God is God;[f] he is the faithful God,[g] keeping his covenant of love[h] to a thousand generations[i] of those who love him and keep his commands.[j] [10]But

> those who hate him he will repay to
> their face by destruction;
> he will not be slow to repay to their
> face those who hate him.[k]

[11]Therefore, take care to follow the commands, decrees and laws I give you today. [12]If you pay attention to these laws and are careful to follow them, then the LORD

your God will keep his covenant of love with you, as he swore to your forefathers.[l] [13]He will love you and bless you[m] and increase your numbers.[n] He will bless the fruit of your womb,[o] the crops of your land—your grain, new wine[p] and oil[q]—the calves of your herds and the lambs of your flocks in the land that he swore to your forefathers to give you.[r] [14]You will be blessed more than any other people; none of your men or women will be childless, nor any of your livestock without young.[s] [15]The LORD will keep you free from every disease.[t] He will not inflict on you the horrible diseases you knew in Egypt,[u] but he will inflict them on all who hate you.[v] [16]You must destroy all the peoples the LORD your God gives over to you.[w] Do not look on them with pity[x] and do not serve their gods,[y] for that will be a snare[z] to you.

[17]You may say to yourselves, "These nations are stronger than we are. How can we drive them out?"[a] [18]But do not be afraid[b] of them; remember well what the LORD your God did to Pharaoh and to all Egypt.[c] [19]You saw with your own eyes the great trials, the miraculous signs and wonders, the mighty hand[d] and outstretched arm, with which the LORD your God brought you out. The LORD your God will do the same to all the peoples you now fear.[e] [20]Moreover, the LORD your God will send the hornet[f] among them until even

---

7:2 /S Dt 2:33
*k*S Dt 2:34
/Nu 31:17;
Dt 33:27;
Jos 11:11
*m*S Ex 23:32 *n*ver 16; Dt 13:8; 19:13; 25:12
7:3
*o*Ex 34:15-16;
Jos 22:16; Da 9:7
7:4 *p*Jdg 3:6
*q*S Dt 4:26
7:5 *r*S Ex 34:13;
Dt 16:21
*s*S Ex 23:24
7:6 *t*Ex 19:6;
S Lev 27:30
*u*Dt 26:19;
Ps 30:4; 37:28;
50:5; 52:9
*v*Dt 14:2;
1Ki 3:8; Isa 41:9;
Eze 20:5
*w*S Ge 17:7;
S Ex 8:22; S 34:9;
Isa 43:1; Ro 9:4;
Tit 2:14
7:7 *x*S Ge 22:17
*y*Ge 34:30
*z*Dt 4:37; 10:22
7:8 *a*S Dt 4:37;
1Ki 10:9;
2Ch 2:11; Ps 44:3
*b*Ex 32:13;
S Nu 14:8;
Ro 11:28
*c*S Ex 3:20
*d*S Ex 13:14
*e*S Ex 13:14
7:9 *f*S Dt 4:35
*g*Ps 18:25; 33:4;
108:4; 145:13;
146:6; Isa 49:7;
Jer 42:5;
Hos 11:12;
S 1Co 1:9 *h*ver 12; 1Ki 8:23;
2Ch 6:14;
Ne 1:5; 9:32
*i*S Ex 20:6
*j*S Dt 5:10
7:10
*k*S Lev 26:28;
S Nu 10:35;
Na 1:2

7:12
/Lev 26:3-13;
Dt 28:1-14;
Ps 105:8-9;
Mic 7:20
7:13 *m*Ps 11:5;
146:8; Pr 15:9;
Isa 51:1; Jn 14:21
*n*S Ge 17:6;
Ex 1:7; Dt 1:10;
13:17; 30:5;
Ps 107:38

*o*S Ge 49:25 *p*S Ge 27:28 *q*S Nu 18:12 *r*Dt 28:4 **7:14** *s*Ex 23:26 **7:15** *t*S Ex 15:26 *u*S Ex 9:9 *v*S Ex 23:25; Dt 30:8-10 **7:16** *w*ver 24; Jos 6:2; 10:26 *x*S ver 2 *y*Jdg 3:6; Ezr 9:1; Ps 106:36 *z*ver 25; S Ex 10:7 **7:17** *a*Nu 33:53 **7:18** *b*S Nu 14:9; S Dt 1:21,29 *c*Ps 105:5; 119:52 **7:19** *d*Ps 136:12 *e*Dt 4:34 **7:20** /S Ex 23:28

*o*2 The Hebrew term refers to the irrevocable giving over of things or persons to the LORD, often by totally destroying them; also in verse 26.   *p*5 That is, symbols of the goddess Asherah; here and elsewhere in Deuteronomy

---

7:2–5 *Make no treaty . . . Do not intermarry . . . Break down their altars.* Israel was to have no association—political, social or religious—with the idol worshipers of Canaan (see v. 16; see also note on 2:34).

7:2 *destroy them totally.* See note on 2:34.

7:4 *turn your sons . . . to serve other gods.* The Lord's command against intermarriage with foreigners was not racially motivated but was intended to prevent spiritual contamination and apostasy (see, e.g., 1Ki 11:1–11; Ne 13:25–27).

7:5 *altars . . . sacred stones . . . Asherah poles.* Cult objects of Canaanite idolatrous worship (see 12:3; 16:21–22). See also NIV text note; Ex 34:13 and note.

7:6 *holy.* Separated from all corrupting people or things and consecrated totally to the Lord (see note on Ex 3:5). *treasured possession.* See note on Ex 19:5.

7:8 *because the LORD loved you.* The "covenant of love" (vv. 9,12) stems from God's love for his people, based on his

character and embodied in his covenant; it does not stem from the numerical greatness of the people or any virtue of theirs. His love must be reciprocated by his people (see vv. 9–10; 9:4–6; see also note on 6:5).

7:9 *Know . . . that the LORD . . . is God.* See Ps 100:3. *thousand generations of those who love him.* See note on Ex 20:6.

7:12–15 The blessings are elaborated in 28:1–14; 30:1–10.

7:13 *grain, new wine and oil.* A common OT summary of the produce of field, vineyard and olive grove (see, e.g., 11:14; 14:23; 18:4; 28:51).

7:15 *not inflict . . . diseases.* See note on 28:60.

7:16 See Introduction to Joshua: The Conquest and the Ethical Question of War.

7:18 *remember.* See note on 4:10.

7:20 *hornet.* See note on Ex 23:28.

the survivors who hide from you have perished. [21]Do not be terrified by them, for the LORD your God, who is among you,[g] is a great and awesome God.[h] [22]The LORD your God will drive out those nations before you, little by little.[i] You will not be allowed to eliminate them all at once, or the wild animals will multiply around you. [23]But the LORD your God will deliver them over to you, throwing them into great confusion until they are destroyed.[j] [24]He will give their kings[k] into your hand,[l] and you will wipe out their names from under heaven. No one will be able to stand up against you;[m] you will destroy them.[n] [25]The images of their gods you are to burn[o] in the fire. Do not covet[p] the silver and gold on them, and do not take it for yourselves, or you will be ensnared[q] by it, for it is detestable[r] to the LORD your God. [26]Do not bring a detestable thing into your house or you, like it, will be set apart for destruction.[s] Utterly abhor and detest it, for it is set apart for destruction.

Do Not Forget the LORD

8 Be careful to follow every command I am giving you today, so that you may live[t] and increase and may enter and possess the land the LORD promised on oath to your forefathers.[u] [2]Remember how the LORD your God led[v] you all the way in the desert these forty years, to humble you and to test[w] you in order to know what was in your heart, whether or not you would keep his commands. [3]He humbled[x] you, causing you to hunger and then feeding you with manna,[y] which neither you nor your fathers had known, to teach[z] that man does not live on bread[a] alone but on every word that comes from the mouth[b] of the LORD.[c] [4]Your clothes did not wear out and your feet did not swell during these forty years.[d] [5]Know then in your heart that as a man disciplines his

son, so the LORD your God disciplines you.[e]

[6]Observe the commands of the LORD your God, walking in his ways[f] and revering him.[g] [7]For the LORD your God is bringing you into a good land[h]—a land with streams and pools of water, with springs flowing in the valleys and hills;[i] [8]a land with wheat and barley,[j] vines[k] and fig trees,[l] pomegranates, olive oil and honey;[m] [9]a land where bread[n] will not be scarce and you will lack nothing;[o] a land where the rocks are iron and you can dig copper out of the hills.[p]

[10]When you have eaten and are satisfied,[q] praise the LORD your God for the good land he has given you. [11]Be careful that you do not forget[r] the LORD your God, failing to observe his commands, his laws and his decrees that I am giving you this day. [12]Otherwise, when you eat and are satisfied, when you build fine houses and settle down,[s] [13]and when your herds and flocks grow large and your silver and gold increase and all you have is multiplied, [14]then your heart will become proud and you will forget[t] the LORD your God, who brought you out of Egypt, out of the land of slavery. [15]He led you through the vast and dreadful desert,[u] that thirsty and waterless land, with its venomous snakes[v] and scorpions. He brought you water out of hard rock.[w] [16]He gave you manna[x] to eat in the desert, something your fathers had never known,[y] to humble and to test[z] you so that in the end it might go well with you. [17]You may say to yourself,[a] "My power and the strength of my hands[b] have produced this wealth for me." [18]But remember the LORD your God, for it is he

---

7:21 [g]S Ge 17:7; Jos 3:10
[h]Dt 10:17; Ne 1:5; 9:32; Ps 47:2; 66:3; 68:35; Isa 9:6; Da 9:4
7:22 [i]Ex 23:28-30
7:23 [j]Ex 23:27; Jos 10:10
7:24 [k]Jos 10:24; Ps 110:5 [l]S ver 16
[m]S Ex 23:31; Dt 11:25; Jos 1:5; 10:8; 23:9
[n]Jos 21:44
7:25 [o]S Ex 4:14; S 32:20
[p]Ex 20:17; Jos 7:21 [q]S ver 16
[r]Dt 17:1
7:26 [s]Lev 27:28-29
8:1 [t]Dt 4:1
[u]S Ex 19:5; Job 36:11; Ps 16:11; Eze 20:19
8:2 [v]Dt 29:5; Ps 136:16; Am 2:10
[w]S Ge 22:1
8:3 [x]2Ch 36:12; Ps 44:9; Pr 18:12; Isa 2:11; Jer 44:10
[y]S Ex 16:4
[z]1Ki 8:36; Ps 25:5; 94:12; 119:171 [a]ver 9; S Ge 3:19;
Job 23:12; Ps 104:15; Pr 28:21; Isa 51:14; Jer 42:14
[b]Job 22:22; Ps 119:13; 138:4
[c]S Ex 16:2-3; Mt 4:4*; Lk 4:4*
8:4 [d]Dt 29:5; Ne 9:21
8:5 [e]Dt 4:36; 2Sa 7:14; Job 5:17; 33:19; Pr 3:11-12; Heb 12:5-11; Rev 3:19
8:6 [f]S Ex 33:13; 1Ki 3:14; Ps 81:13; 95:10
[g]Dt 5:33
8:7 [h]Ps 106:24; Jer 3:19; Eze 20:6
[i]Dt 11:9-12; Jer 2:7
8:8 [j]S Ex 9:31
[k]S Ge 49:11
[l]S Nu 13:23;
S 1Ki 4:25

[m]Dt 32:13; Ps 81:16 8:9 [n]S ver 3 [o]Jdg 18:10 [p]Job 28:2 8:10 [q]Dt 6:10-12 8:11 [r]Dt 4:9 8:12 [s]Pr 30:9; Hos 13:6 8:14 [t]ver 11; Ps 78:7; 106:21 8:15 [u]S Dt 1:19; S 32:10 [v]Nu 21:6; Isa 14:29; 30:6 [w]Ex 17:6; Dt 32:13; Job 28:9; Ps 78:15; 114:8 8:16 [x]S Ex 16:14 [y]Ex 16:15 [z]S Ge 22:1 8:17 [a]Dt 9:4, 7,24; 31:27 [b]Jdg 7:2; Ps 44:3; Isa 10:13

7:22 *God will drive out.* See note on 3:22.
7:25–26 Cf. the story of Achan (Jos 6:17–19; 7:1,20–25).
7:26 *set apart for destruction.* See note on 2:34.
8:2 *Remember.* See note on 4:10. *test.* See v. 16; see also note on Ge 22:1.
8:3 *manna.* See v. 16; see also note on Nu 11:7. *man does not live on bread alone.* See note on 6:13; quoted by Jesus in response to the devil's temptation (see Mt 4:4; Lk 4:4). Bread sustains but does not guarantee life, which is God's gift to those who trust in and live by his word: his commands and promises (see vv. 1,18). God's "discipline" (v. 5) of his people by bringing them through the desert taught them this fundamental truth. There they were humbled (cf. v. 14) by being cast in total dependence on the Lord.
8:7–9 A concise description of the rich and fertile land of promise that the Israelites were about to enter and possess

(see 11:8–12). See map No. 2 at the end of the Study Bible.
8:9 *iron . . . copper.* The mountains of southern Lebanon and the regions east of the Sea of Galilee and south of the Dead Sea contain iron. Both copper and iron were plentiful in the part of the Arabah south of the Dead Sea. Some of the copper mines date to the time of Solomon and earlier. Zarethan was a center for bronze works in Solomon's time (1Ki 7:45–46). Some bronze objects from this site precede the Solomonic period, and today there are copper works at Timnah in the Negev.
8:11,14,19 *forget.* See note on 4:10.
8:15 *water out of hard rock.* See Ex 17:6 and note.
8:16 *test.* See v. 2; see also note on Ge 22:1.
8:17–18 See Zec 4:6 and note.
8:18 *remember.* See note on 4:10.

who gives you the ability to produce wealth,[c] and so confirms his covenant, which he swore to your forefathers, as it is today.

[19]If you ever forget the LORD your God and follow other gods[d] and worship and bow down to them, I testify against you today that you will surely be destroyed.[e] [20]Like the nations[f] the LORD destroyed before you, so you will be destroyed for not obeying the LORD your God.[g]

Not Because of Israel's Righteousness

9 Hear, O Israel. You are now about to cross the Jordan[h] to go in and dispossess nations greater and stronger than you,[i] with large cities[j] that have walls up to the sky.[k] [2]The people are strong and tall—Anakites! You know about them and have heard it said: "Who can stand up against the Anakites?"[l] [3]But be assured today that the LORD your God is the one who goes across ahead of you[m] like a devouring fire.[n] He will destroy them; he will subdue them before you. And you will drive them out and annihilate them quickly,[o] as the LORD has promised you.

[4]After the LORD your God has driven them out before you, do not say to yourself,[p] "The LORD has brought me here to take possession of this land because of my righteousness." No, it is on account of the wickedness[q] of these nations[r] that the LORD is going to drive them out before you. [5]It is not because of your righteousness or your integrity[s] that you are going in to take possession of their land; but on account of the wickedness[t] of these nations,[u] the LORD your God will drive them out[v] before you, to accomplish what he swore[w] to your fathers, to Abraham, Isaac and Jacob.[x] [6]Understand, then, that it is not because of your righteousness that the LORD your God is giving you this good land to possess, for you are a stiff-necked people.[y]

The Golden Calf

[7]Remember this and never forget how you provoked[z] the LORD your God to an-

ger in the desert. From the day you left Egypt until you arrived here, you have been rebellious[a] against the LORD.[b] [8]At Horeb you aroused the LORD's wrath[c] so that he was angry enough to destroy you.[d] [9]When I went up on the mountain to receive the tablets of stone, the tablets of the covenant[e] that the LORD had made with you, I stayed on the mountain forty days[f] and forty nights; I ate no bread and drank no water.[g] [10]The LORD gave me two stone tablets inscribed by the finger of God.[h] On them were all the commandments the LORD proclaimed to you on the mountain out of the fire, on the day of the assembly.[i]

[11]At the end of the forty days and forty nights,[j] the LORD gave me the two stone tablets,[k] the tablets of the covenant. [12]Then the LORD told me, "Go down from here at once, because your people whom you brought out of Egypt have become corrupt.[l] They have turned away quickly[m] from what I commanded them and have made a cast idol for themselves."

[13]And the LORD said to me, "I have seen this people[n], and they are a stiff-necked people indeed! [14]Let me alone,[o] so that I may destroy them and blot out[p] their name from under heaven.[q] And I will make you into a nation stronger and more numerous than they."

[15]So I turned and went down from the mountain while it was ablaze with fire. And the two tablets of the covenant were in my hands.[q][r] [16]When I looked, I saw that you had sinned against the LORD your God; you had made for yourselves an idol cast in the shape of a calf.[s] You had turned aside quickly from the way that the LORD had commanded you. [17]So I took the two tablets and threw them out of my hands, breaking them to pieces before your eyes.

[18]Then once again I fell[t] prostrate before the LORD for forty days and forty nights; I ate no bread and drank no water,[u] because of all the sin you had committed,[v] doing what was evil in the

Cross references (center column)

8:18 [c]Ge 26:13; Dt 26:10; 28:4; 1Sa 2:7; Ps 25:13; 112:3; Pr 8:18; 10:22; Ecc 9:11; Hos 2:8
8:19 [d]Dt 6:14; Ps 16:4; Jer 7:6; 13:10; 25:6
[e]Dt 4:26; 30:18
8:20 [f]2Ki 21:2; Ps 10:16
[g]Eze 5:5-17
9:1 [h]S Nu 35:10
[i]Dt 4:38
[j]S Nu 13:28
[k]S Ge 11:4
9:2 [l]Nu 13:22; Jos 11:22
9:3 [m]Dt 31:3; Jos 3:11
[n]S Ex 15:7; S 19:18; Heb 12:29
[o]S Ex 23:31
9:4 [p]S Dt 8:17
[q]2Ki 16:3; 17:8; 21:2; Ezr 9:11
[r]S Ex 23:24; S Lev 18:21, 24-30; Dt 18:9-14
9:5 [s]S Eph 2:9
[t]Dt 18:9
[u]S Lev 18:25
[v]Dt 4:38; 11:23
[w]S Ge 12:7
[x]Eze 36:32
9:6 [y]S Ex 32:9; Ac 7:51
9:7 [z]S Nu 11:33

[a]S Ex 23:21
[b]S Ex 14:11
9:8 [c]Nu 16:46; 1Sa 28:18; Job 20:28; Ps 2:12; 7:11; 69:24; 110:5; Isa 9:19; Eze 20:13
[d]Ex 32:7-10; Ezr 9:14; Ps 106:19
9:9 [e]S Dt 4:13
[f]S Ge 7:4
[g]S Ex 24:12
9:10 [h]S Ex 31:18
[i]Dt 10:4; 18:16
9:11 [j]S Ge 7:4
[k]S Ex 24:12
9:12 [l]S Dt 4:16
[m]Jdg 2:17
9:13 [n]ver 6; Dt 10:16
9:14 [o]Ex 32:10
[p]S Nu 14:12
[q]Jer 7:16
9:15 [r]S Ex 32:15
9:16 [s]S Ex 32:4
9:18 [t]S Ex 34:28
[u]ver 9
[v]S Ex 32:31

[q]15 Or And I had the two tablets of the covenant with me, one in each hand

---

9:1 *Hear, O Israel.* See note on 4:1.
9:2 *Anakites.* See note on 1:28.
9:3 *devouring fire.* See 4:24; see also note on Ex 24:17. *he will subdue them before you . . . you will drive them out.* The Lord not only went ahead of the Israelites, but he also exerted his power alongside them and through them to assure victory. The Lord's involvement, together with that of the Israelite armies, continues throughout Deuteronomy and the conquest narratives.
9:4 *because of my righteousness.* See note on 7:8. *wicked-*

ness of these nations. See note on Ge 15:16.
9:6,13 *stiff-necked.* See 10:16; 31:27; see also note on Ex 32:9.
9:7,27 *Remember.* See note on 4:10.
9:9 *tablets of stone . . . of the covenant.* See notes on Ex 20:1; 34:28.
9:10 *two stone tablets.* See note on Ex 31:18. *finger of God.* See note on Ex 8:19.
9:11–21 See Ex 31:18–32:20.

Lord's sight and so provoking him to anger. [19]I feared the anger and wrath of the Lord, for he was angry enough with you to destroy you.[w] But again the Lord listened to me.[x] [20]And the Lord was angry enough with Aaron to destroy him, but at that time I prayed for Aaron too. [21]Also I took that sinful thing of yours, the calf you had made, and burned it in the fire. Then I crushed it and ground it to powder as fine as dust[y] and threw the dust into a stream that flowed down the mountain.[z]

[22]You also made the Lord angry[a] at Taberah,[b] at Massah[c] and at Kibroth Hattaavah.[d]

[23]And when the Lord sent you out from Kadesh Barnea,[e] he said, "Go up and take possession[f] of the land I have given you." But you rebelled[g] against the command of the Lord your God. You did not trust[h] him or obey him. [24]You have been rebellious against the Lord ever since I have known you.[i]

[25]I lay prostrate before the Lord those forty days and forty nights[j] because the Lord had said he would destroy you.[k] [26]I prayed to the Lord and said, "O Sovereign Lord, do not destroy your people,[l] your own inheritance[m] that you redeemed[n] by your great power and brought out of Egypt with a mighty hand.[o] [27]Remember your servants Abraham, Isaac and Jacob. Overlook the stubbornness[p] of this people, their wickedness and their sin. [28]Otherwise, the country[q] from which you brought us will say, 'Because the Lord was not able to take them into the land he had promised them, and because he hated them,[r] he brought them out to put them to death in the desert.'[s] [29]But they are your people,[t] your inheritance[u] that you brought out by your great power and your outstretched arm.[v] "

Tablets Like the First Ones

10 At that time the Lord said to me, "Chisel out two stone tablets[w] like the first ones and come up to me on the

mountain. Also make a wooden chest.[r] [2]I will write on the tablets the words that were on the first tablets, which you broke. Then you are to put them in the chest."[x]

[3]So I made the ark out of acacia wood[y] and chiseled[z] out two stone tablets like the first ones, and I went up on the mountain with the two tablets in my hands. [4]The Lord wrote on these tablets what he had written before, the Ten Commandments[a] he had proclaimed[b] to you on the mountain, out of the fire, on the day of the assembly.[c] And the Lord gave them to me. [5]Then I came back down the mountain[d] and put the tablets in the ark[e] I had made,[f] as the Lord commanded me, and they are there now.[g]

[6](The Israelites traveled from the wells of the Jaakanites to Moserah.[h] There Aaron died[i] and was buried, and Eleazar[j] his son succeeded him as priest.[k] [7]From there they traveled to Gudgodah and on to Jotbathah, a land with streams of water.[l] [8]At that time the Lord set apart the tribe of Levi[m] to carry the ark of the covenant[n] of the Lord, to stand before the Lord to minister[o] and to pronounce blessings[p] in his name, as they still do today.[q] [9]That is why the Levites have no share or inheritance among their brothers; the Lord is their inheritance,[r] as the Lord your God told them.)

[10]Now I had stayed on the mountain forty days and nights, as I did the first time, and the Lord listened to me at this time also. It was not his will to destroy you.[s] [11]"Go," the Lord said to me, "and lead the people on their way, so that they may enter and possess the land that I swore to their fathers to give them."

Fear the Lord

[12]And now, O Israel, what does the Lord your God ask of you[t] but to fear[u] the Lord your God, to walk[v] in all his

9:19
wS Ex 32:14;
Heb 12:21* xver
26; Ex 34:10;
S Nu 11:2;
1Sa 7:9; Jer 15:1
9:21 yPs 18:42;
Isa 29:5; 40:15
zEx 32:20;
Isa 2:18; Mic 1:7
9:22 aS Nu 1:53
bNu 11:3
cS Ex 17:7
dNu 11:34
9:23 eS Dt 1:2
fDt 1:21
gS Nu 14:9
hS Dt 1:32;
Ps 106:24
9:24 iS Dt 8:17
9:25 jS Ge 7:4
kver 18;
S Ex 33:17
9:26 lS Ex 33:13
mS Ex 34:9
nS Ex 6:6;
Dt 15:15;
2Sa 7:23;
Ps 78:35 over
19; S Ex 32:11
9:27 pver 6;
S Ex 32:9
9:28 qDt 32:27
rS Dt 1:27
sS Ex 32:12;
Jos 7:9
9:29 tS Ex 33:13
uS Ex 34:9;
Dt 32:9 vDt 4:34;
Ne 1:10; Jer 27:5;
32:17
10:1 wEx 34:1-2

10:2 xEx 25:16,
21; 2Ch 5:10;
6:11
10:3 yEx 37:1-9
zEx 34:4
10:4
aS Ex 24:12;
S 34:28 bEx 20:1
cS Dt 9:10
10:5 dS Ex 19:11
eS Ex 25:10;
S 1Sa 3:3
fS Ex 25:21
gS 1Ki 8:9
10:6 hNu 33:30
iS Nu 27:13
jS Ex 6:23
kS Nu 20:25-28
10:7
lNu 33:32-34;
Ps 42:1; SS 5:12;
Isa 32:2
10:8 mS Nu 3:6
nS Nu 10:33
oS Nu 16:9
pS Ge 48:20
q1Ch 23:26
10:9 rS Nu 18:20
10:10
sS Ex 33:17
10:12 tMic 6:8
uS Ex 20:20
v1Ki 2:3; 3:3; 9:4

r / That is, an ark

9:19 *But again the Lord listened to me.* Moses' intercessory prayer on this occasion (vv. 26–29) ranks among the great prayers for Israel's national survival (see 1Sa 7:5,8–9; Jer 15:1).

9:22 *Taberah.* See Nu 11:3 and NIV text note. *Massah.* See 6:16; 33:8; see also note on Ex 17:7. *Kibroth Hattaavah.* See Nu 11:34 and NIV text note.

9:23 *Kadesh Barnea.* See note on Ge 14:7.

9:27 *Overlook.* See note on Ac 17:30.

10:1–3 *chest . . . ark.* Both words translate the same Hebrew word, which means "chest" or "box." After initially translating "chest" for clarity, the NIV reverts to the more traditional and familiar rendering "ark."

10:1 *two stone tablets.* See note on Ex 31:18.

10:2 *put them in the chest.* See notes on Ex 16:34; 25:16.

10:3 Ex 34–37 shows that the order of events here is different from that in Exodus (see Introduction: Structure and Outline).

10:6–9 A historical parenthesis, apparently stemming from Moses' prayer for Aaron and the Israelites (9:26–29) and the reference to the ark (vv. 1–5).

10:8 *carry the ark.* See note on Nu 1:50. *to minister.* See note on 21:5.

10:9 See Nu 18:20,24.

10:12 *fear the Lord.* See note on Ge 20:11. *love him.* See notes on 4:29,37; 6:5.

ways, to love him,[w] to serve the LORD[x] your God with all your heart[y] and with all your soul,[z] [13]and to observe the LORD's commands[a] and decrees that I am giving you today for your own good?[b]

[14]To the LORD your God belong the heavens,[cde] even the highest heavens,[f g] the earth and everything in it.[h] [15]Yet the LORD set his affection on your forefathers and loved[i] them, and he chose you,[j] their descendants, above all the nations, as it is today.[k] [16]Circumcise[l] your hearts,[m] therefore, and do not be stiff-necked[n] any longer. [17]For the LORD your God is God of gods[o] and Lord of lords,[p] the great God, mighty and awesome,[q] who shows no partiality[r] and accepts no bribes.[s] [18]He defends the cause of the fatherless and the widow,[t] and loves the alien, giving him food and clothing.[u] [19]And you are to love[v] those who are aliens,[w] for you yourselves were aliens in Egypt.[x] [20]Fear the LORD your God and serve him.[y] Hold fast[z] to him and take your oaths in his name.[a] [21]He is your praise;[b] he is your God, who performed for you those great[c] and awesome wonders[d] you saw with your own eyes. [22]Your forefathers who went down into Egypt were seventy in all,[e] and now the LORD your God has made you as numerous as the stars in the sky.[f]

Love and Obey the LORD

11 Love[g] the LORD your God and keep his requirements, his decrees, his laws and his commands always.[h] [2]Remember today that your children[i] were not the ones who saw and experienced the discipline of the LORD your God:[j] his majesty,[k] his mighty hand, his outstretched arm;[l] [3]the signs he performed and the things he did in the heart of Egypt, both to Pharaoh king of Egypt and to his whole country;[m] [4]what he did to the Egyptian army, to its horses and chariots,[n] how he overwhelmed them with the waters of the Red Sea[s o] as they were pursuing you, and how the LORD brought lasting ruin on them. [5]It was not

your children who saw what he did for you in the desert until you arrived at this place, [6]and what he did[p] to Dathan and Abiram, sons of Eliab the Reubenite, when the earth opened[q] its mouth right in the middle of all Israel and swallowed them up with their households, their tents and every living thing that belonged to them. [7]But it was your own eyes that saw all these great things the LORD has done.[r]

[8]Observe therefore all the commands[s] I am giving you today, so that you may have the strength to go in and take over the land that you are crossing the Jordan to possess,[t] [9]and so that you may live long[u] in the land that the LORD swore[v] to your forefathers to give to them and their descendants, a land flowing with milk and honey.[w] [10]The land you are entering to take over is not like the land of Egypt,[x] from which you have come, where you planted your seed and irrigated it by foot as in a vegetable garden. [11]But the land you are crossing the Jordan to take possession of is a land of mountains and valleys[y] that drinks rain from heaven.[z] [12]It is a land the LORD your God cares for; the eyes[a] of the LORD your God are continually on it from the beginning of the year to its end.

[13]So if you faithfully obey[b] the commands I am giving you today—to love[c] the LORD your God and to serve him with all your heart and with all your soul[d]— [14]then I will send rain[e] on your land in its season, both autumn and spring rains,[f] so that you may gather in your grain, new wine and oil. [15]I will provide grass[g] in the fields for your cattle, and you will eat and be satisfied.[h]

[16]Be careful, or you will be enticed to turn away and worship other gods and

---

10:12 [w]Dt 5:33; 6:13; Mt 22:37; 1Ti 1:5
[x]Dt 11:13; 28:47; Ps 100:2
[y]S Dt 6:5; Ps 119:2
[z]S Dt 5:32
10:13 [a]S Dt 4:2
[b]Dt 5:33; 6:24
10:14 [c]Ps 148:4; Isa 19:1; Hab 3:8
[d]Ne 9:6; Job 35:5; Ps 8:3; 89:11; 104:3
[e]Dt 33:26
[f]Ps 115:16
[g]1Ki 8:27
[h]Ex 19:5;
10:15 [i]S Dt 4:37
Ps 105:6; 135:4
[j]S Nu 14:8;
Ro 11:28; 1Pe 2:9
10:16 [l]S Ge 17:11
[m]S Lev 26:41; Dt 30:6; Jer 32:39
[n]S Ex 32:9; S Dt 9:13
10:17 [o]Jos 22:22; Ps 135:5; 136:2; Da 2:47; 11:36
[p]Ps 136:3; S 1Ti 6:15
[q]S Dt 7:21
[r]Dt 1:17; Mal 2:9
[s]S Ex 23:8; S Lev 19:16
10:18 [t]Ex 22:21, 22-24; 23:9; Lev 19:33; Dt 27:19; Job 29:13; Ps 94:6; Isa 10:2; Jer 49:11
[u]S Nu 10:32
10:19 [v]Dt 7:12
[w]S Ex 22:21;
S Dt 24:19
[x]S Lev 19:34; Eze 47:22-23
10:20 [y]Mt 4:10
[z]Dt 11:22; 13:4; 30:20; 2os 23:8; Ru 1:14; 2Ki 18:6; Ps 119:31; Isa 38:3
[a]S Ex 20:7
10:21 [b]S Ex 15:2
[c]1Sa 12:24; Ps 126:2
[d]2Sa 7:23
10:22
[e]S Ge 34:30;
S 46:26; Ac 7:14
[f]S Ge 12:2;
S Nu 10:36
11:1 [g]S Dt 6:5
[h]S Lev 8:35
11:2 [i]Dt 31:13; Ps 78:6 [j]S Dt 5:24
[k]S Dt 3:24
[l]Ps 136:12

11:3 [m]Ex 7:8-21 11:4 [n]S Ex 15:1 [o]S Ex 14:27; S Nu 21:4
11:6 [p]Nu 16:1-35; Ps 106:16-18 [q]Isa 24:19 11:7 [r]Dt 5:3
11:8 [s]Ezr 9:10 [t]Dt 31:6-7,23; Jos 1:7 11:9 [u]S Dt 5:16
[v]Dt 9:5 [w]S Ex 3:8 11:10 [x]Isa 11:15; 37:25 11:11 [y]Eze 36:4
[z]Dt 8:7; Ne 9:25 11:12 [a]1Ki 8:29; 9:3 11:13 [b]S Dt 6:17
[c]S Dt 10:12 [d]Dt 4:29; Jer 17:24 11:14 [e]S Lev 26:4;
Ac 14:17 [f]Ps 147:8; Jer 3:3; 5:24; Joel 2:23; Jas 5:7 11:15
[g]Ps 104:14 [h]S Lev 26:5

[s]4 Hebrew *Yam Suph*; that is, Sea of Reeds

10:13 *for your own good.* See 6:24; see also note on 6:2.
10:16 *Circumcise your hearts.* See note on Ge 17:10. *stiff-necked.* See 9:6,13; 31:27; see also note on Ex 32:9.
10:20 *Hold fast.* As a man is "united" to his wife (Ge 2:24), and as Ruth "clung" to Naomi (Ru 1:14). See 4:4; 11:22; 13:4; 30:20.
10:22 *seventy.* See notes on Ge 46:26-27; see also Ex 1:5. *as the stars in the sky.* See note on 1:10.
11:2–7 Moses continually emphasizes the involvement of his listeners in the Lord's works of providence and deliverance. In 5:3 it was not the fathers but they themselves with whom the covenant was made. Here it is not their children

but they themselves who saw God's great deeds.
11:2 *Remember.* See note on 4:10.
11:8–12 See note on 8:7–9.
11:9 *live long.* See note on 6:2.
11:10 *irrigated it by foot.* Irrigation channels dug by foot and/or fed by devices powered by foot brought the water of the Nile to the gardens in Egypt, in contrast to the rains that watered Canaan (v. 11).
11:13 See note on 4:29.
11:14 *autumn and spring rains.* The rainy season in Palestine begins in October and ends in April.

bow down to them.[i] 17Then the LORD's anger[j] will burn against you, and he will shut[k] the heavens so that it will not rain and the ground will yield no produce,[l] and you will soon perish[m] from the good land the LORD is giving you. 18Fix these words of mine in your hearts and minds; tie them as symbols on your hands and bind them on your foreheads.[n] 19Teach them to your children,[o] talking about them when you sit at home and when you walk along the road, when you lie down and when you get up.[p] 20Write them on the doorframes of your houses and on your gates,[q] 21so that your days and the days of your children may be many[r] in the land that the LORD swore to give your forefathers, as many as the days that the heavens are above the earth.[s]

22If you carefully observe[t] all these commands I am giving you to follow—to love[u] the LORD your God, to walk in all his ways and to hold fast[v] to him— 23then the LORD will drive out[w] all these nations[x] before you, and you will dispossess nations larger and stronger than you.[y] 24Every place where you set your foot will be yours:[z] Your territory will extend from the desert to Lebanon, and from the Euphrates River[a] to the western sea.[t] 25No man will be able to stand against you. The LORD your God, as he promised you, will put the terror[b] and fear of you on the whole land, wherever you go.[c]

26See, I am setting before you today a blessing[d] and a curse[e]— 27the blessing[f] if you obey the commands of the LORD your God that I am giving you today; 28the curse if you disobey[g] the commands of the LORD your God and turn from the way that I command you today by following other gods,[h] which you have not known. 29When the LORD your God has brought you into the land you are entering to possess, you are to proclaim on Mount Gerizim[i] the blessings, and on Mount Ebal[j]

the curses.[k] 30As you know, these mountains are across the Jordan, west of the road,[u] toward the setting sun, near the great trees of Moreh,[l] in the territory of those Canaanites living in the Arabah in the vicinity of Gilgal.[m] 31You are about to cross the Jordan to enter and take possession[n] of the land the LORD your God is giving[o] you. When you have taken it over and are living there, 32be sure that you obey all the decrees and laws I am setting before you today.

The One Place of Worship

12 These are the decrees[p] and laws you must be careful to follow in the land that the LORD, the God of your fathers, has given you to possess—as long as you live in the land.[q] 2Destroy completely all the places on the high mountains[r] and on the hills and under every spreading tree[s] where the nations you are dispossessing worship their gods. 3Break down their altars, smash[t] their sacred stones and burn[u] their Asherah[v] poles in the fire; cut down the idols of their gods and wipe out their names[w] from those places.

4You must not worship the LORD your God in their way.[x] 5But you are to seek the place the LORD your God will choose from among all your tribes to put his Name[y] there for his dwelling.[z] To that place you must go; 6there bring your burnt offerings and sacrifices, your tithes[a] and special gifts, what you have vowed[b] to give and your freewill offerings, and the firstborn of your herds and flocks.[c] 7There, in the presence[d] of the LORD your God,

Cross references

11:16 /Dt 4:19; 8:19; 29:18; Job 31:9,27
11:17 /Dt 6:15; 9:19 k1Ki 17:1; 2Ch 6:26; 7:13 /S Lev 26:20 mDt 4:26; 28:12, 24
11:18 nS Ex 13:9; Dt 6:6-8
11:19 oS Ex 12:26; Dt 6:7; Ps 145:4; Isa 38:19; Jer 32:39 pDt 4:9-10
11:20 qDt 6:9
11:21 rJob 5:26; Pr 3:2; 4:10; 9:11 sPs 72:5
11:22 tS Dt 6:17 uS Dt 6:5
11:23 vS Dt 10:20 wS Dt 9:5 xS Ex 23:28 yDt 9:1
11:24 zGe 15:18; Dt 1:36; 12:20; 19:8; Jos 1:3; 14:9 aS Ge 2:14
11:25 bS Dt 2:25 cEx 23:27; Dt 7:24
11:26 dPs 24:5 eLev 26:14-17; Dt 27:13-26; 30:1,15,19; La 2:17; Da 9:11; Hag 1:11; Mal 2:2; 3:9; 4:6
11:27 /Dt 28:1-14; Ps 24:5
11:28 g2Ch 24:20; Jer 42:13; 44:16 hS Dt 4:28; 13:6, 13; 29:26; 1Sa 26:19
11:29 /Jdg 9:7 /Dt 27:4; Jos 8:30
11:30 /S Ge 12:6 mJos 4:19; 5:9; 9:6; 10:6; 14:6; 15:7; Jdg 2:1; 2Ki 2:1; Mic 6:5
11:31 nS Nu 33:53 oDt 12:10; Jos 11:23
12:1 pPs 119:5 qDt 4:9-10; 6:15; 1Ki 8:40; Eze 20:19
12:2 rS Nu 21:28 s1Ki 14:23; 2Ki 17:10; Isa 57:5; Jer 2:20;
3:6,13 12:3 t2Ki 11:18 uS Ex 32:20 vEx 34:13; 1Ki 14:15,23 wS Ex 23:13 12:4 xver 30; 2Ki 17:15; Jer 10:2 12:5 yS Ex 20:24; S 2Sa 7:13 zver 11,13; Dt 14:23; 15:20; 16:2, 7:12,16; Ezr 6:12; 7:15; Ps 26:8; 78:68; Zec 2:12 12:6 aS Lev 27:30 bS Ge 28:20 cJos 22:27; Isa 66:20 12:7 dS Ex 18:12

t24 That is, the Mediterranean   u30 Or Jordan, westward

Notes

11:17 shut the heavens. The all-important seasonal rains (see v. 14) were controlled by the Lord—not by Baal, as the inhabitants of Canaan thought (cf. Hos 2:8,17).

11:18–20 See note on 6:8–9.

11:22 hold fast. See note on 10:20.

11:24 Every place where you set your foot. See note on 1:7.

11:26–30 The blessings and curses proclaimed on Mount Gerizim and Mount Ebal are detailed in chs. 27–28.

11:28 known. Experienced or acknowledged (see 13:2,6, 13; 28:64; 29:26; 32:17; see also note on Ex 6:3).

11:30 road. Probably the north-south road that ran parallel to the Jordan between the Sea of Galilee and the Dead Sea. great trees of Moreh. See note on Ge 12:6. Arabah. See note on 1:1. The Canaanites who lived there controlled the terri-

tory around Gerizim and Ebal.

12:3 altars . . . sacred stones . . . Asherah poles. See note on 7:5.

12:4 in their way. The rituals and accessories of idolatrous worship were not to be used to worship the Lord, the one true God (cf. vv. 29–31).

12:5 the place the LORD . . . will choose . . . to put his Name. The tabernacle, the Lord's dwelling place during the desert journey, will be located in the city in Canaan where the Lord would choose to dwell. Moses stresses the importance of centralizing the place of worship as he prepares the people for settlement in the promised land, where the Canaanites had established many places of worship. See vv. 11,14,18,21,26; 14:23–24; 16:2,6,11; 26:2.

12:6 See v. 11 and chart on "OT Sacrifices," p. 150.

you and your families shall eat and shall rejoice[e] in everything you have put your hand to, because the LORD your God has blessed you.

[8]You are not to do as we do here today, everyone as he sees fit,[f] [9]since you have not yet reached the resting place[g] and the inheritance[h] the LORD your God is giving you. [10]But you will cross the Jordan and settle in the land the LORD your God is giving[i] you as an inheritance, and he will give you rest[j] from all your enemies around you so that you will live in safety. [11]Then to the place the LORD your God will choose as a dwelling for his Name[k]—there you are to bring everything I command you: your burnt offerings and sacrifices, your tithes and special gifts, and all the choice possessions you have vowed to the LORD.[l] [12]And there rejoice[m] before the LORD your God, you, your sons and daughters, your menservants and maidservants, and the Levites[n] from your towns, who have no allotment or inheritance[o] of their own. [13]Be careful not to sacrifice your burnt offerings anywhere you please.[p] [14]Offer them only at the place the LORD will choose[q] in one of your tribes, and there observe everything I command you.

[15]Nevertheless, you may slaughter your animals in any of your towns and eat as much of the meat as you want, as if it were gazelle or deer,[r] according to the blessing the LORD your God gives you. Both the ceremonially unclean and the clean may eat it. [16]But you must not eat the blood;[s] pour[t] it out on the ground like water.[u] [17]You must not eat in your own towns the tithe[v] of your grain and new wine and oil,[w] or the firstborn of your herds and flocks, or whatever you have vowed to give,[x] or your freewill offerings or special gifts.[y] [18]Instead, you are to eat[z] them in the presence of the LORD your God at the place the LORD your God will choose[a]—you, your sons and daughters, your menservants and maidservants, and the Levites from your towns—and you are to rejoice[b] before the LORD your God in

everything you put your hand to. [19]Be careful not to neglect the Levites[c] as long as you live in your land. [d]

[20]When the LORD your God has enlarged your territory[e] as he promised[f] you, and you crave meat[g] and say, "I would like some meat," then you may eat as much of it as you want. [21]If the place where the LORD your God chooses to put his Name[h] is too far away from you, you may slaughter animals from the herds and flocks the LORD has given you, as I have commanded you, and in your own towns you may eat as much of them as you want.[i] [22]Eat them as you would gazelle or deer.[j] Both the ceremonially unclean and the clean may eat. [23]But be sure you do not eat the blood,[k] because the blood is the life, and you must not eat the life with the meat.[l] [24]You must not eat the blood; pour it out on the ground like water.[m] [25]Do not eat it, so that it may go well[n] with you and your children after you, because you will be doing what is right[o] in the eyes of the LORD.

[26]But take your consecrated things and whatever you have vowed to give,[p] and go to the place the LORD will choose. [27]Present your burnt offerings[q] on the altar of the LORD your God, both the meat and the blood. The blood of your sacrifices must be poured beside the altar of the LORD your God, but you may eat[r] the meat. [28]Be careful to obey all these regulations I am giving you, so that it may always go well[s] with you and your children after you, because you will be doing what is good and right in the eyes of the LORD your God.

[29]The LORD your God will cut off[t] before you the nations you are about to invade and dispossess. But when you have driven them out and settled in their land,[u] [30]and after they have been destroyed before you, be careful not to be ensnared[v] by inquiring about their gods, saying, "How do these nations serve their gods? We will do the same."[w] [31]You must not worship the LORD your God in their way, because in worshiping their gods, they do all kinds

---

12:7
[e]S Lev 23:40;
Ecc 3:12-13;
5:18-20;
S Isa 62:9
12:8 [f]Jdg 17:6;
21:25
12:9
[g]S Ex 33:14;
Dt 3:20;
Ps 95:11;
Mic 2:10
[h]Dt 4:21
12:10
[i]S Dt 11:31
[j]S Ex 33:14
12:11 [k]S ver 5
[l]S Lev 1:3;
Jos 22:23
12:12 [m]ver 7
[n]Dt 26:11-13
[o]S Nu 18:20
12:13 [p]S ver 5
12:14 [q]ver 11
12:15 [r]ver 22;
Dt 14:5; 15:22
12:16 [s]S Ge 9:4;
Ac 15:20 [t]ver
23-24;
S Ge 35:14;
1Ch 11:18;
Jer 7:18
[u]S Lev 17:13;
S Dt 15:23;
Jn 19:34
12:17
[v]S Lev 27:30
[w]S Nu 18:12 [x]ver
26; Nu 18:19
[y]Dt 14:23; 15:20
12:18 [z]Dt 14:23;
15:20 [a]ver 5 [b]ver
7,12; Dt 14:26;
Ne 8:10;
Ecc 3:12-13;
5:18-20
12:19 [c]ver 12;
Dt 14:27;
Ne 13:10
[d]Mal 3:8
12:20
[e]S Ex 34:24
[f]S Ge 15:8;
S Dt 11:24
[g]S Ex 16:3
12:21 [h]Dt 14:24
[i]Lev 17:4
12:22 [j]S ver 15
12:23
[k]S Lev 7:26
[l]Eze 33:25
12:24 [m]ver 16
12:25 [n]S Dt 4:40
[o]ver 28;
Ex 15:26;
Dt 13:10;
1Ki 11:38;
2Ki 12:2
12:26 [p]S ver 17;
Nu 5:9-10
12:27
[q]S Lev 1:13
[r]Lev 3:1-17
12:28 [s]Dt 4:40;
Ecc 8:12
12:29 [t]Jos 23:4
[u]S Dt 6:10
12:30 [v]S Ex 10:7
[w]S ver 4

12:8 *as we do here today.* Israel was not able to follow all the procedures of the sacrificial system during the desert wandering and conquest periods. Moses was giving directives for their worship and way of life when settled in the land (vv. 10–14). *as he sees fit.* See note on Jdg 17:6.
12:9 *resting place.* See note on 3:20.
12:11 *dwelling for his Name.* Equivalent to "dwelling for himself." See notes on Ex 3:13–14.
12:12 *rejoice before the LORD.* Joy, based on the Lord's blessings, was to be a major feature of Hebrew life and

worship in the promised land (vv. 7,18). *Levites... have no ... inheritance.* See 10:9; Nu 18:20,24.
12:13 *not... anywhere you please.* Sacrifices and offerings to the Lord were to be brought only to the central sanctuary, not to the various Canaanite worship sites.
12:16,24 *you must not eat the blood.* See notes on Ge 9:4; Lev 17:11.
12:31 *burn... sons and daughters... as sacrifices.* See 18:10; see also note on Lev 18:21.

of detestable things the LORD hates.[x] They
even burn their sons[y] and daughters in the
fire as sacrifices to their gods.[z]
32 See that you do all I command you; do
not add[a] to it or take away from it.

Worshiping Other Gods

13 If a prophet,[b] or one who foretells
by dreams,[c] appears among you
and announces to you a miraculous sign or
wonder, 2 and if the sign[d] or wonder of
which he has spoken takes place, and he
says, "Let us follow other gods"[e] (gods
you have not known) "and let us worship
them," 3 you must not listen to the words
of that prophet[f] or dreamer.[g] The LORD
your God is testing[h] you to find out
whether you love[i] him with all your heart
and with all your soul. 4 It is the LORD your
God you must follow,[j] and him you must
revere.[k] Keep his commands and obey
him; serve him and hold fast[l] to him.
5 That prophet or dreamer must be put to
death,[m] because he preached rebellion
against the LORD your God, who brought
you out of Egypt and redeemed you from
the land of slavery; he has tried to turn[n]
you from the way the LORD your God commanded you to follow. You must purge the
evil[o] from among you.
6 If your very own brother, or your son
or daughter, or the wife you love, or your
closest friend secretly entices[p] you, saying,
"Let us go and worship other gods"[q] (gods
that neither you nor your fathers have
known, 7 gods of the peoples around you,
whether near or far, from one end of the
land to the other), 8 do not yield[r] to him or
listen to him. Show him no pity.[s] Do not
spare him or shield him. 9 You must certainly put him to death.[t] Your hand[u]
must be the first in putting him to death,
and then the hands of all the people.
10 Stone him to death, because he tried to
turn you away[v] from the LORD your God,
who brought you out of Egypt, out of the
land of slavery. 11 Then all Israel will hear
and be afraid,[w] and no one among you will
do such an evil thing again.
12 If you hear it said about one of the
towns the LORD your God is giving you to
live in 13 that wicked men[x] have arisen
among you and have led the people of
their town astray, saying, "Let us go and
worship other gods" (gods you have not
known), 14 then you must inquire, probe
and investigate it thoroughly.[y] And if it is
true and it has been proved that this detestable thing has been done among you,[z]
15 you must certainly put to the sword all
who live in that town. Destroy it completely,[v][a] both its people and its livestock.[b] 16 Gather all the plunder of the
town into the middle of the public square
and completely burn the town[c] and all its
plunder as a whole burnt offering to the
LORD your God.[d] It is to remain a ruin[e]
forever, never to be rebuilt. 17 None of
those condemned things[v] shall be found in
your hands, so that the LORD will turn
from his fierce anger;[f] he will show you
mercy,[g] have compassion[h] on you, and
increase your numbers,[i] as he promised[j]
on oath to your forefathers, 18 because you
obey the LORD your God, keeping all his
commands that I am giving you today and
doing what is right[k] in his eyes.

Clean and Unclean Food

14:3-20pp — Lev 11:1-23

14 You are the children[l] of the LORD
your God. Do not cut yourselves or
shave the front of your heads for the dead,
2 for you are a people holy[m] to the LORD
your God.[n] Out of all the peoples on the

12:31 [x]S Lev 18:25 [y]S Lev 18:21 [z]S 2Ki 3:27 **12:32** [a]S Dt 4:2; Rev 22:18-19 **13:1** [b]Mt 24:24; Mk 13:22; 2Th 2:9 [c]S Ge 20:3; Jer 23:25; 27:9; 29:8 **13:2** [d]Dt 18:22; 1Sa 2:34; 10:9; 2Ki 19:29; 20:9; Isa 7:11 [e]S Dt 11:28 **13:3** [f]2Pe 2:1 [g]1Sa 28:6,15 [h]S Ge 22:1; 1Ki 13:18; 22:22-23; Jer 29:31; 43:2; Eze 13:9; 1Co 11:19 [i]Dt 6:5 **13:4** [j]2Ki 23:3; 2Ch 34:31; 2Jn 1:6 [k]S Dt 6:13; S Ps 5:7 [l]S Dt 10:20 **13:5** [m]S Ex 21:12; S 22:20 [n]ver 10; Dt 4:19 [o]Dt 17:7, 12; 19:19; 24:7; Jdg 20:13; S 1Co 5:13 **13:6** [p]Dt 17:2-7; 29:18 [q]S Dt 11:28 **13:8** [r]Pr 1:10 [s]S Dt 7:2 **13:9** [t]ver 5 [u]S Lev 24:14 **13:10** [v]S Ex 20:3 **13:11** [w]Dt 17:13; 19:20; 21:21; 1Ti 5:20 **13:13** [x]Jdg 19:22; 20:13; 1Sa 2:12; 10:27; 11:12; 25:17; 1Ki 21:10 **13:14** [y]Jdg 20:12 [z]Dt 17:4 **13:15** [a]Isa 24:6; 34:5; 43:28; 47:6; La 2:6; Da 9:11; Zec 8:13; Mal 4:6 [b]Ex 22:20 **13:16** [c]2Ki 25:9; Jer 39:8; 52:13; Eze 16:41 [d]Dt 7:25,26; Jos 6:24 [e]Jos 8:28; Isa 7:16; 17:1; 24:10; 25:2; 27:10; 32:14,19; 37:26; Jer 49:2; Mic 1:6 **13:17** [f]Ex 32:12; Nu 25:4 [g]S Ge 43:14 [h]Dt 30:3 [i]S Dt 7:13 [j]S Ge 12:2; S 13:14; S 26:24 **13:18** [k]S Dt 12:25 **14:1** [l]S Jn 1:12; S Ro 8:14; 9:8 **14:2** [m]S Ge 28:14; Ex 22:31; Isa 6:13; Mal 2:15 [n]S Lev 20:26; Ro 12:1

[v] *15,17* The Hebrew term refers to the irrevocable giving over of things or persons to the LORD, often by totally destroying them.

12:32 *do not add . . . or take away.* See note on 4:2.
13:1–5 Eventual fulfillment is one test of true prophecy (18:21–22), but the more stringent rule given here guards against intelligent foresight masquerading as prophecy and against coincidental fulfillment of the predictions of false prophets.
13:3 *testing.* See note on Ge 22:1. *all your heart.* See note on 4:29.
13:4 *hold fast.* See note on 10:20.
13:5 *prophet . . . must be put to death.* See 18:20; Jer 28:15–17. *You must purge the evil from among you.* Repeated in 17:7; 19:19; 21:21; 22:21,24; 24:7, and quoted in 1Co 5:13. The purpose was to eliminate the evildoers as well as the evil itself.
13:13 *wicked.* See 1Sa 1:16; 2:12; 25:17. The same Hebrew word is also used, e.g., in 1Sa 10:27; 30:22 ("troublemakers"); 1Ki 21:10,13 ("scoundrels"); Pr 6:12 ("scoundrel"). Later, this word (*Belial* in Hebrew) was used as a name for Satan (2Co 6:15), who is the personification of wickedness and lawlessness.
13:15 *Destroy it completely.* See note on 2:34.
14:1 *cut yourselves.* A pagan religious custom (see 1Ki 18:28). *shave the front of your heads.* Shaving the forehead was a practice of mourners in Canaan.
14:2,21 *holy to the LORD.* See note on Lev 11:44. The regulations regarding clean and unclean foods were intended to separate Israel from things the Lord had identified as detestable and ceremonially unclean.
14:2 *treasured possession.* See note on Ex 19:5.

face of the earth, the LORD has chosen you to be his treasured possession. *o*

³Do not eat any detestable thing. *p* ⁴These are the animals you may eat: *q* the ox, the sheep, the goat, *r* ⁵the deer, *s* the gazelle, the roe deer, the wild goat, *t* the ibex, the antelope and the mountain sheep. *w* ⁶You may eat any animal that has a split hoof divided in two and that chews the cud. ⁷However, of those that chew the cud or that have a split hoof completely divided you may not eat the camel, the rabbit or the coney. *x* Although they chew the cud, they do not have a split hoof; they are ceremonially unclean for you. ⁸The pig is also unclean; although it has a split hoof, it does not chew the cud. You are not to eat their meat or touch their carcasses. *u*

⁹Of all the creatures living in the water, you may eat any that has fins and scales. ¹⁰But anything that does not have fins and scales you may not eat; for you it is unclean.

¹¹You may eat any clean bird. ¹²But these you may not eat: the eagle, the vulture, the black vulture, ¹³the red kite, the black kite, any kind *v* of falcon, *w* ¹⁴any kind of raven, *x* ¹⁵the horned owl, the screech owl, the gull, any kind of hawk, ¹⁶the little owl, the great owl, the white owl, ¹⁷the desert owl, *y* the osprey, the cormorant, ¹⁸the stork, any kind of heron, the hoopoe and the bat.

¹⁹All flying insects that swarm are unclean to you; do not eat them. ²⁰But any winged creature that is clean you may eat. *z*

²¹Do not eat anything you find already dead. *a* You may give it to an alien living in any of your towns, and he may eat it, or you may sell it to a foreigner. But you are a people holy to the LORD your God. *b*

Do not cook a young goat in its mother's milk. *c*

Tithes

²²Be sure to set aside a tenth *d* of all that

your fields produce each year. ²³Eat *e* the tithe of your grain, new wine *f* and oil, and the firstborn of your herds and flocks in the presence of the LORD your God at the place he will choose as a dwelling for his Name, *g* so that you may learn *h* to revere *i* the LORD your God always. ²⁴But if that place is too distant and you have been blessed by the LORD your God and cannot carry your tithe (because the place where the LORD will choose to put his Name is so far away), ²⁵then exchange *j* your tithe for silver, and take the silver with you and go to the place the LORD your God will choose. ²⁶Use the silver to buy whatever you like: cattle, sheep, wine or other fermented drink, *k* or anything you wish. Then you and your household shall eat there in the presence of the LORD your God and rejoice. *l* ²⁷And do not neglect the Levites *m* living in your towns, for they have no allotment or inheritance of their own. *n*

²⁸At the end of every three years, bring all the tithes *o* of that year's produce and store it in your towns, *p* ²⁹so that the Levites (who have no allotment *q* or inheritance *r* of their own) and the aliens, *s* the fatherless and the widows who live in your towns may come and eat and be satisfied, *t* and so that the LORD your God may bless *u* you in all the work of your hands.

The Year for Canceling Debts

15:1–11Ref — Lev 25:8–38

15 At the end of every seven years you must cancel debts. *v* ²This is how it is to be done: Every creditor shall cancel the loan he has made to his fellow Israelite. He shall not require payment from his fellow Israelite or brother, because the LORD's time for canceling debts has been proclaimed. ³You may require payment from a foreigner, *w* but you must cancel any

Cross references (center column)

14:2 *o*S Ex 8:22;
S Dt 7:6
14:3 *p*Eze 4:14
14:4 *q*Ac 10:14
*r*S Lev 7:23
14:5 *s*S Dt 12:15
*t*Job 39:1;
Ps 104:18
14:8 *u*S Lev 5:2
14:13 *v*S Ge 1:11
*w*Isa 34:15
14:14 *x*S Ge 8:7
14:17 *y*Ps 102:6;
Isa 13:21; 14:23;
34:11; Zep 2:14
14:20
*z*S Lev 20:25
14:21
*a*S Lev 11:39 *b*ver
2 *c*S Ex 23:19
14:22
*d*S Ge 14:20;
S Lev 27:30;
S Nu 18:21

14:23
*e*S Dt 12:17,18
*f*Ps 4:7
*g*S Dt 12:5;
1Ki 3:2
*h*S Dt 4:10
*i*Ps 22:23; 33:8;
Mal 2:5
14:25 *j*Mt 21:12;
Jn 2:14
14:26
*k*S Lev 10:9;
Ecc 10:16-17
*l*S Lev 23:40;
S Dt 12:18
14:27
*m*S Dt 12:19
*n*S Nu 18:20;
26:62; Dt 18:1-2
14:28
*o*S Lev 27:30
*p*Dt 26:12
14:29 *q*Ge 47:22
*r*Nu 26:62
*s*Dt 16:11;
24:19-21;
Ps 94:6; Isa 1:17;
58:6 *t*S Dt 6:11
*u*Dt 15:10;
Ps 41:1; Pr 22:9;
Mal 3:10
15:1 *v*Dt 31:10;
Ne 10:31
15:3
*w*S Ge 31:15;
Dt 23:20; 28:12;
Ru 2:10

w 5 The precise identification of some of the birds and animals in this chapter is uncertain.   *x 7* That is, the hyrax or rock badger

---

14:3–21 The subject of clean and unclean food is discussed in greater detail in Lev 11 (see notes there).
14:21 *Do not eat . . . already dead.* Because of the prohibition against eating blood, since the dead animal's blood would not be properly drained (see 12:16,24; see also notes on Ge 9:4; Lev 17:11). *Do not cook a young goat in its mother's milk.* See note on Ex 23:19.
14:22–29 See Nu 18:21–29. Taken together, the two passages suggest the following: 1. Annually, a tenth of all Israelite produce was to be taken to the city of the central sanctuary for distribution to the Levites. 2. At that time, at an initial festival, all Israelites ate part of the tithe. 3. The rest, which would be by far the major part of it, belonged to the Levites. 4. Every third year the tithe was gathered in the

towns and stored for distribution to the Levites and the less fortunate: aliens, fatherless and widows (see 26:12). 5. The Levites were to present to the Lord a tenth of their tithe. See note on Lev 27:30.
14:22 *set aside a tenth.* See notes on Ge 14:20; 28:22.
14:23 *dwelling for his Name.* See note on 12:5.
14:25 *silver.* Pieces of silver of various weights were a common medium of exchange, but not in the form of coins (see note on Ge 20:16).
15:1 *every seven years.* See Ex 23:10–11; Lev 25:1–7.
15:3 *require payment from a foreigner.* Since he was not subject to the command to allow his fields to lie fallow during the seventh year, a foreigner would probably be financially able to pay his debts if asked to do so.

debt your brother owes you. 4However,
there should be no poor among you, for in
the land the LORD your God is giving you
to possess as your inheritance, he will richly bless[x] you, 5if only you fully obey the
LORD your God and are careful to follow[y]
all these commands I am giving you today.
6For the LORD your God will bless you as
he has promised, and you will lend to
many nations but will borrow from none.
You will rule over many nations but none
will rule over you.[z]

7If there is a poor man[a] among your
brothers in any of the towns of the land
that the LORD your God is giving you, do
not be hardhearted or tightfisted[b] toward
your poor brother. 8Rather be openhanded[c] and freely lend him whatever he
needs. 9Be careful not to harbor this
wicked thought: "The seventh year, the
year for canceling debts,[d] is near," so that
you do not show ill will[e] toward your
needy brother and give him nothing. He
may then appeal to the LORD against you,
and you will be found guilty of sin.[f]
10Give generously to him and do so without a grudging heart;[g] then because of this
the LORD your God will bless[h] you in all
your work and in everything you put your
hand to. 11There will always be poor
people[i] in the land. Therefore I command
you to be openhanded toward your brothers and toward the poor and needy in your
land.[j]

Freeing Servants

15:12–18pp — Ex 21:2–6
15:12–18Ref — Lev 25:38–55

12If a fellow Hebrew, a man or a
woman, sells himself to you and serves you
six years, in the seventh year you must let
him go free.[k] 13And when you release
him, do not send him away empty-handed.
14Supply him liberally from your flock,
your threshing floor[l] and your winepress.
Give to him as the LORD your God has
blessed you. 15Remember that you were
slaves[m] in Egypt and the LORD your God
redeemed you.[n] That is why I give you
this command today.

16But if your servant says to you, "I do
not want to leave you," because he loves
you and your family and is well off with
you, 17then take an awl and push it
through his ear lobe into the door, and he
will become your servant for life. Do the
same for your maidservant.

18Do not consider it a hardship to set
your servant free, because his service to
you these six years has been worth twice
as much as that of a hired hand. And the
LORD your God will bless you in everything
you do.

The Firstborn Animals

19Set apart for the LORD[o] your God
every firstborn male[p] of your herds and
flocks.[q] Do not put the firstborn of your
oxen to work, and do not shear the firstborn of your sheep.[r] 20Each year you and
your family are to eat them in the presence
of the LORD your God at the place he will
choose.[s] 21If an animal has a defect,[t] is
lame or blind, or has any serious flaw, you
must not sacrifice it to the LORD your
God.[u] 22You are to eat it in your own
towns. Both the ceremonially unclean and
the clean may eat it, as if it were gazelle or
deer.[v] 23But you must not eat the blood;
pour it out on the ground like water.[w]

Passover

16:1–8pp — Ex 12:14–20; Lev 23:4–8; Nu 28:16–25

16 Observe the month of Abib[x] and
celebrate the Passover[y] of the
LORD your God, because in the month of

15:4 [x]Dt 28:8 **15:5** [y]S Ex 15:26; Dt 7:12; 28:1 **15:6** [z]Dt 28:12-13,44 **15:7** [a]ver 11; Mt 26:11 [b]1Jn 3:17 **15:8** [c]Mt 5:42; Lk 6:34; S Ac 24:17 **15:9** [d]ver 1 [e]Mt 20:15 [f]S Ex 22:23; S Job 5:15; Jas 5:4 **15:10** [g]2Co 9:5 [h]S Dt 14:29 **15:11** [i]S ver 7 [j]Mt 26:11; Mk 14:7; Jn 12:8 **15:12** [k]Jer 34:14 **15:14** [l]S Nu 18:27 **15:15** [m]Ex 13:3; Jer 34:13 [n]Ex 20:2; S Dt 4:34; S 9:26; 16:12; 24:18; Jer 16:14; 23:7 **15:19** [o]S Lev 27:9 [p]S Ex 13:2 [q]S Ge 4:4 [r]S Ex 22:30 **15:20** [s]S Lev 7:15-18; Dt 12:5-7,17,18 **15:21** [t]S Ex 12:5 [u]S Lev 22:19-25; Dt 17:1; Mal 1:8, 13 **15:22** [v]S Dt 12:15 **15:23** [w]S Ge 9:4; Dt 12:16; Eze 33:25 **16:1** [x]S Ex 12:2 [y]S Ex 12:11; 2Ki 23:21; Mt 26:17-29

15:4 *there should be no poor among you.* Because of the Lord's reward for obedience (vv. 4–6), and because of the sabbath-year arrangement (vv. 7–11). This "year for canceling debts" (v. 9) gave Israelites who had experienced economic reverses a way to gain release from indebtedness and so, in a measure, a way to equalize wealth. Cf. the provisions of the Year of Jubilee (Lev 25:8–38).
15:6 *you will lend.* If Israel failed to follow the Lord's commands, the reverse would be true (see 28:43–44).
15:11 *There will always be poor people.* See also Jesus' statement in Mt 26:11. Even in the best of societies under the most enlightened laws, the uncertainties of life and the variations among citizens result in some people becoming poor. In such cases the Lord commands that generosity and kindness be extended to them.
15:15 *Remember.* See note on 4:10.
15:16 *because he loves you.* In Ex 21:5–6 an additional reason is given: The servant may want to stay with his family.
15:17 *take an awl and push it through his ear lobe.* See note on Ex 21:6.
15:18 *worth twice as much as.* A Hebrew servant worked twice as many years as the Code of Hammurapi, e.g., required for release from debt (see chart on "Ancient Texts Relating to the OT," p. 5). Other ancient legal texts, however, support "equivalent to" as a possible translation of the phrase.
15:19 *Set apart . . . every firstborn male.* Because the Lord saved his people from the plague of death on the firstborn in Egypt (see Ex 12:12,29; 13:2 and note; 13:15).
15:21 *If an animal has a defect . . . you must not sacrifice it.* See note on Lev 1:3.
15:23 See 12:16,24; see also notes on Ge 9:4; Lev 17:11.
16:1–17 See chart on "OT Feasts and Other Sacred Days," p. 176; see also Ex 23:14–19 and notes; 34:18–26; Lev 23:4–44 and notes; Nu 28:16–29:40.
16:1–8 See Ex 12:1–28; 13:1–16 and notes.
16:1 *Abib.* See chart on "Hebrew Calendar," p. 102.

Abib he brought you out of Egypt by night. [2]Sacrifice as the Passover to the LORD your God an animal from your flock or herd at the place the LORD will choose as a dwelling for his Name.[z] [3]Do not eat it with bread made with yeast, but for seven days eat unleavened bread, the bread of affliction,[a] because you left Egypt in haste[b]—so that all the days of your life you may remember the time of your departure from Egypt.[c] [4]Let no yeast be found in your possession in all your land for seven days. Do not let any of the meat you sacrifice on the evening[d] of the first day remain until morning.[e]

[5]You must not sacrifice the Passover in any town the LORD your God gives you [6]except in the place he will choose as a dwelling for his Name. There you must sacrifice the Passover in the evening, when the sun goes down, on the anniversary[y] [f] of your departure from Egypt. [7]Roast[g] it and eat it at the place the LORD your God will choose. Then in the morning return to your tents. [8]For six days eat unleavened bread and on the seventh day hold an assembly[h] to the LORD your God and do no work.[i]

Feast of Weeks

16:9–12pp — Lev 23:15–22; Nu 28:26–31

[9]Count off seven weeks[j] from the time you begin to put the sickle to the standing grain.[k] [10]Then celebrate the Feast of Weeks to the LORD your God by giving a freewill offering in proportion to the blessings the LORD your God has given you. [11]And rejoice[l] before the LORD your God at the place he will choose as a dwelling for his Name[m]—you, your sons and daughters, your menservants and maidservants, the Levites[n] in your towns, and the aliens,[o] the fatherless and the widows living among you.[p] [12]Remember that you were slaves in Egypt,[q] and follow carefully these decrees.

Feast of Tabernacles

16:13–17pp — Lev 23:33–43; Nu 29:12–39

[13]Celebrate the Feast of Tabernacles for seven days after you have gathered the produce of your threshing floor[r] and your winepress.[s] [14]Be joyful[t] at your Feast—you, your sons and daughters, your menservants and maidservants, and the Levites, the aliens, the fatherless and the widows who live in your towns. [15]For seven days celebrate the Feast to the LORD your God at the place the LORD will choose. For the LORD your God will bless you in all your harvest and in all the work of your hands, and your joy[u] will be complete.

[16]Three times a year all your men must appear[v] before the LORD your God at the place he will choose: at the Feast of Unleavened Bread,[w] the Feast of Weeks and the Feast of Tabernacles.[x] No man should appear before the LORD empty-handed:[y] [17]Each of you must bring a gift in proportion to the way the LORD your God has blessed you.

Judges

[18]Appoint judges[z] and officials for each of your tribes in every town the LORD your God is giving you, and they shall judge the people fairly.[a] [19]Do not pervert justice[b] or show partiality.[c] Do not accept a bribe,[d] for a bribe blinds the eyes of the wise and twists the words of the righteous. [20]Follow justice and justice alone, so that you may live and possess the land the LORD your God is giving you.

Worshiping Other Gods

[21]Do not set up any wooden Asherah pole[z] [e] beside the altar you build to the LORD your God,[f] [22]and do not erect a sacred stone,[g] for these the LORD your God hates.

17 Do not sacrifice to the LORD your God an ox or a sheep that has any

16:2 [z]Dt 12:5,26
16:3 [a]Ex 12:8, 39; 34:18; 1Co 5:8
[b]S Ex 12:11
[c]Dt 4:9
16:4 [d]S Ex 12:6
[e]S Ex 12:8;
Mk 14:12
16:6 [f]S Ex 12:42
16:7 [g]S Ex 12:8
16:8 [h]S Lev 23:8
[i]Mt 26:17;
Lk 2:41; 22:7;
Jn 2:13
16:9 [j]Ac 2:1
[k]S Ex 23:16
16:11 [l]Dt 12:7
[m]S Ex 20:24;
S 2Sa 7:13
[n]Dt 12:12
[o]S Dt 14:29
[p]Ne 8:10
16:12
[q]S Dt 15:15

16:13 [r]S Lev 2:14
[s]S Ge 27:37;
S Ex 23:16
16:14 [t]ver 11
16:15 [u]Job 38:7;
Ps 4:7; 28:7;
30:11
16:16 [v]Dt 31:11;
Ps 84:7
[w]S Ex 12:17
[x]S Ex 23:14,16;
Ezr 3:4
[y]S Ex 34:20
16:18
[z]S Ex 18:21,26
[a]S Ge 31:37
16:19 [b]S Ex 23:2
[c]S Lev 19:15
[d]S Ex 18:21;
S 1Sa 8:3
16:21 [e]S Dt 7:5
[f]Ex 34:13;
1Ki 14:15;
2Ki 17:16; 21:3;
2Ch 33:3
16:22
[g]S Ex 23:24

[y]6 Or *down, at the time of day*   [z]21 Or *Do not plant any tree dedicated to Asherah*

16:3,12 *remember.* See note on 4:10.
16:6 *on the anniversary.* Referring either to the time of day (see NIV text note), as the preceding phrases do, or to the anniversary of the day it first occurred, as the NIV has translated.
16:7 *to your tents.* To wherever they were staying while at the festival, whether in permanent or temporary quarters.
16:8 *assembly.* The Hebrew for this word probably means "closing assembly," as the NIV translates it in Lev 23:36.
16:9 *the time you begin to put the sickle to the standing grain.* Abib 16, the second day of the Passover Feast.

16:15 *your joy will be complete.* As a result of God's blessing (cf. Jn 3:29; 15:11; 16:24; Php 2:2; 1Jn 1:4; 2Jn 12).
16:16 *Three times a year.* The three annual pilgrimage festivals (see Ex 23:14,17; 34:23).
16:17 *bring a gift in proportion.* See v. 10; cf. 2Co 8:12.
16:18–20 Cf. 1:9–18; Ex 18:13–26.
16:19 See Ex 23:8 and note.
16:21–22 *Asherah pole . . . sacred stone.* See note on 7:5.
17:1 *defect or flaw.* See note on Lev 1:3.

defect[h] or flaw in it, for that would be detestable[i] to him.[j]

[2]If a man or woman living among you in one of the towns the LORD gives you is found doing evil in the eyes of the LORD your God in violation of his covenant,[k] [3]and contrary to my command[l] has worshiped other gods,[m] bowing down to them or to the sun[n] or the moon or the stars of the sky,[o] [4]and this has been brought to your attention, then you must investigate it thoroughly. If it is true[p] and it has been proved that this detestable thing has been done in Israel,[q] [5]take the man or woman who has done this evil deed to your city gate and stone that person to death.[r] [6]On the testimony of two or three witnesses a man shall be put to death, but no one shall be put to death on the testimony of only one witness.[s] [7]The hands of the witnesses must be the first in putting him to death,[t] and then the hands of all the people.[u] You must purge the evil[v] from among you.

Law Courts

[8]If cases come before your courts that are too difficult for you to judge[w] —whether bloodshed, lawsuits or assaults[x]—take them to the place the LORD your God will choose.[y] [9]Go to the priests, who are Levites,[z] and to the judge[a] who is in office at that time. Inquire of them and they will give you the verdict.[b] [10]You must act according to the decisions they give you at the place the LORD will choose. Be careful to do everything they direct you to do. [11]Act according to the law they teach you and the decisions they give you. Do not turn aside from what they tell you, to the right or to the left.[c] [12]The man who shows contempt[d] for the judge or for the priest who stands ministering[e] there to the LORD your God must be put to death.[f] You must purge the

evil from Israel.[g] [13]All the people will hear and be afraid, and will not be contemptuous again.[h]

The King

[14]When you enter the land the LORD your God is giving you and have taken possession[i] of it and settled in it,[j] and you say, "Let us set a king over us like all the nations around us,"[k] [15]be sure to appoint[l] over you the king the LORD your God chooses. He must be from among your own brothers.[m] Do not place a foreigner over you, one who is not a brother Israelite. [16]The king, moreover, must not acquire great numbers of horses[n] for himself[o] or make the people return to Egypt[p] to get more of them,[q] for the LORD has told you, "You are not to go back that way again."[r] [17]He must not take many wives,[s] or his heart will be led astray.[t] He must not accumulate[u] large amounts of silver and gold.[v]

[18]When he takes the throne[w] of his kingdom, he is to write[x] for himself on a scroll a copy[y] of this law, taken from that of the priests, who are Levites. [19]It is to be with him, and he is to read it all the days of his life[z] so that he may learn to revere the LORD his God and follow carefully all the words of this law and these decrees[a] [20]and not consider himself better than his brothers and turn from the law[b] to the right or to the left.[c] Then he and his descendants will reign a long time over his kingdom in Israel.[d]

Offerings for Priests and Levites

18 The priests, who are Levites[e]—indeed the whole tribe of

17:1 [h]S Ex 12:5; S Lev 22:20
[i]Dt 7:25
[j]S Dt 15:21
17:2 [k]Dt 13:6-11
17:3 [l]Jer 7:31
[m]Ex 22:20
[n]S Ge 1:16
[o]S Ge 2:1; S 37:9
17:4 [p]Dt 22:20
[q]Dt 13:12-14
17:5 [r]S Lev 24:14
17:6 [s]Nu 35:30; Dt 19:15; S Mt 18:16
17:7 [t]Jn 8:7
[u]S Lev 24:14; Ac 7:58
[v]S Dt 13:5; 1Co 5:13*
17:8 [w]Ex 21:6
[x]2Ch 19:10
[y]Dt 12:5; Ps 122:3-5
17:9 [z]Dt 24:8; 27:9 [a]S Ex 21:6
[b]S Ge 25:22; Dt 19:17; Eze 44:24; Hag 2:11
17:11 [c]S Lev 10:11; S Dt 5:32
17:12 [d]Nu 15:30 [e]S Nu 16:9 /ver 13; S Ge 17:14; Dt 13:11; 18:20; 19:20; 1Ki 18:40; Jer 14:14; Hos 4:4; Zec 13:3
[g]S Dt 13:5
17:13 [h]S ver 12
17:14 [i]S Nu 33:53 [j]Jos 21:43 [k]1Sa 8:5,19-20; 10:19
17:15 [l]1Sa 16:3; 2Sa 5:3 [m]Jer 30:21
17:16 [n]Isa 2:7; 30:16 [o]1Sa 8:11; 1Ki 4:26; 9:19; 10:26; 2Ch 1:14; Ps 20:7 [p]1Ki 10:29; Isa 31:1; Jer 42:14 [q]1Ki 10:28; Isa 31:1; Eze 17:15 [r]S Ex 13:17
17:17 [s]S Ex 34:16; 2Sa 5:13; 12:11; 1Ki 11:3; 2Ch 11:21 [t]1Ki 11:2; Pr 31:3 [u]1Ki 10:27 [v]2Ch 1:11;
Isa 2:7 17:18 [w]1Ki 1:46; 1Ch 29:23 [x]Dt 31:22,24; Jos 24:26; 1Sa 10:25 [y]2Ch 23:11 17:19 [z]Dt 4:9-10; Jos 1:8 [a]Dt 11:13; 1Ki 3:3; 11:38; 2Ki 22:2 17:20 [b]Jos 23:6; Job 23:12; Ps 119:102 [c]S Dt 5:32; S 1Ki 9:4 [d]1Sa 8:5; 10:25; 1Ki 2:3; 1Ch 28:8 18:1 [e]Jer 33:18,21

17:3 *bowing down to . . . the sun or the moon or the stars.* See 2Ki 17:16; 21:3,5; 23:4–5.

17:6 *two or three witnesses.* A further specification of the law set forth in Nu 35:30. See 19:15; cf. Mt 18:16; 2Co 13:1; 1Ti 5:19; Heb 10:28.

17:7 *You must purge the evil from among you.* See v. 12; see also note on 13:5.

17:14 *a king . . . like all the nations around us.* Moses, Joshua and a succession of judges were chosen directly by the Lord to govern Israel on his behalf. As Gideon later said, "The LORD will rule over you" (Jdg 8:23; see note there). Moses here, however, anticipates a time when the people would ask for a king (see 1Sa 8:4–9) contrary to the Lord's ideal for them (see notes on 7:2–5; 1Sa 8:1–12:25; see also Lev 20:23). So Moses gives guidance concerning the eventual selection of a king.

17:16–17a The very things that later kings were guilty of,

beginning especially with Solomon (1Ki 4:26; 11:1–4)—except that they did not make Israel return to Egypt (but see Jer 42:13–43:7).

17:18 *write for himself . . . a copy of this law.* As a sign of submission to the Lord as his King, and as a guide for his rule in obedience to his heavenly Suzerain. This was required procedure for vassal kings under the suzerainty treaties among the Hittites and others before and during this period (see note on 31:9). See chart on "Major Covenants in the OT," p. 19.

17:20 *not consider himself better.* The king was not above God's law, any more than were the humblest of his subjects.

18:1 *no allotment or inheritance.* No private ownership of land. Towns and surrounding pasturelands were set aside for the use of the Levites (Jos 21:41–42), as were the tithes and parts of sacrifices (see 14:22–29 and note; Lev 27:30 and note; Nu 18:21–29).

Levi—are to have no allotment or inheritance with Israel. They shall live on the offerings[f] made to the LORD by fire, for that is their inheritance.[g] [2]They shall have no inheritance among their brothers; the LORD is their inheritance,[h] as he promised them.[i]

[3]This is the share due the priests[j] from the people who sacrifice a bull[k] or a sheep: the shoulder, the jowls and the inner parts.[l] [4]You are to give them the firstfruits of your grain, new wine and oil, and the first wool from the shearing of your sheep,[m] [5]for the LORD your God has chosen them[n] and their descendants out of all your tribes to stand and minister[o] in the LORD's name always.[p]

[6]If a Levite moves from one of your towns anywhere in Israel where he is living, and comes in all earnestness to the place the LORD will choose,[q] [7]he may minister in the name[r] of the LORD his God like all his fellow Levites who serve there in the presence of the LORD. [8]He is to share equally in their benefits, even though he has received money from the sale of family possessions.[s]

Detestable Practices

[9]When you enter the land the LORD your God is giving you, do not learn to imitate[t] the detestable ways[u] of the nations there. [10]Let no one be found among you who sacrifices his son or daughter in[a] the fire,[v] who practices divination[w] or sorcery,[x] interprets omens, engages in witchcraft,[y] [11]or casts spells,[z] or who is a medium or spiritist[a] or who consults the dead. [12]Anyone who does these things is detestable to the LORD, and because of these detestable practices the LORD your God will drive out those nations before you.[b] [13]You must be blameless[c] before the LORD your God.[d]

The Prophet

[14]The nations you will dispossess listen to those who practice sorcery or divination.[e] But as for you, the LORD your God has not permitted you to do so. [15]The LORD your God will raise up for you a prophet like me from among your own brothers.[f] You must listen to him. [16]For this is what you asked of the LORD your God at Horeb on the day of the assembly when you said, "Let us not hear the voice of the LORD our God nor see this great fire anymore, or we will die."[g]

[17]The LORD said to me: "What they say is good. [18]I will raise up for them a prophet[h] like you from among their brothers; I will put my words[i] in his mouth,[j] and he will tell them everything I command him.[k] [19]If anyone does not listen[l] to my words that the prophet speaks in my name,[m] I myself will call him to account.[n] [20]But a prophet who presumes to speak in my name anything I have not commanded him to say, or a prophet who speaks in the name of other gods,[o] must be put to death."[p]

[21]You may say to yourselves, "How can we know when a message has not been spoken by the LORD?" [22]If what a prophet proclaims in the name of the LORD does not take place or come true,[q] that is a message the LORD has not spoken.[r] That prophet has spoken presumptuously.[s] Do not be afraid of him.

Cities of Refuge

19:1–14Ref — Nu 35:6–34; Dt 4:41–43; Jos 20:1–9

19 When the LORD your God has destroyed the nations whose land he is giving you, and when you have driven

18:1 /S Nu 18:8
gS Nu 18:20;
1Co 9:13
18:2 hNu 18:20
/Jos 13:14
18:3 /S Ex 29:27
kS Lev 1:5
/Lev 7:28-34;
Nu 18:12
18:4 mEx 22:29;
Nu 18:12
18:5 nS Ex 28:1
oDt 10:8
pS Ex 29:9
18:6
qS Nu 35:2-3;
S Dt 12:5
18:7 rver 19;
1Ki 18:32; 22:16;
Ps 118:26
18:8 sNu 18:24;
2Ch 31:4;
Ne 12:44,47;
13:12
18:9 tDt 9:5;
12:29-31
uS Lev 18:3;
2Ki 21:2;
2Ch 28:3; 33:2;
34:33; Ezr 6:21;
9:11; Jer 44:4
18:10
vS Lev 18:21
wISa 15:23
xS Ex 7:11
yS Lev 19:31
18:11 zIsa 47:9
aS Ex 22:18;
S 1Sa 28:13
18:12
bS Lev 18:24
18:13 cS Ge 6:9;
Ps 119:1
dMt 5:48

18:14 e2Ki 21:6
18:15
/S Mt 21:11;
Lk 2:25-35;
Jn 1:21;
Ac 3:22*; 7:37*
18:16
gS Ex 20:19;
Dt 5:23-27
18:18 hS Ge 20:7
/Isa 2:3; 26:8;
51:4; Mic 4:2
/S Ex 4:12
kJn 4:25-26;
S 14:24; Ac 3:22*
18:19
/S Ex 23:21
mS ver 7;
S Lev 19:12;
2Ki 2:24
nJos 22:23;
Ac 3:23*;
Heb 12:25
18:20
oS Ex 23:13
pDt 13:1-5;
S 17:12

18:22 qS Dt 13:2; 1Sa 3:20 r1Ki 22:28; Jer 28:9 sver 20

a 10 Or who makes his son or daughter pass through

18:4 firstfruits. See Ex 23:19 and note; 34:26; Lev 23:10–11; Nu 15:18–20; 18:12–13.
18:5 See note on 21:5.
18:9 detestable ways of the nations. What follows is the most complete list of magical or spiritistic arts in the OT. All were practiced in Canaan, and all are condemned and prohibited. The people are not to resort to such sources for their information, guidance or revelation. Rather, they are to listen to the Lord's true prophets (see vv. 14–22).
18:10 sacrifices his son or daughter. See 12:31; see also note on Lev 18:21.
18:15 prophet like me. Verse 16, as well as the general context (see especially vv. 20–22), indicates that a series of prophets is meant. At Mount Horeb the people requested that Moses take the message from God and deliver it to them (see Ex 20:19 and note). But now that Moses is to leave

them, he says that another spokesman will take his place, and then another will be necessary for the next generation. This is therefore a collective reference to the prophets who will follow. As such, it is also the basis for Messianic expectation and receives a unique fulfillment in Jesus (see Jn 1:21, 25,45; 5:46; 6:14; 7:40; Ac 3:22–26; 7:37).
18:16 See Ex 20:18–19; Heb 12:18–21.
18:18 my words in his mouth. See Ex 4:15–16; see also note on Ex 7:1–2.
18:20 prophet who presumes to speak. See note on 13:1–5. must be put to death. See 13:5; Jer 28:15–17.
18:21–22 This negative form of statement is always true. But the positive statement, "If the prophecy comes true, it is from the Lord," may not always be true (see note on 13:1–5).
19:1–13 See 4:41–43; Nu 35:9–28; Jos 20.

them out and settled in their towns and houses,^{t} ^{2}then set aside for yourselves three cities centrally located in the land the LORD your God is giving you to possess. ^{3}Build roads to them and divide into three parts the land the LORD your God is giving you as an inheritance, so that anyone who kills a man may flee there.

^{4}This is the rule concerning the man who kills another and flees there to save his life—one who kills his neighbor unintentionally, without malice aforethought. ^{5}For instance, a man may go into the forest with his neighbor to cut wood, and as he swings his ax to fell a tree, the head may fly off and hit his neighbor and kill him. That man may flee to one of these cities and save his life. ^{6}Otherwise, the avenger of blood^u might pursue him in a rage, overtake him if the distance is too great, and kill him even though he is not deserving of death, since he did it to his neighbor without malice aforethought. ^{7}This is why I command you to set aside for yourselves three cities.

^{8}If the LORD your God enlarges your territory,^{v} as he promised^w on oath to your forefathers, and gives you the whole land he promised them, ^{9}because you carefully follow all these laws I command you today—to love the LORD your God and to walk always in his ways^x—then you are to set aside three more cities. ^{10}Do this so that innocent blood^y will not be shed in your land, which the LORD your God is giving you as your inheritance, and so that you will not be guilty of bloodshed. ^{z}

^{11}But if a man hates his neighbor and lies in wait for him, assaults and kills him,^{a} and then flees to one of these cities, ^{12}the elders of his town shall send for him, bring him back from the city, and hand him over to the avenger of blood to die. ^{13}Show him no pity. ^{b} You must purge from Israel the guilt of shedding innocent blood,^{c} so that it may go well with you.

^{14}Do not move your neighbor's boundary stone set up by your predecessors in the inheritance you receive in the land the LORD your God is giving you to possess. ^{d}

Witnesses

^{15}One witness is not enough to convict a man accused of any crime or offense he may have committed. A matter must be established by the testimony of two or three witnesses. ^{e}

^{16}If a malicious witness^f takes the stand to accuse a man of a crime, ^{17}the two men involved in the dispute must stand in the presence of the LORD before the priests and the judges^g who are in office at the time. ^{18}The judges must make a thorough investigation,^{h} and if the witness proves to be a liar, giving false testimony against his brother, ^{19}then do to him as he intended to do to his brother.^{i} You must purge the evil from among you. ^{20}The rest of the people will hear of this and be afraid,^{j} and never again will such an evil thing be done among you. ^{21}Show no pity:^{k} life for life, eye for eye, tooth for tooth, hand for hand, foot for foot. ^{l}

Going to War

20 When you go to war against your enemies and see horses and chariots and an army greater than yours,^{m} do not be afraid^n of them,^{o} because the LORD your God, who brought you up out of Egypt, will be with^p you. ^{2}When you are about to go into battle, the priest shall come forward and address the army. ^{3}He shall say: "Hear, O Israel, today you are going into battle against your enemies. Do not be fainthearted^q or afraid; do not be terrified or give way to panic before them. ^{4}For the LORD your God is the one who goes with you^r to fight^s for you against your enemies to give you victory. ^{t}"

^{5}The officers shall say to the army: "Has anyone built a new house and not dedicated^u it? Let him go home, or he may die in battle and someone else may dedicate it. ^{6}Has anyone planted^v a vineyard and not begun to enjoy it?^{w} Let him go home, or he may die in battle and someone else enjoy it. ^{7}Has anyone become pledged to a woman and not married her? Let him go home, or he may die in battle and someone else marry her.^{x}" ^{8}Then the officers

---

19:1 ^{r}Dt 6:10-11
19:6 ^{u}S Nu 35:12
19:8 ^{v}S Ex 34:24
^{w}S Ge 15:8;
S Dt 11:24
19:9 ^{x}Dt 6:5
19:10 ^{y}Pr 6:17;
Jer 7:6; 26:15
^{z}Dt 21:1-9
19:11
^{a}S Ex 21:12;
1Jn 3:15
19:13 ^{b}Dt 7:2
^{c}Dt 21:9;
1Ki 2:31
19:14 ^{d}Dt 27:17;
Job 24:2; Ps 16:6;
Pr 15:25; 22:28;
23:10; Isa 1:23;
Hos 5:10

19:15
^{e}S Dt 17:6;
S Mt 18:16*;
26:60; 2Co 13:1*;
Pr 6:19
19:16 ^{f}Ex 23:1;
19:17 ^{g}S Ex 21:6
19:18 ^{h}S Ex 23:7
19:19 ^{i}Pr 19:5,9;
1Co 5:13*
19:20
/S Dt 13:11
19:21 ^{k}ver 13
^{l}S Ex 21:24;
Mt 5:38*
20:1 ^{m}Ps 20:7;
Isa 31:1
^{n}S Nu 14:9
^{o}S Dt 3:22;
S 1Sa 17:45
^{p}Isa 41:10
20:3 ^{q}1Sa 17:32;
Job 23:16;
Ps 22:14; Isa 7:4;
35:4; Jer 51:46
20:4
^{r}2Ch 20:14-22
^{s}S Ex 14:14;
1Ch 5:22;
Ne 4:20
^{t}Jdg 12:3; 15:18;
Ps 44:7; 144:10
20:5 ^{u}Ne 12:27
20:6 ^{v}Jer 31:5;
Eze 28:26;
Mic 1:6 ^{w}1Co 9:7
20:7 ^{x}Dt 24:5;
Pr 5:18

19:14 *boundary stone.* Such stones were set up to indicate the perimeters of fields and landed estates. Moving them illegally to increase one's own holdings was considered a serious crime.
19:15 See note on 17:6.
19:18 *giving false testimony.* See 5:20; Lev 19:11–13; 1Ki 21:10,13.
19:19 *You must purge the evil from among you.* See note on 13:5.
19:21 *life for life.* See notes on Ex 21:24–25; Lev 24:20;

see also Mt 5:38–42.
20:2 *priest shall . . . address.* Not merely a recitation or ritual. Priests sometimes accompanied the army when it went into battle (see, e.g., Jos 6:4–21; 2Ch 20:14–22).
20:3 *Hear, O Israel.* See note on 4:1.
20:4 See note on 3:22.
20:5–8 *Let him go home.* See the curses in 28:30. Israel was not to trust in the size of its army but in the Lord. Exemptions from military duty were sometimes extensive (see, e.g., Jdg 7:2–8).

shall add, "Is any man afraid or fainthearted? Let him go home so that his brothers will not become disheartened too."[y] [9]When the officers have finished speaking to the army, they shall appoint commanders over it.

[10]When you march up to attack a city, make its people an offer of peace.[z] [11]If they accept and open their gates, all the people in it shall be subject[a] to forced labor[b] and shall work for you. [12]If they refuse to make peace and they engage you in battle, lay siege to that city. [13]When the LORD your God delivers it into your hand, put to the sword all the men in it.[c] [14]As for the women, the children, the livestock[d] and everything else in the city,[e] you may take these as plunder[f] for yourselves. And you may use the plunder the LORD your God gives you from your enemies. [15]This is how you are to treat all the cities that are at a distance[g] from you and do not belong to the nations nearby.

[16]However, in the cities of the nations the LORD your God is giving you as an inheritance, do not leave alive anything that breathes.[h] [17]Completely destroy[b] them—the Hittites, Amorites, Canaanites, Perizzites, Hivites and Jebusites—as the LORD your God has commanded you. [18]Otherwise, they will teach you to follow all the detestable things they do in worshiping their gods,[i] and you will sin[j] against the LORD your God.

[19]When you lay siege to a city for a long time, fighting against it to capture it, do not destroy its trees by putting an ax to them, because you can eat their fruit. Do not cut them down. Are the trees of the field people, that you should besiege them?[c] [20]However, you may cut down trees that you know are not fruit trees[k] and use them to build siege works until the city at war with you falls.

Atonement for an Unsolved Murder

21 If a man is found slain, lying in a field in the land the LORD your God is giving you to possess, and it is not

known who killed him,[l] [2]your elders and judges shall go out and measure the distance from the body to the neighboring towns. [3]Then the elders of the town nearest the body shall take a heifer that has never been worked and has never worn a yoke[m] [4]and lead her down to a valley that has not been plowed or planted and where there is a flowing stream. There in the valley they are to break the heifer's neck. [5]The priests, the sons of Levi, shall step forward, for the LORD your God has chosen them to minister and to pronounce blessings[n] in the name of the LORD and to decide all cases of dispute and assault.[o] [6]Then all the elders of the town nearest the body shall wash their hands[p] over the heifer whose neck was broken in the valley, [7]and they shall declare: "Our hands did not shed this blood, nor did our eyes see it done. [8]Accept this atonement for your people Israel, whom you have redeemed, O LORD, and do not hold your people guilty of the blood of an innocent man." And the bloodshed will be atoned for.[q] [9]So you will purge[r] from yourselves the guilt of shedding innocent blood, since you have done what is right in the eyes of the LORD.

Marrying a Captive Woman

[10]When you go to war against your enemies and the LORD your God delivers them into your hands[s] and you take captives,[t] [11]if you notice among the captives a beautiful[u] woman and are attracted to her,[v] you may take her as your wife. [12]Bring her into your home and have her shave her head,[w] trim her nails [13]and put aside the clothes she was wearing when captured. After she has lived in your house and mourned her father and mother for a full month,[x] then you may go to her and be her husband and she shall be your wife. [14]If you are not pleased with her, let her go

Cross references (center column)

20:8 yJdg 7:3
20:10 zS Dt 2:26; Lk 14:31-32
20:11 aver 15; 2Ki 6:22
20:12 b1Ki 9:21; 1Ch 22:2; Isa 31:8
20:13 cNu 31:7
20:14 dJos 8:2; 22:8 eS Nu 31:11 fS Nu 31:53
20:15 gS ver 11; Jos 9:9
20:16 hEx 23:31-33; Nu 21:2-3; S Dt 7:2; Jos 6:21; 10:1; 11:14
20:18 iS Ex 34:16 jS Ex 10:7
20:20 kJer 6:6

21:1 lS Nu 25:17
21:3 mS Nu 19:2
21:5 nS Ge 48:20; S Ex 39:43 oDt 17:8-11
21:6 pMt 27:24
21:8 qNu 35:33-34
21:9 rDt 19:13
21:10 sJos 21:44 t1Ki 8:46; 1Ch 9:1; Ezr 5:2; Jer 40:1; Eze 1:1; 17:12; Da 2:25; Mic 4:10
21:11 uGe 6:2 vS Ge 34:8
21:12 wS Lev 14:9; S Nu 8:7; 1Co 11:5
21:13 xPs 45:10

[b]*17* The Hebrew term refers to the irrevocable giving over of things or persons to the LORD, often by totally destroying them. [c]*19* Or *down* to use in the siege, for the fruit trees are for the benefit of man.

20:10–15 Rules regarding warfare against nations outside the promised land.

20:11 *subject to forced labor.* A fulfillment of Noah's curse on Canaan (see Ge 9:25 and note).

20:17 *Hittites . . . Jebusites.* See 7:1; see also notes on Ge 10:6,15–18; 13:7.

20:19 *do not destroy its trees.* The failure of later armies to follow this wise rule stripped bare much of Palestine (though the absence of woodlands there today is of relatively recent origin).

21:5 *to minister.* To officiate at the place of worship before the Lord on behalf of the people (see 10:8; 18:5). *to pro-*

nounce blessings. See Nu 6:22–27.

21:6 *wash their hands.* Symbolic of a declaration of innocence (v. 7; see Mt 27:24).

21:10 *against your enemies.* The enemies here are those outside Canaan (see 20:14–15); so the woman (v. 11) could be taken captive and would not be subject to total destruction.

21:12 *shave her head.* Indicative of leaving her former life and beginning a new life, or perhaps symbolic of mourning (v. 13; see, e.g., Jer 47:5; Mic 1:16) or of humiliation (see note on Isa 7:20). For cleansing rites see Lev 14:8; Nu 8:7; cf. 2Sa 19:24.

wherever she wishes. You must not sell her or treat her as a slave, since you have dishonored her. *y*

The Right of the Firstborn

15If a man has two wives, *z* and he loves one but not the other, and both bear him sons but the firstborn is the son of the wife he does not love, *a* 16when he wills his property to his sons, he must not give the rights of the firstborn to the son of the wife he loves in preference to his actual firstborn, the son of the wife he does not love. *b* 17He must acknowledge the son of his unloved wife as the firstborn by giving him a double *c* share of all he has. That son is the first sign of his father's strength. *d* The right of the firstborn belongs to him. *e*

A Rebellious Son

18If a man has a stubborn and rebellious *f* son *g* who does not obey his father and mother *h* and will not listen to them when they discipline him, 19his father and mother shall take hold of him and bring him to the elders at the gate of his town. 20They shall say to the elders, "This son of ours is stubborn and rebellious. He will not obey us. He is a profligate and a drunkard." 21Then all the men of his town shall stone him to death. *i* You must purge the evil *j* from among you. All Israel will hear of it and be afraid. *k*

Various Laws

22If a man guilty of a capital offense *l* is put to death and his body is hung on a tree, 23you must not leave his body on the tree overnight. *m* Be sure to bury *n* him that same day, because anyone who is hung on a tree is under God's curse. *o* You must not

desecrate *p* the land the LORD your God is giving you as an inheritance.

22 If you see your brother's ox or sheep straying, do not ignore it but be sure to take it back to him. *q* 2If the brother does not live near you or if you do not know who he is, take it home with you and keep it until he comes looking for it. Then give it back to him. 3Do the same if you find your brother's donkey or his cloak or anything he loses. Do not ignore it.

4If you see your brother's donkey *r* or his ox fallen on the road, do not ignore it. Help him get it to its feet. *s*

5A woman must not wear men's clothing, nor a man wear women's clothing, for the LORD your God detests anyone who does this.

6If you come across a bird's nest beside the road, either in a tree or on the ground, and the mother is sitting on the young or on the eggs, do not take the mother with the young. *t* 7You may take the young, but be sure to let the mother go, *u* so that it may go well with you and you may have a long life. *v*

8When you build a new house, make a parapet around your roof so that you may not bring the guilt of bloodshed on your house if someone falls from the roof. *w*

9Do not plant two kinds of seed in your vineyard; *x* if you do, not only the crops you plant but also the fruit of the vineyard will be defiled. *d*

10Do not plow with an ox and a donkey yoked together. *y*

11Do not wear clothes of wool and linen woven together. *z*

12Make tassels on the four corners of the cloak you wear. *a*

d 9 Or *be forfeited to the sanctuary*

Cross references (center column)

21:14 *y*S Ge 34:2
21:15 *z*S Ge 4:19
*a*Ge 29:33
21:16
*b*1Ch 26:10
21:17 *c*2Ki 2:9; Isa 40:2; 61:7; Zec 9:12
*d*S Ge 49:3
*e*Ge 25:31; Lk 15:12
21:18 *f*Ps 78:8; Jer 5:23; Zep 3:1
*g*Pr 30:17
*h*S Ge 31:35; Pr 1:8; Isa 30:1; Eph 6:1-3
21:21 *i*S Lev 20:9 /Dt 19:19
*k*S Dt 13:11
21:22 /Dt 22:26; Mt 26:66; Mk 14:64; Ac 23:29
21:23 *m*Jos 8:29; 10:27; Jn 19:31
*n*Eze 39:12
*o*Ezr 6:11; Est 2:23; 7:9; 8:7; 9:13,25; Isa 50:11; Gal 3:13*

*p*S Lev 18:25
22:1 *q*Ex 23:4-5; Pr 27:10; Zec 7:9
22:4 *r*Ex 23:5
*s*1Co 9:9
22:6 *t*Lev 22:28
22:7
*u*S Lev 22:28
*v*S Dt 5:29
22:8 *w*Jos 2:8; 1Sa 9:25; 2Sa 11:2
22:9 *x*Lev 19:19
22:10 *y*2Co 6:14
22:11 *z*Lev 19:19
22:12
*a*Nu 15:37-41; Mt 23:5

21:14 *dishonored.* Twelve other times the Hebrew for this word is used of men forcing women to have sexual intercourse with them (22:24,29; Ge 34:2; Jdg 19:24; 20:5; 2Sa 13:12,14,22,32; La 5:11; Eze 22:10–11).

21:15 *two wives.* See notes on Ge 4:19; 25:6.

21:16 *in preference to.* The order of birth rather than parental favoritism governed succession, though the rule was sometimes set aside with divine approval (cf., e.g., Jacob or Solomon).

21:17 *double share.* In Israel the oldest son enjoyed a double share of the inheritance. Parallels to this practice come from Nuzi, Larsa in the Old Babylonian period, and Assyria in the Middle Assyrian period (see chart on "Ancient Texts Relating to the OT," p. 5). Receiving a double portion of an estate was also tantamount to succession. Thus Elisha succeeded Elijah (2Ki 2:9). *first sign of his father's strength.* The first result of a man's procreative ability.

21:18 *stubborn and rebellious . . . does not obey.* In wicked defiance of the fifth commandment (see 5:16; Ex 20:12 and note).

21:21 *stone him to death.* See 5:16; 27:16; Ex 21:15,17. *You must purge the evil from among you.* See note on 13:5.

21:22 *put to death and . . . hung on a tree.* The offender was first executed, then "hung on a tree" (see Ge 40:19) or, as the Hebrew for this phrase doubtless intends, "impaled on a pole" (see NIV text notes on Ge 40:19; Est 2:23).

21:23 *not leave his body on the tree overnight.* Prolonged exposure gives undue attention to the crime and the criminal. *under God's curse.* God had condemned murder, and hanging on a tree symbolized divine judgment and rejection. Christ accepted the full punishment of our sins, thus becoming "a curse for us" (Gal 3:13).

22:1 *do not ignore it.* See vv. 3–4. The Biblical legislation was intended not only to punish criminal behavior but also to express concern for people and their possessions. See note on "Major Social Concerns in the Covenant," p. 271.

22:5 Probably intended to prohibit such perversions as transvestism and homosexuality, especially under religious auspices. The God-created differences between men and women are not to be disregarded (see Lev 18:22; 20:13).

Marriage Violations

[13] If a man takes a wife and, after lying with her[b], dislikes her [14] and slanders her and gives her a bad name, saying, "I married this woman, but when I approached her, I did not find proof of her virginity," [15] then the girl's father and mother shall bring proof that she was a virgin to the town elders at the gate.[c] [16] The girl's father will say to the elders, "I gave my daughter in marriage to this man, but he dislikes her. [17] Now he has slandered her and said, 'I did not find your daughter to be a virgin.' But here is the proof of my daughter's virginity." Then her parents shall display the cloth before the elders of the town, [18] and the elders[d] shall take the man and punish him. [19] They shall fine him a hundred shekels of silver[e] and give them to the girl's father, because this man has giv-

en an Israelite virgin a bad name. She shall continue to be his wife; he must not divorce her as long as he lives.

[20] If, however, the charge is true[e] and no proof of the girl's virginity can be found, [21] she shall be brought to the door of her father's house and there the men of her town shall stone her to death. She has done a disgraceful thing[f] in Israel by being promiscuous while still in her father's house. You must purge the evil from among you.

[22] If a man is found sleeping with another man's wife, both the man who slept[g] with her and the woman must die.[h] You must purge the evil from Israel.

[23] If a man happens to meet in a town a virgin pledged to be married and he sleeps with her, [24] you shall take both of them to

Cross references (center column):
22:13 *b* Dt 24:1
22:15 *c* S Ge 23:10
22:18 *d* Ex 18:21; Dt 1:9-18
22:20 *e* Dt 17:4
22:21 *f* S Ge 34:7; S 38:24; S Lev 19:29; Dt 23:17-18; 1Co 5:13*
22:22 *g* 2Sa 11:4 *h* S Ge 38:24; S Ex 21:12; Mt 5:27-28; Jn 8:5; 1Co 6:9; Heb 13:4

e19 That is, about 2 1/2 pounds (about 1 kilogram)

22:14 *proof of her virginity.* A blood-stained cloth or garment (see vv. 15,17,20).
22:15 *elders at the gate.* See 25:7; see also notes on Ge 19:1; Ru 4:1.
22:19 *hundred shekels of silver.* A heavy fine—several times what Hosea paid to buy Gomer back (Hos 3:2) or what Jeremiah paid for the field at Anathoth (Jer 32:9). It may have been about twice the average bride-price (see note on v. 29). The high fine, in addition to the no-divorce rule, was intended to restrain not only a husband's charges against his wife but also easy divorce.
22:21,24 *You must purge the evil from among you.* See v.

Major Social Concerns in the Covenant

1. Personhood
Everyone's person is to be secure (Ex 20:13; Dt 5:17; Ex 21:16-21,26-31; Lev 19:14; Dt 24:7; 27:18).

2. False Accusation
Everyone is to be secure against slander and false accusation (Ex 20:16; Dt 5:20; Ex 23:1-3; Lev 19:16; Dt 19:15-21).

3. Woman
No woman is to be taken advantage of within her subordinate status in society (Ex 21:7-11,20, 26-32; 22:16-17; Dt 21:10-14; 22:13-30; 24:1-5).

4. Punishment
Punishment for wrongdoing shall not be excessive so that the culprit is dehumanized (Dt 25:1-5).

5. Dignity
Every Israelite's dignity and right to be God's freedman and servant are to be honored and safeguarded (Ex 21:2,5-6; Lev 25; Dt 15:12-18).

6. Inheritance
Every Israelite's inheritance in the promised land is to be secure (Lev 25; Nu 27:5-7; 36:1-9; Dt 25:5-10).

7. Property
Everyone's property is to be secure (Ex 20:15; Dt 5:19; Ex 21:33-36; 22:1-15; 23:4-5; Lev 19:35-36; Dt 22:1-4; 25:13-15).

8. Fruit of Labor
Everyone is to receive the fruit of his labors (Lev 19:13; Dt 24:14; 25:4).

9. Fruit of the Ground
Everyone is to share the fruit of the ground (Ex 23:10-11; Lev 19:9-10; 23:22; 25:3-55; Dt 14:28-29; 24:19-21).

10. Rest on Sabbath
Everyone, down to the humblest servant and the resident alien, is to share in the weekly rest of God's Sabbath (Ex 20:8-11; Dt 5:12-15; Ex 23:12).

11. Marriage
The marriage relationship is to be kept inviolate (Ex 20:14; Dt 5:18; see also Lev 18:6-23; 20:10-21; Dt 22:13-30).

12. Exploitation
No one, however disabled, impoverished or powerless, is to be oppressed or exploited (Ex 22:21-27; Lev 19:14,33-34; 25:35-36; Dt 23:19; 24:6,12-15,17; 27:18).

13. Fair Trial
Everyone is to have free access to the courts and is to be afforded a fair trial (Ex 23:6,8; Lev 19:15; Dt 1:17; 10:17-18; 16:18-20; 17:8-13; 19:15-21).

14. Social Order
Every person's God-given place in the social order is to be honored (Ex 20:12; Dt 5:16; Ex 21:15,17; 22:28; Lev 19:3,32; 20:9; Dt 17:8-13; 21:15-21; 27:16).

15. Law
No one shall be above the law, not even the king (Dt 17:18-20).

16. Animals
Concern for the welfare of other creatures is to be extended to the animal world (Ex 23:5,11; Lev 25:7; Dt 22:4,6-7; 25:4).

the gate of that town and stone them to death—the girl because she was in a town and did not scream for help, and the man because he violated another man's wife. You must purge the evil from among you.[t]

25But if out in the country a man happens to meet a girl pledged to be married and rapes her, only the man who has done this shall die. 26Do nothing to the girl; she has committed no sin deserving death. This case is like that of someone who attacks and murders his neighbor, 27for the man found the girl out in the country, and though the betrothed girl screamed,[j] there was no one to rescue her.

28If a man happens to meet a virgin who is not pledged to be married and rapes her and they are discovered,[k] 29he shall pay the girl's father fifty shekels of silver.[f] He must marry the girl, for he has violated her. He can never divorce her as long as he lives.

30A man is not to marry his father's wife; he must not dishonor his father's bed.[l]

Exclusion From the Assembly

23 No one who has been emasculated[m] by crushing or cutting may enter the assembly of the LORD.

2No one born of a forbidden marriage[g] nor any of his descendants may enter the assembly of the LORD, even down to the tenth generation.

3No Ammonite[n] or Moabite or any of his descendants may enter the assembly of the LORD, even down to the tenth generation.[o] 4For they did not come to meet you with bread and water[p] on your way when you came out of Egypt, and they hired Balaam[q] son of Beor from Pethor in Aram Naharaim[h][r] to pronounce a curse on you.[s] 5However, the LORD your God would not listen to Balaam but turned the

curse[t] into a blessing for you, because the LORD your God loves[u] you. 6Do not seek a treaty[v] of friendship with them as long as you live.[w]

7Do not abhor an Edomite,[x] for he is your brother.[y] Do not abhor an Egyptian, because you lived as an alien in his country.[z] 8The third generation of children born to them may enter the assembly of the LORD.

Uncleanness in the Camp

9When you are encamped against your enemies, keep away from everything impure.[a] 10If one of your men is unclean because of a nocturnal emission, he is to go outside the camp and stay there.[b] 11But as evening approaches he is to wash himself, and at sunset[c] he may return to the camp.[d]

12Designate a place outside the camp where you can go to relieve yourself. 13As part of your equipment have something to dig with, and when you relieve yourself, dig a hole and cover up your excrement. 14For the LORD your God moves[e] about in your camp to protect you and to deliver your enemies to you. Your camp must be holy,[f] so that he will not see among you anything indecent and turn away from you.

Miscellaneous Laws

15If a slave has taken refuge[g] with you, do not hand him over to his master.[h] 16Let him live among you wherever he likes and in whatever town he chooses. Do not oppress[i] him.

17No Israelite man[j] or woman is to become a shrine prostitute.[k] 18You must not bring the earnings of a female prostitute or of a male prostitute[i] into the house

Cross references (center column)

22:24 [i]1Co 5:13*
22:27
[s]S Ge 39:14
22:28 [k]Ex 22:16
22:30
[s]S Ge 29:29;
S Lev 18:8;
S 20:9; 1Co 5:1
23:1
[m]S Lev 21:20
23:3 [n]S Ge 19:38
[o]ver 4; Ne 13:2
23:4 [p]Dt 2:28
[q]S Nu 23:7;
S 2Pe 2:15
[r]S Ge 24:10
[s]S ver 3

23:5 [t]Nu 24:10;
Jos 24:10; Pr 26:2
[u]S Dt 4:37
23:6
[v]S Nu 24:17;
Isa 15:1; 25:10;
Jer 25:21; 27:3;
48:1; Eze 25:8;
Zep 2:9
[w]Ezr 9:12;
Mt 5:43
23:7 [x]S Ge 25:30
[y]S Ge 25:26
[z]S Lev 19:34
23:9
[a]Lev 15:1-33
23:10 [b]Lev 15:16
23:11
[c]S Lev 15:16
[d]1Sa 21:5
23:14 [e]S Ge 3:8
[f]Ex 3:5
23:15 [g]2Sa 22:3;
Ps 2:12; 71:1
[h]1Sa 30:15
23:16 [i]Ex 22:21;
S 23:6
23:17
[j]1Ki 14:24;
15:12; 22:46;
2Ki 23:7;
Job 36:14
[k]S Ge 38:21

[t]29 That is, about 1 1/4 pounds (about 0.6 kilogram) [g]2 Or *one of illegitimate birth* [h]4 That is, Northwest Mesopotamia [i]18 Hebrew *of a dog*

Study notes

22; see also note on 13:5.
22:22 See Lev 20:10.
22:29 *fifty shekels of silver.* Probably equaled the average bride-price, which must have varied with the economic status of the participants (see note on Ex 22:16).
22:30 *his father's wife.* Refers to a wife other than his mother (see 27:20). *dishonor his father's bed.* Lit. "uncover the corner of his father's garment" (see notes on Ru 3:9; Eze 16:8).
23:1 For blessings on eunuchs in later times see Isa 56:4–5; Ac 8:26–39.
23:2–3 *down to the tenth generation.* Perhaps forever, since ten is symbolic of completeness or finality. In v. 6 the equivalent expression is "as long as you live" (lit. "all your days forever").
23:3 Ruth is an outstanding exception to Moabite exclusion from Israel (see Introduction to Ruth: Theme and

Theology).
23:4 *Balaam son of Beor.* See Nu 22:4–24:25.
23:6 *Do not seek a treaty of friendship with them.* See the prophets' denunciation of Moab, Ammon and Edom (Isa 15–16; Jer 48:1–49:6; Eze 25:1–11; Am 1:13–2:3; Zep 2:8–11).
23:7 *Edomite . . . your brother.* Edom (Esau) is often condemned for his hostility against his brother Jacob (Israel; see Am 1:11; Ob 10; see also notes on Ge 25:22,26).
23:9–14 Sanitary rules for Israel's military camps. For similar rules for the people in general see Lev 15.
23:15 *If a slave has taken refuge.* A foreign slave seeking freedom in Israel (see v. 16). Cf. 24:7.
23:17–18 See notes on Ex 34:15–16.
23:18 *male prostitute.* Lit. "dog" (see NIV text note), a word often associated with moral or spiritual impurity (cf. Mt 7:6; 15:26; Php 3:2).

of the LORD your God to pay any vow, because the LORD your God detests them both. [l]

[19]Do not charge your brother interest, whether on money or food or anything else that may earn interest. [m] [20]You may charge a foreigner [n] interest, but not a brother Israelite, so that the LORD your God may bless [o] you in everything you put your hand to in the land you are entering to possess.

[21]If you make a vow to the LORD your God, do not be slow to pay it, [p] for the LORD your God will certainly demand it of you and you will be guilty of sin. [q] [22]But if you refrain from making a vow, you will not be guilty. [r] [23]Whatever your lips utter you must be sure to do, because you made your vow freely to the LORD your God with your own mouth.

[24]If you enter your neighbor's vineyard, you may eat all the grapes you want, but do not put any in your basket. [25]If you enter your neighbor's grainfield, you may pick kernels with your hands, but you must not put a sickle to his standing grain. [s]

24 If a man marries a woman who becomes displeasing to him [t] because he finds something indecent about her, and he writes her a certificate of divorce, [u] gives it to her and sends her from his house, [2]and if after she leaves his house she becomes the wife of another man, [3]and her second husband dislikes her and writes her a certificate of divorce, gives it to her and sends her from his house, or if he dies, [4]then her first husband, who divorced her, is not allowed to marry her again after she has been defiled. That would be detestable in the eyes of the LORD. Do not bring sin upon the land the LORD [v] your God is giving you as an inheritance.

[5]If a man has recently married, he must not be sent to war or have any other duty laid on him. For one year he is to be free to stay at home and bring happiness to the wife he has married. [w]

[6]Do not take a pair of millstones—not even the upper one—as security for a debt, because that would be taking a man's livelihood as security. [x]

[7]If a man is caught kidnapping one of his brother Israelites and treats him as a slave or sells him, the kidnapper must die. [y] You must purge the evil from among you. [z]

[8]In cases of leprous[j] diseases be very careful to do exactly as the priests, who are Levites, [a] instruct you. You must follow carefully what I have commanded them. [b] [9]Remember what the LORD your God did to Miriam along the way after you came out of Egypt. [c]

[10]When you make a loan of any kind to your neighbor, do not go into his house to get what he is offering as a pledge. [d] [11]Stay outside and let the man to whom you are making the loan bring the pledge out to you. [12]If the man is poor, do not go to sleep with his pledge [e] in your possession. [13]Return his cloak to him by sunset [f] so that he may sleep in it. [g] Then he will thank you, and it will be regarded as a righteous act in the sight of the LORD your God. [h]

[14]Do not take advantage of a hired man who is poor and needy, whether he is a brother Israelite or an alien living in one of your towns. [i] [15]Pay him his wages each day before sunset, because he is poor [j] and is counting on it. [k] Otherwise he may cry to the LORD against you, and you will be guilty of sin. [l]

[16]Fathers shall not be put to death for their children, nor children put to death for their fathers; each is to die for his own sin. [m]

[17]Do not deprive the alien or the fatherless [n] of justice, [o] or take the cloak of the widow as a pledge. [18]Remember that you were slaves in Egypt [p] and the LORD your God redeemed you from there. That is why I command you to do this.

[19]When you are harvesting in your field and you overlook a sheaf, do not go back

---

j 8 The Hebrew word was used for various diseases affecting the skin—not necessarily leprosy.

23:18 *l* S Ge 19:5; S Lev 20:13; Rev 22:15
23:19 *m* S Lev 25:35-37, 36; Ne 5:2-7
23:20 *n* S Ge 31:15; S Dt 15:3; *o* Dt 15:10
23:21 *p* S Nu 6:21; Jdg 11:35; Ps 15:4
23:22 *q* Nu 30:1-2; Job 22:27; Ps 61:8; 65:1; 76:11; Ecc 5:4-5; Isa 19:21; S Mt 5:33; Ac 5:3
23:22 *r* Ac 5:4
23:25 *s* Mt 12:1; Mk 2:23; Lk 6:1
24:1 *t* Dt 22:13; *u* ver 3; 2Ki 17:6; Isa 50:1; Jer 3:8; Mal 2:16; Mt 1:19; 5:31*; 19:7-9; Mk 10:4-5
24:4 *v* Jer 3:1
24:5 *w* S Dt 20:7

24:6 *x* S Ex 22:22
24:7 *y* S Ex 21:16 *z* 1Co 5:13*
24:8 *a* S Dt 17:9 *b* Lev 13:1-46; S 14:2
24:9 *c* S Nu 12:10
24:10
24:12
24:12 *d* Ex 22:25-27
24:12 *e* S Ex 22:26
24:13 *f* Ex 22:26 *g* S Ex 22:27 *h* Dt 6:25; Ps 106:31; Da 4:27
24:14 *i* Lev 19:13; 25:35-43; Dt 15:12-18; Job 24:4; Pr 14:31; 19:17; Am 4:1; 1Ti 5:18
24:15 *j* S Lev 25:35 *k* S Lev 19:13; Mt 20:8 *l* S Ex 22:23; S Job 12:19; Jas 5:4
24:16 *m* S Nu 26:11; Jer 31:29-30
24:17 *n* Ex 22:22; Job 6:27; 24:9; 29:12; Ps 10:18; 82:3; Pr 23:10; Eze 22:7 *o* S Ex 22:21; S 23:2; S Dt 10:18
24:18 *p* S Dt 15:15

23:19 *interest.* See notes on Ex 22:25–27; Lev 25:36.
23:20 *charge a foreigner.* A foreign businessman would come into Israel for financial advantage and so would be subject to paying interest.
23:21–23 See notes on Nu 30; see also Ecc 5:4–6.
24:1–4 In the books of Moses divorce was permitted and regulated (see Lev 21:7,14; 22:13; Nu 30:9). Jesus conditioned the law of 24:1 in the Sermon on the Mount (Mt 5:31–32) and cited the higher law of creation (Mt 19:3–9).
24:5 *happiness.* Marital bliss was held in high regard.
24:6 *millstones.* Used for grinding grain for flour and daily food (see note on Jdg 9:53).

24:7 *as a slave.* Cf. 23:15. *You must purge the evil from among you.* See note on 13:5.
24:8 *leprous diseases.* See NIV text note; see also note on Lev 13:2.
24:9,18,22 *Remember.* See note on 4:10.
24:10–13 See note on Ex 22:26–27.
24:16 *each is to die for his own sin.* See Eze 18:4 and note.
24:17–18 When the Israelites were in trouble, the Lord helped them. Therefore they were not to take advantage of others in difficulty.
24:19–21 See note on Lev 19:9–10.

to get it. *q* Leave it for the alien, *r* the fatherless and the widow, *s* so that the LORD your God may bless *t* you in all the work of your hands. 20When you beat the olives from your trees, do not go over the branches a second time. *u* Leave what remains for the alien, the fatherless and the widow. 21When you harvest the grapes in your vineyard, do not go over the vines again. Leave what remains for the alien, the fatherless and the widow. 22Remember that you were slaves in Egypt. That is why I command you to do this. *v*

25 When men have a dispute, they are to take it to court and the judges *w* will decide the case, *x* acquitting *y* the innocent and condemning the guilty. *z* 2If the guilty man deserves to be beaten, *a* the judge shall make him lie down and have him flogged in his presence with the number of lashes his crime deserves, 3but he must not give him more than forty lashes. *b* If he is flogged more than that, your brother will be degraded in your eyes. *c*

4Do not muzzle an ox while it is treading out the grain. *d*

5If brothers are living together and one of them dies without a son, his widow must not marry outside the family. Her husband's brother shall take her and marry her and fulfill the duty of a brother-in-law to her. *e* 6The first son she bears shall carry on the name of the dead brother so that his name will not be blotted out from Israel. *f*

7However, if a man does not want to marry his brother's wife, *g* she shall go to the elders at the town gate *h* and say, "My husband's brother refuses to carry on his brother's name in Israel. He will not fulfill the duty of a brother-in-law to me." *i* 8Then the elders of his town shall summon him and talk to him. If he persists in saying, "I do not want to marry her," 9his brother's widow shall go up to him in the presence of the elders, take off one of his sandals, *j* spit in his face *k* and say, "This is what is done to the man who will not

build up his brother's family line." 10That man's line shall be known in Israel as The Family of the Unsandaled.

11If two men are fighting and the wife of one of them comes to rescue her husband from his assailant, and she reaches out and seizes him by his private parts, 12you shall cut off her hand. Show her no pity. *l*

13Do not have two differing weights in your bag—one heavy, one light. *m* 14Do not have two differing measures in your house—one large, one small. 15You must have accurate and honest weights and measures, so that you may live long *n* in the land the LORD your God is giving you. 16For the LORD your God detests anyone who does these things, anyone who deals dishonestly. *o*

17Remember what the Amalekites *p* did to you along the way when you came out of Egypt. 18When you were weary and worn out, they met you on your journey and cut off all who were lagging behind; they had no fear of God. *q* 19When the LORD your God gives you rest *r* from all the enemies *s* around you in the land he is giving you to possess as an inheritance, you shall blot out the memory of Amalek *t* from under heaven. Do not forget!

Firstfruits and Tithes

26 When you have entered the land the LORD your God is giving you as an inheritance and have taken possession of it and settled in it, 2take some of the firstfruits *u* of all that you produce from the soil of the land the LORD your God is giving you and put them in a basket. Then go to the place the LORD your God will choose as a dwelling for his Name *v* 3and say to the priest in office at the time, "I declare today to the LORD your God that I have come to the land the LORD swore to our forefathers to give us." 4The priest shall take the basket from your hands and set it down in front of the altar of the LORD your God. 5Then you shall declare before the

Cross references (center column)

24:19
q S Lev 19:9
r Dt 10:19; 27:19;
Eze 47:22;
Zec 7:10; Mal 3:5
s ver 20; Dt 14:29
t S Dt 14:29;
Pr 19:17; 28:27;
Ecc 11:1
24:20 *u* Lev 19:10
24:22 *v* ver 18
25:1 *w* S Ex 21:6
x Dt 17:8-13;
19:17; Ac 23:3
y 1Ki 8:32
z S Ex 23:7;
Dt 1:16-17
25:2 *a* Pr 10:13;
19:29;
Lk 12:47-48
25:3 *b* Mt 27:26;
Jn 19:1;
2Co 11:24
c Jer 20:2
25:4
d S Nu 22:29;
1Co 9:9*;
1Ti 5:18*
25:5 *e* Ru 4:10,
13; Mt 22:24;
Mk 12:19;
Lk 20:28
25:6 *f* Ge 38:9;
Ru 4:5,10
25:7 *g* Ru 1:15
h S Ge 23:10
i Ru 4:1-2,5-6
25:9 *j* Jos 24:22;
Ru 4:7-8,11
k Nu 12:14;
Job 17:6; 30:10;
Isa 50:6

25:12 *l* S Dt 7:2
25:13 *m* Pr 11:1;
20:23; Mic 6:11
25:15
n S Ge 20:12
25:16 *o* Pr 11:1
25:17
p S Ge 36:12
25:18 *q* Ps 36:1;
Ro 3:18
25:19
r S Ex 33:14;
Heb 3:18-19
s Est 9:16
t S Ge 36:12
26:2 *u* S Ex 22:29
v S Ex 20:24;
S Dt 12:5

Footnotes

25:3 *not . . . more than forty lashes.* Beating could subject the culprit to abuse, so the law kept the punishment from becoming inhumane. Cf. Paul's experience (2Co 11:24).
25:4 Applied to ministers of Christ in 1Co 9:9–10; 1Ti 5:17–18. *treading out the grain.* See notes on Ge 50:10; Ru 1:22.
25:5–6 The continuity of each family and the decentralized control of land through family ownership were basic to the Mosaic economy (see note on Ge 38:8).
25:7 *if a man does not want to marry his brother's wife.* See vv. 8–10; note the experiences, with some variations, described in Ge 38:8–10; Ru 4:1–12. *elders at the town gate.* See 22:15; see also notes on Ge 19:1; Ru 4:1.
25:11–12 Cf. Ex 21:22–25.

25:13–16 See note on Lev 19:35.
25:14 *measures.* Of quantity.
25:17 *Remember.* See note on 4:10. *Amalekites.* See Ex 17:8–16; Nu 14:45.
25:18 *fear of God.* See note on Ge 20:11.
25:19 *rest.* See note on 3:20.
26:1 *inheritance.* See note on Ex 32:13.
26:2 *firstfruits.* The offering described here occurred only once and must not be confused with the annual offerings of firstfruits (see 18:4 and note). *the place the LORD . . . will choose as a dwelling for his Name.* See note on 12:5.
26:5 *wandering Aramean.* A reference to Jacob, who had wandered from southern Canaan to Haran and back (Ge 27–35) and who later migrated to Egypt (see Ge 46:3–7).

LORD your God: "My father was a wandering[w] Aramean,[x] and he went down into Egypt with a few people[y] and lived there and became a great nation,[z] powerful and numerous. [6]But the Egyptians mistreated us and made us suffer,[a] putting us to hard labor.[b] [7]Then we cried out to the LORD, the God of our fathers, and the LORD heard our voice[c] and saw[d] our misery,[e] toil and oppression.[f] [8]So the LORD brought us out of Egypt[g] with a mighty hand and an outstretched arm,[h] with great terror and with miraculous signs and wonders.[i] [9]He brought us to this place and gave us this land, a land flowing with milk and honey;[j] [10]and now I bring the firstfruits of the soil that you, O LORD, have given me.[k]" Place the basket before the LORD your God and bow down before him. [11]And you and the Levites[l] and the aliens among you shall rejoice[m] in all the good things the LORD your God has given to you and your household.

[12]When you have finished setting aside a tenth[n] of all your produce in the third year, the year of the tithe,[o] you shall give it to the Levite, the alien, the fatherless and the widow, so that they may eat in your towns and be satisfied. [13]Then say to the LORD your God: "I have removed from my house the sacred portion and have given it to the Levite, the alien, the fatherless and the widow, according to all you commanded. I have not turned aside from your commands nor have I forgotten any of them.[p] [14]I have not eaten any of the sacred portion while I was in mourning, nor have I removed any of it while I was unclean,[q] nor have I offered any of it to the dead. I have obeyed the LORD my God; I have done everything you commanded me. [15]Look down from heaven,[r] your holy dwelling place, and bless[s] your people Israel and the land you have given us as you promised on oath to our forefathers, a land flowing with milk and honey."

Follow the LORD's Commands

[16]The LORD your God commands you

26:5 wS Ge 20:13
xS Ge 25:20
yS Ge 34:30;
43:14 zS Ge 12:2
26:6 aS Nu 20:15
bS Ex 1:13
26:7 cS Ge 21:17
dEx 3:9;
eS Ge 16:11
fPs 42:9; 44:24;
72:14
26:8 gS Nu 20:16
hS Ex 3:20
iS Dt 4:34;
34:11-12
26:9 jS Ex 3:8
26:10 kS Dt 8:18
26:11 lDt 12:12
mS Dt 16:11
26:12
nS Ge 14:20
oS Nu 18:24;
Dt 14:28-29;
Heb 7:5,9
26:13
pPs 119:141,153,
176
26:14 qLev 7:20;
Hos 9:4
26:15 rPs 68:5;
80:14; 102:19;
Isa 63:15;
Zec 2:13
sS Ex 39:43

26:16 tDt 4:29
26:17 uEx 19:8;
Ps 48:14
26:18 vEx 6:7;
Dt 7:6
26:19 wIsa 62:7;
Zep 3:20
xDt 4:7-8; 28:1,
13,44; 1Ch 14:2;
Ps 148:14;
Isa 40:11
yS Dt 7:6
27:1 zPs 78:7
27:2 aJos 4:1
bEx 24:4;
Jos 24:26;
1Sa 7:12
cJos 8:31
27:3 dS Ex 3:8
27:4 eS Dt 11:29
27:5 fS Ex 20:24
gEx 20:25
27:7 hS Ex 32:6
iS Dt 16:11
jJos 8:31
27:8 kIsa 8:1;
30:8; Hab 2:2
lJos 8:32
27:9 mS Dt 17:9

this day to follow these decrees and laws; carefully observe them with all your heart and with all your soul.[t] [17]You have declared this day that the LORD is your God and that you will walk in his ways, that you will keep his decrees, commands and laws, and that you will obey him.[u] [18]And the LORD has declared this day that you are his people, his treasured possession[v] as he promised, and that you are to keep all his commands. [19]He has declared that he will set you in praise,[w] fame and honor high above all the nations[x] he has made and that you will be a people holy[y] to the LORD your God, as he promised.

The Altar on Mount Ebal

27 Moses and the elders of Israel commanded the people: "Keep all these commands[z] that I give you today. [2]When you have crossed the Jordan[a] into the land the LORD your God is giving you, set up some large stones[b] and coat them with plaster.[c] [3]Write on them all the words of this law when you have crossed over to enter the land the LORD your God is giving you, a land flowing with milk and honey,[d] just as the LORD, the God of your fathers, promised you. [4]And when you have crossed the Jordan, set up these stones on Mount Ebal,[e] as I command you today, and coat them with plaster. [5]Build there an altar[f] to the LORD your God, an altar of stones. Do not use any iron tool[g] upon them. [6]Build the altar of the LORD your God with fieldstones and offer burnt offerings on it to the LORD your God. [7]Sacrifice fellowship offerings[k][h] there, eating them and rejoicing[i] in the presence of the LORD your God.[j] [8]And you shall write very clearly all the words of this law on these stones[k] you have set up."[l]

Curses From Mount Ebal

[9]Then Moses and the priests, who are Levites,[m] said to all Israel, "Be silent, O Israel, and listen! You have now become

k[7] Traditionally *peace offerings*

He also married two Aramean women (see Ge 28:5; 29:16, 28). *with a few people . . . became a great nation.* See Ex 1:5; 1:7 and note.
26:11 *rejoice.* See note on 12:12.
26:12 See note on 14:22–29.
26:16 *with all your heart . . . soul.* See note on 4:29.
26:17 The terminology is that of a covenant or treaty, involving a renewal of Israel's vow that the Lord was God and that they would obey him (see note on Ex 19:8).
26:18 *treasured possession.* See note on Ex 19:5.
27:2–8 Setting up stones inscribed with messages to be remembered was a common practice in the ancient Near East.

27:2,4 *coat them with plaster.* So that the writing inscribed on them would stand out clearly (see v. 8).
27:3,8 *all the words of this law.* The stipulations (see note on Ex 20:1) of the covenant that Moses' reaffirmation contained.
27:5 *Build . . . an altar of stones.* Different from the altars of the tabernacle, both in form and in use (see note on Ex 20:25).
27:9 *You have now become the people of the LORD.* The language of covenant renewal.

the people of the LORD your God. *n* ¹⁰Obey the LORD your God and follow his commands and decrees that I give you today."

¹¹On the same day Moses commanded the people:

¹²When you have crossed the Jordan, these tribes shall stand on Mount Gerizim *o* to bless the people: Simeon, Levi, Judah, Issachar, *p* Joseph and Benjamin. *q* ¹³And these tribes shall stand on Mount Ebal *r* to pronounce curses: Reuben, Gad, Asher, Zebulun, Dan and Naphtali.

¹⁴The Levites shall recite to all the people of Israel in a loud voice:

¹⁵"Cursed is the man who carves an image or casts an idol *s*—a thing detestable *t* to the LORD, the work of the craftsman's hands—and sets it up in secret."

Then all the people shall say, "Amen!" *u*

¹⁶"Cursed is the man who dishonors his father or his mother." *v*

Then all the people shall say, "Amen!"

¹⁷"Cursed is the man who moves his neighbor's boundary stone." *w*

Then all the people shall say, "Amen!"

¹⁸"Cursed is the man who leads the blind astray on the road." *x*

Then all the people shall say, "Amen!"

¹⁹"Cursed is the man who withholds justice from the alien, *y* the fatherless or the widow." *z*

Then all the people shall say, "Amen!"

²⁰"Cursed is the man who sleeps with his father's wife, for he dishonors his father's bed." *a*

Then all the people shall say, "Amen!"

²¹"Cursed is the man who has sexual relations with any animal." *b*

Then all the people shall say, "Amen!"

²²"Cursed is the man who sleeps with his sister, the daughter of his father or the daughter of his mother." *c*

Then all the people shall say, "Amen!"

²³"Cursed is the man who sleeps with his mother-in-law." *d*

Then all the people shall say, "Amen!"

²⁴"Cursed is the man who kills *e* his neighbor secretly." *f*

Then all the people shall say, "Amen!"

²⁵"Cursed is the man who accepts a bribe to kill an innocent person." *g*

Then all the people shall say, "Amen!"

²⁶"Cursed is the man who does not uphold the words of this law by carrying them out." *h*

Then all the people shall say, "Amen!" *i*

Blessings for Obedience

28 If you fully obey the LORD your God and carefully follow *j* all his commands *k* I give you today, the LORD your God will set you high above all the nations on earth. *l* ²All these blessings will come upon you *m* and accompany you if you obey the LORD your God:

³You will be blessed *n* in the city and blessed in the country. *o*

⁴The fruit of your womb will be blessed, and the crops of your land and the young of your livestock—the calves of your herds and the lambs of your flocks. *p*

⁵Your basket and your kneading trough will be blessed.

Cross references column

27:9 *n* Dt 26:18
27:12 *o* S Dt 11:29; *p* S Ge 30:18; *q* Jos 8:35
27:13 *r* S Dt 11:29
27:15 *s* S Ex 20:4; *t* 1Ki 11:5,7; 2Ki 23:13; Isa 44:19; 66:3; *u* Nu 5:22; S 1Co 14:16
27:16 *v* S Ge 31:35; S Ex 21:12; S Dt 5:16
27:17 *w* S Dt 19:14
27:18 *x* S Lev 19:14
27:19 *y* S Ex 22:21; S Dt 24:19; *z* S Ex 23:2; S Dt 10:18
27:20 *a* S Ge 34:5; S Lev 18:7
27:21 *b* S Ex 22:19
27:22 *c* S Lev 18:9
27:23 *d* S Lev 20:14
27:24 *e* S Ge 4:23; *f* Ex 21:12
27:25 *g* Ex 23:7-8; S Lev 19:16
27:26 *h* S Lev 26:14; Dt 28:15; Ps 119:21; Jer 11:3; Gal 3:10*; *i* Jer 11:5
28:1 *j* S Dt 15:5; *k* S Lev 26:3; *l* S Nu 24:7; S Dt 26:19
28:2 *m* Jer 32:24; Zec 1:6
28:3 *n* Ps 144:15; *o* S Ge 39:5
28:4 *p* S Ge 49:25; S Dt 8:18

27:12 *these tribes shall stand on Mount Gerizim.* All six were descendants of Jacob by Leah and Rachel (see Ge 35:23–24). See 11:30 and note. *to bless.* No blessings appear in vv. 15–26, which consist entirely of 12 curses (see 28:15–68). Blessings, however, are listed and described in 28:1–14.

27:13 *these tribes shall stand on Mount Ebal.* Reuben and Zebulun were descendants of Jacob by Leah; the rest were his descendants by the maidservants Zilpah and Bilhah (see Ge 35:23,25–26).

27:15 *carves an image . . . casts an idol.* In violation of the first and second commandments of the Decalogue (see note on Ex 20:1). See 4:28; 5:6–10; 31:29; Isa 40:19–20; 41:7; 44:9–20; 45:16; Jer 10:3–9; Hos 8:4–6; 13:2. *Amen!* Not simply approval but a solemn, formal assertion that the people accept and agree to the covenant and its curses and blessings (see vv. 16–26).

27:16 See 5:16; Ex 20:12 and note.
27:17 See note on 19:14.
27:19 See 24:17–18 and note.
27:20 Cf. 22:30; see Lev 18:8.
27:21 See Ex 22:19 and note; Lev 18:23; 20:15–16.
27:22 See Lev 18:9.
27:23 See Lev 18:8.
27:24–25 See 5:17; Ex 20:13; 21:12; Lev 24:17,21.
27:26 Quoted in Gal 3:10 to prove that mankind is under a curse because no one follows the law of God fully. *by carrying them out.* It is not enough to assert allegiance to the law; one must live according to its stipulations.
28:1–14 These blessings are the opposites of the curses in vv. 15–44 (compare especially vv. 3–6 with vv. 16–19).
28:5,17 *basket . . . kneading trough.* Used at home for storage and for the preparation of foods, particularly bread.

⁶You will be blessed when you come in and blessed when you go out. *q*

⁷The LORD will grant that the enemies *r* who rise up against you will be defeated before you. They will come at you from one direction but flee from you in seven. *s*

⁸The LORD will send a blessing on your barns and on everything you put your hand to. The LORD your God will bless *t* you in the land he is giving you.

⁹The LORD will establish you as his holy people, *u* as he promised you on oath, if you keep the commands *v* of the LORD your God and walk in his ways. ¹⁰Then all the peoples on earth will see that you are called by the name *w* of the LORD, and they will fear you. ¹¹The LORD will grant you abundant prosperity—in the fruit of your womb, the young of your livestock *x* and the crops of your ground—in the land he swore to your forefathers to give you. *y*

¹²The LORD will open the heavens, the storehouse *z* of his bounty, *a* to send rain *b* on your land in season and to bless *c* all the work of your hands. You will lend to many nations but will borrow from none. *d* ¹³The LORD will make you the head, not the tail. If you pay attention to the commands of the LORD your God that I give you this day and carefully follow *e* them, you will always be at the top, never at the bottom. *f* ¹⁴Do not turn aside from any of the commands I give you today, to the right or to the left, *g* following other gods and serving them.

Curses for Disobedience

¹⁵However, if you do not obey *h* the LORD your God and do not carefully follow all his commands and decrees I am giving you today, *i* all these curses will come upon you and overtake you: *j*

¹⁶You will be cursed in the city and cursed in the country. *k*

¹⁷Your basket and your kneading trough will be cursed. *l*

¹⁸The fruit of your womb will be cursed, and the crops of your land, and the calves of your herds and the lambs of your flocks. *m*

¹⁹You will be cursed when you

come in and cursed when you go out. *n*

²⁰The LORD will send on you curses, *o* confusion and rebuke *p* in everything you put your hand to, until you are destroyed and come to sudden ruin *q* because of the evil *r* you have done in forsaking him. ¹ ²¹The LORD will plague you with diseases until he has destroyed you from the land you are entering to possess. *s* ²²The LORD will strike you with wasting disease, *t* with fever and inflammation, with scorching heat and drought, *u* with blight *v* and mildew, which will plague *w* you until you perish. *x* ²³The sky over your head will be bronze, the ground beneath you iron. *y* ²⁴The LORD will turn the rain *z* of your country into dust and powder; it will come down from the skies until you are destroyed.

²⁵The LORD will cause you to be defeated *a* before your enemies. You will come at them from one direction but flee from them in seven, *b* and you will become a thing of horror *c* to all the kingdoms on earth. *d* ²⁶Your carcasses will be food for all the birds of the air *e* and the beasts of the earth, and there will be no one to frighten them away. *f* ²⁷The LORD will afflict you with the boils of Egypt *g* and with tumors, festering sores and the itch, from which you cannot be cured. ²⁸The LORD will afflict you with madness, blindness and confusion of mind. ²⁹At midday you will grope *h* about like a blind man in the dark. You will be unsuccessful in everything you do; day after day you will be oppressed and robbed, with no one to rescue *i* you.

³⁰You will be pledged to be married to a woman, but another will take her and ravish her. *j* You will build a house, but you will not live in it. *k* You will plant a vineyard, but you will not even begin to enjoy its fruit. *l* ³¹Your ox will be slaughtered before your eyes, but you will eat none of it. Your donkey will be forcibly taken from

28:6 *q*Ps 121:8
28:7 *r*2Ch 6:34
*s*S Lev 26:8,17
28:8 *t*Dt 15:4
28:9 *u*S Ex 19:6
*v*S Lev 26:3
28:10 *w*S Nu 6:27;
1Ki 8:43;
Jer 25:29;
Da 9:18
28:11 *x*S Ge 30:27 *y*ver 4; Dt 30:9
28:12 *z*Job 38:22;
Ps 135:7;
Jer 10:13; 51:16
*a*Ps 65:11; 68:10;
Jer 31:12
*b*S Lev 26:4;
1Ki 8:35-36;
18:1; Ps 104:13;
Isa 5:6; 30:23;
32:20 *c*Isa 61:9;
65:23;
Jer 32:38-41;
Mal 3:12 *d*ver 44;
S Lev 25:19;
S Dt 15:3,6;
Eze 34:26
28:13 *e*Jer 11:6
*f*S Dt 26:19
28:14 *g*S Dt 5:32;
Jos 1:7
28:15 *h*1Ki 9:6;
2Ch 7:19
*i*S Dt 27:26
*j*Dt 29:27;
Jos 23:15;
2Ch 12:5;
Da 9:11; Mal 2:2
28:16 *k*ver 3
28:17 *l*ver 5
28:18 *m*ver 4
28:19 *n*ver 6
28:20 *o*ver 8,15;
Lev 26:16;
Jer 42:18;
Mal 2:2; 3:9; 4:6
*p*Ps 39:11; 76:6;
80:16; Isa 17:13;
51:20; 54:9;
66:15; Eze 5:15
*q*Dt 4:26
*r*S Ex 32:22
28:21 *s*Lev 26:25;
Nu 14:12;
Jer 24:10;
Am 4:10
28:22 *t*ver 48;
Dt 32:24
*u*Lev 26:16;
2Ki 8:1;
Job 12:15;
Ps 105:16;
Jer 14:1;
Hag 1:11; Mal 3:9
*v*Hag 2:17
*w*S Lev 26:25
*x*Dt 4:26; Am 4:9
28:23 *y*S Lev 26:19
28:24 *z*Lev 26:19;
Dt 11:17;
1Ki 8:35; 17:1;
Isa 5:6; Jer 14:1;
Hag 1:10
28:25 *a*1Sa 4:10;
Ps 78:62
*b*S Lev 26:17 *c*ver

37 *d*2Ch 29:8; 30:7; Jer 15:4; 24:9; 26:6; 29:18; 44:12;
Eze 23:46 **28:26** *e*S Ge 40:19 *f*Ps 79:2; Isa 18:6; Jer 7:33;
12:9; 15:2; 16:4; 19:7; 34:20 **28:27** *g*Dt 7:15 **28:29**
*h*Ge 19:11; Ex 10:21; Job 5:14; 12:25; 24:13; 38:15;
Isa 59:10 *i*Jdg 3:9; 2Ki 13:5; Est 4:14; Isa 19:20; 43:11;
Hos 13:4; Ob 1:21 **28:30** *j*Job 31:10 *k*Isa 65:22; Am 5:11
*l*Jer 12:13

¹20 Hebrew *me*

28:7 For the reverse see v. 25.
28:12 *the heavens, the storehouse.* For the heavens as the storehouse of rain, snow, hail and wind see Job 38:22; Ps 135:7; Jer 10:13; 51:16. *You will lend.* For the opposite see v. 44; see also note on 15:6.
28:13 *the head, not the tail.* For the reverse see v. 44.

28:23 *sky . . . bronze . . . ground . . . iron.* No rain would pierce the sky or penetrate the ground.
28:25 For the reverse see v. 7.
28:27 *boils of Egypt.* See note on Ex 9:9.
28:30 See 20:5–7.

you and will not be returned. Your sheep will be given to your enemies, and no one will rescue them. ³²Your sons and daughters will be given to another nation, *m* and you will wear out your eyes watching for them day after day, powerless to lift a hand. ³³A people that you do not know will eat what your land and labor produce, and you will have nothing but cruel oppression *n* all your days. *o* ³⁴The sights you see will drive you mad. *p* ³⁵The LORD will afflict your knees and legs with painful boils *q* that cannot be cured, spreading from the soles of your feet to the top of your head. *r*

³⁶The LORD will drive you and the king *s* you set over you to a nation unknown to you or your fathers. *t* There you will worship other gods, gods of wood and stone. *u* ³⁷You will become a thing of horror *v* and an object of scorn *w* and ridicule *x* to all the nations where the LORD will drive you. *y*

³⁸You will sow much seed in the field but you will harvest little, *z* because locusts *a* will devour *b* it. ³⁹You will plant vineyards and cultivate them but you will not drink the wine *c* or gather the grapes, because worms will eat *d* them. *e* ⁴⁰You will have olive trees throughout your country but you will not use the oil, because the olives will drop off. *f* ⁴¹You will have sons and daughters but you will not keep them, because they will go into captivity. *g* ⁴²Swarms of locusts *h* will take over all your trees and the crops of your land.

⁴³The alien who lives among you will rise above you higher and higher, but you will sink lower and lower. *i* ⁴⁴He will lend to you, but you will not lend to him. *j* He will be the head, but you will be the tail. *k*

⁴⁵All these curses will come upon you. They will pursue you and overtake you *l* until you are destroyed, *m* because you did not obey the LORD your God and observe the commands and decrees he gave you. ⁴⁶They will be a sign and a wonder to you and your descendants forever. *n* ⁴⁷Because you did not serve *o* the LORD your God joyfully and gladly *p* in the time of prosperity, ⁴⁸therefore in hunger and thirst, *q* in

nakedness and dire poverty, you will serve the enemies the LORD sends against you. He will put an iron yoke *r* on your neck *s* until he has destroyed you.

⁴⁹The LORD will bring a nation against you *t* from far away, from the ends of the earth, *u* like an eagle *v* swooping down, a nation whose language you will not understand, *w* ⁵⁰a fierce-looking nation without respect for the old *x* or pity for the young. ⁵¹They will devour the young of your livestock and the crops of your land until you are destroyed. They will leave you no grain, new wine *y* or oil, *z* nor any calves of your herds or lambs of your flocks until you are ruined. *a* ⁵²They will lay siege *b* to all the cities throughout your land until the high fortified walls in which you trust fall down. They will besiege all the cities throughout the land the LORD your God is giving you. *c*

⁵³Because of the suffering that your enemy will inflict on you during the siege, you will eat the fruit of the womb, the flesh of the sons and daughters the LORD your God has given you. *d* ⁵⁴Even the most gentle and sensitive man among you will have no compassion on his own brother or the wife he loves or his surviving children, ⁵⁵and he will not give to one of them any of the flesh of his children that he is eating. It will be all he has left because of the suffering your enemy will inflict on you during the siege of all your cities. *e* ⁵⁶The most gentle and sensitive *f* woman among you—so sensitive and gentle that she would not venture to touch the ground with the sole of her foot—will begrudge the husband she loves and her own son or daughter *g* ⁵⁷the afterbirth from her womb and the children she bears. For she intends to eat them *h* secretly during the siege and in the distress that your enemy will inflict on you in your cities.

⁵⁸If you do not carefully follow all the words of this law, *i* which are written in

---

28:32 *m* ver 41
28:33 *n* Jer 6:6; 22:17
o Jer 5:15-17; Eze 25:4
28:34 *p* Dt 7:15;
28:35 *q* Dt 7:15; Rev 16:2 *r* Job 2:7; 7:5; 13:28; 30:17,30; Isa 1:6
28:36 *s* 1Sa 12:25 *t* S Dt 4:27; 2Ki 24:14; 25:7, 11; 2Ch 33:11; 36:21; Ezr 5:12; Jer 15:14; 16:13; 27:20; 39:1-9; 52:28; La 1:3 *u* S Dt 4:28
28:37 *v* ver 25; Jer 42:18; Eze 5:15 *w* Ps 22:7; 39:8; 44:13; 64:8; Jer 18:16; 48:27; Mic 6:16 *x* 2Ch 7:20; Ezr 9:7; Jer 44:8 *y* 1Ki 9:7; Ps 44:14; Jer 19:8; 24:9; 25:9,18; 29:18; La 2:15
28:38 *z* Lev 26:20; Ps 129:7; Isa 5:10; Jer 12:13; Hos 8:7; Mic 6:15; Hag 1:6,9; 2:16 *a* S Ex 10:4 *b* S Ex 10:15
28:39 *c* S Lev 10:9 *d* Joel 1:4; 2:25; Mal 3:11 *e* Isa 5:10; 17:10-11; Zep 1:13
28:40 *f* Jer 11:16; Mic 6:15
28:41 *g* ver 32
28:42 *h* ver 38; Jdg 6:5; 7:12; Jer 46:23
28:43 *i* ver 13
28:44 *j* S ver 12 *k* S Dt 26:19
28:45 *l* S Ex 15:9 *m* ver 15; Dt 4:25-26
28:46 *n* S Nu 16:38; Ps 71:7; Isa 8:18; 20:3; Eze 5:15; Zec 3:8
28:47 *o* S Dt 10:12 *p* S Lev 23:40; Ne 9:35
28:48 *q* Jer 14:3; La 4:4
r Jer 28:13-14; La 1:14 *s* Ge 49:8
28:49 *t* S Lev 26:44 *u* Isa 5:26-30,26; 7:18-20; 39:3; Jer 4:16; 5:15;
6:22; 25:32; 31:8; Hab 1:6 *v* 2Sa 1:23; Jer 4:13; 48:40; 49:22; La 4:19; Eze 17:3; Hos 8:1 *w* S Ge 11:7; 1Co 14:21*
28:50 *x* Isa 47:6 28:51 *y* Ps 4:7; Isa 36:17; Hag 1:11
z S Nu 18:12 *a* ver 33; Jdg 6:4 28:52 *b* 2Ki 6:24 *c* Jer 10:18; Eze 6:10; Zep 1:14-16,17 28:53 *d* ver 57; Lev 26:29; 2Ki 6:28-29; La 2:20 28:55 *e* 2Ki 6:29 28:56 *f* Isa 47:1
g La 4:10 28:57 *h* S ver 53 28:58 *i* Dt 31:24

28:35 See note on Ex 9:11.
28:44 See notes on vv. 12–13.
28:49 *ends of the earth.* An indefinite figurative expression meaning "far away"—anywhere from the horizon to the perimeter of the then-known world. *eagle swooping down.* Symbolic of the speed and power of the Assyrians (see Hos 8:1) and Babylonians (see Jer 48:40; 49:22). *whose language you will not understand.* Though related to Hebrew, the languages of Assyria and Babylonia were not understood

by the average Israelite (see Isa 28:11; 33:19 and note; 1Co 14:21).
28:53 *suffering that your enemy will inflict on you during the siege.* See vv. 55, 57. The repetition of the clause emphasizes the distress that the Israelites would suffer if they refused to obey the Lord. *you will eat . . . sons and daughters.* For the actualizing of this curse see 2Ki 6:24–29; La 2:20; 4:10.
28:58 *words of this law.* See note on 31:24. *this glorious*

this book, and do not revere[i] this glorious and awesome name[k]—the LORD your God— [59]the LORD will send fearful plagues on you and your descendants, harsh and prolonged disasters, and severe and lingering illnesses. [60]He will bring upon you all the diseases of Egypt[l] that you dreaded, and they will cling to you. [61]The LORD will also bring on you every kind of sickness and disaster not recorded in this Book of the Law, [m] until you are destroyed. [n] [62]You who were as numerous as the stars in the sky[o] will be left but few[p] in number, because you did not obey the LORD your God. [63]Just as it pleased[q] the LORD to make you prosper and increase in number, so it will please[r] him to ruin and destroy you. [s] You will be uprooted[t] from the land you are entering to possess.

[64]Then the LORD will scatter[u] you among all nations, [v] from one end of the earth to the other. [w] There you will worship other gods—gods of wood and stone, which neither you nor your fathers have known. [x] [65]Among those nations you will find no repose, no resting place[y] for the sole of your foot. There the LORD will give you an anxious mind, eyes[z] weary with longing, and a despairing heart. [a] [66]You will live in constant suspense, filled with dread both night and day, never sure of your life. [67]In the morning you will say, "If only it were evening!" and in the evening, "If only it were morning!"—because of the terror that will fill your hearts and the sights that your eyes will see. [b] [68]The LORD will send you back in ships to Egypt on a journey I said you should never make again. [c] There you will offer yourselves for sale to your enemies as male and female slaves, but no one will buy you.

Renewal of the Covenant

29 These are the terms of the covenant the LORD commanded Moses

to make with the Israelites in Moab, [d] in addition to the covenant he had made with them at Horeb. [e]

[2]Moses summoned all the Israelites and said to them:

Your eyes have seen all that the LORD did in Egypt to Pharaoh, to all his officials and to all his land. [f] [3]With your own eyes you saw those great trials, those miraculous signs and great wonders. [g] [4]But to this day the LORD has not given you a mind that understands or eyes that see or ears that hear. [h] [5]During the forty years that I led[i] you through the desert, your clothes did not wear out, nor did the sandals on your feet. [j] [6]You ate no bread and drank no wine or other fermented drink. [k] I did this so that you might know that I am the LORD your God. [l]

[7]When you reached this place, Sihon[m] king of Heshbon[n] and Og king of Bashan came out to fight against us, but we defeated them. [o] [8]We took their land and gave it as an inheritance[p] to the Reubenites, the Gadites and the half-tribe of Manasseh. [q]

[9]Carefully follow[r] the terms of this covenant, [s] so that you may prosper in everything you do. [t] [10]All of you are standing today in the presence of the LORD your God—your leaders and chief men, your elders and officials, and all the other men of Israel, [11]together with your children and your wives, and the aliens living in your camps who chop your wood and carry your water. [u] [12]You are standing here in order to enter into a covenant with the LORD your God, a covenant the LORD is making with you this day and sealing with an oath, [13]to confirm you this day as his people, [v] that he may be your God[w] as he promised you and as he swore to your fa-

Center cross-reference column

28:58 JPs 96:4; Jer 5:22; Mal 1:14; 2:5; 3:5,16; 4:2
kS Ex 3:15; S Jos 7:9
28:60 lEx 15:26
28:61 mDt 29:21; 30:10; 31:26; Jos 1:8; 8:34; 23:6; 24:26; 2Ki 14:6; 22:8; 2Ch 17:9; 25:4; Ne 8:1,18; Mal 4:4
nDt 4:25-26
28:62 oS Ge 22:17; Dt 4:27; 10:22
pS Lev 26:22
28:63 qDt 30:9; Isa 62:5; 65:19; Jer 32:41; Zep 3:17 rPr 1:26
sS Ge 6:7
tPs 52:5; Jer 12:14; 31:28; 45:4
28:64 uS Dt 4:27; Ezr 9:12; Jer 6:12; Jer 32:23; 43:11; 52:27 vNe 1:8; Ps 44:11; Jer 13:24; 18:17; 22:22
wS Dt 4:32; S Jer 8:19
xDt 11:28; 32:17
28:65 yLa 1:3
zJob 11:20
aLev 26:16,36; Hos 9:17
28:67 bver 34
28:68 cS Ex 13:14
29:1 dS Lev 7:38
eS Ex 3:1
29:2 fEx 19:4
29:3 gS Dt 4:34
29:4 hIsa 6:10; 32:3; 48:8; Jer 5:21; Eze 12:2; S Mt 13:15; Ro 11:8*; Eph 4:18
29:5 iS Dt 8:2
jS Dt 8:4
29:6 kS Lev 10:9
lDt 8:3
29:7 mS Nu 21:26
nS Nu 21:25
oNu 21:21-24, 33-35; Dt 2:26-3:11
29:8 pPs 78:55; 135:12; 136:22
qNu 32:33;

Dt 3:12-13 29:9 rS Dt 4:6; S Jos 1:7 sEx 19:5; Ps 25:10; 103:18 tJos 1:8; 2Ch 31:21 29:11 uJos 9:21,23,27; 1Ch 20:3 29:13 vS Ge 6:18; S Ex 19:6 wS Ge 17:7

---

and awesome name—the LORD. See note and NIV text note on Ex 3:15. One of the oddities of history and revelation is the loss of the proper pronunciation of the Hebrew word YHWH, the most intimate and personal name of God in the OT (see note on Ge 2:4). "Jehovah" is a spelling that developed from combining the consonants of the name with the vowels of a word for "Lord" (*Adonai*). "Yahweh" is probably the original pronunciation. The name eventually ceased to be pronounced because later Jews thought it too holy to be uttered and feared violating Ex 20:7 and Lev 24:16. It is translated "LORD" in this version (see Preface to the NIV).
28:60 *diseases of Egypt.* Those brought on the Egyptians during the plagues (see 7:15; Ex 15:26).
28:61 *Book of the Law.* See note on 31:24.
28:62 *as the stars in the sky.* See 1:10; see also notes on Ge 13:16; 15:5.

28:64 *will scatter you.* Experienced by Israel in the Assyrian (722–721 B.C.) and Babylonian (586 B.C.) exiles (see 2Ki 17:6; 25:21).
28:68 *a journey I said you should never make again.* See 17:16; Ex 13:17; Nu 14:3–4.
29:1 See notes on 5:2–3.
29:2 *Your eyes have seen.* Only those who were less than 20 years old (Nu 14:29) when Israel followed the majority spy report at Kadesh Barnea and refused to enter Canaan would have actually experienced life in Egypt before the exodus. But Moses is speaking to the people as a nation and referring to the national experience (see note on 5:3).
29:4 Quoted in Ro 11:8 and applied to hardened Israel.
29:8 *gave it as an inheritance.* See 3:12–17.
29:9–15 A clear summary of the nature of covenant reaffirmation.

thers, Abraham, Isaac and Jacob. 14I am making this covenant, x with its oath, not only with you 15who are standing here with us today in the presence of the LORD our God but also with those who are not here today. y

16You yourselves know how we lived in Egypt and how we passed through the countries on the way here. 17You saw among them their detestable images and idols of wood and stone, of silver and gold. z 18Make sure there is no man or woman, clan or tribe among you today whose heart turns a away from the LORD our God to go and worship the gods of those nations; make sure there is no root among you that produces such bitter poison. b

19When such a person hears the words of this oath, he invokes a blessing c on himself and therefore thinks, "I will be safe, even though I persist in going my own way.' d This will bring disaster on the watered land as well as the dry. m 20The LORD will never be willing to forgive e him; his wrath and zeal f will burn g against that man. All the curses written in this book will fall upon him, and the LORD will blot h out his name from under heaven. 21The LORD will single him out from all the tribes of Israel for disaster, i according to all the curses of the covenant written in this Book of the Law. j

22Your children who follow you in later generations and foreigners who come from distant lands will see the calamities that have fallen on the land and the diseases with which the LORD has afflicted it. k 23The whole land will be a burning waste l of salt m and sulfur—nothing planted, nothing sprouting, no vegetation growing on it. It will be like the destruction of Sodom and Gomorrah, n Admah and Zeboiim, which the LORD overthrew in fierce anger. o 24All the nations will ask: "Why has the LORD done this to this land? p Why this fierce, burning anger?"

25And the answer will be: "It is because this people abandoned the covenant of the LORD, the God of their fathers, the covenant he made with them when he brought them out of Egypt. q 26They went off and worshiped other gods and bowed down to them, gods they did not know, gods he had not given them. 27Therefore the LORD's anger burned against this land, so that he brought on it all the curses written in this book. r 28In furious anger and in great wrath s the LORD uprooted t them from their land and thrust them into another land, as it is now."

29The secret things belong to the LORD our God, u but the things revealed belong to us and to our children forever, that we may follow all the words of this law. v

Prosperity After Turning to the LORD

30 When all these blessings and curses w I have set before you come upon you and you take them to heart wherever the LORD your God disperses you among the nations, x 2and when you and your children return y to the LORD your God and obey him with all your heart z and with all your soul according to everything I command you today, 3then the LORD your God will restore your fortunes n a and have compassion b on you and gather c you again from all the nations where he scattered d you. e 4Even if you have been banished to the most distant land under the heavens, f from there the LORD your God will gather g you and bring you back. h 5He will bring i you to the land that belonged to your fathers, and you will take possession of it. He will make you more prosperous and numerous j than your fathers. 6The LORD your God will circumcise your hearts and the hearts of your descendants, k so that you may love l him with all your heart and with all your soul, and live. 7The LORD your God will put all these curses m on your enemies who hate

Cross references (center column):

29:14 xEx 19:5; Isa 59:21; Jer 31:31; 32:40; 50:5; Eze 16:62; 37:26; Heb 8:7-8
29:15 yS Ge 6:18; Ac 2:39
29:17 zEx 20:23; Dt 4:28
29:18 aS Dt 13:6 bS Dt 11:16; Heb 12:15
29:19 cPs 72:17; Isa 65:16 dPs 36:2
29:20 eS Ex 23:21 fEx 34:14; Eze 23:25; Zep 1:18 gPs 74:1; 79:5; 80:4; Eze 36:5 h2Ki 13:23; 14:27; Rev 3:5
29:21 iDt 32:23; Eze 7:26 jS Dt 28:61
29:22 kJer 19:8; 49:17; 50:13
29:23 lIsa 1:7; 6:11; 9:18; 64:10; Jer 12:11; 44:2,6; Mic 5:11 mS Ge 13:10; Eze 47:11 nS Ge 19:24,25; Zep 2:9; S Mt 10:15; Ro 9:29 oS Ge 14:8
29:24 p1Ki 9:8; 2Ch 36:19; Jer 16:10; 22:8-9; 52:13
29:25 q2Ki 17:23; 2Ch 36:21
29:27 rS Dt 28:15
29:28 sPs 7:11 t1Ki 14:15; 2Ch 7:20; Ps 9:6; 52:5; Pr 2:22; Jer 12:14; 31:28; 42:10; Eze 19:12
29:29 uAc 1:7 vJn 5:39; Ac 17:11; 2Ti 3:16
30:1 wS Dt 11:26 xLev 26:40-45; S Dt 4:32; 29:28
30:2 yS Dt 4:30 zDt 4:29; Ps 119:2
30:3 aPs 14:7; 53:6; 85:1; 126:4; Jer 30:18; 33:11; Eze 16:53; Joel 3:1; Zep 2:7 bDt 13:17 cS Ge 48:21 dS Ge 11:4; Dt 4:27 eIsa 11:11; Jer 12:15; 16:15; 24:6; 29:14;
48:47; 49:6 30:4 fPs 19:6 gIsa 17:6; 24:13; 27:12; 40:11; 49:5; 56:8; Eze 20:34,41; 34:13 hNe 1:8-9; Isa 11:12; 41:5; 42:10; 43:6; 48:20; 62:11; Jer 31:8,10; 50:2 30:5 iJer 29:14 jS Dt 7:13 30:6 kS Dt 6:24; S 10:16 lDt 6:5 30:7 mS Ge 12:3

m19 Or way, in order to add drunkenness to thirst."
n3 Or will bring you back from captivity

Footnotes (bottom):

29:18 root ... that produces such bitter poison. The poison of idolatry, involving the rejection of the Lord.
29:20 The LORD will never be willing to forgive him. Not to be taken as contradictory to 2Pe 3:9 ("not wanting anyone to perish"). Peter, too, says that those who deny the "sovereign Lord" bring "swift destruction on themselves" (2Pe 2:1). this book. See note on 31:24. blot out his name. See 9:14; Ex 32:32-33; Rev 3:5.
29:21 Book of the Law. See note on 31:24.
29:23 destruction of Sodom. See Ge 19:24-25; see also notes on Ge 10:19; 13:10.

29:27 this book. See note on 31:24.
29:28 as it is now. This would be said when Israel was in exile (see v. 25).
29:29 secret things. The hidden events of Israel's future relative to the blessings and curses; but the phrase can also have wider application. things revealed. Primarily the "words of this law."
30:2,6,10 with all your heart ... soul. See note on 4:29.
30:3 restore your fortunes. See NIV text note.
30:6 circumcise your hearts. See note on Ge 17:10.
30:7 curses on your enemies. Fulfilling Ge 12:3.

and persecute you. n 8You will again obey the LORD and follow all his commands I am giving you today. 9Then the LORD your God will make you most prosperous in all the work of your hands and in the fruit of your womb, the young of your livestock and the crops of your land. o The LORD will again delight p in you and make you prosperous, just as he delighted in your fathers, 10if you obey the LORD your God and keep his commands and decrees that are written in this Book of the Law q and turn to the LORD your God with all your heart and with all your soul. r

The Offer of Life or Death

11Now what I am commanding you today is not too difficult for you or beyond your reach. s 12It is not up in heaven, so that you have to ask, "Who will ascend into heaven t to get it and proclaim it to us so we may obey it?" u 13Nor is it beyond the sea, v so that you have to ask, "Who will cross the sea to get it and proclaim it to us so we may obey it?" w 14No, the word is very near you; it is in your mouth and in your heart so you may obey it. x

15See, I set before you today life y and prosperity, z death a and destruction. b 16For I command you today to love c the LORD your God, to walk in his ways, and to keep his commands, decrees and laws; then you will live d and increase, and the LORD your God will bless you in the land you are entering to possess.

17But if your heart turns away and you are not obedient, and if you are drawn away to bow down to other gods and worship them, 18I declare to you this day that you will certainly be destroyed. e You will not live long in the land you are crossing the Jordan to enter and possess.

19This day I call heaven and earth as witnesses against you f that I have set be-

fore you life and death, blessings and curses. g Now choose life, so that you and your children may live 20and that you may love h the LORD your God, listen to his voice, and hold fast to him. For the LORD is your life, i and he will give j you many years in the land k he swore to give to your fathers, Abraham, Isaac and Jacob.

Joshua to Succeed Moses

31 Then Moses went out and spoke these words to all Israel: 2"I am now a hundred and twenty years old l and I am no longer able to lead you. m The LORD has said to me, 'You shall not cross the Jordan.' n 3The LORD your God himself will cross o over ahead of you. p He will destroy these nations q before you, and you will take possession of their land. Joshua also will cross r over ahead of you, as the LORD said. 4And the LORD will do to them what he did to Sihon and Og, s the kings of the Amorites, whom he destroyed along with their land. 5The LORD will deliver t them to you, and you must do to them all that I have commanded you. 6Be strong and courageous. u Do not be afraid or terrified v because of them, for the LORD your God goes with you; w he will never leave you x nor forsake y you."

7Then Moses summoned Joshua and said z to him in the presence of all Israel, "Be strong and courageous, for you must go with this people into the land that the LORD swore to their forefathers to give them, a and you must divide it among them as their inheritance. 8The LORD himself goes before you and will be with you; b he will never leave you nor forsake you. c Do not be afraid; do not be discouraged."

The Reading of the Law

9So Moses wrote d down this law and

Cross references (center column)

30:7 nDt 7:15
30:9 oJer 1:10; 24:6; 31:28; 32:41; 42:10; 45:4 pS Dt 28:63
30:10 qS Dt 28:61 rS Dt 4:29
30:11 sPs 19:8; Isa 45:19,23; 63:1
30:12 tPr 30:4 uRo 10:6*
30:13 vJob 28:14 wRo 10:7*
30:14 xS Dt 6:6; Ro 10:8*
30:15 yPr 10:16; 11:19; 12:28; Jer 21:8 zDt 28:11; Ps 25:13; 106:5; Pr 3:1-2 aS Ge 2:17 bS Dt 11:26
30:16 cDt 6:5 dver 19; Dt 4:1; 32:47; Ne 9:29
30:18 eS Dt 8:19
30:19 fDt 4:26

gS Dt 11:26
30:20 hDt 6:5 iDt 4:1; S 8:3; 32:47; Ps 27:1; Pr 3:22; S Jn 5:26; Ac 17:28 jGe 12:7 kPs 37:3
31:2 lS Ex 7:7 mNu 27:17; 1Ki 3:7 nS Dt 3:23,26
31:3 oNu 27:18 pS Dt 9:3 qS Dt 7:1 rS Dt 3:28
31:4 sS Nu 21:33
31:5 tS Dt 2:33
31:6 uver 7,23; Jos 1:6,9,18; 10:25; 1Ch 22:13; 28:20; 2Ch 32:7 vJer 1:8,17; Eze 2:6 wS Ge 28:15; S Dt 1:29; 20:4; S Mt 28:20 xPs 56:9; 118:6 yS Dt 4:31; 1Sa 12:22; 1Ki 6:13; Ps 94:14; Isa 41:17; Heb 13:5*
31:7 zver 23; Nu 27:23 aJos 1:6
31:8 bS Ex 13:21 cS Ge 28:15;

S Dt 4:31 31:9 dS Ex 17:14

30:9 your fathers. The patriarchs (see v. 20).

30:10 Book of the Law. See note on 31:24.

30:12,14 It is not up in heaven . . . the word is very near you. Moses declares that understanding, believing and obeying the covenant were not beyond them. Paul applies this passage to the availability of the "word of faith" (Ro 10:6–10).

30:19 I call heaven and earth as witnesses. The typical ancient covenant outside the OT contained a list of gods who served as "witnesses" to its provisions. The covenant in Deuteronomy was "witnessed" by heaven and earth (see 31:28; 32:1; see also notes on Ps 50:1; Isa 1:2).

30:20 hold fast. See note on 10:20. the LORD is your life. When they chose the Lord, they chose life (v. 19). In 32:46–47 "all the words of this law" are said to be their life. The law, the Lord and life are bound together. "Life" in this context refers to all that makes life rich, full and produc-

tive—as God created it to be.

31:2 no longer able to lead. Not a reference to physical disability (see 34:7). The Lord did not allow Moses to lead the people into Canaan because of his sin (see 1:37; 3:23–27; 4:21–22; 32:48–52; Nu 20:2–13).

31:4 what he did to Sihon and Og. See 2:26–3:11.

31:6 Be strong and courageous. The Lord's exhortation, often through his servants, to the people of Israel (Jos 10:25), to Joshua (vv. 7,23; Jos 1:6–7,9,18), to Solomon (1Ch 22:13; 28:20) and to Hezekiah's military officers (2Ch 32:7). By trusting in the Lord and obeying him, his followers would be victorious in spite of great obstacles. he will never leave you nor forsake you. See v. 8; Jos 1:5; 1Ki 8:57; see also note on Ge 28:15.

31:9 wrote down this law and gave it to the priests. Ancient treaties specified that a copy of the treaty was to be placed before the gods at the religious centers of the nations

gave it to the priests, the sons of Levi, who carried[e] the ark of the covenant of the LORD, and to all the elders of Israel. [10]Then Moses commanded them: "At the end of every seven years, in the year for canceling debts,[f] during the Feast of Tabernacles,[g] [11]when all Israel comes to appear[h] before the LORD your God at the place he will choose,[i] you shall read this law[j] before them in their hearing. [12]Assemble the people—men, women and children, and the aliens living in your towns—so they can listen and learn[k] to fear[l] the LORD your God and follow carefully all the words of this law. [13]Their children,[m] who do not know this law, must hear it and learn to fear the LORD your God as long as you live in the land you are crossing the Jordan to possess."

Israel's Rebellion Predicted

[14]The LORD said to Moses, "Now the day of your death[n] is near. Call Joshua[o] and present yourselves at the Tent of Meeting, where I will commission him.[p]" So Moses and Joshua came and presented themselves at the Tent of Meeting. [q]

[15]Then the LORD appeared at the Tent in a pillar of cloud, and the cloud stood over the entrance to the Tent. [r] [16]And the LORD said to Moses: "You are going to rest with your fathers, [s] and these people will soon prostitute[t] themselves to the foreign gods of the land they are entering. They will forsake[u] me and break the covenant I made with them. [17]On that day I will become angry[v] with them and forsake[w] them; I will hide[x] my face[y] from them, and they will be destroyed. Many disasters[z] and difficulties will come upon them, and on that day they will ask, 'Have not these disasters come upon us because our God is not with us?'[a] [18]And I will certainly hide my face on that day because of all their wickedness in turning to other gods.

[19]"Now write[b] down for yourselves this song and teach it to the Israelites and have them sing it, so that it may be a witness[c] for me against them. [20]When I have

brought them into the land flowing with milk and honey, the land I promised on oath to their forefathers, [d] and when they eat their fill and thrive, they will turn to other gods[e] and worship them,[f] rejecting me and breaking my covenant.[g] [21]And when many disasters and difficulties come upon them, [h] this song will testify against them, because it will not be forgotten by their descendants. I know what they are disposed to do,[i] even before I bring them into the land I promised them on oath." [22]So Moses wrote[j] down this song that day and taught it to the Israelites.

[23]The LORD gave this command[k] to Joshua son of Nun: "Be strong and courageous, [l] for you will bring the Israelites into the land I promised them on oath, and I myself will be with you."

[24]After Moses finished writing[m] in a book the words of this law[n] from beginning to end, [25]he gave this command to the Levites who carried[o] the ark of the covenant of the LORD: [26]"Take this Book of the Law and place it beside the ark of the covenant of the LORD your God. There it will remain as a witness against you.[p] [27]For I know how rebellious[q] and stiff-necked[r] you are. If you have been rebellious against the LORD while I am still alive and with you, how much more will you rebel after I die! [28]Assemble before me all the elders of your tribes and all your officials, so that I can speak these words in their hearing and call heaven and earth to testify against them. [s] [29]For I know that after my death you are sure to become utterly corrupt[t] and to turn from the way I have commanded you. In days to come, disaster[u] will fall upon you because you will do evil in the sight of the LORD and provoke him to anger by what your hands have made."

The Song of Moses

[30]And Moses recited the words of this

31:9 ever 25; 1Ch 15:2
31:10 /S Dt 15:1 sS Ex 23:16; Dt 16:13
31:11 hS Dt 16:16 /Dt 12:5 /Jos 8:34-35; 2Ki 23:2; Ne 8:2
31:12 kDt 4:10 /Hag 1:12; Mal 1:6; 3:5,16
31:13 mS Dt 11:2
31:14 nS Ge 25:8; S Nu 27:13 oNu 27:23; Dt 34:9; Jos 1:1-9 pS Nu 27:19 qEx 33:9-11
31:15 rS Ex 33:9
31:16 sS Ge 15:15 tS Ex 34:15; Dt 4:25-28; Jdg 2:12 uJdg 10:6,13; 1Ki 9:9; 18:18; 19:10; Jer 2:13; 5:19; 19:4
31:17 vDt 32:16; Jdg 2:14,20; 10:7; 2Ki 13:3; 22:13; Ps 106:29, 40; Jer 7:18; 21:5; 36:7 wJdg 6:13; 2Ch 15:2; 24:20; Ezr 8:22; Ps 44:9; Isa 2:6 xDt 32:20; Isa 1:15; 45:15; 53:3; 54:8 yJob 13:24; Ps 13:1; 27:9; 30:7; 104:29; Isa 50:6; Jer 33:5; Eze 39:29; Mic 3:4 zJer 4:20; Eze 7:26 aNu 14:42; Hos 9:12
31:19 bver 22 cS Ge 31:50
31:20 dDt 6:10-12 ePs 4:2; 16:4; 40:4; Jer 13:25; Da 3:28; Am 2:4 /Dt 8:19; 11:16-17 gver 16
31:21 hS Dt 4:30 /1Ch 28:9; Hos 5:3; Jn 2:24-25
31:22 /ver 19
31:23 kS ver 7 /Jos 1:6
31:24 mDt 17:18; 2Ki 22:8 nDt 28:58
31:25 oS ver 9
31:26 pver 19
31:27 qS Ex 23:21

rS Dt 9:27 31:28 sDt 4:26; 30:19; 32:1; Job 20:27; Isa 26:21 31:29 tS Dt 4:16; Rev 9:20 uKi 9:9; 22:23; 2Ki 22:16

involved. For Israel, that meant to place it in the ark of the covenant (see 33:9; see also notes on Ex 16:34; 31:18).
31:10 every seven years. See 15:4 and note; Ex 23:10–11; Lev 25:17; see also chart on "OT Feasts and Other Sacred Days," p. 176.
31:11 place he will choose. See note on 12:5. read this law before them. Reading the law to the Israelites (and teaching it to them) was one of the main duties of the priests (see 33:10; Mal 2:4–9).
31:14 I will commission him. See v. 23; cf. Nu 27:18–23.
31:19 write down . . . this song and teach it. See v. 22; 31:30–32:43.

31:23 Be strong and courageous. See note on v. 6.
31:24 words of this law from beginning to end. The book of Deuteronomy up to this place (see note on v. 9).
31:26 place it beside the ark. See note on v. 9.
31:27 stiff-necked. See 9:6,13; 10:16; see also note on Ex 32:9.
31:28 heaven and earth to testify. See note on 30:19.
31:29 what your hands have made. A reference to idols (see 4:28; 27:15 and note).
31:30—32:43 The song of Moses (see notes on Ex 15:1–18; Rev 15:3).

song from beginning to end in the hearing
of the whole assembly of Israel:

32 Listen,[v] O heavens,[w] and I will
speak;
hear, O earth, the words of my
mouth.[x]
[2]Let my teaching fall like rain[y]
and my words descend like dew,[z] [a]
like showers[b] on new grass,
like abundant rain on tender plants.

[3]I will proclaim[c] the name of the
LORD.[d]
Oh, praise the greatness[e] of our God!
[4]He is the Rock,[f] his works are
perfect,[g]
and all his ways are just.
A faithful God[h] who does no wrong,
upright[i] and just is he.[j]

[5]They have acted corruptly toward him;
to their shame they are no longer his
children,
but a warped and crooked
generation.[o] [k]
[6]Is this the way you repay[l] the LORD,
O foolish[m] and unwise people?[n]
Is he not your Father,[o] your Creator,[p]
who made you and formed you?[p]

[7]Remember the days of old;[q]
consider the generations long past.[r]
Ask your father and he will tell you,
your elders, and they will explain to
you.[s]
[8]When the Most High[t] gave the nations
their inheritance,
when he divided all mankind,[u]
he set up boundaries[v] for the peoples
according to the number of the sons
of Israel.[q] [w]
[9]For the LORD's portion[x] is his people,
Jacob his allotted inheritance.[y]

[10]In a desert[z] land he found him,
in a barren and howling waste.[a]
He shielded[b] him and cared for him;
he guarded him as the apple of his
eye,[c]
[11]like an eagle that stirs up its nest

and hovers over its young,[d]
that spreads its wings to catch them
and carries them on its pinions.[e]
[12]The LORD alone led[f] him;[g]
no foreign god was with him.[h]

[13]He made him ride on the heights[i] of
the land
and fed him with the fruit of the
fields.
He nourished him with honey from the
rock,[j]
and with oil[k] from the flinty crag,
[14]with curds and milk from herd and
flock
and with fattened lambs and goats,
with choice rams of Bashan[l]
and the finest kernels of wheat.[m]
You drank the foaming blood of the
grape.[n]

[15]Jeshurun[r] [o] grew fat[p] and kicked;
filled with food, he became heavy
and sleek.
He abandoned[q] the God who made
him
and rejected the Rock[r] his Savior.
[16]They made him jealous[s] with their
foreign gods
and angered[t] him with their
detestable idols.
[17]They sacrificed[u] to demons,[v] which are
not God—
gods they had not known,[w]
gods that recently appeared,[x]
gods your fathers did not fear.
[18]You deserted the Rock, who fathered
you;
you forgot[y] the God who gave you
birth.

32:1 [v]Ps 49:1; Mic 1:2 [w]Jer 2:12 [x]S Dt 4:26
32:2 [y]2Sa 23:4 [z]Ps 107:20; Isa 9:8; 55:11 [a]Mic 5:7 [b]Ps 65:10; 68:9; 72:6; 147:8
32:3 [c]Ps 118:17; 145:6 [d]Ex 33:19; 34:5-6 [e]S Dt 3:24
32:4 [f]S Ge 49:24 [g]2Sa 22:31; Ps 18:30; 19:7 [h]S Dt 4:35 [i]Ps 92:15 [j]S Ge 18:25
32:5 [k]ver 20; Mt 17:17; Lk 9:41; Ac 2:40
32:6 [l]Ps 116:12 [m]Ps 94:8; Jer 5:21 [n]ver 28 [o]S Ex 4:22; 2Sa 7:24 [p]ver 15
32:7 [q]Ps 44:1; 74:2; 77:5; Isa 51:9; 63:9 [r]Dt 4:32; Job 8:8; 20:4; Ps 78:4; Isa 46:9 [s]S Ex 10:2; Job 15:18
32:8 [t]Ps 7:8 [u]S Ge 11:8; Ac 8:1 [v]Ps 74:17 [w]Nu 23:9; Dt 33:12,28; Jer 23:6
32:9 [x]Ps 16:5; 73:26; 119:57; 142:5; Jer 10:16 [y]S Dt 9:29; S 1Sa 26:19
32:10 [z]S Dt 1:19 [a]Dt 8:15; Job 12:24; Ps 107:40 [b]Ps 32:10; Jer 31:22 [c]Ps 17:8; Pr 7:2; Hos 13:5; Zec 2:8
32:11 [d]S Ex 19:4 [e]Ps 17:8; 18:10-19; 61:4
32:12 [f]Ps 106:9; Isa 63:13; Jer 31:32 [g]Dt 4:35 [h]ver 39; Jdg 2:12; Ps 18:31; 81:9; Isa 43:12; 45:5
32:13 [i]Dt 33:29; 2Sa 22:34; Ps 18:33; Isa 33:16; 58:14; Eze 36:2; Hab 3:19 [j]S Dt 8:8 [k]Dt 33:24; Job 29:6
32:14 [l]S Nu 21:33 [m]Ps 65:9; 81:16;
147:14 [n]S Ge 49:11 **32:15** [o]Dt 33:5,26; Isa 44:2 [p]Dt 31:20; Jer 5:28 [q]Dt 31:16; Isa 1:4,28; 58:2; 65:11; Jer 15:6; Eze 14:5 [r]S Ge 49:24 **32:16** [s]S Nu 25:11; S 1Co 10:22 [t]S Dt 31:17; S 1Ki 14:9 **32:17** [u]S Ex 32:8 [v]S Ex 22:20; 1Co 10:20 [w]S Dt 28:64 [x]Jdg 5:8 **32:18** [y]Jdg 3:7; 1Sa 12:9; Ps 44:17,20; 106:21; Jer 2:32; Eze 23:35; Hos 8:14; 13:6

[o]5 Or *Corrupt are they and not his children,* / *a generation warped and twisted to their shame* [p]6 Or *Father, who bought you* [q]8 Masoretic Text; Dead Sea Scrolls (see also Septuagint) *sons of God* [r]15 *Jeshurun* means *the upright one,* that is, Israel.

32:1 *Listen, O heavens.* For similar introductions see Isa 1:2 and note; 34:1; Mic 1:2; 6:1–2.
32:4 *He is the Rock.* A major theme of the song of Moses (see vv. 4,15,18,30–31; see also note on Ge 49:24).
32:5 *warped and crooked generation.* See Php 2:15.
32:6 *Father.* See Isa 63:16; 64:8.
32:7 *Remember the days of old.* See note on 4:10.
32:8 *Most High.* The only occurrence in Deuteronomy of this name for God (see note on Ge 14:19). It emphasizes the Lord's sovereignty over all creation. *gave the nations their inheritance.* See Ge 10. *according to the number of the sons of Israel.* Perhaps referring to the Lord's grant of Canaan to Israel as sufficient to sustain their expected population (see

note on Ge 10:2).
32:10 *apple of his eye.* Lit. "little man of his eye," referring to the pupil, a delicate part of the eye that is essential for vision and that therefore must be protected at all costs.
32:11 *hovers over.* See note on Ge 1:2.
32:13 *honey from the rock.* See Ps 81:16. In Canaan, bees sometimes built their hives in clefts of rocks (cf. Isa 7:18–19). *oil from the flinty crag.* Olive trees often grew on rocky hillsides, as on the Mount of Olives east of Jerusalem.
32:14 *Bashan.* See note on Eze 39:18. *foaming blood of the grape.* Wine (see Ge 49:11).
32:15 *Jeshurun.* See NIV text note; see also Isa 44:2 and note. *Rock.* See v. 18 and note on v. 4.

¹⁹The Lord saw this and rejected them ^z
    because he was angered by his sons
    and daughters. ^a
²⁰"I will hide my face ^b from them," he
    said,
    "and see what their end will be;
for they are a perverse generation, ^c
    children who are unfaithful. ^d
²¹They made me jealous ^e by what is no
    god
    and angered me with their worthless
    idols. ^f
I will make them envious by those who
    are not a people;
I will make them angry by a nation
    that has no understanding. ^g
²²For a fire has been kindled by my
    wrath, ^h
    one that burns to the realm of death ^s
    below. ⁱ
It will devour ^j the earth and its
    harvests ^k
and set afire the foundations of the
    mountains. ^l

²³"I will heap calamities ^m upon them
    and spend my arrows ⁿ against them.
²⁴I will send wasting famine ^o against
    them,
    consuming pestilence ^p and deadly
    plague; ^q
I will send against them the fangs of
    wild beasts, ^r
    the venom of vipers ^s that glide in the
    dust. ^t
²⁵In the street the sword will make them
    childless;
    in their homes terror ^u will reign. ^v
Young men and young women will
    perish,
    infants and gray-haired men. ^w
²⁶I said I would scatter ^x them
    and blot out their memory from
    mankind, ^y
²⁷but I dreaded the taunt of the enemy,
    lest the adversary misunderstand ^z
and say, 'Our hand has triumphed;
    the Lord has not done all this.' " ^a

²⁸They are a nation without sense,
    there is no discernment ^b in them.
²⁹If only they were wise and would
    understand this ^c
    and discern what their end will be! ^d

³⁰How could one man chase a thousand,
    or two put ten thousand to flight, ^e
unless their Rock had sold them, ^f
    unless the Lord had given them
    up? ^g
³¹For their rock is not like our Rock, ^h
    as even our enemies concede. ⁱ
³²Their vine comes from the vine of
    Sodom ^j
    and from the fields of Gomorrah.
Their grapes are filled with poison, ^k
    and their clusters with bitterness. ^l
³³Their wine is the venom of serpents,
    the deadly poison of cobras. ^m

³⁴"Have I not kept this in reserve
    and sealed it in my vaults? ⁿ
³⁵It is mine to avenge; ^o I will repay. ^p
    In due time their foot will slip; ^q
    their day of disaster is near
    and their doom rushes upon them. ^r "

³⁶The Lord will judge his people ^s
    and have compassion ^t on his
    servants ^u
when he sees their strength is gone
    and no one is left, slave ^v or free.
³⁷He will say: "Now where are their
    gods,
    the rock they took refuge in, ^w
³⁸the gods who ate the fat of their
    sacrifices
    and drank the wine of their drink
    offerings? ^x
Let them rise up to help you!
    Let them give you shelter!

³⁹"See now that I myself am He! ^y
    There is no god besides me. ^z
I put to death ^a and I bring to life, ^b
    I have wounded and I will heal, ^c
    and no one can deliver out of my
    hand. ^d

32:19
^zLev 26:30;
Ps 78:59 ^aAm 6:8
32:20 ^bDt 31:17,
29; Ps 4:6; 44:24
^cS ver 5 ^dDt 9:23
32:21
^eS Nu 25:11;
S 1Co 10:22 ^fver
17; 1Ki 16:13,26;
2Ki 17:15;
Ps 31:6; Jer 2:5;
8:19; 10:8;
16:19; Jnh 2:8
^gRo 10:19*
32:22 ^hPs 7:11
ⁱNu 16:31-35;
Ps 18:7-8;
Jer 15:14; La 4:11
^jAm 7:4
^kLev 26:20
^lPs 83:14
32:23
^mDt 29:21 ⁿver
42; 2Sa 22:15;
Job 6:4; Ps 7:13;
18:14; 45:5;
77:17; 120:4;
Isa 5:28; 49:2;
Eze 5:16;
Hab 3:9,11
32:24 ^oGe 26:1;
S 41:55; 42:5;
2Sa 24:13;
1Ch 21:12
^pS Dt 28:22
^qPs 91:6
^rS Ge 37:20 ^sver
33; Job 20:16;
Ps 58:4; Jer 8:17;
Am 5:18-19;
Mic 7:17
^tJob 20:16
32:25 ^uIsa 24:17
^vJer 14:18;
La 1:20;
Eze 7:15; 2Co 7:5
^w2Ch 36:17;
Isa 13:18;
Jer 4:31; La 2:21
32:26 ^xDt 4:27
^yS Nu 14:12;
Job 18:17;
Ps 34:16; 37:28;
109:15; Isa 14:20
32:27
^zDt 9:26-28
^aPs 140:8;
Isa 10:13;
Jer 40:2-3
32:28 ^bIsa 1:3;
5:13; 27:11;
Jer 8:7
32:29 ^cDt 5:29;
Ps 81:13
^dIsa 47:7; La 1:9

32:30
^eS Lev 26:8
^fJdg 2:14; 3:8;
4:2; 10:7;
1Sa 12:9
^gNu 21:34;
1Sa 23:7; Ps 31:8;
44:12; 106:41;
Isa 50:1; 54:6
32:31
^hS Ge 49:24
ⁱS Ex 14:25
32:32 ^jJer 23:14
^kJob 6:4; 20:16
^lDt 29:18
32:33 ^mS ver 24

32:34 ⁿJob 14:17; Jer 2:22; Hos 13:12 **32:35** ^oS ver 41;
S Ge 4:24; S Jer 51:6 ^pS Ge 30:2; S Ex 32:34; S Ps 54:5;
S Ro 12:19*; Heb 10:30* ^qPs 17:5; 35:6; 37:31; 38:16;
66:9; 73:2,18; 94:18; 121:3; Pr 4:19; Jer 23:12 ^rEze 7:8-9
32:36 ^sHeb 10:30* ^tAm 7:3 ^uEze 46:43-45; Dt 30:1-3;
Jdg 2:18; Ps 90:13; 102:13; 103:13; 106:45; 135:14;
Joel 2:14 ^v1Ki 14:10; 21:21; 2Ki 9:8 **32:37** ^wJdg 10:14;
Jer 2:28; 11:12 **32:38** ^xNu 25:1-2; Jer 11:12; 44:8,25 **32:39**
^yIsa 41:4; 43:10; 44:7; 46:4; 48:12 ^zS ver 12 ^a1Sa 2:6
^b1Sa 2:6; 2Ki 5:7; Ps 68:20; Jn 11:25-26 ^cEx 15:26;
Job 5:18; 15:11; Ps 147:3; Isa 6:10; 19:22; 30:26; 53:5;
57:18; Jer 33:6; Hos 6:1; Mal 4:2; 1Pe 2:24 ^dJob 9:12; 10:7;
Ps 7:2; 50:22; Isa 43:13; Da 4:35; Hos 5:14

^s22 Hebrew *to Sheol*

32:21 Quoted in part in Ro 10:19 to illustrate Israel's
failure to understand the good news about Christ.
32:22 *realm of death below.* See note on Ge 37:35.
32:30 *their Rock.* Israel's God.
32:31 *their rock.* The god of Israel's enemy.
32:34 *sealed it in my vaults.* The Lord's plans for the future
are fixed and certain. Sin will be punished in due time.

32:35—36 Quoted in part in Heb 10:30 as a warning
against rejecting the Son of God.
32:35 *It is mine to avenge; I will repay.* Quoted in Ro
12:19 to affirm that avenging is God's prerogative.
32:39 *no god besides me.* See note on 4:35. *I put to death
and I bring to life.* See Isa 45:7 and note.

⁴⁰I lift my hand^e to heaven and declare:
　As surely as I live forever,^f
⁴¹when I sharpen my flashing sword^g
　and my hand grasps it in judgment,
　I will take vengeance^h on my
　　adversaries
　and repay those who hate me.ⁱ
⁴²I will make my arrows drunk with
　　blood,^j
　while my sword devours flesh:^k
　the blood of the slain and the captives,
　the heads of the enemy leaders."

⁴³Rejoice,^l O nations, with his people,^{t,u}
　for he will avenge the blood of his
　　servants;^m
　he will take vengeance on his enemiesⁿ
　and make atonement for his land and
　　people.^o

⁴⁴Moses came with Joshua^{v,p} son of
Nun and spoke all the words of this song in
the hearing of the people. ⁴⁵When Moses
finished reciting all these words to all Israel, ⁴⁶he said to them, "Take to heart all
the words I have solemnly declared to you
this day,^q so that you may command^r
your children to obey carefully all the
words of this law. ⁴⁷They are not just idle
words for you—they are your life.^s By
them you will live long^t in the land you
are crossing the Jordan to possess."

Moses to Die on Mount Nebo

⁴⁸On that same day the LORD told
Moses,^u ⁴⁹"Go up into the Abarim^v Range
to Mount Nebo^w in Moab, across from
Jericho,^x and view Canaan,^y the land I
am giving the Israelites as their own
possession. ⁵⁰There on the mountain that
you have climbed you will die^z and be
gathered to your people, just as your broth-
er Aaron died^a on Mount Hor^b and was
gathered to his people. ⁵¹This is because
both of you broke faith with me in the
presence of the Israelites at the waters of
Meribah Kadesh^c in the Desert of Zin^d
and because you did not uphold my holi-
ness among the Israelites.^e ⁵²Therefore,

32:40
^eS Ge 14:22
^fS Ge 21:33;
Rev 1:18
32:41 ^gJdg 7:20;
Ps 7:12; 45:3;
Isa 27:1; 34:6;
66:16; Jer 12:12;
Eze 21:9-10 ^hver
35; Ps 149:7;
Jer 46:10; Na 1:2
ⁱPs 137:8;
Jer 25:14; 50:29;
51:24,56
32:42 ^jS ver 23
^k2Sa 2:26;
Jer 12:12; 44:1;
46:10,14
32:43 ^lPs 137:6;
Isa 25:9; 65:18;
66:10; Ro 15:10*
^m2Ki 9:7;
S Rev 6:10
ⁿIsa 1:24; Jer 9:9
^oPs 65:3; 79:9
32:44 ^pNu 13:8,
16
32:46 ^qS Dt 6:6;
Jn 1:17; 7:19
^rDt 6:7
32:47
^sS Dt 30:20
32:48 ^tS Ex 23:26;
Dt 33:25;
Isa 65:22
32:48 ^uNu 27:12
32:49 ^vNu 27:12
^wS Nu 32:3
^xS Nu 22:1
^yS Lev 14:34
32:50
^zS Ge 25:8;
S Nu 27:13
^aNu 20:29
^bS Nu 20:22
32:51 ^cEze 47:19
^dS Nu 13:21;
20:11-13
^eNu 27:14

32:52 ^fDt 34:1-3
^gS Dt 3:27
33:1 ^hS Ge 27:4
ⁱJos 14:6;
1Sa 2:27; 9:6;
1Ki 12:22; 13:1;
2Ki 1:9-13; 5:8;
Jer 35:4
33:2 ^jEx 19:18;
Ps 68:8
^kJos 11:17;
Jdg 5:4 ^lPs 50:2;
80:1; 94:1
^mS Nu 10:12
ⁿPs 89:7;
Da 4:13; 7:10;
8:13; Zec 14:5;
Ac 7:53;
Gal 3:19;
Heb 2:2; Rev 5:11
33:3 ^oS Dt 4:37
^pDt 7:6
^qLk 10:39;
Rev 4:10
33:4 ^rDt 4:2;
Jn 1:17; 7:19

---

you will see the land only from a dis-
tance;^f you will not enter^g the land I am
giving to the people of Israel."

Moses Blesses the Tribes

33:1–29Ref — Ge 49:1–28

33 This is the blessing^h that Moses
　the man of Godⁱ pronounced on
the Israelites before his death. ²He said:

"The LORD came from Sinai^j
　and dawned over them from Seir;^k
　he shone forth^l from Mount Paran.^m
He came with^w myriads of holy onesⁿ
　from the south, from his mountain
　　slopes.^x
³Surely it is you who love^o the people;
　all the holy ones are in your hand.^p
At your feet they all bow down,^q
　and from you receive instruction,
⁴the law that Moses gave us,^r
　the possession of the assembly of
　　Jacob.^s
⁵He was king^t over Jeshurun^{y u}
　when the leaders of the people
　　assembled,
　along with the tribes of Israel.

⁶"Let Reuben live and not die,
　nor^z his men be few."^v

⁷And this he said about Judah:^w

"Hear, O LORD, the cry of Judah;
　bring him to his people.
With his own hands he defends his
　　cause.
　Oh, be his help against his foes!"

⁸About Levi^x he said:

"Your Thummim and Urim^y belong

---

^sPs 119:111 **33:5** ^tS Ex 16:8; 1Sa 10:19; Ps 10:16; 149:2
^uS Nu 23:21; S Dt 32:15 **33:6** ^vS Ge 34:5 **33:7** ^wS Ge 49:10
33:8 ^xS Ge 29:34 ^yEx 28:30

^t43 Or *Make his people rejoice, O nations*
^u44 Masoretic Text; Dead Sea Scrolls (see also
Septuagint) *people, / and let all the angels worship him /*
^v44 Hebrew *Hoshea,* a variant of *Joshua*   ^w2 Or *from*
^x2 The meaning of the Hebrew for this phrase is
uncertain.   ^y5 *Jeshurun* means *the upright one,* that is,
Israel; also in verse 26.   ^z6 *or but let*

32:43 *Rejoice, O nations, with his people.* One of the
Dead Sea Scrolls adds a clause in Deuteronomy (see NIV text
note), and the clause is quoted in Heb 1:6.
32:47 *they are your life.* See note on 30:20.
32:50 *gathered to your people.* See note on Ge 25:8.
Aaron died on Mount Hor. See 10:6; Nu 20:22–29.
32:51 *you broke faith with me.* See 1:37; 3:23–26;
4:21–22; 31:2; Nu 20:12. *Meribah Kadesh in the Desert of
Zin.* See 33:8; see also notes on Ex 17:7; Nu 20:13.
33:1 *blessing.* See Ge 12:1–3; 22:15–18; 27:27–29;
28:10–15; 49:1–28. Moses' blessings on the tribes (vv.
6–25) should be compared particularly with Jacob's blessings
on his sons in Ge 49. *man of God.* The first occurrence of this

title. It appears next in Jos 14:6 (also of Moses; see Ps 90
title). Later it designates other messengers of God (see note
on 1Sa 2:27).
33:2 *Sinai . . . Seir . . . Paran.* Mountains associated with
the giving of the law (see Ge 21:21 and note; Jdg 5:4–5; Hab
3:3). *holy ones.* Angels.
33:3 *holy ones.* Israelites (see 7:6; 14:2; 26:19; 28:9).
33:5 *king.* The Lord, not an earthly monarch, was to be
king over Israel (see Jdg 8:23 and note). *Jeshurun.* See NIV
text note; see also Isa 44:2 and note.
33:8 *Thummim and Urim.* See note on Ex 28:30. *Massah.*
See 6:16; 9:22; see also note on Ex 17:7. *Meribah.* See
32:51; see also note on Ex 17:7.

to the man you favored. [z]
You tested[a] him at Massah;
  you contended with him at the
    waters of Meribah. [b]
[9]He said of his father and mother, [c]
  'I have no regard for them.'
He did not recognize his brothers
  or acknowledge his own children,
but he watched over your word
  and guarded your covenant. [d]
[10]He teaches[e] your precepts to Jacob
  and your law to Israel.[f]
He offers incense before you[g]
  and whole burnt offerings on your
    altar. [h]
[11]Bless all his skills, O LORD,
  and be pleased with the work of his
    hands. [i]
Smite the loins of those who rise up
    against him;
  strike his foes till they rise no more.''

[12]About Benjamin[j] he said:

"Let the beloved of the LORD rest
    secure in him, [k]
  for he shields him all day long, [l]
  and the one the LORD loves[m] rests
    between his shoulders. [n]''

[13]About Joseph[o] he said:

"May the LORD bless his land
  with the precious dew from heaven
    above
  and with the deep waters that lie
    below;[p]
[14]with the best the sun brings forth
  and the finest the moon can yield;
[15]with the choicest gifts of the ancient
    mountains[q]
  and the fruitfulness of the everlasting
    hills;
[16]with the best gifts of the earth and its
    fullness
  and the favor of him who dwelt in
    the burning bush. [r]
Let all these rest on the head of Joseph,
  on the brow of the prince among[a]
    his brothers. [s]

[17]In majesty he is like a firstborn bull;
  his horns[t] are the horns of a wild
    ox. [u]
With them he will gore[v] the nations,
  even those at the ends of the earth.
Such are the ten thousands of
    Ephraim;[w]
such are the thousands of
    Manasseh. [x] ''

[18]About Zebulun[y] he said:

"Rejoice, Zebulun, in your going out,
  and you, Issachar, [z] in your tents.
[19]They will summon peoples to the
    mountain[a]
  and there offer sacrifices of
    righteousness; [b]
they will feast on the abundance of the
    seas, [c]
  on the treasures hidden in the sand.''

[20]About Gad[d] he said:

"Blessed is he who enlarges Gad's
    domain! [e]
Gad lives there like a lion,
  tearing at arm or head.
[21]He chose the best land for himself;[f]
  the leader's portion was kept for
    him.[g]
When the heads of the people
    assembled,
  he carried out the LORD's righteous
    will, [h]
  and his judgments concerning Israel.''

[22]About Dan[i] he said:

"Dan is a lion's cub,
  springing out of Bashan.''

[23]About Naphtali[j] he said:

"Naphtali is abounding with the favor of
    the LORD
  and is full of his blessing;
he will inherit southward to the
    lake.''

[24]About Asher[k] he said:

Cross references (center column):

33:8 [z]Ps 106:16
[a]S Nu 14:22
[b]S Ex 17:7
33:9
[c]Ex 32:26-29
[d]Ps 61:5; Mal 2:5
33:10 [e]Ezr 7:10;
Ne 8:18;
Ps 119:151;
Jer 23:22; Mal 2:6
[f]S Lev 10:11;
Dt 17:8-11;
31:9-13
[g]S Ex 30:7;
Lev 16:12-13
[h]Ps 51:19
33:11
[i]2Sa 24:23;
Ps 20:3; 51:19
33:12
[j]S Ge 35:18
[k]Dt 4:37-38;
12:10; S 32:8
[l]S Nu 19:4
[m]Ps 60:5; 127:2;
Isa 5:1
[n]S Ex 28:12
33:13
[o]S Ge 30:24
[p]Ge 27:28;
Ps 148:7
33:15 [q]Hab 3:6
33:16 [r]S Ex 3:2
[s]S Ge 37:8

33:17 [t]1Sa 2:10;
2Sa 22:3;
Eze 34:21
[u]S Nu 23:22
[v]1Ki 22:11;
Ps 44:5
[w]S Ge 41:52
[x]S Ge 41:51
33:18
[y]S Ge 30:20
[z]S Ge 30:18
33:19
[a]S Ex 15:17;
Ps 48:1; Isa 2:3;
65:11; 66:20;
Jer 31:6 [b]Ps 4:5;
51:19 [c]Isa 18:7;
23:18; 45:14;
60:5,11; 61:6;
Hag 2:7;
Zec 14:14
33:20 [d]Ge 30:11
[e]Dt 3:12-17
33:21
[f]Nu 32:1-5,31-32
[g]S Nu 34:14
[h]Jos 22:1-3
33:22 [i]Ge 49:16;
S Nu 1:38
33:23 [j]S Ge 30:8
33:24
[k]S Ge 30:13

[a]16 Or of the one separated from

33:9 *he watched over your word.* The Levites had charge of the tabernacle with its ark, in which the Book of the Law was placed (see note on 31:9).
33:10 *teaches your precepts to Jacob.* See note on 31:11.
33:13 *About Joseph.* Moses included the blessing on the two tribes of Ephraim and Manasseh (v. 17), Joseph's sons, with that of Joseph himself. *dew from heaven ... deep waters.* See note on Ge 49:25.
33:15-16 See Ge 49:26 and note.
33:16 *best gifts of the earth.* Under the Lord's blessing, Joseph's land in the central part of Canaan was to be unusually fertile and productive. *who dwelt in the burning bush.* See Ex 3:1-6.

33:19 *abundance of the seas ... treasures hidden in the sand.* References to maritime wealth (see note on Ge 49:13).
33:21 *He chose the best land.* For his livestock (see 3:12-20).
33:22 *springing out of Bashan.* The lion's cub, not Dan, is the subject. Another possible translation is "keeping away from the viper." Although someday he would be like a viper himself (see Ge 49:17), the early history of Dan pictured him as being somewhat more timid.
33:23 *lake.* The Sea of Galilee. Naphtali's area extended from north of the Waters of Merom to south of the Sea of Galilee.

"Most blessed of sons is Asher;
   let him be favored by his brothers,
   and let him bathe his feet in oil. *l*
25The bolts of your gates will be iron and
   bronze, *m*
   and your strength will equal your
   days. *n*

26"There is no one like the God of
   Jeshurun, *o*
   who rides *p* on the heavens to help
   you *q*
   and on the clouds *r* in his majesty. *s*
27The eternal *t* God is your refuge, *u*
   and underneath are the everlasting *v*
   arms.
He will drive out your enemy before
   you, *w*
   saying, 'Destroy him!' *x*
28So Israel will live in safety alone; *y*
   Jacob's spring is secure
in a land of grain and new wine,
   where the heavens drop dew. *z*
29Blessed are you, O Israel! *a*
   Who is like you, *b*
   a people saved by the Lord? *c*
He is your shield and helper *d*
   and your glorious sword.
Your enemies will cower before you,
   and you will trample down their high
   places. *b e*"

The Death of Moses

34 Then Moses climbed Mount
Nebo *f* from the plains of Moab to
the top of Pisgah, *g* across from Jericho. *h*
There the Lord showed *i* him the whole
land—from Gilead to Dan, *j* 2all of Naphtali, the territory of Ephraim and Manasseh, all the land of Judah as far as the
western sea, *c k* 3the Negev *l* and the
whole region from the Valley of Jericho,
the City of Palms, *m* as far as Zoar. *n* 4Then
the Lord said to him, "This is the land I
promised on oath *o* to Abraham, Isaac and
Jacob *p* when I said, 'I will give it *q* to your
descendants.' I have let you see it with
your eyes, but you will not cross *r* over
into it."

5And Moses the servant of the Lord *s*
died *t* there in Moab, as the Lord had said.
6He buried him *d* in Moab, in the valley
opposite Beth Peor, *u* but to this day no
one knows where his grave is. *v* 7Moses
was a hundred and twenty years old *w*
when he died, yet his eyes were not
weak *x* nor his strength gone. *y* 8The Israelites grieved for Moses in the plains of
Moab *z* thirty days, *a* until the time of
weeping and mourning *b* was over.

9Now Joshua son of Nun was filled with
the spirit *e* of wisdom *c* because Moses had
laid his hands on him. *d* So the Israelites
listened to him and did what the Lord had
commanded Moses.

10Since then, no prophet *e* has risen in
Israel like Moses, *f* whom the Lord knew
face to face, *g* 11who did all those miraculous signs and wonders *h* the Lord sent
him to do in Egypt—to Pharaoh and to all
his officials *i* and to his whole land. 12For
no one has *j* ever shown the mighty power
or performed the awesome deeds *k* that
Moses did in the sight of all Israel.

33:24 *l*S Ge 49:20;
S Dt 32:13
33:25 *m*Ne 3:3;
7:3; Ps 147:13
*n*S Dt 32:47
33:26
*o*S Dt 32:15
*p*Ps 18:10; 68:33
*q*S Dt 10:14;
S Ps 104:3
*r*2Sa 22:10;
Ps 18:9; 68:4;
Da 7:13
*s*S Ex 15:7
33:27 *t*Ex 15:18;
Isa 40:28; 57:15
*u*Ps 9:9; 84:1;
90:1; 91:9
*v*S Ge 21:33
*w*Ex 34:11;
Jos 24:18
*x*S Dt 7:2
33:28
*y*S Ex 33:16;
S Lev 25:18;
S Dt 32:8;
Ps 16:9; Pr 1:33;
Isa 14:30 *z*ver 13;
Ge 27:28
33:29 *a*Ps 1:1;
32:1-2; 144:15
*b*2Sa 22:45;
Ps 18:44; 66:3;
81:15 *c*Dt 4:7
*d*Ge 15:1;
Ex 18:4;
Ps 10:14; 18:1;
27:1,9; 30:10;
54:4; 70:5;
115:9-11; 118:7;
Isa 45:24;
Hos 13:9;
Hab 3:19
*e*S Nu 33:52;
S Dt 32:13
34:1 *f*S Nu 32:3
*g*S Nu 21:20
*h*Dt 32:49
*i*Dt 32:52
*j*S Ge 14:14
34:2 *k*S Ex 23:31
34:3 *l*S Ge 12:9

*m*Jdg 1:16; 3:13;
2Ch 28:15
*n*S Ge 13:10
34:4 *o*Ge 28:13
*p*Jos 21:43
*q*Ge 12:7
*r*S Dt 3:23
34:5 *s*S Nu 12:7
*t*S Ge 25:8
34:6 *u*S Dt 3:29
*v*Jude 1:9

34:7 *w*S Ex 7:7 *x*S Ge 27:1 *y*S Ge 15:15 **34:8** *z*S Nu 21:11
*a*S Ge 37:34; S Dt 1:3 *b*2Sa 11:27 **34:9** *c*S Ge 41:38;
S Ex 28:3; Isa 11:2 *d*S Dt 31:14; Ac 6:6 **34:10** *e*S Ge 20:7
*f*Dt 18:15,18 *g*S Ex 33:11 **34:11** *h*Dt 4:34 *i*S Ex 11:3 **34:12**
*j*Heb 3:1-6 *k*S Dt 4:34

*b*29 Or *will tread upon their bodies*   *c*2 That is, the
Mediterranean   *d*6 Or *He was buried*   *e*9 Or *Spirit*

33:26 *Jeshurun.* See note on 32:15. *rides ... on the clouds.* See note on Ps 68:4.
33:29 *shield.* See note on Ge 15:1. *high places.* See note on 1Ki 3:2.
34:1 *Moses climbed Mount Nebo.* In obedience to the Lord's command in 32:48–52.
34:4 *land I promised.* See 1:8; Ge 12:1; 15:18 and note; Ex 33:1.
34:5 *servant of the Lord.* A special title used to refer to those whom the Lord, as the Great King, has taken into his service; they serve as members of God's royal administration. For example, it was used especially of Abraham (Ge 26:24), Moses (Ex 14:31), Joshua (Jos 24:29), David (2Sa 7:5), the prophets (2Ki 9:7), Israel collectively (Isa 41:8),
and even a foreign king the Lord used to carry out his purposes (Jer 25:9). See notes on Ex 14:31; Isa 42:1–4.
34:6 *Beth Peor.* See note on 3:29.
34:7 *a hundred and twenty years old.* See 31:2; perhaps a round number, indicating three generations of about 40 years each.
34:8 *grieved ... thirty days.* See Ge 50:3 and note.
34:10 *no prophet has risen in Israel like Moses.* See note on 18:15. *face to face.* See Nu 12:8 and note.
34:12 *no one has ever.* Until Jesus came, no one was superior to Moses. See Heb 3:1–6, where Moses the "servant" (Heb 3:5) is contrasted with Christ the "son" (Heb 3:6).

JOSHUA

Title and Theme

Joshua is a story of conquest and fulfillment for the people of God. After many years of slavery in Egypt and 40 years in the desert, the Israelites were finally allowed to enter the land promised to their fathers. Abraham, always a migrant, never possessed the country to which he was sent, but he left to his children the legacy of God's covenant that made them the eventual heirs of all of Canaan (see Ge 15:13,16,18; 17:8). Joshua was destined to turn that promise into reality.

Where Deuteronomy ends, the book of Joshua begins: The tribes of Israel are still camped on the east side of the Jordan River. The narrative opens with God's command to move forward and pass through the river on dry land. Then it relates the series of victories in central, southern and northern Canaan that gave the Israelites control of all the hill country and the Negev. It continues with a description of the tribal allotments and ends with Joshua's final addresses to the people. The theme of the book, therefore, is the establishment of Israel in the promised land.

Earlier in his life Joshua was called simply Hoshea (Nu 13:8,16), meaning "salvation." But later Moses changed his name to Joshua, meaning "The LORD saves" (or "The LORD gives victory"). When this same name (the Greek form of which is Jesus; see NIV text note on Mt 1:21) was given to Mary's firstborn son, it became the most loved of names.

In the Hebrew Bible the book of Joshua initiates a division called the Former Prophets, including also Judges, Samuel and Kings—all historical in content but written from a prophetic standpoint. They do more than merely record the nation's development from Moses to the fall of Judah in 586 B.C. They prophetically interpret God's covenant ways with Israel in history—how he fulfills and remains true to his promises (especially through his servants such as Joshua, the judges, Samuel and David) and how he deals with the waywardness of the Israelites. In Joshua it was the Lord who won the victories and "gave Israel all the land he had sworn to give their forefathers" (21:43).

Author and Date

In the judgment of many scholars Joshua was not written until the end of the period of the kings, some 800 years after the actual events. But there are significant reasons to question this conclusion and to place the time of composition much earlier. The earliest Jewish traditions (Talmud) claim that Joshua wrote his own book except for the final section about his funeral, which is attributed to Eleazar son of Aaron (the last verse must have been added by a later editor).

On at least two occasions the text reports writing at Joshua's command or by Joshua himself. When the tribes received their territories, Joshua instructed his men "to make a survey of the land and write a description of it" (18:8). Then in the last scene of the book, when Joshua led Israel in a renewal of the covenant with the Lord, "he drew up decrees and laws" (24:25). On yet another occasion the one telling the story appears also to have been a participant in the event; he uses the pronouns "we" and "us" (5:1,6).

Moreover, the author's observations are accurate and precise. He is thoroughly at ease with the antiquated names of cities, such as "the Jebusite city" (15:8; 18:16,28) for Jerusalem, Kiriath Arba (14:15; 15:54; 20:7; 21:11) for Hebron, and Greater Sidon (11:8; 19:28) for what later became simply Sidon. Tyre is never mentioned because in the days of Joshua it had not yet developed into a port of major importance.

But if some features suggest Joshua's own lifetime, others point to a time somewhat later. The account of the long day when the sun stood still at Aijalon is substantiated by a quotation from another source, the Book of Jashar (10:13). This would hardly be natural for an eyewitness of the miracle, writing shortly after it happened. Also, there are 12 instances where the phrase "until this day" is employed by the author.

It seems safe to conclude that the book, at least in its early form, dates from the beginning of the monarchy. Some think that Samuel may have had a hand in shaping or compiling the materials of the book, but in fact we are unsure who the final author or editor was.

The Life of Joshua

Joshua's remarkable life was filled with excitement, variety, success and honor. He was known for his deep trust in God and as "a man in whom is the spirit" (Nu 27:18). As a youth he lived through the bitter realities of slavery in Egypt, but he also witnessed the supernatural plagues and the miracle of Israel's escape from the army of the Egyptians when the waters of the sea opened before them. In the Sinai peninsula it was Joshua who led the troops of Israel to victory over the Amalekites (Ex 17:8-13). He alone was allowed to accompany Moses up the holy mountain where the tablets of the law were received (Ex 24:13-14). And it was he who stood watch at the temporary tent of meeting Moses set up before the tabernacle was erected (Ex 33:11).

Joshua was elected to represent his own tribe of Ephraim when the 12 spies were sent into Canaan to look over the land. Only Joshua and his friend Caleb were ready to follow God's will and take immediate possession of the land (see Nu 14:26-34). The rest were condemned to die in the desert. Even Moses died short of the goal and was told to turn everything over to Joshua. God promised to guide and strengthen Joshua, just as he had Moses (Dt 31:23).

Joshua proved to be not only a military strategist in the battles that followed, but also a statesman in the way he governed the tribes. Above all, he was God's chosen servant (see 24:29 and note on Dt 34:5) to bring Moses' work to completion and establish Israel in the promised land. In that role he was a striking OT type (foreshadowing) of Christ (see notes on Heb 4:1,6-8).

Historical Setting

At the time of the Israelite migration into Canaan the superpowers of the ancient Near East were relatively weak. The Hittites had faded from the scene. Neither Babylon nor Egypt could maintain a military presence in Canaan, and the Assyrians would not send in their armies until centuries later.

As the tribes circled east of the Dead Sea, only the stronghold of Edom offered any resistance. Moab was forced to let Israel pass through her territory and camp in her plains. When Og and Sihon, two regional Amorite kings of Transjordan, tried to stop the Israelites, they were easily defeated and their lands occupied.

Biblical archaeologists call this period the Late Bronze Age (1550-1200 B.C.). Today thousands of artifacts give testimony to the richness of the Canaanite material culture, which was in many ways superior to that of the Israelites. When the ruins of the ancient kingdom of Ugarit were discovered at modern Ras Shamra on the northern coast of Syria (see chart on "Ancient Texts Relating to the OT," p. 5), a wealth of new information came to light concerning the domestic, commercial and religious life of the Canaanites. From a language close to Hebrew came stories of ancient kings and gods that revealed their immoral behavior and cruelty. In addition, pagan temples, altars, tombs and ritual vessels have been uncovered, throwing more light on the culture and customs of the peoples surrounding Israel.

Excavations at the ancient sites of Megiddo, Beth Shan and Gezer show how powerfully fortified these cities were and why they were not captured and occupied by Israel in Joshua's day. Many other fortified towns were taken, however, so that Israel became firmly established in the land as the dominant power. Apart from Jericho and Ai, Joshua is reported to have burned only Hazor (11:13), so attempts to date these events by destruction levels in the mounds of Canaan's ancient cities are questionable undertakings. It must also be remembered that other groups were involved in campaigns in the region about this time, among whom were Egyptian rulers and the Sea Peoples (including the Philistines). There had also been much intercity warfare among the Canaanites, and afterward the period of the judges was marked by general turbulence.

Much of the data from archaeology appears to support a date for Joshua's invasion c. 1250 B.C. This fits well with an exodus that would then have taken place 40 years earlier under the famous Rameses II, who ruled from the Nile delta at a city with the same name (Ex 1:11). It also places Joseph in Egypt in a favorable situation. Four hundred years before Rameses II the pharaohs were the Semitic Hyksos, who also ruled from the delta near the land of Goshen.

On the other hand, a good case can be made for the traditional viewpoint that the invasion occurred c. 1406 B.C. The oppression would have taken place under Amunhotep II after the death of his father Thutmose III, who is known to have used slave labor in his building projects. The earlier date also fits

better with the two numbers found in Jdg 11:26 and 1Ki 6:1, since it allows for an additional 150 years between Moses and the monarchy. See also the Introductions to Genesis: Author and Date of Writing; Exodus: Chronology; and Judges: Background.

The Conquest and the Ethical Question of War

Many readers of Joshua (and other OT books) are deeply troubled by the role that warfare plays in this account of God's dealings with his people. Not a few relieve their ethical scruples by ascribing the author's perspective to a pre-Christian (and sub-Christian) stage of moral development that the Christian, in the light of Christ's teaching, must repudiate and transcend. Hence the main thread of the narrative line of Joshua is an offense to them.

It must be remembered, however, that the book of Joshua does not address itself to the abstract ethical question of war as a means for gaining human ends. It can only be understood in the context of the history of redemption unfolding in the Pentateuch, with its interplay of divine grace and judgment. Of that story it is the direct continuation.

Joshua is not an epic account of Israel's heroic generation or the story of Israel's conquest of Canaan with the aid of her national deity. It is rather the story of how God, to whom the whole world belongs, at one stage in the history of redemption reconquered a portion of the earth from the powers of this world that had claimed it for themselves, defending their claims by force of arms and reliance on their false gods. It tells how God commissioned his people, under his servant Joshua, to take Canaan in his name out of the hands of the idolatrous and dissolute Canaanites (whose measure of sin was now full; see Ge 15:16). It tells how he aided them in that enterprise and gave them conditional tenancy in his land in fulfillment of the ancient pledge.

Joshua is the story of the kingdom of God breaking into the world of nations at a time when national and political entities were viewed as the creation of the gods and living proofs of their power. Thus the Lord's triumph over the Canaanites testified to the world that the God of Israel is the one true and living God, whose claim on the world is absolute. It was also a warning to the nations that the irresistible advance of the kingdom of God would ultimately disinherit all those who opposed it, giving place in the earth only to those who acknowledge and serve the Lord. At once an act of redemption and of judgment, it gave notice of the outcome of history and anticipated the eschatological destiny of mankind and the creation.

The battles for Canaan were therefore the Lord's holy war, undertaken at a particular time in the program of redemption. God gave his people under Joshua no commission or license to conquer the world with the sword but a particular, limited mission. The conquered land itself would not become Israel's national possession by right of conquest, but it belonged to the Lord. So the land had to be cleansed of all remnants of paganism. Its people and their wealth were not for Israel to seize as the booty of war from which to enrich themselves (as Achan tried to do, ch. 7) but were placed under God's ban (were to be devoted to God to dispense with as he pleased). On that land Israel was to establish a commonwealth faithful to the righteous rule of God and thus be a witness (and a blessing) to the nations. If she herself became unfaithful and conformed to Canaanite culture and practice, she would in turn lose her place in the Lord's land—as she almost did in the days of the judges, and as she did eventually in the exile.

War is a terrible curse that the human race brings on itself as it seeks to possess the earth by its own unrighteous ways. But it pales before the curse that awaits all those who do not heed God's testimony to himself or his warnings—those who oppose the rule of God and reject his offer of grace. The God of the second Joshua (Jesus) is the God of the first Joshua also. Although now for a time he reaches out to the whole world with the gospel (and commissions his people urgently to carry his offer of peace to all nations), the sword of his judgment waits in the wings—and his second Joshua will wield it (Rev 19:11-16).

Outline

   1. The victory at Jericho (5:13-6:27)
   2. The failure at Ai because of Achan's sin (ch. 7)
   3. The victory at Ai (8:1-29)
   4. The covenant renewed at Shechem (8:30-35)
 B. The Campaign in the South (chs. 9-10)
   1. The treaty with the Gibeonites (ch. 9)
   2. The long day of Joshua (10:1-15)
   3. The southern cities conquered (10:16-43)
 C. The Campaign in the North (ch. 11)
 D. The Defeated Kings of Canaan (ch. 12)
III. The Distribution of the Land (chs. 13-21)
 A. Areas Yet to Be Conquered (13:1-7)
 B. The Land East of the Jordan for Reuben, Gad and Half of Manasseh (13:8-33)
 C. The Lands Given to Judah and "Joseph" at Gilgal (chs. 14-17)
 D. The Lands Given to the Remaining Tribes at Shiloh (chs. 18-19)
   1. The tabernacle at Shiloh (18:1-10)
   2. The allotments for Benjamin, Simeon, Zebulun, Issachar, Asher, Naphtali and Dan (18:11-19:48)
   3. The town given to Joshua (19:49-51)
 E. The Cities Assigned to the Levites (chs. 20-21)
   1. The 6 cities of refuge (ch. 20)
   2. The 48 cities of the priests (ch. 21)
IV. Epilogue: Tribal Unity and Loyalty to the Lord (chs. 22-24)
 A. The Altar of Witness by the Jordan (ch. 22)
 B. Joshua's Farewell Exhortation (ch. 23)
 C. The Renewal of the Covenant at Shechem (24:1-28)
 D. The Death and Burial of Joshua and Eleazar (24:29-33)

The LORD Commands Joshua

1 After the death of Moses the servant of the LORD,[a] the LORD said to Joshua[b] son of Nun, Moses' aide: [2]"Moses my servant is dead. Now then, you and all these people, get ready to cross the Jordan River[cd] into the land[e] I am about to give to them[f]—to the Israelites. [3]I will give you every place where you set your foot,[g] as I promised Moses.[h] [4]Your territory will extend from the desert to Lebanon,[i] and from the great river, the Euphrates[j]—all the Hittite[k] country—to the Great Sea[a] on the west.[l] [5]No one will be able to stand up against you[m] all the days of your life. As I was with[n] Moses, so I will be with you; I will never leave you nor forsake[o] you.

[6]"Be strong[p] and courageous,[q] because you will lead these people to inherit the land I swore to their forefathers[r] to give them. [7]Be strong and very courageous. Be careful to obey[s] all the law[t] my servant Moses[u] gave you; do not turn from it to the right or to the left,[v] that you may be successful wherever you go.[w] [8]Do not let this Book of the Law[x] depart from your mouth;[y] meditate[z] on it day and night, so that you may be careful to do everything written in it. Then you will be prosperous and successful.[a] [9]Have I not commanded you? Be strong and courageous. Do not be terrified;[b] do not be discouraged,[c] for the LORD your God will be with you wherever you go."[d]

[10]So Joshua ordered the officers of the people:[e] [11]"Go through the camp[f] and tell the people, 'Get your supplies[g] ready. Three days[h] from now you will cross the Jordan[i] here to go in and take possession[j] of the land the LORD your God is giving you for your own.'"

[12]But to the Reubenites, the Gadites and the half-tribe of Manasseh,[k] Joshua said, [13]"Remember the command that Moses the servant of the LORD gave you: 'The LORD your God is giving you rest[l] and has granted you this land.' [14]Your wives,[m] your children and your livestock may stay in the land[n] that Moses gave you east of the Jordan, but all your fighting men, fully armed,[o] must cross over ahead of your brothers.[p] You are to help your brothers

1:1 [a]Ex 14:31; Dt 34:5; Rev 15:3 [b]S Ex 17:9
1:2 [c]S Nu 13:29 [d]S Nu 35:10 [e]S Ge 15:14 [f]Ge 12:7; Dt 1:25
1:3 [g]S Dt 11:24 [h]Ge 50:24; Nu 13:2; Dt 1:8
1:4 [i]S Dt 3:25 [j]S Ge 2:14 [k]S Ge 10:15; 23:10; Ex 3:8 [l]Nu 34:2-12; Ezr 4:20
1:5 [m]S Dt 7:24 [n]ver 17; S Ge 26:3; S 39:2; Jdg 6:12; 30:11 [o]S Ge 28:15; S Dt 4:31
1:6 [p]2Sa 2:7; 1Ki 2:2; Isa 41:6; Joel 3:9-10 [q]S Dt 1:21; S 31:6; S Jdg 5:21 [r]Jer 3:18; 7:7
1:7 [s]Dt 29:9; 1Ki 2:3; 3:3 [t]Ezr 7:26; Ps 78:10; 119:136; Isa 42:24; Jer 26:4-6; 32:23; 44:10 [u]ver 2,15; S Nu 12:7; Job 1:8; 42:7 [v]S Dt 5:32; Jos 23:6 [w]ver 9; S Dt 4:2; 5:33; S 11:8; Jos 1:15
1:8 [x]S Dt 28:61; S Ps 147:19 [y]S Ex 4:15; Isa 59:21 [z]S Ge 24:63 [a]Dt 29:9; 1Sa 18:14; Ps 1:1-3; Isa 52:13; 53:10; Jer 23:5
1:9 [b]S Dt 31:6; Jos 10:8; 2Ki 19:6; Isa 35:4; 37:6 [c]S Dt 1:21; Job 4:5 [d]S ver 7; Dt 31:8; Jer 1:8
1:10 [e]S Dt 1:15
1:11 [f]Jos 3:2 [g]1Sa 17:22; Isa 10:28 [h]S Ge 40:13 [i]S Nu 35:10 [j]S Nu 33:53
1:12 [k]Nu 32:33
1:13 [l]S Ex 33:14; Ps 55:6; Isa 11:10; 28:12; 30:15; 32:18; 40:31; Jer 6:16; 45:3; La 5:5
1:14 [m]Dt 3:19 [n]S Nu 32:26 [o]S Ex 13:18 [p]Jos 4:12

[a]4 That is, the Mediterranean

1:1–18 The Lord initiates the action by charging Joshua, his chosen replacement for Moses (see Dt 31:1–8), to lead Israel across the Jordan and take possession of the promised land. He urges courage and promises success—but only if Israel obeys the law of God that Moses has given them. The chapter consists of speeches significant in their content and order: The Lord commands Joshua as his appointed leader over his people (vv. 1–9); Joshua, as the Lord's representative, addresses Israel (vv. 10–15); Israel responds to Joshua as the Lord's representative and successor to Moses (vv. 16–18). Thus the events of the book are set in motion and the roles of the main actors indicated.

1:1 *After the death of Moses.* Immediately the time and occasion of the action are set forth, showing that the story will continue where Deuteronomy ended, with the death of Moses. Cf. "After the death of Joshua" (Jdg 1:1). *servant of the LORD.* See notes on Ex 14:31; Dt 34:5; Ps 18 title; Isa 41:8–9; 42:1. *Moses' aide.* The title by which Joshua served for many years as second in command (see Nu 11:28; see also Ex 24:13; 33:11; Dt 1:38).

1:2 *Jordan River.* The flow of the Jordan near Jericho was not large during most of the year (only 80–100 feet wide), but at flood stage in the spring it filled its wider bed, which at places was a mile wide and far more treacherous to cross. *land I am about to give to them.* A central theme of the Pentateuch (see Ge 12:1; 50:24; Ex 3:8; 23:31; Dt 1:8). Joshua records the fulfillment of this promise of God.

1:3–5 See Dt 11:24–25.

1:4 The dimensions of the land promised to Israel vary (compare this text and Ge 15:18 with Dt 34:1–4) since these are the farthest limits—conquered and held only by David and Solomon. Canaan was still called "Hatti-land" centuries after the Hittites had withdrawn to the north. But Joshua was to take all he set out to conquer; wherever he set his foot was

his. His victories gave to the 12 tribes most of the central hill country and much of the Negev.

1:5 *I will be with you.* To direct, sustain and assure success.

1:6 *land I swore to their forefathers.* The long-awaited inheritance pledged to the descendants of Abraham (Ge 15:7,8–21) and of Jacob (Ge 28:13).

1:7 *Be careful to obey.* Success was not guaranteed unconditionally (see Dt 8:1; 11:8,22–25).

1:8 *Book of the Law.* A documentary form of the laws from Sinai was already extant. *mouth.* See Dt 4:9–10; 6:6–7; 11:19. The law was usually read orally (cf. Dt 30:9–14; Ac 8:30). *meditate.* See Ps 1:2.

1:9 *Have I not commanded you?* A rhetorical question that emphasizes the authority of the speaker.

1:10 *Joshua ordered.* At this point Joshua assumes full command. *officers.* May refer to those whom Moses had appointed over the divisions within the tribes (Ex 18:21; Dt 1:15).

1:11 *supplies.* Foodstuffs needed for the next several days of march.

1:12–15 The threat from the two kings of Transjordan was overcome by military victory and the occupation of the lands north of Moab and east of the Jordan River. The two and a half tribes who asked to remain had been charged by Moses to send their fighting men across with the rest to conquer Canaan (Nu 21:21–35; 32:1–27). The conquest of the promised land must be an undertaking by all Israel.

1:13 *rest.* An important OT concept (see notes on Dt 3:20; 2Sa 7:1,11), implying secure borders, peace with neighboring countries and absence of threat to life and well-being within the land (see note on 1Ki 5:4).

1:14 *your fighting men, fully armed.* Those over 20 (see, e.g., Ex 38:26), known for their valor and able to equip themselves with the weapons of war.

[15]until the LORD gives them rest, as he has done for you, and until they too have taken possession of the land that the LORD your God is giving them. After that, you may go back and occupy your own land, which Moses the servant of the LORD gave you east of the Jordan toward the sunrise."[q]

[16]Then they answered Joshua, "Whatever you have commanded us we will do, and wherever you send us we will go.[r] [17]Just as we fully obeyed Moses, so we will obey you.[s] Only may the LORD your God be with you as he was with Moses. [18]Whoever rebels against your word and does not obey[t] your words, whatever you may command them, will be put to death. Only be strong and courageous![u]"

Rahab and the Spies

2 Then Joshua son of Nun secretly sent two spies[v] from Shittim.[w] "Go, look over[x] the land," he said, "especially Jericho.[y]" So they went and entered the house of a prostitute[b] named Rahab[z] and stayed there.

[2]The king of Jericho was told, "Look! Some of the Israelites have come here tonight to spy out the land." [3]So the king of Jericho sent this message to Rahab:[a] "Bring the men who came to you and entered your house, because they have come to spy out the whole land."

[4]But the woman had taken the two men[b] and hidden them.[c] She said, "Yes,

the men came to me, but I did not know where they had come from. [5]At dusk, when it was time to close the city gate,[d] the men left. I don't know which way they went. Go after them quickly. You may catch up with them."[e] [6](But she had taken them up to the roof and hidden them under the stalks of flax[f] she had laid out on the roof.) [7]So the men set out in pursuit of the spies on the road that leads to the fords of the Jordan,[h] and as soon as the pursuers[i] had gone out, the gate was shut.

[8]Before the spies lay down for the night, she went up on the roof[j] [9]and said to them, "I know that the LORD has given this land to you and that a great fear[k] of you has fallen on us, so that all who live in this country are melting in fear because of you. [10]We have heard how the LORD dried up[l] the water of the Red Sea[c] for you when you came out of Egypt,[m] and what you did to Sihon and Og,[n] the two kings of the Amorites[o] east of the Jordan,[p] whom you completely destroyed.[d][q] [11]When we heard of it, our hearts melted[r] and everyone's courage failed[s] because of you,[t] for the LORD your God[u] is God in heaven above and on the earth[v] below. [12]Now

---

Cross references:

1:15 [q]Nu 32:20-22; Jos 22:1-4
1:16 [r]S Nu 27:20; S 32:25
1:17 [s]S Nu 27:20
1:18 [t]S Nu 32:25 [u]S Dt 1:21; S 31:6
2:1 [v]S ver 4; S Ge 42:9 [w]S Nu 25:1; Jos 3:1; Joel 3:18 [x]S Nu 21:32; Jdg 18:2 [y]S Nu 33:48 [z]Jos 6:17,25; S Heb 11:31
2:3 [a]Jos 6:23
2:4 [b]ver 1; Jos 6:22 [c]Jos 6:17
2:5 [d]Jdg 5:8; 9:35; 16:2 [e]S Heb 11:31
2:6 [f]Jdg 15:14; Pr 31:13; Isa 19:9 [g]S Ex 1:19; Jos 6:25; 2Sa 17:19
2:7 [h]Nu 22:1; Jdg 3:28; 7:24; 12:5,6; Isa 16:2 [i]ver 16,22
2:8 [j]S Dt 22:8; Jdg 16:27; 2Sa 16:22; Ne 8:16; Isa 15:3; 22:1; Jer 32:29
2:9 [k]S Ge 35:5; S Ex 15:14
2:10 [l]S Ge 8:1; Ex 14:21; Jos 3:17; Ps 74:15 [m]S Nu 23:22 [n]S Nu 21:21 [o]S Ge 10:16; S 14:7 [p]Jos 9:10 [q]S Nu 21:2
2:11 [r]S Ge 42:28 [s]S Dt 2:25; Ps 107:26; Jnh 1:5 [t]Ex 15:14;

Jos 5:1; 7:5; 2Sa 4:1; Ps 22:14; Isa 13:7; 19:1; Jer 51:30; Na 2:10 [u]2Ki 5:15; 19:15; Da 6:26 [v]S Ge 14:19; S Nu 20:14

Footnotes:

[b]1 Or possibly an innkeeper   [c]10 Hebrew Yam Suph; that is, Sea of Reeds   [d]10 The Hebrew term refers to the irrevocable giving over of things or persons to the LORD, often by totally destroying them.

1:18 Whoever rebels. Having just taken the oath of allegiance to Joshua, they now agree to the death penalty for any act of treason (e.g., the sin of Achan, 7:15). be strong and courageous. The people's words of encouragement to Joshua echo and reinforce those from the Lord (vv. 6–7,9).

2:1–24 The mission of the two spies and the account of Rahab. The practice of reconnaissance and espionage is as old as war itself (cf. Jdg 7:10–11; 1Sa 26:16). Rahab became a convert to the God of Israel and a famous woman among the Hebrews. She is honored in the NT for her faith (Heb 11:31) and for her good works (Jas 2:25).

2:1 sent . . . from Shittim. The invasion point was in the plains of Moab facing toward the Jordan and Jericho (Nu 33:48–49). The Hebrew word Shittim means "acacia trees," which grow in the semi-arid conditions of the desert. especially Jericho. The primary focus of the spies. It was a fortified city, was well supplied by strong springs, which helped to make it an oasis, and was located just five miles west of the Jordan. Its name probably means "moon city," and archaeological excavations there reveal continuous occupation back to at least 7000 B.C. prostitute. Josephus and other early sources refer to Rahab as an "innkeeper" (see NIV text note), but see Heb 11:31; Jas 2:25.

2:2 king of Jericho. The major cities of Canaan were in reality small kingdoms, each ruled by a local king (attested also in the Amarna letters of the 14th century B.C.; see chart on "Ancient Texts Relating to the OT," p. 5).

2:6 hidden . . . under the stalks of flax. Rooftops in the Near East are still used for drying grain or stalks. Rahab's

cunning saved the lives of the two Israelites but put her own life in jeopardy.

2:7 fords of the Jordan. Shallow crossings of the Jordan, where the depth of normal flow averages only three feet.

2:8–11 Rahab's confession has a significant concentric structure:

a. "I know";

b. "a great fear . . . has fallen on us . . . all who live in this country";

c. "We have heard";

bb. "our hearts melted and everyone's courage failed";

aa. "the LORD your God is God."

Rahab's personal confession forms the outer frame (a.-aa.); the inner frame (b.-bb.) offers the military intelligence that the spies report back to Joshua; the center (c., v. 10) sums up the news about the Lord that occasioned both the Canaanite fear and also Rahab's abandonment of Canaan and its gods for the Lord and Israel. Her confession of faith in the Lord and her accurate information about the Lord's triumphs over powerful enemies are astounding. That the hearts of the Canaanites were "melting in fear" (v. 9) was vital information to the spies.

2:10 completely destroyed. See NIV text note.

2:12 show kindness to my family. The Hebrew for "kindness" is frequently translated "love" or "unfailing love" and often summarizes God's covenant favor toward his people or the love that people are to show to others. Rahab had acted toward the spies as though she were an Israelite, and now she asks that Israel treat her similarly. sure sign. Their oath to

then, please swear to me[w] by the LORD that you will show kindness[x] to my family, because I have shown kindness to you. Give me a sure sign[y] ¹³that you will spare the lives of my father and mother, my brothers and sisters, and all who belong to them,[z] and that you will save us from death."

¹⁴"Our lives for your lives!"[a] the men assured her. "If you don't tell what we are doing, we will treat you kindly and faithfully[b] when the LORD gives us the land."

¹⁵So she let them down by a rope[c] through the window,[d] for the house she lived in was part of the city wall. ¹⁶Now she had said to them, "Go to the hills[e] so the pursuers[f] will not find you. Hide yourselves there three days[g] until they return, and then go on your way."[h]

¹⁷The men said to her, "This oath[i] you made us swear will not be binding on us ¹⁸unless, when we enter the land, you have tied this scarlet cord[j] in the window[k] through which you let us down, and unless you have brought your father and mother, your brothers and all your family[l] into your house. ¹⁹If anyone goes outside your house into the street, his blood will be on his own head;[m] we will not be responsible. As for anyone who is in the house with you, his blood will be on our head[n] if a hand is laid on him. ²⁰But if you tell what we are doing, we will be released from the oath you made us swear.[o]"

²¹"Agreed," she replied. "Let it be as

you say." So she sent them away and they departed. And she tied the scarlet cord[p] in the window.[q]

²²When they left, they went into the hills and stayed there three days,[r] until the pursuers[s] had searched all along the road and returned without finding them. ²³Then the two men started back. They went down out of the hills, forded the river and came to Joshua son of Nun and told him everything that had happened to them. ²⁴They said to Joshua, "The LORD has surely given the whole land into our hands;[t] all the people are melting in fear[u] because of us."

Crossing the Jordan

3 Early in the morning Joshua and all the Israelites set out from Shittim[v] and went to the Jordan,[w] where they camped before crossing over. ²After three days[x] the officers[y] went throughout the camp,[z] ³giving orders to the people: "When you see the ark of the covenant[a] of the LORD your God, and the priests,[b] who are Levites,[c] carrying it, you are to move out from your positions and follow it. ⁴Then you will know which way to go, since you have never been this way before. But keep a distance of about a thousand yards[e] [d] between you and the ark; do not go near it."

⁵Joshua told the people, "Consecrate

[e]4 Hebrew *about two thousand cubits* (about 900 meters)

Cross references (center column)

2:12 wS Ge 24:8; S 47:31
xS Ge 24:12; Ru 3:10
yS Ge 24:14; S Ex 3:12; Jos 4:6; 1Sa 2:34; 2Ki 19:29
2:13 zver 18; Jos 6:23
2:14 a1Ki 20:39, 42; 2Ki 10:24
bS Ge 47:29
2:15 cJer 38:6,11
dver 18,21;
Ge 26:8; Jdg 5:28;
1Sa 19:12
2:16 eS Ge 14:10
fS ver 7 gver 22
hS Heb 11:31
2:17 iS Ge 24:8
2:18 jver 21
kS ver 15 lS ver 13
2:19 mS Lev 20:9
nMt 27:25
2:20 oS Ge 24:8;
S 47:31
2:21 pver 18
qS ver 15
2:22 rver 16
sS ver 7
2:24 tJos 10:8;
11:6; Jdg 3:28;
7:9,14; 20:28;
1Sa 14:10
uS Ex 15:15
3:1 vS Jos 2:1
wS Ge 13:10;
Job 40:23
3:2 xS Ge 40:13;
Jos 2:16
yS Dt 1:15
zJos 1:11
3:3 aS Nu 10:33
bver 8,17;
Nu 4:15; Dt 31:9;
1Ki 8:3 cISa 6:15
3:4 dNu 35:5

Notes (bottom section)

spare the whole family (v. 14).

2:14 *kindly and faithfully.* The terms of the pledge made by the spies echo Rahab's request (v. 12). *when the LORD gives us the land.* All were convinced of the inevitable victory of the Israelites over the city of Jericho.

2:15 *the house . . . was part of the city wall.* There is archaeological evidence that the people of Jericho would occasionally build their houses onto the city wall. Although this evidence predates the time of Joshua, it may still serve to illumine this verse. Alternatively, the Late Bronze fortifications at Jericho may have included a casemate wall (a hollow wall with partitions), and Rahab may have occupied one or more rooms inside it.

2:18 *scarlet cord in the window.* The function of the red marker was similar to that of the blood of the Passover lamb when the Lord struck down the firstborn of Egypt (see Ex 12:13,22–23). The early church viewed the blood-colored cord as a type (symbol) of Christ's atonement.

2:19 *his blood will be on our head.* A vow that accepted responsibility for the death of another, with its related guilt and the retribution meted out by either relatives or the state.

2:22 *into the hills.* Directly west of ancient Jericho were the high, rugged hills of the central mountain ridge in Palestine. They are honeycombed with caves, making the concealment and escape of the two spies relatively easy.

3:1–4:24 Details of the river crossing and the memorial of 12 stones set up in the camp at Gilgal. The great significance of this account can hardly be overemphasized, since it marks

the crossing of the boundary into the promised land and parallels the miracle of the "Red Sea" crossing in the exodus (Ex 14–15). The Israelites' faith in the God of their fathers was renewed and strengthened when it was about to be most severely challenged, while at the same time the Canaanites' fear was greatly increased (5:1). In this account the author uses an "overlay" technique in which, having narrated the crossing to its conclusion (ch. 3), he returns to various points in the event to enlarge on several details: the stones for a memorial (4:1–9); the successful crossing by all Israel (4:10–14); the renewed flow of the river after the crossing was completed (4:15–18). The final paragraph of ch. 4 (vv. 19–24) picks up the story again from 3:17 and completes the account by noting Israel's encampment at Gilgal and the erecting of the stone memorial.

3:3 *ark of the covenant.* The most sacred of the tabernacle furnishings (see Ex 25:10–22). Since it signified the Lord's throne, the Lord himself went into the Jordan ahead of his people as he led them into the land of rest (see Nu 10:33–36).

3:4 *distance of about a thousand yards.* There was evidently a line of march, with the priests and ark leading the way. Respect for the sacred symbol of the Lord's holy presence accounts for this gap between the people and the priests bearing the ark.

3:5 *Consecrate yourselves.* Before their meeting with God at Sinai this had involved washing all their garments as well as their bodies, and also abstinence from sexual intercourse

yourselves, [e] for tomorrow the LORD will do amazing things[f] among you."

[6]Joshua said to the priests, "Take up the ark of the covenant and pass on ahead of the people." So they took it up and went ahead of them.

[7]And the LORD said to Joshua, "Today I will begin to exalt you[g] in the eyes of all Israel, so they may know that I am with you as I was with Moses.[h] [8]Tell the priests[i] who carry the ark of the covenant: 'When you reach the edge of the Jordan's waters, go and stand in the river.'"

[9]Joshua said to the Israelites, "Come here and listen to the words of the LORD your God. [10]This is how you will know that the living God[j] is among you[k] and that he will certainly drive out before you the Canaanites, Hittites,[l] Hivites, Perizzites,[m] Girgashites, Amorites and Jebusites. [n] [11]See, the ark of the covenant of the Lord of all the earth[o] will go into the Jordan ahead of you.[p] [12]Now then, choose twelve men[q] from the tribes of Israel, one from each tribe. [13]And as soon as the priests who carry the ark of the LORD—the Lord of all the earth[r]—set foot in the Jordan, its waters flowing downstream[s] will be cut off[t] and stand up in a heap. [u]"

[14]So when the people broke camp to cross the Jordan, the priests carrying the ark of the covenant[v] went ahead[w] of them. [15]Now the Jordan[x] is at flood stage[y] all during harvest.[z] Yet as soon as the priests who carried the ark reached the Jordan and their feet touched the water's edge, [16]the water from upstream stopped flowing.[a] It piled up in a heap[b] a great distance away, at a town called Adam in the vicinity of Zarethan,[c] while the water flowing down[d] to the Sea of the Arabah[e] (the Salt Sea[f]) was completely cut off.[g] So the people crossed over opposite Jericho.[h] [17]The priests[i] who carried the ark of the covenant of the LORD stood firm on dry ground in the middle of the Jordan,[j] while all Israel passed by until the whole nation had completed the crossing on dry ground.[k]

4 When the whole nation had finished crossing the Jordan,[l] the LORD said to Joshua, [2]"Choose twelve men[m] from among the people, one from each tribe, [3]and tell them to take up twelve stones[n] from the middle of the Jordan[o] from right where the priests stood and to carry them over with you and put them down at the place where you stay tonight.[p]"

[4]So Joshua called together the twelve men[q] he had appointed from the Israelites, one from each tribe, [5]and said to them,

---

3:5 [e]S Ex 29:1; S Lev 11:44
[f]Jdg 6:13; 1Ch 16:9,24; Ps 26:7; 75:1
3:7 [g]Jos 4:14; 1Ch 29:25
[h]Jos 1:5
3:8 [i]S ver 3
3:10 [j]Dt 5:26; 1Sa 17:26,36; 2Ki 19:4,16; Ps 18:46; 42:2; 84:2; Isa 37:4,17; Jer 10:10; 23:36; Da 6:26;
Hos 1:10; S Mt 16:16
[k]S Dt 7:21
[l]S Ge 26:34
[m]Jos 17:15; 24:11; Jdg 1:4; 3:5 [n]S Ex 3:8;
S 23:23; S Dt 7:1; Jos 9:1; 11:3; 12:8; Jdg 19:11; 1Ch 11:4
3:11 [o]ver 13; Ex 19:5;
Dt 10:14; Job 9:10; 28:24; 41:11; Ps 50:12; 97:5; Zec 6:5
[p]S Dt 9:3
3:12 [q]Jos 4:2,4
3:13 [r]S ver 11
[s]ver 16 [t]Jos 4:7
[u]S Ex 14:22;
S Isa 11:15
3:14 [v]Ps 132:8
[w]Ac 7:44-45

3:15 [x]2Ki 2:6
[y]Jos 4:18; 1Ch 12:15; Isa 8:7 [z]S Ge 8:22
3:16 [a]Ps 66:6; 74:15; 114:3
[b]Job 38:37; Ps 33:7
[c]1Ki 4:12; 7:46
[d]ver 13 [e]S Dt 1:1
[f]S Ge 14:3

[g]S Ge 8:1; S Ex 14:22 [h]2Ki 2:4 3:17 [i]S ver 3 [j]Jos 4:3,5,8,9, 10 [k]S Jos 4:1; S Jos 2:10 4:1 [l]Dt 27:2 4:2 [m]S Jos 3:12 4:3 [n]ver 20 [o]S Jos 3:17 [p]ver 19 4:4 [q]S Jos 3:12

[f]16 That is, the Dead Sea

(see Ex 19:10,14–15).
3:7 *I will begin to exalt you.* A prime objective for the divine intervention at the Jordan was to validate the leadership of Joshua. With a miraculous event so much like that of the "Red Sea" crossing, Joshua's position as the Lord's servant would be shown to be comparable to that of Moses.
3:10 *This is how you will know.* The manner by which God is about to bring Israel across the Jordan River, the watery boundary of the promised land, will bring assurance that the one true God is with them and that he will surely dislodge the present inhabitants of Canaan. Two fundamental issues are at stake: 1. Who is the true and mighty God—the God of Israel or the god on whom the Canaanites depend (Baal, who was believed to reign as king among the gods because he had triumphed over the sea-god)? By opening the way through the flooded Jordan the Lord would show both Israel and the Canaanites that he is Lord over the waters (as he was at the "Red Sea," at the flood and at creation) and that that he is able to establish his own order in the world. See 1Ki 20:23; 2Ki 18:32–35. 2. Who has the rightful claim to the land—the Lord or the Canaanites? (For the juridical aspect of such wars see Jdg 11:27.) By passing safely through the Jordan at the head of his army the Lord showed the rightness of his claim on the land. In the ancient Near East a common way for obtaining the judicial verdict of the gods was by compelling the accused to submit to trial by water ordeal. Usually this involved casting him into a river (if the accused drowned, the gods had found him guilty; if not, the gods had declared him innocent). In Israel, however, another form of water ordeal was practiced (see Nu 5:16–28). Significantly, the Lord

would enter the Jordan first and then remain there until his whole army had crossed safely over. Thus his claim to the land was vindicated before the eyes of all who heard about it. And it was his claim, not Israel's; she came through the Jordan only with him and as his army, "baptized" to his service. *Canaanites . . . Jebusites.* See notes on Ge 9:25; 10:6,15–16; 13:7; 15:16; 23:3; Ex 3:8; Jdg 3:3; 6:10.
3:12 *choose twelve men.* Joshua seems to anticipate the Lord's instructions concerning a stone monument of the event (see 4:2–3).
3:13 *cut off.* Blocked, stopped in its flow. *stand up in a heap.* The Hebrew for "heap" is found here, in v. 16 and also in the poetic accounts of the "Red Sea" crossing (Ex 15:8; Ps 78:13). It is possible that God used a physical means (such as a landslide) to dam up the Jordan at the place called Adam (v. 16), near the entrance of the Jabbok. (As recently as 1927 a blockage of the water in this area was recorded that lasted over 20 hours.) But if so, the miraculous element is not diminished (see Ex 14:21).
3:15 *at flood stage.* Because of the spring rains and the melting of snow on Mount Hermon. *harvest.* Grain harvest took place in April and May. *as soon as.* The stoppage nearly 20 miles upstream (v. 16) would have happened several hours earlier to make the events coincide.
3:17 *The priests who carried the ark . . . stood firm on dry ground in the middle of the Jordan.* Signifying that the Lord himself remained in the place of danger until all Israel had crossed the Jordan.
4:3 *at the place where you stay tonight.* Indicating that the entire nation made the crossing in one day.

"Go over before the ark of the LORD your God into the middle of the Jordan.[r] Each of you is to take up a stone on his shoulder, according to the number of the tribes of the Israelites, [6]to serve as a sign[s] among you. In the future, when your children[t] ask you, 'What do these stones mean?'[u] [7]tell them that the flow of the Jordan was cut off[v] before the ark of the covenant of the LORD. When it crossed the Jordan, the waters of the Jordan were cut off. These stones are to be a memorial[w] to the people of Israel forever."

[8]So the Israelites did as Joshua commanded. They took twelve stones[x] from the middle of the Jordan,[y] according to the number of the tribes of the Israelites, as the LORD had told Joshua;[z] and they carried them over with them to their camp, where they put them down. [9]Joshua set up the twelve stones[a] that had been[g] in the middle of the Jordan at the spot where the priests who carried the ark of the covenant had stood. And they are there to this day.[b]

[10]Now the priests who carried the ark remained standing in the middle of the Jordan until everything the LORD had commanded Joshua was done by the people, just as Moses had directed Joshua. The people hurried over, [11]and as soon as all of them had crossed, the ark of the LORD and the priests came to the other side while the people watched. [12]The men of Reuben,[c] Gad[d] and the half-tribe of Manasseh[e] crossed over, armed, in front of the Israelites,[f] as Moses had directed them.[g] [13]About forty thousand armed for battle[h] crossed over[i] before the LORD to the plains of Jericho for war.

[14]That day the LORD exalted[j] Joshua in the sight of all Israel; and they revered him all the days of his life, just as they had revered Moses.

[15]Then the LORD said to Joshua, [16]"Command the priests carrying the ark of the Testimony[k] to come up out of the Jordan."

[17]So Joshua commanded the priests, "Come up out of the Jordan."

[18]And the priests came up out of the river carrying the ark of the covenant of the LORD. No sooner had they set their feet on the dry ground than the waters of the Jordan returned to their place[l] and ran at flood stage[m] as before.

[19]On the tenth day of the first month the people went up from the Jordan and camped at Gilgal[n] on the eastern border of Jericho. [20]And Joshua set up at Gilgal the twelve stones[o] they had taken out of the Jordan. [21]He said to the Israelites, "In the future when your descendants ask their fathers, 'What do these stones mean?'[p] [22]tell them, 'Israel crossed the Jordan on dry ground.'[q] [23]For the LORD your God dried up the Jordan before you until you had crossed over. The LORD your God did to the Jordan just what he had done to the Red Sea[h] when he dried it up before us until we had crossed over.[r] [24]He did this so that all the peoples of the earth might know[s] that the hand of the LORD is powerful[t] and so that you might always fear the LORD your God.[u] "

Circumcision at Gilgal

5 Now when all the Amorite kings west of the Jordan and all the Canaanite kings along the coast[v] heard how the LORD had dried up the Jordan before the Israelites until we had crossed over, their

4:5 [r]S Jos 3:17
4:6 [s]S Jos 2:12
[t]S Ex 10:2 [u]ver 21; Ex 12:26; S 13:14
4:7 [v]Jos 3:13 [w]S Ex 28:12
4:8 [x]Ex 28:21 [y]S Jos 3:17 [z]ver 20
4:9 [a]S Ge 28:18; Jos 24:26; 1Sa 7:12
[b]S Ge 35:20
4:12 [c]S Ge 29:32 [d]S Ge 30:11 [e]S Ge 41:51 [f]S Nu 32:27 [g]Nu 32:29
4:13 [h]S Ex 13:18 [i]S Nu 32:17
4:14 [j]S Jos 3:7

4:16 [k]Ex 25:22
4:18 [l]Ex 14:27 [m]S Jos 3:15
4:19 [n]S Dt 11:30
4:20 [o]ver 3,8
4:21 [p]S ver 6
4:22 [q]S Ex 14:22
4:23
[r]Ex 14:19-22
4:24 [s]1Ki 8:60; 18:36; 2Ki 5:15; Ps 67:2; 83:18; 106:8; Isa 37:20; 52:10 [t]Ex 15:16; 1Ch 29:12; Ps 44:3; 89:13; 98:1; 118:15-16 [u]S Ex 14:31
5:1 [v]S Nu 13:29

[g]9 Or Joshua also set up twelve stones   [h]23 Hebrew Yam Suph; that is, Sea of Reeds

---

4:6 *What do these stones mean?* A stone monument was commonly used as a memorial to remind future generations of what had happened at that place (24:26; 1Sa 7:12).
4:9 *Joshua set up the twelve stones.* Each tribe brought a stone for the monument from the riverbed to the new campsite at Gilgal, and Joshua constructed the monument there. An alternative translation suggests that Joshua set up a second pile in the middle of the river (see NIV text note).
4:13 *About forty thousand.* Seems too few for the number of men listed in Nu 26 for Reuben, Gad and half of Manasseh; the contingents were very likely representative since it would have been imprudent to leave the people undefended who settled in Transjordan (cf. 22:8, "brothers"; Nu 32:17).
4:19 *tenth day of the first month.* The day the Passover lamb was to be selected (Ex 12:3). *Gilgal.* Usually identified with the ruins at Khirbet el-Mafjer, two miles northeast of Jericho.
4:23 *God dried up the Jordan.* Still another descriptive phrase for the miracle, along with "the water . . . cut off,"

"piled up in a heap" and "stopped flowing" (3:16).
4:24 *so that all . . . might know.* The Lord's revelation of his power to the Israelites was a public event that all the Canaanites heard about (see 5:1), just as they had heard of the crossing of the "Red Sea" and defeat of Sihon and Og (2:10). *you.* The Hebrew can also be read as "they." *fear the LORD.* Worship and serve him according to his commandments.
5:1–12 Two covenantal ceremonies were resumed at Gilgal in accordance with the laws from Sinai: the rite of circumcision and the Feast of the Passover. Both were significant preparations for the conquest of the promised land.
5:1 *Amorite . . . Canaanite.* Usually interchangeable, these general names included the many smaller nations in the land. Amorite meant "westerner," and Canaanite referred to the people living along the Mediterranean coast. This verse perhaps concludes the account of the crossing since it notes the effect of that event on the peoples of Canaan (see note on 3:10).

hearts melted ^{w} and they no longer had the courage to face the Israelites.

^{2}At that time the LORD said to Joshua, "Make flint knives ^{x} and circumcise ^{y} the Israelites again." ^{3}So Joshua made flint knives and circumcised the Israelites at Gibeath Haaraloth. ^{i}

^{4}Now this is why he did so: All those who came out of Egypt—all the men of military age ^{z}—died in the desert on the way after leaving Egypt. ^{a} ^{5}All the people that came out had been circumcised, but all the people born in the desert during the journey from Egypt had not. ^{6}The Israelites had moved about in the desert ^{b} forty years ^{c} until all the men who were of military age when they left Egypt had died, since they had not obeyed the LORD. For the LORD had sworn to them that they would not see the land that he had solemnly promised their fathers to give us, ^{d} a land flowing with milk and honey. ^{e} ^{7}So he raised up their sons in their place, and these were the ones Joshua circumcised. They were still uncircumcised because they had not been circumcised on the way. ^{8}And after the whole nation had been circumcised, they remained where they were in camp until they were healed. ^{f}

^{9}Then the LORD said to Joshua, "Today I have rolled away the reproach of Egypt from you." So the place has been called Gilgal ^{g} to this day.

^{10}On the evening of the fourteenth day of the month, ^{h} while camped at Gilgal on the plains of Jericho, the Israelites celebrated the Passover. ^{i} ^{11}The day after the Passover, that very day, they ate some of the produce of the land: ^{j} unleavened bread ^{k} and roasted grain. ^{l} ^{12}The manna stopped the day after ^{k} they ate this food from the land; there was no longer any manna for the Israelites, but that year they ate of the produce of Canaan. ^{m}

The Fall of Jericho

^{13}Now when Joshua was near Jericho, he looked up and saw a man ^{n} standing in front of him with a drawn sword ^{o} in his hand. Joshua went up to him and asked, "Are you for us or for our enemies?"

^{14}"Neither," he replied, "but as commander of the army of the LORD I have now come." Then Joshua fell facedown ^{p} to the ground ^{q} in reverence, and asked him, "What message does my Lord^1 have for his servant?"

^{15}The commander of the LORD's army replied, "Take off your sandals, for the place where you are standing is holy." ^{r} And Joshua did so.

5:1 ^{w}S Ge 42:28
5:2 ^{x}S Ex 4:25
^{y}S Ge 17:10,12,14
5:4 ^{z}S Nu 1:3
^{a}Dt 2:14
5:6 ^{b}Nu 32:13; Jos 14:10; Ps 107:4
^{c}S Ex 16:35
^{d}Nu 14:23,29-35; Dt 2:14 ^{e}S Ex 3:8
5:8 ^{f}Ge 34:25
5:9 ^{g}S Dt 11:30

5:10 ^{h}S Ex 12:6
^{i}S Ex 12:11
5:11 ^{j}S Nu 15:19
^{k}Ex 12:15
^{l}S Lev 23:14
5:12 ^{m}Ex 16:35
5:13 ^{n}S Ge 18:2
^{o}Nu 22:23
5:14 ^{p}S Ge 17:3
^{q}S Ge 19:1
5:15
^{r}S Ge 28:17; Ex 3:5; Ac 7:33

13 Gibeath Haaraloth means hill of foreskins.
19 Gilgal sounds like the Hebrew for roll. ^{k}12 Or the day ^{l}14 Or lord

---

5:2 flint knives. Metal knives were available, but flint made a more efficient surgical tool, as modern demonstrations have shown. Israel had to be consecrated to the Lord's service before she could undertake the Lord's warfare and take possession of the land (cf. Ex 4:24–26). circumcise. Circumcision marked every male as a son of Abraham (Ge 17:10–11) bound to the service of the Lord, and it was a prerequisite for the Passover (Ex 12:48).
5:3 Gibeath Haaraloth. See NIV text note.
5:6 forty years. The time between their departure from Egypt and the crossing of the Jordan. Only 38 years had passed since they turned back at Kadesh Barnea (Nu 14:20–22; Dt 2:14).
5:9 reproach of Egypt. Although the reference may be to Egypt's enslavement of Israel, it is much more likely that the author had in mind the reproach the Egyptians would have cast upon her and her God if Israel had perished in the desert (see Ex 32:12; Nu 14:13; Dt 9:28). Now that the desert journey is over and Israel is safely in the promised land as his special people consecrated to him by circumcision, the reproach of Egypt is rolled away.
5:10 Passover. The ceremonies took place in the month of Abib, the first month of the year (Ex 12:2). At twilight on the 14th day of the month the Passover lamb was to be slaughtered, then roasted and eaten that same night (Ex 12:5–8). Israel had not celebrated Passover since Sinai, one year after her release from Egypt (Nu 9:1–5). Before the next season she had rebelled at the border of Canaan, and the generation of the exodus had been condemned to die in the desert (Nu 14:21–23,29–35). For that generation the celebration of Passover (deliverance from judgment) could have had little

meaning.
5:11 unleavened bread. Bread baked without yeast. It was to be eaten during the seven feast days that followed (Ex 12:15; Lev 23:6).
5:12 manna stopped. This transition from eating manna to eating the "produce of the land" (v. 11) ended 40 years of dependence on God's special provision. Manna was God's gift for the desert journey; from now on he provided Israel with food from the promised land.
5:13—6:5 The narration of the conquest is introduced by the sudden appearance of a heavenly figure who calls himself the "commander of the army of the LORD" (5:14).
5:13 Joshua was near Jericho. The leader of God's army went to scout the nearest Canaanite stronghold, but another warrior was already on the scene. a man standing. The experience is taken by many to be an encounter with God in human form (theophany), or with Christ (Christophany). But angels also were sent on missions of this kind (Jdg 6:11; 13:3), and some were identified as captains over the heavenly armies (Da 10:5,20; 12:1).
5:14 Neither. Joshua and Israel must know their place—it is not that God is on their side; rather, they must fight God's battles. commander of the army of the LORD. God has sent the commander of his heavenly armies to take charge of the battle on earth. Joshua must take orders from him (6:2–5), and he can also know that the armies of heaven are committed to this war—as later events confirm. my Lord. A term of respect for a superior.
5:15 Joshua is commissioned to undertake the Lord's battles for Canaan, just as Moses had been commissioned to confront Pharaoh (Ex 3:5).

6 Now Jerichoˢ was tightly shut up because of the Israelites. No one went out and no one came in.

²Then the LORD said to Joshua, "See, I have deliveredᵗ Jericho into your hands, along with its king and its fighting men. ³March around the city once with all the armed men. Do this for six days. ⁴Have seven priests carry trumpets of rams' hornsᵘ in front of the ark. On the seventh day, march around the city seven times, with the priests blowing the trumpets.ᵛ ⁵When you hear them sound a long blastʷ on the trumpets, have all the people give a loud shout;ˣ then the wall of the city will collapse and the people will go up, every man straight in."

⁶So Joshua son of Nun called the priests and said to them, "Take up the ark of the covenant of the LORD and have seven priests carry trumpets in front of it."ʸ ⁷And he ordered the people, "Advanceᶻ! March around the city, with the armed guard going ahead of the arkᵃ of the LORD."

⁸When Joshua had spoken to the people, the seven priests carrying the seven trumpets before the LORD went forward, blowing their trumpets, and the ark of the LORD's covenant followed them. ⁹The armed guard marched ahead of the priests who blew the trumpets, and the rear guardᵇ followed the ark. All this time the trumpets were sounding. ¹⁰But Joshua had commanded the people, "Do not give a war cry, do not raise your voices, do not say a word until the day I tell you to shout. Then shout!ᶜ" ¹¹So he had the ark of the LORD carried around the city, circling it once. Then the people returned to camp and spent the night there.

¹²Joshua got up early the next morning and the priests took up the ark of the LORD. ¹³The seven priests carrying the seven trumpets went forward, marching before the ark of the LORD and blowing the trumpets. The armed men went ahead of them and the rear guard followed the ark of the LORD, while the trumpets kept sounding. ¹⁴So on the second day they marched around the city once and returned to the camp. They did this for six days.

¹⁵On the seventh day, they got up at daybreak and marched around the city seven times in the same manner, except that on that day they circled the city seven times.ᵈ ¹⁶The seventh time around, when the priests sounded the trumpet blast, Joshua commanded the people, "Shout! For the LORD has given you the city!ᵉ ¹⁷The city and all that is in it are to be

Cross references

6:1 ˢJos 24:11
6:2 ᵗver 16; Dt 7:24; Jos 8:1
6:4 ᵘS Ex 19:13 ᵛS Lev 25:9
6:5 ʷEx 19:13 ˣver 20; 1Sa 4:5; 2Sa 6:15; Ezr 3:11; 10:12; Ps 42:4; 95:1; Isa 8:9; 42:13
6:6 ʸver 4
6:7 ᶻEx 14:15 ᵃNu 10:35; 1Sa 4:3; 7:1
6:9 ᵇver 13; S Nu 2:31; Isa 52:12
6:10 ᶜver 20; 1Sa 4:5; Ezr 3:11
6:15 ᵈ1Ki 18:44; 2Ki 4:35; 5:14
6:16 ᵉS ver 2

Study notes

6:1 *Jericho.* Modern Tell es-Sultan, site of more than two dozen ancient cities, built and destroyed, one above the other. Many had powerful, double walls, but none of the levels has been positively identified as the one that fell under Joshua. The tell (mound) is roughly 400 by 200 yards in size. Since Jericho may have been a center for the worship of the moon-god (Jericho probably means "moon city"), God was destroying not only Canaanite cities, but also Canaanite religion. See map No. 3 at the end of the Study Bible.

6:2 *the LORD.* The Lord's command no doubt comes to Joshua through the "commander of the army of the LORD" (5:14), who orders the first conquest of a Canaanite city.

6:3 *March around the city.* A ritual act, signifying a siege of the city, that was to be repeated for six days.

6:4 *trumpets of rams' horns.* Instruments not of music but of signaling, in both religious and military contexts (which appear to come together here). The trumpets were to be sounded (v. 8), as on the seventh day, announcing the presence of the Lord (see 2Sa 6:15; 1Ch 15:28; Zec 9:14). *ark.* Signified that the Lord was laying siege to the city. *seventh day.* No note is taken of the Sabbath during this seven-day siege, but perhaps that was the day the Lord gave the city to Israel as the first pledge of the land of rest. To arrive at the goal of a long march on the seventh day is a motif found also in other ancient Near Eastern literature. In any event, the remarkable constellation of sevens (seven priests with trumpets, seven days, seven encirclements on the seventh day) underscores the sacred significance of the event (see Introduction to Revelation: Distinctive Feature) and is, perhaps, a deliberate evoking of the seven days of creation to signal the beginning of God's new order in the world.

6:5 *long blast . . . loud shout.* Signaling the onset of the attack—psychological warfare, intended to create panic and confusion (see Jdg 7). In the Dead Sea Scroll of "The War of the Sons of Light against the Sons of Darkness," the Levites are instructed to blow in unison a great battle fanfare to melt the heart of the enemy. (For Dead Sea Scrolls see "The Time between the Testaments," p. 1431.) *every man straight in.* Not a breach here and there but a general collapse of the walls, giving access to the city from all sides.

6:7 *armed guard.* The Hebrew for this term differs from that in v. 3 but may be synonymous with it. It is to be expected that the ark led the procession. If so, the present reference may be to a kind of royal guard (but see v. 9 and note).

6:8—14 Throughout these verses the ark of the Lord is made the center of focus, highlighting the fact that it was the Lord himself who besieged the city.

6:9 *rear guard.* If the rear guard was made up of the final contingents of the army (see Nu 10:25), the armed guard of vv. 7,9 constituted the main body of troops.

6:12—14 Literary repetition reflects repetition in action, a common feature in ancient Near Eastern literature.

6:17 *devoted.* See NIV text note. The ban placed all of Jericho's inhabitants under the curse of death and all of the city's treasures that could not be destroyed under consignment to the Lord's house (v. 19). According to the law of Moses this ban could be applied to animals for sacrifice, to property given to God, or to any person found worthy of death (Lev 27:28–29). It was Moses himself who ruled that all the inhabitants of Canaan be "devoted" by execution for their idolatry and all its accompanying moral corruption (Dt 20:16–18). See note on Dt 2:34. *Rahab . . . and . . . her house shall be spared.* Honoring the pledge made by the two spies (2:14).

devoted[m]f to the LORD. Only Rahab the prostitute[n]g and all who are with her in her house shall be spared, because she hid[h] the spies we sent. [18]But keep away from the devoted things,[i] so that you will not bring about your own destruction by taking any of them. Otherwise you will make the camp of Israel liable to destruction[j] and bring trouble[k] on it. [19]All the silver and gold and the articles of bronze and iron[l] are sacred to the LORD and must go into his treasury."

[20]When the trumpets sounded,[m] the people shouted, and at the sound of the trumpet, when the people gave a loud shout,[n] the wall collapsed; so every man charged straight in, and they took the city.[o] [21]They devoted[p] the city to the LORD and destroyed[q] with the sword every living thing in it—men and women, young and old, cattle, sheep and donkeys.

[22]Joshua said to the two men[r] who had spied out[s] the land, "Go into the prostitute's house and bring her out and all who belong to her, in accordance with your oath to her." [23]So the young men who had done the spying went in and brought out Rahab, her father and mother and brothers and all who belonged to her.[u] They brought out her entire family and put them in a place outside the camp of Israel.

[24]Then they burned the whole city[v] and everything in it, but they put the silver and gold and the articles of bronze and iron[w] into the treasury of the LORD's house.[x] [25]But Joshua spared[y] Rahab the prostitute,[z] with her family and all who belonged to her, because she hid the men Joshua had sent as spies to Jericho[a]—and she lives among the Israelites to this day.

[26]At that time Joshua pronounced this solemn oath:[b] "Cursed[c] before the LORD is the man who undertakes to rebuild this city, Jericho:

"At the cost of his firstborn son
    will he lay its foundations;
at the cost of his youngest
    will he set up its gates."[d]

[27]So the LORD was with Joshua,[e] and his fame spread[f] throughout the land.

Achan's Sin

7 But the Israelites acted unfaithfully in regard to the devoted things[o];[g] Achan[h] son of Carmi, the son of Zimri,[p] the son of Zerah,[i] of the tribe of Judah,[j] took some of them. So the LORD's anger burned[k] against Israel.[l]

[2]Now Joshua sent men from Jericho to Ai,[m] which is near Beth Aven[n] to the east of Bethel,[o] and told them, "Go up and spy out[p] the region." So the men went up and spied out Ai.

[3]When they returned to Joshua, they said, "Not all the people will have to go up against Ai. Send two or three thousand men to take it and do not weary all the people, for only a few men are there." [4]So about three thousand men went up; but they were routed by the men of Ai,[q] [5]who killed about thirty-six[r] of them. They chased the Israelites from the city gate as

Cross references (center column)

6:17 /ver 21; Lev 27:28; Dt 20:17; Isa 13:5; 24:1; 34:2,5; Mal 4:6
gS Jos 2:1 hver 25; Jos 2:4
6:18 iJos 7:1; 1Ch 2:7 /Jos 7:12 kJos 7:25,26
6:19 lver 24; Nu 31:22
6:20 mLev 25:9; Jdg 6:34; 7:22; 1Ki 1:41; Isa 18:3; 27:13; Jer 4:21; 42:14; Am 2:2 nS ver 5, S 10 oHeb 11:30
6:21 pS ver 17 qS Dt 20:16
6:22 rS Ge 42:9; S Jos 2:4 sS Nu 21:32 tJos 2:14; Heb 11:31
6:23 uS Jos 2:13 vS Nu 31:10 wS ver 19 xS Dt 13:16
6:25 yJdg 1:25 zS Jos 2:1 aS ver 17; S Jos 2:6

6:26 b1Sa 14:24 cS Nu 5:21 d1Ki 16:34
6:27 eS Ge 39:2; S Nu 14:43 fJos 9:1; 1Ch 14:17
7:1 gS Jos 6:18 hver 26; 1Ch 2:7 iJos 22:20 /ver 18; Nu 1:4 kS Ex 4:14; S 32:20 lS Lev 10:6
7:2 mS Ge 12:8; S Jos 8:1,28 nJos 18:12; 1Sa 13:5; 14:23; Hos 4:15; 5:8; 10:5 oGe 12:8; Jos 12:16; 16:1; Jdg 1:22; 1Sa 30:27; 2Ki 23:15; Jer 48:13; Am 3:14; 4:4; 5:5-6; 7:10,13 pS Nu 21:32
7:4 qS Lev 26:17; S Dt 28:25

7:5 rJos 22:20

Footnotes

m17 The Hebrew term refers to the irrevocable giving over of things or persons to the LORD, often by totally destroying them; also in verses 18 and 21.   n17 Or possibly innkeeper; also in verses 22 and 25   o1 The Hebrew term refers to the irrevocable giving over of things or persons to the LORD, often by totally destroying them; also in verses 11, 12, 13 and 15.   p1 See Septuagint and 1 Chron. 2:6; Hebrew Zabdi; also in verses 17 and 18.

Study notes (bottom)

6:18 *your own destruction.* See NIV text note on v. 17. If Israel took for herself anything that was under God's ban, she herself would fall under the ban.

6:25 *she lives among the Israelites.* The faith of Rahab is noted twice in the NT (Heb 11:31; Jas 2:25).

6:26 *Cursed ... is the man.* Jericho itself was to be devoted to the Lord as a perpetual sign of God's judgment on the wicked Canaanites and as a firstfruits offering of the land. This was a way of signifying that the conquered land belonged to the Lord. The curse was fulfilled in the rebellious days of King Ahab (1Ki 16:34).

7:1—26 The tragic story of Achan, which stands in sharp contrast to the story of Rahab. In the earlier event a Canaanite prostitute, because of her courageous allegiance to Israel and her acknowledgment of the Lord, was spared and received into Israel. She abandoned Canaan and its gods on account of the Lord and Israel, and so received Canaan back. In the present event an Israelite (of the tribe of Judah, no less), because of his disloyalty to the Lord and Israel, is executed as the Canaanites were. He stole the riches of

Canaan from the Lord, and so lost his inheritance in the promised land. This also is a story of how one man's sin adversely affected the entire nation. Throughout this account (as often in the OT) Israel is considered a corporate unity in covenant with and in the service of the Lord. Thus even in the acts of one (Achan) or a few (the 3,000 defeated at Ai) all Israel is involved (see vv. 1,11; 22:20).

7:2 *from Jericho to Ai.* An uphill march of some 15 miles through a ravine to the top of the central Palestinian ridge. Strategically, an advance from Gilgal to Ai would bring Israel beyond the Jordan Valley and provide them with a foothold in the central highlands. Ai in Hebrew means "the ruin." It is usually identified with et-Tell (meaning "the ruin" in Arabic), just two miles east of Bethel, but some dispute this precise identification. *Beth Aven.* Means "house of wickedness," a derogatory designation of either Bethel itself or a pagan shrine nearby (see 1Sa 13:5; Hos 4:15; Am 5:5). *spy out the region.* See note on 2:1–24.

7:5 *stone quarries.* Or a place called Shebarim (see NIV text note), meaning "breaks," a fitting term for the rocky bluffs overlooking the Jordan Valley.

far as the stone quarries^q and struck them down on the slopes. At this the hearts of the people melted^s and became like water.

^{6}Then Joshua tore his clothes^t and fell facedown^u to the ground before the ark of the LORD, remaining there till evening.^{v} The elders of Israel^w did the same, and sprinkled dust^x on their heads. ^{7}And Joshua said, "Ah, Sovereign LORD, why^y did you ever bring this people across the Jordan to deliver us into the hands of the Amorites to destroy us?^{z} If only we had been content to stay on the other side of the Jordan! ^{8}O Lord, what can I say, now that Israel has been routed by its enemies? ^{9}The Canaanites and the other people of the country will hear about this and they will surround us and wipe out our name from the earth.^{a} What then will you do for your own great name?^{b}"

^{10}The LORD said to Joshua, "Stand up! What are you doing down on your face? ^{11}Israel has sinned;^{c} they have violated my covenant,^{d} which I commanded them to keep. They have taken some of the devoted things; they have stolen, they have lied,^{e} they have put them with their own possessions.^{f} ^{12}That is why the Israelites cannot stand against their enemies;^{g} they turn their backs^h and run^i because they have been made liable to destruction.^{j} I will not be with you anymore^k unless you destroy whatever among you is devoted to destruction.

^{13}"Go, consecrate the people. Tell them, 'Consecrate yourselves^l in preparation for tomorrow; for this is what the LORD, the God of Israel, says: That which is devoted is among you, O Israel. You cannot stand against your enemies until you remove it. ^{14}"'In the morning, present^m yourselves tribe by tribe. The tribe that the LORD

takes^n shall come forward clan by clan; the clan that the LORD takes shall come forward family by family; and the family that the LORD takes shall come forward man by man. ^{15}He who is caught with the devoted things^o shall be destroyed by fire,^{p} along with all that belongs to him.^{q} He has violated the covenant^r of the LORD and has done a disgraceful thing in Israel!'"^{s}

^{16}Early the next morning Joshua had Israel come forward by tribes, and Judah was taken. ^{17}The clans of Judah came forward, and he took the Zerahites.^{t} He had the clan of the Zerahites come forward by families, and Zimri was taken. ^{18}Joshua had his family come forward man by man, and Achan son of Carmi, the son of Zimri, the son of Zerah, of the tribe of Judah,^{u} was taken.^{v}

^{19}Then Joshua said to Achan, "My son, give glory^w to the LORD,^{r} the God of Israel, and give him the praise.^{s} Tell^x me what you have done; do not hide it from me."

^{20}Achan replied, "It is true! I have sinned against the LORD, the God of Israel. This is what I have done: ^{21}When I saw in the plunder^y a beautiful robe from Babylonia,^{t} two hundred shekels^u of silver and a wedge of gold weighing fifty shekels,^{v} I coveted^z them and took them. They are hidden in the ground inside my tent, with the silver underneath."

^{22}So Joshua sent messengers, and they ran to the tent, and there it was, hidden in his tent, with the silver underneath.

7:5 ^{s}S Ge 42:28;
Ps 22:14;
Isa 13:7;
Eze 21:7; Na 2:10
7:6 ^{t}S Ge 37:29
^{u}S Ge 17:3;
1Ch 21:16;
Eze 9:8
^{v}Jdg 20:23
^{w}Jos 8:10; 9:11;
20:4; 23:2
^{x}1Sa 4:12;
2Sa 13:19; 15:32;
Ne 9:1; Job 2:12;
La 2:10;
Eze 27:30;
Rev 18:19
7:7 ^{y}1Sa 4:3
^{z}S Ex 5:22;
S Nu 14:16
7:9 ^{a}Ex 32:12;
S Dt 9:28
^{b}Dt 28:58;
1Sa 12:22;
Ps 48:10; 106:8;
Jer 14:21
7:11 ^{c}S Ex 9:27;
Dt 29:27;
Jos 24:16-27;
2Ki 17:7;
Hos 10:9 ^{d}ver 15;
Jos 6:17-19;
23:16; Jdg 2:20;
1Sa 15:24;
Ps 78:10
^{e}Ac 5:1-2 ^{f}ver 21
7:12 ^{g}Lev 26:37
^{h}Ps 18:40; 21:12
^{i}S Lev 26:17
^{j}Jos 6:18
^{k}Ps 44:9; 60:10
7:13 ^{l}S Lev 11:44
7:14 ^{m}1Sa 10:19
^{n}Pr 16:33
7:15 ^{o}Jos 6:18
^{p}Dt 7:25;
2Ki 25:9;
1Ch 14:12;
Isa 37:19;
Jer 43:12;
Eze 30:16
^{q}1Sa 14:39 ^{r}S ver
11 ^{s}Ge 34:7
7:17 ^{t}Nu 26:20
7:18 ^{u}S ver 1;
S Lev 24:11
^{v}Jnh 1:7
7:19 ^{w}Ex 14:17;
1Sa 6:5; Ps 96:8;
Isa 42:12;
Jer 13:16;
Jn 9:24*
^{x}S Lev 5:5;
1Sa 14:43
7:21
^{y}S Ge 34:29;
S 49:27

^{q}5 Or *as far as Shebarim* ^{r}19 A solemn charge to tell the truth ^{s}19 Or *and confess to him* ^{t}21 Hebrew *Shinar* ^{u}21 That is, about 5 pounds (about 2.3 kilograms) ^{v}21 That is, about 1 1/4 pounds (about 0.6 kilogram)

^{z}S Dt 7:25; Eph 5:5; 1Ti 6:10

7:6 *Joshua tore his clothes.* A sign of great distress (see Ge 37:29,34; 44:13; Jdg 11:35). Joshua's dismay (and that of the people), as indicated by his prayer, arose from his recognition that the Lord had not been with Israel's troops in the battle. And without the Lord the whole venture for which Israel had crossed the Jordan would be impossible. Moreover, the Canaanites would now judge that neither Israel nor her God was invincible. They would pour out of their fortified cities, combine forces and descend on Israel in the Jordan Valley, from which Israel could not escape across the flooding Jordan.
7:9 *your own great name.* Joshua pleads, as Moses had (Nu 14:13–16; Dt 9:28–29), that God's honor in the eyes of all the world was at stake in the fortunes of his people.
7:11 *Israel has sinned.* One soldier's theft of the devoted goods brought collective guilt on the entire nation (see 22:20). *violated my covenant.* See v. 15. This is the main indictment; what follows is further specification.
7:12 *devoted to destruction.* See note on 6:18.

7:13 *Consecrate yourselves.* A series of purifications to be undertaken by every Israelite in preparation for meeting with God, as before a solemn religious feast or a special assembly called by the Lord (see note on 3:5). Here God summons his people before him for his judgment.
7:14 *tribe that the LORD takes.* When the lots are cast, one of the tribes is "taken by the LORD" so that the search is narrowed until the Lord exposes the guilty persons. The lots may have been the Urim and Thummim from the ephod of the high priest (see notes on Ex 28:30; 1Sa 2:28; see also NIV text note on 1Sa 14:41).
7:15 *disgraceful thing in Israel.* An act that within Israel, as the covenant people of the Lord, is an outrage of utter folly (see Dt 22:21; Jdg 19:23–24; 20:6,10; 2Sa 13:12).
7:19 *My son.* Joshua took a fatherly attitude toward Achan. *give glory to the LORD.* See NIV text note. *give him the praise.* See NIV text note.
7:21 *robe from Babylonia.* A valuable import. *two hundred shekels . . . fifty shekels.* See NIV text notes.

23They took the things from the tent, brought them to Joshua and all the Israelites and spread them out before the LORD.

24Then Joshua, together with all Israel, took Achan son of Zerah, the silver, the robe, the gold wedge, his sons^a and daughters, his cattle, donkeys and sheep, his tent and all that he had, to the Valley of Achor.^b 25Joshua said, "Why have you brought this trouble^c on us? The LORD will bring trouble on you today."

Then all Israel stoned him,^d and after they had stoned the rest, they burned them.^e 26Over Achan they heaped^f up a large pile of rocks, which remains to this day.^g Then the LORD turned from his fierce anger.^h Therefore that place has been called the Valley of Achor^w ⁱ ever since.

Ai Destroyed

8 Then the LORD said to Joshua, "Do not be afraid;^j do not be discouraged.^k Take the whole army^l with you, and go up and attack Ai. ^m For I have deliveredⁿ into your hands the king of Ai, his people, his city and his land. 2You shall do to Ai and its king as you did to Jericho and its king, except that you may carry off their plunder^o and livestock for yourselves.^p Set an ambush^q behind the city."

3So Joshua and the whole army moved out to attack Ai. He chose thirty thousand of his best fighting men and sent them out at night 4with these orders: "Listen carefully. You are to set an ambush behind the city. Don't go very far from it. All of you be on the alert. 5I and all those with me will advance on the city, and when the men come out against us, as they did before, we will flee from them. 6They will pursue us until we have lured them away from the city, for they will say, 'They are running away from us as they did before.' So when

we flee from them, 7you are to rise up from ambush and take the city. The LORD your God will give it into your hand.^r 8When you have taken the city, set it on fire.^s Do what the LORD has commanded.^t See to it; you have my orders."

9Then Joshua sent them off, and they went to the place of ambush^u and lay in wait between Bethel and Ai, to the west of Ai—but Joshua spent that night with the people.

10Early the next morning^v Joshua mustered his men, and he and the leaders of Israel^w marched before them to Ai. 11The entire force that was with him marched up and approached the city and arrived in front of it. They set up camp north of Ai, with the valley between them and the city. 12Joshua had taken about five thousand men and set them in ambush between Bethel and Ai, to the west of the city. 13They had the soldiers take up their positions—all those in the camp to the north of the city and the ambush to the west of it. That night Joshua went into the valley.

14When the king of Ai saw this, he and all the men of the city hurried out early in the morning to meet Israel in battle at a certain place overlooking the Arabah.^x But he did not know^y that an ambush had been set against him behind the city. 15Joshua and all Israel let themselves be driven back^z before them, and they fled toward the desert.^a 16All the men of Ai were called to pursue them, and they pursued Joshua and were lured away^b from the city. 17Not a man remained in Ai or Bethel who did not go after Israel. They left the city open and went in pursuit of Israel.

18Then the LORD said to Joshua, "Hold out toward Ai the javelin^c that is in your

w26 *Achor* means *trouble*.

Cross references (center column)

7:24 ^aS Nu 16:27
^bver 26; Jos 15:7; Isa 65:10; Hos 2:15
7:25 ^cS Jos 6:18
^dS Lev 20:2; Dt 17:5; 1Ki 12:18; 2Ch 10:18; 24:21; Ne 9:26
^eS Ge 38:24
7:26 ^f2Sa 18:17
^gS Ge 35:20
^hS Nu 25:4 ⁱS ver 24
8:1 ^jGe 26:24; Dt 31:6
^kS Nu 14:9; S Dt 1:21
^lJos 10:7
^mJos 7:2; 9:3; 10:1; 12:9
ⁿS Jos 6:2
8:2 ^oS Ge 49:27
^pver 27; Dt 20:14
^qver 4,12; Jdg 9:43; 20:29

8:7 ^rJdg 7:7; 1Sa 23:4
8:8 ^sJdg 20:29-38
^tver 19
8:9 ^u2Ch 13:13
8:10 ^vGe 22:3
^wS Jos 7:6
8:14 ^xS Dt 1:1
^yJdg 20:34
8:15 ^zJdg 20:36
^aJos 15:61; 16:1; 18:12
8:16 ^bJdg 20:31
8:18 ^cJob 41:26; Ps 35:3

7:23 *before the LORD.* Who is here the Judge.

7:24 *Joshua . . . all Israel.* Joshua and all Israel were God's agents for executing his judgment on both the Canaanites and this violator of the covenant. *all that he had.* As the head of (and example for) his family, Achan involved his whole household in his guilt and punishment. This is in accordance with the principle of corporate solidarity—the whole community is represented in one member (especially the head of that community).

7:25 *stoned him.* Because he had been found guilty of violating the covenant of the holy Lord (see Ex 19:13; Lev 24:23; Nu 15:36). Afterward the bodies were burned to purge the land of the evil.

7:26 *large pile of rocks.* A second monument in the land to the events of the conquest—alongside the memorial at Gilgal (4:20). *Achor.* See NIV text note. Achor was also another form of Achan's name (see 1Ch 2:7, "Achar," and NIV text note there).

8:1-29 Renewal of the conquest and the taking of Ai.

8:1 *Do not be afraid.* Now that Israel is purged, the Lord reassures Joshua once more (see 1:3-5; 3:11-13; 6:2-5).

8:2 *you may carry off their plunder.* The Lord now assigns the wealth of Canaan to his troops who fight his battles. *Set an ambush.* Still in command, the Lord directs the attack.

8:12 *five thousand.* Verse 3 speaks of a contingent of 30,000 assigned to the ambush. Perhaps Joshua assigned two different units to the task to assure success. Or from the original 30,000 a unit of 5,000 may have been designated to attack Ai itself while the remaining 25,000 served as a covering force to block the threat from Bethel (see v. 17).

8:13 *the camp to the north.* In full visibility Joshua's main force moved north of the city, then pretended to flee to the east, drawing out the entire army of defenders.

8:17 *Ai or Bethel.* Their joint action indicates that the two cities were closely allied, though each is said to have had a king (12:9,16).

hand,[d] for into your hand I will deliver the city." So Joshua held out his javelin[e] toward Ai. [19]As soon as he did this, the men in the ambush rose quickly[f] from their position and rushed forward. They entered the city and captured it and quickly set it on fire.[g]

[20]The men of Ai looked back and saw the smoke of the city rising against the sky,[h] but they had no chance to escape in any direction, for the Israelites who had been fleeing toward the desert had turned back against their pursuers. [21]For when Joshua and all Israel saw that the ambush had taken the city and that smoke was going up from the city, they turned around[i] and attacked the men of Ai. [22]The men of the ambush also came out of the city against them, so that they were caught in the middle, with Israelites on both sides. Israel cut them down, leaving them neither survivors nor fugitives.[j] [23]But they took the king of Ai alive[k] and brought him to Joshua.

[24]When Israel had finished killing all the men of Ai in the fields and in the desert where they had chased them, and when every one of them had been put to the sword, all the Israelites returned to Ai and killed those who were in it. [25]Twelve thousand men and women fell that day—all the people of Ai.[l] [26]For Joshua did not draw back the hand that held out

his javelin[m] until he had destroyed[x n] all who lived in Ai.[o] [27]But Israel did carry off for themselves the livestock and plunder of this city, as the LORD had instructed Joshua.[p]

[28]So Joshua burned[q] Ai[r] and made it a permanent heap of ruins,[s] a desolate place to this day.[t] [29]He hung the king of Ai on a tree and left him there until evening. At sunset,[u] Joshua ordered them to take his body from the tree and throw it down at the entrance of the city gate. And they raised a large pile of rocks[v] over it, which remains to this day.

The Covenant Renewed at Mount Ebal

[30]Then Joshua built on Mount Ebal[w] an altar[x] to the LORD, the God of Israel, [31]as Moses the servant of the LORD had commanded the Israelites. He built it according to what is written in the Book of the Law of Moses—an altar of uncut stones, on which no iron tool[y] had been used. On it they offered to the LORD burnt offerings and sacrificed fellowship offerings.[y z] [32]There, in the presence of the Israelites, Joshua copied on stones the law of Moses, which he had written.[a] [33]All Israel, aliens and citizens[b] alike, with their elders, offi-

Cross references (center column)

8:18 [d]S Ex 4:2; 17:9-12 [e]ver 26
8:19 [f]Jdg 20:33 [g]S ver 8
8:20 [h]Jdg 20:40
8:21 [i]Jdg 20:41
8:22 [j]Dt 7:2; Jos 10:1
8:23 [k]1Sa 15:8
8:25 [l]Dt 20:16-18
8:26 [m]ver 18 [n]S Nu 21:2 [o]Ex 17:12
8:27 [p]S ver 2
8:28 [q]S Nu 31:10 [r]Jos 7:2; Jer 49:3 [s]S Dt 13:16; Jos 10:1 [t]S Ge 35:20
8:29 [u]S Dt 21:23; Jn 19:31 [v]2Sa 18:17
8:30 [w]ver 33; S Dt 11:29 [x]S Ex 20:24
8:31 [y]S Ex 20:25 [z]Dt 27:6-7
8:32 [a]Dt 27:8
8:33 [b]S Lev 16:29

[x]26 The Hebrew term refers to the irrevocable giving over of things or persons to the LORD, often by totally destroying them.   [y]31 Traditionally *peace offerings*

8:26 *he had destroyed.* For the second time Joshua ordered the holy ban on the inhabitants of a Canaanite city (see NIV text note).

8:28 *burned Ai.* As he had Jericho (6:24) and would later do to Hazor (11:11). *desolate place to this day.* If the ruins of Ai have been correctly identified (see note on 7:2), the site shows signs of later occupation only from c. 1200 to 1100 B.C.

8:29 *hung the king of Ai on a tree.* The Israelites did not execute by hanging. "Tree" may refer to a pole on which the king's body was impaled after execution (see note on Dt 21:22). *until evening.* According to Mosaic instructions (see Dt 21:22–23). *large pile of rocks.* A third monument in the land (see note on 7:26).

8:30–35 The renewal of the covenant with the Lord as Moses had ordered (Dt 11:26–30; 27:1–8) concludes the account of the initial battles (see Introduction: Outline). The conquest of Canaan has already been put into rich theological perspective. This final event (see also Joshua's final official act, ch. 24) underscores Israel's servant relationship to the Lord. In conquest and occupation she must faithfully acknowledge her one identity as the people of the kingdom of God, subject to his commission and rule (see note on 5:14).

How Israel could assemble peacefully between Mount Ebal and Mount Gerizim without further conquest is a worrisome question—and has led to some radical reconstructions of Israel's history. It must be noted, however, that Biblical narrators at times followed a thematic rather than a strictly chronological order of events. That may be the case here, since it is clear that the story of the Gibeonite deception

and submission (ch. 9) is included in the thematic development of how Israel came into possession of the rest of Canaan (see the author's introduction in 9:1–2). The Shechemites (Shechem was a major city lying between the two mountains mentioned) were Hivites (or were under Hivite domination; see Ge 34:2) and thus were related to the people of the Gibeonite cities (9:7; 11:19). Also, there was no important town between Gibeon and Shechem (Bethel and Ai had been subdued). Perhaps the treaty of submission established between Israel and the Gibeonites (ch. 9) applied also to the Hivites of Shechem, and the covenant renewal ceremony that concludes ch. 8 (and the previous narrative section) actually took place chronologically after the events narrated in ch. 9. If this suggestion is correct, the Gibeonites or their representatives would have been among the "aliens" who participated with Israel in the covenant event (vv. 33, 35).

8:30 *Mount Ebal.* At the foot of this peak was the fortress city of Shechem, where Abraham had built an altar (Ge 12:6–7).

8:31 *burnt offerings.* See Lev 1:1–17. *fellowship offerings.* See Lev 3:1–17; 7:11–18.

8:32 *copied on stones.* Moses had ordered the people first to plaster the stones, then to inscribe on them the words of the law (Dt 27:2–4). These stones are the fourth monument in the land (see note on v. 29).

8:33 *aliens and citizens alike.* Israel now included the "other people" (Ex 12:38) who had come out of Egypt, plus others who had associated with them during the desert wanderings (see note on vv. 30–35).

cials and judges, were standing on both sides of the ark of the covenant of the LORD, facing those who carried it—the priests, who were Levites. *c* Half of the people stood in front of Mount Gerizim and half of them in front of Mount Ebal, *d* as Moses the servant of the LORD had formerly commanded when he gave instructions to bless the people of Israel.

34Afterward, Joshua read all the words of the law—the blessings and the curses—just as it is written in the Book of the Law. *e* 35There was not a word of all that Moses had commanded that Joshua did not read to the whole assembly of Israel, including the women and children, and the aliens who lived among them. *f*

The Gibeonite Deception

9 Now when all the kings west of the Jordan heard about these things —those in the hill country, *g* in the western foothills, and along the entire coast of the Great Sea *z h* as far as Lebanon *i* (the kings of the Hittites, Amorites, Canaanites, Perizzites, *j* Hivites *k* and Jebusites) *l*— 2they came together to make war against Joshua and Israel.

3However, when the people of Gibeon *m* heard what Joshua had done to Jericho and Ai, *n* 4they resorted to a ruse: They went as a delegation whose donkeys were loaded *a* with worn-out sacks and old wineskins, cracked and mended. 5The men put worn and patched sandals on their feet and wore old clothes. All the bread of their food supply was dry and moldy. 6Then they went to Joshua in the camp at Gilgal *o* and said to him and the men of Israel, "We have come from a distant country; *p* make a treaty *q* with us."

7The men of Israel said to the Hivites, *r*

8:33 *c*Dt 31:12
*d*Dt 11:29;
Jn 4:20
8:34 *e*S Dt 28:61;
31:11
8:35 *f*S Ex 12:38;
Dt 31:12
9:1 *g*S Nu 13:17
*h*S Nu 34:6
*i*S Dt 3:25
*j*Ge 13:7;
S Jos 3:10 *k*ver 7;
Jos 11:19
*l*S Jos 3:10
9:3 *m*ver 17;
Jos 10:10; 11:19;
18:25; 21:17;
2Sa 2:12; 5:25;
20:8; 1Ki 3:4;
9:2; 1Ch 8:29;
14:16; 16:39;
21:29; 2Ch 1:3;
Ne 3:7; Isa 28:21;
Jer 28:1; 41:12
*n*Ge 12:8;
S Jos 8:1
9:6 *o*S Dt 11:30
*p*ver 22
*q*S Ge 26:28
9:7 *r*S ver 1

*s*S Ex 23:32;
S 1Ki 5:12
9:8 *t*2Ki 10:5
9:9 *u*S Dt 20:15
*v*ver 24
*w*S Nu 23:22
9:10 *x*S Nu 21:25
*y*S Nu 21:33
*z*S Nu 21:24,35;
Jos 2:10
9:14
*a*S Ex 16:28;
S Nu 27:21
9:15 *b*S ver 3,7;
Jos 10:1,4; 11:19;
2Sa 21:2; 24:1
*c*ver 21; Jdg 1:21;
Ps 106:34
9:16 *d*ver 22
9:17 *e*Jos 18:25;
2Sa 4:2; 23:37
*f*Jos 15:9,60;
18:14,15;
Jdg 18:12;
1Sa 6:21; 7:2;
Ps 132:6;
Jer 26:20

"But perhaps you live near us. How then can we make a treaty *s* with you?"

8"We are your servants, *t*" they said to Joshua.

But Joshua asked, "Who are you and where do you come from?"

9They answered: "Your servants have come from a very distant country *u* because of the fame of the LORD your God. For we have heard reports *v* of him: all that he did in Egypt, *w* 10and all that he did to the two kings of the Amorites east of the Jordan—Sihon king of Heshbon, *x* and Og king of Bashan, *y* who reigned in Ashtaroth. *z* 11And our elders and all those living in our country said to us, 'Take provisions for your journey; go and meet them and say to them, "We are your servants; make a treaty with us." ' 12This bread of ours was warm when we packed it at home on the day we left to come to you. But now see how dry and moldy it is. 13And these wineskins that we filled were new, but see how cracked they are. And our clothes and sandals are worn out by the very long journey."

14The men of Israel sampled their provisions but did not inquire *a* of the LORD. 15Then Joshua made a treaty of peace *b* with them to let them live, *c* and the leaders of the assembly ratified it by oath.

16Three days after they made the treaty with the Gibeonites, the Israelites heard that they were neighbors, living near *d* them. 17So the Israelites set out and on the third day came to their cities: Gibeon, Kephirah, Beeroth *e* and Kiriath Jearim. *f* 18But the Israelites did not attack them,

z 1 That is, the Mediterranean   *a 4* Most Hebrew manuscripts; some Hebrew manuscripts, Vulgate and Syriac (see also Septuagint) *They prepared provisions and loaded their donkeys*

8:34 *the blessings and the curses.* See Dt 27–28 and notes.

9:1–27 The account of how the Gibeonites deceived the leaders of the tribes and obtained a treaty of submission to Israel. It is the first of three sections telling how Israel came into possession of the bulk of the land. Verses 1–2 introduce the three units.

9:1 *kings west of the Jordan.* Small, independent city-kingdoms were scattered over Canaan, inhabited by a variety of peoples who had come earlier from outside the land (compare vv. 1–2 with Ge 15:19).

9:3 *Gibeon.* A site just north of Jerusalem called el-Jib, showing the remains of a Late Bronze Age city with an excellent water supply. The Gibeonites were in league with a number of neighboring towns (v. 17) but seem to have been dominant in the confederation.

9:4 *they resorted to a ruse.* Motivated by their fear of Israel's God, the Gibeonites used pretense to trick Joshua into a treaty that would allow them to live.

9:6 *make a treaty with us.* In this request they were offering

to submit themselves by treaty to be subjects of the Israelites (see v. 11, where they call themselves "your servants"—unmistakable language in the international diplomacy of that day). They chose submission rather than certain death (v. 24).

9:7 *Hivites.* Possibly Horites, an ethnic group living in Canaan related to the Hurrians of northern Mesopotamia (11:19; Ge 10:17; Ex 23:23; Jdg 3:3).

9:9 *heard reports of him.* The same reports that had been heard in Jericho (see 2:10).

9:14 *did not inquire of the LORD.* Did not consult their King, whose mission they were on.

9:15 *treaty of peace.* A covenant to let them live was sworn by the heads of the tribes—i.e., an oath was taken in the holy name of God. All such oaths were binding in Israel (see Ex 20:7; Lev 19:12; 1Sa 14:24).

9:18 *The whole assembly grumbled.* Perhaps the people feared the consequences of not following through on the earlier divine order to destroy all the Canaanites, but more likely they grumbled because they could not take over the

because the leaders of the assembly had sworn an oath^g to them by the LORD, the God of Israel.

The whole assembly grumbled^h against the leaders, ^{19}but all the leaders answered, "We have given them our oath by the LORD, the God of Israel, and we cannot touch them now. ^{20}This is what we will do to them: We will let them live, so that wrath will not fall on us for breaking the oath^i we swore to them." ^{21}They continued, "Let them live,^{j} but let them be woodcutters and water carriers^k for the entire community." So the leaders' promise to them was kept.

^{22}Then Joshua summoned the Gibeonites and said, "Why did you deceive us by saying, 'We live a long way^l from you,' while actually you live near^m us? ^{23}You are now under a curse:^{n} You will never cease to serve as woodcutters and water carriers for the house of my God."

^{24}They answered Joshua, "Your servants were clearly told^o how the LORD your God had commanded his servant Moses to give you the whole land and to wipe out all its inhabitants from before you. So we feared for our lives because of you, and that is why we did this. ^{25}We are now in your hands.^{p} Do to us whatever seems good and right^q to you."

^{26}So Joshua saved them from the Israelites, and they did not kill them. ^{27}That day he made the Gibeonites^r woodcutters and water carriers^s for the community and for the altar of the LORD at the place the LORD would choose.^{t} And that is what they are to this day.

The Sun Stands Still

10 Now Adoni-Zedek^u king of Jerusalem^v heard that Joshua had taken Ai^w and totally destroyed$^{b\,x}$ it, doing to Ai and its king as he had done to Jericho and its king, and that the people of Gibeon^y had made a treaty of peace^z with Israel and were living near them. ^{2}He and his people were very much alarmed at this, because Gibeon was an important city, like one of the royal cities; it was larger than Ai, and all its men were good fighters. ^{3}So Adoni-Zedek king of Jerusalem appealed to Hoham king of Hebron,^{a} Piram king of Jarmuth,^{b} Japhia king of Lachish^c and Debir^d king of Eglon.^{e} ^{4}"Come up and help me attack Gibeon," he said, "because it has made peace^f with Joshua and the Israelites."

^{5}Then the five kings^g of the Amorites^h—the kings of Jerusalem, Hebron, Jarmuth, Lachish and Eglon—joined forces. They moved up with all their troops and took up positions against Gibeon and attacked it.

^{6}The Gibeonites then sent word to Joshua in the camp at Gilgal:^{i} "Do not abandon your servants. Come up to us quickly and save us! Help us, because all the Amorite kings from the hill country have joined forces against us."

^{7}So Joshua marched up from Gilgal with his entire army,^{j} including all the best fighting men. ^{8}The LORD said to Joshua, "Do not be afraid^k of them; I have given

Cross references

9:18 ^{g}ver 15; Jdg 21:1,7,18; 1Sa 20:17; Ps 15:4 ^{h}Ex 15:24
9:20 ^{i}S Ge 24:8
9:21 ^{j}S ver 15 ^{k}S Dt 29:11
9:22 ^{l}ver 6 ^{m}ver 16
9:23 ^{n}S Ge 9:25
9:24 ^{o}ver 9
9:25 ^{p}Ge 16:6 ^{q}Jer 26:14
9:27 ^{r}S Ex 1:11 ^{s}S Dt 29:11 ^{t}Dt 12:5

10:1 ^{u}ver 3 ^{v}Jos 12:10; 15:8, 63; 18:28; Jdg 1:7 ^{w}S Jos 8:1 ^{x}S Dt 20:16; S Jos 8:22 ^{y}Jos 9:3 ^{z}S Jos 9:15
10:3 ^{a}S Ge 13:18 ^{b}ver 5; Jos 12:11; 15:35; 21:29; Ne 11:29 ^{c}ver 5, 31; Jos 12:11; 15:39; 2Ki 14:19; 2Ch 11:9; 25:27; 32:9; Ne 11:30; Isa 36:2; 37:8; Jer 34:7; Mic 1:13 ^{d}ver 38; Jos 11:21; 12:13; 13:26; 15:7,49; 21:15; Jdg 1:11; 1Ch 6:58 ^{e}ver 23, 34,36; Jos 12:12; 15:39
10:4 ^{f}S Jos 9:15
10:5 ^{g}ver 16 ^{h}Nu 13:29; S Dt 1:7
10:6 ^{i}S Dt 11:30
10:7 ^{j}Jos 8:1
10:8 ^{k}S Dt 3:2; S Jos 1:9

^{b}^{l} The Hebrew term refers to the irrevocable giving over of things or persons to the LORD, often by totally destroying them; also in verses 28, 35, 37, 39 and 40.

Gibeonite cities and possessions.

9:21 *woodcutters and water carriers.* A conventional phrase for household servants.

9:23 *under a curse.* Noah's prediction that Canaan would someday "be the slave of Shem" (Ge 9:25–26) has part of its fulfillment in this event. *for the house of my God.* Probably specifies how the Gibeonites were to serve "the entire community" (v. 21). Worship at the tabernacle (and later at the temple) required much wood and water (for sacrifices and washing) and consequently a great deal of menial labor. From now on, that labor was to be supplied by the Gibeonites, perhaps on a rotating basis. In this way they entered the Lord's service. When Solomon became king, the tabernacle and altar were at Gibeon (2Ch 1:3,5).

9:27 *the place the LORD would choose.* Joshua moved the tabernacle (and its altar) to Shiloh, and there it would reside at least until the days of Samuel (1Sa 4:3). Later, the Lord chose Jerusalem (1Ki 9:3).

10:1–43 The army under Joshua comes to the defense of Gibeon and defeats the coalition of southern kings at Aijalon, then subdues all the southern cities of Judah and the Negev.

10:1 *Adoni-Zedek.* Means "lord of righteousness" or "My (divine) lord is righteous." An earlier king of Jerusalem had a

similar name (Melchizedek; see Ge 14:18 and note). *Jerusalem.* City of the Jebusites.

10:2 *important city.* Gibeon was not only larger in size than Bethel or Ai, but also closer to Jerusalem. With Bethel and Ai conquered and the Gibeonite league in submission, the Israelites were well established in the central highlands, virtually cutting the land in two. Naturally the king of Jerusalem felt threatened, and he wanted to reunite all the Canaanites against Israel. Perhaps he also held (or claimed) some political dominion over the Gibeonite cities and viewed their submission to Israel as rebellion. *good fighters.* Men famous for their courage in battle, yet wise enough to have made peace with the Israelites.

10:5 *five kings of the Amorites.* Rulers over five of the major cities in the southern mountains. The Amorites of the hills are here distinguished from the Canaanites along the coast.

10:6 *Come . . . and save us!* An urgent appeal for deliverance to a man whose name means "The LORD saves." A treaty such as Joshua had made with the Gibeonites usually obliged the ruling nation to come to the aid of the subject peoples if they were attacked.

them into your hand.[l] Not one of them will be able to withstand you." [m]

[9]After an all-night march from Gilgal, Joshua took them by surprise. [10]The LORD threw them into confusion[n] before Israel,[o] who defeated them in a great victory at Gibeon.[p] Israel pursued them along the road going up to Beth Horon[q] and cut them down all the way to Azekah[r] and Makkedah.[s] [11]As they fled before Israel on the road down from Beth Horon to Azekah, the LORD hurled large hailstones[t] down on them from the sky,[u] and more of them died from the hailstones than were killed by the swords of the Israelites.

[12]On the day the LORD gave the Amorites[v] over to Israel, Joshua said to the LORD in the presence of Israel:

"O sun, stand still over Gibeon,
    O moon, over the Valley of
        Aijalon. [w]"
[13]So the sun stood still,[x]
    and the moon stopped,
till the nation avenged itself on[c] its
    enemies,

as it is written in the Book of Jashar.[y]

The sun stopped[z] in the middle of the sky and delayed going down about a full day. [14]There has never been a day like it before or since, a day when the LORD listened to a man. Surely the LORD was fighting[a] for Israel!

[15]Then Joshua returned with all Israel to the camp at Gilgal.[b]

Five Amorite Kings Killed

[16]Now the five kings had fled[c] and hidden in the cave at Makkedah. [17]When Joshua was told that the five kings had been found hiding in the cave at Makkedah, [18]he said, "Roll large rocks up to

the mouth of the cave, and post some men there to guard it. [19]But don't stop! Pursue your enemies, attack them from the rear and don't let them reach their cities, for the LORD your God has given them into your hand."

[20]So Joshua and the Israelites destroyed them completely[d]—almost to a man—but the few who were left reached their fortified cities. [e] [21]The whole army then returned safely to Joshua in the camp at Makkedah, and no one uttered a word against the Israelites.

[22]Joshua said, "Open the mouth of the cave and bring those five kings out to me." [23]So they brought the five kings out of the cave—the kings of Jerusalem, Hebron, Jarmuth, Lachish and Eglon. [24]When they had brought these kings[f] to Joshua, he summoned all the men of Israel and said to the army commanders who had come with him, "Come here and put your feet[g] on the necks of these kings." So they came forward and placed their feet[h] on their necks.

[25]Joshua said to them, "Do not be afraid; do not be discouraged. Be strong and courageous.[i] This is what the LORD will do to all the enemies you are going to fight." [26]Then Joshua struck and killed the kings and hung them on five trees, and they were left hanging on the trees until evening.

[27]At sunset[j] Joshua gave the order and they took them down from the trees and threw them into the cave where they had been hiding. At the mouth of the cave they placed large rocks, which are there to this day.[k]

[28]That day Joshua took Makkedah. He

10:8 [l]S Jos 2:24
[m]S Dt 7:24
10:10 [n]S Ex 14:24
[o]S Dt 7:23
[p]S Jos 9:3
[q]Jos 16:3,5;
18:13,14; 21:22;
1Sa 13:18;
1Ki 9:17;
1Ch 6:68; 7:24;
2Ch 8:5; 25:13
[r]Jos 15:35;
1Sa 17:1;
2Ch 11:9;
Ne 11:30;
Jer 34:7 [s]ver 16,
17,21; Jos 12:16;
15:41
10:11 [t]S Ex 9:18;
Ps 18:12;
32:19; Eze 13:11,
13 [u]Jdg 5:20
10:12 [v]Am 2:9
[w]Jos 19:42;
21:24; Jdg 1:35;
12:12; 1Sa 14:31;
1Ch 6:69; 8:13;
2Ch 11:10; 28:18
10:13 [x]Hab 3:11
[y]2Sa 1:18
[z]Isa 38:8
10:14 [a]ver 42;
S Ex 14:14;
Ps 106:43;
136:24;
Isa 63:10;
Jer 21:5
10:15 [b]ver 43
10:16 [c]Ps 68:12

10:20 [d]Dt 20:16
[e]2Ch 11:10;
Jer 4:5; 5:17;
8:14; 35:11
10:24 [f]S Dt 7:24
[g]Mal 4:3
[h]2Sa 22:40;
Ps 110:1;
Isa 51:23
10:25 [i]S Dt 31:6
10:27
[j]S Dt 21:23
[k]S Ge 35:20

[c]13 Or nation triumphed over

10:9 all-night march. Gilgal was about 20 miles east of Gibeon, a steep uphill climb for Joshua's men. by surprise. Joshua attacked early in the morning, perhaps while the moon was still up (v. 12).
10:10 confusion. The Hebrew for this word implies terror or panic.
10:11 down from Beth Horon. A long descent to the plain of Aijalon below, following the main east-west crossroad just north of Jerusalem. large hailstones. For the Lord's use of the elements of nature as his armaments see Jdg 5:20; 1Sa 7:10; Job 38:22.
10:13 Book of Jashar. An early account of Israel's wars (perhaps all in poetic form; see 2Sa 1:18; see also note on Jdg 5:1–31), but never a part of canonical Scripture. delayed going down. Some believe that God extended the hours of daylight for the Israelites to defeat their enemies. Others suggest that the sun remained cool (perhaps as the result of an overcast sky) for an entire day, allowing the fighting to continue through the afternoon. The fact is we do not know what happened, except that it involved divine intervention.

10:16 Makkedah. A town near Azekah (v. 10) in the western foothills where Joshua's troops made their camp.
10:19 Pursue your enemies. Most of the fighting men defending the southern cities were caught and killed before they could reach the safety of their fortresses.
10:21 no one uttered a word. The thought here appears to be that no one dared even to raise his voice against the Israelites anymore.
10:24 put your feet on the necks. Public humiliation of defeated enemy chieftains was the usual climax of warfare in the ancient Near East.
10:26 hung them on five trees. See note on Dt 21:22.
10:27 they placed large rocks. A fifth monument in the land to the events of the conquest (see note on 8:32).
10:28 totally destroyed everyone. The holy ban was placed on the people of Makkedah, meaning they were "devoted to death" for their wicked deeds (see NIV text note on v. 1). The same fate came to the other major cities of the south (vv. 29–42).

put the city and its king to the sword and totally destroyed everyone in it. He left no survivors.[l] And he did to the king of Makkedah as he had done to the king of Jericho.[m]

Southern Cities Conquered

[29]Then Joshua and all Israel with him moved on from Makkedah to Libnah[n] and attacked it. [30]The LORD also gave that city and its king into Israel's hand. The city and everyone in it Joshua put to the sword. He left no survivors there. And he did to its king as he had done to the king of Jericho.

[31]Then Joshua and all Israel with him moved on from Libnah to Lachish;[o] he took up positions against it and attacked it. [32]The LORD handed Lachish over to Israel, and Joshua took it on the second day. The city and everyone in it he put to the sword, just as he had done to Libnah. [33]Meanwhile, Horam king of Gezer[p] had come up to help Lachish, but Joshua defeated him and his army—until no survivors were left.

[34]Then Joshua and all Israel with him moved on from Lachish to Eglon;[q] they took up positions against it and attacked it. [35]They captured it that same day and put it to the sword and totally destroyed everyone in it, just as they had done to Lachish.

[36]Then Joshua and all Israel with him went up from Eglon to Hebron[r] and attacked it. [37]They took the city and put it to the sword, together with its king, its villages and everyone[s] in it. They left no survivors. Just as at Eglon, they totally destroyed it and everyone in it.

[38]Then Joshua and all Israel with him turned around and attacked Debir.[t] [39]They took the city, its king and its villages, and put them to the sword. Everyone in it they totally destroyed. They left no survivors. They did to Debir and its

king as they had done to Libnah and its king and to Hebron.[u]

[40]So Joshua subdued the whole region, including the hill country, the Negev,[v] the western foothills and the mountain slopes,[w] together with all their kings.[x] He left no survivors. He totally destroyed all who breathed, just as the LORD, the God of Israel, had commanded.[y] [41]Joshua subdued them from Kadesh Barnea[z] to Gaza[a] and from the whole region of Goshen[b] to Gibeon. [42]All these kings and their lands Joshua conquered in one campaign, because the LORD, the God of Israel, fought[c] for Israel.

[43]Then Joshua returned with all Israel to the camp at Gilgal.[d]

Northern Kings Defeated

11 When Jabin[e] king of Hazor[f] heard of this, he sent word to Jobab king of Madon, to the kings of Shimron[g] and Acshaph,[h] [2]and to the northern kings who were in the mountains, in the Arabah[i] south of Kinnereth,[j] in the western foothills and in Naphoth Dor[d k] on the west; [3]to the Canaanites in the east and west; to the Amorites, Hittites, Perizzites[l] and Jebusites in the hill country;[m] and to the Hivites[n] below Hermon[o] in the region of Mizpah.[p] [4]They came out with all their troops and a large number of horses and chariots—a huge army, as numerous as the sand on the seashore.[q] [5]All these kings joined forces[r] and made camp together at the Waters of Merom,[s] to fight against Israel.

[6]The LORD said to Joshua, "Do not be afraid of them, because by this time tomor-

Cross references (center column)

10:28 [l]Dt 20:16 [m]ver 30,32,35, 39; Jos 6:21
10:29 [n]S Nu 33:20
10:31 [o]S ver 3
10:33 [p]Jos 12:12; 16:3, 10; 21:21; Jdg 1:29; 2Sa 5:25; 1Ki 9:15; 1Ch 6:67
10:34 [q]S ver 3
10:36 [r]S Ge 13:18; Jos 14:13; 15:13; 20:7; 21:11; Jdg 16:3
10:37 [s]S ver 28
10:38 [t]S ver 3
10:39 [u]S ver 28
10:40 [v]S Ge 12:9; Jos 12:8; 15:19, 21; 18:25; 19:8; 1Sa 30:27 [w]S Dt 1:7 [x]Dt 7:24 [y]Dt 20:16-17
10:41 [z]S Ge 14:7 [a]S Ge 10:19 [b]Jos 11:16; 15:51
10:42 [c]S ver 14
10:43 [d]ver 15; Jos 5:9; 1Sa 7:16; 10:8; 11:14; 13:12
11:1 [e]Jdg 4:2,7, 23; Ps 83:9 [f]ver 10; Jos 12:19; 15:23,25; 19:36; Jdg 4:2,17; 1Sa 12:9; 1Ki 9:15; 2Ki 15:29; Ne 11:33; Jer 49:28,33 [g]Jos 19:15 [h]Jos 12:20; 19:25
11:2 [i]ver 16; S Dt 1:1; Jos 12:1; 18:18 [j]S Nu 34:11; Dt 3:17; Jos 19:35; 1Ki 15:20 [k]Jos 12:23; 17:11; Jdg 1:27; 1Ki 4:11; 1Ch 7:29
11:3 [l]S Jos 3:10 [m]Nu 13:17 [n]S Ex 3:8; Dt 7:1; Jdg 3:3,5; 1Ki 9:20 [o]S Dt 3:8 [p]ver 8;

S Ge 31:49; Jos 15:38; 18:26; Jdg 11:11; 20:1; 21:1; 1Sa 7:5,6; 1Ki 15:22; 2Ki 25:23 **11:4** [q]S Ge 12:2; Jdg 7:12; 1Sa 13:5 **11:5** [r]Jdg 5:19 [s]ver 7

[d]2 Or *in the heights of Dor*

10:33 *Horam king of Gezer.* An important detail: the defeat of the king of the most powerful city in the area. Gezer was eventually taken over by the Egyptians and given to King Solomon as a wedding gift (see 1Ki 9:16).
10:38 *Debir.* In the past, Debir (also known as Kiriath Sepher, 15:15) was identified with Tell Beit Mirsim. More recently, however, it has been equated with Khirbet Rabud, about five miles southwest of Hebron.
10:41 *Kadesh Barnea to Gaza.* The south-to-north limits in the western part of the region. *Goshen.* A seldom-used name for the eastern Negev, not to be confused with the Goshen in the delta of Egypt; it is also the name of a town (15:51). Goshen and Gibeon mark the south-to-north limits in the eastern part of the region.
11:1–23 Only the northern cities remained to be conquered. The major battle for the hills of Galilee is fought and won against Hazor and the coalition of other northern city-states. A summary follows of all Joshua's victories in the southern and central regions as well.

11:1 *Jabin king of Hazor.* Jabin is perhaps a dynastic name, used again in the days of Deborah (Jdg 4:2). The archaeological excavation of Hazor shows that it was the largest and best fortified of all the Canaanite cities. Its lower city measured 175 acres.
11:2 *Kinnereth.* Means "harp"; the Sea of Galilee.
11:4 *as numerous as the sand.* A widely used figure of speech for indicating large numbers (see note on Ge 22:17).
11:5 *All these kings.* Jabin's muster extended as far as the Arabah (v. 2) in the Jordan Valley and as far as Dor on the Mediterranean, south of Mount Carmel. *Merom.* Probably modern Meirun, just northwest of Safed near the source of the Wadi Ammud (Marun)—some eight miles northwest of the Sea of Galilee.
11:6 *hamstring their horses.* Done by cutting the tendon above the hock or ankle, crippling the horse so that it cannot walk again. *burn their chariots.* These advanced implements of war were not used by the armies of Israel until the time of Solomon (see 1Ki 9:22; 10:26–29).

row I will hand all of them over[t] to Israel, slain. You are to hamstring[u] their horses and burn their chariots."[v]

[7]So Joshua and his whole army came against them suddenly at the Waters of Merom and attacked them, [8]and the LORD gave them into the hand of Israel. They defeated them and pursued them all the way to Greater Sidon,[w] to Misrephoth Maim,[x] and to the Valley of Mizpah on the east, until no survivors were left. [9]Joshua did to them as the LORD had directed: He hamstrung their horses and burned their chariots.

[10]At that time Joshua turned back and captured Hazor and put its king to the sword.[y] (Hazor had been the head of all these kingdoms.) [11]Everyone in it they put to the sword. They totally destroyed[e] them,[z] not sparing anything that breathed,[a] and he burned up[b] Hazor itself.

[12]Joshua took all these royal cities and their kings and put them to the sword. He totally destroyed them, as Moses the servant of the LORD had commanded.[c] [13]Yet Israel did not burn any of the cities built on their mounds—except Hazor, which Joshua burned. [14]The Israelites carried off for themselves all the plunder and livestock of these cities, but all the people they put to the sword until they completely destroyed them, not sparing anyone that breathed.[d] [15]As the LORD commanded his servant Moses, so Moses commanded Joshua, and Joshua did it; he left nothing undone of all that the LORD commanded Moses.[e]

[16]So Joshua took this entire land: the hill country,[f] all the Negev,[g] the whole region of Goshen, the western foothills,[h] the Arabah and the mountains of Israel with their foothills, [17]from Mount Halak, which rises toward Seir,[i] to Baal Gad[j] in the Valley of Lebanon[k] below Mount Hermon.[l] He captured all their kings and struck them down, putting them to death.[m] [18]Joshua waged war against all these kings for a long time. [19]Except for the Hivites[n] living in Gibeon,[o] not one city made a treaty of peace[p] with the Israelites, who took them all in battle. [20]For it was the LORD himself who hardened their hearts[q] to wage war against Israel, so that he might destroy them totally, exterminating them without mercy, as the LORD had commanded Moses.[r]

[21]At that time Joshua went and destroyed the Anakites[s] from the hill country: from Hebron, Debir[t] and Anab,[u] from all the hill country of Judah, and from all the hill country of Israel. Joshua totally destroyed them and their towns. [22]No Anakites were left in Israelite territory; only in Gaza,[v] Gath[w] and Ashdod[x] did any survive. [23]So Joshua took the entire land,[y] just as the LORD had directed Moses, and he gave it as an inheritance[z] to Israel according to their tribal divisions.[a][b]

Then the land had rest[c] from war.[d]

List of Defeated Kings

12 These are the kings of the land whom the Israelites had defeated

[e]*11* The Hebrew term refers to the irrevocable giving over of things or persons to the LORD, often by totally destroying them; also in verses 12, 20 and 21.

Cross references (center column):

11:6 [t]S Jos 2:24; [u]S Ge 49:6; [v]ver 9
11:8 [w]S Ge 10:15; S Jdg 18:7; [x]Jos 13:6
11:10 [y]Isa 3:25; Jer 41:2; 44:18
11:11 [z]S Dt 7:2; [a]Dt 20:16-17; [b]S Nu 31:10
11:12 [c]Nu 33:50-52; Dt 7:2
11:14 [d]S Dt 20:16
11:15 [e]Ex 34:11; Dt 7:2; S Jos 1:7
11:16 [f]Nu 13:17; [g]S Dt 1:7; [h]S Jos 10:41
11:17 [i]S Ge 14:6; S Nu 24:18; S Dt 33:2; [j]Jos 13:5; [k]S Dt 3:25; Jos 12:7; [l]Dt 3:9; Jos 12:8; [m]Dt 7:24
11:19 [n]S Jos 9:1; [o]S Jos 9:3; [p]S Jos 9:15
11:20 [q]S Ex 4:21; S 14:17; Ro 9:18; [r]Dt 7:16; Jdg 14:4
11:21 [s]S Nu 13:22,33; [t]S Jos 10:3; [u]Jos 15:50
11:22 [v]S Ge 10:19; [w]Jos 12:17; 19:13; 1Sa 5:8; 17:4; 1Ki 2:39; 2Ki 14:25; [x]1Ch 8:13; Am 6:2; Jos 15:47; 1Sa 5:1; Isa 20:1
11:23 [y]Jos 21:43-45; Ne 9:24; [z]S Dt 1:38; 12:9-10; S 25:19; S Jos 13:7; [a]S Nu 26:53; [b]Ps 105:44; [c]S Ex 33:14; [d]Jos 14:15

Study notes (bottom):

11:10 *Joshua ... captured Hazor.* Perhaps his greatest victory. Hazor's armed forces, however, had been defeated earlier at Merom. The archaeological site reveals extensive damage and the burning of the Canaanite city c. 1400 B.C., c. 1300 and again c. 1230. Since the destruction level at c. 1300 probably indicates the burning of the city by Pharaoh Seti I, this leaves the destruction levels at c. 1400 and c. 1230 for Joshua's conquest. Those who hold to the late date of the conquest opt for the 1230 level; those who hold to the early date opt for 1400 (see Introduction: Historical Setting). Once again the ban of total destruction was applied (v. 11).
11:13 *mounds.* The Hebrew word is *tel* (Arabic *tell*), a hill formed by the accumulated debris of many ancient settlements one above the other (see note on 7:2).
11:15 *he left nothing undone.* Joshua's success should be measured in the light of the specific orders given by God, which he carried out fully, rather than by the total area that eventually would have to be occupied by Israel.
11:16 *this entire land.* A lesson in the geography of Canaan follows.
11:17 *Mount Halak.* A desert peak to the east of Kadesh Barnea marking Israel's southern extremity. *Baal Gad.* The first valley west of Mount Hermon.

11:18 *for a long time.* An estimation of the duration of Joshua's conquests can be made from the life-span of Caleb: Seven years had elapsed from the beginning of the conquest (age 78; compare 14:7 with Dt 2:14) until he took Hebron (age 85; see 14:10).
11:20 *the LORD ... hardened their hearts.* God has sovereign control of history, yet his will never denies our personal and moral freedom (cf. the case of Pharaoh, Ex 8:32; 9:12).
11:21 *Anakites.* Had been reported by the 12 spies to be a people "of great size" (Nu 13:32), whom the Israelites had feared so much that they had refused to undertake the conquest. They were related to the Nephilim (see note on Ge 6:4) and were named after their forefather, Anak. Joshua shared with Caleb his victory over the Anakites (14:12–15).
12:1–24 A conclusion to the first section of Joshua, and a summary of the victories of the Israelites and the cities whose kings had been defeated (see map No. 3 at the end of the Study Bible).
12:1 *territory ... east of the Jordan.* The unity of the nation is reaffirmed by the inclusion of these lands in Transjordan. *Arnon Gorge.* Marked the border with Moab to the south. *Mount Hermon.* The upper limits of Israel's land to the north.

and whose territory they took[e] over east of the Jordan,[f] from the Arnon[g] Gorge to Mount Hermon,[h] including all the eastern side of the Arabah:[i]

[2]Sihon king of the Amorites, who reigned in Heshbon.[j] He ruled from Aroer[k] on the rim of the Arnon Gorge—from the middle of the gorge—to the Jabbok River,[l] which is the border of the Ammonites.[m] This included half of Gilead.[n] [3]He also ruled over the eastern Arabah from the Sea of Kinnereth[o] to the Sea of the Arabah (the Salt Sea[g,p]), to Beth Jeshimoth,[q] and then southward below the slopes of Pisgah.[r]

[4]And the territory of Og king of Bashan,[s] one of the last of the Rephaites,[t] who reigned in Ashtaroth[u] and Edrei. [5]He ruled over Mount Hermon, Salecah,[v] all of Bashan[w] to the border of the people of Geshur[x] and Maacah,[y] and

half of Gilead[z] to the border of Sihon king of Heshbon.

[6]Moses, the servant of the LORD, and the Israelites conquered them.[a] And Moses the servant of the LORD gave their land to the Reubenites, the Gadites and the half-tribe of Manasseh to be their possession.[b]

[7]These are the kings of the land that Joshua and the Israelites conquered on the west side of the Jordan, from Baal Gad in the Valley of Lebanon[c] to Mount Halak, which rises toward Seir (their lands Joshua gave as an inheritance to the tribes of Israel according to their tribal divisions— [8]the hill country, the western foothills, the Arabah, the mountain slopes, the desert and the Negev[d]—the lands of the Hittites,

12:1	*e* Ps 136:21
	f S Nu 32:19
	g S Nu 21:13
	h S Dt 3:8
	i S Jos 11:2
12:2	*j* ver 5;
	S Nu 21:21,25;
	Jos 13:10;
	Jdg 11:19
	k S Nu 32:34;
	S Jos 13:16
	l S Ge 32:22
	m S Ge 19:38
	n S Ge 31:21;
	S Nu 32:26;
	Dt 2:36; S 3:15;
	Jos 13:11,25;
	17:1; 20:8;
	21:38; Jdg 5:17;
	7:3; 10:8
12:3	*o* Jos 11:2
	p S Ge 14:3
	q S Nu 33:49;
	Jos 13:20
	r S Nu 21:20
12:4	
	s S Nu 21:21,33;
	Jos 13:30
	t S Ge 14:5
	u S Dt 1:4
12:5	*v* S Dt 3:10
	w Nu 32:33;
	Jos 17:1; 20:8;
	21:27; 22:7
	x Jos 13:2,13;
	1Sa 27:8

y S Dt 3:14 *z* ver 2 **12:6** *a* S Dt 3:8 *b* Nu 32:29,33; Jos 13:8
12:7 *c* S Jos 11:17 **12:8** *d* S Dt 1:7

f 3 That is, Galilee   *g 3* That is, the Dead Sea

12:4 *Og king of Bashan.* Og and Sihon (v. 2) met defeat under the command of Moses, a long-remembered tribute to God's mighty power (see Ne 9:22; Ps 135:11).

12:7 *the land . . . on the west side.* Canaan proper (9:1; 11:16–17; 24:11; Ge 15:18–19).

---

4. THE NORTHERN CAMPAIGN

Late Bronze Age Hazor was burned by Joshua (Jos 11:13). Excavations have revealed three clearly datable destruction layers, one of which may provide the strongest evidence yet for a historically verifiable date for the conquest.

The excavator thought Joshua burned the latest level (c. 1230 B.C.), but others argue that it must actually have been the earliest of the three levels, c. 1400 B.C.

Conquest of Canaan

1. ENTRY INTO CANAAN

When the Israelite tribes approached Canaan after four decades of desert existence, they had to overcome the two Amorite kingdoms on the Medeba plateau and in Bashan. Under Moses' leadership, they also subdued the Midianites in order to consolidate their control over the Transjordanian region.

The conquest of Canaan followed a course that in retrospect appears as though it had been planned by a brilliant strategist. Taking Jericho gave Israel control of its strategic plains, fords and roads as a base of operations. When Israel next gained control of the Bethel, Gibeon and the Upper Beth Horon region, she dominated the center of the north-south Palestinian ridge. Subsequently, she was able to break the power of the allied urban centers in separate campaigns south and north.

Amorites, Canaanites, Perizzites, Hivites and Jebusites): *e*

⁹the king of Jericho *f* — one
the king of Ai *g* (near Bethel *h*) — one
¹⁰the king of Jerusalem *i* — one
the king of Hebron — one
¹¹the king of Jarmuth — one
the king of Lachish *j* — one
¹²the king of Eglon *k* — one
the king of Gezer *l* — one
¹³the king of Debir *m* — one
the king of Geder — one
¹⁴the king of Hormah *n* — one
the king of Arad *o* — one
¹⁵the king of Libnah *p* — one
the king of Adullam *q* — one
¹⁶the king of Makkedah *r* — one
the king of Bethel *s* — one
¹⁷the king of Tappuah *t* — one
the king of Hepher *u* — one
¹⁸the king of Aphek *v* — one
the king of Lasharon — one
¹⁹the king of Madon — one

the king of Hazor *w* — one
²⁰the king of Shimron Meron — one
the king of Acshaph *x* — one
²¹the king of Taanach *y* — one
the king of Megiddo *z* — one
²²the king of Kedesh *a* — one
the king of Jokneam *b* in Carmel *c* — one
²³the king of Dor (in Naphoth Dor *h d*) — one
the king of Goyim in Gilgal — one
²⁴the king of Tirzah *e* — one
thirty-one kings in all. *f*

Land Still to Be Taken

13 When Joshua was old and well advanced in years, *g* the LORD said to him, "You are very old, and there are still

Cross-references (center column):

12:8 *e*S Jos 3:10; S 11:17; Ezr 9:1
12:9 *f*S Nu 33:48 *g*S Ge 12:8; S Jos 8:1 *h*S Jos 7:2; 8:9; 18:13; Jdg 1:23; 4:5; 20:18; 21:2; Ne 11:31
12:10 *i*S Jos 10:1
12:11 *j*S Jos 10:3
12:12 *k*S Jos 10:3 *i*S Jos 10:33
12:13 *m*S Jos 10:3
12:14 *n*S Nu 14:45 *o*S Nu 21:1
12:15 *p*S Nu 33:20 *q*S Ge 38:1; Jos 15:35; Mic 1:15
12:16 *r*S Jos 10:10 *s*S Jos 7:2
12:17 *t*Jos 15:34; 16:8; 17:8 *u*S Jos 11:22; 1Ki 4:10
12:18 *v*Jos 13:4; 19:30; Jdg 1:31; 1Sa 4:1; 29:1
12:19 *w*S Jos 11:1
12:20 *x*S Jos 11:1

12:21 *y*Jos 17:11; 21:25 *z*Jdg 1:27; 5:19; 1Ki 4:12 **12:22** *a*Jos 15:23; 19:37; 20:7; 21:32; Jdg 4:6,9 *b*Jos 19:11; 21:34 *c*Jos 15:55; 19:26; 1Sa 15:12; 2Sa 23:35 **12:23** *d*S Jos 11:2 **12:24** *e*1Ki 14:17; 15:33; 16:8,23; SS 6:4 *f*Ps 135:11; 136:18 **13:1** *g*Ge 24:1; Jos 14:10; 23:1,2; 1Ki 1:1

*h*23 Or *in the heights of Dor*

12:12 *king of Gezer.* Had been defeated in the siege of Lachish (10:33), but the city itself was not captured by Joshua, nor were the cities of Aphek, Taanach, Megiddo or Dor (vv. 18–23; see Jdg 1:27–31).

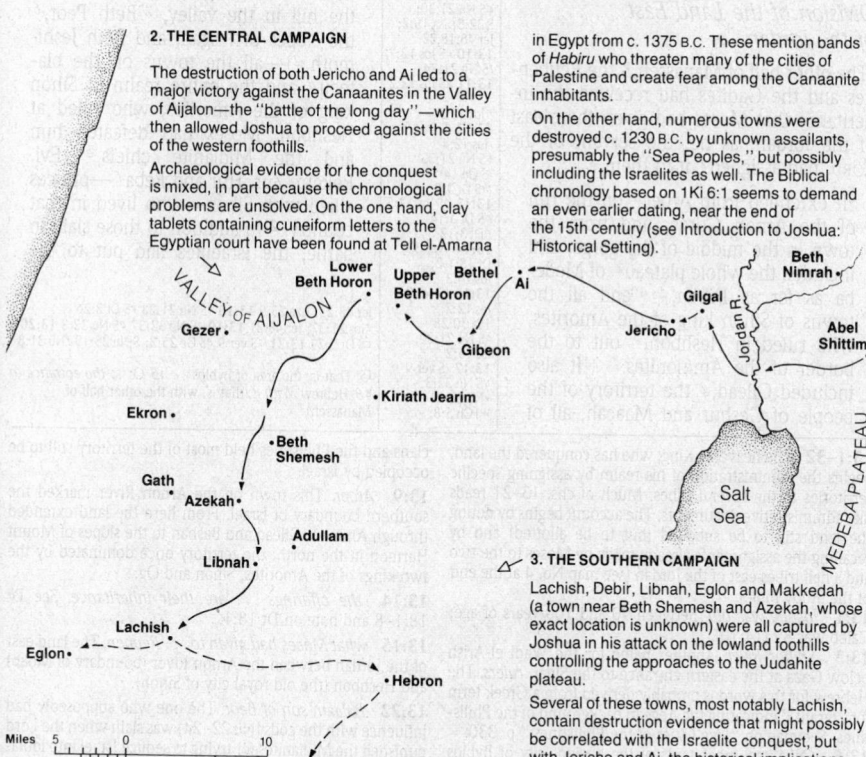

2. THE CENTRAL CAMPAIGN

The destruction of both Jericho and Ai led to a major victory against the Canaanites in the Valley of Aijalon—the "battle of the long day"—which then allowed Joshua to proceed against the cities of the western foothills.

Archaeological evidence for the conquest is mixed, in part because the chronological problems are unsolved. On the one hand, clay tablets containing cuneiform letters to the Egyptian court have been found at Tell el-Amarna

in Egypt from c. 1375 B.C. These mention bands of *Habiru* who threaten many of the cities of Palestine and create fear among the Canaanite inhabitants.

On the other hand, numerous towns were destroyed c. 1230 B.C. by unknown assailants, presumably the "Sea Peoples," but possibly including the Israelites as well. The Biblical chronology based on 1Ki 6:1 seems to demand an even earlier dating, near the end of the 15th century (see Introduction to Joshua: Historical Setting).

3. THE SOUTHERN CAMPAIGN

Lachish, Debir, Libnah, Eglon and Makkedah (a town near Beth Shemesh and Azekah, whose exact location is unknown) were all captured by Joshua in his attack on the lowland foothills controlling the approaches to the Judahite plateau.

Several of these towns, most notably Lachish, contain destruction evidence that might possibly be correlated with the Israelite conquest, but with Jericho and Ai, the historical implications are not clear.

Map labels: VALLEY OF AIJALON, Lower Beth Horon, Upper Beth Horon, Bethel, Ai, Gilgal, Beth Nimrah, Jordan R., Gezer, Gibeon, Jericho, Abel Shittim, Kiriath Jearim, Ekron, Beth Shemesh, Gath, Azekah, Adullam, Libnah, Lachish, Eglon, Hebron, Debir, Salt Sea, MEDEBA PLATEAU

Miles 5 0 10
Kms 5 0 10

very large areas of land to be taken over.

2"This is the land that remains: all the regions of the Philistines[h] and Geshurites: [i] 3from the Shihor River[j] on the east of Egypt to the territory of Ekron[k] on the north, all of it counted as Canaanite (the territory of the five Philistine rulers[l] in Gaza, Ashdod, [m] Ashkelon, [n] Gath and Ekron—that of the Avvites); [o] 4from the south, all the land of the Canaanites, from Arah of the Sidonians as far as Aphek, [p] the region of the Amorites, [q] 5the area of the Gebalites[i]; [r] and all Lebanon[s] to the east, from Baal Gad below Mount Hermon[t] to Lebo[j] Hamath. [u]

6"As for all the inhabitants of the mountain regions from Lebanon to Misrephoth Maim, [v] that is, all the Sidonians, I myself will drive them out[w] before the Israelites. Be sure to allocate this land to Israel for an inheritance, as I have instructed you, [x] 7and divide it as an inheritance[y] among the nine tribes and half of the tribe of Manasseh."

Division of the Land East of the Jordan

8The other half of Manasseh, [k] the Reubenites and the Gadites had received the inheritance that Moses had given them east of the Jordan, as he, the servant of the Lord, had assigned[z] it to them. [a]

9It extended from Aroer[b] on the rim of the Arnon Gorge, and from the town in the middle of the gorge, and included the whole plateau[c] of Medeba as far as Dibon, [d] 10and all the towns of Sihon king of the Amorites, who ruled in Heshbon, [e] out to the border of the Ammonites.[f] 11It also included Gilead, [g] the territory of the people of Geshur and Maacah, all of

Mount Hermon and all Bashan as far as Salecah[h]— 12that is, the whole kingdom of Og in Bashan, [i] who had reigned in Ashtaroth[j] and Edrei[k] and had survived as one of the last of the Rephaites. [l] Moses had defeated them and taken over their land. [m] 13But the Israelites did not drive out the people of Geshur[n] and Maacah, [o] so they continue to live among the Israelites to this day. [p]

14But to the tribe of Levi he gave no inheritance, since the offerings made by fire to the Lord, the God of Israel, are their inheritance, as he promised them. [q]

15This is what Moses had given to the tribe of Reuben, clan by clan:

16The territory from Aroer[r] on the rim of the Arnon Gorge, and from the town in the middle of the gorge, and the whole plateau past Medeba[s] 17to Heshbon and all its towns on the plateau, [t] including Dibon, [u] Bamoth Baal, [v] Beth Baal Meon, [w] 18Jahaz, [x] Kedemoth, [y] Mephaath, [z] 19Kiriathaim, [a] Sibmah, [b] Zereth Shahar on the hill in the valley, 20Beth Peor, [c] the slopes of Pisgah, and Beth Jeshimoth 21—all the towns on the plateau[d] and the entire realm of Sihon king of the Amorites, who ruled at Heshbon. Moses had defeated him and the Midianite chiefs, [e] Evi, Rekem, Zur, Hur and Reba[f]—princes allied with Sihon—who lived in that country. 22In addition to those slain in battle, the Israelites had put to the

13:2
hS Ge 10:14;
S Jdg 3:31
iS Jos 12:5
13:3 /1Ch 13:5;
Isa 23:3; Jer 2:18
kJos 15:11,45;
19:43; Jdg 1:18;
1Sa 5:10; 7:14
/Jdg 3:3; 16:5,18;
1Sa 6:4,17;
Isa 14:29;
Jer 25:20;
Eze 25:15
mS Jos 11:22;
Am 3:9
nJdg 1:18; 14:19;
2Sa 1:20
oS Dt 2:23
13:4 pS Jos 12:18
qS Ge 14:7;
S 15:16; Am 2:10
13:5 r1Ki 5:18;
Ps 83:7; Eze 27:9
sS Jos 11:17
tS Dt 3:8
uS Nu 13:21;
34:8; Jdg 3:3
13:6 vJos 11:8
wPs 80:8
xNu 33:54;
S 34:13
13:7
yS Jos 11:23;
Ps 78:55
13:8 zS Jos 12:6
aJos 18:7
13:9 bver 16;
S Nu 32:34;
Dt 2:36;
Jdg 11:26;
2Sa 24:5 cver 17,
21; Jer 48:8,21
dS Nu 21:30;
S 32:3; Isa 15:2;
Jer 48:18,22
13:10 eS Jos 12:2
fS Nu 21:24
13:11 gS Jos 12:2

hJos 12:5
13:12 iS Dt 1:4
/Jos 12:4
kS Nu 21:33
lS Ge 14:5
mS Dt 3:8
13:13 nS Jos 12:5
oS Dt 3:14
pDt 3:12
13:14 qver 33;
Dt 18:1-2;
Jos 14:3
13:16 rver 9;
Jos 12:2;
1Sa 30:28
sS Nu 21:30;
Isa 15:2
13:17 tS ver 9
uS Nu 32:3
vNu 22:41
w1Ch 5:8;

Jer 48:23; Eze 25:9 **13:18** xS Nu 21:23 yS Dt 2:26
z Jos 21:37; Jer 48:21 **13:19** aS Nu 32:37 bS Nu 32:3 **13:20**
cS Dt 3:29 **13:21** dS ver 9 eS Ge 25:2; S Nu 25:15 /Nu 31:8

i5 That is, the area of Byblos   j5 Or to the entrance to
k8 Hebrew With it (that is, with the other half of Manasseh)

13:1–32 The heavenly King, who has conquered the land, begins the administration of his realm by assigning specific territories to the several tribes. Much of chs. 13–21 reads like administrative documents. The account begins by noting the land still to be subdued (but to be allotted) and by recalling the assignments already made by Moses to the two and a half tribes east of the Jordan (see map No. 4 at the end of the Study Bible).
13:1 *Joshua was old.* Between 90 and 100 years of age; Caleb was 85 (14:10).
13:3 *Shihor River.* Another name for the Wadi el-Arish below Gaza at the eastern entrance to the Sinai. *rulers.* The Hebrew for this word is probably derived from a Greek term for "tyrant," indicating the Aegean background of the Philistines. See map on "Five Cities of the Philistines," p. 330.
13:5 *Gebalites.* Inhabitants of the ancient city of Byblos (see NIV text note) just north of modern Beirut. The Phoeni-

cians and the Philistines held most of the territory still to be occupied by Israel.
13:9 *Aroer.* This town on the Arnon River marked the southern boundary of Israel. From here the land extended through Ammon, Gilead and Bashan to the slopes of Mount Hermon in the north, the territory once dominated by the two kings of the Amorites, Sihon and Og.
13:14 *the offerings . . . are their inheritance.* See Dt 18:1–8 and note on Dt 18:1.
13:15 *what Moses had given to . . . Reuben.* The land east of the Jordan between the Arnon River (boundary of Moab) and Heshbon (the old royal city of Sihon).
13:22 *Balaam son of Beor.* The one who supposedly had influence with the gods (Nu 22–24) was slain when the Lord punished the Midianites for trying to seduce Israel into idolatry and sexual immorality (see Nu 25; 31:8).

sword Balaam son of Beor,^{g} who practiced divination.^{h} ^{23}The boundary of the Reubenites was the bank of the Jordan. These towns and their villages were the inheritance of the Reubenites, clan by clan.^{i}

^{24}This is what Moses had given to the tribe of Gad, clan by clan:

^{25}The territory of Jazer,^{j} all the towns of Gilead^k and half the Ammonite country as far as Aroer, near Rabbah;^{l} ^{26}and from Heshbon^m to Ramath Mizpah and Betonim, and from Mahanaim^n to the territory of Debir;^{o} ^{27}and in the valley, Beth Haram, Beth Nimrah,^{p} Succoth^q and Zaphon^r with the rest of the realm of Sihon king of Heshbon (the east side of the Jordan, the territory up to the end of the Sea of Kinnereth^{1s}). ^{28}These towns and their villages were the inheritance of the Gadites,^{t} clan by clan.

^{29}This is what Moses had given to the half-tribe of Manasseh, that is, to half the family of the descendants of Manasseh, clan by clan:

^{30}The territory extending from Mahanaim^u and including all of Bashan,^{v} the entire realm of Og king of Bashan^w—all the settlements of Jair^x in Bashan, sixty towns, ^{31}half of Gilead, and Ashtaroth and Edrei (the royal cities of Og in Bashan).^{y} This was for the descendants of Makir^z son of Manasseh—for half of the sons of Makir, clan by clan.^{a}

^{32}This is the inheritance Moses had given when he was in the plains of Moab^b across the Jordan east of Jericho.^{c} ^{33}But to the tribe of Levi, Moses had given no inheritance;^{d} the LORD, the God of Israel, is their inheritance,^{e} as he promised them.^{f}

Cross References

13:22 ^{g}S Nu 22:5
^{h}S Ge 30:27;
S Nu 23:23
13:23 ^{i}1Ch 5:7
13:25
^{j}S Nu 21:32;
Jos 21:39
^{k}S Jos 12:2
^{l}S Dt 3:11
13:26
^{m}S Nu 21:25;
Jer 49:3
^{n}S Ge 32:2
^{o}S Jos 10:3
13:27 ^{p}S Nu 32:3
^{q}S Ge 33:17
^{r}Jdg 12:1; Ps 48:2
^{s}S Nu 34:11
13:28 ^{t}Ge 46:16;
S Nu 32:33;
Eze 48:27
13:30 ^{u}S Ge 32:2
^{v}S Nu 21:33
^{w}S Jos 12:4
^{x}S Nu 32:41
13:31 ^{y}Nu 21:33
^{z}S Ge 50:23
^{a}Jos 17:5
13:32 ^{b}S Nu 26:3
^{c}S Nu 22:1
13:33 ^{d}Nu 26:62
^{e}S Nu 18:20
^{f}S ver 14;
Jos 18:7;
Eze 44:28

14:1
^{g}S Jos 11:23;
Ps 16:6; 136:21
^{h}S Ex 6:23
^{i}Jos 21:1
^{j}S Nu 26:53
^{k}Nu 34:17-18;
Jos 19:51
14:2 ^{l}S Lev 16:8
^{m}Nu 34:13
14:3
^{n}S Nu 32:33;
S 34:14
^{o}S Nu 35:2;
S Jos 13:14
14:4
^{p}S Ge 41:52;
S Jdg 1:29
^{q}S Nu 35:2-3;
Jos 21:2
14:5 ^{r}S Nu 34:13
14:6 ^{s}S Dt 11:30
^{t}Nu 13:6; 14:30
^{u}S Dt 33:1
^{v}Nu 13:26
^{w}S Nu 14:38
14:7 ^{x}Jos 15:3
^{y}S Nu 13:17
^{z}Nu 13:30;
S 14:6-9
14:8 ^{a}S Nu 13:31
^{b}S Nu 14:24;
S 32:12
14:9 ^{c}S Dt 11:24
^{d}S Nu 14:24
14:10
^{e}S Nu 11:28;
14:30 ^{f}S Jos 5:6

Division of the Land West of the Jordan

14 Now these are the areas the Israelites received as an inheritance^g in the land of Canaan, which Eleazar^h the priest, Joshua son of Nun and the heads of the tribal clans of Israel^i allotted^j to them.^{k} ^{2}Their inheritances were assigned by lot^l to the nine-and-a-half tribes, ^{m} as the LORD had commanded through Moses. ^{3}Moses had granted the two-and-a-half tribes their inheritance east of the Jordan^n but had not granted the Levites an inheritance among the rest,^{o} ^{4}for the sons of Joseph had become two tribes—Manasseh and Ephraim.^{p} The Levites received no share of the land but only towns to live in, with pasturelands for their flocks and herds.^{q} ^{5}So the Israelites divided the land, just as the LORD had commanded Moses.^{r}

Hebron Given to Caleb

^{6}Now the men of Judah approached Joshua at Gilgal,^{s} and Caleb son of Jephunneh^t the Kenizzite said to him, "You know what the LORD said to Moses the man of God^u at Kadesh Barnea^v about you and me.^{w} ^{7}I was forty years old when Moses the servant of the LORD sent me from Kadesh Barnea^x to explore the land.^{y} And I brought him back a report according to my convictions,^{z} ^{8}but my brothers who went up with me made the hearts of the people melt with fear.^{a} I, however, followed the LORD my God wholeheartedly.^{b} ^{9}So on that day Moses swore to me, 'The land on which your feet have walked will be your inheritance^c and that of your children^d forever, because you have followed the LORD my God wholeheartedly.'^{m}

^{10}"Now then, just as the LORD promised,^{e} he has kept me alive for forty-five years since the time he said this to Moses, while Israel moved^f about in the desert.

^{1}27 That is, Galilee ^{m}9 Deut. 1:36

13:24 *what Moses had given to . . . Gad.* The central area, beginning near Heshbon on the south and reaching, along the Jordan, to the southern end of the Sea of Galilee. It included most of Gilead, but the exact boundary between Gad and the half-tribe of Manasseh remains somewhat uncertain since not all the places named can now be located.
13:29 *what Moses had given to the half-tribe of Manasseh.* The lands east and north of the Sea of Galilee, but also including the upper part of Gilead. Makir led in the occupation of these lands (see Nu 32:32,39–42).
13:33 *the LORD . . . is their inheritance.* See v.14; see also Dt 18:1–8 and note on Dt 18:1.
14:1–15 A short introductory chapter for the following

section (chs. 15–19), with a special note on the Lord's faithfulness to Caleb.
14:1 *Eleazar the priest.* Son of Aaron, Eleazar as high priest was the highest official over the casting of the lots. The Urim and Thummim (see notes on Ex 28:30; 1Sa 2:28) may have been used.
14:4 *Manasseh and Ephraim.* Sons of Joseph. Since Jacob had adopted them as his own sons (Ge 48:5), they constituted two separate tribes. This made possible the 12-part nation, with the Levites serving as a nonpolitical tribe.
14:6 *what the LORD said.* Caleb now recalls the promise from the Lord 38 years earlier at Kadesh Barnea when he brought back a good report of the land (Nu 13:30; 14:6–9; Dt 1:34–36).

So here I am today, eighty-five years old![g] [11]I am still as strong[h] today as the day Moses sent me out; I'm just as vigorous[i] to go out to battle now as I was then. [12]Now give me this hill country that the LORD promised me that day.[j] You yourself heard then that the Anakites[k] were there and their cities were large and fortified,[l] but, the LORD helping me, I will drive them out just as he said."

[13]Then Joshua blessed[m] Caleb son of Jephunneh[n] and gave him Hebron[o] as his inheritance.[p] [14]So Hebron has belonged to Caleb son of Jephunneh the Kenizzite ever since, because he followed the LORD, the God of Israel, wholeheartedly.[q] [15](Hebron used to be called Kiriath Arba[r] after Arba,[s] who was the greatest man among the Anakites.)

Then the land had rest[t] from war.

Allotment for Judah

15:15-19pp — Jdg 1:11-15

15 The allotment for the tribe of Judah, clan by clan, extended down to the territory of Edom,[u] to the Desert of Zin[v] in the extreme south.[w]

[2]Their southern boundary started from the bay at the southern end of the Salt Sea,[n][x] [3]crossed south of Scorpion[o] Pass,[y] continued on to Zin and went over to the south of Kadesh Barnea.[z] Then it ran past Hezron up to Addar and curved around to Karka. [4]It then passed along to Azmon[a] and joined the Wadi of Egypt,[b] ending at the sea. This is their[p] southern boundary.

[5]The eastern boundary[c] is the Salt Sea[d] as far as the mouth of the Jordan.

The northern boundary[e] started from the bay of the sea at the mouth of the Jordan, [6]went up to Beth Hoglah[f] and continued north of Beth Arabah[g] to the Stone of Bohan[h] son of Reuben. [7]The boundary then went up

to Debir[i] from the Valley of Achor[j] and turned north to Gilgal,[k] which faces the Pass of Adummim south of the gorge. It continued along to the waters of En Shemesh[l] and came out at En Rogel.[m] [8]Then it ran up the Valley of Ben Hinnom[n] along the southern slope of the Jebusite[o] city (that is, Jerusalem[p]). From there it climbed to the top of the hill west of the Hinnom Valley[q] at the northern end of the Valley of Rephaim.[r] [9]From the hilltop the boundary headed toward the spring of the waters of Nephtoah,[s] came out at the towns of Mount Ephron and went down toward Baalah[t] (that is, Kiriath Jearim).[u] [10]Then it curved westward from Baalah[v] to Mount Seir,[w] ran along the northern slope of Mount Jearim (that is, Kesalon), continued down to Beth Shemesh[x] and crossed to Timnah.[y] [11]It went to the northern slope of Ekron,[z] turned toward Shikkeron, passed along to Mount Baalah[a] and reached Jabneel.[b] The boundary ended at the sea.

[12]The western boundary is the coastline of the Great Sea.[q][c]

These are the boundaries around the people of Judah by their clans.

[13]In accordance with the LORD's command to him, Joshua gave to Caleb[d] son of Jephunneh a portion in Judah—Kiriath Arba[e], that is, Hebron.[f] (Arba was the forefather of Anak.)[g] [14]From Hebron Caleb drove out the three Anakites[h]—Sheshai, Ahiman and Talmai[i]—descendants of Anak.[j] [15]From there he marched against the people living

---

14:10 [g]S Jos 13:1
14:11 [h]S Dt 34:7
/S Ge 15:15
14:12
/S Nu 14:24
[k]S Nu 13:33
/Nu 13:28
14:13 [m]Jos 22:6,
7 [n]1Sa 25:3;
30:14
[o]S Ge 23:19;
S Jos 10:36
[p]Jdg 1:20;
1Ch 6:56
14:14
[q]S Nu 14:24
14:15 [r]S Ge 23:2
[s]Jos 15:13
[t]Jos 11:23;
Jdg 3:11;
1Ki 4:24; 5:4;
1Ch 22:9
15:1 [u]Nu 34:3
[v]S Nu 13:21
[w]Jos 18:5
15:2 [x]S Ge 14:3
15:3 [y]S Nu 34:4
[z]S Dt 1:2
15:4 [a]Nu 34:4
[b]S Ge 15:18
15:5 [c]Nu 34:10
[d]S Ge 14:3
[e]Jos 18:15-19
15:6 [f]Jos 18:19,
21 [g]ver 61;
Jos 18:18
[h]Jos 18:17

15:7 [i]S Jos 10:3
/S Jos 7:24
[k]S Dt 11:30
/Jos 18:17
[m]Jos 18:16;
2Sa 17:17;
1Ki 1:9
15:8 [n]2Ch 28:3;
Jer 19:6 [o]ver 63;
Jos 18:16,28;
Jdg 1:21; 19:10;
2Sa 5:6;
1Ch 11:4; Ezr 9:1
[p]S Jos 10:1
[q]2Ki 23:10;
Jer 7:31; 19:2
[r]2Sa 5:18,22;
1Ch 14:9;
Isa 17:5
15:9 [s]Jos 18:15
[t]ver 10,11,29;
2Sa 6:2; 1Ch 13:6
[u]S Jos 9:17
15:10 [v]S ver 9
[w]S Nu 24:18
[x]Jos 19:22,38;
21:16; Jdg 1:33;
1Sa 6:9; 1Ki 4:9;
2Ki 14:11
[y]S Ge 38:12
15:11 [z]S Jos 13:3
[a]S ver 9
[b]Jos 19:33
15:12 [c]S Nu 34:6

15:13 [d]1Sa 25:3; 30:14 [e]S Ge 23:2 /S Jos 10:36; 21:12;
1Ch 6:56 [g]S Nu 13:22 15:14 [h]S Nu 13:33 [i]S Nu 13:22
/Jdg 1:10,20

[n]2 That is, the Dead Sea; also in verse 5   [o]3 Hebrew
Akrabbim   [p]4 Hebrew your   [q]12 That is, the
Mediterranean; also in verse 47

14:12 *this hill country.* Hebron is situated high in the Judahite hill country, about 25 miles south of Jerusalem. *Anakites.* See note on 11:21.
14:15 *Kiriath Arba.* Means "the town of Arba" and was named for Arba, the father of the Anakites (15:13; 21:11). It can also mean "the town of four." Hebron means "union." *Then the land had rest from war.* Since the Judahites and Caleb approached Joshua concerning their territory while he was still headquartered at Gilgal, it may be that they did so shortly before the wars fought under Joshua were ended (see 11:23).
15:1–63 Judah is the first of the west bank tribes to have its territory delineated. First the outer limits are listed, then the area apportioned to Caleb and Othniel; finally the Canaanite cities allotted to the clans of Judah are named region by

region.
15:1 *tribe of Judah.* Judah's priority is anchored in the oracle of Jacob (Ge 49:8–12) and upheld in the history of the nation (2Ki 17:18).
15:4 *southern boundary.* The points listed formed a curved line beginning at the lower tip of the Dead Sea and moving under Kadesh Barnea to join the Mediterranean coast at the mouth of the Wadi el-Arish (see note on 13:3).
15:5 *northern boundary.* Judah's border with Benjamin ran in a westerly line from the mouth of the Jordan through the Hinnom Valley, just south of Jerusalem, over to Timnah, then northwest to the coastal city of Jabneel (later called Jamnia), about ten miles south of Joppa.
15:15 *he marched against . . . Debir.* See note on 10:38.

in Debir (formerly called Kiriath Sepher). [16]And Caleb said, "I will give my daughter Acsah[k] in marriage to the man who attacks and captures Kiriath Sepher." [17]Othniel[l] son of Kenaz, Caleb's brother, took it; so Caleb gave his daughter Acsah to him in marriage.

[18]One day when she came to Othniel, she urged him[r] to ask her father for a field. When she got off her donkey, Caleb asked her, "What can I do for you?"

[19]She replied, "Do me a special favor. Since you have given me land in the Negev,[m] give me also springs of water." So Caleb gave her the upper and lower springs.[n]

[20]This is the inheritance of the tribe of Judah, clan by clan:

[21]The southernmost towns of the tribe of Judah in the Negev[o] toward the boundary of Edom were:

Kabzeel,[p] Eder,[q] Jagur, [22]Kinah, Dimonah, Adadah, [23]Kedesh,[r] Hazor,[s] Ithnan, [24]Ziph,[t] Telem, Bealoth, [25]Hazor Hadattah, Kerioth Hezron (that is, Hazor),[u] [26]Amam, Shema, Moladah,[v] [27]Hazar Gaddah, Heshmon, Beth Pelet, [28]Hazar Shual,[w] Beersheba,[x] Biziothiah, [29]Baalah,[y] Iim, Ezem,[z] [30]Eltolad,[a] Kesil, Hormah,[b] [31]Ziklag,[c] Madmannah,[d] Sansannah, [32]Lebaoth, Shilhim, Ain[e] and Rimmon[f]—a total of twenty-nine towns and their villages.

[33]In the western foothills:

Eshtaol,[g] Zorah,[h] Ashnah,[i] [34]Zanoah,[j] En Gannim,[k] Tappuah,[l] Enam, [35]Jarmuth,[m] Adullam,[n] Socoh,[o] Azekah,[p] [36]Shaaraim,[q] Adithaim and Gederah[r] (or Gederothaim)[s]—fourteen towns and their villages.

[37]Zenan, Hadashah, Migdal Gad, [38]Dilean, Mizpah,[s] Joktheel,[t] [39]Lachish,[u] Bozkath,[v] Eglon,[w] [40]Cabbon, Lahmas, Kitlish, [41]Gederoth,[x] Beth Dagon,[y] Naamah and Makkedah[z]—sixteen towns and their villages.

[42]Libnah,[a] Ether, Ashan,[b] [43]Iphtah, Ashnah,[c] Nezib, [44]Keilah,[d] Aczib[e] and Mareshah[f]—nine towns and their villages.

[45]Ekron,[g] with its surrounding settlements and villages; [46]west of Ekron, all that were in the vicinity of Ashdod,[h] together with their villages; [47]Ashdod,[i] its surrounding settlements and villages; and Gaza, its settlements and villages, as far as the Wadi of Egypt[j] and the coastline of the Great Sea.[k]

[48]In the hill country:

Shamir,[l] Jattir,[m] Socoh,[n] [49]Dannah, Kiriath Sannah (that is, Debir[o]), [50]Anab,[p] Eshtemoh,[q] Anim, [51]Goshen,[r] Holon[s] and Giloh[t]—eleven towns and their villages.

[52]Arab, Dumah,[u] Eshan, [53]Janim, Beth Tappuah, Aphekah, [54]Humtah, Kiriath Arba[v] (that is, Hebron) and Zior—nine towns and their villages.

[55]Maon,[w] Carmel,[x] Ziph,[y] Juttah,[z] [56]Jezreel,[a] Jokdeam, Zanoah,[b] [57]Kain, Gibeah[c] and Timnah[d]—ten towns and their villages.

[58]Halhul, Beth Zur,[e] Gedor,[f] [59]Maarath, Beth Anoth and Eltekon—six towns and their villages.

[60]Kiriath Baal[g] (that is, Kiriath Jearim[h]) and Rabbah[i]—two towns and their villages.

[61]In the desert:[j]

Beth Arabah,[k] Middin, Secacah, [62]Nibshan, the City of Salt and En

---

Cross-references (center column):

15:16 [k]1Ch 2:49
15:17 [l]Jdg 3:9, 11; 1Ch 4:13; 27:15
15:19 [m]S Jos 10:40 [n]Ge 36:24
15:21 [o]S Jos 10:40 [p]2Sa 23:20; 1Ch 11:22 [q]Ge 35:21
15:23 [r]S Jos 12:22 [s]S Jos 11:1
15:24 [t]ver 55; 1Sa 23:14; 2Ch 11:8
15:25 [u]S Jos 11:1
15:26 [v]Jos 19:2; 1Ch 4:28; Ne 11:26
15:28 [w]Jos 19:3; 1Ch 4:28 [x]S Ge 21:14 [y]S ver 9 [z]Jos 19:3; 1Ch 4:29
15:30 [a]Jos 19:4 [b]S Nu 14:45
15:31 [c]Jos 19:5; 1Sa 27:6; 1Ch 4:30; 12:1; Ne 11:28 [d]1Ch 2:49
15:32 [e]S Nu 34:11 [f]Jos 19:7; Jdg 20:45; 21:13; Zec 14:10
15:33 [g]Jos 19:41; Jdg 13:25; 16:31; 18:2 [h]Jdg 13:2; 18:11; 2Ch 11:10; Ne 11:29 [i]ver 43
15:34 [j]ver 56; 1Ch 4:18; Ne 3:13; 11:30 [k]Jos 19:21; 21:29 [l]S Jos 12:17
15:35 [m]S Jos 10:3 [n]S Ge 38:1 [o]ver 48; 1Ki 4:10 [p]S Jos 10:10
15:36 [q]1Sa 17:52; 1Ch 4:31 [r]1Ch 12:4
15:38 [s]S Jos 11:3 [t]2Ki 14:7
15:39 [u]S Jos 10:3 [v]2Ki 22:1 [w]S Jos 10:3
15:41 [x]2Ch 28:18 [y]Jos 19:27 [z]S Jos 10:10
15:42 [a]S Nu 33:20 [b]Jos 19:7; 1Sa 30:30; 1Ch 4:32; 6:59
15:43 [c]ver 33
15:44 [d]1Sa 23:1-2,1; 1Ch 4:19; Ne 3:17,18

[e]Jos 19:29; Jdg 1:31; Mic 1:14 [f]Mic 1:15 **15:45** [g]S Jos 13:3 **15:46** [h]Jos 11:22 **15:47** [i]S Jos 11:22 [j]S Ge 15:18 [k]S Nu 34:6 **15:48** [l]Jdg 10:1 [m]Jos 21:14; 1Sa 30:27; 1Ch 6:57 [n]S ver 35 **15:49** [o]S Jos 10:3 **15:50** [p]Jos 11:21 [q]Jos 21:14; 1Sa 30:28 **15:51** [r]S Jos 10:41 [s]Jos 21:15; Jer 48:21 [t]2Sa 15:12 **15:52** [u]S Ge 25:14 **15:54** [v]S Ge 35:27 **15:55** [w]Jdg 10:12; 1Sa 23:24,25; 25:1,2; 1Ch 2:45 [x]S Jos 12:22 [y]S ver 24 [z]Jos 21:16 **15:56** [a]Jos 17:16; 19:18; Jdg 6:33; 1Sa 25:43; 1Ki 18:45; 1Ch 3:1; Hos 1:5 [b]S ver 34 **15:57** [c]Jos 18:28; 24:33; Jdg 19:12; 20:4; 2Sa 23:29; 1Ch 11:31 [d]S Ge 38:12 **15:58** [e]1Ch 2:45; 2Ch 11:7; Ne 3:16 [f]1Ch 4:39; 12:7 **15:60** [g]ver 9 [h]S Jos 9:17 [i]S Dt 3:11 **15:61** [j]S Jos 8:15 [k]S ver 6

[r]18 Hebrew and some Septuagint manuscripts; other Septuagint manuscripts (see also note at Judges 1:14) *Othniel, he urged her*   [s]36 Or *Gederah and Gederothaim*

Study notes (bottom):

15:17 *Othniel.* See Jdg 3:7–11 for his service as judge in Israel.

15:19 *upper and lower springs.* They still water the local farms in Hebron.

15:21 *southernmost towns.* Most of the first 29 villages were assigned to the tribe of Simeon (cf. 19:1–9).

15:33 *western foothills.* The Hebrew term for this term is *Shephelah,* meaning "lowland." This area between the highlands of central Judah and the Philistine coast was for the most part not occupied by Israel until the victories of King

David. Some of the places on this list were reassigned to the tribe of Dan (cf. 19:41–43).

15:48 *hill country.* The high region south of Jerusalem. The Septuagint adds 11 names, including Tekoa and Bethlehem, to this list.

15:61 *desert.* The chalky, dry region east and south of Jerusalem that borders the Dead Sea.

15:62 Only En Gedi can be positively located, though the "City of Salt" is believed by many to be Qumran, where, centuries later, the scribes who produced the Dead Sea

Gedi[l]—six towns and their villages.
63Judah could not[m] dislodge the Jebusites[n], who were living in Jerusalem;[o] to
this day the Jebusites live there with the
people of Judah.[p]

Allotment for Ephraim and Manasseh

16 The allotment for Joseph began at the Jordan of Jericho,[t]
east of the waters of Jericho, and went
up from there through the desert[q]
into the hill country of Bethel.[r] 2It
went on from Bethel (that is, Luz[s]),[u]
crossed over to the territory of the Arkites[t] in Ataroth,[u] 3descended westward to the territory of the Japhletites
as far as the region of Lower Beth Horon[v] and on to Gezer,[w] ending at the
sea.
4So Manasseh and Ephraim, the descendants of Joseph, received their inheritance.[x]
5This was the territory of Ephraim, clan by
clan:
The boundary of their inheritance
went from Ataroth Addar[y] in the east
to Upper Beth Horon[z] 6and continued
to the sea. From Micmethath[a] on the
north it curved eastward to Taanath
Shiloh, passing by it to Janoah[b] on the
east. 7Then it went down from Janoah[c] to Ataroth[d] and Naarah,
touched Jericho and came out at the
Jordan. 8From Tappuah[e] the border
went west to the Kanah Ravine[f] and
ended at the sea. This was the inheritance of the tribe of the Ephraimites,
clan by clan. 9It also included all the
towns and their villages that were set
aside for the Ephraimites within the
inheritance of the Manassites.[g]
10They did not dislodge the Canaanites living in Gezer; to this day the Canaanites
live among the people of Ephraim but are
required to do forced labor.[h]

15:62 [l]1Sa 23:29; 24:1; Eze 47:10 **15:63** [m]Jos 16:10; 17:12; Jdg 1:21; 1Ki 9:21 [n]S ver 8 [o]S Jos 10:1 [p]Eze 48:7 **16:1** [q]S Jos 8:15 [r]S Jos 12:9 **16:2** [s]S Ge 28:19 [t]2Sa 15:32 [u]S ver 5; S Nu 32:3 **16:3** [v]S Jos 10:10 [w]S Jos 10:33 **16:4** [x]Jos 18:5 **16:5** [y]ver 2; Jos 18:13 [z]S Jos 10:10 **16:6** [a]Jos 17:7 [b]ver 7; 2Ki 15:29 **16:7** [c]S ver 6 [d]S Nu 32:3 **16:8** [e]S Jos 12:17 [f]Jos 17:9; 19:28 **16:9** [g]Eze 48:5 **16:10** [h]S Jos 15:63; 17:13; Jdg 1:28-29; 1Ki 9:16

17:1 [i]S Nu 1:34; 1Ch 7:14 [j]S Ge 41:51 [k]S Ge 50:23 [l]S Jos 12:2 [m]S Jos 12:5 **17:2** [n]Jos 22:7 [o]S Nu 26:30; Jdg 6:11,34; 8:2; 1Ch 7:18 [p]1Ch 7:14 [q]S Nu 27:1 [r]1Ch 7:19 **17:3** [s]S Nu 27:1 [t]S Nu 26:33 **17:4** [u]Nu 27:5-7 **17:5** [v]Jos 13:30-31 **17:7** [w]ver 10; Jos 19:24,31; 21:6,30; Jdg 1:31; 5:17; 6:35; 7:23 [x]Jos 16:6 [y]S Ge 12:6; Jos 21:21; 24:25; Jdg 9:1 **17:8** [z]S Jos 12:17 **17:9** [a]S Jos 16:8

17 This was the allotment for the tribe
of Manasseh[i] as Joseph's firstborn,[j] that is, for Makir,[k] Manasseh's
firstborn. Makir was the ancestor of the
Gileadites, who had received Gilead[l] and
Bashan[m] because the Makirites were great
soldiers. 2So this allotment was for the rest
of the people of Manasseh[n]—the clans of
Abiezer,[o] Helek, Asriel,[p] Shechem, Hepher[q] and Shemida.[r] These are the other
male descendants of Manasseh son of Joseph by their clans.
3Now Zelophehad son of Hepher,[s] the
son of Gilead, the son of Makir, the son of
Manasseh, had no sons but only daughters,[t] whose names were Mahlah, Noah,
Hoglah, Milcah and Tirzah. 4They went to
Eleazar the priest, Joshua son of Nun, and
the leaders and said, "The LORD commanded Moses to give us an inheritance
among our brothers." So Joshua gave them
an inheritance along with the brothers of
their father, according to the LORD's command.[u] 5Manasseh's share consisted of ten
tracts of land besides Gilead and Bashan
east of the Jordan,[v] 6because the daughters of the tribe of Manasseh received an
inheritance among the sons. The land of
Gilead belonged to the rest of the descendants of Manasseh.
7The territory of Manasseh extended from Asher[w] to Micmethath[x]
east of Shechem.[y] The boundary ran
southward from there to include the
people living at En Tappuah. 8(Manasseh had the land of Tappuah, but
Tappuah[z] itself, on the boundary of
Manasseh, belonged to the Ephraimites.) 9Then the boundary continued
south to the Kanah Ravine.[a] There
were towns belonging to Ephraim lying among the towns of Manasseh,

[t]*1 Jordan of Jericho* was possibly an ancient name for the Jordan River. [u]*2* Septuagint; Hebrew *Bethel to Luz*

Scrolls lived.

15:63 *Jebusites.* A victory over the city of the Jebusites by the men of Judah is recorded in Jdg 1:8, but evidently this did not result in its permanent occupation. Both Benjamin and Judah failed to take the Jebusite fortress of Jerusalem (Jdg 1:21).

16:1–17:18 Two chapters are devoted to the lands given to the "house of Joseph" (Ephraim and the half-tribe of Manasseh that settled west of the Jordan). Following Judah, the Joseph tribes were given priority.

16:1 *allotment for Joseph.* Ephraim's southern border moved west from Jericho past Bethel and down to Gezer and the Mediterranean coast.

16:5 *boundary.* Ephraim's northern border began down by the Jordan and ran west near Shiloh, but south of Shechem, then followed the Wadi Kanah down to the Mediterranean Sea.

16:10 *Gezer.* See note on 10:33. *but are required to do forced labor.* Since Gezer does not appear to have come under Israelite control until the days of Solomon (1Ki 9:15–16), this may be a note added after that event (but see 2Sa 5:25).

17:1 *Manasseh as Joseph's firstborn.* A reminder to the proud Ephraimites that Manasseh had been the firstborn, though Jacob gave priority to Ephraim when he adopted Joseph's two sons (Ge 48:14,19).

17:3 *Zelophehad . . . had . . . only daughters.* Before Moses died, he promised the daughters an allotment along with their relatives (see Nu 26:33; 27:1–7).

17:5 *ten tracts of land.* Manasseh's territory was second only to Judah's in size. Then ten portions went to the five brothers (minus Hepher) and to the five daughters of Hepher. For the law protecting the inheritance rights of a daughter without brothers see Nu 27:8–11.

but the boundary of Manasseh was the northern side of the ravine and ended at the sea. ¹⁰On the south the land belonged to Ephraim, on the north to Manasseh. The territory of Manasseh reached the sea and bordered Asher ᵇ on the north and Issachar ᶜ on the east. ᵈ

¹¹Within Issachar ᵉ and Asher, Manasseh also had Beth Shan,ᶠ Ibleam ᵍ and the people of Dor,ʰ Endor,ⁱ Taanach ʲ and Megiddo,ᵏ together with their surrounding settlements (the third in the list is Naphoth ᵛ).ᶦ

¹²Yet the Manassites were not able ᵐ to occupy these towns, for the Canaanites were determined to live in that region. ¹³However, when the Israelites grew stronger, they subjected the Canaanites to forced labor but did not drive them out completely.ⁿ

¹⁴The people of Joseph said to Joshua, "Why have you given us only one allotment and one portion for an inheritance? We are a numerous people and the LORD has blessed us abundantly." ᵒ

¹⁵"If you are so numerous," Joshua answered, "and if the hill country of Ephraim is too small for you, go up into the forest ᵖ and clear land for yourselves there in the land of the Perizzites ᑫ and Rephaites. ʳ "

¹⁶The people of Joseph replied, "The hill country is not enough for us, and all the Canaanites who live in the plain have iron chariots,ˢ both those in Beth Shan ᵗ and its settlements and those in the Valley of Jezreel." ᵘ

¹⁷But Joshua said to the house of Jo-

seph—to Ephraim and Manasseh—"You are numerous and very powerful. You will have not only one allotment ᵛ ¹⁸but the forested hill country ʷ as well. Clear it, and its farthest limits will be yours; though the Canaanites have iron chariots ˣ and though they are strong, you can drive them out."

Division of the Rest of the Land

18 The whole assembly of the Israelites gathered at Shiloh ʸ and set up the Tent of Meeting ᶻ there. The country was brought under their control, ²but there were still seven Israelite tribes who had not yet received their inheritance.

³So Joshua said to the Israelites: "How long will you wait before you begin to take possession of the land that the LORD, the God of your fathers, has given you? ⁴Appoint three men from each tribe. I will send them out to make a survey of the land and to write a description of it, ᵃ according to the inheritance of each. ᵇ Then they will return to me. ⁵You are to divide the land into seven parts. Judah is to remain in its territory on the south ᶜ and the house of Joseph in its territory on the north. ᵈ ⁶After you have written descriptions of the seven parts of the land, bring them here to me and I will cast lots ᵉ for you in the presence of the LORD our God. ⁷The Levites, however, do not get a portion among you, because the priestly service of the LORD is their inheritance.ᶠ And Gad, Reuben and the half-tribe of Manasseh have already received their inheritance on the east side of

Cross references (center column)

17:10 ᵇS ver 7; ᶜS Ge 30:18
ᵈEze 48:5
17:11 ᵉver 10; ᶠver 16; Jdg 1:27; 1Sa 31:10; 2Sa 21:12; 1Ki 4:12; 1Ch 7:29; ᵍ2Ki 9:27; ʰS Jos 11:2; ⁱ1Sa 28:7; Ps 83:10; ʲS Jos 12:21; ᵏ1Ki 9:15; ᶦEze 48:4
17:12 ᵐS Jos 15:63
17:13 ⁿJdg 1:27-28
17:14 ᵒNu 26:28-37
17:15 ᵖ2Sa 18:6; ᑫS Jos 3:10; ʳS Ge 14:5; Jos 15:8; 18:16; 2Sa 5:18; 23:13; Isa 17:5
17:16 ˢver 18; Jdg 1:19; 4:3,13; ᵗS ver 11; ᵘS Jos 15:56; S 1Sa 29:1
17:17 ᵛEze 48:5
17:18 ʷ1Sa 1:1; ˣS ver 16
18:1 ʸver 8; Jos 19:51; 21:2; Jdg 18:31; 21:12; 19; 1Sa 1:3; 3:21; 4:3; 1Ki 14:2; Ps 78:60; Jer 7:12; 26:6; 41:5 ᶻS ver 10; S Ex 27:21; S 40:2; Ac 7:45
18:4 ᵃver 8; ᵇMic 2:5
18:5 ᶜJos 15:1
ᵈJos 16:1-4
18:6 ᵉS Lev 16:8
18:7 ᶠS Jos 13:33

ᵛ11 That is, Naphoth Dor

17:11 *Beth Shan ... Megiddo.* These powerfully fortified cities, and others along Manasseh's common border with Issachar and Asher, were not conquered until later. When King Saul died in battle, the victorious Philistines fastened his body to the wall of Beth Shan (see 1Sa 31:10), which suggests that that city was in league with the Philistines.

17:13 *when the Israelites grew stronger.* Possibly referring to the days of David and Solomon (see note on 16:10).

17:14 *people of Joseph ... numerous.* The reference is to both Ephraim and Manasseh (see v. 17). The allotment to the Joseph tribes are handled as one (see 16:1,4)—though the two subdivisions are then described separately (16:5–17:11).

17:15 *hill country of Ephraim.* The territory of the Joseph tribes—under the name of the legal firstborn (see note on v. 1). *clear land for yourselves.* This region of Canaan was still heavily forested. It seems that the Israelites viewed their assigned territories primarily in terms of the number of cities that had their land cleared for farming and pasturage, not in terms of the size of the region in which these cities were located. The region assigned to the Joseph tribes was at the time not as heavily populated as others. *Perizzites and Rephaites.* Here listed as neighboring peoples, though elsewhere the Perizzites are said to have lived on the west bank in Canaan (3:10; 12:8) and the Rephaites in the Transjordan

kingdom of Og (12:4; 13:12). See notes on Ge 13:7; Dt 2:11.

17:16 *in the plain.* Only in the plains were chariots effective. *iron chariots.* Chariots with certain parts made of iron (see note on 2Sa 8:7), perhaps the axles—the use of iron was a new development (see note on 11:6).

18:1–19:51 Seven tribes remained to be assigned land: Benjamin, Simeon, Zebulun, Issachar, Asher, Naphtali and Dan. Their lots were cast at Shiloh, after which a special portion was awarded to Joshua.

18:1 *Shiloh.* About ten miles northeast of Bethel, a little east of the main road between Bethel to Shechem. *Tent of Meeting.* The tabernacle (see note on Ex 27:21) with its sacred ark of the covenant. It would remain at Shiloh until the time of Samuel (1Sa 4:3).

18:3 *take possession.* Conquest had to be followed by settlement, which required a survey, then a fair distribution, and then a full occupation of the land. A distinction must therefore be made between the national wars of conquest (Joshua) and the tribal wars of occupation (Jdg 1–2).

18:5 *north.* Relative to the territory of Judah.

18:6 *I will cast lots for you.* See note on 14:1.

18:7 *priestly service of the LORD is their inheritance.* See 13:14; see also Dt 18:1–8 and note on Dt 18:1.

the Jordan. Moses the servant of the LORD gave it to them. *g* "

8As the men started on their way to map out the land, Joshua instructed them, "Go and make a survey of the land and write a description of it. *h* Then return to me, and I will cast lots for you here at Shiloh *i* in the presence of the LORD." 9So the men left and went through the land. They wrote its description on a scroll, town by town, in seven parts, and returned to Joshua in the camp at Shiloh. 10Joshua then cast lots *j* for them in Shiloh in the presence *k* of the LORD, and there he distributed the land to the Israelites according to their tribal divisions. *l*

Allotment for Benjamin

11The lot came up for the tribe of Benjamin, clan by clan. Their allotted territory lay between the tribes of Judah and Joseph:

12On the north side their boundary began at the Jordan, passed the northern slope of Jericho and headed west into the hill country, coming out at the desert *m* of Beth Aven. *n* 13From there it crossed to the south slope of Luz *o* (that is, Bethel *p*) and went down to Ataroth Addar *q* on the hill south of Lower Beth Horon.

14From the hill facing Beth Horon *r* on the south the boundary turned south along the western side and came out at Kiriath Baal (that is, Kiriath Jearim), *s* a town of the people of Judah. This was the western side.

15The southern side began at the outskirts of Kiriath Jearim on the west, and the boundary came out at the spring of the waters of Nephtoah. *t* 16The boundary went down to the foot of the hill facing the Valley of Ben Hinnom, north of the Valley of Rephaim. *u* It continued down the Hinnom Valley *v* along the southern slope of the Jebusite city and so to En Rogel. *w* 17It then curved north, went to En Shemesh, continued to Geliloth, *x* which faces the Pass of Adummim, *y* and ran down to the Stone of Bohan *z* son of Reuben. 18It continued to the northern slope of Beth Arabah *w a* and on down into the Arabah. *b* 19It then

18:7 *g*Jos 13:8
18:8 *h*ver 4 *i*S ver 1
18:10 /S Nu 34:13
*k*S ver 1; Jer 7:12
/Nu 33:54;
Jos 19:51
18:12 *m*S Jos 8:15
*n*S Jos 7:2
18:13 *o*S Ge 28:19
*p*S Jos 12:9
*q*S Nu 32:3;
S Jos 16:5
18:14 *r*Jos 10:10
*s*S Jos 9:17
18:15 *t*Jos 15:9
18:16 *u*S Jos 17:15
*v*Jos 15:8
*w*S Jos 15:7
18:17 *x*Jos 22:10
*y*Jos 15:7
*z*Jos 15:6
18:18 *a*S Jos 15:6
*b*S Jos 11:2

18:19 *c*S Jos 15:6
*d*S Ge 14:3
18:20 *e*1Sa 9:1
18:21 /S Jos 15:6
18:22 *g*Jos 15:6
*h*2Ch 13:4
/Jos 16:1
18:23 /S Dt 2:23
*k*Jdg 6:11,24;
8:27,32; 9:5;
1Sa 13:17
18:24 /Jos 21:17;
1Sa 13:3,16;
14:5; 1Ki 15:22;
2Ki 23:8;
Isa 10:29
18:25 *m*Jos 9:3
*n*S Jos 10:40;
Jdg 4:5; 19:13;
1Sa 1:1,19; 2:11;
7:17; 25:1;
1Ki 15:17,21;
Ezr 2:26;
Ne 11:33;
Isa 10:29;
Jer 31:15; 40:1
*o*S Jos 9:17;
Ezr 2:25; Ne 7:29
18:26 *p*S Jos 11:3
*q*Jos 9:17;
Ezr 2:25; Ne 7:29
18:28 *r*2Sa 21:14
*s*S Jos 15:8
*t*S Jos 10:1
*u*S Jos 15:57
*v*S Jos 9:17
*w*Eze 48:23
19:1 *x*S Ge 49:7
19:2
*y*S Ge 21:14;
1Ki 19:3
*z*S Jos 15:26
19:3 *a*S Jos 15:28
*b*S Jos 15:29
19:4 *c*Jos 15:30
*d*S Nu 14:45
19:5 *e*S Jos 15:31
19:7 /S Jos 15:32
*g*S Jos 15:42
19:8 *h*S Jos 10:40
19:9 /S Ge 49:7

went to the northern slope of Beth Hoglah *c* and came out at the northern bay of the Salt Sea, *x d* at the mouth of the Jordan in the south. This was the southern boundary.

20The Jordan formed the boundary on the eastern side.

These were the boundaries that marked out the inheritance of the clans of Benjamin on all sides. *e*

21The tribe of Benjamin, clan by clan, had the following cities:

Jericho, Beth Hoglah, *f* Emek Keziz, 22Beth Arabah, *g* Zemaraim, *h* Bethel, *i* 23Avvim, *j* Parah, Ophrah, *k* 24Kephar Ammoni, Ophni and Geba *l* —twelve towns and their villages.

25Gibeon, *m* Ramah, *n* Beeroth, *o* 26Mizpah, *p* Kephirah, *q* Mozah, 27Rekem, Irpeel, Taralah, 28Zelah, *r* Haeleph, the Jebusite city *s* (that is, Jerusalem *t*), Gibeah *u* and Kiriath —fourteen towns and their villages. *v*

This was the inheritance of Benjamin for its clans. *w*

Allotment for Simeon

19:2-10pp — 1Ch 4:28-33

19 The second lot came out for the tribe of Simeon, clan by clan. Their inheritance lay within the territory of Judah. *x* 2It included:

Beersheba *y* (or Sheba), *y* Moladah, *z* 3Hazar Shual, *a* Balah, Ezem, *b* 4Eltolad, *c* Bethul, Hormah, *d* 5Ziklag, *e* Beth Marcaboth, Hazar Susah, 6Beth Lebaoth and Sharuhen —thirteen towns and their villages;

7Ain, Rimmon, *f* Ether and Ashan *g*—four towns and their villages— 8and all the villages around these towns as far as Baalath Beer (Ramah in the Negev). *h*

This was the inheritance of the tribe of the Simeonites, clan by clan. 9The inheritance of the Simeonites was taken from the share of Judah, *i* because Judah's portion was more than they needed. So the Simeonites

w 18 Septuagint; Hebrew slope facing the Arabah
x 19 That is, the Dead Sea   *y 2 Or Beersheba, Sheba; 1 Chron. 4:28 does not have Sheba.*

18:9 *scroll.* Presumed form of the document; the Hebrew for this word is not specific.
18:11 *lot . . . for . . . Benjamin.* A buffer zone between Judah and Ephraim, the two dominant tribes. Its northern line was the same as Ephraim's southern border (see note on 16:1), and its southern line the same as Judah's northern-

most boundary (see note on 15:5).

18:23 *Avvim.* The people of Ai.

19:1 *second lot . . . for . . . Simeon.* Cities within the borders of Judah (15:21) in the Negev along Judah's southern border (1Ch 4:24–42).

received their inheritance within the territory of Judah. *i*

Allotment for Zebulun

[10]The third lot came up for Zebulun, *k* clan by clan:

The boundary of their inheritance went as far as Sarid. *l* [11]Going west it ran to Maralah, touched Dabbesheth, and extended to the ravine near Jokneam. *m* [12]It turned east from Sarid *n* toward the sunrise to the territory of Kisloth Tabor and went on to Daberath *o* and up to Japhia. [13]Then it continued eastward to Gath Hepher *p* and Eth Kazin; it came out at Rimmon *q* and turned toward Neah. [14]There the boundary went around on the north to Hannathon and ended at the Valley of Iphtah El. *r* [15]Included were Kattath, Nahalal, *s* Shimron, *t* Idalah and Bethlehem. *u* There were twelve towns and their villages. [16]These towns and their villages were the inheritance of Zebulun, *v* clan by clan. *w*

Allotment for Issachar

[17]The fourth lot came out for Issachar, *x* clan by clan. [18]Their territory included:

Jezreel, *y* Kesulloth, Shunem, *z* [19]Hapharaim, Shion, Anaharath, [20]Rabbith, Kishion, *a* Ebez, [21]Remeth, En Gannim, *b* En Haddah and Beth Pazzez. [22]The boundary touched Tabor, *c* Shahazumah and Beth Shemesh, *d* and ended at the Jordan. There were sixteen towns and their villages. [23]These towns and their villages were the inheritance of the tribe of Issachar, *e* clan by clan. *f*

Allotment for Asher

[24]The fifth lot came out for the tribe of Asher, *g* clan by clan. [25]Their territory included:

Helkath, Hali, Beten, Acshaph, *h* [26]Allammelech, Amad and Mishal. *i* On the west the boundary touched Carmel *j* and Shihor Libnath. [27]It then turned east toward Beth Dagon, *k*

touched Zebulun *l* and the Valley of Iphtah El, *m* and went north to Beth Emek and Neiel, passing Cabul *n* on the left. [28]It went to Abdon, *z o* Rehob, *p* Hammon *q* and Kanah, *r* as far as Greater Sidon. *s* [29]The boundary then turned back toward Ramah *t* and went to the fortified city of Tyre, *u* turned toward Hosah and came out at the sea *v* in the region of Aczib, *w* [30]Ummah, Aphek *x* and Rehob. *y* There were twenty-two towns and their villages.

[31]These towns and their villages were the inheritance of the tribe of Asher, *z* clan by clan.

Allotment for Naphtali

[32]The sixth lot came out for Naphtali, clan by clan:

[33]Their boundary went from Heleph and the large tree in Zaanannim, *a* passing Adami Nekeb and Jabneel *b* to Lakkum and ending at the Jordan. [34]The boundary ran west through Aznoth Tabor and came out at Hukkok. *c* It touched Zebulun *d* on the south, Asher on the west and the Jordan *a* on the east. [35]The fortified cities were Ziddim, Zer, Hammath, *e* Rakkath, Kinnereth, *f* [36]Adamah, Ramah, *g* Hazor, *h* [37]Kedesh, *i* Edrei, *j* En Hazor, [38]Iron, Migdal El, Horem, Beth Anath *k* and Beth Shemesh. *l* There were nineteen towns and their villages.

[39]These towns and their villages were the inheritance of the tribe of Naphtali, clan by clan. *m*

Allotment for Dan

[40]The seventh lot came out for the tribe of Dan, clan by clan. [41]The territory of their inheritance included:

Zorah, Eshtaol, *n* Ir Shemesh, [42]Shaalabbin, Aijalon, *o* Ithlah, [43]Elon,

19:9 /Eze 48:24
19:10 kver 16,27, 34; Jos 21:7,34
iver 12
19:11
mS Jos 12:22
19:12 nver 10
oJos 21:28;
1Ch 6:72
19:13
pS Jos 11:22
qJos 15:32
19:14 rver 27
19:15 sJos 21:35
tJos 11:1
uS Ge 35:19
19:16 vS ver 10
wEze 48:26
19:17
xS Ge 30:18
19:18
yS Jos 15:56
z1Sa 28:4;
1Ki 1:3; 2Ki 4:8
19:20 aJos 21:28
19:21
bS Jos 15:34
19:22 cJdg 4:6, 12; 8:18;
Ps 89:12;
Jer 46:18
dS Jos 15:10
19:23 eJos 17:10
/Ge 49:15;
Eze 48:25
19:24 gS Jos 17:7
19:25 hS Jos 11:1
19:26 iJos 21:30
/S Jos 12:22;
1Ki 18:19;
2Ki 2:25
19:27 kJos 15:41

/S ver 10 mver 14
n1Ki 9:13
19:28
oJos 21:30;
1Ch 6:74 pver 30; Nu 13:21;
Jos 21:31;
Jdg 1:31
q1Ch 6:76
rS Jos 16:8
sS Ge 10:19
19:29 tJos 18:25
u2Sa 5:11; 24:7;
Ezr 3:7; Ps 45:12;
Isa 23:1;
Jer 25:22;
Eze 26:2
vJdg 5:17
wS Jos 15:44
19:30
xS Jos 12:18
yS ver 28
19:31
zS Ge 30:13;
S Jos 17:7;
Eze 48:2
19:33 aJdg 4:11
bJos 15:11
19:34 c1Ch 6:75
dS ver 10
19:35 e1Ch 2:55
/S Jos 11:2
19:36 gJos 18:25
hS Jos 11:1
19:37
iS Jos 12:22
/S Nu 21:33

19:38 kJdg 1:33 lS Jos 15:10 19:39 mEze 48:3 19:41
nS Jos 15:33 19:42 oS Jos 10:12

z28 Some Hebrew manuscripts (see also Joshua 21:30); most Hebrew manuscripts Ebron   a34 Septuagint; Hebrew west, and Judah, the Jordan,

---

19:10 *third lot . . . for Zebulun.* To this tribe went a portion of lower Galilee west of the Sea of Galilee and in the vicinity of NT Nazareth.

19:17 *fourth lot . . . for Issachar.* Southwest of the Sea of Galilee reaching down to Beth Shan and west to the Jezreel Valley. Mount Tabor marked its northern border.

19:24 *fifth lot . . . for . . . Asher.* Asher was given the coastal area as far north as Sidon in Phoenicia and as far south as Mount Carmel.

19:32 *sixth lot . . . for Naphtali.* An area mostly to the north of the Sea of Galilee, taking in the modern Huleh Valley and the mountains bordering on Asher to the west. Its southernmost point was at the lower edge of the Sea of Galilee.

19:40 *seventh lot . . . for . . . Dan.* An elbow of land squeezed between Ephraim and Judah and west of Benjamin. The port of Joppa marked the northwestern corner of Dan.

Timnah,[p] Ekron,[q] 44Eltekeh, Gibbethon,[r] Baalath,[s] 45Jehud, Bene Berak,
Gath Rimmon,[t] 46Me Jarkon and
Rakkon, with the area facing Joppa.[u]
47(But the Danites had difficulty taking
possession of their territory,[v] so they went
up and attacked Leshem[w], took it, put it to
the sword and occupied it. They settled in
Leshem and named[x] it Dan after their
forefather.)[y]
48These towns and their villages were the
inheritance of the tribe of Dan,[z] clan by
clan.

Allotment for Joshua

49When they had finished dividing the
land into its allotted portions, the Israelites
gave Joshua son of Nun an inheritance
among them, 50as the LORD had commanded. They gave him the town he asked
for—Timnath Serah[b][a] in the hill country
of Ephraim. And he built up the town and
settled there.
51These are the territories that Eleazar
the priest, Joshua son of Nun and the
heads of the tribal clans of Israel assigned
by lot at Shiloh in the presence of the LORD
at the entrance to the Tent of Meeting.
And so they finished dividing[b] the land.[c]

Cities of Refuge

20:1–9Ref — Nu 35:9–34; Dt 4:41–43; 19:1–14

20 Then the LORD said to Joshua:
2"Tell the Israelites to designate
the cities of refuge, as I instructed you
through Moses, 3so that anyone who kills a
person accidentally and unintentionally[d]
may flee there and find protection from the
avenger of blood.[e]
4"When he flees to one of these cities,
he is to stand in the entrance of the city
gate[f] and state his case before the elders[g]
of that city. Then they are to admit him
into their city and give him a place to live
with them. 5If the avenger of blood pursues him, they must not surrender the one
accused, because he killed his neighbor
unintentionally and without malice aforethought. 6He is to stay in that city until he
has stood trial before the assembly[h] and
until the death of the high priest who is
serving at that time. Then he may go back
to his own home in the town from which
he fled."
7So they set apart Kedesh[i] in Galilee in
the hill country of Naphtali, Shechem[j] in
the hill country of Ephraim, and Kiriath
Arba[k] (that is, Hebron[l]) in the hill country of Judah.[m] 8On the east side of the Jordan of Jericho[c] they designated Bezer[n] in
the desert on the plateau in the tribe of
Reuben, Ramoth in Gilead[o][p] in the tribe
of Gad, and Golan in Bashan[q] in the tribe
of Manasseh. 9Any of the Israelites or any
alien living among them who killed some-

19:43 [p]S Ge 38:12 [q]S Jos 13:3 **19:44** [r]Jos 21:23; 1Ki 15:27; 16:15 [s]1Ki 9:18; 2Ch 8:6 **19:45** [t]Jos 21:24; 1Ch 6:69 **19:46** [u]2Ch 2:16; Ezr 3:7; Jnh 1:3; Ac 9:36 **19:47** [v]Jdg 18:1 [w]Jdg 18:7,14 [x]S Dt 3:14 [y]Jdg 18:27,29 **19:48** [z]S Ge 30:6 **19:50** [a]Jos 24:30; Jdg 2:9 **19:51** [b]Jos 23:4 [c]S Jos 14:1; S 18:10; Ac 13:19

20:3 [d]S Lev 4:2 [e]S Nu 35:12 **20:4** [f]S Ge 23:10; Jer 38:7 [g]S Jos 7:6 **20:6** [h]S Nu 35:12 **20:7** [i]S Jos 12:22 [j]S Ge 12:6 [k]S Ge 35:27 [l]S Jos 10:36 [m]Lk 1:39 **20:8** [n]Jos 21:36; 1Ch 6:78 [o]1Ch 6:80 [p]S Jos 12:2 [q]S Jos 12:5; 1Ch 6:71

[b]*50* Also known as *Timnath Heres* (see Judges 2:9)
[c]*8 Jordan of Jericho* was possibly an ancient name for the Jordan River.

19:47 *Danites had difficulty.* The Amorites of this area "confined the Danites to the hill country" (Jdg 1:34), so most of the tribe migrated to the upper Jordan Valley, where they seized the town of Leshem (or Laish, Jdg 18:2–10, 27–29) and renamed it Dan.

19:49 *gave Joshua . . . an inheritance.* In the account of the distribution of the promised land (the territory west of the Jordan), the assignment to Caleb is treated first (14:6–15), the assignment to Joshua last. Thus the allotting of inheritance to these two dauntless servants of the Lord from the desert generation (see Nu 13:30; 14:6,24,30) frames the whole account—and both received the territory they asked for. Appropriately, Joshua's allotment came last; he was not a king or a warlord but the servant of God commissioned to bring the Lord's people into the promised land.

19:50 *Timnath Serah.* Located in the southwestern corner of Ephraim, facing out to the sea. Here Joshua was also buried (24:30).

20:1–9 Having distributed the land to the tribes, the Lord's next administrative regulation (see note on 13:1–32) provided an elementary system of government, specifically a system of regional courts to deal with capital offenses having to do with manslaughter. Thus this most inflammatory of cases was removed from local jurisdiction, and a safeguard was created against the easy miscarriage of justice (with its potential for endless blood feuds) when retribution for manslaughter was left in the hands of family members. The cities chosen were among those also assigned to the Levites, where ideally the law of Moses would especially be known and honored.

20:2 *as I instructed you through Moses.* See Nu 35:6–34.

20:3 *avenger of blood.* Also translated "kinsman-redeemer" (Ru 3:9), or "Redeemer" (Ps 19:14). The avenger was a near relative with the obligation of exacting retribution (see Lev 24:17; Nu 35:16–28).

20:4 *city gate.* Traditional place for trials, where the elders sat to hold court (see Ru 4:1 and note; see also Job 29:7).

20:6 *assembly.* Made up of the adult males of the city. Their function in the trial before the elders (v. 4) is not clear, but perhaps they witnessed the trial to see that it was fair (closed courts are notoriously corruptible). *and.* Or "or." *death of the high priest.* See Nu 35:25–28. Either an atoning effect or a kind of amnesty was achieved by the high priest's death.

20:7 *they set apart Kedesh.* A wordplay in the Hebrew: "they consecrated (the town of) consecration." The other two cities west of the Jordan already had sacred associations: For Shechem see 8:30–35 and note; Ge 12:6–7; for Hebron see Ge 23:2; 49:29–32. The geographical distribution of the cities was important: one in the north, one in the midlands and one in the south. (See v. 8, where the order of the three cities of refuge that served in Transjordan is reversed: Bezer in the south, Ramoth in the midlands and Golan in the north.) See "Cities of Refuge," p. 241.

20:9 *or any alien.* Evidence of the equal protection granted to the foreigners living in Israel (cf. Lev 19:33–34; Dt 10:18–19).

one accidentally[r] could flee to these designated cities and not be killed by the avenger of blood prior to standing trial before the assembly.[s]

Towns for the Levites

21:4–39pp — 1Ch 6:54–80

21 Now the family heads of the Levites approached Eleazar the priest, Joshua son of Nun, and the heads of the other tribal families of Israel[t] ²at Shiloh[u] in Canaan and said to them, "The LORD commanded through Moses that you give us towns[v] to live in, with pasturelands for our livestock."[w] ³So, as the LORD had commanded, the Israelites gave the Levites the following towns and pasturelands out of their own inheritance:

⁴The first lot came out for the Kohathites,[x] clan by clan. The Levites who were descendants of Aaron the priest were allotted thirteen towns from the tribes of Judah, Simeon and Benjamin.[y] ⁵The rest of Kohath's descendants were allotted ten towns from the clans of the tribes of Ephraim, Dan and half of Manasseh.[z]

⁶The descendants of Gershon[a] were allotted thirteen towns from the clans of the tribes of Issachar,[b] Asher,[c] Naphtali and the half-tribe of Manasseh in Bashan.

⁷The descendants of Merari,[d] clan by clan, received twelve[e] towns from the tribes of Reuben, Gad and Zebulun.[f]

⁸So the Israelites allotted to the Levites these towns and their pasturelands, as the LORD had commanded through Moses.

⁹From the tribes of Judah and Simeon they allotted the following towns by name ¹⁰(these towns were assigned to the descendants of Aaron who were from the Kohathite clans of the Levites, because the first lot fell to them):

¹¹They gave them Kiriath Arba[g] (that is, Hebron[h]), with its surrounding pastureland, in the hill country of Judah. (Arba was the forefather of Anak.) ¹²But the fields and villages around the city they had given to Caleb son of Jephunneh as his possession.[i]

¹³So to the descendants of Aaron the priest they gave Hebron (a city of refuge[j] for one accused of murder), Libnah,[k] ¹⁴Jattir,[l] Eshtemoa,[m] ¹⁵Holon,[n] Debir,[o] ¹⁶Ain,[p] Juttah[q] and Beth Shemesh,[r] together with their pasturelands—nine towns from these two tribes.

¹⁷And from the tribe of Benjamin they gave them Gibeon,[s] Geba,[t] ¹⁸Anathoth[u] and Almon, together with their pasturelands—four towns.

¹⁹All the towns[v] for the priests, the descendants of Aaron, were thirteen, together with their pasturelands.[w]

²⁰The rest of the Kohathite clans of the Levites were allotted towns from the tribe of Ephraim:

²¹In the hill country of Ephraim they were given Shechem[x] (a city of refuge for one accused of murder) and Gezer,[y] ²²Kibzaim and Beth Horon,[z] together with their pasturelands—four towns.[a]

²³Also from the tribe of Dan they received Eltekeh, Gibbethon,[b] ²⁴Aijalon[c] and Gath Rimmon,[d] together with their pasturelands—four towns.

²⁵From half the tribe of Manasseh they received Taanach[e] and Gath Rimmon, together with their pasturelands—two towns.

²⁶All these ten towns and their pasturelands were given to the rest of the Kohathite clans.[f]

²⁷The Levite clans of the Gershonites were given:

from the half-tribe of Manasseh,
Golan in Bashan[g] (a city of refuge for one accused of murder[h]) and Be Eshtarah, together with their pasturelands—two towns;

²⁸from the tribe of Issachar,[i]
Kishion,[j] Daberath,[k] ²⁹Jarmuth[l] and En Gannim,[m] together with their pasturelands—four towns;

³⁰from the tribe of Asher,[n]
Mishal,[o] Abdon,[p] ³¹Helkath and Rehob,[q] together with their pasturelands—four towns;

³²from the tribe of Naphtali,
Kedesh[r] in Galilee (a city of refuge for one accused of murder[s]), Hammoth

---

Cross references (center column)

20:9 [r]S Lev 4:2
[s]S Ex 21:13
21:1 [t]Jos 14:1
21:2 [u]S Jos 18:1
[v]S Lev 25:32
[w]S Nu 35:2-3;
S Jos 14:4
21:4 [x]Nu 3:17
[y]ver 19
21:5 [z]ver 26
21:6 [a]Nu 3:17
[b]S Ge 30:18
[c]S Jos 17:7
21:7 [d]S Ex 6:16
[e]ver 40
[f]S Jos 19:10
21:11 [g]S Ge 23:2
[h]S Jos 10:36
21:12
[i]S Jos 15:13

21:13 [j]Nu 35:6
[k]S Nu 33:20
21:14
[l]S Jos 15:48
[m]S Jos 15:50
21:15
[n]S Jos 15:51
[o]S Jos 10:3
21:16
[p]S Nu 34:11
[q]Jos 15:55
[r]S Jos 15:10
21:17 [s]S Jos 9:3
[t]S Jos 18:24;
S Ne 11:31
21:18
[u]2Sa 23:27;
1Ki 2:26;
Ezr 2:23;
Ne 7:27; 11:32;
Isa 10:30; Jer 1:1;
11:21; 32:7
21:19
[v]2Ch 31:15
[w]ver 4
21:21 [x]S Jos 17:7
[y]S Jos 10:33
21:22
[z]S Jos 10:10
[a]1Sa 1:1
21:23
[b]S Jos 19:44
21:24
[c]S Jos 10:12
[d]S Jos 19:45
21:25
[e]S Jos 12:21
21:26 [f]ver 5
21:27 [g]S Jos 12:5
[h]Nu 35:6
21:28
[i]S Ge 30:18
[j]Jos 19:20
[k]S Jos 19:12
21:29 [l]S Jos 10:3
[m]S Jos 15:34
21:30 [n]S Jos 17:7
[o]Jos 19:26
[p]S Jos 19:28
21:31
[q]S Jos 19:28
21:32
[r]S Jos 12:22
[s]Nu 35:6

21:1–45 Finally the Levites are allotted their towns and adjoining pasturelands—with the priestly families being given precedence (see v. 10).
21:4 Kohathites. The three sons of Levi were Kohath, Gershon and Merari (Ex 6:16; Nu 3:17). Judah, Simeon and Benjamin. Tribal areas close to Jerusalem, which would later be the site of the temple. The remaining Kohathites received

cities in adjoining tribes.
21:11 Hebron. Caleb's city (14:13–15). The priests and Levites were to be given space in their assigned cities along with the other inhabitants.
21:27 Gershonites. Received cities in the northern tribes of Asher, Naphtali and Issachar.

Dor and Kartan, together with their pasturelands—three towns.

³³All the towns of the Gershonite^t clans were thirteen, together with their pasturelands.

³⁴The Merarite clans (the rest of the Levites) were given:

from the tribe of Zebulun,^u

Jokneam,^v Kartah, ³⁵Dimnah and Nahalal,^w together with their pasturelands—four towns;

³⁶from the tribe of Reuben,

Bezer,^x Jahaz,^y ³⁷Kedemoth and Mephaath,^z together with their pasturelands—four towns;

³⁸from the tribe of Gad,

Ramoth^a in Gilead^b (a city of refuge for one accused of murder), Mahanaim,^c ³⁹Heshbon and Jazer,^d together with their pasturelands—four towns in all.

⁴⁰All the towns allotted to the Merarite clans, who were the rest of the Levites, were twelve.^e

⁴¹The towns of the Levites in the territory held by the Israelites were forty-eight in all, together with their pasturelands.^f ⁴²Each of these towns had pasturelands surrounding it; this was true for all these towns.

⁴³So the LORD gave Israel all the land he had sworn to give their forefathers,^g and they took possession^h of it and settled there.ⁱ ⁴⁴The LORD gave them rest^j on every side, just as he had sworn to their forefathers. Not one of their enemies^k withstood them; the LORD handed all their enemies^l over to them.^m ⁴⁵Not one of all the LORD's good promisesⁿ to the house of Israel failed; every one was fulfilled.

Eastern Tribes Return Home

22 Then Joshua summoned the Reubenites, the Gadites and the half-

tribe of Manasseh ²and said to them, "You have done all that Moses the servant of the LORD commanded,^o and you have obeyed me in everything I commanded. ³For a long time now—to this very day—you have not deserted your brothers but have carried out the mission the LORD your God gave you. ⁴Now that the LORD your God has given your brothers rest^p as he promised, return to your homes^q in the land that Moses the servant of the LORD gave you on the other side of the Jordan.^r ⁵But be very careful to keep the commandment^s and the law that Moses the servant of the LORD gave you: to love the LORD^t your God, to walk in all his ways, to obey his commands,^u to hold fast to him and to serve him with all your heart and all your soul.^v"

⁶Then Joshua blessed^w them and sent them away, and they went to their homes. ⁷(To the half-tribe of Manasseh Moses had given land in Bashan,^x and to the other half of the tribe Joshua gave land on the west side^y of the Jordan with their brothers.) When Joshua sent them home, he blessed them,^z ⁸saying, "Return to your homes with your great wealth—with large herds of livestock,^a with silver, gold, bronze and iron,^b and a great quantity of clothing—and divide^c with your brothers the plunder^d from your enemies."

⁹So the Reubenites, the Gadites and the half-tribe of Manasseh left the Israelites at Shiloh^e in Canaan to return to Gilead,^f their own land, which they had acquired in accordance with the command of the LORD through Moses.

¹⁰When they came to Geliloth^g near the Jordan in the land of Canaan, the Reubenites, the Gadites and the half-tribe of Manasseh built an imposing altar^h there by the Jordan. ¹¹And when the Israelites heard that they had built the altar on the border of Canaan at Geliloth near the Jor-

Cross references (center column)

21:33 ^tver 6
21:34
^uS Jos 19:10
^vS Jos 12:22
21:35 ^wJos 19:15
21:36 ^xS Jos 20:8
^yS Nu 21:23;
Dt 2:32;
Jdg 11:20
21:37
^zS Jos 13:18
21:38 ^aS Dt 4:43
^bS Jos 12:2
^cS Ge 32:2
21:39
^dS Jos 13:25
21:40 ^ever 7
21:41 ^fNu 35:7
21:43 ^gDt 34:4
^hDt 1:31
ⁱS Dt 17:14
21:44
^jS Ex 33:14
^kS Dt 6:19
^lS Ex 23:31
^mDt 21:10
21:45
ⁿJos 23:14;
Ne 9:8

22:2 ^oS Nu 32:25
22:4 ^pS Ex 33:14
^qNu 32:22;
Dt 3:20
^rNu 32:18;
S Jos 1:13-15
22:5 ^sIsa 43:22;
Mal 3:14
^tJos 23:11
^uS Dt 5:29
^vS Dt 6:5
22:6
^wS Ge 24:60;
S Ex 39:43
22:7
^xS Nu 32:19;
S Jos 12:5
^yJos 17:2
^zS Jos 14:13;
Lk 24:50
22:8 ^aS Dt 20:14
^bS Nu 31:22
^cS Nu 31:27
^dS Ge 49:27;
1Sa 30:16;
2Sa 1:1; Isa 9:3
22:9 ^eJos 18:1
^fS Nu 32:26
22:10 ^gJos 18:17
^hver 19,26-27;
Isa 19:19; 56:7

21:34 *Merarite clans.* Their 12 cities were scattered over Reuben, Gad and Zebulun.

21:43–45 A concluding summary statement of how the Lord had fulfilled his sworn promise to give Israel this land (see Ge 15:18–21). The occupation of the land was not yet complete (see 23:4–5; Jdg 1–2), but the national campaign was over and Israel was finally established in the promised land. No power was left in Canaan that could threaten to dislodge her.

21:44 *rest on every side.* See note on 1:13.

22:1–34 The two and a half tribes from east of the Jordan, faithful in battle, are now commended by Joshua and sent to their homes. But their "altar of witness" (see vv. 26–27,34) was misunderstood, and disciplinary action against them was narrowly averted.

22:2 *all that Moses ... commanded.* Moses had ordered

them to join the other tribes in the conquest of Canaan (Nu 32:16–27; Dt 3:18).

22:5 *love the LORD ... serve him with all your heart.* Both Moses and Joshua saw that obedience to the laws of God would require love and service from the heart. In the ancient Near East, "love" was also a political term, indicating true-hearted loyalty to one's king.

22:8 *divide with your brothers.* Moses also had seen the need for a fair sharing of the spoils of war (Nu 31:25–27).

22:10 *Geliloth.* Understood in the Septuagint to be Gilgal, next to Jericho; more likely it was a site east of Shiloh along the Jordan River (18:17).

22:11 *when the Israelites heard.* Anxiety about apostasy led to hasty conclusions. They thought the altar had been set up as a rival to the true altar at Shiloh.

dan on the Israelite side, [12]the whole assembly of Israel gathered at Shiloh[i] to go to war against them.

[13]So the Israelites sent Phinehas[j] son of Eleazar,[k] the priest, to the land of Gilead—to Reuben, Gad and the half-tribe of Manasseh. [14]With him they sent ten of the chief men, one for each of the tribes of Israel, each the head of a family division among the Israelite clans.[l]

[15]When they went to Gilead—to Reuben, Gad and the half-tribe of Manasseh—they said to them: [16]"The whole assembly of the LORD says: 'How could you break faith[m] with the God of Israel like this? How could you turn away from the LORD and build yourselves an altar in rebellion[n] against him now? [17]Was not the sin of Peor[o] enough for us? Up to this very day we have not cleansed ourselves from that sin, even though a plague fell on the community of the LORD! [18]And are you now turning away from the LORD?

" 'If you rebel against the LORD today, tomorrow he will be angry with the whole community[p] of Israel. [19]If the land you possess is defiled, come over to the LORD's land, where the LORD's tabernacle[q] stands, and share the land with us. But do not rebel against the LORD or against us by building an altar[r] for yourselves, other than the altar of the LORD our God. [20]When Achan son of Zerah acted unfaithfully regarding the devoted things,[d][s] did not wrath[t] come upon the whole community[u] of Israel? He was not the only one who died for his sin.' "[v]

[21]Then Reuben, Gad and the half-tribe of Manasseh replied to the heads of the clans of Israel: [22]"The Mighty One, God, the LORD! The Mighty One, God,[w] the LORD![x] He knows![y] And let Israel know! If this has been in rebellion or disobedience to the LORD, do not spare us this day. [23]If we have built our own altar to turn away from the LORD and to offer burnt offerings and grain offerings,[z] or to sacrifice fellowship offerings[e] on it, may the LORD himself call us to account.[a]

[24]"No! We did it for fear that some day your descendants might say to ours, 'What do you have to do with the LORD, the God of Israel? [25]The LORD has made the Jordan a boundary between us and you—you Reubenites and Gadites! You have no share in the LORD.' So your descendants might cause ours to stop fearing the LORD.

[26]"That is why we said, 'Let us get ready and build an altar—but not for burnt offerings or sacrifices.' [27]On the contrary, it is to be a witness[b] between us and you and the generations that follow, that we will worship the LORD at his sanctuary with our burnt offerings, sacrifices and fellowship offerings.[c] Then in the future your descendants will not be able to say to ours, 'You have no share in the LORD.'

[28]"And we said, 'If they ever say this to us, or to our descendants, we will answer: Look at the replica of the LORD's altar, which our fathers built, not for burnt offerings and sacrifices, but as a witness[d] between us and you.'

[29]"Far be it from us to rebel[e] against the LORD and turn away from him today by building an altar for burnt offerings, grain offerings and sacrifices, other than the altar of the LORD our God that stands before his tabernacle.[f] "

[30]When Phinehas the priest and the leaders of the community—the heads of the clans of the Israelites—heard what Reuben, Gad and Manasseh had to say, they were pleased. [31]And Phinehas son of Eleazar, the priest, said to Reuben, Gad and Manasseh, "Today we know that the LORD is with us,[g] because you have not

---

Cross references (center column):

22:12 *i*Jos 18:1
22:13 *j*S Nu 25:7
*k*Nu 3:32;
Jos 24:33
22:14 *l*ver 32;
S Nu 1:4
22:16 *m*S Dt 7:3;
1Sa 13:13; 15:11
*n*Dt 12:13-14
22:17
*o*S Nu 23:28;
25:1-9
22:18
*p*S Lev 10:6
22:19 *q*S Ex 26:1
*r*S ver 10
22:20 *s*Jos 7:1
*t*Ps 7:11
*u*Lev 10:6
*v*Jos 7:5
22:22
*w*S Dt 10:17
*x*Ps 50:1
*y*1Sa 2:3; 16:7;
1Ki 8:39;
1Ch 28:9;
Ps 11:4; 40:9;
44:21; 139:4;
Jer 17:10

22:23 *z*Jer 41:5
*a*S Dt 12:11;
S 18:19;
1Sa 20:16
22:27
*b*S Ge 21:30;
Jos 24:27;
Isa 19:20
*c*S Dt 12:6
22:28
*d*S Ge 21:30
22:29 *e*Jos 24:16
*f*S Ex 26:1
22:31 *g*2Ch 15:2

*d*20 The Hebrew term refers to the irrevocable giving over of things or persons to the LORD, often by totally destroying them. *e*23 Traditionally *peace offerings;* also in verse 27

22:12 *gathered at Shiloh.* In the presence of God at the tabernacle. *to go to war against them.* To take disciplinary action (cf. Dt 13:12–18; Jdg 20).

22:13–14 A prestigious delegation is sent to try to turn the Transjordan tribes from their (supposed) act of rebellion against the Lord.

22:16 *How could you . . . ?* The accusations were very grave: You have committed apostasy and rebellion.

22:17 *Peor.* Where some of the Israelites became involved in the Moabite worship of Baal of Peor (Nu 25:1–5).

22:19 *is defiled.* By pagan worship, corrupting its inhabitants. *the LORD's land.* The promised land proper had never included Transjordan territory. Canaan was the land the Lord especially claimed as his own and promised to the descendants of Abraham, Isaac and Jacob.

22:20 *Achan . . . the whole community of Israel.* See note on 7:1–26.

22:22 *The Mighty One, God, the LORD!* See note on Ps 50:1. The repetition of the sacred names gives an oath-like quality to this strong denial of any wrongdoing.

22:27 *witness.* The altar, presumably of uncut stone (see 8:31; Ex 20:25), was to serve as a testimony to the commitment of the Transjordan tribes to remain loyal to the Lord, and to their continued right to worship the Lord at the tabernacle—even though they lived outside the land of promise. It constitutes the sixth memorial monument in the land noted by the author of Joshua (see note on 10:27).

22:31 *you have rescued the Israelites.* Their words prevented a terrible punishment that the other tribes were about to inflict as a divine act of judgment (consider the implications of v. 20).

acted unfaithfully toward the LORD in this matter. Now you have rescued the Israelites from the LORD's hand."

³²Then Phinehas son of Eleazar, the priest, and the leaders returned to Canaan from their meeting with the Reubenites and Gadites in Gilead and reported to the Israelites.ʰ ³³They were glad to hear the report and praised God.ⁱ And they talked no more about going to war against them to devastate the country where the Reubenites and the Gadites lived.

³⁴And the Reubenites and the Gadites gave the altar this name: A Witnessʲ Between Us that the LORD is God.

Joshua's Farewell to the Leaders

23 After a long time had passed and the LORD had given Israel restᵏ from all their enemies around them, Joshua, by then old and well advanced in years,ˡ ²summoned all Israel—their elders,ᵐ leaders, judges and officialsⁿ—and said to them: "I am old and well advanced in years.ᵒ ³You yourselves have seen everything the LORD your God has done to all these nations for your sake; it was the LORD your God who fought for you.ᵖ ⁴Remember how I have allotted�q as an inheritanceʳ for your tribes all the land of the nations that remain—the nations I conquered—between the Jordan and the Great Seaᶠˢ in the west. ⁵The LORD your God himself will drive them outᵗ of your way. He will push them outᵘ before you, and you will take possession of their land, as the LORD your God promised you.ᵛ

⁶"Be very strong; be careful to obey all that is written in the Book of the Lawʷ of Moses, without turning asideˣ to the right or to the left.ʸ ⁷Do not associate with these nations that remain among you; do not invoke the names of their gods or swearᶻ by them. You must not serve them

or bow downᵃ to them. ⁸But you are to hold fast to the LORDᵇ your God, as you have until now.

⁹"The LORD has driven out before you great and powerful nations;ᶜ to this day no one has been able to withstand you.ᵈ ¹⁰One of you routs a thousand,ᵉ because the LORD your God fights for you,ᶠ just as he promised. ¹¹So be very carefulᵍ to love the LORDʰ your God.

¹²"But if you turn away and ally yourselves with the survivors of these nations that remain among you and if you intermarry with themⁱ and associate with them,ʲ ¹³then you may be sure that the LORD your God will no longer drive outᵏ these nations before you. Instead, they will become snaresˡ and traps for you, whips on your backs and thorns in your eyes,ᵐ until you perish from this good land,ⁿ which the LORD your God has given you.

¹⁴"Now I am about to go the way of all the earth.ᵒ You know with all your heart and soul that not one of all the good promises the LORD your God gave you has failed. Every promiseᵖ has been fulfilled; not one has failed.q ¹⁵But just as every good promiseʳ of the LORD your God has come true, so the LORD will bring on you all the evilˢ he has threatened, until he has destroyed youᵗ from this good land he has given you.ᵘ ¹⁶If you violate the covenant of the LORD your God, which he commanded you, and go and serve other gods and bow down to them, the LORD's anger will burn against you, and you will quickly perish from the good land he has given you.ᵛ"

The Covenant Renewed at Shechem

24 Then Joshua assembledʷ all the tribes of Israel at Shechem.ˣ He summonedʸ the elders,ᶻ leaders, judges

22:32 ʰS ver 14
22:33
ⁱ1Ch 29:20;
Da 2:19; Lk 2:28
22:34
ʲS Ge 21:30
23:1 ᵏS Dt 12:9;
Jos 21:44
ˡS Jos 13:1
23:2 ᵐS Jos 7:6
ⁿJos 24:1
ᵒS Jos 13:1
23:3
ᵖS Ex 14:14;
S Dt 20:4
23:4 qJos 19:51
ʳS Nu 34:2;
Ps 78:55
ˢS Nu 34:6
23:5 ᵗver 13;
Jdg 2:21
ᵘPs 44:5;
Jer 46:15
ᵛEx 23:30
23:6 ʷS Dt 28:61
ˣS Dt 17:20
ʸJos 1:7
23:7 ᶻEx 23:13;
Jer 5:7; 12:16

ᵃS Ex 20:5
23:8 ᵇS Dt 10:20
23:9 ᶜDt 11:23
ᵈDt 7:24
23:10 ᵉLev 26:8;
Jdg 3:31
ᶠS Ex 14:14
23:11 ᵍS Dt 4:15
ʰJos 22:5
23:12 ⁱS Ge 34:9
ʲS Ex 34:16;
Ps 106:34-35
23:13 ᵏS ver 5
ˡS Ex 10:7
ᵐS Nu 33:55
ⁿDt 1:8; 1Ki 9:7;
2Ki 25:21
23:14 ᵒ1Ki 2:2
ᵖPs 119:140;
145:13
qS Jos 21:45
23:15 ʳ1Ki 8:56;
Jer 33:14
ˢ1Ki 14:10;
2Ki 22:16;
Isa 24:6; 34:5;
43:28; Jer 6:19;
11:8; 35:17;
39:16; Mal 4:6
ᵗJos 24:20
ᵘLev 26:17;
Dt 28:15; Jer 40:2
23:16
ᵛDt 4:25-26
24:1 ʷGe 49:2
ˣS Ge 12:6
ʸ1Sa 12:7;
1Ki 8:14 ᶻJos 7:6

ᶠ4 That is, the Mediterranean

22:34 *name.* Such extended names were common in the ancient Near East.

23:1–16 Joshua, the Lord's servant, delivers a farewell address recalling the victories the Lord has given, but also reminding the people of areas yet to be possessed and of the need to be loyal to God's covenant laws. Their mission remains—to be the people of God's kingdom in the world.

23:1 *rest.* See note on 1:13. *well advanced in years.* Joshua was approaching the age of 110 (24:29).

23:6 *be careful to obey.* Echoing the Lord's instructions at the beginning (1:7–8; see 22:5). *Book of the Law.* A reference to canonical written materials from the time of Moses (cf. Dt 30:10,19; 31:9,24,26).

23:11 *love the LORD your God.* A concluding summation (see note on 22:5).

23:12 *But if you turn away.* Remaining in the promised

land was conditioned on faithfulness to the Lord and separation from the idolaters still around them. Failure to meet these conditions would bring Israel's banishment from the land (cf. vv. 13,15–16; 2Ki 17:7–8; 2Ch 7:14–20). *ally yourselves . . . intermarry.* The Lord prohibited alliances, either national or domestic, with the peoples of Canaan because such alliances would tend to compromise Israel's loyalty to the Lord (see Ex 34:15–16; Dt 7:2–4).

23:13 *snares and traps.* Joshua's warning echoes Ex 23:33; 34:12; Dt 7:16.

24:1–33 Once more Joshua assembled the tribes at Shechem to call Israel to a renewal of the covenant (see 8:30–35). It was his final official act as the Lord's servant, mediator of the Lord's rule over his people. In this he followed the example of Moses, whose final official act was also a call to covenant renewal—of which Deuteronomy is the preserved document.

and officials of Israel,[a] and they presented themselves before God.

[2]Joshua said to all the people, "This is what the LORD, the God of Israel, says: 'Long ago your forefathers, including Terah the father of Abraham and Nahor,[b] lived beyond the River[g] and worshiped other gods.[c] [3]But I took your father Abraham from the land beyond the River and led him throughout Canaan[d] and gave him many descendants.[e] I gave him Isaac,[f] [4]and to Isaac I gave Jacob and Esau.[g] I assigned the hill country of Seir[h] to Esau, but Jacob and his sons went down to Egypt.[i]

[5]" 'Then I sent Moses and Aaron,[j] and I afflicted the Egyptians by what I did there, and I brought you out.[k] [6]When I brought your fathers out of Egypt, you came to the sea,[l] and the Egyptians pursued them with chariots and horsemen[h] [m] as far as the Red Sea.[i] [n] [7]But they cried[o] to the LORD for help, and he put darkness[p] between you and the Egyptians; he brought the sea over them and covered them.[q] You saw with your own eyes what I did to the Egyptians.[r] Then you lived in the desert for a long time.[s]

[8]" 'I brought you to the land of the Amorites[t] who lived east of the Jordan. They fought against you, but I gave them into your hands. I destroyed them from before you, and you took possession of their land.[u] [9]When Balak son of Zippor,[v] the king of Moab, prepared to fight against Israel, he sent for Balaam son of Beor[w] to put a curse on you.[x] [10]But I would not listen to Balaam, so he blessed you[y] again and again, and I delivered you out of his hand.

[11]" 'Then you crossed the Jordan[z] and came to Jericho.[a] The citizens of Jericho fought against you, as did also the Amorites, Perizzites,[b] Canaanites, Hittites, Girgashites, Hivites and Jebusites,[c] but I gave them into your hands.[d] [12]I sent the hornet[e] ahead of you, which drove them out[f] before you—also the two Amorite kings. You did not do it with your own sword and bow.[g] [13]So I gave you a land[h] on which you did not toil and cities you did not build; and you live in them and eat from vineyards and olive groves that you did not plant.'[i]

[14]"Now fear the LORD[j] and serve him with all faithfulness.[k] Throw away the gods[l] your forefathers worshiped beyond the River and in Egypt,[m] and serve the LORD. [15]But if serving the LORD seems undesirable to you, then choose for yourselves this day whom you will serve, whether the gods your forefathers served beyond the River, or the gods of the Amorites,[n] in whose land you are living. But as for me and my household,[o] we will serve the LORD."[p]

[16]Then the people answered, "Far be it from us to forsake[q] the LORD to serve other gods! [17]It was the LORD our God himself who brought us and our fathers up out of Egypt, from that land of slavery,[r] and performed those great signs[s] before our eyes. He protected us on our entire journey and among all the nations through which we traveled. [18]And the LORD drove out[t] before us all the nations,[u] including the Amorites, who lived in the land.[v] We too will serve the LORD, because he is our God."[w]

[19]Joshua said to the people, "You are not able to serve the LORD. He is a holy

24:1 aJos 23:2
24:2 bGe 11:26
cGe 11:32
24:3 dS Ge 12:1
eS Ge 1:28;
S 12:2 fS Ge 21:3
24:4 gS Ge 25:26
hS Ge 14:6;
S Nu 24:18
iGe 46:5-6
24:5 jS Ex 3:10
kEx 12:51
24:6 lS Ex 14:22
mS Ex 14:9
nEx 14:23
24:7 oS Ex 14:10
pEx 14:20
qS Ex 14:28
rS Ex 19:4
sDt 1:46
24:8 tS Ex 23:23
uS Nu 21:31
24:9 vNu 22:2
xS Nu 23:7
24:10
yS Nu 23:11;
S Dt 23:5
24:11
zS Ex 14:29
aJos 6:1

bS Jos 3:10
cS Ge 15:18-21
dEx 23:23; Dt 7:1
24:12
eS Ex 23:28;
Ps 44:3,6-7
fS Ex 23:31
gPs 135:11
24:13 hEx 6:8
iDt 6:10-11
24:14
jISa 12:14;
Job 23:15;
Ps 19:9; 119:120
kDt 10:12; 18:13;
1Sa 12:24;
2Co 1:12 lver 23;
S Ge 31:19;
Ex 12:12; 18:11;
20:3; Nu 25:2;
Dt 11:28;
Jdg 10:16;
Ru 1:15; Isa 55:7
mEze 23:3
24:15 nJdg 6:10;
Ru 1:15
oS Ge 35:2
pRu 1:16; 2:12;
1Ki 18:21;
Da 3:18
24:16 qJos 22:29
24:17 rJdg 6:8
sS Ex 10:1
24:18
tS Ex 23:31
uS Dt 33:27

vAc 7:45 wS Ge 28:21

g2 That is, the Euphrates; also in verses 3, 14 and 15
h6 Or charioteers   i6 Hebrew Yam Suph; that is, Sea of Reeds

---

24:2 *This is what the LORD . . . says.* Only a divinely appointed mediator would dare to speak for God with direct discourse, as in vv. 2–13. *Long ago.* In accordance with the common ancient Near Eastern practice of making treaties (covenants), a brief recital of the past history of the relationship precedes the making of covenant commitments. Joshua here focuses on the separation of Abraham from his polytheistic family, the deliverance of Israel from Egypt and the Lord's establishment of his people in Canaan. *the River.* See NIV text note.

24:6 *Red Sea.* See NIV text note.

24:10 *I would not listen to Balaam.* Not only did the Lord reject Balaam's prayers; he also turned his curse into a blessing (see Nu 23–24).

24:12 *the hornet.* Lower (northern) Egypt had long used the hornet as a national symbol, so Egypt's military campaigns in Canaan may have been in mind. But "the hornet" may also refer to the reports about Israel that spread panic among the Canaanites (2:11; 5:1; 9:24). See note on Ex 23:28.

24:14 *fear the LORD.* Trust, serve and worship him. *gods your forefathers worshiped beyond the River and in Egypt.* See v. 2. Joshua appealed to the Israelites to put away the gods their forefathers had worshiped in Mesopotamia and Egypt. In Ur and Haran, Terah's family would have been exposed to the worship of the moon-god, Nanna(r) or Sin. The golden calf of Ex 32:4 may be an example of their worship of the gods of Egypt. It was probably patterned after Apis, the sacred bull of Egypt; see note on Ex 32:4. (Jeroboam's golden calves at Bethel and Dan, on the other hand, probably represented mounts or pedestals for a riding or standing deity; see 1Ki 12:28–29.)

24:15 *as for me.* Joshua publicly makes his commitment, hoping to elicit the same from Israel.

24:17–18 A creedal statement based on the miraculous events of the exodus and ending with "he is our God."

24:19 *You are not able.* Strong words to emphasize the danger of overconfidence.

God;[x] he is a jealous God.[y] He will not forgive[z] your rebellion[a] and your sins. [20]If you forsake the LORD[b] and serve foreign gods, he will turn[c] and bring disaster[d] on you and make an end of you,[e] after he has been good to you."

[21]But the people said to Joshua, "No! We will serve the LORD."

[22]Then Joshua said, "You are witnesses[f] against yourselves that you have chosen[g] to serve the LORD."

"Yes, we are witnesses,[h]" they replied.

[23]"Now then," said Joshua, "throw away the foreign gods[i] that are among you and yield your hearts[j] to the LORD, the God of Israel."

[24]And the people said to Joshua, "We will serve the LORD our God and obey him."[k]

[25]On that day Joshua made a covenant[l] for the people, and there at Shechem[m] he drew up for them decrees and laws.[n] [26]And Joshua recorded[o] these things in the Book of the Law of God.[p] Then he took a large stone[q] and set it up there under the oak[r] near the holy place of the LORD.

[27]"See!" he said to all the people. "This stone[s] will be a witness[t] against us. It has heard all the words the LORD has said to us. It will be a witness against you if you are untrue[u] to your God."[v]

Buried in the Promised Land
24:29–31pp — Jdg 2:6–9

[28]Then Joshua sent the people away, each to his own inheritance.[w]

[29]After these things, Joshua son of Nun, the servant of the LORD, died[x] at the age of a hundred and ten.[y] [30]And they buried him in the land of his inheritance, at Timnath Serah[z] in the hill country of Ephraim, north of Mount Gaash.[a]

[31]Israel served the LORD throughout the lifetime of Joshua and of the elders[b] who outlived him and who had experienced everything the LORD had done for Israel.

[32]And Joseph's bones,[c] which the Israelites had brought up from Egypt,[d] were buried at Shechem in the tract of land[e] that Jacob bought for a hundred pieces of silver[k] from the sons of Hamor, the father of Shechem. This became the inheritance of Joseph's descendants.

[33]And Eleazar son of Aaron[f] died and was buried at Gibeah,[g] which had been allotted to his son Phinehas[h] in the hill country[i] of Ephraim.

24:19
xS Lev 11:44;
S 20:26
yS Ex 20:5
zS Ex 34:7
aS Ex 23:21
24:20 b1Ch 28:9,
20; 2Ch 24:18
cAc 7:42
d1Sa 12:25;
Hos 13:11
eJos 23:15
24:22 /ver 27;
Ru 4:10; Isa 8:2;
43:10; 44:8;
Jer 42:5; Mal 2:14
gPs 119:30,173
hS Dt 25:9
24:23 /S ver 14
/1Ki 8:58;
Ps 119:36; 141:4;
Jer 31:33
24:24 kEx 19:8;
Jer 42:6
24:25 /S Ex 24:8
mS Jos 17:7
nEx 15:25
24:26
oS Dt 17:18
pS Dt 28:61;
S 31:24
qS Ge 28:18;
S Dt 27:2
rS Ge 12:6;
S Jdg 4:11
24:27
sS Ge 28:18;
Hab 2:11 tS ver
22; S Ge 21:30;
S Jos 22:27
uS Jos 7:11
vS Nu 11:20;
S Pr 30:9

24:28
wJdg 21:23,24
24:29 xJdg 1:1
yS Ge 50:22
24:30
zS Jos 19:50

a2Sa 23:30 24:31 bJos 7:6 24:32 cHeb 11:22
dS Ge 47:29-30 eGe 33:19; Jn 4:5; Ac 7:16 24:33
fS Jos 22:13 gS Jos 15:57 hS Ex 6:25 i1Sa 9:4; 1Ki 4:8

i30 Also known as Timnath Heres (see Judges 2:9)
k32 Hebrew hundred kesitahs; a kesitah was a unit of money of unknown weight and value.

24:22 witnesses. See v. 27; a normal part of treaty/covenant-making (see Dt 30:19).

24:23 foreign gods. The other gods were represented by idols of wood and metal, which could be thrown away and destroyed.

24:25 covenant for the people. Consisting of the pledges they had agreed to and the decrees and laws from God.

24:26 large stone. Set up as a witness to the covenant renewal that closed Joshua's ministry, this is the seventh memorial in the land reminding Israel of what the Lord had done for them through his servant (see note on 22:27). To these memorials were added the perpetual ruins of Jericho (6:26). Thus the promised land itself bore full testimony to Israel (seven being the number of completeness)—how she had come into possession of the land and how she would remain in the land only by fulfilling the covenant conditions. The land shouted its own story. oak. See note on Ge 12:6.

24:29–33 Three burials. Since it was a deep desire of the ancients to be buried in their homeland, these notices not only mark the conclusion of the story and the close of an era

but also underscore the fact that Israel had indeed been established in the promised homeland—the Lord had kept his covenant.

24:29 a hundred and ten. For the significance of this number see note on Ge 50:26.

24:30 buried him ... at Timnath Serah. See 19:50 and note.

24:31 The story told in Joshua is a testimony to Israel's faithfulness in that generation. The author anticipates the quite different story that would follow.

24:32 Joseph's bones. Returning his bones to Shechem was significant not only because of the ancient plot of land Jacob bought from Hamor (Ge 33:19), but also because Shechem was to be the center of the tribes of Ephraim and Manasseh, the two sons of Joseph. Also, the return fulfilled an oath sworn to Joseph on his deathbed (Ge 50:25; Ex 13:19).

24:33 Eleazar. The high priest who served Joshua, as Aaron had served Moses. Gibeah. Not the Benjamite city, but a place in Ephraim near Shiloh.

JUDGES

Title

The title describes the leaders Israel had from the time of the elders who outlived Joshua until the time of the monarchy. Their principal purpose is best expressed in 2:16: "Then the LORD raised up judges, who saved them out of the hands of . . . raiders." Since it was God who permitted the oppressions and raised up deliverers, he himself was Israel's ultimate Judge and Deliverer (11:27; see 8:23, where Gideon, a judge, insists that the Lord is Israel's true ruler).

Author and Date

Although, according to tradition, Samuel wrote the book, authorship is actually uncertain. It is possible that Samuel assembled some of the accounts from the period of the judges and that such prophets as Nathan and Gad, both of whom were associated with David's court, had a hand in shaping and editing the material (see 1Ch 29:29).

The date of composition is also unknown, but it was undoubtedly during the monarchy. The frequent expression "In those days Israel had no king" (17:6; 18:1; 19:1; 21:25) suggests a date after the establishment of the monarchy. The observation that the Jebusites still controlled Jerusalem (1:21) has been taken to indicate a time before David's capture of the city c. 1000 B.C. (see 2Sa 5:6-10). But the new conditions in Israel alluded to in chs. 17-21 suggest a time after the Davidic dynasty had been effectively established (tenth century B.C.).

Theme and Theology

The book of Judges characterizes the life of Israel in the promised land from the death of Joshua to the rise of the monarchy. On the one hand, it is an account of frequent apostasy, provoking divine chastening. On the other hand, it tells of urgent appeals to God in times of crisis, moving the Lord to raise up leaders (judges) through whom he throws off foreign oppressors and restores the land to peace.

After Israel was established in the promised land through the ministry of Joshua, her pilgrimage ended. Many of the covenant promises God had given to the patriarchs in Canaan and to the fathers in the desert had now been fulfilled. The Lord's land, where Israel was to enter into rest, lay under her feet; it remained only for her to occupy it, to displace the Canaanites and to cleanse it of paganism. The time had come for Israel to be the kingdom of God in the form of an established commonwealth on earth.

But in Canaan Israel quickly forgot the acts of God that had given her birth and had established her in the land. Consequently she lost sight of her unique identity as God's people, chosen and called to be his army and the loyal citizens of his emerging kingdom. She settled down and attached herself to Canaan's peoples, morals, gods, and religious beliefs and practices as readily as to Canaan's agriculture and social life.

Throughout Judges the fundamental issue is the lordship of God in Israel—i.e., Israel's acknowledgment of and loyalty to his rule. His kingship over Israel had been uniquely established by the covenant at Sinai (Ex 19-24), which was later renewed by Moses on the plains of Moab (Dt 29) and by Joshua at Shechem (Jos 24). The author accuses Israel of having rejected the kingship of the Lord again and again. She stopped fighting the Lord's battles, turned to the gods of Canaan to secure the blessings of family, flocks and fields, and abandoned God's laws for daily living. In the very center of the cycle of the judges (see Outline), Gideon had to remind Israel that the Lord was her King (see note on 8:23). The recurring lament, and indictment, of chs. 17-21 (see Outline) is: "In those days Israel had no king; everyone did as he saw fit" (see note on 17:6). The primary reference here is doubtless to the earthly mediators of the Lord's rule (i.e., human kings), but the implicit charge is that Israel did not truly acknowledge or obey her heavenly King either.

Only by the Lord's sovereign use of foreign oppression to chasten his people—thereby implementing the covenant curses (see Lev 26:14-45; Dt 28:15-68)—and by his raising up deliverers when his people cried out to him did he maintain his kingship in Israel and preserve the embryonic kingdom from extinction. Israel's flawed condition was graphically exposed; she continued to need new saving acts by God in order to enter into the promised rest (see note on Jos 1:13).

Out of the recurring cycles of disobedience, foreign oppression, cries of distress, and deliverance (see 2:11-19; Ne 9:26-31) emerges another important theme—the covenant faithfulness of the Lord. The amazing patience and long-suffering of God are no better demonstrated than during this unsettled period.

Remarkably, this age of Israel's failure, following directly on the redemptive events that came through Moses and Joshua, is in a special way the OT age of the Spirit. God's Spirit enabled men to accomplish feats of victory in the Lord's holy war against the powers that threatened his kingdom (see 3:10; 6:34; 11:29; 13:25; 14:6,19; 15:14; see also 1Sa 10:6,10; 11:6; 16:13). This same Spirit, poured out on the church following the redemptive work of the second Joshua (Jesus), empowered the people of the Lord to begin the task of preaching the gospel to all nations and of advancing the kingdom of God (see notes on Ac 1:2,8).

Background

Fixing precise dates for the judges is difficult and complex. The dating system followed here is based primarily on 1Ki 6:1, which speaks of an interval of 480 years between the exodus and the fourth year of Solomon's reign. This would place the exodus c. 1446 B.C. and the period of the judges between c. 1380 and the rise of Saul, c. 1050. Jephthah's statement that Israel had occupied Heshbon for 300 years (11:26) generally agrees with these dates.

Some maintain, however, that the number 480 in 1Ki 6:1 is somewhat artificial, arrived at by multiplying 12 (perhaps in reference to the 12 judges) by 40 (a conventional number of years for a generation). They point out the frequent use of the round numbers 10, 20, 40 and 80 in the book of Judges itself. A later date for the exodus would of course require a much shorter period of time for the judges (see Introduction to Exodus: Chronology).

Literary Features

Even a quick reading of Judges discloses its basic threefold division: (1) a prologue (1:1-3:6), (2) a main body (3:7-16:31) and (3) an epilogue (chs. 17-21). Closer study brings to light a more complex structure, with interwoven themes that bind the whole into an intricately designed portrayal of the character of an age.

The prologue (1:1-3:6) has two parts, and each serves a different purpose. They are not chronologically related, nor does either offer a strict chronological scheme of the time as a whole. The first part (1:1-2:5) sets the stage historically for the narratives that follow. It describes Israel's occupation of the promised land—from her initial success to her large-scale failure and divine rebuke.

The second part (2:6-3:6) indicates a basic perspective on the period from the time of Joshua to the rise of the monarchy, a time characterized by recurring cycles of apostasy, oppression, cries of distress and gracious divine deliverance. The author summarizes and explains the Lord's dealings with his rebellious people and introduces some of the basic vocabulary and formulas he will use in the later narratives: "did evil in the eyes of the LORD," 2:11 (see 3:7,12; 4:1; 6:1; 10:6); "handed them over to," 2:14 (see 6:1; 13:1); and "sold them," 2:14 (see 3:8; 4:2; 10:7).

The main body of the book (3:7-16:31), which gives the actual accounts of the recurring cycles (apostasy, oppression, distress, deliverance), has its own unique design. Each cycle has a similar beginning ("the Israelites did evil in the eyes of the LORD"; see note on 3:7) and a recognizable conclusion ("the land had peace . . . years" or "led Israel . . . years"; see note on 3:11). The first of these cycles (Othniel; see 3:7-11 and note) provides the "report form" used for each successive story of oppression and deliverance.

The remaining five cycles form the following narrative units, built around the rest of the major judges:

1. Ehud (3:12-30), a lone hero from the tribe of Benjamin who delivers Israel from oppression from the east.

2. Deborah (chs. 4-5), a woman from one of the Joseph tribes (Ephraim, west of the Jordan) who judges at a time when Israel is being overrun by a coalition of Canaanites under Sisera.

3. Gideon and his son Abimelech (chs. 6-9), who form the central account. In many ways Gideon

is the ideal judge, evoking memory of Moses, while his son is the very antithesis of a responsible and faithful judge.

4. Jephthah (10:6-12:7), a social outcast from the other Joseph tribe (Manasseh, east of the Jordan) who judges at a time when Israel is being threatened by a coalition of powers under the king of Ammon.

5. Samson (chs. 13-16), a lone hero from the tribe of Dan who delivers Israel from oppression from the west.

The arrangement of these narrative units is significant. The central accounts of Gideon (the Lord's ideal judge) and Abimelech (the anti-judge) are bracketed by the parallel narratives of the woman Deborah and the social outcast Jephthah—which in turn are framed by the stories of the lone heroes Ehud and Samson. In this way even the structure focuses attention on the crucial issue of the period of the judges: Israel's attraction to the Baals of Canaan (shown by Abimelech; see note on 9:1-57) versus the Lord's kingship over his people (encouraged by Gideon; see note on 8:23).

The epilogue (chs. 17-21) characterizes the era in yet another way, depicting religious and moral corruption on the part of individuals, cities and tribes. Like the introduction, it has two divisions that are neither chronologically related nor expressly dated to the careers of specific judges. The events must have taken place, however, rather early in the period of the judges (see notes on 18:30; 20:1,28).

By dating the events of the epilogue only in relationship to the monarchy (see the recurring refrain in 17:6; 18:1; 19:1; 21:25), the author contrasts the age of the judges with the better time that the monarchy inaugurated, undoubtedly having in view the rule of David and his dynasty (see note on 17:1-21:25). The book mentions two instances of the Lord's assigning leadership to the tribe of Judah: (1) in driving out the Canaanites (1:1-2), and (2) in disciplining a tribe in Israel (20:18). The author views the ruler from the tribe of Judah as the savior of the nation.

The first division of the epilogue (chs. 17-18) relates the story of Micah's development of a paganized place of worship and tells of the tribe of Dan abandoning their allotted territory while adopting Micah's corrupted religion. The second division (chs. 19-21) tells the story of a Levite's sad experience at Gibeah in Benjamin and records the disciplinary removal of the tribe of Benjamin because it had defended the degenerate town of Gibeah.

The two divisions have several interesting parallels:

1. Both involve a Levite's passing between Bethlehem (in Judah) and Ephraim across the Benjamin-Dan corridor.

2. Both mention 600 warriors—those who led the tribe of Dan and those who survived from the tribe of Benjamin.

3. Both conclude with the emptying of a tribal area in that corridor (Dan and Benjamin).

Not only are these Benjamin-Dan parallels significant within the epilogue, but they also form a notable link to the main body of the book. The tribe of Benjamin, which in the epilogue undertook to defend gross immorality, setting ties of blood above loyalty to the Lord, was the tribe from which the Lord raised the deliverer Ehud (3:15). The tribe of Dan, which in the epilogue retreated from its assigned inheritance and adopted pagan religious practices, was the tribe from which the Lord raised the deliverer Samson (13:2,5). Thus the tribes that in the epilogue depict the religious and moral corruption of Israel are the very tribes from which the deliverers were chosen whose stories frame the central account of the book (Gideon-Abimelech).

The whole design of the book from prologue to epilogue, the unique manner in which each section deals with the age as a whole, and the way the three major divisions are interrelated clearly portray an age gone awry—an age when "Israel had no king" and "everyone did as he saw fit" (see note on 17:6). Of no small significance is the fact that the story is in episodes and cycles. It is given as the story of all Israel, though usually only certain areas are directly involved. The book portrays the centuries after Joshua as a time of Israelite unfaithfulness to the Lord and of her surrender to the allurements of Canaan. Only by the mercies of God was Israel not overwhelmed and absorbed by the pagan nations around her. Meanwhile, however, the history of redemption virtually stood still—awaiting the forward thrust of the Lord's servant David and the establishment of his dynasty.

Outline

I. Prologue: Incomplete Conquest and Apostasy (1:1-3:6)
   A. First Episode: Israel's Failure to Purge the Land (1:1-2:5)
   B. Second Episode: God's Dealings with Israel's Rebellion (2:6-3:6)
II. Oppression and Deliverance (3:7-16:31)

Major Judges	*Minor Judges*
A. Othniel Defeats Aram Naharaim (3:7-11)	
B. Ehud Defeats Moab (3:12-30)	
	1. Shamgar (3:31)
C. Deborah Defeats Canaan (chs. 4-5)	
D. Gideon Defeats Midian (chs. 6-8)	
(Abimelech, the anti-judge, ch. 9)	
	2. Tola (10:1-2)
	3. Jair (10:3-5)
E. Jephthah Defeats Ammon (10:6-12:7)	
	4. Ibzan (12:8-10)
	5. Elon (12:11-12)
	6. Abdon (12:13-15)
F. Samson Checks Philistia (chs. 13-16)	

III. Epilogue: Religious and Moral Disorder (chs. 17-21)
   A. First Episode (chs. 17-18; see 17:6; 18:1)
      1. Micah's corruption of religion (ch. 17)
      2. The Danites' departure from their tribal territory (ch. 18)
   B. Second Episode (chs. 19-21; see 19:1; 21:25)
      1. Gibeah's corruption of morals (ch. 19)
      2. The Benjamites' removal from their tribal territory (chs. 20-21)

Israel Fights the Remaining Canaanites

1:11–15pp — Jos 15:15–19

1 After the death[a] of Joshua, the Israelites asked the LORD, "Who will be the first[b] to go up and fight for us against the Canaanites?[c]"

2The LORD answered, "Judah[d] is to go; I have given the land into their hands.[e]"

3Then the men of Judah said to the Simeonites their brothers, "Come up with us into the territory allotted to us, to fight against the Canaanites. We in turn will go with you into yours." So the Simeonites[f] went with them.

4When Judah attacked, the LORD gave the Canaanites and Perizzites[g] into their hands and they struck down ten thousand men at Bezek.[h] 5It was there that they found Adoni-Bezek[i] and fought against him, putting to rout the Canaanites and Perizzites. 6Adoni-Bezek fled, but they chased him and caught him, and cut off his thumbs and big toes.

7Then Adoni-Bezek said, "Seventy kings with their thumbs and big toes cut off have picked up scraps under my table. Now God has paid me back[j] for what I did to them." They brought him to Jerusalem,[k] and he died there.

8The men of Judah attacked Jerusalem[l]

also and took it. They put the city to the sword and set it on fire.

9After that, the men of Judah went down to fight against the Canaanites living in the hill country,[m] the Negev[n] and the western foothills. 10They advanced against the Canaanites living in Hebron[o] (formerly called Kiriath Arba[p]) and defeated Sheshai, Ahiman and Talmai.[q]

11From there they advanced against the people living in Debir[r] (formerly called Kiriath Sepher). 12And Caleb said, "I will give my daughter Acsah in marriage to the man who attacks and captures Kiriath Sepher." 13Othniel son of Kenaz, Caleb's younger brother, took it; so Caleb gave his daughter Acsah to him in marriage.

14One day when she came to Othniel, she urged him[a] to ask her father for a field. When she got off her donkey, Caleb asked her, "What can I do for you?"

15She replied, "Do me a special favor. Since you have given me land in the Negev, give me also springs of water." Then Caleb gave her the upper and lower springs.[s]

16The descendants of Moses' father-in-law,[t] the Kenite,[u] went up from the City of Palms[b][v] with the men of Judah to live

Cross references (center column)

1:1 aJos 24:29
bS Nu 2:3-9;
Jdg 20:18;
1Ki 20:14 cver
27; S Ge 10:18;
Jdg 3:1-6
1:2 dS Ge 49:10
ever 4; Jdg 3:28;
4:7,14; 7:9
1:3 fver 17
1:4 gS Ge 13:7;
S Jos 3:10
h1Sa 11:8
1:5 iver 6,7
1:7 jLev 24:19;
Jer 25:12
kS Jos 10:1
1:8 lver 21;
Jos 15:63; 2Sa 5:6

1:9 mS Nu 13:17
nS Ge 12:9;
S Nu 21:1;
Isa 30:6
1:10 oS Ge 13:18
pS Ge 35:27 qver
20; S Nu 13:22;
Jos 15:14
1:11 rJos 10:38
1:15 sS Nu 13:6
1:16 tNu 10:29
uS Ge 15:19
vDt 34:3;
Jdg 3:13;
2Ch 28:15

a14 Hebrew; Septuagint and Vulgate *Othniel, he urged her*   b16 That is, Jericho

---

1:1—3:6 An introduction in two parts: (1) an account of Israel's failure to lay claim completely to the promised land as the Lord had directed (1:1–36) and of his rebuke for their disloyalty (2:1–5); (2) an overview of the main body of the book (3:7–16:31), portraying Israel's rebellious ways in the centuries after Joshua's death and showing how the Lord dealt with him in that period (2:6–3:6). See Introduction: Literary Features.

1:1—36 Judah is assigned leadership in occupying the land (v. 2; see 20:18). Her vigorous efforts (together with those of Simeon) highlight by contrast the sad story of failure that follows. Only Ephraim's success at Bethel (vv. 22–26) breaks the monotony of that story.

1:1 *After the death of Joshua.* The book of Judges, like that of Joshua, tells of an era following the death of a leading figure in the history of redemption (see Jos 1:1). Joshua probably died c. 1390 B.C. The battles under his leadership broke the power of the Canaanites to drive the Israelites out of the land. The task that now confronted Israel was the actual occupation of Canaanite territory (see notes on Jos 18:3; 21:43–45). *asked the LORD.* Probably by the priestly use of Urim and Thummim (see notes on Ex 28:30; 1Sa 2:28). *go up.* The main Israelite encampment was at Gilgal, near Jericho in the Jordan Valley (about 800 feet below sea level), while the Canaanite cities were mainly located in the central hill country (about 2,500–3,500 feet above sea level).

1:2 *Judah is to go.* See 20:18. Judah was also the first to be assigned territory west of the Jordan (Jos 15). The leadership role of the tribe of Judah had been anticipated in the blessing of Jacob (Ge 49:8–12).

1:3 *Simeonites.* Joshua assigned to Simeon cities within the territory of Judah (Jos 19:1,9; see Ge 49:5–7).

1:4 *Canaanites.* See note on Ge 10:6. *Perizzites.* See note on Ge 13:7. *Bezek.* Location unknown. Saul marshaled his army there before going to Jabesh Gilead (1Sa 11:8).

1:5 *Adoni-Bezek.* Means "lord of Bezek."

1:6 *cut off his thumbs and big toes.* Physically mutilating prisoners of war was a common practice in the ancient Near East (see note on 16:21). It rendered them unfit for military service.

1:7 *Seventy kings.* Canaan was made up of many small city-states, each of which was ruled by a king. "Seventy" may be a round number, or it may be symbolic of a large number. *under my table.* Humiliating treatment, like that given to a dog (see Mt 15:27; Lk 16:21). *God has paid me back.* See note on Ex 21:23–25.

1:8 *attacked Jerusalem.* Although the city was defeated, it was not occupied by the Israelites at this time (see v. 21). Israel did not permanently control the city until David captured it c. 1000 B.C. (2Sa 5:6–10).

1:10 *Kiriath Arba.* See note on Jos 14:15.

1:11 *Debir.* See note on Jos 10:38.

1:12 *Caleb.* He and Joshua had brought back an optimistic report about the prospects of conquering Canaan (Nu 14:6–9). *daughter . . . in marriage.* Victory in battle was one way to pay the bride-price for a girl (see 1Sa 18:25).

1:13 *Othniel.* First major judge (see 3:7–11).

1:15 *upper and lower springs.* They still water the local farms in Hebron.

1:16 *Moses' father-in-law.* See note on Ex 2:16.

among the people of the Desert of Judah in the Negev near Arad. *w*

17Then the men of Judah went with the Simeonites *x* their brothers and attacked the Canaanites living in Zephath, and they totally destroyed *c* the city. Therefore it was called Hormah. *d y* 18The men of Judah also took *e* Gaza, *z* Ashkelon *a* and Ekron—each city with its territory.

19The LORD was with *b* the men of Judah. They took possession of the hill country, *c* but they were unable to drive the people from the plains, because they had iron chariots. *d* 20As Moses had promised, Hebron *e* was given to Caleb, who drove from it the three sons of Anak. *f* 21The Benjamites, however, failed *g* to dislodge the Jebusites, who were living in Jerusalem; *h* to this day the Jebusites live there with the Benjamites.

22Now the house of Joseph *i* attacked Bethel, *j* and the LORD was with them. 23When they sent men to spy out Bethel (formerly called Luz), *k* 24the spies saw a man coming out of the city and they said to him, "Show us how to get into the city and we will see that you are treated well. *l*" 25So he showed them, and they put the city to the sword but spared *m* the man and his whole family. 26He then went to the land of the Hittites, *n* where he built a city and called it Luz, *o* which is its name to this day.

27But Manasseh did not *p* drive out the people of Beth Shan or Taanach or Dor *q* or Ibleam *r* or Megiddo *s* and their surrounding settlements, for the Canaanites *t* were

1:16 *w*Nu 21:1; Jos 12:14	
1:17 *x*ver 3 *y*S Nu 14:45	
1:18 *z*Jos 11:22 *a*S Jos 13:3	
1:19 *b*S Nu 14:43 *c*Nu 13:17	
1:20 *d*S Jos 17:16 *e*Jos 10:36 *f*S ver 10; S Jos 14:13	
1:21 *g*S Jos 9:15; S 15:63 *h*S ver 8	
1:22 *i*Jdg 10:9 *j*S Jos 7:2	
1:23 *k*S Ge 28:19	
1:24 *l*S Ge 47:29	
1:25 *m*Jos 6:25	
1:26 *n*S Dt 7:1; Eze 16:3 *o*S Ge 28:19	
1:27 *p*1Ki 9:21 *q*S Jos 11:2 *r*S Jos 17:11 *s*S Jos 12:21 *t*S ver 1	

c 17 The Hebrew term refers to the irrevocable giving over of things or persons to the LORD, often by totally destroying them.   *d 17* *Hormah* means *destruction.*
e 18 Hebrew; Septuagint *Judah did not take*

1:17 *men of Judah . . . Simeonites.* Judah was fulfilling her commitment (v. 3).
1:18 *Gaza, Ashkelon and Ekron.* Three of the five main cities inhabited by the Philistines (see map below).
1:19 *unable to drive the people from.* Israel failed to comply with God's commands (Dt 7:1–5; 20:16–18) to

drive the Canaanites out of the land. Five factors were involved in that failure: (1) The Canaanites possessed superior weapons (v. 19); (2) Israel disobeyed God by making treaties with the Canaanites (2:1–3); (3) Israel violated the covenant the Lord had made with their forefathers (2:20–21); (4) God was testing Israel's faithfulness to obey his commands

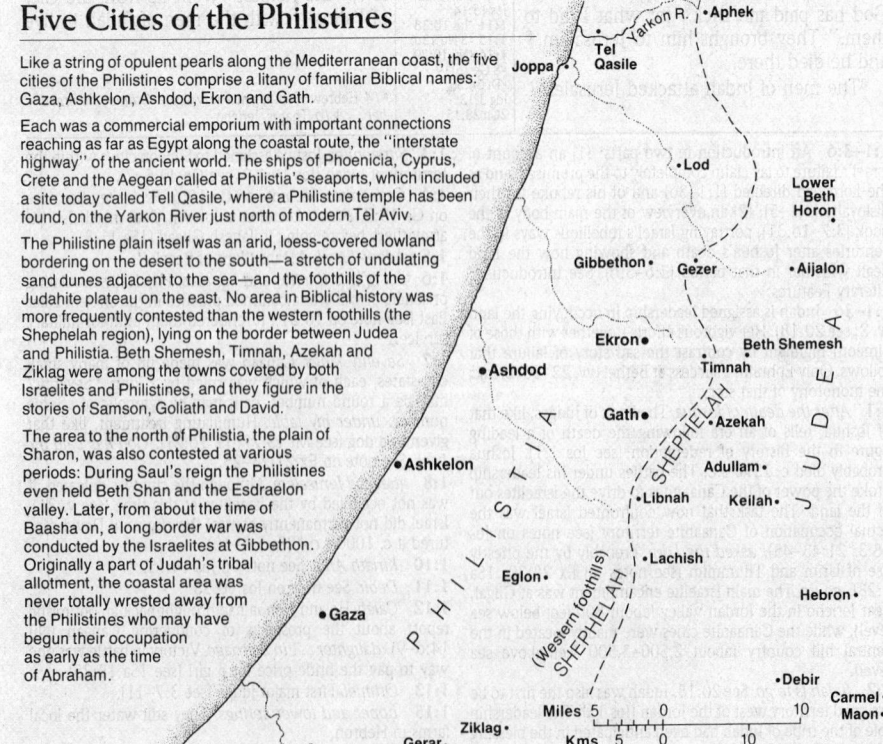

Five Cities of the Philistines

Like a string of opulent pearls along the Mediterranean coast, the five cities of the Philistines comprise a litany of familiar Biblical names: Gaza, Ashkelon, Ashdod, Ekron and Gath.

Each was a commercial emporium with important connections reaching as far as Egypt along the coastal route, the "interstate highway" of the ancient world. The ships of Phoenicia, Cyprus, Crete and the Aegean called at Philistia's seaports, which included a site today called Tell Qasile, where a Philistine temple has been found, on the Yarkon River just north of modern Tel Aviv.

The Philistine plain itself was an arid, loess-covered lowland bordering on the desert to the south—a stretch of undulating sand dunes adjacent to the sea—and the foothills of the Judahite plateau on the east. No area in Biblical history was more frequently contested than the western foothills (the Shephelah region), lying on the border between Judea and Philistia. Beth Shemesh, Timnah, Azekah and Ziklag were among the towns coveted by both Israelites and Philistines, and they figure in the stories of Samson, Goliath and David.

The area to the north of Philistia, the plain of Sharon, was also contested at various periods: During Saul's reign the Philistines even held Beth Shan and the Esdraelon valley. Later, from about the time of Baasha on, a long border war was conducted by the Israelites at Gibbethon. Originally a part of Judah's tribal allotment, the coastal area was never totally wrested away from the Philistines who may have begun their occupation as early as the time of Abraham.

determined to live in that land. 28When Israel became strong, they pressed the Canaanites into forced labor but never drove them out completely.[u] 29Nor did Ephraim[v] drive out the Canaanites living in Gezer,[w] but the Canaanites continued to live there among them.[x] 30Neither did Zebulun drive out the Canaanites living in Kitron or Nahalol, who remained among them; but they did subject them to forced labor. 31Nor did Asher[y] drive out those living in Acco or Sidon[z] or Ahlab or Aczib[a] or Helbah or Aphek[b] or Rehob,[c] 32and because of this the people of Asher lived among the Canaanite inhabitants of the land. 33Neither did Naphtali drive out those living in Beth Shemesh[d] or Beth Anath[e]; but the Naphtalites too lived among the Canaanite inhabitants of the land, and those living in Beth Shemesh and Beth Anath became forced laborers for them. 34The Amorites[f] confined the Danites[g] to the hill country, not allowing them to come down into the plain.[h] 35And the Amorites were determined also to hold out in Mount Heres,[i] Aijalon[j] and Shaalbim,[k] but when the power of the house of Joseph increased, they too were pressed into forced labor. 36The boundary of the Amorites was from Scorpion[f] Pass[l] to Sela[m] and beyond.[n]

1:28
[u]Jos 17:12-13
1:29 [v]Jos 14:4;
Jdg 5:14
[w]S Jos 10:33
[x]Jos 16:10
1:31 [y]S Jos 17:7
[z]S Ge 49:13
[a]S Jos 15:44
[b]S Jos 12:18
[c]S Nu 13:21
1:33 [d]S Jos 15:10
[e]Jos 19:38
1:34 [f]Nu 13:29;
Jdg 10:11;
1Sa 7:14
[g]S Ge 30:6
[h]Jdg 18:1
1:35 [i]Jdg 8:13
[j]Jos 19:42
[k]1Ki 4:9
1:36 [l]Jos 15:3
[m]2Ki 14:7;
Isa 16:1; 42:11
[n]Ps 106:34

2:1 [o]S Ge 16:7
[p]S Dt 11:30 [q]ver
5 [r]Ex 20:2;
Jdg 6:8 [s]Ge 17:8
[t]S Lev 26:42-44;
Dt 7:9
2:2 [u]S Ex 23:32;
S 34:12; Dt 7:2
[v]S Ex 23:24;
34:13; Dt 7:5;
2Ch 14:3
[w]Jer 7:28
2:3 [x]Jos 23:13
[y]S Nu 33:55
[z]S Ex 10:7
2:4 [a]S Ge 27:38;
S Nu 25:6;
2Ki 17:13
2:5 [b]ver 1
2:7 [c]ver 17
2:8 [d]Jos 1:1

The Angel of the Lord at Bokim

2 The angel of the Lord[o] went up from Gilgal[p] to Bokim[q] and said, "I brought you up out of Egypt[r] and led you into the land that I swore to give to your forefathers.[s] I said, 'I will never break my covenant with you,[t] 2and you shall not make a covenant with the people of this land,[u] but you shall break down their altars.[v] Yet you have disobeyed[w] me. Why have you done this? 3Now therefore I tell you that I will not drive them out before you;[x] they will be ⌊thorns⌋[y] in your sides and their gods will be a snare[z] to you.'"

4When the angel of the Lord had spoken these things to all the Israelites, the people wept aloud,[a] 5and they called that place Bokim.[g][b] There they offered sacrifices to the Lord.

Disobedience and Defeat

2:6–9pp — Jos 24:29–31

6After Joshua had dismissed the Israelites, they went to take possession of the land, each to his own inheritance. 7The people served the Lord throughout the lifetime of Joshua and of the elders who outlived him and who had seen all the great things the Lord had done for Israel.[c] 8Joshua son of Nun,[d] the servant of the

[f]36 Hebrew *Akrabbim* [g]5 *Bokim* means *weepers.*

(2:22–23; 3:4); (5) God was giving Israel, as his army, the opportunity to develop her skills in warfare (3:1–2). *iron chariots.* Wooden vehicles with certain iron fittings, perhaps axles.

1:20 *As Moses had promised.* See Nu 14:24; Dt 1:36; Jos 14:9–14. *Anak.* See note on Nu 13:22.

1:21 *Benjamites . . . failed to dislodge.* See note on v. 8. Jerusalem lay on the border between Benjamin and Judah but was allotted to Benjamin (Jos 18:28). *Jebusites.* See note on Ge 10:16.

1:22 *house of Joseph.* Ephraim and West Manasseh. *Bethel.* See note on Ge 12:8. There is archaeological evidence of a destruction in the 13th century B.C. that may reflect the battle mentioned in this verse.

1:23 *spy out.* See note on Nu 13:2.

1:25 *spared the man.* Cf. the treatment of Rahab (Jos 6:25).

1:26 *land of the Hittites.* A name for Aram (Syria) at the time of the conquest (see note on Ge 10:15).

1:27–29 See Jos 17:16–18.

1:28 *forced labor.* See note on 1Ki 5:13.

1:33 *Beth Shemesh.* Location unknown. The name means "house of the sun(-god)." There was also a Beth Shemesh in Judah (see note on v. 35). *Beth Anath.* Means "house of (the goddess) Anath" (see note on 3:31).

1:34 *Amorites.* See note on Ge 10:16. *confined the Danites.* Joshua had defeated the Amorites earlier (Jos 10:5–11), but they were still strong enough to withstand the Danites. For this reason a large number of Danites migrated northward a short time later (see ch. 18).

1:35 *Mount Heres.* Means "mountain of the sun(-god)"; probably the Beth Shemesh in Judah, which is also called Ir Shemesh, "city of the sun(-god)" (Jos 19:41).

1:36 *boundary of the Amorites.* Their southern boundary (see Jos 15:2–3).

2:1–5 Because Israel had not zealously laid claim to the land as the Lord had directed (see 1:27–36), he withdrew his helping hand. On this note the first half of the introduction ends. Although the actual time of the Lord's rebuke is not indicated, it was probably early in the period of the judges and may even have been connected with the event in Jos 9 (or possibly Jos 18:1–3).

2:1 *angel of the Lord.* See note on Ge 16:7. The role of the angel of the Lord in this passage parallels that of the unnamed prophet in 6:8–10 and the word of the Lord in 10:11–14, calling his people to account. *Gilgal.* The place where Israel first became established in the land under Joshua (see Jos 4:19–5:12). *out of Egypt.* The theme of Exodus, frequently referred to as the supreme evidence of God's redemptive love for his people (see Ex 20:2). *swore to give.* See Ge 15:18; see also note on Heb 6:13.

2:2 *not make a covenant.* To have done so would have broken their covenant with the Lord (see Ex 23:32).

2:6–3:6 The second half of the introduction continues the narrative of Jos 24:28–31. It is a preliminary survey of the accounts narrated in Jdg 3:7–16:31, showing that Israel's first centuries in the promised land are a recurring cycle of apostasy, oppression, cries of distress and gracious deliverance (see Introduction: Literary Features). The author reminds Israel that she will enjoy God's promised rest in the promised land only when she is loyal to him and to his covenant.

2:6 *take possession of the land.* See note on 1:1.

2:8 *servant of the Lord.* Joshua is identified as the Lord's

LORD, died at the age of a hundred and ten. ⁹And they buried him in the land of his inheritance, at Timnath Heres^h^e in the hill country of Ephraim, north of Mount Gaash.

¹⁰After that whole generation had been gathered to their fathers, another generation grew up, who knew neither the LORD nor what he had done for Israel.^f ¹¹Then the Israelites did evil^g in the eyes of the LORD^h and served the Baals.^i ¹²They forsook the LORD, the God of their fathers, who had brought them out of Egypt. They followed and worshiped various gods^j of the peoples around them.^k They provoked^l the LORD to anger^m ¹³because they forsook^n him and served Baal and the Ashtoreths.^o ¹⁴In his anger^p against Israel the LORD handed them over^q to raiders who plundered^r them. He sold them^s to their enemies all around, whom they were no longer able to resist.^t ¹⁵Whenever Israel went out to fight, the hand of the LORD was against them^u to defeat them, just as he had sworn to them. They were in great distress.^v

¹⁶Then the LORD raised up judges,^i ^w who saved^x them out of the hands of these raiders. ¹⁷Yet they would not listen to their judges but prostituted^y themselves to other gods^z and worshiped them.^a Unlike their fathers, they quickly turned^b from the way in which their fathers had walked, the way of obedience to the LORD's commands.^c ¹⁸Whenever the LORD

raised up a judge for them, he was with the judge and saved^d them out of the hands of their enemies as long as the judge lived; for the LORD had compassion^e on them as they groaned^f under those who oppressed and afflicted^g them. ¹⁹But when the judge died, the people returned to ways even more corrupt^h than those of their fathers,^i following other gods and serving and worshiping them.^j They refused to give up their evil practices and stubborn^k ways.

²⁰Therefore the LORD was very angry^l with Israel and said, "Because this nation has violated the covenant^m that I laid down for their forefathers and has not listened to me, ²¹I will no longer drive out^n before them any of the nations Joshua left when he died. ²²I will use them to test^o Israel and see whether they will keep the way of the LORD and walk in it as their forefathers did." ²³The LORD had allowed those nations to remain; he did not drive them out at once by giving them into the hands of Joshua.^p

3 These are the nations the LORD left to test^q all those Israelites who had not experienced any of the wars in Canaan

Cross references

2:9 ^e S Jos 19:50
2:10 ^f S Ex 5:2; Gal 4:8
2:11 ^g 1Ki 15:26 ^h Jdg 3:12; 4:1; 6:1; 10:6 ^i Jdg 3:7; 8:33; 1Ki 16:31; 22:53; 2Ki 10:18; 17:16
2:12 ^j S Dt 32:12; Ps 106:36 ^k S Dt 31:16; Jdg 10:6 ^l S Nu 11:33 ^m Dt 4:25; Ps 78:58; 106:40
2:13 ^n 1Sa 7:3; 1Ki 11:5,33; 2Ki 23:13 ^o Jdg 3:7; 5:8; 6:25; 8:33; 10:6; 1Sa 31:10; Ne 9:26; Ps 78:56; Jer 11:10
2:14 ^p S Dt 31:17 ^q Ne 9:27; Ps 106:41 ^r Ps 44:10; 89:41; Eze 34:8 ^s S Dt 32:30; S Jdg 3:8 ^t S Dt 28:25; Job 19:21;
2:15 ^u Ru 1:13; Ps 32:4 ^v Ge 35:3; 2Sa 22:7; 2Ch 15:4; Job 5:5; 20:22; Ps 4:1; 18:6
2:16 ^w Ru 1:1; 1Sa 4:18; 7:6,15; 2Sa 7:11; 1Ch 17:10; Ac 13:20 ^x 1Sa 11:3; Ps 106:43
2:17 ^y S Ex 34:15; S Nu 15:39 ^z S Ps 4:2 ^a Ne 9:28; Ps 106:36 ^b Dt 9:12 ^c ver 7
2:18 ^d 1Sa 7:3; 2Ki 13:5;

2:17 ^y S Ex 34:15; ^e S Dt 32:36 ^f S Ex 2:23 ^g S Nu 10:9 2:19 ^h S Ge 6:11; S Dt 4:16 ^i Dt 32:17; Ne 9:2; Ps 78:57; Jer 44:3,9 ^j Jdg 4:1; 8:33 ^k S Ex 32:9 2:20 ^l S Dt 31:17; Jos 23:16 ^m S Jos 7:11; S 2Ki 17:15 2:21 ^n S Jos 23:5 2:22 ^o S Ge 22:1; S Ex 15:25 2:23 ^p Jdg 1:1 3:1 ^q S Ex 15:25

^h 9 Also known as *Timnath Serah* (see Joshua 19:50 and 24:30) ^i 16 Or *leaders*; similarly in verses 17-19

Study notes

official representative (see notes on Ex 14:31; Ps 18 title; Isa 41:8–9; 42:1). *a hundred and ten.* For the significance of this number see note on Ge 50:26.

2:10–15 The Lord withdraws his help because of Israel's apostasy. He "sells" the people he had "bought" (Ex 15:16) and redeemed (Ex 15:13; cf. Ps 74:2).

2:10 *gathered to their fathers.* See Ge 15:15; see also note on Ge 25:8. *who knew neither the LORD . . . Israel.* They had no direct experience of the Lord's acts (see Ex 1:8).

2:11 *did evil in the eyes of the LORD.* The same expression is used in 3:7,12; 4:1; 6:1; 10:6. *Baals.* The many local forms of this Canaanite deity (see note on v. 13).

2:12 *provoked the LORD to anger.* See Dt 4:25; see also note on Zec 1:2.

2:13 *Baal.* Means "lord." Baal, the god worshiped by the Canaanites and Phoenicians, was variously known to them as the son of Dagon and the son of El. In Aram (Syria) he was called Hadad and in Babylonia Adad. Believed to give fertility to the womb and life-giving rain to the soil, he is pictured as standing on a bull, a popular symbol of fertility and strength (see 1Ki 12:28). The storm cloud was his chariot, thunder his voice, and lightning his spear and arrows. The worship of Baal involved sacred prostitution and sometimes even child sacrifice (see Jer 19:5). The stories of Elijah and Elisha (1Ki 17–2Ki 13), as well as many other OT passages, directly or indirectly protest Baalism (e.g., Ps 29:3–9; 68:1–4,32–34; 93:1–5; 97:1–5; Jer 10:12–16; 14:22; Hos 2:8,16–17; Am 5:8). *Ashtoreths.* Female deities such as Ashtoreth (con-

sort of Baal) and Asherah (consort of El, the chief god of the Canaanite pantheon). Ashtoreth was associated with the evening star and was the beautiful goddess of war and fertility. She was worshiped as Ishtar in Babylonia and as Athtart in Aram. To the Greeks she was Astarte or Aphrodite, and to the Romans, Venus. Worship of the Ashtoreths involved extremely lascivious practices (1Ki 14:24; 2Ki 23:7).

2:14 *handed them over to.* The same expression is used in 6:1; 13:1. *sold them.* The same expression is used in 3:8; 4:2; 10:7.

2:16–19 The Lord was merciful to his people in times of distress, sending deliverers to save them from oppression. But Israel continually forgot these saving acts, just as she had those he had performed through Moses and Joshua.

2:16 *judges.* See Introduction: Title. There were six major judges (Othniel, Ehud, Deborah, Gideon, Jephthah and Samson) and six minor ones (Shamgar, Tola, Jair, Ibzan, Elon and Abdon).

2:17 *prostituted themselves.* Since the Hebrew for Baal (meaning "lord") was also used by women to refer to their husbands, it is understandable that the metaphor of adultery was commonly used in connection with Israelite worship of Baal (see Hos 2:2–3,16–17).

2:18 *groaned . . . oppressed.* The language of the Egyptian bondage (see Ex 2:24; 3:9; 6:5).

2:20–23 The Lord decided to leave the remaining nations to test Israel's loyalty.

3:1–6 The list of nations the Lord left roughly describes an

2(he did this only to teach warfare to the descendants of the Israelites who had not had previous battle experience): 3the five *r* rulers of the Philistines,*s* all the Canaanites, the Sidonians, and the Hivites *t* living in the Lebanon mountains from Mount Baal Hermon *u* to Lebo¡ Hamath. *v* 4They were left to test *w* the Israelites to see whether they would obey the LORD's commands, which he had given their forefathers through Moses.

5The Israelites lived *x* among the Canaanites, Hittites, Amorites, Perizzites,*y* Hivites and Jebusites.*z* 6They took their daughters *a* in marriage and gave their own daughters to their sons, and served their gods.*b c*

Othniel

7The Israelites did evil in the eyes of the LORD; they forgot the LORD *d* their God and served the Baals and the Asherahs.*e* 8The anger of the LORD burned against Israel so that he sold *f* them into the hands of Cushan-Rishathaim *g* king of Aram Naharaim,*k h* to whom the Israelites were subject for eight years. 9But when they cried out *i* to the LORD, he raised up for them a deliverer,*j* Othniel *k* son of Kenaz, Caleb's younger brother, who saved them.

10The Spirit of the LORD came upon him,*l* so that he became Israel's judge¡ and went to war. The LORD gave Cushan-Rishathaim *m* king of Aram *n* into the hands of Othniel, who overpowered him. 11So the land had peace *o* for forty years,*p* until Othniel son of Kenaz *q* died.

Ehud

12Once again the Israelites did evil in the eyes of the LORD,*r* and because they did this evil the LORD gave Eglon king of Moab *s* power over Israel. 13Getting the Ammonites *t* and Amalekites *u* to join him, Eglon came and attacked Israel, and they took possession of the City of Palms.*m v* 14The Israelites were subject to Eglon king of Moab *w* for eighteen years.

15Again the Israelites cried out to the LORD, and he gave them a deliverer *x*—Ehud,*y* a left-handed *z* man, the son of Gera the Benjamite. The Israelites sent him with tribute *a* to Eglon king of Moab.

Cross references

3:3 *r*S Jos 13:3
*s*S Ge 10:14
*t*S Ge 10:17;
S Ex 3:8 *u*S Dt 3:8
*v*S Nu 13:21
3:4 *w*S Ex 15:25
3:5 *x*Ps 106:35
*y*S Jos 3:10
*z*S Jos 11:3;
Ezr 9:1
3:6 *a*Ezr 10:18;
Ne 13:23;
Mal 2:11
*b*S Ex 34:16;
Dt 7:3-4
*c*S Dt 7:16
3:7 *d*Dt 4:9;
S 32:18; Jdg 8:34;
Ps 78:11,42;
106:7; Jer 23:27
*e*S Ex 34:13;
S Jdg 2:11,13;
1Ki 16:33;
Isa 17:8
3:8 *f*Jdg 2:14;
Ps 44:12;
Isa 50:1; 52:3
*g*ver 10
*h*S Ge 24:10
3:9 *i*ver 15;
Jdg 6:6,7; 10:10;
1Sa 12:10;
Ps 106:44;
107:13
*j*S Dt 28:29;
Ne 9:27
*k*S Jos 15:17

3:10
*l*S Nu 11:25;
Jdg 6:34; 11:29;
13:25; 14:6,19;
15:14; 1Sa 11:6;
16:13; 1Ki 18:46;
1Ch 12:18;
2Ch 24:20;
Isa 11:2 *m*ver 8

*n*S Ge 10:22 3:11 *o*ver 30; S Jos 14:15; Jdg 5:31; 8:28
*p*S Ex 16:35 *q*S Jos 15:17 3:12 *r*S Jdg 2:11 *s*1Sa 12:9 3:13
*t*S Ge 19:38; Jdg 10:11 *u*S Ge 14:7 *v*S Jdg 1:16 3:14
*w*Jer 48:1 3:15 *x*S ver 9; Jdg 4:1 *z*Jdg 20:16;
1Ch 12:2 *a*ver 17,18; 2Sa 8:2,6; 1Ki 4:21; 2Ki 17:3;
Est 10:1; Ps 68:29; 72:10; 89:22; Ecc 2:8; Isa 60:5; Hos 10:6

¡3 Or *to the entrance to*   *k8* That is, Northwest
Mesopotamia   ¡10 Or *leader*   *m13* That is, Jericho

---

arc along the western and northern boundaries of the area actually occupied by Israel at the death of Joshua (vv. 1–4). Within Israelite-occupied territory there were large groups of native peoples (v. 5; see 1:27–36) with whom the Israelites intermingled, often adopting their religions (v. 6).
3:2 *only to teach warfare.* As his covenant servant, Israel was the Lord's army for fighting against the powers of the world that were settled in his land. In view of the incomplete conquest, succeeding generations in Israel needed to become capable warriors. "Only" probably here means "especially."
3:3 *five rulers.* The Hebrew for "rulers" is related to the word "tyrant" (see note on Jos 13:3) and is used only of Philistine rulers. These rulers had control of a five-city confederacy. At one point Judah defeated three of these cities (1:18) but was unable to hold them. *Sidonians.* Here used collectively of the Phoenicians. *Hivites.* Here identified with a region in northern Canaan reaching all the way to Hamath (see also Jos 11:3). *Mount Baal Hermon.* Probably Mount Hermon (see 1Ch 5:23).
3:6 *took their daughters . . . and served their gods.* See note on Jos 23:12. The degenerating effect of such intermarriage is well illustrated in Solomon's experience (1Ki 11:1–8).
3:7–11 In the account of Othniel's judgeship the author provides the basic literary form he uses in his accounts of the major judges (i.e., beginning statement; cycle of apostasy, oppression, distress, deliverance; recognizable conclusion), adding only the brief details necessary to complete the report (see Introduction: Literary Features).
3:7 *did evil in the eyes of the LORD.* A recurring expression (see v. 12; 4:1; 6:1; 10:6; 13:1) used to introduce the cycles of the judges (see Introduction: Literary Features). *Baals.* See note on 2:13. *Asherahs.* See notes on 2:13; Ex 34:13.
3:8 *Cushan-Rishathaim.* Probably means "doubly wicked

Cushan," perhaps a caricature of his actual name (see note on 10:6 regarding Baal-Zebub). *Aram Naharaim.* See note on Ge 24:10.
3:9 *they cried out to the LORD.* The Israelites' cries of distress occurred in each recurring cycle of the judges (see Introduction: Literary Features). *Othniel.* See 1:13.
3:10 *Spirit of the LORD came upon him.* The Spirit empowered Othniel to deliver his people, as he did Gideon (6:34), Jephthah (11:29), Samson (14:6,19) and also David (1Sa 16:13). Cf. Nu 11:25–29.
3:11 *the land had peace . . . years.* A recognizable conclusion to the cycle of a judge (noted only here and in v. 30; 5:31; 8:28). After the judgeship of Gideon this formula is replaced by "led Israel . . . years" (12:7; 15:20; 16:31). See Introduction: Literary Features. *forty years.* A conventional number of years for a generation (see Introduction: Background).
3:12–30 Ehud's triumph over Eglon king of Moab. The left-handed Benjamite was an authentic hero. All alone, and purely by his wits, he cut down the king of Moab, who had established himself in Canaan near Jericho. This account balances that of Samson in the five narrative units central to the book of Judges (see Introduction: Literary Features).
3:12 *Moab.* See note on Ge 19:33.
3:13 *Ammonites.* See note on Ge 19:33. *Amalekites.* These descendants of Esau (Ge 36:12,16) lived in the Negev (Nu 13:29). See note on Ge 14:7.
3:14 *Israelites.* Here mainly Benjamin and Ephraim.
3:15 *left-handed man.* Left-handedness was noteworthy among Benjamites (see 20:15–16)—which is ironic since Benjamin means "son of (my) right hand." Being left-handed, Ehud could conceal his dagger on the side where it was not expected (see v. 21). *tribute.* An annual payment, perhaps of agricultural products (cf. 2Ki 3:4).

16Now Ehud *b* had made a double-edged sword about a foot and a half *n* long, which he strapped to his right thigh under his clothing. 17He presented the tribute *c* to Eglon king of Moab, who was a very fat man. *d* 18After Ehud had presented the tribute, he sent on their way the men who had carried it. 19At the idols *o* near Gilgal he himself turned back and said, "I have a secret message for you, O king."

The king said, "Quiet!" And all his attendants left him.

20Ehud then approached him while he was sitting alone in the upper room of his summer palace *p* *e* and said, "I have a message from God for you." As the king rose *f* from his seat, 21Ehud reached with his left hand, drew the sword *g* from his right thigh and plunged it into the king's belly. 22Even the handle sank in after the blade, which came out his back. Ehud did not pull the sword out, and the fat closed in over it. 23Then Ehud went out to the porch *q*; he shut the doors of the upper room behind him and locked them.

24After he had gone, the servants came and found the doors of the upper room locked. They said, "He must be relieving himself *h* in the inner room of the house." 25They waited to the point of embarrassment, *i* but when he did not open the doors of the room, they took a key and unlocked them. There they saw their lord fallen to the floor, dead.

26While they waited, Ehud got away. He passed by the idols and escaped to Seirah. 27When he arrived there, he blew a trumpet *j* in the hill country of Ephraim, and the Israelites went down with him from the hills, with him leading them.

28"Follow me," he ordered, "for the LORD has given Moab, *k* your enemy, into your hands. *l*" So they followed him down and, taking possession of the fords of the Jordan *m* that led to Moab, they allowed no one to cross over. 29At that time they struck down about ten thousand Moabites, all vigorous and strong; not a man escaped. 30That day Moab *n* was made subject to Israel, and the land had peace *o* for eighty years.

Shamgar

31After Ehud came Shamgar son of Anath, *p* who struck down six hundred *q* Philistines *r* with an oxgoad. He too saved Israel.

Deborah

4 After Ehud *s* died, the Israelites once again did evil *t* in the eyes of the LORD. *u* 2So the LORD sold them *v* into the hands of Jabin, a king of Canaan, who reigned in Hazor. *w* The commander of his army was Sisera, *x* who lived in Harosheth Haggoyim. 3Because he had nine hundred iron chariots *y* and had cruelly oppressed *z*

3:16 *b* S ver 15
3:17 *c* S ver 15
d Job 15:27;
Ps 73:4
3:20 *e* Am 3:15
f Ne 8:5
3:21 *g* 2Sa 2:16;
3:27 20:10
3:24 *h* 1Sa 24:3
3:25 *i* 2Ki 2:17;
8:11

3:27 *j* S Lev 25:9;
Jdg 6:34; 7:18;
2Sa 2:28;
Isa 18:3;
Jer 42:14
3:28 *k* S Ge 19:37
l S Jos 2:24;
S Jdg 1:2
m S Nu 13:29;
S Jos 2:7
3:30 *n* S Ge 36:35
o S ver 11
3:31 *p* Jdg 5:6
q S Jos 23:10
r Jos 13:2;
Jdg 10:11; 13:1;
1Sa 5:1; 31:1;
2Sa 8:1;
Jer 25:20; 47:1
4:1 *s* S Jdg 3:15
t S Jdg 2:19
u S Jdg 2:11
4:2 *v* S Dt 32:30
w S Jos 11:1
x 1Sa 12:9;
Ps 83:9
4:3 *y* S Jos 17:16
z Jdg 10:12;
Ps 106:42

n 16 Hebrew *a cubit* (about 0.5 meter)   *o 19* Or *the stone quarries;* also in verse 26   *p 20* The meaning of the Hebrew for this phrase is uncertain.   *q 23* The meaning of the Hebrew for this word is uncertain.

3:16 *made a double-edged sword.* During the period of the judges, Israelite weapons were often fashioned or improvised for the occasion: Shamgar's oxgoad (v. 31), Jael's tent peg (4:22), Gideon's jars and torches (7:20), the woman's millstone (9:53) and Samson's donkey jawbone (15:15). See 1Sa 13:19.

3:19 *idols.* Lit. "carved (stone) things," a frequent Hebrew word for stone idols (see NIV text note). But here the reference may be to carved stone statues of Eglon, marking the boundary of the territory he now claims as part of his expanded realm—a common practice in the ancient Near East.

3:20 *upper room.* Rooms were built on the flat roofs of houses (2Ki 4:10–11) and palaces (Jer 22:13–14), and had latticed windows (2Ki 1:2) that provided comfort in the heat of summer.

3:22 *which came out his back.* Or "and the offal in his belly came out."

3:28 *taking possession of the fords.* This move prevented the Moabites from sending reinforcements and also enabled the Israelites to cut off the Moabites fleeing Jericho.

3:30 *eighty years.* Round numbers are frequently used in Judges (see Introduction: Background).

3:31 *Shamgar.* The first of six minor judges and a contemporary of Deborah (see 5:6–7). His name is foreign, so he was probably not an Israelite. *son of Anath.* Indicates either that Shamgar came from the town of Beth Anath (see 1:33) or that his family worshiped the goddess Anath. Since Anath, Baal's sister, was a goddess of war who fought for Baal, the

expression "son of Anath" may have been a military title, meaning "a warrior." *oxgoad.* A long, wooden rod, sometimes having a metal tip, used for driving draft animals (see 1Sa 13:21).

4:1–5:31 Deborah's triumph over Sisera (commander of a Canaanite army)—first narrated in prose (ch. 4), then celebrated in song (ch. 5). At the time of the Canaanite threat from the north, Israel remained incapable of united action until a woman (Deborah) summoned them to the Lord's battle. Because the warriors of Israel lacked the courage to rise up and face the enemy, the glory of victory went to a woman (Jael)—and she may not have been an Israelite.

4:1–2 Except for the Canaanites, Israel's enemies came from outside the territory she occupied. Nations like Aram Naharaim, Moab, Midian and Ammon were mainly interested in plunder, but the Canaanite uprising of chs. 4–5 was an attempt to restore Canaanite power in the north. The Philistines engaged in continual struggle with Israel for permanent control of the land in the southern and central regions.

4:2 *Jabin.* See Ps 83:9–10. The name was possibly royal rather than personal. Joshua is credited with having earlier slain a king by the same name (Jos 11:1,10). *Hazor.* The original royal city of the Jabin dynasty; it may still have been in ruins (see note on Jos 11:10). Sisera sought to recover the territory once ruled by the kings of Hazor. *Sisera.* His name suggests he was not a Canaanite.

4:3 *nine hundred.* The number probably represents a coali-

the Israelites for twenty years, they cried to the LORD for help.

[4]Deborah,[a] a prophetess,[b] the wife of Lappidoth, was leading[r] Israel at that time. [5]She held court[c] under the Palm of Deborah between Ramah[d] and Bethel[e] in the hill country of Ephraim, and the Israelites came to her to have their disputes decided. [6]She sent for Barak son of Abinoam[f] from Kedesh[g] in Naphtali and said to him, "The LORD, the God of Israel, commands you: 'Go, take with you ten thousand men of Naphtali[h] and Zebulun[i] and lead the way to Mount Tabor.[j] [7]I will lure Sisera, the commander of Jabin's[k] army, with his chariots and his troops to the Kishon River[l] and give him into your hands.[m] '"

[8]Barak said to her, "If you go with me, I will go; but if you don't go with me, I won't go."

[9]"Very well," Deborah said, "I will go with you. But because of the way you are going about this,[s] the honor will not be yours, for the LORD will hand Sisera over to a woman." So Deborah went with Barak to Kedesh,[n] [10]where he summoned[o] Zebulun and Naphtali. Ten thousand men followed him, and Deborah also went with him.

[11]Now Heber the Kenite had left the other Kenites,[p] the descendants of Hobab,[q] Moses' brother-in-law,[t] and

pitched his tent by the great tree[r] in Zaanannim[s] near Kedesh.

[12]When they told Sisera that Barak son of Abinoam had gone up to Mount Tabor,[t] [13]Sisera gathered together his nine hundred iron chariots[u] and all the men with him, from Harosheth Haggoyim to the Kishon River.[v]

[14]Then Deborah said to Barak, "Go! This is the day the LORD has given Sisera into your hands.[w] Has not the LORD gone ahead[x] of you?" So Barak went down Mount Tabor, followed by ten thousand men. [15]At Barak's advance, the LORD routed[y] Sisera and all his chariots and army by the sword, and Sisera abandoned his chariot and fled on foot. [16]But Barak pursued the chariots and army as far as Harosheth Haggoyim. All the troops of Sisera fell by the sword; not a man was left.[z]

[17]Sisera, however, fled on foot to the tent of Jael,[a] the wife of Heber the Kenite,[b] because there were friendly relations between Jabin king of Hazor[c] and the clan of Heber the Kenite.

[18]Jael[d] went out to meet Sisera and said to him, "Come, my lord, come right in. Don't be afraid." So he entered her tent, and she put a covering over him.

[19]"I'm thirsty," he said. "Please give me

Cross references (center column):

4:4 [a]Jdg 5:1,7,12, 15 [b]S Ex 15:20
4:5 [c]1Sa 14:2; 22:6 [d]S Jos 18:25 [e]S Jos 12:9
4:6 [f]Jdg 5:1,12, 15; 1Sa 12:11; Heb 11:32 [g]S Jos 12:22 [h]S Ge 30:8 [i]Jdg 5:18; 6:35 [j]S Jos 19:22
4:7 [k]S Jos 11:1 [l]ver 13; Jdg 5:21; 1Ki 18:40; Ps 83:9 [m]S Jdg 1:2
4:9 [n]S Jos 12:22
4:10 [o]2Ch 36:23; Ezr 1:2; Isa 41:2; 42:6; 45:3; 46:11; 48:15 [p]S Ge 15:19 [q]Nu 10:29

[r]Jos 24:26; Jdg 9:6 [s]Jos 19:33
4:12 [t]S Jos 19:22
4:13 [u]S Jos 17:16 [v]S ver 7; Jdg 5:19
4:14 [w]S Jdg 1:2 [x]Dt 9:3; 1Sa 8:20; 2Sa 5:24; Ps 68:7 [y]S Ex 14:24;
4:15 [y]S Ex 14:24; Ps 18:14
4:16 [z]S Ex 14:28; Ps 83:9
4:17 [a]ver 18,21, 22; Jdg 5:6,24 [b]S Ge 15:19 [c]S Jos 11:1
4:18 [d]S ver 17

[r]4 Traditionally *judging*   [s]9 Or *But on the expedition you are undertaking*   [t]11 Or *father-in-law*

Study notes (bottom):

tion rather than the chariot force of one city. In the 15th century B.C., Pharaoh Thutmose III boasted of having captured 924 chariots at the battle of Megiddo. *Israelites.* Mainly Zebulun and Naphtali, but West Manasseh, Issachar and Asher were also affected.
4:4 *Deborah.* Means "bee"; cf. Dt 1:44. She is the only judge said to have been a prophet(ess). Other women spoken of as prophetesses are Miriam (Ex 15:20), Huldah (2Ki 22:14), Noadiah (Ne 6:14) and Anna (Lk 2:36), but see also Ac 21:9.
4:6 *Barak.* Means "thunderbolt"—which suggests that he is summoned to be the Lord's "flashing sword" (Dt 32:41). He is named among the heroes of faith in Heb 11:32. *Kedesh in Naphtali.* A town affected by the Canaanite oppression. *Naphtali and Zebulun.* Issachar, a near neighbor of these tribes, is not mentioned here but is included in the poetic description of the battle in 5:15. In all, six tribes are mentioned as having participated in the battle. *Mount Tabor.* A mountain about 1,300 feet high, northeast of the battle site.
4:7 With the Israelites encamped on the slopes of Mount Tabor, safe from chariot attack, the Lord's strategy was to draw Sisera into a trap. For the battle site, Sisera cleverly chose the Valley of Jezreel along the Kishon River, where his chariot forces would have ample maneuvering space to range the battlefield and attack in numbers from any quarter. But that was his undoing, for he did not know the power of the Lord, who would fight from heaven for Israel with storm and flood (see 5:20–21), as he had done in the days of Joshua (10:11–14). Even in modern times storms have rendered the plain along the Kishon virtually impassable. In April of 1799 the flooded Kishon River aided Napoleon's victory over a

Turkish army.
4:9 *a woman.* Barak's timidity (and that of Israel's other warriors, whom he exemplified) was due to lack of trust in the Lord and was thus rebuked (see note on 9:54).
4:11 *Heber the Kenite.* Since one meaning of Heber's name is "ally," and since "Kenite" identifies him as belonging to a clan of metalworkers, the author hints at the truth that this member of a people allied with Israel since the days of Moses has moved from south to north to ally himself (see v. 17) with the Canaanite king who is assembling a large force of "iron chariots." It is no doubt he who informs Sisera of Barak's military preparations. *other Kenites.* Settled in the south not far from Kadesh Barnea in the Negev (see 1:16). *Hobab.* See Nu 10:29.
4:14 *gone ahead of you.* As a king at the head of his army (see 1Sa 8:20). See also Ex 15:3 ("the LORD is a warrior"); Jos 10:10–11; 2Sa 5:24; 2Ch 20:15–17,22–24. *Barak went down Mount Tabor.* The Lord's "thunderbolt" (see note on v. 6) descends the mountain to attack the Canaanite army.
4:15 *routed.* See note on v. 7. The Hebrew for this word is also used of the panic that overcame the Egyptians at the "Red Sea" (Ex 14:24) and the Philistines at Mizpah (1Sa 7:10).
4:18 *he entered her tent.* Since ancient Near Eastern custom prohibited any man other than a woman's husband or father from entering her tent, Jael seemed to offer Sisera an ideal hiding place.
4:19 *skin.* Containers for liquids were normally made from the skins of goats or lambs. *milk.* See note on 5:25. Jael, whose name means "mountain goat," gave him milk to drink—and it was most likely goat's milk (see Ex 23:19; Pr

some water." She opened a skin of milk, [e]
gave him a drink, and covered him up.

[20]"Stand in the doorway of the tent," he
told her. "If someone comes by and asks
you, 'Is anyone here?' say 'No.' "

[21]But Jael,[f] Heber's wife, picked up a
tent peg and a hammer and went quietly to
him while he lay fast asleep,[g] exhausted.
She drove the peg through his temple into
the ground, and he died. [h]

[22]Barak came by in pursuit of Sisera, and
Jael[i] went out to meet him. "Come," she
said, "I will show you the man you're
looking for." So he went in with her, and
there lay Sisera with the tent peg through
his temple—dead.[j]

[23]On that day God subdued[k] Jabin,[l]
the Canaanite king, before the Israelites.
[24]And the hand of the Israelites grew
stronger and stronger against Jabin, the Canaanite king, until they destroyed him. [m]

The Song of Deborah

5 On that day Deborah[n] and Barak son
of Abinoam[o] sang this song:[p]

[2]"When the princes in Israel take the
lead,
   when the people willingly offer[q]
      themselves—
   praise the LORD![r]

[3]"Hear this, you kings! Listen, you
rulers!
   I will sing to[u] the LORD, I will sing;[s]

I will make music to[v] the LORD, the
God of Israel. [t]

[4]"O LORD, when you went out[u] from
Seir,[v]
   when you marched from the land of
Edom,
   the earth shook,[w] the heavens poured,
      the clouds poured down water.[x]
[5]The mountains quaked[y] before the
LORD, the One of Sinai,
   before the LORD, the God of Israel.

[6]"In the days of Shamgar son of Anath,[z]
   in the days of Jael,[a] the roads[b] were
abandoned;
   travelers took to winding paths.[c]
[7]Village life[w] in Israel ceased,
   ceased until I,[x] Deborah,[d] arose,
   arose a mother in Israel.
[8]When they chose new gods,[e]
   war came to the city gates,[f]
   and not a shield or spear[g] was seen
      among forty thousand in Israel.
[9]My heart is with Israel's princes,
   with the willing volunteers[h] among
      the people.
   Praise the LORD!

[10]"You who ride on white donkeys,[i]
   sitting on your saddle blankets,
   and you who walk along the road,
   consider [11]the voice of the singers[v] at
      the watering places.

Cross references (center column)

4:19 [e]S Ge 18:8
4:21 [f]S ver 17
[g]Ge 2:21; 15:12;
1Sa 26:12;
Isa 29:10; Jnh 1:5
[h]Jdg 5:26
4:22 [i]S ver 17
[j]Jdg 5:27
4:23 [k]Ne 9:24;
Ps 18:47; 44:2;
47:3; 144:2
[l]S Jos 11:1
4:24 [m]Ps 83:9;
106:43
5:1 [n]S Jdg 4:4
[o]S Jdg 4:6
[p]S Ex 15:1;
Ps 32:7
5:2 [q]2Ch 17:16;
Ps 110:3 [r]ver 9
5:3 [s]S Ex 15:1

[t]Ps 27:6
[u]:4 [u]S Ex 13:21
[v]S Nu 24:18;
S Dt 33:2
[w]2Sa 22:8;
Ps 18:7; 77:18;
82:5; Isa 2:19,21;
13:13; 24:18;
64:3; Jer 10:10;
50:46; 51:29;
Joel 3:16; Na 1:5;
Hab 3:6 [x]Ps 68:8;
77:17
5:5 [y]S Ex 19:18;
Ps 29:6; 46:3;
77:18; 114:4;
Isa 64:3
5:6 [z]Jdg 3:31
[a]S Jdg 4:17
[b]Lev 26:22;
Isa 33:8
[c]Ps 125:5;
Isa 59:8
5:7 [d]S Jdg 4:4
5:8 [e]Dt 32:17;
S Jdg 2:13 [f]ver
11; S Jos 2:5
[g]S Nu 25:7
5:9 [h]S ver 2
5:10 [i]S Ge 49:11;
Jdg 12:14

[u]3 Or of   [v]3 Or / with song I will praise   [w]7 Or
Warriors   [x]7 Or you   [y]11 Or archers; the meaning
of the Hebrew for this word is uncertain.

Bottom notes

27:27).
4:21 *drove the peg through his temple.* The laws of hospitality normally meant that one tried to protect a guest from
any harm (see 19:23; Ge 19:8). Jael remained true to her
family's previous alliance with Israel (she may have been an
Israelite) and so undid her husband's deliberate breach of
faith. Armed only with domestic implements, this dauntless
woman destroyed the great warrior whom Barak had earlier
feared.
4:22 *there lay Sisera . . . dead.* With Sisera dead the kingdom of Jabin was no longer a threat. The land "flowing with
milk and honey" had been saved by the courage and faithfulness of "Bee" (see note on v. 4) and "Mountain Goat" (see
note on v. 19).
5:1–31 To commemorate a national victory with songs
was a common practice (see Ex 15:1–18; Nu 21:27–30; Dt
32:1–43; 1Sa 18:7). The "Book of the Wars of the LORD"
(see note on Nu 21:14) and the "Book of Jashar" (see note
on Jos 10:13) were probably collections of such songs.
   The song was probably written by Deborah or a contemporary (see v. 7 and NIV text note) and is thus one of the oldest
poems in the Bible. It highlights some of the central themes
of the narrative (cf. Ex 15:1–18; 1Sa 2:1–10; 2Sa 22;
23:1–7; Lk 1:46–55,68–79). In particular, it celebrates before the nations (v. 3) the righteous acts of the Lord and of his
warriors (v. 11). The song may be divided into the following
sections: (1) the purpose of the song (praise) and the occasion for the deeds it celebrates (vv. 2–9); (2) the exhortation

to Israel to act in accordance with her heroic past (vv.
10–11a); (3) the people's appeal to Deborah (vv. 11b–12);
(4) the gathering of warriors (vv. 13–18); (5) the battle (vv.
19–23); (6) the crafty triumph of Jael over Sisera (vv.
24–27); (7) the anxious waiting of Sisera's mother (vv.
28–30); and (8) the conclusion (v. 31).
5:4–5 Poetic recalling of the Lord's terrifying appearance in
a storm cloud many years before, when he had brought Israel
through the desert into Canaan (see Dt 33:2; Ps 68:7–8;
Mic 1:3–4; see also Ps 18:7–15).
5:4 *Seir.* Edom. For a similar association of Seir (and Mount
Paran) with Sinai see Dt 33:2. *the heavens poured.* See Ps
68:7–10.
5:5 *the One of Sinai.* See Ps 68:8. An earthquake and
thunderstorm occurred when God appeared at Mount Sinai
(Ex 19:16–18).
5:6 *Shamgar.* See note on 3:31. *roads were abandoned.*
Because of enemy garrisons and marauding bands (see note
on 4:1–2) the roads were unsafe.
5:7 *Village life . . . ceased.* The inhabitants of villages fled
to walled towns for protection.
5:8 *not a shield or spear was seen.* Either because Israel
had made peace with the native Canaanites (see 3:5–6) or
because she had been disarmed (see 1Sa 13:19–22).
5:10 *who ride on white donkeys.* An allusion to the nobles
and the wealthy (see 10:4; 12:14).
5:11 *voice of the singers.* The leaders are encouraged by
the songs of the minstrels at the watering places—songs that

They recite the righteous acts[j] of the
LORD,
the righteous acts of his warriors[z] in
Israel.

"Then the people of the LORD
went down to the city gates.[k]
12"Wake up,[l] wake up, Deborah![m]
Wake up, wake up, break out in
song!
Arise, O Barak![n]
Take captive your captives,[o] O son of
Abinoam.'

13"Then the men who were left
came down to the nobles;
the people of the LORD
came to me with the mighty.
14Some came from Ephraim,[p] whose
roots were in Amalek;[q]
Benjamin[r] was with the people who
followed you.
From Makir[s] captains came down,
from Zebulun those who bear a
commander's staff.
15The princes of Issachar[t] were with
Deborah;[u]
yes, Issachar was with Barak,[v]
rushing after him into the valley.
In the districts of Reuben
there was much searching of heart.
16Why did you stay among the
campfires[a][w]
to hear the whistling for the flocks?[x]
In the districts of Reuben
there was much searching of heart.
17Gilead[y] stayed beyond the Jordan.

And Dan, why did he linger by the
ships?
Asher[z] remained on the coast[a]
and stayed in his coves.
18The people of Zebulun[b] risked their
very lives;
so did Naphtali[c] on the heights of
the field.[d]

19"Kings came[e], they fought;
the kings of Canaan fought
at Taanach by the waters of Megiddo,[f]
but they carried off no silver, no
plunder.[g]
20From the heavens[h] the stars fought,
from their courses they fought against
Sisera.
21The river Kishon[i] swept them away,
the age-old river, the river Kishon.
March on, my soul; be strong![j]
22Then thundered the horses' hoofs—
galloping, galloping go his mighty
steeds.[k]
23'Curse Meroz,' said the angel of the
LORD.
'Curse its people bitterly,
because they did not come to help the
LORD,
to help the LORD against the mighty.'

24"Most blessed of women[l] be Jael,[m]
the wife of Heber the Kenite,[n]
most blessed of tent-dwelling
women.
25He asked for water, and she gave him
milk;[o]

Cross references (center column):

5:11 [j]1Sa 12:7;
Da 9:16; Mic 6:5
[k]S ver 8
5:12 [l]Ps 44:23;
57:8; Isa 51:9,17
[m]S Jdg 4:4
[n]S Jdg 4:6
[o]Ps 68:18;
Eph 4:8
5:14
[p]S Ge 41:52;
S Jdg 1:29
[q]Jdg 3:13
[r]S Nu 34:21
[s]S Ge 50:23
5:15 [t]S Ge 30:18
[u]S Jdg 4:4
[v]S Jdg 4:6
5:16 [w]S Ge 49:14
[x]S Nu 32:1
5:17 [y]S Jos 12:2

[z]S Gen 17:7
[a]Jos 19:29
5:18 [b]S Ge 30:20
[c]S Ge 30:8;
Ps 68:27
[d]S Jdg 4:6
5:19 [e]Jos 11:5;
S Jdg 4:13;
Rev 16:16
[f]S Jos 12:21 [g]ver
30
5:20 [h]S Jos 10:11
5:21 [i]S Jdg 4:7
[j]Jos 1:6
5:22 [k]Jer 8:16
5:24 [l]Lk 1:42
[m]S Jdg 4:17
[n]S Ge 15:19
5:25 [o]S Ge 18:8

[z]11 Or villagers   [a]16 Or saddlebags

---

rehearse the past heroic achievements of the Lord and his
warriors.
5:12 *Wake up.* A plea to take action (see Ps 44:23; Isa
51:9). *Take captive your captives.* The same action is applied
to God in Ps 68:18 and to Christ in Eph 4:8.
5:13–18 The warriors of the Lord who gathered for the
battle. The tribes who came were Ephraim, Benjamin, Manasseh ("Makir" is possibly both East and West Manasseh;
see Dt 3:15; Jos 13:29–31; 17:1), Zebulun (vv. 14,18),
Issachar (v. 15) and Naphtali (v. 18). Especially involved
were Zebulun and Naphtali (v. 18; see 4:10), the tribes most
immediately affected by Sisera's tyranny. Reuben (vv.
15–16) and Gad (here referred to as Gilead, v. 17), from east
of the Jordan, and Dan and Asher, from along the coast (v.
17), are rebuked for not responding. Judah and Simeon are
not even mentioned, perhaps because they were already
engaged with the Philistines. Levi is not mentioned because
it did not have military responsibilities in the theocracy
(kingdom of God).
5:14 *roots . . . in Amalek.* Some Amalekites apparently
once lived in the hill country of Ephraim (see 12:15). *Makir.*
The firstborn son of Manasseh (Jos 17:1). Although the
descendants of Makir settled on both sides of the Jordan (see
Dt 3:15; Jos 13:29–31; 17:1; 1Ch 7:14–19), reference
here is to those west of the Jordan (see v. 17; Jos 17:5).
5:18 *on the heights of the field.* Perhaps connected to Ge

49:21, where Naphtali is described as a "doe set free."
5:19 *Megiddo.* Megiddo and Taanach dominated the main
pass that runs northeast through the hill country from the
plain of Sharon to the Valley of Jezreel. Because of its strategic location, the "plain of Megiddo" (2Ch 35:22) has been a
frequent battleground from the earliest times. There Pharaoh
Thutmose III defeated a Canaanite coalition in 1468 B.C.,
and there in A.D. 1917 the British under General Allenby
ended the rule of the Turks in Palestine by vanquishing them
in the Valley of Jezreel opposite Megiddo. In Biblical history
the forces of Israel under Deborah and Barak crushed the
Canaanites "by the waters of Megiddo" (v. 19), and then
Judah's good king Josiah died in battle against Pharaoh Neco
II in 609 B.C. (2Ki 23:29). See also the reference in Rev
16:16 to "the place that in Hebrew is called Armageddon"
(i.e., "Mount Megiddo") as the site of the "battle on the
great day of God Almighty" (Rev 16:14).
5:20 *stars fought.* A poetic way of saying that the powers of
heaven fought in Israel's behalf (see note on 4:7).
5:21 *swept them away.* See note on 4:7.
5:23 *Meroz.* Because of its refusal to help the army of the
Lord, this Israelite town in Naphtali was cursed. Other cities
were also punished severely for refusing to participate in the
wars of the Lord (see 8:15–17; 21:5–10).
5:25 *curdled milk.* Artificially soured milk made by shaking
milk in a skin-bottle and then allowing it to ferment (due to

in a bowl fit for nobles she brought
   him curdled milk.
26Her hand reached for the tent peg,
   her right hand for the workman's
      hammer.
She struck Sisera, she crushed his head,
   she shattered and pierced his
      temple. p
27At her feet he sank,
   he fell; there he lay.
At her feet he sank, he fell;
   where he sank, there he fell—dead q

28"Through the window r peered Sisera's
      mother;
   behind the lattice she cried out, s
'Why is his chariot so long in coming?
   Why is the clatter of his chariots
      delayed?'
29The wisest of her ladies answer her;
   indeed, she keeps saying to herself,
30'Are they not finding and dividing the
      spoils: t
   a girl or two for each man,
   colorful garments as plunder for
      Sisera,
   colorful garments embroidered,
   highly embroidered garments u for my
      neck—
all this as plunder? v '

31"So may all your enemies perish, w
   O LORD!
But may they who love you be like
      the sun x
   when it rises in its strength." y

Then the land had peace z forty years.

Cross references (center column):
5:26 pJdg 4:21
5:27 qJdg 4:22
5:28 rS Jos 2:15
   sPr 7:6
5:30 tEx 15:9;
   1Sa 30:24;
   Ps 68:12
   uPs 45:14;
   Eze 16:10 vver
   19; 2Sa 1:24
5:31
   wS Nu 10:35
   x2Sa 23:4;
   Job 37:21;
   Ps 19:4; 89:36;
   Isa 18:4
   y2Sa 18:32
   zS Jdg 3:11

6:1 aS Jdg 2:11
   bS Ge 25:2
6:2 c1Sa 13:6;
   Isa 5:30; 8:21;
   26:16; 37:3
   dIsa 2:19;
   Jer 48:28; 49:8,
   30 eJob 24:8;
   Jer 41:9;
   Heb 11:38
6:3 fNu 13:29
   gS Ge 25:6;
   Isa 11:14;
   Jer 49:28
6:4 hLev 26:16;
   Dt 28:30,51;
   Isa 10:6; 39:6;
   42:22
   iS Ge 10:19
6:5 jS Dt 28:42
   kJdg 8:10;
   Isa 21:7; 60:6;
   Jer 49:32
6:6 lS Jdg 3:9
6:7 mS Jdg 3:9
6:8 nDt 18:15;
   1Ki 20:13,22;
   2Ki 17:13,23;
   Ne 9:29;
   Job 36:10;
   Jer 25:5;
   Eze 18:30-31
   oS Jdg 2:1
   pJos 24:17
6:9 qS Nu 10:9;
   Ps 136:24
   rPs 44:2
6:10 sS Ex 20:5
   tS Jos 24:15
6:11 uS Ge 16:7

Gideon

6 Again the Israelites did evil in the eyes of the LORD, a and for seven years he gave them into the hands of the Midianites. b 2Because the power of Midian was so oppressive, c the Israelites prepared shelters for themselves in mountain clefts, caves d and strongholds. e 3Whenever the Israelites planted their crops, the Midianites, Amalekites f and other eastern peoples g invaded the country. 4They camped on the land and ruined the crops h all the way to Gaza i and did not spare a living thing for Israel, neither sheep nor cattle nor donkeys. 5They came up with their livestock and their tents like swarms of locusts. j It was impossible to count the men and their camels; k they invaded the land to ravage it. 6Midian so impoverished the Israelites that they cried out l to the LORD for help.

7When the Israelites cried m to the LORD because of Midian, 8he sent them a prophet, n who said, "This is what the LORD, the God of Israel, says: I brought you up out of Egypt, o out of the land of slavery. p 9I snatched you from the power of Egypt and from the hand of all your oppressors. q I drove them from before you and gave you their land. r 10I said to you, 'I am the LORD your God; do not worship s the gods of the Amorites, t in whose land you live.' But you have not listened to me."

11The angel of the LORD u came and sat

---

bacteria that remained in the skin from previous use).

5:28 This graphic picture of the anxious waiting of Sisera's mother heightens the triumph of Jael over the powerful Canaanite general and presents a contrast between this mother in Canaan and the triumphant Deborah, "a mother in Israel" (v. 7).

5:31 The song ends with a prayer that the present victory would be the pattern for all future battles against the Lord's enemies (see Nu 10:35; Ps 68:1–2). *your enemies . . . they who love you.* The two basic attitudes of people toward the Lord. As Lord of the covenant and royal Head of his people Israel, he demanded their love (see Ex 20:6), just as kings in the ancient Near East demanded the love of their subjects. *forty years.* A conventional number of years for a generation (see Introduction: Background).

6:1–9:57 The Gideon and Abimelech narratives are a literary unit and constitute the center account of the judges. They are bracketed by the stories of Deborah (from Ephraim, a son of Joseph; west of the Jordan) and Jephthah (from Manasseh, the other son of Joseph; east of the Jordan)—which in turn are bracketed by the stories of the heroes Ehud (from Benjamin) and Samson (from Dan). In this center narrative, the crucial issues of the period of the judges are emphasized: the worship of Baal, and the Lord's kingship over his covenant people Israel.

6:1 *Midianites.* See notes on Ge 37:25; Ex 2:15. Since

they were apparently not numerous enough to wage war against the Israelites alone, they often formed coalitions with surrounding peoples—as with the Moabites (Nu 22:4–6; 25:6–18), the Amalekites and other tribes from the east (v. 3). Their defeat was an event long remembered in Hebrew history (see Ps 83:9; Isa 9:4; 10:26; Hab 3:7).

6:3 *Amalekites.* See note on Ge 14:7. Normally they were a people of the Negev, but they are in coalition here with the Midianites and other eastern peoples, who were nomads from the desert east of Moab and Ammon.

6:5 *swarms of locusts.* A vivid picture of the marauders who swarmed across the land, leaving it stripped bare (see 7:12; Ex 10:13–15; Joel 1:4). *camels.* The earliest OT reference to the use of mounted camels in warfare.

6:7 *cried to the LORD.* The Israelites' cries of distress occurred in each recurring cycle of the judges (see Introduction: Literary Features).

6:8 *prophet.* See notes on 2:1; 10:11. The unnamed prophet rebuked Israel for forgetting that the Lord had saved them from Egyptian bondage and had given them the land (vv. 9–10).

6:10 *Amorites.* Probably here includes all the inhabitants of Canaan (see note on Ge 10:16).

6:11 *angel of the LORD.* See note on Ge 16:7. *Ophrah.* To be distinguished from the Benjamite Ophrah (Jos 18:23). *Abiezrite.* The Abiezrites (v. 24) were from the tribe of

down under the oak in Ophrah[v] that belonged to Joash[w] the Abiezrite,[x] where his son Gideon[y] was threshing[z] wheat in a winepress[a] to keep it from the Midianites. [12]When the angel of the LORD appeared to Gideon, he said, "The LORD is with you,[b] mighty warrior.[c]"

[13]"But sir," Gideon replied, "if the LORD is with us, why has all this happened to us? Where are all his wonders[d] that our fathers told[e] us about when they said, 'Did not the LORD bring us up out of Egypt?' But now the LORD has abandoned[f] us and put us into the hand of Midian."

[14]The LORD turned to him and said, "Go in the strength you have[g] and save[h] Israel out of Midian's hand. Am I not sending you?"

[15]"But Lord,[b]" Gideon asked, "how can I save Israel? My clan[i] is the weakest in Manasseh, and I am the least in my family.[j]"

[16]The LORD answered, "I will be with you[k], and you will strike down all the Midianites together."

[17]Gideon replied, "If now I have found favor in your eyes, give me a sign[l] that it is really you talking to me. [18]Please do not go away until I come back and bring my offering and set it before you."

And the LORD said, "I will wait until you return."

[19]Gideon went in, prepared a young goat,[m] and from an ephah[c][n] of flour he made bread without yeast. Putting the meat in a basket and its broth in a pot, he brought them out and offered them to him under the oak.[o]

[20]The angel of God said to him, "Take the meat and the unleavened bread, place them on this rock,[p] and pour out the broth." And Gideon did so. [21]With the tip of the staff[q] that was in his hand, the angel of the LORD touched the meat and the un-

leavened bread.[r] Fire flared from the rock, consuming the meat and the bread. And the angel of the LORD disappeared. [22]When Gideon realized[s] that it was the angel of the LORD, he exclaimed, "Ah, Sovereign LORD! I have seen the angel of the LORD face to face!"[t]

[23]But the LORD said to him, "Peace! Do not be afraid.[u] You are not going to die."[v]

[24]So Gideon built an altar to the LORD there and called[w] it The LORD is Peace. To this day it stands in Ophrah[x] of the Abiezrites.

[25]That same night the LORD said to him, "Take the second bull from your father's herd, the one seven years old.[d] Tear down your father's altar to Baal and cut down the Asherah pole[e][y] beside it. [26]Then build a proper kind of[f] altar to the LORD your God on the top of this height. Using the wood of the Asherah pole that you cut down, offer the second[g] bull as a burnt offering.[z]"

[27]So Gideon took ten of his servants and did as the LORD told him. But because he was afraid of his family and the men of the town, he did it at night rather than in the daytime.

[28]In the morning when the men of the town got up, there was Baal's altar,[a] demolished, with the Asherah pole beside it cut down and the second bull sacrificed on the newly built altar!

[29]They asked each other, "Who did this?"

When they carefully investigated, they were told, "Gideon son of Joash[b] did it."

[30]The men of the town demanded of Joash, "Bring out your son. He must die, because he has broken down Baal's altar[c]

6:11 [v]S Jos 18:23
[w]ver 29;
[x]S Nu 26:30
[y]Jdg 7:1; 8:1;
Heb 11:32
[z]Ru 2:17; 3:2;
1Sa 23:1;
1Ch 21:20
[a]Ne 13:15;
Isa 16:10; 63:3;
La 1:15; Joel 3:13
6:12 [b]S Jos 1:5;
Ru 2:4; 1Sa 10:7;
Ps 129:8
[c]Jdg 11:1
6:13 [d]S Jos 3:5
[e]2Sa 7:22;
Ps 44:1; 78:3
/S Dt 31:17
6:14 [g]Heb 11:34
[h]ver 36; Jdg 10:1;
2Ki 14:27
6:15 [i]Isa 60:22
[j]1Sa 9:21
6:16 [k]Ex 3:12;
S Nu 14:43;
Jos 1:5
6:17 [l]ver 36-37;
S Ge 24:14;
S Ex 3:12; S 4:8
6:19 [m]Jdg 13:15
[n]S Lev 19:36
[o]Ge 18:7-8
6:20 [p]Jdg 13:19
6:21 [q]S Ex 4:2

[r]S Lev 9:24
6:22 [s]Jdg 13:16,
21 [t]Ge 32:30;
Jdg 13:22
6:23 [u]Da 10:19
[v]S Ge 16:13;
S Dt 5:26
6:24 [w]S Ge 22:14
[x]S Jos 18:23
6:25 [y]ver 26,28,
30; Ex 34:13;
S Jdg 2:13
6:26 [z]S Ge 8:20
6:28 [a]ver 30;
1Ki 16:32;
2Ki 21:3
6:29 [b]S ver 11
6:30 [c]S ver 28

---

[b]15 Or sir   [c]19 That is, probably about 3/5 bushel (about 22 liters)   [d]25 Or Take a full-grown, mature bull from your father's herd   [e]25 That is, a symbol of the goddess Asherah; here and elsewhere in Judges   [f]26 Or build with layers of stone an   [g]26 Or full-grown; also in verse 28

Manasseh (Jos 17:2). *threshing wheat in a winepress.* Rather than in the usual, exposed area (see note on Ru 1:22), Gideon felt more secure threshing in this better protected but very confined space.

6:12 *mighty warrior.* Apparently Gideon belonged to the upper class, perhaps a kind of aristocracy (see v. 27), in spite of his disclaimer in v. 15.

6:14 *Lord turned.* See vv. 22–23. Apparently this appearance of the "angel of the Lord" (v. 11) was a theophany (a manifestation of God). *Go . . . Am I not sending you?* Gideon was commissioned to deliver Israel as Moses had been (see Ex 3:7–10).

6:15 *how can I . . . ?* The Lord usually calls the lowly rather than the mighty to act for him (see notes on Ge 25:23; 1Sa 9:21).

6:17 *give me a sign.* See vv. 36–40; cf. the signs the Lord

gave Moses as assurance that he would be with him in his undertaking (see Ex 3:12; 4:1–17).

6:21 *consuming the meat.* Indicating that Gideon's offering was accepted (see Lev 9:24).

6:23 *not going to die.* See 13:22 and notes on Ge 16:13; 32:30.

6:25 *Tear down . . . altar.* Gideon's first task as the Lord's warrior was to tear down an altar to Baal, as Israel had been commanded to do (see 2:2; Ex 34:13; Dt 7:5). *Baal.* See note on 2:13. *Asherah pole.* See NIV text note; see also notes on 2:13; Ex 34:13.

6:26 *proper kind of altar.* See Ex 20:25.

6:30 *He must die.* The Israelites were so apostate that they were willing to kill one of their own people for the cause of Baal (contrast Dt 13:6–10, where God told Moses that idolaters must be stoned).

and cut down the Asherah pole beside it."
31But Joash replied to the hostile crowd
around him, "Are you going to plead Baal's
cause?[d] Are you trying to save him? Whoever fights for him shall be put to death by
morning! If Baal really is a god, he can
defend himself when someone breaks
down his altar." 32So that day they called
Gideon "Jerub-Baal,[h][e]" saying, "Let Baal
contend with him," because he broke
down Baal's altar.
33Now all the Midianites, Amalekites[f]
and other eastern peoples[g] joined forces
and crossed over the Jordan and camped in
the Valley of Jezreel.[h] 34Then the Spirit of
the LORD came upon[i] Gideon, and he
blew a trumpet,[j] summoning the Abiezrites[k] to follow him. 35He sent messengers
throughout Manasseh, calling them to
arms, and also into Asher,[l] Zebulun and
Naphtali,[m] so that they too went up to
meet them.[n]
36Gideon said to God, "If you will save[o]
Israel by my hand as you have promised—
37look, I will place a wool fleece[p] on the
threshing floor.[q] If there is dew only on
the fleece and all the ground is dry, then I
will know[r] that you will save Israel by my
hand, as you said." 38And that is what happened. Gideon rose early the next day; he
squeezed the fleece and wrung out the
dew—a bowlful of water.
39Then Gideon said to God, "Do not be
angry with me. Let me make just one more
request.[s] Allow me one more test with the
fleece. This time make the fleece dry and
the ground covered with dew." 40That
night God did so. Only the fleece was dry;
all the ground was covered with dew.[t]

Gideon Defeats the Midianites

7 Early in the morning, Jerub-Baal[u]
(that is, Gideon[v]) and all his men
camped at the spring of Harod.[w] The camp
of Midian[x] was north of them in the valley
near the hill of Moreh.[y] 2The LORD said to
Gideon, "You have too many men for me
to deliver Midian into their hands. In order
that Israel may not boast against me that
her own strength[z] has saved her, 3an-
nounce now to the people, 'Anyone who
trembles with fear may turn back and
leave Mount Gilead.[a]'" So twenty-two
thousand men left, while ten thousand remained.
4But the LORD said to Gideon, "There
are still too many[b] men. Take them down
to the water, and I will sift them for you
there. If I say, 'This one shall go with you,'
he shall go; but if I say, 'This one shall not
go with you,' he shall not go."
5So Gideon took the men down to the
water. There the LORD told him, "Separate
those who lap the water with their tongues
like a dog from those who kneel down to
drink." 6Three hundred men[c] lapped with
their hands to their mouths. All the rest got
down on their knees to drink.
7The LORD said to Gideon, "With the
three hundred men that lapped I will save
you and give the Midianites into your
hands.[d] Let all the other men go, each to
his own place."[e] 8So Gideon sent the rest
of the Israelites to their tents but kept the
three hundred, who took over the provisions and trumpets of the others.
Now the camp of Midian lay below him
in the valley. 9During that night the LORD
said to Gideon, "Get up, go down against
the camp, because I am going to give it
into your hands.[f] 10If you are afraid to attack, go down to the camp with your servant Purah 11and listen to what they are
saying. Afterward, you will be encouraged
to attack the camp." So he and Purah his
servant went down to the outposts of the
camp. 12The Midianites, the Amalekites[g]

6:31 [d]1Sa 24:15; Ps 43:1; Jer 30:13 **6:32** [e]Jdg 7:1; 8:29,35; 9:1; 1Sa 12:11 **6:33** [f]Nu 13:29 [g]S Ge 25:6 [h]S Jos 15:56; Eze 25:4; Hos 1:5 **6:34** [i]S Jdg 3:10 [j]S Jos 6:20; S Jdg 3:27 [k]S Jos 17:2 **6:35** [l]S Jos 17:7 [m]S Jdg 4:6 [n]Jdg 7:23 **6:36** [o]S ver 14 **6:37** [p]Job 31:20 [q]S Nu 18:27; 2Sa 6:6; 24:16 [r]S Ge 24:14 **6:39** [s]Ge 18:32 **6:40** [t]Ex 4:3-7; Isa 38:7 **7:1** [u]S Jdg 6:32 [v]S Jdg 6:11 [w]2Sa 23:25 [x]S Ge 25:2 [y]S Ge 12:6 **7:2** [z]S Dt 8:17; 2Co 4:7 **7:3** [a]Dt 20:8; S Jos 12:2 **7:4** [b]1Sa 14:6 **7:6** [c]Ge 14:14 **7:7** [d]S Jos 8:7 [e]1Sa 14:6 **7:9** [f]ver 13-15; S Jos 2:24; S Jdg 1:2 **7:12** [g]Nu 13:29

[h]32 *Jerub-Baal* means *let Baal contend.*

6:32 *Jerub-Baal.* See NIV text note. This name later occurs as Jerub-Besheth (2Sa 11:21) by substituting a degrading term (Hebrew *bosheth,* "shameful thing") for the name of Baal, as in the change of the names Esh-Baal and Merib-Baal (1Ch 8:33–34) to Ish-Bosheth and Mephibosheth (see notes on 2Sa 2:8; 4:4). *Let Baal contend with him.* Let Baal defend himself against Gideon.

6:33 *Valley of Jezreel.* See note on 5:19.

6:34 *Spirit . . . came upon.* Lit. "Spirit . . . clothed himself with." This vivid figure, used only three times (here; 1Ch 12:18; 2Ch 24:20), emphasizes that the Spirit of the Lord empowered the human agent and acted through him (see note on 3:10).

6:35 *Manasseh.* West Manasseh. *Asher.* This tribe earlier had failed to answer the call to arms (5:17).

6:39 *just one more request.* Cf. Abraham's words in Ge 18:32.

7:1–8 As supreme commander of Israel, the Lord reduced the army so that Israel would know that the victory was by his power, not theirs.

7:1 *Harod.* Means "trembling" and may refer to either the timidity of the Israelites (v. 3) or the great panic of the Midianites when Gideon attacked (v. 21). The Hebrew verb form is translated "routing" in 8:12. *hill of Moreh.* Located across the Valley of Jezreel, approximately four miles from the Israelite army.

7:3 *may turn back.* Those who were afraid to fight the Lord's battle were not to go out with his army so that they would not demoralize the others (Dt 20:8). *Mount Gilead.* Perhaps used here as another name for Mount Gilboa.

7:6 *lapped.* The 300 remained on their feet, prepared for any emergency.

7:8–14 The Lord provided Gideon with encouraging intelligence information for the battle.

and all the other eastern peoples had settled in the valley, thick as locusts.[h] Their camels[i] could no more be counted than the sand on the seashore.[j]

13Gideon arrived just as a man was telling a friend his dream. "I had a dream," he was saying. "A round loaf of barley bread came tumbling into the Midianite camp. It struck the tent with such force that the tent overturned and collapsed."

14His friend responded, "This can be nothing other than the sword of Gideon son of Joash,[k] the Israelite. God has given the Midianites and the whole camp into his hands."

15When Gideon heard the dream and its interpretation, he worshiped God.[l] He returned to the camp of Israel and called out, "Get up! The LORD has given the Midianite camp into your hands."[m] 16Dividing the three hundred men[n] into three companies,[o] he placed trumpets[p] and empty jars[q] in the hands of all of them, with torches[r] inside.

17"Watch me," he told them. "Follow my lead. When I get to the edge of the camp, do exactly as I do. 18When I and all who are with me blow our trumpets,[s] then from all around the camp blow yours and shout, 'For the LORD and for Gideon.'"

19Gideon and the hundred men with him reached the edge of the camp at the beginning of the middle watch, just after they had changed the guard. They blew their trumpets and broke the jars[t] that were in their hands. 20The three companies blew the trumpets and smashed the jars. Grasping the torches[u] in their left hands and holding in their right hands the

7:12 hS Dt 28:42; Jer 46:23 iJer 49:29 jS Jos 11:4 7:14 kS Jdg 6:11 7:15 lI Sa 15:31 mS ver 9
7:16 nGe 14:15 oJdg 9:43; 1Sa 11:11; 2Sa 18:2 pS Lev 25:9 qver 19; Ge 24:14 rS Ge 15:17 7:18 sS Jdg 3:27 7:19 tS ver 16 7:20 uS Ge 15:17

7:13–14 Although revelations by dreams are frequently mentioned in the OT, here both dreamer and interpreter are non-Israelite. Contrast Joseph, who interpreted dreams in Egypt (Ge 40:1–22; 41:1–32), and Daniel, who interpreted dreams in Babylon (Da 2:1–45; 4:4–27).
7:13 round loaf of barley bread. Since barley was considered an inferior grain and only one-half the value of wheat (see 2Ki 7:1), it is a fitting symbol for Israel, which was inferior in numbers.
7:16 three companies. A strategy adopted by Israel on several occasions (9:43; 1Sa 11:11; 2Sa 18:2). trumpets. Rams' horns (see Ex 19:13).

Gideon's Battles

The story of Gideon begins with a graphic portrayal of one of the most striking facts of life in the Fertile Crescent: the periodic migration of nomadic people from the Aramean desert into the settled areas of Palestine. Each spring the tents of the bedouin herdsmen appear overnight almost as if by magic, scattered on the hills and fields of the farming districts. Conflict between these two ways of life (herdsmen and farmers) was inevitable.

In the Biblical period, the vast numbers and warlike practice of the herdsmen reduced the village people to near vassalage. Gideon's answer was twofold: (1) religious reform, starting with his own family; and (2) military action, based on a coalition of northern Israelite tribes. The location of Gideon's hometown, "Ophrah of the Abiezrites," is not known with certainty, but probably was ancient Aper (modern Afula) in the Valley of Jezreel.

The battle at the spring of Harod is justly celebrated for its strategic brilliance. Denied the use of the only local water source, the Midianites camped in the valley and fell victim to the small band of Israelites, who attacked them from the heights of the hill of Moreh.

The main battle took place north of the hill near the village of Endor at the foot of Mount Tabor. Fleeing by way of the Jordan Valley, the Midianites were trapped when the Ephraimites seized the fords of the Jordan from below Beth Shan to Beth Barah near Adam.

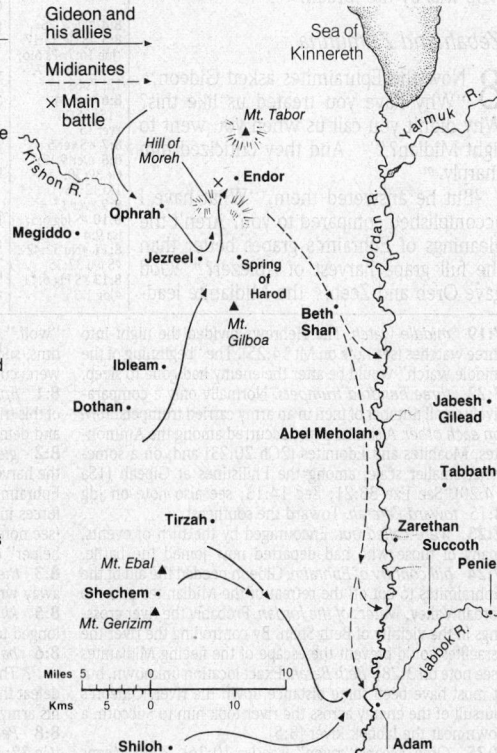

trumpets they were to blow, they shouted, "A sword[v] for the Lord and for Gideon!" [21]While each man held his position around the camp, all the Midianites ran, crying out as they fled.[w]

[22]When the three hundred trumpets sounded,[x] the Lord caused the men throughout the camp to turn on each other[y] with their swords.[z] The army fled to Beth Shittah toward Zererah as far as the border of Abel Meholah[a] near Tabbath. [23]Israelites from Naphtali, Asher[b] and all Manasseh were called out,[c] and they pursued the Midianites.[d] [24]Gideon sent messengers throughout the hill country of Ephraim, saying, "Come down against the Midianites and seize the waters of the Jordan[e] ahead of them as far as Beth Barah."

So all the men of Ephraim were called out and they took the waters of the Jordan as far as Beth Barah. [25]They also captured two of the Midianite leaders, Oreb and Zeeb[f]. They killed Oreb at the rock of Oreb,[g] and Zeeb at the winepress of Zeeb. They pursued the Midianites[h] and brought the heads of Oreb and Zeeb to Gideon, who was by the Jordan.[i]

Zebah and Zalmunna

8 Now the Ephraimites asked Gideon,[j] "Why have you treated us like this? Why didn't you call us when you went to fight Midian?"[k][l] And they criticized him sharply.[m]

[2]But he answered them, "What have I accomplished compared to you? Aren't the gleanings of Ephraim's grapes better than the full grape harvest of Abiezer?[n] [3]God gave Oreb and Zeeb,[o] the Midianite lead-

ers, into your hands. What was I able to do compared to you?" At this, their resentment against him subsided.

[4]Gideon and his three hundred men, exhausted yet keeping up the pursuit, came to the Jordan[p] and crossed it. [5]He said to the men of Succoth,[q] "Give my troops some bread; they are worn out,[r] and I am still pursuing Zebah and Zalmunna,[s] the kings of Midian."

[6]But the officials of Succoth[t] said, "Do you already have the hands of Zebah and Zalmunna in your possession? Why should we give bread[u] to your troops?"[v]

[7]Then Gideon replied, "Just for that, when the Lord has given Zebah and Zalmunna[w] into my hand, I will tear your flesh with desert thorns and briers."

[8]From there he went up to Peniel[i][x] and made the same request of them, but they answered as the men of Succoth had. [9]So he said to the men of Peniel, "When I return in triumph, I will tear down this tower."[y]

[10]Now Zebah and Zalmunna were in Karkor with a force of about fifteen thousand men, all that were left of the armies of the eastern peoples; a hundred and twenty thousand swordsmen had fallen.[z] [11]Gideon went up by the route of the nomads east of Nobah[a] and Jogbehah[b] and fell upon the unsuspecting army. [12]Zebah and Zalmunna, the two kings of Midian, fled, but he pursued them and captured them, routing their entire army.

[13]Gideon son of Joash[c] then returned from the battle by the Pass of Heres.[d] [14]He caught a young man of Succoth and ques-

[i]8 Hebrew *Penuel,* a variant of *Peniel;* also in verses 9 and 17

Cross references (center column)

7:20 [v]S Dt 32:41
7:21 [w]2Ki 7:7
7:22 [x]S Jos 6:20
[y]1Sa 14:20;
2Ch 20:23;
Isa 9:21; 19:2;
Eze 38:21;
Hag 2:22;
Zec 14:13
[z]Hab 3:14
[a]1Sa 18:19;
1Ki 4:12; 19:16
7:23 [b]S Jos 17:7
[c]Jdg 6:35
[d]Ps 83:9
7:24 [e]S Jos 2:7
7:25 [f]Jdg 8:3;
Ps 83:11
[g]Isa 10:26
[h]Isa 9:4 [i]Jdg 8:4;
Ps 106:43
8:1 [i]S Jdg 6:11
[k]S Ge 25:2
[l]Jdg 12:1
[m]2Sa 19:41
8:2 [n]S Nu 26:30
8:3 [o]S Jdg 7:25

8:4 [p]Jdg 7:25
8:5 [q]S Ge 33:17
[r]Job 16:7; Ps 6:6;
Jer 45:3 [s]ver 7,
12; Ps 83:11
8:6 [t]ver 14
[u]1Sa 25:11
[v]ver 15
8:7 [w]S ver 5
8:8 [x]ver 9,17;
Ge 32:30;
1Ki 12:25
8:9 [y]ver 17
8:10 [z]S Jdg 6:5;
Isa 9:4
8:11 [a]Nu 32:42
[b]S Nu 32:35
8:13 [c]S Jdg 6:11
[d]Jdg 1:35

7:19 *middle watch.* The Hebrews divided the night into three watches (see note on Mt 14:25). The "beginning of the middle watch" would be after the enemy had gone to sleep.
7:22 *three hundred trumpets.* Normally only a comparatively small number of men in an army carried trumpets. *turn on each other.* A similar panic occurred among the Ammonites, Moabites and Edomites (2Ch 20:23) and, on a somewhat smaller scale, among the Philistines at Gibeah (1Sa 14:20). See Eze 38:21; Zec 14:13; see also note on Jdg 4:15. *toward Zererah.* Toward the southeast.
7:23 *were called out.* Encouraged by the turn of events, many of those who had departed now joined the battle.
7:24 *hill country of Ephraim.* Gideon needed the aid of the Ephraimites to cut off the retreat of the Midianites into the Jordan Valley. *waters of the Jordan.* Probably the river crossings in the vicinity of Beth Shan. By controlling the river the Israelites could prevent the escape of the fleeing Midianites (see note on 3:28). *Beth Barah.* Exact location unknown, but it must have been some distance down the river. Gideon's pursuit of the enemy across the river took him to Succoth, a town near the Jabbok River (8:5).
7:25 *Oreb.* Means "raven" (see Isa 10:26). *Zeeb.* Means

"wolf." *heads.* Frequently parts of the bodies of dead victims, such as heads, hands (8:6) and foreskins (1Sa 18:25), were cut off and brought back as a kind of body count.
8:1 *Ephraimites.* Contrast Gideon, who placates the wrath of this tribe (vv. 2–3), with Jephthah, who brings humiliation and defeat to it (12:1–6).
8:2 *gleanings.* Leftover grain after the main gathering of the harvest (see note on Ru 1:22). Here Gideon implies that Ephraim has accomplished more than he and all the other forces involved in the initial attack. *Abiezer.* Gideon's clan (see note on 6:11). The name means "My (divine) Father is helper" or "My (divine) Father is strong."
8:3 *their resentment . . . subsided.* "A gentle answer turns away wrath" (Pr 15:1).
8:5 *kings of Midian.* Zebah and Zalmunna may have belonged to different Midianite tribes (see Nu 31:8).
8:6 *hands.* See note on 7:25. *Why should we give bread . . . ?* The officials of Succoth doubted Gideon's ability to defeat the Midianite coalition and feared reprisal if they gave his army food.
8:8 *Peniel.* The place where Jacob had wrestled with God (Ge 32:30–31).

tioned him, and the young man wrote down for him the names of the seventy-seven officials of Succoth, *e* the elders *f* of the town. ¹⁵Then Gideon came and said to the men of Succoth, "Here are Zebah and Zalmunna, about whom you taunted me by saying, 'Do you already have the hands of Zebah and Zalmunna in your possession? Why should we give bread to your exhausted men? *g* '" ¹⁶He took the elders of the town and taught the men of Succoth a lesson *h* by punishing them with desert thorns and briers. ¹⁷He also pulled down the tower of Peniel *i* and killed the men of the town. *j*

¹⁸Then he asked Zebah and Zalmunna, "What kind of men did you kill at Tabor? *k* "

"Men like you," they answered, "each one with the bearing of a prince."

¹⁹Gideon replied, "Those were my brothers, the sons of my own mother. As surely as the LORD lives, *l* if you had spared their lives, I would not kill you." ²⁰Turning to Jether, his oldest son, he said, "Kill them!" But Jether did not draw his sword, because he was only a boy and was afraid.

²¹Zebah and Zalmunna said, "Come, do it yourself. 'As is the man, so is his strength.'" So Gideon stepped forward and killed them, and took the ornaments *m* off their camels' necks.

Gideon's Ephod

²²The Israelites said to Gideon, "Rule over us—you, your son and your grandson—because you have saved us out of the hand of Midian."

²³But Gideon told them, "I will not rule over you, nor will my son rule over you. The LORD will rule *n* over you." ²⁴And he

said, "I do have one request, that each of you give me an earring *o* from your share of the plunder. *p* " (It was the custom of the Ishmaelites *q* to wear gold earrings.)

²⁵They answered, "We'll be glad to give them." So they spread out a garment, and each man threw a ring from his plunder onto it. ²⁶The weight of the gold rings he asked for came to seventeen hundred shekels, *i* not counting the ornaments, the pendants and the purple garments worn by the kings of Midian or the chains *r* that were on their camels' necks. ²⁷Gideon made the gold into an ephod, *s* which he placed in Ophrah, *t* his town. All Israel prostituted themselves by worshiping it there, and it became a snare *u* to Gideon and his family. *v*

Gideon's Death

²⁸Thus Midian was subdued before the Israelites and did not raise its head *w* again. During Gideon's lifetime, the land enjoyed peace *x* forty years.

²⁹Jerub-Baal *y* son of Joash *z* went back home to live. ³⁰He had seventy sons *a* of his own, for he had many wives. ³¹His concubine, *b* who lived in Shechem, also bore him a son, whom he named Abimelech. *c* ³²Gideon son of Joash died at a good old age *d* and was buried in the tomb of his father Joash in Ophrah of the Abiezrites.

³³No sooner had Gideon died than the Israelites again prostituted themselves to the Baals. *e* They set up Baal-Berith *f* as their god *g* and ³⁴did not remember *h* the LORD their God, who had rescued them from the hands of all their enemies on every side. ³⁵They also failed to show kind-

Cross references (center column):

8:14 *e* ver 6
    /S Ex 3:16
8:15 *g* ver 6
8:16 *h*1Sa 14:12
8:17 *i*S ver 8 /ver 9
8:18 *k*S Jos 19:22
8:19 *l*S Nu 14:21
8:21 *m*ver 26; Isa 3:18
8:23 *n*S Ex 16:8; S Nu 11:20; 1Sa 12:12

8:24 *o*S Ge 35:4
    *p*S Ge 49:27
    *q*S Ge 16:11
8:26 *r*S ver 21
8:27 *s*S Ge 25:7; Jdg 17:5; 18:14
    *t*S Jos 18:23
    *u*S Ex 10:7
    *v*S Ex 32:2
8:28 *w*Ps 83:2
    *x*S Jdg 3:11
8:29 *y*S Jdg 6:32
    *z*S Jdg 6:11
8:30 *a*Jdg 9:2,5, 18,24; 2Ki 10:1
8:31 *b*S Ge 22:24
    *c*Jdg 9:1; 10:1; 2Sa 11:21
8:32 *d*S Ge 15:15
8:33 *e*S Jdg 2:11, 13,19 /Jdg 9:4
    *g*Jdg 9:27,46
8:34 *h*S Jdg 3:7; S Ne 9:17

i26 That is, about 43 pounds (about 19.5 kilograms)

8:19 *sons of my own mother.* In an age when men often had several wives it was necessary to distinguish between full brothers and half brothers.

8:21 *do it yourself.* Dying at the hands of a boy may have been considered a disgrace (see 1Sa 17:42). *ornaments.* Crescent necklaces, as in Isa 3:18.

8:23 *I will not rule . . . The LORD will rule.* Gideon, like Samuel (1Sa 8:4–20), rejected the establishment of a monarchy because he regarded it as a replacement of the Lord's rule. God's rule over Israel (theocracy) is a central issue in Judges.

8:24 *earring.* Or possibly "nose ring" (see Ge 24:47; Eze 16:12). *Ishmaelites.* Related to the Midianites (Ge 25:1–2) and sometimes identified with them (vv. 22,24; Ge 37:25–28; 39:1). See note on Ge 37:25.

8:27 *ephod.* Sometimes a holy garment associated with the priesthood (Ex 28:6–30; 39:2–26; Lev 8:7), at other times a pagan object associated with idols (17:5; 18:14,17).

8:28 *forty years.* A conventional number of years for a generation (see Introduction: Background).

8:29 *Jerub-Baal.* See note on 6:32.

8:30 *seventy sons.* A sign of power and prosperity (see 12:14; 2Ki 10:1).

8:31 *concubine.* She was originally a slave in his household (9:18; see note on Ge 16:2). *Abimelech.* Appears elsewhere as a royal title (Ge 20:2; 26:1; Ps 34 title) and means "My (divine) Father is King." Gideon, in naming his son, acknowledges that the Lord (here called "Father") is King.

8:32 *at a good old age.* A phrase used elsewhere only of Abraham (Ge 15:15; 25:8) and David (1Ch 29:28).

8:33 *Baals.* See notes on 2:11,13. *Baal-Berith.* Means "lord of the covenant"; the same deity is called El-Berith ("god of the covenant") in 9:46. There was a temple dedicated to him (see 9:4) in Shechem. The word "covenant" in his name probably refers to a solemn treaty that bound together a league of Canaanite cities whose people worshiped him as their god. Ironically, Shechem (v. 31), near Mount Ebal, was the site at which Joshua had twice renewed the Lord's covenant with Israel after they had entered Canaan (Jos 8:30–35; 24:25–27). See also note on 2:11.

ness to the family of Jerub-Baal[i] (that is, Gideon) for all the good things he had done for them.[j]

Abimelech

9 Abimelech[k] son of Jerub-Baal[l] went to his mother's brothers in Shechem and said to them and to all his mother's clan, 2"Ask all the citizens of Shechem, 'Which is better for you: to have all seventy of Jerub-Baal's sons rule over you, or just one man?' Remember, I am your flesh and blood.[m]"

3When the brothers repeated all this to the citizens of Shechem, they were inclined to follow Abimelech, for they said, "He is our brother." 4They gave him seventy shekels[k] of silver from the temple of Baal-Berith,[n] and Abimelech used it to hire reckless adventurers,[o] who became his followers. 5He went to his father's home in Ophrah and on one stone murdered his seventy brothers,[p] the sons of Jerub-Baal. But Jotham,[q] the youngest son of Jerub-Baal, escaped by hiding.[r] 6Then all the citizens of Shechem and Beth Millo[s] gathered beside the great tree[t] at the pillar in Shechem to crown Abimelech king.

7When Jotham[u] was told about this, he climbed up on the top of Mount Gerizim[v] and shouted to them, "Listen to me, citi-

zens of Shechem, so that God may listen to you. 8One day the trees went out to anoint a king for themselves. They said to the olive tree, 'Be our king.'

9"But the olive tree answered, 'Should I give up my oil, by which both gods and men are honored, to hold sway over the trees?'

10"Next, the trees said to the fig tree, 'Come and be our king.'

11"But the fig tree replied, 'Should I give up my fruit, so good and sweet, to hold sway over the trees?'

12"Then the trees said to the vine, 'Come and be our king.'

13"But the vine answered, 'Should I give up my wine,[w] which cheers both gods and men, to hold sway over the trees?'

14"Finally all the trees said to the thornbush, 'Come and be our king.'

15"The thornbush said to the trees, 'If you really want to anoint me king over you, come and take refuge in my shade;[x] but if not, then let fire come out[y] of the thornbush and consume the cedars of Lebanon!'[z]

16"Now if you have acted honorably and in good faith when you made Abimelech king, and if you have been fair to Jerub-Baal and his family, and if you have treated

Cross references

8:35 /S Jdg 6:32; /Jdg 9:16
9:1 kS Jdg 8:31; /S Jdg 6:32
9:2 mS Ge 29:14
9:4 nS Jdg 8:33; oJdg 11:3; 1Sa 25:25; 2Ch 13:7; Job 30:8
9:5 pS Jdg 8:30; qver 7,21,57; r2Ki 11:2; 2Ch 22:9
9:6 sver 20; 2Ki 12:20; tS Ge 12:6; S Jdg 4:11
9:7 uS ver 5; vS Dt 11:29; Jn 4:20

9:13 wS Ge 14:18; Ecc 2:3; SS 4:10
9:15 xIsa 30:2; yver 20; zS Dt 3:25; 1Ki 5:6; Ps 29:5; 92:12; Isa 2:13

k4 That is, about 1 3/4 pounds (about 0.8 kilogram)

9:1–57 The stories of Gideon and Abimelech form the literary center of Judges (see Introduction: Literary Features). Abimelech, who tried to set himself up like a Canaanite city king with the help of Baal (v. 4), stands in sharp contrast to his father Gideon (Jerub-Baal), who had attacked Baal worship and insisted that the Lord ruled over Israel. Abimelech attempted this Canaanite revival in the very place where Joshua had earlier reaffirmed Israel's allegiance to the Lord (Jos 24:14–27). In every respect Abimelech was the antithesis of the Lord's appointed judges.
9:1 Shechem. See note on Ge 33:18. Ruins dating from the Canaanite era give evidence of a sacred area, probably to be associated with the temple of Baal-Berith or El-Berith (vv. 4,46). Archaeological evidence, which is compatible with the destruction of Shechem by Abimelech, indicates that its sacred area was never rebuilt after this time.
9:2 citizens. The singular form of the Hebrew for this word is ba'al. It means "lord" or "owner" and probably refers here to the aristocracy or landowners of the city. flesh and blood. Being half-Canaanite, Abimelech intimated that it was in their best interest to make him king rather than be under the rule of Gideon's 70 sons. The following he gathered was based on this relationship and became a threat to the people of Israel.
9:4 from the temple. Ancient temples served as depositories for personal and civic funds. The payments of vows and penalties, as well as gifts, were also part of the temple treasury. The temple of Baal-Berith is probably to be identified with a large building found at Shechem by archaeologists. reckless adventurers. Use of mercenaries to accomplish political or military goals was common in ancient times. Others who used them are Jephthah (11:3), David (1Sa

22:1–2), Absalom (2Sa 15:1), Adonijah (1Ki 1:5), Rezon (1Ki 11:23–24) and Jeroboam (2Ch 13:6–7).
9:5 on one stone. Abimelech's 70 brothers were slaughtered like sacrificial animals (see 13:19–20; 1Sa 14:33–34). In effect he inaugurated his kingship by using his Israelite half brothers as his coronation sacrifices (see 2Sa 15:10,12; 1Ki 1:5,9; 3:4).
9:6 Beth Millo. "Millo" is derived from a Hebrew verb meaning "to fill" and probably refers to the earthen fill used to erect a platform on which walls and other large structures were built. Beth Millo may be identical to the "stronghold" of v. 46. great tree. See Jos 24:25–26; see also note on Ge 12:6.
9:7 top. Probably a ledge that overlooked the city.
9:8 trees went out. Fables of this type, in which inanimate objects speak and act, were popular among Eastern peoples of that time (see 2Ki 14:9).
9:9–13 The olive tree, the fig tree and the vine were all plants that produced fruit of great importance to the people of the Near East.
9:13 gods. It was commonly believed that the gods participated in such human experiences as drinking wine.
9:14 thornbush. Probably the well-known buckthorn, a scraggly bush common in the hills of Palestine and a constant menace to farming. It produced nothing of value and was an apt figure for Abimelech.
9:15 shade. Ironically, in offering shade to the trees, the thornbush symbolized the traditional role of kings as protectors of their subjects (see Isa 30:2–3; 32:1–2; Da 4:12). cedars of Lebanon. The most valuable of Near Eastern trees, here symbolic of the leading men of Shechem (see v. 20).

him as he deserves— [17]and to think that my father fought for you, risked[a] his life to rescue you from the hand of Midian [18](but today you have revolted against my father's family, murdered his seventy sons[b] on a single stone, and made Abimelech, the son of his slave girl, king over the citizens of Shechem because he is your brother)— [19]if then you have acted honorably and in good faith toward Jerub-Baal and his family today,[c] may Abimelech be your joy, and may you be his, too! [20]But if you have not, let fire come out[d] from Abimelech and consume you, citizens of Shechem[e] and Beth Millo,[f] and let fire come out from you, citizens of Shechem and Beth Millo, and consume Abimelech!"

[21]Then Jotham[g] fled, escaping to Beer,[h] and he lived there because he was afraid of his brother Abimelech.

[22]After Abimelech had governed Israel three years, [23]God sent an evil spirit[i] between Abimelech and the citizens of Shechem, who acted treacherously against Abimelech. [24]God did this in order that the crime against Jerub-Baal's seventy sons,[j] the shedding[k] of their blood, might be avenged[l] on their brother Abimelech and on the citizens of Shechem, who had helped him[m] murder his brothers. [25]In opposition to him these citizens of Shechem set men on the hilltops to ambush and rob everyone who passed by, and this was reported to Abimelech.

[26]Now Gaal son of Ebed[n] moved with his brothers into Shechem, and its citizens put their confidence in him. [27]After they had gone out into the fields and gathered the grapes and trodden[o] them, they held a festival in the temple of their god.[p] While they were eating and drinking, they cursed Abimelech. [28]Then Gaal son of Ebed[q] said, "Who[r] is Abimelech, and who is Shechem, that we should be subject to him? Isn't he Jerub-Baal's son, and isn't Zebul his deputy? Serve the men of Hamor,[s] Shechem's father! Why should we serve

Abimelech? [29]If only this people were under my command![t] Then I would get rid of him. I would say to Abimelech, 'Call out your whole army!' "[1][u]

[30]When Zebul the governor of the city heard what Gaal son of Ebed said, he was very angry. [31]Under cover he sent messengers to Abimelech, saying, "Gaal son of Ebed and his brothers have come to Shechem and are stirring up the city against you. [32]Now then, during the night you and your men should come and lie in wait[v] in the fields. [33]In the morning at sunrise, advance against the city. When Gaal and his men come out against you, do whatever your hand finds to do.[w]"

[34]So Abimelech and all his troops set out by night and took up concealed positions near Shechem in four companies. [35]Now Gaal son of Ebed had gone out and was standing at the entrance to the city gate[x] just as Abimelech and his soldiers came out from their hiding place.[y]

[36]When Gaal saw them, he said to Zebul, "Look, people are coming down from the tops of the mountains!"

Zebul replied, "You mistake the shadows of the mountains for men."

[37]But Gaal spoke up again: "Look, people are coming down from the center of the land, and a company is coming from the direction of the soothsayers' tree."

[38]Then Zebul said to him, "Where is your big talk now, you who said, 'Who is Abimelech that we should be subject to him?' Aren't these the men you ridiculed?[z] Go out and fight them!"

[39]So Gaal led out[m] the citizens of Shechem and fought Abimelech. [40]Abimelech chased him, and many fell wounded in the flight—all the way to the entrance to the gate. [41]Abimelech stayed in Arumah, and Zebul drove Gaal and his brothers out of Shechem.

9:17 *a*Jdg 12:3; 1Sa 19:5; 28:21; Job 13:14; Ps 119:109
9:18 *b*S Jdg 8:30
9:19 *c*ver 16
9:20 *d*ver 15 *e*ver 45 *f*S ver 6
9:21 *g*S ver 5 *h*Nu 21:16
9:23 *i*1Sa 16:14, 23; 18:10; 19:9; 1Ki 22:22
9:24 *j*S Jdg 8:30 *k*S Ge 9:6; Nu 35:33; 1Ki 2:32 *l*ver 56-57 *m*Dt 27:25
9:26 *n*ver 28,31, 41
9:27 *o*Isa 16:10; Am 5:11; 9:13 *p*S Jdg 8:33 *r*1Sa 25:10 *s*S Ge 33:19

9:29 *t*2Sa 15:4 *u*ver 38
9:32 *v*Jos 8:2
9:33 *w*1Sa 10:7
9:28 *q*S Jos 2:5 *y*Ps 32:7; Isa 28:15,17; Jer 49:10
9:38 *z*ver 28-29

[1]29 Septuagint; Hebrew *him." Then he said to Abimelech, "Call out your whole army!"* [m]39 Or *Gaal went out in the sight of*

9:20 *fire come out . . . and consume.* A grim prediction that Abimelech and the people of Shechem would destroy each other. Fire spreads rapidly through bramble bushes and brings about swift destruction (see Ex 22:6; Isa 9:18).
9:21 *Beer.* A very common name, meaning "a well."
9:22 *Israel.* Those Israelites who recognized Abimelech's authority, mainly in the vicinity of Shechem.
9:23 *evil spirit.* Perhaps a spirit of distrust and bitterness. The Hebrew for "spirit" is often used to describe an attitude or disposition. *acted treacherously.* The one who founded his kingdom by treachery is himself undone by treachery.
9:26 *put their confidence in him.* Just as the fickle population had followed Abimelech, so they are now swayed by the deceptive proposals of Gaal.

9:27 *held a festival.* The vintage harvest was one of the most joyous times of the year (see Isa 16:9–10; Jer 25:30), but festivals and celebrations held at pagan temples often degenerated into debauched drinking affairs.
9:28 *Hamor.* The Hivite ruler who had founded the city of Shechem (Ge 33:19; 34:2; Jos 24:32).
9:32 *lie in wait.* Ambush succeeded against Gibeah in Benjamin (20:37) and against Ai (Jos 8:2).
9:34 *four companies.* Smaller segments meant less chance of detection. Also, attack from several directions was good strategy.
9:37 *center of the land.* See note on Eze 38:12. *soothsayers' tree.* Probably a sacred tree in some way related to the temple of Baal-Berith (see note on Ge 12:6).

42The next day the people of Shechem went out to the fields, and this was reported to Abimelech. 43So he took his men, divided them into three companies[a] and set an ambush[b] in the fields. When he saw the people coming out of the city, he rose to attack them. 44Abimelech and the companies with him rushed forward to a position at the entrance to the city gate. Then two companies rushed upon those in the fields and struck them down. 45All that day Abimelech pressed his attack against the city until he had captured it and killed its people. Then he destroyed the city[c] and scattered salt[d] over it.

46On hearing this, the citizens in the tower of Shechem went into the stronghold of the temple[e] of El-Berith. 47When Abimelech heard that they had assembled there, 48he and all his men went up Mount Zalmon.[f] He took an ax and cut off some branches, which he lifted to his shoulders. He ordered the men with him, "Quick! Do what you have seen me do!" 49So all the men cut branches and followed Abimelech. They piled them against the stronghold and set it on fire over the people inside. So all the people in the tower of Shechem, about a thousand men and women, also died.

50Next Abimelech went to Thebez[g] and besieged it and captured it. 51Inside the city, however, was a strong tower, to which all the men and women—all the people of the city—fled. They locked themselves in and climbed up on the tower roof. 52Abimelech went to the tower and stormed it. But as he approached the en-

trance to the tower to set it on fire, 53a woman dropped an upper millstone on his head and cracked his skull.[h]

54Hurriedly he called to his armor-bearer, "Draw your sword and kill me,[i] so that they can't say, 'A woman killed him.'" So his servant ran him through, and he died. 55When the Israelites saw that Abimelech was dead, they went home.

56Thus God repaid the wickedness that Abimelech had done to his father by murdering his seventy brothers. 57God also made the men of Shechem pay for all their wickedness.[j] The curse of Jotham[k] son of Jerub-Baal came on them.

Tola

10 After the time of Abimelech[l] a man of Issachar,[m] Tola son of Puah,[n] the son of Dodo, rose to save[o] Israel. He lived in Shamir,[p] in the hill country of Ephraim. 2He led[n] Israel twenty-three years; then he died, and was buried in Shamir.

Jair

3He was followed by Jair[q] of Gilead, who led Israel twenty-two years. 4He had thirty sons, who rode thirty donkeys.[r] They controlled thirty towns in Gilead, which to this day are called Havvoth Jair.[o][s] 5When Jair[t] died, he was buried in Kamon.

Jephthah

6Again the Israelites did evil in the eyes

Cross references
9:43 aS Jdg 7:16
bJos 8:2
9:45 cver 20
dJer 48:9
9:46 eS Jdg 8:33
9:48 fPs 68:14
9:50 g2Sa 11:21

9:53 h2Sa 11:21
9:54 i1Sa 31:4; 2Sa 1:9
9:57 jver 24; Ps 94:23 kS ver 5
10:1 lS Jdg 8:31 mS Ge 30:18 nS Ge 46:13 oS Jdg 6:14 pJos 15:48
10:3 qS Nu 32:41
10:4 rS Ge 49:11; S 1Ki 1:33 sS Nu 32:41
10:5 tS Nu 32:41

n2 Traditionally *judged*; also in verse 3   o4 Or *called the settlements of Jair*

9:43 *three companies.* See note on 7:16.
9:45 *scattered salt over it.* To condemn it to perpetual barrenness and desolation (see Dt 29:23; Ps 107:33–34; Jer 17:6; Zep 2:9).
9:46 *stronghold.* Probably the Beth Millo of v. 6. *El-Berith.* Baal-Berith (v. 4).
9:49 *set it on fire.* In fulfillment of Jotham's curse (v. 20).
9:53 *woman.* While the men used bows, arrows and spears, women helped to defend the tower by dropping heavy stones on those who came near it. *upper millstone.* See note on 3:16. The upper, revolving stone of a mill was circular, with a hole in the center. Grinding grain was women's work (see Ex 11:5), usually considered too lowly for men to perform (see 16:21). Abimelech was killed by a woman using a domestic implement (see also 4:21).
9:54 *armor-bearer.* A military leader usually had a young man carry his shield and spear (see 1Sa 14:6; 31:4). *A woman killed him.* It was considered a disgrace for a soldier to die at the hands of a woman. Abimelech's shameful death was long remembered (2Sa 11:21).
9:56 *God repaid.* God was in control of events. As Israel's true King, he brought Abimelech's wickedness to a quick and shameful end.
9:57 *curse of Jotham.* See v. 20.
10:1 *a man of Issachar, Tola son of Puah.* Tola and Puah

bear names of two of the sons of Issachar (Ge 46:13; Nu 26:23; 1Ch 7:1).
10:3 *Jair.* Since Jair came from Gilead (the territory assigned to Manasseh) and since a descendant of Manasseh bore the same name (Nu 32:41; Dt 3:14; 1Ki 4:13), it appears that Jair was a Manassite.
10:4 *thirty sons . . . thirty donkeys . . . thirty towns.* Evidence of wealth and position. *Havvoth Jair.* See NIV text note.
10:6–12:7 Israel now turned to Jephthah, a social outcast whom they had driven from the land and caused to become an outlaw without an inheritance in Israel. The author notes this to Israel's shame. The account of Jephthah's judgeship balances that of Deborah in the story of the judges (see note on 4:1–5:31; see also Introduction: Literary Features).
10:6 *gods of Aram.* The chief gods were Hadad (Baal), Mot, Anath and Rimmon. *gods of Sidon.* The Sidonians worshiped essentially the same gods as the Canaanites (see notes on 2:11,13). *gods of Moab.* The chief deity of Moab was Chemosh. *gods of the Ammonites.* Molech was the chief Ammonite deity (see 1Ki 11:7) and was sometimes worshiped by the offering of human sacrifice (Lev 18:21; 20:2–5; 2Ki 23:10). This god is also called Milcom (see NIV text notes on 1Ki 11:5; 2Ki 23:13). Both Molech and Milcom are forms of a Semitic word for "king." *gods of the*

of the LORD.[u] They served the Baals and the Ashtoreths,[v] and the gods of Aram,[w] the gods of Sidon,[x] the gods of Moab, the gods of the Ammonites[y][z] and the gods of the Philistines.[a] And because the Israelites forsook the LORD[b] and no longer served him, [7]he became angry[c] with them. He sold them[d] into the hands of the Philistines and the Ammonites, [8]who that year shattered and crushed them. For eighteen years they oppressed all the Israelites on the east side of the Jordan in Gilead,[e] the land of the Amorites. [9]The Ammonites also crossed the Jordan to fight against Judah,[f] Benjamin and the house of Ephraim;[g] and Israel was in great distress. [10]Then the Israelites cried[h] out to the LORD, "We have sinned[i] against you, forsaking our God and serving the Baals."[j]

[11]The LORD replied, "When the Egyptians,[k] the Amorites,[l] the Ammonites,[m] the Philistines,[n] [12]the Sidonians, the Amalekites[o] and the Maonites[p][p] oppressed you[q] and you cried to me for help, did I not save you from their hands? [13]But you have forsaken[r] me and served other gods,[s] so I will no longer save you. [14]Go and cry out to the gods you have chosen. Let them save[t] you when you are in trouble![u]"

[15]But the Israelites said to the LORD, "We have sinned. Do with us whatever you think best,[v] but please rescue us now." [16]Then they got rid of the foreign gods among them and served the LORD.[w] And he could bear Israel's misery[x] no longer.[y]

[17]When the Ammonites were called to arms and camped in Gilead, the Israelites assembled and camped at Mizpah.[z] [18]The leaders of the people of Gilead said to each other, "Whoever will launch the attack against the Ammonites will be the head[a] of all those living in Gilead."

11
Jephthah[b] the Gileadite was a mighty warrior.[c] His father was Gilead;[d] his mother was a prostitute.[e] [2]Gilead's wife also bore him sons, and when they were grown up, they drove Jephthah away. "You are not going to get any inheritance in our family," they said, "because you are the son of another woman." [3]So Jephthah fled from his brothers and settled in the land of Tob,[f] where a group of adventurers[g] gathered around him and followed him.

[4]Some time later, when the Ammonites[h] made war on Israel, [5]the elders of Gilead went to get Jephthah from the land of Tob. [6]"Come," they said, "be our commander, so we can fight the Ammonites."

[7]Jephthah said to them, "Didn't you hate me and drive me from my father's house?[i] Why do you come to me now, when you're in trouble?"

[8]The elders of Gilead said to him, "Nevertheless, we are turning to you now; come with us to fight the Ammonites, and you will be our head[j] over all who live in Gilead."

[9]Jephthah answered, "Suppose you take me back to fight the Ammonites and the LORD gives them to me—will I really be your head?"

[10]The elders of Gilead replied, "The LORD is our witness;[k] we will certainly do as you say." [11]So Jephthah went with the elders[l] of Gilead, and the people made him head and commander over them. And he repeated[m] all his words before the LORD in Mizpah.[n]

[12]Then Jephthah sent messengers to the

10:6 [u]S Jdg 2:11
[v]S Jdg 2:13
[w]Eze 27:16
[x]S Ge 10:15
[y]S Ge 19:38
[z]S Nu 21:29
[a]S Ge 26:1;
S Jdg 2:12
10:7 [b]S Dt 32:15
[c]S Dt 31:17
[d]S Dt 32:30
10:8 [e]S Jos 12:2
10:9 [f]ver 17;
Jdg 11:4
[g]Jdg 1:22
10:10 [h]S Jdg 3:9
[i]S Ex 9:27;
Ps 32:5; Jer 3:25;
8:14; 14:20
[j]Jer 2:27
10:11 [k]Ex 14:30
[l]S Ge 14:7
[m]S Jdg 3:13
[n]S Jdg 3:31
10:12 [o]S Ge 14:7
[p]S Jos 15:55
[q]S Jdg 4:3
10:13 [r]S Dt 32:15
[s]Jer 11:10; 13:10
10:14 [t]Isa 44:17;
57:13 [u]Dt 32:37;
Jer 2:28; 11:12;
Hab 2:18
10:15 [v]1Sa 3:18;
2Sa 10:12; 15:26;
Job 1:21; Isa 39:8
10:16
[w]Jos 24:23;
Jer 18:8 [x]Isa 63:9
[y]S Dt 32:36
10:17
[z]S Ge 31:49;
Jdg 11:29
10:18 [a]Jdg 11:8,9
11:1 [b]Jdg 12:1;
1Sa 12:11;
Heb 11:32
[c]Jdg 6:12
[d]Nu 26:29
[e]S Ge 38:15
11:3 [f]ver 5;
2Sa 10:6,8
[g]S Jdg 9:4
11:4 [h]S Jdg 10:9
11:7 [i]S Ge 26:16
11:8 [j]S Jdg 10:18
11:10
[k]S Ge 31:50;
S Isa 1:2
11:11 [l]1Sa 8:4;
2Sa 3:17
[m]Ex 19:9;
1Sa 8:21
[n]S Jos 11:3

[p] 12 Hebrew; some Septuagint manuscripts Midianites

Philistines. While the Philistines worshiped most of the Canaanite gods, their most popular deities appear to have been Dagon and Baal-Zebub. The name Dagon is the same as a Hebrew word for "grain," suggesting that he was a vegetation deity. He was worshiped in Babylonia as early as the second millennium B.C. Baal-Zebub was worshiped in Ekron (2Ki 1:2–3,6,16). The name means "lord of the flies," a deliberate change by followers of the Lord (Yahweh) to ridicule and protest the worship of Baal-Zebul ("Baal the prince"), a name known from ancient Canaanite texts (see Mt 10:25; 12:24 and NIV text notes).

10:7 *Philistines.* The account of Philistine oppression is resumed in 13:1.

10:11 *The LORD replied.* See note on 2:1. The Lord rebuked Israel for forgetting that he had delivered them from their oppressors in Canaan (see notes on 2:16–19; 6:8).

10:12 *Maonites.* See NIV text note; or perhaps the same as the Meunites, who along with the Philistines and Arabs opposed Israel (2Ch 26:7).

10:17 *Mizpah.* Means "watchtower." Several places bore

this name. Jephthah's headquarters was a town or fortress in Gilead (11:11) called "Mizpah of Gilead" (11:29). It may have been the same as Ramath Mizpah (Jos 13:26), located about 30 miles east of Beth Shan.

10:18 The Gileadites wanted to resist the Ammonite incursion but lacked the courageous military leadership to press their cause. *people.* Fighting men.

11:1 *his mother was a prostitute.* Therefore Jephthah was a social outcast.

11:3 *Tob.* The men of Tob were later allied with the Ammonites against David (2Sa 10:6–8). *adventurers.* See note on 9:4.

11:8 *be our head.* In addition to their initial offer of military command during the war with Ammon (v. 6), the Gileadites now also offer to make Jephthah regional head after the fighting is over.

11:11 The proposal of the elders was ratified by the people, a process followed in the election of Saul (1Sa 11:15), Rehoboam (1Ki 12:1) and Jeroboam (1Ki 12:20).

Ammonite king with the question: "What do you have against us that you have attacked our country?"

13The king of the Ammonites answered Jephthah's messengers, "When Israel came up out of Egypt, they took away my land from the Arnon[o] to the Jabbok,[p] all the way to the Jordan. Now give it back peaceably."

14Jephthah sent back messengers to the Ammonite king, 15saying:

"This is what Jephthah says: Israel did not take the land of Moab[q] or the land of the Ammonites.[r] 16But when they came up out of Egypt, Israel went through the desert to the Red Sea[q][s] and on to Kadesh.[t] 17Then Israel sent messengers[u] to the king of Edom, saying, 'Give us permission to go through your country,'[v] but the king of Edom would not listen. They sent also to the king of Moab,[w] and he refused.[x] So Israel stayed at Kadesh.

18"Next they traveled through the desert, skirted the lands of Edom[y] and Moab, passed along the eastern side[z] of the country of Moab, and camped on the other side of the Arnon.[a] They did not enter the territory of Moab, for the Arnon was its border.

19"Then Israel sent messengers[b] to Sihon king of the Amorites, who ruled in Heshbon,[c] and said to him, 'Let us pass through your country to our own place.'[d] 20Sihon, however, did not trust Israel[r] to pass through his territory. He mustered all his men and encamped at Jahaz and fought with Israel.[e]

21"Then the LORD, the God of Israel, gave Sihon and all his men into

Israel's hands, and they defeated them. Israel took over all the land of the Amorites who lived in that country, 22capturing all of it from the Arnon to the Jabbok and from the desert to the Jordan.[f]

23"Now since the LORD, the God of Israel, has driven the Amorites out before his people Israel, what right have you to take it over? 24Will you not take what your god Chemosh[g] gives you? Likewise, whatever the LORD our God has given us,[h] we will possess. 25Are you better than Balak son of Zippor,[i] king of Moab? Did he ever quarrel with Israel or fight with them?[j] 26For three hundred years Israel occupied[k] Heshbon, Aroer,[l] the surrounding settlements and all the towns along the Arnon. Why didn't you retake them during that time? 27I have not wronged you, but you are doing me wrong by waging war against me. Let the LORD, the Judge,[s][m] decide[n] the dispute this day between the Israelites and the Ammonites.[o]"

28The king of Ammon, however, paid no attention to the message Jephthah sent him.

29Then the Spirit[p] of the LORD came upon Jephthah. He crossed Gilead and Manasseh, passed through Mizpah[q] of Gilead, and from there he advanced against the Ammonites.[r] 30And Jephthah made a vow[s] to the LORD: "If you give the Ammonites into my hands, 31whatever comes out of the door of my house to meet me

Cross references (center column):

11:13
oS Nu 21:13
pS Nu 21:24
11:15 qDt 2:9
rDt 2:19
11:16
sNu 14:25;
S Dt 1:40
tS Ge 14:7
11:17 uver 19;
S Ge 32:3;
Nu 20:14
vS Nu 20:17
wJer 48:1
xS Jos 24:9
11:18
yS Nu 20:21
zDt 2:8
aS Nu 21:13
11:19 bS ver 17
cS Jos 12:2
dNu 21:21-22
11:20 eNu 21:23

11:22
fNu 21:21-26;
S Dt 2:26
11:24
gS Nu 21:29;
S Jos 3:10
hDt 2:36
11:25 iNu 22:2
jS Jos 24:9
11:26 kNu 21:25
lS Nu 32:34;
S Jos 13:9
11:27
mS Ge 18:25
nS Ge 16:5
oS 2Ch 20:12
11:29 pS Jdg 3:10
qS Ge 31:49
rS Jdg 10:17
11:30
sS Ge 28:20;
Nu 30:10;
1Sa 1:11; Pr 31:2

q16 Hebrew *Yam Suph*; that is, Sea of Reeds   r20 Or however, would not make an agreement for Israel   s27 Or Ruler

---

11:13 *my land.* When the Israelites had first approached Canaan, this area was ruled by the Amorite king Sihon, who had taken it from the Moabites (Nu 21:29). The Ammonites had since become dominant over Moab and now claimed all previous Moabite territory.

11:14–27 Jephthah responded in accordance with international policies of the time; his letter is a classic example of contemporary international correspondence. It also reflects— and appeals to—the common recognition that the god(s) of a people established and protected their political boundaries and decided all boundary disputes. Jephthah's defense of Israel's claim to the land is threefold: (1) Israel took it from Sihon king of the Amorites, not from the Ammonites (vv. 15–22); (2) the Lord gave the land to Israel (vv. 23–25); (3) Israel had long possessed it (vv. 26–27).

11:16 *Kadesh.* Kadesh Barnea; see note on Nu 20:1.

11:21 *LORD, the God of Israel.* War was viewed not only in military terms but also as a contest between deities (see v. 24; Ex 12:12; Nu 33:4).

11:24 *Chemosh.* Reference to Chemosh, the chief deity of the Moabites, indicates either that at this time the king of

Ammon also ruled Moab or that there was a military confederacy of the two peoples.

11:25 *Balak.* See Nu 22–24.

11:26 *three hundred years.* For the relevance of this phrase in establishing the time span for Judges see Introduction: Background.

11:27 *Judge.* See 1Sa 24:15. As the divine Judge, the Lord is the final court of appeal. It is significant that in the book of Judges the singular noun "judge" is found only here, where it is used of the Lord, Israel's true Judge.

11:29 *Spirit of the LORD.* See note on 3:10. In the OT the unique empowering of the Spirit was given to an individual primarily to enable him to carry out the special responsibilities God had given him.

11:30 *made a vow.* A common practice among the Israelites (see Ge 28:20; 1Sa 1:11; 2Sa 15:8). The precise nature of this vow has been the subject of wide speculation, but v. 31 indicates the promise of a burnt offering and leads to the conclusion that Jephthah probably offered his daughter as a human sacrifice (v. 39). A vow was not to be broken (see Nu 30:2; Dt 23:21–23; see also Ecc 5:4–5).

when I return in triumph[t] from the Ammonites will be the LORD's, and I will sacrifice it as a burnt offering.[u]"

[32]Then Jephthah went over to fight the Ammonites, and the LORD gave them into his hands. [33]He devastated twenty towns from Aroer to the vicinity of Minnith,[v] as far as Abel Keramim. Thus Israel subdued Ammon.

[34]When Jephthah returned to his home in Mizpah, who should come out to meet him but his daughter, dancing[w] to the sound of tambourines![x] She was an only child.[y] Except for her he had neither son nor daughter. [35]When he saw her, he tore his clothes[z] and cried, "Oh! My daughter! You have made me miserable and wretched, because I have made a vow to the LORD that I cannot break.[a]"

[36]"My father," she replied, "you have given your word to the LORD. Do to me just as you promised,[b] now that the LORD has avenged you[c] of your enemies,[d] the Ammonites. [37]But grant me this one request," she said. "Give me two months to roam the hills and weep with my friends, because I will never marry."

[38]"You may go," he said. And he let her go for two months. She and the girls went into the hills and wept because she would never marry. [39]After the two months, she returned to her father and he did to her as he had vowed. And she was a virgin. From this comes the Israelite custom [40]that each year the young women of Israel go out for four days to commemorate the daughter of Jephthah the Gileadite.

Jephthah and Ephraim

12 The men of Ephraim called out their forces, crossed over to Zaphon[e] and said to Jephthah,[f] "Why did you go to fight the Ammonites without calling us to go with you?[g] We're going to burn down your house over your head."

[2]Jephthah answered, "I and my people

were engaged in a great struggle with the Ammonites, and although I called, you didn't save me out of their hands. [3]When I saw that you wouldn't help, I took my life in my hands[h] and crossed over to fight the Ammonites, and the LORD gave me the victory[i] over them. Now why have you come up today to fight me?"

[4]Jephthah then called together the men of Gilead[j] and fought against Ephraim. The Gileadites struck them down because the Ephraimites had said, "You Gileadites are renegades from Ephraim and Manasseh.[k]" [5]The Gileadites captured the fords of the Jordan[l] leading to Ephraim, and whenever a survivor of Ephraim said, "Let me cross over," the men of Gilead asked him, "Are you an Ephraimite?" If he replied, "No," [6]they said, "All right, say 'Shibboleth.'" If he said, "Sibboleth," because he could not pronounce the word correctly, they seized him and killed him at the fords of the Jordan. Forty-two thousand Ephraimites were killed at that time.

[7]Jephthah led[t] Israel six years. Then Jephthah the Gileadite died, and was buried in a town in Gilead.

Ibzan, Elon and Abdon

[8]After him, Ibzan of Bethlehem[m] led Israel. [9]He had thirty sons and thirty daughters. He gave his daughters away in marriage to those outside his clan, and for his sons he brought in thirty young women as wives from outside his clan. Ibzan led Israel seven years. [10]Then Ibzan died, and was buried in Bethlehem.

[11]After him, Elon the Zebulunite led Israel ten years. [12]Then Elon died, and was buried in Aijalon[n] in the land of Zebulun.

[13]After him, Abdon son of Hillel, from Pirathon,[o] led Israel. [14]He had forty sons and thirty grandsons,[p] who rode on seventy donkeys.[q] He led Israel eight years. [15]Then Abdon son of Hillel died, and was

Cross references (center column)

11:31 [t]Ge 28:21
[u]S Ge 8:20;
Lev 1:3;
Jdg 13:16
11:33 [v]Eze 27:17
11:34
[w]S Ex 15:20
[x]S Ge 31:27;
S Ex 15:20
[y]Zec 12:10
11:35 [z]S Nu 14:6
[a]Nu 30:2;
S Dt 23:21;
Ecc 5:2,4,5
11:36 [b]Lk 1:38
[c]S Nu 31:3
[d]2Sa 18:19
12:1 [e]S Jos 13:27
[f]S Jdg 11:1
[g]Jdg 8:1

12:3 [h]S Jdg 9:17
[i]S Dt 20:4
12:4 [j]1Ki 17:1
[k]S Ge 46:20;
Isa 9:21; 19:2
12:5 [l]S Jos 2:7
12:8
[m]S Ge 35:19
12:12
[n]S Jos 10:12
12:13 [o]ver 15;
2Sa 23:30;
1Ch 11:31; 27:14
12:14 [p]S Jdg 8:30
[q]S Jdg 5:10

[t][7] Traditionally *judged*; also in verses 8-14

11:34 *dancing.* It was customary for women to greet armies returning victoriously from battle in this way (see Ex 15:20; 1Sa 18:6).

11:35 *tore his clothes.* A common practice for expressing extreme grief (see Ge 37:34 and note).

11:37 *I will never marry.* To be kept from marrying and rearing children was a bitter prospect for an Israelite girl.

11:39 *Israelite custom.* Probably a local custom, since no other mention of it is found in the OT.

12:1 *burn down your house.* The Philistines issued a similar threat to Samson's wife (14:15). See also 20:48.

12:2 *answered.* Again Jephthah tried diplomacy first (see 11:12,14; see also note on 8:1). *I called.* New information on the sequence of events.

12:6 *Shibboleth.* Ironically, the word meant "floods" (see,

e.g., Ps 69:2,15). Apparently the Israelites east of the Jordan pronounced its initial letter with a strong "sh" sound, while those in Canaan gave it a softer "s" sound. (Peter was similarly betrayed by his accent; see Mt 26:73.)

12:7 *led Israel . . . years.* A new formula for closing out the account of a judge (see note on 3:11; see also Introduction: Literary Features).

12:8 *Bethlehem.* Probably the Bethlehem in western Zebulun.

12:9 *thirty sons and thirty daughters.* See note on 10:4.

12:11 *Elon.* Also the name of a clan in the tribe of Zebulun (Ge 46:14; Nu 26:26).

12:14 *forty sons and thirty grandsons.* A total of 70 (see notes on 8:30; 10:4).

12:15 *hill country of the Amalekites.* See note on 5:14.

buried at Pirathon in Ephraim, in the hill country of the Amalekites.[r]

The Birth of Samson

13 Again the Israelites did evil in the eyes of the LORD, so the LORD delivered them into the hands of the Philistines[s] for forty years.[t]

[2] A certain man of Zorah,[u] named Manoah,[v] from the clan of the Danites,[w] had a wife who was sterile and remained childless.[x] [3] The angel of the LORD[y] appeared to her[z] and said, "You are sterile and childless, but you are going to conceive and have a son.[a] [4] Now see to it that you drink no wine or other fermented drink[b] and that you do not eat anything unclean,[c] [5] because you will conceive and give birth to a son.[d] No razor[e] may be used on his head, because the boy is to be a Nazirite,[f] set apart to God from birth, and he will begin[g] the deliverance of Israel from the hands of the Philistines."

[6] Then the woman went to her husband and told him, "A man of God[h] came to me. He looked like an angel of God,[i] very awesome.[j] I didn't ask him where he came from, and he didn't tell me his name. [7] But he said to me, 'You will conceive and give birth to a son. Now then, drink no wine[k] or other fermented drink[l] and do not eat anything unclean, because the boy will be a Nazirite of God from birth until the day of his death.'[m]"

[8] Then Manoah[n] prayed to the LORD: "O Lord, I beg you, let the man of God[o]

you sent to us come again to teach us how to bring up the boy who is to be born."

[9] God heard Manoah, and the angel of God came again to the woman while she was out in the field; but her husband Manoah was not with her. [10] The woman hurried to tell her husband, "He's here! The man who appeared to me[p] the other day!"

[11] Manoah got up and followed his wife. When he came to the man, he said, "Are you the one who talked to my wife?"

"I am," he said.

[12] So Manoah asked him, "When your words are fulfilled, what is to be the rule for the boy's life and work?"

[13] The angel of the LORD answered, "Your wife must do all that I have told her. [14] She must not eat anything that comes from the grapevine, nor drink any wine or other fermented drink[q] nor eat anything unclean.[r] She must do everything I have commanded her."

[15] Manoah said to the angel of the LORD, "We would like you to stay until we prepare a young goat[s] for you."

[16] The angel of the LORD replied, "Even though you detain me, I will not eat any of your food. But if you prepare a burnt offering,[t] offer it to the LORD." (Manoah did not realize[u] that it was the angel of the LORD.)

[17] Then Manoah inquired of the angel of the LORD, "What is your name,[v] so that we may honor you when your word comes true?"

[18] He replied, "Why do you ask my

Cross references

12:15 [r]Jdg 5:14
13:1 [s]S Jdg 3:31
[t]Jdg 14:4
13:2 [u]S Jos 15:33
[v]ver 8; Jdg 16:31
[w]S Ge 30:6
[x]S Ge 11:30
13:3 [y]S Ge 16:7
[z]ver 10 [a]Isa 7:14;
Lk 1:13
13:4 [b]S Lev 10:9
[c]ver 14;
Nu 6:2-4;
S Lk 1:15
13:5 [d]S Ge 3:15
[e]1Sa 1:11
[f]S Nu 6:2,13;
Am 2:11,12;
[g]1Sa 7:13
13:6 [h]ver 8;
1Sa 2:27; 9:6;
1Ki 13:1; 17:18
[i]S Nu 22:22
[j]Ps 66:5
13:7 [k]Jer 35:6
[l]Lev 10:9
[m]1Sa 1:11,28
13:8 [n]S ver 2
[o]S ver 6

13:10 [p]ver 3
13:14 [q]Lev 10:9
[r]S ver 4
13:15 [s]Jdg 6:19
13:16
[t]S Jdg 11:31
[u]S Jdg 6:22
13:17
[v]S Ge 32:29

The background of this reference is unknown; the Amalekites are otherwise associated with the Negev (Nu 13:29).
13:1—16:31 Samson (from the tribe of Dan), like Ehud (from the tribe of Benjamin), was a loner, whose heroic exploits involved single-handed triumphs over powerful enemies. His story therefore balances that of Ehud (3:12–30). He typifies the nation of Israel—born by special divine provision, consecrated to the Lord from birth and endowed with unique power among his fellowmen. The likeness is even more remarkable in light of his foolish chasing of foreign women, some of ill repute, until he was cleverly subdued by one of them. In this he exemplified Israel, who during the period of the judges constantly prostituted herself to Canaanite gods to her own destruction.
13:1 *did evil in the eyes of the LORD.* See note on 3:7.
13:2 *Zorah.* A town first assigned to Judah (Jos 15:33), but later given to Dan (Jos 19:41). It became the point of departure for the Danite migration northward (18:2,8,11). *Danites.* See 1:34 and note. *sterile . . . childless.* The same condition, before divine intervention, as that of Sarah, the mother of Isaac (Ge 11:30; 16:1); Rebekah, the mother of Jacob (Ge 25:21); Hannah, the mother of Samuel (1Sa 1:2); and Elizabeth, the mother of John the Baptist (Lk 1:7).
13:3 *angel of the LORD.* See note on Ge 16:7. *you are going to . . . have a son.* Cf. the announcements of the births of Ishmael (Ge 16:11), Isaac (Ge 18:10), Immanuel (Isa 7:14), John the Baptist (Lk 1:13) and Jesus (Lk 1:31).

13:5 *Nazirite.* From the Hebrew word meaning "separated" or "dedicated." For the stipulations of this vow see Nu 6:1–21 and notes. Samson's vow was not voluntary, and it applied to his whole lifetime (v. 7). The same was true of Samuel (1Sa 1:11) and John the Baptist (Lk 1:15). *begin the deliverance . . . from . . . the Philistines.* The deliverance was continued in the time of Samuel (1Sa 7:10–14) and completed under David (2Sa 5:17–25; 8:1).
13:6 *man of God.* An expression often used of prophets (see Dt 33:1; 1Sa 2:27; 9:6–10; 1Ki 12:22), though it is clear from vv. 3,21 that this messenger was not a prophet but the angel of the Lord.
13:8 *teach us.* Not the usual parental concern, but a special concern based on the boy's special calling.
13:12 *When your words are fulfilled.* A declaration of faith. To Manoah it was not a matter of whether these events would occur, but of when (v. 17).
13:15 *stay until we prepare a young goat.* Such food was considered a special delicacy. Hospitality of this kind was common in the ancient Near East (see 6:18–19; Ge 18:1–8).
13:17 *What is your name . . . ?* A messenger's identity was considered very important. *when your word comes true.* Fulfilled prophecy was a sign of the authenticity of a prophet (Dt 18:21–22; 1Sa 9:6).
13:18 *beyond understanding.* See NIV text note. In Isa 9:6 the Hebrew for this phrase (translated "Wonderful") applies

name?[w] It is beyond understanding.[u]
[19]Then Manoah took a young goat, together with the grain offering, and sacrificed it on a rock[x] to the LORD. And the
LORD did an amazing thing while Manoah
and his wife watched: [20]As the flame[y]
blazed up from the altar toward heaven,
the angel of the LORD ascended in the
flame. Seeing this, Manoah and his wife
fell with their faces to the ground.[z]
[21]When the angel of the LORD did not
show himself again to Manoah and his
wife, Manoah realized[a] that it was the angel of the LORD.

[22]"We are doomed[b] to die!" he said to
his wife. "We have seen[c] God!"

[23]But his wife answered, "If the LORD
had meant to kill us, he would not have
accepted a burnt offering and grain offering
from our hands, nor shown us all these
things or now told us this."[d]

[24]The woman gave birth to a boy and
named him Samson.[e] He grew[f] and the
LORD blessed him,[g] [25]and the Spirit of the
LORD began to stir[h] him while he was in
Mahaneh Dan,[i] between Zorah and Esh-
taol.

Samson's Marriage

14 Samson[j] went down to Timnah[k]
and saw there a young Philistine
woman. [2]When he returned, he said to his
father and mother, "I have seen a Philistine woman in Timnah; now get her for
me as my wife."[l]

[3]His father and mother replied, "Isn't
there an acceptable woman among your
relatives or among all our people?[m] Must
you go to the uncircumcised[n] Philistines
to get a wife?[o]"

But Samson said to his father, "Get her
for me. She's the right one for me." [4](His
parents did not know that this was from
the LORD,[p] who was seeking an occasion
to confront the Philistines;[q] for at that
time they were ruling over Israel.)[r] [5]Sam-
son went down to Timnah together with
his father and mother. As they approached
the vineyards of Timnah, suddenly a young
lion came roaring toward him. [6]The Spirit
of the LORD came upon him in power[s] so
that he tore the lion apart[t] with his bare
hands as he might have torn a young goat.
But he told neither his father nor his
mother what he had done. [7]Then he went
down and talked with the woman, and he
liked her.

[8]Some time later, when he went back to
marry her, he turned aside to look at the
lion's carcass. In it was a swarm of bees
and some honey, [9]which he scooped out
with his hands and ate as he went along.
When he rejoined his parents, he gave
them some, and they too ate it. But he did
not tell them that he had taken the honey
from the lion's carcass.

[10]Now his father went down to see the
woman. And Samson made a feast[u] there,
as was customary for bridegrooms. [11]When
he appeared, he was given thirty companions.

[12]"Let me tell you a riddle,[v]" Samson

Cross references (center column)

13:18 wS Ge 32:29
13:19 xJdg 6:20
13:20 yS Lev 9:24
zS Ge 17:3
13:21 aS Jdg 6:22
13:22 bS Nu 17:12; S Dt 5:26
cS Ge 16:13; S Ex 3:6; S 24:10; S Jdg 6:22
13:23 dPs 25:14
13:24 eJdg 14:1; 15:1; 16:1; Heb 11:32
fISa 2:21,26; 3:19 gLk 1:80
13:25 hS Jdg 3:10
iJdg 18:12
14:1 jS Jdg 13:24
kS Ge 38:12
14:2 lS Ge 21:21

14:3 mS Ge 24:4
nS Ge 34:14; S 1Sa 14:6
oS Ex 34:16
14:4 pS Dt 2:30
qS Jos 11:20
rJdg 13:1; 15:11
14:6 sS Jdg 3:10
tS 1Sa 17:35
14:10
uS Ge 29:22
14:12
vS Nu 12:8; Eze 17:2; 20:49; 24:3; Hos 12:10

u 18 Or is wonderful

Footnotes (bottom)

to One who would come as "Mighty God."

13:22 *doomed to die.* See 6:23 and notes on Ge 16:13; 32:30.

13:24 *Samson.* The name is derived from a Hebrew word meaning "sun" or "brightness," and is used here either as an expression of joy over the birth of the child or as a reference to the nearby town of Beth Shemesh, "house of the sun(-god)." *He grew and the LORD blessed him.* Cf. 1Sa 2:26 (Samuel) and Lk 2:52 (Jesus).

13:25 *began to stir him.* See notes on 3:10; 11:29. *Maha-neh Dan.* Means "Dan's camp" (see NIV text note on 18:12).

14:1 *Timnah.* Identified as Tell Batash in the Sorek Valley, west of Beth Shemesh. Archaeologists have uncovered the Philistine layer of the town. *young Philistine woman.* The disappointment of Samson's parents (v. 3; cf. Esau, Ge 26:35; 27:46; 28:1) is understandable in light of the prohi-bition against marriage with the peoples of Canaan (Ex 34:11,16; Dt 7:1,3; see also Jdg 3:5–6).

14:2 *get her for me.* See Ge 34:4. As the head of the family, the father exercised authority in all matters, often including the choice of wives for his sons (see 12:9; Ge 24:3–9; Ne 10:30).

14:3 *uncircumcised.* A term of scorn, referring to those not bound by covenant to the Lord, used especially of the Philis-tines (see note on 1Sa 14:6). *right one for me.* The Hebrew

for this expression is similar to that translated "did as he saw fit" in 17:6; 21:25. The author anticipates this theme, which recurs in chs. 17–21.

14:4 *this was from the LORD.* See Jos 11:20; 1Ki 12:15. The Lord uses even the sinful weaknesses of men to accom-plish his purposes and bring praise to his name (see Ge 45:8; 50:20; 2Ch 25:20; Ac 2:23; 4:28; Ro 8:28–29).

14:5 *vineyards of Timnah.* The Sorek Valley (in which Timnah was located) and its surrounding areas were noted for their luxurious vineyards. *young lion.* Lions were once common in southern Canaan (see 1Sa 17:34; 2Sa 23:20; 1Ki 13:24; 20:36).

14:6 *Spirit . . . came upon him.* See 13:25; 14:19; 15:14; see also notes on 3:10; 11:29. *tore the lion apart.* David (1Sa 17:34–37) and Benaiah (2Sa 23:20) later performed similar feats.

14:10 *feast.* Such a special feast was common in the an-cient Near East (see Ge 29:22) and here lasted seven days (v. 12; see Ge 29:27). Since it would have included drinking wine, Samson may have violated his Nazirite vow (see 13:4, 7).

14:11 *companions.* These are the "guests of the bride-groom" (cf. Mt 9:15). They were probably charged with protecting the wedding party against marauders.

14:12 *riddle.* The use of riddles at feasts and special occa-sions was popular in the ancient world. *sets of clothes.*

said to them. "If you can give me the answer within the seven days of the feast, *w* I will give you thirty linen garments and thirty sets of clothes. *x* 13If you can't tell me the answer, you must give me thirty linen garments and thirty sets of clothes."

"Tell us your riddle," they said. "Let's hear it."

14He replied,

"Out of the eater, something to eat;
out of the strong, something
sweet." *y*

For three days they could not give the answer.

15On the fourth *v* day, they said to Samson's wife, "Coax *z* your husband into explaining the riddle for us, or we will burn you and your father's household to death. *a* Did you invite us here to rob us?"

16Then Samson's wife threw herself on him, sobbing, "You hate me! You don't really love me. *b* You've given my people a riddle, but you haven't told me the answer."

"I haven't even explained it to my father or mother," he replied, "so why should I explain it to you?" 17She cried the whole seven days *c* of the feast. So on the seventh day he finally told her, because she continued to press him. She in turn explained the riddle to her people.

18Before sunset on the seventh day the men of the town said to him,

"What is sweeter than honey?
What is stronger than a lion?" *d*

Samson said to them,

"If you had not plowed with my heifer,
you would not have solved my
riddle."

19Then the Spirit of the Lord came upon him in power. *e* He went down to Ashke-

lon, *f* struck down thirty of their men, stripped them of their belongings and gave their clothes to those who had explained the riddle. Burning with anger, *g* he went up to his father's house. 20And Samson's wife was given to the friend *h* who had attended him at his wedding.

Samson's Vengeance on the Philistines

15 Later on, at the time of wheat harvest, *i* Samson *j* took a young goat *k* and went to visit his wife. He said, "I'm going to my wife's room." *l* But her father would not let him go in.

2"I was so sure you thoroughly hated her," he said, "that I gave her to your friend. *m* Isn't her younger sister more attractive? Take her instead."

3Samson said to them, "This time I have a right to get even with the Philistines; I will really harm them." 4So he went out and caught three hundred foxes *n* and tied them tail to tail in pairs. He then fastened a torch *o* to every pair of tails, 5lit the torches *p* and let the foxes loose in the standing grain of the Philistines. He burned up the shocks *q* and standing grain, together with the vineyards and olive groves.

6When the Philistines asked, "Who did this?" they were told, "Samson, the Timnite's son-in-law, because his wife was given to his friend. *r* "

So the Philistines went up and burned her *s* and her father to death. *t* 7Samson said to them, "Since you've acted like this, I won't stop until I get my revenge on you." 8He attacked them viciously and slaughtered many of them. Then he went down and stayed in a cave in the rock *u* of Etam. *v*

9The Philistines went up and camped in

Cross references (center column)

14:12 *w*Ge 29:27
*x*S Ge 45:22;
S 2Ki 5:5
14:14 *y*ver 18
14:15 *z*Jdg 16:5;
Ecc 7:26
*a*S Lev 20:14;
Jdg 15:6
14:16 *b*Jdg 16:15
14:17 *c*Est 1:5
14:18 *d*ver 14
14:19 *e*S Jdg 3:10

*f*S Jos 13:3
*g*1Sa 11:6
14:20 *h*Jdg 15:2,
6; Jn 3:29
15:1 *i*S Ge 30:14
*j*S Jdg 13:24
*k*S Ge 38:17
*l*Ge 29:21
15:2
*m*S Jdg 14:20
15:4 *n*SS 2:15
*o*S Ge 15:17
15:5 *p*S Ge 15:17
*q*Ex 22:6;
2Sa 14:30-31
15:6 *r*S Jdg 14:20
*s*S Ge 38:24
*t*S Jdg 14:15
15:8 *u*Isa 2:21
*v*ver 11

v 15 Some Septuagint manuscripts and Syriac; Hebrew seventh

Study notes (bottom)

Mentioned, together with silver, as gifts of great value in Ge 45:22; 2Ki 5:22 (see also Zec 14:14).
14:16 *don't really love me.* Delilah used the same tactics (16:15).
14:18 *my heifer.* Samson's wife (see v. 15). Since heifers were not used for plowing, Samson is accusing them of unfairness.
14:19 *Spirit... came upon him.* God's purposes for Samson included humbling the Philistines. *Ashkelon.* One of the five principal cities of the Philistines (see map, p. 330).
14:20 *friend.* See 15:2; probably the young man who had attended Samson (cf. Jn 3:29), in all likelihood one of his 30 companions (v. 11).
15:1 *time of wheat harvest.* Near the end of May or the beginning of June (see note on Ru 1:22). *young goat.* Such a gift was customary, as with Judah and Tamar (Ge 38:17).
15:2 *younger sister.* Samson's father-in-law felt he had to

make a counterproposal because he had received the bride-price from Samson. Similar marital transactions were made by Laban and Jacob (Ge 29:16–28) and Saul and David (1Sa 18:19–21).
15:4 *foxes.* The Hebrew word may refer to foxes or jackals, both of which are still found in modern Israel.
15:5 *burned up.* The wheat harvest (v. 1) comes at the end of a long dry season, thus making the fields extremely vulnerable to fire.
15:7 *revenge.* A common feature of life in the ancient Near East. Six cities of refuge were designated by the Lord to prevent endless killings (Jos 20:1–9).
15:9 *Lehi.* Means "jawbone." This locality probably did not receive the name until after the events described here; the author uses the name in anticipation of those events—a common device in Hebrew narrative. The exact site of Lehi is not known.

Judah, spreading out near Lehi.[w] [10]The men of Judah asked, "Why have you come to fight us?"

"We have come to take Samson prisoner," they answered, "to do to him as he did to us."

[11]Then three thousand men from Judah went down to the cave in the rock of Etam and said to Samson, "Don't you realize that the Philistines are rulers over us?[x] What have you done to us?"

He answered, "I merely did to them what they did to me."

[12]They said to him, "We've come to tie you up and hand you over to the Philistines."

Samson said, "Swear to me[y] that you won't kill me yourselves."

[13]"Agreed," they answered. "We will only tie you up and hand you over to them. We will not kill you." So they bound him with two new ropes[z] and led him up from the rock. [14]As he approached Lehi,[a] the Philistines came toward him shouting. The Spirit of the LORD came upon him in power.[b] The ropes on his arms became like charred flax,[c] and the bindings dropped from his hands. [15]Finding a fresh jawbone of a donkey, he grabbed it and struck down a thousand men.[d]

[16]Then Samson said,

"With a donkey's jawbone
 I have made donkeys of them.[w][e]
With a donkey's jawbone
 I have killed a thousand men."

[17]When he finished speaking, he threw away the jawbone; and the place was called Ramath Lehi.[x][f]

[18]Because he was very thirsty, he cried out to the LORD,[g] "You have given your servant this great victory.[h] Must I now die of thirst and fall into the hands of the uncircumcised?" [19]Then God opened up the hollow place in Lehi, and water came out of it. When Samson drank, his strength returned and he revived.[i] So the spring[j] was called En Hakkore,[y] and it is still there in Lehi.

[20]Samson led[z] Israel for twenty years[k] in the days of the Philistines.

Samson and Delilah

16 One day Samson[l] went to Gaza,[m] where he saw a prostitute.[n] He went in to spend the night with her. [2]The people of Gaza were told, "Samson is here!" So they surrounded the place and lay in wait for him all night at the city gate.[o] They made no move during the night, saying, "At dawn[p] we'll kill him."

[3]But Samson lay there only until the middle of the night. Then he got up and took hold of the doors of the city gate, together with the two posts, and tore them loose, bar and all. He lifted them to his shoulders and carried them to the top of the hill that faces Hebron.[q]

[4]Some time later, he fell in love[r] with a woman in the Valley of Sorek whose name was Delilah.[s] [5]The rulers of the Philistines[t] went to her and said, "See if you can lure[u] him into showing you the secret

---

Cross references (center column):

15:9 [w]ver 14,17, 19
15:11 [x]S Jdg 14:4; Ps 106:40-42
15:12 [y]S Ge 47:31
15:13 [z]Jdg 16:11, 12
15:14 [a]S ver 9 [b]S Jdg 3:10 [c]S Jos 2:6
15:15 [d]S Lev 26:8
15:16 [e]Jer 22:19
15:17 [f]S ver 9
15:18 [g]Jdg 16:28 [h]S Dt 20:4
15:19 [i]Ge 45:27; 1Sa 30:12; Isa 40:29 [j]S Ex 17:6
15:20 [k]Jdg 16:31
16:1 [l]S Jdg 13:24 [m]S Ge 10:19 [n]S Ge 38:15
16:2 [o]S Jos 2:5 [p]1Sa 19:11
16:3 [q]S Jos 10:36
16:4 [r]S Ge 24:67; S 34:3 [s]ver 6
16:5 [t]S Jos 13:3 [u]S Ex 10:7; S Jdg 14:15

Footnotes (center column bottom):

[w]16 Or made a heap or two; the Hebrew for donkey sounds like the Hebrew for heap.   [x]17 Ramath Lehi means jawbone hill.   [y]19 En Hakkore means caller's spring.   [z]20 Traditionally judged

---

15:11 *three thousand men from Judah.* The only time a force from Judah is explicitly mentioned in connection with any of the judges (but see note on 1:2). The men of Judah were well aware of Samson's capabilities, and even with a large force they did not attempt to tie him up without his consent (vv. 12–13). *Philistines are rulers over us.* Much of Judah was under Philistine rule, and the tribe was apparently content to accept it. They mustered a force, not to support Samson, but to capture him for the Philistines.
15:14 *shouting.* A battle cry (see 1Sa 17:52). They came shouting against Samson as the lion had come roaring against him (14:5). *Spirit of the LORD.* See notes on 3:10; 11:29; 14:19.
15:15 *struck down a thousand men.* Cf. the exploits of Shamgar, who struck down 600 Philistines with an oxgoad (3:31).
15:18 *Must I now die of thirst . . . ?* Mighty Samson was, after all, only a mortal man.
15:19 *water came out of it.* God provided for Samson as he had for Israel in the desert. See Ex 17:1–7 (Massah and Meribah); Nu 20:2–13 (Meribah).
15:20 *led Israel . . . years.* See note on 12:7. *twenty years.* Round numbers are frequently used in Judges (see Introduction: Background).
16:1 *Gaza.* An important Philistine seaport on the Mediterranean coast of southwest Palestine. *prostitute.* While Samson certainly possessed physical strength, he lacked moral strength, which ultimately led to his ruin.
16:2 *dawn.* By that time they expected Samson to be exhausted and sleeping soundly.
16:3 *bar.* Probably made of bronze (1Ki 4:13) or iron (Ps 107:16; Isa 45:2). *faces Hebron.* That is, in the direction of Hebron, which was 38 miles away in the hill country. Since Hebron was the chief city of Judah, this must be seen as Samson's response to what the men of Judah had done to him (see 15:11–13).
16:5 *rulers of the Philistines.* See note on 3:3. *subdue him.* The Philistines were not interested in killing him quickly; they sought revenge by a prolonged period of torture. *eleven hundred shekels.* An extraordinarily generous payment in light of 17:10 (see note there). (The total amount paid by the five Philistines would have been equivalent to the price of 275 slaves, at the rate offered for Joseph centuries earlier; see Ge 37:28.) Micah stole a similar amount of silver from his mother (17:2).

of his great strength[v] and how we can overpower him so we may tie him up and subdue him. Each one of us will give you eleven hundred shekels[a] of silver."[w]

[6]So Delilah[x] said to Samson, "Tell me the secret of your great strength and how you can be tied up and subdued."

[7]Samson answered her, "If anyone ties me with seven fresh thongs[b] that have not been dried, I'll become as weak as any other man."

[8]Then the rulers of the Philistines brought her seven fresh thongs that had not been dried, and she tied him with them. [9]With men hidden in the room,[y] she called to him, "Samson, the Philistines are upon you!"[z] But he snapped the thongs as easily as a piece of string snaps when it comes close to a flame. So the secret of his strength was not discovered.

[10]Then Delilah said to Samson, "You have made a fool of me;[a] you lied to me. Come now, tell me how you can be tied."

[11]He said, "If anyone ties me securely with new ropes[b] that have never been used, I'll become as weak as any other man."

[12]So Delilah took new ropes and tied him with them. Then, with men hidden in the room, she called to him, "Samson, the Philistines are upon you!"[c] But he snapped the ropes off his arms as if they were threads.

[13]Delilah then said to Samson, "Until now, you have been making a fool of me and lying to me. Tell me how you can be tied."

He replied, "If you weave the seven braids of my head into the fabric on the loom, and tighten it with the pin, I'll become as weak as any other man." So while he was sleeping, Delilah took the seven braids of his head, wove them into the fabric [14]and[c] tightened it with the pin.

Again she called to him, "Samson, the Philistines are upon you!"[d] He awoke

from his sleep and pulled up the pin and the loom, with the fabric.

[15]Then she said to him, "How can you say, 'I love you,'[e] when you won't confide in me? This is the third time[f] you have made a fool of me and haven't told me the secret of your great strength.[g]" [16]With such nagging she prodded him day after day until he was tired to death.

[17]So he told her everything.[h] "No razor has ever been used on my head," he said, "because I have been a Nazirite[i] set apart to God since birth. If my head were shaved, my strength would leave me, and I would become as weak as any other man."

[18]When Delilah saw that he had told her everything, she sent word to the rulers of the Philistines[j] "Come back once more; he has told me everything." So the rulers of the Philistines returned with the silver in their hands.[k] [19]Having put him to sleep on her lap, she called a man to shave off the seven braids of his hair, and so began to subdue him.[d] And his strength left him.[l]

[20]Then she called, "Samson, the Philistines are upon you!"[m]

He awoke from his sleep and thought, "I'll go out as before and shake myself free." But he did not know that the LORD had left him.[n]

[21]Then the Philistines[o] seized him, gouged out his eyes[p] and took him down to Gaza.[q] Binding him with bronze shackles, they set him to grinding[r] in the prison. [22]But the hair on his head began to grow again after it had been shaved.

The Death of Samson

[23]Now the rulers of the Philistines assembled to offer a great sacrifice to Da-

Cross references

16:5 [v]ver 6,15 [w]ver 18
16:6 [x]ver 4
16:9 [y]ver 12 [z]ver 14
16:10 [a]ver 13
16:11
16:12 [b]S Jdg 15:13
[c]ver 14
16:14 [d]ver 9,20

16:15 [e]Jdg 14:16 [f]Nu 24:10 [g]S ver 5
16:17 [h]ver 18; Mic 7:5 [i]S Nu 6:2
16:18 [j]S Jos 13:3; 1Sa 5:8 [k]ver 5
16:19 [l]Pr 7:26-27
16:20 [m]S ver 14 [n]Nu 14:42; Jos 7:12; 1Sa 16:14; 18:12; 28:15
16:21 [o]Jer 47:1 [p]S Nu 16:14 [q]S Ge 10:19 [r]Job 31:10; Isa 47:2

Footnotes

a 5 That is, about 28 pounds (about 13 kilograms)   **b** 7 Or *bowstrings*; also in verses 8 and 9   **c** 13,14 Some Septuagint manuscripts; Hebrew *"I can, if you weave the seven braids of my head into the fabric on the loom."* [14]So she   **d** 19 Hebrew; some Septuagint manuscripts *and he began to weaken*

16:7 *seven fresh thongs.* The number seven had special significance to the ancients, symbolizing completeness or fullness. Note that Samson's hair was divided into seven braids (v. 13).

16:11 *new ropes.* The Philistines apparently did not know that this method had already been tried and had failed (15:13–14).

16:13 Out of disdain, Samson arrogantly played with his Philistine adversaries. *tighten it with the pin.* Probably from a weaver's shuttle. The details of the account suggest that the loom in question was the vertical type with a crossbeam from which warp threads were suspended. Samson's long hair was woven into the warp and beaten up into the web with the pin, thus forming a tight fabric.

16:19–20 *his strength left him . . . the LORD had left him.*

The source of Samson's strength was ultimately God himself. **16:20** *he did not know.* One of the most tragic statements in the OT. Samson was unaware that he had betrayed his calling. He had permitted a Philistine woman to rob him of the sign of his special consecration to the Lord. The Lord's champion lay asleep and helpless in the arms of his paramour.

16:21 *gouged out his eyes.* Brutal treatment of prisoners of war to humiliate and incapacitate them was common (see 1Sa 11:2; 2Ki 25:7; see also note on Jdg 1:6). *to Gaza.* In shame and weakness, Samson was led to Gaza, the place where he had displayed great strength (vv. 1–3). *set him to grinding.* See note on 9:53.

16:23 *Dagon.* See note on 10:6. *Our god has delivered.* It was common to attribute a victory to the national deities.

gon s their god and to celebrate, saying, "Our god has delivered Samson, our enemy, into our hands."

24When the people saw him, they praised their god, t saying,

"Our god has delivered our enemy
into our hands, u
the one who laid waste our land
and multiplied our slain."

25While they were in high spirits, v they shouted, "Bring out Samson to entertain us." So they called Samson out of the prison, and he performed for them.

When they stood him among the pillars, 26Samson said to the servant who held his hand, "Put me where I can feel the pillars that support the temple, so that I may lean against them." 27Now the temple was crowded with men and women; all the rulers of the Philistines were there, and on the roof w were about three thousand men and women watching Samson perform. 28Then Samson prayed to the LORD, x "O Sovereign LORD, remember me. O God, please strengthen me just once more, and let me with one blow get revenge y on the Philistines for my two eyes." 29Then Samson reached toward the two central pillars on which the temple stood. Bracing himself against them, his right hand on the one and his left hand on the other, 30Samson said, "Let me die with the Philistines!" Then he pushed with all his might, and down came the temple on the rulers and all the people in it. Thus he killed many

more when he died than while he lived. 31Then his brothers and his father's whole family went down to get him. They brought him back and buried him between Zorah and Eshtaol in the tomb of Manoah z his father. He had led e a Israel twenty years. b

Micah's Idols

17 Now a man named Micah c from the hill country of Ephraim 2said to his mother, "The eleven hundred shekels f of silver that were taken from you and about which I heard you utter a curse—I have that silver with me; I took it."

Then his mother said, "The LORD bless you, d my son!"

3When he returned the eleven hundred shekels of silver to his mother, she said, "I solemnly consecrate my silver to the LORD for my son to make a carved image and a cast idol. e I will give it back to you."

4So he returned the silver to his mother, and she took two hundred shekels g of silver and gave them to a silversmith, who made them into the image and the idol. f And they were put in Micah's house.

5Now this man Micah had a shrine, g and he made an ephod h and some idols i and installed j one of his sons as his priest. k 6In those days Israel had no king; l everyone did as he saw fit. m

7A young Levite n from Bethlehem in

Cross references (center column)

16:23 sISa 5:2; 1Ch 10:10
16:24 rDa 5:4 uISa 31:9; 1Ch 10:9
16:25 vJdg 9:27; 19:6,9,22; Ru 3:7; Est 1:10
16:27 wS Jos 2:8
16:28 xJdg 15:18 yJer 15:15

16:31 zS Jdg 13:2 aRu 1:1; 1Sa 4:18; 7:6 bJdg 15:20
17:1 cJdg 18:2,13
17:2 dRu 2:20; 3:10; 1Sa 15:13; 23:21; 2Sa 2:5
17:3 eS Ex 20:4
17:4 fS Ex 32:4; S Isa 17:8
17:5 gIsa 44:13; Eze 8:10 hS Jdg 8:27 iS Ge 31:19 jS Nu 16:10 kS Ex 29:9
17:6 lJdg 18:1; 19:1; 21:25 mS Dt 12:8
17:7 nJdg 18:3

e31 Traditionally judged   f2 That is, about 28 pounds (about 13 kilograms)   g4 That is, about 5 pounds (about 2.3 kilograms)

16:27 *on the roof.* The temple complex probably surrounded an open court and had a flat roof where a large number of people had gathered to get a glimpse of the fallen champion.

16:30 *pushed.* Samson pushed the wooden pillars from their stone bases. Archaeologists have discovered a Philistine temple with a pair of closely spaced pillar bases. *killed many more.* Samson previously had slain well over 1,000 people (see 15:15; see also 14:19; 15:8).

16:31 *went down to get him.* The freedom of his family to secure his body and give it a burial indicates that the Philistines had no intention of further dishonoring him (contrast Saul's death, 1Sa 31:9–10). *led Israel . . . years.* See note on 12:7. *twenty years.* Round numbers are frequently used in Judges (see Introduction: Background).

17:1–21:25 Two episodes forming an epilogue to the story of the judges (see Introduction: Literary Features). The events narrated evidently took place fairly early in the period of the judges (see notes on 18:30; 20:1,28). They illustrate the religious and moral degeneracy that characterized the age—when "Israel had no king" and "everyone did as he saw fit" (17:6; 21:25). Writing at a time when the monarchy under the Davidic dynasty had brought cohesion and order to the land and had reestablished a center for the worship of the Lord, the author portrays this earlier era of the judges as a dismal period of national decay, from which it was to be rescued by the house of David.

17:1–18:31 The first episode illustrates corruption in Israelite worship by telling of Micah's establishment of a local place of worship in Ephraim, aided by a Levite claiming descent from Moses. This paganized worship of the Lord is taken over by the tribe of Dan when that tribe abandons its appointed inheritance and migrates to Israel's northern frontier.

17:2 *eleven hundred shekels.* See note on 16:5. *I heard you utter a curse.* Fear of the curse seems to have motivated his returning the stolen money. *The LORD bless you.* A blessing to counteract the curse.

17:3 *mother . . . son.* With their paganized view of the God of Israel, both were idolaters in disobedience to the law (Ex 20:4,23; Dt 4:16). *a carved image and a cast idol.* The image was probably made of wood overlaid with silver; the idol was made of solid silver or of cheaper metal overlaid with silver.

17:4 *silversmith.* A maker of idols, as in Ac 19:24 (cf. Isa 40:19 and Jer 10:9, where the Hebrew for this word is translated "goldsmith").

17:5 *ephod.* See 8:27 and note on Ex 28:6. *idols.* Household gods, used in this case for divining (cf. Eze 21:21; Zec 10:2). Some of them were in human form (1Sa 19:13).

17:6 *had no king.* See 18:1; 19:1; 21:25; suggests that Judges was written after the establishment of the monarchy (see Introduction: Author and Date). *did as he saw fit.* The expression implies that Israel had departed from the cov-

Judah,*o* who had been living within the clan of Judah, [8]left that town in search of some other place to stay. On his way*h* he came to Micah's house in the hill country of Ephraim.

[9]Micah asked him, "Where are you from?"

"I'm a Levite from Bethlehem in Judah,*p*" he said, "and I'm looking for a place to stay."

[10]Then Micah said to him, "Live with me and be my father*q* and priest,*r* and I'll give you ten shekels*i* of silver a year, your clothes and your food." [11]So the Levite agreed to live with him, and the young man was to him like one of his sons. [12]Then Micah installed*s* the Levite, and the young man became his priest*t* and lived in his house. [13]And Micah said, "Now I know that the LORD will be good to me, since this Levite has become my priest."*u*

Danites Settle in Laish

18 In those days Israel had no king.*v* And in those days the tribe of the Danites was seeking a place of their own where they might settle, because they had not yet come into an inheritance among the tribes of Israel.*w* [2]So the Danites*x* sent five warriors*y* from Zorah and Eshtaol to spy out*z* the land and explore it. These men represented all their clans. They told them, "Go, explore the land."*a*

The men entered the hill country of Ephraim and came to the house of Micah,*b* where they spent the night. [3]When they were near Micah's house,

they recognized the voice of the young Levite;*c* so they turned in there and asked him, "Who brought you here? What are you doing in this place? Why are you here?"

[4]He told them what Micah had done for him, and said, "He has hired me and I am his priest.*d*"

[5]Then they said to him, "Please inquire of God*e* to learn whether our journey will be successful."

[6]The priest answered them, "Go in peace*f*. Your journey has the LORD's approval."

[7]So the five men*g* left and came to Laish,*h* where they saw that the people were living in safety, like the Sidonians, unsuspecting and secure.*i* And since their land lacked nothing, they were prosperous.*j* Also, they lived a long way from the Sidonians*j* and had no relationship with anyone else.*k*

[8]When they returned to Zorah and Eshtaol, their brothers asked them, "How did you find things?"

[9]They answered, "Come on, let's attack them! We have seen that the land is very good. Aren't you going to do something? Don't hesitate to go there and take it over.*k* [10]When you get there, you will find an unsuspecting people and a spacious land that God has put into your hands, a land that lacks nothing*l* whatever.*m*"

[11]Then six hundred men*n* from the clan

Cross references

17:7 *o*S Ge 35:19; Mt 2:1
17:9 *p*Ru 1:1
17:10 *q*S Ge 45:8 *r*Jdg 18:19
17:12 *s*S Nu 16:10 *t*Jdg 18:4
17:13 *u*Nu 18:7
18:1 *v*S Jdg 17:6 *w*Jos 19:47; Jdg 1:34
18:2 *x*S Ge 30:6 *y*ver 17 *z*S Nu 21:32 *a*S Jos 2:1 *b*S Jdg 17:1

18:3 *c*Jdg 17:7
18:4 *d*Jdg 17:12
18:5 *e*S Ge 25:22; Jdg 20:18,23,27; 1Sa 14:18; 2Sa 5:19; 2Ki 1:2; 8:8
18:6 *f*1Ki 22:6
18:7 *g*ver 17 *h*S Jos 19:47 *i*S Ge 34:25 *j*ver 28; Jos 11:8
18:9 *k*Nu 13:30; 1Ki 22:3
18:10 *l*Dt 8:9
*m*1Ch 4:40
18:11 *n*ver 16,17

*h*8 Or *To carry on his profession*   *i*10 That is, about 4 ounces (about 110 grams)   *j*7 The meaning of the Hebrew in this clause is uncertain.   *k*7 Hebrew; some Septuagint manuscripts *with the Arameans*

---

enant standards of conduct found in the law (see Dt 12:8).
17:7 *Bethlehem in Judah.* Not among the 48 designated Levitical cities (Jos 21).
17:8 *left that town.* The failure of the Israelites to obey the law probably resulted in a lack of support for the Levites, which explains the man's wandering in search of his fortune.
17:10 *father.* A term of respect used also for Elijah (2Ki 2:12) and Elisha (2Ki 6:21; 13:14). See Ge 45:8; Mt 23:9.
ten shekels. See NIV text note. In the light of this remuneration for a year's service, the stated amounts in 16:5 and 17:2 take on special significance. The offer of wages, clothing and food was more than this Levite could resist (v. 11). Clearly material concerns were at the root of his decision, because later he accepts an even more attractive offer (18:19–20).
17:12 *installed the Levite.* An attempt to make his shrine legitimate and give it prestige. Micah probably removed his son (see v. 5).
18:1 *seeking a place.* The Danite allotment was at the west end of the strip of land between Judah and Ephraim (Jos 19:41–46), but, due to the opposition of the Amorites (Jdg 1:34) and the Philistines, they were unable to occupy that territory (see note on 13:2).
18:2 *spy out.* See 1:23 and note on Nu 13:2.
18:3 *recognized the voice.* Perhaps they recognized him by his dialect or accent.

18:5 *inquire of God.* The request is for an oracle, probably by using the ephod and household gods (see note on 17:5). God had already revealed his will by the allotments given to the various tribes (Jos 14–20). They were searching for an oracle that would guarantee the success of their journey.
18:6 *Go in peace.* The Levite gave them the message they wanted to hear. He was even careful to use the name of the Lord to give the message credibility and authority.
18:7 *Laish.* The journey northward was about 100 miles from Zorah and Eshtaol (v. 2). This town is called Leshem in Jos 19:47. After its capture by the Danites, Laish was renamed Dan (v. 29), and it was Israel's northernmost settlement (see 20:1; 1Sa 3:20; 2Sa 3:10). Excavations there have disclosed that the earliest Israelite occupation of Dan was in the 12th century B.C. and that the first Israelite inhabitants apparently lived in tents or temporary huts. Occupation of the site continued into the Assyrian period, but the town was destroyed and rebuilt many times. A large high place attached to the city was often extensively rebuilt and refurbished and was in use into the Hellenistic period. *Sidonians.* A peaceful Phoenician people who engaged in commerce throughout the Mediterranean world. *had no relationship.* They did not feel threatened by other powers and therefore sought no treaties for mutual defense.
18:11 *six hundred men.* As leaders of the tribe of Dan, they

of the Danites,[o] armed for battle, set out from Zorah and Eshtaol. [12]On their way they set up camp near Kiriath Jearim[p] in Judah. This is why the place west of Kiriath Jearim is called Mahaneh Dan[1][q] to this day. [13]From there they went on to the hill country of Ephraim and came to Micah's house.[r]

[14]Then the five men who had spied out the land of Laish[s] said to their brothers, "Do you know that one of these houses has an ephod,[t] other household gods, a carved image and a cast idol?[u] Now you know what to do." [15]So they turned in there and went to the house of the young Levite at Micah's place and greeted him. [16]The six hundred Danites,[v] armed for battle, stood at the entrance to the gate. [17]The five men who had spied out the land went inside and took the carved image, the ephod, the other household gods[w] and the cast idol while the priest and the six hundred armed men[x] stood at the entrance to the gate.

[18]When these men went into Micah's house and took[y] the carved image, the ephod, the other household gods[z] and the cast idol, the priest said to them, "What are you doing?"

[19]They answered him, "Be quiet![a] Don't say a word. Come with us, and be our father and priest.[b] Isn't it better that you serve a tribe and clan[c] in Israel as priest rather than just one man's household?" [20]Then the priest was glad. He took the ephod, the other household gods and the carved image and went along with the people. [21]Putting their little children, their livestock and their possessions in front of them, they turned away and left.

[22]When they had gone some distance from Micah's house, the men who lived near Micah were called together and over-

took the Danites. [23]As they shouted after them, the Danites turned and said to Micah, "What's the matter with you that you called out your men to fight?"

[24]He replied, "You took[d] the gods I made, and my priest, and went away. What else do I have? How can you ask, 'What's the matter with you?' "

[25]The Danites answered, "Don't argue with us, or some hot-tempered men will attack you, and you and your family will lose your lives." [26]So the Danites went their way, and Micah, seeing that they were too strong for him,[e] turned around and went back home.

[27]Then they took what Micah had made, and his priest, and went on to Laish, against a peaceful and unsuspecting people.[f] They attacked them with the sword and burned[g] down their city.[h] [28]There was no one to rescue them because they lived a long way from Sidon[i] and had no relationship with anyone else. The city was in a valley near Beth Rehob.[j]

The Danites rebuilt the city and settled there. [29]They named it Dan[k] after their forefather Dan, who was born to Israel—though the city used to be called Laish.[l] [30]There the Danites set up for themselves the idols, and Jonathan son of Gershom,[m] the son of Moses,[m] and his sons were priests for the tribe of Dan until the time of the captivity of the land. [31]They continued to use the idols Micah had made,[n] all the time the house of God[o] was in Shiloh.[p]

A Levite and His Concubine

19 In those days Israel had no king. Now a Levite who lived in a

---

Cross references (center column):

18:11 [o]Jdg 13:2
18:12 [p]S Jos 9:17
[q]Jdg 13:25
18:13 [r]S Jdg 17:1
18:14 [s]S Jos 19:47
[t]S Jdg 8:27
[u]S Ge 31:19
18:16 [v]S ver 11
18:17
[w]S Ge 31:19;
Mic 5:13 [x]ver 11
18:18 [y]ver 24;
Isa 46:2;
Jer 43:11; 48:7;
49:3; Hos 10:5
[z]S Ge 31:19
18:19 [a]Job 13:5;
21:5; 29:9; 40:4;
Isa 52:15;
Mic 7:16
[b]Jdg 17:10
[c]Nu 26:42

18:24 [d]S ver 17-18
18:26 [e]2Sa 3:39; Ps 18:17; 35:10
18:27 [f]S Ge 34:25
[g]S Nu 31:10
[h]Ge 49:17; S Jos 19:47
18:28 [i]S ver 7; S Ge 10:19
[j]S Nu 13:21
18:29 [k]S Ge 14:14
[l]S Jos 19:47; 1Ki 15:20
18:30 [m]Ex 2:22
18:31 [n]ver 17
[o]Jdg 19:18; 20:18
[p]S Jos 18:1; Jer 7:14

---

[1]12 Mahaneh Dan means Dan's camp.   [m]30 An ancient Hebrew scribal tradition, some Septuagint manuscripts and Vulgate; Masoretic Text Manasseh

---

represented the entire tribe's migration to its new location in the north. Cf. the 600 men who constituted the remnant of the tribe of Benjamin (20:47).

18:19 father. See note on 17:10. a tribe and clan. Only one clan from the tribe of Dan is ever mentioned—Shuham (Nu 26:42; called Hushim in Ge 46:23). The Danites appealed to the Levite's vanity and materialism.

18:21 in front of them. For protection in case of attack; see Ge 33:2–3 (Jacob and Esau).

18:24 You took the gods. Micah was concerned about the loss of gods that could not even protect themselves. What else do I have? The agonizing cry of one whose faith is centered in helpless gods.

18:28 Beth Rehob. Probably the same as Rehob in Nu 13:21.

18:30 Jonathan. The Levite is here identified as Jonathan son of Gershom, the son of Moses (Ex 2:22; 18:3; 1Ch 23:14–15). In an effort to prevent desecration of the name of Moses, later scribes modified the name slightly, making it

read "Manasseh" (see NIV text note). If Jonathan was the grandson of Moses, the events in this chapter must have occurred early in the period of the judges (see notes on 20:1,28). captivity of the land. The date of this captivity has not been determined (see note on v. 7 regarding Laish).

18:31 all the time the house of God was in Shiloh. See Jos 18:1. For Shiloh's destruction see Ps 78:60; Jer 7:12,14; 26:6. Archaeological work at Shiloh indicates that the site was destroyed c. 1050 B.C. and was left uninhabited for many centuries.

19:1–21:25 The second episode of the epilogue (see note on 17:1–18:31). It illustrates Israel's moral corruption by telling of the degenerate act of the men of Gibeah—an act remembered centuries later (Hos 9:9; 10:9). Although that town showed itself to be as wicked as any Canaanite town, it was defended by the rest of the tribe of Benjamin against the Lord's discipline through the Israelites, until nearly the whole tribe was destroyed.

19:1–30 An account of an Israelite town that revived the

remote area in the hill country of Ephraim[q] took a concubine from Bethlehem in Judah.[r] 2But she was unfaithful to him. She left him and went back to her father's house in Bethlehem, Judah. After she had been there four months, 3her husband went to her to persuade her to return. He had with him his servant and two donkeys. She took him into her father's house, and when her father saw him, he gladly welcomed him. 4His father-in-law, the girl's father, prevailed upon him to stay; so he remained with him three days, eating and drinking,[s] and sleeping there.

5On the fourth day they got up early and he prepared to leave, but the girl's father said to his son-in-law, "Refresh yourself[t] with something to eat; then you can go." 6So the two of them sat down to eat and drink together. Afterward the girl's father said, "Please stay tonight and enjoy yourself.[u]" 7And when the man got up to go, his father-in-law persuaded him, so he stayed there that night. 8On the morning of the fifth day, when he rose to go, the girl's father said, "Refresh yourself. Wait till afternoon!" So the two of them ate together.

9Then when the man, with his concubine and his servant, got up to leave, his father-in-law, the girl's father, said, "Now look, it's almost evening. Spend the night here; the day is nearly over. Stay and enjoy yourself. Early tomorrow morning you can get up and be on your way home." 10But, unwilling to stay another night, the man left and went toward Jebus[v] (that is, Jerusalem), with his two saddled donkeys and his concubine.

11When they were near Jebus and the day was almost gone, the servant said to his master, "Come, let's stop at this city of the Jebusites[w] and spend the night."

12His master replied, "No. We won't go into an alien city, whose people are not Israelites. We will go on to Gibeah." 13He added, "Come, let's try to reach Gibeah or Ramah[x] and spend the night in one of those places." 14So they went on, and the sun set as they neared Gibeah in Benjamin.[y] 15There they stopped to spend the night.[z] They went and sat in the city square,[a] but no one took them into his home for the night.

16That evening[b] an old man from the hill country of Ephraim,[c] who was living in Gibeah (the men of the place were Benjamites), came in from his work in the fields. 17When he looked and saw the traveler in the city square, the old man asked, "Where are you going? Where did you come from?"[d]

18He answered, "We are on our way from Bethlehem in Judah to a remote area in the hill country of Ephraim where I live. I have been to Bethlehem in Judah and now I am going to the house of the LORD.[e] No one has taken me into his house. 19We have both straw and fodder[f] for our donkeys[g] and bread and wine[h] for ourselves your servants—me, your maidservant, and the young man with us. We don't need anything."

20"You are welcome at my house," the old man said. "Let me supply whatever you need. Only don't spend the night in the square." 21So he took him into his house and fed his donkeys. After they had washed their feet, they had something to eat and drink.[i]

22While they were enjoying themselves,[j] some of the wicked men[k] of the city surrounded the house. Pounding on the door, they shouted to the old man who owned the house, "Bring out the man who came to your house so we can have sex with him.[l]"

23The owner of the house went outside[m] and said to them, "No, my friends,

Cross references (center column):

19:1 [q]ver 16,18
[r]Ru 1:1
19:4 [s]ver 6,8; S Ex 32:6
19:5 [t]ver 8; Ge 18:5
19:6 [u]S Jdg 16:25
19:10 [v]S Ge 10:16; S Jos 15:8
19:11 [w]S Ge 10:16; S Jos 3:10

19:13 [x]S Jos 18:25
19:14 [y]Jos 15:57; 1Sa 10:26; 11:4; 13:2; 15:34; Isa 10:29
19:15 [z]S Ge 24:23
[a]S Ge 19:2
19:16 [b]Ps 104:23
[c]S ver 1
19:17 [d]S Ge 29:4
19:18 [e]S Jdg 18:31
19:19 [f]Ge 24:25
[g]S Ge 42:27
[h]S Ge 14:18
19:21 [i]Ge 24:32-33; Lk 7:44
19:22 [j]S Jdg 16:25
[k]S Dt 13:13
[l]Ge 19:4-5; Jdg 20:5; Ro 1:26-27
19:23 [m]Ge 19:6

---

ways of Sodom (see Ge 19).
19:1 *Levite.* Unlike the Levite of chs. 17–18, this man is not named. *concubine.* See note on Ge 25:6.
19:3 *gladly welcomed him.* The separation of the concubine from the Levite was probably a matter of family disgrace, and so his father-in-law was glad for the prospect of the two being reunited.
19:10 *Jebus.* See 1:21; see also note on Ge 10:16.
19:12 *alien city.* With the city under the control of the Jebusites, the Levite was afraid that he would receive no hospitality and might be in mortal danger.
19:14 *Gibeah in Benjamin.* Distinguished from the Gibeah in Judah (Jos 15:20,57) and the Gibeah in the hill country of Ephraim (Jos 24:33). As the political capital of Saul's kingdom, it is called Gibeah of Saul in 1Sa 11:4; see also 1Sa 13:15.
19:15 *took them into his home.* See notes on 13:15; Ge 18:2.

19:18 *house of the LORD.* Apparently the Levite was planning to go to Shiloh (see 18:31; Jos 18:1) to present a thank offering to the Lord or a sin offering for himself and his concubine.
19:21 *washed their feet.* An evidence of hospitality in the ancient Near East, where travelers commonly wore sandals as they walked the dusty roads (see Ge 18:4; 24:32; 43:24; Lk 7:44; Jn 13:5–14).
19:22 *wicked men.* The Hebrew for this expression refers to the morally depraved (see note on Dt 13:13). Elsewhere the expression is associated with idolatry (Dt 13:13), drunkenness (1Sa 1:16) and rebellion (1Sa 2:12). Here the reference is to homosexuality. *Bring out the man.* The sexual perversion of these wicked men is yet another example of the decadence of an age when "everyone did as he saw fit" (17:6; 21:25). A similar request was made by the men of Sodom (Ge 19:5). Homosexuality was common among the Canaanites.

don't be so vile. Since this man is my guest, don't do this disgraceful thing. *n* 24Look, here is my virgin daughter, *o* and his concubine. I will bring them out to you now, and you can use them and do to them whatever you wish. But to this man, don't do such a disgraceful thing."

25But the men would not listen to him. So the man took his concubine and sent her outside to them, and they raped her *p* and abused her *q* throughout the night, and at dawn they let her go. 26At daybreak the woman went back to the house where her master was staying, fell down at the door and lay there until daylight.

27When her master got up in the morning and opened the door of the house and stepped out to continue on his way, there lay his concubine, fallen in the doorway of the house, with her hands on the threshold. 28He said to her, "Get up; let's go." But there was no answer. Then the man put her on his donkey and set out for home.

29When he reached home, he took a knife *r* and cut up his concubine, limb by limb, into twelve parts and sent them into all the areas of Israel. *s* 30Everyone who saw it said, "Such a thing has never been seen or done, not since the day the Israelites came up out of Egypt. *t* Think about it! Consider it! Tell us what to do! *u* "

Israelites Fight the Benjamites

20 Then all the Israelites *v* from Dan to Beersheba *w* and from the land of Gilead came out as one man *x* and assembled *y* before the Lord in Mizpah. *z* 2The leaders of all the people of the tribes of

Israel took their places in the assembly of the people of God, four hundred thousand soldiers *a* armed with swords. 3(The Benjamites heard that the Israelites had gone up to Mizpah.) Then the Israelites said, "Tell us how this awful thing happened."

4So the Levite, the husband of the murdered woman, said, "I and my concubine came to Gibeah *b* in Benjamin to spend the night. *c* 5During the night the men of Gibeah came after me and surrounded the house, intending to kill me. *d* They raped my concubine, and she died. *e* 6I took my concubine, cut her into pieces and sent one piece to each region of Israel's inheritance, *f* because they committed this lewd and disgraceful act *g* in Israel. 7Now, all you Israelites, speak up and give your verdict. *h* "

8All the people rose as one man, saying, "None of us will go home. No, not one of us will return to his house. 9But now this is what we'll do to Gibeah: We'll go up against it as the lot directs. *i* 10We'll take ten men out of every hundred from all the tribes of Israel, and a hundred from a thousand, and a thousand from ten thousand, to get provisions for the army. Then, when the army arrives at Gibeah *n* in Benjamin, it can give them what they deserve for all this vileness done in Israel." 11So all the men of Israel got together and united as one man *j* against the city.

12The tribes of Israel sent men throughout the tribe of Benjamin, saying, "What about this awful crime that was committed among you? *k* 13Now surrender those

---

n *10* One Hebrew manuscript; most Hebrew manuscripts *Geba,* a variant of *Gibeah*

Cross references (center column)

19:23
n S Ge 34:7;
S Lev 19:29;
S Jos 7:15;
S Jdg 20:6;
Ro 1:27
19:24 *o* Ge 19:8
19:25 *p* Jdg 20:5
q 1Sa 31:4
19:29 *r* S Ge 22:6
s Jdg 20:6;
1Sa 11:7
19:30 *t* Hos 9:9
u Jdg 20:7;
Pr 13:10
20:1 *v* Jdg 21:5
w S Ge 21:14;
1Sa 3:20;
2Sa 3:10; 17:11;
24:15; 1Ki 4:25;
2Ch 30:5 *x* ver
11; 1Sa 11:7
y 1Sa 7:5
z S Jos 11:3

20:2 *a* 1Sa 11:8
20:4 *b* S Jos 15:57
c S Ge 24:23
20:5 *d* S Jdg 19:22
e Jdg 19:25-26
20:6 *f* S Jdg 19:29
g S Jdg 19:23;
2Sa 13:12
20:7 *h* S Jdg 19:30
20:9 *i* S Lev 16:8
20:11 *j* S ver 1
20:12 *k* Dt 13:14

Study notes

19:23 *don't be so vile.* An expression of outrage at the willful perversion of what is right and natural (see Ge 19:7; 2Sa 13:12; see also Ro 1:27).
19:24 *my virgin daughter, and his concubine.* The tragedy of this story lies not only in the decadence of Gibeah, but also in the callous selfishness of men who would betray defenseless women to be brutally violated for a whole night. Cf. Ge 19:8, where Lot offered his two daughters to the men of Sodom.
19:25 *took.* Here the Hebrew for this verb suggests taking by force.
19:29 *cut up his concubine.* Dismembering the concubine's body and sending parts to each of the 12 tribes was intended to awaken Israel from its moral lethargy and to marshal the tribes to face up to their responsibility. It is ironic that the one who issued such a call was himself so selfish and insensitive. See also Saul's similar action in 1Sa 11:7.
20:1–48 All Israel (except Jabesh Gilead; see 21:8–9) assembled before the Lord to deal with the moral outrage committed by the men of Gibeah. Having first inquired of God for divine direction, they marched against Gibeah and the Benjamites as the disciplinary arm of the Lord (see Jos 22:11–34), following him as their King.

20:1 *Dan to Beersheba.* A conventional way of speaking of all Israel from north (Dan) to south (Beersheba); see 1Sa 3:20; 2Sa 3:10; 24:2; 1Ch 21:2; 2Ch 30:5. The use of this expression, however, does not mean that the events of this chapter occurred after Dan's move to the north (18:27–29); rather, it indicates the author's perspective at the time of writing (Judges was probably written after the Davidic dynasty was fully established; see Introduction: Author and Date). Here the expression refers to the disciplinary action of all Israel (except Jabesh Gilead; see 21:8–9) against Gibeah and the rest of the Benjamites. Such a united response must have occurred early in the time of the judges, before the period of foreign domination of various parts of the land. *as one man.* Cf. vv. 8,11; 1Sa 11:7. *assembled . . . in Mizpah.* A gathering place of the tribes during the days of Saul (1Sa 7:5–17; 10:17).
20:9 *lot.* Casting lots was a common method of determining the will of God (see notes on Ex 28:30; Jnh 1:7; Ac 1:26).
20:10 *ten men.* Support for the large army had to be well organized and efficient. One man was responsible for providing food for nine men fighting at the front.
20:13 *surrender those wicked men.* The demand of Israel

wicked men *l* of Gibeah so that we may put them to death and purge the evil from Israel. *m*"

But the Benjamites would not listen to their fellow Israelites. ¹⁴From their towns they came together at Gibeah to fight against the Israelites. ¹⁵At once the Benjamites mobilized twenty-six thousand swordsmen from their towns, in addition to seven hundred chosen men from those living in Gibeah. ¹⁶Among all these soldiers there were seven hundred chosen men who were left-handed, *n* each of whom could sling a stone at a hair and not miss.

¹⁷Israel, apart from Benjamin, mustered four hundred thousand swordsmen, all of them fighting men.

¹⁸The Israelites went up to Bethel*o o* and inquired of God. *p* They said, "Who of us shall go first*q* to fight*r* against the Benjamites?"

The LORD replied, "Judah*s* shall go first."

¹⁹The next morning the Israelites got up and pitched camp near Gibeah. ²⁰The men of Israel went out to fight the Benjamites and took up battle positions against them at Gibeah. ²¹The Benjamites came out of Gibeah and cut down twenty-two thousand Israelites*t* on the battlefield that day. ²²But the men of Israel encouraged one another and again took up their positions where they had stationed themselves the first day. ²³The Israelites went up and wept before the LORD*u* until evening, *v* and they inquired of the LORD. *w* They said, "Shall we go up again to battle*x* against the Benjamites, our brothers?"

The LORD answered, "Go up against them."

²⁴Then the Israelites drew near to Benjamin the second day. ²⁵This time, when the Benjamites came out from Gibeah to oppose them, they cut down another eighteen thousand Israelites,*y* all of them armed with swords.

²⁶Then the Israelites, all the people, went up to Bethel, and there they sat weeping before the LORD. *z* They fasted*a* that day until evening and presented burnt offerings*b* and fellowship offerings*P c* to the LORD. *d* ²⁷And the Israelites inquired of the LORD. *e* (In those days the ark of the covenant of God*f* was there, ²⁸with Phinehas son of Eleazar, *g* the son of Aaron, ministering before it.)*h* They asked, "Shall we go up again to battle with Benjamin our brother, or not?"

The LORD responded, "Go, for tomorrow I will give them into your hands. *i*"

²⁹Then Israel set an ambush*j* around Gibeah. ³⁰They went up against the Benjamites on the third day and took up positions against Gibeah as they had done before. ³¹The Benjamites came out to meet them and were drawn away*k* from the city. They began to inflict casualties on the Israelites as before, so that about thirty men fell in the open field and on the roads—the one leading to Bethel*l* and the other to Gibeah.

³²While the Benjamites were saying, "We are defeating them as before," *m* the Israelites were saying, "Let's retreat and draw them away from the city to the roads."

³³All the men of Israel moved from their places and took up positions at Baal Tamar, and the Israelite ambush charged out of its place*n* on the west*o* of Gibeah.*r* ³⁴Then ten thousand of Israel's finest men made a frontal attack on Gibeah. The fighting was so heavy that the Benjamites did not realize*o* how near disaster was. *p* ³⁵The LORD defeated Benjamin*q* before Israel, and on that day the Israelites struck down 25,100 Benjamites, all armed with swords. ³⁶Then the Benjamites saw that they were beaten.

20:13
l S Dt 13:13
m S Dt 13:5;
S 1Co 5:13
20:16 *n* S Jdg 3:15
20:18
o S Jos 12:9;
S Jdg 18:31
p S Jdg 18:5
q S Jdg 1:1 *r*ver 23,28
s S Ge 49:10
20:21 *t*ver 25
20:23 *u* S Nu 14:1
v Jos 7:6
w S Jdg 18:5
x S ver 18
20:25 *y*ver 21

20:26 *z* S Nu 14:1
a 2Sa 12:21
b Lev 1:3
c S Ex 32:6
d Jdg 21:4
20:27 *e* S Jdg 18:5
f S Nu 10:33
20:28 *g* Nu 25:7
h Dt 18:5
i S Jos 2:24
20:29 *j* S Jos 8:2
20:31 *k* Jos 8:16
l Jos 16:1
20:32 *m* ver 39
20:33 *n* Jos 8:19
20:34 *o* Jos 8:14
p ver 41
20:35 *q* 1Sa 9:21

o 18 Or *to the house of God*; also in verse 26
p 26 Traditionally *peace offerings*   *q 33* Some Septuagint manuscripts and Vulgate; the meaning of the Hebrew for this word is uncertain.   *r 33* Hebrew *Geba*, a variant of *Gibeah*

---

was not unreasonable. They wanted to punish only those directly involved in the crime. *wicked men.* See note on Dt 13:13. *put them to death.* The sin of the men of Gibeah called for the death penalty, and Israel had to punish the sin if she was to avoid guilt herself (see Dt 13:5; 17:7; 19:19–20).
20:16 *left-handed.* The Benjamite Ehud was also left-handed (3:15). *sling a stone.* Cf. Zec 9:15. The sling was a very effective weapon, as David later demonstrated in his encounter with Goliath (1Sa 17:49). A slingstone, weighing one pound or more, could be hurled at 90–100 miles an hour. *miss.* In other contexts the Hebrew for this verb is translated "to sin."
20:18 *Bethel.* At this time the ark of the covenant and the high priest Phinehas were at Bethel (see vv. 26–28). *in-*

quired of God. Probably by priestly use of Urim and Thummim (see notes on Ex 28:30; 1Sa 2:28). *Who of us shall go first . . . ?* See 1:1–36. *Judah.* See note on 1:2.
20:21 *twenty-two thousand Israelites.* A rousing victory for the Benjamites, who numbered 25,700 and therefore had slain nearly one man apiece.
20:27 *ark.* The only mention of the ark in Judges.
20:28 *Phinehas.* Phinehas was the priest in the tabernacle in the days of Joshua (Jos 22:13), and the fact that he was still serving is further evidence that these events took place early in the days of the judges (see notes on v. 1; 18:30).
20:29 *set an ambush.* See 9:32; Jos 8:2.
20:33 *Baal Tamar.* Location unknown.
20:36b–45 Details of the account in vv. 29–36a.

Now the men of Israel had given way[r] before Benjamin, because they relied on the ambush[s] they had set near Gibeah. [37]The men who had been in ambush made a sudden dash into Gibeah, spread out and put the whole city to the sword.[t] [38]The men of Israel had arranged with the ambush that they should send up a great cloud of smoke[u] from the city,[v] [39]and then the men of Israel would turn in the battle.

The Benjamites had begun to inflict casualties on the men of Israel (about thirty), and they said, "We are defeating them as in the first battle."[w] [40]But when the column of smoke began to rise from the city, the Benjamites turned and saw the smoke of the whole city going up into the sky.[x] [41]Then the men of Israel turned on them,[y] and the men of Benjamin were terrified, because they realized that disaster had come[z] upon them. [42]So they fled before the Israelites in the direction of the desert, but they could not escape the battle. And the men of Israel who came out of the towns cut them down there. [43]They surrounded the Benjamites, chased them and easily[s] overran them in the vicinity of Gibeah on the east. [44]Eighteen thousand Benjamites fell, all of them valiant fighters.[a] [45]As they turned and fled toward the desert to the rock of Rimmon,[b] the Israelites cut down five thousand men along the roads. They kept pressing after the Benjamites as far as Gidom and struck down two thousand more.

[46]On that day twenty-five thousand Benjamite[c] swordsmen fell, all of them valiant fighters. [47]But six hundred men turned and fled into the desert to the rock of Rimmon, where they stayed four months. [48]The men of Israel went back to Benjamin and put all the towns to the sword, including the animals and every-

thing else they found. All the towns they came across they set on fire.[d]

Wives for the Benjamites

21 The men of Israel had taken an oath[e] at Mizpah:[f] "Not one of us will give[g] his daughter in marriage to a Benjamite."

[2]The people went to Bethel,[t] where they sat before God until evening, raising their voices and weeping bitterly. [3]"O LORD, the God of Israel," they cried, "why has this happened to Israel? Why should one tribe be missing[h] from Israel today?"

[4]Early the next day the people built an altar and presented burnt offerings and fellowship offerings.[u] [i]

[5]Then the Israelites asked, "Who from all the tribes of Israel[i] has failed to assemble before the LORD?" For they had taken a solemn oath that anyone who failed to assemble before the LORD at Mizpah should certainly be put to death.

[6]Now the Israelites grieved for their brothers, the Benjamites. "Today one tribe is cut off from Israel," they said. [7]"How can we provide wives for those who are left, since we have taken an oath[k] by the LORD not to give them any of our daughters in marriage?" [8]Then they asked, "Which one of the tribes of Israel failed to assemble before the LORD at Mizpah?" They discovered that no one from Jabesh Gilead[l] had come to the camp for the assembly. [9]For when they counted the people, they found that none of the people of Jabesh Gilead were there.

[10]So the assembly sent twelve thousand fighting men with instructions to go to Jabesh Gilead and put to the sword those living there, including the women and children. [11]"This is what you are to do,"

Cross-references

20:36 [r]Jos 8:15 [s]Jos 8:2
20:37 [t]Jos 8:19
20:38 [u]Jos 8:20
[v]Jos 8:4-8
20:39 [w]ver 32; Ps 78:9
20:40 [x]Jos 8:20
20:41 [y]Jos 8:21
[z]ver 34
20:44 [a]1Sa 10:26; Ps 76:5
20:45 [b]S Jos 15:32
20:46 [c]1Sa 9:21

20:48 [d]Jdg 21:23
21:1 [e]S Jos 9:18
[f]S Jos 11:3 [g]ver 18,22
21:3 [h]ver 6,17
21:4 [i]Jdg 20:26
21:5 [j]Jdg 20:1
21:7 [k]S Jos 9:18
21:8 [l]1Sa 11:1; 31:11; 2Sa 2:4; 21:12; 1Ch 10:11

Footnotes

[s]43 The meaning of the Hebrew for this word is uncertain.   [t]2 Or *to the house of God*   [u]4 Traditionally *peace offerings*

Study notes

20:46 *twenty-five thousand.* A round number for 25,100 (v. 35).

20:47 *six hundred men.* If these had not escaped, the tribe of Benjamin would have been annihilated. The same number of Danites went to Laish (18:11).

21:1–25 Second thoughts about the slaughter of their Benjamite brothers caused the Israelites to grieve over the loss. Only 600 Benjamites were left alive, and the men of Israel decided to provide wives for them in order to keep the tribe from disappearing. After slaughtering most of the people of Jabesh Gilead, the Israelites took 400 girls from the survivors and gave them to 400 Benjamites. Shortly afterward, each of the remaining Benjamites seized a wife from the girls of Shiloh, and Benjamin began to be restored.

21:1 *taken an oath.* This vow, probably taken in the name of the Lord, was not an ordinary vow but invoked a curse on oneself if the vow was broken (v. 18; see also Ac 23:12–15).

21:2 *Bethel.* See 20:18,26–27. *weeping bitterly.* Earlier the Israelites wept because they were defeated by the Benjamites (20:23,26). Now they weep because the disciplinary action against the Benjamites has nearly annihilated one of the tribes (see v. 3).

21:5 *failed to assemble.* The tribes had a mutual responsibility in times of military action (see note on 5:13–18). Those who failed to participate were often singled out and sometimes punished (5:15–17,23). *solemn oath.* Complicating the situation for Israel was the fact that they had taken a second oath, calling for the death of those who did not participate in the battle.

21:10 *twelve thousand.* A thousand from each tribe (see Nu 31:6), with 1,000 supplied to represent the tribe of Benjamin.

21:11 *Kill every male.* The punishment of Jabesh Gilead seems brutal, but the covenant bond between the tribes was

they said. "Kill every male [m] and every woman who is not a virgin. [n]" 12They found among the people living in Jabesh Gilead four hundred young women who had never slept with a man, and they took them to the camp at Shiloh [o] in Canaan.

13Then the whole assembly sent an offer of peace [p] to the Benjamites at the rock of Rimmon. [q] 14So the Benjamites returned at that time and were given the women of Jabesh Gilead who had been spared. But there were not enough for all of them.

15The people grieved for Benjamin, [r] because the LORD had made a gap in the tribes of Israel. 16And the elders of the assembly said, "With the women of Benjamin destroyed, how shall we provide wives for the men who are left? 17The Benjamite survivors must have heirs," they said, "so that a tribe of Israel will not be wiped out. [s] 18We can't give them our daughters as wives, since we Israelites have taken this oath: [t] 'Cursed be anyone who gives [u] a wife to a Benjamite.' 19But look, there is the annual festival of the LORD in Shiloh, [v] to the north of Bethel [w], and east of the road that goes from Bethel

to Shechem, [x] and to the south of Lebonah."

20So they instructed the Benjamites, saying, "Go and hide in the vineyards 21and watch. When the girls of Shiloh come out to join in the dancing, [y] then rush from the vineyards and each of you seize a wife from the girls of Shiloh and go to the land of Benjamin. 22When their fathers or brothers complain to us, we will say to them, 'Do us a kindness by helping them, because we did not get wives for them during the war, and you are innocent, since you did not give [z] your daughters to them.'"

23So that is what the Benjamites did. While the girls were dancing, [a] each man caught one and carried her off to be his wife. Then they returned to their inheritance [b] and rebuilt the towns and settled in them. [c]

24At that time the Israelites left that place and went home to their tribes and clans, each to his own inheritance.

25In those days Israel had no king; everyone did as he saw fit. [d]

Cross references (center column)

21:11
[m]S Nu 31:7
[n]Nu 31:17-18
21:12 [o]S Jos 18:1
21:13 [p]S Dt 2:26
[q]S Jos 15:32
21:15 [r]ver 6
21:17 [s]S ver 3
21:18 [t]S Jos 9:18
[u]S ver 1
21:19 [v]S Jos 18:1
[w]Jos 16:1

[x]S Jos 17:7
21:21
[y]S Ex 15:20
21:22 [z]S ver 1
21:23 [a]ver 21
[b]S Jos 24:28
[c]Jdg 20:48
21:25 [d]S Dt 12:8

---

extremely important. Even though delinquency on some occasions was not punished (5:15-17), the nature of the crime in this case, coupled with Benjamin's refusal to turn over the criminals, caused Israel to take this oath (v. 5).
21:12 *in Canaan.* Emphasizes the fact that the women were brought across the Jordan from the east.
21:19 *festival of the LORD.* In light of the mention of vineyards (v. 20), it is likely that this reference is to the Feast of Tabernacles (see note on 1Sa 1:3), though it may have been a local festival. *north of Bethel ... south of Lebonah.* This detailed description of Shiloh's location may indicate that this material was written at a time when Shiloh was in ruins, perhaps after its destruction during the battle of Aphek

(1Sa 4:1-11).
21:21 *seize a wife.* With the Benjamites securing wives in this manner, the other tribes were not actually "giving" their daughters to them (see note on v. 22).
21:22 *When their fathers or brothers complain.* It was customary for the brothers of a girl who had been abducted to demand satisfaction (see Ge 34:7-31; 2Sa 13:20-38). It was therefore important that the elders anticipate this response and be prepared to get cooperation from the girls' families.
21:24 *went home.* These soldiers had probably been away from home at least five months (see 20:47).
21:25 *Israel had no king.* See note on 17:6.

RUTH

Title

The book is named after one of its main characters, a young woman of Moab, the great-grandmother of David and an ancestress of Jesus (Mt 1:1,5). The only other Biblical book bearing the name of a woman is Esther.

Background

The story is set in the time of the judges, a time characterized in the book of Judges as a period of religious and moral degeneracy, national disunity and general foreign oppression. The book of Ruth reflects a temporary time of peace between Israel and Moab (contrast Jdg 3:12-30). Like 1Sa 1-2, it gives a series of intimate glimpses into the private lives of the members of an Israelite family. It also presents a delightful account of the remnant of true faith and piety in the period of the judges, relieving an otherwise wholly dark picture of that era.

Author and Date of Writing

The author is unknown. Jewish tradition points to Samuel, but it is unlikely that he is the author because the mention of David (4:17,22) implies a later date. Further, the literary style of Hebrew used in Ruth suggests that it was written during the period of the monarchy.

Theme and Theology

The author focuses on Ruth's unswerving and selfless devotion to desolate Naomi (1:16-17; 2:11-12; 3:10; 4:15) and on Boaz's kindness to these two widows (chs. 2-4). He presents striking examples of lives that embody in their daily affairs the self-giving love that fulfills God's law (Lev 19:18; cf. Ro 13:10). Such love also reflects God's love, in a marvelous joining of man's actions with God's (compare 2:12 with 3:9). In God's benevolence such lives are blessed and are made a blessing.

It may seem surprising that one who reflects God's love so clearly is a Moabitess (see map on "The Book of Ruth," p. 365). Yet her complete loyalty to the Israelite family into which she has been received by marriage and her total devotion to her desolate mother-in-law mark her as a true daughter of Israel and a worthy ancestress of David. She strikingly exemplifies the truth that participation in the coming kingdom of God is decided, not by blood and birth, but by the conformity of one's life to the will of God through the "obedience that comes from faith" (Ro 1:5). Her place in the ancestry of David signifies that all nations will be represented in the kingdom of David's greater Son.

As an episode in the ancestry of David, the book of Ruth sheds light on his role in the history of redemption. Redemption is a key concept throughout the account; the Hebrew word in its various forms occurs 23 times. The book is primarily a story of Naomi's transformation from despair to happiness through the selfless, God-blessed acts of Ruth and Boaz. She moves from emptiness to fullness (1:21; 3:17; see notes on 1:1,3,5-6,12,21-22; 3:17; 4:15), from destitution (1:1-5) to security and hope (4:13-17). Similarly, Israel was transformed from national desperation at the death of Eli (1Sa 4:18) to peace and prosperity in the early days of Solomon (1Ki 4:20-34; 5:4) through the selfless devotion of David, a true descendant of Ruth and Boaz. The author thus reminded Israel that the reign of the house of David, as the means of God's benevolent rule in Israel, held the prospect of God's promised peace and rest. But this rest would continue only so long as those who participated in the kingdom—prince and people alike—reflected in their daily lives the selfless love exemplified by Ruth and Boaz. In Jesus, the great "son of David" (Mt 1:1), and his redemptive work, the promised blessings of the kingdom of God find their fulfillment.

Literary Features

The book of Ruth is a Hebrew short story, told with consummate skill. Among historical narratives in Scripture it is unexcelled in its compactness, vividness, warmth, beauty and dramatic effectiveness—an exquisitely wrought jewel of Hebrew narrative art.

Marvelously symmetrical throughout (see Outline), the action moves from a briefly sketched account of distress (1:1-5; 71 words in Hebrew) through four episodes to a concluding account of relief and hope that is drawn with equal brevity (4:13-17; 71 words in Hebrew). The crucial turning point occurs exactly midway (see note on 2:20). The opening line of each of the four episodes signals its main development (1:6, the return; 2:1, the meeting with Boaz; 3:1, finding a home for Ruth; 4:1, the decisive event at the gate), while the closing line of each episode facilitates transition to what follows (see notes on 1:22; 2:23; 3:18; 4:12). Contrast is also used to good effect: pleasant (the meaning of "Naomi") and bitter (1:20), full and empty (1:21), and the living and the dead (2:20). Most striking is the contrast between two of the main characters, Ruth and Boaz: The one is a young, alien, destitute widow, while the other is a middle-aged, well-to-do Israelite securely established in his home community. For each there is a corresponding character whose actions highlight, by contrast, his or her selfless acts: Ruth—Orpah, Boaz—the unnamed kinsman.

When movements in space, time and circumstance all correspond in some way, a harmony results that both satisfies the reader's artistic sense and helps open doors to understanding. The author of Ruth keeps his readers from being distracted from the central story—Naomi's passage from emptiness to fullness through the selfless acts of Ruth and Boaz (see Theme and Theology). That passage, or restoration, first takes place in connection with her return from Moab to the promised land and to Bethlehem ("house of food"; see note on 1:1). It then progresses with the harvest season, when the fullness of the land is gathered in. All aspects of the story keep the reader's attention focused on the central issue. Consideration of these and other literary devices (mentioned throughout the notes) will aid understanding of the book of Ruth.

Outline

Naomi and Ruth

1 In the days when the judges ruled,[a] [a]
there was a famine in the land,[b] and a
man from Bethlehem in Judah,[c] together
with his wife and two sons, went to live
for a while[d] in the country of Moab.[e]
2The man's name was Elimelech,[f] his
wife's name Naomi, and the names of his
two sons were Mahlon and Kilion.[g] They
were Ephrathites[h] from Bethlehem,[i]
Judah. And they went to Moab and lived
there.

3Now Elimelech, Naomi's husband,
died, and she was left with her two sons.
4They married Moabite women,[j] one
named Orpah and the other Ruth.[k] After
they had lived there about ten years, 5both
Mahlon and Kilion[l] also died,[m] and
Naomi was left without her two sons and
her husband.

6When she heard in Moab[n] that the
LORD had come to the aid of his people[o]
by providing food[p] for them, Naomi and
her daughters-in-law[q] prepared to return
home from there. 7With her two daughters-
in-law she left the place where she had
been living and set out on the road that
would take them back to the land of Judah.

8Then Naomi said to her two daughters-
in-law, "Go back, each of you, to your
mother's home.[r] May the LORD show
kindness[s] to you, as you have shown to
your dead[t] and to me. 9May the LORD
grant that each of you will find rest[u] in the
home of another husband."

Then she kissed[v] them and they wept
aloud[w] 10and said to her, "We will go back
with you to your people."

1:1 [a]Jdg 2:16-18 [b]S Ge 12:10; 2Ki 6:25; Ps 105:16; Hag 1:11 [c]S Ge 35:19 [d]Ge 47:4 [e]S Ge 36:35 **1:2** [f]ver 3; Ru 2:1; 4:3 [g]ver 5; Ru 4:9 [h]S Ge 35:16 [i]Ge 35:19; 1Sa 16:18 **1:4** [j]1Ki 11:1; 2Ch 24:26; Ezr 9:2; Ne 13:23 [k]ver 14; Ru 4:13; Mt 1:5 **1:5** [l]S ver 2 [m]ver 8; Ru 2:11 **1:6** [n]S Ge 36:35 [o]S Ge 50:24; Ex 4:31; Jer 29:10; Zep 2:7 [p]Ps 132:15; Mt 6:11 [q]S Ge 11:31; S 38:16 **1:8** [r]Ge 38:11 [s]S Ge 19:19; 2Ti 1:16 [t]S ver 5 **1:9** [u]Ru 3:1 [v]S Ge 27:27; S 29:11 [w]S Ge 27:38; S Nu 25:6

[a] *1* Traditionally *judged*

1:1 *when the judges ruled.* Probably from c. 1380 to c. 1050 B.C. (see Introduction to Judges: Background). By mentioning the judges, the author calls to mind that period of Israel's apostasy, moral degradation and oppression. *famine.* Not mentioned in Judges. *Bethlehem in Judah.* David's hometown (1Sa 16:18). Bethlehem (the name suggests "house of food") is empty.
1:2 *Elimelech.* Means "(My) God is King" (see note on Jdg 8:23). *Naomi.* See NIV text note on v. 20. *Ephrathites.* Ephrathah was a name for the area around Bethlehem (see 4:11; Ge 35:19; 1Sa 17:12; Mic 5:2).
1:3 *Elimelech, Naomi's husband, died.* Naomi's emptying begins (see v. 21).
1:4 *They married.* Prospect of continuing the family line remained. *Moabite women.* See Ge 19:36–37. Marriage with Moabite women was not forbidden, though no Moabite—or his sons to the tenth generation—was allowed to "enter the assembly of the LORD" (Dt 23:3). *Ruth.* The name sounds like the Hebrew for "friendship." Ruth is one of four women in Matthew's genealogy of Jesus. The others are Tamar, Rahab and Bathsheba (Mt 1:3,5–6).
1:5 *Mahlon.* Ruth's husband (4:10), whose name probably means "weakling." *Naomi was left.* Naomi's emptiness is complete: She has neither husband nor sons. She has only two young daughters-in-law, both of them foreigners and childless.
1:6 *the LORD had come to the aid of his people.* At several points in the account, God's sovereign control of events is acknowledged (here; vv. 13,21; 2:20; 4:12–15). *food.* Bethlehem ("house of food") again has food. *prepared to return home.* Empty Naomi returns to the newly filled land of promise.
1:8 *Go back.* Desolate Naomi repeatedly urges her daughters-in-law to return to their original homes in Moab (here; vv. 11–12,15); she has nothing to offer them. *show kindness.* See 2:20; 3:10.

The Book of Ruth

Set in the dark and bloody days of the judges, the story of Ruth is silent about the underlying hostility and suspicion the two peoples—Judahites and Moabites—felt for each other. The original onslaught of the invading Israelite tribes against towns that were once Moabite had never been forgotten or forgiven, while the Hebrew prophets denounced Moab's pride and arrogance for trying to bewitch, seduce and oppress Israel from the time of Balaam on. The Mesha stele (c. 830 B.C.) boasts of the massacre of entire Israelite towns.

Moab encompassed the expansive, grain-filled plateau between the Dead Sea and the eastern desert on both sides of the enormous rift of the Arnon River gorge. Much of eastern Moab was steppeland—semi-arid wastes not profitable for cultivation, but excellent for grazing flocks of sheep and goats. The tribute Moab paid to Israel in the days of Ahab was 100,000 lambs and the wool of 100,000 rams.

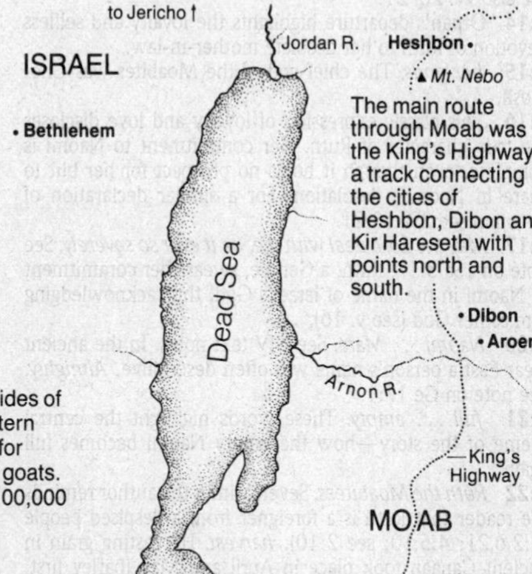
to Jericho
Jordan R.
Heshbon
ISRAEL
Mt. Nebo
The main route through Moab was the King's Highway, a track connecting the cities of Heshbon, Dibon and Kir Hareseth with points north and south.
Bethlehem
Dead Sea
Dibon
Aroer
Arnon R.
King's Highway
MOAB
Kir Hareseth
Miles 10 5 0 10 20
Kms 10 5 0 10 20 30

11 But Naomi said, "Return home, my
daughters. Why would you come with me?
Am I going to have any more sons, who
could become your husbands?[x] 12 Return
home, my daughters; I am too old to have
another husband. Even if I thought there
was still hope for me—even if I had a husband tonight and then gave birth to sons—
13 would you wait until they grew up?[y]
Would you remain unmarried for them?
No, my daughters. It is more bitter[z] for
me than for you, because the LORD's hand
has gone out against me![a]"

14 At this they wept[b] again. Then Orpah
kissed her mother-in-law[c] good-by,[d] but
Ruth clung to her.[e]

15 "Look," said Naomi, "your sister-in-
law[f] is going back to her people and her
gods.[g] Go back with her."

16 But Ruth replied, "Don't urge me to
leave you[h] or to turn back from you.
Where you go I will go,[i] and where you
stay I will stay. Your people will be my
people[j] and your God my God.[k] 17 Where
you die I will die, and there I will be buried. May the LORD deal with me, be it ever
so severely,[l] if anything but death separates you and me."[m] 18 When Naomi realized that Ruth was determined to go with
her, she stopped urging her.[n]

19 So the two women went on until they
came to Bethlehem.[o] When they arrived
in Bethlehem, the whole town was
stirred[p] because of them, and the women
exclaimed, "Can this be Naomi?"

20 "Don't call me Naomi,[b]" she told
them. "Call me Mara,[c] because the Almighty[d][q] has made my life very bitter.[r]
21 I went away full, but the LORD has
brought me back empty.[s] Why call me
Naomi? The LORD has afflicted[e] me;[t] the
Almighty has brought misfortune upon
me."

22 So Naomi returned from Moab accompanied by Ruth the Moabitess,[u] her
daughter-in-law,[v] arriving in Bethlehem
as the barley harvest[w] was beginning.[x]

Ruth Meets Boaz

2 Now Naomi had a relative[y] on her
husband's side, from the clan of
Elimelech,[z] a man of standing,[a] whose
name was Boaz.[b]

2 And Ruth the Moabitess[c] said to
Naomi, "Let me go to the fields and pick

1:11 [x]Ge 38:11; Dt 25:5
1:13 [y]Ge 38:11 [z]ver 20; Ex 1:14; 15:23; 1Sa 30:6 [a]S Jdg 2:15; S Job 4:5
1:14 [b]ver 9 [c]Ru 2:11; 3:1; Mic 7:6 [d]S Ge 31:28 [e]S Dt 10:20
1:15 [f]Dt 25:7 [g]S Jos 24:14
1:16 [h]2Ki 2:2 [i]Ge 24:58 [j]Ps 45:10 [k]S Jos 24:15
1:17 [l]1Sa 3:17; 14:44; 20:13; 25:22; 2Sa 3:9, 35; 19:13; 1Ki 2:23; 19:2; 20:10; 2Ki 6:31 [m]2Sa 15:21
1:18 [n]Ac 21:14
1:19 [o]S Jdg 17:7 [p]Mt 21:10
1:20 [q]S Ge 15:1; S 17:1; Ps 91:1 [r]S ver 13
1:21 [s]Job 1:21 [t]Job 30:11; Ps 88:7; Isa 53:4
1:22 [u]Ru 2:2,6, 21; 4:5,10 [v]S Ge 11:31 [w]S Ex 9:31; S Lev 19:9 [x]2Sa 21:9
2:1 [y]Ru 3:2; Pr 7:4 [z]S Ru 1:2 [a]1Sa 9:1; 1Ki 11:28 [b]Ru 4:21; 1Ch 2:12; Mt 1:5; Lk 3:32
2:2 [c]S Ru 1:22

[b]20 *Naomi* means *pleasant*; also in verse 21.
[c]20 *Mara* means *bitter.*
[d]20 Hebrew *Shaddai*; also in verse 21
[e]21 Or *has testified against*

1:11 *sons, who could become your husbands.* Naomi alludes to the Israelite law (Dt 25:5–6) regarding levirate marriage (see notes on Ge 38:8; Dt 25:5–10; see also Mk 12:18–23), which was given to protect the widow and guarantee continuance of the family line.
1:12 *I am too old.* Naomi can have no more sons; even her womb is empty.
1:13 *the LORD's hand . . . against me.* See notes on vv. 5–6; see also vv. 20–21.
1:14 Orpah's departure highlights the loyalty and selfless devotion of Ruth to her desolate mother-in-law.
1:15 *her gods.* The chief god of the Moabites was Chemosh.
1:16 This classic expression of loyalty and love discloses the true character of Ruth. Her commitment to Naomi is complete, even though it holds no prospect for her but to share in Naomi's desolation. For a similar declaration of devotion see 2Sa 15:21.
1:17 *May the LORD deal with me, be it ever so severely.* See note on 1Sa 3:17. Ruth, a Gentile, swears her commitment to Naomi in the name of Israel's God, thus acknowledging him as her God (see v. 16).
1:20 *Naomi . . . Mara.* See NIV text notes. In the ancient Near East a person's name was often descriptive. *Almighty.* See note on Ge 17:1.
1:21 *full . . . empty.* These words highlight the central theme of the story—how the empty Naomi becomes full again.
1:22 *Ruth the Moabitess.* Several times the author reminds the reader that Ruth is a foreigner from a despised people (2:2,6,21; 4:5,10; see 2:10). *harvest.* Harvesting grain in ancient Canaan took place in April and May (barley first, wheat a few weeks later; see 2:23). It involved the following steps: (1) cutting the ripened standing grain with hand sickles (Dt 16:9; 23:25; Jer 50:16; Joel 3:13)—usually done by men; (2) binding the grain into sheaves—usually done by women; (3) gleaning, i.e., gathering stalks of grain left behind (2:7); (4) transporting the sheaves to the threshing floor—often by donkey, sometimes by cart (Am 2:13); (5) threshing, i.e., loosening the grain from the straw—usually done by the treading of cattle (Dt 25:4; Hos 10:11), but sometimes by toothed threshing sledges (Isa 41:15; Am 1:3) or the wheels of carts (Isa 28:28); (6) winnowing—done by tossing the grain into the air with winnowing forks (Jer 15:7) so that the wind, which usually came up for a few hours in the afternoon, blew away the straw and chaff (Ps 1:4), leaving the grain at the winnower's feet; (7) sifting the grain (Am 9:9) to remove any residual foreign matter; (8) bagging for transportation and storage (Ge 42–44). Threshing floors, where both threshing and winnowing occurred, were hard, smooth, open places, prepared on either rock or clay and carefully chosen for favorable exposure to the prevailing winds. They were usually on the east side—i.e., downwind—of the village. *was beginning.* Naomi and Ruth arrive in Bethlehem just as the renewed fullness of the land is beginning to be harvested—an early hint that Naomi will be full again. Reference to the barley harvest also prepares the reader for the next major scene in the harvest fields (see Introduction: Literary Features).
2:1 *relative.* A sign of hope (see note on v. 20). *Boaz.* Probably means "In him is strength." Boaz is included in both genealogies of Jesus (Mt 1:5; Lk 3:32).
2:2 *Let me go.* Although Ruth is an alien and, as a young woman alone, obviously quite vulnerable in the harvest fields, she undertakes to provide for her mother-in-law. In 3:1 Naomi undertakes to provide for Ruth. *pick up the leftover grain.* The law of Moses instructed landowners to leave what the harvesters missed so that the poor, the alien,

up the leftover grain*d* behind anyone in whose eyes I find favor.*e*"

Naomi said to her, "Go ahead, my daughter." ³So she went out and began to glean in the fields behind the harvesters.*f* As it turned out, she found herself working in a field belonging to Boaz, who was from the clan of Elimelech.*g*

⁴Just then Boaz arrived from Bethlehem and greeted the harvesters, "The LORD be with you!*h*"

"The LORD bless you!*i*" they called back.

⁵Boaz asked the foreman of his harvesters, "Whose young woman is that?"

⁶The foreman replied, "She is the Moabitess*j* who came back from Moab with Naomi. ⁷She said, 'Please let me glean and gather among the sheaves*k* behind the harvesters.' She went into the field and has worked steadily from morning till now, except for a short rest*l* in the shelter."

⁸So Boaz said to Ruth, "My daughter, listen to me. Don't go and glean in another field and don't go away from here. Stay here with my servant girls. ⁹Watch the field where the men are harvesting, and follow along after the girls. I have told the men not to touch you. And whenever you are thirsty, go and get a drink from the water jars the men have filled."

¹⁰At this, she bowed down with her face to the ground.*m* She exclaimed, "Why have I found such favor in your eyes that you notice me*n*—a foreigner?*o*"

¹¹Boaz replied, "I've been told all about what you have done for your mother-in-law*p* since the death of your husband*q*—how you left your father and mother and your homeland and came to live with a people you did not know*r* before.*s* ¹²May the LORD repay you for what

you have done. May you be richly rewarded by the LORD,*t* the God of Israel,*u* under whose wings*v* you have come to take refuge.*w*"

¹³"May I continue to find favor in your eyes,*x* my lord," she said. "You have given me comfort and have spoken kindly to your servant—though I do not have the standing of one of your servant girls."

¹⁴At mealtime Boaz said to her, "Come over here. Have some bread*y* and dip it in the wine vinegar."

When she sat down with the harvesters,*z* he offered her some roasted grain.*a* She ate all she wanted and had some left over.*b* ¹⁵As she got up to glean, Boaz gave orders to his men, "Even if she gathers among the sheaves,*c* don't embarrass her. ¹⁶Rather, pull out some stalks for her from the bundles and leave them for her to pick up, and don't rebuke*d* her."

¹⁷So Ruth gleaned in the field until evening. Then she threshed*e* the barley she had gathered, and it amounted to about an ephah.*f* ¹⁸She carried it back to town, and her mother-in-law saw how much she had gathered. Ruth also brought out and gave her what she had left over*g* after she had eaten enough.

¹⁹Her mother-in-law asked her, "Where did you glean today? Where did you work? Blessed be the man who took notice of you!*h*"

Then Ruth told her mother-in-law about the one at whose place she had been working. "The name of the man I worked with today is Boaz," she said.

²⁰"The LORD bless him!*i*" Naomi said to her daughter-in-law.*j* "He has not stopped showing his kindness*k* to the liv-

*f*17 That is, probably about 3/5 bushel (about 22 liters)

Cross references (center column):

2:2 *d*S Lev 19:9; S 23:22
*e*S Ge 6:8; S 18:3
2:3 *f*ver 14; 2Ki 4:18; Jer 9:22; Am 9:13
*g*ver 1
2:4 *h*S Jdg 6:12; Lk 1:28; 2Th 3:16
*i*S Ge 28:3; S Nu 6:24
2:6 *j*S Ru 1:22
2:7 *k*S Ge 37:7; S Lev 19:9 /2Sa 4:5
2:10 *m*S Ge 19:1; S 1Sa 20:41 *n*ver 19; Ps 41:1 *o*S Ge 31:15; S Dt 15:3
2:11 *p*S Ru 1:14 *q*S Ru 1:5 *r*Isa 55:5 *s*Ru 1:16-17

2:12 *t*1Sa 24:19; 26:23,25; Ps 18:20; Pr 25:22; Jer 31:16 *u*S Jos 24:15 *v*Ps 17:8; 36:7; 57:1; 61:4; 63:7; 91:4 *w*Ps 71:1
2:13 *x*S Ge 18:3
2:14 *y*S Ge 3:19 *z*S ver 3 *a*S Lev 23:14 *b*ver 18
2:15 *c*S Ge 37:7; S Lev 19:9
2:16 *d*S Ge 37:10
2:17 *e*S Jdg 6:11 /S Lev 19:36
2:18 *g*ver 14
2:19 *h*S ver 10
2:20 *i*S Ge 37:2; S 1Sa 23:21 /S Ge 11:31 *k*S Ge 19:19

---

the widow and the fatherless could glean for their needs (Lev 19:9; 23:22; Dt 24:19).

2:3 *As it turned out.* Divine providence is at work (vv. 19–20).

2:4 The exchange of greetings between Boaz and his laborers characterizes Boaz as a godly man with a kind spirit.

2:9 *follow along after the girls.* It was customary for the men to cut the grain and for the servant girls to go behind them to bind the grain into sheaves. Then Ruth could glean what they had left behind (see note on 1:22).

2:11 Ruth's commitment to care for her desolate mother-in-law remains the center of attention throughout the book.

2:12 *under whose wings.* A figure of a bird protecting her young under her wings (see Mt 23:37; see also note on 3:9).

2:13 *your servant.* A polite reference to herself.

2:15 *gave orders to his men.* Boaz goes beyond the requirement of the law in making sure that Ruth's labors are abundantly productive (see 3:15).

2:17 *threshed.* See note on 1:22. In Ruth's case, as in that

of Gideon (Jdg 6:11), the amount was small and could be threshed by hand simply by beating it with a club or stick. *ephah.* See NIV text note; an unusually large amount for one day's gleaning.

2:20 *The LORD . . . has not stopped showing his kindness.* See 1:8. In 3:10 Boaz credits Ruth with demonstrating this same virtue. *kinsman-redeemers.* Redemption is a key concept in Ruth (see Introduction: Theme and Theology). The kinsman-redeemer was responsible for protecting the interests of needy members of the extended family—e.g., to provide an heir for a brother who had died (Dt 25:5–10), to redeem land that a poor relative had sold outside the family (Lev 25:25–28), to redeem a relative who had been sold into slavery (Lev 25:47–49) and to avenge the killing of a relative (Nu 35:19–21; "avenger" and "kinsman-redeemer" are translations of the same Hebrew word). Naomi is encouraged when she hears that the Lord has led Ruth to the fields of a relative who might serve as their kinsman-redeemer. This moment of Naomi's awakened hope is the crucial turning point of the story.

ing and the dead." She added, "That man is our close relative; [l] he is one of our kinsman-redeemers. [m]"

21Then Ruth the Moabitess [n] said, "He even said to me, 'Stay with my workers until they finish harvesting all my grain.' "

22Naomi said to Ruth her daughter-in-law, "It will be good for you, my daughter, to go with his girls, because in someone else's field you might be harmed."

23So Ruth stayed close to the servant girls of Boaz to glean until the barley [o] and wheat harvests [p] were finished. And she lived with her mother-in-law.

Ruth and Boaz at the Threshing Floor

3 One day Naomi her mother-in-law [q] said to her, "My daughter, should I not try to find a home [g] [r] for you, where you will be well provided for? 2Is not Boaz, with whose servant girls you have been, a kinsman [s] of ours? Tonight he will be winnowing barley on the threshing floor. [t] 3Wash [u] and perfume yourself, [v] and put on your best clothes. [w] Then go down to the threshing floor, but don't let him know you are there until he has finished eating and drinking. [x] 4When he lies down, note the place where he is lying. Then go and uncover his feet and lie down. He will tell you what to do."

5"I will do whatever you say," [y] Ruth answered. 6So she went down to the threshing floor [z] and did everything her mother-in-law told her to do.

7When Boaz had finished eating and drinking and was in good spirits, [a] he went over to lie down at the far end of the grain

pile. [b] Ruth approached quietly, uncovered his feet and lay down. 8In the middle of the night something startled the man, and he turned and discovered a woman lying at his feet.

9"Who are you?" he asked.

"I am your servant Ruth," she said. "Spread the corner of your garment [c] over me, since you are a kinsman-redeemer. [d]"

10"The LORD bless you, [e] my daughter," he replied. "This kindness is greater than that which you showed earlier: [f] You have not run after the younger men, whether rich or poor. 11And now, my daughter, don't be afraid. I will do for you all you ask. All my fellow townsmen know that you are a woman of noble character. [g] 12Although it is true that I am near of kin, there is a kinsman-redeemer [h] nearer than [i] I. 13Stay here for the night, and in the morning if he wants to redeem, [j] good; let him redeem. But if he is not willing, as surely as the LORD lives [k] I will do it. [l] Lie here until morning."

14So she lay at his feet until morning, but got up before anyone could be recognized; and he said, "Don't let it be known that a woman came to the threshing floor. [m]" [n]

15He also said, "Bring me the shawl [o] you are wearing and hold it out." When she did so, he poured into it six measures of barley and put it on her. Then he [h] went back to town.

16When Ruth came to her mother-in-

2:20 [l]S Lev 25:25;
[m]Ru 3:9,12; 4:1,
14
2:21 [n]S Ru 1:22
2:23 [o]S Ex 9:31
[p]S Ge 30:14;
S 1Sa 6:13
3:1 [q]S Ru 1:14
[r]Ru 1:9
3:2 [s]S Ru 2:1
[t]S Lev 2:14;
S Nu 18:27;
S Jdg 6:11
3:3 [u]2Sa 12:20;
2Ki 5:10; Ps 26:6;
51:2; Isa 1:16;
Jer 4:14; Eze 16:9
[v]2Sa 14:2;
Isa 61:3
[w]S Ge 41:14
[x]S Ex 32:6;
S Ecc 2:3;
S Jer 15:17
3:5 [y]Eph 6:1;
Col 3:20
3:6 [z]S Nu 18:27
3:7 [a]Jdg 19:6,22;
1Sa 25:36;
2Sa 13:28;
1Ki 21:7; Est 1:10

[b]2Ch 31:6;
SS 7:2; Jer 50:26;
Hag 2:16
3:9 [c]Eze 16:8
[d]S Ru 2:20
3:10 [e]S Jdg 17:2
[f]S Jos 2:12
3:11 [g]Pr 12:4;
14:1; 31:10
3:12 [h]S Ru 2:20
[i]Ru 4:1
3:13 [j]Dt 25:5;
Ru 4:15; Mt 22:24
[k]S Nu 14:21;
Hos 4:15 [l]Ru 4:6
3:14
[m]S Nu 18:27
[n]Ro 14:16;
2Co 8:21
3:15 [o]Isa 3:22

[g][l] Hebrew find rest (see Ruth 1:9)   [h]15 Most
Hebrew manuscripts; many Hebrew manuscripts, Vulgate
and Syriac she

2:23 *until the barley and wheat harvests were finished.* This phrase rounds out the harvest episode and prepares for the next major scene on the threshing floor (see Introduction: Literary Features).

3:1 Naomi's awakened hope (cf. 1:8–13) now moves her to undertake provision for Ruth's future (see note on 2:2).

3:2 *Tonight he will be winnowing.* See note on 1:22. In the threshing season it was customary for the landowner to spend the night near the threshing floor to protect his grain from theft.

3:3 Ruth is instructed to prepare herself like a bride (see Eze 16:9–12). *go down to the threshing floor.* Women were not normally present at the evening revelries of the threshers (v. 14). *eating and drinking.* Harvest was a time of festivity (Isa 9:3; 16:9–10; Jer 48:33).

3:4 *uncover his feet and lie down.* Although Naomi's instructions may appear forward, the moral integrity of Naomi and Ruth is never in doubt (see v. 11). Naomi's advice to Ruth is clearly for the purpose of appealing to Boaz's kinsman obligation. Ruth's actions were a request for marriage. Tamar, the mother of Perez (4:12), had also laid claim to the provision of the levirate (or kinsman-redeemer) law (Ge 38:13–30).

3:9 *Spread the corner of your garment over me.* A request

for marriage (see Eze 16:8); a similar custom is still practiced in some parts of the Middle East today. There is a play on the words "wings" of the Lord (2:12) and "corners" (lit. "wings") of the garment (here), both signifying protection. Boaz is vividly reminded that he must serve as the Lord's protective wing to watch over Ruth.

3:10 *kindness . . . you showed earlier.* See 2:11–12.

3:11 *woman of noble character.* See Pr 31:10. The Hebrew for this expression is similar to that used of Boaz in 2:1; thus the author maintains a balance between his descriptions of Ruth and Boaz.

3:12 *a kinsman-redeemer nearer than I.* How Boaz was related to Ruth's former husband (Mahlon) is unknown, but the closest male relative had the primary responsibility to marry a widow. Naomi instructed Ruth to approach Boaz because he had already shown himself willing to be Ruth's protector. Boaz, however, would not bypass the directives of the law, which clearly gave priority to the nearest relative.

3:13 *as surely as the LORD lives.* Boaz commits himself by oath (cf. 1:17) to redeem the family property and to arrange Ruth's honorable marriage.

3:15 Boaz goes beyond the requirement of the law in supplying Ruth with grain from the threshing floor (see 2:15).

law, Naomi asked, "How did it go, my daughter?"

Then she told her everything Boaz had done for her [17]and added, "He gave me these six measures of barley, saying, 'Don't go back to your mother-in-law empty-handed.' "

[18]Then Naomi said, "Wait, my daughter, until you find out what happens. For the man will not rest until the matter is settled today."[p]

Boaz Marries Ruth

4 Meanwhile Boaz went up to the town gate[q] and sat there. When the kinsman-redeemer[r] he had mentioned[s] came along, Boaz said, "Come over here, my friend, and sit down." So he went over and sat down. [2]Boaz took ten of the elders[t] of the town and said, "Sit here," and they did so.[u] [3]Then he said to the kinsman-redeemer, "Naomi, who has come back from Moab, is selling the piece of land that belonged to our brother Elimelech.[v] [4]I thought I should bring the matter to your attention and suggest that you buy it in the presence of these seated here and in the presence of the elders of my people. If you will redeem it, do so. But if you[i] will not, tell me, so I will know. For no one has the right to do it except you,[w] and I am next in line."

"I will redeem it," he said.

[5]Then Boaz said, "On the day you buy the land from Naomi and from Ruth the Moabitess,[x] you acquire[j] the dead man's widow, in order to maintain the name of the dead with his property."[y]

[6]At this, the kinsman-redeemer said, "Then I cannot redeem[z] it because I might endanger my own estate. You redeem it yourself. I cannot do it."[a]

[7](Now in earlier times in Israel, for the redemption[b] and transfer of property to become final, one party took off his sandal[c] and gave it to the other. This was the method of legalizing transactions[d] in Israel.)[e]

[8]So the kinsman-redeemer said to Boaz, "Buy it yourself." And he removed his sandal.[f]

[9]Then Boaz announced to the elders and all the people, "Today you are witnesses[g] that I have bought from Naomi all the property of Elimelech, Kilion and Mahlon. [10]I have also acquired Ruth the Moabitess,[h] Mahlon's widow, as my wife,[i] in order to maintain the name of the dead with his property, so that his name will not disappear from among his family or from the town records.[j] Today you are witnesses![k]"

[11]Then the elders and all those at the gate[l] said, "We are witnesses.[m] May the LORD make the woman who is coming into your home like Rachel and Leah,[n] who together built up the house of Israel. May

Cross references (center column)

3:18 pPs 37:3-5
4:1 qS Ge 18:1;
S 23:10
rS Ru 2:20
sRu 3:12
4:2 tS Ex 3:16
uS Dt 25:7
4:3 vS Lev 25:25;
S Ru 1:2
4:4
wS Lev 25:25;
Jer 32:7-8

4:5 xS Ru 1:22
yS Ge 38:8;
S Ru 3:13
4:6 zLev 25:25;
Ru 3:13
aS Dt 25:7
4:7 bS Lev 25:24;
cver 8 dIsa 8:1-2,
16,20 eDt 25:7-9
4:8 fDt 25:9
4:9 gIsa 8:2;
Jer 32:10,44
4:10 hS Ru 1:22
iS Dt 25:5
jS Dt 25:6
kS Jos 24:22
4:11 lS Ge 23:10
mS Dt 25:9
nS Ge 4:19;
S 29:16

i4 Many Hebrew manuscripts, Septuagint, Vulgate and Syriac; most Hebrew manuscripts he   i5 Hebrew; Vulgate and Syriac Naomi, you acquire Ruth the Moabitess,

---

3:17 empty-handed. Again the empty-full motif (see note on 1:21).

3:18 Wait. The Hebrew underlying this word is translated "sat" in 4:1. Thus the author prepares the reader for the next major scene, in which Boaz sits at the town gate to see the matter through.

4:1 town gate. The "town hall" of ancient Israel, the normal place for business and legal transactions, where witnesses were readily available (vv. 9-12; see note on Ge 19:1). my friend. The other kinsman remains unnamed.

4:2 ten of the elders. A full court for legal proceedings.

4:3 selling the piece of land. See note on 2:20. Two interpretations are possible: 1. Naomi owns the land but is so destitute that she is forced to sell. It was the duty of the kinsman-redeemer to buy any land in danger of being sold outside the family. 2. Naomi does not own the land—it had been sold by Elimelech before the family left for Moab—but by law she retains the right of redemption to buy the land back. Lacking funds to do so herself, she is dependent on a kinsman-redeemer to do it for her. It is the right of redemption that Naomi is "selling." brother. Used in the broader sense of "relative."

4:5 you acquire the dead man's widow. Now Boaz reveals the other half of the obligation—the acquisition of Ruth. Levirate law (Dt 25:5-6) provided that Ruth's firstborn son would keep Mahlon's name alive and would possess the right of ownership of the family inheritance.

4:6 I cannot redeem it. Possibly he fears that, if he has a son by her and if that son is his only surviving heir, his own property will transfer to the family of Elimelech (see note on Ge 38:9). In that case his risk was no greater than that assumed by Boaz. This kinsman's refusal to assume the kinsman-redeemer's role highlights the kindness and generosity of Boaz toward the two widows—just as Orpah's return to her family highlights Ruth's selfless devotion and loyalty to Naomi.

4:7 one party took off his sandal. The process of renouncing one's property rights and passing them to another was publicly attested by taking off a sandal and transferring it to the new owner (cf. Am 2:6; 8:6). The Nuzi documents (see chart on "Ancient Texts Relating to the OT," p. 5) refer to a similar custom.

4:9 witnesses. The role of public witnesses was to attest to all legal transactions and other binding agreements.

4:10 name of the dead. See Dt 25:6.

4:11 Rachel and Leah . . . built up the house of Israel. Cf. Dt 25:9. The Israelite readers of Ruth would have associated the house of Jacob (Israel), built up by Rachel and Leah, with the house of Israel, rebuilt by David, the descendant of Ruth and Boaz, after it had been threatened with extinction (1Sa 4). They also knew that the Lord had covenanted to "build" the house of David as an enduring dynasty, through which Israel's blessed destiny would be assured (see 2Sa 7:27-29). Ephrathah. See note on 1:2.

you have standing in Ephrathah[o] and be famous in Bethlehem.[p] 12Through the offspring the LORD gives you by this young woman, may your family be like that of Perez,[q] whom Tamar[r] bore to Judah."

The Genealogy of David

4:18–22pp — 1Ch 2:5–15; Mt 1:3–6; Lk 3:31–33

13So Boaz took Ruth and she became his wife. Then he went to her, and the LORD enabled her to conceive,[s] and she gave birth to a son.[t] 14The women[u] said to Naomi: "Praise be to the LORD,[v] who this day has not left you without a kinsman-redeemer.[w] May he become famous throughout Israel! 15He will renew your life and sustain you in your old age. For your daughter-in-law,[x] who loves you and who is better to you than seven sons,[y] has given him birth."

16Then Naomi took the child, laid him in her lap and cared for him. 17The women living there said, "Naomi has a son." And they named him Obed. He was the father of Jesse,[z] the father of David.[a]

18This, then, is the family line of Perez[b]:

Perez was the father of Hezron,[c]
19Hezron the father of Ram,
 Ram the father of Amminadab,[d]
20Amminadab the father of Nahshon,[e]
 Nahshon the father of Salmon,[k]
21Salmon the father of Boaz,[f]
 Boaz the father of Obed,
22Obed the father of Jesse,
 and Jesse the father of David.

k 20 A few Hebrew manuscripts, some Septuagint manuscripts and Vulgate (see also verse 21 and Septuagint of 1 Chron. 2:11); most Hebrew manuscripts *Salma*

Cross references (center column):
4:11 oS Ge 35:16; pRu 1:19
4:12 qS Ge 38:29; rGe 38:6,24
4:13 sS Ge 8:1; S 29:31
tS Ge 29:32; S 30:6; Lk 1:57
4:14 uLk 1:58; vS Ge 24:27; wS Ru 2:20
4:15 xS Ge 11:31; y1Sa 1:8; 2:5; Job 1:2
4:17 zver 22; 1Sa 16:1,18; 17:12,17,58; 1Ch 2:12,13; Ps 72:20; a1Sa 16:13; 1Ch 2:15
4:18 bS Ge 38:29; cNu 26:21
4:19 dS Ex 6:23
4:20 eS Nu 7:12
4:21 fS Ru 2:1

4:12 *Perez, whom Tamar bore to Judah.* Perez was Boaz's ancestor (vv. 18–21; Mt 1:3; Lk 3:33). His birth to Judah was from a union based on the levirate practice (Ge 38:27–30; see note on 1:11). Perez was therefore an appropriate model within Boaz's ancestry for the blessing the elders gave to Boaz. Moreover, the descendants of Perez had raised the tribe of Judah to a prominent place in Israel. So the blessing of the elders—that, through the offspring Ruth would bear to Boaz, his family would be like that of Perez—was fully realized in David and his dynasty. Thus also v. 12 prepares the reader for the events briefly narrated in the conclusion.

4:13–17 The conclusion of the story balances the introduction (1:1–5): (1) In the Hebrew both have the same number of words; (2) both compress much into a short space; (3) both focus on Naomi; (4) the introduction emphasizes Naomi's emptiness, and the conclusion portrays her fullness.

4:13 *the LORD enabled her to conceive.* See note on 1:6.
4:14 *kinsman-redeemer.* The child Obed, as v. 15 makes clear. *May he become famous.* This same wish is expressed concerning Boaz in v. 11.
4:15 *better to you than seven sons.* See 1Sa 1:8. Since

seven was considered a number of completeness, to have seven sons was the epitome of all family blessings in Israel (see 1Sa 2:5; Job 1:2; 42:13). Ruth's selfless devotion to Naomi receives its climactic acknowledgment.

4:16 *laid him in her lap.* Possibly symbolizing adoption (see note on Ge 30:3).
4:17 *Naomi has a son.* Through Ruth, aged Naomi, who can no longer bear children, obtains an heir in place of Mahlon. *Obed.* The name means "servant," in its full form possibly "servant of the LORD."
4:18–22 See 1Ch 2:5–15; Mt 1:3–6; Lk 3:31–33. Like the genealogies of Ge 5:3–32; 11:10–26, this genealogy has ten names (see note on Ge 5:5). It brings to mind the reign of David, during which, in contrast to the turbulent period of the judges recalled in 1:1, Israel finally entered into rest in the promised land (see 1Ki 5:4). It signifies that, just as Naomi was brought from emptiness to fullness through the selfless love of Ruth and Boaz, so the Lord brought Israel from unrest to rest through their descendant David, who selflessly gave himself to fight Israel's battles on the Lord's behalf. The ultimate end of this genealogy is Jesus Christ, the great "son of David" (Mt 1:1), who fulfills prophecy and will bring the Lord's people into final rest.

1 SAMUEL

Title

1 and 2 Samuel are named after the person God used to establish kingship in Israel. Samuel not only anointed both Saul and David, Israel's first two kings, but he also gave definition to the new order of God's rule over Israel that began with the incorporation of kingship into its structure. Samuel's importance as God's representative in this period of Israel's history is close to that of Moses (see Ps 99:6; Jer 15:1) since he, more than any other person, provided for covenant continuity in the transition from the rule of the judges to that of the monarchy.

1 and 2 Samuel were originally one book. It was divided into two parts by the translators of the Septuagint (the Greek translation of the OT)—a division subsequently followed by Jerome (the Latin Vulgate) and by modern versions. The title of the book has varied from time to time, having been designated "The First and Second Books of Kingdoms" (Septuagint), "First and Second Kings" (Vulgate) and "First and Second Samuel" (Hebrew tradition and most modern versions).

Literary Features, Authorship and Date

Many questions have arisen pertaining to the literary character, authorship and date of 1,2 Samuel. Certain literary characteristics of the book suggest that it was compiled with the use of a number of originally independent sources, which the author may have incorporated into his own composition as much as possible in their original, unedited form.

Who the author was cannot be known with certainty since the book itself gives no indication of his identity. Some have suggested Zabud, son of Nathan the prophet, who is referred to in 1 Ki 4:5 as the "personal adviser" to King Solomon. He would have had access to information about David's reign from his father Nathan, as well as from court records. Whoever the author was, he must have lived shortly after Solomon's death (930 B.C.) and the division of the kingdom (see references to "Israel and Judah" in 11:8; 17:52; 18:16; 2Sa 5:5; 24:1-9 and the expression "kings of Judah" in 1Sa 27:6). Also, he doubtless had access to records of the life and times of Samuel, Saul and David. Explicit reference in the book itself is made to only one such source (the Book of Jashar, 2Sa 1:18), but the writer of Chronicles refers to four others that pertain to this period (the book of the annals of King David, 1Ch 27:24; the records of Samuel the seer; the records of Nathan the prophet; the records of Gad the seer, 1Ch 29:29).

Contents and Theme: Kingship and Covenant

1 Samuel portrays the establishment of kingship in Israel. Before the author describes this momentous change in the structure of the theocracy (God's rule), he effectively depicts the complexity of its context. The following events provide both historical and theological context for the birth of the monarchy:

1. *The birth, youth and calling of Samuel (chs. 1-3).* In a book dealing for the most part with the reigns of Israel's first two kings, Saul and David, it is significant that the author chose not to include a birth narrative of either of these men, but to describe the birth of their forerunner and anointer, the prophet Samuel. This in itself accentuates the importance the author attached to Samuel's role in the events that follow. He seems to be saying in a subtle way that flesh and blood are to be subordinated to word and Spirit in the process of the establishment of kingship. For this reason chs. 1-3 should be viewed as integrally related to what follows, not as a more likely component of the book of Judges or as a loosely attached prefix to the rest of 1,2 Samuel. Kingship is given its birth and then nurtured by the prophetic word and work of the prophet Samuel. Moreover, the events of Samuel's nativity thematically anticipate the story of God's working that is narrated in the rest of the book.

2. *The "ark narratives" (chs. 4-6).* This section describes how the ark of God was captured by the Philistines and then, after God wreaked havoc on several Philistine cities, how it was returned to Israel. These narratives reveal the folly of Israel's notion that possession of the ark automatically guaranteed

victory over her enemies. They also display the awesome power of the Lord (Yahweh, the God of Israel) and his superiority over the Philistine god Dagon. The Philistines were forced to confess openly their helplessness against God's power by their return of the ark to Israel. The entire ark episode performs a vital function in placing Israel's subsequent sinful desire for a human king in proper perspective.

3. *Samuel as a judge and deliverer (ch. 7)*. When Samuel called Israel to repentance and renewed dedication to the Lord, the Lord intervened mightily in Israel's behalf and gave victory over the Philistines. This narrative reaffirms the authority of Samuel as a divinely ordained leader; at the same time it provides evidence of divine protection and blessing for God's people when they place their confidence in the Lord and live in obedience to their covenant obligations.

All the material in chs. 1-7 serves as a necessary preface for the narratives of chs. 8-12, which describe the rise and establishment of kingship in Israel. The author has masterfully arranged the stories in chs. 8-12 in order to accentuate the serious theological conflict surrounding the historical events. In the study of these chapters, scholars have often noted the presence of a tension or ambivalence in the attitude toward the monarchy: On the one hand, Samuel is commanded by the Lord to give the people a king (8:7,9,22; 9:16-17; 10:24; 12:13); on the other hand, their request for a king is considered a sinful rejection of the Lord (8:7; 10:19; 12:12,17,19-20). These seemingly conflicting attitudes toward the monarchy must be understood in the context of Israel's covenant relationship with the Lord.

Moses had anticipated Israel's desire for a human king (Dt 17:18-20), but Israelite kingship was to be compatible with the continued rule of the Lord over his people as their Great King. Instead, when the elders asked Samuel to give them a king (8:5,19-20), they rejected the Lord's kingship over them (8:7; 10:19; 12:17,19). Their desire was for a king such as the nations around them had—to lead them in battle and give them a sense of national security and unity. The request for a king constituted a denial of their covenant relationship to the Lord, who was their King. Moreover, the Lord not only had promised to be their protector but had also repeatedly demonstrated his power in their behalf, most recently in the ark narratives (chs. 4-6), as well as in the great victory won over the Philistines under the leadership of Samuel (ch. 7).

Nevertheless the Lord instructed Samuel to give the people a king (8:7,9,22). By divine appointment Saul was brought into contact with Samuel, and Samuel was directed to anoint him privately as king (9:1-10:16). Subsequently, Samuel gathered the people at Mizpah, where, after again admonishing them concerning their sin in desiring a king (10:18-19), he presided over the selection of a king by lot. The lot fell on Saul and publicly designated him as the one whom God had chosen (10:24). Saul did not immediately assume his royal office, but returned home to work his fields (11:5,7). When the inhabitants of Jabesh Gilead were threatened by Nahash the Ammonite, Saul rose to the challenge, gathered an army and led Israel to victory in battle. His success placed a final seal of divine approval on Saul's selection to be king (cf. 10:24; 11:12-13) and occasioned the inauguration of his reign at Gilgal (11:14-12:25).

The question that still needed resolution, then, was not so much whether Israel should have a king (it was clearly the Lord's will to give them a king), but rather how they could maintain their covenant with God (i.e., preserve the theocracy) now that they had a human king. The problem was resolved when Samuel called the people to repentance and renewal of their allegiance to the Lord on the very occasion of the inauguration of Saul as king (11:14-12:25; see note on 10:25). By establishing kingship in the context of covenant renewal, Samuel placed the monarchy in Israel on a radically different footing from that in surrounding nations. The king in Israel was not to be autonomous in his authority and power; rather, he was to be subject to the law of the Lord and the word of the prophet (10:25; 12:23). This was to be true not only for Saul but also for all the kings who would occupy the throne in Israel in the future. The king was to be an instrument of the Lord's rule over his people, and the people as well as the king were to continue to recognize the Lord as their ultimate Sovereign (12:14-15).

Saul very quickly demonstrated that he was unwilling to submit to the requirements of his theocratic office (chs. 13-15). When he disobeyed the instructions of the prophet Samuel in preparation for battle against the Philistines (13:13), and when he refused to totally destroy the Amalekites as he had been commanded to do by the word of the Lord through Samuel (ch. 15), he ceased to be an instrument of the Lord's rule over his people. These abrogations of the requirements of his theocratic office led to his rejection as king (15:23).

The remainder of 1 Samuel (chs. 16-31) depicts the Lord's choice of David to be Saul's successor, and then describes the long road by which David is prepared for accession to the throne. Although Saul's rule became increasingly anti-theocratic in nature, David refused to usurp the throne by forceful means but left his accession to office in the Lord's hands. Eventually Saul was wounded in a battle

with the Philistines and, fearing capture, took his own life. Three of Saul's sons, including David's loyal friend Jonathan, were killed in the same battle (ch. 31).

Chronology

Even though the narratives of 1,2 Samuel contain some statements of chronological import (see, e.g., 1Sa 6:1; 7:2; 8:1,5; 13:1; 25:1; 2Sa 2:10-11; 5:4-5; 14:28; 15:7), the data are insufficient to establish a precise chronology for the major events of this period of Israel's history. Except for the dates of David's birth and the duration of his reign, which are quite firm (see 2Sa 5:4-5), most other dates can only be approximated. The textual problem with the chronological data on the age of Saul when he became king and the length of his reign (see NIV text notes on 1Sa 13:1) contributes to uncertainty concerning the precise time of his birth and the beginning of his reign. No information is given concerning the time of Samuel's birth (1Sa 1:1) or death (25:1). His lifetime must have spanned, at least in part, that of Samson and that of Obed, son of Ruth and Boaz and grandfather of David. It is indicated that he was well along in years when the elders of Israel asked him to give them a king (see 8:1,5). One other factor contributing to chronological uncertainty is that the author has not always arranged his material in strict chronological sequence. It seems clear, for example, that 2Sa 7 is to be placed chronologically after David's conquests described in 2Sa 8:1-14 (see notes on 2Sa 7:1; 8:1). The story of the famine sent by God on Israel during the reign of David because of Saul's violation of a treaty with the Gibeonites is found in 2Sa 21:1-4, though chronologically it occurred prior to the time of Absalom's rebellion recorded in 2Sa 15-18 (see further the notes on 2Sa 21:1-2). The following dates, however, provide an approximate chronological framework for the times of Samuel, Saul and David.

1105 B.C.	Birth of Samuel (1Sa 1:20)
1080	Birth of Saul
1050	Saul anointed to be king (1Sa 10:1)
1040	Birth of David
1025	David anointed to be Saul's successor (1Sa 16:1-13)
1010	Death of Saul and beginning of David's reign over Judah in Hebron (2Sa 1:1; 2:1,4,11)
1003	Beginning of David's reign over all Israel and capture of Jerusalem (2Sa 5)
997-992	David's wars (2Sa 8:1-14)
991	Birth of Solomon (2Sa 12:24; 1Ki 3:7; 11:42)
980	David's census (2Sa 24:1)
970	End of David's reign (2Sa 5:4-5; 1Ki 2:10-11)

Outline

I. Historical Setting for the Establishment of Kingship in Israel (1Sa 1-7)
   A. Samuel's Birth, Youth and Calling to Be a Prophet; Judgment on the House of Eli (1Sa 1-3)
   B. Israel Defeated by the Philistines, the Ark of God Taken and the Ark Restored; Samuel's Role as Judge and Deliverer (1Sa 4-7)
II. The Establishment of Kingship in Israel under the Guidance of Samuel the Prophet (1Sa 8-12)
   A. The People's Sinful Request for a King and God's Intent to Give Them a King (1Sa 8)
   B. Samuel Anoints Saul Privately to Be King (1Sa 9:1-10:16)
   C. Saul Chosen to Be King Publicly by Lot at Mizpah (1Sa 10:17-27)
   D. The Choice of Saul as King Confirmed by Victory over the Ammonites (1Sa 11:1-13)
   E. Saul's Reign Inaugurated at a Covenant Renewal Ceremony Convened by Samuel at Gilgal (1Sa 11:14-12:25)
III. Saul's Kingship a Failure (1Sa 13-15)
IV. David's Rise to the Throne; Progressive Deterioration and End of Saul's Reign (1Sa 16:1-2Sa 5:5)
   A. David Is Anointed Privately, Enters the Service of King Saul and Flees for His Life (1Sa 16-26)
   B. David Seeks Refuge in Philistia, and Saul and His Sons Are Killed in Battle (1Sa 27-31)
   C. David Becomes King over Judah (2Sa 1-4)
   D. David Becomes King over All Israel (2Sa 5:1-5)
V. David's Kingship in Its Accomplishments and Glory (2Sa 5:6-9:12)
   A. David Conquers Jerusalem and Defeats the Philistines (2Sa 5:6-25)
   B. David Brings the Ark to Jerusalem (2Sa 6)
   C. God Promises David an Everlasting Dynasty (2Sa 7)

The Birth of Samuel

1 There was a certain man from Rama-thaim,[a] a Zuphite[a][b] from the hill country[c] of Ephraim,[d] whose name was Elkanah[e] son of Jeroham, the son of Elihu, the son of Tohu, the son of Zuph, an Ephraimite. [2]He had two wives;[f] one was called Hannah and the other Peninnah. Peninnah had children, but Hannah had none.

[3]Year after year[g] this man went up from his town to worship[h] and sacrifice to the LORD Almighty at Shiloh,[i] where Hophni and Phinehas, the two sons of Eli,[j] were priests of the LORD. [4]Whenever the day came for Elkanah to sacrifice,[k] he would give portions of the meat to his wife Penin-nah and to all her sons and daughters. [l] [5]But to Hannah he gave a double portion[m] because he loved her, and the LORD had closed her womb. [n] [6]And because the LORD had closed her womb, her rival kept provoking her in order to irritate her.[o] [7]This went on year after year. Whenever Hannah went up to the house of the LORD, her rival provoked her till she wept and

would not eat.[p] [8]Elkanah her husband would say to her, "Hannah, why are you weeping? Why don't you eat? Why are you downhearted? Don't I mean more to you than ten sons?[q]"

[9]Once when they had finished eating and drinking in Shiloh, Hannah stood up. Now Eli the priest was sitting on a chair by the doorpost of the LORD's temple.[b][r] [10]In bitterness of soul[s] Hannah wept much and prayed to the LORD. [11]And she made a vow,[t] saying, "O LORD Almighty[u], if you will only look upon your servant's misery and remember[v] me, and not forget your servant but give her a son, then I will give him to the LORD for all the days of his life,[w] and no razor[x] will ever be used on his head."

[12]As she kept on praying to the LORD, Eli observed her mouth. [13]Hannah was pray-ing in her heart, and her lips were moving but her voice was not heard. Eli thought she was drunk [14]and said to her, "How long will you keep on getting drunk? Get rid of your wine."

Cross references (center column)

1:1 [a]S Jos 18:25
[b]1Sa 9:5
[c]Jos 17:17-18
[d]Jos 21:20-22
[e]1Ch 6:27,34
1:2 [f]S Ge 4:19
1:3 [g]ver 21;
Ex 23:14;
1Sa 2:19; 20:6,
29; Lk 2:41
[h]Dt 12:5-7
[i]S Jos 18:1
[j]1Sa 2:31; 14:3
1:4 [k]Lev 7:15-18;
Dt 12:17-18
[l]S Ge 29:34
1:5 [m]S Ge 37:3
[n]S Ge 11:30;
S 29:31
1:6 [o]S Ge 16:4
1:7 [p]2Sa 12:17;
Ps 102:4
1:8 [q]S Ru 4:15
1:9 [r]1Sa 3:3
1:10 [s]Job 3:20;
7:11; 10:1;
25:21; 23:2;
27:2; Isa 38:15;
Jer 20:18
1:11 [t]S Jdg 11:30
[u]S Ge 17:1;
Ps 24:10; 46:7;
Isa 1:9 [v]S Ge 8:1
[w]S Jdg 13:7
[x]Nu 6:1-21;
Jdg 13:5; Lk 1:15

1:1 *Ramathaim.* The name occurs only here in the OT and appears to be another name for Ramah (see 1:19; 2:11; 7:17; 19:18; 25:1). It is perhaps to be identified with the Ramah of Benjamin (see Jos 18:25) located in the hill country about five miles north of Jerusalem, between the territories of Ephraim and Benjamin. *Zuphite.* See NIV text note. It is not entirely clear whether this word refers to the man or the place. If it refers to the man, it indicates his descent from Zuph (see 1Ch 6:34-35). If it refers to the place, it designates the general area in which Ramathaim is located (see 9:5). *Ephraimite.* Although Elkanah is here called an Ephraimite, he was probably a Levite whose family belonged to the Kohathite clans that had been allotted towns in Ephraim (see Jos 21:20-21; 1Ch 6:22-26).

1:2 *two wives.* See notes on Ge 4:19; 16:2; 25:6.

1:3 *Year after year this man went up.* Three times a year every Israelite male was required to appear before the Lord at the central sanctuary (Ex 23:14-19; 34:23; Dt 16:16-17). The festival referred to here was probably the Feast of Taber-nacles, which not only commemorated God's care for his people during the desert journey to Canaan (see Lev 23:43) but more especially celebrated, with joy and feasting, God's blessing on the year's crops (see Dt 16:13-15). On such festive occasions Hannah's deep sorrow because of her own barrenness was the more poignant. *the LORD Almighty.* Tradi-tionally "the LORD of hosts." This is the first time in the Bible that God is designated by this title. The Hebrew for "host(s)" can refer to (1) human armies (Ex 7:4; Ps 44:9); (2) the celestial bodies such as the sun, moon and stars (Ge 2:1; Dt 4:19; Isa 40:26); or (3) the heavenly creatures such as angels (Jos 5:14; 1Ki 22:19; Ps 148:2). The title, "the LORD of hosts," is perhaps best understood as a general reference to the sovereignty of God over all powers in the universe (hence the NIV rendering, "the LORD Almighty"). In the account of the establishment of kingship in Israel it became particularly appropriate as a reference to God as the God of armies—both of the heavenly army (Dt 33:2; Jos 5:14; Ps 68:17; Hab 3:8) and of the army of Israel (1Sa 17:45). *Shiloh.* The town in

Ephraim between Bethel and Shechem where the central sanctuary and the ark of the covenant were located (see Jos 18:1; Jdg 21:19).

1:4 *sacrifice.* Here refers to a sacrifice that was combined with a festive meal signifying fellowship and communion with the Lord and grateful acknowledgment of his mercies (see Lev 7:11-18; Dt 12:7,17-18).

1:5 *the LORD had closed her womb.* The Lord gives and withholds children (see Ge 18:10; 29:31; 30:2,22).

1:6 *her rival.* See note on Ge 16:4.

1:9 *temple.* Here and in 3:3 the central sanctuary, the tabernacle (see NIV text note), is referred to as "the LORD's temple." It is also called "the house of the LORD" (v. 7; 3:15), "the Tent of Meeting" (2:22) and "my dwelling" (2:32). The references to the tabernacle as a "house" and a "temple," as well as those to sleeping quarters and doors (3:2,15), give the impression that at this time the tabernacle was part of a larger, more permanent building complex to which the term "temple" could legitimately be applied (cf. Jer 7:12,14; 26:6).

1:11 *vow.* See Ge 28:20-22; Nu 21:2; Ps 50:14; 76:11; 116:14,18; 132:2-5; Pr 20:25; 31:2. Regulations for the making of vows by women are found in Nu 30. *remember.* To remember is more than simply to recall that Hannah existed. It is to go into action in her behalf (see v. 19; see also note on Ge 8:1). *all the days of his life.* In contrast to the normal period of service for Levites, which was from age 25 to 50 (see Nu 8:23-26), Hannah voluntarily vows for her son that which God had required of Samson (Jdg 13:5). Long hair was a symbol of dedication to the service of the Lord and was one of the characteristics of the Nazirite vow (see Nu 6:1-21). The vow was normally taken for a limited time rather than for life.

1:13 *drunk.* Eli's mistake suggests that in those days it was not uncommon for drunken people to enter the sanctuary. Further evidence of the religious and moral deterioration of the time is found in the stories of Jdg 17-21.

15"Not so, my lord," Hannah replied, "I am a woman who is deeply troubled.[y] I have not been drinking wine or beer; I was pouring[z] out my soul to the LORD. 16Do not take your servant for a wicked woman; I have been praying here out of my great anguish and grief."[a]

17Eli answered, "Go in peace,[b] and may the God of Israel grant you what you have asked of him.[c]"

18She said, "May your servant find favor in your eyes.[d]" Then she went her way and ate something, and her face was no longer downcast.[e]

19Early the next morning they arose and worshiped before the LORD and then went back to their home at Ramah.[f] Elkanah lay with Hannah his wife, and the LORD remembered[g] her. 20So in the course of time Hannah conceived and gave birth to a son.[h] She named[i] him Samuel,[c][j] saying, "Because I asked the LORD for him."

Hannah Dedicates Samuel

21When the man Elkanah went up with all his family to offer the annual[k] sacrifice to the LORD and to fulfill his vow,[l] 22Hannah did not go. She said to her husband, "After the boy is weaned, I will take him and present[m] him before the LORD, and he will live there always."

23"Do what seems best to you," Elkanah her husband told her. "Stay here until you have weaned him; only may the LORD make good[n] his[d] word." So the woman stayed at home and nursed her son until she had weaned[o] him.

24After he was weaned, she took the boy with her, young as he was, along with a three-year-old bull,[e][p] an ephah[f] of flour and a skin of wine, and brought him to the house of the LORD at Shiloh. 25When they had slaughtered the bull, they brought the boy to Eli, 26and she said to him, "As surely as you live, my lord, I am the woman who stood here beside you praying to the LORD. 27I prayed[q] for this child, and the LORD has granted me what I asked of him. 28So now I give him to the LORD. For his whole life[r] he will be given over to the LORD." And he worshiped the LORD there.

Hannah's Prayer

2 Then Hannah prayed and said:[s]

"My heart rejoices[t] in the LORD;
    in the LORD my horn[g][u] is lifted high.
My mouth boasts[v] over my enemies,[w]
    for I delight in your deliverance.

2"There is no one holy[h][x] like[y] the
        LORD;
    there is no one besides you;
    there is no Rock[z] like our God.

3"Do not keep talking so proudly
    or let your mouth speak such
        arrogance,[a]
for the LORD is a God who knows,[b]
    and by him deeds[c] are weighed.[d]

Cross references

1:15 [y]2Ki 4:27 [z]Ps 42:4; 62:8; La 2:19
1:16 [a]Ps 55:2
1:17 [b]Nu 6:26; 1Sa 20:42; 2Ki 5:19; S Ac 15:33 [c]S Ge 25:21; Ps 20:3-5
1:18 [d]S Ge 18:3; Ru 2:13 [e]Ro 15:13
1:19 [f]S Jos 18:25 [g]S Ge 8:1; S 29:31
1:20 [h]S Ge 17:19; S 29:32; S 30:6 [i]Ex 2:10; Mt 1:21 [j]1Sa 7:5; 12:23; 1Ch 6:27; Jer 15:1; Heb 11:32
1:21 [k]S ver 3 [l]S Ge 28:20; Nu 30:2; Dt 12:11
1:22 [m]Ex 13:2; Lk 2:22
1:23 [n]S Ge 25:21 [o]Ge 21:8
1:24 [p]Nu 15:8-10
1:27 [q]1Sa 2:20; Ps 66:19-20
1:28 [r]S Jdg 13:7
2:1 [s]Lk 1:46-55 [t]Ps 13:5; 33:21; Zec 10:7 [u]Ps 18:2; 89:17, 24; 148:14 [v]Ps 6:8 [w]S Nu 10:35; Ps 6:10
2:2 [x]S Ex 15:11; S Lev 11:44 [y]S Ex 8:10; Isa 40:25; 46:5 [z]S Ge 49:24; S Ex 33:22; Dt 32:37; 2Sa 22:2,32; 23:3; Ps 31:3; 71:3
2:3 [a]Ps 17:10; 31:18; 73:8; 75:4; 94:4 [b]S Jos 22:22 [c]1Sa 16:7;
1Ki 8:39; 1Ch 28:9; 2Ch 6:30; Pr 15:11; Jer 11:20; 17:10 [d]Pr 16:2; 24:11-12

[c]20 Samuel sounds like the Hebrew for heard of God.
[d]23 Masoretic Text; Dead Sea Scrolls, Septuagint and Syriac your   [e]24 Dead Sea Scrolls, Septuagint and Syriac; Masoretic Text with three bulls   [f]24 That is, probably about 3/5 bushel (about 22 liters)   [g]1 Horn here symbolizes strength; also in verse 10.   [h]2 Or no Holy One

---

1:16 *wicked.* See note on Dt 13:13.
1:20 *Samuel.* See NIV text note.
1:21 *annual sacrifice.* See notes on vv. 3–4. *his vow.* Making vows to God was a common feature of OT piety, usually involving thank offerings and praise (see Lev 7:16; Ps 50:14; 56:12; 66:13–15; 116:17–18; Isa 19:21). Elkanah no doubt annually made vows to the Lord as he prayed for God's blessing on his crops and flocks, and fulfilled those vows at the Feast of Tabernacles (see note on v. 3).
1:22 *weaned.* It was customary in the East to nurse children for three years or longer (in the Apocrypha see 2 Maccabees 7:27) since there was no way to keep milk sweet.
1:23 *his word.* No previous word from God is mentioned, unless this refers to the pronouncement of Eli in v. 17. The Dead Sea Scrolls, Septuagint (the Greek translation of the OT) and Syriac version (see NIV text note) resolve this problem by reading "your word."
1:26 *As surely as you live.* A customary way of emphasizing the truthfulness of one's words.
2:1 *prayed.* Hannah's prayer is a song of praise and thanksgiving to God (see Ps 72:20, where the psalms of David are designated "prayers"). This song has sometimes been termed the "Magnificat of the OT" because it is so similar to the Magnificat of the NT (Mary's song, Lk 1:46–55). It also

has certain resemblances to the "Benedictus" (the song of Zechariah, Lk 1:67–79). Hannah's song of praise finds many echoes in David's song near the end of the book (2Sa 22). These two songs frame the main narrative, and their themes highlight the ways of God that the narrative relates—they contain the theology of the book in the form of praise. Hannah speaks prophetically at a time when Israel is about to enter an important new period of her history with the establishment of kingship through her son, Samuel. *rejoices in the LORD.* The supreme source of Hannah's joy is not in the child, but in the God who has answered her prayer. *my horn is lifted high.* See NIV text note; cf. Dt 33:17; Ps 75:5,10; 92:10; 112:9; Lk 1:69. To have one's horn lifted up by God is to be delivered from disgrace to a position of honor and strength.
2:2 *no one besides you.* See 2Sa 7:22; Dt 4:39; Isa 45:6. *Rock.* A metaphor to depict the strength and stability of the God of Israel as the unfailing source of security for his people (see 2Sa 22:32; Dt 32:4,31; Ps 18:31; Isa 30:29; 44:8).
2:3 *so proudly . . . such arrogance.* After the manner of Peninnah and others in the narratives of 1,2 Samuel—Eli's sons, the Philistines, Saul, Nabal, Goliath, Absalom, Shimei and Sheba). *the LORD is a God who knows.* See 16:7; 1Ki 8:39; Ps 139:1–6.

4"The bows of the warriors are broken, *e*
  but those who stumbled are armed
    with strength.*f*
5Those who were full hire themselves
    out for food,
  but those who were hungry*g* hunger
    no more.
She who was barren*h* has borne seven
    children,
  but she who has had many sons pines
    away.

6"The LORD brings death and makes
    alive;*i*
  he brings down to the grave*i* and
    raises up.*j*
7The LORD sends poverty and wealth;*k*
  he humbles and he exalts.*l*
8He raises*m* the poor*n* from the dust*o*
  and lifts the needy*p* from the ash
    heap;
he seats them with princes
  and has them inherit a throne of
    honor.*q*

"For the foundations*r* of the earth are
    the LORD'S;
  upon them he has set the world.
9He will guard the feet*s* of his saints,*t*
  but the wicked will be silenced in
    darkness.*u*

"It is not by strength*v* that one prevails;

10 those who oppose the LORD will be
      shattered.*w*
He will thunder*x* against them from
      heaven;
  the LORD will judge*y* the ends of the
      earth.

"He will give strength*z* to his king
  and exalt the horn*a* of his anointed."

11Then Elkanah went home to Ramah,*b*
but the boy ministered*c* before the LORD
under Eli the priest.

Eli's Wicked Sons

12Eli's sons were wicked men; they had
no regard*d* for the LORD. 13Now it was the
practice*e* of the priests with the people
that whenever anyone offered a sacrifice
and while the meat*f* was being boiled, the
servant of the priest would come with a
three-pronged fork in his hand. 14He
would plunge it into the pan or kettle or
caldron or pot, and the priest would take
for himself whatever the fork brought up.
This is how they treated all the Israelites
who came to Shiloh. 15But even before the

2:4 *e*2Sa 1:27;
Ps 37:15; 46:9;
76:3 *f*Job 17:9;
Isa 40:31; 41:1;
52:1; 57:10
2:5 *g*Lk 1:53
*h*Ps 113:9;
Isa 54:1; Jer 15:9
2:6 *i*Dt 32:39
*j*Isa 26:19;
Eze 37:3,12
2:7 *k*S Dt 8:18
*l*Job 5:11; 40:12;
Ps 75:7; Isa 2:12;
13:11; 22:19;
Da 4:37
2:8 *m*Ps 113:7-8
*n*Jas 2:5
*o*1Ki 16:2
*p*Ps 72:12;
107:41; 145:14;
146:8;
S Mt 23:12
*q*2Sa 7:8;
Job 36:7;
Isa 22:23;
Eze 21:26
*r*Job 15:7; 38:4;
Ps 104:5; Pr 8:29;
Isa 40:12;
Jer 10:12
2:9 *s*Ps 91:12;
121:3; Pr 3:26
*t*Pr 2:8
*u*Job 10:22;
Isa 5:30; 8:22;
59:9; 60:2;
Jer 13:16;
Am 5:18,20;
Zep 1:14-15;
Mt 8:12
*v*1Sa 17:47;
Ps 33:16-17;
Zec 4:6

Job 37:4,5; 38:1; Ps 18:13; 29:3; Isa 66:6 *y*Ps 96:13; 98:9;
Mt 25:31-32 *z*Ps 18:1; 21:1; 59:16 *a*S Dt 33:17; Ps 89:24;
2:10 *w*S Ex 15:6   S Lk 1:69 **2:11** *b*S Jos 18:25 *c*ver 18; S Nu 16:9; 1Sa 3:1
*x*S Ex 19:16;   **2:12** *d*Jer 2:8; 9:6 **2:13** *e*Dt 18:3 *f*Lev 7:35-36
1Sa 7:10; 12:17;
2Sa 22:14;

16 Hebrew *Sheol*

2:4–5 In a series of examples derived from everyday life
Hannah shows that God often works contrary to natural
expectations and brings about surprising reversals—seen frequently in the stories that follow.
2:5 *seven children.* See note on Ru 4:15.
2:6–8 Hannah declares that life and death, prosperity and
adversity, are determined by the sovereign power of
God—another theme richly illustrated in the following narrative (see Dt 32:39; 1Ki 17:20–24; 2Ki 4:32–35; Jn 5:21;
11:41–44).
2:6 *grave.* See NIV text note; see also note on Ge 37:35.
2:8 *foundations of the earth.* A common figure in the OT
for the solid base on which the earth (the dry land on which
man lives, not planet earth; Ge 1:10) is founded. The phrase
does not teach a particular theory of the structure of the
universe (see Job 9:6; 38:6; Ps 75:3; 104:5; Zec 12:1).
2:9 *guard the feet.* Travel in ancient Israel was for the most
part by foot over trails that were often rocky and dangerous
(see Ps 91:11–12; 121:3). *saints.* People who are faithful to
the Lord. The Hebrew root underlying this word is used of
both God and his people in 2Sa 22:26 (see also Ps 18:25) to
characterize the nature of their mutual relationship. The
word is also translated "godly" (Ps 12:1; 32:6) and "faithful
ones" (Pr 2:8).
2:10 *judge.* Impose his righteous rule upon (see Ps 96:13;
98:9). *ends of the earth.* All nations and peoples (see Dt
33:17; Isa 45:22). *his king.* Hannah's prayer is here prophetic, anticipating the establishment of kingship in Israel and the
initial realization of the Messianic ideal in David (Lk 1:69).
Ultimately her expectation finds fulfillment in Christ and his
complete triumph over the enemies of God. *horn.* See note
on v. 1. *anointed.* The first reference in the Bible to the
Lord's anointed—i.e., his anointed king. (Priests were also

anointed for God's service; see Ex 28:41; Lev 4:3.) The
word is often synonymous with "king" (as here) and provides part of the vocabulary basis for the Messianic idea in
the Bible. "Anointed" and "Messiah" are the translation and
transliteration respectively of the same Hebrew word. The
Greek translation of this Hebrew term is *Christos,* from
which comes the English word "Christ" (see NIV text note
on Mt 1:17). A king (coming from the tribe of Judah) is first
prophesied by Jacob (Ge 49:10); kingship is further anticipated in the oracles of Balaam in Nu 24:7,17. Also Dt
17:14–20 looks forward to the time when the Lord will
place a king of his choice over his people after they enter the
promised land. 1,2 Samuel shows how this expectation of
the theocratic king is realized in the person of David. Hannah's prophetic anticipation of a king at the time of the
dedication of her son Samuel, who was to be God's agent for
establishing kingship in Israel, is entirely appropriate.
2:11 *ministered.* Performed such services as a boy might
render while assisting the high priest. *before the LORD.* At the
"house of the LORD" (1:24).
2:12 *wicked.* See note on Dt 13:13. *had no regard for.* Lit.
"did not know." In OT usage, to "know" the Lord is not just
intellectual or theoretical recognition. To know the Lord is to
enter into fellowship with him and acknowledge his claims
on one's life. The term often has a covenantal connotation
(see Jer 31:34; Hos 13:4, "acknowledge").
2:13–16 Apparently vv. 13–14 describe the practice that
had come to be accepted for determining the priests' portion
of the fellowship offerings (Lev 7:31–36; 10:14–15; Dt
18:1–5)—a tradition presumably based on the assumption
that a random thrust of the fork would providentially determine a fair portion. Verses 15–16 then describe how Eli's
sons arrogantly violated that custom and the law.

fat was burned, the servant of the priest
would come and say to the man who was
sacrificing, "Give the priest some meat to
roast; he won't accept boiled meat from
you, but only raw."
16 If the man said to him, "Let the fat[g]
be burned up first, and then take whatever
you want," the servant would then answer, "No, hand it over now; if you don't,
I'll take it by force."
17 This sin of the young men was very
great in the LORD's sight, for they[j] were
treating the LORD's offering with contempt.[h]
18 But Samuel was ministering[i] before
the LORD—a boy wearing a linen ephod.[j]
19 Each year his mother made him a little
robe and took it to him when she went up
with her husband to offer the annual[k] sacrifice. 20 Eli would bless Elkanah and his
wife, saying, "May the LORD give you children by this woman to take the place of
the one she prayed[l] for and gave to the
LORD." Then they would go home. 21 And
the LORD was gracious to Hannah;[m] she
conceived and gave birth to three sons and
two daughters. Meanwhile, the boy Samuel grew[n] up in the presence of the LORD.
22 Now Eli, who was very old, heard
about everything[o] his sons were doing to
all Israel and how they slept with the
women[p] who served at the entrance to
the Tent of Meeting. 23 So he said to them,
"Why do you do such things? I hear from
all the people about these wicked deeds of
yours. 24 No, my sons; it is not a good report that I hear spreading among the
LORD's people. 25 If a man sins against another man, God[k] may mediate for him;
but if a man sins against the LORD, who
will[q] intercede[r] for him?" His sons, however, did not listen to their father's rebuke,
for it was the LORD's will to put them to
death.
26 And the boy Samuel continued to
grow[s] in stature and in favor with the
LORD and with men.[t]

Prophecy Against the House of Eli

27 Now a man of God[u] came to Eli and
said to him, "This is what the LORD says:
'Did I not clearly reveal myself to your father's house when they were in Egypt under Pharaoh? 28 I chose[v] your father out of
all the tribes of Israel to be my priest, to go
up to my altar, to burn incense,[w] and to
wear an ephod[x] in my presence. I also
gave your father's house all the offerings[y]
made with fire by the Israelites. 29 Why do
you[l] scorn my sacrifice and offering[z] that
I prescribed for my dwelling?[a] Why do
you honor your sons more than me by fat-

2:16 [g]Lev 3:3, 14-16; 7:29-34 **2:17** [h]ver 22,29; S Nu 14:11; Jer 7:21; Eze 22:26; Mal 2:7-9 **2:18** [i]S ver 11 [j]ver 28; 1Sa 22:18; 23:9; 2Sa 6:14; 1Ch 15:27 **2:19** [k]S 1Sa 1:3 **2:20** [l]S 1Sa 1:27 **2:21** [m]Ge 21:1 [n]S Jdg 13:24; Lk 1:80; 2:40 **2:22** [o]S ver 17 [p]S Ex 38:8 **2:25** [q]Ex 4:21; Jos 11:20 [r]S Ex 32:10; S Nu 11:2; 1Sa 3:14; 1Ki 13:6; Job 9:33; Ps 106:30; Isa 1:18; 22:14; Jer 15:1; Heb 10:26 **2:26** [s]S Jdg 13:24; Lk 2:52 [t]Pr 3:4 **2:27** [u]S Dt 33:1; S Jdg 13:6 **2:28** [v]S Ex 28:1 [w]S Ex 30:7 [x]1Sa 22:18; 23:6, 9; 30:7 [y]Lev 7:35-36 **2:29** [z]ver 12-17 [a]S Dt 12:5

j*17* Or *men* k*25* Or *the judges* l*29* The Hebrew is plural.

2:15 *before the fat was burned.* On the altar as the Lord's portion, which he was to receive first (see Lev 3:16; 4:10, 26,31,35; 7:28,30–31; 17:6). *roast.* Boiling is the only form of cooking specified in the law for the priests' portion (Nu 6:19–20). Roasting this portion is nowhere expressly forbidden in the law, but it is specified only for the Passover lamb (Ex 12:8–9; Dt 16:7). The present passage seems to imply that for the priests to roast their portion of the sacrifices was unlawful.

2:16 *by force.* Presenting the priests' portion was to be a voluntary act on the part of the worshipers (see Lev 7:28–36; Dt 18:3).

2:18 *But Samuel.* Between 2:11 and 4:1 the author presents a series of sharp contrasts between Samuel and Eli's sons. *linen ephod.* A priestly garment worn by those who served before the Lord at his sanctuary (see 22:18; 2Sa 6:14). It was a close-fitting, sleeveless pullover, usually of hip length, and is to be distinguished from the special ephod worn by the high priest (see note on v. 28; cf. Ex 39:1–26).

2:19 *little robe.* A sleeveless garment reaching to the knees, worn over the undergarment and under the ephod (see 15:27; 18:4). *annual sacrifice.* See note on 1:3.

2:22 *slept with the women who served.* See Ex 38:8. There is no further reference to such women in the OT. Perhaps these women performed various menial tasks, but certainly their service is not to be confused with that of the Levites, which is prescribed in the Pentateuch (Nu 1:50; 3:6–8; 8:15; 16:9; 18:2–3). The immoral acts of Eli's sons are reminiscent of the religious prostitution (fertility rites) at the Canaanite sanctuaries (see 1Ki 14:24; 15:12; 22:46)—acts that were an abomination to the Lord and a desecration of his house (Dt 23:17–18).

2:23 *he said to them.* Eli rebuked his sons but did not remove them from office. God would do that.

2:25 *God.* See NIV text note. Eli's argument is that when someone commits an offense against another man, there is recourse to a third party to decide the issue (whether this be understood as God or as God's representatives, the judges; see NIV text notes on Ex 22:8–9); but when the offense is against the Lord, there is no recourse, for God is both the one wronged and the judge. *the LORD's will to put them to death.* This comment by the author of the narrative is not intended to excuse Eli's sons, but to indicate that Eli's warning was much too late. Eli's sons had persisted in their evil ways for so long that God's judgment on them was determined (v. 34; see Jos 11:20).

2:26 *grow in stature and in favor with the LORD and with men.* Cf. Luke's description of Jesus (Lk 2:52).

2:27 *man of God.* Often a designation for a prophet (see 9:6,10; Dt 33:1; Jos 14:6; 1Ki 13:1,6–8; 17:18,24; 2Ki 4:7). *father's house.* The descendants of Aaron.

2:28 *to be my priest.* Three tasks of the priests are mentioned: 1. *to go up to my altar.* To perform the sacrificial rites at the altar of burnt offering in the courtyard of the tabernacle. 2. *to burn incense.* At the altar of incense in the Holy Place (Ex 30:1–10). 3. *to wear an ephod.* See note on v. 18. It would appear that the reference here is to the special ephod of the high priest (see Ex 28:4–13). The breastplate containing the Urim and Thummim was attached to the ephod of the high priest. The Urim and Thummim were a divinely ordained means of communication with God, placed in the custody of the high priest (see Ex 28:30 and note; see also 1Sa 23:9–12; 30:7–8).

tening yourselves on the choice parts of
every offering made by my people Israel?’
30“Therefore the LORD, the God of Israel, declares: ‘I promised that your house
and your father’s house would minister before me forever.[b]’ But now the LORD declares: ‘Far be it from me! Those who hon-
or me I will honor,[c] but those who despise[d] me will be disdained.[e] 31The time
is coming when I will cut short your
strength and the strength of your father’s
house, so that there will not be an old man
in your family line[f] 32and you will see distress[g] in my dwelling. Although good will
be done to Israel, in your family line there
will never be an old man.[h] 33Every one of
you that I do not cut off from my altar will
be spared only to blind your eyes with
tears and to grieve your heart, and all your
descendants[i] will die in the prime of life.
34“ ‘And what happens to your two
sons, Hophni and Phinehas, will be a sign[j]
to you—they will both die[k] on the same
day.[l] 35I will raise up for myself a faithful
priest,[m] who will do according to what is
in my heart and mind. I will firmly establish his house, and he will minister before
my anointed[n] one always. 36Then everyone left in your family line will come and
bow down before him for a piece of silver
and a crust of bread and plead,[o] “Appoint
me to some priestly office so I can have
food to eat.[p]” ’ ”

The LORD Calls Samuel

3 The boy Samuel ministered[q] before
the LORD under Eli. In those days the
word of the LORD was rare;[r] there were
not many visions.[s]
2One night Eli, whose eyes[t] were becoming so weak that he could barely see,[u]
was lying down in his usual place. 3The
lamp[v] of God had not yet gone out, and
Samuel was lying down in the temple[m][w] of
the LORD, where the ark[x] of God was.
4Then the LORD called Samuel.
Samuel answered, “Here I am.[y]” 5And
he ran to Eli and said, “Here I am; you
called me.”
But Eli said, “I did not call; go back and
lie down.” So he went and lay down.
6Again the LORD called, “Samuel!” And
Samuel got up and went to Eli and said,
“Here I am; you called me.”
“My son,” Eli said, “I did not call; go
back and lie down.”
7Now Samuel did not yet know[z] the

2:30 [b]S Ex 29:9 [c]Ps 50:23; 91:15; Pr 8:17 [d]Isa 53:3; Na 3:6; Mal 2:9 [e]Jer 18:10
2:31 [f]1Sa 4:11-18; 22:16
2:32 [g]1Sa 4:3; 22:17-20; Jer 7:12,14 [h]1Ki 2:26-27
2:33 [i]Jer 29:32; Mal 2:12
2:34 [j]S Dt 13:2 [k]1Sa 4:11 [l]1Ki 13:3
2:35 [m]2Sa 8:17; 20:25; 1Ki 1:8, 32; 2:35; 4:4; 1Ch 16:39; 29:22; Eze 44:15-16 [n]1Sa 9:16; 10:1; 16:13; 2Sa 2:4; 12:7; 23:1; 1Ki 1:34; Ps 89:20
2:36 [o]Eze 44:10-14 [p]1Sa 3:12; 1Ki 2:27
3:1 [q]S 1Sa 2:11 [r]Ps 74:9; La 2:9; Eze 7:26 [s]Am 8:11
3:2 [t]1Sa 4:15 [u]S Ge 27:1
3:3 [v]Ex 25:31-38; Lev 24:1-4 [w]1Sa 1:9 [x]Dt 10:1-5; 1Ki 6:19; 8:1
3:4 [y]S Ge 22:1; S Ex 3:4
3:7 [z]1Sa 2:12

[m]*3* That is, tabernacle

2:30 *I promised.* See Ex 29:9; Lev 8–9; Nu 16–17; 25:13. *Far be it from me!* This is not to say that the promise of the priesthood to Aaron's house has been annulled, but rather that Eli and his house are to be excluded from participation in this privilege because of their sin. *Those who honor me I will honor.* See v. 29. Spiritual privileges bring responsibilities and obligations; they are not to be treated as irrevocable rights (see 2Sa 22:26–27).
2:31 *strength . . . strength.* Lit. "arm . . . arm," symbolic of strength. Eli's "arm" and that of his priestly family will be cut off (contrast David, 2Sa 22:35). *not be an old man in your family line.* A prediction of the decimation of Eli's priestly family in the death of his sons (4:11), in the massacre of his descendants by Saul at Nob (22:18–19) and in the removal of Abiathar from his priestly office (1Ki 2:26–27).
2:32 *distress in my dwelling.* Including the capture of the ark by the Philistines (4:1–10), the destruction of Shiloh (Jer 7:14) and the relocation of the tabernacle to Nob (21:1–6; see note on 21:1).
2:33 A reference apparently to Abiathar, who was expelled from office by Solomon (see 1Ki 2:26–27) after an unsuccessful attempt to make Adonijah king as the successor to David.
2:34 *a sign to you.* The death of Hophni and Phinehas (4:11) will confirm the longer-term predictions. Such confirmation of a prophetic word was not uncommon (see 10:7–9; 1Ki 13:3; Jer 28:15–17; Lk 1:18–20).
2:35 *I will raise up for myself a faithful priest.* Initially fulfilled in the person of Zadok, who served as a priest during the time of David (see 2Sa 8:17; 15:24,35; 20:25) and who eventually replaced Abiathar as high priest in the time of Solomon (see 1Ki 2:35; 1Ch 29:22). *firmly establish his house.* Lit. "build for him a faithful house"; the faithful priest will be given a "faithful" (i.e., enduring) priestly family. See the similar word spoken concerning David (25:28, "lasting dynasty"; see also 2Sa 7:16; 1Ki 11:38). The line of Zadok was continued by his son Azariah (see 1Ki 4:1) and was still on the scene at the time of the return from the exile (see 1Ch 6:14–15; Ezr 3:2). It continued in intertestamental times until Antiochus IV Epiphanes (175–164 B.C.) sold the priesthood to Menelaus (in the Apocrypha see 2 Maccabees 4:23–50), who was not of the priestly line. *my anointed one.* David and his successors (see note on v. 10).
3:1 *boy Samuel.* See 2:11,18. Samuel is now no longer a little child (see 2:21,26). The Jewish historian Josephus places his age at 12 years; he may have been older. *the word of the LORD was rare.* See Pr 29:18; Am 8:11. During the entire period of the judges, apart from the prophet of 2:27–36, we are told of only two prophets (Jdg 4:4; 6:8) and of five revelations (Jdg 2:1–3; 6:11–23; 7:2–11; 10:11–14; 13:3–21). Possibly 2Ch 15:3 also refers to this period. *visions.* Cf. Ge 15:1.
3:3 *The lamp of God had not yet gone out.* The reference is to the golden lampstand, which stood opposite the table of the bread of the Presence (Ex 25:31–40) in the Holy Place. It was still night, but the early morning hours were approaching when the flame grew dim or went out (see Ex 27:20–21; 30:7–8; Lev 24:3–4; 2Ch 13:11; Pr 31:18). For the lamp to be permitted to go out before morning was a violation of the Pentateuchal regulations. *temple.* See NIV text note and note on 1:9.
3:5 *Eli said.* Eli's failure to recognize at once that the Lord had called Samuel may be indicative of his own unfamiliarity with the Lord.
3:7 *did not yet know the LORD.* In the sense of having a direct experience of him (see Ex 1:8), such as receiving a revelation from God (see the last half of the verse).

LORD: The word[a] of the LORD had not yet been revealed[b] to him.

⁸The LORD called Samuel a third time, and Samuel got up and went to Eli and said, "Here I am; you called me."

Then Eli realized that the LORD was calling the boy. ⁹So Eli told Samuel, "Go and lie down, and if he calls you, say, 'Speak, LORD, for your servant is listening.'" So Samuel went and lay down in his place.

¹⁰The LORD came and stood there, calling as at the other times, "Samuel! Samuel![c]"

Then Samuel said, "Speak, for your servant is listening."

¹¹And the LORD said to Samuel: "See, I am about to do something in Israel that will make the ears of everyone who hears of it tingle.[d] ¹²At that time I will carry out against Eli everything[e] I spoke against his family—from beginning to end. ¹³For I told him that I would judge his family forever because of the sin he knew about; his sons made themselves contemptible,[n] and he failed to restrain[f] them. ¹⁴Therefore, I swore to the house of Eli, 'The guilt of Eli's house will never be atoned[g] for by sacrifice or offering.'"

¹⁵Samuel lay down until morning and then opened the doors of the house of the LORD. He was afraid to tell Eli the vision, ¹⁶but Eli called him and said, "Samuel, my son."

Samuel answered, "Here I am."

¹⁷"What was it he said to you?" Eli asked. "Do not hide[h] it from me. May God deal with you, be it ever so severely,[i] if you hide from me anything he told you." ¹⁸So Samuel told him everything, hiding nothing from him. Then Eli said, "He is the LORD; let him do what is good in his eyes."[j]

¹⁹The LORD was with[k] Samuel as he grew[l] up, and he let none[m] of his words fall to the ground. ²⁰And all Israel from Dan to Beersheba[n] recognized that Samuel was attested as a prophet of the LORD.[o] ²¹The LORD continued to appear at Shiloh, and there he revealed[p] himself to Samuel through his word.

4 And Samuel's word came to all Israel.

The Philistines Capture the Ark

Now the Israelites went out to fight against the Philistines. The Israelites camped at Ebenezer,[q] and the Philistines at Aphek.[r] ²The Philistines deployed their forces to meet Israel, and as the battle spread, Israel was defeated by the Philistines, who killed about four thousand of them on the battlefield. ³When the soldiers returned to camp, the elders of Israel asked, "Why[s] did the LORD bring defeat upon us today before the Philistines? Let us bring the ark[t] of the LORD's covenant from Shiloh,[u] so that it[o] may go with us[v] and save us from the hand of our enemies."

⁴So the people sent men to Shiloh, and they brought back the ark of the covenant

---

3:7 [a]Jer 1:2
[b]S Nu 12:6;
Am 3:7
3:10 [c]Ex 3:4
3:11 [d]2Ki 21:12;
Job 15:21;
Jer 19:3
3:12 [e]S 1Sa 2:27-36
3:13 [f]1Ki 1:6
3:14 [g]S 1Sa 2:25
3:17 [h]1Ki 22:14;
Jer 23:28; 38:14;
42:4

[i]S Ru 1:17
3:18 [j]S Jdg 10:15
3:19
[k]S Ge 21:22;
S Nu 14:43
[l]S Jdg 13:24
[m]1Sa 9:6
3:20 [n]S Jdg 20:1
[o]S Dt 18:22;
Eze 33:33
3:21 [p]S Nu 12:6
4:1 [q]1Sa 5:1;
7:12 [r]Jos 12:18;
1Sa 29:1;
1Ki 20:26
4:3 [s]Jos 7:7
[t]S Jos 6:7
[u]S Jos 18:1;
S 1Sa 2:32
[v]2Ch 13:8

---

[n]13 Masoretic Text; an ancient Hebrew scribal tradition and Septuagint *sons blasphemed God*   [o]3 Or *he*

3:11–14 The Lord's first revelation to Samuel repeats the message Eli had already received from the "man of God" (2:27–36), thus confirming the fact that the youth had indeed received a revelation from God.

3:13 *contemptible.* See NIV text note and Lev 24:14.

3:15 *doors of the house of the LORD.* See note on 1:9. The tabernacle itself did not have doors. This may refer to an enclosure in which it stood. *vision.* See note on vv. 11–14.

3:17 *May God deal with you, be it ever so severely.* A curse formula (see 14:44; 20:13; 25:22; 2Sa 3:9,35; 19:13; Ru 1:17; 1Ki 2:23; 2Ki 6:31), usually directed against the speaker but here used by Eli against Samuel if he conceals anything the Lord said (see also note on 14:24).

3:18 *let him do what is good in his eyes.* Eli bows before God, accepting the judgment as righteous (see Ex 34:5–7).

3:19 *he let none of his words fall to the ground.* Because none of Samuel's words proved unreliable, he was recognized as a prophet who spoke the word of the Lord (see vv. 20–21).

3:20 *Dan to Beersheba.* A conventional expression often used in Samuel, Kings and Chronicles to denote the entire land (Dan was located in the far north and Beersheba in the far south).

3:21 *at Shiloh.* But not after the events narrated in chs. 4–6 (see Jer 7:12–14; 26:6).

4:1 *Samuel's word came to all Israel.* Contrast 3:1. *Ebenezer.* Means "stone of help." The precise location is unknown, but it was probably a short distance (see v. 6) to the east of Aphek—not to be confused with the location of the stone named Ebenezer that was later erected by Samuel between Mizpah and Shen (see 7:12) to commemorate a victory over the Philistines. *Aphek.* A town about 12 miles northeast of the coastal city of Joppa. Philistine presence this far north suggests an attempt to spread their control over the Israelite tribes of central Canaan (see v. 9; Jdg 15:11).

4:3 *Why did the LORD bring defeat . . . ?* The elders understood that their defeat was more an indication of God's displeasure than it was of Philistine military might. Israel's pagan neighbors also believed that the outcome of battle was decided by the gods. *so that it may go with us and save us.* See NIV text note. In an attempt to secure the Lord's presence with them in the struggle against the Philistines, the elders sent for the ark of the covenant. They were correct in thinking there was a connection between God's presence with his people and the ark (cf. v. 4), and no doubt they remembered the presence of the ark at notable victories in Israel's past history (see Nu 10:33–36; Jos 3:3,11,14–17; 6:6,12–20). But they incorrectly believed that the Lord's presence with the ark was guaranteed, rather than being subject to his free decision. They reflect the pagan notion that the deity is identified with the symbol of his presence, and that God's favor could automatically be gained by manipulating the symbol.

4:4 *enthroned between the cherubim.* On each end of the

of the LORD Almighty, who is enthroned between the cherubim. *w* And Eli's two sons, Hophni and Phinehas, were there with the ark of the covenant of God.

⁵When the ark of the LORD's covenant came into the camp, all Israel raised such a great shout *x* that the ground shook. ⁶Hearing the uproar, the Philistines asked, "What's all this shouting in the Hebrew *y* camp?"

When they learned that the ark of the LORD had come into the camp, ⁷the Philistines were afraid. *z* "A god has come into the camp," they said. "We're in trouble! Nothing like this has happened before. ⁸Woe to us! Who will deliver us from the hand of these mighty gods? They are the gods who struck *a* the Egyptians with all kinds of plagues *b* in the desert. ⁹Be strong, Philistines! Be men, or you will be subject to the Hebrews, as they *c* have been to you. Be men, and fight!"

¹⁰So the Philistines fought, and the Israelites were defeated *d* and every man fled to his tent. The slaughter was very great; Israel lost thirty thousand foot soldiers. ¹¹The ark of God was captured, and Eli's two sons, Hophni and Phinehas, died. *e*

Death of Eli

¹²That same day a Benjamite *f* ran from the battle line and went to Shiloh, his clothes torn and dust *g* on his head. ¹³When he arrived, there was Eli *h* sitting on his chair by the side of the road, watching, because his heart feared for the ark of

God. When the man entered the town and told what had happened, the whole town sent up a cry.

¹⁴Eli heard the outcry and asked, "What is the meaning of this uproar?"

The man hurried over to Eli, ¹⁵who was ninety-eight years old and whose eyes *i* were set so that he could not see. ¹⁶He told Eli, "I have just come from the battle line; I fled from it this very day."

Eli asked, "What happened, my son?"

¹⁷The man who brought the news replied, "Israel fled before the Philistines, and the army has suffered heavy losses. Also your two sons, Hophni and Phinehas, are dead, *j* and the ark of God has been captured." *k*

¹⁸When he mentioned the ark of God, Eli fell backward off his chair by the side of the gate. His neck was broken and he died, for he was an old man and heavy. He had led *p l* Israel forty years. *m*

¹⁹His daughter-in-law, the wife of Phinehas, was pregnant and near the time of delivery. When she heard the news that the ark of God had been captured and that her father-in-law and her husband were dead, she went into labor and gave birth, but was overcome by her labor pains. ²⁰As she was dying, the women attending her said, "Don't despair; you have given birth to a son." But she did not respond or pay any attention.

²¹She named the boy Ichabod, *q n* say-

4:4 *w* S Ge 3:24; S Ex 25:22
4:5 *x* S Jos 6:5,10
4:6 *y* S Ge 14:13
4:7 *z* S Ex 15:14
4:8 *a* Ex 12:30; 1Sa 5:12
b Rev 11:6
4:9 *c* S Jdg 13:1
4:10 *d* S Dt 28:25
4:11 *e* Ps 78:64; Jer 7:12
4:12 *f* Eze 24:26; 33:21 *g* S Jos 7:6; S 2Sa 1:2
4:13 *h* ver 18

4:15 *i* S 1Sa 3:2
4:17 *j* 1Sa 22:18; Ps 78:64
k Ps 78:61
4:18 *l* S Jdg 2:16; S 16:31
m 1Sa 2:31
4:21 *n* S Ge 35:18

p 18 Traditionally *judged*   *q 21* *Ichabod* means *no glory.*

---

atonement cover of the ark of the covenant were golden cherubim with their wings spread upward over the ark (see Ex 25:17–22). In the space between these cherubim God's presence with his people was localized in a special way, so that the atonement cover of the ark came to be viewed as the throne of Israel's divine King (see 2Sa 6:2; Ps 80:1; 99:1). *Hophni and Phinehas.* These wicked priests (see 2:12) did not restrain the army from its improper use of the ark but actually accompanied the ark to the battlefield.
4:6 *Hebrew.* See note on Ge 14:13.
4:7 *A god has come into the camp.* The Philistines also identified the God of Israel with the symbol of his presence (see note on v. 3).
4:8 *mighty gods.* The Philistines could think only in polytheistic terms. *Egyptians . . . plagues.* See note on 6:6.
4:11 *The ark of God was captured.* This phrase or a variation of it occurs five times in the chapter (here, vv. 17,19,21–22) and is the focal point of the narrative. In this disastrous event, God's word in 3:11 finds a swift fulfillment. *Hophni and Phinehas, died.* The fulfillment of 2:34; 3:12.
4:12 *his clothes torn and dust on his head.* A sign of grief and sorrow, here marking the messenger as a bearer of bad news (see 2Sa 1:2; 13:19; 15:32).
4:13 *his heart feared for the ark of God.* Eli had sufficient spiritual sensitivity to be aware of the danger inherent in the sinful and presumptuous act of taking the ark of God into the battle. And he seems to have been even more concerned for

the ark than for his sons (see v. 18).
4:18 *he died.* The death of Eli marked the end of an era that had begun with the death of Joshua and the elders who served with him (see Jos 24:29,31). Incapable of restraining Israel or his sons from their wicked ways, and weakened and blinded by age, the old priest is an apt symbol of the flawed age now coming to its tragic close. He is also a striking contrast to the reign of David, which is the main focus of this narrative. *heavy.* A bit of information that not only helps explain why Eli's fall was fatal but also links his death with the judgment announced earlier: "Why do you honor your sons more than me by fattening yourselves . . .?" (2:29). *He had led Israel forty years.* See NIV text note. Eli is here included among the judges (see 2Sa 7:11; Jdg 2:16–19; Ru 1:1), who served as leaders of Israel in the period between the deaths of Joshua and of the elders who outlived him and the establishment of kingship. It is likely that Eli's leadership of 40 years overlapped that of Jephthah, Ibzan, Elon and Abdon (Jdg 12:7–14), as well as that of Samson (Jdg 13–16).
4:21 *The glory has departed.* The glory of Israel was Israel's God, not the ark, and loss of the ark did not mean that God had abandoned his people—God was not inseparably bound to the ark (see Jer 3:16–17). Yet the removal of the ark from Israel did signal estrangement in the relationship between God and his people, and it demonstrated the gravity of their error in thinking that in spite of their wickedness they had the power to coerce God into doing their will simply

ing, "The glory[o] has departed from Israel"—because of the capture of the ark of God and the deaths of her father-in-law and her husband. [22]She said, "The glory[p] has departed from Israel, for the ark of God has been captured."[q]

The Ark in Ashdod and Ekron

5 After the Philistines had captured the ark of God, they took it from Ebenezer[r] to Ashdod.[s] [2]Then they carried the ark into Dagon's temple and set it beside Dagon.[t] [3]When the people of Ashdod rose early the next day, there was Dagon, fallen[u] on his face on the ground before the ark of the LORD! They took Dagon and put him back in his place. [4]But the following morning when they rose, there was Dagon, fallen on his face on the ground before the ark of the LORD! His head and hands had been broken[v] off and were lying on the threshold; only his body remained. [5]That is why to this day neither the priests of Dagon nor any others who enter Dagon's temple at Ashdod step on the threshold.[w]

[6]The LORD's hand[x] was heavy upon the people of Ashdod and its vicinity; he brought devastation[y] upon them and afflicted them with tumors.[rz] [7]When the men of Ashdod saw what was happening, they said, "The ark of the god of Israel must not stay here with us, because his hand is heavy upon us and upon Dagon

our god." [8]So they called together all the rulers[a] of the Philistines and asked them, "What shall we do with the ark of the god of Israel?"

They answered, "Have the ark of the god of Israel moved to Gath.[b]" So they moved the ark of the God of Israel.

[9]But after they had moved it, the LORD's hand was against that city, throwing it into a great panic.[c] He afflicted the people of the city, both young and old, with an outbreak of tumors.[s] [10]So they sent the ark of God to Ekron.[d]

As the ark of God was entering Ekron, the people of Ekron cried out, "They have brought the ark of the god of Israel around to us to kill us and our people." [11]So they called together all the rulers[e] of the Philistines and said, "Send the ark of the god of Israel away; let it go back to its own place, or it[t] will kill us and our people." For death had filled the city with panic; God's hand was very heavy upon it. [12]Those who did not die[f] were afflicted with tumors, and the outcry of the city went up to heaven.

The Ark Returned to Israel

6 When the ark of the LORD had been in Philistine territory seven months, [2]the Philistines called for the priests and the di-

Cross references

4:21
[o]S Ex 24:16; Ps 106:20; Jer 2:11; Eze 1:28; 9:3; 10:18
4:22
[p]S Ex 24:16; Ps 78:61
[q]Jer 7:12
5:1 [r]S 1Sa 4:1
[s]S Jos 11:22; S 13:3
5:2 [t]S Jdg 16:23; Isa 2:18; 19:1; 46:1
5:3 [u]Isa 40:20; 41:7; 46:7; Jer 10:4
5:4 [v]Eze 6:6; Mic 1:7
5:5 [w]Zep 1:9
5:6 [x]S Ex 9:3; Ac 13:11
[y]2Sa 6:7; Ps 78:66
[z]S Ex 15:26; 1Sa 6:5
5:8 [a]S Jdg 16:18
[b]S Jos 11:22
5:9 [c]S Ex 14:24
5:10 [d]S Jos 13:3
5:11 [e]ver 8
5:12 [f]S 1Sa 4:8

[r]6 Hebrew; Septuagint and Vulgate *tumors. And rats appeared in their land, and death and destruction were throughout the city*   [s]9 Or *with tumors in the groin* (see Septuagint)   [t]11 Or *he*

---

because they possessed the ark.

5:1 *Ashdod.* One of the five major cities of the Philistines (Jos 13:3), it was located near the Mediterranean coast about 35 miles west of Jerusalem. See map, p. 330.

5:2 *Dagon.* In Canaanite mythology the son (or brother) of El and the father of Baal. He was the principal god of the Philistines and was worshiped in temples at Gaza (Jdg 16:21,23,26), Ashdod (here) and Beth Shan (31:10–12; 1Ch 10:10). Veneration of this deity was widespread in the ancient world, extending from Mesopotamia to the Aramean and Canaanite area and attested in non-Biblical sources dating from the late third millennium B.C. until Maccabee times (second century B.C.; in the Apocrypha see 1 Maccabees 10:83–85). The precise nature of the worship of Dagon is obscure. Some have considered Dagon to be a fish god, but more recent evidence suggests either a storm or grain god. His name is related to a Hebrew word for "grain."

5:3 *Dagon, fallen on his face.* The ark was placed next to the image of Dagon by the Philistines in order to demonstrate Dagon's superiority over the God of Israel, but the symbolism was reversed when Dagon was toppled to a position of homage before the ark of the Lord.

5:5 *this day.* The time of the writing of 1,2 Samuel (see Introduction: Literary Features, Authorship and Date). *step on the threshold.* Apparently the threshold was considered to possess supernatural power because of its contact with parts of the fallen image of Dagon. Zep 1:9 appears to be a reference to a more general and rather widespread pagan idea that the threshold was the dwelling place of spirits.

5:6 *The LORD's hand was heavy.* Dagon's broken hand lay on the ground (v. 4), but the Lord shows the reality and strength of his own hand by bringing a plague (see note on 6:4) on the people of Ashdod and the surrounding area (see vv. 9,11). God would not be manipulated by his own people (see note on 4:3), nor would he permit the Philistines to think that their victory over the Israelites and the capture of the ark demonstrated the superiority of their god over the God of Israel.

5:8 *rulers.* Of the five major cities of the Philistines (see 6:16; Jos 13:3; Jdg 3:3). *Have the ark of the god of Israel moved to Gath.* Evidently the leaders of the Philistines did not share the opinion of the Ashdodites that there was a direct connection between what had happened in Ashdod and the presence of the ark; they seem to have suspected that the sequence of events was merely coincidental (see 6:9). The removal of the ark to Gath put the matter to a test.

5:10 *Ekron.* The northernmost of the five major Philistine cities, located 11 miles northeast of Ashdod and close to Israelite territory (see map, p. 330).

5:11 *Send the ark of the god of Israel away.* After three successive towns had been struck by disease upon the arrival of the ark, there was little doubt in the people's minds that the power of the God of Israel was the cause of their distress.

6:2 *priests and . . . diviners.* The experts on religious matters (priests) and the discerners of hidden knowledge by interpretation of omens (diviners) were consulted (see Dt 18:10; Isa 2:6; Eze 21:21).

viners*g* and said, "What shall we do with the ark of the LORD? Tell us how we should send it back to its place."

³They answered, "If you return the ark of the god of Israel, do not send it away empty,*h* but by all means send a guilt offering*i* to him. Then you will be healed, and you will know why his hand*j* has not been lifted from you."

⁴The Philistines asked, "What guilt offering should we send to him?"

They replied, "Five gold tumors and five gold rats, according to the number*k* of the Philistine rulers, because the same plague*l* has struck both you and your rulers. ⁵Make models of the tumors*m* and of the rats that are destroying the country, and pay honor*n* to Israel's god. Perhaps he will lift his hand from you and your gods and your land. ⁶Why do you harden*o* your hearts as the Egyptians and Pharaoh did? When he*u* treated them harshly,*p* did they*q* not send the Israelites out so they could go on their way?

⁷"Now then, get a new cart*r* ready, with two cows that have calved and have never been yoked.*s* Hitch the cows to the cart, but take their calves away and pen them up. ⁸Take the ark of the LORD and put it on the cart, and in a chest beside it put the gold objects you are sending back to him as a guilt offering. Send it on its way, ⁹but keep watching it. If it goes up to its own territory, toward Beth Shemesh,*t* then the LORD has brought this great disaster on us. But if it does not, then we will know that it was not his hand that struck us and that it happened to us by chance."

¹⁰So they did this. They took two such cows and hitched them to the cart and penned up their calves. ¹¹They placed the ark of the LORD on the cart and along with it the chest containing the gold rats and the models of the tumors. ¹²Then the cows went straight up toward Beth Shemesh, keeping on the road and lowing all the way; they did not turn to the right or to the left. The rulers of the Philistines followed them as far as the border of Beth Shemesh.

¹³Now the people of Beth Shemesh were harvesting their wheat*u* in the valley, and when they looked up and saw the ark, they rejoiced at the sight. ¹⁴The cart came to the field of Joshua of Beth Shemesh, and there it stopped beside a large rock. The people chopped up the wood of the cart and sacrificed the cows as a burnt offering*v* to the LORD. ¹⁵The Levites*w* took down the ark of the LORD, together with the chest containing the gold objects, and placed them on the large rock.*x* On that day the people of Beth Shemesh*y* offered burnt offerings and made sacrifices to the LORD. ¹⁶The five rulers of the Philistines saw all this and then returned that same day to Ekron.

¹⁷These are the gold tumors the Philistines sent as a guilt offering to the LORD—one each*z* for Ashdod, Gaza, Ashkelon, Gath and Ekron. ¹⁸And the number of the gold rats was according to the number of Philistine towns belonging to the five rulers—the fortified towns with their country villages. The large rock, on which*v* they set the ark of the LORD, is a witness to this day in the field of Joshua of Beth Shemesh.

¹⁹But God struck down*a* some of the

6:2 *g*S Ex 7:11;
S Isa 44:25
6:3 *h*S Ex 22:29;
S 34:20
*i*S Lev 5:15 /ver 9
6:4 *k*S Jos 13:3
/2Sa 24:25
6:5 *m*S 1Sa 5:6
*n*S Jos 7:19;
Rev 14:7
6:6 *o*S Ex 4:21
*p*Ex 10:2
*q*S Ex 12:33
6:7 *r*2Sa 6:3;
1Ch 13:7
*s*S Nu 19:2
6:9 *t*S Jos 15:10;
21:16

6:13
*u*S Ge 30:14;
Ru 2:23;
1Sa 12:17
6:14 *v*1Sa 11:7;
2Sa 24:22;
1Ki 19:21
6:15 *w*Jos 3:3
*x*ver 18
*y*Jos 21:16
6:17 *z*S Jos 13:3
6:19 *a*2Sa 6:7

*u*6 That is, God   *v*18 A few Hebrew manuscripts (see also Septuagint); most Hebrew manuscripts *villages as far as Greater Abel, where*

6:3 *guilt offering.* The priests and diviners suggest returning the ark with a gift, signifying recognition of guilt in taking the ark from Israel and compensation for this violation of the Lord's honor (see v. 5). For the guilt offering in Israel see Lev 5:14–6:7.

6:4 *Five gold tumors.* Corresponding to the symptoms of the plague (see 5:6). *five gold rats.* The disease was accompanied by a plague of rats (v. 5). The Greek translation of the OT (the Septuagint) includes this information earlier in the narrative (see NIV text note on 5:6). It is likely that the rats were carriers of the disease, which may have been a form of the plague.

6:5 *Make models . . . and pay honor to Israel's god.* The golden models were an acknowledgment that the disease and the rats were a judgment from the hand of the God of Israel (see note on v. 3).

6:6 *the Egyptians and Pharaoh.* The plagues that God inflicted on the Egyptians at the time of the exodus made a lasting impression on the surrounding nations (see 4:8; Jos 2:10).

6:7 *have never been yoked.* Have not been trained to pull

a cart. *take their calves away.* Normally cows do not willingly leave their suckling calves.

6:9 *Beth Shemesh.* A town near the Philistine border, belonging to Judah (see Jos 15:10). Its name means "house (or sanctuary) of the sun(-god)."

6:13 *harvesting their wheat.* The time of wheat harvest is from mid-April until mid-June.

6:14–15 The termination of the trip at Beth Shemesh is just as much a revelation of the hand of God as the journey itself, because it was one of the towns of Judah assigned to the priests at the time of the conquest (see Jos 21:13–16).

6:17 *guilt offering.* See note on v. 3.

6:18 *witness.* A kind of monument to the event. *this day.* The time of the writing of 1,2 Samuel (see Introduction: Literary Features, Authorship and Date).

6:19 *seventy.* The additional 50,000 in most Hebrew manuscripts (see NIV text note) is apparently a copyist's mistake because it is added in an ungrammatical way (no conjunction). Furthermore, this small town could not have contained that many inhabitants. *looked into the ark.* The men of Beth Shemesh (Levites and priests among them) were

men of Beth Shemesh, putting seventy[w] of them to death because they had looked[b] into the ark of the LORD. The people mourned because of the heavy blow the LORD had dealt them, [20]and the men of Beth Shemesh asked, "Who can stand[c] in the presence of the LORD, this holy[d] God? To whom will the ark go up from here?"

[21]Then they sent messengers to the people of Kiriath Jearim,[e] saying, "The Philistines have returned the ark of the LORD. Come down and take it up to your place." [1]So the men of Kiriath Jearim came and took up the ark[f] of the LORD. They took it to Abinadab's[g] house on the hill and consecrated Eleazar his son to guard the ark of the LORD.

Samuel Subdues the Philistines at Mizpah

[2]It was a long time, twenty years in all, that the ark remained at Kiriath Jearim,[h] and all the people of Israel mourned and sought after the LORD.[i] [3]And Samuel said to the whole house of Israel, "If you are returning[j] to the LORD with all your hearts, then rid[k] yourselves of the foreign gods and the Ashtoreths[l] and commit[m] yourselves to the LORD and serve him only,[n] and he will deliver[o] you out of the hand of the Philistines." [4]So the Israelites put away their Baals and Ashtoreths, and served the LORD only.

[5]Then Samuel[p] said, "Assemble all Is-

rael at Mizpah[q] and I will intercede[r] with the LORD for you." [6]When they had assembled at Mizpah,[s] they drew water and poured[t] it out before the LORD. On that day they fasted and there they confessed, "We have sinned against the LORD." And Samuel was leader[x][u] of Israel at Mizpah.

[7]When the Philistines heard that Israel had assembled at Mizpah, the rulers of the Philistines came up to attack them. And when the Israelites heard of it, they were afraid[v] because of the Philistines. [8]They said to Samuel, "Do not stop crying[w] out to the LORD our God for us, that he may rescue us from the hand of the Philistines." [9]Then Samuel[x] took a suckling lamb and offered it up as a whole burnt offering to the LORD. He cried out to the LORD on Israel's behalf, and the LORD answered him.[y]

[10]While Samuel was sacrificing the burnt offering, the Philistines drew near to engage Israel in battle. But that day the LORD thundered[z] with loud thunder against the Philistines and threw them into such a panic[a] that they were routed before the Israelites. [11]The men of Israel rushed out of Mizpah and pursued the Philistines, slaughtering them along the way to a point below Beth Car.

[12]Then Samuel took a stone[b] and set it

Cross references

6:19 [b]S Ex 19:21
6:20 [c]2Sa 6:9; Ps 130:3; Mal 3:2; Rev 6:17 [d]S Lev 11:45
6:21 [e]S Jos 9:17; 7:1 [f]S Jos 6:7 [g]2Sa 6:3; 1Ch 13:7
7:2 [h]1Ch 13:5; Ps 132:6 [i]1Ch 13:3
7:3 [j]Dt 30:10; 2Ki 18:5; 23:25; Jer 24:7 [k]S Ge 31:19; S Jos 24:14 [l]S Jdg 2:12-13; 1Sa 12:10; 31:10 [m]Joel 2:12 [n]S Dt 6:13; Mt 4:10; Lk 4:8 [o]S Jdg 2:18
7:5 [p]S 1Sa 1:20; Ps 99:6; Jer 15:1

[q]S Jos 11:3; Jdg 21:5; 1Sa 10:17 [r]S ver 8; S Ge 20:7; S Dt 9:19
7:6 [s]S Jos 11:3 [t]La 2:19 [u]S Jdg 2:16; S 16:31
7:7 [v]1Sa 17:11
7:8 [w]ver 5; S Ex 32:30; S Nu 21:7; 1Sa 12:19,23; 1Ki 18:24; Isa 37:4; Jer 15:1; 27:18
7:9 [x]Ps 99:6 [y]S Ex 32:11; S Dt 9:19
7:10 [z]S Ex 9:23; S 1Sa 2:10 [a]S Ge 35:5; S Ex 14:24
7:12 [b]S Ge 28:22; S Dt 27:2; Jos 4:9

Text notes

[w] 19 A few Hebrew manuscripts; most Hebrew manuscripts and Septuagint 50,070   [x] 6 Traditionally judge

Study notes

judged by God for their irreverent curiosity. Because God had so closely linked the manifestation of his own presence among his people with the ark, it was to be treated with great honor and respect (see 2Sa 6:7; Nu 4:17–20). This attitude of respect, however, is quite different from the superstitious attitude that led the elders to take the ark into battle against the Philistines, thus treating it as an object with magical power (see note on 4:3).

6:20 *To whom will the ark go up from here?* The inhabitants of Beth Shemesh respond to God's judgment in much the same way as the inhabitants of Ashdod, Gath and Ekron (see 5:8–10).

7:1 *Abinadab's house.* The ark remained in relative obscurity at Abinadab's house until David brought it to Jerusalem (2Sa 6:2–3). Somehow the Tent of Meeting (and the altar of burnt offering) escaped the destruction of Shiloh (Jer 7:12,14; 26:6). It apparently was first moved to Nob (21:1–9). In David's and Solomon's days it was located at Gibeon (1Ch 16:39; 21:29; 2Ch 1:3,13), the city whose people had been condemned to be menial laborers at the Lord's sanctuary (Jos 9:23,27). Later, we are told, Solomon brought the "Tent of Meeting" to the completed temple (see notes on 1Ki 3:4; 8:4).

7:2 *twenty years in all.* Probably the 20-year interval between the return of the ark to Israel and the assembly called by Samuel at Mizpah (see v. 5).

7:3 *Ashtoreths.* Ashtoreth was a goddess of love, fertility and war, worshiped in various forms by many peoples of the ancient Near East, including the Canaanites (see note on Jdg

2:13). The worship of Ashtoreth is frequently combined with the worship of Baal (see v. 4; 12:10; Jdg 2:13; 3:7; 10:6), in accordance with the common practice in fertility cults to associate male and female deities.

7:5 *Mizpah.* A town in the territory of Benjamin (Jos 18:26), located about seven and a half miles north of Jerusalem. It was here that the Israelites had previously gathered to undertake disciplinary action against Benjamin (Jdg 20:1; 21:1) after the abuse and murder of the concubine of a traveling Levite in Gibeah of Benjamin. Several other places bore the same name (see 2Sa 22:3; Ge 31:49; Jos 11:3,8; 15:38). *I will intercede.* See 7:8–9; 8:6; 12:17–19,23; 15:11. Samuel, like Moses, was later remembered as a great intercessor (see Ps 99:6; Jer 15:1). Both were appointed by God to mediate his rule over his people, representing God to Israel and speaking on Israel's behalf to God.

7:6 *they drew water and poured it out before the LORD.* There is no other reference to this type of ceremony in the OT. It appears to symbolize the pouring out of one's heart in repentance and humility before the Lord. For related expressions see 1:15; Ps 62:8; La 2:19. *Samuel was leader.* See NIV text note and v. 15; see also note on 4:18.

7:10 *the LORD thundered with loud thunder.* The Lord had promised to be the protector of his people when they were obedient to their covenant obligations (see Ex 23:22; Dt 20:1–4; see also 2Sa 5:19–25; Jos 10:11–14; Jdg 5:20–21; 2Ki 7:6; 19:35; 2Ch 20:17,22).

7:12 *Ebenezer.* See NIV text note and note on 4:1.

up between Mizpah and Shen. He named it Ebenezer,[yc] saying, "Thus far has the LORD helped us." [13]So the Philistines were subdued[d] and did not invade Israelite territory again.

Throughout Samuel's lifetime, the hand of the LORD was against the Philistines. [14]The towns from Ekron[e] to Gath that the Philistines had captured from Israel were restored to her, and Israel delivered the neighboring territory from the power of the Philistines. And there was peace between Israel and the Amorites.[f]

[15]Samuel[g] continued as judge[h] over Israel all[i] the days of his life. [16]From year to year he went on a circuit from Bethel[j] to Gilgal[k] to Mizpah, judging[l] Israel in all those places. [17]But he always went back to Ramah,[m] where his home was, and there he also judged[n] Israel. And he built an altar[o] there to the LORD.

Israel Asks for a King

8 When Samuel grew old, he appointed[p] his sons as judges for Israel. [2]The name of his firstborn was Joel and the name of his second was Abijah,[q] and they served at Beersheba.[r] [3]But his sons[s] did not walk in his ways. They turned aside[t] after dishonest gain and accepted bribes[u] and perverted[v] justice.

[4]So all the elders[w] of Israel gathered together and came to Samuel at Ramah.[x] [5]They said to him, "You are old, and your sons do not walk in your ways; now appoint a king[y] to lead[zz] us, such as all the other nations[a] have."

[6]But when they said, "Give us a king[b] to lead us," this displeased[c] Samuel; so he prayed to the LORD. [7]And the LORD told him: "Listen[d] to all that the people are saying to you; it is not you they have rejected,[e] but they have rejected me as their king.[f] [8]As they have done from the day I brought them up out of Egypt until this day, forsaking[g] me and serving other gods, so they are doing to you. [9]Now listen to them; but warn them solemnly and let them know[h] what the king who will reign over them will do."

[10]Samuel told[i] all the words of the LORD to the people who were asking him for a king. [11]He said, "This is what the king who will reign over you will do: He will take[j] your sons and make them serve[k] with his chariots and horses, and they will run in front of his chariots.[l] [12]Some he will assign to be commanders[m] of thousands and commanders of fifties, and others to plow his ground and reap his harvest, and still others to make weapons of war and equipment for his chariots. [13]He will take your daughters to be perfumers and cooks and bakers. [14]He will take the best of your[n] fields and vineyards[o] and olive groves and give them to his attendants.[p] [15]He will take a tenth[q] of your grain and of your vintage and give it

---

7:12 cS 1Sa 4:1
7:13 dJdg 13:5
7:14 eS Jos 13:3
/S Jdg 1:34
7:15 gver 6;
1Sa 12:11
hS Jdg 2:16
iJdg 2:18
7:16 /S Ge 12:8
kS Jos 10:43;
S 1Sa 10:8;
Am 5:5 lver 6;
Ac 13:20
7:17
mS Jos 18:25;
1Sa 8:4; 15:34;
19:18; 25:1; 28:3
nver 6 o1Sa 9:12;
14:35; 20:6;
2Sa 24:25
8:1 pDt 16:18-19
8:2 qICh 6:28
rGe 22:19;
1Ki 19:3;
Am 5:4-5
8:3 s1Sa 2:12
tNe 9:29;
Job 34:27;
Ps 14:3; 58:3;
Isa 53:6
uEx 23:8;
1Sa 12:3;
Job 8:22;
Pr 17:23
vS Ex 23:2
8:4 wS Jdg 11:11;
1Sa 11:3
xS 1Sa 7:17
8:5 yver 19;
S Dt 17:14-20;
1Sa 10:19; 12:12,
13; Hos 13:11
z1Sa 3:20; 12:2
aver 20

8:6 bHos 13:10
c1Sa 12:17;
15:11; 16:1
8:7 dver 22;
1Sa 12:1
eS Nu 11:20
/S Ex 16:8
8:8 g1Sa 8:12:10;
2Ki 21:22;
Jer 2:17
8:9 hver 11-18;
S Dt 17:14-20;
1Sa 10:25

8:10 /S Ex 19:7 8:11 /1Sa 14:52 kS Ge 41:46 /S Dt 17:16;
2Sa 15:1; 1Ki 1:5; 2Ch 1:14; 9:25; SS 3:7 8:12 mS Dt 1:15
8:14 nEze 46:18 o1Ki 21:7,15; Mic 2:2 p2Ki 22:12 8:15
qS Ge 41:34; 1Sa 17:25

y12 Ebenezer means stone of help.   z5 Traditionally
judge; also in verses 6 and 20

7:13 *did not invade Israelite territory again.* Some interpreters see a contradiction between this statement and subsequent references to the Philistines in 9:16; 10:5; 13:3,5; 17:1; 23:27. This statement, however, only indicates that the Philistines did not immediately counterattack. See 2Ki 6:23–24 for a similar situation.
7:15 A summary statement marking the end of the author's account of Samuel's ministry as Israel's leader (see v. 6).
7:16 *judging Israel.* See note on 4:18.
7:17 *Ramah.* See note on 1:1.
8:1–12:25 See Introduction: Contents and Theme.
8:1 *When Samuel grew old.* Probably about 20 years after the victory at Mizpah, when Samuel was approximately 65 years old (see Introduction: Chronology).
8:3 *accepted bribes.* Perversion of justice through bribery was explicitly forbidden in Pentateuchal law (see Ex 23:8; Dt 16:19).
8:5 *appoint a king to lead us.* The elders cite Samuel's age and the misconduct of his sons as justifications for their request for a king. It soon becomes apparent, however, that the more basic reason for their request was a desire to be like the surrounding nations—to have a human king as a symbol of national power and unity who would lead them in battle and guarantee their security (see v. 20; 10:19; 12:12; see also Introduction: Contents and Theme).
8:7 *Listen to all that the people are saying to you.* Anticipa-

tions of kingship in Israel are present already in the Pentateuch (Ge 49:10; Nu 24:7,17; Dt 17:14–20); Samuel is therefore instructed to listen to the people's request (see vv. 9,22). *it is not you they have rejected, but they have rejected me as their king.* Cf. Jdg 8:23. The sin of Israel in requesting a king (see 10:19; 12:12,17,19–20) did not rest in any evil inherent in kingship itself, but rather in the kind of kingship the people envisioned and their reasons for requesting it (see Introduction: Contents and Theme). Their desire was for a form of kingship that denied their covenant relationship with the Lord, who himself was pledged to be their savior and deliverer. In requesting a king "like all the other nations" (v. 20) they broke the covenant, rejected the Lord who was their King (12:12; Nu 23:21; Dt 33:5) and forgot his constant provision for their protection in the past (10:18; 12:8–11).
8:11 *what the king . . . will do.* Using a description of the policies of contemporary Canaanite kings (vv. 11–17), Samuel warns the people of the burdens associated with the type of kingship they long for.
8:15 *tenth.* This king's portion would be over and above the tenth Israel was to devote to the Lord (Lev 27:30–32; Nu 18:26; Dt 14:22,28; 26:12). In fact, the demands of the king would parallel all that Israel was to consecrate to the Lord as her Great King (persons, lands, crops, livestock)—even the whole population (v. 17).

to his officials and attendants. ¹⁶Your men-servants and maidservants and the best of your cattle ᵃ and donkeys he will take for his own use. ¹⁷He will take a tenth of your flocks, and you yourselves will become his slaves. ¹⁸When that day comes, you will cry out for relief from the king you have chosen, and the LORD will not answer ʳ you in that day. ˢ "

¹⁹But the people refused ᵗ to listen to Samuel. "No!" they said. "We want ᵘ a king ᵛ over us. ²⁰Then we will be like all the other nations, ʷ with a king to lead us and to go out before us and fight our bat-tles."

²¹When Samuel heard all that the people said, he repeated ˣ it before the LORD. ²²The LORD answered, "Listen ʸ to them and give them a king."

Then Samuel said to the men of Israel, "Everyone go back to his town."

Samuel Anoints Saul

9 There was a Benjamite, ᶻ a man of standing, ᵃ whose name was Kish ᵇ son of Abiel, the son of Zeror, the son of Becorath, the son of Aphiah of Benjamin. ²He had a son named Saul, an impressive ᶜ young man without equal ᵈ among the Is-raelites—a head taller ᵉ than any of the others.

³Now the donkeys ᶠ belonging to Saul's father Kish were lost, and Kish said to his son Saul, "Take one of the servants with you and go and look for the donkeys." ⁴So he passed through the hill ᵍ country of Ephraim and through the area around Shalisha, ʰ but they did not find them.

They went on into the district of Shaalim, but the donkeys ⁱ were not there. Then he passed through the territory of Benjamin, but they did not find them.

⁵When they reached the district of Zuph, ʲ Saul said to the servant who was with him, "Come, let's go back, or my fa-ther will stop thinking about the donkeys and start worrying ᵏ about us."

⁶But the servant replied, "Look, in this town there is a man of God; ˡ he is highly respected, and everything ᵐ he says comes true. Let's go there now. Perhaps he will tell us what way to take."

⁷Saul said to his servant, "If we go, what can we give the man? The food in our sacks is gone. We have no gift ⁿ to take to the man of God. What do we have?"

⁸The servant answered him again. "Look," he said, "I have a quarter of a shekel ᵇ of silver. I will give it to the man of God so that he will tell us what way to take." ⁹(Formerly in Israel, if a man went to inquire ᵒ of God, he would say, "Come, let us go to the seer," because the prophet of today used to be called a seer.) ᵖ

¹⁰"Good," Saul said to his servant. "Come, let's go." So they set out for the town where the man of God was.

¹¹As they were going up the hill to the town, they met some girls coming out to draw ᵠ water, and they asked them, "Is the seer here?"

¹²"He is," they answered. "He's ahead of you. Hurry now; he has just come to our town today, for the people have a sacri-

ᵃ16 Septuagint; Hebrew young men   ᵇ8 That is, about 1/10 ounce (about 3 grams)

Cross references (center column)

8:18 ʳ1Sa 28:6; Job 27:9; 35:12, 13; Ps 18:41; 66:18; Pr 1:28; Isa 1:15; 58:4; 59:2; Jer 14:12; Eze 8:18; Mic 3:4 ˢ1Sa 10:25; 1Ki 12:4
8:19 ᵗPr 1:24; Isa 50:2; 66:4; Jer 7:13; 8:12; 13:10; 44:16 ᵘAc 13:21 ᵛS ver 5
8:20 ʷS ver 5
8:21 ˣS Jdg 11:11
8:22 ʸS ver 7
9:1 ᶻJos 18:11-20 ᵃS Ru 2:1 ᵇ1Sa 14:51; 1Ch 8:33; 9:39; Est 2:5; Ac 13:21
9:2 ᶜS Ge 39:6 ᵈ1Sa 10:24 ᵉ1Sa 10:23
9:3 ᶠver 20; 1Sa 10:14,16
9:4 ᵍS Jos 24:33 ʰ2Ki 4:42

9:5 ʲ1Sa 10:2 ᵏ1Sa 1:1 ˡ1Sa 10:2
9:6 ˡS Dt 33:1; S Jdg 13:6 ᵐ1Sa 3:19
9:7 ⁿS Ge 32:20; 1Ki 13:7; 14:3; 2Ki 4:42; 5:5,15; Jer 40:5
9:9 ᵒS Ge 25:22 ᵖ2Sa 15:27; 24:11; 2Ki 17:13; 1Ch 9:22; 21:9; 26:28; 29:29; 2Ch 19:2; Isa 29:10; 30:10; Am 7:12
9:11 ᵠS Ge 24:11,13

Study notes (bottom)

8:18 *cry out for relief from the king.* See 1Ki 12:4; Jer 22:13–17.

8:20 *like all the other nations.* See notes on vv. 5,7.

9:2 *a head taller than any of the others.* Physically of kingly stature (see 10:23).

9:3 *donkeys . . . were lost.* Saul is introduced as a donkey wrangler sent in search of donkeys that had strayed from home—perhaps symbolizing Saul and the rebellious people who had asked for a king (cf. Isa 1:3). David would be introduced as a shepherd caring for his father's flock and later pictured as the shepherd over the Lord's flock (2Sa 5:2; 7:7–8; Ps 78:71–72).

9:6 *the servant replied.* Saul's ignorance of Samuel is in-dicative of his character. *this town.* Probably Ramah (see 7:17), the hometown of Samuel, to which he had just re-turned from a journey (see v. 12; 7:16). *man of God.* See note on 2:27; here a reference to Samuel. *everything he says comes true.* See 3:19 and note.

9:7 *what can we give the man?* Other examples of gifts offered to prophets are found in 1Ki 14:3; 2Ki 4:42; 5:15–16; 8:8–9. Whether Samuel accepted the gift and whether he was dependent on such gifts for a livelihood are not clear. Elisha refused the gift of Naaman (2Ki 5:16). In later times false prophets adjusted their message to the de-

sires of those who supported them (1Ki 22:6,8,18; Mic 3:5,11).

9:8 *a quarter of a shekel of silver.* See NIV text note. Before the use of coins, gold or silver was weighed out for each monetary transaction (see 13:21; Job 28:15). The value of that amount of silver in Saul's time is not known.

9:9 *the prophet of today used to be called a seer.* There was no essential difference between a seer and a prophet. The person popularly designated as a prophet at the time of the writing of 1,2 Samuel was termed a seer in the time of Saul. This need not mean that the term "prophet" was unknown in the time of Saul or that the term "seer" was unknown in later times (see Isa 30:10). The reference is to popular usage.

9:12 *high place.* See Lev 26:30. After entrance into the promised land, the Israelites often followed the custom of the Canaanites in building local altars on hills. (At this time the central sanctuary was not functioning because the ark of God was separated from the tabernacle; Shiloh had been de-stroyed, and the priestly family, after the death of Eli's sons, was apparently still inactive.) In later times, worship at these "high places" provided a means for the entrance of pagan practices into Israel's religious observances and, for this rea-son, it was condemned (see note on 1Ki 3:2).

fice[r] at the high place.[s] 13As soon as you enter the town, you will find him before he goes up to the high place to eat. The people will not begin eating until he comes, because he must bless[t] the sacrifice; afterward, those who are invited will eat. Go up now; you should find him about this time.''

14They went up to the town, and as they were entering it, there was Samuel, coming toward them on his way up to the high place.

15Now the day before Saul came, the LORD had revealed this to Samuel: 16''About this time tomorrow I will send you a man from the land of Benjamin. Anoint[u] him leader[v] over my people Israel; he will deliver[w] my people from the hand of the Philistines.[x] I have looked upon my people, for their cry[y] has reached me.''

17When Samuel caught sight of Saul, the LORD said to him, ''This[z] is the man I spoke to you about; he will govern my people.''

18Saul approached Samuel in the gateway and asked, ''Would you please tell me where the seer's house is?''

19''I am the seer,'' Samuel replied. ''Go up ahead of me to the high place, for today you are to eat with me, and in the morning I will let you go and will tell you all that is in your heart. 20As for the donkeys[a] you lost three days ago, do not worry about them; they have been found. And to whom is all the desire[b] of Israel turned, if not to you and all your father's family?''

21Saul answered, ''But am I not a Benjamite, from the smallest tribe[c] of Israel, and is not my clan the least[d] of all the clans of

the tribe of Benjamin?[e] Why do you say such a thing to me?''

22Then Samuel brought Saul and his servant into the hall and seated them at the head of those who were invited—about thirty in number. 23Samuel said to the cook, ''Bring the piece of meat I gave you, the one I told you to lay aside.''

24So the cook took up the leg[f] with what was on it and set it in front of Saul. Samuel said, ''Here is what has been kept for you. Eat, because it was set aside for you for this occasion, from the time I said, 'I have invited guests.' '' And Saul dined with Samuel that day.

25After they came down from the high place to the town, Samuel talked with Saul on the roof[g] of his house. 26They rose about daybreak and Samuel called to Saul on the roof, ''Get ready, and I will send you on your way.'' When Saul got ready, he and Samuel went outside together. 27As they were going down to the edge of the town, Samuel said to Saul, ''Tell the servant to go on ahead of us''—and the servant did so—''but you stay here awhile, so that I may give you a message from God.''

10 Then Samuel took a flask[h] of oil and poured it on Saul's head and kissed him, saying, ''Has not the LORD anointed[i] you leader over his inheritance?[c/] 2When you leave me today, you will meet two men near Rachel's tomb,[k] at Zelzah on the border of Benjamin. They will say to you, 'The donkeys[l] you set out to look for have been found. And now your father has stopped thinking about them

c/ Hebrew; Septuagint and Vulgate over his people Israel? You will reign over the LORD's people and save them from the power of their enemies round about. And this will be a sign to you that the LORD has anointed you leader over his inheritance:

Cross references

9:12 rNu 28:11-15; S 1Sa 7:17; sS Lev 26:30
9:13 tS Mt 14:19; 1Co 10:16; 1Ti 4:3-5
9:16 uEx 30:25; S 1Sa 2:35; 12:3; 15:1; 26:9; 2Ki 11:12; Ps 2:2 v2Sa 7:8; 1Ki 8:16; 1Ch 5:2 wEx 3:8 x1Sa 23:4; 2Sa 3:18 yGe 16:11; Ps 102:1
9:17 z1Sa 16:12
9:20 aS ver 3
b1Sa 12:13; Ezr 6:8; Isa 60:4-9; Da 2:44; Hag 2:7; Mal 3:1
9:21 cPs 68:27 dS Ex 3:11; Mt 2:6; 1Co 15:9
eJdg 6:15; 20:35, 46; 1Sa 18:18
9:24 fS Lev 7:34
9:25 gS Dt 22:8; S Jos 2:8; S Mt 24:17; Lk 5:19
10:1 h1Sa 16:1; 2Ki 9:1 iS Ex 29:7; S 1Sa 9:16; S 1Ki 1:39 jS Ex 34:9; 2Sa 20:19; Ps 78:62,71
10:2 kGe 35:20 l1Sa 9:4

9:13 *he must bless the sacrifice.* Samuel presided over the sacrificial meal (see 1:4; 2:13–16), at which he gave a prayer, probably similar to those referred to in the NT (see Mt 26:26–27; Jn 6:11, 23; 1Ti 4:3–5).

9:16 *Anoint him.* Priests were also anointed (see Ex 29:7; 40:12–15; Lev 4:3; 8:12), but from this point in the OT it is usually the king who is referred to as ''the anointed of the LORD'' (see note on 2:10; cf. 12:3; 24:6; 26:9,11,16; 2Sa 1:14,16; 19:21; 22:51; 23:1; Ps 2:2,6; but see also Zec 4:14). Anointing signifies separation to the Lord for a particular task and divine equipping for the task (see v. 6; 16:13; Isa 61:1). *leader.* The Hebrew for this word indicates one designated (here by the Lord) to be the chief in rank. It served as a useful term to ease the transition between the time of the judges and that of the kings. *Philistines.* See note on 7:13.

9:20 *all the desire of Israel.* A reference to Israel's desire for a king.

9:21 *smallest tribe . . . least of all the clans.* Saul's origins were among the humblest in Israel (Benjamin was the last of

Jacob's sons, and the tribe had been greatly reduced in time of the judges; see Jdg 20:46–48). His elevation to king shows that God ''raises the poor'' (2:8), which is one of the central themes running throughout Samuel. God's use of the powerless to promote his kingdom in the world is a common feature in the Biblical testimony and underscores the truth that his kingdom is not of this world.

9:24 *leg.* The Hebrew for this word specifies the thigh, which was normally reserved for the Lord's consecrated priest (see Ex 29:22,27; Lev 7:32–33,35; Nu 6:20; 18:18). The presentation of this choice piece of the sacrificial animal to Saul was a distinct honor and anticipated his being designated the Lord's anointed.

10:1 *oil.* Perhaps spiced olive oil (see Ex 30:22–33). *Has not the LORD anointed you . . . ?* See note on 9:16. *leader.* See 9:16 and note. *his inheritance.* ''My people Israel'' (9:16). The Lord's inheritance includes both the people (see Ex 34:9) and the land (see Ex 15:17). After departing from Samuel, Saul is to receive three signs (see vv. 2–7) to authenticate Samuel's words and to assure him that the Lord has indeed chosen him to be king.

and is worried[m] about you. He is asking, "What shall I do about my son?"'

3"Then you will go on from there until you reach the great tree of Tabor. Three men going up to God at Bethel[n] will meet you there. One will be carrying three young goats, another three loaves of bread, and another a skin of wine. 4They will greet you and offer you two loaves of bread,[o] which you will accept from them.

5"After that you will go to Gibeah[p] of God, where there is a Philistine outpost.[q] As you approach the town, you will meet a procession of prophets[r] coming down from the high place[s] with lyres, tambourines,[t] flutes[u] and harps[v] being played before them, and they will be prophesying.[w] 6The Spirit[x] of the LORD will come upon you in power, and you will prophesy with them; and you will be changed[y] into a different person. 7Once these signs are fulfilled, do whatever[z] your hand[a] finds to do, for God is with[b] you.

8"Go down ahead of me to Gilgal.[c] I will surely come down to you to sacrifice burnt offerings and fellowship offerings,[d] but you must wait seven[d] days until I come to you and tell you what you are to do."

Saul Made King

9As Saul turned to leave Samuel, God changed[e] Saul's heart, and all these signs[f] were fulfilled[g] that day. 10When they arrived at Gibeah, a procession of prophets met him; the Spirit[h] of God came upon him in power, and he joined in their prophesying.[i] 11When all those who had

formerly known him saw him prophesying with the prophets, they asked each other, "What is this[j] that has happened to the son of Kish? Is Saul also among the prophets?"[k]

12A man who lived there answered, "And who is their father?" So it became a saying: "Is Saul also among the prophets?"[l] 13After Saul stopped prophesying,[m] he went to the high place.

14Now Saul's uncle[n] asked him and his servant, "Where have you been?"

"Looking for the donkeys,[o]" he said. "But when we saw they were not to be found, we went to Samuel."

15Saul's uncle said, "Tell me what Samuel said to you."

16Saul replied, "He assured us that the donkeys[p] had been found." But he did not tell his uncle what Samuel had said about the kingship.

17Samuel summoned the people of Israel to the LORD at Mizpah[q] 18and said to them, "This is what the LORD, the God of Israel, says: 'I brought Israel up out of Egypt, and I delivered you from the power of Egypt and all the kingdoms that oppressed[r] you.' 19But you have now rejected[s] your God, who saves[t] you out of all your calamities and distresses. And you have said, 'No, set a king[u] over us.'[v] So now present[w] yourselves before the LORD by your tribes and clans."

20When Samuel brought all the tribes of

10:2 m1Sa 9:5
10:3 nS Ge 35:8
10:4 over 27;
1Sa 16:20;
Pr 18:16
10:5 pver 26;
1Sa 11:4; 15:34
q1Sa 13:3
rS Nu 11:29;
1Ki 20:35;
2Ki 2:3,15; 4:1;
6:1; 9:1;
Am 7:14
sS Lev 26:30
tS Ge 31:27;
Jer 31:4
u1Ki 1:40;
Isa 30:29
v1Sa 16:16;
18:10; 19:9;
2Ki 3:15; Ps 92:3
wver 10;
1Sa 19:20;
1Ch 25:1;
1Co 14:1
10:6 xS Nu 11:25
yver 9
10:7 z2Sa 7:3;
1Ki 8:17;
1Ch 22:7; 28:2;
2Ch 6:7; Ecc 9:10
aJdg 9:33
bS Jos 1:5;
Lk 1:28; Heb 13:5
10:8 cJos 4:20;
S 10:43;
1Sa 7:16; 11:14
d1Sa 13:8
10:9 ever 6
/S Dt 13:2 gver 7
10:10
hS Nu 11:25;
1Sa 11:6 /S ver 5
10:11 /Mt 13:54;
Jn 7:15 kver 12;
1Sa 19:24;
2Ki 9:11;
Jer 29:26; Hos 9:7
10:12 /S ver 11
10:13
m1Sa 19:23
10:14 n1Sa 14:50
oS 1Sa 9:3
10:16 pS 1Sa 9:3
10:17 qS 1Sa 7:5
10:18 rS Ex 1:14;
S Nu 10:9
10:19
sS Nu 11:20;

S Dt 33:5 tPs 7:10; 18:48; 68:20; 145:19 uS 1Sa 8:5
vS Dt 17:14 wJos 7:14

d8 Traditionally peace offerings

10:5 *Gibeah of God.* Gibeah was Saul's hometown (see v. 26; 11:4), located in the tribal area of Benjamin (Jos 18:28; Jdg 19:12–14). It was usually called "Gibeah" or "Gibeah of Benjamin" (as in 13:2,15), but twice "Gibeah of Saul" (15:34; 2Sa 21:6). The present designation (used only here) may have been Samuel's way of reminding Saul that the land of Canaan belonged to God and not to the Philistines (see Dt 32:43; Isa 14:2; Hos 9:3). *prophets.* The bands of prophets with which Samuel was associated (as also the "sons of the prophets" with whom Elijah and Elisha were associated; see note on 1Ki 20:35) appear to have been small communities of men who banded together in spiritually decadent times for mutual cultivation of their religious zeal. *prophesying.* Here (and in vv. 6,10–11,13) appears to designate an enthusiastic praising of God inspired by the Holy Spirit (see Nu 11:24–30 for similar use of the term).
10:7 *do whatever your hand finds to do.* Saul is to take whatever action is appropriate when the situation presents itself to manifest publicly his royal leadership (see 11:4–11).
10:8 *Go down ahead of me to Gilgal.* At some unspecified future time, perhaps previously discussed (see 9:25), Saul is to go to Gilgal and wait seven days for Samuel's arrival (see 13:7–14).
10:11 *Is Saul also among the prophets?* An expression of surprise at Saul's behavior (see note on v. 5) by those who

had known him previously—another subtle indication of his character (see notes on 9:3,6).
10:12 *who is their father?* Some understand the question as an expression of contempt for prophets generally, others as implying the recognition that prophetic inspiration comes from God and therefore could be imparted to whomever God chose. However, since leading prophets were sometimes called "father" (2Ki 2:12; 6:21; 13:14), the speaker may have intended a disdainful reference to Samuel or an ironical gibe at Saul.
10:17 *Samuel summoned the people.* After the private designation and anointing of Saul to be king (9:1–10:16), an assembly is called by Samuel to make the Lord's choice known to the people (v. 21) and to define the king's task (v. 25). *Mizpah.* See note on 7:5.
10:18 *I delivered you.* Speaking through Samuel, the Lord emphasizes to the people that he has been their deliverer throughout their history. He brought them out of Egypt and delivered them from all their enemies during the time of the judges. Although the judges themselves are sometimes referred to as Israel's deliverers (see Jdg 3:9,15,31; 6:14; 10:1; 13:5), this was true only in a secondary sense, for they were instruments of the Lord's deliverance (see Jdg 2:18). It was the Lord who sent them (see 12:11; Jdg 6:14).
10:19 *rejected your God.* See note on 8:7.

Israel near, the tribe of Benjamin was chosen. [21]Then he brought forward the tribe of Benjamin, clan by clan, and Matri's clan was chosen.[x] Finally Saul son of Kish was chosen. But when they looked for him, he was not to be found. [22]So they inquired[y] further of the LORD, "Has the man come here yet?"

And the LORD said, "Yes, he has hidden himself among the baggage."

[23]They ran and brought him out, and as he stood among the people he was a head taller[z] than any of the others. [24]Samuel said to all the people, "Do you see the man the LORD has chosen?[a] There is no one like[b] him among all the people."

Then the people shouted, "Long live[c] the king!"

[25]Samuel explained[d] to the people the regulations[e] of the kingship.[f] He wrote them down on a scroll and deposited it before the LORD. Then Samuel dismissed the people, each to his own home.

[26]Saul also went to his home in Gibeah,[g] accompanied by valiant men[h] whose hearts God had touched. [27]But some troublemakers[i] said, "How can this fellow save us?" They despised him and brought him no gifts.[j] But Saul kept silent.

Saul Rescues the City of Jabesh

11 Nahash[k] the Ammonite went up and besieged Jabesh Gilead.[l] And all the men of Jabesh said to him, "Make a treaty[m] with us, and we will be subject to you."

[2]But Nahash the Ammonite replied, "I will make a treaty with you only on the condition[n] that I gouge[o] out the right eye of every one of you and so bring disgrace[p] on all Israel."

[3]The elders[q] of Jabesh said to him, "Give us seven days so we can send messengers throughout Israel; if no one comes to rescue[r] us, we will surrender[s] to you."

[4]When the messengers came to Gibeah[t] of Saul and reported these terms to the people, they all wept[u] aloud. [5]Just then Saul was returning from the fields, behind his oxen, and he asked, "What is wrong with the people? Why are they weeping?" Then they repeated to him what the men of Jabesh had said.

[6]When Saul heard their words, the Spirit[v] of God came upon him in power, and he burned with anger. [7]He took a pair of oxen,[w] cut them into pieces, and sent the pieces by messengers throughout Israel,[x] proclaiming, "This is what will be done to the oxen of anyone[y] who does not follow Saul and Samuel." Then the terror of the LORD fell on the people, and they turned out as one man.[z] [8]When Saul mustered[a] them at Bezek,[b] the men of Israel numbered three hundred thousand and the men of Judah thirty thousand.

[9]They told the messengers who had come, "Say to the men of Jabesh Gilead, 'By the time the sun is hot tomorrow, you will be delivered.' " When the messengers went and reported this to the men of Jabesh, they were elated. [10]They said to the

Cross references (center column)

10:21 *Est 3:7; Pr 16:33
10:22 *Ge 25:22; S Jdg 18:5
10:23 *1Sa 9:2
10:24 *Dt 17:15; 2Sa 21:6 *1Sa 9:2
*1Ki 1:25,34,39; 2Ki 11:12
10:25 *S 1Sa 8:9 *S Dt 17:14-20; S 1Sa 8:11-18; 2Ki 11:12 *1Sa 11:14
10:26 *S ver 5; S Jdg 19:14 *S Jdg 20:44
10:27 *S Dt 13:13; S 1Sa 20:7 *S ver 4; 1Ki 10:25; 2Ch 17:5; 32:23; Ps 68:29
11:1 *S Ge 19:38; 1Sa 12:12; 2Sa 10:2; 17:27; 1Ch 19:1 *Jdg 21:8; 1Sa 31:11; 2Sa 2:4,5; 21:12 *S Ex 23:32; S Jer 37:1
11:2 *Ge 34:15 *S Nu 16:14 *1Sa 17:26
11:3 *S 1Sa 8:4 *S Jdg 2:16 *ver 10
11:4 *S 1Sa 10:5, 26 *S Ge 27:38; S Nu 25:6
11:6 *S Jdg 3:10
11:7 *S Jdg 6:14 *S Jdg 19:29 *Jdg 21:5 *S Jdg 20:1
11:8 *Jdg 20:2 *Jdg 1:4

Study notes (bottom)

10:20 *tribe of Benjamin was chosen.* Probably by casting lots (see 14:41–42; Jos 7:15–18). The Urim and Thummim were used for this purpose (see notes on 2:28; Ex 28:30).
10:24 *Long live the king!* See 2Sa 16:16.
10:25 *regulations of the kingship.* Samuel here takes the first step toward resolving the tension that existed between Israel's misdirected desire for a king (and their misconceived notion of what the king's role and function should be) and the Lord's intent to give them one (see Introduction: Contents and Theme). This description of the duties and prerogatives of the Israelite king was given for the benefit of both the people and the king-designate. It was intended to clearly distinguish Israelite kingship from that of the surrounding nations and to ensure that the king's role in Israel was compatible with the continued rule of the Lord over Israel as her Great King (see Dt 17:14–20). *deposited it before the LORD.* The written constitutional-legal document defining the role of the king in governing God's covenant people was preserved at the sanctuary (the tabernacle, later the temple). Other written documents defining Israel's covenant relationship with the Lord are referred to in Ex 24:7; Dt 31:26; Jos 24:26.
10:27 *troublemakers.* See note on Dt 13:13. *How can this fellow save us?* Reflects the people's continued apostate idea that national security was to be sought in the person of the human king (see note on v. 18; cf. 8:20).
11:1 *Ammonite.* The Ammonites were descended from

Lot (see Ge 19:38; Dt 2:19) and lived east of the tribal territory of Gad near the upper regions of the Jabbok River (see Dt 2:37; Jos 12:2). Previous attempts by the Ammonites to occupy Israelite territory are referred to in Jdg 3:13; 11:4–32. The Philistine threat to Israel in the west presented the Ammonites with an opportunity to move against Israel from the east with supposed impunity. *Jabesh Gilead.* A town east of the Jordan in the tribal area of Manasseh.
11:2 *gouge out the right eye.* Besides causing humiliation (see note on Jdg 16:21), the loss of the right eye would destroy the military capability of the archers.
11:4 *Gibeah of Saul.* See 10:26 and note on 10:5. Close family ties undoubtedly prompted the inhabitants of Jabesh to seek help from the tribe of Benjamin (see Jdg 21:12–14).
11:5 *Saul was returning from the fields.* After Saul's public selection as the king-designate at Mizpah (10:17–27), he returned home (10:26) to resume his normal private activities and to wait for the Lord's leading for the next step in his elevation to the throne (see notes on v. 15; 10:7).
11:6 *the Spirit of God came upon him in power.* For similar endowment of Israel's deliverers with extraordinary vigor by God's Spirit see 10:6,10; Jdg 14:6,19; 15:14.
11:7 *sent the pieces by messengers throughout Israel.* For a similar case see Jdg 19:29.
11:8 *Bezek.* Located north of Shechem, west of the Jordan River but within striking distance of Jabesh Gilead.

Ammonites, "Tomorrow we will surrender^c to you, and you can do to us whatever seems good to you."

¹¹The next day Saul separated his men into three divisions; ^d during the last watch of the night they broke into the camp of the Ammonites^e and slaughtered them until the heat of the day. Those who survived were scattered, so that no two of them were left together.

Saul Confirmed as King

¹²The people then said to Samuel, "Who^f was it that asked, 'Shall Saul reign over us?' Bring these men to us and we will put them to death."

¹³But Saul said, "No one shall be put to death today,^g for this day the LORD has rescued^h Israel."

¹⁴Then Samuel said to the people, "Come, let us go to Gilgalⁱ and there reaffirm the kingship.^j" ¹⁵So all the people went to Gilgal^k and confirmed Saul as king^l in the presence of the LORD. There they sacrificed fellowship offerings^e before the LORD, and Saul and all the Israelites held a great celebration.

Samuel's Farewell Speech

12 Samuel said to all Israel, "I have listened^m to everything you said to me and have set a kingⁿ over you. ²Now

you have a king as your leader.^o As for me, I am old and gray, and my sons^p are here with you. I have been your leader from my youth until this day. ³Here I stand. Testify against me in the presence of the LORD and his anointed.^q Whose ox have I taken? Whose donkey^r have I taken? Whom have I cheated? Whom have I oppressed? From whose hand have I accepted a bribe^s to make me shut my eyes? If I have done^t any of these, I will make it right."^u

⁴"You have not cheated or oppressed us," they replied. "You have not taken anything from anyone's hand."

⁵Samuel said to them, "The LORD is witness^v against you, and also his anointed is witness this day, that you have not found anything^w in my hand.^x"

"He is witness," they said.

⁶Then Samuel said to the people, "It is the LORD who appointed Moses and Aaron and brought^y your forefathers up out of Egypt. ⁷Now then, stand^z here, because I am going to confront^a you with evidence before the LORD as to all the righteous acts^b performed by the LORD for you and your fathers.

⁸"After Jacob^c entered Egypt, they cried^d to the LORD for help, and the LORD sent^e Moses and Aaron, who brought your

---

11:10 ^cver 3
11:11 ^dS Jdg 7:16
^eS Ge 19:38
11:12
^fS Dt 13:13;
Lk 19:27
11:13 ^g2Sa 19:22
^h1Sa 19:5;
1Ch 11:14
11:14
ⁱS Jos 10:43;
S 1Sa 10:8
^j1Sa 10:25
11:15 ^kS Jos 5:9;
2Sa 19:15
^l1Sa 12:1
12:1 ^mS 1Sa 8:7
ⁿ1Sa 11:15
12:2 ^oS 1Sa 8:5

^p1Sa 8:3
12:3 ^qS 1Sa 9:16;
24:6; 26:9,11;
2Sa 1:14; 19:21;
Ps 105:15
^rNu 16:15
^sS Ex 18:21;
S 1Sa 8:3
^tEx 20:17;
Ac 20:33
^uS Lev 25:14
12:5 ^vS Ge 31:50
^wAc 23:9; 24:20
^xEx 22:4
12:6 ^yS Ex 3:10;
Mic 6:4
12:7 ^zS Jos 24:1
^aIsa 1:18; 3:14;
Jer 2:9; 25:31;
Eze 17:20; 20:35;
Mic 6:1-5
^bS Jdg 5:11
12:8 ^cS Ge 46:6
^dS Ex 2:23
^eS Ex 3:10; 4:16

e *15* Traditionally *peace offerings*

11:11 *last watch of the night.* The third watch, from about 2:00 A.M. until about 6:00 A.M. (see note on Mt 14:25). **11:13** *the LORD has rescued Israel.* Saul recognizes Israel's true deliverer (see note on 10:18). The victory, in combination with Saul's confession, places yet another seal of divine approval on Saul as the man the Lord has chosen to be king. **11:14** *let us go to Gilgal and there reaffirm the kingship.* Samuel perceives that it is now the appropriate time for the people to renew their allegiance to the Lord. The kingship of which he speaks is the Lord's, not Saul's. Samuel calls for an assembly to restore the covenant relationship between the Lord and his people. He wants to inaugurate Saul's rule in a manner demonstrating that the continued rule of the Lord as Israel's Great King is in no way diminished or violated in the new era of the monarchy (see Introduction: Contents and Theme). Verses 14-15 are a brief synopsis of the Gilgal assembly and are prefaced to the more detailed account of the same assembly in ch. 12. *Gilgal.* Located east of Jericho near the Jordan River. It was a particularly appropriate place for Israel to renew her allegiance to the Lord (see Jos 4:19-5:11; 10:8-15). **11:15** *confirmed Saul as king in the presence of the LORD.* Saul had previously been anointed in private by Samuel at Ramah (10:1) and publicly selected as the king-designate at Mizpah (10:17-27). In the subsequent Ammonite crisis (vv. 1-13) his leadership did not rest on public recognition of his royal authority, but on the military victory. Now at Gilgal Saul is inaugurated as God's chosen king and formally assumes the privileges and responsibilities of this office. *fellowship offerings.* This type of offering was an important element in the original ceremony of covenant ratification at

Sinai (Ex 24:5,11). It represented the communion or peace between the Lord and his people when the people lived in conformity with their covenant obligations (see Lev 7:11-17; 22:21-23). *held a great celebration.* Rejoicing is the expression of people who have renewed their commitment to the Lord, confessed their sin (see 12:19) and been given a king. **12:3** *Testify against me.* When Samuel presents the newly inaugurated king to the people, he seeks to establish publicly his own past faithfulness to the covenant as leader of the nation. His purpose is to exonerate himself and provide an example for Saul in his new responsibilities. *Whose ox have I taken? Whose donkey have I taken?* See Ex 20:17; 22:1,4, 9. Samuel has not used his position for personal gain (see Nu 16:15). *Whom have I cheated? Whom have I oppressed?* See Lev 19:13; Dt 24:14. *From whose hand have I accepted a bribe . . .?* See Ex 23:8; Dt 16:19. **12:6** *Samuel said to the people.* Samuel turns from consideration of his previous leadership to the matter of the people's request for a king, which he views as a covenant-breaking act and a serious apostasy. *It is the LORD.* Samuel emphasizes that in the past the Lord had provided the necessary leadership for the nation. **12:7** *confront you with evidence.* The terminology is that of a legal proceeding, as in vv. 2-5, but now the relationship of the parties is reversed. This time Samuel is the accuser, the people are the defendants, and the Lord is the Judge. *righteous acts performed by the LORD.* These righteous acts (see vv. 8-11) demonstrate the constancy of the Lord's covenant faithfulness toward his people in the past and, by way of contrast, serve as an indictment of their present apostasy.

forefathers out of Egypt and settled them in this place.

9"But they forgot[f] the LORD their God; so he sold them[g] into the hand of Sisera,[h] the commander of the army of Hazor,[i] and into the hands of the Philistines[j] and the king of Moab,[k] who fought against them. 10They cried[l] out to the LORD and said, 'We have sinned; we have forsaken[m] the LORD and served the Baals and the Ashtoreths.[n] But now deliver us from the hands of our enemies, and we will serve you.' 11Then the LORD sent Jerub-Baal,[f] [o] Barak,[g] [p] Jephthah[q] and Samuel,[h] [r] and he delivered you from the hands of your enemies on every side, so that you lived securely.

12"But when you saw that Nahash[s] king[t] of the Ammonites was moving against you, you said to me, 'No, we want a king to rule[u] over us'—even though the LORD your God was your king. 13Now here is the king[v] you have chosen, the one you asked[w] for; see, the LORD has set a king over you. 14If you fear[x] the LORD and serve and obey him and do not rebel[y] against his commands, and if both you and the king who reigns over you follow the LORD your God—good! 15But if you do not obey the LORD, and if you rebel against[z] his commands, his hand will be against you, as it was against your fathers.

16"Now then, stand still[a] and see[b] this great thing the LORD is about to do before your eyes! 17Is it not wheat harvest[c] now? I will call[d] upon the LORD to send thunder[e] and rain.[f] And you will realize what an evil[g] thing you did in the eyes of the LORD when you asked for a king."

18Then Samuel called upon the LORD,[h] and that same day the LORD sent thunder and rain. So all the people stood in awe[i] of the LORD and of Samuel.

19The people all said to Samuel, "Pray[j] to the LORD your God for your servants so that we will not die,[k] for we have added to all our other sins the evil of asking for a king."

20"Do not be afraid," Samuel replied. "You have done all this evil;[l] yet do not turn away from the LORD, but serve the LORD with all your heart. 21Do not turn away after useless[m] idols.[n] They can do you no good, nor can they rescue you, because they are useless. 22For the sake[o] of his great name[p] the LORD will not reject[q] his people, because the LORD was pleased to make[r] you his own. 23As for me, far be it from me that I should sin against the LORD by failing to pray[s] for you. And I will teach[t] you the way that is good and right.

12:9 [f]S Dt 32:18; S Jdg 3:7
[g]S Dt 32:30
[h]Jdg 4:2
[i]S Jos 11:1
[j]Jdg 10:7
[k]Jdg 3:12
12:10 [l]S Jdg 3:9
[m]S 1Sa 8:8
[n]S 1Sa 7:3
12:11 [o]Jdg 6:32
[p]S Jdg 4:6
[q]S Jdg 11:1
[r]S 1Sa 7:15
12:12 [s]S 1Sa 11:1
[t]S 1Sa 8:5
[u]1Sa 25:30; 2Sa 5:2; 1Ch 5:2
12:13 [v]S 1Sa 8:5
[w]S 1Sa 9:20
12:14 [x]S Jos 24:14
[y]Jer 4:17; La 1:18
12:15 [z]Lev 26:16; Jos 24:20; Isa 1:20; Jer 4:17; 26:4
12:16 [a]S Ex 14:14
[b]S Ex 14:13
12:17 [c]S Ge 30:14; S 1Sa 6:13
[d]1Ki 18:42; Jas 5:18
[e]S Ex 9:23; S 1Sa 2:10
[f]Ge 7:12; Ex 9:18; Job 37:13; Pr 26:1
[g]S 1Sa 8:6
12:18 [h]Ps 99:6
[i]S Ge 3:10; S Ex 14:31
12:19 [j]S Ex 8:8; S 1Sa 7:8; S Jer 37:3; Jas 5:18; 1Jn 5:16
[k]S Dt 9:19
12:20 [l]S Ex 32:30
12:21 [m]Isa 40:20; 41:24,29; 44:9; Jer 2:5,11; 14:22; 16:19; Jnh 2:8; Hab 2:18; Ac 14:15 [n]Dt 11:16 12:22 [o]Ps 25:11; 106:8; Isa 48:9,11; Jer 14:7; Da 9:19 [p]S Jos 7:9; 2Sa 7:23; Jn 17:12 [q]S Lev 26:11; S Dt 31:6 [r]Dt 7:7; 1Pe 2:9 12:23 [s]S Nu 11:2; S 1Sa 1:20; S 7:8; Ro 1:10 [t]1Ki 8:36; Ps 25:4; 34:11; 86:11; 94:12; Pr 4:11

[f] 11 Also called Gideon   [g] 11 Some Septuagint manuscripts and Syriac; Hebrew Bedan   [h] 11 Hebrew; some Septuagint manuscripts and Syriac Samson

---

12:11 *he delivered you.* The Lord repeatedly delivered Israel from her enemies right up to Samuel's own lifetime (see 7:3,8,10,12), demonstrating again the people's apostasy in desiring a king.

12:12 *when you saw that Nahash . . . was moving against you.* In the face of the combined threat from the Philistines in the west (9:16) and the Ammonites in the east (11:1–13), the Israelites sought to find security in the person of a human king. *the LORD your God was your king.* The Israelite desire for and trust in a human leader constituted a rejection of the kingship of the Lord and betrayed a loss of confidence in his care, in spite of his faithfulness during the time of the exodus, conquest and judges (see note on 8:7).

12:13 *the LORD has set a king over you.* In spite of the sinfulness of the people's request, the Lord had chosen to incorporate kingship into the structure of the theocracy (his kingdom). Kingship was given by the Lord to his people and was to function as an instrument of his rule over them (see Introduction: Contents and Theme).

12:14 *If you fear the LORD.* Samuel relates the old covenant condition (see Ex 19:5–6; Dt 8:19; 11:13–15,22–28; 28; 30:17–18; Jos 24:20) to the new era Israel is entering with the establishment of the monarchy. *if both you and the king . . . follow the LORD your God—good!* Israel and her king are to demonstrate that although human kingship has been established, they will continue to recognize the Lord as their true King. In this new era where potential for divided loyalty between the Lord and the human king arises, Israel's loyalty to the Lord must remain inviolate. For similar use of the expression "to follow" see 2Sa 2:10; 15:13; 1Ki 12:20; 16:21.

12:15 *But if you do not obey.* Samuel confronts Israel with the same alternatives Moses had expressed centuries earlier (see Dt 28; 30:15–20). The introduction of kingship into Israel's socio-political structure has not changed the fundamental nature of Israel's relationship to the Lord.

12:16 *see this great thing.* Samuel calls the people to observe as the Lord himself demonstrates his existence and power and authenticates the truthfulness and seriousness of Samuel's words.

12:17 *wheat harvest.* See note on 6:13.

12:19 *Pray to the LORD your God.* Samuel's indictment (vv. 6–15) combined with the awesome sign of thunder and rain in the dry season (vv. 16–18) prompted the people to confess their sin and request Samuel's intercession for them.

12:20 *yet do not turn away from the LORD.* Samuel again brings into focus the central issue in the controversy surrounding the establishment of kingship in Israel.

12:21 *useless idols.* No rivals to the Lord can deliver or guarantee security.

12:23 *I will teach you the way that is good and right.* Samuel is not retiring from his prophetic role when he presents the people with their king. He will continue to intercede for the people (see v. 19; 7:8–9) and will instruct them in their covenant obligations (see Dt 6:18; 12:28). Saul and all future kings are to be subject to instruction and correction by the Lord's prophets.

²⁴But be sure to fear ᵘ the Lᴏʀᴅ and serve him faithfully with all your heart; ᵛ consider ʷ what great ˣ things he has done for you. ²⁵Yet if you persist ʸ in doing evil, both you and your king ᶻ will be swept ᵃ away."

Samuel Rebukes Saul

13 Saul was ˏthirty,ⁱ years old when he became king, and he reigned over Israel ˏforty-ʲ two years.

²Saul ᵏ chose three thousand men from Israel; two thousand ᵇ were with him at Micmash ᶜ and in the hill country of Bethel, and a thousand were with Jonathan at Gibeah ᵈ in Benjamin. The rest of the men he sent back to their homes.

³Jonathan attacked the Philistine outpost ᵉ at Geba,ᶠ and the Philistines heard about it. Then Saul had the trumpet ᵍ blown throughout the land and said, "Let the Hebrews hear!" ⁴So all Israel heard the news: "Saul has attacked the Philistine outpost ʰ to the Philistines." And the people were summoned to join Saul at Gilgal.

⁵The Philistines assembled ⁱ to fight Israel, with three thousand¹ chariots, six thousand charioteers, and soldiers as numerous as the sand ʲ on the seashore. They went up and camped at Micmash, ᵏ east of Beth Aven.ˡ ⁶When the men of Israel saw that their situation was critical and that their army was hard pressed, they hid ᵐ in caves and thickets, among the rocks, and in pits and cisterns. ⁿ ⁷Some Hebrews even crossed the Jordan to the land of Gad ᵒ and Gilead.

Saul remained at Gilgal, and all the troops with him were quaking ᵖ with fear. ⁸He waited seven ᑫ days, the time set by Samuel; but Samuel did not come to Gilgal, and Saul's men began to scatter. ⁹So he said, "Bring me the burnt offering and the fellowship offerings. ᵐ" And Saul offered ʳ up the burnt offering. ¹⁰Just as he finished making the offering, Samuel ˢ arrived, and Saul went out to greet ᵗ him.

¹¹"What have you done?" asked Samuel.

Saul replied, "When I saw that the men were scattering, and that you did not come at the set time, and that the Philistines were assembling at Micmash, ᵘ ¹²I thought, 'Now the Philistines will come down against me at Gilgal, ᵛ and I have not sought the Lᴏʀᴅ's favor. ʷ So I felt compelled to offer the burnt offering."

¹³"You acted foolishly, ˣ" Samuel said. "You have not kept ʸ the command the Lᴏʀᴅ your God gave you; if you had, he would have established your kingdom over Israel for all time. ᶻ ¹⁴But now your kingdom ᵃ will not endure; the Lᴏʀᴅ has sought out a man after his own heart ᵇ and appointed ᶜ him leader ᵈ of his people, because you have not kept ᵉ the Lᴏʀᴅ's command."

12:24 ᵘDt 6:2; Ecc 12:13
ᵛDt 6:5;
ˢ Jos 24:14
ʷJob 34:27;
Isa 5:12; 22:11; 26:10
ˣS Dt 10:21
12:25
ʸ1Sa 31:1-5
ᶻDt 28:36
ᵃS Jos 24:20;
S 1Ki 14:10
13:2 ᵇver 15 ᶜver 5,11,23;
Ne 11:31;
Isa 10:28
ᵈS Jdg 19:14
13:3 ᵉS 1Sa 10:5
ᶠS Jos 18:24
ᵍS Lev 25:9;
S Jdg 3:27
13:4 ʰS Ge 34:30
13:5 ⁱ1Sa 17:1
ʲS Jos 11:4;
Rev 20:8 ᵏS ver 2
ˡS Jos 7:2
13:6 ᵐ1Sa 14:11, 22 ⁿS Jdg 6:2;
Eze 33:27
13:7 ᵒS Nu 32:33

ᵖS Ge 35:5;
S Ex 19:16
13:8 ᑫS Jos 10:8
13:9
ʳDt 12:5-14;
2Sa 24:25;
1Ki 3:4
13:10 ˢ1Sa 15:13
ᵗ1Sa 25:14
13:11 ᵘS ver 2
13:12
ᵛS Jos 10:43
ʷS Dt 4:29;
Ps 119:58;
Jer 26:19
13:13 ˣ2Ch 16:9
ʸver 14;
S Jos 22:16;
1Sa 15:23,24;
2Sa 7:15;
1Ch 10:13
ᶻPs 72:5
13:14
ᵃ1Sa 15:28; 18:8;
24:20; 1Ch 10:14
ᵇAc 7:46; 13:22
ᶜ2Sa 6:21
ᵈ1Sa 25:30;

2Sa 5:2; Ps 18:43; Isa 16:5; 55:4; Jer 30:9; Eze 34:23-24; 37:24; Da 9:25; Hos 3:5; Mic 5:2 ᵉ1Sa 15:26; 16:1;
2Sa 12:9; 1Ki 13:21; Hos 13:11

i1 A few late manuscripts of the Septuagint; Hebrew does not have thirty. *j1 See the round number in Acts 13:21; Hebrew does not have forty-.* *k1,2 Or and when he had reigned over Israel two years,* *2he 15 Some Septuagint manuscripts and Syriac; Hebrew thirty thousand* *m9 Traditionally peace offerings*

12:24 *fear the Lᴏʀᴅ.* Samuel summarizes Israel's obligation of loyalty to the Lord as an expression of gratitude for the great things he has done for them.

12:25 *you and your king will be swept away.* Should the nation persist in covenant-breaking conduct, it will bring upon itself its own destruction.

13:1 *ˏthirty, years old . . . ˏforty-˒ two years.* See NIV text notes. The wording of the verse follows the regularly used formula that introduces the reigns of later kings (see, e.g., 2Sa 2:10; 5:4; 1Ki 14:21; 2Ki 8:26).

13:2 *Micmash.* Located southeast of Bethel and northeast of Gibeah near a pass (see v. 23). *Jonathan.* Saul's oldest son (see 14:49), mentioned here for the first time.

13:3 *Geba.* Located across a ravine and south of Micmash.

13:4 *stench.* A metaphor depicting an object of strong hostility, as in 2Sa 10:6; 16:21; Ge 34:30; Ex 5:21. *Gilgal.* See note on 11:14. By prearrangement Saul had been instructed to wait for Samuel there (see notes on v. 8; 10:8).

13:5 *three thousand chariots.* See NIV text note. The Canaanites under Sisera (see Jdg 4:13) had 900 chariots. The Israelites did not acquire chariots until the time of Solomon (see 1Ki 4:26).

13:8 *time set by Samuel.* See note on 10:8. Saul is fully aware that Samuel's previous instructions had reference to this gathering at Gilgal. *Saul's men began to scatter.* The

seven-day delay heightened the fear of the Israelite soldiers.

13:9 *Saul offered up the burnt offering.* Samuel had promised to make these offerings himself (see 10:8) before Israel went to battle (see 7:9), and he had directed Saul to await his arrival and instructions.

13:13 *You acted foolishly.* The foolish and sinful aspect (see 26:21; 2Sa 24:10; 1Ch 21:8; 2Ch 16:9) of Saul's act was that he thought he could strengthen Israel's chances against the Philistines while disregarding the instruction of the Lord's prophet Samuel. *You have not kept the command the Lᴏʀᴅ your God gave you.* Saul was to recognize the word of the prophet Samuel as the word of the Lord (see 3:20; 15:1; Ex 20:18-19; see also note on Ex 7:1-2). In disobeying Samuel's instructions, Saul violated a fundamental requirement of his theocratic office. His kingship was not to function independently of the law and the prophets (see notes on 12:14,23; 15:11).

13:14 *your kingdom will not endure.* Saul will not be followed by his sons; there will be no dynasty bearing his name (contrast the Lord's word to David, 2Sa 7:11-16). There is a striking parallel in the word of the Lord to Eli (see 2:30,35). *the Lᴏʀᴅ has sought out a man after his own heart and appointed him.* Paul quotes from this passage at Antioch (Ac 13:22). *leader.* See note on 9:16.

15Then Samuel left Gilgal[n] and went up
to Gibeah[f] in Benjamin, and Saul counted
the men who were with him. They numbered about six hundred.[g]

Israel Without Weapons

16Saul and his son Jonathan and the men
with them were staying in Gibeah[o][h] in
Benjamin, while the Philistines camped at
Micmash. 17Raiding[i] parties went out
from the Philistine camp in three detach-
ments. One turned toward Ophrah[j] in the
vicinity of Shual, 18another toward Beth
Horon,[k] and the third toward the border-
land overlooking the Valley of Zeboim[l]
facing the desert.
19Not a blacksmith[m] could be found in
the whole land of Israel, because the Philistines had said, "Otherwise the Hebrews
will make swords or spears![n]" 20So all Israel went down to the Philistines to have
their plowshares, mattocks, axes and sickles[p] sharpened. 21The price was two thirds
of a shekel[q] for sharpening plowshares and
mattocks, and a third of a shekel[r] for
sharpening forks and axes and for repoint-
ing goads.
22So on the day of the battle not a soldier with Saul and Jonathan[o] had a sword
or spear[p] in his hand; only Saul and his
son Jonathan had them.

Jonathan Attacks the Philistines

23Now a detachment of Philistines had
gone out to the pass[q] at Micmash.[r] 1One
14 day Jonathan son of Saul said
to the young man bearing his ar-
mor, "Come, let's go over to the Philistine
outpost on the other side." But he did not
tell his father.
2Saul was staying[s] on the outskirts of
Gibeah[t] under a pomegranate tree[u] in
Migron.[v] With him were about six hundred men, 3among whom was Ahijah, who
was wearing an ephod. He was a son of
Ichabod's[w] brother Ahitub[x] son of Phinehas, the son of Eli,[y] the LORD's priest in
Shiloh.[z] No one was aware that Jonathan
had left.
4On each side of the pass[a] that Jonathan
intended to cross to reach the Philistine
outpost was a cliff; one was called Bozez,
and the other Seneh. 5One cliff stood to
the north toward Micmash, the other to
the south toward Geba.[b]
6Jonathan said to his young armor-bearer, "Come, let's go over to the outpost of
those uncircumcised[c] fellows. Perhaps the
LORD will act in our behalf. Nothing[d] can
hinder the LORD from saving, whether by
many[e] or by few.[f]"
7"Do all that you have in mind," his
armor-bearer said. "Go ahead; I am with
you heart and soul."
8Jonathan said, "Come, then; we will
cross over toward the men and let them
see us. 9If they say to us, 'Wait there until
we come to you,' we will stay where we
are and not go up to them. 10But if they
say, 'Come up to us,' we will climb up,
because that will be our sign[g] that the
LORD has given them into our hands.[h]"
11So both of them showed themselves to
the Philistine outpost. "Look!" said the
Philistines. "The Hebrews[i] are crawling
out of the holes they were hiding[j] in."
12The men of the outpost shouted to Jonathan and his armor-bearer, "Come up to
us and we'll teach you a lesson.[k]"
So Jonathan said to his armor-bearer,
"Climb up after me; the LORD has given
them into the hand[l] of Israel."
13Jonathan climbed up, using his hands

13:15 [f]1Sa 14:2 [g]ver 2
13:16 [h]S Jos 18:24
13:17 [i]1Sa 14:15 [j]S Jos 18:23
13:18 [k]S Jos 10:10 [l]Ne 11:34
13:19 [m]S Ge 4:22 [n]S Nu 25:7
13:22 [o]1Ch 9:39 [p]S Nu 25:7; 1Sa 14:6; 17:47; Zec 4:6
13:23 [q]1Sa 14:4 [r]S ver 2
14:2 [s]S Jdg 4:5 [t]1Sa 13:15 [u]S Ex 28:33 [v]Isa 10:28
14:3 [w]S Ge 35:18 [x]1Sa 22:11,20 [y]S 1Sa 1:3 [z]Ps 78:60
14:4 [a]1Sa 13:23
14:5 [b]S Jos 18:24
14:6 [c]Jdg 14:3; 1Sa 17:26,36; 31:4; Jer 9:26; Eze 28:10 [d]S 1Sa 13:22; S 1Ki 19:12; S Mt 19:26; Heb 11:34 [e]Jdg 7:4 [f]Ps 33:16
14:10 [g]S Ge 24:14 [h]S Jos 2:24
14:11 [i]S Ge 14:13 [j]S 1Sa 13:6
14:12 [k]Jdg 8:16 [l]1Sa 17:46; 2Sa 5:24

[n]*15* Hebrew; Septuagint *Gilgal and went his way; the rest of the people went after Saul to meet the army, and they went out of Gilgal* [o]*16* Two Hebrew manuscripts; most Hebrew manuscripts *Geba,* a variant of *Gibeah* [p]*20* Septuagint; Hebrew *plowshares* [q]*21* Hebrew *pim;* that is, about 1/4 ounce (about 8 grams) [r]*21* That is, about 1/8 ounce (about 4 grams)

13:15 *six hundred.* The seven-day delay had greatly depleted Saul's forces (see vv. 2,4,6–8).
13:17 *Raiding parties.* The purpose of these Philistine contingents was not to engage the Israelites in battle, but to plunder the land and demoralize its inhabitants.
13:18 *Valley of Zeboim.* Located to the east toward the Jordan Valley.
13:19 *Not a blacksmith.* A Philistine monopoly on the technology of iron production placed the Israelites at a great disadvantage in the fashioning and maintenance of agricultural implements and military weapons.
13:22 *not . . . a sword or spear.* The Israelites fought with bow and arrow and slingshot.
14:1 *on the other side.* The Philistines were encamped to the north of the pass and the Israelites to the south.
14:2 *Gibeah.* Saul had retreated farther south from Geba (13:3) to Gibeah. *under a pomegranate tree.* It appears to have been customary for leaders in early Israel to hold court under well-known trees (see 22:6; Jdg 4:5).
14:3 *Ahijah.* Either the brother and predecessor of Ahimelech son of Ahitub (referred to in 21:1; 22:9,11) or an alternate name for Ahimelech. *wearing an ephod.* See note on 2:28. *Ichabod's brother.* See 4:21.
14:6 *uncircumcised fellows.* A term of contempt (see 17:26,36; 31:4; 2Sa 1:20; Jdg 14:3; 15:18; 1Ch 10:4), which draws attention to Israel's covenant relationship to the Lord (see note on Ge 17:10) and, by implication, to the illegitimacy of the Philistine presence in the land. *by many or by few.* See note on 17:47. Jonathan's bold plan is undertaken as an act of faith (cf. Heb 11:33–34) founded on God's promise (9:16).
14:10 *our sign.* See Jdg 6:36–40; Isa 7:11.
14:11 *Hebrews.* See 4:6; 13:3,7 and note on Ge 14:13.

and feet, with his armor-bearer right behind him. The Philistines fell before Jonathan, and his armor-bearer followed and killed behind him. [14]In that first attack Jonathan and his armor-bearer killed some twenty men in an area of about half an acre. [s]

Israel Routs the Philistines

[15]Then panic [m] struck the whole army—those in the camp and field, and those in the outposts and raiding [n] parties—and the ground shook. It was a panic sent by God. [t]

[16]Saul's lookouts [o] at Gibeah in Benjamin saw the army melting away in all directions. [17]Then Saul said to the men who were with him, "Muster the forces and see who has left us." When they did, it was Jonathan and his armor-bearer who were not there.

[18]Saul said to Ahijah, "Bring [p] the ark [q] of God." (At that time it was with the Israelites.) [u] [19]While Saul was talking to the priest, the tumult in the Philistine camp increased more and more. So Saul said to the priest, [r] "Withdraw your hand."

[20]Then Saul and all his men assembled and went to the battle. They found the Philistines in total confusion, striking [s] each other with their swords. [21]Those Hebrews who had previously been with the Philistines and had gone up with them to their camp went [t] over to the Israelites who were with Saul and Jonathan. [22]When all the Israelites who had hidden [u] in the

hill country of Ephraim heard that the Philistines were on the run, they joined the battle in hot pursuit. [23]So the LORD rescued [v] Israel that day, and the battle moved on beyond Beth Aven. [w]

Jonathan Eats Honey

[24]Now the men of Israel were in distress that day, because Saul had bound the people under an oath, [x] saying, "Cursed be any man who eats food before evening comes, before I have avenged myself on my enemies!" So none of the troops tasted food.

[25]The entire army [v] entered the woods, and there was honey on the ground. [26]When they went into the woods, they saw the honey oozing out, yet no one put his hand to his mouth, because they feared the oath. [27]But Jonathan had not heard that his father had bound the people with the oath, so he reached out the end of the staff that was in his hand and dipped it into the honeycomb. [y] He raised his hand to his mouth, and his eyes brightened. [w] [28]Then one of the soldiers told him, "Your father bound the army under a strict oath, saying, 'Cursed be any man who eats food today!' That is why the men are faint."

[29]Jonathan said, "My father has made trouble [z] for the country. See how my eyes

---

14:15
[m]S Ge 35:5;
S Ex 14:24;
S 19:16;
2Ki 7:5-7
[n]1Sa 13:17
14:16
[o]2Sa 18:24;
2Ki 9:17;
Isa 52:8; Eze 33:2
14:18 [p]1Sa 30:7
[q]S Jdg 18:5
14:19 [r]Nu 27:21
14:20
[s]S Jdg 7:22;
Eze 38:21;
Zec 14:13
14:21 [t]1Sa 29:4
14:22
[u]S 1Sa 13:6

14:23
[v]S Ex 14:30
[w]S Jos 7:2
14:24 [x]Jos 6:26
14:27 [y]ver 43;
Ps 19:10;
Pr 16:24; 24:13
14:29 [z]Jos 7:25;
1Ki 18:18

s *14* Hebrew *half a yoke;* a "yoke" was the land plowed by a yoke of oxen in one day.   t *15* Or *a terrible panic*   u *18* Hebrew; Septuagint *"Bring the ephod."* (At that time he wore the ephod before the Israelites.)   v *25* Or *Now all the people of the land*   w *27* Or *his strength was renewed*

14:15 *ground shook.* See 7:10; Jos 10:11–14; Ps 77:18 for other instances of divine intervention in nature to bring deliverance to Israel.

14:18 *Bring the ark of God.* Saul decides to seek God's will before entering into battle with the Philistines (see Nu 27:21; Dt 20:2). Here the Septuagint (the Greek translation of the OT) may preserve the original text (see NIV text note) for the following reasons: 1. In 7:1 the ark was located at Kiriath Jearim, where it remained until David brought it to Jerusalem (2Sa 6), but the ephod was present in Saul's camp at Gibeah (see v. 3). 2. Nowhere else in the OT is the ark used to determine God's will, but the ephod (with the Urim and Thummim) was given for this purpose (see 23:9; 30:7 and notes on 2:18,28). 3. The command to the priest to withdraw his hand (v. 19) is more appropriate with the ephod than with the ark.

14:19 *Withdraw your hand.* Due to the urgency of the moment, Saul decides that to wait for the word of the Lord might jeopardize his military advantage. As in 13:8–12, his decision rests on his own insight rather than on dependence upon the Lord and a commitment to obey him.

14:23 *So the LORD rescued Israel that day.* The writer attributes the victory to the Lord, not to either Saul or Jonathan (see vv. 6,10,15; 11:13).

14:24–46 Following the account of the great victory the Lord had given, the author relates Saul's actions that strikingly illustrated his lack of fitness to be king. This foolish curse

before the battle (see note on v. 24) brought "distress" to the army and, as Jonathan tellingly observed, "made trouble for the country" (v. 29) rather than contributing to the victory. And later, when hindered from taking advantage of the battle's outcome by the Lord's refusal to answer (v. 37), Saul was ready to execute Jonathan as the cause, though Jonathan had contributed most to the victory, as everyone else recognized (v. 45). Saul's growing egocentrism was turning into an all-consuming passion that threatened the very welfare of the nation. Rather than serving the cause of the Lord and his people, he was in fact becoming a king "such as all the other nations have" (8:5).

14:24 *in distress.* Saul's rash action in requiring his troops to fast placed them at an unnecessary disadvantage in the battle (see vv. 29–30). *Cursed.* Thus Saul as king "bound the army under a strict oath" (v. 28), a most serious matter because an oath directly invoked God's involvement, whether it concerned giving testimony (Ex 20:7; Lev 19:12), making commitments (Ge 21:23–24; 24:3–4) or prohibiting action (here; Jos 6:24). It appealed to God as the supreme enforcement power and the all-knowing Judge of human actions. *I have avenged myself on my enemies.* Saul perceives the conflict with the Philistines more as a personal vendetta (see note on 15:12) than as a battle for the honor of the Lord and the security of the Lord's people (note the contrast between his attitude and that of Jonathan in vv. 6,10,12).

brightened^x when I tasted a little of this honey. ³⁰How much better it would have been if the men had eaten today some of the plunder they took from their enemies. Would not the slaughter of the Philistines have been even greater?"

³¹That day, after the Israelites had struck down the Philistines from Micmash^a to Aijalon,^b they were exhausted. ³²They pounced on the plunder^c and, taking sheep, cattle and calves, they butchered them on the ground and ate them, together with the blood.^d ³³Then someone said to Saul, "Look, the men are sinning against the LORD by eating meat that has blood^e in it."

"You have broken faith," he said. "Roll a large stone over here at once." ³⁴Then he said, "Go out among the men and tell them, 'Each of you bring me your cattle and sheep, and slaughter them here and eat them. Do not sin against the LORD by eating meat with blood still^f in it.' "

So everyone brought his ox that night and slaughtered it there. ³⁵Then Saul built an altar^g to the LORD; it was the first time he had done this.

³⁶Saul said, "Let us go down after the Philistines by night and plunder them till dawn, and let us not leave one of them alive."

"Do whatever seems best to you," they replied.

But the priest said, "Let us inquire^h of God here."

³⁷So Saul asked God, "Shall I go down after the Philistines? Will you give them into Israel's hand?" But God did not answerⁱ him that day.

³⁸Saul therefore said, "Come here, all you who are leaders of the army, and let us find out what sin has been committed^j today. ³⁹As surely as the LORD who rescues Israel lives,^k even if it lies with my son Jonathan,^l he must die." ^m But not one of the men said a word.

⁴⁰Saul then said to all the Israelites, "You stand over there; I and Jonathan my son will stand over here."

"Do what seems best to you," the men replied.

⁴¹Then Saul prayed to the LORD, the God of Israel, "Giveⁿ me the right^o answer." ^v And Jonathan and Saul were taken by lot, and the men were cleared. ⁴²Saul said, "Cast the lot^p between me and Jonathan my son." And Jonathan was taken.

⁴³Then Saul said to Jonathan, "Tell me what you have done." ^q

So Jonathan told him, "I merely tasted a little honey^r with the end of my staff. And now must I die?"

⁴⁴Saul said, "May God deal with me, be it ever so severely,^s if you do not die, Jonathan.^t "

⁴⁵But the men said to Saul, "Should Jonathan die—he who has brought about this great deliverance in Israel? Never! As surely as the LORD lives, not a hair^u of his head will fall to the ground, for he did this today with God's help." So the men rescued^v Jonathan, and he was not put to death.

⁴⁶Then Saul stopped pursuing the Philistines, and they withdrew to their own land.

⁴⁷After Saul had assumed rule over Israel, he fought against their enemies on every side: Moab,^w the Ammonites,^x Edom,^y the kings^z of Zobah,^z and the Philistines. Wherever he turned, he inflicted punishment on them.^a ⁴⁸He fought valiantly and defeated the Amalekites,^a delivering Israel from the hands of those who had plundered them.

14:31 ^aver 5
^bS Jos 10:12
14:32 ^c1Sa 15:19;
Est 9:10
^dS Ge 9:4
14:33 ^eS Ge 9:4
14:34 ^fLev 19:26
14:35 ^gS 1Sa 7:17
14:36 ^hS Ge 25:22;
S Jdg 18:5
14:37 ⁱ1Sa 28:6,
15; 2Sa 22:42;
Ps 18:41
14:38 ^jJos 7:11
14:39 ^kS Nu 14:21;
2Sa 12:5;
Job 19:25;
Ps 18:46; 42:2
^lver 44 ^mJos 7:15

14:41 ⁿAc 1:24
^oPr 16:33
14:42 ^pJnh 1:7
14:43 ^qS Jos 7:19
^rS ver 27
14:44 ^sS Ru 1:17
^tver 39
14:45 ^u1Ki 1:52;
S Mt 10:30
^v2Sa 14:11
14:47 ^wS Ge 19:37
^xS Ge 19:38;
2Sa 12:31
^y1Sa 21:7
^z2Sa 8:3; 10:6;
23:36
14:48 ^aS Ge 36:12;
Nu 13:29;
Jdg 3:13;
1Sa 15:2,7; 27:8;
28:18; 30:13;
2Sa 1:13;
1Ch 4:43

^x29 Or *my strength was renewed*   ^y41 Hebrew; Septuagint *"Why have you not answered your servant today? If the fault is in me or my son Jonathan, respond with Urim, but if the men of Israel are at fault, respond with Thummim."*   ^z47 Masoretic Text; Dead Sea Scrolls and Septuagint *king*   ^a47 Hebrew; Septuagint *he was victorious*

14:31 *Aijalon.* Located to the west near the Philistines' own territory (see Jos 10:12).

14:33 *eating meat that has blood in it.* The Israelites were not permitted to eat blood (see Ge 9:4; Lev 17:11; 19:26; Dt 12:16; Eze 33:25; Ac 15:20 and notes). *broken faith.* See Mal 2:10–11. The same Hebrew term is translated "faithless" (Ps 78:57; Jer 3:8–11) and "treacherous" (Isa 48:8).

14:35 *first time he had done this.* Another indication of Saul's personal lack of interest in religious matters (see notes on 9:6; 10:11).

14:36 *priest.* Ahijah (see v. 3).

14:37 *Saul asked God.* The means of ascertaining God's will appears to have been the ephod with its Urim and Thummim (see v. 3 and note on v. 18). *God did not answer.* Because an oath had been broken in the battle, God refused

to answer Saul's inquiry concerning further military action.

14:39 *As surely as the LORD . . . lives.* An oath formula (see note on v. 24; see also 19:6; Jer 4:2; Hos 4:15).

14:41 *taken by lot.* See 10:20–21; Jos 7:14–18; Pr 16:33.

14:44 A curse formula (see note on v. 24; see also 3:17 and note).

14:45 *he did this today with God's help.* The men of Saul's army recognize the inappropriateness of taking the life of the one through whom God has delivered his people.

14:47–48 A summary of Saul's military victories to the east (Moab and the Ammonites), south (Edom), west (Philistines) and north (Zobah).

14:47 *Ammonites.* See Dt 2:19–21,37.

14:48 *Amalekites.* See note on 15:2.

Saul's Family

⁴⁹Saul's sons were Jonathan, Ishvi and Malki-Shua.ᵇ The name of his older daughter was Merab, and that of the younger was Michal.ᶜ ⁵⁰His wife's name was Ahinoam daughter of Ahimaaz. The name of the commander of Saul's army was Abnerᵈ son of Ner, and Ner was Saul's uncle.ᵉ ⁵¹Saul's father Kishᶠ and Abner's father Ner were sons of Abiel.

⁵²All the days of Saul there was bitter war with the Philistines, and whenever Saul saw a mighty or brave man, he tookᵍ him into his service.

The LORD Rejects Saul as King

15 Samuel said to Saul, "I am the one the LORD sent to anointʰ you king over his people Israel; so listen now to the message from the LORD. ²This is what the LORD Almighty says: 'I will punish the Amalekitesⁱ for what they did to Israel when they waylaid them as they came up from Egypt. ³Now go, attack the Amalekites and totallyʲ destroyᵇ everything that belongs to them. Do not spare them; put to death men and women, children and infants, cattle and sheep, camels and donkeys.' "

⁴So Saul summoned the men and mustered them at Telaim—two hundred thousand foot soldiers and ten thousand men

from Judah. ⁵Saul went to the city of Amalek and set an ambush in the ravine. ⁶Then he said to the Kenites,ᵏ "Go away, leave the Amalekites so that I do not destroy you along with them; for you showed kindness to all the Israelites when they came up out of Egypt." So the Kenites moved away from the Amalekites.

⁷Then Saul attacked the Amalekitesˡ all the way from Havilah to Shur,ᵐ to the east of Egypt. ⁸He took Agagⁿ king of the Amalekites alive,ᵒ and all his people he totally destroyed with the sword. ⁹But Saul and the army sparedᵖ Agag and the best of the sheep and cattle, the fat calvesᶜ and lambs—everything that was good. These they were unwilling to destroy completely, but everything that was despised and weak they totally destroyed.

¹⁰Then the word of the LORD came to Samuel: ¹¹"I am grievedᑫ that I have made Saul king, because he has turnedʳ away from me and has not carried out my instructions."ˢ Samuel was troubled,ᵗ and he cried out to the LORD all that night.

¹²Early in the morning Samuel got up and went to meet Saul, but he was told,

14:49 ᵇ1Sa 31:2; 1Ch 8:33 ᶜS Ge 29:26
14:50 ᵈ2Sa 2:8; 3:6; 1Ki 2:5 ᵉ1Sa 10:14
14:51 ᶠS 1Sa 9:1
14:52 ᵍ1Sa 8:11
15:1 ʰS 1Sa 9:16
15:2 ⁱS Ge 14:7; S 1Sa 14:48; S 2Sa 1:8
15:3 ʲver 9,19; S Ge 14:23; Jos 6:17; 1Sa 22:19; 27:9; 28:18; Est 3:13; 9:5

15:6 ᵏS Ge 15:19; Nu 24:22; Jdg 1:16; 1Sa 30:29
15:7 ˡS 1Sa 14:48 ᵐS Ge 16:7
15:8 ⁿEx 17:8-16; S Nu 24:7 ᵒS Jos 8:23
15:9 ᵖS ver 3
15:11 ᑫS Ge 6:6; S Ex 32:14; rS Jos 22:16; 34:27; Ps 28:5; Isa 5:12; 53:6; Jer 48:10; Eze 18:24 ˢS ver 35; S 1Sa 8:6

ᵇ3 The Hebrew term refers to the irrevocable giving over of things or persons to the LORD, often by totally destroying them; also in verses 8, 9, 15, 18, 20 and 21.
ᶜ9 Or the grown bulls; the meaning of the Hebrew for this phrase is uncertain.

14:49 *Saul's sons.* See 2Sa 2:8,10; 1Ch 9:39; 10:2. *Merab...Michal.* See 18:17,20,27; 19:11–17; 25:44; 2Sa 6:16–23.

14:50 *Ahinoam.* The only reference to a wife of Saul. His concubine Rizpah is mentioned in 2Sa 3:7; 21:8–11.

14:52 *All the days of Saul.* Closes the main account of Saul's reign. *he took him into his service.* Saul developed a special cadre of professional soldiers bound to himself, much as David was to do later (see 22:2; 23:13; 25:13; 27:2–3; 29:2; 30:1,9; 2Sa 2:3; 5:6; 8:18; 15:18; 23:8–39).

15:1–35 The event that occasioned Saul's rejection. Although no time designation is given, it evidently occurred after the conflicts of 14:47, in a time of relative peace and security. It is likely that David was anointed (16:1–13) shortly after the rejection of Saul (vv. 22,26,28), thus c. 1025 B.C.

15:2 *Amalekites.* A Bedouin people descended from Esau (see Ge 36:12,16) usually located in the Negev and Sinai regions (see 27:8; 30:1; Ge 14:7; Ex 17:8; Nu 13:29). *what they did to Israel.* See Ex 17:8–13; Nu 14:43, 45; Dt 25:17–19; cf. Jdg 3:13; 6:3–5,33; 7:12; 10:12.

15:3 *totally destroy.* See NIV text note and Lev 27:28–29; Dt 13:12–18; see also notes on Jos 6:17–18. Saul is given an opportunity as king to demonstrate his allegiance to the Lord by obedience in this assigned task.

15:4 *Telaim.* Probably the same as Telem in Jos 15:24, located in the southern part of Judah.

15:5 *city of Amalek.* A settlement of Amalekites, most likely located between Telaim and Kadesh Barnea, possibly the residence of their king.

15:6 *Kenites.* A Bedouin people of the Sinai, closely related to the Midianites. Moses had married a Kenite woman (see

Ex 2:16,21–22; Nu 10:29; Jdg 1:16; 4:11), and some of the Kenites had accompanied the Israelites when they settled in the land of Canaan (see 27:10; Jdg 1:16; 4:17–23; 5:24; 1Ch 2:55).

15:7 *Havilah to Shur.* The location of Havilah is uncertain. Shur was on the eastern frontier of Egypt (see 27:8; Ge 16:7; 20:1). Ishmael's descendants occupied this area (see Ge 25:18).

15:8 *all his people.* All the Amalekites they encountered. Some Amalekites survived (see 27:8; 30:1,18; 2Sa 8:12; 1Ch 4:43).

15:9 When Israel refused to obey the Lord's command (v. 3), their holy war against the Amalekites degenerated into personal aggrandizement, much like that of Achan at the time of the conquest of Canaan (see Jos 7:1). Giving to the Lord by destruction only what was despised and weak was a contemptible act (see Mal 1:7–12), not to be excused (see v. 19) by the protestation that the best had been preserved for sacrifice to the Lord (vv. 15,21).

15:11 *grieved.* See note on v. 29. *he has turned away from me.* A violation of the fundamental requirement of his office as king (see notes on 12:14–15).

15:12 *Carmel.* Located about seven miles south of Hebron (see 25:2; Jos 15:55). *monument in his own honor.* Saul's self-glorification here contrasts sharply with his self-abasement after the victory over the Ammonites (see note on 11:13; cf. v. 17; 2Sa 18:18). *Gilgal.* Saul returns to the place where he was inaugurated and instructed in the responsibilities of his office (see 11:14–12:25). This was also the place where he had been told that he would not have a continuing dynasty because of his disobedience (see 13:13–14).

"Saul has gone to Carmel. *u* There he has set up a monument *v* in his own honor and has turned and gone on down to Gilgal."

13When Samuel reached him, Saul said, "The LORD bless you! I have carried out the LORD's instructions."

14But Samuel said, "What then is this bleating of sheep in my ears? What is this lowing of cattle that I hear?"

15Saul answered, "The soldiers brought them from the Amalekites; they spared the best of the sheep and cattle to sacrifice to the LORD your God, but we totally destroyed the rest."

16"Stop!" Samuel said to Saul. "Let me tell you what the LORD said to me last night."

"Tell me," Saul replied.

17Samuel said, "Although you were once small *w* in your own eyes, did you not become the head of the tribes of Israel? The LORD anointed you king over Israel. 18And he sent you on a mission, saying, 'Go and completely destroy those wicked people, the Amalekites; make war on them until you have wiped them out.' 19Why did you not obey the LORD? Why did you pounce on the plunder *x* and do evil in the eyes of the LORD?"

20"But I did obey *y* the LORD," Saul said. "I went on the mission the LORD assigned me. I completely destroyed the Amalekites and brought back Agag their king. 21The soldiers took sheep and cattle from the plunder, the best of what was devoted to God, in order to sacrifice them to the LORD your God at Gilgal."

22But Samuel replied:

"Does the LORD delight in burnt
    offerings and sacrifices
as much as in obeying the voice of
    the LORD?
To obey is better than sacrifice, *z*
    and to heed is better than the fat of
        rams.
23For rebellion is like the sin of
    divination, *a*
    and arrogance like the evil of idolatry.
Because you have rejected *b* the word of
    the LORD,
    he has rejected you as king."

24Then Saul said to Samuel, "I have sinned. *c* I violated *d* the LORD's command and your instructions. I was afraid *e* of the people and so I gave in to them. 25Now I beg you, forgive *f* my sin and come back with me, so that I may worship the LORD."

26But Samuel said to him, "I will not go back with you. You have rejected *g* the word of the LORD, and the LORD has rejected you as king over Israel!"

27As Samuel turned to leave, Saul caught hold of the hem of his robe, *h* and it tore. *i* 28Samuel said to him, "The LORD has torn *j* the kingdom *k* of Israel from you today and has given it to one of your neighbors—to one better than you. *l* 29He who is the Glory of Israel does not lie *m* or change *n* his mind; for he is not a man, that he should change his mind."

Cross references (center column):

15:12 *u*Jos 15:55
  *v*S Nu 32:42
15:17 *w*S Ex 3:11
15:19
  *x*S Ge 14:23;
  S 1Sa 14:32
15:20 *y*1Sa 28:18

15:22
  *z*Ps 40:6-8;
  51:16; Pr 21:3;
  Isa 1:11-15;
  Jer 7:22; Hos 6:6;
  Am 5:25;
  Mic 6:6-8;
  S Mk 12:33
15:23 *a*Dt 18:10
  *b*S 1Sa 13:13
15:24
  *c*S Ex 9:27;
  S Nu 22:34;
  Ps 51:4
  *d*S 1Sa 13:13
  *e*Pr 29:25;
  Isa 51:12-13;
  Jer 42:11
15:25 *f*Ex 10:17
15:26
  *g*S Nu 15:31;
  S 1Sa 13:14;
  S 1Ki 14:10
15:27 *h*1Sa 28:14
  *i*1Ki 11:11,31;
  14:8; 2Ki 17:21
15:28 *j*1Sa 28:17
  *k*S 1Sa 13:14
  *l*2Sa 6:21; 7:15
15:29 *m*Tit 1:2
  *n*S Nu 23:19;
  Heb 7:21

15:13 *I have carried out the LORD's instructions.* Here and in v. 20 Saul is clearly less than honest in his statements to Samuel.
15:15 *The soldiers ... spared the best ... to sacrifice.* Saul attempts to shift responsibility from himself to the army and to excuse their action by claiming pious intentions. *the LORD your God.* Saul's use of the pronoun "your" instead of "my" here and in vv. 21,30 indicates an awareness of his own alienation from the Lord (see 12:19 for a similar case), even though he speaks of obedience and the intent to honor God by sacrifice.
15:17 *you were once small in your own eyes.* See 9:21; 10:22.
15:22 Samuel does not suggest that sacrifice is unimportant but that it is acceptable only when brought with an attitude of obedience and devotion to the Lord (see Ps 15; Isa 1:11–17; Hos 6:6; Am 5:21–27; Mic 6:6–8). *fat of rams.* The fat of sacrificed animals belonged to the Lord (see 2:15; Ex 23:18; Lev 3:14–16; 7:30).
15:23 *rebellion.* Samuel charges Saul with violating the central requirement of the covenant condition given to him when he became king (see 12:14–15). *sin of divination.* A serious offense against the Lord (see Lev 19:26; Dt 18:9–12), which Saul himself condemned (28:3,9). *you have rejected the word of the LORD.* A king who sets his own will above the command of the Lord ceases to be an instrument of the Lord's rule over his people, violating the very nature of his theocratic office. *he has rejected you as king.* The judgment here goes beyond the one given earlier (see note on 13:14). Now Saul himself is to be set aside as king. Although this did not happen immediately, as chs. 16–31 show, the process began that led to his death. It included in its relentless course the removal of God's Spirit and favor from him (16:14), the defection of his son Jonathan and daughter Michal to David, and the insubordination of his own officials (22:17).
15:24 Saul's confession retains an element of self-justification and a shift of blame (contrast David's confession, 2Sa 12:13; Ps 51). Previously (vv. 15,21) he had attempted to justify his soldiers' actions.
15:25 *come back with me.* Saul's greatest concern was not to worship God but to avoid an open break with the prophet Samuel, a break that would undermine his authority as king (see v. 30).
15:28 *one of your neighbors.* David (see note on 13:14).
15:29 *Glory of Israel.* A title of God used elsewhere only in Mic 1:15, though in Ps 106:20; Jer 2:11; Hos 4:7 he is called "Glory" (see note on 4:21). Cf. 2Sa 1:19; Ps 89:17; Isa 13:19. *does not lie or change his mind.* See Nu 23:19; Ps 110:4; Jer 4:28; Mal 3:6 and notes. There is no conflict between this statement and vv. 11,35, where the Lord is said to "grieve" that he had made Saul king. God has real emotions (one of the marks of personality).

30 Saul replied, "I have sinned.[o] But
please honor[p] me before the elders of my
people and before Israel; come back with
me, so that I may worship the LORD your
God." 31 So Samuel went back with Saul,
and Saul worshiped the LORD.

32 Then Samuel said, "Bring me Agag
king of the Amalekites."

Agag came to him confidently,[d] thinking, "Surely the bitterness of death is
past."

33 But Samuel said,

"As your sword has made women
childless,
so will your mother be childless
among women."[q]

And Samuel put Agag to death before the
LORD at Gilgal.

34 Then Samuel left for Ramah,[r] but Saul
went up to his home in Gibeah[s] of Saul.
35 Until the day Samuel[t] died, he did not
go to see Saul again, though Samuel
mourned[u] for him. And the LORD was
grieved[v] that he had made Saul king over
Israel.

Samuel Anoints David

16 The LORD said to Samuel, "How
long will you mourn[w] for Saul,
since I have rejected[x] him as king over
Israel? Fill your horn with oil[y] and be on
your way; I am sending you to Jesse[z] of
Bethlehem. I have chosen[a] one of his sons
to be king."

2 But Samuel said, "How can I go? Saul
will hear about it and kill me."

The LORD said, "Take a heifer with you
and say, 'I have come to sacrifice to the
LORD.' 3 Invite Jesse to the sacrifice, and I
will show[b] you what to do. You are to
anoint[c] for me the one I indicate."

4 Samuel did what the LORD said. When
he arrived at Bethlehem,[d] the elders of the
town trembled[e] when they met him. They
asked, "Do you come in peace?[f]"

5 Samuel replied, "Yes, in peace; I have
come to sacrifice to the LORD. Consecrate[g]
yourselves and come to the sacrifice with
me." Then he consecrated Jesse and his
sons and invited them to the sacrifice.

6 When they arrived, Samuel saw Eliab[h]
and thought, "Surely the LORD's anointed
stands here before the LORD."

7 But the LORD said to Samuel, "Do not
consider his appearance or his height, for I
have rejected him. The LORD does not look
at the things man looks at. Man looks at
the outward appearance,[i] but the LORD
looks at the heart."[j]

8 Then Jesse called Abinadab[k] and had
him pass in front of Samuel. But Samuel
said, "The LORD has not chosen this one
either." 9 Jesse then had Shammah[l] pass
by, but Samuel said, "Nor has the LORD
chosen this one." 10 Jesse had seven of his
sons pass before Samuel, but Samuel said
to him, "The LORD has not chosen these."
11 So he asked Jesse, "Are these all[m] the
sons you have?"

"There is still the youngest," Jesse answered, "but he is tending the sheep."[n]

Samuel said, "Send for him; we will not
sit down[e] until he arrives."

12 So he[o] sent and had him brought in.
He was ruddy, with a fine appearance and
handsome[p] features.

15:30 [o]S Nu 22:34 [p]Isa 29:13; Jn 12:43
15:33 [q]Est 9:7-10; Jer 18:21
15:34 [r]S 1Sa 7:17 [s]S Jdg 19:14; S 1Sa 10:5
15:35 [t]1Sa 19:24 [u]ver 11; 1Sa 16:1 [v]S Ge 6:6
16:1 [w]S 1Sa 8:6; S 15:35 [x]S 1Sa 13:14 [y]S 1Sa 10:1 [z]S Ru 4:17 [a]2Sa 5:2; 7:8; 1Ki 8:16; 1Ch 12:23; Ps 78:70; Ac 13:22
16:3 [b]Ex 4:15 [c]S Dt 17:15
16:4 [d]S Ge 48:7; Lk 2:4 [e]1Sa 21:1 [f]1Ki 2:13; 2Ki 9:17
16:5 [g]S Ex 19:10, 22
16:6 [h]1Sa 17:13; 1Ch 2:13
16:7 [i]Ps 147:10 [j]S 1Sa 2:3; 2Sa 7:20; S Ps 44:21; S 139:23; S Rev 2:23
16:8 [k]1Sa 17:13
16:9 [l]1Sa 17:13; 2Sa 13:3; 21:21
16:11 [m]1Sa 17:12 [n]S Ge 37:2; 2Sa 7:8
16:12 [o]1Sa 9:17 [p]S Ge 39:6

[d]32 Or *him trembling, yet* [e]11 Some Septuagint manuscripts; Hebrew *not gather around*

15:31 *So Samuel went back with Saul.* Samuel's purpose in agreeing to Saul's request is not to honor Saul, but to carry out the divine sentence on Agag and in so doing to reemphasize Saul's neglect of duty.

15:34 *Ramah.* Samuel's home (see 7:17). *Gibeah of Saul.* See note on 10:5.

15:35 *Samuel mourned.* Samuel regarded Saul as if dead (see the use of "mourned" in 6:19). Even though his love for him remained (see v. 11; 16:1), he sought no further contact with him because God had rejected him as king. Saul did come to Samuel on one other occasion (see 19:24).

16:1 *The LORD said to Samuel.* Probably c. 1025 B.C. (see note on 15:1–35). *Jesse.* For Jesse's genealogy see Ru 4:18–22; Mt 1:3–6. *Bethlehem.* A town five miles south of Jerusalem, formerly known as Ephrath (Ge 48:7). It was later to become renowned as the "town of David" (Lk 2:4) and the birthplace of Christ (Mic 5:2; Mt 2:1; Lk 2:4–7). *I have chosen one of his sons to be king.* See notes on 13:14; 15:28.

16:2 *Saul will . . . kill me.* The road from Ramah (where Samuel was, 15:34) to Bethlehem passed through Gibeah of Saul. Saul already knew that the Lord had chosen someone to replace him as king (see 15:28). Samuel fears that jealousy will incite Saul to violence. Later incidents (18:10–11; 19:10; 20:33) demonstrate that Samuel's fears were well-founded. *say, 'I have come to sacrifice to the LORD.'* This response is true but incomplete, and it was intended to deceive Saul.

16:3 *anoint.* See note on 9:16.

16:5 *Consecrate yourselves.* Involves preparing oneself spiritually as well as making oneself ceremonially clean by washing and putting on clean clothes (see Ex 19:10,14; Lev 15; Nu 19:11–22).

16:6 *Eliab.* Jesse's oldest son (17:13).

16:7 *his appearance or his height.* Samuel is not to focus on these outward features, which had characterized Saul (see 9:2; 10:23–24). *heart.* The Lord is concerned with man's inner disposition and character (see 1Ki 8:39; 1Ch 28:9; Lk 16:15; Jn 2:25; Ac 1:24).

16:8 *Abinadab.* Jesse's second son.

16:9 *Shammah.* Jesse's third son.

16:11 *he is tending the sheep.* The Lord's chosen one is a shepherd (see note on 9:3; see also 2Sa 7:7–8; Ps 78:71–72).

Then the LORD said, "Rise and anoint him; he is the one."

¹³So Samuel took the horn of oil and anointed⁹ him in the presence of his brothers, and from that day on the Spirit of the LORDʳ came upon David in power.ˢ Samuel then went to Ramah.

David in Saul's Service

¹⁴Now the Spirit of the LORD had departedᵗ from Saul, and an evilᶠ spiritᵘ from the LORD tormented him.ᵛ

¹⁵Saul's attendants said to him, "See, an evil spirit from God is tormenting you. ¹⁶Let our lord command his servants here to search for someone who can play the harp.ʷ He will play when the evil spirit from God comes upon you, and you will feel better."

¹⁷So Saul said to his attendants, "Find someone who plays well and bring him to me."

¹⁸One of the servants answered, "I have seen a son of Jesseˣ of Bethlehem who knows how to play the harp. He is a brave man and a warrior.ʸ He speaks well and is a fine-looking man. And the LORD is withᶻ him."

¹⁹Then Saul sent messengers to Jesse and said, "Send me your son David, who is with the sheep.ᵃ" ²⁰So Jesse took a donkey loaded with bread,ᵇ a skin of wine and a young goat and sent them with his son David to Saul.

²¹David came to Saul and entered his service.ᶜ Saul liked him very much, and David became one of his armor-bearers. ²²Then Saul sent word to Jesse, saying,

16:13
⁹S 1Sa 2:35;
S 2Sa 22:51
ʳ1Sa 18:12
ˢS 1Sa 11:6
16:14
ᵗS Jdg 16:20 ᵘver
23; S Jdg 9:23;
1Sa 18:10
ᵛ2Sa 7:15
16:16 ʷver 23;
S 1Sa 10:5,6;
2Ch 29:26-27;
Ps 49:4

16:18 ˣS Ru 4:17
ʸS Ge 39:2;
1Ch 22:11;
Mt 1:23
16:19 ᵃ1Sa 17:15
16:20
ᵇS Ge 32:13;
S 1Sa 10:4
16:21
ᶜS Ge 41:46

ᶠ14 Or *injurious*; also in verses 15, 16 and 23

16:13 *in the presence of his brothers.* The small circle of witnesses to David's anointing assured its confidentiality, but also provided ample testimony for the future that David had been anointed by Samuel and that he was not merely a usurper of Saul's office. *the Spirit of the LORD came upon David in power.* See 10:5–6,10; 11:6; Jdg 15:14.

16:14–17:58 In the next two episodes, David is introduced to Saul's court and to Israel as a gifted musician and warrior. With these two gifts he would become famous in Israel and would lead the nation to spiritual and political vigor (see 2Sa 22; 23:1–7). Also through these two gifts Saul would become dependent upon David.

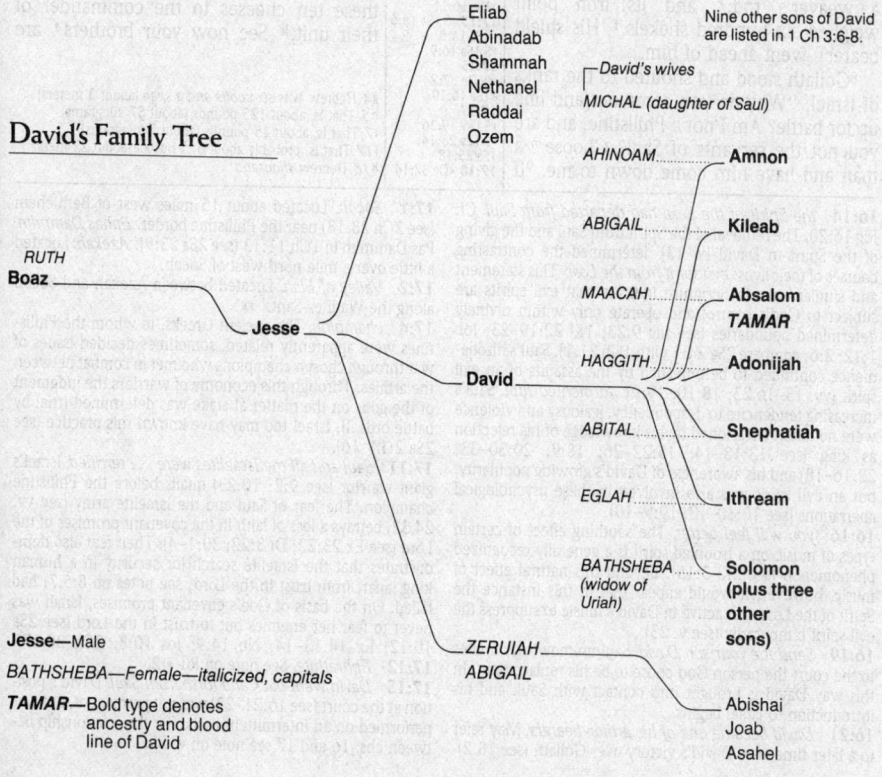

David's Family Tree

Eliab
Abinadab
Shammah
Nethanel
Raddai
Ozem

RUTH
Boaz

Jesse

David

David's wives
MICHAL (daughter of Saul)

AHINOAM .... **Amnon**

ABIGAIL .... **Kileab**

MAACAH .... **Absalom**
                 TAMAR

HAGGITH .... **Adonijah**

ABITAL .... **Shephatiah**

EGLAH .... **Ithream**

BATHSHEBA .... **Solomon**
(widow of   **(plus three**
Uriah)   **other**
                   sons)

ZERUIAH ....
ABIGAIL

                   Abishai
                   Joab
                   Asahel

Nine other sons of David
are listed in 1 Ch 3:6-8.

Jesse—Male
BATHSHEBA—Female—italicized, capitals
TAMAR—Bold type denotes
          ancestry and blood
          line of David

"Allow David to remain in my service, for I am pleased with him."

23Whenever the spirit from God came upon Saul, David would take his harp and play. Then relief would come to Saul; he would feel better, and the evil spirit*d* would leave him.

David and Goliath

17 Now the Philistines gathered their forces for war and assembled*e* at Socoh in Judah. They pitched camp at Ephes Dammim, between Socoh*f* and Azekah.*g* 2Saul and the Israelites assembled and camped in the Valley of Elah*h* and drew up their battle line to meet the Philistines. 3The Philistines occupied one hill and the Israelites another, with the valley between them.

4A champion named Goliath,*i* who was from Gath, came out of the Philistine camp. He was over nine feet*g* tall. 5He had a bronze helmet on his head and wore a coat of scale armor of bronze weighing five thousand shekels*h*; 6on his legs he wore bronze greaves, and a bronze javelin*i* was slung on his back. 7His spear shaft was like a weaver's rod,*k* and its iron point weighed six hundred shekels.*i* His shield bearer*l* went ahead of him.

8Goliath stood and shouted to the ranks of Israel, "Why do you come out and line up for battle? Am I not a Philistine, and are you not the servants of Saul? Choose*m* a man and have him come down to me. 9If

he is able to fight and kill me, we will become your subjects; but if I overcome him and kill him, you will become our subjects and serve us." 10Then the Philistine said, "This day I defy*n* the ranks of Israel! Give me a man and let us fight each other.*o*" 11On hearing the Philistine's words, Saul and all the Israelites were dismayed and terrified.

12Now David was the son of an Ephrathite*p* named Jesse,*q* who was from Bethlehem*r* in Judah. Jesse had eight*s* sons, and in Saul's time he was old and well advanced in years. 13Jesse's three oldest sons had followed Saul to the war: The firstborn was Eliab;*t* the second, Abinadab;*u* and the third, Shammah.*v* 14David was the youngest. The three oldest followed Saul, 15but David went back and forth from Saul to tend*w* his father's sheep*x* at Bethlehem.

16For forty days the Philistine came forward every morning and evening and took his stand.

17Now Jesse said to his son David, "Take this ephah*j**y* of roasted grain*z* and these ten loaves of bread for your brothers and hurry to their camp. 18Take along these ten cheeses to the commander of their unit.*k* See how your brothers*a* are

---

16:23 *d*S ver 14; S Jdg 9:23
17:1 *e*1Sa 13:5 *f*Jos 15:35; 2Ch 28:18 *g*S Jos 10:10,11
17:2 *h*1Sa 21:9
17:4 *i*1Sa 21:9; 2Sa 21:19
17:6 *j*ver 45; 1Sa 18:10
17:7 *k*2Sa 21:19; 1Ch 11:23; 20:5 *l*ver 41
17:8 *m*2Sa 2:12-17

17:10 *n*ver 26, 45; 2Sa 21:21 *o*ver 23
17:12 *p*S Ge 35:16; S 48:7; Ps 132:6 *q*S Ru 4:17 *r*S Ge 35:19 *s*1Sa 16:11
17:13 *t*S 1Sa 16:6 *u*1Sa 16:8 *v*S 1Sa 16:9
17:15 *w*S Ge 37:2 *x*1Sa 16:19
17:17 *y*S Lev 19:36 *z*S Lev 23:14; 1Sa 25:18
17:18 *a*Ge 37:14

*g*4 Hebrew *was six cubits and a span* (about 3 meters)
*h*5 That is, about 125 pounds (about 57 kilograms)
*i*7 That is, about 15 pounds (about 7 kilograms)
*j*17 That is, probably about 3/5 bushel (about 22 liters)
*k*18 Hebrew *thousand*

16:14 *the Spirit of the LORD had departed from Saul.* Cf. Jdg 16:20. The removal of the Spirit from Saul and the giving of the Spirit to David (v. 13) determined the contrasting courses of their lives. *evil spirit from the LORD.* This statement and similar ones in Scripture indicate that evil spirits are subject to God's control and operate only within divinely determined boundaries (see Jdg 9:23; 1Ki 22:19–23; Job 1:12; 2:6; compare 2Sa 24:1 with 1Ch 21:1). Saul's disobedience continued to be punished by the assaults of an evil spirit (vv. 15–16,23; 18:10; 19:9). *tormented him.* Saul's increasing tendencies to despondency, jealousy and violence were no doubt occasioned by his knowledge of his rejection as king (see 13:13–14; 15:22–26; 18:9; 20:30–33; 22:16–18) and his awareness of David's growing popularity, but an evil spirit was also involved in these psychological aberrations (see 18:10–12; 19:9–10).

16:16 *you will feel better.* The soothing effect of certain types of music on a troubled spirit is a generally recognized phenomenon (see 2Ki 3:15). Beyond this natural effect of music, however, it would appear that in this instance the Spirit of the Lord was active in David's music to suppress the evil spirit temporarily (see v. 23).

16:19 *Send me your son David.* Saul unknowingly invites to the court the person God chose to be his replacement. In this way David is brought into contact with Saul, and his introduction to Israel begins.

16:21 *David became one of his armor-bearers.* May refer to a later time after David's victory over Goliath (see 18:2).

17:1 *Socoh.* Located about 15 miles west of Bethlehem (see 2Ch 28:18) near the Philistine border. *Ephes Dammim.* Pas Dammim in 1Ch 11:13 (see 2Sa 23:9). *Azekah.* Located a little over a mile northwest of Socoh.

17:2 *Valley of Elah.* Located between Azekah and Socoh along the Wadi es-Sant.

17:4 *champion.* The ancient Greeks, to whom the Philistines were apparently related, sometimes decided issues of war through chosen champions who met in combat between the armies. Through this economy of warriors the judgment of the gods on the matter at stake was determined (trial by battle ordeal). Israel too may have known this practice (see 2Sa 2:14–16).

17:11 *Saul and all the Israelites were ... terrified.* Israel's giant warrior (see 9:2; 10:23) quails before the Philistine champion. The fear of Saul and the Israelite army (see vv. 24,32) betrays a loss of faith in the covenant promises of the Lord (see Ex 23:22; Dt 3:22; 20:1–4). Their fear also demonstrates that the Israelite search for security in a human king (apart from trust in the Lord; see notes on 8:5,7) had failed. On the basis of God's covenant promises, Israel was never to fear her enemies but to trust in the Lord (see 2Sa 10:12; Ex 14:13–14; Nu 14:9; Jos 10:8; 2Ch 20:17).

17:12 *Ephrathite.* See note on Ru 1:2.

17:15 *David went back and forth from Saul.* David's position at the court (see 16:21–23) was not permanent, but was performed on an intermittent basis. For the relationship between chs. 16 and 17 see note on v. 55.

and bring back some assurance[1] from them. [19]They are with Saul and all the men of Israel in the Valley of Elah, fighting against the Philistines."

[20]Early in the morning David left the flock with a shepherd, loaded up and set out, as Jesse had directed. He reached the camp as the army was going out to its battle positions, shouting the war cry. [21]Israel and the Philistines were drawing up their lines facing each other. [22]David left his things with the keeper of supplies,[b] ran to the battle lines and greeted his brothers. [23]As he was talking with them, Goliath, the Philistine champion from Gath, stepped out from his lines and shouted his usual[c] defiance, and David heard it. [24]When the Israelites saw the man, they all ran from him in great fear.

[25]Now the Israelites had been saying, "Do you see how this man keeps coming out? He comes out to defy Israel. The king will give great wealth to the man who kills him. He will also give him his daughter[d] in marriage and will exempt his father's family from taxes[e] in Israel."

[26]David asked the men standing near him, "What will be done for the man who kills this Philistine and removes this disgrace[f] from Israel? Who is this uncircumcised[g] Philistine that he should defy[h] the armies of the living[i] God?"

[27]They repeated to him what they had been saying and told him, "This is what will be done for the man who kills him."

[28]When Eliab, David's oldest brother, heard him speaking with the men, he burned with anger[j] at him and asked, "Why have you come down here? And with whom did you leave those few sheep in the desert? I know how conceited you are and how wicked your heart is; you came down only to watch the battle."

[29]"Now what have I done?" said David.

"Can't I even speak?" [30]He then turned away to someone else and brought up the same matter, and the men answered him as before. [31]What David said was overheard and reported to Saul, and Saul sent for him.

[32]David said to Saul, "Let no one lose heart[k] on account of this Philistine; your servant will go and fight him."

[33]Saul replied,[l] "You are not able to go out against this Philistine and fight him; you are only a boy, and he has been a fighting man from his youth."

[34]But David said to Saul, "Your servant has been keeping his father's sheep. When a lion[m] or a bear came and carried off a sheep from the flock, [35]I went after it, struck it and rescued the sheep from its mouth. When it turned on me, I seized[n] it by its hair, struck it and killed it. [36]Your servant has killed both the lion[o] and the bear; this uncircumcised Philistine will be like one of them, because he has defied the armies of the living God. [37]The LORD who delivered[p] me from the paw of the lion[q] and the paw of the bear will deliver me from the hand of this Philistine."

Saul said to David, "Go, and the LORD be with[r] you."

[38]Then Saul dressed David in his own[s] tunic. He put a coat of armor on him and a bronze helmet on his head. [39]David fastened on his sword over the tunic and tried walking around, because he was not used to them.

"I cannot go in these," he said to Saul, "because I am not used to them." So he took them off. [40]Then he took his staff in his hand, chose five smooth stones from the stream, put them in the pouch of his shepherd's bag and, with his sling in his hand, approached the Philistine.

17:22 [b]S Jos 1:11
17:23 [c]ver 8-10
17:25 [d]1Sa 18:17
    [e]S 1Sa 8:15
17:26 [f]1Sa 11:2
    [g]S 1Sa 14:6
    [h]S ver 10
    [i]Dt 5:26;
    S Jos 3:10;
    2Ki 18:35
17:28 [j]S Ge 27:41;
    Pr 18:19
17:32 [k]S Dt 20:3;
    Ps 18:45; Isa 7:4;
    Jer 4:9; 38:4;
    Da 11:30
17:33 [l]Nu 13:31
17:34 [m]Job 10:16;
    Isa 31:4;
    Jer 49:19;
    Hos 13:8;
    Am 3:12
17:35 [n]Jdg 14:6
17:36 [o]1Ch 11:22
17:37 [p]2Co 1:10
    [q]2Ti 4:17
    [r]S 1Sa 16:18;
    S 18:12
17:38 [s]S Ge 41:42

[1] 18 Or some token; or some pledge of spoils

17:24 great fear. See note on v. 11.

17:25 The king will give great wealth. See 8:14; 22:7. give him his daughter in marriage. See 18:17–26; cf. Jos 15:16.

17:26 Who is this . . .? David sees the issues clearly—which sets him apart from Saul and all the other Israelites on that battlefield.

17:28 he burned with anger. Eliab's anger may arise from jealousy toward his brother and a sense of guilt for the defeatist attitude of the Israelites. He recognizes, but does not comprehend, David's indomitable spirit (see 16:13).

17:32 Let no one lose heart on account of this Philistine. David's confidence does not rest in his own prowess (see vv. 37,47) but in the power of the living God, whose honor has been violated by the Philistines and whose covenant promises have been scorned by the Israelites.

17:33 You are not able. Saul does not take into account the power of God (see vv. 37,47).

17:34 lion. For the presence of lions in Canaan at that time

see 2Sa 23:20; Jdg 14:5–18; 1Ki 13:24–26; Am 3:12. bear. See 2Sa 17:8; 2Ki 2:24; Am 5:19.

17:36 this uncircumcised Philistine. See note on 14:6.

17:37 The LORD . . . will deliver me. Reliance on the Lord was essential for the true theocratic king (see notes on 10:18; 11:13). Here David's faith contrasts sharply with Saul's loss of faith (see 11:6–7 for Saul's earlier fearlessness). Saul said to David, "Go." Saul is now dependent on David not only for his sanity (see note on 16:16) but also for the security of his realm.

17:40 his staff. God's newly appointed shepherd of his people (see 2Sa 5:2; 7:7; Ps 78:72) goes to defend the Lord's threatened and frightened flock. stones. Usually the stones chosen were round and smooth and somewhat larger than a baseball. When hurled by a master slinger, they probably traveled at close to 100 miles per hour. his sling. For the Benjamites' skill with a sling see Jdg 20:16.

⁴¹Meanwhile, the Philistine, with his shield bearer *t* in front of him, kept coming closer to David. ⁴²He looked David over and saw that he was only a boy, ruddy and handsome, *u* and he despised *v* him. ⁴³He said to David, "Am I a dog, *w* that you come at me with sticks?" And the Philistine cursed David by his gods. ⁴⁴"Come here," he said, "and I'll give your flesh to the birds of the air *x* and the beasts of the field! *y* "

⁴⁵David said to the Philistine, "You come against me with sword and spear and javelin, *z* but I come against you in the name *a* of the LORD Almighty, the God of the armies of Israel, whom you have defied. *b* ⁴⁶This day the LORD will hand *c* you over to me, and I'll strike you down and cut off your head. Today I will give the carcasses *d* of the Philistine army to the birds of the air and the beasts of the earth, and the whole world *e* will know that there is a God in Israel. *f* ⁴⁷All those gathered here will know that it is not by sword *g* or spear that the LORD saves; *h* for the battle *i* is the LORD's, and he will give all of you into our hands."

⁴⁸As the Philistine moved closer to attack him, David ran quickly toward the battle line to meet him. ⁴⁹Reaching into his bag and taking out a stone, he slung it and struck the Philistine on the forehead. The stone sank into his forehead, and he fell facedown on the ground.

⁵⁰So David triumphed over the Philistine with a sling *j* and a stone; without a sword in his hand he struck down the Philistine and killed him.

⁵¹David ran and stood over him. He took hold of the Philistine's sword and drew it from the scabbard. After he killed him, he cut *k* off his head with the sword. *l*

When the Philistines saw that their hero was dead, they turned and ran. ⁵²Then the men of Israel and Judah surged forward with a shout and pursued the Philistines to the entrance of Gath *m* and to the gates of Ekron. *m* Their dead were strewn along the Shaaraim *n* road to Gath and Ekron. ⁵³When the Israelites returned from chasing the Philistines, they plundered their camp. ⁵⁴David took the Philistine's head and brought it to Jerusalem, and he put the Philistine's weapons in his own tent.

⁵⁵As Saul watched David *o* going out to meet the Philistine, he said to Abner, commander of the army, "Abner, *p* whose son is that young man?"

Abner replied, "As surely as you live, O king, I don't know."

⁵⁶The king said, "Find out whose son this young man is."

⁵⁷As soon as David returned from killing the Philistine, Abner took him and brought him before Saul, with David still holding the Philistine's head.

⁵⁸"Whose son are you, young man?" Saul asked him.

David said, "I am the son of your servant Jesse *q* of Bethlehem."

Saul's Jealousy of David

18 After David had finished talking with Saul, Jonathan *r* became one in spirit with David, and he loved *s* him as himself. *t* ²From that day Saul kept David with him and did not let him return to his

m 52 Some Septuagint manuscripts; Hebrew *a valley*

Cross references (center column)

17:41 *t* ver 7
17:42 *u* 1Sa 16:12; *v* Ps 123:3-4; Pr 16:18
17:43 *w* 1Sa 24:14; 2Sa 3:8; 9:8; 2Ki 8:13
17:44 *x* S Ge 40:19; Rev 19:17; *y* 2Sa 21:10; Jer 34:20
17:45 *z* S ver 6; *a* Dt 20:1; 2Ch 13:12; 14:11; 32:8; Ps 20:7-8; 124:8; Heb 11:32-34; *b* S ver 10
17:46 *c* S 1Sa 14:12; *d* S Dt 28:26; *e* S Jos 4:24; S Isa 11:9; *f* 1Ki 18:36; 2Ki 5:8; 19:19; Isa 37:20
17:47 *g* Hos 1:7; *h* 1Sa 14:6; 2Ch 14:11; Jer 39:18; *i* S Ex 14:14; S Nu 21:14; S 1Sa 2:9; 2Ch 20:15; Ps 44:6-7
17:50 *j* 1Sa 25:29
17:51 *k* Heb 11:34; *l* 1Sa 21:9; 22:10
17:52 *m* Jos 15:11; *n* S Jos 15:36
17:55 *o* 1Sa 16:21
17:58 *p* 1Sa 26:5; *q* S Ru 4:17
18:1 *r* 1Sa 19:1; 20:16; 31:2; 2Sa 4:4; *s* 2Sa 1:26; *t* S Ge 44:30

Study notes (bottom)

17:43 *Am I a dog . . . ?* See note on 2Sa 9:8.
17:45 *in the name of the LORD Almighty.* David's strength was his reliance on the Lord (see Ps 9:10; Pr 18:10). For the expression "name of the LORD" see notes on Ex 3:13–14; Dt 12:11.
17:46 *the whole world will know.* The victory that David anticipates will demonstrate to all the world the existence and power of Israel's God (see Ex 7:17; 9:14,16,29; Dt 4:34–35; Jos 2:10–11; 4:23–24; 1Ki 8:59–60; 18:36–39; 2Ki 5:15; 19:19).
17:47 *the battle is the LORD's.* Both the Israelite and the Philistine armies will be shown the error of placing trust in human devices for personal or national security (see 2:10; 14:6; 2Ch 14:11; 20:15; Ps 33:16–17; 44:6–7; Ecc 9:11; Hos 1:7; Zec 4:6).
17:51 *they turned and ran.* Most likely the Philistines saw the fall of their champion as the judgment of the gods, but they did not honor Goliath's original proposal (see v. 9).
17:54 *brought it to Jerusalem.* Jerusalem had not at this time been conquered by the Israelites. David may have kept Goliath's head as a trophy of victory and brought the skull with him to Jerusalem when he took that city and made it his capital (see 2Sa 5:1–9). Or, having grown up almost under

the shadow of the Jebusite city, he may have displayed Goliath's head to its defiant inhabitants as a warning of what the God of Israel was able to do and eventually would do. *put the Philistine's weapons in his own tent.* As his personal spoils of the battle. Since Goliath's sword is later in the custody of the priest at Nob (see 21:9), he must have dedicated it to the Lord, the true victor in the fight (cf. 31:10).
17:55 *whose son is that young man?* The seeming contradiction between vv. 55–58 and 16:14–23 may be resolved by noting that prior to this time David was not a permanent resident at Saul's court (see v. 15; 18:2; see also note on 16:21), so that Saul's knowledge of David and his family may have been minimal. Further, Saul may have been so incredulous at David's courage that he was wondering if his family background and social standing might explain his extraordinary conduct.
18:1 It appears that David spoke with Saul at length, and he may have explained his actions as an expression of his faith in the Lord, thus attracting the love and loyalty of Jonathan (see v. 3; 14:6; 19:5). Their friendship endured even when it became clear that David was to replace him as the successor to his father's throne.
18:2 *Saul kept David with him.* See note on 17:15.

father's house. ³And Jonathan made a covenant[u] with David because he loved him as himself. ⁴Jonathan took off the robe[v] he was wearing and gave it to David, along with his tunic, and even his sword, his bow and his belt.[w]

⁵Whatever Saul sent him to do, David did it so successfully[n][x] that Saul gave him a high rank in the army.[y] This pleased all the people, and Saul's officers as well.

⁶When the men were returning home after David had killed the Philistine, the women came out from all the towns of Israel to meet King Saul with singing and dancing,[z] with joyful songs and with tambourines[a] and lutes. ⁷As they danced, they sang:[b]

"Saul has slain his thousands,
    and David his tens[c] of thousands."

⁸Saul was very angry; this refrain galled him. "They have credited David with tens of thousands," he thought, "but me with only thousands. What more can he get but the kingdom?[d]" ⁹And from that time on Saul kept a jealous[e] eye on David.

¹⁰The next day an evil[o] spirit[f] from God came forcefully upon Saul. He was prophesying in his house, while David was playing the harp,[g] as he usually[h] did. Saul had a spear[i] in his hand ¹¹and he hurled it, saying to himself,[j] "I'll pin David to the wall." But David eluded[k] him twice.[l]

¹²Saul was afraid[m] of David, because the LORD[n] was with[o] David but had left[p] Saul. ¹³So he sent David away from him and gave him command over a thousand men, and David led[q] the troops in their campaigns.[r] ¹⁴In everything he did he had great success,[p][s] because the LORD was

with[t] him. ¹⁵When Saul saw how successful[q] he was, he was afraid of him. ¹⁶But all Israel and Judah loved David, because he led them in their campaigns.[u]

¹⁷Saul said to David, "Here is my older daughter[v] Merab. I will give her to you in marriage;[w] only serve me bravely and fight the battles[x] of the LORD." For Saul said to himself,[y] "I will not raise a hand against him. Let the Philistines do that!"

¹⁸But David said to Saul, "Who am I,[z] and what is my family or my father's clan in Israel, that I should become the king's son-in-law?" ¹⁹So[r] when the time came for Merab,[b] Saul's daughter, to be given to David, she was given in marriage to Adriel of Meholah.[c]

²⁰Now Saul's daughter Michal[d] was in love with David, and when they told Saul about it, he was pleased.[e] ²¹"I will give her to him," he thought, "so that she may be a snare[f] to him and so that the hand of the Philistines may be against him." So Saul said to David, "Now you have a second opportunity to become my son-in-law."

²²Then Saul ordered his attendants: "Speak to David privately and say, 'Look, the king is pleased with you, and his attendants all like you; now become his son-in-law.'"

²³They repeated these words to David. But David said, "Do you think it is a small matter to become the king's son-in-law?[g] I'm only a poor man and little known."

²⁴When Saul's servants told him what David had said, ²⁵Saul replied, "Say to David, 'The king wants no other price[h] for

---

Cross references (center column):

18:3 [u]1Sa 20:8, 16,17,42; 22:8; 23:18; 24:21; 2Sa 21:7
18:4 [v]S Ge 41:42 [w]2Sa 18:11
18:5 [x]ver 30 [y]2Sa 5:2
18:6 [z]S Ex 15:20; 2Sa 1:20 [a]Ps 68:25
18:7 [b]Ex 15:21 c1Sa 21:11; 29:5; 2Sa 18:3
18:8 [d]S 1Sa 13:14
18:9 [e]1Sa 19:1
18:10 [f]S Jdg 9:23; S 1Sa 16:14 [g]S 1Sa 10:5 [h]1Sa 16:21; 19:7 [i]S 1Sa 17:6 [j]1Sa 20:7,33 [k]1Sa 19:10 [l]Ps 132:1
18:12 [m]ver 29 [n]1Sa 16:13 [o]Jos 1:5; 1Sa 17:37; 20:13; 1Ch 22:11 [p]S Jdg 16:20
18:13 [q]Nu 27:17 [r]2Sa 5:2
18:14 [s]S Ge 39:3
[t]S Ge 39:2; S Nu 14:43; 2Sa 7:9
18:16 [u]2Sa 5:2
18:17 [v]1Sa 17:25 [w]S Ge 29:26 [x]S Nu 21:14 [y]ver 25; 1Sa 20:33
18:18 [z]S Ex 3:11; S 1Sa 9:21 [a]ver 23
18:19 [b]2Sa 21:8 [c]S Jdg 7:22
18:20 [d]ver 28; S Ge 29:26 [e]ver 29
18:21 [f]S Ex 10:7; S Dt 7:16
18:23 [g]ver 18
18:25
[h]S Ge 34:12

[n]5 Or wisely   [o]10 Or injurious   [p]14 Or he was very wise   [q]15 Or wise   [r]19 Or However,

---

18:3 *Jonathan made a covenant with David.* The initiative comes from Jonathan. The terms of the agreement are not here specified (see further 19:1; 20:8,13–16,41–42; 23:18) but would appear to involve a pledge of mutual loyalty and friendship. At the very least, Jonathan accepts David as his equal.

18:4 *took off the robe . . . and gave it to David.* Jonathan ratifies the covenant in an act that symbolizes giving himself to David. His act may even signify his recognition that David was to assume his place as successor to Saul (see 20:14–15, 31; 23:17)—a possibility that seems the more likely in that he also gave David "even his sword, his bow and his belt" (cf. 13:22).

18:5 *Whatever Saul sent him to do.* During the rest of the campaign.

18:7 *David his tens of thousands.* In accordance with the normal conventions of Hebrew poetry, this was the women's way of saying "Saul and David have slain thousands" (10,-000 was normally used as the parallel of 1,000—see Dt 32:30; Ps 91:7; Mic 6:7; also in Canaanite poetry found at Ugarit). It is a measure of Saul's insecurity and jealousy that he read their intentions incorrectly and took offense. His

resentment may have been initially triggered by the mention of David's name alongside his own. See note on 21:11 for how the Philistines interpreted the song.

18:10 *evil spirit from God.* See note on 16:14. *prophesying.* The Hebrew for this word is sometimes used to indicate uncontrolled ecstatic behavior (see note on 1Ki 18:29) and is best understood in that sense in this context (see also note on 10:5). *as he usually did.* See 16:14,23.

18:12 *the LORD was with David but had left Saul.* See 16:14 and note.

18:13 *he sent David away.* His apparent motive was the hope that David would be killed in battle (see vv. 17, 21, 25; 19:1), but the result was greater acclaim for David (see vv. 14,16,30).

18:17 *Here is my older daughter.* David was entitled to have Saul's daughter as his wife because of his victory over Goliath (see 17:25). This promise had not been kept and is now made conditional on further military service, in which Saul hoped David would be killed. *battles of the LORD.* See 25:28.

18:25 *no other price.* Normally a bride-price was paid by the bridegroom to the father of the bride (see Ge 34:12; Ex

the bride than a hundred Philistine fore-skins, to take revenge[i] on his enemies.' " Saul's plan[j] was to have David fall by the hands of the Philistines.

26When the attendants told David these things, he was pleased to become the king's son-in-law. So before the allotted time elapsed, 27David and his men went out and killed two hundred Philistines. He brought their foreskins and presented the full number to the king so that he might become the king's son-in-law. Then Saul gave him his daughter Michal[k] in marriage.

28When Saul realized that the LORD was with David and that his daughter Michal[l] loved David, 29Saul became still more afraid[m] of him, and he remained his enemy the rest of his days.

30The Philistine commanders continued to go out to battle, and as often as they did, David met with more success[s][n] than the rest of Saul's officers, and his name became well known.

Saul Tries to Kill David

19 Saul told his son Jonathan[o] and all the attendants to kill[p] David. But Jonathan was very fond of David 2and warned him, "My father Saul is looking for a chance to kill you. Be on your guard tomorrow morning; go into hiding[q] and stay there. 3I will go out and stand with my father in the field where you are. I'll speak[r] to him about you and will tell you what I find out."

4Jonathan spoke[s] well of David to Saul his father and said to him, "Let not the king do wrong[t] to his servant David; he has not wronged you, and what he has done has benefited you greatly. 5He took his life[u] in his hands when he killed the Philistine. The LORD won a great victory[v] for all Israel, and you saw it and were glad. Why then would you do wrong to an inno-

cent[w] man like David by killing him for no reason?"

6Saul listened to Jonathan and took this oath: "As surely as the LORD lives, David will not be put to death."

7So Jonathan called David and told him the whole conversation. He brought him to Saul, and David was with Saul as before.[x]

8Once more war broke out, and David went out and fought the Philistines. He struck them with such force that they fled before him.

9But an evil[t] spirit[y] from the LORD came upon Saul as he was sitting in his house with his spear in his hand. While David was playing the harp,[z] 10Saul tried to pin him to the wall with his spear, but David eluded[a] him as Saul drove the spear into the wall. That night David made good his escape.

11Saul sent men to David's house to watch[b] it and to kill him in the morning.[c] But Michal, David's wife, warned him, "If you don't run for your life tonight, tomorrow you'll be killed." 12So Michal let David down through a window,[d] and he fled and escaped. 13Then Michal took an idol[u][e] and laid it on the bed, covering it with a garment and putting some goats' hair at the head.

14When Saul sent the men to capture David, Michal said,[f] "He is ill."

15Then Saul sent the men back to see David and told them, "Bring him up to me in his bed so that I may kill him." 16But when the men entered, there was the idol in the bed, and at the head was some goats' hair.

17Saul said to Michal, "Why did you deceive me like this and send my enemy away so that he escaped?"

Michal told him, "He said to me, 'Let me get away. Why should I kill you?' "

Cross references (center column):

18:25 *i* Ps 8:2; 44:16; Jer 20:10 /S ver 11,S 17
18:27 *k* 2Sa 3:14; 6:16
18:28 /S ver 20
18:29 *m* ver 12
18:30 *n* ver 5
19:1 *o* S 1Sa 18:1 *p* 1Sa 18:9
19:2 *q* 1Sa 20:5, 19
19:3 *r* 1Sa 20:12
19:4 *s* 1Sa 20:32; 22:14; Pr 31:8,9; Jer 18:20 *t* 1Sa 25:21; Pr 17:13
19:5 *u* S Jdg 9:17; S 12:3 *v* S 1Sa 11:13
w S Ge 31:36; Dt 19:10-13
19:7 *x* S 1Sa 18:10
19:9 *y* S Jdg 9:23 *z* S 1Sa 10:5
19:10 *a* 1Sa 18:11
19:11 *b* Ps 59 Title *c* Jdg 16:2
19:12 *d* S Jos 2:15; Ac 9:25; 2Co 11:33
19:13 *e* S Ge 31:19
19:14 /S Ex 1:19; Jos 2:4

Text notes (bottom of columns):

*s*30 Or *David acted more wisely*   *t*9 Or *injurious*   *u*13 Hebrew *teraphim*; also in verse 16

22:16) as compensation for the loss of his daughter and insurance for her support if widowed. Saul requires David instead to pass a test appropriate for a great warrior, hoping that he will "fall" (see vv. 17,21).

18:28 *Michal loved David.* God's favor on David is revealed not only in his military accomplishments, but also in Michal's love for him—now added to that of Jonathan. Everything Saul seeks to use against David turns to David's advantage.

18:29 *Saul became still more afraid of him.* Saul's perception that God's hand was on David did not lead him to repentance and acceptance of his own lot (see 15:26) but into greater fear and jealousy toward David.

19:1 *Saul told his son . . . to kill David.* Saul now abandons his indirect attempts on David's life (see 18:13,17,25) and adopts a more direct approach, leading to David's departure

from the court and from service to Saul (see vv. 12,18; 20:42).

19:4 *Jonathan spoke well of David.* Jonathan does not let his own personal ambition distort his perception of David's true theocratic spirit (see v. 5 and notes on 14:6; 17:11; 18:1).

19:6 *Saul listened to Jonathan and took this oath.* See 14:24,44 for previous oaths that Saul did not keep (see note on 14:39).

19:9 *evil spirit from the LORD.* See note on 16:14; cf. 18:10-11.

19:10 *with his spear.* See 18:10-11; 20:33.

19:12 *through a window.* For similar escapes see Jos 2:15; Ac 9:25.

19:13 *idol.* See NIV text note and note on Ge 31:19.

18When David had fled and made his escape, he went to Samuel at Ramah*g* and told him all that Saul had done to him. Then he and Samuel went to Naioth and stayed there. 19Word came to Saul: "David is in Naioth at Ramah"; 20so he sent men to capture him. But when they saw a group of prophets*h* prophesying, with Samuel standing there as their leader, the Spirit of God came upon*i* Saul's men and they also prophesied.*j* 21Saul was told about it, and he sent more men, and they prophesied too. Saul sent men a third time, and they also prophesied. 22Finally, he himself left for Ramah and went to the great cistern at Secu. And he asked, "Where are Samuel and David?"

"Over in Naioth at Ramah," they said.

23So Saul went to Naioth at Ramah. But the Spirit of God came even upon him, and he walked along prophesying*k* until he came to Naioth. 24He stripped*l* off his robes and also prophesied in Samuel's*m* presence. He lay that way all that day and

night. This is why people say, "Is Saul also among the prophets?"*n*

David and Jonathan

20 Then David fled from Naioth at Ramah and went to Jonathan and asked, "What have I done? What is my crime? How have I wronged*o* your father, that he is trying to take my life?"*p*

2"Never!" Jonathan replied. "You are not going to die! Look, my father doesn't do anything, great or small, without confiding in me. Why would he hide this from me? It's not so!"

3But David took an oath*q* and said, "Your father knows very well that I have found favor in your eyes, and he has said to himself, 'Jonathan must not know this or he will be grieved.' Yet as surely as the LORD lives and as you live, there is only a step between me and death."

4Jonathan said to David, "Whatever you want me to do, I'll do for you."

5So David said, "Look, tomorrow is the New Moon festival,*r* and I am supposed to

19:18
g S 1Sa 7:17
19:20
h S Nu 11:29
i S Nu 11:25
j S 1Sa 10:5
19:23 *k* 1Sa 10:13
19:24 *l* 2Sa 6:20;
Isa 20:2
m 1Sa 15:35

n S 1Sa 10:11
20:1 *o* 1Sa 24:9
p 1Sa 22:23;
23:15; 24:11;
25:29; Ps 40:14;
54:3; 63:9; 70:2
20:3 *q* Dt 6:13
20:5 *r* S Nu 10:10

19:18 *Ramah.* Samuel's home (see 7:17 and note on 1:1). *Naioth.* Means "habitations" or "dwellings." The term appears to designate a complex of houses in a certain section of Ramah where a company of prophets resided (see vv. 19–20,22–23).
19:20 *group of prophets.* See 10:5 and note. *prophesying.* See notes on 10:5; 18:10.
19:24 *He lay that way all that day and night.* Saul was so overwhelmed by the power of the Spirit of God that he was prevented from carrying out his intention to take David's life. His frustrated attempts to kill David—his own inability to harm David and the thwarting of his plans by Jonathan's loyalty, by Michal's deception and by David's own clever-

ness—all reach their climax here. *Is Saul also among the prophets?* This second occasion reinforced the first (see 10:11 and note). Its repetition underscores how alien Saul's spirit was from that of these zealous servants of the Lord.
20:1 *Naioth at Ramah.* See note on 19:18.
20:3 *as surely as the LORD lives.* See note on 14:39.
20:5 *New Moon festival.* Each month of the year was consecrated to the Lord by the bringing of special sacrifices (Nu 28:11–15) and the blowing of trumpets (Nu 10:10; Ps 81:3). This observance also involved cessation from normal work, especially at the beginning of the seventh month (Lev 23:24–25; Nu 29:1–6; 2Ki 4:23; Isa 1:13; Am 8:5).

David the Fugitive

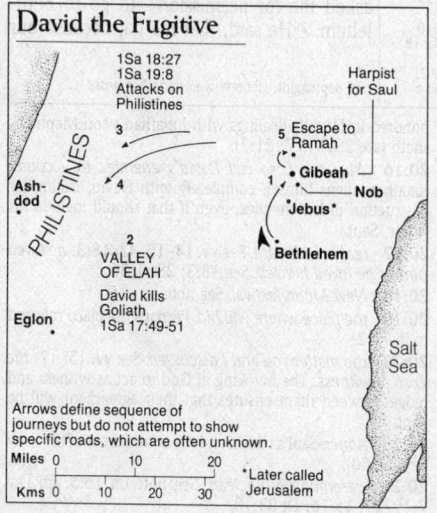

1Sa 18:27
1Sa 19:8
Attacks on
Philistines

Harpist
for Saul

3

5 Escape to
   Ramah

• Gibeah

1

• Nob

Ash-
dod

4

•Jebus•

2

Bethlehem•

VALLEY
OF ELAH

David kills
Goliath
1Sa 17:49-51

Eglon

PHILISTINES

Salt
Sea

Arrows define sequence of
journeys but do not attempt to show
specific roads, which are often unknown.

Miles 0   10   20

Kms 0   10   20   30

*Later called
Jerusalem

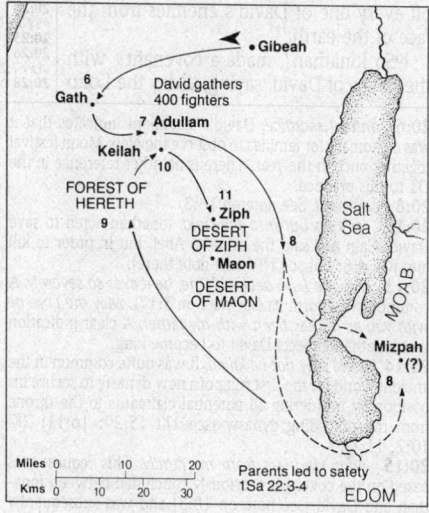

• Gibeah

6
Gath •

David gathers
400 fighters

7 Adullam

Keilah •

10

FOREST OF
HERETH

9

11
• Ziph

DESERT
OF ZIPH

• Maon

DESERT
OF MAON

8

Salt
Sea

MOAB

Mizpah
•(?)

8

Miles 0   10   20

Kms 0   10   20   30

Parents led to safety
1Sa 22:3-4

EDOM

dine with the king; but let me go and hide^s in the field until the evening of the day after tomorrow. ^{6}If your father misses me at all, tell him, 'David earnestly asked my permission^t to hurry to Bethlehem,^{u} his hometown, because an annual^v sacrifice is being made there for his whole clan.' ^{7}If he says, 'Very well,' then your servant is safe. But if he loses his temper,^{w} you can be sure that he is determined^x to harm me. ^{8}As for you, show kindness to your servant, for you have brought him into a covenant^y with you before the Lord. If I am guilty, then kill^z me yourself! Why hand me over to your father?"

^{9}"Never!" Jonathan said. "If I had the least inkling that my father was determined to harm you, wouldn't I tell you?"

^{10}David asked, "Who will tell me if your father answers you harshly?"

^{11}"Come," Jonathan said, "let's go out into the field." So they went there together.

^{12}Then Jonathan said to David: "By the Lord, the God of Israel, I will surely sound^a out my father by this time the day after tomorrow! If he is favorably disposed toward you, will I not send you word and let you know? ^{13}But if my father is inclined to harm you, may the Lord deal with me, be it ever so severely,^{b} if I do not let you know and send you away safely. May the Lord be with^c you as he has been with my father. ^{14}But show me unfailing kindness^d like that of the Lord as long as I live, so that I may not be killed, ^{15}and do not ever cut off your kindness from my family^e—not even when the Lord has cut off every one of David's enemies from the face of the earth."

^{16}So Jonathan^f made a covenant^g with the house of David, saying, "May the Lord

call David's enemies to account.^{h}" ^{17}And Jonathan had David reaffirm his oath^i out of love for him, because he loved him as he loved himself.

^{18}Then Jonathan said to David: "Tomorrow is the New Moon festival. You will be missed, because your seat will be empty.^{j} ^{19}The day after tomorrow, toward evening, go to the place where you hid^k when this trouble began, and wait by the stone Ezel. ^{20}I will shoot three arrows^l to the side of it, as though I were shooting at a target. ^{21}Then I will send a boy and say, 'Go, find the arrows.' If I say to him, 'Look, the arrows are on this side of you; bring them here,' then come, because, as surely as the Lord lives, you are safe; there is no danger. ^{22}But if I say to the boy, 'Look, the arrows are beyond^m you,' then you must go, because the Lord has sent you away. ^{23}And about the matter you and I discussed—remember, the Lord is witness^n between you and me forever."

^{24}So David hid in the field, and when the New Moon festival^o came, the king sat down to eat. ^{25}He sat in his customary place by the wall, opposite Jonathan,^{v} and Abner sat next to Saul, but David's place was empty.^{p} ^{26}Saul said nothing that day, for he thought, "Something must have happened to David to make him ceremonially unclean—surely he is unclean.^{q}" ^{27}But the next day, the second day of the month, David's place was empty again. Then Saul said to his son Jonathan, "Why hasn't the son of Jesse come to the meal, either yesterday or today?"

^{28}Jonathan answered, "David earnestly asked me for permission^r to go to Bethlehem. ^{29}He said, 'Let me go, because our

Cross references

20:5 ^{s}S 1Sa 19:2
20:6 ^{t}ver 28
^{u}1Sa 17:58
^{v}S 1Sa 1:3
20:7 ^{w}1Sa 10:27; 25:17
^{x}S 1Sa 18:11
20:8 ^{y}S 1Sa 18:3
^{z}2Sa 14:32
20:12 ^{a}1Sa 19:3
20:13 ^{b}S Ru 1:17
^{c}S 1Sa 16:18; S 18:12
20:14 ^{d}S Ge 40:14
20:15 ^{e}1Sa 24:21; 2Sa 9:7
20:16 ^{f}S 1Sa 18:1
^{g}S 1Sa 18:3

20:17 ^{h}S Jos 22:23
^{i}S Jos 9:18;
S 1Sa 18:3
20:18 ^{j}ver 25
20:19 ^{k}S 1Sa 19:2
20:20 ^{l}2Ki 13:15
20:22 ^{m}ver 37
20:23 ^{n}S Ge 31:50
20:24 ^{o}S Nu 10:10
20:25 ^{p}ver 18
20:26 ^{q}Lev 7:20-21
20:28 ^{r}ver 6

^{v}25 Septuagint; Hebrew *wall. Jonathan arose*

20:6 *annual sacrifice.* David's statement indicates that it was customary for families to observe the New Moon festival together once in the year. There is no other reference in the OT to this practice.

20:8 *covenant.* See note on 18:3.

20:11 *let's go out into the field.* Jonathan acted to save David. Cain had said the same to Abel, but in order to kill him (Ge 4:8; but see NIV text note there).

20:13 *may the Lord deal with me, be it ever so severely.* A common curse formula (see note on 3:17). *May the Lord be with you as he has been with my father.* A clear indication that Jonathan expects David to become king.

20:14 *that I may not be killed.* It was quite common in the ancient world for the first ruler of a new dynasty to secure his position by murdering all potential claimants to the throne from the preceding dynasty (see 1Ki 15:29; 16:11; 2Ki 10:7; 11:1).

20:15 *your kindness from my family.* This request was based on the covenant previously concluded between Jonathan and David (see note on 18:3) and was subsequently

honored in David's dealings with Jonathan's son Mephibosheth (see 2Sa 9:3,7; 21:7).

20:16 *May the Lord call David's enemies to account.* Jonathan aligns himself completely with David, calling for destruction of his enemies, even if that should include his father, Saul.

20:17 *reaffirm his oath.* See vv. 14–15, 42; 18:3. *he loved him as he loved himself.* See 18:3; 2Sa 1:26.

20:18 *New Moon festival.* See note on v. 5.

20:19 *the place where you hid.* Perhaps the place referred to in 19:2.

20:23 *the matter you and I discussed.* See vv. 15–17. *the Lord is witness.* The invoking of God to act as witness and judge between them ensures that their agreement will be kept.

20:25 *Abner.* Saul's cousin and the commander of his army (see 14:50).

20:26 *ceremonially unclean.* See note on 16:5; cf. Lev 7:19–21; 15:16; Dt 23:10.

family is observing a sacrifice^s in the town and my brother has ordered me to be there. If I have found favor in your eyes, let me get away to see my brothers.' That is why he has not come to the king's table."

^{30}Saul's anger flared up at Jonathan and he said to him, "You son of a perverse and rebellious woman! Don't I know that you have sided with the son of Jesse to your own shame and to the shame of the mother who bore you? ^{31}As long as the son of Jesse lives on this earth, neither you nor your kingdom^t will be established. Now send and bring him to me, for he must die!"

^{32}"Why^u should he be put to death? What^v has he done?" Jonathan asked his father. ^{33}But Saul hurled his spear at him to kill him. Then Jonathan knew that his father intended^w to kill David.

^{34}Jonathan got up from the table in fierce anger; on that second day of the month he did not eat, because he was grieved at his father's shameful treatment of David.

^{35}In the morning Jonathan went out to the field for his meeting with David. He had a small boy with him, ^{36}and he said to the boy, "Run and find the arrows I shoot." As the boy ran, he shot an arrow beyond him. ^{37}When the boy came to the place where Jonathan's arrow had fallen, Jonathan called out after him, "Isn't the arrow beyond^x you?" ^{38}Then he shouted, "Hurry! Go quickly! Don't stop!" The boy picked up the arrow and returned to his master. ^{39}(The boy knew nothing of all this; only Jonathan and David knew.) ^{40}Then Jonathan gave his weapons to the boy and said, "Go, carry them back to town."

^{41}After the boy had gone, David got up from the south side of the stone, and bowed down before Jonathan three times, with his face to the ground.^{y} Then they kissed each other and wept together—but David wept the most.

^{42}Jonathan said to David, "Go in peace,^{z} for we have sworn friendship^a with each other in the name of the LORD,^{b} saying, 'The LORD is witness^c between you and me, and between your descendants and my descendants forever.^{d}'" Then David left, and Jonathan went back to the town.

David at Nob

21 David went to Nob,^{e} to Ahimelech the priest. Ahimelech trembled^f when he met him, and asked, "Why are you alone? Why is no one with you?"

^{2}David answered Ahimelech the priest, "The king charged me with a certain matter and said to me, 'No one is to know anything about your mission or your instructions.' As for my men, I have told them to meet me at a certain place. ^{3}Now then, what do you have on hand? Give me five loaves of bread, or whatever you can find."

^{4}But the priest answered David, "I don't have any ordinary bread^g on hand; however, there is some consecrated^h bread here—provided the men have kept^i themselves from women."

^{5}David replied, "Indeed women have been kept from us, as usual^j whenever^w I set out. The men's things^x are holy^k even on missions that are not holy. How much more so today!" ^{6}So the priest gave him

Cross references

20:29 ^{s}S Ge 8:20
20:31 ^{t}1Sa 23:17; 24:20
20:32 ^{u}S 1Sa 19:4;
Mt 27:23
^{v}S Ge 31:36
20:33 ^{w}S 1Sa 18:11,17
20:37 ^{x}ver 22

20:41 ^{y}S Ge 33:3;
Ru 2:10;
1Sa 24:8; 25:23;
2Sa 1:2
20:42 ^{z}S 1Sa 1:17;
S Ac 15:33
^{a}S Ge 40:14;
2Sa 1:26;
Pr 18:24
^{b}Isa 48:1
^{c}S Ge 31:50;
S 1Sa 18:3
^{d}2Sa 9:1
21:1 ^{e}1Sa 22:9,
19; Ne 11:32;
Isa 10:32
^{f}1Sa 16:4
21:4 ^{g}Lev 24:8-9
^{h}Mt 12:4
^{i}S Ex 19:15;
S Lev 15:18
21:5 ^{j}Dt 23:9-11;
Jos 3:5; 2Sa 11:11
^{k}1Th 4:4

^{w}5 Or *from us in the past few days since* ^{x}5 Or *bodies*

20:30 *son of a perverse and rebellious woman.* The Hebrew idiom intends to characterize Jonathan, not his mother.

20:31 *neither you nor your kingdom will be established.* Saul is now convinced that David will succeed him if David is not killed (see notes on 18:13,17,29; 19:1), and he is incapable of understanding Jonathan's lack of concern for his own succession to the throne.

20:33 *hurled his spear.* See 18:11; 19:10.

20:41 *bowed ... three times.* A sign of submission and respect (see Ge 33:3; 42:6).

20:42 *sworn friendship.* See vv. 14–15,23; 18:3. *the town.* Gibeah (see 10:26).

21:1 *Nob.* A town northeast of Jerusalem and south of Gibeah where the tabernacle was relocated after the destruction of Shiloh (4:2–3; Jer 7:12). Although it appears that no attempt was made to bring the ark to this sanctuary (see note on 7:1), Ahimelech the high priest, 85 other priests (22:17–18), the ephod (v. 9) and the table of consecrated bread (v. 6) are mentioned in connection with it. *Ahimelech the priest.* See note on 14:3. It appears from 22:10,15 that

David's purpose in coming to Nob was to seek the Lord's guidance by means of the Urim and Thummim (see notes on 2:28; Ex 28:30).

21:2 It is not clear why David resorts to deception in his response to Ahimelech. Perhaps it was an attempt to protect Ahimelech from the charge of involvement in David's escape from Saul. If so, his strategy was not successful (see 22:13–18).

21:4 *consecrated bread.* The "bread of the Presence" (see v. 6; Ex 25:30), which was placed in the Holy Place in the tabernacle and later in the temple as a thank offering to the Lord, symbolizing his provision of daily bread. *provided the men have kept themselves from women.* Although the bread was to be eaten only by the priests (see Lev 24:9), Ahimelech agreed to give it to David and his men on the condition that they were ceremonially clean (see Ex 19:15; Lev 15:18). Jesus uses this incident to illustrate the principle that the ceremonial law was not to be viewed in a legalistic manner (see Mt 12:3–4). He also teaches that it is always lawful to do good and to save life (see Lk 6:9). Such compassionate acts are within the true spirit of the law.

the consecrated bread,[l] since there was no bread there except the bread of the Presence that had been removed from before the LORD and replaced by hot bread on the day it was taken away.

[7]Now one of Saul's servants was there that day, detained before the LORD; he was Doeg[m] the Edomite,[n] Saul's head shepherd.

[8]David asked Ahimelech, "Don't you have a spear or a sword here? I haven't brought my sword or any other weapon, because the king's business was urgent."

[9]The priest replied, "The sword[o] of Goliath[p] the Philistine, whom you killed in the Valley of Elah,[q] is here; it is wrapped in a cloth behind the ephod. If you want it, take it; there is no sword here but that one."

David said, "There is none like it; give it to me."

David at Gath

[10]That day David fled from Saul and went[r] to Achish king of Gath. [11]But the servants of Achish said to him, "Isn't this David, the king of the land? Isn't he the one they sing about in their dances:

" 'Saul has slain his thousands,
    and David his tens of thousands'?"[s]

[12]David took these words to heart and was very much afraid of Achish king of Gath. [13]So he pretended to be insane[t] in their presence; and while he was in their hands he acted like a madman, making marks on the doors of the gate and letting saliva run down his beard.

[14]Achish said to his servants, "Look at the man! He is insane! Why bring him to me? [15]Am I so short of madmen that you have to bring this fellow here to carry on like this in front of me? Must this man come into my house?"

David at Adullam and Mizpah

22 David left Gath and escaped to the cave[u] of Adullam.[v] When his brothers and his father's household heard about it, they went down to him there. [2]All those who were in distress or in debt or discontented gathered[w] around him, and he became their leader. About four hundred men were with him.

[3]From there David went to Mizpah in Moab and said to the king of Moab, "Would you let my father and mother come and stay with you until I learn what God will do for me?" [4]So he left them with the king of Moab,[x] and they stayed with him as long as David was in the stronghold.

[5]But the prophet Gad[y] said to David, "Do not stay in the stronghold. Go into the land of Judah." So David left and went to the forest of Hereth.[z]

Saul Kills the Priests of Nob

[6]Now Saul heard that David and his men had been discovered. And Saul, spear in hand, was seated[a] under the tamarisk[b] tree on the hill at Gibeah, with all his officials standing around him. [7]Saul said to them, "Listen, men of Benjamin! Will the son of Jesse give all of you fields and vineyards? Will he make all of you commanders[c] of thousands and commanders of hundreds? [8]Is that why you have all conspired[d] against me? No one tells me when my son makes a covenant[e] with the son of

21:6 [l]S Ex 25:30; 1Sa 22:10; Mt 12:3-4; Mk 2:25-28; Lk 6:1-5
21:7 [m]1Sa 22:9, 22 [n]1Sa 14:47; Ps 52 Title
21:9 [o]S 1Sa 17:51 [p]S 1Sa 17:4 [q]1Sa 17:2
21:10 [r]1Sa 25:13; 27:2
21:11 [s]S 1Sa 18:7
21:13 [t]Ps 34 Title

22:1 [u]Ps 57 Title; 142 Title [v]S Ge 38:1
22:2 [w]1Sa 23:13; 25:13; 2Sa 15:20
22:4 [x]S Ge 19:37
22:5 [y]2Sa 24:11; 1Ch 21:9; 29:29; 2Ch 29:25 [z]2Sa 23:14
22:6 [a]S Jdg 4:5 [b]S Ge 21:33
22:7 [c]S Dt 1:15
22:8 [d]ver 13 [e]S 1Sa 18:3

21:9 *sword of Goliath.* See note on 17:54. *ephod.* See note on 2:28.
21:10 *Achish.* See note on Ps 34 title. *Gath.* One of the five major towns of the Philistines (Jos 13:3).
21:11 *king of the land.* The designation of David as "king" by the Philistines may be understood as a popular exaggeration expressing an awareness of the enormous success and popularity of David among the Israelite people.
22:1 *cave of Adullam.* See 2Sa 23:13; Ge 38:1; Jos 12:15; 15:35; 1Ch 11:15 and note on Ps 142 title.
22:2 *four hundred men were with him.* David, officially an outlaw, was joined by others in similar circumstances, so that he began to develop the power base that would sustain him throughout his later years as king.
22:3 *Mizpah in Moab.* Precise location unknown. *let my father and mother come and stay with you.* The king of Moab was a natural ally for David because Saul had warred against him (see 14:47) and David's own great-grandmother was a Moabitess (see Ru 4:13,22).
22:4 *stronghold.* Perhaps a specific fortress, but more likely a reference to a geographical area in which it was easy to hide (see 23:14; 2Sa 5:17; 23:14).

22:5 *prophet Gad.* The king-designate is now served also by a prophet. Later a priest would come to him (v. 20) and complete the basic elements of a royal entourage—and they were all refugees from Saul's administration. This is the first appearance of the prophet who later assisted David in musical arrangements for the temple services (see 2Ch 29:25), wrote a history of David's reign (see 1Ch 29:29) and confronted David with the Lord's rebuke for his sin of numbering the Israelites (see 2Sa 24:11-25). *forest of Hereth.* Located in the tribal area of Judah.

22:6 *tamarisk tree.* See note on 14:2. *Gibeah.* See note on 10:5.

22:7 *men of Benjamin.* Saul, a Benjamite (9:1-2; 10:21), seeks to strengthen his position with his own officials by emphasizing tribal loyalty. David was from the tribe of Judah (see note on 16:1; 2Sa 2:4). *give all of you fields and vineyards.* Saul does exactly what Samuel had warned him that he would do—become as the kings of other nations (see 8:14). His actions are contrary to the covenantal ideal for kingship (see notes on 8:7; 10:25). *commanders of thousands and of hundreds.* See 8:12.

Jesse.[f] None of you is concerned[g] about me or tells me that my son has incited my servant to lie in wait for me, as he does today."

[9]But Doeg[h] the Edomite, who was standing with Saul's officials, said, "I saw the son of Jesse come to Ahimelech son of Ahitub[i] at Nob.[j] [10]Ahimelech inquired[k] of the LORD for him; he also gave him provisions[l] and the sword[m] of Goliath the Philistine."

[11]Then the king sent for the priest Ahimelech son of Ahitub and his father's whole family, who were the priests at Nob, and they all came to the king. [12]Saul said, "Listen now, son of Ahitub."

"Yes, my lord," he answered.

[13]Saul said to him, "Why have you conspired[n] against me, you and the son of Jesse, giving him bread and a sword and inquiring of God for him, so that he has rebelled against me and lies in wait for me, as he does today?"

[14]Ahimelech answered the king, "Who[o] of all your servants is as loyal as David, the king's son-in-law, captain of your bodyguard and highly respected in your household? [15]Was that day the first time I inquired of God for him? Of course not! Let not the king accuse your servant or any of his father's family, for your servant knows nothing at all about this whole affair."

[16]But the king said, "You will surely die, Ahimelech, you and your father's whole family.[p]"

[17]Then the king ordered the guards at his side: "Turn and kill the priests of the LORD, because they too have sided with David. They knew he was fleeing, yet they did not tell me."

But the king's officials were not willing[q] to raise a hand to strike the priests of the LORD.

[18]The king then ordered Doeg, "You turn and strike down the priests."[r] So Doeg the Edomite turned and struck them down. That day he killed eighty-five men who wore the linen ephod.[s] [19]He also put to the sword[t] Nob,[u] the town of the priests, with its men and women, its chil-

dren and infants, and its cattle, donkeys and sheep.

[20]But Abiathar,[v] a son of Ahimelech son of Ahitub,[w] escaped and fled to join David.[x] [21]He told David that Saul had killed the priests of the LORD. [22]Then David said to Abiathar: "That day, when Doeg[y] the Edomite was there, I knew he would be sure to tell Saul. I am responsible for the death of your father's whole family. [23]Stay with me; don't be afraid; the man who is seeking your life[z] is seeking mine also. You will be safe with me."

David Saves Keilah

23 When David was told, "Look, the Philistines are fighting against Keilah[a] and are looting the threshing floors,"[b] [2]he inquired[c] of the LORD, saying, "Shall I go and attack these Philistines?"

The LORD answered him, "Go, attack the Philistines and save Keilah."

[3]But David's men said to him, "Here in Judah we are afraid. How much more, then, if we go to Keilah against the Philistine forces!"

[4]Once again David inquired[d] of the LORD, and the LORD answered him, "Go down to Keilah, for I am going to give the Philistines[e] into your hand."[f] [5]So David and his men went to Keilah, fought the Philistines and carried off their livestock. He inflicted heavy losses on the Philistines and saved the people of Keilah. [6](Now Abiathar[g] son of Ahimelech had brought the ephod[h] down with him when he fled to David at Keilah.)

Saul Pursues David

[7]Saul was told that David had gone to Keilah, and he said, "God has handed him over[i] to me, for David has imprisoned himself by entering a town with gates and bars."[j] [8]And Saul called up all his forces for battle, to go down to Keilah to besiege David and his men.

[9]When David learned that Saul was plotting against him, he said to Abiathar[k] the priest, "Bring the ephod."[l] [10]David

---

Cross references (center column):

22:8 [f]2Sa 20:1; [g]1Sa 23:21
22:9 [h]S 1Sa 21:7
[i]1Sa 14:3
[j]S 1Sa 21:1
22:10 [k]S Ge 25:22; S 1Sa 23:2
[l]S 1Sa 21:6
[m]S 1Sa 17:51
22:13 [n]ver 8
22:14 [o]S 1Sa 19:4
22:16 [p]S 1Sa 2:31
22:17 [q]S Ex 1:17
22:18 [r]S 1Sa 4:17; [s]S 1Sa 2:18
22:19 [t]S 1Sa 15:3; [u]S 1Sa 21:1

22:20 [v]1Sa 23:6, 9; 30:7; 2Sa 15:24; 20:25; 1Ki 1:7; 2:22,26, 27; 4:4; 1Ch 15:11; 27:34; [w]S 1Sa 14:3; [x]S 1Sa 2:32
22:22 [y]S 1Sa 21:7
22:23 [z]S 1Sa 20:1
23:1 [a]S Jos 15:44; [b]S Nu 18:27; S Jdg 6:11
23:2 [c]ver 4,12; 1Sa 22:10; 30:8; 2Sa 2:1; 5:19; Ps 50:15
23:4 [d]S ver 2; [e]S 1Sa 9:16; [f]S Jos 8:7
23:6 [g]S 1Sa 22:20; [h]S 1Sa 2:28
23:7 [i]S Dt 32:30; [j]Ps 31:21
23:9 [k]S 1Sa 22:20; [l]S 1Sa 2:18

22:10 *Ahimelech inquired of the LORD for him.* See note on 21:1.

22:17 *They knew he was fleeing.* How much the priests really knew is not clear. David himself had not told them (see 21:2–3,8).

22:18 *linen ephod.* See note on 2:18.

22:19 *put to the sword Nob.* Thus the prophecy of judgment against the house of Eli is fulfilled (see 2:31).

22:20 *Abiathar . . . escaped and fled to join David.* See note on v. 5. Abiathar brought the high priestly ephod with him (see 23:6) and subsequently "inquired of the LORD" for David (see 23:2 and note; see also 23:4,9; 30:7–8; 2Sa 2:1; 5:19,23). He served as high priest until removed from office by Solomon for participating in the rebellion of Adonijah (see 1Ki 2:26–27).

23:2 *he inquired of the LORD.* By means of the Urim and Thummim through the high priest Abiathar (see vv. 6,9 and note on 2:28).

23:9 *Bring the ephod.* See note on v. 2.

said, "O LORD, God of Israel, your servant has heard definitely that Saul plans to come to Keilah and destroy the town on account of me. [11]Will the citizens of Keilah surrender me to him? Will Saul come down, as your servant has heard? O LORD, God of Israel, tell your servant."

And the LORD said, "He will."

[12]Again David asked, "Will the citizens of Keilah surrender[m] me and my men to Saul?"

And the LORD said, "They will."

[13]So David and his men,[n] about six hundred in number, left Keilah and kept moving from place to place. When Saul was told that David had escaped from Keilah, he did not go there.

[14]David stayed in the desert[o] strongholds and in the hills of the Desert of Ziph.[p] Day after day Saul searched[q] for him, but God did not[r] give David into his hands.

[15]While David was at Horesh in the Desert of Ziph, he learned that Saul had come out to take his life.[s] [16]And Saul's son Jonathan went to David at Horesh and helped him find strength[t] in God. [17]"Don't be afraid," he said. "My father Saul will not lay a hand on you. You will be king[u] over Israel, and I will be second to you. Even my father Saul knows this." [18]The two of them made a covenant[v] before the LORD. Then Jonathan went home, but David remained at Horesh.

[19]The Ziphites[w] went up to Saul at Gibeah and said, "Is not David hiding among us[x] in the strongholds at Horesh, on the hill of Hakilah,[y] south of Jeshimon? [20]Now, O king, come down whenever it pleases you to do so, and we will be responsible for handing[z] him over to the king."

[21]Saul replied, "The LORD bless[a] you for your concern[b] for me. [22]Go and make further preparation. Find out where David usually goes and who has seen him there. They tell me he is very crafty. [23]Find out

about all the hiding places he uses and come back to me with definite information.[y] Then I will go with you; if he is in the area, I will track[c] him down among all the clans of Judah."

[24]So they set out and went to Ziph ahead of Saul. Now David and his men were in the Desert of Maon,[d] in the Arabah south of Jeshimon.[e] [25]Saul and his men began the search, and when David was told about it, he went down to the rock and stayed in the Desert of Maon. When Saul heard this, he went into the Desert of Maon in pursuit of David.

[26]Saul[f] was going along one side of the mountain, and David and his men were on the other side, hurrying to get away from Saul. As Saul and his forces were closing in on David and his men to capture them, [27]a messenger came to Saul, saying, "Come quickly! The Philistines are raiding the land." [28]Then Saul broke off his pursuit of David and went to meet the Philistines. That is why they call this place Sela Hammahlekoth.[z] [29]And David went up from there and lived in the strongholds[g] of En Gedi.[h]

David Spares Saul's Life

24 After Saul returned from pursuing the Philistines, he was told, "David is in the Desert of En Gedi.[i]" [2]So Saul took three thousand chosen men from all Israel and set out to look[j] for David and his men near the Crags of the Wild Goats.

[3]He came to the sheep pens along the way; a cave[k] was there, and Saul went in to relieve[l] himself. David and his men were far back in the cave. [4]The men said, "This is the day the LORD spoke[m] of when he said[a] to you, 'I will give your enemy into your hands for you to deal with as you wish.' "[n] Then David crept up unnoticed and cut[o] off a corner of Saul's robe.

[5]Afterward, David was conscience-

(center cross-reference column)

23:12 [m]ver 20
23:13
[n]S 1Sa 22:2
23:14 [o]Ps 55:7
[p]S Jos 15:24
[q]Ps 54:3-4
[r]Ps 32:7
23:15
[s]S 1Sa 20:1
23:16 [t]1Sa 30:6;
Ps 18:2; 27:14
23:17
[u]S 1Sa 20:31
23:18
[v]S 1Sa 18:3;
2Sa 9:1
23:19 [w]1Sa 26:1
[x]Ps 54 Title
[y]1Sa 26:3
23:20 [z]ver 12
23:21 [a]Ru 2:20;
2Sa 2:5 [b]1Sa 22:8

23:23
[c]S Ge 31:36
23:24
[d]S Jos 15:55
[e]1Sa 26:1
23:26 [f]Ps 17:9
23:29 [g]1Sa 24:22
[h]S Jos 15:62;
2Ch 20:2; SS 1:14
24:1 [i]S Jos 15:62
24:2 [j]1Sa 26:2
24:3 [k]Ps 57 Title;
142 Title
[l]Jdg 3:24
24:4
[m]1Sa 25:28-30
[n]2Sa 4:8 [o]ver 10, 11

[y]23 Or me at Nacon   [z]28 Sela Hammahlekoth means rock of parting.   [a]4 Or "Today the LORD is saying

---

23:13 *about six hundred.* The number of David's men has grown significantly (cf. 22:2).
23:14 *desert strongholds.* Inaccessible places (see note on 22:4). *Desert of Ziph.* Located south of Hebron. *God did not give David into his hands.* The reality of God's protection over David portrayed here contrasts sharply with the wishful thinking of Saul in v. 7.
23:17 *You will be king over Israel.* See notes on 18:4; 20:13,16,31. *I will be second to you.* Jonathan's love and respect for David enable him to accept a role subordinate to David without any sign of resentment or jealousy (see notes on 18:3; 19:4). This is the last recorded meeting between Jonathan and David. *Saul knows this.* See 18:8 and note on 20:31.

23:18 *covenant.* See notes on 18:3; 20:14–15.
23:19 *strongholds.* Inaccessible places (see note on 22:4).
24:4 *This is the day the LORD spoke of when he said.* There is no previous record of the divine revelation here alluded to by David's men. Perhaps this was their own interpretation of the anointing of David to replace Saul (see 16:13–14), or of assurances given to David that he would survive Saul's vendetta against him and ultimately become king (see 20:14–15; 23:17). If the alternative given in the NIV text note is taken, the reference would not be to a verbal communication from the Lord but to the providential nature of the incident itself, which David's men understood as a revelation from God that David should not ignore.

stricken[p] for having cut off a corner of his robe. [6]He said to his men, "The LORD forbid that I should do such a thing to my master, the LORD's anointed,[q] or lift my hand against him; for he is the anointed of the LORD." [7]With these words David rebuked his men and did not allow them to attack Saul. And Saul left the cave and went his way.

[8]Then David went out of the cave and called out to Saul, "My lord the king!" When Saul looked behind him, David bowed down and prostrated himself with his face to the ground.[r] [9]He said to Saul, "Why do you listen[s] when men say, 'David is bent on harming[t] you'? [10]This day you have seen with your own eyes how the LORD delivered you into my hands in the cave. Some urged me to kill you, but I spared[u] you; I said, 'I will not lift my hand against my master, because he is the LORD's anointed.' [11]See, my father, look at this piece of your robe in my hand! I cut[v] off the corner of your robe but did not kill you. Now understand and recognize that I am not guilty[w] of wrongdoing[x] or rebellion. I have not wronged[y] you, but you are hunting[z] me down to take my life.[a] [12]May the LORD judge[b] between you and me. And may the LORD avenge[c] the wrongs you have done to me, but my hand will not touch you. [13]As the old saying goes, 'From evildoers come evil deeds,[d]' so my hand will not touch you.

[14]"Against whom has the king of Israel come out? Whom are you pursuing? A dead dog?[e] A flea?[f] [15]May the LORD be our judge[g] and decide[h] between us. May

he consider my cause and uphold[i] it; may he vindicate[j] me by delivering[k] me from your hand."

[16]When David finished saying this, Saul asked, "Is that your voice,[l] David my son?" And he wept aloud. [17]"You are more righteous than I,"[m] he said. "You have treated me well,[n] but I have treated you badly.[o] [18]You have just now told me of the good you did to me; the LORD delivered[p] me into your hands, but you did not kill me. [19]When a man finds his enemy, does he let him get away unharmed? May the LORD reward[q] you well for the way you treated me today. [20]I know that you will surely be king[r] and that the kingdom[s] of Israel will be established in your hands. [21]Now swear[t] to me by the LORD that you will not cut off my descendants or wipe out my name from my father's family."[u]

[22]So David gave his oath to Saul. Then Saul returned home, but David and his men went up to the stronghold.[v]

David, Nabal and Abigail

25 Now Samuel died,[w] and all Israel assembled and mourned[x] for him; and they buried him at his home in Ramah.[y]

Then David moved down into the Desert of Maon.[b] [2]A certain man in Maon,[z] who had property there at Carmel, was very wealthy.[a] He had a thousand goats and three thousand sheep, which he was shearing[b] in Carmel. [3]His

---

Cross references (center column)

24:5 [p]1Sa 26:9; 2Sa 24:10
24:6 [q]S Ge 26:11; S 1Sa 12:3
24:8 [r]S 1Sa 20:41
24:9 [s]1Sa 26:19
[t]1Sa 20:1
24:10 [u]S ver 4
24:11 [v]S ver 4
[w]Ps 7:3
[x]1Sa 25:28
[y]Ps 35:7
[z]S Ge 31:36; 1Sa 26:20
24:12 [a]S 1Sa 20:1
[b]S Ge 16:5; S 1Sa 25:38; S Job 9:15
[c]S Nu 31:3
24:13 [d]Mt 7:20
24:14 [e]S 1Sa 17:43
[f]1Sa 26:20
24:15 [g]ver 12
[h]S Ge 16:5

[i]Ps 35:1,23; Isa 49:25
[j]Ps 26:1; 35:24; 43:1; 50:4; 54:1; 135:14
[k]Ps 119:134,154
24:16 [l]1Sa 26:17
24:17 [m]Ge 38:26
[n]Mt 5:44
[o]S Ex 9:27
24:18 [p]1Sa 26:23
24:19 [q]S Ru 2:12; S 2Ch 15:7
24:20 [r]S 1Sa 20:31
[s]S 1Sa 13:14
24:21 [t]Ge 21:23; S 47:31; S 1Sa 18:3; 2Sa 21:1-9
[u]S Ge 20:14-15
24:22 [v]1Sa 23:29
25:1 [w]1Sa 28:3
[x]S Lev 10:6; Dt 34:8
[y]S 1Sa 7:17
25:2 [z]S Jos 15:55
[a]2Sa 19:32
[b]S Ge 31:19

b[1] Some Septuagint manuscripts; Hebrew *Paran*

24:6 *for he is the anointed of the LORD.* Because Saul's royal office carried divine sanction by virtue of his anointing (see note on 9:16), David is determined not to wrest the kingship from Saul but to leave its disposition to the Lord who gave it (see vv. 12,15; 26:10).

24:11 *my father.* Saul was David's father-in-law (see 18:27).

24:16 *he wept aloud.* Saul experiences temporary remorse (see 26:21) for his actions against David but quickly reverts to his former determination to kill him (see 26:2).

24:21 *not cut off my descendants.* See notes on 20:14–15.

24:22 *stronghold.* An inaccessible place (see note on 22:4). From previous experience David did not place any confidence in Saul's words of repentance.

25:1 *all Israel . . . mourned for him.* Samuel was recognized as a leader of national prominence who played a key role in the restructuring of the theocracy with the establishment of the monarchy (see chs. 8–12). The loss of his leadership was mourned much like that of other prominent figures in Israel's past history, including Jacob (Ge 50:10), Aaron (Nu 20:29) and Moses (Dt 34:8). *Ramah.* See 7:17 and note on 1:1.

25:2–44 Nabal, the "fool" (see v. 25), lived near Carmel, where Saul had erected a monument in his own honor (see 15:12) and had committed the act that led to his rejection

(see 15:26). The account of Nabal effectively serves the author's purpose in a number of ways: 1. Nabal's general character, his disdainful attitude toward David though David had guarded his flocks, and his sudden death at the Lord's hand all parallel Saul (whose "flock" David had also protected). This allows the author indirectly to characterize Saul as a fool (see 13:13; 26:21) and to foreshadow his end. 2. David's vengeful attitude toward Nabal displays his natural tendency and highlights his restraint toward Saul, the Lord's anointed (this event is sandwiched between the two instances in which David spared Saul in spite of the urging of his men). 3. Abigail's prudent action prevents David from using his power as leader for personal vengeance (the very thing Saul was doing). In this way the Lord (who avenged his servant) keeps David's sword clean, teaching him a lesson he does not forget. 4. Abigail's confident acknowledgment of David's future accession to the throne foreshadows that event and even anticipates the Lord's commitment to establish David's house as a "lasting dynasty" (v. 28; cf. 2Sa 7:11–16). 5. Abigail's marriage to David provides him with a wise and worthy wife, while Saul gives away David's wife Michal to another, illustrating how the Lord counters every move Saul makes against David.

25:3 *Calebite.* A descendant of Caleb (see Nu 14:24), who settled at Hebron (see Jos 14:13) after the conquest of Ca-

name was Nabal and his wife's name was Abigail.^c She was an intelligent and beautiful woman, but her husband, a Calebite,^d was surly and mean in his dealings.

⁴While David was in the desert, he heard that Nabal was shearing sheep. ⁵So he sent ten young men and said to them, "Go up to Nabal at Carmel and greet him in my name. ⁶Say to him: 'Long life to you! Good health^e to you and your household! And good health to all that is yours!^f

⁷" 'Now I hear that it is sheep-shearing time. When your shepherds were with us, we did not mistreat^g them, and the whole time they were at Carmel nothing of theirs was missing. ⁸Ask your own servants and they will tell you. Therefore be favorable toward my young men, since we come at a festive time. Please give your servants and your son David whatever^h you can find for them.' "

⁹When David's men arrived, they gave Nabal this message in David's name. Then they waited.

¹⁰Nabal answered David's servants, "Whoⁱ is this David? Who is this son of Jesse? Many servants are breaking away from their masters these days. ¹¹Why should I take my bread^j and water, and the meat I have slaughtered for my shearers, and give it to men coming from who knows where?"

¹²David's men turned around and went back. When they arrived, they reported every word. ¹³David said to his men^k, "Put on your swords!" So they put on their swords, and David put on his. About four hundred men went^l up with David, while two hundred stayed with the supplies.^m

¹⁴One of the servants told Nabal's wife Abigail: "David sent messengers from the desert to give our master his greetings,ⁿ but he hurled insults at them. ¹⁵Yet these men were very good to us. They did not mistreat^o us, and the whole time we were out in the fields near them nothing was

missing.^p ¹⁶Night and day they were a wall^q around us all the time we were herding our sheep near them. ¹⁷Now think it over and see what you can do, because disaster is hanging over our master and his whole household. He is such a wicked^r man that no one can talk to him."

¹⁸Abigail lost no time. She took two hundred loaves of bread, two skins of wine, five dressed sheep, five seahs^c of roasted grain,^s a hundred cakes of raisins^t and two hundred cakes of pressed figs, and loaded them on donkeys.^u ¹⁹Then she told her servants, "Go on ahead;^v I'll follow you." But she did not tell^w her husband Nabal.

²⁰As she came riding her donkey into a mountain ravine, there were David and his men descending toward her, and she met them. ²¹David had just said, "It's been useless—all my watching over this fellow's property in the desert so that nothing of his was missing.^x He has paid^y me back evil^z for good. ²²May God deal with David,^d be it ever so severely,^a if by morning I leave alive one male^b of all who belong to him!"

²³When Abigail saw David, she quickly got off her donkey and bowed down before David with her face to the ground.^c ²⁴She fell at his feet and said: "My lord, let the blame^d be on me alone. Please let your servant speak to you; hear what your servant has to say. ²⁵May my lord pay no attention to that wicked man Nabal. He is just like his name—his name is Fool^e,^f and folly goes with him. But as for me, your servant, I did not see the men my master sent.

²⁶"Now since the LORD has kept you, my master, from bloodshed^g and from avenging^h yourself with your own hands, as surely as the LORD lives and as you live, may your enemies and all who intend to harm my master be like Nabal.ⁱ ²⁷And let this gift,^j which your servant has brought

25:3 ^cPr 31:10
^dS Jos 14:13;
S 15:13
25:6 ^ePs 122:7;
Mt 10:12
^f1Ch 12:18
25:7 ^gver 15
25:8 ^hNe 8:10
25:10 ⁱJdg 9:28
25:11 ^jJdg 8:6
25:13
^kS 1Sa 22:2
^lS 1Sa 21:10
^mS Nu 31:27
25:14 ⁿ1Sa 13:10
25:15 ^over 7
^pver 21

25:16 ^qEx 14:22;
Job 1:10;
Ps 139:5
25:17
^rS Dt 13:13;
S 1Sa 20:7
25:18
^sS Lev 23:14;
S 1Sa 17:17
^t1Ch 12:40
^uS Ge 42:26;
2Sa 16:1; Isa 30:6
25:19 ^vGe 32:20
^wver 36
25:21 ^xver 15
^yPs 109:5
^zS 1Sa 19:4
25:22 ^aS Ru 1:17
^b1Ki 14:10;
21:21; 2Ki 9:8
25:23
^cS Ge 19:1;
S 1Sa 20:41
25:24 ^d2Sa 14:9
25:25 ^ePr 17:12
^fPr 12:16; 14:16;
20:3; Isa 32:5
25:26 ^gver 33
^hHeb 10:30 ⁱver
34; 2Sa 18:32
25:27
^jS Ge 33:11

^c18 That is, probably about a bushel (about 37 liters)
^d22 Some Septuagint manuscripts; Hebrew *with David's enemies*

---

naan. Since Caleb's name can mean "dog," Nabal is subtly depicted as a dog as well as a fool. He would soon be a dead dog (see note on 2Sa 9:8), when the Lord would avenge his acts of contempt toward David. The hint is strong that, when the Lord avenges Saul's sins against David (see 24:12,15), the king will no longer pursue a dead dog (see 24:14) but will himself become one—a case of biting irony.

25:4 *shearing sheep.* A festive occasion (see v. 8; 2Sa 13:23–24).

25:8 *whatever you can find for them.* David and his men ask for some remuneration for their protection of Nabal's shepherds and flocks against pillage (see vv. 15–16,21).

25:17 *wicked man.* See note on Dt 13:13. *no one can talk*

to him. In this way, too, Nabal is like Saul (cf., e.g., 20:27–33).

25:19 *did not tell her husband.* Cf. Michal's treatment of Saul (19:11–14).

25:22 *May God deal with David, be it ever so severely.* See note on 3:17. David invokes a curse on himself if he should fail to kill every male in Nabal's household and so obliterate Nabal's family.

25:25 *wicked man.* See note on Dt 13:13. *He is just like his name.* In ancient times a person's name was believed to reflect his nature and character. *his name is Fool.* In Hebrew the name Nabal means "fool."

25:26 *as surely as the LORD lives.* See note on 14:39.

to my master, be given to the men who follow you. ²⁸Please forgive^k your servant's offense, for the LORD will certainly make a lasting^l dynasty for my master, because he fights the LORD's battles.^m Let no wrongdoingⁿ be found in you as long as you live. ²⁹Even though someone is pursuing you to take your life,^o the life of my master will be bound securely in the bundle of the living by the LORD your God. But the lives of your enemies he will hurl^p away as from the pocket of a sling.^q ³⁰When the LORD has done for my master every good thing he promised concerning him and has appointed him leader^r over Israel, ³¹my master will not have on his conscience the staggering burden of needless bloodshed or of having avenged himself. And when the LORD has brought my master success, remember^s your servant."^t

³²David said to Abigail, "Praise^u be to the LORD, the God of Israel, who has sent you today to meet me. ³³May you be blessed for your good judgment and for keeping me from bloodshed^v this day and from avenging myself with my own hands. ³⁴Otherwise, as surely as the LORD, the God of Israel, lives, who has kept me from harming you, if you had not come quickly to meet me, not one male belonging to Nabal^w would have been left alive by daybreak."

³⁵Then David accepted from her hand what she had brought him and said, "Go home in peace. I have heard your words and granted^x your request."

³⁶When Abigail went to Nabal, he was in the house holding a banquet like that of a king. He was in high^y spirits and very drunk.^z So she told^a him nothing until daybreak. ³⁷Then in the morning, when Nabal was sober, his wife told him all these things, and his heart failed him and he

became like a stone.^b ³⁸About ten days later, the LORD struck^c Nabal and he died.

³⁹When David heard that Nabal was dead, he said, "Praise be to the LORD, who has upheld my cause against Nabal for treating me with contempt. He has kept his servant from doing wrong and has brought Nabal's wrongdoing down on his own head."

Then David sent word to Abigail, asking her to become his wife. ⁴⁰His servants went to Carmel and said to Abigail, "David has sent us to you to take you to become his wife."

⁴¹She bowed down with her face to the ground and said, "Here is your maidservant, ready to serve you and wash the feet of my master's servants." ⁴²Abigail^d quickly got on a donkey and, attended by her five maids, went with David's messengers and became his wife. ⁴³David had also married Ahinoam^e of Jezreel, and they both were his wives.^f ⁴⁴But Saul had given his daughter Michal, David's wife, to Paltiel^{eg} son of Laish, who was from Gallim.^h

David Again Spares Saul's Life

26 The Ziphitesⁱ went to Saul at Gibeah and said, "Is not David hiding^j on the hill of Hakilah, which faces Jeshimon?^k"

²So Saul went down to the Desert of Ziph, with his three thousand chosen men of Israel, to search^l there for David. ³Saul made his camp beside the road on the hill of Hakilah^m facing Jeshimon, but David stayed in the desert. When he saw that Saul had followed him there, ⁴he sent out scouts and learned that Saul had definitely arrived.^f

⁵Then David set out and went to the

25:28 ^kver 24; 2Sa 14:9
^l2Sa 7:11,26
^m1Sa 18:17
ⁿ1Sa 24:11
25:29 ^oS 1Sa 20:1
^pJer 10:18; 22:26
^q1Sa 17:50; 2Sa 4:8
25:30 ^rS 1Sa 12:12; S 13:14
25:31 ^sS Ge 40:14
^t2Sa 3:10
25:32 ^uS Ge 24:27
25:33 ^vver 26
25:34 ^wS ver 26
25:35
^xS Ge 19:21
25:36 ^yS Ru 3:7
^zPr 20:1;
Ecc 10:17;
Isa 5:11,22;
22:13; 28:7;
56:12; Hos 4:11
^aver 19

25:37 ^bEx 15:16
25:38 ^cDt 32:35;
1Sa 24:12; 26:10;
2Sa 6:7; 12:15
25:42 ^d2Sa 2:2;
3:3; 1Ch 3:1
25:43 ^e2Sa 3:2;
1Ch 3:1
^f1Sa 27:3; 30:5;
2Sa 2:2
25:44 ^g2Sa 3:15
^hIsa 10:30
26:1 ⁱ1Sa 23:19
^jPs 54 Title
^k1Sa 23:24
26:2 ^l1Sa 24:2
26:3 ^m1Sa 23:19

^e44 Hebrew *Palti*, a variant of *Paltiel*   ^f4 Or *had come to Nacon*

25:28 *the LORD will certainly make a lasting dynasty.* While the idea that David was destined to become king in place of Saul may have spread among the general populace, Abigail's assessment of David contrasts sharply with that of her husband (see v. 10). *he fights the LORD's battles.* Abigail is familiar with David's victories over the Philistines, in which he sought to glorify the Lord rather than advance his own honor (see 17:26,45–47; 18:16–17). *Let no wrongdoing be found in you.* Abigail shows concern for the preservation of David's integrity in view of the office he was later to assume (see vv. 30–31,39).
25:29 *bound securely in the bundle of the living.* Using the figure of placing a valuable possession in a carefully wrapped package for safekeeping, Abigail assures David that the Lord will preserve his life in the midst of danger.
25:30 *leader.* See note on 9:16.
25:31 *needless bloodshed.* See note on v. 28.
25:32 *who has sent you.* David recognizes the providential

leading of the Lord in his encounter with Abigail (see v. 39).
25:36 *holding a banquet.* See Pr 30:21–22. *like that of a king.* Another clue that the author is using Nabal as a subtle portrayal of Saul.
25:37 *became like a stone.* Perhaps he suffered a stroke—he who was without moral sensitivity (was a *nabal;* see v. 25 and note) became as senseless as a stone.
25:43 *Ahinoam.* David's first wife (see 27:3; 30:5; 2Sa 2:2) and mother of his first son, Amnon (see 2Sa 3:2). *Jezreel.* Located near Carmel (see v. 2; Jos 15:55) and not to be confused with the northern town of the same name, where Israel camped against the Philistines (see 29:1,11) and where Ahab resided in later times (see 1Ki 18:45–46).
25:44 *Michal, David's wife.* See 18:27.
26:1 *Ziphites.* See notes on 23:14,19. *Gibeah.* Saul's residence (see 10:26).
26:2 *three thousand.* Apparently Saul's standing army (see 24:2).

place where Saul had camped. He saw where Saul and Abner[n] son of Ner, the commander of the army, had lain down. Saul was lying inside the camp, with the army encamped around him.

[6]David then asked Ahimelech the Hittite[o] and Abishai[p] son of Zeruiah,[q] Joab's brother, "Who will go down into the camp with me to Saul?"

"I'll go with you," said Abishai.

[7]So David and Abishai went to the army by night, and there was Saul, lying asleep inside the camp with his spear stuck in the ground near his head. Abner and the soldiers were lying around him.

[8]Abishai said to David, "Today God has delivered your enemy into your hands. Now let me pin him to the ground with one thrust of my spear; I won't strike him twice."

[9]But David said to Abishai, "Don't destroy him! Who can lay a hand on the LORD's anointed[r] and be guiltless?[s] [10]As surely as the LORD lives," he said, "the LORD himself will strike[t] him; either his time[u] will come and he will die,[v] or he will go into battle and perish. [11]But the LORD forbid that I should lay a hand on the LORD's anointed. Now get the spear and water jug that are near his head, and let's go."

[12]So David took the spear and water jug near Saul's head, and they left. No one saw or knew about it, nor did anyone wake up. They were all sleeping, because the LORD had put them into a deep sleep.[w]

[13]Then David crossed over to the other side and stood on top of the hill some distance away; there was a wide space between them. [14]He called out to the army and to Abner son of Ner, "Aren't you going to answer me, Abner?"

Abner replied, "Who are you who calls to the king?"

[15]David said, "You're a man, aren't you? And who is like you in Israel? Why didn't you guard your lord the king? Someone came to destroy your lord the king. [16]What you have done is not good. As surely as the LORD lives, you and your men deserve to die, because you did not guard your master, the LORD's anointed. Look around you. Where are the king's spear and water jug that were near his head?"

[17]Saul recognized David's voice and said, "Is that your voice,[x] David my son?"

David replied, "Yes it is, my lord the king." [18]And he added, "Why is my lord pursuing his servant? What have I done, and what wrong[y] am I guilty of? [19]Now let my lord the king listen[z] to his servant's words. If the LORD has incited you against me, then may he accept an offering.[a] If, however, men have done it, may they be cursed before the LORD! They have now driven me from my share in the LORD's inheritance[b] and have said, 'Go, serve other gods.'[c] [20]Now do not let my blood[d] fall to the ground far from the presence of the LORD. The king of Israel has come out to look for a flea[e]—as one hunts a partridge in the mountains.[f] "

[21]Then Saul said, "I have sinned.[g] Come back, David my son. Because you considered my life precious[h] today, I will not try to harm you again. Surely I have acted like a fool and have erred greatly."

[22]"Here is the king's spear," David answered. "Let one of your young men come over and get it. [23]The LORD rewards[i] every man for his righteousness[j] and faithfulness. The LORD delivered[k] you into my hands today, but I would not lay a hand on the LORD's anointed. [24]As surely

---

26:5 *n* 1Sa 17:55
26:6 *o* S Ge 10:15
p 2Sa 2:18; 10:10;
16:9; 18:2;
19:21; 23:18;
1Ch 11:20; 19:11
q 1Ch 2:16
26:9 *r* ver 16;
S Ge 26:11;
S 1Sa 9:16;
2Sa 1:14; 19:21;
La 4:20
s S 1Sa 24:5
26:10
t S Ge 16:5;
S 1Sa 25:38;
S Ro 12:19
u Dt 31:14;
Ps 37:13
v 1Sa 31:6;
2Sa 1:1
26:12
w S Jdg 4:21

26:17 *x* 1Sa 24:16
26:18
y Job 13:23;
Jer 37:18
26:19 *z* 1Sa 24:9
a 2Sa 16:11
b Dt 20:16; 32:9;
2Sa 14:16; 20:19;
21:3 *c* S Dt 4:28;
S 11:28
26:20
d S 1Sa 24:11
e 1Sa 24:14
f Jer 4:29; 16:16;
Am 9:3
26:21 *g* S Ex 9:27
h Ps 72:14
26:23 *i* S Ge 16:5;
S Ru 2:12;
Ps 62:12
j 2Sa 22:21,25;
Ps 7:8; 18:20,24
k 1Sa 24:18

26:5 *lain down.* David arrived at Saul's camp during the night when the men were sleeping. *Abner.* Saul's cousin (see 14:50).

26:6 *Ahimelech the Hittite.* Not referred to elsewhere. Hittites had long resided in Canaan (see note on Ge 10:15; see also Ge 15:20; 23:3–20; Dt 7:1; 20:17). Another Hittite in David's service was Uriah (see 2Sa 11:3; 23:39). *Abishai son of Zeruiah, Joab's brother.* Zeruiah was an older sister of David (1Ch 2:16), so Abishai and Joab (and their brother Asahel, 2Sa 2:18) were David's nephews as well as trusted military leaders. Joab would long serve as the commander of his army.

26:9 See note on 24:6.
26:10 *As surely as the LORD lives.* See note on 14:39.
26:12 *David took the spear and water jug.* In this way he sought to prove again to Saul that he did not seek his life.
26:19 *may he accept an offering.* David knows no reason why God should be angry with him; but if for some reason God is behind Saul's determined effort to kill him, David

appeals for God to accept an offering of appeasement (cf. 16:5)—in any event, to let the matter be settled between David and God, without Saul's involvement. *may they be cursed before the LORD!* David commits any such men to the judgment of God. *the LORD's inheritance.* See note on 10:1. David appeals to Saul's conscience by describing his present exclusion from the fellowship of God's people and from living at peace in the Lord's land. *Go, serve other gods.* In their view, to be expelled from the Lord's land was to be separated from the Lord's sanctuary (an OT form of excommunication) and left to serve the gods of whatever land one may settle in (see Jos 22:24–27).

26:20 *look for a flea.* See 24:14. David suggests that Saul is making a fool of himself in his fanatical pursuit of an innocent and undesigning man.

26:21 *I have sinned.* See 24:17. *I have acted like a fool.* Saul confesses that his behavior has been not only unwise but also ungodly (see notes on 13:13; 25:2–44).

26:23 *I would not lay a hand on the LORD's anointed.* See v. 9 and note on 24:6.

as I valued your life today, so may the LORD value my life and deliver[l] me from all trouble."

25Then Saul said to David, "May you be blessed,[m] my son David; you will do great things and surely triumph."

So David went on his way, and Saul returned home.

David Among the Philistines

27 But David thought to himself, "One of these days I will be destroyed by the hand of Saul. The best thing I can do is to escape to the land of the Philistines. Then Saul will give up searching for me anywhere in Israel, and I will slip out of his hand."

2So David and the six hundred men[n] with him left and went[o] over to Achish[p] son of Maoch king of Gath. 3David and his men settled in Gath with Achish. Each

man had his family with him, and David had his two wives:[q] Ahinoam of Jezreel and Abigail of Carmel, the widow of Nabal. 4When Saul was told that David had fled to Gath, he no longer searched for him.

5Then David said to Achish, "If I have found favor in your eyes, let a place be assigned to me in one of the country towns, that I may live there. Why should your servant live in the royal city with you?"

6So on that day Achish gave him Ziklag,[r] and it has belonged to the kings of Judah ever since. 7David lived[s] in Philistine territory a year and four months.

8Now David and his men went up and raided the Geshurites,[t] the Girzites and the Amalekites.[u] (From ancient times these peoples had lived in the land extending to Shur[v] and Egypt.) 9Whenever

Cross references (center column)

26:24 [l]Ps 54:7
26:25
27:2 [m]S Ru 2:12
[n]1Sa 30:9;
2Sa 2:3
[o]S 1Sa 21:10
[p]1Ki 2:39

27:3
[q]S 1Sa 25:43
27:6 [r]Jos 15:31;
19:5; 1Sa 30:1;
1Ch 12:20;
Ne 11:28
27:7 [s]1Sa 29:3
27:8 [t]S Jos 12:5
[u]S Ex 17:14;
30:1; 2Sa 1:8;
8:12 [v]S Ge 16:7

Study notes

26:25 *you will . . . triumph.* Saul makes a veiled reference to his own conviction that David will replace him as king (see 24:20).

27:1 *I will be destroyed by the hand of Saul.* David falters in his faith (see 23:14; 25:29) and under pressure of Saul's superior forces feels compelled to seek security outside Israel's borders. *land of the Philistines.* For the second time David seeks refuge in the land of the Philistines (see 21:10–15).

27:2 *Achish . . . king of Gath.* See 21:10. In contrast to David's previous excursion into Philistia, Achish is now ready to receive him because he has become known as a formidable adversary of Saul. Moreover, to offer sanctuary under the circumstances would obligate David and his men to serve at his call in any military venture (see 28:1).

27:3 *Ahinoam.* See note on 25:43. *Abigail.* See 25:39–42.

27:4 *he no longer searched for him.* Saul did not have sufficient military strength to make incursions into Philistine

territory, and with David out of the country he no longer faced an internal threat to his throne.

27:5 *in one of the country towns.* David desired more independence and freedom of movement than was possible while residing under the very eyes of the king of Gath. *Why should your servant live in the royal city with you?* David implies that he is not worthy of this honor.

27:6 *Ziklag.* Location unknown, but it is included in a list of towns in southern Judah (see Jos 15:31). It was given to the tribe of Simeon (see Jos 19:1–5) and was presumably occupied by them (cf. Jdg 1:17–18), only to be lost to the Philistines at a later, undisclosed time. *it has belonged to the kings of Judah ever since.* As royal property. This comment implies that the book of Samuel was written after the time of the division of Israel into the northern and southern kingdoms—an important consideration in determining the date of the writing of the book (see Introduction: Literary Features, Authorship and Date).

Exploits of David

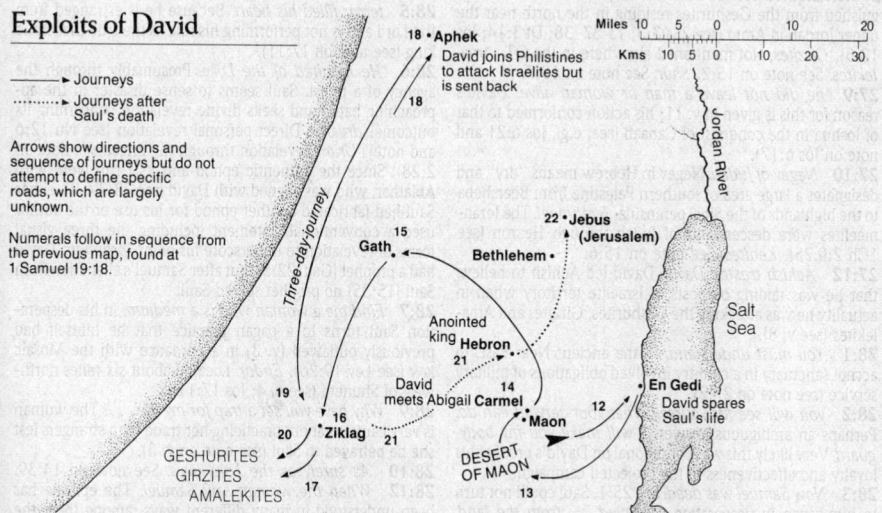

— ► Journeys
.... ► Journeys after Saul's death

Arrows show directions and sequence of journeys but do not attempt to define specific roads, which are largely unknown.

Numerals follow in sequence from the previous map, found at 1 Samuel 19:18.

Miles 10   5   0   10   20
Kms 10 5 0   10   20   30

18 • Aphek
David joins Philistines to attack Israelites but is sent back
18

Three-day journey

Gath 15
Bethlehem •
22 • Jebus (Jerusalem)

Anointed king Hebron 21

David meets Abigail Carmel 14
• Maon

19
16 • Ziklag 21
20
17

GESHURITES
GIRZITES
AMALEKITES

DESERT OF MAON 13

Jordan River

Salt Sea

• En Gedi 12
David spares Saul's life

David attacked an area, he did not leave a
man or woman alive,[w] but took sheep and
cattle, donkeys and camels, and clothes.
Then he returned to Achish.
10When Achish asked, "Where did you
go raiding today?" David would say,
"Against the Negev of Judah" or "Against
the Negev of Jerahmeel[x]" or "Against the
Negev of the Kenites.[y]" 11He did not leave
a man or woman alive to be brought to
Gath, for he thought, "They might inform
on us and say, 'This is what David did.' "
And such was his practice as long as he
lived in Philistine territory. 12Achish
trusted David and said to himself, "He has
become so odious[z] to his people, the Israelites, that he will be my servant forever.[a]"

Saul and the Witch of Endor

28 In those days the Philistines gathered[b] their forces to fight against
Israel. Achish said to David, "You must
understand that you and your men will accompany me in the army."
2David said, "Then you will see for
yourself what your servant can do."
Achish replied, "Very well, I will make
you my bodyguard[c] for life."
3Now Samuel was dead,[d] and all Israel
had mourned for him and buried him in
his own town of Ramah.[e] Saul had expelled[f] the mediums and spiritists[g] from
the land.
4The Philistines assembled and came
and set up camp at Shunem,[h] while Saul
gathered all the Israelites and set up camp
at Gilboa.[i] 5When Saul saw the Philistine
army, he was afraid; terror[j] filled his
heart. 6He inquired[k] of the LORD, but the
LORD did not answer him by dreams[l] or
Urim[m] or prophets.[n] 7Saul then said to his
attendants, "Find me a woman who is a
medium,[o] so I may go and inquire of her."
"There is one in Endor,[p]" they said.
8So Saul disguised[q] himself, putting on
other clothes, and at night he and two men
went to the woman. "Consult[r] a spirit for
me," he said, "and bring up for me the one
I name."
9But the woman said to him, "Surely
you know what Saul has done. He has cut
off[s] the mediums and spiritists from the
land. Why have you set a trap[t] for my life
to bring about my death?"
10Saul swore to her by the LORD, "As
surely as the LORD lives, you will not be
punished for this."
11Then the woman asked, "Whom shall
I bring up for you?"
"Bring up Samuel," he said.
12When the woman saw Samuel, she

27:9 [w]S 1Sa 15:3
27:10 [x]1Sa 30:29 [y]Jdg 1:16
27:12 [z]S Ge 34:30 [a]1Sa 29:6
28:1 [b]1Sa 29:1
28:2 [c]1Sa 29:2
28:3 [d]1Sa 25:1 [e]S 1Sa 7:17 [f]ver 9 [g]S Ex 22:18
28:4 [h]S Jos 19:18 [i]1Sa 31:1,3; 2Sa 1:6,21; 21:12
28:5 [j]S Ex 19:16
28:6 [k]S 1Sa 8:18; 14:37 [l]S Dt 13:3 [m]S Ex 28:30; S Lev 8:8 [n]Eze 20:3; Am 8:11; Mic 3:7
28:7 [o]1Ch 10:13; Ac 16:16 [p]Jos 17:11; Ps 83:10
28:8 [q]1Ki 22:30; 2Ch 18:29; 35:22 [r]2Ki 1:3; Isa 8:19
28:9 [s]ver 3 [t]Job 18:10; Ps 31:4; 69:22; Isa 8:14

27:7 *David lived in Philistine territory a year and four months.* It was not until after the death of Saul that David moved his residence from Ziklag (see 2Sa 1:1; 2:1–3) to Hebron.
27:8 *Geshurites.* A people residing in the area south of Philistia who were not defeated by the Israelites at the time of the conquest (see Jos 13:1–3) and who are to be distinguished from the Geshurites residing in the north near the upper Jordan in Aram (see 2Sa 3:3; 13:37–38; Dt 3:14; Jos 12:5). *Girzites.* Not mentioned elsewhere in the OT. *Amalekites.* See note on 15:2. *Shur.* See note on 15:7.
27:9 *he did not leave a man or woman alive.* David's reason for this is given in v. 11; his action conformed to that of Joshua in the conquest of Canaan (see, e.g., Jos 6:21 and note on Jos 6:17).
27:10 *Negev of Judah.* Negev in Hebrew means "dry" and designates a large area of southern Palestine from Beersheba to the highlands of the Sinai peninsula. *Jerahmeel.* The Jerahmeelites were descendants of Judah through Hezron (see 1Ch 2:9,25). *Kenites.* See note on 15:6.
27:12 *Achish trusted David.* David led Achish to believe that he was raiding outposts of Israelite territory when in actuality he was attacking the Geshurites, Girzites and Amalekites (see v. 8).
28:1 *You must understand.* In the ancient Near East, to accept sanctuary in a country involved obligations of military service (see note on 27:2).
28:2 *you will see for yourself what your servant can do.* Perhaps an ambiguous answer. *I will make you my bodyguard.* Very likely this was conditional on David's proof of his loyalty and effectiveness in the projected campaign.
28:3 *Now Samuel was dead.* See 25:1. Saul could not turn to him, even in desperation. *expelled . . . from the land.* Possibly a euphemism for "put to death," in agreement with Pentateuchal law (see vv. 9,21). *mediums and spiritists.* See Lev 19:31; 20:6,27; Dt 18:11.
28:4 *Shunem.* The Philistines assembled their forces far to the north, along the plain of Jezreel in the territory of Issachar (see Jos 19:18). *Gilboa.* A range of mountains east of the plain of Jezreel.
28:5 *terror filled his heart.* Because he is estranged from the Lord and is not performing his role as the true theocratic king (see note on 17:11).
28:6 *He inquired of the LORD.* Presumably through the agency of a priest. Saul seems to sense disaster in the approaching battle and seeks divine revelation concerning its outcome. *dreams.* Direct personal revelation (see Nu 12:6 and note). *Urim.* Revelation through the priest (see note on 2:28). Since the authentic ephod and its Urim were with Abiathar, who was aligned with David (see 23:2,6,9), either Saul had fabricated another ephod for his use or the author used a conventional statement including the three visual forms of revelation to underscore his point. *prophets.* David had a prophet (Gad, 22:5), but after Samuel's alienation from Saul (15:35) no prophet served Saul.
28:7 *Find me a woman who is a medium.* In his desperation Saul turns to a pagan practice that he himself had previously outlawed (v. 3) in accordance with the Mosaic law (see Lev 19:26). *Endor.* Located about six miles northwest of Shunem (see v. 4; Jos 17:11).
28:9 *Why have you set a trap for my life . . . ?* The woman is very cautious about practicing her trade with strangers lest she be betrayed to Saul (see note on v. 3).
28:10 *As surely as the LORD lives.* See note on 14:39.
28:12 *When the woman saw Samuel.* The episode has been understood in many different ways, among them the

cried out at the top of her voice and said to Saul, "Why have you deceived me? *u* You are Saul!"

13The king said to her, "Don't be afraid. What do you see?"

The woman said, "I see a spirit *g* coming up out of the ground." *v*

14"What does he look like?" he asked.

"An old man wearing a robe *w* is coming up," she said.

Then Saul knew it was Samuel, and he bowed down and prostrated himself with his face to the ground.

15Samuel said to Saul, "Why have you disturbed me by bringing me up?"

"I am in great distress," Saul said. "The Philistines are fighting against me, and God has turned *x* away from me. He no longer answers *y* me, either by prophets or by dreams. *z* So I have called on you to tell me what to do."

16Samuel said, "Why do you consult me, now that the LORD has turned away from you and become your enemy? 17The LORD has done what he predicted through me. The LORD has torn *a* the kingdom out of your hands and given it to one of your neighbors—to David. 18Because you did not obey *b* the LORD or carry out his fierce wrath *c* against the Amalekites, *d.* the LORD has done this to you today. 19The LORD will hand over both Israel and you to the Philistines, and tomorrow you and your sons *e* will be with me. The LORD will also hand over the army of Israel to the Philistines."

20Immediately Saul fell full length on the ground, filled with fear because of Samuel's words. His strength was gone, for he had eaten nothing all that day and night.

21When the woman came to Saul and saw that he was greatly shaken, she said, "Look, your maidservant has obeyed you. I took my life *f* in my hands and did what

you told me to do. 22Now please listen to your servant and let me give you some food so you may eat and have the strength to go on your way."

23He refused *g* and said, "I will not eat."

But his men joined the woman in urging him, and he listened to them. He got up from the ground and sat on the couch.

24The woman had a fattened calf *h* at the house, which she butchered at once. She took some flour, kneaded it and baked bread without yeast. 25Then she set it before Saul and his men, and they ate. That same night they got up and left.

Achish Sends David Back to Ziklag

29 The Philistines gathered *i* all their forces at Aphek, *j* and Israel camped by the spring in Jezreel. *k* 2As the Philistine rulers marched with their units of hundreds and thousands, David and his men were marching at the rear *l* with Achish. 3The commanders of the Philistines asked, "What about these Hebrews?"

Achish replied, "Is this not David, *m* who was an officer of Saul king of Israel? He has already been with me for over a year, *n* and from the day he left Saul until now, I have found no fault in him."

4But the Philistine commanders were angry with him and said, "Send *o* the man back, that he may return to the place you assigned him. He must not go with us into battle, or he will turn *p* against us during the fighting. How better could he regain his master's favor than by taking the heads of our own men? 5Isn't this the David they sang about in their dances:

" 'Saul has slain his thousands,
    and David his tens of thousands'?" *q*

6So Achish called David and said to him,

Cross references (center column)

28:12 *u*S Ge 27:36; 1Ki 14:6
28:13 *v*ver 15; S Lev 19:31; 2Ch 33:6
28:14 *w*1Sa 15:27
28:15 *x*S Jdg 16:20 *y*S 1Sa 14:37 *z*S Dt 13:3
28:17 *a*1Sa 15:28
28:18 *b*1Sa 15:20 *c*S Dt 9:8; S 1Sa 15:3 *d*S Ge 14:7; S 1Sa 14:48
28:19 *e*1Sa 31:2; 1Ch 8:33
28:21 *f*S Jdg 9:17; S 12:3

28:23 *g*1Ki 21:4
28:24 *h*S Ge 18:7
29:1 *i*1Sa 28:1 *j*S 1Sa 4:1 *k*Jos 17:16; 1Ki 18:45; 21:1, 23; 2Ki 9:30; Jer 50:5; Hos 1:4, 5,11; 2:22
29:2 *l*1Sa 28:2
29:3 *m*1Ch 12:19 *n*1Sa 27:7
29:4 *o*1Ch 12:19 *p*1Sa 14:21
29:5 *q*S 1Sa 18:7

g13 Or *see spirits;* or *see gods*

---

following: 1. God permitted the spirit of Samuel to appear to the woman. 2. The woman had contact with an evil or devilish spirit in the form of Samuel by whom she was deceived and controlled. 3. By using parapsychological powers such as telepathy or clairvoyance, the woman was able to discern Saul's thoughts and picture Samuel in her own mind. Whatever the explanation of this mysterious affair, the medium was used in some way to convey to Saul that the impending battle would bring death, would dash his hopes for a dynasty and would conclude his reign with a devastating defeat of Israel that would leave the nation at the mercy of the Philistines, the very people against whom he had struggled all his years as king. And this would come, as Samuel had previously announced (15:26,28), because of his unfaithfulness to the Lord. *she cried out . . . You are Saul!* By whatever means, the medium suddenly becomes aware that she is dealing with Saul.
28:14 *An old man wearing a robe.* Saul remembers Samuel

as customarily dressed in this apparel (see 15:27).
28:21 *When the woman came to Saul.* This statement suggests that the woman removed herself from the direct view of Saul while she gave her oracles.
29:1 *The Philistines gathered all their forces.* The narrative flow broken at 28:2 is resumed. *Aphek.* A place in the vicinity of Shunem (28:4), to be distinguished from another place of the same name referred to in 4:1 (see 1 Ki 20:26,30; 2 Ki 13:17).
29:2 *Philistine rulers.* See note on 5:8.
29:3 *I have found no fault in him.* David's tactics described in 27:10–12 were highly successful.
29:4 *the place you assigned him.* See 27:6. *he will turn against us during the fighting.* The Philistines had experienced just such a reversal on a previous occasion (see 14:21).
29:6 *As surely as the LORD lives.* See note on 14:39. Achish swears by the God of Israel apparently as a means of proving his sincerity to David.

"As surely as the LORD lives, you have been reliable, and I would be pleased to have you serve with me in the army. From the day[r] you came to me until now, I have found no fault in you, but the rulers[s] don't approve of you. [7]Turn back and go in peace; do nothing to displease the Philistine rulers."

[8]"But what have I done?" asked David. "What have you found against your servant from the day I came to you until now? Why can't I go and fight against the enemies of my lord the king?"

[9]Achish answered, "I know that you have been as pleasing in my eyes as an angel[t] of God; nevertheless, the Philistine commanders[u] have said, 'He must not go up with us into battle.' [10]Now get up early, along with your master's servants who have come with you, and leave[v] in the morning as soon as it is light."

[11]So David and his men got up early in the morning to go back to the land of the Philistines, and the Philistines went up to Jezreel.

David Destroys the Amalekites

30 David and his men reached Ziklag[w] on the third day. Now the Amalekites[x] had raided the Negev and Ziklag. They had attacked Ziklag and burned[y] it, [2]and had taken captive the women and all who were in it, both young and old. They killed none of them, but carried them off as they went on their way.

[3]When David and his men came to Ziklag, they found it destroyed by fire and their wives and sons and daughters taken captive.[z] [4]So David and his men wept[a] aloud until they had no strength left to weep. [5]David's two wives[b] had been captured—Ahinoam of Jezreel and Abigail, the widow of Nabal of Carmel. [6]David was greatly distressed because the men were talking of stoning[c] him; each one was bitter[d] in spirit because of his sons and daughters. But David found strength[e] in the LORD his God.

29:6
r 1Sa 27:8-12 s ver 3
29:9 t 2Sa 14:17, 20; 19:27 u ver 4
29:10 v 1Ch 12:19
30:1 w S 1Sa 27:6 x S 1Sa 27:8 y ver 14
30:3 z S Ge 31:26
30:4 a S Ge 27:38
30:5 b S 1Sa 25:43
30:6 c S Ex 17:4; Jn 8:59 d S Ru 1:13 e S 1Sa 23:16; Ro 4:20

30:7 f S 1Sa 22:20 g S 1Sa 2:28
30:8 h S 1Sa 23:2 i S Ge 14:16 j S Ex 2:17
30:9 k S 1Sa 27:2
30:10 l ver 21
30:12 m S Jdg 15:19
30:13 n S 1Sa 14:48
30:14 o 2Sa 8:18; 15:18; 20:7,23; 1Ki 1:38,44; 1Ch 18:17; Eze 25:16; Zep 2:5 p S Jos 14:13; S 15:13 q ver 1
30:15 r Dt 23:15
30:16 s Lk 12:19 t S ver 17; S Jos 22:8
30:17 u ver 16; 1Sa 11:11; 2Sa 1:1 v 2Sa 1:8
30:18 w S Ge 14:16

[7]Then David said to Abiathar[f] the priest, the son of Ahimelech, "Bring me the ephod.[g]" Abiathar brought it to him, [8]and David inquired[h] of the LORD, "Shall I pursue this raiding party? Will I overtake them?"

"Pursue them," he answered. "You will certainly overtake them and succeed[i] in the rescue.[j]"

[9]David and the six hundred men[k] with him came to the Besor Ravine, where some stayed behind, [10]for two hundred men were too exhausted[l] to cross the ravine. But David and four hundred men continued the pursuit.

[11]They found an Egyptian in a field and brought him to David. They gave him water to drink and food to eat— [12]part of a cake of pressed figs and two cakes of raisins. He ate and was revived,[m] for he had not eaten any food or drunk any water for three days and three nights.

[13]David asked him, "To whom do you belong, and where do you come from?"

He said, "I am an Egyptian, the slave of an Amalekite.[n] My master abandoned me when I became ill three days ago. [14]We raided the Negev of the Kerethites[o] and the territory belonging to Judah and the Negev of Caleb.[p] And we burned[q] Ziklag."

[15]David asked him, "Can you lead me down to this raiding party?"

He answered, "Swear to me before God that you will not kill me or hand me over to my master,[r] and I will take you down to them."

[16]He led David down, and there they were, scattered over the countryside, eating, drinking and reveling[s] because of the great amount of plunder[t] they had taken from the land of the Philistines and from Judah. [17]David fought[u] them from dusk until the evening of the next day, and none of them got away, except four hundred young men who rode off on camels and fled.[v] [18]David recovered[w] everything the Amalekites had taken, including his two

---

29:8 *But what have I done?* David pretends disappointment in order to keep intact his strategy of deception. In reality this turn of events rescued David from a serious dilemma. *Why can't I go and fight against the enemies of my lord the king?* David again uses an ambiguous statement (see 28:2). To whom was he referring as "my lord the king"—Achish or Saul or the Lord?
29:9 *as an angel of God.* A common simile.
29:11 *Jezreel.* The place of Israel's camp (see v. 1).
30:1–31:13 While Saul goes to his death at the hands of the Philistines, David is drawn into and pursues the Lord's continuing war with the Amalekites (see 15:2–3 and notes).
30:1 *Ziklag.* See note on 27:6. *Amalekites.* See 27:8 and

note on 15:2. The absence of David and his warriors gave the Amalekites opportunity for revenge. *Negev.* See note on 27:10.
30:5 *Ahinoam.* See note on 25:43. *Abigail.* See 25:42.
30:7 *Abiathar the priest.* See note on 22:20. *ephod.* See note on 2:28.
30:14 *Negev.* See note on 27:10. *Kerethites.* Along with the Pelethites, they later contributed contingents of professional warriors to David's private army (see 2Sa 15:18; 20:7; 1Ki 1:38). The name may indicate that they originally came from the island of Crete (see Am 9:7 and NIV text note there). *Negev of Caleb.* The area south of Hebron (see Jos 14:13).

wives. [19]Nothing was missing: young or old, boy or girl, plunder or anything else they had taken. David brought everything back. [20]He took all the flocks and herds, and his men drove them ahead of the other livestock, saying, "This is David's plunder."

[21]Then David came to the two hundred men who had been too exhausted[x] to follow him and who were left behind at the Besor Ravine. They came out to meet David and the people with him. As David and his men approached, he greeted them. [22]But all the evil men and troublemakers among David's followers said, "Because they did not go out with us, we will not share with them the plunder we recovered. However, each man may take his wife and children and go."

[23]David replied, "No, my brothers, you must not do that with what the LORD has given us. He has protected us and handed over to us the forces that came against us. [24]Who will listen to what you say? The share of the man who stayed with the supplies is to be the same as that of him who went down to the battle. All will share alike.[y]" [25]David made this a statute and ordinance for Israel from that day to this.

[26]When David arrived in Ziklag, he sent some of the plunder to the elders of Judah, who were his friends, saying, "Here is a present[z] for you from the plunder of the LORD's enemies."

[27]He sent it to those who were in Bethel,[a] Ramoth[b] Negev and Jattir;[c] [28]to those in Aroer,[d] Siphmoth,[e] Eshtemoa[f] [29]and Racal; to those in the towns of the Jerahmeelites[g] and the Kenites;[h] [30]to those in Hormah,[i] Bor Ashan,[j] Athach [31]and Hebron;[k] and to those in all the other places where David and his men had roamed.

Reference column:

30:21 [x]ver 10
30:24 [y]S Nu 31:27; [S]Jdg 5:30
30:26 [z]S Ge 33:11
30:27 [a]S Jos 7:2 [b]S Jos 10:40 [c]S Jos 15:48
30:28 [d]S Nu 32:34; S Jos 13:16 [e]1Ch 27:27 [f]S Jos 15:50
30:29 [g]1Sa 27:10 [h]S 1Sa 15:6
30:30 [i]S Nu 14:45; S 21:3 [j]S Jos 15:42
30:31 [k]Nu 13:22; S Jos 10:36; 2Sa 2:1,4

31:1 [l]S 1Sa 28:4
31:2 [m]S 1Sa 28:19 [n]S 1Sa 18:1 [o]S 1Sa 14:49
31:3 [p]S 1Sa 28:4
31:4 [q]S Jdg 9:54 [r]S Ge 34:14; S 1Sa 14:6
31:6 [s]S 1Sa 26:10
31:8 [t]2Sa 1:20
31:9 [u]2Sa 1:20; 4:4 [v]S Jdg 16:24
31:10 [w]S Jdg 2:12-13; S 1Sa 7:3 [x]S Jos 17:11
31:11 [y]S Jdg 21:8; S 1Sa 11:1
31:12 [z]Ps 76:5

Saul Takes His Life

31:1–13pp — 2Sa 1:4–12; 1Ch 10:1–12

31 Now the Philistines fought against Israel; the Israelites fled before them, and many fell slain on Mount Gilboa.[l] [2]The Philistines pressed hard after Saul and his sons,[m] and they killed his sons Jonathan,[n] Abinadab and Malki-Shua.[o] [3]The fighting grew fierce around Saul, and when the archers overtook him, they wounded[p] him critically.

[4]Saul said to his armor-bearer, "Draw your sword and run me through,[q] or these uncircumcised[r] fellows will come and run me through and abuse me."

But his armor-bearer was terrified and would not do it; so Saul took his own sword and fell on it. [5]When the armor-bearer saw that Saul was dead, he too fell on his sword and died with him. [6]So Saul and his three sons and his armor-bearer and all his men died[s] together that same day.

[7]When the Israelites along the valley and those across the Jordan saw that the Israelite army had fled and that Saul and his sons had died, they abandoned their towns and fled. And the Philistines came and occupied them.

[8]The next day, when the Philistines[t] came to strip the dead, they found Saul and his three sons fallen on Mount Gilboa. [9]They cut off his head and stripped off his armor, and they sent messengers throughout the land of the Philistines to proclaim the news[u] in the temple of their idols and among their people.[v] [10]They put his armor in the temple of the Ashtoreths[w] and fastened his body to the wall of Beth Shan.[x]

[11]When the people of Jabesh Gilead[y] heard of what the Philistines had done to Saul, [12]all their valiant men[z] journeyed

---

30:22 *troublemakers.* See note on Dt 13:13.
30:23 *what the LORD has given us.* David gently but firmly rejects the idea that their victory is to be attributed to their own prowess. Because the Lord gave the victory, no segment of David's men could claim any greater right to the spoils than any other.
30:26 *elders of Judah, who were his friends.* David sent the plunder as an expression of gratitude to those who had assisted him during his flight from Saul (see v. 31), thus preparing the way for his later elevation to kingship in Judah (see 2Sa 2:1–4).
30:29 *Jerahmeelites.* See note on 27:10. *Kenites.* See note on 15:6.
30:31 *Hebron.* The most important city in the southern part of Judah. The other locations mentioned are to the southwest and southeast of Hebron.
31:2 *Jonathan, Abinadab and Malki-Shua.* See note on 14:49. The surviving son, Ish-Bosheth or Esh-Baal (1Ch 8:33; 9:39), was afterward promoted by Abner, who some-

how survived the battle, to succeed his father as king (2Sa 2:8–9).
31:4 *uncircumcised fellows.* See 14:6 and note. *abuse me.* A practice that was not uncommon; previously the Philistines had mutilated and humiliated Samson after his capture (see Jdg 16:23–25). *took his own sword and fell on it.* The culmination of a long process of self-destruction.
31:6 *all his men.* Those who had served around him in his administration (but see note on v. 2).
31:9 *They cut off his head.* David had done the same to Goliath (see 17:51). *sent messengers throughout the land.* Probably bearing Saul's head and armor as proof and trophies of their victory.
31:10 *They put his armor in the temple.* Symbolic of ascribing the victory to the Philistine gods.
31:11 *Jabesh Gilead.* See note on 11:1.
31:12 *They took down the bodies of Saul and his sons.* The men of Jabesh Gilead had not forgotten how Saul had come to their defense when they were threatened by the

through the night to Beth Shan. They took down the bodies of Saul and his sons from the wall of Beth Shan and went to Jabesh, where they burned[a] them. [13]Then they

took their bones[b] and buried them under a tamarisk[c] tree at Jabesh, and they fasted[d] seven days.[e]

31:12
aS Ge 38:24;
Am 6:10

31:13
b2Sa 21:12-14
cS Ge 21:33

d2Sa 3:35; 12:19-23 eS Ge 50:10

Ammonites (see ch. 11). *burned them.* Cremation was not customary in ancient Israel and here appears to have been done to prevent any further abuse of the bodies of Saul and his sons by the Philistines.

31:13 *took their bones and buried them.* David later had

their remains removed from Jabesh and placed in the family burial grounds of Zela in Benjamin (see 2Sa 21:12–14). *fasted seven days.* As an indication of their mourning for Saul (cf. 2Sa 1:12; 3:35; 12:16,21–23).

2 SAMUEL

Title

1 and 2 Samuel were originally one book (see Introduction to 1 Samuel: Title).

Literary Features, Authorship and Date

See Introduction to 1 Samuel: Literary Features, Authorship and Date.

Contents and Theme: Kingship and Covenant

2 Samuel depicts David as a true (though imperfect) representative of the ideal theocratic king. David was initially acclaimed king at Hebron by the tribe of Judah (chs. 1-4), and subsequently was accepted by the remaining tribes after the murder of Ish-Bosheth, one of Saul's surviving sons (5:1-5). David's leadership was decisive and effective. He captured Jerusalem from the Jebusites and made it his royal city and residence (5:6-14). Shortly afterward he brought the ark of the Lord from the house of Abinadab to Jerusalem, publicly acknowledging the Lord's kingship and rule over himself and the nation (ch. 6; Ps 132:3-5).

Under David's rule the Lord caused the nation to prosper, to defeat its enemies and, in fulfillment of his promise (see Ge 15:18), to extend its borders from Egypt to the Euphrates (ch. 8). David wanted to build a temple for the Lord—as his royal house, as a place for his throne (the ark) and as a place for Israel to worship him. But the prophet Nathan told David that he was not to build the Lord a house (temple); rather, the Lord would build David a house (dynasty). Ch. 7 announces the Lord's promise that this Davidic dynasty would endure forever. This climactic chapter also describes the establishment of the Davidic covenant (see Ps 89:34-37), a covenant that promises ultimate victory over the evil one through the offspring of Eve (see Ge 3:15 and note). This promise—which had come to be focused on Shem and his descendants (see Ge 9:26-27 and notes), then on Abraham and his descendants (see Ge 12:2-3; 13:16; 15:5 and notes) and then on Judah and his (royal) descendants (see Ge 49:8-11 and notes)—is now focused specifically on the royal family of David. Later the prophets make clear that a descendant of David who sits on David's throne will perfectly fulfill the role of the theocratic king. He will complete the redemption of God's people (see Isa 9:6-7; 11:1-16; Jer 23:5-6; 30:8-9; 33:14-16; Eze 34:23-24; 37:24-25), thus enabling them to achieve the promised victory with him (Ro 16:20).

After the description of David's rule in its glory and success, chs. 10-20 depict the darker side of his reign and describe David's weaknesses and failures. Even though David remained a king after God's own heart because he was willing to acknowledge his sin and repent (12:13), he nevertheless fell far short of the theocratic ideal and suffered the disciplinary results of his disobedience (12:10-12). His sin with Bathsheba (chs. 11-12) and his leniency both with the wickedness of his sons (13:21; 14:1,33; 19:4-6) and with the insubordination of Joab (3:29,39; 20:10,23) led to intrigue, violence and bloodshed within his own family and the nation. It eventually drove him from Jerusalem at the time of Absalom's rebellion. Nonetheless the Lord was gracious to David, and his reign became a standard by which the reigns of later kings were measured (see 2Ki 18:3; 22:2).

The book ends with David's own words of praise to God, who had delivered him from all his enemies (22:31-51), and with words of expectation for the fulfillment of God's promise that a king will come from the house of David and rule "over men in righteousness" (23:3-5). These songs echo many of the themes of Hannah's song (1Sa 2:1-10), and together they frame (and interpret) the basic narrative.

Chronology

See Introduction to 1 Samuel: Chronology.

Outline

Below is an abbreviated outline for 2 Samuel. For the complete outline see Introduction to 1 Samuel: Outline.

David Hears of Saul's Death

1:4–12pp — 1Sa 31:1–13; 1Ch 10:1–12

1 After the death[a] of Saul, David returned from defeating[b] the Amalekites[c] and stayed in Ziklag two days. [2]On the third day a man[d] arrived from Saul's camp, with his clothes torn and with dust on his head.[e] When he came to David, he fell[f] to the ground to pay him honor.[g]

[3]"Where have you come from?" David asked him.

He answered, "I have escaped from the Israelite camp."

[4]"What happened?" David asked. "Tell me."

He said, "The men fled from the battle. Many of them fell and died. And Saul and his son Jonathan are dead."

[5]Then David said to the young man who brought him the report, "How do you know that Saul and his son Jonathan are dead?"

[6]"I happened to be on Mount Gilboa,[h]" the young man said, "and there was Saul, leaning on his spear, with the chariots and riders almost upon him. [7]When he turned around and saw me, he called out to me, and I said, 'What can I do?'

[8]"He asked me, 'Who are you?'

" 'An Amalekite,[i]' I answered.

[9]"Then he said to me, 'Stand over me and kill me![j] I am in the throes of death, but I'm still alive.'

[10]"So I stood over him and killed him, because I knew that after he had fallen he could not survive. And I took the crown[k]

that was on his head and the band on his arm and have brought them here to my lord."

[11]Then David and all the men with him took hold of their clothes and tore[l] them. [12]They mourned and wept and fasted till evening for Saul and his son Jonathan, and for the army of the LORD and the house of Israel, because they had fallen by the sword.

[13]David said to the young man who brought him the report, "Where are you from?"

"I am the son of an alien, an Amalekite,[m]" he answered.

[14]David asked him, "Why were you not afraid to lift your hand to destroy the LORD's anointed?[n]"

[15]Then David called one of his men and said, "Go, strike him down!"[o] So he struck him down, and he died.[p] [16]For David had said to him, "Your blood be on your own head.[q] Your own mouth testified against you when you said, 'I killed the LORD's anointed.' "

David's Lament for Saul and Jonathan

[17]David took up this lament[r] concerning Saul and his son Jonathan,[s] [18]and ordered that the men of Judah be taught this lament of the bow (it is written in the Book of Jashar):[t]

[19]"Your glory, O Israel, lies slain on your heights.

Cross references

1:1 aS 1Sa 26:10; 1Ch 10:13
bS Jos 22:8; S 1Sa 30:17
cS Ge 14:7; Nu 13:29
1:2 d2Sa 4:10
eS 1Sa 4:12; Job 2:12; Eze 27:30
fS 1Sa 20:41
gS Ge 37:7
1:6 hver 21; S 1Sa 28:4
1:8 iver 13; S 1Sa 15:2; S 27:8; 30:13,17
1:9 jS Jdg 9:54
1:10 k2Ki 11:12

1:11 lS Ge 37:29; S Nu 14:6
1:13 mS ver 8; S 1Sa 14:48
1:14 nS 1Sa 12:3; S 26:9
1:15 o2Sa 4:12
p2Sa 4:10
1:16 qS Lev 20:9; Mt 27:24-25; Ac 18:6
1:17 rS Ge 50:10; S Eze 32:2 sver 26
1:18 tJos 10:13

Study notes

1:1 *After the death of.* See Jos 1:1; Jdg 1:1. The narrative thread of 1 Samuel is continued. 1 and 2 Samuel were originally one book (see Introduction to 1 Samuel: Title). *David returned from defeating the Amalekites.* See 1Sa 30:26. *Ziklag.* See note on 1Sa 27:6.
1:2 *his clothes torn . . . dust on his head.* See note on 1Sa 4:12; see also Jos 7:6; Ac 14:14.
1:8 *Amalekite.* It is not necessary to conclude from v. 3 that this Amalekite was a member of Saul's army. His statement that he "happened to be on Mount Gilboa" (v. 6) is probably not as innocent as it appears. He may have been there as a scavenger to rob the fallen soldiers of their valuables and weapons. It is ironic that Saul's death is reported by an Amalekite (see 1Sa 15).
1:10 *I stood over him and killed him.* The Amalekite's story conflicts with 1Sa 31:3–6, where Saul is depicted as taking his own life. It appears that the Amalekite fabricated this version of Saul's death, expecting David to reward him (see 4:10). His miscalculation of David's response cost him his life (see v. 15). *I took the crown.* Apparently he got to Saul before the Philistines did (see 1Sa 31:8–9).
1:11 *took hold of their clothes and tore them.* See note on 1Sa 4:12.
1:12 *mourned and wept.* David and his men expressed their grief in typical Near Eastern fashion (see Ge 23:2; 1Ki 13:30; Jer 22:18). *fasted.* See 3:35; 1Sa 31:13.
1:13 *Amalekite.* The man was probably unaware of David's

recent hostile encounters with the Amalekites (see v. 1; 1Sa 30; see also note on 1Sa 15:2).
1:14 The Amalekite understood nothing of the deep significance that David attached to the sanctity of the royal office in Israel (see note on 1Sa 24:6). *the LORD's anointed.* See note on 1Sa 9:16.
1:15 *strike him down!* David displays no personal satisfaction over Saul's death and condemns to death the one he believes to be his murderer (see note on v. 10; see also 4:10).
1:16 *Your blood be on your own head.* The Amalekite's own testimony brought about his execution (see Jos 2:19; 1Ki 2:37).
1:17 *lament.* It was a common practice in the ancient Near East to compose laments for fallen leaders and/or heroes.
1:18 *lament of the bow.* Perhaps David taught his men to sing this lament while they practiced the bow (Israel's most common weapon; see, e.g., 22:35) as a motivation to master the weapon thoroughly so they would not experience a similar defeat (see note on Eze 21:9). *Book of Jashar.* See note on Jos 10:13.
1:19 *Your glory.* A reference to Saul and Jonathan as divinely designated leaders of God's covenant people, who had achieved many significant victories over Israel's enemies (see 1Sa 14:47–48 and note). *heights.* Of Gilboa (see vv. 21,25; 1Sa 31:1). *How the mighty have fallen!* The theme of David's lament (see v. 27). David's words contain no suggestion of bitterness toward Saul but rather recall the good qualities

How the mighty[u] have fallen![v]

20"Tell it not in Gath,[w]
  proclaim it not in the streets of
    Ashkelon,[x]
  lest the daughters of the Philistines[y] be
    glad,
  lest the daughters of the
    uncircumcised rejoice.[z]

21"O mountains of Gilboa,[a]
  may you have neither dew[b] nor
    rain,[c]
  nor fields that yield offerings[d] of
    grain.
  For there the shield of the mighty was
    defiled,
  the shield of Saul—no longer rubbed
    with oil.[e]

22From the blood[f] of the slain,
  from the flesh of the mighty,
  the bow[g] of Jonathan did not turn
    back,
  the sword of Saul did not return
    unsatisfied.

23"Saul and Jonathan—
  in life they were loved and gracious,
  and in death they were not parted.
  They were swifter than eagles,[h]
  they were stronger than lions.[i]

24"O daughters of Israel,
  weep for Saul,
  who clothed you in scarlet and finery,
  who adorned your garments with
    ornaments of gold.[j]

25"How the mighty have fallen in battle!

Jonathan lies slain on your heights.
26I grieve[k] for you, Jonathan[l] my
    brother;[m]
  you were very dear to me.
  Your love for me was wonderful,[n]
  more wonderful than that of women.

27"How the mighty have fallen!
  The weapons of war have
    perished!"[o]

David Anointed King Over Judah

2 In the course of time, David inquired[p]
  of the LORD. "Shall I go up to one of
the towns of Judah?" he asked.
  The LORD said, "Go up."
  David asked, "Where shall I go?"
  "To Hebron,"[q] the LORD answered.
  2So David went up there with his two
wives,[r] Ahinoam of Jezreel and Abigail,[s]
the widow of Nabal of Carmel. 3David also
took the men who were with him,[t] each
with his family, and they settled in Hebron[u] and its towns. 4Then the men of
Judah came to Hebron[v] and there they
anointed[w] David king over the house of
Judah.
  When David was told that it was the
men of Jabesh Gilead[x] who had buried
Saul, 5he sent messengers to say to them, "The LORD
bless[y] you for showing this kindness to
Saul your master by burying him. 6May the
LORD now show you kindness and faithfulness,[z] and I too will show you the same
favor because you have done this. 7Now
then, be strong[a] and brave, for Saul your

Cross references (center column):

1:19 [u]2Sa 23:8;
Ps 29:1; 45:3
[v]2Sa 3:38
1:20 [w]Mic 1:10
[x]S Jos 13:3
[y]1Sa 31:8
[z]S 1Sa 18:6
1:21 [a]S ver 6
[b]S Ge 27:28;
S Isa 18:4
[c]Dt 11:17;
1Ki 8:35; 17:1;
18:1; 2Ch 6:26;
Job 36:27; 38:28;
Ps 65:10; 147:8;
Isa 5:6; Jer 5:24;
14:4; Am 1:2
[d]Jer 12:4;
Eze 31:15
[e]Isa 21:5
1:22 [f]Isa 34:3,7;
49:26 [g]Dt 32:42
1:23 [h]S Dt 28:49
[i]Jdg 14:18
1:24 [j]S Jdg 5:30
1:26 [k]Jer 22:18;
34:5 [l]ver 17
[m]S 1Sa 20:42
[n]S 1Sa 18:1
1:27 [o]S 1Sa 2:4
2:1 [p]S 1Sa 23:2,
11-12
[q]S Ge 13:18;
S 23:19
2:2 [r]S 1Sa 25:43
[s]S 1Sa 25:42
2:3 [t]S 1Sa 27:2;
1Ch 12:22
[u]S Ge 13:18;
23:2; 37:14
2:4 [v]S 1Sa 30:31
[w]S 1Sa 2:35;
2Sa 5:3-5;
1Ch 12:23-40
[x]S Jdg 21:8;
S 1Sa 11:1
2:5 [y]S Jdg 17:2;
S 1Sa 23:21;
2Ti 1:16
2:6 [z]Ex 34:6
2:7 [a]S Jos 1:6;
S Jdg 5:21

---

and accomplishments of Saul and Jonathan.
1:20 Tell it not in Gath . . . Ashkelon. As the major Philistine cities located the closest and farthest from Israel's borders, Gath and Ashkelon represent the entire Philistine nation. David does not want the enemies of God's covenant
people to take pleasure in Israel's defeat (as he knew they
would; see 1Sa 31:9–10) and thus bring reproach on the
name of the Lord (see Ex 32:12; Nu 14:13–19; Dt 9:28; Jos
7:9; Mic 1:10). uncircumcised. See note on 1Sa 14:6.
1:21 O mountains of Gilboa. As an expression of profound
grief, David rhetorically pronounces a curse on the place
where Israel was defeated and Saul and Jonathan were killed
(for other such rhetorical curses see Job 3:3–26; Jer
20:14–18). no longer rubbed with oil. Leather shields were
rubbed with oil to preserve them (but see note on Isa 21:5).
1:23 in death they were not parted. Even though Jonathan
opposed his father's treatment of David, he gave his life
beside his father in Israel's defense.
1:26 more wonderful than that of women. David is not
suggesting that marital love is inferior to that of friendship,
nor do his remarks have any sexual implications. He is simply
calling attention to Jonathan's nearly inexplicable self-denying commitment to David, whom he had long recognized
as the Lord's choice to succeed his father rather than himself
(see notes on 1Sa 20:13–16).
1:27 weapons of war. Probably a metaphor for Saul and
Jonathan.

2:1 David inquired of the LORD. By means of the ephod
through the priest Abiathar (see notes on Ex 28:30; 1Sa
2:28; 23:2). one of the towns of Judah. Even though Saul
was dead and David had many friends and contacts among
the people of his own tribe (see 1Sa 30:26–31), David did
not presume to return from Philistine territory to assume the
kingship promised to him without first seeking the Lord's
guidance. Hebron. An old and important city (see Ge 13:18;
23:2; Jos 15:13–15; see also note on 1Sa 30:31) centrally
located in the tribe of Judah.
2:2 Ahinoam of Jezreel. See note on 1Sa 25:43. Abigail.
See 1Sa 25.
2:3 men who were with him. See 1Sa 22:2; 23:13; 30:3,9.
2:4 anointed David king. See notes on 1Sa 2:10; 9:16.
David had previously been anointed privately by Samuel in
the presence of his own family (see note on 1Sa 16:13). Here
the anointing ceremony is repeated as a public recognition by
his own tribe of his divine calling to be king. over the house
of Judah. Very likely the tribe of Simeon was also involved
(see Jos 19:1; Jdg 1:3), but the Judahites in every way
dominated the area. men of Jabesh Gilead. See notes on 1Sa
11:1; 31:12. buried Saul. See note on 1Sa 31:13.
2:7 your master is dead, and the house of Judah has
anointed me king over them. David's concluding statement
to the men of Jabesh Gilead is a veiled invitation to them to
recognize him as their king just as the tribe of Judah had
done. This appeal for their support, however, was ignored

master is dead, and the house of Judah has anointed me king over them."

War Between the Houses of David and Saul

3:2–5pp — 1Ch 3:1–4

[8]Meanwhile, Abner[b] son of Ner, the commander of Saul's army, had taken Ish-Bosheth[c] son of Saul and brought him over to Mahanaim.[d] [9]He made him king over Gilead,[e] Ashuri[a][f] and Jezreel, and also over Ephraim, Benjamin and all Israel.[g]

[10]Ish-Bosheth son of Saul was forty years old when he became king over Israel, and he reigned two years. The house of Judah, however, followed David. [11]The length of time David was king in Hebron over the house of Judah was seven years and six months.[h]

[12]Abner son of Ner, together with the men of Ish-Bosheth son of Saul, left Mahanaim and went to Gibeon.[i] [13]Joab[j] son of Zeruiah and David's men went out and met them at the pool of Gibeon. One group sat down on one side of the pool and one group on the other side.

[14]Then Abner said to Joab, "Let's have some of the young men get up and fight hand to hand in front of us."

"All right, let them do it," Joab said.

[15]So they stood up and were counted off—twelve men for Benjamin and Ish-Bosheth son of Saul, and twelve for David. [16]Then each man grabbed his opponent by the head and thrust his dagger[k] into his opponent's side, and they fell down together. So that place in Gibeon was called Helkath Hazzurim.[b]

[17]The battle that day was very fierce, and Abner and the men of Israel were defeated[l] by David's men.[m]

[18]The three sons of Zeruiah[n] were there: Joab,[o] Abishai[p] and Asahel.[q] Now Asahel was as fleet-footed as a wild gazelle.[r] [19]He chased Abner, turning neither to the right nor to the left as he pursued him. [20]Abner looked behind him and asked, "Is that you, Asahel?"

"It is," he answered.

[21]Then Abner said to him, "Turn aside to the right or to the left; take on one of the young men and strip him of his weapons." But Asahel would not stop chasing him.

[22]Again Abner warned Asahel, "Stop chasing me! Why should I strike you down? How could I look your brother Joab in the face?"[s]

[23]But Asahel refused to give up the pur-

2:8 [b]S 1Sa 14:50; S 2Sa 3:27
[c]2Sa 4:5;
1Ch 8:33; 9:39
[d]S Ge 32:2
2:9 [e]S Nu 32:26
[f]S Jos 19:24-31
[g]1Ch 12:29
2:11 [h]2Sa 5:5
2:12 [i]S Jos 9:3
2:13 [j]2Sa 8:16; 19:13; 1Ki 1:7; 1Ch 2:16; 11:6; 27:34

2:16 [k]S Jdg 3:21
2:17 [l]2Sa 3:1
[m]S 1Sa 17:8
2:18 [n]2Sa 3:39; 16:10; 19:22
[o]2Sa 3:30; 10:7; 11:1; 14:1; 18:14; 20:8; 24:3; 1Ki 1:7; 2:5,34
[p]S 1Sa 26:6
[q]2Sa 23:24; 1Ch 2:16; 11:26; 27:7 [r]1Ch 12:8; Pr 6:5; SS 2:9
2:22 [s]2Sa 3:27

[a]9 Or *Asher*   [b]16 *Helkath Hazzurim* means *field of daggers* or *field of hostilities.*

(see 1Sa 2:8–9).

2:8 *Abner son of Ner.* See note on 1Sa 14:50. *Saul's army.* His small standing army of professionals loyal to him and his family (see 1Sa 13:2,15; 14:2,52). *Ish-Bosheth.* The name was originally Ish-(or Esh-)Baal (1Ch 8:33) but was changed by the author of Samuel to Ish-Bosheth, meaning "man of the shameful thing" (see note on 4:4). Evidently Baal (meaning "lord" or "master") was at this time still used to refer to the Lord. Later this was discontinued because of confusion with the Canaanite god Baal, and the author of Samuel reflects the later sensitivity. *son of Saul.* See notes on 1Sa 14:49; 31:2. *brought him.* Abner takes the initiative in the power vacuum created by Saul's death, using the unassertive Ish-Bosheth as a pawn for his own ambitions (see 3:11; see also note on 4:1). There is no evidence that Ish-Bosheth had strong support among the Israelites generally. *Mahanaim.* A Gileadite town in Transjordan and thus beyond the sphere of Philistine domination—a kind of refugee capital.

2:9 *He made him king.* As a nephew of Saul (see note on 1Sa 14:50), Abner had both a family and a career interest in ensuring dynastic succession for Saul's house. *Gilead . . . all Israel.* This delineation of Ish-Bosheth's realm suggests that his actual rule, while involving territory both east and west of the Jordan, was quite limited and that the last entry ("all Israel") was more claim than reality. David ruled over Judah and Simeon, and the Philistines controlled large sections of the northern tribal regions.

2:11 *seven years and six months.* Cf. Ish-Bosheth's two-year reign in Mahanaim (v. 10). Because it appears that David was made king over all Israel shortly after Ish-Bosheth's death (5:1–5) and moved his capital to Jerusalem not long afterward (5:6–12), reconciling the lengths of David's and Ish-Bosheth's reigns is difficult. The difficulty is

best resolved by assuming that it took Ish-Bosheth a number of years to be recognized as his father's successor, and that the two years of his reign roughly correspond to the last two or three years of David's reign in Hebron.

2:12 Abner initiates an action to prevent Ish-Bosheth's sphere of influence from spreading northward out of Judah. Gibeon was located in the tribal area of Benjamin, to which Saul and his family belonged, and which the Philistines had not occupied.

2:13 *Joab son of Zeruiah.* See note on 1Sa 26:6. Joab became a figure of major importance during David's reign as a competent but ruthless military leader (see 10:7–14; 11:1; 12:26; 1Ki 11:15–16). At times David was unable to control him (3:39; 18:5,14; 1Ki 2:5–6), and he was eventually executed for his wanton assassinations and his part in the conspiracy to place Adonijah rather than Solomon on David's throne (1Ki 2:28–34). *David's men.* Some, at least, of David's small force of professionals that had gathered around him (see 1Sa 22:1–2; 23:13; 27:2; 30:9).

2:15 *Benjamin.* At this time Ish-Bosheth seems to have been supported mainly by his own tribesmen.

2:17 *The battle that day was very fierce.* Because the representative combat (see note on 1Sa 17:4) by 12 men from each side was indecisive, a full-scale battle ensued in which David's forces were victorious. The attempt to use representative combat to avoid the decimation of civil war failed (see 3:1).

2:21 *Turn aside.* Abner tried unsuccessfully to avoid the necessity of killing Asahel.

2:22 *How could I look your brother Joab in the face?* Abner did not want the hostility between himself and Joab to be intensified by the practice of blood revenge (see note on 3:27).

suit; so Abner thrust the butt of his spear into Asahel's stomach,[t] and the spear came out through his back. He fell there and died on the spot. And every man stopped when he came to the place where Asahel had fallen and died.[u]

24But Joab and Abishai pursued Abner, and as the sun was setting, they came to the hill of Ammah, near Giah on the way to the wasteland of Gibeon. 25Then the men of Benjamin rallied behind Abner. They formed themselves into a group and took their stand on top of a hill.

26Abner called out to Joab, "Must the sword devour[v] forever? Don't you realize that this will end in bitterness? How long before you order your men to stop pursuing their brothers?"

27Joab answered, "As surely as God lives, if you had not spoken, the men would have continued the pursuit of their brothers until morning.[c]"

28So Joab[w] blew the trumpet,[x] and all the men came to a halt; they no longer pursued Israel, nor did they fight anymore.

29All that night Abner and his men marched through the Arabah.[y] They crossed the Jordan, continued through the whole Bithron[d] and came to Mahanaim.[z]

30Then Joab returned from pursuing Abner and assembled all his men. Besides Asahel, nineteen of David's men were found missing. 31But David's men had killed three hundred and sixty Benjamites who were with Abner. 32They took Asahel and buried him in his father's tomb[a] at Bethlehem. Then Joab and his men marched all night and arrived at Hebron by daybreak.

3 The war between the house of Saul and the house of David lasted a long time.[b] David grew stronger and stronger,[c]

while the house of Saul grew weaker and weaker.[d]

2Sons were born to David in Hebron:

His firstborn was Amnon[e] the son of Ahinoam[f] of Jezreel;

3his second, Kileab the son of Abigail[g] the widow of Nabal of Carmel;

the third, Absalom[h] the son of Maacah daughter of Talmai king of Geshur;[i]

4the fourth, Adonijah[j] the son of Haggith;

the fifth, Shephatiah the son of Abital;

5and the sixth, Ithream the son of David's wife Eglah.

These were born to David in Hebron.

Abner Goes Over to David

6During the war between the house of Saul and the house of David, Abner[k] had been strengthening his own position in the house of Saul. 7Now Saul had had a concubine[l] named Rizpah[m] daughter of Aiah. And Ish-Bosheth said to Abner, "Why did you sleep with my father's concubine?"

8Abner was very angry because of what Ish-Bosheth said and he answered, "Am I a dog's head[n]—on Judah's side? This very day I am loyal to the house of your father Saul and to his family and friends. I haven't handed you over to David. Yet now you accuse me of an offense involving this woman! 9May God deal with Abner, be it ever so severely, if I do not do for David

2:23 [r]2Sa 3:27; 4:6 [u]2Sa 20:12
2:26 [v]S Dt 32:42; Jer 46:10,14; Na 2:13; 3:15
2:28 [w]2Sa 18:16; 20:23 [x]S Jdg 3:27
2:29 [y]S Dt 3:17 [z]S Ge 32:2
2:32 [a]S Ge 49:29
3:1 [b]1Ki 14:30 [c]2Sa 5:10

[d]2Sa 2:17; 22:44; Est 9:4
3:2 [e]2Sa 13:1 [f]S 1Sa 25:43
3:3 [g]S 1Sa 25:42 [h]2Sa 13:1,28 [i]2Sa 13:37; 14:32; 15:8
3:4 [j]1Ki 1:5,11; 2:13,22
3:6 [k]S 1Sa 14:50 3:7 [l]S Ge 22:24; 2Sa 16:21-22; S 1Ki 1:3
[m]2Sa 21:8-11
3:8 [n]S 1Sa 17:43; 2Sa 9:8; 16:9; 2Ki 8:13

c27 Or spoken this morning, the men would not have taken up the pursuit of their brothers; or spoken, the men would have given up the pursuit of their brothers by morning   d29 Or morning; or ravine; the meaning of the Hebrew for this word is uncertain.

2:26 Must the sword devour forever? Abner proposes an armistice as a means of avoiding the awful consequences of civil war.
2:27 As surely as God lives. An oath formula (see note on 1Sa 14:39).
2:28 nor did they fight anymore. For the present the open conflict ceased, but the hostility remained (see 3:1).
2:29 Arabah. See note on Dt 1:1.
3:2–5 The list of six sons born to David in Hebron is given as an evidence of the strengthening of David's house in contrast to that of Saul (v. 1). That these six sons were each born of a different mother indirectly informs us that David married four additional wives (see 2:2) during his time in Hebron. The writer does not offer any direct criticism of this polygamous practice (see 5:13), which conflicts with Dt 17:17, but he lets the disastrous results in David's family life speak for themselves (see chs. 13–19; 1Ki 1–2). Amnon. Later raped his sister Tamar and was killed by his brother Absalom (see ch. 13). Ahinoam of Jezreel. See note on 1Sa 25:43.
3:3 Kileab. Called Daniel in 1Ch 3:1. Abigail. See 1Sa 25.

Absalom. Later avenged the rape of Tamar by killing Amnon, and conspired against his father David in an attempt to make himself king (see chs. 13–18). Maacah daughter of Talmai. David's marriage to Maacah undoubtedly had political implications. With Talmai as an ally on Ish-Bosheth's northern border, David flanked the northern kingdom both south and north. Geshur. A small Aramean city kingdom (see 15:8) located northeast of the Sea of Galilee (see Jos 12:5; 13:11–13).
3:4 Adonijah. Was put to death for attempting to take over the throne before Solomon could be crowned (see 1Ki 1–2).
3:7 Rizpah. See 21:8–11. Why did you sleep with my father's concubine? Ish-Bosheth suspects that Abner's act was part of a conspiracy to seize the kingship (cf. v. 6). Great significance was attached to taking the concubine of a former king (see note on 12:8; see also 16:21; 1Ki 2:22).
3:9 May God deal with Abner, be it ever so severely. A curse formula (see note on 1Sa 3:17). what the LORD promised him on oath. The knowledge of David's divine designation as successor to Saul had spread widely (see notes on 2:4; 1Sa 16:13; 25:28).

what the LORD promised[o] him on oath [10]and transfer the kingdom from the house of Saul and establish David's throne over Israel and Judah from Dan to Beersheba."[p] [11]Ish-Bosheth did not dare to say another word to Abner, because he was afraid of him.

[12]Then Abner sent messengers on his behalf to say to David, "Whose land is it? Make an agreement with me, and I will help you bring all Israel over to you."

[13]"Good," said David. "I will make an agreement with you. But I demand one thing of you: Do not come into my presence unless you bring Michal daughter of Saul when you come to see me."[q] [14]Then David sent messengers to Ish-Bosheth son of Saul, demanding, "Give me my wife Michal,[r] whom I betrothed to myself for the price of a hundred Philistine foreskins."

[15]So Ish-Bosheth gave orders and had her taken away from her husband[s] Paltiel[t] son of Laish. [16]Her husband, however, went with her, weeping behind her all the way to Bahurim.[u] Then Abner said to him, "Go back home!" So he went back.

[17]Abner conferred with the elders[v] of Israel and said, "For some time you have wanted to make David your king. [18]Now do it! For the LORD promised David, 'By my servant David I will rescue my people Israel from the hand of the Philistines[w] and from the hand of all their enemies.[x]'"

[19]Abner also spoke to the Benjamites in person. Then he went to Hebron to tell David everything that Israel and the whole

house of Benjamin[y] wanted to do. [20]When Abner, who had twenty men with him, came to David at Hebron, David prepared a feast[z] for him and his men. [21]Then Abner said to David, "Let me go at once and assemble all Israel for my lord the king, so that they may make a compact[a] with you, and that you may rule over all that your heart desires."[b] So David sent Abner away, and he went in peace.

Joab Murders Abner

[22]Just then David's men and Joab returned from a raid and brought with them a great deal of plunder. But Abner was no longer with David in Hebron, because David had sent him away, and he had gone in peace. [23]When Joab and all the soldiers with him arrived, he was told that Abner son of Ner had come to the king and that the king had sent him away and that he had gone in peace.

[24]So Joab went to the king and said, "What have you done? Look, Abner came to you. Why did you let him go? Now he is gone! [25]You know Abner son of Ner; he came to deceive you and observe your movements and find out everything you are doing."

[26]Joab then left David and sent messengers after Abner, and they brought him back from the well of Sirah. But David did not know it. [27]Now when Abner[c] returned to Hebron, Joab took him aside into the gateway, as though to speak with him privately. And there, to avenge the blood

Cross references (center column)

3:9 [o]S 1Sa 15:28
3:10 [p]S Jdg 20:1; 1Sa 25:28-31; 2Sa 24:2
3:13 [q]S Ge 43:5
3:14 [r]S 1Sa 18:27
3:15 [s]Dt 24:1-4
[t]1Sa 25:44
3:16 [u]2Sa 16:5; 17:18
3:17 [v]S Jdg 11:11
3:18 [w]S 1Sa 9:16
[x]2Sa 8:6
3:19 [y]1Ch 12:2, 16,29
3:20 [z]1Ch 12:39
3:21 [a]2Sa 5:3
[b]1Ki 11:37
3:27 [c]2Sa 2:8; 4:1; 1Ki 2:5,32

3:10 *transfer the kingdom.* Abner was the real power behind the throne. *Dan to Beersheba.* See note on 1Sa 3:20.
3:12 *Whose land is it?* Possibly a rhetorical question that presumed that the land belonged either to Abner or to David. The former seems more likely from the following sentence. *Make an agreement with me.* Abner wants assurance that he will face no reprisals for his past loyalty to the house of Saul.
3:13 *Michal daughter of Saul.* Although Saul had given Michal to David (1Sa 18:27), he later gave her to another man after David fled from his court (1Sa 25:44). In the minds of the northern elders, the reunion of David and Michal would strengthen David's claim to the throne as a legitimate son-in-law of Saul.
3:14 *David sent messengers to Ish-Bosheth.* David wanted Michal returned as an open and official act of Ish-Bosheth himself, rather than as part of a subterfuge planned by Abner. David knew that Ish-Bosheth would not dare to defy Abner's wishes (see v. 11). *a hundred Philistine foreskins.* See 1Sa 18:25. Saul had required 100 Philistine foreskins; David presented him with 200 (1Sa 18:27).
3:16 *Bahurim.* The last Benjamite city on the way to Hebron (see 16:5; 17:18).
3:17 *elders of Israel.* The collective leadership of the various tribes comprised an informal national ruling body (see notes on Ex 3:16; Joel 1:2; Mt 15:2; Ac 24:1; see also 1Sa 8:4; 2Sa 5:3; 1Ki 8:1,3; 20:7; 2Ki 10:1; 23:1). *you have*

wanted to make David your king. Apparently Ish-Bosheth's support came mainly from the tribe of Benjamin (see 2:15 and note) and from Gilead in Transjordan (see 2:8; 1Sa 11:9–11; 31:11–13).
3:18 *the LORD promised David.* By this time Samuel's anointing of David must have become common knowledge (see 5:2). Abner probably interpreted the anointing as a promise from the Lord, since Samuel was the Lord's much-revered prophet.
3:19 *Abner also spoke to the Benjamites in person.* Because Saul and his family were from the tribe of Benjamin, Abner was careful to consult the Benjamites concerning the transfer of kingship to the tribe of Judah. Apparently they consented, but Abner was not above representing matters in a way that was favorable to his purpose.
3:21 *make a compact with you.* See 5:3 and note.
3:25 *he came to deceive you.* Joab despised Abner for killing his brother (2:18,23; 3:27) and sought to discredit him in David's eyes as a mere opportunist. Perhaps he also sensed that his own position of leadership would be threatened if Abner joined forces with David, since Abner was obviously a power among the northern tribes.
3:27 *Joab stabbed him in the stomach, and he died.* Joab's murder of Abner is not to be excused either as an act of war or as justifiable blood revenge (cf. Nu 35:12; Dt 19:11–13). Asahel had been killed by Abner in the course of battle (see 2:23; see also note on 2:21).

of his brother Asahel, Joab stabbed him *d* in the stomach, and he died. *e*

28Later, when David heard about this, he said, "I and my kingdom are forever innocent *f* before the LORD concerning the blood of Abner son of Ner. 29May his blood *g* fall upon the head of Joab and upon all his father's house! *h* May Joab's house never be without someone who has a running sore *i* or leprosy *e* or who leans on a crutch or who falls by the sword or who lacks food."

30(Joab and his brother Abishai murdered Abner because he had killed their brother Asahel in the battle at Gibeon.)

31Then David said to Joab and all the people with him, "Tear your clothes and put on sackcloth *j* and walk in mourning *k* in front of Abner." King David himself walked behind the bier. 32They buried Abner in Hebron, and the king wept *l* aloud at Abner's tomb. All the people wept also.

33The king sang this lament *m* for Abner:

"Should Abner have died as the lawless die?
34 Your hands were not bound,
    your feet were not fettered. *n*
You fell as one falls before wicked men."

And all the people wept over him again.

35Then they all came and urged David to eat something while it was still day; but David took an oath, saying, "May God deal with me, be it ever so severely, *o* if I taste bread *p* or anything else before the sun sets!"

36All the people took note and were pleased; indeed, everything the king did pleased them. 37So on that day all the people and all Israel knew that the king

had no part *q* in the murder of Abner son of Ner.

38Then the king said to his men, "Do you not realize that a prince and a great man has fallen *r* in Israel this day? 39And today, though I am the anointed king, I am weak, and these sons of Zeruiah *s* are too strong *t* for me. *u* May the LORD repay *v* the evildoer according to his evil deeds!"

Ish-Bosheth Murdered

4 When Ish-Bosheth son of Saul heard that Abner *w* had died in Hebron, he lost courage, and all Israel became alarmed. 2Now Saul's son had two men who were leaders of raiding bands. One was named Baanah and the other Recab; they were sons of Rimmon the Beerothite from the tribe of Benjamin—Beeroth *x* is considered part of Benjamin, 3because the people of Beeroth fled to Gittaim *y* and have lived there as aliens to this day.

4(Jonathan *z* son of Saul had a son who was lame in both feet. He was five years old when the news *a* about Saul and Jonathan came from Jezreel. His nurse picked him up and fled, but as she hurried to leave, he fell and became crippled. *b* His name was Mephibosheth.) *c*

5Now Recab and Baanah, the sons of Rimmon the Beerothite, set out for the house of Ish-Bosheth, *d* and they arrived there in the heat of the day while he was taking his noonday rest. *e* 6They went into the inner part of the house as if to get some wheat, and they stabbed *f* him in the stomach. Then Recab and his brother Baanah slipped away.

7They had gone into the house while he

Cross references (center column)

3:27 *d*S Ex 21:14; S Jdg 3:21; S 2Sa 2:23
*e*2Sa 2:22
3:28 *f*ver 37; Dt 21:9
3:29 *g*S Lev 20:9 *h*1Ki 2:31-33 *i*S Lev 15:2
3:31 *j*Ps 30:11; 35:13; 69:11; Isa 20:2 *k*S Ge 37:34
3:32 *l*S Nu 14:1; Pr 24:17
3:33 *m*S Ge 50:10
3:34 *n*Job 36:8; Ps 2:3; 149:8; Isa 45:14; Na 3:10
3:35 *o*S Ru 1:17 *p*S 1Sa 31:13; 2Sa 12:17; Jer 16:7

3:37 *q*S ver 28
3:38 *r*2Sa 1:19
3:39 *s*S 2Sa 2:18 *t*2Sa 16:9; 18:11 *u*S Jdg 18:26 *v*1Ki 2:32; Ps 41:10; 101:8
4:1 *w*S 2Sa 3:27
4:2 *x*S Jos 9:17
4:3 *y*Ne 11:33
4:4 *z*S 1Sa 18:1 *a*S 1Sa 31:9 *b*S Lev 21:18 *c*2Sa 9:8,12; 16:1-4; 19:24; 21:7-8; 1Ch 8:34; 9:40
4:5 *d*S 2Sa 2:8 *e*Ru 2:7
4:6 *f*S 2Sa 2:23

*e*29 The Hebrew word was used for various diseases affecting the skin—not necessarily leprosy.

3:29 *May his blood fall upon the head of Joab and upon all his father's house!* After disclaiming any personal or official involvement in the plot to assassinate Abner (v. 28), David cursed Joab and thereby called on God to judge his wicked act. In this crucial hour when David's relationship to the northern tribes hung in the balance, he appears not to have felt sufficiently secure in his own position to bring Joab publicly to justice (see v. 39). The crime went unpunished until early in the reign of Solomon (1Ki 2:5-6,29-35).
3:31 *Joab.* He too was compelled to join the mourners. It may be that Joab's involvement was not widely known and that David hoped to keep the matter secret for the time being.
3:32 *Hebron.* David's royal city at the time. *the king wept aloud at Abner's tomb.* Because Abner's murder had the potential of destroying the union of the nation under David's rule, David did everything possible to demonstrate his innocence to the people. In this he was successful (see vv. 36-37).
3:35 *May God deal with me, be it ever so severely.* A curse formula (see note on 1Sa 3:17).

3:39 *May the LORD repay the evildoer.* See note on v. 29.
4:1 *he lost courage.* Ish-Bosheth was very much aware of his dependence on Abner (see note on 2:8). *all Israel became alarmed.* Civil strife threatened, and the northern tribes were now without a strong leader.
4:2 *Beeroth.* One of the Gibeonite cities (Jos 9:17) assigned to Benjamin (Jos 18:25).
4:3 *Gittaim.* Its location is not known (but see Ne 11:33), so it is possible that the "because" at the beginning of the verse is unwarranted.
4:4 *Jonathan son of Saul had a son who was lame in both feet.* The writer emphasizes that with the death of Ish-Bosheth (see v. 6) there was no other viable claimant to the throne from the house of Saul. *news about Saul and Jonathan.* See 1:4; 1Sa 31:2-4. *Mephibosheth.* See 9:1-13; 16:1-4; 19:24-30; 21:7-8. The name was originally Merib-Baal (apparently meaning "opponent of Baal"; see 1Ch 8:34), perhaps to be spelled "Meri-Baal" (meaning "loved by Baal"), but was changed by the author of Samuel to Mephibosheth (meaning "from the mouth of the shameful thing"). See note on 2:8.

was lying on the bed in his bedroom. After they stabbed and killed him, they cut off his head. Taking it with them, they traveled all night by way of the Arabah.^g ⁸They brought the head^h of Ish-Bosheth to David at Hebron and said to the king, "Here is the head of Ish-Bosheth son of Saul,ⁱ your enemy, who tried to take your life. This day the LORD has avenged^j my lord the king against Saul and his offspring."

⁹David answered Recab and his brother Baanah, the sons of Rimmon the Beerothite, "As surely as the LORD lives, who has delivered^k me out of all trouble, ¹⁰when a man told me, 'Saul is dead,' and thought he was bringing good news, I seized him and put him to death in Ziklag.^l That was the reward I gave him for his news! ¹¹How much more—when wicked men have killed an innocent man in his own house and on his own bed—should I not now demand his blood^m from your hand and rid the earth of you!"

¹²So David gave an order to his men, and they killed them.ⁿ They cut off their hands and feet and hung the bodies by the pool in Hebron. But they took the head of

4:7 *g*S Dt 3:17
4:8 *h*2Sa 20:21; 2Ki 10:7 *i*1Sa 24:4; 25:29 *j*S Nu 31:3
4:9 *k*S Ge 48:16; 1Ki 1:29
4:10 *l*2Sa 1:2-16
4:11 *m*S Ge 4:10; 9:5; Ps 9:12; 72:14
4:12 *n*2Sa 1:15
5:1 *o*2Sa 19:43 *p*S Ge 29:14; 35:26
5:2 *q*1Sa 18:5,13, 16 *r*S 1Sa 11:6 *s*S Ge 48:15; S 1Sa 16:1; 2Sa 7:7; Mt 2:6; Jn 21:16 *t*S 1Sa 12:12; S 13:14; S 2Sa 6:21
5:3 *u*2Sa 3:21 *v*S Dt 17:15; 2Sa 2:4
5:4 *w*S Ge 37:2; Lk 3:23 *x*1Ki 2:11; 1Ch 3:4 *y*1Ch 26:31
5:5 *z*2Sa 2:11; 1Ki 2:11; 1Ch 3:4

Ish-Bosheth and buried it in Abner's tomb at Hebron.

David Becomes King Over Israel

5:1–3pp — 1Ch 11:1–3

5 All the tribes of Israel^o came to David at Hebron and said, "We are your own flesh and blood.^p ²In the past, while Saul was king over us, you were the one who led Israel on their military campaigns.^q And the LORD said^r to you, 'You will shepherd^s my people Israel, and you will become their ruler.^t '"

³When all the elders of Israel had come to King David at Hebron, the king made a compact^u with them at Hebron before the LORD, and they anointed^v David king over Israel.

⁴David was thirty years old^w when he became king, and he reigned^x forty^y years. ⁵In Hebron he reigned over Judah seven years and six months,^z and in Jerusalem he reigned over all Israel and Judah thirty-three years.

David Conquers Jerusalem

5:6–10pp — 1Ch 11:4–9
5:11–16pp — 1Ch 3:5–9; 14:1–7

⁶The king and his men marched to

4:7 *Arabah.* See note on Dt 1:1.
4:8 *This day the LORD has avenged my lord the king against Saul.* Recab and Baanah depict their assassination of Ish-Bosheth in pious terms, expecting David to commend them for their act—a serious miscalculation.
4:9 *As surely as the LORD lives.* An oath formula (see note on 1Sa 14:39).
4:11 *demand his blood from your hand.* An expression for the death penalty (see Ge 9:5–6). David here does what he was unable to do with Joab (see note on 3:29).
4:12 *their hands and feet.* The hands that had assassinated Ish-Bosheth and the feet that had run with the news.
5:1–24:25 Beginning with ch. 5 there are sections of 2 Samuel that have parallel passages in 1 Chronicles (they are listed at the sectional headings). In some instances these parallel accounts are nearly identical; in others they are variations.
5:1 *All the tribes of Israel.* Representatives of each tribe, including elders and armed soldiers (see 1Ch 12:23–40). *your own flesh and blood.* The representatives of the various tribes cite three reasons for recognizing David as their king. The first of these is the acknowledgment that David is an Israelite. Even though national unity had been destroyed in the civil strife following Saul's death (2:8–3:1), this blood relationship had not been forgotten.
5:2 *the one who led Israel on their military campaigns.* The second reason (see note on v. 1) for recognizing David as king (see 1Sa 18:5,13–14,16,30). *the LORD said to you.* The third and most important reason (see 1Sa 13:13–14; 16:1, 13; 23:17; 25:26–31).
5:3 *the king made a compact with them . . . before the LORD.* David and Israel entered into a covenant in which both the king and the people obligated themselves before the Lord to carry out their mutual responsibilities (see 2Ki 11:17 and note). Thus, while David was king over Judah as the one

elevated to that position by his tribe and later became king over Jerusalem by conquest (vv. 6–10), his rule over the northern tribes was by virtue of a treaty (covenant) of submission. That treaty was not renewed with David's grandson Rehoboam because he refused to negotiate its terms at the time of his accession to the throne (1Ki 12:1–16). *they anointed David king over Israel.* The third time David was anointed (see note on 2:4).
5:5 *In Hebron he reigned . . . seven years and six months.* See 2:11. *Israel and Judah.* The specific relationship of David to these two segments of his realm appears to have remained distinct (see note on v. 3).
5:6 *Jerusalem.* One of the most significant accomplishments of David's reign was the establishment of Jerusalem as his royal city and the nation's capital (see Introduction: Contents and Theme). The site was first occupied in the third millennium B.C. and was a royal city in the time of Abraham (see note on Ge 14:18). It was located on the border between Judah and Benjamin but was controlled by neither tribe. At the time of the conquest both Judah and Benjamin had attacked the city (see notes on Jdg 1:8,21), but it was quickly lost again to the Jebusites (Jos 15:63) and was sometimes referred to by the name Jebus (see Jdg 19:10; 1Ch 11:4). The city David conquered covered somewhat less than 11 acres and could have housed not many more than 3,500 inhabitants. By locating his royal city in a newly conquered town on the border between the two segments of his realm, David united the kingdom under his rule without seeming to subordinate one part to the other. *Jebusites.* A Canaanite people (Ge 10:15–16) inhabiting the area in (Jos 15:8; 18:16) and around (Nu 13:29; Jos 11:3) Jerusalem. *the blind and lame can ward you off.* Jerusalem was a natural fortress because of its location on a rise surrounded on three sides by deep valleys; so the Jebusites were confident that their walls could easily be defended.

Jerusalem*a* to attack the Jebusites,*b* who lived there. The Jebusites said to David, "You will not get in here; even the blind and the lame can ward you off." They thought, "David cannot get in here." 7Nevertheless, David captured the fortress of Zion,*c* the City of David.*d e*

8On that day, David said, "Anyone who conquers the Jebusites will have to use the water shaft*f/* to reach those 'lame and blind'*g* who are David's enemies.*g*" That is why they say, "The 'blind and lame' will not enter the palace."

9David then took up residence in the fortress and called it the City of David. He built up the area around it, from the supporting terraces*h h* inward. 10And he became more and more powerful,*i* because the LORD God Almighty*j* was with him.*k*

11Now Hiram*l* king of Tyre sent mes-

sengers to David, along with cedar logs and carpenters and stonemasons, and they built a palace for David. 12And David knew that the LORD had established him as king over Israel and had exalted his kingdom*m* for the sake of his people Israel.

13After he left Hebron, David took more concubines and wives*n* in Jerusalem, and more sons and daughters were born to him. 14These are the names of the children born to him there:*o* Shammua, Shobab, Nathan,*p* Solomon, 15Ibhar, Elishua, Nepheg, Japhia, 16Elishama, Eliada and Eliphelet.

David Defeats the Philistines

5:17–25pp — 1Ch 14:8–17

17When the Philistines heard that David had been anointed king over Israel, they

5:6 *a*S Jdg 1:8	
*b*S Jos 15:8	
5:7 *c*Ps 76:2	
*d*Jer 21:13	
*e*2Sa 6:12,16; 1Ki 2:10; 8:1; Isa 29:1; Jer 25:29	
5:8 *f*2Ki 20:20; 2Ch 32:30	
*g*Mt 21:14	
5:9 *h*1Ki 9:15,24	
5:10 *i*2Sa 3:1	
*j*Ps 24:10	
*k*2Sa 7:9	
5:11 *l*1Ki 5:1,18; 2Ch 2:3	
5:12 *m*S Nu 24:7	
5:13 *n*S Dt 17:17	
5:14 *o*1Ch 3:5	
*p*Lk 3:31	

*f*8 Or *use scaling hooks*   *g*8 Or *are hated by David*
*h*9 Or *the Millo*

5:7 *fortress.* Probably the fortified city itself. *Zion.* The first occurrence of the name in the OT (its meaning is unknown). Originally the name appears to have been given to the southernmost hill of the city on which the Jebusite fortress was located. As the city expanded (from the days of Solomon onward), the name continued to be applied to the entire city (see Isa 1:8; 2:3). **5:8** *On that day, David said.* 1Ch 11:6 may be combined with this verse for a more complete account. Joab's part in the conquest of the city demonstrated again his military prowess and reconfirmed him in the position of commander of David's armies. *water shaft.* Although the Hebrew for this term is obscure (see NIV text note), it appears that David knew of a secret tunnel—perhaps running from the Gihon spring outside the city into the fortress—that gave access to water when the city was under siege (see 2Ch 32:30). *lame and blind.* An ironic reference to the Jebusites (cf. v. 6). *The 'blind and lame' will not enter the palace.* The proverb may

mean that the Jebusites did not have access to the royal palace, though they were allowed to remain in the city and its environs. **5:9** *supporting terraces.* Stone terraces on the steep slopes of the hill, creating additional space for buildings (but see NIV text note; see also note on Jdg 9:6). **5:11** *Hiram king of Tyre.* This Phoenician king was the first to accord the newly established King David international recognition. It was vital to him that he have good relations with the king of Israel since Israel dominated the inland trade routes to Tyre, and Tyre was dependent on Israelite agriculture for much of its food (also true in the first century A.D.; see Ac 12:20). A close relationship existed between these two realms until the Babylonian invasions. *Tyre.* An important Phoenician seaport on the Mediterranean coast north of Israel (see Eze 26–27). **5:12** *David knew that the LORD had established him as king.* In the ideology of the ancient Near East the king's

---

Substantial historical evidence, both Biblical and extra-Biblical, places the temple of Herod (and before it the temples of Zerubbabel and of Solomon) on the holy spot where King David built an altar to the Lord. David had purchased the land from Araunah the Jebusite, who was using the exposed

bedrock as a threshing floor (2Sa 24:18-25). Tradition claims a much older sanctity for the site, associating it with the altar of Abraham on Mount Moriah (Ge 22:1-19). The writer of Genesis equates Moriah with "the Mountain of the LORD," and other OT shrines originated in altars erected by Abraham.

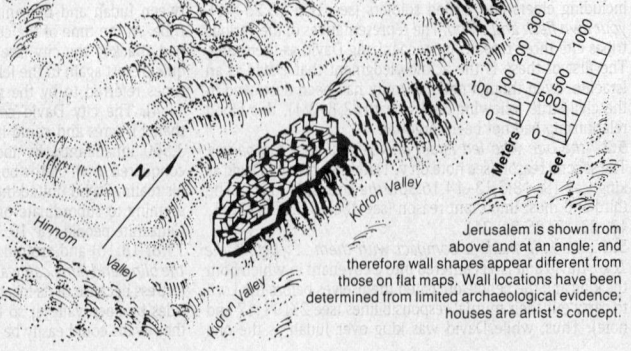

1. The City of the Jebusites
2. David's Jerusalem

c. 1000 B.C.

Barely 12 acres in size, Jebus, a Canaanite city, could well defend itself against attack, with walls atop steep canyons and shafts reaching an underground water source. David captured the stronghold, c. 1000 B.C. and made it his capital.

Jerusalem is shown from above and at an angle; and therefore wall shapes appear different from those on flat maps. Wall locations have been determined from limited archaeological evidence; houses are artist's concept.

went up in full force to search for him, but David heard about it and went down to the stronghold.*q* *18*Now the Philistines had come and spread out in the Valley of Rephaim;*r* *19*so David inquired*s* of the LORD, "Shall I go and attack the Philistines? Will you hand them over to me?"

The LORD answered him, "Go, for I will surely hand the Philistines over to you."

*20*So David went to Baal Perazim, and there he defeated them. He said, "As waters break out, the LORD has broken out against my enemies before me." So that place was called Baal Perazim.*i t* *21*The Philistines abandoned their idols there, and David and his men carried them off.*u*

*22*Once more the Philistines came up and spread out in the Valley of Rephaim; *23*so David inquired of the LORD, and he answered, "Do not go straight up, but circle around behind them and attack them in front of the balsam trees. *24*As soon as you hear the sound*v* of marching in the tops of the balsam trees, move quickly, because that will mean the LORD has gone out in front*w* of you to strike the Philistine army." *25*So David did as the LORD commanded him, and he struck down the Philistines*x* all the way from Gibeon*j y* to Gezer.*z*

The Ark Brought to Jerusalem

6:1–11pp — 1Ch 13:1–14
6:12–19pp — 1Ch 15:25–16:3

6 David again brought together out of Israel chosen men, thirty thousand in all. *2*He and all his men set out from Baalah*a* of Judah*k* to bring up from there the ark*b* of God, which is called by the Name,*l c* the name of the LORD Almighty, who is enthroned*d* between the cherubim*e* that are on the ark. *3*They set the ark of God on a new cart*f* and brought it from the house of Abinadab, which was on the hill.*g* Uzzah and Ahio, sons of Abinadab, were guiding the new cart *4*with the ark of God on it,*m* and Ahio was walking in front of it. *5*David and the whole house of Israel were celebrating*h* with all their might before the LORD, with songs*n* and with harps, lyres, tambourines, sistrums and cymbals.*i*

*6*When they came to the threshing floor of Nacon, Uzzah reached out and took hold of*j* the ark of God, because the oxen

Cross references (center column):

5:17 *q*2Sa 23:14; 1Ch 11:16
5:18 *r*S Jos 15:8; S 17:15
5:19 *s*S Jdg 18:5; S 1Sa 23:2
5:20 *t*S Ge 38:29
5:21 *u*Dt 7:5; Isa 46:2
5:24 *v*S Ex 14:24 *w*Jdg 4:14
5:25 *x*2Sa 8:12; 21:15 *y*Isa 28:21 *z*S Jos 10:33

6:2 *a*S Jos 15:9 *b*1Sa 4:4; 7:1 *c*Lev 24:16; Dt 28:10; Isa 63:14 *d*Ps 99:1; 132:14 *e*S Ge 3:24; S Ex 25:22
6:3 *f*ver 7; Nu 7:4-9; S 1Sa 6:7 *g*2Sa 7:1
6:5 *h*S Ex 15:20 *i*Ezr 3:10; Ne 12:27; Ps 150:5
6:6 *j*S Nu 4:15, 19-20

Footnotes (center column):

i20 *Baal Perazim* means *the lord who breaks out.*
j25 Septuagint (see also 1 Chron. 14:16); Hebrew *Geba*
k2 That is, Kiriath Jearim; Hebrew *Baale Judah,* a variant of *Baalah of Judah*   *l2* Hebrew; Septuagint and Vulgate do not have *the Name.*   *m3,4* Dead Sea Scrolls and some Septuagint manuscripts; Masoretic Text *cart* *d*and they brought it with the ark of God from the house of Abinadab, which was on the hill   *n5* See Dead Sea Scrolls, Septuagint and 1 Chronicles 13:8; Masoretic Text *celebrating before the LORD with all kinds of instruments made of pine.*

---

possession of a palace was the chief symbolic indication of his status. *for the sake of his people Israel.* David acknowledged that his elevation to kingship over all Israel was the Lord's doing and that it was an integral part of his continuing redemptive program for Israel—just as the ministries of Moses, Joshua, the judges and Samuel had been.

5:13 *David took more concubines and wives.* See note on 3:2.

5:14 *Shammua, Shobab, Nathan, Solomon.* 1Ch 3:5 designates Bathsheba as their mother.

5:17 *When the Philistines heard that David had been anointed king.* Chronologically it is likely that the Philistine attack followed immediately after the events of v. 3 and before the capture of Jerusalem (vv. 6–14). (The author arranged his narrative by topics; see note on 7:1.) The Philistines had not been disturbed by David's reign over Judah, but now they acted to protect their interests in the north, much of which they dominated after the defeat of Saul (1Sa 31). *stronghold.* Probably a reference to the desert area in southern Judah where David had hidden from Saul (see notes on 1Sa 22:4; 23:14). This action of David suggests that he had not yet taken Jerusalem.

5:19 *David inquired of the LORD.* See notes on 2:1; 1Sa 2:28; 22:20; 23:2.

5:20 *the LORD has broken out . . . Baal Perazim.* See NIV text note. As a true theocratic king, David attributes the victory to the Lord and does not claim the glory for himself (see notes on 1Sa 10:18,27; 11:13; 12:11; 14:23; 17:11, 45–47).

5:21 *abandoned their idols there.* As the Israelites had taken the ark into battle (see note on 1Sa 4:3), so the Philistines carried images of their deities into battle in the hope that this would ensure victory. *carried them off.* In compliance with the instruction of Dt 7:5, they also burned them (1Ch 14:12).

5:23 *he answered.* As had been true in the case of the conquest under Joshua, the Lord ordered the battle and he himself marched against the enemy with his heavenly host (see Jos 6:2–5; 8:1–2; 10:8,14; 11:6). David's wars were a continuation and completion of the wars fought by Joshua.

5:24 *sound of marching.* The heavenly host of the Lord going into battle.

6:2 *Baalah of Judah.* See NIV text note; see also Jos 15:60; 18:14; 1Sa 7:1. *ark of God.* See Ex 25:10–22; see also notes on 1Sa 4:3–4,21. The ark had remained at Kiriath Jearim during the reign of Saul. *called by the Name.* Used elsewhere to designate ownership (see 12:28; Dt 28:10; Isa 4:1; 63:19). *LORD Almighty.* See note on 1Sa 1:3. *enthroned between the cherubim.* See note on 1Sa 4:4; see also 1Ch 28:2 ("footstool of our God"). David recognized the great significance of the ark as the earthly throne of Israel's God. As a true theocratic king, he wished to acknowledge the Lord's kingship and rule over both himself and the people by restoring the ark to a place of prominence in the nation.

6:3 *new cart.* David follows the example of the Philistines (see 1Sa 6:7) rather than the instructions of Ex 25:12–14; Nu 4:5–6,15, which require that the ark be carried on the shoulders of the Levites (see 1Ch 15:13–15). *from the house of Abinadab.* See 1Sa 7:1. *Uzzah and Ahio, sons of Abinadab.* 1Sa 7:1 speaks of Eleazar as the son of Abinadab. The Hebrew word for "son" can have the broader meaning of "descendant."

stumbled. ⁷The LORD's anger burned against Uzzah because of his irreverent act;ᵏ therefore God struck him downˡ and he died there beside the ark of God.

⁸Then David was angry because the LORD's wrathᵐ had broken out against Uzzah, and to this day that place is called Perez Uzzah.ᵒ ⁿ

⁹David was afraid of the LORD that day and said, "Howᵒ can the ark of the LORD ever come to me?" ¹⁰He was not willing to take the ark of the LORD to be with him in the City of David. Instead, he took it aside to the house of Obed-Edomᵖ the Gittite. ¹¹The ark of the LORD remained in the house of Obed-Edom the Gittite for three months, and the LORD blessed him and his entire household.�q

¹²Now King Davidʳ was told, "The LORD has blessed the household of Obed-Edom and everything he has, because of the ark of God." So David went down and brought up the ark of God from the house of Obed-Edom to the City of David with rejoicing. ¹³When those who were carrying the ark of the LORD had taken six steps, he sacrificedˢ a bull and a fattened calf. ¹⁴David, wearing a linen ephod,ᵗ dancedᵘ before the LORD with all his might, ¹⁵while he and the entire house of Israel brought up the ark of the LORD with shoutsᵛ and the sound of trumpets.ʷ

¹⁶As the ark of the LORD was entering the City of David,ˣ Michalʸ daughter of Saul watched from a window. And when she saw King David leaping and dancing before the LORD, she despised him in her heart.

¹⁷They brought the ark of the LORD and set it in its place inside the tent that David had pitched for it,ᶻ and David sacrificed burnt offeringsᵃ and fellowship offeringsᴾ before the LORD. ¹⁸After he had finished sacrificingᵇ the burnt offerings and fellowship offerings, he blessedᶜ the people in the name of the LORD Almighty. ¹⁹Then he gave a loaf of bread, a cake of dates and a cake of raisinsᵈ to each person in the whole crowd of Israelites, both men and women.ᵉ And all the people went to their homes.

²⁰When David returned home to bless his household, Michal daughter of Saul came out to meet him and said, "How the king of Israel has distinguished himself today, disrobingᶠ in the sight of the slave girls of his servants as any vulgar fellow would!"

²¹David said to Michal, "It was before the LORD, who chose me rather than your father or anyone from his house when he appointedᵍ me rulerʰ over the LORD's people Israel—I will celebrate before the LORD. ²²I will become even more undignified than this, and I will be humiliated in my own eyes. But by these slave girls you spoke of, I will be held in honor."

²³And Michal daughter of Saul had no children to the day of her death.

God's Promise to David

7:1–17pp — 1Ch 17:1–15

7 After the king was settled in his palaceⁱ and the LORD had given him rest

6:7
ᵏ1Ch 15:13-15
ˡS Ex 19:22;
S 1Sa 5:6; 6:19;
S 25:38
6:8 ᵐPs 7:11
ⁿS Ge 38:29
6:9 ᵒS 1Sa 6:20
6:10
ᵖ1Ch 15:18;
26:4-5
6:11
qS Ge 30:27;
39:5
6:12 ʳ1Ki 8:1
6:13 ˢ1Ki 8:5,62;
Ezr 6:17
6:14 ᵗEx 19:6;
S 1Sa 2:18
ᵘS Ex 15:20
6:15 ᵛS Jos 6:5
ʷPs 47:5; 98:6
6:16 ˣS 2Sa 5:7
ʸS 1Sa 18:27

6:17 ᶻ1Ki 8:6;
1Ch 15:1;
2Ch 1:4
ᵃLev 1:1-17;
1Ki 8:62-64
6:18 ᵇ1Ki 8:22
ᶜS Ex 39:43
6:19 ᵈHos 3:1
ᵉDt 26:13;
Ne 8:10
6:20 ᶠS 1Sa 19:24
6:21 ᵍ1Sa 13:14;
S 15:28 ʰ2Sa 5:2;
7:8; 1Ch 5:2;
17:7; Mic 5:2
7:1 ⁱ2Sa 6:3

ᵒ8 *Perez Uzzah* means *outbreak against Uzzah.*
ᴾ17 Traditionally *peace offerings*; also in verse 18

6:7 *his irreverent act.* Although Uzzah's intent may have been good, he violated the clear instructions the Lord had given for handling the ark (see note on v. 3; cf. Ex 25:15; Nu 4:5–6,15; 1Ch 15:13–15; see also note on 1Sa 6:19). At this important new beginning in Israel's life with the Lord, the Lord gives a shocking and vivid reminder to David and Israel that those who claim to serve him must acknowledge his rule with absolute seriousness (see Lev 10:1–3; Jos 7:24–25; 24:19–20; Ac 5:1–11).
6:8 *David was angry.* David's initial reaction was resentment that his attempt to honor the Lord had resulted in a display of God's wrath. *to this day.* Until the time of the writing of 2 Samuel. *Perez Uzzah.* See NIV text note. The place-name memorialized a divine warning that was not soon forgotten (see Jos 7:26 and NIV text note).
6:9 *David was afraid of the LORD.* David's anger was accompanied by fear—not the wholesome fear of proper honor and respect for the Lord (1Sa 12:24; Jos 24:14) but an anxiety arising from an acute sense of his own guilt (Ge 3:10; Dt 5:5).
6:10 *Obed-Edom.* Perhaps means "servant of man." *Gittite.* He appears to have been a Levite (see note on 1Ch 13:13; cf. 1Ch 15:18,24; 16:5; 26:4–8,15; 2Ch 25:24), though many think the term "Gittite" fixes his place of birth

at the Philistine city of Gath (see 15:18). However, Gittite may be a reference to the Levitical city Gath Rimmon in Dan or Manasseh (Jos 21:20–25).
6:12 *David . . . brought up the ark.* God's blessing on the household of Obed-Edom showed David that God's anger had been appeased.
6:13 *those . . . carrying the ark.* David had become aware of his previous error (1Ch 15:13–15). *six steps.* Sufficient to show that now God's blessing was on the Levites (see 1Ch 15:26).
6:14 *linen ephod.* See note on 1Sa 2:18.
6:16 *she despised him.* Michal had no appreciation for the significance of the event and deeply resented David's public display as unworthy of the dignity of a king (see vv. 20–23).
6:17 *burnt offerings.* See Lev 1. *fellowship offerings.* See note on 1Sa 11:15.
6:18 *he blessed the people.* As Solomon would later do at the dedication of the temple (1Ki 8:55–61).
6:20 *disrobing.* An allusion to David's having worn only a linen ephod (v. 14) rather than his royal robe.
6:23 *Michal . . . had no children.* Probably a punishment for her pride and at the same time another manifestation of God's judgment on the house of Saul.
7:1–29 God's great promise to David (see Introduction:

from all his enemies[j] around him,[k] [2]he said to Nathan[l] the prophet, "Here I am, living in a palace[m] of cedar, while the ark of God remains in a tent."[n]

[3]Nathan replied to the king, "Whatever you have in mind,[o] go ahead and do it, for the LORD is with you."

[4]That night the word of the LORD came to Nathan, saying:

[5]"Go and tell my servant David, 'This is what the LORD says: Are you[p] the one to build me a house to dwell in?[q] [6]I have not dwelt in a house from the day I brought the Israelites up out of Egypt to this day.[r] I have been moving from place to place with a tent[s] as my dwelling.[t] [7]Wherever I have moved with all the Israelites,[u] did I ever say to any of their rulers whom I commanded to shepherd[v] my people Israel, "Why have you not built me a house[w] of cedar?[x]" '

[8]"Now then, tell my servant David, 'This is what the LORD Almighty says: I took you from the pasture and from following the flock[y] to be ruler[z] over my people Israel.[a] [9]I have been with you wherever you have gone,[b] and I have cut off all your enemies from be-

fore you.[c] Now I will make your name great, like the names of the greatest men of the earth.[d] [10]And I will provide a place for my people Israel and will plant[e] them so that they can have a home of their own and no longer be disturbed.[f] Wicked[g] people will not oppress them anymore,[h] as they did at the beginning [11]and have done ever since the time I appointed leaders[q][i] over my people Israel. I will also give you rest from all your enemies.[j]

" 'The LORD declares[k] to you that the LORD himself will establish[l] a house[m] for you: [12]When your days are over and you rest[n] with your fathers, I will raise up your offspring to succeed you, who will come from your own body,[o] and I will establish his kingdom.[p] [13]He is the one who will build a house[q] for my Name,[r] and I will establish the throne of his kingdom

7:1 /ver 11
kICh 22:18
7:2 /2Sa 12:1;
1Ki 1:8,22;
1Ch 29:29;
2Ch 9:29
m2Sa 5:11;
1Ki 3:1; 7:1,2,7;
9:1; 2Ch 8:1;
Jer 22:14;
Hag 1:4
nS Ex 26:1;
Ps 132:3;
Ac 7:45-46
7:3 oS 1Sa 10:7;
Ps 132:1-5
7:5 p1Ki 8:19;
1Ch 22:8
q1Ki 5:3-5;
1Ch 28:3
7:6 rAc 7:45
sEx 40:18,34;
Jos 18:1 t1Ki 8:16
7:7 uDt 23:14
vS 2Sa 5:2
w1Ki 8:27;
Isa 66:1
xLev 26:11-12
7:8 yS 1Sa 16:11;
1Ch 21:17;
Ps 74:1; Am 7:15
zS 1Sa 2:7-8;
S 9:16; S 16:1;
S 2Sa 6:21
aPs 78:70-72;
2Co 6:18*
7:9 bS 1Sa 18:14;
2Sa 5:10

cPs 18:37-42
dS Ex 11:3
7:10
eS Ex 15:17;
Isa 5:1-7
f2Ki 21:8;
2Ch 33:8
gPs 89:22-23

hPs 147:14; Isa 54:14; 60:18 7:11 iS Jdg 2:16; 1Sa 12:9-11
/ver 1 k1Ki 2:24 l1Sa 25:28; Ps 89:35-37; S Mt 1:1;
Lk 1:32-33; Ac 13:22-23; 2Ti 2:8 mS Ex 1:21; 1sa 7:2 7:12
nS Ge 15:15; 1Ki 2:1; Ac 13:36 o1Ki 8:20; Ps 132:11-12;
Jer 30:21; 33:15 p2Ch 23:3 7:13 qS Dt 12:5; 1Ki 6:12
rDt 16:11; 1Ki 5:5; 8:19,29; 2Ki 21:4,7

q11 Traditionally judges

Contents and Theme). Although it is not expressly called a covenant here, it is elsewhere (23:5; Ps 89:3,28,34,39; cf. Ps 132:11), and David responds with language suggesting his recognition that a covenant had been made (see notes on vv. 20,28).

7:1 *After the king was settled in his palace.* See 5:11; see also note on 5:12. *and the LORD had given him rest from all his enemies.* Chronologically the victories noted in 8:1–14 probably preceded the events of this chapter. The arrangement of material is topical (see also note on 5:17)—ch. 6 records the bringing of the ark to Jerusalem; ch. 7 tells of David's desire to build a temple in Jerusalem in which to house the ark.

7:2 *Nathan.* The first reference to this prophet (see 12:1–14; 1Ki 1). *tent.* See v. 6; 6:17. Now that he himself had a royal palace (symbolic of his established kingship), a tent did not seem to David to be an appropriate place for the throne of Israel's divine King (see note on 6:2; see also Ps 132:2–5; Ac 7:46). He wanted to build Israel's heavenly King a royal house in the capital city of his kingdom.

7:3 *Nathan replied.* In consulting a prophet, David sought God's will, but Nathan boldly voiced approval of David's plans in the Lord's name before he had received a revelation from the Lord.

7:5 *Are you the one . . . ?* David's desire was commendable (1Ki 8:18–19), but his gift and mission were to fight the Lord's battles until Israel was securely at rest in the promised land (see v. 10; 1Ki 5:3).

7:7 *did I ever say . . . "Why have you not built me a house . . . ?"* David misunderstood the Lord's priorities. He reflected the pagan notion that the gods were interested in human beings only as builders and maintainers of their temples and as practitioners of their cult. Instead, the Lord had raised up rulers in Israel only to shepherd his people (that is also why he had brought David "from the pasture," v. 8).

7:9 *I have cut off all your enemies.* See note on v. 1.

7:10 *I will provide a place for my people Israel.* It is for this purpose that the Lord has made David king, and through David he will do it. *at the beginning.* In Egypt.

7:11 *leaders.* During the period of the judges (see NIV text note). *I will also give you rest from all your enemies.* See vv. 1,9. David's victories over threatening powers will be complete, so that the rest already enjoyed will be assured for the future. *the LORD himself will establish a house for you.* Compare this statement with the rhetorical question of v. 5. In a beautiful play on words God says that David is not to build him a house (temple); rather, God will build David a house (royal dynasty) that will last forever (v. 16). God has been building Israel ever since the days of Abraham, and now he commits himself to build David's royal house so that the promise to Israel may be fulfilled—rest in the promised land. It is God's building that effects his kingdom. This covenant with David is unconditional, like those with Noah, Abram and Phinehas (see note on Ge 9:9; see also chart on "Major Covenants in the OT," p. 19), grounded only in God's firm and gracious purpose. It finds its ultimate fulfillment in the kingship of Christ, who was born of the tribe of Judah and the house of David (see Ps 89:30–38; Isa 9:1–7; Mt 1:1; Lk 1:32–33,69; Ac 2:30; 13:23; Ro 1:2–3; 2Ti 2:8; Rev 3:7; 22:16).

7:12 *raise up your offspring to succeed you.* The royal line of David, in contrast to that of Saul, would continue after David's death by dynastic succession.

7:13 *He is the one who will build a house for my Name.* God's priorities are that his own royal house, where his throne (the ark) can finally come to rest (1Ch 6:31; 28:2), will wait until Israel is at rest and David's dynasty (in the person of his son) is secure. "Name" is equivalent to "me" in v. 5 (see note on 1Sa 25:25).

forever.^{s} ^{14}I will be his father, and he will be my son.^{t} When he does wrong, I will punish him^u with the rod^v of men, with floggings inflicted by men. ^{15}But my love will never be taken away from him,^{w} as I took it away from Saul,^{x} whom I removed from before you. ^{16}Your house and your kingdom will endure forever before me^r; your throne^y will be established^z forever.^{a}' "

^{17}Nathan reported to David all the words of this entire revelation.

David's Prayer

7:18–29pp — 1Ch 17:16–27

^{18}Then King David went in and sat before the LORD, and he said:

"Who am I,^{b} O Sovereign LORD, and what is my family, that you have brought me this far? ^{19}And as if this were not enough in your sight, O Sovereign LORD, you have also spoken about the future of the house of your servant. Is this your usual way of dealing with man,^{c} O Sovereign LORD? ^{20}"What more can David say^d to you? For you know^e your servant,^{f} O Sovereign LORD. ^{21}For the sake of your word and according to your will, you have done this great thing and made it known to your servant.

^{22}"How great^g you are,^{h} O Sovereign LORD! There is no one like^i you,

and there is no God^j but you, as we have heard with our own ears.^{k} ^{23}And who is like your people Israel^l—the one nation on earth that God went out to redeem as a people for himself, and to make a name^m for himself, and to perform great and awesome wonders^n by driving out nations and their gods from before your people, whom you redeemed^o from Egypt?^{s} ^{24}You have established your people Israel as your very own^p forever, and you, O LORD, have become their God. ^{q}

^{25}"And now, LORD God, keep forever the promise^r you have made concerning your servant and his house. Do as you promised, ^{26}so that your name^s will be great forever. Then men will say, 'The LORD Almighty is God over Israel!' And the house of your servant David will be established^t before you.

^{27}"O LORD Almighty, God of Israel, you have revealed this to your servant, saying, 'I will build a house for you.' So your servant has found courage to offer you this prayer. ^{28}O Sovereign

Cross references (center column)

7:13 ^{s}ver 16;
^{t}Ge 9:16;
2Sa 22:51;
1Ki 2:4,45;
1Ch 22:10; 28:6;
2Ch 6:16; 7:18;
13:5; 21:7;
Ps 89:3-4,29,
35-37; Pr 25:5;
Isa 9:7; 16:5;
Jer 17:25; 33:17,
21; Da 7:27
7:14 ^{t}Ps 2:7;
89:26; Jer 3:19;
^{s}Mt 3:17;
Jn 1:49;
2Co 6:18*;
Heb 1:5*;
Rev 21:7
^{u}S Dt 8:5;
1Ki 11:34;
1Ch 22:10;
Heb 12:7
^{v}Ps 89:30-33;
Pr 13:24
7:15 ^{w}ver 25;
1Ki 2:4; 6:12;
8:25; 9:5; 11:13,
32; 2Ki 19:34;
2Ch 6:16; 7:18;
21:7; Ps 89:24,
33; Jer 33:17
^{x}S 1Sa 13:13;
S 15:28; 16:14
7:16
^{y}Ps 89:36-37;
S Lk 1:33 ^{z}Ps 9:7;
93:2; 103:19
^{a}S ver 13
7:18 ^{b}S Ex 3:11
7:19 ^{c}Isa 55:8-9
7:20 ^{d}Isa 38:15
^{e}Jn 21:17
^{f}S 1Sa 16:7
7:22 ^{g}Ps 48:1;
77:13; 86:10;
Jer 10:6 ^{h}Dt 3:24
^{i}S Ex 9:14

^{j}S Ex 8:10; S 20:4
^{k}Ex 10:2;
S Jdg 6:13;
Ps 44:1
7:23 ^{l}Dt 4:32-38;
S 33:29;
S 1Sa 12:22

^{m}S Nu 6:27 ^{n}Dt 10:21 ^{o}Dt 7:7-8; S 9:26 ^{p}Dt 26:18 ^{q}Ex 6:6-7; Ps 48:14 ^{r}2S ver 15; S Nu 23:19; 2Ch 1:9 7:26 ^{s}S Ex 6:3; Ne 9:5; Ps 72:19; 96:8; Mt 6:9 ^{t}S 1Sa 25:28

^{r}16 Some Hebrew manuscripts and Septuagint; most Hebrew manuscripts *you* ^{s}23 See Septuagint and 1 Chron. 17:21; Hebrew *wonders for your land and before your people, whom you redeemed from Egypt, from the nations and their gods.*

Study notes (bottom)

7:14 *his father . . . my son.* This familial language expresses the special relationship God promises to maintain with the descendant(s) of David whom he will establish on David's throne. It marks him as the one God has chosen and enthroned to rule in his name as the official representative of God's rule over his people (see notes on Ps 2:7; 45:6; 89:27). In Jesus Christ this promise comes to ultimate fulfillment (see Mt 1:1; Mk 1:11; Heb 1:5).
7:15 *my love.* God's special and unfailing favor (see note on Ps 6:4).
7:16 *your throne will be established forever.* See note on v. 11; see also Introduction: Contents and Theme. The promise of an everlasting kingdom for the house of David became the focal point for many later prophecies and powerfully influenced the development of the Messianic hope in Israel.
7:18–29 David's prayer expresses wonder that God would make such commitments to him and his descendants. But he also acknowledges that what God had pledged to him is for Israel's sake, that its purpose is the fulfillment of God's covenanted promises to his people—and that its ultimate effect will be the honor and praise of God throughout the world.
7:18 *went in.* Presumably into the tent (6:17) in which the ark was kept. *sat before the LORD.* The ark was the symbol of God's presence with his people (see Ex 25:22; see also notes on 1Sa 4:3–4,21).
7:19 *Is this your usual way of dealing with man, O Sovereign LORD?* The meaning of this clause is uncertain (cf. 1Ch

17:17). It has also been taken as an exclamation ("This is your law for man, O Sovereign LORD!") and understood as a summation of the divine decree concerning David and his house.
7:20 *know.* Or "especially acknowledge" or "choose" (see Ge 18:19, "chosen"; Am 3:2, "chosen"). David recognizes God's promise as a covenant (23:5).
7:21 *your word.* Probably God's covenant word of promise to his people.
7:22 *no God but you.* See 22:32; 1Sa 2:2.
7:23 *the one nation on earth that God went out to redeem as a people for himself.* Israel's uniqueness did not consist in her national achievements but in God's choice of her to be his own people (see Dt 7:6–8; 33:26–29). *to make a name for himself.* The basis for God's electing love, revealed in his dealings with Israel, did not lie in any meritorious characteristic of the Israelite people but in his own sovereign purposes (see Dt 7:6–8; 9:4–5; 1Sa 12:22; Ne 9:10; Isa 63:12; Jer 32:20–21; Eze 36:22–38).
7:24 *you, O LORD, have become their God.* What God has pledged to David, he has pledged as the God of Israel.
7:27 *your servant has found courage to offer you this prayer.* David's prayer lays claim on God's promise.
7:28 *good things.* A common summary expression for covenant benefits from God (see, e.g., 1Sa 2:32, "good"; Nu 10:29,32; Dt 26:11; Jos 21:45; 23:14, "good promises"; Isa 63:7; Jer 29:32; 32:40–41, "good"; 33:9).

LORD, you are God! Your words are trustworthy, [u] and you have promised these good things to your servant. [29]Now be pleased to bless the house of your servant, that it may continue forever in your sight; for you, O Sovereign LORD, have spoken, and with your blessing [v] the house of your servant will be blessed forever."

David's Victories

8:1–14pp — 1Ch 18:1–13

8 In the course of time, David defeated the Philistines [w] and subdued [x] them, and he took Metheg Ammah from the control of the Philistines.

[2]David also defeated the Moabites. [y] He made them lie down on the ground and measured them off with a length of cord. Every two lengths of them were put to death, and the third length was allowed to live. So the Moabites became subject to David and brought tribute. [z]

[3]Moreover, David fought Hadadezer [a] son of Rehob, king of Zobah, [b] when he went to restore his control along the Euphrates [c] River. [4]David captured a thousand of his chariots, seven thousand charioteers [t] and twenty thousand foot soldiers. He hamstrung [d] all but a hundred of the chariot horses.

[5]When the Arameans of Damascus [e] came to help Hadadezer king of Zobah, David struck down twenty-two thousand of them. [6]He put garrisons [f] in the Aramean kingdom of Damascus, and the Arameans became subject [g] to him and brought tribute. The LORD gave David victory wherever he went. [h]

[7]David took the gold shields [i] that belonged to the officers of Hadadezer and brought them to Jerusalem. [8]From Tebah [u] and Berothai, [i] towns that belonged to Hadadezer, King David took a great quantity of bronze.

[9]When Tou [v] king of Hamath [k] heard that David had defeated the entire army of Hadadezer, [l] [10]he sent his son Joram [w] to King David to greet him and congratulate him on his victory in battle over Hadadezer, who had been at war with Tou. Joram brought with him articles of silver and gold and bronze.

[11]King David dedicated [m] these articles to the LORD, as he had done with the silver and gold from all the nations he had subdued: [12]Edom [x] [n] and Moab, [o] the Ammonites [p] and the Philistines, [q] and Amalek. [r] He also dedicated the plunder taken from Hadadezer son of Rehob, king of Zobah.

[13]And David became famous [s] after he returned from striking down eighteen thousand Edomites [y] in the Valley of Salt. [t]

[14]He put garrisons throughout Edom, and all the Edomites [u] became subject to David. [v] The LORD gave David victory [w] wherever he went. [x]

David's Officials

8:15–18pp — 1Ch 18:14–17

[15]David reigned over all Israel, doing what was just and right [y] for all his people. [16]Joab [z] son of Zeruiah was over the army;

Cross references (center column)

7:28 [u]Ex 34:6; Jn 17:17
7:29 [v]Nu 6:23-27
8:1 [w]Ps 60:8; 87:4; 108:9
[x]Heb 11:32-33
8:2 [y]S Ge 19:37; S Nu 21:29
[z]S Jdg 3:15; S Isa 45:14
8:3 [a]2Sa 10:16, 19; 1Ki 11:23
[b]S 1Sa 14:47
[c]S Ge 2:14
8:4 [d]S Ge 49:6; Jos 11:9
8:5 [e]S Ge 14:15; 2Sa 10:6; 1Ki 11:24; 2Ki 8:7; 14:28
8:6 [f]1Ki 20:34
[g]2Sa 10:19
[h]2Sa 3:18
8:7 [i]1Ki 10:16; 14:26; 2Ki 11:10
8:8 [j]Eze 47:16
8:9 [k]1Ki 8:65; 2Ki 14:28; 2Ch 8:4
[l]Lk 14:31-32
8:11 [m]ver 12; 1Ki 7:51; 15:15; 1Ch 26:26; 2Ch 5:1
8:12 [n]S Nu 24:18
[o]ver 2
[p]2Sa 10:14
[q]S 2Sa 5:25
[r]S Nu 24:20; S 1Sa 27:8
8:13 [s]2Sa 7:9
[t]2Ki 14:7; 1Ch 18:12; Ps 60 Title
8:14 [u]Nu 24:17-18; Ps 108:9; Isa 34:5; 63:1; Jer 49:7; Eze 25:12
[v]S Ge 27:29, 37-40; [w]Ps 144:10
[x]2Sa 22:44; Ps 18:43
8:15 [y]S Ge 18:19; 1Ki 11:38; 14:8; 15:11; 22:43; 2Ki 12:2; Job 29:14; Ps 5:12; 119:121; Heb 11:33
8:16 [z]S 2Sa 2:13

Text notes (center column, lower)

[t]4 Septuagint (see also Dead Sea Scrolls and 1 Chron. 18:4); Masoretic Text *captured seventeen hundred of his charioteers*   [u]8 See some Septuagint manuscripts (see also 1 Chron. 18:8); Hebrew *Betah*.   [v]9 Hebrew *Toi*, a variant of *Tou*; also in verse 10   [w]10 A variant of *Hadoram*   [x]12 Some Hebrew manuscripts, Septuagint and Syriac (see also 1 Chron. 18:11); most Hebrew manuscripts *Aram*   [y]13 A few Hebrew manuscripts, Septuagint and Syriac (see also 1 Chron. 18:12); most Hebrew manuscripts *Aram* (that is, Arameans)

Study notes (bottom)

8:1 *In the course of time.* Chronologically the events of this chapter, or many of them, are probably to be placed between chs. 5 and 6 (see 7:1 and note). *Metheg Ammah.* An unknown site, perhaps near Gath (see 1Ch 18:1).
8:2 *Moabites.* Descendants of Lot (Ge 19:37), occupying territory east of the Dead Sea. Saul fought with the Moabites (1Sa 14:47), and David sought refuge in Moab for his parents during his exile from Israel (1Sa 22:3–4). See note on Ru 1:22.
8:3 *Hadadezer.* Means "Hadad is (my) help." Hadad was an Aramean deity equivalent to the Canaanite Baal. *Zobah.* Saul had previously fought against the kings of Zobah (1Sa 14:47), whose territory was apparently located in the Beqaa Valley between the Lebanon and Anti-Lebanon mountains, thus on Israel's northern border. *restore.* Saul's earlier victories over the kings of Zobah had extended Israelite control, if only briefly, as far as the fringes of the Euphrates Valley. *Euphrates River.* The land promised to Abraham had included borders from Egypt to the Euphrates (Ge 15:18–21; Dt 1:7; 11:24; Jos 1:4). Here is at least another provisional fulfillment of this promise (see 1Ki 4:21–24; see also Ge

17:8; Jos 21:43–45). See map No. 5 at the end of the Study Bible.
8:4 See NIV text note. *hamstrung . . . the chariot horses.* See Jos 11:6 and note. David may not have understood the value of the chariot as a military weapon.
8:5 *came to help Hadadezer.* They feared Israelite expansion to the north.
8:7 *gold shields.* Shields adorned with gold—the phrase is similar to "iron chariots" (see Jos 17:16 and note).
8:8 *bronze.* Later used by Solomon in the construction of the temple (1Ch 18:8).
8:9 *Hamath.* A kingdom centered on the Orontes River, north of Zobah (see v. 3 and note).
8:13 *Valley of Salt.* See 2Ki 14:7; see also Ps 60 title.
8:15 *just and right.* As a true theocratic king, David's reign was characterized by adherence to God's standards of right rule (see notes on 1Sa 8:3; 12:3), as no doubt laid down in Samuel's "regulations of the kingship" (see 1Sa 10:25 and note; 1Ki 2:3–4).
8:16 *Joab son of Zeruiah was over the army.* See notes on 2:13; 5:8. *recorder.* The precise duties of this official are not

Jehoshaphat[a] son of Ahilud was recorder;[b] [17]Zadok[c] son of Ahitub and Ahimelech son of Abiathar[d] were priests; Seraiah was secretary;[e] [18]Benaiah[f] son of Jehoiada was over the Kerethites[g] and Pelethites; and David's sons were royal advisers.[z]

David and Mephibosheth

9 David asked, "Is there anyone still left of the house of Saul to whom I can show kindness for Jonathan's sake?"[h]

[2]Now there was a servant of Saul's household named Ziba.[i] They called him to appear before David, and the king said to him, "Are you Ziba?"

"Your servant," he replied.

[3]The king asked, "Is there no one still left of the house of Saul to whom I can show God's kindness?"

Ziba answered the king, "There is still a son of Jonathan;[j] he is crippled[k] in both feet."

[4]"Where is he?" the king asked.

Ziba answered, "He is at the house of Makir[l] son of Ammiel in Lo Debar."

[5]So King David had him brought from Lo Debar, from the house of Makir son of Ammiel.

[6]When Mephibosheth son of Jonathan, the son of Saul, came to David, he bowed down to pay him honor.[m]

David said, "Mephibosheth!"

"Your servant," he replied.

[7]"Don't be afraid," David said to him, "for I will surely show you kindness for the sake of your father Jonathan.[n] I will restore to you all the land that belonged to your grandfather Saul, and you will always eat at my table.[o]

[8]Mephibosheth[p] bowed down and said, "What is your servant, that you should notice a dead dog[q] like me?"

[9]Then the king summoned Ziba, Saul's servant, and said to him, "I have given

Cross references

8:16 [a]2Sa 20:24; 1Ki 4:3 [b]Isa 36:3, 22
8:17 [c]S 1Sa 2:35; 2Sa 15:24,29; 20:25; 1Ki 1:8; 4:4; 1Ch 6:8,53; 16:39; 24:3; 27:17; 2Ch 31:10; Eze 40:46; 43:19; 44:15; 48:11 [d]Mk 2:26 [e]1Ki 4:3; 2Ki 12:10; 19:2; Jer 36:12
8:18 [f]2Sa 20:23; 23:20; 1Ki 1:8, 38; 2:25,35,46; 4:4 [g]S 1Sa 30:14
9:1 [h]S 1Sa 20:14-17, 42; S 23:18
9:2 [i]2Sa 16:1-4; 19:17,26,29
9:3 [j]1Ch 8:34 [k]S Lev 21:18
9:4 [l]2Sa 17:27-29
9:6 [m]S Ge 37:7
9:7 [n]S 1Sa 20:14-15 [o]ver 13; 2Sa 19:28; 21:7; 1Ki 2:7; 2Ki 25:29; Jer 52:33
9:8 [p]S 2Sa 4:4 [q]S 2Sa 3:8

[z]18 Or were priests

---

indicated, though the position was an important one in the court and was maintained throughout the period of the monarchy (see 2Ki 18:18,37; 2Ch 34:8; Isa 36:3,11,22). He may have been a kind of chancellor or chief administrator of royal affairs, responsible among other things for the royal chronicles and annals.

8:17 *Zadok son of Ahitub.* First mentioned here, Zadok was a descendant of Eleazar son of Aaron (see 1Ch 6:4–8, 50–52; 24:1–3). His father, Ahitub, is not to be identified with Ichabod's brother of the same name (1Sa 14:3). Zadok remained loyal to David throughout his reign (15:24–29; 17:15–16; 19:11) and eventually anointed Solomon as David's successor (1Ki 1:8,45; 2:35; 4:4). *Ahimelech son of Abiathar.* It appears that a copyist's error may have occurred here (repeated in 1Ch 24:3,6,31) in which these two names have been transposed. Abiathar is referred to as son of Ahimelech in 1Sa 22:20. While it is true that the Abiathar of 1Sa 22:20 could have had a son named Ahimelech (after his grandfather), such a person does not appear elsewhere in the narratives of Samuel and Kings as a colleague of Zadok, but Abiathar consistently does (15:29,35; 17:15; 19:11; 20:25; 1Ki 1:7–8,19; 2:27,35; 4:4). Abiathar was a descendant of Aaron through Ithamar (1Ch 24:3) in the line of Eli (see notes on 1Sa 2:31,33). *Seraiah.* Also called Sheva (20:25), Shisha (1Ki 4:3) and Shavsha (1Ch 18:16). *secretary.* His duties presumably included domestic and foreign correspondence, perhaps keeping records of important political events, and various administrative functions (2Ki 12:10–12).

8:18 *Kerethites and Pelethites.* See note on 1Sa 30:14. Under the leadership of Benaiah, they formed a sort of special royal guard for David (23:22–23). "Pelethite" is probably an alternate form of "Philistine." *royal advisers.* The Hebrew has the common word for "priests" (see NIV text note; see also 20:26), but the usage is obscure since that sense appears unlikely. Chronicles has "chief officials at the king's side" (see 1Ch 18:17 and note), which supports the meaning "royal advisers."

9:1–20:26 These chapters, together with 1Ki 1:1–2:46, are often referred to as the "Court History of David" and hailed as one of the finest examples of historical narrative to have been produced in the ancient world. Their intimate and precise detail marks them as the work of an eyewitness. **9:1–13** The events of this chapter cannot be dated precisely, but they occurred a number of years after David's capture of Jerusalem. Mephibosheth was five years old at the time of his father's death (4:4); now he has a son of his own (v. 12). **9:1** *I can show kindness for Jonathan's sake.* David has not forgotten his promise to Jonathan (see 1Sa 20:15,42). **9:2** *Ziba.* The chief steward of Saul's estate, which had been inherited by Mephibosheth son of Jonathan, Saul's firstborn (see 16:1–4; 19:17). **9:3** *There is still a son of Jonathan.* Saul had other descendants (see 21:8), but Ziba mentions only the one in whom David would be chiefly interested. **9:4** *Makir.* Apparently a wealthy benefactor of Mephibosheth who later also came to David's aid (17:27). *Lo Debar.* A town deep in Gileadite territory in Transjordan (Jos 13:26, "Debir"), far from the family estate and from David's court (see note on 2:8). **9:7** *restore to you.* The property Saul had acquired as king had either been taken over by David, or Ziba as steward had virtually taken possession of it and was profiting from its income (see 16:1–4; 19:26–30). *you will always eat at my table.* More a matter of high honor than economic assistance. Mephibosheth's general financial needs were to be cared for by the produce of Saul's estate (v. 10). **9:8** *dead dog like me.* An expression of deep self-abasement. The author has used the "dead dog" motif with great effect. First Goliath, scornfully disdaining the young warrior David, asks, "Am I a dog . . . ?" (1Sa 17:43)—and unwittingly foreshadows his own end. Then David, in a self-deprecating manner, describes himself as a "dead dog" (1Sa 24:14) to suggest to Saul that the king of Israel should not consider him worth so much attention. In the Nabal episode, that "dog" (a Calebite) and his sudden death characterize Saul and foreshadow his unhappy end (see note on 1Sa 25:3). Here a grandson of Saul and in 16:9 a relative of the dead king who curses David are similarly described. For the author, "dead dog" fittingly characterizes those who foolishly scorn or oppose the Lord's anointed, while David's own self-depreciation (see 1Sa 18:18; 2Sa 7:18) is conducive to his exaltation.

your master's grandson everything that belonged to Saul and his family. [10]You and your sons and your servants are to farm the land for him and bring in the crops, so that your master's grandson[r] may be provided for. And Mephibosheth, grandson of your master, will always eat at my table." (Now Ziba had fifteen sons and twenty servants.)

[11]Then Ziba said to the king, "Your servant will do whatever my lord the king commands his servant to do." So Mephibosheth ate at David's[a] table like one of the king's sons.[s]

[12]Mephibosheth had a young son named Mica, and all the members of Ziba's household were servants of Mephibosheth.[t] [13]And Mephibosheth lived in Jerusalem, because he always ate at the king's table, and he was crippled in both feet.

David Defeats the Ammonites

10:1–19pp — 1Ch 19:1–19

10 In the course of time, the king of the Ammonites died, and his son Hanun succeeded him as king. [2]David thought, "I will show kindness to Hanun son of Nahash,[u] just as his father showed kindness to me." So David sent a delegation to express his sympathy to Hanun concerning his father.

When David's men came to the land of the Ammonites, [3]the Ammonite nobles said to Hanun their lord, "Do you think David is honoring your father by sending men to you to express sympathy? Hasn't David sent them to you to explore the city and spy it out[v] and overthrow it?" [4]So Hanun seized David's men, shaved off half of each man's beard,[w] cut off their garments in the middle at the buttocks,[x] and sent them away.

[5]When David was told about this, he sent messengers to meet the men, for they were greatly humiliated. The king said, "Stay at Jericho till your beards have grown, and then come back."

[6]When the Ammonites realized that

they had become a stench[y] in David's nostrils, they hired twenty thousand Aramean[z] foot soldiers from Beth Rehob[a] and Zobah,[b] as well as the king of Maacah[c] with a thousand men, and also twelve thousand men from Tob.[d]

[7]On hearing this, David sent Joab[e] out with the entire army of fighting men. [8]The Ammonites came out and drew up in battle formation at the entrance to their city gate, while the Arameans of Zobah and Rehob and the men of Tob and Maacah were by themselves in the open country.

[9]Joab saw that there were battle lines in front of him and behind him; so he selected some of the best troops in Israel and deployed them against the Arameans. [10]He put the rest of the men under the command of Abishai[f] his brother and deployed them against the Ammonites. [11]Joab said, "If the Arameans are too strong for me, then you are to come to my rescue; but if the Ammonites are too strong for you, then I will come to rescue you. [12]Be strong[g] and let us fight bravely for our people and the cities of our God. The LORD will do what is good in his sight."[h]

[13]Then Joab and the troops with him advanced to fight the Arameans, and they fled before him. [14]When the Ammonites[i] saw that the Arameans were fleeing, they fled before Abishai and went inside the city. So Joab returned from fighting the Ammonites and came to Jerusalem.

[15]After the Arameans saw that they had been routed by Israel, they regrouped. [16]Hadadezer had Arameans brought from beyond the River[b]; they went to Helam, with Shobach the commander of Hadadezer's army leading them.

[17]When David was told of this, he gathered all Israel, crossed the Jordan and went to Helam. The Arameans formed their battle lines to meet David and fought against him. [18]But they fled before Israel, and Da-

Cross references (center column)

9:10 *r*2Sa 16:3
9:11 *s*Job 36:7; Ps 113:8
9:12 *t*S 2Sa 4:4
10:2 *u*S 1Sa 11:1
10:3 *v*S Nu 21:32
10:4 *w*S Lev 19:27; Isa 7:20; 15:2; 50:6; 52:14; Jer 48:37; Eze 5:1 *x*Isa 20:4

10:6 *y*S Ge 34:30 *z*S 2Sa 8:5 *a*S Nu 13:21 *b*S 1Sa 14:47 *c*S Dt 3:14 *d*Jdg 11:3-5
10:7 *e*S 2Sa 2:18
10:10 *f*S 1Sa 26:6
10:12 *g*S Dt 1:21; 31:6; S Eph 6:10 *h*S Jdg 10:15; Ne 4:14
10:14 *i*2Sa 8:12

a 11 Septuagint; Hebrew *my*   *b 16* That is, the Euphrates

9:12 *Mica.* See 1Ch 8:35–39 for his descendants.

10:1 *king.* Nahash (see v. 2; 1Sa 11). *Ammonites.* See note on 1Sa 11:1.

10:2 *show kindness.* The Hebrew for this expression suggests that a formal treaty existed between the Israelites and the Ammonites. Perhaps this explains why there is no account of a war against the Ammonites in ch. 8, and why the Ammonites did not come to the assistance of the Moabites (8:2).

10:3 *city.* Rabbah, the capital (11:1; 12:26).

10:4 *shaved off half of each man's beard.* In the Eastern world of that time this was considered an insult of the most serious kind. A beard was shaved only as a sign of deep mourning (see Isa 15:2; Jer 41:5; Eze 5:1). *cut off their*

garments in the middle at the buttocks. A customary way of degrading prisoners of war (see Isa 20:4).

10:5 *Jericho.* See notes on Jos 6:1,26; 1Ki 16:34. Jericho remained unrestored during the centuries between Joshua's conquest and the time of Ahab.

10:6 *Beth Rehob.* See Nu 13:21; Jdg 18:28. *Zobah.* See note on 8:3. *Maacah.* See Dt 3:14; Jos 12:5; 13:13. *Tob.* See Jdg 11:3,5.

10:10 *Abishai.* See note on 1Sa 26:6.

10:16 *Hadadezer.* See note on 8:3. *Helam.* A town close to the northern border of Gilead.

10:18 *seven hundred.* Evidently a copyist's mistake; in 1Ch 19:18 the figure is 7,000.

vid killed seven hundred of their charioteers and forty thousand of their foot soldiers.^c He also struck down Shobach the commander of their army, and he died there. ¹⁹When all the kings who were vassals of Hadadezer saw that they had been defeated by Israel, they made peace with the Israelites and became subject^j to them.

So the Arameans^k were afraid to help the Ammonites anymore.

David and Bathsheba

11 In the spring,^l at the time when kings go off to war, David sent Joab^m out with the king's men and the whole Israelite army.ⁿ They destroyed the Ammonites and besieged Rabbah.^o But David remained in Jerusalem.

²One evening David got up from his bed and walked around on the roof^p of the palace. From the roof he saw^q a woman bathing. The woman was very beautiful, ³and David sent someone to find out about her. The man said, "Isn't this Bathsheba,^r the daughter of Eliam^s and the wife of Uriah^t the Hittite?" ⁴Then David sent messengers to get her.^u She came to him, and he slept^v with her. (She had purified herself from her uncleanness.)^w Then^d she went back home. ⁵The woman conceived and sent word to David, saying, "I am pregnant."

⁶So David sent this word to Joab: "Send me Uriah^x the Hittite." And Joab sent him to David. ⁷When Uriah came to him, David asked him how Joab was, how the soldiers were and how the war was going. ⁸Then David said to Uriah, "Go down to your house and wash your feet."^y So Uriah left the palace, and a gift from the king was sent after him. ⁹But Uriah slept at the entrance to the palace with all his master's servants and did not go down to his house.

¹⁰When David was told, "Uriah did not go home," he asked him, "Haven't you just come from a distance? Why didn't you go home?"

¹¹Uriah said to David, "The ark^z and Israel and Judah are staying in tents, and my master Joab and my lord's men are camped in the open fields. How could I go to my house to eat and drink and lie^a with my wife? As surely as you live, I will not do such a thing!"

¹²Then David said to him, "Stay here one more day, and tomorrow I will send you back." So Uriah remained in Jerusalem that day and the next. ¹³At David's invitation, he ate and drank with him, and David made him drunk. But in the evening Uriah went out to sleep on his mat among his master's servants; he did not go home.

Cross references

10:19 /2Sa 8:6
k 1Ki 11:25;
22:31; 2Ki 5:1
11:1 /1Ki 20:22,
26 mS 2Sa 2:18
n 1Ch 20:1
o S Dt 3:11
11:2 p S Dt 22:8;
S Jos 2:8
q Mt 5:28
11:3 r 1Ch 3:5
s 2Sa 23:34
t 2Sa 23:39
11:4
u S Lev 20:10;
Ps 51 Title;
Jas 1:14-15
v Dt 22:22
w S Lev 15:25-30

11:6 x 1Ch 11:41
11:8 y S Ge 18:4
11:11 z 2Sa 7:2
a S 1Sa 21:5

c 18 Some Septuagint manuscripts (see also 1 Chron. 19:18); Hebrew horsemen   d 4 Or with her. When she purified herself from her uncleanness,

---

10:19 *they made peace with the Israelites.* There is no indication that Hadadezer himself made peace with Israel as his vassals did in the aftermath of this defeat. These events represent David's last major campaign against combined foreign powers.
11:1 *the spring.* Of the year following the events reported in ch. 10. The time must have been about ten years after David became established in Jerusalem. *the time when kings go off to war.* Directly after the grain harvest in April and May. *Rabbah.* See note on 10:3. Though now alone (see 10:19), the Ammonites had not yet been subjugated.
11:2 *walked around on the roof.* The roofs were flat (see 1Sa 9:25). David had probably gone there to enjoy the cool evening air.
11:3 *Eliam.* Perhaps the same Eliam who was a member of David's personal bodyguard (23:34) and a son of his counselor Ahithophel. *Uriah.* Also listed among those comprising David's royal guard (23:39). His name suggests that even though he was a Hittite, he had adopted the Israelite faith (Uriah means "My light is the LORD"). *Hittite.* See note on 1Sa 26:6.
11:4 *David sent messengers to get her.* Through this action David eventually becomes guilty of breaking the sixth, seventh, ninth and tenth commandments (Ex 20:13–17). *She came to him, and he slept with her.* Bathsheba appears to have been an unprotesting partner in this adulterous relationship with David. (*She had purified herself from her uncleanness.*) The purpose of this parenthetical statement is to indicate Bathsheba's condition at the time of her sexual relations with David. She had just become ceremonially

clean (Lev 15:28–30) after the seven-day period of monthly impurity due to menstruation (Lev 15:19–30). The significance of this in the context is to make it clear that she was not already pregnant by her own husband when David took her.
11:5 *I am pregnant.* Bathsheba leaves the next step up to David. The law prescribed the death penalty for both David and Bathsheba (Lev 20:10; Dt 22:22), as they well knew.
11:6 *Send me Uriah.* Under the pretense of seeking information about the course of the war, David brings Uriah back to Jerusalem.
11:8 *Go down to your house and wash your feet.* In essence, David tells Uriah to go home and relax. What he does not say specifically is what is most important, and well understood by Uriah (v. 11). *a gift from the king was sent after him.* The Hebrew word for "gift" has the meaning of "food" in Ge 43:34 ("portions" from the king's table). David wanted Uriah and Bathsheba to enjoy their evening together.
11:11 *ark.* Uriah's statement suggests that the ark was in the field camp with the army rather than in the tent that David had set up for it in Jerusalem (6:17). If so, it was probably there for purposes of worship and to seek guidance for the war. But then the circumstances are even more damning for David—the Lord is in the field with his army while David stays at home in leisure. *How could I go to my house . . . ?* Uriah's devotion to duty exposes by sharp contrast David's dalliance at home while his men are in the field. *As surely as you live.* See note on 1Sa 1:26.
11:13 *David made him drunk.* In the hope that in this condition he would relent and go to Bathsheba.

14In the morning David wrote a letter[b]
to Joab and sent it with Uriah. 15In it he
wrote, "Put Uriah in the front line where
the fighting is fiercest. Then withdraw
from him so he will be struck down[c] and
die.[d]"
16So while Joab had the city under siege,
he put Uriah at a place where he knew the
strongest defenders were. 17When the men
of the city came out and fought against
Joab, some of the men in David's army fell;
moreover, Uriah the Hittite died.
18Joab sent David a full account of the
battle. 19He instructed the messenger:
"When you have finished giving the king
this account of the battle, 20the king's anger may flare up, and he may ask you,
'Why did you get so close to the city to
fight? Didn't you know they would shoot
arrows from the wall? 21Who killed
Abimelech[e] son of Jerub-Besheth[e]? Didn't
a woman throw an upper millstone on him
from the wall,[f] so that he died in Thebez?
Why did you get so close to the wall?' If he
asks you this, then say to him, 'Also, your
servant Uriah the Hittite is dead.' "
22The messenger set out, and when he
arrived he told David everything Joab had
sent him to say. 23The messenger said to
David, "The men overpowered us and
came out against us in the open, but we
drove them back to the entrance to the city
gate. 24Then the archers shot arrows at
your servants from the wall, and some of
the king's men died. Moreover, your servant Uriah the Hittite is dead."
25David told the messenger, "Say this to
Joab: 'Don't let this upset you; the sword
devours one as well as another. Press the
attack against the city and destroy it.' Say
this to encourage Joab."
26When Uriah's wife heard that her husband was dead, she mourned for him.
27After the time of mourning[g] was over,
David had her brought to his house, and
she became his wife and bore him a son.
But the thing David had done displeased[h]
the LORD.

Nathan Rebukes David

11:1; 12:29–31pp — 1Ch 20:1–3

12 The LORD sent Nathan[i] to David.[j]
When he came to him,[k] he said,
"There were two men in a certain town,
one rich and the other poor. 2The rich man
had a very large number of sheep and cattle, 3but the poor man had nothing except
one little ewe lamb he had bought. He
raised it, and it grew up with him and his
children. It shared his food, drank from his
cup and even slept in his arms. It was like
a daughter to him.
4"Now a traveler came to the rich man,
but the rich man refrained from taking one
of his own sheep or cattle to prepare a
meal for the traveler who had come to
him. Instead, he took the ewe lamb that
belonged to the poor man and prepared it
for the one who had come to him."
5David[l] burned with anger[m] against the
man[n] and said to Nathan, "As surely as
the LORD lives,[o] the man who did this deserves to die! 6He must pay for that lamb
four times over,[p] because he did such a
thing and had no pity."
7Then Nathan said to David, "You are
the man![q] This is what the LORD, the God
of Israel, says: 'I anointed[r] you[s] king over
Israel, and I delivered you from the hand of
Saul. 8I gave your master's house to you,[t]
and your master's wives into your arms. I
gave you the house of Israel and Judah.
And if all this had been too little, I would
have given you even more. 9Why did you

11:14 [b]1Ki 21:8 **11:15** [c]ver 14-17; 2Sa 12:9 [d]2Sa 12:12 **11:21** [e]S Jdg 8:31 [f]Jdg 9:50-54 **11:27** [g]Dt 34:8 [h]2Sa 12:9; Ps 51:4-5 **12:1** [i]S 2Sa 7:2 [j]Ps 51 Title [k]2Sa 14:4 **12:5** [l]1Ki 20:40 [m]S Ge 34:7 [n]Ro 2:1 [o]S 1Sa 14:39 **12:6** [p]Ex 22:1 **12:7** [q]2Sa 14:13; Da 4:22 [r]S 1Sa 2:35 [s]1Ki 20:42 **12:8** [t]S 2Sa 9:7

e *21* Also known as *Jerub-Baal* (that is, Gideon)

11:15 *so he will be struck down and die.* Unsuccessful in making it appear that Uriah was the father of Bathsheba's child, David plotted Uriah's death so he could marry Bathsheba himself as quickly as possible.
11:21 *Jerub-Besheth.* Another possible spelling is "Jerub-Bosheth." In Judges he is called Jerub-Baal (see note on Jdg 6:32; see also NIV text note here). For similar name changes by the author of Samuel see notes on 2:8; 4:4. *millstone.* See Jdg 9:52–53. *Uriah . . . is dead.* Joab knows that this news is of great importance to David, and he uses it to squelch any criticism David might otherwise have had of the battle tactics.
11:25 *David told the messenger.* David hid his satisfaction over the news with a hypocritical statement that war is war and the death of Uriah should not be a discouragement.
11:27 *time of mourning was over.* Presumably a period of seven days (Ge 50:10; 1Sa 31:13). *she became his wife.* See notes on 3:2–5; 5:14. *the thing David had done displeased the LORD.* Not only had David brazenly violated God's laws (see note on v. 4) but, even worse, he had shamelessly abused his royal power, which the Lord had entrusted to him to shepherd the Lord's people (5:2; 7:7–8).
12:1 *The LORD sent.* Prophets were messengers from the Lord. Here the Great King sends his emissary to rebuke and announce judgment on the king he had enthroned over his people. *Nathan.* See note on 7:2. *There were two men.* Nathan begins one of the most striking parables in the OT.
12:5 *As surely as the LORD lives.* See note on 1Sa 14:39.
12:6 *four times over.* In agreement with the requirements of Ex 22:1.
12:8 *your master's wives.* Earlier narratives refer to only one wife of Saul (Ahinoam, 1Sa 14:50) and one concubine (Rizpah, 2Sa 3:7; 21:8). This statement suggests that there were others. But since it was customary for new kings to assume the harem of their predecessors (see note on 3:7), it may be that Nathan merely uses conventional language to emphasize that the Lord had placed David on Saul's throne. *I gave you the house of Israel and Judah.* See 2:4; 5:2–3.

despise[u] the word of the LORD by doing what is evil in his eyes? You struck down[v] Uriah[w] the Hittite with the sword and took his wife to be your own. You killed[x] him with the sword of the Ammonites. 10Now, therefore, the sword[y] will never depart from your house, because you despised me and took the wife of Uriah the Hittite to be your own.'

11"This is what the LORD says: 'Out of your own household[z] I am going to bring calamity upon you. [a] Before your very eyes I will take your wives and give them to one who is close to you, and he will lie with your wives in broad daylight. [b] 12You did it in secret, [c] but I will do this thing in broad daylight[d] before all Israel.' "

13Then David said to Nathan, "I have sinned[e] against the LORD."

Nathan replied, "The LORD has taken away[f] your sin.[g] You are not going to die.[h] 14But because by doing this you have made the enemies of the LORD show utter contempt,[f][i] the son born to you will die."

15After Nathan had gone home, the LORD struck[j] the child that Uriah's wife had borne to David, and he became ill. 16David pleaded with God for the child. He fasted and went into his house and spent the nights lying[k] on the ground. 17The elders of his household stood beside him to get him up from the ground, but he refused,[l] and he would not eat any food with them. [m]

18On the seventh day the child died. David's servants were afraid to tell him that the child was dead, for they thought, "While the child was still living, we spoke to David but he would not listen to us.

How can we tell him the child is dead? He may do something desperate."

19David noticed that his servants were whispering among themselves and he realized the child was dead. "Is the child dead?" he asked.

"Yes," they replied, "he is dead."

20Then David got up from the ground. After he had washed,[n] put on lotions and changed his clothes,[o] he went into the house of the LORD and worshiped. Then he went to his own house, and at his request they served him food, and he ate.

21His servants asked him, "Why are you acting this way? While the child was alive, you fasted and wept,[p] but now that the child is dead, you get up and eat!"

22He answered, "While the child was still alive, I fasted and wept. I thought, 'Who knows?[q] The LORD may be gracious to me and let the child live.'[r] 23But now that he is dead, why should I fast? Can I bring him back again? I will go to him,[s] but he will not return to me."[t]

24Then David comforted his wife Bathsheba,[u] and he went to her and lay with her. She gave birth to a son, and they named him Solomon.[v] The LORD loved him; 25and because the LORD loved him, he sent word through Nathan the prophet to name him Jedidiah.[g][w]

26Meanwhile Joab fought against Rabbah[x] of the Ammonites and captured the royal citadel. 27Joab then sent messengers to David, saying, "I have fought against Rabbah and taken its water supply. 28Now muster the rest of the troops and besiege

---

12:9
[u]S Nu 15:31;
S 1Sa 13:14
[v]S 2Sa 11:15
[w]1Ki 15:5
[x]Ps 26:9; 51:14
12:10
[y]2Sa 13:28;
18:14-15;
1Ki 2:25
12:11 [z]2Sa 16:11
[a]Dt 28:30;
2Sa 16:21-22
[b]S Dt 17:17
12:12
[c]2Sa 11:4-15
[d]2Sa 16:22
12:13
[e]S Ge 13:13;
S 20:6;
S Nu 22:34
[f]Ps 32:1-5; 51:1,
9; 103:12;
Isa 43:25; 44:22;
Zec 3:4,9
[g]Pr 28:13;
Jer 2:35;
Mic 7:18-19
[h]Lev 20:10;
24:17
12:14 [f]Isa 52:5;
Ro 2:24
12:15
[i]S 1Sa 25:38
12:16 [k]Ps 5:7;
95:6
12:17
[l]S Ge 37:35;
S 1Sa 1:7
[m]S 2Sa 3:35;
Da 6:18

12:20 [n]Mt 6:17
[o]S Ge 41:14
12:21 [p]Jdg 20:26
12:22 [q]Jnh 3:9
[r]Isa 38:1-5
12:23 [s]Ge 37:35
[t]S 1Sa 31:13;
2Sa 13:39;
Job 7:10; 10:21
12:24 [u]1Ki 1:11
[v]1Ki 1:10;
1Ch 22:9; 28:5;
Mt 1:6
12:25 [w]Ne 13:26
12:26 [x]S Dt 3:11

[f]14 Masoretic Text; an ancient Hebrew scribal tradition *this you have shown utter contempt for the LORD*
[g]25 *Jedidiah* means *loved by the LORD.*

12:9 *despise the word of the LORD.* See notes on 11:4,27. *You killed him.* David is held directly responsible for Uriah's death even though he fell in battle (see 11:15).

12:10 *the sword will never depart from your house.* Three of David's sons came to violent deaths: Amnon (13:28–29), Absalom (18:14) and Adonijah (1Ki 2:25).

12:11 *Out of your own household I am going to bring calamity upon you.* David was driven from Jerusalem by Absalom's conspiracy to seize the kingship from his own father (15:1–15). *he will lie with your wives in broad daylight.* Fulfilled at the time of Absalom's rebellion (see note on 16:22).

12:13 *I have sinned against the LORD.* David recognizes his guilt and confesses his sin in response to Nathan's rebuke (see Ps 51). Notice the contrast between David's confession and Saul's (see note on 1Sa 15:24). *The LORD has taken away your sin.* David experienced the joy of knowing his sin was forgiven (see Ps 32:1,5; cf. Ps 51:8,12). *You are not going to die.* The Lord, in his grace, released David from the customary death penalty for adultery and murder (Lev 20:10; 24:17).

12:14 *you have made the enemies of the LORD show utter*

contempt. David is required to suffer the disciplinary results of his sin in a manner open to public view. But see NIV text note.

12:20 *he went into the house of the LORD and worshiped.* In this way David clearly demonstrated his humble acceptance of the disciplinary results of his sin. Notice again (see note on v. 13) the contrast between David's attitude and Saul's (see note on 1Sa 15:25).

12:23 *I will go to him.* Like the child, David will die and join him in the grave (see note on Ge 37:35).

12:24 *Solomon.* See 1Ch 22:9 and NIV text note.

12:25 *Jedidiah.* See NIV text note. The giving of this name suggests that the Lord's special favor rested on Solomon from his birth. And since the name also contained an echo of David's name, it provided assurance to David that the Lord also loved him and would continue his dynasty.

12:26 *Joab fought against Rabbah.* The writer now returns to the outcome of the attack against the Ammonites (11:1, 25), which provided the background for the story of David and Bathsheba. Even while the Lord was displeased with David, he gave the Israelites victory over a people that had abused them.

the city and capture it. Otherwise I will take the city, and it will be named after me."

²⁹So David mustered the entire army and went to Rabbah, and attacked and captured it. ³⁰He took the crown[y] from the head of their king[h]—its weight was a talent[i] of gold, and it was set with precious stones—and it was placed on David's head. He took a great quantity of plunder from the city ³¹and brought out the people who were there, consigning them to labor with saws and with iron picks and axes, and he made them work at brickmaking.[j] He did this to all the Ammonite[z] towns. Then David and his entire army returned to Jerusalem.

Amnon and Tamar

13 In the course of time, Amnon[a] son of David fell in love with Tamar,[b] the beautiful sister of Absalom[c] son of David.

²Amnon became frustrated to the point of illness on account of his sister Tamar, for she was a virgin, and it seemed impossible for him to do anything to her.

³Now Amnon had a friend named Jonadab son of Shimeah,[d] David's brother. Jonadab was a very shrewd man. ⁴He asked Amnon, "Why do you, the king's son, look so haggard morning after morning? Won't you tell me?"

Amnon said to him, "I'm in love with Tamar, my brother Absalom's sister."

⁵"Go to bed and pretend to be ill," Jonadab said. "When your father comes to see you, say to him, 'I would like my sister Tamar to come and give me something to eat. Let her prepare the food in my sight so I may watch her and then eat it from her hand.'"

⁶So Amnon lay down and pretended to be ill. When the king came to see him, Amnon said to him, "I would like my sister Tamar to come and make some special

bread in my sight, so I may eat from her hand."

⁷David sent word to Tamar at the palace: "Go to the house of your brother Amnon and prepare some food for him." ⁸So Tamar went to the house of her brother Amnon, who was lying down. She took some dough, kneaded it, made the bread in his sight and baked it. ⁹Then she took the pan and served him the bread, but he refused to eat.

"Send everyone out of here,"[e] Amnon said. So everyone left him. ¹⁰Then Amnon said to Tamar, "Bring the food here into my bedroom so I may eat from your hand." And Tamar took the bread she had prepared and brought it to her brother Amnon in his bedroom. ¹¹But when she took it to him to eat, he grabbed[f] her and said, "Come to bed with me, my sister."[g]

¹²"Don't, my brother!" she said to him. "Don't force me. Such a thing should not be done in Israel![h] Don't do this wicked thing.[i] ¹³What about me?[j] Where could I get rid of my disgrace? And what about you? You would be like one of the wicked fools in Israel. Please speak to the king; he will not keep me from being married to you." ¹⁴But he refused to listen to her, and since he was stronger than she, he raped her.[k]

¹⁵Then Amnon hated her with intense hatred. In fact, he hated her more than he had loved her. Amnon said to her, "Get up and get out!"

¹⁶"No!" she said to him. "Sending me away would be a greater wrong than what you have already done to me."

But he refused to listen to her. ¹⁷He called his personal servant and said, "Get this woman out of here and bolt the door after her." ¹⁸So his servant put her out and bolted the door after her. She was wearing

Cross references

12:30 [y]Est 8:15; Ps 21:3; 132:18
12:31
13:1 [a]2Sa 3:2
[b]2Sa 14:27; 1Ch 3:9
[c]2Sa 3:3
13:3 [d]1Sa 16:9
[z]S 1Sa 14:47

13:9 [e]Ge 45:1
13:11
[f]S Ge 39:12
[g]S Ge 38:16
13:12 [h]Lev 20:17
[i]S Ge 34:7
13:13
[j]S Lev 18:9;
S Dt 22:21,23-24
13:14
[k]S Ge 34:2;
Eze 22:11

[h]30 Or *of Milcom* (that is, Molech)   [i]30 That is, about 75 pounds (about 34 kilograms)   [j]31 The meaning of the Hebrew for this clause is uncertain.

Footnotes

12:30 *the crown . . . was placed on David's head.* A crown of such weight (see NIV text note) would have been worn only briefly and on very special occasions. Perhaps it was worn only once in a symbolic act of transferring to David sovereignty over Ammon.

12:31 *consigning them to labor.* Victorious kings often used prisoners of war as menial laborers in royal building projects (see 1Ki 9:20–21; cf. also Ex 1:11).

13:1–39 The trouble within David's family begins (see note on 12:10).

13:1 *Amnon.* David's oldest son (3:2). *Tamar.* David's daughter by Maacah of Geshur (3:3), and Absalom's full sister.

13:3 *Shimeah.* Called Shammah in 1Sa 16:9.

13:13 *what about you?* This act would jeopardize Amnon's position as crown prince and heir to the throne. *he will not keep me from being married to you.* Possibly a futile attempt by Tamar to escape Amnon's immediate designs rather than a serious proposal, since such a marriage was prohibited in Israel (see Lev 18:9; 20:17; Dt 27:22).

13:15 *Amnon hated her.* The reversal in Amnon's feelings toward Tamar demonstrates that his former "love" (v. 1) was nothing but sensual desire.

13:16 *Sending me away would be a greater wrong.* No longer a virgin, she could not be offered by her father to any other potential husband (see v. 21 and note).

13:18 *richly ornamented robe.* See Ge 37:3 and note.

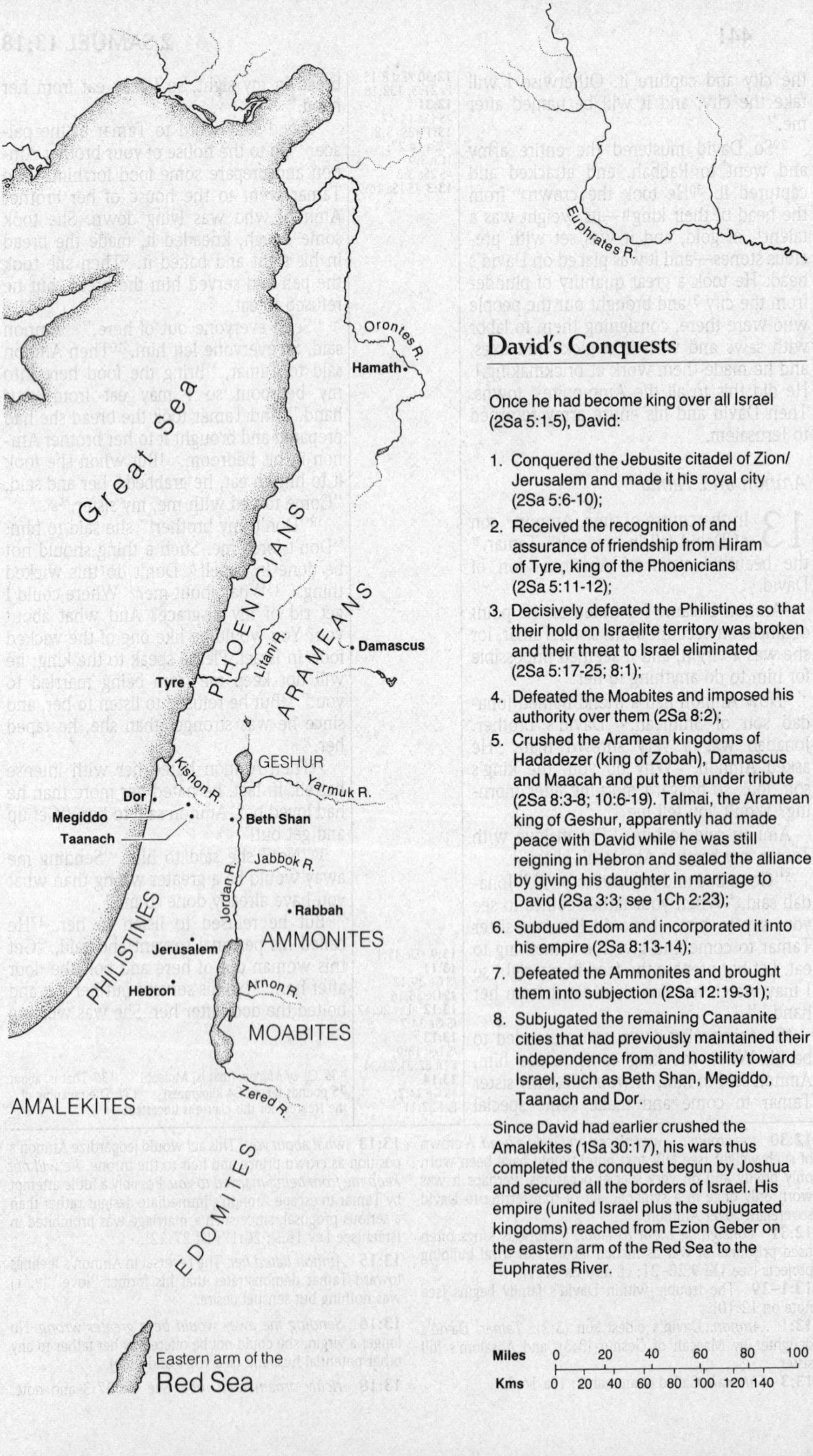

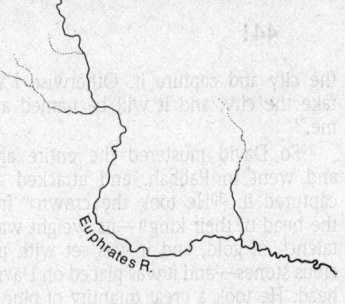

David's Conquests

Once he had become king over all Israel (2Sa 5:1-5), David:

1. Conquered the Jebusite citadel of Zion/Jerusalem and made it his royal city (2Sa 5:6-10);

2. Received the recognition of and assurance of friendship from Hiram of Tyre, king of the Phoenicians (2Sa 5:11-12);

3. Decisively defeated the Philistines so that their hold on Israelite territory was broken and their threat to Israel eliminated (2Sa 5:17-25; 8:1);

4. Defeated the Moabites and imposed his authority over them (2Sa 8:2);

5. Crushed the Aramean kingdoms of Hadadezer (king of Zobah), Damascus and Maacah and put them under tribute (2Sa 8:3-8; 10:6-19). Talmai, the Aramean king of Geshur, apparently had made peace with David while he was still reigning in Hebron and sealed the alliance by giving his daughter in marriage to David (2Sa 3:3; see 1Ch 2:23);

6. Subdued Edom and incorporated it into his empire (2Sa 8:13-14);

7. Defeated the Ammonites and brought them into subjection (2Sa 12:19-31);

8. Subjugated the remaining Canaanite cities that had previously maintained their independence from and hostility toward Israel, such as Beth Shan, Megiddo, Taanach and Dor.

Since David had earlier crushed the Amalekites (1Sa 30:17), his wars thus completed the conquest begun by Joshua and secured all the borders of Israel. His empire (united Israel plus the subjugated kingdoms) reached from Ezion Geber on the eastern arm of the Red Sea to the Euphrates River.

Great Sea

Euphrates R.

Orontes R.

Hamath

PHOENICIANS

ARAMEANS

Damascus

Litani R.

Tyre

Kishon R.

GESHUR

Yarmuk R.

Dor

Megiddo

Beth Shan

Taanach

Jabbok R.

Jordan R.

Rabbah

Jerusalem

AMMONITES

Hebron

Arnon R.

MOABITES

PHILISTINES

Zered R.

AMALEKITES

EDOMITES

Eastern arm of the
Red Sea

Miles	0	20	40	60	80	100
Kms	0 20 40 60 80 100 120 140					

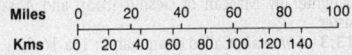

a richly ornamented[k] robe,[l] for this was the kind of garment the virgin daughters of the king wore. [19]Tamar put ashes[m] on her head and tore the ornamented[l] robe she was wearing. She put her hand on her head and went away, weeping aloud as she went.

[20]Her brother Absalom said to her, "Has that Amnon, your brother, been with you? Be quiet now, my sister; he is your brother. Don't take this thing to heart." And Tamar lived in her brother Absalom's house, a desolate woman.

[21]When King David heard all this, he was furious.[n] [22]Absalom never said a word to Amnon, either good or bad;[o] he hated[p] Amnon because he had disgraced his sister Tamar.

Absalom Kills Amnon

[23]Two years later, when Absalom's sheepshearers[q] were at Baal Hazor near the border of Ephraim, he invited all the king's sons to come there. [24]Absalom went to the king and said, "Your servant has had shearers come. Will the king and his officials please join me?"

[25]"No, my son," the king replied. "All of us should not go; we would only be a burden to you." Although Absalom urged him, he still refused to go, but gave him his blessing.

[26]Then Absalom said, "If not, please let my brother Amnon come with us."

The king asked him, "Why should he go with you?" [27]But Absalom urged him, so he sent with him Amnon and the rest of the king's sons.

[28]Absalom[r] ordered his men, "Listen! When Amnon is in high[s] spirits from drinking wine and I say to you, 'Strike Amnon down,' then kill him. Don't be afraid. Have not I given you this order? Be strong and brave.[t]" [29]So Absalom's men did to Amnon what Absalom had ordered. Then all the king's sons got up, mounted their mules and fled.

[30]While they were on their way, the report came to David: "Absalom has struck down all the king's sons; not one of them is left." [31]The king stood up, tore[u] his clothes and lay down on the ground; and all his servants stood by with their clothes torn.

[32]But Jonadab son of Shimeah, David's brother, said, "My lord should not think that they killed all the princes; only Amnon is dead. This has been Absalom's expressed intention ever since the day Amnon raped his sister Tamar. [33]My lord the king should not be concerned about the report that all the king's sons are dead. Only Amnon is dead."

[34]Meanwhile, Absalom had fled.

Now the man standing watch looked up and saw many people on the road west of him, coming down the side of the hill. The watchman went and told the king, "I see men in the direction of Horonaim, on the side of the hill."[m]

[35]Jonadab said to the king, "See, the king's sons are here; it has happened just as your servant said."

[36]As he finished speaking, the king's sons came in, wailing loudly. The king, too, and all his servants wept very bitterly.

[37]Absalom fled and went to Talmai[v] son

13:18
/S Ge 37:23
13:19 m S Jos 7:6;
Est 4:1; Da 9:3
13:21 n S Ge 34:7
13:22 o Ge 31:24
p Lev 19:17-18;
1Jn 2:9-11
13:23 q 1Sa 25:7
13:28 r S 2Sa 3:3
s S Ru 3:7

t S 2Sa 12:10
13:31 u S Nu 14:6
13:37 v S 2Sa 3:3

k 18 The meaning of the Hebrew for this phrase is uncertain.   l 19 The meaning of the Hebrew for this word is uncertain.   m 34 Septuagint; Hebrew does not have this sentence.

13:19 *put ashes on her head.* A sign of great mourning. *tore the ornamented robe.* Thus expressing her anguish and announcing that her virginity had been violated. *put her hand on her head.* Also a sign of grief (see Jer 2:37).

13:20 *Be quiet now, my sister . . . Don't take this thing to heart.* Absalom urges his sister not to make the matter a public scandal, and attempts to quiet her by minimizing its significance. Meanwhile, he formulates his own secret plans for revenge (see vv. 22,28,32).

13:21 *he was furious.* Although David was incensed by Amnon's rape of Tamar, there is no record that he took any punitive action against him. Perhaps the memory of his own sin with Bathsheba adversely affected his judicious handling of the matter. Whatever the reason, David abdicated his responsibility both as king and as father. This disciplinary leniency toward his sons (see notes on 14:33; 1Ki 1:6) eventually led to the death of Amnon and the revolts of Absalom and Adonijah.

13:22 *Absalom never said a word to Amnon . . . he hated Amnon.* He quietly bided his time.

13:23 *he invited all the king's sons.* The time of sheepshearing was a festive occasion (see 1Sa 25:4,8).

13:26 *let my brother Amnon come.* Upon David's refusal of the invitation, Absalom diplomatically requested that Amnon, the crown prince and oldest son, be his representative. *Why should he go with you?* David's question suggests some misgivings because of the strained relationship between the two half brothers (see v. 22).

13:28 *kill him.* Absalom arranged for the murder of his half brother in violation of Eastern hospitality. In the wicked acts of Amnon and Absalom, David's oldest sons became guilty of sexual immorality and murder, as their father had before them. With the murder of Amnon, Absalom not only avenged the rape of his sister but also secured for himself the position of successor to the throne (see 3:3; 15:1–6). Kileab, David's second son (3:3), may have died in his youth since there is no reference to him beyond the announcement of his birth.

13:29 *mules.* Apparently the normal mount for royalty in David's kingdom (see 18:9; 1Ki 1:33,38,44; see also note on 1Ki 1:33).

13:31 *tore his clothes and lay down on the ground.* Common ways of expressing grief (see Jos 7:6; 1Ki 21:27; Est 4:1,3; Job 1:20; 2:8).

of Ammihud, the king of Geshur. But King David mourned for his son every day.

³⁸After Absalom fled and went to Geshur, he stayed there three years. ³⁹And the spirit of the kingⁿ longed to go to Absalom,^w for he was consoled^x concerning Amnon's death.

Absalom Returns to Jerusalem

14 Joab^y son of Zeruiah knew that the king's heart longed for Absalom. ²So Joab sent someone to Tekoa^z and had a wise woman^a brought from there. He said to her, "Pretend you are in mourning. Dress in mourning clothes, and don't use any cosmetic lotions.^b Act like a woman who has spent many days grieving for the dead. ³Then go to the king and speak these words to him." And Joab^c put the words in her mouth.

⁴When the woman from Tekoa went^o to the king, she fell with her face to the ground to pay him honor, and she said, "Help me, O king!"

⁵The king asked her, "What is troubling you?"

She said, "I am indeed a widow; my husband is dead. ⁶I your servant had two sons. They got into a fight with each other in the field, and no one was there to separate them. One struck the other and killed him. ⁷Now the whole clan has risen up against your servant; they say, 'Hand over the one who struck his brother down, so that we may put him to death^d for the life

of his brother whom he killed; then we will get rid of the heir^e as well.' They would put out the only burning coal I have left,^f leaving my husband neither name nor descendant on the face of the earth."

⁸The king said to the woman, "Go home,^g and I will issue an order in your behalf."

⁹But the woman from Tekoa said to him, "My lord the king, let the blame^h rest on me and on my father's family,ⁱ and let the king and his throne be without guilt.^j"

¹⁰The king replied, "If anyone says anything to you, bring him to me, and he will not bother you again."

¹¹She said, "Then let the king invoke the LORD his God to prevent the avenger^k of blood from adding to the destruction, so that my son will not be destroyed."

"As surely as the LORD lives," he said, "not one hair^l of your son's head will fall to the ground.^m"

¹²Then the woman said, "Let your servant speak a word to my lord the king."

"Speak," he replied.

¹³The woman said, "Why then have you devised a thing like this against the people of God? When the king says this, does he not convict himself,ⁿ for the king has not brought back his banished son?^o ¹⁴Like water^p spilled on the ground, which can-

Cross references

13:39
w 2Sa 14:13
x S 2Sa 12:19-23
14:1 y S 2Sa 2:18
14:2 z Ne 3:5;
Jer 6:1; Am 1:1
a 2Sa 20:16
b S Ru 3:3;
S Isa 1:6
14:3 c ver 19
14:7 d Nu 35:19

e Mt 21:38
f Dt 19:10-13
14:8 g 1Sa 25:35
14:9 h 1Sa 25:24
i Mt 27:25
14:11
k S Nu 35:12,21
l S Mt 10:30
m S 1Sa 14:45
14:13
n S 2Sa 12:7;
1Ki 20:40
o 2Sa 13:38-39
14:14
p Job 14:11;
Ps 58:7; Isa 19:5

ⁿ39 Dead Sea Scrolls and some Septuagint manuscripts; Masoretic Text *But the spirit of David the king*
^o4 Many Hebrew manuscripts, Septuagint, Vulgate and Syriac; most Hebrew manuscripts *spoke*

13:37 *Talmai son of Ammihud, the king of Geshur.* Absalom's grandfather (see 3:3).

13:39 *longed to go to Absalom.* With Absalom a refugee, David had lost both of his oldest living sons.

14:1 *Joab son of Zeruiah.* See note on 2:13. *the king's heart longed for Absalom.* Torn between anger and love (and perhaps remorse), David again leaves the initiative to others.

14:2 *So Joab sent.* Joab appears to have been motivated by a concern for the political implications of the unresolved dispute between David and the son in line for the throne. He attempts to move David to action by means of a story designed to elicit a response clearly applicable, by analogy, to David's own predicament. A similar technique was used by Nathan the prophet (12:1–7; see 1Ki 20:38–43). *Tekoa.* A town a few miles south of Bethlehem, from which the prophet Amos also came (Am 1:1).

14:7 *the whole clan has risen up against your servant.* It was customary in Israel for a murder victim's next of kin to avenge the blood of his relative by putting the murderer to death (see note on 3:27; see also Nu 35:12; Dt 19:11–13). In the case presented, however, blood revenge would wipe out the family line, which was something Israelite law and custom tried to avoid if at all possible (see notes on Dt 25:5–6; Ru 2:20). *we will get rid of the heir as well.* The woman suggests that the motivation for blood revenge was more a selfish desire to acquire the family inheritance than a desire for justice (see Nu 27:11). *leaving my husband*

neither name nor descendant. The implication is that it would be a more serious offense to terminate the woman's family line than to permit a murder to go unpunished by blood revenge. Apparently Joab hoped subtly to suggest to David that if he did not restore Absalom, a struggle for the throne would eventually ensue.

14:8 *I will issue an order in your behalf.* David's judicial action may have rested on the legal ground that the murder was not premeditated (see Dt 19:4–6).

14:9 *blame.* For the unpunished crime.

14:11 *let the king invoke the LORD his God.* The woman wants David to confirm his promise by an oath in the Lord's name. *As surely as the LORD lives.* An oath formula (see notes on Ge 42:15; 1Sa 14:39) that solemnly binds David to his commitment.

14:13 *against the people of God.* The woman's suggestion is that David has done the same thing to Israel that her family members have done to her. The people of Israel want their crown prince returned safely to them. *does he not convict himself . . . ?* The argument is that when David exempted the fictitious murderer from blood revenge, he in effect rendered himself guilty for not doing the same in the case of Absalom. The analogy places David in the position of the blood avenger.

14:14 *Like water spilled on the ground.* Blood revenge will not return the victim of murder to life, just as water spilled on the ground cannot be recovered. *God does not take away life.* In the suggestion that the avenging of blood is contrary

not be recovered, so we must die.*q* But God does not take away life; instead, he devises ways so that a banished person*r* may not remain estranged from him.

15"And now I have come to say this to my lord the king because the people have made me afraid. Your servant thought, 'I will speak to the king; perhaps he will do what his servant asks. 16Perhaps the king will agree to deliver his servant from the hand of the man who is trying to cut off both me and my son from the inheritance*s* God gave us.'

17"And now your servant says, 'May the word of my lord the king bring me rest, for my lord the king is like an angel*t* of God in discerning*u* good and evil. May the LORD your God be with you.' "

18Then the king said to the woman, "Do not keep from me the answer to what I am going to ask you."

"Let my lord the king speak," the woman said.

19The king asked, "Isn't the hand of Joab*v* with you in all this?"

The woman answered, "As surely as you live, my lord the king, no one can turn to the right or to the left from anything my lord the king says. Yes, it was your servant Joab who instructed me to do this and who put all these words into the mouth of your servant. 20Your servant Joab did this to change the present situation. My lord has wisdom*w* like that of an angel of God—he knows everything that happens in the land.*x* "

21The king said to Joab, "Very well, I will do it. Go, bring back the young man Absalom."

22Joab fell with his face to the ground to pay him honor, and he blessed the king.*y* Joab said, "Today your servant knows that he has found favor in your eyes, my lord

the king, because the king has granted his servant's request."

23Then Joab went to Geshur and brought Absalom back to Jerusalem. 24But the king said, "He must go to his own house; he must not see my face." So Absalom went to his own house and did not see the face of the king.

25In all Israel there was not a man so highly praised for his handsome appearance as Absalom. From the top of his head to the sole of his foot there was no blemish in him. 26Whenever he cut the hair of his head*z*—he used to cut his hair from time to time when it became too heavy for him—he would weigh it, and its weight was two hundred shekels*p* by the royal standard.

27Three sons*a* and a daughter were born to Absalom. The daughter's name was Tamar,*b* and she became a beautiful woman.

28Absalom lived two years in Jerusalem without seeing the king's face. 29Then Absalom sent for Joab in order to send him to the king, but Joab refused to come to him. So he sent a second time, but he refused to come. 30Then he said to his servants, "Look, Joab's field is next to mine, and he has barley*c* there. Go and set it on fire." So Absalom's servants set the field on fire.

31Then Joab did go to Absalom's house and he said to him, "Why have your servants set my field on fire?*d* "

32Absalom said to Joab, "Look, I sent word to you and said, 'Come here so I can send you to the king to ask, "Why have I come from Geshur?*e* It would be better for me if I were still there!" ' Now then, I want to see the king's face, and if I am guilty of anything, let him put me to death."*f*

33So Joab went to the king and told him

Cross references (center column):

14:14 *q*Job 10:8; 17:13; 30:23; Ps 22:15; Heb 9:27
14:16 *s*S Ex 34:9; S 1Sa 26:19
14:17 *t*S 1Sa 29:9 *u*1Ki 3:9; Da 2:21
14:19 *v*ver 3
14:20 *w*1Ki 3:12, 28; 10:23-24; Isa 28:6 *x*2Sa 18:13
14:22 *y*S Ge 47:7

14:26 *z*2Sa 18:9
14:27 *a*2Sa 18:18 *b*S 2Sa 13:1
14:30 *c*S Ex 9:31
14:31 *d*S Jdg 15:5
14:32 *e*S 2Sa 3:3
*f*1Sa 20:8

P26 That is, about 5 pounds (about 2.3 kilograms)

---

to God's ways of dealing with people, the woman apparently distorts Biblical teaching of God's justice (see note on Ge 9:6). But she dwells on the mercy of God, who would rather preserve life than take it (see Eze 18:23,32; 33:11). David's own guilt and subsequent experience of God's mercy appear to give added weight to the woman's argument (see notes on 12:13; 13:21).
14:15 *the people have made me afraid.* The woman reverts to her own fabricated story. "The people" are evidently those of her own family who are seeking blood revenge.
14:17 *like an angel of God in discerning good and evil.* Possessing superhuman powers of discernment—as a king ideally should (see v. 20; 19:27).
14:21 *Joab.* He appears to have been present the whole time.
14:23 *Joab went to Geshur.* See 13:37.
14:24 *he must not see my face.* David still vacillates (see note on v. 1); he does not offer forgiveness and restoration.

14:25 *not a man so highly praised.* Absalom's handsomeness brought him attention and popular favor—which he was soon to cultivate.
14:26 *hair of his head.* For the people of that time, hair was apparently a sign of vigor. Kings and heroic figures were usually portrayed with abundant locks, while baldness was a disgrace (see 2Ki 2:23). In this, too, Absalom seemed destined for the throne. *royal standard.* The royal shekel was perhaps heavier than the sanctuary shekel (see Ex 30:13; Lev 5:15; Nu 3:47).
14:27 *Three sons.* Their names are unknown; 18:18 suggests that they died in their youth. *Tamar.* Absalom named his daughter after his sister (13:1). Maacah (1Ki 15:2) was probably a daughter of Tamar, and Absalom's granddaughter (see note on 2Ch 11:20).
14:32 *if I am guilty of anything, let him put me to death.* Absalom demands either full pardon and restoration or death, but he still gives no sign of repentance.

this. Then the king summoned Absalom,
and he came in and bowed down with his
face to the ground before the king. And the
king kissed[g] Absalom.

Absalom's Conspiracy

15 In the course of time,[h] Absalom
provided himself with a chariot[i]
and horses and with fifty men to run ahead
of him. 2He would get up early and stand
by the side of the road leading to the city
gate.[j] Whenever anyone came with a
complaint to be placed before the king for
a decision, Absalom would call out to him,
"What town are you from?" He would answer, "Your servant is from one of the
tribes of Israel." 3Then Absalom would say
to him, "Look, your claims are valid and
proper, but there is no representative of
the king to hear you."[k] 4And Absalom
would add, "If only I were appointed judge
in the land![l] Then everyone who has a
complaint or case could come to me and I
would see that he gets justice."

5Also, whenever anyone approached
him to bow down before him, Absalom
would reach out his hand, take hold of him
and kiss him. 6Absalom behaved in this
way toward all the Israelites who came to
the king asking for justice, and so he stole
the hearts[m] of the men of Israel.

7At the end of four[q] years, Absalom said
to the king, "Let me go to Hebron and
fulfill a vow I made to the LORD. 8While
your servant was living at Geshur[n] in
Aram, I made this vow:[o] 'If the LORD
takes me back to Jerusalem, I will worship
the LORD in Hebron.[r]' "

9The king said to him, "Go in peace."
So he went to Hebron.

10Then Absalom sent secret messengers
throughout the tribes of Israel to say, "As
soon as you hear the sound of the trumpets,[p] then say, 'Absalom is king in Hebron.' " 11Two hundred men from Jerusalem had accompanied Absalom. They had
been invited as guests and went quite innocently, knowing nothing about the matter. 12While Absalom was offering sacrifices, he also sent for Ahithophel[q] the
Gilonite, David's counselor,[r] to come
from Giloh,[s] his hometown. And so the
conspiracy gained strength, and Absalom's
following kept on increasing.[t]

David Flees

13A messenger came and told David,
"The hearts of the men of Israel are with
Absalom."

14Then David said to all his officials who
were with him in Jerusalem, "Come! We
must flee,[u] or none of us will escape from
Absalom.[v] We must leave immediately, or
he will move quickly to overtake us and
bring ruin upon us and put the city to the
sword."

15The king's officials answered him,
"Your servants are ready to do whatever
our lord the king chooses."

16The king set out, with his entire
household following him; but he left ten
concubines[w] to take care of the palace.
17So the king set out, with all the people
following him, and they halted at a place

q7 Some Septuagint manuscripts, Syriac and Josephus; Hebrew *forty* r8 Some Septuagint manuscripts; Hebrew does not have *in Hebron.*

14:33 [g]Lk 15:20
15:1 [h]S 2Sa 12:11 [i]S 1Sa 8:11
15:2 [j]S Ge 23:10; 2Sa 19:8
15:3 [k]Pr 12:2
15:4 [l]Jdg 9:29
15:6 [m]Ro 16:18
15:8 [n]S 2Sa 3:3 [o]S Ge 28:20
15:10 [p]1Ki 1:34, 39; 2Ki 9:13
15:12 [q]ver 31, 34; 2Sa 16:15,23; 17:14; 23:34; 1Ch 27:33 [r]Job 19:14; Ps 41:9; 55:13; Jer 9:4 [s]Jos 15:51 [t]Ps 3:1
15:14 [u]1Ki 2:26; Ps 132:1; Ps 3 Title [v]2Sa 19:9
15:16 [w]2Sa 16:21-22; 20:3

14:33 *the king kissed Absalom.* Signifying his forgiveness and Absalom's reconciliation with the royal family. David sidesteps repentance and justice, and in this way he probably contributes to the fulfillment of the prophecy of Nathan (12:10–12).
15:1 *chariot and horses.* As far as is known, Absalom was the first Israelite leader to acquire a chariot and horses (cf. Dt 17:16). *fifty men.* They probably functioned as bodyguards and provided a display of royal pomp that appealed to the masses. Adonijah later followed Absalom's example (1Ki 1:5).
15:3 *your claims are valid.* Absalom seeks to ingratiate himself with the people by endorsing their grievances apart from any investigation into their legitimacy.
15:4 *If only I were appointed judge in the land!* Absalom presents himself as the solution to the people's legal grievances. In the case of Amnon, he had taken matters into his own hands because of his father's laxity. He has found, he believes, the weakness in his father's reign, and he capitalizes on it with political astuteness.
15:7 *four years.* After his return to the court (14:33). By this time Absalom must have been about 30 years old, so his revolt must be dated early in the last decade of David's reign. *Hebron.* Where David was first proclaimed king (see notes on 2:1,4; 5:3,5) and where Absalom was born (3:2–3). Absalom may have had reason to believe that he could count on some local resentment over David's transfer of the capital to Jerusalem. Hebron was also the site of an important sanctuary.
15:8 *Geshur.* See 13:37.
15:12 *Ahithophel.* Bathsheba's grandfather (see 11:3; 23:34) and a wise and respected counselor (16:23). He appears to have secretly aligned himself with Absalom's rebellion in its planning stage, perhaps in retaliation against David for his treatment of Bathsheba and Uriah. This unsuspected betrayal by a trusted friend may have prompted David's statements in Ps 41:9; 55:12–14. *Gilonite.* Giloh was near Hebron (see Jos 15:51).
15:14 *none of us will escape from Absalom.* Uncertain of the extent of Absalom's support (see v. 13), David fears being trapped in Jerusalem, and he wants to spare the city a bloodbath.
15:16 *he left ten concubines to take care of the palace.* See 5:13; see also note on 3:2. David unknowingly arranges for the fulfillment of one of Nathan's prophecies (see note on 12:11; see also 20:3).

some distance away. [18]All his men marched past him, along with all the Kerethites[x] and Pelethites; and all the six hundred Gittites who had accompanied him from Gath marched before the king.

[19]The king said to Ittai[y] the Gittite, "Why should you come along with us? Go back and stay with King Absalom. You are a foreigner,[z] an exile from your homeland. [20]You came only yesterday. And today shall I make you wander[a] about with us, when I do not know where I am going? Go back, and take your countrymen. May kindness and faithfulness[b] be with you."

[21]But Ittai replied to the king, "As surely as the LORD lives, and as my lord the king lives, wherever my lord the king may be, whether it means life or death, there will your servant be."[c]

[22]David said to Ittai, "Go ahead, march on." So Ittai the Gittite marched on with all his men and the families that were with him.

[23]The whole countryside wept aloud[d] as all the people passed by. The king also crossed the Kidron Valley,[ef] and all the people moved on toward the desert.

[24]Zadok[g] was there, too, and all the Levites who were with him were carrying the ark[h] of the covenant of God. They set down the ark of God, and Abiathar[i] offered sacrifices[s] until all the people had finished leaving the city.

[25]Then the king said to Zadok, "Take the ark of God back into the city. If I find favor in the LORD's eyes, he will bring me back and let me see it and his dwelling place[j] again. [26]But if he says, 'I am not

pleased with you,' then I am ready; let him do to me whatever seems good to him.[k]"

[27]The king also said to Zadok the priest, "Aren't you a seer?[l] Go back to the city in peace, with your son Ahimaaz and Jonathan[m] son of Abiathar. You and Abiathar take your two sons with you. [28]I will wait at the fords[n] in the desert until word comes from you to inform me." [29]So Zadok and Abiathar took the ark of God back to Jerusalem and stayed there.

[30]But David continued up the Mount of Olives, weeping[o] as he went; his head[p] was covered and he was barefoot. All the people with him covered their heads too and were weeping as they went up. [31]Now David had been told, "Ahithophel[q] is among the conspirators with Absalom." So David prayed, "O LORD, turn Ahithophel's counsel into foolishness."

[32]When David arrived at the summit, where people used to worship God, Hushai[r] the Arkite[s] was there to meet him, his robe torn and dust[t] on his head. [33]David said to him, "If you go with me, you will be a burden[u] to me. [34]But if you return to the city and say to Absalom, 'I will be your servant, O king; I was your father's servant in the past, but now I will be your servant,'[v] then you can help me by frustrating[w] Ahithophel's advice. [35]Won't the priests Zadok and Abiathar be there with you? Tell them anything you hear in the king's palace.[x] [36]Their two sons, Ahimaaz[y] son of Zadok and Jonathan[z] son of Abiathar, are there with them. Send them to me with anything you hear."

[37]So David's friend Hushai[a] arrived at Jerusalem as Absalom[b] was entering the city.

Cross-references (center column):

15:18
xS 1Sa 30:14;
2Sa 20:7,23;
1Ki 1:38,44;
1Ch 18:17
15:19 y2Sa 18:2
zS Ge 31:15
15:20
aS 1Sa 22:2
b2Sa 2:6
15:21
cRu 1:16-17;
Pr 17:17
15:23 d1Sa 11:4;
Job 2:12
e1Ki 2:37;
2Ki 23:12;
2Ch 15:16;
29:16; 30:14;
Jer 31:40 fJn 18:1
15:24
gS 2Sa 8:17;
19:11 hNu 4:15;
S 10:33; 1Ki 2:26
iS 1Sa 22:20
15:25 jEx 15:13;
S Lev 15:31;
Ps 43:3; 46:4;
84:1; 132:7
15:26
kS Jdg 10:15;
2Sa 22:20

15:27 lS 1Sa 9:9
mver 36;
2Sa 17:17;
1Ki 1:42
15:28 n2Sa 17:16
15:30
oS Nu 25:6;
S Ps 30:5
pEst 6:12
15:31 qS ver 12
15:32 rver 37;
2Sa 16:16; 17:5;
1Ki 4:16 sJos 16:2
tS Jos 7:6
15:33 u2Sa 19:35
15:34 v2Sa 16:19
w2Sa 17:14;
Pr 11:14
15:35
x2Sa 17:15-16
15:36 y2Sa 18:19
zS ver 27;
2Sa 17:17;
1Ki 1:42
15:37
a1Ch 27:33
b2Sa 16:15

s24 Or Abiathar went up

15:18 *Kerethites and Pelethites.* See note on 8:18. *six hundred Gittites.* Philistine soldiers from Gath under the command of Ittai who for some unknown reason had joined David's personal military force (see 18:2).

15:19 *Go back and stay with King Absalom.* David releases the Philistine contingent from further obligations to him.

15:21 *As surely as the LORD lives.* An oath of loyalty and devotion taken in the name of Israel's God (see note on 1Sa 14:39). For a similar oath see Ru 1:16-17.

15:24 *Zadok.* See note on 8:17. *Abiathar.* See note on 8:17; see also 1Sa 22:20-23.

15:25 *Take the ark of God back into the city.* David reveals a true understanding of the connection between the ark and God's presence with his people. He knows that possession of the ark does not guarantee God's blessing (see notes on 1Sa 4:3,21). He also recognizes that the ark belongs in the capital city as a symbol of the Lord's rule over the nation (see note on 6:2), no matter who the king might be.

15:26 *let him do to me whatever seems good to him.* David confesses that he has no exclusive claim to the throne and that Israel's divine King is free to confer the kingship on

whomever he chooses.

15:27 *Aren't you a seer?* Perhaps an allusion to the high priest's custody of the Urim and Thummim as a means of divine revelation (see notes on Ex 28:30; 1Sa 2:28). See also note on 1Sa 9:9.

15:28 *fords in the desert.* Fords across the Jordan in the vicinity of Gilgal.

15:30 *his head was covered.* A sign of sorrow (see Est 6:12; Jer 14:3-4). *he was barefoot.* Another sign of sorrow (see Isa 20:2,4; Eze 24:17; Mic 1:8).

15:31 *Ahithophel.* See note on v. 12.

15:32 *Hushai the Arkite.* The Arkites were a clan (some think non-Israelite) that inhabited an area southwest of Bethel (Jos 16:2). Since Hushai was a trusted member of David's court (see note on v. 37), his appearance was the beginning of an answer to David's prayer (v. 31).

15:37 *David's friend Hushai.* 1Ch 27:33 calls him the "king's friend," which seems to be an official title for the king's most trusted adviser (see 1Ki 4:5, where the Hebrew for "king's friend" is translated "personal adviser to the king").

David and Ziba

16 When David had gone a short distance beyond the summit, there was Ziba, [c] the steward of Mephibosheth, waiting to meet him. He had a string of donkeys saddled and loaded with two hundred loaves of bread, a hundred cakes of raisins, a hundred cakes of figs and a skin of wine. [d]

[2] The king asked Ziba, "Why have you brought these?"

Ziba answered, "The donkeys are for the king's household to ride on, the bread and fruit are for the men to eat, and the wine is to refresh [e] those who become exhausted in the desert."

[3] The king then asked, "Where is your master's grandson?" [f]

Ziba [g] said to him, "He is staying in Jerusalem, because he thinks, 'Today the house of Israel will give me back my grandfather's kingdom.'"

[4] Then the king said to Ziba, "All that belonged to Mephibosheth [h] is now yours."

"I humbly bow," Ziba said. "May I find favor in your eyes, my lord the king."

Shimei Curses David

[5] As King David approached Bahurim, [i] a man from the same clan as Saul's family came out from there. His name was Shimei [j] son of Gera, and he cursed [k] as he came out. [6] He pelted David and all the king's officials with stones, though all the troops and the special guard were on David's right and left. [7] As he cursed, Shimei said, "Get out, get out, you man of blood, you scoundrel! [8] The LORD has repaid you for all the blood you shed in the household of Saul, in whose place you have reigned. [l] The LORD has handed the kingdom over to your son Absalom. You have come to ruin because you are a man of blood!" [m]

[9] Then Abishai [n] son of Zeruiah said to the king, "Why should this dead dog [o] curse my lord the king? Let me go over and cut off his head." [p]

[10] But the king said, "What do you and I have in common, you sons of Zeruiah? [q] If he is cursing because the LORD said to him, 'Curse David,' who can ask, 'Why do you do this?'" [r]

[11] David then said to Abishai and all his officials, "My son, [s] who is of my own flesh, is trying to take my life. How much more, then, this Benjamite! Leave him alone; let him curse, for the LORD has told him to. [t] [12] It may be that the LORD will see my distress [u] and repay me with good [v] for the cursing I am receiving today." [w]

[13] So David and his men continued along the road while Shimei was going along the hillside opposite him, cursing as he went and throwing stones at him and showering him with dirt. [14] The king and all the people with him arrived at their destination exhausted. [x] And there he refreshed himself.

The Advice of Hushai and Ahithophel

[15] Meanwhile, Absalom [y] and all the men of Israel came to Jerusalem, and Ahithophel [z] was with him. [16] Then Hushai [a] the Arkite, David's friend, went to Absalom and said to him, "Long live the king! Long live the king!"

[17] Absalom asked Hushai, "Is this the love you show your friend? Why didn't you go with your friend?" [b]

[18] Hushai said to Absalom, "No, the one chosen by the LORD, by these people, and by all the men of Israel—his I will be, and I will remain with him. [19] Furthermore, whom should I serve? Should I not serve the son? Just as I served your father, so I will serve you." [c]

[20] Absalom said to Ahithophel, "Give us your advice. What should we do?"

[21] Ahithophel answered, "Lie with your

Cross references (center column)

16:1 [c] 2Sa 9:1-13
[d] S 1Sa 25:18;
1Ch 12:40
16:2 [e] 2Sa 17:27-29
16:3 [f] 2Sa 9:9-10
[g] S 2Sa 9:2
16:4 [h] S 2Sa 4:4
16:5 [i] S 2Sa 3:16
[j] 2Sa 19:16-23;
1Ki 2:8-9,36,44
[k] S Ge 22:28
16:8 [l] 2Sa 19:28;
21:9 [m] 2Sa 19:19;
Ps 55:3
16:9 [n] S 1Sa 26:6

[o] S 2Sa 3:8
[p] S 2Sa 3:39;
Lk 9:54
16:10
[q] S 2Sa 2:18;
19:22 [r] Ro 9:20
16:11 [s] 2Sa 12:11
[t] S Ge 45:5;
1Sa 26:19
16:12 [u] Ps 4:1;
25:18 [v] Dt 23:5;
Ro 8:28
[w] Ps 109:28
16:14 [x] 2Sa 17:2
16:15
[y] S 2Sa 15:37
[z] S 2Sa 15:12
16:16
[a] S 2Sa 15:32
16:17 [b] 2Sa 19:25
16:19 [c] 2Sa 15:34

16:1 *Ziba.* See ch. 9. *Mephibosheth.* See note on 4:4.
16:2 *Ziba answered.* Since David assumed control of Saul's estate (9:7–10), Ziba, always the opportunist, seeks to profit from the political crisis.
16:3 *your master's grandson.* Mephibosheth (see 9:3,9).
16:4 *All that belonged to Mephibosheth is now yours.* Because the revolt was so widespread and loyalties so uncertain, David was quick to assume the worst.
16:5 *Bahurim.* On the eastern slope of the Mount of Olives (see note on 3:16). *same clan as Saul's family.* The clan of Matri (see 1Sa 10:21). *Gera.* His exact relation to Saul is unknown (see note on 1Ki 2:8).
16:6 *troops and special guard.* The Kerethites, Pelethites and 600 Gittites (see 15:18).
16:7 *scoundrel.* See note on Dt 13:13.
16:8 *blood you shed in the household of Saul.* Shimei may

be referring to the executions reported in 21:1–14, but the time of that event is uncertain (see note on 21:1).
16:9 *Abishai.* See note on 1Sa 26:6. *this dead dog.* An expression of absolute contempt (see note on 9:8).
16:10 *If . . . because the LORD said to him, 'Curse David.'* David leaves open the possibility that God has seen fit to terminate his rule—the verdict is not yet in (see 15:26). For David's later actions regarding Shimei see 19:18–23; 1Ki 2:8–9.
16:15 *Ahithophel.* See note on 15:12.
16:16 *Hushai the Arkite, David's friend.* See notes on 15:32,37.
16:21 *Lie with your father's concubines.* This would signify Absalom's assumption of royal power; it would also be a definitive and irreversible declaration of the break between father and son (see notes on 3:7; 12:8; 1Ki 2:22).

father's concubines whom he left to take care of the palace. Then all Israel will hear that you have made yourself a stench in your father's nostrils, and the hands of everyone with you will be strengthened." [22]So they pitched a tent for Absalom on the roof, and he lay with his father's concubines in the sight of all Israel. [d]

[23]Now in those days the advice[e] Ahithophel gave was like that of one who inquires of God. That was how both David[f] and Absalom regarded all of Ahithophel's advice.

17 Ahithophel said to Absalom, "I would[t] choose twelve thousand men and set out tonight in pursuit of David. [2]I would[u] attack him while he is weary and weak.[g] I would[u] strike him with terror, and then all the people with him will flee. I would[u] strike down only the king[h] [3]and bring all the people back to you. The death of the man you seek will mean the return of all; all the people will be unharmed." [4]This plan seemed good to Absalom and to all the elders of Israel.

[5]But Absalom said, "Summon also Hushai[i] the Arkite, so we can hear what he has to say." [6]When Hushai came to him, Absalom said, "Ahithophel has given this advice. Should we do what he says? If not, give us your opinion."

[7]Hushai replied to Absalom, "The advice Ahithophel has given is not good this time. [8]You know your father and his men; they are fighters, and as fierce as a wild bear robbed of her cubs.[j] Besides, your father is an experienced fighter;[k] he will not spend the night with the troops. [9]Even now, he is hidden in a cave or some other place.[l] If he should attack your troops first,[v] whoever hears about it will say, 'There has been a slaughter among the troops who follow Absalom.' [10]Then even the bravest soldier, whose heart is like the heart of a lion,[m] will melt[n] with fear, for all Israel knows that your father is a fighter and that those with him are brave.[o]

[11]"So I advise you: Let all Israel, from Dan to Beersheba[p]—as numerous as the sand[q] on the seashore—be gathered to you, with you yourself leading them into battle. [12]Then we will attack him wherever he may be found, and we will fall on him as dew settles on the ground. Neither he nor any of his men will be left alive. [13]If he withdraws into a city, then all Israel will bring ropes to that city, and we will drag it down to the valley[r] until not even a piece of it can be found."

[14]Absalom and all the men of Israel said, "The advice[s] of Hushai the Arkite is better than that of Ahithophel."[t] For the LORD had determined to frustrate[u] the good advice of Ahithophel in order to bring disaster[v] on Absalom.[w]

[15]Hushai told Zadok and Abiathar, the priests, "Ahithophel has advised Absalom and the elders of Israel to do such and such, but I have advised them to do so and so. [16]Now send a message immediately and tell David, 'Do not spend the night at the fords in the desert;[x] cross over without fail, or the king and all the people with him will be swallowed up.[y] ' "

[17]Jonathan[z] and Ahimaaz were staying at En Rogel.[a] A servant girl was to go and inform them, and they were to go and tell King David, for they could not risk being seen entering the city. [18]But a young man saw them and told Absalom. So the two of them left quickly and went to the house of a man in Bahurim.[b] He had a well in his courtyard, and they climbed down into it. [19]His wife took a covering and spread it out over the opening of the well and scattered grain over it. No one knew anything about it.[c]

[20]When Absalom's men came to the woman[d] at the house, they asked, "Where are Ahimaaz and Jonathan?"

The woman answered them, "They

Cross references (center column):

16:22 [d]S 2Sa 3:7;
12:11-12;
S 15:16
16:23
[e]2Sa 17:14,23
[f]S 2Sa 15:12
17:2 [g]2Sa 16:14
[h]1Ki 22:31;
Zec 13:7
17:5 [i]S 2Sa 15:32
17:8 [j]Hos 13:8
[k]1Sa 16:18
17:9 [l]Jer 41:9
17:10 [m]1Ch 12:8
[n]Jos 2:9,11;
Eze 21:15
[o]2Sa 23:8;
1Ch 11:11

17:11 [p]S Jdg 20:1
[q]S Ge 12:2;
S Jos 11:4
17:13 [r]Mic 1:6
17:14
[s]S 2Sa 16:23
[t]S 2Sa 15:12
[u]S 2Sa 15:34;
Ne 4:15 [v]Ps 9:16
[w]2Ch 10:8
17:16 [x]2Sa 15:28
[y]2Sa 15:35
17:17
[z]S 2Sa 15:27,36
[a]Jos 15:7; 18:16;
1Ki 1:9
17:18
[b]S 2Sa 3:16
17:19 [c]S Jos 2:6
17:20 [d]S Ex 1:19

Footnotes:

[t]1 Or Let me   [u]2 Or will   [v]9 Or When some of the men fall at the first attack

---

16:22 *he lay with his father's concubines.* A fulfillment of Nathan's prophecy (12:11–12). For additional significance see note on v. 21.

17:1–3 Ahithophel's advice to Absalom envisioned a cheap and easy victory that would not leave the nation weakened.

17:4 *all the elders of Israel.* See note on 3:17. Absalom's rebellion appears to have gained extensive backing from prominent tribal leaders.

17:5 *Hushai the Arkite.* See 16:16–19; see also notes on 15:32,37.

17:7–13 Hushai's advice subtly capitalizes on Absalom's uncertainty, his fear and his egotism.

17:12 *we . . . we.* Hushai carefully links himself with the revolt.

17:14 *the LORD had determined to frustrate the good advice of Ahithophel.* An answer to David's prayer (see 15:31; cf. Ps 33:10; Pr 21:30).

17:15 *Zadok and Abiathar.* See 15:24–29,35–36.

17:16 *fords in the desert.* See 15:28 and note. *cross over.* Hushai advises David to cross the Jordan River, knowing that Absalom might change his mind and immediately set out after him.

17:17 *Jonathan and Ahimaaz.* See 15:36. *En Rogel.* A spring in the Kidron Valley just outside the walls of Jerusalem. *A servant girl.* A servant girl going to the spring for water would attract no attention.

17:18 *Bahurim.* See note on 16:5.

crossed over the brook." w The men searched but found no one, so they returned to Jerusalem.

21After the men had gone, the two climbed out of the well and went to inform King David. They said to him, "Set out and cross the river at once; Ahithophel has advised such and such against you." 22So David and all the people with him set out and crossed the Jordan. By daybreak, no one was left who had not crossed the Jordan.

23When Ahithophel saw that his advice e had not been followed, he saddled his donkey and set out for his house in his hometown. He put his house in order f and then hanged himself. So he died and was buried in his father's tomb.

24David went to Mahanaim, g and Absalom crossed the Jordan with all the men of Israel. 25Absalom had appointed Amasa h over the army in place of Joab. Amasa was the son of a man named Jether, x i an Israelite y who had married Abigail, z the daughter of Nahash and sister of Zeruiah the mother of Joab. 26The Israelites and Absalom camped in the land of Gilead.

27When David came to Mahanaim, Shobi son of Nahash j from Rabbah k of the Ammonites, and Makir l son of Ammiel from Lo Debar, and Barzillai m the Gileadite n from Rogelim 28brought bedding and bowls and articles of pottery. They also brought wheat and barley, flour and roasted grain, beans and lentils, a 29honey and curds, sheep, and cheese from cows' milk for David and his people to eat. o For they said, "The people have become hungry and tired and thirsty in the desert. p"

Absalom's Death

18 David mustered the men who were with him and appointed over them commanders of thousands and commanders of hundreds. 2David sent the troops out q—a third under the command of Joab, a third under Joab's brother Abishai r son of Zeruiah, and a third under Ittai s the Gittite. The king told the troops, "I myself will surely march out with you."

3But the men said, "You must not go out; if we are forced to flee, they won't care about us. Even if half of us die, they won't care; but you are worth ten t thousand of us. b It would be better now for you to give us support from the city." u

4The king answered, "I will do whatever seems best to you."

So the king stood beside the gate while all the men marched out in units of hundreds and of thousands. 5The king commanded Joab, Abishai and Ittai, "Be gentle with the young man Absalom for my sake." And all the troops heard the king giving orders concerning Absalom to each of the commanders.

6The army marched into the field to fight Israel, and the battle took place in the forest v of Ephraim. 7There the army of Israel was defeated by David's men, and the casualties that day were great—twenty thousand men. 8The battle spread out over the whole countryside, and the forest claimed more lives that day than the sword.

9Now Absalom happened to meet David's men. He was riding his mule, and as

Cross references (center column)

17:23
e S 2Sa 16:23
f 2Ki 20:1
17:24 g S Ge 32:2
17:25
h 2Sa 19:13; 20:4,
9-12; 1Ki 2:5,32;
1Ch 12:18
i 1Ch 2:13-17
17:27 j S 1Sa 11:1
k S Dt 3:11
l 2Sa 9:4
m 2Sa 19:31-39;
1Ki 2:7
n 2Sa 19:31;
Ezr 2:61
17:29
o 1Ch 12:40
p 2Sa 16:2;
S Ro 12:13

18:2 q S Jdg 7:16;
1Sa 11:11
r S 1Sa 26:6
s 2Sa 15:19
18:3 t S 1Sa 18:7
u 2Sa 21:17
18:6 v S Jos 17:15

Textual notes

w 20 Or "They passed by the sheep pen toward the water." x 25 Hebrew Ithra, a variant of Jether y 25 Hebrew and some Septuagint manuscripts; other Septuagint manuscripts (see also 1 Chron. 2:17) Ishmaelite or Jezreelite z 25 Hebrew Abigal, a variant of Abigail a 28 Most Septuagint manuscripts and Syriac; Hebrew lentils, and roasted grain b 3 Two Hebrew manuscripts, some Septuagint manuscripts and Vulgate; most Hebrew manuscripts care; for now there are ten thousand like us

Study notes

17:23 his hometown. Giloh (see note on 15:12). hanged himself. Ahithophel was convinced that the rebellion would fail and that he would be found guilty of treason as a co-conspirator.
17:24 Mahanaim. Ironically the same place where Ish-Bosheth had sought refuge after Saul's death (2:8).
17:25 Amasa. Nephew of David and cousin of both Absalom and Joab son of Zeruiah. Abigail, the daughter of Nahash and sister of Zeruiah. Zeruiah was David's sister (1Ch 2:16). Since the father of Abigail and Zeruiah is Nahash rather than Jesse, it would appear that their unnamed mother married Jesse after the death of Nahash.
17:27 Shobi son of Nahash. Apparently the brother of Hanun (see 10:2-4), whom David had defeated earlier in his reign (12:26-31). Rabbah of the Ammonites. See note on 10:3. Makir. See note on 9:4. Barzillai. A wealthy benefactor of David during his flight to Mahanaim (see 19:32; 1Ki 2:7). After the Babylonian exile, there were claimants to the priesthood among his descendants (Ezr 2:61-63; Ne 7:63).
18:2 Ittai the Gittite. See 15:18-22.

18:3 You must not go out. In addition to the reason given, David was growing old and was no longer the warrior he had been (see note on 15:7). This is essentially the same idea that Ahithophel had expressed to Absalom (see 17:2).
18:5 Be gentle with . . . Absalom for my sake. David's love for his (now) oldest son was undying—and almost his undoing (see 19:5-7).
18:6 Israel. Absalom's army (see 15:13; 16:15; 17:4,11, 24-26). forest of Ephraim. The battle was apparently fought in Gilead, east of the Jordan (see 17:24,26). Why this area is termed the "forest of Ephraim" is not clear (perhaps it comes from an Ephraimite claim on the area; see Jdg 12:1-4).
18:8 The battle spread out. The armies apparently became dispersed, and many of the men got lost in the forest.
18:9 his mule. See note on 13:29. Absalom's head got caught in the tree. Whether by the entanglement of his abundant hair (14:26) or by some other means is not stated, but his handsome head (see 14:25) was in the end—ironically—his undoing.

the mule went under the thick branches of a large oak, Absalom's head[w] got caught in the tree. He was left hanging in midair, while the mule he was riding kept on going.

[10]When one of the men saw this, he told Joab, "I just saw Absalom hanging in an oak tree."

[11]Joab said to the man who had told him this, "What! You saw him? Why didn't you strike[x] him to the ground right there? Then I would have had to give you ten shekels[c] of silver and a warrior's belt.[y]"

[12]But the man replied, "Even if a thousand shekels[d] were weighed out into my hands, I would not lift my hand against the king's son. In our hearing the king commanded you and Abishai and Ittai, 'Protect the young man Absalom for my sake.[e]' [13]And if I had put my life in jeopardy[f]—and nothing is hidden from the king[z]—you would have kept your distance from me."

[14]Joab[a] said, "I'm not going to wait like this for you." So he took three javelins in his hand and plunged them into Absalom's heart while Absalom was still alive in the oak tree. [15]And ten of Joab's armor-bearers surrounded Absalom, struck him and killed him.[b]

[16]Then Joab[c] sounded the trumpet, and the troops stopped pursuing Israel, for Joab halted them. [17]They took Absalom, threw him into a big pit in the forest and piled up[d] a large heap of rocks[e] over him. Meanwhile, all the Israelites fled to their homes.

[18]During his lifetime Absalom had taken a pillar and erected it in the King's Valley[f] as a monument[g] to himself, for he thought, "I have no son[h] to carry on the memory of my name." He named the pillar after himself, and it is called Absalom's Monument to this day.

David Mourns

[19]Now Ahimaaz[i] son of Zadok said, "Let me run and take the news to the king

that the LORD has delivered him from the hand of his enemies.[j]"

[20]"You are not the one to take the news today," Joab told him. "You may take the news another time, but you must not do so today, because the king's son is dead."

[21]Then Joab said to a Cushite, "Go, tell the king what you have seen." The Cushite bowed down before Joab and ran off.

[22]Ahimaaz son of Zadok again said to Joab, "Come what may, please let me run behind the Cushite."

But Joab replied, "My son, why do you want to go? You don't have any news that will bring you a reward."

[23]He said, "Come what may, I want to run."

So Joab said, "Run!" Then Ahimaaz ran by way of the plain[g] and outran the Cushite.

[24]While David was sitting between the inner and outer gates, the watchman[k] went up to the roof of the gateway by the wall. As he looked out, he saw a man running alone. [25]The watchman called out to the king and reported it.

The king said, "If he is alone, he must have good news." And the man came closer and closer.

[26]Then the watchman saw another man running, and he called down to the gatekeeper, "Look, another man running alone!"

The king said, "He must be bringing good news,[l] too."

[27]The watchman said, "It seems to me that the first one runs like[m] Ahimaaz son of Zadok."

"He's a good man," the king said. "He comes with good news."

[28]Then Ahimaaz called out to the king, "All is well!" He bowed down before the

Cross references (center column)

18:9 [w]2Sa 14:26
18:11 [x]S 2Sa 3:39
[y]1Sa 18:4
18:13 [z]2Sa 14:19-20
18:14 [a]S 2Sa 2:18
18:15 [b]S 2Sa 12:10
18:16 [c]S 2Sa 2:28
18:17 [d]Jos 7:26
[e]Jos 8:29
18:18 [f]Ge 14:17
[g]S Ge 50:5; S Nu 32:42
[h]2Sa 14:27
18:19 [i]S 2Sa 15:36

[j]Jdg 11:36
18:24 [k]S 1Sa 14:16; S Jer 51:12
18:26 [l]1Ki 1:42; Isa 52:7; 61:1
18:27 [m]2Ki 9:20

Footnotes

[c]11 That is, about 4 ounces (about 115 grams)
[d]12 That is, about 25 pounds (about 11 kilograms)
[e]12 A few Hebrew manuscripts, Septuagint, Vulgate and Syriac; most Hebrew manuscripts may be translated *Absalom, whoever you may be.*   [f]13 Or *Otherwise, if I had acted treacherously toward him*   [g]23 That is, the plain of the Jordan

---

18:11 *I would have had to give you.* Joab must be referring to an announced intent on his part to reward anyone killing Absalom. His actions and interests did not always coincide with David's wishes (see note on 2:13).
18:15 *killed him.* The easiest and most certain way of ending the rebellion—but the brutal overkill is indicative of the deep animosity felt by David's men against Absalom.
18:17 *large heap of rocks.* A mound of rocks that mocked the monument Absalom himself had erected (v. 18). *all the Israelites.* See note on v. 6.
18:18 *erected it ... as a monument to himself.* As Saul had done (1Sa 15:12). *King's Valley.* Thought to be located near Jerusalem (see Ge 14:17; Josephus, *Antiquities,*

7.10.3). *I have no son.* See 14:27 and note. *Absalom's Monument.* Not to be confused with the much later monument of the same name that is still visible today in the valley east of Jerusalem.
18:19 *Ahimaaz son of Zadok.* See 15:27; 17:17–21.
18:20 *not the one to take the news.* The choice of a messenger depended on the content of the message (see v. 27 and note).
18:21 *Cushite.* An alien (see notes on Ge 10:6–8; Am 9:7).
18:27 *He comes with good news.* David presumed that Joab would not have sent someone like Ahimaaz to carry bad news (see v. 20 and note).

king with his face to the ground and said, "Praise be to the LORD your God! He has delivered up the men who lifted their hands against my lord the king."

29The king asked, "Is the young man Absalom safe?"

Ahimaaz answered, "I saw great confusion just as Joab was about to send the king's servant and me, your servant, but I don't know what it was."

30The king said, "Stand aside and wait here." So he stepped aside and stood there.

31Then the Cushite arrived and said, "My lord the king, hear the good news! The LORD has delivered you today from all who rose up against you."

32The king asked the Cushite, "Is the young man Absalom safe?"

The Cushite replied, "May the enemies of my lord the king and all who rise up to harm you be like that young man." n

33The king was shaken. He went up to the room over the gateway and wept. As he went, he said: "O my son Absalom! My son, my son Absalom! If only I had died o instead of you—O Absalom, my son, my son!" p

19 Joab was told, "The king is weeping and mourning for Absalom." 2And for the whole army the victory that day was turned into mourning, because on that day the troops heard it said, "The king is grieving for his son." 3The men stole into the city that day as men steal in who are ashamed when they flee from battle. 4The king covered his face and cried aloud, "O my son Absalom! O Absalom, my son, my son!"

5Then Joab went into the house to the king and said, "Today you have humiliated all your men, who have just saved your life and the lives of your sons and daughters and the lives of your wives and concubines. 6You love those who hate you and hate those who love you. You have made it

clear today that the commanders and their men mean nothing to you. I see that you would be pleased if Absalom were alive today and all of us were dead. 7Now go out and encourage your men. I swear by the LORD that if you don't go out, not a man will be left with you by nightfall. This will be worse for you than all the calamities that have come upon you from your youth till now." q

8So the king got up and took his seat in the gateway. When the men were told, "The king is sitting in the gateway," r they all came before him.

David Returns to Jerusalem

Meanwhile, the Israelites had fled to their homes. 9Throughout the tribes of Israel, the people were all arguing with each other, saying, "The king delivered us from the hand of our enemies; he is the one who rescued us from the hand of the Philistines. s But now he has fled the country because of Absalom; t 10and Absalom, whom we anointed to rule over us, has died in battle. So why do you say nothing about bringing the king back?"

11King David sent this message to Zadok u and Abiathar, the priests: "Ask the elders of Judah, 'Why should you be the last to bring the king back to his palace, since what is being said throughout Israel has reached the king at his quarters? 12You are my brothers, my own flesh and blood. So why should you be the last to bring back the king?' 13And say to Amasa, v 'Are you not my own flesh and blood? w May God deal with me, be it ever so severely, x if from now on you are not the commander of my army in place of Joab.' y ' "

14He won over the hearts of all the men of Judah as though they were one man. They sent word to the king, "Return, you and all your men." 15Then the king returned and went as far as the Jordan.

Now the men of Judah had come to Gil-

18:32 nJdg 5:31; S 1Sa 25:26
18:33 oEx 32:32
pS Ge 43:14; 2Sa 19:4

19:7 qPr 14:28
19:8 rS 2Sa 15:2
19:9 s2Sa 8:1-14
t2Sa 15:14
19:11 uS 2Sa 15:24
19:13 vS 2Sa 17:25
wS Ge 29:14
xS Ru 1:17
yS 2Sa 2:13

18:29 *I saw great confusion.* Ahimaaz avoids a direct answer to David's question, though he knew Absalom was dead.

18:33 *O my son Absalom!* One of the most moving expressions in all literature of a father's love for a son—in spite of all that Absalom had done.

19:5 *Joab went . . . to the king.* Apparently confident that the king was unaware of his part in Absalom's death. David never indicates that he learned of it (see 1Ki 2:5). *you have humiliated all your men.* Joab boldly rebukes David for allowing his personal grief to keep him from expressing his appreciation for the loyalty of those who risked their lives to preserve his throne. Joab warns David that his love for Absalom can still undo him.

19:9 *The king delivered us.* With Absalom dead, the north-

ern tribes remember what David had done for them (see 3:17–18; 5:2).

19:11 *Ask the elders of Judah.* Even though the rebellion had begun in Hebron in Judah (see 15:9–12), David appeals to the elders of his own tribe to take the initiative in restoring him to the throne in Jerusalem (see 2:4; 1Sa 30:26). This appeal produced the desired result, but it also led to the arousal of tribal jealousies (see vv. 41–42).

19:13 *Amasa.* See 17:25 and note. Although Amasa deserved death for treason, David appointed him commander of his army in place of Joab, hoping to secure the allegiance of those who had followed Amasa, especially the Judahites (see 20:5). *May God deal with me, be it ever so severely.* A curse formula (see note on 1Sa 3:17).

19:15 *Gilgal.* See note on Jos 4:19.

gal[z] to go out and meet the king and bring him across the Jordan. [16]Shimei[a] son of Gera, the Benjamite from Bahurim, hurried down with the men of Judah to meet King David. [17]With him were a thousand Benjamites, along with Ziba,[b] the steward of Saul's household,[c] and his fifteen sons and twenty servants. They rushed to the Jordan, where the king was. [18]They crossed at the ford to take the king's household over and to do whatever he wished.

When Shimei son of Gera crossed the Jordan, he fell prostrate before the king [19]and said to him, "May my lord not hold me guilty. Do not remember how your servant did wrong on the day my lord the king left Jerusalem.[d] May the king put it out of his mind. [20]For I your servant know that I have sinned, but today I have come here as the first of the whole house of Joseph to come down and meet my lord the king."

[21]Then Abishai[e] son of Zeruiah said, "Shouldn't Shimei be put to death for this? He cursed[f] the LORD's anointed."[g]

[22]David replied, "What do you and I have in common, you sons of Zeruiah?[h] This day you have become my adversaries! Should anyone be put to death in Israel today?[i] Do I not know that today I am king over Israel?" [23]So the king said to Shimei, "You shall not die." And the king promised him on oath.[j]

[24]Mephibosheth,[k] Saul's grandson, also went down to meet the king. He had not taken care of his feet or trimmed his mustache or washed his clothes from the day the king left until the day he returned safely. [25]When he came from Jerusalem to meet the king, the king asked him, "Why didn't you go with me,[l] Mephibosheth?"

[26]He said, "My lord the king, since I your servant am lame,[m] I said, 'I will have

my donkey saddled and will ride on it, so I can go with the king.' But Ziba[n] my servant betrayed me. [27]And he has slandered your servant to my lord the king. My lord the king is like an angel[o] of God; so do whatever pleases you. [28]All my grandfather's descendants deserved nothing but death[p] from my lord the king, but you gave your servant a place among those who eat at your table.[q] So what right do I have to make any more appeals to the king?"

[29]The king said to him, "Why say more? I order you and Ziba to divide the fields."

[30]Mephibosheth said to the king, "Let him take everything, now that my lord the king has arrived home safely."

[31]Barzillai[r] the Gileadite also came down from Rogelim to cross the Jordan with the king and to send him on his way from there. [32]Now Barzillai was a very old man, eighty years of age. He had provided for the king during his stay in Mahanaim, for he was a very wealthy[s] man. [33]The king said to Barzillai, "Cross over with me and stay with me in Jerusalem, and I will provide for you."

[34]But Barzillai answered the king, "How many more years will I live, that I should go up to Jerusalem with the king? [35]I am now eighty[t] years old. Can I tell the difference between what is good and what is not? Can your servant taste what he eats and drinks? Can I still hear the voices of men and women singers?[u] Why should your servant be an added[v] burden to my lord the king? [36]Your servant will cross over the Jordan with the king for a short distance, but why should the king reward me in this way? [37]Let your servant return, that I may die in my own town near the tomb of my father[w] and mother. But here is your servant Kimham.[x] Let him cross

---

Cross references (center column):

19:15
[z]S 1Sa 11:15
19:16
[a]2Sa 16:5-13
19:17 [b]S 2Sa 9:2
[c]S Ge 43:16
19:19
[d]S 2Sa 16:6-8
19:21
[e]S 1Sa 26:6
[f]S Ex 22:28
[g]S 1Sa 12:3;
S 26:9
19:22
[h]S 2Sa 2:18;
S 16:10
[i]1Sa 11:13
19:23 /1Ki 2:8,42
19:24 [k]S 2Sa 4:4
19:25 [l]2Sa 16:17
19:26
[m]S Lev 21:18

[n]S 2Sa 9:2
19:27
[o]S 1Sa 29:9
19:28
[p]S 2Sa 16:8
[q]S 2Sa 9:7,13
19:31
[r]S 2Sa 17:27-29,
27; 1Ki 2:7
19:32 [s]1Sa 25:2
19:35 [t]Ps 90:10
[u]2Ch 35:25;
Ezr 2:65; Ecc 2:8;
12:1 [v]2Sa 15:33
19:37
[w]S Ge 49:29
[x]Jer 41:17

19:17 *a thousand Benjamites.* No doubt fearing they would be suspected by the king of being implicated in Shimei's deed.

19:20 *I your servant know that I have sinned.* Shimei's guilt was common knowledge; he could only seize the most appropriate time to plead for mercy. *house of Joseph.* A common way of referring to the northern tribes (see 1Ki 11:28; Eze 37:19; Am 5:6; Zec 10:6)—of which Ephraim and Manasseh (sons of Joseph) were the most prominent (see Nu 26:28; Jos 18:5; Jdg 1:22).

19:21 *Abishai.* See 16:9; see also note on 1Sa 26:6. *the LORD's anointed.* See note on 1Sa 9:16; see also 1Sa 24:6; 26:9–11; Ex 22:28; 1Ki 21:10.

19:22 *Should anyone be put to death in Israel today?* It was a day for general amnesty (see 1Sa 11:13).

19:23 *You shall not die.* David kept his pledge; he would not himself avenge the wrong committed against him (see note on 1Sa 25:2–44). But on his deathbed he instructed

Solomon to take Shimei's case in hand (see 1Ki 2:8–9, 36–46).

19:24 *Mephibosheth.* See 9:6–13.

19:25 *Why didn't you go with me . . . ?* David remembers Ziba's previous allegations (see 16:3).

19:26 *lame.* See 4:4; 9:3.

19:27 *he has slandered your servant.* See 16:3. *like an angel of God.* See 14:17 and note. *do whatever pleases you.* Mephibosheth discreetly requests David to reconsider the grant of his property to Ziba (see 16:4).

19:29 *divide the fields.* Faced with conflicting testimony that could not be corroborated, David withholds judgment and orders the division of Saul's estate.

19:31 *Barzillai.* See note on 17:27.

19:35 *difference between what is good and what is not.* At his age, he would be indifferent to all the pleasures of the court.

19:37 *Kimham.* Likely a son of Barzillai (see 1Ki 2:7).

over with my lord the king. Do for him whatever pleases you."

38The king said, "Kimham shall cross over with me, and I will do for him whatever pleases you. And anything you desire from me I will do for you."

39So all the people crossed the Jordan, and then the king crossed over. The king kissed Barzillai and gave him his blessing,*y* and Barzillai returned to his home.

40When the king crossed over to Gilgal, Kimham crossed with him. All the troops of Judah and half the troops of Israel had taken the king over.

41Soon all the men of Israel were coming to the king and saying to him, "Why did our brothers, the men of Judah, steal the king away and bring him and his household across the Jordan, together with all his men?"*z*

42All the men of Judah answered the men of Israel, "We did this because the king is closely related to us. Why are you angry about it? Have we eaten any of the king's provisions? Have we taken anything for ourselves?"

43Then the men of Israel*a* answered the men of Judah, "We have ten shares in the king; and besides, we have a greater claim on David than you have. So why do you treat us with contempt? Were we not the first to speak of bringing back our king?"

But the men of Judah responded even more harshly than the men of Israel.

Sheba Rebels Against David

20 Now a troublemaker named Sheba son of Bicri, a Benjamite, happened to be there. He sounded the trumpet and shouted,

19:39 *y*S Ge 47:7
19:41 *z*Jdg 8:1;
12:1
19:43 *a*S 2Sa 5:1

"We have no share*b* in David,*c*
  no part in Jesse's son!*d*
Every man to his tent, O Israel!"

2So all the men of Israel deserted David to follow Sheba son of Bicri. But the men of Judah stayed by their king all the way from the Jordan to Jerusalem.

3When David returned to his palace in Jerusalem, he took the ten concubines*e* he had left to take care of the palace and put them in a house under guard. He provided for them, but did not lie with them. They were kept in confinement till the day of their death, living as widows.

4Then the king said to Amasa,*f* "Summon the men of Judah to come to me within three days, and be here yourself." 5But when Amasa went to summon Judah, he took longer than the time the king had set for him.

6David said to Abishai,*g* "Now Sheba son of Bicri will do us more harm than Absalom did. Take your master's men and pursue him, or he will find fortified cities and escape from us." 7So Joab's men and the Kerethites*h* and Pelethites and all the mighty warriors went out under the command of Abishai. They marched out from Jerusalem to pursue Sheba son of Bicri.

8While they were at the great rock in Gibeon,*i* Amasa came to meet them. Joab*j* was wearing his military tunic, and strapped over it at his waist was a belt with a dagger in its sheath. As he stepped forward, it dropped out of its sheath.

9Joab said to Amasa, "How are you, my brother?" Then Joab took Amasa by the beard with his right hand to kiss him. 10Amasa was not on his guard against the dagger*k* in Joab's hand, and Joab plunged

20:1 *b*S Ge 31:14
*c*S Ge 29:14;
1Ki 12:16
*d*1Sa 22:7-8
20:3
*e*S 2Sa 15:16
20:4 *f*S 2Sa 17:25
20:6 *g*2Sa 21:17
20:7
*h*S 1Sa 30:14;
S 2Sa 15:18
20:8 *i*S Jos 9:3
*j*S 2Sa 2:18
20:10 *k*S Jdg 3:21
*l*1Ki 2:5

19:41 *Why did . . . the men of Judah, steal the king away and bring him . . . across the Jordan . . . ?* It seems that the Jordan was a kind of psychological border to the land of Israel (see Jos 22:19,25; Jdg 12:4)—which may also explain why Ish-Bosheth (2:8), Mephibosheth (9:4) and even David himself (17:22) had sought refuge in Transjordan. That being the case, the protest of the Israelites may be that the Judahites had not waited for all Israel to assemble before bringing David across the Jordan, thus leaving the Israelites in a bad light—as though they were reluctant to receive the king back (see v. 43).
19:43 *ten shares.* The ten tribes, excluding Judah and Simeon (see note on 2:4). *we have a greater claim on David.* The grounds for this assertion may be that the Lord had chosen David to reign in the place of Saul (see 3:17–18; 5:2).
20:1 *troublemaker.* See note on Dt 13:13. *Bicri.* Benjamin's second son (Beker, Ge 46:21; 1Ch 7:6–9). *Benjamite.* Tribal jealousy still simmered over the transfer of the royal house from Benjamin (Saul's tribe) to Judah. *there.* In Gilgal (19:40–43). *We have no share in David.* Sheba appeals to the Israelite suspicion that David favored his own tribe Judah

over the other tribes (see 1Ki 12:16).
20:2 *all the men of Israel.* Those referred to in 19:41–43.
20:3 *ten concubines.* See notes on 15:16; 16:22.
20:4 *Amasa.* See notes on 17:25; 19:13. David bypasses Joab.
20:6 *Abishai.* David bypasses Joab a second time (see v. 7). *your master's men.* "Joab's men" (v. 7).
20:7 *Joab's men.* See 18:2. It becomes clear that Joab also accompanied the soldiers and, though not in command (by the king's order), he was obviously the leader recognized by the soldiers (see vv. 7,11,15). *Kerethites and Pelethites.* See note on 8:18. *mighty warriors.* See 23:8–39. Once more in a time of crisis David depended mainly on the small force of professionals (many of them non-Israelite) who made up his private army.
20:8 *Gibeon.* See note on 2:12. *Amasa came.* Apparently with some troops (see v. 11 and note).
20:10 *into his belly.* See 2:23; 3:27. For the second time Joab commits murder to secure his position as commander of David's army (see 1Ki 2:5–6). *Joab and his brother Abishai.* In defiance of David's order, Joab reassumes command on his own initiative (see v. 23).

it into his belly, and his intestines spilled out on the ground. Without being stabbed again, Amasa died. Then Joab and his brother Abishai pursued Sheba son of Bicri.

[11]One of Joab's men stood beside Amasa and said, "Whoever favors Joab, and whoever is for David, let him follow Joab!" [12]Amasa lay wallowing in his blood in the middle of the road, and the man saw that all the troops came to a halt [m] there. When he realized that everyone who came up to Amasa stopped, he dragged him from the road into a field and threw a garment over him. [13]After Amasa had been removed from the road, all the men went on with Joab to pursue Sheba son of Bicri.

[14]Sheba passed through all the tribes of Israel to Abel Beth Maacah [h] and through the entire region of the Berites, [n] who gathered together and followed him. [15]All the troops with Joab came and besieged Sheba in Abel Beth Maacah. [o] They built a siege ramp [p] up to the city, and it stood against the outer fortifications. While they were battering the wall to bring it down, [16]a wise woman [q] called from the city, "Listen! Listen! Tell Joab to come here so I can speak to him." [17]He went toward her, and she asked, "Are you Joab?"

"I am," he answered.

She said, "Listen to what your servant has to say."

"I'm listening," he said.

[18]She continued, "Long ago they used to say, 'Get your answer at Abel,' and that settled it. [19]We are the peaceful [r] and

faithful in Israel. You are trying to destroy a city that is a mother in Israel. Why do you want to swallow up the LORD's inheritance?" [s]

[20]"Far be it from me!" Joab replied, "Far be it from me to swallow up or destroy! [21]That is not the case. A man named Sheba son of Bicri, from the hill country of Ephraim, has lifted up his hand against the king, against David. Hand over this one man, and I'll withdraw from the city."

The woman said to Joab, "His head [t] will be thrown to you from the wall."

[22]Then the woman went to all the people with her wise advice, [u] and they cut off the head of Sheba son of Bicri and threw it to Joab. So he sounded the trumpet, and his men dispersed from the city, each returning to his home. And Joab went back to the king in Jerusalem.

[23]Joab [v] was over Israel's entire army; Benaiah son of Jehoiada was over the Kerethites and Pelethites; [24]Adoniram [i] [w] was in charge of forced labor; Jehoshaphat [x] son of Ahilud was recorder; [25]Sheva was secretary; Zadok [y] and Abiathar were priests; [26]and Ira the Jairite was David's priest.

The Gibeonites Avenged

21 During the reign of David, there was a famine [z] for three successive years; so David sought [a] the face of the

20:12
[m]S 2Sa 2:23
20:14 [n]Nu 21:16
20:15
[o]1Ki 15:20;
2Ki 15:29
[p]Isa 37:33;
Jer 6:6; 32:24
20:16 [q]2Sa 14:2
20:19 [r]S Dt 2:26

[s]S 1Sa 26:19
20:21 [t]S 2Sa 4:8
20:22 [u]Ecc 9:13
20:23
[v]S 2Sa 2:28;
8:16-18; 24:2
20:24 [w]1Ki 4:6;
5:14; 12:18;
2Ch 10:18
[x]S 2Sa 8:16
20:25
[y]S 1Sa 2:35;
S 2Sa 8:17
21:1
[z]S Ge 12:10;
S Dt 32:24
[a]S Ex 32:11

[h]14 Or Abel, even Beth Maacah; also in verse 15
[i]24 Some Septuagint manuscripts (see also 1 Kings 4:6 and 5:14); Hebrew Adoram

---

20:11 *Whoever favors Joab, and whoever is for David.* To dispel any idea that Joab was aligned with Sheba's conspiracy, an appeal is made to Amasa's troops to support Joab if they are truly loyal to David.
20:14 *Abel Beth Maacah.* See NIV text note; located to the north of Dan (see 1Ki 15:20; 2Ch 16:4). Sheba's strategy was to gather as many volunteers for his revolt as possible, but he was obviously afraid to assemble his ragtag army anywhere within close reach of David's men. *Berites.* Otherwise unknown.
20:18 *Get your answer at Abel.* The city was famous for the wisdom of its inhabitants.
20:19 *a mother in Israel.* A town that produced faithful Israelites—cities were commonly personified as women (see Jer 50:12; Gal 4:26). *the LORD's inheritance.* See note on 1Sa 10:1.
20:21 *hill country of Ephraim.* Either Sheba, a Benjamite (see v. 1), lived in the tribal territory of Ephraim or this was the designation of a geographical, rather than a strictly tribal, region.
20:22 *Joab went back to the king in Jerusalem.* See notes on vv. 7,10.
20:23–26 These royal officials apparently served David during most of his reign (see 8:15–18).
20:23 *Joab was over Israel's entire army.* Though in some disfavor, he held this position until he participated in Adonijah's conspiracy (1Ki 1:7; 2:28–35). *Kerethites and Pele-*

thites. See note on 8:18.
20:24 *Adoniram was in charge of forced labor.* A position not established in the early years of David's reign (see 8:15–16). Adoniram must have been a late appointee of David since he continued to serve under Solomon (1Ki 4:6; 5:14) and was eventually killed in the early days of the reign of Rehoboam (1Ki 12:18; 2Ch 10:18). *forced labor.* Labor performed for the most part by prisoners of war from defeated nations (see 12:31; Jos 9:21; 1Ki 9:15,20–21). *recorder.* See note on 8:16.
20:25 *Sheva.* See note on 8:17 ("Seraiah"). *secretary.* See note on 8:17. *Zadok and Abiathar.* See note on 8:17.
20:26 *Jairite.* A reference either to Jair of the tribe of Manasseh (Nu 32:41) or to a judge from Gilead (Jdg 10:3,5). *priest.* See note on 8:18.
21:1—24:25 This concluding section forms an appendix to 1,2 Samuel and contains additional materials (without concern for chronology) relating to David's reign. While its topical arrangement is striking, it also employs a literary pattern, *a-b-c-c-b-a*, frequently found elsewhere in OT literature. The first and last units (21:1–14; 24:1–25) are narratives of two events in which David had to deal with God's wrath against Israel (the first occasioned by an act of Saul, the second by his own). The second and fifth units (21:15–22; 23:8–39) are accounts of David's warriors (the second much longer than the first). At the center (22:1–23:7) are two songs of David (the first much longer than the second), one of

LORD. The LORD said, "It is on account of Saul and his blood-stained house; it is because he put the Gibeonites to death."

²The king summoned the Gibeonitesᵇ and spoke to them. (Now the Gibeonites were not a part of Israel but were survivors of the Amorites; the Israelites had sworn to spare them, but Saul in his zeal for Israel and Judah had tried to annihilate them.) ³David asked the Gibeonites, "What shall I do for you? How shall I make amends so that you will bless the LORD's inheritance?"ᶜ

⁴The Gibeonites answered him, "We have no right to demand silver or gold from Saul or his family, nor do we have the right to put anyone in Israel to death."ᵈ

"What do you want me to do for you?" David asked.

⁵They answered the king, "As for the man who destroyed us and plotted against us so that we have been decimated and have no place anywhere in Israel, ⁶let seven of his male descendants be given to us to be killed and exposedᵉ before the LORD at Gibeah of Saul—the Lord's chosenᶠ one."

So the king said, "I will give them to you."

⁷The king spared Mephiboshethᵍ son of Jonathan, the son of Saul, because of the oathʰ before the LORD between David and Jonathan son of Saul. ⁸But the king took Armoni and Mephibosheth, the two sons

of Aiah's daughter Rizpah,ⁱ whom she had borne to Saul, together with the five sons of Saul's daughter Merab,ʲ whom she had borne to Adriel son of Barzillai the Meholathite.ʲ ⁹He handed them over to the Gibeonites, who killed and exposed them on a hill before the LORD. All seven of them fell together; they were put to deathᵏ during the first days of the harvest, just as the barley harvest was beginning.ˡ

¹⁰Rizpah daughter of Aiah took sackcloth and spread it out for herself on a rock. From the beginning of the harvest till the rain poured down from the heavens on the bodies, she did not let the birds of the air touch them by day or the wild animals by night. ᵐ ¹¹When David was told what Aiah's daughter Rizpah, Saul's concubine, had done, ¹²he went and took the bones of Saulⁿ and his son Jonathan from the citizens of Jabesh Gilead.ᵒ (They had taken them secretly from the public square at Beth Shan,ᵖ where the Philistines had hungᵠ them after they struck Saul down on Gilboa.)ʳ ¹³David brought the bones of Saul and his son Jonathan from there, and the bones of those who had been killed and exposed were gathered up.

¹⁴They buried the bones of Saul and his son Jonathan in the tomb of Saul's father Kish, at Zelaˢ in Benjamin, and did every-

Cross references (center column)

21:2 ᵇS Jos 9:15
21:3 ᶜS 1Sa 26:19
21:4 ᵈNu 35:33-34
/S 1Sa 10:24
21:6 ᵉNu 25:4
21:7 ᵍ2Sa 4:4
ʰS 1Sa 18:3;
S 2Sa 9:7

21:8 ⁱ2Sa 3:7
/1Sa 18:19
21:9 ᵏS 2Sa 16:8
/S Ru 1:22
21:10 ᵐS Ge 40:19;
S 1Sa 17:44
21:12 ⁿ1Sa 31:11-13
ᵒS Jdg 21:8;
S 1Sa 11:1
ᵖS Jos 17:11
ᵠ1Sa 31:10
ʳS 1Sa 28:4
21:14 ˢJos 18:28

i8 Two Hebrew manuscripts, some Septuagint manuscripts and Syriac (see also 1 Samuel 18:19); most Hebrew and Septuagint manuscripts *Michal*

---

which celebrates David's victories as warrior-king while the other recalls his role as psalmist (see note on 1Sa 16:14–17:58). It is unknown if motivation for this arrangement went beyond aesthetic considerations. The triumph song of ch. 22 and the song of Hannah in 1Sa 2:1–10 clearly form a literary frame enclosing the main composition (see note on 1Sa 2:1).
21:1–14 This event appears to have occurred after David's kindness was extended to Mephibosheth (ch. 9) and before Absalom's rebellion (16:7–8; 18:28; see note on 16:8).
21:1 *he put the Gibeonites to death.* Saul's action against the Gibeonites is not related elsewhere but appears to have been instituted early in his reign, motivated by an excessive nationalism (if not tribalism—the Gibeonites occupied territory partly assigned to Benjamin, and Saul's great-grandfather was known as the "father of Gibeon," 1Ch 8:29; 9:35).
21:2 *Amorites.* A comprehensive name sometimes used to designate all the pre-Israelite inhabitants of Canaan (Ge 15:16; Jos 24:18; Jdg 6:10; Am 2:10). More precisely, the Gibeonites were called Hivites (Jos 9:7; 11:19). *the Israelites had sworn to spare them.* A pledge sworn in the name of the Lord (Jos 9:15,18–26). *tried to annihilate them.* The reason Saul was unsuccessful is not known.
21:3 *bless.* Since the oath sworn to them had been violated, they could rightly call down God's curse on the land. *the LORD's inheritance.* See note on 1Sa 10:1.
21:4 *nor do we have the right to put anyone in Israel to death.* Bloodguilt could only be redressed by the shedding of blood, but as subject aliens the Gibeonites had no right to

legal redress against an Israelite. This restriction must have been Saul's since it is contrary to the Mosaic law (see Ex 22:21; Lev 19:34; 24:22; Dt 1:16–17; 24:17; 27:19).
21:5 *the man.* Saul. *no place anywhere in Israel.* Those who escaped Saul's attack had been driven from their towns and lands (see 4:2–3 and notes).
21:6 *seven.* Because it would represent a full number (seven symbolized completeness)—though many more Gibeonites had been slain. *Gibeah.* The place of Saul's residence (see 1Sa 10:26).
21:7 *oath before the LORD between David and Jonathan.* See 4:4; 9:1–13; 1Sa 18:3; 20:15.
21:8 *Rizpah.* See 3:7. *Merab.* See 1Sa 18:19. *Barzillai the Meholathite.* Not to be confused with Barzillai the Gileadite (17:27; 19:31).
21:9 *All seven of them fell together.* This nearly extinguished the house of Saul, which God had rejected (see 1Sa 13:13–14; 15:23–26). In 1Ch 8:29–39; 9:35–44 no descendants of Saul are listed other than from the line of Jonathan. *barley harvest was beginning.* About the middle of April (see note on Ru 1:22).
21:10 *sackcloth.* See note on Ge 37:34. *rain poured down.* An indication that the famine was caused by drought and evidence that the judgment on Israel for breaking the oath sworn to the Gibeonites (see v. 1) was now over.
21:12 *bones of Saul and his son Jonathan.* See 1Sa 31:11–13. David's final act toward Saul and Jonathan was a deed of deep respect for the king he had honored and the friend he had loved.

thing the king commanded. After that,[t] God answered prayer[u] in behalf of the land.[v]

Wars Against the Philistines

21:15–22pp — 1Ch 20:4–8

15Once again there was a battle between the Philistines[w] and Israel. David went down with his men to fight against the Philistines, and he became exhausted. 16And Ishbi-Benob, one of the descendants of Rapha, whose bronze spearhead weighed three hundred shekels[k] and who was armed with a new ¸sword¸, said he would kill David. 17But Abishai[x] son of Zeruiah came to David's rescue; he struck the Philistine down and killed him. Then David's men swore to him, saying, "Never again will you go out with us to battle, so that the lamp[y] of Israel will not be extinguished.[z]"

18In the course of time, there was another battle with the Philistines, at Gob. At that time Sibbecai[a] the Hushathite killed Saph, one of the descendants of Rapha.

19In another battle with the Philistines at Gob, Elhanan son of Jaare-Oregim[l] the Bethlehemite killed Goliath[m] the Gittite,[b] who had a spear with a shaft like a weaver's rod.[c]

20In still another battle, which took place at Gath, there was a huge man with six fingers on each hand and six toes on each foot—twenty-four in all. He also was descended from Rapha. 21When he taunt-

ed[d] Israel, Jonathan son of Shimeah,[e] David's brother, killed him.

22These four were descendants of Rapha in Gath, and they fell at the hands of David and his men.

David's Song of Praise

22:1–51pp — Ps 18:1–50

22 David sang[f] to the LORD the words of this song when the LORD delivered him from the hand of all his enemies and from the hand of Saul. 2He said:

"The LORD is my rock,[g] my fortress[h]
        and my deliverer;[i]
3   my God is my rock, in whom I take
            refuge,[j]
    my shield[k] and the horn[n l] of my
            salvation.
    He is my stronghold,[m] my refuge and
            my savior—
    from violent men you save me.
4I call to the LORD, who is worthy[n] of
            praise,
    and I am saved from my enemies.
5"The waves[o] of death swirled about
            me;
        the torrents of destruction
            overwhelmed me.
6The cords of the grave[o p] coiled around
            me;
        the snares of death confronted me.

Cross references (center column)

21:14 [t]Jos 7:26; [u]2Sa 24:25; [v]1Ch 8:34
21:15 [w]S 2Sa 5:25
21:17 [x]2Sa 20:6; [y]1Ki 11:36; 15:4; 2Ki 8:19; 2Ch 21:7; Ps 132:17; [z]2Sa 18:3
21:18 [a]1Ch 11:29; 27:11
21:19 [b]S 1Sa 17:4; [c]S 1Sa 17:7
21:21 [d]S 1Sa 17:10; [e]S 1Sa 16:9
22:1 [f]S Ex 15:1
22:2 [g]S 1Sa 2:2; [h]Ps 31:3; 91:2; [i]Ps 144:2
22:3 [j]S Dt 23:15; S 32:37; Ps 14:6; 31:2; 59:16; 71:7; 91:2; 94:22; Pr 10:29; Isa 25:4; Jer 16:19; Joel 3:16; [k]S Ge 15:1; [l]S Dt 33:17; S Lk 1:69; [m]Ps 9:9; 52:7
22:4 [n]Ps 48:1; 96:4; 145:3
22:5 [o]Ps 69:14-15; Jnh 2:3
22:6 [p]Ps 116:3; Ac 2:24

k16 That is, about 7 1/2 pounds (about 3.5 kilograms)   l19 Or *son of Jair the weaver*   m19 Hebrew and Septuagint; 1 Chron. 20:5 *son of Jair killed Lahmi the brother of Goliath*   n3 *Horn* here symbolizes strength.   o6 Hebrew *Sheol*

21:15–22 These four Philistine episodes (vv. 15–17, 18, 19, 20–21) cannot be chronologically located with any certainty (see note on 21:1–24:25). Each involves a heroic accomplishment by one of David's mighty men, resulting in the death of a "descendant of Rapha" (see vv. 16,18,20,22).
21:16 *Rapha.* In calling the four formidable enemy warriors referred to in this series "descendants of Rapha" (v. 22), the writer most likely identifies them as giants, as suggested by Dt 2:10–11,20–21. In that case, they may have been related to the Anakites (see Jos 11:21–22). Cf. Ge 15:19–20, which in its list of ten peoples of Canaan mentions Rephaites but not Anakites, though the Anakites (but not Rephaites) figure significantly in the accounts of the conquest (Nu 13:22,28,33; Dt 1:28; 9:2; Jos 14:12,15; Jdg 1:20).
21:17 *Abishai.* See note on 1Sa 26:6. *so that the lamp of Israel will not be extinguished.* A striking metaphor depicting Israel's dependence on David for its security and continuing existence as a nation—its national hope (see 22:29; 23:3–4; 1Ki 11:36).
21:18 *Gob.* Probably in the near vicinity of Gezer, where 1Ch 20:4 locates this same battle. *Saph.* Called Sippai in 1Ch 20:4.
21:19 *Elhanan . . . killed Goliath.* See NIV text note. Since it is clear from 1Sa 17 that David killed Goliath, it is possible that an early copyist misread the Hebrew for "Lahmi the brother of " (see 1Ch 20:5) as "the Bethlehemite" (in He-

brew the word for "killed" stands first in the clause).
21:21 *taunted Israel.* As Goliath had done (see 1Sa 17:10, 25). *Shimeah.* Also called Shammah (1Sa 16:9; 17:13).
22:1 *this song.* Preserved also as Ps 18 (see notes on that psalm). Besides an introduction (vv. 2–4) and conclusion (vv. 47–51), the song consists of three major sections: the first describes David's deliverance from mortal danger at the hands of his enemies (vv. 5–20); the second sets forth the moral grounds for God's saving help (vv. 21–30); the third recounts the help that the Lord gave him (vv. 31–46). The song was probably composed shortly after David's victories over foreign enemies (8:1–14) and before his sin with Bathsheba (compare vv. 21–25 with 1Ki 15:5). *from . . . all his enemies.* See 8:1–14. *from . . . Saul.* See 1Sa 18–31.
22:2 *my rock.* A figure particularly appropriate to David's experience (see vv. 32,47; 23:3; Dt 32:4,15,18,31; Ps 28:1; 31:2; 61:2; 78:35; 89:36; 94:22; 95:1). He had often taken refuge among the rocks of the desert (1Sa 23:25; 24:2), but he realized that true security was found only in the Lord. *fortress.* The Hebrew for this word occurs in 5:17; 23:14; 1Sa 22:4–5; 24:22, referring to places where David sought refuge.
22:3 *my shield.* See vv. 31,36; Ge 15:1; Dt 33:29. *horn.* See NIV text note; Dt 33:17; Jer 48:25.
22:5 *waves of death.* In vv. 5–6 David depicts his experiences in poetic figures of mortal danger.
22:6 *grave.* See note on Jnh 2:2.

⁷In my distress⁹ I called ʳ to the LORD;
    I called out to my God.
From his temple he heard my voice;
    my cry came to his ears.

⁸"The earth ˢ trembled and quaked, ᵗ
    the foundations ᵘ of the heavensᵖ
    shook;
they trembled because he was angry.
⁹Smoke rose from his nostrils;
    consuming fire ᵛ came from his
    mouth,
    burning coals ʷ blazed out of it.
¹⁰He parted the heavens and came down;
    dark clouds ˣ were under his feet.
¹¹He mounted the cherubimʸ and flew;
    he soared⁹ on the wings of the
    wind. ᶻ
¹²He made darkness ᵃ his canopy around
    him—
    the dark ʳ rain clouds of the sky.
¹³Out of the brightness of his presence
    bolts of lightning ᵇ blazed forth.
¹⁴The LORD thundered ᶜ from heaven;
    the voice of the Most High
    resounded.
¹⁵He shot arrows ᵈ and scattered ͵the
    enemies,͵
    bolts of lightning and routed them.
¹⁶The valleys of the sea were exposed
    and the foundations of the earth laid
    bare
at the rebuke ᵉ of the LORD,
    at the blastᶠ of breath from his
    nostrils.
¹⁷"He reached down from on highᵍ and
    took hold of me;
he drew ʰ me out of deep waters.
¹⁸He rescued ⁱ me from my powerful
    enemy,
    from my foes, who were too strong
    for me.
¹⁹They confronted me in the day of my
    disaster,

but the LORD was my support.ʲ
²⁰He brought me out into a spacious ᵏ
    place;
he rescued ˡ me because he
    delighted ᵐ in me. ⁿ

²¹"The LORD has dealt with me according
    to my righteousness; ᵒ
    according to the cleanness ᵖ of my
    hands ⁹ he has rewarded me.
²²For I have kept ʳ the ways of the LORD;
    I have not done evil by turning from
    my God.
²³All his laws are before me; ˢ
    I have not turned ᵗ away from his
    decrees.
²⁴I have been blameless ᵘ before him
    and have kept myself from sin.
²⁵The LORD has rewarded me according
    to my righteousness, ᵛ
    according to my cleanness ˢ in his
    sight.

²⁶"To the faithful you show yourself
    faithful,
    to the blameless you show yourself
    blameless,
²⁷to the pure ʷ you show yourself pure,
    but to the crooked you show yourself
    shrewd. ˣ
²⁸You save the humble,ʸ
    but your eyes are on the haughtyᶻ to
    bring them low. ᵃ
²⁹You are my lamp, ᵇ O LORD;
    the LORD turns my darkness into
    light.

22:7 ᵃGe 35:3;
S Jdg 2:15;
2Ch 15:4; Ps 4:1;
77:2; 120:1;
Isa 26:16
ʳPs 34:6,15;
116:4
22:8 ˢJdg 5:4;
Ps 97:4
ᵗS Ex 19:18;
S Jdg 5:4;
Ps 68:8; 77:18;
Jer 10:10
ᵘJob 9:6; 26:11;
Ps 75:3
22:9 ᵛPs 50:3;
97:3; Heb 12:29;
S Rev 11:5
ʷIsa 6:6;
Eze 1:13; 10:2
22:10
ˣS Ex 19:9;
Lev 16:2;
S Dt 33:26;
1Ki 8:12;
Job 26:9;
Ps 104:3;
Isa 19:1; Jer 4:13;
Na 1:3
22:11
ʸS Ge 3:24;
S Ex 25:22
ᶻPs 104:3
22:12 ᵃS Ex 19:9
22:13 ᵇJob 37:3;
Ps 77:18
22:14
ᶜS 1Sa 2:10
22:15
ᵈS Dt 32:23
22:16 ᵉPs 6:1;
50:8,21; 106:9;
Na 1:4
ᶠS Ex 14:21;
Isa 30:33; 40:24
22:17 ᵍPs 144:7
ʰEx 2:10
22:18 ⁱLk 1:71

22:19 ʲPs 23:4
22:20
ᵏJob 36:16;
Ps 31:8 ˡPs 118:5
ᵐPs 22:8;
Isa 42:1;
Mt 12:18
ⁿS 2Sa 15:26
22:21
ᵒS 1Sa 26:23
ᵖPs 26:6
⁹Job 17:9; 22:30;
42:7-8; Ps 24:4
22:22 ʳGe 18:19;
Ps 128:1; Pr 8:32
22:23 ˢDt 6:4-9;
Ps 119:30-33
ᵗPs 119:102
22:24 ᵘS Ge 6:9;
Eph 1:4

22:25 ᵛS 1Sa 26:23 **22:27** ʷMt 5:8 ˣLev 26:23-24 **22:28**
ʸS Ex 3:8; 1Sa 2:8-9; Ps 72:12-13 ᶻPs 131:1; Pr 30:13;
Da 4:31; Zep 3:11 ᵃIsa 2:12,17; 5:15; S Lk 1:51 **22:29**
ᵇPs 27:1; Isa 2:5; Mic 7:8; Rev 21:23; 22:5

ᵖ8 Hebrew; Vulgate and Syriac (see also Psalm 18:7)
mountains   ⁹11 Many Hebrew manuscripts (see also
Psalm 18:10); most Hebrew manuscripts *appeared*
ʳ12 Septuagint and Vulgate (see also Psalm 18:11);
Hebrew *massed*   ˢ25 Hebrew; Septuagint and Vulgate
(see also Psalm 18:24) *to the cleanness of my hands*

22:7 *his temple.* Heaven, where the Lord is enthroned as
King (see Ps 11:4; Isa 6:1; Jnh 2:7).
22:8–16 See note on Ps 18:7–15.
22:9 *Smoke rose from his nostrils.* God's power is portrayed in terms similar to those applied to the awesome
beast, the leviathan (Job 41:19–21).
22:11 *cherubim.* See Eze 1 and 10, where cherubim are
said to be the bearers of the throne of God; see also notes on
Ge 3:24; 1Sa 4:4; Eze 1:5.
22:14 *The LORD thundered.* The reference to thunder as
the voice of God is common in the OT (see Ps 29; Job
37:2–5). Thunder is particularly suited to expressing God's
power and majesty.
22:17 *He reached down from on high.* In vv. 17–20 David
describes his deliverance, initially in figurative terms (v. 17;
cf. v. 5) and subsequently in more literal language (vv.
18–20).
22:20 *delighted in.* The Hebrew underlying this expres-

sion is used in 15:26 ("pleased"); Ps 22:8 (cf. Mt 3:17,
"well pleased") and expresses the idea of the sovereign good
pleasure and favor of God toward his anointed one (v. 51).
22:21 *according to my righteousness.* In vv. 21–25 David
refers to the Lord's deliverances as a reward for his own
righteousness. While these statements may give the impression of self-righteous boasting and a meritorious basis for
divine favor, they should be understood in their context as:
(1) David's desire to please the Lord in his service as the
Lord's anointed (see note on v. 51); (2) his recognition that
the Lord rewards those who faithfully seek to serve him.
22:26–30 Because God responds to man in kind (see Job
34:11; Pr 3:34), David has experienced the Lord's favor.
22:28 *the haughty to bring them low.* The words of this
verse fit well with David's experience in his conflict with
Saul (see Hannah's song, 1Sa 2:3–8).
22:29 *You are my lamp.* The Lord causes David's life and
undertakings to flourish (see Job 18:5–6; 21:17; see also

³⁰With your help I can advance against a
    troopᵗ ;
  with my God I can scale a wall.

³¹"As for God, his way is perfect; ᶜ
  the word of the LORD is flawless. ᵈ
  He is a shieldᵉ
  for all who take refuge in him.
³²For who is God besides the LORD?
  And who is the Rockᶠ except our
    God? ᵍ
³³It is God who arms me with strengthᵘ
  and makes my way perfect.
³⁴He makes my feet like the feet of a
    deer; ʰ
  he enables me to stand on the
    heights. ⁱ
³⁵He trains my handsʲ for battle;
  my arms can bend a bowᵏ of bronze.
³⁶You give me your shieldˡ of victory;
  you stoop down to make me great.
³⁷You broaden the pathᵐ beneath me,
  so that my ankles do not turn.

³⁸"I pursued my enemies and crushed
    them;
  I did not turn back till they were
    destroyed.
³⁹I crushedⁿ them completely, and they
    could not rise;
  they fell beneath my feet.
⁴⁰You armed me with strength for battle;
  you made my adversaries bow at my
    feet. ᵒ
⁴¹You made my enemies turn their
    backsᵖ in flight,
  and I destroyed my foes.
⁴²They cried for help, ᑫ but there was no
    one to save them—ʳ
  to the LORD, but he did not answer. ˢ
⁴³I beat them as fine as the dustᵗ of the
    earth;
  I pounded and trampledᵘ them like
    mudᵛ in the streets.

⁴⁴"You have deliveredʷ me from the
    attacks of my people;

you have preservedˣ me as the head
    of nations.
Peopleʸ I did not know are subject to
    me,
⁴⁵ and foreigners come cringingᶻ to me;
  as soon as they hear me, they obey
    me. ᵃ
⁴⁶They all lose heart;
  they come tremblingᵛ ᵇ from their
    strongholds.

⁴⁷"The LORD lives! Praise be to my Rock!
  Exaltedᶜ be God, the Rock, my
    Savior! ᵈ
⁴⁸He is the God who avengesᵉ me, ᶠ
  who puts the nations under me,
⁴⁹ who sets me free from my enemies. ᵍ
  You exalted meʰ above my foes;
  from violent men you rescued me.
⁵⁰Therefore I will praise you, O LORD,
    among the nations;
  I will sing praisesⁱ to your name. ʲ
⁵¹He gives his king great victories; ᵏ
  he shows unfailing kindness to his
    anointed, ˡ
  to Davidᵐ and his descendants
    forever." ⁿ

The Last Words of David

23 These are the last words of David:

"The oracle of David son of Jesse,
  the oracle of the man exaltedᵒ by the
    Most High,
  the man anointedᵖ by the God of Jacob,
  Israel's singer of songsʷ:

²"The Spiritᑫ of the LORD spoke through
    me;
  his word was on my tongue.
³The God of Israel spoke,

22:31 ᶜS Dt 32:4;
Mt 5:48 ᵈPs 12:6;
119:140;
Pr 30:5-6
ᵉS Ge 15:1
22:32 ᶠS 1Sa 2:2
ᵍS 2Sa 7:22
22:34 ʰIsa 35:6;
Hab 3:19
ⁱS Dt 32:13
22:35 ʲPs 144:1
ᵏPs 7:12; 11:2;
Zec 9:13
22:36 ˡEph 6:16
22:37 ᵐPr 4:11
22:39 ⁿPs 44:5;
110:6; Mal 4:3
22:40
ᵒJos 10:24;
S 1Ki 5:3
22:41
ᵖS Ex 23:27
22:42 ᑫIsa 1:15
ʳPs 50:22
ˢS 1Sa 14:37
22:43
ᵗ1Ki 20:10;
2Ki 13:7;
Isa 41:2; Am 1:3
ᵘPs 7:5;
Isa 41:25;
Mic 7:10;
Zec 10:5
ᵛIsa 5:25; 10:6;
22:5; Mic 7:10
22:44
ʷS Ex 11:3;
S 2Sa 3:1

ˣDt 28:13
ʸS 2Sa 8:1-14;
Isa 55:3-5
22:45 ᶻPs 66:3;
81:15
ᵃS Dt 33:29
22:46 ᵇMic 7:17
22:47 ᶜS Ex 15:2
ᵈDt 32:15;
Ps 18:31; 89:26;
95:1
22:48 ᵉS Nu 31:3
ᶠPs 144:2
22:49 ᵍPs 140:1,
4 ʰPs 27:6
22:50 ⁱPs 9:11;
47:6; 68:4
ʲRo 15:9*
22:51 ᵏPs 21:1;
144:9-10
ˡ1Sa 16:13;
Ps 89:20;
Ac 13:23
ᵐS 2Sa 7:13
ⁿPs 89:24,29
23:1 ᵒS Ex 11:3;
Ps 78:70-71;
89:27 ᵖ1Sa 2:10,
35; Ps 18:50;
20:6; 84:9;
Isa 45:1;
Hab 3:13

23:2 ᑫMt 22:43; Mk 12:36; 2Pe 1:21

ᵗ30 Or can run through a barricade   ᵘ33 Dead Sea
Scrolls, some Septuagint manuscripts, Vulgate and Syriac
(see also Psalm 18:32); Masoretic Text who is my strong
refuge   ᵛ46 Some Septuagint manuscripts and Vulgate
(see also Psalm 18:45); Masoretic Text they arm
themselves.   ʷ1 Or Israel's beloved singer

note on Ps 27:1].
22:31 *his way is perfect.* The remainder of the song (vv.
31–51) accentuates David's praise to God for his deliverances.
22:32 *Rock.* See note on v. 2.
22:47 *The LORD lives!* God's interventions and blessings in
David's behalf have shown him to be the living God (see Dt
5:26).
22:50 *I will praise you, O LORD, among the nations.* For
Paul's reference to this vow see Ro 15:9.
22:51 *his king . . . his anointed.* See notes on 1Sa 10:25;
12:14–15. David refers to himself in the third person in a
way that acknowledges the covenantal character of his kingship. It is in the context of David's official capacity as the
Lord's anointed that the entire song is to be read and understood (see note on v. 21). *his descendants forever.* David

speaks of God's promise through Nathan (see 7:12–16).
23:1 *last words of David.* Probably to be understood as
David's last poetic testimony (in the manner of his psalms),
perhaps composed at the time of his final instructions and
warnings to his son Solomon (see 1Ki 2:1–10).
23:2 *The Spirit of the LORD spoke through me.* David was
conscious of God's Spirit at work in him enabling him to
speak under the Spirit's guidance (see notes on 2Ti 3:16; 2Pe
1:21).
23:3 *Rock.* See note on 22:2; see also 1Sa 2:2; Dt 32:4,
15,18,30–31. *When one rules over men in righteousness.*
In brief and vivid strokes David portrays the ideal theocratic
king—to be fully realized only in the rule of David's greater
son, Jesus Christ. This prophetic utterance complements that
of 7:12–16 and anticipates those of Isa 9:7; 11:1–5; Jer
23:5–6; 33:15–16; Zec 9:9.

the Rock[r] of Israel said to me:
'When one rules over men in
　righteousness,[s]
when he rules in the fear[t] of God,[u]
[4]he is like the light[v] of morning[w] at
　sunrise[x]
on a cloudless morning,
like the brightness after rain[y]
that brings the grass from the earth.'

[5]"Is not my house right with God?
Has he not made with me an
　everlasting covenant,[z]
arranged and secured in every part?
Will he not bring to fruition my
　salvation
and grant me my every desire?
[6]But evil men are all to be cast aside like
　thorns,[a]
which are not gathered with the
　hand.
[7]Whoever touches thorns
uses a tool of iron or the shaft of a
　spear;
they are burned up where they lie."

David's Mighty Men

23:8–39pp — 1Ch 11:10–41

[8]These are the names of David's mighty
men:[b]

Josheb-Basshebeth,[x][c] a Tahkemonite,[y]
was chief of the Three; he raised his spear
against eight hundred men, whom he
killed[z] in one encounter.

[9]Next to him was Eleazar son of Dodai[d]
the Ahohite.[e] As one of the three mighty
men, he was with David when they taunted the Philistines gathered at Pas Dammim,[a] for battle. Then the men of Israel
retreated, [10]but he stood his ground and
struck down the Philistines till his hand
grew tired and froze to the sword. The
LORD brought about a great victory that
day. The troops returned to Eleazar, but
only to strip the dead.

[11]Next to him was Shammah son of
Agee the Hararite. When the Philistines
banded together at a place where there
was a field full of lentils, Israel's troops fled
from them. [12]But Shammah took his stand
in the middle of the field. He defended it
and struck the Philistines down, and the
LORD brought about a great victory.

[13]During harvest time, three of the
thirty chief men came down to David at
the cave of Adullam,[f] while a band of
Philistines was encamped in the Valley of
Rephaim.[g] [14]At that time David was in the
stronghold,[h] and the Philistine garrison
was at Bethlehem.[i] [15]David longed for
water and said, "Oh, that someone would
get me a drink of water from the well near
the gate of Bethlehem!" [16]So the three
mighty men broke through the Philistine
lines, drew water from the well near the
gate of Bethlehem and carried it back to
David. But he refused to drink it; instead,
he poured[j] it out before the LORD. [17]"Far
be it from me, O LORD, to do this!" he
said. "Is it not the blood[k] of men who
went at the risk of their lives?" And David
would not drink it.

Such were the exploits of the three
mighty men.

[18]Abishai[l] the brother of Joab son of
Zeruiah was chief of the Three.[b] He raised
his spear against three hundred men,
whom he killed, and so he became as famous as the Three. [19]Was he not held in
greater honor than the Three? He became

Cross references

23:3 [r]Dt 32:4; S 1Sa 2:2; Ps 18:31 [s]Ps 72:3 [t]S Ge 42:18 [u]Isa 11:1-5
23:4 [v]Jn 1:5; [w]Ps 119:147; 130:6; Pr 4:18 [x]S Jdg 5:31; Mt 13:43 [y]S Dt 32:2
23:5 [z]S Ge 9:16; Ps 89:29
23:6 [a]Isa 5:6; 9:18; 10:17; 27:4; 33:12; Mic 7:4; Na 1:10; Mt 13:40-41
23:8 [b]S 2Sa 17:10 [c]1Ch 27:2
23:9 [d]1Ch 27:4 [e]1Ch 8:4
23:13 [f]S Ge 38:1; S Jos 12:15 [g]S Jos 17:15
23:14 [h]1Sa 22:4-5; S 2Sa 5:17
23:16 [i]Ru 1:19
23:16 [j]S Ge 35:14
23:17 [k]Lev 17:10-12
23:18 [l]S 1Sa 26:6

Text notes

[x]8 Hebrew; some Septuagint manuscripts suggest *Ish-Bosheth,* that is, *Esh-Baal* (see also 1 Chron. 11:11 *Jashobeam*). [y]8 Probably a variant of *Hacmonite* (see 1 Chron. 11:11) [z]8 Some Septuagint manuscripts (see also 1 Chron. 11:11); Hebrew and other Septuagint manuscripts *Three; it was Adino the Eznite who killed eight hundred men* [a]9 See 1 Chron. 11:13; Hebrew *gathered there.* [b]18 Most Hebrew manuscripts (see also 1 Chron. 11:20); two Hebrew manuscripts and Syriac *Thirty*

23:4 *like the light of morning.* See notes on Ps 27:1; 36:9.
23:5 *Is not my house right with God?* A rhetorical question recalling God's covenant with him and his dynasty (see 7:12–16). *everlasting covenant.* David expressly calls God's promise to him a covenant that will not be abrogated (see notes on 7:20,28; Isa 55:3; see also Ps 89:3,28,34,39; 132:11). *bring to fruition.* Through David's promised descendants.
23:6 *evil men . . . cast aside.* Godless people who have no interest in the righteous king will be destroyed (see Ps 2:9; 110:5–6).
23:8–39 See note on 21:1–24:25. This list of 37 (see v. 39) of David's most valiant warriors and the description of some of their exploits are paralleled in 1Ch 11:11–41. There the list is expanded by 16 names (1Ch 11:41–47).
23:8 *Tahkemonite.* 1Ch 11:11 reads "Hacmonite" (see NIV text note here), derived from an unknown place-name.

Three. Two groups of three warriors (vv. 8–12 and 13–23) and one group of 30 warriors (vv. 23–39) are mentioned (see note on v. 39 for the total number of warriors).
23:9 *Ahohite.* A descendant of Ahoah from the tribe of Benjamin (1Ch 8:4).
23:13 *harvest time.* See 11:1 and note. The circumstances of this event suggest that it happened shortly after David had fled from Saul, when men first began to gather to his cause (see 1Sa 22:1–4), or shortly after his conquest of Jerusalem (see 2Sa 5:17–18). *three.* Not the same as the three mighty men of v. 9. *thirty chief men.* See vv. 23–24,39. *cave of Adullam.* See 1Sa 22:1. *Rephaim.* See 5:18.
23:14 *stronghold.* See note on 1Sa 22:4.
23:15–16 See note on 1Ch 11:15–19.
23:18 *Abishai.* See 10:10,14; 18:2; see also note on 1Sa 26:6. *Three.* Presumably those referred to in vv. 13–17.

their commander, even though he was not included among them.

20Benaiah [m] son of Jehoiada was a valiant fighter from Kabzeel, [n] who performed great exploits. He struck down two of Moab's best men. He also went down into a pit on a snowy day and killed a lion. 21And he struck down a huge Egyptian. Although the Egyptian had a spear in his hand, Benaiah went against him with a club. He snatched the spear from the Egyptian's hand and killed him with his own spear. 22Such were the exploits of Benaiah son of Jehoiada; he too was as famous as the three mighty men. 23He was held in greater honor than any of the Thirty, but he was not included among the Three. And David put him in charge of his bodyguard.

24Among the Thirty were:

Asahel [o] the brother of Joab,
Elhanan son of Dodo from Bethlehem,
25Shammah the Harodite, [p]
Elika the Harodite,
26Helez [q] the Paltite,
Ira [r] son of Ikkesh from Tekoa,
27Abiezer [s] from Anathoth, [t]
Mebunnai [c] the Hushathite,
28Zalmon the Ahohite,
Maharai [u] the Netophathite, [v]
29Heled [d][w] son of Baanah the Netophathite,
Ithai son of Ribai from Gibeah [x] in Benjamin,
30Benaiah the Pirathonite, [y]

Hiddai [e] from the ravines of Gaash, [z]
31Abi-Albon the Arbathite,
Azmaveth the Barhumite, [a]
32Eliahba the Shaalbonite,
the sons of Jashen,
Jonathan 33son of [f] Shammah the Hararite,
Ahiam son of Sharar [g] the Hararite,
34Eliphelet son of Ahasbai the Maacathite, [b]
Eliam [c] son of Ahithophel [d] the Gilonite,
35Hezro the Carmelite, [e]
Paarai the Arbite,
36Igal son of Nathan from Zobah, [f]
the son of Hagri, [h]
37Zelek the Ammonite,
Naharai the Beerothite, [g] the armor-bearer of Joab son of Zeruiah,
38Ira the Ithrite, [h]
Gareb the Ithrite
39and Uriah [i] the Hittite.
There were thirty-seven in all.

David Counts the Fighting Men

24:1–17pp — 1Ch 21:1–17

24 Again [j] the anger of the Lord burned against Israel, [k] and he in-

23:20 *mS* 2Sa 8:18; 1Ch 27:5
n Jos 15:21
23:24
o S 2Sa 2:18
23:25 *p* Jdg 7:1
23:26
q 1Ch 27:10
r 1Ch 27:9
23:27
s 1Ch 27:12
t S Jos 21:18
23:28
u 1Ch 27:13
v 2Ki 25:23; Ezr 2:22; Ne 7:26; Jer 40:8
23:29
w 1Ch 27:15
x S Jos 15:57
23:30
y S Jdg 12:13

z Jos 24:30
23:31 *a* 2Sa 3:16
23:34 *b* S Dt 3:14
c S 2Sa 11:3
d S 2Sa 15:12
23:35
e S Jos 12:22
23:36
f S 1Sa 14:47
23:37 *g* S Jos 9:17
23:38 *h* 1Ch 2:53
23:39 *i* 2Sa 11:3
24:1 *j* S Jos 9:15
k Job 1:6; Zec 3:1

c 27 Hebrew; some Septuagint manuscripts (see also 1 Chron. 11:29) *Sibbecai*   *d* 29 Some Hebrew manuscripts and Vulgate (see also 1 Chron. 11:30); most Hebrew manuscripts *Heleb*   *e* 30 Hebrew; some Septuagint manuscripts (see also 1 Chron. 11:32) *Hurai*   *f* 33 Some Septuagint manuscripts (see also 1 Chron. 11:34); Hebrew does not have *son of.*   *g* 33 Hebrew; some Septuagint manuscripts (see also 1 Chron. 11:35) *Sacar*   *h* 36 Some Septuagint manuscripts (see also 1 Chron. 11:38); Hebrew *Haggadi*

23:20 *Benaiah son of Jehoiada.* Commander of the Kerethites and Pelethites (8:18; 20:23; see v. 23 below) and of the division of troops for the third month of the year (1Ch 27:5). He supported Solomon's succession to the throne (1Ki 1–2) and eventually replaced Joab as commander of the army (1Ki 2:35).
23:24 *Thirty.* Twenty-nine names are listed in vv. 24–39. Since the three of vv. 13–17 are also included in the thirty (see v. 13), the total number of warriors mentioned is 32. 1Ch 11:26–47 lists 16 additional names for this group, so it appears that the list includes the names of replacements for vacancies when a warrior either dropped out or died. *Asahel.* See 2:18–23.
23:34 *Eliam.* Father of Bathsheba (see 11:3) and son of David's counselor Ahithophel, who joined in Absalom's conspiracy (see 15:12,31,34; 16:20–23; 17:1–23).
23:39 *Uriah.* Husband of Bathsheba (see 11:3–27). *thirty-seven.* The total number of warriors referred to in vv. 8–39, including the Three of vv. 8–12, the Three of vv. 13–17, Abishai (vv. 18–19), Benaiah (vv. 20–23) and the 29 whose names are recorded in vv. 24–39 (see note on v. 24).
24:1 *Again.* The previous occasion may have been the famine of 21:1. *the anger of the Lord burned against Israel.* The specific reason for the Lord's displeasure is not stated. Because the anger is said to be directed against Israel rather

than David, some have concluded that it was occasioned by the widespread support among the people for the rebellions of Absalom and Sheba against David (see 15:12; 17:11, 24–26; 18:7; 20:1–2), the divinely chosen and anointed theocratic king. This would mean that the events of this chapter are to be placed chronologically shortly after those of chs. 15–20 and so after 980 B.C. (see note on 15:7). *the Lord . . . incited David against them.* 1Ch 21:1 says that Satan inspired David to take the census. Although Scripture is clear that God does not cause anyone to sin (Jas 1:13–15), it is also clear that man's—and Satan's—evil acts are under God's sovereign control (see Ex 4:21; 7:3; 9:12; 10:1,20,27; 11:10; 14:4; Jos 11:20; 1Ki 22:22–23; Job 1:12; 2:10; Eze 3:20; 14:9; Ac 4:28). *take a census of Israel and Judah.* David's military census (see vv. 2–3) does not appear to have been prompted by any immediate external threat. Since he wanted to "know how many there are" (v. 2), it is evident that his action was motivated either by pride in the size of the empire he had acquired or by reliance for his security on the size of the reserve of manpower he could muster in an emergency or, more likely, both. The mere taking of a census was hardly sinful (see Nu 1:2–3; 26:2–4), but in this instance it represented an unwarranted glorying in and dependence on human power rather than the Lord (not much different from Israel's initial desire to have a king for their

cited David against them, saying, "Go and take a census of[l] Israel and Judah."

[2] So the king said to Joab[m] and the army commanders[i] with him, "Go throughout the tribes of Israel from Dan to Beersheba[n] and enroll[o] the fighting men, so that I may know how many there are."

[3] But Joab[p] replied to the king, "May the LORD your God multiply the troops a hundred times over,[q] and may the eyes of my lord the king see it. But why does my lord the king want to do such a thing?"

[4] The king's word, however, overruled Joab and the army commanders; so they left the presence of the king to enroll the fighting men of Israel.

[5] After crossing the Jordan, they camped near Aroer,[r] south of the town in the gorge, and then went through Gad and on to Jazer.[s] [6] They went to Gilead and the region of Tahtim Hodshi, and on to Dan Jaan and around toward Sidon.[t] [7] Then they went toward the fortress of Tyre[u] and all the towns of the Hivites[v] and Canaanites. Finally, they went on to Beersheba[w] in the Negev[x] of Judah.

[8] After they had gone through the entire land, they came back to Jerusalem at the end of nine months and twenty days.

[9] Joab reported the number of the fighting men to the king: In Israel there were eight hundred thousand able-bodied men who could handle a sword, and in Judah five hundred thousand.[y]

[10] David was conscience-stricken[z] after he had counted the fighting men, and he said to the LORD, "I have sinned[a] greatly in what I have done. Now, O LORD, I beg you, take away the guilt of your servant. I have done a very foolish thing.[b]"

[11] Before David got up the next morning, the word of the LORD had come to Gad[c] the prophet, David's seer:[d] [12] "Go and tell

David, 'This is what the LORD says: I am giving you three options. Choose one of them for me to carry out against you.' "

[13] So Gad went to David and said to him, "Shall there come upon you three[j] years of famine[e] in your land? Or three months of fleeing from your enemies while they pursue you? Or three days of plague[f] in your land? Now then, think it over and decide how I should answer the one who sent me."

[14] David said to Gad, "I am in deep distress. Let us fall into the hands of the LORD, for his mercy[g] is great; but do not let me fall into the hands of men."

[15] So the LORD sent a plague on Israel from that morning until the end of the time designated, and seventy thousand of the people from Dan to Beersheba died.[h] [16] When the angel stretched out his hand to destroy Jerusalem, the LORD was grieved[i] because of the calamity and said to the angel who was afflicting the people, "Enough! Withdraw your hand." The angel of the LORD[j] was then at the threshing floor of Araunah the Jebusite.

[17] When David saw the angel who was striking down the people, he said to the LORD, "I am the one who has sinned and done wrong. These are but sheep.[k] What have they done?[l] Let your hand fall upon me and my family." [m]

David Builds an Altar

24:18–25pp — 1Ch 21:18–26

[18] On that day Gad went to David and said to him, "Go up and build an altar to the LORD on the threshing floor of Araunah[n] the Jebusite." [19] So David went up, as the LORD had commanded through Gad.

---

l 2 Septuagint (see also verse 4 and 1 Chron. 21:2);
Hebrew *Joab the army commander*   *i* 13 Septuagint
(see also 1 Chron. 21:12); Hebrew *seven*

24:1 *l* S Ex 30:12;
1Ch 27:23
24:2
m S 2Sa 20:23
n S 2Sa 3:10
o 2Ch 2:17;
17:14; 25:5
24:3 *p* S 2Sa 2:18
q S Dt 1:11
24:5 *r* S Jos 13:9
s S Nu 21:32
24:6 *t* S Ge 10:19;
Jdg 1:31
24:7 *u* S Jos 19:29
v S Ex 3:8
w Ge 21:31
x S Dt 1:7
24:9
y S Nu 1:44-46
24:10
z S 1Sa 24:5
a S Nu 22:34
b S Nu 12:11
24:11
c S 1Sa 22:5
d 1Sa 9:9

24:13
e Dt 28:38-42,48;
S 32:24;
Eze 14:21
f S Ex 5:3;
S 30:12;
S Lev 26:25;
Dt 28:21-22,
27-28,35
24:14 *g* Ne 9:28;
Ps 4:1; 51:1;
86:5; 103:8,13;
119:132; 130:4;
Isa 54:7; 55:7;
Jer 33:8; 42:12;
Da 9:9
24:15
h 1Ch 27:24
24:16 *i* S Ge 6:6
/S Ge 16:7;
S 19:13;
S Ex 12:23;
Ac 12:23
24:17 *k* Ps 74:1;
100:3; Jer 49:20
/S Ge 18:23
m Jnh 1:12
24:18 *n* Ge 22:2;
2Ch 3:1

---

security; see 1Sa 8–12). The act was uncharacteristic of David (see 1Sa 17:26,37,45–47; 2Sa 22:2–4,47–51).

24:2   *Dan to Beersheba.* See note on 1Sa 3:20.

24:3   *But why . . . ?* David's directive does not go unchallenged. The fact that he does not answer suggests that he knew his reasons were highly questionable. In any event, Joab's challenge renders David the more guilty.

24:5–8   The military census was begun in southern Transjordan and moved northward, then back across the Jordan, moving from north to south.

24:9   *eight hundred thousand . . . five hundred thousand.* These figures differ from those of 1Ch 21:5 (see notes on 1Ch 21:5–6).

24:10   *I have sinned greatly.* See note on v. 1.

24:11   *Gad the prophet, David's seer.* See notes on 1Sa 9:9; 22:5.

24:12   *Go and tell David.* See 12:1 and note. *three options.* The three alternative judgments were all included in the curses that Moses said would come on God's people when

they failed to adhere to their covenant obligations (see Dt 28:15–25).

24:14   *not . . . into the hands of men.* David, who knew both God and war, knew that even in his anger God is more merciful than man let loose in the rampages of war (see Ps 30:5).

24:15   *Dan to Beersheba.* See note on 1Sa 3:20.

24:16   *angel.* Angels appear elsewhere in Scripture as instruments of God's judgment (see Ex 33:2; 2Ki 19:35; Ps 35:5–6; 78:49; Mt 13:41; Ac 12:23). *the LORD was grieved.* See note on 1Sa 15:29. *threshing floor of Araunah.* Located on Mount Moriah, immediately north of David's city and overlooking it. Later it would become the site of the temple (see 1Ch 22:1; 2Ch 3:1). *Jebusite.* See note on 5:6.

24:17   *Let your hand fall upon me and my family.* Although the people of Israel were not without guilt (see v. 1), David assumes full blame for his own act and acknowledges his responsibility as king for the well-being of the Lord's people (see 5:2; 7:7–8).

20When Araunah looked and saw the king and his men coming toward him, he went out and bowed down before the king with his face to the ground.

21Araunah said, "Why has my lord the king come to his servant?"

"To buy your threshing floor," David answered, "so I can build an altar to the LORD, that the plague on the people may be stopped."o

22Araunah said to David, "Let my lord the king take whatever pleases him and offer it up. Here are oxenp for the burnt offering, and here are threshing sledges and ox yokes for the wood. 23O king, Araunah givesq all this to the king." Arau-

nah also said to him, "May the LORD your God accept you."

24But the king replied to Araunah, "No, I insist on paying you for it. I will not sacrifice to the LORD my God burnt offerings that cost me nothing."r

So David bought the threshing floor and the oxen and paid fifty shekelsk s of silver for them. 25David built an altart to the LORD there and sacrificed burnt offerings and fellowship offerings.l Then the LORD answered prayeru in behalf of the land, and the plague on Israel was stopped.

24:21
oNu 16:44-50
24:22
pS 1Sa 6:14
24:23 qGe 23:11

24:24
rMal 1:13-14
sS Ge 23:16
24:25 tS 1Sa 7:17
u2Sa 21:14

k24 That is, about 1 1/4 pounds (about 0.6 kilogram)
l25 Traditionally peace offerings

24:19 as the LORD had commanded. The Lord himself appointed the atoning sacrifice in answer to David's prayer.
24:21 To buy your threshing floor. David does not simply expropriate the property for his royal purposes (see 1Sa 8:14).
24:24 burnt offerings. See Lev 1:1–17. David bought the threshing floor. Thus the later site of the temple (see note on

v. 16) became the royal property of the house of David. and the oxen. David's haste could not wait for oxen to be brought some distance from his own herds. fifty shekels. See note on 1Ch 21:25.
24:25 fellowship offerings. See note on 1Sa 11:15. Reconciliation and restoration of covenant fellowship were obtained by the king's repentance, intercessory prayer and the offering of sacrifices.

1 KINGS

Title

1 and 2 Kings (like 1 and 2 Samuel and 1 and 2 Chronicles) are actually one literary work, called in Hebrew tradition simply "Kings." The division of this work into two books was introduced by the translators of the Septuagint (the Greek translation of the OT) and subsequently followed in the Latin Vulgate and most modern versions. In 1448 the division into two sections also appeared in a Hebrew manuscript and was perpetuated in later printed editions of the Hebrew text. Both the Septuagint and the Latin Vulgate further designated Samuel and Kings in a way that emphasized the relationship of these two works (Septuagint: First, Second, Third and Fourth Book of Kingdoms; Latin Vulgate: First, Second, Third and Fourth Kings). Together Samuel and Kings relate the whole history of the monarchy, from its rise under the ministry of Samuel to its fall at the hands of the Babylonians.

The division between 1 and 2 Kings has been made at an appropriate but somewhat arbitrary place, shortly after the deaths of Ahab of the northern kingdom (22:37) and Jehoshaphat of the southern kingdom (22:50). Placing the division at this point causes the account of the reign of Ahaziah of Israel to overlap the end of 1 Kings (22:51-53) and the beginning of 2 Kings (ch. 1). The same is true of the narration of the ministry of Elijah, which for the most part appears in 1 Kings (chs. 17-19). However, his final act of judgment and the passing of his cloak to Elisha at the moment of his ascension to heaven in a whirlwind are contained in 2 Kings (1:1-2:17).

Author, Sources and Date

There is little conclusive evidence as to the identity of the author of 1,2 Kings. Although Jewish tradition credits Jeremiah, few today accept this as likely. Whoever the author was, it is clear that he was familiar with the book of Deuteronomy—as were many of Israel's prophets. It is also clear that he used a variety of sources in compiling his history of the monarchy. Three such sources are named: "the book of the annals of Solomon" (11:41), "the book of the annals of the kings of Israel" (14:19), "the book of the annals of the kings of Judah" (14:29). It is likely that other written sources were also employed (such as those mentioned in Chronicles; see below).

Although some scholars have concluded that the three sources specifically cited in 1,2 Kings are to be viewed as official court annals from the royal archives in Jerusalem and Samaria, this is by no means certain. It seems at least questionable whether official court annals would have included details of conspiracies such as those referred to in 16:20; 2Ki 15:15. It is also questionable whether official court annals would have been readily accessible for public scrutiny, as the author clearly implies in his references to them. Such considerations have led some scholars to conclude that these sources were records of the reigns of the kings of Israel and Judah compiled by the succession of Israel's prophets spanning the kingdom period. 1,2 Chronicles makes reference to a number of such writings: "the records of Samuel the seer, the records of Nathan the prophet and the records of Gad the seer" (1Ch 29:29), "the prophecy of Ahijah the Shilonite" and "the visions of Iddo the seer" (2Ch 9:29), "the records of Shemaiah the prophet" (2Ch 12:15), "the annals of Jehu son of Hanani," (2Ch 20:34), "the annotations on the book of the kings" (2Ch 24:27), the "events of Uzziah's reign . . . recorded by the prophet Isaiah son of Amoz" (2Ch 26:22; see also 2Ch 32:32)—and there may have been others. It is most likely, for example, that for the ministries of Elijah and Elisha the author depended on a prophetic source (perhaps from the eighth century) that had drawn up an account of those two prophets in which they were already compared with Moses and Joshua.

Some scholars place the date of composition of 1,2 Kings in the time subsequent to Jehoiachin's release from prison (562 B.C.; 2Ki 25:27-30) and prior to the end of the Babylonian exile in 538. This position is challenged by others on the basis of statements in 1,2 Kings that speak of certain things in the preexilic period that are said to have continued in existence "to this day" (see, e.g., 8:8, the poles

used to carry the ark; 9:20-21, conscripted labor; 12:19, Israel in rebellion against the house of David; 2Ki 8:22, Edom in rebellion against the kingdom of Judah). From such statements it is argued that the writer must have been a person living in Judah in the preexilic period rather than in Babylon in postexilic times. If this argument is accepted, one must conclude that the original book was composed about the time of the death of Josiah and that the material pertaining to the time subsequent to his reign was added during the exile c. 550. While this "two-edition" viewpoint is possible, it rests largely on the "to this day" statements.

An alternative is to understand these statements as those of the original source used by the author rather than statements of the author himself. A comparison of 2Ch 5:9 with 1Ki 8:8 suggests that this is a legitimate conclusion. Chronicles is clearly a postexilic writing, yet the wording of the statement concerning the poles used to carry the ark ("they are still there today") is the same in Chronicles as it is in Kings. Probably the Chronicler was simply quoting his source, namely, 1Ki 8:8. There is no reason that the author of 1,2 Kings could not have done the same thing in quoting from his earlier sources. This explanation allows for positing a single author living in exile and using the source materials at his disposal.

Theme: Kingship and Covenant

1,2 Kings contains no explicit statement of purpose or theme. Reflection on its content, however, reveals that the author has selected and arranged his material in a manner that provides a sequel to the history found in 1,2 Samuel—a history of kingship regulated by covenant. In general, 1,2 Kings describes the history of the kings of Israel and Judah in the light of God's covenants. The guiding thesis of the book is that the welfare of Israel and her kings depended on their obedience to their obligations as defined in the Mosaic covenant.

It is clearly not the author's intention to present a socio-politico-economic history of Israel's monarchy in accordance with the principles of modern historiography. The author repeatedly refers the reader to other sources for more detailed information about the reigns of the various kings (see, e.g., 11:41; 14:19,29; 15:7,31; 16:5,14,20,27), and he gives a covenantal rather than a social or political or economic assessment of their reigns. From the standpoint of a political historian, Omri would be considered one of the more important rulers in the northern kingdom. He established a powerful dynasty and made Samaria the capital city. According to the Moabite Stone (see chart on "Ancient Texts Relating to the OT," p. 5), Omri was the ruler who subjugated the Moabites to the northern kingdom. Long after Omri's death, Assyrian rulers referred to Jehu as the "son of Omri" (either mistakenly or merely in accordance with their literary conventions when speaking of a later king of a realm). Yet in spite of Omri's political importance, his reign is dismissed in six verses (16:23-28) with the statement that he "did evil in the eyes of the LORD and sinned more than all those before him" (16:25). Similarly, the reign of Jeroboam II, who presided over the northern kingdom during the time of its greatest political and economic power, is treated only briefly (2Ki 14:23-29).

Another example of the writer's covenantal rather than merely political or economic interest can be seen in the description of the reign of Josiah of Judah. Nothing is said about the early years of his reign, but a detailed description is given of the reformation and renewal of the covenant that he promoted in his 18th year as king (2Ki 22:3-23:28). Nor is anything said of the motives leading Josiah to oppose Pharaoh Neco of Egypt at Megiddo, or of the major shift in geopolitical power from Assyria to Babylon that was connected with this incident (see notes on 2Ki 23:29-30).

It becomes apparent, then, that the kings who receive the most attention in 1,2 Kings are those during whose reigns there was either notable deviation from or affirmation of the covenant (or significant interaction between a king and God's prophet; see below). Ahab son of Omri is an example of the former (17:1-22:39). His reign is given extensive treatment, not so much because of its extraordinary political importance, but because of the serious threat to covenant fidelity and continuity that arose in the northern kingdom during his reign. Ultimately the pagan influence of Ahab's wife Jezebel through Ahab's daughter Athaliah (whether she was Jezebel's daughter is unknown) nearly led to the extermination of the house of David in Judah (see 2Ki 11:1-3).

Manasseh (2Ki 21:1-18) is an example of a similar sort. Here again it is deviation from the covenant that is emphasized in the account of his reign rather than political features, such as involvement in the Assyrian-Egyptian conflict (mentioned in Assyrian records but not in 2 Kings). The extreme apostasy characterizing Manasseh's reign made exile for Judah inevitable (2Ki 21:10-15; 23:26-27).

On the positive side, Hezekiah (2Ki 18:1-20:21) and Josiah (2Ki 22:1-23:29) are given extensive treatment because of their involvement in covenant renewal. These are the only two kings given

unqualified approval by the writer for their loyalty to the Lord (2Ki 18:3; 22:2). It is noteworthy that all the kings of the northern kingdom are said to have done evil in the eyes of the Lord and walked in the ways of Jeroboam, who caused Israel to sin (see, e.g., 16:26,31; 22:52; 2Ki 3:3; 10:29). It was Jeroboam who established the golden calf worship at Bethel and Dan shortly after the division of the kingdom (see 12:26-33; 13:1-6).

While the writer depicts Israel's obedience or disobedience to the Sinai covenant as decisive for her historical destiny, he also recognizes the far-reaching historical significance of the Davidic covenant, which promised that David's dynasty would endure forever. This is particularly noticeable in references to the "lamp" that the Lord had promised David (see 11:36; 15:4; 2Ki 8:19; see also note on 2Sa 21:17). It also appears in more general references to the promise to David (8:20,25) and its consequences for specific historical developments in Judah's later history (11:12-13,32; 2Ki 19:34; 20:6). In addition, the writer uses the life and reign of David as a standard by which the lives of later kings are measured (see, e.g., 9:4; 11:4,6,33,38; 14:8; 15:3,5,11; 2Ki 16:2; 18:3; 22:2).

Another prominent feature of the narratives of 1,2 Kings is the emphasis on the relationship between prophecy and fulfillment in the historical developments of the monarchy. On at least 11 occasions a prophecy is recorded that is later said to have been fulfilled (see, e.g., 2Sa 7:13 and 1Ki 8:20; 1Ki 11:29-39 and 1Ki 12:15; 1Ki 13 and 2Ki 23:16-18). The result of this emphasis is that the history of the kingdom is not presented as a chain of chance occurrences or the mere interplay of human actions but as the unfolding of Israel's historical destiny under the guidance of an omniscient and omnipotent God—Israel's covenant Lord, who rules all history in accordance with his sovereign purposes (see 8:56; 2Ki 10:10).

The author also stresses the importance of the prophets themselves in their role as official emissaries from the court of Israel's covenant Lord, the Great King to whom Israel and her king were bound in service through the covenant. The Lord sent a long succession of such prophets to call king and people back to covenant loyalty (2Ki 17:13). For the most part their warnings and exhortations fell on deaf ears. Many of these prophets and prophetesses are mentioned in the narratives of 1,2 Kings (see, e.g., Ahijah, 11:29-40; 14:5-18; Shemaiah, 12:22-24; Micaiah, 22:8-28; Jonah, 2Ki 14:25; Isaiah, 2Ki 19:1-7,20-34; Huldah, 2Ki 22:14-20), but particular attention is given to the ministries of Elijah and Elisha (1Ki 17-19; 2Ki 1-13).

Reflection on these features of 1,2 Kings suggests that it was written to explain to a people in exile that the reason for their condition of humiliation was their stubborn persistence in breaking the covenant. In bringing the exile upon his people, God, after much patience, imposed the curses of the covenant, which had stood as a warning to them from the beginning (see Lev 26:27-45; Dt 28:64-68). This is made explicit with respect to the captivity of the northern kingdom in 2Ki 17:7-23; 18:10-12, and with respect to the southern kingdom in 2Ki 21. The reformation under Josiah in the southern kingdom is viewed as too little, too late (see 2Ki 23:26-27; 24:3).

The book, then, provides a retrospective analysis of Israel's history. It explains the reasons both for the destruction of Samaria and Jerusalem and their respective kingdoms and for the bitter experience of being forced into exile. This does not mean, however, that there is no hope for the future. The writer consistently keeps the promise to David in view as a basis on which Israel in exile may look to the future with hope rather than with despair. In this connection the final four verses of the book, reporting Jehoiachin's release from prison in Babylon and his elevation to a place of honor in the court there (2Ki 25:27-30), take on added significance. The future remains open for a new work of the Lord in faithfulness to his promise to the house of David.

It is important to note that, although the author was undoubtedly a Judahite exile, and although the northern kingdom had been dispersed for well over a century and a half at the time of his writing, the scope of his concern was all Israel—the whole covenant people. Neither he nor the prophets viewed the division of the kingdom as an excommunication of the ten tribes, nor did they see the earlier exile of the northern kingdom as a final exclusion of the northern tribes from Israel's future.

Chronology

1,2 Kings presents the reader with abundant chronological data. Not only is the length of the reign of each king given, but during the period of the divided kingdom the beginning of the reign of each king is synchronized with the regnal year of the ruling king in the opposite kingdom. Often additional data, such as the age of the ruler at the time of his accession, are also provided.

By integrating Biblical data with those derived from Assyrian chronological records, the year 853 B.C. can be fixed as the year of Ahab's death, and the year 841 as the year Jehu began to reign. The

years in which Ahab and Jehu had contacts with Shalmaneser III of Assyria can also be given definite dates (by means of astronomical calculations based on an Assyrian reference to a solar eclipse). With these fixed points, it is then possible to work both forward and backward in the lines of the kings of Israel and Judah to give dates for each king. By the same means it can be determined that the division of the kingdom occurred in 930, that Samaria fell to the Assyrians in 722-721 and that Jerusalem fell to the Babylonians in 586.

The synchronistic data correlating the reigns of the kings of Israel and Judah present some knotty problems, which have long been considered nearly insoluble. In more recent times, most of these problems have been resolved in a satisfactory way through recognizing such possibilities as overlapping reigns, co-regencies of sons with their fathers, differences in the time of the year in which the reign of a king officially began, and differences in the way a king's first year was reckoned (e.g., see notes on 15:33; 2Ki 8:25; see also chart on "Rulers of Israel and Judah," p. 502).

Content

1,2 Kings describes the history of Israel's monarchy from the closing days of the rule of David until the time of the Babylonian exile. After an extensive account of Solomon's reign, the narrative records the division of the kingdom and then, by means of its synchronistic accounts, presents an interrelated picture of developments within the two kingdoms.

Kingship in the northern kingdom was plagued with instability and violence. Twenty rulers represented nine different dynasties during the approximately 210 years from the division of the kingdom in 930 B.C. until the fall of Samaria in 722-721. In the southern kingdom there were also 20 rulers, but these were all descendants of David (except Athaliah, whose usurping of the throne interrupted the sequence for a few years) and spanned a period of about 345 years from the division of the kingdom until the fall of Jerusalem in 586.

Outline

1,2 Kings can be broadly outlined by relating its contents to the major historical periods it describes and to the ministries of Elijah and Elisha.

I. The Solomonic Era (1:1-12:24)
  A. Solomon's Succession to the Throne (1:1-2:12)
  B. Solomon's Throne Consolidated (2:13-46)
  C. Solomon's Wisdom (ch. 3)
  D. Solomon's Reign Characterized (ch. 4)
  E. Solomon's Building Projects (5:1-9:9)
    1. Preparation for building the temple (ch. 5)
    2. Building the temple (ch. 6)
    3. Building the palace (7:1-12)
    4. The temple furnishings (7:13-51)
    5. Dedication of the temple (ch. 8)
    6. The Lord's response and warning (9:1-9)
  F. Solomon's Reign Characterized (9:10-10:29)
  G. Solomon's Folly (11:1-13)
  H. Solomon's Throne Threatened (11:14-43)
  I. Rehoboam's Succession to the Throne (12:1-24)
II. Israel and Judah from Jeroboam I/Rehoboam to Ahab/Asa (12:25-16:34)
  A. Jeroboam I of Israel (12:25-14:20)
  B. Rehoboam of Judah (14:21-31)
  C. Abijah of Judah (15:1-8)
  D. Asa of Judah (15:9-24)
  E. Nadab of Israel (15:25-32)
  F. Baasha of Israel (15:33-16:7)
  G. Elah of Israel (16:8-14)
  H. Zimri of Israel (16:15-20)
  I. Omri of Israel (16:21-28)
  J. Ahab of Israel (16:29-34)

III. The Ministries of Elijah and Elisha and Other Prophets from Ahab/Asa to Joram/Jehoshaphat (17:1-2Ki 8:15)
   A. Elijah (and Other Prophets) in the Reign of Ahab (17:1-22:40)
      1. Elijah and the drought (ch. 17)
      2. Elijah on Mount Carmel (ch. 18)
      3. Elijah's flight to Horeb (ch. 19)
      4. A prophet condemns Ahab for sparing Ben-Hadad (ch. 20)
      5. Elijah condemns Ahab for seizing Naboth's vineyard (ch. 21)
      6. Micaiah prophesies Ahab's death; its fulfillment (22:1-40)
   B. Jehoshaphat of Judah (22:41-50)
   C. Ahaziah of Israel; Elijah's Last Prophecy (22:51-2Ki 1:18)
   D. Elijah's Translation; Elisha's Inauguration (2Ki 2:1-18)
   E. Elisha in the Reign of Joram (2:19-8:15)
      1. Elisha's initial miraculous signs (2:19-25)
      2. Elisha during the campaign against Moab (ch. 3)
      3. Elisha's ministry to needy ones in Israel (ch. 4)
      4. Elisha heals Naaman (ch. 5)
      5. Elisha's deliverance of one of the prophets (6:1-7)
      6. Elisha's deliverance of Joram from Aramean raiders (6:8-23)
      7. Aramean siege of Samaria lifted, as Elisha prophesied (6:24-7:20)
      8. The Shunammite's land restored (8:1-6)
      9. Elisha prophesies Hazael's oppression of Israel (8:7-15)
IV. Israel and Judah from Joram/Jehoram to the Exile of Israel (2Ki 8:16-17:41)
   A. Jehoram of Judah (8:16-24)
   B. Ahaziah of Judah (8:25-29)
   C. Jehu's Revolt and Reign (chs. 9-10)
      1. Elisha orders Jehu's anointing (9:1-13)
      2. Jehu's assassination of Joram and Ahaziah (9:14-29)
      3. Jehu's execution of Jezebel (9:30-37)
      4. Jehu's slaughter of Ahab's family (10:1-17)
      5. Jehu's eradication of Baal worship (10:18-36)
   D. Athaliah and Joash of Judah; Repair of the Temple (chs. 11-12)
   E. Jehoahaz of Israel (13:1-9)
   F. Jehoash of Israel; Elisha's Last Prophecy (13:10-25)
   G. Amaziah of Judah (14:1-22)
   H. Jeroboam II of Israel (14:23-29)
   I. Azariah of Judah (15:1-7)
   J. Zechariah of Israel (15:8-12)
   K. Shallum of Israel (15:13-16)
   L. Menahem of Israel (15:17-22)
   M. Pekahiah of Israel (15:23-26)
   N. Pekah of Israel (15:27-31)
   O. Jotham of Judah (15:32-38)
   P. Ahaz of Judah (ch. 16)
   Q. Hoshea of Israel (17:1-6)
   R. Exile of Israel; Resettlement of the Land (17:7-41)
V. Judah from Hezekiah to the Babylonian Exile (2Ki 18-25)
   A. Hezekiah (chs. 18-20)
      1. Hezekiah's good reign (18:1-8)
      2. The Assyrian threat and deliverance (18:9-19:37)
      3. Hezekiah's illness and alliance with Babylon (ch. 20)
   B. Manasseh (21:1-18)
   C. Amon (21:19-26)
   D. Josiah (22:1-23:30)
      1. Repair of the temple; discovery of the Book of the Law (ch. 22)
      2. Renewal of the covenant; end of Josiah's reign (23:1-30)
   E. Jehoahaz Exiled to Egypt (23:31-35)

Adonijah Sets Himself Up as King

1 When King David was old and well advanced in years, he could not keep warm even when they put covers over him. [2]So his servants said to him, "Let us look for a young virgin to attend the king and take care of him. She can lie beside him so that our lord the king may keep warm."

[3]Then they searched throughout Israel for a beautiful girl and found Abishag,[a] a Shunammite,[b] and brought her to the king. [4]The girl was very beautiful; she took care of the king and waited on him, but the king had no intimate relations with her.

[5]Now Adonijah,[c] whose mother was Haggith, put himself forward and said, "I will be king." So he got chariots[d] and horses[a] ready, with fifty men to run ahead of him. [6](His father had never interfered[e] with him by asking, "Why do you behave as you do?" He was also very handsome and was born next after Absalom.)

[7]Adonijah conferred with Joab[f] son of Zeruiah and with Abiathar[g] the priest, and they gave him their support. [8]But Zadok[h] the priest, Benaiah[i] son of Jehoiada, Nathan[j] the prophet, Shimei[k] and Rei[b] and

David's special guard[l] did not join Adonijah.

[9]Adonijah then sacrificed sheep, cattle and fattened calves at the Stone of Zoheleth near En Rogel. [m] He invited all his brothers, the king's sons,[n] and all the men of Judah who were royal officials, [10]but he did not invite[o] Nathan the prophet or Benaiah or the special guard or his brother Solomon.[p]

[11]Then Nathan asked Bathsheba,[q] Solomon's mother, "Have you not heard that Adonijah,[r] the son of Haggith, has become king without our lord David's knowing it? [12]Now then, let me advise[s] you how you can save your own life and the life of your son Solomon. [13]Go in to King David and say to him, 'My lord the king, did you not swear[t] to me your servant: "Surely Solomon your son shall be king after me, and he will sit on my throne"? Why then has Adonijah become king?' [14]While you are still there talking to the king, I will come in and confirm what you have said."

[15]So Bathsheba went to see the aged king in his room, where Abishag[u] the Shunammite was attending him. [16]Bathsheba bowed low and knelt before the king.

a5 Or charioteers   b8 Or and his friends

1:3 aVer 15; S 2Sa 3:7; 1Ki 2:17,22
bS Jos 19:18
1:5 cS 2Sa 3:4
dS 1Sa 8:11
1:6 eISa 3:13
1:7 fS 2Sa 2:13, 18 gS 1Sa 22:20
1:8 hS 1Sa 2:35; S 2Sa 8:17
iS 2Sa 8:18
jS 2Sa 7:2
k1Ki 4:18
l2Sa 23:8
1:9 mS 2Sa 17:17
n1Ch 29:24
1:10 over 26
pS 2Sa 12:24
1:11 q2Sa 12:24
rS 2Sa 3:4
1:12 sPr 15:22
1:13 tver 17,30
1:15 uS ver 3

1:1—12:24 The narrative of the Solomonic era is an exquisite example of literary inversion, in this case consisting of nine sections. The first and last are parallel, as well as the second and eighth, etc.—and the fifth section, which occupies the central position in the structure, is the longest of the nine and describes Solomon's building projects (see Introduction: Outline).

1:1 *advanced in years.* 2Sa 5:4 indicates that David died at about 70 years of age (cf. 1Ki 2:11).

1:3 *Shunammite.* Abishag came from Shunem (2Ki 4:8; Jos 19:18; 1Sa 28:4), located near the plain of Jezreel in the tribal territory of Issachar.

1:4 *had no intimate relations with her.* Significant in connection with Adonijah's request to be given Abishag as his wife after the death of David (see notes on 2:17,22).

1:5 *Adonijah.* The fourth son of David (see 2Sa 3:4), who was at this time approximately 35 years of age. It is likely that he was the oldest surviving son of David (see note on 2Sa 13:28; see also 2Sa 18:14). *put himself forward.* A unilateral attempt to usurp the throne, bypassing King David's right to designate his own successor (Adonijah must at least have known that his father favored Solomon; see v. 10). If successful, it would have thwarted God's and David's choice of Solomon (see vv. 13,17,30; 1Ch 22:9–10; see also note on 2Sa 12:25). *fifty men to run ahead of him.* Adonijah here follows the example of Absalom before him (see note on 2Sa 15:1).

1:6 *never interfered.* David appears to have been consistently negligent in disciplining his sons (see notes on 2Sa 13:21; 14:33). *very handsome.* Attractive physical appearance was an important asset to an aspirant to the throne (see 1Sa 9:2; 16:12; 2Sa 14:25).

1:7 *Joab son of Zeruiah.* See notes on 1Sa 26:6; 2Sa 2:13; 19:13; 20:10,23. Joab's alignment with Adonijah may have

been motivated by a struggle for power with Benaiah (see v. 8; 2Sa 8:18; 20:23; 23:20–23). Joab held his position more by his standing with the army than by the favor and confidence of David (see 2:5–6). *Abiathar the priest.* See note on 2Sa 8:17.

1:8 *Zadok the priest.* See note on 2Sa 8:17. *Benaiah son of Jehoiada.* See note on 2Sa 23:20. *Nathan the prophet.* See 2Sa 12:1–25. *Shimei.* Not the Shimei of 2:8,46; 2Sa 16:5–8; perhaps the same as Shimei son of Ela (4:18). *Rei.* See NIV text note. There is no other OT reference to Rei if taken as a proper name. *David's special guard.* See 2Sa 23:8–39.

1:9 *Adonijah then sacrificed.* Here also (see note on v. 5) Adonijah followed the example of Absalom (see 2Sa 15:7–12). *En Rogel.* Means "the spring of Rogel"; located just south of Jerusalem in the Kidron Valley. Apparently the site of a spring had some kind of symbolic significance for the business at hand (see v. 33 and note).

1:11 *Bathsheba, Solomon's mother.* The queen mother held an important and influential position in the royal court (see 2:19; 15:13; 2Ki 10:13; 2Ch 15:16). *has become king.* Although the preceding narrative does not relate the actual proclamation of Adonijah's kingship, it can be assumed from v. 25; 2:15; cf. 2Sa 15:10).

1:12 *save your own life and the life of your son Solomon.* It was common in the ancient Near East for a usurper to liquidate all potential claimants to the throne in an attempt to secure his own position (see 15:29; 2Ki 10:11; 11:1).

1:13 *did you not swear to me ...?* Although 2 Samuel does not record David's oath concerning the succession of Solomon, it does suggest that Solomon was the son through whom the Lord's promise to David for an eternal dynasty would be carried forward (see note on v. 5).

"What is it you want?" the king asked. ¹⁷She said to him, "My lord, you yourself swore^v to me your servant by the LORD your God: 'Solomon your son shall be king after me, and he will sit on my throne.' ¹⁸But now Adonijah has become king, and you, my lord the king, do not know about it. ¹⁹He has sacrificed^w great numbers of cattle, fattened calves, and sheep, and has invited all the king's sons, Abiathar the priest and Joab the commander of the army, but he has not invited Solomon your servant. ²⁰My lord the king, the eyes of all Israel are on you, to learn from you who will sit on the throne of my lord the king after him. ²¹Otherwise, as soon as my lord the king is laid to rest^x with his fathers, I and my son Solomon will be treated as criminals."

²²While she was still speaking with the king, Nathan the prophet arrived. ²³And they told the king, "Nathan the prophet is here." So he went before the king and bowed with his face to the ground.

²⁴Nathan said, "Have you, my lord the king, declared that Adonijah shall be king after you, and that he will sit on your throne? ²⁵Today he has gone down and sacrificed great numbers of cattle, fattened calves, and sheep. He has invited all the king's sons, the commanders of the army and Abiathar the priest. Right now they are eating and drinking with him and saying, 'Long live King Adonijah!' ²⁶But me your servant, and Zadok the priest, and Benaiah son of Jehoiada, and your servant Solomon he did not invite.^y ²⁷Is this something my lord the king has done without letting his servants know who should sit on the throne of my lord the king after him?"

David Makes Solomon King

1:28–53pp — 1Ch 29:21–25

²⁸Then King David said, "Call in Bathsheba." So she came into the king's presence and stood before him.

²⁹The king then took an oath: "As surely as the LORD lives, who has delivered me out of every trouble,^z ³⁰I will surely carry out today what I swore^a to you by the LORD, the God of Israel: Solomon your son shall be king after me, and he will sit on my throne in my place."

³¹Then Bathsheba bowed low with her face to the ground and, kneeling before the king, said, "May my lord King David live forever!"

³²King David said, "Call in Zadok^b the priest, Nathan the prophet and Benaiah son of Jehoiada." When they came before the king, ³³he said to them: "Take your lord's servants with you and set Solomon my son on my own mule^c and take him down to Gihon.^d ³⁴There have Zadok the priest and Nathan the prophet anoint^e him king over Israel. Blow the trumpet^f and shout, 'Long live King Solomon!' ³⁵Then you are to go up with him, and he is to come and sit on my throne and reign in my place. I have appointed him ruler over Israel and Judah."

³⁶Benaiah son of Jehoiada answered the king, "Amen! May the LORD, the God of my lord the king, so declare it. ³⁷As the LORD was with my lord the king, so may he be with^g Solomon to make his throne even greater^h than the throne of my lord King David!"

³⁸So Zadokⁱ the priest, Nathan the prophet, Benaiah son of Jehoiada, the Kerethites^j and the Pelethites went down and put Solomon on King David's mule

Cross references (center column)

1:17 ^vS ver 13
1:19 ^wver 9
1:21 ^xS Ge 15:15; 1Ki 2:10
1:26 ^yver 10

1:29 ^zS 2Sa 4:9
1:30 ^aS ver 13; 1Ch 23:1
1:32 ^bS 1Sa 2:35
1:33 ^cJdg 10:4; Zec 9:9 ^dver 38; 2Ch 32:30; 33:14
1:34 ^eS 1Sa 2:35; 10:1 ^fS 2Sa 15:10
1:37 ^gJos 1:5,17 ^hver 47
1:38 ⁱver 8 /S 1Sa 30:14; S 2Sa 15:18

1:17 *you yourself swore to me . . . by the LORD your God.* An oath taken in the Lord's name was inviolable (see Ex 20:7; Lev 19:12; Jos 9:15,18,20; Jdg 11:30,35; Ecc 5:4–7).
1:21 *laid to rest with his fathers.* A conventional expression for death (see Ge 47:30; Dt 31:16).
1:24 Nathan approached David diplomatically by raising a question that revealed the dilemma. Either David had secretly encouraged Adonijah to claim the throne and thereby had broken his oath to Bathsheba and Solomon (see v. 27), or he had been betrayed by Adonijah.
1:25 *Long live King Adonijah!* An expression of recognition and acclamation of the new king (see 1Sa 10:24; 2Sa 16:16; 2Ki 11:12).
1:31 *May my lord King David live forever!* An expression of Bathsheba's thanks in the stereotyped hyperbolic language of the court (see Ne 2:3; Da 2:4; 3:9; 5:10; 6:21).
1:33 *your lord's servants.* Presumably including the Kerethites and Pelethites (see v. 38). *my own mule.* Although crossbreeding was forbidden in the Mosaic law (Lev 19:19), mules (perhaps imported; see Eze 27:14) were used in the

time of David, at least as mounts for royalty (see 2Sa 13:29; 18:9). To ride on David's own mule was a public proclamation that Solomon's succession to the throne was sanctioned by David (see Ge 41:43 and first NIV text note; Est 6:7–8). *Gihon.* The site of a spring on the eastern slope of Mount Zion (see notes on v. 9; 2Sa 5:8).
1:34 *anoint him.* See notes on 1Sa 2:10; 9:16. *Blow the trumpet.* See 2Ki 9:13; 2Sa 15:10; 20:1. *Long live King Solomon!* See note on v. 25.
1:35 *Israel and Judah.* The distinction between Israel and Judah was rooted in the separate arrangements by which David became king over these two tribal units (see 2Sa 2:4; 5:3).
1:36 *Amen! May the LORD . . . so declare it.* See Jer 28:6.
1:37 *even greater.* Not a deprecation of David's accomplishments, but an expression of total loyalty to David and Solomon. Benaiah shared David's own desire for his chosen successor (see vv. 47–48).
1:38 *the Kerethites and the Pelethites.* See note on 2Sa 8:18.

and escorted him to Gihon.[k] [39]Zadok the priest took the horn of oil[l] from the sacred tent[m] and anointed Solomon. Then they sounded the trumpet[n] and all the people shouted,[o] "Long live King Solomon!" [40]And all the people went up after him, playing flutes[p] and rejoicing greatly, so that the ground shook with the sound.

[41]Adonijah and all the guests who were with him heard it as they were finishing their feast. On hearing the sound of the trumpet, Joab asked, "What's the meaning of all the noise in the city?"[q]

[42]Even as he was speaking, Jonathan[r] son of Abiathar the priest arrived. Adonijah said, "Come in. A worthy man like you must be bringing good news."[s]

[43]"Not at all!" Jonathan answered. "Our lord King David has made Solomon king. [44]The king has sent with him Zadok the priest, Nathan the prophet, Benaiah son of Jehoiada, the Kerethites and the Pelethites, and they have put him on the king's mule, [45]and Zadok the priest and Nathan the prophet have anointed him king at Gihon. From there they have gone up cheering, and the city resounds[t] with it. That's the noise you hear. [46]Moreover, Solomon has taken his seat[u] on the royal throne. [47]Also, the royal officials have come to congratulate our lord King David, saying, 'May your God make Solomon's name more famous than yours and his throne greater[v] than yours!' And the king bowed in worship on his bed [48]and said,

'Praise be to the LORD, the God of Israel, who has allowed my eyes to see a successor[w] on my throne today.' "

[49]At this, all Adonijah's guests rose in alarm and dispersed. [50]But Adonijah, in fear of Solomon, went and took hold of the horns[x] of the altar. [51]Then Solomon was told, "Adonijah is afraid of King Solomon and is clinging to the horns of the altar. He says, 'Let King Solomon swear to me today that he will not put his servant to death with the sword.' "

[52]Solomon replied, "If he shows himself to be a worthy man, not a hair[y] of his head will fall to the ground; but if evil is found in him, he will die." [53]Then King Solomon sent men, and they brought him down from the altar. And Adonijah came and bowed down to King Solomon, and Solomon said, "Go to your home."

David's Charge to Solomon

2:10–12pp — 1Ch 29:26–28

2 When the time drew near for David to die,[z] he gave a charge to Solomon his son.

[2]"I am about to go the way of all the earth,"[a] he said. "So be strong,[b] show yourself a man, [3]and observe[c] what the LORD your God requires: Walk in his ways, and keep his decrees and commands, his laws and requirements, as written in the Law of Moses, so that you may prosper[d] in all you do and wherever you go, [4]and that the LORD may keep his promise[e] to me: 'If

1:38 [k]S ver 33
1:39 [l]S Ex 29:7;
S 1Sa 10:1;
2Ki 11:12;
Ps 89:20
[m]S Ex 26:1;
S 27:21
[n]S 2Sa 15:10;
2Ki 11:14 [o]ver 34; Nu 23:21;
Ps 47:5; Zec 9:9
1:40 [p]S 1Sa 10:5
1:41
[q]2Ch 23:12-13
1:42
[r]S 2Sa 15:27,36
[s]S 2Sa 18:26
1:45 [t]ver 40
1:46 [u]S Dt 17:18
1:47 [v]ver 37

1:48 [w]1Ki 3:6
1:50 [x]S Ex 27:2
1:52
[y]S 1Sa 14:45
2:1 [z]S Ge 27:2;
S Nu 27:13
2:2 [a]Jos 23:14
[b]S Jos 1:6
2:3 [c]S Dt 4:6;
S 10:12;
S 17:14-20;
S Jos 1:7
[d]1Ch 22:13
2:4 [e]S 2Sa 7:13,
15; 2Ch 23:3

1:39 *Zadok ... anointed Solomon.* Kings chosen by God to rule over his people who were not in a line of dynastic succession were anointed by prophets (Saul, 1Sa 9:16; David, 1Sa 16:12; Jehu, 2Ki 9). Kings who assumed office in the line of dynastic succession were anointed by priests (Solomon, here; Joash, 2Ki 11:12). The distinction seems to be that the priest worked within the established order while the prophets introduced new divine initiatives. *horn of oil.* Perhaps containing the anointing oil described in Ex 30:22–33. *sacred tent.* The tent David had erected in Jerusalem to house the ark (see 2Sa 6:17) rather than the tabernacle at Gibeon (see 3:4 and note; 2Ch 1:3).

1:41 *heard it.* Although Gihon may not have been visible from En Rogel, the distance was not great and the sound would carry down the Kidron Valley.

1:42 *Jonathan son of Abiathar.* See 2Sa 17:17–21.

1:47 *more famous.* See note on v. 37.

1:48 *successor.* In Solomon's succession to the throne David sees a fulfillment of the promise in 2Sa 7:12,16.

1:49 *dispersed.* No one wanted to be identified with Adonijah's abortive coup now that it appeared certain to fail.

1:50 *took hold of the horns of the altar.* The horns of the altar were vertical projections at each corner. The idea of seeking asylum at the altar was rooted in the Pentateuch (see Ex 21:13–14). The priest smeared the blood of the sacrifice on the horns of the altar (see Ex 29:12; Lev 4:7,18,25,30, 34) during the sacrificial ritual. Adonijah thus seeks to place his own destiny under the protection of God.

1:52 *worthy man.* Who recognizes and submits to Solomon's office and authority. *if evil is found in him.* If he shows evidence of continuing opposition to Solomon's succession to the throne.

2:1 *he gave a charge.* Moses (Dt 31:1–8), Joshua (Jos 23:1–16) and Samuel (1Sa 12:1–25), as representatives of the Lord's rule, had all given final instructions and admonitions shortly before their deaths.

2:2 *the way of all the earth.* To the grave (see Jos 23:14). *be strong.* See Dt 31:7,23; Jos 1:6–7,9,18.

2:3 *observe what the LORD your God requires.* See Ge 26:5; Lev 18:30; Dt 11:1. *Walk in his ways.* A characteristic expression of Deuteronomy for obedience to covenant obligations (Dt 5:33; 8:6; 10:12; 11:22; 19:9; 26:17; 28:9; 30:16). *his decrees and commands, his laws and requirements.* Four generally synonymous terms for covenant obligations (see 6:12; 8:58; 2Ki 17:37; Dt 8:11; 11:1; 26:17; 28:15,45; 30:10,16). *that you may prosper.* See Dt 29:9.

2:4 *that the LORD may keep his promise to me.* David here alludes to the covenanted promise of an everlasting dynasty given to him by God through Nathan the prophet (see notes on 2Sa 7:11–16). Although the covenant promise to David was unconditional, individual participation in its blessing on the part of David's royal descendants was conditioned on obedience to the obligations of the Mosaic covenant (see 2Ch 7:17–22). *with all their heart and soul.* See Dt 4:29; 6:5; 10:12; 30:6. *you will never fail to have a man on the*

your descendants watch how they live, and if they walk faithfully[f] before me with all their heart and soul, you will never fail to have a man on the throne of Israel.'

⁵"Now you yourself know what Joab[g] son of Zeruiah did to me—what he did to the two commanders of Israel's armies, Abner[h] son of Ner and Amasa[i] son of Jether. He killed them, shedding their blood in peacetime as if in battle, and with that blood stained the belt around his waist and the sandals on his feet. ⁶Deal with him according to your wisdom,[j] but do not let his gray head go down to the grave[c] in peace.

⁷"But show kindness[k] to the sons of Barzillai[l] of Gilead and let them be among those who eat at your table.[m] They stood by me when I fled from your brother Absalom.

⁸"And remember, you have with you Shimei[n] son of Gera, the Benjamite from Bahurim, who called down bitter curses on me the day I went to Mahanaim.[o] When he came down to meet me at the Jordan, I swore[p] to him by the LORD: 'I will not put you to death by the sword.' ⁹But now, do not consider him innocent. You are a man of wisdom;[q] you will know what to do to him. Bring his gray head down to the grave in blood."

¹⁰Then David rested with his fathers and was buried[r] in the City of David.[s] ¹¹He had reigned[t] forty years over Israel—seven years in Hebron and thirty-three in Jerusalem. ¹²So Solomon sat on the throne[u] of his father David, and his rule was firmly established.[v]

Solomon's Throne Established

¹³Now Adonijah,[w] the son of Haggith, went to Bathsheba, Solomon's mother.

Cross references
2:4 /2Ki 18:3-6; 20:3; Ps 26:1-3; 132:12
2:5 gS 2Sa 2:18 hS 1Sa 14:50; S 2Sa 17:25 iS 2Sa 17:25
2:6 /ver 9
2:7 kS Ge 40:14 lS 2Sa 17:27; 19:31-39 mS 2Sa 9:7
2:8 nver 36-46; 2Sa 16:5-13
oS Ge 32:2
p2Sa 19:18-23
2:9 qver 6
2:10 rAc 2:29 sS 2Sa 5:7
2:11 tS 2Sa 5:4,5
2:12 uICh 17:14; 29:23; 2Ch 9:8 vver 46; 2Ch 1:1; 12:13; 17:1; 21:4
2:13 wS 2Sa 3:4

c6 Hebrew *Sheol*; also in verse 9

---

throne of Israel. Both Solomon and his descendants fell short of their covenant obligations. This led to the division of the kingdom and eventually to the exile of both the northern and southern kingdoms. It was only in the coming of Christ that the fallen tent of David would be restored (see notes on Am 9:11–15; Ac 15:16) and the promise of David's eternal dynasty ultimately fulfilled. When the nation and its king turned away from the requirements of the Sinai covenant, they experienced the covenant curses rather than blessings; but in all this God remained faithful to his covenant promises to Abraham and to David (see Lev 26:42–45; Isa 9:6–7; 11:1–16; 16:5; 55:3; Jer 23:5–6; 30:9; 33:17,20–22, 25–26; Eze 34:23–24; 37:24–28).

2:5 *Joab son of Zeruiah.* See note on 1:7. *Abner son of Ner.* See notes on 2Sa 3:25–32. *Amasa son of Jether.* See 2Sa 20:10. *shedding their blood in peacetime.* Joab's actions were unlawful assassinations (see Dt 19:1–13; 21:1–9) and

only served his own self-interest.
2:7 *sons of Barzillai.* See note on 2Sa 17:27. *eat at your table.* A position of honor that brought with it other benefits (see 18:19; 2Ki 25:29; 2Sa 9:7; 19:28; Ne 5:17).
2:8 See 2Sa 16:5–13. *Shimei son of Gera, the Benjamite.* Gera was probably the ancestor of Shimei's particular line of descent rather than his immediate father (see Ge 46:21; Jdg 3:15). See NIV text notes on Ge 10:2; Da 5:22.
2:9 *do not consider him innocent.* The Mosaic law prohibited cursing a ruler (21:10; Ex 22:28).
2:10 *rested with his fathers.* See note on 1:21. *City of David.* See 2Sa 5:7 and note. Peter implies that David's tomb is still known in his day (Ac 2:29).
2:11 *forty years.* See 2Sa 5:4–5. David ruled c. 1010–970 B.C. (see Introduction to 1Samuel: Chronology).
2:13 *Adonijah, the son of Haggith.* See note on 1:5. *Do you come peacefully?* The question (see 1Sa 16:4; 2Ki 9:22)

Solomon's Jerusalem

c. 950 B.C.

Solomon extended the city northward from the original site and there built his magnificent temple.

His royal residence was nearby; however, its architecture and location are unknown.

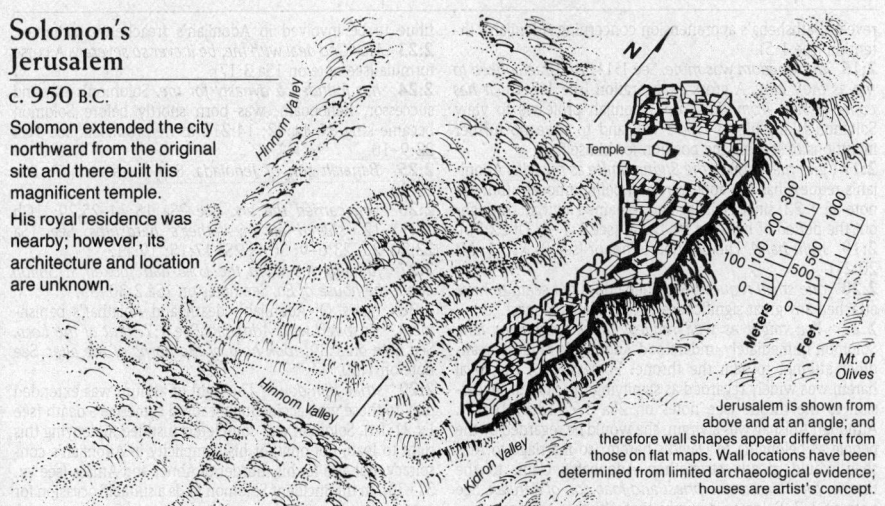

Jerusalem is shown from above and at an angle; and therefore wall shapes appear different from those on flat maps. Wall locations have been determined from limited archaeological evidence; houses are artist's concept.

Bathsheba asked him, "Do you come
peacefully?"[x]
He answered, "Yes, peacefully." 14Then
he added, "I have something to say to
you."
"You may say it," she replied.
15"As you know," he said, "the kingdom was mine. All Israel looked to me as
their king. But things changed, and the
kingdom has gone to my brother; for it has
come to him from the LORD. 16Now I have
one request to make of you. Do not refuse
me."
"You may make it," she said.
17So he continued, "Please ask King
Solomon—he will not refuse you—to give
me Abishag[y] the Shunammite as my
wife."
18"Very well," Bathsheba replied, "I
will speak to the king for you."
19When Bathsheba went to King Solomon to speak to him for Adonijah, the king
stood up to meet her, bowed down to her
and sat down on his throne. He had a
throne brought for the king's mother,[z]
and she sat down at his right hand.[a]
20"I have one small request to make of
you," she said. "Do not refuse me."
The king replied, "Make it, my mother;
I will not refuse you."
21So she said, "Let Abishag[b] the Shunammite be given in marriage to your
brother Adonijah."
22King Solomon answered his mother,
"Why do you request Abishag[c] the Shunammite for Adonijah? You might as well
request the kingdom for him—after all, he
is my older brother[d]—yes, for him and for
Abiathar[e] the priest and Joab son of Zeruiah!"
23Then King Solomon swore by the
LORD: "May God deal with me, be it ever
so severely,[f] if Adonijah does not pay with
his life for this request! 24And now, as
surely as the LORD lives—he who has
established me securely on the throne of
my father David and has founded a dynasty
for me as he promised[g]—Adonijah shall
be put to death today!" 25So King Solomon
gave orders to Benaiah[h] son of Jehoiada,
and he struck down Adonijah and he
died.[i]
26To Abiathar[j] the priest the king said,
"Go back to your fields in Anathoth.[k] You
deserve to die, but I will not put you to
death now, because you carried the ark[l]
of the Sovereign LORD before my father
David and shared all my father's hardships."[m] 27So Solomon removed Abiathar
from the priesthood of the LORD, fulfilling[n]
the word the LORD had spoken at Shiloh
about the house of Eli.
28When the news reached Joab, who
had conspired with Adonijah though not
with Absalom, he fled to the tent of the
LORD and took hold of the horns[o] of the
altar. 29King Solomon was told that Joab
had fled to the tent of the LORD and was
beside the altar.[p] Then Solomon ordered
Benaiah[q] son of Jehoiada, "Go, strike him
down!"
30So Benaiah entered the tent[r] of the
LORD and said to Joab, "The king says,
'Come out![s]'"
But he answered, "No, I will die here."

2:13 [x]S 1Sa 16:4
2:17 [y]S 1Ki 1:3
2:19 [z]1Ki 15:13; 2Ki 10:13; 24:15; 2Ch 15:16; Jer 13:18; 22:26; 29:2 [a]Ps 45:9
2:21 [b]1Ki 1:3
2:22 [c]S Ge 22:24; S 1Ki 1:3 [d]1Ch 3:2 [e]S 1Sa 22:20
2:23 [f]S Ru 1:17
2:24 [g]2Sa 7:11
2:25 [h]S 2Sa 8:18 [i]S 2Sa 12:10
2:26 [j]S 1Sa 22:20 [k]S Jos 21:18 [l]S 2Sa 15:24 [m]S 2Sa 15:14
2:27 [n]S 1Sa 2:27-36
2:28 [o]S Ex 27:2
2:29 [p]Ex 21:14 [q]ver 25
2:30 [r]2Ki 11:15 [s]Ex 21:14

---

reveals Bathsheba's apprehension concerning Adonijah's intention (see 1:5).
2:15 *the kingdom was mine.* See 1:11. *All Israel looked to me as their king.* A gross exaggeration (see 1:7–8). *it has come to him from the LORD.* Adonijah professes to view Solomon's kingship as God's will and to have no further intentions of seeking the position for himself.
2:17 *give me Abishag the Shunammite as my wife.* Adonijah's request has the appearance of being innocent (but see note on v. 22) since Abishag had remained a virgin throughout the period of her care for David (see 1:1–4; Dt 22:30).
2:19 *right hand.* The position of honor (see Ps 110:1; Mt 20:21).
2:20 *one small request.* Bathsheba does not seem to have attached any great significance to Adonijah's request.
2:22 *You might as well request the kingdom for him.* Solomon immediately understood Adonijah's request as another attempt to gain the throne. Possession of the royal harem was widely regarded as signifying the right of succession to the throne (see notes on 2Sa 3:7; 12:8; 16:21). Although Abishag was a virgin, she would be regarded by the people as belonging to David's harem; so marriage to Abishag would greatly strengthen Adonijah's claim to the throne. *for Abiathar the priest and Joab son of Zeruiah.* See note on 1:7. Solomon assumes that Abiathar and Joab continue to be involved in Adonijah's treacherous schemes.
2:23 *May God deal with me, be it ever so severely.* A curse formula (see note on 1Sa 3:17).
2:24 *has founded a dynasty for me.* Solomon's son and successor, Rehoboam, was born shortly before Solomon became king (cf. 11:42; 14:21). *as he promised.* See 1Ch 22:9–10.
2:25 *Benaiah son of Jehoiada.* See notes on 1:7; 2Sa 23:20.
2:26 *you carried the ark.* See 2Sa 15:24–25,29; 1Ch 15:11–12. *shared all my father's hardships.* See 1Sa 22:20–23; 23:6–9; 30:7; 2Sa 17:15; 19:11.
2:27 *fulfilling the word the LORD had spoken at Shiloh about the house of Eli.* See notes on 1Sa 2:30–35.
2:28 *news.* Of Adonijah's death and Abiathar's banishment. *conspired with Adonijah.* See 1:7. *tent of the LORD.* See note on 1:39. *took hold of the horns of the altar.* See note on 1:50.
2:29 *strike him down!* The right of asylum was extended only to those who accidentally caused someone's death (see Ex 21:14). Solomon was completely justified in denying this right to Joab, not only for his complicity in Adonijah's conspiracy, but also for his murder of Abner and Amasa (see vv. 31–33). In this incident Solomon finds a suitable occasion for carrying out his father's instruction (see vv. 5–6).

Benaiah reported to the king, "This is how Joab answered me."

31Then the king commanded Benaiah, "Do as he says. Strike him down and bury him, and so clear me and my father's house of the guilt of the innocent blood[t] that Joab shed. 32The LORD will repay[u] him for the blood he shed,[v] because without the knowledge of my father David he attacked two men and killed them with the sword. Both of them—Abner son of Ner, commander of Israel's army, and Amasa[w] son of Jether, commander of Judah's army—were better[x] men and more upright than he. 33May the guilt of their blood rest on the head of Joab and his descendants forever. But on David and his descendants, his house and his throne, may there be the LORD's peace forever."

34So Benaiah[y] son of Jehoiada went up and struck down Joab[z] and killed him, and he was buried on his own land[d] in the desert. 35The king put Benaiah[a] son of Jehoiada over the army in Joab's position and replaced Abiathar with Zadok[b] the priest.

36Then the king sent for Shimei[c] and said to him, "Build yourself a house in Jerusalem and live there, but do not go anywhere else. 37The day you leave and cross the Kidron Valley,[d] you can be sure you will die; your blood will be on your own head."[e]

38Shimei answered the king, "What you say is good. Your servant will do as my lord the king has said." And Shimei stayed in Jerusalem for a long time.

39But three years later, two of Shimei's slaves ran off to Achish[f] son of Maacah,

king of Gath, and Shimei was told, "Your slaves are in Gath." 40At this, he saddled his donkey and went to Achish at Gath in search of his slaves. So Shimei went away and brought the slaves back from Gath.

41When Solomon was told that Shimei had gone from Jerusalem to Gath and had returned, 42the king summoned Shimei and said to him, "Did I not make you swear by the LORD and warn[g] you, 'On the day you leave to go anywhere else, you can be sure you will die'? At that time you said to me, 'What you say is good. I will obey.' 43Why then did you not keep your oath to the LORD and obey the command I gave you?"

44The king also said to Shimei, "You know in your heart all the wrong[h] you did to my father David. Now the LORD will repay you for your wrongdoing. 45But King Solomon will be blessed, and David's throne will remain secure[i] before the LORD forever."

46Then the king gave the order to Benaiah[j] son of Jehoiada, and he went out and struck Shimei[k] down and killed him.

The kingdom was now firmly established[l] in Solomon's hands.

Solomon Asks for Wisdom

3:4–15pp — 2Ch 1:2–13

3 Solomon made an alliance with Pharaoh king of Egypt and married[m] his daughter.[n] He brought her to the City of David[o] until he finished building his palace[p] and the temple of the LORD, and the

2:31 [t]S Dt 19:13
2:32 [u]Jdg 9:57
[v]S Ge 4:14;
S Jdg 9:24
2:34 [w]S 2Sa 17:25
[x]2Ch 21:13
[y]ver 25
2:35 [z]S 2Sa 2:18
[a]S 2Sa 8:18
[b]S 1Sa 2:35
2:36 [c]S 2Sa 16:5
2:37
[d]S 2Sa 15:23;
Jn 18:1
[e]S Lev 20:9
2:39 [f]1Sa 27:2

2:42
[g]S 2Sa 19:23
2:44
[h]2Sa 16:5-13
2:45 [i]S 2Sa 7:13
2:46 [j]S 2Sa 8:18
[k]S ver 8 /S ver 12
3:1 [m]1Ki 7:8;
11:1-13
[n]1Ki 9:24;
2Ch 8:11
[o]2Sa 5:7;
1Ki 2:10
[p]S 2Sa 7:2;
1Ki 9:10

d34 Or buried in his tomb

2:32 he attacked two men and killed them. See 2Sa 3:27; 20:9–10. Israel's army. See 2Sa 2:8–9. Judah's army. See 2Sa 20:4.

2:34 on his own land. See NIV text note. The tomb of Joab's father was located near Bethlehem (see 2Sa 2:32). desert. Of Judah, east of Bethlehem.

2:35 Benaiah son of Jehoiada. See note on 2Sa 23:20. Zadok the priest. See notes on 1Sa 2:35; 2Sa 8:17.

2:36 do not go anywhere else. Confinement to Jerusalem would greatly reduce the possibility of Shimei's (see v. 8) conspiring with any remaining followers of Saul against Solomon's rule.

2:39 Achish son of Maacah, king of Gath. Gath was a major Philistine city (see Jos 13:3; 1Sa 6:16–17). It is likely that Gath was ruled successively by Maoch, Achish the elder (1Sa 27:2), Maacah and Achish the younger (here).

2:46 struck Shimei down and killed him. The third execution carried out by Benaiah (see vv. 25,34). It brought to completion the tasks assigned to Solomon by David just before his death (vv. 6,9).

3:1 made an alliance with Pharaoh. It appears likely that Solomon established his marriage alliance with either Siamun or Psusennes II, the last kings of the 21st Egyptian

dynasty (the first Egyptian pharaoh mentioned by name in the OT is Shishak—11:40; 14:25–26—who established the 22nd Egyptian dynasty c. 945 B.C.). Such an alliance attests Egyptian recognition of the growing importance and strength of the Israelite state. 1 Ki 9:16 indicates that the pharaoh gave his daughter the Canaanite town of Gezer as a dowry at the time of her marriage to Solomon. Gezer was located near the crossing of two important trade routes. One, to the west of Gezer, went from Egypt to the north and was very important for Egypt's commercial interests. The other, to the north of Gezer, went from Jerusalem to the Mediterranean Sea and the port of Joppa and was important to Solomon as a supply line for his building projects. The marriage alliance enabled both Solomon and the pharaoh to accomplish important economic and political objectives. No precise date is given for the conclusion of the marriage alliance, though it appears to have occurred in the third or fourth year of Solomon's reign (see 2:39). Solomon began construction of the temple in his fourth year (6:1), and control of the Gezer area was important to him for the beginning of this project. City of David. The Egyptian princess was given a temporary residence in the old fortress (see 2Sa 5:7 and note) until a separate palace of her own could be constructed some 20 years later (7:8; 9:10; 2Ch 8:11).

wall around Jerusalem. 2The people, however, were still sacrificing at the high
places,[q] because a temple had not yet
been built for the Name[r] of the LORD.
3Solomon showed his love[s] for the LORD
by walking[t] according to the statutes[u] of
his father David, except that he offered
sacrifices and burned incense on the high
places.[v]
4The king went to Gibeon[w] to offer sacrifices, for that was the most important
high place, and Solomon offered a thousand burnt offerings on that altar. 5At
Gibeon the LORD appeared[x] to Solomon
during the night in a dream,[y] and God
said, "Ask[z] for whatever you want me to
give you."
6Solomon answered, "You have shown
great kindness to your servant, my father
David, because he was faithful[a] to you and
righteous and upright in heart. You have
continued this great kindness to him and
have given him a son[b] to sit on his throne
this very day.
7"Now, O LORD my God, you have
made your servant king in place of my father David. But I am only a little child[c]
and do not know how to carry out my
duties. 8Your servant is here among the
people you have chosen,[d] a great people,
too numerous to count or number.[e] 9So
give your servant a discerning[f] heart to
govern your people and to distinguish[g] between right and wrong. For who is able[h]
to govern this great people of yours?"
10The Lord was pleased that Solomon
had asked for this. 11So God said to him,
"Since you have asked[i] for this and not
for long life or wealth for yourself, nor
have asked for the death of your enemies
but for discernment[j] in administering
justice, 12I will do what you have asked.[k] I
will give you a wise[l] and discerning heart,
so that there will never have been anyone
like you, nor will there ever be. 13More-
over, I will give you what you have not[m]
asked for—both riches and honor[n]—so
that in your lifetime you will have no
equal[o] among kings. 14And if you walk[p] in
my ways and obey my statutes and commands as David your father did, I will give
you a long life."[q] 15Then Solomon
awoke[r]—and he realized it had been a
dream.[s]
He returned to Jerusalem, stood before
the ark of the Lord's covenant and sacrificed burnt offerings[t] and fellowship offerings.[e][u] Then he gave a feast[v] for all his
court.

3:2 [q]Lev 17:3-5; S 26:30; Dt 12:14; 1Ki 15:14; 22:43 [r]S Dt 14:23 **3:3** [s]Dt 6:5; Ps 31:23; 145:20 [t]S Dt 10:12; S Jos 1:7 [u]S Dt 17:19; S 1Ki 14:8 [v]S ver 2; Lev 17:3-5; 2Ki 12:3; 15:4, 35; 16:4; 21:3 **3:4** [w]S Jos 9:3 **3:5** [x]1Ki 9:2; 11:9 [y]S Mt 27:19 [z]S Mt 7:7 **3:6** [a]S Ge 17:1 [b]1Ki 1:48 **3:7** [c]Nu 27:17; 1Ch 22:5; 29:1; Jer 1:6 **3:8** [d]S Dt 7:6 [e]S Ge 12:2; S 1Ch 27:23 **3:9** [f]S 2Sa 14:17; Jas 1:5 [g]S Dt 1:16; Heb 5:14 [h]2Co 2:16 **3:11** [i]Jas 4:3 [j]1Ch 22:12 **3:12** [k]1Jn 5:14-15 [l]S 2Sa 14:20; 1Ki 4:29,30,31; 5:12; 10:23; Ecc 1:16 **3:13** [m]Mt 6:33; Eph 3:20 [n]Pr 3:1-2,16; 8:18 [o]1Ki 10:23; 2Ch 9:22; Ne 13:26 **3:14** [p]1Ki 9:4; Ps 25:13; 101:2; 128:1; Pr 3:1-2, 16 [q]Ps 61:6 **3:15** [r]S Ge 28:16 [s]ver 5 [t]Lev 6:8-13 [u]Lev 7:11-21 [v]Est 1:3, 9; 2:18; 5:8; 6:14; 9:17; Da 5:1

[e]*15* Traditionally *peace offerings*

3:2 *high places.* Upon entering Canaan, the Israelites often followed the Canaanite custom of locating their altars on high hills, probably on the old Baal sites. The question of the legitimacy of Israelite worship at these high places has long been a matter of debate. It is clear that the Israelites were forbidden to take over pagan altars and high places and use them for the worship of the Lord (Nu 33:52; Dt 7:5; 12:3). It is also clear that altars were to be built only at divinely sanctioned sites (see Ex 20:24; Dt 12:5,8,13–14). It is not so clear whether multiplicity of altars was totally forbidden provided the above conditions were met (see 19:10,14; Lev 26:30–31; Dt 12; 1Sa 9:12). It seems, however, that these conditions were not followed even in the time of Solomon, and pagan high places were being used for the worship of the Lord. This would eventually lead to religious apostasy and syncretism and was strongly condemned (2Ki 17:7–18; 21:2–9; 23:4–25). *because a temple had not yet been built.* Worship at a variety of places was apparently considered normal prior to the building of the temple (see Jdg 6:24; 13:19; 1Sa 7:17; 9:12–13).
3:3 *except.* Solomon's one major fault early in his reign was inconsistency in meeting the Mosaic requirements concerning places of legitimate worship.
3:4 *Gibeon.* The Gibeonites tricked Joshua and Israel into a peace treaty at the time of the conquest of Canaan (see Jos 9:3–27). The city was subsequently given to the tribe of Benjamin and set apart for the Levites (Jos 18:25; 21:17). David avenged Saul's violation of the Gibeonite treaty by the execution of seven of Saul's descendants (see 2Sa 21:1–9). *most important high place.* The reason for Gibeon's importance was the presence there of the tabernacle and the ancient bronze altar (see 1Ch 21:29; 2Ch 1:2–6). These must have been salvaged after the destruction of Shiloh by the Philistines (see note on 1Sa 7:1).
3:5 *dream.* Revelation through dreams is found elsewhere in the OT (see Ge 28:12; 31:11; 46:2; Nu 12:6; Jdg 7:13; Da 2:4; 7:1), as well as in the NT (see, e.g., Mt 1:20; 2:12,22).
3:6 *kindness.* The Hebrew for this word refers to God's covenant favors (see note on 2Sa 7:15). Solomon is praising the Lord for faithfulness to his promises to David (2Sa 7:8–16). *because.* See note on 2Sa 22:21.
3:7 *I am only a little child.* The birth of Solomon is generally placed in approximately the middle of David's 40-year reign, meaning that Solomon was about 20 years old at the beginning of his own reign (see 2:11–12) and lacked experience in assuming the responsibilities of his office (cf. Jer 1:6).
3:8 *great people, too numerous to count.* From the small beginnings of a single family living in Egypt (see Ge 46:26–27; Dt 7:7), the Israelites had increased to an extent approaching that anticipated in the promise given to Abraham (Ge 13:16; 22:17–18) and Jacob (Ge 32:12). See 4:20.
3:11 *long life . . . wealth . . . death of your enemies.* Typical desires of ancient Near Eastern monarchs.
3:12 *never . . . anyone like you.* See 4:29–34; 10:1–13.
3:13 *I will give you what you have not asked for.* Cf. Jesus' promise in Lk 12:31.
3:14 *if you walk in my ways . . . I will give you a long life.* Echoes Dt 6:2; 17:20; 22:7. Unfortunately Solomon did not remain obedient to the covenant as his father David had (11:6), and he did not live to be much more than 60 years of age (see note on v. 7; cf. 11:42).
3:15 *ark of the Lord's covenant.* See notes on 6:19; 2Sa 6:2. *fellowship offerings.* See note on 1Sa 11:15.

A Wise Ruling

16Now two prostitutes came to the king and stood before him. 17One of them said, "My lord, this woman and I live in the same house. I had a baby while she was there with me. 18The third day after my child was born, this woman also had a baby. We were alone; there was no one in the house but the two of us.

19"During the night this woman's son died because she lay on him. 20So she got up in the middle of the night and took my son from my side while I your servant was asleep. She put him by her breast and put her dead son by my breast. 21The next morning, I got up to nurse my son—and he was dead! But when I looked at him closely in the morning light, I saw that it wasn't the son I had borne."

22The other woman said, "No! The living one is my son; the dead one is yours."

But the first one insisted, "No! The dead one is yours; the living one is mine." And so they argued before the king.

23The king said, "This one says, 'My son is alive and your son is dead,' while that one says, 'No! Your son is dead and mine is alive.' "

24Then the king said, "Bring me a sword." So they brought a sword for the king. 25He then gave an order: "Cut the living child in two and give half to one and half to the other."

26The woman whose son was alive was filled with compassion w for her son and said to the king, "Please, my lord, give her the living baby! Don't kill him!"

But the other said, "Neither I nor you shall have him. Cut him in two!"

27Then the king gave his ruling: "Give the living baby to the first woman. Do not kill him; she is his mother."

28When all Israel heard the verdict the king had given, they held the king in awe, because they saw that he had wisdom x from God to administer justice.

Solomon's Officials and Governors

4 So King Solomon ruled over all Israel. 2And these were his chief officials: y

Azariah z son of Zadok—the priest;
3Elihoreph and Ahijah, sons of Shisha—secretaries; a
Jehoshaphat b son of Ahilud—recorder;
4Benaiah c son of Jehoiada—commander in chief;
Zadok d and Abiathar—priests;
5Azariah son of Nathan—in charge of the district officers;
Zabud son of Nathan—a priest and personal adviser to the king;
6Ahishar—in charge of the palace; e
Adoniram f son of Abda—in charge of forced labor. g

7Solomon also had twelve district governors h over all Israel, who supplied provisions for the king and the royal household. Each one had to provide supplies for one month in the year. 8These are their names:

Ben-Hur—in the hill country i of Ephraim;
9Ben-Deker—in Makaz, Shaalbim, j Beth Shemesh k and Elon Bethhanan;
10Ben-Hesed—in Arubboth (Socoh l and all the land of Hepher m were his);

Cross references (margin)

3:26 wPs 102:13; Isa 49:15; 63:15; Jer 3:12; 31:20; Hos 11:8
3:28 xS 2Sa 14:20; Col 2:3
4:2 y1Ki 12:6; Job 12:12
z1Ch 6:10; 2Ch 26:17
4:3 aS 2Sa 8:17
bS 2Sa 8:16
4:4 cS 2Sa 8:18
dS 2Sa 8:17
4:6 eS Ge 41:40
fS 2Sa 20:24
gS Ge 49:15
4:7 hver 27
4:8 iS Jos 24:33
4:9 jJdg 1:35
kS Jos 15:10
4:10 lS Jos 15:35
mS Jos 12:17

Footnotes

3:16 two prostitutes. It is not known if these two were Israelites or Jebusites— possibly the latter. came to the king. It was possible for Israelites (and others within the realm) to bypass lower judicial officials (Dt 16:18) and appeal directly to the king (see 2Ki 8:3; 2Sa 15:2).
3:17 live in the same house. Brothels were common in ancient Near Eastern cities.
3:28 they saw that he had wisdom from God. This episode strikingly demonstrated that the Lord had answered Solomon's prayer for a discerning heart (vv. 9,12).
4:1 ruled over all Israel. Solomon ruled over an undivided kingdom, as his father had before him (see 2Sa 8:15).
4:2 son. According to 2Sa 15:27,36 and 1Ch 6:8–9, Azariah was the son of Ahimaaz and the grandson of Zadok (see note on 2:8). Apparently Zadok's son Ahimaaz had died, so that Zadok was succeeded by his grandson Azariah. Zadok. See 2:27,35.
4:3 Shisha. See note on 2Sa 8:17. secretaries. See note on 2Sa 8:17. Jehoshaphat son of Ahilud. The same person who served in David's court (see 2Sa 8:16). recorder. See note on 2Sa 8:16.
4:4 Benaiah. Replaced Joab as commander of the army (see

2:35; 2Sa 8:18). Zadok and Abiathar. Abiathar was banished at the beginning of Solomon's reign (2:27,35), and Zadok was succeeded by his grandson Azariah (v. 2).
4:5 Nathan. Either the prophet (1:11) or the son of David (2Sa 5:14). district officers. See vv. 7–19. priest. See note on 2Sa 8:18 ("royal advisers"). personal adviser to the king. See note on 2Sa 15:37.
4:6 in charge of the palace. The first OT reference to an office mentioned frequently in 1,2 Kings (1Ki 16:9; 18:3; 2Ki 18:18,37; 19:2). It is likely that this official was administrator of the palace and steward of the king's properties. Adoniram. Served not only under Solomon, but also under David before him (2Sa 20:24) and Rehoboam after him (1Ki 12:18). forced labor. See notes on 9:15; 2Sa 20:24.
4:7 Solomon . . . had twelve district governors. The 12 districts were not identical to tribal territories, possibly because the tribes varied greatly in agricultural productivity. But Solomon's administrative decision violated traditional tribal boundaries and probably stirred up ancient tribal loyalties, eventually contributing to the disruption of the united kingdom.
4:8 Ben-Hur. Hebrew Ben means "son of."

11Ben-Abinadab—in Naphoth Dor[f] [n] (he was married to Taphath daughter of Solomon);

12Baana son of Ahilud—in Taanach and Megiddo, and in all of Beth Shan[o] next to Zarethan[p] below Jezreel, from Beth Shan to Abel Meholah[q] across to Jokmeam;[r]

13Ben-Geber—in Ramoth Gilead (the settlements of Jair[s] son of Manasseh in Gilead[t] were his, as well as the district of Argob in Bashan and its sixty large walled cities[u] with bronze gate bars);

14Ahinadab son of Iddo—in Mahanaim;[v]

15Ahimaaz[w]—in Naphtali (he had married Basemath daughter of Solomon);

16Baana son of Hushai[x]—in Asher and in Aloth;

17Jehoshaphat son of Paruah—in Issachar;

18Shimei[y] son of Ela—in Benjamin;

19Geber son of Uri—in Gilead (the country of Sihon[z] king of the Amorites and the country of Og[a] king of Bashan). He was the only governor over the district.

Solomon's Daily Provisions

20The people of Judah and Israel were as numerous as the sand[b] on the seashore; they ate, they drank and they were happy.[c] 21And Solomon ruled[d] over all the kingdoms from the River[g][e] to the land of the Philistines, as far as the border of Egypt.[f] These countries brought tribute[g]

and were Solomon's subjects all his life.

22Solomon's daily provisions[h] were thirty cors[h] of fine flour and sixty cors[i] of meal, 23ten head of stall-fed cattle, twenty of pasture-fed cattle and a hundred sheep and goats, as well as deer, gazelles, roebucks and choice fowl.[i] 24For he ruled over all the kingdoms west of the River, from Tiphsah[j] to Gaza, and had peace[k] on all sides. 25During Solomon's lifetime Judah and Israel, from Dan to Beersheba,[l] lived in safety,[m] each man under his own vine and fig tree.[n]

26Solomon had four[j] thousand stalls for chariot horses,[o] and twelve thousand horses.[k]

27The district officers,[p] each in his month, supplied provisions for King Solomon and all who came to the king's table. They saw to it that nothing was lacking. 28They also brought to the proper place their quotas of barley and straw for the chariot horses and the other horses.

Solomon's Wisdom

29God gave Solomon wisdom[q] and very great insight, and a breadth of understanding as measureless as the sand[r] on the seashore. 30Solomon's wisdom was greater than the wisdom of all the men of the East,[s] and greater than all the wisdom of Egypt.[t] 31He was wiser[u] than any other man, including Ethan the Ezrahite—wiser

Cross references

4:11 [n]S Jos 11:2
4:12 [o]S Jos 17:11
[p]S Jos 3:16
[q]S Jdg 7:22
[r]1Ch 6:68
4:13 [s]S Nu 32:41
[t]Nu 32:40
[u]Dt 3:4
4:14 [v]Jos 13:26
4:15 [w]2Sa 15:27
4:16
[x]S 2Sa 15:32
4:18 [y]1Ki 1:8
4:19 [z]S Jos 12:2
[a]Dt 3:8-10;
S Jos 12:4
4:20 [b]S Ge 12:2;
S 32:12
[c]1Ch 22:9
4:21 [d]2Ch 9:26;
Ezr 4:20;
Ps 72:11; La 1:1
[e]S Ge 2:14;
Ps 72:8
[f]S Ex 23:31
[g]S Jdg 3:15;
Eze 16:13

4:22 [h]1Ki 10:5
4:23 [i]Ne 5:18
4:24 [j]2Ki 15:16
[k]S Jos 14:15
4:25 [l]S Jdg 20:1
[m]1Ch 22:9;
Jer 23:6;
Eze 28:26; 39:26
[n]Dt 8:8;
2Ki 18:31;
Ps 105:33;
Isa 36:16;
Jer 5:17;
Joel 2:22;
Mic 4:4; Zec 3:10
4:26 [o]S Dt 17:16
4:27 [p]ver 7
4:29 [q]S 1Ki 3:12
[r]S Ge 32:12
4:30 [s]S Ge 25:6;
S Jdg 6:3;
Da 1:20; Mt 2:1
[t]Isa 19:11;
Ac 7:22
4:31 [u]S 1Ki 3:12

Footnotes

[f]11 Or in the heights of Dor   [g]21 That is, the Euphrates; also in verse 24   [h]22 That is, probably about 185 bushels (about 6.6 kiloliters)   [i]22 That is, probably about 375 bushels (about 13.2 kiloliters)   [j]26 Some Septuagint manuscripts (see also 2 Chron. 9:25); Hebrew forty   [k]26 Or charioteers

---

4:11 *Ben-Abinadab.* Most likely the "son of" David's brother Abinadab (see 1Sa 16:8; 17:13), making him Solomon's first cousin (he was also his son-in-law).

4:12 *Baana son of Ahilud.* Probably a brother of Jehoshaphat the recorder (v. 3).

4:16 *Baana son of Hushai.* Perhaps the son of David's trusted adviser (see notes on 2Sa 15:32,37).

4:18 *Shimei son of Ela.* Perhaps the same Shimei mentioned in 1:8.

4:20 *as numerous as the sand on the seashore.* See 3:8 and note; see also v. 29; Ge 22:17; 2Sa 17:11; Isa 10:22; Jer 33:22; Hos 1:10; cf. Ge 41:49; Jos 11:4; Jdg 7:12; Ps 78:27. *they ate, they drank and they were happy.* Judah and Israel prospered (see 5:4).

4:21 *from the River to the land of the Philistines, as far as the border of Egypt.* The borders of Solomon's empire extended to the limits originally promised to Abraham (see note on 2Sa 8:3). However, rebellion was brewing in Edom (11:14–21) and Damascus (11:23–25).

4:22 *Solomon's daily provisions.* For all his household, his palace servants and his court officials and their families.

4:24 *Tiphsah.* A city on the west bank of the Euphrates River. *Gaza.* The southernmost city of the Philistines on the Mediterranean coast.

4:26 *four thousand.* See NIV text note. 1Ki 10:26 and 2Ch 1:14 indicate that Solomon had 1,400 chariots, meaning he maintained stalls for two horses for each chariot, with places for about 1,200 reserve horses. By way of comparison, an Assyrian account of the battle of Qarqar in 853 B.C. (about a century after Solomon) speaks of 1,200 chariots from Damascus, 700 chariots from Hamath and 2,000 chariots from Israel (the northern kingdom).

4:29 *as measureless as the sand on the seashore.* See note on v. 20.

4:30 *men of the East.* The phrase is general and appears to refer to the peoples of Mesopotamia (see Ge 29:1) and Arabia (see Jer 49:28; Eze 25:4,10)—those associated with Israel's northeastern and eastern horizons, just as Egypt was the main region on her southwestern horizon. Many examples of Mesopotamian wisdom literature have been recovered. *wisdom of Egypt.* See Ge 41:8; Ex 7:11; Ac 7:22. Examples of Egyptian wisdom literature are to be found in the proverbs of Ptahhotep (c. 2450 B.C.) and Amenemope (see Introduction to Proverbs: Date).

4:31 *He was wiser than any other man.* Until Jesus came (see Lk 11:31). *Ethan the Ezrahite.* See Ps 89 title. *Heman, Calcol and Darda.* See note on 1Ch 2:6–7.

than Heman, Calcol and Darda, the sons of Mahol. And his fame spread to all the surrounding nations. 32He spoke three thousand proverbs[v] and his songs[w] numbered a thousand and five. 33He described plant life, from the cedar of Lebanon to the hyssop[x] that grows out of walls. He also taught about animals and birds, reptiles and fish. 34Men of all nations came to listen to Solomon's wisdom, sent by all the kings[y] of the world, who had heard of his wisdom.

Preparations for Building the Temple

5:1–16pp — 2Ch 2:1–18

5 When Hiram[z] king of Tyre heard that Solomon had been anointed king to succeed his father David, he sent his envoys to Solomon, because he had always been on friendly terms with David. 2Solomon sent back this message to Hiram:

3"You know that because of the wars[a] waged against my father David from all sides, he could not build[b] a temple for the Name of the LORD his God until the LORD put his enemies under his feet.[c] 4But now the LORD my God has given me rest[d] on every side, and there is no adversary[e] or disaster. 5I intend, therefore, to build a temple[f] for the Name of the LORD my God, as the LORD told my father David, when he said, 'Your son whom I will put on the throne in your place will build the temple for my Name.'[g]

6"So give orders that cedars[h] of

Lebanon be cut for me. My men will work with yours, and I will pay you for your men whatever wages you set. You know that we have no one so skilled in felling timber as the Sidonians."

7When Hiram heard Solomon's message, he was greatly pleased and said, "Praise be to the LORD[i] today, for he has given David a wise son to rule over this great nation."

8So Hiram sent word to Solomon:

"I have received the message you sent me and will do all you want in providing the cedar and pine logs. 9My men will haul them down from Lebanon to the sea[j], and I will float them in rafts by sea to the place you specify. There I will separate them and you can take them away. And you are to grant my wish by providing food[k] for my royal household."

10In this way Hiram kept Solomon supplied with all the cedar and pine logs he wanted, 11and Solomon gave Hiram twenty thousand cors[l] of wheat as food[l] for his household, in addition to twenty thousand baths[m,n] of pressed olive oil. Solomon continued to do this for Hiram year after year. 12The LORD gave Solomon wisdom,[m] just as he had promised him. There were peaceful relations between

Cross references (center column)

4:32 [v]Pr 1:1; 10:1; 25:1; Ecc 12:9
[w]Ps 78:63; SS 1:1; Eze 33:32
4:33 [x]S Lev 14:49
4:34 [y]2Ch 9:23
5:1 [z]S 2Sa 5:11
5:3 [a]1Ch 22:8; 28:3 [b]S 2Sa 7:5 [c]2Sa 22:40; Ps 8:6; 110:1; S Mt 22:44; 1Co 15:25
5:4 [d]S Jos 14:15; 1Ch 22:9; Lk 2:14 [e]1Ki 11:14,23
5:5 [f]S Dt 12:5; 1Ch 17:12; 1Co 3:16; Rev 21:22 [g]Dt 12:5; 2Sa 7:13
5:6 [h]1Ch 14:1; 22:4
5:7 [i]1Ki 10:9; Isa 60:6
5:9 [j]Ezr 3:7 [k]ver 11; Eze 27:17; Ac 12:20
5:11 [l]S ver 9
5:12 [m]S 1Ki 3:12

[l] / / That is, probably about 125,000 bushels (about 4,400 kiloliters)   [m] / / Septuagint (see also 2 Chron. 2:10); Hebrew twenty cors   [n] / / That is, about 115,000 gallons (about 440 kiloliters)

4:32 three thousand proverbs. Only some of these are preserved in the book of Proverbs.
4:33 animals and birds, reptiles and fish. Examples of Solomon's knowledge of these creatures are found in Pr 6:6–8; 26:2–3,11; 27:8; 28:1,15.
4:34 all nations . . . all the kings of the world. A general statement referring to the Near Eastern world (cf. Ge 41:57).
5:1 Hiram king of Tyre. Hiram ruled over Tyre c. 978–944 B.C. He may have also served as co-regent with his father Abibaal as early as 993. Before Solomon was born, Hiram provided timber and workmen for the building of David's palace (see 2Sa 5:11).
5:3 he could not build a temple. Although David was denied the privilege of building the temple, he did make plans and provisions for its construction (see 1Ch 22:2–5; 28:2; cf. also Ps 30 title).
5:4 rest. Described here as "no adversary or disaster." God's promises to his people (see Ex 33:14; Dt 25:19; Jos 1:13,15) and to David (2Sa 7:11) have now been fulfilled (see 8:56), so that the Israelites are free to concentrate their strength and resources on building their Great King's royal house (see note on 2Sa 7:11).
5:5 Name. Signifies God's revealed character or self-revelation as a person (see, e.g., 8:16; Ex 20:24; Dt 12:5; 2Sa 6:2; 7:13). as the LORD told my father David. See 2Sa 7:12–13; 1Ch 22:8–10.

5:6 So give orders. A more detailed account of Solomon's request is found in 2Ch 2:3–10. cedars of Lebanon. Widely used in the ancient Near East in the construction of royal houses and temples.
5:7 Praise be to the LORD. In polytheistic cultures it was common practice for the people of one nation to recognize the deities of another nation (see 10:9; 11:5) and even to ascribe certain powers to them (see 2Ki 18:25; see also 2Ch 2:12).
5:9 place you specify. Joppa (2Ch 2:16; see note on 1Ki 3:1). providing food for my royal household. Provision of food for Hiram's court personnel appears to cover only the cost of the wood itself. In addition, Solomon would have to provide for the wages of the Phoenician laborers (v. 6). Comparison of v. 11 with 2Ch 2:10 indicates that besides wheat and olive oil for Hiram's court, Solomon also sent barley and wine for labor costs. Hiram may have sold some of these provisions in order to pay the laborers.
5:11 twenty thousand cors of wheat. See NIV text note. By way of comparison, Solomon's court received 10,950 cors of flour and 21,900 cors of meal on an annual basis (see 4:22). Solomon's whole grain payment to Hiram of 20,000 cors of wheat and 20,000 cors of barley (2Ch 2:10) would probably yield about 26,666 cors of refined flour and meal, or about 20 percent less than the requirements of Solomon's own court.

Hiram and Solomon, and the two of them made a treaty. [n]

[13]King Solomon conscripted laborers[o] from all Israel—thirty thousand men. [14]He sent them off to Lebanon in shifts of ten thousand a month, so that they spent one month in Lebanon and two months at home. Adoniram[p] was in charge of the forced labor. [15]Solomon had seventy thousand carriers and eighty thousand stonecutters in the hills, [16]as well as thirty-three hundred[o] foremen[q] who supervised the project and directed the workmen. [17]At the king's command they removed from the quarry[r] large blocks of quality stone[s] to provide a foundation of dressed stone for the temple. [18]The craftsmen of Solomon and Hiram[t] and the men of Gebal[p] [u] cut and prepared the timber and stone for the building of the temple.

Solomon Builds the Temple

6:1–29pp — 2Ch 3:1–14

6 In the four hundred and eightieth[q] year after the Israelites had come out of Egypt, in the fourth year of Solomon's reign over Israel, in the month of Ziv, the second month,[v] he began to build the temple of the LORD. [w]

[2]The temple[x] that King Solomon built for the LORD was sixty cubits long, twenty wide and thirty high.[r] [3]The portico[y] at the front of the main hall of the temple extended the width of the temple, that is twenty cubits,[s] and projected ten cubits[t]

from the front of the temple. [4]He made narrow clerestory windows[z] in the temple. [5]Against the walls of the main hall and inner sanctuary he built a structure around the building, in which there were side rooms. [a] [6]The lowest floor was five cubits[u] wide, the middle floor six cubits[v] and the third floor seven.[w] He made offset ledges around the outside of the temple so that nothing would be inserted into the temple walls.

[7]In building the temple, only blocks dressed[b] at the quarry were used, and no hammer, chisel or any other iron tool[c] was heard at the temple site while it was being built.

[8]The entrance to the lowest[x] floor was on the south side of the temple; a stairway led up to the middle level and from there to the third. [9]So he built the temple and completed it, roofing it with beams and cedar[d] planks. [10]And he built the side rooms all along the temple. The height of each was five cubits, and they were attached to the temple by beams of cedar.

[11]The word of the LORD came[e] to Solo-

Cross references (center column)

5:12 nJos 9:7;
1Ki 15:19;
Am 1:9
5:13 oS Ge 49:15;
S Lev 25:39;
1Ki 9:15
5:14 pS 2Sa 20:24;
1Ki 4:6;
2Ch 10:18
5:16 q1Ki 9:23
5:17 r1Ki 6:7
s1Ch 22:2
5:18 tS 2Sa 5:11
uS Jos 13:5
6:1 vEzr 3:8
wEzr 5:11
6:2 xEx 26:1
6:3 yEze 40:49

6:4 zEze 41:16
6:5 aJer 35:2;
Eze 41:5-6
6:7 bS Ex 20:25
cS Dt 27:5
6:9 dSS 1:17
6:11 e1Ki 12:22;
13:20; 16:1,7;
17:2; 21:17;
Jer 40:1

o 16 Hebrew; some Septuagint manuscripts (see also 2 Chron. 2:2, 18) thirty-six hundred   p 18 That is, Byblos   q 1 Hebrew; Septuagint four hundred and fortieth   r 2 That is, about 90 feet (about 27 meters) long and 30 feet (about 9 meters) wide and 45 feet (about 13.5 meters) high   s 3 That is, about 30 feet (about 9 meters)   t 3 That is, about 15 feet (about 4.5 meters)   u 6 That is, about 7 1/2 feet (about 2.3 meters); also in verses 10 and 24   v 6 That is, about 9 feet (about 2.7 meters)   w 6 That is, about 10 1/2 feet (about 3.1 meters)   x 8 Septuagint; Hebrew middle

---

5:13 *conscripted laborers.* See notes on 9:15; 2Sa 20:24. Resentment among the people toward this sort of forced labor eventually led to a civil uprising and the division of Solomon's kingdom immediately after his death (12:1–18).
5:15 *seventy thousand carriers and eighty thousand stonecutters.* Conscripted from the non-Israelite population that David had subdued and incorporated into his kingdom (see 2Ch 2:17–18). *hills.* The limestone hills of Palestine where the stone was quarried.
5:16 *thirty-three hundred foremen.* 1Ki 9:23 refers to 550 supervisors. If these are two different categories of supervisory personnel, the total is 3,850 men. 2Ch 2:2 refers to 3,600 foremen, and 2Ch 8:10 speaks of 250 supervisors, which again yields a total of 3,850 men in a supervisory capacity.
5:17 *large blocks of quality stone.* For the size of these stones see 7:10. Transportation of such stones to Jerusalem would require enormous manpower.
5:18 *men of Gebal.* See NIV text note; see also Eze 27:9.
6:1–38 See drawing of "Solomon's Temple," p. 481.
6:1 *four hundred and eightieth year . . . fourth year.* Synchronizations between certain events in the reigns of later Israelite kings and Assyrian chronological records fix the fourth year of Solomon's reign at c. 966 B.C. (see Introduction: Chronology). If Israel's exodus is placed 480 years prior to 966, it would have occurred c. 1446 (the chronology followed in this Study Bible) during the rule of the 18th-dynasty Egyptian pharaoh, Amunhotep II. On the basis of Ex 1:11 and certain other historical considerations, however,

some have concluded that the exodus could not have occurred prior to the rule of the 19th-dynasty pharaoh, Rameses II—thus not until c. 1290 (see note on Ge 47:11). This would mean that the 480 years of this verse would be understood as either a schematic (perhaps representative of 12 generations multiplied by the conventional, but not always actual, 40-year length of a generation) or aggregate figure (the combined total of a number of subsidiary time periods, which in reality were partly concurrent, examples of which are to be found in Egyptian and Mesopotamian records).
6:2 *temple that King Solomon built.* The temple was patterned after the tabernacle (and, in general, other temples of the time) and was divided into three major areas: the Most Holy Place, the Holy Place and the outer courtyard. The Most Holy Place in the temple was cubical, as it probably was in the tabernacle. The dimensions of the temple in most instances seem to be double those of the tabernacle (see Ex 26:15–30; 36:20–34).
6:6 *offset ledges.* To avoid making holes in the temple wall, it was built with a series of ledges on which the beams for the three floors of side chambers rested. This accounts for the different widths of the rooms on each floor.
6:8 *entrance to the lowest floor.* Of the side chambers.
6:11 *The word of the LORD came to Solomon.* As the temple neared completion the Lord spoke to Solomon, perhaps through an unnamed prophet (but see 3:5,11–14; 9:2–9).

mon: [12]"As for this temple you are building, if you follow my decrees, carry out my
regulations and keep all my commands[f]
and obey them, I will fulfill through you
the promise[g] I gave to David your father.
[13]And I will live among the Israelites and
will not abandon[h] my people Israel."

[14]So Solomon[i] built the temple and
completed[j] it. [15]He lined its interior walls
with cedar boards, paneling them from the
floor of the temple to the ceiling,[k] and
covered the floor of the temple with planks
of pine.[l] [16]He partitioned off twenty cubits[y] at the rear of the temple with cedar
boards from floor to ceiling to form within
the temple an inner sanctuary, the Most
Holy Place.[m] [17]The main hall in front of
this room was forty cubits[z] long. [18]The inside of the temple was cedar,[n] carved with

gourds and open flowers. Everything was
cedar; no stone was to be seen.

[19]He prepared the inner sanctuary[o]
within the temple to set the ark of the covenant[p] of the LORD there. [20]The inner
sanctuary[q] was twenty cubits long, twenty
wide and twenty high.[a] He overlaid the
inside with pure gold, and he also overlaid
the altar of cedar.[r] [21]Solomon covered the
inside of the temple with pure gold, and he
extended gold chains across the front of
the inner sanctuary, which was overlaid
with gold. [22]So he overlaid the whole interior with gold. He also overlaid with gold
the altar that belonged to the inner sanctuary.

[23]In the inner sanctuary he made a pair

6:12 /1Ki 11:10
g2Sa 7:12-16;
1Ki 9:5
6:13
hS Lev 26:11;
S Dt 31:6;
Jn 14:18;
Heb 13:5
6:14 iAc 7:47
/1Ch 28:20;
2Ch 5:1
6:15 k1Ki 7:7
/Eze 41:15-16
6:16 mS Ex 26:33
6:18 nver 29;
Ps 74:6;
Eze 41:18

6:19 o1Ki 8:6
pS Ex 25:10;
S 1Sa 3:3
6:20 qEze 41:3-4
rS Ex 30:1

y16 That is, about 30 feet (about 9 meters)   z17 That
is, about 60 feet (about 18 meters)   a20 That is, about
30 feet (about 9 meters) long, wide and high

6:12 *if you follow my decrees . . . I will fulfill through you
the promise.* In words similar to those spoken by David (see
notes on 2:1-4), the Lord assures Solomon of a continuing
dynasty (see 2Sa 7:12-16) if he is faithful to the covenant.
6:13 *I will live among the Israelites.* In the temple being
built (see 9:3). To avoid any apprehension among the Israel-

ites concerning his presence with them (cf. Ps 78:60; Jer
26:6,9; see note on 1Sa 7:1), the Lord gives assurance that
he will dwell in their midst (see 8:10-13; Lev 26:11).
6:16 *Most Holy Place.* The same terminology was used for
the inner sanctuary housing the ark in the tabernacle (see Ex
26:33-34; Lev 16:2,16-17, 20, 23).

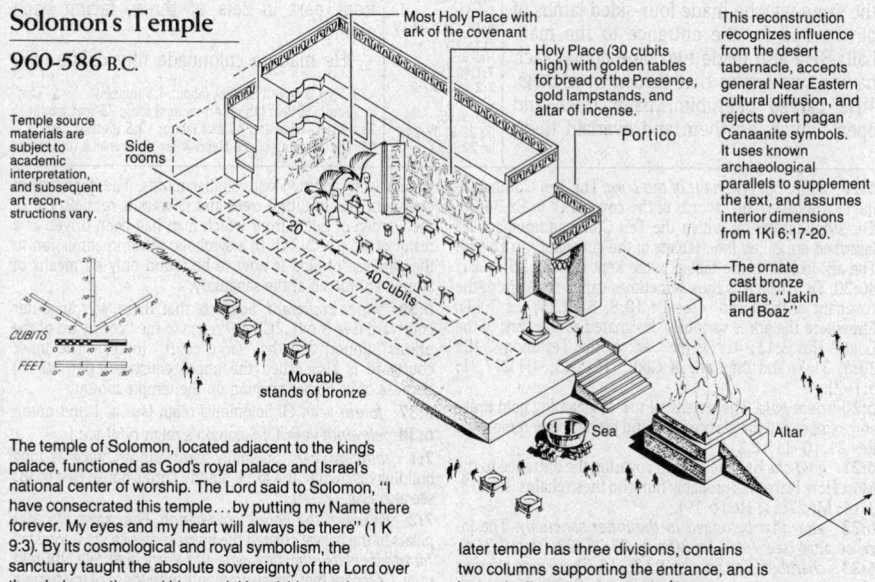

Solomon's Temple
960-586 B.C.

Temple source materials are subject to academic interpretation, and subsequent art reconstructions vary.

Side rooms

Most Holy Place with ark of the covenant

Holy Place (30 cubits high) with golden tables for bread of the Presence, gold lampstands, and altar of incense.

Portico

This reconstruction recognizes influence from the desert tabernacle, accepts general Near Eastern cultural diffusion, and rejects overt pagan Canaanite symbols. It uses known archaeological parallels to supplement the text, and assumes interior dimensions from 1Ki 6:17-20.

20
40 cubits

CUBITS
FEET

Movable stands of bronze

The ornate cast bronze pillars, "Jakin and Boaz"

Sea   Altar
N

The temple of Solomon, located adjacent to the king's
palace, functioned as God's royal palace and Israel's
national center of worship. The Lord said to Solomon, "I
have consecrated this temple . . . by putting my Name there
forever. My eyes and my heart will always be there" (1 K
9:3). By its cosmological and royal symbolism, the
sanctuary taught the absolute sovereignty of the Lord over
the whole creation and his special headship over Israel.

The floor plan is a type that has a long history in Semitic
religion, particularly among the West Semites. An early
example of the tripartite division into *'ulam, hekal,* and
debir (portico, main hall, and inner sanctuary) has been
found at Syrian Ebla (c. 2300 B.C.) and, much later but
more contemporaneous with Solomon, at Tell Tainat
in the Orontes basin (c. 900 B.C.). Like Solomon's, the

later temple has three divisions, contains
two columns supporting the entrance, and is
located adjacent to the royal palace.

Many archaeological parallels can be drawn to the
methods of construction used in the temple, e.g., the
"stone and cedar beam" technique described in 1Ki 6:36.
Interestingly, evidence for the largest bronze-casting
industry ever found in Palestine comes from the same locale
and period as that indicated in Scripture: Zarethan in the
Jordan Valley c. 1000 B.C.

© Hugh Claycombe 1986

of cherubim[s] of olive wood, each ten cubits[b] high. 24One wing of the first cherub was five cubits long, and the •other wing five cubits—ten cubits from wing tip to wing tip. 25The second cherub also measured ten cubits, for the two cherubim were identical in size and shape. 26The height of each cherub was ten cubits. 27He placed the cherubim[t] inside the innermost room of the temple, with their wings spread out. The wing of one cherub touched one wall, while the wing of the other touched the other wall, and their wings touched each other in the middle of the room. 28He overlaid the cherubim with gold.

29On the walls[u] all around the temple, in both the inner and outer rooms, he carved cherubim,[v] palm trees and open flowers. 30He also covered the floors of both the inner and outer rooms of the temple with gold.

31For the entrance of the inner sanctuary he made doors of olive wood with five-sided jambs. 32And on the two olive wood doors[w] he carved cherubim, palm trees and open flowers, and overlaid the cherubim and palm trees with beaten gold. 33In the same way he made four-sided jambs of olive wood for the entrance to the main hall. 34He also made two pine doors, each having two leaves that turned in sockets. 35He carved cherubim, palm trees and open flowers on them and overlaid them

with gold hammered evenly over the carvings.

36And he built the inner courtyard[x] of three courses[y] of dressed stone and one course of trimmed cedar beams.

37The foundation of the temple of the LORD was laid in the fourth year, in the month of Ziv. 38In the eleventh year in the month of Bul, the eighth month, the temple was finished in all its details[z] according to its specifications.[a] He had spent seven years building it.

Solomon Builds His Palace

7 It took Solomon thirteen years, however, to complete the construction of his palace.[b] 2He built the Palace[c] of the Forest of Lebanon[d] a hundred cubits long, fifty wide and thirty high,[c] with four rows of cedar columns supporting trimmed cedar beams. 3It was roofed with cedar above the beams that rested on the columns—forty-five beams, fifteen to a row. 4Its windows were placed high in sets of three, facing each other. 5All the doorways had rectangular frames; they were in the front part in sets of three, facing each other.[d]

6He made a colonnade fifty cubits long

Cross references

6:23 [s]S Ex 37:7
6:27 [t]S Ge 3:24;
S Ex 25:18
6:29 [u]S ver 18
[v]ver 32,35;
Eze 41:18,25
6:32 [w]Eze 41:23

6:36 [x]2Ch 4:9
[y]1Ki 7:12;
Ezr 6:4
6:38 [z]1Ch 28:19
[a]Ex 25:9;
Heb 8:5
7:1 [b]S 2Sa 7:2
7:2 [c]S 2Sa 7:2
[d]1Ki 10:17;
2Ch 9:16;
Isa 22:8; 37:24;
Jer 22:6,23

Footnotes

[b]23 That is, about 15 feet (about 4.5 meters)   [c]2 That is, about 150 feet (about 46 meters) long, 75 feet (about 23 meters) wide and 45 feet (about 13.5 meters) high   [d]5 The meaning of the Hebrew for this verse is uncertain.

6:19 *ark of the covenant of the LORD.* The Ten Commandments are called the "words of the covenant" in Ex 34:28. The stone tablets on which the Ten Commandments were inscribed are called the "tablets of the covenant" in Dt 9:9. The ark in which the tablets were kept (see Ex 25:16,21; 40:20; Dt 10:1–5) is thus sometimes called the "ark of the covenant of the LORD" (see Dt 10:8; 31:9,25; Jos 3:11). Elsewhere the ark is variously designated as the "ark of the LORD" (Jos 3:13; 4:11), the "ark of the Testimony" (Ex 30:6; 31:7) and the "ark of God" (1Sa 3:3; 4:11,17,21; 5:1–2).

6:20 *pure gold.* The extensive use of gleaming gold probably symbolized the glory of God and his heavenly temple (cf. Rev 21:10–11,18,21).

6:21 *gold chains.* The curtain covering the entrance to the Most Holy Place was probably hung on these chains (see 2Ch 3:14; Mt 27:51; Heb 6:19).

6:22 *altar that belonged to the inner sanctuary.* The incense altar (see 7:48; Ex 30:1,6; 37:25–28; Heb 9:3–4).

6:23 *cherubim.* See note on Ex 25:18. They were to stand as sentries on either side of the ark (8:6–7; 2Ch 3:10–13). Two additional cherubim stood on the ark—one on each end of its atonement cover (Ex 25:17–22). *ten cubits high.* The Most Holy Place, where the cherubim stood, was 20 cubits high (v. 16).

6:29 *he carved cherubim.* Not a violation of the second commandment, which prohibited making anything to serve as a representation of God and worshiping it (see note on Ex 20:4). *palm trees and open flowers.* Early Jewish syna-

gogues were adorned with similar motifs. The depiction of cherubim and beautiful trees and flowers is reminiscent of the Garden of Eden, from which man had been driven as a result of sin (Ge 3:24). In a symbolic sense, readmission to the paradise of God is now to be found only by means of atonement for sin at the sanctuary.

6:36 *inner courtyard.* Suggests that there was an outer courtyard (see 8:64). 2Ch 4:9 refers to the "courtyard of the priests" (inner) and the "large court" (outer). The inner courtyard is also called the upper courtyard (Jer 36:10) because of its higher position on the temple mount.

6:37 *fourth year.* Of Solomon's reign (see v. 1 and note).

6:38 *eleventh year.* Of Solomon's reign (959 B.C.).

7:1 *thirteen years.* Solomon spent almost twice as long building his own house as he did the Lord's house (see 6:38; see also Hag 1:2–4).

7:2 *Palace of the Forest of Lebanon.* Four rows of cedar pillars in the palace created the impression of a great forest. *a hundred cubits long, fifty wide and thirty high.* See NIV text note. Compare these measurements with those of the temple in 6:2.

7:3 *forty-five beams, fifteen to a row.* Suggests that there were three floors in the building above the main hall on the ground level. The building included storage area for weaponry (see 10:16–17).

7:6 *colonnade.* Apparently an entrance hall to the Palace of the Forest of Lebanon. Its length (50 cubits) corresponds to the width of the palace.

and thirty wide.[e] In front of it was a portico, and in front of that were pillars and
an overhanging roof.
7He built the throne hall, the Hall of
Justice, where he was to judge,[e] and he
covered it with cedar from floor to ceiling.[f][f] 8And the palace in which he was to
live, set farther back, was similar in design.
Solomon also made a palace like this hall
for Pharaoh's daughter, whom he had married.[g]
9All these structures, from the outside to
the great courtyard and from foundation to
eaves, were made of blocks of high-grade
stone cut to size and trimmed with a saw
on their inner and outer faces. 10The foundations were laid with large stones of good
quality, some measuring ten cubits[g] and
some eight.[h] 11Above were high-grade
stones, cut to size, and cedar beams. 12The
great courtyard was surrounded by a wall
of three courses[h] of dressed stone and one
course of trimmed cedar beams, as was the
inner courtyard of the temple of the LORD
with its portico.

The Temple's Furnishings

7:23–26pp — 2Ch 4:2–5
7:38–51pp — 2Ch 4:6,10–5:1

13King Solomon sent to Tyre and
brought Huram,[i][i] 14whose mother was a
widow from the tribe of Naphtali and
whose father was a man of Tyre and a
craftsman in bronze. Huram was highly
skilled[j] and experienced in all kinds of
bronze work. He came to King Solomon
and did all[k] the work assigned to him.
15He cast two bronze pillars,[l] each
eighteen cubits high and twelve cubits
around,[j] by line. 16He also made two capitals[m] of cast bronze to set on the tops of
the pillars; each capital was five cubits[k]
high. 17A network of interwoven chains
festooned the capitals on top of the pillars,
seven for each capital. 18He made pomegranates in two rows[l] encircling each network to decorate the capitals on top of the
pillars.[m] He did the same for each capital.
19The capitals on top of the pillars in the
portico were in the shape of lilies, four cubits[n] high. 20On the capitals of both pillars,
above the bowl-shaped part next to the
network, were the two hundred pomegranates[n] in rows all around. 21He erected
the pillars at the portico of the temple. The
pillar to the south he named Jakin[o] and
the one to the north Boaz.[p][o] 22The capitals on top were in the shape of lilies. And
so the work on the pillars[p] was completed.
23He made the Sea[q] of cast metal, circular in shape, measuring ten cubits[g] from
rim to rim and five cubits high. It took a
line[r] of thirty cubits[q] to measure around
it. 24Below the rim, gourds encircled
it—ten to a cubit. The gourds were cast in
two rows in one piece with the Sea.
25The Sea stood on twelve bulls,[s] three
facing north, three facing west, three facing south and three facing east. The Sea
rested on top of them, and their hindquarters were toward the center. 26It was a

7:7 [e]1Sa 7:15; Ps 122:5; Pr 20:8 [f]1Ki 6:15 **7:8** [g]S 1Ki 3:1 **7:12** [h]S 1Ki 6:36 **7:13** [i]ver 45; 2Ch 2:13; 4:16 **7:14** [j]Ex 31:2-5; S 35:31 [k]2Ch 4:11 **7:15** [l]2Ki 11:14; 23:3; 25:17; 2Ch 3:15; 23:13; 34:31; Jer 27:19; 52:17,21; Eze 40:49 **7:16** [m]ver 20,42; 2Ki 25:17; Jer 52:22 **7:20** [n]ver 18; 2Ch 3:16; 4:13 **7:21** [o]2Ch 3:17 **7:22** [p]2Ki 25:17 **7:23** [q]ver 47; 2Ki 25:13; 1Ch 18:8; 2Ch 4:18; Jer 52:17; Rev 4:6 [r]Jer 31:39; Zec 2:1 **7:25** [s]Jer 52:20

[e]*6* That is, about 75 feet (about 23 meters) long and 45 feet (about 13.5 meters) wide [f]*7* Vulgate and Syriac; Hebrew *floor* [g]*10,23* That is, about 15 feet (about 4.5 meters) [h]*10* That is, about 12 feet (about 3.6 meters) [i]*13* Hebrew *Hiram,* a variant of *Huram;* also in verses 40 and 45 [j]*15* That is, about 27 feet (about 8.1 meters) high and 18 feet (about 5.4 meters) around [k]*16* That is, about 7 1/2 feet (about 2.3 meters); also in verse 23 [l]*18* Two Hebrew manuscripts and Septuagint; most Hebrew manuscripts *made the pillars, and there were two rows* [m]*18* Many Hebrew manuscripts and Syriac; most Hebrew manuscripts *pomegranates* [n]*19* That is, about 6 feet (about 1.8 meters); also in verse 38 [o]*21* *Jakin* probably means *he establishes.* [p]*21* *Boaz* probably means *in him is strength.* [q]*23* That is, about 45 feet (about 13.5 meters)

7:7 *throne hall.* It is not clear whether the throne hall, the Hall of Justice, Solomon's own living quarters (v. 8) and the palace for Pharaoh's daughter (v. 8) were separate buildings or locations within the Palace of the Forest of Lebanon.
7:9 *trimmed with a saw.* The pinkish white limestone of Palestine is easily cut when originally quarried, but gradually hardens with exposure.
7:12 *great courtyard.* Constructed in the same way as the inner courtyard of the temple (6:36).
7:13 *King Solomon sent.* Prior to the completion of the temple and the construction of Solomon's palace (see 2Ch 2:7,13–14). *Huram.* See NIV text note. His full name is Huram-Abi (2Ch 2:13).
7:14 *widow from the tribe of Naphtali.* 2Ch 2:14 indicates that Huram-Abi's mother was from Dan. Apparently she was born in the city of Dan in northern Israel close to the tribe of Naphtali, from which came her first husband. After he died, she married a man from Tyre. *all kinds of bronze work.* Huram-Abi had a much wider range of skills as well (see 2Ch 2:7,14).
7:15 *two bronze pillars.* One was placed on each side of the main entrance to the temple (v. 21). Surely decorative, they may also have embodied a symbolism not known to us. It has been suggested that they were not freestanding but supported a roof (forming a portico to the temple) and an architrave.
7:21 *pillar to the south.* The temple, like the tabernacle before it, faced east (see Eze 8:16).
7:23 *Sea of cast metal.* This enormous reservoir of water corresponded to the bronze basin made for the tabernacle (see Ex 30:17–21; 38:8). Its water was used by the priests for ritual cleansing (2Ch 4:6). *thirty cubits.* Technically speaking, this should be 31.416 cubits because of the ten-cubit diameter of the circular top. Thirty may be a round number here, or perhaps the measurement was taken a bit below the rim or on the inside circumference (see v. 26).
7:24 *ten to a cubit.* With ten gourds to a cubit it took 300 gourds to span the entire reservoir, or 600 gourds counting both rows.

handbreadth r in thickness, and its rim was like the rim of a cup, like a lily blossom. It held two thousand baths. s

27He also made ten movable stands t of bronze; each was four cubits long, four wide and three high. t 28This is how the stands were made: They had side panels attached to uprights. 29On the panels between the uprights were lions, bulls and cherubim—and on the uprights as well. Above and below the lions and bulls were wreaths of hammered work. 30Each stand u had four bronze wheels with bronze axles, and each had a basin resting on four supports, cast with wreaths on each side. 31On the inside of the stand there was an opening that had a circular frame one cubit u deep. This opening was round, and with its basework it measured a cubit and a half. v Around its opening there was engraving. The panels of the stands were square, not round. 32The four wheels were under the

panels, and the axles of the wheels were attached to the stand. The diameter of each wheel was a cubit and a half. 33The wheels were made like chariot wheels; the axles, rims, spokes and hubs were all of cast metal.

34Each stand had four handles, one on each corner, projecting from the stand. 35At the top of the stand there was a circular band half a cubit w deep. The supports and panels were attached to the top of the stand. 36He engraved cherubim, lions and palm trees on the surfaces of the supports and on the panels, in every available space, with wreaths all around. 37This is the way

7:27 r2Ki 16:17
7:30 u2Ki 16:17

r26 That is, about 3 inches (about 8 centimeters)
s26 That is, probably about 11,500 gallons (about 44 kiloliters); the Septuagint does not have this sentence.
t27 That is, about 6 feet (about 1.8 meters) long and wide and about 4 1/2 feet (about 1.3 meters) high
u31 That is, about 1 1/2 feet (about 0.5 meter)
v31 That is, about 2 1/4 feet (about 0.7 meter); also in verse 32   w35 That is, about 3/4 foot (about 0.2 meter)

7:27 *ten movable stands.* These movable bronze stands were designed to hold water basins (see v. 38) of much smaller dimensions than the bronze Sea. The water from the basins was used to wash certain prescribed parts of the animals that were slaughtered for burnt offerings (see Lev 1:9,13; 2Ch 4:6).

7:36 *He engraved cherubim, lions and palm trees.* See note on 6:29.

Temple Furnishings

Glimpses of the rich ornamentation of Solomon's temple can be gained through recent discoveries that illumine the text of 1 Ki 6-7.

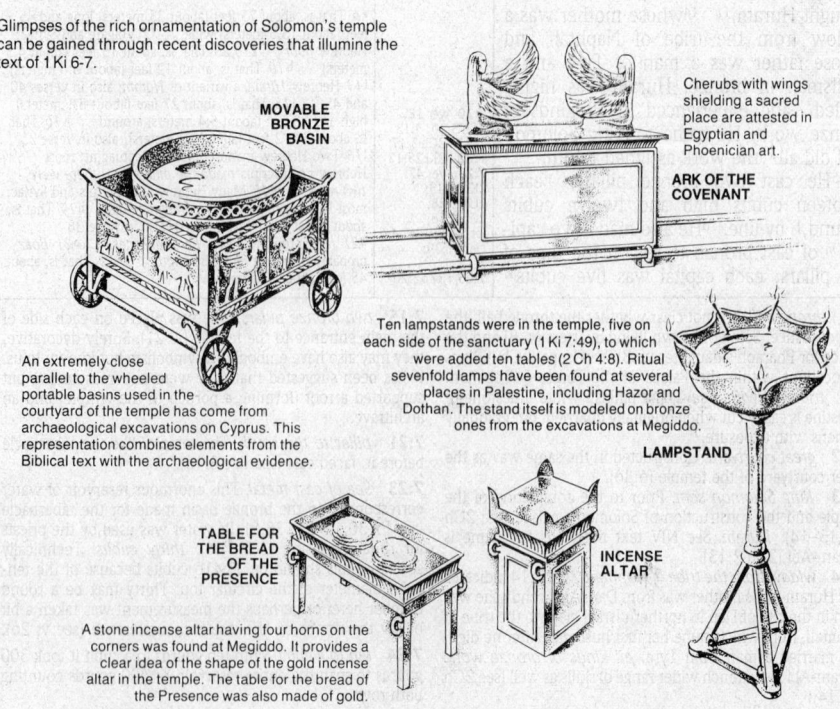

MOVABLE BRONZE BASIN

An extremely close parallel to the wheeled portable basins in the courtyard of the temple has come from archaeological excavations on Cyprus. This representation combines elements from the Biblical text with the archaeological evidence.

Cherubs with wings shielding a sacred place are attested in Egyptian and Phoenician art.

ARK OF THE COVENANT

Ten lampstands were in the temple, five on each side of the sanctuary (1 Ki 7:49), to which were added ten tables (2 Ch 4:8). Ritual sevenfold lamps have been found at several places in Palestine, including Hazor and Dothan. The stand itself is modeled on bronze ones from the excavations at Megiddo.

LAMPSTAND

TABLE FOR THE BREAD OF THE PRESENCE

INCENSE ALTAR

A stone incense altar having four horns on the corners was found at Megiddo. It provides a clear idea of the shape of the gold incense altar in the temple. The table for the bread of the Presence was also made of gold.

he made the ten stands. They were all cast in the same molds and were identical in size and shape.

³⁸He then made ten bronze basins,ᵛ each holding forty bathsˣ and measuring four cubits across, one basin to go on each of the ten stands. ³⁹He placed five of the stands on the south side of the temple and five on the north. He placed the Sea on the south side, at the southeast corner of the temple. ⁴⁰He also made the basins and shovels and sprinkling bowls.ʷ

So Huram finished all the work he had undertaken for King Solomon in the temple of the LORD:

⁴¹the two pillars;
    the two bowl-shaped capitals on top
        of the pillars;
    the two sets of network decorating
        the two bowl-shaped capitals on
        top of the pillars;
⁴²the four hundred pomegranates for
        the two sets of network (two rows
        of pomegranates for each network,
        decorating the bowl-shaped capi-
        talsˣ on top of the pillars);
⁴³the ten stands with their ten basins;
⁴⁴the Sea and the twelve bulls under it;
⁴⁵the pots, shovels and sprinkling
        bowls.ʸ

All these objects that Huramᶻ made for King Solomon for the temple of the LORD were of burnished bronze. ⁴⁶The king had them cast in clay molds in the plainᵃ of the Jordan between Succothᵇ and Zarethan.ᶜ ⁴⁷Solomon left all these things un-weighed,ᵈ because there were so many;ᵉ the weight of the bronzeᶠ was not deter-mined.

Marginal references (left column):

7:38 ᵛS Ex 30:18
7:40 ʷS Ex 27:3; Jer 52:18
7:42 ˣS ver 16
7:45 ʸS Ex 27:3; Jer 52:18 ᶻS ver 13
7:46 ᵃS Ge 13:10 ᵇS Ge 33:17 ᶜJos 3:16
7:47 ᵈ1Ch 22:3; Jer 52:20 ᵉEx 36:5-7 ᶠS ver 23

7:48 ᵍEx 39:32-43 ʰS Ex 25:23 ⁱS Ex 25:30
7:49 ʲS Ex 25:31
7:50 ᵏS Nu 7:14 ˡ2Ki 25:13; Jer 52:19
7:51 ᵐS 2Sa 8:11 ⁿ2Ki 12:13; 24:13; Jer 27:19
8:1 ᵒNu 7:2 ᵖS 1Sa 3:3; Rev 11:19 ᑫS 2Sa 5:7
8:2 ʳver 65; S Lev 23:36; Ne 8:17 ˢS Lev 23:34; S Nu 29:12
8:3 ᵗS Jos 3:3

⁴⁸Solomon also made allᵍ the fur-nishings that were in the LORD's temple:

    the golden altar;
    the golden tableʰ on which was the
        bread of the Presence;ⁱ
⁴⁹the lampstandsʲ of pure gold (five on
        the right and five on the left, in
        front of the inner sanctuary);
    the gold floral work and lamps and
        tongs;
⁵⁰the pure gold basins, wick trimmers,
        sprinkling bowls, dishesᵏ and cen-
        sers;ˡ
    and the gold sockets for the doors of
        the innermost room, the Most
        Holy Place, and also for the doors
        of the main hall of the temple.

⁵¹When all the work King Solomon had done for the temple of the LORD was fin-ished, he brought in the things his father David had dedicatedᵐ—the silver and gold and the furnishingsⁿ—and he placed them in the treasuries of the LORD's temple.

The Ark Brought to the Temple
8:1–21pp — 2Ch 5:2–6:11

8 Then King Solomon summoned into his presence at Jerusalem the elders of Israel, all the heads of the tribes and the chiefsᵒ of the Israelite families, to bring up the arkᵖ of the LORD's covenant from Zion, the City of David.ᑫ ²All the men of Israel came together to King Solomon at the time of the festivalʳ in the month of Ethanim, the seventh month.ˢ

³When all the elders of Israel had ar-rived, the priestsᵗ took up the ark, ⁴and they brought up the ark of the LORD and

ˣ38 That is, about 230 gallons (about 880 liters)

7:40 *basins.* Perhaps used for cooking meat to be eaten in connection with the fellowship offerings (see Lev 7:11–17; 22:21–23). *shovels.* Used for removing ashes from the altar. *sprinkling bowls.* For use by the priests in various rites involving the sprinkling of blood or water (see Ex 27:3).
7:41 *two sets of network.* See v. 17.
7:42 *four hundred pomegranates.* See vv. 18,20.
7:43 *ten stands with their ten basins.* See vv. 27–37.
7:44 *the Sea and the twelve bulls.* See vv. 23–26.
7:45 *pots, shovels and sprinkling bowls.* See v. 40.
7:46 *Succoth.* Located on the east side of the Jordan (Ge 33:17; Jos 13:27; Jdg 8:4–5) just north of the Jabbok River. Excavations in this area have confirmed that Succoth was a center of metallurgy during the period of the monarchy. *Zarethan.* Located near Adamah (see Jos 3:16) and Abel Meholah (4:12).
7:48 *golden altar.* See 6:22. *golden table.* The bread of the Presence was placed on this table (see Ex 25:23–30; 1Ch 9:32; 2Ch 13:11; 29:18). Ten such golden tables are men-tioned in 1Ch 28:16 and 2Ch 4:8,19, five placed on the north and five on the south side of the temple.
7:49 *lampstands of pure gold.* Only one lampstand with

seven arms had stood in the tabernacle, opposite the table for the bread of the Presence (Ex 25:31–40; 26:35). The ten lampstands in the temple, five on the north and five on the south side, created a lane of light in the Holy Place. *gold floral work.* See Ex 25:33. *lamps.* See Ex 25:37. *tongs.* See 2Ch 4:21; Isa 6:6.
7:50 *censers.* See 2Ki 25:15; 2Ch 4:22; Jer 52:18–19.
7:51 *things his father David had dedicated.* Valuable ob-jects of silver and gold, either taken as booty in war or received as tribute from kings seeking David's favor (see 2Sa 8:9–12; 1Ch 18:7–11; 2Ch 5:1). *treasuries of the LORD's temple.* See 15:18; 2Ki 12:18; 1Ch 9:26; 26:20–26; 28:12.
8:1 *bring up the ark of the LORD's covenant.* David had previously brought the ark from the house of Obed-Edom to Jerusalem (see 2Sa 6). *Zion, the City of David.* See note on 2Sa 5:7.
8:2 *festival.* It is probable that Solomon waited 11 months (see 6:38) to dedicate the temple during the Feast of Taber-nacles, which was observed in the seventh month of the year (Lev 23:34; Dt 16:13–15). *seventh month.* Presumably in the 12th year of Solomon's reign.

the Tent of Meeting[u] and all the sacred furnishings in it. The priests and Levites[v] carried them up, [5]and King Solomon and the entire assembly of Israel that had gathered about him were before the ark, sacrificing[w] so many sheep and cattle that they could not be recorded or counted.

[6]The priests then brought the ark of the LORD's covenant[x] to its place in the inner sanctuary of the temple, the Most Holy Place,[y] and put it beneath the wings of the cherubim.[z] [7]The cherubim spread their wings over the place of the ark and overshadowed[a] the ark and its carrying poles. [8]These poles were so long that their ends could be seen from the Holy Place in front of the inner sanctuary, but not from outside the Holy Place; and they are still there today.[b] [9]There was nothing in the ark except the two stone tablets[c] that Moses had placed in it at Horeb, where the LORD made a covenant with the Israelites after they came out of Egypt.

[10]When the priests withdrew from the Holy Place, the cloud[d] filled the temple of the LORD. [11]And the priests could not perform their service[e] because of the cloud, for the glory[f] of the LORD filled his temple.

[12]Then Solomon said, "The LORD has said that he would dwell in a dark cloud;[g] [13]I have indeed built a magnificent temple for you, a place for you to dwell[h] forever."

[14]While the whole assembly of Israel was standing there, the king turned around and blessed[i] them. [15]Then he said:

"Praise be to the LORD,[j] the God of Israel, who with his own hand has fulfilled what he promised with his own mouth to my father David. For he said, [16]'Since the day I brought my people Israel out of Egypt,[k] I have not chosen a city in any tribe of Israel to have a temple built for my Name[l] to be there, but I have chosen[m] David[n] to rule my people Israel.'

[17]"My father David had it in his heart[o] to build a temple[p] for the Name of the LORD, the God of Israel. [18]But the LORD said to my father David, 'Because it was in your heart to build a temple for my Name, you did well to have this in your heart. [19]Nevertheless, you[q] are not the one to build the temple, but your son, who is your own flesh and blood—he is the one who will build the temple for my Name.'[r]

[20]"The LORD has kept the promise he made: I have succeeded[s] David my father and now I sit on the throne of Israel, just as the LORD promised, and I have built[t] the temple for the Name of the LORD, the God of Israel. [21]I have provided a place there for the ark, in which is the covenant of the LORD that he made with our fathers when he brought them out of Egypt."

Solomon's Prayer of Dedication

8:22–53pp — 2Ch 6:12–40

[22]Then Solomon stood before the altar of the LORD in front of the whole assembly of Israel, spread out his hands[u] toward heaven [23]and said:

"O LORD, God of Israel, there is no God like[v] you in heaven above or on earth below—you who keep your covenant of love[w] with your servants who continue wholeheartedly in your way. [24]You have kept your promise to your servant David my father; with your mouth you have promised and with your hand you have fulfilled it—as it is today.

[25]"Now LORD, God of Israel, keep for your servant David my father the promises[x] you made to him when you said, 'You shall never fail to have a man to sit before me on the throne of Israel, if only your sons are careful in

Cross references (center column)

8:4 [u]S Lev 17:4
[v]1Ch 15:13
8:5 [w]S 2Sa 6:13;
S 2Ch 30:24
8:6 [x]S Ex 26:33;
S 2Sa 6:17;
Rev 11:19
[y]S Ex 26:33
[z]S Ge 3:24;
S Ex 25:18
8:7 [a]S Ex 25:20
8:8 [b]Ex 25:13-15
8:9 [c]S Ex 16:34;
S 25:16; Heb 9:4
8:10
[d]S Ex 16:10;
S Lev 16:2;
Rev 15:8
8:11 [e]2Ch 7:2;
Rev 15:8
[f]S Ex 16:7;
S 29:43
8:12
[g]S Ex 40:34;
S 2Sa 22:10
8:13 [h]Ex 15:17;
Ps 132:13;
135:21; Mt 23:21
8:14 [i]S Ex 39:43
8:15 [j]1Ch 16:36;
Lk 1:68
8:16 [k]S Ex 3:10
[l]S Dt 12:5
[m]S 1Sa 9:16;
S 16:1 [n]Ps 89:3-4

8:17 [o]S 1Sa 10:7;
Ac 7:46
[p]2Sa 7:27;
1Ch 22:7;
Ps 26:8; 132:5
8:19 [q]S 2Sa 7:5
[r]S 2Sa 7:13
8:20 [s]S 2Sa 7:12
[t]1Ch 28:6
8:22 [u]S Ex 9:29
8:23 [v]S Ex 9:14
[w]S Dt 7:9,12;
Ne 1:5; 9:32;
Da 9:4
8:25 [x]S 2Sa 7:15;
1Ch 17:23;
2Ch 1:9

8:4 *Tent of Meeting.* The tabernacle, which had been preserved at Gibeon (see notes on 3:4; 1Sa 7:1; see also 2Ch 5:4–5).

8:6 *put it beneath the wings of the cherubim.* See 6:23–28.

8:8 *their ends could be seen.* The carrying poles were always to remain in the gold rings of the ark (Ex 25:15). *they are still there today.* These words must be those of the original author of this description of the dedication of the temple rather than those of the final compiler of the books of Kings (see Introduction: Author, Sources and Date; see also 2Ch 5:9).

8:9 *two stone tablets.* See Ex 25:16; 40:20. *the LORD made a covenant.* See Ex 24.

8:10 *the cloud filled the temple.* Just as a visible manifestation of the presence of the Lord had descended on the

tabernacle at Sinai, so now the Lord came to take up his abode in the temple (see Ex 40:33–35; Eze 10:3–5,18–19; 43:4–5).

8:12 *he would dwell in a dark cloud.* See Ex 19:9; 24:15, 18; 33:9–10; 34:5; Lev 16:2; Dt 4:11; 5:22; Ps 18:10–11.

8:15 *what he promised.* See 2Sa 7:5–16.

8:16 *my Name.* Equivalent to the Lord himself (see note on 5:5).

8:23 *no God like you.* No other god has acted in history as has the God of Israel, performing great miracles and directing the course of events so that his long-range covenant promises are fulfilled (see Ex 15:11; Dt 4:39; 7:9; Ps 86:8–10).

8:24 *your promise.* See v. 15; 2Sa 7:5–16.

8:25 *if only your sons . . . walk before me.* See 9:4–9; 2Ch 7:17–22; see also note on 1Ki 2:4.

all they do to walk before me as you have done.' 26And now, O God of Israel, let your word that you promised *y* your servant David my father come true.

27"But will God really dwell *z* on earth? The heavens, even the highest heaven, *a* cannot contain *b* you. How much less this temple I have built! 28Yet give attention to your servant's prayer and his plea for mercy, O LORD my God. Hear the cry and the prayer that your servant is praying in your presence this day. 29May your eyes be open *c* toward *d* this temple night and day, this place of which you said, 'My Name *e* shall be there,' so that you will hear the prayer your servant prays toward this place. 30Hear the supplication of your servant and of your people Israel when they pray *f* toward this place. Hear *g* from heaven, your dwelling place, and when you hear, forgive. *h*

31"When a man wrongs his neighbor and is required to take an oath and he comes and swears the oath *i* before your altar in this temple, 32then hear from heaven and act. Judge between your servants, condemning the guilty and bringing down on his own head what he has done. Declare the innocent not guilty, and so establish his innocence. *j*

8:26 *y* S 2Sa 7:25
8:27 *z* Ac 7:48; 17:24 *a* S Dt 10:14 *b* 2Ch 2:6; Ps 139:7-16; Isa 66:1; Jer 23:24
8:29 *c* ver 52; 2Ki 19:16; 2Ch 7:15; Ne 1:6; Ps 5:1; 31:2; 102:17; 130:2; Isa 37:17 *d* Ps 28:2; 138:2; Da 6:10 *e* S Dt 11:12; 12:11; S 2Sa 7:13
8:30 *f* ver 47; Lev 26:40; Ne 1:6; Jer 29:12; Da 9:4 *g* ver 39; Ps 34:6 *h* S Ex 34:7,9; Lev 26:40-42; Ps 85:2
8:31 *i* S Ex 22:11
8:32 *j* Dt 25:1; Eze 18:20
8:33 *k* S Lev 26:17 *l* Lev 26:39 *m* Isa 37:1,14,38
8:35 *n* S Dt 28:24; S 2Sa 1:21 *o* Jer 5:25
8:36 *p* S Dt 8:3; S 1Sa 12:23 *q* Ps 5:8; 27:11; 107:7; Pr 11:5; Isa 45:13; Jer 6:16; 7:23; 31:21 *r* ver 35; 1Ki 17:1; 18:1, 45; Jer 5:24; 10:3; 14:22; Zec 10:1
8:37 *s* S Lev 26:26 *t* S Ex 30:12; S Lev 26:25 *u* S Dt 28:22 *v* S Ex 10:13;

33"When your people Israel have been defeated *k* by an enemy because they have sinned *l* against you, and when they turn back to you and confess your name, praying and making supplication to you in this temple, *m* 34then hear from heaven and forgive the sin of your people Israel and bring them back to the land you gave to their fathers.

35"When the heavens are shut up and there is no rain *n* because your people have sinned *o* against you, and when they pray toward this place and confess your name and turn from their sin because you have afflicted them, 36then hear from heaven and forgive the sin of your servants, your people Israel. Teach *p* them the right way *q* to live, and send rain *r* on the land you gave your people for an inheritance.

37"When famine *s* or plague *t* comes to the land, or blight *u* or mildew, locusts or grasshoppers, *v* or when an enemy besieges them in any of their cities, whatever disaster or disease may come, 38and when a prayer or plea is made by any of your people Israel—each one aware of the afflictions of his own heart, and spreading out his hands *w* toward this temple— 39then hear *x* from heaven, your dwelling place. Forgive *y* and act;

Ps 105:34 8:38 *w* S Ex 9:29 8:39 *x* S ver 30 *y* Ps 130:4

8:27 *How much less this temple I have built!* With the construction of the temple and the appearance of a visible manifestation of the presence of God within its courts, the erroneous notion that God was irreversibly and exclusively bound to the temple in a way that guaranteed his assistance to Israel no matter how the people lived could very easily arise (see Jer 7:4–14; Mic 3:11). Solomon confessed that even though God had chosen to dwell among his people in a special and localized way, he far transcended containment by anything in all creation.

8:29 *My Name.* I the Lord (see note on 5:5).

8:30 *pray toward this place.* When an Israelite was unable to pray in the temple itself, he was to direct his prayers toward the place where God had pledged to be present among his people (see Da 6:10). *heaven, your dwelling place.* See note on v. 27.

8:31 *required to take an oath.* In cases such as default in pledges (Ex 22:10–12) or alleged adultery (Nu 5:11–31), when there was insufficient evidence to establish the legitimacy of the charge, the supposed offender was required to take an oath of innocence at the sanctuary. Such an oath, with its attendant blessings and curses, was considered a divinely given means of determining innocence or guilt since the consequences of the oath became apparent in the life of the individual either by his experiencing the blessing or the curse or by direct divine revelation through the Urim and Thummim (see Ex 28:29–30; Lev 8:8; Nu 27:21).

8:32 *hear from heaven.* It is clear that Solomon viewed the oath as an appeal to God to act and not as an automatic

power that worked in a magical way.

8:33 *defeated by an enemy because they have sinned against you.* Defeat by enemies was listed in Dt 28:25 as one of the curses that would come on Israel if she disobeyed the covenant. Solomon's prayer reflects an awareness of the covenant obligations the Lord had placed on his people and a knowledge of the consequences that disobedience would entail.

8:34 *bring them back to the land.* A reference to prisoners taken in battle.

8:35 *no rain.* Drought was another of the covenant curses listed in Dt 28:22–24.

8:36 *right way to live.* In accordance with covenant obligations (see Dt 6:18; 12:25; 13:18; 1Sa 12:23).

8:37 *famine.* See Dt 32:24. *plague.* See Dt 28:21–22; 32:24. *locusts or grasshoppers.* See Dt 28:38,42. *an enemy besieges them in any of their cities.* See Dt 28:52. *disaster.* See Dt 28:61; 31:29; 32:23–25. *disease.* See Dt 28:22.

8:38 *aware of the afflictions of his own heart.* Conscious of one's guilt before God, with an attitude of repentance and the desire for God's forgiveness and grace (see 2Ch 6:29; Ps 38:17–18; Jer 17:9).

8:39 *deal with each man according to all he does.* Not to be viewed as a request for retribution for the wrong committed (forgiveness and retribution are mutually exclusive), but as a desire for whatever discipline God in his wisdom may use to correct his people and to instruct them in the way of the covenant (see v. 40; Pr 3:11; Heb 12:5–15).

deal with each man according to all he does, since you know[z] his heart (for you alone know the hearts of all men), [40]so that they will fear[a] you all the time they live in the land[b] you gave our fathers.

[41]"As for the foreigner[c] who does not belong to your people Israel but has come from a distant land because of your name— [42]for men will hear[d] of your great name and your mighty hand[e] and your outstretched arm—when he comes and prays toward this temple, [43]then hear from heaven, your dwelling place, and do whatever the foreigner asks of you, so that all the peoples of the earth may know[f] your name and fear[g] you, as do your own people Israel, and may know that this house I have built bears your Name.[h]

[44]"When your people go to war against their enemies, wherever you send them, and when they pray[i] to the LORD toward the city you have chosen and the temple I have built for your Name, [45]then hear from heaven their prayer and their plea, and uphold their cause.[j]

[46]"When they sin against you—for there is no one who does not sin[k]—and you become angry with them and give them over to the enemy, who takes them captive[l] to his own land, far away or near; [47]and if they have a change of heart in the land where they are held captive, and repent and plead[m] with you in the land of their conquerors and say, 'We have sinned, we have done wrong, we have acted wickedly'; [n] [48]and if they turn back[o] to you with all their heart[p] and soul in the land of their

enemies who took them captive, and pray[q] to you toward the land you gave their fathers, toward the city you have chosen and the temple[r] I have built for your Name; [s] [49]then from heaven, your dwelling place, hear their prayer and their plea, and uphold their cause. [50]And forgive your people, who have sinned against you; forgive all the offenses they have committed against you, and cause their conquerors to show them mercy; [t] [51]for they are your people and your inheritance, [u] whom you brought out of Egypt, out of that iron-smelting furnace. [v]

[52]"May your eyes be open[w] to your servant's plea and to the plea of your people Israel, and may you listen to them whenever they cry out to you. [x] [53]For you singled them out from all the nations of the world to be your own inheritance, [y] just as you declared through your servant Moses when you, O Sovereign LORD, brought our fathers out of Egypt."

[54]When Solomon had finished all these prayers and supplications to the LORD, he rose from before the altar of the LORD, where he had been kneeling with his hands spread out toward heaven. [55]He stood and blessed[z] the whole assembly of Israel in a loud voice, saying:

[56]"Praise be to the LORD, who has given rest[a] to his people Israel just as he promised. Not one word has failed of all the good promises[b] he gave through his servant Moses. [57]May the LORD our God be with us as he was with our fathers; may he never leave us nor forsake[c] us. [58]May he turn our

---

Cross-reference column:

8:39
zS Jos 22:22;
S Ps 44:21;
Jn 2:24;
S Rev 2:23
8:40 aver 39-40;
Dt 6:13;
Ps 103:11; 130:4
bS Dt 12:1
8:41
cS Ge 31:15;
Isa 56:3,6; 61:5
8:42 d1Ki 10:1;
Isa 60:3; Ac 8:27
eDt 3:24
8:43 fS Jos 4:24;
S 1Sa 17:46
gPs 102:15
hS Dt 28:10
8:44 i1Ch 5:20;
2Ch 14:11
8:45 jPs 9:4;
140:12
8:46 kPs 130:3;
143:2; Pr 20:9;
S Ro 3:9
lLev 26:33-39;
S Dt 4:27;
S 21:10; S 28:64;
2Ki 25:21
8:47 mS ver 30;
S Lev 5:5;
Ezr 9:15; Ne 1:6;
Jer 14:20
nEzr 9:7;
Ps 106:6; Jer 3:25
8:48 oS Dt 4:30
pS Dt 4:29

qJn 1:8-10
rPs 5:7; 11:4;
Jnh 2:4
sDt 12:11-14;
Ne 1:9; Jer 23:3;
31:8
8:50 t2Ki 25:28;
2Ch 30:9;
Ps 106:46; Da 1:9
8:51 uS Ex 34:9;
S Dt 9:29
vS Ex 1:13;
Isa 48:10;
Jer 11:4
8:52 wS ver 29
xJob 30:20;
Ps 3:4; 22:2;
77:1; 142:1
8:53 yEx 19:5;
S 34:9
8:55
zS Ex 39:43;
Nu 6:23
8:56
aS Ex 33:14;
Dt 12:10; Heb 4:8
bS Jos 23:15;
S Jer 29:10

8:57 cS Dt 4:31; S 31:6; S Mt 28:20; Heb 13:5

8:40 *fear you.* Honor and obediently serve you (see Dt 5:29; 6:1–2; 8:6; 31:13; 2Ch 6:31; Ps 130:4).
8:41 *foreigner who does not belong to your people Israel.* One who comes from a foreign land to pray to Israel's God at the temple, as distinguished from a resident alien.
8:42 *men will hear.* See 9:9 (foreign nations generally); 10:1 (queen of Sheba); Jos 2:9–11 (Rahab); 1Sa 4:6–8 (Philistines). *your great name and your mighty hand and your outstretched arm.* God's great power, demonstrated by his interventions in the history of his people (see Dt 4:34; 5:15; 7:19; 11:2; 26:8).
8:44 *go to war ... wherever you send them.* Military initiatives undertaken with divine sanction (see, e.g., Lev 26:7; Dt 20; 21:10; 1Sa 15:3; 23:2,4; 30:8; 2Sa 5:19,24). *toward the city you have chosen.* See note on v. 30.
8:46 *the enemy, who takes them captive.* On the basis of Lev 26:33–45; Dt 28:64–68; 30:1–5 Solomon knew that stubborn disobedience would lead to exile from the promised land.

8:51 *iron-smelting furnace.* See Dt 4:20 and note.
8:53 *you singled them out . . . to be your own inheritance.* Solomon began his prayer with an appeal to the Davidic covenant (vv. 23–30), and he closes with an appeal to the Sinaitic covenant (see Ex 19:5; Lev 20:24,26; Dt 7:6; 32:9).
8:54 *he had been kneeling.* Cf. v. 22; 2Sa 7:18; 2Ch 6:13; Lk 22:41; Eph 3:14.
8:56 *Praise be to the LORD.* Solomon understood this historic day to be a testimony to God's covenant faithfulness. *rest to his people.* After the conquest of Canaan under the leadership of Joshua, the Lord gave the Israelites a period of rest from their enemies (Jos 11:23; 21:44; 22:4), even though there remained much land to be possessed (Jos 13:1; Jdg 1). It was only with David's victories that the rest was made durable and complete (see 2Sa 7:1; see also note on 1Ki 5:4).
8:58 *turn our hearts to him.* Solomon asks for a divine work of grace within his people that will enable them to be faithful to the covenant (see Dt 30:6; Ps 51:10; Php 2:13).

hearts[d] to him, to walk in all his ways and to keep the commands, decrees and regulations he gave our fathers. [59]And may these words of mine, which I have prayed before the LORD, be near to the LORD our God day and night, that he may uphold the cause of his servant and the cause of his people Israel according to each day's need, [60]so that all the peoples[e] of the earth may know that the LORD is God and that there is no other.[f] [61]But your hearts[g] must be fully committed[h] to the LORD our God, to live by his decrees and obey his commands, as at this time."

The Dedication of the Temple

8:62–66pp — 2Ch 7:1–10

[62]Then the king and all Israel with him offered sacrifices[i] before the LORD. [63]Solomon offered a sacrifice of fellowship offerings[y] to the LORD: twenty-two thousand cattle and a hundred and twenty thousand sheep and goats. So the king and all the Israelites dedicated[j] the temple of the LORD.

[64]On that same day the king consecrated the middle part of the courtyard in front of the temple of the LORD, and there he offered burnt offerings, grain offerings and the fat[k] of the fellowship offerings, because the bronze altar[l] before the LORD was too small to hold the burnt offerings, the grain offerings and the fat of the fellowship offerings.[m]

[65]So Solomon observed the festival[n] at that time, and all Israel with him—a vast assembly, people from Lebo[z] Hamath[o] to the Wadi of Egypt.[p] They celebrated it before the LORD our God for seven days and seven days more, fourteen days in all. [66]On

the following day he sent the people away. They blessed the king and then went home, joyful and glad in heart for all the good[q] things the LORD had done for his servant David and his people Israel.

The LORD Appears to Solomon

9:1–9pp — 2Ch 7:11–22

9 When Solomon had finished[r] building the temple of the LORD and the royal palace, and had achieved all he had desired to do, [2]the LORD appeared[s] to him a second time, as he had appeared to him at Gibeon. [3]The LORD said to him:

"I have heard[t] the prayer and plea you have made before me; I have consecrated this temple, which you have built, by putting my Name[u] there forever. My eyes[v] and my heart will always be there.

[4]"As for you, if you walk before me in integrity of heart[w] and uprightness, as David[x] your father did, and do all I command and observe my decrees and laws,[y] [5]I will establish[z] your royal throne over Israel forever, as I promised David your father when I said, 'You shall never fail[a] to have a man on the throne of Israel.'

[6]"But if you[a] or your sons turn away[b] from me and do not observe the commands and decrees I have given you[a] and go off to serve other gods[c] and worship them, [7]then I will cut off Israel from the land[d] I have given them and will reject this temple I have consecrated for my Name.[e] Israel will then become a byword[f] and an object of ridicule[g] among all peo-

Cross references (center column)

8:58 [d]S Jos 24:23
8:60 [e]S Jos 4:24
　　　[f]S Dt 4:35
8:61 [g]Dt 6:5
　　　[h]1Ki 9:4; 11:4;
　　　15:3,14; 22:43;
　　　2Ki 20:3;
　　　1Ch 28:9; 29:19;
　　　2Ch 16:9; 17:6;
　　　25:2; Ps 119:80;
　　　Isa 38:3
8:62 [i]S 2Sa 6:13;
　　　1Ch 29:21;
　　　Eze 45:17
8:63 [j]Ezr 6:16
8:64 [k]S Ex 29:13
　　　[l]S Ex 27:1;
　　　2Ki 16:14;
　　　2Ch 4:1; 8:12;
　　　15:8;
　　　Eze 43:13-17
　　　[m]S 2Sa 6:17
8:65 [n]S ver 2
　　　[o]S Nu 13:21
　　　[p]S Ge 15:18

8:66 [q]S Ex 18:9
9:1 [r]S 2Sa 7:2
9:2 [s]S 1Ki 3:5
9:3 [t]S 1Sa 9:16;
　　　2Ki 19:20; 20:5;
　　　Ps 10:17; 34:17
　　　[u]S Ex 20:24;
　　　S Dt 12:5
　　　[v]S Dt 11:12
9:4 [w]S Ge 17:1
　　　[x]Dt 17:20;
　　　1Ki 14:8; 15:5
　　　[y]S 1Ki 3:14;
　　　1Ch 28:9; Pr 4:4
9:5 [z]1Ch 22:10
　　　[a]S 2Sa 7:15
9:6 [b]Dt 28:15;
　　　2Sa 7:14;
　　　2Ki 18:12;
　　　Jer 17:27; 26:4;
　　　32:23; 44:23
　　　[c]1Ki 11:10
9:7
　　　[d]Lev 18:24-28;
　　　Dt 4:26;
　　　S Jos 23:13;
　　　2Ki 17:23;
　　　Jer 24:10
　　　[e]Dt 12:5; Jer 7:14
　　　[f]Job 17:6;
　　　Ps 44:14;
　　　Jer 24:9; Joel 2:17
　　　[g]S Dt 28:37;
　　　Eze 5:15

[y]63 Traditionally *peace offerings*; also in verse 64　[z]65 Or *from the entrance to*　[a]6 The Hebrew is plural.

8:59 *his servant.* The king, who, as the Lord's anointed, serves as the earthly representative of God's rule over his people (see notes on Ps 2:2,7).

8:60 *so that all . . . may know.* See note on Ps 46:10.

8:63 *fellowship offerings.* Involved a communion meal (see note on 1Sa 11:15). *twenty-two thousand cattle and a hundred and twenty thousand sheep and goats.* Although these numbers may seem large, there were vast numbers of people who participated in the dedication ceremony, which lasted 14 days (see vv. 1–2; see also v. 65).

8:65 *Lebo Hamath.* See note on Eze 47:15. *Wadi of Egypt.* Probably Wadi el-Arish (see note on Ge 15:18). People came to Jerusalem for the dedication of the temple from nearly the entire area of Solomon's dominion (see note on 4:21). *seven days and seven days more, fourteen days in all.* It appears that the seven-day celebration for the dedication of the temple was followed by the seven-day Feast of Tabernacles (see note on v. 2), which was observed from the 15th to the 21st of the seventh month. According to Chronicles, this was followed by a final assembly on the next day, in accordance

with Lev 23:33–36; then on the 23rd of the month the people were sent to their homes (see 2Ch 7:8–10).

9:1 *When Solomon had finished.* At the earliest this would be in the 24th year $(4 + 7 + 13 = 24)$ of Solomon's reign—946 B.C. (see 6:1,37–38; 7:1; 9:10).

9:2 *he had appeared to him at Gibeon.* See 3:4–15.

9:3 *putting my Name there forever.* See 8:10–13. *My eyes and my heart will always be there.* See 8:29.

9:4–5 *if you walk before me in integrity of heart . . . I will establish your royal throne over Israel forever.* See 8:25 and note on 2:4. The Lord reemphasizes to Solomon the importance of obedience to the covenant in order to experience its blessings rather than its curses. This was particularly necessary as Solomon's kingdom grew in influence and wealth, with all the potential for covenant-breaking that prosperity brought (see Dt 8:12–14,17; 31:20; 32:15).

9:6 *serve other gods and worship them.* See 11:4–8.

9:7 *a byword and an object of ridicule among all peoples.* See the covenant curse in Dt 28:37.

ples. [8]And though this temple is now imposing, all who pass by will be appalled[h] and will scoff and say, 'Why has the LORD done such a thing to this land and to this temple?'[i] [9]People will answer,[j] 'Because they have forsaken[k] the LORD their God, who brought their fathers out of Egypt, and have embraced other gods, worshiping and serving them—that is why the LORD brought all this disaster[l] on them.'"

Solomon's Other Activities

9:10–28pp — 2Ch 8:1–18

[10]At the end of twenty years, during which Solomon built these two buildings—the temple of the LORD and the royal palace— [11]King Solomon gave twenty towns in Galilee to Hiram king of Tyre, because Hiram had supplied him with all the cedar and pine and gold[m] he wanted. [12]But when Hiram went from Tyre to see the towns that Solomon had given him, he was not pleased with them. [13]"What kind of towns are these you have given me, my brother?" he asked. And he called them the Land of Cabul,[b][n] a name they have to this day. [14]Now Hiram had sent to the king 120 talents[c] of gold.[o]

[15]Here is the account of the forced labor King Solomon conscripted[p] to build the LORD's temple, his own palace, the supporting terraces,[d][q] the wall of Jerusalem, and Hazor,[r] Megiddo and Gezer.[s] [16](Pharaoh king of Egypt had attacked and captured Gezer. He had set it on fire. He

9:8 [h]S Lev 26:32; [i]S Dt 29:24; Jer 7:4-15; Mt 23:38 **9:9** [j]Dt 29:25; 2Ki 22:17; Jer 5:19; 13:22; 16:11,13; 22:9 [k]S Nu 25:3; Jer 40:3; 44:23; La 4:12 [l]S Dt 31:29 **9:11** [m]ver 14 **9:13** [n]Jos 19:27 **9:14** [o]ver 11 **9:15** [p]1Ki 5:13 [q]S 2Sa 5:9 [r]Jos 11:10-11 [s]S Jos 10:33

9:16 [t]1Ki 3:1; Ps 45:12; 68:29; 72:10 **9:17** [u]S Jos 10:10 **9:18** [v]S Jos 19:44 **9:19** [w]S Ex 1:11 [x]S Dt 17:16; 1Ki 4:26; 2Ch 1:14; 9:25 **9:20** [y]S Nu 13:29 [z]S Jos 11:3 **9:21** [a]S Ge 9:25-26 [b]S Jos 15:63 [c]S Ge 49:15; S Ex 1:11; S Dt 20:11 **9:22** [d]S Lev 25:39 **9:23** [e]1Ki 5:16 **9:24** [f]S 1Ki 3:1; [g]2Sa 5:9; 1Ki 11:27 **9:25** [h]S Ex 23:14

killed its Canaanite inhabitants and then gave it as a wedding gift to his daughter,[t] Solomon's wife. [17]And Solomon rebuilt Gezer.) He built up Lower Beth Horon,[u] [18]Baalath,[v] and Tadmor[e] in the desert, within his land, [19]as well as all his store cities[w] and the towns for his chariots[x] and for his horses[f]—whatever he desired to build in Jerusalem, in Lebanon and throughout all the territory he ruled.

[20]All the people left from the Amorites, Hittites,[y] Perizzites, Hivites and Jebusites[z] (these peoples were not Israelites), [21]that is, their descendants[a] remaining in the land, whom the Israelites could not exterminate[g][b]—these Solomon conscripted for his slave labor force,[c] as it is to this day. [22]But Solomon did not make slaves[d] of any of the Israelites; they were his fighting men, his government officials, his officers, his captains, and the commanders of his chariots and charioteers. [23]They were also the chief officials[e] in charge of Solomon's projects—550 officials supervising the men who did the work.

[24]After Pharaoh's daughter[f] had come up from the City of David to the palace Solomon had built for her, he constructed the supporting terraces.[g]

[25]Three[h] times a year Solomon sacrificed burnt offerings and fellowship offer-

[b]13 *Cabul* sounds like the Hebrew for *good-for-nothing.*
[c]14 That is, about 4 1/2 tons (about 4 metric tons)
[d]15 Or *the Millo;* also in verse 24   [e]18 The Hebrew may also be read *Tamar.*   [f]19 Or *charioteers*
[g]21 The Hebrew term refers to the irrevocable giving over of things or persons to the LORD, often by totally destroying them.

9:9 *that is why the LORD brought all this disaster on them.* See Dt 29:22–28; Jer 22:8–30.
9:10–28 See map No. 5 at the end of the Study Bible.
9:11 *Solomon gave twenty towns in Galilee to Hiram king of Tyre.* Comparison of vv. 10–14 with 5:1–12 suggests that during Solomon's 20 years of building activity he became more indebted to Hiram than anticipated in their original agreement (see note on 5:9), which had provided for payment for labor (5:6) and wood (5:10–11). From vv. 11,14 it is evident that in addition to wood and labor Solomon had also acquired great quantities of gold from Hiram. It appears that Solomon gave Hiram the 20 towns in the Phoenician-Galilee border area as a surety for repayment of the gold. 2Ch 8:1–2 indicates that at some later date when Solomon's gold reserves were increased, perhaps after the return of the expedition to Ophir (1Ki 9:26–28; 10:11) or the visit of the queen of Sheba (10:1–13), he settled his debt with Hiram and recovered the 20 towns held as collateral.
9:15 *forced labor.* Non-Israelite slave labor of a permanent nature (in contrast to the temporary conscription of Israelite workmen described in 5:13–16). *supporting terraces.* Probably for Solomon's expansion of Jerusalem on the ridge north from David's city (see note on 2Sa 5:9). *Hazor.* Solomon's building activity at Hazor, Megiddo and Gezer was intended to strengthen the fortifications of these ancient, strategically located towns (Solomonic gates, probably built by the same

masons, have been found at all three sites). Hazor was the most important fortress in the northern Galilee area, controlling the trade route running from the Euphrates River to Egypt. *Megiddo.* Another fortress along the great north-south trade route; it commanded the pass through the Carmel range from the plain of Jezreel to the coastal plain of Sharon. *Gezer.* See note on 3:1.
9:16 *killed its Canaanite inhabitants.* Although Joshua had killed the king of Gezer at the time of the conquest (Jos 10:33; 12:12), the tribe of Ephraim had been unable to drive out its inhabitants (Jos 16:10; Jdg 1:29).
9:17 *Lower Beth Horon.* Located about eight miles northwest of Jerusalem at a pass giving entrance to the Judahite highlands and Jerusalem from the coastal plain.
9:18 *Baalath.* To be identified with either the Bealoth of Jos 15:24 located to the south of Hebron in the tribe of Judah or the Baalath southwest of Beth Horon in the tribe of Dan (Jos 19:44). *Tadmor.* See NIV text note; see also 2Ch 8:4; Eze 47:19.
9:20 *Amorites . . . Jebusites.* See Dt 7:1; 20:17; see also notes on Ge 10:15–18; 13:7; 15:16; 23:9; Jos 5:1; Jdg 3:3; 6:10; 2Sa 21:2.
9:22 *Solomon did not make slaves of any of the Israelites.* See note on v. 15.
9:23 *550 officials.* See note on 5:16.
9:25 *Three times a year.* On the occasion of the three

ings[h] on the altar he had built for the Lord, burning incense before the Lord along with them, and so fulfilled the temple obligations.

26King Solomon also built ships[i] at Ezion Geber,[j] which is near Elath[k] in Edom, on the shore of the Red Sea.[i] 27And Hiram sent his men—sailors[l] who knew the sea—to serve in the fleet with Solomon's men. 28They sailed to Ophir[m] and brought back 420 talents[j] of gold,[n] which they delivered to King Solomon.

The Queen of Sheba Visits Solomon

10:1–13pp — 2Ch 9:1–12

10 When the queen of Sheba[o] heard about the fame[p] of Solomon and his relation to the name of the Lord, she came to test him with hard questions.[q] 2Arriving at Jerusalem with a very great caravan[r]—with camels carrying spices, large quantities of gold, and precious stones—she came to Solomon and talked with him about all that she had on her mind. 3Solomon answered all her questions; nothing was too hard for the king to explain to her. 4When the queen of Sheba saw all the wisdom of Solomon and the palace he had built, 5the food on his table,[s] the seating of his officials, the attending servants in their robes, his cupbearers, and the burnt offerings he made at[k] the temple of the Lord, she was overwhelmed.

6She said to the king, "The report I

heard in my own country about your achievements and your wisdom is true. 7But I did not believe[t] these things until I came and saw with my own eyes. Indeed, not even half was told me; in wisdom and wealth[u] you have far exceeded the report I heard. 8How happy your men must be! How happy your officials, who continually stand before you and hear[v] your wisdom! 9Praise[w] be to the Lord your God, who has delighted in you and placed you on the throne of Israel. Because of the Lord's eternal love[x] for Israel, he has made you king, to maintain justice[y] and righteousness."

10And she gave the king 120 talents[1] of gold,[z] large quantities of spices, and precious stones. Never again were so many spices brought in as those the queen of Sheba gave to King Solomon.

11(Hiram's ships brought gold from Ophir;[a] and from there they brought great cargoes of almugwood[m] and precious stones. 12The king used the almugwood to make supports for the temple of the Lord and for the royal palace, and to make harps and lyres for the musicians. So much almugwood has never been imported or seen since that day.)

13King Solomon gave the queen of

Cross-references (center column)

9:26 [i]1Ki 10:22; 22:48; 2Ch 20:37; Isa 2:16 /S Nu 33:35
[k]2Ki 14:22; 16:6
9:27 [l]Eze 27:8
9:28 [m]S Ge 10:29 [n]ver 14; 1Ki 10:10,11, 14,21; 2Ch 1:15; Ecc 2:8
10:1 [o]S Ge 10:7, 28; S 25:3; Mt 12:42; Lk 11:31
[p]Eze 16:14 [q]S Nu 12:8; S Jdg 14:12
10:2 [r]S Ge 24:10
10:5 [s]1Ki 4:22

10:7 [t]S Ge 45:26 [u]1Ch 29:25
10:8 [v]Pr 8:34
10:9 [w]S 1Ki 5:7; S Isa 42:10 [x]S Dt 7:8 [y]Ps 11:7; 33:5; 72:2; 99:4; 103:6
10:10 [z]S 1Ki 9:28; Isa 60:6
10:11 [a]S Ge 10:29

Footnotes (center column)

[h]25 Traditionally *peace offerings* [i]26 Hebrew *Yam Suph;* that is, Sea of Reeds [j]28 That is, about 16 tons (about 14.5 metric tons) [k]5 Or *the ascent by which he went up to* [l]10 That is, about 4 1/2 tons (about 4 metric tons) [m]11 Probably a variant of *algumwood;* also in verse 12

---

important annual festivals: the Feast of Unleavened Bread, the Feast of Weeks, and the Feast of Tabernacles (see Ex 23:14–17; 2Ch 8:13).

9:26 *ships.* Used in a large trading business that brought great wealth to Solomon's court (see v. 28; 10:11). *Ezion Geber.* Located at the northern tip of the Gulf of Aqaba (see 22:48; Nu 33:35; Dt 2:8). *Red Sea.* The Hebrew for this term, normally read as *Yam Suph* ("sea of reeds"; see NIV text note), refers to the body of water through which the Israelites passed at the time of the exodus (see notes on Ex 13:18; 14:2). It can also be read, however, as *Yam Soph* ("sea of land's end"), a more likely reading when referring to the Red Sea, and especially (as here) to its eastern arm (the Gulf of Aqaba).

9:28 *Ophir.* A source for gold (2Ch 8:18; Job 28:16; Ps 45:9; Isa 13:12), almugwood and precious stones (10:11), and silver, ivory, apes and baboons (10:22). Its location is disputed: Southeastern Arabia, southwestern Arabia, the northeastern African coast (in the area of Somalia), India and Zimbabwe have all been suggested. If Ophir was located in Arabia, it was probably a trading center for goods from farther east as well as from east Africa. But the three-year voyages of Solomon's merchant vessels (10:22) suggest a more distant location than the Arabian coast.

10:1 *Sheba.* Archaeological evidence suggests that Sheba is to be identified with a mercantile kingdom that flourished in southwest Arabia (see notes on Ge 10:28; Joel 3:8) c. 900–450 B.C. It profited from the sea trade of India and east

Africa by transporting luxury commodities north to Damascus and Gaza on caravan routes through the Arabian Desert. It is possible that Solomon's fleet of ships threatened Sheba's continued dominance of this trading business. *his relation to the name of the Lord.* The queen of Sheba recognized a connection between the wisdom of Solomon and the God he served. Jesus used her example to condemn the people of his own day who had not recognized that "one greater than Solomon" was in their midst (Mt 12:42; Lk 11:31).

10:9 *Praise be to the Lord your God.* The queen of Sheba's confession is beautifully worded and reflects a profound understanding of Israel's covenant relationship with the Lord. However, it does not necessarily imply anything more than her recognition of the Lord as Israel's national God in conformity with the ideas of polytheistic paganism (see note on 5:7; see also 2Ch 2:12; Da 3:28–29). There is no confession that Solomon's God has become her God to the exclusion of all others.

10:10 *120 talents of gold.* See notes on 9:11,28.

10:11 *Hiram's ships.* See 9:26–28. Hiram had supplied the wood, the sailors and the expertise in construction that Israel lacked. *almugwood.* See NIV text note and 2Ch 9:10–11. Its identity is unknown, though some suggest it is juniper. It was apparently available from Lebanon as well as Ophir (2Ch 2:8).

10:13 *all she desired and asked for.* The exchange of gifts between Solomon and the queen may have signified the effecting of a trade agreement (see note on v. 1). There is no

Sheba all she desired and asked for, besides what he had given her out of his royal bounty. Then she left and returned with her retinue to her own country.

Solomon's Splendor

10:14–29pp — 2Ch 1:14–17; 9:13–28

[14]The weight of the gold[b] that Solomon received yearly was 666 talents,[n] [15]not including the revenues from merchants and traders and from all the Arabian kings and the governors of the land.

[16]King Solomon made two hundred large shields[c] of hammered gold; six hundred bekas[o] of gold went into each shield. [17]He also made three hundred small shields of hammered gold, with three minas[p] of gold in each shield. The king put them in the Palace of the Forest of Lebanon.[d]

[18]Then the king made a great throne inlaid with ivory and overlaid with fine gold. [19]The throne had six steps, and its back had a rounded top. On both sides of the seat were armrests, with a lion standing beside each of them. [20]Twelve lions stood on the six steps, one at either end of each step. Nothing like it had ever been made for any other kingdom. [21]All King Solomon's goblets were gold, and all the household articles in the Palace of the Forest of Lebanon were pure gold.[e] Nothing was made of silver, because silver was considered of little value in Solomon's days. [22]The king had a fleet of trading ships[q,f] at sea along with the ships[g] of Hiram. Once every three years it returned, carrying gold, silver and ivory, and apes and baboons.

[23]King Solomon was greater in riches[h] and wisdom[i] than all the other kings of the earth. [24]The whole world sought audience with Solomon to hear the wisdom[j] God had put in his heart. [25]Year after year, everyone who came brought a gift[k]—articles of silver and gold, robes, weapons and spices, and horses and mules.

[26]Solomon accumulated chariots and horses;[l] he had fourteen hundred chariots and twelve thousand horses,[r] which he kept in the chariot cities and also with him in Jerusalem. [27]The king made silver as common[m] in Jerusalem as stones,[n] and cedar as plentiful as sycamore-fig[o] trees in the foothills. [28]Solomon's horses were imported from Egypt[s] and from Kue[t]—the royal merchants purchased them from Kue. [29]They imported a chariot from Egypt for six hundred shekels[u] of silver, and a horse for a hundred and fifty.[v] They also exported them to all the kings of the Hittites[p] and of the Arameans.

Solomon's Wives

11 King Solomon, however, loved many foreign women[q] besides Pharaoh's daughter—Moabites, Ammonites,[r] Edomites, Sidonians and Hittites. [2]They were from nations about which the LORD had told the Israelites, "You must not intermarry[s] with them, because they will surely turn your hearts after their gods." Nevertheless, Solomon held fast to them in love. [3]He had seven hundred wives of royal birth and three hundred

Cross references

10:14
b S 1Ki 9:28
10:16 c S 2Sa 8:7
10:17 d S 1Ki 7:2
10:21 e Isa 60:17
10:22 f S 1Ki 9:26
g 1Ki 9:27;
Ps 48:7; Isa 2:16;
23:1,14; 60:6,9
10:23 h 1Ki 3:13;
Mt 6:29
i S 1Ki 3:12;
Mt 12:42

10:24
j S 2Sa 14:20
10:25
k S 1Sa 10:27
10:26
l S Dt 17:16
10:27 m Dt 17:17
n Job 27:16;
Isa 60:17
o 1Ch 27:28;
Am 7:14
10:29
p S Nu 13:29
11:1 q S ver 3;
S Ex 34:16
r 1Ki 14:21,31
11:2 s S Ex 34:16;
1Ki 16:31

Footnotes

n 14 That is, about 25 tons (about 23 metric tons)
o 16 That is, about 7 1/2 pounds (about 3.5 kilograms)
p 17 That is, about 3 3/4 pounds (about 1.7 kilograms)
q 22 Hebrew *of ships of Tarshish*   r 26 Or *charioteers*
s 28 Or possibly *Muzur,* a region in Cilicia; also in verse
29   t 28 Probably *Cilicia*   u 29 That is, about 15
pounds (about 7 kilograms)   v 29 That is, about 3 3/4
pounds (about 1.7 kilograms)

---

basis for the idea sometimes suggested that she desired offspring fathered by Solomon and left Jerusalem carrying his child.
10:15 *revenues from . . . Arabian kings.* Tribute from Bedouin sheiks for passage of their caravans into Israelite territory. *governors of the land.* See 4:7–19.
10:16 *large shields.* Rectangular shields that afforded maximum protection (in distinction from the smaller round shields). These gold shields were probably not intended for battle but for ceremonial use, symbolizing Israel's wealth and glory. They were probably made of wood overlaid with gold. Shishak of Egypt carried them off as plunder in the fifth regnal year of Solomon's son Rehoboam (see 14:25–26).
10:22 *fleet of trading ships.* See NIV text note; 2Ch 9:21. The same fleet is referred to in v. 11; 9:26–28. "Ships of Tarshish" are not necessarily ships that sail to Tarshish (see note on Jnh 1:3) but can designate large trading vessels.
10:26 *chariots and horses.* See note on 4:26. Accumulation of chariots and horses by the king was forbidden in the Mosaic law (Dt 17:16).
10:29 *exported them.* Through his agents Solomon was the middleman in a lucrative trading business. It appears that

he acquired horses from the north (Muzur and Kue in Asia Minor; see NIV text notes on v. 28) and sold them in the south, while at the same time acquiring chariots from the south (Egypt) and selling them in the north. See inset to map No. 4 at the end of the Study Bible.

11:1 *loved many foreign women.* Many of Solomon's marriages were no doubt for the purpose of sealing international relationships with various kingdoms, large and small—a common practice in the ancient Near East. But this violated not only Dt 17:17 with respect to the multiplicity of wives, but also the prohibition against taking wives from the pagan peoples among whom Israel settled (see Ex 34:16; Dt 7:1–3; Jos 23:12–13; Ezr 9:2; 10:2–3; Ne 13:23–27). *Moabites.* See note on Ge 19:36–38. *Ammonites.* See note on Ge 19:36–38; see also 14:21; Dt 23:3. *Edomites.* See notes on Ge 25:26; 36:1; Am 1:11; 9:12; see also Dt 23:7–8. *Sidonians.* See 16:31.

11:2 *they will surely turn your hearts after their gods.* An example in Israel's earlier history is found in Nu 25:1–15.

11:3 *seven hundred . . . three hundred.* Cf. SS 6:8, but see note there.

concubines,[t] and his wives led him astray.[u] [4]As Solomon grew old, his wives turned his heart after other gods,[v] and his heart was not fully devoted[w] to the LORD his God, as the heart of David his father had been. [5]He followed Ashtoreth[x] the goddess of the Sidonians, and Molech[w][y] the detestable god of the Ammonites. [6]So Solomon did evil[z] in the eyes of the LORD; he did not follow the LORD completely, as David his father had done.

[7]On a hill east[a] of Jerusalem, Solomon built a high place for Chemosh[b] the detestable god of Moab, and for Molech[c] the detestable god of the Ammonites. [8]He did the same for all his foreign wives, who burned incense and offered sacrifices to their gods.

[9]The LORD became angry with Solomon because his heart had turned away from the LORD, the God of Israel, who had appeared[d] to him twice. [10]Although he had forbidden Solomon to follow other gods,[e] Solomon did not keep the LORD's command.[f] [11]So the LORD said to Solomon, "Since this is your attitude and you have not kept my covenant and my decrees,[g] which I commanded you, I will most certainly tear[h] the kingdom away from you and give it to one of your subordinates. [12]Nevertheless, for the sake of David[i] your father, I will not do it during your lifetime. I will tear it out of the hand of your son. [13]Yet I will not tear the whole kingdom from him, but will give him one tribe[j] for the sake[k] of David my servant

and for the sake of Jerusalem, which I have chosen."[l]

Solomon's Adversaries

[14]Then the LORD raised up against Solomon an adversary,[m] Hadad the Edomite, from the royal line of Edom. [15]Earlier when David was fighting with Edom, Joab the commander of the army, who had gone up to bury the dead, had struck down all the men in Edom.[n] [16]Joab and all the Israelites stayed there for six months, until they had destroyed all the men in Edom. [17]But Hadad, still only a boy, fled to Egypt with some Edomite officials who had served his father. [18]They set out from Midian and went to Paran.[o] Then taking men from Paran with them, they went to Egypt, to Pharaoh king of Egypt, who gave Hadad a house and land and provided him with food.

[19]Pharaoh was so pleased with Hadad that he gave him a sister of his own wife, Queen Tahpenes, in marriage. [20]The sister of Tahpenes bore him a son named Genubath, whom Tahpenes brought up in the royal palace. There Genubath lived with Pharaoh's own children.

[21]While he was in Egypt, Hadad heard that David rested with his fathers and that Joab the commander of the army was also dead. Then Hadad said to Pharaoh, "Let me go, that I may return to my own country."

[22]"What have you lacked here that you

Cross references (center column)

11:3 [t]S Ge 22:24; S Est 2:14 [u]ver 1; Dt 17:17; Ne 13:26; Pr 31:3
11:4 [v]S Ex 34:16 [w]S 1Ki 8:61; S 1Ch 29:19
11:5 [x]S Jdg 2:13 [y]ver 7; S Lev 18:21; Isa 57:9; Zep 1:5
11:6 [z]S Dt 4:25
11:7 [a]2Ki 23:13 [b]S Nu 21:29 [c]S Lev 18:21; 20:2-5; Ac 7:43
11:9 [d]S 1Ki 3:5
11:10 [e]S 1Ki 9:6 /1Ki 6:12
11:11 [g]S Lev 18:4 [h]ver 31; S 1Sa 15:27; 2Ki 17:21; Mt 21:43
11:12 [i]Ps 89:33
11:13 [j]1Ki 12:20 [k]S 2Sa 7:15
11:14 [m]S 1Ki 5:4
11:15
11:18 [o]Nu 10:12

[l]Dt 12:11

[n]1Ch 18:12

[w]5 Hebrew Milcom; also in verse 33

11:4 *his heart was not fully devoted to the LORD his God.* See 8:61. The atmosphere of paganism and idolatry introduced into Solomon's court by his foreign wives gradually led Solomon into syncretistic religious practices.

11:5 *Ashtoreth.* See v. 33; 14:15; 2Ki 23:13; see also note on Jdg 2:13. *Molech.* See 2Sa 12:30 and NIV text note. Molech and Milcom (see NIV text note) are alternate names for the same pagan deity. Worship of this god not only severely jeopardized the continued recognition of the absolute kingship of the Lord over his people, but also involved (on rare occasions) the abomination of child sacrifice (see 2Ki 16:3; 17:17; 21:6; Lev 18:21; 20:2-5; see also note on Jdg 10:6).

11:6 *as David his father had done.* Although David committed grievous sins, he was repentant, and he was never involved in idolatrous worship.

11:7 *high place.* See note on 3:2. *Chemosh.* See 2Ki 3:26-27.

11:9 *appeared to him twice.* See 3:4-5; 9:1-9.

11:11 *not kept my covenant.* Solomon had broken the most basic demands of the covenant (see Ex 20:2-5) and thereby severely undermined the entire covenant relationship between God and his people.

11:12 *for the sake of David your father.* Because of David's unwavering loyalty to the Lord and God's covenant with him (see 2Sa 7:11-16).

11:13 *one tribe.* Judah (see note on vv. 31-32; see also

12:20). *for the sake of Jerusalem, which I have chosen.* Now that Jerusalem contained the temple built by David's son in accordance with 2Sa 7:13, the destiny of Jerusalem and the Davidic dynasty were closely linked (see 2Ki 19:34; 21:7-8; Ps 132). The temple represented God's royal palace, where his earthly throne (the ark) was situated and where he had pledged to be present as Israel's Great King (9:3).

11:14 *Hadad.* A familiar name among Edomite kings (see Ge 36:35,39).

11:15 *David was fighting with Edom.* See 2Sa 8:13-14.

11:16 *all the Israelites . . . all the men in Edom.* All those, on both sides, who took part in the campaign.

11:17 *only a boy.* Probably in his early teens.

11:18 *Midian.* At this time Midianites inhabited a region on the eastern borders of Moab and Edom. *Paran.* A desert area southeast of Kadesh in the central area of the Sinai peninsula (see Nu 10:12; 12:16; 13:3). *Pharaoh king of Egypt.* See note on 3:1. *gave Hadad a house and land and . . . food.* In a time of Israel's growing strength it was in Egypt's interest to befriend those who would harass Israel and keep her power in check.

11:21 *Let me go.* It appears that Hadad returned to Edom during the early days of Solomon's reign.

11:22 *What have you lacked here . . . ?* Because Egypt had by this time established relatively good relations with Israel (see note on 3:1), the pharaoh was reluctant to see Hadad return to Edom and provoke trouble with Solomon.

want to go back to your own country?" Pharaoh asked.

"Nothing," Hadad replied, "but do let me go!"

23And God raised up against Solomon another adversary,p Rezon son of Eliada, who had fled from his master, Hadadezerq king of Zobah. 24He gathered men around him and became the leader of a band of rebels when David destroyed the forcesx ,of Zobah,; the rebels went to Damascus,r where they settled and took control. 25Rezon was Israel's adversary as long as Solomon lived, adding to the trouble caused by Hadad. So Rezon ruled in Arams and was hostile toward Israel.

Jeroboam Rebels Against Solomon

26Also, Jeroboam son of Nebat rebelledt against the king. He was one of Solomon's officials, an Ephraimite from Zeredah, and his mother was a widow named Zeruah. 27Here is the account of how he rebelled against the king: Solomon had built the supporting terracesyu and had filled in the gap in the wall of the city of David his father. 28Now Jeroboam was a man of standing,v and when Solomon saw how wellw the young man did his work, he put him in charge of the whole labor force of the house of Joseph.

29About that time Jeroboam was going out of Jerusalem, and Ahijahx the prophet of Shiloh met him on the way, wearing a new cloak. The two of them were alone out in the country, 30and Ahijah took hold of the new cloak he was wearing and torey it into twelve pieces. 31Then he said to Jeroboam, "Take ten pieces for yourself, for this is what the LORD, the God of Israel, says: 'See, I am going to tearz the kingdom out of Solomon's hand and give you ten tribes. 32But for the sakea of my servant David and the city of Jerusalem, which I have chosen out of all the tribes of Israel, he will have one tribe. 33I will do this because they havez forsaken me and worshipedb Ashtoreth the goddess of the Sidonians, Chemosh the god of the Moabites, and Molech the god of the Ammonites, and have not walkedc in my ways, nor done what is right in my eyes, nor kept my statutesd and laws as David, Solomon's father, did.

34" 'But I will not take the whole kingdom out of Solomon's hand; I have made him ruler all the days of his life for the sake of David my servant, whom I chose and who observed my commands and statutes. 35I will take the kingdom from his son's hands and give you ten tribes. 36I will give one tribee to his son so that David my servant may always have a lampf before me in Jerusalem, the city where I chose to

---

Cross references (center column):

11:23 pS 1Ki 5:4
qS 2Sa 8:3
11:24 rS 2Sa 8:5
11:25
sS Ge 10:22;
S 2Sa 10:19
11:26 t2Ch 13:6
11:27
uS 1Ki 9:24
11:28 vS Ru 2:1
wS Ge 39:4;
Pr 22:29
11:29
x1Ki 12:15; 14:2;
2Ch 9:29; 10:15

11:30 y1Sa 15:27
11:31 zS ver 11;
S 1Sa 15:27
11:32
aS 2Sa 7:15
11:33 bS Jdg 2:13
c2Ki 21:22
d1Ki 3:3
11:36 e1Ki 12:17
fS 2Sa 21:17

x24 Hebrew destroyed them   y27 Or the Millo
z33 Hebrew; Septuagint, Vulgate and Syriac because he has

11:24 leader of a band of rebels. As David had been (1Sa 22:1–2), and Jephthah before him (Jdg 11:3). rebels went to Damascus, where they settled and took control. Presumably this took place in the early part of Solomon's reign (see 2Sa 8:6 for the situation in Damascus during the time of David). It is likely that Solomon's expedition (2Ch 8:3) against Hamath Zobah (the kingdom formerly ruled by Hadadezer, 2Sa 8:3–6) was provoked by opposition led by Rezon. Even though Solomon was able to retain control of the territory north of Damascus to the Euphrates (4:21,24), he was not able to drive Rezon from Damascus itself.

11:26 rebelled against the king. See note on v. 40.

11:27 supporting terraces. See 9:15 and note.

11:28 whole labor force of the house of Joseph. See 5:13–18. Jeroboam's supervision of the conscripted laborers from the tribes of Ephraim and Manasseh made him aware of the smoldering discontent among the people over Solomon's policies (see 12:4).

11:31–32 ten tribes . . . one tribe. The tradition of considering the ten northern tribes as a unit distinct from the southern tribes (Judah and Simeon—Levi received no territorial inheritance; see Jos 21) goes back to the period of the judges (see Jdg 5:14–16). The reason, no doubt, was the continuing presence of a non-Israelite corridor (Jerusalem, Gibeonite league, Gezer) that separated the two Israelite regions (see map No. 3 at the end of the Study Bible). Political division along the same line during the early years of David's reign and the different arrangements that brought the southern and northern segments under David's rule (see 2Sa 2:4; 5:3) reinforced this sense of division. With the conquest of Jerusalem by David (2Sa 5:6–7) and the pharaoh's gift of Gezer to Solomon's wife (9:16–17), all Israel was for the first time territorially united. (Now that Jerusalem and Gezer were under Israelite control, the Gibeonite league, which had submitted already to Joshua—see Jos 9—could be effectively absorbed politically.) In the division here announced, the "one tribe" refers to the area dominated by Judah (but including Simeon; see Jos 19:1–9), and the "ten tribes" refers to the region that came under David's rule at the later date (Ephraim and Manasseh, Joseph's sons, being counted as two tribes; see Ge 48:5; see also note on Jos 14:4). For further refinement of the new boundaries that came about see note on 12:21.

11:33 forsaken me. See vv. 5–7. have not walked in my ways. See vv. 1–2; 3:14.

11:34 I have made him ruler all the days of his life. See vv. 12–13.

11:35 from his son's hands. From Rehoboam (see 12:1–24).

11:36 a lamp before me in Jerusalem. Symbolizes the continuance of the Davidic dynasty in the city where God had chosen to cause his Name to dwell (see v. 13 and note). In a number of passages, the burning or snuffing out of one's lamp signifies the flourishing or ceasing of one's life (Job 18:6; 21:17; Pr 13:9; 20:20; 24:20). Here (and in 15:4; 2Ki 8:19; 2Ch 21:7) this same figure is applied to David's dynasty (see especially Ps 132:17, where "set up a lamp for my anointed" is parallel to "make a horn grow for David"). In David's royal sons his "lamp" continues to burn before the Lord in Jerusalem.

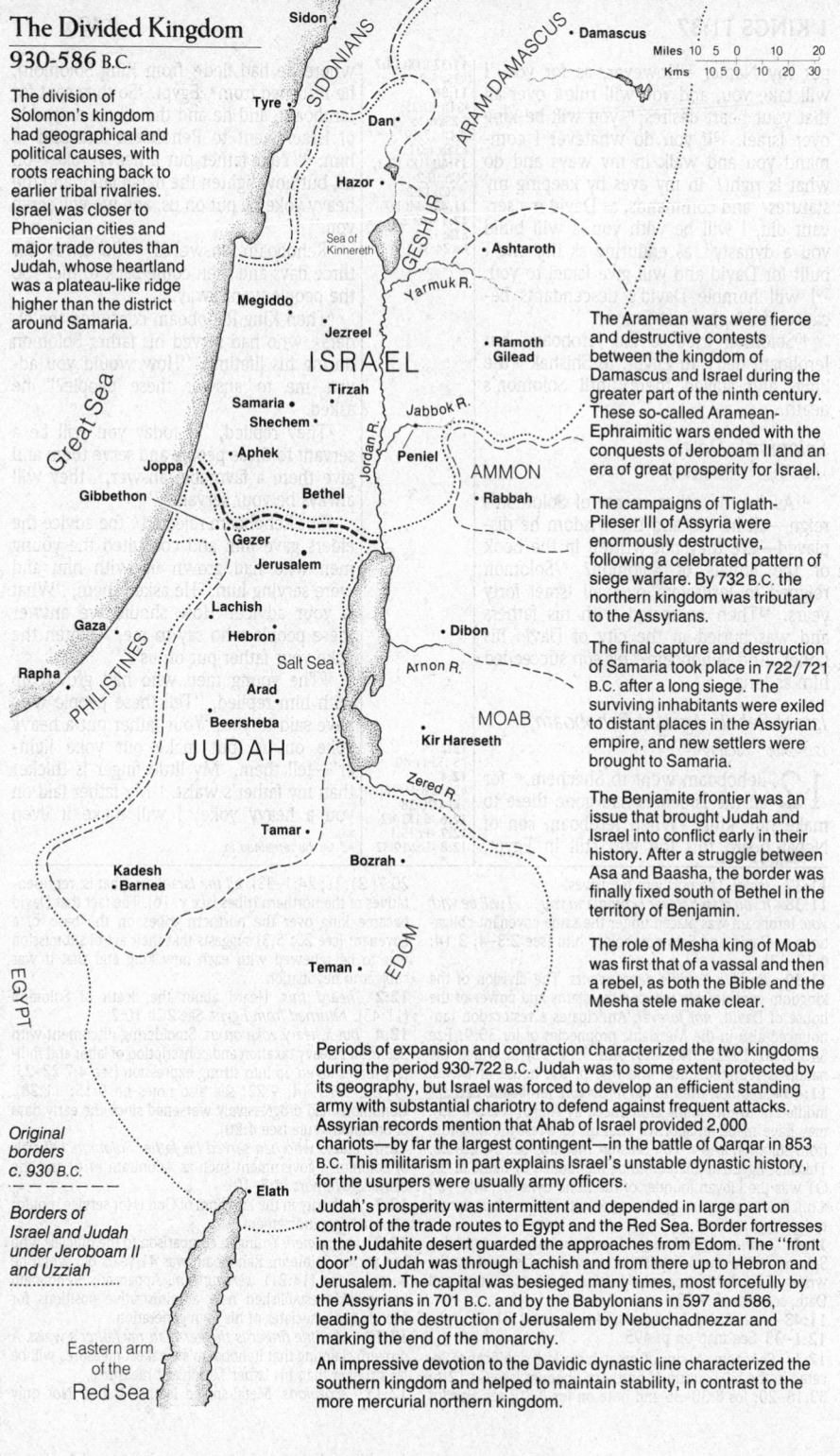

The Divided Kingdom
930-586 B.C.

The division of Solomon's kingdom had geographical and political causes, with roots reaching back to earlier tribal rivalries. Israel was closer to Phoenician cities and major trade routes than Judah, whose heartland was a plateau-like ridge higher than the district around Samaria.

The Aramean wars were fierce and destructive contests between the kingdom of Damascus and Israel during the greater part of the ninth century. These so-called Aramean-Ephraimitic wars ended with the conquests of Jeroboam II and an era of great prosperity for Israel.

The campaigns of Tiglath-Pileser III of Assyria were enormously destructive, following a celebrated pattern of siege warfare. By 732 B.C. the northern kingdom was tributary to the Assyrians.

The final capture and destruction of Samaria took place in 722/721 B.C. after a long siege. The surviving inhabitants were exiled to distant places in the Assyrian empire, and new settlers were brought to Samaria.

The Benjamite frontier was an issue that brought Judah and Israel into conflict early in their history. After a struggle between Asa and Baasha, the border was finally fixed south of Bethel in the territory of Benjamin.

The role of Mesha king of Moab was first that of a vassal and then a rebel, as both the Bible and the Mesha stele make clear.

Periods of expansion and contraction characterized the two kingdoms during the period 930-722 B.C. Judah was to some extent protected by its geography, but Israel was forced to develop an efficient standing army with substantial chariotry to defend against frequent attacks. Assyrian records mention that Ahab of Israel provided 2,000 chariots—by far the largest contingent—in the battle of Qarqar in 853 B.C. This militarism in part explains Israel's unstable dynastic history, for the usurpers were usually army officers.

Judah's prosperity was intermittent and depended in large part on control of the trade routes to Egypt and the Red Sea. Border fortresses in the Judahite desert guarded the approaches from Edom. The "front door" of Judah was through Lachish and from there up to Hebron and Jerusalem. The capital was besieged many times, most forcefully by the Assyrians in 701 B.C. and by the Babylonians in 597 and 586, leading to the destruction of Jerusalem by Nebuchadnezzar and marking the end of the monarchy.

An impressive devotion to the Davidic dynastic line characterized the southern kingdom and helped to maintain stability, in contrast to the more mercurial northern kingdom.

Original borders c. 930 B.C.

Borders of Israel and Judah under Jeroboam II and Uzziah

Eastern arm of the Red Sea

Map labels: Sidon, Tyre, Dan, Hazor, SIDONIANS, ARAM-DAMASCUS, Damascus, Miles, Kms, Sea of Kinnereth, GESHUR, Ashtaroth, Yarmuk R., Megiddo, Jezreel, Ramoth Gilead, ISRAEL, Tirzah, Samaria, Shechem, Jabbok R., Aphek, Joppa, Jordan R., Peniel, AMMON, Gibbethon, Bethel, Rabbah, Gezer, Jerusalem, Great Sea, Lachish, Gaza, Hebron, Dibon, Salt Sea, Rapha, Arnon R., Arad, MOAB, Beersheba, Kir Hareseth, JUDAH, Zered R., Tamar, Bozrah, Kadesh Barnea, EDOM, Teman, EGYPT, Philistines, Elath, Red Sea

put my Name. 37However, as for you, I will take you, and you will rule*g* over all that your heart desires;*h* you will be king over Israel. 38If you do whatever I command you and walk in my ways and do what is right*i* in my eyes by keeping my statutes*j* and commands, as David my servant did, I will be with you. I will build you a dynasty*k* as enduring as the one I built for David and will give Israel to you. 39I will humble David's descendants because of this, but not forever.'"

40Solomon tried to kill Jeroboam, but Jeroboam fled*l* to Egypt, to Shishak*m* the king, and stayed there until Solomon's death.

Solomon's Death

11:41–43pp — 2Ch 9:29–31

41As for the other events of Solomon's reign—all he did and the wisdom he displayed—are they not written in the book of the annals of Solomon? 42Solomon reigned in Jerusalem over all Israel forty years. 43Then he rested with his fathers and was buried in the city of David his father. And Rehoboam*n* his son succeeded him as king.

Israel Rebels Against Rehoboam

12:1–24pp — 2Ch 10:1–11:4

12 Rehoboam went to Shechem,*o* for all the Israelites had gone there to make him king. 2When Jeroboam son of Nebat heard this (he was still in Egypt,

where he had fled*p* from King Solomon), he returned from*a* Egypt. 3So they sent for Jeroboam, and he and the whole assembly of Israel went to Rehoboam and said to him: 4"Your father put a heavy yoke*q* on us, but now lighten the harsh labor and the heavy yoke he put on us, and we will serve you."

5Rehoboam answered, "Go away for three days and then come back to me." So the people went away.

6Then King Rehoboam consulted the elders*r* who had served his father Solomon during his lifetime. "How would you advise me to answer these people?" he asked.

7They replied, "If today you will be a servant to these people and serve them and give them a favorable answer,*s* they will always be your servants."

8But Rehoboam rejected*t* the advice the elders gave him and consulted the young men who had grown up with him and were serving him. 9He asked them, "What is your advice? How should we answer these people who say to me, 'Lighten the yoke your father put on us'?"

10The young men who had grown up with him replied, "Tell these people who have said to you, 'Your father put a heavy yoke on us, but make our yoke lighter'—tell them, 'My little finger is thicker than my father's waist. 11My father laid on you a heavy yoke; I will make it even

Cross references

11:37 *g*1Ki 14:7
*h*2Sa 3:21
11:38 *i*S Dt 12:25;
S 2Sa 8:15
*j*S Dt 17:19
*k*S Ex 1:21
11:40 *l*1Ki 12:2;
2Ch 10:2
*m*2Ch 12:2
11:43 *n*Mt 1:7
12:1 *o*ver 25;
S Ge 12:6;
Jos 24:32

12:2
*p*S 1Ki 11:40
12:4
*q*S 1Sa 8:11–18;
1Ki 4:20-28
12:6 *r*S 1Ki 4:2
12:7 *s*Pr 15:1
12:8 *t*Lev 19:32

*a*2 Or *he remained in*

11:37 *Israel.* The northern ten tribes.
11:38 *If you do whatever I command you . . . I will be with you.* Jeroboam was placed under the same covenant obligations as David and Solomon before him (see 2:3–4; 3:14; 6:12–13).
11:39 *humble David's descendants.* The division of the kingdom considerably reduced the status and power of the house of David. *not forever.* Anticipates a restoration (announced also in the Messianic prophecies of Jer 30:9; Eze 34:23; 37:15–28; Hos 3:5; Am 9:11–12) in which the nation is reunited under the rule of the house of David.
11:40 *Solomon tried to kill Jeroboam.* Jeroboam, perhaps indifferent to the timing announced by Ahijah (vv. 34–35), may have made an abortive attempt to wrest the kingdom from Solomon (see v. 26). *Shishak the king.* See 14:25–26. This first Egyptian pharaoh to be mentioned by name in the OT was the Libyan founder of the 22nd dynasty (945–924 B.C.). Solomon's marriage ties were with the previous dynasty (see note on 3:1).
11:41 *annals of Solomon.* A written source concerning Solomon's life and administration, which was used by the writer of 1,2 Kings (see Introduction: Author, Sources and Date; see also 15:7,23).
11:43 *rested with his fathers.* See note on 1:21.
12:1–33 See map on p. 495.
12:1 *Shechem.* A city of great historical significance located in the hill country of northern Ephraim (see Ge 12:6; 33:18–20; Jos 8:30–35 and note on Jos 8:30; see also Jos

20:7; 21:21; 24:1–33). *all the Israelites.* That is, representatives of the northern tribes (see v. 16). The fact that David became king over the northern tribes on the basis of a covenant (see 2Sa 5:3) suggests that their act of submission was to be renewed with each new king and that it was subject to negotiation.
12:2 *heard this.* Heard about the death of Solomon (11:43). *returned from Egypt.* See 2Ch 10:2.
12:4 *put a heavy yoke on us.* Smoldering discontent with Solomon's heavy taxation and conscription of labor and military forces flared up into strong expression (see 4:7,22–23, 27–28; 5:13–14; 9:22; see also notes on 9:15; 11:28). Conditions had progressively worsened since the early days of Solomon's rule (see 4:20).
12:6 *elders who had served his father Solomon.* Officials of Solomon's government such as Adoniram (4:6) and the district governors (4:7–19).
12:7 Authority in the kingdom of God is for service, not for personal aggrandizement.
12:8 *young men.* Young in comparison to the officials who had served Solomon. Rehoboam was 41 years old when he became king (14:21). *serving him.* Apparently Rehoboam had quickly established new administrative positions for friends and associates of his own generation.
12:10 *My little finger is thicker than my father's waist.* A proverb claiming that Rehoboam's weakest measures will be far stronger than his father's strongest measures.
12:11 *scorpions.* Metal-spiked leather lashes. Not only

heavier. My father scourged you with whips; I will scourge you with scorpions.' "

¹²Three days later Jeroboam and all the people returned to Rehoboam, as the king had said, "Come back to me in three days." ¹³The king answered the people harshly. Rejecting the advice given him by the elders, ¹⁴he followed the advice of the young men and said, "My father made your yoke heavy; I will make it even heavier. My father scourged ᵘ you with whips; I will scourge you with scorpions." ¹⁵So the king did not listen to the people, for this turn of events was from the LORD, ᵛ to fulfill the word the LORD had spoken to Jeroboam son of Nebat through Ahijah ʷ the Shilonite.

¹⁶When all Israel saw that the king refused to listen to them, they answered the king:

"What share ˣ do we have in David,
    what part in Jesse's son?
To your tents, O Israel! ʸ
    Look after your own house,
        O David!"

So the Israelites went home. ᶻ ¹⁷But as for the Israelites who were living in the towns of Judah, ᵃ Rehoboam still ruled over them.

¹⁸King Rehoboam sent out Adoniram, ᵇ ᵇ who was in charge of forced labor, but all

12:14 ᵘEx 1:14
12:15 ᵛS Dt 2:30;
2Ch 25:20
ʷS 1Ki 11:29
12:16
ˣS Ge 31:14
ʸS 2Sa 20:1
ᶻIsa 7:17
12:17 ᵃ1Ki 11:36
12:18
ᵇS 2Sa 20:24

ᶜS Jos 7:25
12:19 ᵈ2Ki 17:21
12:20
ᵉ1Ki 11:13;
Eze 37:16
12:21
ᶠ1Ki 14:30; 15:6,
16; 2Ch 11:1
12:22
ᵍ2Ch 12:5-7
ʰS Dt 33:1;
2Ki 4:7
12:25 ⁱS ver 1

Israel stoned him to death. ᶜ King Rehoboam, however, managed to get into his chariot and escape to Jerusalem. ¹⁹So Israel has been in rebellion against the house of David ᵈ to this day.

²⁰When all the Israelites heard that Jeroboam had returned, they sent and called him to the assembly and made him king over all Israel. Only the tribe of Judah remained loyal to the house of David. ᵉ

²¹When Rehoboam arrived in Jerusalem, he mustered the whole house of Judah and the tribe of Benjamin—a hundred and eighty thousand fighting men—to make war ᶠ against the house of Israel and to regain the kingdom for Rehoboam son of Solomon.

²²But this word of God came to Shemaiah ᵍ the man of God: ʰ ²³"Say to Rehoboam son of Solomon king of Judah, to the whole house of Judah and Benjamin, and to the rest of the people, ²⁴'This is what the LORD says: Do not go up to fight against your brothers, the Israelites. Go home, every one of you, for this is my doing.' " So they obeyed the word of the LORD and went home again, as the LORD had ordered.

Golden Calves at Bethel and Dan

²⁵Then Jeroboam fortified Shechem ⁱ in

ᵇ*18* Some Septuagint manuscripts and Syriac (see also 1 Kings 4:6 and 5:14); Hebrew *Adoram*

---

will governmental burdens on the people be increased, but the punishment for not complying with the government's directives will also be intensified.
12:14 *followed the advice of the young men.* Rehoboam's answer reflects a despotic spirit completely contrary to the covenantal character of Israelite kingship (see Dt 17:14–20; see also note on 1Sa 10:25).
12:15 *this turn of events was from the LORD.* By this statement the writer of Kings does not condone either the foolish act of Rehoboam or the revolutionary spirit of the northern tribes, but he reminds the reader that all these things occurred to bring about the divinely announced punishment on the house of David for Solomon's idolatry and breach of the covenant (11:9–13). For the relationship between divine sovereignty over all things and human responsibility for evil acts see note on 2Sa 24:1. *the word the LORD had spoken to Jeroboam . . . through Ahijah.* See 11:29–39.
12:16 *all Israel.* The northern tribes (see note on v. 1). *David.* The Davidic dynasty (see 2Sa 20:1 for an earlier expression of the same sentiment).
12:17 *Israelites who were living in the towns of Judah.* People originally from the northern tribes who had settled in Judah. They were later to be joined by others from the north who desired to serve the Lord and worship at the temple (see 2Ch 11:16–17).
12:18 *Adoniram, who was in charge of forced labor.* He had served in the same capacity under both David (2Sa 20:24) and Solomon (1Ki 4:6; 5:14).
12:19 *this day.* The time of the writing of the source from which the author of 1 Kings derived this account (see Intro-

duction: Author, Sources and Date).
12:21 *tribe of Benjamin.* Although the bulk of Benjamin was aligned with the northern tribes (see note on 11:31–32), the area around Jerusalem remained under Rehoboam's control (as did the Gibeonite cities and Gezer). The northern boundary of Judah must have reached almost to Bethel (12 miles north of Jerusalem)—which Abijah, Rehoboam's son, even held for a short while (see 2Ch 13:19). *a hundred and eighty thousand fighting men.* Probably includes all support personnel together with those who would actually be committed to battle.
12:22 *Shemaiah.* Wrote a history of Rehoboam's reign (2Ch 12:15). Another of his prophecies is recorded in 2Ch 12:5–8. *man of God.* A common way of referring to a prophet (see, e.g., 13:1; Dt 18:18; 33:1; 1Sa 2:27; 9:9–10).
12:23 *rest of the people.* See note on v. 17.
12:24 *went home again.* Although full-scale civil war was averted, intermittent skirmishes and battles between Israel and Judah continued throughout the reigns of Rehoboam, Abijah and Asa, until political instability in Israel after the death of Baasha finally brought the conflict to a halt. Asa's son Jehoshaphat entered into an alliance with Ahab and sealed the relationship by the marriage of his son Jehoram to Ahab's daughter Athaliah (see 14:30; 15:6,16; 22:2,44; 2Ki 8:18).
12:25 *Peniel.* A town in Transjordan (see Ge 32:31; Jdg 8:9,17) of strategic importance for defense against the Arameans of Damascus (see 11:23–25) and the Ammonites.

the hill country of Ephraim and lived there. From there he went out and built up Peniel. c /

26Jeroboam thought to himself, "The kingdom will now likely revert to the house of David. 27If these people go up to offer sacrifices at the temple of the LORD in Jerusalem, k they will again give their allegiance to their lord, Rehoboam king of Judah. They will kill me and return to King Rehoboam."

28After seeking advice, the king made two golden calves. l He said to the people, "It is too much for you to go up to Jerusalem. Here are your gods, O Israel, who brought you up out of Egypt." m 29One he set up in Bethel, n and the other in Dan. o 30And this thing became a sin; p the people went even as far as Dan to worship the one there.

31Jeroboam built shrines q on high places and appointed priests r from all sorts of people, even though they were not Levites. 32He instituted a festival on the fifteenth day of the eighth s month, like the festival held in Judah, and offered sacrifices on the altar. This he did in Bethel, t sacrificing to the calves he had made. And at Bethel he also installed priests at the high places he had made. 33On the fifteenth day of the eighth month, a month of his own choosing, he offered sacrifices on the altar he

had built at Bethel. u So he instituted the festival for the Israelites and went up to the altar to make offerings.

The Man of God From Judah

13 By the word of the LORD a man of God v came from Judah to Bethel, w as Jeroboam was standing by the altar to make an offering. 2He cried out against the altar by the word of the LORD: "O altar, altar! This is what the LORD says: 'A son named Josiah x will be born to the house of David. On you he will sacrifice the priests of the high places y who now make offerings here, and human bones will be burned on you.' " 3That same day the man of God gave a sign: z "This is the sign the LORD has declared: The altar will be split apart and the ashes on it will be poured out."

4When King Jeroboam heard what the man of God cried out against the altar at Bethel, he stretched out his hand from the altar and said, "Seize him!" But the hand he stretched out toward the man shriveled up, so that he could not pull it back. 5Also, the altar was split apart and its ashes poured out according to the sign given by the man of God by the word of the LORD.

6Then the king said to the man of God,

Cross-references column:
12:25 /S Jdg 8:8
12:27 kDt 12:5-6
12:28 lS Ex 32:4; S 2Ch 11:15
mS Ex 32:8
12:29 nS Ge 12:8; S Jos 7:2
oJdg 18:27-31; Am 8:14
12:30 pl Ki 13:34; 14:16; 15:26,30; 16:2; 2Ki 3:3; 10:29; 13:2; 17:21
12:31 qS Lev 26:30; 1Ki 13:32; 2Ki 17:29 rS Ex 29:9; 1Ki 13:33; 2Ki 17:32; 2Ch 11:14-15; 13:9
12:32 sS Nu 29:12 t2Ki 10:29

12:33 u2Ki 23:15; Am 7:13
13:1 vS Dt 33:1; S Jdg 13:6 wAm 7:13
13:2 x2Ki 23:15-16,20; 2Ch 34:5 yS Lev 26:30
13:3 zS Ge 24:14; S Ex 4:8; S Jn 2:11

c25 Hebrew Penuel, a variant of Peniel

12:26 *revert to the house of David.* Jeroboam did not have confidence in the divine promise given to him through Ahijah (see 11:38) and thus took action that forfeited the theocratic basis for his kingship.
12:28 *two golden calves.* Pagan gods of the Arameans and Canaanites were often represented as standing on calves or bulls as symbols of their strength and fertility (see note on Jdg 2:13). *Here are your gods, O Israel, who brought you up out of Egypt.* Like Aaron (Ex 32:4-5), Jeroboam attempted to combine the pagan calf symbol with the worship of the Lord, though he attempted no physical representation of the Lord—no "god" stood on the backs of his bulls.
12:29 *Bethel.* Located about 12 miles north of Jerusalem close to the border of Ephraim but within the territory of Benjamin (Jos 18:11-13,22). Bethel held a prominent place in the history of Israel's worship of the Lord (see Ge 12:8; 28:11-19; 35:6-7; Jdg 20:26-28; 1Sa 7:16). *Dan.* Located in the far north of the land near Mount Hermon. A similarly paganized worship was practiced here during the period of the judges (Jdg 18:30-31).
12:30 *this thing became a sin.* Jeroboam's royal policy promoted violation of the second commandment (Ex 20:4-6). It inevitably led to Israel's violation of the first commandment also (Ex 20:3) and opened the door for the entrance of fully pagan practices into Israel's religious rites (especially in the time of Ahab). Jeroboam foolishly abandoned religious principle for political expediency and in so doing forfeited the promise given him by the prophet Ahijah (see 11:38).
12:31 *Jeroboam built shrines on high places.* See note on 3:2. *not Levites.* Many of the priests and Levites of the northern kingdom migrated to Judah because Jeroboam

bypassed them when appointing cult personnel in the north (see 2Ch 11:13-14).
12:32 *festival held in Judah.* Apparently the Feast of Tabernacles, observed in Judah on the 15th to the 21st of the seventh month (see 8:2; Lev 23:34). *offered sacrifices on the altar.* Jeroboam overstepped the limits of his prerogatives as king and assumed the role of a priest (see 2Ch 26:16-21).
13:1 *man of God.* See note on 12:22. *from Judah to Bethel.* God sent a prophet from the southern kingdom to Bethel in the northern kingdom. Possibly he did this to emphasize that the divinely appointed political division (11:11,29-39; 12:15,24) was not intended to establish rival religious systems in the two kingdoms. Two centuries later the prophet Amos from Tekoa in Judah also went to Bethel in the northern kingdom to pronounce God's judgment on Jeroboam II (Am 7:10-17).
13:2 *Josiah.* A prophetic announcement of the rule of King Josiah, who came to the throne in Judah nearly 300 years after the division of the kingdom. *will sacrifice the priests of the high places.* Fulfilled in 2Ki 23:15-20.
13:3 *sign.* The immediate fulfillment of a short-term prediction would serve to authenticate the reliability of the longer-term prediction (see Dt 18:21-22).
13:5 *its ashes poured out.* Visibly demonstrating God's power to fulfill the words of the prophet (see note on v. 3) and providing a clear sign that Jeroboam's offering was unacceptable to the Lord (see Lev 6:10-11).
13:6 *your God.* Should not be taken as implying that Jeroboam no longer considered the Lord as his own God (cf. 2:3; Ge 27:20), but as suggesting that he recognized the prophet as his superior in the theocratic order. *king's hand*

"Intercede[a] with the LORD your God and pray for me that my hand may be restored." So the man of God interceded with the LORD, and the king's hand was restored and became as it was before.

[7]The king said to the man of God, "Come home with me and have something to eat, and I will give you a gift."[b]

[8]But the man of God answered the king, "Even if you were to give me half your possessions,[c] I would not go with you, nor would I eat bread[d] or drink water here. [9]For I was commanded by the word of the LORD: 'You must not eat bread or drink water or return by the way you came.'" [10]So he took another road and did not return by the way he had come to Bethel.

[11]Now there was a certain old prophet living in Bethel, whose sons came and told him all that the man of God had done there that day. They also told their father what he had said to the king. [12]Their father asked them, "Which way did he go?" And his sons showed him which road the man of God from Judah had taken. [13]So he said to his sons, "Saddle the donkey for me." And when they had saddled the donkey for him, he mounted it [14]and rode after the man of God. He found him sitting under an oak tree and asked, "Are you the man of God who came from Judah?"

"I am," he replied.

[15]So the prophet said to him, "Come home with me and eat."

[16]The man of God said, "I cannot turn back and go with you, nor can I eat bread[e] or drink water with you in this place. [17]I have been told by the word of the LORD: 'You must not eat bread or drink water there or return by the way you came.'"

[18]The old prophet answered, "I too am a prophet, as you are. And an angel said to me by the word of the LORD:[f] 'Bring him back with you to your house so that he may eat bread and drink water.'" (But he was lying[g] to him.) [19]So the man of God returned with him and ate and drank in his house.

[20]While they were sitting at the table, the word of the LORD came to the old prophet who had brought him back. [21]He cried out to the man of God who had come from Judah, "This is what the LORD says: 'You have defied[h] the word of the LORD and have not kept the command the LORD your God gave you. [22]You came back and ate bread and drank water in the place where he told you not to eat or drink. Therefore your body will not be buried in the tomb of your fathers.'"

[23]When the man of God had finished eating and drinking, the prophet who had brought him back saddled his donkey for him. [24]As he went on his way, a lion[i] met him on the road and killed him, and his body was thrown down on the road, with both the donkey and the lion standing beside it. [25]Some people who passed by saw the body thrown down there, with the lion standing beside the body, and they went and reported it in the city where the old prophet lived.

[26]When the prophet who had brought him back from his journey heard of it, he said, "It is the man of God who defied[j] the word of the LORD. The LORD has given him over to the lion, which has mauled him and killed him, as the word of the LORD had warned him."

[27]The prophet said to his sons, "Saddle the donkey for me," and they did so. [28]Then he went out and found the body

---

Cross references (center column):

13:6 [a]S Ge 20:7; S Nu 11:2; S Jer 37:3; Ac 8:24
13:7 [b]S 1Sa 9:7
13:8 [c]Nu 22:18
[d]ver 16
13:16 [e]ver 8

13:18 [f]1Ki 22:6, 12; 2Ch 35:21; Isa 36:10
[g]S Ge 19:14; S Dt 13:3
13:21 [h]ver 26; S 1Sa 13:14; 1Ki 20:35
13:24 [i]1Ki 20:36
13:26 [j]S ver 21

Footnotes / commentary:

was restored. The Lord's gracious response to Jeroboam's request is to be seen as an additional sign (see v. 3) given to confirm the word of the prophet and to move Jeroboam to repentance.

13:7 *Come home with me.* Jeroboam attempted to renew his prestige in the eyes of the people by creating the impression that there was no fundamental break between himself and the prophetic order (see 1Sa 15:30 for a similar situation).

13:9 *You must not.* The prophet's refusal of Jeroboam's invitation rested on a previously given divine command. It underscored God's extreme displeasure with the apostate worship at Bethel.

13:18 *I too am a prophet, as you are.* A half-truth. It is likely that the old prophet in Bethel had faithfully proclaimed the word of the Lord in former days, but those days had long since passed.

13:19 *the man of God returned with him.* Neither the old prophet's lie nor his own need justified disobedience to the direct and explicit command of the Lord. His public action in this matter undermined respect for the divine authority of all

he had said at Bethel.

13:20 *the word of the LORD came to the old prophet.* The fundamental distinction between a true and a false prophecy here becomes apparent. The false prophecy arises from one's own imagination (Jer 23:16; Eze 13:2,7) while the true prophecy is from God (Ex 4:16; Dt 18:18; Jer 1:9; 2Pe 1:21).

13:22 *your body will not be buried in the tomb of your fathers.* The man of God from Judah will die far from his own home and family burial plot.

13:24 *killed him.* A stern warning to Jeroboam that God takes his word very seriously. *the donkey and the lion standing beside it.* The remarkable fact that the donkey did not run and the lion did not attack the donkey or disturb the man's body (v. 28) clearly stamped the incident as a divine judgment. This additional miracle was reported in Bethel (v. 25) and provided yet another sign authenticating the message that the man of God from Judah had delivered at Jeroboam's altar. But Jeroboam was still not moved to repentance (v. 33).

thrown down on the road, with the donkey and the lion standing beside it. The lion had neither eaten the body nor mauled the donkey. [29]So the prophet picked up the body of the man of God, laid it on the donkey, and brought it back to his own city to mourn for him and bury him. [30]Then he laid the body in his own tomb, [k] and they mourned over him and said, "Oh, my brother!" [l]

[31]After burying him, he said to his sons, "When I die, bury me in the grave where the man of God is buried; lay my bones [m] beside his bones. [32]For the message he declared by the word of the LORD against the altar in Bethel and against all the shrines on the high places [n] in the towns of Samaria [o] will certainly come true." [p]

[33]Even after this, Jeroboam did not change his evil ways, [q] but once more appointed priests for the high places from all sorts [r] of people. Anyone who wanted to become a priest he consecrated for the high places. [34]This was the sin [s] of the house of Jeroboam that led to its downfall and to its destruction [t] from the face of the earth.

Ahijah's Prophecy Against Jeroboam

14 At that time Abijah son of Jeroboam became ill, [2]and Jeroboam said to his wife, "Go, disguise yourself, so you won't be recognized as the wife of Jeroboam. Then go to Shiloh. Ahijah [u] the prophet is there—the one who told me I

would be king over this people. [3]Take ten loaves of bread [v] with you, some cakes and a jar of honey, and go to him. He will tell you what will happen to the boy." [4]So Jeroboam's wife did what he said and went to Ahijah's house in Shiloh.

Now Ahijah could not see; his sight was gone because of his age. [5]But the LORD had told Ahijah, "Jeroboam's wife is coming to ask you about her son, for he is ill, and you are to give her such and such an answer. When she arrives, she will pretend to be someone else."

[6]So when Ahijah heard the sound of her footsteps at the door, he said, "Come in, wife of Jeroboam. Why this pretense? [w] I have been sent to you with bad news. [7]Go, tell Jeroboam that this is what the LORD, the God of Israel, says: [x] 'I raised you up from among the people and made you a leader [y] over my people Israel. [8]I tore [z] the kingdom away from the house of David and gave it to you, but you have not been like my servant David, who kept my commands and followed me with all his heart, doing only what was right [a] in my eyes. [9]You have done more evil [b] than all who lived before you. [c] You have made for yourself other gods, idols [d] made of metal; you have provoked [e] me to anger and thrust me behind your back. [f]

[10]" 'Because of this, I am going to bring disaster [g] on the house of Jeroboam. I will cut off from Jeroboam every last male in Israel—slave or free. [h] I will burn up the

Cross references (center column)

13:30 [k]2Ki 23:17
/Jer 22:18
13:31
[m]2Ki 23:18
13:32
[n]S Lev 26:30;
S 1Ki 12:31
[o]1Ki 16:24,28;
20:1; 2Ki 10:1;
15:13 [p]2Ki 23:16
13:33 [q]1Ki 15:26
[r]S 1Ki 12:31
13:34
[s]S 1Ki 12:30
[t]1Ki 14:10;
15:29; 2Ki 9:9;
Jer 35:17; Am 7:9
14:2
[u]S 1Ki 11:29

14:3 [v]S 1Sa 9:7
14:6
[w]S 1Sa 28:12
14:7 [x]1Ki 15:29
[y]1Ki 11:37
14:8
[z]S 1Sa 15:27
[a]S 2Sa 8:15;
1Ki 3:3; 15:5;
2Ki 14:3; 15:3,
34; 16:2; 18:3;
20:3; 22:2
14:9 [b]1Ki 16:30,
33; 21:25;
2Ki 21:9,11; 24:3
[c]1Ki 16:2
[d]S Ex 20:4;
S 32:4;
2Ch 11:15
[e]Dt 32:16;
1Ki 16:2;
Jer 7:18; 8:19;
32:32; 44:3;
Eze 8:17; 16:26
/Ne 9:26;
Ps 50:17;
Jer 2:27; 32:33;
Eze 23:35
14:10
[g]S Jos 23:15;
S 1Ki 13:34
[h]S Dt 32:36;
2Ki 9:8-9

13:30 *laid the body in his own tomb.* See v. 22. The old prophet did the only thing left for him to do in order to make amends for his deliberate and fatal deception.

13:31 *grave where the man of God is buried.* The old prophet chose in this way to identify himself with the message that the man of God from Judah had given at Bethel.

13:32 *Samaria.* As the capital of the northern kingdom, Samaria is used to designate the entire territory of the northern ten tribes (see note on 16:24). However, Samaria was not established until about 50 years after this (16:23–24). The use of the name here reflects the perspective of the author of Kings (see note on Ge 14:14 for a similar instance of the use of a place-name—Dan—of later origin than the historical incident with which it is connected).

13:33 *appointed priests . . . from all sorts of people.* See 12:31 and note.

13:34 *sin.* The sin in 12:30 was the establishment of a paganized worship; here it is persistence in this worship with all its attendant evils.

14:1 *At that time.* Probably indicating a time not far removed from the event narrated in ch. 13. *Abijah.* Means "My (divine) Father is the LORD," suggesting that Jeroboam, at least to some degree, desired to be regarded as a worshiper of the Lord.

14:2 *disguise yourself.* Jeroboam's attempt to mislead the prophet Ahijah into giving a favorable prophecy concerning the sick boy indicates (1) his consciousness of his own guilt, (2) his superstition that prophecy worked in a magical way

and (3) his confused but real respect for the power of the Lord's prophet. *who told me I would be king over this people.* See 11:29–39.

14:3 *ten loaves of bread.* The gift of an ordinary farmer (like Saul in 1Sa 9:7–8) rather than that of a king (see 2Ki 8:7–9).

14:5 *the LORD had told Ahijah.* See 1Sa 9:15–17; 2Ki 6:32 for other examples of divine revelation concerning an imminent visit.

14:6 *Come in, wife of Jeroboam.* Ahijah's recognition of the woman and his knowledge of the purpose of her visit served to authenticate his message as truly being the word of the Lord.

14:7–8 *raised you . . . made you a leader . . . tore the kingdom away.* Jeroboam is first reminded of the gracious acts of the Lord in his behalf (see 11:26,30–38).

14:8 *you have not been like my servant David.* Jeroboam had not responded to God's gracious acts and had ignored the requirements given when Ahijah told him he would become king (see 11:38).

14:9 *all who lived before you.* Jeroboam's wickedness surpassed that of Saul, David and Solomon in that he implemented a paganized system of worship for the entire populace of the northern kingdom. *other gods.* See notes on 12:28,30.

14:10 *slave or free.* Without exception (see 21:21; 2Ki 9:8; 14:26).

house of Jeroboam as one burns dung, until it is all gone.[i] [11]Dogs[j] will eat those belonging to Jeroboam who die in the city, and the birds of the air[k] will feed on those who die in the country. The LORD has spoken!'

[12]"As for you, go back home. When you set foot in your city, the boy will die. [13]All Israel will mourn for him and bury him. He is the only one belonging to Jeroboam who will be buried, because he is the only one in the house of Jeroboam in whom the LORD, the God of Israel, has found anything good.[l]

[14]"The LORD will raise up for himself a king over Israel who will cut off the family of Jeroboam. This is the day! What? Yes, even now.[d] [15]And the LORD will strike Israel, so that it will be like a reed swaying in the water. He will uproot[m] Israel from this good land that he gave to their forefathers and scatter them beyond the River,[e] because they provoked[n] the LORD to anger by making Asherah[o] poles.[f] [16]And he will give Israel up because of the sins[p] Jeroboam has committed and has caused Israel to commit."

[17]Then Jeroboam's wife got up and left and went to Tirzah.[q] As soon as she stepped over the threshold of the house, the boy died. [18]They buried him, and all Israel mourned for him, as the LORD had said through his servant the prophet Ahijah.

[19]The other events of Jeroboam's reign, his wars and how he ruled, are written in the book of the annals of the kings of Israel. [20]He reigned for twenty-two years and then rested with his fathers. And Nadab his son succeeded him as king.

Rehoboam King of Judah

14:21,25–31pp — 2Ch 12:9–16

[21]Rehoboam son of Solomon was king in Judah. He was forty-one years old when he became king, and he reigned seventeen years in Jerusalem, the city the LORD had chosen out of all the tribes of Israel in which to put his Name. His mother's name was Naamah; she was an Ammonite.[r]

[22]Judah[s] did evil in the eyes of the LORD. By the sins they committed they stirred up his jealous anger[t] more than their fathers had done. [23]They also set up for themselves high places, sacred stones[u] and Asherah poles[v] on every high hill and

Cross references (center column):

14:10
[i]1Sa 12:25;
15:26; 1Ki 15:29;
Hos 13:11
14:11 /1Ki 16:4;
21:24
[k]S Ge 40:19;
S Dt 28:26
14:13
[l]2Ch 12:12; 19:3
14:15
[m]S Dt 29:28;
S 2Ch 7:20
[n]Jer 44:3
[o]S Dt 12:3
14:16
[p]S 1Ki 12:30;
S 15:26
14:17
[q]S Jos 12:24;
S 1Ki 15:33

14:21 [r]S 1Ki 11:1
14:22
[s]2Ki 17:19;
2Ch 12:1
[t]Dt 32:21;
Ps 78:58;
Jer 44:3;
S 1Co 10:22
14:23
[u]S Ex 23:24;
Dt 16:22;
Hos 10:1
[v]S Dt 12:3

[d]14 The meaning of the Hebrew for this sentence is uncertain. [e]15 That is, the Euphrates [f]15 That is, symbols of the goddess Asherah; here and elsewhere in 1 Kings

---

14:11 *birds of the air will feed on those who die in the country.* See note on 16:4. The covenant curse of Dt 28:26 is applied to Jeroboam's male descendants, none of whom will receive an honorable burial.

14:12 *boy.* The Hebrew for this word allows for wide latitude in age (the same term is used for the young advisers of Rehoboam; see 12:8 and note). *will die.* Although the death of Abijah was a severe disappointment to Jeroboam and his wife, it was an act of God's mercy to the prince, sparing him the disgrace and suffering that were to come on his father's house (see Isa 57:1–2).

14:13 *All Israel will mourn for him and bury him.* Perhaps an indication that Abijah was the crown prince, and was well known and loved by the people. *buried.* He alone of Jeroboam's descendants would receive an honorable burial.

14:14 *a king . . . who will cut off the family of Jeroboam.* Ahijah looked beyond the brief reign of Nadab, Jeroboam's son (15:25–26), to the revolt of Baasha (15:27–16:7).

14:15 *like a reed swaying in the water.* Descriptive of the instability of the royal house in the northern kingdom, which was to be characterized by assassinations and revolts (see 15:27–28; 16:16; 2Ki 9:24; 15:10,14,25,30). *He will uproot Israel.* The list of curses for covenant breaking found in Deuteronomy climaxes in forced exile for God's people from the land of promise (Dt 28:63–64; 29:25–28). *Asherah poles.* See NIV text note. Ahijah perceived that Jeroboam's use of golden bulls in worship would inevitably lead to the adoption of other elements of Canaanite nature religion. The goddess Asherah was the consort of Baal (cf. Jdg 3:7; 2Ki 23:4), and the Asherah poles were probably wooden representations of the goddess (see note on Ex 34:13).

14:16 *sins Jeroboam has committed.* See 12:26–33; 13:33–34. *caused Israel to commit.* A phrase repeated often in 1,2 Kings (e.g., 15:26; 16:2,13,19,26).

14:17 *Tirzah.* Used by the kings of Israel as the royal city until Omri purchased and built up Samaria to serve that purpose (16:24). It is probably modern Tell el-Far'ah, about seven miles north of Shechem (see note on SS 6:4).

14:19 *his wars.* See v. 30; 15:6; 2Ch 13:2–20. *annals of the kings of Israel.* A record of the reigns of the kings of the northern kingdom used by the author of 1,2 Kings and apparently accessible to those interested in further details of the history of the reigns of Israelite kings. It is not to be confused with the canonical book of 1,2 Chronicles, which was written later than 1,2 Kings and contains the history of the reigns of the kings of Judah only (see Introduction: Author, Sources and Date).

14:20 *twenty-two years.* 930–909 B.C. *rested with his fathers.* See note on 1:21. *Nadab.* See 15:25–32.

14:21 *forty-one years old.* Rehoboam was born shortly before David's death (see 11:42; see also note on 2:24). *seventeen years.* 930–913 B.C. *city the LORD had chosen . . . to put his Name.* See 9:3; Ps 132:13.

14:22 *Judah did evil in the eyes of the LORD.* The reign of Rehoboam is described in greater detail in 2Ch 11–12. The priests and Levites who immigrated to Judah from the north led the country to follow the way of David and Solomon for the first three years of Rehoboam's reign (see 12:24; 2Ch 11:17). In later years Rehoboam and the people of Judah turned away from the Lord (2Ch 12:1).

14:23 *high places.* See note on 3:2. *sacred stones.* Stone pillars, bearing a religious significance, that were placed next to the altars. The use of such pillars was common among the Canaanites and was explicitly forbidden to the Israelites in the Mosaic law (Ex 23:24; Lev 26:1; Dt 16:21–22). It is likely that the pillars were intended to be representations of the deity (2Ki 3:2). For legitimate uses of stone pillars see Ge 28:18; 31:45; Ex 24:4. *Asherah poles.* See note on v. 15.

Rulers of Israel and Judah

DATA AND DATES IN
ORDER OF SEQUENCE

Adapted from: *A Chronology of the Hebrew Kings* by Edwin R. Thiele.
© 1977 by The Zondervan Corporation. Used by permission.

1. 1Ki 12:1-24 14:21-31	**Rehoboam** *(Judah)*		17 years		**930-913**
2. 1Ki 12:25—14:20	**Jeroboam I** (Israel)		22 years		**930-909**
3. 1Ki 15:1-8	**Abijah** *(Judah)*	18th of Jeroboam	3 years		**913-910**
4. 1Ki 15:9-24	**Asa** *(Judah)*	20th of Jeroboam	41 years		**910-869**
5. 1Ki 15:25-31	**Nadab** (Israel)	2nd of Asa	2 years		**909-908**
6. 1Ki 15:32—16:7	**Baasha** (Israel)	3rd of Asa	24 years		**908-886**
7. 1Ki 16:8-14	**Elah** (Israel)	26th of Asa	2 years		**886-885**
8. 1Ki 16:15-20	**Zimri** (Israel)	27th of Asa	7 days		**885**
9. 1Ki 16:21-22	**Tibni** (Israel)			Overlap with Omri	**885-880**
10. 1Ki 16:23-28	**Omri** (Israel)	27th of Asa		Made king by the people	885
				Overlap with Tibni	**885-880**
		31st of Asa	12 years	Official reign = 11 actual years Beginning of sole reign	**885-874** 880
11. 1Ki 16:29—22:40	**Ahab** (Israel)	38th of Asa	22 years	Official reign = 21 actual years	**874-853**
12. 1Ki 22:41-50	**Jehoshaphat** *(Judah)*			Co-regency with Asa	872-869
			25 years	Official reign	872-848
		4th of Ahab		Beginning of sole reign Has Jehoram as regent	869 853-848
13. 1Ki 22:51— 2Ki 1:18	**Ahaziah** (Israel)	17th of Jehoshaphat	2 years	Official reign = 1 yr. actual reign	**853-852**
14. 2Ki 1:17 2Ki 3:1—8:15	**Joram** (Israel)	2nd of Jehoram 18th of Jehoshaphat	12 years	Official reign = 11 actual years	852 **852-841**
15. 2Ki 8:16-24	**Jehoram** *(Judah)*	5th of Joram		Beginning of sole reign	848
			8 years	Official reign = 7 actual years	**848-841**
16. 2Ki 8:25-29 2Ki 9:29	**Ahaziah** *(Judah)*	12th of Joram 11th of Joram	1 year	Nonaccession-year reckoning Accession-year reckoning	841 841
17. 2Ki 9:30—10:36	**Jehu** (Israel)		28 years		**841-814**
18. 2Ki 11	**Athaliah** *(Judah)*		7 years		**841-835**
19. 2Ki 12	**Joash** *(Judah)*	7th of Jehu	40 years		**835-796**
20. 2Ki 13:1-9	**Jehoahaz** (Israel)	23rd of Joash	17 years		**814-798**
21. 2Ki 13:10-25	**Jehoash** (Israel)	37th of Joash	16 years		**798-782**

22. 2Ki 14:1-22	Amaziah (Judah)	2nd of Jehoash	29 years		796-767
				Overlap with Azariah	792-767
23. 2Ki 14:23-29	Jeroboam II (Israel)			Co-regency with Jehoash	793-782
			41 years	Total reign	793-753
		15th of Amaziah		Beginning of sole reign	782
24. 2Ki 15:1-7	Azariah (Judah)			Overlap with Amaziah	792-767
			52 years	Total reign	792-740
		27th of Jeroboam		Beginning of sole reign	767
25. 2Ki 15:8-12	Zechariah (Israel)	38th of Azariah	6 months		753
26. 2Ki 15:13-15	Shallum (Israel)	39th of Azariah	1 month		752
27. 2Ki 15:16-22	Menahem (Israel)	39th of Azariah	10 years	Ruled in Samaria	752-742
28. 2Ki 15:23-26	Pekahiah (Israel)	50th of Azariah	2 years		742-740
29. 2Ki 15:27-31	Pekah (Israel)			In Gilead; overlapping years	752-740
			20 years	Total reign	752-732
		52nd of Azariah		Beginning of sole reign	740
30. 2Ki 15:32-38	Jotham (Judah)			Co-regency with Azariah	750-740
2Ki 15:30			16 years	Official reign	750-735
				Reign to his 20th year	750-732
		2nd of Pekah		Beginning of co-regency	750
31. 2Ki 16	Ahaz (Judah)			Total reign	735-715
		17th of Pekah			735
			16 years	From 20th of Jotham	732-715
32. 2Ki 15:30	Hoshea (Israel)			20th of Jotham	732
2Ki 17		12th of Ahaz*	9 years		732-722
33. 2Ki 18:1—20:21	Hezekiah (Judah)	3rd of Hoshea*	29 years		715-686
34. 2Ki 21:1-18	Manasseh (Judah)			Co-regency with Hezekiah	697-686
			55 years	Total reign	697-642
35. 2Ki 21:19-26	Amon (Judah)		2 years		642-640
36. 2Ki 22:1—23:30	Josiah (Judah)		31 years		640-609
37. 2Ki 23:31-33	Jehoahaz (Judah)		3 months		609
38. 2Ki 23:34—24:7	Jehoiakim (Judah)		11 years		609-598
39. 2Ki 24:8-17	Jehoiachin (Judah)		3 months		598-597
40. 2Ki 24:18—25:26	Zedekiah (Judah)		11 years		597-586

* These data arise when the reign of Hoshea
is thrown 12 years in advance of its historical position.

Italics denote kings of Judah.
Non-italic type denotes kings of **Israel**.

under every spreading tree. *w* 24There were even male shrine prostitutes *x* in the land; the people engaged in all the detestable *y* practices of the nations the LORD had driven out before the Israelites.

25In the fifth year of King Rehoboam, Shishak king of Egypt attacked *z* Jerusalem. 26He carried off the treasures of the temple *a* of the LORD and the treasures of the royal palace. He took everything, including all the gold shields *b* Solomon had made. 27So King Rehoboam made bronze shields to replace them and assigned these to the commanders of the guard on duty at the entrance to the royal palace. *c* 28Whenever the king went to the LORD's temple, the guards bore the shields, and afterward they returned them to the guardroom.

29As for the other events of Rehoboam's reign, and all he did, are they not written in the book of the annals of the kings of Judah? 30There was continual warfare *d* between Rehoboam and Jeroboam. 31And Rehoboam rested with his fathers and was buried with them in the City of David. His mother's name was Naamah; she was an Ammonite. *e* And Abijah *g* his son succeeded him as king.

Abijah King of Judah

15:1–2,6–8pp —2Ch 13:1–2,22–14:1

15 In the eighteenth year of the reign of Jeroboam son of Nebat, Abijah *h* became king of Judah, 2and he reigned in

Jerusalem three years. His mother's name was Maacah *f* daughter of Abishalom. *i*

3He committed all the sins his father had done before him; his heart was not fully devoted *g* to the LORD his God, as the heart of David his forefather had been. 4Nevertheless, for David's sake the LORD his God gave him a lamp *h* in Jerusalem by raising up a son to succeed him and by making Jerusalem strong. 5For David had done what was right in the eyes of the LORD and had not failed to keep *i* any of the LORD's commands all the days of his life—except in the case of Uriah *j* the Hittite.

6There was war *k* between Rehoboam *j* and Jeroboam throughout ˌAbijah'sˌ lifetime. 7As for the other events of Abijah's reign, and all he did, are they not written in the book of the annals of the kings of Judah? There was war between Abijah and Jeroboam. 8And Abijah rested with his fathers and was buried in the City of David. And Asa his son succeeded him as king.

Asa King of Judah

15:9–22pp — 2Ch 14:2–3; 15:16–16:6
15:23–24pp — 2Ch 16:11–17:1

9In the twentieth year of Jeroboam king of Israel, Asa became king of Judah, 10and he reigned in Jerusalem forty-one years.

Cross references

14:23
w S Dt 12:2;
Eze 6:13
14:24
x S Dt 23:17
y 1Ki 11:5-7;
2Ki 21:2;
Ezr 9:11;
Pr 21:27;
Isa 1:13;
Jer 16:18; 32:35;
44:4
14:25 *z* 2Ch 12:2
14:26
a 1Ki 15:15,18
b S 2Sa 8:7
14:27 *c* 2Ki 11:5
14:30 *d* 2Sa 3:1;
S 1Ki 12:21
14:31
e S 1Ki 11:1

15:2 *f* ver 10,13;
2Ch 11:20
15:3 *g* S 1Ki 8:61
15:4
h S 2Sa 21:17
15:5 *i* S Dt 5:32;
S 1Ki 9:4
j 2Sa 11:2-27;
12:9
15:6 *k* ver 16,32;
S 1Ki 12:21;
2Ch 16:9

g *31* Some Hebrew manuscripts and Septuagint (see also 2 Chron. 12:16); most Hebrew manuscripts *Abijam*
h *1* Some Hebrew manuscripts and Septuagint (see also 2 Chron. 12:16); most Hebrew manuscripts *Abijam*; also in verses 7 and 8 *i* *2* A variant of *Absalom*; also in verse 10 *16* Most Hebrew manuscripts; some Hebrew manuscripts and Syriac *Abijam* (that is, Abijah)

14:24 *male shrine prostitutes.* Ritual prostitution was an important feature of Canaanite fertility religion. The Israelites had been warned by Moses not to engage in this abominable practice (see Dt 23:17–18; see also 1Ki 15:12; 2Ki 23:7; Hos 4:14).

14:25 *fifth year of King Rehoboam.* 926 B.C. *Shishak.* See notes on 3:1; 11:40. *attacked Jerusalem.* Shishak's invasion is described in more detail in 2Ch 12:2–4 and is also attested in a victory inscription found on the walls of the temple of Amun in Thebes, where numerous cities that Shishak plundered in both Judah and the northern kingdom are listed. 2Ch 12:5–8 indicates that fear of the impending invasion led to a temporary reformation in Judah.

14:26 *gold shields Solomon had made.* See 10:16–17.
14:27 *bronze shields.* The reduced realm could not match the great wealth Solomon had accumulated in Jerusalem (see 10:21,23,27).
14:29 *annals of the kings of Judah.* A record of the reigns of the kings of Judah similar to the one for the kings of the northern kingdom (see note on v. 19; see also Introduction: Author, Sources and Date).
14:30 *continual warfare.* See notes on v. 19; 12:24.
14:31 *rested with his fathers.* See note on 1:21.
15:1 *eighteenth year of the reign of Jeroboam.* The first of numerous synchronisms in 1,2 Kings between the reigns of the kings in the north and those in Judah (see, e.g., vv. 9,25, 33; 16:8,15,29; see also Introduction: Chronology). *Abijah.* See note on 14:1. Both Rehoboam and Jeroboam had sons by

this name.
15:2 *three years.* 913–910 B.C. *Maacah daughter of Abishalom.* See NIV text note. Abijah's mother is said to be a daughter of Uriel of Gibeah in 2Ch 13:2. It is likely that Maacah was the granddaughter of Absalom and the daughter of a marriage between Tamar (Absalom's daughter; see 2Sa 14:27) and Uriel. Absalom's mother was also named Maacah (2Sa 3:3).
15:3 *sins his father had done.* See 14:22–24. *not fully devoted to the LORD his God, as . . . David his forefather had been.* Although David fell into grievous sin, his heart was never divided between serving the Lord and serving the nature deities of the Canaanites.
15:4 *lamp in Jerusalem.* See note on 11:36.
15:5 *Uriah the Hittite.* See 2Sa 11.
15:6 *Rehoboam.* See NIV text note; see also note on 12:24.
15:7 *other events of Abijah's reign.* See 2Ch 13. *annals of the kings of Judah.* See note on 14:29. *war between Abijah and Jeroboam.* Cf. v. 6; 14:30. From 2Ch 13 it is clear that the chronic hostile relations of preceding years flared into serious combat in which Abijah defeated Jeroboam and took several towns from him, including Bethel (2Ch 13:19).
15:8 *rested with his fathers.* See note on 1:21.
15:9 *twentieth year of Jeroboam.* 910 B.C. (see note on 14:20).
15:10 *forty-one years.* 910–869 B.C. *Maacah daughter of Abishalom.* See note on v. 2.

His grandmother's name was Maacah[l] daughter of Abishalom.

[11]Asa did what was right in the eyes of the LORD, as his father David[m] had done. [12]He expelled the male shrine prostitutes[n] from the land and got rid of all the idols[o] his fathers had made. [13]He even deposed his grandmother Maacah[p] from her position as queen mother,[q] because she had made a repulsive Asherah pole. Asa cut the pole down[r] and burned it in the Kidron Valley. [14]Although he did not remove[s] the high places, Asa's heart was fully committed[t] to the LORD all his life. [15]He brought into the temple of the LORD the silver and gold and the articles that he and his father had dedicated.[u]

[16]There was war[v] between Asa and Baasha king of Israel throughout their reigns. [17]Baasha king of Israel went up against Judah and fortified Ramah[w] to prevent anyone from leaving or entering the territory of Asa king of Judah.

[18]Asa then took all the silver and gold that was left in the treasuries of the LORD's temple[x] and of his own palace. He entrusted it to his officials and sent[y] them to

Ben-Hadad[z] son of Tabrimmon, the son of Hezion, the king of Aram, who was ruling in Damascus. [19]"Let there be a treaty[a] between me and you," he said, "as there was between my father and your father. See, I am sending you a gift of silver and gold. Now break your treaty with Baasha king of Israel so he will withdraw from me."

[20]Ben-Hadad agreed with King Asa and sent the commanders of his forces against the towns of Israel. He conquered[b] Ijon, Dan, Abel Beth Maacah and all Kinnereth in addition to Naphtali. [21]When Baasha heard this, he stopped building Ramah[c] and withdrew to Tirzah. [d] [22]Then King Asa issued an order to all Judah—no one was exempt—and they carried away from Ramah[e] the stones and timber Baasha had been using there. With them King Asa[f] built up Geba[g] in Benjamin, and also Mizpah. [h]

[23]As for all the other events of Asa's reign, all his achievements, all he did and the cities he built, are they not written in the book of the annals of the kings of Judah? In his old age, however, his feet became diseased. [24]Then Asa rested with

---

Cross references (center column):

15:10 /S ver 2
15:11 mIKi 9:4
15:12 nIKi 14:24
o2Ch 15:8
15:13 pS ver 2
qS 1Ki 2:19
rS Ex 34:13
15:14 s2Ch 14:5;
17:6 tS 1Ki 8:61
15:15 uS 2Sa 8:11
15:16 vS ver 6;
S 1Ki 12:21
15:17 wS Jos 18:25
15:18 xS 1Ki 14:26
y2Ki 12:18; 16:8;
18:14-16,15;
Joel 3:5

zver 18-20;
1Ki 20:1;
2Ki 6:24; 13:3;
Jer 49:27
15:19 aS Ex 23:32;
S 1Ki 5:12
15:20 b1Ki 20:34
15:21 cS Jos 18:25
d1Ki 16:15-17
15:22 ever 17
fver 9-24;
Jer 41:9
gS Jos 18:24;
2Ki 23:8
hS Jos 11:3

15:12 *male shrine prostitutes.* See note on 14:24. *got rid of all the idols his fathers had made.* See 14:23.
15:13 *deposed his grandmother Maacah.* 2Ch 14:1–15:16 indicates that a progression in Asa's reform over a period of years. Although Asa had destroyed pagan idols and altars early in his reign (2Ch 14:2–3), it was not until after a victory over Zerah the Cushite (2Ch 14:8–15) that Asa responded to the message of the prophet Azariah son of Oded by calling for a covenant renewal assembly in Jerusalem in the 15th year of his reign (2Ch 15:10). After this assembly Asa deposed his grandmother Maacah because of her idolatry (2Ch 15:16). *made a repulsive Asherah pole.* See note on 14:15. It appears that Maacah's action was a deliberate attempt to counter Asa's reform.
15:14 *did not remove the high places.* The reference here and in 2Ch 15:17 is to those high places where the Lord was worshiped (for the question of legitimacy of worship of the Lord at high places see note on 3:2). When 2Ch 14:3 indicates that Asa removed the high places, it is to be taken as a reference to the high places that were centers of pagan Canaanite worship (see 2Ch 17:6; 20:33 for the same distinction). This same statement of qualified approval that is made of Asa is made of five other kings of Judah prior to the time of Hezekiah (Jehoshaphat, 22:43; Joash, 2Ki 12:3; Amaziah, 2Ki 14:4; Azariah, 2Ki 15:4; Jotham, 2Ki 15:35). *fully committed to the LORD.* See note on v. 3.
15:15 *silver and gold and the articles.* Most likely consisting of war booty that Abijah had taken from Jeroboam (2Ch 13) and that Asa acquired from Zerah the Cushite (2Ch 14:8–15).
15:16 *war between Asa and Baasha . . . throughout their reigns.* A reference to the chronic hostile relations that had existed ever since the division of the kingdom, rather than to full-scale combat (see notes on v. 7; 12:24; see also 2Ch 15:19).
15:17 *fortified Ramah.* Baasha had recaptured the territory previously taken from Jeroboam by Abijah (see note on v. 7; see also 2Ch 13:19) since Ramah was located south of Bethel

and only about five miles north of Jerusalem. *prevent anyone from leaving or entering the territory of Asa.* See 2Ch 15:9–10.
15:18 *silver and gold that was left.* That which remained after the plundering of Jerusalem by Shishak of Egypt (see 14:25). *Hezion.* It is not clear whether Hezion is to be identified with Rezon of Damascus (see 11:23–25) or regarded as the founder of a new dynasty.
15:19 *treaty . . . between my father and your father.* A reference to a previously unmentioned treaty between Abijah and Tabrimmon of Aram. When Tabrimmon died, Baasha succeeded in establishing a treaty with his successor Ben-Hadad. Asa saw no hope for success against Baasha without the assistance provided by a renewal of the old treaty with Aram. Although his plan seemed to be successful, it was condemned by Hanani the prophet as a foolish act and a denial of reliance on the Lord (see 2Ch 16:7–10). The true theocratic king was never to fear his enemies but to trust in the God of the covenant for security and protection (see note on 1Sa 17:11). Ahaz was later to follow Asa's bad example and seek Assyria's help when he was attacked by Israel and Aram (see 2Ki 16:5–9; Isa 7).
15:20 *Naphtali.* The cities that Ben-Hadad conquered in Naphtali were of particular importance because the major trade routes from Damascus going west to Tyre and southwest through the plain of Jezreel to the coastal plain and Egypt transversed this area. This same territory was later seized by the Assyrian ruler Tiglath-Pileser III (2Ki 15:29).
15:21 *Tirzah.* See note on 14:17.
15:22 *order to all Judah.* Asa's action is reminiscent of the labor force conscripted by Solomon (5:13–14; 11:28). *Geba . . . Mizpah.* Asa established two border fortresses to check Baasha's desire to expand his territory southward. Geba was east of Ramah, and Mizpah was southwest of Ramah.
15:23 *other events of Asa's reign.* See 2Ch 14:2–16:14. *annals of the kings of Judah.* See note on 14:29. *feet became diseased.* See 2Ch 16:12.
15:24 *rested with his fathers.* See note on 1:21. *Jehosha-*

his fathers and was buried with them in the city of his father David. And Jehoshaphat[i] his son succeeded him as king.

Nadab King of Israel

25Nadab son of Jeroboam became king of Israel in the second year of Asa king of Judah, and he reigned over Israel two years. 26He did evil[j] in the eyes of the LORD, walking in the ways of his father[k] and in his sin, which he had caused Israel to commit.

27Baasha son of Ahijah of the house of Issachar plotted against him, and he struck him down[l] at Gibbethon,[m] a Philistine town, while Nadab and all Israel were besieging it. 28Baasha killed Nadab in the third year of Asa king of Judah and succeeded him as king.

29As soon as he began to reign, he killed Jeroboam's whole family.[n] He did not leave Jeroboam anyone that breathed, but destroyed them all, according to the word of the LORD given through his servant Ahijah the Shilonite— 30because of the sins[o] Jeroboam had committed and had caused[p] Israel to commit, and because he provoked the LORD, the God of Israel, to anger.

31As for the other events of Nadab's reign, and all he did, are they not written in the book of the annals[q] of the kings of Israel? 32There was war[r] between Asa and

Baasha king of Israel throughout their reigns.

Baasha King of Israel

33In the third year of Asa king of Judah, Baasha son of Ahijah became king of all Israel in Tirzah,[s] and he reigned twenty-four years. 34He did evil[t] in the eyes of the LORD, walking in the ways of Jeroboam and in his sin, which he had caused Israel to commit.

16 Then the word of the LORD came to Jehu[u] son of Hanani[v] against Baasha: 2"I lifted you up from the dust[w] and made you leader[x] of my people Israel, but you walked in the ways of Jeroboam and caused[y] my people Israel to sin and to provoke me to anger by their sins. 3So I am about to consume Baasha[z] and his house,[a] and I will make your house like that of Jeroboam son of Nebat. 4Dogs[b] will eat those belonging to Baasha who die in the city, and the birds of the air[c] will feed on those who die in the country."

5As for the other events of Baasha's reign, what he did and his achievements, are they not written in the book of the annals[d] of the kings of Israel? 6Baasha rested with his fathers and was buried in Tirzah.[e] And Elah his son succeeded him as king.

7Moreover, the word of the LORD came[f] through the prophet Jehu[g] son of

Cross references (center column)

15:24 [i]Mt 1:8
15:26 [j]S Dt 4:25
[k]S 1Ki 12:30
15:27 [l]1Ki 14:14
[m]S Jos 19:44
15:29 [n]S 1Ki 13:34
15:30 [o]S 1Ki 12:30
[p]1Ki 16:26;
2Ki 3:3; 14:24;
15:28; 21:16
15:31 [q]1Ki 11:41
15:32 [r]S ver 6

15:33 [s]1Ki 14:17; 16:6,
23; 2Ki 15:14;
SS 6:4
15:34 [t]ver 26
16:1 [u]ver 7;
2Ch 19:2; 20:34
[v]2Ch 16:7
16:2 [w]1Sa 2:8
[x]S 1Ki 14:7-9
[y]S 1Ki 12:30
16:3 [z]2Ki 9:9
[a]ver 11;
1Ki 21:22
16:4 [b]S 1Ki 14:11
[c]S Ge 40:19
16:5 [d]1Ki 15:31
16:6 [e]S 1Ki 15:33
16:7 [f]S 1Ki 6:11
[g]S ver 1

---

phat his son succeeded him. For the reign of Jehoshaphat see 22:41–50; 2Ch 17:1–21:1.

15:25 *second year of Asa.* See note on v. 1. The second year of Asa of Judah corresponded to the 22nd and last year of Jeroboam of Israel (see v. 9; 14:20). *two years.* 909–908 B.C.

15:26 *his sin, which he had caused Israel to commit.* Jeroboam's sin (see note on 14:16). Although Abijah of Judah occupied Bethel during the reign of Jeroboam (see note on v. 7), it is probable that the paganized worship Jeroboam initiated was continued elsewhere until control of Bethel was regained by Baasha.

15:27 *Gibbethon.* A town located between Jerusalem and Joppa (probably a few miles west of Gezer) in the territory originally assigned to Dan (Jos 19:43–45). This Levitical city (Jos 21:23) probably fell into Philistine hands at the time of the Philistine expansion in the period of the judges.

15:28 *third year of Asa.* 908 B.C. (see note on v. 10). It is likely that Baasha was a commander in Nadab's army and was able to secure the support of the military for his revolt.

15:29 *the word ... given through ... Ahijah.* See 14:10–11.

15:30 *sins Jeroboam had committed and had caused Israel to commit.* See note on 14:16.

15:31 *annals of the kings of Israel.* See note on 14:19.

15:32 *war ... throughout their reigns.* See note on v. 16. The demise of Jeroboam's dynasty did not improve relations between the two kingdoms.

15:33 *third year of Asa.* 908 B.C. (see note on v. 10). *Tirzah.* See note on 14:17. *twenty-four years.* 908–886 B.C.

His official years were counted as 24, though his actual years were 23 (see 16:8; see also Introduction: Chronology).

15:34 *his sin, which he had caused Israel to commit.* See note on 14:16. The assessment of Baasha's reign indicates no improvement over the reign of Nadab, whom he replaced (see v. 26).

16:1 *Jehu.* Like his father before him (see 2Ch 16:7–10), Jehu brought God's word of condemnation to a king. Much as the man of God from Judah (see note on 13:1) and later the prophet Amos, he was sent from the south to a northern king. His ministry continued for about 50 years until the reign of Jehoshaphat of Judah (2Ch 19:2; 20:34).

16:2 *I lifted you up from the dust.* Cf. 14:7. *walked in the ways of Jeroboam.* See note on 14:16.

16:3 *consume Baasha and his house.* Cf. 14:10 (the house of Jeroboam); 21:21 (the house of Omri and Ahab).

16:4 Identical to the prophecy against Jeroboam's dynasty in 14:11.

16:5 *his achievements.* For the purposes of the writer of Kings (see Introduction: Theme), it was not necessary to list any of Baasha's achievements. He may have been a very successful ruler from a military-political point of view. *annals of the kings of Israel.* See note on 14:19.

16:6 *rested with his fathers.* See note on 1:21.

16:7 *evil he had done ... like the house of Jeroboam.* See v. 2; 15:34. *he destroyed it.* Although Baasha fulfilled God's purpose (14:10,14) in destroying the house of Jeroboam, he remained responsible for this violent and unlawful act (cf. Ge 50:20; Isa 10:5–7,12).

Hanani to Baasha and his house, because of all the evil he had done in the eyes of the LORD, provoking him to anger by the things he did, and becoming like the house of Jeroboam—and also because he destroyed it.

Elah King of Israel

[8]In the twenty-sixth year of Asa king of Judah, Elah son of Baasha became king of Israel, and he reigned in Tirzah two years.

[9]Zimri, one of his officials, who had command of half his chariots, plotted against him. Elah was in Tirzah at the time, getting drunk[h] in the home of Arza, the man in charge[i] of the palace at Tirzah. [10]Zimri came in, struck him down and killed him in the twenty-seventh year of Asa king of Judah. Then he succeeded him as king.[j]

[11]As soon as he began to reign and was seated on the throne, he killed off Baasha's whole family.[k] He did not spare a single male, whether relative or friend. [12]So Zimri destroyed the whole family of Baasha, in accordance with the word of the LORD spoken against Baasha through the prophet Jehu— [13]because of all the sins Baasha and his son Elah had committed and had caused Israel to commit, so that they provoked the LORD, the God of Israel, to anger by their worthless idols.[l]

[14]As for the other events of Elah's reign, and all he did, are they not written in the book of the annals of the kings of Israel?

Zimri King of Israel

[15]In the twenty-seventh year of Asa king of Judah, Zimri reigned in Tirzah seven days. The army was encamped near Gibbethon,[m] a Philistine town. [16]When the Israelites in the camp heard that Zimri had plotted against the king and murdered him, they proclaimed Omri, the commander of the army, king over Israel that very day there in the camp. [17]Then Omri and all the Israelites with him withdrew from Gibbethon and laid siege to Tirzah. [18]When Zimri saw that the city was taken, he went into the citadel of the royal palace and set the palace on fire around him. So he died, [19]because of the sins he had committed, doing evil in the eyes of the LORD and walking in the ways of Jeroboam and in the sin he had committed and had caused Israel to commit.

[20]As for the other events of Zimri's reign, and the rebellion he carried out, are they not written in the book of the annals of the kings of Israel?

Omri King of Israel

[21]Then the people of Israel were split into two factions; half supported Tibni son of Ginath for king, and the other half supported Omri. [22]But Omri's followers proved stronger than those of Tibni son of Ginath. So Tibni died and Omri became king.

[23]In the thirty-first year of Asa king of Judah, Omri became king of Israel, and he reigned twelve years, six of them in Tirzah.[n] [24]He bought the hill of Samaria from Shemer for two talents[k] of silver and built

16:9 [h]1Ki 20:12, 16; Pr 31:4-5
[i]1Ki 18:3
16:10 [j]2Ki 9:31
16:11 [k]S ver 3
16:13 [l]S Dt 32:21

16:15 [m]S Jos 19:44
16:23 [n]S Jos 12:24; S 1Ki 15:33

[k]*24* That is, about 150 pounds (about 70 kilograms)

16:8 *twenty-sixth year of Asa.* 886 B.C. (see note on 15:10; see also Introduction: Chronology). *two years.* 886–885 B.C.
16:9 *getting drunk.* The fact that Elah was carousing at Tirzah while the army was laying siege to Gibbethon (v. 15) indicates he had little perception of his responsibilities as king.
16:10 *twenty-seventh year of Asa.* 885 B.C.
16:11 *killed off Baasha's whole family.* See 15:29; 2Ki 10:1-7; 11:1. *friend.* Probably the chief adviser to the king (see note on 2Sa 15:37).
16:12 *word of the LORD . . . through the prophet Jehu.* See vv. 1–4. Zimri did not consciously decide to fulfill Jehu's prophecy, but unwittingly he became the instrument by which Jehu's prediction was fulfilled (see note on v. 7) when he conspired against Elah and destroyed the dynasty of Baasha.
16:13 *sins Baasha and his son Elah had committed.* See 15:34. *worthless idols.* A reference to all the paganism in Israel's religious observances, including the use of the golden calves in worship (see 12:28; 14:9).
16:14 *annals of the kings of Israel.* See note on 14:19.
16:15 *twenty-seventh year of Asa.* 885 B.C. (see notes on 15:1,10). *Gibbethon.* See notes on v. 9; 15:27.
16:16 *plotted against the king and murdered him.* See vv. 9–12. *Omri, the commander of the army.* He held a higher

rank than Zimri did under Elah (v. 9).
16:17 *Tirzah.* The royal residence (see vv. 8–10; see also note on 14:17).
16:19 *ways of Jeroboam.* See note on 14:16.
16:20 *annals of the kings of Israel.* See note on 14:19.
16:22 *Tibni died.* It is not clear whether Tibni's death was due to natural causes or the result of the military struggle for control of the land.
16:23 *thirty-first year of Asa.* 880 B.C. (see note on 15:10; see also Introduction: Chronology). *became king.* Became sole king. The struggle for control of the northern kingdom between Omri and Tibni lasted four years (compare this verse with v. 15). *twelve years.* 885–874. The 12 years of Omri's reign include the four years of struggle between Omri and Tibni (cf. vv. 15,29). *Tirzah.* See note on 14:17. Omri had been able to capture Tirzah in a matter of days (vv. 15–19).
16:24 *Samaria.* Seven miles northwest of Shechem, Samaria rose about 300 feet above the surrounding fertile valleys (referred to as a "wreath" in Isa 28:1). The original owner may have been persuaded to sell his property (see 21:3) on the condition that the city be named after him (cf. Ru 4:5). The site provided an ideal location for a nearly impregnable capital city for the northern kingdom (see 20:1–21; 2Ki 6:25; 18:9–10). With the establishment of

a city on the hill, calling it Samaria,[o] after Shemer, the name of the former owner of the hill.

[25]But Omri did evil[p] in the eyes of the LORD and sinned more than all those before him. [26]He walked in all the ways of Jeroboam son of Nebat and in his sin, which he had caused[q] Israel to commit, so that they provoked the LORD, the God of Israel, to anger by their worthless idols.[r]

[27]As for the other events of Omri's reign, what he did and the things he achieved, are they not written in the book of the annals of the kings of Israel? [28]Omri rested with his fathers and was buried in Samaria.[s] And Ahab his son succeeded him as king.

Ahab Becomes King of Israel

[29]In the thirty-eighth year of Asa king of Judah, Ahab son of Omri became king of Israel, and he reigned in Samaria over Israel twenty-two years. [30]Ahab son of Omri

did more[t] evil in the eyes of the LORD than any of those before him. [31]He not only considered it trivial to commit the sins of Jeroboam son of Nebat, but he also married[u] Jezebel daughter[v] of Ethbaal king of the Sidonians, and began to serve Baal[w] and worship him. [32]He set up an altar[x] for Baal in the temple[y] of Baal that he built in Samaria. [33]Ahab also made an Asherah pole[z] and did more[a] to provoke the LORD, the God of Israel, to anger than did all the kings of Israel before him.

[34]In Ahab's time, Hiel of Bethel rebuilt Jericho. He laid its foundations at the cost of his firstborn son Abiram, and he set up its gates at the cost of his youngest son Segub, in accordance with the word of the LORD spoken by Joshua son of Nun.[b]

Elijah Fed by Ravens

17 Now Elijah[c] the Tishbite, from Tishbe[1] in Gilead,[d] said to Ahab,

[1] Or Tishbite, of the settlers

Cross-reference column

16:24 oS 1Ki 13:32; S Mt 10:5
16:25 pver 25-26; S Dt 4:25; Mic 6:16
16:26 qS 1Ki 15:30 rS Dt 32:21
16:28 sS 1Ki 13:32
16:30 tS 1Ki 14:9
16:31 uS 1Ki 11:2 vS Jdg 3:6; 2Ki 9:34 wS Jdg 2:11
16:32 xS Jdg 6:28 y2Ki 10:27; 11:18; Jer 43:12
16:33 zS Jdg 3:7; 2Ki 13:6 aS 1Ki 14:9; 21:25
16:34 bJos 6:26
17:1 cMal 4:5; Mt 11:14; 17:3 dJdg 12:4

---

this royal city, the kings of the north came to possess a royal citadel-city like that of the Davidic dynasty (see 2Sa 5:6–12). Archaeologists have discovered that Omri and Ahab also adorned it with magnificent structures to rival those Solomon had erected in Jerusalem. From this time on, the northern kingdom could be designated by the name of the royal city, just as the southern kingdom could be designated by its capital, Jerusalem (see, e.g., 21:1; Isa 10:10; Am 6:1).

16:25 sinned more than all. Omri's alliance with Ethbaal of Tyre and Sidon (Omri's son Ahab married Ethbaal's daughter Jezebel to seal the alliance) led to widespread Baal worship in the northern kingdom (vv. 31–33) and eventually to the near extinction of the Davidic line in the southern kingdom (see 2Ki 11; see also note on 2Ki 8:18). This marriage alliance must have been established in the early years of Omri's reign (see note on v. 23), perhaps to strengthen his hand against Tibni (see vv. 21–22).

16:26 sin, which he had caused Israel to commit. See 12:26–33; see also note on 14:16. worthless idols. See note on v. 13.

16:27 things he achieved. Omri's military and political accomplishments were not of importance for the purposes of the writer of Kings (see Introduction: Theme). Apart from establishing Samaria as the capital of the northern kingdom, about all that is known of him is that he organized a governmental structure in the northern kingdom that was in place during the rule of his son, Ahab (see 20:14–15). Omri's dynasty, however, endured for over 40 years. A century and a half later (732 B.C.) Tiglath-Pileser III of Assyria referred to Israel as the "house of Omri" in his annals. annals of the kings of Israel. See note on 14:19.

16:28 rested with his fathers. See note on 1:21.

16:29 thirty-eighth year of Asa. 874 B.C. (see notes on 15:9–10). twenty-two years. 874–853 B.C.

16:30 more evil . . . than any. Omri sinned more than those before him (see v. 25), and Ahab sinned more than his father had. Evil became progressively worse in the royal house of the northern kingdom. Nearly a third of the narrative material in 1,2 Kings concerns the 34-year period of the reigns of Ahab and his two sons, Ahaziah and Joram. In this period the struggle between the kingdom of God (championed especially by Elijah and Elisha) and the kingdom of

Satan was especially intense.

16:31 married Jezebel daughter of Ethbaal. The Jewish historian Josephus refers to Ethbaal as a king-priest who ruled over Tyre and Sidon for 32 years. Ahab had already married Jezebel during the reign of his father (see note on v. 25). Baal. Perhaps Melqart, the local manifestation of Baal in Tyre, whose worship was brought to Israel by Jezebel. It is probable that Ahab participated in the worship of this deity at the time of his marriage. The names of Ahab's sons (Ahaziah, "The LORD grasps"; Joram, "The LORD is exalted") suggest that Ahab did not intend to replace the worship of the Lord with the worship of Baal but to worship both deities in a syncretistic way.

16:32 temple of Baal that he built in Samaria. Ahab imported the Phoenician Baal worship of his wife Jezebel into the northern kingdom by constructing a temple of Baal in Samaria, just as Solomon had erected the temple of the Lord in Jerusalem. This pagan temple and its sacred stone (see note on 14:23) were later destroyed by Jehu (2Ki 10:21–27).

16:33 Asherah pole. See note on 14:15. than did all the kings of Israel. See note on v. 30. Ahab elevated the worship of Baal to an official status in the northern kingdom at the beginning of his reign.

16:34 rebuilt Jericho. Does not mean that Jericho had remained uninhabited since its destruction by Joshua (see Jos 18:21; Jdg 1:16; 3:13; 2Sa 10:5), but that it had remained an unwalled town or village. During the rule of Ahab, Hiel fortified the city by reconstructing its walls and gates (see 9:17 for a similar use of "rebuild"). This violated God's intention that the ruins of Jericho (Jos 6:26) be a perpetual reminder that Israel had received the land of Canaan from God's hand as a gift of grace. Accordingly, Hiel suffered the curse Joshua had pronounced.

17:1 Elijah. Elijah's name (meaning "The LORD is my God") was the essence of his message (18:21,39). He was sent to oppose vigorously, by word and action, both Baal worship and those who engaged in it. from Tishbe in Gilead. See NIV text note. Gilead was in the northern Transjordan area. The precise location of Tishbe is unknown. whom I serve. Lit. "before whom I stand," a technical expression indicating one who stands in the service of a king. Kings and

"As the LORD, the God of Israel, lives, whom I serve, there will be neither dew nor rain *e* in the next few years except at my word."

2Then the word of the LORD came to Elijah: 3"Leave here, turn eastward and hide *f* in the Kerith Ravine, east of the Jordan. 4You will drink from the brook, and I have ordered the ravens *g* to feed you there."

5So he did what the LORD had told him. He went to the Kerith Ravine, east of the Jordan, and stayed there. 6The ravens brought him bread and meat in the morning *h* and bread and meat in the evening, and he drank from the brook.

The Widow at Zarephath

7Some time later the brook dried up because there had been no rain in the land. 8Then the word of the LORD came to him: 9"Go at once to Zarephath *i* of Sidon and stay there. I have commanded a widow *j* in that place to supply you with food." 10So he went to Zarephath. When he came to the town gate, a widow was there gathering sticks. He called to her and asked,

"Would you bring me a little water in a jar so I may have a drink?" *k* 11As she was going to get it, he called, "And bring me, please, a piece of bread."

12"As surely as the LORD your God lives," she replied, "I don't have any bread—only a handful of flour in a jar and a little oil *l* in a jug. I am gathering a few sticks to take home and make a meal for myself and my son, that we may eat it—and die."

13Elijah said to her, "Don't be afraid. Go home and do as you have said. But first make a small cake of bread for me from what you have and bring it to me, and then make something for yourself and your son. 14For this is what the LORD, the God of Israel, says: 'The jar of flour will not be used up and the jug of oil will not run dry until the day the LORD gives rain *m* on the land.'"

15She went away and did as Elijah had told her. So there was food every day for Elijah and for the woman and her family. 16For the jar of flour was not used up and the jug of oil did not run dry, in keeping

Cross references (center column)

17:1 *e*S Dt 11:17; S 28:24; S 2Sa 1:21; S 1Ki 8:36; Job 12:15; S Lk 4:25
17:3 *f*1Ki 18:4, 10; Jer 36:19,26
17:4 *g*S Ge 8:7
17:6 *h*Ex 16:8
17:9 *i*Ob 1:20 /Lk 4:26
17:10 *k*S Ge 24:17; Jn 4:7
17:12 *l*2Ki 4:2
17:14 *m*ver 1

Study notes

priests in Israel were supposed to be anointed to serve as official representatives of the Lord, Israel's Great King, leading Israel in the way of faithfulness to the Lord and channeling his covenantal care and blessings to them. Since the days of Jeroboam the northern kingdom had not had such a priest (12:31), and its kings had all been unfaithful. Now, in the great crisis brought on by Ahab's promotion of Baal worship, the Lord sent Elijah (and after him Elisha) to serve as his representative (instead of king and priest), much as Moses had done long ago. The author of Kings highlights many parallels between the ministries of Elijah and Moses. *neither dew nor rain.* The drought was not only a divine judgment on a nation that had turned to idolatry, but also a demonstration that even though Baal was considered the god of fertility and lord of the rain clouds, he was powerless to give rain (cf. Lev 26:3–4; Hos 2:5,8).

17:3 *Leave here.* With this command God withdrew his prophet from his land and people to leave them isolated from his word and blessings. The absence of the prophet confirmed and intensified the judgment. *Kerith Ravine, east of the Jordan.* The location of Kerith is uncertain. Perhaps it was a gorge formed by one of the northern tributaries to the Yarmuk River.

17:4 *ravens to feed you there.* The Lord's faithful servant Elijah was miraculously sustained beyond the Jordan (like Israel in the desert in the time of Moses) while Israel in the promised land was going hungry—a clear testimony against Israel's reliance on Baal. The fact that Elijah was sustained in a miraculous way apart from living among his own people demonstrated that the word of God was not dependent on the people, but the people were dependent on the word of God.

17:9 *Zarephath of Sidon.* A coastal town located between Tyre and Sidon in the territory ruled by Jezebel's father Ethbaal (16:31). Elijah is commanded to go and reside in the heart of the very land from which the Baal worship now being promoted in Israel had come. *I have commanded a widow in that place to supply you with food.* Elijah, as the

bearer of God's word, was now to be sustained by human hands, but they were the hands of a poor widow facing starvation (v. 12). She was, moreover, from outside the circle of God's own people (cf. Lk 4:25–26)—in fact, she was from the pagan nation that at that time (much like Egypt earlier and Babylon later) represented the forces arrayed against God's kingdom.

17:10 *So he went.* Elijah's reliance on the Lord demonstrated the faith in the Lord that Israel should have been living by.

17:12 *As surely as the LORD your God lives.* Her oath in the name of the Lord was either an accommodation to Elijah, whom she recognized as an Israelite (see notes on 5:7; 10:9), or a genuine expression of previous knowledge of and commitment to the God of Israel.

17:13 *first make a small cake of bread for me . . . then make something for yourself and your son.* As a prophet, Elijah's words are the command of the Lord. The widow is asked to give all she has to sustain the bearer of the word of God. The demand to give her all is in essence the demand of the covenant that Israel had broken.

17:14 *what the LORD, the God of Israel, says.* Elijah can tell the widow "Don't be afraid" (v. 13) because the demand of the covenant is not given without the promise of the covenant. The Lord does not ask more than he promises to give.

17:15 *did as Elijah had told her.* By an act of faith the woman received the promised blessing. Israel had forsaken the covenant and followed Baal and Asherah in search of prosperity. Now in the midst of a pagan kingdom a widow realized that trustful obedience to the word of God is the way that leads to life.

17:16 *jar of flour was not used up.* God miraculously provided for this non-Israelite who, in an act of faith in the Lord's word, had laid her life on the line. He gave her "manna" from heaven even while he was withholding food from his unfaithful people in the promised land. The warning of Dt 32:21 was being fulfilled (cf. Ro 10:19; 11:11,14).

with the word of the LORD spoken by Elijah.

[17]Some time later the son of the woman who owned the house became ill. He grew worse and worse, and finally stopped breathing. [18]She said to Elijah, "What do you have against me, man of God? Did you come to remind me of my sin[n] and kill my son?"

[19]"Give me your son," Elijah replied. He took him from her arms, carried him to the upper room where he was staying, and laid him on his bed. [20]Then he cried[o] out to the LORD, "O LORD my God, have you brought tragedy also upon this widow I am staying with, by causing her son to die?" [21]Then he stretched[p] himself out on the boy three times and cried to the LORD, "O LORD my God, let this boy's life return to him!"

[22]The LORD heard Elijah's cry, and the boy's life returned to him, and he lived. [23]Elijah picked up the child and carried him down from the room into the house. He gave him to his mother[q] and said, "Look, your son is alive!"

[24]Then the woman said to Elijah, "Now I know[r] that you are a man of God[s] and that the word of the LORD from your mouth is the truth."[t]

Elijah and Obadiah

18 After a long time, in the third[u] year, the word of the LORD came to Elijah: "Go and present[v] yourself to Ahab, and I will send rain[w] on the land." [2]So Elijah went to present himself to Ahab.

Now the famine was severe[x] in Samaria, [3]and Ahab had summoned Obadiah, who was in charge[y] of his palace. (Obadiah was a devout believer[z] in the LORD. [4]While Jezebel[a] was killing off the LORD's prophets, Obadiah had taken a hundred prophets and hidden[b] them in two caves, fifty in each, and had supplied[c] them with food and water.) [5]Ahab had said to Obadiah, "Go through the land to all the springs[d] and valleys. Maybe we can find some grass to keep the horses and mules alive so we will not have to kill any of our animals."[e] [6]So they divided the land they were to cover, Ahab going in one direction and Obadiah in another.

[7]As Obadiah was walking along, Elijah met him. Obadiah recognized[f] him, bowed down to the ground, and said, "Is it really you, my lord Elijah?"

[8]"Yes," he replied. "Go tell your master, 'Elijah is here.' "

[9]"What have I done wrong," asked Obadiah, "that you are handing your servant over to Ahab to be put to death? [10]As surely as the LORD your God lives, there is not a nation or kingdom where my master has not sent someone to look[g] for you. And whenever a nation or kingdom claimed you were not there, he made them swear they could not find you. [11]But now you tell me to go to my master and say, 'Elijah is here.' [12]I don't know where the

---

Cross references (center column):

17:18 [n]Lk 5:8
17:20 [o]2Ki 4:33
17:21 [p]2Ki 4:34;
Ac 20:10
17:23 [q]Heb 11:35
17:24 [r]Jn 16:30
[s]ver 18
[t]1Ki 22:16;
Ps 119:43;
Jn 17:17
18:1 [u]1Ki 17:1;
Lk 4:25 [v]ver 15

[w]S Dt 28:12
18:2
[x]S Lev 26:26
18:3 [y]1Ki 16:9
[z]Ne 7:2
18:4 [a]1Ki 21:23;
2Ki 9:7
[b]S 1Ki 17:3;
Isa 16:3; 25:4;
32:2; Ob 1:14
[c]Jer 26:24
18:5 [d]Jer 14:3
[e]S Ge 47:4
18:7 [f]2Ki 1:8;
Zec 13:4
18:10
[g]S 1Ki 17:3

17:18 *Did you come to remind me of my sin and kill my son?* The widow concluded that Elijah's presence in her house had called God's attention to her sin, and that the death of her son was a divine punishment for this sin. Although her sense of guilt seems to have been influenced by pagan ideas, both she and Elijah are confronted with the question: Why did the God who promised life bring death instead?

17:21 *stretched himself out on the boy three times.* The apparent intent of this physical contact was to transfer the bodily warmth and stimulation of the prophet to the child. Elijah's prayer, however, makes it clear that he expected the life of the child to return as an answer to prayer, not as a result of bodily contact. *let this boy's life return to him.* Moved by a faith like that of Abraham (Ro 4:17; Heb 11:19), Elijah prayed for the child's return to life so that the veracity and trustworthiness of God's word might be demonstrated.

17:22 *the boy's life returned to him.* The first instance of raising the dead recorded in Scripture. This non-Israelite widow was granted the supreme covenant blessing, the gift of life rescued from the power of death. This blessing came in the person of her son, the only hope for a widow in ancient society (see 2Ki 4:14; Ru 1:11–12; 4:15–17; Lk 7:12).

17:24 *you are a man of God.* The widow had addressed Elijah as a man of God previously (v. 18), but now she knew in a much more experiential way that he truly was a prophet of the Lord (see note on 12:22). *the word of the LORD from your mouth is the truth.* God used this experience to con-

vince the Phoenician widow that his word was completely reliable. Her confession was one that the Lord's own people in Israel had failed to make.

18:1 *third year.* Apparently of the drought. Later Jewish tradition indicates that the drought lasted three and a half years (cf. Lk 4:25; Jas 5:17), but that probably represents a symbolic number for a drought cut short (half of seven years; see Ge 41:27; 2Ki 8:1). *present yourself to Ahab, and I will send rain on the land.* Elijah's return is not occasioned by repentance in Israel but by the command of the Lord, who in his sovereign grace determined to reveal himself anew to his people.

18:3 *Obadiah.* A common OT name, meaning "servant of the LORD." *in charge of his palace.* See note on 4:6.

18:5 The famine did not move Ahab to repentance (contrast Ahab's response to the famine with that of David years earlier, 2Sa 21:1). But when his military strength seemed to be jeopardized, he scoured the land for food and water (see 10:26; according to the annals of the Assyrian ruler Shalmaneser III, Ahab had a force of at least 2,000 chariots).

18:8 *tell your master, 'Elijah is here.'* This action would publicly identify Obadiah with Elijah in contrast to his previous clandestine support of the prophets sought by Jezebel (see vv. 4,13).

18:12 *I don't know where the Spirit of the LORD may carry you.* Elijah's disappearance earlier and now his sudden reappearance suggested to Obadiah that God's Spirit was miraculously transporting the prophet about (see 2Ki 2:16).

Spirit[h] of the LORD may carry you when I leave you. If I go and tell Ahab and he doesn't find you, he will kill me. Yet I your servant have worshiped the LORD since my youth. [13]Haven't you heard, my lord, what I did while Jezebel was killing the prophets of the LORD? I hid a hundred of the LORD's prophets in two caves, fifty in each, and supplied them with food and water. [14]And now you tell me to go to my master and say, 'Elijah is here.' He will kill me!"

[15]Elijah said, "As the LORD Almighty lives, whom I serve, I will surely present[i] myself to Ahab today."

Elijah on Mount Carmel

[16]So Obadiah went to meet Ahab and told him, and Ahab went to meet Elijah. [17]When he saw Elijah, he said to him, "Is that you, you troubler[j] of Israel?"

[18]"I have not made trouble for Israel," Elijah replied. "But you[k] and your father's family have. You have abandoned[l] the LORD's commands and have followed the Baals. [19]Now summon[m] the people from all over Israel to meet me on Mount Carmel.[n] And bring the four hundred and fifty prophets of Baal and the four hundred prophets of Asherah, who eat at Jezebel's table."[o]

[20]So Ahab sent word throughout all Israel and assembled the prophets on Mount Carmel.[p] [21]Elijah went before the people and said, "How long will you waver[q] between two opinions? If the LORD[r] is God, follow him; but if Baal is God, follow him."

But the people said nothing.

[22]Then Elijah said to them, "I am the only one of the LORD's prophets left,[s] but Baal has four hundred and fifty prophets.[t] [23]Get two bulls for us. Let them choose one for themselves, and let them cut it into pieces and put it on the wood but not set fire to it. I will prepare the other bull and put it on the wood but not set fire to it. [24]Then you call[u] on the name of your god, and I will call on the name of the LORD.[v] The god who answers by fire[w]—he is God."

Then all the people said, "What you say is good."

[25]Elijah said to the prophets of Baal, "Choose one of the bulls and prepare it first, since there are so many of you. Call on the name of your god, but do not light the fire." [26]So they took the bull given them and prepared it.

Then they called[x] on the name of Baal from morning till noon. "O Baal, answer us!" they shouted. But there was no response;[y] no one answered. And they danced around the altar they had made.

[27]At noon Elijah began to taunt them. "Shout louder!" he said. "Surely he is a god! Perhaps he is deep in thought, or busy, or traveling. Maybe he is sleeping and must be awakened."[z] [28]So they shouted louder and slashed[a] themselves with swords and spears, as was their custom, until their blood flowed. [29]Midday passed, and they continued their frantic prophesying until the time for the evening

Cross references

18:12 [h]2Ki 2:16; Eze 3:14; Ac 8:39
18:15 [i]ver 1
18:17 [j]Jos 7:25; 1Sa 14:29; 1Ki 21:20; Jer 38:4
18:18 [k]1Ki 16:33; 21:25 [l]S Dt 31:16
18:19 [m]2Ki 10:19 [n]S Jos 19:26 [o]2Ki 9:22
18:20 [p]2Ki 2:25; 4:25
18:21 [q]Jos 24:15; 2Ki 17:41; Ps 119:113; Mt 6:24 [r]ver 39; Ps 100:3; 118:27
18:22 [s]1Ki 19:10 [t]Jer 2:8; 23:13
18:24 [u]S 1Sa 7:8 [v]S Ge 4:26 [w]S ver 38; S Ex 19:18; S Lev 9:24
18:26 [x]Isa 44:17; 45:20 [y]Ps 115:4-5; 135:16; Isa 41:26,28; 46:7; Jer 10:5; 1Co 8:4; 12:2
18:27 [z]Hab 2:19
18:28 [a]S Lev 19:28

18:13 *Jezebel was killing the prophets.* Possibly in an attempt to please Baal so he would send rain. *prophets of the LORD.* Probably members of the communities of "prophets" that had sprung up in Israel during this time of apostasy (see note on 20:35).

18:17 *you troubler of Israel.* Ahab holds Elijah to account for the drought and charges him with a crime against the state worthy of death (he calls him a "trouble bringer"; see Jos 7:25).

18:18 *You have abandoned the LORD's commands and have followed the Baals.* The source of Israel's trouble was not Elijah or even the drought, but the breach of covenantal loyalty.

18:19 *Mount Carmel.* A high ridge next to the Mediterranean Sea, where the effects of the drought would be most apparent (see Am 1:2) and the power of Baal to nurture life would seem to be strongest. *prophets of Baal . . . prophets of Asherah.* See v. 29 and note. *Asherah.* See note on 14:15. *eat at Jezebel's table.* See note on 2:7.

18:21 *waver.* The Hebrew for this word is the same as that used for "danced" in v. 26 (see note there). Elijah speaks with biting irony: In her religious ambivalence Israel is but engaging in a wild and futile religious "dance." *If the LORD is God, follow him; but if Baal is God, follow him.* Elijah placed a clear choice before the people. He drew a sharp contrast between the worship of the Lord and that of Baal, to elimi-

nate the apostate idea that both deities could be worshiped in a syncretistic way.

18:22 *only one . . . left.* At least the only one to stand boldly and publicly against the king and the prophets of Baal (but see v. 4; 19:10,14; 20:13,28,35; 22:6,8).

18:24 *The god who answers by fire—he is God.* Both the Lord and Baal were said to ride the thunderstorm as their divine chariot (see Ps 104:3 and note); thunder was their voice (see Ps 29:3-9 and note) and lightning their weapon (see Ps 18:14 and note). Elijah's challenge is direct. Cf. Lev 9:24.

18:26 *danced around the altar.* The ecstatic cultic dance was part of the pagan ritual intended to arouse the deity to perform some desired action.

18:27 *deep in thought . . . sleeping.* Elijah ridicules, but as he does he shows knowledge of the Baal myths. *until their blood flowed.* Self-inflicted wounds (causing blood to flow) were symbolic of self-sacrifice as an extreme method of arousing the deity to action. Such mutilation of the body was strictly forbidden in the Mosaic law (Lev 19:28; Dt 14:1).

18:29 *frantic prophesying.* Indicative of ecstatic raving, in which the ritual reached its climax (see notes on 1Sa 10:5; 18:10). *time for the evening sacrifice.* See Ex 29:38-41; Nu 28:3-8. *no response.* Dramatic demonstration of Baal's impotence (see Ps 115:5-8; 135:15-18; Jer 10:5).

sacrifice.[b] But there was no response, no one answered, no one paid attention.[c]

30Then Elijah said to all the people, "Come here to me." They came to him, and he repaired the altar[d] of the LORD, which was in ruins. 31Elijah took twelve stones, one for each of the tribes descended from Jacob, to whom the word of the LORD had come, saying, "Your name shall be Israel."[e] 32With the stones he built an altar in the name[f] of the LORD, and he dug a trench around it large enough to hold two seahs[m] of seed. 33He arranged[g] the wood, cut the bull into pieces and laid it on the wood. Then he said to them, "Fill four large jars with water and pour it on the offering and on the wood."

34"Do it again," he said, and they did it again.

"Do it a third time," he ordered, and they did it the third time. 35The water ran down around the altar and even filled the trench.

36At the time[h] of sacrifice, the prophet Elijah stepped forward and prayed: "O LORD, God of Abraham,[i] Isaac and Israel, let it be known[j] today that you are God in Israel and that I am your servant and have done all these things at your command.[k] 37Answer me, O LORD, answer me, so these people will know[l] that you, O LORD, are God, and that you are turning their hearts back again."

38Then the fire[m] of the LORD fell and burned up the sacrifice, the wood, the stones and the soil, and also licked up the water in the trench.

39When all the people saw this, they fell prostrate[n] and cried, "The LORD—he is God! The LORD—he is God!"[o]

40Then Elijah commanded them, "Seize the prophets of Baal. Don't let anyone get away!" They seized them, and Elijah had them brought down to the Kishon Valley[p] and slaughtered[q] there.

41And Elijah said to Ahab, "Go, eat and drink, for there is the sound of a heavy rain." 42So Ahab went off to eat and drink, but Elijah climbed to the top of Carmel, bent down to the ground and put his face between his knees.[r]

43"Go and look toward the sea," he told his servant. And he went up and looked.

"There is nothing there," he said.

Seven times Elijah said, "Go back."

44The seventh time[s] the servant reported, "A cloud[t] as small as a man's hand is rising from the sea."

So Elijah said, "Go and tell Ahab, 'Hitch up your chariot and go down before the rain stops you.'"

45Meanwhile, the sky grew black with clouds, the wind rose, a heavy rain[u] came on and Ahab rode off to Jezreel.[v] 46The power[w] of the LORD came upon Elijah and, tucking his cloak into his belt,[x] he ran ahead of Ahab all the way to Jezreel.

Elijah Flees to Horeb

19 Now Ahab told Jezebel[y] everything Elijah had done and how he had killed[z] all the prophets with the sword. 2So Jezebel sent a messenger to Elijah to say, "May the gods deal with me, be it ever so severely,[a] if by this time tomor-

Cross references:

18:29
bS Ex 29:41
c2Ki 19:12;
Isa 16:12;
Jer 10:5
18:30 d1Ki 19:10
18:31
eS Ge 17:5;
2Ki 17:34
18:32 fS Dt 18:7;
Col 3:17
18:33 gS Ge 22:9
18:36
hS Ex 29:39,41
iS Ge 24:12;
S Ex 4:5;
Mt 22:32
jS Jos 4:24;
S 1Sa 17:46;
S Ps 46:10
kNu 16:28
18:37 lS Jos 4:24
18:38 mver 24;
S Ex 19:18;
S Lev 9:24;
2Ki 1:10;
1Ch 21:26;
2Ch 7:1; Job 1:16

18:39
nS Lev 9:24
oS ver 21;
S Ps 46:10
18:40 pS Jdg 4:7
qS Ex 22:20;
S Dt 17:12;
S 2Ki 11:18
18:42
rS 1Sa 12:17;
Jas 5:18
18:44 sS Jos 6:15
tLk 12:54
18:45
uS 1Ki 8:36;
Job 37:13
vS 1Sa 29:1;
S Hos 1:4
18:46
wS Jdg 3:10;
S 1Sa 11:6;
Lk 1:35; 4:14
x2Ki 4:29; 9:1
19:1 y1Ki 16:31
zS Ex 22:20
19:2 aS Ru 1:17

m 32 That is, probably about 13 quarts (about 15 liters)

18:30 *altar of the LORD, which was in ruins.* It is possible that the altar had been built by people of the northern ten tribes after the division of the kingdom (see note on 3:2) and that it had been destroyed by the agents of Jezebel (vv. 4,13; 19:10,14).

18:31 *twelve stones, one for each of the tribes.* In this way Elijah called attention to the covenant unity of Israel as the people of God in spite of her political division. What was about to happen concerned the entire nation, not just the northern ten tribes.

18:33 *water.* By drenching the whole installation Elijah showed to all that he was using no tricks.

18:36 *prayed.* Elijah's simple but earnest prayer stands in sharp contrast to the frantic shouts and "dancing" and self-mutilation of the Baal prophets. *God of Abraham, Isaac and Israel.* An appeal to the Lord to remember his ancient covenant with the patriarchs, and to Israel to remember all that the Lord has done for her since the days of her forefathers.

18:38 *fire of the LORD fell.* See note on v. 24.

18:40 *slaughtered there.* Elijah, acting on the authority of the Lord, who sent him, carried out the sentence pronounced in the Mosaic law for prophets of pagan deities (Dt 13:13–18; 17:2–5).

18:41 *sound of a heavy rain.* Now that Baal worship has been struck a devastating blow, there is the promise of rain (see 17:1). Significantly, Ahab takes no action—either to carry out the Mosaic sentence or to halt Elijah.

18:42 *Elijah . . . bent down to the ground and put his face between his knees.* Now that the people had confessed that the Lord alone was God, Elijah prayed for the covenant curse to be lifted (see note on 17:1) by the coming of rain (see 8:35; 2Ch 7:13–14).

18:43 *Seven times.* The number symbolic of completeness.

18:44 *rising from the sea.* Appearing on the western horizon.

18:46 *ran ahead of Ahab all the way to Jezreel.* Divinely energized by extraordinary strength, Elijah ran before Ahab's chariot to Jezreel. This dramatic scene, with the Lord's prophet running before the king and the Lord himself racing behind him riding his mighty thundercloud chariot (see note on v. 24), served as a powerful appeal to Ahab to break once for all with Baal and henceforth to rule as the servant of the Lord.

19:2 *May the gods deal with me, be it ever so severely.* A curse formula (see note on 1Sa 3:17). *one of them.* The dead prophets of Baal (v. 1).

row I do not make your life like that of one of them." [b]

[3]Elijah was afraid[n] and ran[c] for his life. [d] When he came to Beersheba[e] in Judah, he left his servant there, [4]while he himself went a day's journey into the desert. He came to a broom tree, [f] sat down under it and prayed that he might die. "I have had enough, LORD," he said. "Take my life; [g] I am no better than my ancestors." [5]Then he lay down under the tree and fell asleep. [h]

All at once an angel [i] touched him and said, "Get up and eat." [6]He looked around, and there by his head was a cake of bread baked over hot coals, and a jar of water. He ate and drank and then lay down again.

[7]The angel of the LORD came back a second time and touched him and said, "Get

up and eat, for the journey is too much for you." [8]So he got up and ate and drank. Strengthened by that food, he traveled forty[j] days and forty nights until he reached Horeb, [k] the mountain of God. [9]There he went into a cave [l] and spent the night.

The LORD Appears to Elijah

And the word of the LORD came to him: "What are you doing here, Elijah?" [m]

[10]He replied, "I have been very zealous[n] for the LORD God Almighty. The Israelites have rejected your covenant, [o] broken down your altars, [p] and put your prophets to death with the sword. I am the only one left, [q] and now they are trying to kill me too."

[11]The LORD said, "Go out and stand on

19:2 [b]Ps 13:4; Jer 20:10; 26:21; 36:26
19:3 [c]S Ge 31:21 [d]S Ge 19:17 [e]S Jos 19:2
19:4 [f]Job 30:4 [g]S Nu 11:15; Job 6:9; 7:16; 10:1; Ps 69:19; Jer 20:18; Jnh 4:8
19:5 [h]Ge 28:11 [i]S Ge 16:7

19:8 [j]Ex 24:18; Mt 4:2 [k]S Ex 3:1
19:9 [l]S Ex 33:22 [m]S Ge 3:9
19:10 [n]S Nu 25:13; Ac 22:3; Gal 4:18 [o]S Dt 31:16 [p]1Ki 18:30 [q]1Ki 18:22; Jer 5:11; 9:2; Ro 11:3*

[n]3 Or *Elijah saw*

19:3 *Elijah was afraid and ran for his life.* In spite of Elijah's great triumph in the trial on Mount Carmel and the dramatic demonstration that Elijah's God is the Lord of heaven and earth and the source of Israel's blessings, Jezebel is undaunted. Hers is no empty threat, and Ahab has shown that he is either unwilling or unable to restrain her. So Elijah knows that one of the main sources of Israel's present apostasy is still spewing out its poison and that his own life is in danger. *Beersheba.* The southernmost city in Judah (see notes on Ge 21:31; Am 5:5; see also Jdg 20:1).
19:4 *broom tree.* A desert shrub, sometimes large enough to offer some shade. *prayed that he might die.* Cf. Jnh 4:3,8.

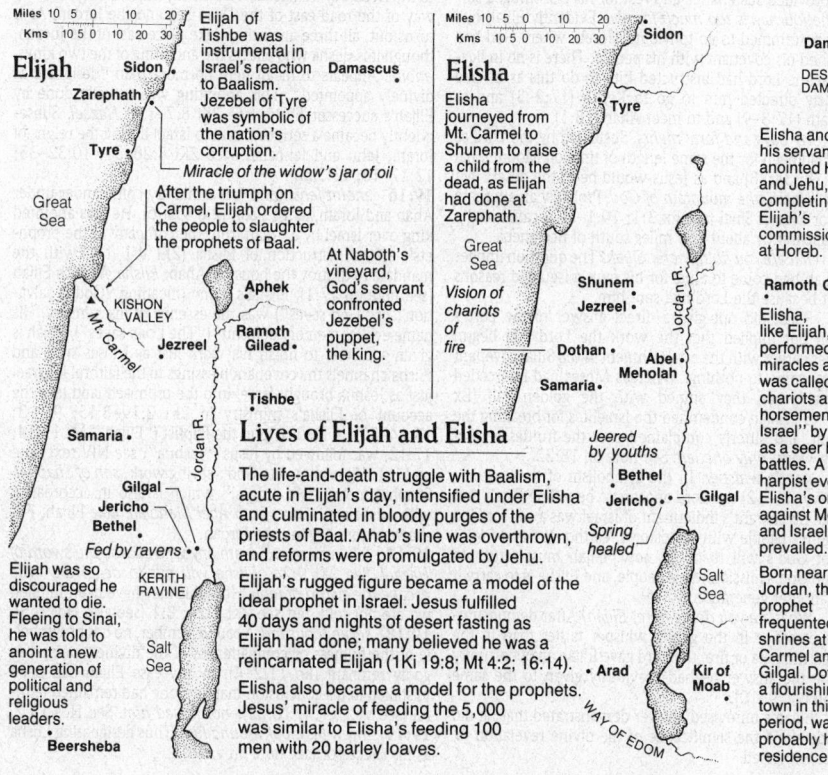

Elijah

Elijah of Tishbe was instrumental in Israel's reaction to Baalism. Jezebel of Tyre was symbolic of the nation's corruption.

Miracle of the widow's jar of oil

After the triumph on Carmel, Elijah ordered the people to slaughter the prophets of Baal.

At Naboth's vineyard, God's servant confronted Jezebel's puppet, the king.

Elijah was so discouraged he wanted to die. Fleeing to Sinai, he was told to anoint a new generation of political and religious leaders.

Elisha

Elisha journeyed from Mt. Carmel to Shunem to raise a child from the dead, as Elijah had done at Zarephath.

Vision of chariots of fire

Lives of Elijah and Elisha

The life-and-death struggle with Baalism, acute in Elijah's day, intensified under Elisha and culminated in bloody purges of the priests of Baal. Ahab's line was overthrown, and reforms were promulgated by Jehu.

Elijah's rugged figure became a model of the ideal prophet in Israel. Jesus fulfilled 40 days and nights of desert fasting as Elijah had done; many believed he was a reincarnated Elijah (1Ki 19:8; Mt 4:2; 16:14).

Elisha also became a model for the prophets. Jesus' miracle of feeding the 5,000 was similar to Elisha's feeding 100 men with 20 barley loaves.

Elisha and his servant anointed Hazael and Jehu, completing Elijah's commission at Horeb.

Elisha, like Elijah, performed miracles and was called "the chariots and horsemen of Israel" by acting as a seer before battles. A harpist evoked Elisha's oracle against Moab, and Israel prevailed.

Born near the Jordan, the prophet frequented shrines at Mt. Carmel and Gilgal. Dothan, a flourishing town in this period, was probably his residence.

the mountain[r] in the presence of the LORD, for the LORD is about to pass by."[s]

Then a great and powerful wind[t] tore the mountains apart and shattered[u] the rocks before the LORD, but the LORD was not in the wind. After the wind there was an earthquake, but the LORD was not in the earthquake. [12]After the earthquake came a fire,[v] but the LORD was not in the fire. And after the fire came a gentle whisper.[w] [13]When Elijah heard it, he pulled his cloak over his face[x] and went out and stood at the mouth of the cave.

Then a voice said to him, "What are you doing here, Elijah?"

[14]He replied, "I have been very zealous for the LORD God Almighty. The Israelites have rejected your covenant, broken down your altars, and put your prophets to death with the sword. I am the only one left,[y] and now they are trying to kill me too."

[15]The LORD said to him, "Go back the

way you came, and go to the Desert of Damascus. When you get there, anoint Hazael[z] king over Aram. [16]Also, anoint[a] Jehu son of Nimshi king over Israel, and anoint Elisha[b] son of Shaphat from Abel Meholah[c] to succeed you as prophet. [17]Jehu will put to death any who escape the sword of Hazael,[d] and Elisha will put to death any who escape the sword of Jehu.[e] [18]Yet I reserve[f] seven thousand in Israel—all whose knees have not bowed down to Baal and all whose mouths have not kissed[g] him."

The Call of Elisha

[19]So Elijah went from there and found Elisha son of Shaphat. He was plowing with twelve yoke of oxen, and he himself was driving the twelfth pair. Elijah went up to him and threw his cloak[h] around him. [20]Elisha then left his oxen and ran after Elijah. "Let me kiss my father and

Cross references (center column)

19:11 [r]Ex 34:2; Mt 17:1-3
[s]Ex 33:19
[t]S Ex 14:21; S 2Ki 2:1 [u]Na 1:6
19:12 [v]S Ex 3:2
[w]ver 11; S 1Sa 14:6; Job 4:16; Zec 4:6; 2Co 12:9
19:13 [x]Ex 3:6
19:14 [y]1Ki 18:22; Ro 11:3*
19:15 [z]2Ki 8:7-15
19:16 [a]2Ki 9:6 [b]ver 21; 2Ki 2:1; 3:11 [c]S Jdg 7:22
19:17 [d]2Ki 8:12, 29; 10:32; 12:17; 13:3,7,22; Am 1:4 [e]Jer 48:44
19:18 [f]Ro 11:4* [g]Hos 13:2
19:19 [h]S Ge 41:42; 2Ki 2:8,14

Elijah concluded that his work was fruitless and consequently that life was not worth living. He had lost his confidence in the triumph of the kingdom of God and was withdrawing from the arena of conflict.

19:7 *angel of the LORD.* See note on Ge 16:7. God in his mercy provided sustenance and rest for his discouraged servant. *the journey is too much for you.* Evidently Elijah had already determined to go to Mount Horeb, where God had established his covenant with his people. There is no indication that the Lord had instructed him to do this as he had previously directed him to go to Kerith (17:2–3) and to Zarephath (17:8–9) and to meet Ahab (18:1).

19:8 *forty days and forty nights.* Sustained by the Lord as Moses had been for the same length of time on Mount Sinai (Ex 24:18; 34:28) and as Jesus would be in the desert (Mt 4:2,11). *Horeb, the mountain of God.* Probably an alternate name for Mount Sinai (see Ex 3:1; 19:1–3), located in the desert apparently about 250 miles south of Beersheba.

19:9 *What are you doing here, Elijah?* The question implies that Elijah had come to Sinai for his own misguided reasons and not because the Lord had sent him.

19:10 Elijah did not give a direct answer to the Lord's question but implied that the work the Lord had begun centuries earlier with the establishment of the Sinai covenant had now come to nothing. Whereas Moses had interceded for Israel when they sinned with the golden calf (Ex 32:11–13), Elijah condemned the Israelites for breaking the covenant, and bitterly complained over the fruitlessness of his own work. *only one left.* See note on 18:22.

19:12 *gentle whisper.* In the symbolism of these occurrences (vv. 11–12) the Lord appears to be telling Elijah that although his servant's indictment of Israel was a call for God to judge his people with windstorm, earthquake and fire, it was not God's will to do so now. Elijah must return to continue God's mission to his people, and Elisha is to carry it on for another generation (v. 16).

19:13 *What are you doing here, Elijah?* After demonstrating his presence in the gentle whisper rather than in the wind, earthquake or fire, the Lord gave Elijah an opportunity to revise the answer he had previously given to the same question (vv. 9–10).

19:14 Elijah's unrevised answer demonstrated that he did not understand the significance of the divine revelation he had just witnessed.

19:15 *The LORD said to him.* Giving instructions to Elijah that revealed his sovereign power over people and nations. Even though Israel would experience divine judgment through Hazael, Jehu and Elisha, God would continue to preserve a remnant faithful to himself among the people. *go to the Desert of Damascus.* Apparently Elijah is to go back by way of the road east of the Dead Sea and the Jordan. As it turns out, all three anointings take place east of the Jordan, though it is Elisha who effects the anointing of the two kings. *anoint.* Appears to mean here no more than "designate as divinely appointed." This anointing was actually done by Elijah's successor Elisha (see 2Ki 8:7–15). *Hazael.* Subsequently became a serious threat to Israel during the reigns of Joram, Jehu and Jehoahaz (see 2Ki 8:28–29; 10:32–33; 12:17–18; 13:3,22).

19:16 *anoint Jehu.* Jehu was a military commander under Ahab and Joram, Ahab's son (2Ki 9:5–6). He was anointed king over Israel by a "man from the company of the prophets" at the instruction of Elisha (2Ki 9:1–16), with the mandate to destroy the house of Ahab. *Elisha.* As with Elijah (see note on 17:1), Elisha's name (meaning "God is salvation" or "God saves") was the essence of his ministry. His name evokes memory of Joshua ("The LORD saves"). Elijah is given someone to finish his work just as Moses was, and Elisha channels the covenant blessings to the faithful in Israel just as Joshua brought Israel into the promised land (see the account of Elisha's ministry in 2Ki 2:19–8:15; 9:1–3; 13:14–20). In the NT John the Baptist ("Elijah," Mt 11:14; 17:12) was followed by Jesus ("Joshua"; see NIV text note on Mt 1:21) to complete God's saving work. *son of Shaphat.* Shaphat means "He judges," which is also in accordance with Elisha's ministry. *from Abel Meholah.* Like Elijah, Elisha was from beyond the Jordan.

19:17 *Jehu will put to death any who escape the sword of Hazael.* See 2Ki 9:24. *Elisha will put to death any who escape the sword of Jehu.* How this may have been fulfilled we are not told, but see 2Ki 2:24; 8:1 (see also Hos 6:5).

19:18 *seven thousand.* A round number, no doubt symbolic of the fullness or completeness of the divinely preserved godly remnant (Ro 11:2–4). In any case Elijah had been mistaken in his conclusion that he alone had remained faithful (see vv. 10,14; 18:22). *not kissed him.* See Hos 13:2.

19:19 *threw his cloak around him.* Thus designating Elisha as his successor (see note on v. 16).

mother good-by," *i* he said, "and then I will come with you."

"Go back," Elijah replied. "What have I done to you?"

21So Elisha left him and went back. He took his yoke of oxen *j* and slaughtered them. He burned the plowing equipment to cook the meat and gave it to the people, and they ate. Then he set out to follow Elijah and became his attendant. *k*

Ben-Hadad Attacks Samaria

20 Now Ben-Hadad *l* king of Aram mustered his entire army. Accompanied by thirty-two kings with their horses and chariots, he went up and besieged Samaria *m* and attacked it. 2He sent messengers into the city to Ahab king of Israel, saying, "This is what Ben-Hadad says: 3'Your silver and gold are mine, and the best of your wives and children are mine.' "

4The king of Israel answered, "Just as you say, my lord the king. I and all I have are yours."

5The messengers came again and said, "This is what Ben-Hadad says: 'I sent to demand your silver and gold, your wives and your children. 6But about this time tomorrow I am going to send my officials to search your palace and the houses of your officials. They will seize everything you value and carry it away.' "

7The king of Israel summoned all the elders *n* of the land and said to them, "See how this man is looking for trouble! *o* When he sent for my wives and my children, my silver and my gold, I did not refuse him."

8The elders and the people all answered, "Don't listen to him or agree to his demands."

9So he replied to Ben-Hadad's messengers, "Tell my lord the king, 'Your servant will do all you demanded the first time, but this demand I cannot meet.' " They left and took the answer back to Ben-Hadad.

10Then Ben-Hadad sent another message to Ahab: "May the gods deal with me, be it ever so severely, if enough dust *p* remains in Samaria to give each of my men a handful."

11The king of Israel answered, "Tell him: 'One who puts on his armor should not boast *q* like one who takes it off.' "

12Ben-Hadad heard this message while he and the kings were drinking *r* in their tents, *o* and he ordered his men: "Prepare to attack." So they prepared to attack the city.

Ahab Defeats Ben-Hadad

13Meanwhile a prophet *s* came to Ahab king of Israel and announced, "This is what the LORD says: 'Do you see this vast army? I will give it into your hand today, and then you will know *t* that I am the LORD.' "

14"But who will do this?" asked Ahab.

The prophet replied, "This is what the LORD says: 'The young officers of the provincial commanders will do it.' "

"And who will start *u* the battle?" he asked.

The prophet answered, "You will."

15So Ahab summoned the young officers of the provincial commanders, 232 men.

Cross references (center column)

19:20 *l* Lk 9:61
19:21 *j* S 1Sa 6:14
  k S ver 16
20:1 *l* S 1Ki 15:18
  m S 1Ki 13:32
20:7 *n* 1Sa 11:3
  o 2Ki 5:7

20:10 *p* S 2Sa 22:43
20:11 *q* Pr 27:1;
Jer 9:23; Am 2:14
20:12 *r* S 1Ki 16:9
20:13 *s* S Jdg 6:8
  t S Ex 6:7
20:14 *u* S Jdg 1:1

o 12 Or in Succoth; also in verse 16

19:21 *slaughtered them . . . burned the plowing equipment.* Elisha's break with his past vocation was complete, though he obviously came from a wealthy family. *attendant.* In Hebrew the same designation as used for Joshua's relationship to Moses ("aide," Ex 24:13; 33:11).

20:1 *Ben-Hadad king of Aram.* Chronological considerations suggest that this was Ben-Hadad II, either a son or a grandson of Ben-Hadad I, who had ruled Aram as early as 900–895 B.C. (see notes on 15:9–10,18–20,33). The events of this chapter span parts of two years (see vv. 22–26) followed by three years of peace between Israel and Aram (see 22:1). Ahab died at the conclusion of the three years of peace in a battle against the Arameans (22:37) in 853. This means that the events of this chapter are to be dated c. 857. *thirty-two kings.* Tribal chieftains or city-state kings who were vassals of Ben-Hadad II.

20:4 *I and all I have are yours.* Ahab's submission to Ben-Hadad's demand suggests that Israel saw little hope for the possibility of a military victory over the Aramean forces. The negotiated settlement would end the siege on Samaria, spare Ahab's life and avoid the plundering of the city.

20:6 *I am going to send my officials to search your palace and the houses of your officials.* Ben-Hadad's new demand

required the surrender of the city to his forces.

20:9 *this demand I cannot meet.* Ahab replied in language conceding Ben-Hadad's superiority ("my lord the king, 'Your servant . . . ' ") but was adamant in refusing to surrender the city.

20:10 *May the gods deal with me, be it ever so severely.* A curse formula (see note on 1Sa 3:17).

20:11 *'One who puts on his armor should not boast like one who takes it off.'* A saying similar to the familiar "Don't count your chickens before they hatch."

20:13 *you will know that I am the LORD.* Although Ahab had not sought God's help in the crisis confronting the city, the Lord graciously chose to reveal himself yet another time (see 18:36–37) to the king and people, this time through a deliverance.

20:14 *young officers of the provincial commanders.* See note on 16:27. Organizational details of the provincial government of the northern kingdom are unknown.

20:15 *232 men . . . 7,000 in all.* Not a large military force (though a significant number for a city under siege) but one of fitting size for demonstrating that the imminent victory was from the Lord rather than from Israel's own military superiority (cf. Jdg 7:2).

Then he assembled the rest of the Israelites, 7,000 in all. 16They set out at noon while Ben-Hadad and the 32 kings allied with him were in their tents getting drunk.v 17The young officers of the provincial commanders went out first.

Now Ben-Hadad had dispatched scouts, who reported, "Men are advancing from Samaria."

18He said, "If they have come out for peace, take them alive; if they have come out for war, take them alive."

19The young officers of the provincial commanders marched out of the city with the army behind them 20and each one struck down his opponent. At that, the Arameans fled, with the Israelites in pursuit. But Ben-Hadad king of Aram escaped on horseback with some of his horsemen. 21The king of Israel advanced and overpowered the horses and chariots and inflicted heavy losses on the Arameans.

22Afterward, the prophetw came to the king of Israel and said, "Strengthen your position and see what must be done, because next springx the king of Aram will attack you again."

23Meanwhile, the officials of the king of Aram advised him, "Their gods are godsy of the hills. That is why they were too strong for us. But if we fight them on the plains, surely we will be stronger than they. 24Do this: Remove all the kings from their commands and replace them with other officers. 25You must also raise an army like the one you lost—horse for horse and chariot for chariot—so we can

fight Israel on the plains. Then surely we will be stronger than they." He agreed with them and acted accordingly.

26The next springz Ben-Hadad mustered the Arameans and went up to Apheka to fight against Israel. 27When the Israelites were also mustered and given provisions, they marched out to meet them. The Israelites camped opposite them like two small flocks of goats, while the Arameans covered the countryside.b

28The man of God came up and told the king of Israel, "This is what the LORD says: 'Because the Arameans think the LORD is a god of the hills and not a godc of the valleys, I will deliver this vast army into your hands, and you will knowd that I am the LORD.' "

29For seven days they camped opposite each other, and on the seventh day the battle was joined. The Israelites inflicted a hundred thousand casualties on the Aramean foot soldiers in one day. 30The rest of them escaped to the city of Aphek,e where the wall collapsedf on twenty-seven thousand of them. And Ben-Hadad fled to the city and hidg in an inner room.

31His officials said to him, "Look, we have heard that the kings of the house of Israel are merciful.h Let us go to the king of Israel with sackclothi around our waists and ropes around our heads. Perhaps he will spare your life."

32Wearing sackcloth around their waists and ropes around their heads, they went to the king of Israel and said, "Your servant Ben-Hadad says: 'Please let me live.' "

Cross references (center column)

20:16 vS 1Ki 16:9
20:22 wS Jdg 6:8
xS 2Sa 11:1
20:23 yver 28; Isa 36:20; Ro 1:21-23

20:26 zS 2Sa 11:1 aver 30; S 1Sa 4:1; 2Ki 13:17
20:27 bJdg 6:6; S 1Sa 13:6
20:28 cS ver 23 dS Ex 6:7; Jer 16:19-21
20:30 eS ver 26 fPs 62:4; Isa 26:21; 30:13 g1Ki 22:25
20:31 hJob 41:3 iS Ge 37:34

20:20 *each one struck down his opponent.* Apparently they were met by a small advance force like their own (see 2Sa 2:15–16). *escaped on horseback with some of his horsemen.* Since fighting on horseback did not come until later, reference must be to chariot horses and charioteers. After their defeat, the Arameans seem to have withdrawn to Damascus.
20:22 *the king of Aram will attack you again.* The anonymous prophet (see v. 13) warned Ahab against undue self-confidence. The prophet's announcement of an impending renewed attack by Ben-Hadad should have driven Ahab to more complete reliance on the God who had revealed himself on Mount Carmel and in the recent military victory.
20:23 *gods of the hills.* An expression of the pagan idea that a deity's power extended only over the limited area of his particular jurisdiction. *That is why they were too strong for us.* The Arameans believed that the outcome of military conflicts depended on the relative strength of the gods of the opposing forces rather than on the inherent strength of the two armies. For this reason, their strategy was to fight the next battle in a way that advantageously maximized the supposed strengths and weaknesses of the deities involved.
20:26 *Aphek.* Presumably the Aphek located a few miles east of the Sea of Galilee. The battle apparently took place in the Jordan Valley near the juncture of the Yarmuk and Jordan rivers.

20:28 *man of God.* Apparently the same prophet mentioned in vv. 13,22. *you will know that I am the LORD.* See note on v. 13. God will again demonstrate that he is the sovereign ruler over all nature and history and that the pagan nature deities are powerless before him.
20:29 *a hundred thousand casualties.* Probably includes all those who were driven from the field and the Aramean encampment, including support personnel.
20:30 *wall collapsed.* The God of Israel not only gave Israel's army a victory in battle but also caused an additional disaster to fall on the Aramean army. *twenty-seven thousand.* Aphek was certainly not so large a city that its wall could literally have collapsed on so many. Perhaps this is the number of troops that had taken refuge in Aphek and were left defenseless when the city walls gave way.
20:31 *kings of the house of Israel are merciful.* The Arameans recognized that Israel's kings were different from, e.g., the ruthless Assyrian kings. *sackcloth . . . ropes.* Perhaps here symbolic of humility and submission.
20:32 *Your servant.* In the diplomatic language of the time, Ben-Hadad acknowledged his inferiority and subordination to Ahab by designating himself Ahab's servant (see note on v. 9). *my brother.* Ahab disregarded Ben-Hadad's concession and responded in terminology used by rulers who considered themselves equals (see 9:13). In doing this, Ahab gave much more than Ben-Hadad had asked or expected.

The king answered, "Is he still alive? He is my brother."

[33]The men took this as a good sign and were quick to pick up his word. "Yes, your brother Ben-Hadad!" they said.

"Go and get him," the king said. When Ben-Hadad came out, Ahab had him come up into his chariot.

[34]"I will return the cities[j] my father took from your father," Ben-Hadad[k] offered. "You may set up your own market areas[l] in Damascus,[m] as my father did in Samaria."

Ahab said,[u] "On the basis of a treaty[n] I will set you free." So he made a treaty with him, and let him go.

A Prophet Condemns Ahab

[35]By the word of the LORD one of the sons of the prophets[o] said to his companion, "Strike me with your weapon," but the man refused.[p]

[36]So the prophet said, "Because you have not obeyed the LORD, as soon as you leave me a lion[q] will kill you." And after the man went away, a lion found him and killed him.

[37]The prophet found another man and said, "Strike me, please." So the man struck him and wounded him. [38]Then the prophet went and stood by the road waiting for the king. He disguised himself with his headband down over his eyes. [39]As the king passed by, the prophet called out to him, "Your servant went into the thick of the battle, and someone came to me with a captive and said, 'Guard this man. If he is missing, it will be your life for his life,[r] or you must pay a talent[p] of silver.' [40]While your servant was busy here and there, the man disappeared."

"That is your sentence,"[s] the king of Israel said. "You have pronounced it yourself."

[41]Then the prophet quickly removed the headband from his eyes, and the king of Israel recognized him as one of the prophets. [42]He said to the king, "This is what the LORD says: 'You[t] have set free a man I had determined should die.[qu] Therefore it is your life for his life,[v] your people for his people.' " [43]Sullen and angry,[w] the king of Israel went to his palace in Samaria.

Naboth's Vineyard

21 Some time later there was an incident involving a vineyard belonging to Naboth[x] the Jezreelite. The vineyard was in Jezreel,[y] close to the palace of Ahab king of Samaria. [2]Ahab said to Naboth, "Let me have your vineyard to use for a vegetable garden, since it is close

---

Cross references (center column):

20:34 /1Ki 15:20
kS Ge 10:22
l2Sa 8:6
mS Ge 14:15;
Jer 49:23-27
nS Ex 23:32
20:35
oS 1Sa 10:5;
Am 7:14
pS 1Ki 13:21
20:36 q1Ki 13:24
20:39 rS Jos 2:14
20:40 s2Sa 12:5;
S 14:13
20:42 tS 2Sa 12:7
uJer 48:10
vS Jos 2:14
20:43 w1Ki 21:4
21:1 x2Ki 9:21
yS 1Sa 29:1;
2Ki 10:1

p39 That is, about 75 pounds (about 34 kilograms)
q42 The Hebrew term refers to the irrevocable giving over of things or persons to the LORD, often by totally destroying them.

20:33 *come up into his chariot.* Not the treatment normally accorded a defeated military opponent.

20:34 *cities my father took from your father.* Perhaps Ramoth Gilead (see 22:3) along with some of the cities Ben-Hadad I had taken from Baasha (15:20) at an even earlier time. *your own market areas.* Outlets for engaging in the lucrative international trade—a distinct economic advantage; usually such privileges were a jealously guarded local monopoly. *made a treaty with him, and let him go.* A parity treaty (a peace treaty between equals) that included among its provisions the political and trade agreements proposed by Ben-Hadad.

20:35 *sons of the prophets.* An expression designating members of prophetic companies (see 2Ki 2:3,5,7,15; 4:1, 38; 5:22; 6:1; 9:1). "Son" is not to be understood here as "male child" or "descendant" but as the member of a group. These companies of prophets were apparently religious communities that sprang up in the face of general indifference and apostasy for the purpose of mutual edification and the cultivation of the experience of God. It seems likely that they were known as prophets because their religious practices (sometimes ecstatic) were called prophesying (see 18:29; Nu 11:25–27; 1Sa 10:5–6,10–11; 18:10; 19:20–24)—to be distinguished from "prophet" in the sense of one bringing ("prophesying") a word from the Lord. The relationship of the Lord's great prophets (such as Samuel, Elijah and Elisha) to these communities was understandably a close one, the Lord's prophets probably being their spiritual mentors.

20:36 *as soon as you leave me a lion will kill you.* A penalty reminiscent of what happened to the man of God from Judah (13:23–24).

20:39 *talent.* See NIV text note. Because few soldiers could have paid such a large sum, it would appear to Ahab that the man's life was at stake.

20:40 *That is your sentence.* Ahab refused to grant clemency. Little did he know that he was pronouncing his own death sentence (cf. the similar technique used by Nathan the prophet, 2Sa 12:1–12).

20:42 *a man I had determined should die.* See NIV text note and notes on Lev 27:28; Jos 6:17. It is not clear whether Ahab violated a previous revelation or erred by simply neglecting to inquire of the Lord before releasing Ben-Hadad. In any case, the Lord had given Ben-Hadad into Ahab's hand (see v. 28), and Ahab was responsible to the Lord for his custody. *your life for his life, your people for his people.* Because Ahab sinned in his official capacity as king, the sentence fell not only on Ahab personally but also on the people of the northern kingdom. Ahab died in battle against the Arameans (22:29–39), and Israel was severely humiliated by them during the reigns of Jehu and Jehoahaz (2Ki 10:32; 13:3).

21:1 *close to the palace of Ahab.* Ahab maintained a residence in Jezreel in addition to his official palace in Samaria (see 18:45; 2Ki 9:30). *Samaria.* The entire northern kingdom is here represented by its capital city (see note on 16:24).

21:2 *Let me have your vineyard.* Because royal power in Israel was limited by covenantal law (see Dt 17:14–20; 1Sa 10:25), Ahab was unable simply to confiscate privately held land, as was customary with Canaanite kings (see note on v. 7; see also 1Sa 8:9–17).

to my palace. In exchange I will give you a better vineyard or, if you prefer, I will pay you whatever it is worth."

³But Naboth replied, "The LORD forbid that I should give you the inheritance*z* of my fathers."

⁴So Ahab went home, sullen and angry*a* because Naboth the Jezreelite had said, "I will not give you the inheritance of my fathers." He lay on his bed sulking and refused*b* to eat.

⁵His wife Jezebel came in and asked him, "Why are you so sullen? Why won't you eat?"

⁶He answered her, "Because I said to Naboth the Jezreelite, 'Sell me your vineyard; or if you prefer, I will give you another vineyard in its place.' But he said, 'I will not give you my vineyard.'"

⁷Jezebel his wife said, "Is this how you act as king over Israel? Get up and eat! Cheer up. I'll get you the vineyard*c* of Naboth the Jezreelite."

⁸So she wrote letters*d* in Ahab's name, placed his seal*e* on them, and sent them to the elders and nobles who lived in Naboth's city with him. ⁹In those letters she wrote:

"Proclaim a day of fasting and seat Naboth in a prominent place among the people. ¹⁰But seat two scoundrels*f* opposite him and have them testify that he has cursed*g* both God and the king. Then take him out and stone him to death."

¹¹So the elders and nobles who lived in Naboth's city did as Jezebel directed in the letters she had written to them. ¹²They proclaimed a fast*h* and seated Naboth in a

prominent place among the people. ¹³Then two scoundrels came and sat opposite him and brought charges against Naboth before the people, saying, "Naboth has cursed both God and the king." So they took him outside the city and stoned him to death.*i* ¹⁴Then they sent word to Jezebel: "Naboth has been stoned and is dead."

¹⁵As soon as Jezebel heard that Naboth had been stoned to death, she said to Ahab, "Get up and take possession of the vineyard*j* of Naboth the Jezreelite that he refused to sell you. He is no longer alive, but dead." ¹⁶When Ahab heard that Naboth was dead, he got up and went down to take possession of Naboth's vineyard.

¹⁷Then the word of the LORD came to Elijah the Tishbite: ¹⁸"Go down to meet Ahab king of Israel, who rules in Samaria. He is now in Naboth's vineyard, where he has gone to take possession of it. ¹⁹Say to him, 'This is what the LORD says: Have you not murdered a man and seized his property?'*k* Then say to him, 'This is what the LORD says: In the place where dogs licked up Naboth's blood,*l* dogs*m* will lick up your blood—yes, yours!'"

²⁰Ahab said to Elijah, "So you have found me, my enemy!"*n*

"I have found you," he answered, "because you have sold*o* yourself to do evil in the eyes of the LORD. ²¹I am going to bring disaster on you. I will consume your descendants and cut off from Ahab every last male*p* in Israel—slave or free.*q* ²²I will make your house*r* like that of Jeroboam son of Nebat and that of Baasha son of Ahijah, because you have provoked me to anger and have caused Israel to sin.'*s*

21:3
z S Lev 25:23
21:4 *a* 1Ki 20:43
b 1Sa 28:23
21:7 *c* S 1Sa 8:14
21:8 *d* 2Sa 11:14
e S Ge 38:18
21:10
f S Dt 13:13;
Ac 6:11
g S Ex 22:28;
Lev 24:15-16
21:12 *h* Isa 58:4

21:13
i S Lev 24:16
21:15 *j* S 1Sa 8:14
21:19 *k* Job 24:6;
31:39 *l* 2Ki 9:26;
Ps 9:12; Isa 14:20
m 1Ki 22:38;
Ps 68:23; Jer 15:3
21:20
n S 1Ki 18:17
o 2Ki 17:17;
Ro 7:14
21:21 *p* Jdg 9:5;
2Ki 10:7
q S Dt 32:36
21:22 *r* 1Ki 16:3
s S 1Ki 12:30

21:3 Naboth's refusal to dispose of his land was based on the conviction that the land was the Lord's, that he had granted a perpetual lease to each Israelite family and that this lease was to be jealously preserved as the family's permanent inheritance in the promised land.

21:7 *Is this how you act as king over Israel?* A sarcastic remark of incredulity spoken by one accustomed to the despotic practices of the Phoenician and Canaanite kings, who would not hesitate a moment to use their power to satisfy personal interests (contrast the attitude and practice of Samuel in the exercise of his civil power, 1Sa 12:3–4).

21:9 *Proclaim a day of fasting.* Jezebel attempted to create the impression that a disaster threatened the people that could be averted only if they would humble themselves before the Lord and remove any person whose sin had brought God's judgment on them (cf. Jdg 20:26; 1Sa 7:5–6; 2Ch 20:2–4).

21:10 *two.* Mosaic law required two witnesses for capital offenses (Nu 35:30; Dt 17:6; 19:15). *scoundrels.* See note on Dt 13:13. *have them testify.* The entire scenario was designed to give an appearance of legitimate judicial procedure (see Ex 20:16; 23:7; Lev 19:16). *he has cursed both*

God and the king. For this the Mosaic law prescribed death by stoning (Lev 24:15–16).

21:13 *outside the city.* In accordance with Mosaic law (Lev 24:14; Nu 15:35–36). Naboth was stoned on his own field (compare v. 19 with 2Ki 9:21,26), and his sons were stoned with him (see 2Ki 9:26; cf. the case of Achan, Jos 7:24–25), thus also eliminating his heirs.

21:19 *Have you not murdered a man and seized his property?* Ahab's willing compliance with Jezebel's scheme made him guilty of murder and theft. *In the place where dogs licked up Naboth's blood, dogs will lick up your blood.* Ahab's subsequent repentance (v. 29) occasioned the postponement of certain aspects of this prophecy until the time of his son Joram, whose body was thrown on the field of Naboth (2Ki 9:25–26). Ahab himself was killed in battle at Ramoth Gilead (22:29–37) and his body brought to Samaria, where the dogs licked the blood being washed from his chariot (22:38).

21:21 *slave or free.* See note on 14:10.

21:22 *like that of Jeroboam.* See 14:10; 15:28–30. *that of Baasha.* See 16:3–4,11–13.

23"And also concerning Jezebel the LORD says: 'Dogs^t will devour Jezebel by the wall of^r Jezreel.'

24"Dogs^u will eat those belonging to Ahab who die in the city, and the birds of the air^v will feed on those who die in the country.

25(There was never^w a man like Ahab, who sold himself to do evil in the eyes of the LORD, urged on by Jezebel his wife. 26He behaved in the vilest manner by going after idols, like the Amorites^x the LORD drove out before Israel.)

27When Ahab heard these words, he tore his clothes, put on sackcloth^y and fasted. He lay in sackcloth and went around meekly.^{z}

28Then the word of the LORD came to Elijah the Tishbite: 29"Have you noticed how Ahab has humbled himself before me? Because he has humbled^a himself, I will not bring this disaster in his day,^{b} but I will bring it on his house in the days of his son."^{c}

Micaiah Prophesies Against Ahab

22:1–28pp — 2Ch 18:1–27

22 For three years there was no war between Aram and Israel. 2But in the third year Jehoshaphat king of Judah went down to see the king of Israel. 3The king of Israel had said to his officials, "Don't you know that Ramoth Gilead^d belongs to us and yet we are doing nothing to retake it from the king of Aram?"

4So he asked Jehoshaphat, "Will you go

with me to fight^e against Ramoth Gilead?"

Jehoshaphat replied to the king of Israel, "I am as you are, my people as your people, my horses as your horses." 5But Jehoshaphat also said to the king of Israel, "First seek the counsel^f of the LORD."

6So the king of Israel brought together the prophets—about four hundred men—and asked them, "Shall I go to war against Ramoth Gilead, or shall I refrain?"

"Go,"^{g} they answered, "for the Lord will give it into the king's hand."^{h}

7But Jehoshaphat asked, "Is there not a prophet^i of the LORD here whom we can inquire^j of?"

8The king of Israel answered Jehoshaphat, "There is still one man through whom we can inquire of the LORD, but I hate^k him because he never prophesies anything good^l about me, but always bad. He is Micaiah son of Imlah."

"The king should not say that," Jehoshaphat replied.

9So the king of Israel called one of his officials and said, "Bring Micaiah son of Imlah at once."

10Dressed in their royal robes, the king of Israel and Jehoshaphat king of Judah were sitting on their thrones at the threshing floor^m by the entrance of the gate of Samaria, with all the prophets prophesying before them. 11Now Zedekiah^n son of Kenaanah had made iron horns^o and he

Cross references

21:23 ^{r}2Ki 9:10, 34-36
21:24 ^{u}1Ki 14:11
^{v}S Ge 40:19; S Dt 28:26
21:25 ^{w}S 1Ki 14:9; S 16:33
21:26 ^{x}S Ge 15:16
21:27 ^{y}S Ge 37:34; S Jer 4:8
^{z}Isa 38:15
21:29 ^{a}S Ex 10:3
^{b}S Ex 32:14; 2Ki 22:20
^{c}Ex 20:5; 2Ki 9:26; 10:6-10
22:3 ^{d}S Dt 4:43

22:4 ^{e}2Ki 3:7
22:5 ^{f}Ex 33:7; 2Ki 3:11; Job 38:2; Ps 32:8; 73:24; 107:11
22:6 ^{g}S Jdg 18:6
^{h}S 1Ki 13:18
22:7 ^{i}Dt 18:15; 2Ki 3:11; 5:8
^{j}S Nu 27:21; 2Ki 3:11
22:8 ^{k}Am 5:10
^{l}ver 13; Isa 5:20; 30:10; Jer 23:17
22:10 ^{m}S Jdg 6:37
22:11 ^{n}ver 24
^{o}Dt 33:17; Jer 27:2; 28:10; Zec 1:18-21

^{r}23 Most Hebrew manuscripts; a few Hebrew manuscripts, Vulgate and Syriac (see also 2 Kings 9:26) *the plot of ground at*

21:24 See notes on 14:11; 16:4.
21:25 *urged on by Jezebel.* See 16:31; 18:4; 19:1–2; 21:7.
21:26 *Amorites.* Here a designation for the entire pre-Israelite population of Canaan (see Ge 15:16; Dt 1:7).
21:27 *sackcloth.* See note on Ge 37:34.
21:29 *in the days of his son.* The judgment was postponed but not rescinded (see note on v. 19).
22:1 *three years.* See note on 20:1. *no war between Aram and Israel.* The annals of the Assyrian ruler Shalmaneser III (859–824 B.C.) record the participation of both "Ahab the Israelite" and Hadadezer (Ben-Hadad) of Damascus in a coalition of 12 rulers that fought against Assyrian forces at Qarqar on the Orontes River in 853. According to the Assyrian records, Ahab contributed 2,000 chariots and 10,000 foot soldiers to the allied forces. Assyrian claims of victory appear exaggerated since they withdrew and did not venture westward again for four or five years.
22:2 *Jehoshaphat king of Judah went down to see the king of Israel.* Perhaps to congratulate him on the success of the western alliance against the Assyrian threat (see notes on v. 1; 2Ch 18:2).
22:3 *Ramoth Gilead.* Located near the Yarmuk River in Transjordan; an Israelite city since the days of Moses (see 4:13; Dt 4:43; Jos 20:8). *belongs to us.* Israel could lay claim to Ramoth Gilead also by virtue of the treaty concluded with Ben-Hadad a few years earlier (see 20:34), the provi-

sions of which he had apparently failed to honor.
22:4 *Will you go with me . . . ?* Even though Ahab had just been allied with the Arameans against the Assyrians, now that the Assyrian threat was over he did not hesitate to seize an opportunity to free Ramoth Gilead from Aramean control. *I am as you are, my people as your people, my horses as your horses.* Jehoshaphat was later to be condemned by the prophet Jehu (2Ch 19:2) for violating the Lord's will by joining forces with Ahab. In this alliance, Jehoshaphat completely reversed the policy of his father Asa, who had entered into an alliance with the Arameans against Baasha of the northern kingdom (see 15:17–23).
22:5 *First seek the counsel of the LORD.* Jehoshaphat hesitated to proceed with the planned action without the assurance of the Lord's favor (see 1Sa 23:1–4; 2Sa 2:1).
22:6 *prophets.* No doubt associated with the paganized worship at Bethel (see notes on 12:28–29), they exercised their "office" by proclaiming messages designed to please the king (see Am 7:10–13).
22:7 *Is there not a prophet of the LORD here . . . ?* Jehoshaphat recognized that the 400 prophets were not to be relied on (see Eze 13:2–3) and asked for consultation with a true prophet of the Lord.
22:8 *never prophesies anything good.* Ahab's assessment of a prophet depended on whether his message was favorable to him (see 18:17; 21:20).
22:11 *Zedekiah.* Evidently the spokesman for the 400

declared, "This is what the LORD says:
'With these you will gore the Arameans
until they are destroyed.' "
12 All the other prophets were prophesying the same thing. "Attack Ramoth Gilead
and be victorious," they said, "for the
LORD will give it into the king's hand."
13 The messenger who had gone to summon Micaiah said to him, "Look, as one
man the other prophets are predicting success for the king. Let your word agree with
theirs, and speak favorably."[p]
14 But Micaiah said, "As surely as the
LORD lives, I can tell him only what the
LORD tells me."[q]
15 When he arrived, the king asked him,
"Micaiah, shall we go to war against
Ramoth Gilead, or shall I refrain?"
"Attack and be victorious," he answered, "for the LORD will give it into the
king's hand."
16 The king said to him, "How many
times must I make you swear to tell me
nothing but the truth in the name of the
LORD?"
17 Then Micaiah answered, "I saw all Israel scattered[r] on the hills like sheep without a shepherd,[s] and the LORD said,
'These people have no master. Let each
one go home in peace.' "
18 The king of Israel said to Jehoshaphat,
"Didn't I tell you that he never prophesies
anything good about me, but only bad?"
19 Micaiah continued, "Therefore hear
the word of the LORD: I saw the LORD sitting on his throne[t] with all the host[u] of
heaven standing around him on his right
and on his left. 20 And the LORD said, 'Who
will entice Ahab into attacking Ramoth
Gilead and going to his death there?'
"One suggested this, and another that.
21 Finally, a spirit came forward, stood before the LORD and said, 'I will entice him.'
22 " 'By what means?' the LORD asked.
" 'I will go out and be a lying[v] spirit in
the mouths of all his prophets,' he said.
" 'You will succeed in enticing him,'
said the LORD. 'Go and do it.'
23 "So now the LORD has put a lying[w]
spirit in the mouths of all these prophets[x]
of yours. The LORD has decreed disaster[y]
for you."
24 Then Zedekiah[z] son of Kenaanah
went up and slapped[a] Micaiah in the face.
"Which way did the spirit from[s] the LORD
go when he went from me to speak[b] to
you?" he asked.
25 Micaiah replied, "You will find out on
the day you go to hide[c] in an inner room."
26 The king of Israel then ordered, "Take
Micaiah and send him back to Amon the
ruler of the city and to Joash the king's son
27 and say, 'This is what the king says: Put
this fellow in prison[d] and give him nothing
but bread and water until I return safely.' "
28 Micaiah declared, "If you ever return
safely, the LORD has not spoken[e] through
me." Then he added, "Mark my words, all
you people!"

Ahab Killed at Ramoth Gilead

22:29–36pp — 2Ch 18:28–34

29 So the king of Israel and Jehoshaphat
king of Judah went up to Ramoth Gilead.
30 The king of Israel said to Jehoshaphat, "I
will enter the battle in disguise,[f] but you
wear your royal robes." So the king of Israel disguised himself and went into battle.
31 Now the king of Aram[g] had ordered
his thirty-two chariot commanders, "Do
not fight with anyone, small or great, ex-

22:13 [p]S ver 8 **22:14** [q]S Nu 22:18; S 1Sa 3:17 **22:17** [r]S Ge 11:4; Na 3:18 [s]Nu 27:17; Isa 13:14; S Mt 9:36 **22:19** [t]Ps 47:8; Isa 6:1; 63:15; Eze 1:26; Da 7:9 [u]Job 1:6; 15:8; 38:7; Ps 103:20-21; 148:2; Jer 23:18, 22; Lk 2:13 **22:22** [v]S Jdg 9:23; 2Th 2:11 **22:23** [w]S Dt 13:3 [x]Eze 14:9 [y]S Dt 31:29 **22:24** [z]ver 11 [a]Ac 23:2 [b]Job 26:4 **22:25** [c]1Ki 20:30 **22:27** [d]2Ch 16:10; Jer 20:2; 26:21; 37:15; Heb 11:36 **22:28** [e]S Dt 18:22 **22:30** [f]S 1Sa 28:8 **22:31** [g]S Ge 10:22; S 2Sa 10:19

[s]24 Or *Spirit of*

prophets. *iron horns.* A symbol of power (see Dt 33:17).
22:13 *Let your word agree with theirs.* A bit of advice reflecting the view that all prophets were merely self-serving.
22:15 *we.* A subtle shift (see v. 6) that seeks a favorable response by including Jehoshaphat as a co-sponsor of the enterprise. *Attack . . . for the LORD will give it into the king's hand.* Micaiah sarcastically mimics the 400 false prophets (see v. 12).
22:16 *tell me nothing but the truth.* Micaiah apparently betrayed his lack of seriousness, and Ahab immediately recognizes this.
22:17 *like sheep without a shepherd . . . These people have no master.* Using the imagery of shepherd and sheep (see Nu 27:16–17; Zec 13:7; Mt 9:36; 26:31), Micaiah depicts Ahab's death in the upcoming battle.
22:19 *I saw the LORD sitting on his throne.* A true prophet was one who had, as it were, been made privy to what had transpired in God's heavenly throne room and so could truthfully declare what God intended to do (see Isa 6:1; Jer 23:16–22).
22:23 *the LORD has put a lying spirit in the mouths of all these prophets.* Some view the lying spirit as Satan or one of his agents. Others have suggested a spirit of God who undertakes the task of a lying spirit (but see 1Sa 15:29). Still others understand the lying spirit as a symbolic picture of the power of the lie. The Lord had given the 400 prophets over to the power of the lie because they did not love the truth and had chosen to speak out of their own hearts (see Jer 14:14; 23:16,26; Eze 13:2–3,17; see also note on 2Sa 24:1).
22:24 *Which way did the spirit from the LORD go when he went from me to speak to you?* By this sarcastic question Zedekiah suggests that one prophet can be a liar just as well as another.
22:25 *hide in an inner room.* Where Zedekiah will seek refuge (cf. 20:30). This will vindicate Micaiah's prophetic authority.
22:30 *disguise.* By this strategy he thought he could direct attention away from himself and so minimize any chance for fulfillment of Micaiah's prediction.
22:31 *except the king of Israel.* If the leader was killed or captured, ancient armies usually fell apart (cf. vv. 35–36).

cept the king[h] of Israel." [32]When the chariot commanders saw Jehoshaphat, they thought, "Surely this is the king of Israel." So they turned to attack him, but when Jehoshaphat cried out, [33]the chariot commanders saw that he was not the king of Israel and stopped pursuing him.

[34]But someone drew his bow[i] at random and hit the king of Israel between the sections of his armor. The king told his chariot driver, "Wheel around and get me out of the fighting. I've been wounded." [35]All day long the battle raged, and the king was propped up in his chariot facing the Arameans. The blood from his wound ran onto the floor of the chariot, and that evening he died. [36]As the sun was setting, a cry spread through the army: "Every man to his town; everyone to his land!"[j]

[37]So the king died and was brought to Samaria, and they buried him there. [38]They washed the chariot at a pool in Samaria (where the prostitutes bathed),[t] and the dogs[k] licked up his blood, as the word of the LORD had declared.

[39]As for the other events of Ahab's reign, including all he did, the palace he built and inlaid with ivory,[l] and the cities he fortified, are they not written in the book of the annals of the kings of Israel? [40]Ahab rested with his fathers. And Ahaziah his son succeeded him as king.

Jehoshaphat King of Judah

22:41–50pp — 2Ch 20:31–21:1

[41]Jehoshaphat son of Asa became king of Judah in the fourth year of Ahab king of Israel. [42]Jehoshaphat was thirty-five years

old when he became king, and he reigned in Jerusalem twenty-five years. His mother's name was Azubah daughter of Shilhi. [43]In everything he walked in the ways of his father Asa[m] and did not stray from them; he did what was right in the eyes of the LORD. The high places,[n] however, were not removed, and the people continued to offer sacrifices and burn incense there. [44]Jehoshaphat was also at peace with the king of Israel.

[45]As for the other events of Jehoshaphat's reign, the things he achieved and his military exploits, are they not written in the book of the annals of the kings of Judah? [46]He rid the land of the rest of the male shrine prostitutes[o] who remained there even after the reign of his father Asa. [47]There was then no king[p] in Edom; a deputy ruled.

[48]Now Jehoshaphat built a fleet of trading ships[u][q] to go to Ophir for gold, but they never set sail—they were wrecked at Ezion Geber.[r] [49]At that time Ahaziah son of Ahab said to Jehoshaphat, "Let my men sail with your men," but Jehoshaphat refused.

[50]Then Jehoshaphat rested with his fathers and was buried with them in the city of David his father. And Jehoram his son succeeded him.

Ahaziah King of Israel

[51]Ahaziah son of Ahab became king of Israel in Samaria in the seventeenth year of Jehoshaphat king of Judah, and he reigned

---

22:31
hS 2Sa 17:2
22:34 *l*2Ki 9:24;
2Ch 35:23
22:36 *j*2Ki 14:12
22:38
kS 1Ki 21:19
22:39 *l*2Ch 9:17;
Ps 45:8; Am 3:15

22:43
mS 1Ki 8:61;
2Ch 17:3
nS 1Ki 3:2
22:46
oS Dt 23:17
22:47
pS 1Ki 11:14-18;
2Ki 3:9; 8:20
22:48
qS 1Ki 9:26
rS Nu 33:35

t*38* Or *Samaria and cleaned the weapons*
u*48* Hebrew *of ships of Tarshish*

22:34 *chariot driver.* A war chariot normally carried two men—a fighter and a driver. Sometimes, it appears, there were three men, but the third seems to have been an officer who commanded a chariot unit (see 9:22; 2Ki 9:25; Ex 14:7; 15:4, where these officers are called lit. "the third"). **22:35** *that evening he died.* Fulfilling Micaiah's prophecy (vv. 17,28).
22:38 *as the word of the LORD had declared.* A partial fulfillment of Elijah's prophecy concerning Ahab's death (see note on 21:19).
22:39 *the palace he built and inlaid with ivory.* Excavators of Samaria have found ivory inlays in some of the buildings dating from this period of Israel's history. Ahab's use of ivory in this way is indicative of the realm's economic prosperity during his reign. *cities he fortified.* Excavators have found evidence that Ahab strengthened the fortifications of Megiddo and Hazor. *annals of the kings of Israel.* See note on 14:19.
22:40 *rested with his fathers.* See note on 1:21. *Ahaziah his son succeeded him.* For the reign of Ahaziah see vv. 51–53; 2Ki 1.
22:41 *Jehoshaphat . . . became king of Judah in the fourth year of Ahab.* Appears to refer to the beginning of Jehoshaphat's reign as sole king in 869 B.C. (see notes on v. 42; 16:29; see also Introduction: Chronology).

22:42 *twenty-five years.* 872–848 B.C. The full span of Jehoshaphat's reign dates from the 39th year of King Asa, when he became co-regent with his father (see note on 15:10; see also 2Ch 16:12).
22:43 *The high places, however, were not removed.* See notes on 3:2; 15:14.
22:44 *king.* Probably to be understood in the collective sense and as including Ahab, Ahaziah and Joram, all of whom ruled in the north during the reign of Jehoshaphat in the south (see note on v. 4).
22:45 *military exploits.* See 2Ki 3; 2Ch 17:11; 20. *annals of the kings of Judah.* See note on 14:29.
22:46 *male shrine prostitutes.* See note on 14:24.
22:47 *no king in Edom.* Suggests that Edom was subject to Judah (see 2Sa 8:14; 2Ki 8:20).
22:48 *Ophir.* See note on 9:28. *wrecked at Ezion Geber.* The destruction of the trading ships was a judgment of God on Jehoshaphat for entering into an alliance with Ahaziah of the northern kingdom (see 2Ch 20:35–37).
22:50 *rested with his fathers.* See note on 1:21. *Jehoram his son succeeded him.* For the reign of Jehoram see 2Ki 8:16–24; 2Ch 21.
22:51 *seventeenth year of Jehoshaphat.* 853 B.C. (see notes on vv. 41–42). *two years.* 853–852 (see note on 2Ki 1:17).

over Israel two years. ⁵²He did evil ˢ in the eyes of the LORD, because he walked in the ways of his father and mother and in the ways of Jeroboam son of Nebat, who caused Israel to sin. ⁵³He served and worshiped Baal ᵗ and provoked the LORD, the God of Israel, to anger, just as his father ᵘ had done.

22:52 ˢ1Ki 15:26

22:53 ᵗS Jdg 2:11 ᵘ1Ki 21:25

22:52 *ways of his father and mother.* See 16:30–33.

ways of Jeroboam. See 12:28–33.

2 KINGS

See Introduction to 1 Kings.

Outline

Below is an abbreviated outline for 2 Kings. For the complete outline see Introduction to 1 Kings: Outline.

The LORD's Judgment on Ahaziah

1 After Ahab's death, Moab[a] rebelled against Israel. [2]Now Ahaziah had fallen through the lattice of his upper room in Samaria and injured himself. So he sent messengers,[b] saying to them, "Go and consult Baal-Zebub,[c] the god of Ekron,[d] to see if I will recover[e] from this injury."

[3]But the angel[f] of the LORD said to Elijah[g] the Tishbite, "Go up and meet the messengers of the king of Samaria and ask them, 'Is it because there is no God in Israel[h] that you are going off to consult Baal-Zebub, the god of Ekron?' [4]Therefore this is what the LORD says: 'You will not leave[i] the bed you are lying on. You will certainly die!'" So Elijah went.

[5]When the messengers returned to the king, he asked them, "Why have you come back?"

[6]"A man came to meet us," they replied. "And he said to us, 'Go back to the king who sent you and tell him, "This is what the LORD says: Is it because there is no God in Israel that you are sending men to consult Baal-Zebub, the god of Ekron? Therefore you will not leave[j] the bed you

are lying on. You will certainly die!'"'"

[7]The king asked them, "What kind of man was it who came to meet you and told you this?"

[8]They replied, "He was a man with a garment of hair[k] and with a leather belt around his waist."

The king said, "That was Elijah the Tishbite."

[9]Then he sent[l] to Elijah a captain[m] with his company of fifty men. The captain went up to Elijah, who was sitting on the top of a hill, and said to him, "Man of God, the king says, 'Come down!'"

[10]Elijah answered the captain, "If I am a man of God, may fire come down from heaven and consume you and your fifty men!" Then fire[n] fell from heaven and consumed the captain and his men.

[11]At this the king sent to Elijah another captain with his fifty men. The captain said to him, "Man of God, this is what the king says, 'Come down at once!'"

[12]"If I am a man of God," Elijah replied, "may fire come down from heaven and consume you and your fifty men!" Then the fire of God fell from heaven and consumed him and his fifty men.

1:1 [a]S Ge 19:37; 2Ki 3:5
1:2 [b]ver 16
[c]S Mk 3:22
[d]1Sa 6:2; Isa 2:6; 14:29 [e]S Jdg 18:5
1:3 [f]ver 15
[g]1Ki 17:1
[h]S 1Sa 28:8
1:4 [i]ver 6,16; Ps 41:8
1:6 [j]S ver 4
1:8 [k]S 1Ki 18:7; Mt 3:4; Mk 1:6
1:9 [l]2Ki 6:14
[m]Ex 18:25; Isa 3:3
1:10
[n]S 1Ki 18:38; S Rev 11:5; S 13:13

1:1 *After Ahab's death.* See 1Ki 22:37. *Moab rebelled.* Moab had been brought into subjection by David (see 2Sa 8:2), but when the northern and Transjordan tribes rebelled and made Jeroboam their king, political domination of Moab probably also shifted to the northern kingdom. An inscription of Mesha king of Moab (see chart on "Ancient Texts Relating to the OT," p. 5) indicates that during the reign of Omri's "son" (probably a reference to his grandson Joram, not to Ahab) the Moabites were able to free the area of Medeba from Israelite control (see map No. 5 at the end of the Study Bible).
1:2 *Baal-Zebub.* See note on Jdg 10:6. *Ekron.* The northernmost of the five major Philistine cities (see Jos 13:3; 1Sa 5:10 and notes). *if I will recover.* Ahaziah appears to have feared that his injury would be fatal. He turned to the pagan deity for a revelatory oracle, not for healing.
1:3 *angel of the LORD.* See 1Ki 19:7; see also note on Ge 16:7. The Lord usually spoke directly to the consciousness of the prophet (1Ki 17:2,8; 18:1; 19:9; 21:17). Perhaps the means of revelation was changed in this instance to heighten the contrast between the messengers of Ahaziah (vv. 2–3,5) and the angel (which means "messenger") of the Lord. *Elijah the Tishbite.* See note on 1Ki 17:1. *king of Samaria.* See note on 1Ki 21:1.
1:4 *You will certainly die!* Ahaziah will receive the oracle he sought, but it will come from the Lord through Elijah, not from Baal-Zebub.
1:5 *Why have you come back?* Ahaziah realized the messengers could not have traveled so quickly to Ekron and back.
1:8 *garment of hair.* See 1Ki 19:19. Elijah's cloak was probably of sheepskin or camel's hair, tied with a simple leather thong (cf. Mt 3:4). His dress contrasted sharply with the fine linen clothing (see Jer 13:1) of his wealthy contemporaries and constituted a protest against the materialistic attitudes of the king and the upper classes (cf. Mt 11:7–8; Lk 7:24–25). *That was Elijah the Tishbite.* Ahaziah was familiar

with Elijah's appearance because of the prophet's many encounters with Ahab, his father.

1:9 *he sent to Elijah a captain with his company of fifty men.* The pagan people of that time thought that the magical power of curses could be nullified either by forcing the pronouncer of the curse to retract his statement or by killing him so that his curse would go with him to the netherworld. It appears that Ahaziah shared this view and desired to take Elijah prisoner in order to counteract the pronouncement of his death. *Man of God, the king says, 'Come down!'* Ahaziah attempted to place the prophet under the authority of the king. This constituted a violation of the covenant nature of Israelite kingship, in which the king's actions were always to be placed under the scrutiny and authority of the word of the Lord spoken by his prophets (see notes on 1Sa 10:25; 12:23).
1:10 *fire fell from heaven and consumed the captain and his men.* See 1Ki 18:38. Another link between the ministries of Elijah and Moses (see Lev 10:2; Nu 16:35). At stake in this incident was the question of who was sovereign in Israel. Would Ahaziah recognize that the king in Israel was only a vice-regent under the authority and kingship of the Lord, or would he exercise despotic power, like pagan kings (see notes on 1Sa 12:14–15)? At Mount Carmel the Lord had revealed himself and authenticated his prophet by fire from heaven (see 1Ki 18:38–39). Now this previous revelation is confirmed to Ahaziah. Jesus' rebuke of his disciples for suggesting that fire be called down from heaven to destroy the Samaritans (Lk 9:51–56) is not to be understood as a disapproval of Elijah's action, but as an indication that the disciples failed to discern the difference between the issue at stake in Elijah's day and the unbelief of the Samaritans in their own day.
1:11 *the king sent to Elijah another captain.* Ahaziah refused to submit to the word of the Lord in spite of the dramatic revelation of God's power.

¹³So the king sent a third captain with his fifty men. This third captain went up and fell on his knees before Elijah. "Man of God," he begged, "please have respect for my life*o* and the lives of these fifty men, your servants! ¹⁴See, fire has fallen from heaven and consumed the first two captains and all their men. But now have respect for my life!"

¹⁵The angel*p* of the LORD said to Elijah, "Go down with him; do not be afraid*q* of him." So Elijah got up and went down with him to the king.

¹⁶He told the king, "This is what the LORD says: Is it because there is no God in Israel for you to consult that you have sent messengers*r* to consult Baal-Zebub, the god of Ekron? Because you have done this, you will never leave*s* the bed you are lying on. You will certainly die!" ¹⁷So he died,*t* according to the word of the LORD that Elijah had spoken.

Because Ahaziah had no son, Joram*a* *u* succeeded him as king in the second year of Jehoram son of Jehoshaphat king of Judah. ¹⁸As for all the other events of Ahaziah's reign, and what he did, are they not written in the book of the annals of the kings of Israel?

Elijah Taken Up to Heaven

2 When the LORD was about to take*v* Elijah up to heaven in a whirlwind,*w* Elijah and Elisha*x* were on their way from Gilgal.*y* ²Elijah said to Elisha, "Stay here;*z* the LORD has sent me to Bethel."

But Elisha said, "As surely as the LORD lives and as you live, I will not leave you."*a* So they went down to Bethel.

³The company*b* of the prophets at Bethel came out to Elisha and asked, "Do you know that the LORD is going to take your master from you today?"

"Yes, I know," Elisha replied, "but do not speak of it."

⁴Then Elijah said to him, "Stay here, Elisha; the LORD has sent me to Jericho.*c*"

And he replied, "As surely as the LORD lives and as you live, I will not leave you." So they went to Jericho.

⁵The company*d* of the prophets at Jericho went up to Elisha and asked him, "Do you know that the LORD is going to take your master from you today?"

"Yes, I know," he replied, "but do not speak of it."

⁶Then Elijah said to him, "Stay here;*e* the LORD has sent me to the Jordan."*f*

And he replied, "As surely as the LORD lives and as you live, I will not leave you."*g* So the two of them walked on.

⁷Fifty men of the company of the prophets went and stood at a distance, facing the place where Elijah and Elisha had stopped at the Jordan. ⁸Elijah took his cloak,*h* rolled it up and struck*i* the water with it. The water divided*j* to the right and to the left, and the two of them crossed over on dry*k* ground.

⁹When they had crossed, Elijah said to Elisha, "Tell me, what can I do for you before I am taken from you?"

"Let me inherit a double*l* portion of your spirit,"*m* Elisha replied.

¹⁰"You have asked a difficult thing," Elijah said, "yet if you see me when I am

Cross references (center column)

1:13 oPs 72:14
1:15 pver 3
qIsa 51:12; 57:11; Jer 1:17; Eze 2:6
1:16 rS ver 2 sver 4
1:17 t2Ki 8:15; Jer 20:6; 28:17
u2Ki 3:1; 8:16
2:1 vS Ge 5:24
wver 11; 1Ki 19:11; Isa 5:28; 66:15; Jer 4:13; Na 1:3
xS 1Ki 19:16
yS Dt 11:30; 2Ki 4:38
2:2 zver 6
aRu 1:16

2:3 bS 1Sa 10:5
2:4 cJos 3:16
2:5 dver 3
2:6 ever 2
fJos 3:15
gRu 1:16
2:8 hS 1Ki 19:19
iver 14
jS Ex 14:21
kEx 14:22,29
2:9 lS Dt 21:17
mS Nu 11:17

a 17 Hebrew *Jehoram*, a variant of *Joram*

1:13 *fell on his knees before Elijah.* The third captain, recognizing that Elijah was the bearer of the word of the Lord, feared for his life and bowed before him with a humble request.

1:15 *The angel of the LORD said to Elijah.* See note on v. 3.

1:17 *died, according to the word of the LORD.* In the end Ahaziah was punished for turning away from the God of Israel to a pagan deity, and the word of the Lord was shown to be both reliable and beyond the power of the king to annul. *Joram.* Ahaziah's younger brother (see 3:1; 1Ki 22:51). *second year of Jehoram son of Jehoshaphat.* Jehoram's reign overlapped that of his father Jehoshaphat from 853 to 848 B.C. (see note on 8:16). The reference here is to the second year of that co-regency. The 18th year of Jehoshaphat (3:1) is therefore the same as the second year of Jehoram's co-regency (852).

1:18 *annals of the kings of Israel.* See note on 1Ki 14:19.

2:2 *I will not leave you.* Elisha was aware that Elijah's ministry was almost finished and that his departure was near (v. 5). He was determined to accompany him until the moment the Lord took him. His commitment to Elijah and to Elijah's ministry was unfailing (see v. 9; 1Ki 19:21).

2:3 *company of.* Lit. "sons of" (see note on 1Ki 20:35).

During the days of Elijah and Elisha, companies of prophets were located at Bethel (here), Jericho (v. 5) and Gilgal (4:38). It appears that Elijah journeyed by divine instruction to Gilgal (v. 1), Bethel (v. 2) and Jericho (v. 4) for a last meeting with each of these companies.

2:7 *Fifty men.* These men were to witness the miracle by which Elijah and Elisha crossed the river.

2:8 *Elijah took his cloak ... and struck the water with it.* Elijah used his cloak much as Moses had used his staff at the time of Israel's passage through the "Red Sea" (see Ex 14:16,21,26).

2:9 *Let me inherit a double portion.* Elisha was not expressing a desire for a ministry twice as great as Elijah's, but he was using terms derived from inheritance law to express his desire to carry on Elijah's ministry. Inheritance law assigned a double portion of a father's possessions to the firstborn son (see Dt 21:17 and note).

2:10 *difficult thing.* Although Elijah had previously been told to anoint Elisha as his successor (1Ki 19:16,19–21), Elijah's response clearly showed that the issue rested solely with the Lord's sovereign good pleasure. *If you see me ... it will be yours—otherwise not.* Elijah left the answer to Elisha's request in the Lord's hands.

taken from you, it will be yours—otherwise not."

[11]As they were walking along and talking together, suddenly a chariot of fire[n] and horses of fire appeared and separated the two of them, and Elijah went up to heaven[o] in a whirlwind.[p] [12]Elisha saw this and cried out, "My father! My father! The chariots[q] and horsemen of Israel!" And Elisha saw him no more. Then he took hold of his own clothes and tore[r] them apart.

[13]He picked up the cloak that had fallen from Elijah and went back and stood on the bank of the Jordan. [14]Then he took the cloak[s] that had fallen from him and struck[t] the water with it. "Where now is the LORD, the God of Elijah?" he asked. When he struck the water, it divided to the right and to the left, and he crossed over.

[15]The company[u] of the prophets from Jericho, who were watching, said, "The spirit[v] of Elijah is resting on Elisha." And they went to meet him and bowed to the ground before him. [16]"Look," they said, "we your servants have fifty able men. Let them go and look for your master. Perhaps the Spirit[w] of the LORD has picked him

up[x] and set him down on some mountain or in some valley."

"No," Elisha replied, "do not send them."

[17]But they persisted until he was too ashamed[y] to refuse. So he said, "Send them." And they sent fifty men, who searched for three days but did not find him. [18]When they returned to Elisha, who was staying in Jericho, he said to them, "Didn't I tell you not to go?"

Healing of the Water

[19]The men of the city said to Elisha, "Look, our lord, this town is well situated, as you can see, but the water is bad and the land is unproductive. [20]"Bring me a new bowl," he said, "and put salt in it." So they brought it to him.

[21]Then he went out to the spring and threw[z] the salt into it, saying, "This is what the LORD says: 'I have healed this water. Never again will it cause death or make the land unproductive.'" [22]And the water has remained wholesome[a] to this day, according to the word Elisha had spoken.

Elisha Is Jeered

[23]From there Elisha went up to Bethel.

Cross references (center column):

2:11 [n]2Ki 6:17; Ps 68:17; 104:3, 4; Isa 66:15; Hab 3:8; Zec 6:1 [o]S Ge 5:24 [p]S ver 1
2:12 [q]2Ki 6:17; 13:14 [r]S Ge 37:29
2:14 [s]S 1Ki 19:19 [t]ver 8
2:15 [u]S 1Sa 10:5 [v]S Nu 11:17
2:16 [w]S 1Ki 18:12

[x]Ac 8:39
2:17 [y]S Jdg 3:25
2:21 [z]S Ex 15:25; 2Ki 4:41; 6:6
2:22 [a]Ex 15:25

2:11 *chariot of fire and horses of fire.* The Lord's heavenly host has accompanied and supported Elijah's ministry (as it had that of Moses; see Ex 15:1–10), and now at his departure Elisha is allowed to see it (cf. 6:17). *Elijah went up to heaven in a whirlwind.* Elijah, like Enoch before him (Ge 5:24), was taken up to heaven bodily without experiencing death; like Moses (Dt 34:4–6), he was taken away outside the promised land.

2:12 *chariots and horsemen of Israel!* Elisha depicted Elijah as embodying the true strength of the nation. He, rather than the apostate king, was the Lord's representative. The same description was later used of Elisha (13:14).

2:13 *He picked up the cloak.* See note on v. 8. Possession of Elijah's cloak symbolized Elisha's succession to Elijah's ministry (see 1Ki 19:19).

2:14 *When he struck the water, it divided.* See v. 8. The Lord authenticated Elisha's succession to Elijah's ministry and demonstrated that the same divine power that had accompanied Elijah's ministry was now operative in the ministry of Elisha. In crossing the Jordan as Joshua had before him, Elisha is shown to be Elijah's "Joshua" (Elisha and Joshua are very similar names, Elisha meaning "God saves" and Joshua "The LORD saves").

2:15 *bowed to the ground before him.* Indicated their recognition of Elisha's succession to Elijah's position. Elisha was now the Lord's official representative in this time of royal apostasy.

2:16 *Perhaps the Spirit of the LORD has picked him up and set him down.* Obadiah expressed the same idea years earlier (see 1Ki 18:12). *do not send them.* Elisha knew their search would be fruitless.

2:17 *Send them.* When the company of prophets refused to be satisfied with Elisha's answer, he permitted them to go so that the authority and truth of his words would be confirmed

to them.

2:19 *city.* Evidently Jericho (see v. 18). *the water is bad and the land is unproductive.* The inhabitants of Jericho were experiencing the effects of the covenant curse (contrast Dt 28:15–18 with Ex 23:25–26; Lev 26:9; Dt 28:1–4). See 1Ki 16:34; Jos 6:26.

2:20 *new bowl.* That which was to be used in the service of the Lord was to be undefiled by profane use (see Lev 1:3,10; Nu 19:2; Dt 21:3; 1Sa 6:7). *put salt in it.* Elisha may have used salt because of its known preservative qualities, but it is more likely that he used it to symbolize the covenant faithfulness of the Lord (see notes on Lev 2:13; Nu 18:19; see also 2Ch 13:5).

2:21 *I have healed this water.* Any idea of a magical effect of the salt in the purification of the water is excluded by the explicit statement that the Lord himself healed the water. In this symbolic way Elisha was able, as the first act of his ministry, to proclaim to the people that in spite of their disobedience the Lord was merciful and was still reaching out to them in his grace (see 13:23).

2:23 *Go on up.* Since Bethel was the royal cult center of the northern kings (1Ki 12:29; Am 7:13) and Elijah and Elisha were known to frequent Samaria (perhaps even as their main residence; see note on 5:3), the youths from Bethel no doubt assumed that Elisha was going up to Samaria to continue Elijah's struggle against royal apostasy. (Some believe that the youths, in their mocking, were telling Elisha to ascend to heaven as Elijah had done.) *you baldhead!* Baldness was uncommon among the ancient Jews, and luxuriant hair seems to have been viewed as a sign of strength and vigor (see note on 2Sa 14:26). By calling Elisha "baldhead," the youths from Bethel expressed that city's utter disdain for the Lord's representative, who, they felt, had no power.

As he was walking along the road, some youths came out of the town and jeered[b] at him. "Go on up, you baldhead!" they said. "Go on up, you baldhead!" [24]He turned around, looked at them and called down a curse[c] on them in the name[d] of the LORD. Then two bears came out of the woods and mauled forty-two of the youths. [25]And he went on to Mount Carmel[e] and from there returned to Samaria.

Moab Revolts

3 Joram[b][f] son of Ahab became king of Israel in Samaria in the eighteenth year of Jehoshaphat king of Judah, and he reigned twelve years. [2]He did evil[g] in the eyes of the LORD, but not as his father[h] and mother had done. He got rid of the sacred stone[i] of Baal that his father had made. [3]Nevertheless he clung to the sins[j] of Jeroboam son of Nebat, which he had caused Israel to commit; he did not turn away from them.

[4]Now Mesha king of Moab[k] raised sheep, and he had to supply the king of Israel with a hundred thousand lambs[l] and with the wool of a hundred thousand rams. [5]But after Ahab died, the king of Moab rebelled[m] against the king of Israel. [6]So at that time King Joram set out from Samaria and mobilized all Israel. [7]He also sent this message to Jehoshaphat king of

Judah: "The king of Moab has rebelled against me. Will you go with me to fight[n] against Moab?"

"I will go with you," he replied. "I am as you are, my people as your people, my horses as your horses."

[8]"By what route shall we attack?" he asked.

"Through the Desert of Edom," he answered.

[9]So the king of Israel set out with the king of Judah and the king of Edom.[o] After a roundabout march of seven days, the army had no more water for themselves or for the animals with them.

[10]"What!" exclaimed the king of Israel. "Has the LORD called us three kings together only to hand us over to Moab?"

[11]But Jehoshaphat asked, "Is there no prophet of the LORD here, that we may inquire[p] of the LORD through him?"

An officer of the king of Israel answered, "Elisha[q] son of Shaphat is here. He used to pour water on the hands of Elijah.[c][r]"

[12]Jehoshaphat said, "The word[s] of the LORD is with him." So the king of Israel and Jehoshaphat and the king of Edom went down to him.

[13]Elisha said to the king of Israel, "What do we have to do with each other? Go to

---

2:23
[b]S Ex 22:28;
2Ch 30:10;
36:16; Job 19:18;
Ps 31:18
2:24 [c]S Ge 4:11
[d]S Dt 18:19
2:25
[e]S 1Ki 18:20
3:1 /S 2Ki 1:17
3:2 [g]1Ki 15:26
[h]1Ki 16:30
[i]S Ex 23:24
3:3 /S 1Ki 12:30
3:4 [k]S Ge 19:37;
2Ki 1:1 /Ezr 7:17;
Isa 16:1
3:5 [m]S 2Ki 1:1

3:7 [n]1Ki 22:4
3:9 [o]S 1Ki 22:47
3:11
[p]S Ge 25:22;
S 1Ki 22:5
[q]S Ge 20:7
[r]S 1Ki 19:16
3:12 [s]S Nu 11:17

[b]/ Hebrew *Jehoram*, a variant of *Joram*; also in verse 6
[c]// That is, he was Elijah's personal servant.

2:24 *called down a curse on them in the name of the LORD.* Elisha pronounced a curse similar to the covenant curse of Lev 26:21–22. The result gave warning of the judgment that would come on the entire nation should it persist in disobedience and apostasy (see 2Ch 36:16). Thus Elisha's first acts were indicative of his ministry that would follow: God's covenant blessings would come to those who looked to him (vv. 19–22), but God's covenant curses would fall on those who turned away from him.

3:1 *Joram son of Ahab became king . . . in the eighteenth year of Jehoshaphat.* See note on 1:17. *twelve years.* 852–841 B.C.

3:2 *not as his father and mother had done.* Not as Ahab (see notes on 1Ki 16:30–34) and Jezebel (see 1Ki 18:4; 19:1–2; 21:7–15). *sacred stone of Baal that his father had made.* Apparently a reference to the stone representation of the male deity (see note on 1Ki 14:23) that Ahab placed in the temple he had constructed for Jezebel in Samaria (see 1Ki 16:32–33). From 10:27 it appears that this stone was later reinstated, perhaps by Jezebel.

3:3 *sins of Jeroboam . . . he had caused Israel to commit.* See note on 1Ki 14:16.

3:4 *Mesha king of Moab.* See note on 1:1. *a hundred thousand lambs and . . . the wool of a hundred thousand rams.* The heavy annual tribute (see Isa 16:1) that Israel required from the Moabites as a vassal state.

3:5 *king of Moab rebelled.* See note on 1:1.

3:7 *Will you go with me to fight against Moab?* Joram wished to attack Moab from the rear (v. 8), but to do that his army had to pass through Judah. *I am as you are, my people as your people, my horses as your horses.* See 1Ki 22:4. Jehoshaphat had already been condemned by prophets of the

Lord for his alliance with the northern kings Ahab (see 2Ch 18:1; 19:1–2) and Ahaziah (2Ch 20:35–37), yet he agreed to join with Joram against Moab. Perhaps he was disturbed by the potential danger to Judah posed by the growing strength of Moab (see 2Ch 20), and he may have considered Joram less evil than his predecessors (see v. 2).

3:8 *Through the Desert of Edom.* This route of attack took the armies of Israel and Judah south of the Dead Sea, enabling them to circumvent the fortifications of Moab's northern frontier and to avoid the possibility of a rearguard action against them by the Arameans of Damascus. The Edomites, who were subject to Judah, were in no position to resist the movement of Israel's army through their territory.

3:9 *king of Edom.* Although then designated a king, he was in reality a governor appointed by Jehoshaphat (see 8:20; 1Ki 22:47).

3:11 *Is there no prophet of the LORD here . . . ?* See 1Ki 22:7. Only after the apparent failure of their own strategies did the three rulers seek the word of the Lord (v. 12). *Elisha son of Shaphat is here.* Since Elijah is reported to have sent a letter to Jehoshaphat's son Jehoram after his father's death (2Ch 21:12–15), it seems that Elisha accompanied the armies on this campaign as the representative of the aged Elijah. The event is narrated here after the account of Elisha's initiation as Elijah's successor and the two events that foreshadowed the character of his ministry. Following this introduction to Elisha's ministry, the present episode is topically associated with the series of Elisha's acts that now occupies the narrative.

3:13 *Go to the prophets of your father and . . . mother.* See 1Ki 22:6.

the prophets of your father and the prophets of your mother."

"No," the king of Israel answered, "because it was the LORD who called us three kings together to hand us over to Moab."

[14]Elisha said, "As surely as the LORD Almighty lives, whom I serve, if I did not have respect for the presence of Jehoshaphat king of Judah, I would not look at you or even notice you. [15]But now bring me a harpist." [t]

While the harpist was playing, the hand [u] of the LORD came upon Elisha [16]and he said, "This is what the LORD says: Make this valley full of ditches. [17]For this is what the LORD says: You will see neither wind nor rain, yet this valley will be filled with water, [v] and you, your cattle and your other animals will drink. [18]This is an easy [w] thing in the eyes of the LORD; he will also hand Moab over to you. [19]You will overthrow every fortified city and every major town. You will cut down every good tree, stop up all the springs, and ruin every good field with stones."

[20]The next morning, about the time [x] for offering the sacrifice, there it was—water flowing from the direction of Edom! And the land was filled with water. [y]

[21]Now all the Moabites had heard that the kings had come to fight against them; so every man, young and old, who could bear arms was called up and stationed on the border. [22]When they got up early in the morning, the sun was shining on the water. To the Moabites across the way, the water looked red—like blood. [23]"That's blood!" they said. "Those kings must have fought and slaughtered each other. Now to the plunder, Moab!"

[24]But when the Moabites came to the camp of Israel, the Israelites rose up and fought them until they fled. And the Israelites invaded the land and slaughtered the Moabites. [25]They destroyed the towns, and each man threw a stone on every good field until it was covered. They stopped up all the springs and cut down every good tree. Only Kir Hareseth [z] was left with its stones in place, but men armed with slings surrounded it and attacked it as well.

[26]When the king of Moab saw that the battle had gone against him, he took with him seven hundred swordsmen to break through to the king of Edom, but they failed. [27]Then he took his firstborn [a] son, who was to succeed him as king, and offered him as a sacrifice on the city wall. The fury against Israel was great; they withdrew and returned to their own land.

The Widow's Oil

4 The wife of a man from the company [b] of the prophets cried out to Elisha, "Your servant my husband is dead, and you know that he revered the LORD. But now his creditor [c] is coming to take my two boys as his slaves."

[2]Elisha replied to her, "How can I help you? Tell me, what do you have in your house?"

"Your servant has nothing there at all," she said, "except a little oil." [d]

Cross references (center column):
3:15 [t]S 1Sa 10:5
[u]Jer 15:17;
Eze 1:3
3:17 [v]Ps 107:35;
Isa 12:3; 32:2;
35:6; 41:18;
65:13
3:18 [w]S Ge 18:14;
2Ki 20:10;
Isa 49:6;
Jer 32:17,27;
Mk 10:27
3:20 [x]S Ex 29:41
[y]S Ex 17:6

3:25 [z]Isa 15:1;
16:7; Jer 48:31,
36
3:27 [a]S Dt 12:31;
2Ki 16:3; 21:6;
2Ch 28:3;
Ps 106:38;
Mic 6:7
Jer 19:4-5;
4:1 [b]S 1Sa 10:5
[c]S Ex 22:26;
Lev 25:39-43;
Ne 5:3-5;
Job 22:6; 24:9
4:2 [d]S 1Ki 17:12

3:14 *if I did not have respect for ... Jehoshaphat ... I would not look at you.* Joram will share in the blessing of the word of God only because of his association with Jehoshaphat.

3:15 *bring me a harpist.* To create a disposition conducive to receiving the word of the Lord.

3:16 *this valley.* The Israelite armies were encamped in the broad valley (the Arabah) between the highlands of Moab on the east and those of Judah on the west, just south of the Dead Sea.

3:17 *will be filled with water.* The word of the Lord contained a promise and a directive. The Lord will graciously provide for his people, but they must respond to his word in faith and obedience (v. 16).

3:19 The two armies will devastate the rebellious country.

3:20 *time for offering.* See Ex 29:38-39; Nu 28:3-4. *water flowing from the direction of Edom.* Flash floods in the distant mountains of Edom caused water to flow north through the broad, usually dry, valley that sloped toward the Dead Sea (see note on v. 16).

3:23 *Those kings must have ... slaughtered each other.* The Moabites would have good reason to suspect that an internal conflict had arisen between the parties of an alliance whose members had previously been mutually hostile.

3:25 *Kir Hareseth.* The capital city of Moab (see Isa 16:7, 11; Jer 48:31,36), usually identified with present-day Kerak,

located about 11 miles east of the Dead Sea and 15 miles south of the Arnon River.

3:26 *break through to the king of Edom.* A desperate attempt by the king of Moab to induce Edom to turn against Israel and Judah.

3:27 *offered him as a sacrifice on the city wall.* King Mesha offered his oldest son, the crown prince, as a burnt offering (see 16:3; Jer 7:31) to the Moabite god Chemosh (see 1Ki 11:7; Nu 21:29; Jer 48:46) in an attempt to induce the deity to come to his aid. *The fury against Israel was great.* The Hebrew underlying this clause would normally refer to a visitation of God's wrath. It may be that just when total victory appeared to be in Israel's grasp, God's displeasure with the Ahab dynasty showed itself in some way that caused the Israelite kings to give up the campaign. Comparing Aramaic and later Hebrew usage, a few scholars suggest that the Hebrew here can be translated, "There was great dismay upon/in Israel."

4:1 *company of the prophets.* See notes on 2:3; 1Ki 20:35. *to take my two boys as his slaves.* Servitude as a means of debt payment by labor was permitted in the Mosaic law (Ex 21:1-2; Lev 25:39-41; Dt 15:1-11). It appears that the practice was much abused (see Ne 5:5,8; Am 2:6; 8:6), even though the law limited the term of such bondage and required that those so held be treated as hired workers.

³Elisha said, "Go around and ask all your neighbors for empty jars. Don't ask for just a few. ⁴Then go inside and shut the door behind you and your sons. Pour oil into all the jars, and as each is filled, put it to one side."

⁵She left him and afterward shut the door behind her and her sons. They brought the jars to her and she kept pouring. ⁶When all the jars were full, she said to her son, "Bring me another one."

But he replied, "There is not a jar left." Then the oil stopped flowing.

⁷She went and told the man of God,ᵉ and he said, "Go, sell the oil and pay your debts. You and your sons can live on what is left."

The Shunammite's Son Restored to Life

⁸One day Elisha went to Shunem.ᶠ And a well-to-do woman was there, who urged him to stay for a meal. So whenever he came by, he stopped there to eat. ⁹She said to her husband, "I know that this man who often comes our way is a holy man of God. ¹⁰Let's make a small room on the roof and put in it a bed and a table, a chair and a lamp for him. Then he can stayᵍ there whenever he comes to us."

¹¹One day when Elisha came, he went up to his room and lay down there. ¹²He said to his servant Gehazi, "Call the Shunammite."ʰ So he called her, and she stood before him. ¹³Elisha said to him, "Tell her, 'You have gone to all this trou-

ble for us. Now what can be done for you? Can we speak on your behalf to the king or the commander of the army?' "

She replied, "I have a home among my own people."

¹⁴"What can be done for her?" Elisha asked.

Gehazi said, "Well, she has no son and her husband is old."

¹⁵Then Elisha said, "Call her." So he called her, and she stood in the doorway. ¹⁶"About this timeⁱ next year," Elisha said, "you will hold a son in your arms."

"No, my lord," she objected. "Don't mislead your servant, O man of God!"

¹⁷But the woman became pregnant, and the next year about that same time she gave birth to a son, just as Elisha had told her.

¹⁸The child grew, and one day he went out to his father, who was with the reapers.ʲ ¹⁹"My head! My head!" he said to his father.

His father told a servant, "Carry him to his mother." ²⁰After the servant had lifted him up and carried him to his mother, the boy sat on her lap until noon, and then he died. ²¹She went up and laid him on the bedᵏ of the man of God, then shut the door and went out.

²²She called her husband and said, "Please send me one of the servants and a donkey so I can go to the man of God quickly and return."

²³"Why go to him today?" he asked. "It's not the New Moonˡ or the Sabbath."

4:7 ᵉS 1Ki 12:22
4:8 ᶠS Jos 19:18
4:10 ᵍMt 10:41; S Ro 12:13
4:12 ʰ2Ki 8:1

4:16 ⁱS Ge 18:10
4:18 ʲS Ru 2:3
4:21 ᵏver 32
4:23 ˡS Nu 10:10; 1Ch 23:31; Ps 81:3

4:4 *shut the door behind you and your sons.* The impending miracle was not intended to be a public sensation but to demonstrate privately God's mercy and grace to this widow (cf. Ps 68:5). She did not hesitate to respond to the instructions of the Lord's prophet in faith and obedience.

4:8 *Shunem.* See note on 1Ki 1:3.

4:9 *holy man of God.* The woman recognized that Elisha was a person set apart to the Lord's work in a very special sense. Nowhere else in the OT is the term "holy" applied to a prophet.

4:10 *he can stay there whenever he comes to us.* By her hospitality the woman was able to assist in sustaining the proclamation of God's word through Elisha.

4:12 *Gehazi.* Referred to here for the first time; he appears to have served Elisha in some of the same ways as Elisha had served Elijah, though the two men were of drastically different character (see 5:19–27; 6:15).

4:13 *I have a home among my own people.* The Shunammite woman felt secure and content in the community of her own family and tribe, and she had no need or desire for favors from high government officials.

4:14 *she has no son and her husband is old.* A great disappointment because it meant that the family's name would cease and its land and possessions would pass on to others. It was also a great threat to this young wife's future in that she faced the likelihood of many years as a widow with no provider or protector—children were a widow's only

social security in old age (see 8:1–6; see also note on 1Ki 17:22).

4:16 *About this time next year.* See Ge 17:21; 18:14. *Don't mislead your servant, O man of God!* The woman's response revealed the depths of her desire for a son and her fear of disappointment more than it showed a lack of confidence in the word of Elisha.

4:17 *just as Elisha had told her.* The trustworthiness of Elisha's word was confirmed, and the birth of the son was shown to be the result of God's gracious intervention in her behalf.

4:20 *he died.* The child, given as an evidence of God's grace and the reliability of his word, was suddenly taken from the woman in a severe test of her faith. Her subsequent actions demonstrate the strength of her faith in the face of great calamity.

4:21 *laid him on the bed of the man of God.* In this way the woman concealed the child's death from the rest of the household while she went to seek the prophet at whose word the child had been born.

4:23 *Why go to him today?* The question suggests that it was not uncommon for the woman to go to Elisha, but that on this occasion the timing of her visit was unusual. *It's not the New Moon or the Sabbath.* The Sabbath and New Moon were observed by cessation from work (see notes on Ge 2:3; Ex 16:23; 20:9–10; 1Sa 20:5; see also Lev 23:3).

"It's all right," she said.

24She saddled the donkey and said to her servant, "Lead on; don't slow down for me unless I tell you." 25So she set out and came to the man of God at Mount Carmel. m

When he saw her in the distance, the man of God said to his servant Gehazi, "Look! There's the Shunammite! 26Run to meet her and ask her, 'Are you all right? Is your husband all right? Is your child all right?' "

"Everything is all right," she said.

27When she reached the man of God at the mountain, she took hold of his feet. Gehazi came over to push her away, but the man of God said, "Leave her alone! She is in bitter distress, n but the LORD has hidden it from me and has not told me why."

28"Did I ask you for a son, my lord?" she said. "Didn't I tell you, 'Don't raise my hopes'?"

29Elisha said to Gehazi, "Tuck your cloak into your belt, o take my staff p in your hand and run. If you meet anyone, do not greet him, and if anyone greets you, do not answer. Lay my staff on the boy's face."

30But the child's mother said, "As surely as the LORD lives and as you live, I will not leave you." So he got up and followed her.

31Gehazi went on ahead and laid the staff on the boy's face, but there was no sound or response. So Gehazi went back to meet Elisha and told him, "The boy has not awakened."

32When Elisha reached the house, there was the boy lying dead on his couch. q 33He went in, shut the door on the two of them and prayed r to the LORD. 34Then he

got on the bed and lay upon the boy, mouth to mouth, eyes to eyes, hands to hands. As he stretched s himself out upon him, the boy's body grew warm. 35Elisha turned away and walked back and forth in the room and then got on the bed and stretched out upon him once more. The boy sneezed seven times t and opened his eyes. u

36Elisha summoned Gehazi and said, "Call the Shunammite." And he did. When she came, he said, "Take your son." v 37She came in, fell at his feet and bowed to the ground. Then she took her son and went out.

Death in the Pot

38Elisha returned to Gilgal w and there was a famine x in that region. While the company of the prophets was meeting with him, he said to his servant, "Put on the large pot and cook some stew for these men."

39One of them went out into the fields to gather herbs and found a wild vine. He gathered some of its gourds and filled the fold of his cloak. When he returned, he cut them up into the pot of stew, though no one knew what they were. 40The stew was poured out for the men, but as they began to eat it, they cried out, "O man of God, there is death in the pot!" And they could not eat it.

41Elisha said, "Get some flour." He put it into the pot and said, "Serve it to the people to eat." And there was nothing harmful in the pot. y

Feeding of a Hundred

42A man came from Baal Shalishah, z bringing the man of God twenty loaves a of

---

Cross references (center column):

4:25
mS 1Ki 18:20
4:27 n1Sa 1:15
4:29
oS 1Ki 18:46
pS Ex 4:2
4:32 qver 21
4:33 r1Ki 17:20;
Mt 6:6

4:34 s1Ki 17:21;
Ac 20:10
4:35 tS Jos 6:15
u2Ki 8:5
4:36 vHeb 11:35
4:38 wS 2Ki 2:1
xS Lev 26:26;
2Ki 8:1
4:41 yS Ex 15:25;
S 2Ki 2:21
4:42 z1Sa 9:4
aMt 14:17; 15:36

4:26 *Everything is all right.* The woman was determined to share her distress with no one but the prophet from whom she had received the promise of the birth of her son.

4:28 *Didn't I tell you, 'Don't raise my hopes'?* The woman struggled with the question of why her Lord would take from her that which she had been given as a special demonstration of his grace and the trustworthiness of his word.

4:29 *Lay my staff on the boy's face.* It appears that Elisha expected the Lord to restore the boy's life when the staff was placed on him. This does not suggest that Elisha attributed magical power to the staff, but that he viewed it as a representation of his own presence and a symbol of divine power (see note on 2:8; cf. Ex 14:16; Ac 19:12).

4:30 *I will not leave you.* The woman was not convinced that Gehazi's mission would be successful and insisted that Elisha himself accompany her to Shunem.

4:33 *shut the door on the two of them and prayed.* Just as Elijah had done in a similar situation years before (see 1Ki 17:20–22), Elisha first turned to the Lord in earnest prayer for restoration of life to the dead child. His prayer is clear evidence that his subsequent actions were not intended as a

magical means of restoring life.

4:34 *lay upon the boy.* See note on 1Ki 17:21. Perhaps Elisha was familiar with the earlier similar action of Elijah.

4:37 *fell at his feet and bowed to the ground.* The woman gratefully acknowledged the special favor granted to her by the Lord through Elisha, and silently reaffirmed the verbal confession of the widow of Zarephath (see 1Ki 17:24).

4:38 *famine in that region.* Perhaps the same famine mentioned in 8:1. Famine was a covenant curse (see Lev 26:19–20,26; Dt 28:18,23–24; 1Ki 8:36–37) and evidence of God's anger with his people's disobedience to their covenant obligations. *company of the prophets.* See note on 2:3.

4:39 *wild vine . . . gourds.* The precise type of plant is not specified.

4:41 *flour.* The flour itself did not make the stew edible (see 2:21 and note). It was simply a means by which the Lord provided for those who were faithful to the covenant, at a time when others suffered under the covenant curse.

4:42 *first ripe grain.* Instead of bringing the firstfruits of the new harvest (see Lev 2:14; 23:15–17; Dt 18:3–5) to the

barley bread[b] baked from the first ripe grain, along with some heads of new grain. "Give it to the people to eat," Elisha said.

[43]"How can I set this before a hundred men?" his servant asked.

But Elisha answered, "Give it to the people to eat.[c] For this is what the LORD says: 'They will eat and have some left over.[d]'" [44]Then he set it before them, and they ate and had some left over, according to the word of the LORD.

Naaman Healed of Leprosy

5 Now Naaman was commander of the army of the king of Aram.[e] He was a great man in the sight of his master and highly regarded, because through him the LORD had given victory to Aram. He was a valiant soldier, but he had leprosy.[d][f]

[2]Now bands[g] from Aram had gone out and had taken captive a young girl from Israel, and she served Naaman's wife. [3]She said to her mistress, "If only my master would see the prophet[h] who is in Samaria! He would cure him of his leprosy."

[4]Naaman went to his master and told him what the girl from Israel had said. [5]"By all means, go," the king of Aram replied. "I will send a letter to the king of Israel." So Naaman left, taking with him

ten talents[e] of silver, six thousand shekels[f] of gold and ten sets of clothing.[i] [6]The letter that he took to the king of Israel read: "With this letter I am sending my servant Naaman to you so that you may cure him of his leprosy."

[7]As soon as the king of Israel read the letter,[j] he tore his robes and said, "Am I God?[k] Can I kill and bring back to life?[l] Why does this fellow send someone to me to be cured of his leprosy? See how he is trying to pick a quarrel[m] with me!"

[8]When Elisha the man of God heard that the king of Israel had torn his robes, he sent him this message: "Why have you torn your robes? Have the man come to me and he will know that there is a prophet[n] in Israel." [9]So Naaman went with his horses and chariots and stopped at the door of Elisha's house. [10]Elisha sent a messenger to say to him, "Go, wash[o] yourself seven times[p] in the Jordan, and your flesh will be restored and you will be cleansed."

[11]But Naaman went away angry and said, "I thought that he would surely come

Cross references

4:42 [b]S 1Sa 9:7
4:43 [c]Lk 9:13
[d]Mt 14:20; Jn 6:12
5:1 [e]S Ge 10:22; S 2Sa 10:19 /S Ex 4:6; S Nu 12:10; Lk 4:27
5:2 [g]2Ki 6:23; 13:20; 24:2
5:3 [h]S Ge 20:7
5:5 [i]ver 22; S Ge 24:53; Jdg 14:12; S 1Sa 9:7
5:7 [j]2Ki 19:14 [k]S Ge 30:2 [l]S Dt 32:39 [m]1Ki 20:7
5:8 [n]S 1Ki 22:7
5:10 [o]Jn 9:7 [p]S Ge 33:3; S Lev 14:7

[d]/ The Hebrew word was used for various diseases affecting the skin—not necessarily leprosy; also in verses 3, 6, 7, 11 and 27.   [e]5 That is, about 750 pounds (about 340 kilograms)   [f]5 That is, about 150 pounds (about 70 kilograms)

---

apostate priests at Bethel and Dan (see 1Ki 12:28–31), godly people in the northern kingdom may have contributed their offerings for the sustenance of Elisha and those associated with him (see note on v. 23). Thus they looked upon Elisha rather than the apostate king and priests as the true representative of their covenant Lord.

4:43 *the LORD says.* The bread was multiplied at the word of the Lord through Elisha apart from any intermediate means (contrast v. 41; 2:20; cf. Mk 6:35–43).

5:1 *king of Aram.* Probably Ben-Hadad II (see notes on 8:7; 13:3; 1Ki 20:1). *the LORD had given victory to Aram.* Probably a reference to an otherwise undocumented Aramean victory over the Assyrians in the aftermath of the battle of Qarqar in 853 B.C. (see note on 1Ki 22:1). In the narrator's theological perspective, this victory is attributable to the sovereignty of the God of Israel, who is seen as the ruler and controller of the destinies of all nations, not just that of Israel (see Eze 30:24; Am 2:1–3; 9:7).

5:2 *bands from Aram.* Although Israel had concluded a peace treaty with the Arameans during the reign of Ahab (see 1Ki 20:34), minor border skirmishes continued between the two states in the aftermath of the battle for control of Ramoth Gilead, in which Ahab had been killed (see note on 1Ki 22:4; see also 1Ki 22:35). *young girl from Israel.* In sharp contrast to the Israelite king in Samaria, this young girl held captive in Damascus was very much aware of God's saving presence with his people through his servant Elisha, and she selflessly shared that knowledge with her Aramean captors.

5:3 *prophet who is in Samaria.* Elisha, who maintained a residence in Samaria (see v. 9; 2:25; 6:19).

5:5 *I will send a letter to the king of Israel.* The border skirmishes had not nullified the official peace between the two nations as established by treaty. The king of Israel was Joram (see 1:17; 3:1; 9:24). *ten talents of silver.* See NIV

text note. An idea of the relative value of this amount of silver can be seen by comparing it with the price Omri paid for the hill of Samaria (see 1Ki 16:24).

5:6 *so that you may cure him of his leprosy.* Ben-Hadad assumed that the prophet described by the Israelite slave girl was subject to the authority of the king and that his services could be bought with a sufficiently large gift. He thought he could buy with worldly wealth one of the chief blessings of God's saving presence among his people.

5:7 *he is trying to pick a quarrel with me!* Joram concluded that the entire incident was an attempt by Ben-Hadad to create a pretext for a declaration of war. So blind was the king to God's saving presence through Elisha that he could think only of international intrigue.

5:8 *Why have you torn your robes?* Elisha chided Joram for his fear (see note on 1Sa 17:11) and for his failure to consult the Lord's prophet (see 3:13–14 for evidence of the tension that existed between Joram and Elisha).

5:9 *with his horses and chariots.* This proud pagan would command the healing by his lordly presence.

5:10 *wash yourself seven times in the Jordan.* The instruction is designed to demonstrate to Naaman that healing would come by the power of the God of Israel, but only if he obeyed the word of the Lord's prophet. The prophet himself was not a healer. Ritual washings were practiced among Eastern religions as a purification rite, and the number seven was generally known as a symbol of completeness. Naaman was to wash in the muddy waters of the Jordan River, demonstrating that there was no natural connection between the washing and the desired healing. Perhaps it also suggested that one needed to pass through the Jordan, as Israel had done (Jos 3–4), in order to obtain healing from the God of Israel.

5:11 *wave his hand over the spot and cure me of my*

out to me and stand and call on the name of the LORD his God, wave his hand *q* over the spot and cure me of my leprosy. [12]Are not Abana and Pharpar, the rivers of Damascus, better than any of the waters *r* of Israel? Couldn't I wash in them and be cleansed?" So he turned and went off in a rage. *s*

[13]Naaman's servants went to him and said, "My father, *t* if the prophet had told you to do some great thing, would you not have done it? How much more, then, when he tells you, 'Wash and be cleansed'!" [14]So he went down and dipped himself in the Jordan seven times, *u* as the man of God had told him, and his flesh was restored *v* and became clean like that of a young boy. *w*

[15]Then Naaman and all his attendants went back to the man of God *x*. He stood before him and said, "Now I know *y* that there is no God in all the world except in Israel. Please accept now a gift *z* from your servant."

[16]The prophet answered, "As surely as the LORD lives, whom I serve, I will not accept a thing." And even though Naaman urged him, he refused. *a*

[17]"If you will not," said Naaman, "please let me, your servant, be given as much earth *b* as a pair of mules can carry, for your servant will never again make burnt offerings and sacrifices to any other god but the LORD. [18]But may the LORD forgive your servant for this one thing: When my master enters the temple of Rimmon to

bow down and he is leaning *c* on my arm and I bow there also—when I bow down in the temple of Rimmon, may the LORD forgive your servant for this."

[19]"Go in peace," *d* Elisha said.

After Naaman had traveled some distance, [20]Gehazi, the servant of Elisha the man of God, said to himself, "My master was too easy on Naaman, this Aramean, by not accepting from him what he brought. As surely as the LORD *e* lives, I will run after him and get something from him."

[21]So Gehazi hurried after Naaman. When Naaman saw him running toward him, he got down from the chariot to meet him. "Is everything all right?" he asked.

[22]"Everything is all right," Gehazi answered. "My master sent me to say, 'Two young men from the company of the prophets have just come to me from the hill country of Ephraim. Please give them a talent *g* of silver and two sets of clothing.' " *f*

[23]"By all means, take two talents," said Naaman. He urged Gehazi to accept them, and then tied up the two talents of silver in two bags, with two sets of clothing. He gave them to two of his servants, and they carried them ahead of Gehazi. [24]When Gehazi came to the hill, he took the things from the servants and put them away in the house. He sent the men away and they left. [25]Then he went in and stood before his master Elisha.

Cross references

5:11 *q* S Ex 7:19
5:12 *r* Isa 8:6
s Pr 14:17,29; 19:11; 29:11
5:13 *t* 2Ki 6:21; 13:14
5:14 *u* S Ge 33:3; S Lev 14:7; S Jos 6:15
v S Ex 4:7
w Job 33:25
5:15 *x* S Jos 2:11
y S Jos 4:24; S 1Sa 17:46
z S 1Sa 9:7
5:16 *a* ver 20,26; Ge 14:23; Da 5:17
5:17 *b* Ex 20:24
5:18 *c* 2Ki 7:2
5:19 *d* 1Sa 1:17; S Ac 15:33
5:20 *e* Ex 20:7
5:22 *f* S ver 5; S Ge 45:22

g 22 That is, about 75 pounds (about 34 kilograms)

---

leprosy. Naaman expected to be healed by the magical technique of the prophet rather than by the power of God operative in connection with his own obedient response to God's word.

5:12 *Abana and Pharpar.* The Abana was termed the Golden River by the Greeks. It is usually identified with the Barada River of today, rising in the Anti-Lebanon mountains and flowing through the city of Damascus. The Pharpar River flows east from Mount Hermon just to the south of Damascus.

5:14 *his flesh was restored and became clean like that of a young boy.* Physically he was reborn (see also v. 15 and note). As he obeyed God's word, Naaman received the gift of God's grace. Naaman is here a sign to disobedient Israel that God's blessing is found only in the path of trustful obedience. When his own people turn away from covenant faithfulness, God will raise up those who will follow his word from outside the covenant nation (see notes on 1Ki 17:9–24; see also Mt 8:10–12; Lk 4:27).

5:15 *no God in all the world except in Israel.* Naaman's confession put to shame the Israelites who continued to waver in their opinion on whether Baal and the Lord (Yahweh) were both gods, or whether Yahweh alone was God (see note on 1Ki 18:21).

5:16 *I will not accept a thing.* Elisha did not seek monetary gain for proclaiming the word of the Lord (see Mt 10:8). Naaman was healed solely by divine grace, not by the power

of Elisha.

5:17 *let me ... be given as much earth as a pair of mules can carry.* In the ancient world it was commonly thought that a deity could be worshiped only on the soil of the nation to which he was bound (see v. 15). For this reason Naaman wanted to take Israelite soil with him in order to have a place in Damascus for the worship of the Lord.

5:18 *my master.* Ben-Hadad, king of Aram. *Rimmon.* Also known as Hadad (and in Canaan and Phoenicia as Baal), this Aramean deity was the god of storm ("Rimmon" means "thunderer") and war. The two names were sometimes combined (see note on Zec 12:11).

5:19 *Go in peace.* Elisha did not directly address Naaman's problem of conscience (v. 18), but commended him to the leading and grace of God as he returned to his pagan environment and official responsibilities.

5:20 *As surely as the LORD lives.* An oath formula (see note on 1Sa 14:39).

5:22 *company of the prophets.* See note on 2:3. *Please give them a talent of silver and two sets of clothing.* Gehazi deceived Naaman in order to satisfy his desire for material gain. The evil of his lie was compounded in that it obscured the gracious character of the Lord's work in Naaman's healing and blurred the distinction between Elisha's function as a true prophet of the Lord and the self-serving actions of false prophets and pagan soothsayers.

5:24 *house.* Of Elisha (see v. 9).

"Where have you been, Gehazi?" Elisha asked.

"Your servant didn't go anywhere," Gehazi answered.

26But Elisha said to him, "Was not my spirit with you when the man got down from his chariot to meet you? Is this the time *g* to take money, or to accept clothes, olive groves, vineyards, flocks, herds, or menservants and maidservants? *h* 27Naaman's leprosy *i* will cling to you and to your descendants forever." Then Gehazi *j* went from Elisha's presence and he was leprous, as white as snow. *k*

An Axhead Floats

6 The company *l* of the prophets said to Elisha, "Look, the place where we meet with you is too small for us. 2Let us go to the Jordan, where each of us can get a pole; and let us build a place there for us to live."

And he said, "Go."

3Then one of them said, "Won't you please come with your servants?"

"I will," Elisha replied. 4And he went with them.

They went to the Jordan and began to cut down trees. 5As one of them was cutting down a tree, the iron axhead fell into the water. "Oh, my lord," he cried out, "it was borrowed!"

6The man of God asked, "Where did it fall?" When he showed him the place, Elisha cut a stick and threw *m* it there, and made the iron float. 7"Lift it out," he said. Then the man reached out his hand and took it.

Elisha Traps Blinded Arameans

8Now the king of Aram was at war with Israel. After conferring with his officers, he said, "I will set up my camp in such and such a place."

9The man of God sent word to the king *n* of Israel: "Beware of passing that place, because the Arameans are going down there." 10So the king of Israel checked on the place indicated by the man of God. Time and again Elisha warned *o* the king, so that he was on his guard in such places.

11This enraged the king of Aram. He summoned his officers and demanded of them, "Will you not tell me which of us is on the side of the king of Israel?"

12"None of us, my lord the king *p*," said one of his officers, "but Elisha, the prophet who is in Israel, tells the king of Israel the very words you speak in your bedroom."

13"Go, find out where he is," the king ordered, "so I can send men and capture him." The report came back: "He is in Dothan." *q* 14Then he sent *r* horses and chariots and a strong force there. They went by night and surrounded the city.

15When the servant of the man of God got up and went out early the next morning, an army with horses and chariots had surrounded the city. "Oh, my lord, what shall we do?" the servant asked.

16"Don't be afraid," *s* the prophet answered. "Those who are with us are more *t* than those who are with them."

17And Elisha prayed, "O LORD, open his

5:26 *g*S ver 16
*h*Jer 45:5
5:27 *i*S Nu 12:10
*j*Col 3:5 *k*S Ex 4:6
6:1 *l*S 1Sa 10:5
6:6 *m*S Ex 15:25;
S 2Ki 2:21

6:9 *n*ver 12
6:10 *o*Jer 11:18
6:12 *p*ver 9
6:13 *q*Ge 37:17
6:14 *r*2Ki 1:9
6:16 *s*S Ge 15:1
*t*2Ch 32:7;
Ps 55:18;
Ro 8:31; 1Jn 4:4

5:26 *Is this the time to take money ... ?* Gehazi sought to use the grace of God granted to another individual for his own material advantage. This was equivalent to making merchandise of God's grace (see note on 2Co 2:17). "Money" here and elsewhere in 2 Kings refers to gold or silver in various weights, not to coins, which were a later invention. *clothes ... maidservants.* Evidently what Gehazi secretly hoped to acquire with the two talents of silver (see note on v. 5).

5:27 *leprosy.* See NIV text note on v. 1. *to you and to your descendants forever.* For the extension of punishment to the children of an offender of God's law see Ex 20:5 and note; see also note on Jos 7:24. *white as snow.* See Ex 4:6.

6:1 *company of the prophets.* See note on 2:3.

6:2 *a place there for us to live.* Some have suggested that the company of prophets lived in a communal housing structure. The Hebrew for this phrase, however, could be translated "a place there for us to sit," referring to some type of assembly hall. It is implied in 4:1–7 that there were separate dwellings for the members of the prophetic companies (see note on 1Sa 19:18).

6:5 *it was borrowed.* At that time an iron axhead was a costly tool, too expensive for the members of the prophetic company to purchase. Having lost it, the borrower faced the prospect of having to work off the value as a bondservant.

6:6 *Elisha cut a stick and threw it there, and made the iron float.* The Lord demonstrated here his concern for the welfare of his faithful ones.

6:8 *king of Aram.* Probably Ben-Hadad II (see note on 5:1). *war with Israel.* A reference to border clashes rather than full-scale hostility (see v. 23; see also note on 5:2). Some indication of Israelite weakness and Aramean strength is seen in the ability of the Arameans to send forces to Dothan (only about 11 miles north of Samaria) without apparent difficulty (see vv. 13–14).

6:9 *man of God.* Elisha (see v. 10). *king of Israel.* Probably Joram (see 1:17; 3:1; 9:24).

6:11 *which of us is on the side of the king of Israel?* Repeated evidence that Israel possessed advance knowledge of Aramean military plans led the king of Aram to suspect that there was a traitor among his top officials.

6:13 *capture him.* The king of Aram thought he could eliminate Elisha's influence by denying him contact with Israel's king. *Dothan.* Located on a hill about halfway between Jezreel and Samaria, where the main royal residences were (see 1:2; 3:1; 8:29; 9:15; 10:1; 1Ki 21:1).

6:16 *Those who are with us are more than those who are with them.* Elisha knew that there was greater strength in the unseen reality of the hosts of heaven than in the visible reality of the Aramean forces (see 2Ch 32:7–8; 1Jn 4:4).

eyes so he may see." Then the LORD opened the servant's eyes, and he looked and saw the hills full of horses and chariots[u] of fire all around Elisha.

18As the enemy came down toward him, Elisha prayed to the LORD, "Strike these people with blindness."[v] So he struck them with blindness, as Elisha had asked.

19Elisha told them, "This is not the road and this is not the city. Follow me, and I will lead you to the man you are looking for." And he led them to Samaria.

20After they entered the city, Elisha said, "LORD, open the eyes of these men so they can see." Then the LORD opened their eyes and they looked, and there they were, inside Samaria.

21When the king of Israel saw them, he asked Elisha, "Shall I kill them, my father?[w] Shall I kill them?"

22"Do not kill them," he answered. "Would you kill men you have captured[x] with your own sword or bow? Set food and water before them so that they may eat and drink and then go back to their master." 23So he prepared a great feast for them, and after they had finished eating and drinking, he sent them away, and they returned to their master. So the bands[y] from Aram stopped raiding Israel's territory.

6:17 uS 2Ki 2:11, 12
6:18 vGe 19:11; Ac 13:11
6:21 wS 2Ki 5:13
6:22 xS Dt 20:11; 2Ch 28:8-15
6:23 yS 2Ki 5:2

6:24 zS 1Ki 15:18; 2Ki 8:7 aDt 28:52
6:25 bS Lev 26:26; S Ru 1:1 cIsa 36:12
6:29 dS Lev 26:29; Dt 28:53-55
6:30 e2Ki 18:37; Isa 22:15 fS Ge 37:34

Famine in Besieged Samaria

24Some time later, Ben-Hadad[z] king of Aram mobilized his entire army and marched up and laid siege[a] to Samaria. 25There was a great famine[b] in the city; the siege lasted so long that a donkey's head sold for eighty shekels[h] of silver, and a quarter of a cab[i] of seed pods[j][c] for five shekels.[k]

26As the king of Israel was passing by on the wall, a woman cried to him, "Help me, my lord the king!"

27The king replied, "If the LORD does not help you, where can I get help for you? From the threshing floor? From the winepress?" 28Then he asked her, "What's the matter?"

She answered, "This woman said to me, 'Give up your son so we may eat him today, and tomorrow we'll eat my son.' 29So we cooked my son and ate[d] him. The next day I said to her, 'Give up your son so we may eat him,' but she had hidden him."

30When the king heard the woman's words, he tore[e] his robes. As he went along the wall, the people looked, and there, underneath, he had sackcloth[f] on his body. 31He said, "May God deal with

h25 That is, about 2 pounds (about 1 kilogram)   i25 That is, probably about 1/2 pint (about 0.3 liter)   j25 Or of dove's dung   k25 That is, about 2 ounces (about 55 grams)

6:17 *saw the hills full of horses and chariots.* In response to Elisha's prayer, his servant was able to see the protecting might of the heavenly hosts gathered about Elisha (see Ge 32:1–2; Ps 34:7; 91:11–12; Mt 18:10; 26:53; see also note on 2Ki 2:11).

6:18 *Strike these people with blindness.* Elisha had prayed for the eyes of his servant to be opened to the unseen reality of the heavenly hosts; now he prays for the eyes of the Aramean soldiers to be closed to earthly reality (see Ge 19:11).

6:19 *This is not the road and this is not the city.* Elisha's statement led the Aramean soldiers to believe that they were being directed to the city where Elisha could be found. Technically this statement was not an untruth, since Elisha accompanied them to Samaria, but it was a means of deceiving the Aramean soldiers into a trap inside Samaria, the fortress-like capital city of the northern kingdom (see Ex 1:19–20; Jos 2:6; 1Sa 16:1–2 for other instances of deception recorded in the OT).

6:20 *there they were, inside Samaria.* The power of the Lord operative through Elisha turned the intended captors into captives.

6:21 *king of Israel.* Joram (see note on v. 9).

6:22 *Do not kill them.* In reality the Aramean soldiers had been taken captive by the power of the Lord, not by Joram's military prowess. The Lord's purpose was to demonstrate to them and their king and to the Israelites and their king that Israel's national security ultimately was grounded in the Lord, not in military forces or strategies.

6:23 *bands from Aram stopped raiding Israel's territory.* See notes on v. 8; 5:2. Temporarily the Arameans recognized the futility of opposition to the power of the God of

Israel.

6:24 *Ben-Hadad.* The same Ben-Hadad who had besieged Samaria on a previous occasion (see notes on 13:3; 1Ki 20:1). This siege is probably to be dated c. 850 B.C.

6:25 *donkey's head.* According to Pentateuchal law the donkey was unclean and not to be eaten (see Lev 11:2–7; Dt 14:4–8). The severity of the famine caused the inhabitants of Samaria not only to disregard the laws of uncleanness, but also to place a high value on the least edible part of the donkey. *eighty shekels of silver.* See NIV text note; see also note on 5:5.

6:27 *If the LORD does not help you, where can I get help for you?* Joram correctly recognized his own inability to assist the woman if the Lord himself did not act in Israel's behalf, but he wrongly implied that the Lord was to be blamed for a situation brought on by Israel's own disobedience and idolatry.

6:28 *tomorrow we'll eat my son.* The sins of the king and people were so great that the covenant curses of Lev 26:29 and Dt 28:53,57 were being inflicted (cf. La 4:10).

6:30 *tore his robes.* More an expression of anger toward Elisha and the Lord (see v. 31) than one of repentance and sorrow for the sins that had provoked the covenant curse. *sackcloth.* A coarse cloth usually worn as a sign of mourning (see note on Ge 37:34). It is not clear why Joram wore sackcloth hidden under his royal robe. Perhaps it was a testing of the Lord, a private ritual to attempt to gain divine favor.

6:31 *May God deal with me, be it ever so severely.* A curse formula (see note on 1Sa 3:17). *if the head of Elisha . . . remains on his shoulders today!* Joram considered Elisha in some way responsible for the conditions in the city. Cf.

me, be it ever so severely, if the head of Elisha son of Shaphat remains on his shoulders today!"

³²Now Elisha was sitting in his house, and the eldersᵍ were sitting with him. The king sent a messenger ahead, but before he arrived, Elisha said to the elders, "Don't you see how this murdererʰ is sending someone to cut off my head?ⁱ Look, when the messenger comes, shut the door and hold it shut against him. Is not the sound of his master's footsteps behind him?"

³³While he was still talking to them, the messenger came down to him. And ˏthe kingˎ said, "This disaster is from the Lord. Why should I waitʲ for the Lord any longer?"

7 Elisha said, "Hear the word of the Lord. This is what the Lord says: About this time tomorrow, a seahˡ of flour will sell for a shekelᵐ and two seahsⁿ of barley for a shekelᵏ at the gate of Samaria."

²The officer on whose arm the king was leaningˡ said to the man of God, "Look, even if the Lord should open the floodgatesᵐ of the heavens, could this happen?"

"You will see it with your own eyes," answered Elisha, "but you will not eatⁿ any of it!"

The Siege Lifted

³Now there were four men with leprosyᵒ ᵒ at the entrance of the city gate. They said to each other, "Why stay here until we die? ⁴If we say, 'We'll go into the city'—the famine is there, and we will die. And if we stay here, we will die. So let's go over to the camp of the Arameans and surrender. If they spare us, we live; if they kill us, then we die."

⁵At dusk they got up and went to the camp of the Arameans. When they reached the edge of the camp, not a man was there, ⁶for the Lord had caused the Arameans to hear the soundᵖ of chariots and horses and a great army, so that they said to one another, "Look, the king of Israel has hiredᵠ the Hittiteʳ and Egyptian kings to attack

us!" ⁷So they got up and fledˢ in the dusk and abandoned their tents and their horses and donkeys. They left the camp as it was and ran for their lives.

⁸The men who had leprosyᵗ reached the edge of the camp and entered one of the tents. They ate and drank, and carried away silver, gold and clothes, and went off and hid them. They returned and entered another tent and took some things from it and hid them also.

⁹Then they said to each other, "We're not doing right. This is a day of good news and we are keeping it to ourselves. If we wait until daylight, punishment will overtake us. Let's go at once and report this to the royal palace."

¹⁰So they went and called out to the city gatekeepers and told them, "We went into the Aramean camp and not a man was there—not a sound of anyone—only tethered horses and donkeys, and the tents left just as they were." ¹¹The gatekeepers shouted the news, and it was reported within the palace.

¹²The king got up in the night and said to his officers, "I will tell you what the Arameans have done to us. They know we are starving; so they have left the camp to hideᵘ in the countryside, thinking, 'They will surely come out, and then we will take them alive and get into the city.'"

¹³One of his officers answered, "Have some men take five of the horses that are left in the city. Their plight will be like that of all the Israelites left here—yes, they will only be like all these Israelites who are doomed. So let us send them to find out what happened."

¹⁴So they selected two chariots with their horses, and the king sent them after the Aramean army. He commanded the drivers, "Go and find out what has hap-

6:32 ᵍEze 8:1; 14:1; 20:1
ʰ1Ki 18:4 ⁱver 31
6:33 ʲLev 24:11; Isa 40:31
7:1 ᵏver 16
7:2 ˡ2Ki 5:18 ᵐver 19; Ge 7:11; Ps 78:23; Mal 3:10 ⁿver 17
7:3 ᵒLev 13:45-46; Nu 5:1-4
7:6 ᵖS Ex 14:24; Eze 1:24 ᵠ2Sa 10:6; Jer 46:21 ʳNu 13:29

7:7 ˢJdg 7:21; Ps 48:4-6; Pr 28:1; Isa 30:17
7:8 ᵗIsa 33:23; 35:6
7:12 ᵘJos 8:4

ˡ *l* That is, probably about 7 quarts (about 7.3 liters); also in verses 16 and 18 ᵐ *l* That is, about 2/5 ounce (about 11 grams); also in verses 16 and 18 ⁿ *l* That is, probably about 13 quarts (about 15 liters); also in verses 16 and 18 ᵒ3 The Hebrew word is used for various diseases affecting the skin—not necessarily leprosy; also in verse 8.

Ahab's attitude toward Elijah (1Ki 18:10,16; 21:20).
6:32 *elders.* Leaders of the city (see notes on Ex 3:16; 2Sa 3:17). They sit with Elisha rather than with the king.
6:33 *Why should I wait for the Lord any longer?* Joram felt himself deceived by Elisha and abandoned by the Lord, whom he blamed for the disastrous conditions in the city.
7:1 *a seah of flour will sell for a shekel.* See NIV text notes. This was about double the normal cost of flour, but a phenomenal improvement.
7:2 *floodgates of the heavens.* See v. 19; Ge 8:2; Isa 24:18.
7:3 *entrance of the city gate.* Pentateuchal law excluded

persons with skin diseases from residence in the community (Lev 13:46; Nu 5:2–3).
7:6 *the Lord had caused the Arameans to hear the sound.* See 2Sa 5:24 and note. *Hittite . . . kings.* Kings of small city-states ruled by dynasties of Hittite origin, which had arisen in northern Aram after the fall of the Hittite empire c. 1200 B.C.
7:12 *what the Arameans have done to us.* Joram's unbelief caused him to conclude that the report of the four leprous men was part of an Aramean war strategy rather than an evidence of the fulfillment of Elisha's prophecy (see v. 1).

pened." [15]They followed them as far as the Jordan, and they found the whole road strewn with the clothing and equipment the Arameans had thrown away in their headlong flight.[v] So the messengers returned and reported to the king. [16]Then the people went out and plundered[w] the camp of the Arameans. So a seah of flour sold for a shekel, and two seahs of barley sold for a shekel,[x] as the LORD had said.

[17]Now the king had put the officer on whose arm he leaned in charge of the gate, and the people trampled him in the gateway, and he died,[y] just as the man of God had foretold when the king came down to his house. [18]It happened as the man of God had said to the king: "About this time tomorrow, a seah of flour will sell for a shekel and two seahs of barley for a shekel at the gate of Samaria."

[19]The officer had said to the man of God, "Look, even if the LORD should open the floodgates[z] of the heavens, could this happen?" The man of God had replied, "You will see it with your own eyes, but you will not eat any of it!" [20]And that is exactly what happened to him, for the people trampled him in the gateway, and he died.

The Shunammite's Land Restored

8 Now Elisha had said to the woman[a] whose son he had restored to life, "Go away with your family and stay for a while wherever you can, because the LORD has decreed a famine[b] in the land that will last

7:15 *v*Job 27:22
7:16 *w*Isa 33:4, 23 *x*ver 1
7:17 *y*S ver 2
7:19 *z*S ver 2
8:1 *a*2Ki 4:8-37 *b*S Lev 26:26; S Dt 28:22; S Ru 1:1

*c*S Ge 12:10
8:5 *d*2Ki 4:35
8:7 *e*S 2Sa 8:5
*f*S 2Ki 6:24
8:8 *g*1Ki 19:15
*h*S Ge 32:20; S 1Sa 9:7
*i*S Jdg 18:5

seven years."[c] [2]The woman proceeded to do as the man of God said. She and her family went away and stayed in the land of the Philistines seven years.

[3]At the end of the seven years she came back from the land of the Philistines and went to the king to beg for her house and land. [4]The king was talking to Gehazi, the servant of the man of God, and had said, "Tell me about all the great things Elisha has done." [5]Just as Gehazi was telling the king how Elisha had restored[d] the dead to life, the woman whose son Elisha had brought back to life came to beg the king for her house and land.

Gehazi said, "This is the woman, my lord the king, and this is her son whom Elisha restored to life." [6]The king asked the woman about it, and she told him.

Then he assigned an official to her case and said to him, "Give back everything that belonged to her, including all the income from her land from the day she left the country until now."

Hazael Murders Ben-Hadad

[7]Elisha went to Damascus,[e] and Ben-Hadad[f] king of Aram was ill. When the king was told, "The man of God has come all the way up here," [8]he said to Hazael,[g] "Take a gift[h] with you and go to meet the man of God. Consult[i] the LORD through him; ask him, 'Will I recover from this illness?'"

[9]Hazael went to meet Elisha, taking with him as a gift forty camel-loads of all

---

7:16–20 *as the LORD had said . . . as the man of God had foretold . . . as the man of God had said . . . that is exactly what happened to him.* Emphasizing the trustworthiness of the prophetic word spoken by Elisha. In the fulfillment of Elisha's prophecy Israel was reminded that deliverance from her enemies was a gift of God's grace and that rejection of God's word provoked the wrath of divine judgment.

8:1 *the LORD has decreed a famine.* The famine should have been perceived by the people of the northern kingdom as a covenant curse sent on them because of their sin (see note on 4:38). *seven years.* It is not clear whether this famine began before or after the Aramean siege of Samaria (see 4:38; 6:24–7:20).

8:2 *She and her family went away.* Elisha's instruction enabled the woman and her family to escape the privations of the famine.

8:3 *went to the king.* See note on 1Ki 3:16. *beg for her house and land.* Either someone had illegally occupied the woman's property during her absence, or it had fallen to the domain of the king by virtue of its abandonment.

8:4 *Gehazi.* See 5:27. *Tell me about all the great things Elisha has done.* The king's lack of familiarity with Elisha's ministry is perhaps an indication that this incident occurred in the early days of the reign of Jehu rather than in the time of Joram, who had had numerous contacts with Elisha (see 3:13–14; 5:7–10; 6:10–23; 6:24–7:20). But see note on 5:7.

8:5 *as Gehazi was telling the king.* The woman's approach to the king providentially coincided with Gehazi's story of her son's miraculous restoration to life through the ministry of Elisha.

8:6 *Give back everything that belonged to her.* The widow and her son were living examples of the Lord's provision and blessing for those who were obedient to the word of the Lord through his prophets.

8:7 *Elisha went to Damascus.* The time had come for Elisha to carry out one of the three tasks originally given to Elijah at Mount Horeb (see notes on 1Ki 19:15–16). The annals of the Assyrian ruler Shalmaneser III record Assyrian victories over Ben-Hadad (Hadadezer) of Damascus in 846 B.C. and Hazael of Damascus in 842. Elisha's visit to Damascus is to be dated c. 843.

8:8 *Consult the LORD through him.* In a reversal of the situation described in 1:1–4, a pagan king seeks an oracle from Israel's God. *Will I recover . . . ?* The question is the same as that of Ahaziah in 1:2.

8:9 *forty camel-loads of all the finest wares of Damascus.* Damascus was the center for trade between Egypt, Asia Minor and Mesopotamia. Ben-Hadad evidently thought a generous gift would favorably influence Elisha's oracle. *Your son Ben-Hadad.* Use of father-son terminology is a tacit acknowledgment by Ben-Hadad of Elisha's superiority (see 6:21; 1Sa 25:8).

the finest wares of Damascus. He went in
and stood before him, and said, "Your son
Ben-Hadad king of Aram has sent me to
ask, 'Will I recover from this illness?' "
10 Elisha answered, "Go and say to him,
'You will certainly recover';[j] but[p] the
LORD has revealed to me that he will in
fact die." 11 He stared at him with a fixed
gaze until Hazael felt ashamed.[k] Then the
man of God began to weep.[l]
12 "Why is my lord weeping?" asked
Hazael.
"Because I know the harm[m] you will do
to the Israelites," he answered. "You will
set fire to their fortified places, kill their
young men with the sword, dash[n] their
little children[o] to the ground, and rip
open[p] their pregnant women."
13 Hazael said, "How could your servant,
a mere dog,[q] accomplish such a feat?"
"The LORD has shown me that you will
become king[r] of Aram," answered Elisha.
14 Then Hazael left Elisha and returned
to his master. When Ben-Hadad asked,
"What did Elisha say to you?" Hazael replied, "He told me that you would certainly recover." 15 But the next day he took
a thick cloth, soaked it in water and spread
it over the king's face, so that he died.[s]
Then Hazael succeeded him as king.

8:10 [j]Isa 38:1 **8:11** [k]S Jdg 3:25 [l]Lk 19:41 **8:12** [m]S 1Ki 19:17 [n]Ps 137:9; Isa 13:16; Hos 13:16; Na 3:10; Lk 19:44 [o]S Ge 34:29 [p]2Ki 15:16; Am 1:13 **8:13** [q]S 1Sa 17:43; S 2Sa 3:8 [r]1Ki 19:15 **8:15** [s]S 2Ki 1:17

8:16 [t]S 2Ki 1:17 [u]2Ch 21:1-4 **8:18** [v]ver 26; 2Ki 11:1 **8:19** [w]S Ge 6:13 [x]S 2Sa 21:17; Rev 21:23 **8:20** [y]S 1Ki 22:47 **8:22** [z]Ge 27:40 [a]S Nu 33:20; Jos 21:13; 2Ki 19:8

Jehoram King of Judah

8:16–24pp — 2Ch 21:5–10,20

16 In the fifth year of Joram[t] son of Ahab
king of Israel, when Jehoshaphat was king
of Judah, Jehoram[u] son of Jehoshaphat began his reign as king of Judah. 17 He was
thirty-two years old when he became king,
and he reigned in Jerusalem eight years.
18 He walked in the ways of the kings of
Israel, as the house of Ahab had done, for
he married a daughter[v] of Ahab. He did
evil in the eyes of the LORD. 19 Nevertheless, for the sake of his servant David, the
LORD was not willing to destroy[w] Judah.
He had promised to maintain a lamp[x] for
David and his descendants forever.
20 In the time of Jehoram, Edom rebelled
against Judah and set up its own king.[y]
21 So Jehoram[q] went to Zair with all his
chariots. The Edomites surrounded him
and his chariot commanders, but he rose
up and broke through by night; his army,
however, fled back home. 22 To this day
Edom has been in rebellion[z] against
Judah. Libnah[a] revolted at the same time.
23 As for the other events of Jehoram's
reign, and all he did, are they not written

[p] *10* The Hebrew may also be read *Go and say, 'You will certainly not recover,' for.* [q] *21* Hebrew *Joram,* a variant of *Jehoram;* also in verses 23 and 24

8:10 *You will certainly recover.* This reading of the Hebrew text (see NIV text note for an alternative reading) is to be preferred (see v. 14) and understood as an assertion that Ben-Hadad's illness was not terminal.

8:12 *harm you will do to the Israelites.* The Lord gave Elisha a clear picture of the severity of the judgment he was about to send on Israel by the hand of Hazael (see 9:14–16; 10:32; 12:17–18; 13:3,22). *set fire . . . rip open their pregnant women.* These actions were characteristic of victorious armies in that time (see 15:16; Hos 10:14; 13:16; Am 1:13). Elisha's words do not sanction such acts but simply describe Hazael's future attacks on Israel.

8:13 *How could your servant, a mere dog, accomplish such a feat?* Hazael did not show repulsion at these violent acts but saw no possibility to gain the power necessary to accomplish them (for this metaphorical use of "dog" see note on 2Sa 9:8). *you will become king of Aram.* Elisha's prophecy suggests that Hazael was not a legitimate successor to Ben-Hadad. In an Assyrian inscription Hazael is designated "the son of a nobody" (i.e., a commoner) who usurped the throne.

8:15 *died.* Elisha's prophecy of Hazael's kingship did not legitimize the assassination. Hazael's murder of Ben-Hadad as well as his future acts of violence against Israel were wicked acts arising out of his own sinful heart (see Isa 10:5–19). His reign extended from c. 842 B.C. to c. 806 or 796, and he was followed by a son he named Ben-Hadad (13:24).

8:16 *fifth year of Joram.* 848 B.C. Jehoram had been co-regent with his father since 853 (see note on 1:17), but he now began his reign as sole king.

8:17 *reigned in Jerusalem eight years.* Jehoram's sole reign is to be dated 848–841 B.C.

8:18 *as the house of Ahab had done.* Jehoram introduced Baal worship in Judah, as Ahab had done in the northern kingdom (see 11:18). Baal worship now spread to the southern kingdom at the same time it was being restricted in the northern kingdom by Ahab's son Joram (see 3:1–2). *married a daughter of Ahab.* Jehoram's wife was Athaliah, a daughter of Ahab but probably not of Jezebel (see v. 26; 2Ch 18:1). Athaliah's influence on Jehoram paralleled that of Jezebel on Ahab (see 1Ki 16:31; 18:4; 19:1–2; 2Ch 21:6).

8:19 *lamp for David.* See note on 1Ki 11:36; see also Ps 132:17. The Lord spared Judah and its royal house the judgment he brought on the house of Ahab because of the covenant he had made with David (see 2Sa 7:16,29; 2Ch 21:7).

8:20 *set up its own king.* Previously Edom had been subject to Judah and had been ruled by a deputy (see note on 3:9; see also 1Ki 22:47).

8:21 *his army . . . fled.* Although Jehoram and his army were able to break through an encirclement by Edomite forces, they were soundly defeated and forced to retreat to their own territory.

8:22 *To this day.* Until the time of the writing of the account of Jehoram's reign used by the author of 1,2 Kings (see Introduction to 1 Kings: Author, Sources and Date; see also note on 1Ki 8:8). Later, Amaziah of Judah was able to inflict a serious defeat on Edom (14:7), and his successor Azariah regained control of the trade route to Elath through Edomite territory (14:22; 2Ch 26:2). *Libnah revolted at the same time.* Libnah appears to have been located close to the Philistine border near Lachish (see 19:8). It is likely that the revolt of Libnah was connected with that of the Philistines and Arabs described in 2Ch 21:16–17.

8:23 *other events of Jehoram's reign.* See 2Ch 21:4–20. *annals of the kings of Judah.* See note on 1Ki 14:29.

in the book of the annals of the kings of Judah? 24Jehoram rested with his fathers and was buried with them in the City of David. And Ahaziah his son succeeded him as king.

Ahaziah King of Judah

8:25–29pp — 2Ch 22:1–6

25In the twelfth *b* year of Joram son of Ahab king of Israel, Ahaziah son of Jehoram king of Judah began to reign. 26Ahaziah was twenty-two years old when he became king, and he reigned in Jerusalem one year. His mother's name was Athaliah, *c* a granddaughter of Omri *d* king of Israel. 27He walked in the ways of the house of Ahab *e* and did evil *f* in the eyes of the LORD, as the house of Ahab had done, for he was related by marriage to Ahab's family.

28Ahaziah went with Joram son of Ahab to war against Hazael king of Aram at Ramoth Gilead. *g* The Arameans wounded Joram; 29so King Joram returned to Jezreel *h* to recover from the wounds the Arameans had inflicted on him at Ramoth *r* in his battle with Hazael *i* king of Aram.

Then Ahaziah *j* son of Jehoram king of Judah went down to Jezreel to see Joram son of Ahab, because he had been wounded.

Jehu Anointed King of Israel

9 The prophet Elisha summoned a man from the company *k* of the prophets and said to him, "Tuck your cloak into your belt, *l* take this flask of oil *m* with you and go to Ramoth Gilead. *n* 2When you get there, look for Jehu son of Jehoshaphat, the son of Nimshi. Go to him, get him away from his companions and take him into an inner room. 3Then take the flask and pour the oil *o* on his head and declare, 'This is

what the LORD says: I anoint you king over Israel.' Then open the door and run; don't delay!"

4So the young man, the prophet, went to Ramoth Gilead. 5When he arrived, he found the army officers sitting together. "I have a message for you, commander," he said.

"For which of us?" asked Jehu.

"For you, commander," he replied.

6Jehu got up and went into the house. Then the prophet poured the oil *p* on Jehu's head and declared, "This is what the LORD, the God of Israel, says: 'I anoint you king over the LORD's people Israel. 7You are to destroy the house of Ahab your master, and I will avenge *q* the blood of my servants *r* the prophets and the blood of all the LORD's servants shed by Jezebel. *s* 8The whole house *t* of Ahab will perish. I will cut off from Ahab every last male *u* in Israel—slave or free. 9I will make the house of Ahab like the house of Jeroboam *v* son of Nebat and like the house of Baasha *w* son of Ahijah. 10As for Jezebel, dogs *x* will devour her on the plot of ground at Jezreel, and no one will bury her.'" Then he opened the door and ran.

11When Jehu went out to his fellow officers, one of them asked him, "Is everything all right? Why did this madman *y* come to you?"

"You know the man and the sort of things he says," Jehu replied.

12"That's not true!" they said. "Tell us."

Jehu said, "Here is what he told me: 'This is what the LORD says: I anoint you king over Israel.'"

13They hurried and took their cloaks and spread *z* them under him on the bare steps.

*r*29 Hebrew *Ramah,* a variant of *Ramoth*

Cross references

8:25 *b*2Ki 9:29
8:26 *c*S ver 18
*d*1Ki 16:23
8:27 *e*1Ki 16:30
*f*1Ki 15:26
8:28 *g*S Dt 4:43;
2Ki 9:1,14
8:29 *h*1Ki 21:29;
2Ki 9:21
*i*1Ki 19:15,17
*j*2Ki 10:13
9:1 *k*S 1Sa 10:5
*l*S 1Ki 18:46
*m*S 1Sa 10:1
*n*S 2Ki 8:28
9:3 *o*1Ki 19:16

9:6 *p*1Ki 19:16
9:7 *q*S Ge 4:24;
S Rev 6:10
*r*S Dt 32:43
*s*S 1Ki 18:4
9:8 *t*2Ki 10:17
*u*S 1Sa 25:22
9:9 *v*S 1Ki 13:34;
S 14:10
*w*1Ki 16:3
9:10 *x*S 1Ki 21:23
9:11 *y*S 1Sa 10:11;
S Jn 10:20
9:13 *z*Mt 21:8;
Lk 19:36

8:24 *rested with his fathers.* See notes on 1Ki 1:21; 2Ch 21:20.

8:25 *twelfth year of Joram.* 841 B.C. In 9:29 the first year of Joram's reign was counted as his accession year and his second year as the first year of his reign, whereas here his accession year was counted as the first year of his reign (see Introduction to 1 Kings: Chronology).

8:26 *twenty-two years old when he became king.* See note on 2Ch 22:2. *Athaliah.* See note on v. 18.

8:27 *ways of the house of Ahab.* See 2Ch 22:3–5.

8:28 *Ahaziah went with Joram . . . to war against Hazael . . . at Ramoth Gilead.* As Jehoshaphat had joined Ahab in battle against the Arameans at Ramoth Gilead (1Ki 22), so now Ahaziah joined his uncle Joram in a similar venture. On the previous occasion Ahab met his death (1Ki 22:37). On this occasion Joram was wounded and, while recuperating in Jezreel (see note on 1Ki 21:1), both he and his nephew Ahaziah were assassinated by Jehu (see 9:14–28).

9:1 *company of the prophets.* See note on 2:3.

9:3 *I anoint you king.* See notes on 1Sa 2:10; 9:16; 1Ki 19:16.

9:7 *destroy the house of Ahab.* Jehu learned that he was the divinely appointed agent to inflict the judgment Elijah had pronounced many years earlier in his own hearing against the house of Ahab (see vv. 25–26; 1Ki 21:21–24). *blood of all the LORD's servants shed by Jezebel.* A reference to people such as Naboth and his family (1Ki 21:13), who were unjustly put to death through Jezebel's influence.

9:8 *slave or free.* See note on 1Ki 14:10.

9:9 *like the house of Jeroboam.* See 1Ki 14:7–11; 15:27–30. *like the house of Baasha.* See 1Ki 16:1–4,8–12. Elijah had spoken the same words to Ahab years before (see 1Ki 21:21–24).

9:11 *this madman.* The epithet betrays a scornful attitude on the part of the military officers of the northern kingdom toward members of the prophetic companies.

Then they blew the trumpet[a] and shouted, "Jehu is king!"

Jehu Kills Joram and Ahaziah

9:21–29pp — 2Ch 22:7–9

[14]So Jehu son of Jehoshaphat, the son of Nimshi, conspired against Joram. (Now Joram and all Israel had been defending Ramoth Gilead[b] against Hazael king of Aram, [15]but King Joram[s] had returned to Jezreel to recover[c] from the wounds the Arameans had inflicted on him in the battle with Hazael king of Aram.) Jehu said, "If this is the way you feel, don't let anyone slip out of the city to go and tell the news in Jezreel." [16]Then he got into his chariot and rode to Jezreel, because Joram was resting there and Ahaziah[d] king of Judah had gone down to see him.

[17]When the lookout[e] standing on the tower in Jezreel saw Jehu's troops approaching, he called out, "I see some troops coming."

"Get a horseman," Joram ordered. "Send him to meet them and ask, 'Do you come in peace?[f]'"

[18]The horseman rode off to meet Jehu and said, "This is what the king says: 'Do you come in peace?'"

"What do you have to do with peace?" Jehu replied. "Fall in behind me."

The lookout reported, "The messenger has reached them, but he isn't coming back."

[19]So the king sent out a second horseman. When he came to them he said, "This is what the king says: 'Do you come in peace?'"

Jehu replied, "What do you have to do with peace? Fall in behind me."

[20]The lookout reported, "He has reached them, but he isn't coming back either. The driving is like[g] that of Jehu son of Nimshi—he drives like a madman."

[21]"Hitch up my chariot," Joram ordered. And when it was hitched up, Joram king of Israel and Ahaziah king of Judah rode out, each in his own chariot, to meet

Jehu. They met him at the plot of ground that had belonged to Naboth[h] the Jezreelite. [22]When Joram saw Jehu he asked, "Have you come in peace, Jehu?"

"How can there be peace," Jehu replied, "as long as all the idolatry and witchcraft of your mother Jezebel[i] abound?"

[23]Joram turned about and fled, calling out to Ahaziah, "Treachery,[j] Ahaziah!"

[24]Then Jehu drew his bow[k] and shot Joram between the shoulders. The arrow pierced his heart and he slumped down in his chariot. [25]Jehu said to Bidkar, his chariot officer, "Pick him up and throw him on the field that belonged to Naboth the Jezreelite. Remember how you and I were riding together in chariots behind Ahab his father when the LORD made this prophecy[l] about him: [26]'Yesterday I saw the blood of Naboth[m] and the blood of his sons, declares the LORD, and I will surely make you pay for it on this plot of ground, declares the LORD.'[t] Now then, pick him up and throw him on that plot, in accordance with the word of the LORD." [n]

[27]When Ahaziah king of Judah saw what had happened, he fled up the road to Beth Haggan.[u] Jehu chased him, shouting, "Kill him too!" They wounded him in his chariot on the way up to Gur near Ibleam,[o] but he escaped to Megiddo[p] and died there. [28]His servants took him by chariot[q] to Jerusalem and buried him with his fathers in his tomb in the City of David. [29](In the eleventh[r] year of Joram son of Ahab, Ahaziah had become king of Judah.)

Jezebel Killed

[30]Then Jehu went to Jezreel. When Jezebel heard about it, she painted[s] her eyes, arranged her hair and looked out of a window. [31]As Jehu entered the gate, she

9:13
aS 2Sa 15:10
9:14 bS Dt 4:43;
S 2Ki 8:28
9:15 cS 2Ki 8:29
9:16 d2Ch 22:7
9:17
eS 1Sa 14:16;
Isa 21:6
fS 1Sa 16:4
9:20 g2Sa 18:27

9:21 h1Ki 21:1
9:22 i1Ki 18:19;
Rev 2:20
9:23 j2Ki 11:14
9:24 kS 1Ki 22:34
9:25
l1Ki 21:19-22
9:26
mS 1Ki 21:19
nS 1Ki 21:29
9:27 oS Jdg 1:27
p2Ki 23:29
9:28 q2Ki 14:20;
23:30
9:29 r2Ki 8:25
9:30 sJer 4:30;
Eze 23:40

s15 Hebrew Jehoram, a variant of Joram; also in verses 17 and 21-24   t26 See 1 Kings 21:19.   u27 Or fled by way of the garden house

---

9:15 don't let anyone . . . go and tell the news in Jezreel. For the success of Jehu's revolt and to avoid a civil conflict it was important to take Joram totally by surprise.

9:16 Jezreel. About 45 miles from Ramoth Gilead. Ahaziah . . . had gone down to see him. See 8:29.

9:21 plot of ground that had belonged to Naboth. See notes on 1Ki 21:2–3,13,19.

9:22 idolatry and witchcraft. Both punishable by death (see Dt 13; 18:10–12). As long as these evils were promoted in the northern kingdom, there could be no peace.

9:26 in accordance with the word of the LORD. Jehu saw himself providentially placed in the position of fulfilling the prophecy of Elijah given years before (see 1Ki 21:18–24).

Even though Ahab's own blood was not shed on Naboth's field (see 1Ki 21:29 and note), Jehu saw in Joram's death the fulfillment of Elijah's prophecy (see note on 1Ki 21:19).

9:27 escaped to Megiddo and died there. It may be questioned whether Jehu was justified in extending the purge of Ahab's house (see Hos 1:4) to the descendants of the house of David through Ahab's daughter Athaliah (see 8:18,26).

9:31 Zimri, you murderer of your master. In bitter sarcasm Jezebel called Jehu by the name Zimri. About 45 years earlier Zimri had seized the throne from Elah by assassination and then had destroyed the whole house of Baasha. He ruled, however, for only seven days before Omri seized power (see 1Ki 16:8–20).

asked, "Have you come in peace, Zimri,[t] you murderer of your master?"[v]

[32]He looked up at the window and called out, "Who is on my side? Who?" Two or three eunuchs looked down at him. [33]"Throw her down!" Jehu said. So they threw her down, and some of her blood spattered the wall and the horses as they trampled her underfoot.[u]

[34]Jehu went in and ate and drank. "Take care of that cursed woman," he said, "and bury her, for she was a king's daughter."[v] [35]But when they went out to bury her, they found nothing except her skull, her feet and her hands. [36]They went back and told Jehu, who said, "This is the word of the LORD that he spoke through his servant Elijah the Tishbite: On the plot of ground at Jezreel dogs[w] will devour Jezebel's flesh.[w][x] [37]Jezebel's body will be like refuse[y] on the ground in the plot at Jezreel, so that no one will be able to say, 'This is Jezebel.' "

Ahab's Family Killed

10 Now there were in Samaria[z] seventy sons[a] of the house of Ahab. So Jehu wrote letters and sent them to Samaria: to the officials of Jezreel,[x][b] to the elders and to the guardians[c] of Ahab's children. He said, [2]"As soon as this letter reaches you, since your master's sons are with you and you have chariots and horses, a fortified city and weapons, [3]choose the best and most worthy of your master's sons and set him on his father's

throne. Then fight for your master's house."

[4]But they were terrified and said, "If two kings could not resist him, how can we?"

[5]So the palace administrator, the city governor, the elders and the guardians sent this message to Jehu: "We are your servants[d] and we will do anything you say. We will not appoint anyone as king; you do whatever you think best."

[6]Then Jehu wrote them a second letter, saying, "If you are on my side and will obey me, take the heads of your master's sons and come to me in Jezreel by this time tomorrow."

Now the royal princes, seventy of them, were with the leading men of the city, who were rearing them. [7]When the letter arrived, these men took the princes and slaughtered all seventy[e] of them. They put their heads[f] in baskets and sent them to Jehu in Jezreel. [8]When the messenger arrived, he told Jehu, "They have brought the heads of the princes."

Then Jehu ordered, "Put them in two piles at the entrance of the city gate until morning."

[9]The next morning Jehu went out. He stood before all the people and said, "You are innocent. It was I who conspired against my master and killed him, but who killed all these? [10]Know then, that not a

---

9:31
[t]1Ki 16:9-10
9:33 [u]Ps 7:5
9:34 [v]S 1Ki 16:31
9:36 [w]Ps 68:23; Jer 15:3
[x]S 1Ki 21:23
9:37 [y]Ps 83:10; Isa 5:25; Jer 8:2; 9:22; 16:4; 25:33; Zep 1:17
10:1 [z]S 1Ki 13:32
[a]S Jdg 8:30
[b]S 1Ki 21:1
[c]ver 5

10:5 [d]Jos 9:8
10:7 [e]S 1Ki 21:21
[f]S 2Sa 4:8

---

[v]31 Or "Did Zimri have peace, who murdered his master?"   [w]36 See 1 Kings 21:23.   [x]1 Hebrew; some Septuagint manuscripts and Vulgate of the city

---

9:36 *the word of the LORD that he spoke through his servant Elijah.* In the manner of Jezebel's death the word of the Lord was confirmed—the word she had defied during her life (see 1 Ki 21:23).

10:1 *Samaria.* In order to consolidate his coup and establish control of the northern kingdom, Jehu still faced the formidable problems of taking the nearly impregnable fortress of Samaria (see note on 1 Ki 16:24) and then of completing the destruction of Ahab's house. *seventy sons of the house of Ahab.* The number of Ahab's wives is unknown (see 1 Ki 20:5). The 70 presumably included both sons and grandsons. *officials.* Officers appointed by the king (see 1 Ki 4:1–6). *elders.* Local leaders by virtue of their position in the tribal and family structure (see notes on Ex 3:16; 2Sa 3:17). *guardians of Ahab's children.* Those entrusted with the care and upbringing of the princes in the royal family.

10:3 *fight for your master's house.* Jehu's strategy was to induce the leaders of Samaria into submission to his rule by bluffing a military confrontation.

10:4 *terrified.* The leaders of Samaria were completely intimidated by Jehu's challenge.

10:5 *palace administrator.* See note on 1 Ki 4:6. *city governor.* Probably an official appointed by the king who served as commander of the militia of the capital city. *the elders and the guardians.* See note on v. 1.

10:6 *take the heads of your master's sons and come to me.* The wording of Jehu's command contains what appears to be

a deliberate ambiguity. The "heads of your master's sons" could be understood as a reference to the leading figures among the 70 descendants of Ahab, such as the crown prince and several other sons of special ability and standing. On the other hand, the expression could be taken as a reference to the literal heads of all 70 princes.

10:7 *slaughtered all seventy.* The leaders of the city understood the communique in the literal sense, as Jehu most certainly had hoped they would. *put their heads in baskets and sent them to Jehu.* The leaders of Samaria did not carry the heads of the princes to Jezreel themselves as they had been ordered to do by Jehu (see v. 6). It is likely that they feared for their lives.

10:8 *Put them in two piles at the entrance of the city gate.* This gruesome procedure imitated the barbaric practice of the Assyrian rulers Ashurnasirpal and Shalmaneser III, whose reigns were characterized by acts of terror.

10:9 *It was I who . . . killed him.* Jehu openly confessed his own part in the overthrow of the government of Joram. *who killed all these?* Because of the ambiguous communique Jehu sent to the leaders of Samaria (see note on v. 6), he can now deny any personal responsibility for the slaughter of the 70 sons of Ahab and can lay the blame for it on the leaders of Samaria.

10:10 *what he promised through his servant Elijah.* See 1 Ki 21:20–24,29. Jehu implies a divine sanction not only for what had already been done but also for his intent to con-

word the LORD has spoken against the house of Ahab will fail. The LORD has done what he promised[g] through his servant Elijah."[h] [11]So Jehu[i] killed everyone in Jezreel who remained of the house of Ahab, as well as all his chief men, his close friends and his priests, leaving him no survivor.[j]

[12]Jehu then set out and went toward Samaria. At Beth Eked of the Shepherds, [13]he met some relatives of Ahaziah king of Judah and asked, "Who are you?"

They said, "We are relatives of Ahaziah,[k] and we have come down to greet the families of the king and of the queen mother.[l]"

[14]"Take them alive!" he ordered. So they took them alive and slaughtered them by the well of Beth Eked—forty-two men. He left no survivor.[m]

[15]After he left there, he came upon Jehonadab[n] son of Recab,[o] who was on his way to meet him. Jehu greeted him and said, "Are you in accord with me, as I am with you?"

"I am," Jehonadab answered.

"If so," said Jehu, "give me your hand."[p] So he did, and Jehu helped him up into the chariot. [16]Jehu said, "Come with me and see my zeal[q] for the LORD." Then he had him ride along in his chariot.

[17]When Jehu came to Samaria, he killed all who were left there of Ahab's family;[r] he destroyed them, according to the word of the LORD spoken to Elijah.

Ministers of Baal Killed

[18]Then Jehu brought all the people together and said to them, "Ahab served[s] Baal a little; Jehu will serve him much. [19]Now summon[t] all the prophets of Baal, all his ministers and all his priests. See that no one is missing, because I am going to hold a great sacrifice for Baal. Anyone who

fails to come will no longer live." But Jehu was acting deceptively in order to destroy the ministers of Baal.

[20]Jehu said, "Call an assembly[u] in honor of Baal." So they proclaimed it. [21]Then he sent word throughout Israel, and all the ministers of Baal came; not one stayed away. They crowded into the temple of Baal until it was full from one end to the other. [22]And Jehu said to the keeper of the wardrobe, "Bring robes for all the ministers of Baal." So he brought out robes for them.

[23]Then Jehu and Jehonadab son of Recab went into the temple of Baal. Jehu said to the ministers of Baal, "Look around and see that no servants of the LORD are here with you—only ministers of Baal." [24]So they went in to make sacrifices and burnt offerings. Now Jehu had posted eighty men outside with this warning: "If one of you lets any of the men I am placing in your hands escape, it will be your life for his life."[v]

[25]As soon as Jehu had finished making the burnt offering, he ordered the guards and officers: "Go in and kill[w] them; let no one escape."[x] So they cut them down with the sword. The guards and officers threw the bodies out and then entered the inner shrine of the temple of Baal. [26]They brought the sacred stone[y] out of the temple of Baal and burned it. [27]They demolished the sacred stone of Baal and tore down the temple[z] of Baal, and people have used it for a latrine to this day.

[28]So Jehu[a] destroyed Baal worship in Israel. [29]However, he did not turn away from the sins[b] of Jeroboam son of Nebat, which he had caused Israel to commit—the worship of the golden calves[c] at Bethel[d] and Dan.

[30]The LORD said to Jehu, "Because you have done well in accomplishing what is

Cross-references (center column)

10:10 gZKi 9:7-10 hS 1Ki 21:29
10:11 iHos 1:4 jver 14; Job 18:19; Mal 4:1
10:13 kZKi 8:29; 2Ch 22:8 lS 1Ki 2:19
10:14 mS ver 11
10:15 nJer 35:6, 14-19 oICh 2:55; Jer 35:2 pEzr 10:19; Eze 17:18
10:16 qS Nu 25:13
10:17 rZKi 9:8
10:18 sS Jdg 2:11
10:19 tIKi 18:19

10:20 uS Ex 32:5
10:24 vS Jos 2:14
10:25 wS Ex 22:20; S 2Ki 11:18 xS 1Ki 18:40
10:26 yS Ex 23:24
10:27 zS 1Ki 16:32
10:28 aIKi 19:17
10:29 bS 1Ki 12:30 cS Ex 32:4 dIKi 12:32

---

tinue the purge of Ahab's house and associates.

10:11 *all his chief men, his close friends and his priests.* Jehu went beyond the responsibility given to him (see 9:7; Hos 1:4) and acted solely on grounds of political self-interest. Jehu himself had been in the service of Ahab (see 9:25).

10:13 *relatives of Ahaziah.* See 2Ch 21:17. *families of the king and of the queen mother.* Members of the royal family from Judah who had not yet heard of the deaths of Joram and Jezebel.

10:15 *Jehonadab son of Recab.* Jehonadab was the leader of a conservative movement among the Israelites that was characterized by strong opposition to Baalism as well as to various practices of a settled agricultural society, including the building of houses, the sowing of crops and the use of wine. His followers still adhered to these principles over 200 years later and were known as Recabites (see Jer 35:6–10).

10:16 *had him ride along.* Public association with Jehonadab gave Jehu added credentials among the rural populace as

a follower of the Lord.

10:18 *Ahab served Baal a little; Jehu will serve him much.* After settling in Samaria, Jehu gave the appearance of having previously appealed to the word of the Lord as a mere political maneuver.

10:19 *will no longer live.* Jehu's reputation made this no idle threat.

10:26 *burned it.* May refer to the Asherah pole (see note on 1Ki 14:15) that usually accompanied a sacred stone (see 1Ki 16:32–33).

10:27 *sacred stone of Baal.* See note on 1Ki 14:23. *to this day.* See note on 8:22.

10:29 *sins of Jeroboam . . . he had caused Israel to commit.* See 1Ki 12:26–32; 13:33–34; 14:16.

10:30 *Because you have done . . . to the house of Ahab all I had in mind.* Jehu was the Lord's instrument to bring judgment on the house of Ahab, for which he was commended. But he was later condemned by the prophet Hosea for the

right in my eyes and have done to the house of Ahab all I had in mind to do, your descendants will sit on the throne of Israel to the fourth generation." *e* ³¹Yet Jehu was not careful *f* to keep the law of the LORD, the God of Israel, with all his heart. He did not turn away from the sins *g* of Jeroboam, which he had caused Israel to commit.

³²In those days the LORD began to reduce *h* the size of Israel. Hazael *i* overpowered the Israelites throughout their territory ³³east of the Jordan in all the land of Gilead (the region of Gad, Reuben and Manasseh), from Aroer *j* by the Arnon *k* Gorge through Gilead to Bashan.

³⁴As for the other events of Jehu's reign, all he did, and all his achievements, are they not written in the book of the annals *l* of the kings of Israel?

³⁵Jehu rested with his fathers and was buried in Samaria. And Jehoahaz his son succeeded him as king. ³⁶The time that Jehu reigned over Israel in Samaria was twenty-eight years.

Athaliah and Joash

11:1–21pp — 2Ch 22:10–23:21

11 When Athaliah *m* the mother of Ahaziah saw that her son was dead, she proceeded to destroy the whole royal family. ²But Jehosheba, the daughter of King Jehoram *y* and sister of Ahaziah,

took Joash *n* son of Ahaziah and stole him away from among the royal princes, who were about to be murdered. She put him and his nurse in a bedroom to hide him from Athaliah; so he was not killed. *o* ³He remained hidden with his nurse at the temple of the LORD for six years while Athaliah ruled the land.

⁴In the seventh year Jehoiada sent for the commanders of units of a hundred, the Carites *p* and the guards and had them brought to him at the temple of the LORD. He made a covenant with them and put them under oath at the temple of the LORD. Then he showed them the king's son. ⁵He commanded them, saying, "This is what you are to do: You who are in the three companies that are going on duty on the Sabbath *q*—a third of you guarding the royal palace, *r* ⁶a third at the Sur Gate, and a third at the gate behind the guard, who take turns guarding the temple— ⁷and you who are in the other two companies that normally go off Sabbath duty are all to guard the temple for the king. ⁸Station yourselves around the king, each man with his weapon in his hand. Anyone who approaches your ranks *z* must be put to death. Stay close to the king wherever he goes."

10:30 *e* 2Ki 15:12
10:31 /Dt 4:9;
Pr 4:23
g 1Ki 12:30
10:32 *h* 2Ki 13:25;
Ps 107:39
i S 1Ki 19:17
10:33 /S Nu 32:34;
Dt 2:36;
Jdg 11:26;
Isa 17:2
k S Nu 21:13
10:34 /1Ki 15:31
11:1 *m* S 2Ki 8:18

11:2 *n* 2Ki 12:1
o S Jdg 9:5
11:4 *p* ver 19
11:5 *q* 1Ch 9:25
r 1Ki 14:27

y2 Hebrew *Joram,* a variant of *Jehoram*   *z8* Or *approaches the precincts*

---

killing of all Ahab's associates, as well as Ahaziah of Judah and the 42 Judahite princes—the "massacre at Jezreel" (Hos 1:4). *fourth generation.* The restriction of this blessing to four generations is reflective of the qualified approval given to Jehu's reign. Nevertheless, his dynasty survived longer than any other dynasty of the northern kingdom, lasting nearly 100 years. It included the reigns of Jehoahaz, Jehoash, Jeroboam II and Zechariah (see note on 15:12).

10:31 *was not careful to keep the law of the LORD . . . with all his heart.* Jehu seems to have been driven more by a political desire to secure his own position on the throne of the northern kingdom than by a desire to serve the Lord. In this he was guilty of using God's judgment on the house of Ahab to satisfy his self-interest.

10:32 *the LORD began to reduce the size of Israel.* The climax of the covenant curses enumerated in Lev 26 and Dt 28 was Israel's expulsion from Canaan. During the rule of Jehu the northern kingdom experienced the beginnings of this curse (see 17:7–18 for its full realization).

10:33 All of Transjordan was lost to Hazael and the Arameans of Damascus.

10:34 *other events of Jehu's reign.* The "Black Obelisk" of the Assyrian ruler Shalmaneser III informs us that Jehu paid tribute to the Assyrians shortly after coming to the throne of the northern kingdom in 841 B.C. In the Assyrian inscription Jehu is incorrectly called the "son of Omri," but this may simply be Shalmaneser's way of identifying Jehu with Samaria (or Israel). There is no reference to this payment of tribute in the Biblical narratives of Jehu's reign. *annals of the kings of Israel.* See note on 1Ki 14:19.

10:35 *rested with his fathers.* See note on 1Ki 1:21. *Jehoahaz his son succeeded him.* For the reign of Jehoahaz

see 13:1–9.

10:36 *twenty-eight years.* 841–814 B.C.

11:1 *Athaliah.* See note on 8:18. *her son was dead.* See 9:27. *destroy the whole royal family.* To secure the throne in Judah for herself. By this time the royal family in Judah had already been reduced to a mere remnant. Jehoram, the late husband of Athaliah and the father of Ahaziah, had killed all his brothers when he succeeded his father Jehoshaphat on the throne (see 2Ch 21:4). Jehu had slain another 42 members of the royal house of Judah, perhaps including many of the sons of Jehoram's brothers (10:12–14; 2Ch 22:8–9), and the brothers of Ahaziah had been killed by marauding Arabs (2Ch 22:1). It is likely that Athaliah's purge focused primarily on the children of Ahaziah, i.e., her own grandchildren. Ahaziah had died at the young age of 22 (see 8:26). This attempt to completely destroy the house of David was an attack on God's redemptive plan—a plan that centered in the Messiah, which the Davidic covenant promised (see notes on 2Sa 7:11,16; 1Ki 8:25).

11:2 *daughter of King Jehoram and sister of Ahaziah.* It is likely that Jehosheba was the daughter of Jehoram by a wife other than Athaliah, and thus she was a half sister of Ahaziah. She was married to the high priest Jehoiada (see 2Ch 22:11). *him and his nurse.* The child was not more than a year old and had not yet been weaned (see vv. 3,21).

11:4 *seventh year.* Of Athaliah's rule. *commanders of units of a hundred.* 2Ch 23:1 lists the names of five commanders, all native Israelites. *Carites.* Mercenary soldiers from Caria in southwest Asia Minor who served as royal bodyguards. *had them brought to him at the temple.* 2Ch 23:2 includes the Levites and family leaders of Judah in the conspiracy.

⁹The commanders of units of a hundred did just as Jehoiada the priest ordered. Each one took his men—those who were going on duty on the Sabbath and those who were going off duty—and came to Jehoiada the priest. ¹⁰Then he gave the commanders the spears and shields ˢ that had belonged to King David and that were in the temple of the LORD. ¹¹The guards, each with his weapon in his hand, stationed themselves around the king—near the altar and the temple, from the south side to the north side of the temple.

¹²Jehoiada brought out the king's son and put the crown on him; he presented him with a copy of the covenant ᵗ and proclaimed him king. They anointed ᵘ him, and the people clapped their hands ᵛ and shouted, "Long live the king!" ʷ

¹³When Athaliah heard the noise made by the guards and the people, she went to the people at the temple of the LORD. ¹⁴She looked and there was the king, standing by the pillar, ˣ as the custom was. The officers and the trumpeters were beside the king, and all the people of the land were rejoicing and blowing trumpets. ʸ Then Athaliah tore ᶻ her robes and called out, "Treason! Treason!" ᵃ

¹⁵Jehoiada the priest ordered the commanders of units of a hundred, who were in charge of the troops: "Bring her out between the ranks ᵃ and put to the sword anyone who follows her." For the priest had said, "She must not be put to death in the temple ᵇ of the LORD." ¹⁶So they seized her as she reached the place where the horses enter ᶜ the palace grounds, and there she was put to death. ᵈ

¹⁷Jehoiada then made a covenant ᵉ be-

tween the LORD and the king and people that they would be the LORD's people. He also made a covenant between the king and the people. ᶠ ¹⁸All the people of the land went to the temple ᵍ of Baal and tore it down. They smashed ʰ the altars and idols to pieces and killed Mattan the priest ⁱ of Baal in front of the altars.

Then Jehoiada the priest posted guards at the temple of the LORD. ¹⁹He took with him the commanders of hundreds, the Carites, ʲ the guards and all the people of the land, and together they brought the king down from the temple of the LORD and went into the palace, entering by way of the gate of the guards. The king then took his place on the royal throne, ²⁰and all the people of the land rejoiced. ᵏ And the city was quiet, because Athaliah had been slain with the sword at the palace.

²¹Joash ᵇ was seven years old when he began to reign.

Joash Repairs the Temple

12:1-21pp — 2Ch 24:1-14; 24:23-27

12 In the seventh year of Jehu, Joash ᶜˡ became king, and he reigned in Jerusalem forty years. His mother's name was Zibiah; she was from Beersheba. ²Joash did what was right ᵐ in the eyes of the LORD all the years Jehoiada the priest instructed him. ³The high places, ⁿ however, were not removed; the people continued to offer sacrifices and burn incense there.

⁴Joash said to the priests, "Collect ᵒ all the money that is brought as sacred offer-

(center reference column)

11:10 ˢS 2Sa 8:7
11:12 ᵗEx 25:16;
2Ki 23:3
ᵘS 1Sa 9:16;
S 1Ki 1:39
ᵛPs 47:1; 98:8;
Isa 55:12
ʷS 1Sa 10:24
11:14
ˣS 1Ki 7:15
ʸS 1Ki 1:39
ᶻS Ge 37:29
ᵃ2Ki 9:23
11:15 ᵇ1Ki 2:30
11:16 ᶜNe 3:28;
Jer 31:40
ᵈS Ge 4:14
11:17
ᵉS Ex 24:8;
2Sa 5:3;
2Ch 15:12; 23:3;
29:10; 34:31;
Ezr 10:3

ᶠ2Ki 23:3;
Jer 34:8
11:18
ᵍS 1Ki 16:32
ʰS Dt 12:3
ⁱ1Ki 18:40;
2Ki 10:25; 23:20
11:19 ʲver 4
11:20 ᵏPr 11:10;
28:12; 29:2
12:1 ʲ2Ki 11:2
12:2
ᵐS Dt 12:25;
S 2Sa 8:15
12:3 ⁿS 1Ki 3:3;
S 2Ki 18:4
12:4 ᵒ2Ki 22:4

ᵃ15 Or *out from the precincts*   ᵇ21 Hebrew *Jehoash*,
a variant of *Joash*   ᶜ1 Hebrew *Jehoash*, a variant of
Joash; also in verses 2, 4, 6, 7 and 18

11:10 *spears and shields that had belonged to King David and that were in the temple.* David had probably taken the spears and gold shields as plunder in his battle with Hadadezer and then dedicated them to the LORD (see 2Sa 8:7–11).
11:12 *covenant.* Either (1) the Ten Commandments, (2) the entire Mosaic covenant or (3) a document dealing more specifically with the covenant responsibilities of the king (see Dt 17:14–20; see also note on 1Sa 10:25). The third option is most likely. *anointed him.* See notes on 1Sa 2:10; 9:16; 1Ki 1:39. *Long live the king!* See 1Sa 10:24; 1Ki 1:34,39.
11:14 *pillar.* Apparently one of the two bronze pillars of the portico of the temple, named Jakin and Boaz (see 23:3; 1Ki 7:15–22; 2Ch 23:13). *all the people of the land.* It is likely that Jehoiada had chosen to stage his coup on a Sabbath during one of the major religious festivals, when many from the realm who were loyal to the Lord would be in Jerusalem.
11:17 *covenant between the LORD and the king and people that they would be the LORD's people.* A renewal of the Mosaic covenant, by which Israel had been constituted as the Lord's people (see Ex 19:5–6; Dt 4:20). The years of apostasy, involving both the royal house and the people of Judah, necessitated a renewal of allegiance to the Lord at the

time of an important new beginning for the southern kingdom (see notes on 1Sa 11:14–15; 12:14–15,24–25). *covenant between the king and the people.* Defined responsibilities and mutual obligations of king and people that were compatible with Israel's covenant relationship with the Lord (see notes on 1Sa 10:25; 2Sa 5:3).
11:18 *idols.* Stone pillars (see note on 1Ki 14:23) and Asherah poles (see note on 1Ki 14:15).
11:19 *commanders of hundreds, the Carites, the guards.* See note on v. 4.
11:21 See v. 3. The Lord had preserved a lamp for David in Jerusalem (see 1Ki 11:36).
12:1 *seventh year of Jehu.* 835 B.C. (see note on 10:36). *forty years.* 835–796.
12:2 *all the years Jehoiada the priest instructed him.* After Jehoiada died, Joash turned away from the Lord (see 2Ch 24:17–27).
12:3 *high places . . . were not removed.* These were high places where the Lord was worshiped rather than pagan deities (see note on 1Ki 15:14). They were nevertheless potential sources for the entrance of pagan practices into Israel's worship (see note on 1Ki 3:2).

ings^p to the temple of the LORD—the money collected in the census,^q the money received from personal vows and the money brought voluntarily^r to the temple. ⁵Let every priest receive the money from one of the treasurers, and let it be used to repair^s whatever damage is found in the temple."

⁶But by the twenty-third year of King Joash the priests still had not repaired the temple. ⁷Therefore King Joash summoned Jehoiada the priest and the other priests and asked them, "Why aren't you repairing the damage done to the temple? Take no more money from your treasurers, but hand it over for repairing the temple." ⁸The priests agreed that they would not collect any more money from the people and that they would not repair the temple themselves.

⁹Jehoiada the priest took a chest and bored a hole in its lid. He placed it beside the altar, on the right side as one enters the temple of the LORD. The priests who guarded the entrance^t put into the chest all the money^u that was brought to the temple of the LORD. ¹⁰Whenever they saw that there was a large amount of money in the chest, the royal secretary^v and the

high priest came, counted the money that had been brought into the temple of the LORD and put it into bags. ¹¹When the amount had been determined, they gave the money to the men appointed to supervise the work on the temple. With it they paid those who worked on the temple of the LORD—the carpenters and builders, ¹²the masons and stonecutters. ^w They purchased timber and dressed stone for the repair of the temple of the LORD, and met all the other expenses of restoring the temple.

¹³The money brought into the temple was not spent for making silver basins, wick trimmers, sprinkling bowls, trumpets or any other articles of gold^x or silver for the temple of the LORD; ¹⁴it was paid to the workmen, who used it to repair the temple. ¹⁵They did not require an accounting from those to whom they gave the money to pay the workers, because they acted with complete honesty.^y ¹⁶The money from the guilt offerings^z and sin offerings^a was not brought into the temple of the LORD; it belonged^b to the priests.

¹⁷About this time Hazael^c king of Aram went up and attacked Gath and captured it. Then he turned to attack Jerusalem.

Cross references (center column):
12:4 ^pNu 18:19
^qS Ex 30:12
^rS Ex 25:2; S 35:29
12:5 ^s2Ki 22:5
12:9 ^t2Ki 25:18; Jer 35:4; 52:24
^uMk 12:41; Lk 21:1
12:10 ^vS 2Sa 8:17
12:12 ^w2Ki 22:5-6
12:13 ^xS 1Ki 7:51
12:15 ^y2Ki 22:7; 1Co 4:2
12:16 ^zLev 5:14-19 ^aLev 4:1-35 ^bS Lev 7:7
12:17 ^c2Ki 8:12

12:4 *money . . . brought as sacred offerings to the temple.* The money was derived from three different sources: 1. *money collected in the census.* At the age of 20, Israelite youths were required to register for military service and to make an offering of half a shekel (see note on 5:26) for use in the service of the central sanctuary (see Ex 30:11–16; 38:25–26; Nu 2:32). 2. *money received from personal vows.* Various types of vows and their equivalence in monetary assessments are described in Lev 27:1–25. 3. *money brought voluntarily to the temple.* For voluntary offerings see Lev 22:18–23; Dt 16:10.

12:5 *treasurers.* Temple functionaries who handled financial matters for the priests relative to the people's sacrifices and offerings. *whatever damage is found in the temple.* Construction of the temple had been completed 124 years before the beginning of the reign of Joash (see notes on v. 1; 1Ki 6:38). In addition to deterioration due to age, it had fallen into disrepair and abuse during the rule of Athaliah (see 2Ch 24:7).

12:6 *twenty-third year of King Joash.* Joash may have instituted his plan for restoration of the temple a few years before the 23rd year of his reign. Now at age 30 he asserts his royal authority and takes charge of the temple repairs.

12:7 *Take no more money from your treasurers.* The proceeds from the sources of revenue mentioned in v. 4 were no longer to be given to the priests.

12:8 *priests agreed.* Apparently a compromise was reached: The priests would no longer take the money received from the people, but neither would they pay for the temple repairs from the money they had already received.

12:9 *priests who guarded the entrance.* Three high-ranking priests charged with protecting the temple from unlawful (profane) entry (see 25:18; Jer 52:24). *put into the chest all the money.* When the people were assured that all their offerings would be used for the temple restoration, they

responded with greater generosity. See 22:3–7 for continuation (or renewal) of this practice in the reign of Josiah.

12:10 *royal secretary.* See note on 2Sa 8:17. Joash arranges for direct royal supervision of the temple's monetary affairs.

12:11 *men appointed.* The whole matter is taken out of the hands of the priests.

12:13 *articles of gold or silver for the temple.* All the money was initially designated for the restoration of the temple. When the restoration was completed, additional funds were used for the acquisition of silver and gold articles for use in the temple service (see 2Ch 24:14).

12:16 *money from the guilt offerings and sin offerings.* See Lev 5:16; 6:5; Nu 5:7–10 for references to priestly income in connection with the bringing of a guilt offering. There is no Pentateuchal reference to priestly income in connection with the bringing of a sin offering (but see Lev 7:7).

12:17 *About this time.* These events must have taken place toward the end of Joash's reign. From 2Ch 24:17–24 it is clear that the Aramean attack was occasioned by Joash's turning away from the Lord after Jehoiada's death. Joash's apostasy reached its climax in the stoning of Jehoiada's son Zechariah (2Ch 24:22). Probably because of Joash's earlier zeal for the temple, the author of Kings did not choose to relate these matters. *Hazael.* See 8:7–15; 10:32–33; 13:3, 22. *Gath.* One of the major Philistine cities (see Jos 13:3) that David had conquered (1Ch 18:1) and that continued to be subject to Judah during the reign of Rehoboam (2Ch 11:8). In the latter years of the reign of Joash of Judah (835–796 B.C.) and during the reign of Jehoahaz of Israel (814–798; see 13:3,7), the Arameans had virtually overrun the northern kingdom, enabling them to advance against the Philistines and the kingdom of Judah with little resistance. *he turned to attack Jerusalem.* See 2Ch 24:23–24.

¹⁸But Joash king of Judah took all the sacred objects dedicated by his fathers—Jehoshaphat, Jehoram and Ahaziah, the kings of Judah—and the gifts he himself had dedicated and all the gold found in the treasuries of the temple of the Lord and of the royal palace, and he sent^d them to Hazael king of Aram, who then withdrew^e from Jerusalem.

¹⁹As for the other events of the reign of Joash, and all he did, are they not written in the book of the annals of the kings of Judah? ²⁰His officials^f conspired against him and assassinated^g him at Beth Millo,^h on the road down to Silla. ²¹The officials who murdered him were Jozabad son of Shimeath and Jehozabad son of Shomer. He died and was buried with his fathers in the City of David. And Amaziah his son succeeded him as king.

Jehoahaz King of Israel

13 In the twenty-third year of Joash son of Ahaziah king of Judah, Jehoahaz son of Jehu became king of Israel in Samaria, and he reigned seventeen years. ²He did evilⁱ in the eyes of the Lord by following the sins of Jeroboam son of Nebat, which he had caused Israel to commit, and he did not turn away from them. ³So the Lord's anger^j burned against Israel, and for a long time he kept

them under the power^k of Hazael king of Aram and Ben-Hadad^l his son.

⁴Then Jehoahaz sought^m the Lord's favor, and the Lord listened to him, for he sawⁿ how severely the king of Aram was oppressing^o Israel. ⁵The Lord provided a deliverer^p for Israel, and they escaped from the power of Aram. So the Israelites lived in their own homes as they had before. ⁶But they did not turn away from the sins^q of the house of Jeroboam, which he had caused Israel to commit; they continued in them. Also, the Asherah pole^{d r} remained standing in Samaria.

⁷Nothing had been left^s of the army of Jehoahaz except fifty horsemen, ten chariots and ten thousand foot soldiers, for the king of Aram had destroyed the rest and made them like the dust^t at threshing time.

⁸As for the other events of the reign of Jehoahaz, all he did and his achievements, are they not written in the book of the annals of the kings of Israel? ⁹Jehoahaz rested with his fathers and was buried in Samaria. And Jehoash^e his son succeeded him as king.

Jehoash King of Israel

¹⁰In the thirty-seventh year of Joash king

Cross references

12:18
^dS 1Ki 15:18;
S 2Ch 21:16-17
^e1Ki 15:21;
2Ki 15:20; 19:36
12:20 /2Ki 14:5
^g2Ki 14:19;
15:10,14,25,30;
21:23; 25:25
^hJdg 9:6
13:2
ⁱ1Ki 12:26-33
13:3 /S Dt 31:17

^kS 1Ki 19:17 /ver 24
13:4 ^mS Dt 4:29
ⁿS Dt 26:7
^oS Nu 10:9;
2Sa 7:10
13:5 ^pS Ge 45:7;
S Dt 28:29;
S Jdg 2:18
13:6 ^q1Ki 12:30
^rS 1Ki 16:33
13:7
^s2Ki 10:32-33
^tS 2Sa 22:43

^d6 That is, a symbol of the goddess Asherah; here and elsewhere in 2 Kings   ^e9 Hebrew Joash, a variant of Jehoash; also in verses 12-14 and 25

12:18 *sacred objects . . . gold . . . he sent them to Hazael.* Years earlier, Asa had sought to secure assistance from the Arameans with a similar gift (see 1Ki 15:18).

12:19 *annals of the kings of Judah.* See note on 1Ki 14:29. A fuller account of the reign of Joash is also found in 2Ch 22:10–24:27.

12:20 *conspired against him.* The conspiracy was aroused in response to Joash's murder of Zechariah son of Jehoiada (see 2Ch 24:25). *Beth Millo.* Beth means "house"; for the meaning of Millo see note on Jdg 9:6. Here the reference may be to a building (perhaps a kind of barracks) built on the "Millo" in the old City of David (see 2Sa 5:9 and note; 1Ki 11:27). Perhaps the king was staying there temporarily with his troops at the time of his assassination; Chronicles says he was killed "in his bed" (2Ch 24:25). *Silla.* Perhaps refers to a steep descent from the City of David down into the Kidron Valley.

12:21 *officials.* Sons of Ammonite and Moabite mothers (2Ch 24:26), suggesting that they may have been mercenary military officers whose services could have been bought by others. *buried with his fathers.* But see 2Ch 24:25. *Amaziah his son succeeded him.* For the reign of Amaziah see 14:1–22.

13:1 *twenty-third year of Joash.* 814 B.C. (see note on 12:1; see also Introduction to 1 Kings: Chronology). *seventeen years.* 814–798.

13:2 *sins of Jeroboam.* See 1Ki 12:26–32; 13:33–34; 14:16.

13:3 *Hazael.* See notes on 8:12,13,15; 10:33. *Ben-Hadad.* See v. 24. His reign began in either 806 or 796 B.C.

13:4 *the Lord listened to him.* Although deliverance did not come during the lifetime of Jehoahaz (see v. 22), the Lord was merciful to his people in spite of their sin, because of his covenant with Abraham, Isaac and Jacob (v. 23).

13:5 *deliverer for Israel.* Probably either (1) the Assyrian ruler Adadnirari III (810–783 B.C.), whose attacks on the Arameans of Damascus in 806 and 804 enabled the Israelites to break Aramean control over Israelite territory (see v. 25; 14:25), or (2) Jehoash son of Jehoahaz (vv. 17,19,25), or (3) Jeroboam II, who was able to extend Israel's boundaries far to the north (see 14:25,27) after the Assyrians had broken the military power of the Arameans.

13:6 *Asherah pole remained standing.* This idol had been set up by Ahab (see 1Ki 16:33) and had either escaped destruction by Jehu when he purged Baal worship from Samaria (see 10:27–28) or had been reintroduced during the reign of Jehoahaz.

13:7 *ten chariots.* In effect, a small police force. According to the Assyrian annals of Shalmaneser III, Ahab had contributed 2,000 chariots to the coalition of forces that opposed the Assyrians at the battle of Qarqar in 853 B.C. (see note on 1Ki 22:1). *ten thousand foot soldiers.* At the battle of Qarqar Ahab had supplied 10,000 foot soldiers to the coalition of forces opposing the Assyrians. At that time this would have represented only a contingent of Israel's army, while now it represented the entire Israelite infantry. In 857 Ahab had inflicted 100,000 casualties on the Aramean foot soldiers in one day (see 1Ki 20:29).

13:8 *annals of the kings of Israel.* See note on 1Ki 14:19.

13:9 *rested with his fathers.* See note on 1Ki 1:21.

13:10 *thirty-seventh year of Joash.* 798 B.C. (see note on

of Judah, Jehoash son of Jehoahaz became king of Israel in Samaria, and he reigned sixteen years. ¹¹He did evil in the eyes of the LORD and did not turn away from any of the sins of Jeroboam son of Nebat, which he had caused Israel to commit; he continued in them.

¹²As for the other events of the reign of Jehoash, all he did and his achievements, including his war against Amaziah ᵘ king of Judah, are they not written in the book of the annals ᵛ of the kings of Israel? ¹³Jehoash rested with his fathers, and Jeroboam ʷ succeeded him on the throne. Jehoash was buried in Samaria with the kings of Israel.

¹⁴Now Elisha was suffering from the illness from which he died. Jehoash king of Israel went down to see him and wept over him. "My father! My father!" he cried. "The chariots ˣ and horsemen of Israel!"

¹⁵Elisha said, "Get a bow and some arrows," ʸ and he did so. ¹⁶"Take the bow in your hands," he said to the king of Israel. When he had taken it, Elisha put his hands on the king's hands.

¹⁷"Open the east window," he said, and he opened it. "Shoot!" ᶻ Elisha said, and he shot. "The LORD's arrow of victory, the arrow of victory over Aram!" Elisha declared. "You will completely destroy the Arameans at Aphek." ᵃ

¹⁸Then he said, "Take the arrows," and the king took them. Elisha told him, "Strike the ground." He struck it three times and stopped. ¹⁹The man of God was angry with him and said, "You should have struck the ground five or six times; then you would have defeated Aram and completely destroyed it. But now you will defeat it only three times." ᵇ

²⁰Elisha died and was buried.

Now Moabite raiders ᶜ used to enter the country every spring. ²¹Once while some Israelites were burying a man, suddenly they saw a band of raiders; so they threw the man's body into Elisha's tomb. When the body touched Elisha's bones, the man came to life ᵈ and stood up on his feet.

²²Hazael king of Aram oppressed ᵉ Israel throughout the reign of Jehoahaz. ²³But the LORD was gracious to them and had compassion and showed concern for them because of his covenant ᶠ with Abraham, Isaac and Jacob. To this day he has been unwilling to destroy ᵍ them or banish them from his presence. ʰ

²⁴Hazael king of Aram died, and Ben-Hadad ⁱ his son succeeded him as king. ²⁵Then Jehoash son of Jehoahaz recaptured from Ben-Hadad son of Hazael the towns he had taken in battle from his father Jehoahaz. Three times ʲ Jehoash defeated him, and so he recovered ᵏ the Israelite towns.

13:12 ᵘ2Ki 14:15
ᵛ1Ki 15:31
13:13 ʷ2Ki 14:23; Hos 1:1
13:14 ˣS 2Ki 2:12
13:15 ʸ1Sa 20:20
13:17 ᶻJos 8:18
ᵃS 1Ki 20:26

13:19 ᵇver 25
13:20 ᶜS 2Ki 5:2
13:21 ᵈMt 27:52
13:22 ᵉS 1Ki 19:17
13:23 ᶠS Ex 2:24
ᵍS Dt 29:20
ʰS Ex 33:15; 2Ki 17:18; 24:3, 20
13:24 ⁱver 3
13:25 ʲver 19
ᵏS 2Ki 10:32

12:1). *sixteen years.* 798–782.
13:11 *sins of Jeroboam.* See 1Ki 12:26–32; 13:33–34; 14:16.
13:12 *war against Amaziah.* See 14:8–14; 2Ch 25:17–24. *annals of the kings of Israel.* See note on 1Ki 14:19.
13:13 *rested with his fathers.* See note on 1Ki 1:21. *Jeroboam succeeded him.* For the reign of Jeroboam II see 14:23–29.
13:14 *Elisha was suffering.* Ch. 9 contains the last previous reference to Elisha. Since Jehu had been anointed in 841 B.C. (see note on 10:36) and Jehoash began to reign in 798 (see note on v. 10), there is at least a 43-year period in which we are told nothing of Elisha's activities. Based on Elisha's relationship with Elijah, he must have been born prior to 880 and he must have lived to be more than 80 years of age. *The chariots and horsemen of Israel!* An expression of recognition by Jehoash that Elisha was of greater significance for Israel's military success than Israel's military forces were (see notes on 2:12; 6:13,16–23).
13:16 *put his hands on the king's hands.* By this symbolic act Elisha indicated that Jehoash was to engage the Arameans in battle with the Lord's blessing on him.
13:17 *east window.* Faced Transjordan, which was controlled by the Arameans (see 10:32–33). *Aphek.* About 60 years earlier Ahab had won a decisive victory at Aphek over the Arameans and Ben-Hadad II (see 1Ki 20:26–30 and note on 1Ki 20:26).
13:18 *struck it three times and stopped.* The moderately

enthusiastic response to Elisha's directive reflected insufficient zeal for accomplishing the announced task.
13:19 *defeat it only three times.* Jehoash's moderate enthusiasm in striking the ground with arrows symbolized the moderate success he would have against the Arameans. It would be left for Jeroboam II son of Jehoash to gain complete victory over them (see 14:25,28).
13:21 *When the body touched Elisha's bones, the man came to life.* The life-giving power of the God Elisha represented is demonstrated once again in this last OT reference to Elisha (for previous demonstrations of this power see 4:32–37 and 1Ki 17:17–24; for Elijah's translation to heaven without dying see 2:11–12).
13:23 *To this day.* Until the time of the writing of the source from which the author derived this account (see note on 1Ki 8:8; see also Introduction to 1 Kings: Author, Sources and Date). *unwilling to destroy them or banish them.* In his mercy and grace the Lord was long-suffering toward his people and refrained from full implementation of the covenant curse of exile from Canaan (see note on 10:32). This postponement of judgment provided Israel with the opportunity to repent and return to covenant faithfulness.
13:24 *Ben-Hadad.* See note on v. 3.
13:25 *towns he had taken...from...Jehoahaz.* Probably towns west of the Jordan, since the area east of the Jordan had been lost already in the time of Jehu (see 10:32–33). It was not until the time of Jeroboam II that the area east of the Jordan was fully recovered for Israel (see 14:25). *Three times.* In fulfillment of Elisha's prophecy (v. 19).

Amaziah King of Judah

14:1–7pp — 2Ch 25:1–4,11–12
14:8–22pp — 2Ch 25:17–26:2

14 In the second year of Jehoash[f] son of Jehoahaz king of Israel, Amaziah son of Joash king of Judah began to reign. ²He was twenty-five years old when he became king, and he reigned in Jerusalem twenty-nine years. His mother's name was Jehoaddin; she was from Jerusalem. ³He did what was right in the eyes of the LORD, but not as his father David had done. In everything he followed the example of his father Joash. ⁴The high places,[l] however, were not removed; the people continued to offer sacrifices and burn incense there.

⁵After the kingdom was firmly in his grasp, he executed[m] the officials[n] who had murdered his father the king. ⁶Yet he did not put the sons of the assassins to death, in accordance with what is written in the Book of the Law[o] of Moses where the LORD commanded: "Fathers shall not be put to death for their children, nor children put to death for their fathers; each is to die for his own sins."[g][p]

⁷He was the one who defeated ten thousand Edomites in the Valley of Salt[q] and captured Sela[r] in battle, calling it Joktheel, the name it has to this day.

⁸Then Amaziah sent messengers to Jehoash son of Jehoahaz, the son of Jehu, king of Israel, with the challenge: "Come, meet me face to face."

⁹But Jehoash king of Israel replied to Amaziah king of Judah: "A thistle[s] in Lebanon sent a message to a cedar in Lebanon, 'Give your daughter to my son in marriage.' Then a wild beast in Lebanon came along and trampled the thistle underfoot. ¹⁰You have indeed defeated Edom and now you are arrogant.[t] Glory in your victory, but stay at home! Why ask for trouble and cause your own downfall and that of Judah also?"

¹¹Amaziah, however, would not listen, so Jehoash king of Israel attacked. He and Amaziah king of Judah faced each other at Beth Shemesh[u] in Judah. ¹²Judah was routed by Israel, and every man fled to his home.[v] ¹³Jehoash king of Israel captured Amaziah king of Judah, the son of Joash, the son of Ahaziah, at Beth Shemesh. Then Jehoash went to Jerusalem and broke down the wall[w] of Jerusalem from the Ephraim Gate[x] to the Corner Gate[y]—a section about six hundred feet long.[h] ¹⁴He took all the gold and silver and all the articles found in the temple of the LORD and in the treasuries of the royal palace. He also took hostages and returned to Samaria.

¹⁵As for the other events of the reign of Jehoash, what he did and his achievements, including his war[z] against Amaziah king of Judah, are they not written in the book of the annals of the kings of Israel? ¹⁶Jehoash rested with his fathers and was

---

14:4 [f]2Ki 12:3
14:5 [m]2Ki 21:24
[n]2Ki 12:20
14:6 [o]S Dt 28:61
[p]S Nu 26:11;
Job 21:20;
Jer 31:30; 44:3;
Eze 18:4,20
14:7 [q]S 2Sa 8:13
[r]S Jdg 1:36

14:9 [s]Jdg 9:8-15
14:10 [t]2Ch 26:16;
32:25
14:11 [u]S Jos 15:10
14:12 [v]1Ki 22:36
14:13 [w]1Ki 3:1;
36:19; Jer 39:2
[x]Ne 8:16; 12:39
[y]2Ch 26:9;
Jer 31:38;
Zec 14:10
14:15 [z]2Ki 13:12

---

[f]1 Hebrew *Joash*, a variant of *Jehoash*; also in verses 13, 23 and 27   [g]6 Deut. 24:16   [h]13 Hebrew *four hundred cubits* (about 180 meters)

14:1 *second year of Jehoash.* 796 B.C. (see note on 13:10).
14:2 *twenty-nine years.* 796–767. Amaziah's 29-year reign included a 24-year co-regency with his son Azariah (see notes on v. 21; 15:1–2).
14:3 *not as his father David.* Amaziah did not remain completely free from involvement with the worship of pagan deities (see 2Ch 25:14–16). His loyalty to the Lord fell short of that of Asa and Jehoshaphat before him (see 1Ki 15:11,14; 22:43; see also 1Ki 9:4; 11:4).
14:4 *high places, however, were not removed.* See note on 1Ki 15:14.
14:7 *defeated ten thousand Edomites.* Amaziah was able to regain temporarily (see 2Ch 28:17) some of Judah's control over the Edomites, which had been lost during the reign of Jehoram (see 8:20–22). *Valley of Salt.* The same battlefield on which David had defeated the Edomites (see 2Sa 8:13; 1Ch 18:12; Ps 60 title), generally identified with the Arabah directly south of the Dead Sea. *Sela.* Means "rock"; often regarded as the Edomite stronghold presently known as Petra (a Greek word meaning "rock"; see Jdg 1:36; Isa 16:1; 42:11; Ob 3). *to this day.* Until the time of the writing of the account of Amaziah's reign used by the author (see note on 1Ki 8:8; see also Introduction to 1 Kings: Author, Sources and Date).
14:8 *meet me face to face.* A challenge amounting to a declaration of war. Perhaps it was provoked by the hostile actions of mercenary troops from the northern kingdom after their dismissal from the Judahite army (see 2Ch 25:10,13)

and by the refusal of Jehoash to establish a marriage alliance with Amaziah (see v. 9).
14:9 *Jehoash . . . replied.* For his reply Jehoash used a fable (see Jdg 9:8–15) in which he represented himself as a strong cedar and Amaziah as an insignificant thistle that could easily be trampled underfoot.
14:11 *would not listen.* See 2Ch 25:20. *Beth Shemesh.* A town about 15 miles west of Jerusalem near the border between Judah and Dan (see Jos 15:10; 1Sa 6:9).
14:13 *Jehoash . . . captured Amaziah.* It is likely that Amaziah was taken back to the northern kingdom as a prisoner, where he remained until being released to return to Judah after the death of Jehoash (see vv. 15–16; see also note on v. 21). *Ephraim Gate to the Corner Gate.* The Corner Gate (see Jer 31:38; Zec 14:10) was at the northwest corner of the wall around Jerusalem. The Ephraim Gate was on the north side of Jerusalem (see Ne 12:39), 600 feet east of the Corner Gate. This northwestern section of the wall of Jerusalem was the point at which the city was most vulnerable to attack.
14:14 *gold and silver and all the articles found in the temple . . . and . . . the royal palace.* The value of the plundered articles was probably not great, because Joash had previously stripped the temple and palace to pay tribute to Hazael of Damascus (see 12:17–18). *took hostages.* The hostages were probably intended to secure additional payments of tribute in view of the meager war booty.
14:15 *annals of the kings of Israel.* See note on 1Ki 14:19.

buried in Samaria with the kings of Israel. And Jeroboam his son succeeded him as king.

[17]Amaziah son of Joash king of Judah lived for fifteen years after the death of Jehoash son of Jehoahaz king of Israel. [18]As for the other events of Amaziah's reign, are they not written in the book of the annals of the kings of Judah?

[19]They conspired[a] against him in Jerusalem, and he fled to Lachish,[b] but they sent men after him to Lachish and killed him there. [20]He was brought back by horse[c] and was buried in Jerusalem with his fathers, in the City of David.

[21]Then all the people of Judah took Azariah,[i][d] who was sixteen years old, and made him king in place of his father Amaziah. [22]He was the one who rebuilt Elath[e] and restored it to Judah after Amaziah rested with his fathers.

Jeroboam II King of Israel

[23]In the fifteenth year of Amaziah son of Joash king of Judah, Jeroboam[f] son of Jehoash king of Israel became king in Samaria, and he reigned forty-one years. [24]He did evil in the eyes of the LORD and

did not turn away from any of the sins of Jeroboam son of Nebat, which he had caused Israel to commit.[g] [25]He was the one who restored the boundaries of Israel from Lebo[j] Hamath[h] to the Sea of the Arabah,[k][i] in accordance with the word of the LORD, the God of Israel, spoken through his servant Jonah[j] son of Amittai, the prophet from Gath Hepher.

[26]The LORD had seen how bitterly everyone in Israel, whether slave or free,[k] was suffering;[l] there was no one to help them.[m] [27]And since the LORD had not said he would blot out[n] the name of Israel from under heaven, he saved[o] them by the hand of Jeroboam son of Jehoash.

[28]As for the other events of Jeroboam's reign, all he did, and his military achievements, including how he recovered for Israel both Damascus[p] and Hamath,[q] which had belonged to Yaudi,[l] are they not written in the book of the annals[r] of the kings of Israel? [29]Jeroboam rested with his fathers, the kings of Israel. And Zechariah his son succeeded him as king.

Cross-references

14:19
[a]S 2Ki 12:20
[b]S Jos 10:3
14:20
[c]S 2Ki 9:28
14:21 [d]2Ki 15:1;
2Ch 26:23;
Isa 1:1; Hos 1:1;
Am 1:1
14:22
[e]S 1Ki 9:26
14:23
[f]S 2Ki 13:13;
1Ch 5:17;
Am 1:1; 7:10

14:24
[g]S 1Ki 15:30
14:25
[h]S Nu 13:21
[i]Dt 3:17 /Jnh 1:1;
Mt 12:39
14:26 [k]Dt 32:36
[l]2Ki 13:4
[m]Ps 18:41;
22:11; 72:12;
107:12; Isa 63:5;
La 1:7
14:27
[n]S Dt 29:20
[o]S Jdg 6:14
14:28 [p]S 2Sa 8:5
[q]S 2Sa 8:9
[r]1Ki 15:31

[i]21 Also called *Uzziah* [j]25 Or *from the entrance to*
[k]25 That is, the Dead Sea [l]28 Or *Judah*

14:16 *rested with his fathers.* See 13:12–13; see also note on 1Ki 1:21.
14:17 *lived for fifteen years after the death of Jehoash.* Jehoash died in 782 B.C. and Amaziah in 767.
14:18 *annals of the kings of Judah.* See note on 1Ki 14:29.
14:19 *conspired against him.* 2Ch 25:27 connects the conspiracy against Amaziah with his turning away from the Lord, but it did not serve the purpose of the author of Kings to note this. *Lachish.* A fortress city in southern Judah 15 miles west of Hebron, presently known as Tell ed-Duweir (see 18:14; 2Ch 11:9).
14:21 *Then all the people of Judah took Azariah, who was.* Or "Now all the people of Judah had taken Azariah, when he was." See NIV text note. *made him king in place of his father Amaziah.* It is likely that this occurred after Amaziah had been taken prisoner by Jehoash (see v. 13). Thus Azariah's reign substantially overlapped that of his father Amaziah (see notes on v. 2; 15:2).
14:22 *rebuilt Elath and restored it to Judah.* Azariah extended the subjection of the Edomites begun by his father (see v. 7) and reestablished Israelite control over the important port city on the Gulf of Aqaba (see 1Ki 9:26).
14:23 *fifteenth year of Amaziah.* 782 B.C. (see note on v. 2). This was the beginning of Jeroboam's sole reign. He had previously served as co-regent with his father Jehoash. *forty-one years.* 793–753 (including the co-regency with his father).
14:24 *sins of Jeroboam.* See 1Ki 12:26–32; 13:33–34; 14:16; Am 3:13–14; 4:4–5; 5:4–6; 7:10–17.
14:25 *from Lebo Hamath.* Jeroboam II was able to free the northern kingdom from the oppression it had suffered at the hands of Hazael and Ben-Hadad (see 10:32; 12:17; 13:3, 22,25). He also extended Israelite political control over the Arameans of Damascus, an undertaking that had been begun by his father Jehoash (see 13:25). Assyrian pressure on the Arameans, including attacks on Damascus by Shalmaneser IV in 773 B.C. and Ashur-Dan III in 772, had weakened the

Arameans enough to enable Jeroboam II to gain the upper hand over them. Meanwhile, Assyria also became too weak to suppress Jeroboam's expansion. *Sea of the Arabah.* See NIV text note. According to Am 6:14 the southern limit of Jeroboam's kingdom in Transjordan was the "valley of the Arabah"—probably to be connected with the Valley of Salt (see note on v. 7). If so, Jeroboam had also subdued Moab and the Ammonites. *Jonah . . . the prophet from Gath Hepher.* See Jnh 1:1. Gath Hepher was located in the tribe of Zebulun, northeast of Nazareth (see Jos 19:13). This reference to Jonah is of help in dating the ministry of the prophet.
14:26 *slave or free.* See note on 1Ki 14:10. *suffering.* At the hands of the Arameans (see 10:32–33; 13:3–7), the Moabites (13:20) and the Ammonites (Am 1:13).
14:27 *had not said.* The sin of the Israelites had not yet reached its full measure, and the Lord mercifully extended to the nation an additional period of grace in which there was opportunity to repent (see note on 13:23). Persistence in apostasy, however, would bring certain judgment (see Am 4:2–3; 6:14). *saved them by the hand of Jeroboam.* See note on 13:5.
14:28 *all he did.* During Jeroboam's reign the northern kingdom enjoyed greater material prosperity than it had at any time since the rule of David and Solomon. Unfortunately, it was also a time of religious formalism and apostasy as well as social injustice (see the books of Amos and Hosea, who prophesied during Jeroboam's reign). *Damascus and Hamath.* See note on v. 25. *Yaudi.* Thought by some to be a place in northern Aram referred to in a few Assyrian inscriptions. Others understand the word as a reference to Judah (see NIV text note) in the sense that Damascus and Hamath were once included in territory ruled by David and Solomon (see 2Sa 8:6; 2Ch 8:3). *annals of the kings of Israel.* See note on 1Ki 14:19.
14:29 *rested with his fathers.* See note on 1Ki 1:21. *Zechariah his son succeeded him.* For the reign of Zechariah see 15:8–12.

Azariah King of Judah

15:1–7pp — 2Ch 26:3–4,21–23

15 In the twenty-seventh year of Jeroboam king of Israel, Azariah[s] son of Amaziah king of Judah began to reign. [2]He was sixteen years old when he became king, and he reigned in Jerusalem fifty-two years. His mother's name was Jecoliah; she was from Jerusalem. [3]He did what was right[t] in the eyes of the LORD, just as his father Amaziah had done. [4]The high places, however, were not removed; the people continued to offer sacrifices and burn incense there.

[5]The LORD afflicted[u] the king with leprosy[m] until the day he died, and he lived in a separate house.[n][v] Jotham[w] the king's son had charge of the palace[x] and governed the people of the land.

[6]As for the other events of Azariah's reign, and all he did, are they not written in the book of the annals of the kings of Judah? [7]Azariah rested[y] with his fathers and was buried near them in the City of David. And Jotham[z] his son succeeded him as king.

Zechariah King of Israel

[8]In the thirty-eighth year of Azariah king of Judah, Zechariah son of Jeroboam became king of Israel in Samaria, and he reigned six months. [9]He did evil[a] in the eyes of the LORD, as his fathers had done. He did not turn away from the sins of Jeroboam son of Nebat, which he had caused Israel to commit.

[10]Shallum son of Jabesh conspired against Zechariah. He attacked him in front of the people,[o] assassinated[b] him and succeeded him as king. [11]The other events of Zechariah's reign are written in the book of the annals[c] of the kings of Israel. [12]So the word of the LORD spoken to Jehu was fulfilled:[d] "Your descendants will sit on the throne of Israel to the fourth generation."[p]

Shallum King of Israel

[13]Shallum son of Jabesh became king in the thirty-ninth year of Uzziah king of Judah, and he reigned in Samaria[e] one month. [14]Then Menahem son of Gadi went from Tirzah[f] up to Samaria. He attacked Shallum son of Jabesh in Samaria, assassinated[g] him and succeeded him as king.

[15]The other events of Shallum's reign, and the conspiracy he led, are written in the book of the annals[h] of the kings of Israel.

[16]At that time Menahem, starting out from Tirzah, attacked Tiphsah[i] and everyone in the city and its vicinity, because they refused to open[j] their gates. He sacked Tiphsah and ripped open all the pregnant women.

Menahem King of Israel

[17]In the thirty-ninth year of Azariah king

Cross references (center column):

15:1 [s]S ver 32; S 2Ki 14:21
15:3 [t]S 1Ki 14:8
15:5 [u]S Ge 12:17 [v]Lev 13:46 [w]ver 7,32; 2Ch 27:1; Mic 1:1
15:6 [x]S Ge 41:40
15:7 [y]Isa 6:1; 14:28 [z]S ver 5
15:9 [a]1Ki 15:26

15:10 [b]S 2Ki 12:20
15:11 [c]1Ki 15:31
15:12 [d]2Ki 10:30
15:13 [e]S 1Ki 13:32
15:14 [f]S 1Ki 15:33 [g]S 2Ki 12:20
15:15 [h]1Ki 15:31
15:16 [i]1Ki 4:24 [j]S 2Ki 8:12; S Hos 13:16

Text notes (center column):

[m]5 The Hebrew word was used for various diseases affecting the skin—not necessarily leprosy.   [n]5 Or *in a house where he was relieved of responsibility*   [o]10 Hebrew; some Septuagint manuscripts *in Ibleam*   [p]12 2 Kings 10:30

15:1 *twenty-seventh year of Jeroboam.* 767 B.C., based on dating the beginning of Jeroboam's co-regency with Jehoash in 793 (see note on 14:23). *Azariah . . . began to reign.* He began his sole reign, after a 24-year co-regency with his father Amaziah (see notes on v. 2; 14:2,21). (His actual years were one less than his official years.)
15:2 *fifty-two years.* 792–740 B.C. (but he was co-regent with his father Amaziah 792–767). See note on v. 1.
15:3 *as his father Amaziah had done.* See note on 14:3.
15:4 *high places, however, were not removed.* See 14:4; see also note on 1Ki 15:14.
15:5 *afflicted the king with leprosy.* A punishment for usurping the priestly function of burning incense on the altar in the temple (see 2Ch 26:16–21; cf. Lev 13:46). *had charge of the palace and governed the people of the land.* Jotham ruled for his father for the remainder of Azariah's life (750–740 B.C.; see note on v. 33).
15:6 *all he did.* A more detailed account of Azariah's accomplishments is found in 2Ch 26:1–15. *annals of the kings of Judah.* See note on 1Ki 14:29.
15:7 *rested with his fathers.* See note on 1Ki 1:21. *Jotham his son succeeded him.* For the reign of Jotham see vv. 32–38.
15:8 *thirty-eighth year of Azariah.* 753 B.C. (see note on v. 2).
15:9 *sins of Jeroboam.* See 1Ki 12:26–32; 13:33–34; 14:16.

15:11 *annals of the kings of Israel.* See note on 1Ki 14:19.
15:12 *word of the LORD . . . was fulfilled.* See NIV text note. With the downfall of Jehu's dynasty, the northern kingdom entered a period of political instability (see Hos 1:4). The remaining five kings of the northern kingdom were all assassinated with the exception of Menahem, who reigned ten years, and Hoshea, who was imprisoned by the Assyrians. From the strength and wealth of the reign of Jeroboam II, the decline and fall of the northern kingdom was swift.
15:13 *thirty-ninth year of Uzziah.* 752 B.C. (see note on v. 2). Uzziah is another name for Azariah (see NIV text note on 14:21).
15:14 *Menahem . . . went from Tirzah up to Samaria.* It is likely that Menahem was the commander of a military garrison at Tirzah, the former capital of the northern kingdom (see 1Ki 14:17; 15:21,33). *succeeded him.* For the reign of Menahem see vv. 17–22.
15:15 *annals of the kings of Israel.* See note on 1Ki 14:19.
15:16 *Tiphsah.* There was a Tiphsah located far to the north of Hamath (see 14:25) on the Euphrates River (see 1Ki 4:24). It is unlikely that this was the city intended. Some interpreters prefer the reading "Tappuah" of the Septuagint. Tappuah was a city on the border between Ephraim and Manasseh (Jos 16:8; 17:7–8). Perhaps there was a Tiphsah in Israel not otherwise mentioned. *ripped open all the pregnant women.* See 8:12 and note.

Assyrian Campaigns against Israel and Judah

The Assyrian invasions of the eighth century B.C. were the most traumatic political events in the entire history of Israel.

The brutal Assyrian style of warfare relied on massive armies, superbly equipped with the world's first great siege machines manipulated by an efficient corps of engineers.

Psychological terror, however, was Assyria's most effective weapon. It was ruthlessly applied, with corpses impaled on stakes, severed heads stacked in heaps, and captives skinned alive.

The shock of bloody military sieges on both Israel and Judah was profound. The prophets did not fail to scream out against their horror, while at the same time pleading with the people to see God's hand in history, to recognize spiritual causes in the present punishment.

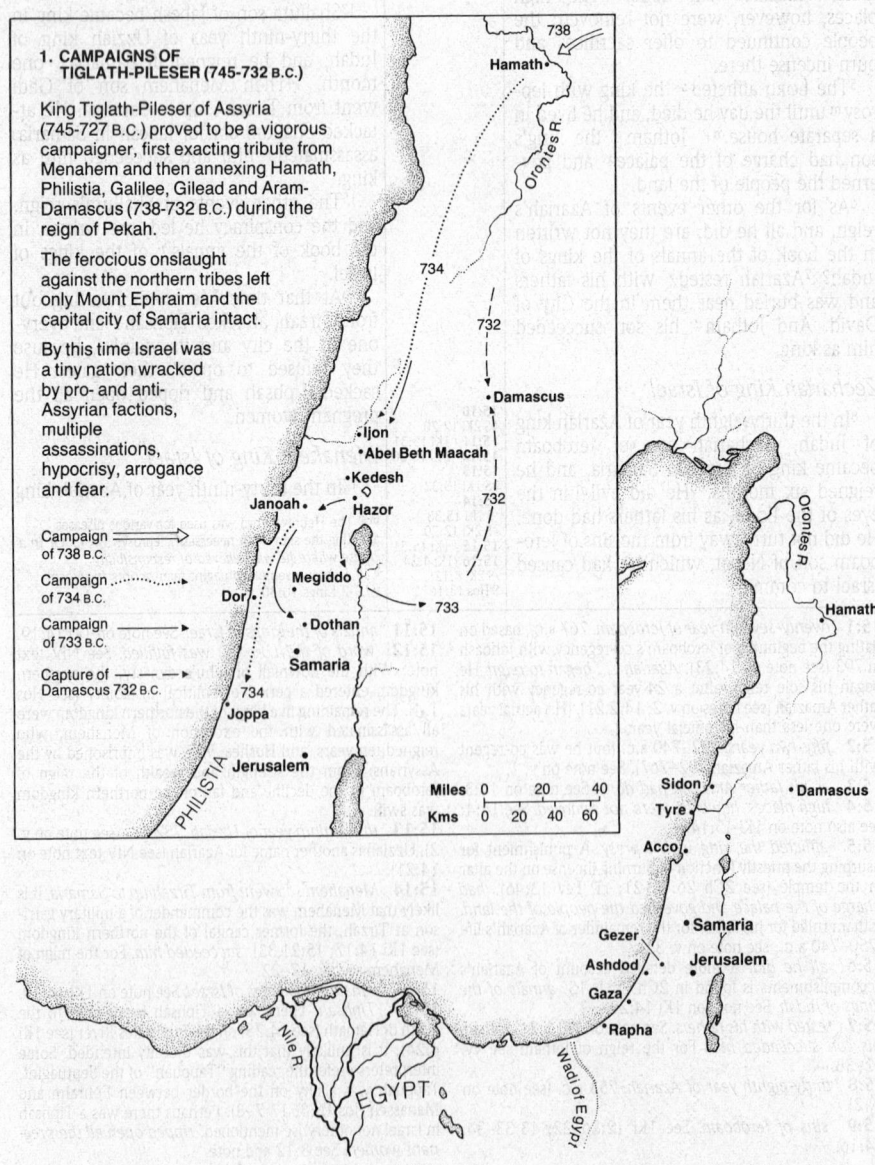

1. CAMPAIGNS OF TIGLATH-PILESER (745-732 B.C.)

King Tiglath-Pileser of Assyria (745-727 B.C.) proved to be a vigorous campaigner, first exacting tribute from Menahem and then annexing Hamath, Philistia, Galilee, Gilead and Aram-Damascus (738-732 B.C.) during the reign of Pekah.

The ferocious onslaught against the northern tribes left only Mount Ephraim and the capital city of Samaria intact.

By this time Israel was a tiny nation wracked by pro- and anti-Assyrian factions, multiple assassinations, hypocrisy, arrogance and fear.

Campaign of 738 B.C.
Campaign of 734 B.C.
Campaign of 733 B.C.
Capture of Damascus 732 B.C.

Miles 0 20 40
Kms 0 20 40 60

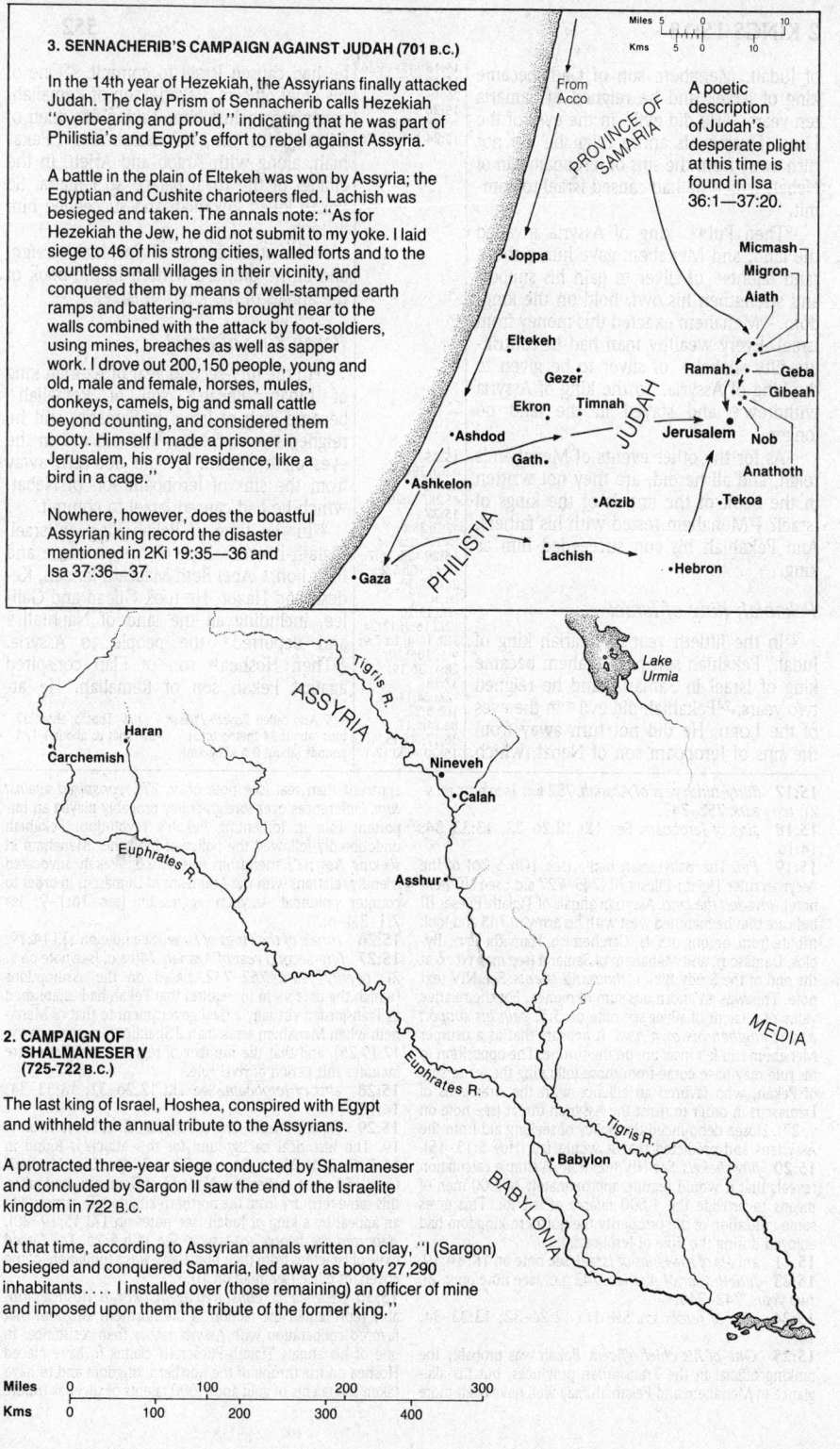

3. SENNACHERIB'S CAMPAIGN AGAINST JUDAH (701 B.C.)

In the 14th year of Hezekiah, the Assyrians finally attacked Judah. The clay Prism of Sennacherib calls Hezekiah "overbearing and proud," indicating that he was part of Philistia's and Egypt's effort to rebel against Assyria.

A battle in the plain of Eltekeh was won by Assyria; the Egyptian and Cushite charioteers fled. Lachish was besieged and taken. The annals note: "As for Hezekiah the Jew, he did not submit to my yoke. I laid siege to 46 of his strong cities, walled forts and to the countless small villages in their vicinity, and conquered them by means of well-stamped earth ramps and battering-rams brought near to the walls combined with the attack by foot-soldiers, using mines, breaches as well as sapper work. I drove out 200,150 people, young and old, male and female, horses, mules, donkeys, camels, big and small cattle beyond counting, and considered them booty. Himself I made a prisoner in Jerusalem, his royal residence, like a bird in a cage."

Nowhere, however, does the boastful Assyrian king record the disaster mentioned in 2Ki 19:35—36 and Isa 37:36—37.

A poetic description of Judah's desperate plight at this time is found in Isa 36:1—37:20.

Miles 5 0 10
Kms 5 10

From Acco

PROVINCE OF SAMARIA

Joppa

Micmash
Migron
Aiath

Eltekeh

Gezer

Ekron   Timnah

Ashdod

Gath.

Ashkelon

Ramah
Geba
Gibeah

JUDAH

Jerusalem   Nob

Anathoth

Aczib

Tekoa

PHILISTIA

Lachish

Gaza

Hebron

---

2. CAMPAIGN OF SHALMANESER V (725-722 B.C.)

The last king of Israel, Hoshea, conspired with Egypt and withheld the annual tribute to the Assyrians.

A protracted three-year siege conducted by Shalmaneser and concluded by Sargon II saw the end of the Israelite kingdom in 722 B.C.

At that time, according to Assyrian annals written on clay, "I (Sargon) besieged and conquered Samaria, led away as booty 27,290 inhabitants.... I installed over (those remaining) an officer of mine and imposed upon them the tribute of the former king."

Tigris R.

ASSYRIA

Haran
Carchemish

Nineveh
Calah

Euphrates R.

Asshur

Lake Urmia

MEDIA

Euphrates R.

Tigris R.

Babylon

BABYLONIA

Miles 0 100 200 300
Kms 0 100 200 300 400

of Judah, Menahem son of Gadi became king of Israel, and he reigned in Samaria ten years. [18]He did evil[k] in the eyes of the LORD. During his entire reign he did not turn away from the sins of Jeroboam son of Nebat, which he had caused Israel to commit.

[19]Then Pul[q][l] king of Assyria invaded the land, and Menahem gave him a thousand talents[r] of silver to gain his support and strengthen his own hold on the kingdom. [20]Menahem exacted this money from Israel. Every wealthy man had to contribute fifty shekels[s] of silver to be given to the king of Assyria. So the king of Assyria withdrew[m] and stayed in the land no longer.

[21]As for the other events of Menahem's reign, and all he did, are they not written in the book of the annals of the kings of Israel? [22]Menahem rested with his fathers. And Pekahiah his son succeeded him as king.

Pekahiah King of Israel

[23]In the fiftieth year of Azariah king of Judah, Pekahiah son of Menahem became king of Israel in Samaria, and he reigned two years. [24]Pekahiah did evil[n] in the eyes of the LORD. He did not turn away from the sins of Jeroboam son of Nebat, which

he had caused Israel to commit. [25]One of his chief officers, Pekah[o] son of Remaliah, conspired against him. Taking fifty men of Gilead with him, he assassinated[p] Pekahiah, along with Argob and Arieh, in the citadel of the royal palace at Samaria. So Pekah killed Pekahiah and succeeded him as king.

[26]The other events of Pekahiah's reign, and all he did, are written in the book of the annals of the kings of Israel.

Pekah King of Israel

[27]In the fifty-second year of Azariah king of Judah, Pekah[q] son of Remaliah[r] became king of Israel in Samaria, and he reigned twenty years. [28]He did evil in the eyes of the LORD. He did not turn away from the sins of Jeroboam son of Nebat, which he had caused Israel to commit.

[29]In the time of Pekah king of Israel, Tiglath-Pileser[s] king of Assyria came and took Ijon,[t] Abel Beth Maacah, Janoah, Kedesh and Hazor. He took Gilead and Galilee, including all the land of Naphtali,[u] and deported[v] the people to Assyria. [30]Then Hoshea[w] son of Elah conspired against Pekah son of Remaliah. He at-

15:18 k1Ki 15:26
15:19 l1Ch 5:6,
26
15:20 mS 2Ki 12:18
15:24 n1Ki 15:26

15:25 o2Ch 28:6;
Isa 7:1
p S 2Ki 12:20
15:27 q2Ch 28:6;
Isa 7:1 rIsa 7:4
15:29 s2Ki 16:7;
17:6; 1Ch 5:26;
2Ch 28:20;
Jer 50:17
t1Ki 15:20
u2Ki 16:9; 17:24;
2Ch 16:4; Isa 7:9;
9:1; 10:9,10;
28:1; 36:19;
37:18
v2Ki 24:14-16;
1Ch 5:22;
Isa 14:6,17;
36:17; 45:13
15:30 w2Ki 17:1

q19 Also called Tiglath-Pileser   r19 That is, about 37 tons (about 34 metric tons)   s20 That is, about 1 1/4 pounds (about 0.6 kilogram)

15:17 thirty-ninth year of Azariah. 752 B.C. (see note on v. 2). ten years. 752–742.

15:18 sins of Jeroboam. See 1Ki 12:26–32; 13:33–34; 14:16.

15:19 Pul. The Babylonian name (see 1Ch 5:26) of the Assyrian ruler Tiglath-Pileser III (745–727 B.C.; see NIV text note). invaded the land. Assyrian annals of Tiglath-Pileser III indicate that he marched west with his army in 743 and took tribute from, among others, Carchemish, Hamath, Tyre, Byblos, Damascus, and Menahem of Samaria (see map No. 6 at the end of the Study Bible). thousand talents. See NIV text note. This was an enormous sum of money. For the relative value of a talent of silver see note on 5:5. gain his support and strengthen his own hold. It appears that as a usurper Menahem still felt insecure on the throne. The opposition to his rule may have come from those following the leadership of Pekah, who favored an alliance with the Arameans of Damascus in order to resist the Assyrian threat (see note on v. 27). Hosea denounced the policy of seeking aid from the Assyrians and predicted that it would fail (Hos 5:13–15).

15:20 fifty shekels. See NIV text note. A simple calculation reveals that it would require approximately 60,000 men of means to provide the 1,000 talents of tribute. This gives some indication of the prosperity the northern kingdom had enjoyed during the time of Jeroboam II.

15:21 annals of the kings of Israel. See note on 1Ki 14:19.

15:23 fiftieth year of Azariah. 742 B.C. (see note on v. 2). two years. 742–740.

15:24 sins of Jeroboam. See 1Ki 12:26–32; 13:33–34; 14:16.

15:25 One of his chief officers. Pekah was probably the ranking official in the Transjordan provinces, but his allegiance to Menahem and Pekahiah may well have been more

apparent than real (see note on v. 27). conspired against him. Differences over foreign policy probably played an important role in fomenting Pekah's revolution. Pekahiah undoubtedly followed the policy of his father Menahem in seeking Assyria's friendship (see v. 20). Pekah advocated friendly relations with the Arameans of Damascus in order to counter potential Assyrian aggression (see 16:1–9; Isa 7:1–2,4–6).

15:26 annals of the kings of Israel. See note on 1Ki 14:19.

15:27 fifty-second year of Azariah. 740 B.C. (see note on v. 2). twenty years. 752–732, based on the assumptions (which the data seem to require) that Pekah had established in Transjordan virtually a rival government to that of Menahem when Menahem assassinated Shallum (see notes on vv. 17,19,25), and that the number of regnal years given here includes this period of rival rule.

15:28 sins of Jeroboam. See 1Ki 12:26–32; 13:33–34; 14:16.

15:29 Tiglath-Pileser king of Assyria came. See note on v. 19. The historical background for this attack is found in 16:5–9; 2Ch 28:16–21; Isa 7:1–17. Ijon . . . Naphtali. Over 150 years earlier Ben-Hadad I of Damascus had taken this same territory from the northern kingdom in response to an appeal by a king of Judah (see notes on 1Ki 15:19–20). deported the people to Assyria. See 1Ch 5:26. The forced exile of Israelites from their homeland was a fulfillment of the covenant curse (see note on 10:32).

15:30 Hoshea . . . conspired against Pekah. Hoshea probably represented the faction in the northern kingdom that favored cooperation with Assyria rather than resistance. In one of his annals Tiglath-Pileser III claims to have placed Hoshea on the throne of the northern kingdom and to have taken ten talents of gold and 1,000 talents of silver as tribute

tacked and assassinated[x] him, and then succeeded him as king in the twentieth year of Jotham son of Uzziah.

[31]As for the other events of Pekah's reign, and all he did, are they not written in the book of the annals[y] of the kings of Israel?

Jotham King of Judah

15:33-38pp — 2Ch 27:1-4,7-9

[32]In the second year of Pekah son of Remaliah king of Israel, Jotham[z] son of Uzziah king of Judah began to reign. [33]He was twenty-five years old when he became king, and he reigned in Jerusalem sixteen years. His mother's name was Jerusha daughter of Zadok. [34]He did what was right[a] in the eyes of the LORD, just as his father Uzziah had done. [35]The high places,[b] however, were not removed; the people continued to offer sacrifices and burn incense there. Jotham rebuilt the Upper Gate[c] of the temple of the LORD.

[36]As for the other events of Jotham's reign, and what he did, are they not written in the book of the annals of the kings of Judah? [37](In those days the LORD began to

send Rezin[d] king of Aram and Pekah son of Remaliah against Judah.) [38]Jotham rested with his fathers and was buried with them in the City of David, the city of his father. And Ahaz his son succeeded him as king.

Ahaz King of Judah

16:1-20pp — 2Ch 28:1-27

16 In the seventeenth year of Pekah son of Remaliah, Ahaz[e] son of Jotham king of Judah began to reign. [2]Ahaz was twenty years old when he became king, and he reigned in Jerusalem sixteen years. Unlike David his father, he did not do what was right[f] in the eyes of the LORD his God. [3]He walked in the ways of the kings of Israel[g] and even sacrificed his son[h] in[t] the fire, following the detestable[i] ways of the nations the LORD had driven out before the Israelites. [4]He offered sacrifices and burned incense[j] at the high places, on the hilltops and under every spreading tree.[k]

[5]Then Rezin[l] king of Aram and Pekah

Cross references (center column):

15:30 [x]S 2Ki 12:20
15:31 [y]1Ki 15:31
15:32 [z]ver 1,S 5; 1Ch 5:17; Isa 1:1;
Hos 1:1
15:34 [a]S 1Ki 14:8
15:35 [b]2Ki 12:3
[c]S Ge 23:10;
2Ch 23:20

15:37 [d]2Ki 16:5;
Isa 7:1; 8:6; 9:11
16:1 [e]Isa 1:1;
7:1; 14:28;
Hos 1:1; Mic 1:1
16:2 [f]S 1Ki 14:8
16:3 [g]2Ki 17:19
[h]S Lev 18:21;
S 2Ki 3:27
[i]S Lev 18:3;
S Dt 9:4
16:4 [j]2Ki 22:17;
23:5 [k]Dt 12:2;
Eze 6:13
16:5 [l]S 2Ki 15:37

[t]3 Or *even made his son pass through*

---

from him. *twentieth year of Jotham.* 732 B.C. (see notes on vv. 32–33). Reference is to his 20th official year, which was his 19th actual year.
15:31 *annals of the kings of Israel.* See note on 1Ki 14:19.
15:32 *second year of Pekah.* 750 B.C. (see note on v. 27).
15:33 *sixteen years.* 750–735 B.C. Jotham was co-regent with his father 750–740 (see note on v. 5). Jotham's reign was in some sense terminated in 735, and his son Ahaz took over. However, Jotham continued to live until at least 732 (see notes on vv. 30,37).
15:34 *as his father Uzziah had done.* See note on v. 3; see also 2Ch 27:2.
15:35 *high places, however, were not removed.* See v. 4; see also note on 1Ki 15:14. *Upper Gate of the temple.* See 2Ch 23:20; Jer 20:2; Eze 8:3; 9:2. Additional information on Jotham's building activities is given in 2Ch 27:3–4.
15:36 *other events of Jotham's reign.* See 2Ch 27:1–6. *annals of the kings of Judah.* See note on 1Ki 14:29.
15:37 This parenthetical statement concerning Jotham's reign supports the idea of an overlap between the reigns of Jotham and Ahaz (see note on v. 33), since 16:5–12; 2Ch 28:5–21; Isa 7:1–17 all place the major effort of Rezin and Pekah in the time of Ahaz.
15:38 *rested with his fathers.* See note on 1Ki 1:21.
16:1 *seventeenth year of Pekah.* 735 B.C. (see note on v. 27). The reign of Ahaz apparently overlapped that of Jotham, with Ahaz serving as a senior partner beginning in 735 (see notes on 15:33,37; see also notes on v. 2; 17:1).
16:2 *twenty years old when he became king.* Perhaps the age at which Ahaz became a senior co-regent with his father Jotham in 735 B.C. (see note on v. 1). Otherwise, according to the ages and dates provided, Ahaz would have been 11 or 12 instead of 14 or 15 years old when his son Hezekiah was born (cf. 18:1–2). *sixteen years.* The synchronizations of the reigns of Ahaz and Hezekiah of Judah with those of Pekah and Hoshea of the northern kingdom present some apparent chronological difficulties (see notes on v. 1; 17:1; 18:1, 9–10). It seems best to take the 16 years specified here as the

number of years Ahaz reigned after the death of Jotham, thus 732–715 (see notes on 15:30,33). The beginning of his reign appears to be dated in a variety of ways in the Biblical text: (1) in 744/743, which presupposes a co-regency with his grandfather Azariah at the tender age of 11 or 12 (see 17:1); (2) in 735, when he became senior co-regent with Jotham (see v. 1); and (3) in 732, when he began his sole reign after the death of Jotham. *Unlike David his father.* Ahaz does not even receive the qualified approval given to Amaziah (14:3), Azariah (15:3) and Jotham (15:34).
16:3 *ways of the kings of Israel.* It is unlikely that Ahaz adhered to the calf worship introduced by Jeroboam I at Bethel and Dan (see 1Ki 12:26–32; 13:33–34; 14:16). The reference here is probably to Baal worship in the spirit of Ahab (see notes on 1Ki 16:31–33; see also 2Ch 28:2). *sacrificed his son.* Israel had been warned by Moses not to engage in this pagan rite (see Lev 18:21; Dt 18:10). In Israel the firstborn son in each household was to be consecrated to the Lord and redeemed by a payment of five shekels to the priests (see Ex 13:1,11–13; Nu 18:16). See also 3:27; 17:17; 21:6; 23:10; 2Ch 28:3; Jer 7:31; 32:35.
16:4 *high places.* See 15:4,35; see also note on 1Ki 15:14. These high places appear to be those assimilated from pagan Baal worship and used for the worship of the Lord in a syncretistic fashion. *under every spreading tree.* Large trees were viewed as symbols of fertility by the pre-Israelite inhabitants of Canaan. Immoral pagan rites were performed at shrines located under such trees. Contrary to the explicit prohibition of the Mosaic covenant, the Israelites adopted this pagan custom (see 17:10; 1Ki 14:23; Dt 12:2; Jer 2:20; 3:6; 17:2; Eze 6:13; 20:28; Hos 4:13–14).
16:5 *Rezin . . . and Pekah . . . marched up to fight against Jerusalem.* See notes on 15:25,37. *could not overpower.* See Isa 7:1–17; 2Ch 28:5–21. Rezin and Pekah desired to replace Ahaz on the throne of the southern kingdom with the son of Tabeel in order to gain another ally in their anti-Assyrian political policy (see notes on 15:19,25). The Lord delivered Judah and Ahaz from this threat in spite of their

son of Remaliah king of Israel marched up to fight against Jerusalem and besieged Ahaz, but they could not overpower him. [6]At that time, Rezin[m] king of Aram recovered Elath[n] for Aram by driving out the men of Judah. Edomites then moved into Elath and have lived there to this day.

[7]Ahaz sent messengers to say to Tiglath-Pileser[o] king of Assyria, "I am your servant and vassal. Come up and save[p] me out of the hand of the king of Aram and of the king of Israel, who are attacking me." [8]And Ahaz took the silver and gold found in the temple of the LORD and in the treasuries of the royal palace and sent it as a gift[q] to the king of Assyria. [9]The king of Assyria complied by attacking Damascus[r] and capturing it. He deported its inhabitants to Kir[s] and put Rezin to death.

[10]Then King Ahaz went to Damascus to meet Tiglath-Pileser king of Assyria. He saw an altar in Damascus and sent to Uriah[t] the priest a sketch of the altar, with detailed plans for its construction. [11]So Uriah the priest built an altar in accordance with all the plans that King Ahaz had sent from Damascus and finished it before King Ahaz returned. [12]When the king came back from Damascus and saw the altar, he approached it and presented offerings[u] [u] on it. [13]He offered up his burnt offering[v] and grain offering,[w] poured out his drink

offering,[x] and sprinkled the blood of his fellowship offerings[v][y] on the altar. [14]The bronze altar[z] that stood before the LORD he brought from the front of the temple—from between the new altar and the temple of the LORD—and put it on the north side of the new altar.

[15]King Ahaz then gave these orders to Uriah the priest: "On the large new altar, offer the morning[a] burnt offering and the evening grain offering, the king's burnt offering and his grain offering, and the burnt offering of all the people of the land, and their grain offering and their drink offering. Sprinkle on the altar all the blood of the burnt offerings and sacrifices. But I will use the bronze altar for seeking guidance."[b] [16]And Uriah the priest did just as King Ahaz had ordered.

[17]King Ahaz took away the side panels and removed the basins from the movable stands. He removed the Sea from the bronze bulls that supported it and set it on a stone base.[c] [18]He took away the Sabbath canopy[w] that had been built at the temple and removed the royal entryway outside the temple of the LORD, in deference to the king of Assyria.[d]

[19]As for the other events of the reign of

Cross references (center column):

16:6 *m*Isa 9:12
*n*S 1Ki 9:26
16:7
*o*S 2Ki 15:29
*p*Isa 2:6; 10:20;
Jer 2:18; 3:1;
Eze 16:28; 23:5;
Hos 10:6
16:8
*q*S 1Ki 15:18;
2Ki 12:18
16:9
*r*S Ge 14:15;
S 2Ki 15:29
*s*Isa 22:6;
Am 1:5; 9:7
16:10 *t*ver 11,15,
16; Isa 8:2
16:12
*u*2Ch 26:16
16:13
*v*Lev 6:8-13
*w*Lev 6:14-23

*x*S Ex 29:40
*y*Lev 7:11-21
16:14
*z*S Ex 20:24;
16:15
S 40:6; S 1Ki 8:64
*a*Ex 29:38-41
*b*1Sa 9:9
16:17 *c*1Ki 7:27
16:18 *d*Eze 16:28

Textual notes:

[u]*12* Or *and went up*   [v]*13* Traditionally *peace offerings*   [w]*18* Or *the dais of his throne* (see Septuagint)

---

wickedness because of the promises of the Davidic covenant (see 1Ki 11:36; 2Sa 7:13; Isa 7:3–7,14).

16:6 *Rezin king of Aram recovered Elath.* See note on 14:22. *Edomites then moved into Elath.* See 2Ch 28:17. The Philistines also took this opportunity to avenge previous defeats (compare 2Ch 26:5–7 with 2Ch 28:18). *to this day.* See note on 1Ki 8:8.

16:7 *Tiglath-Pileser.* See notes on 15:19, 29. *your servant and vassal.* Ahaz preferred to seek security for Judah by means of a treaty with Assyria rather than by obedience to the Lord and trust in his promises (see Ex 23:22; Isa 7:10–16).

16:8 *silver and gold found in the temple.* The temple treasure must have been restored to some degree by Jotham (see 12:18; 14:14). The name "Jehoahaz of Judah" (Ahaz) appears on a list of rulers (including those of the Philistines, Ammonites, Moabites and Edomites) who brought tribute to Tiglath-Pileser in 734 B.C.

16:9 *attacking Damascus and capturing it.* In 732 B.C. Tiglath-Pileser III moved against Damascus and destroyed it (see the prophecies of Isa 7:16; Am 1:3–5). *deported its inhabitants to Kir.* The Arameans were sent back to the place from which they had come (Am 9:7) in fulfillment of the prophecy of Amos (Am 1:5). The location of Kir is unknown, though it is mentioned in connection with Elam in Isa 22:6.

16:10 *Ahaz went to Damascus to meet Tiglath-Pileser.* As a vassal king to express his gratitude and loyalty to the victorious Assyrian ruler. *altar in Damascus.* Perhaps that of the god Rimmon (see 5:18; 2Ch 28:23), but more likely a royal altar of Tiglath-Pileser. Ahaz's reproduction of such an altar would have been a further sign of submission to the Assyrians.

16:13 *burnt offering . . . grain offering . . . drink offering . . . fellowship offerings.* With the exception of the drink offering, these same sacrifices were offered at the dedication of the temple (1Ki 8:64).

16:14 *north side of the new altar.* Ahaz removed the bronze altar from its prominent place in front of the temple and gave it a place alongside the new stone altar.

16:15 *large new altar.* Even though fire from heaven had inaugurated and sanctioned the use of the bronze altar for the worship of the Lord (see 2Ch 7:1), Ahaz now replaced it with an altar built on the pattern of the pagan altar from Damascus. Although the bronze altar was quite large (see 2Ch 4:1), the new altar was larger. *morning burnt offering.* See 3:20; Ex 29:38–39; Nu 28:3–4. *evening grain offering.* See note on 1Ki 18:29. *king's burnt offering and his grain offering.* There is no other reference to these special offerings of the king in the OT, with the possible exception of Ezekiel's depiction of the offerings of a future prince (Eze 46:12). *I will use the bronze altar for seeking guidance.* Seeking omens by the examination of the entrails of sacrificed animals is well attested in ancient Near Eastern texts. Here Ahaz states his intention to follow an Assyrian divination technique in an attempt to secure the Lord's guidance.

16:17 *side panels and . . . basins from the movable stands.* See 1Ki 7:27–39. *removed the Sea from the bronze bulls.* See 1Ki 7:23–26. Perhaps the bronze was needed for tribute required by Tiglath-Pileser III.

16:18 *in deference to the king of Assyria.* As a vassal of Tiglath-Pileser, Ahaz was forced to relinquish some of the symbols of his own royal power.

16:19 *other events of the reign of Ahaz.* See 2Ch 28, where, among other things, it is said that Ahaz went so far as to

Ahaz, and what he did, are they not written in the book of the annals of the kings of Judah? ²⁰Ahaz rested ^e with his fathers and was buried with them in the City of David. And Hezekiah his son succeeded him as king.

Hoshea Last King of Israel

17:3–7pp — 2Ki 18:9–12

17 In the twelfth year of Ahaz king of Judah, Hoshea^f son of Elah became king of Israel in Samaria, and he reigned nine years. ²He did evil^g in the eyes of the LORD, but not like the kings of Israel who preceded him.

³Shalmaneser^h king of Assyria came up to attack Hoshea, who had been Shalmaneser's vassal and had paid him tribute.ⁱ ⁴But the king of Assyria discovered that Hoshea was a traitor, for he had sent envoys to So^x king of Egypt,^j and he no longer paid tribute to the king of Assyria, as he had done year by year. Therefore Shalmaneser seized him and put him in prison.^k ⁵The king of Assyria invaded the entire land, marched against Samaria and laid siege^l to it for three years. ⁶In the ninth year of Hoshea, the king of Assyria^m captured Samariaⁿ and deported^o the Isra-

elites to Assyria. He settled them in Halah, in Gozan^p on the Habor River and in the towns of the Medes.

Israel Exiled Because of Sin

⁷All this took place because the Israelites had sinned^q against the LORD their God, who had brought them up out of Egypt^r from under the power of Pharaoh king of Egypt. They worshiped other gods ⁸and followed the practices of the nations^s the LORD had driven out before them, as well as the practices that the kings of Israel had introduced. ⁹The Israelites secretly did things against the LORD their God that were not right. From watchtower to fortified city^t they built themselves high places in all their towns. ¹⁰They set up sacred stones^u and Asherah poles^v on every high hill and under every spreading tree.^w ¹¹At every high place they burned incense, as the nations whom the LORD had driven out before them had done. They did wicked things that provoked the LORD to anger. ¹²They worshiped idols,^x though the LORD had said, "You shall not do this."^y ¹³The LORD warned^z Israel and Judah through

Cross references (center column)

16:20 *e*Isa 14:28
17:1 *f*2Ki 15:30
17:2 *g*S Dt 4:25
17:3 *h*Hos 10:14
/S Jdg 3:15
17:4 /Ps 146:3;
Isa 30:1,7; 36:6;
Jer 2:36; Hos 12:1
*k*Hos 13:10
17:5 /Hos 13:16
17:6 *m*ver 20;
S 2Ki 15:29;
Isa 42:24
*n*Isa 10:9
*o*S Dt 4:27;
S 24:1;
S 2Ki 15:29;
Am 7:17

*p*1Ch 5:26
17:7 *q*S Jos 7:11
*r*Ex 14:15-31
17:8 *s*S Ex 34:15;
S Lev 18:3;
S Dt 9:4
17:9 *t*2Ki 18:8
17:10
*u*S Ex 23:24
*v*Ex 34:13;
Isa 17:8; Mic 5:14
*w*S Dt 12:2
17:12 *x*S Ex 20:4
17:13 *y*S Jdg 6:8;
S 2Ch 7:14;
S Job 34:33;
Eze 3:17-19

x4 Or *to Sais, to the; So* is possibly an abbreviation for *Osorkon.*   **y12** Exodus 20:4, 5

---

to "shut the doors of the temple" (2Ch 28:24). *annals of the kings of Judah.* See note on 1Ki 14:29.
16:20 *rested with his fathers.* See note on 1Ki 1:21; see also 2Ch 28:27. *Hezekiah his son succeeded him.* For the reign of Hezekiah see 18:1–20:21.
17:1 *twelfth year of Ahaz.* 732 B.C. (see note on 15:30), on the assumption that Ahaz began a co-regency with Azariah in 744/743 (see notes on 16:1–2). Some interpreters prefer to place the beginning of the reign of Ahaz in 735 on the assumption that the "twelfth" year of his reign in this text is a copyist's error for the "fourth" year of his reign (i.e., 732). *nine years.* 732–723 (see Introduction to 1 Kings: Chronology).
17:3 *Shalmaneser.* Hoshea had become a vassal to Assyria under the rule of Tiglath-Pileser III (see note on 15:30). The latter was succeeded on the Assyrian throne by Shalmaneser V, who ruled 727–722 B.C.
17:5 *three years.* 725–722 B.C. Samaria was a strongly fortified city and extremely difficult to subdue (see note on 1Ki 16:24).
17:6 *ninth year of Hoshea.* 722 B.C. (see note on v. 1). *king of Assyria captured Samaria.* In the winter (December) of 722–721 Shalmaneser V died (possibly by assassination), and the Assyrian throne was seized by Sargon II (722/721–705). In his annals Sargon II lays claim to the capture of Samaria at the beginning of his reign, but it was hardly more than a mopping-up operation. *deported the Israelites.* Because the northern kingdom refused to be obedient to their covenant obligations, the Lord brought on them the judgment pronounced already by Ahijah during the reign of the northern kingdom's first king, Jeroboam I (see note on 1Ki 14:15). In his annals Sargon II claims to have deported 27,290 Israelites. He then settled other captured people in the vacated towns of the northern kingdom (see v. 24). *Halah.* Location uncertain. *Gozan on the Habor River.* An Assyrian provincial

capital located on a tributary of the Euphrates River. *towns of the Medes.* Towns located in the area south of the Caspian Sea and northeast of the Tigris River.
17:7–23 A theological explanation for the downfall of the northern kingdom. Israel had repeatedly spurned the Lord's gracious acts, had refused to heed the prophets' warnings of impending judgment (vv. 13–14,23) and had failed to keep her covenant obligations (v. 15). The result was the implementation of the covenant curse precisely as it had been presented to the Israelites by Moses before they entered into Canaan (Dt 28:49–68; 32:1–47).
17:7 *brought them up out of Egypt.* The deliverance from Egypt was the fundamental redemptive event in Israel's history. She owed her very existence as a nation to this gracious and mighty act of the Lord (see Ex 20:2; Dt 5:15; 26:8; Jos 24:5–7,17; Jdg 10:11; 1Sa 12:6; Ne 9:9–13; Mic 6:4). *worshiped other gods.* A violation of the most basic obligation of Israel's covenant with the Lord (see v. 35; Dt 5:7; 6:14; Jos 24:14–16,20; Jer 25:2–6; 25:6; 35:15).
17:8 *practices of the nations.* See Dt 18:9; Jdg 2:12–13. *practices that the kings of Israel had introduced.* See, e.g., 10:31 (Jehu); 14:24 (Jeroboam II); 1Ki 12:28–33 (Jeroboam I); 16:25–26 (Omri); 16:30–34 (Ahab).
17:9 *high places in all their towns.* See 14:4; 15:4,35; see also notes on 16:4; 1Ki 3:2; 15:14.
17:10 *sacred stones.* See note on 1Ki 14:23. *Asherah poles.* See note on 1Ki 14:15. *on every high hill and under every spreading tree.* See 16:4; 1Ki 14:23; Jer 2:20; 3:6,13; 17:2.
17:11 *wicked things.* Perhaps a reference to ritual prostitution (see note on 1Ki 14:24; see also Hos 4:13–14).
17:12 *You shall not do this.* See NIV text note; see also Ex 23:13; Lev 26:1; Dt 5:6–10.
17:13 *warned Israel and Judah through all his prophets.* Israel not only violated the requirements of the Sinai cov-

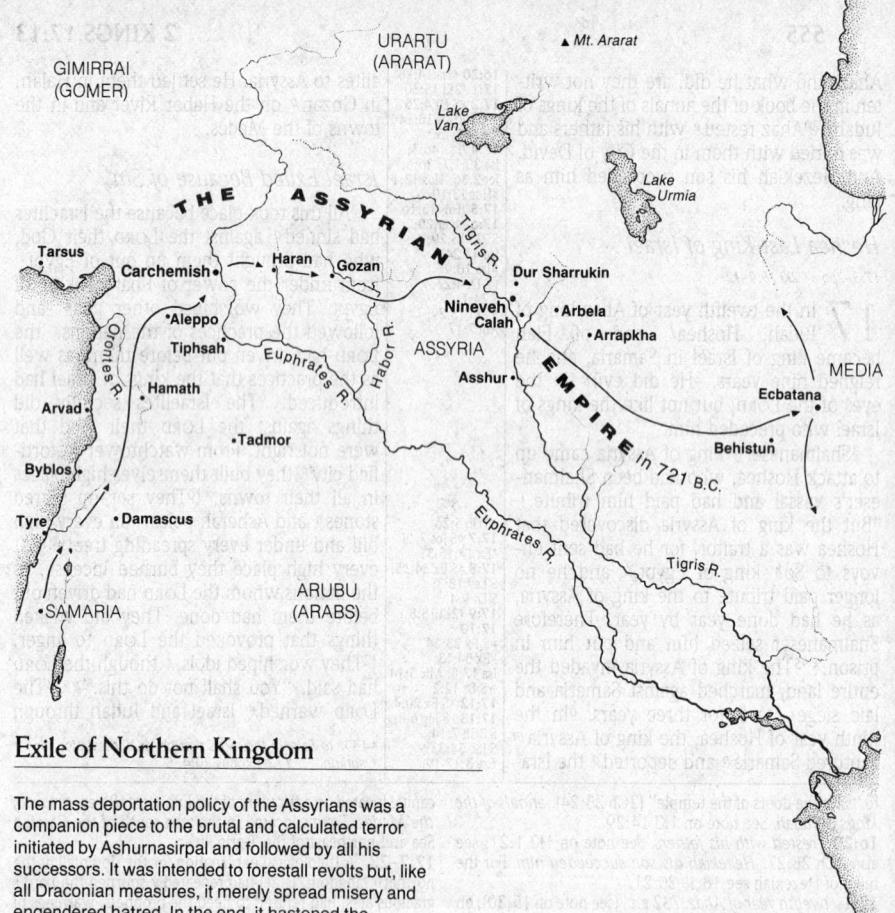

GIMIRRAI
(GOMER)

URARTU
(ARARAT)

▲ Mt. Ararat

Lake
Van

Lake
Urmia

THE ASSYRIAN EMPIRE in 721 B.C.

Tarsus

Carchemish • — Haran → Gozan

Dur Sharrukin

Nineveh • • Arbela
Calah

• Arrapkha

• Aleppo

Tiphsah

Euphrates R.

Habor R.

ASSYRIA

Asshur •

MEDIA

Hamath

Arvad •

Orontes R.

• Tadmor

Ecbatana •

Behistun

Byblos •

Tyre

• Damascus

Euphrates R.

Tigris R.

• SAMARIA

ARUBU
(ARABS)

Miles 0 — 100 — 200 — 300
Kms 0 — 100 — 200 — 300 — 400

Exile of Northern Kingdom

The mass deportation policy of the Assyrians was a companion piece to the brutal and calculated terror initiated by Ashurnasirpal and followed by all his successors. It was intended to forestall revolts but, like all Draconian measures, it merely spread misery and engendered hatred. In the end, it hastened the disintegration of the Assyrian empire.

There is some evidence that Israel experienced its first deportations under Tiglath-Pileser III (745-727 B.C.), a cruelty repeated by Sargon II (722-705 B.C.) at the time of the fall of Samaria. The latter king's inscriptions boast of carrying away 27,290 inhabitants of the city "as booty." According to 2Ki 17:6, they were sent to Assyria, to Halah (Calah?), to Gozan on the Habor River, and apparently to the eastern frontiers of the empire (to the towns of the Medes, most probably somewhere in the vicinity of Ecbatana, the modern Hamadan).

The sequel is provided by the inscriptions of Sargon: "The Arabs who live far away in the desert, who know neither overseers nor officials, and who had not yet brought their tribute to any king, I deported . . . and settled them in Samaria."

Much mythology has developed around the theme of the so-called ten lost tribes of Israel. A close examination of Assyrian records reveals that the deportations approximated only a limited percentage of the population, usually consisting of noble families. Agricultural workers, no doubt the majority, were deliberately left to care for the crops (cf. the Babylonian practice, 2Ki 24:14; 25:12).

all his prophets and seers:[z] "Turn from your evil ways.[a] Observe my commands and decrees, in accordance with the entire Law that I commanded your fathers to obey and that I delivered to you through my servants the prophets."[b]

[14]But they would not listen and were as stiff-necked[c] as their fathers, who did not trust in the LORD their God. [15]They rejected his decrees and the covenant[d] he had made with their fathers and the warnings he had given them. They followed worthless idols[e] and themselves became worthless.[f] They imitated the nations[g] around them although the LORD had ordered them, "Do not do as they do," and they did the things the LORD had forbidden them to do.

[16]They forsook all the commands of the LORD their God and made for themselves two idols cast in the shape of calves,[h] and an Asherah[i] pole. They bowed down to all the starry hosts,[j] and they worshiped Baal.[k] [17]They sacrificed[l] their sons and daughters in[z] the fire. They practiced divination and sorcery[m] and sold[n] themselves to do evil in the eyes of the LORD, provoking him to anger.

[18]So the LORD was very angry with Israel and removed them from his presence.[o] Only the tribe of Judah was left, [19]and even Judah did not keep the commands of the LORD their God. They followed the practices Israel had introduced.[p] [20]Therefore the LORD rejected all the people of Israel; he afflicted them and gave them into the hands of plunderers,[q] until he thrust them from his presence.[r]

[21]When he tore[s] Israel away from the house of David, they made Jeroboam son of Nebat their king.[t] Jeroboam enticed Israel away from following the LORD and caused them to commit a great sin.[u] [22]The Israelites persisted in all the sins of Jeroboam and did not turn away from them [23]until the LORD removed them from his presence,[v] as he had warned[w] through all his servants the prophets. So the people of Israel were taken from their homeland[x] into exile in Assyria, and they are still there.

Samaria Resettled

[24]The king of Assyria[y] brought people from Babylon, Cuthah, Avva, Hamath and Sepharvaim[z] and settled them in the towns of Samaria to replace the Israelites. They took over Samaria and lived in its towns. [25]When they first lived there, they

---

Cross-references (center column):

17:13 [z]S 1Sa 9:9; [a]Jer 4:1; 18:11; 23:22; 25:5; 35:15; 36:3; Zec 1:4
17:14 [b]Mt 23:34
17:15 [c]S Ex 32:9; Ac 7:51
17:16 [d]S Lev 26:11; Dt 29:25; Jdg 2:20; 1Ki 11:11; 2Ki 18:12; Ps 78:10; Eze 5:6; Mal 2:10
17:16 [e]S Dt 32:21; Hos 11:2; Ro 1:21-23
17:16 [f]Je 2:5; [g]S Dt 12:4
17:16 [h]S Ex 32:4; [i]S Dt 16:21
17:16 [j]S Ge 2:1; Isa 40:26; Jer 19:13
17:16 [k]S Jdg 2:11
17:17 [l]S Dt 12:31; 18:10-12; 2Ki 16:3; Eze 16:21
17:17 [m]S Lev 19:26
17:18 [n]S 1Ki 21:20; Ro 7:14
17:18 [o]S Ge 4:14; S Ex 33:15; S 2Ki 13:23; 2Th 1:9
17:19 [p]2Ki 16:3; Jer 3:6-10; Eze 23:13
17:20 [q]S ver 6
17:21 [r]Jer 7:15; 15:1
17:21 [s]S 1Sa 15:27; S 1Ki 11:11
17:21 [t]1Ki 12:20

[u]S 1Ki 12:30 17:23 [v]Eze 39:23-24 [w]S Jdg 6:8 [x]S 1Ki 9:7
17:24 [y]2Ki 19:37; Ezr 4:2,10; Isa 37:38 [z]ver 31;
S 2Ki 15:29; 18:34; Isa 36:19; 37:13; Am 6:2

[z]17 Or They made their sons and daughters pass through

---

enant, but she also spurned the words of prophets the Lord had graciously sent to call his people back to the covenant (see, e.g., 1Ki 13:1–3; 14:6–16; Jdg 6:8–10; 1Sa 3:19–21 as well as the ministries of Elijah, Elisha, Amos and Hosea).
seers. See note on 1Sa 9:9.
17:14 *stiff-necked.* A figure derived from the obstinate resistance of an ox to being placed under a yoke (see Dt 10:16; Jer 2:20; 7:26; 17:23; 19:15; Hos 4:16).
17:15 *followed worthless idols.* See Dt 32:21; Jer 2:5; 8:19; 10:8; 14:22; 51:18.
17:16 *two idols cast in the shape of calves.* The golden calves of Bethel and Dan (see 1Ki 12:28–30). *Asherah pole.* See note on 1Ki 14:15. *all the starry hosts.* Israel had been commanded not to follow the astral cults of her pagan neighbors (see Dt 4:19; 17:3). Although this form of idolatry is not mentioned previously in 1,2 Kings, the prophet Amos apparently alludes to its practice in the northern kingdom during the reign of Jeroboam II (see note on Am 5:26). It was later introduced in the southern kingdom during the reign of Manasseh (see 21:3,5) and abolished during the reformation of Josiah (see 23:4–5,12; see also Eze 8:16).
17:17 *sacrificed their sons and daughters.* See note on 16:3. *divination and sorcery.* Such practices were forbidden in the Mosaic covenant (see note on 16:15; see also Lev 19:26; Dt 18:10).
17:18 *removed them from his presence.* The exile of the northern kingdom (see v. 6; 23:27). *Only the tribe of Judah was left.* The southern kingdom included elements of the tribes of Simeon and Benjamin, but Judah was the only tribe in the south to retain its complete integrity (see notes on 1Ki 11:31–32; see also note on 2Ki 19:4).
17:20 *afflicted them and gave them into the hands of*

plunderers. See 10:32–33; 13:3,20; 24:2; 2Ch 21:16; 28:18; Am 1:13.
17:21 *tore Israel away from the house of David.* See 1Ki 11:11,31; 12:24. The division of the kingdom was of the Lord, but it came to the nation as a punishment for their sins. *Jeroboam . . . caused them to commit a great sin.* See 1Ki 12:26–32; 13:33–34.
17:23 *warned through all his servants the prophets.* See 1Ki 14:15–16; Hos 10:1–7; 11:5; Am 5:27.
17:24 *king of Assyria.* Primarily Sargon II (722–705 B.C.), though later Assyrian rulers, including Esarhaddon (681–669) and Ashurbanipal (669–627), settled additional non-Israelites in Samaria (see Ezr 4:2,9–10). *Babylon, Cuthah.* Babylon and Cuthah (located about eight miles northeast of Babylon) were forced to submit to Assyrian rule by Sargon II in 709. *Avva.* Probably the same as Ivvah (see 18:34; 19:13). Its association with Hamath, Arpad and Sepharvaim suggests a location somewhere in Aram (Syria). *Hamath.* Located on the Orontes River (see 14:25; 18:34; see also note on Eze 47:15). In 720 Sargon II made the kingdom of Hamath into an Assyrian province. *Sepharvaim.* Perhaps located in Aramean territory, possibly between Damascus and Hamath. *Samaria.* Here a designation for the entire northern kingdom (see note on 1Ki 13:32).
17:25 *did not worship the LORD.* They worshiped their own national deities. *sent lions among them.* Lions had always been present in Canaan (see 1Ki 13:24; 20:36; Jdg 14:5; 1Sa 17:34; Am 3:12). In the aftermath of the disruption and depopulation caused by the conflict with the Assyrians, the lions greatly increased in number (see Ex 23:29). This was viewed by the inhabitants of the land and the writer of Kings as a punishment from the Lord (see Lev 26:21–22).

did not worship the LORD; so he sent lions[a] among them and they killed some of the people. 26It was reported to the king of Assyria: "The people you deported and resettled in the towns of Samaria do not know what the god of that country requires. He has sent lions among them, which are killing them off, because the people do not know what he requires."

27Then the king of Assyria gave this order: "Have one of the priests you took captive from Samaria go back to live there and teach the people what the god of the land requires." 28So one of the priests who had been exiled from Samaria came to live in Bethel and taught them how to worship the LORD.

29Nevertheless, each national group made its own gods in the several towns[b] where they settled, and set them up in the shrines[c] the people of Samaria had made at the high places. [d] 30The men from Babylon made Succoth Benoth, the men from Cuthah made Nergal, and the men from Hamath made Ashima; 31the Avvites made Nibhaz and Tartak, and the Sepharvites burned their children in the fire as sacrifices to Adrammelech[e] and Anammelech, the gods of Sepharvaim.[f] 32They worshiped the LORD, but they also appointed all sorts[g] of their own people to officiate for them as priests in the shrines at the high places. 33They worshiped the LORD, but they also served their own gods in accordance with the customs of the nations from which they had been brought.

34To this day they persist in their former practices. They neither worship the LORD

nor adhere to the decrees and ordinances, the laws and commands that the LORD gave the descendants of Jacob, whom he named Israel.[h] 35When the LORD made a covenant with the Israelites, he commanded them: "Do not worship[i] any other gods or bow down to them, serve them or sacrifice to them.[j] 36But the LORD, who brought you up out of Egypt with mighty power and outstretched arm,[k] is the one you must worship. To him you shall bow down and to him offer sacrifices. 37You must always be careful[l] to keep the decrees[m] and ordinances, the laws and commands he wrote for you. Do not worship other gods. 38Do not forget[n] the covenant I have made with you, and do not worship other gods. 39Rather, worship the LORD your God; it is he who will deliver you from the hand of all your enemies."

40They would not listen, however, but persisted in their former practices. 41Even while these people were worshiping the LORD,[o] they were serving their idols. To this day their children and grandchildren continue to do as their fathers did.

Hezekiah King of Judah

18:2–4pp — 2Ch 29:1–2; 31:1
18:5–7pp — 2Ch 31:20–21
18:9–12pp — 2Ki 17:3–7

18 In the third year of Hoshea son of Elah king of Israel, Hezekiah[p] son of Ahaz king of Judah began to reign. 2He was twenty-five years old when he became king, and he reigned in Jerusalem twenty-nine years.[q] His mother's name was Abi-

Cross references (center column):

17:25
aS Ge 37:20;
Isa 5:29; 15:9;
Jer 50:17
17:29 bJer 2:28;
11:13
cS Lev 26:30;
S 1Ki 12:31
dMic 4:5
17:31 e2Ki 19:37
fS ver 24
17:32
gS 1Ki 12:31

17:34
hS Ge 17:5;
S 1Ki 18:31
17:35 iS Ex 20:5
jS Ex 20:3
17:36
kS Ex 3:20;
Ps 136:12
17:37 lDt 5:32
mS Lev 19:37
17:38 nS Dt 6:12
17:41
oS 1Ki 18:21;
Ezr 4:2; Mt 6:24
18:1 pIsa 1:1;
Hos 1:1; Mic 1:1
18:2 qver 13;
Isa 38:5

17:26 *king of Assyria.* Sargon II. *what the god of that country requires.* According to the religious ideas of that time, each regional deity required special ritual observances, which, if ignored or violated, would bring disaster on the land.

17:27 *one of the priests.* Of the golden calf cult established in the northern kingdom by Jeroboam I (see 1Ki 12:31 and note).

17:28 *came to live in Bethel.* Bethel continued to be the center for the apostate form of Yahweh worship that had been promoted in the northern kingdom since the time of Jeroboam I (see notes on 1Ki 12:28–30).

17:29 *people of Samaria.* The mixed population of the former territory of the northern kingdom. These people of mixed ancestry eventually came to be known as Samaritans. In later times the Samaritans rejected the idolatry of their polytheistic origins and followed the teachings of Moses, including monotheism. In NT times Jesus testified to a Samaritan woman (Jn 4:4–26), and many Samaritans were converted under the ministry of Philip (Ac 8:4–25).

17:32 *officiate for them as priests.* See note on 1Ki 12:31.

17:33 *They worshiped the LORD, but they also served their own gods.* A classic statement of syncretistic religion.

17:34 *To this day.* Until the time of the writing of

1,2 Kings. *worship the LORD.* Here used in the sense of faithful worship. In vv. 32–33 "worship the LORD" refers to a paganized worship.

17:35 *Do not worship any other gods.* The Mosaic covenant demanded exclusive worship of the Lord (Ex 20:5; Dt 5:9). This was the first and great commandment, and it was to distinguish Israel from all other peoples.

17:36 *the LORD, who brought you up out of Egypt . . . you must worship.* Here, as in v. 7, the deliverance from Egypt is cited as the gracious act of the Lord par excellence that entitled him to exclusive claim on Israel's loyalty.

17:39 *will deliver you from . . . all your enemies.* See Ex 23:22; Dt 20:1–4; 23:14.

17:41 *To this day.* See note on v. 34.

18:1 *third year of Hoshea . . . Hezekiah . . . began to reign.* 729 B.C. (see 17:1). Hezekiah was co-regent with his father Ahaz from 729 to 715 (see note on 16:2).

18:2 *became king.* Became sole king of Judah. *twenty-nine years.* 715–686 B.C. See also 2Ch 29–32 and Isa 36–39 for a description of the events of his reign, including a more detailed account of the reformation he led (2Ch 29–31). One of his first acts was to reopen the temple, which had been closed by his father Ahaz (see note on 16:19; see also 2Ch 29:3).

jah[a] daughter of Zechariah. [3]He did what was right[r] in the eyes of the LORD, just as his father David[s] had done. [4]He removed[t] the high places, [u] smashed the sacred stones[v] and cut down the Asherah poles. He broke into pieces the bronze snake[w] Moses had made, for up to that time the Israelites had been burning incense to it. (It was called[b] Nehushtan.[c])

[5]Hezekiah trusted[x] in the LORD, the God of Israel. There was no one like him among all the kings of Judah, either before him or after him. [6]He held fast[y] to the LORD and did not cease to follow him; he kept the commands the LORD had given Moses. [7]And the LORD was with him; he was successful[z] in whatever he undertook. He rebelled[a] against the king of Assyria and did not serve him. [8]From watchtower to fortified city,[b] he defeated the Philistines, as far as Gaza and its territory.

[9]In King Hezekiah's fourth year,[c] which was the seventh year of Hoshea son of Elah king of Israel, Shalmaneser king of Assyria marched against Samaria and laid siege to it. [10]At the end of three years the Assyrians took it. So Samaria was captured in Hezekiah's sixth year, which was the ninth year

of Hoshea king of Israel. [11]The king[d] of Assyria deported Israel to Assyria and settled them in Halah, in Gozan on the Habor River and in towns of the Medes. [e] [12]This happened because they had not obeyed the LORD their God, but had violated his covenant[f]—all that Moses the servant of the LORD commanded.[g] They neither listened to the commands[h] nor carried them out.

[13]In the fourteenth year[i] of King Hezekiah's reign, Sennacherib king of Assyria attacked all the fortified cities of Judah[j] and captured them. [14]So Hezekiah king of Judah sent this message to the king of Assyria at Lachish:[k] "I have done wrong.[l] Withdraw from me, and I will pay whatever you demand of me." The king of Assyria exacted from Hezekiah king of Judah three hundred talents[d] of silver and thirty talents[e] of gold. [15]So Hezekiah gave[m] him all the silver that was found in the temple of the LORD and in the treasuries of the royal palace.

Cross references

18:3 [r]S 1Ki 14:8; [s]Isa 38:5
18:4 [t]2Ch 31:1; Isa 36:7; [u]2Ki 12:3; 21:3; [v]S Ex 23:24; [w]Nu 21:9
18:5 [x]ver 19; S 1Sa 7:3; 2Ki 19:10; Ps 21:7; 125:1; Pr 3:26
18:6 [y]S Dt 6:18; S 10:20
18:7 [z]S Ge 39:3; S Job 22:25; [a]2Ki 24:1; Ezr 4:19; Isa 36:5
18:8 [b]2Ki 17:9
18:9 [c]Isa 1:1; 36:1

18:11 [d]Isa 37:12; [e]Eze 16:39; 23:9
18:12 [f]S 2Ki 17:15; [g]2Ki 21:8; Da 9:6,10; [h]S 1Ki 9:6
18:13 [i]S ver 2
18:14 [j]2Ki 19:8; [i]Isa 24:5; 33:8
18:15 [m]S 1Ki 15:18; Isa 39:2

Text notes

[a]2 Hebrew Abi, a variant of Abijah   [b]4 Or He called it   [c]4 Nehushtan sounds like the Hebrew for bronze and snake and unclean thing.   [d]14 That is, about 11 tons (about 10 metric tons)   [e]14 That is, about 1 ton (about 1 metric ton)

18:3 right . . . as his father David. Hezekiah is one of the few kings who is compared favorably with David. The others are Asa (1Ki 15:11), Jehoshaphat (1Ki 22:43) and Josiah (2Ki 22:2). A qualification is introduced, however, with both Asa and Jehoshaphat: They did not remove the high places (see 1Ki 15:14; 22:43).

18:4 removed the high places. Hezekiah was not the first king to destroy high places (see notes on 1Ki 3:2; 15:14), but he was the first to destroy high places dedicated to the worship of the Lord (see 12:3; 14:4; 15:4,35; 17:9; 1Ki 22:43). This became known even to the Assyrian king, Sennacherib (see v. 22). sacred stones. See 3:2; 10:26–27; 17:10; see also note on 1Ki 14:23. Asherah poles. See 13:6; 17:10,16; 1Ki 16:23; see also note on 1Ki 14:15. Israelites had been burning incense to it. It is unlikely that the bronze snake had been an object of worship all through the centuries of Israel's existence as a nation. Just when an idolatrous significance was attached to it is not known, but perhaps it occurred during the reign of Hezekiah's father Ahaz (see ch. 16). Snake worship of various types was common among ancient Near Eastern peoples.

18:5 no one like him . . . either before him or after him. A difference of emphasis is to be seen in this statement when compared to that of 23:25. Hezekiah's uniqueness is to be found in his trust in the Lord, while Josiah's uniqueness is to be found in his scrupulous observance of the Mosaic law.

18:7 rebelled against the king of Assyria. Judah had become a vassal to Assyria under Ahaz (see 16:7)—which required at least formal recognition of Assyrian deities. Hezekiah reversed the policy of his father Ahaz and sought independence from Assyrian dominance. It is likely that sometime shortly after 705 B.C., when Sennacherib replaced Sargon II on the Assyrian throne, Hezekiah refused to pay the annual tribute due the Assyrians.

18:8 defeated the Philistines. In a reversal of the conditions existing during the time of Ahaz, in which the Philis-

tines captured Judahite cities in the hill country and Negev (see 2Ch 28:18), Hezekiah was able once again to subdue the Philistines. Probably Hezekiah tried to coerce the Philistines into joining his anti-Assyrian policy. In one of his annals Sennacherib tells of forcing Hezekiah to release Padi, king of the Philistine city of Ekron, whom Hezekiah held prisoner in Jerusalem. This occurred in connection with Sennacherib's military campaign in 701 B.C.

18:9 Hezekiah's fourth year. 725 B.C., the fourth year of Hezekiah's co-regency with Ahaz (see notes on v. 1; 17:1).

18:10 three years. See note on 17:5. ninth year of Hoshea. See note on 17:6.

18:11 king of Assyria deported Israel. See note on 17:6.

18:12 violated his covenant. See 17:7–23.

18:13 fourteenth year. Of Hezekiah's sole reign: 701 B.C. (see note on v. 2). Sennacherib . . . attacked. Verses 13–16 correspond very closely with Sennacherib's own account of his 701 campaign against Phoenicia, Judah and Egypt. captured them. In his annals, Sennacherib claims to have captured 46 of Hezekiah's fortified cities, as well as numerous open villages, and to have taken 200,150 of the people captive. He says he made Hezekiah "a prisoner in Jerusalem his royal residence, like a bird in a cage," but he does not say he took Jerusalem.

18:14 three hundred talents of silver and thirty talents of gold. See NIV text notes. The Assyrian and Biblical reports of the amount of tribute paid by Hezekiah to Sennacherib agree with respect to the 30 talents of gold, but Sennacherib claims to have received 800 talents of silver rather than the 300 specified in the Biblical text. This discrepancy may be the result of differences in the weight of Assyrian and Israelite silver talents, or it may simply be due to the Assyrian propensity for exaggeration. For the relative value of this amount of silver and gold see note on 5:5.

18:15 silver . . . in the temple . . . and in the treasuries of the royal palace. See 12:10,18; 14:14; 16:8; 1Ki 7:51; 14:26; 15:18.

16At this time Hezekiah king of Judah stripped off the gold with which he had covered the doors[n] and doorposts of the temple of the LORD, and gave it to the king of Assyria.

Sennacherib Threatens Jerusalem

18:13, 17–37pp — Isa 36:1–22
18:17–35pp — 2Ch 32:9–19

17The king of Assyria sent his supreme commander,[o] his chief officer and his field commander with a large army, from Lachish to King Hezekiah at Jerusalem. They came up to Jerusalem and stopped at the aqueduct of the Upper Pool,[p] on the road to the Washerman's Field. 18They called for the king; and Eliakim[q] son of Hilkiah the palace administrator, Shebna[r] the secretary, and Joah son of Asaph the recorder went out to them.

19The field commander said to them, "Tell Hezekiah:

" 'This is what the great king, the king of Assyria, says: On what are you basing this confidence[s] of yours? 20You say you have strategy and military strength—but you speak only empty words. On whom are you depending, that you rebel against me? 21Look now, you are depending on Egypt,[t] that splintered reed of a staff,[u] which pierces a man's hand and wounds him if he leans on it! Such is Pharaoh king of Egypt to all who depend on him. 22And if you say to me, "We are depending on the LORD our God"—isn't he the one whose high places and altars Hezekiah removed, saying to Judah and Jerusalem, "You must worship before this altar in Jerusalem"?

23" 'Come now, make a bargain with my master, the king of Assyria: I will give you two thousand horses—if you can put riders on them! 24How can you repulse one officer[v] of the least of my master's officials, even though you are depending on Egypt for chariots and horsemen[f]? 25Furthermore, have I come to attack and destroy this place without word from the LORD?[w] The LORD himself told me to march against this country and destroy it.' "

26Then Eliakim son of Hilkiah, and Shebna and Joah said to the field commander, "Please speak to your servants in Aramaic,[x] since we understand it. Don't speak to us in Hebrew in the hearing of the people on the wall."

27But the commander replied, "Was it only to your master and you that my master sent me to say these things, and not to the men sitting on the wall—who, like you, will have to eat their own filth and drink their own urine?"

28Then the commander stood and called out in Hebrew: "Hear the word of the great king, the king of Assyria! 29This is what the king says: Do not let Hezekiah deceive[y] you. He cannot deliver you from my hand. 30Do not let Hezekiah persuade

---

18:16 [n]2Ch 29:3
18:17 [o]Isa 20:1
[p]2Ki 20:20;
2Ch 32:4,30;
Ne 2:14; Isa 22:9
18:18 [q]2Ki 19:2;
Isa 22:20; 36:3,
11,22; 37:2 [r]ver
26,37; Isa 22:15
18:19 [s]S ver 5;
S Job 4:6
18:21 [t]Isa 20:5;
31:1; Eze 29:6
[u]2Ki 24:7;
Isa 20:6; 30:5,7;
Jer 25:19; 37:7;
46:2

18:24 [v]Isa 10:8
18:25 [w]2Ki 19:6,
22; 24:3;
2Ch 35:21
18:26 [x]Ezr 4:7
18:29 [y]2Ki 19:10   [f]24 Or *charioteers*

18:17–19:37 See Isa 36–37; cf. 2Ch 32.
18:17 *Lachish.* See note on Isa 36:2. *aqueduct ... Field.* See note on Isa 7:3. It is ironic that the Assyrian officials demand Judah's surrender on the very spot where Isaiah had warned Ahaz to trust in the Lord rather than in an alliance with Assyria for deliverance from the threat against him from Aram and the northern kingdom of Israel (see 16:5–10; Isa 7:1–17).
18:18 *palace administrator.* See note on 1Ki 4:6. *secretary.* See note on 2Sa 8:17. *recorder.* See note on 2Sa 8:16.
18:19 *great king.* A frequently used title of the Assyrian rulers—and occasionally of the Lord (Ps 47:2; 48:2; 95:3; Mal 1:14; Mt 5:35). *says.* The following address is a masterpiece of calculated intimidation and psychological warfare designed to break the resistance of the inhabitants of Jerusalem (see vv. 26–27).
18:21 *depending on Egypt.* See 19:9; Isa 30:1–5; 31:1–3.
18:22 *isn't he the one whose high places and altars Hezekiah removed ... ?* The Assyrians cleverly attempted to drive a wedge between Hezekiah and the people. They attempted to exploit any resentment that may have existed among those who opposed Hezekiah's reformation and his destruction of the high places (see note on v. 4).
18:23 *if you can put riders on them!* With this sarcastic taunt, the Assyrians undoubtedly accurately suggest that the

Judahites were so weak in military personnel that they could not even take advantage of such a generous offer. In contrast with the Assyrians, the army of Judah at the time consisted largely of foot soldiers. The city under siege would have contained few chariots, and it is not known whether the Israelites ever employed mounted men in combat.
18:25 *The LORD himself told me.* Possibly Assyrian spies had informed Sennacherib of the prophecies of Isaiah and Micah.
18:26 *Aramaic.* Had become the international language of the Near East, known and used by those experienced in diplomacy and commerce. It is surprising that the Assyrian officials were able to speak the Hebrew dialect of the common people of Judah (see 2Ch 32:18).
18:27 *men sitting on the wall.* The Assyrian strategy was to negotiate in the hearing of the people in order to demoralize them and turn them against Hezekiah. *eat their own filth and drink their own urine.* A vivid portrayal of the potential hardship of a prolonged siege.
18:29 *the king says.* The Assyrian officials now address their remarks directly to the populace rather than to the officials of Hezekiah, as in vv. 19–27. *Do not let Hezekiah deceive you.* Here and in vv. 30–31 the people are urged three times to trust in Hezekiah.
18:30 *this city will not be given into the hand of the king of Assyria.* Hezekiah could say this on the basis of God's

you to trust in the LORD when he says, 'The LORD will surely deliver us; this city will not be given into the hand of the king of Assyria.'

31"Do not listen to Hezekiah. This is what the king of Assyria says: Make peace with me and come out to me. Then every one of you will eat from his own vine and fig tree*z* and drink water from his own cistern,*a* 32until I come and take you to a land like your own, a land of grain and new wine, a land of bread and vineyards, a land of olive trees and honey. Choose life*b* and not death!

"Do not listen to Hezekiah, for he is misleading you when he says, 'The LORD will deliver us.' 33Has the god*c* of any nation ever delivered his land from the hand of the king of Assyria? 34Where are the gods of Hamath*d* and Arpad?*e* Where are the gods of Sepharvaim, Hena and Ivvah? Have they rescued Samaria from my hand? 35Who of all the gods of these countries has been able to save his land from me? How then can the LORD deliver Jerusalem from my hand?"*f*

36But the people remained silent and said nothing in reply, because the king had commanded, "Do not answer him."

37Then Eliakim*g* son of Hilkiah the palace administrator, Shebna the secretary and Joah son of Asaph the recorder went to Hezekiah, with their clothes torn,*h* and

Center reference column

18:31
*z*S Nu 13:23;
S 1Ki 4:25
*a*Jer 14:3; La 4:4
18:32 *b*Dt 30:19
18:33 *c*2Ki 19:12
18:34
*d*S 2Ki 17:24;
S Jer 49:23
*e*Isa 10:9
18:35 *f*Ps 2:1-2
18:37 *g*S ver 18;
Isa 33:7; 36:3,22
*h*S 2Ki 6:30

19:1 *i*S Ge 37:34;
S Nu 14:6
19:2 *j*S 2Ki 18:18
*k*Jer 19:1
*l*S Ge 37:34
*m*Isa 1:1
19:3 *n*Hos 13:13
19:4
*o*S 1Sa 17:26
*p*2Sa 16:12
*q*S Ge 45:7;
S Jer 37:3
19:6 *r*S Dt 3:2;
S Jos 1:9
*s*2Ki 18:25
19:7 *t*S Ex 14:24;
Jer 51:46

told him what the field commander had said.

Jerusalem's Deliverance Foretold

19:1–13pp — Isa 37:1-13

19 When King Hezekiah heard this, he tore*i* his clothes and put on sackcloth and went into the temple of the LORD. 2He sent Eliakim*j* the palace administrator, Shebna the secretary and the leading priests,*k* all wearing sackcloth,*l* to the prophet Isaiah*m* son of Amoz. 3They told him, "This is what Hezekiah says: This day is a day of distress and rebuke and disgrace, as when children come to the point*n* of birth and there is no strength to deliver them. 4It may be that the LORD your God will hear all the words of the field commander, whom his master, the king of Assyria, has sent to ridicule*o* the living God, and that he will rebuke*p* him for the words the LORD your God has heard. Therefore pray for the remnant*q* that still survives."

5When King Hezekiah's officials came to Isaiah, 6Isaiah said to them, "Tell your master, 'This is what the LORD says: Do not be afraid*r* of what you have heard—those words with which the underlings of the king of Assyria have blasphemed*s* me. 7Listen! I am going to put such a spirit in him that when he hears a certain report,*t* he will return to his own

---

promise to him (see 20:6; see also note on Isa 38:6).
18:31 *eat from his own vine and fig tree and drink water from his own cistern.* Depicting peaceful and prosperous times (see 1Ki 4:25; Mic 4:4; Zec 3:10).
18:32 *until I come and take you to a land like your own.* Ultimately surrender meant deportation, but Sennacherib pictured it as something desirable. *Choose life and not death!* The alternatives depicted for the people are: (1) Trust in the Lord and Hezekiah and die, or (2) trust in the Assyrians and enjoy prosperity and peace. These words directly contradict the alternatives placed before Israel by Moses in Dt 30:15–20.
18:33–35 *Has the god of any nation ever delivered his land from the hand of the king of Assyria? . . . How then can the LORD deliver Jerusalem from my hand?* The flaw in the Assyrian reasoning was to equate the one true and living God with the no-gods (Dt 32:21) of the pagan peoples the Assyrians had defeated (see 19:4,6; 2Ch 32:13–19; Isa 10:9–11).
18:34 *Hamath.* See notes on 14:25; 17:24. *Arpad.* A city located near Hamath and taken by the Assyrians in 740 B.C. (see 19:13; Isa 10:9; Jer 49:23). *Sepharvaim.* See note on 17:24. *Hena.* Probably located in the vicinity of the other cities mentioned. *Ivvah.* See note on 17:24.
18:36 *because the king had commanded, "Do not answer him."* The Assyrian attempt to stir up a popular revolt against the leadership and authority of Hezekiah had failed.
18:37 *clothes torn.* An expression of great emotion (see 6:30; 1Ki 21:27). Perhaps in this instance it was motivated by the Assyrian blasphemy against the true God (see 19:4,6; Mt 26:65; Mk 14:63–64).

19:1 *sackcloth.* See note on 6:30.
19:2 *palace administrator.* See note on 1Ki 4:6. *secretary.* See note on 2Sa 8:17. *leading priests.* Probably the oldest members of various priestly families (see Jer 19:1). The crisis involved not only the city of Jerusalem, but also the temple. *prophet Isaiah.* The first reference to Isaiah in the book of Kings, though he had been active in the reigns of Uzziah, Jotham and Ahaz (see Isa 1:1).
19:3 *as when children come to the point of birth and there is no strength to deliver them.* Depicts the critical nature of the threat facing the city.
19:4 *living God.* In contrast to the no-gods of 18:33–35. See 1Sa 17:26,36,45 for another example of ridiculing the living and true God. *pray.* Intercessory prayer was an important aspect of the ministry of the prophets (see, e.g., the intercession of Moses and Samuel: Ex 32:31–32; 33:12–17; Nu 14:13–19; 1Sa 7:8–9; 12:19,23; Ps 99:6; Jer 15:1). *remnant.* Those left in Judah after Sennacherib's capture of many towns and numerous people (see note on 18:13; cf. Isa 10:28–32). Archaeological evidence reveals that many Israelites fled the northern kingdom during the Assyrian assaults and settled in Judah, so that the nation of Judah became the remnant of all Israel.
19:7 *spirit.* Of insecurity and fear. *report.* Some interpreters link this "report" with the challenge to Sennacherib from Tirhakah of Egypt (v. 9). Others regard it as disturbing information from Sennacherib's homeland. *cut down with the sword.* See v. 37. Here the eventual murder of Sennacherib is connected with his blasphemy against the living God.

country, and there I will have him cut down with the sword. u ' "

8When the field commander heard that the king of Assyria had left Lachish, v he withdrew and found the king fighting against Libnah. w

9Now Sennacherib received a report that Tirhakah, the Cushite g king of Egypt, was marching out to fight against him. So he again sent messengers to Hezekiah with this word: 10"Say to Hezekiah king of Judah: Do not let the god you depend x on deceive y you when he says, 'Jerusalem will not be handed over to the king of Assyria.' 11Surely you have heard what the kings of Assyria have done to all the countries, destroying them completely. And will you be delivered? 12Did the gods of the nations that were destroyed by my forefathers deliver z them: the gods of Gozan, a Haran, b Rezeph and the people of Eden who were in Tel Assar? 13Where is the king of Hamath, the king of Arpad, the king of the city of Sepharvaim, or of Hena or Ivvah?" c

Hezekiah's Prayer

19:14–19pp — Isa 37:14–20

14Hezekiah received the letter d from the messengers and read it. Then he went up to the temple of the LORD and spread it out before the LORD. 15And Hezekiah prayed to the LORD: "O LORD, God of Israel, enthroned between the cherubim, e you alone f are God over all the kingdoms of the earth. You have made heaven and earth. 16Give ear, g O LORD, and hear; h open your eyes, i O LORD, and see; listen to the words Sennacherib has sent to insult the living God.

17"It is true, O LORD, that the Assyrian kings have laid waste these nations and their lands. 18They have thrown their gods into the fire and destroyed them, for they were not gods j but only wood and stone, fashioned by men's hands. k 19Now, O LORD our God, deliver l us from his hand, so that all kingdoms m on earth may know n that you alone, O LORD, are God."

Isaiah Prophesies Sennacherib's Fall

19:20–37pp — Isa 37:21–38
19:35–37pp — 2Ch 32:20–21

20Then Isaiah son of Amoz sent a message to Hezekiah: "This is what the LORD, the God of Israel, says: I have heard o your prayer concerning Sennacherib king of Assyria. 21This is the word that the LORD has spoken against p him:

" 'The Virgin Daughter q of Zion
    despises r you and mocks s you.
The Daughter of Jerusalem
    tosses her head t as you flee.
22Who is it you have insulted and
    blasphemed? u
Against whom have you raised your
    voice
and lifted your eyes in pride?
    Against the Holy One v of Israel!
23By your messengers
    you have heaped insults on the Lord.
And you have said, w
    "With my many chariots x
I have ascended the heights of the
    mountains,
    the utmost heights of Lebanon.
I have cut down y its tallest cedars,
    the choicest of its pines.
I have reached its remotest parts,
    the finest of its forests.
24I have dug wells in foreign lands
    and drunk the water there.
With the soles of my feet
    I have dried up all the streams of
        Egypt."

25" 'Have you not heard? z

19:7 uver 37; 2Ch 32:21; Isa 10:12
19:8 v2Ki 18:14 wS Nu 33:20; S 2Ki 8:22
19:10 xS 2Ki 18:5 y2Ki 18:29
19:12 z2Ki 18:33; 2Ch 32:17 a2Ki 17:6 bS Ge 11:31
19:13 cIsa 10:9-11; Jer 49:23 d2Ki 5:7
19:14 eS Ge 3:24; S Ex 25:22 fS Ge 1:1; S Jos 2:11
19:16 gPs 31:2; 71:2; 88:2; 102:2 hS 1Ki 8:29 iS Ex 3:16
19:18 jIsa 44:9-11; Jer 10:3-10 kDt 4:28; Ps 115:4; Ac 17:29
19:19 lIsa 12:10; Job 6:23; Ps 3:7; 71:4 mS 1Ki 8:43; 1Ch 16:8 nS Jos 4:24; S 1Sa 17:46
19:20 oS 1Ki 9:3
19:21 pIsa 10:5; 33:1 qIsa 47:1; Jer 14:17; 18:13; 31:4; 46:11; La 2:13; Am 5:2 rPs 53:5 sPr 1:26; 3:34 tJob 16:4; Ps 44:14; 64:8; 109:25; Jer 18:16
19:22 uS 2Ki 18:25 vLev 19:2; 1Sa 2:2; Job 6:10; Ps 16:10; 22:3; 71:22; 78:41; 89:18; Isa 1:4; 6:3; 57:15; Hos 11:9
19:23 wIsa 10:18; Jer 21:14; Eze 20:47 xPs 20:7; Jer 50:37 yIsa 10:34; 14:8; 33:9; Eze 31:3
19:25 zIsa 40:21, 28

g9 That is, from the upper Nile region

19:8 *Lachish.* See 18:17 (see also note on Isa 36:2). *Libnah.* See note on 8:22.
19:9 *Tirhakah.* See note on Isa 37:9. *Cushite.* See NIV text note.
19:12 *Gozan.* See note on 17:6. *Haran.* See note on Ge 11:31. It is not known just when Haran was taken by the Assyrians. *Rezeph.* Located south of the Euphrates River and northeast of Hamath. *Eden.* See Eze 27:23; Am 1:5; a district along the Euphrates River south of Haran. It was incorporated into the Assyrian empire by Shalmaneser III in 855 B.C. *Tel Assar.* Location unknown.
19:13 *Hamath . . . Ivvah.* See note on 18:34.
19:14 *letter.* See 2Ch 32:17.
19:15 *enthroned between the cherubim.* See notes on Ex 25:18; 1Sa 4:4. *you alone are God.* See notes on 18:33–35; Dt 6:4.
19:18 *fashioned by men's hands.* For the foolishness and

futility of idolatry see Ps 115:3–8; 135:15–18; Isa 2:20; 40:19–20; 41:7; 44:9–20.
19:20 *heard your prayer.* On this occasion Isaiah's message to Hezekiah was unsolicited by the king (contrast v. 2).
19:21–28 The arrogance of the Assyrians and their ridicule of the Israelites and their God are countered with a derisive pronouncement of judgment (cf. Ps 2) on the misconceived Assyrian pride (see Isa 10:5–34).
19:21 *Virgin Daughter of Zion.* A personification of Jerusalem and its inhabitants.
19:22 *Holy One of Israel.* A designation of the God of Israel characteristic of Isaiah (see note on Isa 1:4).
19:24 *dried up all the streams of Egypt.* A presumptuous boast for one who had not even conquered Egypt.
19:25 *I ordained it . . . now I have brought it to pass.* The God of Israel is the ruler of all nations and history. The Assyrians attributed their victories to their own military su-

Long ago I ordained it.
In days of old I planned[a] it;
    now I have brought it to pass,
that you have turned fortified cities
    into piles of stone.[b]
26Their people, drained of power,[c]
    are dismayed[d] and put to shame.
They are like plants in the field,
    like tender green shoots,[e]
like grass sprouting on the roof,
    scorched[f] before it grows up.

27" 'But I know[g] where you stay
    and when you come and go
    and how you rage against me.
28Because you rage against me
    and your insolence has reached my
        ears,
I will put my hook[h] in your nose
    and my bit[i] in your mouth,
and I will make you return[j]
    by the way you came.'

29"This will be the sign[k] for you,
O Hezekiah:

"This year you will eat what grows by
    itself,[l]
and the second year what springs
    from that.
But in the third year sow and reap,
    plant vineyards[m] and eat their fruit.
30Once more a remnant[n] of the house of
        Judah
    will take root[o] below and bear fruit
        above.
31For out of Jerusalem will come a
        remnant,[p]

and out of Mount Zion a band of
    survivors.[q]

The zeal[r] of the LORD Almighty will accomplish this.

32"Therefore this is what the LORD says
concerning the king of Assyria:

"He will not enter this city
    or shoot an arrow here.
He will not come before it with shield
    or build a siege ramp against it.
33By the way that he came he will
        return;[s]
    he will not enter this city,
        declares the LORD.
34I will defend[t] this city and save it,
    for my sake and for the sake of
        David[u] my servant."

35That night the angel of the LORD[v]
went out and put to death a hundred and
eighty-five thousand men in the Assyrian
camp. When the people got up the next
morning—there were all the dead bodies![w] 36So Sennacherib king of Assyria
broke camp and withdrew.[x] He returned
to Nineveh[y] and stayed there.

37One day, while he was worshiping in
the temple of his god Nisroch, his sons
Adrammelech[z] and Sharezer cut him
down with the sword,[a] and they escaped
to the land of Ararat.[b] And Esarhaddon[c]
his son succeeded him as king.

Hezekiah's Illness

20:1-11pp — 2Ch 32:24-26; Isa 38:1-8

20 In those days Hezekiah became ill
and was at the point of death. The

19:25 aIsa 22:11; bMic 1:6 **19:26** cIsa 13:7; Eze 7:17; Zep 3:16 dPs 6:10; 71:24; 83:17; Isa 41:23; Jer 8:9 eIsa 4:2; 11:1; 53:2; Jer 23:5 fJob 8:12; Ps 37:2; 129:6 **19:27** gPs 139:1-4 **19:28** h2Ch 33:11; Eze 19:9; 29:4; 38:4; Am 4:2 iIsa 30:28 jver 33 **19:29** kS Ex 7:9; Lk 2:12 lLev 25:5 mPs 107:37; Isa 65:21; Am 9:14 **19:30** nS Ge 45:7 oIsa 5:24; 11:1; 27:6; Eze 17:22; Am 2:9 **19:31** pS Ge 45:7

qIsa 66:19; Zep 2:9; Zec 14:16 rIsa 9:7 **19:33** sver 28 **19:34** t2Ki 20:6 uS 2Sa 7:15 **19:35** vS Ge 19:13; S Dt 13:2; S Ex 12:23 wJob 24:24; Isa 17:14; 41:12; Na 3:3 **19:36** xS 2Ki 12:18 yS Ge 10:11 **19:37** z2Ki 17:31 aS ver 7 bS Ge 8:4 cS 2Ki 17:24

periority. However, Isaiah said that God alone ordained these victories (see Isa 10:5–19; cf. Eze 30:24–26).
19:27 *I know.* See Ps 121:8.
19:28 *hook in your nose.* At the top of an Assyrian obelisk an Assyrian king (probably Esarhaddon, 681–669 B.C.) is pictured holding ropes attached to rings in the noses of four of his enemies. Here Isaiah portrays the same thing happening to Sennacherib (see note on Isa 37:29; cf. Eze 38:4; Am 4:2).
19:29 *This year you will eat what grows by itself.* Sennacherib had apparently either destroyed or confiscated the entire harvest that had been sown the previous fall. The people would only have use of the later, second growth that came from seeds dropped from the previous year's harvest (see Lev 25:5). This suggests that Sennacherib came to Judah in March or April about the time of harvest. *the second year what springs from that.* Sennacherib's departure would be too late in the fall (October) for new crops to be planted for the coming year. In Palestine crops are normally sown in September and October. *in the third year sow and reap.* The routine times for sowing and harvesting could be observed in the following year. The third year is likely a reference to the third year of harvests detrimentally affected by the Assyrian presence.
19:30–31 *remnant.* See note on v. 4. For use of the term

"remnant" as a designation for those who will participate in the future unfolding of God's redemptive program see Isa 11:11,16; 28:5; Mic 4:7; Ro 11:5.
19:32 *not enter this city.* Sennacherib, who was presently at Libnah (see v. 8; see also note on 8:22), would not be able to carry out his threats against Jerusalem (see note on 18:13).
19:34 *for the sake of David my servant.* See note on 1Ki 11:13.
19:35 *angel of the LORD.* See note on Ge 16:7. *a hundred and eighty-five thousand.* See Isa 37:36.
19:36 *Nineveh.* The capital of the Assyrian empire.
19:37 *Nisroch.* The name of this deity does not appear in preserved Assyrian records. *his sons Adrammelech and Sharezer.* Ancient records refer to the murder of Sennacherib by an unnamed son on the 20th of the month of Tebet in the 23rd year of Sennacherib's reign. *Ararat.* See note on Ge 8:4. *Esarhaddon his son succeeded him.* And reigned 681–669 B.C. Assyrian inscriptions speak of a struggle among Sennacherib's sons for the right of succession to the Assyrian throne. Sennacherib's designation of Esarhaddon as heir apparent, even though he was younger than several of his brothers, may have sparked the abortive attempt at a coup by Adrammelech and Sharezer.
20:1 *In those days.* Hezekiah's illness (vv. 1–11) as well as his reception of envoys from Babylon (vv. 12–19) must have

prophet Isaiah son of Amoz went to him and said, "This is what the LORD says: Put your house in order, because you are going to die; you will not recover."

²Hezekiah turned his face to the wall and prayed to the LORD, ³"Remember,ᵈ O LORD, how I have walkedᵉ before you faithfullyᶠ and with wholehearted devotion and have done what is good in your eyes." And Hezekiah wept bitterly.

⁴Before Isaiah had left the middle court, the word of the LORD came to him: ⁵"Go back and tell Hezekiah, the leader of my people, 'This is what the LORD, the God of your father David, says: I have heardᵍ your prayer and seen your tears;ʰ I will heal you. On the third day from now you will go up to the temple of the LORD. ⁶I will add fifteen years to your life. And I will deliver you and this city from the hand of the king of Assyria. I will defendⁱ this city for my sake and for the sake of my servant David.' "

⁷Then Isaiah said, "Prepare a poultice of figs." They did so and applied it to the boil,ʲ and he recovered.

⁸Hezekiah had asked Isaiah, "What will be the sign that the LORD will heal me and that I will go up to the temple of the LORD on the third day from now?"

⁹Isaiah answered, "This is the LORD's signᵏ to you that the LORD will do what he has promised: Shall the shadow go forward ten steps, or shall it go back ten steps?"

¹⁰"It is a simpleˡ matter for the shadow to go forward ten steps," said Hezekiah. "Rather, have it go back ten steps."

¹¹Then the prophet Isaiah called upon the LORD, and the LORD made the shadow go backᵐ the ten steps it had gone down on the stairway of Ahaz.

Envoys From Babylon

20:12–19pp — Isa 39:1–8
20:20–21pp — 2Ch 32:32–33

¹²At that time Merodach-Baladan son of Baladan king of Babylon sent Hezekiah letters and a gift, because he had heard of Hezekiah's illness. ¹³Hezekiah received the messengers and showed them all that was in his storehouses—the silver, the gold, the spices and the fine oil—his armory and everything found among his treasures. There was nothing in his palace or in all his kingdom that Hezekiah did not show them.

¹⁴Then Isaiah the prophet went to King Hezekiah and asked, "What did those men say, and where did they come from?"

"From a distant land," Hezekiah replied. "They came from Babylon."

¹⁵The prophet asked, "What did they see in your palace?"

"They saw everything in my palace," Hezekiah said. "There is nothing among my treasures that I did not show them."

¹⁶Then Isaiah said to Hezekiah, "Hear the word of the LORD: ¹⁷The time will

surely come when everything in your palace, and all that your fathers have stored up until this day, will be carried off to Babylon. [n] Nothing will be left, says the LORD. [18]And some of your descendants, [o] your own flesh and blood, that will be born to you, will be taken away, and they will become eunuchs in the palace of the king of Babylon." [p]

[19]"The word of the LORD you have spoken is good," Hezekiah replied. For he thought, "Will there not be peace and security in my lifetime?"

[20]As for the other events of Hezekiah's reign, all his achievements and how he made the pool [q] and the tunnel [r] by which he brought water into the city, are they not written in the book of the annals of the kings of Judah? [21]Hezekiah rested with his fathers. And Manasseh his son succeeded him as king.

Manasseh King of Judah

21:1–10pp — 2Ch 33:1–10
21:17–18pp — 2Ch 33:18–20

21 Manasseh was twelve years old when he became king, and he reigned in Jerusalem fifty-five years. His mother's name was Hephzibah. [s] [2]He did evil [t] in the eyes of the LORD, following the detestable practices [u] of the nations the LORD had driven out before the Israelites. [3]He rebuilt the high places [v] his father Hezekiah had destroyed; he also erected altars to Baal [w] and made an Asherah pole, [x] as Ahab king of Israel had done. He bowed down to all the starry hosts [y] and worshiped them. [4]He built altars [z] in the temple of the LORD, of which the LORD had said, "In Jerusalem I will put my Name." [a] [5]In both courts [b] of the temple of the LORD, he built altars to all the starry hosts. [6]He sacrificed his own son [c] in [h] the fire, practiced sorcery and divination, [d] and consulted mediums and spiritists. [e] He did much evil in the eyes of the LORD, provoking [f] him to anger.

[7]He took the carved Asherah pole [g] he had made and put it in the temple, [h] of which the LORD had said to David and to his son Solomon, "In this temple and in Jerusalem, which I have chosen out of all the tribes of Israel, I will put my Name [i] forever. [8]I will not again [j] make the feet of the Israelites wander from the land I gave their forefathers, if only they will be careful to do everything I commanded them and will keep the whole Law that my servant Moses [k] gave them." [9]But the people did not listen. Manasseh led them astray, so that they did more evil [l] than the nations [m] the LORD had destroyed before the Israelites.

[10]The LORD said through his servants the prophets: [11]"Manasseh king of Judah has committed these detestable sins. He has done more evil [n] than the Amorites [o]

[h]6 Or He made his own son pass through

Cross-references

20:17
[n]2Ki 24:13;
2Ch 36:10;
Jer 20:5; 27:22;
52:17-23
20:18
[o]2Ki 24:15;
Da 1:3 [p]Mic 4:10
20:20
[q]S 2Ki 18:17
[r]S 2Sa 5:8
21:1 [s]Isa 62:4
21:2 [t]ver 16;
S Dt 4:25;
Jer 15:4 [u]Dt 9:4;
S 18:9;
S 1Ki 14:24;
2Ki 16:3
21:3 [v]S 1Ki 3:3;
S 2Ki 18:4
[w]S Jdg 6:28
[x]S Dt 16:21
[y]S Ge 2:1;
Dt 17:3; Jer 19:13
21:4 [z]Isa 66:4;
Jer 4:1; 7:30;
23:11; 32:34;
Eze 23:39
[a]S Ex 20:24;
S 2Sa 7:13
21:5 [b]1Ki 7:12;
2Ki 23:12
21:6
[c]S Lev 18:21;
S Dt 18:10;
S 2Ki 3:27
[d]Dt 18:14
[e]S Lev 19:31
/2Ki 23:26
21:7 [g]Dt 16:21;
2Ki 23:4
[h]S Lev 15:31
/S Ex 20:24;
S 2Sa 7:13
21:8 [i]S 2Sa 7:10
[k]S 2Ki 18:12
21:9 [l]S 1Ki 14:9;
Eze 5:7 [m]Dt 9:4
21:11
[n]S 1Ki 14:9
[o]S Ge 15:16

20:17 *carried off to Babylon.* Hezekiah's reception of the Babylonians would bring the exact opposite of what he desired and expected. Isaiah's prediction of Babylonian exile at least 115 years before it happened is all the more remarkable because, when he spoke, it appeared that Assyria rather than Babylon was the world power from whom Judah had the most to fear.
20:18 *some of your descendants . . . will be taken away.* Hezekiah's own son Manasseh was taken by the Assyrians and held prisoner for a while in Babylon (see 2Ch 33:11); later, many more from the house of David were to follow (see 24:15; 25:7; Da 1:3).
20:19 *word . . . is good.* Although it is possible to understand Hezekiah's statement as a selfish expression of relief that he himself would not experience the announced adversity, it seems better to take it as a humble acceptance of the Lord's judgment (see 2Ch 32:26) and as gratefulness for the intervening time of peace that the Lord in his mercy was granting to his people.
20:20 *the pool and the tunnel.* Hezekiah built a tunnel from the Gihon spring (see 1Ki 1:33,38) to a cistern (2Ch 32:30) within the city's walls (see diagram No. 9 at the end of the Study Bible). This greatly reduced Jerusalem's vulnerability to siege by guaranteeing a continuing water supply. In 1880 an inscription (the Siloam inscription; see chart on "Ancient Texts Relating to the OT," p. 5) was found in the rock wall at the entrance to this tunnel, describing the method of its construction. The tunnel, cut through solid rock, is over 1,700 feet long; its height varies from 3 2/3 feet to 11 1/2 feet and it averages 2 feet in width. *annals of the kings of Judah.* See note on 1Ki 14:29.
20:21 *rested with his fathers.* See note on 1Ki 1:21.
21:1 *twelve years old.* Manasseh was born after Hezekiah's serious illness (see 20:6). *fifty-five years.* 697–642 B.C., including a ten-year co-regency (697–686) with his father Hezekiah. This was the longest reign of any king in either Israel or Judah.
21:2 *detestable practices.* Manasseh reversed the religious policies of his father Hezekiah (see 18:3–5) and reverted to those of Ahaz (see 16:3).
21:3 *high places . . . Hezekiah had destroyed.* See note on 18:4; see also 2Ch 31:1. *Asherah pole.* See 1Ki 14:15,23; 15:13; 16:33. *as Ahab.* Manasseh was the Ahab of Judah (see 1Ki 16:30–33). *bowed down to all the starry hosts.* See note on 17:16.
21:4 *In Jerusalem I will put my Name.* See 1Ki 8:20,29; 9:3.
21:6 *sacrificed his own son.* See note on 16:3; see also 17:17. *practiced sorcery and divination.* See notes on 16:15; 17:17. *consulted mediums and spiritists.* See Lev 19:31; Dt 18:11; 1Sa 28:3,7–9 and notes.
21:7 *carved Asherah pole.* See note on 1Ki 14:15. *David.* See 2Sa 7:13. *Solomon.* See 1Ki 9:3. *chosen out of all the tribes.* See 1Ki 11:13,32,36.
21:9 *nations the LORD had destroyed.* See 1Ki 14:24; Dt 12:29–31; 31:3.
21:10 *his servants the prophets.* See 2Ch 33:10,18.
21:11 *more evil than the Amorites.* See note on 1Ki 21:26.

who preceded him and has led Judah into sin with his idols. *p* 12Therefore this is what the LORD, the God of Israel, says: I am going to bring such disaster *q* on Jerusalem and Judah that the ears of everyone who hears of it will tingle. *r* 13I will stretch out over Jerusalem the measuring line used against Samaria and the plumb line *s* used against the house of Ahab. I will wipe *t* out Jerusalem as one wipes a dish, wiping it and turning it upside down. 14I will forsake *u* the remnant *v* of my inheritance and hand them over to their enemies. They will be looted and plundered by all their foes, 15because they have done evil *w* in my eyes and have provoked *x* me to anger from the day their forefathers came out of Egypt until this day."

16Moreover, Manasseh also shed so much innocent blood *y* that he filled Jerusalem from end to end—besides the sin that he had caused Judah *z* to commit, so that they did evil in the eyes of the LORD.

17As for the other events of Manasseh's reign, and all he did, including the sin he committed, are they not written in the book of the annals of the kings of Judah? 18Manasseh rested with his fathers and was buried in his palace garden, *a* the garden of Uzza. And Amon his son succeeded him as king.

Amon King of Judah

21:19–24pp — 2Ch 33:21–25

19Amon was twenty-two years old when

he became king, and he reigned in Jerusalem two years. His mother's name was Meshullemeth daughter of Haruz; she was from Jotbah. 20He did evil *b* in the eyes of the LORD, as his father Manasseh had done. 21He walked in all the ways of his father; he worshiped the idols his father had worshiped, and bowed down to them. 22He forsook *c* the LORD, the God of his fathers, and did not walk *d* in the way of the LORD.

23Amon's officials conspired against him and assassinated *e* the king in his palace. 24Then the people of the land killed *f* all who had plotted against King Amon, and they made Josiah *g* his son king in his place.

25As for the other events of Amon's reign, and what he did, are they not written in the book of the annals of the kings of Judah? 26He was buried in his grave in the garden *h* of Uzza. And Josiah his son succeeded him as king.

The Book of the Law Found

22:1–20pp — 2Ch 34:1–2,8–28

22 Josiah *i* was eight years old when he became king, and he reigned in Jerusalem thirty-one years. His mother's name was Jedidah daughter of Adaiah; she was from Bozkath. *j* 2He did what was right *k* in the eyes of the LORD and walked in all the ways of his father David, not turning aside to the right *l* or to the left.

3In the eighteenth year of his reign, King Josiah sent the secretary, Shaphan *m* son of

Cross references (center column)

21:11 *p*Eze 18:12
21:12 *q*2Ki 23:26; 24:3; Jer 15:4; Eze 7:5
*r*S 1Sa 3:11
21:13 *s*Isa 28:17; 34:11; La 2:8; Am 7:7-9
*t*2Ki 23:27
21:14 *u*Ps 78:60; Jer 12:7; 23:33
*v*2Ki 19:4; Ezr 9:8; Ne 1:2; Isa 1:9; 10:21; Jer 6:9; 40:15; 42:2; 44:7,28; 50:20; Mic 2:12
21:15 *w*S Ex 32:22
*x*Jer 25:7
21:16 *y*2Ki 24:4; Job 22:14; Ps 10:11; 94:7; 106:38; Isa 29:15; 47:10; 59:3,7; Jer 2:34; 7:6; 19:4; 22:17; La 4:13; Eze 7:23; 8:12; 9:9; 22:3-4; Hos 4:2; Zep 1:12
*z*S ver 2,11
21:18 *a*ver 26; Est 1:5; 7:7

21:20 *b*1Ki 15:26
21:22 *c*S 1Sa 8:8
*d*1Ki 11:33
21:23 *e*S 2Ki 12:20
21:24 *f*2Ki 14:5
*g*2Ch 33:21; Zep 1:1
21:26 *h*S ver 18
22:1 *i*Jer 1:2; 25:3 /Jos 15:39
22:2 *k*S Dt 17:19; S 1Ki 14:8
*l*S Dt 5:32
22:3 *m*2Ch 34:20; Jer 39:14

21:12 *ears of everyone who hears of it will tingle.* See Jer 19:3.
21:13 *measuring line . . . plumb line.* Instruments normally associated with construction are used here as symbols of destruction (see Isa 34:11; Am 7:7–9,17).
21:14 *I will forsake.* In the sense of giving over to judgment (see Jer 12:7), not in the sense of abrogation of the covenant (see 1Sa 12:22; Isa 43:1–7). *remnant of my inheritance.* Upon the destruction of the northern kingdom, Judah had become the remnant of the Lord's inheritance (see 1Ki 8:51; Dt 4:20; 1Sa 10:1; Ps 28:9; see also note on 2Ki 19:4).
21:15 The history of Israel was a history of covenant breaking. With the reign of Manasseh the cup of God's wrath overflowed, and the judgment of exile from the land of promise (see note on 17:7) became inevitable (see 24:1–4).
21:16 *innocent blood.* A reference to godly people and perhaps even prophets who were martyred for opposition to Manasseh's evil practices (see vv. 10–11). According to a Jewish tradition (not otherwise substantiated) Isaiah was sawed in two during Manasseh's reign (cf. Heb 11:37).
21:17 *other events of Manasseh's reign.* See 2Ch 33:12–19. *annals of the kings of Judah.* See note on 1Ki 14:29.
21:18 *rested with his fathers.* See note on 1Ki 1:21. *Uzza.* Probably a shortened form of Uzziah (see 14:21–22 and 15:1–7, Azariah; 2Ch 26, Uzziah).
21:19 *two years.* 642–640 B.C. *Jotbah.* Some identify it

with the Jotbathah of Nu 33:33–34 and Dt 10:7, near Ezion Geber. Others, including the church father Jerome, have located it in Judah.
21:20 *did evil.* Amon did not share in the change of heart that characterized his father Manasseh in the last days of his life (see 2Ch 33:12–19). He must have restored the idolatrous practices that Manasseh abolished because these were again in existence in the time of Josiah (see 23:5–7,12).
21:23 *conspired against him.* Whether this palace revolt was motivated by religious or political considerations is not known.
21:24 *people of the land.* The citizenry in general (see 11:14,18; 14:21; 23:30). *killed all who had plotted against King Amon.* It is not clear whether this counterinsurgency was motivated simply by loyalty to the house of David or by other factors.
21:25 *annals of the kings of Judah.* See note on 1Ki 14:29.
21:26 *Uzza.* See note on v. 18.
22:1 *thirty-one years.* 640–609 B.C. (see note on 21:19).
Bozkath. Located in Judah in the vicinity of Lachish (see Jos 15:39).
22:2 *ways of his father David.* See note on 18:3. Josiah was the last godly king of the Davidic line prior to the exile. Jeremiah, who prophesied during the time of Josiah (see Jer 1:2), spoke highly of him (Jer 22:15–16). Zephaniah also prophesied in the early days of his reign (Zep 1:1).
22:3 *eighteenth year.* 622 B.C. Josiah was then 26 years old

Azaliah, the son of Meshullam, to the temple of the LORD. He said: [4]"Go up to Hilkiah[n] the high priest and have him get ready the money that has been brought into the temple of the LORD, which the doorkeepers have collected[o] from the people. [5]Have them entrust it to the men appointed to supervise the work on the temple. And have these men pay the workers who repair[p] the temple of the LORD— [6]the carpenters, the builders and the masons. Also have them purchase timber and dressed stone to repair the temple.[q] [7]But they need not account for the money entrusted to them, because they are acting faithfully."[r]

[8]Hilkiah the high priest said to Shaphan the secretary, "I have found the Book of the Law[s] in the temple of the LORD." He gave it to Shaphan, who read it. [9]Then Shaphan the secretary went to the king and reported to him: "Your officials have paid out the money that was in the temple of the LORD and have entrusted it to the workers and supervisors at the temple." [10]Then Shaphan the secretary informed the king, "Hilkiah the priest has given me a book." And Shaphan read from it in the presence of the king.[t]

[11]When the king heard the words of the Book of the Law,[u] he tore his robes. [12]He gave these orders to Hilkiah the priest, Ahikam[v] son of Shaphan, Acbor son of Micaiah, Shaphan the secretary and Asaiah the king's attendant:[w] [13]"Go and inquire[x] of the LORD for me and for the people and for all Judah about what is written in this book that has been found. Great is the

LORD's anger[y] that burns against us because our fathers have not obeyed the words of this book; they have not acted in accordance with all that is written there concerning us."

[14]Hilkiah the priest, Ahikam, Acbor, Shaphan and Asaiah went to speak to the prophetess[z] Huldah, who was the wife of Shallum son of Tikvah, the son of Harhas, keeper of the wardrobe. She lived in Jerusalem, in the Second District.

[15]She said to them, "This is what the LORD, the God of Israel, says: Tell the man who sent you to me, [16]This is what the LORD says: I am going to bring disaster[a] on this place and its people, according to everything written in the book[b] the king of Judah has read. [17]Because they have forsaken[c] me and burned incense to other gods and provoked me to anger by all the idols their hands have made,[i] my anger will burn against this place and will not be quenched.' [18]Tell the king of Judah, who sent you to inquire[d] of the LORD, 'This is what the LORD, the God of Israel, says concerning the words you heard: [19]Because your heart was responsive and you humbled[e] yourself before the LORD when you heard what I have spoken against this place and its people, that they would become accursed[f] and laid waste,[g] and because you tore your robes and wept in my presence, I have heard you, declares the LORD. [20]Therefore I will gather you to your fathers, and you will be buried in peace.[h] Your eyes[i] will not see all the

---

22:4 [n]Ezr 7:1
[o]2Ki 12:4-5
22:5 [p]2Ki 12:5
22:6
[q]2Ki 12:11-12
22:7 [r]S 2Ki 12:15
22:8 [s]S Dt 28:61;
S 31:24; Gal 3:10
22:10 [t]Jer 36:21
22:11 [u]ver 8
22:12
[v]2Ki 25:22;
Jer 26:24; 39:14
[w]1Sa 8:14
22:13
[x]S Ge 25:22;
S 1Sa 9:9

[y]Dt 29:24-28;
S 31:17; Isa 5:25;
42:25; Am 2:4
22:14
[z]S Ex 15:20
22:16
[a]S Dt 31:29;
S Jos 23:15;
Jer 6:19; 11:11;
18:11; 35:17
[b]Da 9:11
22:17 [c]S 1Ki 9:9
22:18 [d]Jer 21:2;
37:3,7
22:19
[e]S Ex 10:3;
Isa 57:15; 61:1;
Mic 6:8 [f]Jer 24:9;
25:18; 26:6
[g]Lev 26:31
22:20 [h]Isa 47:11;
57:1; Jer 18:11
[i]S 1Ki 21:29

[i]17 Or *by everything they have done*

(see v. 1). He had begun to serve the Lord faithfully at the age of 16 (the 8th year of his reign, 2Ch 34:3). When he was 20 years old (the 12th year of his reign, 2Ch 34:3), he had already begun to purge the land of its idolatrous practices. *secretary, Shaphan.* See note on 2Sa 8:17. Two additional individuals are mentioned as accompanying Shaphan in 2Ch 34:8.

22:4 *Hilkiah.* Father of Azariah and grandfather of Seraiah, the high priest executed at the destruction of Jerusalem by the Babylonians (see 25:18–20). It is unlikely that this Hilkiah was also the father of Jeremiah (see Jer 1:1). *money . . . the doorkeepers have collected.* Josiah used the method devised by Joash for collecting funds for the restoration of the temple (see 12:1–16; 2Ch 34:9).

22:5 *men appointed to supervise.* See 2Ch 34:12–13.

22:8 *Book of the Law.* Some interpreters hold that this refers to a copy of the entire Pentateuch, while others understand it as a reference to a copy of part or all of Deuteronomy alone (see Dt 31:24,26; 2Ch 34:14).

22:11 *tore his robes.* See note on 18:37; contrast Josiah's reaction with that of Jehoiakim to the words of the scroll written by Jeremiah (see Jer 36:24). Perhaps the covenant curses of Lev 26 and/or Dt 28, climaxing with the threat of exile, were the statements that especially disturbed Josiah.

22:12 *Ahikam.* Father of Gedaliah, who was later to be

appointed governor of Judah by Nebuchadnezzar (see 25:22; Jer 39:14). He was also the protector of Jeremiah when his life was threatened during the reign of Jehoiakim (see Jer 26:24). *Acbor.* His son Elnathan is mentioned in 24:8; Jer 26:22; 36:12. *Shaphan the secretary.* See note on v. 3.

22:14 *prophetess Huldah.* Why the delegation sought out Huldah rather than Jeremiah or Zephaniah is not known. Perhaps it was merely a matter of her accessibility in Jerusalem. *Shallum . . . keeper of the wardrobe.* Perhaps the same Shallum who was the uncle of Jeremiah (see Jer 32:7). *Second District.* A section of the city (the Hebrew for this phrase is translated "New Quarter" in Zep 1:10) probably located in a newly developed area between the first and second walls in the northwest part of Jerusalem (see 2Ch 33:14).

22:16 *this place.* Jerusalem.

22:19 *your heart was responsive.* See v. 11.

22:20 *gather you to your fathers.* See note on 1Ki 21:1. *you will be buried in peace.* This prediction refers to Josiah's death before God's judgment on Jerusalem through Nebuchadnezzar and so is not contradicted by his death in battle with Pharaoh Neco of Egypt (see 23:29–30). Josiah was assured that the final judgment on Judah and Jerusalem would not come in his own days.

disaster I am going to bring on this place.' "

So they took her answer back to the king.

Josiah Renews the Covenant

23:1–3pp — 2Ch 34:29–32
23:4–20Ref — 2Ch 34:3–7,33
23:21–23pp — 2Ch 35:1,18–19
23:28–30pp — 2Ch 35:20–36:1

23 Then the king called together all the elders of Judah and Jerusalem. ²He went up to the temple of the LORD with the men of Judah, the people of Jerusalem, the priests and the prophets—all the people from the least to the greatest. He read/ in their hearing all the words of the Book of the Covenant,ᵏ which had been found in the temple of the LORD. ³The king stood by the pillar/ and renewed the covenantᵐ in the presence of the LORD—to followⁿ the LORD and keep his commands, regulations and decrees with all his heart and all his soul, thus confirming the words of the covenant written in this book. Then all the people pledged themselves to the covenant.

⁴The king ordered Hilkiah the high priest, the priests next in rank and the doorkeepersᵒ to removeᵖ from the temple of the LORD all the articles made for Baal and Asherah and all the starry hosts. He burned them outside Jerusalem in the fields of the Kidron Valley and took the ashes to Bethel. ⁵He did away with the pagan priests appointed by the kings of Judah to burn incense on the high places of the towns of Judah and on those around Jerusalem—those who burned incense q to Baal, to the sun and moon, to the constellations and to all the starry hosts.ʳˢ ⁶He took the Asherah pole from the temple of the LORD to the Kidron Valleyᵗ outside Jerusalem and burned it there. He ground it to powderᵘ and scattered the dust over the gravesᵛ of the common people.ʷ ⁷He also tore down the quarters of the male shrine prostitutes,ˣ which were in the temple of the LORD and where women did weaving for Asherah.

⁸Josiah brought all the priests from the towns of Judah and desecrated the high places, from Gebaʸ to Beersheba, where the priests had burned incense. He broke down the shrinesʲ at the gates—at the entrance to the Gate of Joshua, the city governor, which is on the left of the city gate. ⁹Although the priests of the high places did not serveᶻ at the altar of the LORD in Jerusalem, they ate unleavened bread with their fellow priests.

¹⁰He desecrated Topheth,ᵃ which was in the Valley of Ben Hinnom,ᵇ so no one could use it to sacrifice his sonᶜ or daughter inᵏ the fire to Molech. ¹¹He removed

Cross references

23:2 /S Dt 31:11
ᵏS Ex 24:7
23:3 /S 1Ki 7:15
ᵐS 2Ki 11:12
ⁿS Dt 13:4
23:4 ᵒ2Ki 25:18;
Jer 35:4
ᵖS 2Ki 21:7

23:5 qS 2Ki 16:4
ʳJer 8:2
ˢJer 43:13
23:6 ᵗJer 31:40
ᵘS Ex 32:20
ᵛS Nu 19:16
ʷJer 26:23
23:7 ˣS Ge 38:21;
1Ki 14:24;
Eze 16:16
23:8 ʸS Jos 18:24;
S 1Ki 15:22
23:9 ᶻEze 44:10-14
23:10 ᵃIsa 30:33;
Jer 7:31,32; 19:6
ᵇS Jos 15:8
ᶜS Lev 18:21;
S Dt 18:10

j8 Or high places   k10 Or to make his son or daughter pass through

---

23:1 *elders.* See note on 10:1.
23:2 *Book of the Covenant.* Although this designation is used in Ex 24:7 with reference to the contents of Ex 20–23, it is here applied to either all or part of the book of Deuteronomy or the entire Mosaic law. Whatever else the scroll contained, it clearly included the covenant curses of Lev 26 and/or Dt 28 (see notes on v. 21; 22:8,11).
23:3 *pillar.* See note on 11:14. *renewed the covenant.* Josiah carries out the function of covenant mediator; cf. Moses (Ex 24:3–8; Dt 1:34), Joshua (Jos 24), Samuel (1Sa 11:14–12:25) and Jehoiada (2Ki 11:17). *follow the LORD.* See notes on 1Sa 12:14,20. ʻpledged themselves to the covenant.* It is likely that some sort of ratification rite was performed, in which the people participated and pledged by oath to be loyal to their covenant obligations. Whether this was done symbolically (see Jer 34:18) or verbally (see Dt 27:11–26) is not clear.
23:4 *doorkeepers.* See 12:9. *Baal and Asherah.* See note on 1Ki 14:15. *starry hosts.* See note on 17:16. *took the ashes to Bethel.* See vv. 15–16. Bethel was located just over the border between Judah and the former northern kingdom in territory nominally under Assyrian control. With a decline in Assyrian power, Josiah was able to exert his own influence in the north. He apparently deposited the ashes at Bethel in order to desecrate (see note on v. 14) the very place where golden calf worship had originally polluted the land (see notes on 1Ki 12:28,30).
23:5 *pagan priests.* See Hos 10:5; Zep 1:4. *kings of Judah.* A reference to Manasseh and Amon, and perhaps to Ahaz before them. *high places.* See note on 18:4.

23:6 *Asherah pole.* See note on 1Ki 14:15. The Asherah poles destroyed by Hezekiah (18:4) were reintroduced by Manasseh (21:7). When Manasseh turned to the Lord, it is likely that he too got rid of the Asherah poles (see 2Ch 33:15) and that they were then again reintroduced by Amon (2Ki 21:21; 2Ch 33:22). *scattered the dust over the graves of the common people.* Intended as a defilement of the goddess, not as a desecration of the graves of the poor (see Jer 26:23).
23:7 *male shrine prostitutes.* See note on 1Ki 14:24.
23:8 *desecrated the high places.* See note on 18:4. *Geba to Beersheba.* Geba was on the northern border of the southern kingdom (see 1Ki 15:22), and Beersheba was on its southern border (see note on 1Sa 3:20).
23:9 *ate unleavened bread with their fellow priests.* Although not permitted to serve at the temple altar, these priests were not to be sustained by a share of the priestly provisions (see Lev 2:10; 6:16–18). They occupied a status similar to that of priests with physical defects (see Lev 21:16–23).
23:10 *Topheth.* The name of an area in the Valley of Hinnom where altars used for child sacrifice were located (see Isa 30:33; Jer 7:31; 19:5–6). *sacrifice his son or daughter.* See 17:17; 21:6; see also note on 16:3. *Molech.* See note on 1Ki 11:5.
23:11 *horses . . . dedicated to the sun.* If live, the horses may have been used to pull chariots bearing images of a sun-god in religious processions. Small images of horses have recently been found in a cult place just outside one of the ancient walls of Jerusalem. *Nathan-Melech.* Perhaps the

from the entrance to the temple of the LORD the horses that the kings of Judah*d* had dedicated to the sun. They were in the court near the room of an official named Nathan-Melech. Josiah then burned the chariots dedicated to the sun. *e*

¹²He pulled down*f* the altars the kings of Judah had erected on the roof*g* near the upper room of Ahaz, and the altars Manasseh had built in the two courts*h* of the temple of the LORD. He removed them from there, smashed them to pieces and threw the rubble into the Kidron Valley. *i* ¹³The king also desecrated the high places that were east of Jerusalem on the south of the Hill of Corruption—the ones Solomon*j* king of Israel had built for Ashtoreth the vile goddess of the Sidonians, for Chemosh the vile god of Moab, and for Molech¹ the detestable*k* god of the people of Ammon. *l* ¹⁴Josiah smashed*m* the sacred stones and cut down the Asherah poles and covered the sites with human bones. *n*

¹⁵Even the altar*o* at Bethel, the high place made by Jeroboam*p* son of Nebat, who had caused Israel to sin—even that altar and high place he demolished. He burned the high place and ground it to powder, and burned the Asherah pole also. ¹⁶Then Josiah*q* looked around, and when he saw the tombs that were there on the hillside, he had the bones removed from them and burned on the altar to defile it, in accordance*r* with the word of the LORD proclaimed by the man of God who foretold these things.

¹⁷The king asked, "What is that tombstone I see?"

The men of the city said, "It marks the tomb of the man of God who came from Judah and pronounced against the altar of Bethel the very things you have done to it."

¹⁸"Leave it alone," he said. "Don't let anyone disturb his bones*s*." So they spared his bones and those of the prophet*t* who had come from Samaria.

¹⁹Just as he had done at Bethel, Josiah removed and defiled all the shrines at the high places that the kings of Israel had built in the towns of Samaria that had provoked the LORD to anger. ²⁰Josiah slaughtered*u* all the priests of those high places on the altars and burned human bones*v* on them. Then he went back to Jerusalem.

²¹The king gave this order to all the people: "Celebrate the Passover*w* to the LORD your God, as it is written in this Book of the Covenant."*x* ²²Not since the days of the judges who led Israel, nor throughout the days of the kings of Israel and the kings of Judah, had any such Passover been observed. ²³But in the eighteenth year of King Josiah, this Passover was celebrated to the LORD in Jerusalem.*y*

²⁴Furthermore, Josiah got rid of the mediums and spiritists,*z* the household gods,*a* the idols and all the other detestable*b* things seen in Judah and Jerusalem. This he did to fulfill the requirements of the law written in the book that Hilkiah the priest had discovered in the temple of the LORD. ²⁵Neither before nor after Josiah was there a king like him who turned*c* to

23:11 *d*ver 5,19; Ne 9:34; Jer 44:9
*e*S Dt 4:19
23:12 /2Ch 33:15
*g*Jer 19:13; Zep 1:5
*h*S 2Ki 21:5
*i*S 2Sa 15:23
23:13 /1Ki 11:7
*k*S Dt 27:15
*l*Jer 11:13
23:14 *m*S Ex 23:24
*n*S Nu 19:16; S Ps 53:5
23:15 *o*S Jos 7:2; 1Ki 13:1-3
*p*S 1Ki 12:33
23:16 *q*S 1Ki 13:2
*r*1Ki 13:32
23:18 *s*1Ki 13:31
*t*1Ki 13:29
23:20 *u*S Ex 22:20; S 2Ki 11:18
*v*S 1Ki 13:2
23:21 *w*S Ex 12:11; Dt 16:1-8
*x*S Ex 24:7
23:23 *y*S Ex 12:11; S Nu 28:16
23:24 *z*S Lev 19:31; S Dt 18:11
*a*S Ge 31:19
*b*Dt 7:26; 2Ki 16:3
23:25 *c*S 1Sa 7:3

¹*13 Hebrew Milcom*

---

official in charge of the chariots.

23:12 *altars . . . on the roof.* Altars dedicated to the worship of all the starry hosts (see Jer 19:13; Zep 1:5)—erected by Ahaz (2Ki 16:3–4,10–16), Manasseh (21:3) and Amon (21:21–22).

23:13 *high places . . . Solomon . . . had built.* See note on 1Ki 11:5.

23:14 *covered the sites with human bones.* The bones would defile these sites and make them unsuitable for cultic use in the future (see Nu 19:16).

23:15 *altar at Bethel.* See 1Ki 12:32–33. Nothing is said of the golden calf, which undoubtedly had been sent to Assyria as tribute at the time of the captivity of the northern kingdom (see Hos 10:5–6).

23:16 *tombs.* Of the priests of the Bethel sanctuary (see 1Ki 13:2). *burned on the altar to defile it.* See notes on vv. 6,14. *the man of God who foretold these things.* See 1Ki 13:1–2, 32.

23:18 *prophet who had come from Samaria.* See 1Ki 13:31–32. Samaria is here not to be understood as the city by that name since the prophet came from Bethel (see 1Ki 13:11), and the city Samaria did not yet exist (see 1Ki 16:24). Rather, it is to be taken as a designation for the entire area of the former northern kingdom (see notes on 17:24, 29; 1Ki 13:32).

23:20 *slaughtered all the priests of those high places.* These were non-Levitical priests of the apostate worship practiced in the area of the former northern kingdom (see notes on 17:27–28,33–34). They were treated like the pagan priests of Judah (see v. 5) in contrast to Josiah's treatment of the priests at the high places in Judah (see vv. 8–9). Josiah's actions in this matter conformed to the requirements of Dt 13; 17:2–7.

23:21 *Celebrate the Passover.* A more complete description of this observance is found in 2Ch 35:1–19. *as it is written in this Book of the Covenant.* See note on v. 2. This appears to refer to Dt 16:1–8, where the Passover is described in a communal setting at a sanctuary (see Ex 23:15–17; 34:23–24; Lev 23:4–14) rather than in the family setting of Ex 12:1–14,43–49.

23:22 The uniqueness of Josiah's Passover celebration seems to be in the fact that all the Passover lambs were slaughtered exclusively by the Levites (see 2Ch 35:1–19; cf. 2Ch 30:2–3,17–20 for the Passover observed in the time of Hezekiah).

23:23 *eighteenth year.* See note on 22:3.

23:24 *household gods.* See note on Ge 31:19. *requirements of the law.* See notes on v. 2; 22:8.

23:25 *was there a king like him.* See note on 18:5. *with all his heart . . . soul and . . . strength.* See Dt 6:5.

the LORD as he did—with all his heart and with all his soul and with all his strength, in accordance with all the Law of Moses. *d*

²⁶Nevertheless, the LORD did not turn away from the heat of his fierce anger, *e* which burned against Judah because of all that Manasseh*f* had done to provoke him to anger. ²⁷So the LORD said, "I will remove*g* Judah also from my presence*h* as I removed Israel, and I will reject*i* Jerusalem, the city I chose, and this temple, about which I said, 'There shall my Name be.'*m*"

²⁸As for the other events of Josiah's reign, and all he did, are they not written in the book of the annals of the kings of Judah?

²⁹While Josiah was king, Pharaoh Neco*j* king of Egypt went up to the Euphrates River to help the king of Assyria. King Josiah marched out to meet him in battle, but Neco faced him and killed him at Megiddo.*k* ³⁰Josiah's servants brought his body in a chariot*l* from Megiddo to Jerusalem and buried him in his own tomb. And the people of the land took Jehoahaz son of Josiah and anointed him and made him king in place of his father.

Jehoahaz King of Judah

23:31–34pp — 2Ch 36:2–4

³¹Jehoahaz *m* was twenty-three years old when he became king, and he reigned in Jerusalem three months. His mother's name was Hamutal *n* daughter of Jeremiah; she was from Libnah. ³²He did evil *o* in the eyes of the LORD, just as his fathers had done. ³³Pharaoh Neco put him in chains at Riblah*p* in the land of Hamath*n q* so that he might not reign in Jerusalem, and he imposed on Judah a levy of a hundred talents*o* of silver and a talent*p* of gold. ³⁴Pharaoh Neco made Eliakim*r* son of Josiah king in place of his father Josiah and changed Eliakim's name to Jehoiakim. But he took Jehoahaz and carried him off to Egypt, and there he died. *s* ³⁵Jehoiakim paid Pharaoh Neco the silver and gold he demanded. In order to do so, he taxed the land and exacted the silver and gold from the people of the land according to their assessments. *t*

Jehoiakim King of Judah

23:36–24:6pp — 2Ch 36:5–8

³⁶Jehoiakim *u* was twenty-five years old when he became king, and he reigned in Jerusalem eleven years. His mother's name was Zebidah daughter of Pedaiah; she was from Rumah. ³⁷And he did evil *v* in the

---

23:25 *d*Jer 22:15
23:26 *e*2Ki 21:6;
Jer 23:20; 30:24
/S 2Ki 21:12
23:27 *g*2Ki 21:13
*h*S Ex 33:15;
2Ki 24:3
*i*Jer 27:10; 32:31
23:29 *j*ver 33-35;
Jer 46:2 *k*2Ki 9:27
23:30 *l*S 2Ki 9:28
23:31
*m*1Ch 3:15;
Jer 22:11

*n*2Ki 24:18
23:32 *o*1Ki 15:26
23:33
*p*S Nu 34:11
*q*1Ki 8:65
23:34 *r*2Ki 24:6;
1Ch 3:15;
2Ch 36:5-8;
Jer 1:3 *s*Jer 22:12
23:35 *t*Jer 2:16
23:36 *u*Jer 26:1
23:37 *v*1Ki 15:26

m*27* 1 Kings 8:29   **n***33* Hebrew; Septuagint (see also 2 Chron. 36:3) *Neco at Riblah in Hamath removed him*   **o***33* That is, about 3 3/4 tons (about 3.4 metric tons)   **p***33* That is, about 75 pounds (about 34 kilograms)

23:26 *Nevertheless, the LORD did not turn away from the heat of his fierce anger.* The judgment against Judah and Jerusalem was postponed but not rescinded because of Josiah's reformation (see notes on 21:15; 22:20).

23:27 *as I removed Israel.* See 17:18–23. *Jerusalem, the city I chose.* See 21:4,7,13. *this temple, about which I said, 'There shall my Name be.'* See note on 1Ki 8:16.

23:28 *annals of the kings of Judah.* See note on 1Ki 14:29.

23:29 *Pharaoh Neco king of Egypt.* Ruled 610–595 B.C. *help the king of Assyria.* Pharaoh Neco intended to help Ashur-Uballit II, the last Assyrian king, in his struggle against the rising power of Babylon under Nabopolassar. The Assyrian capital, Nineveh, had already fallen to the Babylonians and Medes in 612 (see the book of Nahum). The remaining Assyrian forces had regrouped at Haran, but in 609 they were forced west of the Euphrates. It appears to be at this time that the Egyptians under Neco were coming to the Assyrians' aid. *King Josiah marched out to meet him in battle.* Perhaps Josiah opposed the passage of Neco's army through the pass at Megiddo (see 2Ch 35:20–24) because he feared that the growth of either Egyptian or Assyrian power would have adverse results for the continued independence of Judah.

23:30 *buried him in his own tomb.* See 2Ch 35:24–25. *people of the land.* See note on 21:24. *Jehoahaz son of Josiah.* Jehoahaz was the fourth and youngest son of Josiah. His name was originally Shallum (see 1Ch 3:15; Jer 22:11), which was probably changed to Jehoahaz at the time of his accession to the throne. Perhaps Jehoahaz was chosen by the people over Jehoiakim because it was known that Jehoiakim favored a pro-Egyptian policy instead of the anti-Egyptian policy of Josiah and Jehoahaz. *anointed him.* See note on 1Sa

9:16.

23:31 *three months.* In 609 B.C. *Jeremiah.* Not the prophet (see Jer 1:1). *Libnah.* See note on 8:22.

23:32 *evil . . . as his fathers.* See 16:3; 21:2,21; Eze 19:3.

23:33 *in chains at Riblah.* By either deception or overt force the Egyptians were able to take Jehoahaz captive and impose tribute on Judah (see 2Ch 36:3). Jehoahaz was imprisoned at Neco's military headquarters established at Riblah on the Orontes River. Nebuchadnezzar was later to make his headquarters at the same place (see 25:6,20).

23:34 *Eliakim son of Josiah.* Eliakim was an older brother of Jehoahaz (see 1Ch 3:15). Perhaps he had been bypassed earlier as a successor to Josiah because of a pro-Egyptian political stance. *changed Eliakim's name to Jehoiakim.* The meaning of these two names is similar (Eliakim, "God has established"; Jehoiakim, "Yahweh has established"). Perhaps Neco wanted to use the name change to imply that his actions were sanctioned by Yahweh, the God of Judah (see 18:25; 2Ch 35:21). In any case, the change in name indicated that Jehoiakim was subject to Neco's authority. *took Jehoahaz . . . to Egypt, and there he died.* See 2Ch 36:4; 22:10–12.

23:35 *from the people of the land.* The tribute for Neco was raised by a graduated tax placed on the very people who had supported the kingship of Jehoahaz (see v. 30). Menahem of the northern kingdom had used a similar method of raising funds for tribute (see 15:20).

23:36 *eleven years.* 609–598 B.C.

23:37 *did evil in the eyes of the LORD.* Jehoiakim was responsible for the murder of the prophet Uriah from Kiriath Jearim (Jer 26:20–24), and his rule was characterized by dishonesty, oppression and injustice (see Jer 22:13–19). He

eyes of the LORD, just as his fathers had
done.

24 During Jehoiakim's reign, Nebuchadnezzar[w] king of Babylon invaded[x] the land, and Jehoiakim became
his vassal for three years. But then he
changed his mind and rebelled[y] against
Nebuchadnezzar. 2The LORD sent Babylonian,[q][z] Aramean,[a] Moabite and Ammonite raiders[b] against him. He sent them to
destroy[c] Judah, in accordance with the
word of the LORD proclaimed by his servants the prophets.[d] 3Surely these things
happened to Judah according to the LORD's
command,[e] in order to remove them from
his presence[f] because of the sins of Manasseh[g] and all he had done, 4including
the shedding of innocent blood.[h] For he
had filled Jerusalem with innocent blood,
and the LORD was not willing to forgive.[i]

5As for the other events of Jehoiakim's
reign,[j] and all he did, are they not written
in the book of the annals of the kings of
Judah? 6Jehoiakim rested[k] with his fathers. And Jehoiachin[l] his son succeeded
him as king.

7The king of Egypt[m] did not march out
from his own country again, because the
king of Babylon[n] had taken all his territory, from the Wadi of Egypt to the Euphrates River.

24:1 [w]ver 10; 2Ki 25:11; Ezr 5:12; Jer 4:7; 25:1,9; 39:1; 40:1; 50:17; 52:15; Eze 32:2; Da 1:1; 7:4 [x]Jer 35:11 [y]S 2Ki 18:7 **24:2** [z]Jer 5:15; Hab 1:6 [a]Jer 35:11 [b]S 2Ki 5:2 [c]Isa 28:18-19 [d]Jer 12:7-9; 25:1; 26:1; 36:1; Eze 23:23; Da 1:2 **24:3** [e]S 2Ki 18:25 [f]S 2Ki 13:23 [g]S 1Ki 14:9; S 2Ki 21:12; Jer 15:4 **24:4** [h]S 2Ki 21:16; Jer 22:3 [i]S Ex 23:21; La 3:42 **24:5** [j]Jer 22:18-19 **24:6** [k]Jer 22:19; 36:30 [l]1Ch 3:16; Jer 22:24,28; Eze 19:1 **24:7** [m]S Ge 15:18; S 2Ki 18:21; S Jer 46:25 [n]Jer 1:14; 25:9; 46:24

24:8 [o]1Ch 3:16; Jer 22:24; 37:1 [p]ver 15; Jer 13:18; 22:26; 29:2 **24:9** [q]1Ki 15:26 **24:10** [r]S ver 1

Jehoiachin King of Judah

24:8–17pp — 2Ch 36:9–10

8Jehoiachin[o] was eighteen years old
when he became king, and he reigned in
Jerusalem three months. His mother's
name was Nehushta[p] daughter of Elnathan; she was from Jerusalem. 9He did
evil[q] in the eyes of the LORD, just as his
father had done.

10At that time the officers of Nebuchadnezzar[r] king of Babylon advanced on
Jerusalem and laid siege to it, 11and Nebuchadnezzar himself came up to the city
while his officers were besieging it.
12Jehoiachin king of Judah, his mother, his
attendants, his nobles and his officials all
surrendered[s] to him.

In the eighth year of the reign of the
king of Babylon, he took Jehoiachin prisoner. 13As the LORD had declared,[t] Nebuchadnezzar removed all the treasures[u]
from the temple of the LORD and from the
royal palace, and took away all the gold
articles[v] that Solomon[w] king of Israel had
made for the temple of the LORD. 14He car-

24:12 [s]2Ki 25:27; Jer 13:18; 22:24-30; 24:1; 29:2 **24:13** [t]2Ki 20:17 [u]2Ki 25:15; Isa 39:6; 42:22 [v]2Ki 25:14; Ezr 1:7; Isa 39:6; Jer 15:13; 17:3; 20:5; 27:16; 28:3; Eze 7:21; Da 1:2; 5:2,23; Zep 1:13 [w]S 1Ki 7:51

[q]*2* Or *Chaldean*

reintroduced idolatrous worship in the temple (see Eze 8:5–17) and refused to accept the word of the Lord through Jeremiah (see Jer 36). *his fathers.* Manasseh (21:1–18) and Amon (21:19–26).

24:1 *Nebuchadnezzar.* Means "O (god) Nabu, protect my son!" He was the son of Nabopolassar (see note on 23:29) and the most powerful king of the Neo-Babylonian empire (612–539 B.C.), reigning 605–562 (see Da 1–4). *invaded the land.* In 605 Nebuchadnezzar, the crown prince and commander of the Babylonian army, defeated Pharaoh Neco and the Egyptians at the battle of Carchemish and again at Hamath (see 23:29; Jer 46:2). These victories had far-reaching implications in the geopolitical power structure of the eastern Mediterranean world. Nebuchadnezzar went on to conquer all of the "Hatti-country," which, according to Babylonian records, included the "city of Judah." Daniel was among the Judahite hostages taken at this time (see Da 1:1). Perhaps as early as Sept. 6, 605, Nebuchadnezzar acceded to the Babylonian throne upon the death of his father. *three years.* Probably 604–602. In 604 Nebuchadnezzar returned to the west and took tribute from "all the kings of Hatti-land." It is likely that Jehoiakim was included among these kings. *changed his mind and rebelled.* In 601 Nebuchadnezzar again marched west against Egypt and was repulsed by strong Egyptian resistance. This may have encouraged Jehoiakim's rebellion, even though Jeremiah had warned against it (see Jer 27:9–11).

24:2 *Babylonian, Aramean, Moabite and Ammonite raiders against him.* Reaction to Jehoiakim's rebellion was swift. Babylonian troops, perhaps garrisoned in Aram, along with troops of other loyal vassals, were sent to put down the Judahite rebellion.

24:3 *sins of Manasseh.* See 21:11–12; 23:26–27; Jer 15:3–4.

24:4 *innocent blood.* See note on 21:16. *not willing to forgive.* See 22:17.

24:5 *annals of the kings of Judah.* See note on 1Ki 14:29. *rested with his fathers.* See note on 1Ki 1:21. Jehoiakim died shortly before Jerusalem fell to the Babylonian siege (see vv. 8–12). Whether his death was due to natural causes or political intrigue is not indicated.

24:7 *The king of Egypt did not march out from his own country again.* This was due to the Egyptian defeat at Carchemish (see Jer 46:2) in 605 B.C., and it explains why Jehoiakim received no help from Egypt in his rebellion against the Babylonians. *Wadi of Egypt.* See note on 1Ki 8:65.

24:8 *three months.* In 598–597 B.C. Babylonian records place the fall of Jerusalem to Nebuchadnezzar on Mar. 16, 597. This means that the three-month and ten-day reign (see 2Ch 36:9–10) of Jehoiachin began in December, 598.

24:9 *as his father.* See 23:37; Jer 22:20–30.

24:11 *Nebuchadnezzar himself came up to the city.* Babylonian records say that Nebuchadnezzar "encamped against the city of Judah, and on the second day of the month of Addaru [i.e., Mar. 16, 597 B.C.] he seized the city and captured the king."

24:12 *eighth year.* April, 597 B.C. (see 2Ch 36:10; see also note on Jer 52:28, where a different system of dating is reflected).

24:13 *As the LORD had declared.* See 20:13,17.

24:14 *ten thousand.* This figure may include the 7,000 fighting men and 1,000 craftsmen mentioned in v. 16 (see note on Jer 52:28, where a different number of captives is mentioned).

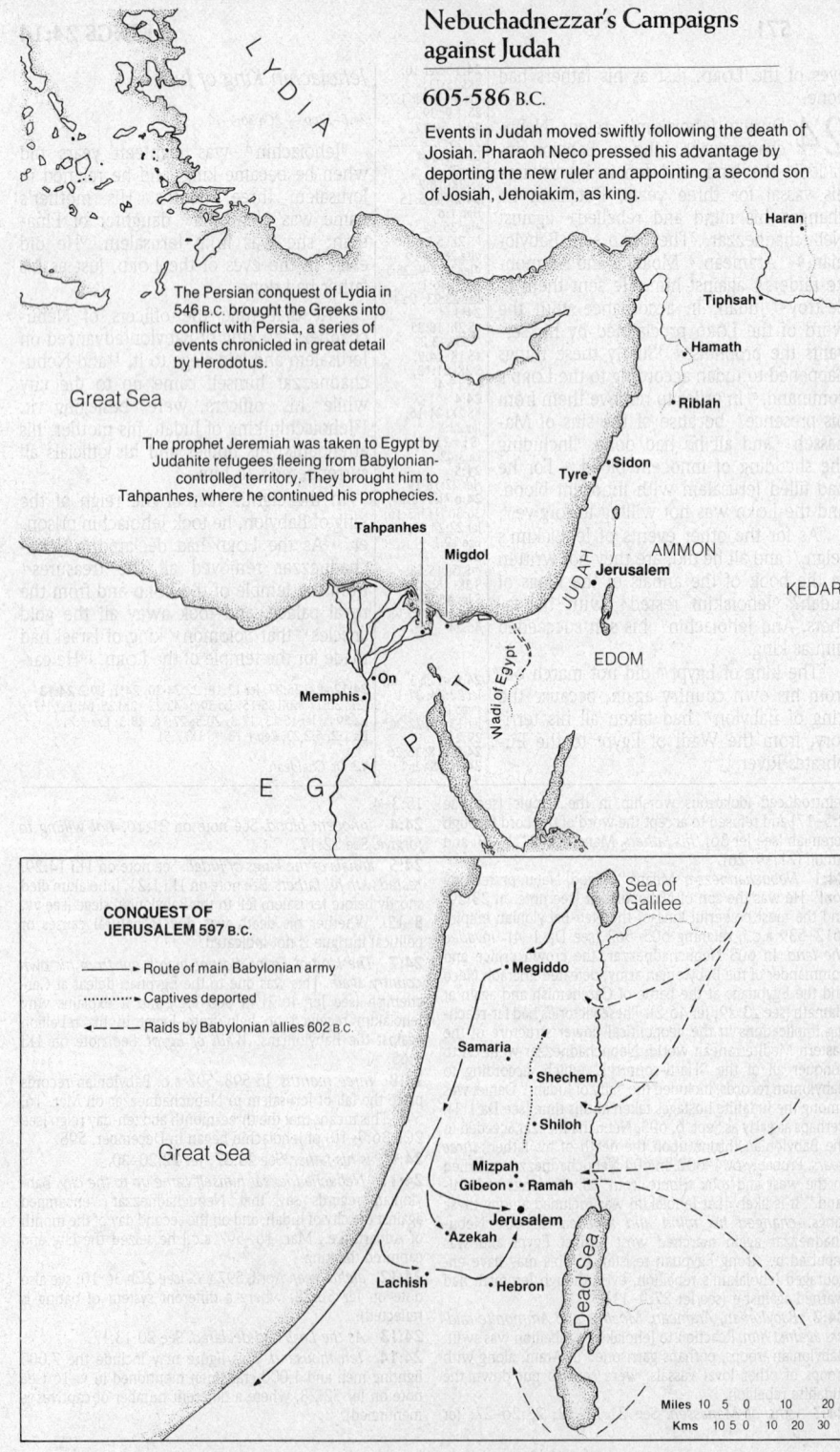

Nebuchadnezzar's Campaigns against Judah

605-586 B.C.

Events in Judah moved swiftly following the death of Josiah. Pharaoh Neco pressed his advantage by deporting the new ruler and appointing a second son of Josiah, Jehoiakim, as king.

The Persian conquest of Lydia in 546 B.C. brought the Greeks into conflict with Persia, a series of events chronicled in great detail by Herodotus.

Great Sea

The prophet Jeremiah was taken to Egypt by Judahite refugees fleeing from Babylonian-controlled territory. They brought him to Tahpanhes, where he continued his prophecies.

LYDIA

Haran

Tiphsah

Hamath

Riblah

Sidon
Tyre

JUDAH

AMMON

Jerusalem

KEDAR

EDOM

Tahpanhes

Migdol

Wadi of Egypt

On
Memphis

E G Y P T

CONQUEST OF JERUSALEM 597 B.C.

→ Route of main Babylonian army

······▶ Captives deported

◄─ ─ Raids by Babylonian allies 602 B.C.

Sea of Galilee

Megiddo

Samaria

Shechem

Shiloh

Mizpah
Gibeon • Ramah

Jerusalem

Azekah

Lachish • Hebron

Great Sea

Dead Sea

Miles 10 5 0   10   20
Kms   10 5 0   10   20   30

Soon a stronger power appeared in the north in the person of Nebuchadnezzar, king of the Chaldeans (Neo-Babylonians), who determined to follow the fierce policies of his Assyrian predecessors.

The tribute of Jehoiakim was paid at a distance when he heard of Nebuchadnezzar's approach. After three years as a Babylonian vassal, he rebelled, bringing a rapid response in the form of small-scale raids from Babylonians, Arameans, Moabites and Ammonites

(c. 602 B.C.). Finally, Nebuchadnezzar's forces controlled all of the coastal territory north of the Wadi of Egypt.

When 18-year-old Jehoiachin had ruled just three months (597 B.C.), the main Babylonian army struck, capturing Jerusalem and exiling the king as a captive in Babylon. Ten thousand persons were deported.

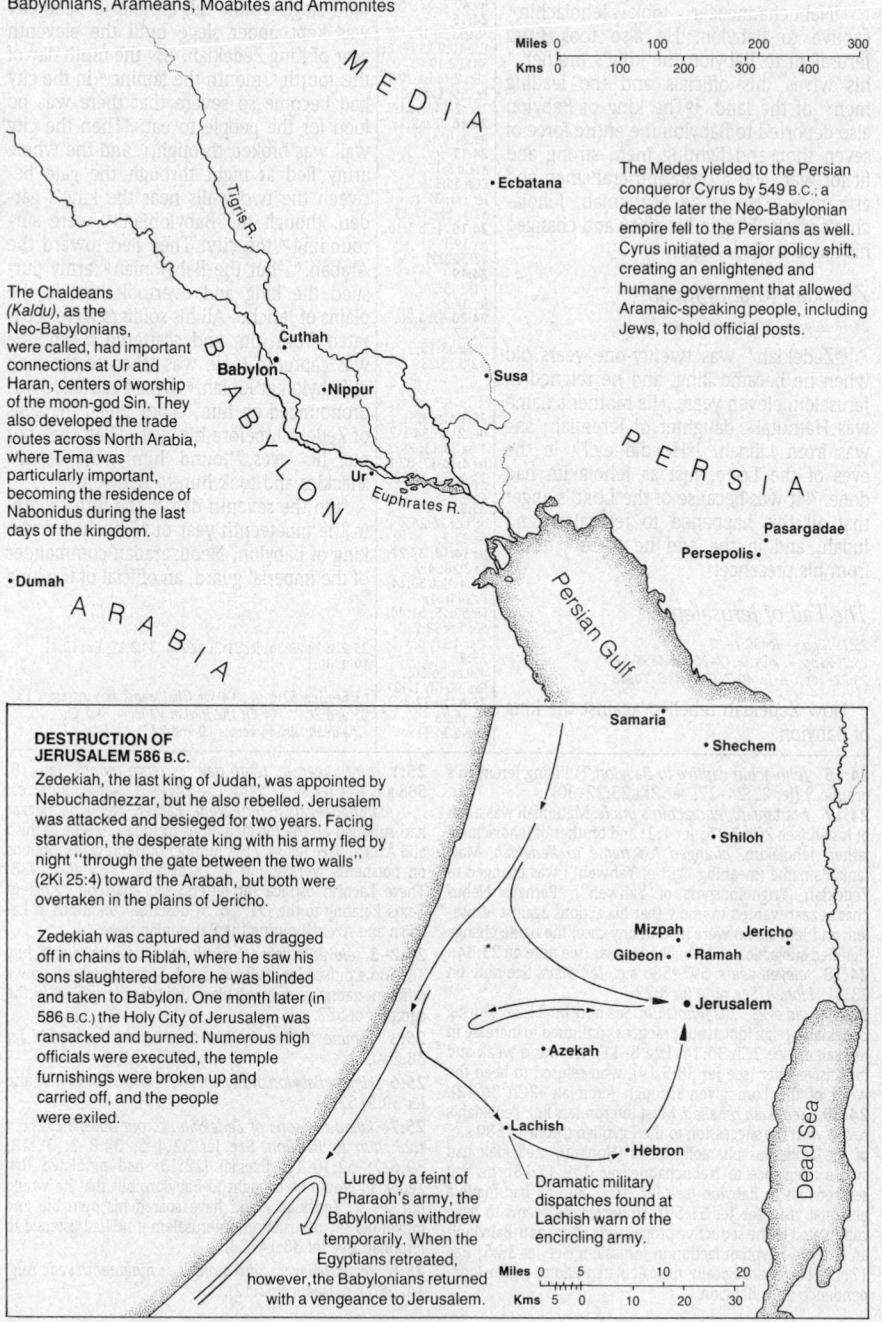

The Medes yielded to the Persian conqueror Cyrus by 549 B.C.; a decade later the Neo-Babylonian empire fell to the Persians as well. Cyrus initiated a major policy shift, creating an enlightened and humane government that allowed Aramaic-speaking people, including Jews, to hold official posts.

The Chaldeans (Kaldu) as the Neo-Babylonians, were called, had important connections at Ur and Haran, centers of worship of the moon-god Sin. They also developed the trade routes across North Arabia, where Tema was particularly important, becoming the residence of Nabonidus during the last days of the kingdom.

DESTRUCTION OF JERUSALEM 586 B.C.

Zedekiah, the last king of Judah, was appointed by Nebuchadnezzar, but he also rebelled. Jerusalem was attacked and besieged for two years. Facing starvation, the desperate king with his army fled by night "through the gate between the two walls" (2Ki 25:4) toward the Arabah, but both were overtaken in the plains of Jericho.

Zedekiah was captured and was dragged off in chains to Riblah, where he saw his sons slaughtered before he was blinded and taken to Babylon. One month later (in 586 B.C.) the Holy City of Jerusalem was ransacked and burned. Numerous high officials were executed, the temple furnishings were broken up and carried off, and the people were exiled.

Lured by a feint of Pharaoh's army, the Babylonians withdrew temporarily. When the Egyptians retreated, however, the Babylonians returned with a vengeance to Jerusalem.

Dramatic military dispatches found at Lachish warn of the encircling army.

ried into exile[x] all Jerusalem: all the officers and fighting men,[y] and all the craftsmen and artisans—a total of ten thousand. Only the poorest[z] people of the land were left.

[15]Nebuchadnezzar took Jehoiachin[a] captive to Babylon. He also took from Jerusalem to Babylon the king's mother,[b] his wives, his officials and the leading men[c] of the land. [16]The king of Babylon also deported to Babylon the entire force of seven thousand fighting men, strong and fit for war, and a thousand craftsmen and artisans.[d] [17]He made Mattaniah, Jehoiachin's uncle, king in his place and changed his name to Zedekiah.[e]

Zedekiah King of Judah

24:18–20pp — 2Ch 36:11–16; Jer 52:1–3

[18]Zedekiah[f] was twenty-one years old when he became king, and he reigned in Jerusalem eleven years. His mother's name was Hamutal[g] daughter of Jeremiah; she was from Libnah. [19]He did evil[h] in the eyes of the LORD, just as Jehoiakim had done. [20]It was because of the LORD's anger that all this happened to Jerusalem and Judah, and in the end he thrust[i] them from his presence.[j]

The Fall of Jerusalem

25:1–12pp — Jer 39:1–10
25:1–21pp — 2Ch 36:17–20; Jer 52:4–27
25:22–26pp — Jer 40:7–9; 41:1–3, 16–18

Now Zedekiah rebelled against the king of Babylon.

25 So in the ninth[k] year of Zedekiah's reign, on the tenth day of the tenth month, Nebuchadnezzar[l] king of Babylon marched against Jerusalem with his whole army. He encamped outside the city and built siege works[m] all around it. [2]The city was kept under siege until the eleventh year of King Zedekiah. [3]By the ninth day of the fourth[r] month the famine[n] in the city had become so severe that there was no food for the people to eat. [4]Then the city wall was broken through,[o] and the whole army fled at night through the gate between the two walls near the king's garden, though the Babylonians[s] were surrounding[p] the city. They fled toward the Arabah,[t] [5]but the Babylonian[u] army pursued the king and overtook him in the plains of Jericho. All his soldiers were separated from him and scattered,[q] [6]and he was captured.[r] He was taken to the king of Babylon at Riblah,[s] where sentence was pronounced on him. [7]They killed the sons of Zedekiah before his eyes. Then they put out his eyes, bound him with bronze shackles and took him to Babylon.[t]

[8]On the seventh day of the fifth month, in the nineteenth year of Nebuchadnezzar king of Babylon, Nebuzaradan commander of the imperial guard, an official of the king

Cross references

24:14
[x]S Dt 28:36;
[y]2Ch 36:20;
S Mt 1:11
[y]Isa 3:1-3
[z]Dt 15:11;
2Ki 25:12;
Job 5:16; Ps 9:18;
Jer 40:7; 52:16
24:15
[a]S 2Ki 20:18;
Eze 19:9 [b]S ver 8;
S 1Ki 2:19
[c]Est 2:6; Isa 39:7;
La 2:9; Eze 1:2;
17:12-14; Da 1:3
24:16 [d]Ezr 2:1;
Jer 24:1
24:17
[e]1Ch 3:15;
2Ch 36:11;
Jer 1:3; 37:1;
52:1; Eze 17:13
24:18 [f]1Ch 3:16;
Jer 39:1
[g]2Ki 23:31
24:19
[h]1Ki 15:26;
Jer 37:2
24:20 [i]Dt 4:26;
29:27
[j]S Ex 33:15;
S 2Ki 13:23

25:1 [k]Jer 32:1
[l]Jer 21:2; 34:1-7
[m]Isa 23:13; 29:3;
Jer 4:16-17; 32:2;
33:4; Eze 21:22;
24:2
25:3
[n]S Lev 26:26;
Isa 22:2;
Jer 14:18; 37:21;
La 2:20; 4:9
25:4 [o]Job 30:14;
Ps 144:14;
Jer 50:15; 51:44,
58; Eze 33:21
[p]Jer 4:17; 6:3
25:5
[q]S Lev 26:36;
Eze 12:14; 17:21
25:6 [r]Isa 22:3;
Jer 38:23
[s]S Nu 34:11

25:7 [t]S Dt 28:36; Jer 21:7; 32:4-5; 34:3,21; Eze 12:11; 19:9; 40:1

[r]3 See Jer. 52:6.   [s]4 Or *Chaldeans*; also in verses 13, 25 and 26   [t]4 Or *the Jordan Valley*   [u]5 Or *Chaldean*; also in verses 10 and 24

Notes

24:15 *Jehoiachin captive to Babylon.* Fulfilling Jeremiah's prophecy (Jer 22:24–27; see 2Ki 25:27–30).

24:17 *Mattaniah, Jehoiachin's uncle.* Mattaniah was a son of Josiah (see 2Ch 3:15; Jer 1:3) and brother of Jehoiachin's father, Jehoiakim. *changed his name to Zedekiah.* Mattaniah's name (meaning "gift of Yahweh") was changed to Zedekiah ("righteousness of Yahweh"). Perhaps Nebuchadnezzar wanted to imply that his actions against Jerusalem and Jehoiachin were just. In any case, the name change signified subjection to Nebuchadnezzar (see note on 23:34).
24:18 *eleven years.* 597–586 B.C. *Jeremiah.* See note on 23:31. *Libnah.* See note on 8:22.
24:19 *did evil . . . as Jehoiakim.* See note on 23:37. During Zedekiah's reign idolatrous practices continued to increase in Jerusalem (see 2Ch 36:14; Eze 8–11). He was a weak and indecisive ruler (see Jer 38:5,19), who refused to heed the word of the Lord given through Jeremiah (2Ch 36:12).
24:20 *Zedekiah rebelled.* Most interpreters link Zedekiah's revolt with the succession to the Egyptian throne in 589 B.C. of the ambitious pharaoh Apries (Hophra). Zedekiah had sworn allegiance to Nebuchadnezzar (Eze 17:13), he had sent envoys to Babylon (see Jer 29:3), and he had made a personal visit (see Jer 51:59). However, he seems to have capitulated to the seductive propaganda of the anti-Babylonian and pro-Egyptian faction in Jerusalem (see Jer 37:5; Eze 17:15–16) in a tragically miscalculated effort to gain independence from Babylon.

25:1 *ninth year . . . tenth day . . . tenth month.* Jan. 15, 588 B.C. (see Jer 39:1; 52:4; Eze 24:1–2). *Nebuchadnezzar . . . marched against Jerusalem.* Earlier, Nebuchadnezzar had subdued all the fortified cities in Judah except Lachish and Azekah (see Jer 34:7). A number of Hebrew inscriptions on potsherds were found at Lachish in 1935 and 1938. These Lachish ostraca (or letters; see chart on "Ancient Texts Relating to the OT," p. 5) describe conditions at Lachish and Azekah during the Babylonian siege.
25:2–3 *eleventh year . . . ninth day . . . fourth month.* July 18, 586 B.C. (see Jer 39:2; 52:5–7). Some scholars follow a different dating system and place the fall of Jerusalem in the summer of 587.
25:3 *famine in the city had become so severe.* See Jer 38:2–9.
25:6 *king of Babylon at Riblah.* See note on 23:33; see also Jer 39:5; 52:9.
25:7 *killed the sons of Zedekiah . . . put out his eyes . . . took him to Babylon.* See Jer 32:4-5; 34:2-3; 38:18; 39:6-7; 52:10–11. Ezekiel (12:13) had predicted that Zedekiah would be brought to Babylon, but that he would not see it. Zedekiah could have spared his own life and prevented the destruction of Jerusalem if he had listened to Jeremiah (see Jer 38:14–28).
25:8 *seventh day . . . fifth month . . . nineteenth year.* Aug. 14, 586 B.C. (see Jer 52:12).

of Babylon, came to Jerusalem. [9]He set fire[u] to the temple of the LORD, the royal palace and all the houses of Jerusalem. Every important building he burned down.[v] [10]The whole Babylonian army, under the commander of the imperial guard, broke down the walls[w] around Jerusalem. [11]Nebuzaradan the commander of the guard carried into exile[x] the people who remained in the city, along with the rest of the populace and those who had gone over to the king of Babylon.[y] [12]But the commander left behind some of the poorest people[z] of the land to work the vineyards and fields.

[13]The Babylonians broke[a] up the bronze pillars, the movable stands and the bronze Sea that were at the temple of the LORD and they carried the bronze to Babylon. [14]They also took away the pots, shovels, wick trimmers, dishes[b] and all the bronze articles[c] used in the temple service. [15]The commander of the imperial guard took away the censers and sprinkling bowls—all that were made of pure gold or silver.[d]

[16]The bronze from the two pillars, the Sea and the movable stands, which Solomon had made for the temple of the LORD, was more than could be weighed. [17]Each pillar[e] was twenty-seven feet[v] high. The bronze capital on top of one pillar was four and a half feet[w] high and was decorated with a network and pomegranates of bronze all around. The other pillar, with its network, was similar.

[18]The commander of the guard took as

prisoners Seraiah[f] the chief priest, Zephaniah[g] the priest next in rank and the three doorkeepers. [h] [19]Of those still in the city, he took the officer in charge of the fighting men and five royal advisers. He also took the secretary who was chief officer in charge of conscripting the people of the land and sixty of his men who were found in the city. [20]Nebuzaradan the commander took them all and brought them to the king of Babylon at Riblah. [21]There at Riblah, [i] in the land of Hamath, the king had them executed.[j]

So Judah went into captivity,[k] away from her land. [l]

[22]Nebuchadnezzar king of Babylon appointed Gedaliah[m] son of Ahikam, [n] the son of Shaphan, to be over the people he had left behind in Judah. [23]When all the army officers and their men heard that the king of Babylon had appointed Gedaliah as governor, they came to Gedaliah at Mizpah—Ishmael son of Nethaniah, Johanan son of Kareah, Seraiah son of Tanhumeth the Netophathite, Jaazaniah the son of the Maacathite, and their men. [24]Gedaliah took an oath to reassure them and their men. "Do not be afraid of the Babylonian officials," he said. "Settle down in the land and serve the king of Babylon, and it will go well with you."

[25]In the seventh month, however, Ishmael son of Nethaniah, the son of Elishama, who was of royal blood, came with ten men and assassinated[o] Gedaliah and also

25:9 [u]Isa 60:7; 63:15,18; 64:11
[v]S Dt 13:16; Ne 1:3; Ps 74:3-8; 79:1; Jer 2:15; 17:27; 21:10; 26:6,18; La 4:11; Am 2:5; Mic 3:12
25:10 [w]Ne 1:3; Jer 50:15
25:11 [x]S Lev 26:44; 2Ki 24:14
[y]S Dt 28:36; S 2Ki 24:1
25:12 [z]S 2Ki 24:14
25:13 [a]S 1Ki 7:50
25:14 [b]S Nu 7:14 [c]S 2Ki 24:13; Ezr 1:7
25:15 [d]S 2Ki 24:13; Jer 15:13; 20:5; 27:16-22
25:17 [e]1Ki 7:15-22

25:18 [f]ver 18-21; 1Ch 6:14; Ezr 7:1; Ne 11:11 [g]Jer 21:1; 29:25; 37:3 [h]S 2Ki 12:9; S 23:4
25:21 [i]S Nu 34:11 [j]Jer 34:21 [k]S 1Ki 8:46 [l]S Ge 12:7; S Jos 23:13
25:22 [m]Jer 39:14; 40:5, 7; 41:18 [n]S 2Ki 22:12
25:25 [o]S 2Ki 12:20

v[17] Hebrew *eighteen cubits* (about 8.1 meters)
w[17] Hebrew *three cubits* (about 1.3 meters)

25:9 *set fire to the temple.* See 2Ch 36:19; Jer 39:8; 52:13.
25:13 *bronze pillars.* See 1Ki 7:15–22. *movable stands.* See 1Ki 7:27–39. *bronze Sea.* See 1Ki 7:23–26.
25:14 *all the bronze articles used in the temple service.* See 1Ki 7:40,45.
25:17 *bronze capital . . . was four and a half feet high.* See NIV text note. In 1Ki 7:16 and Jer 52:22 the height of the capital is given as seven and a half feet (five cubits). The three-cubit difference may be due to a copyist's error.
25:18 *Seraiah the chief priest.* Seraiah was the grandson of Hilkiah (see note on 22:4; see also 22:8; 1Ch 6:13–14). His son Jehozadak was taken captive to Babylon. Ezra was one of Jehozadak's descendants (see Ezr 7:1).
25:20 *brought them to the king of Babylon at Riblah.* See v. 6 and note.
25:21 *Judah went into captivity, away from her land.* Judah's exile from Canaan fulfilled the prediction of judgment given during the reign of Manasseh (see 23:27). Exile was the most dire of the covenant curses (see Lev 26:33; Dt 28:36; see also Jer 25:8–11).
25:22 *Gedaliah.* See note on 22:12. Gedaliah shared Jeremiah's nonresistance approach to the Babylonians (see v. 24) and won their confidence as a trustworthy governor of Judah

(see Jer 41:10).
25:23 *Mizpah.* Had been a town of important political significance in the time just before the establishment of the monarchy (see note on 1Sa 7:5). Jeremiah found Gedaliah there (see Jer 40:1–6). *Ishmael son of Nethaniah.* Verse 25 gives a fuller genealogy. Elishama, Ishmael's grandfather, was the royal secretary under Jehoiakim (Jer 36:12). *Jaazaniah the son of the Maacathite.* In 1932 an agate seal was found at Tell en-Nasbeh (Mizpah) bearing the name of Jaazaniah (perhaps the man mentioned here) with the inscription: "Belonging to Jaazaniah the servant of the king."
25:24 Gedaliah urged submission to the Babylonians as the judgment of God. He advocated the restoration of the normal pursuits of a peacetime society (see Jer 27). A similar message had been given by Jeremiah to the captives taken to Babylon in 597 B.C. (see Jer 29:4–7).
25:25 *seventh month.* October, 586 B.C. *assassinated Gedaliah.* A more complete account of the assassination of Gedaliah is given in Jer 40:13–41:15. Ishmael appears to have had personal designs on the throne, to have resented Gedaliah's ready submission to the Babylonians, and to have been manipulated by the Ammonites, who also chafed under Babylonian domination (see Jer 40:14; 41:10,15).

the men of Judah and the Babylonians who
were with him at Mizpah.[p] 26At this, all
the people from the least to the greatest,
together with the army officers, fled to
Egypt[q] for fear of the Babylonians.

Jehoiachin Released

25:27–30pp — Jer 52:31–34

27In the thirty-seventh year of the exile
of Jehoiachin king of Judah, in the year
Evil-Merodach[x] became king of Babylon,
he released Jehoiachin[r] from prison on the
twenty-seventh day of the twelfth month.
28He spoke kindly[s] to him and gave him a
seat of honor[t] higher than those of the

25:25 [p]Zec 7:5
25:26 [q]Isa 30:2; Jer 43:7
25:27 [r]S 2Ki 24:12
25:28 [s]S 1Ki 8:50 [t]Ezr 5:5; 7:6,28; 9:9; Ne 2:1; Da 2:48

[x]27 Also called *Amel-Marduk*

25:26 *fled to Egypt.* Pharaoh Apries (Hophra) was then ruler in Egypt (see note on 24:20).
25:27 *thirty-seventh year . . . twenty-seventh day . . . twelfth month.* Mar. 22, 561 B.C. *in the year Evil-Merodach became king of Babylon.* 561 (some scholars place Evil-Merodach's succession to the throne in October, 562; see note on 24:1). His name means "man of (the god) Marduk." *released Jehoiachin from prison.* Babylonian administrative tablets (see chart on "Ancient Texts Relating to the OT," p. 5), recording the payment of rations in oil and barley to prisoners held in Babylon, mention Yaukin (Jehoiachin) king of Iahudu (Judah) and five of his sons (cf. 24:15). No reason is given for Jehoiachin's release. Perhaps it was part of a general amnesty proclaimed at the beginning of Evil-

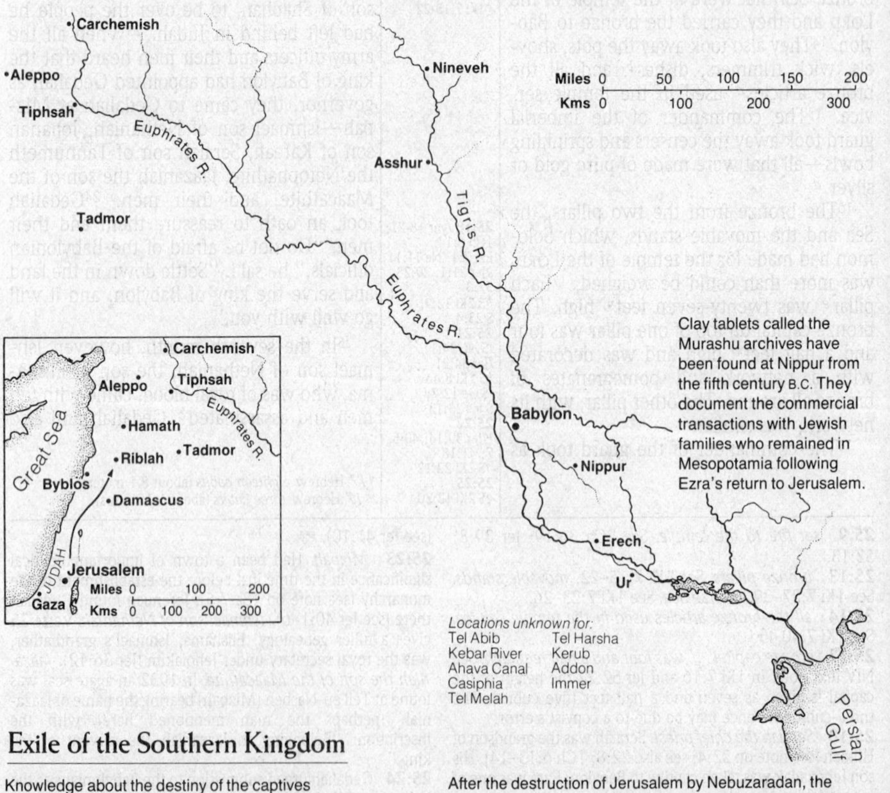
Carchemish
Aleppo
Tiphsah
Euphrates R.
Nineveh
Miles 0 50 100 150 200
Kms 0 100 200 300
Asshur
Tigris R.
Tadmor
Euphrates R.
Babylon
Nippur
Erech
Ur
Persian Gulf
Carchemish
Aleppo
Tiphsah
Hamath
Tadmor
Riblah
Great Sea
Byblos
Damascus
JUDAH
Jerusalem
Gaza
Miles 0 100 200
Kms 0 100 200 300
Clay tablets called the Murashu archives have been found at Nippur from the fifth century B.C. They document the commercial transactions with Jewish families who remained in Mesopotamia following Ezra's return to Jerusalem.
Locations unknown for:
Tel Abib
Kebar River
Ahava Canal
Casiphia
Tel Melah
Tel Harsha
Kerub
Addon
Immer

Exile of the Southern Kingdom

Knowledge about the destiny of the captives from Israel and Judah is sparse in the period following the capture of Samaria and the later destruction of Jerusalem.

Assyrians and Babylonians treated their subject peoples essentially the same: overwhelming military force used in a manner inspiring psychological terror, along with mass deportations and heavy tribute.

Three deportations are mentioned in Jer 52:28-30, the largest one consisting of 3,023 Jews who were taken to Babylon along with King Jehoiachin in 597 B.C.

After the destruction of Jerusalem by Nebuzaradan, the commander of the Babylonian army, hundreds of exiles were taken to Riblah "in the land of Hamath," where, in addition to Zedekiah's sons, at least 61 were executed.

Jehoiachin and his family were kept in Babylon, where clay ration receipts bearing his name have been found in a dramatic archaeological confirmation of Biblical history.

Eze 1:1-3 and 3:15 indicate that other captives were placed at Tel Abib and at the Kebar River, both probably in the locale of Nippur, as were other villages mentioned in Ezr 2:59; 8:15, 17; Ne 7:61.

other kings who were with him in Babylon. ²⁹So Jehoiachin put aside his prison clothes and for the rest of his life ate regu-

25:29 uS 2Sa 9:7
25:30 vGe 43:34; Est 2:9; 9:22; Jer 28:4

larly at the king's table. ^u ³⁰Day by day the king gave Jehoiachin a regular allowance as long as he lived. ^v

---

Merodach's reign.
25:28 *spoke kindly to him and gave him a seat of honor.* The book of Kings ends on a hopeful note. The judgment of

exile will not destroy the people of Israel or the line of David. God's promise concerning David's house remains (see 2Sa 7:14–16).

1 CHRONICLES

Title

The Hebrew title (*dibre hayyamim*) can be translated "the events (or annals) of the days (or years)." The same phrase occurs in references to sources used by the author or compiler of Kings (translated "annals" in, e.g., 1Ki 14:19,29; 15:7,23,31; 16:5,14,20,27; 22:46). The Septuagint translators (translators of the OT into Greek) called the book "the things omitted," indicating that they regarded it as a supplement to Samuel and Kings. Jerome (A.D. 347-420), translator of the Latin Vulgate, suggested that a more appropriate title would be "chronicle of the whole sacred history." Luther took over this suggestion in his German version, and others have followed him. Chronicles was first divided into two books by the Septuagint translators.

Author, Date and Sources

According to ancient Jewish tradition, Ezra wrote Chronicles, Ezra and Nehemiah (see Introduction to Ezra: Literary Form and Authorship), but this cannot be established with certainty. A growing consensus dates Chronicles in the latter half of the fifth century B.C., thus possibly within Ezra's lifetime. And it must be acknowledged that the author, if not Ezra himself, at least shared many basic concerns with that reforming priest—though Chronicles is not so narrowly "priestly" in its perspective as was long affirmed.

Some believe the text contains evidence here and there of later expansions after the basic work had been composed. While editorial revisions are not unlikely, all specific proposals regarding them remain tentative.

In his recounting of history long past the Chronicler relied on many written sources. About half his work was taken from Samuel and Kings; he also drew on the Pentateuch, Judges, Ruth, Psalms, Isaiah, Jeremiah, Lamentations and Zechariah (though he used texts of these books that varied somewhat from those that have been preserved in the later standardized Hebrew texts). And there are frequent references to still other sources: "the book of the kings of Israel" (9:1; 2Ch 20:34; cf. 2Ch 33:18), "the book of the annals of King David" (27:24), "the book of the kings of Judah and Israel" or ". . . of Israel and Judah" (2Ch 16:11; 25:26; 27:7; 28:26; 32:32; 35:27; 36:8), "the annotations on the book of the kings" (2Ch 24:27). It is unclear whether these all refer to the same source or to different sources, and what their relationship is to Samuel and Kings or to the royal annals referred to in Kings. In addition, the author cites a number of prophetic writings: those of "Samuel the seer" (29:29), "Nathan the prophet" (29:29; 2Ch 9:29), "Gad the seer" (29:29), "Ahijah the Shilonite" (2Ch 9:29), "Iddo the seer" (2Ch 9:29; 12:15; 13:22), "Shemaiah the prophet" (2Ch 12:15), "the prophet Isaiah" (2Ch 26:22), "the seers" (2Ch 33:19). All these he used, often with only minor changes, to tell his own story of the past. He did not invent, but he did select, arrange and integrate his sources to compose a narrative "sermon" for postexilic Israel as she struggled to reorient herself as the people of God in a new situation.

Purpose and Themes

Just as the author of Kings had organized and interpreted the data of Israel's history to address the needs of the exiled community, so the Chronicler wrote for the restored community. The burning issue was the question of continuity with the past: Is God still interested in us? Are his covenants still in force? Now that we have no Davidic king and are subject to Persia, do God's promises to David still have meaning for us? After the great judgment (the dethroning of the house of David, the destruction of the nation, of Jerusalem and of the temple, and the exile to Babylon), what is our relationship to Israel of old? Several elements go into the Chronicler's answer:

1. Continuity with the past is signified by the temple in Jerusalem, rebuilt by the Lord's sovereign

influence over a Persian imperial edict (2Ch 36:22-23). For a generation that had no independent political status and no Davidic king the author takes great pains to show that the temple of the Lord and its service (including its book of prayer and praise, an early edition of the Psalms) are supreme gifts of God given to Israel through the Davidic dynasty. For that reason his account of the reigns of David and Solomon is largely devoted to David's preparation for and Solomon's building of the temple, and David's instructions for the temple service (with the counsel of Gad the seer and Nathan the prophet, 2Ch 29:25, and also of the Levites Asaph, Heman and Jeduthun, 2Ch 35:15). See also the Chronicler's accounts of the reigns of Asa, Jehoshaphat, Joash, Hezekiah and Josiah. The temple of the Lord in the ancient holy city and its service (including the Psalms) were the chief legacy left to the restored community by the house of David.

2. The value of this legacy is highlighted by the author's emphasis on God's furtherance of his gracious purposes toward Israel through his sovereign acts of election: (1) of the tribe of Levi to serve before the ark of the covenant (15:2; see 23:24-32), (2) of David to be king over Israel (28:4; 2Ch 6:6), (3) of Solomon his son to be king and to build the temple (28:5-6,10; 29:1), (4) of Jerusalem (2Ch 6:6,34,38; 12:13; 33:7) and (5) of the temple (2Ch 7:12,16; 33:7) to be the place where God's Name would be present among his people. These divine acts give assurance to postexilic Israel that her rebuilt temple in Jerusalem and its continuing service mark her as God's people whose election has not been annulled.

3. In addition to the temple, Israel has the law and the prophets as a major focus of her covenant life under the leadership of the house of David. Neither the Davidic kings nor the temple had in themselves assured Israel's security and blessing. All had been conditional on Israel's and the king's faithfulness to the law (28:7; 2Ch 6:16; 7:17; 12:1; 33:8). In the Chronicler's account, a primary feature of the reign of every faithful Davidic king was his attempt to bring about compliance with the law: David (6:49; 15:13,15; 16:40; 22:12-13; 29:19), Asa (2Ch 14:4; 15:12-14), Jehoshaphat (2Ch 17:3-9; 19:8-10), Joash (2Ch 24:6,9), Hezekiah (2Ch 29:10,31; 30:15-16; 31:3-4,21), Josiah (2Ch 34:19-21,29-33; 35:6,12,26). And to heed God's prophetic word was no less crucial. The faithful kings, such as David, Asa, Jehoshaphat, Hezekiah and Josiah—and even Rehoboam (2Ch 11:4; 12:6) and Amaziah (2Ch 25:7-10)—honored it; the unfaithful kings disregarded it to their destruction (Jehoram, 2Ch 21:12-19; Joash, 2Ch 24:19-25; Amaziah, 2Ch 25:15-16,20; Manasseh, 2Ch 33:10-11; see 36:15-16). Chronicles, in fact, notes the ministries of more prophets than do Samuel and Kings. Jehoshaphat's word to Israel expresses the Chronicler's view succinctly: "Have faith in the LORD your God and you will be upheld; have faith in his prophets and you will be successful" (2Ch 20:20). In the Chronicler's account of Israel's years under the kings, her response to the law and the prophets was more decisive for her destiny than the reigns of kings.

Thus the law and the prophets, like the temple, are more crucial to Israel's continuing relationship with the Lord than the presence or absence of a king, the reigns of the Davidic kings themselves being testimony.

4. The Chronicler further underscores the importance of obedience to the law and the prophets by emphasizing the theme of immediate retribution. See the express statements of David (28:9), of the Lord (2Ch 7:14) and of the prophets (2Ch 12:5; 15:2,7; 16:7,9; 19:2-3; 21:14-15; 24:20; 25:15-16; 28:9; 34:24-28). In writing his accounts of individual reigns, he never tires of demonstrating how sin always brings judgment in the form of disaster (usually either illness or defeat in war), whereas repentance, obedience and trust yield peace, victory and prosperity.

5. Clearly the author of Chronicles wished to sustain Israel's hope for the promised Messiah, son of David, in accordance with the Davidic covenant (2Sa 7) and the assurances of the prophets, including those near to him (Haggai, Zechariah and Malachi). He was careful to recall the Lord's pledge to David (1Ch 17) and to follow this with many references back to it (see especially his account of Solomon's reign and also 2Ch 13:5; 21:7; 23:3). But perhaps even more indicative are his idealized depictions of David, Solomon, Asa, Jehoshaphat, Hezekiah and Josiah. While not portrayed as flawless, these kings are presented as prime examples of the Messianic ideal, i.e., as royal servants of the Lord whose reigns promoted godliness and covenant faithfulness in Israel. They were crowned with God's favor toward his people in the concrete forms of victories, deliverances and prosperity. They sat, moreover, on the "throne of the LORD" (29:23; see 28:5; 2Ch 9:8) and ruled over the Lord's kingdom (17:14; 2Ch 13:8). Thus they served as types, foreshadowing the David to come of whom the prophets had spoken, and their remembrance nurtured hope in the face of much discouragement (see the book of Malachi). See further the next section on "Portrait of David and Solomon."

6. Yet another major theme of the Chronicler's history is his concern with "all Israel" (see, e.g., 9:1; 11:1-4; 12:38-40; 16:1-3; 18:14; 21:1-5; 28:1-8; 29:21-26; 2Ch 1:1-3; 7:8-10; 9:30; 10:1-3,16; 12:1; 18:16; 28:23; 29:24; 30:1-13,23-27; 34:6-9,33). As a matter of fact, he viewed the restored community as the remnant of all Israel, both north and south (9:2-3). This was more than a theological conceit. His narrative makes frequent note of movements of godly people from Israel to Judah for specifically religious reasons. The first were Levites in the time of Rehoboam (2Ch 11:14). In the reign of Asa others followed from Ephraim and Manasseh (2Ch 15:9). Shortly after the Assyrian destruction of the northern kingdom, many from that devastated land resettled in Judah at Hezekiah's invitation (2Ch 30). Presumably not all who came for Hezekiah's great Passover remained, but archaeology has shown a sudden large increase in population in the region around Jerusalem at this time, and the Chronicler specifically mentions "men of Israel . . . who lived in the towns of Judah" (2Ch 31:6). He also speaks of "the people of Manasseh, Ephraim and the entire remnant of Israel" who joined with "the people of Judah and Benjamin and the inhabitants of Jerusalem" in restoring the temple in the days of Josiah (2Ch 34:9). These were also present at Josiah's Passover (2Ch 35:17-18). So the kingdom of "Judah" had absorbed many from the northern kingdom through the years, and the Chronicler viewed it as the remnant of all Israel from the time of Samaria's fall.

7. The genealogies also demonstrate continuity with the past. To the question "Is God still interested in us?" the Chronicler answers, "He has always been." God's grace and love for the restored community did not begin with David or the conquest or the exodus—but with creation (1:1). For the genealogies see below.

8. The Chronicler often introduces speeches not found in Samuel and Kings, using them to convey some of his main emphases. Of the 165 speeches in Chronicles of varying lengths, only 95 are found in the parallel texts of Samuel and Kings. Cf., e.g., the speeches of Abijah (2Ch 13:4-12), Asa (2Ch 14:11) and Jehoshaphat (2Ch 20:5-12).

Portrait of David and Solomon

The bulk of the Chronicler's history is devoted to the reigns of David (chs. 11-29) and Solomon (2Ch 1-9). His portraits of these two kings are quite distinctive and provide a key to his concerns:

1. The Chronicler has idealized David and Solomon. Anything in his source material (mainly Samuel and Kings) that might tarnish his picture of them is omitted. He makes no reference to the seven-year reign in Hebron before the uniting of the kingdom, the wars between Saul's house and David, the negotiations with Abner, the difficulties over David's wife Michal, or the murders of Abner and Ish-Bosheth (2Sa 1-4). The Chronicler presents David as being immediately anointed king over all Israel after the death of Saul (ch. 11) and enjoying the total support of the people (11:10-12:40; see note on 3:1-9). Subsequent difficulties for David are also not recounted. No mention is made of David's sin with Bathsheba, the crime and death of Amnon, the fratricide by Absalom and his plot against his father, the flight of David from Jerusalem, the rebellions of Sheba and Shimei, and other incidents that might diminish the glory of David's reign (2Sa 11-20). David is presented without blemish, apart from the incident of the census (the Chronicler had a special purpose for including it; see ch. 21 and notes).

The Chronicler handles Solomon similarly. Solomon is specifically named in a divine oracle as David's successor (22:7-10; 28:6). His accession to the throne is announced publicly by David and is greeted with the unanimous support of all Israel (chs. 28-29). No mention is made of the bedridden David, who must overturn the attempted coup by Adonijah at the last moment to secure the throne for Solomon. Nor is there mention that the military commander Joab and the high priest Abiathar supported Adonijah's attempt (1Ki 1). Solomon's execution of those who had wronged David (1Ki 2) is also omitted. The accession of Solomon is without competition or detracting incident. The account of his reign is devoted almost wholly to the building of the temple (2Ch 2-8), and no reference to his failures is included. No mention is made of his idolatry, his foreign wives or of the rebellions against his rule (1Ki 11). Even the blame for the schism is removed from Solomon (1Ki 11:26-40; 12:1-4) and placed on the scheming of Jeroboam. Solomon's image in Chronicles is such that he can be paired with David in the most favorable light (2Ch 11:17).

The David and Solomon of the Chronicler, then, must be seen not only as the David and Solomon of history, but also as typifying the Messianic king of the Chronicler's expectation.

2. Not only is there idealization of David and Solomon, but the author also appears to consciously adopt the account of the succession of Moses and Joshua as a model for the succession of David and Solomon:

a. Both David and Moses fail to attain their goals—one to build the temple and the other to enter

the promised land. In both cases the divine prohibition is related to the appointment of a successor (22:5-13; 28:2-8; Dt 1:37-38; 31:2-8).

b. Both Solomon and Joshua bring the people of God into rest (22:8-9; Jos 11:23; 21:44).

c. There are a number of verbal parallels in the appointments of Solomon and Joshua (compare 22:11-13,16; 28:7-10,20; 2Ch 1:1 with Dt 31:5-8,23; Jos 1:5,7-9).

d. There are both private and public announcements of the appointment of the successors: private (22:6; Dt 31:23); public (28:8; Dt 31:7—both "in the presence/sight of all Israel").

e. Both enjoy the immediate and wholehearted support of the people (29:23-24; Dt 34:9; Jos 1:16-18).

f. It is twice reported that God "exalted" or "made great" Solomon and Joshua (29:25; 2Ch 1:1; Jos 3:7; 4:14).

The Chronicler also uses other models from Pentateuchal history in his portrayal of David and Solomon. Like Moses, David received the plans for the temple from God (28:11-19; Ex 25:9) and called on the people to bring voluntary offerings for its construction (29:1-9; Ex 25:1-7). Solomon's relationship to Huram-Abi, the craftsman from Tyre (2Ch 2:13-14), echoes the role of Bezalel and Oholiab in the building of the tabernacle (Ex 35:30-36:7). See note on 2Ch 1:5.

Genealogies

Analysis of genealogies, both inside and outside the Bible, has disclosed that they serve a variety of functions (with different principles governing the lists), that they vary in form (some being segmented, others linear) and depth (number of generations listed), and that they are often fluid (subject to change).

There are three general areas in which genealogies function: the familial or domestic, the legal-political, and the religious. In the domestic area an individual's social status, privileges and obligations may be reflected in his placement in the lineage (see 7:14-19); the rights of the firstborn son and the secondary status of the children of concubines are examples from the Bible. In the political sphere genealogies substantiate claims to hereditary office or settle competing claims when the office is contested. Land organization and territorial groupings of social units may also be determined by genealogical reckoning—e.g., the division of the land among the 12 tribes. In Israel military levies also proceeded along genealogical lines; several of the genealogies in Chronicles reflect military conscription (5:1-26; 7:1-12,30-40; 8:1-40). Genealogies function in the religious sphere primarily by establishing membership among the priests and Levites (6:1-30; 9:10-34; Ne 7:61-65).

As to form, some genealogical lists trace several lines of descent (segmented genealogies) while others are devoted to a single line (linear genealogies).

Comparison of genealogical lists of the same tribal or family line often brings to light surprising differences. This fluidity of the lists may reflect variation in function. But sometimes changes in the status or relations of social structures are reflected in genealogies by changes in the relationships of names in the genealogy (see 1:35-42; 6:22,27) or by the addition of names or segments to a lineage (see 5:11-22; 6:27; 7:6-12). The most common type of fluidity in Biblical materials is telescoping, the omission of names from the list. Unimportant names are left out in order to relate an individual to a prominent ancestor, or possibly to achieve the desired number of names in the genealogy. Some Biblical genealogies, for example, omit names to achieve multiples of 7: For the period from David to the exile Matthew gives 14 generations (2 times 7), while Luke gives 21 (3 times 7), and the same authors give similar multiples of 7 for the period from the exile to Jesus (Mt 1:1-17; Lk 3:23-38).

The genealogies of Chronicles show variation in all these properties; the arrangements often reflect the purpose for which the genealogies were composed prior to their being adopted by the Chronicler as part of his record.

Outline

Historical Records From Adam to Abraham

To Noah's Sons

1 Adam,[a] Seth, Enosh, [2]Kenan,[b] Mahalalel,[c] Jared,[d] [3]Enoch,[e] Methuselah,[f] Lamech,[g] Noah.[h]

[4]The sons of Noah:[a][i]
Shem, Ham and Japheth.[j]

The Japhethites

1:5–7pp — Ge 10:2–5

[5]The sons[b] of Japheth:
Gomer, Magog, Madai, Javan, Tubal, Meshech and Tiras.
[6]The sons of Gomer:
Ashkenaz, Riphath[c] and Togarmah.
[7]The sons of Javan:
Elishah, Tarshish, the Kittim and the Rodanim.

The Hamites

1:8–16pp — Ge 10:6–20

[8]The sons of Ham:
Cush, Mizraim,[d] Put and Canaan.
[9]The sons of Cush:
Seba, Havilah, Sabta, Raamah and Sabteca.
The sons of Raamah:
Sheba and Dedan.
[10]Cush was the father[e] of
Nimrod, who grew to be a mighty warrior on earth.

[11]Mizraim was the father of
the Ludites, Anamites, Lehabites, Naphtuhites, [12]Pathrusites, Casluhites (from whom the Philistines came) and Caphtorites.
[13]Canaan was the father of
Sidon his firstborn,[f] and of the Hittites, [14]Jebusites, Amorites, Girgashites, [15]Hivites, Arkites, Sinites, [16]Arvadites, Zemarites and Hamathites.

The Semites

1:17–23pp — Ge 10:21–31; 11:10–27

[17]The sons of Shem:
Elam, Asshur, Arphaxad, Lud and Aram.
The sons of Aram[g]:
Uz, Hul, Gether and Meshech.
[18]Arphaxad was the father of Shelah,
and Shelah the father of Eber.
[19]Two sons were born to Eber:
One was named Peleg,[h] because in his time the earth was divided; his brother was named Joktan.
[20]Joktan was the father of

1:1 *a*Ge 5:1-32; Lk 3:36-38 **1:2** *b*S Ge 5:9 *c*S Ge 5:12 *d*S Ge 5:15 **1:3** *e*S Ge 5:18; Jude 1:14 *f*S Ge 5:21 *g*S Ge 5:25 *h*S Ge 5:29 **1:4** *i*Ge 6:10; 10:1 *j*S Ge 5:32

a4 Septuagint; Hebrew does not have *The sons of Noah:* b5 *Sons* may mean *descendants* or *successors* or *nations*; also in verses 6-10, 17 and 20. c6 Many Hebrew manuscripts and Vulgate (see also Septuagint and Gen. 10:3); most Hebrew manuscripts *Diphath* d8 That is, Egypt; also in verse 11 e10 *Father* may mean *ancestor* or *predecessor* or *founder*; also in verses 11, 13, 18 and 20. f13 Or *of the Sidonians, the foremost* g17 One Hebrew manuscript and some Septuagint manuscripts (see also Gen. 10:23); most Hebrew manuscripts do not have this line. h19 *Peleg* means *division*.

1:1–9:44 The genealogies succinctly show the restored community's continuity with the past. The great deeds of God on Israel's behalf prior to the rise of David are passed over in silence, but the genealogies serve as a skeleton of history to show that the Israel of the restoration stands at the center of the divine purpose from the beginning (from Adam, v. 1). And the genealogies also serve the very practical purpose of legitimizing the present. They provide the framework by which the ethnic and religious purity of the people can be maintained. They also establish the continuing line of royal succession and the legitimacy of the priests for the postexilic temple service. (See Introduction: Genealogies.)
1:1–2:1 The Chronicler here covers the period from Adam to Jacob, and the materials are drawn almost entirely from Genesis. The subsidiary lines of descent are presented first: Japheth and Ham (vv. 5–16) are given before Shem (vv. 17–27), the sons of Shem other than those in Abraham's ancestry (vv. 17–23) before that line (vv. 24–27), the sons of Abraham's concubines (vv. 28–33) before Isaac's line (v. 34), the descendants of Esau and the Edomite ruling houses (vv. 35–54) before the sons of Israel (2:1). In each case the elect lineage is given last.

Several features of this genealogy are striking when compared with non-Biblical materials. The genealogy begins without an introduction. Two sections of the genealogy have no kinship terms and are only lists of names: the first 13 names (vv. 1–4; see note on v. 4) and vv. 24–27. In vv. 5–16 (and following v. 27) kinship terms are used. Both segmented (those tracing several lines of descent) and linear (those tracing a single line) genealogies are included. This identical structure is found in a copy of the Assyrian King List: There is no introduction, and the scribe has drawn lines across the tablet dividing it into four sections, two of which are lists of names without kinship terms, alternating with two lists in which relations are specified; both segmented and linear genealogies are used. This suggests that the Chronicler was following a known literary pattern for his composition.
1:1–4 From creation to the flood. This list is taken from Ge 5:1–32 (see notes there). The omission of Cain and Abel demonstrates the Chronicler's interest in the chosen line (see Ge 4:17–25).
1:4 *The sons of Noah.* The phrase is not found in the Hebrew text (see NIV text note); this omission parallels the Assyrian King List (see note on 1:1–2:1). The Chronicler's readers would have known that these were the sons of Noah and would not have needed the kinship notice; the Septuagint (the Greek translation of the OT) and most modern translations insert the phrase to clarify the relationship.
1:5–23 This genealogy is drawn from the table of nations in Ge 10:2–29 (see notes there). The arrangement is primarily geographical and cultural rather than biological. Omitting the Philistines (v. 11) as a parenthesis, a total of 70 nations is achieved: Japheth, 14; Ham, 30; Shem, 26 (see note on Ge 10:2)—an example of a genealogy telescoped to attain multiples of 7 (see Introduction: Genealogies).

Almodad, Sheleph, Hazarmaveth, Jerah, [21]Hadoram, Uzal, Diklah, [22]Obal,[i] Abimael, Sheba, [23]Ophir, Havilah and Jobab. All these were sons of Joktan.

[24]Shem,[k] Arphaxad,[j] Shelah,
[25]Eber, Peleg, Reu,
[26]Serug, Nahor, Terah
[27]and Abram (that is, Abraham).

The Family of Abraham

[28]The sons of Abraham:
Isaac and Ishmael.

Descendants of Hagar

1:29–31pp — Ge 25:12–16

[29]These were their descendants:
Nebaioth the firstborn of Ishmael, Kedar, Adbeel, Mibsam, [30]Mishma, Dumah, Massa, Hadad, Tema, [31]Jetur, Naphish and Kedemah. These were the sons of Ishmael.

Descendants of Keturah

1:32–33pp — Ge 25:1–4

[32]The sons born to Keturah, Abraham's concubine:[l]
Zimran, Jokshan, Medan, Midian, Ishbak and Shuah.
The sons of Jokshan:
Sheba and Dedan.[m]
[33]The sons of Midian:
Ephah, Epher, Hanoch, Abida and Eldaah.
All these were descendants of Keturah.

Descendants of Sarah

1:35–37pp — Ge 36:10–14

[34]Abraham[n] was the father of Isaac.[o]
The sons of Isaac:
Esau and Israel.[p]

Esau's Sons

[35]The sons of Esau:[q]
Eliphaz, Reuel,[r] Jeush, Jalam and Korah.

[36]The sons of Eliphaz:
Teman, Omar, Zepho,[k] Gatam and Kenaz;
by Timna: Amalek.[l] [s]
[37]The sons of Reuel:[t]
Nahath, Zerah, Shammah and Mizzah.

The People of Seir in Edom

1:38–42pp — Ge 36:20–28

[38]The sons of Seir:
Lotan, Shobal, Zibeon, Anah, Dishon, Ezer and Dishan.
[39]The sons of Lotan:
Hori and Homam. Timna was Lotan's sister.
[40]The sons of Shobal:
Alvan,[m] Manahath, Ebal, Shepho and Onam.
The sons of Zibeon:
Aiah and Anah.[u]
[41]The son of Anah:
Dishon.
The sons of Dishon:
Hemdan,[n] Eshban, Ithran and Keran.
[42]The sons of Ezer:
Bilhan, Zaavan and Akan.[o]
The sons of Dishan[p]:
Uz and Aran.

The Rulers of Edom

1:43–54pp — Ge 36:31–43

[43]These were the kings who reigned in

Cross references (center column)

1:24 [k]S Ge 10:21-25; Lk 3:34-36
1:32 [l]S Ge 22:24
[m]S Ge 10:7
1:34 [n]Lk 3:34
[o]Mt 1:2; Ac 7:8
[p]S Ge 17:5
1:35 [q]Ge 36:19
[r]S Ge 36:4

1:36 [s]S Ex 17:14
1:37 [t]Ge 36:17
1:40 [u]S Ge 36:2

Text notes

[i]22 Some Hebrew manuscripts and Syriac (see also Gen. 10:28); most Hebrew manuscripts *Ebal* [j]24 Hebrew; some Septuagint manuscripts *Arphaxad, Cainan* (see also note at Gen. 11:10) [k]36 Many Hebrew manuscripts, some Septuagint manuscripts and Syriac (see also Gen. 36:11); most Hebrew manuscripts *Zephi* [l]36 Some Septuagint manuscripts (see also Gen. 36:12); Hebrew *Gatam, Kenaz, Timna and Amalek* [m]40 Many Hebrew manuscripts and some Septuagint manuscripts (see also Gen. 36:23); most Hebrew manuscripts *Alian* [n]41 Many Hebrew manuscripts and some Septuagint manuscripts (see also Gen. 36:26); most Hebrew manuscripts *Hamran* [o]42 Many Hebrew and Septuagint manuscripts (see also Gen. 36:27); most Hebrew manuscripts *Zaavan, Jaakan* [p]42 Hebrew *Dishon,* a variant of *Dishan*

1:24–27 See notes on 1:1–2:1; Ge 11:10–26.
1:28–34 See notes on Ge 25:1–18.
1:35–42 See Ge 36:10–28 and notes.
1:36 *sons of Eliphaz.* These correspond to Ge 36:11–12, but with one difficulty: The Hebrew text of Chronicles (see second NIV text note on this verse) lists Timna as a son of Eliphaz, while Ge 36:12 designates Timna as the concubine of Eliphaz and mother of Amalek. The NIV follows the Septuagint, which regarded Timna as the mother of Amalek, not as the son of Eliphaz. This solution says that the Hebrew text is here in error, or perhaps that the Chronicler has once again omitted kinship terminology (see notes on 1:1–2:1;

v. 4). Alternatively, some regard this as an example of genealogical fluidity (see Introduction: Genealogies): Since the name Timna also became the name of a chiefdom in Edom (v. 51; Ge 36:40), during the course of time Timna was "promoted" in the Edomite genealogies to the position of a son of Eliphaz and brother of Amalek.
1:43–54 See Ge 36:31–43. The Chronicler continues with extensive coverage of Edom. This is striking in contrast to his omission of the line of Cain and the brief treatment of the line of Ishmael. It probably reflects the fact that the Edomites were important in the Chronicler's own day (see 18:11–13; 2Ch 8:17; 21:8; 25:20; 28:17).

Edom before any Israelite king reigned[q]:

Bela son of Beor, whose city was named Dinhabah.
[44]When Bela died, Jobab son of Zerah from Bozrah succeeded him as king.
[45]When Jobab died, Husham from the land of the Temanites[y] succeeded him as king.
[46]When Husham died, Hadad son of Bedad, who defeated Midian in the country of Moab, succeeded him as king. His city was named Avith.
[47]When Hadad died, Samlah from Masrekah succeeded him as king.
[48]When Samlah died, Shaul from Rehoboth on the river[r] succeeded him as king.
[49]When Shaul died, Baal-Hanan son of Acbor succeeded him as king.
[50]When Baal-Hanan died, Hadad succeeded him as king. His city was named Pau,[s] and his wife's name was Mehetabel daughter of Matred, the daughter of Me-Zahab.
[51]Hadad also died.

The chiefs of Edom were:

Timna, Alvah, Jetheth, [52]Oholibamah, Elah, Pinon, [53]Kenaz, Teman, Mibzar, [54]Magdiel and Iram. These were the chiefs of Edom.

Israel's Sons

2:1–2pp — Ge 35:23–26

2 These were the sons of Israel: Reuben, Simeon, Levi, Judah, Issachar, Zebulun, [2]Dan, Joseph, Benjamin, Naphtali, Gad and Asher.

Judah

2:5–15pp — Ru 4:18–22; Mt 1:3–6

To Hezron's Sons

[3]The sons of Judah:[w]

Er, Onan and Shelah.[x] These three were born to him by a Canaanite woman, the daughter of Shua.[y] Er, Judah's firstborn, was wicked in the LORD's sight; so the LORD put him to death.[z] [4]Tamar,[a] Judah's daughter-in-law,[b] bore him Perez[c] and Zerah. Judah had five sons in all.

[5]The sons of Perez:[d]

Hezron[e] and Hamul.
[6]The sons of Zerah:

Zimri, Ethan, Heman, Calcol and Darda[t]—five in all.
[7]The son of Carmi:

Achar,[u][f] who brought trouble on Israel by violating the ban on taking devoted things.[v][g]
[8]The son of Ethan:

Azariah.
[9]The sons born to Hezron[h] were:

Jerahmeel, Ram and Caleb.[w]

From Ram Son of Hezron

[10]Ram[i] was the father of Amminadab,[j] and Amminadab

Cross-references: 1:45 /S Ge 36:11 | 2:3 wS Ge 29:35; 38:2-10 xS Ge 38:5 yS Ge 38:2 zS Nu 26:19 | 2:4 aGe 38:11-30 bS Ge 11:31 cS Ge 38:29 | 2:5 dS Ge 46:12 eNu 26:21 | 2:7 fS Jos 7:1 gS Jos 6:18 | 2:9 hS Nu 26:21 | 2:10 iLk 3:32-33 jS Ex 6:23

[q]43 Or *before an Israelite king reigned over them*   [r]48 Possibly the Euphrates   [s]50 Many Hebrew manuscripts, Vulgate and Syriac (see also Gen. 36:39); most Hebrew manuscripts *Pai*   [t]6 Many Hebrew manuscripts, some Septuagint manuscripts and Syriac (see also 1 Kings 4:31); most Hebrew manuscripts *Dara*   [u]7 *Achar* means *trouble*; *Achar* is called *Achan* in Joshua.   [v]7 The Hebrew term refers to the irrevocable giving over of things or persons to the LORD, often by totally destroying them.   [w]9 Hebrew *Kelubai,* a variant of *Caleb*

2:1–2 Although there are numerous lists of the 12 tribes in the OT, only four are given in genealogical form: (1) Ge 29:31–30:24; 35:16–20; (2) Ge 35:22–26; (3) Ge 46:8–27; (4) here. Other lists of the tribes are found in 12:24–37; 27:16–22; Ex 1:2–5; Dt 27:12–13; 33; Eze 48:31–34. In other lists the tribe of Levi is omitted, and the number 12 is achieved by dividing Joseph into the tribes of Ephraim and Manasseh (Nu 1:5–15; 1:20–43; 2:3–31; 7:12–83; 10:14–28; 13:4–15; 26:5–51). In this passage the Chronicler appears to follow Ge 35:22–26 except for the position of the tribe of Dan, which is found in seventh instead of ninth place. The list here does not set the order in which the Chronicler will take up the tribes; rather, he moves immediately to his major concern with the house of David and the tribe of Judah (2:3–4:23), even though Judah is fourth in the genealogy. In the lists of these chapters the Chronicler maintains the number 12, but with the following names: Judah, Simeon, Reuben, Gad, half of Manasseh, Levi, Issachar, Benjamin, Naphtali, Ephraim, Manasseh and Asher. Zebulun and Dan are omitted.
2:3–9 The lineage of Judah is traced to Hezron's sons (v. 9), whose descendants are given in 2:10–3:24. Of Judah's

five sons, the first two (Er and Onan) died as the result of sin recorded in Ge 38. The lineage of the third son, Shelah, is taken up in 4:21; this section focuses on the remaining two (see Ge 46:12; Nu 26:19–22).
2:6 *Ethan, Heman, Calcol and Darda.* Not immediate descendants of Zerah; rather, they are from the later period of the reign of Solomon (1Ki 4:31). A Heman and an Ethan were David's musicians (see 15:19; Ps 88–89 titles), but whether these are the same individuals is uncertain. If they are the same, the fact that in 6:33–42 and 15:19 Heman and Ethan are assigned to the tribe of Levi may be another example of genealogical fluidity, where these men's musical skills brought them into the Levitical lineage. Or the reverse may have occurred: As Levites associated with Judah, they were brought into that lineage.
2:7 *Achar.* The change from Achan to Achar (meaning "trouble"; see NIV text note) is probably a play on words reflecting the trouble he brought to Israel (Jos 7).
2:10–3:24 That the Chronicler's primary concern in the genealogy of Judah is with the line of David is seen in his arrangement of this section's material as an inversion:
Descendants of Ram (David's ancestry), 2:10–17

the father of Nahshon,[k] the leader of the people of Judah. [11]Nahshon was the father of Salmon,[x] Salmon the father of Boaz, [12]Boaz[l] the father of Obed and Obed the father of Jesse.[m]

[13]Jesse[n] was the father of Eliab[o] his firstborn; the second son was Abinadab, the third Shimea, [14]the fourth Nethanel, the fifth Raddai, [15]the sixth Ozem and the seventh David. [16]Their sisters were Zeruiah[p] and Abigail. Zeruiah's[q] three sons were Abishai, Joab[r] and Asahel. [17]Abigail was the mother of Amasa,[s] whose father was Jether the Ishmaelite.

Caleb Son of Hezron

[18]Caleb son of Hezron had children by his wife Azubah (and by Jerioth). These were her sons: Jesher, Shobab and Ardon. [19]When Azubah died, Caleb[t] married Ephrath, who bore him Hur. [20]Hur was the father of Uri, and Uri the father of Bezalel.[u]

[21]Later, Hezron lay with the daughter of Makir the father of Gilead[v] (he had married her when he was sixty years old), and she bore him Segub. [22]Segub was the father of Jair, who controlled twenty-three towns in Gilead. [23](But Geshur and Aram captured Havvoth Jair,[v][w] as well as Kenath[x] with its surrounding settlements—sixty towns.) All these were descendants of Makir the father of Gilead.

[24]After Hezron died in Caleb Ephrathah, Abijah the wife of Hezron

bore him Ashhur[y] the father[z] of Tekoa.

Jerahmeel Son of Hezron

[25]The sons of Jerahmeel the firstborn of Hezron:
Ram his firstborn, Bunah, Oren, Ozem and[a] Ahijah. [26]Jerahmeel had another wife, whose name was Atarah; she was the mother of Onam.

[27]The sons of Ram the firstborn of Jerahmeel:
Maaz, Jamin and Eker.
[28]The sons of Onam:
Shammai and Jada.
The sons of Shammai:
Nadab and Abishur.
[29]Abishur's wife was named Abihail, who bore him Ahban and Molid.
[30]The sons of Nadab:
Seled and Appaim. Seled died without children.
[31]The son of Appaim:
Ishi, who was the father of Sheshan.
Sheshan was the father of Ahlai.
[32]The sons of Jada, Shammai's brother:
Jether and Jonathan. Jether died without children.
[33]The sons of Jonathan:
Peleth and Zaza.
These were the descendants of Jerahmeel.
[34]Sheshan had no sons—only daughters.
He had an Egyptian servant named

2:10 [k]S Nu 1:7
2:12 [l]S Ru 2:1
[m]S Ru 4:17
2:13 [n]S Ru 4:17
[o]1Sa 16:6
2:16 [p]1Sa 26:6
[q]2Sa 2:18
[r]S 2Sa 2:13
2:17 [s]2Sa 17:25
2:19 [t]ver 42,50
2:20 [u]S Ex 31:2
2:21 [v]S Nu 27:1
2:23
[w]S Nu 32:41;
Dt 3:14
[x]Nu 32:42

2:24 [y]1Ch 4:5

---

[x]11 Septuagint (see also Ruth 4:21); Hebrew *Salma*
[y]23 Or *captured the settlements of Jair*   [z]24 *Father* may mean *civic leader* or *military leader*; also in verses 42, 45, 49-52 and possibly elsewhere.   [a]25 Or *Oren and Jonathan, by*

Descendants of Caleb, 2:18-24
Descendants of Jerahmeel, 2:25-33
Supplementary material on Jerahmeel, 2:34-41
Supplementary material on Caleb, 2:42-55
Supplementary material on Ram (David's descendants), ch. 3

The Chronicler has structured this central portion of the Judah genealogy to highlight the Davidic ancestry and descent, which frame this section and emphasize the position of David—in line with the Chronicler's interests in the historical portions that follow (see note on 4:1-23).
2:10-17 Verses 10-12 are a linear genealogy from Ram to Jesse; then Jesse's lineage is segmented, reminiscent of 1Sa 16:1-13. The source for most of the material is Ru 4:19-22. In 1Sa 16:10-13 David was the eighth of Jesse's sons to appear before Samuel; in this passage only seven are named, enabling David to occupy the favored place of the seventh son (v. 15; see Introduction: Genealogies). David was the half-uncle of his famous warriors Abishai, Joab, Asahel and Amasa (11:6,20,26; 2Sa 2:13,18; 17:25; 19:13).
2:18-24 For the Chronicler the important name in this

genealogy of the Calebites is Bezalel (v. 20), the wise master craftsman who supervised the building of the tabernacle (Ex 31:1-5). He is mentioned in the Bible only in Exodus and Chronicles. The Chronicler uses Bezalel and Oholiab (Ex 31:6) as a model for his portrait of Solomon and Huram-Abi in the building of the temple (see note on 2Ch 1:5). By inserting a reference to the builder of the tabernacle next to the genealogy of David in vv. 10-17, the Chronicler characteristically juxtaposes the themes of king and temple—so important to his historical narrative.
2:25-33 This section is identified as a separate entity from the supplementary material by its opening and closing formulas: "The sons of Jerahmeel" (v. 25) and "These were the descendants of Jerahmeel" (v. 33). Verses 25-41 are the only genealogical materials on the Jerahmeelites in the Bible. 1Sa 27:10 and 30:27-29 place their settlements in the Negev.
2:34-41 Supplementary material on the line of Sheshan (v. 31); it is a linear genealogy to a depth of 13 generations. The generation of Elishama (v. 41) would be the 23rd since Judah, if there has been no telescoping in this lineage. If no

Jarha. [35]Sheshan gave his daughter in marriage to his servant Jarha, and she bore him Attai.

[36]Attai was the father of Nathan, Nathan the father of Zabad,[z]

[37]Zabad the father of Ephlal, Ephlal the father of Obed,

[38]Obed the father of Jehu, Jehu the father of Azariah,

[39]Azariah the father of Helez, Helez the father of Eleasah,

[40]Eleasah the father of Sismai, Sismai the father of Shallum,

[41]Shallum the father of Jekamiah, and Jekamiah the father of Elishama.

The Clans of Caleb

[42]The sons of Caleb[a] the brother of Jerahmeel:
Mesha his firstborn, who was the father of Ziph, and his son Mareshah,[b] who was the father of Hebron.

[43]The sons of Hebron:
Korah, Tappuah, Rekem and Shema. [44]Shema was the father of Raham, and Raham the father of Jorkeam. Rekem was the father of Shammai. [45]The son of Shammai was Maon,[b] and Maon was the father of Beth Zur.[c]

[46]Caleb's concubine Ephah was the mother of Haran, Moza and Gazez. Haran was the father of Gazez.

[47]The sons of Jahdai:
Regem, Jotham, Geshan, Pelet, Ephah and Shaaph.

[48]Caleb's concubine Maacah was the mother of Sheber and Tirhanah. [49]She also gave birth to Shaaph the father of Madmannah[d] and to

Sheva the father of Macbenah and Gibea. Caleb's daughter was Acsah.[e] [50]These were the descendants of Caleb.

The sons of Hur,[f] the firstborn of Ephrathah:
Shobal the father of Kiriath Jearim,[g] [51]Salma the father of Bethlehem, and Hareph the father of Beth Gader.

[52]The descendants of Shobal the father of Kiriath Jearim were:
Haroeh, half the Manahathites, [53]and the clans of Kiriath Jearim: the Ithrites,[h] Puthites, Shumathites and Mishraites. From these descended the Zorathites and Eshtaolites.

[54]The descendants of Salma:
Bethlehem, the Netophathites,[i] Atroth Beth Joab, half the Manahathites, the Zorites, [55]and the clans of scribes[c] who lived at Jabez: the Tirathites, Shimeathites and Sucathites. These are the Kenites[j] who came from Hammath,[k] the father of the house of Recab.[d][l]

The Sons of David

3:1–4pp — 2Sa 3:2–5
3:5–8pp — 2Sa 5:14–16; 1Ch 14:4–7

3 These were the sons of David[m] born to him in Hebron:
The firstborn was Amnon the son of Ahinoam[n] of Jezreel;[o] the second, Daniel the son of Abigail[p] of Carmel;

[2]the third, Absalom the son of Maacah daughter of Talmai king of Geshur;

Cross references

2:36 z1Ch 11:41
2:42 aS ver 19
2:45 bS Jos 15:55
cS Jos 15:58
2:49 dJos 15:31

eJos 15:16
2:50 f1Ch 4:4
gS ver 19
2:53 h2Sa 23:38
2:54 iEzr 2:22;
Ne 7:26; 12:28
2:55 jS Ge 15:19;
S Jdg 4:11
kJos 19:35
l2Ki 10:15,23;
Jer 35:2-19
3:1 m1Ch 14:3;
28:5
nS 1Sa 25:43
oS Jos 15:56
pS 1Sa 25:42

b42 The meaning of the Hebrew for this phrase is uncertain.   c55 Or of the Sopherites   d55 Or father of Beth Recab

---

names are omitted, Elishama would likely be contemporary with David, though we know nothing of him.

2:42–55 The same opening and closing formulas noted in vv. 25,33 occur in vv. 42,50a: "The sons of Caleb . . . These were the descendants of Caleb." The list in this section is a mixture of personal and place-names; the phrase "father of" must often be understood as "founder of" or "leader of" a city (see NIV text notes on 1:10; 4:4).

2:50b–55 Resumes the genealogy of Hur (v. 20). The same formulas for identifying the genealogical sections in vv. 25, 33 and in vv. 42,50a are used in v. 50b and 4:4: "The sons of Hur . . . These were the descendants of Hur." The presence of these formulas suggests that this section and 4:1–4 were once a unit; the Chronicler has inserted his record of the Davidic descent (ch. 3) into the middle of this other genealogy, apparently to balance the sections of his material (see notes on 2:10–3:24; 4:1–23). Otherwise the disruption of the genealogy of Hur may have already occurred in the Chronicler's sources.

2:55 *Tirathites, Shimeathites and Sucathites.* May refer to three families, as translated here, or possibly to three different classes of scribes, perhaps those who (1) read, (2) copied and (3) checked the work. *Kenites.* Originally a foreign people, many of the Kenites were incorporated into Judah (see Nu 10:29–32; Jdg 1:16; 4:11).

3:1–24 See note on 2:10–3:24.

3:1–9 This list of David's children is largely drawn from 2Sa 3:2–5; 5:13–16; 13:1 (see notes there). The sons born in Jerusalem are repeated in 1Ch 14:3–7. The name Eliphelet occurs twice (vv. 6,8); in 14:5,7 two spellings of the name are given (only one son having this name is mentioned in 2Sa 5:14–16). The reference to David's seven-year rule in Hebron (v. 4) is repeated in 29:27, though the Chronicler does not deal with this period in his narrative. The references to Absalom, Tamar, Adonijah, Amnon and Bathsheba all recall unhappy incidents in the life of David, incidents the Chronicler has omitted from his later narrative (see 2Sa 11–15; 17–18; 1Ki 1).

the fourth, Adonijah q the son of Haggith;

3 the fifth, Shephatiah the son of Abital;

and the sixth, Ithream, by his wife Eglah.

4 These six were born to David in Hebron, r where he reigned seven years and six months. s David reigned in Jerusalem thirty-three years, 5 and these were the children born to him there:

Shammua, e Shobab, Nathan and Solomon. These four were by Bathsheba ft daughter of Ammiel. 6 There were also Ibhar, Elishua, g Eliphelet, 7 Nogah, Nepheg, Japhia, 8 Elishama, Eliada and Eliphelet—nine in all. 9 All these were the sons of David, besides his sons by his concubines. And Tamar u was their sister. v

The Kings of Judah

10 Solomon's son was Rehoboam, w

Abijah x his son,

Asa y his son,

Jehoshaphat z his son,

11 Jehoram ha his son,

Ahaziah b his son,

Joash c his son,

12 Amaziah d his son,

Azariah e his son,

Jotham f his son,

13 Ahaz g his son,

Hezekiah h his son,

Manasseh i his son,

14 Amon j his son,

Josiah k his son.

15 The sons of Josiah:

Johanan the firstborn,

Jehoiakim l the second son,

Zedekiah m the third,

Shallum n the fourth.

16 The successors of Jehoiakim:

Jehoiachin io his son,

and Zedekiah. p

The Royal Line After the Exile

17 The descendants of Jehoiachin the captive:

Shealtiel q his son, 18 Malkiram, Pedaiah, Shenazzar, r Jekamiah, Hoshama and Nedabiah. s

19 The sons of Pedaiah:

Zerubbabel t and Shimei.

The sons of Zerubbabel:

Meshullam and Hananiah. Shelomith was their sister.

20 There were also five others: Hashubah, Ohel, Berekiah, Hasadiah and Jushab-Hesed.

21 The descendants of Hananiah:

Cross references (center column):

3:2 q1Ki 2:22
3:4 rS 2Sa 5:4; 1Ch 29:27
sS 2Sa 5:5
3:5 t2Sa 11:3
3:9 uS 2Sa 13:1
v1Ch 14:4
3:10 w1Ki 14:21-31; 2Ch 12:16
x1Ki 15:1-8; 2Ch 13:1
y1Ki 15:9-24
z2Ch 17:1-21:3
3:11 a2Ki 8:16-24; 2Ch 21:1
b2Ki 8:25-10:14; 2Ch 22:1-10
c2Ki 11:1-12:21; 2Ch 22:11-24:27
3:12 d2Ki 14:1-22; 2Ch 25:1-28
e2Ki 15:1-7; 2Ch 26:1-23
f2Ki 15:32-38; 2Ch 27:1; Isa 1:1; Hos 1:1; Mic 1:1
3:13 g2Ki 16:1-20; 2Ch 28:1; Isa 7:1
h2Ki 18:1-20:21; 2Ch 29:1; Isa 1:1; Jer 26:19; Hos 1:1; Mic 1:1
i2Ki 21:1-18; 2Ch 33:1
3:14 j2Ki 21:19-26; 2Ch 33:21; Zep 1:1
k2Ki 22:1; 2Ch 34:1; Jer 1:2; 3:6; 25:3
3:15 lS 2Ki 23:34
mJer 37:1
nS 2Ki 23:31
3:16 oS 2Ki 24:6, 8
pS 2Ki 24:18
3:17 qEzr 3:2
3:18 rEzr 1:8; 5:14
sJer 22:30
3:19 tEzr 2:2; 3:2; 5:2; Ne 7:7; 12:1; Hag 1:1; 2:2; Zec 4:6

e5 Hebrew *Shimea*, a variant of *Shammua* f5 One Hebrew manuscript and Vulgate (see also Septuagint and 2 Samuel 11:3); most Hebrew manuscripts *Bathshua* g6 Two Hebrew manuscripts (see also 2 Samuel 5:15 and 1 Chron. 14:5); most Hebrew manuscripts *Elishama* h11 Hebrew *Joram*, a variant of *Jehoram* i16 Hebrew *Jeconiah*, a variant of *Jehoiachin*; also in verse 17

3:10 *Rehoboam.* See 2Ch 10–12. *Abijah.* See 2Ch 13:1–14:1. *Asa.* See 2Ch 14–16. *Jehoshaphat.* See 1Ki 22. **3:11** *Jehoram.* See 2Ch 21. **3:13** *Ahaz.* See 2Ch 28. *Hezekiah.* See 2Ch 29–32. *Manasseh.* See 2Ch 33:1–20. **3:14** *Amon.* See 2Ch 33:21–25. *Josiah.* See 2Ki 22:1–23:30; 2Ch 34:1–36:1.

3:15–16 "Johanan the firstborn" is not mentioned elsewhere and may have died before Josiah. The genealogy is segmented at this point, instead of linear as in vv. 10–14. Since Josiah's other three sons would all occupy the throne, the succession was not uniformly father to son. Shallum/Jehoahaz (2Ch 36:2–4; 2Ki 23:30–35) was replaced by Jehoiakim (2Ch 36:5–8; 2Ki 23:34–24:6); Jehoiakim was succeeded by his son Jehoiachin (2Ch 36:9–10; 2Ki 24:8–16). After Jehoiachin was taken captive to Babylon by Nebuchadnezzar, Josiah's third son Zedekiah (2Ki 24:18–20; 2Ch 36:11–14) became the last king of Judah. **3:17–20** Seven sons are attributed to Jehoiachin, but not one succeeded him (see notes on vv. 15–16; Jer 22:30). Tablets found in Babylon dating from the 10th to the 35th year of Nebuchadnezzar (595–570 B.C.) and listing deliveries of rations mention Jehoiachin and five sons as well as other Judahites held in Babylon. Jehoiachin received similar largess from Nebuchadnezzar's successor Evil-Merodach (562–560 B.C.; see 2Ki 25:27–30). **3:18** *Shenazzar.* May be another spelling of the name Sheshbazzar. If so, the treasures of the temple were con-

signed to his care for return to Judah (Ezr 1:11). He also served for a short time as the first governor of the returnees and made an initial attempt at rebuilding the temple (Ezr 5:14–16). Little is known of him; he soon disappeared from the scene and was overshadowed by his nephew Zerubbabel, who assumes such importance in Ezra, Haggai and Zechariah. But see note on Ezr 1:8.

3:19 *Pedaiah.* Other texts name Shealtiel (v. 17) as Zerubbabel's father (Ezr 3:2,8; Ne 12:1; Hag 1:12,14; 2:2,23). Suggestions offered to resolve this difficulty are: 1. Shealtiel may have died early, and Pedaiah became the head of the family. 2. Pedaiah may have married the childless widow of Shealtiel. 2. Zerubbabel would then be regarded as the son of Shealtiel according to the law of levirate marriage (Dt 25:5–6). In Lk 3:27 Neri instead of Jehoiachin (v. 17) is identified as the father of Shealtiel. Similar suggestions to those above could be made in this instance as well. It is also interesting to note that the genealogies of Jesus in Mt 1 and Lk 3 both trace his descent to Zerubbabel, but that none of the names subsequent to Zerubbabel (vv. 19–24) is found in the NT genealogies.

3:20 *five others.* May have been sons of Zerubbabel, but no kinship terms are provided. Since the sons of Hananiah (v. 19) are specified in v. 21, they could also be the sons of Meshullam (v. 19).

3:21 *sons of Rephaiah . . . Shecaniah.* Probably other Davidic families at the time of Zerubbabel (v. 19) or Pelatiah and Jeshaiah. If they are understood as contemporary with

Pelatiah and Jeshaiah, and the sons of Rephaiah, of Arnan, of Obadiah and of Shecaniah.

²²The descendants of Shecaniah:
Shemaiah and his sons:
Hattush,^u Igal, Bariah, Neariah and Shaphat—six in all.
²³The sons of Neariah:
Elioenai, Hizkiah and Azrikam—three in all.
²⁴The sons of Elioenai:
Hodaviah, Eliashib, Pelaiah, Akkub, Johanan, Delaiah and Anani—seven in all.

Other Clans of Judah

4 The descendants of Judah:^v
Perez, Hezron,^w Carmi, Hur and Shobal.

²Reaiah son of Shobal was the father of Jahath, and Jahath the father of Ahumai and Lahad. These were the clans of the Zorathites.

³These were the sons^j of Etam:
Jezreel, Ishma and Idbash. Their sister was named Hazzelelponi.
⁴Penuel was the father of Gedor, and Ezer the father of Hushah.

These were the descendants of Hur,^x the firstborn of Ephrathah and father^k of Bethlehem.^y

⁵Ashhur^z the father of Tekoa had two wives, Helah and Naarah.

⁶Naarah bore him Ahuzzam, Hepher, Temeni and Haahashtari. These were the sons of Naarah.
⁷The sons of Helah:
Zereth, Zohar, Ethnan, ⁸and Koz, who was the father of Anub and

3:22 ^uEzr 8:2-3
4:1 ^vS Ge 29:35;
S 1Ch 2:3
^wNu 26:21
4:4 ^x1Ch 2:50
^yRu 1:19
4:5 ^z1Ch 2:24

4:13 ^aS Jos 15:17

Hazzobebah and of the clans of Aharhel son of Harum.

⁹Jabez was more honorable than his brothers. His mother had named him Jabez,^l saying, "I gave birth to him in pain." ¹⁰Jabez cried out to the God of Israel, "Oh, that you would bless me and enlarge my territory! Let your hand be with me, and keep me from harm so that I will be free from pain." And God granted his request.

¹¹Kelub, Shuhah's brother, was the father of Mehir, who was the father of Eshton. ¹²Eshton was the father of Beth Rapha, Paseah and Tehinnah the father of Ir Nahash.^m These were the men of Recah.

¹³The sons of Kenaz:
Othniel^a and Seraiah.
The sons of Othniel:
Hathath and Meonothai.ⁿ
¹⁴Meonothai was the father of Ophrah.
Seraiah was the father of Joab,
the father of Ge Harashim.^o It was called this because its people were craftsmen.

¹⁵The sons of Caleb son of Jephunneh:
Iru, Elah and Naam.
The son of Elah:
Kenaz.
¹⁶The sons of Jehallelel:

j3 Some Septuagint manuscripts (see also Vulgate); Hebrew father   k4 Father may mean civic leader or military leader; also in verses 12, 14, 17, 18 and possibly elsewhere.   l9 Jabez sounds like the Hebrew for pain.   m12 Or of the city of Nahash   n13 Some Septuagint manuscripts and Vulgate; Hebrew does not have and Meonothai.   o14 Ge Harashim means valley of craftsmen.

Zerubbabel, his genealogy was carried only two generations (his sons and grandsons) and a date for Chronicles as early as 450 B.C. is possible (see Introduction: Author, Date and Sources).

3:22 *six.* Shemaiah appears to have five sons, but the total is given as six. Either one of the six names is missing, or Shemaiah is to be understood as the brother of the five persons named (in which case there should be a semicolon after "sons" instead of a colon)—all six then being sons of Shecaniah.

4:1–23 None of the genealogies of Judah in this section appears elsewhere in Scripture. Although the section may have the appearance of miscellaneous notes, the careful shaping of the Chronicler is evident in light of the overall inverted structure of the genealogies of Judah:

2:3	Shelah
2:4-8	Perez
2:9-3:24	Hezron
4:1-20	Perez
4:21-23	Shelah

This balancing of the material in inverse order shows the centrality of the section of the lineage of Hezron and the house of David; the same balancing in inverse order is

observed within the Hezron section (see note on 2:10–3:24). The record of Judah's oldest surviving son, Shelah, frames the entire genealogy of Judah. There are 15 fragmentary genealogies in this section, with two to six generations in each.

4:1–2 The descendants of Judah here are not brothers; rather, the genealogy is linear.

4:1 *Carmi.* Either a scribal confusion or an alternative name for Caleb (2:9); the confusion may have been induced by 2:7.

4:2 *Reaiah.* A variant of Haroeh (2:52).

4:5–8 Supplementary to 2:24.

4:9–10 The practice of inserting short historical notes into genealogical records is amply attested in non-Biblical genealogical texts from the ancient Near East as well as in other Biblical genealogies (Ge 4:19–24; 10:8–12).

4:13 *Othniel.* The first of Israel's judges (Jos 15:17; Jdg 1:13; 3:9–11).

4:16–20 This portion of the genealogy is from preexilic times; several of the places named were not included in the province of Judah in the restoration period (e.g., Ziph and Eshtemoa).

Ziph, Ziphah, Tiria and Asarel.
[17]The sons of Ezrah:

Jether, Mered, Epher and Jalon. One of Mered's wives gave birth to Miriam,[b] Shammai and Ishbah the father of Eshtemoa. [18](His Judean wife gave birth to Jered the father of Gedor, Heber the father of Soco, and Jekuthiel the father of Zanoah.[c]) These were the children of Pharaoh's daughter Bithiah, whom Mered had married.

[19]The sons of Hodiah's wife, the sister of Naham:

the father of Keilah[d] the Garmite, and Eshtemoa the Maacathite.[e]

[20]The sons of Shimon:

Amnon, Rinnah, Ben-Hanan and Tilon.

The descendants of Ishi:
Zoheth and Ben-Zoheth.

[21]The sons of Shelah[f] son of Judah:

Er the father of Lecah, Laadah the father of Mareshah and the clans of the linen workers at Beth Ashbea, [22]Jokim, the men of Cozeba, and Joash and Saraph, who ruled in Moab and Jashubi Lehem. (These records are from ancient times.) [23]They were the potters who lived at Netaim and Gederah; they stayed there and worked for the king.

Simeon

4:28–33pp — Jos 19:2–10

[24]The descendants of Simeon:[g]

Nemuel, Jamin, Jarib,[h] Zerah and Shaul;

[25]Shallum was Shaul's son, Mibsam his son and Mishma his son.

[26]The descendants of Mishma:

Hammuel his son, Zaccur his son and Shimei his son.

[27]Shimei had sixteen sons and six daughters, but his brothers did not have many children; so their entire clan did not

become as numerous as the people of Judah. [28]They lived in Beersheba,[i] Moladah,[j] Hazar Shual, [29]Bilhah, Ezem,[k] Tolad, [30]Bethuel, Hormah,[l] Ziklag,[m] [31]Beth Marcaboth, Hazar Susim, Beth Biri and Shaaraim.[n] These were their towns until the reign of David. [32]Their surrounding villages were Etam, Ain,[o] Rimmon, Token and Ashan[p]—five towns— [33]and all the villages around these towns as far as Baalath.[p] These were their settlements. And they kept a genealogical record.

[34]Meshobab, Jamlech, Joshah son of Amaziah, [35]Joel, Jehu son of Joshibiah, the son of Seraiah, the son of Asiel, [36]also Elioenai, Jaakobah, Jeshohaiah, Asaiah, Adiel, Jesimiel, Benaiah, [37]and Ziza son of Shiphi, the son of Allon, the son of Jedaiah, the son of Shimri, the son of Shemaiah.

[38]The men listed above by name were leaders of their clans. Their families increased greatly, [39]and they went to the outskirts of Gedor[q] to the east of the valley in search of pasture for their flocks. [40]They found rich, good pasture, and the land was spacious, peaceful and quiet.[r] Some Hamites had lived there formerly.

[41]The men whose names were listed came in the days of Hezekiah king of Judah. They attacked the Hamites in their dwellings and also the Meunites[s] who were there and completely destroyed[q] them, as is evident to this day. Then they settled in their place, because there was pasture for their flocks. [42]And five hundred of these Simeonites, led by Pelatiah, Neariah, Rephaiah and Uzziel, the sons of Ishi, invaded the hill country of Seir.[t] [43]They killed the remaining Amalekites[u] who had escaped, and they have lived there to this day.

Cross references

4:17 [b]S Ex 15:20
4:18 [c]S Jos 15:34
4:19 [d]S Jos 15:44
[e]S Dt 3:14
4:21 [f]S Ge 38:5
4:24 [g]S Ge 29:33
[h]Nu 26:12

4:28 [i]S Ge 21:14
[j]S Jos 15:26
4:29 [k]S Jos 15:29
4:30 [l]S Nu 14:45
[m]S Jos 15:31
4:31 [n]S Jos 15:36
4:32 [o]S Nu 34:11
[p]S Jos 15:42
4:39 [q]S Jos 15:58
4:40 [r]Jdg 18:7-10
4:41 [s]2Ch 20:1; 26:7
4:42 [t]S Ge 14:6
4:43 [u]S Ge 14:7; Est 3:1; 9:16

p.33 Some Septuagint manuscripts (see also Joshua 19:8); Hebrew *Baal*   q.41 The Hebrew term refers to the irrevocable giving over of things or persons to the LORD, often by totally destroying them.

4:17 *One of Mered's wives.* Pharaoh's daughter (v. 18). Mered is otherwise unknown; the fact that he married a daughter of Pharaoh suggests his prominence. The event may be associated with the fortunes of Israel in Egypt under Joseph.

4:21,23 This section accurately reflects a feature of ancient Near Eastern society. Clans were often associated not only with particular localities but also with special trades or guilds, such as linen workers (v. 21), potters (v. 23), royal patronage (v. 23) and scribes (2:55).

4:24–43 The genealogy of Simeon is also found in Ge 46:10; Ex 6:15; Nu 26:12–13. Simeon settled in part of the territory of Judah; the list of occupied towns should be compared with Jos 15:26–32,42; 19:2–7. Since Simeon

occupied areas allotted to Judah, this tribe was politically incorporated into Judah and appears to have lost much of its own identity in history (see Ge 34:24–31; 49:5–7; see also notes on Ge 34:25; 49:7). Geographical and historical notes are inserted in the genealogy (see note on vv. 9–10). Apparently two genealogies are included here: vv. 24–33— ending with the formula, "they kept a genealogical record"—and vv. 34–43. Overpopulation (v. 38) caused them to expand toward Gedor and east toward Edom at the time of Hezekiah (vv. 39–43). The long hostility between Israel and Amalek surfaced once again (v. 43; cf. Ex 17:8–16; Dt 25:17–19; 1Sa 15; see Introduction to Esther: Purpose and Theme).

Reuben

5 The sons of Reuben[v] the firstborn of Israel (he was the firstborn, but when he defiled his father's marriage bed,[w] his rights as firstborn were given to the sons of Joseph[x] son of Israel;[y] so he could not be listed in the genealogical record in accordance with his birthright,[z] [2]and though Judah[a] was the strongest of his brothers and a ruler[b] came from him, the rights of the firstborn[c] belonged to Joseph)— [3]the sons of Reuben[d] the firstborn of Israel:

Hanoch, Pallu,[e] Hezron[f] and Carmi.

[4]The descendants of Joel:

Shemaiah his son, Gog his son, Shimei his son, [5]Micah his son, Reaiah his son, Baal his son,

[6]and Beerah his son, whom Tiglath-Pileser[r][g] king of Assyria took into exile. Beerah was a leader of the Reubenites.

[7]Their relatives by clans,[h] listed according to their genealogical records:

Jeiel the chief, Zechariah, [8]and Bela son of Azaz, the son of Shema, the son of Joel. They settled in the area from Aroer[i] to Nebo[j] and Baal Meon.[k] [9]To the east they occupied the land up to the edge of the desert that extends to the Euphrates[l] River, because their livestock had increased in Gilead.[m]

[10]During Saul's reign they waged war against the Hagrites[n], who were defeated at their hands; they occupied the dwellings of the Hagrites throughout the entire region east of Gilead.

Gad

[11]The Gadites[o] lived next to them in Bashan, as far as Salecah: [p]

[12]Joel was the chief, Shapham the second, then Janai and Shaphat, in Bashan.

[13]Their relatives, by families, were:

Michael, Meshullam, Sheba, Jorai, Jacan, Zia and Eber—seven in all.

[14]These were the sons of Abihail son of Huri, the son of Jaroah, the son of Gilead, the son of Michael, the son of Jeshishai, the son of Jahdo, the son of Buz.

[15]Ahi son of Abdiel, the son of Guni, was head of their family.

[16]The Gadites lived in Gilead, in Bashan and its outlying villages, and on all the pasturelands of Sharon as far as they extended.

[17]All these were entered in the genealogical records during the reigns of Jotham[q] king of Judah and Jeroboam[r] king of Israel.

[18]The Reubenites, the Gadites and the half-tribe of Manasseh had 44,760 men ready for military service[s] —able-bodied men who could handle shield and sword, who could use a bow, and who were trained for battle. [19]They waged war against the Hagrites, Jetur,[t] Naphish and Nodab. [20]They were helped[u] in fighting them, and God handed the Hagrites and all their allies over to them, because they cried[v] out to him during the battle. He answered their prayers, because they trusted[w] in him. [21]They seized the live-

[r][6] Hebrew *Tilgath-Pilneser*, a variant of *Tiglath-Pileser*, also in verse 26

Cross references

5:1 [v]S Ge 29:32
[w]Ge 35:22; 49:4
[x]S Ge 48:16;
S 49:26 [y]Ge 48:5
[z]1Ch 26:10
5:2 [a]S Ge 49:10,
12 [b]S 1Sa 9:16;
S 12:12;
S 2Sa 6:21;
1Ch 11:2;
S 2Ch 7:18;
Mt 2:6
[c]S Ge 25:31
5:3 [d]S Ge 29:32;
46:9; Ex 6:14;
Nu 26:5-11
[e]S Nu 26:5
[f]S Nu 26:6
5:6 [g]ver 26;
S 2Ki 15:19;
16:10; 2Ch 28:20
5:7 [h]Jos 13:15-23
5:8 [i]S Nu 32:34;
Jdg 11:26
[j]S Nu 32:3
[k]S Jos 13:17
5:9 [l]S Ge 2:14
[m]S Nu 32:26
5:10 [n]ver 22;
1Ch 27:31

5:11
[o]S Ge 30:11;
S Nu 1:25;
S Jos 13:24-28
[p]S Dt 3:10
5:17
[q]S 2Ki 15:32
[r]S 2Ki 14:23
5:18 [s]S Nu 1:3
5:19 [t]Ge 25:15
5:20 [u]Ps 37:40;
46:5; 54:4
[v]1Ki 8:44;
2Ch 6:34; 13:14;
14:11; Ps 20:7-9;
22:5; 107:6
[w]Ps 26:1;
Isa 26:3; Da 6:23

5:1–26 The genealogical records of the Transjordan tribes: Reuben, Gad and half of Manasseh (see Nu 32:33–42). The Chronicler's concern with "all Israel" includes incorporating the genealogical records of these tribes that were no longer significant entities in Israel's life in the restoration period, having been swept away in the Assyrian conquests.
5:1–10 The necessity to explain why the birthright of the firstborn did not remain with Reuben (see Ge 35:22; 49:4 for Reuben's sin) interrupts the initial statement (v. 1), which is then repeated after the explanation (v. 3). The parenthetical material (vv. 1–2) shows the writer's partiality for Judah, even though Joseph received the double portion (Ephraim and Manasseh) of the firstborn. The Hebrew term translated "ruler" (v. 2) is used of David in 11:2; 17:7; 2Sa 5:2; 6:21; 7:8; cf. 1Ch 28:4. The use of military titles (vv. 6–7) and a battle account (v. 10) suggest that this genealogy may have functioned in military organization (see Introduction: Genealogies). The source for some of this material on Reuben is Nu 26:5–11. The Chronicler has omitted reference to Eliab and his three sons who perished in the rebellion of Korah (see Nu 26:8–10) and so were not relevant to his purpose.

5:6 *Tiglath-Pileser.* This Assyrian king (745–727 B.C.) attacked Israel (v. 26; 2Ki 15:29) and also imposed tribute on Ahaz of Judah (2Ch 28:19–20; 2Ki 16:7–10).
5:10 *Hagrites.* See vv. 19–22. Named among the enemies of Israel (Ps 83:6), this tribe is apparently associated with Hagar, the mother of Ishmael (Ge 16), but see note on Ps 83:6.

5:11–22 The materials in this list for the tribe of Gad have no parallels in the Bible. The other genealogies of Gad are organized around his seven sons (Ge 46:16; Nu 26:15–18); here four names are given, none found in the other lists. The Chronicler states (v. 17) that these records came from the period of Jotham of Judah (750–732 B.C.) and Jeroboam of Israel (793–753). The presence of military titles and narratives (vv. 12,18–22) suggests that this genealogy originated as part of a military census. The territory of Gad is delineated in Dt 3:12.
5:18–22 The first example of the Chronicler's theme of immediate retribution (see Introduction: Purpose and Themes). Success in warfare is attributed to their crying out to God (v. 20; cf. 2Ch 6:24–25,34–39; 12:7–12; 13:13–16; 14:9–15; 18:31; 20:1–30; 32:1–23).

stock of the Hagrites—fifty thousand camels, two hundred fifty thousand sheep and two thousand donkeys. They also took one hundred thousand people captive, 22and many others fell slain, because the battle x was God's. And they occupied the land until the exile. y

The Half-Tribe of Manasseh

23The people of the half-tribe of Manasseh z were numerous; they settled in the land from Bashan to Baal Hermon, that is, to Senir (Mount Hermon). a

24These were the heads of their families: Epher, Ishi, Eliel, Azriel, Jeremiah, Hodaviah and Jahdiel. They were brave warriors, famous men, and heads of their families. 25But they were unfaithful b to the God of their fathers and prostituted c themselves to the gods of the peoples of the land, whom God had destroyed before them. 26So the God of Israel stirred up the spirit d of Pul e king of Assyria (that is, Tiglath-Pileser f king of Assyria), who took the Reubenites, the Gadites and the half-tribe of Manasseh into exile. He took them to Halah, g Habor, Hara and the river of Gozan, where they are to this day.

Levi

6 The sons of Levi: h
Gershon, Kohath and Merari.
2The sons of Kohath:

Amram, Izhar, Hebron and Uzziel. i
3The children of Amram:
Aaron, Moses and Miriam. j
The sons of Aaron:
Nadab, Abihu, k Eleazar l and Ithamar. m
4Eleazar was the father of Phinehas, n
Phinehas the father of Abishua,
5Abishua the father of Bukki,
Bukki the father of Uzzi,
6Uzzi the father of Zerahiah,
Zerahiah the father of Meraioth,
7Meraioth the father of Amariah,
Amariah the father of Ahitub,
8Ahitub the father of Zadok, o
Zadok the father of Ahimaaz,
9Ahimaaz the father of Azariah,
Azariah the father of Johanan,
10Johanan the father of Azariah p (it was he who served as priest in the temple Solomon built in Jerusalem),
11Azariah the father of Amariah,
Amariah the father of Ahitub,
12Ahitub the father of Zadok,
Zadok the father of Shallum,
13Shallum the father of Hilkiah, q
Hilkiah the father of Azariah,
14Azariah the father of Seraiah, r
and Seraiah the father of Jehozadak.

5:22 xS Dt 20:4; 2Ch 32:8 yS ver 10; S 2Ki 15:29
5:23 z1Ch 7:14 aS Dt 3:8,9; SS 4:8
5:25 bDt 32:15-18; 1Ch 9:1; 10:13; 2Ch 12:2; 26:16; 28:19; 29:6; 30:7; 36:14 cS Ex 34:15; S Lev 18:3
5:26 dIsa 37:7 eS 2Ki 15:19 fS ver 6; S 2Ki 15:29 g2Ki 17:6
6:1 hS Ge 29:34; S Nu 3:17

6:2 iS Ex 6:18
6:3 jS Ex 15:20 kS Lev 10:1; S 10:1-20:2 lLev 10:6 mS Ex 6:23
6:4 nEzr 7:5
6:8 oS 2Sa 8:17; S 1Ch 12:28; S Ezr 7:2
6:10 pS 1Ki 4:2
6:13 q2Ki 22:1-20; 2Ch 34:9; 35:8
6:14 rS 2Ki 25:18; S Ezr 2:2

5:23–26 Manasseh is treated further in 7:14–19; the half-tribe that settled in Transjordan is dealt with here since it shared the same fate as Reuben and Gad, and possibly also so that the Chronicler could keep the total of 12 for his tribal genealogies (see note on 2:1–2). Again immediate retribution is apparent: Just as trust in God can bring victory (vv. 18–22), so also defeat comes to the unfaithful (vv. 25–26). The use of the retributive theme in these two accounts argues for the unity of the genealogies with the historical portions of Chronicles. The list of names given here is not properly a genealogy but a list of clans. Since they are described as brave warriors in connection with a battle report (vv. 24–26), this section too is likely derived from records of military conscription (see note on vv. 1–10; see also 2Ki 15:19,29; 17:6; 18:11).
5:26 *Pul.* Probably Tiglath-Pileser's throne name in Babylon (the Babylonians called him Pulu).
6:1–81 This chapter is devoted to a series of lists, all pertaining to the tribe of Levi. The first section (vv. 1–15) records the line of the high priests down to the exile; the clans of Levi follow (vv. 16–30). David's appointees as temple musicians came from the three clans of Levi: Gershon, Kohath and Merari (vv. 31–47). The generations between Aaron and Ahimaaz are given a separate listing (vv. 49–53), reinforcing the separate duties of priests and Levites (see note on Ex 32:26). The listing of the Levitical possessions among the tribes concludes the chapter (vv. 54–81).
6:1–3 A short segmented genealogy narrows the descendants of Levi to the lineage of Eleazar, in whose line the high priests are presented in linear form (vv. 4–15). The sons of Levi (v. 1) always appear in this order, based on age (v. 16;

Ge 46:11; Ex 6:16; Nu 3:17; 26:57). Of Aaron's four sons (v. 3), the first two died as a result of sacrilege (Lev 10:2; Nu 26:61); succeeding generations of priests would trace their lineage to either Eleazar or Ithamar.
6:4–15 This list of high priests from the time of Eleazar to the exile has been sharply telescoped. The following high priests known from the OT are not mentioned: Jehoiada (2Ch 12:2), Uriah (2Ki 16:10–16), possibly two other Azariahs (2Ch 26:17,20; 31:10–13), Eli (1Sa 1:9; 14:3) and Abiathar (2Sa 8:17). The list is repeated with some variation in Ezr 7:1–5 (see notes there).
6:8 *Ahitub the father of Zadok.* This Zadok was one of David's two priests (18:16; 2Sa 8:17). When David's other priest, Abiathar (see note on vv. 4–15), supported the rebellion of Adonijah, Zadok supported Solomon (1Ki 1). After the expulsion of Abiathar (1Ki 2:26–27), Zadok alone held the office (1Ch 29:22), which continued in his line (1Ki 4:2). The Ahitub mentioned here should not be confused with the priest who was the grandson of Eli (1Sa 14:3) and grandfather of Abiathar (1Sa 22:20); the line of Zadok replaced the line of Eli (1Sa 2:27–36; 1Ki 2:26–27). For the importance of the line of Zadok see Eze 40:46; 43:19; 44:15; 48:11. Ezra was concerned to trace his own priestly lineage to this house (Ezr 7:1–5).
6:13 *Hilkiah.* Discovered the Book of the Law in the temple at the time of Josiah (2Ki 22; 2Ch 34).
6:14 *Seraiah.* Executed by the Babylonians after the conquest of Jerusalem in 586 B.C. (2Ki 25:18–21). *Jehozadak.* Father of Jeshua, the high priest in the first generation of the restoration (Ezr 3:2; 5:2; 10:18; Hag 1:1; 2:2; Zec 3:1; 6:11); his name is also spelled "Jozadak."

15Jehozadak[s] was deported when the LORD sent Judah and Jerusalem into exile by the hand of Nebuchadnezzar.

16The sons of Levi:[t]
Gershon,[s] Kohath and Merari.[u]
17These are the names of the sons of Gershon:
Libni and Shimei.[v]
18The sons of Kohath:
Amram, Izhar, Hebron and Uzziel.[w]
19The sons of Merari:[x]
Mahli and Mushi.[y]

These are the clans of the Levites listed according to their fathers:
20Of Gershon:
Libni his son, Jehath his son,
Zimmah his son, 21Joah his son,
Iddo his son, Zerah his son
and Jeatherai his son.
22The descendants of Kohath:
Amminadab his son, Korah[z] his son,
Assir his son, 23Elkanah his son,
Ebiasaph his son, Assir his son,
24Tahath his son, Uriel[a] his son,
Uzziah his son and Shaul his son.
25The descendants of Elkanah:
Amasai, Ahimoth,
26Elkanah his son,[t] Zophai his son,
Nahath his son, 27Eliab his son,
Jeroham his son, Elkanah[b] his son
and Samuel[c] his son.[u]
28The sons of Samuel:
Joel[v][d] the firstborn
and Abijah the second son.
29The descendants of Merari:
Mahli, Libni his son,
Shimei his son, Uzzah his son,
30Shimea his son, Haggiah his son

and Asaiah his son.

The Temple Musicians

6:54–80pp — Jos 21:4–39

31These are the men[e] David put in charge of the music[f] in the house of the LORD after the ark came to rest there. 32They ministered with music before the tabernacle, the Tent of Meeting, until Solomon built the temple of the LORD in Jerusalem. They performed their duties according to the regulations laid down for them.

33Here are the men who served, together with their sons:
From the Kohathites:
Heman,[g] the musician,
the son of Joel,[h] the son of Samuel,
34the son of Elkanah,[i] the son of Jeroham,
the son of Eliel, the son of Toah,
35the son of Zuph, the son of Elkanah,
the son of Mahath, the son of Amasai,
36the son of Elkanah, the son of Joel,
the son of Azariah, the son of Zephaniah,
37the son of Tahath, the son of Assir,
the son of Ebiasaph, the son of Korah,[j]

6:15 [s]Ne 12:1; Hag 1:1,14; 2:2, 4; Zec 6:11
6:16 [t]S Ge 29:34; S Nu 3:17-20 [u]S Nu 26:57
6:17 [v]S Ex 6:17
6:18 [w]S Ex 6:18
6:19 [x]S Ge 46:11; 1Ch 23:21; 24:26 [y]S Ex 6:19
6:22 [z]S Ex 6:24
6:24 [a]1Ch 15:5
6:27 [b]S 1Sa 1:1
6:28 [d]ver 33; 1Sa 8:2

6:31 [e]1Ch 25:1; 2Ch 29:25-26; Ne 12:45 [f]1Ch 9:33; 15:19; Ezr 3:10; Ps 68:25
6:33 [g]1Ki 4:31; 1Ch 15:17; 25:1 [h]S ver 28
6:34 [i]S 1Sa 1:1
6:37 [i]S Ex 6:24

[s]16 Hebrew *Gershom*, a variant of *Gershon*; also in verses 17, 20, 43, 62 and 71 [t]26 Some Hebrew manuscripts, Septuagint and Syriac; most Hebrew manuscripts *Ahimoth* 26*and Elkanah. The sons of Elkanah:* [u]27 Some Septuagint manuscripts (see also 1 Samuel 1:19,20 and 1 Chron. 6:33,34); Hebrew does not have *and Samuel his son.* [v]28 Some Septuagint manuscripts and Syriac (see also 1 Samuel 8:2 and 1 Chron. 6:33); Hebrew does not have *Joel.*

6:16–19a Repeated from Ex 6:16–19; Nu 3:17–20; 26:57–61.

6:22–23 *Assir . . . Elkanah . . . Ebiasaph.* Ex 6:24 names these men as sons of Korah, but here they are presented in the form ordinarily used for a linear genealogy of successive generations (see vv. 20–21,25–26,29–30). Either this is another example of genealogical fluidity, or one must understand "his son" as referring to Kohath and not to the immediately preceding name.

6:22 *Amminadab.* The almost parallel genealogy later in this chapter lists Izhar in the place of Amminadab—who is nowhere else listed as a son of Kohath, while every other list includes Izhar (vv. 2,37–38; Ex 6:18,21). Either Amminadab is an otherwise unattested alternative name of Izhar, or he is an otherwise unknown son. Or this may be another example of genealogical fluidity in which the Levites are linked with the tribe of Judah and the lineage of David (see Ru 4:18–22; see also Mt 1:4; Lk 3:33) in view of Aaron's marriage to the daughter of Amminadab of Judah (Ex 6:23; see 1Ch 2:10).

6:24 *Uriel.* Possibly the one who led the Kohathites in David's day (15:5).

6:26–27 *Zophai . . . Nahath . . . Eliab.* Apparently variant names for Zuph, Toah and Eliel (vv. 34–35).

6:27 *Samuel.* His lineage is also given in 1Sa 1:1, where his family is identified as Ephraimite (see note there). Either this is an example of genealogical fluidity, in which Samuel's involvement in the tabernacle (1Sa 3) and performance of priestly duties (9:22; 1Sa 2:18; 3:1) resulted in his incorporation into the Levites, or the term "Ephraimite" is to be understood as a place of residence, not as a statement of lineage.

6:31–48 Each of the three Levitical clans contributed musicians for the temple: Heman from the family of Kohath, Asaph from Gershon, and Ethan from Merari. The Chronicler makes frequent reference to the appointment of the musical guilds by David (15:16,27; 25:1–31; 2Ch 29:25–26; see Ne 12:45–47). The frequent mention of the role of the Levites has led many to assume that the author was a member of the musicians. Non-Biblical literature also attests to guilds of singers and musicians in Canaanite temples. This genealogy appears to function as a means of legitimizing the Levites of the restoration period (Ezr 2:40–41; Ne 7:43–44; 10:9–13, 28–29; 11:15–18; 12:24–47).

38the son of Izhar,[k] the son of Kohath,

the son of Levi, the son of Israel; 39and Heman's associate Asaph,[l] who served at his right hand:

Asaph son of Berekiah, the son of Shimea,[m]

40the son of Michael, the son of Baaseiah,[w]

the son of Malkijah, 41the son of Ethni,

the son of Zerah, the son of Adaiah,

42the son of Ethan, the son of Zimmah,

the son of Shimei, 43the son of Jahath,

the son of Gershon, the son of Levi;

44and from their associates, the Merarites,[n] at his left hand:

Ethan son of Kishi, the son of Abdi, the son of Malluch, 45the son of Hashabiah,

the son of Amaziah, the son of Hilkiah,

46the son of Amzi, the son of Bani, the son of Shemer, 47the son of Mahli,

the son of Mushi, the son of Merari,

the son of Levi.

48Their fellow Levites[o] were assigned to all the other duties of the tabernacle, the house of God. 49But Aaron and his descendants were the ones who presented offerings on the altar[p] of burnt offering and on the altar of incense[q] in connection with all that was done in the Most Holy Place, making atonement for Israel, in accordance with all that Moses the servant of God had commanded.

50These were the descendants of Aaron:

Eleazar his son, Phinehas his son, Abishua his son, 51Bukki his son, Uzzi his son, Zerahiah his son,

52Meraioth his son, Amariah his son, Ahitub his son, 53Zadok[r] his son and Ahimaaz his son.

54These were the locations of their settlements[s] allotted as their territory (they were assigned to the descendants of Aaron

6:38 [k]Ex 6:21
6:39 [l]1Ch 25:1, 9; 2Ch 29:13; Ne 11:17
[m]1Ch 15:17
6:44 [n]1Ch 15:17
6:48 [o]1Ch 23:32
6:49 [p]Ex 27:1-8
[q]S Ex 30:7; 2Ch 26:18
6:53 [r]S 2Sa 8:17
6:54 [s]S Nu 31:10

6:56 [t]S Jos 14:13; S 15:13
6:57 [u]S Nu 33:20
[v]S Jos 15:48
6:58 [w]S Jos 10:3
6:59 [x]S Jos 15:42
6:60 [y]Jer 1:1
6:64 [z]Nu 35:1-8
6:67 [a]S Jos 10:33
6:68 [b]1Ki 4:12
[c]S Jos 10:10
6:69 [d]S Jos 10:12
[e]S Jos 19:45

who were from the Kohathite clan, because the first lot was for them):

55They were given Hebron in Judah with its surrounding pasturelands. 56But the fields and villages around the city were given to Caleb son of Jephunneh.[t]

57So the descendants of Aaron were given Hebron (a city of refuge), and Libnah,[x][u] Jattir,[v] Eshtemoa, 58Hilen, Debir,[w] 59Ashan,[x] Juttah[y] and Beth Shemesh, together with their pasturelands. 60And from the tribe of Benjamin they were given Gibeon,[z] Geba, Alemeth and Anathoth,[y] together with their pasturelands.

These towns, which were distributed among the Kohathite clans, were thirteen in all.

61The rest of Kohath's descendants were allotted ten towns from the clans of half the tribe of Manasseh.

62The descendants of Gershon, clan by clan, were allotted thirteen towns from the tribes of Issachar, Asher and Naphtali, and from the part of the tribe of Manasseh that is in Bashan.

63The descendants of Merari, clan by clan, were allotted twelve towns from the tribes of Reuben, Gad and Zebulun.

64So the Israelites gave the Levites these towns[z] and their pasturelands. 65From the tribes of Judah, Simeon and Benjamin they allotted the previously named towns.

66Some of the Kohathite clans were given as their territory towns from the tribe of Ephraim.

67In the hill country of Ephraim they were given Shechem (a city of refuge), and Gezer,[aa] 68Jokmeam,[b] Beth Horon,[c] 69Aijalon[d] and Gath Rimmon,[e] together with their pasturelands.

70And from half the tribe of Manasseh the Israelites gave Aner and Bileam, together with their pasturelands, to the rest of the Kohathite clans.

[w]40 Most Hebrew manuscripts; some Hebrew manuscripts, one Septuagint manuscript and Syriac Maaseiah   [x]57 See Joshua 21:13; Hebrew given the cities of refuge: Hebron, Libnah.   [y]59 Syriac (see also Septuagint and Joshua 21:16); Hebrew does not have Juttah.   [z]60 See Joshua 21:17; Hebrew does not have Gibeon.   [aa]67 See Joshua 21:21; Hebrew given the cities of refuge: Shechem, Gezer.

6:49–53 Repeats vv. 4–8 but presumably serves a different function: to legitimize the line of Zadok, which is traced down to Solomon's time, as the only Levitical division authorized to offer sacrifices.

6:54–81 This list of Levitical possessions is taken from Jos 21 with only minor differences (see notes there). The Levites, who were given no block of territory of their own, were distributed throughout Israel.

⁷¹The Gershonites* received the following:

From the clan of the half-tribe of Manasseh
they received Golan in Bashan*
and also Ashtaroth, together with
their pasturelands;
⁷²from the tribe of Issachar
they received Kedesh, Daberath,*
⁷³Ramoth and Anem, together
with their pasturelands;
⁷⁴from the tribe of Asher
they received Mashal, Abdon,*
⁷⁵Hukok* and Rehob,* together
with their pasturelands;
⁷⁶and from the tribe of Naphtali
they received Kedesh in Galilee,
Hammon* and Kiriathaim,* together with their pasturelands.

⁷⁷The Merarites (the rest of the Levites)
received the following:
From the tribe of Zebulun
they received Jokneam, Kartah,*
Rimmono and Tabor, together
with their pasturelands;
⁷⁸from the tribe of Reuben across the
Jordan east of Jericho
they received Bezer* in the desert,
Jahzah, ⁷⁹Kedemoth* and Mephaath, together with their pasturelands;
⁸⁰and from the tribe of Gad
they received Ramoth in Gilead,*
Mahanaim,* ⁸¹Heshbon and Jazer,* together with their pasturelands.*

Issachar

7 The sons of Issachar:*
Tola, Puah,* Jashub and Shimron—four in all.
²The sons of Tola:
Uzzi, Rephaiah, Jeriel, Jahmai, Ibsam and Samuel—heads of their
families. During the reign of David,
the descendants of Tola listed as
fighting men in their genealogy
numbered 22,600.
³The son of Uzzi:
Izrahiah.

The sons of Izrahiah:
Michael, Obadiah, Joel and Isshiah. All five of them were chiefs.
⁴According to their family genealogy, they had 36,000 men ready
for battle, for they had many wives
and children.
⁵The relatives who were fighting men
belonging to all the clans of Issachar, as listed in their genealogy,
were 87,000 in all.

Benjamin

⁶Three sons of Benjamin:*
Bela, Beker and Jediael.
⁷The sons of Bela:
Ezbon, Uzzi, Uzziel, Jerimoth and
Iri, heads of families—five in all.
Their genealogical record listed
22,034 fighting men.
⁸The sons of Beker:
Zemirah, Joash, Eliezer, Elioenai,
Omri, Jeremoth, Abijah, Anathoth
and Alemeth. All these were the
sons of Beker. ⁹Their genealogical
record listed the heads of families
and 20,200 fighting men.
¹⁰The son of Jediael:
Bilhan.
The sons of Bilhan:
Jeush, Benjamin, Ehud, Kenaanah,
Zethan, Tarshish and Ahishahar.
¹¹All these sons of Jediael were
heads of families. There were 17,-
200 fighting men ready to go out
to war.
¹²The Shuppites and Huppites were the
descendants of Ir, and the Hushites
the descendants of Aher.

Naphtali

¹³The sons of Naphtali:*
Jahziel, Guni, Jezer and Shillem*—the descendants of Bilhah.

Manasseh

¹⁴The descendants of Manasseh:*

6:71 *1Ch 23:7
*S Jos 20:8
6:72 *S Jos 19:12
6:74 *S Jos 19:28
6:75 *Jos 19:34
*S Nu 13:21
6:76 *Jos 19:28
*S Nu 32:37
6:78 *S Jos 20:8
6:79 *S Dt 2:26
6:80 *Jos 20:8
*S Ge 32:2
6:81 *S Nu 21:32
*2Ch 11:14
7:1 *S Ge 30:18
*S Ge 46:13

7:6 *S Nu 26:38
7:13 *S Ge 30:8
7:14
*S Ge 41:51;
S Jos 17:1;
1Ch 5:23

b *77* See Septuagint and Joshua 21:34; Hebrew does not
have *Jokneam, Kartah.*   **c** *13* Some Hebrew and
Septuagint manuscripts (see also Gen. 46:24 and Num.
26:49); most Hebrew manuscripts *Shallum*

7:1–5 Parts of the genealogy of Issachar are taken from Ge 46:13; Nu 1:28; 26:23–25, though many of the names are otherwise unattested. This list of the clans appears to come from a military muster (vv. 2,4–5) from the time of David (v. 2), perhaps reflecting the census of ch. 21 and 2Sa 24. **7:6–12** There is considerable fluidity among the Biblical sources listing the sons of Benjamin. This list gives three sons; Ge 46:21 records ten; Nu 26:38–39 and 1Ch 8:1–2 both list five (the only name appearing in all these sources is Bela, the firstborn). The variations reflect different origins

and functions for these genealogies. The list here appears to function in the military sphere (vv. 7,9,11). **7:13** Repeats Ge 46:24; Nu 26:48–50. *descendants of Bilhah.* Dan and Naphtali were the actual "sons" of Jacob's concubine Bilhah (Ge 30:3–8), so Naphtali's sons are Bilhah's "descendants." **7:14–19** See note on 5:23–26. The sources for this genealogy are Nu 26:29–34; Jos 17:1–18. The daughters of Zelophehad (v. 15) prompted the rulings on the inheritance rights of women (Nu 26:29–34; 27:1–11; 36:1–12; Jos

Asriel was his descendant through his Aramean concubine. She gave birth to Makir the father of Gilead.*y* [15]Makir took a wife from among the Huppites and Shuppites. His sister's name was Maacah.

Another descendant was named Zelophehad,*z* who had only daughters.

[16]Makir's wife Maacah gave birth to a son and named him Peresh. His brother was named Sheresh, and his sons were Ulam and Rakem.

[17]The son of Ulam:

Bedan.

These were the sons of Gilead*a* son of Makir, the son of Manasseh. [18]His sister Hammoleketh gave birth to Ishhod, Abiezer*b* and Mahlah.

[19]The sons of Shemida*c* were:

Ahian, Shechem, Likhi and Aniam.

Ephraim

[20]The descendants of Ephraim:*d*

Shuthelah, Bered his son,
Tahath his son, Eleadah his son,
Tahath his son, [21]Zabad his son
and Shuthelah his son.

Ezer and Elead were killed by the native-born men of Gath, when they went down to seize their livestock. [22]Their father Ephraim mourned for them many days, and his relatives came to comfort him. [23]Then he lay with his wife again, and she became pregnant and gave birth to a son. He named him Beriah,*d* because there had been misfortune in his family. [24]His daughter was Sheerah, who built Lower and Upper Beth Horon*e* as well as Uzzen Sheerah.

[25]Rephah was his son, Resheph his son,*e*

Telah his son, Tahan his son,
[26]Ladan his son, Ammihud his son,
Elishama his son, [27]Nun his son
and Joshua his son.

[28]Their lands and settlements included

Bethel and its surrounding villages, Naaran to the east, Gezer*f* and its villages to the west, and Shechem and its villages all the way to Ayyah and its villages. [29]Along the borders of Manasseh were Beth Shan,*g* Taanach, Megiddo and Dor,*h* together with their villages. The descendants of Joseph son of Israel lived in these towns.

Asher

[30]The sons of Asher:*i*

Imnah, Ishvah, Ishvi and Beriah.
Their sister was Serah.

[31]The sons of Beriah:

Heber and Malkiel, who was the father of Birzaith.

[32]Heber was the father of Japhlet, Shomer and Hotham and of their sister Shua.

[33]The sons of Japhlet:

Pasach, Bimhal and Ashvath.
These were Japhlet's sons.

[34]The sons of Shomer:

Ahi, Rohgah,*f* Hubbah and Aram.

[35]The sons of his brother Helem:

Zophah, Imna, Shelesh and Amal.

[36]The sons of Zophah:

Suah, Harnepher, Shual, Beri, Imrah, [37]Bezer, Hod, Shamma, Shilshah, Ithran*g* and Beera.

[38]The sons of Jether:

Jephunneh, Pispah and Ara.

[39]The sons of Ulla:

Arah, Hanniel and Rizia.

[40]All these were descendants of Asher—heads of families, choice men, brave warriors and outstanding leaders. The number of men ready for battle, as listed in their genealogy, was 26,000.

The Genealogy of Saul the Benjamite

8:28-38pp — 1Ch 9:34-44

8 Benjamin*j* was the father of Bela his firstborn,

7:14 *y*S Nu 26:30
7:15 *z*S Nu 26:33; 36:1-12
7:17 *a*S Nu 26:30
7:18 *b*S Jos 17:2
7:19 *c*Jos 17:2
7:20 *d*S Ge 41:52; S Nu 1:33
7:24 *e*S Jos 10:10

7:28 *f*Jos 10:33
7:29 *g*S Jos 17:11
*h*S Jos 11:2
7:30 *i*S Nu 1:40
8:1 *j*S Ge 46:21

*d*23 *Beriah* sounds like the Hebrew for *misfortune.*
*e*25 Some Septuagint manuscripts; Hebrew does not have *his son.* *f*34 Or *of his brother Shomer: Rohgah*
*g*37 Possibly a variant of *Jether*

17:3–4). Of the 13 different clans of the tribe of Manasseh known from these genealogies, seven are mentioned in the Samaria ostraca (about 65 inscribed potsherds containing records of deliveries of wine, oil, barley and other commodities in the eighth century B.C.). The prominence of women in this genealogy is unusual; this suggests that it may have functioned in the domestic sphere, perhaps as a statement of the social status of the various clans of Manasseh (see Introduction: Genealogies).

7:20–29 The source for part of the genealogy of Ephraim is Nu 26:35. If Rephah (v. 25) is the grandson of Ephraim, ten generations are recorded from Ephraim to Joshua, a number

that fits very well the 400-year interval when Israel was in Egypt. Joshua's Ephraimite ancestry is also mentioned in Nu 13:8 (where he is called "Hoshea"; see Nu 13:16). The raid against Gath (vv. 21–22) must have taken place well before the conquest of Canaan and must have originated in Egypt. The list of settlements (vv. 28–29) summarizes Jos 16–17.

7:30–40 The genealogy of Asher follows Ge 46:17 for the first three generations; it is also parallel to Nu 26:44–46, except that the name Ishvah (v. 30) is missing there. This genealogy too reflects a military function (v. 40).

8:1–40 The inclusion of a second and even more extensive genealogy of Benjamin (see note on 7:6–12) reflects both the

Ashbel the second son, Aharah the third,
²Nohah the fourth and Rapha the fifth.
³The sons of Bela were:
Addar,ᵏ Gera, Abihud,ʰ ⁴Abishua, Naaman, Ahoah,ˡ ⁵Gera, Shephuphan and Huram.
⁶These were the descendants of Ehud,ᵐ who were heads of families of those living in Geba and were deported to Manahath:
⁷Naaman, Ahijah, and Gera, who deported them and who was the father of Uzza and Ahihud.
⁸Sons were born to Shaharaim in Moab after he had divorced his wives Hushim and Baara. ⁹By his wife Hodesh he had Jobab, Zibia, Mesha, Malcam, ¹⁰Jeuz, Sakia and Mirmah. These were his sons, heads of families. ¹¹By Hushim he had Abitub and Elpaal.
¹²The sons of Elpaal:
Eber, Misham, Shemed (who built Onoⁿ and Lod with its surrounding villages), ¹³and Beriah and Shema, who were heads of families of those living in Aijalonᵒ and who drove out the inhabitants of Gath.ᵖ
¹⁴Ahio, Shashak, Jeremoth, ¹⁵Zebadiah, Arad, Eder, ¹⁶Michael, Ishpah and Joha were the sons of Beriah.
¹⁷Zebadiah, Meshullam, Hizki, Heber, ¹⁸Ishmerai, Izliah and Jobab were the sons of Elpaal.
¹⁹Jakim, Zicri, Zabdi, ²⁰Elienai, Zillethai, Eliel, ²¹Adaiah, Beraiah and Shimrath were the sons of Shimei.
²²Ishpan, Eber, Eliel, ²³Abdon, Zicri, Hanan, ²⁴Hananiah, Elam, Anthothijah, ²⁵Iphdeiah and Penuel were the sons of Shashak.
²⁶Shamsherai, Shehariah, Athaliah, ²⁷Jaareshiah, Elijah and Zicri were the sons of Jeroham.
²⁸All these were heads of families, chiefs

as listed in their genealogy, and they lived in Jerusalem.

²⁹Jeielⁱ the fatherʲ of Gibeon lived in Gibeon. ꟼ
His wife's name was Maacah, ³⁰and his firstborn son was Abdon, followed by Zur, Kish, Baal, Ner,ᵏ Nadab, ³¹Gedor, Ahio, Zeker ³²and Mikloth, who was the father of Shimeah. They too lived near their relatives in Jerusalem.
³³Nerʳ was the father of Kish,ˢ Kish the father of Saulᵗ, and Saul the father of Jonathan, Malki-Shua, Abinadab and Esh-Baal.ˡ ᵘ
³⁴The son of Jonathan:ᵛ
Merib-Baal,ᵐ ʷ who was the father of Micah.
³⁵The sons of Micah:
Pithon, Melech, Tarea and Ahaz.
³⁶Ahaz was the father of Jehoaddah, Jehoaddah was the father of Alemeth, Azmaveth and Zimri, and Zimri was the father of Moza.
³⁷Moza was the father of Binea; Raphah was his son, Eleasah his son and Azel his son.
³⁸Azel had six sons, and these were their names:
Azrikam, Bokeru, Ishmael, Sheariah, Obadiah and Hanan. All these were the sons of Azel.
³⁹The sons of his brother Eshek:
Ulam his firstborn, Jeush the second son and Eliphelet the third.
⁴⁰The sons of Ulam were brave warriors who could handle the bow. They had many sons and grandsons—150 in all.
All these were the descendants of Benjamin.ˣ

8:3 ᵏS Ge 46:21
8:4 ˡ2Sa 23:9
8:6 ᵐJdg 3:12-30
8:12 ⁿEzr 2:33; Ne 6:2; 7:37; 11:35
8:13 ᵒS Jos 10:12 ᵖS Jos 11:22

8:29 ꟼS Jos 9:3
8:33 ʳS 1Sa 28:19 ˢS 1Sa 9:1 ᵗ1Sa 14:49 ᵘS 2Sa 2:8
8:34 ᵛS 2Sa 9:12 ʷS 2Sa 4:4; S 21:7-14
8:40 ˣS Nu 26:38

ʰ3 Or Gera the father of Ehud   ⁱ29 Some Septuagint manuscripts (see also 1 Chron. 9:35); Hebrew does not have Jeiel.   ʲ29 Father may mean civic leader or military leader.   ᵏ30 Some Septuagint manuscripts (see also 1 Chron. 9:36); Hebrew does not have Ner.   ˡ33 Also known as Ish-Bosheth   ᵐ34 Also known as Mephibosheth

importance of this tribe and the Chronicler's interest in Saul. Judah, Simeon and part of Benjamin had composed the southern kingdom (1Ki 12:1–21), and their territory largely comprised the restoration province of Judah in the Chronicler's own time. The genealogy of Benjamin is more extensive than that of all the other tribes except Judah and Levi. The Chronicler is also concerned with the genealogy of Saul (vv. 29–38) in order to set the stage for the historical narrative that begins with the end of his reign (ch. 10). Saul's genealogy is repeated in 9:35–44. Several references suggest that this genealogy also originated in the military sphere (vv. 6,10,13,28,40).

8:1–5   Cf. the lists in 7:6–12; Ge 46:21–22; Nu 26:38–41.
8:6–27   Unique to Chronicles.
8:29–38   Essentially the same as the list in 9:35–44.
8:33   For the sons of Saul see 1Sa 14:49; 31:2. Jonathan. The firstborn and the best known of the sons of Saul, both for his military prowess and for his friendship with David (1Sa 13–14; 18:1–4; 19:1–7; 20:1–42; 23:16–18; 2Sa 21:13–14). Esh-Baal. See NIV text note; see also note on 2Sa 2:8.
8:34   Merib-Baal. See NIV text note; see also note on 2Sa 4:4.

9 All Israel[y] was listed in the genealogies recorded in the book of the kings of Israel.

The People in Jerusalem

9:1–17pp — Ne 11:3–19

The people of Judah were taken captive to Babylon[z] because of their unfaithfulness.[a] ²Now the first to resettle on their own property in their own towns[b] were some Israelites, priests, Levites and temple servants.[c]

³Those from Judah, from Benjamin, and from Ephraim and Manasseh who lived in Jerusalem were:

⁴Uthai son of Ammihud, the son of Omri, the son of Imri, the son of Bani, a descendant of Perez son of Judah.[d]

⁵Of the Shilonites:

Asaiah the firstborn and his sons.

⁶Of the Zerahites:

Jeuel.

The people from Judah numbered 690.

⁷Of the Benjamites:

Sallu son of Meshullam, the son of Hodaviah, the son of Hassenuah;
⁸Ibneiah son of Jeroham; Elah son of Uzzi, the son of Micri; and Meshullam son of Shephatiah, the son of Reuel, the son of Ibnijah.

⁹The people from Benjamin, as listed in their genealogy, numbered 956. All these men were heads of their families.

¹⁰Of the priests:

Jedaiah; Jehoiarib; Jakin;
¹¹Azariah son of Hilkiah, the son of Meshullam, the son of Zadok, the son of Meraioth, the son of Ahitub, the official in charge of the house of God;

¹²Adaiah son of Jeroham, the son of Pashhur,[e] the son of Malkijah; and Maasai son of Adiel, the son of Jahzerah, the son of Meshullam, the son of Meshillemith, the son of Immer.

¹³The priests, who were heads of families, numbered 1,760. They were able men, responsible for ministering in the house of God.

¹⁴Of the Levites:

Shemaiah son of Hasshub, the son of Azrikam, the son of Hashabiah, a Merarite; ¹⁵Bakbakkar, Heresh, Galal and Mattaniah[f] son of Mica, the son of Zicri, the son of Asaph; ¹⁶Obadiah son of Shemaiah, the son of Galal, the son of Jeduthun; and Berekiah son of Asa, the son of Elkanah, who lived in the villages of the Netophathites.[g]

¹⁷The gatekeepers:[h]

Shallum, Akkub, Talmon, Ahiman and their brothers, Shallum their chief ¹⁸being stationed at the King's Gate[i] on the east, up to the present time. These were the gatekeepers belonging to the camp of the Levites. ¹⁹Shallum[j] son of Kore, the son of Ebiasaph, the son of Korah, and his fellow gatekeepers from his family (the Korahites) were responsible for guarding the thresholds of the Tent[n] just as their fathers had been responsible for guarding the entrance to the dwelling of the LORD. ²⁰In earlier times Phinehas[k] son of Eleazar was in charge of the gatekeepers, and the LORD was with him. ²¹Zechariah[l] son of Meshelemiah

[n] 19 That is, the temple; also in verses 21 and 23

Cross references

9:1 [y]1Ch 11:1, 10; 12:38; 14:8; 15:3,28; 18:14; 19:17; 21:5; 28:4,8; 29:21,23; 2Ch 1:2; 5:3; 7:8; 10:3,16; 12:1; 13:4,15; 18:16; 24:5; 28:23; 29:24; 30:1 [z]S Dt 21:10 [a]S 1Ch 5:25
9:2 [b]Jos 9:27; Ezr 2:70 [c]Ezr 2:43,58; 8:20; Ne 7:60
9:4 [d]S Ge 38:29; 46:12
9:12 [e]Ezr 2:38; 10:22; Ne 10:3; Jer 21:1; 38:1
9:15 [f]2Ch 20:14; Ne 11:22
9:16 [g]Ne 12:28
9:17 [h]ver 22; 1Ch 26:1; 2Ch 8:14; 31:14; Ezr 2:42; Ne 7:45
9:18 [i]1Ch 26:14; Eze 43:1; 46:1
9:19 [j]Jer 35:4
9:20 [k]Nu 25:11
9:21 [l]1Ch 26:2, 14

Footnotes

9:1 *All Israel.* The Chronicler's concern with "all Israel" is one key to why he included the genealogies (see Introduction: Purpose and Themes).

9:2–34 This list of the members of the restored community reflects the Chronicler's concern with the institutions of his own day, especially the legitimacy of officeholders. He lists laity ("Israelites," v. 2) in vv. 3–9, priests in vv. 10–13 and Levites in vv. 14–34. He mentions a fourth class of returnees—the temple servants (v. 2)—but does not give them separate listing in the material that follows. They may have been originally foreigners who were incorporated into the Levites (Jos 9:23; Ezr 8:20) and so are not listed apart from that tribe. A similar office is known in the temple at ancient Ugarit. The list here is related to the one in Ne 11, but less than half the names are the same in the two lists.

9:3 *Ephraim and Manasseh.* Again reflecting his concern with "all Israel," the Chronicler shows that the returnees were not only from Judah and Benjamin but also from the northern tribes.

9:4–6 See 2:3–6; 4:21. The returnees of Judah are traced to Judah's sons Perez, Zerah and Shelah—if the word "Shilonites" (v. 5) is read as "Shelanites" (Nu 26:20). If the reading "Shilonites" is retained, the reference is to Shiloh, the important sanctuary city (Jdg 18:31; Jer 7:12–14; 26:9).

9:10–13 The list of priests is essentially the same as that in Ne 11:10–14. Since it is tied to the list of priests earlier in the genealogies (6:1–15,50–53), contemporary Israel's continuity with her past is shown.

9:15–16 *Asaph . . . Jeduthun.* Leaders of musical groups (6:39; 16:41). Later the Chronicler also lists the musicians (ch. 25) before the gatekeepers (ch. 26).

9:16 *Netophathites.* See note on Ne 12:28.

9:17–21 The Chronicler gives the names of four gatekeepers, while Ne 11:19 mentions only two. The chief of the gatekeepers had the honor of responsibility for the gate used by the king (Eze 46:1–2). The gatekeepers are also listed in ch. 26; Ezr 2:42. These officers traced their origin to Phinehas (v. 20; 6:4; Nu 3:32; 25:6–13).

was the gatekeeper at the entrance to the Tent of Meeting.

²²Altogether, those chosen to be gate-keepers ^m at the thresholds numbered 212. They were registered by genealogy in their villages. The gatekeepers had been assigned to their positions of trust by David and Samuel the seer. ⁿ ²³They and their descendants were in charge of guarding the gates of the house of the LORD—the house called the Tent. ²⁴The gatekeepers were on the four sides: east, west, north and south. ²⁵Their brothers in their villages had to come from time to time and share their duties for seven-day ^o periods. ²⁶But the four principal gatekeepers, who were Levites, were entrusted with the responsibility for the rooms and treasuries ^p in the house of God. ²⁷They would spend the night stationed around the house of God, ^q because they had to guard it; and they had charge of the key ^r for opening it each morning.

²⁸Some of them were in charge of the articles used in the temple service; they counted them when they were brought in and when they were taken out. ²⁹Others were assigned to take care of the furnishings and all the other articles of the sanctuary, ^s as well as the flour and wine, and the oil, incense and spices. ³⁰But some ^t of the priests took care of mixing the spices. ³¹A Levite named Mattithiah, the firstborn son of Shallum the Korahite, was entrusted with the responsibility for baking the offering bread. ³²Some of their Kohathite brothers were in charge of preparing for every Sabbath the bread set out on the table. ^u

³³Those who were musicians, ^v heads of Levite families, stayed in the rooms of the temple and were exempt from other duties because they were responsible for the work day and night. ^w

³⁴All these were heads of Levite families, chiefs as listed in their genealogy, and they lived in Jerusalem.

9:22 mS ver 17
nS 1Sa 9:9
9:25 o2Ki 11:5
9:26 p1Ch 26:22
9:27 qS Nu 3:38
rIsa 22:22
9:29 sS Nu 3:28; 1Ch 23:29
9:30 tS Ex 30:25
9:32 uLev 24:5-8; 1Ch 23:29; 2Ch 13:11
9:33 vS 1Ch 6:31; 25:1-31; S 2Ch 5:12 wPs 134:1

The Genealogy of Saul
9:34–44pp — 1Ch 8:28–38

³⁵Jeiel ^x the father ^o of Gibeon lived in Gibeon.

His wife's name was Maacah, ³⁶and his firstborn son was Abdon, followed by Zur, Kish, Baal, Ner, Nadab, ³⁷Gedor, Ahio, Zechariah and Mikloth. ³⁸Mikloth was the father of Shimeam. They too lived near their relatives in Jerusalem.

³⁹Ner ^y was the father of Kish, ^z Kish the father of Saul, and Saul the father of Jonathan, ^a Malki-Shua, Abinadab and Esh-Baal. ^{p b}

⁴⁰The son of Jonathan:

Merib-Baal, ^{q c} who was the father of Micah.

⁴¹The sons of Micah:

Pithon, Melech, Tahrea and Ahaz. ^r

⁴²Ahaz was the father of Jadah, Jadah ^s was the father of Alemeth, Azmaveth and Zimri, and Zimri was the father of Moza. ⁴³Moza was the father of Binea; Rephaiah was his son, Eleasah his son and Azel his son.

⁴⁴Azel had six sons, and these were their names:

Azrikam, Bokeru, Ishmael, Sheariah, Obadiah and Hanan. These were the sons of Azel.

Saul Takes His Life
10:1–12pp — 1Sa 31:1–13; 2Sa 1:4–12

10 Now the Philistines fought against Israel; the Israelites fled before them, and many fell slain on Mount Gilboa. ²The Philistines pressed hard after Saul and his sons, and they killed his sons Jonathan, Abinadab and Malki-Shua. ³The fighting grew fierce around Saul, and when the archers overtook him, they wounded him.

o35 *Father* may mean *civic leader* or *military leader.*
p39 Also known as *Ish-Bosheth* q40 Also known as *Mephibosheth* r41 Vulgate and Syriac (see also Septuagint and 1 Chron. 8:35); Hebrew does not have *and Ahaz.* s42 Some Hebrew manuscripts and Septuagint (see also 1 Chron. 8:36); most Hebrew manuscripts *Jarah, Jarah*

9:35 x1Ch 8:29
9:39 yS 1Ch 8:33
zS 1Sa 9:1
a1Sa 13:22
b5 2Sa 2:8
9:40 c5 2Sa 4:4

9:22–27 Twenty-four guard stations were manned in three shifts around the clock; 72 men would be needed for each week. With a total of 212 men, each would have a tour of duty approximately every three weeks (26:12–18).
9:28–34 The Levites not only were responsible for the temple precincts and for opening the gates in the morning, but they also had charge of the chambers and supply rooms (23:28; 26:20–29) as well as the implements, supplies and furnishings (28:13–18; Ezr 1:9–11). In addition they were responsible for the preparation of baked goods (Ex 25:30; Lev 2:5–7; 7:9). The priests alone prepared the perfumed anointing oil and spices (Ex 30:23–33).
9:35–44 The genealogy of Saul is duplicated here (see 8:29–38) as a transition to the short account of his reign that begins the Chronicler's narration (ch. 10).
10:2 For the strategy of pursuing the king in battle see note on 1Ki 22:31.

4Saul said to his armor-bearer, "Draw
your sword and run me through, or these
uncircumcised fellows will come and
abuse me."

But his armor-bearer was terrified and
would not do it; so Saul took his own
sword and fell on it. 5When the armor-
bearer saw that Saul was dead, he too fell
on his sword and died. 6So Saul and his
three sons died, and all his house died together.

7When all the Israelites in the valley saw
that the army had fled and that Saul and
his sons had died, they abandoned their
towns and fled. And the Philistines came
and occupied them.

8The next day, when the Philistines
came to strip the dead, they found Saul
and his sons fallen on Mount Gilboa. 9They
stripped him and took his head and his
armor, and sent messengers throughout
the land of the Philistines to proclaim the
news among their idols and their people.
10They put his armor in the temple of their
gods and hung up his head in the temple of
Dagon.[d]

11When all the inhabitants of Jabesh Gilead[e] heard of everything the Philistines
had done to Saul, 12all their valiant men
went and took the bodies of Saul and his
sons and brought them to Jabesh. Then
they buried their bones under the great
tree in Jabesh, and they fasted seven
days.

13Saul died[f] because he was unfaithful[g]
to the LORD; he did not keep[h] the word of
the LORD and even consulted a medium[i]
for guidance, 14and did not inquire of the
LORD. So the LORD put him to death and
turned[j] the kingdom[k] over to David son
of Jesse.

10:10 [d]S Jdg 16:23 **10:11** [e]S Jdg 21:8 **10:13** [f]S 2Sa 1:1 [g]S 1Ch 5:25 [h]S 1Sa 13:13 [i]S Lev 19:31; S 20:6; Dt 18:9-14 **10:14** [j]1Ch 12:23 [k]S 1Sa 13:14

David Becomes King Over Israel

11:1–3pp — 2Sa 5:1–3

11 All Israel[l] came together to David
at Hebron[m] and said, "We are your
own flesh and blood. 2In the past, even
while Saul was king, you were the one
who led Israel on their military campaigns.[n] And the LORD your God said to
you, 'You will shepherd[o] my people Israel,
and you will become their ruler.[p]' "

3When all the elders of Israel had come
to King David at Hebron, he made a compact with them at Hebron before the LORD,
and they anointed[q] David king over Israel,
as the LORD had promised through Samuel.

David Conquers Jerusalem

11:4–9pp — 2Sa 5:6–10

4David and all the Israelites marched to
Jerusalem (that is, Jebus). The Jebusites[r]
who lived there 5said to David, "You will
not get in here." Nevertheless, David captured the fortress of Zion, the City of David.

6David had said, "Whoever leads the attack on the Jebusites will become commander-in-chief." Joab[s] son of Zeruiah
went up first, and so he received the command.

7David then took up residence in the
fortress, and so it was called the City of
David. 8He built up the city around it, from
the supporting terraces[t][t] to the surrounding wall, while Joab restored the rest of the
city. 9And David became more and more
powerful,[u] because the LORD Almighty
was with him.

David's Mighty Men

11:10–41pp — 2Sa 23:8–39

10These were the chiefs of David's

11:1 [l]S 1Ch 9:1 [m]S Ge 13:18; S 23:19 **11:2** [n]S 1Sa 18:5, 16 [o]Ps 78:71; Mt 2:6 [p]S 1Ch 5:2 **11:3** [q]1Sa 16:1-13 **11:4** [r]S Ge 10:16; S 15:18-21; S Jos 3:10; S 15:8 **11:6** [s]S 2Sa 2:13 **11:8** [t]S 2Sa 5:9; 2Ch 32:5 **11:9** [u]Est 9:4

[t]8 Or *the Millo*

10:6 *his three sons.* See v. 2 (Ish-Bosheth survived; see note on 1Sa 31:2). *all his house.* His three sons and his chief officials (his official "house"), not all his descendants (see 8:33–34 and notes; 1Sa 31:6).

10:13–14 These verses are not paralleled in the Samuel account; they were put here by the Chronicler in line with his concern with immediate retribution (see Introduction: Purpose and Themes). Seeking mediums was forbidden (Dt 18:9–14) and brought death to Saul. The Chronicler is obviously writing to an audience already familiar with Samuel and Kings, and he frequently assumes that knowledge. Here the consultation with the medium at Endor is alluded to (see 1Sa 28), but the Chronicler does not recount the incident.

11:1–2Ch 9:31 See Introduction: Portrait of David and Solomon.

11:1–3 The material here parallels that in 2Sa 5:1–3, but is recast by the Chronicler in accordance with his emphasis on the popular support given David by "all Israel" (v. 1). While the Chronicler twice mentions the seven-year reign at Hebron before the death of Ish-Bosheth and the covenant with the northern tribes (3:4; 29:27), these incidents are bypassed in the narrative portion of the book. Most striking is the elimination at this point of the information in 2Sa 5:4–5. Rather, the Chronicler paints a picture of immediate accession over "all Israel," followed by the immediate conquest of Jerusalem (see Introduction: Portrait of David and Solomon). The author once again assumes the reader's knowledge of the parallel account.

11:4–9 See 2Sa 5:6–10 and notes. The "all Israel" theme appears in v. 4 as a substitute for "the king and his men" (2Sa 5:6).

11:10–41a See 2Sa 23:8–39 and notes. In the Samuel account this list of David's mighty men is given near the end of his reign. The Chronicler has moved the list to the beginning of his reign and has greatly expanded it (11:41b–12:40), again as part of his emphasis on the broad support of "all Israel" for the kingship of David (v. 10).

mighty men—they, together with all Israel,ᵛ gave his kingship strong support to extend it over the whole land, as the LORD had promisedʷ— ¹¹this is the list of David's mighty men:ˣ

Jashobeam,ᵘ a Hacmonite, was chief of the officersᵛ; he raised his spear against three hundred men, whom he killed in one encounter.

¹²Next to him was Eleazar son of Dodai the Ahohite, one of the three mighty men. ¹³He was with David at Pas Dammim when the Philistines gathered there for battle. At a place where there was a field full of barley, the troops fled from the Philistines. ¹⁴But they took their stand in the middle of the field. They defended it and struck the Philistines down, and the LORD brought about a great victory.ʸ

¹⁵Three of the thirty chiefs came down to David to the rock at the cave of Adullam, while a band of Philistines was encamped in the Valleyᶻ of Rephaim. ¹⁶At that time David was in the stronghold,ᵃ and the Philistine garrison was at Bethlehem. ¹⁷David longed for water and said, "Oh, that someone would get me a drink of water from the well near the gate of Bethlehem!" ¹⁸So the Three broke through the Philistine lines, drew water from the well near the gate of Bethlehem and carried it back to David. But he refused to drink it; instead, he pouredᵇ it out before the LORD. ¹⁹"God forbid that I should do this!" he said. "Should I drink the blood of these men who went at the risk of their lives?" Because they risked their lives to bring it back, David would not drink it. Such were the exploits of the three mighty men.

²⁰Abishaiᶜ the brother of Joab was chief of the Three. He raised his spear against three hundred men, whom he killed, and so he became as famous as the Three. ²¹He was doubly honored above the Three and became their commander, even though he was not included among them.

²²Benaiah son of Jehoiada was a valiant fighter from Kabzeel,ᵈ who performed great exploits. He struck down two of Moab's best men. He also went down into a pit on a snowy day and killed a lion.ᵉ ²³And he struck down an Egyptian who was seven and a half feetʷ tall. Although

the Egyptian had a spear like a weaver's rodᶠ in his hand, Benaiah went against him with a club. He snatched the spear from the Egyptian's hand and killed him with his own spear. ²⁴Such were the exploits of Benaiah son of Jehoiada; he too was as famous as the three mighty men. ²⁵He was held in greater honor than any of the Thirty, but he was not included among the Three. And David put him in charge of his bodyguard.

²⁶The mighty men were:
　　Asahelᵍ the brother of Joab,
　　Elhanan son of Dodo from Bethlehem,
²⁷Shammothʰ the Harorite,
　　Helez the Pelonite,
²⁸Ira son of Ikkesh from Tekoa,
　　Abiezerⁱ from Anathoth,
²⁹Sibbecaiʲ the Hushathite,
　　Ilai the Ahohite,
³⁰Maharai the Netophathite,
　　Heled son of Baanah the Netophathite,
³¹Ithai son of Ribai from Gibeah in Benjamin,
　　Benaiahᵏ the Pirathonite,ˡ
³²Hurai from the ravines of Gaash,
　　Abiel the Arbathite,
³³Azmaveth the Baharumite,
　　Eliahba the Shaalbonite,
³⁴the sons of Hashem the Gizonite,
　　Jonathan son of Shagee the Hararite,
³⁵Ahiam son of Sacar the Hararite,
　　Eliphal son of Ur,
³⁶Hepher the Mekerathite,
　　Ahijah the Pelonite,
³⁷Hezro the Carmelite,
　　Naarai son of Ezbai,
³⁸Joel the brother of Nathan,
　　Mibhar son of Hagri,
³⁹Zelek the Ammonite,
　　Naharai the Berothite, the armorbearer of Joab son of Zeruiah,
⁴⁰Ira the Ithrite,
　　Gareb the Ithrite,
⁴¹Uriahᵐ the Hittite,
　　Zabadⁿ son of Ahlai,
⁴²Adina son of Shiza the Reubenite,

11:10 ʳver 1
ʷ1Ch 12:23
11:11
ˣS 2Sa 17:10
11:14
ʸS Ex 14:30;
S 1Sa 11:13
11:15 ᶻ1Ch 14:9;
Isa 17:5
11:16
ᵃS 2Sa 5:17
11:18
ᵇS Dt 12:16
11:20
ᶜS 1Sa 26:6
11:22
ᵈS Jos 15:21
ᵉ1Sa 17:36

11:23 ᶠS 1Sa 17:7
11:26
ᵍS 2Sa 2:18
11:27 ʰ1Ch 27:8
11:28
ⁱ1Ch 27:12
11:29
ʲS 2Sa 21:18
11:31
ᵏ1Ch 27:14
ˡS Jdg 12:13
11:41 ᵐ2Sa 11:6
ⁿ1Ch 2:36

ᵘ11 Possibly a variant of Jashob-Baal　ᵛ11 Or Thirty; some Septuagint manuscripts Three (see also 2 Samuel 23:8)　ʷ23 Hebrew five cubits (about 2.3 meters)

11:12–14 See 2Sa 23:9b–11a.
11:15–19 David recognizes that he is not worthy of such devotion and makes the water a drink offering to the Lord (see Ge 35:14; 2Ki 16:13; Jer 7:18; Hos 9:4).
11:41b–12:40 See note on vv. 10–41a. The list in 2Sa 23

ends with Uriah the Hittite (2Sa 11); the source for the additional names is not known. The emphasis continues to be on the support of "all Israel"—even Saul's own kinsmen recognized the legitimacy of David's kingship before Saul's death (12:1–7,16–18,23,29).

who was chief of the Reubenites,
and the thirty with him,
43Hanan son of Maacah,
Joshaphat the Mithnite,
44Uzzia the Ashterathite,[o]
Shama and Jeiel the sons of Hotham the Aroerite,
45Jediael son of Shimri,
his brother Joha the Tizite,
46Eliel the Mahavite,
Jeribai and Joshaviah the sons of Elnaam,
Ithmah the Moabite,
47Eliel, Obed and Jaasiel the Mezobaite.

Warriors Join David

12 These were the men who came to
David at Ziklag,[p] while he was
banished from the presence of Saul son of
Kish (they were among the warriors who
helped him in battle; 2they were armed
with bows and were able to shoot arrows
or to sling stones right-handed or left-
handed;[q] they were kinsmen of Saul[r]
from the tribe of Benjamin):

3Ahiezer their chief and Joash the sons
of Shemaah the Gibeathite; Jeziel and
Pelet the sons of Azmaveth; Beracah,
Jehu the Anathothite, 4and Ishmaiah
the Gibeonite, a mighty man among
the Thirty, who was a leader of the
Thirty; Jeremiah, Jahaziel, Johanan,
Jozabad the Gederathite,[s] 5Eluzai,
Jerimoth, Bealiah, Shemariah and
Shephatiah the Haruphite; 6Elkanah,
Isshiah, Azarel, Joezer and Jashobeam
the Korahites; 7and Joelah and Zebadiah the sons of Jeroham from Gedor.[t]

8Some Gadites[u] defected to David at his
stronghold in the desert. They were brave
warriors, ready for battle and able to handle the shield and spear. Their faces were
the faces of lions,[v] and they were as swift
as gazelles[w] in the mountains.

9Ezer was the chief,
Obadiah the second in command,
Eliab the third,
10Mishmannah the fourth, Jeremiah the fifth,
11Attai the sixth, Eliel the seventh,
12Johanan the eighth, Elzabad the ninth,
13Jeremiah the tenth and Macbannai the eleventh.

14These Gadites were army commanders; the least was a match for a hundred,[x]
and the greatest for a thousand.[y] 15It was
they who crossed the Jordan in the first
month when it was overflowing all its
banks,[z] and they put to flight everyone
living in the valleys, to the east and to the
west.

16Other Benjamites[a] and some men
from Judah also came to David in his
stronghold. 17David went out to meet
them and said to them, "If you have come
to me in peace, to help me, I am ready to
have you unite with me. But if you have
come to betray me to my enemies when
my hands are free from violence, may the
God of our fathers see it and judge you."
18Then the Spirit[b] came upon Amasai,[c]
chief of the Thirty, and he said:

"We are yours, O David!
We are with you, O son of Jesse!
Success,[d] success to you,
and success to those who help you,
for your God will help you."

So David received them and made them
leaders of his raiding bands.

19Some of the men of Manasseh defected to David when he went with the Philistines to fight against Saul. (He and his men
did not help the Philistines because, after
consultation, their rulers sent him away.
They said, "It will cost us our heads if he
deserts to his master Saul.")[e] 20When David went to Ziklag,[f] these were the men of
Manasseh who defected to him: Adnah,
Jozabad, Jediael, Michael, Jozabad, Elihu
and Zillethai, leaders of units of a thousand
in Manasseh. 21They helped David against
raiding bands, for all of them were brave
warriors, and they were commanders in
his army. 22Day after day men came to
help David, until he had a great army, like
the army of God.[x]

Others Join David at Hebron

23These are the numbers of the men

11:44 [o]S Dt 1:4
12:1 [p]S Jos 15:31
12:2 [q]S Jdg 3:15 [r]S 2Sa 3:19
12:4 [s]Jos 15:36
12:7 [t]S Jos 15:58
12:8 [u]S Ge 30:11 [v]2Sa 17:10 [w]S 2Sa 2:18
12:14 [x]S Lev 26:8 [y]S Dt 32:30
12:15 [z]S Jos 3:15
12:16 [a]S 2Sa 3:19
12:18 [b]S Jdg 3:10; 1Ch 28:12; 2Ch 15:1; 20:14; 24:20 [c]S 2Sa 17:25 [d]1Sa 25:5-6
12:19 [e]1Sa 29:2-11
12:20 [f]S 1Sa 27:6

[x]22 Or *a great and mighty army*

12:1 The Chronicler assumes the reader's knowledge of the events at Ziklag (1Sa 27); see vv. 19–20.
12:8–15 The men of Gad were from Transjordan. Melting snows to the north would have brought the Jordan to flood stage in the first month (March-April) at the time of their crossing (v. 15). The most appropriate time for this incident would have been in the period of David's wandering in the region of the Dead Sea (1Sa 23:14; 24:1; 25:1; 26:1).
12:23–37 The emphasis remains on "all Israel" (v. 38). Though 13 tribes are named, they are grouped in order to maintain the traditional number of 12 (see note on 2:1–2). The northernmost and the Transjordan tribes send the largest number of men (vv. 33–37), reinforcing the degree of support that David enjoyed not only in Judah and Benjamin

armed for battle who came to David at Hebron[g] to turn[h] Saul's kingdom over to him, as the LORD had said:[i]

24men of Judah, carrying shield and spear—6,800 armed for battle;
25men of Simeon, warriors ready for battle—7,100;
26men of Levi—4,600, 27including Jehoiada, leader of the family of Aaron, with 3,700 men, 28and Zadok,[j] a brave young warrior, with 22 officers from his family;
29men of Benjamin,[k] Saul's kinsmen—3,000, most[l] of whom had remained loyal to Saul's house until then;
30men of Ephraim, brave warriors, famous in their own clans—20,800;
31men of half the tribe of Manasseh, designated by name to come and make David king—18,000;
32men of Issachar, who understood the times and knew what Israel should do[m]—200 chiefs, with all their relatives under their command;
33men of Zebulun, experienced soldiers prepared for battle with every type of weapon, to help David with undivided loyalty—50,000;
34men of Naphtali—1,000 officers, together with 37,000 men carrying shields and spears;
35men of Dan, ready for battle—28,600;
36men of Asher, experienced soldiers prepared for battle—40,000;
37and from east of the Jordan, men of

Reuben, Gad and the half-tribe of Manasseh, armed with every type of weapon—120,000.

38All these were fighting men who volunteered to serve in the ranks. They came to Hebron fully determined to make David king over all Israel.[n] All the rest of the Israelites were also of one mind to make David king. 39The men spent three days there with David, eating and drinking,[o] for their families had supplied provisions for them. 40Also, their neighbors from as far away as Issachar, Zebulun and Naphtali came bringing food on donkeys, camels, mules and oxen. There were plentiful supplies[p] of flour, fig cakes, raisin[q] cakes, wine, oil, cattle and sheep, for there was joy[r] in Israel.

Bringing Back the Ark

13:1–14pp — 2Sa 6:1–11

13 David conferred with each of his officers, the commanders of thousands and commanders of hundreds. 2He then said to the whole assembly of Israel, "If it seems good to you and if it is the will of the LORD our God, let us send word far and wide to the rest of our brothers throughout the territories of Israel, and also to the priests and Levites who are with them in their towns and pasturelands, to come and join us. 3Let us bring the ark of our God back to us,[s] for we did not inquire[t] of[y] it[z] during the reign of Saul."

12:23 *g*2Sa 2:3-4
*h*1Ch 10:14
*i*S 1Sa 16:1;
1Ch 11:10
12:28 *j*1Ch 6:8;
15:11; 16:39;
27:17
12:29
*k*S 2Sa 3:19
*l*2Sa 2:8-9
12:32 *m*Est 1:13

12:38 *n*S 1Ch 9:1
12:39 *o*2Sa 3:20;
Isa 25:6-8
12:40
*p*S 2Sa 16:1;
17:29 *q*1Sa 25:18
*r*1Ch 29:22
13:3 *s*1Sa 7:1-2
*t*2Ch 1:5

*y*3 Or *we neglected*   *z*3 Or *him*

but throughout the other tribes as well. The numbers in this section seem quite high. Essentially two approaches are followed on this question: 1. It is possible to explain the numbers so that a lower figure is actually attained. The Hebrew word for "thousand" may represent a unit of a tribe, each having its own commander (13:1; see Nu 31:14,48,52,54). In this case the numbers would be read not as a total figure, but as representative commanders. For example, the 6,800 from Judah (v. 24) would be read either as six commanders of 1,000 and eight commanders of 100 (see 13:1), or possibly as six commanders of thousands and 800 men. Reducing the numbers in this fashion fits well with 13:1 and with the list of commanders alone found for Zadok's family (v. 28) and the tribe of Issachar (v. 32). Taking the numbers as straight totals would require the presence of 340,800 persons in Hebron for a feast at the same time. 2. Another approach is to allow the numbers to stand and to view them as hyperbole on the part of the Chronicler to achieve a number "like the army of God" (v. 22). This approach would fit well with the Chronicler's glorification of David and with the banquet scene that follows.
12:38–40 The Chronicler's portrait of David is influenced by his Messianic expectations (see Introduction: Purpose and Themes). In the presence of a third of a million people (see note on vv. 23–37) David's coronation banquet typifies the future Messianic feast (Isa 25:6–8). The imagery of the

Messianic banquet became prominent in the intertestamental literature (*Apocalypse of Baruch* 29:4–8; *Enoch* 62:14) and in the NT (see Mt 8:11–12 and Lk 13:28–30; Mt 22:1–10 and Lk 14:16–24; see also Mt 25:1–13; Lk 22:28–30; Rev 19:7–9). The Lord's Supper anticipates that coming banquet (Mt 26:29; Mk 14:25; Lk 22:15–18; 1Cor 11:23–26).
13:1–14 See 2Sa 6:1–11 and notes. The author abandons the chronological order as given in 2Sa 5–6 and puts the transfer of the ark first, delaying his account of the palace building and the Philistine campaign until later (ch. 14). This is in accordance with his portrayal of David; David's concern with the ark was expressed immediately upon his accession—his consultation with the leaders appears to be set in the context of the coronation banquet (12:38–40).
13:1–4 These verses are not found in Samuel and reflect the Chronicler's own concerns with "all Israel." The semi-military expedition to retrieve the ark in 2Sa 6:1 is here broadened by consultation with and support from the whole assembly of Israel, "throughout the territories" (v. 2), including the priests and Levites—an important point for the Chronicler since only they are allowed to move the ark (15:2,13; 23:25–27; Dt 10:8).
13:3 *we did not inquire of it during the reign of Saul.* 1Sa 14:18 may be an exception (but see NIV text note there).

4The whole assembly agreed to do this, because it seemed right to all the people.

5So David assembled all the Israelites, *u* from the Shihor River *v* in Egypt to Lebo *a* Hamath, *w* to bring the ark of God from Kiriath Jearim. *x* 6David and all the Israelites with him went to Baalah *y* of Judah (Kiriath Jearim) to bring up from there the ark of God the LORD, who is enthroned between the cherubim *z*—the ark that is called by the Name.

7They moved the ark of God from Abinadab's *a* house on a new cart, with Uzzah and Ahio guiding it. 8David and all the Israelites were celebrating with all their might before God, with songs and with harps, lyres, tambourines, cymbals and trumpets. *b*

9When they came to the threshing floor of Kidon, Uzzah reached out his hand to steady the ark, because the oxen stumbled. 10The LORD's anger *c* burned against Uzzah, and he struck him down *d* because he had put his hand on the ark. So he died there before God.

11Then David was angry because the LORD's wrath had broken out against Uzzah, and to this day that place is called Perez Uzzah. *b* *e*

12David was afraid of God that day and asked, "How can I ever bring the ark of God to me?" 13He did not take the ark to be with him in the City of David. Instead, he took it aside to the house of Obed-Edom *f* the Gittite. 14The ark of God remained with the family of Obed-Edom in his house for three months, and the LORD

blessed his household *g* and everything he had.

David's House and Family

14:1–7pp — 2Sa 5:11–16; 1Ch 3:5–8

14 Now Hiram king of Tyre sent messengers to David, along with cedar logs, *h* stonemasons and carpenters to build a palace for him. 2And David knew that the LORD had established him as king over Israel and that his kingdom had been highly exalted *i* for the sake of his people Israel.

3In Jerusalem David took more wives and became the father of more sons *j* and daughters. 4These are the names of the children born to him there: *k* Shammua, Shobab, Nathan, Solomon, 5Ibhar, Elishua, Elpelet, 6Nogah, Nepheg, Japhia, 7Elishama, Beeliada *c* and Eliphelet.

David Defeats the Philistines

14:8–17pp — 2Sa 5:17–25

8When the Philistines heard that David had been anointed king over all Israel, *l* they went up in full force to search for him, but David heard about it and went out to meet them. 9Now the Philistines had come and raided the Valley *m* of Rephaim; 10so David inquired of God: "Shall I go and attack the Philistines? Will you hand them over to me?"

The LORD answered him, "Go, I will hand them over to you."

11So David and his men went up to Baal Perazim, *n* and there he defeated them. He

Cross references

13:5 *u* 1Ch 11:1;
15:3 *v* S Jos 13:3
w S Nu 13:21
x S 1Sa 7:2
13:6 *y* S Jos 15:9
z S Ex 25:22;
2Ki 19:15
13:7 *a* S 1Sa 7:1
13:8 *b* 1Ch 15:16,
19,24; 2Ch 5:12;
Ps 92:3
13:10
c 1Ch 15:13
d S Lev 10:2
13:11
e 1Ch 15:13;
Ps 7:11
13:13
f 1Ch 15:18,24;
16:38; 26:4-5,15

13:14
g S 2Sa 6:11
14:1 *h* S 1Ki 5:6;
1Ch 17:6; 22:4;
2Ch 2:3; Ezr 3:7;
Hag 1:8
14:2 *i* S Nu 24:7;
S Dt 26:19
14:3 *j* S 1Ch 3:1
14:4 *k* S 1Ch 3:9
14:8 *l* 1Ch 11:1
14:9 *m* ver 13;
S Jos 15:8;
S 1Ch 11:15
14:11 *n* Ps 94:16;
Isa 28:21

a 5 Or *to the entrance to* *b* 11 *Perez Uzzah* means *outbreak against Uzzah.* *c* 7 A variant of *Eliada*

13:5–6 The emphasis remains on the united action of "all Israel." Israelites came to participate in this venture all the way from Lebo Hamath in the north and from the Shihor River in the south.

13:5 *Shihor.* An Egyptian term meaning "the pool of Horus." It appears to be a part of the Nile or one of the major canals of the Nile (see Jos 13:3; Isa 23:3; Jer 2:18 and notes).

13:6 *Baalah.* The Canaanite name for Kiriath Jearim, also known as Kiriath Baal (Jos 18:14). The Chronicler assumes that his readers are familiar with the account of how the ark came to be at Kiriath Jearim (1Sa 6:1–7:1).

13:7 *Uzzah and Ahio.* Sons or descendants of Abinadab (2Sa 6:3).

13:10 *because he had put his hand on the ark.* The ark was to be moved only by Levites, who carried it with poles inserted through rings in the sides of the ark (Ex 25:12–15). None of the holy things was to be touched, on penalty of death (Nu 4:15). These strictures were observed in the second and successful attempt to move the ark to Jerusalem (15:1–15). It cannot be known whether Uzzah and Ahio were Levites—the Samuel account does not mention the presence of Levites, but the Chronicler's careful inclusion of Levites in this expedition suggests that they were (see note on vv. 1–4). In any case, the ark should not have been moved on a cart (as done by the Philistines, 1Sa 6) or

touched.

13:13 *Obed-Edom.* Perhaps the same man mentioned in 15:18,21,24. In 26:4 God's blessing on Obed-Edom included numerous sons. This reference also establishes that Obed-Edom was a Levite and that the ark was properly left in his care.

14:1–17 The Chronicler backtracks to pick up material from 2Sa 5 deferred to this point (see note on 13:1–14). The three-month period that the ark remained with Obed-Edom (13:14) was filled with incidents showing God's blessing on David: the building of his royal house (vv. 1–2), his large family (vv. 3–7) and his success in warfare (vv. 8–16)—all because of the Lord's blessing (vv. 2,17).

14:1–2 See 2Sa 5:11–12 and notes.

14:1 *Hiram.* Later provided materials and labor for building the temple (2Ch 2). His mention here implies international recognition of David as king over Israel and a treaty between David and Hiram.

14:3–7 See 3:5–9; 2Sa 5:13–16. David's children born in Hebron are omitted (3:1–4; 2Sa 3:2–5; see note on 11:1–3).

14:7 *Beeliada.* Eliada (see NIV text note) in 3:8; 2Sa 5:16.

14:8–12 See 2Sa 5:17–21 and notes.

14:11 *break out . . . Perazim.* The Hebrew underlying the name of this place where the Lord broke out against the Philistines is the same as that underlying the word used in

said, "As waters break out, God has broken out against my enemies by my hand." So that place was called Baal Perazim.[d] [12]The Philistines had abandoned their gods there, and David gave orders to burn[o] them in the fire.[p]

[13]Once more the Philistines raided the valley;[q] [14]so David inquired of God again, and God answered him, "Do not go straight up, but circle around them and attack them in front of the balsam trees. [15]As soon as you hear the sound of marching in the tops of the balsam trees, move out to battle, because that will mean God has gone out in front of you to strike the Philistine army." [16]So David did as God commanded him, and they struck down the Philistine army, all the way from Gibeon[r] to Gezer.[s]

[17]So David's fame[t] spread throughout every land, and the LORD made all the nations fear[u] him.

The Ark Brought to Jerusalem

15:25–16:3pp — 2Sa 6:12–19

15 After David had constructed buildings for himself in the City of David, he prepared[v] a place for the ark of God and pitched[w] a tent for it. [2]Then David said, "No one but the Levites[x] may carry[y] the ark of God, because the LORD chose them to carry the ark of the LORD and to minister[z] before him forever."

[3]David assembled all Israel[a] in Jerusalem to bring up the ark of the LORD to the place he had prepared for it. [4]He called together the descendants of Aaron and the Levites:[b]

[5]From the descendants of Kohath,
    Uriel[c] the leader and 120 relatives;

---

[6]from the descendants of Merari,
    Asaiah the leader and 220 relatives;
[7]from the descendants of Gershon,[e]
    Joel the leader and 130 relatives;
[8]from the descendants of Elizaphan,[d]
    Shemaiah the leader and 200 relatives;
[9]from the descendants of Hebron,[e]
    Eliel the leader and 80 relatives;
[10]from the descendants of Uzziel,
    Amminadab the leader and 112 relatives.

[11]Then David summoned Zadok[f] and Abiathar[g] the priests, and Uriel, Asaiah, Joel, Shemaiah, Eliel and Amminadab the Levites. [12]He said to them, "You are the heads of the Levitical families; you and your fellow Levites are to consecrate[h] yourselves and bring up the ark of the LORD, the God of Israel, to the place I have prepared for it. [13]It was because you, the Levites,[i] did not bring it up the first time that the LORD our God broke out in anger against us.[j] We did not inquire of him about how to do it in the prescribed way.[k]" [14]So the priests and Levites consecrated themselves in order to bring up the ark of the LORD, the God of Israel. [15]And the Levites carried the ark of God with the poles on their shoulders, as Moses had commanded[l] in accordance with the word of the LORD.[m]

[16]David[n] told the leaders of the Levites[o] to appoint their brothers as singers[p] to sing joyful songs, accompanied by musical instruments: lyres, harps and cymbals.[q]

[17]So the Levites appointed Heman[r] son

Cross references (center column)

14:12
o S Ex 32:20
p S Jos 7:15
14:13 q S ver 9
14:16 r S Jos 9:3
s Jos 10:33
14:17 t S Jos 6:27
u Ex 15:14-16;
S Dt 2:25;
Ps 2:1-12
15:1
v Ps 132:1-18
w S 2Sa 6:17;
1Ch 16:1; 17:1
15:2 x S Nu 3:6;
4:15; Dt 10:8;
31:25; 2Ch 5:5
y S Dt 31:9
z 1Ch 16:4;
23:13;
2Ch 29:11; 31:2;
Ps 134:1; 135:2
15:3 a S 1Ch 13:5
15:4
b S Nu 3:17-20
15:5 c 1Ch 6:24

15:8 d S Ex 6:22
15:9 e Ex 6:18
15:11
f S 1Ch 12:28
g S 1Sa 22:20
15:12
h S Ex 29:1;
30:19-21,30;
40:31-32;
S Lev 11:44
15:13 i 1Ki 8:4
j S 1Ch 13:11
k S Lev 5:10
15:15
l S Ex 25:14
m 2Sa 6:7
15:16 n 1Ch 6:31
o 2Ch 7:6
p Ezr 2:41;
Ne 11:23;
Ps 68:25
q S 1Ch 13:8;
23:5; 2Ch 29:26;
Ne 12:27,36;
Job 21:12;
Ps 150:5; Am 6:5
15:17
r S 1Ch 6:33

---

[d] *11 Baal Perazim* means *the lord who breaks out.*
[e] *7* Hebrew *Gershom,* a variant of *Gershon*

13:11 when the Lord broke out against Uzzah (see NIV text notes).

14:12 *gave orders to burn them.* 2Sa 5:21 does not mention burning but says that David and his men carried the idols away. Many have seen here an intentional change on the part of the Chronicler in order to bring David's actions into strict conformity with the law, which required that pagan idols be burned (Dt 7:5,25). However, some Septuagint (the Greek translation of the OT) manuscripts of Samuel agree with Chronicles that David burned the idols. This would indicate that the Chronicler was not innovating for theological reasons but was carefully reproducing the text he had before him, which differed from the Masoretic (traditional Hebrew) text of Samuel.

14:13–16 See 2Sa 5:22–25 and notes.

14:17 *the LORD made all the nations fear him.* Here and elsewhere the Chronicler uses an expression that refers to an incapacitating terror brought on by the sense that the awful power of God is present in behalf of his people (see Ex 15:16). Thus David is seen by the nations as the very representative of God (similarly Asa, 2Ch 14:14; Jehoshaphat,

2Ch 17:10; 20:29).

15:1–16:3 This account of the successful attempt to move the ark to Jerusalem is greatly expanded over the material in 2 Samuel. Only 15:25–16:3 has a parallel (2Sa 6:12–19); the rest of the material is unique to the Chronicler and reflects his own interests, especially in the Levites and cultic musicians (vv. 3–24; see Introduction: Purpose and Themes). Ps 132 should also be read in connection with this account.

15:1 *constructed buildings for himself.* See 14:1–2 and note on 13:1–14.

15:2–3 See note on 13:10.

15:4–10 The three clans of Levi are represented (Kohath, Merari and Gershon), as well as three distinct subgroups within Kohath (Elizaphan, Hebron and Uzziel)—862 in all.

15:12 *consecrate yourselves.* Through ritual washings and avoidance of ceremonial defilement (Ex 29:1–37; 30:19–21; 40:31–32; Lev 8:5–35).

15:13–15 The Chronicler provides the explanation for the failure in the first attempt to move the ark, an explanation not found in the Samuel account (see note on 13:10).

of Joel; from his brothers, Asaph[s] son of Berekiah; and from their brothers the Merarites,[t] Ethan son of Kushaiah; [18]and with them their brothers next in rank: Zechariah,[f] Jaaziel, Shemiramoth, Jehiel, Unni, Eliab, Benaiah, Maaseiah, Mattithiah, Eliphelehu, Mikneiah, Obed-Edom[u] and Jeiel,[g] the gatekeepers.

[19]The musicians Heman,[v] Asaph and Ethan were to sound the bronze cymbals, [20]Zechariah, Aziel, Shemiramoth, Jehiel, Unni, Eliab, Maaseiah and Benaiah were to play the lyres according to *alamoth*,[h] [21]and Mattithiah, Eliphelehu, Mikneiah, Obed-Edom, Jeiel and Azaziah were to play the harps, directing according to *sheminith*.[h] [22]Kenaniah the head Levite was in charge of the singing; that was his responsibility because he was skillful at it.

[23]Berekiah and Elkanah were to be doorkeepers for the ark. [24]Shebaniah, Joshaphat, Nethanel, Amasai, Zechariah, Benaiah and Eliezer the priests were to blow trumpets[w] before the ark of God. Obed-Edom and Jehiah were also to be doorkeepers for the ark.

[25]So David and the elders of Israel and the commanders of units of a thousand went to bring up the ark[x] of the covenant of the LORD from the house of Obed-Edom, with rejoicing. [26]Because God had helped the Levites who were carrying the ark of the covenant of the LORD, seven bulls and seven rams[y] were sacrificed. [27]Now David was clothed in a robe of fine linen, as were all the Levites who were carrying the ark, and as were the singers, and Kenaniah, who was in charge of the singing of the choirs. David also wore a linen ephod.[z] [28]So all Israel[a] brought up the ark of the covenant of the LORD with shouts,[b] with the sounding of rams' horns[c] and trumpets, and of cymbals, and the playing of lyres and harps.

[29]As the ark of the covenant of the LORD was entering the City of David, Michal daughter of Saul watched from a window. And when she saw King David dancing and celebrating, she despised him in her heart.

16 They brought the ark of God and set it inside the tent that David had pitched[d] for it, and they presented burnt offerings and fellowship offerings[i] before God. [2]After David had finished sacrificing the burnt offerings and fellowship offerings, he blessed[e] the people in the name of the LORD. [3]Then he gave a loaf of bread, a cake of dates and a cake of raisins[f] to each Israelite man and woman.

[4]He appointed some of the Levites to minister[g] before the ark of the LORD, to make petition, to give thanks, and to praise the LORD, the God of Israel: [5]Asaph was the chief, Zechariah second, then Jeiel, Shemiramoth, Jehiel, Mattithiah, Eliab, Benaiah, Obed-Edom and Jeiel. They were to play the lyres and harps, Asaph was to sound the cymbals, [6]and Benaiah and Jahaziel the priests were to blow the trumpets regularly before the ark of the covenant of God.

David's Psalm of Thanks

16:8–22pp — Ps 105:1–15
16:23–33pp — Ps 96:1–13
16:34–36pp — Ps 106:1,47–48

[7]That day David first committed to Asaph and his associates this psalm[h] of thanks to the LORD:

[8]Give thanks[i] to the LORD, call on his
    name;

Cross references (center column):

15:17 [s]1Ch 6:39
  [t]1Ch 6:44
15:18 [u]2Sa 6:10;
  1Ch 26:4-5
15:19 [v]1Ch 16:41; 25:6
15:24 [w]2Ch 5:12; 7:6;
  29:26
15:25 [x]2Ch 1:4;
  5:2; Jer 3:16
15:26 [y]Nu 23:1-4,29
15:27 [z]S 1Sa 2:18
15:28 [a]S 1Ch 9:1
  [b]S 1Ki 1:39;
  Zec 4:7
  [c]S Ex 19:13

16:1 [d]S 1Ch 15:1
16:2 [e]S Ex 39:43;
  Nu 6:23-27
16:3 [f]Isa 16:7
16:4 [g]S 1Ch 15:2
16:7 [h]Ps 47:7
16:8 [i]ver 34;
  Ps 107:1; 118:1;
  136:1

---

f18 Three Hebrew manuscripts and most Septuagint manuscripts (see also verse 20 and 1 Chron. 16:5); most Hebrew manuscripts *Zechariah son and* or *Zechariah, Ben and*   g18 Hebrew; Septuagint (see also verse 21) *Jeiel and Azaziah*   h20,21 Probably a musical term   i1 Traditionally *peace offerings*; also in verse 2

15:18,21,24 *Obed-Edom.* See note on 13:13.
15:24 *priests were to blow trumpets.* See 16:6; Nu 10:1–10.
15:27 Both 2Sa 6:14 and the Chronicler mention David's wearing a linen ephod, a garment worn by priests (1Sa 2:18; 22:18). The Chronicler adds, however, that David (as well as the rest of the Levites in the procession) was wearing a robe of fine linen, further associating him with the dress of the cultic functionaries. Apparently the Chronicler viewed David as a priest-king, a kind of Messianic figure (see Ps 110; Zec 6:9–15).
15:29 Parallel to 2Sa 6:16, but the Chronicler omits the remainder of this incident recorded there (2Sa 6:20–23). Some interpreters regard this omission as part of the Chronicler's positive view of David, so that a possibly unseemly account is omitted. On the other hand, it is equally plausible that the Chronicler here simply assumes the reader's knowledge of the other account (see notes on 10:13–14; 11:1–3;

12:1; 13:6).
16:1–3 David is further associated with the priests in his supervision of the sacrifices and his exercising the priestly prerogative of blessing the people (Nu 6:22–27; see note on 15:27). The baked goods provided by David were for the sacrificial meal following the fellowship offerings (Lev 3:1–17; 7:11–21,28–36).
16:8–36 Similar to various parts of the book of Psalms (for vv. 8–22 see Ps 105:1–15; for vv. 23–33, Ps 96; for vv. 34–36, Ps 106:1,47–48). This psalm is not found in the Samuel account. The use of the lengthy historical portion from Ps 105 emphasizing the promises to Abraham would be particularly relevant to the Chronicler's postexilic audience, for whom the faithfulness of God was a fresh reality in their return to the land. The citation from Ps 106 would also be of immediate relevance to the Chronicler's audience as those who had been gathered and delivered from the nations (v. 35).

make known among the nations[j]
   what he has done.
[9]Sing to him, sing praise[k] to him;
   tell of all his wonderful acts.
[10]Glory in his holy name;[l]
   let the hearts of those who seek the
   LORD rejoice.
[11]Look to the LORD and his strength;
   seek[m] his face always.
[12]Remember[n] the wonders[o] he has done,
   his miracles,[p] and the judgments he
   pronounced,
[13]O descendants of Israel his servant,
   O sons of Jacob, his chosen ones.

[14]He is the LORD our God;
   his judgments[q] are in all the earth.
[15]He remembers[r] his covenant forever,
   the word he commanded, for a
   thousand generations,
[16]the covenant[s] he made with Abraham,
   the oath he swore to Isaac.
[17]He confirmed it to Jacob[t] as a decree,
   to Israel as an everlasting covenant:
[18]"To you I will give the land of Canaan[u]
   as the portion you will inherit."

[19]When they were but few in number,[v]
   few indeed, and strangers in it,
[20]they[k] wandered[w] from nation to
   nation,
   from one kingdom to another.
[21]He allowed no man to oppress them;
   for their sake he rebuked kings:[x]
[22]"Do not touch my anointed ones;
   do my prophets[y] no harm."

[23]Sing to the LORD, all the earth;
   proclaim his salvation day after day.
[24]Declare his glory[z] among the nations,
   his marvelous deeds among all
   peoples.
[25]For great is the LORD and most worthy
   of praise;[a]
   he is to be feared[b] above all gods.[c]
[26]For all the gods of the nations are idols,
   but the LORD made the heavens.[d]
[27]Splendor and majesty are before him;
   strength and joy in his dwelling place.
[28]Ascribe to the LORD, O families of
   nations,
   ascribe to the LORD glory and
   strength,[e]
[29] ascribe to the LORD the glory due his
   name.[f]
   Bring an offering and come before him;

   worship the LORD in the splendor of
   his[l] holiness.[g]
[30]Tremble[h] before him, all the earth!
   The world is firmly established; it
   cannot be moved.[i]
[31]Let the heavens rejoice, let the earth be
   glad;[j]
   let them say among the nations, "The
   LORD reigns![k]"
[32]Let the sea resound, and all that is in
   it;[l]
   let the fields be jubilant, and
   everything in them!
[33]Then the trees[m] of the forest will sing,
   they will sing for joy before the LORD,
   for he comes to judge[n] the earth.

[34]Give thanks[o] to the LORD, for he is
   good;[p]
   his love endures forever.[q]
[35]Cry out, "Save us, O God our Savior;[r]
   gather us and deliver us from the
   nations,
   that we may give thanks to your holy
   name,
   that we may glory in your praise."
[36]Praise be to the LORD, the God of
   Israel,[s]
   from everlasting to everlasting.

Then all the people said "Amen" and
"Praise the LORD."

[37]David left Asaph and his associates before the ark of the covenant of the LORD to
minister there regularly, according to each
day's requirements.[t] [38]He also left Obed-
Edom[u] and his sixty-eight associates to
minister with them. Obed-Edom son of
Jeduthun, and also Hosah,[v] were gatekeepers.

[39]David left Zadok[w] the priest and his
fellow priests before the tabernacle of the
LORD at the high place in Gibeon[x] [40]to
present burnt offerings to the LORD on the
altar of burnt offering regularly, morning
and evening, in accordance with everything written in the Law[y] of the LORD,
which he had given Israel. [41]With them

Center column cross-references:

16:8 /S 2Ki 19:19
16:9 kS Ex 15:1;
Ps 7:17
16:10 lPs 8:1;
29:2; 66:2
16:11 mver 10;
1Ch 28:9;
2Ch 7:14; 14:4;
15:2,12; 16:12;
18:4; 20:4; 34:3;
Ps 24:6; 27:8;
105:4; 119:2,58;
Pr 8:17
16:12 nPs 77:11
oS Dt 4:34
pPs 78:43
16:14 qIsa 4:4;
26:9
16:15 rS Ge 8:1;
Ps 98:3; 111:5;
115:12; 136:23
16:16
sS Ge 12:7;
S 15:18;
22:16-18
16:17
tGe 35:9-12
16:18
uGe 13:14-17
16:19 vDt 7:7
16:20
wS Ge 20:13
16:21 xGe 12:17;
S 20:3;
Ex 7:15-18;
Ps 9:5
16:22 yS Ge 20:7
16:24 zIsa 42:12;
66:19
16:25 aPs 18:3;
48:1 bPs 76:7;
89:7 cEx 18:11;
Dt 32:39;
2Ch 2:5;
Ps 135:5;
Isa 40:25
16:26 dPs 8:3;
102:25
16:28 ePs 29:1-2
16:29 fPs 8:1

gZCh 20:21;
Ps 29:1-2
16:30 hPs 2:11;
33:8; 76:8; 99:1;
114:7 iPs 93:1
16:31 jIsa 44:23;
49:13 kPs 9:7;
47:8; 93:1; 97:1;
99:1; 146:10;
Isa 52:7; La 5:19
16:32 lEx 20:11;
Isa 42:10
16:33 mIsa 14:8;
55:12 nIsa 2:10;
Ps 7:8; 96:10;
98:9; 110:6;
Isa 2:4
16:34 oS ver 8;
Ps 105:1; Isa 12:4
pPs 25:7; 34:8;
100:5; 135:3;
145:9; Na 1:7
qZCh 5:13; 7:3;
Ezr 3:11
16:35 rDt 32:15;
Ps 18:46; 38:22;
Mic 7:7
16:36
sS 1Ki 8:15;
Ps 72:18-19
16:37 tZCh 8:14
16:38
uS 1Ch 13:13;
26:4-5

v1Ch 26:10 16:39 wS 1Sa 2:35; S 2Sa 8:17; S 1Ch 12:28
x S Jos 9:3; 2Ch 1:3 16:40 yS Ex 29:38; Nu 28:1-8

j15 Some Septuagint manuscripts (see also Psalm 105:8);
Hebrew Remember k 18-20 One Hebrew manuscript,
Septuagint and Vulgate (see also Psalm 105:12); most
Hebrew manuscripts inherit, / 19though you are but few
in number, / few indeed, and strangers in it." / 20They
l 29 Or LORD with the splendor of

16:29 splendor of his holiness. See note on Ps 29:2.
16:39 tabernacle . . . in Gibeon. The tabernacle remained
at Gibeon until Solomon's construction of the temple in
Jerusalem (2Ch 1:13; 5:5), when it was stored within the
temple. The existence of these two shrines—the tabernacle
and the temporary structure for the ark in Jerusalem (v.
1)—accounts for the two high priests: Zadok serving in
Gibeon and Abiathar in Jerusalem (18:16; 27:34; see note
on 6:8).

were Heman[z] and Jeduthun and the rest of those chosen and designated by name to give thanks to the LORD, "for his love endures forever." [42]Heman and Jeduthun were responsible for the sounding of the trumpets and cymbals and for the playing of the other instruments for sacred song.[a] The sons of Jeduthun[b] were stationed at the gate.

[43]Then all the people left, each for his own home, and David returned home to bless his family.

God's Promise to David

17:1–15pp — 2Sa 7:1–17

17 After David was settled in his palace, he said to Nathan the prophet, "Here I am, living in a palace of cedar, while the ark of the covenant of the LORD is under a tent.[c]"

[2]Nathan replied to David, "Whatever you have in mind,[d] do it, for God is with you."

[3]That night the word of God came to Nathan, saying:

[4]"Go and tell my servant David, 'This is what the LORD says: You[e] are not the one to build me a house to dwell in. [5]I have not dwelt in a house from the day I brought Israel up out of Egypt to this day. I have moved from one tent site to another, from one dwelling place to another. [6]Wherever I have moved with all the Israelites, did I ever say to any of their leaders[m] whom I commanded to shepherd my people, "Why have you not built me a house of cedar?[f]" '

[7]"Now then, tell my servant David, 'This is what the LORD Almighty says: I took you from the pasture and from following the flock, to be ruler[g] over my people Israel. [8]I have been with

you wherever you have gone, and I have cut off all your enemies from before you. Now I will make your name like the names of the greatest men of the earth. [9]And I will provide a place for my people Israel and will plant them so that they can have a home of their own and no longer be disturbed. Wicked people will not oppress them anymore, as they did at the beginning [10]and have done ever since the time I appointed leaders[h] over my people Israel. I will also subdue all your enemies.

"'I declare to you that the LORD will build a house for you: [11]When your days are over and you go to be with your fathers, I will raise up your offspring to succeed you, one of your own sons, and I will establish his kingdom. [12]He is the one who will build[i] a house for me, and I will establish his throne forever.[j] [13]I will be his father,[k] and he will be my son.[l] I will never take my love away from him, as I took it away from your predecessor. [14]I will set him over my house and my kingdom forever; his throne[m] will be established forever.[n]'"

[15]Nathan reported to David all the words of this entire revelation.

David's Prayer

17:16–27pp — 2Sa 7:18–29

[16]Then King David went in and sat before the LORD, and he said:

"Who am I, O LORD God, and what is my family, that you have brought me this far? [17]And as if this were not enough in your sight, O God, you have spoken about the future of the

16:41
[z]S 1Ch 15:19
16:42 [a]2Ch 7:6
[b]1Ch 25:3
17:1 [c]S 1Ch 15:1
17:2 [d]1Ch 22:7; 28:2; 2Ch 6:7
17:4 [e]1Ch 22:10; 28:3
17:6 [f]S 1Ch 14:1
17:7 [g]S 2Sa 6:21

17:10 [h]S Jdg 2:16
17:12 [i]S 1Ki 5:5 /1Ch 22:10; 2Ch 7:18; 13:5
17:13 [k]2Co 6:18 /1Ch 28:6; Lk 1:32; Heb 1:5
17:14 [m]S 1Ki 2:12; 1Ch 28:5; 29:23; 2Ch 9:8 [n]Ps 132:11; Jer 33:17

m6 Traditionally judges; also in verse 10

16:42 *sounding the trumpets.* See Nu 10:1–10.

17:1–27 See 2Sa 7 and notes.

17:1,10 In these verses the Chronicler omits the statement that David had rest from his enemies (2Sa 7:1,11). Several factors may be at work in his omission: 1. The account of David's major wars is yet to come (chs. 18–20). Chronologically, this passage should follow the account of the wars (v. 8), but the author has placed it here to continue his concern with the ark and the building of the temple (vv. 4–6,12). 2. The Chronicler also views David as a man of war through most of his life (22:6–8), in contrast to Solomon, who is the man of "peace and rest" (22:9) and who will build the temple (22:10). For the Chronicler, David has rest from enemies only late in his life (22:18). 3. As part of his concern to parallel David and Solomon to Moses and Joshua, Solomon (like Joshua) brings the people to rest from enemies (see Introduction: Portrait of David and Solomon).

17:12–14 Though in this context these words refer to

Solomon, the NT applies them to Jesus (Mk 1:11; Lk 1:32–33; Heb 1:5).

17:13 The Chronicler omits from his source (2Sa 7:14) any reference to "punishment with the rod" or "flogging" as discipline for Solomon. This omission reflects his idealization of Solomon as a Messianic figure, for whom such punishment would not be appropriate (see Introduction: Portrait of David and Solomon).

17:14 The Chronicler introduces his own concerns by the changes in the pronouns found in his source (2Sa 7:16); instead of "Your house and your kingdom," the Chronicler reads "my house and my kingdom." This same emphasis on theocracy (God's rule) is found in several other passages unique to Chronicles (28:5–6; 29:23; 2Ch 1:11; 9:8; 13:4–8).

17:16 *sat.* Aside from its parallel in 2Sa 7:18, this is the only reference in the OT to sitting as a posture for prayer.

house of your servant. You have looked on me as though I were the most exalted of men, O LORD God.

[18] "What more can David say to you for honoring your servant? For you know your servant, [19] O LORD. For the sake[o] of your servant and according to your will, you have done this great thing and made known all these great promises.[p]

[20] "There is no one like you, O LORD, and there is no God but you,[q] as we have heard with our own ears. [21] And who is like your people Israel—the one nation on earth whose God went out to redeem[r] a people for himself, and to make a name for yourself, and to perform great and awesome wonders by driving out nations from before your people, whom you redeemed from Egypt? [22] You made your people Israel your very own forever,[s] and you, O LORD, have become their God.

[23] "And now, LORD, let the promise[t] you have made concerning your servant and his house be established forever. Do as you promised, [24] so that it will be established and that your name will be great forever. Then men will say, 'The LORD Almighty, the God over Israel, is Israel's God!' And the house of your servant David will be established before you.

[25] "You, my God, have revealed to your servant that you will build a house for him. So your servant has found courage to pray to you. [26] O LORD, you are God! You have promised these good things to your servant. [27] Now you have been pleased to bless the house of your servant, that it may continue forever in your sight;[u] for

17:19
o2Sa 7:16-17;
2Ki 20:6; Isa 9:7;
37:35; 55:3
pS 2Sa 7:25
17:20
qS Ex 8:10;
S 9:14; S 15:11;
Isa 44:6; 46:9
17:21 rS Ex 6:6
17:22 sEx 19:5-6
17:23 tS 1Ki 8:25
17:27 uPs 16:11;
21:6

18:2 vS Nu 21:29
18:3 w 1Ch 19:6
xS Ge 2:14
18:4 yS Ge 49:6
18:5 zZki 16:9
18:8 aS 1Ki 7:23;
2Ch 4:2-5

you, O LORD, have blessed it, and it will be blessed forever."

David's Victories

18:1-13pp — 2Sa 8:1-14

18 In the course of time, David defeated the Philistines and subdued them, and he took Gath and its surrounding villages from the control of the Philistines.

[2] David also defeated the Moabites,[v] and they became subject to him and brought tribute.

[3] Moreover, David fought Hadadezer king of Zobah,[w] as far as Hamath, when he went to establish his control along the Euphrates River.[x] [4] David captured a thousand of his chariots, seven thousand charioteers and twenty thousand foot soldiers. He hamstrung[y] all but a hundred of the chariot horses.

[5] When the Arameans of Damascus[z] came to help Hadadezer king of Zobah, David struck down twenty-two thousand of them. [6] He put garrisons in the Aramean kingdom of Damascus, and the Arameans became subject to him and brought tribute. The LORD gave David victory everywhere he went.

[7] David took the gold shields carried by the officers of Hadadezer and brought them to Jerusalem. [8] From Tebah[n] and Cun, towns that belonged to Hadadezer, David took a great quantity of bronze, which Solomon used to make the bronze Sea,[a] the pillars and various bronze articles.

[9] When Tou king of Hamath heard that David had defeated the entire army of Hadadezer king of Zobah, [10] he sent his son Hadoram to King David to greet him and congratulate him on his victory in battle

[n]8 Hebrew *Tibhath*, a variant of *Tebah*

17:21–22 The references to the exodus from Egypt would remind the Chronicler's audience of the second great exodus, the release of the restoration community from the period of Babylonian captivity.

18:1–20:8 The accounts of David's wars serve to show the blessing of God on his reign; God keeps his promise to subdue David's enemies (17:10). These accounts are also particularly relevant to a theme developed in the postexilic prophets: that the silver and gold of the nations would flow to Jerusalem; the tribute of enemy peoples builds the temple of God (18:7–8,11; 22:2–5,14–15; cf. Hag 2:1–9,20–23; Zec 2:7–13; 6:9–15; 14:12–14). While this passage of Chronicles portrays God's blessing on David, it simultaneously explains the Chronicler's report later (22:6–8; 28:3) that David could not build the temple because he was a man of war. The material in these chapters essentially follows the Chronicler's source in 2 Samuel. The major differences are not changes the Chronicler introduces into the text, but

items he chooses not to deal with—in particular 2Sa 9; 11:2–12:25, where accounts not compatible with his portrait of David occur.

18:1–13 See 2Sa 8:1–14 and notes.

18:2 The Chronicler omits the harsh treatment of the Moabites recorded in 2Sa 8:2, perhaps so that no unnecessary cruelty or brutality would tarnish his portrait of David.

18:5 *Arameans.* Mentioned also among the enemies of Saul (1Sa 14:47, "Zobah"). By the time of David they were united north (Zobah) and south (Beth Rehob, 2Sa 10:6) under Hadadezer. They persisted as a foe of Israel for two centuries until they fell to Assyria shortly before the northern kingdom likewise fell (2Ki 16:7–9).

18:8 *Tebah and Cun.* Located in the valley between the Lebanon and Anti-Lebanon mountain ranges. *which Solomon used to make . . . various bronze articles.* See 2Ch 4:2–5,18.

over Hadadezer, who had been at war with Tou. Hadoram brought all kinds of articles of gold and silver and bronze.

[11] King David dedicated these articles to the LORD, as he had done with the silver and gold he had taken from all these nations: Edom [b] and Moab, the Ammonites and the Philistines, and Amalek. [c]

[12] Abishai son of Zeruiah struck down eighteen thousand Edomites [d] in the Valley of Salt. [13] He put garrisons in Edom, and all the Edomites became subject to David. The LORD gave David victory everywhere he went.

David's Officials

18:14–17pp — 2Sa 8:15–18

[14] David reigned [e] over all Israel, [f] doing what was just and right for all his people. [15] Joab [g] son of Zeruiah was over the army; Jehoshaphat son of Ahilud was recorder; [16] Zadok [h] son of Ahitub and Ahimelech [o] [i] son of Abiathar were priests; Shavsha was secretary; [17] Benaiah son of Jehoiada was over the Kerethites and Pelethites; [j] and David's sons were chief officials at the king's side.

The Battle Against the Ammonites

19:1–19pp — 2Sa 10:1–19

19 In the course of time, Nahash king of the Ammonites [k] died, and his son succeeded him as king. [2] David thought, "I will show kindness to Hanun son of Nahash, because his father showed kindness to me." So David sent a delegation to express his sympathy to Hanun concerning his father.

When David's men came to Hanun in the land of the Ammonites to express sympathy to him, [3] the Ammonite nobles said to Hanun, "Do you think David is honoring your father by sending men to you to express sympathy? Haven't his men come to you to explore and spy out [l] the country and overthrow it?" [4] So Hanun seized David's men, shaved them, cut off their garments in the middle at the buttocks, and sent them away.

[5] When someone came and told David about the men, he sent messengers to meet them, for they were greatly humiliated. The king said, "Stay at Jericho till your beards have grown, and then come back."

[6] When the Ammonites realized that they had become a stench [m] in David's nostrils, Hanun and the Ammonites sent a thousand talents [p] of silver to hire chariots and charioteers from Aram Naharaim, [q] Aram Maacah and Zobah. [n] [7] They hired thirty-two thousand chariots and charioteers, as well as the king of Maacah with his troops, who came and camped near Medeba, [o] while the Ammonites were mustered from their towns and moved out for battle.

[8] On hearing this, David sent Joab out with the entire army of fighting men. [9] The Ammonites came out and drew up in battle formation at the entrance to their city,

Cross-references (center column)

18:11
b S Nu 24:18
c Nu 24:20
18:12 *d* 1Ki 11:15
18:14
e 1Ch 29:26
f 1Ch 11:1
18:15 *g* 2Sa 5:6-8
18:16 *h* 1Ch 6:8
i 1Ch 24:6
18:17
j S 1Sa 30:14;
S 2Sa 15:18
19:1
k S Ge 19:38;
Jdg 10:17-11:33;
2Ch 20:1-2;
Zep 2:8-11

19:3 *l* S Nu 21:32
19:6
m S Ge 34:30
n S 1Ch 18:3
19:7 *o* S Nu 21:30

o16 Some Hebrew manuscripts, Vulgate and Syriac (see also 2 Samuel 8:17); most Hebrew manuscripts *Abimelech* *p6* That is, about 37 tons (about 34 metric tons) *q6* That is, Northwest Mesopotamia

---

18:12 *Abishai.* 2Sa 8:13 speaks only of David (see 1Ki 11:15–16; Ps 60 title).

18:15–17 The titles and duties of these officers at David's court appear to be modeled on the organization of Egyptian functionaries serving Pharaoh.

18:15 For the account of how Joab attained his position over the army see 11:4–6; 2Sa 5:6–8.

18:16 *Zadok . . . Ahimelech son of Abiathar.* See notes on 6:8; 16:39; 2Sa 8:17.

18:17 *Kerethites and Pelethites.* Apparently a group of foreign mercenaries who constituted part of the royal bodyguard (2Sa 8:18; 20:23; see note on 1Sa 30:14). They remained loyal to David at the time of the rebellions of Absalom (2Sa 15:18) and Sheba (2Sa 20:7) and supported the succession of Solomon against his rival Adonijah (1Ki 1:38,44). *chief officials.* The earlier narrative at this point uses the Hebrew term ordinarily translated "priests" (see note on 2Sa 8:18). The Chronicler has used a term for civil service instead of sacral service. Two approaches to this passage are ordinarily followed: 1. Some scholars see here an attempt by the Chronicler to keep the priesthood restricted to the Levitical line as part of his larger concern with legitimacy of cultic institutions in his own day. 2. Others argue that the Hebrew term used in 2Sa 8:18 could earlier have had a broader meaning than "priest" and could be used

of some other types of officials (cf. 2Sa 20:26; 1Ki 4:5). The Chronicler used an equivalent term, since by his day the Hebrew term for "priest" was restricted to cultic functionaries. The Septuagint, Targum, Old Latin and Josephus all translate the term in Samuel by some word other than "priest."

19:1–20:3 The Chronicler follows 2Sa 10–12 closely (see notes there), apart from his omission of the account of David's sin with Bathsheba (11:2–12:25). The Ammonites were a traditional enemy of Israel (2Ch 20:1–2,23; 27:5; Jdg 3:13; 10:7–9; 10:17–11:33; 1Sa 11:1–13; 14:47; 2Ki 10:32–33; Jer 49:1–6; Zep 2:8–11). Even during the postexilic period Tobiah the Ammonite troubled Jerusalem (Ne 2:19; 4:3,7; 6:1,12,14; 13:4–9).

19:1 *Nahash.* Possibly the same as Saul's foe (1Sa 11:1), or perhaps his descendant.

19:6 *Aram Naharaim, Aram Maacah and Zobah.* 2Sa 10:6 also mentions Beth Rehob and Tob. All these states were north and northeast of Israel and formed a solid block from the region of Lake Huleh through the Anti-Lebanons to beyond the Euphrates.

19:7 *Medeba.* A town in Moab apparently in the hands of Ammon.

19:9 *their city.* The capital city, Rabbah, to which Joab would lay siege the following year (20:1–3).

while the kings who had come were by themselves in the open country.

¹⁰Joab saw that there were battle lines in front of him and behind him; so he selected some of the best troops in Israel and deployed them against the Arameans. ¹¹He put the rest of the men under the command of Abishai ᵖ his brother, and they were deployed against the Ammonites. ¹²Joab said, "If the Arameans are too strong for me, then you are to rescue me; but if the Ammonites are too strong for you, then I will rescue you. ¹³Be strong and let us fight bravely for our people and the cities of our God. The LORD will do what is good in his sight."

¹⁴Then Joab and the troops with him advanced to fight the Arameans, and they fled before him. ¹⁵When the Ammonites saw that the Arameans were fleeing, they too fled before his brother Abishai and went inside the city. So Joab went back to Jerusalem.

¹⁶After the Arameans saw that they had been routed by Israel, they sent messengers and had Arameans brought from beyond the River, ʳ with Shophach the commander of Hadadezer's army leading them.

¹⁷When David was told of this, he gathered all Israel �q and crossed the Jordan; he advanced against them and formed his battle lines opposite them. David formed his lines to meet the Arameans in battle, and they fought against him. ¹⁸But they fled before Israel, and David killed seven thousand of their charioteers and forty thousand of their foot soldiers. He also killed Shophach the commander of their army.

¹⁹When the vassals of Hadadezer saw that they had been defeated by Israel, they made peace with David and became subject to him.

So the Arameans were not willing to help the Ammonites anymore.

The Capture of Rabbah
20:1–3pp — 2Sa 11:1; 12:29–31

20 In the spring, at the time when kings go off to war, Joab led out the armed forces. He laid waste the land of the Ammonites and went to Rabbah ʳ and besieged it, but David remained in Jerusalem. Joab attacked Rabbah and left it in ruins. ˢ ²David took the crown from the head of their king ˢ—its weight was found to be a talent ᵗ of gold, and it was set with precious stones—and it was placed on David's head. He took a great quantity of plunder from the city ³and brought out the people who were there, consigning them to labor with saws and with iron picks and axes. ᵗ David did this to all the Ammonite towns. Then David and his entire army returned to Jerusalem.

War With the Philistines
2:4–8pp — 2Sa 21:15–22

⁴In the course of time, war broke out with the Philistines, at Gezer. ᵘ At that time Sibbecai the Hushathite killed Sippai, one of the descendants of the Rephaites, ᵛ and the Philistines were subjugated.

⁵In another battle with the Philistines, Elhanan son of Jair killed Lahmi the brother of Goliath the Gittite, who had a spear with a shaft like a weaver's rod. ʷ

⁶In still another battle, which took place at Gath, there was a huge man with six fingers on each hand and six toes on each foot—twenty-four in all. He also was descended from Rapha. ⁷When he taunted Israel, Jonathan son of Shimea, David's brother, killed him.

⁸These were descendants of Rapha in Gath, and they fell at the hands of David and his men.

David Numbers the Fighting Men
21:1–26pp — 2Sa 24:1–25

21 Satan ˣ rose up against Israel and incited David to take a census ʸ of

19:11 ᵖS 1Sa 26:6
19:17 qS 1Ch 9:1

20:1 ʳS Dt 3:11
ˢAm 1:13-15
20:3 ᵗS Dt 29:11
20:4 ᵘJos 10:33
ᵛS Ge 14:5
20:5 ʷS 1Sa 17:7
21:1 ˣS 2Ch 18:21; S Ps 109:6 ʸ2Ch 14:8; 25:5

ʳ16 That is, the Euphrates   ˢ2 Or of Milcom, that is, Molech   ᵗ2 That is, about 75 pounds (about 34 kilograms)

19:18 *seven thousand.* 2Sa 10:18 has 700, which is evidently a copyist's mistake.
20:1 *when kings go off to war.* Immediately following the spring harvest when there was some relaxation of agricultural labors and armies on the move could live off the land. *Rabbah.* See note on 19:9. Rabbah is the site of modern Amman, Jordan.
20:2–3 The Chronicler assumes that the reader is familiar with 2Sa 12:26–29; he does not offer an explanation of how David, who had remained in Jerusalem (v. 1), came to be at Rabbah.

20:4 *Sibbecai.* See 11:29; 27:11. *Rephaites.* Ancient people known for their large size (see Ge 14:5; Dt 2:11; see also note on 2Sa 21:16).
20:5 See note on 2Sa 21:19. *weaver's rod.* See 11:23; 1Sa 17:7.
20:6 *Rapha.* See note on 2Sa 21:16.
21:1–22:1 See 2Sa 24 and notes. Although the story of David's census is quite similar in both narratives, the two accounts function differently. In Samuel the account belongs to the appendix (2Sa 21–24), which begins and ends with accounts of the Lord's anger against Israel during the reign of

Israel. [2]So David said to Joab and the commanders of the troops, "Go and count[z] the Israelites from Beersheba to Dan. Then report back to me so that I may know how many there are."

[3]But Joab replied, "May the LORD multiply his troops a hundred times over.[a] My lord the king, are they not all my lord's subjects? Why does my lord want to do this? Why should he bring guilt on Israel?"

[4]The king's word, however, overruled Joab; so Joab left and went throughout Israel and then came back to Jerusalem. [5]Joab reported the number of the fighting men to David: In all Israel[b] there were one million one hundred thousand men who could handle a sword, including four hundred and seventy thousand in Judah.

[6]But Joab did not include Levi and Benjamin in the numbering, because the king's command was also evil in the sight of God; so he punished Israel.

[8]Then David said to God, "I have sinned greatly by doing this. Now, I beg you, take away the guilt of your servant. I have done a very foolish thing."

[9]The LORD said to Gad,[c] David's seer,[d] [10]"Go and tell David, 'This is what the LORD says: I am giving you three options. Choose one of them for me to carry out against you.' "

[11]So Gad went to David and said to him, "This is what the LORD says: 'Take your choice: [12]three years of famine,[e] three months of being swept away[u] before your enemies, with their swords overtaking you, or three days of the sword[f] of the

LORD[g]—days of plague in the land, with the angel of the LORD ravaging every part of Israel.' Now then, decide how I should answer the one who sent me."

[13]David said to Gad, "I am in deep distress. Let me fall into the hands of the LORD, for his mercy[h] is very great; but do not let me fall into the hands of men."

[14]So the LORD sent a plague on Israel, and seventy thousand men of Israel fell dead.[i] [15]And God sent an angel[j] to destroy Jerusalem.[k] But as the angel was doing so, the LORD saw it and was grieved[l] because of the calamity and said to the angel who was destroying[m] the people, "Enough! Withdraw your hand." The angel of the LORD was then standing at the threshing floor of Araunah[v] the Jebusite.

[16]David looked up and saw the angel of the LORD standing between heaven and earth, with a drawn sword in his hand extended over Jerusalem. Then David and the elders, clothed in sackcloth, fell facedown.[n]

[17]David said to God, "Was it not I who ordered the fighting men to be counted? I am the one who has sinned and done wrong. These are but sheep.[o] What have they done? O LORD my God, let your hand fall upon me and my family,[p] but do not let this plague remain on your people."

[18]Then the angel of the LORD ordered Gad to tell David to go up and build an altar to the LORD on the threshing floor[q] of Araunah the Jebusite. [19]So David went up

21:2
[z]1Ch 27:23-24
21:3 [a]S Dt 1:11
21:5 [b]S 1Ch 9:1
21:9 [c]S 1Sa 22:5
[d]S 1Sa 9:9
21:12
[e]S Dt 32:24
[f]Eze 30:25

[g]S Ge 19:13
21:13 [h]Ps 6:4; 86:15; 130:4,7
21:14
[i]1Ch 27:24
21:15 [j]S Ge 32:1
[k]Ps 125:2
[l]S Ge 6:6;
S Ex 32:14
[m]S Ge 19:13
21:16
[n]S Nu 14:5;
S Jos 7:6
21:17 [o]S 2Sa 7:8
[p]Jnh 1:12
21:18 [q]2Ch 3:1

[u]12 Hebrew; Septuagint and Vulgate (see also 2 Samuel 24:13) of fleeing   [v]15 Hebrew Ornan, a variant of Araunah; also in verses 18-28

David because of actions by her kings (in ch. 21, an act of Saul; in ch. 24, an act of David). See note on 2Sa 21:1–24:25. The Chronicler appears to include it in order to account for the purchase of the ground on which the temple would be built. The additional material in Chronicles that is not found in Samuel (21:28–22:1) makes this interest clear. The census is the preface to David's preparations for the temple (chs. 22–29).

21:1 See note on 2Sa 24:1. *Satan.* See NIV text notes on Job 1:6; Zec 3:1.

21:4 The Chronicler abridges the more extensive account of Joab's itinerary found in 2Sa 24:4–8; he does not mention that the census required nine months and 20 days (2Sa 24:8).

21:5 *In all Israel . . . one million one hundred thousand men . . . including four hundred and seventy thousand in Judah.* 2Sa 24:9 has 800,000 in Israel and 500,000 (which could be a round number for 470,000) in Judah. The reason for the difference is unclear. Perhaps it is to be related to the unofficial and incomplete nature of the census (see 27:23–24), with the differing figures representing the inclusion or exclusion of certain unspecified groupings among the people (see v. 6). Or perhaps it is simply due to a copyist's mistake. The NIV relieves the problem somewhat by translating the conjunction here as "including" instead of "and."

21:6 The Chronicler adds the note that Joab exempted Levi and Benjamin from the counting. This additional note reflects the Chronicler's concern with the Levites and with the worship of Israel. The tabernacle in Gibeon and the ark in Jerusalem both fell within the borders of Benjamin.

21:9 *Gad.* A longtime friend of David, having been with him when he was a fugitive from Saul (1Sa 22:3–5; cf. 1Ch 29:29; 2Ch 29:25).

21:12 *three years of famine.* See NIV text note on 2Sa 24:13.

21:16 The verse has no parallel in the traditional Hebrew text of 2Sa 24, so some scholars regard it as an addition by the Chronicler reflecting the more developed doctrine of angels in the postexilic period. However, a fragmentary Hebrew text of Samuel from the third century B.C., discovered at Qumran, contains the verse. It now appears that the Chronicler was carefully copying the Samuel text at his disposal, which differed in some respects from the Masoretic (traditional Hebrew) text. Josephus, who appears to be following the text of Samuel, also reported this information. Presumably, he too used a text of Samuel similar to that followed by the Chronicler.

in obedience to the word that Gad had spoken in the name of the LORD.

²⁰While Araunah was threshing wheat,ʳ he turned and saw the angel; his four sons who were with him hid themselves. ²¹Then David approached, and when Araunah looked and saw him, he left the threshing floor and bowed down before David with his face to the ground.

²²David said to him, "Let me have the site of your threshing floor so I can build an altar to the LORD, that the plague on the people may be stopped. Sell it to me at the full price."

²³Araunah said to David, "Take it! Let my lord the king do whatever pleases him. Look, I will give the oxen for the burnt offerings, the threshing sledges for the wood, and the wheat for the grain offering. I will give all this."

²⁴But King David replied to Araunah, "No, I insist on paying the full price. I will not take for the LORD what is yours, or sacrifice a burnt offering that costs me nothing."

²⁵So David paid Araunah six hundred shekelsʷ of gold for the site. ²⁶David built an altar to the LORD there and sacrificed burnt offerings and fellowship offerings.ˣ He called on the LORD, and the LORD answered him with fireˢ from heaven on the altar of burnt offering.

²⁷Then the LORD spoke to the angel, and he put his sword back into its sheath. ²⁸At that time, when David saw that the LORD had answered him on the threshing floor of Araunah the Jebusite, he offered sacrifices there. ²⁹The tabernacle of the LORD, which

Moses had made in the desert, and the altar of burnt offering were at that time on the high place at Gibeon.ᵗ ³⁰But David could not go before it to inquire of God, because he was afraid of the sword of the angel of the LORD.

22 Then David said, "The house of the LORD Godᵘ is to be here, and also the altar of burnt offering for Israel."

Preparations for the Temple

²So David gave orders to assemble the aliensᵛ living in Israel, and from among them he appointed stonecuttersʷ to prepare dressed stone for building the house of God. ³He provided a large amount of iron to make nails for the doors of the gateways and for the fittings, and more bronze than could be weighed.ˣ ⁴He also provided more cedar logsʸ than could be counted, for the Sidonians and Tyrians had brought large numbers of them to David.

⁵David said, "My son Solomon is youngᶻ and inexperienced, and the house to be built for the LORD should be of great magnificence and fame and splendorᵃ in the sight of all the nations. Therefore I will make preparations for it." So David made extensive preparations before his death.

⁶Then he called for his son Solomon and charged him to buildᵇ a house for the LORD, the God of Israel. ⁷David said to Solomon: "My son, I had it in my heartᶜ to buildᵈ a house for the Nameᵉ of the LORD my God. ⁸But this word of the LORD came to me: 'You have shed much blood

---

21:20 ʳS Jdg 6:11
21:26
⁵S Ex 19:18;
S Jdg 6:21

21:29 ᵗS Jos 9:3
22:1 ᵘS Ge 28:17
22:2 ᵛS Ex 1:11;
S Dt 20:11;
2Ch 8:10;
S Isa 56:6
ʷ1Ki 5:17-18;
Ezr 3:7
22:3 ˣS 1Ki 7:47;
1Ch 29:2-5
22:4 ʸS 1Ki 5:6
22:5 ᶻS 1Ki 3:7;
1Ch 29:1
ᵃ2Ch 2:5
22:6 ᵇAc 7:47
22:7 ᶜS 1Ch 17:2
ᵈS 1Ki 8:17
ᵉDt 12:5,11

ʷ25 That is, about 15 pounds (about 7 kilograms)
ˣ26 Traditionally peace offerings

21:20-21 The Chronicler reports that Araunah was threshing wheat as the king approached—information not found in 2Sa 24:20. However, Josephus and the fragmentary text of Samuel from Qumran both mention this information (see note on v. 16).

21:25 six hundred shekels of gold. 2Sa 24:24 says 50 shekels of silver were paid for the threshing floor and oxen. The difference has been explained by some as the Chronicler's attempt to glorify David and the temple by inflating the price. However, the difference is more likely explained by the Chronicler's statement that this was the price for the "site," i.e., for a much larger area than the threshing floor alone.

21:26 fire from heaven. Underscores the divine approval and the sanctity of the site (see 2Ch 7:1; Lev 9:24; 1Ki 18:37-38).

21:28-22:1 This material is not found in 2Sa 24. It reflects the Chronicler's main concern in reporting this narrative (see note on 21:1-22:1).

21:30 it. The tabernacle.

22:1-29:30 This material is unique to Chronicles and displays some of the Chronicler's most characteristic interests: the preparations for the building of the temple, the legitimacy of the priests and Levites, and the royal succession. The chapters portray a theocratic "Messianic" kingdom

as it existed under David and Solomon.

22:1 David dedicates this property (21:18-30) as the site for the temple (see vv. 2-6).

22:2-19 Solomon's appointment to succeed David was twofold: (1) a private audience, with David and some leaders in attendance (vv. 17-19), and (2) a public announcement to the people (ch. 28), similar to when Joshua succeeded Moses (see Introduction: Portrait of David and Solomon).

22:2 aliens . . . stonecutters. 2Sa 20:24 confirms the use of forced labor by David, but does not specify that these laborers were aliens, not Israelites. Solomon used Israelites in conscripted labor (1Ki 5:13-18; 9:15-23; 11:28), but the Chronicler mentions only his use of aliens (2Ch 8:7-10). Though they were personally free, aliens were without political rights and could be easily exploited. The OT frequently warns that they were not to be oppressed (Ex 22:21; 23:9; Lev 19:33; Dt 24:14; Jer 7:6; Zec 7:10). Isaiah prophesies the participation of foreigners in the building of Jerusalem's walls in the future (Isa 60:10-12).

22:3 bronze. See note on 18:8.

22:5 young. Solomon's age at the time of his accession is not known with certainty. He came to the throne in 970 B.C. and was likely born c. 991.

22:8-9 See note on 17:1. In 1Ki 5:3 Solomon explains that David could not build the temple because he was too busy

and have fought many wars.^{f} You are not to build a house for my Name,^{g} because you have shed much blood on the earth in my sight. ^{9}But you will have a son who will be a man of peace^h and rest,^{i} and I will give him rest from all his enemies on every side. His name will be Solomon,^{v}^{j} and I will grant Israel peace and quiet^k during his reign. ^{10}He is the one who will build a house for my Name.^{l} He will be my son,^{m} and I will be his father. And I will establish^n the throne of his kingdom over Israel forever.'^{o}

^{11}"Now, my son, the LORD be with^p you, and may you have success and build the house of the LORD your God, as he said you would. ^{12}May the LORD give you discretion and understanding^q when he puts you in command over Israel, so that you may keep the law of the LORD your God. ^{13}Then you will have success^r if you are careful to observe the decrees and laws^s that the LORD gave Moses for Israel. Be strong and courageous.^{t} Do not be afraid or discouraged.

^{14}"I have taken great pains to provide for the temple of the LORD a hundred thousand talents^z of gold, a million talents^a of silver, quantities of bronze and iron too great to be weighed, and wood and stone. And you may add to them.^{u} ^{15}You have many workmen: stonecutters, masons and carpenters,^{v} as well as men skilled in every kind of work ^{16}in gold and silver, bronze and iron—craftsmen^w beyond number. Now begin the work, and the LORD be with you."

^{17}Then David ordered^x all the leaders of Israel to help his son Solomon. ^{18}He said to them, "Is not the LORD your God with you? And has he not granted you rest^y on every side?^{z} For he has handed the inhabitants of the land over to me, and the land

is subject to the LORD and to his people. ^{19}Now devote your heart and soul to seeking the LORD your God.^{a} Begin to build the sanctuary of the LORD God, so that you may bring the ark of the covenant belonging to the LORD and the sacred articles belonging to God into the temple that will be built for the Name of the LORD."

The Levites

23 When David was old and full of years, he made his son Solomon^b king over Israel.^{c}

^{2}He also gathered together all the leaders of Israel, as well as the priests and Levites. ^{3}The Levites thirty years old or more^d were counted,^{e} and the total number of men was thirty-eight thousand.^{f} ^{4}David said, "Of these, twenty-four thousand are to supervise^g the work^h of the temple of the LORD and six thousand are to be officials and judges.^{i} ^{5}Four thousand are to be gatekeepers and four thousand are to praise the LORD with the musical instruments^j I have provided for that purpose."^{k}

^{6}David divided^l the Levites into groups corresponding to the sons of Levi:^{m} Gershon, Kohath and Merari.

Gershonites

^{7}Belonging to the Gershonites:^{n}
  Ladan and Shimei.
^{8}The sons of Ladan:
  Jehiel the first, Zetham and Joel—three in all.
^{9}The sons of Shimei:
  Shelomoth, Haziel and Haran—three in all.

Cross references (center column)

22:8 /S 1Ki 5:3
  g1Ch 28:3
22:9
  hS Jos 14:15;
  S 1Ki 5:4 /ver 18;
  1Ch 23:25;
  2Ch 14:6,7;
  15:15; 20:30;
  36:21
  /S 2Sa 12:24;
  S 1Ch 23:1
  k1Ki 4:20
22:10
  /S 1Ch 17:12
  mS 2Sa 7:13
  n1Ki 9:5
  oS 2Sa 7:14;
  S 1Ch 17:4;
  2Ch 6:15
22:11
  pS 1Sa 16:18;
  S 18:12
22:12 q1Ki 3:11
22:13 r1Ki 2:3
  s1Ch 28:7
  /S Dt 31:6
22:14
  u1Ch 29:2-5,19
22:15 vEzr 3:7
22:16 w2Ch 2:7
22:17 x1Ch 28:1
22:18 yS ver 9
  z2Sa 7:1

22:19 a2Ch 7:14
23:1 b1Ch 22:9;
  28:5; 2Ch 1:8
  cS 1Ki 1:30;
  1Ch 29:28
23:3 dNu 8:24
  e1Ch 21:7
  /Nu 4:3-49
23:4 gEzr 3:8
  h2Ch 34:13;
  Ne 4:10
  i1Ch 26:29;
  2Ch 19:8;
  Eze 44:24
23:5
  /S 1Ch 15:16;
  Ps 92:3
  kNe 12:45
23:6 l2Ch 8:14;
  23:18; 29:25
  mS Nu 3:17;
  1Ch 24:20
23:7 n1Ch 6:71

v9 *Solomon* sounds like and may be derived from the Hebrew for *peace*. z14 That is, about 3,750 tons (about 3,450 metric tons) a14 That is, about 37,500 tons (about 34,500 metric tons)

---

with wars. The Chronicler's nuance is slightly different—not just that wars took so much of his time, but that David was in some sense defiled by them because of the bloodshed. A pun on Solomon's name is woven into the divine oracle (see NIV text note on v. 9).
22:10 See note on 17:12–14.
22:12–13 See Introduction: Portrait of David and Solomon.
22:19 See 2Ch 5:7.
23:1–27:34 David's preparations for the temple were not restricted to amassing materials for the building; he also arranged for its administration and worship. Unique to Chronicles (see note on 22:1–29:30), these details of the organization of the theocracy (God's kingdom) were of vital concern in the Chronicler's own day. Characteristically for the Chronicler, details about religious and cultic matters (chs. 23–26) take precedence over those that are civil and secular (ch. 27). David's arrangements provided the basis and authority for the practices of the restored community.

23:1 *made his son Solomon king.* The account of Solomon's succession is resumed in chs. 28–29. The Chronicler omits the accounts of disputed succession and bloody consolidation recorded in 1Ki 1–2 (see note on 28:1–29:30) since these would not be in accord with his overall portrait of David and Solomon (see Introduction: Portrait of David and Solomon).

23:2–5 The Levites were not counted in the census that had provoked the wrath of God (21:6–7).

23:3 *Levites thirty years old or more.* The census of Levites was made first in accordance with the Mosaic prescription (Nu 4:1–3). Apparently soon after this count, David instructed that the age be lowered to 20 years (vv. 24,27); a similar adjustment to age 25 had been made under Moses (Nu 8:23–24, but see note on Nu 8:24).

23:6 *Gershon, Kohath and Merari.* The Levites were organized by their three clans (ch. 6; Ex 6:16–19; Nu 3). This list parallels those in 6:16–30; 24:20–30.

These were the heads of the families of Ladan.

10And the sons of Shimei:

Jahath, Ziza,b Jeush and Beriah. These were the sons of Shimei—four in all.

11Jahath was the first and Ziza the second, but Jeush and Beriah did not have many sons; so they were counted as one family with one assignment.

Kohathites

12The sons of Kohath:o

Amram, Izhar, Hebron and Uzziel—four in all.

13The sons of Amram:p

Aaron and Moses.

Aaron was set apart,q he and his descendants forever, to consecrate the most holy things, to offer sacrifices before the Lord, to ministerr before him and to pronounce blessingss in his name forever. 14The sons of Moses the mant of God were counted as part of the tribe of Levi.

15The sons of Moses:

Gershom and Eliezer.u

16The descendants of Gershom:v

Shubael was the first.

17The descendants of Eliezer:

Rehabiahw was the first. Eliezer had no other sons, but the sons of Rehabiah were very numerous.

18The sons of Izhar:

Shelomithx was the first.

19The sons of Hebron:y

Jeriah the first, Amariah the second, Jahaziel the third and Jekameam the fourth.

20The sons of Uzziel:

Micah the first and Isshiah the second.

Merarites

21The sons of Merari:z

Mahli and Mushi.a

The sons of Mahli:

Eleazar and Kish.

22Eleazar died without having sons: he had only daughters. Their cous-

ins, the sons of Kish, married them.b

23The sons of Mushi:

Mahli, Eder and Jerimoth—three in all.

24These were the descendants of Levi by their families—the heads of families as they were registered under their names and counted individually, that is, the workers twenty years old or morec who served in the temple of the Lord. 25For David had said, "Since the Lord, the God of Israel, has granted restd to his people and has come to dwell in Jerusalem forever, 26the Levites no longer need to carry the tabernacle or any of the articles used in its service."e 27According to the last instructions of David, the Levites were counted from those twenty years old or more.

28The duty of the Levites was to help Aaron's descendants in the service of the temple of the Lord: to be in charge of the courtyards, the side rooms, the purificationf of all sacred things and the performance of other duties at the house of God. 29They were in charge of the bread set out on the table,g the flour for the grain offerings,h the unleavened wafers, the baking and the mixing, and all measurements of quantity and size.i 30They were also to stand every morning to thank and praise the Lord. They were to do the same in the eveningj 31and whenever burnt offerings were presented to the Lord on Sabbaths and at New Moonk festivals and at appointed feasts.l They were to serve before the Lord regularly in the proper number and in the way prescribed for them.

32And so the Levitesm carried out their responsibilities for the Tent of Meeting,n for the Holy Place and, under their brothers the descendants of Aaron, for the service of the temple of the Lord.o

The Divisions of Priests

24 These were the divisionsp of the sons of Aaron:q

The sons of Aaron were Nadab, Abihu, Eleazar and Ithamar.r 2But Nadab and

23:12
oS Ge 46:11;
S Ex 6:18
23:13 pEx 6:20
qEx 30:7-10
rS 1Ch 15:2
sS Nu 6:23
23:14 tDt 33:1
23:15 uEx 18:4
23:16
vlCh 26:24-28
23:17
w1Ch 24:21
23:18
x1Ch 26:25
23:19
y1Ch 24:23;
26:31
23:21
zS 1Ch 6:19
aS Ex 6:19

23:22 bNu 36:8
23:24 cS Nu 4:3
23:25
dS 1Ch 22:9
23:26 eNu 4:5,
15; 7:9; Dt 10:8
23:28
f2Ch 29:15;
Ne 13:9; Mal 3:3
23:29
gS Ex 25:30
hLev 2:4-7;
6:20-23
iLev 19:35-36;
S 1Ch 9:29,32
23:30
jS 1Ch 9:33;
Ps 134:1
23:31
kS 2Ki 4:23
lNu 28:9-29:39;
Col 2:16
23:32 m1Ch 6:48
nNu 3:6-8,38
o2Ch 23:18;
31:2; Eze 44:14
24:1 p1Ch 23:6;
28:13; 2Ch 5:11;
8:14; 23:8; 31:2;
35:4,5; Ezr 6:18
qNu 3:2-4
rS Ex 6:23

b10 One Hebrew manuscript, Septuagint and Vulgate (see also verse 11); most Hebrew manuscripts Zina

---

23:24,27 twenty years old or more. See note on v. 3.
23:28–32 See note on 9:28–34. The function of the Levites was to assist the priests. In addition to the care of the precincts and implements, baked goods and music (mentioned as Levitical duties in 9:22–34), the Chronicler adds details on the role of the Levites assisting in sacrifices.
23:30 morning . . . evening. See Ex 29:38–41; Nu

28:3–8.
24:1–19 There are several lists of priests from the postexilic period (see 6:3–15; 9:10–13; Ezr 2:36–39; Ne 10:1–8; 11:10–12; 12:1–7,12–21).
24:2 Nadab and Abihu died. The Chronicler alludes to the events recorded in Lev 10:1–3 (see note on 6:1–3).

Abihu died before their father did,^{s} and they had no sons; so Eleazar and Ithamar served as the priests. ^{3}With the help of Zadok^t a descendant of Eleazar and Ahimelech a descendant of Ithamar, David separated them into divisions for their appointed order of ministering. ^{4}A larger number of leaders were found among Eleazar's descendants than among Ithamar's, and they were divided accordingly: sixteen heads of families from Eleazar's descendants and eight heads of families from Ithamar's descendants. ^{5}They divided them impartially by drawing lots,^{u} for there were officials of the sanctuary and officials of God among the descendants of both Eleazar and Ithamar.

^{6}The scribe Shemaiah son of Nethanel, a Levite, recorded their names in the presence of the king and of the officials: Zadok the priest, Ahimelech^v son of Abiathar and the heads of families of the priests and of the Levites—one family being taken from Eleazar and then one from Ithamar.

^{7}The first lot fell to Jehoiarib,
  the second to Jedaiah,^{w}
^{8}the third to Harim,^{x}
  the fourth to Seorim,
^{9}the fifth to Malkijah,
  the sixth to Mijamin,
^{10}the seventh to Hakkoz,
  the eighth to Abijah,^{y}
^{11}the ninth to Jeshua,
  the tenth to Shecaniah,
^{12}the eleventh to Eliashib,
  the twelfth to Jakim,
^{13}the thirteenth to Huppah,
  the fourteenth to Jeshebeab,
^{14}the fifteenth to Bilgah,
  the sixteenth to Immer,^{z}
^{15}the seventeenth to Hezir,^{a}
  the eighteenth to Happizzez,
^{16}the nineteenth to Pethahiah,
  the twentieth to Jehezkel,
^{17}the twenty-first to Jakin,
  the twenty-second to Gamul,
^{18}the twenty-third to Delaiah
  and the twenty-fourth to Maaziah.

^{19}This was their appointed order of min-

istering when they entered the temple of the LORD, according to the regulations prescribed for them by their forefather Aaron, as the LORD, the God of Israel, had commanded him.

The Rest of the Levites

^{20}As for the rest of the descendants of Levi:^{b}

  from the sons of Amram: Shubael;
    from the sons of Shubael: Jehdeiah.
  ^{21}As for Rehabiah,^{c} from his sons:
    Isshiah was the first.
^{22}From the Izharites: Shelomoth;
    from the sons of Shelomoth: Jahath.
^{23}The sons of Hebron:^{d} Jeriah the first,^{c} Amariah the second, Jahaziel the third and Jekameam the fourth.
^{24}The son of Uzziel: Micah;
    from the sons of Micah: Shamir.
  ^{25}The brother of Micah: Isshiah;
    from the sons of Isshiah: Zechariah.
^{26}The sons of Merari:^{e} Mahli and Mushi.
    The son of Jaaziah: Beno.
^{27}The sons of Merari:
    from Jaaziah: Beno, Shoham, Zaccur and Ibri.
^{28}From Mahli: Eleazar, who had no sons.
^{29}From Kish: the son of Kish: Jerahmeel.
^{30}And the sons of Mushi: Mahli, Eder and Jerimoth.

These were the Levites, according to their families. ^{31}They also cast lots,^{f} just as their brothers the descendants of Aaron did, in the presence of King David and of Zadok, Ahimelech, and the heads of families of the priests and of the Levites. The families of the oldest brother were treated the same as those of the youngest.

^{c}*23* Two Hebrew manuscripts and some Septuagint manuscripts (see also 1 Chron. 23:19); most Hebrew manuscripts *The sons of Jeriah:*

24:2 ^{s}Lev 10:1-2
24:3 ^{t}S 2Sa 8:17
24:5 ^{u}ver 31;
1Ch 25:8; 26:13
24:6 ^{v}1Ch 18:16
Ne 12:6
24:7 ^{w}Ezr 2:36;
24:8 ^{x}Ezr 2:39;
10:21; Ne 10:5
24:10 ^{y}Ne 12:4,
17; Lk 1:5
24:14 ^{z}Ezr 2:37;
10:20; Jer 20:1
24:15 ^{a}Ne 10:20

24:20
^{b}S 1Ch 23:6
24:21
^{c}1Ch 23:17
24:23
^{d}S 1Ch 23:19
24:26
^{e}S 1Ch 6:19
24:31 ^{f}S ver 5

24:3 *Zadok . . . Ahimelech.* Zadok and Abiathar had served as David's high priests. Here, late in David's life, Abiathar's son Ahimelech appears to have taken over some of his father's duties (see note on 6:8), but see note on 2Sa 8:17.
24:4 *sixteen . . . eight.* A total of 24 divisions was selected by lot. This would allow for service either in monthly shifts, as was done by priests in Egyptian mortuary temples, or for two-week shifts once each year as found in NT times. The names of the first, second, fourth, ninth and 24th divisions have been found in a Dead Sea scroll from the fourth cave at Qumran (see "The Time between the Testaments," p.

1431).
24:7 *Jehoiarib.* Mattathias, father of the Maccabees, was a member of the Jehoiarib division (in the Apocrypha see 1 Maccabees 2:1).
24:10 *Abijah.* The father of John the Baptist "belonged to the priestly division of Abijah" (Lk 1:5).
24:15 *Hezir.* The division from the family of Hezir was prominent in intertestamental times; the name appears on one of the large tombs in the Kidron Valley, east of Jerusalem.
24:20-31 This list supplements 23:7-23 by extending some of the lines mentioned there.

The Singers

25 David, together with the commanders of the army, set apart some of the sons of Asaph,[g] Heman[h] and Jeduthun[i] for the ministry of prophesying,[j] accompanied by harps, lyres and cymbals.[k] Here is the list of the men[l] who performed this service:[m]

[2]From the sons of Asaph:

Zaccur, Joseph, Nethaniah and Asarelah. The sons of Asaph were under the supervision of Asaph, who prophesied under the king's supervision.

[3]As for Jeduthun, from his sons:[n]

Gedaliah, Zeri, Jeshaiah, Shimei,[d] Hashabiah and Mattithiah, six in all, under the supervision of their father Jeduthun, who prophesied, using the harp[o] in thanking and praising the LORD.

[4]As for Heman, from his sons:

Bukkiah, Mattaniah, Uzziel, Shubael and Jerimoth; Hananiah, Hanani, Eliathah, Giddalti and Romamti-Ezer; Joshbekashah, Mallothi, Hothir and Mahazioth. [5]All these were sons of Heman the king's seer. They were given him through the promises of God to exalt him.[e] God gave Heman fourteen sons and three daughters.

[6]All these men were under the supervision of their fathers[p] for the music of the temple of the LORD, with cymbals, lyres and harps, for the ministry at the house of God. Asaph, Jeduthun and Heman[q] were under the supervision of the king.[r] [7]Along with their relatives—all of them trained and skilled in music for the LORD—they numbered 288. [8]Young and old alike, teacher as well as student, cast lots[s] for their duties.

[9]The first lot, which was for Asaph,[t] fell to Joseph,

his sons and relatives,[f]   12[g]

the second to Gedaliah,

he and his relatives and sons, 12

[10]the third to Zaccur,

his sons and relatives,   12

[11]the fourth to Izri,[h]

his sons and relatives,	12
[12]the fifth to Nethaniah,	
his sons and relatives,	12
[13]the sixth to Bukkiah,	
his sons and relatives,	12
[14]the seventh to Jesarelah,[i]	
his sons and relatives,	12
[15]the eighth to Jeshaiah,	
his sons and relatives,	12
[16]the ninth to Mattaniah,	
his sons and relatives,	12
[17]the tenth to Shimei,	
his sons and relatives,	12
[18]the eleventh to Azarel,[j]	
his sons and relatives,	12
[19]the twelfth to Hashabiah,	
his sons and relatives,	12
[20]the thirteenth to Shubael,	
his sons and relatives,	12
[21]the fourteenth to Mattithiah,	
his sons and relatives,	12
[22]the fifteenth to Jerimoth,	
his sons and relatives,	12
[23]the sixteenth to Hananiah,	
his sons and relatives,	12
[24]the seventeenth to Joshbekashah,	
his sons and relatives,	12
[25]the eighteenth to Hanani,	
his sons and relatives,	12
[26]the nineteenth to Mallothi,	
his sons and relatives,	12
[27]the twentieth to Eliathah,	
his sons and relatives,	12
[28]the twenty-first to Hothir,	
his sons and relatives,	12
[29]the twenty-second to Giddalti,	
his sons and relatives,	12
[30]the twenty-third to Mahazioth,	
his sons and relatives,	12
[31]the twenty-fourth to Romamti-Ezer,	
his sons and relatives,	12[u]

25:1 [g]S 1Ch 6:39
[h]S 1Ch 6:33
[f]1Ch 16:41,42; Ne 11:17
[i]S 1Sa 10:5; 2Ki 3:15
[k]S 1Ch 15:16
[l]S 1Ch 6:31
[m]2Ch 5:12; 8:14; 34:12; 35:15; Ezr 3:10
25:3 [n]1Ch 16:41-42
[o]S Ge 4:21; Ps 33:2
25:6 [p]S 1Ch 15:16
[q]S 1Ch 15:19
[r]2Ch 23:18; 29:25
25:8 [s]1Ch 26:13
25:9 [t]S 1Ch 6:39

25:31 [u]S 1Ch 9:33

[d]3 One Hebrew manuscript and some Septuagint manuscripts (see also verse 17); most Hebrew manuscripts do not have *Shimei.*   [e]5 Hebrew *exalt the horn*   [f]9 See Septuagint; Hebrew does not have *his sons and relatives.*   [g]9 See the total in verse 7; Hebrew does not have *twelve.*   [h]11 A variant of *Zeri*   [i]14 A variant of *Asarelah*   [j]18 A variant of *Uzziel*

25:1 *commanders of the army.* David often sought the counsel of military leaders (11:10; 12:32; 28:1), even in cultic affairs (13:1; 15:25). *Asaph, Heman and Jeduthun.* See note on 6:31–48. *ministry of prophesying.* There are several passages in Chronicles, largely in portions unique to these books, where cultic personnel are designated prophets (here; 2Ch 20:14–17; 29:30; 35:15; cf. 2Ki 23:2; 2Ch 34:30). Zechariah the priest also appears to function as a prophet, though he is not so named (2Ch 24:19–22). This may reflect postexilic interest in the prophet-priest-king fig-

ure of Messianic expectation: In Chronicles not only do priests prophesy, but kings also function as priests (see notes on 15:27; 16:1–3). David's organizing of the temple musicians may reflect his overall interest in music (1Sa 16:23; 18:10; 19:9; 2Sa 1:17–27; 6:5,14).

25:5 *fourteen sons and three daughters.* Numerous progeny are a sign of divine blessing (see Job 1:2; 42:13). This is specifically stated for Heman as the result of the promises of God to exalt him. See 3:1–9; 14:2–7; 26:4–5; 2Ch 11:18–21; 13:21; 21:2; 24:3.

The Gatekeepers

26 The divisions of the gatekeepers:

From the Korahites: Meshelemiah son of Kore, one of the sons of Asaph.

[2]Meshelemiah had sons:

Zechariah [w] the firstborn,
Jediael the second,
Zebadiah the third,
Jathniel the fourth,
[3]Elam the fifth,
Jehohanan the sixth
and Eliehoenai the seventh.

[4]Obed-Edom also had sons:

Shemaiah the firstborn,
Jehozabad the second,
Joah the third,
Sacar the fourth,
Nethanel the fifth,
[5]Ammiel the sixth,
Issachar the seventh
and Peullethai the eighth.

(For God had blessed Obed-Edom. [x])

[6]His son Shemaiah also had sons, who were leaders in their father's family because they were very capable men. [7]The sons of Shemaiah: Othni, Rephael, Obed and Elzabad; his relatives Elihu and Semakiah were also able men. [8]All these were descendants of Obed-Edom; they and their sons and their relatives were capable men with the strength to do the work—descendants of Obed-Edom, 62 in all.

[9]Meshelemiah had sons and relatives, who were able men—18 in all.

[10]Hosah the Merarite had sons: Shimri the first (although he was not the firstborn, his father had appointed him the first), [y] [11]Hilkiah the sec-

ond, Tabaliah the third and Zechariah the fourth. The sons and relatives of Hosah were 13 in all.

[12]These divisions of the gatekeepers, through their chief men, had duties for ministering [z] in the temple of the LORD, just as their relatives had. [13]Lots [a] were cast for each gate, according to their families, young and old alike.

[14]The lot for the East Gate [b] fell to Shelemiah. [k] Then lots were cast for his son Zechariah, [c] a wise counselor, and the lot for the North Gate fell to him. [15]The lot for the South Gate fell to Obed-Edom, [d] and the lot for the storehouse fell to his sons. [16]The lots for the West Gate and the Shalleketh Gate on the upper road fell to Shuppim and Hosah.

Guard was alongside of guard: [17]There were six Levites a day on the east, four a day on the north, four a day on the south and two at a time at the storehouse. [18]As for the court to the west, there were four at the road and two at the court itself.

[19]These were the divisions of the gatekeepers who were descendants of Korah and Merari. [e]

The Treasurers and Other Officials

[20]Their fellow Levites [f] were[1] in charge of the treasuries of the house of God and the treasuries for the dedicated things. [g]

[21]The descendants of Ladan, who were Gershonites through Ladan and who were heads of families belonging to Ladan the Gershonite, [h] were Jehieli, [22]the sons of Jehieli, Zetham and his brother Joel. They were in charge of the treasuries [i] of the temple of the LORD.

[23]From the Amramites, the Izharites, the Hebronites and the Uzzielites: [j]

26:1 [v]S 1Ch 9:17
26:2 [w]S 1Ch 9:21
26:5 [x]S 2Sa 6:10; S 1Ch 13:13; S 16:38
26:10 [y]Dt 21:16; 1Ch 5:1

26:12 [z]1Ch 9:22
26:13 [a]S 1Ch 24:5
26:14 [b]S 1Ch 9:18 [c]S 1Ch 9:21
26:15 [d]S 1Ch 13:13; 2Ch 25:24
26:19 [e]2Ch 35:15; Ne 7:1; Eze 44:11
26:20 [f]2Ch 24:5 [g]1Ch 28:12
26:21 [h]1Ch 23:7; 29:8
26:22 [i]1Ch 9:26
26:23 [j]S Nu 3:27

[k]14 A variant of *Meshelemiah*   [l]20 Septuagint; Hebrew *As for the Levites, Ahijah was*

26:1–19 The most extensive of the Chronicler's lists of gatekeepers (see 9:17–27; 16:37–38). A list of gatekeepers in the postexilic period is found in Ezr 2:42 (Ne 7:45).
26:1 *Asaph.* This name appears to be an abbreviation of Ebiasaph (6:23; 9:19); he should not be confused with the temple musician (25:1–2,6).
26:4–5 Numerous sons are again a sign of divine blessing (see note on 25:5).
26:4 *Obed-Edom.* Had cared for the ark when it was left at his house (see note on 13:13).
26:12 *duties.* Elaborated in 9:22–29.
26:14 *East Gate.* The main entrance; it had six guard posts, as opposed to four at the other gates (v. 17).
26:15 *South Gate.* The palaces of David and Solomon were south of the temple mount. The southern gate would be the main one used by the king, and this assignment probably reflects a particular honor for Obed-Edom (see notes on 26:4–5; see also Eze 46:1–10).

26:16 *Shalleketh Gate.* The only reference to a gate by this name; presumably it was on the western side. The Chronicler writes to an audience familiar with these topographical details.
26:20 *treasuries of the house of God.* The Levites in charge of these treasuries received the offerings of the people and cared for the valuable temple equipment (9:28–29). *treasuries for the dedicated things.* Received the plunder from warfare (vv. 27–28). Texts from Mesopotamian temples confirm the presence of temple officers who served as assayers to handle and refine the precious metals received as revenue and offerings. The procedure with reference to the offerings of the people may be seen in the reign of Joash (2Ch 24:4–14; 2Ki 12:4–16). Numerous passages reflect on the wealth collected in the temple (see, e.g., 29:1–9; 2Ch 4:1–22; 34:9–11; 36:7,10,18–19; 1Ki 14:25–28; 15:15, 18; 2Ki 12:4–18; 14:14; 16:8; 25:13–17).

24 Shubael,[k] a descendant of Gershom
son of Moses, was the officer in
charge of the treasuries. 25 His relatives through Eliezer: Rehabiah his
son, Jeshaiah his son, Joram his
son, Zicri his son and Shelomith[l]
his son. 26 Shelomith and his relatives were in charge of all the treasuries for the things dedicated[m] by
King David, by the heads of families who were the commanders of
thousands and commanders of
hundreds, and by the other army
commanders. 27 Some of the plunder taken in battle they dedicated
for the repair of the temple of the
LORD. 28 And everything dedicated
by Samuel the seer[n] and by Saul
son of Kish, Abner son of Ner and
Joab son of Zeruiah, and all the
other dedicated things were in the
care of Shelomith and his relatives.
29 From the Izharites: Kenaniah and his
sons were assigned duties away
from the temple, as officials and
judges[o] over Israel.
30 From the Hebronites: Hashabiah[p]
and his relatives—seventeen hundred able men—were responsible
in Israel west of the Jordan for all
the work of the LORD and for the
king's service. 31 As for the Hebronites,[q] Jeriah was their chief according to the genealogical records
of their families. In the fortieth[r]
year of David's reign a search was
made in the records, and capable
men among the Hebronites were
found at Jazer in Gilead. 32 Jeriah
had twenty-seven hundred relatives, who were able men and
heads of families, and King David
put them in charge of the Reubenites, the Gadites and the half-tribe
of Manasseh for every matter pertaining to God and for the affairs of
the king.

Army Divisions

27 This is the list of the Israelites—heads of families, commanders of thousands and commanders of hundreds, and their officers, who served the
king in all that concerned the army divisions that were on duty month by month
throughout the year. Each division consisted of 24,000 men.

2 In charge of the first division, for the first
month, was Jashobeam[s] son of Zab-
diel. There were 24,000 men in his
division. 3 He was a descendant of
Perez and chief of all the army officers for the first month.
4 In charge of the division for the second
month was Dodai[t] the Ahohite;
Mikloth was the leader of his division. There were 24,000 men in his
division.
5 The third army commander, for the third
month, was Benaiah[u] son of Jehoiada the priest. He was chief and
there were 24,000 men in his division. 6 This was the Benaiah who
was a mighty man among the Thirty
and was over the Thirty. His son
Ammizabad was in charge of his
division.
7 The fourth, for the fourth month, was
Asahel[v] the brother of Joab; his son
Zebadiah was his successor. There
were 24,000 men in his division.
8 The fifth, for the fifth month, was the
commander Shamhuth[w] the Izra-
hite. There were 24,000 men in his
division.
9 The sixth, for the sixth month, was Ira[x]

26:24 [k] 1Ch 23:16
26:25 [l] 1Ch 23:18
26:26 [m] S 2Sa 8:11
26:28 [n] S 1Sa 9:9
26:29 [o] Dt 17:8-13; S 1Ch 23:4
26:30 [p] 1Ch 27:17
26:31 [q] S 1Ch 23:19 [r] S 2Sa 5:4
27:2 [s] 2Sa 23:8
27:4 [t] S 2Sa 23:9
27:5 [u] S 2Sa 23:20
27:7 [v] S 2Sa 2:18
27:8 [w] 1Ch 11:27
27:9 [x] 2Sa 23:26

26:26 *things dedicated by King David.* See note on 18:1–20:8; see also 2Ch 5:1.
26:27 *plunder taken in battle they dedicated.* Cf. Ge 14:17–20.
26:29–32 These verses designate the 6,000 officials and judges (23:4) who would work outside Jerusalem; they are drawn from two sub-clans of Kohath (6:18). Dt 17:8–13 envisages a judicial function for the priests and Levites (see 2Ch 19:4–11).
26:30,32 *for all the work of the LORD and for the king's service . . . for every matter pertaining to God and for the affairs of the king.* In the theocracy (kingdom of God) there is no division between secular and sacred, no tension in serving God and the king (cf. Mt 22:15–22; Lk 16:10–13; Ro 13:1–7; 1Ti 2:1–4; 1Pe 2:13–17).
26:31 *fortieth year.* The last year of David's reign.
27:1–15 The names of the commanders of David's army are the same as those found in the list of his mighty men (see 11:11–47; see also 2Sa 23:8–39 and notes). Those who had served David while he fled from Saul became commanders in the regular army.
27:1 *24,000.* See note on 12:23–37. Although a national militia consisting of 12 units of 24,000 each (a total of 288,000) is not unreasonable, the stress in this passage on unit commanders and divisions suggests that here too the Hebrew word for "1,000" should perhaps be taken as the designation of a military unit. To designate a division as "1,000" would be to give the upper limit of the number of men in such a unit, though such units would ordinarily not have a full complement of men. If this approach is followed, the figures in the following verses would be read as "24 units" instead of 24,000.
27:2 *Jashobeam.* See 11:11.
27:4 *Dodai.* See 11:12.
27:5 *Benaiah.* See 11:22–25; 18:17.
27:7 *Asahel.* See 11:26; 2Sa 2:18–23.

the son of Ikkesh the Tekoite. There were 24,000 men in his division.

¹⁰The seventh, for the seventh month, was Helez ʸ the Pelonite, an Ephraimite. There were 24,000 men in his division.

¹¹The eighth, for the eighth month, was Sibbecai ᶻ the Hushathite, a Zerahite. There were 24,000 men in his division.

¹²The ninth, for the ninth month, was Abiezer ᵃ the Anathothite, a Benjamite. There were 24,000 men in his division.

¹³The tenth, for the tenth month, was Maharai ᵇ the Netophathite, a Zerahite. There were 24,000 men in his division.

¹⁴The eleventh, for the eleventh month, was Benaiah ᶜ the Pirathonite, an Ephraimite. There were 24,000 men in his division.

¹⁵The twelfth, for the twelfth month, was Heldai ᵈ the Netophathite, from the family of Othniel. ᵉ There were 24,000 men in his division.

Officers of the Tribes

¹⁶The officers over the tribes of Israel:

over the Reubenites: Eliezer son of Zicri;

over the Simeonites: Shephatiah son of Maacah;

¹⁷over Levi: Hashabiah ᶠ son of Kemuel;

over Aaron: Zadok; ᵍ

¹⁸over Judah: Elihu, a brother of David;

over Issachar: Omri son of Michael;

¹⁹over Zebulun: Ishmaiah son of Obadiah;

over Naphtali: Jerimoth son of Azriel;

²⁰over the Ephraimites: Hoshea son of Azaziah;

over half the tribe of Manasseh: Joel son of Pedaiah;

²¹over the half-tribe of Manasseh in Gilead: Iddo son of Zechariah;

over Benjamin: Jaasiel son of Abner;

²²over Dan: Azarel son of Jeroham.

These were the officers over the tribes of Israel.

²³David did not take the number of the men twenty years old or less, ʰ because the LORD had promised to make Israel as numerous as the stars ⁱ in the sky. ²⁴Joab son of Zeruiah began to count the men but did not finish. Wrath came on Israel on account of this numbering, ʲ and the number was not entered in the book ᵐ of the annals of King David.

The King's Overseers

²⁵Azmaveth son of Adiel was in charge of the royal storehouses.

Jonathan son of Uzziah was in charge of the storehouses in the outlying districts, in the towns, the villages and the watchtowers.

²⁶Ezri son of Kelub was in charge of the field workers who farmed the land.

²⁷Shimei the Ramathite was in charge of the vineyards.

Zabdi the Shiphmite was in charge of the produce of the vineyards for the wine vats.

²⁸Baal-Hanan the Gederite was in charge of the olive and sycamore-fig ᵏ trees in the western foothills.

Joash was in charge of the supplies of olive oil.

²⁹Shitrai the Sharonite was in charge of the herds grazing in Sharon. ˡ

Shaphat son of Adlai was in charge of the herds in the valleys.

³⁰Obil the Ishmaelite was in charge of the camels.

Cross references (center column)

27:10 ʸ2Sa 23:26
27:11 ᶻS 2Sa 21:18
27:12 ᵃ2Sa 23:27
27:13 ᵇ2Sa 23:28
27:14 ᶜS 1Ch 11:31
27:15 ᵈ2Sa 23:29
 ᵉS Jos 15:17
27:17 ᶠ1Ch 26:30
 ᵍ2Sa 8:17;
 S 1Ch 12:28

27:23 ʰS 2Sa 24:1;
 1Ch 21:2-5
 ⁱS Ge 12:2
27:24 ʲS 2Sa 24:15;
 1Ch 21:14
27:28 ᵏS 1Ki 10:27
27:29 ˡSS 2:1;
 Isa 33:9; 35:2;
 65:10

ᵐ24 Septuagint; Hebrew *number*

27:9–15 The remainder of the commanders were selected from among the Thirty (see the names listed in 11:27–31). **27:16–22** The Chronicler's interest in "all Israel" appears in this list of officers who were over the 12 tribes (see Introduction: Purpose and Themes). The number is kept at 12 by omitting Gad and Asher (see note on 2:1–2). **27:17** *Zadok.* See note on 6:8; see also 12:28; 16:39. **27:18** *Elihu.* Not named elsewhere among the brothers of David. Perhaps he is the unnamed son from the list in 2:10–17 (see note there). Elihu could also be a variant of the name of Jesse's oldest son, Eliab, or the term "brother" could be taken in the sense of "relative," in which case Elihu would be a more distant kinsman. **27:21** *Abner.* A relative of King Saul (see 26:28; 1Sa 14:50–51; 17:55–58; 26:5–16; 2Sa 2:8–4:1). **27:23–24** *number.* Refers to the census narrative in ch. 21 (2Sa 24).

27:23 *twenty years old or less.* The figures reported in ch. 21 and 2Sa 24 were the numbers of those older than 20 years. *promised to make Israel as numerous as the stars.* The patriarchal promises of numerous descendants (Ge 12:2; 13:16; 15:5; 22:17) appear to have been the basis for the objections of Joab (v. 24) to the taking of a census (21:3; 2Sa 24:3). **27:24** *did not finish.* Joab did not count those under age 20, nor did he include the tribes of Levi and Benjamin (21:6). **27:25–31** A list of the administrators of David's property (v. 31). The large cities of the ancient Near East had three basic economic sectors: (1) royal, (2) temple and (3) private. There is no evidence of direct taxation during the reign of David; his court appears to have been financed by extensive landholdings, commerce, plunder from his many wars, and tribute from subjugated kingdoms.

Jehdeiah the Meronothite was in charge of the donkeys.

[31] Jaziz the Hagrite *m* was in charge of the flocks.

All these were the officials in charge of King David's property.

[32] Jonathan, David's uncle, was a counselor, a man of insight and a scribe. Jehiel son of Hacmoni took care of the king's sons.

[33] Ahithophel *n* was the king's counselor. Hushai *o* the Arkite was the king's friend. [34] Ahithophel was succeeded by Jehoiada son of Benaiah and by Abiathar. *p*

Joab *q* was the commander of the royal army.

David's Plans for the Temple

28 David summoned *r* all the officials *s* of Israel to assemble at Jerusalem: the officers over the tribes, the commanders of the divisions in the service of the king, the commanders of thousands and commanders of hundreds, and the officials in charge of all the property and livestock belonging to the king and his sons, together with the palace officials, the mighty men and all the brave warriors.

[2] King David rose to his feet and said: "Listen to me, my brothers and my people. I had it in my heart *t* to build a house as a place of rest *u* for the ark of the covenant of the LORD, for the footstool *v* of our God, and I made plans to build it. *w* [3] But God said to me, *x* 'You are not to build a house for my Name, *y* because you are a warrior and have shed blood.' *z*

[4] "Yet the LORD, the God of Israel, chose me *a* from my whole family *b* to be king over Israel forever. He chose Judah *c* as leader, and from the house of Judah he

chose my family, and from my father's sons he was pleased to make me king over all Israel. *d* [5] Of all my sons—and the LORD has given me many *e*—he has chosen my son Solomon *f* to sit on the throne *g* of the kingdom of the LORD over Israel. [6] He said to me: 'Solomon your son is the one who will build *h* my house and my courts, for I have chosen him to be my son, *i* and I will be his father. [7] I will establish his kingdom forever if he is unswerving in carrying out my commands and laws, *j* as is being done at this time.'

[8] "So now I charge you in the sight of all Israel *k* and of the assembly of the LORD, and in the hearing of our God: Be careful to follow all the commands *l* of the LORD your God, that you may possess this good land and pass it on as an inheritance to your descendants forever. *m*

[9] "And you, my son Solomon, acknowledge the God of your father, and serve him with wholehearted devotion *n* and with a willing mind, for the LORD searches every heart *o* and understands every motive behind the thoughts. If you seek him, *p* he will be found by you; but if you forsake *q* him, he will reject *r* you forever. [10] Consider now, for the LORD has chosen you to build a temple as a sanctuary. Be strong and do the work."

[11] Then David gave his son Solomon the plans *s* for the portico of the temple, its buildings, its storerooms, its upper parts, its inner rooms and the place of atonement. [12] He gave him the plans of all that the Spirit *t* had put in his mind for the courts of the temple of the LORD and all the surrounding rooms, for the treasuries of the temple of God and for the treasuries for the dedicated things. *u* [13] He gave him instructions for the divisions *v* of the priests

Cross references (center column)

27:31
m S 1Ch 5:10
27:33
n S 2Sa 15:12
o S 2Sa 15:37
27:34
p S 1Sa 22:20
q S 2Sa 2:13
28:1 *r* 1Ch 22:17
s 1Ch 27:1-31;
29:6
28:2 *t* S 1Sa 10:7;
S 1Ch 17:2
u 2Ch 6:41
v Ps 99:5; 132:7;
Isa 60:13
w Ps 132:1-5
28:3 *x* S 2Sa 7:5
y 1Ch 22:8
z S 1Ki 5:3;
S 1Ch 17:4
28:4 *a* 2Ch 6:6
b 1Sa 16:1-13
Nu 24:17-19

d 1Ch 11:1
28:5 *e* S 1Ch 3:1
f S 2Sa 12:24;
S 1Ch 23:1
g S 1Ch 17:14
28:6 *h* 1Ki 8:20
i S 2Sa 7:13;
S 1Ch 17:13
28:7 *j* 1Ch 22:13
28:8 *k* S 1Ch 9:1
l Dt 6:1 *m* Dt 4:1;
S 17:14-20
28:9
n S 1Ch 29:19
o S 1Sa 2:3;
2Ch 6:30; Ps 7:9
p S 1Ch 16:11;
S Ps 40:16
q S Dt 4:31;
S Jos 24:20;
S 2Ch 7:19; 15:2
r 1Ki 9:7;
Ps 44:23; 74:1;
77:7
28:11
s S Ex 25:9;
Ac 7:44; Heb 8:5
28:12
t S 1Ch 12:18
u 1Ch 26:20
28:13
v S 1Ch 24:1

27:32–34 A list of David's cabinet members, supplementary to that in 18:14–17.
27:33 *Ahithophel.* Was replaced after he committed suicide, following his support of Absalom's rebellion (2Sa 15:12,31–37; 16:20–17:23).
27:34 *Benaiah.* See v. 5.
28:1–29:30 The account of the transition from the reign of David to that of Solomon is one of the clearest demonstrations of the Chronicler's idealization of their reigns when it is compared with the succession account in 1Ki 1–2. The Chronicler makes no mention of the infirmities of the aged David (1Ki 1:1–4), the rebellion of Adonijah and the king's sons (1Ki 1:5–10), the court intrigue to secure Solomon's succession (1Ki 1:11–31) or David's charge to Solomon to punish his enemies after his death (1Ki 2:1–9). His selection of material presents a transition of power that is smooth and peaceful and receives the support of "all Israel" (29:25), the officials and the people (28:1–2; 29:6–9,21–25). Instead of the bedridden David who sends others to anoint Solomon (1Ki 1:32–35), David himself is present and in charge of the

ceremonies (see 23:1 and note).
28:1 The assembly is composed largely of the groups named in ch. 27. This public announcement (v. 5) follows the private announcement of Solomon's succession in ch. 22 (see note on 22:2–19).
28:3 *you are a warrior and have shed blood.* See note on 22:8–9.
28:5 *chosen my son Solomon.* See vv. 6,10; 29:1. These are the only uses in the OT of the Hebrew verb for "chosen" with reference to any king after David (see Introduction: Purpose and Themes). The Chronicler's application of this term to Solomon is consistent with his depiction of that king. *kingdom of the LORD.* See note on 17:14.
28:6 *my son.* See 17:12–14 and note; see also 22:10.
28:8–9 See Introduction: Portrait of David and Solomon.
28:12 David provides Solomon with the plans for the temple. This reflects the Chronicler's modeling David after Moses: Just as Moses received the plans for the tabernacle from God (Ex 25–30), so also David received the plans for the temple.

and Levites, and for all the work of serving in the temple of the LORD, as well as for all the articles to be used in its service. ¹⁴He designated the weight of gold for all the gold articles to be used in various kinds of service, and the weight of silver for all the silver articles to be used in various kinds of service: ¹⁵the weight of gold for the gold lampstands ʷ and their lamps, with the weight for each lampstand and its lamps; and the weight of silver for each silver lampstand and its lamps, according to the use of each lampstand; ¹⁶the weight of gold for each table ˣ for consecrated bread; the weight of silver for the silver tables; ¹⁷the weight of pure gold for the forks, sprinkling bowls ʸ and pitchers; the weight of gold for each gold dish; the weight of silver for each silver dish; ¹⁸and the weight of the refined gold for the altar of incense. ᶻ He also gave him the plan for the chariot, ᵃ that is, the cherubim of gold that spread their wings and shelter ᵇ the ark of the covenant of the LORD.

¹⁹"All this," David said, "I have in writing from the hand of the LORD upon me, and he gave me understanding in all the details ᶜ of the plan. ᵈ "

²⁰David also said to Solomon his son, "Be strong and courageous, ᵉ and do the work. Do not be afraid or discouraged, for the LORD God, my God, is with you. He will not fail you or forsake ᶠ you until all the work for the service of the temple of the LORD is finished. ᵍ ²¹The divisions of the priests and Levites are ready for all the work on the temple of God, and every willing man skilled ʰ in any craft will help you in all the work. The officials and all the people will obey your every command."

Gifts for Building the Temple

29 Then King David said to the whole assembly: "My son Solomon, the one whom God has chosen, is young and inexperienced. ⁱ The task is great, because this palatial structure is not for man but for the LORD God. ²With all my resources I have provided for the temple of my God—gold ʲ for the gold work, silver for

the silver, bronze for the bronze, iron for the iron and wood for the wood, as well as onyx for the settings, turquoise, ⁿ ᵏ stones of various colors, and all kinds of fine stone and marble—all of these in large quantities. ˡ ³Besides, in my devotion to the temple of my God I now give my personal treasures of gold and silver for the temple of my God, over and above everything I have provided ᵐ for this holy temple: ⁴three thousand talents ᵒ of gold (gold of Ophir) ⁿ and seven thousand talents ᵖ of refined silver, ᵒ for the overlaying of the walls of the buildings, ⁵for the gold work and the silver work, and for all the work to be done by the craftsmen. Now, who is willing to consecrate himself today to the LORD?"

⁶Then the leaders of families, the officers of the tribes of Israel, the commanders of thousands and commanders of hundreds, and the officials ᵖ in charge of the king's work gave willingly. ᵠ ⁷They ʳ gave toward the work on the temple of God five thousand talents ᵠ and ten thousand darics ʳ of gold, ten thousand talents ˢ of silver, eighteen thousand talents ᵗ of bronze and a hundred thousand talents ᵘ of iron. ⁸Any who had precious stones ˢ gave them to the treasury of the temple of the LORD in the custody of Jehiel the Gershonite. ᵗ ⁹The people rejoiced at the willing response of their leaders, for they had given freely and wholeheartedly ᵘ to the LORD. David the king also rejoiced greatly.

David's Prayer

¹⁰David praised the LORD in the presence of the whole assembly, saying,

"Praise be to you, O LORD,
God of our father Israel,
from everlasting to everlasting.

Cross references

28:15 ʷEx 25:31
28:16 ˣS Ex 25:23
28:17 ʸS Ex 27:3
28:18 ᶻEx 30:1-10; ᵃS Ex 25:22; ᵇS Ex 25:20
28:19 ᶜ1Ki 6:38; ᵈS Ex 25:9
28:20 ᵉS Dt 31:6; 1Ch 22:13; 2Ch 19:11; Hag 2:4; ᶠS Dt 4:31; S Jos 24:20; ᵍS 1Ki 6:14; 2Ch 7:11
28:21 ʰEx 35:25-36:5
29:1 ⁱ1Ki 3:7; 1Ch 22:5; 2Ch 13:7
29:2 ʲver 7,14,16; Ezr 1:4; 6:5; Hag 2:8

ᵏIsa 54:11
ˡ1Ch 22:2-5
29:3 ᵐ2Ch 24:10; 31:3; 35:8
29:4 ⁿS Ge 10:29
ᵒ1Ch 22:14
29:6 ᵖ1Ch 27:1; S 28:1 ᵠver 9; Ex 25:1-8; 35:20-29; 36:2; 2Ch 24:10; Ezr 7:15
29:7 ʳS Ex 25:2; Ne 7:70-71
29:8 ˢEx 35:27
ᵗS 1Ch 26:21
29:9 ᵘ1Ki 8:61

Footnotes

ⁿ2 The meaning of the Hebrew for this word is uncertain.
ᵒ4 That is, about 110 tons (about 100 metric tons)
ᵖ4 That is, about 260 tons (about 240 metric tons)
ᵠ7 That is, about 190 tons (about 170 metric tons)
ʳ7 That is, about 185 pounds (about 84 kilograms)
ˢ7 That is, about 375 tons (about 345 metric tons)
ᵗ7 That is, about 675 tons (about 610 metric tons)
ᵘ7 That is, about 3,750 tons (about 3,450 metric tons)

28:19 *I have in writing from the hand of the LORD upon me.* The Chronicler may intend no more than the ordinary process of inspiration whereby David wrote under divine influence. On the other hand, he may imply a parallel with Moses, who also received documents from the hand of the Lord (Ex 25:40; 27:8; 31:18; 32:16).

28:20 See Introduction: Portrait of David and Solomon.

29:1 *chosen.* See note on 28:5. *young.* See note on 22:5.

29:2-9 After donating his personal fortune to the construc-

tion of the temple, David appeals to the people for their voluntary gifts. The Chronicler again appears to be modeling his account of David on events from the life of Moses (Ex 25:1-8; 35:4-9,20-29). The willing response of the people aided the building of both tabernacle and temple.

29:7 *darics.* The daric was a Persian coin, apparently named for Darius I (522-486 B.C.) in whose reign it first appears (see Ezr 8:27). Since the Chronicler's readers were familiar with it, he could use it as an up-to-date standard of value for an earlier treasure of gold.

[11]Yours, O Lord, is the greatness and the power[v]

and the glory and the majesty and the splendor,

for everything in heaven and earth is yours. [w]

Yours, O Lord, is the kingdom;

you are exalted as head over all. [x]

[12]Wealth and honor[y] come from you;

you are the ruler[z] of all things.

In your hands are strength and power

to exalt and give strength to all.

[13]Now, our God, we give you thanks,

and praise your glorious name.

[14]"But who am I, and who are my people, that we should be able to give as generously as this?[a] Everything comes from you, and we have given you only what comes from your hand. [b] [15]We are aliens and strangers[c] in your sight, as were all our forefathers. Our days on earth are like a shadow,[d] without hope. [16]O Lord our God, as for all this abundance that we have provided for building you a temple for your Holy Name, it comes from your hand, and all of it belongs to you. [17]I know, my God, that you test the heart[e] and are pleased with integrity. All these things have I given willingly and with honest intent. And now I have seen with joy how willingly your people who are here have given to you.[f] [18]O Lord, God of our fathers Abraham, Isaac and Israel, keep this desire in the hearts of your people forever, and keep their hearts loyal to you. [19]And give my son Solomon the wholehearted devotion[g] to keep your commands, requirements and decrees[h] and to do everything to build the palatial structure for which I have provided." [i]

[20]Then David said to the whole assembly, "Praise the Lord your God." So they all praised the Lord, the God of their fathers; they bowed low and fell prostrate before the Lord and the king.

Solomon Acknowledged as King

29:21–25pp — 1Ki 1:28–53

[21]The next day they made sacrifices to the Lord and presented burnt offerings to him:[j] a thousand bulls, a thousand rams and a thousand male lambs, together with their drink offerings, and other sacrifices in abundance for all Israel.[k] [22]They ate and drank with great joy[l] in the presence of the Lord that day.

Then they acknowledged Solomon son of David as king a second time, anointing him before the Lord to be ruler and Zadok[m] to be priest. [23]So Solomon sat[n] on the throne[o] of the Lord as king in place of his father David. He prospered and all Israel obeyed him. [24]All the officers and mighty men, as well as all of King David's sons,[p] pledged their submission to King Solomon.

[25]The Lord highly exalted[q] Solomon in the sight of all Israel and bestowed on him royal splendor[r] such as no king over Israel ever had before.[s]

The Death of David

29:26–28pp — 1Ki 2:10–12

[26]David son of Jesse was king[t] over all Israel. [u] [27]He ruled over Israel forty years—seven in Hebron[v] and thirty-three in Jerusalem. [w] [28]He died[x] at a good old age, having enjoyed long life, wealth and honor. His son Solomon succeeded him as king. [y]

[29]As for the events of King David's reign, from beginning to end, they are written in the records of Samuel the seer,[z] the records of Nathan[a] the prophet and the records of Gad[b] the seer, [30]together with the details of his reign and power, and the circumstances that surrounded him and Israel and the kingdoms of all the other lands.

Cross references (center column):

29:11 [v]Ps 24:8; 59:17; 62:11 [w]Ps 89:11 [x]Rev 5:12-13
29:12 [y]2Ch 1:12; 32:27; Ezr 7:27; Ecc 5:19 [z]2Ch 20:6
29:14 [a]Ps 8:4; 144:3 [b]S ver 2
29:15 [c]S Ge 17:8; S 23:4; Ps 39:12; S Heb 11:13 [d]Job 7:6; 8:9; 14:2; 32:7; Ps 102:11; 144:4; Ecc 6:12
29:17 [e]Ps 139:23; Pr 15:11; 17:3; Jer 11:20; 17:10 [f]1Ch 28:9; Pr 15:1-5; Pr 11:20
29:19 [g]S 1Ki 8:61; 11:4; 1Ch 28:9; Isa 38:3 [h]Ps 72:1 [i]S 1Ch 22:14
29:21 [j]S 1Ki 8:62 [k]1Ch 11:1
29:22 [l]1Ch 12:40 [m]S 1Sa 2:35
29:23 [n]S Dt 17:18 [o]S 1Ki 2:12; S 1Ch 17:14
29:24 [p]1Ki 1:9 [q]S Jos 3:7 [r]1Ch 10:7; 2Ch 1:1,12 [s]Ecc 2:9
29:26 [t]1Ch 18:14 [u]1Ch 11:1
29:27 [v]S Ge 23:19 [w]2Sa 5:4-5; S 1Ch 3:4
29:28 [x]S Ge 15:15; Ac 13:36 [y]S 1Ch 23:1
29:29 [z]S 1Sa 9:9 [a]S 2Sa 7:2 [b]1Sa 22:5

29:22 *ate and drank.* See 12:38–40 and note. The anointing of both Solomon and Zadok portrays the harmony between them (see Zec 4:14; 6:13 and notes). *second time.* Perhaps the first time was Solomon's anointing recorded in 1Ki 1:32–36, but omitted by the Chronicler (see note on 28:1–29:30). However, the phrase "second time" is missing in the Septuagint, suggesting that it may have been an addition to the Hebrew text of this passage by an ancient scribe after the Septuagint had already been translated, in order to harmonize the Chronicles account with Kings. Multiple anointings are found in the cases of both Saul (1Sa 10:1,24; 11:14–15) and David (1Sa 16:13; 2Sa 2:4; 5:3).

29:24 *all . . . pledged their submission.* But compare the rebellion of Adonijah, in which the officers and sons of the king had assisted the attempted coup (1Ki 1:9,19,25). Again the Chronicler has bypassed a negative event that would tarnish his image of David and Solomon.

29:25 *all Israel.* See 11:1,10; 12:38–40; see also Introduction: Purpose and Themes.

29:27 See note on 3:1–9.

29:28 *long life, wealth and honor.* As a feature of the Chronicler's theme of immediate retribution (see Introduction: Purpose and Themes), the righteous enjoy these blessings (cf. Ps 128; Pr 3:2,4,9–10,16,22,33–35).

29:29 See Introduction: Author, Date and Sources.

29:30 *kingdoms of all the other lands.* Those immediately surrounding David's kingdom.

2 CHRONICLES

See Introduction to 1 Chronicles.

The Building of the Temple in Chronicles

The Chronicler has used the Pentateuchal history as a model for his account of the reigns of David and Solomon. Similarly, the Pentateuchal record of the building of the tabernacle affects his account of the building of the temple:

1. The building of the tabernacle was entrusted to Bezalel and Oholiab (Ex 35:30-36:7), and they provide the Chronicler's model for the relationship of Solomon and Huram-Abi (2Ch 2:13). It is significant that the only references to Bezalel outside the book of Exodus are in Chronicles (1Ch 2:20; 2Ch 1:5).

Solomon is the new Bezalel: (1) Both Solomon and Bezalel are designated by name for their tasks by God; they are the only workers on their projects to be chosen by name (Ex 31:2; 35:30-36:2; 38:22–23; 1Ch 28:6). (2) Both are from the tribe of Judah (Ex 31:2; 35:30; 1Ch 2:20; 3:10). (3) Both receive the Spirit to endow them with wisdom (Ex 31:3; 35:30-31; 2Ch 1:1-13), and Solomon's vision at Gibeon (2Ch 1:3-13) dominates the preface to the account of the temple construction (2Ch 2-7). (4) Both build a bronze altar for the sanctuary (2Ch 1:5; 4:1; 7:7)—significantly, the bronze altar is not mentioned in the summary list of Huram-Abi's work (4:12-16). (5) Both make the sanctuary furnishings (Ex 31:1-10; 37:10-29; 2Ch 4:19-22).

Similarly, Huram-Abi becomes the new Oholiab: (1) In the account of the temple building in Kings, Huram-Abi is not mentioned until after the story of the main construction of temple and palace has been told (1Ki 7:13-45); in Chronicles he is introduced as being involved in the building work from the beginning, just as Oholiab worked on the tabernacle from the beginning (Ex 31:6; 2Ch 2:13). (2) Kings speaks only of Huram-Abi's skill in casting bronze (1Ki 7:14); in Chronicles, however, his list of skills is the same as Oholiab's (Ex 31:1-6; 35:30-36:2; 38:22-23; 2Ch 2:14). (3) Kings reports that the mother of Huram-Abi was a widow from the tribe of Naphtali (1Ki 7:14); Chronicles, however, states that she was a widow from the tribe of Dan (2Ch 2:14), thus giving Huram-Abi the same ancestry as Oholiab (Ex 31:6; 35:34; 38:23). See note on 2Ch 2:14.

2. The plans for both tabernacle and temple are given by God (Ex 25:1-30:37; see Ex 25:9,40; 27:8; see also 1Ch 28:11-19—not mentioned in Samuel and Kings).

3. The spoils of war are used as building materials for both tabernacle and temple (Ex 3:21-22; 12:35-36; see 1Ch 18:6-11—not mentioned in Samuel and Kings).

4. The people contribute willingly and generously for both structures (Ex 25:1-7; 36:3-7; see 1Ch 29:1-9—not mentioned in Samuel and Kings).

5. The glory cloud appears at the dedication of both structures (Ex 40:34-35; 2Ch 7:1-3).

Solomon Asks for Wisdom

1:2–13pp — 1Ki 3:4–15
1:14–17pp — 1Ki 10:26–29; 2Ch 9:25–28

1 Solomon son of David established[a] himself firmly over his kingdom, for the LORD his God was with[b] him and made him exceedingly great. [c]

[2] Then Solomon spoke to all Israel[d] —to the commanders of thousands and commanders of hundreds, to the judges and to all the leaders in Israel, the heads of families— [3] and Solomon and the whole assembly went to the high place at Gibeon, [e] for God's Tent of Meeting[f] was there, which Moses[g] the LORD's servant had made in the desert. [4] Now David had brought up the ark[h] of God from Kiriath Jearim to the place he had prepared for it, because he had pitched a tent[i] for it in Jerusalem. [5] But the bronze altar[j] that Bezalel[k] son of Uri, the son of Hur, had made was in Gibeon in front of the tabernacle of the LORD; so Solomon and the assembly inquired[l] of him there. [6] Solomon went up to the bronze altar before the LORD in the Tent of Meeting and offered a thousand burnt offerings on it.

[7] That night God appeared[m] to Solomon and said to him, "Ask for whatever you want me to give you."

[8] Solomon answered God, "You have shown great kindness to David my father and have made me[n] king in his place. [9] Now, LORD God, let your promise[o] to my father David be confirmed, for you have made me king over a people who are as numerous as the dust of the earth. [p] [10] Give me wisdom and knowledge, that I may lead[q] this people, for who is able to govern this great people of yours?"

[11] God said to Solomon, "Since this is your heart's desire and you have not asked for wealth, [r] riches or honor, nor for the death of your enemies, and since you have not asked for a long life but for wisdom and knowledge to govern my people over whom I have made you king, [12] therefore wisdom and knowledge will be given you. And I will also give you wealth, riches and honor, [s] such as no king who was before you ever had and none after you will have. [t] "

[13] Then Solomon went to Jerusalem from the high place at Gibeon, from before the Tent of Meeting. And he reigned over Israel.

[14] Solomon accumulated chariots[u] and horses; he had fourteen hundred chariots and twelve thousand horses, [a] which he kept in the chariot cities and also with him in Jerusalem. [15] The king made silver and gold[v] as common in Jerusalem as stones, and cedar as plentiful as sycamore-fig trees in the foothills. [16] Solomon's horses were imported from Egypt[b] and from Kue[c]—the royal merchants purchased them from Kue. [17] They imported a chariot[w] from Egypt for six hundred shekels[d] of silver, and a horse for a hundred and fifty. [e] They also exported them to all the kings of the Hittites and of the Arameans.

Preparations for Building the Temple

2:1–18pp — 1Ki 5:1–16

2 Solomon gave orders to build a temple[x] for the Name of the LORD and a royal palace for himself. [y] [2] He conscripted

---

Cross references

1:1 [a]S 1Ki 2:12; S 2Ch 1:2:1; [b]S Ge 21:22; S 39:2; S Nu 14:43; [c]S 1Ch 29:25
1:2 [d]S 1Ch 9:1
1:3 [e]S Jos 9:3; [f]S Lev 17:4; [g]Ex 40:18
1:4 [h]S 1Ch 15:25; [i]2Sa 6:17
1:5 [j]Ex 38:2; [k]S Ex 31:2
1:6 [l]1Ch 13:3
1:7 [m]2Ch 7:12
1:8 [n]S 1Ch 23:1
1:9 [o]S 2Sa 7:25; S 1Ki 8:25
1:10 [q]Nu 27:17; 2Sa 5:2; Pr 8:15-16
1:11 [r]S Dt 17:17
1:12 [s]S 1Ch 29:12; [t]S 1Ch 29:25; 2Ch 9:22; Ne 13:26
1:14 [u]S 1Sa 8:11; S 1Ki 9:19
1:15 [v]S 1Ki 9:28; Isa 60:5
1:17 [w]SS 1:9
2:1 [x]S Dt 12:5; [y]Ecc 2:4

---

[a] 14 Or *charioteers*   [b] 16 Or possibly *Muzur,* a region in Cilicia; also in verse 17   [c] 16 Probably Cilicia   [d] 17 That is, about 15 pounds (about 7 kilograms)   [e] 17 That is, about 3 3/4 pounds (about 1.7 kilograms)

1:1—9:31 The account of the reign of Solomon is primarily devoted to his building of the temple (chs. 2–7); his endowment with wisdom is mainly to facilitate the building work. Much of the material in Kings that does not bear on building the temple is omitted by the Chronicler; e.g., he does not mention the judgment between the prostitutes (1Ki 3:16–28) or the building of the royal palace (1Ki 7:1–12).
1:1 *established himself.* This expression, or a variation of it, is common in Chronicles (12:13; 13:7–8,21; 15:8; 16:9; 17:1; 21:4; 23:1; 25:11; 27:6; 32:5; 1Ch 11:10; 19:13). Here and in 21:4 it includes the elimination of enemies and rivals to the throne (see 1Ki 2, especially v. 46).
1:2–13 See 1Ki 3:4–15 and notes. Verses 2–6 are largely unique to Chronicles and show some of the writer's concerns: 1. The support of "all Israel" (v. 2) is emphasized (see Introduction to 1 Chronicles: Purpose and Themes). 2. While the writer of Kings is somewhat apologetic about Solomon's visit to a high place (1Ki 3:3), the Chronicler adds the note that this was the location of the tabernacle made by Moses in the desert (v. 3), bringing Solomon's action into line with the provisions of the law (Lev 17:8–9).
1:5 *Bezalel.* See Introduction: The Building of the Temple

in Chronicles. It is specifically in connection with his offering on the altar built by Bezalel (Ex 31:1–11; 38:1–2) that Solomon receives the wisdom from God to reign. In the account that follows, Solomon devotes his gift of wisdom primarily to building the temple, just as Bezalel had been gifted by God to serve as the master craftsman of the tabernacle.
1:7 *God . . . said to him.* Both David and Solomon function as prophets (7:1; 29:25; 1Ch 22:8; 28:6,19).
1:9 *numerous as the dust.* In provisional fulfillment of the promise to Abraham (Ge 13:16; 22:17; see note on 1Ch 27:23; cf. Ge 28:14).
1:14–17 The Chronicler does not include the material in 1Ki 3:16–4:34. He moves rather to the account of Solomon's wealth in 1Ki 10:26–29; part of this material is repeated in 2Ch 9:25–28. Recounting Solomon's wealth at this point shows the fulfillment of God's promise (v. 12).
1:16 *Egypt.* See NIV text note; see also note on 1Ki 10:29.
2:1 *palace.* Although the Chronicler frequently mentions the palace Solomon built (7:11; 8:1; 9:11), he gives no details of its construction (see 1Ki 7:1–12).
2:2 See vv. 17–18.

seventy thousand men as carriers and eighty thousand as stonecutters in the hills and thirty-six hundred as foremen over them. *z*

[3]Solomon sent this message to Hiram*f* *a* king of Tyre:

"Send me cedar logs*b* as you did for my father David when you sent him cedar to build a palace to live in. [4]Now I am about to build a temple*c* for the Name of the LORD my God and to dedicate it to him for burning fragrant incense*d* before him, for setting out the consecrated bread*e* regularly, and for making burnt offerings*f* every morning and evening and on Sabbaths*g* and New Moons*h* and at the appointed feasts of the LORD our God. This is a lasting ordinance for Israel.

[5]"The temple I am going to build will be great,*i* because our God is greater than all other gods.*j* [6]But who is able to build a temple for him, since the heavens, even the highest heavens, cannot contain him?*k* Who then am I*l* to build a temple for him, except as a place to burn sacrifices before him?

[7]"Send me, therefore, a man skilled to work in gold and silver, bronze and iron, and in purple, crimson and blue yarn, and experienced in the art of engraving, to work in Judah and Jerusalem with my skilled craftsmen,*m* whom my father David provided.

[8]"Send me also cedar, pine and algum*g* logs from Lebanon, for I know that your men are skilled in cutting timber there. My men will work with yours [9]to provide me with plenty of lumber, because the temple I build must be large and magnificent. [10]I will give your servants, the woodsmen

who cut the timber, twenty thousand cors*h* of ground wheat, twenty thousand cors of barley, twenty thousand baths*i* of wine and twenty thousand baths of olive oil. *n*"

[11]Hiram king of Tyre replied by letter to Solomon:

"Because the LORD loves*o* his people, he has made you their king."

[12]And Hiram added:

"Praise be to the LORD, the God of Israel, who made heaven and earth!*p* He has given King David a wise son, endowed with intelligence and discernment, who will build a temple for the LORD and a palace for himself.

[13]"I am sending you Huram-Abi,*q* a man of great skill, [14]whose mother was from Dan*r* and whose father was from Tyre. He is trained*s* to work in gold and silver, bronze and iron, stone and wood, and with purple and blue*t* and crimson yarn and fine linen. He is experienced in all kinds of engraving and can execute any design given to him. He will work with your craftsmen and with those of my lord, David your father.

[15]"Now let my lord send his servants the wheat and barley and the olive oil*u* and wine he promised, [16]and we will cut all the logs from Lebanon that you need and will float them in rafts by sea down to Joppa.*v* You can then take them up to Jerusalem."

[17]Solomon took a census of all the

2:2 *z*2Ch 10:4
2:3 *a*S 2Sa 5:11
*b*S 1Ch 14:1
2:4 *c*S Dt 12:5
*d*S Ex 30:7
*e*Ex 25:30
*f*Ex 29:42;
2Ch 13:11; 29:28
*g*S Lev 23:38
*h*S Nu 28:14
2:5 *i*1Ch 22:5
*j*S Ex 12:12;
S 1Ch 16:25
2:6 *k*S 1Ki 8:27;
Jer 23:24
*l*S Ex 3:11
2:7 *m*S Ex 35:31;
1Ch 22:16

2:10 *n*Ezr 3:7
2:11 *o*1Ki 10:9;
2Ch 9:8
2:12 *p*Ne 9:6;
Ps 8:3; 33:6;
96:5; 102:25;
146:6
2:13 *q*S 1Ki 7:13
2:14 *r*S Ex 31:6
*s*S Ex 35:31
*t*Ex 35:35
2:15 *u*Ezr 3:7
2:16
*v*S Jos 19:46;
Jnh 1:3

*f*3 Hebrew *Huram*, a variant of *Hiram*; also in verses 11 and 12   *g*8 Probably a variant of *almug*; possibly juniper   *h*10 That is, probably about 125,000 bushels (about 4,400 kiloliters)   *i*10 That is, probably about 115,000 gallons (about 440 kiloliters)

2:3–10 The Chronicler's theological interests appear in his handling of Solomon's correspondence with Hiram of Tyre. In the Kings account the correspondence was initiated by Hiram (1Ki 5:11). The Chronicler omits this (and also the material in 1Ki 5:3–5) but adds his own material, reflecting his concerns with the temple worship in vv. 3–7.
2:4 See 1Ch 23:28–31.
2:7 See Introduction: The Building of the Temple in Chronicles. In the Kings account Solomon's request for a master craftsman is found late in the narrative (1Ki 7:13); to carry out his parallel between Oholiab and Huram-Abi, the Chronicler includes it in the initial correspondence. Furthermore, here and in vv. 13–14 the list of Huram-Abi's skills is expanded and matches that of Bezalel and Oholiab (Kings is concerned only with casting bronze).
2:10 The payment here differs from that reported in 1Ki 5:11, but the texts speak of two different payments: In Kings the payment is an annual sum delivered to the royal house-

hold of Hiram, while Chronicles speaks of one payment to the woodsmen. The goods paid are also not identical; the oil specified in Kings is of a finer quality.
2:11–16 See 1Ki 5:7–9; 7:13–14 and notes.
2:13 *Huram-Abi.* See note on v. 7. Kings reports that the ancestry of Huram-Abi was through a widow of Naphtali (1Ki 7:14); Chronicles strengthens the parallel between Huram-Abi and Oholiab by assigning him Danite ancestry. These statements are not necessarily contradictory: (1) The mother's ancestry may have been Danite, though she lived in the territory of Naphtali; or (2) her parents may have been from Dan and Naphtali, allowing her descent to be reckoned to either. The Danites had been previously associated with the Phoenicians (Jdg 18:7).
2:17–18 See 1Ki 5:13–18 and notes. The Chronicler specifies that this levy of forced laborers was from aliens resident in the land, not from Israelites. This is not stated in the parallel passage in Kings, though 1Ki 9:20–22 confirms

aliens[w] who were in Israel, after the census[x] his father David had taken; and they were found to be 153,600. [18]He assigned[y] 70,000 of them to be carriers and 80,000 to be stonecutters in the hills, with 3,600 foremen over them to keep the people working.

Solomon Builds the Temple

3:1–14pp — 1Ki 6:1–29

3 Then Solomon began to build[z] the temple of the LORD[a] in Jerusalem on Mount Moriah, where the LORD had appeared to his father David. It was on the threshing floor of Araunah[j][b] the Jebusite, the place provided by David. [2]He began building on the second day of the second month in the fourth year of his reign. [c]

[3]The foundation Solomon laid for building the temple of God was sixty cubits long and twenty cubits wide[k][d] (using the cubit of the old standard). [4]The portico at the front of the temple was twenty cubits[l] long across the width of the building and twenty cubits[m] high.

He overlaid the inside with pure gold. [5]He paneled the main hall with pine and covered it with fine gold and decorated it with palm tree[e] and chain designs. [6]He adorned the temple with precious stones. And the gold he used was gold of Parvaim. [7]He overlaid the ceiling beams, doorframes, walls and doors of the temple with gold, and he carved cherubim[f] on the walls.

[8]He built the Most Holy Place,[g] its length corresponding to the width of the

temple—twenty cubits long and twenty cubits wide. He overlaid the inside with six hundred talents[n] of fine gold. [9]The gold nails[h] weighed fifty shekels.[o] He also overlaid the upper parts with gold.

[10]In the Most Holy Place he made a pair[i] of sculptured cherubim and overlaid them with gold. [11]The total wingspan of the cherubim was twenty cubits. One wing of the first cherub was five cubits[p] long and touched the temple wall, while its other wing, also five cubits long, touched the wing of the other cherub. [12]Similarly one wing of the second cherub was five cubits long and touched the other temple wall, and its other wing, also five cubits long, touched the wing of the first cherub. [13]The wings of these cherubim[j] extended twenty cubits. They stood on their feet, facing the main hall.[q]

[14]He made the curtain[k] of blue, purple and crimson yarn and fine linen, with cherubim[l] worked into it.

[15]In the front of the temple he made two pillars, [m] which together, were thirty-five cubits[r] long, each with a capital[n] on top measuring five cubits. [16]He made inter-

Cross references (center column)

2:17 [w]1Ch 22:2
[x]S 2Sa 24:2
2:18 [y]1Ch 22:2;
2Ch 8:8
3:1 [z]Ac 7:47
[a]S Ge 28:17
[b]S 2Sa 24:18
3:2 [c]Ezr 5:11
3:3 [d]Eze 41:2
3:5 [e]Eze 40:16
3:7 [f]Ge 3:24;
Eze 41:18
3:8 [g]S Ex 26:33

3:9 [h]Ex 26:32
3:10 [i]Ex 25:18
3:13 [j]S Ex 25:18
3:14 [k]S Ex 26:31,
33 [l]Ge 3:24
3:15 [m]S 1Ki 7:15;
Rev 3:12
[n]1Ki 7:22

Footnotes

[j]1 Hebrew Ornan, a variant of Araunah   [k]3 That is, about 90 feet (about 27 meters) long and 30 feet (about 9 meters) wide   [l]4 That is, about 30 feet (about 9 meters); also in verses 8, 11 and 13   [m]4 Some Septuagint and Syriac manuscripts; Hebrew and a hundred and twenty   [n]8 That is, about 23 tons (about 21 metric tons)   [o]9 That is, about 1 1/4 pounds (about 0.6 kilogram)   [p]11 That is, about 7 1/2 feet (about 2.3 meters); also in verse 15   [q]13 Or facing inward   [r]15 That is, about 52 feet (about 16 meters)

---

that alien labor was used (see 8:8).

2:18 *3,600 foremen.* See v. 2. The number given in 1Ki 5:16 is 3,300; however, some manuscripts of the Septuagint (the Greek translation of the OT) also have 3,600. The Chronicler may have been following a different text of Kings from the present Masoretic (traditional Hebrew) text at this point (but see note on 1Ki 5:16).

3:1–17 The Chronicler has considerably curtailed the description of the temple's construction found in Kings, omitting completely 1Ki 6:4–20. This abridgment probably indicates that the Chronicler's audience was familiar with the details of the earlier history and that the temple of the restoration period was less elaborate than the original Solomonic structure (Hag 2:3). On the other hand, the Chronicler goes into more detail on the furnishings and implements (3:6–9; 4:1,6–9).

3:1 *Mount Moriah.* The only passage in the OT where Mount Zion is identified with Mount Moriah, the place where Abraham was commanded to offer Isaac (Ge 22:2, 14). *place provided by David.* See 1Ch 21:18–22:1.

3:2 *second month in the fourth year.* In the spring of 966 B.C. See note on 1Ki 6:1).

3:4 *overlaid.* Or "inlaid," which perhaps gives a more correct picture: not that the entire interior was covered with gold leaf, but that designs (palm trees, chains) were inlaid with gold leaf (v. 5).

3:6 *Parvaim.* Designates either the source of the gold (perhaps southeast Arabia) or a particular quality of fine gold.

3:7 *cherubim.* See vv. 10–14; see also notes on Ge 3:24; Eze 1:5.

3:8 *twenty cubits long and twenty cubits wide.* It was also 20 cubits high (1Ki 6:20), making the dimensions of the Most Holy Place a perfect cube, as probably also in the tabernacle. In the New Jerusalem there is no temple (Rev 21:22); rather, the whole city is in the shape of a cube (Rev 21:16), for the whole city becomes "the Most Holy Place."

3:9 *gold nails.* The fact that gold is such a soft metal would make it unlikely that nails were made of this substance. It is probable that this small amount (only 1 1/4 pounds; see NIV text note) represents gold leaf or sheeting used to gild the nail heads.

3:10–13 See 1Ki 6:23–27 and notes.

3:14 *curtain.* Also separated the two rooms of the tabernacle (Ex 26:31). Wooden doors could also be closed across the opening (4:22; 1Ki 6:31–32; cf. Mt 27:51; Heb 9:8).

3:15 *together, were thirty-five cubits long.* Supplying the word "together" represents an attempt to harmonize this measurement with the 18 cubits found in 1Ki 7:15 (also confirmed by 2Ki 25:17—see NIV text note there; Jer 52:21, though the Septuagint at Jer 52:21 has 35). Alternatively, 35 may be the result of a copyist's mistake.

woven chains[s][o] and put them on top of the pillars. He also made a hundred pomegranates[p] and attached them to the chains. [17]He erected the pillars in the front of the temple, one to the south and one to the north. The one to the south he named Jakin[t] and the one to the north Boaz.[u]

The Temple's Furnishings

4:2–6,10–5:1pp — 1Ki 7:23–26,38–51

4 He made a bronze altar[q] twenty cubits long, twenty cubits wide and ten cubits high.[v] [2]He made the Sea[r] of cast metal, circular in shape, measuring ten cubits from rim to rim and five cubits[w] high. It took a line of thirty cubits[x] to measure around it. [3]Below the rim, figures of bulls encircled it—ten to a cubit.[y] The bulls were cast in two rows in one piece with the Sea.

[4]The Sea stood on twelve bulls, three facing north, three facing west, three facing south and three facing east.[s] The Sea rested on top of them, and their hindquarters were toward the center. [5]It was a handbreadth[z] in thickness, and its rim was like the rim of a cup, like a lily blossom. It held three thousand baths.[a]

[6]He then made ten basins[t] for washing and placed five on the south side and five on the north. In them the things to be used for the burnt offerings[u] were rinsed, but the Sea was to be used by the priests for washing.

[7]He made ten gold lampstands[v] according to the specifications[w] for them and placed them in the temple, five on the south side and five on the north.

[8]He made ten tables[x] and placed them in the temple, five on the south side and five on the north. He also made a hundred gold sprinkling bowls.[y]

[9]He made the courtyard[z] of the priests, and the large court and the doors for the court, and overlaid the doors with bronze. [10]He placed the Sea on the south side, at the southeast corner.

[11]He also made the pots and shovels and sprinkling bowls.

So Huram finished[a] the work he had undertaken for King Solomon in the temple of God:

[12]the two pillars;
  the two bowl-shaped capitals on top of the pillars;
  the two sets of network decorating the two bowl-shaped capitals on top of the pillars;
[13]the four hundred pomegranates for the two sets of network (two rows of pomegranates for each network, decorating the bowl-shaped capitals on top of the pillars);
[14]the stands[b] with their basins;
[15]the Sea and the twelve bulls under it;
[16]the pots, shovels, meat forks and all related articles.

All the objects that Huram-Abi[c] made for King Solomon for the temple of the LORD were of polished bronze. [17]The king had them cast in clay molds in the plain of the Jordan between Succoth[d] and Zarethan.[b] [18]All these things that Solomon made amounted to so much that the

Cross references (center column)

3:16 o1Ki 7:17
p S 1Ki 7:20
4:1 q S Ex 20:24;
S 40:6; S 1Ki 8:64
4:2 r Rev 4:6;
15:2
4:4 s Nu 2:3-25;
Eze 48:30-34;
Rev 21:13
4:6 t S Ex 30:18
u Ne 13:5,9;
Eze 40:38
4:7 v S Ex 25:31
w Ex 25:40
4:8 x S Ex 25:23
y S Nu 4:14

4:9 z 1Ki 6:36;
2Ch 33:5
4:11 a 1Ki 7:14
4:14
b 1Ki 7:27-30
4:16 c S 1Ki 7:13
4:17 d S Ge 33:17

Footnotes

s 16 Or possibly *made chains in the inner sanctuary*; the meaning of the Hebrew for this phrase is uncertain.
t 17 Jakin probably means *he establishes.*   u 17 Boaz probably means *in him is strength.*   v 1 That is, about 30 feet (about 9 meters) long and wide, and about 15 feet (about 4.5 meters) high   w 2 That is, about 7 1/2 feet (about 2.3 meters)   x 2 That is, about 45 feet (about 13.5 meters)   y 3 That is, about 1 1/2 feet (about 0.5 meter)   z 5 That is, about 3 inches (about 8 centimeters)   a 5 That is, about 17,500 gallons (about 66 kiloliters)   b 17 Hebrew *Zeredatha,* a variant of *Zarethan*

Study notes (bottom)

3:17 *pillars.* Remains of such pillars have been found in the excavations of numerous temples in Palestine. Cf. Rev 3:12. *Jakin . . . Boaz.* See NIV text notes.

4:1 *bronze altar.* The parallel text in Kings does not mention the main altar of the temple described here (1Ki 7:22–23), though several other passages in Kings do refer to it (1Ki 8:64; 9:25; 2Ki 16:14). The main altar of Solomon's temple was similar to the altar with steps that is described in Eze 43:13–17.

4:2 *Sea of cast metal.* Replaced the bronze basin of the tabernacle (Ex 30:18); it was used by the priests for their ceremonial washing (v. 6; Ex 30:21). The NT views these rituals as foreshadowing the cleansing provided by Christ (Tit 3:5; Heb 9:11–14). In the temple of Ezekiel, the Sea, which was on the south side in front of the temple (v. 10), has been replaced by a life-giving river that flows from the south side of the temple (Eze 47:1–12; cf. Joel 3:18; Zec 14:8; Jn 4:9–15; Rev 22:1–2).

4:3 *bulls.* 1Ki 7:24 has "gourds." The Hebrew for the two words is very similar, so the difference may well be due to a

copyist's mistake.

4:4 *twelve bulls.* Possibly symbolic of the 12 tribes, which also encamped three on each side of the tabernacle during the desert journeys (Nu 2; cf. Eze 48:30–35).

4:5 *three thousand baths.* 1Ki 7:26 has 2,000 baths. These figures could easily have been misread by the ancient scribes.

4:6 *ten basins.* See 1Ki 7:38–39.

4:7 *ten gold lampstands.* Instead of one, as in the tabernacle (Ex 25:31–40). *specifications.* See 1Ch 28:15. These lamps were not necessarily of the same shape as described in Ex 25:31–40, but could have resembled the style of lamp depicted in Zec 4:2–6.

4:8 *ten tables.* Instead of one, as in the tabernacle (Ex 25:23–30; 40:4; Lev 24:5–9; 1Sa 21:1–6; Eze 41:22; Heb 9:2; cf. 2Ch 13:11; 29:18).

4:11–16 See 1Ki 7:40–45.

4:17–22 See 1Ki 7:46–50.

4:17 *clay molds.* The clay beds of the Jordan plain made it possible to dig molds for these bronze castings.

weight of the bronze[e] was not determined.

[19]Solomon also made all the furnishings that were in God's temple:

the golden altar;
the tables[f] on which was the bread of the Presence;
[20]the lampstands[g] of pure gold with their lamps, to burn in front of the inner sanctuary as prescribed;
[21]the gold floral work and lamps and tongs (they were solid gold);
[22]the pure gold wick trimmers, sprinkling bowls, dishes[h] and censers;[i] and the gold doors of the temple: the inner doors to the Most Holy Place and the doors of the main hall.

5 When all the work Solomon had done for the temple of the LORD was finished,[j] he brought in the things his father David had dedicated[k]—the silver and gold and all the furnishings—and he placed them in the treasuries of God's temple.

The Ark Brought to the Temple

5:2–6:11pp — 1Ki 8:1–21

[2]Then Solomon summoned to Jerusalem the elders of Israel, all the heads of the tribes and the chiefs of the Israelite families, to bring up the ark[l] of the LORD's covenant from Zion, the City of David. [3]And all the men of Israel[m] came together to the king at the time of the festival in the seventh month.

[4]When all the elders of Israel had arrived, the Levites took up the ark, [5]and they brought up the ark and the Tent of Meeting and all the sacred furnishings in it. The priests, who were Levites,[n] carried them up; [6]and King Solomon and the entire assembly of Israel that had gathered about him were before the ark, sacrificing so many sheep and cattle that they could not be recorded or counted.

[7]The priests then brought the ark[o] of the LORD's covenant to its place in the inner sanctuary of the temple, the Most Holy Place, and put it beneath the wings of the cherubim. [8]The cherubim[p] spread their wings over the place of the ark and covered the ark and its carrying poles. [9]These poles were so long that their ends, extending from the ark, could be seen from in front of the inner sanctuary, but not from outside the Holy Place; and they are still there today. [10]There was nothing in the ark except[q] the two tablets[r] that Moses had placed in it at Horeb, where the LORD made a covenant with the Israelites after they came out of Egypt.

[11]The priests then withdrew from the Holy Place. All the priests who were there had consecrated themselves, regardless of their divisions.[s] [12]All the Levites who were musicians[t]—Asaph, Heman, Jeduthun and their sons and relatives—stood on the east side of the altar, dressed in fine linen and playing cymbals, harps and lyres. They were accompanied by 120 priests sounding trumpets.[u] [13]The trumpeters and singers joined in unison, as with one voice, to give praise and thanks to the LORD. Accompanied by trumpets, cymbals and other instruments, they raised their voices in praise to the LORD and sang:

"He is good;
his love endures forever."[v]

Then the temple of the LORD was filled with a cloud,[w] [14]and the priests could not perform[x] their service because of the cloud,[y] for the glory[z] of the LORD filled the temple of God.

6 Then Solomon said, "The LORD has said that he would dwell in a dark cloud;[a] [2]I have built a magnificent temple for you, a place for you to dwell forever.[b]"

[3]While the whole assembly of Israel was standing there, the king turned around and blessed them. [4]Then he said:

Cross references (center column)

4:18 [e]S 1Ki 7:23
4:19 [f]S Ex 25:23
4:20 [g]Ex 25:31
4:22 [h]S Nu 7:14
5:1 [i]Lev 10:1
5:1 [j]S 1Ki 6:14
[k]S 2Sa 8:11
5:2 [l]S Nu 3:31; S 1Ch 15:25
5:3 [m]S 1Ch 9:1
5:5 [n]S Nu 3:31; S 1Ch 15:2

5:7 [o]Rev 11:19
5:8 [p]S Ge 3:24
5:10 [q]Heb 9:4
[r]S Ex 16:34; S Dt 10:2
5:11 [s]S 1Ch 24:1
5:12 [t]1Ki 10:12; 1Ch 9:33; S 25:1; Ps 68:25
[u]S 1Ch 13:8
5:13 [v]S 1Ch 16:34; 2Ch 7:3; 20:21; Ezr 3:11; Ps 100:5; 106:1; 107:1; 118:1; 136:1; Jer 33:11
[w]S Ex 40:34
5:14 [x]Ex 40:35; Rev 15:8
[y]Ex 19:16
[z]S Ex 29:43; S 40:35
6:1 [a]S Ex 19:9
6:2 [b]Ezr 6:12; 7:15; Ps 135:21

Footnotes (bottom)

5:1 *things his father David had dedicated.* See notes on 1Ch 18:1–20:8; 22:2–16; 29:2–5; see also 1Ch 26:26.
5:2–14 See 1Ki 8:1–11 and notes.
5:2 *ark.* Had been in a tent provided for it 40 years earlier when David brought it to Jerusalem (1Ch 15:1–16:6).
5:3 *festival in the seventh month.* The Feast of Tabernacles. The month is designated by its Canaanite name Ethanim in 1Ki 8:2; the Hebrew name is Tishri. According to 1Ki 6:38 the temple was completed in the eighth month of Solomon's 11th year, i.e., September-October, 959 B.C. This celebration of dedication took place either a month before the completion of the work or 11 months after, probably the latter (see note on 1Ki 8:2).
5:6 Cf. David's bringing of the ark to Jerusalem (1Ch 15:26; 16:1–3).

5:9 *still there today.* See note on 1Ki 8:8; see also 8:8; 10:19; 20:26; 21:10; 35:25; 1Ch 4:41,43; 5:26; 13:11; 17:5.
5:10 *two tablets.* See Ex 31:18 and note; see also Ex 32:15–16. The ark had earlier contained also the gold jar of manna (Ex 16:32–34) and Aaron's staff (Nu 17:10–11; Heb 9:4). These items were presumably lost, perhaps while the ark was in Philistine hands.
5:12 *fine linen.* See 1Ch 15:27 and note.
5:14 *cloud … glory of the LORD.* Cf. 7:1–3. The glory cloud represented the presence of God. It had guided Israel out of Egypt and through the desert, and was present above the tabernacle (Ex 13:21–22; 40:34–38; cf. Eze 43:1–5; Hag 2:9; Zec 1:16; 2:10; 8:3).
6:1–11 See notes on 1Ki 8:12–21.

"Praise be to the LORD, the God of Israel, who with his hands has fulfilled what he promised with his mouth to my father David. For he said, 5'Since the day I brought my people out of Egypt, I have not chosen a city in any tribe of Israel to have a temple built for my Name to be there, nor have I chosen anyone to be the leader over my people Israel. 6But now I have chosen Jerusalem c for my Name d to be there, and I have chosen David e to rule my people Israel.'

7"My father David had it in his heart f to build a temple for the Name of the LORD, the God of Israel. 8But the LORD said to my father David, 'Because it was in your heart to build a temple for my Name, you did well to have this in your heart. 9Nevertheless, you are not the one to build the temple, but your son, who is your own flesh and blood—he is the one who will build the temple for my Name.'

10"The LORD has kept the promise he made. I have succeeded David my father and now I sit on the throne of Israel, just as the LORD promised, and I have built the temple for the Name of the LORD, the God of Israel. 11There I have placed the ark, in which is the covenant g of the LORD that he made with the people of Israel."

Solomon's Prayer of Dedication

6:12–40pp — 1Ki 8:22–53
6:41–42pp — Ps 132:8–10

12Then Solomon stood before the altar of the LORD in front of the whole assembly of Israel and spread out his hands. 13Now he had made a bronze platform, h five cubits c long, five cubits wide and three cubits d high, and had placed it in the center of the outer court. He stood on the platform and then knelt down i before the whole assembly of Israel and spread out his hands toward heaven. 14He said:

"O LORD, God of Israel, there is no God like you j in heaven or on earth—you who keep your covenant of love k with your servants who con-

tinue wholeheartedly in your way. 15You have kept your promise to your servant David my father; with your mouth you have promised l and with your hand you have fulfilled it—as it is today.

16"Now LORD, God of Israel, keep for your servant David my father the promises you made to him when you said, 'You shall never fail m to have a man to sit before me on the throne of Israel, if only your sons are careful in all they do to walk before me according to my law, n as you have done.' 17And now, O LORD, God of Israel, let your word that you promised your servant David come true.

18"But will God really dwell o on earth with men? The heavens, p even the highest heavens, cannot contain you. How much less this temple I have built! 19Yet give attention to your servant's prayer and his plea for mercy, O LORD my God. Hear the cry and the prayer that your servant is praying in your presence. 20May your eyes q be open toward this temple day and night, this place of which you said you would put your Name r there. May you hear s the prayer your servant prays toward this place. 21Hear the supplications of your servant and of your people Israel when they pray toward this place. Hear from heaven, your dwelling place; and when you hear, forgive. t

22"When a man wrongs his neighbor and is required to take an oath u and he comes and swears the oath before your altar in this temple, 23then hear from heaven and act. Judge between your servants, repaying v the guilty by bringing down on his own head what he has done. Declare the innocent not guilty and so establish his innocence.

24"When your people Israel have been defeated w by an enemy because they have sinned against you and

---

6:6 cS Dt 12:5; S Isa 14:1
dS Ex 20:24
eS 1Ch 28:4
6:7 fS 1Sa 10:7; S 1Ch 17:2; Ac 7:46
6:11 gS Dt 10:2; Ps 25:10; 50:5
6:13 hNe 8:4
iPs 95:6
6:14 jS Ex 8:10; 15:11 kS Dt 7:9

6:15 lS 1Ch 22:10
6:16 mS 2Sa 7:13,15; 2Ch 23:3
nPs 132:12
6:18 oS Rev 21:3
pPs 11:4; Isa 40:22; 66:1
6:20 qS Ex 3:16; Ps 34:15
rDt 12:11
sZCh 7:14; 30:20
6:21 tPs 51:1; Isa 33:24; 40:2; 43:25; 44:22; 55:7; Mic 7:18
6:22 uS Ex 22:11
6:23 vIsa 3:11; 65:6; S Mt 16:27
6:24 wS Lev 26:17

c13 That is, about 7 1/2 feet (about 2.3 meters)
d13 That is, about 4 1/2 feet (about 1.3 meters)

6:8–9 Cf. David's speech in 1Ch 28:2–3.
6:12–21 See notes on 1Ki 8:22–30.
6:13 Not in 1Ki 8. Some think that the Chronicler may have wished to clarify the fact that Solomon was not "before the altar" (v. 12) exercising priestly duties. On the other hand, the verse may have been dropped from Kings by a copying error: The phrase "spread out his hands" occurs in vv. 12–13; it is possible that the scribe copying Kings looked back to the second occurrence of the phrase, thus omitting the verse. The verse would then be present in Chronicles because it was in the particular text of Kings used by the Chronicler.
6:18 Cf. 2:6.
6:22–39 See notes on 1Ki 8:31–46.
6:22–23 See Ex 22:10–11; Lev 6:3–5.
6:24–25 See Lev 26:17,23; Dt 28:25,36–37,48–57,64; Jos 7:11–12.

when they turn back and confess your
name, praying and making supplication before you in this temple, 25then
hear from heaven and forgive the sin
of your people Israel and bring them
back to the land you gave to them and
their fathers.

26"When the heavens are shut up
and there is no rain[x] because your
people have sinned against you, and
when they pray toward this place and
confess your name and turn from their
sin because you have afflicted them,
27then hear from heaven and forgive[y]
the sin of your servants, your people
Israel. Teach them the right way to
live, and send rain on the land you
gave your people for an inheritance.

28"When famine[z] or plague comes
to the land, or blight or mildew, locusts or grasshoppers, or when enemies besiege them in any of their cities, whatever disaster or disease may
come, 29and when a prayer or plea is
made by any of your people Israel—each one aware of his afflictions
and pains, and spreading out his hands
toward this temple— 30then hear
from heaven, your dwelling place.
Forgive,[a] and deal with each man according to all he does, since you know
his heart (for you alone know the
hearts of men),[b] 31so that they will
fear you[c] and walk in your ways all
the time they live in the land you gave
our fathers.

32"As for the foreigner who does
not belong to your people Israel but
has come[d] from a distant land because of your great name and your
mighty hand[e] and your outstretched
arm—when he comes and prays
toward this temple, 33then hear from
heaven, your dwelling place, and do
whatever the foreigner[f] asks of you,
so that all the peoples of the earth may
know your name and fear you, as do
your own people Israel, and may
know that this house I have built
bears your Name.

34"When your people go to war
against their enemies,[g] wherever you
send them, and when they pray[h] to
you toward this city you have chosen
and the temple I have built for your
Name, 35then hear from heaven their
prayer and their plea, and uphold their
cause.

36"When they sin against you—for
there is no one who does not
sin[i]—and you become angry with
them and give them over to the enemy, who takes them captive[j] to a
land far away or near; 37and if they
have a change of heart[k] in the land
where they are held captive, and repent and plead with you in the land of
their captivity and say, 'We have
sinned, we have done wrong and acted wickedly'; 38and if they turn back
to you with all their heart and soul in
the land of their captivity where they
were taken, and pray toward the land
you gave their fathers, toward the city
you have chosen and toward the temple I have built for your Name; 39then
from heaven, your dwelling place,
hear their prayer and their pleas, and
uphold their cause. And forgive[l] your
people, who have sinned against you.

40"Now, my God, may your eyes be
open and your ears attentive[m] to the
prayers offered in this place.

41"Now arise,[n] O LORD God, and
come to your resting
place,[o]
you and the ark of your might.
May your priests,[p] O LORD God, be
clothed with salvation,
may your saints rejoice in your
goodness.[q]
42O LORD God, do not reject your
anointed one.[r]
Remember the great love[s]
promised to David your
servant."

6:26 [x]Lev 26:19; S Dt 11:17; 28:24; S 2Sa 1:21 **6:27** [y]ver 30,39; 2Ch 7:14 **6:28** [z]2Ch 20:9 **6:30** [a]S ver 27 [b]S 1Sa 2:3; Ps 7:9; 44:21; Pr 16:2; 17:3 **6:31** [c]S Dt 6:13; Ps 34:7,9; 103:11,13; Pr 8:13 **6:32** [d]2Ch 9:6 [e]S Ex 3:19,20 **6:33** [f]S Ex 12:43

6:34 [g]Dt 28:7 [h]S 1Ch 5:20 **6:36** [i]S 1Ki 8:46; Job 11:12; 15:14; Ps 143:2; Ecc 7:20; Jer 9:5; 13:23; 17:9; S Ro 3:9; Eph 2:3 [j]S Lev 26:44 **6:37** [k]1Ki 8:48; 2Ch 7:14; 12:6, 12; 30:11; 33:12, 19,23; 34:27; 36:12; Isa 58:3; Jer 24:7; 29:13 **6:39** [l]S ver 27; 2Ch 30:9 **6:40** [m]S 1Ki 8:29,52; 2Ch 7:15; Ne 1:6, 11; Ps 17:6; 116:1; 130:2; Isa 37:17 **6:41** [n]Ps 3:7; 7:6; 59:4; Isa 33:10 [o]1Ch 28:2 [p]Ps 132:16 [q]Ps 13:6; 27:13; 116:12; 142:7 **6:42** [r]Ps 2:2 [s]Ps 89:24,28

6:26–27 See Lev 26:19; Dt 11:10–15; 28:18,22–24.
6:28–31 See Lev 26:16,20,25–26; Dt 28:20–22,27–28, 35,42.
6:32–33 The prophets also envisaged the Gentiles as coming to Jerusalem to worship the Lord (Isa 56:6–8; Zec 8:20–23; 14:16–21; cf. Ps 87).
6:34–35 See Lev 26:7–8; Dt 28:6–7. The Chronicler repeatedly demonstrates God's answer to prayer in time of battle (ch. 13; 14:9–15; 18:31; 20:1–29; 25:5–13; 32:20–22).
6:36 *no one who does not sin.* See Jer 13:23; Ro 3:23. *captive to a land far away.* See 36:15–20; Lev 26:33, 44–45; Dt 28:49–52; 2Ki 17:7–20; 25:1–21.
6:40–42 The Chronicler replaces the ending of Solomon's prayer in Kings (1Ki 8:50–53) with a repetition of Ps 132:8–10, a psalm that deals with bringing the ark to the temple, the theme of this section in Chronicles (5:2–14). The prayer in Kings ends with an appeal to the exodus deliverance under Moses, while in Chronicles the appeal is on the basis of the eternal promises to David.

The Dedication of the Temple

7:1–10pp — 1Ki 8:62–66

7 When Solomon finished praying, fire[t] came down from heaven and consumed the burnt offering and the sacrifices, and the glory of the LORD filled[u] the temple.[v] 2The priests could not enter[w] the temple of the LORD because the glory[x] of the LORD filled it. 3When all the Israelites saw the fire coming down and the glory of the LORD above the temple, they knelt on the pavement with their faces to the ground, and they worshiped and gave thanks to the LORD, saying,

"He is good;
his love endures forever."[y]

4Then the king and all the people offered sacrifices before the LORD. 5And King Solomon offered a sacrifice of twenty-two thousand head of cattle and a hundred and twenty thousand sheep and goats. So the king and all the people dedicated the temple of God. 6The priests took their positions, as did the Levites[z] with the LORD's musical instruments,[a] which King David had made for praising the LORD and which were used when he gave thanks, saying, "His love endures forever." Opposite the Levites, the priests blew their trumpets, and all the Israelites were standing.

7Solomon consecrated the middle part of the courtyard in front of the temple of the LORD, and there he offered burnt offerings and the fat[b] of the fellowship offerings,[e] because the bronze altar he had made could not hold the burnt offerings, the grain offerings and the fat portions.

8So Solomon observed the festival[c] at that time for seven days, and all Israel[d] with him—a vast assembly, people from Lebo[f] Hamath[e] to the Wadi of Egypt.[f] 9On the eighth day they held an assembly,

7:1 [t]S Ex 19:18;
[s]Lev 9:24;
[s]1Ki 18:38
[u]S Ex 16:10
[v]Ps 26:8
7:2 [w]S 1Ki 8:11
[x]S Ex 29:43;
[s]40:35
7:3
[y]S 1Ch 16:34;
2Ch 5:13;
Ezr 3:11
7:6 [z]1Ch 15:16
[a]S 1Ch 15:24
7:7 [b]S Ex 29:13
7:8 [c]2Ch 30:26;
Ne 8:17
[d]S 1Ch 9:1
[e]S Nu 13:21
[f]S Ge 15:18

7:9 [g]2Ch 30:23
[h]S Lev 23:36
7:11
[i]S 1Ch 28:20
7:12 [j]2Ch 1:7
[k]Dt 12:11
[l]S Dt 12:5
7:13
[m]S Dt 11:17;
Am 4:7
7:14 [n]S Nu 6:27
[o]S Ex 10:3;
S Lev 26:41;
S 2Ch 6:37
[p]S 1Ch 16:11
[q]S 2Ki 17:13;
Isa 55:7;
Eze 18:32;
Zec 1:4
[r]S 2Ch 6:20
[s]S 2Ch 6:27
[t]S Ex 15:26;
2Ch 30:20;
Ps 60:2;
Isa 30:26; 53:5;
57:18; Jer 33:6;
Mal 4:2
7:15 [u]S 1Ki 8:29;
S 2Ch 6:40;
Ne 1:6
7:16 [v]S Dt 12:5;
2Ch 33:7
7:17 [w]S 1Ki 9:4
[x]S Lev 19:37
7:18 [y]Isa 9:7;
Jer 33:17,21

for they had celebrated[g] the dedication of the altar for seven days and the festival[h] for seven days more. 10On the twenty-third day of the seventh month he sent the people to their homes, joyful and glad in heart for the good things the LORD had done for David and Solomon and for his people Israel.

The LORD Appears to Solomon

7:11–22pp — 1Ki 9:1–9

11When Solomon had finished[i] the temple of the LORD and the royal palace, and had succeeded in carrying out all he had in mind to do in the temple of the LORD and in his own palace, 12the LORD appeared[j] to him at night and said:

"I have heard your prayer and have chosen[k] this place for myself[l] as a temple for sacrifices.

13"When I shut up the heavens so that there is no rain,[m] or command locusts to devour the land or send a plague among my people, 14if my people, who are called by my name,[n] will humble[o] themselves and pray and seek my face[p] and turn[q] from their wicked ways, then will I hear[r] from heaven and will forgive[s] their sin and will heal[t] their land. 15Now my eyes will be open and my ears attentive to the prayers offered in this place.[u] 16I have chosen[v] and consecrated this temple so that my Name may be there forever. My eyes and my heart will always be there.

17"As for you, if you walk before me[w] as David your father did, and do all I command, and observe my decrees[x] and laws, 18I will establish your royal throne, as I covenanted[y] with

[e]7 Traditionally *peace offerings*   [f]8 Or *from the entrance to*

7:1–22 See 1Ki 8:54–9:9 and notes.
7:1–3 Not found in 1Ki 8. The addition of the fire descending from heaven to consume the sacrifices provides the same sign of divine acceptance as was given at the dedication of the tabernacle (Lev 9:23–24) and David's offering at the threshing floor of Araunah the Jebusite (1Ch 21:26; cf. 1Ki 18:38). While vv. 1–3 are unique to Chronicles, the Chronicler has omitted Solomon's blessing of the congregation (1Ki 8:55–61).
7:1 *glory of the LORD.* See 5:14 and note.
7:3 *He is good . . . forever.* See v. 6; 5:13.
7:6 The verse is unique to Chronicles and reflects the author's overall interest in the Levites, especially the musicians (cf. 29:26–27; see note on 1Ch 6:31–48). *all the Israelites.* See Introduction to 1 Chronicles: Purpose and Themes.
7:8 *from Lebo Hamath to the Wadi of Egypt.* Not only were the patriarchal promises of descendants provisionally fulfilled

under David and Solomon (see 1:9; 1Ch 27:23–24 and notes), but also the promises of land (Ge 15:18–21).
7:9 *eighth day.* The final day of the Feast of Tabernacles (see 5:3 and note; Lev 23:36; Nu 29:35). *seven days . . . seven days.* The dedication had run from the 8th to the 14th day of the month, and the Feast of Tabernacles from the 15th to the 22nd day. The Day of Atonement was on the 10th day of the 7th month (Lev 16; cf. 1Ki 8:65–66).
7:12 *appeared to him.* The second time God appeared to Solomon; the first was at Gibeon (1:3–13; 1Ki 9:2).
7:13–15 Unique to Chronicles. These verses illustrate the writer's emphasis on immediate retribution (see Introduction to 1 Chronicles: Purpose and Themes). The Chronicler subsequently portrays the kings in a way that demonstrates this principle (see v. 22).
7:14 See, e.g., 12:6–7,12.
7:17–18 See 1Ki 9:4–5. Such words as these reinforced ancient Israel's Messianic hopes.

David your father when I said, 'You shall never fail to have a man[z] to rule over Israel.'[a]

[19]"But if you[g] turn away[b] and forsake[c] the decrees and commands I have given you[g] and go off to serve other gods and worship them, [20]then I will uproot[d] Israel from my land,[e] which I have given them, and will reject this temple I have consecrated for my Name. I will make it a byword and an object of ridicule[f] among all peoples. [21]And though this temple is now so imposing, all who pass by will be appalled[g] and say,[h] 'Why has the LORD done such a thing to this land and to this temple?' [22]People will answer, 'Because they have forsaken the LORD, the God of their fathers, who brought them out of Egypt, and have embraced other gods, worshiping and serving them[i]—that is why he brought all this disaster on them.' "

Solomon's Other Activities
8:1–18pp — 1Ki 9:10–28

8 At the end of twenty years, during which Solomon built the temple of the LORD and his own palace,[j] [2]Solomon rebuilt the villages that Hiram[h] had given him, and settled Israelites in them. [3]Solomon then went to Hamath Zobah and captured it. [4]He also built up Tadmor in the desert and all the store cities he had built in Hamath.[k] [5]He rebuilt Upper Beth Horon[l] and Lower Beth Horon as fortified cities, with walls and with gates and bars, [6]as well as Baalath[m] and all his store cities, and all the cities for his chariots and for his horses[i]—whatever he desired to build in Jerusalem, in Lebanon and throughout all the territory he ruled.

[7]All the people left from the Hittites,

Amorites, Perizzites, Hivites and Jebusites[n] (these peoples were not Israelites), [8]that is, their descendants remaining in the land, whom the Israelites had not destroyed—these Solomon conscripted[o] for his slave labor force, as it is to this day. [9]But Solomon did not make slaves of the Israelites for his work; they were his fighting men, commanders of his captains, and commanders of his chariots and charioteers. [10]They were also King Solomon's chief officials—two hundred and fifty officials supervising the men.

[11]Solomon brought Pharaoh's daughter[p] up from the City of David to the palace he had built for her, for he said, "My wife must not live in the palace of David king of Israel, because the places the ark of the LORD has entered are holy."

[12]On the altar[q] of the LORD that he had built in front of the portico, Solomon sacrificed burnt offerings to the LORD, [13]according to the daily requirement[r] for offerings commanded by Moses for Sabbaths,[s] New Moons[t] and the three[u] annual feasts—the Feast of Unleavened Bread,[v] the Feast of Weeks[w] and the Feast of Tabernacles.[x] [14]In keeping with the ordinance of his father David, he appointed the divisions[y] of the priests for their duties, and the Levites[z] to lead the praise and to assist the priests according to each day's requirement. He also appointed the gatekeepers[a] by divisions for the various gates, because this was what David the man of God[b] had ordered.[c] [15]They did not deviate from the king's commands to the priests or to the Levites in any matter, including that of the treasuries.

[16]All Solomon's work was carried out, from the day the foundation of the temple

Cross references (center column)

7:18 zS 1Ch 5:2; Isa 55:4; Mic 5:2
aS 2Sa 7:13; S 1Ch 17:12; 2Ch 13:5; 23:3
7:19 bS Dt 28:15
cS 1Ch 28:9; 2Ch 12:1; 24:18; Jer 9:13; 11:8
7:20 dS Dt 29:28
eI Ki 14:15; Jer 12:14; 16:13; 50:11 fS Dt 28:37
7:21 gJer 19:8
7:22 iJer 16:11
8:1 jS 2Sa 7:2
8:4 kS 2Sa 8:9
8:5 lS Jos 10:10
8:6 mS Jos 19:44

8:7 nS Ge 10:16; S 15:18-21; Ezr 9:1
8:8 oS 2Ch 2:18
8:11 pS 1Ki 3:1
8:12 qS 1Ki 8:64; 2Ch 15:8
8:13 rS Ex 29:38
sNu 28:9
tS Nu 10:10
uS Ex 23:14
vS Ex 12:17; Nu 28:16-25
wS Ex 23:16
xNu 29:12-38; Ne 8:17
8:14 yS 1Ch 24:1
zS 1Ch 25:1
aS 1Ch 9:17
bNe 12:24,36
cS 1Ch 23:6; Ne 12:45

g*19* The Hebrew is plural.   h*2* Hebrew *Huram*, a variant of *Hiram*; also in verse 18   i*6* Or *charioteers*

7:19–22 See 1Ki 9:6–9.
8:1–18 See 1Ki 9:10–18 and notes. Verses 13–16 are unique to Chronicles and underscore the Chronicler's concern to show continuity with the past and his association of David with Moses (see Introduction to 1 Chronicles: Purpose and Themes).
8:1–2 In 1Ki 9:10–14 the cities were given to Hiram by Solomon, whereas in Chronicles the reverse is true. Perhaps as part of his effort to idealize Solomon, the Chronicler does not record the fact that Hiram found these cities unacceptable payment (1Ki 9:11–13); he mentions only the sequel to the story, the return of the cities to Solomon and their subsequent improvement. They may also have served as a kind of collateral against the monies owed Hiram, who returned them when the debt was satisfied (see note on 1Ki 9:11). The Chronicler also says nothing about Pharaoh's gift of Gezer to Solomon (1Ki 9:16).
8:3–4 The Chronicler records an additional military campaign to the north, not mentioned in Kings. David had also

campaigned in the north against Zobah (1Ch 18:3–9; 19:6; 2Sa 8:3–12; 10:6–8; cf. 1Ki 11:23–24).
8:5 The two Beth Horons were situated on a strategic road from the coastal plain to the area just north of Jerusalem.
8:7 *not Israelites.* See 2:17; 1Ch 22:2; 1Ki 9:21.
8:8 *to this day.* See note on 5:9.
8:11 *holy.* Both 1Ki 9:24 and Chronicles record the transfer of Pharaoh's daughter to special quarters, but only Chronicles adds the reason: Not only the temple but also David's palace was regarded as holy, because of the presence of the ark.
8:12–16 In line with his overall interests, the Chronicler considerably elaborates on the sacrificial and temple provisions made by Solomon. While 1Ki 9:25 mentions only the sacrifices at the three annual feasts, the Chronicler adds the offerings on Sabbaths and New Moons to conform these provisions fully to Mosaic prescription (Lev 23:1–37; Nu 28–29).

of the LORD was laid until its completion. So the temple of the LORD was finished.

17Then Solomon went to Ezion Geber and Elath on the coast of Edom. 18And Hiram sent him ships commanded by his own officers, men who knew the sea. These, with Solomon's men, sailed to Ophir and brought back four hundred and fifty talentsi of gold,d which they delivered to King Solomon.

The Queen of Sheba Visits Solomon

9:1–12pp — 1Ki 10:1–13

9 When the queen of Shebae heard of Solomon's fame, she came to Jerusalem to test him with hard questions. Arriving with a very great caravan—with camels carrying spices, large quantities of gold, and precious stones—she came to Solomon and talked with him about all she had on her mind. 2Solomon answered all her questions; nothing was too hard for him to explain to her. 3When the queen of Sheba saw the wisdom of Solomon,f as well as the palace he had built, 4the food on his table, the seating of his officials, the attending servants in their robes, the cupbearers in their robes and the burnt offerings he made atk the temple of the LORD, she was overwhelmed.

5She said to the king, "The report I heard in my own country about your achievements and your wisdom is true. 6But I did not believe what they said until I cameg and saw with my own eyes. Indeed, not even half the greatness of your wisdom was told me; you have far exceeded the report I heard. 7How happy your men must be! How happy your officials, who continually stand before you and hear your wisdom! 8Praise be to the LORD your God, who has delighted in you and placed you on his throneh as king to rule for the LORD your God. Because of the love of your God for Israel and his desire to uphold them forever, he has made you kingi over them, to maintain justice and righteousness."

9Then she gave the king 120 talentsl of

gold,j large quantities of spices, and precious stones. There had never been such spices as those the queen of Sheba gave to King Solomon.

10(The men of Hiram and the men of Solomon brought gold from Ophir;k they also brought algumwoodm and precious stones. 11The king used the algumwood to make steps for the temple of the LORD and for the royal palace, and to make harps and lyres for the musicians. Nothing like them had ever been seen in Judah.)

12King Solomon gave the queen of Sheba all she desired and asked for; he gave her more than she had brought to him. Then she left and returned with her retinue to her own country.

Solomon's Splendor

9:13–28pp — 1Ki 10:14–29; 2Ch 1:14–17

13The weight of the gold that Solomon received yearly was 666 talents,n 14not including the revenues brought in by merchants and traders. Also all the kings of Arabial and the governors of the land brought gold and silver to Solomon.

15King Solomon made two hundred large shields of hammered gold; six hundred bekaso of hammered gold went into each shield. 16He also made three hundred small shieldsm of hammered gold, with three hundred bekasp of gold in each shield. The king put them in the Palace of the Forest of Lebanon.n

17Then the king made a great throne inlaid with ivoryo and overlaid with pure gold. 18The throne had six steps, and a footstool of gold was attached to it. On both sides of the seat were armrests, with a lion standing beside each of them. 19Twelve lions stood on the six steps, one at either end of each step. Nothing like it had ever been made for any other king-

8:18 d2Ch 9:9
9:1 eS Ge 10:7;
Eze 23:42;
Mt 12:42;
Lk 11:31
9:3 f1Ki 5:12
9:6 g2Ch 6:32
9:8 hS 1Ki 2:12;
S 1Ch 17:14;
2Ch 13:8
i2Ch 2:11

9:9 j2Ch 8:18
9:10 k2Ch 8:18
9:14 l2Ch 17:11;
Isa 21:13;
Jer 25:24;
Eze 27:21; 30:5
9:16 m2Ch 12:9
nS 1Ki 7:2
9:17
oS 1Ki 22:39

j18 That is, about 17 tons (about 16 metric tons)
k4 Or the ascent by which he went up to   19 That is, about 4 1/2 tons (about 4 metric tons)   m10 Probably a variant of almugwood   n13 That is, about 25 tons (about 23 metric tons)   o15 That is, about 7 1/2 pounds (about 3.5 kilograms)   p16 That is, about 3 3/4 pounds (about 1.7 kilograms)

8:17–18 See 1Ki 9:26–28. This joint venture between Solomon and Hiram secured for these kings the lucrative trade routes through the Mediterranean to the south Arabian peninsula; Solomon became the middleman between these economic spheres.

8:18 Hiram sent him ships. Presumably ships crafted in Phoenicia and assembled at the port of Ezion Geber after being shipped overland (see 9:21).

9:1–12 See 1Ki 10:1–13 and notes. The visit of the queen of Sheba portrays the fulfillment of God's promise to give Solomon wisdom and wealth (1:12). Although the themes of Solomon's wisdom and wealth are here put to the fore, a

major motive for the queen's visit may have been commercial, perhaps prompted by Solomon's naval operations toward south Arabia (8:17–18).

9:1 Sheba. See note on 1Ki 10:1; see also Job 1:15; 6:19; Ps 72:10–11,15; Isa 60:6; Jer 6:20; Eze 27:22; 38:13; Joel 3:8.

9:8 his throne. The most significant variation from the account of the queen's visit in 1 Kings (10:9) is found here. The queen's speech becomes the vehicle for the Chronicler's conviction that the throne of Israel is the throne of God, for whom the king ruled (see 13:18; see also note on 1Ch 17:14).

dom. ²⁰All King Solomon's goblets were gold, and all the household articles in the Palace of the Forest of Lebanon were pure gold. Nothing was made of silver, because silver was considered of little value in Solomon's day. ²¹The king had a fleet of trading ships^q manned by Hiram's^r men. Once every three years it returned, carrying gold, silver and ivory, and apes and baboons.

²²King Solomon was greater in riches and wisdom than all the other kings of the earth.^p ²³All the kings^q of the earth sought audience with Solomon to hear the wisdom God had put in his heart. ²⁴Year after year, everyone who came brought a gift^r—articles of silver and gold, and robes, weapons and spices, and horses and mules.

²⁵Solomon had four thousand stalls for horses and chariots,^s and twelve thousand horses,^s which he kept in the chariot cities and also with him in Jerusalem. ²⁶He ruled^t over all the kings from the River^t ^u to the land of the Philistines, as far as the border of Egypt.^v ²⁷The king made silver as common in Jerusalem as stones, and cedar as plentiful as sycamore-fig trees in the foothills. ²⁸Solomon's horses were imported from Egypt^u and from all other countries.

Solomon's Death

9:29–31pp — 1Ki 11:41–43

²⁹As for the other events of Solomon's reign, from beginning to end, are they not written in the records of Nathan^w the prophet, in the prophecy of Ahijah^x the Shilonite and in the visions of Iddo the seer concerning Jeroboam^y son of Nebat? ³⁰Solomon reigned in Jerusalem over all Israel forty years. ³¹Then he rested with his fathers and was buried in the city of David^z his father. And Rehoboam his son succeeded him as king.

Cross references column

9:22 ^pS 1Ki 3:13; S 2Ch 1:12
9:23 ^qI Ki 4:34
9:24 ^rZCh 32:23; Ps 45:12; 68:29; 72:10; Isa 18:7
9:25 ^sS 1Sa 8:11
9:26 ^tS 1Ki 4:21 ^uPs 72:8-9 ^vGe 15:18-21
9:29 ^wS 2Sa 7:2 ^xS 1Ki 11:29 ^y2Ch 10:2
9:31 ^z1Ki 2:10

10:2 ^aS 2Ch 9:29 ^bS 1Ki 11:40
10:3 ^cS 1Ch 9:1
10:4 ^dZCh 2:2
10:6 ^eJob 8:8-9; 12:12; 15:10; 32:7
10:7 ^fPr 15:1
10:8 ^gS 2Sa 17:14 ^hPr 13:20

Israel Rebels Against Rehoboam

10:1–11:4pp — 1Ki 12:1–24

10 Rehoboam went to Shechem, for all the Israelites had gone there to make him king. ²When Jeroboam^a son of Nebat heard this (he was in Egypt, where he had fled^b from King Solomon), he returned from Egypt. ³So they sent for Jeroboam, and he and all Israel^c went to Rehoboam and said to him: ⁴"Your father put a heavy yoke on us,^d but now lighten the harsh labor and the heavy yoke he put on us, and we will serve you."

⁵Rehoboam answered, "Come back to me in three days." So the people went away.

⁶Then King Rehoboam consulted the elders^e who had served his father Solomon during his lifetime. "How would you advise me to answer these people?" he asked.

⁷They replied, "If you will be kind to these people and please them and give them a favorable answer,^f they will always be your servants."

⁸But Rehoboam rejected^g the advice the elders^h gave him and consulted the young men who had grown up with him and were serving him. ⁹He asked them, "What is your advice? How should we answer these people who say to me, 'Lighten the yoke your father put on us'?"

¹⁰The young men who had grown up with him replied, "Tell the people who have said to you, 'Your father put a heavy yoke on us, but make our yoke lighter'—tell them, 'My little finger is thicker than my father's waist. ¹¹My father laid on you a heavy yoke; I will make it even heavier. My father scourged you with

^q21 Hebrew *of ships that could go to Tarshish* ^r21 Hebrew *Huram,* a variant of *Hiram* ^s25 Or *charioteers* ^t26 That is, the Euphrates ^u28 Or possibly *Muzur,* a region in Cilicia

---

9:26 See 7:8 and note.
9:27 See 1:15.
9:28 The Chronicler omits the accounts of Solomon's wives and the rebellions at the end of his reign (1Ki 11:1–40), both of which would detract from his uniformly positive portrayal of Solomon. *horses . . . Egypt.* See note on 1:16.
9:29–31 See 1Ki 11:41–43.
10:1–36:23 The material covering the divided monarchy in Chronicles is considerably shorter than that in Kings: 27 chapters compared to 36 (1Ki 12–2Ki 25). Moreover, about half of this material is unique to Chronicles and shows no dependence on Kings. The most obvious reason for this is that the Chronicler has written a history of the Davidic dynasty in Judah; the history of the northern kingdom is passed over in silence except where it impinges on that of

Judah. At least two considerations prompt this treatment of the divided kingdom: 1. The Chronicler is concerned to trace God's faithfulness to his promise to give David an unbroken line of descent on the throne of Israel. 2. At the time of the Chronicler the restored community was confined to the returnees of the kingdom of Judah, who were actually the remnant of all Israel (see Introduction to 1 Chronicles: Purpose and Themes).
10:1–19 See 1Ki 12:1–20 and notes. Somewhat in line with his idealization of Solomon, the Chronicler places most of the blame for the schism on the rebellious Jeroboam (cf. 13:6–7).
10:1 *Rehoboam.* Reigned 930–913 B.C.
10:2 *Jeroboam.* His second mention in Chronicles (see 9:29). The Chronicler assumes the reader's familiarity with 1Ki 11:26–40.

whips; I will scourge you with scorpions.' "

12Three days later Jeroboam and all the people returned to Rehoboam, as the king had said, "Come back to me in three days." 13The king answered them harshly. Rejecting the advice of the elders, 14he followed the advice of the young men and said, "My father made your yoke heavy; I will make it even heavier. My father scourged you with whips; I will scourge you with scorpions." 15So the king did not listen to the people, for this turn of events was from God, *i* to fulfill the word the LORD had spoken to Jeroboam son of Nebat through Ahijah the Shilonite. *j*

16When all Israel *k* saw that the king refused to listen to them, they answered the king:

"What share do we have in David, *l*
  what part in Jesse's son?
To your tents, O Israel!
  Look after your own house,
    O David!"

So all the Israelites went home. 17But as for the Israelites who were living in the towns of Judah, Rehoboam still ruled over them.

18King Rehoboam sent out Adoniram, *v* *m* who was in charge of forced labor, but the Israelites stoned him to death. King Rehoboam, however, managed to get into his chariot and escape to Jerusalem. 19So Israel has been in rebellion against the house of David to this day.

11 When Rehoboam arrived in Jerusalem, *n* he mustered the house of Judah and Benjamin—a hundred and eighty thousand fighting men—to make war against Israel and to regain the kingdom for Rehoboam.

2But this word of the LORD came to Shemaiah *o* the man of God: 3"Say to Rehoboam son of Solomon king of Judah and to all the Israelites in Judah and Benjamin, 4'This is what the LORD says: Do not go up to fight against your brothers. *p* Go home, every one of you, for this is my doing.' " So they obeyed the words of the LORD and turned back from marching against Jeroboam.

Rehoboam Fortifies Judah

5Rehoboam lived in Jerusalem and built up towns for defense in Judah: 6Bethlehem, Etam, Tekoa, 7Beth Zur, Soco, Adullam, 8Gath, Mareshah, Ziph, 9Adoraim, Lachish, Azekah, 10Zorah, Aijalon and Hebron. These were fortified cities *q* in Judah and Benjamin. 11He strengthened their defenses and put commanders in them, with supplies of food, olive oil and wine. 12He put shields and spears in all the cities, and made them very strong. So Judah and Benjamin were his.

13The priests and Levites from all their districts throughout Israel sided with him. 14The Levites *r* even abandoned their pasturelands and property, *s* and came to Judah and Jerusalem because Jeroboam and his sons had rejected them as priests of the LORD. 15And he appointed *t* his own priests *u* for the high places and for the goat *v* and calf *w* idols he had made. 16Those from every tribe of Israel *x* who set their hearts on seeking the LORD, the God of Israel, followed the Levites to Jerusalem to offer sacrifices to the LORD, the God of their fathers. 17They strengthened *y* the kingdom of Judah and supported Rehoboam son of Solomon three years, walking

---

Cross references (center column):

10:15 *l*2Ch 11:4;
25:16-20
*j*S 1Ki 11:29
10:16 *k*S 1Ch 9:1
*l*S 2Sa 20:1
10:18
*m*S 2Sa 20:24;
S 1Ki 5:14
11:1
*n*S 1Ki 12:21
11:2
*o*S 1Ki 12:22;
2Ch 12:5-7,15
11:4
*p*2Ch 28:8-11
11:10
*q*S Jos 10:20;
2Ch 12:4; 17:2,
19; 21:3
11:14
*r*S Nu 35:2-5
*s*1Ch 6:81
11:15
*t*S 1Ki 13:33
*u*S 1Ki 12:31
*v*Lev 17:7
*w*1Ki 12:28;
2Ch 13:8
11:16 *x*2Ch 15:9
11:17 *y*2Ch 12:1

v 18 Hebrew *Hadoram*, a variant of *Adoniram*

10:15 *Ahijah.* The Chronicler assumes the reader's familiarity with 1Ki 11:29–33.

10:18 *Adoniram . . . in charge of forced labor.* Had held the same office under Solomon (1Ki 4:6; 5:14).

10:19 *to this day.* See note on 5:9.

11:1–23 Verses 1–4 are parallel to 1Ki 12:21–24; vv. 5–23 are largely unique to Chronicles. The Chronicler's account of Rehoboam is a good example of his emphasis on immediate retribution (see Introduction to 1 Chronicles: Purpose and Themes). Ch. 11 traces the rewards for obedience to the command of God (vv. 1–4): Rehoboam enjoys prosperity and power (vv. 5–12), popular support (vv. 13–17) and progeny (vv. 18–23). Ch. 12 demonstrates the reverse: Disobedience brings judgment.

11:2 *Shemaiah.* The function of the prophets as guardians of the theocracy (God's kingdom) is prominent in Chronicles; most of Judah's kings are portrayed as receiving advice from prophets (see Introduction to 1 Chronicles: Purpose and Themes).

11:3 *the Israelites in Judah and Benjamin.* A variation from the wording found in 1Ki 12:23, in accordance with the

Chronicler's interest in "all Israel."

11:4 *my doing.* See 10:15.

11:5–10 This list of cities is not found in Kings. Rehoboam fortified his eastern, western and southern borders, but not the north, perhaps demonstrating his hope of reunification of the kingdoms, as well as the threat of invasion from Egypt.

11:13–17 The Chronicler assumes the reader's familiarity with 1Ki 12:26–33. This material is unique to Chronicles and reflects the author's concern both with the temple and its personnel and with showing that the kingdom of Judah was the remnant of all Israel.

11:14 *pasturelands and property.* See 1Ch 6:54–80; Lev 25:32–34; Nu 35:1–5; see also Introduction to 1 Chronicles: Purpose and Themes.

11:15 *goat and calf idols.* The account in Kings mentions only the golden calves (for the worship of goat idols or satyrs see Lev 17:7).

11:17 *three years.* See note on 12:2. *ways of David and Solomon.* Characteristic of the Chronicler's idealization of Solomon; contrast the portrait of Solomon in 1Ki 11:1–13.

in the ways of David and Solomon during
this time.

Rehoboam's Family

18 Rehoboam married Mahalath, who
was the daughter of David's son Jerimoth
and of Abihail, the daughter of Jesse's son
Eliab. 19 She bore him sons: Jeush, Shemariah and Zaham. 20 Then he married Maacah[z] daughter of Absalom, who bore him
Abijah,[a] Attai, Ziza and Shelomith.
21 Rehoboam loved Maacah daughter of
Absalom more than any of his other wives
and concubines. In all, he had eighteen
wives[b] and sixty concubines, twenty-eight
sons and sixty daughters.
22 Rehoboam appointed Abijah[c] son of
Maacah to be the chief prince among his
brothers, in order to make him king. 23 He
acted wisely, dispersing some of his sons
throughout the districts of Judah and Benjamin, and to all the fortified cities. He
gave them abundant provisions[d] and took
many wives for them.

Shishak Attacks Jerusalem

12:9–16pp — 1Ki 14:21, 25–31

12 After Rehoboam's position as king
was established[e] and he had
become strong,[f] he and all Israel[w][g] with
him abandoned[h] the law of the LORD. 2 Because they had been unfaithful[i] to the
LORD, Shishak[j] king of Egypt attacked
Jerusalem in the fifth year of King Rehoboam. 3 With twelve hundred chariots and
sixty thousand horsemen and the innumerable troops of Libyans,[k] Sukkites and
Cushites[x][l] that came with him from
Egypt, 4 he captured the fortified cities[m] of
Judah and came as far as Jerusalem.
5 Then the prophet Shemaiah[n] came to
Rehoboam and to the leaders of Judah who
had assembled in Jerusalem for fear of Shishak, and he said to them, "This is what
the LORD says, 'You have abandoned me;
therefore, I now abandon[o] you to Shishak.' "
6 The leaders of Israel and the king humbled[p] themselves and said, "The LORD is
just."[q]
7 When the LORD saw that they humbled
themselves, this word of the LORD came to
Shemaiah: "Since they have humbled
themselves, I will not destroy them but
will soon give them deliverance.[r] My
wrath[s] will not be poured out on Jerusalem through Shishak. 8 They will, however,
become subject[t] to him, so that they may
learn the difference between serving me
and serving the kings of other lands."
9 When Shishak king of Egypt attacked
Jerusalem, he carried off the treasures of
the temple of the LORD and the treasures of
the royal palace. He took everything, including the gold shields[u] Solomon had
made. 10 So King Rehoboam made bronze
shields to replace them and assigned these
to the commanders of the guard on duty at
the entrance to the royal palace. 11 Whenever the king went to the LORD's temple,
the guards went with him, bearing the
shields, and afterward they returned them
to the guardroom.
12 Because Rehoboam humbled[v] him-

11:20 [z]S 1Ki 15:2 [a]2Ch 12:16; 13:2
11:21 [b]S Dt 17:17
11:22 [c]Dt 21:15-17
11:23 [d]2Ch 21:3
12:1 [e]ver 13; 2Ch 1:1 [f]2Ch 11:17 [g]S 1Ch 9:1 [h]S 2Ch 7:19
12:2 [i]1Ki 14:22-24; S 1Ch 5:25 [j]1Ki 11:40
12:3 [k]Da 11:43 [l]S Ge 10:6; 2Ch 14:9; 16:8; Isa 18:2; Am 9:7; Na 3:9
12:4 [m]S 2Ch 11:10
12:5 [n]2Ch 11:2 [o]S Dt 28:15
12:6 [p]S Lev 26:41; S 2Ch 6:37 [q]Ex 9:27; Ezr 9:15; Ps 11:7; 116:5; Da 9:14
12:7 [r]Ps 78:38 [s]Dt 9:19; Ps 69:24; Jer 7:20; 42:18; Eze 5:13
12:8 [t]Dt 28:48
12:9 [u]2Ch 9:16
12:12 [v]S 2Ch 6:37

[w] *1* That is, Judah, as frequently in 2 Chronicles
[x] *3* That is, people from the upper Nile region

11:18–22 The report on the size of Rehoboam's family is placed here as part of the Chronicler's effort to show God's blessing on his obedience (see note on 11:1–23). The material is not in chronological sequence with the surrounding context but summarizes events throughout his reign. The Chronicler uses numerous progeny as a sign of divine blessing (see 13:21; see also notes on 21:2; 1Ch 25:5).
11:20 *Maacah daughter of Absalom.* See note on 1Ki 15:2. She was likely the granddaughter of Absalom, through his daughter Tamar (2Sa 14:27; 18:18), who was married to Uriel (2Ch 13:2).
11:21–22 These verses explain why the eldest son was not appointed Rehoboam's successor.
11:23 *dispersing some of his sons.* Rehoboam may have sought to secure the succession of Abijah by assigning other sons to outlying posts, perhaps to avoid the difficulties faced by David, whose sons at court (Adonijah and Absalom) had attempted to seize power.
12:1–14 See note on 11:1–23. Whereas obedience to the prophetic word (11:1–4) had brought blessing (11:5–23), now the prophet comes to announce judgment for disobedience (see 1Ki 14:25–28). While the writer of Kings also reports the attack of Shishak, the Chronicler alone adds the rationale that the invasion was because of forsaking the commands of God (vv. 1–2,5).
12:1 *all Israel.* Used in a variety of ways in 2 Chronicles: (1) of both kingdoms (9:30), (2) of the northern kingdom (10:16; 11:13) or (3) of the southern kingdom alone (as here; 11:3). *abandoned.* The opposite of "seeking the LORD" (v. 14); see v. 5; see also note on 24:18,20,24.
12:2 *Shishak.* Founder of the 22nd dynasty of Egypt, he ruled c. 945–924 B.C. The Bible mentions this invasion only as it affected Jerusalem, but Shishak's own inscription on the wall of the temple of Amun at Karnak (Thebes) indicates that his armies also swept as far north as the plain of Jezreel and Megiddo. *fifth year.* 925 B.C. The Chronicler often introduces chronological notes not found in Kings (e.g., 11:17; 15:10,19; 16:1,12–13; 17:7; 21:20; 24:15,17,23; 26:16; 27:5,8; 29:3; 34:3; 36:21). These become a vehicle for his emphasis on immediate retribution by dividing the reigns of individual kings into cycles of obedience-blessing and disobedience-punishment. This sequence is clear for Rehoboam: Three years of obedience and blessing (11:17) are followed by rebellion, presumably in the fourth year (12:1), and punishment in the fifth (here).
12:3 *Sukkites.* Probably a group of mercenary soldiers of Libyan origin who are known from Egyptian texts.
12:5 See notes on vv. 1–14; v. 1.
12:6–7 See v. 12. The Chronicler has in mind God's promise in 7:14.

self, the LORD's anger turned from him, and he was not totally destroyed. Indeed, there was some good ^{w} in Judah.

^{13}King Rehoboam established ^{x} himself firmly in Jerusalem and continued as king. He was forty-one years old when he became king, and he reigned seventeen years in Jerusalem, the city the LORD had chosen out of all the tribes of Israel in which to put his Name.^{y} His mother's name was Naamah; she was an Ammonite. ^{14}He did evil because he had not set his heart on seeking the LORD.

^{15}As for the events of Rehoboam's reign, from beginning to end, are they not written in the records of Shemaiah ^{z} the prophet and of Iddo the seer that deal with genealogies? There was continual warfare between Rehoboam and Jeroboam. ^{16}Rehoboam ^{a} rested with his fathers and was buried in the City of David. And Abijah ^{b} his son succeeded him as king.

Abijah King of Judah

13:1–2,22–14:1pp — 1Ki 15:1–2,6–8

13 In the eighteenth year of the reign of Jeroboam, Abijah became king of Judah, ^{2}and he reigned in Jerusalem three years. His mother's name was Maacah,^{y} ^{c} a daughter^z of Uriel of Gibeah.

There was war between Abijah ^{d} and Jeroboam. ^{e} ^{3}Abijah went into battle with a force of four hundred thousand able fighting men, and Jeroboam drew up a battle line against him with eight hundred thousand able troops.

^{4}Abijah stood on Mount Zemaraim,^{f} in the hill country of Ephraim, and said, "Jeroboam and all Israel,^{g} listen to me! ^{5}Don't you know that the LORD, the God of Israel, has given the kingship of Israel to David and his descendants forever ^{h} by a covenant of salt?^{i} ^{6}Yet Jeroboam son of

Nebat, an official of Solomon son of David, rebelled^j against his master. ^{7}Some worthless scoundrels ^{k} gathered around him and opposed Rehoboam son of Solomon when he was young and indecisive^l and not strong enough to resist them.

^{8}"And now you plan to resist the kingdom of the LORD, which is in the hands of David's descendants. ^{m} You are indeed a vast army and have with you ^{n} the golden calves^o that Jeroboam made to be your gods. ^{9}But didn't you drive out the priests^p of the LORD,^{q} the sons of Aaron, and the Levites, and make priests of your own as the peoples of other lands do? Whoever comes to consecrate himself with a young bull^r and seven rams^s may become a priest of what are not gods.^{t}

^{10}"As for us, the LORD is our God, and we have not forsaken him. The priests who serve the LORD are sons of Aaron, and the Levites assist them. ^{11}Every morning and evening ^{u} they present burnt offerings and fragrant incense^v to the LORD. They set out the bread on the ceremonially clean table^w and light the lamps^x on the gold lampstand every evening. We are observing the requirements of the LORD our God. But you have forsaken him. ^{12}God is with us; he is our leader. His priests with their trumpets will sound the battle cry against you.^{y} Men of Israel, do not fight against the LORD,^{z} the God of your fathers, for you will not succeed."^{a}

^{13}Now Jeroboam had sent troops around to the rear, so that while he was in front of Judah the ambush ^{b} was behind them. ^{14}Judah turned and saw that they were being attacked at both front and rear. Then they cried out^c to the LORD. The priests blew their trumpets ^{15}and the men of

12:12
^{w}S 1Ki 14:13;
2Ch 19:3
12:13 ^{x}S ver 1;
S 1Ki 2:12
^{y}S Ex 20:24;
Dt 12:5
12:15
^{z}S 2Ch 11:2
12:16
^{a}S 1Ch 3:10
^{b}S 2Ch 11:20
13:2 ^{c}2Ch 15:16
^{d}S 2Ch 11:20
^{e}1Ki 15:6
13:4 ^{f}Jos 18:22
^{g}1Ch 11:1
13:5 ^{h}S 2Sa 7:13;
S 1Ch 17:12
^{i}S Lev 2:13

13:6 ^{j}1Ki 11:26
13:7 ^{k}S Jdg 9:4
^{l}S 1Ch 29:1
13:8 ^{m}S 2Ch 9:8
^{n}1Sa 4:3
^{o}S Ex 32:4;
S 2Ch 11:15
13:9
^{p}S 1Ki 12:31
^{q}2Ch 11:14-15
^{r}Ex 29:35-36
^{s}S Ex 29:31
^{t}Jer 2:11; Gal 4:8
13:11
^{u}S Ex 29:39;
S 2Ch 2:4
^{v}S Ex 25:6
^{w}S 1Ch 9:32
^{x}S Ex 25:37
13:12
^{y}S Nu 10:8-9
^{z}S Jdg 2:15;
Ac 5:39 ^{a}Job 9:4;
Pr 21:30; 29:1
13:13 ^{b}Jos 8:9;
2Ch 20:22
13:14
^{c}S 1Ch 5:20;
2Ch 14:11; 18:31

^{y}2 Most Septuagint manuscripts and Syriac (see also 2 Chron. 11:20 and 1 Kings 15:2); Hebrew *Micaiah* ^{z}2 Or *granddaughter*

12:13 *seventeen years.* See note on 10:1.
12:15–16 See 1Ki 14:29–31.
13:1–14:1 The Chronicler's account of Abijah's reign is about three times longer than that in 1Ki 15:1–8, largely due to Abijah's lengthy speech (13:4–12; see note on 28:1–27). The most striking difference in the accounts of Abijah's reign in Kings and in Chronicles is the evaluation given in each: Kings offers a negative evaluation (1Ki 15:3), for which there was no doubt warrant, while the assessment in Chronicles is positive, in view of what the Chronicler is able to report of him. The kings' reigns, like the lives of common people, were often a mixture of good and evil.
13:2 *three years.* 913–910 B.C. *Maacah.* See note on 11:20.
13:3 *four hundred thousand . . . eight hundred thousand.* Surprisingly large figures but in line with those in 1Ch 21:5 (see note there). Apparently this was all-out war.
13:4 *Mount Zemaraim.* Location uncertain. The town

Zemaraim was in the territory of Benjamin (Jos 18:22); presumably the battle was along the common border of Benjamin and Israel. *all Israel.* See note on 12:1; here and in v. 15 the reference is to the northern kingdom.
13:5 See 7:17–18; 1Ch 17:13–14. *covenant of salt.* See notes on Lev 2:13; Nu 18:19; 2Ki 2:20.
13:6 See note on 10:1–19.
13:7 Not all in the northern kingdom are rebuked, only the leadership—a subtle appeal to those in the north who had been led into rebellion. *scoundrels.* See note on Dt 13:13. *young and indecisive.* Cf. 1Ch 22:5; 29:1. Rehoboam was 41 years old at the time of the schism (12:13).
13:8 *kingdom of the LORD.* The house of David represents the kingdom of God (see 9:8 and note).
13:9 See 1Ki 12:25–33. *consecrate himself.* Cf. Ex 29:1.
13:10–12 The Chronicler's concern with acceptable worship focuses on the legitimate priests and the observance of prescribed worship (cf. 1Ch 23:28–31).

Judah raised the battle cry. At the sound of their battle cry, God routed Jeroboam and all Israel ^{d} before Abijah and Judah. ^{16}The Israelites fled before Judah, and God delivered ^{e} them into their hands. ^{17}Abijah and his men inflicted heavy losses on them, so that there were five hundred thousand casualties among Israel's able men. ^{18}The men of Israel were subdued on that occasion, and the men of Judah were victorious because they relied ^{f} on the LORD, the God of their fathers.

^{19}Abijah pursued Jeroboam and took from him the towns of Bethel, Jeshanah and Ephron, with their surrounding villages. ^{20}Jeroboam did not regain power during the time of Abijah. And the LORD struck him down and he died.

^{21}But Abijah grew in strength. He married fourteen wives and had twenty-two sons and sixteen daughters.

^{22}The other events of Abijah's reign, what he did and what he said, are written in the annotations of the prophet Iddo.

14 And Abijah rested with his fathers and was buried in the City of David. Asa his son succeeded him as king, and in his days the country was at peace for ten years.

Asa King of Judah

14:2–3pp — 1Ki 15:11–12

^{2}Asa did what was good and right in the eyes of the LORD his God. ^{g} ^{3}He removed the foreign altars ^{h} and the high places,

smashed the sacred stones ^{i} and cut down the Asherah poles. $^{a\,j}$ ^{4}He commanded Judah to seek the LORD, ^{k} the God of their fathers, and to obey his laws and commands. ^{5}He removed the high places ^{l} and incense altars ^{m} in every town in Judah, and the kingdom was at peace under him. ^{6}He built up the fortified cities of Judah, since the land was at peace. No one was at war with him during those years, for the LORD gave him rest. ^{n}

^{7}"Let us build up these towns," he said to Judah, "and put walls around them, with towers, gates and bars. The land is still ours, because we have sought the LORD our God; we sought him and he has given us rest ^{o} on every side." So they built and prospered.

^{8}Asa had an army of three hundred thousand ^{p} men from Judah, equipped with large shields and with spears, and two hundred and eighty thousand from Benjamin, armed with small shields and with bows. All these were brave fighting men.

^{9}Zerah the Cushite ^{q} marched out against them with a vast army ^{b} and three hundred chariots, and came as far as Mareshah. ^{r} ^{10}Asa went out to meet him, and they took up battle positions in the Valley of Zephathah near Mareshah.

^{11}Then Asa called ^{s} to the LORD his God and said, "LORD, there is no one like you

Cross references (margin)

13:15 ^{d}S 1Ch 9:1
13:16 ^{e}2Ch 16:8
13:18
^{f}2Ch 14:11;
16:7; Ps 22:5
14:2 ^{g}2Ch 21:12
14:3 ^{h}S Jdg 2:2
14:4 ^{k}S 1Ch 16:11
14:5 ^{l}S 1Ki 15:14
^{m}Isa 27:9;
Eze 6:4
14:6 ^{n}S 1Ch 22:9
14:7 ^{o}S 1Ch 22:9
14:8 ^{p}S 1Ch 21:1
14:9 ^{q}S 2Ch 12:3
^{r}S Ge 10:8-9;
2Ch 11:8; 24:24
14:11
^{s}S 1Ki 8:44;
S 2Ch 13:14;
25:8

14 ^{i}S Ex 23:24
^{j}S Ex 34:13

^{a}3 That is, symbols of the goddess Asherah; here and elsewhere in 2 Chronicles ^{b}9 Hebrew with an army of a thousand thousands or with an army of thousands upon thousands

---

13:21 See note on 11:18–22.

14:1 *peace for ten years.* For the Chronicler peace and prosperity go hand in hand with righteous rule. This first decade of Asa's reign (910–900 B.C.) preceded the invasion by Zerah (14:9–15) and was followed by 20 more years of peace, from the 15th (15:10) to the 35th years (15:19). Contrast this account with the statement that there was war between Asa and Baasha throughout their reigns (see 1Ki 15:16 and note). The tensions between the two kingdoms may have accounted for Asa's fortifications (14:7–8), though actual combat was likely confined to raids until the major campaign was launched in Asa's 36th year (16:1). See 15:8 and note.

14:2–16:14 The account of Asa's reign (910–869 B.C.) here is greatly expanded over the one in 1Ki 15:9–24. The expansions characteristically express the Chronicler's view concerning the relationship between obedience and blessing, disobedience and punishment. The author introduces chronological notes into his account to divide Asa's reign into these periods (see note on 12:2): For ten years Asa did what was right and prospered (14:1–7), and an invasion by a powerful Cushite force was repulsed because he called on the Lord (14:8–15). There followed further reforms (15:1–9) and a covenant renewal in Asa's 15th year (15:10–18), and so he enjoyed peace until his 35th year (15:19). But then came a change: When confronted by an invasion from the northern kingdom in his 36th year (16:1), he hired Aramean reinforcements rather than trusting in the

Lord (16:2–6), and imprisoned the prophet who rebuked him (16:7–10). In his 39th year he was afflicted with a disease (16:12), but still steadfastly refused to seek the Lord. In his 41st year he died (16:13).

14:3 *sacred stones.* See note on 1Ki 14:23.

14:5 *removed the high places.* 1Ki 15:14 states that Asa did not remove the high places. This difficulty is best resolved by the Chronicler's own statement in 15:17, which is properly parallel to 1Ki 15:14: Early in his reign Asa did attempt to remove the high places, but pagan worship was extremely resilient, and ultimately his efforts were unsuccessful (15:17). Statements that the high places both were and were not removed are also found in the reign of Jehoshaphat (17:6; 20:33). Cf. Dt 12:2–3.

14:7 *rest on every side.* See note on 20:30.

14:9 *Zerah the Cushite.* Many identify him with Pharaoh Osorkon I, second pharaoh of the 22nd Egyptian dynasty. However, since he is not called "king" or "pharaoh," and is known as the "Cushite" or "Nubian," some prefer to identify him as an otherwise unknown general serving the pharaoh. The invasion appears to have been an attempt to duplicate the attack of Shishak 30 years earlier (12:1–12), but the results against Asa were quite different.

14:10 *Valley of Zephathah.* Marked the entrance to a road leading to the hills of Judah and Jerusalem. *Mareshah.* Earlier fortified by Rehoboam (11:8) to protect the route mentioned here.

to help the powerless against the mighty.
Help us,[t] O LORD our God, for we rely[u]
on you, and in your name[v] we have come
against this vast army. O LORD, you are our
God; do not let man prevail[w] against you."
12The LORD struck down[x] the Cushites
before Asa and Judah. The Cushites fled,
13and Asa and his army pursued them as
far as Gerar.[y] Such a great number of
Cushites fell that they could not recover;
they were crushed[z] before the LORD and
his forces. The men of Judah carried off a
large amount of plunder.[a] 14They destroyed all the villages around Gerar, for
the terror[b] of the LORD had fallen upon
them. They plundered all these villages,
since there was much booty there. 15They
also attacked the camps of the herdsmen
and carried off droves of sheep and goats
and camels. Then they returned to Jerusalem.

Asa's Reform

15:16–19pp — 1Ki 15:13–16

15 The Spirit of God came upon[c]
Azariah son of Oded. 2He went out
to meet Asa and said to him, "Listen to
me, Asa and all Judah and Benjamin. The
LORD is with you[d] when you are with
him.[e] If you seek[f] him, he will be found
by you, but if you forsake him, he will forsake you.[g] 3For a long time Israel was
without the true God, without a priest to
teach[h] and without the law.[i] 4But in their
distress they turned to the LORD, the God
of Israel, and sought him,[j] and he was
found by them. 5In those days it was not
safe to travel about,[k] for all the inhabitants
of the lands were in great turmoil. 6One
nation was being crushed by another and
one city by another,[l] because God was
troubling them with every kind of distress.
7But as for you, be strong[m] and do not give
up, for your work will be rewarded."[n]
8When Asa heard these words and the
prophecy of Azariah son of[c] Oded the
prophet, he took courage. He removed the
detestable idols[o] from the whole land of
Judah and Benjamin and from the towns
he had captured[p] in the hills of Ephraim.
He repaired the altar[q] of the LORD that
was in front of the portico of the LORD's
temple.
9Then he assembled all Judah and Benjamin and the people from Ephraim, Manasseh and Simeon who had settled among
them, for large numbers[r] had come over
to him from Israel when they saw that the
LORD his God was with him.
10They assembled at Jerusalem in the
third month[s] of the fifteenth year of Asa's
reign. 11At that time they sacrificed to the
LORD seven hundred head of cattle and
seven thousand sheep and goats from the
plunder[t] they had brought back. 12They
entered into a covenant[u] to seek the
LORD,[v] the God of their fathers, with all
their heart and soul. 13All who would not
seek the LORD, the God of Israel, were to
be put to death,[w] whether small or great,
man or woman. 14They took an oath to the
LORD with loud acclamation, with shouting and with trumpets and horns. 15All
Judah rejoiced about the oath because they
had sworn it wholeheartedly. They sought
God[x] eagerly, and he was found by them.
So the LORD gave them rest[y] on every
side.
16King Asa also deposed his grandmother Maacah[z] from her position as
queen mother,[a] because she had made a
repulsive Asherah pole.[b] Asa cut the pole
down, broke it up and burned it in the
Kidron Valley.[c] 17Although he did not remove the high places from Israel, Asa's
heart was fully committed ⌊to the LORD⌋ all

14:11 [t]Ps 60:11-12; 79:9 [u]S 2Ch 13:18 [v]S 1Sa 17:45 [w]Ps 9:19 **14:12** [x]1Ki 8:45 **14:13** [y]Ge 10:19 [z]2Sa 22:38; Ne 9:24; Ps 44:2, 19; 135:10 [a]2Ch 15:11,18 **14:14** [b]S Ge 35:5; S Dt 2:25; 11:25 **15:1** [c]S Nu 11:25,26 **15:2** [d]2Ch 20:17 [e]Jas 4:8 [f]2Ch 7:14; Ps 78:34; Isa 45:19; 55:6; Jer 29:13; Hos 3:5 [g]S Dt 31:17; S 1Ch 28:9 **15:3** [h]S Lev 10:11 [i]La 2:9; Am 8:11 **15:4** [j]S Dt 4:29 **15:5** [k]S Jdg 5:6; 19:20; Zec 8:10 **15:6** [l]Isa 19:2; Mt 24:7; Mk 13:8; Lk 21:10 **15:7** [m]Jos 1:7,9 [n]1Sa 24:19; Ps 18:20; 58:11; Pr 14:14; Jer 31:16 **15:8** [o]1Ki 15:12 [p]2Ch 17:2 [q]S 1Ki 8:64; S 2Ch 8:12 **15:9** [r]2Ch 11:16-17 **15:10** [s]S Lev 23:15-21 **15:11** [t]S 2Ch 14:13 **15:12** [u]S 2Ki 11:17 [v]S 1Ch 16:11 **15:13** [w]S Ex 22:20; Dt 13:9-16 **15:15** [x]Dt 4:29 [y]S 1Ch 22:9 **15:16** [z]2Ch 13:2 [a]S 1Ki 2:19 [b]S Ex 34:13 [c]S 2Sa 15:23

[c]8 Vulgate and Syriac (see also Septuagint and verse 1); Hebrew does not have *Azariah son of.*

14:13 *Gerar.* See note on Ge 20:1. *plunder.* Much of this booty (v. 14) made its way to the storehouses of the temple (15:18; see note on 1Ch 18:1–20:8).
14:14 *terror of the LORD.* See note on 1Ch 14:17.
15:1–19 This chapter appears to recount a second stage in the reforms introduced by Asa, beginning with the victory over Zerah and encouraged by the preaching of Azariah (v. 1).
15:3 *priest to teach.* The duties of the priests were not only to officiate at the altar, but also to teach the law (see 17:7–9; Lev 10:11).
15:8 *towns he had captured in . . . Ephraim.* A tacit admission that there had been some fighting between Baasha and Asa prior to Asa's 36th year (16:1); see 17:1.
15:9 *large numbers had come over to him.* Cf. the defection from the northern kingdom that also occurred under Rehoboam (11:13–17).
15:10 *third month of the fifteenth year.* Spring, 895 B.C., the year after Zerah's invasion (v. 19). The Feast of Weeks (or Pentecost) was held in the third month (Lev 23:15–21) and may have been the occasion for this assembly.
15:12 *covenant.* A renewal of the covenant made at Sinai, similar to the covenant renewals on the plain of Moab (Dt 29:1), at Mount Ebal (Jos 8:30–35), at Shechem (Jos 24:25) and at Gilgal (1Sa 11:14; see note there). Later the priest Jehoiada (23:16), as well as Hezekiah (29:10) and Josiah (34:31), would also lead in renewals of the covenant—events of primary significance in the view of the Chronicler.
15:13 *would not seek the LORD.* Would turn to other gods. *were to be put to death.* In accordance with basic covenant law (Ex 22:20; Dt 13:6–9).
15:15 *rest.* See note on 20:30.
15:16 *Asherah pole.* See NIV text note on 14:3.

his life. [18]He brought into the temple of God the silver and gold and the articles that he and his father had dedicated. [d]

[19]There was no more war until the thirty-fifth year of Asa's reign.

Asa's Last Years

16:1–6pp — 1Ki 15:17–22
16:11–17:1pp — 1Ki 15:23–24

16 In the thirty-sixth year of Asa's reign Baasha[e] king of Israel went up against Judah and fortified Ramah to prevent anyone from leaving or entering the territory of Asa king of Judah.

[2]Asa then took the silver and gold out of the treasuries of the LORD's temple and of his own palace and sent it to Ben-Hadad king of Aram, who was ruling in Damascus.[f] [3]"Let there be a treaty[g] between me and you," he said, "as there was between my father and your father. See, I am sending you silver and gold. Now break your treaty with Baasha king of Israel so he will withdraw from me."

[4]Ben-Hadad agreed with King Asa and sent the commanders of his forces against the towns of Israel. They conquered Ijon, Dan, Abel Maim[d] and all the store cities of Naphtali.[h] [5]When Baasha heard this, he stopped building Ramah and abandoned his work. [6]Then King Asa brought all the men of Judah, and they carried away from Ramah the stones and timber Baasha had been using. With them he built up Geba and Mizpah. [i]

[7]At that time Hanani[j] the seer came to Asa king of Judah and said to him: "Because you relied[k] on the king of Aram and not on the LORD your God, the army of the king of Aram has escaped from your hand.

[8]Were not the Cushites[e] [l] and Libyans a mighty army with great numbers[m] of chariots and horsemen[f]? Yet when you relied on the LORD, he delivered[n] them into your hand. [9]For the eyes[o] of the LORD range throughout the earth to strengthen those whose hearts are fully committed to him. You have done a foolish[p] thing, and from now on you will be at war. [q]"

[10]Asa was angry with the seer because of this; he was so enraged that he put him in prison. [r] At the same time Asa brutally oppressed some of the people.

[11]The events of Asa's reign, from beginning to end, are written in the book of the kings of Judah and Israel. [12]In the thirty-ninth year of his reign Asa was afflicted[s] with a disease in his feet. Though his disease was severe, even in his illness he did not seek[t] help from the LORD, [u] but only from the physicians. [13]Then in the forty-first year of his reign Asa died and rested with his fathers. [14]They buried him in the tomb that he had cut out for himself[v] in the City of David. They laid him on a bier covered with spices and various blended perfumes, [w] and they made a huge fire[x] in his honor.

Jehoshaphat King of Judah

17 Jehoshaphat his son succeeded him as king and strengthened[y] himself against Israel. [2]He stationed troops in all the fortified cities[z] of Judah and put garrisons in Judah and in the towns of Ephraim that his father Asa had captured. [a]

[3]The LORD was with Jehoshaphat be-

Cross references (center column)

15:18 [d]S 2Ch 14:13
16:1 [e]2Ki 9:9; Jer 41:9
16:2 [f]2Ch 19:1-20:37; 22:1-9
16:3 [g]2Ch 20:35; 25:7
16:4 [h]S 2Ki 15:29
16:6 [i]Jer 41:9
16:7 [j]1Ki 16:1
[k]S 2Ch 13:18

16:8 [l]S Ge 10:6, 8-9; S 2Ch 12:3
[m]2Ch 24:24
[n]2Ch 13:16
16:9 [o]Job 24:23; Ps 33:13-15; Pr 15:3; Jer 16:17; Zec 3:9; 4:10
[p]1Sa 13:13
[q]S 1Ki 15:6;
2Ch 19:2; 25:7; 28:16-21
16:10 [r]S 1Ki 22:27
16:12 [s]2Ch 21:18; 26:19; Ps 103:3
[t]2Ch 7:14
[u]Jer 17:5-6
16:14 [v]S Ge 50:5
[w]S Ge 50:2
[x]2Ch 21:19; Jer 34:5
17:1 [y]S 1Ki 2:12
17:2 [z]S 2Ch 11:10
[a]2Ch 15:8

Footnotes (bottom of columns)

[d]4 Also known as *Abel Beth Maacah*   [e]8 That is, people from the upper Nile region   [f]8 Or *charioteers*

15:17 *did not remove the high places.* See 14:5 and note.
16:1 *thirty-sixth year of Asa's reign Baasha.* According to Kings, Baasha ruled for 24 years and was succeeded by Elah in the 26th year of Asa (1Ki 15:33; 16:8). Obviously Baasha could not have been alive in the 36th year of Asa, where this passage places him—he had been dead for a decade. In order to solve this difficulty, some suggest that the Chronicler here and in 15:19 is dating from the schism in Israel rather than from the year number of Asa's reign: Since Rehoboam had reigned 17 years and Abijah 3, 20 years are deducted with the result that the 35th and 36th years of Asa are in fact the 15th and 16th years of his reign. This would make Baasha's attack come as a possible response to the defections from the northern kingdom (15:9). While this solution may be possible, it has not met with general acceptance. The action described here is not dated in 1Ki 15:17. Perhaps the dates here and in 15:19 are the result of a copyist's error (possibly for an original 25th and 26th).
16:2-9 *Hiring foreign troops* brought Asa into a foreign alliance, which showed lack of trust in the Lord. Other examples of condemned foreign alliances are found in the reigns of Jehoshaphat (20:35-37), Ahaziah (22:1-9) and Ahaz (28:16-21). By hiring Ben-Hadad to the north, Asa

opened a two-front war for Baasha and forced his withdrawal.

16:12 *disease in his feet.* For other examples of disease as punishment for sin see 21:16-20; 26:16-23; Ac 12:23. Cf. 2Ki 15:5.

17:1-21:3 The Chronicler's account of Jehoshaphat's reign is more than twice as long as that in Kings, where the interest in Ahab and Elijah overshadows the space allotted to Jehoshaphat (1Ki 22:1-46). The Chronicler has also used Jehoshaphat's reign to emphasize immediate retribution. This theme is specifically announced in 19:10 and is illustrated in the blessing of Jehoshaphat's obedient faith and in the reproof for his wrongdoing (19:2-3; 20:35-37). Jehoshaphat reigned 872-848 B.C., from 872 to 869 likely as co-regent with his father Asa (see 20:31 and note). The details of his reign may not be in chronological order; the teaching mission of 17:7-9 may have been part of the reforms noted in 19:4-11.

17:2 *cities of Judah . . . towns of Ephraim.* See note on 15:8. Abijah (13:19), Asa (15:8) and now Jehoshaphat had managed to hold these cities; they would be lost under Amaziah (25:17-24).

cause in his early years he walked in the ways his father David[b] had followed. He did not consult the Baals [4]but sought[c] the God of his father and followed his commands rather than the practices of Israel. [5]The LORD established the kingdom under his control; and all Judah brought gifts[d] to Jehoshaphat, so that he had great wealth and honor.[e] [6]His heart was devoted[f] to the ways of the LORD; furthermore, he removed the high places[g] and the Asherah poles[h] from Judah.[i]

[7]In the third year of his reign he sent his officials Ben-Hail, Obadiah, Zechariah, Nethanel and Micaiah to teach[j] in the towns of Judah. [8]With them were certain Levites[k]—Shemaiah, Nethaniah, Zebadiah, Asahel, Shemiramoth, Jehonathan, Adonijah, Tobijah and Tob-Adonijah—and the priests Elishama and Jehoram. [9]They taught throughout Judah, taking with them the Book of the Law[l] of the LORD; they went around to all the towns of Judah and taught the people.

[10]The fear[m] of the LORD fell on all the kingdoms of the lands surrounding Judah, so that they did not make war with Jehoshaphat. [11]Some Philistines brought Jehoshaphat gifts and silver as tribute, and the Arabs[n] brought him flocks:[o] seven thousand seven hundred rams and seven thousand seven hundred goats.

[12]Jehoshaphat became more and more powerful; he built forts and store cities in Judah [13]and had large supplies in the towns of Judah. He also kept experienced fighting men in Jerusalem. [14]Their enrollment[p] by families was as follows:

From Judah, commanders of units of 1,000:

Adnah the commander, with 300,000 fighting men;

[15]next, Jehohanan the commander, with 280,000;

[16]next, Amasiah son of Zicri, who volunteered[q] himself for the service of the LORD, with 200,000.

[17]From Benjamin:[r]

Eliada, a valiant soldier, with 200,000 men armed with bows and shields;

[18]next, Jehozabad, with 180,000 men armed for battle.

[19]These were the men who served the king, besides those he stationed in the fortified cities[s] throughout Judah.[t]

Micaiah Prophesies Against Ahab

18:1–27pp — 1Ki 22:1–28

18 Now Jehoshaphat had great wealth and honor,[u] and he allied[v] himself with Ahab[w] by marriage. [2]Some years later he went down to visit Ahab in Samaria. Ahab slaughtered many sheep and cattle for him and the people with him and urged him to attack Ramoth Gilead. [3]Ahab king of Israel asked Jehoshaphat king of Judah, "Will you go with me against Ramoth Gilead?"

Jehoshaphat replied, "I am as you are, and my people as your people; we will join you in the war." [4]But Jehoshaphat also said to the king of Israel, "First seek the counsel of the LORD."

[5]So the king of Israel brought together the prophets—four hundred men—and asked them, "Shall we go to war against Ramoth Gilead, or shall I refrain?"

"Go," they answered, "for God will give it into the king's hand."

[6]But Jehoshaphat asked, "Is there not a

Cross references (center column)

17:3 [b]S 1Ki 22:43
17:4 [c]2Ch 22:9
17:5 [d]S 1Sa 10:27
[e]2Ch 18:1
17:6 [f]S 1Ki 8:61
[g]S 1Ki 15:14; 2Ch 19:3; 20:33
[h]S Ex 34:13
[i]2Ch 21:12
17:7 [j]S Lev 10:11; Dt 6:4-9; 2Ch 19:4-11; 35:3; Ne 8:7; Mal 2:7
17:8 [k]2Ch 19:8; Ne 8:7-8; Hos 4:6
17:9 [l]S Dt 28:61
17:10
[m]S Ge 35:5; S Dt 2:25
17:11 [n]S 2Ch 9:14
[o]2Ch 21:16
17:14 [p]S 2Sa 24:2

17:16 [q]S Jdg 5:9
17:17 [r]S Nu 1:36
17:19 [s]S 2Ch 11:10
[t]2Ch 25:5
18:1 [u]2Ch 17:5
[v]2Ch 19:1-3;
22:3 [w]2Ch 21:6

17:6 *removed the high places.* Just as his father Asa had attempted to remove the high places, only to have them be restored (14:5; 15:17), so also Jehoshaphat removed them initially, only to have them revive and persist (20:33; cf. 1Ki 22:43). But see notes on 1Ki 3:2; 15:14. *Asherah poles.* See NIV text note on 14:3.

17:7–9 This incident may be part of the reform more fully detailed in 19:4–11. In the theocracy, the law of the Lord was supposed to be an integral part of the law of the land; the king and his officials, as well as the priests and prophets, were representatives of the Lord's kingship over his people. **17:7** *third year.* Perhaps the first year of his sole reign after a co-regency of three years with his father Asa (see 20:31 and note).

17:10–11 See note on 1Ch 18:1–20:8.

17:10 *fear of the LORD.* See note on 1Ch 14:17.

17:14–18 *300,000 ... 280,000 ... 200,000 ... 200,000 ... 180,000.* Or "300 units ... 280 units ... 200 units ... 200 units ... 180 units" (see notes on 1Ch 12:23–37; 27:1).

18:1–19:3 See 1Ki 22:1–40 and notes. To conform with

his interest in the southern kingdom and Jehoshaphat, the Chronicler omits elaboration on the death of Ahab and his succession (1Ki 22:36–40) and adds the material on the prophetic condemnation of Jehoshaphat's involvement (19:1–3).

18:1 Not found in 1Ki 22. The verse enhances the status of Jehoshaphat by mentioning the blessing of wealth for his fidelity, and also sets the stage for an entangling foreign alliance condemned by the prophet in 19:2–3. *allied himself with Ahab by marriage.* This marriage alliance to Athaliah, daughter of Ahab, resulted later in an attempt to exterminate the Davidic line (22:10–23:21).

18:2 The Chronicler further enhances the status of Jehoshaphat by noting the large number of animals Ahab slaughtered in his honor, a note not found in 1Ki 22. *urged him.* Also not used in the parallel text. The Hebrew for this verb is often used in the sense of "inciting to evil" (e.g., 1Ch 21:1) and may express the Chronicler's attitude toward Jehoshaphat's involvement.

18:4 *seek the counsel of the LORD.* This request fits the Chronicler's overall positive portrait of Jehoshaphat.

prophet of the LORD here whom we can inquire of?"

⁷The king of Israel answered Jehoshaphat, "There is still one man through whom we can inquire of the LORD, but I hate him because he never prophesies anything good about me, but always bad. He is Micaiah son of Imlah."

"The king should not say that," Jehoshaphat replied.

⁸So the king of Israel called one of his officials and said, "Bring Micaiah son of Imlah at once."

⁹Dressed in their royal robes, the king of Israel and Jehoshaphat king of Judah were sitting on their thrones at the threshing floor by the entrance to the gate of Samaria, with all the prophets prophesying before them. ¹⁰Now Zedekiah son of Kenaanah had made iron horns, and he declared, "This is what the LORD says: 'With these you will gore the Arameans until they are destroyed.' "

¹¹All the other prophets were prophesying the same thing. "Attack Ramoth Gileadˣ and be victorious," they said, "for the LORD will give it into the king's hand."

¹²The messenger who had gone to summon Micaiah said to him, "Look, as one man the other prophets are predicting success for the king. Let your word agree with theirs, and speak favorably."

¹³But Micaiah said, "As surely as the LORD lives, I can tell him only what my God says."ʸ

¹⁴When he arrived, the king asked him, "Micaiah, shall we go to war against Ramoth Gilead, or shall I refrain?"

"Attack and be victorious," he answered, "for they will be given into your hand."

¹⁵The king said to him, "How many times must I make you swear to tell me nothing but the truth in the name of the LORD?"

¹⁶Then Micaiah answered, "I saw all Israelᶻ scattered on the hills like sheep without a shepherd,ᵃ and the LORD said, 'These people have no master. Let each one go home in peace.' "

¹⁷The king of Israel said to Jehoshaphat, "Didn't I tell you that he never prophesies anything good about me, but only bad?"

¹⁸Micaiah continued, "Therefore hear

the word of the LORD: I saw the LORD sitting on his throneᵇ with all the host of heaven standing on his right and on his left. ¹⁹And the LORD said, 'Who will entice Ahab king of Israel into attacking Ramoth Gilead and going to his death there?'

"One suggested this, and another that. ²⁰Finally, a spirit came forward, stood before the LORD and said, 'I will entice him.'

" 'By what means?' the LORD asked.

²¹" 'I will go and be a lying spiritᶜ in the mouths of all his prophets,' he said.

" 'You will succeed in enticing him,' said the LORD. 'Go and do it.'

²²"So now the LORD has put a lying spirit in the mouths of these prophets of yours.ᵈ The LORD has decreed disaster for you."

²³Then Zedekiah son of Kenaanah went up and slappedᵉ Micaiah in the face. "Which way did the spirit fromᵍ the LORD go when he went from me to speak to you?" he asked.

²⁴Micaiah replied, "You will find out on the day you go to hide in an inner room."

²⁵The king of Israel then ordered, "Take Micaiah and send him back to Amon the ruler of the city and to Joash the king's son, ²⁶and say, 'This is what the king says: Put this fellow in prisonᶠ and give him nothing but bread and water until I return safely.' "

²⁷Micaiah declared, "If you ever return safely, the LORD has not spoken through me." Then he added, "Mark my words, all you people!"

Ahab Killed at Ramoth Gilead

18:28–34pp — 1Ki 22:29–36

²⁸So the king of Israel and Jehoshaphat king of Judah went up to Ramoth Gilead. ²⁹The king of Israel said to Jehoshaphat, "I will enter the battle in disguise, but you wear your royal robes." So the king of Israel disguisedᵍ himself and went into battle.

³⁰Now the king of Aram had ordered his chariot commanders, "Do not fight with anyone, small or great, except the king of Israel." ³¹When the chariot commanders saw Jehoshaphat, they thought, "This is the king of Israel." So they turned to attack him, but Jehoshaphat cried out,ʰ and the

18:11 ˣ2Ch 22:5
18:13 ʸNu 22:18, 20,35
18:16 ᶻS 1Ch 9:1
ᵃS Nu 27:17

18:18 ᵇDa 7:9
18:21 ᶜ1Ch 21:1; Job 1:6; Zec 3:1; Jn 8:44
18:22 ᵈJob 12:16; Eze 14:9
18:23 ᵉAc 23:2
18:26 ᶠHeb 11:36
18:29 ᵍS 1Sa 28:8
18:31 ʰS 2Ch 13:14

ᵍ23 Or *Spirit of*

18:29 The fact that Ahab disguises himself while directing Jehoshaphat into battle in royal regalia, thus making Jehoshaphat the logical target for attack, is consistent with Israel's dominant position at this time.
18:31 *the LORD helped him. God drew them away from*

him. Not found in 1Ki 22:32. However, some Septuagint (the Greek translation of the OT) manuscripts of Kings do contain the statement that "the LORD helped him," suggesting that the Chronicler was following a Hebrew text of Kings that had these words.

LORD helped him. God drew them away from him, [32]for when the chariot commanders saw that he was not the king of Israel, they stopped pursuing him.

[33]But someone drew his bow at random and hit the king of Israel between the sections of his armor. The king told the chariot driver, "Wheel around and get me out of the fighting. I've been wounded." [34]All day long the battle raged, and the king of Israel propped himself up in his chariot facing the Arameans until evening. Then at sunset he died. [i]

19 When Jehoshaphat king of Judah returned safely to his palace in Jerusalem, [2]Jehu[j] the seer, the son of Hanani, went out to meet him and said to the king, "Should you help the wicked[k] and love[h] those who hate the LORD?[l] Because of this, the wrath[m] of the LORD is upon you. [3]There is, however, some good[n] in you, for you have rid the land of the Asherah poles[o] and have set your heart on seeking God.[p]"

Jehoshaphat Appoints Judges

[4]Jehoshaphat lived in Jerusalem, and he went out again among the people from Beersheba to the hill country of Ephraim and turned them back to the LORD, the God of their fathers. [5]He appointed judges[q] in the land, in each of the fortified cities of Judah. [6]He told them, "Consider carefully what you do,[r] because you are not judging for man[s] but for the LORD, who is with you whenever you give a verdict. [7]Now let the fear of the LORD be upon

18:34 [i]2Ch 22:5
19:2 [j]S 1Ki 16:1
[k]S 2Ch 16:2-9
[l]Ps 139:21-22
[m]2Ch 24:18;
32:25; Ps 7:11
19:3
[n]S 1Ki 14:13
[o]S 2Ch 17:6
[p]S 2Ch 18:1;
20:35; 25:7
19:5 [q]S Ge 47:6;
S Ex 18:26
19:6 [r]S Lev 19:15
[s]Dt 16:18-20;
17:8-13

19:7 [t]S Ge 18:25;
S Job 8:3
[u]S Ex 18:16;
Dt 10:17;
Job 13:10; 32:21;
34:19
19:8 [v]S 1Ch 23:4
[w]Eze 44:24
[x]2Ch 17:8-9
19:10
[y]Dt 17:8-13
19:11
[z]S 1Ch 28:20
20:1 [a]Ps 83:6
[b]S 1Ch 4:41
20:2 [c]2Ch 24:24

you. Judge carefully, for with the LORD our God there is no injustice[t] or partiality[u] or bribery."

[8]In Jerusalem also, Jehoshaphat appointed some of the Levites,[v] priests[w] and heads of Israelite families to administer[x] the law of the LORD and to settle disputes. And they lived in Jerusalem. [9]He gave them these orders: "You must serve faithfully and wholeheartedly in the fear of the LORD. [10]In every case that comes before you from your fellow countrymen who live in the cities—whether bloodshed or other concerns of the law, commands, decrees or ordinances—you are to warn them not to sin against the LORD;[y] otherwise his wrath will come on you and your brothers. Do this, and you will not sin.

[11]"Amariah the chief priest will be over you in any matter concerning the LORD, and Zebadiah son of Ishmael, the leader of the tribe of Judah, will be over you in any matter concerning the king, and the Levites will serve as officials before you. Act with courage,[z] and may the LORD be with those who do well."

Jehoshaphat Defeats Moab and Ammon

20 After this, the Moabites[a] and Ammonites with some of the Meunites[i][b] came to make war on Jehoshaphat.

[2]Some men came and told Jehoshaphat, "A vast army[c] is coming against you from

[h]2 Or and make alliances with   [i]1 Some Septuagint manuscripts; Hebrew Ammonites

---

19:1–3 Not found in 1Ki 22.

19:2 Should you help the wicked . . . ? Jehu's father Hanani had earlier given Jehoshaphat's father Asa the same warning (see 16:7–9). Jehoshaphat later committed the same sin again and suffered for it (20:35–37).

19:3 Asherah poles. See NIV text note on 14:3.

19:4 Jehoshaphat . . . went . . . among the people. The king traveled throughout the realm personally to promote religious reformation.

19:5 appointed judges. The name Jehoshaphat (meaning "The LORD judges") is appropriate for the king who instituted this judicial reform. The arrangement of the courts under Jehoshaphat (vv. 5–11) would be of particular interest to the Chronicler's audience in the postexilic period, when the courts of the restored community would have their own existence and structure legitimized by this precedent.

19:6 Cf. Dt 16:18–20; 17:8–13.

19:7 let the fear of the LORD be upon you. Let a terrifying sense of God's presence restrain you from any injustice (see note on 1Ch 14:17).

19:8 Levites, priests . . . to administer the law. See note on 1Ch 26:29–32. One effect of this judicial reform appears to be the bringing of the traditional system of justice administered by the elders of the city under closer royal and priestly supervision.

19:11 any matter concerning the LORD . . . any matter

concerning the king. This division into the affairs of religion and the affairs of the king reflects the postexilic structure of the Chronicler's day. Cf. the anointing of Solomon and Zadok (1Ch 29:22) and the administration of the postexilic community by Zerubbabel, a Davidic descendant, and Joshua, the high priest (Zec 4:14; 6:9–15).

20:1–30 This episode held special interest for the Chronicler since the restored community was being harassed by the descendants of these same peoples (see Ne 2:19; 4:1–3, 7–9; 6:1–4; 13). He uses it to encourage his contemporaries to trust in the Lord and his prophets, as Jehoshaphat son of David had exhorted (v. 20). The account is significantly structured. Apart from the outer frame, which highlights the reversal of circumstances (vv. 1–4,28–30), it falls into three divisions: (1) Jehoshaphat's prayer (vv. 5–13), (2) the Lord's response (vv. 14–19), (3) the great victory (vv. 20–27). At the center of each is its crucial statement, and these are all linked by a key word: v. 9, "we will stand in your presence before this temple"; v. 17, "stand firm and see the deliverance the LORD will give you"; v. 23, "The men of Ammon and Moab rose up (lit. 'stood up') against the men from Mount Seir to destroy . . . them."

20:1 Meunites. A people from the region of Mount Seir in Edom (26:7; 1Ch 4:41; cf. 2Ch 20:10,22–23).

20:2 Edom. See NIV text note. Since the Arameans are well to the north and not mentioned among the attackers

Edom,[j] from the other side of the Sea.[k] It
is already in Hazazon Tamar[d]" (that is, En
Gedi).[e] 3Alarmed, Jehoshaphat resolved to
inquire of the LORD, and he proclaimed a
fast[f] for all Judah. 4The people of Judah[g]
came together to seek help from the LORD;
indeed, they came from every town in
Judah to seek him.

5Then Jehoshaphat stood up in the assembly of Judah and Jerusalem at the temple of the LORD in the front of the new
courtyard 6and said:

"O LORD, God of our fathers,[h] are
you not the God who is in heaven?[i]
You rule over all the kingdoms[j] of the
nations. Power and might are in your
hand, and no one can withstand
you.[k] 7O our God, did you not drive
out the inhabitants of this land[l] before your people Israel and give it forever to the descendants of Abraham
your friend?[m] 8They have lived in it
and have built in it a sanctuary[n] for
your Name, saying, 9'If calamity
comes upon us, whether the sword of
judgment, or plague or famine,[o] we
will stand in your presence before this
temple that bears your Name and will
cry out to you in our distress, and you
will hear us and save us.'

10"But now here are men from Ammon, Moab and Mount Seir, whose
territory you would not allow Israel to
invade when they came from Egypt;[p]
so they turned away from them and
did not destroy them. 11See how they
are repaying us by coming to drive us
out of the possession[q] you gave us as
an inheritance. 12O our God, will you
not judge them?[r] For we have no
power to face this vast army that is
attacking us. We do not know what to
do, but our eyes are upon you.[s]"

13All the men of Judah, with their wives
and children and little ones, stood there
before the LORD.

14Then the Spirit[t] of the LORD came
upon Jahaziel son of Zechariah, the son of
Benaiah, the son of Jeiel, the son of Mattaniah,[u] a Levite and descendant of Asaph,
as he stood in the assembly.

15He said: "Listen, King Jehoshaphat
and all who live in Judah and Jerusalem!
This is what the LORD says to you: 'Do not
be afraid or discouraged[v] because of this
vast army. For the battle[w] is not yours, but
God's. 16Tomorrow march down against
them. They will be climbing up by the Pass
of Ziz, and you will find them at the end of
the gorge in the Desert of Jeruel. 17You will
not have to fight this battle. Take up your
positions; stand firm and see[x] the deliverance the LORD will give you, O Judah and
Jerusalem. Do not be afraid; do not be discouraged. Go out to face them tomorrow,
and the LORD will be with you.'"

18Jehoshaphat bowed[y] with his face to
the ground, and all the people of Judah and
Jerusalem fell down in worship before the
LORD. 19Then some Levites from the Kohathites and Korahites stood up and
praised the LORD, the God of Israel, with
very loud voice.

20Early in the morning they left for the
Desert of Tekoa. As they set out, Jehoshaphat stood and said, "Listen to me, Judah
and people of Jerusalem! Have faith[z] in
the LORD your God and you will be
upheld; have faith in his prophets and you
will be successful.[a]" 21After consulting the
people, Jehoshaphat appointed men to sing
to the LORD and to praise him for the
splendor of his[l] holiness[b] as they went
out at the head of the army, saying:

"Give thanks to the LORD,
for his love endures forever."[c]

22As they began to sing and praise, the
LORD set ambushes[d] against the men of
Ammon and Moab and Mount Seir who
were invading Judah, and they were defeated. 23The men of Ammon[e] and Moab

20:2 [d]S Ge 14:7 [e]S 1Sa 23:29; SS 1:14 **20:3** [f]1Sa 7:6; Ezr 8:23; Ne 1:4; Est 4:16; Isa 58:6; Jer 36:9; Da 9:3; Joel 1:14; 2:15; Jnh 3:5,7 **20:4** [g]Jer 36:6 **20:6** [h]Mt 6:9 [i]Dt 4:39 [j]1Ch 29:11-12 [k]2Ch 25:8; Job 25:2; 41:10; 42:2; Isa 14:27; Jer 32:27; 49:19 **20:7** [l]S Ge 12:7 [m]Isa 41:8; Jas 2:23 **20:8** [n]2Ch 6:20 **20:9** [o]S 2Ch 6:28 **20:10** [p]Nu 20:14-21; Dt 2:4-6,9,18-19 **20:11** [q]Ps 83:1-12 **20:12** [r]Jdg 11:27 [s]Ps 25:15; Isa 30:15; 45:22; Mic 7:7 **20:14** [t]S 1Ch 12:18 [u]S 1Ch 9:15 **20:15** [v]2Ch 32:7 [w]S 1Sa 17:47; Ps 91:8 **20:17** [x]S Ex 14:13 **20:18** [y]S Ge 24:26; 2Ch 29:29 **20:20** [z]Isa 7:9 [a]S Ge 39:3; Pr 16:3 **20:21** [b]S 1Ch 16:29 [c]S 2Ch 5:13; Ps 136:1 **20:22** [d]S 2Ch 13:13 **20:23** [e]S Ge 19:38

[j]2 One Hebrew manuscript; most Hebrew manuscripts, Septuagint and Vulgate *Aram* [k]2 That is, the Dead Sea [l]21 Or *him with the splendor of*

named in v. 1, the NIV has followed the reading "Edom." The difference between "Aram" and "Edom" in Hebrew is only one letter, which is very similar in shape and was often confused in the process of copying manuscripts.

20:5–12 Jehoshaphat's prayer shows him to be a true theocratic king, a worthy son of David and type (foreshadowing) of the awaited Messiah (see Introduction to 1 Chronicles: Purpose and Themes).

20:9 An apparent reference to Solomon's prayer and the divine promise of response (6:14–42; 7:12–22).

20:15 See Ex 14:13–14.

20:16 *Pass of Ziz.* Began seven miles north of En Gedi and wound inland, emerging west of Tekoa. *Jeruel.* Southeast of Tekoa.

20:19 *Levites.* The Chronicler's interest in the priests and Levites is apparent throughout the account (vv. 14,21–22, 28).

20:20 *Have faith in the LORD your God and . . . in his prophets.* A particularly apt word for the Chronicler's contemporaries to hear from this son of David—at a time when their only hope for the future lay with the Lord and the reassuring words of his prophets.

20:21 *splendor of his holiness.* See note on Ps 29:2.

20:22 *ambushes.* The nature of this "ambush" is indicated in v. 23: Israel's foes destroyed each other in the confusion of battle, similar to the victory under Gideon (Jdg 7:22).

rose up against the men from Mount Seir[f] to destroy and annihilate them. After they finished slaughtering the men from Seir, they helped to destroy one another.[g]

24When the men of Judah came to the place that overlooks the desert and looked toward the vast army, they saw only dead bodies lying on the ground; no one had escaped. 25So Jehoshaphat and his men went to carry off their plunder, and they found among them a great amount of equipment and clothing[m] and also articles of value—more than they could take away. There was so much plunder that it took three days to collect it. 26On the fourth day they assembled in the Valley of Beracah, where they praised the LORD. This is why it is called the Valley of Beracah[n] to this day.

27Then, led by Jehoshaphat, all the men of Judah and Jerusalem returned joyfully to Jerusalem, for the LORD had given them cause to rejoice over their enemies. 28They entered Jerusalem and went to the temple of the LORD with harps and lutes and trumpets.

29The fear[h] of God came upon all the kingdoms of the countries when they heard how the LORD had fought[i] against the enemies of Israel. 30And the kingdom of Jehoshaphat was at peace, for his God had given him rest[j] on every side.

The End of Jehoshaphat's Reign

20:31–21:1pp — 1Ki 22:41–50

31So Jehoshaphat reigned over Judah. He was thirty-five years old when he became king of Judah, and he reigned in Jerusalem twenty-five years. His mother's name was Azubah daughter of Shilhi. 32He walked in the ways of his father Asa and did not stray from them; he did what was right in the eyes of the LORD. 33The high places,[k] however, were not removed, and the people still had not set their hearts on the God of their fathers.

34The other events of Jehoshaphat's reign, from beginning to end, are written in the annals of Jehu[l] son of Hanani, which are recorded in the book of the kings of Israel.

35Later, Jehoshaphat king of Judah made an alliance[m] with Ahaziah king of Israel, who was guilty of wickedness.[n] 36He agreed with him to construct a fleet of trading ships.[o] After these were built at Ezion Geber, 37Eliezer son of Dodavahu of Mareshah prophesied against Jehoshaphat, saying, "Because you have made an alliance with Ahaziah, the LORD will destroy what you have made." The ships[o] were wrecked and were not able to set sail to trade.[p]

21 Then Jehoshaphat rested with his fathers and was buried with them in the City of David. And Jehoram[p] his son succeeded him as king. 2Jehoram's brothers, the sons of Jehoshaphat, were Azariah, Jehiel, Zechariah, Azariahu, Michael and Shephatiah. All these were sons of Jehoshaphat king of Israel.[q] 3Their father had given them many gifts[q] of silver and gold and articles of value, as well as fortified cities[r] in Judah, but he had given the kingdom to Jehoram because he was his firstborn son.

Jehoram King of Judah

21:5–10,20pp — 2Ki 8:16–24

4When Jehoram established[s] himself

20:23 /2Ch 21:8
gS Jdg 7:22;
1Sa 14:20;
Eze 38:21
20:29
hS Ge 35:5;
S Dt 2:25
iS Ex 14:14
20:30
/S 1Ch 22:9

20:33
kS 2Ch 17:6
20:34 /S 1Ki 16:1
20:35
mS 2Ch 16:3
nS 2Ch 19:1-3
20:37
oS 1Ki 9:26
21:1 pS 1Ch 3:11
21:3 q2Ch 11:23
rS 2Ch 11:10
21:4 sS 1Ki 2:12

---

m25 Some Hebrew manuscripts and Vulgate; most Hebrew manuscripts *corpses*   n26 *Beracah* means *praise.*   o36 Hebrew *of ships that could go to Tarshish*   p37 Hebrew *sail for Tarshish*   q2 That is, Judah, as frequently in 2 Chronicles

---

20:26 *to this day.* See note on 5:9.
20:29 *The fear of God.* See note on 1Ch 14:17.
20:30 *rest on every side.* Rest from enemies is part of God's blessing for obedience in Chronicles (14:5–7; 15:15; 1Ch 22:8–9,18). Righteous kings have victory in warfare (Abijah, Asa, Jehoshaphat, Uzziah, Hezekiah), while wicked rulers experience defeat (Jehoram, Ahaz, Joash, Zedekiah).
20:31 *twenty-five years.* Kings reports 22 (18 in 2Ki 3:1, and 4 more in 8:16). These figures are reconciled by suggesting a co-regency with his father Asa for three years, probably due to the severity of his father's illness and the need to arrange for a secure succession (16:10–14). The author of Kings speaks only of his years of sole reign after his father's death.
20:33 *high places . . . were not removed.* See note on 17:6.
20:34 *Jehu son of Hanani.* See note on 19:2.
20:35–37 See 1Ki 22:48–49. The lucrative maritime trade through the Gulf of Aqaba no doubt tempted Jehoshaphat to enter into this improper alliance (see 19:2 and note).

Solomon's earlier alliance for the same purpose had been with a non-Israelite king (8:17–18).
20:35 *Ahaziah.* Reigned 853–852 B.C. (see 1Ki 22:51–2Ki 1:18 for the account of his reign).
21:2 *sons of Jehoshaphat.* The Chronicler shows the blessing of God on Jehoshaphat by mentioning his large family, particularly his seven sons (see 11:18–22; 1Ch 25:5 and notes). Jehoshaphat's large number of sons is in striking contrast to the wicked Jehoram who, after murdering his brothers (v. 4), is left with but one son (v. 17). Jehoram's wife Athaliah would later perform a similar slaughter (22:10).
21:3 Cf. the similar actions of Rehoboam (11:23).
21:4–20 See 2Ki 8:16–24.
21:4 This bloody assassination of all potential rivals is not reported in Kings, but it fits the pattern of the northern kings (see v. 6). The princes of Israel were probably leading men in the southern kingdom who opposed having a king married to a daughter of Ahab. For this use of "Israel" see note on 12:1.

firmly over his father's kingdom, he put all his brothers[t] to the sword along with some of the princes of Israel. [5]Jehoram was thirty-two years old when he became king, and he reigned in Jerusalem eight years. [6]He walked in the ways of the kings of Israel, [u] as the house of Ahab had done, for he married a daughter of Ahab.[v] He did evil in the eyes of the LORD. [7]Nevertheless, because of the covenant the LORD had made with David,[w] the LORD was not willing to destroy the house of David.[x] He had promised to maintain a lamp[y] for him and his descendants forever.

[8]In the time of Jehoram, Edom[z] rebelled against Judah and set up its own king. [9]So Jehoram went there with his officers and all his chariots. The Edomites surrounded him and his chariot commanders, but he rose up and broke through by night. [10]To this day Edom has been in rebellion against Judah.

Libnah[a] revolted at the same time, because Jehoram had forsaken the LORD, the God of his fathers. [11]He had also built high places on the hills of Judah and had caused the people of Jerusalem to prostitute themselves and had led Judah astray.

[12]Jehoram received a letter from Elijah[b] the prophet, which said:

"This is what the LORD, the God of your father[c] David, says: 'You have not walked in the ways of your father Jehoshaphat or of Asa[d] king of Judah. [13]But you have walked in the ways of the kings of Israel, and you have led Judah and the people of Jerusalem to prostitute themselves, just as the house of Ahab did.[e] You have also

murdered your own brothers, members of your father's house, men who were better[f] than you. [14]So now the LORD is about to strike your people, your sons, your wives and everything that is yours, with a heavy blow. [15]You yourself will be very ill with a lingering disease[g] of the bowels, until the disease causes your bowels to come out.' "

[16]The LORD aroused against Jehoram the hostility of the Philistines and of the Arabs[h] who lived near the Cushites. [17]They attacked Judah, invaded it and carried off all the goods found in the king's palace, together with his sons and wives. Not a son was left to him except Ahaziah,[r] the youngest.[i]

[18]After all this, the LORD afflicted Jehoram with an incurable disease of the bowels. [19]In the course of time, at the end of the second year, his bowels came out because of the disease, and he died in great pain. His people made no fire in his honor,[j] as they had for his fathers.

[20]Jehoram was thirty-two years old when he became king, and he reigned in Jerusalem eight years. He passed away, to no one's regret, and was buried[k] in the City of David, but not in the tombs of the kings.

Ahaziah King of Judah

22:1–6pp — 2Ki 8:25–29
22:7–9pp — 2Ki 9:21–29

22 The people[l] of Jerusalem[m] made Ahaziah, Jehoram's youngest son, king in his place, since the raiders,[n] who

---

Cross references (center column):

21:4 [t]Jdg 9:5
21:6
[u]1Ki 12:28-30
[v]2Ch 18:1; 22:3
21:7 [w]S 2Sa 7:13
[x]S 2Sa 7:15;
2Ch 23:3
[y]S 2Sa 21:17
21:8
[z]2Ch 20:22-23
21:10
[a]S Nu 33:20
21:12
[b]2Ki 1:16-17
[c]2Ch 17:3-6
[d]2Ch 14:2
21:13
[e]1Ki 16:29-33

[f]1Ki 2:32
21:15
[g]S Nu 12:10
21:16
[h]2Ch 17:10-11;
22:1; 26:7
21:17
[i]2Ki 12:18;
2Ch 22:1;
Joel 3:5
21:19
[j]S 2Ch 16:14
21:20
[k]2Ch 24:25;
28:27; 33:20
22:1 [l]2Ch 33:25;
36:1
[m]2Ch 23:20-21;
26:1
[n]S 2Ch 21:16-17

[r]17 Hebrew *Jehoahaz*, a variant of *Ahaziah*

21:5 *eight years.* 848–841 B.C. The period 853–848 was probably a co-regency of Jehoram with his father Jehoshaphat—Jehoshaphat's 18th year was also Jehoram's second year (cf. 2Ki 1:17; 3:1).
21:6 *married a daughter of Ahab.* Probably the marriage referred to in 18:1, used to cement the alliance between Jehoshaphat and Ahab. Such political marriages were common. Many of Solomon's marriages sealed international relationships, as did Ahab's marriage to Jezebel.
21:8–10 The pious Jehoshaphat had enjoyed victory over Edom (20:1–30), while the wicked Jehoram is defeated in his attempt to keep Edom in subjection to Judah (see note on 20:30).
21:10 *To this day.* See note on 5:9. *Libnah.* Located between Judah and Philistia. *because Jehoram had forsaken the LORD.* Not found in 2Ki 8:22. The Chronicler introduces this judgment as an indication of immediate retribution (see notes on 12:1–14; 12:2; see also Introduction to 1 Chronicles: Purpose and Themes).
21:12–20a Not found in the parallel text in 2Ki 8.
21:12–15 This reference to a letter from Elijah is the only mention in Chronicles of that prophet, to whom the books of Kings give so much attention (1Ki 17–2Ki 2). Elijah's letter

specifically announces the immediate consequences of Jehoram's disobedience—further defeat in war, which will cost Jehoram his wives and sons; and disease, which will lead to his death (see note on 16:12). Cf. also the foot disease of Asa (16:12–14) and the leprosy of Uzziah (26:16–23). Kings does not mention the nature of Jehoram's death. Some have argued that this letter could not be authentic because, they claim, Elijah was taken to heaven before Jehoram became king. But this is not a necessary conclusion (see 2Ki 1:17; see also note on 2Ki 3:11). Elijah's translation may well have taken place as late as 848 B.C.
21:16 *Cushites.* See NIV text note on 16:8.
21:20 *eight years.* See note on v. 5. This is the first time that the Chronicler does not refer his readers to other sources for additional details on the reign of a king. *not in the tombs of the kings.* Only the Chronicler mentions the refusal of the people to accord Jehoram the customary burial honors of a tomb with the other kings of Judah (cf. 24:25).
22:1–9 The Chronicler's account of Ahaziah's reign is much shorter than the parallel in 2Ki 8:24–9:29, probably due to the fact that the Kings account focuses on the rebellion of Jehu and the downfall of the dynasty of Omri (see 2Ki 8:26; see also 1Ki 16:21–28)—events in the northern king-

came with the Arabs into the camp, had killed all the older sons. So Ahaziah son of Jehoram king of Judah began to reign.

²Ahaziah was twenty-two^s years old when he became king, and he reigned in Jerusalem one year. His mother's name was Athaliah, a granddaughter of Omri.

³He too walked^o in the ways of the house of Ahab,^{p} for his mother encouraged him in doing wrong. ⁴He did evil in the eyes of the LORD, as the house of Ahab had done, for after his father's death they became his advisers, to his undoing. ⁵He also followed their counsel when he went with Joram^t son of Ahab king of Israel to war against Hazael king of Aram at Ramoth Gilead.^{q} The Arameans wounded Joram; ⁶so he returned to Jezreel to recover from the wounds they had inflicted on him at Ramoth^u in his battle with Hazael^r king of Aram.

Then Ahaziah^v son of Jehoram king of Judah went down to Jezreel to see Joram son of Ahab because he had been wounded.

⁷Through Ahaziah's^s visit to Joram, God brought about Ahaziah's downfall. When Ahaziah arrived, he went out with Joram to meet Jehu son of Nimshi, whom the LORD had anointed to destroy the house of Ahab. ⁸While Jehu was executing judgment on the house of Ahab,^{t} he found the princes of Judah and the sons of Ahaziah's relatives, who had been attending Ahaziah, and he killed them. ⁹He then

22:3 ^{o}S 2Ch 18:1
^{p}S 2Ch 21:6
22:5 ^{q}2Ch 18:11, 34
22:6 ^{r}1Ki 19:15; 2Ki 8:13-15
22:7 ^{s}2Ki 9:16
22:8 ^{t}S 2Ki 10:13

22:9 ^{u}S Jdg 9:5
^{v}2Ch 17:4

went in search of Ahaziah, and his men captured him while he was hiding^u in Samaria. He was brought to Jehu and put to death. They buried him, for they said, "He was a son of Jehoshaphat, who sought^v the LORD with all his heart." So there was no one in the house of Ahaziah powerful enough to retain the kingdom.

Athaliah and Joash

22:10–23:21pp — 2Ki 11:1–21

¹⁰When Athaliah the mother of Ahaziah saw that her son was dead, she proceeded to destroy the whole royal family of the house of Judah. ¹¹But Jehosheba,^{w} the daughter of King Jehoram, took Joash son of Ahaziah and stole him away from among the royal princes who were about to be murdered and put him and his nurse in a bedroom. Because Jehosheba,^{w} the daughter of King Jehoram and wife of the priest Jehoiada, was Ahaziah's sister, she hid the child from Athaliah so she could not kill him. ¹²He remained hidden with them at the temple of God for six years while Athaliah ruled the land.

23 In the seventh year Jehoiada showed his strength. He made a covenant with the commanders of units of

$^s2$ Some Septuagint manuscripts and Syriac (see also 2 Kings 8:26); Hebrew *forty-two* $^t5$ Hebrew *Jehoram,* a variant of *Joram;* also in verses 6 and 7 $^u6$ Hebrew *Ramah,* a variant of *Ramoth* $^v6$ Some Hebrew manuscripts, Septuagint, Vulgate and Syriac (see also 2 Kings 8:29); most Hebrew manuscripts *Azariah* $^w11$ Hebrew *Jehoshabeath,* a variant of *Jehosheba*

---

dom, in which the Chronicler is not interested. The Chronicler's account again shows his interest in immediate retribution: Ahaziah's personal wickedness and his involvement in a foreign alliance result in immediate judgment and a reign of only one year (see note on 16:2–9; see also Introduction to 1 Chronicles: Purpose and Themes).
22:1 *had killed all the older sons.* Emphasizes divine retribution: Jehoram, who murdered all his brothers, had to watch the death of his own sons (21:4,13,16–17).
22:2 *twenty-two.* See NIV text note. The Hebrew reading of "42" would make Ahaziah older than his father (21:20). *one year.* 841 B.C.
22:3–4 The great influence of the dynasty of Omri in Judah is indicated by the power of Athaliah and the presence of advisers from the northern kingdom (see note on 18:29).
22:5 *went with Joram . . . to war.* An action similar to that for which Jehoshaphat had been rebuked (see 19:2 and note). *Hazael.* Had been anointed by Elisha; he later killed his master in a coup to seize the throne (2Ki 8:13–15; cf. 1Ki 19:15 and note). *Ramoth Gilead.* Located in the Transjordan border area between Israel and Aram. More than ten years earlier Jehoshaphat had participated with Ahab in a battle there that cost Ahab his life (ch. 18; 1Ki 22).
22:6 *returned to Jezreel.* Joram apparently recovered Ramoth Gilead and left Jehu in charge (2Ki 8:28–9:28).
22:7 *God brought about Ahaziah's downfall.* The Chronicler assumes that the reader is familiar with the account of Jehu's anointing and the additional details of the coup, which

resulted in the deaths of Joram and Ahaziah (2Ki 8:28–9:28). While the writer of Kings primarily portrays the end of the dynasty of Omri as a result of the judgment of God (1Ki 21:20–29; 2Ki 9:24–10:17), the Chronicler notes that the assassination of Ahaziah was also brought about by God.
22:9 The account of Ahaziah's death appears to be somewhat different in the two histories (cf. 2Ki 9:21–27; 10:12–14). Since the writer of Chronicles presumes the reader's familiarity with the other account (see note on v. 7), it is best to take the details of Chronicles as supplementary to Kings, not contradictory, though it is difficult to know the precise sequence and location of events. Apart from the Chronicler's statement that Ahaziah received a decent burial because of his father's piety rather than his own, the differences in the two accounts do not appear to be theologically motivated. There is no summary statement about the reign of Ahaziah in either history.
22:10–12 See 2Ki 11:1–3. In the history of Judah, Athaliah represents the only break in the continuity of the Davidic dynasty; she is the only queen of Judah to rule in her own name (841–835 B.C.). Her attempt to wipe out the royal family repeated the action of her husband Jehoram (21:4). It threatened the continuity of the Davidic dynasty, and if she had succeeded, Judah may have been claimed by the dynasty of Omri in the north since Athaliah was from that dynasty and had no living son and heir.
22:11 *wife of the priest Jehoiada.* Not noted in Kings.
23:1–24:27 See 2Ki 11:4–12:21 and notes. The Chroni-

a hundred: Azariah son of Jeroham, Ishmael son of Jehohanan, Azariah son of Obed, Maaseiah son of Adaiah, and Elishaphat son of Zicri. [2]They went throughout Judah and gathered the Levites[w] and the heads of Israelite families from all the towns. When they came to Jerusalem, [3]the whole assembly made a covenant[x] with the king at the temple of God.

Jehoiada said to them, "The king's son shall reign, as the LORD promised concerning the descendants of David.[y] [4]Now this is what you are to do: A third of you priests and Levites who are going on duty on the Sabbath are to keep watch at the doors, [5]a third of you at the royal palace and a third at the Foundation Gate, and all the other men are to be in the courtyards of the temple of the LORD. [6]No one is to enter the temple of the LORD except the priests and Levites on duty; they may enter because they are consecrated, but all the other men are to guard[z] what the LORD has assigned to them.[x] [7]The Levites are to station themselves around the king, each man with his weapons in his hand. Anyone who enters the temple must be put to death. Stay close to the king wherever he goes."

[8]The Levites and all the men of Judah did just as Jehoiada the priest ordered.[a] Each one took his men—those who were going on duty on the Sabbath and those who were going off duty—for Jehoiada the priest had not released any of the divisions.[b] [9]Then he gave the commanders of units of a hundred the spears and the large and small shields that had belonged to King David and that were in the temple of God. [10]He stationed all the men, each with his weapon in his hand, around the king—near the altar and the temple, from the south side to the north side of the temple.

[11]Jehoiada and his sons brought out the king's son and put the crown on him; they presented him with a copy[c] of the covenant and proclaimed him king. They anointed him and shouted, "Long live the king!"

[12]When Athaliah heard the noise of the people running and cheering the king, she went to them at the temple of the LORD. [13]She looked, and there was the king,[d] standing by his pillar[e] at the entrance. The officers and the trumpeters were beside the king, and all the people of the land were rejoicing and blowing trumpets, and singers with musical instruments were leading the praises. Then Athaliah tore her robes and shouted, "Treason! Treason!"

[14]Jehoiada the priest sent out the commanders of units of a hundred, who were in charge of the troops, and said to them: "Bring her out between the ranks[y] and put to the sword anyone who follows her." For the priest had said, "Do not put her to death at the temple of the LORD." [15]So they seized her as she reached the entrance of the Horse Gate[f] on the palace grounds, and there they put her to death.

[16]Jehoiada then made a covenant[g] that he and the people and the king[z] would be the LORD's people. [17]All the people went to the temple of Baal and tore it down. They smashed the altars and idols and killed[h] Mattan the priest of Baal in front of the altars.

23:2
[w]S Nu 35:2-5
23:3 [x]S 2Ki 11:17
[y]S 2Sa 7:12;
S 1Ki 2:4;
S 2Ch 6:16;
S 7:18; S 21:7
23:6 [z]Zec 3:7
23:8 [a]2Ki 11:9
[b]S 1Ch 24:1

23:11 [c]Dt 17:18
23:13 [d]1Ki 1:41
[e]S 1Ki 7:15
23:15 [f]Jer 31:40
23:16
[g]2Ch 29:10;
34:31; Ne 9:38
23:17 [h]Dt 13:6-9

[x]6 Or *to observe the LORD's command not to enter*
[y]14 Or *out from the precincts*   [z]16 Or *covenant between the LORD and the people and the king that they* (see 2 Kings 11:17)

---

cler divides the reign of Joash (835–796 B.C.) into three parts: (1) the recovery of the throne for the house of David (ch. 23); (2) Joash and Jehoiada—the good years (24:1–16); (3) Joash alone—the bad years (24:17–27). The last section is largely unique to Chronicles and further develops the theme of immediate retribution: Once again chronological notes provide the framework for cycles of obedience and disobedience (24:15–17,23); see notes on 12:2; 14:2–16:14.
23:1–21 See 2Ki 11:4–20. The Chronicler has followed his source rather closely but has introduced material reflecting his own concerns in three areas: 1. The account in Kings has more to say about the participation of the military in the coup; the Chronicler adds material emphasizing the presence of temple officials and their role (vv. 2,6,8,13,18–19). 2. The Chronicler stresses the widespread popular support for the coup by mentioning the presence of large groups of people, such as "all the people" or "the whole assembly" (vv. 3,5–6,8,10,16–17). 3. The Chronicler shows additional concern for the sanctity of the temple area by inserting notes showing the steps taken to ensure that only qualified personnel enter the temple precincts (vv. 5–6,19).
23:1 *Azariah . . . Elishaphat.* The Chronicler names the commanders, which was not done in Kings, but he does not mention the Carites, mercenaries who served as a royal guard (see note on 2Ki 11:4). Verse 20 exhibits the same omission (cf. 2Ki 11:19), the motive for which may have been the Chronicler's concern that only authorized persons enter the temple precincts.
23:2 *the Levites and the heads of Israelite families.* Reflects both the Chronicler's concerns with the temple personnel and the widespread support for the coup against Athaliah.
23:3 *as the LORD promised.* See 2Sa 7:11–16.
23:11 *copy of the covenant.* May refer to the covenant sworn by the assembly (vv. 1,3; cf. v. 16) or to the law of God, by which the king was to rule (see Dt 17:18–20). See note on 2Ki 11:12.
23:13 *singers with musical instruments.* The Chronicler adds a note (not found in 2Ki 11:14) about the presence of Levitical musicians, who were leading the praises (see note on 1Ch 6:31–48).

[18]Then Jehoiada placed the oversight of the temple of the LORD in the hands of the priests, who were Levites,[i] to whom David had made assignments in the temple,[j] to present the burnt offerings of the LORD as written in the Law of Moses, with rejoicing and singing, as David had ordered. [19]He also stationed doorkeepers[k] at the gates of the LORD's temple so that no one who was in any way unclean might enter.

[20]He took with him the commanders of hundreds, the nobles, the rulers of the people and all the people of the land and brought the king down from the temple of the LORD. They went into the palace through the Upper Gate[l] and seated the king on the royal throne, [21]and all the people of the land rejoiced. And the city was quiet, because Athaliah had been slain with the sword.[m]

Joash Repairs the Temple

24:1–14pp — 2Ki 12:1–16
24:23–27pp — 2Ki 12:17–21

24 Joash was seven years old when he became king, and he reigned in Jerusalem forty years. His mother's name was Zibiah; she was from Beersheba. [2]Joash did what was right in the eyes of the LORD[n] all the years of Jehoiada the priest. [3]Jehoiada chose two wives for him, and he had sons and daughters.

[4]Some time later Joash decided to restore the temple of the LORD. [5]He called together the priests and Levites and said to them, "Go to the towns of Judah and collect the money[o] due annually from all Israel,[p] to repair the temple of your God. Do it now." But the Levites[q] did not act at once.

[6]Therefore the king summoned Jehoiada the chief priest and said to him, "Why haven't you required the Levites to bring in from Judah and Jerusalem the tax imposed by Moses the servant of the LORD and by the assembly of Israel for the Tent of the Testimony?"[r]

[7]Now the sons of that wicked woman Athaliah had broken into the temple of God and had used even its sacred objects for the Baals.

[8]At the king's command, a chest was made and placed outside, at the gate of the temple of the LORD. [9]A proclamation was then issued in Judah and Jerusalem that they should bring to the LORD the tax that Moses the servant of God had required of Israel in the desert. [10]All the officials and all the people brought their contributions gladly,[s] dropping them into the chest until it was full. [11]Whenever the chest was brought in by the Levites to the king's officials and they saw that there was a large amount of money, the royal secretary and the officer of the chief priest would come and empty the chest and carry it back to its place. They did this regularly and collected a great amount of money. [12]The king and Jehoiada gave it to the men who carried out the work required for the temple of the LORD. They hired[t] masons and carpenters to restore the LORD's temple, and also workers in iron and bronze to repair the temple.

[13]The men in charge of the work were diligent, and the repairs progressed under them. They rebuilt the temple of God according to its original design and reinforced it. [14]When they had finished, they brought the rest of the money to the king and Jehoiada, and with it were made articles for the LORD's temple: articles for the service and for the burnt offerings, and also dishes and other objects of gold and silver. As long as Jehoiada lived, burnt offerings were presented continually in the temple of the LORD.

[15]Now Jehoiada was old and full of

Cross references (center column)

23:18
[i] S 1Ch 23:28-32
[j] S 1Ch 23:6;
S 25:6
23:19 [k] 1Ch 9:22
23:20
[l] S 2Ki 15:35
23:21
[m] S 2Ch 22:1
24:2 [n] 2Ch 25:2;
26:5
24:5
[o] S Ex 30:16;
Ne 10:32-33;
Mt 17:24
[p] 1Ch 11:1
[q] S 1Ch 26:20

24:6 [r] S Ex 38:21
24:10
[s] S Ex 25:2;
S 1Ch 29:3,6,9
24:12
[t] 2Ch 34:11

23:18–19 The Chronicler adds information on the cultic ritual and the guards at the gates (see note on vv. 1–21).
23:20 See note on v. 1.
24:1–14 See 2Ki 12:1–17.
24:1 forty years. 835–796 B.C.
24:2 Provides the outline for the Chronicler's treatment of Joash—the good years while Jehoiada was alive (vv. 1–16), and the turn to evil after his death (vv. 17–27). See note on 25:2.
24:3 Another expression of the Chronicler's conviction that large families represent the blessing of God (see v. 27; see also note on 1Ch 25:5).
24:4 restore the temple. The vandalism and atrocities of Athaliah (v. 7) required the refurbishing of the temple.
24:5 The writer of 2 Kings speaks of three different sources of revenue (2Ki 12:4–5), whereas the Chronicler mentions only the census tax (see Ex 30:14; 38:26; Mt 17:24). The reason for the tardiness of the priests is not stated (see 2Ki

12:6–8). The writer of Kings notes that the audience with the priests takes place in the 23rd year of Joash's reign, when he is presumably no longer the ward of Jehoiada. Resistance on the part of the priests to the reassignment of the temple revenues for repair work may be the underlying cause.
24:8 chest. Mesopotamian texts speak of a similar offering box placed in temples. Representatives of both the king and the temple officials administered temple revenues (see note on 1Ch 26:20).
24:14 See 2Ki 12:13–14. As long as Jehoiada lived. An additional note on the part of the Chronicler to introduce the turn to the worse in the reign of Joash upon Jehoiada's death (vv. 15–16).
24:15–22 This section is unique to the Chronicler and shows his emphasis on immediate retribution (see note on 23:1–24:27). After a period of righteous rule until the death of Jehoiada, Joash turns to idolatry and murders Jehoiada's son. In the following year he is invaded and defeated by

years, and he died at the age of a hundred and thirty. ¹⁶He was buried with the kings in the City of David, because of the good he had done in Israel for God and his temple.

The Wickedness of Joash

¹⁷After the death of Jehoiada, the officials of Judah came and paid homage to the king, and he listened to them. ¹⁸They abandoned^u the temple of the LORD, the God of their fathers, and worshiped Asherah poles and idols.^{v} Because of their guilt, God's anger^w came upon Judah and Jerusalem. ¹⁹Although the LORD sent prophets to the people to bring them back to him, and though they testified against them, they would not listen.^{x}

²⁰Then the Spirit^y of God came upon Zechariah^z son of Jehoiada the priest. He stood before the people and said, "This is what God says: 'Why do you disobey the LORD's commands? You will not prosper.^{a} Because you have forsaken the LORD, he has forsaken^b you.'"

²¹But they plotted against him, and by order of the king they stoned^c him to death^d in the courtyard of the LORD's temple.^{e} ²²King Joash did not remember the kindness Zechariah's father Jehoiada had shown him but killed his son, who said as he lay dying, "May the LORD see this and call you to account."^{f}

²³At the turn of the year,^{a} the army of Aram marched against Joash; it invaded Judah and Jerusalem and killed all the leaders of the people.^{g} They sent all the plunder to their king in Damascus. ²⁴Although the Aramean army had come with only a few men,^{h} the LORD delivered into

their hands a much larger army.^{i} Because Judah had forsaken the LORD, the God of their fathers, judgment was executed on Joash. ²⁵When the Arameans withdrew, they left Joash severely wounded. His officials conspired against him for murdering the son of Jehoiada the priest, and they killed him in his bed. So he died and was buried^j in the City of David, but not in the tombs of the kings.

²⁶Those who conspired against him were Zabad,^{b} son of Shimeath an Ammonite woman, and Jehozabad, son of Shimrith^{ck} a Moabite woman.^{l} ²⁷The account of his sons, the many prophecies about him, and the record of the restoration of the temple of God are written in the annotations on the book of the kings. And Amaziah his son succeeded him as king.

Amaziah King of Judah

25:1–4pp — 2Ki 14:1–6
25:11–12pp — 2Ki 14:7
25:17–28pp — 2Ki 14:8–20

25 Amaziah was twenty-five years old when he became king, and he reigned in Jerusalem twenty-nine years. His mother's name was Jehoaddin^d; she was from Jerusalem. ²He did what was right in the eyes of the LORD, but not wholeheartedly.^{m} ³After the kingdom was firmly in his control, he executed the officials who had murdered his father the king. ⁴Yet he did not put their sons to death, but acted in accordance with what is written in the Law, in the Book of Moses,^{n} where the LORD commanded: "Fathers shall not be put to death for their

---

Cross references

24:18 ^{u}S Jos 24:20; ^{v}S 2Ch 7:19 ^{w}S Ex 34:13; 2Ch 33:3; Jer 17:2 ^{w}S 2Ch 19:2
24:19 ^{x}S Nu 11:29; Jer 7:25; Zec 1:4
24:20 ^{y}S Jdg 3:10; ^{z}S 1Ch 12:18 ^{z}Mt 23:35; Lk 11:51 ^{a}Nu 14:41 ^{b}S Dt 31:17
24:21 ^{c}S Jos 7:25 ^{d}Jer 26:21 ^{e}Jer 20:2
24:22 ^{f}S Ge 9:5 ^{g}2Ki 12:17-18
24:23 ^{h}S 2Ch 14:9; 16:8; 20:2,12
24:25 ^{l}Lev 26:23-25; Dt 28:25 ^{g}S 2Ch 21:20
24:26 ^{k}2Ki 12:21 ^{l}S Ru 1:4
25:2 ^{m}S 1Ki 8:61; S 2Ch 24:2
25:4 ^{n}S Dt 28:61

^{a}23 Probably in the spring ^{b}26 A variant of *Jozabad* ^{c}26 A variant of *Shomer* ^{d}1 Hebrew *Jehoaddan,* a variant of *Jehoaddin*

Aram because Judah, under his leadership, "had forsaken the LORD" (v. 24).

24:18,20,24 *abandoned . . . forsaken . . . forsaken . . . forsaken.* The Hebrew word is the same in these verses; it is a verb frequently used by the Chronicler to denote the reason for divine punishment (see note on 12:1; see also 7:19,22; 12:5; 13:10–11; 15:2; 21:10; 24:18,20,24; 28:6; 29:6; 34:25; 1Ch 28:9,20).

24:19 *Although the LORD sent prophets.* Israel's failure to heed the Lord's prophets ultimately led to her destruction (see 36:16; cf. 20:20; see also Introduction to 1 Chronicles: Purpose and Themes).

24:20 *Zechariah.* See note on Mt 23:35.

24:24 *only a few men.* Just as God had helped the small army of Judah against overwhelming odds when the king and people were faithful to him (14:8–9; 20:2,12), so now in their unfaithfulness they are defeated by a much smaller force of invaders (see note on 20:30).

24:25 *for murdering . . . they killed him.* Only the Chronicler mentions that this assassination was revenge for the murder of Zechariah. *not in the tombs of the kings.* Burial in the tombs of the kings was an honor accorded to Jehoiada (v.

16), but withheld from his rebellious ward Joash (see note on 21:20).

24:26 *an Ammonite . . . a Moabite.* Information not given in Kings but important to the Chronicler (see note on 20:1–30).

25:1–28 Typically, the Chronicler has divided the reign of Amaziah into two parts: (1) the good years, marked by obedience, divine blessing and victory (vv. 1–13), and (2) the bad years of idolatry, defeat and regicide (vv. 14–28). See 2Ki 14:1–20 and notes.

25:1 *twenty-nine years.* 796–767 B.C.

25:2 The Chronicler does not indicate that Amaziah failed to remove the high places, which continued to be used as places for sacrifice by the people (see 2Ki 14:4). Also compare 24:2 with 2Ki 12:4, and 26:4 with 2Ki 15:4. The writer appears to be motivated by his outline, which covered the good years first and then the reversion to evil. Negative comments about these kings are held to the second half of the account of their reigns, whereas in Kings the summary judgment about their reigns and the high places is given immediately.

children, nor children put to death for their fathers; each is to die for his own sins." e o

5Amaziah called the people of Judah together and assigned them according to their families to commanders of thousands and commanders of hundreds for all Judah and Benjamin. He then mustered p those twenty years old q or more and found that there were three hundred thousand men ready for military service, r able to handle the spear and shield. 6He also hired a hundred thousand fighting men from Israel for a hundred talents f of silver.

7But a man of God came to him and said, "O king, these troops from Israel s must not march with you, for the LORD is not with Israel—not with any of the people of Ephraim. 8Even if you go and fight courageously in battle, God will overthrow you before the enemy, for God has the power to help or to overthrow." t

9Amaziah asked the man of God, "But what about the hundred talents I paid for these Israelite troops?"

The man of God replied, "The LORD can give you much more than that." u

10So Amaziah dismissed the troops who had come to him from Ephraim and sent them home. They were furious with Judah and left for home in a great rage. v

11Amaziah then marshaled his strength and led his army to the Valley of Salt, where he killed ten thousand men of Seir. 12The army of Judah also captured ten thousand men alive, took them to the top of a cliff and threw them down so that all were dashed to pieces. w

13Meanwhile the troops that Amaziah had sent back and had not allowed to take part in the war raided Judean towns from Samaria to Beth Horon. They killed three thousand people and carried off great quantities of plunder.

14When Amaziah returned from slaughtering the Edomites, he brought back the gods of the people of Seir. He set them up

as his own gods, x bowed down to them and burned sacrifices to them. 15The anger of the LORD burned against Amaziah, and he sent a prophet to him, who said, "Why do you consult this people's gods, which could not save y their own people from your hand?"

16While he was still speaking, the king said to him, "Have we appointed you an adviser to the king? Stop! Why be struck down?"

So the prophet stopped but said, "I know that God has determined to destroy you, because you have done this and have not listened to my counsel."

17After Amaziah king of Judah consulted his advisers, he sent this challenge to Jehoash g son of Jehoahaz, the son of Jehu, king of Israel: "Come, meet me face to face."

18But Jehoash king of Israel replied to Amaziah king of Judah: "A thistle z in Lebanon sent a message to a cedar in Lebanon, 'Give your daughter to my son in marriage.' Then a wild beast in Lebanon came along and trampled the thistle underfoot. 19You say to yourself that you have defeated Edom, and now you are arrogant and proud. But stay at home! Why ask for trouble and cause your own downfall and that of Judah also?"

20Amaziah, however, would not listen, for God so worked that he might hand them over to Jehoash, because they sought the gods of Edom. a 21So Jehoash king of Israel attacked. He and Amaziah king of Judah faced each other at Beth Shemesh in Judah. 22Judah was routed by Israel, and every man fled to his home. 23Jehoash king of Israel captured Amaziah king of Judah, the son of Joash, the son of Ahaziah, h at Beth Shemesh. Then Jehoash

---

Cross references (center column):

25:4 oS Nu 26:11
25:5 pS 2Sa 24:2
qS Ex 30:14
rS 1Ch 21:1;
2Ch 17:14-19
25:7
sS 2Ch 16:2-9,3;
S 19:1-3
25:8
tS 2Ch 14:11;
S 20:6
25:9 uDt 8:18;
Pr 10:22
25:10 vver 13
25:12 wPs 141:6;
Ob 1:3

25:14 xEx 20:3;
2Ch 28:23;
Isa 44:15
25:15 yIsa 36:20
25:18
zJdg 9:8-15
25:20
aS 2Ch 10:15

e4 Deut. 24:16   f6 That is, about 3 3/4 tons (about 3.4 metric tons); also in verse 9   g17 Hebrew Joash, a variant of Jehoash; also in verses 18, 21, 23 and 25   h23 Hebrew Jehoahaz, a variant of Ahaziah

---

25:5–16 An expansion of 2Ki 14:7. The author of Kings mentions the successful war with Edom only as a prelude to Amaziah's challenge to Jehoash, but the Chronicler sets it in the framework of his emphasis on immediate retribution: Obedience brings victory over Edom, while the subsequent idolatry (vv. 14–16) brings defeat in the campaign against Israel. By expanding his account the Chronicler gives the theological reason for both the victory over Edom and the defeat before Israel.

25:7 troops from Israel must not march with you. Another instance of the Chronicler's condemnation of alliances that imply lack of trust in the Lord (see notes on 16:2–9; 22:5). Cf. other prophetic speeches that call on the people to trust in God (20:15–17,20; 32:7–8).

25:13 May be the inciting incident for the later war with

the north. Samaria. A town by this name in the southern kingdom is not otherwise known. The reference may be a copyist's error.

25:14–25 The Chronicler's account of the war with the north is close to the parallel in 2Ki 14:8–14, except for some additions in line with his theme of immediate retribution. The Chronicler mentions Amaziah's foolish idolatry and the prophetic speech of judgment, neither of which is found in Kings. He also adds notes in vv. 20,27 to emphasize that the idolatry of Amaziah was being punished.

25:18 Cf. the parable in Jdg 9:7–15.

25:23 Ephraim Gate to the Corner Gate. Both gates were located in the northern wall of the city, the Ephraim Gate at the northwest and the Corner Gate at the northeast.

brought him to Jerusalem and broke down the wall of Jerusalem from the Ephraim Gate[b] to the Corner Gate[c]—a section about six hundred feet[i] long. [24]He took all the gold and silver and all the articles found in the temple of God that had been in the care of Obed-Edom,[d] together with the palace treasures and the hostages, and returned to Samaria.

[25]Amaziah son of Joash king of Judah lived for fifteen years after the death of Jehoash son of Jehoahaz king of Israel. [26]As for the other events of Amaziah's reign, from beginning to end, are they not written in the book of the kings of Judah and Israel? [27]From the time that Amaziah turned away from following the LORD, they conspired against him in Jerusalem and he fled to Lachish[e], but they sent men after him to Lachish and killed him there. [28]He was brought back by horse and was buried with his fathers in the City of Judah.

Uzziah King of Judah

26:1–4pp — 2Ki 14:21–22; 15:1–3
26:21–23pp — 2Ki 15:5–7

26 Then all the people of Judah[f] took Uzziah,[j] who was sixteen years old, and made him king in place of his father Amaziah. [2]He was the one who rebuilt Elath and restored it to Judah after Amaziah rested with his fathers.

[3]Uzziah was sixteen years old when he became king, and he reigned in Jerusalem fifty-two years. His mother's name was Jecoliah; she was from Jerusalem. [4]He did what was right in the eyes of the LORD, just as his father Amaziah had done. [5]Amaziah sought God during the days of Zechariah, who instructed him in the fear[k] of God.[g] As long as he sought the LORD, God gave him success.[h]

[6]He went to war against the Philistines[i] and broke down the walls of Gath, Jabneh and Ashdod.[j] He then rebuilt towns near Ashdod and elsewhere among the Philistines. [7]God helped him against the Philistines and against the Arabs[k] who lived in Gur Baal and against the Meunites.[l] [8]The Ammonites[m] brought tribute to Uzziah, and his fame spread as far as the border of Egypt, because he had become very powerful.

[9]Uzziah built towers in Jerusalem at the Corner Gate,[n] at the Valley Gate[o] and at the angle of the wall, and he fortified them. [10]He also built towers in the desert and dug many cisterns, because he had much livestock in the foothills and in the plain. He had people working his fields and vineyards in the hills and in the fertile lands, for he loved the soil.

[11]Uzziah had a well-trained army, ready to go out by divisions according to their numbers as mustered by Jeiel the secretary and Maaseiah the officer under the direction of Hananiah, one of the royal officials. [12]The total number of family leaders over the fighting men was 2,600. [13]Under their

---

Cross references (center column):

25:23 [b]2Ki 14:13; Ne 8:16; 12:39 [c]2Ch 26:9; Jer 31:38
25:24 [d]S 1Ch 26:15
25:27 [e]S Jos 10:3
26:1 [f]S 2Ch 22:1
26:5 [g]S 2Ch 24:2 [h]2Ch 27:6
26:6 [i]Isa 2:6; 11:14; 14:29; Jer 25:20 [j]Am 1:8; 3:9
26:7 [k]S 2Ch 21:16 [l]2Ch 20:1
26:8 [m]S Ge 19:38
26:9 [n]S 2Ki 14:13; S 2Ch 25:23 [o]Ne 2:13; 3:13

NIV text notes:
[i]23 Hebrew *four hundred cubits* (about 180 meters)
[j]1 Also called *Azariah*   [k]5 Many Hebrew manuscripts, Septuagint and Syriac; other Hebrew manuscripts *vision*

25:24 The family of Obed-Edom was the Levitical family into whose care the temple storehouse had been entrusted (1Ch 26:15).

25:27 See note on vv. 14–25.

26:1–23 See 2Ki 15:1–7 and notes. The Chronicler has characteristically divided his account of Uzziah's reign into two parts: the good years, then the bad; cf. his treatment of Uzziah's father Amaziah and his grandfather Joash (see notes on 24:2; 25:1–28). The Chronicler elaborates on the blessings and divine help that flowed from Uzziah's obedience and fidelity (vv. 4–15), whereas the author of Kings only alludes to his fidelity (2Ki 15:3). Where Kings only mentions Uzziah's leprosy (2Ki 15:5), the Chronicler gives additional details to show that the disease was a result of unfaithfulness (vv. 16–21). Under Uzziah and his contemporary in the north, Jeroboam II, the borders of Israel and Judah briefly reached the extent they had attained under David and Solomon (vv. 6–8; 2Ki 14:25). In part, this flourishing of the two kingdoms was facilitated by the removal of the Aramean threat by Assyria under Adadnirari III (802 B.C.), following which Assyria herself went into a period of weakness.

26:1 *Uzziah.* See NIV text note (see also, e.g., 2Ki 15:6–7; 1Ch 3:12). It is likely that Uzziah was a throne name, while Azariah was his personal name.

26:3 *fifty-two years.* 792–740 B.C., including a co-regency with Amaziah from 792 to 767.

26:4 The Chronicler has constructed his account of Uzziah's reign to give it the same outline as that for Amaziah and Joash (see note on vv. 1–23). He has also once again bypassed the statement in the parallel account that the king did not remove the high places (2Ki 15:4), just as he did in the accounts of the other two kings (see note on 25:2).

26:5 *days of Zechariah.* The author again uses chronological notes to portray the cycles of blessing and judgment associated with the individual king's response to God's commands (see note on 12:2).

26:6–8 Uzziah's conquests were toward the southeast and the southwest; Israel's powerful Jeroboam II was in control to the north of Judah.

26:7 *Meunites.* See note on 20:1.

26:9 *Corner Gate . . . Valley Gate.* Found at the northeast and southwest portions of the walls. *fortified.* This construction along the wall of Jerusalem may reflect, in part, repair of the damage done by Jehoash during the reign of Amaziah (25:23).

26:10 *towers . . . cisterns.* Towers and cisterns have been found in several excavations (Qumran, Gibeah, Beersheba). A seal bearing Uzziah's name has been found in a cistern at Tell Beit Mirsim.

26:11 *Uzziah had a well-trained army.* Tiglath-Pileser III of Assyria states that he was opposed in his advance toward the west (743 B.C.) by a coalition headed by "Azriau of Yaudi," perhaps Azariah (Uzziah) of Judah.

command was an army of 307,500 men trained for war, a powerful force to support the king against his enemies. [14]Uzziah provided shields, spears, helmets, coats of armor, bows and slingstones for the entire army.[p] [15]In Jerusalem he made machines designed by skillful men for use on the towers and on the corner defenses to shoot arrows and hurl large stones. His fame spread far and wide, for he was greatly helped until he became powerful.

[16]But after Uzziah became powerful, his pride[q] led to his downfall.[r] He was unfaithful[s] to the LORD his God, and entered the temple of the LORD to burn incense[t] on the altar of incense. [17]Azariah[u] the priest with eighty other courageous priests of the LORD followed him in. [18]They confronted him and said, "It is not right for you, Uzziah, to burn incense to the LORD. That is for the priests,[v] the descendants[w] of Aaron,[x] who have been consecrated to burn incense.[y] Leave the sanctuary, for you have been unfaithful; and you will not be honored by the LORD God."

[19]Uzziah, who had a censer in his hand ready to burn incense, became angry. While he was raging at the priests in their presence before the incense altar in the LORD's temple, leprosy[1][z] broke out on his forehead. [20]When Azariah the chief priest and all the other priests looked at him, they saw that he had leprosy on his forehead, so they hurried him out. Indeed, he himself was eager to leave, because the LORD had afflicted him.

[21]King Uzziah had leprosy until the day he died. He lived in a separate house[m][a] —leprous, and excluded from the temple of the LORD. Jotham his son had charge of the palace and governed the people of the land.

[22]The other events of Uzziah's reign, from beginning to end, are recorded by the prophet Isaiah[b] son of Amoz. [23]Uzziah[c] rested with his fathers and was buried near them in a field for burial that belonged to the kings, for people said, "He had leprosy." And Jotham his son succeeded him as king.[d]

Jotham King of Judah

27:1–4,7–9pp — 2Ki 15:33–38

27 Jotham[e] was twenty-five years old when he became king, and he reigned in Jerusalem sixteen years. His mother's name was Jerusha daughter of Zadok. [2]He did what was right in the eyes of the LORD, just as his father Uzziah had done, but unlike him he did not enter the temple of the LORD. The people, however, continued their corrupt practices. [3]Jotham rebuilt the Upper Gate of the temple of the LORD and did extensive work on the wall at the hill of Ophel.[f] [4]He built towns in the Judean hills and forts and towers in the wooded areas.

[5]Jotham made war on the king of the Ammonites[g] and conquered them. That year the Ammonites paid him a hundred talents[n] of silver, ten thousand cors[o] of wheat and ten thousand cors of barley. The Ammonites brought him the same amount also in the second and third years.

[6]Jotham grew powerful[h] because he walked steadfastly before the LORD his God.

[7]The other events in Jotham's reign, including all his wars and the other things he did, are written in the book of the kings of Israel and Judah. [8]He was twenty-five years old when he became king, and he

Cross references (center column)

26:14 [p]Jer 46:4
26:16 [q]S 2Ki 14:10; [r]Dt 32:15; [s]S 1Ch 5:25; [t]2Ki 16:12
26:17 [u]S 1Ki 4:2
26:18 [v]Nu 16:39; [w]Nu 18:1-7; [x]S Ex 30:7; [y]S 1Ch 6:49
26:19 [z]S Nu 12:10
26:21 [a]S Ex 4:6; Lev 13:46; S 14:8; Nu 5:2; S 19:12

26:22 [b]2Ki 15:1; Isa 1:1; 6:1
26:23 [c]Isa 1:1; 6:1 [d]S 2Ki 14:21; Am 1:1
27:1 [e]S 2Ki 15:5, 32; S 1Ch 3:12
27:3 [f]2Ch 33:14; Ne 3:26
27:5 [g]S Ge 19:38
27:6 [h]2Ch 26:5

Footnotes (center column)

[1][19] The Hebrew word was used for various diseases affecting the skin—not necessarily leprosy; also in verses 20, 21 and 23.   [m][21] Or *in a house where he was relieved of responsibilities*   [n][5] That is, about 3 3/4 tons (about 3.4 metric tons)   [o][5] That is, probably about 62,000 bushels (about 2,200 kiloliters)

26:15 *machines . . . to shoot arrows and hurl large stones.* Since the catapult was not known in the military technology of the period, and since torsion-operated devices for shooting arrows did not appear for approximately another three centuries, the devices mentioned here may refer to defensive constructions to protect those shooting arrows and hurling stones from the tops of the walls.

26:16 *after Uzziah became powerful.* See note on v. 5.

26:19 *leprosy.* For disease as a punishment for sin see notes on 16:12; 21:12–15.

26:21 *Uzziah . . . died.* See Isa 6:1 and note. *separate house.* See NIV text note; the same phrase in the Canaanite texts from Ugarit suggests a kind of quarantine or separation.

26:22 *recorded by . . . Isaiah.* Not a reference to the canonical book but to some other work no longer in existence.

26:23 *buried . . . in a field . . . that belonged to the kings.* Cf. 2Ki 15:7. Apparently due to his leprosy, Uzziah was buried in a cemetery belonging to the kings, though not in the tombs of the kings.

27:1–9 See 2Ki 15:32–38 and notes.

27:1 *sixteen years.* 750–735 B.C., including a co-regency with Uzziah (750–740). His reign also overlapped that of his successor Ahaz from 735 to 732.

27:2 *did not enter the temple.* The Chronicler commends Jotham for not making the same error Uzziah did (26:16). *corrupt practices.* Appears to refer to the flourishing high places (2Ki 15:35).

27:3–6 Unique to the Chronicler and an elaboration of his thesis that fidelity to God's commands brings blessing: in construction, military victory and prosperity—all "because he walked steadfastly before the LORD" (v. 6). Judah's relationship with the Ammonites held particular interest for the Chronicler (see notes on 20:1–30; 24:26).

27:7 *all his wars.* See, e.g., 2Ki 15:37.

reigned in Jerusalem sixteen years. 9Jo-
tham rested with his fathers and was buried in the City of David. And Ahaz his son
succeeded him as king.

Ahaz King of Judah

28:1–27pp — 2Ki 16:1–20

28 Ahaz[i] was twenty years old when
he became king, and he reigned in
Jerusalem sixteen years. Unlike David his
father, he did not do what was right in the
eyes of the LORD. 2He walked in the ways
of the kings of Israel and also made cast
idols[j] for worshiping the Baals. 3He
burned sacrifices in the Valley of Ben Hinnom[k] and sacrificed his sons[l] in the fire,
following the detestable[m] ways of the nations the LORD had driven out before the
Israelites. 4He offered sacrifices and burned
incense at the high places, on the hilltops
and under every spreading tree.

5Therefore the LORD his God handed
him over to the king of Aram.[n] The Arameans defeated him and took many of his
people as prisoners and brought them to
Damascus.

He was also given into the hands of the
king of Israel, who inflicted heavy casualties on him. 6In one day Pekah[o] son of
Remaliah killed a hundred and twenty
thousand soldiers in Judah[p]—because
Judah had forsaken the LORD, the God of
their fathers. 7Zicri, an Ephraimite warrior,
killed Maaseiah the king's son, Azrikam
the officer in charge of the palace, and Elkanah, second to the king. 8The Israelites
took captive from their kinsmen[q] two
hundred thousand wives, sons and daughters. They also took a great deal of plunder,
which they carried back to Samaria.[r]

9But a prophet of the LORD named Oded
was there, and he went out to meet the
army when it returned to Samaria. He said
to them, "Because the LORD, the God of
your fathers, was angry[s] with Judah, he
gave them into your hand. But you have
slaughtered them in a rage that reaches to
heaven.[t] 10And now you intend to make
the men and women of Judah and Jerusalem your slaves.[u] But aren't you also guilty
of sins against the LORD your God? 11Now
listen to me! Send back your fellow countrymen you have taken as prisoners, for the
LORD's fierce anger rests on you.[v]"

12Then some of the leaders in
Ephraim—Azariah son of Jehohanan,
Berekiah son of Meshillemoth, Jehizkiah
son of Shallum, and Amasa son of Had-
lai—confronted those who were arriving
from the war. 13"You must not bring those
prisoners here," they said, "or we will be
guilty before the LORD. Do you intend to
add to our sin and guilt? For our guilt is
already great, and his fierce anger rests on
Israel."

14So the soldiers gave up the prisoners
and plunder in the presence of the officials
and all the assembly. 15The men designated by name took the prisoners, and
from the plunder they clothed all who
were naked. They provided them with
clothes and sandals, food and drink,[w] and
healing balm. All those who were weak
they put on donkeys. So they took them
back to their fellow countrymen at Jericho,
the City of Palms,[x] and returned to Samaria.[y]

16At that time King Ahaz sent to the
king[p] of Assyria[z] for help. 17The Edomites[a] had again come and attacked Judah

28:1 [i]S 1Ch 3:13; Isa 1:1
28:2 [j]Ex 34:17
28:3 [k]S Jos 15:8 [l]S Lev 18:21; S 2Ki 3:27; Eze 20:26 [m]S Dt 18:9; 2Ch 33:2
28:5 [n]Isa 7:1
28:6 [o]S 2Ki 15:25,27 [p]ver 8; Isa 9:21; 11:13
28:8 [q]Dt 28:25-41 [r]2Ch 29:9
28:9 [s]Isa 10:6; 47:6; Zec 1:15 [t]Ezr 9:6; Rev 18:5
28:10 [u]Lev 25:39-46
28:11 [v]2Ch 11:4
28:15 [w]2Ki 6:22; Pr 25:21-22 [x]S Dt 34:3; S Jdg 1:16 [y]Lk 10:25-37
28:16 [z]S 2Ki 16:7; Eze 23:12
28:17 [a]Ps 137:7; Isa 34:5; 63:1; Jer 25:21; Eze 16:57; 25:12; Am 1:11

p*16* One Hebrew manuscript, Septuagint and Vulgate (see also 2 Kings 16:7); most Hebrew manuscripts *kings*

28:1–27 See 2Ki 16:1–20 and notes, though only the introduction and conclusion in the two accounts are strictly parallel. The reign of Ahaz is the only one for which the Chronicler does not mention a single redeeming feature. In his account the Chronicler appears to adopt explicit parallels from the speech of Abijah condemning the northern kingdom (ch. 13) in order to show that under Ahaz the southern kingdom had sunk to the same depths of apostasy. Judah's religious fidelity, of which Abijah had boasted, was completely overthrown under Ahaz.
28:1 *sixteen years.* 732–715 B.C., not including the coregency with Jotham (735–732).
28:2 *made cast idols.* Cf. 13:8.
28:3 *Valley of Ben Hinnom.* Cf. 33:6. Josiah put an end to the pagan practices observed there (2Ki 23:10). *sacrificed his sons.* See Lev 20:1–5; Jer 7:31–32. 2Ki 16:3 has the singular "son." Some have regarded the plural as a deliberate inflation on the part of the Chronicler to heighten the wickedness of Ahaz. However, some manuscripts of the Septuagint (the Greek translation of the OT) also have a plural in 2Ki 16:3, suggesting that the Chronicler may have faithfully copied the text before him.
28:5 Cf. 13:16–17. *God handed him over.* According to the Chronicler's view on immediate retribution, defeat in war is one of the results of disobedience (see note on 20:30). *also given into the hands of the king of Israel.* 2Ki 16:5–6 and Isa 7 make it clear that Rezin (king of Aram) and Pekah acted together against Judah. The Chronicler has chosen either to treat them separately or to report on two different episodes of the Aram-Israel coalition.
28:6 *Pekah.* Reigned over the northern kingdom 752–732 B.C. (see 2Ki 15:27–31). *had forsaken the LORD.* The same charge Abijah made against the northern kingdom (13:11).
28:9–15 The kindness of the northern captors to their captives from Judah, especially as recorded in vv. 14–15, may be the background for Jesus' parable of the Good Samaritan (Lk 10:25–37). Oded's attitude to the north is shown by his willingness to call them "fellow countrymen" (v. 11). In this case, too, the record of ch. 13 has been reversed: The northern tribes are more righteous than the south.
28:17–18 *Edomites . . . attacked Judah . . . Philistines had*

and carried away prisoners,[b] 18while the Philistines[c] had raided towns in the foothills and in the Negev of Judah. They captured and occupied Beth Shemesh, Aijalon[d] and Gederoth,[e] as well as Soco,[f] Timnah[g] and Gimzo, with their surrounding villages. 19The LORD had humbled Judah because of Ahaz king of Israel,[q] for he had promoted wickedness in Judah and had been most unfaithful[h] to the LORD. 20Tiglath-Pileser[r][i] king of Assyria[j] came to him, but he gave him trouble[k] instead of help.[l] 21Ahaz[m] took some of the things from the temple of the LORD and from the royal palace and from the princes and presented them to the king of Assyria, but that did not help him.[n]

22In his time of trouble King Ahaz became even more unfaithful[o] to the LORD. 23He offered sacrifices to the gods[p] of Damascus, who had defeated him; for he thought, "Since the gods of the kings of Aram have helped them, I will sacrifice to them so they will help me."[q] But they were his downfall and the downfall of all Israel.[r]

24Ahaz gathered together the furnishings[s] from the temple of God[t] and took them away.[s] He shut the doors[u] of the LORD's temple and set up altars[v] at every street corner in Jerusalem. 25In every town in Judah he built high places to burn sacrifices to other gods and provoked the LORD, the God of his fathers, to anger.

26The other events of his reign and all his ways, from beginning to end, are written in the book of the kings of Judah and Israel. 27Ahaz rested[w] with his fathers and was buried[x] in the city of Jerusalem, but he was not placed in the tombs of the kings of Israel. And Hezekiah his son succeeded him as king.

Hezekiah Purifies the Temple

29:1–2pp — 2Ki 18:2–3

29 Hezekiah[y] was twenty-five years old when he became king, and he reigned in Jerusalem twenty-nine years. His mother's name was Abijah daughter of Zechariah. 2He did what was right in the eyes of the LORD, just as his father David[z] had done.

3In the first month of the first year of his reign, he opened the doors of the temple of the LORD and repaired[a] them. 4He brought in the priests and the Levites, assembled them in the square on the east side 5and

Cross references (center column)

28:17 [b]2Ch 29:9
28:18 [c]Isa 9:12; 11:14; Jer 25:20; Eze 16:27,57; 25:15
[d]S Jos 10:12
[e]Jos 15:41
[f]S 1Sa 17:1
[g]S Ge 38:12
28:19 [h]S 1Ch 5:25
28:20 [i]S 2Ki 15:29; S 1Ch 5:6
[j]Isa 7:17; 8:7; 10:5-6; 36:1
[k]Isa 10:20
[l]S 2Ki 16:7
28:21 [m]S 2Ch 16:2-9
[n]Jer 2:36
28:22 [o]Jer 5:3; 15:7; 17:23
28:23 [p]S 2Ch 25:14
[q]Isa 10:20; Jer 44:17-18
[r]1Ch 11:1; Jer 18:15
28:24 [s]2Ch 29:19
[t]S 2Ki 16:18
[u]Mal 1:10
[v]2Ch 30:14
28:27 [w]Isa 14:28-32
[x]S 2Ch 21:20
29:1 [y]S 1Ch 3:13
29:2 [z]2Ch 34:2
29:3 [a]2Ki 18:16

Footnotes (center column)

[q]19 That is, Judah, as frequently in 2 Chronicles
[r]20 Hebrew *Tilgath-Pilneser*, a variant of *Tiglath-Pileser*
[s]24 Or *and cut them up*

---

raided. Foreign alliances (v. 16) led to further defeats for Ahaz (see note on 16:2–9).

28:19 *The LORD had humbled Judah because of Ahaz.* The same formula used to describe the defeat of the northern tribes in 13:18, though under Ahaz it is Judah that is subdued.

28:20 *Tiglath-Pileser.* King of Assyria 745–727 B.C. (see 1Ch 5:26 and note). *trouble instead of help.* Appears on the surface to contradict the statement in 2Ki 16:9 that Tiglath-Pileser III responded to Ahaz's request by attacking and capturing Damascus, exiling its population and killing Rezin. The Chronicler assumes the reader's familiarity with the other account and knows of the temporary respite for Judah gained by Assyrian intervention against Damascus and the northern kingdom of Israel. But he focuses on the long-range results, in which Judah herself was reduced to vassalage to Assyria.

28:22–23 The Chronicler presumes the reader's familiarity with Ahaz's trip to Damascus and his copying of the altar and practices there (2Ki 16:10–16).

28:24–25 Additional details on Ahaz's alterations are found in 2Ki 16:17–18. The Chronicler also adds details in his description of Hezekiah's reforming activities to correct some of the abuses under Ahaz: Not only had the doors been shut, but also the lamps were put out and offerings were not made at the sanctuary (29:7); the altar and utensils were desecrated, and the table for the consecrated bread was neglected (29:18–19). It is precisely these accoutrements of proper temple service about which Abijah had boasted when he proclaimed the faithfulness of Judah in contrast to that of the northern kingdom (13:11). Now these orthodox furnishings are lacking under Ahaz and make the southern kingdom just like the north (see note on vv. 1–27).

28:27 *not placed in the tombs of the kings.* The third king

whose wickedness resulted in the loss of this honor at death. The others were Jehoram (21:20) and Joash (24:25). Uzziah's sin and leprosy brought the same result, though it is not reported in exactly the same terms (26:23). Cf. also Manasseh (33:20).

29:1–32:33 The Chronicler devotes more attention to Hezekiah than to any other post-Solomonic king. Although the parallel text (2Ki 18–20) has about the same amount of material, only about a fourth of the total relates the same or similar material; only a few verses are strict literary parallels (29:1–2; 32:32–33). In Kings preeminence among the post-Solomonic kings is given to Josiah (2Ki 22–23; cf. 1Ki 13:2), and the record of Hezekiah is primarily devoted to his confrontation with Sennacherib of Assyria. By contrast, the Chronicler highlights almost exclusively Hezekiah's religious reform and his devotion to matters of ceremony and ritual. The parallel passage (2Ki 18:1–6) touches the religious reform only briefly. The numerous parallels in these chapters with the account of Solomon's reign suggest that the Chronicler viewed Hezekiah as a "second Solomon" in his celebration of the Passover (30:2,5,23,25–26), his cultic arrangements (29:7,18,35; 31:2–3), his wealth (32:27–29), the honor accorded him by the Gentiles (32:23) and the extent of his dominion (30:25).

29:1 *twenty-nine years.* 715–686 B.C. (but see note on Isa 36:1), including a 15-year extension of life granted by God (2Ki 20:6) but not mentioned by the Chronicler.

29:3–30:27 Not found in Kings.

29:3 *first year.* 715 B.C., another example of the Chronicler's practice of introducing chronological materials into his narrative (see note on 12:2). *opened the doors of the temple.* Necessary after the actions of Ahaz (28:24). *repaired them.* The repairs to the doors included new gold overlay (2Ki 18:16).

said: "Listen to me, Levites! Consecrate[b] yourselves now and consecrate the temple of the LORD, the God of your fathers. Remove all defilement from the sanctuary. [6]Our fathers[c] were unfaithful;[d] they did evil in the eyes of the LORD our God and forsook him. They turned their faces away from the LORD's dwelling place and turned their backs on him. [7]They also shut the doors of the portico and put out the lamps. They did not burn incense[e] or present any burnt offerings at the sanctuary to the God of Israel. [8]Therefore, the anger of the LORD has fallen on Judah and Jerusalem; he has made them an object of dread and horror[f] and scorn,[g] as you can see with your own eyes. [9]This is why our fathers have fallen by the sword and why our sons and daughters and our wives are in captivity.[h] [10]Now I intend to make a covenant[i] with the LORD, the God of Israel, so that his fierce anger[j] will turn away from us. [11]My sons, do not be negligent now, for the LORD has chosen you to stand before him and serve him,[k] to minister[l] before him and to burn incense."

[12]Then these Levites[m] set to work:
from the Kohathites,
      Mahath son of Amasai and Joel son of Azariah;
from the Merarites,
      Kish son of Abdi and Azariah son of Jehallel;
from the Gershonites,
      Joah son of Zimmah and Eden[n] son of Joah;
[13]from the descendants of Elizaphan,[o]
      Shimri and Jeiel;
from the descendants of Asaph,[p]
      Zechariah and Mattaniah;
[14]from the descendants of Heman,
      Jehiel and Shimei;
from the descendants of Jeduthun,
      Shemaiah and Uzziel.

[15]When they had assembled their brothers and consecrated themselves, they went in to purify[q] the temple of the LORD, as the king had ordered, following the word

of the LORD. [16]The priests went into the sanctuary of the LORD to purify it. They brought out to the courtyard of the LORD's temple everything unclean that they found in the temple of the LORD. The Levites took it and carried it out to the Kidron Valley.[r] [17]They began the consecration on the first day of the first month, and by the eighth day of the month they reached the portico of the LORD. For eight more days they consecrated the temple of the LORD itself, finishing on the sixteenth day of the first month.

[18]Then they went in to King Hezekiah and reported: "We have purified the entire temple of the LORD, the altar of burnt offering with all its utensils, and the table for setting out the consecrated bread, with all its articles. [19]We have prepared and consecrated all the articles[s] that King Ahaz removed in his unfaithfulness while he was king. They are now in front of the LORD's altar."

[20]Early the next morning King Hezekiah gathered the city officials together and went up to the temple of the LORD. [21]They brought seven bulls, seven rams, seven male lambs and seven male goats[t] as a sin offering[u] for the kingdom, for the sanctuary and for Judah. The king commanded the priests, the descendants of Aaron, to offer these on the altar of the LORD. [22]So they slaughtered the bulls, and the priests took the blood and sprinkled it on the altar; next they slaughtered the rams and sprinkled their blood on the altar; then they slaughtered the lambs and sprinkled their blood[v] on the altar. [23]The goats[w] for the sin offering were brought before the king and the assembly, and they laid their hands[x] on them. [24]The priests then slaughtered the goats and presented their blood on the altar for a sin offering to atone[y] for all Israel, because the king had ordered the burnt offering and the sin offering for all Israel.[z]

[25]He stationed the Levites in the temple of the LORD with cymbals, harps and lyres

29:5
[b]S Lev 11:44; Ne 13:9
29:6 [c]Ezr 9:7; Ps 106:6-47; Jer 2:27; 18:17; Eze 23:35; Da 9:5-6
[d]S 1Ch 5:25
29:7 [e]S Ex 30:7
29:8 [f]S Dt 28:25
[g]S Lev 26:32; Jer 18:16; 19:8; 25:9,18
29:9 [h]2Ch 28:5-8,17
29:10 [i]S 2Ki 11:17; S 2Ch 23:16
[j]S Nu 25:4; 2Ch 30:8; Ezr 10:14
29:11 [k]S Nu 3:6; 8:6,14
[l]S 1Ch 15:2
29:12 [m]S Nu 3:17-20
[n]2Ch 31:15
29:13 [o]S Ex 6:22
[p]S 1Ch 6:39
29:15 [q]S 1Ch 23:28; S Isa 1:25

29:16 [r]S 2Sa 15:23
29:19 [s]2Ch 28:24
29:21 [t]Ezr 6:17; 8:35
[u]S Lev 4:13-14
29:22 [v]S Lev 4:18; Nu 18:17
29:23 [w]S Lev 16:5
[x]Lev 4:15
29:24 [y]S Ex 29:36; Lev 4:26
[z]1Ch 11:1; Ezr 8:35

29:5–11 Hezekiah's speech demonstrates again the Chronicler's convictions about the coherence of action and effect: The sins of the past brought difficulty and judgment, but renewed fidelity brings relief.
29:7 Hezekiah reinstitutes these temple arrangements—following the pattern of Solomon (2:4; 4:7).
29:8 *object of dread and horror and scorn.* Echoes the language of the prophets, especially Jeremiah (see Jer 19:8; 25:9,18; 29:18; 51:37). Reference is to the Assyrian devastation of the northern kingdom and much of Judah.
29:12 *Kohathites . . . Merarites . . . Gershonites.* The three clans of Levi (1Ch 6:1).
29:13–14 *Asaph . . . Heman . . . Jeduthun.* Founders of

the three families of Levitical musicians (1Ch 6:31–48; 25:1–31).
29:13 *Elizaphan.* A leader of the Kohathites (Nu 3:30), whose family had achieved status almost as a sub-clan (see 1Ch 15:8 and note on 1Ch 15:4–10).
29:16 *carried it out to the Kidron Valley.* Asa also burned pagan cult objects there (15:16; cf. 30:14).
29:18 These actions under Hezekiah mirror those of Solomon (2:4).
29:21 *sin offering.* See Lev 4:1–5:13.
29:22 *sprinkled their blood.* See Lev 17:6; Nu 18:17.
29:23 *laid their hands on them.* See Lev 4:13–15; 8:14–15; Nu 8:12.

in the way prescribed by David[a] and Gad[b] the king's seer and Nathan the prophet; this was commanded by the LORD through his prophets. 26So the Levites stood ready with David's instruments,[c] and the priests with their trumpets.[d]

27Hezekiah gave the order to sacrifice the burnt offering on the altar. As the offering began, singing to the LORD began also, accompanied by trumpets and the instruments[e] of David king of Israel. 28The whole assembly bowed in worship, while the singers sang and the trumpeters played. All this continued until the sacrifice of the burnt offering[f] was completed.

29When the offerings were finished, the king and everyone present with him knelt down and worshiped.[g] 30King Hezekiah and his officials ordered the Levites to praise the LORD with the words of David and of Asaph the seer. So they sang praises with gladness and bowed their heads and worshiped.

31Then Hezekiah said, "You have now dedicated yourselves to the LORD. Come and bring sacrifices[h] and thank offerings to the temple of the LORD." So the assembly brought sacrifices and thank offerings, and all whose hearts were willing[i] brought burnt offerings.

32The number of burnt offerings[j] the assembly brought was seventy bulls, a hundred rams and two hundred male lambs—all of them for burnt offerings to the LORD. 33The animals consecrated as sacrifices amounted to six hundred bulls and three thousand sheep and goats. 34The priests, however, were too few to skin all the burnt offerings;[k] so their kinsmen the

Levites helped them until the task was finished and until other priests had been consecrated,[l] for the Levites had been more conscientious in consecrating themselves than the priests had been. 35There were burnt offerings in abundance, together with the fat[m] of the fellowship offerings[t] [n] and the drink offerings[o] that accompanied the burnt offerings.

So the service of the temple of the LORD was reestablished. 36Hezekiah and all the people rejoiced at what God had brought about for his people, because it was done so quickly.[p]

Hezekiah Celebrates the Passover

30 Hezekiah sent word to all Israel[q] and Judah and also wrote letters to Ephraim and Manasseh,[r] inviting them to come to the temple of the LORD in Jerusalem and celebrate the Passover[s] to the LORD, the God of Israel. 2The king and his officials and the whole assembly in Jerusalem decided to celebrate[t] the Passover in the second month. 3They had not been able to celebrate it at the regular time because not enough priests had consecrated[u] themselves and the people had not assembled in Jerusalem. 4The plan seemed right both to the king and to the whole assembly. 5They decided to send a proclamation throughout Israel, from Beersheba to Dan,[v] calling the people to come to Jerusalem and celebrate the Passover to the LORD, the God of Israel. It had not been celebrated in large numbers according to what was written.

6At the king's command, couriers went

t 35 Traditionally peace offerings

Cross references (center column)

29:25
a S 1Ch 25:6;
28:19 b S 1Sa 22:5
29:26
c S 1Ch 15:16
d S 1Ch 15:24
29:27
e S 1Sa 16:16
29:28 f S 2Ch 2:4
29:29
g S 2Ch 20:18
29:31
h Heb 13:15-16
i S Ex 25:2; 35:22
29:32
j Lev 1:1-17
29:34 k Eze 44:11

l 2Ch 30:3,15
29:35 m S Ge 4:4;
S Ex 29:13
n Lev 7:11-21
o S Ge 35:14
29:36 p 2Ch 35:8
30:1 q S 1Ch 9:1
r S Ge 41:52
s S Ex 12:11;
S Nu 28:16
30:2 t Nu 9:10
30:3 u Nu 9:6-13;
S 2Ch 29:34
30:5 v S Jdg 20:1

29:25 *David and Gad . . . and Nathan . . . prophets.* The Chronicler considers David among the prophets (see notes on 1:7; 1Ch 28:19).

29:26 *David's instruments.* See 1Ch 23:5.

29:35 *burnt offerings in abundance . . . fellowship offerings . . . drink offerings.* Reminiscent of the dedication of the temple under Solomon (7:4–6). For the laws regarding the fellowship offerings see Lev 3; 7:11–21; for the drink offerings see Nu 15:1–12. *service of the temple of the LORD was reestablished.* Similar to the formula used in 8:16 with reference to Solomon's work.

30:1–27 Unique to the Chronicler; cf. the famous Passover under Josiah (35:1–19; 2Ki 23:21–23). Hezekiah allowed two deviations from the law (Ex 12; Dt 16:1–8) in this observance: (1) the date in the second month (v. 2) and (2) exemption from some ritual requirements (vv. 18–19).

30:1 *all Israel and Judah.* See Introduction to 1 Chronicles: Purpose and Themes. With the northern kingdom now ended as the result of the Assyrian invasion and deportation (which surprisingly is not mentioned), the Chronicler shows "all Israel" once again united around the Davidic king and the temple (see vv. 5,18–19,25).

30:2 *second month.* After the division of the kingdom, Jeroboam deferred the sacral calendar of the northern kingdom by one month (1Ki 12:32), possibly to further wean the subjects in the north away from devotion to Jerusalem. By delaying the celebration of Passover one month, Hezekiah not only allows time for the priests to consecrate themselves (v. 3) and for the people to gather (vv. 3,13), but also achieves unity between the kingdoms on the date of the Passover for the first time since the schism more than two centuries earlier. Delaying the date reflects Hezekiah's concern to involve "all Israel." For the first time since Solomon the entire nation observes Passover together, reflecting the Chronicler's view that Hezekiah is a "second Solomon." Passover was prescribed for the 14th day of the first month (Ex 12:2,6; Dt 16:1–8), but could not be celebrated at that time due to the defilement of the temple and the purification rites under way (29:3,17). For celebration of Passover by the restored community shortly after the dedication of the rebuilt temple see Ezr 6:16–22.

30:5 *large numbers.* Another comparison with the time of Solomon (see v. 26). At the time of its inception, Passover was primarily a family observance (Ex 12). It later became a national celebration at the temple (v. 8; see Dt 16:1–8).

throughout Israel and Judah with letters from the king and from his officials, which read:

"People of Israel, return to the LORD, the God of Abraham, Isaac and Israel, that he may return to you who are left, who have escaped from the hand of the kings of Assyria. [7]Do not be like your fathers[w] and brothers, who were unfaithful[x] to the LORD, the God of their fathers, so that he made them an object of horror,[y] as you see. [8]Do not be stiff-necked,[z] as your fathers were; submit to the LORD. Come to the sanctuary, which he has consecrated forever. Serve the LORD your God, so that his fierce anger[a] will turn away from you. [9]If you return[b] to the LORD, then your brothers and your children will be shown compassion[c] by their captors and will come back to this land, for the LORD your God is gracious and compassionate.[d] He will not turn his face from you if you return to him."

[10]The couriers went from town to town in Ephraim and Manasseh, as far as Zebulun, but the people scorned and ridiculed[e] them. [11]Nevertheless, some men of Asher, Manasseh and Zebulun humbled[f] themselves and went to Jerusalem.[g] [12]Also in Judah the hand of God was on the people to give them unity[h] of mind to carry out what the king and his officials had ordered, following the word of the LORD.

[13]A very large crowd of people assembled in Jerusalem to celebrate the Feast of Unleavened Bread[i] in the second month. [14]They removed the altars[j] in Jerusalem and cleared away the incense altars and threw them into the Kidron Valley.[k]

[15]They slaughtered the Passover lamb on the fourteenth day of the second month. The priests and the Levites were ashamed and consecrated[l] themselves and

brought burnt offerings to the temple of the LORD. [16]Then they took up their regular positions[m] as prescribed in the Law of Moses the man of God. The priests sprinkled the blood handed to them by the Levites. [17]Since many in the crowd had not consecrated themselves, the Levites had to kill[n] the Passover lambs for all those who were not ceremonially clean and could not consecrate their lambs to the LORD. [18]Although most of the many people who came from Ephraim, Manasseh, Issachar and Zebulun had not purified themselves,[o] yet they ate the Passover, contrary to what was written. But Hezekiah prayed for them, saying, "May the LORD, who is good, pardon everyone [19]who sets his heart on seeking God—the LORD, the God of his fathers—even if he is not clean according to the rules of the sanctuary." [20]And the LORD heard[p] Hezekiah and healed[q] the people.[r]

[21]The Israelites who were present in Jerusalem celebrated the Feast of Unleavened Bread[s] for seven days with great rejoicing, while the Levites and priests sang to the LORD every day, accompanied by the LORD's instruments of praise.[u]

[22]Hezekiah spoke encouragingly to all the Levites, who showed good understanding of the service of the LORD. For the seven days they ate their assigned portion and offered fellowship offerings[v] and praised the LORD, the God of their fathers.

[23]The whole assembly then agreed to celebrate[t] the festival seven more days; so for another seven days they celebrated joyfully. [24]Hezekiah king of Judah provided[u] a thousand bulls and seven thousand sheep and goats for the assembly, and the officials provided them with a thousand bulls and ten thousand sheep and goats. A great number of priests consecrated themselves.

30:7 wPs 78:8, 57; 106:6; Jer 11:10; Eze 20:18 xS 1Ch 5:25 yS Dt 28:25
30:8 zS Ex 32:9 aS Nu 25:4; S 2Ch 29:10
30:9 bDt 30:2-5; Isa 1:16; 55:7; Jer 25:5; Eze 33:11 cS Ex 3:21; S 1Ki 8:50 dS Ex 22:27; S Dt 4:31; S 2Ch 6:39; Mic 7:18
30:10 e2Ch 36:16
30:11 fS 2Ch 6:37 gver 25
30:12 hJer 32:39; Eze 11:19
30:13 iS Nu 28:16
30:14 j2Ch 28:24 kS 2Sa 15:23
30:15 lS 2Ch 29:34
30:16 m2Ch 35:10
30:17 n2Ch 35:11; Ezr 6:20
30:18 oEx 12:43-49; Nu 9:6-10
30:20 pS 2Ch 6:20 qS 2Ch 7:14; Mal 4:2 rJas 5:16 17; 13:6
30:23 t2Ch 7:9
30:24 u1Ki 8:5; 2Ch 35:7; Ezr 6:17; 8:35

u21 Or *priests praised the LORD every day with resounding instruments belonging to the LORD*
v22 Traditionally *peace offerings*

30:8 *Come to the sanctuary.* Passover was one of three annual pilgrim feasts requiring attendance at the temple (see Nu 28:9–29:39).
30:9 *shown compassion by their captors.* In Solomon's prayer in 6:39 the Chronicler omitted the phrase found in the parallel account (1Ki 8:50) that their conquerors would "show them mercy." Here the phrase is found in the speech of Hezekiah, again portraying him as a kind of "second Solomon" (see Lev 26:40–42). *will come back to this land.* Those who repent will have hope of return, even those from the Assyrian captivity.
30:14 *threw them into the Kidron Valley.* See 29:16 and note.
30:15 *The priests and the Levites . . . consecrated themselves.* The reproach previously directed against the priests

(v. 3; 29:34) is here broadened to include also the Levites—an exhortation to the priests and Levites of the restored community to be faithful.
30:17 *Levites had to kill the Passover lambs.* See Ex 12:6; Dt 16:6. According to the law the heads of families were to slay the Passover sacrifice. The Levites perhaps acted for the recent arrivals from the northern kingdom who were not ceremonially clean. Cf. Jn 11:55.
30:18–19 Faith and obedience take precedence over ritual (see Mk 7:1–23; Jn 7:22–23; 9:14–16).
30:20 The response to Hezekiah's prayer recalls the prayer of Solomon (7:14).
30:23 *another seven days.* The festival was observed for two weeks, just as the observance of the dedication of Solomon's temple had been (7:8–9).

25The entire assembly of Judah rejoiced, along with the priests and Levites and all who had assembled from Israel[v], including the aliens who had come from Israel and those who lived in Judah. 26There was great joy in Jerusalem, for since the days of Solomon[w] son of David king of Israel there had been nothing like this in Jerusalem. 27The priests and the Levites stood to bless[x] the people, and God heard them, for their prayer reached heaven, his holy dwelling place.

31 When all this had ended, the Israelites who were there went out to the towns of Judah, smashed the sacred stones and cut down[y] the Asherah poles. They destroyed the high places and the altars throughout Judah and Benjamin and in Ephraim and Manasseh. After they had destroyed all of them, the Israelites returned to their own towns and to their own property.

Contributions for Worship

31:20–21pp — 2Ki 18:5–7

2Hezekiah[z] assigned the priests and Levites to divisions[a]—each of them according to their duties as priests or Levites—to offer burnt offerings and fellowship offerings,[w] to minister,[b] to give thanks and to sing praises[c] at the gates of the LORD's dwelling.[d] 3The king contributed[e] from his own possessions for the morning and evening burnt offerings and for the burnt offerings on the Sabbaths, New Moons and appointed feasts as written in the Law of the LORD.[f] 4He ordered the people living in Jerusalem to give the portion[g] due the priests and Levites so they could devote themselves to the Law of the LORD. 5As soon as the order went out, the Israelites generously gave the firstfruits[h] of their grain, new wine,[i] oil and honey and all

that the fields produced. They brought a great amount, a tithe of everything. 6The men of Israel and Judah who lived in the towns of Judah also brought a tithe[j] of their herds and flocks and a tithe of the holy things dedicated to the LORD their God, and they piled them in heaps.[k] 7They began doing this in the third month and finished in the seventh month.[l] 8When Hezekiah and his officials came and saw the heaps, they praised the LORD and blessed[m] his people Israel.

9Hezekiah asked the priests and Levites about the heaps; 10and Azariah the chief priest, from the family of Zadok,[n] answered, "Since the people began to bring their contributions to the temple of the LORD, we have had enough to eat and plenty to spare, because the LORD has blessed his people, and this great amount is left over."[o]

11Hezekiah gave orders to prepare storerooms in the temple of the LORD, and this was done. 12Then they faithfully brought in the contributions, tithes and dedicated gifts. Conaniah,[p] a Levite, was in charge of these things, and his brother Shimei was next in rank. 13Jehiel, Azaziah, Nahath, Asahel, Jerimoth, Jozabad,[q] Eliel, Ismakiah, Mahath and Benaiah were supervisors under Conaniah and Shimei his brother, by appointment of King Hezekiah and Azariah the official in charge of the temple of God.

14Kore son of Imnah the Levite, keeper of the East Gate, was in charge of the freewill offerings given to God, distributing the contributions made to the LORD and also the consecrated gifts. 15Eden,[r] Miniamin, Jeshua, Shemaiah, Amariah and Shecaniah assisted him faithfully in the towns[s] of the priests, distributing to their fellow priests

Cross references

30:25 vver 11
30:26 wS 2Ch 7:8
30:27 xS Ex 39:43
31:1 yS 2Ki 18:4; 2Ch 32:12; Isa 36:7
31:2 zS 2Ch 29:9 aS 1Ch 24:1 bS 1Ch 15:2 cPs 7:17; 9:2; 47:6; 71:22 dS 1Ch 23:28-32
31:3 eS 1Ch 29:3; 2Ch 35:7; Eze 45:17 fNu 28:1-29:40
31:4 gS Nu 18:8; S Dt 18:8; Ne 13:10
31:5 hS Nu 18:12,24; Ne 13:12; Eze 44:30 iDt 12:17
31:6 jS Lev 27:30; Ne 13:10-12 kS Ru 3:7
31:7 lEx 23:16
31:8 mPs 144:13-15
31:10 nS 2Sa 8:17 oS Ex 36:5; Eze 44:30; Mal 3:10-12
31:12 pS 2Ch 35:9
31:13 qS 2Ch 35:9
31:15 rS 2Ch 29:12 sJos 21:9-19

w2 Traditionally *peace offerings*

Study notes

30:26 *since the days of Solomon.* An explicit indication of the Chronicler's modeling of the reign of Hezekiah after that of Solomon (see note on 29:1–32:33).

30:27 *prayer reached heaven, his holy dwelling place.* Another echo of Solomon's dedication prayer (6:21,30,33, 39).

31:1–21 Apart from the first verse, which parallels 2Ki 18:4, the material of this chapter is unique to the Chronicler, whose interest in the Levites and the temple predominates. Hezekiah's efforts to ensure the material support of the Levites (v. 4) probably had relevance to the postexilic audience for whom the Chronicler wrote.

31:1 *the Israelites . . . the Israelites.* Lit. "all Israel . . . all the Israelites." The Chronicler's interest in "all Israel" as united under Hezekiah is again apparent. *sacred stones.* See note on 1Ki 14:23. *Asherah poles.* See NIV text note on 14:3.

31:2 Echoes 8:14. The Chronicler continues to model Hezekiah as a "second Solomon" (see notes on 29:7,18).

31:3 *king contributed.* The king's giving from his own wealth prompted a generous response from the people, as it had also under David (1Ch 29:3–9).

31:5–6 See Dt 12:5–19; 14:22–27. The grain, new wine and oil had to be brought to the temple (Dt 12:17). Those coming from a distance, however, could bring the value of their offerings and purchase them on arrival (Dt 14:24). Only those who actually lived in Judah brought the tithe of their herds and flocks, a difficult procedure for those who lived farther away. For the restored community's commitment to bring their firstfruits, tithes and offerings see Ne 10:35–39. For their failure to do so see Ne 13:10–13; Mal 3:8–10.

31:7 *third month.* May-June, the time of the Feast of Pentecost and the grain harvest. *seventh month.* September-October, the time of the Feast of Tabernacles and the fruit and vine harvest (see Ex 23:16).

according to their divisions, old and young alike.

[16]In addition, they distributed to the males three years old or more whose names were in the genealogical records [t]—all who would enter the temple of the LORD to perform the daily duties of their various tasks, according to their responsibilities and their divisions. [17]And they distributed to the priests enrolled by their families in the genealogical records and likewise to the Levites twenty years old or more, according to their responsibilities and their divisions. [18]They included all the little ones, the wives, and the sons and daughters of the whole community listed in these genealogical records. For they were faithful in consecrating themselves.

[19]As for the priests, the descendants of Aaron, who lived on the farm lands around their towns or in any other towns, [u] men were designated by name to distribute portions to every male among them and to all who were recorded in the genealogies of the Levites.

[20]This is what Hezekiah did throughout Judah, doing what was good and right and faithful [v] before the LORD his God. [21]In everything that he undertook in the service of God's temple and in obedience to the law and the commands, he sought his God and worked wholeheartedly. And so he prospered. [w]

Sennacherib Threatens Jerusalem

32:9–19pp — 2Ki 18:17–35; Isa 36:2–20
32:20–21pp — 2Ki 19:35–37; Isa 37:36–38

32 After all that Hezekiah had so faithfully done, Sennacherib [x] king of Assyria came and invaded Judah. He laid siege to the fortified cities, thinking to conquer them for himself. [2]When Hezekiah saw that Sennacherib had come and that he intended to make war on Jerusalem, [y]

Cross-references column
31:16 [t]1Ch 23:3
31:19
[u]S Nu 35:2-5
31:20
[v]S 2Ki 20:3
31:21 [w]S Dt 29:9
32:1 [x]Isa 36:1; 37:9,17,37
32:2 [y]Isa 22:7; Jer 1:15

32:4
[z]S 2Ki 18:17; Isa 22:9,11; Na 3:14
32:5 [a]Isa 22:10
[b]S 1Ch 11:8
[c]Isa 22:8
32:7 [d]S Dt 31:6
[e]2Ch 20:15
[f]S Nu 14:9; 2Ki 6:16
32:8 [g]Job 40:9; Isa 52:10;
Jer 17:5; 32:21
[h]S Dt 3:22; S 1Sa 17:45
[i]S 1Ch 5:22; Ps 20:7; Isa 28:6
32:9 [j]S Jos 10:3,31
32:10 [k]Eze 29:16
32:11 [l]Isa 37:10

[3]he consulted with his officials and military staff about blocking off the water from the springs outside the city, and they helped him. [4]A large force of men assembled, and they blocked all the springs [z] and the stream that flowed through the land. "Why should the kings [x] of Assyria come and find plenty of water?" they said. [5]Then he worked hard repairing all the broken sections of the wall [a] and building towers on it. He built another wall outside that one and reinforced the supporting terraces [y][b] of the City of David. He also made large numbers of weapons [c] and shields.

[6]He appointed military officers over the people and assembled them before him in the square at the city gate and encouraged them with these words: [7]"Be strong and courageous. [d] Do not be afraid or discouraged [e] because of the king of Assyria and the vast army with him, for there is a greater power with us than with him. [f] [8]With him is only the arm of flesh, [g] but with us [h] is the LORD our God to help us and to fight our battles." [i] And the people gained confidence from what Hezekiah the king of Judah said.

[9]Later, when Sennacherib king of Assyria and all his forces were laying siege to Lachish, [j] he sent his officers to Jerusalem with this message for Hezekiah king of Judah and for all the people of Judah who were there:

[10]"This is what Sennacherib king of Assyria says: On what are you basing your confidence, [k] that you remain in Jerusalem under siege? [11]When Hezekiah says, 'The LORD our God will save us from the hand of the king of Assyria,' he is misleading [l] you, to let you die of hunger and thirst. [12]Did not Hezekiah himself remove this god's high places and altars, saying to Judah

[x]4 Hebrew; Septuagint and Syriac *king*   [y]5 Or the *Millo*

31:16 *three years.* Although no ancient versions or manuscripts disagree with this figure, it may represent a copyist's mistake for "30 years," the age at which duties were assigned in the temple (1Ch 23:3).

31:20–21 Another brief indication of the Chronicler's emphasis on immediate retribution: Not only does disobedience bring immediate chastening, but obedience and seeking God bring prosperity.

32:1–23 The record of Sennacherib's invasion is much more detailed in 2 Kings and Isaiah (see note on 29:1–32:33).

32:1 The Chronicler omits the date of the invasion (701 B.C., Hezekiah's 14th year; see 2Ki 18:13; Isa 36:1).

32:2–8 Unique to the Chronicler, but normal preparations for invasion.

32:3–4 See v. 30.

32:9 The Chronicler bypasses 2Ki 18:14–16, which records Hezekiah's suit for peace with its accompanying bribe stripped from the temple treasures. These acts were apparently out of accord with the Chronicler's portrait of Hezekiah. He also omits 2Ki 18:17b–18.

32:10 The Chronicler omits 2Ki 18:20–21 (and Isa 36:5–6), containing a portion of the Assyrian commander's speech ridiculing Hezekiah and the citizens of Jerusalem for trusting in Egypt and Pharaoh. This, too, may be theologically motivated, in light of the Chronicler's attitude toward foreign alliances (see note on 16:2–9). The same concern with foreign alliances is also likely the reason for the omission of the material in 2Ki 18:23–27 (and Isa 36:8–12), where mention is again made of the hope of Egyptian intervention (see 2Ki 19:9 for the incursion of Tirhakah).

and Jerusalem, 'You must worship before one altar *m* and burn sacrifices on it'?

13"Do you not know what I and my fathers have done to all the peoples of the other lands? Were the gods of those nations ever able to deliver their land from my hand? *n* 14Who of all the gods of these nations that my fathers destroyed has been able to save his people from me? How then can your god deliver you from my hand? 15Now do not let Hezekiah deceive *o* you and mislead you like this. Do not believe him, for no god of any nation or kingdom has been able to deliver *p* his people from my hand or the hand of my fathers. *q* How much less will your god deliver you from my hand!"

16Sennacherib's officers spoke further against the LORD God and against his servant Hezekiah. 17The king also wrote letters *r* insulting *s* the LORD, the God of Israel, and saying this against him: "Just as the gods *t* of the peoples of the other lands did not rescue their people from my hand, so the god of Hezekiah will not rescue his people from my hand." 18Then they called out in Hebrew to the people of Jerusalem who were on the wall, to terrify them and make them afraid in order to capture the city. 19They spoke about the God of Jerusalem as they did about the gods of the other peoples of the world—the work of men's hands. *u*

20King Hezekiah and the prophet Isaiah son of Amoz cried out in prayer *v* to heaven about this. 21And the LORD sent an angel, *w* who annihilated all the fighting men and the leaders and officers in the camp of the Assyrian king. So he withdrew to his own land in disgrace. And when he went into the temple of his god, some of his sons cut him down with the sword. *x* 22So the LORD saved Hezekiah and the

people of Jerusalem from the hand of Sennacherib king of Assyria and from the hand of all others. He took care of them *z* on every side. 23Many brought offerings to Jerusalem for the LORD and valuable gifts *y* for Hezekiah king of Judah. From then on he was highly regarded by all the nations.

Hezekiah's Pride, Success and Death
32:24–33pp — 2Ki 20:1–21; Isa 37:21–38; 38:1–8

24In those days Hezekiah became ill and was at the point of death. He prayed to the LORD, who answered him and gave him a miraculous sign. *z* 25But Hezekiah's heart was proud *a* and he did not respond to the kindness shown him; therefore the LORD's wrath *b* was on him and on Judah and Jerusalem. 26Then Hezekiah repented *c* of the pride of his heart, as did the people of Jerusalem; therefore the LORD's wrath did not come upon them during the days of Hezekiah. *d*

27Hezekiah had very great riches and honor, *e* and he made treasuries for his silver and gold and for his precious stones, spices, shields and all kinds of valuables. 28He also made buildings to store the harvest of grain, new wine and oil; and he made stalls for various kinds of cattle, and pens for the flocks. 29He built villages and acquired great numbers of flocks and herds, for God had given him very great riches. *f*

30It was Hezekiah who blocked *g* the upper outlet of the Gihon *h* spring and channeled *i* the water down to the west side of the City of David. He succeeded in everything he undertook. 31But when envoys were sent by the rulers of Babylon *j* to ask him about the miraculous sign *k* that had occurred in the land, God left him to test *l* him and to know everything that was in his heart.

32The other events of Hezekiah's reign

z 22 Hebrew; Septuagint and Vulgate He gave them rest

32:12
m S 2Ch 31:1
32:13 *n* ver 15
32:15 *o* Isa 37:10
p Da 3:15 *q* Ex 5:2
32:17 *r* Isa 37:14
s Ps 74:22;
Isa 37:4,17
t S 2Ki 19:12
32:19 *u* Ps 115:4,
4-8; Isa 2:8;
17:8; 37:19;
Jer 1:16
32:20 *v* Isa 1:15;
37:15
32:21
w S Ge 19:13
x S 2Ki 19:7;
Isa 37:7,38;
Jer 41:2

32:23
y S 1Sa 10:27;
S 2Ch 9:24;
Ps 68:18,29;
76:11; Isa 16:1;
18:7; 45:14;
Zep 3:10;
Zec 14:16-17
32:24 *z* ver 31
32:25
a S 2Ki 14:10
b S 2Ch 19:2
32:26
c Jer 26:18-19
d 2Ch 34:27,28;
Isa 39:8
32:27
e S 1Ch 29:12;
S 2Ch 9:24
32:29 *f* Isa 39:2
32:30
g S 2Ki 18:17
h S 1Ki 1:33
i S 2Sa 5:8
32:31 *j* Isa 13:1;
39:1 *k* S ver 24;
Isa 38:7
l S Ge 22:1;
Dt 8:16

32:16 *spoke further.* The Chronicler appears to assume his reader's familiarity with the longer account of the Assyrian taunts found in Kings and Isaiah.

32:18 *called out in Hebrew.* Assumes knowledge of the fuller story (2Ki 18:26–28; Isa 36:11–13).

32:20 This brief reference to the prayers of Hezekiah and Isaiah abridges the much longer narrative in 2Ki 19:1–34 (and Isa 37:1–35).

32:21 See 2Ki 19:35–37; Isa 37:36–38. The Chronicler and the parallel accounts telescope events somewhat: Sennacherib's invasion of Judah was in 701 B.C., while his death at the hand of his sons was in 681.

32:23 *highly regarded by all the nations.* Another effort to compare Hezekiah with Solomon (see 9:23–24).

32:24 The Chronicler again abridges the narrative in 2Ki 20:1–11 (and Isa 38:1–8), assuming the reader's familiarity

with the role of Isaiah and the miraculous sign of the shadow reversing ten steps.

32:25–30 Not found in the parallel texts.

32:25–26 *proud . . . pride.* The Chronicler does not specify the nature of Hezekiah's pride (however, see v. 31; 2Ki 20:12–13; Isa 39:1–2). Even for a "second Solomon" like Hezekiah, disobedience brings anger from the Lord.

32:27–29 The Chronicler likens Hezekiah to Solomon also by recounting his wealth (9:13–14).

32:30 See vv. 2–4; 2Ki 20:20.

32:31 See v. 25. The Chronicler assumes the reader's knowledge of the fuller account in 2Ki 20:12–19 (and Isa 39:1–8). The envoys from Babylon were apparently interested in joint efforts against the Assyrians, hoping to open two fronts against them simultaneously.

and his acts of devotion are written in the vision of the prophet Isaiah son of Amoz in the book of the kings of Judah and Israel. [33]Hezekiah rested with his fathers and was buried on the hill where the tombs of David's descendants are. All Judah and the people of Jerusalem honored him when he died. And Manasseh his son succeeded him as king.

Manasseh King of Judah

33:1–10pp — 2Ki 21:1–10
33:18–20pp — 2Ki 21:17–18

33 Manasseh [m] was twelve years old when he became king, and he reigned in Jerusalem fifty-five years. [2]He did evil in the eyes of the LORD, [n] following the detestable [o] practices of the nations the LORD had driven out before the Israelites. [3]He rebuilt the high places his father Hezekiah had demolished; he also erected altars to the Baals and made Asherah poles. [p] He bowed down [q] to all the starry hosts and worshiped them. [4]He built altars in the temple of the LORD, of which the LORD had said, "My Name [r] will remain in Jerusalem forever." [5]In both courts of the temple of the LORD, [s] he built altars to all the starry hosts. [6]He sacrificed his sons [t] in [a] the fire in the Valley of Ben Hinnom, practiced sorcery, divination and witchcraft, and consulted mediums [u] and spiritists. [v] He did much evil in the eyes of the LORD, provoking him to anger.

[7]He took the carved image he had made and put it in God's temple, [w] of which God had said to David and to his son Solomon,

"In this temple and in Jerusalem, which I have chosen out of all the tribes of Israel, I will put my Name forever. [8]I will not again make the feet of the Israelites leave the land [x] I assigned to your forefathers, if only they will be careful to do everything I commanded them concerning all the laws, decrees and ordinances given through Moses." [9]But Manasseh led Judah and the people of Jerusalem astray, so that they did more evil than the nations the LORD had destroyed before the Israelites. [y]

[10]The LORD spoke to Manasseh and his people, but they paid no attention. [11]So the LORD brought against them the army commanders of the king of Assyria, who took Manasseh prisoner, [z] put a hook [a] in his nose, bound him with bronze shackles [b] and took him to Babylon. [12]In his distress he sought the favor of the LORD his God and humbled [c] himself greatly before the God of his fathers. [13]And when he prayed to him, the LORD was moved by his entreaty and listened to his plea; so he brought him back to Jerusalem and to his kingdom. Then Manasseh knew that the LORD is God.

[14]Afterward he rebuilt the outer wall of the City of David, west of the Gihon [d] spring in the valley, as far as the entrance of the Fish Gate [e] and encircling the hill of Ophel; [f] he also made it much higher. He stationed military commanders in all the fortified cities in Judah.

[15]He got rid of the foreign gods and re-

Cross references (center column)

33:1 [m] 1Ch 3:13
33:2 [n] Jer 15:4
[o] S Dt 18:9
33:3 [p] Dt 16:21-22; S 2Ch 24:18
[q] Dt 17:3
33:4 [r] 2Ch 7:16
33:5 [s] S 2Ch 4:9
33:6 [t] S Lev 18:21; S Dt 18:10
[u] S Ex 22:18; S Lev 19:31
[v] 1Sa 28:13
33:7 [w] S 2Ch 7:16
33:8 [x] S 2Sa 7:10
33:9 [y] Jer 15:4; Eze 5:7
33:11 [z] S Dt 28:36
[a] S 2Ki 19:28; Isa 37:29; Eze 29:4; 38:4; Am 4:2 [b] Ps 149:8
33:12 [c] S 2Ch 6:37
33:14 [d] S 1Ki 1:33
[e] Ne 3:3; 12:39; Zep 1:10
[f] 2Ch 27:3; Ne 3:26

[a] 6 Or *He made his sons pass through*

33:1–20 See 2Ki 21:1–18 and notes. Manasseh had the longest reign of any of the kings of Judah, a total of 55 years (v. 1). The emphasis in the two accounts differs: While both histories report at length the evil done in Manasseh's reign, only the Chronicler mentions his journey to Babylon and his repentance and restoration to rule. For the writer of Kings, the picture is only a bad one in which Manasseh could be considered almost single-handedly the cause of the exile (2Ki 21:10–15; 23:26). Some scholars regard the record of Manasseh's repentance in Chronicles as motivated by the author's emphasis on immediate retribution: Length of reign is viewed as a blessing for obedience, so that the Chronicler deliberately records some good in Manasseh as a ground for his long reign. However, it must be noted that length of reign is not elsewhere used by the Chronicler as an indication of divine blessing. The usual indicators for such blessing in his account are peace and prosperity, building projects, success in warfare and large families.
33:1 *fifty-five years.* 697–642 B.C.
33:3 *Asherah poles.* See NIV text note on 14:3.
33:6 *sacrificed his sons.* See 28:3–4.
33:10 See note on vv. 1–20. The Chronicler abridges what the Lord said to Manasseh and the people through the prophets; the fuller record is found in 2Ki 21:10–15.
33:11–17 Unique to the Chronicler, showing his stress on immediate retribution: Manasseh's evil brings invasion and

defeat, while his repentance brings restoration to rule.
33:11 *took him to Babylon.* In extant non-Biblical records there is no reference as yet to Manasseh being taken to Babylon by an Assyrian king. Esarhaddon (681–669 B.C.) lists him among 22 kings required to forward materials for his building projects, and Ashurbanipal (669–627) names him as one of a number of vassals supporting his campaign against Egypt. The fact that an Assyrian king would have him taken to Babylon suggests that this incident may have taken place during the rebellion of Shamash-Shum-Ukin against his brother and overlord Ashurbanipal. This rebellion lasted from 652 to 648, and Manasseh may have joined or at least have been suspected of assisting in the Babylonian defection from Assyria. Manasseh may have been found innocent, or he may have been pardoned on the basis of a renewed pledge of loyalty. Egypt had also bolted from the Assyrian yoke under the new 26th dynasty, and the return of Manasseh to rule may reflect the Assyrian need of a vassal near the border of Egypt.
33:12 The language is reminiscent of Solomon's prayer (7:14).
33:14 *rebuilt the outer wall.* For the Chronicler such building programs are a sign of divine blessing (8:1–6; 11:5–12; 14:6–7; 26:9–10,14–15; 32:1–5,27–30; 1Ch 11:7–9; 15:1).
33:15–16 Whatever the precise nature of Manasseh's re-

moved[g] the image from the temple of the LORD, as well as all the altars he had built on the temple hill and in Jerusalem; and he threw them out of the city. [16]Then he restored the altar of the LORD and sacrificed fellowship offerings[b] and thank offerings[h] on it, and told Judah to serve the LORD, the God of Israel. [17]The people, however, continued to sacrifice at the high places, but only to the LORD their God.

[18]The other events of Manasseh's reign, including his prayer to his God and the words the seers spoke to him in the name of the LORD, the God of Israel, are written in the annals of the kings of Israel.[c] [19]His prayer and how God was moved by his entreaty, as well as all his sins and unfaithfulness, and the sites where he built high places and set up Asherah poles and idols before he humbled[i] himself—all are written in the records of the seers.[d] [20]Manasseh rested with his fathers and was buried[k] in his palace. And Amon his son succeeded him as king.

Amon King of Judah

33:21–25pp — 2Ki 21:19–24

[21]Amon[l] was twenty-two years old when he became king, and he reigned in Jerusalem two years. [22]He did evil in the eyes of the LORD, as his father Manasseh had done. Amon worshiped and offered sacrifices to all the idols Manasseh had made. [23]But unlike his father Manasseh, he

did not humble[m] himself before the LORD; Amon increased his guilt.

[24]Amon's officials conspired against him and assassinated him in his palace. [25]Then the people[n] of the land killed all who had plotted against King Amon, and they made Josiah his son king in his place.

Josiah's Reforms

34:1–2pp — 2Ki 22:1–2
34:3–7Ref — 2Ki 23:4–20
34:8–13pp — 2Ki 22:3–7

34 Josiah[o] was eight years old when he became king,[p] and he reigned in Jerusalem thirty-one years. [2]He did what was right in the eyes of the LORD and walked in the ways of his father David,[q] not turning aside to the right or to the left.

[3]In the eighth year of his reign, while he was still young, he began to seek the God[r] of his father David. In his twelfth year he began to purge Judah and Jerusalem of high places, Asherah poles, carved idols and cast images. [4]Under his direction the altars of the Baals were torn down; he cut to pieces the incense altars that were above them, and smashed the Asherah poles,[s] the idols and the images. These he broke to pieces and scattered over the graves of those who had sacrificed to them.[t] [5]He burned[u] the bones of the

Cross references (center column)

33:15 g2Ki 23:12
33:16
hLev 7:11-18
33:19
iS 2Ch 6:37
j2Ki 21:17
33:20
k2Ki 21:18;
S 2Ch 21:20
33:21
iS 1Ch 3:14

33:23
mS Ex 10:3;
2Ch 7:14;
Ps 18:27; 147:6;
Pr 3:34
33:25
nS 2Ch 22:1
34:1 oS 1Ch 3:14
pZep 1:1
34:2 q2Ch 29:2
34:3
rS 1Ch 16:11
34:4 sS Ex 34:13
tEx 32:20;
S Lev 26:30;
2Ki 23:11;
Mic 1:5
34:5 uS 1Ki 13:2

b16 Traditionally *peace offerings*   c18 That is, Judah, as frequently in 2 Chron.   d19 One Hebrew manuscript and Septuagint; most Hebrew manuscripts *of Hozai*

---

forms, Josiah would later still need to remove "the altars Manasseh had built in the two courts of the temple" (2Ki 23:12).

33:19 *Asherah poles.* See NIV text note on 14:3.

33:20 *buried in his palace.* Cf. 2Ki 21:18. His burial in the palace garden makes Manasseh the fifth king the Chronicler names who was not buried in the tombs of the kings (see note on 28:27).

33:21–25 See 2Ki 21:19–26. The Chronicler's account of the reign of Amon (642–640 B.C.) is quite similar to that in Kings, apart from (1) the additional note that Amon was not repentant like his father Manasseh, a note based on a passage unique to the Chronicler (vv. 12–13), and (2) the absence of the death formula.

34:1–36:1 See 2Ki 22:1–23:30 and notes. Both accounts of Josiah's reign are about the same length and treat the same subjects, but with considerable variation in emphasis. Both deal with three different aspects of Josiah's reform: (1) the removal of foreign cults, (2) the finding of the Book of the Law and the covenant renewal that followed and (3) the celebration of Passover. On the second item the two histories are quite similar. On the first item the writer of Kings goes to great lengths (2Ki 23:4–20), while the Chronicler summarizes it only briefly (34:3–7,33). The account of the Passover is greatly expanded in Chronicles (35:1–19), while only alluded to in 2 Kings (23:21–23). Not only are these items treated at different lengths, but the order is also changed. In Kings the finding of the Book of the Law in the temple in Josiah's 18th year is the first incident mentioned. The writer

appears to have organized his material geographically, i.e., beginning with the temple and spreading through the city, then into the rest of the nation. The Chronicler, on the other hand, has arranged the incidents in order of their occurrence and has characteristically introduced a number of chronological notes into the text: 34:3 (two notes without parallel in Kings); 34:8 (see 2Ki 22:3); 35:19 (see 2Ki 23:23; see also note on 2Ch 12:2). Chronicles makes it clear that the reform began in Josiah's 12th year (34:3), six years before the discovery of the Book of the Law.

34:1–2 See 2Ki 22:1–2.

34:1 *thirty-one years.* 640–609 B.C.

34:3–7 The writer of Kings covers this aspect of Josiah's reform in much greater detail (2Ki 23:4–20). He also delays his account of the removal of pagan cults until after the discovery of the Book of the Law, while the Chronicler places it before.

34:3 Some scholars have sought to tie the events of Josiah's 8th (v. 3), 12th (v. 3) and 18th (v. 8) years to stages in the progressive decline and fall of the Assyrian empire, which had dominated the area for about two centuries. The demise of Assyrian control in Aram and Palestine undoubtedly facilitated and encouraged Josiah's reassertion of Davidic authority over former Assyrian provinces (vv. 6–7). However, one must not undercut religious motives in Josiah's reforms. Otherwise, the reform is reduced to merely a religious expression of an essentially political rebellion. *Asherah poles.* See NIV text note on 14:3.

priests on their altars, and so he purged Judah and Jerusalem. [6]In the towns of Manasseh, Ephraim and Simeon, as far as Naphtali, and in the ruins around them, [7]he tore down the altars and the Asherah poles and crushed the idols to powder[v] and cut to pieces all the incense altars throughout Israel. Then he went back to Jerusalem.

[8]In the eighteenth year of Josiah's reign, to purify the land and the temple, he sent Shaphan son of Azaliah and Maaseiah the ruler of the city, with Joah son of Joahaz, the recorder, to repair the temple of the LORD his God.

[9]They went to Hilkiah[w] the high priest and gave him the money that had been brought into the temple of God, which the Levites who were the doorkeepers had collected from the people of Manasseh, Ephraim and the entire remnant of Israel and from all the people of Judah and Benjamin and the inhabitants of Jerusalem. [10]Then they entrusted it to the men appointed to supervise the work on the LORD's temple. These men paid the workers who repaired and restored the temple. [11]They also gave money[x] to the carpenters and builders to purchase dressed stone, and timber for joists and beams for the buildings that the kings of Judah had allowed to fall into ruin.[y]

[12]The men did the work faithfully.[z] Over them to direct them were Jahath and Obadiah, Levites descended from Merari, and Zechariah and Meshullam, descended from Kohath. The Levites—all who were skilled in playing musical instruments—[a] [13]had charge of the laborers[b] and supervised all the workers from job to job. Some of the Levites were secretaries, scribes and doorkeepers.

The Book of the Law Found

34:14–28pp — 2Ki 22:8–20
34:29–32pp — 2Ki 23:1–3

[14]While they were bringing out the money that had been taken into the temple of the LORD, Hilkiah the priest found the Book of the Law of the LORD that had been given through Moses. [15]Hilkiah said to Shaphan the secretary, "I have found the

Book of the Law[c] in the temple of the LORD." He gave it to Shaphan.

[16]Then Shaphan took the book to the king and reported to him: "Your officials are doing everything that has been committed to them. [17]They have paid out the money that was in the temple of the LORD and have entrusted it to the supervisors and workers." [18]Then Shaphan the secretary informed the king, "Hilkiah the priest has given me a book." And Shaphan read from it in the presence of the king.

[19]When the king heard the words of the Law,[d] he tore[e] his robes. [20]He gave these orders to Hilkiah, Ahikam son of Shaphan[f], Abdon son of Micah,[e] Shaphan the secretary and Asaiah the king's attendant: [21]"Go and inquire of the LORD for me and for the remnant in Israel and Judah about what is written in this book that has been found. Great is the LORD's anger that is poured out[g] on us because our fathers have not kept the word of the LORD; they have not acted in accordance with all that is written in this book."

[22]Hilkiah and those the king had sent with him[f] went to speak to the prophetess[h] Huldah, who was the wife of Shallum son of Tokhath,[g] the son of Hasrah,[h] keeper of the wardrobe. She lived in Jerusalem, in the Second District.

[23]She said to them, "This is what the LORD, the God of Israel, says: Tell the man who sent you to me, [24]'This is what the LORD says: I am going to bring disaster[i] on this place and its people[j]—all the curses[k] written in the book that has been read in the presence of the king of Judah. [25]Because they have forsaken me[l] and burned incense to other gods and provoked me to anger by all that their hands have made,[i] my anger will be poured out on this place and will not be quenched.' [26]Tell the king of Judah, who sent you to inquire of the LORD, 'This is what the LORD, the God of Israel, says concerning the words you heard: [27]Because your heart was responsive[m] and you humbled[n] yourself before

---

34:7 [v]S Ex 32:20
34:9 [w]S 1Ch 6:13
34:11 [x]2Ch 24:12
[y]2Ch 33:4-7
34:12 [z]2Ki 12:15
[a]S 1Ch 25:1
34:13 [b]S 1Ch 23:4

34:15 [c]S 2Ki 22:8; Ezr 7:6; Ne 8:1
34:19 [d]Dt 28:3-68
[e]Isa 36:22; 37:1
34:20 [f]S 2Ki 22:3
34:21 [g]La 2:4; 4:11; Eze 36:18
34:22 [h]S Ex 15:20; Ne 6:14
34:24 [i]Pr 16:4; Isa 3:9; Jer 40:2; 42:10; 44:2,11
[j]2Ch 36:14-20
[k]Dt 28:15-68
34:25 [l]2Ch 33:3-6; Jer 22:9
[m]S 2Ch 32:26
[n]S Ex 10:3; S 2Ch 6:37

[e]20 Also called *Acbor son of Micaiah*   [f]22 One Hebrew manuscript, Vulgate and Syriac; most Hebrew manuscripts do not have *had sent with him.*   [g]22 Also called *Tikvah*   [h]22 Also called *Harhas*   [i]25 Or *by everything they have done*

34:6 *Manasseh, Ephraim and Simeon, as far as Naphtali.* The Chronicler's concern for "all Israel" (see Introduction to 1 Chronicles: Purpose and Themes) is apparent in his recording the involvement of the northern tribes in Josiah's reform (see also vv. 9,21,33). The Chronicler again shows all Israel united under a Davidic king, just as he did under Hezekiah (see note on 30:1). *Simeon.* Perhaps some Simeonites had migrated from Judah to the north.

34:7 *throughout Israel.* Defined by the list of tribes in v. 6.
34:8–21 See 2Ki 22:3–13 and notes.
34:9 *Manasseh, Ephraim and the entire remnant of Israel.* Again as part of his concern with "all Israel," the Chronicler notes that worshipers from the north also brought gifts to the temple (not explicitly indicated in 2Ki 22:4).
34:10–13 Cf. 24:8–12.
34:22–28 See 2Ki 22:14–20 and notes.

God when you heard what he spoke against this place and its people, and because you humbled yourself before me and tore your robes and wept in my presence, I have heard you, declares the LORD. [28]Now I will gather you to your fathers,[o] and you will be buried in peace. Your eyes will not see all the disaster I am going to bring on this place and on those who live here.' " [p]

So they took her answer back to the king.

[29]Then the king called together all the elders of Judah and Jerusalem. [30]He went up to the temple of the LORD [q] with the men of Judah, the people of Jerusalem, the priests and the Levites—all the people from the least to the greatest. He read in their hearing all the words of the Book of the Covenant, which had been found in the temple of the LORD. [31]The king stood by his pillar[r] and renewed the covenant[s] in the presence of the LORD—to follow[t] the LORD and keep his commands, regulations and decrees with all his heart and all his soul, and to obey the words of the covenant written in this book.

[32]Then he had everyone in Jerusalem and Benjamin pledge themselves to it; the people of Jerusalem did this in accordance with the covenant of God, the God of their fathers.

[33]Josiah removed all the detestable[u] idols from all the territory belonging to the Israelites, and he had all who were present in Israel serve the LORD their God. As long as he lived, they did not fail to follow the LORD, the God of their fathers.

Josiah Celebrates the Passover

35:1,18–19pp — 2Ki 23:21–23

35 Josiah celebrated the Passover[v] to the LORD in Jerusalem, and the Passover lamb was slaughtered on the fourteenth day of the first month. [2]He appointed the priests to their duties and encouraged them in the service of the LORD's temple. [3]He said to the Levites, who instructed[w] all Israel and who had been con-

secrated to the LORD: "Put the sacred ark in the temple that Solomon son of David king of Israel built. It is not to be carried about on your shoulders. Now serve the LORD your God and his people Israel. [4]Prepare yourselves by families in your divisions,[x] according to the directions written by David king of Israel and by his son Solomon.

[5]"Stand in the holy place with a group of Levites for each subdivision of the families of your fellow countrymen, the lay people. [6]Slaughter the Passover lambs, consecrate yourselves[y] and prepare the lambs for your fellow countrymen, doing what the LORD commanded through Moses."

[7]Josiah provided for all the lay people who were there a total of thirty thousand sheep and goats for the Passover offerings,[z] and also three thousand cattle—all from the king's own possessions.[a]

[8]His officials also contributed[b] voluntarily to the people and the priests and Levites. Hilkiah,[c] Zechariah and Jehiel, the administrators of God's temple, gave the priests twenty-six hundred Passover offerings and three hundred cattle. [9]Also Conaniah[d] along with Shemaiah and Nethanel, his brothers, and Hashabiah, Jeiel and Jozabad,[e] the leaders of the Levites, provided five thousand Passover offerings and five hundred head of cattle for the Levites.

[10]The service was arranged and the priests stood in their places with the Levites in their divisions[f] as the king had ordered.[g] [11]The Passover lambs were slaughtered,[h] and the priests sprinkled the blood handed to them, while the Levites skinned the animals. [12]They set aside the burnt offerings to give them to the subdivisions of the families of the people to offer to the LORD, as is written in the Book of Moses. They did the same with the cattle. [13]They roasted the Passover animals over the fire as prescribed,[i] and boiled the holy offerings in pots, caldrons and pans and served them quickly to all the people. [14]Af-

---

34:28
[o]2Ch 35:20-25
[p]S 2Ch 32:26
34:30
[q]S 2Ki 23:2
34:31 [r]S 1Ki 7:15
[s]S 2Ki 11:17;
S 2Ch 23:16
[t]S Dt 13:4
34:33 [u]S Dt 18:9
35:1
[v]Ex 12:1-30;
S Nu 28:16
35:3
[w]S 2Ch 17:7

35:4 [x]ver 10;
S 1Ch 24:1;
Ezr 6:18
35:6
[y]S Lev 11:44
35:7
[z]S 2Ch 30:24
[a]S 2Ch 31:3
35:8
[b]S 1Ch 29:3;
2Ch 29:31-36
[c]S 1Ch 6:13
35:9 [d]2Ch 31:12
[e]2Ch 31:13
35:10 [f]S ver 4
[g]2Ch 30:16
35:11
[h]S 2Ch 30:17
35:13
[i]Ex 12:2-11

34:28 *will be buried in peace.* See the death and burial account (35:20–25).

34:29–31 See 2Ki 23:1–3.

34:30 *the priests and the Levites.* Cf. 2Ki 23:2, which has "the priests and the prophets."

34:33 *all the territory belonging to the Israelites ... all who were present in Israel.* See note on v. 6.

35:1–19 The Chronicler gives much more extensive coverage to Josiah's Passover celebration than is found in the brief allusion in Kings (2Ki 23:21–23).

35:1 *first month.* The traditional month; contrast the Passover of Hezekiah (see note on 30:2).

35:3 *Put the sacred ark in the temple.* Implies that it had been removed, perhaps for protection during the evil reigns of Manasseh and Amon, who preceded Josiah.

35:4 *David ... Solomon.* The Chronicler specifically parallels David and Solomon in three cases: 7:10 (contrast 1Ki 8:66, where only David is mentioned); 11:17; and here. This tendency reflects his glorification and idealization of both (see Introduction to 1 Chronicles: Portrait of David and Solomon).

35:7–9 The emphasis in Chronicles on voluntary and joyful giving (24:8–14; 29:31–36; 31:3–21; 1Ch 29:3–9) presumably had direct relevance to the postexilic readers for whom the Chronicler wrote.

ter this, they made preparations for themselves and for the priests, because the priests, the descendants of Aaron, were sacrificing the burnt offerings and the fat portions/ until nightfall. So the Levites made preparations for themselves and for the Aaronic priests.

15The musicians,k the descendants of Asaph, were in the places prescribed by David, Asaph, Heman and Jeduthun the king's seer. The gatekeepers at each gate did not need to leave their posts, because their fellow Levites made the preparations for them.

16So at that time the entire service of the LORD was carried out for the celebration of the Passover and the offering of burnt offerings on the altar of the LORD, as King Josiah had ordered. 17The Israelites who were present celebrated the Passover at that time and observed the Feast of Unleavened Bread for seven days. 18The Passover had not been observed like this in Israel since the days of the prophet Samuel; and none of the kings of Israel had ever celebrated such a Passover as did Josiah, with the priests, the Levites and all Judah and Israel who were there with the people of Jerusalem. 19This Passover was celebrated in the eighteenth year of Josiah's reign.

The Death of Josiah

35:20–36:1pp — 2Ki 23:28–30

20After all this, when Josiah had set the temple in order, Neco king of Egypt went up to fight at Carchemish/ on the Euphrates, m and Josiah marched out to meet him in battle. 21But Neco sent messengers to him, saying, "What quarrel is there between you and me, O king of Judah? It is not you I am attacking at this time, but the

house with which I am at war. God has told n me to hurry; so stop opposing God, who is with me, or he will destroy you."

22Josiah, however, would not turn away from him, but disguised o himself to engage him in battle. He would not listen to what Neco had said at God's command but went to fight him on the plain of Megiddo.

23Archersp shot King Josiah, and he told his officers, "Take me away; I am badly wounded." 24So they took him out of his chariot, put him in the other chariot he had and brought him to Jerusalem, where he died. He was buried in the tombs of his fathers, and all Judah and Jerusalem mourned for him.

25Jeremiah composed laments for Josiah, and to this day all the men and women singers commemorate Josiah in the laments. q These became a tradition in Israel and are written in the Laments. r

26The other events of Josiah's reign and his acts of devotion, according to what is written in the Law of the LORD— 27all the events, from beginning to end, are written in the book of the kings of Israel and

36 Judah. 1And the peoples of the land took Jehoahaz son of Josiah and made him king in Jerusalem in place of his father.

Jehoahaz King of Judah

36:2–4pp — 2Ki 23:31–34

2Jehoahazj was twenty-three years old when he became king, and he reigned in Jerusalem three months. 3The king of Egypt dethroned him in Jerusalem and imposed on Judah a levy of a hundred talentsk of silver and a talentl of gold. 4The

Cross references (center column)

35:14 /S Ex 29:13
35:15 kS 1Ch 25:1; S 26:12-19; 2Ch 29:30; Ne 12:46; Ps 68:25
35:20 /Isa 10:9; Jer 46:2
mS Ge 2:14

35:21 nS 1Ki 13:18; S 2Ki 18:25
35:22 oS 1Sa 28:8
35:23 pS 1Ki 22:34
35:25 qS Ge 50:10; Jer 22:10,15-16
r2Ch 34:28
36:1 sS 2Ch 22:1

j2 Hebrew *Joahaz*, a variant of *Jehoahaz*; also in verse 4
k3 That is, about 3 3/4 tons (about 3.4 metric tons)
l3 That is, about 75 pounds (about 34 kilograms)

35:18 *since the days of the prophet Samuel.* Instead of "since the days of the judges" (2Ki 23:22).

35:19 *eighteenth year.* The same year as the discovery of the Book of the Law (34:8,14).

35:20–27 See 2Ki 23:28–30. In 609 B.C. Pharaoh Neco "went up to the Euphrates River to help the king of Assyria" (2Ki 23:29) against the Babylonians.

35:20 *at Carchemish.* Not found in Kings.

35:21–22 Unique to the Chronicler, showing his view on retribution once again: Josiah's death in battle comes as a result of his disobedience to the word of God as heard even in the mouth of the pagan pharaoh.

35:21 *house with which I am at war.* A reference to the Babylonians; Nabopolassar was on the throne of Babylon, while his son Nebuchadnezzar was commanding the armies in the field. Nebuchadnezzar would succeed his father after another battle at Carchemish against Egypt in 605 B.C. Josiah may have been an ally of Babylon (see 32:31; 33:11 and notes).

35:22 *disguised himself.* Cf. Ahab and Jehoshaphat (see

18:29 and note). *plain of Megiddo.* See note on Jdg 5:19.

35:24b–25 Unique to Chronicles.

35:25 *Jeremiah composed laments for Josiah.* Jeremiah held Josiah in high esteem (Jer 22:15–16). The laments he composed are no longer extant. The statement that he composed laments is one of the reasons the book of Lamentations has been traditionally associated with him. *to this day.* See note on 5:9.

36:2–14 Josiah is the only king of Judah to be succeeded by three of his sons (Jehoahaz, Jehoiakim and Zedekiah). The Chronicler's account of the reigns of the remaining kings of Judah is quite brief.

36:2 See 2Ki 23:31–35. With the death of Josiah at the hands of Pharaoh Neco, Judah slipped into a period of Egyptian domination (vv. 3–4). *three months.* In 609 B.C. Neco's assertion of authority over Judah ended the brief 20 years of Judahite independence under Josiah. The Chronicler makes no moral judgment on this brief reign, though the author of Kings does (2Ki 23:32).

36:4 Just as Neco took Jehoahaz into captivity and replaced

king of Egypt made Eliakim, a brother of Jehoahaz, king over Judah and Jerusalem and changed Eliakim's name to Jehoiakim. But Neco[t] took Eliakim's brother Jehoahaz and carried him off to Egypt. [u]

Jehoiakim King of Judah

36:5–8pp — 2Ki 23:36–24:6

[5]Jehoiakim[v] was twenty-five years old when he became king, and he reigned in Jerusalem eleven years. He did evil in the eyes of the LORD his God. [6]Nebuchadnezzar[w] king of Babylon attacked him and bound him with bronze shackles to take him to Babylon.[x] [7]Nebuchadnezzar also took to Babylon articles from the temple of the LORD and put them in his temple[m] there.[y]

[8]The other events of Jehoiakim's reign, the detestable things he did and all that was found against him, are written in the book of the kings of Israel and Judah. And Jehoiachin his son succeeded him as king.

Jehoiachin King of Judah

36:9–10pp — 2Ki 24:8–17

[9]Jehoiachin[z] was eighteen[n] years old when he became king, and he reigned in Jerusalem three months and ten days. He did evil in the eyes of the LORD. [10]In the spring, King Nebuchadnezzar sent for him and brought him to Babylon,[a] together with articles of value from the temple of the LORD, and he made Jehoiachin's uncle,[o] Zedekiah, king over Judah and Jerusalem.

Zedekiah King of Judah

36:11–16pp — 2Ki 24:18–20; Jer 52:1–3

[11]Zedekiah[b] was twenty-one years old when he became king, and he reigned in Jerusalem eleven years. [12]He did evil in the eyes of the LORD[c] his God and did not humble[d] himself before Jeremiah the

prophet, who spoke the word of the LORD. [13]He also rebelled against King Nebuchadnezzar, who had made him take an oath[e] in God's name. He became stiffnecked[f] and hardened his heart and would not turn to the LORD, the God of Israel. [14]Furthermore, all the leaders of the priests and the people became more and more unfaithful,[g] following all the detestable practices of the nations and defiling the temple of the LORD, which he had consecrated in Jerusalem.

The Fall of Jerusalem

36:17–20pp — 2Ki 25:1–21; Jer 52:4–27
36:22–23pp — Ezr 1:1–3

[15]The LORD, the God of their fathers, sent word to them through his messengers[h] again and again,[i] because he had pity on his people and on his dwelling place. [16]But they mocked God's messengers, despised his words and scoffed[j] at his prophets until the wrath[k] of the LORD was aroused against his people and there was no remedy.[l] [17]He brought up against them the king of the Babylonians,[p] [m] who killed their young men with the sword in the sanctuary, and spared neither young man[n] nor young woman, old man or aged.[o] God handed all of them over to Nebuchadnezzar.[p] [18]He carried to Babylon all the articles[q] from the temple of God, both large and small, and the treasures of the LORD's temple and the treasures of the king and his officials. [19]They set fire[r] to God's temple[s] and broke down the wall[t] of Jerusalem; they burned

36:4
[t]Jer 22:10-12
[u]Eze 19:4
36:5 [v]Jer 22:18;
25:1; 26:1; 35:1;
36:1; 45:1; 46:2
36:6 [w]Jer 25:9;
27:6; Eze 29:18
[x]Eze 19:9; Da 1:1
36:7 [y]ver 18;
Ezr 1:7;
Jer 27:16; Da 1:2
36:9
[z]Jer 22:24-28;
24:1; 27:20;
29:21; 52:31
36:10 [a]ver 18;
S 2Ki 20:17;
Ezr 1:7;
Isa 52:11;
Jer 14:18; 21:7;
22:25; 24:1;
27:16,20,22;
29:1; 34:21;
40:1; Eze 17:12;
Da 5:2
36:11
[b]S 2Ki 24:17;
Jer 27:1; 28:1;
34:2; 37:1; 39:1
36:12
[c]Jer 37:1-39:18
[d]S Dt 8:3;
2Ch 7:14;
Jer 44:10
36:13 [e]Eze 17:13
[f]S Ex 32:9;
S Dt 9:27
36:14
[g]S 1Ch 5:25
36:15 [h]Isa 5:4;
44:26; Jer 7:25;
Hag 1:13;
Zec 1:4; Mal 2:7;
3:1; S Mt 5:12
[i]Jer 7:13,25;
11:7; 25:3-4;
35:14,15; 44:4-6
36:16
[j]S 2Ki 2:23;
Job 8:2; Isa 28:14,
22; 29:20; 57:4;
Jer 5:13; 43:2;
Mic 2:11
[k]Ezr 5:12;
Pr 1:30-31;
Jer 44:3 [l]Ne 9:30;
Pr 29:1; Jer 7:26;
20:8; 25:4;
30:12; Da 9:6;
Zec 1:2
36:17
[m]S Ge 10:10
[n]Jer 6:11; 9:21;
18:21; 44:7
[o]S Dt 32:25;
Jer 51:22
[p]Ezr 5:12;
Jer 32:28;
La 2:21; Eze 9:6;

23:47 36:18 [q]S ver 7,S 10; Jer 27:20 36:19 [r]Jer 11:16;
17:27; 21:10,14; 22:7; 32:29; 39:8; La 4:11; Eze 20:47;
Am 2:5; Zec 11:1 [s]1Ki 9:8-9 [t]S 2Ki 14:13

[m]7 Or palace   [n]9 One Hebrew manuscript, some Septuagint manuscripts and Syriac (see also 2 Kings 24:8); most Hebrew manuscripts eight   [o]10 Hebrew brother, that is, relative (see 2 Kings 24:17)   [p]17 Or Chaldeans

---

him with Eliakim, whose name he changed to Jehoiakim, so also Nebuchadnezzar would later take Jehoiachin to Babylon, replacing him with Mattaniah, whose name he changed to Zedekiah (2Ki 24:15–17). Each conqueror wanted to place his own man on the throne; the change of name implied authority over him.

36:5–8 See 2Ki 23:36–24:7. Jehoiakim persecuted the prophets and is the object of scathing denunciation by Jeremiah (Jer 25–26; 36). After the Egyptian defeat at Carchemish (Jer 46:2) in 605 B.C., Jehoiakim transferred allegiance to Nebuchadnezzar of Babylon. When he later rebelled and again allied himself with Egypt, Nebuchadnezzar sent a punitive army against him. But Jehoiakim died before the army arrived, and Nebuchadnezzar took his son Jehoiachin into captivity.

36:5 eleven years. 609–598 B.C.

36:9–10 See 2Ki 24:8–17; see also Jer 22:24–28; 24:1;

29:2; 52:31. Although Jehoiachin was taken into captivity (597 B.C.) with a large retinue, including the queen mother and high officials, and was succeeded by Zedekiah, the exiles continued to date in terms of his reign (Jer 52:31; Eze 1:2; cf. Est 2:5–6).

36:9 three months and ten days. 598–597 B.C.

36:11–14 See 2Ki 24:18–20; Jer 52:1–3. Verses 13b–14 are unique to the Chronicler (cf. Jer 1:3; 21:1–7; 24:8; 27:1–15; 32:1–5; 34:1–7,21; 37:1–39:7). Zedekiah succumbed to the temptation to look to Egypt for help and rebelled against Nebuchadnezzar. Babylonian reaction was swift. Jerusalem was besieged (Jer 21:3–7) in 588 B.C. and held out for almost two years before being destroyed in the summer of 586.

36:11 eleven years. 597–586 B.C.

36:15–16 See 24:19 and note.

all the palaces and destroyed[u] everything of value there.[v]

20He carried into exile[w] to Babylon the remnant, who escaped from the sword, and they became servants[x] to him and his sons until the kingdom of Persia came to power. 21The land enjoyed its sabbath rests;[y] all the time of its desolation it rested,[z] until the seventy years[a] were completed in fulfillment of the word of the LORD spoken by Jeremiah.

22In the first year of Cyrus[b] king of Persia, in order to fulfill the word of the LORD spoken by Jeremiah, the LORD

moved the heart of Cyrus king of Persia to make a proclamation throughout his realm and to put it in writing:

23"This is what Cyrus king of Persia says:

" 'The LORD, the God of heaven, has given me all the kingdoms of the earth and he has appointed[c] me to build a temple for him at Jerusalem in Judah. Anyone of his people among you—may the LORD his God be with him, and let him go up.' "

36:19 [u]La 2:6
[v]Ps 79:1-3
36:20
[w]S Lev 26:44;
S 2Ki 24:14;
Ezr 2:1; Ne 7:6
[x]Jer 27:7
36:21
[y]S Lev 25:4
[z]S 1Ch 22:9
[a]Jer 1:1; 25:11;
27:22; 29:10;
40:1; Da 9:2;
Zec 1:12; 7:5
36:22 [b]Isa 44:28;
45:1,13; Da 1:21;
6:28; 10:1

36:23 [c]S Jdg 4:10

36:20–21 The conclusion of the two Biblical histories is interestingly different: The writer(s) of Samuel and Kings had sought to show why the exile occurred and had traced the sad history of Israel's disobedience to the exile, the time in which the writer(s) of those books lived. With the state at an end, he could still show God's faithfulness to his promises to David (2Ki 25:27–30) by reporting the favor bestowed on his descendants. The Chronicler, whose vantage point was after the exile, was able to look back to the exile not only as judgment, but also as containing hope for the future. For him the purified remnant had returned to a purified land (vv. 22–23), and a new age was beginning. The exile was not judgment alone, but also blessing, for it allowed the land to catch up on its sabbath rests (Lev 26:40–45). And God had

remembered his covenant (Lev 26:45) and restored his people to the land (see next note).
36:22–23 The writer of Kings concluded his history before the restoration, so this text is not paralleled in his account. It is repeated, however, at the beginning of Ezra (1:1–4), which resumes the history at the point where Chronicles ends—indicating that Chronicles and Ezra may have been written by the same author. See the prophecy of Jeremiah (Jer 25:1–14; cf. Da 9). Cyrus also issued decrees for other captive peoples, allowing them to return to their lands. Under God's sovereignty, this effort by a Persian king to win the favor of peoples treated harshly by the Babylonians also inaugurated the restoration period. See notes on Ezr 1: 1–4.

EZRA

Ezra and Nehemiah

Although the caption to Ne 1:1, "The words of Nehemiah son of Hacaliah," indicates that Ezra and Nehemiah were originally two separate compositions, they were combined as one in the earliest Hebrew manuscripts. Josephus (c. A.D. 37-100) and the Jewish Talmud refer to the book of Ezra but not to a separate book of Nehemiah. The oldest manuscripts of the Septuagint (the Greek translation of the OT) also treat Ezra and Nehemiah as one book.

Origen (A.D. 185-253) is the first writer known to distinguish between two books, which he called I Ezra and II Ezra. In translating the Latin Vulgate (A.D. 390-405), Jerome called Nehemiah the second book of Esdrae (Ezra). The English translations by Wycliffe (1382) and Coverdale (1535) also called Ezra "I Esdras" and Nehemiah "II Esdras." The same separation first appeared in a Hebrew manuscript in 1448.

Literary Form and Authorship

As in the closely related books of 1 and 2 Chronicles, one notes the prominence of various lists in Ezra and Nehemiah, which have evidently been obtained from official sources. Included are lists of (1) the temple articles (Ezr 1:9-11), (2) the returned exiles (Ezr 2, which is virtually the same as Ne 7:6-73), (3) the genealogy of Ezra (Ezr 7:1-5), (4) the heads of the clans (Ezr 8:1-14), (5) those involved in mixed marriages (Ezr 10:18-43), (6) those who helped rebuild the wall (Ne 3), (7) those who sealed the covenant (Ne 10:1-27), (8) residents of Jerusalem and other towns (Ne 11:3-36) and (9) priests and Levites (Ne 12:1-26).

Also included in Ezra are seven official documents or letters (all in Aramaic except the first, which is in Hebrew): (1) the decree of Cyrus (1:2-4), (2) the accusation of Rehum and others against the Jews (4:11-16), (3) the reply of Artaxerxes I (4:17-22), (4) the report from Tattenai (5:7-17), (5) the memorandum of Cyrus's decree (6:2b-5), (6) Darius's reply to Tattenai (6:6-12) and (7) the authorization given by Artaxerxes I to Ezra (7:12-26). The documents compare favorably with contemporary non-Biblical documents of the Persian period.

Certain materials in Ezra are first-person extracts from his memoirs: 7:27-28; 8:1-34; 9. Other sections are written in the third person: 7:1-26; 10; see also Ne 8. Linguistic analysis has shown that the first-person and third-person extracts resemble each other, making it likely that the same author wrote both.

Most scholars conclude that the author/compiler of Ezra and Nehemiah was also the author of 1,2 Chronicles. This viewpoint is based on certain characteristics common to both Chronicles and Ezra-Nehemiah. The verses at the end of Chronicles and at the beginning of Ezra are virtually identical. Both Chronicles and Ezra-Nehemiah exhibit a fondness for lists, for the description of religious festivals and for such phrases as "heads of families" and "the house of God." Especially striking in these books is the prominence of Levites and temple personnel. The words for "singer," "gatekeeper" and "temple servants" are used almost exclusively in Ezra-Nehemiah and Chronicles. See Introduction to 1 Chronicles: Author, Date and Sources.

Date

We may date the composition of Ezra c. 440 B.C. and the Nehemiah memoirs c. 430.

The Order of Ezra and Nehemiah

According to the traditional view, Ezra arrived in Jerusalem in the seventh year (Ezr 7:8) of Artaxerxes I (458 B.C.), followed by Nehemiah, who arrived in the king's 20th year (445; Ne 2:1).

Some have proposed a reverse order in which Nehemiah arrived in 445 B.C., while Ezra arrived in the seventh year of Artaxerxes II (398). By amending "seventh" (Ezr 7:8) to either "27th" or "37th," others place Ezra after Nehemiah but maintain that they were contemporaries.

These alternative views, however, present more problems than the traditional position. As the text stands, Ezra arrived before Nehemiah and they are found together in Ne 8:9 (at the reading of the Law) and Ne 12:26,36 (at the dedication of the wall). See chart on "Chronology: Ezra-Nehemiah," p. 674.

Languages

Ezra and Nehemiah were written in a form of late Hebrew with the exception of Ezr 4:8-6:18; 7:12-26, which were written in Aramaic, the international language during the Persian period. Of these 67 Aramaic verses, 52 are in records or letters. Ezra evidently found these documents in Aramaic and copied them, inserting connecting verses in Aramaic.

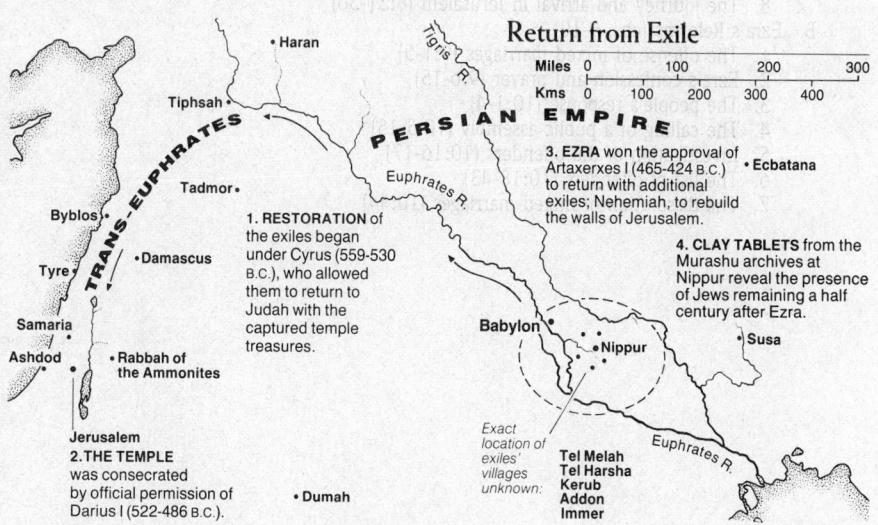

Outline

I. First Return from Exile and Rebuilding of the Temple (chs. 1-6)
A. First Return of the Exiles (ch. 1)
    1. The edict of Cyrus (1:1-4)
    2. The return under Sheshbazzar (1:5-11)
B. List of Returning Exiles (ch. 2)
C. Revival of Temple Worship (ch. 3)
    1. The rebuilding of the altar (3:1-3)
    2. The Feast of Tabernacles (3:4-6)
    3. The beginning of temple reconstruction (3:7-13)
D. Opposition to Rebuilding (4:1-23)
    1. Opposition during the reign of Cyrus (4:1-5)
    2. Opposition during the reign of Xerxes (4:6)
    3. Opposition during the reign of Artaxerxes (4:7-23)
E. Completion of the Temple (4:24-6:22)
    1. Resumption of work under Darius (4:24)
    2. A new beginning inspired by Haggai and Zechariah (5:1-2)
    3. Intervention of the governor, Tattenai (5:3-5)
    4. Report to Darius (5:6-17)
    5. Search for the decree of Cyrus (6:1-5)

Cyrus Helps the Exiles to Return

1:1–3pp — 2Ch 36:22–23

1 In the first year of Cyrus king of Persia, in order to fulfill the word of the LORD spoken by Jeremiah,[a] the LORD moved the heart[b] of Cyrus king of Persia to make a proclamation throughout his realm and to put it in writing:

2"This is what Cyrus king of Persia says:

" 'The LORD, the God of heaven, has given me all the kingdoms of the earth and he has appointed[c] me to build[d] a temple for him at Jerusalem in Judah. 3Anyone of his people among you—may his God be with him, and let him go up to Jerusalem in Judah and build the temple of the LORD, the God of Israel, the God who is in Jerusalem. 4And the people of any place where survivors[e] may now be living are to provide him with silver and gold,[f] with goods and livestock, and with freewill offerings[g] for the temple of God[h] in Jerusalem.' "[i]

5Then the family heads of Judah and Benjamin,[j] and the priests and Levites—everyone whose heart God had moved[k]—prepared to go up and build the house[l] of the LORD in Jerusalem. 6All their neighbors assisted them with articles of silver and gold,[m] with goods and livestock, and with valuable gifts, in addition to all the freewill offerings. 7Moreover, King Cyrus brought out the articles belonging to the temple of the LORD, which Nebuchadnezzar had carried away from Jerusalem and had placed in the temple of his god.[a][n] 8Cyrus king of Persia had them brought by Mithredath the treasurer, who counted them out to Sheshbazzar[o] the prince of Judah.

9This was the inventory:

gold dishes	30
silver dishes	1,000

1:1
a Jer 25:11-12; 29:10-14; Zec 1:12-16
b Ezr 6:22; 7:27
1:2 c S Jdg 4:10; Ps 72:11; Isa 41:2,25; 44:28; 45:13; 46:11; 49:7,23; 60:3,10 d Hag 1:2
1:4 e Isa 10:20-22 f S Ex 3:22
g Nu 15:3; Ps 50:14; 54:6; 116:17 h Ps 72:8-11; Rev 21:24 i Ezr 3:7; 4:3; 5:13; 6:3,14
1:5 j 2Ch 11:1,3, 10,12,23; 15:2, 8-9; 25:5; 31:1; 34:9; Ezr 4:1; 10:9; Ne 11:4; 12:34 k ver 1; Ex 35:20-22; 2Ch 36:22; Hag 1:14; S Php 2:13 l Ps 127:1
1:6 m S Ex 3:22
1:7 n S 2Ki 24:13; S 2Ch 36:7,10; Ezr 5:14; 6:5; Jer 52:17-19
1:8 o S 1Ch 3:18
a 7 Or *gods*

1:1–3a Virtually identical with the last two verses of 2 Chronicles. This fact has been used to argue that Chronicles and Ezra-Nehemiah were written and/or edited by the same person, the so-called Chronicler. However, the repetition may have been a device of the author of Chronicles (or less probably of Ezra) to dovetail the narratives chronologically.

1:1 *first year.* Of the reign of Cyrus over Babylon, beginning in March, 538 B.C., after he captured Babylon in October, 539. Cyrus, the founder of the Persian empire, reigned over the Persians from 559 until 530. Isa 44:28; 45:1 speak of him as the Lord's "shepherd" and his "anointed." *to fulfill the word of the LORD spoken by Jeremiah.* Jeremiah prophesied a 70-year Babylonian captivity (Jer 25:11–12; 29:10). The first deportation began in 605, the third year of Jehoiakim (Da 1:1); in 538, approximately 70 years later, the people began to return.

1:2–4 This oral proclamation of Cyrus's decree was written in Hebrew, the language of the Israelite captives, in contrast to the copy of the decree in 6:3–5, which was an Aramaic memorandum for the archives.

1:2 *God of heaven.* Of the 22 OT occurrences of the phrase, 17 occur in Ezra, Nehemiah and Daniel. *temple . . . at Jerusalem.* Jerusalem and the house of God are prominent subjects in Ezra and Nehemiah.

1:3 Cyrus instituted the policy of placating the gods of his subject peoples instead of carrying off their cult images as the Assyrians and the Babylonians had done earlier. His generosity to the Jews was paralleled by his benevolence to the Babylonians.

1:4 *people of any place.* Probably designates the many Jews who did not wish to leave Mesopotamia. *freewill offerings.* A key to the restoration of God's temple and its services (see 2:68; 3:5; 8:28).

1:5 *family heads.* In ancient times families were extended families—more like clans than modern nuclear families. The authority figure was the patriarch, who was the "family head." See 10:16; see also 2:59; Ne 7:61; 10:34. *Judah and Benjamin.* The two main tribes of the kingdom of Judah, which the Babylonians had exiled. *Levites.* See Introduction to Leviticus: Title.

1:7 It was the custom for conquerors to carry off the images of the gods of conquered cities. Since the Jews did not have an image of the Lord (see note on Ex 20:4), Nebuchadnezzar carried away only the temple articles.

1:8 *Mithredath.* A Persian name meaning "given by/to Mithra," a Persian god who became popular among Roman soldiers in the second century A.D. *Sheshbazzar.* A Babylonian name meaning either "Sin, protect the father" or "Shamash/Shashu, protect the father." Sin was the moon-god, and Shamash (Shashu is a variant) was the sun-god. In spite of his Babylonian name, Sheshbazzar was probably a Jewish official who served as a deputy governor of Judah under the satrap in Samaria (see 5:14). Some believe that Sheshbazzar and Zerubbabel were the same person and give the following reasons: 1. Both were governors (5:14; Hag 1:1; 2:2). 2. Both are said to have laid the foundation of the temple (3:2–8; 5:16; Hag 1:14–15; Zec 4:6–10). 3. Jews in Babylon were often given "official" Babylonian names (cf. Da 1:7). 4. Josephus (*Antiquities*, 11.1.3) seems to identify Sheshbazzar with Zerubbabel.

Others point out, however, that the Apocrypha distinguishes between the two men (1 Esdras 6:18). Furthermore, it is likely that Sheshbazzar was an elderly man at the time of the return, while Zerubbabel was probably a younger contemporary. Sheshbazzar also may have been viewed as the official governor, while Zerubbabel served as the popular leader (3:8–11). Whereas the high priest Jeshua is associated with Zerubbabel, no priest is associated with Sheshbazzar. Although Sheshbazzar presided over the foundation of the temple in 536 B.C., so little was accomplished that Zerubbabel had to preside over a second foundation some 16 years later (see Hag 1:14–15; Zec 4:6–10).

Still others hold that Sheshbazzar is to be identified with Shenazar (1Ch 3:18), the fourth son of King Jehoiachin. Zerubbabel would then have been Sheshbazzar's nephew (compare 3:2 with 1Ch 3:18).

1:9–11 When Assyrian and Babylonian conquerors carried off plunder, their scribes made a careful inventory of all the goods seized. The total of the figures in vv. 9–10 adds up to 2,499 rather than the 5,400 of v. 11. It may be that only the larger and more valuable vessels were specified.

silver pans[b]	29
[10]gold bowls	30
matching silver bowls	410
other articles	1,000

[11]In all, there were 5,400 articles of gold and of silver. Sheshbazzar brought all these along when the exiles came up from Babylon to Jerusalem.

The List of the Exiles Who Returned

2:1–70pp — Ne 7:6–73

2 Now these are the people of the province who came up from the captivity of the exiles,[p] whom Nebuchadnezzar king of Babylon[q] had taken captive to Babylon (they returned to Jerusalem and Judah, each to his own town,[r] [2]in company with Zerubbabel,[s] Jeshua,[t] Nehemiah, Seraiah,[u] Reelaiah, Mordecai, Bilshan, Mispar, Bigvai, Rehum and Baanah):

Cross references (center column):
2:1 pS 2Ch 36:20
qS 2Ki 24:16;
25:12 rver 70;
1Ch 9:2;
Ne 7:73; 11:3
2:2 sS 1Ch 3:19;
Mt 1:12; Lk 3:27
tEzr 3:2; 5:2;
10:18; Ne 12:1,8;
Hag 1:1,12; 2:4;
Zec 3:1-10;
6:9-15
uCh 6:14;
Ne 10:2; 11:11;
12:1
2:3 vEzr 8:3;
10:25; Ne 3:25
2:13 wEzr 8:13

The list of the men of the people of Israel:

[3]the descendants of Parosh[v]	2,172
[4]of Shephatiah	372
[5]of Arah	775
[6]of Pahath-Moab (through the line of Jeshua and Joab)	2,812
[7]of Elam	1,254
[8]of Zattu	945
[9]of Zaccai	760
[10]of Bani	642
[11]of Bebai	623
[12]of Azgad	1,222
[13]of Adonikam[w]	666
[14]of Bigvai	2,056
[15]of Adin	454
[16]of Ater (through Hezekiah)	98
[17]of Bezai	323
[18]of Jorah	112

b9 The meaning of the Hebrew for this word is uncertain.

1:11 We are not told anything about the details of Sheshbazzar's journey, which probably took place in 537 B.C. Judging from Ezra's later journey (7:8–9), the trip took about four months. See inset to map No. 7 at the end of the Study Bible.

2:1–70 The list of returning exiles in ch. 2 almost exactly parallels the list in Ne 7:6–73 (see also 1 Esdras 5:4–46 in the Apocrypha). The list of localities indicates that people retained the memories of their homes and that exiles from a wide background of tribes, villages and towns returned. In comparing the list here with that in Ne 7, one notes many differences in the names and numbers listed. About 20 percent of the numbers, e.g., are not the same in Ezra and Nehemiah. Many of these differences may be explained, however, by assuming that a cipher notation was used with vertical strokes for units and horizontal strokes for tens, which led to copying errors.

2:1 *province.* Probably Judah (cf. 5:8, where the Aramaic

word for "province" is translated "district"; see also Ne 1:3).

2:2 *Zerubbabel.* See notes on 3:2; 5:2. *Jeshua.* Means "The LORD saves" and is an Aramaic variant of Hebrew "Joshua." The Greek form is "Jesus" (see NIV text note on Mt 1:21). Jeshua is the same as the Joshua of Hag 1:1, the son of the high priest Jehozadak (Jozadak, Ezr 3:2), who was taken into exile (1Ch 6:15). *Nehemiah.* Not the Nehemiah of the book by that name. *Mordecai.* A Babylonian name based on that of Marduk the god of Babylon (cf. Jer 50:2). Esther's cousin had the same name (Est 2:7).

2:3 *Parosh.* Means "flea" (Israelites were often named after insects and animals). Members of this family, as well as of several other families named in vv. 6–14, also returned with Ezra (8:3–14).

2:5 *Arah.* Probably means "wild ox." Since the name is rare in the OT and has been found in documents from Mesopotamia, it may have been adopted during the exile.

Chronology: Ezra-Nehemiah

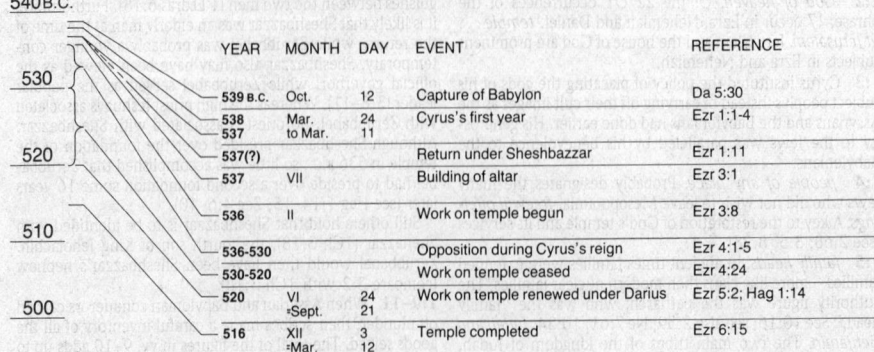

Dates below are given according to a Nisan-to-Nisan Jewish calendar (see chart on "Hebrew Calendar," p. 102).
Roman numerals represent months; Arabic numerals represent days.

540 B.C.

	YEAR	MONTH	DAY	EVENT	REFERENCE
530	539 B.C.	Oct.	12	Capture of Babylon	Da 5:30
	538	Mar.	24	Cyrus's first year	Ezr 1:1-4
	537	to Mar.	11		
520	537(?)			Return under Sheshbazzar	Ezr 1:11
	537	VII		Building of altar	Ezr 3:1
510	536	II		Work on temple begun	Ezr 3:8
	536-530			Opposition during Cyrus's reign	Ezr 4:1-5
	530-520			Work on temple ceased	Ezr 4:24
500	520	VI =Sept.	24 21	Work on temple renewed under Darius	Ezr 5:2; Hag 1:14
	516	XII =Mar.	3 12	Temple completed	Ezr 6:15

490

¹⁹of Hashum   223
²⁰of Gibbar   95

²¹the men of Bethlehem*   123
²²of Netophah   56
²³of Anathoth   128
²⁴of Azmaveth   42
²⁵of Kiriath Jearim,ᶜ Kephirah
   and Beeroth   743
²⁶of Ramahʸ and Geba   621
²⁷of Micmash   122
²⁸of Bethel and Aiᶻ   223
²⁹of Nebo   52
³⁰of Magbish   156
³¹of the other Elam   1,254
³²of Harim   320
³³of Lod, Hadid and Ono   725
³⁴of Jerichoᵃ   345
³⁵of Senaah   3,630

³⁶The priests:

2:21 ˣMic 5:2
2:26 ʸS Jos 18:25
2:28 ᶻS Ge 12:8
2:34 ᵃ1Ki 16:34;
2Ch 28:15

the descendants of Jedaiahᵇ
   (through the family
   of Jeshua)   973
   ³⁷of Immerᶜ   1,052
   ³⁸of Pashhurᵈ   1,247
   ³⁹of Harimᵉ   1,017

⁴⁰The Levites:ᶠ

the descendants of Jeshuaᵍ and
   Kadmiel (through the line of
   Hodaviah)   74
⁴¹The singers: ʰ

the descendants of Asaph   128
⁴²The gatekeepersⁱ of the temple:

the descendants of
   Shallum, Ater, Talmon,
   Akkub, Hatita and Shobai   139

2:36 ᵇS 1Ch 24:7
2:37 ᶜS 1Ch 24:14
2:38 ᵈS 1Ch 9:12
2:39 ᵉS 1Ch 24:8
2:40 ᶠGe 29:34;
Nu 3:9;
Dt 18:6-7;
1Ch 16:4;
Ezr 7:7; 8:15;
Ne 12:24
ᵍEzr 3:9
2:41
ʰS 1Ch 15:16
2:42 ⁱ1Sa 3:15;
S 1Ch 9:17

ᶜ25 See Septuagint (see also Neh. 7:29); Hebrew Kiriath Arim.

2:6 *Pahath-Moab.* Means "governor of Moab" and may have once designated an official title.
2:12 *Azgad.* Cf. 8:12; means "Gad is strong." It is a reference either to Gad (the god of fortune, referred to in Isa 65:11) or to the Transjordanian tribe of Gad.
2:16 *Ater.* Means "left-handed," as in Jdg 3:15; 20:16.
2:21–35 Whereas the names in vv. 3–20 are of families, vv. 21–35 present a series of villages and towns, many of which were in Benjamite territory north of Jerusalem. It is significant that there are no references to towns in the Negev, south of Judah. When Nebuchadnezzar overran Judah in 597 B.C. (Jer 13:19), the Edomites (see the book of Obadiah) took advantage of the situation and occupied that area.
2:21 *men of Bethlehem.* The ancestors of Jesus may have been among the returnees.
2:23 *Anathoth.* See note on Jer 1:1.
2:28 *Bethel.* See note on Ge 12:8. Towns such as Bethel,

Mizpah, Gibeon and Gibeah seem to have escaped the Babylonian assault. Bethel, however, was destroyed in the transition between the Babylonian and Persian periods. Archaeological excavations reveal that there was a small town on the site in Ezra's day.
2:31 See v. 7.
2:33 *Lod.* Modern Lydda.
2:35 *Senaah.* The largest number of returnees—3,630 (3,930 in Ne 7:38)—is associated with Senaah. It has therefore been suggested that they did not come from a specific locality or family, but represented low-caste people, as inferred from the meaning of the name.
2:36–39 Four clans of priests numbering 4,289, about a tenth of the total.
2:40 *Levites.* See Introduction to Leviticus: Title. *74.* The number of Levites who returned was relatively small (cf. 8:15). Since the Levites had been entrusted with the menial tasks of temple service, many of them may have found a

	YEAR	MONTH	DAY	EVENT	REFERENCE
	458	I =Apr.	1 8	Ezra departs from Babylon	Ezr 7:6-9
480		V =Aug.	1 4	Ezra arrives in Jerusalem	Ezr 7:8-9
		IX =Dec.	20 19	People assemble	Ezr 10:9
470		X =Dec.	1 29	Committee begins investigation	Ezr 10:16
	457	I =Mar.	1 27	Committee ends investigation	Ezr 10:17
460	445 444	Apr. to Apr.	13 2	20th year of Artaxerxes I	Ne 1:1
	445	I =Mar.-Apr.		Nehemiah approaches king	Ne 2:1
		Aug.(?)		Nehemiah arrives in Jerusalem	Ne 2:11
450		VI =Oct.	25 2	Completion of wall	Ne 6:15
		VII =Oct. to Nov.	8 5	Public assembly	Ne 7:73-8:1
440		VII =Oct.	15-22 22-28	Feast of Tabernacles	Ne 8:14
		VII =Oct.	24 30	Fast	Ne 9:1
430 B.C.	433 432	Apr. to Apr.	1 19	32nd year of Artaxerxes; Nehemiah's recall and return	Ne 5:14; 13:6

43 The temple servants:[l]

the descendants of
Ziha, Hasupha, Tabbaoth,
44 Keros, Siaha, Padon,
45 Lebanah, Hagabah, Akkub,
46 Hagab, Shalmai, Hanan,
47 Giddel, Gahar, Reaiah,
48 Rezin, Nekoda, Gazzam,
49 Uzza, Paseah, Besai,
50 Asnah, Meunim, Nephussim,
51 Bakbuk, Hakupha, Harhur,
52 Bazluth, Mehida, Harsha,
53 Barkos, Sisera, Temah,
54 Neziah and Hatipha

55 The descendants of the servants of Solomon:

the descendants of
Sotai, Hassophereth, Peruda,
56 Jaala, Darkon, Giddel,
57 Shephatiah, Hattil,
Pokereth-Hazzebaim and Ami

58 The temple servants[k] and the descendants of the servants of Solomon 392

59 The following came up from the towns of Tel Melah, Tel Harsha, Kerub, Addon and Immer, but they could not show that their families were descended[l] from Israel:

60 The descendants of
Delaiah, Tobiah and Nekoda 652

61 And from among the priests:

The descendants of
Hobaiah, Hakkoz and Barzillai (a man who had married a daughter of Barzillai the Gileadite[m] and was called by that name).

62 These searched for their family records, but they could not find them and so were excluded from the priesthood[n] as unclean.
63 The governor ordered them not to eat any of the most sacred food[o] until there was a priest ministering with the Urim and Thummim.[p]

64 The whole company numbered 42,360,
65 besides their 7,337 menservants and maidservants; and they also had 200 men and women singers.[q]
66 They had 736 horses,[r] 245

2:43 [l]S 1Ch 9:2; Ne 11:21
2:58 [k]S 1Ch 9:2
2:59 [l]S Nu 1:18
2:61 [m]S 2Sa 17:27
2:62 [n]Nu 3:10; 16:39-40
2:63 [o]Lev 2:3,10 [p]S Ex 28:30
2:65 [q]S 2Sa 19:35
2:66 [r]Isa 66:20

more comfortable way of life in exile.
2:41 *Asaph.* One of the three Levites appointed by David over the temple singers (1Ch 25:1; 2Ch 5:12; 35:15), whose duties are detailed in 1Ch 15:16–24.
2:42 *gatekeepers.* Usually Levites (1Ch 9:26; 2Ch 23:4; 35:15; Ne 12:25; 13:22). They are mentioned 16 times in Ezra-Nehemiah and 19 times in Chronicles. Their primary function was to tend the doors and gates of the temple (1Ch 9:17–27) and to perform other menial tasks (1Ch 9:28–32; 2Ch 31:14).
2:43–57 The temple servants and the descendants of Solomon's servants together numbered 392 (v. 58), which was more than the total of the Levites, singers and gatekeepers together (vv. 40–42).
2:46 *Hanan.* Means "(God) is gracious." The verb "to be gracious" and its derivatives are the components of numerous personal names in the OT—e.g., Johanan ("The LORD is gracious"; see 8:12), which has given us the English name John.
2:51 *Bakbuk.* Means "jar." It may have originally been a nickname for a fat man with a protruding belly. Cf. Jer 19:1,10, where the same Hebrew word is translated "jar"; see NIV text note on Jer 19:7.
2:53 *Barkos.* Means "son of Kos" (or Qos, an Edomite god).
2:55,58 *descendants of the servants of Solomon.* The phrase occurs only here and in Ne 7:57,60; 11:3. These may be the descendants of the Canaanites whom Solomon enslaved (1Ki 9:20–21).
2:55 *Hassophereth.* Probably means "the scribal office/function" and may have once been an official title.
2:59–63 Individuals who lacked evidence of their ancestry.
2:59 *towns.* Places in Mesopotamia where the Jews were settled by their Babylonian captors. *Tel Melah.* Means "mound of salt," possibly a mound on which salt had been scattered (see Jdg 9:45 and note). The Hebrew word *tel* designates a hill-like mound (see note on Jos 11:13) formed by the remains of a ruined city. The Jewish exiles had been settled along the Kebar River (Eze 1:1), perhaps near Nippur, a city in southern Mesopotamia that was the stronghold of rebels. The Jews had probably been settled on the mounds of ruined cities that had been depopulated by the Babylonians.
2:61 *Barzillai.* Means "man of iron." For another Barzillai see 2Sa 17:27–29; 19:31–39; 1Ki 2:7.
2:63 *governor.* Probably either Sheshbazzar or Zerubbabel (see note on 1:8). *Urim and Thummim.* See note on Ex 28:30.
2:64 *42,360.* Considerably more than the sum of the other figures given:

Categories	*Ezra*	*Nehemiah*	*1 Esdras*
Men of Israel	24,144	25,406	25,947
Priests	4,289	4,289	5,288
Levites, singers, gatekeepers	341	360	341
Temple servants, descendants of Solomon's servants	392	392	372
Men of unproven origin	652	642	652
Totals	29,818	31,089	32,600

It is difficult to account for the difference of about 10,000–12,000. The figure may refer to an unspecified 10,000–12,000 women and/or children, and it doubtless includes the priests of unproven origin referred to in vv. 61–63. Some suggest that the groups explicitly counted were returnees from Judah and Benjamin, while the remainder were from other tribes.
2:65 *menservants and maidservants.* The ratio of servants to others (one to six) is relatively high. The fact that so many returned with their masters speaks highly of the benevolent treatment of servants by the Jews. *singers.* The men and women singers listed here may be secular singers who sang at social events such as weddings and funerals (2Ch 35:25), as distinct from the temple singers of v. 41, who were all male.
2:66 *horses.* Perhaps a donation from Cyrus for the nobility. *mules.* Often used by royalty and the wealthy (1Ki 1:33;

mules, [67]435 camels and 6,720 donkeys.

[68]When they arrived at the house of the LORD in Jerusalem, some of the heads of the families[s] gave freewill offerings toward the rebuilding of the house of God on its site. [69]According to their ability they gave to the treasury for this work 61,000 drachmas[d] of gold, 5,000 minas[e] of silver and 100 priestly garments.

[70]The priests, the Levites, the singers, the gatekeepers and the temple servants settled in their own towns, along with some of the other people, and the rest of the Israelites settled in their towns.[t]

Rebuilding the Altar

3 When the seventh month came and the Israelites had settled in their towns,[u] the people assembled[v] as one man in Jerusalem. [2]Then Jeshua[w] son of Jozadak[x] and his fellow priests and Zerubbabel son of Shealtiel[y] and his associates began to build the altar of the God of Israel to sacrifice burnt offerings on it, in accordance with what is written in the Law of Moses[z] the man of God. [3]Despite their fear[a] of the peoples around them, they built the altar on its foundation and sacrificed burnt offerings on it to the LORD, both the morning and evening sacrifices.[b] [4]Then in accordance with what is written, they celebrated the Feast of Tabernacles[c] with the required number of burnt offerings prescribed for each day. [5]After that, they presented the regular burnt offerings,

the New Moon[d] sacrifices and the sacrifices for all the appointed sacred feasts of the LORD,[e] as well as those brought as freewill offerings to the LORD. [6]On the first day of the seventh month they began to offer burnt offerings to the LORD, though the foundation of the LORD's temple had not yet been laid.

Rebuilding the Temple

[7]Then they gave money to the masons and carpenters,[f] and gave food and drink and oil to the people of Sidon and Tyre, so that they would bring cedar logs[g] by sea from Lebanon[h] to Joppa, as authorized by Cyrus[i] king of Persia.

[8]In the second month[j] of the second year after their arrival at the house of God in Jerusalem, Zerubbabel[k] son of Shealtiel, Jeshua son of Jozadak and the rest of their brothers (the priests and the Levites and all who had returned from the captivity to Jerusalem) began the work, appointing Levites twenty[l] years of age and older to supervise the building of the house of the LORD. [9]Jeshua[m] and his sons and brothers and Kadmiel and his sons (descendants of Hodaviah[f]) and the sons of Henadad and their sons and brothers—all Levites—joined together in supervising those working on the house of God.

[10]When the builders laid[n] the founda-

Cross references
2:68 sS Ex 25:2
2:70 tS ver 1; S 1Ch 9:2; Ne 11:3-4
3:1 uNe 7:73
vS Lev 23:24
3:2 wS Ezr 2:2
xHag 1:1; Zec 6:11
yCh 3:17
zS Ex 20:24; Dt 12:5-6
3:3 aEzr 4:4; Da 9:25
bS Ex 29:39; Nu 28:1-8
3:4 cS Ex 23:16; Nu 29:12-38; Ne 8:14-18; Zec 14:16-19
3:5 dS Nu 28:14; Col 2:16
eLev 23:1-44; S Nu 29:39
3:7 f1Ch 22:15
gS 1Ch 14:1
hIsa 35:2; 60:13
iS Ezr 1:2-4
3:8 j1Ki 6:1
kZec 4:9
lS Nu 4:3
3:9 mEzr 2:40
3:10 nEzr 5:16; 6:3; Hag 2:15

d69 That is, about 1,100 pounds (about 500 kilograms) e69 That is, about 3 tons (about 2.9 metric tons) f9 Hebrew Yehudah, probably a variant of Hodaviah

---

Isa 66:20).
2:67 *donkeys.* Were used to carry loads, women or children. Sheep, goats and cattle are not mentioned. They would have slowed the caravan.
2:68 *arrive... Jerusalem.* For the route of the return from exile see inset to map No. 7 at the end of the Study Bible.
2:69 The parallel passage (Ne 7:70–72) gives a fuller description than the account in Ezra. In Ezra the gifts come from the heads of the families (v. 68), while in Nehemiah the gifts are credited to three sources: the governor, the heads of the families, and the rest of the people. *drachmas.* The drachma was a Greek silver coin. Some believe that the coin intended here was the Persian *daric*, a gold coin. *minas.* In the sexagesimal system (based on the number 60) that originated in Mesopotamia, there were 60 shekels in a mina and 60 minas in a talent. A shekel, which was about two-fifths of an ounce of silver, was the average wage for a month's work. Thus a mina would be the equivalent of five years' wages, and a talent would be 300 years' wages.
2:70 Later, Nehemiah (11:1–2) would be compelled to move people by lot to reinforce the population of Jerusalem.
3:1 *seventh month.* Tishri (September-October), about three months after the arrival of the exiles in Judah (in 537 B.C.). Tishri was one of the most sacred months of the Jewish year (see Lev 23:23–43 and notes).
3:2 *Jeshua ... Zerubbabel.* The priest takes precedence over the civil leader in view of the nature of the occasion

(contrast 3:8; 4:3; 5:2; Hag 1:1).
3:4 *Feast of Tabernacles.* See Lev 23:33–43 and notes.
3:5 *New Moon.* See note on 1Sa 20:5. *appointed sacred feasts.* See note on Lev 23:2. *freewill offerings.* See note on 1:4. It is noteworthy that the restoration of the sacrifices preceded the erection of the temple itself.
3:7 *cedar logs.* As in the case of the first temple, the Phoenicians cooperated by sending timbers and workmen (1Ki 5:6–12).
3:8 *second month.* The same month (April-May) in which Solomon had begun his temple (1Ki 6:1). *second year.* Since the Jews probably returned to Judah in the spring of 537 B.C., the second year would be the spring of 536. *twenty years.* In earlier times the lower age limit for Levites was 30 (Nu 4:3) or 25 years (Nu 8:24). It was later reduced to 20 (1Ch 23:24,27; 2Ch 31:17), probably because there were so few Levites.
3:10 *trumpets.* Made of hammered silver (see Nu 10:2 and note). According to Josephus (*Antiquities*, 3.12.6—written c. A.D. 93), the trumpet was "in length a little short of a cubit; it is a narrow tube, slightly thicker than a flute." With the possible exception of their use at the coronation of Joash (2Ki 11:14; 2Ch 23:13), the trumpets were always blown by priests. They were most often used on joyous occasions, such as here and at the dedication of the rebuilt walls of Jerusalem (Ne 12:35; cf. 2Ch 5:13; Ps 98:6). *cymbals.* The Hebrew for this word occurs 13 times in the OT, all in Chronicles except

tion of the temple of the LORD, the priests in their vestments and with trumpets,[o] and the Levites (the sons of Asaph) with cymbals, took their places to praise[p] the LORD, as prescribed by David[q] king of Israel.[r] ¹¹With praise and thanksgiving they sang to the LORD:

"He is good;
  his love to Israel endures forever."[s]

And all the people gave a great shout[t] of praise to the LORD, because the foundation[u] of the house of the LORD was laid. ¹²But many of the older priests and Levites and family heads, who had seen the former temple,[v] wept[w] aloud when they saw the foundation of this temple being laid, while many others shouted for joy. ¹³No one could distinguish the sound of the shouts of joy[x] from the sound of weeping, be-

cause the people made so much noise. And the sound was heard far away.

Opposition to the Rebuilding

4 When the enemies of Judah and Benjamin heard that the exiles were building[y] a temple for the LORD, the God of Israel, ²they came to Zerubbabel and to the heads of the families and said, "Let us help you build because, like you, we seek your God and have been sacrificing to him since the time of Esarhaddon[z] king of Assyria, who brought us here."[a]

³But Zerubbabel, Jeshua and the rest of the heads of the families of Israel answered, "You have no part with us in building a temple to our God. We alone will build it for the LORD, the God of Israel, as King Cyrus, the king of Persia, commanded us."[b]

3:10 oS Nu 10:2;
S 2Sa 6:5;
1Ch 16:6;
2Ch 5:13;
Ne 12:35
pS 1Ch 25:1
qS 1Ch 6:31
rZec 6:12
3:11 sS 1Ch 16:34,
41; S 2Ch 7:3;
Ps 30:5; 107:1;
118:1; 138:8
tS Jos 6:5,10
uHag 2:18;
Zec 4:9; 8:9
3:12 vHag 2:3,9
wJer 31:9; 50:4
3:13 xJob 8:21;
33:26; Ps 27:6;
42:4; Isa 16:9;
Jer 48:33

4:1 yNe 2:20
4:2 zS 2Ki 17:24
aS 2Ki 17:41
4:3 bEzr 1:1-4

here and Ne 12:27.
3:11 *sang.* May mean "sang responsively," referring to antiphonal singing by a choir divided into two groups. *He is good . . . endures forever.* See, e.g., 1Ch 16:34; 2Ch 5:13; Ps 100:5. *great shout.* See Jos 6:5,20; 1Sa 4:5; Ps 95:1.
3:13 *shouts of joy . . . sound of weeping.* The people of

Israel were accustomed to showing their emotions in visible and audible ways (10:1; Ne 1:4; 8:9). The same God who had permitted judgment had now brought them back and would enable them to complete the project. A Babylonian cornerstone reads: "I started the work weeping, I finished it rejoicing." Cf. Ps 126:5–6.

Zerubbabel's Temple

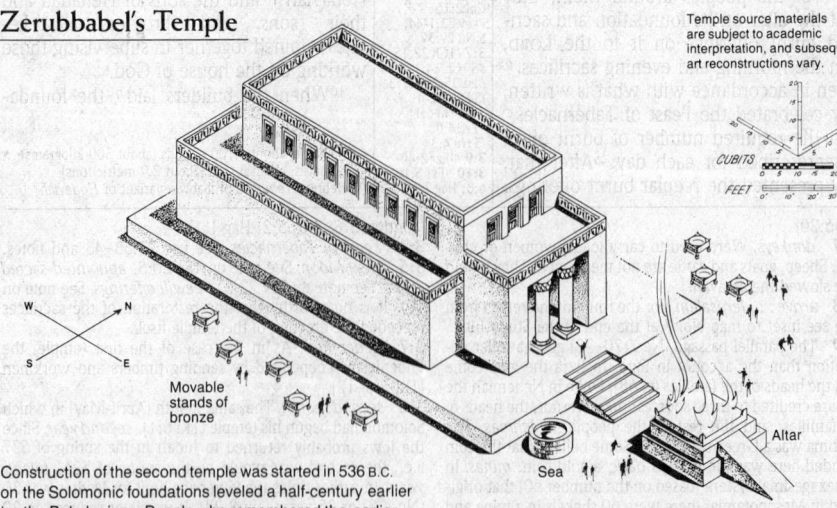

Temple source materials are subject to academic interpretation, and subsequent art reconstructions vary.

CUBITS

FEET

W N S E

Movable stands of bronze

Sea

Altar

Construction of the second temple was started in 536 B.C. on the Solomonic foundations leveled a half-century earlier by the Babylonians. People who remembered the earlier temple wept at the comparison (Ezr 3:12). Not until 516 B.C., the 6th year of the Persian emperor Darius I (522-486), was the temple finally completed at the urging of Haggai and Zechariah (Ezr 6:13-15).

Archaeological evidence confirms that the Persian period in Palestine was a comparatively impoverished one in terms of material culture. Later Aramaic documents from Elephantine in Upper Egypt illustrate the official process of gaining permission to construct a Jewish place of worship, and the opposition engendered by the presence of various foes during this period.

Of the temple and its construction, little is known. Among the few contemporary buildings, the Persian palace at Lachish and the Tobiad monument at Iraq el-Amir may be compared in terms of technique.

Unlike the more famous structures razed in 586 B.C. and A.D. 70, the temple begun by Zerubbabel suffered no major hostile destruction, but was gradually repaired and reconstructed over a long period. Eventually it was replaced entirely by Herod's magnificent edifice.

© Hugh Claycombe 1986

⁴Then the peoples around them set out to discourage the people of Judah and make them afraid to go on building.^{g c} ⁵They hired counselors to work against them and frustrate their plans during the entire reign of Cyrus king of Persia and down to the reign of Darius king of Persia.

Later Opposition Under Xerxes and Artaxerxes

⁶At the beginning of the reign of Xerxes,^{h d} they lodged an accusation against the people of Judah and Jerusalem. ^e

⁷And in the days of Artaxerxes^f king of Persia, Bishlam, Mithredath, Tabeel and the rest of his associates wrote a letter to Artaxerxes. The letter was written in Aramaic script and in the Aramaic^g language.^{i,j}

⁸Rehum the commanding officer and Shimshai the secretary wrote a letter against Jerusalem to Artaxerxes the king as follows:

⁹Rehum the commanding officer and Shimshai the secretary, together with the rest of their associates^h—the judges and officials over the men from Tripolis, Persia,^k Erechⁱ and Babylon, the Elamites of Susa,^j ¹⁰and the other people whom the great and honorable Ashurbanipal^{l k} deported and settled in the city of Samaria and elsewhere in Trans-Euphrates.^l

¹¹(This is a copy of the letter they sent him.)

To King Artaxerxes,

From your servants, the men of Trans-Euphrates:

¹²The king should know that the Jews who came up to us from you

Cross references:
4:4 ^cS Ezr 3:3
4:6 ^dEst 1:1; Da 9:1 ^eEst 3:13; 9:5
4:7 ^fEzr 7:1; Ne 2:1 ^g2Ki 18:26; Isa 36:11; Da 1:4; 2:4
4:9 ^hver 23; Ezr 5:6; 6:6,13 ⁱGe 10:10 ^jNe 1:1; Est 1:2; Da 8:2
4:10 ^kS 2Ki 17:24 ^lver 17; Ne 4:2

Footnotes:
^g4 Or *and troubled them as they built*   ^h6 Hebrew *Ahasuerus,* a variant of Xerxes' Persian name   ⁱ7 Or *written in Aramaic and translated*   ^j7 The text of Ezra 4:8—6:18 is in Aramaic.   ^k9 Or *officials, magistrates and governors over the men from*   ^l10 Aramaic *Osnappar,* a variant of Ashurbanipal

---

4:1–23 A summary of various attempts to thwart the efforts of the Jews. In vv. 1–5 the author describes events in the reign of Cyrus (559–530 B.C.), in v. 6 the reign of Xerxes (486–465) and in vv. 7–23 the reign of Artaxerxes I (465–424). He then reverts in v. 24 to the time of Darius I (522–486), during whose reign the temple was completed (see 5:1–2; 6:13–15; Haggai; Zec 1:1–17; 4:9).

4:1 *enemies.* The people who offered their "help" (v. 2) were from Samaria. *Judah and Benjamin.* See notes on 1:5; 1Ki 12:21.

4:2 After the fall of Samaria in 722–721 B.C., the Assyrian kings brought in people from Mesopotamia and Aram. These people served their own gods but also took up the worship of the Lord as the god of the land (2Ki 17:24–41). *Esarhaddon.* See note on 2Ki 19:37.

4:4 *peoples around them.* Josephus (*Antiquities,* 11.2.1) singles out especially the Cutheans (see 2Ki 17:24,30). *make them afraid.* The Hebrew for this verb often describes the fear aroused in a battle situation (Jdg 20:41; 2Sa 4:1; 2Ch 32:18).

4:5 *hired.* Cf. the hiring of Balaam (Dt 23:4–5; Ne 13:2) and the hiring of a prophet to intimidate Nehemiah (Ne 6:12–13).

4:6 *Xerxes.* See the book of Esther. When Darius died in 486 B.C., Egypt rebelled, and Xerxes, the son of Darius, had to march west to suppress the revolt.

4:7 *Artaxerxes.* Three Persian kings bore this name: Artaxerxes I (465–424 B.C.), II (404–358) and III (358–338). The king here is Artaxerxes I. *Mithredath.* See 1:8 and note. *Tabeel.* An Aramaic name (see Isa 7:6 and note). *wrote a letter.* Near Eastern kings employed an elaborate system of informers and spies. Egyptian sources speak of the "ears and eyes" of Pharaoh. Sargon II of Assyria had agents in Urartu whom he ordered: "Write me whatever you see and hear." The King's Eye and the King's Ear were two officials who reported to the Persian monarch.

4:8–6:18 For this passage the author draws upon Aramaic documents; a further Aramaic section is 7:12–26.

4:8 *commanding officer.* An official who had the role of a chancellor or commissioner. Perhaps Rehum dictated, and Shimshai wrote the letter in Aramaic. (Alternatively, Shim-

shai may have been a high official rather than a scribe.) The letter would then be read in a Persian translation before the king (v. 18). According to Herodotus (3.128), royal scribes were attached to each governor to report directly to the Persian king.

4:9 *associates.* See vv. 17,23; 5:3,6; 6:6 ("fellow officials"); 6:13. One of the striking characteristics of Persian bureaucracy was that each responsibility was shared among colleagues. *Erech.* See note on Ge 10:10. *Babylon.* During the reign of the Assyrian king Ashurbanipal (669–627 B.C.), a major revolt had taken place (652–648), involving Shamash-Shum-Ukin, the brother of the king and the ruler over Babylonia. After a long siege Shamash-Shum-Ukin hurled himself into the flames. Doubtless these men of Babylon and the other cities mentioned were the descendants of the rebels, whom the Assyrians deported to the west. *Susa.* The major city of Elam (in southwest Iran). Because of Susa's part in the revolt, Ashurbanipal brutally destroyed it in 640 (two centuries before Rehum's letter).

4:10 *Ashurbanipal.* The last great Assyrian king, famed for his library at Nineveh. He is not named elsewhere in the Bible, but he is probably the king who freed Manasseh from exile (2Ch 33:11–13). *deported.* Ashurbanipal may be the unnamed Assyrian king who brought people to Samaria according to 2Ki 17:24. It is characteristic of such deportations that the descendants of populations that had been removed from their homelands nearly two centuries earlier should still stress their origins. *Samaria.* The murder of Amon king of Judah (642–640 B.C.; see 2Ki 21:23; 2Ch 33:24) was probably the result of an anti-Assyrian movement inspired by the revolt in Elam and Babylonia. The Assyrians may then have deported the rebellious Samaritans and replaced them with the rebellious Elamites and Babylonians. *Trans-Euphrates.* Lit. "beyond the River," i.e., the Euphrates River. From the Palestinian point of view the land "beyond the River" was Mesopotamia (Jos 24:2–3,14–15; 2Sa 10:16). From the Mesopotamian point of view the land "beyond the River" included the areas of Aram, Phoenicia and Palestine (1Ki 4:24). The Persians also called this area Athura.

4:12 *restoring the walls and repairing the foundations.* As Isaiah had foretold (Isa 58:13–14).

have gone to Jerusalem and are rebuilding that rebellious and wicked city. They are restoring the walls and repairing the foundations. [m]

[13]Furthermore, the king should know that if this city is built and its walls are restored, no more taxes, tribute or duty[n] will be paid, and the royal revenues will suffer. [14]Now since we are under obligation to the palace and it is not proper for us to see the king dishonored, we are sending this message to inform the king, [15]so that a search may be made in the archives[o] of your predecessors. In these records you will find that this city is a rebellious city, troublesome to kings and provinces, a place of rebellion from ancient times. That is why this city was destroyed. [p] [16]We inform the king that if this city is built and its walls are restored, you will be left with nothing in Trans-Euphrates.

[17]The king sent this reply:

To Rehum the commanding officer, Shimshai the secretary and the rest of their associates living in Samaria and elsewhere in Trans-Euphrates: [q]

Greetings.

[18]The letter you sent us has been read and translated in my presence. [19]I issued an order and a search was made, and it was found that this city

has a long history of revolt[r] against kings and has been a place of rebellion and sedition. [20]Jerusalem has had powerful kings ruling over the whole of Trans-Euphrates,[s] and taxes, tribute and duty were paid to them. [21]Now issue an order to these men to stop work, so that this city will not be rebuilt until I so order. [22]Be careful not to neglect this matter. Why let this threat grow, to the detriment of the royal interests? [t]

[23]As soon as the copy of the letter of King Artaxerxes was read to Rehum and Shimshai the secretary and their associates, [u] they went immediately to the Jews in Jerusalem and compelled them by force to stop.

[24]Thus the work on the house of God in Jerusalem came to a standstill until the second year of the reign of Darius[v] king of Persia.

Tattenai's Letter to Darius

5 Now Haggai[w] the prophet and Zechariah[x] the prophet, a descendant of Iddo, prophesied[y] to the Jews in Judah and Jerusalem in the name of the God of Israel, who was over them. [2]Then Zerubbabel[z] son of Shealtiel and Jeshua[a] son of Jozadak set to work[b] to rebuild the house of God in Jerusalem. And the prophets of God were with them, helping them.

[3]At that time Tattenai,[c] governor of

4:12 [m]Ezr 5:3,9
4:13 [n]Ezr 7:24; Ne 5:4
4:15 [o]Ezr 5:17; 6:1 [p]Est 3:8
4:17 [q]S ver 10
4:19 [r]S 2Ki 18:7
4:20 [s]Ge 15:18-21; S Ezr 23:31; S Jos 1:4; S 1Ki 4:21; 1Ch 18:3; Ps 72:8-11
4:22 [t]Da 6:2
4:23 [u]S ver 9
4:24 [v]Ne 2:1-8; Da 9:25; Hag 1:1, 15; Zec 1:1
5:1 [w]Ezr 6:14; Hag 1:1,3,12; 2:1, 10,20 [x]Zec 1:1; 7:1 [y]Hag 1:14-2:9; Zec 4:9-10; 8:9
5:2 [z]S 1Ch 3:19; Hag 1:14; 2:21; Zec 4:6-10 [a]S Ezr 2:2 [b]ver 8; Hag 2:2-5
5:3 [c]Ezr 6:6

4:13 Most of the gold and silver coins that came into Persia's treasury were melted down to be stored as bullion. Very little of the taxes returned to benefit the provinces.
4:14 *we are under obligation to the palace.* Lit. "we eat the salt of the palace." Salt was made a royal monopoly by the Ptolemies in Egypt, and perhaps by the Persians as well.
4:15 *archives.* See 5:17; 6:1; Est 2:23; 6:1–2. There were several repositories of such documents at the major capitals. These royal archives preserved documents for centuries. In the third century B.C. the Babylonian priest Berossus made use of the Babylonian Chronicles in his history of Babylon, which covered events from the Assyrian to the Hellenistic (beginning with Alexander's conquest of Babylon in 330 B.C.) eras.
4:18 *read.* Since the king probably could not read Aramaic, he would have had the document read to him. *translated.* From Aramaic into Persian (see NIV text notes on v. 7; Ne 8:8).
4:19 *rebellion.* There is some truth in the accusation. Jerusalem had rebelled against the Assyrians in 701 B.C. (2Ki 18:7) and against the Babylonians in 600 and 589 (2Ki 24:1,20).
4:21–23 As a result of the intervention of the provincial authorities, Artaxerxes I (see v. 11 and note on v. 7) ordered that the Jews stop rebuilding the walls of Jerusalem (see note on Ne 1:3). The events of vv. 7–23 probably occurred prior to 445 B.C. The forcible destruction of these recently rebuilt

walls rather than the destruction by Nebuchadnezzar would then be the basis of the report made to Nehemiah (Ne 1:3).
4:24 After this long digression describing the opposition to Jewish efforts, the writer returns to his original subject of the rebuilding of the temple (vv. 1–5). *second year of the reign of Darius.* According to Persian reckoning, the second regnal year of Darius I began on Nisan 1 (Apr. 3), 520 B.C., and lasted until Feb. 21, 519. In that year the prophet Haggai (Hag 1:1–5) exhorted Zerubbabel to begin rebuilding the temple on the first day of the sixth month (Aug. 29). Work began on the temple on the 24th day of the month, Sept. 21 (Hag 1:15). During his first two years, Darius had to establish his right to the throne by fighting numerous rebels, as recounted in his famous Behistun (Bisitun) inscription. It was only after the stabilization of the Persian empire that efforts to rebuild the temple could be permitted.
5:1 *Haggai . . . Zechariah.* Beginning on Aug. 29, 520 B.C. (Hag 1:1), and continuing until Dec. 18 (Hag 2:1,10,20), the prophet Haggai delivered a series of messages to stir up the people to resume work on the temple. Two months after Haggai's first speech, Zechariah joined him (Zec 1:1).
5:2 *Zerubbabel.* A Babylonian name meaning "offspring of Babylon," referring to his birth in exile. He was the son of Shealtiel and the grandson of Jehoiachin (1Ch 3:17), the next-to-last king of Judah. Zerubbabel was the last of the Davidic line to be entrusted with political authority by the occupying powers. He was also an ancestor of Jesus (Mt 1:12–13; Lk 3:27). *Jeshua.* See note on 2:2.

Trans-Euphrates, and Shethar-Bozenai[d] and their associates went to them and asked, "Who authorized you to rebuild this temple and restore this structure?"[e] [4]They also asked, "What are the names of the men constructing this building?"[m] [5]But the eye of their God[f] was watching over the elders of the Jews, and they were not stopped until a report could go to Darius and his written reply be received.

[6]This is a copy of the letter that Tattenai, governor of Trans-Euphrates, and Shethar-Bozenai and their associates, the officials of Trans-Euphrates, sent to King Darius. [7]The report they sent him read as follows:

To King Darius:

Cordial greetings.

[8]The king should know that we went to the district of Judah, to the temple of the great God. The people are building it with large stones and placing the timbers in the walls. The work[g] is being carried on with diligence and is making rapid progress under their direction.

[9]We questioned the elders and asked them, "Who authorized you to rebuild this temple and restore this structure?"[h] [10]We also asked them their names, so that we could write down the names of their leaders for your information.

[11]This is the answer they gave us:

"We are the servants of the God of heaven and earth, and we are rebuilding the temple[i] that was built many years ago, one that a great king of Israel built and finished. [12]But because our fathers angered[j] the God of heaven, he handed them over to Nebuchadnezzar the Chaldean, king

of Babylon, who destroyed this temple and deported the people to Babylon.[k]

[13]"However, in the first year of Cyrus king of Babylon, King Cyrus issued a decree[l] to rebuild this house of God. [14]He even removed from the temple[n] of Babylon the gold and silver articles of the house of God, which Nebuchadnezzar had taken from the temple in Jerusalem and brought to the temple[n] in Babylon.[m]

"Then King Cyrus gave them to a man named Sheshbazzar,[n] whom he had appointed governor, [15]and he told him, 'Take these articles and go and deposit them in the temple in Jerusalem. And rebuild the house of God on its site.' [16]So this Sheshbazzar came and laid the foundations of the house of God[o] in Jerusalem. From that day to the present it has been under construction but is not yet finished."

[17]Now if it pleases the king, let a search be made in the royal archives[p] of Babylon to see if King Cyrus did in fact issue a decree to rebuild this house of God in Jerusalem. Then let the king send us his decision in this matter.

The Decree of Darius

6 King Darius then issued an order, and they searched in the archives[q] stored in the treasury at Babylon. [2]A scroll was found in the citadel of Ecbatana in the province of Media, and this was written on it:

Memorandum:

[3]In the first year of King Cyrus, the

Cross-references (center column):

5:3 [d]Ezr 6:6
[e]S Ezr 4:12
5:5 [f]S 2Ki 25:28; Ezr 7:6,9,28; 8:18,22,31; Ne 2:8,18; Ps 33:18; Isa 66:14
5:8 [g]S ver 2
5:9 [h]S Ezr 4:12
5:11 [i]1Ki 6:1; 2Ch 3:1-2
5:12 [j]S 2Ch 36:16

[k]S Dt 21:10; S 28:36; S 2Ki 24:1; S Jer 1:3
5:13 [l]S Ezr 1:2-4
5:14 [m]Ezr 1:7
[n]S 1Ch 3:18
5:16 [o]S Ezr 3:10
5:17 [p]S Ezr 4:15
6:1 [q]S Ezr 4:15

Textual footnotes:

[m]4 See Septuagint; Aramaic *4We told them the names of the men constructing this building.*　[n]14 Or *palace*

Study notes:

5:3 *Tattenai.* Probably a Babylonian name. *Shethar-Bozenai.* Perhaps a Persian official.

5:5 *not stopped.* The Persian governor gave the Jews the benefit of the doubt by not stopping the work while the inquiry was proceeding.

5:6–7 *sent to King Darius . . . sent him.* Texts found in the royal city of Persepolis vividly confirm that such inquiries were sent directly to the king himself, revealing the close attention he paid to minute details.

5:8 *timbers.* May refer to interior paneling (1Ki 6:15–18) or to logs alternating with the brick or stone layers in the walls (see note on 6:4).

5:11 *great king of Israel.* According to 1Ki 6:1 Solomon began building the temple in the fourth year of his reign (966 B.C.). The project lasted seven years (1Ki 6:38).

5:12 *Chaldean.* The Chaldeans were the inhabitants of the southern regions of Mesopotamia who established the Neo-Babylonian empire (612–539 B.C.). Their origins are obscure. In the late seventh century B.C. the Chaldeans, led by

Nebuchadnezzar's father Nabopolassar, overthrew the Assyrians.

5:14 *Sheshbazzar . . . governor.* See note on 1:8.

6:1 *archives . . . in the treasury at Babylon.* Many documents have also been found in the so-called "treasury" area of Persepolis (see map on p. 573).

6:2 *Ecbatana.* One of the four capitals (along with Babylon, Persepolis and Susa) of the Persian empire. Located in what is today the Iranian city of Hamadan, its remains have not yet been excavated. This is the only reference to the site in the OT, though there are numerous references in the Apocryphal books (Judith 1:1–4; Tobit 3:7; 7–1; 14:12–14; 2 Maccabees 9:3). *Media.* The homeland of the Medes in northwestern Iran. The Medes were an Indo-European tribe related to the Persians. After the rise of Cyrus in 550 B.C., they became subordinate to the Persians. The name of the area was retained as late as the NT era (Ac 2:9).

6:3–5 Compare this Aramaic memorandum of the decree of Cyrus with the Hebrew version in 1:2–4. The Aramaic is

king issued a decree concerning the temple of God in Jerusalem:

Let the temple be rebuilt as a place to present sacrifices, and let its foundations be laid.[r] It is to be ninety feet[o] high and ninety feet wide, [4]with three courses[s] of large stones and one of timbers. The costs are to be paid by the royal treasury.[t] [5]Also, the gold[u] and silver articles of the house of God, which Nebuchadnezzar took from the temple in Jerusalem and brought to Babylon, are to be returned to their places in the temple in Jerusalem; they are to be deposited in the house of God.[v]

[6]Now then, Tattenai,[w] governor of Trans-Euphrates, and Shethar-Bozenai[x] and you, their fellow officials of that province, stay away from there. [7]Do not interfere with the work on this temple of God. Let the governor of the Jews and the Jewish elders rebuild this house of God on its site.

[8]Moreover, I hereby decree what you are to do for these elders of the Jews in the construction of this house of God:

The expenses of these men are to be fully paid out of the royal treasury,[y] from the revenues[z] of Trans-Euphrates, so that the work will not stop. [9]Whatever is needed—young bulls, rams, male lambs for burnt offerings[a] to the God of heaven, as well as wheat, salt, wine and oil, as requested by the priests in Jerusalem—must be given them daily without fail, [10]so that they may offer sacrifices pleasing to the God of heaven and pray for the well-being of the king and his sons.[b]

[11]Furthermore, I decree that if anyone changes this edict, a beam is to be pulled from his house and he is to be lifted up and impaled[c] on it. And for this crime his house is to be made a pile of rubble.[d] [12]May God, who has caused his Name to dwell there,[e] overthrow any king or people who lifts a hand to change this decree or to destroy this temple in Jerusalem.

I Darius[f] have decreed it. Let it be carried out with diligence.

Completion and Dedication of the Temple

[13]Then, because of the decree King Darius had sent, Tattenai, governor of Trans-Euphrates, and Shethar-Bozenai and their associates[g] carried it out with dili-

Cross references

6:3 [r]S Ezr 3:10; Hag 2:3
6:4 [s]S 1Ki 6:36
[t]ver 8; Ezr 7:20
6:5 [u]S 1Ch 29:2
[v]S Ezr 1:7
6:6 [w]Ezr 5:3
[x]Ezr 5:3
6:8 [y]S ver 4
[z]S 1Sa 9:20

6:9 [a]Lev 1:3,10
6:10 [b]Ezr 7:23; 1Ti 2:1-2
6:11 [c]S Dt 21:22-23; Est 2:23; 5:14; 9:14 [d]Ezr 7:26; Da 2:5; 3:29
6:12 [e]S Ex 20:24; S Dt 12:5; S 2Ch 6:2 [f]ver 14
6:13 [g]S Ezr 4:9

[o]3 Aramaic *sixty cubits* (about 27 meters)

written in a more sober administrative style without any reference to the Lord (Yahweh). A similar memorandum dealing with permission to rebuild the Jewish temple at Elephantine in Upper Egypt was found among fifth-century B.C. Aramaic papyri recovered at that site.
6:3 *ninety feet high and ninety feet wide.* These dimensions, which contrast with those of Solomon's temple (see NIV text note on 1Ki 6:2), are probably not specifications of the temple as built but of the outer limits of a building the Persians were willing to subsidize. The second temple was not as grandiose as the first (3:12; Hag 2:3).
6:4 *large stones . . . timbers.* The same kind of construction is mentioned in 1Ki 6:36; 7:12. Such a design was possibly intended to cushion the building against earthquake shocks. *costs are to be paid by the royal treasury.* In 1973 archaeologists discovered at Xanthos in southwest Turkey a cult foundation charter from the late Persian period that provides some striking parallels with this decree of Cyrus. As in Ezra, amounts of sacrifices, names of priests and the responsibility for the upkeep of the cult are specified. The Persian king seems to have known details of the cult.
6:8 *paid out of the royal treasury.* It was a consistent policy of Persian kings to help restore sanctuaries in their empire. For example, a memorandum concerning the rebuilding of the Jewish temple at Elephantine was written by the Persian governors of Judah and Samaria. Also from non-Biblical sources we learn that Cyrus repaired temples at Uruk (Erech) and Ur. Cambyses, successor to Cyrus, gave funds for the temple at Sais in Egypt. The temple of Amun in the Khargah Oasis was rebuilt by order of Darius.
6:9 That the Persian monarchs were interested in the details of foreign cults is shown clearly by the ordinances of Cambyses and Darius I, regulating the temples and priests in Egypt. On the authority of Darius II (423–404 B.C.) a letter was written to the Jews at Elephantine concerning the keeping of the Feast of Unleavened Bread.
6:10 *pray for the well-being of the king and his sons.* In the inscription on the Cyrus Cylinder (made of baked clay), the king asks: "May all the gods whom I have resettled in their sacred cities ask Bel and Nebo daily for a long life for me." The Jews of Elephantine offered to pray for the Persian governor of Judah. The daily synagogue services included a prayer for the royal family (cf. 1Ti 2:1–2).
6:11 *if anyone changes this edict.* It was customary at the end of decrees and treaties to append a long list of curses against anyone who might disregard them. *impaled.* According to Herodotus (3.159), Darius I impaled 3,000 Babylonians when he took the city of Babylon. See NIV text note on Est 2:23.
6:12 *May God . . . overthrow any king or people.* At the end of his famous Behistun (Bisitun) inscription Darius I warned: "If you see this inscription or these sculptures, and destroy them and do not protect them as long as you have strength, may Ahuramazda strike you, and may you not have a family, and what you do . . . may Ahuramazda utterly destroy." *caused his Name to dwell.* See note on Dt 12:5.
6:13–14 Work on the temple had made little progress not only because of opposition but also because of the preoccupation of the returnees with their own homes (Hag 1:2–9). Because they had placed their own interests first, God sent them famine as a judgment (Hag 1:5–6,10–11). Spurred by the preaching of Haggai and Zechariah, and under the leadership of Zerubbabel and Jeshua, a new effort was begun (Hag 1:12–15).

gence. [14]So the elders of the Jews continued to build and prosper under the preaching[h] of Haggai the prophet and Zechariah, a descendant of Iddo. They finished building the temple according to the command of the God of Israel and the decrees of Cyrus,[i] Darius[j] and Artaxerxes,[k] kings of Persia. [15]The temple was completed on the third day of the month Adar, in the sixth year of the reign of King Darius.[l]

[16]Then the people of Israel—the priests, the Levites and the rest of the exiles—celebrated the dedication[m] of the house of God with joy. [17]For the dedication of this house of God they offered[n] a hundred bulls, two hundred rams, four hundred male lambs and, as a sin offering for all Israel, twelve male goats, one for each of the tribes of Israel. [18]And they installed the priests in their divisions[o] and the Levites in their groups[p] for the service of God at Jerusalem, according to what is written in the Book of Moses.[q]

The Passover

[19]On the fourteenth day of the first month, the exiles celebrated the Passover.[r] [20]The priests and Levites had purified themselves and were all ceremonially clean. The Levites slaughtered[s] the Passover lamb for all the exiles, for their brothers the priests and for themselves. [21]So the Israelites who had returned from the exile ate it, together with all who had separated themselves[t] from the unclean practices[u] of their Gentile neighbors in order to seek the LORD,[v] the God of Israel. [22]For seven days they celebrated with joy the Feast of Unleavened Bread,[w] because the LORD had filled them with joy by changing the attitude[x] of the king of Assyria, so that he assisted them in the work on the house of God, the God of Israel.

Ezra Comes to Jerusalem

7 After these things, during the reign of Artaxerxes[y] king of Persia, Ezra son of Seraiah,[z] the son of Azariah, the son of Hilkiah,[a] [2]the son of Shallum, the son of

Cross references (center column):
6:14 [h]S Ezr 5:1
[i]S Ezr 1:2-4 /ver 12 [k]Ezr 7:1;
Ne 2:1
6:15 [l]Zec 1:1; 4:9
6:16 [m]S 1Ki 8:63
6:17 [n]S 2Sa 6:13; 2Ch 29:21; S 30:24
6:18 [o]S 2Ch 35:4; Lk 1:5 [p]S 1Ch 24:1 [q]Nu 3:6-9; 8:9-11; 18:1-32

6:19 [r]S Ex 12:11; S Nu 28:16
6:20
[s]2Ch 30:17
6:21 [t]Ezr 9:1; Ne 9:2 [u]S Dt 18:9; Eze 36:25 [v]1Ch 22:19; Ps 14:2
6:22 [w]S Ex 12:17 [x]S Ezr 1:1
7:1 [y]S Ezr 4:7; S 6:14 [z]S 2Ki 25:18 [a]2Ki 22:4

6:14 *Artaxerxes.* The reference to him seems out of place, because he did not contribute to rebuilding the temple. He may have been inserted here since he contributed to the work of the temple at a later date under Ezra (7:21–24).
6:15 *temple was completed.* On Mar. 12, 516 B.C., almost 70 years after its destruction. The renewed work on the temple had begun on Sept. 21, 520 (Hag 1:15), and sustained effort had continued for almost three and a half years. According to Hag 2:3, the older members who could remember the splendor of Solomon's temple were disappointed when they saw the smaller size of Zerubbabel's temple (cf. Ezr 3:12). Yet in the long run the second temple, though not as grand as the first, enjoyed a much longer life. The general plan of the second temple was similar to that of Solomon's, but the Most Holy Place was left empty because the ark of the covenant had been lost through the Babylonian conquest. According to Josephus, on the Day of Atonement the high priest placed his censer on the slab of stone that marked the former location of the ark. The Holy Place was furnished with a table for the bread of the Presence, the incense altar, and one lampstand (in the Apocrypha cf. 1 Maccabees 1:21–22; 4:49–51) instead of Solomon's ten (1Ki 7:49).
6:16 *exiles . . . dedication.* Cf. the dedication of Solomon's temple (1Ki 8). The leaders of those who returned from exile were responsible for the completion of the temple. "Dedication" translates the Aramaic word *hanukkah.* The Jewish holiday in December that celebrates the recapture of the temple from the Seleucids and its rededication (165 B.C.) is also known as Hanukkah.
6:17 *hundred . . . two hundred . . . four hundred.* The number of animals sacrificed was small in comparison with similar services in the reigns of Solomon (1Ki 8:5,63), Hezekiah (2Ch 30:24) and Josiah (2Ch 35:7), when thousands rather than hundreds were offered.
6:18 *divisions.* The priests were separated into 24 divisions (1Ch 24:1–19), each of which served at the temple for a week at a time (cf. Lk 1:5,8). In 1962 fragments of a synagogue inscription listing the 24 divisions were found at Caesarea. *written in the Book of Moses.* Perhaps referring to such

passages as Ex 29; Lev 8; Nu 3; 8:5–26; 18.
6:19 *fourteenth day . . . first month . . . Passover.* The date would have been about Apr. 21, 516 B.C.
6:20 *purified themselves . . . ceremonially clean.* See note on Lev 4:12. Priests and Levites had to be ceremonially clean to fulfill their ritual functions.
6:21 *with all who had separated themselves.* The returning exiles were willing to accept those who separated themselves from the paganism of the foreigners who had been introduced into the area by the Assyrians.
6:22 *king of Assyria.* A surprising title for Darius, the Persian king. But even after the fall of Nineveh in 612 B.C., the term "Assyria" continued to be used for former territories the Assyrians had occupied (even Syria is an abbreviation of Assyria). Persian kings adopted a variety of titles, including "king of Babylon" (cf. 5:13; Ne 13:6).
7:1–5 The genealogy of Ezra given here lists 16 ancestors back to Aaron, the brother of Moses.
7:1 *After these things.* The events of the preceding chapter concluded with the completion of the temple in 516 B.C. *Artaxerxes.* The identity of the king mentioned in this chapter has been disputed. If this was Artaxerxes I, which seems likely, Ezra would have arrived in Judah in 458, and there would be a gap of almost 60 years between the events of ch. 6 and those of ch. 7. The only recorded event during this interval is the opposition to the rebuilding of Jerusalem in the reign of Xerxes (486–465) in 4:6. *Ezra.* Perhaps a shortened form of Azariah, a name that occurs twice in the list of his ancestors. The Greek form is Esdras, as in the Apocrypha. *Seraiah.* Means "The LORD is prince." He was the high priest under Zedekiah who was killed in 586 by Nebuchadnezzar (2Ki 25:18–21) some 128 years before Ezra's arrival. He was therefore the ancestor rather than the father of Ezra; "son" often means "descendant" (see 1Ch 6:14–15). *Azariah.* Means "The LORD helps." *Hilkiah.* Means "My portion is the LORD." He was the high priest under Josiah (2Ki 22:4).
7:2 *Zadok.* Means "righteous." He was a priest under David (2Sa 8:17). Solomon appointed Zadok as high priest in place of Abiathar, who supported the rebel Adonijah (1Ki 1:7–8; 2:35). Ezekiel regarded the Zadokites as free from

Zadok,[b] the son of Ahitub,[c] [3]the son of Amariah, the son of Azariah, the son of Meraioth, [4]the son of Zerahiah, the son of Uzzi, the son of Bukki, [5]the son of Abishua, the son of Phinehas,[d] the son of Eleazar, the son of Aaron the chief priest— [6]this Ezra[e] came up from Babylon. He was a teacher well versed in the Law of Moses, which the LORD, the God of Israel, had given. The king had granted[f] him everything he asked, for the hand of the LORD his God was on him.[g] [7]Some of the Israelites, including priests, Levites, singers, gatekeepers and temple servants, also came up to Jerusalem in the seventh year of King Artaxerxes.[h]

[8]Ezra arrived in Jerusalem in the fifth month of the seventh year of the king. [9]He had begun his journey from Babylon on the first day of the first month, and he arrived in Jerusalem on the first day of the fifth month, for the gracious hand of his God was on him.[i] [10]For Ezra had devoted himself to the study and observance of the Law of the LORD, and to teaching[j] its decrees and laws in Israel.

7:2 [b]1Ki 1:8; 2:35; 1Ch 6:8; Eze 40:46; 43:19; 44:15 [c]Ne 11:11
7:5 [d]1Ch 6:4
7:6 [e]Ne 12:36 /S 2Ki 25:28 [g]S Ezr 5:5; S Isa 41:20
7:7 [h]Ezr 8:1
7:9 [i]ver 6
7:10 /S Dt 33:10

7:12 [k]Eze 26:7; Da 2:37
7:14 [l]Est 1:14
7:15 [m]S 1Ch 29:6 [n]S Dt 12:5; S 2Ch 6:2
7:16 [o]S Ex 3:22

King Artaxerxes' Letter to Ezra

[11]This is a copy of the letter King Artaxerxes had given to Ezra the priest and teacher, a man learned in matters concerning the commands and decrees of the LORD for Israel:

[12][p]Artaxerxes, king of kings,[k]

To Ezra the priest, a teacher of the Law of the God of heaven:

Greetings.

[13]Now I decree that any of the Israelites in my kingdom, including priests and Levites, who wish to go to Jerusalem with you, may go. [14]You are sent by the king and his seven advisers[l] to inquire about Judah and Jerusalem with regard to the Law of your God, which is in your hand. [15]Moreover, you are to take with you the silver and gold that the king and his advisers have freely given[m] to the God of Israel, whose dwelling[n] is in Jerusalem, [16]together with all the silver and gold[o] you may obtain from the province of Babylon, as well as the freewill

P 12 The text of Ezra 7:12-26 is in Aramaic.

---

idolatry (Eze 44:15). They held the office of high priest until 171 B.C. The Sadducees may have been named after Zadok, and the Qumran community (see "The Time between the Testaments," p. 1431) looked for the restoration of the Zadokite priesthood. *Ahitub.* Probably means "My (divine) brother is good." He was actually the grandfather of Zadok (Ne 11:11).
7:5 *Eleazar.* Means "God helps." The Greek form of the name is Lazarus (Jn 11:1).
7:6 *teacher.* Lit. "scribe" (as in Ne 8:1,4,9,13; 12:26,36). Earlier, scribes served kings as secretaries, such as Shaphan under Josiah (2Ki 22:3, where the Hebrew word for "scribe" is translated "secretary"). Other scribes took dictation—such as Baruch, who wrote down what Jeremiah spoke (Jer 36:32). From the exilic period on, the "scribes" were scholars who studied and taught the Scriptures (cf. the "teachers of the law" in the NT; see notes on Mt 2:4; Lk 5:17). In the NT period they were addressed as "rabbis" (cf. Mt 23:7). *well versed.* The Hebrew for this phrase is translated "skillful" in Ps 45:1 and "skilled" in Pr 22:29. *hand of the LORD.* For this striking expression of God's favor cf. also vv. 9,28; 8:18,22,31; Ne 2:8,18.
7:7–9 *seventh year . . . first day of the first month . . . first day of the fifth month.* Ezra began his journey on the first of Nisan (Apr. 8, 458 B.C.) and arrived in Jerusalem on the first of Ab (Aug. 4, 458). The journey took four months, including an 11-day delay indicated by the comparison of v. 9 with 8:31. The spring was the most auspicious time for such journeys; most armies went on campaigns at this time of the year. Although the actual distance between Babylon and Jerusalem is about 500 miles, the travelers had to cover a total of about 900 miles, going northwest along the Euphrates River and then south. The relatively slow pace was caused by the presence of the elderly and the children. See inset to map No. 7 at the end of the Study Bible.
7:10 *study . . . observance . . . teaching.* See Ne 8.

7:11 *letter.* Many regard the letter of Artaxerxes I as the beginning point of Daniel's first 69 "sevens" (Da 9:24–27). Others regard the commission of Nehemiah by the same king as the starting point of this prophecy (Ne 1:1,11; 2:1–8). By using either a solar calendar with the former date (458 B.C.) or a lunar calendar with the latter date (445), one can arrive remarkably close to the date of Jesus' public ministry.
7:12 See NIV text note. *king of kings.* The phrase was originally used by Assyrian kings, since their empires incorporated many kingdoms. It was then used by the later Babylonian (Eze 26:7; Da 2:37) and Persian kings. Cf. 1Ti 6:15; Rev 17:14; 19:16.
7:13 *Israelites.* It is noteworthy that "Israel" is used rather than "Judah." It was Ezra's aim to make one Israel of all who returned. The markedly Jewish coloring of this decree may have resulted from the king's use of Jewish officials, quite possibly Ezra himself, to help him compose it.
7:14 *seven advisers.* Cf. Est 1:14, which refers to the seven nobles who "had special access to the king." This corresponds with Persian practice as reported by the early Greek historians Herodotus and Xenophon. *Law of your God.* Perhaps the complete Pentateuch (the five books of Moses) in its present form (see v. 6).
7:15 *silver and gold.* Cf. Hag 2:8. *freely given.* The Persian treasury had ample funds, and benevolence was a well-attested policy of Persian kings.
7:16 *offerings of the people.* The custom of sending gifts to Jerusalem from the Jews who lived outside Palestine continued until the Jewish-Roman War, when the Romans forced the Jews to send such contributions to the temple of Jupiter instead (Josephus, *Antiquities,* 18.9.1). There are close parallels to such directives in the contemporary letters from the Jewish garrison at Elephantine in Egypt, including a papyrus in which Darius II ordered: "Let grain offering, incense and burnt offering be offered" on the altar of the god Yahu "in your name."

offerings of the people and priests for the temple of their God in Jerusalem. *p* ¹⁷With this money be sure to buy bulls, rams and male lambs, *q* together with their grain offerings and drink offerings, *r* and sacrifice *s* them on the altar of the temple of your God in Jerusalem.

¹⁸You and your brother Jews may then do whatever seems best with the rest of the silver and gold, in accordance with the will of your God. ¹⁹Deliver *t* to the God of Jerusalem all the articles entrusted to you for worship in the temple of your God. ²⁰And anything else needed for the temple of your God that you may have occasion to supply, you may provide from the royal treasury. *u*

²¹Now I, King Artaxerxes, order all the treasurers of Trans-Euphrates to provide with diligence whatever Ezra the priest, a teacher of the Law of the God of heaven, may ask of you— ²²up to a hundred talents *q* of silver, a hundred cors *r* of wheat, a hundred baths *s* of wine, a hundred baths *s* of olive oil, and salt without limit. ²³Whatever the God of heaven has prescribed, let it be done with diligence for the temple of the God of heaven. Why should there be wrath against the realm of the king and of his sons? *v* ²⁴You are also to know that you have no authority to impose taxes, tribute or duty *w* on any of the

priests, Levites, singers, gatekeepers, temple servants or other workers at this house of God. *x*

²⁵And you, Ezra, in accordance with the wisdom of your God, which you possess, appoint *y* magistrates and judges to administer justice to all the people of Trans-Euphrates—all who know the laws of your God. And you are to teach *z* any who do not know them. ²⁶Whoever does not obey the law of your God and the law of the king must surely be punished by death, banishment, confiscation of property, or imprisonment. *a*

²⁷Praise be to the LORD, the God of our fathers, who has put it into the king's heart *b* to bring honor *c* to the house of the LORD in Jerusalem in this way ²⁸and who has extended his good favor *d* to me before the king and his advisers and all the king's powerful officials. Because the hand of the LORD my God was on me, *e* I took courage and gathered leading men from Israel to go up with me.

List of the Family Heads Returning With Ezra

8 These are the family heads and those registered with them who came up with me from Babylon during the reign of King Artaxerxes: *f*

Cross references (center column):

7:16 *p* Zec 6:10
7:17 *q* Ki 3:4
r Nu 15:5-12
7:19 *r* Ezr 5:14;
Jer 27:22
7:20 *u* S Ezr 6:4
7:23 *v* S Ezr 6:10
7:24 *w* S Ezr 4:13

x Ezr 8:36
7:25 *y* S Ex 18:21,
26 *z* S Lev 10:11
7:26 *a* S Ezr 6:11
7:27 *b* S Ezr 1:1
c S 1Ch 29:12
7:28
d S 2Ki 25:28
e S Ezr 5:5
8:1 *f* Ezr 7:7

Footnotes (center column):

q 22 That is, about 3 3/4 tons (about 3.4 metric tons)   *r* 22 That is, probably about 600 bushels (about 22 kiloliters)   *s* 22 That is, probably about 600 gallons (about 2.2 kiloliters)

7:20 *provide from the royal treasury.* Texts from the treasury at Persepolis also record the disbursement of supplies and funds from the royal purse.

7:22 *hundred talents.* An enormous amount (see NIV text note). *hundred cors.* The total was relatively small (see NIV text note). The wheat would be used in grain offerings. *salt without limit.* See note on 4:14. A close parallel is the benefaction of Antiochus III as recorded by Josephus (*Antiquities,* 12.3.3): "In the first place we have decided, on account of their piety, to furnish for their sacrifices an allowance of sacrificial animals, wine, oil and frankincense to the value of 20,000 pieces of silver, and sacred artabae of fine flour in accordance with their native law, and 1,460 medimni of wheat and 375 medimni of salt."

7:23 *wrath against the realm of the king.* Egypt had revolted against the Persians in 460 B.C. and had expelled the Persians with the help of the Athenians in 459. In 458, when Ezra traveled to Jerusalem, the Persians were involved in suppressing this revolt. *his sons.* We do not know how many sons the king had at this time, but he ultimately had 18, according to Ctesias (a Greek physician who wrote an extensive history of Persia).

7:24 *no ... taxes ... or duty on any of the priests ... temple servants.* Priests and other temple personnel were often given exemptions from enforced labor or taxes. A close parallel is found in the Gadates Inscription of Darius I to a governor in western Turkey, granting exemptions to the

priests of Apollo. Antiochus III granted similar exemptions to the Jews: "The priests, the scribes of the temple and the temple singers shall be relieved from the poll tax, the crown tax and the salt tax that they pay" (Josephus, *Antiquities,* 12.3.3).

7:26 *Whoever does not obey ... must surely be punished.* The extensive powers given to Ezra are striking and extend to secular fields. Perhaps the implementation of these provisions involved Ezra in a great deal of traveling, which would explain the silence about his activities between his arrival and the arrival of Nehemiah 13 years later. A close parallel to the king's commission of Ezra may be found in an earlier commission by Darius I, who sent Udjahorresenet, a priest and scholar, back to Egypt. He ordered the codification of the Egyptian laws by the chief men of Egypt—a task that took from 518 to 503 B.C.

7:28 *me.* The first occurrence of the first person for Ezra—a trait that characterizes the "Ezra Memoirs," which begin in v. 27 and continue to the end of ch. 9.

8:1–21 In vv. 1–14 Ezra lists those who accompanied him in his return from Mesopotamia, including the descendants of 15 individuals. The figures of the men given total 1,496 in addition to the individuals named. There were also women and children (see note on v. 21). About 40 Levites (vv. 18–19) are also included, as are 220 "temple servants" (v. 20).

²of the descendants of Phinehas, Gershom;

of the descendants of Ithamar, Daniel;

of the descendants of David, Hattush ³of the descendants of Shecaniah; *g*

of the descendants of Parosh, *h* Zechariah, and with him were registered 150 men;

⁴of the descendants of Pahath-Moab, *i* Eliehoenai son of Zerahiah, and with him 200 men;

⁵of the descendants of Zattu, *t* Shecaniah son of Jahaziel, and with him 300 men;

⁶of the descendants of Adin, *j* Ebed son of Jonathan, and with him 50 men;

⁷of the descendants of Elam, Jeshaiah son of Athaliah, and with him 70 men;

⁸of the descendants of Shephatiah, Zebadiah son of Michael, and with him 80 men;

⁹of the descendants of Joab, Obadiah son of Jehiel, and with him 218 men;

¹⁰of the descendants of Bani, *u* Shelomith son of Josiphiah, and with him 160 men;

¹¹of the descendants of Bebai, Zechariah son of Bebai, and with him 28 men;

¹²of the descendants of Azgad, Johanan son of Hakkatan, and with him 110 men;

¹³of the descendants of Adonikam, *k* the last ones, whose names were Eliphelet, Jeuel and Shemaiah, and with them 60 men;

¹⁴of the descendants of Bigvai, Uthai and Zaccur, and with them 70 men.

The Return to Jerusalem

¹⁵I assembled them at the canal that flows toward Ahava, *l* and we camped there three days. When I checked among the people and the priests, I found no Levites *m* there. ¹⁶So I summoned Eliezer, Ariel, Shemaiah, Elnathan, Jarib, Elnathan, Nathan, Zechariah and Meshullam, who were leaders, and Joiarib and Elnathan, who were men of learning, ¹⁷and I sent them to Iddo, the leader in Casiphia. I told them what to say to Iddo and his kinsmen, the temple servants *n* in Casiphia, so that they might bring attendants to us for the house of our God. ¹⁸Because the gracious hand of our God was on us, *o* they brought us Sherebiah, *p* a capable man, from the descendants of Mahli son of Levi, the son of Israel, and Sherebiah's sons and brothers, 18 men; ¹⁹and Hashabiah, together with Jeshaiah from the descendants of Merari, and his brothers and nephews, 20 men. ²⁰They also brought 220 of the temple servants *q*—a body that David and the

---

8:3 *g* 1Ch 3:22
h S Ezr 2:3
8:4 *i* Ezr 2:6
8:6 *j* Ezr 2:15;
Ne 7:20; 10:16

8:13 *k* Ezr 2:13
8:15 *l* ver 21,31
m S Ezr 2:40
8:17 *n* Ezr 2:43
8:18 *o* S Ezr 5:5
p ver 24
8:20 *q* S 1Ch 9:2

t 5 Some Septuagint manuscripts (also 1 Esdras 8:32); Hebrew does not have *Zattu*. **u** *10* Some Septuagint manuscripts (also 1 Esdras 8:36); Hebrew does not have *Bani*.

8:2 *Gershom.* For the meaning of the name see NIV text note on Ex 2:22, where we learn that Gershom was also the name of the firstborn son of Moses and Zipporah. *Ithamar.* Also the name of the fourth son of Aaron (Ex 6:23).
8:3 *Zechariah.* Cf. v. 11. The name means "The LORD remembers"; it was the name of about 30 individuals mentioned in the Bible, including both the OT prophet and the father of John the Baptist (Lk 1:5–67).
8:4 *Eliehoenai.* Means "On the LORD are my eyes"; the name occurs only here and in 1Ch 26:3. Cf. Ps 25:15.
8:6 *Ebed.* May be a shortened form of Obadiah (cf. v. 9), meaning "servant of the LORD." *Jonathan.* Means "The LORD gives"; it was the name of 15 OT individuals.
8:7 *Athaliah.* Also the name of a famous queen, daughter of Ahab (2Ki 11).
8:8 *Michael.* Means "Who is like God?" It was the name of ten other Biblical personages, including the archangel (Da 10:13; Jude 9; Rev 12:7).
8:10 *Shelomith.* Although it is a feminine form (see also note on SS 6:13), it is often a man's name, as here. The Greek equivalent is Salome.
8:12 *Azgad.* See note on 2:12. *Johanan.* See note on 2:46. *Hakkatan.* Means "the little one"; the name occurs only here.
8:15 *canal that flows toward Ahava.* Probably flows into either the Euphrates or the Tigris (the Kebar "River" in Eze 1:1 was also a canal). *three days.* Perhaps from the 9th to the

12th day of Nisan; the journey began on the 12th (see v. 31). *no Levites.* Since they were entrusted with many menial tasks, they may have found a more comfortable way of life in exile. A rabbinic midrash (comment) on Ps 137 relates the legend that Levites were in the caravan but that they were not qualified to officiate because when Nebuchadnezzar had ordered them to sing for him the songs of Zion, "they refused and bit off the ends of their fingers, so that they could not play on the harps." In the Hellenistic era (following Alexander's conquest of Palestine in 333 B.C.) the role of the Levites declined sharply, though the "Temple Scroll" among the Dead Sea Scrolls from Qumran (see "The Time between the Testaments," p. 1431) assigns important roles to them.
8:16 *Ariel.* Means "lion of God" or "altar hearth" (see note on Isa 29:1,2,7). It occurs only here as a personal name. *Meshullam.* Perhaps means "rewarded." Some assume that he is the same as the Meshullam who opposed the marriage reforms (10:15). *men of learning.* Lit. "those who cause to understand." The Hebrew for this phrase is translated "teacher" in 1Ch 25:8 and "instructed" or "instructing" in 2Ch 35:3; Ne 8:7,9.
8:17 *Casiphia.* Some have located it at the site that was later to become the Parthian capital of Ctesiphon on the Tigris River, north of Babylon.
8:18–19 *18 men . . . 20 men.* Only about 40 Levites from two families were found who were willing to join Ezra's caravan.

officials had established to assist the Levites. All were registered by name.

21There, by the Ahava Canal,[r] I proclaimed a fast, so that we might humble ourselves before our God and ask him for a safe journey[s] for us and our children, with all our possessions. 22I was ashamed to ask the king for soldiers[t] and horsemen to protect us from enemies on the road, because we had told the king, "The gracious hand of our God is on everyone[u] who looks to him, but his great anger is against all who forsake him.[v]" 23So we fasted[w] and petitioned our God about this, and he answered our prayer.

24Then I set apart twelve of the leading priests, together with Sherebiah,[x] Hashabiah and ten of their brothers, 25and I weighed out[y] to them the offering of silver and gold and the articles that the king, his advisers, his officials and all Israel present there had donated for the house of our God. 26I weighed out to them 650 talents[v] of silver, silver articles weighing 100 talents,[w] 100 talents[w] of gold, 2720 bowls of gold valued at 1,000 darics,[x] and two fine articles of polished bronze, as precious as gold.

28I said to them, "You as well as these articles are consecrated to the LORD.[z] The silver and gold are a freewill offering to the LORD, the God of your fathers. 29Guard them carefully until you weigh them out in the chambers of the house of the LORD in Jerusalem before the leading priests and the Levites and the family heads of Israel." 30Then the priests and Levites received the silver and gold and sacred articles that had

been weighed out to be taken to the house of our God in Jerusalem.

31On the twelfth day of the first month we set out from the Ahava Canal[a] to go to Jerusalem. The hand of our God was on us,[b] and he protected us from enemies and bandits along the way. 32So we arrived in Jerusalem, where we rested three days.[c]

33On the fourth day, in the house of our God, we weighed out[d] the silver and gold and the sacred articles into the hands of Meremoth[e] son of Uriah, the priest. Eleazar son of Phinehas was with him, and so were the Levites Jozabad[f] son of Jeshua and Noadiah son of Binnui.[g] 34Everything was accounted for by number and weight, and the entire weight was recorded at that time.

35Then the exiles who had returned from captivity sacrificed burnt offerings to the God of Israel: twelve bulls[h] for all Israel,[i] ninety-six rams, seventy-seven male lambs and, as a sin offering, twelve male goats.[j] All this was a burnt offering to the LORD. 36They also delivered the king's orders[k] to the royal satraps and to the governors of Trans-Euphrates,[l] who then gave assistance to the people and to the house of God.[m]

Ezra's Prayer About Intermarriage

9 After these things had been done, the leaders came to me and said, "The people of Israel, including the priests and

Cross references

8:21 [r]S ver 15; [s]Ps 5:8; 27:11; 107:7
8:22 [t]Ne 2:9; Jer 41:16; [u]S Ezr 5:5; [v]S Dt 31:17
8:23 [w]S 2Ch 20:3; Ac 14:23
8:24 [x]ver 18
8:25 [y]ver 33
8:28 [z]S Lev 21:6; 22:2-3
8:31 [a]S ver 15; [b]S Ezr 5:5
8:32 [c]S Ge 40:13
8:33 [d]ver 25; [e]Ne 3:4,21; [f]Ne 11:16; [g]Ne 3:24
8:35 [h]S Lev 1:3; [i]S 2Ch 29:24; [j]S 2Ch 29:21; S 30:24
8:36 [k]Ezr 7:21-24; [l]Ne 2:7 [m]Est 9:3

Footnotes

[v]26 That is, about 25 tons (about 22 metric tons)
[w]26 That is, about 3 3/4 tons (about 3.4 metric tons)
[x]27 That is, about 19 pounds (about 8.5 kilograms)

8:20 temple servants. See note on 2:43–57.

8:21 safe journey. Lit. "straight way"—unimpeded by obstacles and dangers (see v. 31; cf. Pr 3:6). children. Elsewhere (e.g., Ge 43:8) the term also includes the elderly and the women. possessions. The vast treasures they were carrying with them offered a tempting bait for robbers.

8:22 I was ashamed. Scripture speaks often of unholy shame (Jer 48:13; 49:23; Mic 3:7) and on occasion, as here, of holy shame. Ezra was quick to blush with such shame (see also 9:6). Having proclaimed his faith in God's ability to protect the caravan, he was embarrassed to ask for human protection. Grave dangers faced travelers going the great distance between Mesopotamia and Palestine. Some 13 years later Nehemiah was accompanied by an armed escort. The difference, however, does not mean that Nehemiah was a man of lesser faith (see note on Ne 2:9).

8:23 fasted and petitioned. For the association of fasting and prayer see Ne 1:4; Da 9:3; Mt 17:21 (NIV text note); Ac 14:23.

8:25 offering. Lit. "what is lifted," i.e., dedicated (cf. Ex 25:2; 35:5; Lev 7:14). In Dt 12:6 the Hebrew for this word is translated "special gifts."

8:26 650 talents . . . 100 talents. Enormous sums, worth millions of dollars today. See also note on 7:22.

8:27 darics. See NIV text note. The word occurs only here

and in 1Ch 29:7 (but see note on 2:69). polished. This kind of bronze may have been orichalc, a bright yellow (the Hebrew for "yellow" in Lev 13:30,32,36 is related to the Hebrew for "polished" here) alloy of copper, which resembles gold and was highly prized in ancient times.

8:31 twelfth day. See notes on v. 15; 7:7–9.

8:32 rested three days. Nehemiah also took a similar rest period after his arrival in Jerusalem (Ne 2:11).

8:33 Meremoth son of Uriah. Probably the same as the man who repaired two sections of the wall (Ne 3:4,21).

8:34 recorded. According to Babylonian practice (e.g., in the law code of Hammurapi) almost every transaction, including sales and marriages, had to be recorded in writing. Ezra may have had to send back to Artaxerxes a signed certification of the delivery of the treasures.

8:35 sacrificed. Except for the identical number of male goats, the offerings here were far fewer than those presented by the returnees under Zerubbabel (6:17), who brought with him a far greater number of families.

9:1 After these things had been done . . . have not kept themselves separate. Ezra had reached Jerusalem in the fifth month (7:9). The measures dealing with the problem of intermarriage were announced in the ninth month (10:9), or four months after his arrival. Those who brought Ezra's attention to the problem were probably the ordinary mem-

the Levites, have not kept themselves separate[n] from the neighboring peoples with their detestable practices, like those of the Canaanites, Hittites, Perizzites, Jebusites,[o] Ammonites,[p] Moabites,[q] Egyptians and Amorites.[r] [2]They have taken some of their daughters[s] as wives for themselves and their sons, and have mingled[t] the holy race[u] with the peoples around them. And the leaders and officials have led the way in this unfaithfulness."[v]

[3]When I heard this, I tore[w] my tunic and cloak, pulled hair from my head and beard and sat down appalled.[x] [4]Then everyone who trembled[y] at the words of the God of Israel gathered around me because of this unfaithfulness of the exiles. And I sat there appalled[z] until the evening sacrifice.

[5]Then, at the evening sacrifice,[a] I rose from my self-abasement, with my tunic and cloak torn, and fell on my knees with my hands[b] spread out to the LORD my God [6]and prayed:

"O my God, I am too ashamed[c] and disgraced to lift up my face to you, my God, because our sins are higher than our heads and our guilt has reached to the heavens.[d] [7]From the days of our forefathers[e] until now, our guilt has been great. Because of our sins, we and our kings and our priests have been subjected to the sword[f] and captivity,[g] to pillage and humiliation[h] at the hand of foreign kings, as it is today.

[8]"But now, for a brief moment, the LORD our God has been gracious[i] in leaving us a remnant[j] and giving us a firm place[k] in his sanctuary, and so our God gives light to our eyes[l] and a little relief in our bondage. [9]Though we are slaves,[m] our God has not deserted us in our bondage. He has shown us kindness[n] in the sight of the

---

Cross references (center column):

9:1 [n]S Ezr 6:21
[o]S Ge 10:16;
S Jos 15:8
[p]Ge 19:38
[q]S Ge 19:37
[r]Ex 13:5; 23:28;
Dt 20:17;
S Jos 3:10;
S Jdg 3:5;
1Ki 9:20;
S 2Ch 8:7; Ne 9:8
9:2 [s]S Ex 34:16;
S Ru 1:4
[t]Ps 106:35
[u]S Ex 22:31;
S Lev 27:30;
S Dt 14:2
[v]Ezr 10:2
9:3 [w]S Nu 14:6
[x]S Ex 32:19;
S 33:4
9:4 [y]Ezr 10:3;
Ps 119:120;
Isa 66:2,5
[z]Ne 1:4;
Ps 119:136;
Da 10:2
9:5 [a]S Ex 29:41
[b]Ne 8:6; Ps 28:2;
134:2

9:6 [c]Jer 31:19
[d]S 2Ch 28:9;
Job 42:6; Ps 38:4;
Isa 59:12;
Jer 3:25; 14:20;
Rev 18:5
9:7 [e]S 2Ch 29:6
[f]Eze 21:1-32

[g]S Dt 28:64 [h]S Dt 28:37 9:8 [i]Ps 25:16; 67:1; 119:58;
Isa 33:2 /S Ge 45:7 [k]Ecc 12:11; Isa 22:23 [l]Ps 13:3; 19:8 9:9
[m]S Ex 1:14; Ne 9:36 [n]S 2Ki 25:28; Ps 106:46

---

bers of the community rather than the leaders, who were themselves guilty (v. 2). Malachi, who prophesied about the same time as Ezra's mission, indicates that some Jews had broken their marriages to marry daughters of a foreign god (Mal 2:10–16), perhaps the daughters of influential landholders. One of the reasons for such intermarriages may have been the shortage of returning Jewish women who were available. What happened to a Jewish community that was lax concerning intermarriage can be seen in the example of the Elephantine settlement in Egypt, which was contemporary with Ezra and Nehemiah. There the Jews who married pagan spouses expressed their devotion to pagan gods in addition to the Lord. The Elephantine community was gradually assimilated and disappeared. *neighboring peoples.* The eight groups mentioned are representative of the original inhabitants of Canaan before the Israelite conquest (see note on Ex 3:8). Only the Ammonites, Moabites and Egyptians were still living there in the postexilic period (cf. 2Ch 8:7–8). *Canaanites.* See note on Ge 10:6. *Hittites.* See note on Ge 10:15. *Perizzites.* See note on Ge 13:7. *Jebusites.* See note on Ge 10:16. *Ammonites, Moabites.* See note on Ge 19:36–38. *Amorites.* See note on Ge 10:16.

9:2 *holy race.* The Hebrew for this phrase is translated "holy seed" in Isa 6:13. *led the way.* In the wrong direction (see 10:18). *unfaithfulness.* See 10:6; Jos 22:16; Da 9:7. Marrying those who did not belong to the Lord was an act of infidelity for the people of Israel.

9:3 *tore my tunic and cloak.* A common way to express grief or distress (see v. 5; Ge 37:29,34; Jos 7:6; Jdg 11:35; 2Sa 13:19; 2Ch 34:27; Est 4:1; Job 1:20; Isa 36:22; Jer 41:5; Mt 26:65). *pulled hair from my head and beard.* Unique in the Bible. Elsewhere we read about the shaving of one's head and/or beard (Job 1:20; Jer 41:5; 47:5; Eze 7:18; Am 8:10). When Nehemiah was confronted with the same problem of intermarriage, instead of pulling out his own hair he pulled out the hair of the offending parties (Ne 13:25).

9:4 *everyone who trembled.* Cf. Ex 19:16; Isa 66:2; Heb 12:21. *appalled.* See v. 3; cf. Da 4:19; 8:27. *evening sacrifice.* See Ex 12:6. The informants had probably visited Ezra in the morning, so that he must have sat appalled for many

hours. The time of the evening sacrifice, usually about 3:00 P.M., was also the appointed time for prayer and confession (Ac 3:1).

9:5 *self-abasement.* The Hebrew for this word later meant "fasting." See note on Lev 16:29,31. *fell on my knees.* Cf. 1Ki 8:54; Ps 95:6; Da 6:10. *with my hands spread out.* See note on Ex 9:29. Ezra's prayer (vv. 6–15) may be compared with those of Nehemiah (Ne 9:5–37) and Daniel (Da 9:4–19).

9:6 *ashamed and disgraced.* See 8:22 and note; Lk 18:13. Ezra felt both an inner shame before God and an outward humiliation before people for his own sins and the sins of his people. The two Hebrew verbs often occur together; see Ps 35:4; Isa 45:16; Jer 31:19 ("ashamed and humiliated"). *our sins . . . our guilt.* Cf. also vv. 7,13,15; 10:10,19; 1Ch 21:3; 2Ch 24:18; Ps 38:4. *has reached to the heavens.* But God's love is more than a match for our guilt (Ps 103:11–12).

9:7 *From the days of our forefathers.* Israelites were conscious of their corporate solidarity with their ancestors. *sword.* Cf. Ne 4:13. In Eze 21 "the sword of the king of Babylon" (21:19) is described as an instrument of divine judgment. *humiliation.* Cf. Da 9:7–8; 2Ch 32:21.

9:8 *remnant.* See Ge 45:7; Isa 1:9; 10:20–22 and notes. *firm place.* Lit. "nail" or "peg," like a nail driven into a wall (see Isa 22:23 and note) or a tent peg driven into the ground (Isa 33:20; 54:2). *light to our eyes.* An increase in light means vitality and joy (Ps 13:3; 19:8; Ecc 8:1).

9:9 *kings of Persia.* The Achaemenid Persian kings were favorably disposed to the Jews: Cyrus (539–530 B.C.) gave them permission to return (ch. 1); his son Cambyses (530–522), though not named in the Bible, also favored the Jews, as we learn from Elephantine papyri; Darius I (522–486) renewed the decree of Cyrus (ch. 6); his son Xerxes (486–465) granted privileges and protection to Jews (Est 8–10); his son Artaxerxes I (465–424) gave authorizations to Ezra (ch. 7) and to Nehemiah (Ne 2). *repair its ruins.* Isaiah had prophesied that the Lord would restore Jerusalem's ruins (Isa 44:26), which would burst into singing (Isa 52:9; cf. 58:12; 61:4). *wall of protection.* Used of a city wall only in Mic 7:11. The use here is metaphorical (cf. Zec 2:4–5).

kings of Persia: He has granted us new life to rebuild the house of our God and repair its ruins, *o* and he has given us a wall of protection in Judah and Jerusalem.

10"But now, O our God, what can we say after this? For we have disregarded the commands *p* 11you gave through your servants the prophets when you said: 'The land you are entering *q* to possess is a land polluted *r* by the corruption of its peoples. By their detestable practices *s* they have filled it with their impurity from one end to the other. 12Therefore, do not give your daughters in marriage to their sons or take their daughters for your sons. Do not seek a treaty of friendship with them *t* at any time, that you may be strong *u* and eat the good things *v* of the land and leave it to your children as an everlasting inheritance.' *w*

13"What has happened to us is a result of our evil *x* deeds and our great guilt, and yet, our God, you have punished us less than our sins have deserved *y* and have given us a remnant like this. 14Shall we again break your commands and intermarry *z* with the peoples who commit such detestable practices? Would you not be angry enough with us to destroy us, *a* leaving us no remnant *b* or survivor? 15O LORD, God of Israel, you are righteous! *c* We are left this day as a rem-

nant. Here we are before you in our guilt, though because of it not one of us can stand *d* in your presence. *e* "

The People's Confession of Sin

10 While Ezra was praying and confessing, *f* weeping *g* and throwing himself down before the house of God, a large crowd of Israelites—men, women and children—gathered around him. They too wept bitterly. 2Then Shecaniah son of Jehiel, one of the descendants of Elam, *h* said to Ezra, "We have been unfaithful *i* to our God by marrying foreign women from the peoples around us. But in spite of this, there is still hope for Israel. *j* 3Now let us make a covenant *k* before our God to send away *l* all these women and their children, in accordance with the counsel of my lord and of those who fear the commands of our God. Let it be done according to the Law. 4Rise up; this matter is in your hands. We will support you, so take courage and do it."

5So Ezra rose up and put the leading priests and Levites and all Israel under oath *m* to do what had been suggested. And they took the oath. 6Then Ezra withdrew from before the house of God and went to the room of Jehohanan son of Eliashib. While he was there, he ate no food and drank no water, *n* because he continued to mourn over the unfaithfulness of the exiles.

7A proclamation was then issued throughout Judah and Jerusalem for all the

Cross references (center column)

9:9 *o*Ps 69:35; Isa 43:1; 44:26; 48:20; 52:9; 63:9; Jer 32:44; Zec 1:16-17
9:10 *p*Dt 11:8; Isa 1:19-20
9:11 *q*Dt 4:5 *r*S Lev 18:25-28 *s*S Dt 9:4; S 18:9; S 1Ki 14:24
9:12 *t*S Ex 34:15 *u*Dt 11:8 *v*S Ge 45:18 *w*Ps 103:17; Eze 37:25; Joel 3:20
9:13 *x*S Ex 32:22 *y*Job 11:6; 15:5; 22:5; 33:27; Ps 103:10
9:14 *z*Ne 13:27 *a*S Dt 9:8 *b*Dt 9:14
9:15 *c*S Ge 18:25; S 2Ch 12:6; Ne 9:8; Ps 51:4; 129:4; 145:17; Isa 24:16; Jer 12:1; 23:6; 33:16; La 1:18; Da 9:7; Zep 3:5

*d*Ps 76:7; 130:3; Mal 3:2 *e*S 1Ki 8:47
10:1 *f*2Ch 20:9; Da 9:20 *g*S Nu 25:6
10:2 *h*ver 26 *i*S Ezr 9:2 *j*Dt 30:8-10
10:3 *k*S 2Ki 11:17 *l*S Ex 34:16
10:5 *m*Ne 5:12; 13:25
10:6 *n*S Ex 34:28; Dt 9:18; Ps 102:4; Jnh 3:7

9:11–12 The references are not to a single OT passage but to several passages, such as Dt 11:8–9; Isa 1:19; Eze 37:25.
9:11 *your servants the prophets.* See notes on Jer 7:25; Zec 1:6. *corruption.* Of Canaanite idolatry and the immoral practices associated with it (Lev 18:3; 2Ch 29:5; La 1:17; Eze 7:20; 36:17). The degrading practices and beliefs of the Canaanites are described in texts from ancient Ugarit (see chart on "Ancient Texts Relating to the OT," p. 5).
9:14 *be angry.* God's anger came upon the Israelites because they had violated his covenant with them (Dt 7:4; 11:16–17; 29:26–28; Jos 23:16; Jdg 2:20).
9:15 *you are righteous.* See note on Ps 4:1. *our guilt.* A proper sense of God's holiness makes us aware of our unworthiness. See Isa 6:1–5; Lk 5:8. For comparable passages of national lament see Ps 44; 60; 74; 79–80; 83; 85; 90; 108; 126; 129; 137.
10:1 *weeping.* Not silently but out loud (see 3:13 and note; Ne 1:4; Joel 2:12). *throwing himself down.* The prophets and other leaders used object lessons, even bizarre actions, to attract people's attention (Isa 7:3; 8:1–4,18; Jer 13:1–11; 19; 27:2–12; Eze 4:1–5:4).
10:2 Ezra, as a wise teacher, waited for his audience to draw their own conclusions about what should be done. *Shecaniah.* Perhaps his father Jehiel is the Jehiel mentioned in v. 26 since he was also of the family of Elam. If so, Shecaniah was doubtless grieved that his father had married a non-Jewish woman. Six members of the clan of Elam were

involved in intermarriage (v. 26).
10:3 *make a covenant.* Lit. "cut a covenant" (see note on Ge 15:18). *women and their children.* Mothers were given custody of their children when marriages were dissolved. When Hagar was dismissed, Ishmael was sent with her (Ge 21:14). In Babylonia divorced women were granted their children and had to wait for them to grow up before remarrying, according to the law code of Hammurapi (see chart on "Ancient Texts Relating to the OT," p. 5). In Greece, however, children from broken homes remained with their fathers.
10:4 *Rise up.* Cf. David's exhortation (1Ch 22:16).
10:5 *oath.* The implied curse attendant upon nonfulfillment of a Biblical oath is often expressed in the vague statement, "May God deal with you, be it ever so severely, if . . ." (see note on 1Sa 3:17). On rare occasions the full implications of the curse are spelled out (Nu 5:19–22; Job 31; Ps 7:4–5; 137:5–6).
10:6 *room.* Such temple chambers were used as storerooms (8:29; Ne 13:4–5). *ate no food and drank no water.* Complete fasting from both food and drink was rare. Moses did it twice (Ex 34:28; Dt 9:18), and the Ninevites also did it (Jnh 3:7). Ordinarily, fasting involved abstaining only from eating (1Sa 1:7; 2Sa 3:35). *mourn.* The Hebrew for this word often describes the reaction of those aware of the threat of deserved judgment (Ex 33:4; Nu 14:39).
10:7–8 While Ezra continued to fast and pray, the officials

exiles to assemble in Jerusalem. 8Anyone
who failed to appear within three days
would forfeit all his property, in accordance with the decision of the officials and
elders, and would himself be expelled from
the assembly of the exiles.

9Within the three days, all the men of
Judah and Benjamin[o] had gathered in
Jerusalem. And on the twentieth day of the
ninth month, all the people were sitting in
the square before the house of God, greatly
distressed by the occasion and because of
the rain. 10Then Ezra[p] the priest stood up
and said to them, "You have been unfaithful; you have married foreign women, adding to Israel's guilt.[q] 11Now make confession to the LORD, the God of your fathers,
and do his will. Separate yourselves from
the peoples around you and from your foreign wives."[r]

12The whole assembly responded with a
loud voice:[s] "You are right! We must do
as you say. 13But there are many people
here and it is the rainy season; so we cannot stand outside. Besides, this matter cannot be taken care of in a day or two, because we have sinned greatly in this thing.
14Let our officials act for the whole assembly. Then let everyone in our towns who
has married a foreign woman come at a set
time, along with the elders and judges[t] of
each town, until the fierce anger[u] of our
God in this matter is turned away from
us." 15Only Jonathan son of Asahel and
Jahzeiah son of Tikvah, supported by Meshullam and Shabbethai[v] the Levite, opposed this.

16So the exiles did as was proposed.
Ezra the priest selected men who were
family heads, one from each family division, and all of them designated by name.
On the first day of the tenth month they
sat down to investigate the cases, 17and by
the first day of the first month they finished
dealing with all the men who had married
foreign women.

Those Guilty of Intermarriage

18Among the descendants of the priests,
the following had married foreign
women:[w]
From the descendants of Jeshua[x] son
of Jozadak, and his brothers: Maaseiah, Eliezer, Jarib and Gedaliah.
19(They all gave their hands[y] in
pledge to put away their wives,
and for their guilt they each
presented a ram from the flock as a
guilt offering.)[z]
20From the descendants of Immer:[a]
Hanani and Zebadiah.
21From the descendants of Harim:[b]
Maaseiah, Elijah, Shemaiah, Jehiel
and Uzziah.
22From the descendants of Pashhur:[c]
Elioenai, Maaseiah, Ishmael, Nethanel, Jozabad and Elasah.
23Among the Levites:[d]
Jozabad, Shimei, Kelaiah (that is,

10:9 [o]S Ezr 1:5 **10:10** [p]Ezr 7:21 [q]2Ch 28:13 **10:11** [r]S Dt 24:1; Ne 9:2; Mal 2:10-16 **10:12** [s]S Jos 6:5 **10:14** [t]Dt 16:18 [u]S Nu 25:4; S 2Ch 29:10
10:15 [v]Ne 11:16 **10:18** [w]S Jdg 3:6 [x]S Ezr 2:2 **10:19** [y]S 2Ki 10:15 [z]S Lev 5:15; 6:6 **10:20** [a]S 1Ch 24:14 **10:21** [b]S 1Ch 24:8 **10:22** [c]S 1Ch 9:12 **10:23** [d]Ne 8:7; 9:4

and elders ordered all the exiles to assemble in Jerusalem. Although Ezra had been invested with great authority (7:25–26), he used it sparingly and influenced the people by his example.

10:8 *within three days.* Since the territory of Judah had been much reduced, the most distant people would not be more than 50 miles from Jerusalem. The borders were Bethel in the north, Beersheba in the south, Jericho in the east and Ono in the west (cf. Ne 7:26–38; 11:25–35). *forfeit.* The Hebrew for this word means "to ban from profane use and to devote to the Lord," either by destruction (see Ex 22:20; Dt 13:12–18 and NIV text notes) or by giving it to the Lord's treasury (cf. Lev 27:28; Jos 6:19; 7:1–15).

10:9,16–17 See chart on "Chronology: Ezra-Nehemiah," p. 674.

10:9 *Judah and Benjamin.* See note on 1:5. *square.* Either the outer court of the temple or the open space before the Water Gate (Ne 8:1). *rain.* The Hebrew for this word is a plural of intensity, indicating heavy torrential rains. The ninth month, Kislev (November-December), is in the middle of the "rainy season" (v. 13), which begins with light showers in October and lasts to mid-April. December and January are also cold months, with temperatures in the 50s and even 40s in Jerusalem. The people shivered not only because they were drenched, but perhaps also because they sensed divine displeasure in the heavy rains (see 1Sa 12:17–18; Eze 13:11,13).

10:10 *adding to Israel's guilt.* See Ex 9:34; Jdg 3:12; 4:1; 2Ch 28:13. The sins and failures of the exiles were great enough, but they added insult to injury by marrying pagan women.

10:11 *Separate yourselves.* See Nu 16:21; 2Co 6:14.

10:12 *with a loud voice.* See Ne 9:4.

10:14 *elders and judges of each town.* See Dt 16:18; 19:12; 21:3,19; Ru 4:2.

10:15 Perhaps these four men opposed the measure because they wanted to protect themselves or their relatives, or they may have viewed it as being too harsh. *Jahzeiah.* Means "May the LORD see" (the name is found only here). *Tikvah.* Means "hope" (found elsewhere only in 2Ki 22:14). *Meshullam.* See note on 8:16. If he is the Meshullam of v. 29, he himself had married a pagan wife. *Shabbethai.* Occurs only here and in Ne 8:7; 11:16; perhaps means "one born on the Sabbath."

10:16–17 The committee completed its work in three months, discovering that about 110 men were guilty of marrying pagan wives.

10:18–22 See 2:36–39.

10:19 *gave their hands.* For the symbolic use of the handshake see 2Ki 10:15; Eze 17:18. *ram.* Guilt offerings were to be made for sins committed unintentionally (Lev 5:14–19) as well as intentionally (Lev 6:1–7), and a ram was the appropriate offering in either case (Lev 5:15; 6:6).

Kelita), Pethahiah, Judah and Eliezer.

²⁴From the singers:
Eliashib. ᵉ

From the gatekeepers:
Shallum, Telem and Uri.

²⁵And among the other Israelites:

From the descendants of Parosh:ᶠ
Ramiah, Izziah, Malkijah, Mijamin, Eleazar, Malkijah and Benaiah.

²⁶From the descendants of Elam:ᵍ
Mattaniah, Zechariah, Jehiel, Abdi, Jeremoth and Elijah.

²⁷From the descendants of Zattu:
Elioenai, Eliashib, Mattaniah, Jeremoth, Zabad and Aziza.

²⁸From the descendants of Bebai:
Jehohanan, Hananiah, Zabbai and Athlai.

²⁹From the descendants of Bani:
Meshullam, Malluch, Adaiah, Jashub, Sheal and Jeremoth.

³⁰From the descendants of Pahath-Moab:
Adna, Kelal, Benaiah, Maaseiah, Mattaniah, Bezalel, Binnui and Manasseh.

³¹From the descendants of Harim:
Eliezer, Ishijah, Malkijah, Shemaiah, Shimeon, ³²Benjamin, Malluch and Shemariah.

³³From the descendants of Hashum:
Mattenai, Mattattah, Zabad, Eliphelet, Jeremai, Manasseh and Shimei.

³⁴From the descendants of Bani:
Maadai, Amram, Uel, ³⁵Benaiah, Bedeiah, Keluhi, ³⁶Vaniah, Meremoth, Eliashib, ³⁷Mattaniah, Mattenai and Jaasu.

³⁸From the descendants of Binnui:ʸ
Shimei, ³⁹Shelemiah, Nathan, Adaiah, ⁴⁰Macnadebai, Shashai, Sharai, ⁴¹Azarel, Shelemiah, Shemariah, ⁴²Shallum, Amariah and Joseph.

⁴³From the descendants of Nebo:
Jeiel, Mattithiah, Zabad, Zebina, Jaddai, Joel and Benaiah.

⁴⁴All these had married foreign women, and some of them had children by these wives.ᶻ

ʸ37,38 See Septuagint (also 1 Esdras 9:34); Hebrew Jaasu ³⁸and Bani and Binnui, ᶻ44 Or and they sent them away with their children

10:24 e Ne 3:1; 12:10; 13:7,28 **10:25** f S Ezr 2:3 **10:26** g S ver 2

10:24 It is striking that only one singer and three gatekeepers were involved. No temple servants (2:43–54) or descendants of Solomon's servants (2:55–57) sinned through intermarriage.

10:25–43 See 2:3–20.

10:30 Bezalel. Cf. Ex 31:2.

10:31 Shimeon. The Hebrew for this name is the same as that for Simeon, Jacob's second son (see NIV text note on Ge 29:33). In Greek the name became Simon.

10:43 Nebo. The Hebrew equivalent of the name of the Babylonian god Nabu (see Isa 46:1); found only here as a personal name.

10:44 Some of the marriages had produced children, but this was not accepted as a reason for halting the divorce proceedings. See NIV text note.

NEHEMIAH

See Introduction to Ezra.

Nehemiah's Prayer

1 The words of Nehemiah son of Hacaliah:

In the month of Kislev[a] in the twentieth year, while I was in the citadel of Susa,[b] [2]Hanani,[c] one of my brothers, came from Judah with some other men, and I questioned them about the Jewish remnant[d] that survived the exile, and also about Jerusalem.

[3]They said to me, "Those who survived the exile and are back in the province are in great trouble and disgrace. The wall of Jerusalem is broken down, and its gates have been burned with fire.[e]"

[4]When I heard these things, I sat down and wept.[f] For some days I mourned and fasted[g] and prayed before the God of heaven. [5]Then I said:

"O LORD, God of heaven, the great and awesome God,[h] who keeps his covenant of love[i] with those who love him and obey his commands, [6]let your ear be attentive and your eyes open to hear[j] the prayer[k] your servant is praying before you day and night for your servants, the people of Israel. I confess[l] the sins we Israelites, including myself and my father's house, have committed against you. [7]We have acted very wickedly[m] toward you. We have not obeyed the commands, decrees and laws you gave your servant Moses.

[8]"Remember[n] the instruction you gave your servant Moses, saying, 'If you are unfaithful, I will scatter[o] you among the nations, [9]but if you return to me and obey my commands, then even if your exiled people are at the farthest horizon, I will gather[p] them from there and bring them to the place I have chosen as a dwelling for my Name.' [10]"They are your servants and your people, whom you redeemed by your great strength and your mighty hand.[r] [11]O Lord, let your ear be attentive[s] to the prayer of this your servant and to the prayer of your servants

1:1 [a]Zec 7:1
[b]S Ezr 4:9;
S Est 2:8
1:2 [c]Ne 7:2
[d]S 2Ki 21:14;
Ne 7:6; Jer 52:28
1:3 [e]S Lev 26:31;
2Ki 25:10;
Ne 2:3,13,17;
Isa 22:9; Jer 39:8;
52:14; La 2:9
1:4 [f]Ps 137:1
[g]S 2Ch 20:3;
S Ezr 9:4; Da 9:3
1:5 [h]S Dt 7:21;
Ne 4:14
[i]S Dt 7:9;
S 1Ki 8:23;
Da 9:4
1:6 [j]S 1Ki 8:29;
S 2Ch 7:15
[k]S 1Ki 8:30
[l]S 1Ki 8:47
1:7 [m]Ps 106:6
1:8 [n]S Ge 8:1;
S 2Ki 20:3;
Ne 4:14; 5:19;
6:14; 13:22,29,
31 [o]S Lev 26:33
1:9 [p]S Dt 30:4;
Ps 106:47; 107:3;
Isa 11:12; 56:8;
Jer 42:12;
Eze 11:17
[q]S 1Ki 8:48;
Jer 29:14;
Eze 11:17;
20:34-38;
36:24-38;
Mic 2:12
1:10 [r]S Ex 32:11;
Isa 51:9-11
1:11 [s]S 2Ch 6:40

1:1 *The words of.* Originally an introduction to the title of a separate composition (see Jer 1:1; Am 1:1), though the books of Ezra and Nehemiah appear as a single work from earliest times (see Introduction to Ezra: Ezra and Nehemiah). *Nehemiah.* Means "The LORD comforts." *Hacaliah.* Perhaps means "Wait for the LORD," though an imperative in a Hebrew name is quite unusual. The name occurs only here and in 10:1. *Kislev . . . twentieth year.* November-December, 446 B.C. See chart on "Chronology: Ezra-Nehemiah," p. 674. *Susa.* See note on Ezr 4:9.
1:2 *Hanani.* Probably a shortened form of Hananiah, which means "The LORD is gracious." *one of my brothers.* See 7:2. The Elephantine papyri mention a Hananiah who was the head of Jewish affairs in Jerusalem. Many believe that he is to be identified with Nehemiah's brother, and that he may have governed between Nehemiah's first and second terms (see NIV text note on 7:2). *remnant.* See note on Ezr 9:8.
1:3 *province.* See note on Ezr 2:1. *wall of Jerusalem is broken down.* The lack of a city wall meant that the people were defenseless against their enemies. Thucydides (1.89) describes the comparable condition of Athens after its devastation by the Persians in 480-479 B.C. Excavations at Jerusalem during 1961-67 revealed that the lack of a wall on the eastern slopes also meant the disintegration of the terraces there. When Nebuchadnezzar assaulted Jerusalem, he battered and broke down the walls around it (2Ki 25:10). Most, however, do not believe that Nehemiah's distress was caused by Nebuchadnezzar's destruction in 586 but by the episode of Ezr 4:7-23. The Jews had attempted to rebuild the walls earlier in the reign of Artaxerxes I; but after the protest of Rehum and Shimshai, the king ordered the Jews to desist. See note on Ezr 4:21-23.
1:4 *sat down.* Cf. Ezr 9:3; Job 2:13. *wept.* See 8:9; Ezr 3:13 and note; 10:1; Est 8:3. *mourned.* See Ezr 10:6; Da 10:2. *fasted and prayed.* See note on Ezr 8:23. During the exile, fasting became a common practice, including solemn fasts to commemorate the fall of Jerusalem and the murder of Gedaliah (see note on Zec 8:19; see also Est 4:16; Da 9:3;

10:3; Zec 7:3-7). *God of heaven.* See note on Ezr 1:2.
1:5 *love.* Or "faithful love," the quality that honors a covenant through thick and thin.
1:6 *praying before you day and night.* Cf. Ps 42:3; 88:1; Jer 9:1; 14:17; La 2:18; Lk 2:37; 1Th 3:10; 1Ti 5:5; 2Ti 1:3. *sins . . . myself and my father's house.* Nehemiah does not exclude himself or members of his own family in his confession of sins. A true sense of the awesomeness of God reveals the depths of our own sinfulness (Isa 6:1-5; Lk 5:8).
1:7 *commands, decrees and laws.* See note on Ge 26:5. *Moses.* For the prominence of the law of Moses in Ezra and Nehemiah see Ezr 3:2; 6:18; 7:6; Ne 1:8; 8:1,14; 9:14; 10:29; 13:1.
1:8 *Remember.* See note on 13:31; a key word in the book (4:14; 5:19; 6:14; 13:14,22,29,31). *unfaithful . . . scatter.* Dispersion was the inescapable consequence of the people's unfaithfulness. By the NT period there were still more Jews in the Diaspora (dispersion) than in Palestine.
1:9 *I will gather them.* See Dt 30:1-5; a frequent promise, especially in the prophets (e.g., Isa 11:12; Jer 23:3; 31:8-10; Eze 20:34,41; 36:24; Mic 2:12). *chosen as a dwelling for my Name.* See Dt 12:5 and note; Ps 132:13.
1:10 *your people . . . you redeemed.* Although they had sinned and failed, they were still God's people by virtue of his redeeming them (see Dt 4:34; 9:29).
1:11 *Give your servant success today.* Cf. Ge 24:12. *cupbearer.* Lit. "one who gives (someone) something to drink." The Hebrew for this word occurs 11 other times in the OT in the sense of "cupbearer" (Ge 40:1-2,5,9,13,20-21,23; 41:9; 1Ki 10:5; 2Ch 9:4). According to the Greek historian Xenophon (*Cyropaedia,* 1.3.9), one of the cupbearer's duties was to choose and taste the king's wine to make certain that it was not poisoned (see 2:1). Thus Nehemiah had to be a man who enjoyed the unreserved confidence of the king. The need for trustworthy court attendants is underscored by the intrigues that characterized the Achaemenid court of Persia. Xerxes, the father of Artaxerxes I, was killed in his own bedchamber by a courtier.

who delight in revering your name. Give your servant success today by granting him favor [t] in the presence of this man."

I was cupbearer [u] to the king.

Artaxerxes Sends Nehemiah to Jerusalem

2 In the month of Nisan in the twentieth year of King Artaxerxes, [v] when wine was brought for him, I took the wine and gave it to the king. I had not been sad in his presence before; [2]so the king asked me, "Why does your face look so sad when you are not ill? This can be nothing but sadness of heart."

I was very much afraid, [3]but I said to the king, "May the king live forever! [w] Why should my face not look sad when the city [x] where my fathers are buried lies in ruins, and its gates have been destroyed by fire? [y] "

[4]The king said to me, "What is it you want?"

Then I prayed to the God of heaven, [5]and I answered the king, "If it pleases the king and if your servant has found favor in his sight, let him send me to the city in Judah where my fathers are buried so that I can rebuild it."

[6]Then the king [z], with the queen sitting beside him, asked me, "How long will your journey take, and when will you get back?" It pleased the king to send me; so I set a time.

[7]I also said to him, "If it pleases the king, may I have letters to the governors of Trans-Euphrates, [a] so that they will provide me safe-conduct until I arrive in Judah? [8]And may I have a letter to Asaph, keeper of the king's forest, so he will give me timber to make beams for the gates of the citadel [b] by the temple and for the city wall and for the residence I will occupy?" And because the gracious hand of my God was upon me, [c] the king granted my requests. [d] [9]So I went to the governors of Trans-Euphrates and gave them the king's letters. The king had also sent army officers and cavalry [e] with me.

[10]When Sanballat [f] the Horonite and

Cross references (center column):

1:11 [t]S Ex 3:21
[u]S Ge 40:1
2:1 [v]S Ezr 4:7; S 6:14
2:3 [w]1Ki 1:31; Da 2:4; 3:9; 5:10; 6:6,21
[x]Ps 137:6
[y]S Ne 1:3
2:6 [z]Ne 5:14; 13:6
2:7 [a]S Ezr 8:36
2:8 [b]Ne 7:2
[c]S Ezr 5:5
[d]S Ezr 4:24
2:9 [e]S Ezr 8:22
2:10 [f]ver 19; Ne 4:1,7; 6:1-2,5, 12,14; 13:28

2:1 *Nisan . . . twentieth year.* March-April, 445 B.C. (see chart on "Chronology: Ezra-Nehemiah," p. 674).There was a delay of four months from Kislev, when Nehemiah first heard the news (1:1), to Nisan, when he approached the king. Various reasons have been suggested: 1. The king may have been in his other winter palace at Babylon. 2. Perhaps the king was not in the right mood. 3. Even though Nehemiah was a favorite of the king, he would not have rashly blurted out his request. *sad in his presence.* No matter what one's personal problems were, the king's servants were expected to keep their feelings to themselves and to display a cheerful disposition before him.
2:3 *May the king live forever!* A common form of address to kings. *city.* Nehemiah does not mention Jerusalem by name (see v. 5); he may have wished to arouse the king's sympathy by stressing first the desecration of ancestral tombs.
2:4 *I prayed to the God of heaven.* Before turning to answer the king, Nehemiah utters a brief, spontaneous prayer to God. One of Nehemiah's striking characteristics is his frequent recourse to prayer (1:4; 4:4,9; 5:19; 6:9,14; 13:14,22,29,31).
2:6 *queen.* The Hebrew for this word is used only here and in Ps 45:9 ("royal bride"). It is a loanword from Akkadian and means lit. "(woman) of the palace." The Aramaic equivalent is found only in Da 5:2–3,23, where it is translated "wives." Ctesias, a Greek who lived at the Achaemenid court, informs us that the name of Artaxerxes's queen was Damaspia and that he had at least three concubines. Like Esther, Damaspia may have used her influence with the king (Est 5). The Achaemenid court was notorious for the great influence exercised by the royal women. Especially domineering was Amestris, the cruel wife of Xerxes and mother of Artaxerxes I. *How long will your journey take . . . ?* Nehemiah probably asked for a brief leave of absence, which he then had extended. We can infer from 5:14 that he spent 12 years on his first term as governor of Judah. In the 32nd year of Artaxerxes, Nehemiah returned to report to the king and then came back to Judah for a second term (13:6–7).
2:7 *letters.* A contemporary document from Arsames, the

satrap of Egypt who was at the Persian court, to one of his officers who was returning to Egypt orders Persian officials to provide him with food and drink on the stages of his journey. *Trans-Euphrates.* See note on Ezr 4:10.
2:8 *forest.* The Hebrew for this word is *pardes,* a loanword from Old Persian meaning "enclosure," a pleasant retreat or park. The word occurs elsewhere in the OT only in Ecc 2:5 ("parks") and SS 4:13 ("orchard"). In the Septuagint (the Greek translation of the OT) the Greek transliteration *paradeisos* is used here. In the period between the OT and the NT, the word acquired the sense of the abode of the blessed dead, i.e., "paradise." It appears three times in the NT (Lk 23:43; 2Co 12:4; Rev 2:7). As to the location of the "king's forest," some believe that it was in Lebanon, which was famed for its forests of cedars and other coniferous trees (see notes on Jdg 9:15; Ezr 3:7). But a more plausible suggestion is that it should be identified with Solomon's gardens at Etham, about six miles south of Jerusalem (see Josephus, *Antiquities,* 8.7.3). For city gates, costly imported cedars from Lebanon would not be used but rather indigenous oak, poplar or terebinth (Hos 4:13). *citadel.* Probably refers to the fortress north of the temple, the forerunner of the Antonia fortress built by Herod the Great (Josephus, *Antiquities,* 15.11.4; see Ac 21:34,37; 22:24).
2:9 *army officers and cavalry.* In striking contrast to Ezra (see note on Ezr 8:22), Nehemiah was accompanied by an armed escort since he was officially Judah's governor.
2:10 *Sanballat.* A Babylonian name, meaning "Sin (the moon-god) has given life." *Horonite.* Identifies him as coming from (1) Hauran (Eze 47:16,18), east of the Sea of Galilee, (2) Horonaim, in Moab (Jer 48:34), or, most probably, (3) either Upper or Lower Beth Horon, two key cities 12 miles northwest of Jerusalem, which guarded the main road to Jerusalem (Jos 10:10; 16:3,5; 1 Maccabees 3:16; 7:39). Sanballat was the chief political opponent of Nehemiah (v. 19; 4:1,7; 6:1–2,5,12,14; 13:28). He held the position of governor over Samaria (cf. 4:1–2). An Elephantine papyrus letter of the late fifth century B.C. to Bagohi (Bigvai), governor of Judah, refers to "Delaiah and Shele-

Tobiah[g] the Ammonite official heard about this, they were very much disturbed that someone had come to promote the welfare of the Israelites.[h]

Nehemiah Inspects Jerusalem's Walls

[11]I went to Jerusalem, and after staying there three days[i] [12]I set out during the night with a few men. I had not told anyone what my God had put in my heart to do for Jerusalem. There were no mounts with me except the one I was riding on.

[13]By night I went out through the Valley Gate[j] toward the Jackal[a] Well and the Dung Gate,[k] examining the walls[l] of Jerusalem, which had been broken down, and its gates, which had been destroyed by fire. [14]Then I moved on toward the Fountain Gate[m] and the King's Pool,[n] but there was not enough room for my mount to get through; [15]so I went up the valley by night, examining the wall. Finally, I turned back and reentered through the Valley Gate. [16]The officials did not know where I had gone or what I was doing, because as yet I had said nothing to the Jews or the priests or nobles or officials or any others who would be doing the work.

[17]Then I said to them, "You see the trouble we are in: Jerusalem lies in ruins, and its gates have been burned with fire.[o] Come, let us rebuild the wall[p] of Jerusalem, and we will no longer be in disgrace.[q]" [18]I also told them about the gracious hand of my God upon me[r] and what the king had said to me.

They replied, "Let us start rebuilding." So they began this good work.

[19]But when Sanballat[s] the Horonite, Tobiah the Ammonite official and Ge-

---

2:10 [g]Ne 4:3; 13:4-7 [h]Est 10:3
2:11 [i]S Ge 40:13
2:13 [j]S 2Ch 26:9 [k]Ne 3:13; 12:31 [l]S Ne 1:3
2:14 [m]Ne 3:15; 12:37 [n]S 2Ki 18:17

2:17 [o]S Ne 1:3 [p]Ps 102:16; Isa 30:13; 58:12 [q]Eze 5:14
2:18 [r]S Ezr 5:5
2:19 [s]S ver 10

[a]13 Or Serpent or Fig

---

miah, the sons of Sanballat, governor of Samaria." In 1962 a fourth-century B.C. papyrus was found in a cave north of Jericho, listing the name Sanballat, probably a descendant of Nehemiah's contemporary. *Tobiah.* Means "The LORD is good." He was probably a worshiper of the Lord (Yahweh), as indicated not only by his name but also by that of his son Jehohanan (6:17–18), meaning "The LORD is gracious." Jehohanan was married to the daughter of Meshullam son of Berekiah, the leader of one of the groups repairing the wall (3:4,30; 6:18). Tobiah also had a close relationship with Eliashib the priest (13:4–7). *Ammonite.* See Ezr 9:1; see also note on Ge 19:33. Tobiah was probably governor of Transjordan under the Persians. In later generations a prominent family bearing the name of Tobiah was sometimes associated with the region of Ammon in non-Biblical texts. *very much disturbed.* The reasons for the opposition of Sanballat and Tobiah were not basically religious but political. The authority of the Samaritan governor in particular was threatened by Nehemiah's arrival.

2:11 *three days.* See note on Ezr 8:32.
2:12 Nehemiah was cautious and discreet as he inspected the city's fortifications. *one I was riding on.* Probably a mule or donkey.
2:13 Nehemiah did not make a complete circuit of the walls, but only of the southern area. Jerusalem was always attacked from the north because it was most vulnerable there, so the walls had probably been completely destroyed in that part of the city. *Valley Gate.* See 3:13. According to 2Ch 26:9 Uzziah fortified towers in the west wall, which overlooked the Tyropoeon Valley, i.e., the central valley between the Hinnom and Kidron valleys. Excavations in 1927–28 uncovered the remains of a gate from the Persian period, which has been identified as the Valley Gate. *Jackal Well.* Many scholars suggest that this was En Rogel (Jos 15:7–8; 18:16; 2Sa 17:17; 1Ki 1:9), a well situated at the junction of the Hinnom and Kidron valleys, 250 yards south

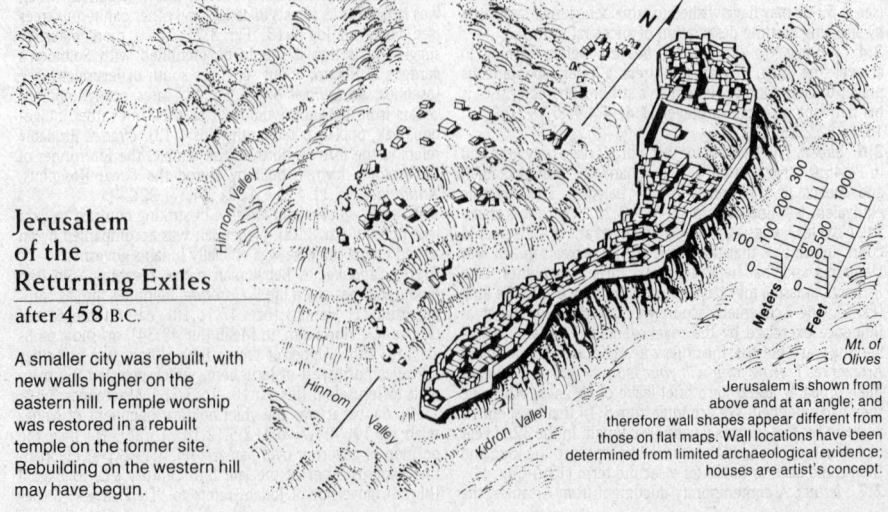

Jerusalem of the Returning Exiles

after 458 B.C.

A smaller city was rebuilt, with new walls higher on the eastern hill. Temple worship was restored in a rebuilt temple on the former site. Rebuilding on the western hill may have begun.

Jerusalem is shown from above and at an angle; and therefore wall shapes appear different from those on flat maps. Wall locations have been determined from limited archaeological evidence; houses are artist's concept.

shem[t] the Arab heard about it, they mocked and ridiculed us.[u] "What is this you are doing?" they asked. "Are you rebelling against the king?"

[20]I answered them by saying, "The God of heaven will give us success. We his servants will start rebuilding,[v] but as for you, you have no share[w] in Jerusalem or any claim or historic right to it."

Builders of the Wall

3 Eliashib[x] the high priest and his fellow priests went to work and rebuilt[y] the Sheep Gate.[z] They dedicated it and set its doors in place, building as far as the Tower of the Hundred, which they dedicated, and as far as the Tower of Hananel.[a] [2]The men of Jericho[b] built the adjoining section, and Zaccur son of Imri built next to them.

[3]The Fish Gate[c] was rebuilt by the sons of Hassenaah. They laid its beams and put its doors and bolts and bars in place. [4]Meremoth[d] son of Uriah, the son of Hakkoz, repaired the next section. Next to him Meshullam son of Berekiah, the son of Meshezabel, made repairs, and next to him Zadok son of Baana also made repairs. [5]The next section was repaired by the men of Tekoa,[e] but their nobles would not put their shoulders to the work under their supervisors.[b]

[6]The Jeshanah[c] Gate[f] was repaired by Joiada son of Paseah and Meshullam son of Besodeiah. They laid its beams and put its doors and bolts and bars in place. [7]Next to them, repairs were made by men from Gibeon[g] and Mizpah—Melatiah of Gibeon and Jadon of Meronoth—places under

Cross references (center column)

2:19 [t]Ne 6:1,2,6 [u]Ps 44:13-16
2:20 [v]Ezr 4:1 [w]Ezr 4:3; Ac 8:21
3:1 [x]S Ezr 10:24 [y]Isa 58:12 [z]ver 32; Ne 12:39;
Jn 5:2 [a]Ne 12:39; Ps 48:12; Jer 31:38; Zec 14:10
3:2 [b]Ne 7:36
3:3 [c]S 2Ch 33:14
3:4 [d]S Ezr 8:33
3:5 [e]ver 27; S 2Sa 14:2
3:6 [f]Ne 12:39
3:7 [g]S Jos 9:3

[b]5 Or *their Lord* or *the governor*   [c]6 Or *Old*

---

of the southeast ridge of Jerusalem. Others suggest that it was the Pool of Siloam. *Dung Gate.* Perhaps the gate leading to the rubbish dump in the Hinnom Valley (cf. 3:13–14; 12:31; 2Ki 23:10). It was situated about 500 yards south of the Valley Gate (3:13).

2:14 *Fountain Gate.* Possibly in the southeast wall facing toward En Rogel (see 3:15; 12:37). *King's Pool.* Hezekiah may have diverted the overflow from his Siloam tunnel (cf. 2Ki 20:20; 2Ch 32:30) to irrigate the royal gardens (2Ki 25:4) located outside the city walls at the junction of the Kidron and Hinnom valleys. The King's Pool was probably therefore the Pool of Siloam (3:15) or the adjacent Birket el-Hamra. *not enough room.* Possibly because of the collapse of the supporting terraces (cf. 2Sa 5:9; 1Ki 9:15,24) on the east side of the city.

2:15 *valley.* The Kidron.

2:16 *nobles.* The Hebrew root for this word means "free" (see 4:14,19; 5:7; 6:17; 7:5; 13:17; see also note on 3:5).

2:17 *ruins.* The condition of the walls and gates of the city since their destruction by Nebuchadnezzar in 586 B.C., in spite of abortive attempts to rebuild them. The leaders and people had evidently become reconciled to this sad state of affairs. It took an outsider to assess the situation and to rally them to renewed efforts.

2:18 *my God . . . and . . . the king.* Nehemiah could personally attest that God was alive and active in his behalf and that he (Nehemiah) had come with royal sanction and authority.

2:19 *Sanballat . . . Tobiah.* See note on v. 10. *Geshem.* Inscriptions from Dedan in northwest Arabia and from Tell el-Maskhutah near Ismailia in Egypt bear the name of Geshem, who may have been in charge of a north Arabian confederacy that controlled vast areas from northeast Egypt to northern Arabia and southern Palestine. Geshem may have been opposed to Nehemiah's development of an independent kingdom because he feared that it might interfere with his lucrative spice trade. *Arab.* See 2Ch 9:14; Isa 21:13; Jer 25:24. Arabs became dominant in Transjordan from the Assyrian to the Persian periods. Sargon II of Assyria resettled some Arabs in Samaria in 715 B.C. Classical sources reveal that the Arabs enjoyed a favored status under the Persians.

3:1–32 One of the most important chapters in the OT for determining the topography of Jerusalem. The narrative be-

gins at the Sheep Gate (northeast corner of the city) and proceeds in a counterclockwise direction around the wall. About 40 key men are named as participants in the reconstruction of about 45 sections. The towns listed as the homes of the builders may have represented the administrative centers of the province of Judah. Ten gates are named: (1) Sheep Gate (v. 1), (2) Fish Gate (v. 3), (3) Jeshanah Gate (v. 6), (4) Valley Gate (v. 13), (5) Dung Gate (v. 14), (6) Fountain Gate (v. 15), (7) Water Gate (v. 26), (8) Horse Gate (v. 28), (9) East Gate (v. 29), (10) Inspection Gate (v. 31). The account suggests that most of the rebuilding was concerned with the gates, where the enemy's assaults were always concentrated. Not all the sections of the walls or buildings in Jerusalem were in the same state of disrepair. A selective policy of destruction seems to be indicated by 2Ki 25:9.

3:1 *Eliashib the high priest.* It was fitting that the high priest should set the example. Among the ancient Sumerians the king himself would carry bricks for the building of a temple. *Sheep Gate.* See v. 32; 12:39. It was known in NT times (Jn 5:2) as located near the Bethesda Pool (in the northeast corner of Jerusalem). Even today a sheep market is held periodically near this area. The Sheep Gate may have replaced the earlier Benjamin Gate (Jer 37:13; 38:7; Zec 14:10). *Tower of the Hundred.* See 12:39. "Hundred" may refer to (1) its height (100 cubits), (2) the number of its steps or (3) a military unit (cf. Dt 1:15). *Tower of Hananel.* The towers were associated with the "citadel by the temple" (2:8) in protecting the vulnerable northern approaches to the city.

3:3 *Fish Gate.* See 12:39. During the days of the first temple, it was one of Jerusalem's main entrances (2Ch 33:14; Zep 1:10). Merchants brought fish from either Tyre or the Sea of Galilee to the fish market (13:16) through this entrance, which may have been located close to the site of the present-day Damascus Gate.

3:4 *Meremoth.* See note on Ezr 8:33. *Meshullam.* Repaired a second section (v. 30). Nehemiah complained that Meshullam had given his daughter in marriage to a son of Tobiah (see 6:17–18 and note on 2:10).

3:5 *Tekoa.* A small town about 6 miles south of Bethlehem and 11 miles from Jerusalem. It was the hometown of the prophet Amos. *nobles.* The Hebrew for this word is different from that in 2:16 (see note there) and means "mighty" or "magnificent" (see 10:29; 2Ch 23:20; Jer 14:3). These

the authority of the governor of Trans-Euphrates. 8Uzziel son of Harhaiah, one of the goldsmiths, repaired the next section; and Hananiah, one of the perfume-makers, made repairs next to that. They restored d Jerusalem as far as the Broad Wall. h 9Rephaiah son of Hur, ruler of a half-district of Jerusalem, repaired the next section. 10Adjoining this, Jedaiah son of Harumaph made repairs opposite his house, and Hattush son of Hashabneiah made repairs next to him. 11Malkijah son of Harim and Hasshub son of Pahath-Moab repaired another section and the Tower of the Ovens. i 12Shallum son of Hallohesh, ruler of a half-district of Jerusalem, repaired the next section with the help of his daughters.

13The Valley Gate j was repaired by Hanun and the residents of Zanoah. k They rebuilt it and put its doors and bolts and bars in place. They also repaired five hundred yards e of the wall as far as the Dung Gate. l

14The Dung Gate was repaired by Malkijah son of Recab, ruler of the district of Beth Hakkerem. m He rebuilt it and put its doors and bolts and bars in place.

15The Fountain Gate was repaired by Shallun son of Col-Hozeh, ruler of the district of Mizpah. He rebuilt it, roofing it over and putting its doors and bolts and

bars in place. He also repaired the wall of the Pool of Siloam, f n by the King's Garden, as far as the steps going down from the City of David. 16Beyond him, Nehemiah son of Azbuk, ruler of a half-district of Beth Zur, o made repairs up to a point opposite the tombs g p of David, as far as the artificial pool and the House of the Heroes.

17Next to him, the repairs were made by the Levites under Rehum son of Bani. Beside him, Hashabiah, ruler of half the district of Keilah, q carried out repairs for his district. 18Next to him, the repairs were made by their countrymen under Binnui h son of Henadad, ruler of the other half-district of Keilah. 19Next to him, Ezer son of Jeshua, ruler of Mizpah, repaired another section, from a point facing the ascent to the armory as far as the angle. 20Next to him, Baruch son of Zabbai zealously repaired another section, from the angle to the entrance of the house of Eliashib the high priest. 21Next to him, Meremoth r son of Uriah, the son of Hakkoz, repaired another section, from the entrance of Eliashib's house to the end of it.

3:8 hNe 12:38
3:11 iNe 12:38
3:13 jS 2Ch 26:9
kS Jos 15:34
lS Ne 2:13
3:14 mJer 6:1

3:15 nIsa 8:6; Jn 9:7
3:16 oS Jos 15:58
pAc 2:29
3:17 qS Jos 15:44
3:21 rS Ezr 8:33

d8 Or They left out part of e13 Hebrew a thousand cubits (about 450 meters) f15 Hebrew Shelah, a variant of Shiloah, that is, Siloam g16 Hebrew; Septuagint, some Vulgate manuscripts and Syriac tomb h18 Two Hebrew manuscripts and Syriac (see also Septuagint and verse 24); most Hebrew manuscripts Bavvai

---

aristocrats disdained manual labor. shoulders. Lit. "back of the neck." The expression is drawn from the imagery of oxen that refuse to yield to the yoke (Jer 27:12).
3:6 Jeshanah Gate. In the northwest corner. Its name has been interpreted to mean Old Gate (see NIV text note), or gate to Jeshanah (lying on the border between Judah and Samaria, 2Ch 13:19), or as a corruption of Mishneh (the Hebrew word for "New Quarter"; see Zep 1:10) Gate. In any case, it may be another name for the Gate of Ephraim (see 12:39), which otherwise is not mentioned in ch. 3.
3:7 authority. Lit. "throne," which symbolizes authority here.
3:8 goldsmiths. See vv. 31–32. perfume-makers. See 1Sa 8:13. Broad Wall. See 12:38. In 1970–71 archaeological excavations in Jerusalem uncovered such a wall west of the temple area. It is dated to the early seventh century B.C. and was probably built by Hezekiah (2Ch 32:5). The expansion to and beyond the Broad Wall may have become necessary because of the influx of refugees fleeing from the fall of Samaria in 722–721.
3:10 Jedaiah . . . made repairs opposite his house. See vv. 23,28–30. It made sense to have him and others repair the sections of the wall nearest their homes.
3:11 Tower of the Ovens. It was on the western wall, perhaps in the same location as one built by Uzziah (2Ch 26:9). The ovens may have been those situated in the "street of the bakers" (Jer 37:21).
3:12 daughters. A unique reference to women working on the wall. When the Athenians attempted to rebuild their walls after the Persians had destroyed them, it was decreed that "the whole population of the city—men, women and

children—should take part in the wall-building" (Thucydides, 1.90.3).
3:13 Valley Gate. See note on 2:13. five hundred yards. An extraordinary length; probably most of the section was relatively intact. Dung Gate. See note on 2:13.
3:14 Beth Hakkerem. Means "house of the vineyard." It was a fire-signal point (Jer 6:1) and is identified with Ramat Rahel, two miles south of Jerusalem. It may have been the residence of a district governor in the Persian period.
3:15 Fountain Gate. See note on 2:14. Pool of Siloam. Perhaps the Lower Pool of Isa 22:9 (see note on Isa 8:6). King's Garden. See note on 2:14. City of David. See 12:37; see also note on 2Sa 5:7.
3:16 Beth Zur. A district capital, 13 miles south of Jerusalem. Excavations in 1931 and 1957 revealed that occupation was sparse during the early Persian period but was resumed in the fifth century B.C. tombs of David. Cf. 2:5. David was buried in the city area (1Ki 2:10; 2Ch 21:20; 32:33; Ac 2:29). The so-called Tomb of David on Mount Zion venerated today by Jewish pilgrims is in the Coenaculum building, erected in the 14th century A.D. Such a site for David's tomb is mentioned no earlier than the ninth century A.D. House of the Heroes. May have been the house of David's mighty men (see 2Sa 23:8–39), which perhaps served later as the barracks or armory.
3:17–18 Keilah. Located about 15 miles southwest of Jerusalem, it played an important role in David's early history (1Sa 23:1–13).
3:19 armory. See note on v. 16.
3:20–21 The residences of the high priest and his fellow priests were located inside the city along the eastern wall.

22The repairs next to him were made by the priests from the surrounding region. 23Beyond them, Benjamin and Hasshub made repairs in front of their house; and next to them, Azariah son of Maaseiah, the son of Ananiah, made repairs beside his house. 24Next to him, Binnui[s] son of Henadad repaired another section, from Azariah's house to the angle and the corner, 25and Palal son of Uzai worked opposite the angle and the tower projecting from the upper palace near the court of the guard.[t] Next to him, Pedaiah son of Parosh[u] 26and the temple servants[v] living on the hill of Ophel[w] made repairs up to a point opposite the Water Gate[x] toward the east and the projecting tower. 27Next to them, the men of Tekoa[y] repaired another section, from the great projecting tower[z] to the wall of Ophel.

28Above the Horse Gate,[a] the priests made repairs, each in front of his own house. 29Next to them, Zadok son of Immer made repairs opposite his house. Next to him, Shemaiah son of Shecaniah, the guard at the East Gate, made repairs. 30Next to him, Hananiah son of Shelemiah, and Hanun, the sixth son of Zalaph, repaired another section. Next to them, Meshullam son of Berekiah made repairs opposite his living quarters. 31Next to him, Malkijah, one of the goldsmiths, made repairs as far as the house of the temple servants and the merchants, opposite the Inspection Gate, and as far as the room above the corner; 32and between the room above the corner and the Sheep Gate[b] the goldsmiths and merchants made repairs.

Cross references (center column)

3:24 sS Ezr 8:33
3:25 tJer 32:2;
37:21; 39:14
uS Ezr 2:3
3:26 vNe 7:46;
11:21
wS 2Ch 33:14
xNe 8:1,3,16;
12:37
3:27 yS ver 5
zPs 48:12
3:28 aS 2Ki 11:16
3:32 bS ver 1;
Jn 5:2

4:1 cS Ne 2:10
4:2 dS Ezr 4:9-10
ePs 79:1;
Jer 26:18
4:3 fS Ne 2:10
gJob 13:12; 15:3
4:4 hPs 44:13;
123:3-4;
Jer 33:24
4:5 iIsa 2:9;
La 1:22
j2Ki 14:27;
Ps 51:1;
69:27-28;
109:14; Jer 18:23
4:7 kS Ne 2:10
4:8 lPs 2:2;
83:1-18

Opposition to the Rebuilding

4 When Sanballat[c] heard that we were rebuilding the wall, he became angry and was greatly incensed. He ridiculed the Jews, 2and in the presence of his associates[d] and the army of Samaria, he said, "What are those feeble Jews doing? Will they restore their wall? Will they offer sacrifices? Will they finish in a day? Can they bring the stones back to life from those heaps of rubble[e]—burned as they are?"

3Tobiah[f] the Ammonite, who was at his side, said, "What they are building—if even a fox climbed up on it, he would break down their wall of stones!"[g]

4Hear us, O our God, for we are despised.[h] Turn their insults back on their own heads. Give them over as plunder in a land of captivity. 5Do not cover up their guilt[i] or blot out their sins from your sight,[j] for they have thrown insults in the face of[i] the builders.

6So we rebuilt the wall till all of it reached half its height, for the people worked with all their heart.

7But when Sanballat, Tobiah,[k] the Arabs, the Ammonites and the men of Ashdod heard that the repairs to Jerusalem's walls had gone ahead and that the gaps were being closed, they were very angry. 8They all plotted together[l] to come and fight against Jerusalem and stir up trouble against it. 9But we prayed to our God and posted a guard day and night to meet this threat.

10Meanwhile, the people in Judah said,

i 5 Or have provoked you to anger before

3:25 *upper palace.* Perhaps the old palace of David (see 12:37). Like Solomon's palace, it would have had a guardhouse (Jer 32:2).
3:26 *Ophel.* See v. 27. The word means "swelling" or "bulge," hence a (fortified) "hill" (as in Mic 4:8; see NIV text note there), specifically the northern part of the southeastern hill of Jerusalem, which formed the original City of David, just south of the temple area (2Ch 27:3). *Water Gate.* So called because it led to the main source of Jerusalem's water, the Gihon spring. It must have opened onto a large area, for the reading of the Law took place there (8:1,3,16; 12:37). *projecting tower.* Perhaps the large tower whose ruins were discovered by archaeologists on the crest of the Ophel hill in 1923–25. Excavations at the base of the tower in 1978 revealed a level dating to the Persian era.
3:27 *men of Tekoa.* The common people of Tekoa did double duty, whereas the nobles of Tekoa shirked their responsibility (see note on v. 5).
3:28 *Horse Gate.* Where Athaliah was slain (2Ch 23:15). It may have been the easternmost point in the city wall—a gate through which one could reach the Kidron Valley (Jer 31:40).
3:29 *East Gate.* May have been the predecessor of the present Golden Gate.

3:31 *goldsmiths.* See v. 8. *Inspection Gate.* In the northern part of the eastern wall.
3:32 *Sheep Gate.* Back to the point of departure (see v. 1).
4:2 *he said.* Disputes between rival Persian governors were frequent. Sanballat asked several derisive questions to taunt the Jews and to discourage them in their efforts. *burned.* Fire had damaged the stones, which were probably limestone, and had caused many of them to crack and crumble.
4:3 *fox.* See Jdg 15:4; SS 2:15. The Hebrew for this word may also mean "jackal" (Ps 63:10; La 5:18; Eze 13:4). The jackal normally hunts in packs, whereas the fox is usually a nocturnal and solitary animal.
4:4–5 As in the so-called imprecatory psalms (Ps 79:12; 83; 94:1–3; 109:14; 137:7–9), Nehemiah does not himself take action against his opponents but calls down on them redress from God. In v. 5 Nehemiah's prayer echoes the language of Jer 18:23.
4:7 *Ashdod.* See note on Isa 20:1. It became a district capital under Persian rule.
4:9 *prayed . . . posted a guard.* Prayer and watchfulness blend faith and action, and also emphasize both the divine side and the human side.
4:10 *giving out.* The picture is of a worker staggering under the weight of his load and ready to fall at any step.

"The strength of the laborers[m] is giving out, and there is so much rubble that we cannot rebuild the wall."

[11]Also our enemies said, "Before they know it or see us, we will be right there among them and will kill them and put an end to the work."

[12]Then the Jews who lived near them came and told us ten times over, "Wherever you turn, they will attack us."

[13]Therefore I stationed some of the people behind the lowest points of the wall at the exposed places, posting them by families, with their swords, spears and bows. [14]After I looked things over, I stood up and said to the nobles, the officials and the rest of the people, "Don't be afraid[n] of them. Remember[o] the Lord, who is great and awesome,[p] and fight[q] for your brothers, your sons and your daughters, your wives and your homes."

[15]When our enemies heard that we were aware of their plot and that God had frustrated it,[r] we all returned to the wall, each to his own work.

[16]From that day on, half of my men did the work, while the other half were equipped with spears, shields, bows and armor. The officers posted themselves behind all the people of Judah [17]who were building the wall. Those who carried materials did their work with one hand and held a weapon[s] in the other, [18]and each of

the builders wore his sword at his side as he worked. But the man who sounded the trumpet[t] stayed with me.

[19]Then I said to the nobles, the officials and the rest of the people, "The work is extensive and spread out, and we are widely separated from each other along the wall. [20]Wherever you hear the sound of the trumpet,[u] join us there. Our God will fight[v] for us!"

[21]So we continued the work with half the men holding spears, from the first light of dawn till the stars came out. [22]At that time I also said to the people, "Have every man and his helper stay inside Jerusalem at night, so they can serve us as guards by night and workmen by day." [23]Neither I nor my brothers nor my men nor the guards with me took off our clothes; each had his weapon, even when he went for water.[j]

Nehemiah Helps the Poor

5 Now the men and their wives raised a great outcry against their Jewish brothers. [2]Some were saying, "We and our sons and daughters are numerous; in order for us to eat and stay alive, we must get grain."

[3]Others were saying, "We are mortgag-

Cross references (center column):

4:10
[m]S 1Ch 23:4
4:14
[n]S Ge 28:15;
S Dt 1:29
[o]S Ne 1:8
[p]S Ne 1:5
[q]S 2Sa 10:12
4:15
[r]S 2Sa 17:14;
Job 5:12
4:17 [s]Ps 149:6

4:18 [t]S Nu 10:2
4:20 [u]Eze 33:3
[v]S Ex 14:14;
S Dt 20:4;
Jos 10:14

[j]23 The meaning of the Hebrew for this clause is uncertain.

4:11 *our enemies said.* Either Nehemiah had friendly informants, or the enemy was spreading unsettling rumors.
4:12 *ten times over.* Many times.
4:13 *lowest points ... exposed places.* Nehemiah posted men conspicuously in the areas that were the most vulnerable along the wall. *spears.* Used as thrusting weapons (Nu 25:7–8; 1Ki 18:28).
4:14 *Don't be afraid of them. Remember the Lord.* See note on 1:8. The best way to dispel fear is to remember the Lord, who alone is to be feared (see Dt 3:22; 20:3; 31:6).
4:16 *shields.* Made primarily of wood or wickerwork and therefore combustible (Eze 39:9). *armor.* The Hebrew for this word designated primarily a breastplate of metal or a coat of mail (see 2Ch 18:33).
4:17 *work with one hand ... weapon in the other.* Means either that the workers carried their materials with one hand and their weapons with the other, or simply that the weapons were kept close at hand.
4:18 *trumpet.* See note on Isa 18:3; see also Jos 6:4,6,8, 13.
4:20 *Our God will fight for us!* For the concept of holy war, in which God fights for his people, see Jos 10:14,42; Jdg 4:14; 20:35; 2Sa 5:24; see also Introduction to Joshua: The Conquest and the Ethical Question of War.
4:21 *till the stars came out.* Indicates the earnestness of their efforts, since the usual time to stop working was at sunset (Dt 24:15; Mt 20:8).
4:22 *guards by night.* Even men from outside Jerusalem stayed in the city at night so that some of them could serve as sentries.
4:23 See NIV text note. Although the precise meaning of

the end of the verse is not clear, the implication is that constant preparedness was the rule. According to Josephus *(Antiquities,* 11.5.8), Nehemiah "himself made the rounds of the city by night, never tiring either through work or lack of food and sleep, neither of which he took for pleasure but as a necessity."
5:1–19 During his major effort to rebuild the walls of Jerusalem, Nehemiah faced an economic crisis. Since the building of the wall took only 52 days (6:15), it is surprising that Nehemiah called a "large meeting" (v. 7) in the midst of such a project. Perhaps the economic pressures created by the rebuilding program brought to light problems that had long been simmering and that had to be dealt with before work could proceed. Among the classes affected by the economic crisis were (1) the landless, who were short of food (v. 2); (2) the landowners, who were compelled to mortgage their properties (v. 3); (3) those forced to borrow money at exorbitant rates and sell their children into slavery (vv. 4–5).
5:1 *wives.* The situation was so serious that the wives joined in the protest as they ran short of funds and supplies to feed their families. They complained not against the foreign authorities but against their own countrymen who were taking advantage of their poorer brothers at a time when all were needed for the defense of the country.
5:2 *grain.* About six to seven bushels would be needed for a man to feed his family for a month.
5:3 *mortgaging.* Even those who had considerable property were forced to mortgage it, benefiting the wealthy few (cf. Isa 5:8). In times of economic stress the rich got richer, and the poor got poorer. *famine.* The economic situation was aggravated by the natural conditions that had produced a

ing our fields,ʷ our vineyards and our homes to get grain during the famine."ˣ

⁴Still others were saying, "We have had to borrow money to pay the king's taxʸ on our fields and vineyards. ⁵Although we are of the same flesh and bloodᶻ as our countrymen and though our sons are as good as theirs, yet we have to subject our sons and daughters to slavery.ᵃ Some of our daughters have already been enslaved, but we are powerless, because our fields and our vineyards belong to others."ᵇ

⁶When I heard their outcry and these charges, I was very angry. ⁷I pondered them in my mind and then accused the nobles and officials. I told them, "You are exacting usuryᶜ from your own countrymen!" So I called together a large meeting to deal with them ⁸and said: "As far as possible, we have boughtᵈ back our Jewish brothers who were sold to the Gentiles. Now you are selling your brothers, only for them to be sold back to us!" They kept quiet, because they could find nothing to say.ᵉ

⁹So I continued, "What you are doing is not right. Shouldn't you walk in the fear of our God to avoid the reproachᶠ of our

Gentile enemies? ¹⁰I and my brothers and my men are also lending the people money and grain. But let the exacting of usury stop!ᵍ ¹¹Give back to them immediately their fields, vineyards, olive groves and houses, and also the usuryʰ you are charging them—the hundredth part of the money, grain, new wine and oil."

¹²"We will give it back," they said. "And we will not demand anything more from them. We will do as you say."

Then I summoned the priests and made the nobles and officials take an oathⁱ to do what they had promised. ¹³I also shookʲ out the folds of my robe and said, "In this way may God shake out of his house and possessions every man who does not keep this promise. So may such a man be shaken out and emptied!"

At this the whole assembly said, "Amen,"ᵏ and praised the Lᴏʀᴅ. And the people did as they had promised.

¹⁴Moreover, from the twentieth year of King Artaxerxes,ˡ when I was appointed to be their governorᵐ in the land of Judah, until his thirty-second year—twelve years—neither I nor my brothers ate the food allotted to the governor. ¹⁵But the

5:3 ʷPs 109:11
ˣGe 47:23
5:4 ʸS Ezr 4:13
5:5 ᶻS Ge 29:14
ᵃLev 25:39-43,
47; S 2Ki 4:1;
Isa 50:1
ᵇDt 15:7-11;
S 2Ki 4:1
5:7 ᶜEx 22:25-27;
S Lev 25:35-37;
Dt 23:19-20;
24:10-13
5:8 ᵈLev 25:47
ᵉJer 34:8
5:9 ᶠIsa 52:5
5:10 ᵍS Ex 22:25
5:11 ʰIsa 58:6
5:12 ⁱS Ezr 10:5
5:13 ʲS Mt 10:14
ᵏDt 27:15-26
5:14 ˡS Ne 2:6
ᵐGe 42:6;
Ezr 6:7; Jer 40:7;
Hag 1:1

famine. Some 75 years earlier the prophet Haggai had referred to a time of drought, when food was insufficient (Hag 1:5–11). Such times of distress were considered to be expressions of God's judgment (Isa 51:19; Jer 14:13–18; Am 4:6). Famines were common in Palestine. They occurred in the time of Abraham (Ge 12:10), Isaac (Ge 26:1), Joseph (Ge 41:27,54), Ruth (Ru 1:1), David (2Sa 21:1), Elijah (1Ki 18:2), Elisha (2Ki 4:38) and Claudius (Ac 11:28).

5:4 *tax.* It is estimated that the Persian king collected the equivalent of 20 million darics a year in taxes. Little was ever returned to benefit the provinces, because most of it was melted down and stored as bullion. Alexander the Great found at Susa alone 9,000 talents (about 340 tons) of coined gold and 40,000 talents (about 1,500 tons) of silver stored as bullion. As coined money was increasingly taken out of circulation by taxes, inflation became rampant. The acquisition of land by the Persians and its removal from production also helped produce a 50 percent rise in prices during the Persian period.

5:5 *slavery.* In times of economic distress families would borrow funds, using family members as collateral. If a man could not repay the loan and its interest, his children, his wife, or even the man himself could be sold into bondage. An Israelite who fell into debt, however, would serve his creditor as a "hired worker" (Lev 25:39–40). He was to be released in the seventh year (Dt 15:12–18), unless he chose to stay voluntarily. During the seven-year famine in Egypt, Joseph was approached by people who asked him to accept their land and their bodies in exchange for food (Ge 47:18–19). The irony for the Israelites was that at least as exiles in Mesopotamia their families were together, but now, because of dire economic necessity, their children were being sold into slavery.

5:6 *I was very angry.* Sometimes it becomes necessary to express indignation against social injustice (cf. Mk 11:15–18; Eph 4:26).

5:7 *usury.* See notes on Ex 22:25–27; Lev 25:36; Dt

23:20. Josephus (*Antiquities,* 4.8.25) explains: "Let it not be permitted to lend upon usury to any Hebrew either meat or drink; for it is not just to draw a revenue from the misfortunes of a fellow countryman. Rather, in consoling him in his distress, you should reckon as gain the gratitude of such persons and the recompense that God has in store for an act of generosity."

5:8 *Jewish brothers who were sold.* An impoverished brother could be hired as a servant, but he was not to be sold as a slave (Lev 25:39–42). *to the Gentiles.* The sale of fellow Hebrews as slaves to foreigners was forbidden (Ex 21:8). *kept quiet.* Their guilt was so obvious that they had no rebuttal or excuse (cf. Jn 8:7–10).

5:9 *not right.* Failure to treat others, especially fellow believers, with compassion is an insult to our Maker and a blot on our testimony (cf. Pr 14:31; 1Pe 2:12–15).

5:10 *let the exacting of usury stop!* The OT condemns the greed that seeks a profit at the expense of people (Ps 119:36; Isa 56:9–12; 57:17; Jer 6:13; 8:10; 22:13–17; Eze 22:12–13; 33:31). In view of the economic crisis facing his people, Nehemiah urges the creditors to relinquish their rights to repayment with interest.

5:11 *grain, new wine and oil.* See notes on 10:37; Dt 7:13.

5:13 *shook out the folds of my robe.* Symbolizing the solemnity of an oath and reinforcing the attendant curses for its nonfulfillment. *Amen.* See 8:6; Nu 5:22; see also note on Dt 27:15.

5:14 *thirty-second year.* From Apr. 1, 433 B.C., to Apr. 19, 432. Nehemiah served his first term as governor for 12 years before being recalled to court (13:6), after which he returned to Jerusalem (13:7) for a second term whose length cannot be determined. *food allotted to the governor.* See v. 18. Provincial governors normally assessed the people in their provinces for their support. But Nehemiah, like Paul (1Co 9; 2Th 3:8–9), sacrificed even what was normally his in order to serve as an example to the people.

earlier governors—those preceding me —placed a heavy burden on the people and took forty shekels[k] of silver from them in addition to food and wine. Their assistants also lorded it over the people. But out of reverence for God[n] I did not act like that. [16]Instead,[o] I devoted myself to the work on this wall. All my men were assembled there for the work; we[l] did not acquire any land.

[17]Furthermore, a hundred and fifty Jews and officials ate at my table, as well as those who came to us from the surrounding nations. [18]Each day one ox, six choice sheep and some poultry[p] were prepared for me, and every ten days an abundant supply of wine of all kinds. In spite of all this, I never demanded the food allotted to the governor, because the demands were heavy on these people.

[19]Remember[q] me with favor, O my God, for all I have done for these people.

Further Opposition to the Rebuilding

6 When word came to Sanballat, Tobiah,[r] Geshem[s] the Arab and the rest of our enemies that I had rebuilt the wall and not a gap was left in it—though up to

5:15 [n]S Ge 20:11
5:16 [o]2Th 3:7-10
5:18 [p]1Ki 4:23
5:19 [q]S Ge 8:1;
S 2Ki 20:3;
S Ne 1:8
6:1 [r]Ne 2:10
[s]S Ne 2:19

6:2 [t]S 1Ch 8:12
6:5 [u]S Ne 2:10
6:6 [v]S Ne 2:19

that time I had not set the doors in the gates— [2]Sanballat and Geshem sent me this message: "Come, let us meet together in one of the villages[m] on the plain of Ono.[t]"

But they were scheming to harm me; [3]so I sent messengers to them with this reply: "I am carrying on a great project and cannot go down. Why should the work stop while I leave it and go down to you?" [4]Four times they sent me the same message, and each time I gave them the same answer.

[5]Then, the fifth time, Sanballat[u] sent his aide to me with the same message, and in his hand was an unsealed letter [6]in which was written:

> "It is reported among the nations—and Geshem[n][v] says it is true—that you and the Jews are plotting to revolt, and therefore you are building the wall. Moreover, according to these reports you are about to become their king [7]and have even ap-

[k]15 That is, about 1 pound (about 0.5 kilogram)
[l]16 Most Hebrew manuscripts; some Hebrew manuscripts, Septuagint, Vulgate and Syriac *I* [m]2 Or *in Kephirim* [n]6 Hebrew *Gashmu,* a variant of *Geshem*

5:15 *governors.* The Hebrew for this word is used of Sheshbazzar (Ezr 5:14) and Zerubbabel (Hag 1:1,14; 2:2) as well as of various Persian officials (Ezr 5:3,6; 6:6–7,13; 8:36; Ne 2:7,9; 3:7). Nehemiah was not referring here to men of the caliber of Zerubbabel. Some believe that Judah did not have governors before Nehemiah and that the reference here is to governors of Samaria. But new archaeological evidence, in the form of seals and seal impressions, confirms the reference to the previous governors of Judah. *heavy burden.* It was customary Persian practice to exempt temple personnel from taxation, which increased the burden on lay people. *assistants.* If the governors themselves used extortion, their underlings often proved even more oppressive (cf. Mt 18:21–35; 20:25–28). *reverence for God.* Those in high positions are in danger of abusing their authority over their subordinates if they forget that they themselves are servants of a superior "Master in heaven" (Col 4:1; cf. Ge 39:9; 2Co 5:11).
5:16 *did not acquire any land.* Nehemiah's behavior as governor was guided by principles of service rather than by opportunism.
5:17 *ate at my table.* As part of his social responsibility, a ruler or governor was expected to entertain lavishly. A text found at Nimrud has Ashurnasirpal II feeding 69,574 guests at a banquet for ten days. When Solomon dedicated the temple, he sacrificed 22,000 cattle and 120,000 sheep and goats, and held a great festival for the assembly for 14 days (1Ki 8:62–65). We are not told how many he fed (cf. 1Ki 4:27).
5:18 *Each day.* The meat listed here would provide one meal for 600–800 persons, including the 150 Jews and officials of v. 18. Cf. Solomon's provisions for one day (1Ki 4:22–23). *choice sheep.* Cf. Mal 1:8. *poultry.* Chickens were domesticated in the Indus River Valley by 2000 B.C. and were brought to Egypt by the time of Thutmose III (15th century B.C.). They were known in Mesopotamia and in

Greece by the eighth century B.C. The earliest inscriptional evidence for Palestine is the seal of Jaazaniah (dated c. 600 B.C.), which depicts a fighting rooster.
5:19 *Remember me.* See note on 1:8; cf. Heb 6:10. Perhaps Nehemiah's memoirs (see Introduction to Ezra: Literary Form and Authorship) were inscribed as a memorial that was set up in the temple. A striking parallel to Nehemiah's prayer is found in a prayer of Nebuchadnezzar: "O Marduk, my lord, do remember my deeds favorably as good [deeds]; may (these) my good deeds be always before your mind."
6:1 *Sanballat, Tobiah, Geshem.* See notes on 2:10,19.
6:2 *Ono.* Located about seven miles southeast of Joppa near Lod (Lydda; see note on Ezr 2:33), in the westernmost area settled by the returning Jews (Ne 7:37; 11:35). It may have been proposed as neutral territory, but Nehemiah recognized the invitation as a trap (cf. Ge 4:8; Jer 41:1–3).
6:3 Nehemiah's sharp reply may seem like a haughty response to a reasonable invitation, but he correctly discerned the insincerity of his enemies. He refused to be distracted by matters that would divert his energies from rebuilding Jerusalem's wall.
6:4 *Four times.* Nehemiah's foes were persistent, but he was equally persistent in resisting them.
6:5 *unsealed letter.* During this period a letter was ordinarily written on a papyrus or leather sheet, which was rolled up, tied with a string and sealed with a clay bulla (seal impression) to guarantee the letter's authenticity. Sanballat apparently wanted the contents of his letter to be made known to the public at large.
6:6 *their king.* The Persian kings did not tolerate the claims of pretenders to kingship, as we can see from the Behistun (Bisitun) inscription of Darius. In NT times the Roman emperor was likewise suspicious of any unauthorized claims to royalty (Jn 19:12; cf. Mt 2:1–13).

pointed prophets to make this proclamation about you in Jerusalem: 'There is a king in Judah!' Now this report will get back to the king; so come, let us confer together."

⁸I sent him this reply: "Nothing like what you are saying is happening; you are just making it up out of your head."

⁹They were all trying to frighten us, thinking, "Their hands will get too weak for the work, and it will not be completed."

But I prayed, "Now strengthen my hands."

¹⁰One day I went to the house of Shemaiah son of Delaiah, the son of Mehetabel, who was shut in at his home. He said, "Let us meet in the house of God, inside the temple ʷ, and let us close the temple doors, because men are coming to kill you—by night they are coming to kill you."

¹¹But I said, "Should a man like me run away? Or should one like me go into the temple to save his life? I will not go!" ¹²I realized that God had not sent him, but that he had prophesied against me ˣ because Tobiah and Sanballat ʸ had hired him. ¹³He had been hired to intimidate me so that I would commit a sin by doing this, and then they would give me a bad name to discredit me. ᶻ

¹⁴Remember ᵃ Tobiah and Sanballat, ᵇ O my God, because of what they have done; remember also the prophetess ᶜ Noadiah

and the rest of the prophets ᵈ who have been trying to intimidate me.

The Completion of the Wall

¹⁵So the wall was completed on the twenty-fifth of Elul, in fifty-two days. ¹⁶When all our enemies heard about this, all the surrounding nations were afraid and lost their self-confidence, because they realized that this work had been done with the help of our God.

¹⁷Also, in those days the nobles of Judah were sending many letters to Tobiah, and replies from Tobiah kept coming to them. ¹⁸For many in Judah were under oath to him, since he was son-in-law to Shecaniah son of Arah, and his son Jehohanan had married the daughter of Meshullam son of Berekiah. ¹⁹Moreover, they kept reporting to me his good deeds and then telling him what I said. And Tobiah sent letters to intimidate me.

7 After the wall had been rebuilt and I had set the doors in place, the gatekeepers ᵉ and the singers ᶠ and the Levites ᵍ were appointed. ²I put in charge of Jerusalem my brother Hanani, ʰ along with° Hananiah ⁱ the commander of the citadel, ʲ because he was a man of integrity and feared ᵏ God more than most men do. ³I said to them, "The gates of Jerusalem are not to be opened until the sun is hot. While the gatekeepers are still on duty, have them shut the doors and bar them. Also appoint residents of Jerusalem as

6:10 ʷNu 18:7
6:12
  ˣEze 13:22-23
  ʸS Ne 2:10
6:13 ᶻJer 20:10
6:14 ᵃS Ne 1:8
  ᵇS Ne 2:10
  ᶜS Ex 15:20;
  Eze 13:17-23;
  S Ac 21:9;
  Rev 2:20

ᵈJer 23:9-40;
  Zec 13:2-3
7:1 ᵉ1Ch 9:27;
  S 26:12-19
ᶠPs 68:25 ᵍNe 8:9
7:2 ʰNe 1:2
  ⁱNe 10:23
ʲNe 2:8 ᵏ1Ki 18:3

°2 Or Hanani, that is,

6:8 *Nothing.* Nehemiah does not mince words. He calls the report a lie. He may have sent his own messenger to the Persian king to assure him of his loyalty.

6:9 *hands will get . . . weak.* Figurative language to express the idea of discouragement. The Hebrew for this phrase is used also in Ezr 4:4; Jer 38:4, as well as on an ostracon from Lachish dated c. 588 B.C.

6:10 *Shemaiah . . . was shut in.* Perhaps as a symbolic action to indicate that his own life is in danger and to suggest that both Nehemiah and he must flee to the temple (for other symbolic actions see 1Ki 22:11; Isa 20:2-4; Jer 27:2-7; 28:10-11; Eze 4:1-17; 12:3-11; Ac 21:11). Since Shemaiah had access to the temple, he may have been a priest. He was clearly a friend of Tobiah (cf. v. 12), and therefore Nehemiah's enemy. It was at least credible for Shemaiah to propose that Nehemiah take refuge in the temple area at the altar of asylum (see Ex 21:13-14 and notes), but not in the "house of God," the temple building itself.

6:11 Even if the threat against his life was real, Nehemiah was not a coward who would run into hiding. Nor would he transgress the law to save his life. As a layman, he was not permitted to enter the sanctuary (Nu 18:7). When King Uzziah entered the temple to burn incense, he was punished by being afflicted with leprosy (2Ch 26:16-21).

6:12 The fact that Shemaiah proposed a course of action contrary to God's word revealed him as a false prophet (cf. Dt 18:20; Isa 8:19-20).

6:13 If Nehemiah had wavered in the face of the threat against him, his leadership would have been discredited and morale among the people would have plummeted.

6:14 *Remember.* See note on 1:8. *prophetess.* See note on Ex 15:20.

6:15 *twenty-fifth of Elul.* Oct. 2, 445 B.C. *fifty-two days.* The walls that lay in ruins for nearly a century and a half were rebuilt in less than two months once the people were galvanized into action by Nehemiah's leadership. Archaeological investigations have shown that the circumference of the wall in Nehemiah's day was much reduced. Josephus states (*Antiquities*, 11.5.8) that the rebuilding of the wall took two years and four months, but he is doubtless including such additional tasks as further strengthening of various sections, embellishing and beautifying, and the like. The dedication of the wall is described in 12:27-47.

6:17-18 Tobiah was related to an influential family in Judah, since his son Jehohanan was married to the daughter of Meshullam, who had helped repair the wall of Jerusalem (3:4,30).

7:2 *in charge of Jerusalem.* Over Rephaiah and Shallum, who were over sections of the city (3:9,12). *Hanani.* See note on 1:2. *citadel.* See notes on 2:8; 3:1.

7:3 *until the sun is hot.* Normally the gates would be opened at dawn, but their opening was to be delayed until the sun was high in the heavens to prevent the enemy from making a surprise attack before most of the people were up.

guards, some at their posts and some near their own houses."

The List of the Exiles Who Returned

7:6-73pp — Ezr 2:1-70

4Now the city was large and spacious, but there were few people in it,[l] and the houses had not yet been rebuilt. 5So my God put it into my heart to assemble the nobles, the officials and the common people for registration by families. I found the genealogical record of those who had been the first to return. This is what I found written there:

6These are the people of the province who came up from the captivity of the exiles[m] whom Nebuchadnezzar king of Babylon had taken captive (they returned to Jerusalem and Judah, each to his own town, 7in company with Zerubbabel,[n] Jeshua, Nehemiah, Azariah, Raamiah, Nahamani, Mordecai, Bilshan, Mispereth, Bigvai, Nehum and Baanah):

The list of the men of Israel:

8the descendants of Parosh	2,172
9of Shephatiah	372
10of Arah	652
11of Pahath-Moab (through the line of Jeshua and Joab)	2,818
12of Elam	1,254
13of Zattu	845
14of Zaccai	760
15of Binnui	648
16of Bebai	628
17of Azgad	2,322
18of Adonikam	667
19of Bigvai	2,067
20of Adin[o]	655
21of Ater (through Hezekiah)	98
22of Hashum	328
23of Bezai	324
24of Hariph	112
25of Gibeon	95
26the men of Bethlehem and Netophah[p]	188
27of Anathoth[q]	128
28of Beth Azmaveth	42
29of Kiriath Jearim, Kephirah[r] and Beeroth[s]	743
30of Ramah and Geba	621
31of Micmash	122
32of Bethel and Ai[t]	123
33of the other Nebo	52

34of the other Elam	1,254
35of Harim	320
36of Jericho[u]	345
37of Lod, Hadid and Ono[v]	721
38of Senaah	3,930

39The priests:

the descendants of Jedaiah (through the family of Jeshua)	973
40of Immer	1,052
41of Pashhur	1,247
42of Harim	1,017

43The Levites:

the descendants of Jeshua (through Kadmiel through the line of Hodaviah)	74

44The singers:[w]

the descendants of Asaph	148

45The gatekeepers:[x]

the descendants of Shallum, Ater, Talmon, Akkub, Hatita and Shobai	138

46The temple servants:[y]

the descendants of
Ziha, Hasupha, Tabbaoth,
47Keros, Sia, Padon,
48Lebana, Hagaba, Shalmai,
49Hanan, Giddel, Gahar,
50Reaiah, Rezin, Nekoda,
51Gazzam, Uzza, Paseah,
52Besai, Meunim, Nephussim,
53Bakbuk, Hakupha, Harhur,
54Bazluth, Mehida, Harsha,
55Barkos, Sisera, Temah,
56Neziah and Hatipha

57The descendants of the servants of Solomon:

the descendants of
Sotai, Sophereth, Perida,
58Jaala, Darkon, Giddel,
59Shephatiah, Hattil,
Pokereth-Hazzebaim and Amon

60The temple servants and the descendants of the servants of Solomon[z]	392

61The following came up from the towns of Tel Melah, Tel Harsha, Kerub, Addon and Immer, but they could not show that their families were descended from Israel:

62the descendants of

Cross references (center column):

7:4 [l]Ne 11:1
7:6 [m]S 2Ch 36:20; S Ne 1:2
7:7 [n]S 1Ch 3:19
7:20 [o]S Ezr 8:6
7:26 [p]S 2Sa 23:28; S 1Ch 2:54
7:27 [q]S Jos 21:18
7:29 [r]S Jos 18:26
   [s]S Jos 18:25
7:32 [t]S Ge 12:8

7:36 [u]Ne 3:2
7:37 [v]S 1Ch 8:12
7:44 [w]Ne 11:23
7:45 [x]S 1Ch 9:17
7:46 [y]S Ne 3:26
7:60 [z]S 1Ch 9:2

7:6–73 Essentially the same as Ezr 2. See notes there for the nature of the list and the reasons for the numerous variations in names and numbers between the two lists.   **7:7** *Nahamani.* Does not occur in Ezr 2:2.   **7:43** *74.* See note on Ezr 2:40.

Delaiah, Tobiah and Nekoda 642
63 And from among the priests:

the descendants of
Hobaiah, Hakkoz and Barzillai (a
man who had married a daughter
of Barzillai the Gileadite and was
called by that name).
64 These searched for their family
records, but they could not find them
and so were excluded from the priesthood as unclean. 65 The governor,
therefore, ordered them not to eat any
of the most sacred food until there
should be a priest ministering with the
Urim and Thummim.[a]

66 The whole company numbered
42,360, 67 besides their 7,337 menservants and maidservants; and they
also had 245 men and women singers.
68 There were 736 horses, 245
mules,[p] 69 435 camels and 6,720 donkeys.

70 Some of the heads of the families
contributed to the work. The governor
gave to the treasury 1,000 drachmas[q]
of gold, 50 bowls and 530 garments
for priests. 71 Some of the heads of the
families[b] gave to the treasury for the
work 20,000 drachmas[r] of gold and
2,200 minas[s] of silver. 72 The total
given by the rest of the people was
20,000 drachmas of gold, 2,000
minas[t] of silver and 67 garments for
priests.[c]

73 The priests, the Levites, the gatekeepers, the singers and the temple
servants,[d] along with certain of the
people and the rest of the Israelites,
settled in their own towns.[e]

Ezra Reads the Law

When the seventh month came and the
Israelites had settled in their towns,[f]
8 1 all the people assembled as one man
in the square before the Water Gate.[g]
They told Ezra the scribe to bring out the
Book of the Law of Moses,[h] which the
LORD had commanded for Israel.
2 So on the first day of the seventh
month[i] Ezra the priest brought the Law[j]
before the assembly, which was made up
of men and women and all who were able
to understand. 3 He read it aloud from daybreak till noon as he faced the square before the Water Gate[k] in the presence of
the men, women and others who could
understand. And all the people listened attentively to the Book of the Law.
4 Ezra the scribe stood on a high wooden
platform[l] built for the occasion. Beside
him on his right stood Mattithiah, Shema,
Anaiah, Uriah, Hilkiah and Maaseiah; and
on his left were Pedaiah, Mishael, Malkijah, Hashum, Hashbaddanah, Zechariah
and Meshullam.
5 Ezra opened the book. All the people
could see him because he was standing[m]
above them; and as he opened it, the
people all stood up. 6 Ezra praised the

7:65 [a]S Ex 28:30 **7:71** [b]S 1Ch 29:7 **7:72** [c]S Ex 25:2 **7:73** [d]Ne 1:10; Ps 34:22; 103:21; 113:1; 135:1 [e]S Ezr 3:1; Ne 11:1 [f]Ezr 3:1 **8:1** [g]S Ne 3:26 [h]S Dt 28:61; S 2Ch 34:15 **8:2** [i]Lev 23:23-25; Nu 29:1-6 [j]S Dt 31:11 **8:3** [k]S Ne 3:26 **8:4** [l]2Ch 6:13 **8:5** [m]Jdg 3:20

[p]68 Some Hebrew manuscripts (see also Ezra 2:66); most Hebrew manuscripts do not have this verse. [q]70 That is, about 19 pounds (about 8.5 kilograms) [r]71 That is, about 375 pounds (about 170 kilograms); also in verse 72 [s]71 That is, about 1 1/3 tons (about 1.2 metric tons) [t]72 That is, about 1 1/4 tons (about 1.1 metric tons)

7:70 *drachmas.* See note on Ezr 2:69.
7:73 *settled in their own towns.* See note on Ezr 2:70. *seventh month.* October-November, 445 B.C.
8:1–18 According to the traditional view, the reading of the Law by Ezra would be the first reference to him in almost 13 years since his arrival in 458 B.C. Since he was commissioned to teach the Law (Ezr 7:6,10,14,25–26), it is surprising that there was such a long delay in its public proclamation.
8:1 *all the people assembled.* See Ezr 3:1, which also refers to an assembly called in the seventh month (Tishri), the beginning of the civil year (see chart on "Hebrew Calendar," p. 102). *square before the Water Gate.* See vv. 3,16; see also notes on 3:26; Ezr 10:9. Squares were normally located near a city gate (2Ch 32:6). *scribe.* See note on Ezr 7:6. *Book of the Law of Moses.* Cf. vv. 2–3,5,8–9,13–15, 18. Four views have been proposed concerning the extent of this Book: (1) a collection of legal materials, (2) the priestly laws of Exodus and Leviticus, (3) the laws of Deuteronomy, (4) the Pentateuch. Surely Ezra could have brought back with him the Torah, i.e., the entire Pentateuch.
8:2 *first day of the seventh month.* Oct. 8, 445 B.C.; the New Year's Day of the civil calendar (see note on Lev 23:24), celebrated as the Feast of Trumpets (Nu 29:1–6), with cessation of labor and a sacred assembly. *women.* See 10:28. Women did not usually participate in assemblies (see note on Ex 10:11), but were brought, together with children, on such solemn occasions (Dt 31:12; Jos 8:35; 2Ki 23:2).
8:3 *read it aloud.* See Ex 24:7; Ac 8:30. *from daybreak till noon.* The people evidently stood (vv. 5,7) for five or six hours, listening attentively to the reading and exposition (vv. 7–8,12) of the Scriptures.
8:5 *book.* Scroll (see note on Ex 17:14). *people all stood up.* The rabbis deduced from this verse that the congregation should stand for the reading of the Torah. It is customary in Eastern Orthodox churches for the congregation to stand throughout the service.
8:6 *lifted their hands.* See Ex 9:29 and note; Ps 28:2; 134:2; 1Ti 2:8. *Amen! Amen!* See notes on Dt 27:15; Ro 1:25. The repetition conveys the intensity of feeling behind the affirmation (for other repetitions see Ge 22:11 and note; cf. 2Ki 11:14; Lk 23:21). *worshiped.* In its original sense the Hebrew for this verb meant "to prostrate oneself on the ground," as the frequently accompanying phrase "to the ground" indicates. Private acts of worship often involved prostration "to the ground," as in the case of Abraham's servant (Ge 24:52), Moses (Ex 34:8), Joshua (Jos 5:14) and Job (Job 1:20). There are three cases of spontaneous communal worship in Exodus (4:31; 12:27; 33:10). In 2Ch 20:18 Jehoshaphat and the people "fell down in worship before the

LORD, the great God; and all the people lifted their hands [n] and responded, "Amen! Amen!" Then they bowed down and worshiped the LORD with their faces to the ground.

[7]The Levites[o]—Jeshua, Bani, Sherebiah, Jamin, Akkub, Shabbethai, Hodiah, Maaseiah, Kelita, Azariah, Jozabad, Hanan and Pelaiah—instructed[p] the people in the Law while the people were standing there. [8]They read from the Book of the Law of God, making it clear[u] and giving the meaning so that the people could understand what was being read.

[9]Then Nehemiah the governor, Ezra the priest and scribe, and the Levites[q] who were instructing the people said to them all, "This day is sacred to the LORD your God. Do not mourn or weep."[r] For all the people had been weeping as they listened to the words of the Law.

[10]Nehemiah said, "Go and enjoy choice food and sweet drinks, and send some to those who have nothing[s] prepared. This day is sacred to our Lord. Do not grieve, for the joy[t] of the LORD is your strength."

[11]The Levites calmed all the people, saying, "Be still, for this is a sacred day. Do not grieve."

[12]Then all the people went away to eat and drink, to send portions of food and to celebrate with great joy,[u] because they now understood the words that had been made known to them.

[13]On the second day of the month, the heads of all the families, along with the priests and the Levites, gathered around Ezra the scribe to give attention to the words of the Law. [14]They found written in the Law, which the LORD had commanded through Moses, that the Israelites were to live in booths[v] during the feast of the seventh month [15]and that they should proclaim this word and spread it throughout their towns and in Jerusalem: "Go out into the hill country and bring back branches from olive and wild olive trees, and from myrtles, palms and shade trees, to make booths"—as it is written.[v]

[16]So the people went out and brought back branches and built themselves booths on their own roofs, in their courtyards, in the courts of the house of God and in the square by the Water Gate[w] and the one by the Gate of Ephraim.[x] [17]The whole company that had returned from exile built booths and lived in them.[y] From the days of Joshua son of Nun until that day, the

---

8:6 [n]S Ezr 9:5; 1Ti 2:8
8:7 [o]S Ezr 10:23 [p]S Lev 10:11; S 2Ch 17:7
8:9 [q]Ne 7:1 [r]Dt 12:7,12; 16:14-15
8:10 [s]1Sa 25:8; S 2Sa 6:19; Est 9:22; Lk 14:12-14 [t]S Lev 23:40; S Dt 12:18; 16:11,14-15
8:12 [u]Est 9:22
8:14 [v]S Ex 23:16
8:16 [w]S Ne 3:26 [x]S 2Ch 25:23
8:17 [y]Hos 12:9

[u]8 Or God, translating it   [v]15 See Lev. 23:37-40.

LORD" when they heard his promise of victory.

8:7 *instructed.* See v. 8; Ezr 8:16 and note; Ps 119:34,73, 130; Isa 40:14.

8:8 *read.* See note on v. 3. *making it clear.* Rabbinic tradition understands the Hebrew for this expression as referring to translation from Hebrew into an Aramaic Targum (see NIV text note). But there is no evidence of Targums (free Aramaic translations of OT books or passages) from such an early date. The earliest extensive Targum is one on Job from Qumran, dated c. 150-100 B.C. Targums exist for every book of the OT except Daniel and Ezra-Nehemiah. *understand.* See v. 12.

8:9 *Nehemiah . . . Ezra.* An explicit reference showing that they were contemporaries (see 12:26,36). *Do not mourn.* See Ezr 10:6 and note; Est 9:22; Isa 57:18-19; Jer 31:13. *weep.* See 1:4; Ezr 3:13 and note; 10:1.

8:10 *choice food.* Delicious festive food prepared with much fat. The fat of sacrificial animals was offered to God as the tastiest element of the burnt offering (Lev 1:8,12), the fellowship offering (Lev 3:9-10), the sin offering (Lev 4:8-10) and the guilt offering (Lev 7:3-4). The fat was not to be eaten in these cases. *send some to those who have nothing.* It was customary for God's people to remember the less fortunate on joyous occasions (2Sa 6:19; Est 9:22; contrast 1Co 11:20-22; Jas 2:14-16).

8:14 *booths.* See notes on Ex 23:16; Lev 23:34,42; Jn 7:37-39.

8:15 *olive.* Widespread in Mediterranean countries. It was growing in Canaan before the conquest (Dt 8:8). Because it takes an olive tree 30 years to mature, its cultivation requires peaceful conditions. *wild olive trees.* Lit. "tree of oil," commonly regarded as the wild olive tree. But this is questionable since the "tree of oil" was used as timber (1Ki 6:23,31-33),

whereas the wood of the wild olive tree would have been of little value for use in the temple's furniture. Also, the wild olive tree contains very little oil. The phrase may refer to a resinous tree like the fir. *myrtles.* Evergreen bushes with a pleasing odor (Isa 41:19; 55:13; Zec 1:8,10-11). *palms.* The date palm was common around Jericho (Dt 34:3; 2Ch 28:15). *shade trees.* Cf. Eze 6:13; 20:28. Later Jewish celebrations of the Feast of Tabernacles include waving the *lulav* (made of branches of palms, myrtles and willows) with the right hand and holding branches of the *ethrog* (a citrus native to Palestine) in the left.

8:16 *courts of the house of God.* See note on 13:7. The temple that Ezekiel saw in his visions had an outer and an inner court (see p. 1284). Ezekiel's temple was to some extent patterned after Solomon's, which had an inner court of priests and an outer court (1Ki 6:36; 7:12; 2Ki 21:5; 23:12; 2Ch 4:9; 33:5). The temple of the NT era had a court of the Gentiles and an inner court, which was subdivided into courts of the women, of Israel and the priests. The Temple Scroll from Qumran has God setting forth in detail an ideal temple. Columns 40-46 describe the outer court as follows: "On the roof of the third story are columns for the constructing of booths for the Feast of Tabernacles, to be occupied by the elders, tribal chieftains and commanders of thousands and hundreds." *Gate of Ephraim.* A gate of the oldest rampart of Jerusalem (see note on 3:6; see also 2Ki 14:13). It was restored by Nehemiah (12:39).

8:17 *From the days of Joshua . . . until that day.* The phrase does not mean that the Feast of Tabernacles had not been celebrated since Joshua's time, because such celebrations took place after the dedication of Solomon's temple (2Ch 7:8-10) and after the return of the exiles (Ezr 3:4). What apparently is meant is that the feast had not been celebrated before with such great joy (cf. 2Ch 30:26; 35:18).

Israelites had not celebrated[z] it like this. And their joy was very great.

[18]Day after day, from the first day to the last, Ezra read[a] from the Book of the Law[b] of God. They celebrated the feast for seven days, and on the eighth day, in accordance with the regulation,[c] there was an assembly.[d]

The Israelites Confess Their Sins

9 On the twenty-fourth day of the same month, the Israelites gathered together, fasting and wearing sackcloth and having dust on their heads.[e] [2]Those of Israelite descent had separated themselves from all foreigners.[f] They stood in their places and confessed their sins and the wickedness of their fathers.[g] [3]They stood where they were and read from the Book of the Law of the LORD their God for a quarter of the day, and spent another quarter in confession and in worshiping the LORD their God. [4]Standing on the stairs were the Levites[h]—Jeshua, Bani, Kadmiel, Shebaniah, Bunni, Sherebiah, Bani and Kenani—who called with loud voices to the LORD their God. [5]And the Levites—Jeshua, Kadmiel, Bani, Hashabneiah, Sherebiah, Hodiah, Shebaniah and Pethahiah—said: "Stand up and praise the LORD your God,[i] who is from everlasting to everlasting.[w]"

"Blessed be your glorious name,[j] and may it be exalted above all blessing and praise. [6]You alone are the LORD.[k] You made the heavens,[l] even the highest heavens, and all their starry host,[m] the earth[n] and all that is on it, the seas[o] and all that is in them.[p] You give life to everything, and the multitudes of heaven[q] worship you.

[7]"You are the LORD God, who chose Abram[r] and brought him out of Ur of the Chaldeans[s] and named him Abraham.[t] [8]You found his heart faithful to you, and you made a covenant with him to give to his descendants the land of the Canaanites, Hittites, Amorites, Perizzites, Jebusites and Girgashites.[u] You have kept your promise[v] because you are righteous.[w]

[9]"You saw the suffering of our forefathers in Egypt;[x] you heard their cry at the Red Sea.[x][y] [10]You sent miraculous signs[z] and wonders[a] against Pharaoh, against all his officials and all the people of his land, for you knew how arrogantly the Egyptians treated them. You made a name[b] for yourself,[c] which remains to this day. [11]You divided the sea before them,[d] so that they passed through it on dry ground, but you hurled their pursuers into the depths,[e] like a stone into mighty waters.[f] [12]By day[g] you led[h] them with a pillar of cloud,[i] and by night with a pillar of fire to give them light on the way they were to take.

[13]"You came down on Mount Sinai;[j] you spoke[k] to them from heaven.[l] You gave them regulations and laws that are just[m] and right, and decrees and commands that are good.[n] [14]You made known to them your holy Sabbath[o] and gave them commands, decrees and laws through your servant Moses. [15]In their hunger you gave them bread from heaven[p] and in their thirst you brought them

---

8:17 [z]S 1Ki 8:2; S 2Ch 7:8; S 8:13
8:18 [a]Dt 31:11; S 33:10
[b]S Dt 28:61
[c]S Lev 23:40; S Ezr 3:4
[d]S Lev 23:36
9:1 [e]Lev 26:40-45; S Jos 7:6; 2Ch 7:14-16
9:2 [f]S Ezr 6:21; Ne 10:28; 13:3, 30 [g]S Lev 26:40; S Ezr 10:11; Ps 106:6
9:4 [h]S Ezr 10:23
9:5 [i]Ps 78:4 [j]S 2Sa 7:26
9:6 [k]S Dt 6:4 [l]S Ex 8:19 [m]Isa 40:26; 45:12 [n]S Ge 1:1; Isa 37:16 [o]Ps 95:5; 146:6; Jnh 1:9 [p]Dt 10:14; Ac 4:24; Rev 10:6 [q]Ps 103:20; 148:2
9:7 [r]S Ge 16:11 [s]S Ge 11:28 [t]S Ge 17:5
9:8 [u]S Ge 15:18-21; S Ezr 9:1 [v]S Jos 21:45 [w]Ge 15:6; S Ezr 9:15
9:9 [x]Ex 2:23-25; 3:7 [y]Ex 14:10-30
9:10 [z]S Ex 10:1; Ps 74:9 [a]S Ex 3:20; S 6:6 [b]Jer 32:20; Da 9:15 [c]S Nu 6:27
9:11 [d]Ps 78:13 [e]S Ex 14:28 [f]Ex 15:4-5,10; Heb 11:29
9:12 [g]S Dt 1:33 [h]S Ex 15:13 [i]S Ex 13:21
9:13 [j]S Ex 19:11 [k]S Ex 19:19 [l]S Ex 20:22 [m]Ps 119:137 [n]S Ex 20:1; Dt 4:7-8
9:14 [o]S Ge 2:3; Ex 20:8-11
9:15 [p]S Ex 16:4; Ps 78:24-25; Jn 6:31

[w]5 Or *God for ever and ever*   [x]9 Hebrew *Yam Suph*; that is, Sea of Reeds

---

8:18 *assembly.* See Nu 29:35.

9:1–37 The ninth chapters of Ezra, Nehemiah and Daniel are devoted to confessions of national sin and to prayers for God's grace.

9:1 *twenty-fourth day.* Oct. 30, 445 B.C.; a day of penance in the spirit of the Day of Atonement, which was held on the tenth day (Lev 16:29–30). *fasting . . . sackcloth . . . dust.* See notes on Ge 37:34; Ezr 8:23; 10:6; Joel 1:13–14.
9:3 *quarter of the day.* About three hours.
9:5–37 One of the most beautiful prayers outside the Psalms, it reviews God's grace and power (1) in creation (v. 6), (2) in the Abrahamic covenant (vv. 7–8), (3) in Egypt and at the Red Sea (vv. 9–11), (4) in the desert and at Sinai (vv. 12–21), (5) during the conquest of Canaan (vv. 22–25), (6) through the judges (vv. 26–28), (7) through the prophets (vv. 29–31) and (8) in the present situation (vv. 32–37). Cf. Ps 78; 105–106.
9:6 *You alone are the LORD.* Though not in the words of Dt 6:4, which expresses the central monotheistic conviction of Israel's faith, the prayer begins with a similar affirmation (cf.

2Ki 19:15; Ps 86:10). *highest heavens.* See Dt 10:14; 1Ki 8:27; 2Ch 2:6; Ps 148:4. *multitudes of heaven worship you.* See Ps 89:5–7.
9:7 *Ur of the Chaldeans.* See note on Ge 11:28. *named him Abraham.* See note on Ge 17:5.
9:8 *faithful.* Compare Ro 4:16–22 with Jas 2:21–23. *made a covenant with him.* See note on Ge 15:18. *Canaanites . . . Girgashites.* See notes on Ge 10:6,15–18; 13:7; Ex 3:8; Ezr 9:1.
9:9 *Red Sea.* See notes on Ex 13:18; 14:2.
9:11 *divided the sea.* See Ex 14:21–22; 1Co 10:1.
9:13 *laws.* The singular form of the Hebrew for this word is *Torah,* which means "instruction," "law," and later the Pentateuch, the five books of Moses.
9:14 *holy Sabbath.* According to the rabbis, "the Sabbath outweighs all the commandments of the Torah." See 10:31–33; 13:15–22.
9:15 *bread from heaven.* See note on Ex 16:4. *water from the rock.* See note on Ex 17:6. *sworn with uplifted hand.* See Ge 14:22 and note; 22:15–17; Ex 6:8; Eze 20:6; 47:14.

water from the rock; *q* you told them to go in and take possession of the land you had sworn with uplifted hand *r* to give them. *s*

16"But they, our forefathers, became arrogant and stiff-necked, *t* and did not obey your commands. *u* 17They refused to listen and failed to remember *v* the miracles *w* you performed among them. They became stiff-necked *x* and in their rebellion appointed a leader in order to return to their slavery. *y* But you are a forgiving God, *z* gracious and compassionate, *a* slow to anger *b* and abounding in love. *c* Therefore you did not desert them, *d* 18even when they cast for themselves an image of a calf *e* and said, 'This is your god, who brought you up out of Egypt,' or when they committed awful blasphemies. *f*

19"Because of your great compassion you did not abandon *g* them in the desert. By day the pillar of cloud *h* did not cease to guide them on their path, nor the pillar of fire by night to shine on the way they were to take. 20You gave your good Spirit *i* to instruct *j* them. You did not withhold your manna *k* from their mouths, and you gave them water *l* for their thirst. 21For forty years *m* you sustained them in the desert; they lacked nothing, *n* their clothes did not wear out nor did their feet become swollen. *o*

22"You gave them kingdoms and nations, allotting to them even the remotest frontiers. They took over the country of Sihon *y p* king of Heshbon and the country of Og king of Bashan. *q* 23You made their sons as numerous as the stars in the sky, *r* and you brought them into the land that you told their fathers to enter and pos-

sess. 24Their sons went in and took possession of the land. *s* You subdued *t* before them the Canaanites, who lived in the land; you handed the Canaanites over to them, along with their kings and the peoples of the land, to deal with them as they pleased. 25They captured fortified cities and fertile land; *u* they took possession of houses filled with all kinds of good things, *v* wells already dug, vineyards, olive groves and fruit trees in abundance. They ate to the full and were well-nourished; *w* they reveled in your great goodness. *x*

26"But they were disobedient and rebelled against you; they put your law behind their backs. *y* They killed *z* your prophets, *a* who had admonished them in order to turn them back to you; they committed awful blasphemies. *b* 27So you handed them over to their enemies, *c* who oppressed them. But when they were oppressed they cried out to you. From heaven you heard them, and in your great compassion *d* you gave them deliverers, *e* who rescued them from the hand of their enemies.

28"But as soon as they were at rest, they again did what was evil in your sight. *f* Then you abandoned them to the hand of their enemies so that they ruled over them. And when they cried out to you again, you heard from heaven, and in your compassion *g* you delivered them *h* time after time.

29"You warned *i* them to return to your law, but they became arrogant *j*

9:15 *q*Ex 17:6; Nu 20:7-13 *r*S Ge 14:22 *s*Dt 1:8,21
9:16 *t*S Ex 32:9; Jer 7:26; 17:23; 19:15 *u*Dt 1:26-33; 31:29
9:17 *v*Jdg 8:34; Ps 78:42 *w*Ps 77:11; 78:12; 105:5; 106:7 *x*Jer 7:26; 19:15 *y*Nu 14:1-4 *z*Ps 130:4; Da 9:9 *a*S Dt 4:31 *b*S Ex 34:6; Ps 103:8; Na 1:3 *c*S Ex 22:27; Nu 14:17-19; Ps 86:15 *d*Ps 78:11; Eze 5:6
9:18 *e*S Ex 32:4 /S Ex 20:23
9:19 *g*Ex 13:22 *h*S Ex 13:21
9:20 *i*Nu 9:17; 11:17; Isa 63:11, 14; Hag 2:5; Zec 4:6 /Ps 23:3; 143:10 *k*S Ex 16:15 /Ex 17:6
9:21 *m*S Ex 16:35 *n*S Dt 2:7 *o*S Dt 8:4
9:22 *p*S Nu 21:21 *q*S Nu 21:33; Dt 2:26-3:11
9:23 *r*S Ge 12:2; S Lev 26:9; S Nu 10:36
9:24 *s*S Jos 11:23 *t*S Jdg 4:23; S 2Ch 14:13
9:25 *u*S Dt 11:11 *v*S Ex 18:9 *w*Dt 6:10-12 *x*Dt 8:8-11; 32:12-15; Ps 23:6; 25:7; 69:16
9:26 *y*S 1Ki 14:9; Jer 44:10 *z*S Jos 7:25 *a*Jer 2:30; 26:8; Mt 21:35-36; 23:29-36; Ac 7:52 *b*S Jdg 2:12-13
9:27 *c*S Nu 25:17; S Jdg 2:14 *d*Ps 51:1; 103:8; 106:45; 119:156 *e*S Jdg 3:9

9:28 /S Ex 32:22; S Jdg 2:17 *g*S 2Sa 24:14 *h*Ps 22:4; 106:43; 136:24 9:29 *i*S Jdg 6:8 /ver 16-17; Ps 5:5; Isa 2:11; Jer 43:2

*y*22 One Hebrew manuscript and Septuagint; most Hebrew manuscripts *Sihon, that is, the country of the*

9:16 *stiff-necked.* See vv. 17,29; see also notes on 3:5; Ex 32:9.

9:17 *appointed a leader.* Their intention to do so is recorded in Nu 14:4. *gracious . . . abounding in love.* See note on Ex 34:6-7.

9:18 *blasphemies.* See v. 26; Eze 35:12.

9:19 *compassion.* See vv. 27-28; a tender, maternal kind of love (see note on Zec 1:16).

9:20 *Spirit to instruct.* See Ex 31:3.

9:21 *clothes did not wear out.* Evidence of the special providence of God (see Dt 8:4; 29:5; contrast Jos 9:13). *swollen.* Or "blistered"; the Hebrew for this word occurs only here and in Dt 8:4.

9:22 *Sihon . . . Og.* See Nu 21:21-35.

9:23 *numerous as the stars.* See notes on Ge 13:16; 15:5; 22:17.

9:25 See Dt 6:10-12 and note; Jos 24:13. *fertile.* See v.

35; cf. Nu 14:7; Dt 8:7; Jos 23:13. *wells already dug.* Because of the lack of rainfall during much of the year, almost every house had its own well or cistern in which to store water from the rainy seasons (2Ki 18:31; Pr 5:15). By 1200 B.C. the technique of waterproofing cisterns was developed, permitting greater occupation of the central hills of Judah. *vineyards, olive groves and fruit trees.* Cf. Dt 8:8. The Egyptian story of Sinuhe (c. 2000 B.C.) describes Canaan as follows: "Figs were in it, and grapes. It had more wine than water. Plentiful was its honey, abundant its olives. Every (kind of) fruit was on its trees." *well-nourished.* Elsewhere the Hebrew for this word always implies physical fullness and spiritual insensitivity.

9:26-28 See note on Jdg 2:6-3:6.

9:27 *deliverers.* See Introduction to Judges: Title.

9:29 *will live if he obeys.* See note on Lev 18:5. *Stubbornly they turned their backs.* See Zec 7:11; cf. the similar expressions in v. 16; 3:5; Hos 4:16.

and disobeyed your commands. They sinned against your ordinances, by which a man will live if he obeys them.[k] Stubbornly they turned their backs[l] on you, became stiff-necked[m] and refused to listen.[n] 30For many years you were patient with them. By your Spirit you admonished them through your prophets.[o] Yet they paid no attention, so you handed them over to the neighboring peoples.[p] 31But in your great mercy you did not put an end[q] to them or abandon them, for you are a gracious and merciful[r] God.

32"Now therefore, O our God, the great, mighty[s] and awesome God,[t] who keeps his covenant of love,[u] do not let all this hardship seem trifling in your eyes—the hardship[v] that has come upon us, upon our kings and leaders, upon our priests and prophets, upon our fathers and all your people, from the days of the kings of Assyria until today. 33In all that has happened to us, you have been just;[w] you have acted faithfully, while we did wrong.[x] 34Our kings,[y] our leaders, our priests and our fathers[z] did not follow your law; they did not pay attention to your commands or the warnings you gave them. 35Even while they were in their kingdom, enjoying your great goodness[a] to them in the spacious and fertile land you gave them, they did not serve you[b] or turn from their evil ways.

36"But see, we are slaves[c] today, slaves in the land you gave our forefathers so they could eat its fruit and the other good things it produces. 37Because of our sins, its abundant harvest goes to the kings you have placed over us. They rule over our bodies and our cattle as they please. We are in great distress.[d]

The Agreement of the People

38"In view of all this, we are making a binding agreement,[e] putting it in writ-

ing,[f] and our leaders, our Levites and our priests are affixing their seals to it."

10 Those who sealed it were:

Nehemiah the governor, the son of Hacaliah.

Zedekiah, 2Seraiah,[g] Azariah, Jeremiah,

3Pashhur,[h] Amariah, Malkijah,
4Hattush, Shebaniah, Malluch,
5Harim,[i] Meremoth, Obadiah,
6Daniel, Ginnethon, Baruch,
7Meshullam, Abijah, Mijamin,
8Maaziah, Bilgai and Shemaiah.

These were the priests.[j]

9The Levites:[k]

Jeshua son of Azaniah, Binnui of the sons of Henadad, Kadmiel,
10and their associates: Shebaniah, Hodiah, Kelita, Pelaiah, Hanan,
11Mica, Rehob, Hashabiah,
12Zaccur, Sherebiah, Shebaniah,
13Hodiah, Bani and Beninu.

14The leaders of the people:

Parosh, Pahath-Moab, Elam, Zattu, Bani,
15Bunni, Azgad, Bebai,
16Adonijah, Bigvai, Adin,[l]
17Ater, Hezekiah, Azzur,
18Hodiah, Hashum, Bezai,
19Hariph, Anathoth, Nebai,
20Magpiash, Meshullam, Hezir,[m]
21Meshezabel, Zadok, Jaddua,
22Pelatiah, Hanan, Anaiah,
23Hoshea, Hananiah,[n] Hasshub,
24Hallohesh, Pilha, Shobek,
25Rehum, Hashabnah, Maaseiah,
26Ahiah, Hanan, Anan,
27Malluch, Harim and Baanah.

28"The rest of the people—priests, Levites, gatekeepers, singers, temple servants[o] and all who separated themselves from the neighboring peoples[p] for the sake of the Law of God, together with their wives and all their sons and daughters who are able to understand— 29all these now join their brothers the nobles, and bind

9:29 kS Dt 30:16
lS 1Sa 8:3
mJer 19:15
nZec 7:11-12
9:30 o2Ki 17:13-18; S 2Ch 36:16
pJer 16:11; Zec 7:12
9:31 qIsa 48:9; 65:9 rS Dt 4:31
9:32 sJob 9:19; Ps 24:8; 89:8; 93:4 tS Dt 7:21 uS Dt 7:9; S 1Ki 8:23; Da 9:4 vS Ex 18:8
9:33 wS Ge 18:25 xJer 44:3; Da 9:7-8,14
9:34 yS 2Ki 23:11 zJer 44:17
9:35 aIsa 63:7 bDt 28:45-48
9:36 cS Ezr 9:9
9:37 dDt 28:33; La 5:5
9:38 eS 2Ch 23:16

fIsa 44:5
10:2 gS Ezr 2:2
10:3 hS 1Ch 9:12
10:5 iS 1Ch 24:8
10:8 jNe 12:1
10:9 kNe 12:1
10:16 lS Ezr 8:6
10:20 mICh 24:15
10:23 nS Ne 7:2
10:28 oPs 135:1 p2Ch 6:26; S Ne 9:2

9:32 kings of Assyria. Including Tiglath-Pileser III, also known as Pul (1Ch 5:26); Shalmaneser V (2Ki 18:9); Sargon II (Isa 20:1); Sennacherib (2Ki 18:13); Esarhaddon (Ezr 4:2); and Ashurbanipal (Ezr 4:10).
9:37 rule over our bodies. See 1Sa 8:11-13. The Persian rulers drafted their subjects into military service. Some Jews may have accompanied Xerxes on his invasion of Greece in 480 B.C.
10:1-27 A legal list, bearing the official seal and containing a roster of 84 names.
10:2-8 About half of these names occur again in 12:1-7.
10:9-13 Most of these names appear also in the lists of Levites in 8:7; 9:4-5.
10:14-27 Almost half of the names in this category are also found in the lists of 7:6-63; Ezr 2:1-61.
10:28 Levites. See Introduction to Leviticus: Title. gatekeepers. See note on Ezr 2:42. wives . . . sons and daughters. See note on 8:2.

themselves with a curse and an oath q to follow the Law of God given through Moses the servant of God and to obey carefully all the commands, regulations and decrees of the LORD our Lord.

30"We promise not to give our daughters in marriage to the peoples around us or take their daughters for our sons. r

31"When the neighboring peoples bring merchandise or grain to sell on the Sabbath, s we will not buy from them on the Sabbath or on any holy day. Every seventh year we will forgo working the land t and will cancel all debts. u

32"We assume the responsibility for carrying out the commands to give a third of a shekel z each year for the service of the house of our God: 33for the bread set out on the table; v for the regular grain offerings and burnt offerings; for the offerings on the Sabbaths, New Moon w festivals and appointed feasts; for the holy offerings; for sin offerings to make atonement for Israel; and for all the duties of the house of our God. x

34"We—the priests, the Levites and the people—have cast lots y to determine when each of our families is to bring to the house of our God at set times each year a contribution of wood z to burn on the altar of the LORD our God, as it is written in the Law.

35"We also assume responsibility

for bringing to the house of the LORD each year the firstfruits a of our crops and of every fruit tree. b

36"As it is also written in the Law, we will bring the firstborn c of our sons and of our cattle, of our herds and of our flocks to the house of our God, to the priests ministering there. d

37"Moreover, we will bring to the storerooms of the house of our God, to the priests, the first of our ground meal, of our grain offerings, of the fruit of all our trees and of our new wine and oil. e And we will bring a tithe f of our crops to the Levites, g for it is the Levites who collect the tithes in all the towns where we work. h 38A priest descended from Aaron is to accompany the Levites when they receive the tithes, and the Levites are to bring a tenth of the tithes i up to the house of our God, to the storerooms of the treasury. 39The people of Israel, including the Levites, are to bring their contributions of grain, new wine and oil to the storerooms where the articles for the sanctuary are kept and where the ministering priests, the gatekeepers and the singers stay.

"We will not neglect the house of our God." j

The New Residents of Jerusalem

11:3–19pp — 1Ch 9:1–17

11 Now the leaders of the people settled in Jerusalem, and the rest of

Cross references (center column)

10:29
qS Nu 5:21;
Ps 119:106
10:30
rS Ex 34:16;
Ne 13:23
10:31 sNe 13:16,
18; Jer 17:27;
Eze 23:38;
Am 8:5
tS Ex 23:11;
Lev 25:1-7
uS Dt 15:1
10:33 vLev 24:6
wNu 10:10;
Ps 81:3; Isa 1:14
xS 2Ch 24:5
10:34
yS Lev 16:8
zNe 13:31

10:35
aS Ex 22:29;
S Nu 18:12
bDt 26:1-11
10:36
cS Ex 13:2;
S Nu 18:14-16
dNe 13:31
10:37
eS Nu 18:12
fS Lev 27:30;
S Nu 18:21
gDt 14:22-29
hEze 44:30
10:38 iNu 18:26
10:39 jNe 13:11,
12

z32 That is, about 1/8 ounce (about 4 grams)

Study notes

10:31–33 Perhaps a code drawn up by Nehemiah to correct the abuses listed in 13:15–22.

10:31 sell on the Sabbath. Though Ex 20:8–11; Dt 5:12–15 do not explicitly prohibit trading on the Sabbath, see Jer 17:19–27; Am 8:5 and note. seventh year . . . forgo working the land . . . cancel all debts. See note on Lev 25:4. The Romans misrepresented the Sabbath and the sabbath year as caused by laziness. According to Tacitus, the Jews "were led by the charms of indolence to give over the seventh year as well to inactivity."

10:32 third of a shekel. Ex 30:13–14 speaks of a "half shekel" as "an offering to the LORD" from each man who was 20 years old or more as a symbolic ransom. Later Joash used the annual contributions for the repair of the temple (2Ch 24:4–14). In the NT period Jewish men from everywhere sent an offering of a half shekel (actually two drachmas, its equivalent; see Josephus, Antiquities, 3.8.2) for the temple in Jerusalem (Mt 17:24). The pledge of a third of a shekel in Nehemiah's time may have been due to economic circumstances.

10:33 bread. See note on Lev 24:8.

10:34 cast lots. See notes on 11:1; Jnh 1:7. contribution of wood. Though there is no specific reference to a wood offering in the Pentateuch, the perpetual burning of fire on the sanctuary altar (Lev 6:12–13) would have required a

continual supply of wood. Josephus mentions "the festival of wood offering" on the 14th day of the fifth month (Ab). The Jewish Mishnah (rabbinic interpretations and applications of Pentateuchal laws) lists nine times when certain families brought wood, and stipulates that all kinds of wood were suitable except the vine and the olive. The Temple Scroll from Qumran describes the celebration of a wood offering festival for six days following a new oil festival.

10:35 firstfruits. Brought to the sanctuary to support the priests and Levites (Ex 23:19; Nu 18:13; Dt 26:1–11; Eze 44:30).

10:36 firstborn. See note on Ex 13:13.

10:37 storerooms. Chambers in the courts of the temple were used as storage rooms for silver, gold and sacred articles (cf. vv. 38–39; 12:44; 13:4–5,9; Ezr 8:28–30). new wine. See note on Dt 7:13. Though the Hebrew for this term can refer to freshly pressed grape juice (Isa 65:8; Mic 6:15), it can also be used of intoxicating wine (Hos 4:11). tithe. See notes on Ge 14:20; 28:22; Lev 27:30; Am 4:4. Levites. Tithes were meant for their support (13:12–13; Nu 18:21–32).

10:39 See 13:11. We will not neglect. Haggai (Hag 1:4–9) had accused the people of neglecting the temple.

11:1 cast lots. See 10:34. Lots were usually made out of small stones or pieces of wood. Sometimes arrows were used

the people cast lots to bring one out of
every ten to live in Jerusalem,[k] the holy
city,[l] while the remaining nine were to
stay in their own towns.[m] 2The people
commended all the men who volunteered
to live in Jerusalem.

3These are the provincial leaders who
settled in Jerusalem (now some Israelites,
priests, Levites, temple servants and descendants of Solomon's servants lived in
the towns of Judah, each on his own property in the various towns,[n] 4while other
people from both Judah and Benjamin[o]
lived in Jerusalem):[p]

From the descendants of Judah:

Athaiah son of Uzziah, the son of
Zechariah, the son of Amariah, the son
of Shephatiah, the son of Mahalalel, a
descendant of Perez; 5and Maaseiah
son of Baruch, the son of Col-Hozeh,
the son of Hazaiah, the son of Adaiah,
the son of Joiarib, the son of Zechariah, a descendant of Shelah. 6The descendants of Perez who lived in
Jerusalem totaled 468 able men.

7From the descendants of Benjamin:

Sallu son of Meshullam, the son of
Joed, the son of Pedaiah, the son of
Kolaiah, the son of Maaseiah, the son
of Ithiel, the son of Jeshaiah, 8and his
followers, Gabbai and Sallai—928
men. 9Joel son of Zicri was their chief
officer, and Judah son of Hassenuah
was over the Second District of the
city.

10From the priests:

Jedaiah; the son of Joiarib; Jakin; 11Se-
raiah[q] son of Hilkiah, the son of Meshullam, the son of Zadok, the son of
Meraioth, the son of Ahitub,[r] super-
visor in the house of God, 12and their
associates, who carried on work for
the temple—822 men; Adaiah son of
Jeroham, the son of Pelaliah, the son
of Amzi, the son of Zechariah, the son
of Pashhur, the son of Malkijah, 13and
his associates, who were heads of
families—242 men; Amashsai son of
Azarel, the son of Ahzai, the son of
Meshillemoth, the son of Immer,
14and his[a] associates, who were able
men—128. Their chief officer was
Zabdiel son of Haggedolim.

15From the Levites:

Shemaiah son of Hasshub, the son of
Azrikam, the son of Hashabiah, the
son of Bunni; 16Shabbethai[s] and Jozabad,[t] two of the heads of the Levites,
who had charge of the outside work of
the house of God; 17Mattaniah[u] son
of Mica, the son of Zabdi, the son of
Asaph,[v] the director who led in
thanksgiving and prayer; Bakbukiah,
second among his associates; and
Abda son of Shammua, the son of Galal, the son of Jeduthun.[w] 18The Levites in the holy city[x] totaled 284.

19The gatekeepers:

Akkub, Talmon and their associates,
who kept watch at the gates—172
men.

20The rest of the Israelites, with the
priests and Levites, were in all the towns of
Judah, each on his ancestral property.

21The temple servants[y] lived on the hill

11:1 [k]Ne 7:4 [l]Isa 48:2; 52:1; 64:10; Zec 14:20-21 [m]S Ne 7:73 **11:3** [n]S Ezr 2:1 **11:4** [o]S Ezr 1:5 [p]S Ezr 2:70 **11:11** [q]S 2Ki 25:18; S Ezr 2:2 [r]S Ezr 7:2 **11:16** [s]Ezr 10:15 [t]S Ezr 8:33 **11:17** [u]S 1Ch 9:15; Ne 12:8 [v]2Ch 5:12 [w]S 1Ch 25:1 **11:18** [x]S Rev 21:2 **11:21** [y]S Ezr 2:43; S Ne 3:26

[a]*14* Most Septuagint manuscripts; Hebrew *their*

(Eze 21:21). *one out of every ten to live in Jerusalem.* Josephus (*Antiquities,* 11.5.8) asserts: "But Nehemiah, seeing that the city had a small population, urged the priests and Levites to leave the countryside and move to the city and remain there, for he had prepared houses for them at his own expense." The practice of redistributing populations was also used to establish Greek and Hellenistic cities. It involved the forcible transfer from rural settlements to urban centers. Tiberias on the Sea of Galilee was populated with Gentiles by such a process by Herod Antipas in A.D. 18. *holy city.* See Isa 48:2 and note; Da 9:24; Mt 4:5; 27:53; Rev 11:2; cf. Joel 3:17.

11:2 In addition to those chosen by lot (v. 1), some volunteered out of a sense of duty. But evidently most preferred to stay in their hometowns.

11:3–19 A census roster that parallels 1Ch 9:2–21, a list of the first residents in Jerusalem after the return from Babylonia. About half the names in the two lists are the same.

11:8 *928.* The men of Benjamin provided twice as many men as Judah (v. 6) to live in and protect the city of Jerusalem.

11:9 *Second District.* See 2Ch 34:22 (in Zep 1:10 the Hebrew for this phrase is translated "New Quarter"). Like the "market district" (Zep 1:11), which was probably the Tyropoeon Valley area, the Second District was a new suburb west of the temple area. Excavations indicate that the city had spread outside the walls in this direction by the late eighth century B.C. before the so-called Broad Wall was built c. 700 by Hezekiah (see note on 3:8).

11:16 *outside work.* Duties outside the temple (cf. 1Ch 26:29) but connected with it.

11:17 *Asaph.* See note on Ezr 2:41; see also titles of Ps 50; 73–83. *Jeduthun.* See 1Ch 16:42; 25:1,3; 2Ch 5:12; titles of Ps 39; 62; 77.

11:18 *284.* The relatively small number of Levites, compared with 1,192 priests (the total of 822, 242 and 128 in vv. 12–13), is striking (see note on Ezr 2:40).

11:20 *ancestral property.* Inalienable hereditary possessions—including land, buildings and movable goods—acquired by either conquest or inheritance (Ge 31:14; Nu 18:21; 27:7; 34:2; 36:3; 1Ki 21:1–4).

11:21 *Ophel.* See note on 3:26.

of Ophel, and Ziha and Gishpa were in charge of them.

22The chief officer of the Levites in Jerusalem was Uzzi son of Bani, the son of Hashabiah, the son of Mattaniah,^{z} the son of Mica. Uzzi was one of Asaph's descendants, who were the singers responsible for the service of the house of God. 23The singers^a were under the king's orders, which regulated their daily activity.

24Pethahiah son of Meshezabel, one of the descendants of Zerah^b son of Judah, was the king's agent in all affairs relating to the people.

25As for the villages with their fields, some of the people of Judah lived in Kiriath Arba^c and its surrounding settlements, in Dibon^d and its settlements, in Jekabzeel and its villages, 26in Jeshua, in Moladah,^{e} in Beth Pelet,^{f} 27in Hazar Shual,^{g} in Beersheba^h and its settlements, 28in Ziklag,^{i} in Meconah and its settlements, 29in En Rimmon, in Zorah,^{j} in Jarmuth,^{k} 30Zanoah,^{l} Adullam^m and their villages, in Lachish^n and its fields, and in Azekah^o and its settlements. So they were living all the way from Beersheba^p to the Valley of Hinnom.

31The descendants of the Benjamites from Geba^q lived in Micmash,^{r} Aija, Bethel^s and its settlements, 32in Anathoth,^{t} Nob^u and Ananiah, 33in Hazor,^{v} Ramah^w and Gittaim,^{x} 34in Hadid, Zeboim^y and Neballat, 35in Lod and Ono,^{z} and in the Valley of the Craftsmen.

36Some of the divisions of the Levites of Judah settled in Benjamin.

Priests and Levites

12 These were the priests^a and Levites^b who returned with Zerubbabel^c son of Shealtiel^d and with Jeshua:^{e} Seraiah,^{f} Jeremiah, Ezra, 2Amariah, Malluch, Hattush, 3Shecaniah, Rehum, Meremoth, 4Iddo,^{g} Ginnethon,^{b} Abijah,^{h} 5Mijamin,^{c} Moadiah, Bilgah, 6Shemaiah, Joiarib, Jedaiah,^{i} 7Sallu, Amok, Hilkiah and Jedaiah. These were the leaders of the priests and their associates in the days of Jeshua.

11:22 ^{z}S 1Ch 9:15
11:23 ^{a}S 1Ch 15:16; Ne 7:44
11:24 ^{b}S Ge 38:30
11:25 ^{c}S Ge 35:27 ^{d}S Nu 21:30
11:26 ^{e}Jos 15:26 ^{f}Jos 15:27
11:27 ^{g}Jos 15:28 ^{h}S Ge 21:14
11:28 ^{i}S 1Sa 27:6
11:29 ^{j}Jos 15:33 ^{k}S Jos 10:3; S 15:35
11:30 ^{l}Jos 15:34 ^{m}Jos 15:35 ^{n}S Jos 10:3; 15:39 ^{o}S Jos 10:10 ^{p}Jos 15:28
11:31 ^{q}Jos 21:17; Isa 10:29 ^{r}S 1Sa 13:2 ^{s}S Jos 12:9
11:32 ^{t}Jos 21:18; Isa 10:30; Jer 1:1 ^{u}S 1Sa 21:1
11:33 ^{v}S Jos 11:1 ^{w}S Jos 18:25 ^{x}2Sa 4:3
11:34 ^{y}1Sa 13:18
11:35 ^{z}S 1Ch 8:12
12:1 ^{a}Ne 10:1-8 ^{b}Ne 10:9 ^{c}S 1Ch 3:19; Ezr 3:2; Zec 4:6-10 ^{d}Ezr 3:2

^{e}S Ezr 2:2 ^{f}S Ezr 2:2 12:4 ^{g}ver 16; Zec 1:1 ^{h}S 1Ch 24:10; Lk 1:5 12:6 ^{i}S 1Ch 24:7

^{b}4 Many Hebrew manuscripts and Vulgate (see also Neh. 12:16); most Hebrew manuscripts *Ginnethoi* ^{c}5 A variant of *Miniamin*

11:23 *king's orders... regulated.* David had regulated the services of the Levites, including the singers (1Ch 25). The Persian king, Darius I, gave a royal stipend so that the Jewish elders might "pray for the well-being of the king and his sons" (Ezr 6:10). Artaxerxes I may have done much the same for the Levite choir.

11:25–30 An important list, corresponding to earlier lists of towns in Judah. All these names also appear in Jos 15 with the exception of Dibon, Jekabzeel (but see Kabzeel in Jos 15:21), Jeshua, Meconah and En Rimmon (but see Ain and Rimmon in Jos 15:32). The list, however, is not comprehensive, since a number of towns listed in ch. 3; Ezr 2:21–22 are lacking. No Judean coins have been found outside the area designated by vv. 25–30.

11:25 *Kiriath Arba.* See note on Ge 23:2. In the Hellenistic era it fell to the Idumeans, together with other Judean towns.

11:26 *Moladah.* Near Beersheba; later occupied by the Idumeans. *Beth Pelet.* Means "house of refuge," a site near Beersheba.

11:27 *Hazar Shual.* Means "enclosure of a fox" (see 1Ch 4:28). *Beersheba.* See note and NIV text note on Ge 21:31. Archaeological excavations reveal that the city was destroyed by Sennacherib in 701 B.C. and only resettled in the Persian period.

11:28 *Ziklag.* Given to David by Achish, king of Gath (1Sa 27:6), and taken by the Amalekites (1Sa 30:1); see Jos 15:31.

11:29 *En Rimmon.* Means "spring of the pomegranate," probably Khirbet Umm er-Ramamin, nine miles north-northeast of Beersheba (see Jos 15:32). *Zorah.* See note on Jdg 13:2. *Jarmuth.* Eight miles north-northeast of Eleutheropolis (Beit Jibrin), it was one of five Canaanite cities in the south that attempted to halt Joshua's invasion (Jos 10:3–5).

11:30 *Zanoah.* A village in the Shephelah district of low hills between Judah and Philistia. The men of Zanoah re-

paired the Valley Gate (3:13). The site has been identified with Khirbet Zanu, three miles south-southeast of Beth Shemesh. *Adullam.* See note on Ge 38:1. *Lachish.* See Jos 10:3; see also notes on Isa 36:2; Mic 1:13. *Azekah.* See note on Jer 34:7. *Hinnom.* The valley west and south of Jerusalem; Gehenna in the NT.

11:31–35 Most of the Benjamite towns listed here appear also in 7:26–38; Ezr 2:23–35.

11:31 *Geba.* See 12:29; see also note on 1Sa 13:3. *Micmash.* See note on 1Sa 13:2. *Aija.* An alternate name for Ai (see note on Jos 7:2). *Bethel.* See notes on Ge 12:8; Jos 7:2; Ezr 2:28; Am 4:4.

11:32 *Anathoth.* See note on Jer 1:1. *Nob.* See note on 1Sa 21:1. *Ananiah.* Probably Bethany, meaning "house of Ananiah" (see note on Mt 21:17).

11:33 *Gittaim.* Its location is not known.

11:34 *Hadid.* Three to four miles northeast of Lod (see 7:37; Ezr 2:33).

11:35 *Lod.* See note on Ezr 2:33. *Ono.* See note on 6:2. *Valley of the Craftsmen.* See 1Ch 4:14 and NIV text note. It may be the broad valley between Lod and Ono. The name may preserve the memory of the Philistine iron monopoly (1Sa 13:19–20).

12:1 *Zerubbabel son of Shealtiel.* See Ezr 3:2,8; 5:2; see also note on Hag 1:1. *Jeshua.* Returned from Babylonian exile in 538 B.C. (see vv. 10,26; 7:7; Ezr 2:2 and note; Hag 1:1; Zec 3:1 and note). *Ezra.* Not the Ezra of the book, who was the leader of the exiles who returned 80 years later.

12:7 *leaders of the priests.* The rotation of 24 priestly houses was established at the time of David (1Ch 24:3, 7–19). Twenty-two heads of priestly houses are mentioned in vv. 1–7. Inscriptions listing the 24 divisions of the priests probably hung in many synagogues in Palestine. So far, only fragments of two such inscriptions have been recovered—from Ashkelon in the 1920s and from Caesarea in the 1960s (dated to the third and fourth centuries A.D.).

[8]The Levites were Jeshua,[j] Binnui, Kadmiel, Sherebiah, Judah, and also Mattaniah,[k] who, together with his associates, was in charge of the songs of thanksgiving. [9]Bakbukiah and Unni, their associates, stood opposite them in the services.

[10]Jeshua was the father of Joiakim, Joiakim the father of Eliashib,[l] Eliashib the father of Joiada, [11]Joiada the father of Jonathan, and Jonathan the father of Jaddua.

[12]In the days of Joiakim, these were the heads of the priestly families:

of Seraiah's family, Meraiah;
of Jeremiah's, Hananiah;
[13]of Ezra's, Meshullam;
of Amariah's, Jehohanan;
[14]of Malluch's, Jonathan;
of Shecaniah's,[d] Joseph;
[15]of Harim's, Adna;
of Meremoth's,[e] Helkai;
[16]of Iddo's,[m] Zechariah;
of Ginnethon's, Meshullam;
[17]of Abijah's,[n] Zicri;
of Miniamin's and of Moadiah's, Piltai;
[18]of Bilgah's, Shammua;
of Shemaiah's, Jehonathan;
[19]of Joiarib's, Mattenai;
of Jedaiah's, Uzzi;
[20]of Sallu's, Kallai;
of Amok's, Eber;
[21]of Hilkiah's, Hashabiah;
of Jedaiah's, Nethanel.

[22]The family heads of the Levites in the days of Eliashib, Joiada, Johanan and Jaddua, as well as those of the priests, were recorded in the reign of Darius the Persian. [23]The family heads among the descendants of Levi up to the time of Johanan son of Eliashib were recorded in the book of the annals. [24]And the leaders of the Levites[o] were Hashabiah, Sherebiah, Jeshua son of Kadmiel, and their associates, who stood opposite them to give praise and thanksgiving, one section responding to the other, as prescribed by David the man of God.[p]

[25]Mattaniah, Bakbukiah, Obadiah, Meshullam, Talmon and Akkub were gatekeepers who guarded the storerooms at the gates. [26]They served in the days of Joiakim son of Jeshua, the son of Jozadak, and in the days of Nehemiah the governor and of Ezra the priest and scribe.

Dedication of the Wall of Jerusalem

[27]At the dedication[q] of the wall of Jerusalem, the Levites were sought out from where they lived and were brought to Jerusalem to celebrate joyfully the dedication with songs of thanksgiving and with the music of cymbals,[r] harps and lyres.[s] [28]The singers also were brought together from the region around Jerusalem—from

---

Cross references (center column):

12:8 /S Ezr 2:2
kS Ne 11:17
12:10
/S Ezr 10:24;
Ne 3:20
12:16 mS ver 4
12:17
nS 1Ch 24:10

12:24
oS Ezr 2:40
pS 2Ch 8:14
12:27 qDt 20:5
rS 2Sa 6:5
sS 1Ch 15:16,28;
25:6; Ps 92:3

Textual notes:

d[14] Very many Hebrew manuscripts, some Septuagint manuscripts and Syriac (see also Neh. 12:3); most Hebrew manuscripts *Shebaniah's*   e[15] Some Septuagint manuscripts (see also Neh. 12:3); Hebrew *Meraioth's*

12:9 *opposite them.* See v. 24; Ezr 3:11 and note; cf. 2Ch 7:6. The singing was antiphonal, with two sections of the choir standing opposite each other. *services.* The Hebrew for this word (*Mishmarot*) is the title of a work from Qumran, which discusses in detail the rotation of the priestly families' service in the temple according to the sect's solar calendar and synchronized with the conventional lunar calendar.

12:10 *Jeshua.* See note on v. 1. *Joiakim.* See vv. 12,26. *Eliashib.* See vv. 22–23; the high priest who assisted in rebuilding the wall (3:1,20–21; 13:28). A priest named Eliashib was guilty of defiling the temple by assigning rooms to Tobiah the Ammonite (13:4,7). It is not known whether this Eliashib was the same as the high priest.

12:11 *Jonathan.* Since v. 22 mentions a Johanan after Joiada and before Jaddua, and v. 23 identifies Johanan as "son" of Eliashib, some believe that "Jonathan" is an error for "Johanan." Further complicating the identification are attempts to identify this high priest with a "Johanan" mentioned in the Elephantine papyri and in Josephus (*Antiquities*, 11.7.1). Such an identification, however, is disputable.

12:12–21 All but one (Hattush, v. 2) of the 22 priestly families listed in vv. 1–7 are repeated (Rehum, v. 3, is a variant of Harim, v. 15; Mijamin, v. 5, is a variant of Miniamin, v. 17) in this later list, which dates to the time of Joiakim (v. 12), high priest in the late sixth and/or early fifth

centuries B.C.

12:22 *Darius the Persian.* Either Darius II Nothus (423–404 B.C.) or Darius III Codomannus (336–331).

12:23 *book of the annals.* Cf. 7:5. This may have been the official temple chronicle, containing various lists and records. Cf. the annals of the Persian kings (Ezr 4:15; Est 2:23; 6:1; 10:2); cf. also the "book of the annals of the kings," mentioned frequently in 1,2 Kings.

12:26 *Nehemiah . . . Ezra.* See note on 8:9.

12:27 *dedication.* See note on Ezr 6:16. *cymbals.* See note on Ezr 3:10. Cymbals were used in religious ceremonies (1Ch 16:42; 25:1; 2Ch 5:12; 29:25). Ancient examples have been found at Beth Shemesh and Tell Abu Hawam. *harps.* See note on Ge 31:27; used mainly in religious ceremonies (1Sa 10:5; 2Sa 6:5; Ps 150:3). Ancient harps have been reconstructed from information derived from the remains of harps at Ur, pictures of harps, and cuneiform texts describing in detail the tuning of harps. *lyres.* Had strings of the same length but of different diameters and tensions (see 1Ch 15:16; Da 3:5).

12:28 *Netophathites.* From Netophah, a town near Bethlehem (7:26).

12:29 *Beth Gilgal.* Perhaps the Gilgal near Jericho (see note on Jos 4:19), or the Gilgal of Elijah (2Ki 2:1), about seven miles north of Bethel.

the villages of the Netophathites, t 29from Beth Gilgal, and from the area of Geba and Azmaveth, for the singers had built villages for themselves around Jerusalem. 30When the priests and Levites had purified themselves ceremonially, they purified the people, u the gates and the wall.

31I had the leaders of Judah go up on topf of the wall. I also assigned two large choirs to give thanks. One was to proceed on topg of the wall to the right, toward the Dung Gate. v 32Hoshaiah and half the leaders of Judah followed them, 33along with Azariah, Ezra, Meshullam, 34Judah, Benjamin, w Shemaiah, Jeremiah, 35as well as some priests with trumpets,x and also Zechariah son of Jonathan, the son of Shemaiah, the son of Mattaniah, the son of Micaiah, the son of Zaccur, the son of Asaph, 36and his associates—Shemaiah, Azarel, Milalai, Gilalai, Maai, Nethanel, Judah and Hanani—with musical instrumentsy prescribed by David the man of God. z Ezraa the scribe led the procession. 37At the Fountain Gateb they continued directly up the steps of the City of David on the ascent to the wall and passed above the house of David to the Water Gatec on the east.

38The second choir proceeded in the opposite direction. I followed them on toph of the wall, together with half the people—past the Tower of the Ovensd to the Broad Wall,e 39over the Gate of Ephraim,f the Jeshanahi Gate,g the Fish Gate,h the Tower of Hananeli and the Tower of the Hundred,j as far as the Sheep Gate.k At the Gate of the Guard they stopped.

40The two choirs that gave thanks then took their places in the house of God; so

did I, together with half the officials, 41as well as the priests—Eliakim, Maaseiah, Miniamin, Micaiah, Elioenai, Zechariah and Hananiah with their trumpets— 42and also Maaseiah, Shemaiah, Eleazar, Uzzi, Jehohanan, Malkijah, Elam and Ezer. The choirs sang under the direction of Jezrahiah. 43And on that day they offered great sacrifices, rejoicing because God had given them great joy. The women and children also rejoiced. The sound of rejoicing in Jerusalem could be heard far away.

44At that time men were appointed to be in charge of the storeroomsl for the contributions, firstfruits and tithes. m From the fields around the towns they were to bring into the storerooms the portions required by the Law for the priests and the Levites, for Judah was pleased with the ministering priests and Levites. n 45They performed the service of their God and the service of purification, as did also the singers and gatekeepers, according to the commands of Davido and his son Solomon. p 46For long ago, in the days of David and Asaph,q there had been directors for the singers and for the songs of praiser and thanksgiving to God. 47So in the days of Zerubbabel and of Nehemiah, all Israel contributed the daily portions for the singers and gatekeepers. They also set aside the portion for the other Levites, and the Levites set aside the portion for the descendants of Aaron.s

Nehemiah's Final Reforms

13 On that day the Book of Moses was read aloud in the hearing of the people and there it was found written that

Cross-references (center column)

12:28
tS 1Ch 2:54; 9:16
12:30 uEx 19:10;
Job 1:5
12:31 vNe 2:13
12:34 wS Ezr 1:5
12:35 xS Ezr 3:10
12:36
yS 1Ch 15:16
zS 2Ch 8:14
aEzr 7:6
12:37 bS Ne 2:14
cS Ne 3:26
12:38 dNe 3:11
eNe 3:8
12:39
fS 2Ki 14:13
gNe 3:6
hS 2Ch 33:14
iS Ne 3:1 /Ne 3:1
kS Ne 3:1

12:44 lNe 13:4,
13 mS Lev 27:30
nS Dt 18:8
12:45
oS 2Ch 8:14
pS 1Ch 6:31;
23:5
12:46
qS 2Ch 35:15,
r2Ch 29:27;
Ps 137:4
12:47 sS Dt 18:8

t31 Or go alongside   g31 Or proceed alongside
h38 Or them alongside   i39 Or Old

12:30 purified. See note on Lev 4:12. The Levites are said to have purified all that was sacred in the temple (1Ch 23:28) and the temple itself (2Ch 29:15) during times of revival. Ritual purity was intended to teach God's holiness and moral purity (Lev 16:30).
12:31 two large choirs. See note on v. 38. The two great processions probably started from the area of the Valley Gate (2:13,15; 3:13) near the center of the western section of the wall. The first procession, led by Ezra (v. 36), moved in a counterclockwise direction upon the wall; the second, with Nehemiah (v. 38), moved in a clockwise direction. Both met between the Water Gate (v. 37) and the Gate of the Guard (v. 39), then entered the temple area. Cf. Ps 48:12–13. to the right. Or "to the south." The Semite oriented himself facing east, so the right hand represented the south (see Jos 17:7; 1Sa 23:24; Job 23:9). Dung Gate. See note on 2:13.
12:35 trumpets. See note on Ezr 3:10. Each choir had priests blowing trumpets, as well as Levites playing other musical instruments. Asaph. See note on 11:17.
12:36 Ezra the scribe. See notes on Ezr 7:1,6.

12:37 Fountain Gate. See note on 2:14. City of David. See 3:15; see also note on 2Sa 5:7. Water Gate. See note on 3:26.
12:38 choir. Lit. "thanks," i.e., "thanksgiving choir" (see v. 40). Tower of the Ovens. See note on 3:11. Broad Wall. See note on 3:8.
12:39 Gate of Ephraim. See notes on 3:6; 8:16. Jeshanah Gate. See note on 3:6. Fish Gate. See note on 3:3. Tower of Hananel . . . Tower of the Hundred . . . Sheep Gate. See note on 3:1. Gate of the Guard. Cf. Jer 32:2.
12:43 God had given them great joy. See 1Ch 29:9; Jnh 4:6. women. See 8:2; Ex 15:20 and notes. heard far away. See on Ezr 3:13; cf. 1Ki 1:40; 2Ki 11:13.
12:44 Judah was pleased. The people cheerfully contributed their offerings to support the priests and Levites (cf. 2Co 9:7). ministering. See Dt 10:8.
12:46 Asaph. See note on 11:17.
12:47 contributed. The Hebrew for this verb implies continued giving.
13:1–2 See Dt 23:3–6.

no Ammonite or Moabite should ever be admitted into the assembly of God, [t] ²because they had not met the Israelites with food and water but had hired Balaam [u] to call a curse down on them. [v] (Our God, however, turned the curse into a blessing.) [w] ³When the people heard this law, they excluded from Israel all who were of foreign descent. [x]

⁴Before this, Eliashib the priest had been put in charge of the storerooms [y] of the house of our God. He was closely associated with Tobiah, [z] ⁵and he had provided him with a large room formerly used to store the grain offerings and incense and temple articles, and also the tithes [a] of grain, new wine and oil prescribed for the Levites, singers and gatekeepers, as well as the contributions for the priests.

⁶But while all this was going on, I was not in Jerusalem, for in the thirty-second year of Artaxerxes [b] king of Babylon I had returned to the king. Some time later I asked his permission ⁷and came back to Jerusalem. Here I learned about the evil thing Eliashib [c] had done in providing Tobiah [d] a room in the courts of the house of God. ⁸I was greatly displeased and threw all Tobiah's household goods out of the room. [e] ⁹I gave orders to purify the rooms, [f] and then I put back into them the

equipment of the house of God, with the grain offerings and the incense. [g]

¹⁰I also learned that the portions assigned to the Levites had not been given to them, [h] and that all the Levites and singers responsible for the service had gone back to their own fields. [i] ¹¹So I rebuked the officials and asked them, "Why is the house of God neglected?" [j] Then I called them together and stationed them at their posts.

¹²All Judah brought the tithes [k] of grain, new wine and oil into the storerooms. [l] ¹³I put Shelemiah the priest, Zadok the scribe, and a Levite named Pedaiah in charge of the storerooms and made Hanan son of Zaccur, the son of Mattaniah, their assistant, because these men were considered trustworthy. They were made responsible for distributing the supplies to their brothers. [m]

¹⁴Remember [n] me for this, O my God, and do not blot out what I have so faithfully done for the house of my God and its services.

¹⁵In those days I saw men in Judah treading winepresses on the Sabbath and bringing in grain and loading it on donkeys, together with wine, grapes, figs and all other kinds of loads. And they were

13:1	[t] ver 23; Dt 23:3
13:2	[u] Nu 22:3-11 [v] S Nu 23:7; S Dt 23:3 [w] S Nu 23:11; Dt 23:4-5
13:3	[x] ver 23; S Ne 9:2
13:4	[y] S Ne 12:44 [z] Ne 2:10
13:5	[a] S Lev 27:30; S Nu 18:21
13:6	[b] S Ne 2:6
13:7	[c] S Ezr 10:24 [d] S Ne 2:10
13:8	[e] Mt 21:12-13; Mk 11:15-17; Lk 19:45-46; Jn 2:13-16
13:9	[f] S 1Ch 23:28; S 2Ch 29:5
13:10	[g] S Lev 2:1 [h] S Dt 12:19 [i] S 2Ch 31:4
13:11	[j] S Ne 10:37-39; Hag 1:1-9; Mal 3:8-9
13:12	[k] S 2Ch 31:6 [l] S Dt 18:8; 1Ki 7:51; S 2Ch 31:5; S Ne 10:37-39; Mal 3:10
13:13	[m] S Ne 12:44; Ac 6:1-5
13:14	[n] S Ge 8:1; S 2Ki 20:3

13:2 *Balaam.* See note on Nu 22:5. An Aramaic inscription of the sixth century B.C. found at Deir 'Alla in Transjordan refers to Balaam.

13:4 *Eliashib.* See note on 12:10. *Tobiah.* See note on 2:10.

13:5 *provided him with a large room.* During Nehemiah's absence from the city to return to the Persian king's court, Tobiah, one of his archenemies, had used his influence with Eliashib to gain entrance into a chamber ordinarily set aside for the storage of tithes and other offerings (see 10:37 and note; cf. Nu 18:21–32; Dt 14:28–29; 26:12–15). Elsewhere we read of the chamber of Meshullam (3:30) and of Jehohanan (Ezr 10:6).

13:6 *thirty-second year of Artaxerxes.* See note on 5:14. *king of Babylon.* The title was assumed by Cyrus after his conquest of Babylon (see Ezr 5:13) and was adopted by subsequent Achaemenid (Persian) kings.

13:7 *came back to Jerusalem.* Nehemiah's second term must have ended before 407 B.C., when Bagohi (Bigvai) was governor of Judah according to the Elephantine papyri. Some have suggested that after Nehemiah's first term he was succeeded by his brother Hanani (see note on 1:2). *courts.* See note on 8:16. Zerubbabel's temple had two courtyards (Zec 3:7; cf. Isa 62:9).

13:8 *displeased . . . threw.* Nehemiah expressed his indignation by taking action (cf. vv. 24–25; 5:6–7). Contrast the reaction of Ezra, who "sat down appalled" (Ezr 9:3). Nehemiah's action reminds us of Christ's expulsion of the money changers from the temple area (Mt 21:12–13).

13:9 *rooms.* Though only a single chamber was mentioned in vv. 5–8, additional rooms were involved. A parallel to the occupation and desecration of the temple by Tobiah comes

from a century earlier in Egypt, where Greek mercenaries had occupied the temple of Neith at Sais. Upon the appeal of the Egyptian priest, Udjahorresnet, the Persian king had the squatters driven out and the temple's ceremonies, processions and revenues restored: "And His Majesty commanded that all the foreigners who had settled in the temple of Neith should be driven out and that all their houses and all their superfluities that were in this temple should be thrown down, and that all their own baggage should be carried for them outside the wall of this temple."

13:10 Nehemiah was apparently correcting an abuse of long standing. Strictly speaking, the Levites had no holdings (Nu 18:20,23–24; Dt 14:29; 18:1), but some may have had private income (Dt 18:8). Therefore the Levites were dependent on the faithful support of the people. This may explain the reluctance of great numbers of Levites to return from exile (see Ezr 8:15–20). For the complaints of those who found little material advantage in serving the Lord see Mal 2:17; 3:13–15.

13:11 *neglected.* See note on 10:39.

13:12 *tithes.* See 12:44. Temples in Mesopotamia also levied tithes for the support of their personnel.

13:13 Of the four treasurers, one was a priest, one a Levite, one a scribe and one a layman of rank. *trustworthy.* Nehemiah appointed honest men to make sure that supplies were distributed equitably, just as the church appointed deacons for this purpose (Ac 6:1–5).

13:15 *treading winepresses.* See notes on Isa 5:2; 16:10. *Sabbath.* The temptation to violate the Sabbath rest was especially characteristic of non-Jewish merchants (see 10:31; Isa 56:1–8). On the other hand, the high regard that many had for the Sabbath was expressed by parents who called their children Shabbethai (see 8:7; 11:16; Ezr 10:15).

bringing all this into Jerusalem on the Sabbath. [o] Therefore I warned them against selling food on that day. [16]Men from Tyre who lived in Jerusalem were bringing in fish and all kinds of merchandise and selling them in Jerusalem on the Sabbath[p] to the people of Judah. [17]I rebuked the nobles of Judah and said to them, "What is this wicked thing you are doing—desecrating the Sabbath day? [18]Didn't your forefathers do the same things, so that our God brought all this calamity upon us and upon this city?[q] Now you are stirring up more wrath against Israel by desecrating the Sabbath."[r]

[19]When evening shadows fell on the gates of Jerusalem before the Sabbath,[s] I ordered the doors to be shut and not opened until the Sabbath was over. I stationed some of my own men at the gates so that no load could be brought in on the Sabbath day. [20]Once or twice the merchants and sellers of all kinds of goods spent the night outside Jerusalem. [21]But I warned them and said, "Why do you spend the night by the wall? If you do this again, I will lay hands on you." From that time on they no longer came on the Sabbath. [22]Then I commanded the Levites to purify themselves and go and guard the gates in order to keep the Sabbath day holy.

Remember[t] me for this also, O my God,

and show mercy to me according to your great love.

[23]Moreover, in those days I saw men of Judah who had married[u] women from Ashdod, Ammon and Moab.[v] [24]Half of their children spoke the language of Ashdod or the language of one of the other peoples, and did not know how to speak the language[w] of Judah. [25]I rebuked them and called curses down on them. I beat some of the men and pulled out their hair. I made them take an oath[x] in God's name and said: "You are not to give your daughters in marriage to their sons, nor are you to take their daughters in marriage for your sons or for yourselves.[y] [26]Was it not because of marriages like these that Solomon king of Israel sinned? Among the many nations there was no king like him.[z] He was loved by his God,[a] and God made him king over all Israel, but even he was led into sin by foreign women.[b] [27]Must we hear now that you too are doing all this terrible wickedness and are being unfaithful to our God by marrying[c] foreign women?"

[28]One of the sons of Joiada son of Eliashib[d] the high priest was son-in-law to Sanballat[e] the Horonite. And I drove him away from me.

[29]Remember[f] them, O my God, because they defiled the priestly office and the covenant of the priesthood and of the Levites.[g]

13:15
[o]Ex 20:8-11;
S 34:21;
Dt 5:12-15
13:16
[p]S Ne 10:31
13:18 [q]Jer 44:23
[r]S Ne 10:31
13:19 [s]Lev 23:32
13:22 [t]S Ge 8:1;
S Ne 1:8
13:23
[u]Ezr 9:1-2;
Mal 2:11 [v]S ver 1,
S 3; Ex 34:16;
S Ru 1:4;
S Ne 10:30

13:24 [w]Est 1:22;
3:12; 8:9
13:25 [x]S Ezr 10:5
[y]S Ex 34:16
13:26
[z]S 1Ki 3:13;
S 2Ch 1:12
[a]2Sa 12:25
[b]S Ex 34:16;
S 1Ki 11:3
13:27 [c]Ezr 9:14
13:28
[d]S Ezr 10:24
[e]S Ne 2:10
13:29 [f]S Ne 1:8
[g]S Nu 3:12

13:16 *Tyre.* See note on Isa 23:1. *fish.* Most of the fish exported by the Tyrians (Eze 26:4–5,14) was dried, smoked or salted. Fish, much of it from the Sea of Galilee, was an important part of the Israelites' diet (Lev 11:9; Nu 11:5; Mt 15:34; Lk 24:42; Jn 21:5–13). It was sold at the market near the Fish Gate (see note on 3:3).
13:17 *rebuked the nobles.* Because they were the leaders. *desecrating.* Turning what is sacred into common use and so profaning it (see Mal 2:10–11).
13:19 *When evening shadows fell on the gates.* Before sunset, when the Sabbath began. The Israelites, like the Babylonians, counted their days from sunset to sunset (the Egyptians reckoned theirs from dawn to dawn). The precise moment when the Sabbath began was heralded by the blowing of a trumpet by a priest. According to the Jewish Mishnah, "On the eve of Sabbath they used to blow six more blasts, three to cause the people to cease from work and three to mark the break between the sacred and the profane." Josephus (*Jewish War,* 4.9.12) speaks of the location on the parapet of the temple where the priests "gave a signal beforehand, with a trumpet, at the beginning of every seventh day, in the evening twilight, and also at the evening when that day was finished, announcing to the people the respective hours for ceasing work and for resuming their labors." Excavators at the temple mount recovered a stone from the southwest corner of the parapet, which had fallen to the ground in Titus's siege, with the inscription "for the place of the blowing (of the trumpet)."
13:22 *Remember me.* See note on 1:8.

13:23 Ezra had dealt with the same problem of intermarriage some 25 years before (see note on Ezr 9:1). *Ashdod.* See 4:7; Isa 20:1 and notes. *Ammon and Moab.* See note on Ge 19:36–38.
13:24 The Israelites recognized other people as foreigners by their languages (see Dt 3:9; Jdg 12:6; Ps 114:1; Isa 33:19; Eze 3:5–6).
13:25 *pulled out their hair.* See Ezr 9:3; Isa 50:6 and notes. *You are not to give.* Nehemiah's action was designed to prevent future intermarriages, whereas Ezra dissolved the existing unions.
13:26 *Solomon.* Israel's outstanding king in terms of wealth and political achievements (1Ki 3:13; 2Ch 1:12). Solomon began his reign by humbly asking for wisdom from the Lord (1Ki 3:5–9). *he was led into sin.* In later years his foreign wives led him to worship other gods, so that he built a high place for Chemosh, the god of the Moabites (1Ki 11:7).
13:28 *son-in-law to Sanballat.* According to Lev 21:14 the high priest was not to marry a foreigner. The expulsion of Joiada's son followed either this special ban or the general prohibition against intermarriage. The union described in this verse was especially rankling to Nehemiah in the light of Sanballat's enmity (see 2:10). Josephus (*Antiquities,* 11.7.2) records that an almost identical episode, involving a marriage between the daughter of a Sanballat of Samaria and the brother of the Jewish high priest, took place a little over a century later in the time of Alexander the Great.

³⁰So I purified the priests and the Levites of everything foreign, *h* and assigned them duties, each to his own task. ³¹I also made

13:30	*h*S Ne 9:2
13:31	*i*Ne 10:34
	*j*Ne 10:35-36
	*k*S Ge 8:1; S Ne 1:8

provision for contributions of wood *i* at designated times, and for the firstfruits. *j* Remember *k* me with favor, O my God.

13:30 *duties.* Or "divisions," referring to the assignment of particular duties to groups of priests and Levites, possibly on a rotating basis (see note on 12:9).
13:31 *wood.* See note on 10:34. *firstfruits.* See note on

10:35. *Remember me with favor.* The last recorded words of Nehemiah recapitulate a theme running through the final chapter (vv. 14,22; see note on 1:8). His motive throughout his ministry was to please and to serve his divine Sovereign.

ESTHER

Author and Date

Although we do not know who wrote the book of Esther, from internal evidence it is possible to make some inferences about the author and the date of composition. It is clear that the author was a Jew, both from his emphasis on the origin of a Jewish festival and from the Jewish nationalism that permeates the story. The author's knowledge of Persian customs, the setting of the story in the city of Susa and the absence of any reference to the land of Judah or to Jerusalem suggest that he was a resident of a Persian city. The earliest date for the book would be shortly after the events narrated, i.e., c. 460 B.C. (before Ezra's return to Jerusalem; see note on 8:12). Internal evidence also suggests that the festival of Purim had been observed for some time prior to the writing of the book (9:19). Several scholars have dated the book in the Hellenistic period; the absence of Greek words and the style of the author's Hebrew dialect, however, suggest that the book must have been written before the Persian empire fell to Greece in 331.

Purpose, Themes and Literary Features

The author's central purpose was to record the institution of the annual festival of Purim and to keep alive for later generations the memory of the great deliverance of the Jewish people during the reign of Xerxes. The book accounts for both the initiation of that observance and the obligation for its perpetual commemoration (see 3:7; 9:24,28-32; see also chart on "OT Feasts and Other Sacred Days," p. 176).

Throughout much of the story the author calls to mind the ongoing conflict of Israel with the Amalekites (see notes on 2:5; 3:1-6; 9:5-10), a conflict that began during the exodus (Ex 17:8-16; Dt 25:17-19) and continued through Israel's history (1Sa 15; 1Ch 4:43; and, of course, Esther). As the first to attack Israel after their deliverance from Egypt, the Amalekites were viewed—and the author of Esther views them—as the epitome of all the powers of the world arrayed against God's people (see Nu 24:20; 1Sa 15:1-3; 28:18). And now that Israel has been released from captivity, Haman's edict is the final major effort in the OT period to destroy them.

Closely associated with the conflict with the Amalekites is the rest that is promised to the people of God (see Dt 25:19). With Haman's defeat the Jews enjoy rest from their enemies (9:16,22).

The author also draws upon the remnant motif that recurs throughout the Bible (natural disasters, disease, warfare or other calamities threaten God's people; those who survive constitute a remnant). Events in the Persian city of Susa threatened the continuity of God's purposes in redemptive history. The future existence of God's chosen people, and ultimately the appearance of the Redeemer-Messiah, were jeopardized by Haman's edict to destroy the Jews. The author of Esther patterned much of his material on the events of the Joseph story (see notes on 2:3-4,9,21-23; 3:4; 4:14; 6:1,8,14; 8:6), in which the remnant motif is also central to the narrative (Ge 45:7).

Feasting is another prominent theme in Esther, as shown in the outline below. Banquets provide the setting for important plot developments. There are ten banquets: (1) 1:3-4, (2) 1:5-8, (3) 1:9, (4) 2:18, (5) 3:15, (6) 5:1-8, (7) 7:1-10, (8) 8:17, (9) 9:17, (10) 9:18-32. The three pairs of banquets that mark the beginning, middle and end of the story are particularly prominent: the two banquets given by Xerxes, the two prepared by Esther and the double celebration of Purim.

Recording duplications appears to be one of the favorite compositional techniques of the writer. In addition to the three groups of banquets that come in pairs there are two lists of the king's servants (1:10,14), two reports that Esther concealed her identity (2:10,20), two gatherings of the women (2:8,19), two houses for the women (2:12-14), two fasts (4:3,16), two consultations of Haman with his wife and friends (5:14; 6:13), two unscheduled appearances of Esther before the king (5:2; 8:3), two investitures for Mordecai (6:7-11; 8:15), two coverings of Haman's face (6:12; 7:8), two references to Haman's sons (5:11; 9:6-10, 13-14), two appearances of Harbona (1:10; 7:9), two royal

edicts (3:12-14; 8:1-13), two references to the subsiding of the king's anger (2:1; 7:10), two references to the irrevocability of the Persian laws (1:19; 8:8), two days for the Jews to take vengeance (9:5-15) and two letters instituting the commemoration of Purim (9:20-32).

An outstanding feature of this book—one that has given rise to considerable discussion—is the complete absence of any explicit reference to God, worship, prayer, or sacrifice. This "secularity" has produced many detractors who have judged the book to be of little religious value. However, it appears that the author has deliberately refrained from mentioning God or any religious activity as a literary device to heighten the fact that it is God who controls and directs all the seemingly insignificant coincidences (see, e.g., note on 6:1) that make up the plot and issue in deliverance for the Jews. God's sovereign rule is assumed at every point (see note on 4:12-16), an assumption made all the more effective by the total absence of reference to him.

Outline

I. The Feasts of Xerxes (1:1-2:18)
   A. Vashti Deposed (ch. 1)
   B. Esther Made Queen (2:1-18)
II. The Feasts of Esther (2:19-7:10)
   A. Mordecai Uncovers a Plot (2:19-23)
   B. Haman's Plot (ch. 3)
   C. Mordecai Persuades Esther to Help (ch. 4)
   D. Esther's Request to the King: The First Banquet (5:1-8)
   E. A Sleepless Night (5:9-6:14)
   F. Haman Hanged: The Second Banquet (ch. 7)
III. The Feasts of Purim (8-10)
   A. The King's Edict in Behalf of the Jews (ch. 8)
   B. The Institution of Purim (ch. 9)
   C. The Promotion of Mordecai (ch. 10)

Queen Vashti Deposed

1 This is what happened during the time of Xerxes,[a] [a] the Xerxes who ruled over 127 provinces[b] stretching from India to Cush[b:] [c] 2At that time King Xerxes reigned from his royal throne in the citadel of Susa,[d] 3and in the third year of his reign he gave a banquet[e] for all his nobles and officials. The military leaders of Persia and Media, the princes, and the nobles of the provinces were present.

4For a full 180 days he displayed the vast wealth of his kingdom and the splendor and glory of his majesty. 5When these days were over, the king gave a banquet, lasting seven days,[f] in the enclosed garden[g] of the king's palace, for all the people from the least to the greatest, who were in the citadel of Susa. 6The garden had hangings of white and blue linen, fastened with cords of white linen and purple material to silver rings on marble pillars. There were couches[h] of gold and silver on a mosaic pavement of porphyry, marble, mother-of-pearl and other costly stones. 7Wine was served in goblets of gold, each one different from the other, and the royal wine was abundant, in keeping with the king's liberality.[i] 8By the king's command each guest was allowed to drink in his own way, for the king instructed all the wine stewards to serve each man what he wished.

9Queen Vashti also gave a banquet[j] for the women in the royal palace of King Xerxes.

10On the seventh day, when King Xerxes was in high spirits[k] from wine,[l] he commanded the seven eunuchs who served him—Mehuman, Biztha, Harbona,[m] Bigtha, Abagtha, Zethar and Carcas— 11to bring[n] before him Queen Vashti, wearing her royal crown, in order to display her beauty[o] to the people and nobles, for she was lovely to look at. 12But when the attendants delivered the king's command, Queen Vashti refused to come. Then the king became furious and burned with anger.[p]

13Since it was customary for the king to consult experts in matters of law and justice, he spoke with the wise men who understood the times[q] 14and were closest to the king—Carshena, Shethar, Admatha, Tarshish, Meres, Marsena and Memucan, the seven nobles[r] of Persia and Media who had special access to the king and were highest in the kingdom.

15"According to law, what must be done to Queen Vashti?" he asked. "She has not obeyed the command of King Xerxes that the eunuchs have taken to her."

16Then Memucan replied in the presence of the king and the nobles, "Queen Vashti has done wrong, not only against the king but also against all the nobles and the peoples of all the provinces of King Xerxes. 17For the queen's conduct will become known to all the women, and so they will despise their husbands and say, 'King Xerxes commanded Queen Vashti to be brought before him, but she would not come.' 18This very day the Persian and

Cross references

1:1 aS Ezr 4:6
bEst 9:30;
Da 3:2; 6:1
cEst 8:9
1:2 dS Ezr 4:9;
S Est 2:8
1:3 eS 1Ki 3:15
1:5 fJdg 14:17
gS 2Ki 21:18
1:6 hEst 7:8;
Eze 23:41;
Am 3:12; 6:4
1:7 iEst 2:18;
Da 5:2
1:9 jS 1Ki 3:15
1:10 kS Jdg 16:25;
Est 3:15; 5:6;
7:2; Pr 31:4-7;
Da 5:1-4
mEst 7:9
1:11 nSS 2:4
oPs 45:11;
Eze 16:14
1:12 pGe 39:19;
Est 2:21; 7:7;
Pr 19:12
1:13 qICh 12:32
1:14 rEzr 7:14

Footnotes

[a] Hebrew *Ahasuerus*, a variant of Xerxes' Persian name; here and throughout Esther [b] That is, the upper Nile region

---

1:1 *Xerxes.* A transliteration of the Greek form of the Persian name Khshayarshan (see note on Ezr 4:6; see also NIV text note here). Xerxes succeeded his father Darius and ruled 486–465 B.C. See 8:9. The Greek historian Herodotus (3.89) records that Xerxes's father Darius had organized the empire into 20 satrapies. (Satraps, the rulers of the satrapies, are mentioned in 3:12; 8:9; 9:3.) The provinces were smaller administrative units.

1:2 *citadel of Susa.* The fortified acropolis and palace complex; it is distinguished from the surrounding city in 3:15; 4:1–2,6; 8:15. Several archaeological investigations have been made at the site since the mid–19th century. Xerxes had made extensive renovations in the palace structures. *Susa.* The winter residence of the Persian kings; the three other capitals were Ecbatana (Ezr 6:2), Babylon and Persepolis. One of Daniel's visions was set in Susa (Da 8:2); Nehemiah also served there (Ne 1:1).

1:3–4 The year (483–482 B.C.), the persons in attendance and the length of the meeting suggest that the gathering may have been to plan for the disastrous campaigns of 482–479 against Greece. Herodotus (7.8) possibly describes this assembly.

1:3 *banquet.* Feasting is a prominent theme in Esther (see Introduction: Purpose, Themes and Literary Features).

1:5–6 The excavations at Susa have unearthed a text in which Xerxes's father Darius describes in some detail the building of his palace. Xerxes continued the work his father had begun.

1:9 *Queen Vashti.* Deposed in 484/483 B.C.; Esther became queen in 479/478 (2:16–17). The Greek historians call Xerxes's queen Amestris; they record her influence during the early part of his reign and as queen mother during the following reign of her son Artaxerxes (Ezr 7:1,7,11–12,21; 8:1; Ne 2:1; 5:14; 13:6) until the time of her own death c. 424. Artaxerxes came to the throne when he was 18 years old; therefore he was born c. 484/483, approximately at the time of Vashti's deposal. Since he was the third son of Amestris, the name Amestris cannot be identified with Esther and must be viewed as a Greek version of the name Vashti. Comparatively little is known of the late portions of Xerxes's reign, nor is it possible to determine the subsequent events of the life of Esther. Apparently after Esther's death or her fall from favor, Vashti was able to reassert her power and to exercise a controlling influence over her son.

1:13–14 Ezr 7:14 and the Greek historian Herodotus indicate that seven men functioned as the immediate advisers to the king.

1:13 *wise men who understood the times.* Court astrologers.

Median women of the nobility who have heard about the queen's conduct will respond to all the king's nobles in the same way. There will be no end of disrespect and discord. *s*

¹⁹"Therefore, if it pleases the king, *t* let him issue a royal decree and let it be written in the laws of Persia and Media, which cannot be repealed, *u* that Vashti is never again to enter the presence of King Xerxes. Also let the king give her royal position to someone else who is better than she. ²⁰Then when the king's edict is proclaimed throughout all his vast realm, all the women will respect their husbands, from the least to the greatest."

²¹The king and his nobles were pleased with this advice, so the king did as Memucan proposed. ²²He sent dispatches to all parts of the kingdom, to each province in its own script and to each people in its own language, *v* proclaiming in each people's tongue that every man should be ruler over his own household.

Esther Made Queen

2 Later when the anger of King Xerxes had subsided, *w* he remembered Vashti and what she had done and what he had

decreed about her. ²Then the king's personal attendants proposed, "Let a search be made for beautiful young virgins for the king. ³Let the king appoint commissioners in every province of his realm to bring all these beautiful girls into the harem at the citadel of Susa. Let them be placed under the care of Hegai, the king's eunuch, who is in charge of the women; and let beauty treatments be given to them. ⁴Then let the girl who pleases the king be queen instead of Vashti." This advice appealed to the king, and he followed it.

⁵Now there was in the citadel of Susa a Jew of the tribe of Benjamin, named Mordecai son of Jair, the son of Shimei, the son of Kish, *x* ⁶who had been carried into exile from Jerusalem by Nebuchadnezzar king of Babylon, among those taken captive with Jehoiachin *c y* king of Judah. *z* ⁷Mordecai had a cousin named Hadassah, whom he had brought up because she had neither father nor mother. This girl, who was also known as Esther, *a* was lovely *b* in form and features, and Mordecai had taken her as his own daughter when her father and mother died.

⁸When the king's order and edict had

c 6 Hebrew *Jeconiah,* a variant of *Jehoiachin*

Cross references

1:18 *s*Pr 19:13; 27:15
1:19 *t*Ecc 8:4
*u*Est 8:8; Da 6:8, 12
1:22 *v*S Ne 13:24
2:1 *w*Est 7:10

2:5 *x*S 1Sa 9:1
2:6 *y*S 2Ki 24:15
*z*Da 1:1-5; 5:13
2:7 *a*Ge 41:45
*b*S Ge 39:6

Notes

1:19 *cannot be repealed.* The irrevocability of the Persian laws is mentioned in 8:8 and Da 6:8. *never again to enter.* The punishment corresponds to the crime: Since Vashti refused to appear before the king, it is decreed that she never appear before him again. Furthermore, from this point on she is no longer given the title "Queen" in the book of Esther.
1:22 *proclaiming ... household.* Or "that every man should be ruler over his own household and that his native language should be used in the home," thus referring to the use of the husband's native language in ethnically mixed marriages as a sign of his rule in the home (see Ne 13:23–24).
2:1 *Later.* Esther was taken to Xerxes "in the seventh year of his reign" (v. 16), i.e., in December, 479 B.C., or January, 478. The Greek wars intervened before a new queen was sought (see note on 1:3–4).
2:2 *virgins for the king.* To add to his harem.
2:3–4 The phraseology here is similar to that in Ge 41:34–37. This and numerous other parallels suggest that the author of Esther modeled his work after the Joseph story. Both accounts are set in the courts of foreign monarchs and portray Israelite heroes who rise to prominence and provide the means by which their people are saved (see notes on vv. 9,21–23; 3:4; 4:14; 6:1,8,14; 8:6).
2:5 *in the citadel of Susa a Jew.* As far back as the fall of the northern kingdom in 722–721 B.C. Israelites had been exiled among the cities of the Medes (2Ki 17:6). After the conquest of Babylon by King Cyrus of Persia in 539, some of the Jewish population taken there by the Babylonians (605–586) probably moved eastward into the cities of Medo-Persia. Only 50,000 returned to Israel in the restoration of 538 (Ezr 2:64–67). The presence of a large Jewish population in Medo-Persia is confirmed by the discovery of an archive of texts in Nippur (southern Mesopotamia) from the period of

Artaxerxes I (465–424) and Darius II (424–405). This archive contains the names of about 100 Jews who lived in that city. Some had attained positions of importance and wealth. Similar Jewish populations are probable in many other Medo-Persian cities. *Mordecai.* The name is derived from that of the Babylonian deity Marduk. There are numerous examples in the Bible of Jews having double names—a Hebrew name and a "Gentile" name. Mordecai likely had a Hebrew name, as did Esther (v. 7), Daniel and his friends (Da 1:6–7), Joseph (Ge 41:45) and others, but the text does not mention Mordecai's Hebrew name. A cuneiform tablet from Borsippa near Babylon mentions a scribe by the name of Mardukaya; he was an accountant or minister at the court of Susa in the early years of Xerxes. Many scholars identify him with Mordecai. *son of Jair, the son of Shimei, the son of Kish.* The persons named could be immediate ancestors, in which case Mordecai would be the great-grandson of Kish, who was among the exiles with Jehoiachin in 597 B.C. It is more likely, however, that the names refer to remote ancestors in the tribe of Benjamin (see 2Sa 16:5–14 for Shimei, 1Sa 9:1 for Kish). This association with the tribe and family of King Saul sets the stage for the ongoing conflict between Israel and the Amalekites (see notes on 3:1–6). If the names are those of remote ancestors, the clause "who had been carried into exile" (v. 6) would not apply to Mordecai, who would have been over 100 years old in that case; rather, it would have to be taken as an elliptical construction in the sense "whose family had been carried into exile."
2:6 *Jehoiachin king of Judah.* See 2Ki 24:8–17; 2Ch 36:9–10.
2:7 *Hadassah.* Esther's Hebrew name, meaning "myrtle." The name Esther is likely derived from the Persian word for "star," though some derive it from the name of the Babylonian goddess Ishtar (see note on Jer 7:18).
2:8 *Esther also was taken.* Neither she nor Mordecai

been proclaimed, many girls were brought to the citadel of Susa [c] and put under the care of Hegai. Esther also was taken to the king's palace and entrusted to Hegai, who had charge of the harem. [9]The girl pleased him and won his favor. [d] Immediately he provided her with her beauty treatments and special food. [e] He assigned to her seven maids selected from the king's palace and moved her and her maids into the best place in the harem.

[10]Esther had not revealed her nationality and family background, because Mordecai had forbidden her to do so. [f] [11]Every day he walked back and forth near the courtyard of the harem to find out how Esther was and what was happening to her.

[12]Before a girl's turn came to go in to King Xerxes, she had to complete twelve months of beauty treatments prescribed for the women, six months with oil of myrrh and six with perfumes [g] and cosmetics. [13]And this is how she would go to the king: Anything she wanted was given her to take with her from the harem to the king's palace. [14]In the evening she would go there and in the morning return to another part of the harem to the care of Shaashgaz, the king's eunuch who was in charge of the concubines. [h] She would not return to the king unless he was pleased with her and summoned her by name. [i]

[15]When the turn came for Esther (the girl Mordecai had adopted, the daughter of his uncle Abihail [j]) to go to the king, [k] she asked for nothing other than what Hegai,

the king's eunuch who was in charge of the harem, suggested. And Esther won the favor [l] of everyone who saw her. [16]She was taken to King Xerxes in the royal residence in the tenth month, the month of Tebeth, in the seventh year of his reign.

[17]Now the king was attracted to Esther more than to any of the other women, and she won his favor and approval more than any of the other virgins. So he set a royal crown on her head and made her queen [m] instead of Vashti. [18]And the king gave a great banquet, [n] Esther's banquet, for all his nobles and officials. [o] He proclaimed a holiday throughout the provinces and distributed gifts with royal liberality. [p]

Mordecai Uncovers a Conspiracy

[19]When the virgins were assembled a second time, Mordecai was sitting at the king's gate. [q] [20]But Esther had kept secret her family background and nationality just as Mordecai had told her to do, for she continued to follow Mordecai's instructions as she had done when he was bringing her up. [r]

[21]During the time Mordecai was sitting at the king's gate, Bigthana [d] and Teresh, two of the king's officers [s] who guarded the doorway, became angry [t] and conspired to assassinate King Xerxes. [22]But Mordecai found out about the plot and told Queen Esther, who in turn reported it to the king, giving credit to Mordecai. [23]And when the report was investigated

Cross references

2:8 cNe 1:1;
Est 1:2; Da 8:2
2:9 dS Ge 39:21
eS Ge 37:3;
1Sa 9:22-24;
S 2Ki 25:30;
Est 9:19;
Eze 16:9-13;
Da 1:5
2:10 fver 20
2:12 gPr 27:9;
SS 1:3; Isa 3:24
2:14 hI Ki 11:3;
SS 6:8; Da 5:2
iEst 4:11
2:15 jEst 9:29
kPs 45:14

2:14 iS Ge 18:3;
S 30:27; Est 5:8;
7:3; 8:5
2:17 mEze 16:9-13
2:18 nS 1Ki 3:15
oS Ge 40:20
pS Est 1:7
2:19 qEst 4:2;
5:13
2:20 rver 10
2:21 sS Ge 40:2
tS Est 1:12; 3:5;
5:9; 7:7

d21 Hebrew *Bigthan*, a variant of *Bigthana*

---

would have had any choice in the matter (cf. 2Sa 11:4).

2:9 *special food.* Lit. "her portions." Unlike Daniel and his friends (Da 1:5-10), Esther does not observe the dietary laws, perhaps in part to conceal her Jewish identity (vv. 10,20). Giving such portions is a sign of special favor (1Sa 9:22-24; 2Ki 25:29-30; Da 1:1-10; negatively, Jer 13:25); in the Joseph narrative cf. Ge 43:34. The motif of giving portions appears later as a practice in observing Purim (9:19,22).

2:10 The fact that Esther concealed her identity is reported twice—here and in v. 20 (for the author's use of duplications see Introduction: Purpose, Themes and Literary Features).

2:14 *to another part of the harem.* To the chambers of the concubines.

2:16 *tenth month . . . seventh year.* December, 479 B.C., or January, 478 (see notes on 1:3-4; 2:1). Esther's tenure as queen continued through the events of the book, i.e., through 473 (see 3:7 and note; see also 8:9-13; 9:1). She may have died or fallen from favor shortly thereafter (see note on 1:11).

2:18 *holiday.* The Hebrew for this word, unique to this verse, may imply a remission of taxes, an emancipation of slaves, a cancellation of debts or a remission of obligatory military service.

2:19 See Introduction: Purpose, Themes and Literary Features. The enlargement of the harem apparently continued

unabated. Perhaps there is a causal connection between the second gathering of women and the assassination plot (vv. 21-23); some have suggested that it reflects palace intrigue in support of the deposed Vashti. *king's gate.* The gate of an ancient city was its major commercial and legal center. Markets were held in the gate; the court sat there to transact its business (see Dt 21:18-20; Jos 20:4; Ru 4:1-11; Ps 69:12). A king might hold an audience in the gate (see 2Sa 19:8; 1Ki 22:10). Daniel was at the king's gate as ruler over all Babylon (Da 2:48-49). Mordecai's sitting in the king's gate confirms his holding a high position in the civil service of the empire (see note on v. 5). From this vantage point he might overhear plans for the murder of the king.

2:21-23 Another point of comparison with the Joseph narrative is the involvement of two chamberlains (Ge 40:1-3; see note on vv. 3-4).

2:23 *hanged.* See NIV text note. Among the Persians this form of execution was impalement, as is confirmed in pictures and statues from the ancient Near East and in the comments of the Greek historian Herodotus (3.125,129; 4.43). According to Herodotus (3.159) Darius I impaled 3,000 Babylonians when he took Babylon, an act that Darius himself recorded in his Behistun (Bisitun) inscription. In Israelite and Canaanite practice, hanging was an exhibition of the corpse and not the means of execution itself (Dt 21:22-23; Jos 8:29; 10:26; 1Sa 31:8-10; 2Sa 4:12; 21:9-10). The execution of a chamberlain in the Joseph

and found to be true, the two officials were hanged[u] on a gallows.[e] All this was recorded in the book of the annals[v] in the presence of the king.[w]

Haman's Plot to Destroy the Jews

3 After these events, King Xerxes honored Haman son of Hammedatha, the Agagite,[x] elevating him and giving him a seat of honor higher than that of all the other nobles. [2]All the royal officials at the king's gate knelt down and paid honor to Haman, for the king had commanded this concerning him. But Mordecai would not kneel down or pay him honor.

[3]Then the royal officials at the king's gate asked Mordecai, "Why do you disobey the king's command?"[y] [4]Day after day they spoke to him but he refused to comply.[z] Therefore they told Haman about it to see whether Mordecai's behavior would be tolerated, for he had told them he was a Jew.

[5]When Haman saw that Mordecai would not kneel down or pay him honor, he was enraged.[a] [6]Yet having learned who

Mordecai's people were, he scorned the idea of killing only Mordecai. Instead Haman looked for a way[b] to destroy[c] all Mordecai's people, the Jews,[d] throughout the whole kingdom of Xerxes.

[7]In the twelfth year of King Xerxes, in the first month, the month of Nisan, they cast the *pur*[e] (that is, the lot[f]) in the presence of Haman to select a day and month. And the lot fell on[f] the twelfth month, the month of Adar.[g]

[8]Then Haman said to King Xerxes, "There is a certain people dispersed and scattered among the peoples in all the provinces of your kingdom whose customs[h] are different from those of all other people and who do not obey[i] the king's laws; it is not in the king's best interest to tolerate them.[j] [9]If it pleases the king, let a decree be issued to destroy them, and I will put ten thousand talents[g] of silver into

2:23 uS Ge 40:19; S Dt 21:22-23; Ps 7:14-16; Pr 26:27; Ecc 10:8 vEst 6:1; 10:2 wEst 6:2
3:1 xS Ex 17:8-16; S Nu 24:7; Dt 25:17-19; 1Sa 14:48 **3:3** yEst 5:9; Da 3:12 **3:4** zGe 39:10 **3:5** aS Est 2:21

3:6 bPr 16:25 cPs 74:8; 83:4 dEst 9:24 **3:7** eEst 9:24,26 fS Lev 16:8; S 1Sa 10:21 gver 13; Est 9:19 **3:8** hAc 16:20-21 iJer 29:7; Da 6:13 jEzr 4:15

e23 Or *were hung* (or *impaled*) *on poles*; similarly elsewhere in Esther   f7 Septuagint; Hebrew does not have *And the lot fell on.*   g9 That is, about 375 tons (about 345 metric tons)

narrative also appears to have been by impalement (Ge 40:19). The sons of Haman were killed by the sword, and then their corpses were displayed in this way (9:5–14). *annals.* The concern of the author of Esther with rhetorical symmetry is seen in the fact that the annals are mentioned in the beginning (here), middle (6:1) and end (10:2) of the narrative. The episode dealing with the plot of Bigthana and Teresh is a good example of the many "coincidences" in the book that later take on crucial significance for the story. **3:1** *After these events.* Four years have elapsed since Esther's selection as queen (v. 7; 2:16–17). The fact that no reason is given for the promotion of Haman provides an ironic contrast between the unrewarded merit of Mordecai (2:21–23; see 6:3) and the unmerited reward of Haman. *son of Hammedatha, the Agagite.* There is some debate about the ancestry of Haman. The name Hammedatha appears to be Persian and probably refers to an immediate ancestor. The title "Agagite" could refer to some other immediate ancestor or to an unknown place; however, it is far more likely that it refers to Agag, king of Amalek (1Sa 15:20). The Amalekites had attacked Israel after she fled from Egypt (Ex 17:8–16; 1Sa 14:47–48); for this reason the Lord would "be at war against the Amalekites from generation to generation" (Ex 17:16). Israel was not to forget, but must "blot out the memory of Amalek from under heaven" (Dt 25:17–19). Saul's attack on Amalek (1Sa 15) resulted in the death of King Agag and most, though not all (1Ch 4:42–43), of the city's population. In Esther, about 500 years after the battle led by the Benjamite Saul, the Benjamite Mordecai (see note on 2:5) continues the war with the Amalekites. **3:2–6** Obedience to the second commandment (Ex 20:4) is not the issue in Mordecai's refusal to bow down to Haman, for the Jews were willing to bow down to kings (see 1Sa 24:8; 2Sa 14:4; 1Ki 1:16) and to other persons (see Ge 23:7; 33:3; 44:14). Only the long-standing enmity between the Jews and the Amalekites accounts both for Mordecai's refusal and for Haman's intent to destroy all the Jews (vv. 5–6). The threat against the Jews "throughout the whole kingdom" (v. 6) is a threat against the ultimate issue of

redemptive history (see Introduction: Purpose, Themes and Literary Features). **3:4** Compare the phraseology with that in the Joseph story (Ge 39:10). **3:7** *twelfth year . . . first month.* April or May, 474 B.C., the fifth year of Esther's reign. *they.* Either indefinite or the astrologers who assisted Haman (5:10,14; 6:12–13). *pur.* See 9:24,26. This word is found in Akkadian texts with the meaning "lot" (as here). The celebration known as Purim takes its name from the plural of this noun (see 9:23–32). There is irony in the fact that the month of the Jews' celebration of the Passover deliverance from Egypt is also the month that Haman begins plotting their destruction (Ex 12:1–11). *twelfth month.* An 11-month delay is contemplated between the securing of the decree and the execution of it in the month Adar (February-March). **3:8–9** The name of the people Haman wishes to destroy is slyly omitted in this blend of the true and the false: The Jews did have their own customs and laws, but they were not disobedient to the king (Jer 29:7). **3:8** *dispersed and scattered.* See 8:11,17; 9:2, 12,16, 19–20,28. **3:9** *ten thousand talents.* Herodotus (3.95) records that the annual income of the Persian empire was 15,000 talents. If this figure is correct, Haman offers two-thirds of that amount—a huge sum. Presumably the money would have come from the plundered wealth of the victims of the decree. Verse 13 implies that those who would take part in the massacre were to be allowed to keep the plunder, perhaps adding financial incentive to the execution of the decree since Xerxes disavows taking the money (v. 11). On the other hand, 4:7 and 7:4 may imply that the king had planned on collecting some of the money. *men who carry out this business.* This clause may represent the title of revenue officers who would bring the money to the treasury, or it could refer to those who carry out the decree. The Amalekites had once before plundered Israel (see note on v. 1); Haman plans a recurrence.

the royal treasury for the men who carry out this business." [k]

[10]So the king took his signet ring [l] from his finger and gave it to Haman son of Hammedatha, the Agagite, the enemy of the Jews. [11]"Keep the money," the king said to Haman, "and do with the people as you please."

[12]Then on the thirteenth day of the first month the royal secretaries were summoned. They wrote out in the script of each province and in the language [m] of each people all Haman's orders to the king's satraps, the governors of the various provinces and the nobles of the various peoples. These were written in the name of King Xerxes himself and sealed [n] with his own ring. [13]Dispatches were sent by couriers to all the king's provinces with the order to destroy, kill and annihilate all the Jews [o]—young and old, women and little children—on a single day, the thirteenth day of the twelfth month, the month of Adar, [p] and to plunder [q] their goods. [14]A copy of the text of the edict was to be issued as law in every province and made known to the people of every nationality so they would be ready for that day. [r]

[15]Spurred on by the king's command, the couriers went out, and the edict was issued in the citadel of Susa. [s] The king and Haman sat down to drink, [t] but the city of Susa was bewildered. [u]

Mordecai Persuades Esther to Help

4 When Mordecai learned of all that had been done, he tore his clothes, [v] put on sackcloth and ashes, [w] and went out into the city, wailing [x] loudly and bitterly. [2]But he went only as far as the king's gate, [y] because no one clothed in sackcloth was allowed to enter it. [3]In every province to which the edict and order of the king

Cross references (center column)

3:9 [k]Est 7:4
3:10 [l]S Ge 41:42
3:12
[m]S Ne 13:24
[n]S Ge 38:18
3:13 [o]S 1Sa 15:3;
S Ezr 4:6 [p]S ver 7
[q]Est 8:11; 9:10
3:14 [r]Est 8:8; 9:1
3:15 [s]Est 8:14
[t]S Est 1:10
[u]Est 8:15
4:1 [v]S Nu 14:6
[w]S 2Sa 13:19;
Eze 27:30-31
[x]S Ex 11:6;
Ps 30:11
4:2 [y]S Est 2:19

4:7 [z]Est 7:4
4:11 [a]Est 2:14
[b]Da 2:9 [c]Est 5:2;
8:4; Ps 125:3
4:14 [d]Job 34:29;
Ps 28:1; 35:22;
Ecc 3:7;
Isa 42:14; 57:11;
62:1; 64:12;
Am 5:13

came, there was great mourning among the Jews, with fasting, weeping and wailing. Many lay in sackcloth and ashes.

[4]When Esther's maids and eunuchs came and told her about Mordecai, she was in great distress. She sent clothes for him to put on instead of his sackcloth, but he would not accept them. [5]Then Esther summoned Hathach, one of the king's eunuchs assigned to attend her, and ordered him to find out what was troubling Mordecai and why.

[6]So Hathach went out to Mordecai in the open square of the city in front of the king's gate. [7]Mordecai told him everything that had happened to him, including the exact amount of money Haman had promised to pay into the royal treasury for the destruction of the Jews. [z] [8]He also gave him a copy of the text of the edict for their annihilation, which had been published in Susa, to show to Esther and explain it to her, and he told him to urge her to go into the king's presence to beg for mercy and plead with him for her people.

[9]Hathach went back and reported to Esther what Mordecai had said. [10]Then she instructed him to say to Mordecai, [11]"All the king's officials and the people of the royal provinces know that for any man or woman who approaches the king in the inner court without being summoned [a] the king has but one law: [b] that he be put to death. The only exception to this is for the king to extend the gold scepter [c] to him and spare his life. But thirty days have passed since I was called to go to the king."

[12]When Esther's words were reported to Mordecai, [13]he sent back this answer: "Do not think that because you are in the king's house you alone of all the Jews will escape. [14]For if you remain silent [d] at this time,

---

3:12 *thirteenth day . . . first month.* In the 12th year of Xerxes's reign (v. 7), i.e., Apr. 17, 474 B.C.
3:13 Haman's decree against Israel is the same destruction that had earlier been decreed against Amalek (1Sa 15:3). *thirteenth day . . . twelfth month.* Mar. 7, 473 B.C. (see 8:12).
3:15 Haman and the king will drink together again in the story when the fate of the Jews is once again being decided (7:1–2), but then it will be at the dissolution of their relationship and the reversal of the decree here celebrated. The celebration here is in sharp contrast to the fasting and mourning of the Jews (4:1–3,15–16).
4:2 *king's gate.* See note on 2:19.
4:3 See note on 3:15. The prominence of feasting throughout the book of Esther sets the fasts of vv. 3,16 in sharp relief; a pair of fasts matches the prominent pairs of banquets (see Introduction: Purpose, Themes and Literary Features; see also note on 9:31).
4:4–12 The fact that the dialogue of Esther and Mordecai

is mediated by Hathach reflects the prohibition against Mordecai's entering the royal citadel dressed in mourning (v. 2) and the isolation of Esther in the harem quarters.
4:7 See note on 3:9. That Mordecai is aware of the amount Haman promised to the king is a reminder of his high position in the bureaucracy at Susa (2:21–23).
4:11 Herodotus (3.118,140) also notes that anyone approaching the Persian king unsummoned would be killed unless the king gave immediate pardon.
4:12–16 The themes of the book of Esther are most clearly expressed in this passage. Mordecai's confidence for the Jews' deliverance is based on God's sovereignty in working out his purposes and fulfilling his promises. Their deliverance will come, even if through some means other than Esther. Yet that sovereignty is not fatalistic: Unless Esther exercises her individual responsibility, she and her family will perish. Cf. Mt 26:24; Ac 2:23 for similar treatments of the relationship between divine sovereignty and human responsibility.
4:14 *such a time as this.* Cf. Ge 45:5–7 in the Joseph

relief[e] and deliverance[f] for the Jews will arise from another place, but you and your father's family will perish. And who knows but that you have come to royal position for such a time as this?"[g]

[15]Then Esther sent this reply to Mordecai: [16]"Go, gather together all the Jews who are in Susa, and fast[h] for me. Do not eat or drink for three days, night or day. I and my maids will fast as you do. When this is done, I will go to the king, even though it is against the law. And if I perish, I perish."[i]

[17]So Mordecai went away and carried out all of Esther's instructions.

Esther's Request to the King

5 On the third day Esther put on her royal robes[j] and stood in the inner court of the palace, in front of the king's[k] hall. The king was sitting on his royal throne in the hall, facing the entrance. [2]When he saw Queen Esther standing in the court, he was pleased with her and held out to her the gold scepter that was in his hand. So Esther approached and touched the tip of the scepter.[l]

[3]Then the king asked, "What is it, Queen Esther? What is your request? Even up to half the kingdom,[m] it will be given you."

[4]"If it pleases the king," replied Esther, "let the king, together with Haman, come today to a banquet I have prepared for him."

[5]"Bring Haman at once," the king said, "so that we may do what Esther asks."

So the king and Haman went to the banquet Esther had prepared. [6]As they were drinking wine,[n] the king again asked Esther, "Now what is your petition? It will be given you. And what is your request? Even up to half the kingdom,[o] it will be granted."[p]

[7]Esther replied, "My petition and my request is this: [8]If the king regards me with favor[q] and if it pleases the king to grant my petition and fulfill my request, let the king and Haman come tomorrow to the banquet[r] I will prepare for them. Then I will answer the king's question."

Haman's Rage Against Mordecai

[9]Haman went out that day happy and in high spirits. But when he saw Mordecai at the king's gate and observed that he neither rose nor showed fear in his presence, he was filled with rage[s] against Mordecai.[t] [10]Nevertheless, Haman restrained himself and went home.

Calling together his friends and Zeresh,[u] his wife, [11]Haman boasted[v] to them about his vast wealth, his many sons,[w] and all the ways the king had honored him and how he had elevated him above the other nobles and officials. [12]"And that's not all," Haman added. "I'm the only person[x] Queen Esther invited to accompany the king to the banquet she gave. And she has invited me along with the king tomorrow. [13]But all this gives me no satisfaction as long as I see that Jew Mordecai sitting at the king's gate.[y]"

[14]His wife Zeresh and all his friends said to him, "Have a gallows built, seventy-five feet[h] high,[z] and ask the king in the morning to have Mordecai hanged[a] on it. Then go with the king to the dinner and be happy." This suggestion delighted Haman, and he had the gallows built.

Mordecai Honored

6 That night the king could not sleep;[b] so he ordered the book of the chronicles,[c] the record of his reign, to be brought in and read to him. [2]It was found

[h]14 Hebrew *fifty cubits* (about 23 meters)

Cross references (center column)

4:14 [e]Est 9:16,22
[f]S Ge 45:7;
S Dt 28:29
[g]S Ge 50:20
4:16
[h]S 2Ch 20:3;
Est 9:31
[i]S Ge 43:14
5:1 [j]Eze 16:13
[k]Pr 21:1
5:2 [l]S Est 4:11
5:3 [m]Est 7:2;
Da 5:16; Mk 6:23
5:6 [n]S Est 1:10
[o]Da 5:16;
Mk 6:23
[p]Est 9:12

5:8 [q]S Est 2:15
[r]S 1Ki 3:15
5:9 [s]S Est 2:21;
Pr 14:17
[t]S Est 3:3
5:10 [u]Est 6:13
5:11 [v]Pr 13:16
[w]Est 9:10,13
5:12 [x]Job 22:29;
Pr 16:18; 29:23
5:13 [y]S Est 2:19
5:14 [z]Est 7:9
[a]S Ezr 6:11
6:1 [b]Da 2:1;
6:18 [c]S Est 2:23

---

narrative.
4:16 *fast.* See note on v. 3. Prayer, which usually accompanied such fasting, was presumably a part of this fast as well (see Jdg 20:26; 1Sa 7:6; 2Sa 12:16; Ezr 8:21–23; Ne 9:1–3; Isa 58:3; Jer 14:12; Joel 1:14; 2:12–17; Jnh 3:6–9). The omission of any reference to prayer or to God is consistent with the author's intention; absence of any distinctively religious concepts or vocabulary is a rhetorical device used to heighten the fact that it is indeed God who has been active in the whole narrative (see Introduction: Purpose, Themes and Literary Features). *I and my maids will fast.* Note the rhetorical symmetry: Where once Esther and her maids had received special foods (2:9), now they share a fast. *if I perish.* Cf. the similar formulation in the Joseph narrative (Ge 43:14).
5:2 See Pr 21:1.
5:6–7 One can only speculate regarding Esther's reasons for delaying her answer to the king's question until he had

asked it a third time (vv. 3,6; 7:2). The author uses these delays as plot retardation devices that sustain the tension and permit the introduction of new material on Haman's self-aggrandizement (vv. 11–12) and Mordecai's reward (6:6–11).
5:9 Haman's rage is kindled when Mordecai does not rise in his presence—an ironic contrast to his earlier refusal to bow (3:2–6).
5:11 *many sons.* Haman had ten sons (9:7–10). Herodotus (1.136) reports that the Persians prized a large number of sons second only to valor in battle; the Persian king sent gifts to the subject with the most sons (cf. Ps 127:3–5).
5:12–13 See Pr 16:18; 29:23.
5:14 *seventy-five feet high.* There may be a note of hyperbole in the height of the gallows. Others have suggested that the gallows was erected atop some other structure to achieve this height, e.g., the city wall (see 1Sa 31:10). *hanged.* See note on 2:23.

recorded there that Mordecai had exposed Bigthana and Teresh, two of the king's officers who guarded the doorway, who had conspired to assassinate King Xerxes. [d]

[3] "What honor and recognition has Mordecai received for this?" the king asked.

"Nothing has been done for him," [e] his attendants answered.

[4] The king said, "Who is in the court?" Now Haman had just entered the outer court of the palace to speak to the king about hanging Mordecai on the gallows he had erected for him.

[5] His attendants answered, "Haman is standing in the court."

"Bring him in," the king ordered.

[6] When Haman entered, the king asked him, "What should be done for the man the king delights to honor?"

Now Haman thought to himself, "Who is there that the king would rather honor than me?" [7] So he answered the king, "For the man the king delights to honor, [8] have them bring a royal robe [f] the king has worn and a horse [g] the king has ridden, one with a royal crest placed on its head. [9] Then let the robe and horse be entrusted to one of the king's most noble princes. Let them robe the man the king delights to honor, and lead him on the horse through the city streets, proclaiming before him, 'This is what is done for the man the king delights to honor! [h] '"

[10] "Go at once," the king commanded Haman. "Get the robe and the horse and do just as you have suggested for Mordecai the Jew, who sits at the king's gate. Do not neglect anything you have recommended."

[11] So Haman got [i] the robe and the

horse. He robed Mordecai, and led him on horseback through the city streets, proclaiming before him, "This is what is done for the man the king delights to honor!"

[12] Afterward Mordecai returned to the king's gate. But Haman rushed home, with his head covered [j] in grief, [13] and told Zeresh [k] his wife and all his friends everything that had happened to him.

His advisers and his wife Zeresh said to him, "Since Mordecai, before whom your downfall [l] has started, is of Jewish origin, you cannot stand against him—you will surely come to ruin!" [m] [14] While they were still talking with him, the king's eunuchs arrived and hurried Haman away to the banquet [n] Esther had prepared.

Haman Hanged

7 So the king and Haman went to dine [o] with Queen Esther, [2] and as they were drinking wine [p] on that second day, the king again asked, "Queen Esther, what is your petition? It will be given you. What is your request? Even up to half the kingdom, [q] it will be granted. [r] "

[3] Then Queen Esther answered, "If I have found favor [s] with you, O king, and if it pleases your majesty, grant me my life—this is my petition. And spare my people—this is my request. [4] For I and my people have been sold for destruction and slaughter and annihilation. [t] If we had merely been sold as male and female slaves, I would have kept quiet, because no such distress would justify disturbing the king. [i] "

[5] King Xerxes asked Queen Esther,

6:2 [d] Est 2:21-23
6:3 [e] Ecc 9:13-16
6:8 [f] S Ge 41:42;
S Isa 52:1
[g] 1 Ki 1:33
6:9 [h] Ge 41:43
6:11 [i] S Ge 41:42

6:12 [j] 2Sa 15:30;
Est 7:8; Jer 14:3,
4; Mic 3:7
6:13 [k] Est 5:10
[l] Ps 57:6;
Pr 26:27; 28:18
[m] Est 7:7
6:14 [n] S 1Ki 3:15
7:1 [o] Ge 40:20-22;
Mt 22:1-14
7:2 [p] S Est 1:10
[q] S Est 5:3
[r] Est 9:12
7:3 [s] S Est 2:15
7:4 [t] Est 3:9;
S 4:7

[i] 4 Or *quiet, but the compensation our adversary offers cannot be compared with the loss the king would suffer*

6:1 This verse marks the literary center of the narrative. When things could not look worse, a series of seemingly trivial coincidences marks a critical turn that brings resolution to the story. The king's inability to sleep, his requesting the reading of the annals, the reading of the passage reporting Mordecai's past kindness, Haman's noisy carpentry in the early hours of the morning (5:14), his sudden entry into the outer court and his assumption that he was the man the king wished to honor—all are events testifying to the sovereignty of God over the events of the narrative. Circumstances that seemed incidental earlier in the narrative take on crucial significance. Just as in the Joseph story (Ge 41:1–45), the hero's personal fortunes are reversed because of the monarch's disturbed sleep (cf. Da 2:1; 6:18).
6:2 The scribe was reading at the time from the annals that recorded events five years earlier (compare 3:7 with 2:16).
6:4–6 Again, the irony is evident: Just as Haman had withheld from the king the identity of the "certain people" (3:8), so now the king unintentionally keeps from Haman the identity of the "man the king delights to honor" (v. 6).
6:8 *royal robe the king has worn.* See 8:15; see also Introduction: Purpose, Themes and Literary Features. Cf. in

the Joseph story Ge 41:41–43. Great significance was attached to the king's garment in ancient times; wearing his garments was a sign of unique favor (1Sa 18:4). To wear another's garments was to partake of his power, stature, honor or sanctity (2Ki 2:13–14; Isa 61:3,10; Zec 3; Mk 5:27). Haman's suggestion is not only a great honor to the recipient, but it is also considerably flattering to the king: Wearing his garment was chosen instead of wealth.
6:13 See Introduction: Purpose, Themes and Literary Features.
6:14 Guests were usually escorted to feasts (see in the Joseph narrative Ge 43:15–26; cf. Mt 22:1–14).
7:2 See 5:3,6.
7:3 See 2:15,17.
7:4 *sold.* Esther refers to the bribe Haman offered to the king (3:9; 4:7); she also paraphrases Haman's edict (3:13). *because no such distress . . . king.* See NIV text note. The statement probably means either (1) that the affliction of the Jews would be less injurious to the king if slavery was all that was involved, or (2) that Esther would not trouble the king if slavery was the only issue.

"Who is he? Where is the man who has
dared to do such a thing?"
6 Esther said, "The adversary and enemy
is this vile Haman."
Then Haman was terrified before the
king and queen. 7 The king got up in a
rage,[u] left his wine and went out into the
palace garden.[v] But Haman, realizing that
the king had already decided his fate,[w]
stayed behind to beg Queen Esther for his
life.
8 Just as the king returned from the palace garden to the banquet hall, Haman was
falling on the couch[x] where Esther was
reclining.[y]
The king exclaimed, "Will he even molest the queen while she is with me in the
house?"[z]
As soon as the word left the king's
mouth, they covered Haman's face.[a]
9 Then Harbona,[b] one of the eunuchs attending the king, said, "A gallows seventy-
five feet[j] high[c] stands by Haman's house.
He had it made for Mordecai, who spoke
up to help the king."
The king said, "Hang him on it!"[d] 10 So
they hanged[e] Haman[f] on the gallows[g] he
had prepared for Mordecai.[h] Then the
king's fury subsided.[i]

The King's Edict in Behalf of the Jews

8 That same day King Xerxes gave
Queen Esther the estate of Haman,[j]
the enemy of the Jews. And Mordecai
came into the presence of the king, for Esther had told how he was related to her.
2 The king took off his signet ring,[k] which
he had reclaimed from Haman, and
presented it to Mordecai. And Esther appointed him over Haman's estate.[l]
3 Esther again pleaded with the king, falling at his feet and weeping. She begged
him to put an end to the evil plan of Haman the Agagite,[m] which he had devised
against the Jews. 4 Then the king extended
the gold scepter[n] to Esther and she arose
and stood before him.
5 "If it pleases the king," she said, "and
if he regards me with favor[o] and thinks it
the right thing to do, and if he is pleased
with me, let an order be written overruling
the dispatches that Haman son of Hammedatha, the Agagite, devised and wrote
to destroy the Jews in all the king's provinces. 6 For how can I bear to see disaster
fall on my people? How can I bear to see
the destruction of my family?"[p]
7 King Xerxes replied to Queen Esther
and to Mordecai the Jew, "Because Haman attacked the Jews, I have given his
estate to Esther, and they have hanged[q]
him on the gallows. 8 Now write another
decree[r] in the king's name in behalf of the
Jews as seems best to you, and seal[s] it
with the king's signet ring[t]—for no document written in the king's name and
sealed with his ring can be revoked."[u]
9 At once the royal secretaries were summoned—on the twenty-third day of the
third month, the month of Sivan. They
wrote out all Mordecai's orders to the
Jews, and to the satraps, governors and nobles of the 127 provinces stretching from
India to Cush.[k][v] These orders were writ-

7:7 [u]S Ge 34:7; S Est 1:12; Pr 19:12; 20:1-2 [v]S 2Ki 21:18 [w]Est 6:13 **7:8** [x]S Est 1:6 [y]Ge 39:14; Jn 13:23 [z]S Ge 34:7 [a]S Est 6:12 **7:9** [b]Est 1:10 [c]Est 5:14 [d]S Dt 21:22-23; Ps 7:14-16; 9:16; Pr 11:5-6; S 26:27; S Mt 7:2 **7:10** [e]Ge 40:22 [f]Pr 10:28 [g]Est 9:25 [h]Da 6:24 [i]Est 2:1 **8:1** [j]Pr 22:22-23 **8:2** [k]S Ge 24:22; S 41:42 [l]S Ge 41:41; Pr 13:22; 14:35; Da 2:48 **8:3** [m]S Ex 17:8-16 **8:4** [n]S Est 4:11 **8:5** [o]S Est 2:15 **8:6** [p]Ge 44:34 **8:7** [q]S Dt 21:22-23 **8:8** [r]S Est 3:12-14 [s]S Ge 38:18 [t]S Ge 41:42 [u]S Est 1:19; Da 6:15 **8:9** [v]Est 1:1

[j]9 Hebrew *fifty cubits* (about 23 meters) [k]9 That is, the upper Nile region

7:8 *falling on the couch where Esther was reclining.* Meals were customarily taken reclining on a couch (Am 6:4–7; Jn 13:23). It is ironic that Haman, who became angry when the Jew Mordecai would not bow down (which set the whole story in motion), now falls before the Jewess Esther (see 6:13). The king's leaving the room sets the stage for the final twist that would seal Haman's fate. *covered Haman's face.* See 6:12; see also Introduction: Purpose, Themes and Literary Features.
7:9 Before this moment there is no evidence that Esther had known of Mordecai's triumph earlier in the day (ch. 6); she has pleaded for the life of her people. Harbona's reference to the gallows in effect introduces a second charge against Haman—his attempt to kill the king's benefactor. *Harbona.* See Introduction: Purpose, Themes and Literary Features. He had been sent earlier to bring Vashti and thus set in motion the events that would lead to her fall and the choice of Esther (1:10); now he is instrumental in the fall of Haman and the rise of Mordecai.
7:10 *subsided.* See 2:1; see also Introduction: Purpose, Themes and Literary Features.
8:1–17 The author achieves considerable literary symmetry by recapitulating much of 3:1–4:3 in almost identical terms.
8:1 *gave Queen Esther the estate of Haman.* Herodotus (3.128–129) and Josephus (*Antiquities*, 11.17) confirm that the property of a traitor reverted to the crown; Xerxes presents Haman's wealth (5:11) to Esther.
8:2 Cf. 3:10, where the king's offer of his ring includes Haman's keeping the money; here Mordecai receives the office and the estate of Haman.
8:3–6 Esther and Mordecai are secure (7:4–5), but the irrevocable decree is still a threat to the rest of the Jews.
8:3 *Agagite.* See note on 3:1.
8:5 *favor.* See 4:11; 5:2.
8:6 Cf. the Joseph story (Ge 44:34).
8:8 See 1:19; see also Introduction: Purpose, Themes and Literary Features. The dilemma is the same as the one that confronted Darius the Mede in Daniel (Da 6:8,12,15). The solution is to issue another decree that in effect counters the original decree of Haman without formally revoking it (see note on 9:2–3).
8:9–13 The phraseology is taken from the parallel in 3:12–14. The extent of the destruction is the same as that earlier decreed against Amalek (see note on 3:13).
8:9 *twenty-third day . . . third month.* In Xerxes's 12th year, i.e., June 25, 474 B.C., two months and ten days after the proclamation of Haman's edict (see note on 3:13).

ten in the script of each province and the language of each people and also to the Jews in their own script and language. [w] [10]Mordecai wrote in the name of King Xerxes, sealed the dispatches with the king's signet ring, and sent them by mounted couriers, who rode fast horses especially bred for the king.

[11]The king's edict granted the Jews in every city the right to assemble and protect themselves; to destroy, kill and annihilate any armed force of any nationality or province that might attack them and their women and children; and to plunder[x] the property of their enemies. [12]The day appointed for the Jews to do this in all the provinces of King Xerxes was the thirteenth day of the twelfth month, the month of Adar. [y] [13]A copy of the text of the edict was to be issued as law in every province and made known to the people of every nationality so that the Jews would be ready on that day[z] to avenge themselves on their enemies.

[14]The couriers, riding the royal horses, raced out, spurred on by the king's command. And the edict was also issued in the citadel of Susa. [a]

[15]Mordecai[b] left the king's presence wearing royal garments of blue and white, a large crown of gold[c] and a purple robe of fine linen. [d] And the city of Susa held a joyous celebration. [e] [16]For the Jews it was a time of happiness and joy,[f] gladness and honor.[g] [17]In every province and in every city, wherever the edict of the king went, there was joy[h] and gladness among the Jews, with feasting and celebrating. And many people of other nationalities became Jews because fear[i] of the Jews had seized them.[j]

Triumph of the Jews

9 On the thirteenth day of the twelfth month, the month of Adar,[k] the edict commanded by the king was to be carried out. On this day the enemies of the Jews had hoped to overpower them, but now the tables were turned and the Jews got the upper hand[l] over those who hated them. [m] [2]The Jews assembled in their cities[n] in all the provinces of King Xerxes to attack those seeking their destruction. No one could stand against them,[o] because the people of all the other nationalities were afraid of them. [3]And all the nobles of the provinces, the satraps, the governors and the king's administrators helped the Jews,[p] because fear of Mordecai had seized them.[q] [4]Mordecai[r] was prominent[s] in the palace; his reputation spread throughout the provinces, and he became more and more powerful. [t]

[5]The Jews struck down all their enemies with the sword, killing and destroying them,[u] and they did what they pleased to those who hated them. [6]In the citadel of Susa, the Jews killed and destroyed five hundred men. [7]They also killed Parshandatha, Dalphon, Aspatha, [8]Poratha, Adalia, Aridatha, [9]Parmashta, Arisai, Aridai and Vaizatha, [10]the ten sons[v] of Haman son of Hammedatha, the enemy of the Jews. [w] But they did not lay their hands on the plunder.[x]

[11]The number of those slain in the citadel of Susa was reported to the king that same day. [12]The king said to Queen Esther, "The Jews have killed and destroyed five hundred men and the ten sons of Haman in the citadel of Susa. What have they done in the rest of the king's provinces? Now what is your petition? It will be given you. What is your request? It will also be granted."[y]

[13]"If it pleases the king," Esther an-

Cross references

8:9 [w]S Ne 13:24
8:11 [x]S Ge 14:23; [y]S Est 3:13; 9:15, 16
8:12 [y]Est 3:13; 9:1
8:13 [z]Est 3:14
8:14 [a]Est 3:15
8:15 [b]Est 9:4; 10:2 [c]S 2Sa 12:30 [d]S Ge 41:42 [e]Est 3:15
8:16 [f]Ps 97:10-12 [g]Est 4:1-3; Ps 112:4; Jer 15:16
8:17 [h]Ps 35:27; 45:15; 51:8; Pr 11:10 [i]S Ex 15:14,16; Dt 11:25; Da 6:26 [j]Est 9:3
9:1 [k]S Est 8:12 [l]Jer 29:4-7 [m]S Est 3:12-14; Pr 22:22-23
9:2 [n]S Ge 22:17 [o]Ps 35:26; 40:14; 70:2; 71:13,24
9:3 [p]S Ezr 8:36 [q]Est 8:17
9:4 [r]S Est 8:15 [s]S Ex 11:3 [t]S 2Sa 3:1; 1Ch 11:9
9:5 [u]Dt 25:17-19; S 1Sa 15:3; S Ezr 4:6
9:10 [v]S Est 5:11; Ps 127:3-5 [w]S 1Sa 15:33 [x]S Ge 14:23; S 1Sa 14:32; S Est 3:13
9:12 [y]Est 5:6; 7:2

Footnotes

8:12 *thirteenth day ... twelfth month.* Mar. 7, 473 B.C. (see 3:13). Some 15 years after this first Purim, Ezra would lead his expedition to Jerusalem (Ezr 7:9).

8:14–17 The phraseology is taken from 3:15–4:3.

8:15 *royal garments.* Mordecai's second investiture (see Introduction: Purpose, Themes and Literary Features; see also note on 6:10).

9:1 See notes on 8:9–13. The Jews carry out the edict of Mordecai eight months and 20 days later. *tables were turned.* The statement that the opposite happened points to the author's concern with literary symmetry: He balances most of the details from the first half of the story with their explicit reversal in the second half.

9:2–3 An illustration of Ge 12:3. Confronted with two conflicting edicts issued in the king's name—the edict of Haman and the edict of Mordecai—the governors follow the edict of the current regime.

9:5–10 The Jews attend to the unfinished business of "blotting out the name of the Amalekites" (Ex 17:16; Dt 25:17–19; see notes on 3:1–6). This incident is presented as the antithesis of 1Sa 15: The narrator is emphatic that the Jews did not take plunder, in spite of the king's permission to do so (8:11). Seizing the plunder 500 years earlier in the battle against Amalek had cost Saul his kingship (1Sa 15:17–19); here, not taking the plunder brings royal power to Mordecai (vv. 20–23). See vv. 15–16; cf. Ge 14:22–24.

9:10 *sons of Haman.* The second reference to Haman's sons (see 5:11; see also Introduction: Purpose, Themes and Literary Features).

9:12 See 5:3,6; 7:2.

9:13 The reference to hanging in this case is to the display of the corpses, not to the means of the execution (see vv. 7–10 and note on 2:23).

swered, "give the Jews in Susa permission to carry out this day's edict tomorrow also, and let Haman's ten sons[z] be hanged[a] on gallows."

[14]So the king commanded that this be done. An edict was issued in Susa, and they hanged[b] the ten sons of Haman. [15]The Jews in Susa came together on the fourteenth day of the month of Adar, and they put to death in Susa three hundred men, but they did not lay their hands on the plunder.[c]

[16]Meanwhile, the remainder of the Jews who were in the king's provinces also assembled to protect themselves and get relief[d] from their enemies.[e] They killed seventy-five thousand of them[f] but did not lay their hands on the plunder.[g] [17]This happened on the thirteenth day of the month of Adar, and on the fourteenth they rested and made it a day of feasting[h] and joy.

Purim Celebrated

[18]The Jews in Susa, however, had assembled on the thirteenth and fourteenth, and then on the fifteenth they rested and made it a day of feasting and joy.

[19]That is why rural Jews—those living in villages—observe the fourteenth of the month of Adar[i] as a day of joy and feasting, a day for giving presents to each other.[j]

[20]Mordecai recorded these events, and he sent letters to all the Jews throughout the provinces of King Xerxes, near and far, [21]to have them celebrate annually the fourteenth and fifteenth days of the month of Adar [22]as the time when the Jews got relief[k] from their enemies, and as the month when their sorrow was turned into joy and their mourning into a day of celebration.[l] He wrote them to observe the days as days of feasting and joy and giving presents of food[m] to one another and gifts to the poor.[n]

[23]So the Jews agreed to continue the

celebration they had begun, doing what Mordecai had written to them. [24]For Haman son of Hammedatha, the Agagite,[o] the enemy of all the Jews, had plotted against the Jews to destroy them and had cast the pur[p] (that is, the lot[q]) for their ruin and destruction.[r] [25]But when the plot came to the king's attention,[1] he issued written orders that the evil scheme Haman had devised against the Jews should come back onto his own head,[s] and that he and his sons should be hanged[t] on the gallows.[u] [26](Therefore these days were called Purim, from the word pur.[v]) Because of everything written in this letter and because of what they had seen and what had happened to them, [27]the Jews took it upon themselves to establish the custom that they and their descendants and all who join them should without fail observe these two days every year, in the way prescribed and at the time appointed. [28]These days should be remembered and observed in every generation by every family, and in every province and in every city. And these days of Purim should never cease to be celebrated by the Jews, nor should the memory of them die out among their descendants.

[29]So Queen Esther, daughter of Abihail,[w] along with Mordecai the Jew, wrote with full authority to confirm this second letter concerning Purim. [30]And Mordecai sent letters to all the Jews in the 127 provinces[x] of the kingdom of Xerxes—words of goodwill and assurance— [31]to establish these days of Purim at their designated times, as Mordecai the Jew and Queen Esther had decreed for them, and as they had established for themselves and their descendants in regard to their times of fasting[y] and lamentation.[z] [32]Esther's decree confirmed these regulations about Purim, and it was written down in the records.

9:13 zS Est 5:11
aS Dt 21:22-23
9:14 bS Ezr 6:11
9:15
cS Ge 14:23;
S Est 8:11
9:16 dS Est 4:14
eDt 25:19
/S 1Ch 4:43
gS Est 8:11
9:17 hS 1Ki 3:15
9:19 iS Est 3:7
/S Est 2:9;
Rev 11:10
9:22 kS Est 4:14
lNe 8:12;
Ps 30:11-12
mS 2Ki 25:30
nS Ne 8:10

9:24
oS Ex 17:8-16
pS Est 3:7
qS Lev 16:8
rEst 3:6
9:25 sPs 7:16
tS Dt 21:22-23
uEst 7:10
9:26 vS Est 3:7
9:29 wEst 2:15
9:30 xS Est 1:1
9:31 yS Est 4:16
zEst 4:1-3

125 Or when Esther came before the king

9:15–16 See note on vv. 5–10.

9:16,22 relief from their enemies. Closely associated with the vengeance on their enemies is the rest promised to Israel (Dt 25:19). The defeat of Haman brings rest to the Jews. Cf. 1Ch 22:6–10; Ps 95:8–11; Isa 32:18; Heb 3:11–4:11.

9:18–19 The author accounts for the tradition of observing Purim on two different days: It is observed on the 14th in most towns, but the Jews of Susa observed it on the 15th. Today it is observed on the 14th except in Jerusalem, where it is observed on the 15th.

9:20 Mordecai recorded these events. Some take this as indicating that Mordecai wrote the book of Esther; however, the more natural understanding is that he recorded the events in the letters he sent.

9:22 presents of food. See note on 2:9; cf. Ne 8:10,12.

9:24,26 pur. See note on 3:7.

9:27 all who join them. Some refer this phrase to a period of Jewish proselytism and regard it as important to dating the book. It is more likely that it refers to those mentioned in 8:17.

9:31 fasting. See notes on 4:3,16. No date is assigned for this fast. Jews traditionally observe the 13th of Adar, Haman's propitious day (see 3:7,13), as a fast ("the fast of Esther") before the celebration of Purim. These three days of victory celebration on the 13th–15th days of Adar rhetorically balance the three days of Esther's fasting prior to interceding with the king (4:16).

The Greatness of Mordecai

10 King Xerxes imposed tribute throughout the empire, to its distant shores.[a] [2]And all his acts of power and might, together with a full account of the greatness of Mordecai[b] to which the king had raised him,[c] are they not written in the book of the annals[d] of the kings of Media and Persia? [3]Mordecai the Jew was second[e] in rank[f] to King Xerxes,[g] preeminent among the Jews, and held in high esteem by his many fellow Jews, because he worked for the good of his people and spoke up for the welfare of all the Jews. [h]

10:1 [a]Ps 72:10; 97:1
10:2 [b]S Est 8:15
[c]S Ge 41:44
[d]S Est 2:23

10:3 [e]Da 5:7
[f]Ge 41:43
[g]Ge 41:40
[h]Ne 2:10;
Jer 29:4-7; Da 6:3

10:1–2 The reference to this taxation may represent material in the author's source, to which he directs the reader for additional information and confirmation (see note on 2:23).

JOB

Author

Although most of the book consists of the words of Job and his counselors, Job himself was not the author. We may be sure that the author was an Israelite, since he (not Job or his friends) frequently uses the Israelite covenant name for God (*Yahweh*; NIV "the LORD"). In the prologue (chs. 1-2), divine discourses (38:1-42:6) and epilogue (42:7-17) "LORD" occurs a total of 25 times (31 times in the Hebrew text), while in the rest of the book (chs. 3-37) it appears only once (12:9).

The unknown author probably had access to oral and/or written sources from which, under divine inspiration, he composed the book that we now have. Of course the subject matter of the prologue had to be divinely revealed to him, since it contains information only God could know. While the author preserves much of the archaic and non-Israelite flavor in the language of Job and his friends, he also reveals his own style as a writer of wisdom literature. The literary structures and the quality of the rhetoric used display the author's literary genius.

Date

Two dates are involved: (1) the date of the man Job and his historical setting, and (2) the date of the inspired writer who composed the book. The latter could be dated anytime from the reign of Solomon to the exile. Although the writer was an Israelite, he mentions nothing of Israelite history. He had a written and/or oral account about the non-Israelite sage Job (1:1), whose setting appears to be during the second millennium B.C. (2000-1000), and probably late in that millennium (see note on 19:24). Like the Hebrew patriarchs, Job lived more than 100 years (42:16). His wealth was measured in cattle (1:3), and he acted as priest for his family (1:5). The raiding of Sabean (1:15) and Chaldean (1:17) tribes fits the second millennium, as does the mention of the *kesitah*, "a piece of silver," in 42:11 (see Ge 33:19; Jos 24:32). The discovery of a Targum (Aramaic paraphrase) on Job from the first or second century B.C. (the earliest written Targum) makes a very late date for authorship highly unlikely.

Language and Text

In many places Job is difficult to translate because of its many unusual words and its style. For that reason, modern translations frequently differ widely. Even the early translator(s) of Job into Greek (the Septuagint) seem(s) often to have been perplexed. The Septuagint of Job is about 400 lines shorter than the accepted Hebrew text, and it may be that the translator(s) simply omitted lines he (they) did not understand. The early Syriac (Peshitta), Aramaic (Targum) and Latin (Vulgate) translators had similar difficulties.

Theme and Message

The book provides a profound statement on the subject of theodicy (the justice of God in light of human suffering). But the manner in which the problem of theodicy is conceived and the solution offered (if it may be called that) is uniquely Israelite. The theodicy question in Greek and later Western thought has been: How can the justice of an almighty God be defended in the face of evil, especially human suffering—and, even more particularly, the suffering of the innocent? In this form of the question, three possible assumptions are left open: (1) that God is not almighty, (2) that God is not just (that there is a "demonic" element in his being) and (3) that man may be innocent. In ancient Israel, however, it was indisputable that God is almighty, that he is perfectly just and that no human is wholly innocent in his sight. These three assumptions were also fundamental to the theology of Job and his friends. Simple logic then dictated the conclusion: Every person's suffering is indicative of the measure of his guilt in the eyes of God. In the abstract, this conclusion appeared inescapable, logically

imperative and theologically satisfying. Hence, in the context of such a theology, theodicy was not a problem because its solution was self-evident.

But what was thus theologically self-evident and unassailable in the abstract was often, as in the case of Job, in radical tension with actual human experience. There were those whose godliness was genuine, whose moral character was upright and who, though not sinless, had kept themselves from great transgression, but who nonetheless were made to suffer bitterly. For these the self-evident theology brought no consolation and offered no guidance. It only gave rise to a great enigma. And the God to whom the sufferer was accustomed to turn in moments of need and distress became himself the overwhelming enigma. In the speeches of chs. 3-37, we hear on the one hand the flawless logic but wounding thrusts of those who insisted on the "orthodox" theology, and on the other hand the writhing of soul of the righteous sufferer who struggles with the great enigma. In addition he suffers from the wounds inflicted by his well-intended friends (see note on 5:27). Here, then, we have a graphic portrayal of the unique form of the problem of theodicy as experienced by righteous sufferers within orthodox Israel.

The "solution" offered is also uniquely Israelite—or, better said, Biblical. The relationship between God and man is not exclusive and closed. A third party intrudes, the great adversary (see chs. 1-2). Incapable of contending with God hand to hand, power pitted against power, he is bent on frustrating God's enterprise embodied in the creation and centered on the God-man relationship. As tempter he seeks to alienate man from God (see Ge 3; Mt 4:1); as accuser (one of the names by which he is called, *śaṭan,* means "accuser") he seeks to alienate God from man (see Zec 3:1; Rev 12:9-10). His all-consuming purpose is to drive an irremovable wedge between God and man, to effect an alienation that cannot be reconciled.

In the story of Job, the author portrays the adversary in his boldest and most radical assault on God and the godly man in the special and intimate relationship that is dearest to them both. When God calls up the name of Job before the accuser and testifies to the righteousness of this one on the earth—this man in whom God delights—Satan attempts with one crafty thrust both to assail God's beloved and to show up God as a fool. True to one of his modes of operation, he accuses Job before God. He charges that Job's godliness is evil. The very godliness in which God takes delight is void of all integrity; it is the worst of all sins. Job's godliness is self-serving; he is righteous only because it pays. If God will only let Satan tempt Job by breaking the link between righteousness and blessing, he will expose the righteous man for the sinner he is.

It is the adversary's ultimate challenge. For if the godliness of the righteous man in whom God delights can be shown to be the worst of all sins, then a chasm of alienation stands between them that cannot be bridged. Then even redemption is unthinkable, for the godliest of men will be shown to be the most ungodly. God's whole enterprise in creation and redemption will be shown to be radically flawed, and God can only sweep it all away in awful judgment.

The accusation, once raised, cannot be removed, not even by destroying the accuser. So God lets the adversary have his way with Job (within specified limits) so that God and the righteous Job may be vindicated and the great accuser silenced. Thus comes the anguish of Job, robbed of every sign of God's favor so that God becomes for him the great enigma. Also his righteousness is assailed on earth through the logic of the "orthodox" theology of his friends. Alone he agonizes. But he knows in his heart that his godliness has been authentic and that someday he will be vindicated (see 13:18; 14:13-17; 16:19; 19:25-27). And in spite of all, though he may curse the day of his birth (ch. 3) and chide God for treating him unjustly (9:28-35)—the uncalculated outcry of a distraught spirit—he will not curse God (as his wife, the human nearest his heart, proposes; see 2:9). In fact, what pains him most is God's apparent alienation from him.

In the end the adversary is silenced. And the astute theologians, Job's friends, are silenced. And Job is silenced. But God is not. And when he speaks, it is to Job that he speaks, bringing the silence of regret for hasty speech in days of suffering and the silence of repose in the ways of the Almighty (see 38:1-42:6). Furthermore, as his heavenly friend, God hears Job's intercessions for his associates (42:8-10), and he restores Job's beatitude (42:10-17).

In summary, the author's pastoral word to the godly sufferer is that his righteousness has such supreme value that God treasures it more than all. And the great adversary knows that if he is to thwart the purposes of God he must assail the righteousness of man. At stake in the suffering of the truly godly is the outcome of the struggle in heaven between the great adversary and God, with the all-encompassing divine purpose in the balance. Thus the suffering of the righteous has a meaning and value commensurate with the titanic spiritual struggle of the ages.

Literary Form and Structure

Like some other ancient compositions, the book of Job has a sandwich literary structure: prologue (prose), main body (poetry), and epilogue (prose), revealing a creative composition, not an arbitrary compilation. Some of Job's words are lament (cf. ch. 3 and many shorter poems in his speeches), but the form of lament is unique to Job and often unlike the regular format of most lament psalms (except Ps 88). Much of the book takes the form of legal disputation. Although the friends come to console him, they end up arguing over the reason for Job's suffering. The argument breaks down in ch. 27, and Job then proceeds to make his final appeal to God for vindication (chs. 29-31). The wisdom poem in ch. 28 appears to be the words of the author, who sees the failure of the dispute as evidence of a lack of wisdom. So in praise of true wisdom he centers his structural apex between the three cycles of dialogue-dispute (chs. 3-27) and the three monologues: Job's (chs. 29-31), Elihu's (chs. 32-37) and God's (38:1-42:6). Job's monologue turns directly to God for a legal decision: that he is innocent of the charges his counselors have leveled against him. Elihu's monologue—another human perspective on why people suffer—rebukes Job but moves beyond the punishment theme to the value of divine chastening and God's redemptive purpose in it. God's monologue gives the divine perspective: Job is not condemned, but neither is a logical or legal answer given to why Job has suffered. That remains a mystery to Job, though the reader is ready for Job's restoration in the epilogue because he has had the heavenly vantage point of the prologue all along. So the literary structure and the theological significance of the book are beautifully tied together.

Outline

Prologue

1 In the land of Uz[a] there lived a man whose name was Job.[b] This man was blameless[c] and upright;[d] he feared God[e] and shunned evil.[f] 2He had seven sons[g] and three daughters,[h] 3and he owned seven thousand sheep, three thousand camels, five hundred yoke of oxen and five hundred donkeys,[i] and had a large number of servants.[j] He was the greatest man[k] among all the people of the East.[l]

4His sons used to take turns holding feasts[m] in their homes, and they would invite their three sisters to eat and drink with them. 5When a period of feasting had run its course, Job would send and have them purified.[n] Early in the morning he would sacrifice a burnt offering[o] for each of them, thinking, "Perhaps my children have sinned[p] and cursed God[q] in their hearts." This was Job's regular custom.

Job's First Test

6One day the angels[a][r] came to present themselves before the LORD, and Satan[b][s] also came with them.[t] 7The LORD said to Satan, "Where have you come from?"

Satan answered the LORD, "From roaming through the earth and going back and forth in it."[u]

8Then the LORD said to Satan, "Have you considered my servant Job?[v] There is

no one on earth like him; he is blameless and upright, a man who fears God[w] and shuns evil."[x]

9"Does Job fear God for nothing?"[y] Satan replied. 10"Have you not put a hedge[z] around him and his household and everything he has?[a] You have blessed the work of his hands, so that his flocks and herds are spread throughout the land.[b] 11But stretch out your hand and strike everything he has,[c] and he will surely curse you to your face."[d]

12The LORD said to Satan, "Very well, then, everything he has[e] is in your hands, but on the man himself do not lay a finger."[f]

Then Satan went out from the presence of the LORD.

13One day when Job's sons and daughters[g] were feasting[h] and drinking wine at the oldest brother's house, 14a messenger came to Job and said, "The oxen were plowing and the donkeys were grazing[i] nearby, 15and the Sabeans[j] attacked and carried them off. They put the servants to the sword, and I am the only one who has escaped to tell you!"

16While he was still speaking, another messenger came and said, "The fire of God

Cross references

1:1 aS Ge 10:23
bEze 14:14,20;
Jas 5:11
cS Ge 6:9;
S Job 23:10
dJob 23:7;
Ps 11:7; 107:42;
Pr 21:29; Mic 7:2
eS Ge 22:12
fver 8; S Dt 4:6;
Job 2:3; 1Th 5:22
1:2 gS Ru 4:15
hver 13,18;
Job 42:13;
Ps 127:3; 144:12
1:3 iS Ge 13:2
jS Ge 12:16
kver 8; Job 29:25
lS Ge 25:6;
Job 42:10;
Ps 103:10
1:4 mver 13,18
1:5 nS Ne 12:30
oS Ge 8:20
pJob 8:4
q1Ki 21:10,13;
Ps 10:3; 74:10
1:6 rS 1Ki 22:19;
fn Ge 6:2
sS 2Sa 24:1;
S 2Ch 18:21;
S Ps 109:6;
Lk 22:31 tJob 2:1
1:7 uS Ge 3:1;
1Pe 5:8
1:8 vS Jos 1:7

wPs 25:12;
112:1; 128:4
xS ver 1;
S Ex 20:20
1:9 y1Ti 6:5
1:10
zS 1Sa 25:16 aver
12; Job 2:4;
Ps 34:7 bver 3;
Job 8:7; 29:6;
42:12,17
1:11 cJob 19:21;
Lk 22:31
dLev 24:11;
Job 2:5; Isa 3:8;

65:3; Rev 12:9-10 1:12 eS ver 10 fJob 2:6; 1Co 10:13 1:13 gS ver 2 hS ver 4 1:14 iGe 36:24 1:15 jS Ge 10:7; S Job 9:24

a6 Hebrew the sons of God   b6 Satan means accuser.

1:1 land of Uz. A large territory east of the Jordan (see v. 3), which included Edom in the south (see Ge 36:28; La 4:21) and the Aramean lands in the north (see Ge 10:23; 22:21). blameless and upright. Spiritually and morally upright. This does not mean that Job was sinless. He later defends his moral integrity but also admits he is a sinner (see 6:24; 7:21). feared God. See 28:28; Pr 3:7; see also note on Ge 20:11.
1:2 seven sons. An ideal number, signifying completeness (see note on Ru 4:15).
1:3 seven thousand sheep. See note on 42:12. Job's enormous wealth was in livestock, not land (see Ge 12:16; 13:2; 26:14). donkeys. The Hebrew for this word is feminine in form. Donkeys that produced offspring were very valuable. people of the East. The Hebrew for this phrase is translated "eastern peoples" in Ge 29:1; Jdg 6:3 (see note there).
1:5 period of feasting. On special occasions, feasts might last a week (see Ge 29:27; Jdg 14:12). he would sacrifice. Before the ceremonial laws of Moses were introduced, the father of the household acted as priest (see Ge 15:9-10). purified. Made ceremonially clean in preparation for the sacrifices he offered for them (see Ex 19:10,14, where the Hebrew for this verb is translated "consecrate").
1:6 angels came to present themselves. See NIV text note here and on 2:1; 38:7. They came as members of the heavenly council who stand in the presence of God (see 1Ki 22:19; Ps 89:5-7; Jer 23:18,22). Satan. Lit. "the accuser" (see NIV text note; see also Rev 12:10). In Job the Hebrew for this word is always preceded by the definite article. In the Hebrew of 1Ch 21:1 the article is not used, because by then "Satan" had become a proper name.

1:7 The LORD. The Israelite covenant name for God (see Introduction: Author).
1:8 Have you considered . . . Job? The Lord, not Satan, initiates the dialogue that leads to the testing of Job. He holds up Job as one against whom "the accuser" can lodge no accusation. my servant. See 42:7-8 and note; a designation for one who stands in a special relationship with God and is loyal in service (e.g., Moses, Nu 12:7; David, 2Sa 7:5; see Isa 42:1; 52:13; 53:11).
1:9 "The accuser" boldly accuses the man God commends: He says Job's righteousness, in which God delights, is self-serving—the heart of Satan's attack on God and his faithful servant in the book of Job.
1:10 hedge. Symbolizes protection (see Isa 5:5; contrast Job 3:23).
1:11 stretch out your hand and strike. See 4:5.
1:12 Satan, the accuser, is given power to afflict (v. 12a) but is kept on a leash (v. 12b). In all his evil among men (vv. 15,17) or in nature (vv. 16,19), Satan is under God's power (compare 1Ch 21:1 with 2Sa 24:1; see 1Sa 16:14; 2Sa 24:16; 1Co 5:5; 2Co 12:7; Heb 2:14). The contest, however, is not a sham. Will Job curse God to his face? If Job does not, the accuser will be proven false and God's delight in Job vindicated.
1:15 Sabeans. Probably south Arabians from Sheba, whose descendants became wealthy traders in spices, gold and precious stones (see the account of the queen of Sheba in 1Ki 10:1-13; see also Ps 72:10,15; Isa 60:6; Jer 6:20; Eze 27:22; Joel 3:8). Job 6:19 calls the Sabeans "traveling merchants" and associates them with Tema (about 350 miles southeast of Jerusalem).

fell from the sky[k] and burned up the sheep and the servants,[l] and I am the only one who has escaped to tell you!"

[17]While he was still speaking, another messenger came and said, "The Chaldeans[m] formed three raiding parties and swept down on your camels and carried them off. They put the servants to the sword, and I am the only one who has escaped to tell you!"

[18]While he was still speaking, yet another messenger came and said, "Your sons and daughters[n] were feasting[o] and drinking wine at the oldest brother's house, [19]when suddenly a mighty wind[p] swept in from the desert and struck the four corners of the house. It collapsed on them and they are dead,[q] and I am the only one who has escaped to tell you![r]"

[20]At this, Job got up and tore his robe[s] and shaved his head.[t] Then he fell to the ground in worship[u] [21]and said:

"Naked I came from my mother's womb,
　and naked I will depart.[c][v]
The LORD gave and the LORD has taken away;[w]
　may the name of the LORD be praised."[x]

[22]In all this, Job did not sin by charging God with wrongdoing.[y]

Job's Second Test

2 On another day the angels[d][z] came to present themselves before the LORD, and Satan also came with them[a] to present himself before him. [2]And the LORD said to Satan, "Where have you come from?"

Satan answered the LORD, "From roaming through the earth and going back and forth in it."[b]

[3]Then the LORD said to Satan, "Have you considered my servant Job? There is no one on earth like him; he is blameless and upright, a man who fears God and shuns evil.[c] And he still maintains his integrity,[d] though you incited me against him to ruin him without any reason."[e]

[4]"Skin for skin!" Satan replied. "A man will give all he has[f] for his own life. [5]But stretch out your hand and strike his flesh and bones,[g] and he will surely curse you to your face."[h]

[6]The LORD said to Satan, "Very well, then, he is in your hands;[i] but you must spare his life."[j]

[7]So Satan went out from the presence of the LORD and afflicted Job with painful sores from the soles of his feet to the top of his head.[k] [8]Then Job took a piece of broken pottery and scraped himself with it as he sat among the ashes.[l]

[9]His wife said to him, "Are you still holding on to your integrity?[m] Curse God and die!"[n]

[10]He replied, "You are talking like a

1:16
[k]S 1Ki 18:38;
2Ki 1:12;
Job 20:26
[l]S Ge 18:17;
S Lev 10:2;
S Nu 11:1-3
1:17
[m]S Ge 11:28;
S Job 9:24
1:18 [n]S ver 2
[o]S ver 4
1:19 [p]Ps 11:6;
Isa 5:28; 21:1;
Jer 4:11; 13:24;
18:17; Eze 17:10;
Hos 13:15;
Mt 7:25
[q]Job 16:7;
19:13-15
[r]Eze 24:26
1:20
[s]S Ge 37:29;
S Mk 14:63
[t]Isa 3:24; 15:2;
22:12; Jer 7:29;
16:6; Eze 27:31;
29:18; Mic 1:16
[u]1Pe 5:6
1:21 [v]Ecc 5:15;
1Ti 6:7 [w]Ru 1:21;
1Sa 2:7
[x]S Jdg 10:15;
Job 2:10;
Ecc 7:14;
Jer 40:2;
S Eph 5:20;
1Th 5:18;
Jas 5:11
1:22 [y]Job 2:10;
Ps 39:1; Pr 10:19;
13:3; Isa 53:7;
Ro 9:20
2:1 [z]fn Ge 6:2
[a]S Job 1:6

2:2 [b]S Ge 3:1
2:3 [c]S Ex 20:20;
S Job 1:1
[d]Job 6:29; 13:18;
27:6; 31:6; 32:1;
40:8 [e]Job 9:17;
Ps 44:17
2:4 [f]S Job 1:10
2:5 [g]Job 16:8;
19:20; 33:21;
Ps 102:5; La 4:8
[h]S Ex 20:7;
S Job 1:11

2:6 [i]2Co 12:7 [j]S Job 1:12 2:7 [k]S Dt 28:35; S Job 16:16 2:8
[l]Ge 18:27; Est 4:3; Job 16:15; 19:9; 30:19; 42:6; Ps 7:5;
Isa 58:5; 61:3; Jer 6:26; La 3:29; Eze 26:16; Jnh 3:5-8,6;
Mt 11:21 2:9 [m]Job 6:29; 13:15; 27:5; 33:9; 35:2; 1Th 5:8
[n]S Ex 20:7; S 2Ki 6:33

[c]21 Or will return there　　[d]1 Hebrew the sons of God

1:16 *fire of God.* Lightning (see Nu 11:1; 1Ki 18:38; 2Ki 1:12).

1:17 *Chaldeans.* A people who were Bedouin until c. 1000 B.C., when they settled in southern Mesopotamia and later became the nucleus of Nebuchadnezzar's empire.

1:19 *mighty wind.* Tornado.

1:20 *At this, Job got up.* He is silent until his children are killed. *tore his robe and shaved his head.* In mourning (see notes on Ge 37:34; Isa 15:2).

1:21 *depart.* See NIV text note; see also Ge 2:7; 3:19 and note. *The LORD gave and the LORD has taken away.* Job's faith leads him to see the sovereign God's hand at work, and that gives him repose even in the face of calamity.

2:1-3 Except for the final sentence, this passage is almost identical to 1:6-8. He who accused Job of having a deceitful motive is now shown to have a deceitful motive himself: to discredit the Lord through Job.

2:3 *you incited me.* God cannot be stirred up to do things against his will. Though it is not always clear how, everything that happens is part of his divine purpose (see 38:2).

2:4 *Skin for skin!* No doubt a proverb—perhaps originally an expression of willingness to barter one animal skin for another of equal value.

2:5 *strike his flesh and bones.* See 1:11-12; cf. Ge 2:23; Lk 24:39.

2:6 *spare his life.* Satan is still limited by God. Should Job die, neither God nor Job could be vindicated.

2:7 The precise nature of Job's sickness is uncertain, but its symptoms were painful festering sores over the whole body (7:5), nightmares (7:14), scabs that peeled and became black (30:28,30), disfigurement and revolting appearance (2:12; 19:19), bad breath (19:17), excessive thinness (17:7; 19:20), fever (30:30) and pain day and night (30:17). *sores.* The Hebrew for this word is translated "boils" in Ex 9:9; Lev 13:18; 2Ki 20:7.

2:8 *ashes.* Symbolic of mourning (see 42:6; Est 4:3; cf. Jnh 3:6, which speaks of sitting in dust).

2:9 *Curse God.* The Hebrew for this expression here and in 1:5 employs a euphemism (lit. "Bless God"). Satan is using Job's wife to tempt Job as he used Eve to tempt Adam. *and die.* Since nothing but death is left for Job, his wife wants him to provoke God to administer the final stroke due to all who curse him (Lev 24:10-16).

2:10 *Shall we accept good from God, and not trouble?* A key theme of the book: Trouble and suffering are not merely punishment for sin; for God's people they may serve as a trial (as here) or as a discipline that culminates in spiritual gain (see 5:17; Dt 8:5; 2Sa 7:14; Ps 94:12; Pr 3:11-12; 1Co 11:32; Heb 12:5-11).

foolish^e woman. Shall we accept good from God, and not trouble?"^o

In all this, Job did not sin in what he said.^p

Job's Three Friends

¹¹When Job's three friends, Eliphaz the Temanite,^q Bildad the Shuhite^r and Zophar the Naamathite,^s heard about all the troubles that had come upon him, they set out from their homes and met together by agreement to go and sympathize with him and comfort him.^t ¹²When they saw him from a distance, they could hardly recognize him;^u they began to weep aloud,^v and they tore their robes^w and sprinkled dust on their heads.^x ¹³Then they sat on the ground^y with him for seven days and seven nights.^z No one said a word to him,^a because they saw how great his suffering was.

Job Speaks

3 After this, Job opened his mouth and cursed the day of his birth.^b ²He said:

³"May the day of my birth perish,
  and the night it was said, 'A boy is
    born!'^c
⁴That day—may it turn to darkness;
  may God above not care about it;
  may no light shine upon it.
⁵May darkness and deep shadow^{f d}
    claim it once more;
  may a cloud settle over it;
  may blackness overwhelm its light.
⁶That night—may thick darkness^e seize
    it;
  may it not be included among the
    days of the year
  nor be entered in any of the months.
⁷May that night be barren;
  may no shout of joy^f be heard in it.

2:10 ^oS Job 1:21; S Ecc 2:24; La 3:38 ^pS Job 1:22; S 6:24; Jas 1:12; 5:11
2:11 ^qS Ge 36:11 ^rS Ge 25:2 ^sJob 11:1; 20:1 ^tS Ge 37:35; S Job 6:10; Jn 11:19
2:12 ^uJob 17:7; Isa 52:14 ^vS 2Sa 15:23 ^wS Ge 37:29; S Mk 14:63 ^xS Jos 7:6; S 2Sa 1:2
2:13 ^yIsa 3:26; 47:1; Jer 48:18; La 2:10; Eze 26:16; Jnh 3:6; Hag 2:22 ^zS Ge 50:10 ^aPr 17:28; Isa 23:2; 47:5
3:1 ^bJer 15:10; 20:14
3:3 ^cver 11,16; Job 10:18-19; Ecc 4:2; 6:3; Jer 20:14-18; Mt 26:24
3:5 ^dJob 10:21, 22; 34:22; 38:17; Ps 23:4; 44:19; 88:12; Jer 2:6; 13:16
3:6 ^eJob 23:17; 30:26
3:7 ^fPs 20:5; 33:3; 65:13; Isa 26:19; Jer 51:48
3:8 ^gJob 10:18; Jer 20:14 ^hS Ge 1:21; Job 41:1,8,10,25; Ps 74:14; 104:26
3:9 ⁱJob 41:18; Hab 3:4
3:11 ^jS ver 3
3:12 ^kS Ge 48:12; Isa 66:12
3:13 ^lJob 17:13; 30:23 ^mver 17; Job 7:8-10,21; 10:22; 13:19; 14:10-12; 19:27; 21:13,23; 27:19; Ps 139:11; Isa 8:22
3:14 ⁿJob 9:24; 12:17; Isa 14:9; Eze 32:28-32

⁸May those who curse days^g curse that
    day,^g
  those who are ready to rouse
    Leviathan.^h
⁹May its morning stars become dark;
  may it wait for daylight in vain
  and not see the first rays of dawn,ⁱ
¹⁰for it did not shut the doors of the
    womb on me
  to hide trouble from my eyes.

¹¹"Why did I not perish at birth,
  and die as I came from the womb?^j
¹²Why were there knees to receive me^k
  and breasts that I might be nursed?
¹³For now I would be lying down^l in
    peace;
  I would be asleep and at rest^m
¹⁴with kings and counselors of the earth,ⁿ
  who built for themselves places now
    lying in ruins,^o
¹⁵with rulers^p who had gold,
  who filled their houses with silver.^q
¹⁶Or why was I not hidden in the ground
    like a stillborn child,^r
  like an infant who never saw the
    light of day?^s
¹⁷There the wicked cease from turmoil,^t
  and there the weary are at rest.^u
¹⁸Captives^v also enjoy their ease;
  they no longer hear the slave
    driver's^w shout.^x
¹⁹The small and the great are there,^y
  and the slave is freed from his
    master.

---

^oJob 15:28; Jer 51:37; Na 3:7 **3:15** ^pJob 12:21; Isa 45:1 ^qJob 15:29; 20:10; 27:17; Ps 49:16-17; Pr 13:22; 28:8; Ecc 2:26; Isa 2:7; Zep 1:11 **3:16** ^rPs 58:8; Ecc 4:3; 6:3 ^sS ver 3; Ps 71:6 **3:17** ^tver 26; Job 30:26; Ecc 4:2; Isa 14:3 ^uS ver 13 **3:18** ^vIsa 51:14 ^wS Ge 15:13 ^xJob 39:7 **3:19** ^yJob 9:22; 17:16; 21:33; 24:24; 30:23; Ecc 12:5

e 10 The Hebrew word rendered *foolish* denotes moral deficiency.   *f* 5 Or *and the shadow of death*   **g** 8 Or *the sea*

2:11 *three friends.* Older than Job (see 15:10). *Eliphaz.* An Edomite name (see Ge 36:11). *Temanite.* Teman was a village in Edom, south of the Dead Sea (see Ge 36:11; Jer 49:7; Eze 25:13; Am 1:12; Ob 9). *Shuhite.* Bildad may have been a descendant of Shuah, the youngest son of Abraham and Keturah (Ge 25:2). *Naamathite.* Apart from 11:1; 20:1; 42:9, this word does not occur elsewhere in the Bible. **2:12** *could hardly recognize him.* Cf. Isa 52:14; 53:3. *tore their robes and sprinkled dust on their heads.* Visible signs of mourning (see note on 1:20). **2:13** *sat on the ground with him.* See Eze 3:15; a commendable expression of sympathy. *seven.* See Ge 50:10; 1Sa 31:13; the number of completeness (see 1:2; see also note on Ru 4:15). *No one said a word to him.* Their mere presence was of more comfort to him than their words of advice would prove to be (see 16:2-3). **3:3** *May the day of my birth perish.* Job's very existence, which has been a joy to him because of God's favor, is now his intolerable burden. He is as close as he will ever come to

cursing God, but he does not do it. **3:4** *may it turn to darkness.* God had said in Ge 1:3, "Let there be light." Job, using similar language, would negate God's creative act. **3:8** *those who curse days.* Eastern soothsayers, like Balaam (see Nu 22-24), who pronounced curses on people, objects and days. *Leviathan.* Using vivid, figurative language, Job wishes that "those who curse days" would arouse the sea monster Leviathan (see note on Isa 27:1) to swallow the day-night of his birth. **3:11-12,16,20-23** A series of rhetorical questions. **3:16** Since in fact his birth had taken place, the next possibility would have been a stillbirth. He would then have lived only in the grave (or Sheol), which he envisions as a place of peace and rest (vv. 13-19; see note on Ge 37:35). Such a situation would be much better than his present intolerable condition, in which he can find neither peace nor rest (v. 26). **3:18** *slave driver's shout.* As in Egypt (see Ex 5:13-14).

20"Why is light given to those in misery,
  and life to the bitter of soul, *z*
21to those who long for death that does
  not come, *a*
  who search for it more than for
  hidden treasure, *b*
22who are filled with gladness
  and rejoice when they reach the
  grave? *c*
23Why is life given to a man
  whose way is hidden, *d*
  whom God has hedged in? *e*
24For sighing *f* comes to me instead of
  food; *g*
  my groans *h* pour out like water. *i*
25What I feared has come upon me;
  what I dreaded *j* has happened to
  me. *k*
26I have no peace, *l* no quietness;
  I have no rest, *m* but only turmoil." *n*

Eliphaz

4 Then Eliphaz the Temanite *o* replied:

2"If someone ventures a word with
  you, will you be impatient?
  But who can keep from speaking? *p*
3Think how you have instructed many, *q*
  how you have strengthened feeble
  hands. *r*
4Your words have supported those who
  stumbled; *s*
  you have strengthened faltering
  knees. *t*
5But now trouble comes to you, and you
  are discouraged; *u*
  it strikes *v* you, and you are
  dismayed. *w*
6Should not your piety be your
  confidence *x*

and your blameless *y* ways your
  hope?

7"Consider now: Who, being innocent,
  has ever perished? *z*
  Where were the upright ever
  destroyed? *a*
8As I have observed, *b* those who plow
  evil *c*
  and those who sow trouble reap it. *d*
9At the breath of God *e* they are
  destroyed;
  at the blast of his anger they perish. *f*
10The lions may roar *g* and growl,
  yet the teeth of the great lions *h* are
  broken. *i*
11The lion perishes for lack of prey, *j*
  and the cubs of the lioness are
  scattered. *k*

12"A word *l* was secretly brought to me,
  my ears caught a whisper *m* of it. *n*
13Amid disquieting dreams in the night,
  when deep sleep falls on men, *o*
14fear and trembling *p* seized me
  and made all my bones shake. *q*
15A spirit glided past my face,
  and the hair on my body stood on
  end. *r*
16It stopped,
  but I could not tell what it was.
  A form stood before my eyes,
  and I heard a hushed voice: *s*
17"Can a mortal be more righteous than
  God? *t*

3:20 *z*S 1Sa 1:10;
Eze 27:30-31
3:21 *a*Rev 9:6
*b*Ps 119:127;
Pr 2:4
3:22 *c*Job 7:16;
Ecc 4:3; Jer 8:3
3:23 *d*Pr 4:19;
Isa 59:10;
Jer 13:16; 23:12
*e*Job 6:4; 16:13;
19:12; Ps 88:8;
La 2:4; 3:7;
Hos 2:6
3:24 *f*Ps 5:1;
38:9; Isa 35:10
*g*Job 6:7; 33:20;
Ps 107:18
*h*Ps 22:1; 32:3;
38:8 *i*Isa 1:15;
Job 30:16; Ps 6:6;
22:14; 42:3,4;
80:5; Isa 53:12;
La 2:12
3:25 *j*Job 7:9;
9:28; 30:15;
Hos 13:3
*k*S Ge 42:36
3:26 *l*Isa 48:22;
Jn 14:27
*m*Job 7:4,14;
Ps 6:6; Da 4:5;
Mt 11:28 *n*S ver
17; S Job 10:18;
S 19:8
4:1 *o*S Ge 36:11;
Job 15:1; 22:1
4:2 *p*Job 32:20;
Jer 4:19; 20:9
4:3 *q*Dt 32:2;
Job 29:23;
Hos 6:3
*r*Job 26:2;
Ps 71:9; Isa 13:7;
35:3; Zep 3:16;
Heb 12:12
4:4 *s*Job 16:5;
29:16,25;
Isa 1:17
*t*Job 29:11,15;
Isa 35:3; Jer 31:8;
Heb 12:12
4:5 *u*S Jos 1:9
*v*Ru 1:13;
Job 1:11; 19:21;
30:21; Ps 38:2;
Isa 53:4
*w*Job 6:14;
Pr 24:10
4:6 *x*2Ki 18:19;
Ps 27:3; 71:5;
Pr 3:26 *y*S Ge 6:9

4:7 *z*Job 5:11;
36:7; Ps 41:12;
2Pe 2:9
*a*Job 8:20;
Ps 37:25;

91:9-10; Pr 12:21; 19:23 **4:8** *b*Job 5:3; 15:17 *c*Jdg 14:18;
Job 5:6; 15:35; Ps 7:14; Isa 59:4 *d*Ps 7:15; 9:15; Pr 11:18;
22:8; Isa 17:11; Hos 8:7; 10:13; Gal 6:7-8 **4:9** *e*S Ex 15:10;
S Job 41:21; 2Th 2:8 *f*S Lev 26:38; Job 40:13; Isa 25:7 **4:10**
*g*Ps 22:13 *h*Ps 17:12; 22:21; Pr 28:15 *i*Job 5:15; 29:17;
36:6; 38:15; Ps 35:10; 58:6 **4:11** *j*Dt 28:41; Job 27:14;
29:17; Ps 34:10; 58:6; Pr 30:14 *k*Job 5:4 **4:12** *l*ver 17-21;
Job 32:13; Jer 9:23 *m*Job 26:14 *n*Job 33:14 **4:13** *o*Job 33:15
4:14 *p*Job 21:6; Ps 48:6; 55:5; 119:120,161; Jer 5:22;
Hab 3:16; S 2Co 7:15 *q*Jer 23:9; Da 10:8; Hab 3:16 **4:15**
*r*Da 5:6; 7:15,28; 10:8; Mt 14:26 **4:16** *s*S 1Ki 19:12 **4:17**
*t*Job 9:2; 13:18; Ps 143:2

3:21–22 Death has become desirable for Job.
3:23 *whom God has hedged in.* God, who had put a hedge
of protection around him (see 1:10 and note), has now, he
feels, hemmed him in with turmoil (see v. 26).
4:1 *Eliphaz the Temanite.* See note on 2:11. Teman was an
Edomite town noted for wisdom (see Jer 49:7). The speeches
of Job's three friends contain elements of truth, but they
must be carefully interpreted in context. The problem is not
so much with what the friends knew but with what they did
not know: God's high purpose in allowing Satan to buffet
Job.
4:2 *ventures a word.* Eliphaz seems to be genuinely concerned with Job's well-being and offers a complimentary
word (vv. 3–4). *impatient.* See note on 9:2–3.
4:5 *strikes you.* See 1:11; 2:5; 19:21.
4:6–7 Eliphaz counsels Job to be confident that his piety
will count with God, that though God is now chastening him
for some sin, it is to a good end (see v. 17; 5:17), and he can
be assured that God will not destroy him along with the

wicked.
4:6 *piety.* Lit. "fear (of God)" (see note on 1:1). The word
is used only by Eliphaz (see 15:4; 22:4).
4:7–9 If Job is truly innocent, he will not be destroyed.
4:8–11 Just as the strongest lions eventually die (vv.
10–11), so the wicked are eventually destroyed (vv. 8–9).
4:9 *blast of his anger.* See Ex 15:7–8. God's judgment is
fearfully severe.
4:12–21 Eliphaz tells of a hair-raising (see v. 15), mystical
experience mediated through a dream (see v. 13), through
which he claims to have received divine revelation and on
which he bases his advice to Job.
4:13 *Amid . . . dreams . . . when deep sleep falls on men.*
Eliphaz's words are echoed by Elihu in 33:15.
4:14 *all my bones shake.* A sign of great distress (see Jer
23:9; Hab 3:16).
4:17–21 All mortals are sinful; therefore God has a right to
punish them. Job should be thankful for the correction God is
giving him (see 5:17).

Can a man be more pure than his
  Maker? [u]
[18]If God places no trust in his servants, [v]
  if he charges his angels with error, [w]
[19]how much more those who live in
  houses of clay, [x]
  whose foundations [y] are in the dust, [z]
  who are crushed [a] more readily than
  a moth! [b]
[20]Between dawn and dusk they are
  broken to pieces;
  unnoticed, they perish forever. [c]
[21]Are not the cords of their tent pulled
  up, [d]
  so that they die [e] without
  wisdom?' [h] [f]

5 "Call if you will, but who will answer
  you? [g]
  To which of the holy ones [h] will you
  turn?
[2]Resentment [i] kills a fool,
  and envy slays the simple. [j]
[3]I myself have seen [k] a fool taking root, [l]
  but suddenly [m] his house was
  cursed. [n]
[4]His children [o] are far from safety, [p]
  crushed in court [q] without a
  defender. [r]
[5]The hungry consume his harvest, [s]
  taking it even from among thorns,
  and the thirsty pant after his wealth.
[6]For hardship does not spring from the
  soil,
  nor does trouble sprout from the
  ground. [t]
[7]Yet man is born to trouble [u]
  as surely as sparks fly upward.

[8]"But if it were I, I would appeal to
  God;
  I would lay my cause before him. [v]

[9]He performs wonders [w] that cannot be
  fathomed, [x]
  miracles that cannot be counted. [y]
[10]He bestows rain on the earth; [z]
  he sends water upon the
  countryside. [a]
[11]The lowly he sets on high, [b]
  and those who mourn [c] are lifted [d] to
  safety.
[12]He thwarts the plans [e] of the crafty,
  so that their hands achieve no
  success. [f]
[13]He catches the wise [g] in their
  craftiness, [h]
  and the schemes of the wily are
  swept away. [i]
[14]Darkness [j] comes upon them in the
  daytime;
  at noon they grope as in the night. [k]
[15]He saves the needy [l] from the sword in
  their mouth;
  he saves them from the clutches of
  the powerful. [m]
[16]So the poor [n] have hope,
  and injustice shuts its mouth. [o]

[17]"Blessed is the man whom God
  corrects; [p]

4:17 [u]Job 8:3;
10:3; 14:4;
15:14; 21:14;
25:4; 31:15;
32:22; 35:10;
36:3,13; 37:23;
40:19; Ps 18:26;
51:5; 119:73;
Pr 20:9; Ecc 7:20;
Isa 51:13;
Mal 2:10;
Ac 17:24
4:18 [v]Heb 1:14
[w]Job 15:15;
21:22; 25:5
4:19 [x]Job 10:9;
33:6; Isa 64:8;
Ro 9:21; 2Co 4:7;
5:1 [y]Job 22:16
[z]S Ge 2:7
[a]Job 5:4
[b]Job 7:17; 15:16;
17:14; 25:6;
Ps 22:6; Isa 41:14
4:20 [c]Job 14:2,
20; 15:33; 20:7;
24:24; Ps 89:47;
90:5-6; Jas 4:14
4:21 [d]Job 8:22;
Isa 38:12 [e]Jn 8:24
[f]Job 18:21;
36:12; Pr 5:23;
Jer 9:3
5:1 [g]Hab 1:2
[h]Job 15:15;
Ps 89:5,7
5:2 [i]Job 21:15;
36:13 [j]Pr 12:16;
Gal 5:26
5:3 [k]S Job 4:8
[l]Ps 37:35;
Isa 40:24;
Jer 12:2; Eze 17:6
[m]Pr 6:15
[n]Job 24:18;
Ps 37:22,35-36;
109:9-10; Pr 3:33
5:4 [o]Job 20:10;
27:14 [p]S Job 4:11
[q]Job 4:19;
Am 5:12
[r]Ps 109:12;
Isa 9:17; 1Jn 2:1
5:5 [s]Lev 26:16;
S Jdg 2:15;
Job 20:18; 31:8;
Mic 6:15
5:6 [t]S Job 4:8
5:7 [u]S Ge 3:17;
Job 10:17; 15:35;
Ps 51:5; 58:3;
90:10; Pr 22:8
5:8 [v]Job 8:5;
11:13; 13:3,15;
23:4; 40:1;

Ps 35:23; 50:15; Jer 12:1; 1Co 4:4 **5:9** [w]Ps 78:4; 111:2
[x]Dt 29:29; Job 9:4,10; 11:7; 25:2; 26:14; 33:12; 36:5,22,
26; 37:5,14,16,23; 42:3; Ps 40:5; 71:17; 72:18; 86:10;
131:1; 139:6,17; 145:3; Isa 40:28; Ro 11:33 [y]Ps 71:15 **5:10**
[z]Mt 5:45 [a]S Lev 26:4; Job 36:28; 37:6,13; 38:28,34;
Ps 135:7; Jer 14:22 **5:11** [b]S 1Sa 2:7-8; S Job 4:7; Ps 75:7;
113:7-8 [c]Isa 61:2; Mt 5:4; Ro 12:15 [d]S Mt 23:12; Jas 4:10
5:12 [e]Ne 4:15; Ps 33:10; Isa 8:10; 19:3; Jer 19:7 [f]Job 12:23;
Ps 78:59; 140:8 **5:13** [g]Job 37:24; Isa 29:14; 44:25; Jer 8:8;
18:18; 51:57 [h]Job 15:5; Ps 36:3; Lk 20:23; 1Co 3:19*;
2Co 11:3; Eph 4:14 [i]Job 9:4; 18:7; Pr 21:30; 29:6; Jer 8:9
5:14 [j]Job 15:22,30; 18:6,18; 20:26; 22:11; 27:20; Isa 8:22;
Jn 12:35 [k]S Dt 28:29; S Job 18:5; Am 8:9 **5:15** [l]S Ex 22:23;
Job 8:6; 22:27; 33:26; 36:15 [m]S Job 4:10; S 31:22 **5:16**
[n]Job 20:19; 31:16; Pr 17:5; 22:22; Isa 11:4; 41:17; 61:1.
[o]Ps 63:11; 107:42; Ro 3:19 **5:17** [p]Dt 8:5; Job 33:19; 36:10;
Zep 3:7; Jas 1:12

[h]21 Some interpreters end the quotation after verse 17.

4:18–19 If the angels, who are not made of dust, can be
guilty in God's sight, how much more man (see 15:15–16)!
4:18 *servants.* Angels.
4:19 *houses of clay.* Bodies made of dust (see 10:9; 33:6;
see also note on Ge 2:7). *moth.* A symbol of fragility (cf.
27:18).
4:20 *Between dawn and dusk.* A vivid picture of the
shortness of life.
4:21 *tent.* A temporary home, like the human body (see
2Co 5:1,4; 2Pe 1:13). *without wisdom.* Needlessly and
senselessly (see v. 20).
5:1 *To which . . . will you turn?* To plead your case with
God. The idea of a mediator, someone to arbitrate between
God and Job, is an important motif in the book (see 9:33;
16:19–20; see also NIV text note on 19:25). *holy ones.* Holy
angels, the "sons of God" in the prologue (see NIV text notes
on 1:6; 2:1).
5:2 Without mentioning him, Eliphaz implies that Job is
resentful against God and that harm will follow. *fool.* One
who pays no attention to God (see NIV text notes on 2:10; Pr
1:7).

5:3 *A fool taking root.* A wicked man prospering like a tree
taking root (see Ps 1:3).
5:6 Unlike a weed, trouble must be sown and cultivated.
5:7 *man is born to trouble.* See 14:1; proof that no one is
righteous in the eyes of God (see 4:17–19). Job should stop
behaving like a fool (see vv. 1–7) and should humble himself.
Then God would bless, and injustice would shut its mouth
(see v. 16). *sparks.* Lit. "sons of Resheph." In Canaanite
mythology, Resheph was a god of plague and destruction.
"(Sons of) Resheph" is used as a poetic image in the OT for
fire (SS 8:6), bolts of lightning (Ps 78:48) and pestilence (Dt
32:24; Hab 3:5).
5:9 Repeated in 9:10.
5:13 Quoted in part in 1Co 3:19 (the only clear quotation
of Job in the NT).
5:17–26 While the preceding hymn (vv. 8–16) spoke of
God's goodness and justice, this poem celebrates the blessedness of the man whom God disciplines (see Pr 1:2,7; 3:12;
23:13,23). Eliphaz believed that discipline is temporary and
is followed by healing (v. 18), and that the good man will
always be rescued. But with Job's wealth gone and his

so do not despise the discipline *q* of the Almighty. *i r*

18For he wounds, but he also binds up; *s* he injures, but his hands also heal. *t*

19From six calamities he will rescue *u* you;
in seven no harm will befall you. *v*

20In famine *w* he will ransom you from death,
and in battle from the stroke of the sword. *x*

21You will be protected from the lash of the tongue, *y*
and need not fear *z* when destruction comes. *a*

22You will laugh *b* at destruction and famine, *c*
and need not fear the beasts of the earth. *d*

23For you will have a covenant *e* with the stones *f* of the field,
and the wild animals will be at peace with you. *g*

24You will know that your tent is secure; *h*
you will take stock of your property and find nothing missing. *i*

25You will know that your children will be many, *j*
and your descendants like the grass of the earth. *k*

26You will come to the grave in full vigor, *l*
like sheaves gathered in season. *m*

27"We have examined this, and it is true. So hear it *n* and apply it to yourself." *o*

Job

6 Then Job replied:

2"If only my anguish could be weighed

and all my misery be placed on the scales! *p*

3It would surely outweigh the sand *q* of the seas—
no wonder my words have been impetuous. *r*

4The arrows *s* of the Almighty *t* are in me, *u*
my spirit drinks *v* in their poison; *w*
God's terrors *x* are marshaled against me. *y*

5Does a wild donkey *z* bray *a* when it has grass,
or an ox bellow when it has fodder? *b*

6Is tasteless food eaten without salt,
or is there flavor in the white of an egg *j* ? *c*

7I refuse to touch it;
such food makes me ill. *d*

8"Oh, that I might have my request,
that God would grant what I hope for, *e*

9that God would be willing to crush *f* me,
to let loose his hand and cut me off! *g*

10Then I would still have this consolation *h*—
my joy in unrelenting pain *i* —
that I had not denied the words *j* of the Holy One. *k*

11"What strength do I have, that I should still hope?
What prospects, that I should be patient? *l*

5:17 *q*Ps 94:12; Pr 3:11; Jer 31:18 *r*S Ge 17:1; S Job 15:11; Heb 12:5-11
5:18 *s*Ps 147:3; Isa 57:15; 61:1; Hos 6:1 *t*S Dt 32:39
5:19 *u*Da 3:17; 6:16 *v*Ps 34:19; 91:10; Pr 3:25-26; 24:15-16
5:20 *w*ver 22; Ps 33:19; 37:19 *x*Ps 22:20; 91:7; 140:7; 144:10; Jer 39:18
5:21 *y*Ps 12:2-4; 31:20 *z*Ps 23:4; 27:1; 91:5 *a*ver 15
5:22 *b*Job 8:21; 39:7,18,22; 41:29 *c*S ver 20 *d*S Lev 25:18; Ps 91:13; Hos 2:18; Mk 1:13
5:23 *e*Isa 28:15; Hos 2:18 *f*2Ki 3:19,25; Ps 91:12; Mt 13:8 *g*Job 40:20; Isa 11:6-9; 65:25; Eze 34:25
5:24 *h*Job 12:6; 21:9 *i*Job 8:6; 22:23
5:25 *j*Dt 28:4; Ps 112:2 *k*Ps 72:16; Isa 44:3-4; 48:19
5:26 *l*S Ge 15:15; S Dt 11:21; S Ecc 8:13 *m*Pr 3:21-26
5:27 *n*Job 32:10, 17 *o*Job 8:5; 11:13; 22:27

6:2 *p*Job 31:6; Pr 11:1; Da 5:27
6:3 *q*1Ki 4:29; Pr 27:3 *r*ver 11, 26; Job 7:11; 16:6; 21:4; 23:2
6:4 *s*S Dt 32:23; Ps 38:2 *t*S Ge 17:1 *u*Job 7:20; 16:12, 13; 19:12; La 3:12 *v*Job 21:20 *w*S Dt 32:32; Job 30:21; 34:6; Jer 15:18; 30:12

*x*Job 9:34; 13:21; 18:11; 23:6; 27:20; 30:15; 33:16 *y*S Job 3:23; Ps 88:15-18 **6:5** *z*S Ge 16:12 *a*Job 30:7 *b*Job 24:6; Isa 30:24 **6:6** *c*Job 33:20; Ps 107:18 **6:7** *d*S Job 3:24 **6:8** *e*Job 14:13 **6:9** *f*Job 19:2 *g*S Nu 11:15; S Ps 31:22 **6:10** *h*S Job 2:11; 15:11; Ps 94:19 *i*Ps 38:17; Jer 4:19; 45:3 *j*Job 22:22; 23:12; Ps 119:102; Mk 8:38 *k*S Lev 11:44; S 2Ki 19:22; S Isa 31:1 **6:11** *l*S ver 3

i 17 Hebrew *Shaddai;* here and throughout Job   *j6* The meaning of the Hebrew for this phrase is uncertain.

---

children dead, these words about security (v. 24) and children (v. 25) must have seemed cruel indeed to him.
5:17 *Almighty.* The first of 31 times that the Hebrew word *Shaddai* is used in Job (see note on Ge 17:1).
5:18–19 See Hos 6:1-2.
5:19 *six . . . seven.* See 33:29; 40:5; Pr 6:16; 30:15,18, 21,29; Ecc 11:2; Am 1:3,6,9,11,13; 2:1,4,6; Mic 5:5. Normally, such number patterns are not to be taken literally but are a poetic way of saying "many."
5:23 *covenant with the stones.* A figurative way of saying that stones will "be at peace with you" and will not ruin the crops (see 2Ki 3:19; Isa 5:2; Mt 13:5).
5:25 *like the grass.* As numerous as blades of grass (see note on Ge 13:16).
5:26 Eliphaz's prediction was more accurate than he realized (see 42:16–17).
5:27 *apply it to yourself.* Eliphaz's conclusion: Job must turn from unrighteousness (4:7) and resentment against God (v. 2) to humility (v. 11) and the acceptance of God's right-

eous discipline (v. 17). Eliphaz's purpose is to offer theological comfort and counsel to Job (2:11), but instead he wounds him with false accusation.
6:2–3 Job appeals for a sympathetic understanding of the harsh words he spoke in ch. 3.
6:4 *arrows of the Almighty.* Job shares Eliphaz's "orthodox" theology and believes that God is aiming his arrows of judgment at him—though he does not know why (see 7:20; 16:12–13; see also La 3:12; cf. Dt 32:23; Ps 7:13; 38:2).
6:5–6 Job claims the right to bray and bellow, since he has been wounded by God and offered tasteless food (words) by his friends.
6:8–9 Job repeats the thoughts of ch. 3.
6:10 *Then.* In the afterlife, Job would have the joy of knowing that he had remained true to God.
6:11–13 With no human resources left, Job considers his condition hopeless.
6:11 *patient.* See note on 9:2–3.

12Do I have the strength of stone?
Is my flesh bronze?[m]
13Do I have any power to help myself,[n]
now that success has been driven
from me?

14"A despairing man[o] should have the
devotion[p] of his friends,[q]
even though he forsakes the fear of
the Almighty.[r]
15But my brothers are as undependable as
intermittent streams,[s]
as the streams that overflow
16when darkened by thawing ice
and swollen with melting snow,[t]
17but that cease to flow in the dry season,
and in the heat[u] vanish from their
channels.
18Caravans turn aside from their routes;
they go up into the wasteland and
perish.
19The caravans of Tema[v] look for water,
the traveling merchants of Sheba[w]
look in hope.
20They are distressed, because they had
been confident;
they arrive there, only to be
disappointed.[x]
21Now you too have proved to be of no
help;
you see something dreadful and are
afraid.[y]
22Have I ever said, 'Give something on
my behalf,
pay a ransom[z] for me from your
wealth,[a]
23deliver me from the hand of the enemy,
ransom me from the clutches of the
ruthless'?[b]

24"Teach me, and I will be quiet;[c]
show me where I have been wrong.[d]
25How painful are honest words![e]
But what do your arguments prove?
26Do you mean to correct what I say,
and treat the words of a despairing
man as wind?[f]
27You would even cast lots[g] for the
fatherless[h]
and barter away your friend.

28"But now be so kind as to look at me.
Would I lie to your face?[i]
29Relent, do not be unjust;[j]
reconsider, for my integrity[k] is at
stake.[k] [l]
30Is there any wickedness on my lips?[m]
Can my mouth not discern[n] malice?

7 "Does not man have hard service[o]
on earth?[p]
Are not his days like those of a hired
man?[q]
2Like a slave longing for the evening
shadows,[r]
or a hired man waiting eagerly for his
wages,[s]
3so I have been allotted months of
futility,
and nights of misery have been
assigned to me.[t]
4When I lie down I think, 'How long
before I get up?'[u]
The night drags on, and I toss till
dawn.[v]
5My body is clothed with worms[w] and
scabs,
my skin is broken and festering.[x]

6"My days are swifter than a weaver's
shuttle,[y]
and they come to an end without
hope.[z]
7Remember, O God, that my life is but a
breath;[a]
my eyes will never see happiness
again.[b]
8The eye that now sees me will see me
no longer;
you will look for me, but I will be no
more.[c]
9As a cloud vanishes[d] and is gone,

6:12 [m]Job 26:2 **6:13** [n]Job 26:2 **6:14** [o]S Job 4:5 [p]1Sa 20:42; Job 15:4 [q]Job 12:4; 17:2, 6; 19:19,21; 21:3; 30:1,10; Ps 38:11; 69:20; 1Jn 3:17 [r]S Ge 17:1 **6:15** [s]Job 13:4; 16:2; 21:34; Ps 22:1; 38:11; Jer 15:18 **6:16** [t]Ps 147:18 **6:17** [u]Job 24:19 **6:19** [v]S Ge 25:15 [w]S Ge 10:7,28 **6:20** [x]Jer 14:3; Joel 1:11 **6:21** [y]Ps 38:11 **6:22** [z]S Nu 35:31; Job 33:24; Ps 49:7 [a]Jer 15:10 **6:23** [b]S 2Ki 19:19 **6:24** [c]S Job 2:10; 33:33; Ps 39:1; 141:3; Pr 10:19; 11:12; 17:27; Ecc 5:2 [d]Job 19:4 **6:25** [e]Ecc 12:11; Isa 22:23 **6:26** [f]S ver 3; S Ge 41:6; Job 8:2; 15:3; 16:3; Jer 5:13 **6:27** [g]Eze 24:6; Joel 3:3; Ob 1:11; Na 3:10 [h]S Ex 22:22,24; Job 31:17,21; Isa 10:2 **6:28** [i]Job 9:15; 24:25; 27:4; 32:10; 33:1,3; 34:6; 36:3,4 **6:29** [j]Job 19:6; 27:2; 40:8; Isa 40:27 [k]S Job 2:3 [l]Job 9:21; 10:7; 11:2; 12:4; 23:7, 10; 33:9,32; 34:5,36; 35:2; 42:6; Ps 66:10; Zec 13:9 **6:30** [m]Job 27:4 [n]Job 12:11 **7:1** [o]Job 14:14; Isa 40:2 [p]S Job 5:7 [q]S Lev 25:50 **7:2** [r]Job 14:1; Ecc 2:23 [s]S Lev 19:13; S Job 14:6 **7:3** [t]Job 16:7; Ps 6:6; 42:3; 56:8; Ecc 4:1; Isa 16:9; Jer 9:1; La 1:2,16 **7:4** [u]Dt 28:67 [v]ver 13-14 **7:5** [w]Job 17:14; 21:26; 24:20; 25:6; Isa 14:11 [x]S Dt 28:35 **7:6** [y]Job 9:25; Ps 39:5; Isa 38:12 [z]Job 13:15; 14:19; 17:11,15; 19:10; Ps 37:4; 52:9 **7:7** [a]ver 16; Ge 27:46; Ps 39:4,5,11; 62:9; 78:39; 89:47; 144:4; Ecc 7:15; S Jas 4:14 [b]Job 10:20 **7:8** [c]S Job 3:13; 8:18; 15:29; 20:7,9,21; 27:17; Ps 37:36; 103:16; Isa 41:12; Jn 16:16; Ac 20:25 **7:9** [d]S Job 3:25

[k]29 Or *my righteousness still stands*

6:14–15 See Gal 6:1. Job needs spiritual help, but his friends are proving to be undependable.
6:15 *brothers.* By calling his friends his "brothers," Job makes their callousness stand out more sharply.
6:19 *Tema.* See note on Isa 21:14. *Sheba.* See note on 1:15.
6:22–23 Job has not asked them for anything except what will cost them nothing: their friendship and counsel.
6:25 *honest words.* Job is referring to his own words.
6:26 *wind.* See 8:2.
6:27 In addition to dishonesty, Job accuses his friends of heartless cruelty.
6:29 Job softens his tone, pleading that his friends take back their false accusations.
7:1–21 Having replied to Eliphaz, Job now addresses his complaint toward God.
7:1 *hard service.* See 14:14. The Hebrew for this expression sometimes implies military service. It is also used in reference to the Babylonian exile in Isa 40:2 (see note there).
7:2 *evening shadows.* End of the workday.
7:5 See note on 2:7.
7:7 *my life is but a breath.* As a chronic sufferer he has lost all sense of purpose in life (see v. 3; see also Ps 144:3–4). He does not anticipate healing and sees death as his only escape.
7:8 *you will look . . . no more.* See v. 21.
7:9 *he who goes down to the grave does not return.* Such

so he who goes down to the grave[l] [e]
  does not return.[f]

[10]He will never come to his house again;
  his place[g] will know him no more. [h]

[11]"Therefore I will not keep silent;[i]
  I will speak out in the anguish[j] of
    my spirit,
  I will complain[k] in the bitterness of
    my soul.[l]
[12]Am I the sea,[m] or the monster of the
    deep,[n]
  that you put me under guard?[o]
[13]When I think my bed will comfort me
  and my couch will ease my
    complaint,[p]
[14]even then you frighten me with dreams
  and terrify[q] me with visions,[r]
[15]so that I prefer strangling and death,[s]
  rather than this body of mine.[t]
[16]I despise my life;[u] I would not live
    forever.[v]
  Let me alone;[w] my days have no
    meaning.[x]

[17]"What is man that you make so much
    of him,
  that you give him so much
    attention,[y]
[18]that you examine him every morning[z]
  and test him[a] every moment?[b]
[19]Will you never look away from me,[c]
  or let me alone even for an instant?[d]
[20]If I have sinned, what have I done to
    you,[e]
  O watcher of men?
  Why have you made me your target?[f]
  Have I become a burden to you?[m][g]
[21]Why do you not pardon my offenses

and forgive my sins?[h]
For I will soon lie down in the dust;[i]
  you will search for me, but I will be
    no more."[j]

Bildad

8 Then Bildad the Shuhite[k] replied:

  [2]"How long will you say such
    things?[l]
  Your words are a blustering wind. [m]
[3]Does God pervert justice?[n]
  Does the Almighty pervert what is
    right?[o]
[4]When your children sinned against him,
  he gave them over to the penalty of
    their sin.[p]
[5]But if you will look to God
  and plead[q] with the Almighty,[r]
[6]if you are pure and upright,
  even now he will rouse himself on
    your behalf[s]
  and restore you to your rightful
    place.[t]
[7]Your beginnings will seem humble,
  so prosperous[u] will your future be.[v]

[8]"Ask the former generations[w]

7:9 [e]S Job 3:13; 11:8; 14:13; 17:16; 26:6; 38:17; Am 9:2 [f]2Sa 12:23
7:10 [g]Job 18:21; 21:18; 27:21,23; Ps 58:9; Jer 18:17; 19:8 [h]S ver 8; Ps 37:10; 104:35
7:11 [i]Job 9:35; 13:13; Ps 22:2; 40:9 /Job 10:1; Ps 6:3; Isa 38:15, 17 [k]ver 13; Job 9:27; 21:4; 23:2 /S 1Sa 1:10; S Job 6:3
7:12 [m]Job 38:8-11 [n]S Ge 1:21 [o]ver 20; Isa 1:14
7:13 [p]S ver 11
7:14 [q]Job 9:34 [r]S Ge 41:8; S Job 3:26
7:15 [s]1Ki 19:4; Jnh 4:3 [t]Job 6:9; Rev 9:6
7:16 [u]S 1Ki 19:4; Job 9:21 [v]S Job 3:22 [w]ver 19; Job 10:20; Ps 39:13 [x]S ver 7
7:17 [y]S Job 4:19; 22:2; Ps 8:4; 144:3; Heb 2:6
7:18 [z]Ps 73:14 [a]Job 23:10; Ps 139:23 [b]Job 14:3; Ps 17:3; 26:2; 66:10; 139:1-6; 143:2
7:19 [c]S ver 16 [d]Job 9:18; 13:26; 14:6; 27:2; Ps 139:7
7:20 [e]Job 35:6; Jer 7:19 /S Job 6:4 [g]S ver 12
7:21 [h]Job 9:28; 10:14; 16:6; Ps 119:120; Isa 43:25; Jer 31:34; Heb 1:3 [i]S Ge 3:19;

Job 10:9; 34:15; Ps 7:5; 22:15; 90:3; 104:29 /S ver 8; S Job 3:13 **8:1** [k]S Ge 25:2; Job 18:1; 25:1 **8:2** [l]Job 11:2; 18:2 [m]S 2Ch 36:16; S Job 6:26 **8:3** [n]S Job 4:17; 34:12; Isa 29:15; Ro 3:5 [o]S Ge 18:25; S Jer 12:1 **8:4** [p]Job 1:19 **8:5** [q]Job 9:15 [r]S Job 5:8,27 **8:6** [s]S Job 5:15; 22:27; 33:26; 34:28; Isa 58:9; 65:24 [t]S Job 5:24 **8:7** [u]Job 21:13; 22:21; 36:11; Ps 25:13 [v]S Job 1:10; Jer 29:11; 31:17 **8:8** [w]S Dt 32:7; S Ps 71:18

[l]9 Hebrew *Sheol*   [m]20 A few manuscripts of the Masoretic Text, an ancient Hebrew scribal tradition and Septuagint; most manuscripts of the Masoretic Text *I have become a burden to myself.*

statements are based on common observation and are not meant to dogmatize about what happens after death. Mesopotamian descriptions of the netherworld refer to it similarly as the "land of no return" (see note on v. 21).
7:11 *not keep silent.* Job is determined to cry out against the apparent injustice of God who, it seems, will not leave him alone (vv. 17–20). *speak out in . . . anguish.* See Jer 4:19. *bitterness of . . . soul.* See 10:1; 21:25; 27:2.
7:12 *the sea, or the monster of the deep.* See 3:8 and NIV text note. The boisterous sea monster was a symbol of chaos (see Ps 74:13–14 and note; Isa 27:1; 51:9), and Job objects to being treated like him.
7:13–14 He thinks that even the nightmares that disturb his much-needed sleep are from God.
7:16 *I despise my life.* See note on 9:21.
7:17 *What is man that you make so much of him . . . ?* See Ps 144:3; cf. Ps 8:4–8, where the answer is given that man is created in God's image to have dominion over the world (see Ge 1:27–28). Job's words (vv. 18–21) are a parody on this theme—as if God's only interest in man is to scrutinize him unmercifully and take quick offense at his slightest fault.
7:19 *even for an instant.* Lit. "long enough for me to swallow my saliva."
7:20 *If I have sinned, what have I done to you . . . ?* I have not been perfect, but what terrible sin have I committed that

deserves this kind of suffering? *watcher.* The Hebrew for this word is used in a favorable sense in Isa 27:3, but here Job complains that God is too critical. *made me your target.* See note on 6:4. *burden to you.* See NIV text note. Ancient Hebrew scribes report that a change in the text had been made from "you" to "myself" because the reading "you" involved too presumptuous a questioning of God's justice.
7:21 *offenses . . . sins.* Job confesses that he is a sinner, but he cannot understand why God refuses to forgive him. *lie down in the dust.* Of the netherworld, as in Mesopotamian descriptions of it (see note on v. 9).
8:2 *How long . . . ?* See 18:1. In contrast to the older Eliphaz, Bildad is impatient.
8:3 *Does God pervert justice?* But Job has not yet blatantly accused God of injustice.
8:5–6 Bildad reasons as follows: God cannot be unjust, so Job and his family must be suffering as a result of sinfulness. Job should plead for mercy, and if he has been upright, God will restore him.
8:6 *if you are pure and upright.* We know God's verdict about Job (1:8; 2:3), but Bildad is confident that Job is a hypocrite (see v. 13).
8:7 See v. 21. Bildad spoke more accurately than he realized (see 42:10–17).
8:8 *Ask the former generations.* Eliphaz appealed to reve-

and find out what their fathers
learned,

[9]for we were born only yesterday and
know nothing, [x]

and our days on earth are but a
shadow. [y]

[10]Will they not instruct [z] you and tell
you?

Will they not bring forth words from
their understanding? [a]

[11]Can papyrus grow tall where there is no
marsh? [b]

Can reeds [c] thrive without water?

[12]While still growing and uncut,

they wither more quickly than
grass. [d]

[13]Such is the destiny [e] of all who forget
God; [f]

so perishes the hope of the godless. [g]

[14]What he trusts in is fragile [n];

what he relies on is a spider's web. [h]

[15]He leans on his web, [i] but it gives way;

he clings to it, but it does not hold. [j]

[16]He is like a well-watered plant in the
sunshine,

spreading its shoots [k] over the
garden; [l]

[17]it entwines its roots around a pile of
rocks

and looks for a place among the
stones.

[18]But when it is torn from its spot,

that place disowns [m] it and says, 'I
never saw you.' [n]

[19]Surely its life withers [o] away,

and [o] from the soil other plants
grow. [p]

[20]"Surely God does not reject a
blameless [q] man

or strengthen the hands of
evildoers. [r]

[21]He will yet fill your mouth with
laughter [s]

and your lips with shouts of joy. [t]

[22]Your enemies will be clothed in
shame, [u]

and the tents [v] of the wicked will be
no more." [w]

Job

9 Then Job replied:

[2]"Indeed, I know that this is true.

But how can a mortal be righteous
before God? [x]

[3]Though one wished to dispute with
him, [y]

he could not answer him one time
out of a thousand. [z]

[4]His wisdom [a] is profound, his power is
vast. [b]

Who has resisted [c] him and come out
unscathed? [d]

[5]He moves mountains [e] without their
knowing it

and overturns them in his anger. [f]

[6]He shakes the earth [g] from its place

and makes its pillars tremble. [h]

[7]He speaks to the sun and it does not
shine; [i]

he seals off the light of the stars. [j]

[8]He alone stretches out the heavens [k]

8:9 [x]S Ge 47:9
[y]S 1Ch 29:15;
S 2Ch 10:6;
S Ps 39:6
8:10 [z]Pr 1:8
[a]Pr 2:1-2; 4:1
8:11 [b]Job 40:21
[c]S Ex 2:3;
Isa 19:6; 35:7
8:12 [d]ver 19;
S 2Ki 19:26;
Job 18:16; 20:5;
Ps 90:5-6;
102:11; Isa 34:4;
40:7,24
8:13 [e]Ps 37:38;
73:17 [f]Ps 91:9;
50:22; Isa 51:13;
Jer 17:6 [g]Job 6:9;
11:20; 13:16;
15:34; 20:5;
27:8; 34:30;
Ps 37:1-2;
112:10; Pr 10:28;
11:7; Jer 15:9
8:14 [h]ver 15;
Job 27:18;
Isa 59:5
8:15 [i]S ver 14
[j]Ps 49:11;
Mt 7:26-27
8:16 [k]Ps 80:11;
Isa 16:8
[l]Ps 37:35;
Jer 11:16
8:18 [m]Job 20:9;
Ps 103:16
[n]S Job 7:8;
S 14:20
8:19 [o]S ver 12;
S Job 15:30
[p]Ps 119:90;
Ecc 1:4
8:20 [q]Job 1:1
[r]S Ge 18:25

8:21 [s]S Job 5:22
[t]S Ezr 3:13;
Job 35:10;
Ps 47:5; 107:22;
118:15; 126:2;
132:16; Isa 35:6
8:22 [u]Job 27:7;
Ps 6:10; 35:26;
44:7; 53:5;
71:13; 86:17;
109:29; 132:18;
Eze 7:27; 26:16
[v]S Job 4:21
[w]S 1Sa 8:3;
Job 18:6,14,21;
21:28; 27:8,18;
34:26; 36:6;
38:13; Ps 52:5;
Pr 14:11

9:2 [x]S Job 4:17; Ro 3:20 **9:3** [y]ver 32; Job 40:5 [z]ver 12,14,
29,32; Job 10:2; 12:14; 13:9,14; 22:4; 23:7,13; 37:19;
40:2; Ps 44:21; Isa 14:24 **9:4** [a]Job 11:6; 28:12,20,23; 38:36;
Ps 51:6; Pr 2:6; Ecc 2:26 [b]ver 19; S Job 5:9; 12:13,16; 23:6;
24:22; 26:12; 30:18; Ps 93:4; 95:3; Pr 8:14; Isa 40:26;
63:1; Da 2:20; 4:35 [c]Jer 50:24 [d]S 2Ch 13:12; S Job 5:13 **9:5**
[e]Mt 17:20 /Ps 18:7; 46:2-3; Isa 13:13; Mic 1:4 **9:6**
[g]S Ex 19:18; Isa 2:21; 13:13; 24:18-20; Am 8:8; Heb 12:26
[h]S 2Sa 22:8; Job 26:14; 30:29; 37:4-5; Ps 75:3; Hab 3:4 **9:7**
[i]Isa 34:4; Jer 4:28; Joel 2:2,10,31; 3:15; Zep 1:15; Zec 14:6
[j]Isa 13:10; Jer 4:23; Eze 32:8 **9:8** [k]S Ge 1:1,8; S Isa 48:13

[n]14 The meaning of the Hebrew for this word is
uncertain. [o]19 Or *Surely all the joy it has / is that*

---

lation from the spirit world (see 4:12–21), while Bildad
appeals to the accumulated wisdom of tradition.
8:9 *our days . . . are but a shadow.* A common motif in
wisdom literature (see 14:2; 1Ch 29:15; Ps 102:11; 144:4;
Ecc 6:12; 8:13).
8:11–19 A practical wisdom poem, giving words of instruction learned from the fathers. It is introduced in v. 10
and applied to Job in vv. 20–22.
8:20 Bildad is blunt about Job's being an evildoer, whereas
Eliphaz had resorted to insinuation (see 4:7–9).
8:21 See note on v. 7.
9:2–3 Job does not believe that he is sinless, but he wishes
to have his day in court so that he can prove he is innocent of
the kind of sin that deserves the suffering he endures. In his
despair he voices awful complaints against God (see vv.
16–20,22–24,29–35; 10:1–7,13–17). Yet he does not
abandon God; he does not curse him (see 10:2,8–12), as
Satan said he would (see 1:11; 2:5). Ch. 42 implies that Job
persevered, but chs. 9–10 show that he did so with impatience (see 4:2; 6:11; 21:4). Cf. Jas 5:11, which speaks of
Job's perseverance, not (as traditionally) his patience.

9:3 *dispute.* See v. 14. Job's speech is filled with the
imagery of the courtroom: "answer him" (vv. 3,15,32),
"argue with him" (v. 14), "innocent . . . plead . . . Judge" (v.
15), "summon(ed)" (vv. 16,19), "pronounce me guilty" (v.
20), "judges" (v. 24), "court" (v. 32), "charges . . . against
me" (10:2), "witnesses" (10:17). Job argues his innocence,
but he feels that because God is so great there is no use in
contending with him (v. 14). Job's innocence does him no
good (v. 15).
9:5–10 A beautiful hymn about God's greatness. But Job is
not blessed by it, for he does not see that God's power is
controlled by goodness and justice.
9:6 *pillars.* See 26:11. The metaphor of the earth resting on
a foundation (see 38:6; 1Sa 2:8; Ps 75:3; 104:5) is changed
in 26:7 to a description of the earth suspended over nothing.
9:8 *stretches out the heavens.* Either (1) creates the heavens (see Isa 44:24), or perhaps (2) causes the dawn to spread,
like a man stretching out a tent (see Ps 104:2). *treads on the
waves.* Canaanite texts describe the goddess Asherah as
walking on the sea (or sea-god) to subdue it. Similarly, God
"treads on the waves" to control the boisterous sea.

and treads on the waves of the sea. [l]

⁹He is the Maker [m] of the Bear and
  Orion,
  the Pleiades and the constellations of
    the south. [n]

¹⁰He performs wonders [o] that cannot be
    fathomed,
  miracles that cannot be counted. [p]

¹¹When he passes me, I cannot see him;
  when he goes by, I cannot perceive
    him. [q]

¹²If he snatches away, who can stop
    him? [r]
  Who can say to him, 'What are you
    doing?' [s]

¹³God does not restrain his anger; [t]
  even the cohorts of Rahab [u] cowered
    at his feet.

¹⁴"How then can I dispute with him?
  How can I find words to argue with
    him? [v]

¹⁵Though I were innocent, I could not
    answer him; [w]
  I could only plead [x] with my Judge [y]
    for mercy. [z]

¹⁶Even if I summoned him and he
    responded,
  I do not believe he would give me a
    hearing. [a]

¹⁷He would crush me [b] with a storm [c]
  and multiply [d] my wounds for no
    reason. [e]

¹⁸He would not let me regain my breath
  but would overwhelm me with
    misery. [f]

¹⁹If it is a matter of strength, he is
    mighty! [g]
  And if it is a matter of justice, who
    will summon him [p] ? [h]

²⁰Even if I were innocent, my mouth
  would condemn me;

if I were blameless, it would
  pronounce me guilty. [i]

²¹"Although I am blameless, [j]
  I have no concern for myself; [k]
  I despise my own life. [l]

²²It is all the same; that is why I say,
  'He destroys both the blameless and
    the wicked.' [m]

²³When a scourge [n] brings sudden death,
  he mocks the despair of the
    innocent. [o]

²⁴When a land falls into the hands of the
    wicked, [p]
  he blindfolds its judges. [q]
  If it is not he, then who is it? [r]

²⁵"My days are swifter than a runner; [s]
  they fly away without a glimpse of
    joy. [t]

²⁶They skim past [u] like boats of papyrus, [v]
  like eagles swooping down on their
    prey. [w]

²⁷If I say, 'I will forget my complaint, [x]
  I will change my expression, and
    smile,'

²⁸I still dread [y] all my sufferings,
  for I know you will not hold me
    innocent. [z]

²⁹Since I am already found guilty,
  why should I struggle in vain? [a]

³⁰Even if I washed myself with soap [q] [b]
  and my hands [c] with washing soda, [d]

³¹you would plunge me into a slime pit [e]

9:8 [l]Job 38:16;
Ps 77:19; Pr 8:28;
Hab 3:15;
Mt 14:25;
Mk 6:48; Jn 6:19
9:9 [m]Job 32:22;
40:15,19
[n]S Ge 1:16
9:10 [o]Dt 6:22;
Ps 72:18; 136:4;
Jer 32:20
[p]S Job 5:9
9:11 [q]Job 23:8-9;
35:14
9:12 [r]Nu 23:20;
Job 11:10;
Isa 14:27; 43:13
[s]S ver 3;
S Dt 32:39;
Isa 29:16; 45:9;
Da 2:21; 4:32;
Ro 9:20
9:13 [t]Nu 14:18;
Job 10:15;
Ps 78:38;
Isa 3:11; 6:5;
48:9 [u]Job 26:12;
Ps 87:4; 89:10;
Isa 30:7; 51:9
9:14 [v]S ver 3
9:15 [w]Job 10:15;
13:19; 34:5-6;
40:5; 42:7
[x]Job 8:5
[y]S Ge 18:25;
1Sa 24:12;
Ps 50:6; 96:13
[z]ver 20,29;
Job 15:6; 23:4;
40:2
9:16 [a]Job 13:22;
Ro 9:20-21
9:17 [b]Job 16:12;
30:16; Ps 10:10;
Isa 38:13
[c]Job 30:22;
Ps 83:15; Jnh 1:4
[d]Job 16:14;
[e]S Job 2:3
9:18 [f]S Job 7:19;
S 10:1
9:19 [g]S ver 4;
S Ne 9:32 [h]ver
33; Jer 49:19

9:20 [i]S ver 15
9:21 [j]S Ge 6:9;
Job 34:6,7 [k]ver
14; S Job 6:29;
10:1; 13:13
[l]S Nu 11:15;
S Job 7:16
9:22 [m]S Job 3:19;
10:8; Ecc 9:2,3;
Eze 21:3
9:23 [n]Heb 11:36
[o]Job 24:1,12;
Ps 64:4; Hab 1:3;

1Pe 1:7 **9:24** [p]Job 1:15,17; 10:3; 16:11; 21:16; 22:18;
27:2; 40:8; Ps 73:3 [q]S Job 3:14; 12:6; 19:7; 21:7; 24:23;
31:35; 35:15; Ps 73:12; Ecc 8:11; Jer 12:1; La 3:9 [r]Job 12:9;
13:1; 24:12; Isa 41:20 **9:25** [s]S Job 7:6 [t]Job 7:7; 10:20 **9:26**
[u]Job 24:18; Ps 46:3 [v]Isa 18:2 [w]Job 39:29; Hab 1:8 **9:27**
[x]S Job 7:11 **9:28** [y]S Job 3:25 [z]S Ex 34:7; S Job 7:21 **9:29**
[a]S ver 3,S 15; Ps 37:33 **9:30** [b]Mal 3:2 [c]Job 17:9; 31:7;
Isa 1:15 [d]Job 14:4,17; 33:9; Isa 1:18; Jer 2:22; Hos 13:12
9:31 [e]Ps 35:7; 40:2; Isa 57:20; Jer 2:22; Na 3:6; Mal 2:3

[p] 19 See Septuagint; Hebrew me. [q] 30 Or snow

9:9 *Bear . . . Orion . . . Pleiades.* These three constellations
are mentioned again in 38:31–32, and the last two are
mentioned in Am 5:8 (see note there). Despite their limited
knowledge of astronomy, the ancient Israelites were awed by
the fact that God had created the constellations.
9:10 The same words are spoken by Eliphaz in 5:9.
9:12 *who can stop him?* Job argues that God has an
unchallengeable, sovereign freedom that works to accomplish everything he pleases.
9:13 *Rahab.* Not the prostitute Rahab of Jos 2 but a mythical sea monster (see 26:12), elsewhere used as symbolic of
Egypt (see Isa 30:7 and note). See 3:8; 7:12 and notes.
9:15 *Judge.* God's fairness is unimpeachable (see Ge 18:25
and note).
9:17 Job does not know that God has allowed Satan to
crush him for a high purpose.
9:20 *mouth would condemn me.* See 15:6.
9:21 *I despise my own life.* See 7:16; words of despairing
resignation that would be partially echoed in Job's final

outpouring of repentance (see 42:6).
9:22–24 God has become Job's great enigma. Job describes
a phantom God—one who does not exist, except in Job's
mind. The God of the Bible is not morally indifferent (cf.
God's words in 38:2; 40:2 and Job's response in 42:3).
9:24 *blindfolds its judges.* Our statues of Lady Justice are
blindfolded, implying that she will judge impartially. But
Job's accusation against God is that he has blindfolded the
judges so that they see neither crimes nor innocence.
9:26 *boats of papyrus.* See note on Ex 2:3.
9:28 *you will not hold me innocent.* Job wants to stand
before God as an innocent man—not sinless, but innocent of
any sin commensurate with his suffering.
9:29 *already found guilty.* As appears from the bitter suffering he is enduring.
9:30 *soda.* A vegetable alkali used as a cleansing agent. The
Hebrew underlying this word is translated "soap" in Jer
2:22; Mal 3:2.

so that even my clothes would detest
  me. *f*

32"He is not a man *g* like me that I might
  answer him, *h*
  that we might confront each other in
  court. *i*
33If only there were someone to arbitrate
  between us, *j*
  to lay his hand upon us both, *k*
34someone to remove God's rod from
  me, *l*
  so that his terror would frighten me
  no more. *m*
35Then I would speak up without fear of
  him, *n*
  but as it now stands with me, I
  cannot. *o*

10 "I loathe my very life; *p*
  therefore I will give free rein to
  my complaint
  and speak out in the bitterness of my
  soul. *q*
2I will say to God: *r* Do not condemn
  me,
  but tell me what charges *s* you have
  against me. *t*
3Does it please you to oppress me, *u*
  to spurn the work of your hands, *v*
  while you smile on the schemes of
  the wicked? *w*
4Do you have eyes of flesh?
  Do you see as a mortal sees? *x*
5Are your days like those of a mortal
  or your years like those of a man, *y*
6that you must search out my faults
  and probe after my sin *z* —
7though you know that I am not guilty *a*
  and that no one can rescue me from
  your hand? *b*

8"Your hands shaped *c* me and made me.
  Will you now turn and destroy me? *d*
9Remember that you molded me like
  clay. *e*

Will you now turn me to dust
  again? *f*
10Did you not pour me out like milk
  and curdle me like cheese,
11clothe me with skin and flesh
  and knit me together *g* with bones
  and sinews?
12You gave me life *h* and showed me
  kindness, *i*
  and in your providence *j* watched
  over *k* my spirit.

13"But this is what you concealed in your
  heart,
  and I know that this was in your
  mind: *l*
14If I sinned, you would be watching me *m*
  and would not let my offense go
  unpunished. *n*
15If I am guilty *o*—woe to me! *p*
  Even if I am innocent, I cannot lift
  my head, *q*
  for I am full of shame
  and drowned in *r* my affliction. *r*
16If I hold my head high, you stalk me
  like a lion *s*
  and again display your awesome
  power against me. *t*
17You bring new witnesses against me *u*
  and increase your anger toward me; *v*
  your forces come against me wave
  upon wave. *w*

18"Why then did you bring me out of the
  womb? *x*
  I wish I had died before any eye saw
  me. *y*
19If only I had never come into being,

9:31 *f*S Job 7:20; 34:9; 35:3; Ps 73:13
9:32 *g*S Nu 23:19 *h*S ver 3; Ro 9:20 *i*Ps 143:2; Ecc 6:10
9:33 *j*S 1Sa 2:25 *k*S ver 19
9:34 *l*Job 21:9; Ps 39:10; 73:5
9:35 *m*S Job 6:4; 7:14; 33:7; Ps 32:4 *n*S Job 7:11 *o*Job 7:15; 13:21
10:1 *p*S Nu 11:15; S 1Ki 19:4 *q*S 1Sa 1:10; S Job 7:11; 9:18, 21
10:2 *r*Job 13:3; 40:1 *s*Isa 3:13; 12:2; Mic 6:2; Ro 8:33 *t*S Job 9:3
10:3 *u*S Job 9:22; 16:9,14; 19:6,21; 22:10; 30:13,21; 31:23; 34:6 *v*ver 8; Ge 1:26; S Job 4:17; 14:15; 34:19; Ps 8:6; 95:6; 100:3; 138:8; 149:2; Isa 60:21; 64:8 *w*S Job 9:24
10:4 *x*1Sa 16:7; Job 11:11; 14:16; 24:23; 28:24; 31:4; 34:21; 41:11; Ps 11:4; 33:15; 119:168; 139:12; Pr 5:21; 15:3; Jer 11:20-23; 16:17
10:5 *y*Job 36:26; Ps 39:5; 90:2,4; 102:24; 2Pe 3:8
10:6 *z*Job 14:16
10:7 *a*ver 15; S Job 6:29; 11:4; 16:17; 27:5,6; 31:6; 32:1; *b*S Dt 32:39
10:8 *c*Ge 2:7; *d*S ver 3; S 2Sa 14:14; S Job 30:15
10:9 *e*S Job 4:19; Isa 29:16

*f*S Ge 2:7; S Job 7:21
10:11 *g*Ps 139:13,15
10:12 *h*S Ge 2:7 *i*S Ge 24:12 *j*S Ge 45:5 *k*1Pe 2:25

10:13 *l*Job 23:13; Ps 115:3 **10:14** *m*Job 13:27 *n*S Ex 34:7; S Job 7:21 **10:15** *o*S ver 7 *p*S Job 9:13 *q*S Job 9:15 *r*Ps 25:16 **10:16** *s*S 1Sa 17:34; Ps 7:2; Isa 38:13; Jer 5:6; 25:38; La 3:10; Hos 5:14; 13:7 *t*Job 5:9; Isa 28:21; 29:14; 65:7 **10:17** *u*1Ki 21:10; Job 16:8 *v*Ru 1:21 *w*S Job 5:7 **10:18** *x*S Job 3:8; S Ps 22:9 *y*Job 3:26; Ecc 4:2; 7:1

r 15 Or and aware of

9:33 *someone to arbitrate between us.* See note on 5:1. God is so immense that Job feels he needs someone who can help him, someone who can argue his case in court. Job's call is not directly predicting the mediatorship of Christ, for Job is not looking for one to forgive him but for one who can testify to his innocence (see 16:20-21; 19:25-26).

9:34 See 13:21. *God's rod.* Symbolic of divine judgment and wrath (see, e.g., Ps 89:32; La 3:1).

10:1 *I loathe my very life.* See note on 9:21. *bitterness of my soul.* Because Job is so bitter, his mind has conjured up a false picture of God.

10:3 Job imagines that God is angry with him, an innocent man (see 9:28 and note), and that he takes delight in the wicked. Such words are a reminder that the sickroom is not the place to argue theology; in times of severe suffering, people may say things that require a response of love and

understanding. Job himself will eventually repent, and God will forgive (42:1-6).

10:4 *eyes of flesh.* Imperfect vision, like that of a man.

10:8-17 Job continues to question God as if he were his adversary in court. He wants to know how God, who so wonderfully formed him in the womb, could all the while have planned (see v. 13) to punish him—even though he may be innocent.

10:8-11 A poetic description of God making a baby in the womb (see Ps 139:13-16).

10:8 See Ps 119:73.

10:9 *molded me like clay.* See note on 4:19. *turn me to dust.* See note on Ge 3:19.

10:15-16 Job says that whether he is guilty or innocent, the all-powerful God will not treat him justly.

10:17 *witnesses against me.* See note on 9:3.

10:18-22 See notes on ch. 3.

or had been carried straight from the
  womb to the grave! *z*
²⁰Are not my few days *a* almost over? *b*
  Turn away from me *c* so I can have a
    moment's joy *d*
²¹before I go to the place of no return, *e*
  to the land of gloom and deep
    shadow, *s f*
²²to the land of deepest night,
  of deep shadow *g* and disorder,
  where even the light is like
    darkness." *h*

Zophar

11 Then Zophar the Naamathite *i* replied:

²"Are all these words to go
    unanswered? *j*
  Is this talker to be vindicated? *k*
³Will your idle talk *l* reduce men to
    silence?
  Will no one rebuke you when you
    mock? *m*
⁴You say to God, 'My beliefs are
    flawless *n*
  and I am pure *o* in your sight.'
⁵Oh, how I wish that God would
    speak, *p*
  that he would open his lips against
    you
⁶and disclose to you the secrets of
    wisdom, *q*
  for true wisdom has two sides.
  Know this: God has even forgotten
    some of your sin. *r*
⁷"Can you fathom *s* the mysteries of
    God?

Can you probe the limits of the
  Almighty?
⁸They are higher *t* than the
    heavens *u*—what can you do?
  They are deeper than the depths of
    the grave *t v*—what can you
    know? *w*
⁹Their measure *x* is longer than the earth
  and wider than the sea. *y*

¹⁰"If he comes along and confines you in
    prison
  and convenes a court, who can
    oppose him? *z*
¹¹Surely he recognizes deceitful men;
  and when he sees evil, does he not
    take note? *a*
¹²But a witless man can no more become
    wise
  than a wild donkey's colt *b* can be
    born a man. *u c*

¹³"Yet if you devote your heart *d* to him
  and stretch out your hands *e* to him, *f*
¹⁴if you put away *g* the sin that is in your
    hand
  and allow no evil *h* to dwell in your
    tent, *i*
¹⁵then you will lift up your face *j* without
    shame;
  you will stand firm *k* and without
    fear. *l*
¹⁶You will surely forget your trouble, *m*

Cross references

10:19 *z*S Job 3:3; Jer 15:10
10:20 *a*Job 14:1; Ecc 6:12
*b*S Job 7:7
*c*S Job 7:16
*d*S Job 9:25
10:21
*e*S 2Sa 12:23; S Job 3:13; 16:22; Ps 39:13; Ecc 12:5
*f*S Job 3:5
10:22 *g*S Job 3:5
*h*S 1Sa 2:9; S Job 3:13
11:1 *i*S Job 2:11
11:2 *j*S Job 8:2; S 16:3
*k*S Ge 41:6; S Job 6:29
11:3 *l*Eph 4:29; 5:4 *m*Job 12:4; 16:10; 17:2; 21:3; 30:1; Ps 1:1
11:4 *n*Job 9:21
*o*S Job 10:7
11:5 *p*Ex 20:19; Job 23:5; 32:13; 38:1
11:6 *q*S Job 9:4; 1Co 2:10
*r*S Ezr 9:13; S Job 15:5
11:7 *s*S Job 5:9; Ecc 3:11

11:8 *t*Eph 3:18
*u*S Ge 15:5; Job 22:12; 25:2; Ps 57:10; Isa 55:9
*v*S Job 7:9
*w*Job 15:13,25; 33:13; 40:2; Ps 139:8
11:9
*x*Eph 3:19-20
*y*Job 22:12; 35:5; 36:26; 37:5,23; Isa 40:26
11:10
*z*S Job 9:12; Rev 3:7
11:11
*a*S Job 10:4; 31:37; 34:11,25; 36:7; Ps 10:14
11:12
*b*S Ge 16:12
*c*S 2Ch 6:36

11:13 *d*1Sa 7:3; Ps 78:8 *e*S Ex 9:29 *f*S Job 5:8,27 **11:14** *g*S Jos 24:14 *h*Ps 101:4 *i*Job 22:23 **11:15** *j*Job 22:26 *k*S 1Sa 2:9; Ps 20:8; 37:23; 40:2; 119:5; Eph 6:14 *l*S Ge 4:7; S Prs 3:6 **11:16** *m*Isa 26:16; 37:3; 65:16

*s*21 Or *and the shadow of death;* also in verse 22   *t*8 Hebrew *than Sheol*   *u*12 Or *wild donkey can be born tame*

Study notes

10:21 *place of no return.* See note on 7:9. *land of gloom and deep shadow.* See 38:17. Ancient Mesopotamian documents refer to the netherworld as the "house of darkness."
11:1–20 Like Eliphaz (see 4:7–11) and Bildad (see 8:3–6), Zophar claims that Job's sins have caused his troubles.
11:2–3 Zophar's failure to put himself in Job's place before condemning him shows a lack of compassion. Nor is Zophar entirely correct in his condemnation: Job has sincerely challenged what he perceives to be God's unjust actions (see 9:14–24), but he has not mocked God (as Zophar accuses him of having done).
11:4 *I am pure.* In 10:7,15 Job had disclaimed being guilty, and in 9:21 he said he was "blameless," the word God used to describe him in 1:8; 2:3. Zophar, however, implies that Job was claiming absolute purity (sinless perfection), but Job nowhere uses such terms of himself.
11:5 Zophar thought God should speak against Job, but eventually God spoke against Zophar himself (see 42:7).
11:6 *true wisdom has two sides.* OT wisdom literature (especially Proverbs) makes abundant use of the term *mashal* ("proverb," "riddle," "parable"), which often had a hidden as well as an obvious meaning. Zophar thinks Job is shallow and lacks an understanding of the true nature of God (see vv.

7–9).
11:7 Unwittingly, Zophar anticipates the Lord's discourses in 38:1–42:6.
11:8–9 In the same way that Zophar speaks of the height, depth, length and width of God's knowledge, Paul speaks of Christ's love (see Eph 3:18).
11:8 *what can you do?* Can you climb into the heavens and explore God's knowledge?
11:11–12 *deceitful . . . witless.* Zophar claims that it would take a miracle to change Job.
11:12 The NIV text note contrasts two related but utterly different Biblical animals—the wild donkey and the domestic donkey.
11:13–20 Zophar assumes that Job's problems are rooted in his sin; all Job has to do is to repent, and then his life will become blessed and happy. But God nowhere guarantees a life "brighter than noonday" (v. 17) simply because we are his children. He has higher purposes for us than our physical prosperity, or people courting our favor (v. 19). Zophar's philosophy is in conflict with Ps 73.
11:13 *stretch out your hands to him.* For help (see Pr 1:24; La 1:17).
11:15 *lift up your face without shame.* Zophar echoes Job's thought in 10:15.

recalling it only as waters gone by. [n]

[17]Life will be brighter than noonday, [o]
and darkness will become like
morning. [p]

[18]You will be secure, because there is
hope;
you will look about you and take
your rest [q] in safety. [r]

[19]You will lie down, with no one to make
you afraid, [s]
and many will court your favor. [t]

[20]But the eyes of the wicked will fail, [u]
and escape will elude them; [v]
their hope will become a dying
gasp." [w]

Job

12 Then Job replied:

[2]"Doubtless you are the people,
and wisdom will die with you! [x]

[3]But I have a mind as well as you;
I am not inferior to you.
Who does not know all these
things? [y]

[4]"I have become a laughingstock [z] to my
friends, [a]
though I called upon God and he
answered [b] —
a mere laughingstock, though
righteous and blameless! [c]

[5]Men at ease have contempt [d] for
misfortune
as the fate of those whose feet are
slipping. [e]

[6]The tents of marauders are
undisturbed, [f]
and those who provoke God are
secure [g] —
those who carry their god in their
hands. [v]

[7]"But ask the animals, and they will
teach you, [h]

or the birds of the air, [i] and they will
tell you; [j]

[8]or speak to the earth, and it will teach
you,
or let the fish of the sea inform you.

[9]Which of all these does not know [k]
that the hand of the LORD has done
this? [l]

[10]In his hand is the life [m] of every creature
and the breath of all mankind. [n]

[11]Does not the ear test words
as the tongue tastes food? [o]

[12]Is not wisdom found among the aged? [p]
Does not long life bring
understanding? [q]

[13]"To God belong wisdom [r] and power; [s]
counsel and understanding are his. [t]

[14]What he tears down [u] cannot be
rebuilt; [v]
the man he imprisons cannot be
released. [w]

[15]If he holds back the waters, [x] there is
drought; [y]
if he lets them loose, they devastate
the land. [z]

[16]To him belong strength and victory; [a]
both deceived and deceiver are his. [b]

[17]He leads counselors away stripped [c]
and makes fools of judges. [d]

[18]He takes off the shackles [e] put on by
kings
and ties a loincloth [w] around their
waist. [f]

[19]He leads priests away stripped [g]

11:16 [n]Jos 7:5;
Job 22:11;
Ps 58:7; 112:10;
Eze 21:7
11:17
[o]Job 22:28;
Ps 37:6; Isa 58:8,
10; 62:1
[p]Job 17:12; 18:6;
29:3; Ps 18:28;
112:4; 119:105;
Isa 5:20; Jn 8:12
11:18 [q]Ps 3:5;
4:8; 127:2;
Ecc 5:12
[r]S Lev 26:6;
Pr 3:24;
Isa 11:10; 14:3;
28:12; 30:15;
32:18; Zec 3:10
11:19
[s]S Lev 26:6
[t]Isa 45:14
11:20 [u]Dt 28:65;
Job 17:5
[v]Job 12:10;
18:18; 27:22;
34:22; 36:6;
Ps 139:11-12;
Jer 11:11; 23:24;
25:35; Am 2:14;
9:2-3 [w]S Job 8:13
12:2 [x]Job 15:8;
17:10
12:3 [y]Job 13:2;
15:9
12:4 [z]S Ge 38:23
[a]S Job 6:14;
S 11:3; S 16:10;
S 19:14 [b]Ps 91:15
[c]S Ge 6:9;
S Job 6:29;
S 15:16
12:5 [d]Ps 123:4
[e]Ps 17:5; 37:31;
38:16; 66:9;
73:2; 94:18
12:6 [f]S Job 5:24
[g]S Job 9:24
12:7
[h]Job 35:11 fn

[i]Mt 6:26
[j]Job 18:3;
Ro 1:20
12:9 [k]Isa 1:3
[l]S Job 9:24
12:10 [m]Da 5:23
[n]S Ge 2:7;
S Nu 16:22;
S Job 11:20;
Ac 17:28
12:11 [o]Job 34:3
12:12 [p]S 1Ki 4:2;
Job 15:10 [q]ver
20; Job 17:4;
32:7,9; 34:4,10
12:13 [r]Pr 21:30;
Isa 45:9

[s]S Job 9:4; S Jer 32:19; 1Co 1:24 [t]S Nu 23:19; 1Ki 3:12;
Job 32:8; 38:36; Pr 2:6; Isa 40:13-14; Da 1:17 **12:14**
[u]Job 16:9; 19:10 [v]Dt 13:16; Ps 127:1; Isa 24:20; 25:2;
Eze 26:14 [w]S Job 9:3; Isa 22:22; Rev 3:7 **12:15** [x]Job 28:25;
Isa 40:12 [y]S Dt 28:22; S 1Ki 17:1 [z]S Ge 7:24 **12:16**
[a]S Job 9:4 [b]2Ch 18:22; Job 13:7,9; 27:4; Ro 2:11 **12:17** [c]ver
19; Job 19:9; Isa 20:4 [d]S Job 3:14; 1Co 1:20 **12:18**
[e]Ps 107:14; 116:16; Na 1:13 [f]ver 21; Job 34:18; Ps 107:40;
Isa 5:27; 40:23 **12:19** [g]S ver 17

[v]6 Or *secure / in what God's hand brings them*
[w]18 Or *shackles of kings / and ties a belt*

11:20 Bildad ended his speech in a similar way (see 8:22).
12:1–14:22 As before, Job's reply is divided into two parts: He speaks to his three friends (12:2–13:19), then to God (13:20–14:22).
12:2 For the first time, Job reacts with sarcasm to the harshness of his counselors (see v. 20).
12:3 *Who does not know . . . ?* See v. 9. The advice of Job's friends is trivial and commonplace.
12:4 *God . . . answered.* In the days before his suffering began (contrast 9:16).
12:5 The prosperous despise those who, like Job, have trouble.
12:6 Such statements (see 9:21–24) irked the counselors and made them brand Job as a man whose feet were slipping (see v. 5).
12:7–12 Job appeals to all creation to prove that God does what he pleases—that he does not use a person's piety as the sole basis for granting freedom from affliction.

12:7 *they will teach you.* That the righteous suffer and the evil are secure.
12:9 *LORD.* The only place in Job's and his friends' speeches (chs. 3–37) where the divine name "LORD" (Hebrew *Yahweh*) is used (see Introduction: Author).
12:11 Echoed by Elihu in 34:3. Cf. 6:6, where Job says that Eliphaz's words are like "tasteless food."
12:12 Job sarcastically chides his counselors for being elders and yet lacking in true wisdom.
12:13–25 The theme of this section is stated in v. 13: God is sovereign in the created world, and especially in history. The rest of the poem dwells on the negative aspects of God's power and wisdom—e.g., the destructive forces of nature (vv. 14–15), how judges become fools (v. 17), how priests become humiliated (v. 19), how trusted advisers are silenced and elders deprived of good sense (v. 20). Contrast the claim of Eliphaz that God always uses his power in ways that make sense (5:10–16).

and overthrows men long
   established. *h*
20He silences the lips of trusted advisers
   and takes away the discernment of
   elders. *i*
21He pours contempt on nobles *j*
   and disarms the mighty. *k*
22He reveals the deep things of darkness *l*
   and brings deep shadows *m* into the
   light. *n*
23He makes nations great, and destroys
   them; *o*
   he enlarges nations, *p* and disperses
   them. *q*
24He deprives the leaders of the earth of
   their reason; *r*
   he sends them wandering through a
   trackless waste. *s*
25They grope in darkness with no light; *t*
   he makes them stagger like
   drunkards. *u*

13 "My eyes have seen all this, *v*
   my ears have heard and
   understood it.
2What you know, I also know;
   I am not inferior to you. *w*
3But I desire to speak to the Almighty *x*
   and to argue my case with God. *y*
4You, however, smear me with lies; *z*
   you are worthless physicians, *a* all of
   you! *b*
5If only you would be altogether silent! *c*
   For you, that would be wisdom. *d*
6Hear now my argument;
   listen to the plea of my lips. *e*
7Will you speak wickedly on God's
   behalf?
   Will you speak deceitfully for him? *f*
8Will you show him partiality? *g*
   Will you argue the case for God?
9Would it turn out well if he examined
   you? *h*
   Could you deceive him as you might
   deceive men? *i*

10He would surely rebuke you
   if you secretly showed partiality. *j*
11Would not his splendor *k* terrify you?
   Would not the dread of him fall on
   you? *l*
12Your maxims are proverbs of ashes;
   your defenses are defenses of clay. *m*

13"Keep silent *n* and let me speak; *o*
   then let come to me what may. *p*
14Why do I put myself in jeopardy
   and take my life in my hands? *q*
15Though he slay me, yet will I hope *r* in
   him; *s*
   I will surely *x* defend my ways to his
   face. *t*
16Indeed, this will turn out for my
   deliverance, *u*
   for no godless *v* man would dare
   come before him! *w*
17Listen carefully to my words; *x*
   let your ears take in what I say.
18Now that I have prepared my case, *y*
   I know I will be vindicated. *z*
19Can anyone bring charges against me? *a*
   If so, I will be silent *b* and die. *c*

20"Only grant me these two things,
   O God,
   and then I will not hide from you:
21Withdraw your hand *d* far from me,
   and stop frightening me with your
   terrors. *e*
22Then summon me and I will answer, *f*
   or let me speak, and you reply. *g*
23How many wrongs and sins have I
   committed? *h*
   Show me my offense and my sin. *i*

12:19
h S Dt 24:15;
S Job 9:24; 14:20;
22:8; 24:12,22;
34:20,28; 35:9;
Isa 2:22; 31:8;
40:17,23;
Jer 25:18;
Da 2:21,34;
Lk 1:52
12:20 *i* S ver 12,
24; Da 4:33-34
12:21 *j* S ver 18;
S Isa 34:12
k S Job 3:15
12:22 *l* 1Co 4:5
m Job 3:5
n Ps 139:12;
Da 2:22
12:23 *o* Ps 2:1;
46:6; Isa 13:4;
Jer 25:9
p S Ex 34:24;
Ps 107:38;
Isa 9:3; 26:15;
54:3 *q* S Ps 5:12;
Ac 17:26
12:24 *r* S ver 20
s Ps 107:40
12:25
t S Dt 28:29;
Job 18:6; 21:17;
29:3 *u* Ps 107:27;
Isa 24:20
13:1 *v* S Job 9:24
13:2 *w* S Job 12:3
13:3 *x* Job 5:17;
40:2 *y* S Job 5:8;
9:14-20; S 10:2
13:4 *z* Ps 119:69;
Isa 9:15;
Jer 23:32
a Jer 8:22
b S Job 6:15
13:5 *c* ver 13;
S Jdg 18:19
d Pr 17:28
13:6 *e* Job 33:1;
34:4
13:7
f S Job 12:16;
S 16:17
13:8
g S Lev 19:15
13:9 *h* S Job 9:3
i S Job 12:16;
Gal 6:7

13:10
j S Lev 19:15;
S 2Ch 19:7
13:11 *k* Job 31:23
l S Ex 3:6
13:12
m S Ne 4:2-3
13:13 *n* S ver 5
o S Job 7:11
p S Job 9:21
13:14 *q* S Jdg 9:17
13:15 *r* S Job 7:6
s Ps 23:4; 27:1;

Pr 14:32; Isa 12:2; Da 3:28 *t* S Job 5:8; 27:5 **13:16** *u* Ps 30:5;
Isa 12:1; 54:7-8; Hos 14:4; Php 1:19 *v* S Job 8:13 *w* S Ge 3:8
13:17 *x* Job 21:2 **13:18** *y* S Job 23:4; 37:19 *z* S Job 2:3;
S 9:21 **13:19** *a* Job 40:4; Isa 50:8; Ro 8:33 *b* S Job 9:15
c S Job 3:13; 10:8 **13:21** *d* S Ex 9:3; Heb 10:31 *e* S Job 6:4
13:22 *f* Job 9:35; 14:15 *g* S Job 9:16 **13:23** *h* S 1Sa 26:18
i Job 7:21; 9:21; 14:17; 33:9

x 15 Or *He will surely slay me; I have no hope — yet I
will*

12:20 See note on v. 2.
12:21a, 24b The Hebrew text of these lines is repeated
verbatim in Ps 107:40.
12:22 God knows even secret, evil plans.
12:25 *grope in darkness.* Job concludes this section with a
parody of Eliphaz's confident assertion in 5:14.
13:1-12 Job feels that his counselors have become completely untrustworthy (see v. 12). He calls them quacks (see
v. 4; see also 16:2) and accuses them of showing partiality to
God (since God is stronger than Job) by telling lies about Job
(see vv. 7-8). Someday God will examine and punish them
for their deception (see vv. 9-11).
13:1 *all this.* God's sovereign actions as described in ch.
12.
13:2 See 15:9. *I am not inferior to you.* Repeated from
12:3.
13:5 See v. 13. The friends' silent presence had ministered

to Job earlier (see 2:13), but Job's current retort is intended
as sarcasm (cf. Pr 17:28).
13:12 *defenses.* Arguments in their defense of God's judgment.
13:15 See NIV text note. Both readings state that no matter
what happens, Job intends to seek vindication from God and
believes that he will receive it (see v. 18).
13:16 *turn out for my deliverance.* See Php 1:19 (perhaps
Paul was reflecting on Job's experience).
13:17 Job asks his friends to listen to what he is going to say
to God in 13:20-14:22.
13:20 *two things.* Job wants God (1) to withdraw his hand
of punishment (v. 21), and (2) to start communicating with
him (v. 22).
13:21 See 9:34.
13:23 Job's words are based on the counselors' point that
suffering always implies sinfulness. He does not yet under-

24Why do you hide your face/
  and consider me your enemy? k
25Will you torment l a windblown leaf? m
  Will you chase n after dry chaff? o
26For you write down bitter things against
    me
  and make me inherit the sins of my
    youth. p
27You fasten my feet in shackles; q
  you keep close watch on all my
    paths r
  by putting marks on the soles of my
    feet.
28"So man wastes away like something
    rotten,
  like a garment s eaten by moths. t

14 "Man born of woman u
  is of few days v and full of
    trouble. w
2He springs up like a flower x and
    withers away; y
  like a fleeting shadow, z he does not
    endure. a
3Do you fix your eye on such a one? b
  Will you bring him y before you for
    judgment? c
4Who can bring what is pure d from the
    impure? e
  No one! f
5Man's days are determined; g
  you have decreed the number of his
    months h
  and have set limits he cannot
    exceed. i
6So look away from him and let him
    alone, j
  till he has put in his time like a hired
    man. k

7"At least there is hope for a tree: l
  If it is cut down, it will sprout again,
  and its new shoots m will not fail. n

8Its roots may grow old in the ground
  and its stump o die in the soil,
9yet at the scent of water p it will bud
  and put forth shoots like a plant. q
10But man dies and is laid low; r
  he breathes his last and is no more. s
11As water disappears from the sea
  or a riverbed becomes parched and
    dry, t
12so man lies down and does not rise; u
  till the heavens are no more, v men
    will not awake
  or be roused from their sleep. w

13"If only you would hide me in the
    grave z x
  and conceal me till your anger has
    passed! y
  If only you would set me a time
    and then remember z me! a
14If a man dies, will he live again?
  All the days of my hard service b
  I will wait for my renewal a c to
    come.
15You will call and I will answer you; d
  you will long for the creature your
    hands have made. e
16Surely then you will count my steps f
  but not keep track of my sin. g
17My offenses will be sealed h up in a
    bag; i
  you will cover over my sin. j

13:24
/S Dt 32:20
kJob 16:9; 19:11;
33:10;
Ps 88:14-15;
Jer 30:14; La 2:5
13:25 /Job 19:2
mLev 26:36
nJob 19:22,28
oJob 21:18;
Ps 1:4; 35:5;
83:13; Isa 17:13;
42:3; 43:17;
Hos 13:3
13:26 pJob 18:7;
20:11; 21:23;
Ps 25:7
13:27
qS Ge 40:15;
Job 33:11;
Jer 20:2;
Ac 16:24
rJob 10:14
13:28
sPs 102:26;
Mk 2:21
tS Dt 28:35;
Ps 39:11;
Isa 50:9; 51:8;
Hos 5:12; Jas 5:2
14:1 uJob 15:14;
Mt 11:11
vS Job 10:20
wS Ge 3:17;
S Job 7:2
14:2 xPs 103:15;
S Jas 1:10
yPs 37:2; 90:5-6;
Isa 40:6-8
zJob 8:9; Ps 39:4;
102:11; 109:23;
144:4; Ecc 6:12
aS Job 4:20;
Ps 49:12
14:3 bPs 8:4;
144:3 cS Job 7:18
14:4 dPs 51:10
eS Job 4:17;
Eph 2:1-3
fS Job 9:30;
Jn 3:6; Ro 5:12;
7:14
14:5 gJob 24:1;
Ps 31:15; 139:16
hJob 21:21;
Ps 39:4; 90:12
iAc 17:26
14:6 jS Job 7:19
kJob 7:1,2;
Ps 39:13;
Isa 16:14; 21:16
14:7 lJob 19:10;
24:20; Ps 52:5
mIsa 11:1; 53:2;
60:21 nIsa 6:13

14:8 oIsa 6:13;

11:1; 53:2 14:9 pJob 29:19; Ps 1:3; Jer 17:8; Eze 31:7
qLev 26:4; Eze 34:27; Zec 10:1 14:10 rver 12 sS Job 10:21;
13:19 14:11 tS 2Sa 14:14 14:12 uver 10 vPs 102:26;
Rev 20:11; 21:1 wAc 3:21 14:13 xS Job 7:9 yPs 30:5;
Isa 26:20; 54:7 zS Ge 8:1 aJob 6:8 14:14 bS Job 7:1
cS 2Ki 6:33 14:15 dS Job 13:22 eS Job 10:3 14:16
/S Job 10:4; Ps 139:1-3; Pr 5:21; Jer 16:17; 32:19 gJob 10:6;
1Co 13:5 14:17 hJer 32:10 iS Dt 32:34 /S Job 9:30; S 13:23

v3 Septuagint, Vulgate and Syriac; Hebrew me
z13 Hebrew Sheol   a14 Or release

stand that God has a higher purpose in his suffering. *wrongs
. . . sins . . . offense.* The three most important OT terms for
sin (see note on Ex 34:7).
13:24 *hide your face.* Withhold your blessing (see note on
Ps 13:1).
13:25 *windblown leaf . . . dry chaff.* See note on Ps 1:4.
13:26 *sins of my youth.* Since Job feels that he is not
presently guilty of a sinful life, God must still be holding the
sins of his youth against him. *write down . . . things against
me.* See Ps 130:3; Hos 13:12; contrast 1Co 13:5.
13:27 *You fasten . . . my paths.* Elihu later quotes Job's
words (see 33:11). *marks on the soles of my feet.* The
Babylonian code of Hammurapi (18th century B.C.) attests to
the practice of putting marks on slaves. Job feels that he is
being harassed by a God who has taken him captive and is
tormenting him (see v. 25).
13:28—14:1 The introduction to ch. 14, expressing the
pessimistic theme that man's legacy is trouble and his destiny
is death.
13:28 *garment eaten by moths.* See Mt 6:19-20; Lk

12:33.
14:1 See 5:7.
14:2–6 A symmetrical poem centered around v. 4; v. 2
corresponds to v. 5, and v. 3 to v. 6. Job expostulates with
God: Given man's insignificance and inherited impurity,
why do you take him so seriously (see 13:25)?
14:2 *He . . . withers away.* Life at best is brief and fragile
(see 8:19; Ps 37:2; Isa 40:7,24). *like a fleeting shadow.* See
note on 8:9.
14:7–12 Man is like a flower that lives its short life and is
gone (v. 2), not like a tree that revives even after it has been
cut down.
14:7 *sprout.* The Hebrew root underlying this word is
translated "renewal" in v. 14.
14:13–17 Job's spirit now appears to rise above the despair
engendered by his rotting body. Although resurrection in the
fullest sense is not taught here, Job is saying that if God so
desires he is able to hide Job in the grave, then raise him back
to life at a time when the divine anger is past.
14:14 *hard service.* See note on 7:1.

18"But as a mountain erodes and
     crumbles k
   and as a rock is moved from its
     place, l
19as water wears away stones
   and torrents m wash away the soil, n
   so you destroy man's hope. o
20You overpower him once for all, and he
     is gone; p
   you change his countenance and send
     him away. q
21If his sons are honored, he does not
     know it;
   if they are brought low, he does not
     see it. r
22He feels but the pain of his own body s
   and mourns only for himself. t "

Eliphaz

15 Then Eliphaz the Temanite u re-
     plied:

2"Would a wise man answer with empty
     notions
   or fill his belly with the hot east
     wind? v
3Would he argue with useless words,
   with speeches that have no value? w
4But you even undermine piety
   and hinder devotion to God. x
5Your sin y prompts your mouth; z
   you adopt the tongue of the crafty. a
6Your own mouth condemns you, not
     mine;
   your own lips testify against you. b

7"Are you the first man ever born? c
   Were you brought forth before the
     hills? d
8Do you listen in on God's council? e

Do you limit wisdom to yourself? f
9What do you know that we do not
     know?
   What insights do you have that we
     do not have? g
10The gray-haired and the aged h are on
     our side,
   men even older than your father. i
11Are God's consolations j not enough for
     you,
   words k spoken gently to you? l
12Why has your heart m carried you away,
   and why do your eyes flash,
13so that you vent your rage n against God
   and pour out such words o from your
     mouth? p

14"What is man, that he could be pure,
   or one born of woman, q that he
     could be righteous? r
15If God places no trust in his holy ones, s
   if even the heavens are not pure in
     his eyes, t
16how much less man, who is vile and
     corrupt, u
   who drinks up evil v like water! w

17"Listen to me and I will explain to you;
   let me tell you what I have seen, x
18what wise men have declared,
   hiding nothing received from their
     fathers y
19(to whom alone the land z was given
   when no alien passed among them):
20All his days the wicked man suffers
     torment, a

14:18 k Eze 38:20; l Job 18:4
14:19 m Eze 13:13; n S Ge 7:23; o S Job 7:6
14:20 p S Job 4:20; q S Job 7:10; 8:18; S 12:19; 27:19; Jas 1:10
14:21 r Job 21:21; Ecc 9:5; Isa 63:16
14:22 s Ps 38:7; Isa 21:3; Jer 4:19; t Job 21:21
15:1 u S Job 4:1
15:2 v S Ge 41:6
15:3 w S Ne 4:2-3; S Job 6:26
15:4 x Job 25:6
15:5 y Job 11:6; 22:5 z Pr 16:23
a S Job 5:13
15:6 b S Job 9:15; 18:7; Ps 10:2; S Mt 12:37; Lk 19:22
15:7 c Job 38:21
d 1Sa 2:8; Ps 90:2; Pr 8:25
15:8 e Job 29:4; Isa 9:6; 40:13; 41:28; Jer 23:18; Ro 11:34; 1Co 2:11
15:9 f S Job 12:2; g S Job 12:3
15:10 h S Job 12:12; i S 2Ch 10:6
15:11 j S Ge 37:35; S Job 6:10; 2Co 1:3-4; k Zec 1:13; l S Dt 8:3; S 32:39; m S Job 5:17; 22:22; 23:12; 36:16; Ps 119:11,72; Jer 15:16
15:12 m Job 11:13; 36:13
15:13 n Pr 29:11; Da 11:30; o Ps 94:4 p S Job 11:8;
22:5; 32:3 **15:14** q S Job 14:1 r S 2Ch 6:36; S Job 4:17 **15:15** s S Job 5:1 t S Job 4:18 **15:16** u S Lev 5:2; S Job 4:19; Ps 14:1 v Job 20:12 w Job 12:4; 34:7; Pr 19:28 **15:17** x S Job 4:8 **15:18** y S Dt 32:7 **15:19** z Ge 12:1; Job 22:8 **15:20** a ver 24; Isa 8:22; 50:11; 66:24

14:18–22 Job's pessimism arises not from skepticism about the possibility of resurrection from the dead but rather from God's apparent unwillingness to do something immediately for a person like him, whose life has become a nightmare of pain and mourning.

15:1–6 Up to this point Eliphaz has been the most sympathetic of the three counselors, but now he has run out of patience with Job and denounces him more severely than before.

15:2 *empty.* The Hebrew for this word is translated "long-winded" in 16:3, where Job hurls Eliphaz's charges back at him. *hot east wind.* See 27:21; 38:24; the sirocco that blows in from the desert (see notes on Ge 41:6; Jer 4:11).

15:4 *piety.* See note on 4:6.

15:5 See Mt 15:11,17–18.

15:6 *mouth condemns you.* See 9:20.

15:7–10 Job, says Eliphaz, presumes to be wise enough to sit among the members of God's council in heaven (see note on 1:6) when in reality he is no wiser than ordinary elders and sages on earth.

15:10 Age, with its tested experience, was equated with wisdom in ancient times—a truism denied by Elihu (see 32:6–9).

15:11–13 Eliphaz chides Job for replying in rage to his

friends' attempts to console him with gentle words, which Eliphaz believes come from God himself (v. 11). But Eliphaz has been guilty of cruel insinuation (ch. 5), and the other two counselors have been even more malicious. Genuine words of comfort for Job have been few indeed (see 4:2–6).

15:14–16 See 25:4–6. Eliphaz repeats what he had already said in 4:17–19, perhaps because he thought the earlier words had come to him through divine revelation (see note on 4:12–21).

15:14 *born of woman.* An echo of Job's words in 14:1.

15:15 *holy ones.* Angels (see note on 5:1).

15:16 *drinks up evil like water.* See Elihu's description of Job in 34:7.

15:17–26 Eliphaz now bolsters his earlier advice with traditional wisdom: The wicked man (a caricature of Job) can never escape the suffering he deserves.

15:20–35 A poem on the fate of the wicked (see 8:11–19). Eliphaz's caricature continues with a variety of figures: a belligerent sinner who attacks God (vv. 24–26); a fat, rich wicked man who finally gets what he deserves (vv. 27–32); a grapevine stripped before the fruit is ripe (v. 33a); "an olive tree shedding its blossoms" (v. 33b). As long as Eliphaz rejects Job's insistence that the wicked go on prospering, he does not have to wrestle with the disturbing

the ruthless through all the years
stored up for him. *b*

[21] Terrifying sounds fill his ears; *c*
when all seems well, marauders
attack him. *d*

[22] He despairs of escaping the darkness; *e*
he is marked for the sword. *f*

[23] He wanders about *g*—food for
vultures *b*; *h*
he knows the day of darkness *i* is at
hand. *j*

[24] Distress and anguish *k* fill him with
terror; *l*
they overwhelm him, like a king *m*
poised to attack,

[25] because he shakes his fist *n* at God
and vaunts himself against the
Almighty, *o*

[26] defiantly charging against him
with a thick, strong shield. *p*

[27] "Though his face is covered with fat
and his waist bulges with flesh, *q*

[28] he will inhabit ruined towns
and houses where no one lives, *r*
houses crumbling to rubble. *s*

[29] He will no longer be rich and his wealth
will not endure, *t*
nor will his possessions spread over
the land. *u*

[30] He will not escape the darkness; *v*
a flame *w* will wither his shoots, *x*
and the breath of God's mouth *y* will
carry him away. *z*

[31] Let him not deceive *a* himself by
trusting what is worthless, *b*
for he will get nothing in return. *c*

[32] Before his time *d* he will be paid in
full, *e*
and his branches will not flourish. *f*

[33] He will be like a vine stripped of its
unripe grapes, *g*
like an olive tree shedding its
blossoms. *h*

[34] For the company of the godless *i* will be
barren,
and fire will consume *j* the tents of
those who love bribes. *k*

[35] They conceive trouble *l* and give birth
to evil; *m*
their womb fashions deceit."

Job

16 Then Job replied:

[2] "I have heard many things like
these;
miserable comforters *n* are you all! *o*

[3] Will your long-winded speeches never
end? *p*
What ails you that you keep on
arguing? *q*

[4] I also could speak like you,
if you were in my place;
I could make fine speeches against you
and shake my head *r* at you.

[5] But my mouth would encourage you;
comfort *s* from my lips would bring
you relief. *t*

[6] "Yet if I speak, my pain is not relieved;
and if I refrain, it does not go away. *u*

[7] Surely, O God, you have worn me
out; *v*
you have devastated my entire
household. *w*

[8] You have bound me—and it has
become a witness;
my gauntness *x* rises up and testifies
against me. *y*

[9] God assails me and tears *z* me in his
anger *a*
and gnashes his teeth at me; *b*
my opponent fastens on me his
piercing eyes. *c*

[10] Men open their mouths *d* to jeer at
me; *e*
they strike my cheek *f* in scorn
and unite together against me. *g*

[11] God has turned me over to evil men

15:20 *b*Job 24:1;
27:13-23;
Isa 2:12;
Jer 46:10;
Ob 1:15; Zep 1:7
15:21 *c*ver 24;
S 1Sa 3:11;
Job 18:11; 20:25;
Jer 6:25; 20:3
*d*Job 22:10;
27:20; Isa 13:3;
Jer 51:25,53,56;
1Th 5:3
15:22 *e*ver 23;
S Job 5:14; 24:17;
38:15; Ps 91:5;
SS 3:8 *f*Job 16:13;
18:19; 19:29;
20:24; 27:14;
33:18; 36:12;
Pr 7:23; Isa 1:20;
Jer 44:27;
Hos 9:13;
Am 5:19
15:23 *g*Ps 109:10
*h*Pr 30:17;
Eze 39:17;
Mt 24:28;
Lk 17:37 *i*S ver
22 *j*Job 18:12
15:24 *k*Isa 8:22;
9:1 *l*S ver 20
*m*Job 18:14
15:25 *n*Ps 44:16;
Isa 10:32; 37:23
*o*S Job 11:8;
35:12; 36:9;
40:8; Ps 2:2-3;
73:9; 75:5;
Pr 21:30;
Isa 3:16; 45:9
15:26 *p*Jer 44:16
15:27 *q*S Jdg 3:17
15:28 *r*Isa 5:9
*s*S Job 3:14
15:29
*t*S Job 3:15; S 7:8
*u*Isa 5:8
15:30 *v*S Job 5:14
*w*ver 34;
Job 16:7; 20:26;
22:20; 31:12 *x*ver
32; Job 8:19;
18:16; 29:19;
Hos 9:1-16;
Mal 4:1
*y*S Ex 15:10
*z*Isa 40:23-24
15:31 *a*Job 31:5;
Pr 1:16; 6:18;
Isa 44:20; 59:7;
Mic 2:11;
S Mk 13:5;
Jas 1:16
*b*Isa 30:12;
47:10; 59:4;
Jer 7:4,8;
S Mt 6:19
*c*Job 20:7; 22:13;
27:9; 35:13;
Pr 15:29;
Isa 1:15;
Jer 11:11; Mic 3:4
15:32 *d*Ecc 7:17
*e*Job 22:16;
36:14; Ps 55:23;
109:8; Pr 10:27
*f*S ver 30
15:33 *g*Hab 3:17
*h*S Job 4:20

15:34 *i*S Job 8:13 *j*S ver 30; Heb 10:27 *k*S Ex 23:8; S 1Sa 8:3
15:35 *l*S Job 5:7 *m*S Job 4:8; S Isa 29:20; Gal 6:7; Jas 1:15
16:2 *n*Ps 69:20 *o*S Job 6:15 *p*Job 11:2; 18:2 *q*S Job 6:26
16:4 *r*S 2Ki 19:21; Ps 22:7; Isa 37:22; Jer 48:27; La 2:15;
Zep 2:15; S Mt 27:39 **16:5** *s*Job 29:25 *t*S Ge 37:35 **16:6**
*u*S Job 6:3; S 7:21 **16:7** *v*S Jdg 8:5; S Job 7:3 *w*S Job 1:19
16:8 *x*Job 17:7; 19:20; 33:21; Ps 6:7; 22:17; 88:9; 102:5;
109:24; La 5:17 *y*S Job 10:17 **16:9** *z*S Job 12:14; Hos 6:1
*a*S Job 9:5; 18:4; 19:11 *b*Job 30:21; Ps 35:16; 37:12;
112:10; La 2:16; Ac 7:54 *c*S Job 13:24 **16:10** *d*Ps 22:13;
35:21 *e*Job 12:4; 19:18; 21:3; 30:1,9; Ps 22:13; 69:12;
119:51 *f*Isa 50:6; La 3:30; Mic 5:1; Ac 23:2 *g*ver 7;
S Job 11:3; 19:12; 30:12; Ps 27:3; 35:15; Ac 7:57

*b*23 Or *about, looking for food*

---

corollary: the mystery of why the innocent sometimes suffer.
15:23,30 *darkness.* Death, characterized by the journey to
the netherworld (see note on 10:21).
15:35 *They conceive trouble and give birth to evil.* Repeated in Isa 59:4 (see note there). Once initiated, sinful
thoughts develop quickly into evil acts.
16:2–5 Helpful advice is usually brief and encouraging, not
lengthy and judgmental.
16:2 *miserable comforters.* See note on 13:1–12. Job
would eventually be comforted, but not by his three friends

(see 42:11).
16:3 *long-winded.* See note on 15:2.
16:4 *shake . . . head.* A gesture of insult and scorn (see Ps
22:7; Jer 48:27; Mt 27:39).
16:9 The figure here is graphic and disturbing: God, like a
ferocious lion (see 10:16), attacks and tears at Job's flesh.
opponent. The Hebrew for this word is translated "enemy"
in 19:11.
16:10–14 Job sees himself as God's target and views his
situation as the reverse of Eliphaz's description in 15:25–26.

and thrown me into the clutches of
the wicked. [h]

12All was well with me, but he shattered
me;
he seized me by the neck and
crushed me. [i]
He has made me his target; [j]

13 his archers surround me. [k]
Without pity, he pierces [l] my kidneys
and spills my gall on the ground.

14Again and again [m] he bursts upon me;
he rushes at me like a warrior. [n]

15"I have sewed sackcloth [o] over my skin
and buried my brow in the dust. [p]

16My face is red with weeping, [q]
deep shadows ring my eyes; [r]

17yet my hands have been free of
violence [s]
and my prayer is pure. [t]

18"O earth, do not cover my blood; [u]
may my cry [v] never be laid to rest! [w]

19Even now my witness [x] is in heaven; [y]
my advocate is on high. [z]

20My intercessor [a] is my friend [c] [b]
as my eyes pour out [c] tears [d] to God;

21on behalf of a man he pleads [e] with God
as a man pleads for his friend.

22"Only a few years will pass
before I go on the journey of no
return. [f]

17 1My spirit [g] is broken,
my days are cut short, [h]
the grave awaits me. [i]

2Surely mockers [j] surround me; [k]
my eyes must dwell on their hostility.

3"Give me, O God, the pledge you
demand. [l]

Who else will put up security [m] for
me? [n]

4You have closed their minds to
understanding; [o]
therefore you will not let them
triumph.

5If a man denounces his friends for
reward, [p]
the eyes of his children will fail. [q]

6"God has made me a byword [r] to
everyone, [s]
a man in whose face people spit. [t]

7My eyes have grown dim with grief; [u]
my whole frame is but a shadow. [v]

8Upright men are appalled at this;
the innocent are aroused [w] against the
ungodly.

9Nevertheless, the righteous [x] will hold
to their ways,
and those with clean hands [y] will
grow stronger. [z]

10"But come on, all of you, try again!
I will not find a wise man among
you. [a]

11My days have passed, [b] my plans are
shattered,
and so are the desires of my heart. [c]

12These men turn night into day; [d]
in the face of darkness they say,
'Light is near.' [e]

13If the only home I hope for is the
grave, [d] [f]

16:11
[h]S Job 9:24
16:12 /S Job 9:17
/S Job 6:4;
La 3:12
16:13 [k]S Job 3:23
/Job 20:24;
Pr 7:23; La 3:13
16:14 [m]Job 9:17
[n]S Job 10:3;
Joel 2:7
16:15
[o]S Ge 37:34
[p]S Job 2:8
16:16 [q]ver 20;
Ps 6:6 /Job 2:7;
17:7; 30:17,30;
33:19; Isa 52:14
16:17 [s]Isa 55:7;
59:6; Jer 18:11;
Jnh 3:8
/S Job 6:28;
S 10:7; 13:7;
Isa 53:9; Zep 3:13
16:18
[u]S Ge 4:10;
Isa 26:21 [v]Ps 5:2;
18:6; 102:1;
119:169
[w]Job 19:24;
Ps 66:18-19;
Heb 11:4
16:19
[x]S Ge 31:50;
S Ro 1:9; 1Th 2:5
[y]Job 22:12; 42:2
[z]Job 19:27;
21:17; 25:2;
27:13; 31:2;
Ps 113:5;
Isa 33:5; 57:15;
58:4; 66:1;
Mk 11:10
16:20 [a]S Ro 8:34
[b]Jn 15:15
[c]La 2:19 [d]S ver
16
16:21 [e]1Ki 8:45;
Ps 9:4; 140:12
16:22
/S Job 10:21
17:1 [g]Ps 143:4
[h]Isa 38:12
/Ps 88:3-4;
Ecc 12:1-7
17:2 /S Job 11:3
[k]S Job 6:14;
Ps 22:7; 119:51;
Jer 20:7; La 3:14
17:3 /Ps 35:27;
119:122

[m]Pr 6:1 [n]Ps 35:2;
40:17; Isa 38:14

17:4 [o]S Job 12:12 17:5 [p]S Ex 22:15 [q]S Job 11:20 17:6
[r]S 1Ki 9:7; Job 30:9; Jer 15:4 [s]S ver 2 [t]S Nu 12:14 17:7
[u]S Job 16:8 [v]S Job 2:12; S 16:16 17:8 [w]S Ex 4:14 17:9
[x]Pr 4:18 [y]S 2Sa 22:21; S Job 9:30 [z]S 1Sa 2:4; Ps 84:7 17:10
[a]S Job 12:2 17:11 [b]ver 15; Isa 38:10 [c]S Job 7:6 17:12
[d]Isa 50:11 [e]Job 5:17-26; S 11:17 17:13 /S 2Sa 14:14;
S Job 3:13

[c]20 Or My friends treat me with scorn   [d]13 Hebrew
Sheol

16:12 All was well . . . but he shattered me. See 2:3 and
note. made me his target. See note on 6:4.

16:15–17 Job summarizes his misery: Though innocent,
he continues to suffer.

16:15 sackcloth . . . dust. Signs of mourning (see notes on
Ge 37:34; Jnh 3:5–6).

16:18–21 Verse 18 (see v. 22; 17:1) indicates that Job
does not think he will live long enough to be vindicated
before his peers. His only hope is that in heaven he has a
friend (v. 20), a holy one (see 5:1), who will be his "witness," his "advocate," his "intercessor," one who will plead
with God on his behalf (v. 21; see 9:33 and note).

16:18 blood . . . cry. Job felt that his blood, like Abel's (see
Ge 4:10 and note), was innocent and would therefore cry
out from the ground after his death.

16:20 intercessor. The Hebrew for this word is translated
"mediator" in 33:23 and "spokesman" in Isa 43:27.

16:22 only a few years will pass. Job does not expect his
death immediately. journey of no return. To the netherworld
(see notes on 7:9; 10:21).

17:1 the grave awaits me. See note on vv. 10–16.

17:3 Give me . . . the pledge you demand. Job is asking

God for a guarantee that he is right, that he is not guilty of
sins that deserve punishment (as his counselors have said).

17:4 their minds. Those of his three friends.

17:5 Job quotes a proverb to counter the false accusations
of his friends.

17:6–9 The guarantee Job asked for is not provided, so he
feels that God is responsible for making him an object of
scorn. If the tone of vv. 8–9 is intended as sarcastic (as v. 10
would seem to indicate), the "upright" and "innocent" are
the counselors.

17:6 byword. See 30:9; an object of scorn and ridicule (see
the covenant curse in Dt 28:37). in whose face people spit.
See 30:10.

17:7 frame is but a shadow. See note on 2:7.

17:10–16 Zophar had promised that Job's repentance
would turn his darkness into light (11:17). Job now makes a
parody on such advice (vv. 12–16). His only hope is the
grave (see v. 1), which will not be as his home had been (vv.
13–15).

17:13 home. See Ecc 12:5. darkness. See 18:18; the
netherworld (see note on 10:21).

if I spread out my bed^g in darkness,^h
14if I say to corruption,^i 'You are my
    father,'
and to the worm,^j 'My mother' or
    'My sister,'
15where then is my hope?^k
    Who can see any hope for me?^l
16Will it go down to the gates of
    death^e?^m
Will we descend together into the
    dust?'"^n

Bildad

18 Then Bildad the Shuhite^o replied:
2"When will you end these
    speeches?^p
Be sensible, and then we can talk.
3Why are we regarded as cattle^q
    and considered stupid in your sight?^r
4You who tear yourself^s to pieces in
    your anger,^t
    is the earth to be abandoned for your
    sake?
    Or must the rocks be moved from
    their place?^u

5"The lamp of the wicked is snuffed
    out;^v
    the flame of his fire stops burning.^w
6The light in his tent^x becomes dark;^y
    the lamp beside him goes out.^z
7The vigor^a of his step is weakened;^b
    his own schemes^c throw him
    down.^d
8His feet thrust him into a net^e
    and he wanders into its mesh.
9A trap seizes him by the heel;
    a snare^f holds him fast.^g
10A noose^h is hidden for him on the
    ground;
    a trap^i lies in his path.^j
11Terrors^k startle him on every side^l
    and dog^m his every step.

12Calamity^n is hungry^o for him;
    disaster^p is ready for him when he
    falls.^q
13It eats away parts of his skin;^r
    death's firstborn devours his limbs.^s
14He is torn from the security of his tent^t
    and marched off to the king^u of
    terrors.^v
15Fire resides^f in his tent;^w
    burning sulfur^x is scattered over his
    dwelling.
16His roots dry up below^y
    and his branches wither above.^z
17The memory of him perishes from the
    earth;^a
    he has no name^b in the land.^c
18He is driven from light into darkness^d
    and is banished^e from the world.^f
19He has no offspring^g or descendants^h
    among his people,
    no survivor^i where once he lived.^j
20Men of the west are appalled^k at his
    fate;^l
    men of the east are seized with
    horror.
21Surely such is the dwelling^m of an evil
    man;^n
    such is the place^o of one who knows
    not God."^p

17:13 gPs 139:8
hPs 88:18
17:14 iJob 13:28;
30:28,30;
Ps 16:10; 49:9
/S Job 4:19; S 7:5
17:15 kS Job 7:6
/Ps 31:22;
La 3:18;
Eze 37:11
17:16
mS Job 7:9;
33:28; Ps 9:13;
30:3; 107:18;
Isa 38:10,17;
Jnh 2:6
nS Ge 2:7;
S Job 3:19; 20:11;
21:26
18:1 oS Job 8:1
18:2 pS Job 8:2;
S 16:3
18:3 qS Job 12:7
rPs 73:22
18:4 sJob 13:14
tS Job 16:9
uJob 14:18
18:5 vJob 21:17;
35:15; Pr 13:9;
20:20; 24:20;
Jer 25:10;
Mt 25:8; Jn 8:12
wS Job 5:14;
12:25; 24:17;
38:15
18:6 xS Job 8:22
yS Job 5:14
zS Job 11:17;
S 12:25
18:7 aS Job 13:26
bPr 4:12
cS Job 5:13
dS Job 15:6
18:8 eJob 19:6;
Ps 9:15; 10:9;
35:7; 57:6;
66:11; 140:5;
La 1:13; Mic 7:2;
Hab 1:15
18:9 fJob 22:10;
30:12; Isa 24:18;
Jer 48:44;
Am 5:19 gPr 5:22
18:10 hPr 7:22;
Isa 51:20
/S 1Sa 28:9
/Ps 140:5
18:11 kver 14;
S Job 6:4; 20:25;
24:17; Ps 55:4;
88:15; Isa 28:19;
Jer 15:8; La 2:22
/S Job 15:21;
Ps 31:13 mver 18;
Job 20:8;
Isa 22:18

18:12 nJob 21:17 oIsa 8:21; 9:20; 65:13 pJob 31:3
qJob 15:23 18:13 rNu 12:12 sZec 14:12 tJob 18:14 18:14 uS Job 8:22
uJob 15:24 vS ver 11 18:15 wver 18; Job 20:26 xS Ge 19:24
18:16 yIsa 5:24; Hos 5:12; Am 2:9 zS Ge 27:28; S Job 8:12;
S 15:30 18:17 aS Dt 32:26 bDt 9:14; Ps 9:5; 69:28; Pr 10:7;
Isa 14:22 cJob 24:20; Ps 34:16; Pr 2:22; 10:7; Isa 49:15
18:18 dS Job 5:14 eS ver 11 /S Job 11:20; 30:8 18:19
gPs 37:28; Isa 1:4; 14:20; Jer 22:30 hPs 21:10; 109:13;
Isa 14:22 /S 2Ki 10:11; S Eze 17:8 /Job 27:14-15 18:20
kPs 22:6-7; Isa 52:14; 53:2-3; Eze 27:35 /Ps 37:13;
Jer 46:21; 50:27,31; Eze 7:7 18:21 mJob 21:28 nIsa 57:20
oS Job 7:10 pS Job 4:21; 1Th 4:5

e16 Hebrew *Sheol*   t15 Or *Nothing he had remains*

17:14 In the grave, one's family consists only of decomposition and maggots.
17:15 *where ... is my hope?* See 14:19.
17:16 *gates of death.* See 38:17; Mt 16:18. In Mesopotamian literature, all who entered the netherworld passed through a series of seven gates. *dust.* See note on 7:21.
18:1-4 Bildad resents what he perceives to be a belittling attitude. He considers Job's emotional reaction as self-centered and irrational.
18:5-21 Another poem on the fate of the wicked (see 8:11-19; 15:20-35). Bildad wants to convince Job that he is wrong when he claims that the righteous suffer and the wicked prosper. Bildad is absolutely certain that every wicked person gets paid in full, in this life, for his wicked deeds.
18:5 *The lamp of the wicked is snuffed out.* See 21:17; repeated in Pr 13:9. Life, symbolized by light, is extinguished.
18:13 *death's firstborn.* See 5:7.

18:14 *king of terrors.* A vivid figure of speech referring to death, which is personified in v. 13. Canaanite literature pictured death as the devouring god Mot. Isaiah reverses the figure and envisions the Lord as swallowing up death forever (Isa 25:8; see 1Co 15:54).
18:15 *burning sulfur.* Reminiscent of the destruction of Sodom and Gomorrah (see Ge 19:24).
18:16 *roots ... and ... branches.* Cf. Am 2:9; figurative for descendants (see, e.g., Isa 11:1,10) and/or ancestors (see, e.g., Jdg 5:14; Isa 14:29).
18:17 *memory of him perishes.* Apparently Bildad knows nothing of punishment in the realm of death. The only retribution beyond the grave is having one's memory (name) cut off by not leaving any heirs (see v. 19).
18:18 *darkness.* See 17:13; the netherworld (see note on 10:21).
18:21 *evil man ... knows not God.* Having no intimate knowledge of God is synonymous with being wicked (see Hos 4:1-2,6).

Job

19

Then Job replied:

2"How long will you torment[q] me
and crush[r] me with words?
3Ten times[s] now you have reproached[t]
me;
shamelessly you attack me.
4If it is true that I have gone astray,
my error[u] remains my concern alone.
5If indeed you would exalt yourselves
above me[v]
and use my humiliation against me,
6then know that God has wronged me[w]
and drawn his net[x] around me.[y]

7"Though I cry, 'I've been wronged!' I
get no response;[z]
though I call for help,[a] there is no
justice.[b]
8He has blocked my way so I cannot
pass;[c]
he has shrouded my paths in
darkness.[d]
9He has stripped[e] me of my honor[f]
and removed the crown from my
head.[g]
10He tears me down[h] on every side till I
am gone;
he uproots my hope[i] like a tree.[j]
11His anger[k] burns against me;
he counts me among his enemies.[l]
12His troops advance in force;[m]
they build a siege ramp[n] against me
and encamp around my tent.[o]

13"He has alienated my brothers[p] from
me;

my acquaintances are completely
estranged from me.[q]
14My kinsmen have gone away;
my friends[r] have forgotten me.
15My guests[s] and my maidservants[t]
count me a stranger;
they look upon me as an alien.
16I summon my servant, but he does not
answer,
though I beg him with my own
mouth.
17My breath is offensive to my wife;
I am loathsome[u] to my own
brothers.
18Even the little boys[v] scorn me;
when I appear, they ridicule me.[w]
19All my intimate friends[x] detest me;[y]
those I love have turned against me.[z]
20I am nothing but skin and bones;[a]
I have escaped with only the skin of
my teeth.[g]

21"Have pity on me, my friends,[b] have
pity,
for the hand of God has struck[c] me.
22Why do you pursue[d] me as God does?[e]
Will you never get enough of my
flesh?[f]

23"Oh, that my words were recorded,
that they were written on a scroll,[g]
24that they were inscribed with an iron
tool[h] on[h] lead,
or engraved in rock forever![i]

19:2 qJob 13:25
rJob 6:9
19:3 sS Ge 31:7
tJob 20:3
19:4 uJob 6:24
19:5 vPs 35:26;
38:16; 55:12
19:6 wS Job 6:29
xS Job 18:8
yS Job 10:3
19:7 zJob 30:20;
Ps 22:2
aJob 30:24,28;
31:35; Ps 5:2
bS Job 9:24;
Hab 1:2-4
19:8 cLa 3:7;
Hos 2:6
dJob 3:26; 23:17;
30:26; Ecc 6:4;
Isa 59:9; Jer 8:15;
14:19; La 3:2
19:9 eS Job 12:17
fGe 43:28;
Ex 12:42;
Ps 15:4; 50:23;
Pr 14:31
gS Job 2:8; 29:14;
Ps 89:39,44;
La 5:16
19:10 hS Job 12:14
iS Job 7:6
jS Job 14:7
19:11 kJob 16:9
lS Job 13:24
19:12 mS Job 16:13
nS Job 16:10
oS Job 3:23
19:13 pPs 69:8

qver-19; Job 16:7;
42:11; Ps 31:11;
38:11; 88:8
19:14 rver 19;
S 2Sa 15:12;
Job 12:4; 16:20;
Ps 88:18;
Jer 20:10; 38:22
19:15 sGe 14:14
tEcc 2:7
19:17 uPs 38:5
19:18 vS 2Ki 2:23
wS Job 16:10
19:19 xS ver 14;
S Job 6:14;
Ps 55:12-13
yJob 30:10 zS ver
13; Jn 13:18

19:20 aS Job 2:5 19:21 bS Job 6:14 cS Jdg 2:15; S Job 4:5;
S 10:3; La 3:1 19:22 dS Job 13:25 ever 6 /S 2Ch 28:9;
Ps 14:4; 27:2; 69:26; Pr 30:14; Isa 53:4 19:23 gS Ex 17:14;
S Ps 40:7; S Isa 8:1 19:24 hJer 17:1 iS Job 16:18

g20 Or only my gums   h24 Or and

19:3 *Ten times.* Several times. Ten is often used as a round number (see, e.g., Ge 31:41; 1Sa 1:8).
19:4 *my concern alone.* Job's friends have no right to interfere or to behave as if they were God (see v. 22).
19:6 *wronged.* Cf. 40:8. The Hebrew for this verb is twice translated "pervert" in 8:3, where Bildad denied that God perverts justice. But Job, struggling with the enigma of his suffering, can only conclude that God is his enemy, though in fact he is his friend who delights in him (see 1:8; 2:3). Job's true enemy, of course, is the Accuser. *drawn his net.* The wicked may get themselves into trouble, as Bildad had pointed out (see 18:8–10), but Job here attributes his suffering to God.
19:7 *I cry, 'I've been wronged!'* Lit. "I cry, 'Violence!'" See Hab 1:2.
19:8–12 In Job's mind, God is at war with him (see 16:12–14).
19:10 *uproots my hope like a tree.* See 24:20; unlike 14:7–9, where Job had used as a symbol of hope a tree that is cut down but later sprouts again.
19:12 *siege ramp.* See 30:12.
19:13–19 See Jer 12:6. Nothing in life hurts more than rejection by one's family and friends. Job's children are gone, and his wife, brothers, friends and servants find him repul-

sive.
19:17 *breath is offensive.* See note on 2:7.
19:18 *little boys scorn me.* An intolerable insult in a patriarchal society, where one's elders were to be honored and respected (see Ex 20:12 and note).
19:20 *skin and bones.* See note on 2:7. *skin of my teeth.* The NIV text note understands the phrase to imply that even Job's teeth are gone.
19:21 *hand of God has struck me.* See 1:11; 2:4–6; see also note on v. 6.
19:23–27 Probably the best-known and most-loved passage in the book of Job, reaching a high point in Job's understanding of his own situation and of his relationship to God. Its position between two sections in which Job pleads with (vv. 21–22) and then warns (vv. 28–29) his friends causes it to stand out even more boldly.
19:23 *my words.* Job would have his complaint and defense recorded so that even after his death they would endure until he is finally vindicated. *scroll.* See note on Ex 17:14.
19:24 *iron.* See also 20:24; 28:2; 40:18; 41:27. Iron did not come into common use in the ancient Near East until the 12th century B.C.

[25]I know that my Redeemer[i][j] lives,[k]
    and that in the end he will stand
      upon the earth.[j]
[26]And after my skin has been destroyed,
    yet[k] in[l] my flesh I will see God;[l]
[27]I myself will see him
    with my own eyes[m]—I, and not
      another.
    How my heart yearns[n] within me!

[28]"If you say, 'How we will hound[o] him,
    since the root of the trouble lies in
      him,[m]'
[29]you should fear the sword yourselves;
    for wrath will bring punishment by
      the sword,[p]
    and then you will know that there is
      judgment.[n]"[q]

Zophar

20 Then Zophar the Naamathite[r] replied:

[2]"My troubled thoughts prompt me to
    answer
    because I am greatly disturbed.[s]
[3]I hear a rebuke[t] that dishonors me,
    and my understanding inspires me to
      reply.

[4]"Surely you know how it has been from
    of old,[u]
    ever since man[o] was placed on the
      earth,
[5]that the mirth of the wicked[v] is brief,
    the joy of the godless[w] lasts but a
      moment.[x]
[6]Though his pride[y] reaches to the
      heavens[z]
    and his head touches the clouds,[a]

[7]he will perish forever,[b] like his own
      dung;
    those who have seen him will say,
      'Where is he?'[c]
[8]Like a dream[d] he flies away,[e] no more
      to be found,
    banished[f] like a vision of the night.[g]
[9]The eye that saw him will not see him
      again;
    his place will look on him no more.[h]
[10]His children[i] must make amends to the
      poor;
    his own hands must give back his
      wealth.[j]
[11]The youthful vigor[k] that fills his bones[l]
    will lie with him in the dust.[m]

[12]"Though evil[n] is sweet in his mouth
    and he hides it under his tongue,[o]
[13]though he cannot bear to let it go
    and keeps it in his mouth,[p]
[14]yet his food will turn sour in his
      stomach;[q]
    it will become the venom of
      serpents[r] within him.
[15]He will spit out the riches[s] he
      swallowed;
    God will make his stomach vomit[t]
      them up.
[16]He will suck the poison[u] of serpents;
    the fangs of an adder will kill him.[v]
[17]He will not enjoy the streams,

19:25 /S Ex 6:6;
S Lev 25:25;
Ps 68:5; 78:35;
Pr 23:11;
Isa 41:14; 43:14;
44:6,24; 47:4;
48:17; 49:26;
54:5; 59:20;
60:16
[k]S 1Sa 14:39;
Job 16:19
19:26
/S Nu 12:8;
S Mt 5:8;
1Co 13:12;
1Jn 3:2
19:27 [m]Lk 2:30
[n]Ps 42:1; 63:1;
84:2
19:28
[o]S Job 13:25
19:29 [p]Job 15:22
[q]Job 27:13-23;
Ps 1:5; 9:7;
58:11; Ecc 3:17;
11:9; 12:14
20:1 [r]S Job 2:11
20:2 [s]Ps 42:5;
La 1:20
20:3 [t]Job 19:3
20:4 [u]Dt 4:32;
S 32:7
20:5 [v]Ps 94:3
[w]S Job 8:13
[x]S Job 8:12;
Ps 37:35-36;
73:19
20:6 [y]Job 33:17;
Isa 16:6
[z]S Ge 11:4
[a]Isa 14:13-14;
Ob 1:3-4

20:7 [b]S Job 4:20
[c]S Job 7:8;
S 14:20
20:8 [d]Ps 73:20;
Ecc 5:3
[e]Ps 90:10;
Ecc 6:12; 12:7
/S Job 18:11
[g]Job 7:20;
34:20; Ps 90:5;
Isa 17:14; 29:7
20:9 [h]S Job 7:8
20:10 /S Job 5:4
/ver 15,18,20;
S Job 3:15; 31:8
20:11
[k]S Job 13:26
/Job 21:24
[m]S Job 17:16

20:12 [n]S Job 15:16 [o]Ps 10:7; 140:3 **20:13** [p]S Nu 11:18-20
20:14 [q]Pr 20:17; Jer 2:19; 4:18; Rev 10:9 [r]S Nu 21:6; **20:15**
[s]S ver 10 [t]S Lev 18:25 **20:16** [u]S Dt 32:32 [v]Dt 32:24

[i]25 Or defender   [j]25 Or upon my grave   [k]26 Or
And after I awake, / though this body has been
destroyed, / then   [l]26 Or / apart from
[m]28 Many Hebrew manuscripts, Septuagint and Vulgate;
most Hebrew manuscripts me   [n]29 Or / that you may
come to know the Almighty   [o]4 Or Adam

19:25 *I know that my Redeemer lives.* This staunch confession of faith has been appropriated by generations of Christians, especially through the medium of Handel's *Messiah*. But these celebrate redemption from guilt and judgment; Job had something else in mind. Although in other contexts he desires a defender (see NIV text note; see also Pr 23:11) as an advocate in heaven who would plead with God on his behalf (see 9:33-34; 16:18-21 and notes; see also note on 5:1), here the Redeemer seems to be none other than God himself (see note on Ru 2:20). Job expresses confidence that ultimately God will vindicate his faithful servants in the face of all false accusations. *in the end.* Lit. "afterward" (after Job's life has ended). *he will stand.* To defend and vindicate me.
19:26 *my skin has been destroyed.* Job senses that the ravages of his disease will eventually bring about his death. *I will see God.* He is absolutely certain, however, that death is not the end of existence and that someday he will stand in the presence of his Redeemer and see him with his own eyes (see v. 27; see also Mt 5:8; 1Jn 3:2). See note on 42:5.
19:28 *hound.* The Hebrew for this verb is translated "pursue" in v. 22. It serves as a clue that Job's tirade against the counselors is being resumed after the intervening section (vv.

23-27).
20:1-29 Yet another poem on the fate of the wicked as held by the "orthodox" theology of Job's friends (see 8:11-19; 15:20-35; 18:5-21).
20:2-3 Zophar takes Job's words, especially his closing words in 19:28-29, as a personal affront. Job has dared to assert that on Zophar's theory of retribution Zophar himself is due for punishment.
20:4-11 Zophar is proud that he is a healthy and prosperous man, for, in his view, that in itself is proof of his goodness and righteousness. But the joy and vigor of the wicked will always be brief and elusive (see Ps 73:18-20 and note).
20:6 *pride reaches to the heavens.* See Ge 11:4 and note.
20:7 *dung.* A symbol of what is temporary and worthless (see 1Ki 14:10).
20:10,19 Oppression of the poor is the mark of the truly wicked (see, e.g., Am 2:6-8; 8:4-8). On this subject, Job had no quarrel with Zophar (see 31:16-23).
20:11 *dust.* See note on 7:21.
20:12-15 An evil man's wicked deeds are like tasty food that pleases his palate but turns sour in his stomach.
20:15 *riches he swallowed.* After taking what belonged to the poor (see note on vv. 10,19).

the rivers *w* flowing with honey *x* and
cream. *y*
18What he toiled for he must give back
uneaten; *z*
he will not enjoy the profit from his
trading. *a*
19For he has oppressed the poor *b* and left
them destitute; *c*
he has seized houses *d* he did not
build.
20"Surely he will have no respite from his
craving; *e*
he cannot save himself by his
treasure. *f*
21Nothing is left for him to devour;
his prosperity will not endure. *g*
22In the midst of his plenty, distress will
overtake him; *h*
the full force of misery will come
upon him. *i*
23When he has filled his belly, *j*
God will vent his burning anger *k*
against him
and rain down his blows upon him. *l*
24Though he flees *m* from an iron weapon,
a bronze-tipped arrow pierces him. *n*
25He pulls it out of his back,
the gleaming point out of his liver.
Terrors *o* will come over him; *p*
26   total darkness *q* lies in wait for his
treasures.
A fire *r* unfanned will consume him *s*
and devour what is left in his tent. *t*
27The heavens will expose his guilt;
the earth will rise up against him. *u*
28A flood will carry off his house, *v*
rushing waters *p* on the day of God's
wrath. *w*
29Such is the fate God allots the wicked,
the heritage appointed for them by
God." *x*

Cross references (center column):

20:17 *w*Ps 36:8
*x*Dt 32:13
*y*Dt 32:14;
Job 29:6
20:18 *z*S ver 10;
S Job 5:5
*a*Ps 109:11
20:19
*b*S Job 5:16;
Ps 10:2; 94:6;
109:16
*c*S Dt 15:11;
24:14; Job 24:4,
14; 35:9;
Pr 14:31; 28:28;
Am 8:4 *d*Isa 5:8
20:20 *e*Ecc 5:12
*f*S ver 10;
Pr 11:4;
Zep 1:18;
Lk 12:15
20:21 *g*S Job 7:8
20:22
*h*S Jdg 2:15;
Lk 12:16-20 *i*ver
29; Job 21:17,30;
31:2-3
20:23
*j*S Nu 11:18-20
*k*La 4:11;
Eze 5:13; 6:12
*l*ver 14;
Ps 78:30-31
20:24
*m*Isa 24:18;
Jer 46:21; 48:44
*n*S Job 15:22
20:25
*o*S Job 18:11
*p*S Job 15:21;
Ps 88:15-16
20:26 *q*S Job 5:14
*r*S Job 1:16
*s*Job 15:34; 26:6;
28:22; 31:12;
Ps 21:9
*t*S Job 18:15
20:27
*u*S Dt 31:28
20:28 *v*Dt 28:31;
Mt 7:26-27 *w*ver
29; Nu 14:28-32;
Job 21:17,20,30;
40:11; Ps 60:3;
75:8; Pr 16:4;
Isa 24:18; 51:17;
Am 5:18; Jn 3:36;
Ro 1:18; Eph 5:6
20:29 *x*S ver 22;
S Job 15:20; 22:5;
31:2; 36:17;
Jer 13:25;
Rev 21:8

21:2 *y*S Job 13:17
*z*ver 34
21:3 *a*S Job 6:14;
S 11:3; S 16:10

Job

21

Then Job replied:

2"Listen carefully to my words; *y*
let this be the consolation you give
me. *z*
3Bear with me while I speak,
and after I have spoken, mock on. *a*

4"Is my complaint *b* directed to man?
Why should I not be impatient? *c*
5Look at me and be astonished;
clap your hand over your mouth. *d*
6When I think about this, I am
terrified; *e*
trembling seizes my body. *f*
7Why do the wicked live on,
growing old and increasing in
power? *g*
8They see their children established
around them,
their offspring before their eyes. *h*
9Their homes are safe and free from
fear; *i*
the rod of God is not upon them. *j*
10Their bulls never fail to breed;
their cows calve and do not
miscarry. *k*
11They send forth their children as a
flock; *l*
their little ones dance about.
12They sing to the music of tambourine
and harp; *m*
they make merry to the sound of the
flute. *n*
13They spend their years in prosperity *o*

Cross references (right column):

21:4 *b*S Job 7:11 *c*S Job 6:3 21:5 *d*S Jdg 18:19 21:6
*e*S Ge 45:3 *f*S Job 4:14 21:7 *g*ver 13; S Job 9:24; 12:19;
Ps 37:1; 73:3; Ecc 7:15; 8:14; Hab 1:13; Mal 3:15 21:8
*h*Ps 17:14; Mal 3:15 21:9 *i*S Job 5:24 /S Job 9:34 21:10
*k*Ex 23:26 21:11 *l*Ps 78:52; 107:41 21:12 *m*Ps 33:2
*n*S Ge 4:21; S 1Ch 15:16; Ps 71:22; 81:2; 108:2; Isa 5:12;
Mt 11:17 21:13 *o*S ver 7; S Job 8:7; Ps 10:1-12; 94:3

*p*28 Or *The possessions in his house will be carried off,*
/ *washed away*

20:18 *What he toiled for . . . he will not enjoy.* A common
theme in wisdom literature (see, e.g., Ecc 2:18–23).
20:20–25 Although a wicked man may fill his belly, when
God vents his anger against him there will be nothing for him
to eat.
20:24 *iron.* See note on 19:24.
20:26 *darkness.* See note on 10:21.
20:27 See Dt 30:19 and note.
20:28 *flood . . . rushing waters.* Caused by intermittent
streams that can overflow and cause extensive damage during the rainy season (see 6:15–16).
20:29 Like Bildad in 18:21, Zophar concludes his speech
with a summary statement in which he claims that all he has
said is in accord with God's plans for judging sinners. *Such is
the fate God allots the wicked.* Repeated almost verbatim by
Job in 27:13.
21:2 *consolation you give me.* See v. 34 ("you console
me"), which, with v. 2, frames Job's reply to Zophar.
21:4 *Is my complaint directed to man?* No, says Job, I am

complaining to God, because he is responsible for my condition—at least Job so perceived it. *impatient.* See note on
9:2–3.
21:5 *Look at me.* Job addresses his three friends.
21:6 *this.* His complaint to God. *I am terrified.* To contemplate the morally upside-down situation in which the wicked
flourish.
21:7–15 Job's counselors have elaborated on the fate of
the wicked (see 8:11–19; 15:20–35; 18:5–21; ch. 20), but
Job insists that experience shows just the reverse of what his
friends have said. The wicked, who want to know nothing of
God's ways and who even consider prayer a useless exercise
(vv. 14–15), flourish in all they do. Far from dying prematurely, as Zophar assumed concerning them (see 20:11),
they live long and increase in power (v. 7). Bildad's claim
that the wicked have no offspring or descendants (see 18:19)
Job flatly denies (vv. 8,11).
21:9 *rod of God.* See note on 9:34.
21:13 *peace.* The Hebrew root underlying this word is

and go down to the grave q p in
peace. r q

¹⁴Yet they say to God, 'Leave us alone! r
We have no desire to know your
ways. s

¹⁵Who is the Almighty, that we should
serve him?
What would we gain by praying to
him?' t

¹⁶But their prosperity is not in their own
hands,
so I stand aloof from the counsel of
the wicked. u

¹⁷"Yet how often is the lamp of the
wicked snuffed out? v
How often does calamity w come
upon them,
the fate God allots in his anger? x

¹⁸How often are they like straw before
the wind,
like chaff y swept away z a by a
gale? b

¹⁹It is said, 'God stores up a man's
punishment for his sons.' c
Let him repay the man himself, so
that he will know it! d

²⁰Let his own eyes see his destruction; e
let him drink f of the wrath of the
Almighty. s g

²¹For what does he care about the family
he leaves behind h
when his allotted months i come to
an end? j

²²"Can anyone teach knowledge to
God, k
since he judges even the highest? l

²³One man dies in full vigor, m
completely secure and at ease, n

²⁴his body t well nourished, o
his bones p rich with marrow. q

²⁵Another man dies in bitterness of soul, r
never having enjoyed anything good.

²⁶Side by side they lie in the dust, s
and worms t cover them both. u

²⁷"I know full well what you are
thinking,

the schemes by which you would
wrong me.

²⁸You say, 'Where now is the great
man's v house,
the tents where wicked men lived?' w

²⁹Have you never questioned those who
travel?
Have you paid no regard to their
accounts—

³⁰that the evil man is spared from the day
of calamity, x
that he is delivered from u the day of
wrath? y

³¹Who denounces his conduct to his face?
Who repays him for what he has
done? z

³²He is carried to the grave,
and watch is kept over his tomb. a

³³The soil in the valley is sweet to him; b
all men follow after him,
and a countless throng goes v before
him. c

³⁴"So how can you console me d with
your nonsense?
Nothing is left of your answers but
falsehood!" e

Eliphaz

22 Then Eliphaz the Temanite f replied:

²"Can a man be of benefit to God? g
Can even a wise man benefit him? h

³What pleasure i would it give the
Almighty if you were
righteous? j
What would he gain if your ways
were blameless? k

21:13 p Job 24:19;
Ps 49:14;
Isa 14:15
q S Job 3:13
21:14 r S Job 4:17;
22:17; Isa 30:11
s S Dt 32:15;
S 1Sa 15:11;
Ps 95:10; Pr 1:29;
Jer 2:20,31
21:15 t S Job 5:2;
34:9; 35:3;
Ps 73:13; 139:20;
Isa 48:5; Jer 9:6;
44:17
21:16 u Job 22:18;
Ps 1:1; 26:5;
36:1
21:17 v S Job 18:5
w Job 18:12
x S Job 20:22,28
21:18 y S Job 13:25
z S Ge 19:15
a S Job 7:10;
Pr 10:25
b S Ge 7:23
21:19 c Ex 20:5;
Jer 31:29;
Eze 18:2; Jn 9:2
d Jer 25:14;
50:29; 51:6,24,
56
21:20 e S Ex 32:33;
Nu 16:22;
S 2Ki 14:6;
Jer 42:16 f Job 6:4
g S Job 20:28;
Jer 25:15;
Rev 14:10
21:21 h Job 14:22
i S Job 14:5
j S Job 14:21;
Ecc 5:5-6
21:22 k Job 35:11;
36:22; 39:17;
Ps 94:12;
Isa 40:13-14;
Jer 32:33;
Ro 11:34
l S Job 4:18;
Ps 82:1; 86:8;
135:5
21:23 m S Ge 15:15;
S Job 13:26
n S Job 3:13
21:24 o Ps 73:4
p Job 20:11
q Pr 3:8
21:25 r S Job 10:1
21:26 s S Job 17:16
t S Job 7:5
u Job 24:20;
Ecc 9:2-3;
Isa 14:11
21:28 v Job 1:3;
12:21; 29:25;
31:37

w S Job 8:22 x Job 31:3 y S Job 20:22,28; S Isa 5:30;
Ro 2:5; 2Pe 2:9 **21:31** z Job 34:11; Ps 62:12; Pr 24:11-12;
Isa 59:18 **21:32** a Isa 14:18 **21:33** b Job 3:22 c S Job 3:19
21:34 d ver 2 e S Job 6:15; 8:20 **22:1** f S Job 4:1 **22:2**
g Job 35:7; Pr 9:12

q 13 Hebrew *Sheol*   r 13 Or *in an instant*
s 17-20 Verses 17 and 18 may be taken as exclamations
and 19 and 20 as declarations.   t 24 The meaning of
the Hebrew for this word is uncertain.   u 30 Or *man is
reserved for the day of calamity, / that he is brought forth
to*   v 33 Or */ as a countless throng went*

---

translated "those who live quietly" in Ps 35:20.
21:16 See 22:18. Job disavows the unholy counsel of the
wicked and knows that God is in control (see v. 17), but such
knowledge makes God all the more of an enigma to him.
21:17 *lamp of the wicked snuffed out.* See 18:5 and note.
21:18 *straw . . . chaff.* See 13:25; see also note on Ps 1:4.
21:20 *drink . . . wrath of the Almighty.* See note on Isa
51:17.
21:22 *Can anyone teach . . . God?* See Isa 40:14. On the
contrary, God is the one who does the teaching (see 35:11;
36:22; chs. 38-41).
21:26 *dust.* See note on 7:21.
21:34 *how can you console me . . . ?* See 16:2 and note.

22:1—26:14 The third cycle of speeches, unlike the first
(chs. 4-14) and second (chs. 15-21), is truncated and abbreviated. Bildad's speech is very brief (25:1-6), and Zophar
does not speak at all. The dialogue between Job and his
friends comes to an end because the friends cannot convince
Job of his guilt—Job cannot acknowledge what is not
true.

22:2—4 Eliphaz's odd reasoning is as follows: Since all
things have their origin in God, man's giving back what God
has given him does not enhance God in any way. Indeed,
God is indifferent to man's goodness, because goodness is
expected of him. It is when man becomes wicked that God is
aroused (v. 4).

4"Is it for your piety that he rebukes you
  and brings charges against you? [l]
5Is not your wickedness great?
  Are not your sins [m] endless? [n]
6You demanded security [o] from your
    brothers for no reason; [p]
  you stripped men of their clothing,
    leaving them naked. [q]
7You gave no water [r] to the weary
  and you withheld food from the
    hungry, [s]
8though you were a powerful man,
    owning land [t] —
  an honored man, [u] living on it. [v]
9And you sent widows [w] away
    empty-handed [x]
  and broke the strength of the
    fatherless. [y]
10That is why snares [z] are all around
    you, [a]
  why sudden peril terrifies you, [b]
11why it is so dark [c] you cannot see,
  and why a flood of water covers
    you. [d]
12"Is not God in the heights of heaven? [e]
  And see how lofty are the highest
    stars!
13Yet you say, 'What does God know? [f]
  Does he judge through such
    darkness? [g]
14Thick clouds [h] veil him, so he does not
    see us [i]
  as he goes about in the vaulted
    heavens.' [i]
15Will you keep to the old path
  that evil men [k] have trod? [l]
16They were carried off before their
    time, [m]
  their foundations [n] washed away by a
    flood. [o]
17They said to God, 'Leave us alone!

What can the Almighty do to us?' [p]
18Yet it was he who filled their houses
    with good things, [q]
  so I stand aloof from the counsel of
    the wicked. [r]
19"The righteous see their ruin and
    rejoice; [s]
  the innocent mock [t] them, saying,
20'Surely our foes are destroyed, [u]
  and fire [v] devours their wealth.'
21"Submit to God and be at peace [w] with
    him; [x]
  in this way prosperity will come to
    you. [y]
22Accept instruction from his mouth [z]
  and lay up his words [a] in your
    heart. [b]
23If you return [c] to the Almighty, you will
    be restored: [d]
  If you remove wickedness far from
    your tent [e]
24and assign your nuggets [f] to the dust,
  your gold [g] of Ophir [h] to the rocks in
    the ravines, [i]
25then the Almighty will be your gold, [i]
  the choicest silver for you. [k]
26Surely then you will find delight in the
    Almighty [l]
  and will lift up your face [m] to God. [n]

Cross references:

22:4 [l]S Job 9:3; 19:29; Ps 143:2; Isa 3:14; Eze 20:35
22:5 [m]S Ezr 9:13; S Job 15:5 [n]S Job 15:13; S 20:29; 29:17
22:6 [o]S Ex 22:26 [p]S 2Ki 4:1 [q]S Ex 22:27; Dt 24:12-13
22:7 [r]Mt 10:42 [s]ver 9; Job 29:12; 31:17,21,31; Isa 58:7,10; Eze 18:7; Mt 25:42
22:8 [t]S Job 15:19 [u]Isa 3:3; 5:13; 9:15 [v]S Job 12:19
22:9 [w]Job 29:13; 31:16; Isa 10:2; Lk 1:53 [x]Job 24:3,21; Isa 10:2; Lk 1:53 [y]S ver 7; S Job 6:27; S Isa 1:17
22:10 [z]S Job 18:9 [a]S Job 10:3 [b]S Job 15:21
22:11 [c]S Job 5:14 [d]S Ge 7:23; Job 36:28; 38:34, 37; Ps 69:1-2; 124:4-5; Isa 58:10-11; La 3:54
22:12 [e]S Job 11:8; S 16:19
22:13 [f]ver 14; Ps 10:11; 59:7; 64:5; 73:11; 94:7; Isa 29:15; Eze 9:9; Zep 1:12 [g]Ps 139:11; Eze 8:12; Eph 6:12
22:14 [h]Job 26:9; Ps 97:2; 105:39 [i]S ver 13; S 2Ki 21:16 [i]Job 37:18; Ps 18:11; Pr 8:27; Isa 40:22; Jer 23:23-24
22:15 [k]Job 23:10; 34:36 [l]Job 34:8; Ps 1:1; 50:18
22:16 [m]S Job 15:32 [n]S Job 4:19

[o]S Ge 7:23; Mt 7:26-27 22:17 [p]Job 21:15 22:18 [q]S Job 12:6 [r]S Job 21:16 22:19 [s]Ps 5:11; 9:2; 32:11; 58:10; 64:10; 97:12; 107:42 [t]Job 21:3; Ps 52:6 22:20 [u]Ps 18:39 [v]S Job 15:30 22:21 [w]Isa 26:3,12; 27:5; Ro 5:1 [x]S Ge 17:1; Jer 9:24 [y]S Job 8:7; Ps 34:8-10; Pr 3:10; 1Pe 5:6 22:22 [z]S Dt 8:3 [a]S Job 6:10 [b]S Job 15:11; 28:23; Ps 37:31; 40:8; Pr 2:6; Eze 3:10 22:23 [c]Isa 31:6; 44:22; 55:7; 59:20; Jer 3:14,22; Eze 18:32; Zec 1:3; Mal 3:7 [d]S Job 5:24; Isa 19:22; Ac 20:32 [e]Job 11:14 22:24 [f]Job 28:6 [g]Ps 19:10 [h]S Ge 10:29 [i]S Job 1:10; 31:25; Isa 2:20; 30:22; 31:7; 40:19-20; Mt 6:19 22:25 [i]Job 31:24; Ps 49:6; 52:7; Pr 11:28 [k]2Ki 18:7; Isa 33:6; Mt 6:20-21 22:26 [l]Job 27:10; Ps 2:8; 16:6; 37:4; Isa 58:14; 61:10 [m]Job 11:15 [n]Job 11:17; 33:26; Ps 27:6; 100:1

22:4 *piety.* See note on 4:6. *brings charges against.* See note on 9:3.
22:5–11 In his earlier speeches, Eliphaz was the least caustic and at first even offered consolation (4:6; 5:17). But despite what he said in 4:3–4, Eliphaz now reprimands Job for gross social sins against the needy, who are naked and hungry (vv. 6–7), and against widows and the fatherless (v. 9). The only proof Eliphaz has for Job's alleged wickedness is his present suffering (vv. 10–11). In ch. 29 Job emphatically denies the kind of behavior of which Eliphaz accuses him.
22:6 *demanded security ... stripped men of their clothing.* Sins condemned by the prophets (see, e.g., Am 2:8 and note).
22:9 *widows ... fatherless.* See 24:3; Isa 1:17 and note; Jas 1:27. *strength.* Lit. "arms" (as in 38:15).
22:10 *snares.* See 19:6 and note.
22:11 *dark ... flood of water.* Two common figures of trouble and distress (see Ps 42:7 and note; Isa 8:7–8,22; 43:2).
22:12–20 Eliphaz finally appears to support the argument of Bildad and Zophar, who were fully convinced that Job was

a wicked man. Eliphaz makes a severe accusation: Job follows the path of the ungodly (v. 15), who defy God's power and say, "What can the Almighty do to us?" (v. 17; see vv. 13–14). They even have contempt for God's goodness (v. 18).
22:18 See 21:16 and note.
22:21–30 Eliphaz makes one last attempt to reach Job. In many ways it is a commendable call to repentance: Submit to God (v. 21), lay up God's words in your heart (v. 22), return to the Almighty and forsake wickedness (v. 23), find your delight in God rather than in gold (vv. 24–26), pray and obey (v. 27) and become concerned about sinners (vv. 29–30). But Eliphaz's advice assumes (1) that Job is a very wicked man and (2) that Job's major concern is the return of his prosperity (see v. 21). Job had already made it clear in 19:25–27 that he deeply yearned to see God and be his friend.
22:22 See Job's response in 23:12. *lay up his words in your heart.* See Ps 119:11.
22:24 *gold of Ophir.* See 28:16; the finest gold (see notes on 1Ki 9:28; 10:11; Ps 45:9; Isa 13:12).

27You will pray to him,[o] and he will hear
      you,[p]
   and you will fulfill your vows. [q]
28What you decide on will be done,[r]
   and light[s] will shine on your ways. [t]
29When men are brought low[u] and you
      say, 'Lift them up!'
   then he will save the downcast. [v]
30He will deliver even one who is not
      innocent,[w]
   who will be delivered through the
      cleanness of your hands." [x]

Job

23 Then Job replied:

2"Even today my complaint[y] is
      bitter;[z]
   his hand[w] is heavy in spite of[x] my
      groaning. [a]
3If only I knew where to find him;
   if only I could go to his dwelling! [b]
4I would state my case[c] before him
   and fill my mouth with arguments. [d]
5I would find out what he would answer
      me,[e]
   and consider what he would say.
6Would he oppose me with great
      power?[f]
   No, he would not press charges
      against me.[g]
7There an upright man[h] could present
      his case before him,[i]
   and I would be delivered forever
      from my judge.[j]

8"But if I go to the east, he is not there;
   if I go to the west, I do not find him.

9When he is at work in the north, I do
      not see him;
   when he turns to the south, I catch
      no glimpse of him. [k]
10But he knows the way that I take;[l]
   when he has tested me,[m] I will come
      forth as gold. [n]
11My feet have closely followed his
      steps;[o]
   I have kept to his way without
      turning aside.[p]
12I have not departed from the commands
      of his lips;[q]
   I have treasured the words of his
      mouth more than my daily
      bread. [r]

13"But he stands alone, and who can
      oppose him?[s]
   He does whatever he pleases. [t]
14He carries out his decree against me,
   and many such plans he still has in
      store. [u]
15That is why I am terrified before him;[v]
   when I think of all this, I fear him. [w]
16God has made my heart faint;[x]
   the Almighty[y] has terrified me. [z]
17Yet I am not silenced by the darkness,[a]
   by the thick darkness that covers my
      face.

24 "Why does the Almighty not set
      times[b] for judgment? [c]

22:27 oS Job 5:27
pS Job 5:15;
S Ps 86:7;
S Isa 30:19
qS Nu 30:2
22:28
rPs 103:11;
145:19
sJob 33:28;
Ps 97:11; Pr 4:18
tS Job 11:17
22:29 uS Est 5:12
vPs 18:27;
S Mt 23:12
22:30 wIsa 1:18;
Ro 4:5
xS 2Sa 22:21
23:2 yS Job 7:11
zS 1Sa 1:10;
S Job 6:3 aPs 6:6;
32:4; Jer 45:3;
Eze 21:7
23:3 bDt 4:29
23:4 cS Job 13:18
dS Job 9:15
23:5 eS Job 11:5
23:6 fS Job 9:4
gS Job 6:4
23:7 hS Job 1:1
iS Ge 3:8;
S Job 9:3; 13:3
jS Job 6:29

23:9 kS Job 9:11
23:10 lJob 1:1;
27:6; 31:6; 36:7;
Ps 7:9; 11:5;
34:15; 37:18;
94:11; 119:168;
146:8
mS Job 7:18;
Ps 139:1-3
nS Job 6:29;
S 22:15;
S Ps 12:6; 1Pe 1:7
23:11 oPs 17:5
pJob 31:7;
Ps 40:4; 44:18;
119:51,59,157;
125:5; Jer 11:20
23:12 qS Job 6:10
rS Job 15:11;
Mt 4:4; Jn 4:32,
34
23:13 sS Job 9:3
tS Job 10:13;
Isa 55:11
23:14 u1Th 3:3;
1Pe 4:12

23:15 vS Ge 45:3; wS Jos 24:14; Ps 34:9; 36:1; 111:10;
Pr 1:7; Ecc 3:14; 12:13; 2Co 5:11 23:16 xS Dt 20:3
yJob 27:2 zS Ex 3:6; Rev 6:16 23:17 aS Job 3:6; S 19:8 24:1
bS Job 14:5 cS Job 9:23; 2Pe 3:7

w2 Septuagint and Syriac; Hebrew / the hand on me
x2 Or heavy on me in

22:28 *light will shine on your ways.* Through obedience to
the word of God (see vv. 22,27; 29:3; Ps 119:105).
22:30 *cleanness of your hands.* See note on Ps 24:4.
23:2 *my complaint.* See 21:4 and note. *his hand is heavy.*
See NIV text notes; 33:7; see also note on 1Sa 5:6.
23:3 *where to find him.* See note on vv. 8-9.
23:6 *not press charges against me.* Job is seeking a fair
trial. In 9:14-20 Job was fearful that he could not find words
to argue with God. Now he is confident that if God would
give him a hearing, he would be acquitted (see 13:13-19;
see also Ps 17:1-3; 26:1-3 and notes).
23:8-9 *east . . . west . . . north . . . south.* Whatever direction Job went, he could not find God (contrast Ps 139:7-10).
23:8,10 *I do not find him . . . But he knows the way that
I take.* Job is frustrated over his apparent inability to have an
audience with God, who knows that he is an upright man.
Job is here answering Eliphaz's admonition beginning in
22:21: "Submit to God and . . . prosperity will come." Job
replies that this is what he has always done (vv. 11-12). He
treasures God's words more than his daily food. He admits
that God is testing him—not to purge away his sinful dross,
but to show that Job is pure gold (see Ps 119:11,101,168;
1Pe 1:7).
23:12 *Job's response to the advice offered by Eliphaz in
22:22. words . . . more than daily bread.* See Dt 8:3.

23:13 *he stands alone.* Lit. "he is one (unique)." Though
Job is not an Israelite, he worships the one true God—there
is no other (see Dt 6:4 and note). *He does whatever he
pleases.* He is sovereign (see Ps 115:3; 135:6; Lk 10:21).
23:15 *I am terrified.* See note on 21:6. A necessary part of
Job's faith is fear of a God who does what he pleases. By
contrast, the counselors tried to make God predictable.
23:17 *I am not silenced by the darkness.* Job responds to
Eliphaz's accusation in 22:11 (see note there).
24:1-12 *Job describes the terrible injustice that often exists in the world. Robbery of both the "haves" (see v. 2) and
the "have-nots" (see vv. 3-4) is equally obnoxious to him.
But perhaps his suffering has enabled him to empathize with
the poor, who must forage for food (v. 5) and "glean in the
vineyards of the wicked" (v. 6). The scene he depicts is
heart-rending: The naked shiver in the cold of night (vv.
7-8), fatherless infants are "snatched from the breast" (v. 9),
field hands harvest food but go hungry (v. 10), vineyard
workers make wine but suffer thirst (v. 11), groans rise from
the dying and wounded (v. 12). Job cannot understand why
God is silent and indifferent (vv. 1,12) in the face of such
misery, but the fact that God waits disproves the counselors'
theory of suffering. Job is no more out of God's favor as one
of the victims than the criminal in vv. 13-17 is in God's favor
because of God's inaction.

Why must those who know him look
in vain for such days? *d*

2Men move boundary stones; *e*
they pasture flocks they have stolen. *f*

3They drive away the orphan's donkey
and take the widow's ox in pledge. *g*

4They thrust the needy *h* from the path
and force all the poor *i* of the land
into hiding. *j*

5Like wild donkeys *k* in the desert,
the poor go about their labor *l* of
foraging food;
the wasteland *m* provides food for
their children.

6They gather fodder *n* in the fields
and glean in the vineyards *o* of the
wicked. *p*

7Lacking clothes, they spend the night
naked;
they have nothing to cover
themselves in the cold. *q*

8They are drenched *r* by mountain rains
and hug *s* the rocks for lack of
shelter. *t*

9The fatherless *u* child is snatched *v* from
the breast;
the infant of the poor is seized *w* for a
debt. *x*

10Lacking clothes, they go about naked; *y*
they carry the sheaves, *z* but still go
hungry.

11They crush olives among the terraces *y*;
they tread the winepresses, *a* yet
suffer thirst. *b*

12The groans of the dying rise from the
city,
and the souls of the wounded cry out
for help. *c*
But God charges no one with
wrongdoing. *d*

13"There are those who rebel against the
light, *e*
who do not know its ways
or stay in its paths. *f*

14When daylight is gone, the murderer
rises up

and kills *g* the poor and needy; *h*
in the night he steals forth like a
thief. *i*

15The eye of the adulterer *j* watches for
dusk; *k*
he thinks, 'No eye will see me,' *l*
and he keeps his face concealed.

16In the dark, men break into houses, *m*
but by day they shut themselves in;
they want nothing to do with the
light. *n*

17For all of them, deep darkness is their
morning *z*;
they make friends with the terrors *o*
of darkness. *a* *p*

18"Yet they are foam *q* on the surface of
the water; *r*
their portion of the land is cursed, *s*
so that no one goes to the
vineyards. *t*

19As heat and drought snatch away the
melted snow, *u*
so the grave *b* *v* snatches away those
who have sinned.

20The womb forgets them,
the worm *w* feasts on them; *x*
evil men are no longer remembered *y*
but are broken like a tree. *z*

21They prey on the barren and childless
woman,
and to the widow show no
kindness. *a*

22But God drags away the mighty by his
power; *b*
though they become established, *c*
they have no assurance of life. *d*

23He may let them rest in a feeling of
security, *e*

24:1
*d*S Job 15:20;
Ac 1:7
24:2 *e*S Dt 19:14
*f*Ex 20:15;
Dt 28:31
24:3 *g*S Job 6:27;
S 22:9
24:4 *h*Job 29:16;
31:19 *i*Job 29:12;
30:25; Ps 12:5;
41:1; 82:3,4;
Isa 11:4
*j*S Job 20:19;
S Pr 28:12
24:5 *k*S Ge 16:12
*l*Ps 104:23
*m*Job 30:3
24:6 *n*S Job 6:5
*o*ver 18
*p*Ru 2:22;
S 1Ki 21:19
24:7 *q*S Ex 22:27
24:8 *r*Da 4:25,33
*s*La 4:5 *t*S Jdg 6:2
24:9 *u*S Dt 24:17
*v*Job 29:17
*w*Ps 14:4;
Pr 30:14;
Isa 3:14; 10:1-2;
Eze 18:12
*x*S Lev 25:47;
S 2Ki 4:1
24:10
*y*Dt 24:12-13
*z*S Lev 19:9
24:11 *a*Isa 5:2;
16:10; Hag 2:16
*b*Mic 6:15
24:12
*c*S Job 12:19;
30:28; Ps 5:2;
22:24; 39:12;
119:147;
Isa 30:19;
Jer 50:46; 51:52,
54; Eze 26:15;
Rev 6:10
*d*S Job 9:23
24:13 *e*ver 16;
Job 38:15;
Jn 3:19-20;
1Th 5:4-5
*f*Job 17:12;
38:20; Ps 18:28;
Isa 5:20;
Eph 5:8-14

24:14 *g*Isa 3:15;
Mic 3:3
*h*S Job 20:19;
Ps 37:32 *i*Ps 10:9
24:15 *j*Job 31:9,
27; Pr 1:10
*k*Pr 7:8-9
*l*Ps 10:11
24:16
*m*S Ex 22:2;
Mt 6:19 *n*S ver 13
24:17
*o*S Job 18:11
*p*S Job 15:22;
S 18:5
24:18
*q*S Job 9:26;

Jude 1:13 *r*Job 22:16; Isa 57:20 *s*S Job 5:3 *t*ver 6 24:19
*u*Job 6:17 *v*S Job 21:13 24:20 *w*S Job 7:5 *x*S Job 21:26
*y*S Job 18:17 *z*S Job 14:7; Ps 31:12; Da 4:14 24:21
*a*S Job 22:9 24:22 *b*S Job 9:4 *c*S Job 12:19 *d*Dt 28:66;
Mt 6:27; Jas 4:14 24:23 *e*S Job 9:24; Am 6:1

*y*11 Or *olives between the millstones;* the meaning of the
Hebrew for this word is uncertain.   *z*17 Or *them, their
morning is like the shadow of death*   *a*17 Or *of the
shadow of death*   *b*19 Hebrew *Sheol*

24:1 See note on vv. 21–24.
24:2 *move boundary stones.* A serious crime in ancient
times (see note on Dt 19:14).
24:3 *orphan's . . . widow's.* See 22:9; Isa 1:17 and note;
Jas 1:27.
24:5 *wild donkeys.* See 39:5–8.
24:6 *glean.* See note on Ru 1:22.
24:7,10 Job implicitly denies the accusation of Eliphaz (see
22:6).
24:13–17 A description of those who cause the suffering
depicted in vv. 2–12: the murderer (v. 14), the adulterer (v.
15), the robber (v. 16). Darkness is their element, the medium in which they thrive (see vv. 14–17). By contrast, God's
law is the light against which they rebel (see v. 13; see also

note on 22:28).

24:18–20 Job seems to agree with the counselors here.
But it is also legitimate to translate the verses as Job's call for
redress against evildoers: "May their portion of the land be
cursed . . . may the grave snatch away . . . May the womb
forget them, may the worm feast on them; may evil men be
no longer remembered but be broken like a tree."

24:20 *worm feasts on them.* See 21:26; Isa 14:11. *broken
like a tree.* See note on 19:10.

24:21–24 By way of summary, Job says that God judges
the wicked, but he does so in his own good time. Job wishes,
however, that God would give the righteous the satisfaction
of seeing it happen (v. 1).

but his eyes*f* are on their ways. *g*

²⁴For a little while they are exalted, and
then they are gone; *h*
they are brought low and gathered up
like all others; *i*
they are cut off like heads of grain. *j*

²⁵"If this is not so, who can prove me
false
and reduce my words to nothing?" *k*

Bildad

25 Then Bildad the Shuhite *l* replied:

²"Dominion and awe belong to
God; *m*
he establishes order in the heights of
heaven. *n*
³Can his forces be numbered?
Upon whom does his light not rise? *o*
⁴How then can a man be righteous
before God?
How can one born of woman be
pure? *p*
⁵If even the moon *q* is not bright
and the stars are not pure in his
eyes, *r*
⁶how much less man, who is but a
maggot—
a son of man, *s* who is only a
worm!" *t*

Job

26 Then Job replied:

²"How you have helped the
powerless! *u*
How you have saved the arm that is
feeble! *v*

³What advice you have offered to one
without wisdom!
And what great insight *w* you have
displayed!
⁴Who has helped you utter these words?
And whose spirit spoke from your
mouth? *x*

⁵"The dead are in deep anguish, *y*
those beneath the waters and all that
live in them.
⁶Death *c z* is naked before God;
Destruction *d a* lies uncovered. *b*
⁷He spreads out the northern ₎skies₍ *c*
over empty space;
he suspends the earth over nothing. *d*
⁸He wraps up the waters *e* in his
clouds, *f*
yet the clouds do not burst under
their weight.
⁹He covers the face of the full moon,
spreading his clouds *g* over it.
¹⁰He marks out the horizon on the face of
the waters *h*
for a boundary between light and
darkness. *i*
¹¹The pillars of the heavens quake, *j*
aghast at his rebuke.
¹²By his power he churned up the sea; *k*
by his wisdom *l* he cut Rahab *m* to
pieces.
¹³By his breath the skies *n* became fair;
his hand pierced the gliding serpent. *o*
¹⁴And these are but the outer fringe of his
works;

24:23
f S 2Ch 16:9
g S Job 10:4
24:24
h S 2Ki 19:35;
S Job 4:20;
Ps 37:10; 83:13;
Isa 5:24; 17:13;
40:24; 41:2,15
i S Job 3:19
j Isa 17:5
24:25
k S Job 6:28;
S 16:17
25:1 *l* S Job 8:1
25:2 *m* S Job 9:4;
Ps 47:9; 89:18;
Zec 9:7; Rev 1:6
n S 2Ch 20:6;
S Job 11:8;
S 16:19
25:3 *o* Mt 5:45;
Jas 1:17
25:4 *p* S Job 4:17
25:5 *q* Job 31:26
r S Job 4:18
25:6 *s* Ps 80:17;
144:3; Eze 2:1
t S Job 4:19; S 7:5
26:2 *u* Job 6:12
v S Job 4:3

26:3 *w* Job 34:35
26:4 *x* 1Ki 22:24
26:5 *y* Ps 88:10;
Isa 14:9; 26:14
26:6 *z* Ps 139:8
a Job 20:26;
S Rev 9:11
b Job 10:22; 11:8;
38:17; 41:11;
Ps 139:11-12;
Pr 15:11;
S Heb 4:13
26:7 *c* Job 9:8
d Job 38:6;
Ps 104:5;
Pr 3:19-20; 8:27;
Isa 40:22
26:8 *e* Pr 30:4
f S Ge 1:2;
Job 36:27; 37:11;
Ps 147:8
26:9
g S 2Sa 22:10;
S Job 22:14
26:10 *h* Pr 8:27;
Isa 40:22
i S Ge 1:4;
S Job 28:3;

38:8-11 **26:11** *j* S 2Sa 22:8 **26:12** *k* S Ex 14:21 *l* Job 12:13
m S Job 9:13 **26:13** *n* Job 9:8 *o* Isa 27:1

c 6 Hebrew *Sheol*   *d* 6 Hebrew *Abaddon*

24:24 *cut off like heads of grain.* A symbol of judgment
(see note on Isa 17:5).
25:1–6 See note on 22:1–26:14. Bildad adds nothing new
here, and Zophar, who has already admitted how emotionally disturbed he was (see 20:2), doesn't even comment.
25:2 *establishes order in the heights of heaven.* Bildad
apparently considered heaven as a place of warfare, where
God must use his celestial troops (see v. 3) to establish order.
25:3 *his forces.* Angels. *his light.* The sun. All that is under
God's dominion pales before him.
25:4–6 Bildad echoes Eliphaz's earlier statements about
human depravity (4:17–19; 15:14–16).
26:2–4 With biting sarcasm, Job responds to Bildad alone
(the Hebrew for the words "you" and "your" in these verses
is singular rather than plural), indicating that Eliphaz and
Zophar have already been silenced.
26:2 *saved the arm that is feeble.* See 4:3–4; Isa 35:3; Heb
12:12.
26:5–14 Job's poem about the vast power of God, the
theme of Bildad's final speech (ch. 25), is written in colorful
language that is often highly figurative.
26:5 *The dead.* The Hebrew for this expression is translated "spirits of the dead" in Pr 2:18, "spirits of the departed" in Isa 14:9 and "departed spirits" in Isa 26:14. The
term is used figuratively of the deceased who inhabit the

netherworld (see 3:13–15,17–19; see also note on 3:16).
waters. Part of the world inhabited by living beings, and
therefore above the netherworld.
26:6 *Death.* See NIV text note; personified elsewhere as
the "king of terrors" (see 18:14 and note). *Destruction.* See
NIV text note; see also 28:22; 31:12; Pr 15:11 and NIV text
notes. In Rev 9:11, Abaddon is the name of the "angel of the
Abyss" (see NIV text note there).
26:7 *He.* God. *spreads out the northern ₎skies.₍* See 37:18.
empty space. The Hebrew for this word is translated "formless" in Ge 1:2. *nothing.* See note on 9:6.
26:11 *pillars of the heavens.* See note on 9:6.
26:12 *churned up the sea.* See Isa 51:15; Jer 31:35.
Rahab. See note on 9:13.
26:13 *gliding serpent.* A description of the sea monster
Leviathan (see notes on 3:8; Isa 27:1).
26:14 *these are but the outer fringe of his works.* What
God has revealed of his dominion over natural and supernatural forces amounts to no more than a whisper. Job is
impressed with the severely limited character of man's
understanding. Zophar had chided Job about his inability to
fathom the mysteries of God (11:7–9), but the knowledge
possessed by Job's friends was not superior to that of Job
himself (see 12:3; 13:2). *thunder of his power.* If it is
difficult for us to comprehend the little that we know about

how faint the whisper[p] we hear of
    him![q]
Who then can understand the
    thunder of his power?"[r]

27 And Job continued his discourse:[s]

²"As surely as God lives, who has
    denied me justice,[t]
the Almighty,[u] who has made me
    taste bitterness of soul,[v]
³as long as I have life within me,
    the breath of God[w] in my nostrils,
⁴my lips will not speak wickedness,
    and my tongue will utter no deceit.[x]
⁵I will never admit you are in the right;
    till I die, I will not deny my
    integrity.[y]
⁶I will maintain my righteousness[z] and
    never let go of it;
my conscience[a] will not reproach me
    as long as I live.[b]

⁷"May my enemies be like the wicked,[c]
    my adversaries[d] like the unjust!
⁸For what hope has the godless[e] when
    he is cut off,
when God takes away his life?[f]
⁹Does God listen to his cry
    when distress comes upon him?[g]
¹⁰Will he find delight in the Almighty?[h]
    Will he call upon God at all times?

¹¹"I will teach you about the power of
    God;
the ways[i] of the Almighty I will not
    conceal.[j]
¹²You have all seen this yourselves.
    Why then this meaningless talk?

¹³"Here is the fate God allots to the
    wicked,
the heritage a ruthless man receives
    from the Almighty:[k]

¹⁴However many his children,[l] their fate
    is the sword;[m]
his offspring will never have enough
    to eat.[n]
¹⁵The plague will bury those who survive
    him,
and their widows will not weep for
    them.[o]
¹⁶Though he heaps up silver like dust[p]
    and clothes like piles of clay,[q]
¹⁷what he lays up[r] the righteous will
    wear,[s]
and the innocent will divide his
    silver.[t]
¹⁸The house[u] he builds is like a moth's
    cocoon,[v]
like a hut[w] made by a watchman.
¹⁹He lies down wealthy, but will do so no
    more;[x]
when he opens his eyes, all is gone.[y]
²⁰Terrors[z] overtake him like a flood;[a]
    a tempest snatches him away in the
    night.[b]
²¹The east wind[c] carries him off, and he
    is gone;[d]
it sweeps him out of his place.[e]
²²It hurls itself against him without
    mercy[f]
as he flees headlong[g] from its
    power.[h]
²³It claps its hands[i] in derision
    and hisses him out of his place.[j]

28 "There is a mine for silver
    and a place where gold is
    refined.[k]
²Iron is taken from the earth,
    and copper is smelted from ore.[l]

26:14 ᵖJob 4:12
qJob 42:5;
Hab 3:2;
1Co 13:12
ʳS Job 9:6
27:1 ˢJob 29:1
27:2 ᵗS Job 6:29;
S 9:24; Isa 45:9;
49:4,14
ᵘJob 23:16
ᵛS 1Sa 1:10;
S Job 7:19; S 10:1
27:3 ʷS Ge 2:7;
Job 32:8; 33:4;
34:14; S Ps 144:4
27:4 ˣS Job 6:28;
S 12:16; S 16:17
27:5 ʸS Job 2:9;
S 10:7; S 32:2
27:6 ᶻJob 29:14;
Ps 119:121;
132:9; Isa 59:17;
61:10 ᵃS Ac 23:1;
Ro 2:15
ᵇS Job 2:3;
S 10:7; S 23:10;
S 34:17
27:7 ᶜS Job 8:22
ᵈJob 31:35
27:8 ᵉS Job 8:13
ᶠS Nu 16:22;
S Job 8:22;
S 11:20; Lk 12:20
27:9 ᵍS Dt 1:45;
S 1Sa 8:18;
S Job 15:31
27:10
ʰS Job 22:26
27:11 ⁱJob 36:23
ʲver 13
27:13
ᵏS Job 16:19;
S 20:29

27:14 ˡS Job 5:4
ᵐS Job 15:22;
S La 2:22
ⁿS Job 4:11
27:15 ᵒPs 78:64
27:16
ᵖS 1Ki 10:27
ᵠZec 9:3
27:17 ʳPs 39:6;
49:10; Ecc 2:26
ˢS Job 7:8;
Pr 13:22; 28:8;
Ecc 2:26
ᵗEx 3:22;
S Job 3:15
27:18 ᵘS Job 8:22
ᵛS Job 8:14
ʷIsa 1:8; 24:20
27:19
ˣS Job 3:13; S 7:8
ʸS Job 14:20

27:20 ᶻS Job 6:4 ᵃS Job 15:21 ᵇS Job 20:8 27:21 ᶜJob 38:24;
Jer 13:24; 22:22 ᵈJob 30:22 ᵉS Job 7:10 27:22 ᶠJer 13:14;
Eze 5:11; 24:14 ᵍ2Ki 7:15 ʰS Job 11:20 27:23 ⁱS Nu 24:10;
Na 3:19 ʲS Job 7:10 28:1 ᵏPs 12:6; 66:10; Jer 9:7; Da 11:35;
Mal 3:3 28:2 ˡDt 8:9

God, how much more impossible it would be to understand
the full extent of his might!

27:1–23 The dialogue-dispute section of the book begins
with Job's opening lament (ch. 3), continues with the three
cycles of speeches (chs. 4–14; 15–21; 22–26) and concludes with Job's closing discourse (ch. 27), in which he
reasserts his own innocence (vv. 2–6) and eloquently describes the ultimate fate of the wicked (vv. 13–23).

27:2 *As surely as God lives.* The most solemn of oaths (see
note on Ge 42:15). Job's faith in God continued despite his
perception of denied justice.

27:5 *you.* The Hebrew for this word is plural. In his summary statement, Job once again speaks to his three friends as
a group.

27:6 *maintain my righteousness.* God had spoken similarly
of Job (see 2:3).

27:7 *May my enemies be like the wicked.* Job calls for his
friends, who had falsely accused him of being wicked, to be
treated as though they themselves were wicked men (cf. Ps
109:6–15; 137:8–9).

27:11 *I will teach you.* Job is about to remind his counsel-

ors about an issue on which they all agree: that the truly
wicked deserve God's wrath (vv. 13–23). The three friends
had falsely put Job in that category.

27:13–23 A poem that dramatizes the effect of Job's earlier
call for redress (v. 7).

27:13 Job echoes the words of Zophar in 20:29 (see note
there).

27:18 *cocoon . . . hut.* Symbols of fragility (see note on
4:19; Isa 1:8 and note; 24:20).

27:21 *east wind.* See note on 15:2.

28:1–28 Job's friends' application of traditional wisdom to
human suffering has been even more unsatisfactory than
Job's untraditional response. Both attempts to penetrate the
mystery have failed, and the dialogue has come to an unsatisfactory conclusion. Therefore Job, or perhaps the unknown
author of the book, inserts a striking wisdom poem that
answers the question, "Where can wisdom be found?" (v.
12; see v. 20). The poem consists of three parts: (1) precious
stones and metals are found in the deepest mines (vv. 1–11);
(2) wisdom is not found in mines, nor can it be bought with
precious stones or metals (vv. 12–19); (3) wisdom is found

³Man puts an end to the darkness; *m*
  he searches the farthest recesses
  for ore in the blackest darkness. *n*
⁴Far from where people dwell he cuts a
      shaft, *o*
  in places forgotten by the foot of
      man;
  far from men he dangles and sways.
⁵The earth, from which food comes, *p*
  is transformed below as by fire;
⁶sapphires *e q* come from its rocks,
  and its dust contains nuggets of
      gold. *r*
⁷No bird of prey knows that hidden path,
  no falcon's eye has seen it. *s*
⁸Proud beasts *t* do not set foot on it,
  and no lion prowls there. *u*
⁹Man's hand assaults the flinty rock *v*
  and lays bare the roots of the
      mountains. *w*
¹⁰He tunnels through the rock; *x*
  his eyes see all its treasures. *y*
¹¹He searches *f* the sources of the rivers *z*
  and brings hidden things *a* to light.

¹²"But where can wisdom be found? *b*
  Where does understanding dwell? *c*
¹³Man does not comprehend its worth; *d*
  it cannot be found in the land of the
      living. *e*
¹⁴The deep *f* says, 'It is not in me';
  the sea *g* says, 'It is not with me.'
¹⁵It cannot be bought with the finest gold,
  nor can its price be weighed in
      silver. *h*
¹⁶It cannot be bought with the gold of
      Ophir, *i*
  with precious onyx or sapphires. *j*
¹⁷Neither gold nor crystal can compare
      with it, *k*
  nor can it be had for jewels of gold. *l*
¹⁸Coral *m* and jasper *n* are not worthy of
      mention;

  the price of wisdom is beyond
      rubies. *o*
¹⁹The topaz *p* of Cush *q* cannot compare
      with it;
  it cannot be bought with pure gold. *r*

²⁰"Where then does wisdom come from?
  Where does understanding dwell? *s*
²¹It is hidden from the eyes of every living
      thing,
  concealed even from the birds of the
      air. *t*
²²Destruction *g u* and Death *v* say,
  'Only a rumor of it has reached our
      ears.'
²³God understands the way to it
  and he alone *w* knows where it
      dwells, *x*
²⁴for he views the ends of the earth *y*
  and sees everything under the
      heavens. *z*
²⁵When he established the force of the
      wind
  and measured out the waters, *a*
²⁶when he made a decree for the rain *b*
  and a path for the thunderstorm, *c*
²⁷then he looked at wisdom and appraised
      it;
  he confirmed it and tested it. *d*
²⁸And he said to man,
  'The fear of the Lord—that is
      wisdom,
  and to shun evil *e* is
      understanding. *f* ' "

28:3 *m*Ecc 1:13; 7:25; 8:17 *n*S Job 26:10; 38:19
28:4 *o*ver 10; 2Sa 5:8
28:5 *p*Ge 1:29; Ps 104:14; 145:15
28:6 *q*ver 16; SS 5:14; Isa 54:11 *r*S Job 22:24
28:7 *s*ver 21
28:8 *t*Job 41:34 *u*Isa 35:9
28:9 *v*S Dt 8:15 *w*Jnh 2:6
28:10 *x*S ver 4 *y*Pr 2:4
28:11 *z*S Ge 7:11 *a*Isa 48:6; Jer 33:3
28:12 *b*ver 28; Pr 1:20; 3:13-20; 8:1; 9:1-3; Ecc 7:24 *c*ver 20, 23
28:13 *d*Pr 3:15; Mt 13:44-46 *e*Dt 29:29; Ps 27:13; 52:5; 116:9; 142:5; Isa 38:11; Jer 11:19; Eze 26:20; 32:24
28:14 *f*Ps 42:7; Ro 10:7 *g*Dt 30:13
28:15 *h*ver 17; Pr 3:13-14; 8:10-11; 16:16; Ac 8:20
28:16 *i*S Ge 10:29 *j*S ver 6; S Ex 24:10
28:17 *k*Ps 119:72; Pr 8:10 *l*S ver 15
28:18 *m*Eze 27:16 *n*Rev 21:11
28:19 *o*Pr 3:15; 8:11 *p*Ex 28:17 *q*Isa 11:11 *r*Pr 3:14-15; 8:10-11,19
28:20 *s*S Job 9:4
28:21 *t*ver 7
28:22 *u*S Job 20:26; S Rev 9:11 *v*Pr 8:32-36
28:23 *w*Ecc 3:11; S 22:22; Pr 8:22-31
28:24 *y*Job 36:32; 37:3; 38:18,24,35; Ps 33:13-14; 66:7; Isa 11:12 *z*S Jos 3:11; S Job 10:4; S Heb 4:13
28:25 *a*S Job 12:15; 38:8-11
28:26 *b*Job 36:28; 37:6; Jer 51:16 *c*Job 36:33; 37:3,8,11; 38:27; Ps 65:12; 104:14; 147:8; Isa 35:7
28:27 *d*Pr 3:19; 8:22-31
28:28 *e*Ps 11:5; 97:10; Pr 3:7; 8:13 *f*S Ex 20:20; S Dt 4:6; S Job 37:24

e 6 Or *lapis lazuli*; also in verse 16   *f* 11 Septuagint, Aquila and Vulgate; Hebrew *He dams up*   *g* 22 Hebrew *Abaddon*

---

only in God and in the fear of him (vv. 20–28). The chapter, then, anticipates the theme of God's speeches (38:1–42:6): God alone is the answer to the mystery that Job and his friends have sought to fathom.
28:1–11 A fascinating, lyrical description of ancient mining techniques.
28:2 *Iron.* See note on 19:24.
28:3 *puts an end to the darkness.* By using an artificial source of light, such as a torch or lamp.
28:4 *dangles and sways.* Mining, then as now, is difficult and dangerous work. Men will hazard everything to dig the earth's treasures.
28:6 *sapphires.* See v. 16; see also notes on SS 5:14; Isa 54:11.
28:9 *roots of the mountains.* A poetic expression emphasizing great depth (cf. Jnh 2:6).
28:10 *tunnels through the rock.* An eighth-century B.C. inscription found at Jerusalem's Pool of Siloam testifies to the

sophistication of ancient tunneling technology.
28:12 The questions, repeated almost verbatim in v. 20, are answered in v. 28.
28:16 *gold of Ophir.* See 22:24 and note.
28:18 *the price of wisdom is beyond rubies.* Cf. the value of a "wife of noble character" (Pr 31:10), who fears the Lord (Pr 31:30) and is therefore wise (see v. 28).
28:19 *Cush.* The upper Nile region, south of Egypt.
28:21 *hidden . . . from the birds.* As are precious stones and metals (see v. 7).
28:22 *Destruction and Death.* See note on 26:6.
28:25–27 Wisdom has been with God from the time of creation itself (see Pr 8:22–31).
28:28 *fear of the Lord . . . shun evil.* See the description of Job's character in 1:1,8; 2:3. *that is wisdom.* "The fear of the LORD is the beginning of wisdom" (Ps 111:10; Pr 9:10; see Pr 1:7).

29

Job continued his discourse: [g]

2"How I long for the months gone by, [h]
for the days when God watched over me, [i]
3when his lamp shone upon my head
and by his light I walked through darkness! [j]
4Oh, for the days when I was in my prime,
when God's intimate friendship [k] blessed my house, [l]
5when the Almighty was still with me
and my children [m] were around me, [n]
6when my path was drenched with cream [o]
and the rock [p] poured out for me streams of olive oil. [q]

7"When I went to the gate [r] of the city
and took my seat in the public square,
8the young men saw me and stepped aside [s]
and the old men rose to their feet; [t]
9the chief men refrained from speaking [u]
and covered their mouths with their hands; [v]
10the voices of the nobles were hushed, [w]
and their tongues stuck to the roof of their mouths. [x]
11Whoever heard me spoke well of me,
and those who saw me commended me, [y]
12because I rescued the poor [z] who cried for help,
and the fatherless [a] who had none to assist him. [b]
13The man who was dying blessed me; [c]
I made the widow's [d] heart sing.
14I put on righteousness [e] as my clothing;
justice was my robe and my turban. [f]

15I was eyes [g] to the blind
and feet to the lame. [h]
16I was a father to the needy; [i]
I took up the case [j] of the stranger. [k]
17I broke the fangs of the wicked
and snatched the victims [l] from their teeth. [m]

18"I thought, 'I will die in my own house,
my days as numerous as the grains of sand. [n]
19My roots will reach to the water, [o]
and the dew will lie all night on my branches. [p]
20My glory will remain fresh [q] in me,
the bow [r] ever new in my hand.' [s]

21"Men listened to me expectantly,
waiting in silence for my counsel. [t]
22After I had spoken, they spoke no more; [u]
my words fell gently on their ears. [v]
23They waited for me as for showers
and drank in my words as the spring rain. [w]
24When I smiled at them, they scarcely believed it;
the light of my face [x] was precious to them. [h] [y]
25I chose the way for them and sat as their chief; [z]
I dwelt as a king [a] among his troops;
I was like one who comforts mourners. [b]

30

"But now they mock me, [c] men younger than I,
whose fathers I would have disdained

Cross references:

29:1 gJob 27:1
29:2 hS Ge 31:30
iJer 1:12; 31:28; 44:27
29:3 jS Job 11:17; S 12:25
29:4 kS Job 15:8
lPs 25:14; Pr 3:32
29:5 mPs 127:3-5; 128:3 nRu 4:1
29:6 oS Job 20:17 pPs 81:16
qGe 49:20; S Dt 32:13
29:7 rver 21; Job 5:4; 31:21; Jer 20:2; 38:7
29:8 sLev 19:32
29:9 uver 21; Job 31:21
vS Jdg 18:19; Job 40:4; Pr 30:32
29:10 wver 22
xPs 137:6
29:11 yS Job 4:4; Heb 11:4
29:12 zS Job 24:4
aS Dt 24:17; Job 31:17,21
bPs 72:12; Pr 21:13
29:13 cJob 31:20
dS Dt 10:18; S Job 22:9
29:14 eS 2Sa 8:15; S Job 27:6; Eph 4:24; 6:14
fS Job 19:9
29:15 gNu 10:31 hS Job 4:4
29:16 iS Job 24:4 /Ex 18:26
kS Job 4:4; Pr 22:22-23
29:17 lJob 24:9
mS Job 4:10,11; S Ps 3:7
29:18 nPs 1:1-3; 15:5; 16:8; 30:6; 62:2; 139:18; Pr 3:1-2
29:19 oS Nu 24:6; S Job 14:9
pS Ge 27:28; S Job 15:30; S Ps 133:3
29:20 qPs 92:14 rJob 30:11; Ps 18:34; Isa 38:12

sGe 49:24 29:21 tS ver 7,S 9 29:22 uver 10 vDt 32:2 29:23 wS Job 4:3 29:24 xS Nu 6:25 yPr 16:14,15 29:25 zS Job 21:28 aS Job 1:3 bS Job 4:4 30:1 cS Job 6:14; S 11:3; S Ps 119:21

h24 The meaning of the Hebrew for this clause is uncertain.

29:1–31:40 Like a lawyer submitting his final brief, Job presents a three-part summation: Part one (ch. 29) is a nostalgic review of his former happiness, wealth and honor; part two (ch. 30) is a lament over the loss of everything, especially his honor; part three (ch. 31) is a final protestation of his innocence.
29:1–25 A classic example of Semitic rhetoric, using the following symmetrical pattern: blessing (vv. 2–6), honor (vv. 7–10), benevolence (vv. 11–17), blessing (vv. 18–20), honor (vv. 21–25).
29:2–6 Words charged with emotion. In earlier days, God had been Job's friend and companion.
29:3 by his light I walked. See note on 22:28.
29:4 when God's intimate friendship blessed my house. Lit. "when God's council was by my tent," or "when God was an intimate in my tent." The clause evokes a situation similar to that in Ge 18, where God and two members of his heavenly council eat and drink at Abraham's tent—and there God discloses to his friend the imminent birth of the promised son and God's intentions concerning Sodom and

Gomorrah.
29:5 my children were around me. See 1:2.
29:6 cream . . . olive oil. Symbols of richness and luxury (see 20:17; Eze 16:19).
29:7 gate of the city. Where the most important business was conducted and the most significant legal cases were tried (see note on Ru 4:1). took my seat. As a city elder, a member of the ruling council (see note on Ge 19:1).
29:12–13 I rescued . . . the fatherless . . . I made the widow's heart sing. Implicitly responding to Eliphaz's accusation in 22:9, Job expresses his concern for the helpless and unfortunate (see 24:9; 31:16–18,21).
29:14 I put on righteousness . . . justice was my robe. For similar imagery see Isa 59:17; 61:10; Eph 6:14,17.
29:18 I thought. Job muses on what might have been the course of his life.
29:21–25 His counsel was valued (vv. 21–23), his approval sought (v. 24) and his civic leadership accepted with gratitude (v. 25).
30:1–31 In contrast to the positive notes of blessing and

to put with my sheep dogs. *d*

2Of what use was the strength of their
hands to me,
since their vigor had gone from
them?

3Haggard from want and hunger,
they roamed*i* the parched land*e*
in desolate wastelands*f* at night.*g*

4In the brush they gathered salt herbs, *h*
and their food*j* was the root of the
broom tree. *i*

5They were banished from their fellow
men,
shouted at as if they were thieves.

6They were forced to live in the dry
stream beds,
among the rocks and in holes in the
ground.*j*

7They brayed*k* among the bushes*l*
and huddled in the undergrowth.

8A base and nameless brood, *m*
they were driven out of the land. *n*

9"And now their sons mock me*o* in
song;*p*
I have become a byword*q* among
them.

10They detest me*r* and keep their
distance;
they do not hesitate to spit in my
face.*s*

11Now that God has unstrung my bow*t*
and afflicted me,*u*
they throw off restraint*v* in my
presence.

12On my right*w* the tribe*k* attacks;
they lay snares*x* for my feet,*y*
they build their siege ramps against
me.*z*

13They break up my road;*a*
they succeed in destroying me*b*—
without anyone's helping them.*l*

14They advance as through a gaping
breach;*c*
amid the ruins they come rolling in.

15Terrors*d* overwhelm me;*e*

my dignity is driven away as by the
wind,
my safety vanishes like a cloud.*f*

16"And now my life ebbs away;*g*
days of suffering grip me. *h*

17Night pierces my bones;
my gnawing pains never rest. *i*

18In his great power*j* God, becomes like
clothing to me*m*;
he binds me like the neck of my
garment.

19He throws me into the mud, *k*
and I am reduced to dust and ashes. *l*

20"I cry out to you, *m* O God, but you do
not answer; *n*
I stand up, but you merely look at
me.

21You turn on me ruthlessly; *o*
with the might of your hand*p* you
attack me. *q*

22You snatch me up and drive me before
the wind; *r*
you toss me about in the storm. *s*

23I know you will bring me down to
death, *t*
to the place appointed for all the
living. *u*

24"Surely no one lays a hand on a broken
man*v*
when he cries for help in his
distress. *w*

25Have I not wept for those in trouble? *x*
Has not my soul grieved for the
poor? *y*

26Yet when I hoped for good, evil came;
when I looked for light, then came
darkness. *z*

27The churning inside me never stops; *a*

Cross references

30:1 *d*Isa 56:10
30:3 *e*Isa 8:21
*f*Job 24:5
*g*Jer 17:6
30:4 *h*Job 39:6
*i*S 1Ki 19:4
30:6 *j*Isa 2:19;
Hos 10:8
30:7 *k*Job 6:5
*l*Job 39:5-6
30:8 *m*S Jdg 9:4
*n*S Job 18:18
30:9
*o*S Job 16:10;
Ps 69:11
*p*Job 12:4;
La 3:14,63
*q*S Job 17:6
30:10 *r*Job 19:19
*s*S Dt 25:9;
Mt 26:67
30:11
*t*S Job 29:20
*u*S Ge 12:17;
S Ru 1:21
*v*Job 41:13;
Ps 32:9
30:12 *w*Ps 109:6;
Zec 3:1
*x*S Job 18:9
*y*Ps 140:4-5
*z*S Job 16:10
30:13 *a*Isa 3:12
*b*S Job 10:3
30:14
*c*S 2Ki 25:4
30:15 *d*S Job 6:4
*e*S Ex 3:6;
Job 10:8; 31:2-3,
23; Ps 55:4-5

*f*S Job 3:25
30:16 *g*S Job 3:24
*h*ver 27;
S Job 9:17
30:17
*i*S Dt 28:35;
S Job 16:16
30:18 *j*S Job 9:4
30:19 *k*Ps 40:2;
69:2,14; 130:1;
Jer 38:6,22
*l*S Ge 3:19;
S Job 2:8
30:20
*m*S 1Ki 8:52;
Ps 34:17; Pr 2:3;
Mic 4:9
*n*S Job 19:7;
La 3:8
30:21 *o*Jer 6:23;
30:14; 50:42
*p*Isa 9:12; 14:26;
31:3; Eze 6:14
*q*S Job 4:5; S 6:4;
S 10:3
30:22 *r*Job 27:21;
Jude 1:12
*s*S Job 9:17
30:23
*t*S 2Sa 14:14;
S Job 3:13; S 10:3
*u*S Job 3:19

30:24 *v*Ps 145:14; Isa 42:3; 57:15 *w*S Job 19:7 30:25
*x*Lk 19:41; Php 3:18 *y*S Job 24:4; Ps 35:13-14; Ro 12:15
30:26 *z*S Job 3:6,17; S 19:8; S Ps 82:5; S Jer 4:23 30:27
*a*Ps 38:8; La 2:11

*i*3 Or *gnawed* *j*4 Or *fuel* *k*12 The meaning of the
Hebrew for this word is uncertain. *l*13 Or *me.* / *'No
one can help him,' they say.* *m*18 Hebrew;
Septuagint *God* *grasps my clothing*

---

honor sounded in ch. 29, Job now bemoans the suffering and
dishonor he has been forced to undergo. God has heaped
overwhelming terrors on him (v. 15). His final, forlorn lament (see v. 31) over his condition shows that his rage has
not yet subsided.
30:1,9 *now . . . mock me.* Earlier both young and old had
deferred to him (see 29:8–11,21–25).
30:4 *salt herbs.* Probably saltwort, which grows in otherwise infertile areas, including the regions east of Sinai where
Job and his friends lived. Cf. 39:6. *broom tree.* A large bush
that grows in the deserts of Palestine and Arabia (see 1Ki
19:4; Ps 120:4).
30:9 *byword.* See note on 17:6.
30:11 *God has unstrung my bow.* In contrast to 29:20,
where Job was confident that his bow would be new and

strong.
30:12 *siege ramps.* See 19:12.
30:14 *breach.* In a city wall.
30:15 *driven . . . as by the wind.* See v. 22.
30:17 *gnawing pains.* See note on 2:7.
30:18 *neck of my garment.* Tight-fitting collar.
30:19 *dust and ashes.* Symbolic of humiliation and insignificance (see note on Ge 18:27). Job would someday use
"dust and ashes" to symbolize repentance (42:6).
30:20–23 Job now directs his thoughts away from men
and toward God. He accuses God of abusing his power by
attacking him despite his pleas for mercy.
30:24 Job feels that he has been treated unjustly, whether
by God or by man.
30:26 Cf. Isa 5:2,7.

days of suffering confront me. [b]

28I go about blackened, [c] but not by the
    sun;
  I stand up in the assembly and cry for
    help. [d]

29I have become a brother of jackals, [e]
  a companion of owls. [f]

30My skin grows black[g] and peels; [h]
  my body burns with fever. [i]

31My harp is tuned to mourning, [j]
  and my flute[k] to the sound of
    wailing.

31 "I made a covenant with my
    eyes[l]
  not to look lustfully at a girl. [m]

2For what is man's lot[n] from God above,
  his heritage from the Almighty on
    high?[o]

3Is it not ruin[p] for the wicked,
  disaster[q] for those who do wrong?[r]

4Does he not see my ways
  and count my every step?[t]

5"If I have walked in falsehood
  or my foot has hurried after
    deceit[u] —

6let God weigh me[v] in honest scales[w]
  and he will know that I am
    blameless[x] —

7if my steps have turned from the path,[y]
  if my heart has been led by my eyes,
  or if my hands[z] have been defiled, [a]

8then may others eat what I have
    sown,[b]
  and may my crops be uprooted. [c]

9"If my heart has been enticed[d] by a
    woman,[e]
  or if I have lurked at my neighbor's
    door,

10then may my wife grind[f] another man's
    grain,
  and may other men sleep with her.[g]

11For that would have been shameful,[h]
  a sin to be judged. [i]

12It is a fire[j] that burns to
    Destruction[n]; [k]
  it would have uprooted my harvest. [l]

13"If I have denied justice to my
    menservants and
    maidservants[m]
  when they had a grievance against
    me, [n]

14what will I do when God confronts
    me?[o]
  What will I answer when called to
    account?[p]

15Did not he who made me in the womb
    make them?[q]
  Did not the same one form us both
    within our mothers?[r]

16"If I have denied the desires of the
    poor[s]
  or let the eyes of the widow[t] grow
    weary, [u]

17if I have kept my bread to myself,
  not sharing it with the fatherless[v] —

18but from my youth I reared him as
    would a father,
  and from my birth I guided the
    widow[w] —

19if I have seen anyone perishing for lack
    of clothing, [x]
  or a needy[y] man without a garment,

20and his heart did not bless me[z]
  for warming him with the fleece[a]
    from my sheep,

21if I have raised my hand against the
    fatherless, [b]
  knowing that I had influence in
    court, [c]

Cross references (center column):

30:27 bS ver 16
30:28 cS Job 17:14; La 4:8 dS Job 19:7; S 24:12
30:29 ePs 44:19; Isa 34:13; Jer 9:11 fPs 102:6; Mic 1:8
30:30 gS Job 17:14 hLa 3:4; 4:8 iS Dt 28:35; S Job 16:16; Ps 102:3; La 1:13; 5:10
30:31 jS Ge 8:8; Ps 137:2; Isa 16:11; 24:8; Eze 26:13 kS Ge 4:21
31:1 lPr 4:25; 17:24; 2Pe 2:14 mEx 20:14,17; Dt 5:18; Mt 5:28
31:2 nNu 26:55; Ps 11:6; 16:5; 50:18; Ecc 3:22; 5:19; 9:9 oS Job 16:19; S 20:29
31:3 pS Job 21:30 qJob 18:12 rJob 34:22; Ro 2:9
31:4 sS 2Ch 16:9; Ps 139:3; Da 4:37; 5:23 tS ver 14; S Job 10:4
31:5 uS Job 15:31
31:6 vPs 139:23 wS Lev 19:36; S Job 6:2 xS Ge 6:9; S Job 2:3; S 23:10
31:7 yS Job 23:11 zS Job 9:30 aPs 7:3
31:8 bS Job 5:5; S 20:10; Jn 4:37 cver 12; Mic 6:15
31:9 dS Dt 11:16; S Job 24:15; Jas 1:14 ePr 5:3; 7:5
31:10 fS Jdg 16:21 gDt 28:30
31:11 hPr 6:32-33 iS Ge 38:24; S Ex 21:12; Jn 8:4-5
31:12 jS Job 15:30 kS Job 26:6 lS ver 8

8 31:13 mS Dt 5:14 n Ex 21:2-11; Lev 25:39-46; Dt 24:14-15 31:14 oJob 33:5 pver 4,37; Ps 10:13,15; 94:7; Isa 10:3; Jer 5:31; Hos 9:7; Mic 7:4; Col 4:1 31:15 qS Job 4:17; Pr 22:2 rS Job 10:3; Eph 6:9 31:16 sS Lev 25:17; S Job 5:16 tS Job 22:9; Jas 1:27 uJob 22:7 31:17 vS Job 6:27; S 22:7 31:18 wIsa 51:18 31:19 xJob 22:6; Isa 58:7 yS Job 24:4 31:20 zJob 29:13 aJdg 6:37 31:21 bS Job 22:7; Jas 1:27 cS Job 29:7,9

n12 Hebrew *Abaddon*

Study notes (bottom):

30:28 *blackened.* See v. 30; see also note on 2:7.

30:29 *brother of jackals . . . companion of owls.* The prophet Micah uses similar imagery of himself in Mic 1:8.

30:30 *fever.* See note on 2:7.

31:1–40 The climactic section of Job's three-part summation (see note on 29:1–31:40). It is negative in the sense that Job denies all the sins listed, but it has the positive purpose of attesting loyalty to God as his sovereign Lord. In the strongest legal terms, using a series of self-maledictory oaths, Job completes his defense. No more can be said (v. 40). He now affixes his signature to the document (v. 35), and the burden of proof that he is a wretched sinner rests with God. Job's call for vindication had reached a climax in 27:2–6. Now he amplifies that statement with the details of his godly life. Each disavowal (vv. 5–7,9,13,16–21,24–27,29–34,38–39) is accompanied by an oath that calls for the punishment the offense deserves (vv. 8,10–12,14–15,22–23,28,40). The

principle at work is the so-called "law of retaliation" (see Ex 21:23–25 and note).

31:1–12 Job begins with sins of the heart, especially sexual lust (vv. 1–4), cheating in business (vv. 5–8) and marital infidelity (vv. 9–12).

31:1 *look lustfully at a girl.* To do so is to sin (see Mt 5:28).

31:4 Echoed by Elihu in 34:21.

31:6 *God weigh me in honest scales.* See 6:2; Pr 16:12; 21:2; 24:12. *blameless.* Does not imply sinless perfection (see note on 1:1).

31:12 *Destruction.* See note on 26:6.

31:13–23 Job reveals genuine understanding concerning matters of social justice: Human equality is based on creation (vv. 13–15), compassion toward those in need is essential (vv. 16–20), and power and influence must not be abused (vv. 21–23).

31:16–17 *widow . . . fatherless.* See note on 29:12–13.

²²then let my arm fall from the shoulder,
  let it be broken off at the joint. *d*
²³For I dreaded destruction from God, *e*
  and for fear of his splendor *f* I could
    not do such things. *g*

²⁴"If I have put my trust in gold *h*
  or said to pure gold, 'You are my
    security,' *i*
²⁵if I have rejoiced over my great
    wealth, *j*
  the fortune my hands had gained, *k*
²⁶if I have regarded the sun *l* in its
    radiance
  or the moon *m* moving in splendor,
²⁷so that my heart was secretly enticed *n*
  and my hand offered them a kiss of
    homage, *o*
²⁸then these also would be sins to be
    judged, *p*
  for I would have been unfaithful to
    God on high. *q*

²⁹"If I have rejoiced at my enemy's
    misfortune *r*
  or gloated over the trouble that came
    to him *s* —
³⁰I have not allowed my mouth to sin
  by invoking a curse against his
    life *t* —
³¹if the men of my household have never
    said,
  'Who has not had his fill of Job's
    meat?' *u* —
³²but no stranger had to spend the night
    in the street,
  for my door was always open to the
    traveler *v* —
³³if I have concealed *w* my sin as men
    do, *o*

by hiding *x* my guilt in my heart
³⁴because I so feared the crowd *y*
  and so dreaded the contempt of the
    clans
  that I kept silent *z* and would not go
    outside

³⁵("Oh, that I had someone to hear me! *a*
  I sign now my defense—let the
    Almighty answer me;
  let my accuser *b* put his indictment in
    writing.
³⁶Surely I would wear it on my
    shoulder, *c*
  I would put it on like a crown. *d*
³⁷I would give him an account of my
    every step; *e*
  like a prince *f* I would approach
    him.)—

³⁸"if my land cries out against me *g*
  and all its furrows are wet *h* with
    tears,
³⁹if I have devoured its yield without
    payment *i*
  or broken the spirit of its tenants, *j*
⁴⁰then let briers *k* come up instead of
    wheat
  and weeds *l* instead of barley."

The words of Job are ended. *m*

Elihu

32 So these three men stopped answering Job, *n* because he was
righteous in his own eyes. *o* 2But Elihu son

Center column references:

31:22
d Nu 15:30;
Job 5:15; 38:15;
Ps 10:15; 37:17;
137:5
31:23
e S Job 10:3;
S 30:15
f Job 13:11
g S Ge 20:11
31:24
h S Job 22:25
i Mt 6:24;
Lk 12:15
31:25
j S Ge 12:16;
Ps 49:6; 52:7;
62:10; Isa 10:14
k S Job 22:24;
Eze 28:5;
Lk 12:20-21
31:26 *l* S Ge 1:16
m Job 25:5
31:27
n S Dt 11:16;
S Job 24:15;
Jas 1:14 *o* Jer 8:2;
16:11
31:28
p S Ge 38:24;
Dt 17:2-7
q S Nu 11:20;
Eze 8:16
31:29
r S Nu 14:1;
Ps 35:15;
Ob 1:12; Mt 5:44
s Pr 17:5;
24:17-18
31:30 *t* Job 5:3;
Ro 12:14
31:31 *u* S Job 22:7
31:32
v Ge 19:2-3;
Jdg 19:20;
Mt 25:35;
S Ro 12:13
31:33 *w* Ps 32:5;
Pr 28:13

x S Ge 3:8
31:34 *y* Ex 23:2
z Ps 32:3; 39:2
31:35
a S Job 9:24;
30:28 *b* Job 27:7
31:36
c S Ex 28:12
d Job 29:14
31:37 *e* S ver 14;
S Job 11:11
f S Job 21:28

31:38 *g* S Ge 4:10 *h* Ps 65:10 31:39 *i* S 1Ki 21:19
j S Lev 19:13; Jas 5:4 31:40 *k* S Ge 3:18; Mt 13:7 *l* Zep 2:9;
Mt 13:26 *m* Ps 72:20; Jer 51:64 32:1 *n* ver 15 *o* S Job 2:3;
S 10:7

o 33 Or *as Adam did*

31:24–28 Covetous greed (vv. 24–25) and idolatry (vv. 26–27) are equally reprehensible in the eyes of God (v. 28; see Mt 6:19–24; Col 3:5).

31:25 *my great wealth.* See 1:3,10.

31:26–27 The sun and moon are not to be objects of worship (see Dt 4:19; 17:3; Eze 8:16–17).

31:27 *kiss.* An ancient gesture of worship (see 1Ki 19:18; Hos 13:2).

31:29–32 The sin of gloating over one's enemy was condemned by Moses (Ex 23:4–5) and by Christ (Mt 5:43–47).

31:33–34 A strong denial of hypocrisy.

31:33 *as men do.* See NIV text note and Ge 3:8–10; Hos 6:7.

31:35–37 Job's final call for justice. His signature endorses every word of the oaths he has just taken.

31:35 *someone to hear me.* See notes on 5:1; 9:33; 16:18–21; 19:25. *let the Almighty answer me.* See note on 38:1. *accuser.* The Hebrew for this word is not the same as that for "Satan" (see note on 1:6). Here Job's accuser is either (1) a human adversary (perhaps one of the three friends) or (2) God himself. In any event, Job assumes that accusations have been lodged against him before the court of heaven to which God has responded with judgments.

31:36 *shoulder.* Inscriptions were sometimes worn on the shoulder as a perpetual reminder of their importance (see Ex 28:12).

31:38–40 A climactic oath that completes an earlier theme and creates a unique emphasis. Job calls for a curse on his land if he has not been fully committed to social justice (see also vv. 13–15).

31:40 *The words of Job are ended.* His complaints and arguments are now over. He will only make brief statements of contrition (40:4–5; 42:2–6) following the divine discourses.

32:1—37:24 A fourth counselor, named Elihu and younger than the other three (32:4,6–7,9), has been standing on the sidelines, giving deference to age and listening to the dialogue-dispute. But now he declares himself ready to show that both Job and the three other counselors are in the wrong. Elihu's four poetic speeches (32:5–33:33; ch. 34; ch. 35; chs. 36–37) are preceded by a prose introduction (32:1–4) written by the author of the book.

32:1 *righteous in his own eyes.* He insisted on his innocence in spite of the terrible suffering that he was experiencing.

32:2–3 *angry.* Elihu considers Job's emphasis on vindicat-

of Barakel the Buzite,[p] of the family of
Ram, became very angry with Job for justifying himself[q] rather than God.[r] 3He was
also angry with the three friends,[s] because
they had found no way to refute Job,[t] and
yet had condemned him.[P][u] 4Now Elihu
had waited before speaking to Job because
they were older than he.[v] 5But when he
saw that the three men had nothing more
to say, his anger was aroused.

6So Elihu son of Barakel the Buzite said:

"I am young in years,
and you are old;[w]
that is why I was fearful,
not daring to tell you what I know.
7I thought, 'Age should speak;
advanced years should teach
wisdom.'[x]
8But it is the spirit[q][y] in a man,
the breath of the Almighty,[z] that
gives him understanding.[a]
9It is not only the old[r] who are wise,[b]
not only the aged[c] who understand
what is right.[d]

10"Therefore I say: Listen to me;[e]
I too will tell you what I know.[f]
11I waited while you spoke,
I listened to your reasoning;
while you were searching for words,
12 I gave you my full attention.
But not one of you has proved Job
wrong;
none of you has answered his
arguments.[g]
13Do not say, 'We have found wisdom;[h]
let God refute[i] him, not man.'
14But Job has not marshaled his words
against me,[j]
and I will not answer him with your
arguments.

15"They are dismayed and have no more
to say;
words have failed them.[k]
16Must I wait, now that they are silent,
now that they stand there with no
reply?
17I too will have my say;
I too will tell what I know.[l]
18For I am full of words,
and the spirit[m] within me compels
me;[n]
19inside I am like bottled-up wine,
like new wineskins ready to burst.[o]
20I must speak and find relief;
I must open my lips and reply.[p]
21I will show partiality[q] to no one,[r]
nor will I flatter any man;[s]
22for if I were skilled in flattery,
my Maker[t] would soon take me
away.[u]

33 "But now, Job, listen[v] to my
words;
pay attention to everything I say.[w]
2I am about to open my mouth;
my words are on the tip of my
tongue.
3My words come from an upright
heart;[x]
my lips sincerely speak what I
know.[y]
4The Spirit[z] of God has made me;[a]
the breath of the Almighty[b] gives me
life.[c]
5Answer me[d] then, if you can;
prepare[e] yourself and confront me.[f]
6I am just like you before God;[g]

32:2 [p]S Ge 22:21 [q]ver 1 [r]S Job 13:19; 27:5; 30:21; 35:2 **32:3** [s]Job 42:7 [t]ver 12-13 [u]S Job 15:13 **32:4** [v]S Lev 19:32 **32:6** [w]Job 15:10 **32:7** [x]S 1Ch 29:15; S 2Ch 10:6 **32:8** [y]ver 18 [z]S Job 27:3 [a]S Job 12:13; S Ps 119:34; Jas 1:5 **32:9** [b]1Co 1:26 [c]Ps 119:100 [d]S Job 12:12,20; Lk 2:47; 1Ti 4:12 **32:10** [e]Job 33:1,31,33; 34:2,16; 37:2,14; Ps 34:11 [f]S Job 5:27 **32:12** [g]ver 3 **32:13** [h]S Job 4:12; S Ecc 9:11 [i]S Job 11:5 **32:14** [j]Job 23:4 **32:15** [k]ver 1 **32:17** [l]S Job 5:27; 33:3; 36:4 **32:18** [m]ver 8 [n]Ac 4:20; 1Co 9:16; 2Co 5:14 **32:19** [o]Jer 20:9; Am 3:8; Mt 9:17 **32:20** [p]S Job 4:2; S Jer 6:11 **32:21** [q]S Lev 19:15; S 2Ch 19:7; S Job 13:10 [r]Mt 22:16 [s]Pr 29:5; 1Th 2:5 **32:22** [t]S Job 4:17; S 9:9 [u]Ps 12:2-4 **33:1** [v]Job 32:10 [w]S Job 6:28; S 13:6 **33:3** [x]1Ki 3:6; Ps 7:10; 11:2; 64:10 [y]S Job 6:28 **33:4** [z]S Ge 1:2 [a]Job 10:3 [b]S Job 27:3 [c]S Nu 16:22; S Job 12:10 **33:5** [d]ver 32 [e]Job 13:18 [f]S Job 31:14 **33:6** [g]Ac 14:15; Jas 5:17

P3 Masoretic Text; an ancient Hebrew scribal tradition *Job, and so had condemned God* q8 Or *Spirit*; also in verse 18 r9 Or *many*; or *great*

ing himself rather than God reprehensible, but he also believes that the friends' inability to refute Job was tantamount to condemning God (see NIV text note on v. 3).
32:2 *Buzite.* An inhabitant of Buz, a desert region in the east (see Jer 25:23).
32:6,10,17 *tell . . . what I know.* Elihu is eager to share his "knowledge" and assumes that he can communicate it effectively (see note on 36:4).
32:6 *young . . . fearful.* See Jer 1:6–8; 1Ti 4:12; 2Ti 1:7.
32:8 *breath of the Almighty.* See 33:4.
32:14 *I will not answer him with your arguments.* Elihu feels that something important has been left out and, where the wisdom of age has failed, he by the Spirit of God (see NIV text note on v. 8) has the understanding to supply the right answers.
32:15–22 Elihu delivers a soliloquy to himself, but it is also for the benefit of those who may be listening.
32:15–16 *words have failed them . . . they stand there with no reply.* See v. 5. The breakdown of the third cycle in the dialogue-dispute cut short Bildad's last word and left Zophar without a third speech (see note on 22:1–26:14).
32:18 *I am full of words.* Elihu's speeches continue unabated through ch. 37. He has a genuine contribution to make, however, to the problems Job is facing. At the same time, he does not stoop to false accusation about Job's earlier life but usually confines his criticism of Job to quotations from Job himself. This is perhaps the reason that God, in the epilogue, does not condemn Elihu along with Job's three friends (see 42:7).
32:19 *new wineskins ready to burst.* Old wineskins might be expected to crack or break (see Mt 9:17), but not new ones. Elihu is obviously eager to speak.
33:1–33 Elihu turns to Job and speaks directly to him. Unlike the three friends, he addresses Job by name (vv. 1,31; see 37:14).
33:1 *pay attention to everything I say.* He is thoroughly convinced of the importance and wisdom of the advice he is about to give (see vv. 31,33).
33:4 *Spirit of God has made me.* See Ge 1:2 and note. *breath of the Almighty.* See 32:8. *gives me life.* See 27:3; see also Ge 2:7 and note.
33:5 *Answer me.* He opens and closes his speech (see v.

I too have been taken from clay. [h]
[7]No fear of me should alarm you,
nor should my hand be heavy upon
you. [i]

[8]"But you have said in my hearing—
I heard the very words—
[9]'I am pure[j] and without sin;[k]
I am clean and free from guilt. [l]
[10]Yet God has found fault with me;
he considers me his enemy. [m]
[11]He fastens my feet in shackles;[n]
he keeps close watch on all my
paths.'[o]

[12]"But I tell you, in this you are not right,
for God is greater than man. [p]
[13]Why do you complain to him[q]
that he answers none of man's
words[s]?[r]
[14]For God does speak[s]—now one way,
now another[t]—
though man may not perceive it. [u]
[15]In a dream,[v] in a vision[w] of the night,[x]
when deep sleep[y] falls on men
as they slumber in their beds,
[16]he may speak[z] in their ears
and terrify them[a] with warnings,[b]
[17]to turn man from wrongdoing
and keep him from pride,[c]
[18]to preserve his soul from the pit,[t] [d]
his life from perishing by the
sword.[u] [e]
[19]Or a man may be chastened[f] on a bed
of pain[g]

with constant distress in his bones, [h]
[20]so that his very being finds food[i]
repulsive
and his soul loathes the choicest
meal.[j]
[21]His flesh wastes away to nothing,
and his bones,[k] once hidden, now
stick out. [l]
[22]His soul draws near to the pit,[v] [m]
and his life to the messengers of
death.[w] [n]
[23]"Yet if there is an angel on his side
as a mediator,[o] one out of a
thousand,
to tell a man what is right for him, [p]
[24]to be gracious to him and say,
'Spare him from going down to the
pit[x]; [q]
I have found a ransom for him'[r]—
[25]then his flesh is renewed[s] like a child's;
it is restored as in the days of his
youth. [t]
[26]He prays to God and finds favor with
him, [u]

33:6 [h]S Job 4:19
33:7 [i]S Job 9:34;
2Co 2:4
33:9 [j]S Job 10:7
[k]S Job 9:30;
S 13:23 [l]S Job 2:9
33:10
[m]S Job 13:24
33:11
[n]S Job 13:27
[o]Job 14:16;
Pr 3:6; Isa 30:21
33:12 [p]S Job 5:9;
Ps 8:4; 50:21;
Ecc 7:20;
Isa 55:8-9
33:13 [q]Job 40:2;
Isa 45:9
[r]S Job 11:8
33:14 [s]Ps 62:11
[t]ver 29 [u]Job 4:12
33:15
[v]S Ge 20:3;
Job 4:13;
S Mt 27:19
[w]Ac 16:9
[x]S Ge 15:1;
Da 2:19
[y]S Ge 2:21
33:16
[z]Job 36:10,15
[a]S Job 6:4
[b]Ps 88:15-16
33:17 [c]S Job 20:6
33:18 [d]ver 22,
24,28,30;
Ps 28:1; 30:9;
69:15; 88:6;
103:4; Pr 1:12;
Isa 14:15; 38:17;
Jnh 2:6; Zec 9:11
[e]S Job 15:22;
Mt 26:52
33:19 [f]S Job 5:17
[g]S Ge 17:1;
S Dt 8:5;
2Co 12:7-10;
Jas 1:3

33:20 [h]Ps 102:4; 107:18 [i]S Job 3:24; S 6:6 **33:21** [k]S Job 2:5
[l]S Job 16:8 **33:22** [m]S ver 18 [n]Job 38:17; Ps 9:13; 88:3;
107:18; 116:3 **33:23** [o]Gal 3:19; Heb 8:6; 9:15
[p]Job 36:9-10; Mic 6:8 **33:24** [q]S ver 18 [r]S Job 6:22 **33:25**
[s]Ps 103:5 [t]2Ki 5:14 **33:26** [u]S Job 5:15; Pr 8:35; 12:2;
18:22; Lk 2:52

[s]13 Or that he does not answer for any of his actions
[t]18 Or preserve him from the grave   [u]18 Or from
crossing the River   [v]22 Or He draws near to the grave
[w]22 Or to the dead   [x]24 Or grave

---

32) with the same plea. *if you can*. His attitude of superiority shows through.
33:6 *I . . . have been taken from clay*. See note on 4:19.
33:7 *hand . . . heavy upon*. The idiom is elsewhere used only of God (see 23:2 and NIV text notes; see also note on 1Sa 5:6).
33:8 *But you have said*. Elihu's method is to quote Job (vv. 9–11; 34:5–6,9; 35:2–3) and then show him where and how he is wrong. The quotations are not always verbatim, which indicates that Elihu is content simply to repeat the substance of Job's arguments.
33:11 Elihu quotes Job's words almost verbatim here (see 13:27).
33:12 *you are not right*. Elihu feels that Job needs to be corrected. Certainly Job's perception of God as his enemy (see v. 10; 13:24; 19:11) is wrong, but Elihu is also offended by what he considers Job's claim to purity (see v. 9). Job, however, had never claimed to be "pure and without sin," though some of his words were also understood that way by Eliphaz (see 15:14–16). Job admits being a sinner (7:21; 13:26) but disclaims the outrageous sins for which he thinks he is being punished. His complaints about God's silence (see v. 13) are also an offense to Elihu. But he imputes to Job the blanket statement that God never speaks to man, whereas Job's point is that God is silent in his present experience.
33:15 *In a dream . . . when deep sleep falls on men*. Elihu echoes Eliphaz (see 4:13).
33:18 *pit*. See vv. 22,24,28,30; a metaphor for the grave (see NIV text note), as often in the Psalms. *perishing by the sword*. See 36:12. The reading in the NIV text note in both

verses refers to the figurative waterway between the land of the living and the realm of the dead. The Hebrew for "River" here is *shelah* (from a root that means "to send") and sometimes means "water channel" (see Ne 3:15 and NIV text note), a conduit through which water is "sent" (see Jn 9:7) by a spring. The "River" therefore is the figurative means of passage between this world and the next.

33:19 *a man may be chastened on a bed of pain*. Dreams and visions (see v. 15) are not the only ways in which God speaks. He can talk to us in ways that we do not perceive (see v. 14). Elihu rightly states that God speaks to man in order to turn him from sin. But he overlooks Job's reason for wanting an audience with God: to find out what sins he is being accused of (see 13:22–23).

33:23–28 Having emphasized the importance of the chastening aspect of suffering, a point mentioned only briefly by Eliphaz (see 5:17), Elihu now moves on to the possibility of redemption based on a mediator (see note on 5:1). He further allows for God's gracious response of forgiveness where sincere repentance is present (vv. 27–28). But Elihu is still ignorant of the true nature of Job's relationship to God, known only in the divine council (chs. 1–2).

33:24 *Spare him from going down to the pit*. See Isa 38:17. *ransom*. See Ps 49:7–9 and note.

33:25 *flesh is renewed like a child's . . . restored*. Similar phrases are used in 2Ki 5:14 with reference to healing from leprosy.

33:26 *sees God's face*. Not literally (see note on Ge 16:13).

he sees God's face and shouts for
  joy; [v]
he is restored by God to his righteous
  state. [w]
27Then he comes to men and says,
  'I sinned, [x] and perverted what was
  right, [y]
  but I did not get what I deserved. [z]
28He redeemed [a] my soul from going
  down to the pit, [v] [b]
  and I will live to enjoy the light.' [c]

29"God does all these things to a man [d] —
  twice, even three times [e] —
30to turn back [f] his soul from the pit, [z] [g]
  that the light of life [h] may shine on
  him. [i]

31"Pay attention, Job, and listen [j] to me; [k]
  be silent, [l] and I will speak.
32If you have anything to say, answer
  me; [m]
  speak up, for I want you to be
  cleared. [n]
33But if not, then listen to me; [o]
  be silent, [p] and I will teach you
  wisdom. [q]"

34 Then Elihu said:
  2"Hear my words, you wise men;
  listen to me, [r] you men of learning.
3For the ear tests words
  as the tongue tastes food. [s]
4Let us discern for ourselves what is
  right; [t]
  let us learn together what is good. [u]

5"Job says, 'I am innocent, [v]
  but God denies me justice. [w]

6Although I am right,
  I am considered a liar; [x]
although I am guiltless, [y]
  his arrow inflicts an incurable
  wound.' [z]
7What man is like Job,
  who drinks scorn like water? [a]
8He keeps company with evildoers;
  he associates with wicked men. [b]
9For he says, 'It profits a man nothing
  when he tries to please God.' [c]

10"So listen to me, [d] you men of
  understanding. [e]
  Far be it from God to do evil, [f]
  from the Almighty to do wrong. [g]
11He repays a man for what he has
  done; [h]
  he brings upon him what his conduct
  deserves. [i]
12It is unthinkable that God would do
  wrong, [j]
  that the Almighty would pervert
  justice. [k]
13Who appointed [l] him over the earth?
  Who put him in charge of the whole
  world? [m]
14If it were his intention
  and he withdrew his spirit [a] [n] and
  breath, [o]
15all mankind would perish [p] together

33:26
[v]S Ezr 3:13;
S Job 22:26
[w]Ps 13:5; 50:15;
51:12; 1Jn 1:9
33:27
[x]S Nu 22:34
[y]Lk 15:21
[z]S Ezr 9:13;
Ps 22:27; 51:13;
Ro 6:21; Jas 2:13
33:28
[a]S Ex 15:13;
Ps 34:22; 107:20
[b]S ver 18;
S Job 17:16
[c]S Job 22:28
33:29
[d]Ps 139:16;
Pr 16:9; 20:24;
Jer 10:23;
1Co 12:6;
Eph 1:11;
Php 2:13 [e]ver 14
[g]S ver 18
33:30 [f]Jas 5:19
[h]Ps 49:19; 56:13;
116:9; Isa 53:11
[i]Isa 60:1;
Eph 5:14
33:31 [j]Jer 23:18
[k]S Job 32:10 [l]ver
33
33:32 [m]ver 6,
[n]S Job 6:29; 35:2
33:33
[o]S Job 32:10 [p]ver
31 [q]S Job 6:24;
Pr 10:8,10,19
34:2 [r]S Job 32:10
34:3 [s]Job 12:11
34:4
[t]S Job 12:12;
Heb 5:14
[u]1Th 5:21
34:5 [v]S Job 10:7
[w]S Job 6:29

34:6 [x]S Job 6:28
[y]S Job 9:21
[z]S Job 6:4;
S 10:3;
S Jer 10:19
34:7 [a]S Job 9:21;
S 15:16
34:8 [b]S Job 22:15
34:9
[c]S Job 9:29-31;
S 21:15

34:10 [d]Job 32:10 [e]ver 16; S Job 12:12 [f]S Ge 18:25 [g]ver 12;
Dt 32:4; Job 8:3; 36:23; Ps 92:15; Ro 3:5; 9:14 **34:11**
[h]S Job 21:31; S Mt 16:27 [i]Jer 17:10; 32:19; Eze 33:20 **34:12**
[j]S ver 10; Tit 1:2; Heb 6:18 [k]S Job 8:3; Ps 9:16; Col 3:25;
2Th 1:6 **34:13** [l]Heb 1:2 [m]Job 36:23; 38:4,6; Isa 40:14
34:14 [n]S Ge 6:3 [o]S Nu 16:22; S Job 27:3 **34:15** [p]S Ge 6:13;
La 3:22; Mal 3:6; Jn 3:16

[v]28 Or redeemed me from going down to the grave
[z]30 Or turn him back from the grave   [a]14 Or Spirit

33:29 *twice . . . three times.* See note on 5:19.
33:30 *to turn back his soul from the pit.* Elihu teaches that God's apparent cruelty in chastening human beings is in reality an act of love, since man is never punished in this life in keeping with what he fully deserves (see v. 27). *light of life.* Spiritual well-being (see Ps 49:19; see also Ps 27:1 and note). In some contexts, the phrase refers to resurrection (see note on Isa 53:11).
33:32 *I want you to be cleared.* But this will happen, Elihu insists, only if Job repents.
34:1-37 The second of Elihu's four speeches (see note on 32:1-37:24), divided into three sections: (1) addressed to a group of wise men (vv. 2-15), doubtless including the three friends; (2) addressed to Job (vv. 16-33); (3) addressed to himself (vv. 34-37), as in 32:15-22 (see note there).
34:2,10 *listen to me.* Although it is possible that Elihu is overly impressed with his own wisdom, it is more likely that he considered himself a messenger of God (see 32:8,18 and NIV text note), especially in the light of his humble attitude in v. 4.
34:2 *wise men . . . men of learning.* Also referred to as "men of understanding" (vv. 10,34).
34:3 Elihu echoes the words of Job in 12:11 (see note there).
34:5,9 *Job says . . . For he says.* Elihu again quotes Job and

then goes on to defend God's justice against what he considers to be Job's false theology (e.g., 9:14-24; 16:11-17; 19:7; 21:17-18; 24:1-12; 27:2). The substance of the quotation in v. 5 is accurate (cf. 12:4; 13:18; 27:6), and much of v. 6 represents Job fairly (see 21:34; 27:5; see also 6:4 and note)—though Job had never claimed to be completely guiltless. Verse 9 is not a direct quotation from Job, who had only imagined the wicked saying something similar (see 21:15). But perhaps Elihu derives it from Job's repeated statement that God treats the righteous and the wicked in the same way (cf. 9:22; 21:17; 24:1-12), leading to the conclusion that it does not pay to please God.
34:7 *drinks scorn like water.* See Eliphaz's description of man in 15:16.
34:10 *Far be it from God to do evil.* See Ge 18:25 and note. Elihu's concern that Job was making God the author of evil is commendable. Job, in his frustration, has come perilously close to charging God with wrongdoing (12:4-6; 24:1-12). He has suggested that this is the only conclusion he can reach on the basis of his knowledge and experience (9:24).
34:11 See 2Co 5:10.
34:13-15 Elihu is zealous for God's glory as the sovereign Sustainer who demonstrates his grace every moment by granting life and breath to man.

and man would return to the dust. *q*

¹⁶"If you have understanding, *r* hear this;
　　listen to what I say. *s*
¹⁷Can he who hates justice govern? *t*
　　Will you condemn the just and
　　　mighty One? *u*
¹⁸Is he not the One who says to kings,
　　'You are worthless,'
　　and to nobles, *v* 'You are wicked,' *w*
¹⁹who shows no partiality *x* to princes
　　and does not favor the rich over the
　　　poor, *y*
　　for they are all the work of his
　　　hands? *z*
²⁰They die in an instant, in the middle of
　　the night; *a*
　　the people are shaken and they pass
　　　away;
　　the mighty are removed without
　　　human hand. *b*

²¹"His eyes are on the ways of men; *c*
　　he sees their every step. *d*
²²There is no dark place, *e* no deep
　　shadow, *f*
　　where evildoers can hide. *g*
²³God has no need to examine men
　　further, *h*
　　that they should come before him for
　　　judgment. *i*
²⁴Without inquiry he shatters *j* the
　　mighty *k*
　　and sets up others in their place. *l*
²⁵Because he takes note of their deeds, *m*
　　he overthrows them in the night *n*
　　and they are crushed. *o*
²⁶He punishes them for their wickedness *p*
　　where everyone can see them,
²⁷because they turned from following
　　him *q*
　　and had no regard for any of his
　　　ways. *r*
²⁸They caused the cry of the poor to
　　come before him,

so that he heard the cry of the
　　　needy. *s*
²⁹But if he remains silent, *t* who can
　　condemn him? *u*
　　If he hides his face, *v* who can see
　　　him?
　　Yet he is over man and nation alike, *w*
³⁰　　to keep a godless *x* man from ruling, *y*
　　from laying snares for the people. *z*

³¹"Suppose a man says to God,
　　'I am guilty *a* but will offend no
　　　more.
³²Teach me what I cannot see; *b*
　　if I have done wrong, I will not do so
　　　again.' *c*
³³Should God then reward you on your
　　terms,
　　when you refuse to repent? *d*
　You must decide, not I;
　　so tell me what you know.

³⁴"Men of understanding declare,
　　wise men who hear me say to me,
³⁵'Job speaks without knowledge; *e*
　　his words lack insight.' *f*
³⁶Oh, that Job might be tested to the
　　utmost
　　for answering like a wicked man! *g*
³⁷To his sin he adds rebellion;
　　scornfully he claps his hands *h* among
　　　us
　　and multiplies his words *i* against
　　　God." *j*

35 Then Elihu said:

²"Do you think this is just?
　　You say, 'I will be cleared *k* by
　　　God. *b*' *l*

34:15 *q*S Ge 2:7;
S Job 7:21; 9:22;
Ps 90:10
34:16 *r*S ver 10
*s*S Job 32:10
34:17 *t*ver 30;
2Sa 23:3-4;
Pr 20:8,26;
24:23-25; 28:28
*u*ver 29;
S Job 10:7; 40:8;
Ro 3:5-6
34:18
*v*S Job 12:18
*w*Ex 22:28;
Isa 40:24
34:19
*x*S Job 13:10;
S Ac 10:34
*y*S Lev 19:15;
Jas 2:5
*z*S Job 10:3
34:20 *a*ver 25;
S Ex 11:4;
S Job 20:8
*b*S Job 12:19
34:21 *c*Jer 32:19
*d*S Job 14:16;
Pr 15:3;
S Heb 4:13
34:22 *e*Ps 74:20
*f*S Job 3:5
*g*S Ge 3:8;
S Job 11:20
34:23 *h*Ps 11:4
*i*Job 11:11
34:24 *j*Isa 8:9;
9:4; Jer 51:20;
Da 2:34
*k*Job 12:19
*l*Da 2:21
34:25
*m*S Job 11:11
*n*S ver 20
*o*Pr 5:21-23
34:26 *p*S Ge 6:5;
S Job 8:22;
S 28:24; Ps 9:5;
Jer 44:5
34:27 *q*Ps 14:3
*r*S 1Sa 15:11

34:28
*s*S Ex 22:23;
S Job 5:15;
S 12:19
34:29 *t*Ps 28:1;
83:1; 109:1
*u*S ver 17;
Ro 8:34 *v*Ps 13:1
*w*Ps 83:18; 97:9
34:30 *x*S Job 8:13
*y*S ver 17
*z*Ps 25:15; 31:4;
91:3; 124:7;
140:5; Pr 29:2-12
34:31 *a*Ps 51:5;
Lk 15:21;
Ro 7:24; 1Jn 1:8,
10

34:32 *b*Ex 33:13; Job 35:11; 38:36; Ps 15:2; 25:4; 27:11;
51:6; 86:11; 139:23-24; 143:8 *c*Job 33:27; S Lk 19:8 **34:33**
*d*S 2Ki 17:13; Job 33:23; 36:10,15,18,21; 41:11; 42:6;
Pr 17:23; Jnh 3:8 **34:35** *e*Job 35:16; 38:2; 42:3 *f*Job 26:3
34:36 *g*S Job 6:29; S 22:15 **34:37** *h*S Job 27:23 *i*Job 35:16
*j*Job 23:2 **35:2** *k*S Job 33:32 *l*S Job 2:9; S 32:2

*b*2 Or *My righteousness is more than God's*

34:15 *return to the dust.* See Ecc 12:7; see also Ge 3:19
and note.
34:16 *hear . . . listen.* The Hebrew for these verbs is singular, addressed to Job. Elihu is concerned that Job's attitude
about God's justice be corrected (see v. 17), so he stresses
God's impartial rule as Lord of all, especially in meting out
justice to the wicked in high places (see vv. 18–20).
34:18 *worthless.* See note on Dt 13:13.
34:21–28 God's omniscience guarantees that he will not
make any mistakes when he punishes evildoers. It is not
necessary for him to set times to examine people for judgment (see v. 23; contrast 24:1).
34:21 Elihu echoes the words of Job in 31:4.
34:29 *if he remains silent, who can condemn him?* Elihu
attempts to answer Job's complaint about God's silence (ch.
23). God watches over men and nations to see that right is
done (vv. 29–30).

34:31–33 First indirectly (vv. 31–32) and then more
directly (v. 33), Elihu condemns Job and calls for his repentance.
34:35 *Job speaks without knowledge.* A motif in the first
discourse of the Lord (see 38:2) and the final response of Job
(see 42:3).
35:1–16 Elihu's third speech (see note on 32:1–37:24),
addressed to Job.
35:2 *cleared.* The Hebrew for this word is translated "vindicated" in Job's statement in 13:18. Elihu thinks that it is
unjust and inconsistent for Job to expect vindication from
God and at the same time imply that God does not care
whether we are righteous (see v. 3). But allowance must be
made for a person to express his feelings. The psalmist who
thirsted for God (Ps 42:1–2) also questioned why God had
forgotten him (Ps 42:9) and rejected him (Ps 43:2).

3Yet you ask him, 'What profit is it to me,[c]
and what do I gain by not sinning?'[m]
4"I would like to reply to you
and to your friends with you.
5Look up at the heavens[n] and see;
gaze at the clouds so high above you.[o]
6If you sin, how does that affect him?
If your sins are many, what does that do to him?[p]
7If you are righteous, what do you give to him,[q]
or what does he receive[r] from your hand?[s]
8Your wickedness affects only a man like yourself,[t]
and your righteousness only the sons of men.[u]

9"Men cry out[v] under a load of oppression;[w]
they plead for relief from the arm of the powerful.[x]
10But no one says, 'Where is God my Maker,[y]
who gives songs[z] in the night,[a]
11who teaches[b] more to[c] us than to[d] the beasts of the earth
and makes us wiser than[e] the birds of the air?'
12He does not answer[d] when men cry out
because of the arrogance[e] of the wicked.[f]
13Indeed, God does not listen to their empty plea;
the Almighty pays no attention to it.[g]
14How much less, then, will he listen
when you say that you do not see him,[h]
that your case[i] is before him
and you must wait for him,[j]
15and further, that his anger never punishes[k]
and he does not take the least notice of wickedness.[f] [l]
16So Job opens his mouth with empty talk;[m]
without knowledge he multiplies words."[n]

36

Elihu continued:
2"Bear with me a little longer and I will show you
that there is more to be said in God's behalf.
3I get my knowledge from afar;[o]
I will ascribe justice to my Maker.[p]
4Be assured that my words are not false;[q]
one perfect in knowledge[r] is with you.[s]

5"God is mighty,[t] but does not despise men;[u]
he is mighty, and firm in his purpose.[v]
6He does not keep the wicked alive[w]
but gives the afflicted their rights.[x]
7He does not take his eyes off the righteous;[y]
he enthrones them with kings[z]
and exalts them forever.[a]

35:3 [m]S Job 9:29-31; S 21:15 **35:5** [n]S Ge 15:5; S Dt 10:14 [o]S Job 11:7-9; Ps 19:1-4 **35:6** [p]S Job 7:20 **35:7** [q]Ro 11:35 [r]1Co 4:7 [s]S Job 22:2-3; Lk 17:10 **35:8** [t]Eze 18:24 [u]Eze 18:5-9; Zec 7:9-10 **35:9** [v]Ex 2:23 [w]S Job 20:19 [x]S Job 5:15; S 12:19 **35:10** [y]S Job 4:17 [z]S Job 8:21 [a]Ps 42:8; 77:6; 119:62; 149:5; Ac 16:25 **35:11** [b]S Job 21:22; Lk 12:24 [c]Job 12:7 **35:12** [d]S 1Sa 8:18 [e]S Job 15:25 [f]Ps 66:18 **35:13** [g]S Dt 1:45; S 1Sa 8:18; S Job 15:31; S Pr 15:8 **35:14** [h]S Job 9:11 [i]Ps 37:6 [j]Job 31:35 **35:15** [k]S Job 9:24 [l]S Job 18:5; Ps 10:11; Hos 7:2; Am 8:7 **35:16** [m]Tit 1:10 [n]S Job 34:35,37; 1Co 4:20; Jude 1:10 **36:3** [o]S Job 6:28 [p]S Job 4:17 **36:4** [q]S Job 6:28; S 13:6 [r]Job 37:5, 16,23 [s]S Job 32:17 **36:5** [t]S Job 9:4 [u]Ps 5:2; 22:24; 31:22; 69:33; 102:17; 103:10 [v]S Nu 23:19; Ro 11:29 **36:6** [w]S Job 34:26 [x]S Job 4:10 **36:7** [y]S Job 11:11; Ps 11:5; 33:18; 34:15; Mt 6:18 [z]Ps 113:8; Isa 22:23 [a]S 1Sa 2:7-8; S Job 4:7

[c]*3* Or *you* [d]*11* Or *teaches us by* [e]*11* Or *us wise by* [f]*15* Symmachus, Theodotion and Vulgate; the meaning of the Hebrew for this word is uncertain.

35:5 *Look up at the heavens and see.* Elihu asserts that God is so far above man that there is really nothing man can do, good or bad, that will affect God's essential nature (see v. 6).
35:9 *Men cry out . . . they plead for relief.* Elihu states that those like Job who pray for help when suffering innocently never seem to get around to trusting the justice and goodness of their Maker, who is also the author of wisdom and joy (see vv. 10–11). Such failure is a sign of arrogance (see v. 12), so Job's complaint against God's justice and about God's silence is meaningless talk (see vv. 13–16).
35:10–11 *gives songs . . . teaches . . . makes us wiser.* God chooses to condescend, to reach out to man in love.
35:12 Is it because of the arrogance of the wicked that men are crying out? A comma after the first line would change the meaning and make more sense of the verse in context: Since men are arrogant, God does not listen (see v. 13). Job himself might not be wicked, but he shares their arrogance. He too receives no answer, because he does not ask rightly (see v. 14).
35:16 The reference here to Job in the third person does not necessarily mean that someone other than Job is being addressed (see note on vv. 1–16). *without knowledge.* See 38:2 and note. *multiplies words.* Against God (see 34:37).
36:1–37:24 Elihu's fourth and final (see 36:2) speech (see note on 32:1–37:24), addressed for the most part to Job (but see note on 37:2).
36:2–4 Elihu desires to strengthen the case for God's goodness and justice.
36:4 *perfect in knowledge.* Here Elihu applies the phrase to himself, while in 37:16 he applies it to God—thus appearing to make himself equal to God. But the Hebrew for "knowledge" is not quite the same here as in 37:16. Elihu is probably referring to his ability as a communicator, i.e., he claims perfection in the knowledge of speech (see note on 32:6,10,17).
36:5 God's power assures the fulfillment of his purpose.
36:6–9 A classic statement of God's justice in rewarding the righteous and punishing sinners (in contrast to what Job has been claiming). In v. 7 Elihu perhaps has in mind Job's complaint that God will not leave him alone (see 7:17–19), and in v. 9 he may be thinking of Job's charge that God will not present his indictment against him (see 31:35–36).

[8]But if men are bound in chains,[b]
　held fast by cords of affliction,[c]
[9]he tells them what they have done—
　that they have sinned arrogantly.[d]
[10]He makes them listen[e] to correction[f]
　and commands them to repent of
　their evil.[g]
[11]If they obey and serve him,[h]
　they will spend the rest of their days
　in prosperity[i]
　and their years in contentment.[j]
[12]But if they do not listen,
　they will perish by the sword[g][k]
　and die without knowledge.[l]
[13]"The godless in heart[m] harbor
　resentment;[n]
　even when he fetters them, they do
　not cry for help.[o]
[14]They die in their youth,[p]
　among male prostitutes of the
　shrines.[q]
[15]But those who suffer[r] he delivers in
　their suffering;[s]
　he speaks[t] to them in their
　affliction.[u]
[16]"He is wooing[v] you from the jaws of
　distress
　to a spacious place[w] free from
　restriction,[x]
　to the comfort of your table[y] laden
　with choice food.[z]
[17]But now you are laden with the
　judgment due the wicked;[a]
　judgment and justice have taken hold
　of you.[b]
[18]Be careful that no one entices you by
　riches;
　do not let a large bribe[c] turn you
　aside.[d]
[19]Would your wealth[e]
　or even all your mighty efforts
　sustain you so you would not be in
　distress?
[20]Do not long for the night,[f]
　to drag people away from their
　homes.[h]

[21]Beware of turning to evil,[g]
　which you seem to prefer to
　affliction.[h]
[22]"God is exalted in his power.[i]
　Who is a teacher like him?[j]
[23]Who has prescribed his ways[k] for
　him,[l]
　or said to him, 'You have done
　wrong'?[m]
[24]Remember to extol his work,[n]
　which men have praised in song.[o]
[25]All mankind has seen it;[p]
　men gaze on it from afar.
[26]How great is God—beyond our
　understanding![q]
　The number of his years is past
　finding out.[r]
[27]"He draws up the drops of water,[s]
　which distill as rain to the
　streams[i] ;[t]
[28]the clouds pour down their moisture
　and abundant showers[u] fall on
　mankind.[v]
[29]Who can understand how he spreads
　out the clouds,
　how he thunders[w] from his
　pavilion?[x]
[30]See how he scatters his lightning[y]
　about him,
　bathing the depths of the sea.[z]
[31]This is the way he governs[j] the
　nations[a]
　and provides food[b] in abundance.[c]
[32]He fills his hands with lightning
　and commands it to strike its mark.[d]

36:8 [b]S 2Sa 3:34;
2Ki 23:33;
Ps 107:10,14 [c]ver
10,15,21;
Ps 119:67,71
36:9 [d]S Job 15:25
36:10
[e]S Job 33:16
[f]S Job 5:17 [g]S ver
8; S Jdg 6:8;
S Job 34:33;
1Th 5:22
36:11
[h]S Lev 26:33;
Dt 28:1; Isa 1:19;
Hag 1:12
[i]S Dt 30:15;
S Job 8:7
[j]S Ex 8:22;
S Dt 8:1;
Jn 14:21; 1Ti 4:8
36:12
[k]S Lev 26:38;
S Job 15:22
[l]S Job 4:21;
Eph 4:18
36:13
[m]S Job 15:12;
Ro 2:5 [n]S Job 5:2
[o]S Job 4:17;
Am 4:11
36:14
[p]S Job 15:32
[q]S Dt 23:17
36:15 [r]S Job 5:15
[s]2Co 12:10
[t]S Job 33:16
[u]S ver 8;
S Job 34:33
36:16 [v]Hos 2:14
[w]S 2Sa 22:20;
Ps 18:19
[x]Ps 118:5
[y]Ps 23:5; 78:19
[z]S Ge 17:1;
S Job 15:11
36:17
[a]S Job 20:29
[b]Job 22:11
36:18
[c]S Ex 23:8;
Am 5:12
[d]S Job 34:33
36:19 [e]Ps 49:6;
Jer 9:23
36:20 [f]Job 34:20,
25
36:21
[g]S Job 34:33;
Ps 66:18 [h]S ver 8;
Heb 11:25
36:22 [i]S Job 5:9;
S 9:4
[j]S Job 21:22;
S Ro 11:34
36:23 [k]Job 27:11;
Ro 11:33
[l]S Job 34:13;
Ro 11:33
[m]S Ge 18:25;
S Job 34:10
36:24
[n]1Ch 16:24;
Ps 35:27; 92:5;
111:2; 138:5;

145:10 [o]S Ex 15:1; Rev 15:3 36:25 [p]Ro 1:20 36:26
[q]S Job 5:9; 1Co 13:12 [r]S Ge 21:33; S Job 10:5; Heb 1:12
36:27 [s]S Job 26:8 [t]S 2Sa 1:21; Job 28:26; 38:28; Isa 55:10
36:28 [u]Ps 65:10; 72:6; Joel 2:23 [v]S Job 5:10; S 22:11;
S 28:26; Mt 5:45 36:29 [w]Ps 29:3; Jer 10:13 [x]S Job 9:6;
37:16; Ps 18:7-15; 19:4,5; 104:2; Pr 8:28; Isa 40:22 36:30
[y]Ex 19:16; Job 37:11,15; Ps 18:12,14; 97:4; Jer 10:13;
Hab 3:11 [z]Ps 68:22; Isa 51:10 36:31 [a]Dt 28:23-24;
1Ki 17:1; Job 37:13; Am 4:7-8 [b]Ps 145:15 [c]Ps 104:14-15,
27-28; Isa 30:23; Ac 14:17 36:32 [d]S Job 28:24; 37:12,15;
Ps 18:14; 29:7-9

[g]12 Or will cross the River　[h]20 The meaning of the
Hebrew for verses 18-20 is uncertain.　[i]27 Or distill
from the mist as rain　[j]31 Or nourishes

36:10 *makes them listen to correction.* Elihu states that
God uses trouble to gain man's attention.
36:12 See NIV text note (see also note on 33:18).
36:13–15 Elihu understands that the basic spiritual need
of man stems from his hardness of heart—his refusal to yield
to God, to cry out to God in his distress (see Ps 107), or to
hear the voice of God in suffering.
36:14 *male prostitutes of the shrines.* See note on 1Ki
14:24.
36:16–21 Elihu warns Job to respond to God's discipline
by turning away from evil (see v. 21). Verse 16 shows that he
still views Job as a man for whom there is hope.
36:16 *He is wooing you.* With tender compassion, God
brings his people back to himself (see Hos 2:14).

36:21 *Beware of turning to evil.* Elihu's evaluation of Job is
the opposite of God's (see 1:8; 2:3).
36:22–33 Elihu anticipates some of God's statements in
the discourses of chs. 38–41.
36:24 *his work, which men have praised in song.* See, e.g.,
Ex 15:1; Jdg 5:1.
36:26 *beyond our understanding.* See 37:5. That God's
ways and thoughts are infinitely higher than ours is an
important theme in chs. 38–41.
36:30 *bathing.* Lit. "covering," here in the sense of "light-
ing up" the depths of the sea.
36:31 *governs.* The NIV text note understands the verse to
mean that the Lord "nourishes" the nations with the showers mentioned in vv. 27–30.

33His thunder announces the coming
storm; e
even the cattle make known its
approach. k f

37 "At this my heart pounds g
and leaps from its place.
2Listen! h Listen to the roar of his voice, i
to the rumbling that comes from his
mouth. j
3He unleashes his lightning k beneath the
whole heaven
and sends it to the ends of the
earth. l
4After that comes the sound of his roar;
he thunders m with his majestic
voice. n
When his voice resounds,
he holds nothing back.
5God's voice thunders o in marvelous
ways; p
he does great things beyond our
understanding. q
6He says to the snow, r 'Fall on the
earth,'
and to the rain shower, 'Be a mighty
downpour.' s
7So that all men he has made may know
his work, t
he stops every man from his labor.1 u
8The animals take cover; v
they remain in their dens. w
9The tempest comes out from its
chamber, x
the cold from the driving winds. y
10The breath of God produces ice,
and the broad waters become
frozen. z
11He loads the clouds with moisture; a
he scatters his lightning b through
them. c
12At his direction they swirl around
over the face of the whole earth
to do whatever he commands them. d
13He brings the clouds to punish men, e

or to water his earth m and show his
love. f
14"Listen g to this, Job;
stop and consider God's wonders. h
15Do you know how God controls the
clouds
and makes his lightning i flash? j
16Do you know how the clouds hang
poised, k
those wonders of him who is perfect
in knowledge? l
17You who swelter in your clothes
when the land lies hushed under the
south wind, m
18can you join him in spreading out the
skies, n
hard as a mirror of cast bronze? o
19"Tell us what we should say to him; p
we cannot draw up our case q
because of our darkness. r
20Should he be told that I want to speak?
Would any man ask to be swallowed
up?
21Now no one can look at the sun, s
bright as it is in the skies
after the wind has swept them clean.
22Out of the north he comes in golden
splendor; t
God comes in awesome majesty. u
23The Almighty is beyond our reach and
exalted in power; v
in his justice w and great
righteousness, he does not
oppress. x
24Therefore, men revere him, y
for does he not have regard for all the
wise z in heart? n "

36:33 eJob 37:5;
40:9 /S Job 28:26
37:1 gPs 38:10;
Isa 15:5; Jer 4:19;
Hab 3:16
37:2 hS Job 32:10
iver 5 /Ps 18:13;
29:3-9
37:3
kS 2Sa 22:13;
Ps 18:14
lS Job 36:32;
Mt 24:27;
Lk 17:24
37:4 mS 1Sa 2:10
nS Ex 20:19
37:5 oS 1Sa 2:10;
Jn 12:29
pS Job 36:33
qS Job 5:9;
S 11:7-9; S 36:4
37:6 rDt 28:12;
Job 38:22
sS Ge 7:4;
S Job 5:10;
S 28:26
37:7 tPs 109:27
uPs 104:19-23;
111:2
37:8 vS Job 28:26
wJob 38:40;
Ps 104:22
37:9 xPs 50:3
yPs 147:17
37:10
zJob 38:29-30;
Ps 147:17
37:11 aS Job 26:8
bS Job 36:30
cS Job 28:26
37:12 dS ver 3;
Ps 147:16; 148:8
37:13 eS Ge 7:4;
Ex 9:22-23;
S 1Sa 12:17

/S 1Ki 18:45;
S Job 5:10;
S 36:31; 38:27
37:14
gS Job 32:10
hS Job 5:9
37:15
iS Job 36:30
/S Job 36:32
37:16
kS Job 36:29
/S Job 5:9; S 36:4
37:17 mAc 27:13
37:18 nS Ge 1:1,
8; S Job 22:14
oDt 28:23
37:19 pRo 8:26
qS Job 13:18
rS Job 9:3
37:21
sS Jdg 5:31;
Ac 22:11; 26:13
37:22 tPs 19:5
uEx 24:17

37:23 vS Job 5:9; S 36:4; Ro 11:33; 1Ti 6:16 wS Job 8:3
xS Job 4:17; Ps 44:1; Isa 63:9; Jer 25:5; La 3:33; Eze 18:23,
32 37:24 yS Ge 22:12; Job 28:28; Ecc 12:13; Mic 6:8;
Mt 10:28 zS Job 5:13; Eph 5:15

k33 Or announces his coming— / the One zealous
against evil 17 Or / he fills all men with fear by his
power m13 Or to favor them n24 Or for he does
not have regard for any who think they are wise.

36:32 his hands. Lit. "both hands." God works with equal
effectiveness with either hand (cf. 1Ch 12:2).
37:1–13 A continuation of Elihu's hymnic description of
God's marvels exhibited in the earth's atmosphere, beginning in 36:27. His heart pounds at the awesome display (see
v. 1). The passage reveals a sophisticated observation of
atmospheric conditions and their effects: the evaporation
and distillation of water for rain (see 36:27 and NIV text
note), the clouds as holders of moisture (see 36:28; 37:11)
and the cyclonic behavior of clouds (see v. 12). Such forces
originate from God's command and always perform his will
for mankind, whether for good or for ill (v. 13).
37:2 Listen. The Hebrew for this verb is plural, indicating
that others (including the three friends) besides Job are being
addressed here (see note on 36:1–37:24). roar of his voice
... rumbling. Thunder (see v. 4).
37:5 beyond our understanding. See note on 36:26.

37:10 breath of God. Here a metaphor for a chilling wind.
37:14–18 Job is challenged to ponder God's power over
the elements. The question format is also used in the divine
discourses (chs. 38–41).
37:16 perfect in knowledge. See note on 36:4.
37:18 spreading out the skies. See 26:7. hard as . . .
bronze. In Dt 28:23, a bronze sky symbolizes unremitting
heat (see note there).
37:19 we cannot draw up our case. Job had dared to sign
his defense and call for an audience with God (see 31:35).
For this, Elihu seeks to shame him. But he softens his tone by
including himself as one equally vulnerable to God's majesty.
37:22 Out of the north he comes. See note on Ps 48:2.
God comes. Elihu prepares Job for the appearance of God in
the storm (chs. 38–41).
37:24 revere. Fear (see 28:28; Ge 20:11 and notes).

The LORD Speaks

38 Then the LORD answered Job[a] out
of the storm.[b] He said:

2"Who is this that darkens my counsel[c]
  with words without knowledge?[d]
3Brace yourself like a man;
  I will question you,
  and you shall answer me.[e]

4"Where were you when I laid the
    earth's foundation?[f]
  Tell me, if you understand.[g]
5Who marked off its dimensions?[h]
    Surely you know!
  Who stretched a measuring line[i]
    across it?
6On what were its footings set,[j]
  or who laid its cornerstone[k]—
7while the morning stars[l] sang
    together[m]
  and all the angels[o n] shouted for
    joy?[o]

8"Who shut up the sea behind doors[p]
  when it burst forth from the womb,[q]
9when I made the clouds its garment
  and wrapped it in thick darkness,[r]
10when I fixed limits for it[s]
  and set its doors and bars in place,[t]
11when I said, 'This far you may come
    and no farther;[u]
  here is where your proud waves
    halt'?[v]

12"Have you ever given orders to the
    morning,[w]
  or shown the dawn its place,[x]

13that it might take the earth by the edges
  and shake the wicked[y] out of it?[z]
14The earth takes shape like clay under a
    seal;[a]
  its features stand out like those of a
    garment.
15The wicked are denied their light,[b]
  and their uplifted arm is broken.[c]

16"Have you journeyed to the springs of
    the sea
  or walked in the recesses of the
    deep?[d]
17Have the gates of death[e] been shown
    to you?
  Have you seen the gates of the
    shadow of death[P ?f]
18Have you comprehended the vast
    expanses of the earth?[g]
  Tell me, if you know all this.[h]

19"What is the way to the abode of light?
  And where does darkness reside?[i]
20Can you take them to their places?
  Do you know the paths[j] to their
    dwellings?
21Surely you know, for you were already
    born![k]
  You have lived so many years!

22"Have you entered the storehouses of
    the snow[l]

Cross references (center column):

38:1 [a]S Job 11:5
[b]S Ex 14:21;
S 1Sa 2:10;
Job 40:6;
Isa 21:1; Eze 1:4
38:2 [c]S 1Ki 22:5;
Isa 40:13
[d]S Job 34:35;
Mk 10:38;
1Ti 1:7
38:3 [e]Job 40:7;
42:4; Mk 11:29
38:4 [f]S ver 5;
S Ge 1:1;
S 1Sa 2:8 [g]ver 18;
S Job 34:13;
Pr 30:4
38:5 [h]ver 4;
Ps 102:25;
Pr 8:29;
Isa 40:12; 48:13;
Jer 31:37
[i]Jer 31:39;
Zec 1:16; 4:9-10
38:6 [j]Pr 8:25
[k]S Job 26:7
38:7 [l]S Ge 1:16
[m]Ps 19:1-4;
148:2-3
[n]S 1Ki 22:19
[o]Dt 16:15
38:8 [p]ver 11;
Ps 33:7; Pr 8:29;
Jer 5:22
[q]S Ge 1:9-10
38:9 [r]S Ge 1:2
38:10
[s]S Job 28:25;
Ps 33:7; 104:9;
Isa 40:12 [t]Ne 3:3;
Job 7:12; 26:10
38:11 [u]S ver 8
[v]Ps 65:7; 89:9;
104:6-9
38:12 [w]Ps 57:8
[x]Ps 74:16;
Am 5:8

38:13 [y]Ps 104:35
[z]S Job 8:22
38:14 [a]Ex 28:11
38:15
[b]S Dt 28:29;
S Job 15:22;
S 18:5
[c]S Ge 17:14;
S Job 4:10;

S 31:22 38:16 [d]S Ge 1:7; S Job 9:8 38:17 [e]S Job 33:22;
Mt 16:18; Rev 1:18 /S Job 7:9 38:18 [g]S Job 28:24; Isa 40:12
[h]S ver 4 38:19 [i]S Ge 1:4; S Job 28:3; Ps 139:11-12 38:20
[j]S Job 24:13 38:21 [k]Job 15:7 38:22 [l]S Job 37:6

[o]7 Hebrew *the sons of God*   [P]17 Or *gates of deep
shadows*

38:1–42:6 The theophany (appearance of God) to Job,
consisting of two discourses by the Lord (38:1–40:2;
40:6–41:34), each of which receives a brief response from
Job (40:3–5; 42:1–6).
38:1 *the LORD.* The Israelite covenant name for God (see
Introduction: Author). *storm.* See 40:6. Elihu had imagined
the appearance of the divine presence as a display of "golden
splendor" and "awesome majesty" (37:22). He also had
anticipated the storm or whirlwind (see note on 37:22), from
which Job would hear the voice of God. Job had said, "Let
the Almighty answer me" (31:35). He now receives the
Lord's answer.
38:2 See 35:16. In 42:3, Job echoes the Lord's words. God
states that Job's complaining and raging against him are
unjustified and proceed from limited understanding.
38:3 Repeated in 40:7 (see also 42:4). The format of God's
response is to ply Job with rhetorical questions, to each of
which Job must plead ignorance. God says nothing about
Job's suffering, nor does he address Job's problem about
divine justice. Job gets neither a bill of indictment nor a
verdict of innocence. But, more important, God does not
humiliate or condemn him—which surely would have been
the case if the counselors had been right. So by implication
Job is vindicated, and later his vindication is directly affirmed
(see 42:7–8). The divine discourses, then, succeed in bringing Job to complete faith in God's goodness without his
receiving a direct answer to his questions.

38:4–38 Inanimate creation testifies to God's sovereignty
and power (the earth, vv. 4–7,18; the sea, vv. 8–11,16; the
sun, vv. 12–15; the netherworld, v. 17; light and darkness,
vv. 19–20; the weather, vv. 22–30,34–38; the constellations, vv. 31–33). See note on 38:39–39:30.
38:4–5 See the similar questions of Agur, and the similar
irony in his demand for a response (Pr 30:4).
38:7 See Ps 148:2–3; see also note on Ps 65:13. When the
earth was created, the angels were there to sing the praises of
the Creator, but Job was not (see vv. 4–5). He should
therefore not expect to be able to understand even lesser
aspects of God's plans for the world and for mankind. *angels.*
See NIV text notes here and on 1:6; 2:1.
38:10–11 See Ps 33:7; Jer 5:22.
38:11 *when I said.* God the Father controls the sea by
speaking to it, as does God the Son (see Lk 8:24–25).
38:12–13 The arrival of the dawn sends the wicked scur-
rying for cover.
38:14 *clay under a seal.* Either a cylinder seal (see note on
Ge 38:18) or a stamp seal.
38:15 *their light.* The night is when the wicked are active
(see Jn 3:19; for the imagery cf. Lk 11:35). *uplifted arm is
broken.* See 22:9 and note.
38:16 *springs of the sea.* See Ge 7:11; 8:2.
38:17 *gates of death.* See note on 17:16; see also 26:5–6.
38:22–23 *hail . . . for days of war.* See, e.g., Jos 10:11; Isa
28:2 and note.

or seen the storehouses ^m of the hail, ⁿ

²³which I reserve for times of trouble, ^o
  for days of war and battle? ^p
²⁴What is the way to the place where the
    lightning is dispersed, ^q
  or the place where the east winds ^r
    are scattered over the earth? ^s
²⁵Who cuts a channel for the torrents of
    rain,
  and a path for the thunderstorm, ^t
²⁶to water ^u a land where no man lives,
  a desert with no one in it, ^v
²⁷to satisfy a desolate wasteland
  and make it sprout with grass? ^w
²⁸Does the rain have a father? ^x
  Who fathers the drops of dew?
²⁹From whose womb comes the ice?
  Who gives birth to the frost from the
    heavens ^y
³⁰when the waters become hard as stone,
  when the surface of the deep is
    frozen? ^z

³¹"Can you bind the beautiful ^q Pleiades?
  Can you loose the cords of Orion? ^a
³²Can you bring forth the constellations ^b
    in their seasons ^r
  or lead out the Bear ^s with its cubs? ^c
³³Do you know the laws ^d of the
    heavens? ^e
  Can you set up ⌊God's⌋ dominion
    over the earth?

³⁴"Can you raise your voice to the clouds
  and cover yourself with a flood of
    water? ^f
³⁵Do you send the lightning bolts on their
    way? ^g
  Do they report to you, 'Here we are'?
³⁶Who endowed the heart ^u with
    wisdom ^h
  or gave understanding ⁱ to the
    mind ^u?
³⁷Who has the wisdom to count the
    clouds?
  Who can tip over the water jars ^j of
    the heavens ^k
³⁸when the dust becomes hard ^l

and the clods of earth stick
    together? ^m
³⁹"Do you hunt the prey for the lioness
  and satisfy the hunger of the lions ⁿ
⁴⁰when they crouch in their dens ^o
  or lie in wait in a thicket? ^p
⁴¹Who provides food ^q for the raven ^r
  when its young cry out to God
  and wander about for lack of food? ^s

39 "Do you know when the
    mountain goats ^t give birth?
  Do you watch when the doe bears
    her fawn? ^u
²Do you count the months till they bear?
  Do you know the time they give
    birth? ^v
³They crouch down and bring forth their
    young;
  their labor pains are ended.
⁴Their young thrive and grow strong in
    the wilds;
  they leave and do not return.

⁵"Who let the wild donkey ^w go free?
  Who untied his ropes?
⁶I gave him the wasteland ^x as his home,
  the salt flats ^y as his habitat. ^z
⁷He laughs ^a at the commotion in the
    town;
  he does not hear a driver's shout. ^b
⁸He ranges the hills ^c for his pasture
  and searches for any green thing.

⁹"Will the wild ox ^d consent to serve
    you? ^e
  Will he stay by your manger ^f at
    night?
¹⁰Can you hold him to the furrow with a
    harness? ^g
  Will he till the valleys behind you?
¹¹Will you rely on him for his great
    strength? ^h

38:22
^mS Dt 28:12
ⁿPs 105:32;
147:17
38:23 ^oPs 27:5;
Isa 28:17; 30:30;
Eze 13:11
^pEx 9:26;
Jos 10:11;
Eze 13:13;
Rev 16:21
38:24
^qS Job 28:24
^rS Job 27:21
^sJer 10:13; 51:16
38:25 ^tJob 28:26
38:26 ^uJob 36:27
^vPs 84:6; 107:35;
Isa 41:18
38:27
^wS Job 28:26;
S 37:13;
S Ps 104:14
38:28
^xS 2Sa 1:21;
S Job 5:10
38:29
^yPs 147:16-17
38:30 ^zJob 37:10
38:31 ^aJob 9:9;
Am 5:8
38:32 ^b2Ki 23:5;
Isa 13:10; 40:26;
45:12; Jer 19:13
^cS Ge 1:16
38:33 ^dPs 148:6;
Jer 31:36
^eS Ge 1:16
38:34
^fS Job 5:10;
S 22:11
38:35
^gS Job 36:32
38:36 ^hS Job 9:4;
S 34:32; Jas 1:5
ⁱS Job 12:13
38:37 ^jS Jos 3:16
^kS Job 22:11
38:38
^lS Lev 26:19

^m1Ki 18:45
38:39 ⁿS Ge 49:9
38:40 ^oS Job 37:8
^pS Ge 49:9
38:41 ^qS Ge 1:30
^rS Ge 8:7;
Lk 12:24
^sPs 147:9;
S Mt 6:26
39:1 ^tS Dt 14:5
^uGe 49:21
39:2
^vS Ge 31:7-9
39:5 ^wS Ge 16:12
39:6 ^xJob 24:5;
Ps 107:34;
Jer 2:24 ^yJob 30:4
^zJob 30:7;
Jer 14:6; 17:6
39:7 ^aS Job 5:22
^bJob 3:18
39:8 ^cIsa 32:20
39:9 ^dS Nu 23:22
^eS Ex 21:6

^fS Ge 42:27 **39:10** ^gJob 41:13; Ps 32:9 **39:11** ^hver 19;
Job 40:16; 41:12,22; Ps 147:10

^q31 Or the twinkling; or the chains of the   ^r32 Or
the morning star in its season   ^s32 Or out Leo
^t33 Or his; or their   ^u36 The meaning of the Hebrew
for this word is uncertain.

38:24 *east winds.* See note on 15:2.
38:31-32 *Pleiades . . . Orion . . . Bear.* See note on 9:9.
38:36 *heart . . . mind.* It is possible that the first word
should be translated "ibis" and the second "rooster," two
birds whose habits were sometimes observed by people who
wished to forecast the weather. If so, the words would serve
as a transition to the next major section of the first divine
discourse.
38:39-39:30 Animate creation testifies to God's sovereignty, power and loving care (the lion, 38:39-40; the
raven, 38:41; the mountain goat, 39:1-4; the wild donkey,
vv. 5-8; the wild ox, vv. 9-12; the ostrich, vv. 13-18; the
horse, vv. 19-25; the hawk, v. 26; the eagle, vv. 27-30).
See note on 38:4-38.

38:41 *provides food for the raven.* God cares for and feeds
all the birds, of which the raven is representative (e.g.,
compare Lk 12:24 with Mt 6:26).
39:5 *wild donkey.* See 24:5; see also the description of
Ishmael in Ge 16:12 and note there.
39:9-12 As there was an implied contrast between the
wild donkey and the domestic donkey (see v. 7), here there
is a more explicit contrast between the wild ox and the
domestic ox.
39:11 *great strength.* In the OT, the wild ox (the now
virtually extinct aurochs) often symbolizes strength (see,
e.g., Nu 23:22; 24:8; Dt 33:17; Ps 29:6). Next to the
elephant and rhinoceros, the wild ox was the largest and
most powerful land animal of the OT world.

Will you leave your heavy work to
  him?
¹²Can you trust him to bring in your grain
  and gather it to your threshing floor?

¹³"The wings of the ostrich flap joyfully,
  but they cannot compare with the
    pinions and feathers of the
    stork. *i*
¹⁴She lays her eggs on the ground
  and lets them warm in the sand,
¹⁵unmindful that a foot may crush them,
  that some wild animal may trample
    them. *j*
¹⁶She treats her young harshly, *k* as if they
    were not hers;
  she cares not that her labor was in
    vain,
¹⁷for God did not endow her with
    wisdom
  or give her a share of good sense. *l*
¹⁸Yet when she spreads her feathers to
    run,
  she laughs *m* at horse and rider.

¹⁹"Do you give the horse his strength *n*
  or clothe his neck with a flowing
    mane?
²⁰Do you make him leap like a locust, *o*
  striking terror *p* with his proud
    snorting? *q*
²¹He paws fiercely, rejoicing in his
    strength, *r*
  and charges into the fray. *s*
²²He laughs *t* at fear, afraid of nothing;
  he does not shy away from the
    sword.
²³The quiver *u* rattles against his side,
  along with the flashing spear *v* and
    lance.
²⁴In frenzied excitement he eats up the
    ground;
  he cannot stand still when the
    trumpet sounds. *w*

²⁵At the blast of the trumpet *x* he snorts,
    'Aha!'
  He catches the scent of battle from
    afar,
  the shout of commanders and the
    battle cry. *y*

²⁶"Does the hawk take flight by your
    wisdom
  and spread his wings toward the
    south? *z*
²⁷Does the eagle soar at your command
  and build his nest on high? *a*
²⁸He dwells on a cliff and stays there at
    night;
  a rocky crag *b* is his stronghold.
²⁹From there he seeks out his food; *c*
  his eyes detect it from afar.
³⁰His young ones feast on blood,
  and where the slain are, there is
    he." *d*

40 The LORD said to Job: *e*

²"Will the one who contends with
    the Almighty *f* correct him? *g*
  Let him who accuses God answer
    him!" *h*

³Then Job answered the LORD:

⁴"I am unworthy *i*—how can I reply to
    you?
  I put my hand over my mouth. *j*
⁵I spoke once, but I have no answer *k* —
    twice, but I will say no more." *l*

⁶Then the LORD spoke to Job out of the
storm: *m*

⁷"Brace yourself like a man;
  I will question you,
  and you shall answer me. *n*

⁸"Would you discredit my justice? *o*
  Would you condemn me to justify
    yourself? *p*

Cross references (center column)

39:13 *l*Zec 5:9
39:15 *j*2Ki 14:9
39:16 *k*ver 17;
La 4:3
39:17 *l*S ver 16;
S Job 21:22
39:18
*m*S Job 5:22
39:19 *n*S ver 11
39:20
*o*Joel 2:4-5;
Rev 9:7
*p*Job 41:25
*q*Jer 8:16
39:21 *r*ver 11
*s*Jer 8:6
39:22 *t*S Job 5:22
39:23 *u*Isa 5:28;
Jer 5:16 *v*Na 3:3
39:24 *w*Nu 10:9;
Jer 4:5,19;
Eze 7:14; Am 3:6

39:25 *x*Jos 6:5
*y*Jer 8:6;
Am 1:14; 2:2
39:26 *z*Jer 8:7
39:27 *a*Jer 49:16;
Ob 1:4; Hab 2:9
39:28 *b*Jer 49:16;
Ob 1:3
39:29 *c*S Job 9:26
39:30
*d*Mt 24:28;
Lk 17:37
40:1 *e*S Job 5:8;
S 10:2
40:2 *f*S Job 13:3
*g*S Job 9:15;
S 11:8; S 33:13;
Ro 9:20
*h*S Job 9:3
40:4 *i*Job 42:6
*j*S Jdg 18:19;
S Job 29:9
40:5 *k*S Job 9:3
*l*S Job 9:15
40:6
*m*S Ex 14:21;
S Job 38:1
40:7 *n*S Job 38:3
40:8
*o*S Job 15:25;
S 27:2; Ro 3:3
*p*S Job 2:3;
S 34:17

39:13–18 This stanza is unique in the discourses, because in it the Lord asks Job no questions. Could it be because the ostrich is so amusing?
39:13 *pinions and feathers of the stork.* A stork's wings were particularly impressive (see Zec 5:9).
39:18 *horse and rider.* Forms a transition to the next paragraph.
39:19–25 The horse is the only domestic animal in the discourses. This fact, though unexpected, serves the Lord's purpose, since it is specifically the war horse that is in view.
39:20 *like a locust.* Horses and locusts are compared also in Jer 51:27; Rev 9:7; cf. Joel 2:4.
39:26 *hawk.* The sparrow hawk, not resident to Palestine, stops there in its migration south for the winter.
39:27 *eagle.* Or possibly "vulture" (see v. 30).
40:1–2 The conclusion of the first divine discourse. Once again, God challenges Job to answer him.
40:3–5 Job, duly chastened and no longer "like a prince"

(31:37), is unwilling to speak another word of complaint.
40:4 *unworthy.* The Hebrew for this word can also mean "small" or "insignificant."
40:5 *once . . . twice.* See note on 5:19.
40:6 See 38:1 and note.
40:7 Repeated from 38:3 (see note there).
40:8–14 The prologue to the second divine discourse, which ends at 41:34. Unlike the first discourse, God here addresses the issues of his own justice and Job's futile attempt at self-justification. In chs. 21 and 24, Job had complained about God's indifference toward the wickedness of evil men. Here the Lord asserts his ability and determination to administer justice—a matter over which Job has no control. Therefore by implication Job is admonished to leave all this, including his own vindication (see v. 14), under the power of God's strong arm (see v. 9).
40:8 *Would you condemn me to justify yourself?* In 19:6, Job had said, "God has wronged me."

⁹Do you have an arm like God's, *q*
and can your voice *r* thunder like
his? *s*

¹⁰Then adorn yourself with glory and
splendor,
and clothe yourself in honor and
majesty. *t*

¹¹Unleash the fury of your wrath, *u*
look at every proud man and bring
him low, *v*

¹²look at every proud *w* man and humble
him, *x*
crush *y* the wicked where they stand.

¹³Bury them all in the dust together; *z*
shroud their faces in the grave. *a*

¹⁴Then I myself will admit to you
that your own right hand can save
you. *b*

¹⁵"Look at the behemoth, *v*
which I made *c* along with you
and which feeds on grass like an ox. *d*

¹⁶What strength *e* he has in his loins,
what power in the muscles of his
belly! *f*

¹⁷His tail *w* sways like a cedar;
the sinews of his thighs are
close-knit. *g*

¹⁸His bones are tubes of bronze,
his limbs *h* like rods of iron. *i*

¹⁹He ranks first among the works of
God, *j*
yet his Maker *k* can approach him
with his sword. *l*

²⁰The hills bring him their produce, *m*
and all the wild animals play *n*
nearby. *o*

²¹Under the lotus plants he lies,
hidden among the reeds *p* in the
marsh. *q*

²²The lotuses conceal him in their
shadow;

the poplars by the stream *r* surround
him.

²³When the river rages, *s* he is not
alarmed;
he is secure, though the Jordan *t*
should surge against his mouth.

²⁴Can anyone capture him by the eyes, *x*
or trap him and pierce his nose? *u*

41 "Can you pull in the leviathan *y* *v*
with a fishhook *w*
or tie down his tongue with a rope?

²Can you put a cord through his nose *x*
or pierce his jaw with a hook? *y*

³Will he keep begging you for mercy? *z*
Will he speak to you with gentle
words?

⁴Will he make an agreement with you
for you to take him as your slave for
life? *a*

⁵Can you make a pet of him like a bird
or put him on a leash for your girls?

⁶Will traders barter for him?
Will they divide him up among the
merchants?

⁷Can you fill his hide with harpoons
or his head with fishing spears? *b*

⁸If you lay a hand on him,
you will remember the struggle and
never do it again! *c*

⁹Any hope of subduing him is false;
the mere sight of him is
overpowering. *d*

¹⁰No one is fierce enough to rouse him. *e*

40:9
*q*S 2Ch 32:8;
S Ps 98:1 *r*Isa 6:8;
Eze 10:5
*s*S Ex 20:19;
S Job 36:33
40:10 *t*Ps 29:1-2;
45:3; 93:1; 96:6;
104:1; 145:5
40:11
*u*S Job 20:28;
Ps 7:11; Isa 5:25;
9:12,19; 10:5;
13:3,5; 30:27;
42:25; 51:20;
Jer 7:20; Na 1:6;
Zep 1:18
*v*Ps 18:27;
Isa 2:11,12,17;
23:9; 24:10;
25:12; 26:5;
32:19
40:12 *w*Ps 10:4;
Isa 25:11;
Jer 48:29; 49:16;
Zep 2:10
*x*S 1Sa 2:7;
S Ps 52:5; 1Pe 5:5
*y*Ps 60:12;
Isa 22:5; 28:3;
63:2-3,6;
Da 5:20; Mic 5:8;
7:10; Zec 10:5;
Mal 4:3
40:13
*z*Nu 16:31-34
*a*S Job 4:9
40:14 *b*Ex 15:6,
12; Ps 18:35;
20:6; 48:10;
60:5; 108:6;
Isa 41:10; 63:5
40:15 *c*S Job 9:9
*d*Isa 11:7; 65:25
40:16
*e*S Job 39:11
*f*Job 41:9
40:17 *g*Job 41:15
40:18 *h*Job 41:12
*i*Isa 11:4; 49:2
40:19 *j*Job 41:33;
Ps 40:5; 139:14;
Isa 27:1
*k*S Job 4:17; S 9:9
*l*S Ge 3:24
40:20
*m*Ps 104:14
*n*Ps 104:26
*o*S Job 5:23
40:21
*p*S Ge 41:2;
Ps 68:30; Isa 35:7
*q*Job 8:11
40:22 *r*Ps 1:3;

Isa 44:4 **40:23** *s*Isa 8:7; 11:15 *t*S Jos 3:1 **40:24** *u*2Ki 19:28;
Job 41:2,7,26; Isa 37:29 **41:1** *v*S Job 3:8 *w*Am 4:2 **41:2**
*x*S Job 40:24 *y*Eze 19:4 **41:3** *z*1Ki 20:31 **41:4** *a*S Ex 21:6
41:7 *b*S Job 40:24 **41:8** *c*S Job 3:8 **41:9** *d*Job 40:16 **41:10**
*e*S Job 3:8

v 15 Possibly the hippopotamus or the elephant
w 17 Possibly trunk   *x 24* Or *by a water hole*
y 1 Possibly the crocodile

40:10 *clothe yourself in honor and majesty.* The Hebrew
underlying this clause describes God in Ps 104:1: "you are
clothed with splendor and majesty." The Lord here challenges Job to take on the appearance of deity—if he can.
40:11–12 See Isa 13:11, where the Lord describes himself
as doing these things.
40:13 *dust.* See note on 7:21.
40:14 *your own right hand can save you.* Contrast Ps
49:7–9 (see note there).
40:15–24 The first of two poems (ch. 41 constitutes the
second) in this discourse, each describing a huge beast and
resuming the animal theme of ch. 39.
40:15 *behemoth.* The word is Hebrew and means "beast
par excellence," referring to a large land animal (for possible
identifications see NIV text note). Much of the language used
to describe him in vv. 16–24 is highly poetic and hyperbolic.
which I made. He is one of God's creatures, not a mythical
being.
40:18 *iron.* See note on 19:24.
40:19 *first among the works of God.* The Hebrew underlying this phrase is translated "first of his works" in Pr 8:22

with reference to the creation of wisdom (see Pr 8:12). Here
the descriptive phrase stresses the importance of the behemoth as an example of a huge animal under the control of a
sovereign God.
40:21–23 *reeds in the marsh . . . poplars . . . Jordan.* The
area described is probably the Huleh region, north of the Sea
of Galilee.
40:24 The proposal to capture the behemoth forms a transition to the similar proposal concerning the leviathan in
41:1.
41:1–34 The second of two poems in the Lord's final
discourse (see note on 40:15–24).
41:1 *leviathan.* The OT uses the word in both a figurative
and a literal sense. For its figurative usage see note on 3:8.
Literally, the leviathan was a large marine animal (see Ps
104:26), here perhaps a crocodile (see NIV text note). His
description in ch. 41 indicates that he is even more terrifying
than the behemoth in ch. 40.
41:10 The leviathan is mighty, but God is infinitely more
powerful.

Who then is able to stand against
me?*f*

¹¹Who has a claim against me that I must
pay?*g*
Everything under heaven belongs to
me. *h*

¹²"I will not fail to speak of his limbs, *i*
his strength*j* and his graceful form.
¹³Who can strip off his outer coat?
Who would approach him with a
bridle? *k*
¹⁴Who dares open the doors of his
mouth, *l*
ringed about with his fearsome teeth?
¹⁵His back has*z* rows of shields
tightly sealed together; *m*
¹⁶each is so close to the next
that no air can pass between.
¹⁷They are joined fast to one another;
they cling together and cannot be
parted.
¹⁸His snorting throws out flashes of light;
his eyes are like the rays of dawn. *n*
¹⁹Firebrands*o* stream from his mouth;
sparks of fire shoot out.
²⁰Smoke pours from his nostrils*p*
as from a boiling pot over a fire of
reeds.
²¹His breath*q* sets coals ablaze,
and flames dart from his mouth. *r*
²²Strength*s* resides in his neck;
dismay goes before him.
²³The folds of his flesh are tightly joined;
they are firm and immovable.
²⁴His chest is hard as rock,
hard as a lower millstone. *t*
²⁵When he rises up, the mighty are
terrified; *u*
they retreat before his thrashing. *v*
²⁶The sword that reaches him has no
effect,
nor does the spear or the dart or the
javelin. *w x*
²⁷Iron he treats like straw*y*
and bronze like rotten wood.
²⁸Arrows do not make him flee; *z*

slingstones are like chaff to him.
²⁹A club seems to him but a piece of
straw; *a*
he laughs*b* at the rattling of the
lance.
³⁰His undersides are jagged potsherds,
leaving a trail in the mud like a
threshing sledge. *c*
³¹He makes the depths churn like a
boiling caldron *d*
and stirs up the sea like a pot of
ointment. *e*
³²Behind him he leaves a glistening wake;
one would think the deep had white
hair.
³³Nothing on earth is his equal*f* —
a creature without fear.
³⁴He looks down on all that are
haughty; *g*
he is king over all that are proud. *h*"

Job

42 Then Job replied to the LORD:

²"I know that you can do all
things; *i*
no plan of yours can be thwarted. *j*
³You asked*L* 'Who is this that obscures
my counsel without
knowledge?' *k*
Surely I spoke of things I did not
understand,
things too wonderful for me to
know. *l*

⁴"You said*L* 'Listen now, and I will
speak;
I will question you,
and you shall answer me.' *m*
⁵My ears had heard of you *n*
but now my eyes have seen you. *o*
⁶Therefore I despise myself*p*
and repent*q* in dust and ashes." *r*

Epilogue

⁷After the LORD had said these things to

Cross references

41:10
f S 2Ch 20:6;
S Isa 46:5;
Jer 50:44;
Rev 6:17
41:11
g S Job 34:33;
Ro 11:35
h S Jos 3:11;
S Job 10:4;
Ac 4:24;
1Co 10:26
41:12 *i* Job 40:18
j S Job 39:11
41:13
k S Job 30:11;
S 39:10
41:14 *l* Ps 22:13
41:15
m Job 40:17
41:18 *n* S Job 3:9
41:19 *o* Da 10:6
41:20 *p* Ps 18:8
41:21 *q* S Job 4:9;
Isa 11:4; 40:7
r Ps 18:8;
Isa 10:17; 30:27;
33:14; 66:14-16;
Jer 4:4
41:22
s S Job 39:11
41:24 *t* Mt 18:6
41:25 *u* Job 39:20
v S Job 3:8
41:26
w S Jos 8:18
x S Job 40:24
41:27 *y* ver 29
41:28 *z* Ps 91:5

41:29 *a* ver 27
b S Job 5:22
41:30 *c* Isa 28:27;
41:15; Am 1:3
41:31 *d* 1Sa 2:14
e Eze 32:2
41:33
f S Job 40:19
41:34 *g* Ps 18:27;
101:5; 131:1;
Pr 6:17; 21:4;
30:13 *h* Job 28:8
42:2 *i* S Ge 18:14;
S Mt 19:26
j S 2Ch 20:6;
S Job 16:19;
Ac 4:28; Eph 1:11
42:3 *k* S Job 34:35
l S Job 5:9
42:4 *m* S Job 38:3
42:5
n S Job 26:14;
Ro 10:17
o Jdg 13:22;
Isa 6:5; S Mt 5:8;
Lk 2:30;
Eph 1:17-18
42:6 *p* Job 40:4;
Eze 6:9; Ro 12:3
q S Job 34:33
r S Ex 10:3;
S Ezr 9:6;
S Job 2:8; S 6:29

z 15 Or *His pride is his*

41:11 Perhaps alluded to, though not directly quoted, by Paul in Ro 11:35.
41:14–15 *doors of his mouth . . . fearsome teeth . . . back has rows of shields.* Characteristic of the crocodile (see NIV text note on v. 1).
41:18–21 Highly figurative, exaggerated poetic imagery.
41:27 *iron.* See note on 19:24.
41:30 *jagged potsherds.* Broken pottery fragments.
41:34 *king over all that is proud.* The Lord alone can humble such creatures. Job cannot be expected to do so, though God challenges him to attempt it—if he so desires (see 40:11–12).
42:1–6 Job's last recorded words are his response to the Lord's second discourse.
42:2 Job finally sees that God and his purposes are

supreme.
42:3 *You asked.* Job quotes the Lord's words in 38:2.
42:4 *You said.* Job quotes the Lord's words in 38:3; 40:7.
42:5 Job—and his three friends, and Elihu—had only heard of God, but now Job has seen God (see Isa 6:5) with the eyes of faith and spiritual understanding. He can therefore accept God's plan for his life (see v. 2)—which includes suffering. *my eyes have seen you.* A down payment on the hope expressed in 19:26 (see note there).
42:6 *I despise myself.* See note on 9:21. To his humility (see 40:4–5) Job adds repentance for the presumptuous words he had spoken to God. *dust and ashes.* See 30:19 and note.
42:7–9 Despite Job's mistakes in word and attitude while he suffered, he is now commended and the counselors are

Job[s], he said to Eliphaz the Temanite, "I am angry with you and your two friends,[t] because you have not spoken of me what is right, as my servant Job has.[u] 8So now take seven bulls and seven rams[v] and go to my servant Job[w] and sacrifice a burnt offering[x] for yourselves. My servant Job will pray for you, and I will accept his prayer[y] and not deal with you according to your folly.[z] You have not spoken of me what is right, as my servant Job has."[a] 9So Eliphaz the Temanite, Bildad the Shuhite and Zophar the Naamathite[b] did what the LORD told them; and the LORD accepted Job's prayer.[c]

10After Job had prayed for his friends, the LORD made him prosperous again[d] and gave him twice as much as he had before.[e] 11All his brothers and sisters and everyone who had known him before[f] came and ate with him in his house. They comforted and consoled him over all the trouble the LORD had brought upon him,[g] and each one gave him a piece of silver[a] and a gold ring.

12The LORD blessed the latter part of Job's life more than the first. He had fourteen thousand sheep, six thousand camels, a thousand yoke of oxen and a thousand donkeys. 13And he also had seven sons and three daughters. 14The first daughter he named Jemimah, the second Keziah and the third Keren-Happuch. 15Nowhere in all the land were there found women as beautiful as Job's daughters, and their father granted them an inheritance along with their brothers.

16After this, Job lived a hundred and forty years; he saw his children and their children to the fourth generation. 17And so he died, old and full of years.[h]

42:7 sS Jos 1:7
tJob 32:3 uver 8;
S Job 9:15
42:8 vNu 23:1,
29; Eze 45:23
wJob 1:8
xS Ge 8:20
yJas 5:15-16;
1Jn 5:16
zGe 20:7;
Job 22:30 aS ver 7
42:9 bJob 2:11
cS Ge 19:21;
S 20:17;
Eze 14:14
42:10 dDt 30:3;
Ps 14:7
eS Job 1:3;
Ps 85:1-3;
126:5-6;
Php 2:8-9;
Jas 5:11
42:11
fS Job 19:13

gS Ge 37:35
42:17
hS Ge 15:15

a 11 Hebrew *him a kesitah*; a kesitah was a unit of money of unknown weight and value.

---

rebuked. Why? Because even in his rage, even when he challenged God, he was determined to speak honestly before him. The counselors, on the other hand, mouthed many correct and often beautiful creedal statements, but without living knowledge of the God they claimed to honor. Job spoke to God; they only spoke about God. Even worse, their spiritual arrogance caused them to claim knowledge they did not possess. They presumed to know why Job was suffering.
42:7–8 *my servant Job.* The phrase is used four times in these two verses (see note on 1:8).
42:10 Job's prayer for those who had abused him is a touching OT illustration of the high Christian virtue our Lord taught in Mt 5:44. Job's prayer marked the turning point back to prosperity for him. *made prosperous again.* The Hebrew for this expression is translated "restores the fortunes of" in Ps 14:7.
42:11 Contrast 16:2; 19:13. *piece of silver.* The Hebrew for this phrase is found elsewhere in the OT only in Ge 33:19 (see note there); Jos 24:32.
42:12–16 The cosmic contest with the Accuser is now over, and Job is restored. No longer is there a reason for Job to experience suffering—unless he was sinful and deserved it, which is not the case. God does not allow us to suffer for no reason, and even though the reason may be hidden in the mystery of his divine purpose (see Isa 55:8–9)—never for us to know in this life—we must trust in him as the God who does only what is right.
42:12 The number of animals is in each case twice as many (see v. 10) as Job had owned before (see 1:3).
42:13 *seven sons and three daughters.* To replace the children he had lost earlier (see 1:2,18–19).
42:14 *Jemimah.* Means "dove." *Keziah.* Means "cinnamon." *Keren-Happuch.* Means "container of antimony," a highly prized eyeshadow (see note on Jer 4:30).
42:15 *granted them an inheritance along with their brothers.* Contrast Nu 27:8.
42:16 *lived a hundred and forty years.* The longevity of a true patriarch (see note on Ex 6:16). *he saw . . . to the fourth generation.* See Ge 50:23.
42:17 *old and full of years.* See 5:26 and note; Ge 25:8.

PSALMS

Name

The names "Psalms" and "Psalter" come from the Septuagint (the Greek translation of the OT), where they originally referred to stringed instruments (such as harp, lyre and lute), then to songs sung with their accompaniment. The traditional Hebrew title is *tehillim* (meaning "praises"; see note on Ps 145 title), even though many of the psalms are *tephillot* (meaning "prayers"). In fact, one of the first collections included in the book was titled "the prayers of David son of Jesse" (72:20).

Collection, Arrangement and Date

The Psalter is a collection of collections and represents the final stage in a process that spanned centuries. It was put into its final form by postexilic temple personnel, who completed it probably in the third century B.C. As such, it served as the prayer book (book of prayer, praise and religious instruction) for the second (Zerubbabel's and Herod's) temple and for use in the synagogues. By the first century A.D. it was referred to as the "Book of Psalms" (Lk 20:42; Ac 1:20). At that time also Psalms was used as a title for the entire section of the Hebrew OT canon known as the "Writings" (see Lk 24:44).

Many collections preceded this final compilation of the Psalms. In fact, the formation of psalters probably goes back to the early days of the first (Solomon's) temple (or even to the time of David), when the temple liturgy began to take shape. Reference has already been made to "the prayers of David." Additional collections expressly referred to in the present Psalter titles are: (1) the songs and/or psalms "of the Sons of Korah" (Ps 42-49; 84-85; 87-88), (2) the psalms and/or songs "of Asaph" (Ps 50; 73-83) and (3) the songs "of ascents" (Ps 120-134).

Other evidence points to further compilations. Ps 1-41 (Book I) make frequent use of the divine name *Yahweh* ("the LORD"), while Ps 42-72 (Book II) make frequent use of *Elohim* ("God"). The reason for the *Elohim* collection in distinction from the *Yahweh* collection remains unexplained, but both of them date, at least essentially in their present form, from the period of the monarchy. Moreover, Ps 93-100 appear to be a traditional collection (see "The LORD reigns" in 93:1; 96:10; 97:1; 99:1). Other apparent groupings include Ps 111-118 (the "Egyptian Hallel"), Ps 138-145 (all of which include "of David" in their titles) and Ps 146-150 (with their frequent "Praise the LORD"; see NIV text note on 111:1). Whether the "Great Hallel" (Ps 120-136) was already a recognized unit is not known. (The seven "penitential psalms" get their name from Christian liturgical usage and so were never a unit in the Jewish Psalter tradition; see introduction to Ps 6.)

In its final edition, the Psalter contained 150 psalms. On this the Septuagint and Hebrew texts agree, though they arrive at this number differently. The Septuagint has an extra psalm at the end (but not numbered separately as Ps 151); it also unites Ps 9-10 (see NIV text note on Ps 9) and Ps 114-115 and divides Ps 116 and Ps 147 each into two psalms. Strangely, both the Septuagint and Hebrew texts number Ps 42-43 as two psalms whereas they were evidently originally one (see NIV text note on Ps 42).

The Psalter was divided into five Books (Ps 1-41; 42-72; 73-89; 90-106; 107-150), and each was provided with an appropriate concluding doxology (see 41:13; 72:18-19; 89:52; 106:48; 150). The first two of these Books, as already noted, were probably preexilic. The division of the remaining psalms into three Books, thus attaining the number five, was possibly in imitation of the five books of Moses (otherwise known simply as the Law). At least one of these divisions (between Ps 106-107) seems arbitrary (see introduction to Ps 107). In spite of this five-book division, the Psalter was clearly thought of as a whole, with an introduction (Ps 1-2) and a conclusion (Ps 146-150). Notes throughout the Psalms give additional indications of conscious arrangement.

Authorship and Titles (or Superscriptions)

Of the 150 psalms, only 34 lack superscriptions of any kind (only 17 in the Septuagint). These

so-called "orphan" psalms are found mainly in Books III-V, where they tend to occur in clusters: Ps 91; 93-97; 99; 104-107; 111-119; 135-137; 146-150. (In Books I-II, only Ps 1-2; 10; 33; 43; 71 lack titles, and Ps 10; 43 are actually continuations of the preceding psalms.)

The contents of the superscriptions vary but fall into a few broad categories: (1) author, (2) name of collection, (3) type of psalm, (4) musical notations, (5) liturgical notations and (6) brief indications of occasion for composition. For details see notes on the titles of the various psalms.

Students of the Psalms are not agreed on the antiquity and reliability of these superscriptions. That many of them are at least preexilic appears evident from the fact that the Septuagint translators were no longer clear as to their meaning. Furthermore, the practice of attaching titles, including the name of the author, is ancient. On the other hand, comparison between the Septuagint and the Hebrew texts shows that the content of some titles was still subject to change well into the postexilic period. Most discussion centers on categories 1 and 6 above.

As for the superscriptions regarding occasion of composition, many of these brief notations of events read as if they had been taken from 1,2 Samuel. Moreover, they are sometimes not easily correlated with the content of the psalms they head. The suspicion therefore arises that they are later attempts to fit the psalms into the real-life events of history. But then why the limited number of such notations, and why the apparent mismatches? The arguments cut both ways.

Regarding authorship, opinions are even more divided. The notations themselves are ambiguous since the Hebrew phraseology used, meaning in general "belonging to," can also be taken in the sense of "concerning" or "for the use of" or "dedicated to." The name may refer to the title of a collection of psalms that had been gathered under a certain name (as "Of Asaph" or "Of the Sons of Korah"). As for Davidic authorship, there can be little doubt that the Psalter contains psalms composed by that noted singer and musician and that there was at one time a "Davidic" psalter. This, however, may have also included psalms written concerning David, or concerning one of the later Davidic kings, or even psalms written in the manner of those he authored. It is also true that the tradition as to which psalms are "Davidic" remains somewhat indefinite, and some "Davidic" psalms seem clearly to reflect later situations (see, e.g., Ps 30 title—but see also note there; and see introduction to Ps 69 and note on Ps 122 title). Moreover, "David" is sometimes used elsewhere as a collective for the kings of his dynasty, and this could also be true in the psalm titles.

The word *Selah* is found in 39 psalms, all but two of which (Ps 140; 143, both "Davidic") are in Books I-III. It is also found in Hab 3, a psalm-like poem. Suggestions as to its meaning abound, but honesty must confess ignorance. Most likely, it is a liturgical notation. The common suggestions that it calls for a brief musical interlude or for a brief liturgical response by the congregation are plausible (the former may be supported by the Septuagint rendering). In some instances its present placement in the Hebrew text is highly questionable.

Psalm Types

Superscriptions to the Psalms acquaint us with an ancient system of classification: (1) *mizmor* ("psalm"); (2) *shiggaion* (see note on Ps 7 title); (3) *miktam* (see note on Ps 16 title); (4) *shir* ("song"); (5) *maśkil* (see note on Ps 32 title); (6) *tephillah* ("prayer"); (7) *tehillah* ("praise"); (8) *lehazkir* ("for being remembered"—i.e., before God, a petition); (9) *letodah* ("for praising" or "for giving thanks"); (10) *lelammed* ("for teaching"); and (11) *shir yedidot* ("song of loves"—i.e., a wedding song). The meaning of many of these terms, however, is uncertain. In addition, some titles contain two of these (especially *mizmor* and *shir*), indicating that the types are diversely based and overlapping.

Analysis of content has given rise to a different classification that has proven useful for study of the Psalms. The main types that can be identified are: (1) prayers of the individual (e.g., Ps 3:7-8); (2) praise from the individual for God's saving help (e.g., Ps 30; 34); (3) prayers of the community (e.g., Ps 12; 44; 79); (4) praise from the community for God's saving help (e.g., Ps 66; 75); (5) confessions of confidence in the Lord (e.g., Ps 11; 16; 52); (6) hymns in praise of God's majesty and virtues (e.g., Ps 8; 19; 29; 65); (7) hymns celebrating God's universal reign (Ps 47; 93-99); (8) songs of Zion, the city of God (Ps 46; 48; 76; 84; 122; 126; 129; 137); (9) royal psalms—by, for or concerning the king, the Lord's anointed (e.g., Ps 2; 18; 20; 45; 72; 89; 110); (10) pilgrimage songs (Ps 120-134); (11) liturgical songs (e.g., Ps 15; 24; 68); (12) didactic (instructional) songs (e.g., Ps 1; 34; 37; 73; 112; 119; 128; 133).

This classification also involves some overlapping. For example, "prayers of the individual" may include prayers of the king (in his special capacity as king) or even prayers of the community speaking in the collective first person singular. Nevertheless, it is helpful to study a psalm in conjunction with

others of the same type. Attempts to fix specific liturgical settings for each type have not been very convincing. For those psalms about which something can be said in this regard see the introductions to the individual psalms.

Of all these psalm types, the prayers (both of the individual and of the community) are the most complex. Several modes of speech combine to form these appeals to God: (1) address to God: "O Lord," "my God," "my deliverer"; (2) initial appeal: "Arise," "Answer me," "Help," "Save me"; (3) description of distress: "Many are rising against me," "The wicked attack," "I am in distress"; (4) complaint against God: "Why have you forsaken me?" "How long will you hide your face from me?"; (5) petition: "Be not far from me," "Vindicate me"; (6) motivation for God to hear: "for I take refuge in you," "for your name's sake"; (7) accusation against the adversary: "There is no truth in their mouths," "Ruthless men seek my life" ("the wicked" are often quoted); (8) call for redress: "Let them be put to shame," "Call him to account for his wickedness"; (9) claims of innocence: "I have walked in my integrity," "They hate me without cause"; (10) confessions of sin: "I have sinned against you," "I confess my iniquity"; (11) professions of trust: "You are a shield about me," "You will answer me"; (12) vows to praise for deliverance: "I will sing your might," "My lips will praise you"; (13) calls to praise: "Magnify the Lord with me," "Sing praise to the Lord"; (14) motivations for praise: "for you have delivered me," "for the Lord hears the needy."

Though not all these appear in every prayer, they all belong to the conventions of prayer in the Psalter, with petition itself being but one (usually brief) element among the rest. On the whole they reflect the conventions of the court, the psalmist(s) presenting his/their case before the heavenly King/Judge. When beset by wicked adversaries, the petitioner describes his situation, pleads his innocence ("righteousness"), lodges accusation against his adversaries, and appeals for deliverance and judicial redress. When suffering at the hands of God (when God is his adversary), he confesses his guilt and pleads for mercy. Giving attention to the various modes of speech in the prayers and to their functions in the judicial appeals they present will significantly aid the reader.

Literary Features

The Psalter is from first to last poetry, even though it contains many prayers and not all OT prayers were poetic (see 1Ki 8:23-53; Ezr 9:6-15; Ne 9:5-37; Da 9:4-19)—nor was all praise poetic, for that matter (see 1Ki 8:15-21). The Psalms are impassioned, vivid and concrete; they are rich in images, in simile and metaphor. Assonance, alliteration and wordplays abound in the Hebrew text. Effective use of repetition and the piling up of synonyms and complements to fill out the picture are characteristic. Key words frequently highlight major themes in prayer or song. Enclosure (repetition of a significant word or phrase at the end that occurs at the beginning) frequently wraps up a composition or a unit within it. The notes on the structure of the individual psalms often call attention to literary frames within which the psalm has been set.

Hebrew poetry lacks rhyme and regular meter. Its most distinctive and pervasive feature is parallelism. Most poetic lines are composed of two (sometimes three) balanced segments (the balance is often loose, with the second segment commonly somewhat shorter than the first). The second segment either echoes (synonymous parallelism), contrasts (antithetic parallelism) or syntactically completes (synthetic parallelism) the first. These three types are generalizations and are not wholly adequate to describe the rich variety that the creativity of the poets has achieved within the basic two-segment line structure. They can serve, however, as rough distinctions that will assist the reader. In the NIV the second and third segments of a line are slightly indented relative to the first.

Determining where the Hebrew poetic lines or line segments begin or end (scanning) is sometimes an uncertain matter. Even the Septuagint at times scans the lines differently from the way the Hebrew texts now available to us do. It is therefore not surprising that modern translations occasionally differ.

A related problem is the extremely concise, often elliptical writing style of the Hebrew poets. The syntactical connection of words must at times be inferred simply from context. Where more than one possibility presents itself, the translator is confronted with ambiguity. He is not always sure with which line segment a border word or phrase is to be read.

The stanza structure of Hebrew poetry is also a matter of dispute. Occasionally, recurring refrains mark off stanzas, as in Ps 42-43; 57. In Ps 110 two balanced stanzas are divided by their introductory oracles (see also introduction to Ps 132), while Ps 119 devotes eight lines to each letter of the Hebrew alphabet. For the most part, however, no such obvious indicators are present. The NIV has used spaces to mark off poetic paragraphs (called "stanzas" in the notes). Usually this could be done with some

confidence, and the reader is advised to be guided by them. But there are a few places where these divisions are questionable—and are challenged in the notes.

Close study of the Psalms discloses that the authors often composed with an overall design in mind. This is true of the alphabetic acrostics, in which the poet devoted to each letter of the Hebrew alphabet one line segment (as in Ps 111-112), or a single line (as in Ps 25; 34; 145), or two lines (as in Ps 37), or eight lines (as in Ps 119). In addition Ps 33; 38; 103 each have 22 lines, no doubt because of the number of letters in the Hebrew alphabet (see Introduction to Lamentations: Literary Features). The oft-voiced notion that this device was used as a memory aid seems culturally prejudiced and quite unwarranted. Actually people of that time were able to memorize far more readily than most people today. It is much more likely that the alphabet—which was relatively recently invented as a simple system of symbols capable of representing in writing the rich and complex patterns of human speech and therefore of inscribing all that man can put into words (one of the greatest intellectual achievements of all time)—commended itself as a framework on which to hang significant phrases.

Other forms were also used. Ps 44 is a prayer fashioned after the design of a ziggurat (a Babylonian stepped pyramid; see note on Ge 11:4). A sense of symmetry is pervasive. There are psalms that devote the same number of lines to each stanza (as Ps 12; 41), or do so with variation only in the introductory or concluding stanza (as Ps 38; 83; 94). Others match the opening and closing stanzas and balance those between (as Ps 33; 86). A particularly interesting device is to place a key thematic line at the very center, sometimes constructing the whole or part of the poem around that center (see note on 6:6). Still other design features are pointed out in the notes. The authors of the psalms crafted their compositions very carefully. They were heirs of an ancient art (in many details showing that they had inherited a poetic tradition that goes back hundreds of years), and they developed it to a state of high sophistication. Their works are best appreciated when carefully studied and pondered.

Theology

The Psalter is for the most part a book of prayer and praise. It speaks to God in prayer and it speaks of God in praise—also in professions of faith and trust. Although occasionally didactic (instructional) in form and purpose (teaching the way of godliness), the Psalter is not a catechism of doctrine. Its "theology" is therefore not abstract or systematic but confessional and doxological. So a summation of that "theology" impoverishes it by translating it into an objective mode.

Furthermore, any summation faces a still greater problem. The Psalter is a large collection of independent pieces of many kinds, serving different purposes and written over the course of many centuries. Not only must a brief summary of its "theology" be selective and incomplete; it will also of necessity be somewhat artificial. It will suggest that each psalm reflects or at least presupposes the "theology" outlined, that there is no "theological" tension or progression within the Psalter. Manifestly this is not so.

Still, the final editors of the Psalter were obviously not eclectic in their selection. They knew that many voices from many times spoke here, but none that in their judgment was incompatible with the Law and the Prophets. No doubt they also assumed that each psalm was to be understood in the light of the collection as a whole. That assumption we may share. Hence something, after all, can be said concerning major theological themes that, while admittedly a bit artificial, need not seriously distort and can be helpful to the student of the Psalms.

At the core of the theology of the Psalter is the conviction that the gravitational center of life (of right human understanding, trust, hope, service, morality, adoration), but also of history and of the whole creation (heaven and earth), is God (*Yahweh*, "the LORD"). He is the Great King over all, the One to whom all things are subject. He created all things and preserves them; they are the robe of glory with which he has clothed himself. Because he ordered them, they have a well-defined and "true" identity (no chaos there). Because he maintains them, they are sustained and kept secure from disruption, confusion or annihilation. Because he alone is the sovereign God, they are governed by one hand and held in the service of one divine purpose. Under God creation is a cosmos—an orderly and systematic whole. What we distinguish as "nature" and history had for them one Lord, under whose rule all things worked together. Through the creation the Great King's majestic glory is displayed. He is good (wise, righteous, faithful, amazingly benevolent and merciful—evoking trust), and he is great (his knowledge, thoughts and works are beyond human comprehension—evoking reverent awe). By his good and lordly rule he is shown to be the Holy One.

As the Great King by right of creation and enduring absolute sovereignty, he ultimately will not tolerate any worldly power that opposes or denies or ignores him. He will come to rule the nations

so that all will be compelled to acknowledge him. This expectation is no doubt the root and broadest scope of the psalmists' long view of the future. Because the Lord is the Great King beyond all challenge, his righteous and peaceable kingdom will come, overwhelming all opposition and purging the creation of all rebellion against his rule—such will be the ultimate outcome of history.

As the Great King on whom all creatures depend, he opposes the "proud," those who rely on their own resources (and/or the gods they have contrived) to work out their own destiny. These are the ones who ruthlessly wield whatever power they possess to attain worldly wealth, status and security; who are a law to themselves and exploit others as they will. In the Psalter, this kind of "pride" is the root of all evil. Those who embrace it, though they may seem to prosper, will be brought down to death, their final end. The "humble," the "poor and needy," those who acknowledge their dependence on the Lord in all things—these are the ones in whom God delights. Hence the "fear of the LORD"—i.e., humble trust in and obedience to the Lord—is the "beginning" of all wisdom (111:10). Ultimately, those who embrace it will inherit the earth. Not even death can hinder their seeing the face of God.

The psalmists' hope for the future—the future of God and his kingdom and the future of the godly—was firm, though somewhat generalized. None of the psalmists gives expression to a two-age vision of the future (the present evil age giving way to a new age of righteousness and peace on the other side of a great eschatological divide). Such a view began to appear in the intertestamental literature—a view that had been foreshadowed by Daniel (see especially 12:2-3) and by Isaiah (see 65:17-25; 66:22-24)—and it later received full expression in the teaching of Jesus and the apostles. But this revelation was only a fuller development consistent with the hopes the psalmists lived by.

Because God is the Great King, he is the ultimate Executor of justice among men (to avenge oneself is an act of the "proud"). God is the court of appeal when persons are threatened or wronged—especially when no earthly court that he has established has jurisdiction (as in the case of international conflicts) or is able to judge (as when one is wronged by public slander) or is willing to act (out of fear or corruption). He is the mighty and faithful Defender of the defenseless and the wronged. He knows every deed and the secrets of every heart. There is no escaping his scrutiny. No false testimony will mislead him in judgment. And he hears the pleas brought to him. As the good and faithful Judge, he delivers those who are oppressed or wrongfully attacked and redresses the wrongs committed against them. This is the unwavering conviction that accounts for the psalmists' impatient complaints when they boldly, yet as "poor and needy," cry to him, "Why (have you not yet delivered me)?" "How long, O LORD (before you act)?"

As the Great King over all the earth, the Lord has chosen Israel to be his servant people, his "inheritance" among the nations. He has delivered them by mighty acts out of the hands of the world powers, he has given them a land of their own (territory that he took from other nations to be his own "inheritance" in the earth), and he has united them with himself in covenant as the initial embodiment of his redeemed kingdom. Thus both their destiny and his honor came to be bound up with this relationship. To them he also gave his word of revelation, which testified of him, made specific his promises and proclaimed his will. By God's covenant, Israel was to live among the nations, loyal only to her heavenly King. She was to trust solely in his protection, hope in his promises, live in accordance with his will and worship him exclusively. She was to sing his praises to the whole world—which in a special sense revealed Israel's anticipatory role in the evangelization of the nations.

As the Great King, Israel's covenant Lord, God chose David to be his royal representative on earth. In this capacity, David was the Lord's "servant"—i.e., a member of the Great King's administration. The Lord himself anointed him and adopted him as his royal "son" to rule in his name. Through him God made his people secure in the promised land and subdued all the powers that threatened them. What is more, he covenanted to preserve the Davidic dynasty. Henceforth the kingdom of God on earth, while not dependent on the house of David, was linked to it by God's decision and commitment. In its continuity and strength lay Israel's security and hope as she faced a hostile world. And since the Davidic kings were God's royal representatives in the earth, in concept seated at God's right hand (110:1), the scope of their rule was potentially worldwide (see Ps 2).

The Lord's anointed, however, was more than a warrior king. He was to be endowed by God to govern his people with godlike righteousness: to deliver the oppressed, defend the defenseless, suppress the wicked, and thus bless the nation with internal peace and prosperity. He was also an intercessor with God in behalf of the nation, the builder and maintainer of the temple (as God's earthly palace and the nation's house of prayer) and the foremost voice calling the nation to worship the Lord. It is perhaps with a view to these last duties that he is declared to be not only king, but also "priest" (see Ps 110 and notes).

As the Great King, Israel's covenant Lord, God (who had chosen David and his dynasty to be his royal representatives) also chose Jerusalem (the City of David) as his own royal city, the earthly seat of his throne. Thus Jerusalem (Zion) became the earthly capital (and symbol) of the kingdom of God. There in his palace (the temple) he sat enthroned among his people. There his people could meet with him to bring their prayers and praise, and to see his power and glory. From there he brought salvation, dispensed blessings and judged the nations. And with him as the city's great Defender, Jerusalem was the secure citadel of the kingdom of God, the hope and joy of God's people.

God's goodwill and faithfulness toward his people were most strikingly symbolized by his pledged presence among them at his temple in Jerusalem, the "city of the Great King" (48:2). But no manifestation of his benevolence was greater than his readiness to forgive the sins of those who humbly confessed them and whose hearts showed him that their repentance was genuine and that their professions of loyalty to him had integrity. As they anguished over their own sinfulness, the psalmists remembered the ancient testimony of their covenant Lord: I am *Yahweh* ("the Lord"), "the compassionate and gracious God, slow to anger, abounding in love and faithfulness, maintaining love to thousands, and forgiving wickedness, rebellion and sin" (Ex 34:6-7). Only so did they dare to submit to him as his people, to "fear" him (see 130:3-4).

Unquestionably the supreme kingship of Yahweh (in which he displays his transcendent greatness and goodness) is the most basic metaphor and most pervasive theological concept in the Psalter—as in the OT generally. It provides the fundamental perspective in which man is to view himself, the whole creation, events in "nature" and history, and the future. The whole creation is his one kingdom. To be a creature in the world is to be a part of his kingdom and under his rule. To be a human being in the world is to be dependent on and responsible to him. To proudly deny that fact is the root of all wickedness—the wickedness that now pervades the world.

God's election of Israel and subsequently of David and Zion, together with the giving of his word, represent the renewed inbreaking of God's righteous kingdom into this world of rebellion and evil. It initiates the great divide between the righteous nation and the wicked nations, and on a deeper level between the righteous and the wicked, a more significant distinction that cuts even through Israel. In the end this divine enterprise will triumph. Human pride will be humbled, and wrongs will be redressed. The humble will be given the whole earth to possess, and the righteous and peaceable kingdom of God will come to full realization. These theological themes, of course, have profound religious and moral implications. Of these, too, the psalmists spoke.

One question that ought yet to be addressed is: Do the Psalms speak of the Christ? Yes, but in a variety of ways—and not as the prophets do. The Psalter is not a book of prophetic oracles and was never numbered among the prophetic books.

When the Psalms speak of the king on David's throne, they speak of the king who is being crowned (as in Ps 2; 72; 110—though some think 110 is an exception) or is reigning (as in Ps 45) at the time. They proclaim his status as God's anointed and declare what God will accomplish through him and his dynasty. Thus they also speak of the sons of David to come—and in the exile and the postexilic era, when there was no reigning king, they spoke to Israel only of the great Son of David whom the prophets had announced as the one in whom God's covenant with David would yet be fulfilled. So the NT quotes these psalms as testimonies to Christ, which in their unique way they are. In them they are truly fulfilled.

When in the Psalms righteous sufferers—who are "righteous" because they are innocent, not having provoked or wronged their adversaries, and because they are among the "humble" who trust in the Lord—when they cry out to God in their distress (as in Ps 22; 69), they give voice to the sufferings of God's servants in a hostile and evil world.

These cries became the prayers of God's oppressed "saints," and as such they were taken up into Israel's book of prayers. When Christ came in the flesh, he identified himself with God's "humble" people in the world. He became for them God's righteous servant par excellence, and he shared their sufferings at the hands of evil men. Thus these prayers became his prayers also—uniquely his prayers. In him the suffering and deliverance of which these prayers speak are fulfilled (though they continue to be the prayers also of those who take up their cross and follow him).

Similarly, in speaking of God's covenant people, of the city of God, and of the temple in which God dwells, the Psalms ultimately speak of Christ's church. The Psalter is not only the prayer book of the second temple; it is also the enduring prayer book of the people of God. Now, however, it must be used in the light of the new era of redemption that dawned with the first coming of the Messiah and that will be consummated at his second coming.

BOOK I

Psalms 1–41

Psalm 1

[1]Blessed is the man[a]
    who does not walk[b] in the counsel
        of the wicked[c]
    or stand in the way[d] of sinners[e]
    or sit[f] in the seat of mockers.[g]
[2]But his delight[h] is in the law of the
        LORD,[i]
    and on his law he meditates[j] day
        and night.
[3]He is like a tree[k] planted by streams[l]
        of water,[m]
    which yields its fruit[n] in season
    and whose leaf[o] does not wither.
    Whatever he does prospers.[p]

[4]Not so the wicked!
    They are like chaff[q]
    that the wind blows away.

[5]Therefore the wicked will not stand[r] in
        the judgment,[s]
    nor sinners in the assembly[t] of the
        righteous.

[6]For the LORD watches over[u] the way of
        the righteous,
    but the way of the wicked will
        perish.[v]

Psalm 2

[1]Why do the nations conspire[a]
    and the peoples plot[w] in vain?
[2]The kings[x] of the earth take their stand
    and the rulers gather together
        against the LORD
    and against his Anointed[y] One.[b][z]
[3]"Let us break their chains,[a]" they say,

1:1 ᵃS Dt 33:29;
Ps 40:4; 128:4
ᵇPs 89:15
ᶜS Job 21:16;
Ps 10:2-11
ᵈS Ge 49:6
ᵉPs 26:9; 37:38;
51:13; 104:35
ᶠPs 26:4
ᵍS Job 11:3;
Pr 1:22;
Isa 28:14; Hos 7:5
1:2 ʰPs 112:1;
119:16,35;
Ro 7:22 ⁱPs 19:7;
119:1; Eze 11:20;
18:17
ⁱS Ge 24:63
1:3 ᵏPs 52:8;
92:12; 128:3;
Jer 11:16; Zec 4:3
ˡPs 46:4; 65:9;
Isa 33:21;
Jer 31:9
ᵐS Nu 24:6;
S Job 14:9;
S Eze 17:5
ⁿPs 92:14;
Eze 47:12
ᵒIsa 1:30; 64:6
ᵖS Ge 39:3
1:4 ᑫS Job 13:25;
Isa 40:24;
Jer 13:24

1:5 ʳPs 5:5

ˢS Job 19:29 ᵗPs 26:12; 35:18; 82:1; 89:5; 107:32; 111:1;
149:1 1:6 ᵘPs 37:18; 121:5; 145:20; Na 1:7 ᵛS Lev 26:38;
Ps 9:6 2:1 ʷPs 21:11; 83:5; Pr 24:2 2:2 ˣPs 48:4
ʸISa 9:16; Jn 1:41 ᶻAc 4:25-26* 2:3 ᵃS Job 36:8

ᵃ1 Hebrew; Septuagint *rage*   ᵇ2 Or *anointed one*

Ps 1 Author and date unknown. Godly wisdom here declares the final outcome of the two "ways": "the way of sinners" (v. 1) and "the way of the righteous" (v. 6). See 34:19–22; 37; Introduction to Proverbs: Wisdom Literature. As an introduction to the book, this psalm reminds the reader (1) that those of whom the Psalms speak (using various terms) as the people of God, those whom he receives in his presence and favors with his salvation and blessing, must be characterized by righteousness—sinners have no place among them (v. 5; see Ps 15; 24)—and (2) that the godly piety that speaks in the Psalms is a faithful response to God's revealed (and written) directives for life—which is the path that leads to blessedness.
1:1 Speaks progressively of association with the ungodly and participation in their ungodly ways. *Blessed.* The happy condition of those who revere the Lord and do his will (see 94:12; 112:1; 119:1–2; 128:1; Pr 29:18; cf. Ps 41:1; 106:3; Pr 14:21; Isa 56:2), who put their trust in him (see 40:4; 84:5,12; 144:15; 146:5; Pr 16:20; Isa 30:18; Jer 17:7; cf. Ps 2:12; 34:8), and so are blessed by God (see especially 41:1–3; 144:12–14; see also Mt 5:3–12). The Psalter begins by proclaiming the blessedness of the godly and ends by calling all living things to praise God in his earthly and heavenly sanctuaries (Ps 150). *walk in.* Order his life according to. *counsel.* Deliberations and advice (see Pr 1:10–19). *stand.* Station oneself. *sinners.* See v. 5; those for whom evil is habitual, for whom wickedness is a way of life. *sit.* Settle oneself. *mockers.* Those who ridicule God and defiantly reject his law (see Pr 1:22).
1:2 *on his law he meditates.* Seeking guidance for life in God's law rather than in the deliberations of the wicked. *day and night.* See Jos 1:8.
1:3 *like a tree . . . does not wither.* See Jer 17:8; a simile of the blessedness of the righteous. Such a tree withstands the buffeting of the winds and, flourishing, it blesses man, animals and birds with its unfailing fruit and shade.
1:4 *like chaff . . . blows away.* A simile of the wretchedness of the wicked. Chaff is carried away by the lightest wind, and its removal brings about cleansing by extracting what is utterly useless (see note on Ru 1:22).
1:5 *will not stand in the judgment.* Will not be able to withstand God's wrath when he judges (see 76:7; 130:3; Ezr 9:15; Mal 3:2; Mt 25:31–46; Rev 6:17). *assembly.* The

worshiping assembly at God's sanctuary (as in 22:25; 26:12; 35:18; 40:9–10; 111:1; 149:1; see Ps 15; 24). *righteous.* One of several terms in the OT for God's people; it presents them as those who honor God and order their lives in all things according to his will. In every human relationship they faithfully fulfill the obligations that the relationship entails, remembering that power and authority (of whatever sort: domestic, social, political, economic, religious, intellectual) are to be used to bless, not to exploit.
1:6 *way . . . way.* Implicit in the destinies of the two life-styles are also the destinies of those who choose them.
Ps 2 Author and date unknown (Peter and John ascribed it to David in Ac 4:25—possibly in accordance with the Jewish practice of honoring David as the primary author of the Psalter). A royal psalm, it was originally composed for the coronation of Davidic kings, in light of the Lord's covenant with David (see 2Sa 7). Later, prophetic words of judgment against the house of David and announcements of God's future redemption of his people through an exalted royal son of David highlighted the Messianic import of this psalm. As the second half of a two-part introduction to the Psalms, it proclaims the blessedness of all who acknowledge the lordship of God and his anointed and "take refuge in him" (v. 12; see note on 1:1)—as does the godly piety that speaks in the Psalms. This psalm is frequently quoted in the NT, where it is applied to Christ as the great Son of David and God's Anointed.
2:1–3 The nations rebel. In the ancient Near East the coronation of a new king was often the occasion for the revolt of peoples and kings who had been subject to the crown. The newly anointed king is here pictured as ruler over an empire.
2:1–2 For a NT application see Ac 4:25–28.
2:1 *Why . . . ?* A rhetorical question that implies "How dare they!"
2:2 *LORD . . . his Anointed One.* To rebel against the Lord's Anointed is also to rebel against the One who anointed him. *Anointed One.* See NIV text notes here and on vv. 6–7. The psalm refers to the Davidic king and is ultimately fulfilled in Christ. The English word "Messiah" comes from the Hebrew word for "anointed one," and the English word "Christ" from the Greek word for "anointed one" (see NIV text note on Mt 1:17).

"and throw off their fetters." *b*

⁴The One enthroned *c* in heaven
laughs; *d*
the Lord scoffs at them.
⁵Then he rebukes them in his anger *e*
and terrifies them in his wrath, *f*
saying,
⁶"I have installed my King *c g*
on Zion, *h* my holy hill. *i* "

⁷I will proclaim the decree of the LORD:

He said to me, "You are my Son *d* ; *j*
today I have become your Father. *e k*
⁸Ask of me,
and I will make the nations *l* your
inheritance, *m*
the ends of the earth *n* your
possession.
⁹You will rule them with an iron
scepter *f* ; *o*
you will dash them to pieces *p* like
pottery. *q* "

¹⁰Therefore, you kings, be wise; *r*
be warned, you rulers *s* of the earth.
¹¹Serve the LORD with fear *t*
and rejoice *u* with trembling. *v*

¹²Kiss the Son, *w* lest he be angry
and you be destroyed in your way,
for his wrath *x* can flare up in a
moment.
Blessed *y* are all who take refuge *z* in
him.

Psalm 3

A psalm of David. When he fled from his
son Absalom. *a*

¹O LORD, how many are my foes!
How many rise up against me!
²Many are saying of me,
"God will not deliver him. *b* " Selah *g*

³But you are a shield *c* around me,
O LORD;
you bestow glory on me and lift *h* up
my head. *d*
⁴To the LORD I cry aloud, *e*

Cross references (center column):

2:3 *b*S 2Sa 3:34
2:4 *c*Isa 37:16;
40:22; 66:1
*d*Ps 37:13;
Pr 1:26
2:5 *e*Ps 6:1;
27:9; 38:1
*f*Ps 21:9; 79:6;
90:7; 110:5
2:6 *g*Ps 10:16;
24:10
*h*2Ki 19:31;
Ps 9:11; 48:2,11;
78:68; 110:2;
133:3 *i*S Ex 15:17
2:7 *j*S Mt 3:17;
S 4:3 *k*S 2Sa 7:14;
Ac 13:33*;
Heb 1:5*; 5:5
2:8 *l*Rev 2:26
*m*S Job 22:26;
Mt 21:38
*n*Ps 22:27; 67:7
2:9 *o*S Ge 49:10;
Rev 12:5
*p*S Ex 15:6
*q*Isa 30:14;
Jer 19:10;
Rev 2:27*; 19:15
2:10 *r*Pr 27:11
*s*Ps 141:6;
Pr 8:15; Am 2:3
2:11 *t*Ps 103:11
*u*Ps 9:2; 35:9;
104:34; Isa 61:10
*v*1Ch 16:30

2:12 *w*ver 7
*x*S Dt 9:8;
Rev 6:16
*y*Ps 84:12
*z*Ps 5:11; 34:8;
64:10

3: *a*3 Title 2Sa 15:14 3:2 *b*Ps 22:8; 71:11; Isa 36:15; 37:20
3:3 *c*S Ge 15:1 *d*Ps 27:6 3:4 *e*S Job 30:20

*c*6 Or *king*   *d*7 Or *son*; also in verse 12   *e*7 Or
have begotten you   *f*9 Or *will break them with a rod
of iron*   *g*2 A word of uncertain meaning, occurring
frequently in the Psalms; possibly a musical term
*h*3 Or *LORD, / my Glorious One, who lifts*

2:4–6 The Lord mocks the rebels. With derisive laughter the Lord meets the confederacy of rebellious world powers with the sovereign declaration that it is he who has established the Davidic king in his own royal city of Zion (Jerusalem).
2:4 See 59:8.
2:5 *anger . . . wrath.* God's anger is always an expression of his righteousness (see 7:11; see also note on 4:1).
2:6 *holy hill.* The site of the Jerusalem temple (see 2Ch 33:15); see also 3:4; 15:1; 43:3 ("holy mountain"); 46:4 ("holy mountain").
2:7–9 The Lord's Anointed proclaims the Lord's coronation decree. For NT application to Jesus' resurrection see Ac 13:33; to his superiority over angels see Heb 1:5; to his appointment as high priest see Heb 5:5.
2:7 *Son . . . Father.* In the ancient Near East the relationship between a great king and one of his subject kings, who ruled by his authority and owed him allegiance, was expressed not only by the words "lord" and "servant" but also by "father" and "son." The Davidic king was the Lord's "servant" and his "son" (2Sa 7:5,14).
2:8 *your inheritance.* Your domain—as the promised land was the Lord's "inheritance" (Ex 15:17; see Jos 22:19; Ps 28:9; 79:1; 82:8). *ends of the earth.* Ultimately the rule of the Lord's Anointed will extend as far as the rule of God himself.
2:9 According to Rev 12:5; 19:15 this word will be fulfilled in the triumphant reign of Christ; in Rev 2:26–27 Christ declares that he will appoint those who remain faithful to him to share in his subjugating rule over the nations. *dash them to pieces like pottery.* See Jer 19:11.
2:10–12 The rebellious rulers are warned.
2:11 *rejoice.* Hail the Lord as King with joy. *trembling.* Awe and reverence.
2:12 *Kiss.* As a sign of submission (see 1Sa 10:1; 1Ki 19:18; Hos 13:2; see also note on Ge 41:40). Submission to an Assyrian king was expressed by kissing his feet. *destroyed in your way.* See 1:6 and note. *Blessed.* See 1:1 and note.

him. The Lord.
Ps 3 Though threatened by many foes, the psalmist prays confidently to the Lord. Ps 3 and 4 are linked by references to glory (see v. 3; 4:2; see NIV text notes on both verses) and to the psalmist's sleep at night (see v. 5; 4:8). In v. 5 David speaks of the assurance of his waking in the morning because the Lord will keep him while he sleeps; in 4:8 he speaks of the inner quietness with which he goes to sleep because of the Lord's care. This juxtaposition of prayers with references to waking (morning) and sleeping (evening) at the beginning of the Psalter suggests that God's faithful care sustains the godly day and night whatever the need or circumstances, many of which will be mentioned in this book of prayers.
3 title *When he fled.* See 2Sa 15:13–17:22. References to events in David's life stand in the superscriptions of 13 psalms (3; 7; 18; 34; 51–52; 54; 56–57; 59–60; 63; 142), all but one (Ps 142) in Books I and II. See Introduction: Authorship and Titles (or Superscriptions).
3:1–2 David's need: threatened by many foes.
3:2 See 22:7–8; 71:10–11. The psalmists frequently quote their wicked oppressors in order to portray how they mock (see note on 1:1) God and his servants (see note on 10:11). *Selah.* See NIV text note; see also Introduction: Authorship and Titles (or Superscriptions).
3:3–4 David's confidence in God, who does not fail to answer his prayers.
3:3 *shield.* That one's king is his shield (protector) was a common concept in ancient Israel (see NIV text notes on 7:10; 47:9; 59:11; 84:9; 89:18; Ge 15:1). That the Lord is the shield of his people is frequently asserted (see 84:11; 91:4; 115:9–11; Dt 33:29; Pr 30:5) or claimed (see 18:2, 30; 28:7; 33:20; 119:114; 144:2). *you bestow glory on me.* The psalmist rejoices in the Lord as his royal provider and protector (see note on 2:11). See NIV text note. *lift up my head.* In victory over his enemies (see 110:7).
3:4 *holy hill.* The place of the Lord's sanctuary, the earthly counterpart of his heavenly throne room (see note on 2:6).

and he answers me from his holy
    hill.*f*   **Selah**

[5]I lie down and sleep;*g*
    I wake again,*h* because the LORD
    sustains me.
[6]I will not fear*i* the tens of thousands
    drawn up against me on every side.*j*

[7]Arise,*k* O LORD!
    Deliver me,*l* O my God!
    Strike*m* all my enemies on the jaw;
    break the teeth*n* of the wicked.

[8]From the LORD comes deliverance.*o*
    May your blessing*p* be on your
    people.   **Selah**

Psalm 4

For the director of music. With stringed
instruments. A psalm of David.

[1]Answer me*q* when I call to you,
    O my righteous God.
    Give me relief from my distress;*r*
    be merciful*s* to me and hear my
    prayer.*t*

[2]How long, O men, will you turn my
    glory*u* into shame*i* ?*v*
    How long will you love delusions and
    seek false gods*j* ?*w*   **Selah**
[3]Know that the LORD has set apart the
    godly*x* for himself;
    the LORD will hear*y* when I call to
    him.

[4]In your anger do not sin;*z*
    when you are on your beds,*a*
    search your hearts and be silent.
                   Selah
[5]Offer right sacrifices
    and trust in the LORD.*b*

[6]Many are asking, "Who can show us
    any good?"
    Let the light of your face shine upon
    us,*c* O LORD.
[7]You have filled my heart*d* with greater
    joy*e*

Cross-references

3:4 /Ps 2:6
3:5 *g*S Lev 26:6
*h*Ps 17:15; 139:18
3:6 /Job 11:15; Ps 23:4; 27:3
/Ps 118:11
3:7 *k*S 2Ch 6:41
/Ps 6:4; 7:1; 59:1; 109:21; 119:153; Isa 25:9; 33:22; 35:4; 36:15; 37:20; Jer 42:11; Mt 6:13
*m*Job 16:10
*n*Job 29:17; Ps 57:4; Pr 30:14; La 3:16
3:8 *o*Ps 27:1; 37:39; 62:1; Isa 43:3,11; 44:6, 8; 45:21; Hos 13:4; Jnh 2:9; Rev 7:10
*p*Nu 6:23; Ps 29:11; 129:8
4:1 *q*Ps 13:3; 27:7; 69:16; 86:7; 102:2
*r*S Ge 32:7; S Jdg 2:15
*s*Ps 30:10
*t*Ps 17:6; 54:2; 84:8; 88:2

4:2 *u*Ex 16:7; 1Sa 4:21
*v*2Ki 19:26; Job 8:22; Ps 35:26

*w*Jdg 2:17; Ps 31:6; 40:4; Jer 13:25; 16:19; Am 2:4 4:3
*x*Ps 12:1; 30:4; 31:23; 79:2; Mic 7:2; 1Ti 4:7; 2Pe 3:11
*y*Ps 6:8; Mic 7:7 4:4 *z*Eph 4:26* *a*Ps 63:6; Da 2:28 4:5
*b*Ps 31:6; 115:9; Pr 3:5; 28:26; Isa 26:4; Jn 14:1 4:6
*c*Nu 6:25 4:7 *d*Ac 14:17 *e*Isa 9:3; 35:10; 65:14,18

i2 Or *you dishonor my Glorious One*   j2 Or *seek lies*

3:5–6 David's sense of security.
3:5 Even while his own watchfulness is surrendered to sleep, the watchful Lord preserves him (see 4:8).
3:7–8 David's prayer.
3:7 *Arise . . . Deliver.* Hebrew idiom frequently prefaces an imperative calling for immediate action with the call to arise (see Ex 12:31, "Up!"; Dt 2:13; Jdg 7:9, "Get up"). In poetry the two imperatives of the idiom are often distributed between the two halves of the poetic line. Hence the psalmist's prayer is: "Arise (and) deliver me." *LORD . . . my God.* That is, LORD my God; the two elements of a compound divine name are also frequently distributed between the two halves of a poetic line. *break the teeth.* Probably likening the enemies to wild animals (see note on 7:2).
3:8 *From the LORD comes deliverance.* A common feature in the prayers of the Psalter is a concluding expression of confidence that the prayer will be or has been heard (as in 6:8–10; 7:10–17; 10:16–18; 12:7; 13:5–6 and often elsewhere; see note on 12:5–6). Here David's confidence becomes a testimony to God's people. *May your blessing be on your people.* See 25:22; 28:8–9; 51:18. The psalmists stood before God, the royal King, as his servants responsible for the well-being of his people.
Ps 4 Perhaps a prayer for relief when some calamity (possibly drought; see v. 7) has fallen and many are turning from the Lord to the gods of Canaan, from whom they hope to receive better. See introduction to Ps 3.
4 title See Hab 3:19. *For the director of music.* Probably a liturgical notation, indicating either that the psalm was to be added to the collection of works to be used by the director of music in Israel's worship services, or that when the psalm was used in the temple worship it was to be spoken by the leader of the Levitical choir—or by the choir itself (see 1Ch 23:5,30; 25; Ne 11:17). In this liturgical activity the Levites functioned as representatives of the worshiping congregation. Following their lead the people probably responded with "Amen" and "Praise the LORD" (Hallelujah); see 1Ch 16:36; Ne 5:13; cf. 1Co 14:16; Rev 5:14; 7:12; 19:4. *With stringed instruments.* See Ps 6; 54–55; 61; 67; 76 titles.

This is a liturgical notation, indicating that the Levites (see previous note) were to accompany the psalm with harp and lyre (see 1Ch 23:5; 25:1,3,6; cf. Ps 33:2; 43:4; 71:22; see also notes on Ps 39; 42 titles).
4:1 Initial request to be heard. *righteous.* Very often the "righteousness" of God in the Psalms (and frequently elsewhere in the OT) refers to the faithfulness with which he acts. This faithfulness is in full accordance with his commitments (both expressed and implied) to his people and with his status as the divine King—to whom the powerless may look for protection, the oppressed for redress and the needy for help. *Give me relief.* Lit. "Make a spacious place for me" (see 18:19 and note).
4:2–3 David rebukes those who turn away from his God to seek relief from the counterfeit gods; he assures them that the Lord will hear him.
4:2 *How long . . . ?* See Introduction: Theology; see also note on 6:3. *my glory.* David's special relationship with the Lord is the source of his glory—or perhaps he here speaks directly of God (see NIV text note here and on 3:3). *Selah.* See NIV text note on 3:2; see also Introduction: Authorship and Titles (or Superscriptions).
4:3 *godly.* Hebrew *hasid,* which occurs 26 times in the Psalms (once of God: 145:17, "loving"; cf. 18:25) and is usually rendered (in the plural) in the NIV as "the godly" or "saints." It is one of several Hebrew words for God's people, referring to them as people who are or should be devoted to God and faithful to him.
4:4–5 An exhortation not to give way to exasperation or anxiety (lit. "tremble" in anger or fear) but to look to the Lord.
4:4 *In your anger do not sin.* Paul uses these words in a different context (see Eph 4:26).
4:6 In the face of widespread uncertainty, David prays for the Lord to bless. *Who . . . ?* Which of the gods . . . ? *face shine upon.* See note on 13:1; a common expression for favor, reminiscent of the Aaronic benediction (see Nu 6:25–26).
4:7–8 David's confidence (see note on 3:8).

than when their grain and new
  wine*f* abound.
8I will lie down and sleep*g* in peace,*h*
  for you alone, O LORD,
  make me dwell in safety.*i*

Psalm 5

For the director of music. For flutes.
A psalm of David.

1Give ear*j* to my words, O LORD,
  consider my sighing.*k*
2Listen to my cry for help,*l*
  my King and my God,*m*
  for to you I pray.
3In the morning,*n* O LORD, you hear my
    voice;
  in the morning I lay my requests
    before you
  and wait in expectation.*o*

4You are not a God who takes pleasure
    in evil;
  with you the wicked*p* cannot dwell.
5The arrogant*q* cannot stand*r* in your
    presence;
  you hate*s* all who do wrong.

6You destroy those who tell lies;*t*
  bloodthirsty and deceitful men
  the LORD abhors.

7But I, by your great mercy,
  will come into your house;
  in reverence*u* will I bow down*v*
  toward your holy temple.*w*
8Lead me, O LORD, in your
    righteousness*x*
  because of my enemies—
  make straight your way*y* before me.

9Not a word from their mouth can be
    trusted;
  their heart is filled with destruction.
  Their throat is an open grave;*z*
  with their tongue they speak deceit.*a*
10Declare them guilty, O God!
  Let their intrigues be their downfall.
  Banish them for their many sins,*b*
  for they have rebelled*c* against you.

11But let all who take refuge in you be
    glad;

4:7 /S Ge 27:28;
S Dt 28:51
4:8 *g*S Lev 26:6
*h*S Nu 6:26;
S Job 11:18
*i*S Dt 33:28;
S Jer 32:37
5:1 /S 1Ki 8:29;
Ps 17:1; 40:1;
116:2; Da 9:18
*k*Ps 38:9;
Isa 35:10; 51:11
5:2 /S Job 19:7;
S 24:12; S 36:5
*m*Ps 44:4; 68:24;
84:3
5:3 *n*Isa 28:19;
50:4; Jer 21:12;
Eze 46:13;
Zep 3:5 *o*Ps 62:1;
119:81; 130:5;
Hab 2:1; Ro 8:19
5:4 *p*Ps 1:5;
11:5; 104:35;
Pr 2:22
5:5 *q*2Ki 19:32;
Ps 73:3; 75:4;
Isa 33:19; 37:33
*r*Ps 1:5 *s*Ps 45:7;
101:3; 119:104;
Pr 8:13
5:6 *t*Pr 19:22;
S Jn 8:44; Ac 5:3;
Rev 21:8
5:7 *u*Dt 13:4;
Jer 44:10;
Da 6:26
*v*S 2Sa 12:16;
Ps 138:2
*w*S 1Ki 8:48
5:8 *x*Ps 23:3;
31:1; 71:2;

85:13; 89:16; Pr 8:20 *y*S 1Ki 8:36; Jn 1:23 **5:9** *z*Jer 5:16;
Lk 11:44 *a*Ps 12:2; 28:3; 36:3; Pr 15:4; Jer 9:8; Ro 3:13*
5:10 *b*La 1:5 *c*Ps 78:40; 106:7; 107:11; La 3:42

4:7 *heart.* In Biblical language the center of the human
spirit, from which spring emotions, thought, motivations,
courage and action—"the wellspring of life" (Pr 4:23).
4:8 See 3:5–6. *in peace.* Without anxiety.
Ps 5 This morning prayer, perhaps offered at the time of the
morning sacrifice, is the psalmist's cry for help when his
enemies spread malicious lies to destroy him.
5 title *For the director of music.* See note on Ps 4 title.
flutes. The Hebrew for this word occurs only here; meaning
uncertain.
5:1–3 Initial appeal to be heard.
5:2 *King.* See Introduction: Theology.
5:4–6 An appeal to the righteousness of God's rule over
mankind.
5:5 *The arrogant.* See note on 31:23.
5:7–8 The psalmist presents his plea to the Lord in humble
reverence (v. 7), trusting in the Lord's great mercy (v. 7) and
righteousness (v. 8).
5:7 *great mercy.* See note on 6:4.
5:8 *Lead me.* As a shepherd (see 23:3). *righteousness.* See
note on 4:1. *make straight your way.* May the way down
which you lead me be straight, level and smooth, free from
obstacles and temptations. The psalmist prays that God will
so direct him that his enemies will have no grounds for their
malicious accusations (see 25:4; 27:11; 139:24;
143:8–10).
5:9–10 Accusation (a common element in the prayers of
the Psalter) and call for redress.
5:9 *word from their mouth.* The most frequent weapon
used against the psalmists is the tongue (for a striking example see Ps 12; see also note on 10:7). The psalmists experienced that the tongue is as deadly as the sword (see 57:4;
64:3–4). Perhaps appeals to God against those who maliciously wield the tongue are frequent in the Psalms because
only in God's courtroom can a person experience redress for
such attacks. *heart.* See note on 4:7. *throat . . . grave.* See
note on 49:14. *they speak deceit.* For the plots and intrigues
of enemies, usually involving lies to discredit the king and

bring him down, see Ps 17; 25; 27–28; 31; 35; 41; 52;
54–57; 59; 63–64; 71; 86; 109; 140–141—all ascribed to
David. Frequently such attacks came when the king was
"low" and seemingly abandoned by God (as in Ps 25; 35;
41; 71; 86; 109). In that case he was viewed as no longer fit
to be king—God was no longer with him (and so he could no
longer secure the safety of the nation; see 1Sa 8:20; 11:12;
12:12; 25:28; 2Sa 3:18; 7:9–11). In any event, he was an
easy prey (see 3:2; 22:7–8; 71:11). See note on 86:17. See
also Paul's use of this verse in Ro 3:13.
5:10 The presence of so-called "imprecations" (curses) in
the Psalms has occasioned endless discussion and has caused
many Christians to wince, in view of Jesus' instructions to
turn the other cheek and to pray for one's enemies (see Mt
5:39,44), and his own example on the cross (see Lk 23:34).
Actually, these "imprecations" are not that at all; rather,
they are appeals to God to redress wrongs perpetrated against
the psalmists by imposing penalties commensurate with the
violence done (see 28:4)—in accordance also with normal
judicial procedure in human courts (see Dt 25:1–3). The
psalmists knew that he who has been wronged is not to right
that wrong by his own hand but is to leave redress to the
Lord, who says, "It is mine to avenge; I will repay" (Dt
32:35; see Pr 20:22; Ro 12:19). Therefore they appeal their
cases to the divine Judge (see Jer 15:15). *Banish them.* From
God's presence, thus from the source of blessing and life (see
Ge 3:23). *rebelled against you.* By their attacks on the
psalmist.
5:11 The psalmist expands his prayer to include all the
godly (see note on 3:8). *your name.* The name of the Lord is
the manifestation of his character (see notes on Ex 3:14–15;
34:6–7). It has no separate existence apart from the Lord,
but is synonymous with the Lord himself in his gracious
manifestation and accessibility to his people. Hence the
Jerusalem temple is the earthly residence of his name among
his people (see 74:7; Dt 12:5,11; 2Sa 7:13), and his people
can pray to him by calling on his name (see 79:6; 80:18;
99:6; 105:1; 116:4,13,17). The name of the Lord protects

let them ever sing for joy. *d*
Spread your protection over them,
    that those who love your name *e* may
        rejoice in you. *f*
12For surely, O LORD, you bless the
        righteous; *g*
    you surround them *h* with your favor
        as with a shield. *i*

Psalm 6

For the director of music. With stringed
instruments. According to *sheminith*.*k*
A psalm of David.

1O LORD, do not rebuke me in your
        anger *j*
    or discipline me in your wrath.
2Be merciful to me, *k* LORD, for I am
        faint; *l*
    O LORD, heal me, *m* for my bones are
        in agony. *n*

3My soul is in anguish. *o*
    How long, *p* O LORD, how long?

4Turn, *q* O LORD, and deliver me;
    save me because of your unfailing
        love. *r*
5No one remembers you when he is
        dead.
    Who praises you from the grave[1] ? *s*

6I am worn out *t* from groaning; *u*
    all night long I flood my bed with
        weeping *v*
    and drench my couch with tears. *w*
7My eyes grow weak *x* with sorrow;
    they fail because of all my foes.

Cross references (center column):

5:11 *d*Ps 33:1;
81:1; 90:14;
92:4; 95:1; 145:7
*e*Ps 69:36;
119:132
*f*S Job 22:19
5:12 *g*Ps 112:2
*h*Ps 32:7
*i*S Ge 15:1
6:1 *j*S Ps 2:5
6:2 *k*Ps 4:1;
26:11; Jer 3:12;
12:15; 31:20
*l*Ps 61:2; 77:3;
142:3; Isa 40:31;
Jer 8:18; Eze 21:7
*m*S Nu 12:13
*n*Ps 22:14; 31:10;
32:3; 38:3;
42:10; 102:3

6:3 *o*S Job 7:11;
Ps 31:7; 38:8;
55:4; S Jn 12:27;
Ro 9:2; 2Co 2:4
*p*1Sa 1:14;
1Ki 18:21; Ps 4:2;
89:46; Isa 6:11;
Jer 4:14; Hab 1:2;
Zec 1:12
6:4 *q*Ps 25:16;
31:2; 69:16;
71:2; 86:16;

88:2; 102:2; 119:132 *r*Ps 13:5; 31:16; 77:8; 85:7; 119:41;
Isa 54:8,10 6:5 *s*Ps 30:9; 88:10-12; 115:17; Ecc 9:10;
Isa 38:18 6:6 *t*S Jdg 8:5 *u*S Job 3:24; S 23:2; Ps 12:5; 77:3;
102:5; La 1:8,11,21,22 *v*S Job 16:16 *w*S Job 7:3; Lk 7:38;
Ac 20:19 6:7 *x*S Job 16:8; Ps 31:9; 69:3; 119:82; Isa 38:14

*k*Title: Probably a musical term   15 Hebrew *Sheol*

(see 20:1; Pr 18:10); the Lord saves by his name (see 54:1);
and his saving acts testify that his name is near (see 52:9).
Accordingly, the godly "trust in" his name (20:7; 33:21),
hope in his name (see 52:9), "sing praise" to his name (7:17;
9:2; 18:49) and "rejoice in" his name (89:16). Both the
"love" and the "fear" that belong alone to God are similarly
directed toward his name (love: 69:36; 119:132; fear:
61:5; 86:11; 102:15).

5:12 See note on 3:8. *righteous.* See note on 1:5.

Ps 6 A prayer in time of severe illness, an occasion seized
upon by David's enemies to vent their animosity. In early
Christian liturgical tradition it was numbered with the seven
penitential psalms (the others: Ps 32; 38; 51; 102; 130;
143).

6 title See note on Ps 4 title. *According to.* Represents a
Hebrew preposition of varied usage (also found in the titles of
Ps 8; 12; 46; 53; 81; 84; 88). *sheminith.* Occurs also in Ps
12 title and in 1Ch 15:21. It perhaps refers to an eight-
stringed instrument (see NIV text note).

6:1-3 Initial appeal for mercy. Though the Lord has sent
him illness to chastise him for his sin (see 32:3-5; 38:1-8,
17-18), the psalmist asks that God would not in anger
impose the full measure of the penalty for sin, for then death
must come (see v. 5; see also 130:3).

6:1 Ps 38 begins similarly. *rebuke . . . discipline.* That is,
rebuke-and-discipline (see 39:11; see also note on 3:7).
anger . . . wrath. See note on 2:5.

6:2 *bones.* As the inner skeleton, they here represent the
whole body.

6:3 *soul.* Not a spiritual aspect in distinction from the
physical, nor the psalmist's "inner" being in distinction from
his "outer" being, but his very self as a living, conscious,
personal being. Its use in conjunction with "bones" (also in
35:9-10: "soul" and "whole being") did not for the Hebrew
writer involve reference to two distinct entities but constituted for him two ways of referring to himself, as is the case
also in the combination "soul" and "body" (31:9; 63:1).
How long . . . how long? See Introduction: Theology. Such
language of impatience and complaint is found frequently in
the prayers of the Psalter (usually "how long?" or "when?"
or "why?"). It expresses the anguish of relief not (yet)
granted and exhibits the boldness with which the psalmists
wrestled with God on the basis of their relationship with him
and their conviction concerning his righteousness (see note
on 4:1).

6:4-5 Earnest prayer for deliverance from death.

6:4 *unfailing love.* The Hebrew for this phrase denotes
befriending. Appeal to God's "(unfailing) love, kindness,
mercy" is frequent in the OT since it summarizes all that the
Lord covenanted to show to Israel (see Dt 7:9,12) as well as
to David and his dynasty (see 89:24,28,33; 2Sa 7:15; Isa
55:3).

6:5 The psalmist urges that God's praise is at stake. It is the
living, not the dead, who remember God's mercies and
celebrate his deliverances. The Israelites usually viewed
death as they saw it—the very opposite of life. And resurrection was not yet a part of their communal experience with
God. The grave brought no escape from God (see 139:8), but
just how they viewed the condition of the godly dead is not
clear. (Non-Biblical documents from the ancient Near East
indicate a general conception that immortality was reserved
for the gods but that the dead continued to have some kind
of shadowy existence in the dismal netherworld.) The OT
writers knew that man was created for life, that God's will
for his people was life and that he had power over death.
They also knew that death was every man's lot, and at its
proper time the godly rested in God and accepted it with
equanimity (see Ge 15:15; 25:8; 47:30; 49:33; 1Ki 2:2).
Death could even be a blessing for the righteous, affording
escape from the greater evil that would overtake the living
(see 2Ki 22:20; Isa 57:1-2). Furthermore, the death of the
righteous was reputedly better than that of the wicked (see
Nu 23:10). It seems clear that there was even an awareness
that death (as observed) was not the end of hope for the
righteous, that God had more in store for them (see especially 16:9-11; 17:15; 49:14-15; 73:24; see also note on
Ge 5:24). But when the psalmists wrestled with God for the
preservation of life, it was death as they saw it, in its radical
contradiction to life, that was evoked.

6:6-7 Anguish at night because of the prolongation of the
illness and the barbs of the enemies.

6:6 *I am worn out from groaning.* The very center of the
poem—thus underscoring the pathos of this prayer. This
literary device—of placing a key thematic line at the very
center of the psalm—was frequently used (see notes on 8:4;
21:7; 23:4; 34:8-14; 42:8; 47:5-6; 48:8; 54:4; 71:14;
74:12; 76:7; 82:5a; 86:9; 92:8; 97:7; 113:5; 138:4-5;
141:5; see also Introduction: Literary Features).

6:7 *eyes grow weak . . . fail.* In the vivid language of the OT
the eyes are dimmed by failing strength (see 38:10; 1Sa

8Away from me,y all you who do evil,z
  for the LORD has heard my weeping.
9The LORD has heard my cry for mercy;a
  the LORD accepts my prayer.
10All my enemies will be ashamed and
    dismayed;b
  they will turn back in sudden
    disgrace.c

Psalm 7

A *shiggaion*m d of David, which he sang
to the LORD concerning Cush, a
Benjamite.

1O LORD my God, I take refugee in you;
  save and deliver mef from all who
    pursue me,g
2or they will tear me like a lionh
  and rip me to pieces with no one to
    rescuei me.

3O LORD my God, if I have done this
  and there is guilt on my handsj —
4if I have done evil to him who is at
    peace with me
  or without causek have robbed my
    foe—
5then let my enemy pursue and
    overtakel me;
  let him trample my life to the
    groundm
  and make me sleep in the dust.n

                                    Selah

6Arise,o O LORD, in your anger;
  rise up against the rage of my
    enemies.p

Awake,q my God; decree justice.
7Let the assembled peoples gather
    around you.
  Rule over them from on high;r
8 let the LORD judges the peoples.
 Judge me, O LORD, according to my
    righteousness,t
  according to my integrity,u O Most
    High.v
9O righteous God,w
  who searches minds and hearts,x
 bring to an end the violence of the
    wicked
  and make the righteous secure.y

10My shieldn z is God Most High,
  who saves the upright in heart.a
11God is a righteous judge,b
  a God who expresses his wrathc
    every day.
12If he does not relent,d
  heo will sharpen his sword;e
  he will bend and string his bow.f
13He has prepared his deadly weapons;
  he makes ready his flaming arrows.g

14He who is pregnant with evil
  and conceives trouble gives birthh to
    disillusionment.
15He who digs a hole and scoops it out
  falls into the piti he has made.j
16The trouble he causes recoils on
    himself;

6:8 yPs 119:115;
139:19 zPs 5:5;
S Mt 7:23
6:9 aPs 28:6;
116:1
6:10
bS 2Ki 19:26
cPs 40:14
7 Title dHab 3:1
7:1 ePs 2:12;
11:1; 31:1
/S Ps 3:7
gPs 31:15;
119:86,157,161
7:2 hS Ge 49:9;
Rev 4:7 iPs 3:2;
71:11
7:3 /Isa 59:4
7:4 kPs 35:7,19;
Pr 24:28
7:5 /S Ex 15:9
mS 2Sa 22:43;
2Ki 9:33;
Isa 10:6; La 3:16
nS Job 7:21
7:6 oS 2Ch 6:41
pPs 138:7

qPs 35:23; 44:23
7:7 rPs 68:18
7:8 sS 1Ch 16:33
tS 1Sa 26:23;
Ps 18:20
uS Ge 20:5
vS Ge 3:5;
S Nu 24:16;
S Mk 5:7
7:9 wJer 11:20
xS 1Ch 28:9;
Ps 26:2; Rev 2:23
yPs 37:23; 40:2
7:10 zPs 3:3
aS Job 33:3
7:11
bS Ge 18:25;
Ps 9:8; 67:4;
75:2; 96:13;
98:9; Isa 11:4;
Jer 11:20
cS Dt 9:8
7:12 dEze 3:19;
33:9 eS Dt 32:41
/S 2Sa 22:35;
Ps 21:12;
Isa 5:28; 13:18

7:13 gPs 11:2; 18:14; 64:3 7:14 hIsa 59:4; Jas 1:15 7:15
iPs 35:7,8; 40:2; 94:13; Pr 26:27 /S Job 4:8

mTitle: Probably a literary or musical term   n10 Or
sovereign   o12 Or *If a man does not repent, / God*

14:27,29 and NIV text notes; Jer 14:6), by grief (often
associated with affliction: 31:9; 88:9; Job 17:7; La 2:11)
and by longings unsatisfied or hope deferred (see 69:3;
119:82,123; Dt 28:32; Isa 38:14). *because of all my foes.*
See note on 5:9.
6:8—10 Concluding expression of buoyant confidence (see
note on 3:8).
6:10 At the psalmist's restoration, his enemies will be
disgraced.
Ps 7 An appeal to the Lord's court of justice when enemies
attack.
7 title *shiggaion.* See NIV text note. The word occurs only
here (but see its plural in Hab 3:1). *Cush.* Not otherwise
known, but as a Benjamite he was probably a supporter of
Saul. Hence the title associates the psalm with Saul's determined attempts on David's life. See Introduction: Authorship
and Titles (or Superscriptions).
7:1—2 Initial summation of David's appeal.
7:2 *like a lion.* As a young shepherd, David had been
attacked by lions (see 1Sa 17:34–35). But it is also a convention in the Psalms to liken the attack of enemies to that of
ferocious animals, especially the lion (see 10:9; 17:12;
22:12–13,16,20–21; 35:17; 57:4; 58:6; 124:6).
7:3—5 David pleads his own innocence; he has given his
enemy no cause to attack him.
7:5 *me.* Lit. "my glory," a way of referring to the core of
one's being (see 16:9; 30:12; 57:8; 108:1 and notes).

7:6—9 An appeal to the Judge of all the earth to execute his
judgment over all peoples, and particularly to adjudicate
David's cause.
7:6 *Arise . . . rise up.* See note on 3:7. *anger.* See v. 11 and
note on 2:5. *Awake.* The Lord does not sleep (see 121:4)
while evil triumphs and the oppressed cry to him in vain (as
they do to Baal; see 1Ki 18:27). But the psalmists' language
of urgent prayer vividly expresses their anguished impatience
with God's inaction in the face of their great need (see 80:2;
see also 78:65; Isa 51:9).
7:8 *my righteousness.* See vv. 3–5.
7:9 *righteous.* See note on 4:1. *minds and hearts.* Lit.
"hearts and kidneys." The Israelites used the words as virtual synonyms (but "heart" most often) to refer to man's
innermost center of conscious life (see note on 4:7). To
"search mind and heart" was a conventional expression for
God's examination of man's hidden character and motives
(see Jer 11:20; 17:10; 20:12). *the righteous.* See note on
1:5.
7:10—13 David's confidence that his prayer will be heard
(see note on 3:8).
7:10 *shield.* See note on 3:3. *heart.* See note on 4:7.
7:11 *every day.* God's judgments are not all kept in store for
some future day.
7:14—16 David comforts himself with the common wisdom that under God's rule "crime does not pay."

his violence comes down on his own head.

[17]I will give thanks to the LORD because of his righteousness[k]
and will sing praise[l] to the name of the LORD Most High.[m]

Psalm 8

For the director of music. According to *gittith*.[p] A psalm of David.

[1]O LORD, our Lord,
how majestic is your name[n] in all the earth!

You have set your glory[o]
above the heavens.[p]

[2]From the lips of children and infants you have ordained praise[q] [q]
because of your enemies,
to silence the foe[r] and the avenger.

[3]When I consider your heavens,[s]
the work of your fingers,[t]
the moon and the stars,[u]
which you have set in place,

[4]what is man that you are mindful of him,
the son of man that you care for him?[v]

[5]You made him a little lower than the heavenly beings[r] [w]
and crowned him with glory and honor.[x]

[6]You made him ruler[y] over the works of your hands;[z]
you put everything under his feet:[a] [b]

[7]all flocks and herds,[c]
and the beasts of the field,[d]

[8]the birds of the air,
and the fish of the sea,[e]
all that swim the paths of the seas.

[9]O LORD, our Lord,
how majestic is your name in all the earth![f]

Psalm 9[s]

For the director of music.
To ˌthe tune of ˌ"The Death of the Son."
A psalm of David.

[1]I will praise you, O LORD, with all my heart;[g]
I will tell of all your wonders.[h]

Cross references (center column):

7:17 [k]Ps 5:8
[l]S 2Ch 31:2;
Ro 15:11;
Heb 2:12
[m]S Ge 14:18
8:1 [n]S 1Ch 16:10
[o]S Ex 15:11;
Lk 2:9 [p]Ps 57:5;
108:5; 113:4;
148:13; Hab 3:3
8:2 [q]Mt 21:16*
[r]Ps 143:12
8:3 [s]S Ge 15:5;
S Dt 10:14
[t]S Ex 8:19;
S 1Ch 16:26;
S 2Ch 2:12;
Ps 102:25
[u]S Ge 1:16;
1Co 15:41
8:4 [v]S 1Ch 29:14

8:5 [w]S Ge 1:26
[x]Ps 21:5; 103:4
8:6 [y]S Ge 1:28
[z]S Job 10:3;
Ps 19:1; 102:25;
145:10;
Isa 26:12; 29:23;
45:11; Heb 1:10
[a]Heb 2:6-8*
[b]S 1Ki 5:3;
1Co 15:25,27;
Eph 1:22
8:7 [c]Ge 13:5;
26:14 [d]S Ge 2:19
8:8 [e]Ge 1:26
8:9 [f]ver 1
9:1 [g]Ps 86:12;
111:1; 119:2,10,
145; 138:1
[h]S Dt 4:34

[p]Title: Probably a musical term　[q]2 Or *strength*
[r]5 Or *than God*　[s]Psalms 9 and 10 may have been originally a single acrostic poem, the stanzas of which begin with the successive letters of the Hebrew alphabet. In the Septuagint they constitute one psalm.

7:17 A vow to praise. Many prayers in the Psalter include such vows in anticipation of the expected answer to prayer. They reflect Israel's religious consciousness that praise must follow deliverance as surely as prayer springs from need—if God is to be truly honored. Such praise was usually offered with thank offerings and involved celebrating God's saving act in the presence of those assembled at the temple (see 50:14–15,23; see also note on 9:1). *name of the LORD.* See note on 5:11. *Most High.* See note on Ge 14:19.
Ps 8 In praise of the Creator (not of man—as is evident from the doxology that encloses it, vv. 1,9; see also note on 9:1) out of wonder over his sovereign ordering of the creation. Ge 1 (particularly vv. 26–28) clearly provides the spectacles, but David speaks out of his present experience of reality (perhaps on a bright, clear night when the vast host of the heavenly lights, stretching from horizon to horizon, erased from his musings small everyday affairs and engaged his mind with deeper thoughts). Two matters especially impressed him: (1) the glory of God reflected in the starry heavens, and (2) the astonishing condescension of God to be mindful of puny man, to crown him with glory almost godlike and to grant him lordly power over his creatures.
8 title *For the director of music.* See note on Ps 4 title. *According to.* See note on Ps 6 title. *gittith.* See Ps 81; 84 titles. The Hebrew word perhaps refers to either the winepress ("song of the winepress") or the Philistine city of Gath ("Gittite lyre or music"; see 2Sa 15:18).
8:1a *name.* See note on 5:11.
8:1b–2 The mighty God, whose glory is displayed across the face of the heavens, appoints (and evokes) the praise of little children to silence the dark powers arrayed against him (for a NT application see Mt 21:16).
8:2 *avenger.* See 44:16; one who strikes back in malicious revenge (not as in 9:12).
8:3–5 The vastness and majesty of the heavens as the

handiwork of God (see 19:1–6; 104:19–23) evoke wonder for what their Maker has done for little man, who is here today and gone tomorrow (see 144:3–4). (See Job 7:17–21 for Job's complaint that God takes man too seriously.)
8:3 *fingers.* See note on Ex 8:19.
8:4–6 Heb 2:6–8, quoting the Septuagint (the Greek translation of the OT), applies these verses to Jesus, who as the incarnate Son of God is both the representative man and the one in whom man's appointed destiny will be fully realized. The author of Hebrews thus makes use of the eschatological implications of these nonprophetic words in his testimony to Christ. Paul does the same with v. 6 in 1Co 15:27 (see also Eph 1:22).
8:4 *what.* The Hebrew for this word is translated "how" in vv. 1,9 and begins the line that serves as the center of the psalm (see note on 6:6). *are mindful of.* Lit. "remember" (see note on Ge 8:1). *son of man.* Often a poetic synonym for "man" (see 80:17; 144:3; see also note on Eze 2:1).
8:5 *heavenly beings.* The exalted angelic creatures that surround God in his heavenly realm (as, e.g., in Isa 6:2); but see NIV text note.
8:6–8 See Ge 1:26–27. Man's rule is real—a part of his "glory and honor" (v. 5)—and it is his destiny (the eschatological import drawn on by Paul and the author of Hebrews; see note on vv. 4–6). But it is not absolute or independent. It is participation, as a subordinate, in God's rule; and it is a gift, not a right.
8:9 Repeated verbatim from v. 1a (see note there).
Ps 9 That Ps 9 and 10 were sometimes viewed (or used) as one psalm is known from the Septuagint (the Greek translation of the OT; see NIV text note). Whether they were originally composed as one psalm is not known, though a number of indicators point in that direction. Ps 10 is the only psalm from Ps 3 to 32 that has no superscription, and the Hebrew text of the two psalms together appears to reflect an

²I will be glad and rejoice *i* in you;
   I will sing praise *j* to your name, *k*
     O Most High.

³My enemies turn back;
   they stumble and perish before you.
⁴For you have upheld my right *l* and my
     cause; *m*
   you have sat on your throne, *n*
     judging righteously. *o*
⁵You have rebuked the nations *p* and
     destroyed the wicked;
   you have blotted out their name *q* for
     ever and ever.
⁶Endless ruin has overtaken the enemy,
   you have uprooted their cities; *r*
   even the memory of them *s* has
     perished.

⁷The LORD reigns forever; *t*
   he has established his throne *u* for
     judgment.
⁸He will judge the world in
     righteousness; *v*
   he will govern the peoples with
     justice. *w*

⁹The LORD is a refuge *x* for the
     oppressed, *y*
   a stronghold in times of trouble. *z*
¹⁰Those who know your name *a* will trust
     in you,
   for you, LORD, have never forsaken *b*
     those who seek you. *c*

¹¹Sing praises *d* to the LORD, enthroned in
     Zion; *e*
   proclaim among the nations *f* what
     he has done. *g*
¹²For he who avenges blood *h* remembers;
   he does not ignore the cry of the
     afflicted. *i*

¹³O LORD, see how my enemies *j*
     persecute me!
   Have mercy *k* and lift me up from the
     gates of death, *l*
¹⁴that I may declare your praises *m*

9:2 /S Job 22:19;
Ps 14:7; 31:7;
70:4; 97:8;
126:3; Pr 23:15;
Isa 25:9;
Jer 30:19;
Joel 2:21;
Zep 3:14;
S Mt 5:12;
Rev 19:7
/S 2Ch 31:2
k Ps 92:1
9:4 /S 1Ki 8:45
m S Job 16:21
n Ps 11:4; 47:8;
Isa 6:1 *o* Ps 7:11;
67:4; 98:9;
1Pe 2:3
9:5 *p* Ge 20:7;
S 37:10;
S 1Ch 16:21;
Ps 59:5; 109:14;
Isa 26:14; 66:15
q S Job 18:17
9:6 *r* S Dt 29:28;
Jer 2:3;
46:1-51:58;
Zep 2:8-10
s Ps 34:16;
109:15; Ecc 9:5;
Isa 14:22; 26:14
9:7 /S 1Ch 16:31;
Rev 19:6
u Ps 11:4; 47:8;
93:2; Isa 6:1;
66:1
9:8 *v* S ver 4;
Ps 7:11 *w* Ps 11:7;
45:6; 72:2

9:9 *x* S Dt 33:27;

S 2Sa 22:3 *y* Ps 10:18; 74:21 *z* Ps 32:7; 121:7 **9:10** *a* Ps 91:14
b S Ge 28:15; S Dt 4:31; Ps 22:1; 37:25; 71:11; Isa 49:14;
Jer 15:18; Heb 13:5 *c* Ps 70:4 **9:11** *d* Ps 7:17 *e* S Ps 2:6
/Ps 18:49; 44:11; 57:9; 106:27; Isa 24:13; Eze 20:23;
1Ti 3:16 *g* Ps 105:1 **9:12** *h* S 2Sa 4:11 *i* ver 18; Ps 10:17;
22:24; 72:4; Isa 49:13 **9:13** /Nu 10:9; Ps 3:7; 18:3 *k* Ps 6:2;
41:4; 51:1; 86:3,16; 119:132 /S Job 17:16; Mt 16:18 **9:14**
m Ps 51:15; 1Pe 2:9

---

incomplete (or broken) acrostic structure. The first letter of each verse or pair of verses tends to follow the order of the Hebrew alphabet near the beginning of Ps 9 and again near the end of Ps 10. The thoughts also tend to be developed in two-verse units throughout. Ps 9 is predominantly praise (by the king) for God's deliverance from hostile nations (the specific occasion is unknown, but since there is no reference to victories on the part of Israel, God's destruction of the nations may have come by other means). It concludes with a short prayer for God's continuing righteous judgments (see v. 4) on the haughty nations. Ps 10 is predominantly prayer against the rapacity of unscrupulous men within the realm—as arrogant and wicked in their dealings with the "weak" (v. 2) as the nations were in their attacks on Israel (vv. 2–11 can serve equally as a description of both). The conjunction of these two within a single psalm is not unthinkable since the attacks of "the wicked" (9:5; 10:4), whether from within or from without, on the godly community are equally threatening to true Israel. Praise of God's past deliverances is often an integral part of prayer in the Psalter (see 3:3–4,8 and notes; 25:6; 40:1–5), as also in other ancient Near Eastern prayers. Such praise expressed the ground of the psalmist's hope that his present prayer would be heard, and it also functioned to motivate the Lord to act once more in his people's (or his servant's) behalf. For other lengthy prefaces to prayer see Ps 40; 44; 89. Probably Ps 9–10 came to be separated for the purpose of separate liturgical use, as did Ps 42–43 (see introduction there).
9 title *For the director of music.* See note on Ps 4 title. *To the tune of.* See titles of Ps 22; 45; 56–60; 69; 75; 80; see also NIV text note on Ps 88 title. Nothing more is known of the apparent tune titles.
9:1–2 Initial announcement of praise.
9:1 *heart.* See note on 4:7. *tell of.* The Hebrew for this phrase is translated "declare" in v. 14. The praise of God in the Psalter is rarely a private matter between the psalmist and the Lord. It is usually a public (at the temple) celebration of God's holy virtues or of his saving acts or gracious bestowal of blessings. In his praise the psalmist proclaims to the assem-

bled throng God's glorious attributes or his righteous (see note on 4:1) deeds (see, e.g., 22:22–31; 56:12–13; 61:8; 65:1; 69:30–33). To this is usually added a call to praise, summoning all who hear to take up the praise—to acknowledge and joyfully celebrate God's glory, his goodness and all his righteous acts. This aspect of praise in the Psalms has rightly been called the OT anticipation of NT evangelism. *wonders.* God's saving acts, sometimes involving miracles—as in the exodus from Egypt, the desert wanderings and the entrance into the promised land—and sometimes not, but always involving the manifestation of God's sovereign lordship over events. Here reference is to the destruction of the enemies celebrated in this psalm.
9:2,10 *your name.* See note on 5:11.
9:2 *Most High.* See note on Ge 14:19.
9:3–6 In destroying the enemies, God has redressed the wrongs committed by them against David (and Israel).
9:4 *throne.* See note on v. 7.
9:5 *blotted out their name.* As if from a register of mankind written on a papyrus scroll (see Nu 5:23; see also Dt 9:14; 25:19; 29:20; 2Ki 14:27).
9:7–10 Celebration of the righteous rule of God (see note on 4:1), which evokes trust in those who look to the Lord.
9:7 *his throne.* In heaven (see 11:4). See also v. 4.
9:8 See Ac 17:31.
9:11–12 A call to the assembly at the temple to take up the praise of God for his righteous judgments (see note on v. 1).
9:11 *enthroned in Zion.* God's heavenly throne (see v. 7) has its counterpart on earth in his temple at Jerusalem, from which center he rules the world (see 2:6; 3:4 and notes; 20:2). For God's election of Zion as the seat of his rule see 132:13.
9:12 *he who avenges blood.* See Dt 32:41,43.
9:13–14 Perhaps a recollection of David's prayer ("the cry of the afflicted," v. 12), which the Lord has now answered.
9:13 *gates of death.* See Job 17:16 and note.
9:14 *declare.* See notes on v. 1; 7:17. *gates.* Having been thrust down by the attacks of his enemies to "the gates of death" (v. 13), David prayed to be lifted up so he could

in the gates of the Daughter of Zion[n]
and there rejoice in your salvation.[o]

[15]The nations have fallen into the pit they
have dug;[p]
their feet are caught in the net they
have hidden.[q]

[16]The LORD is known by his justice;
the wicked are ensnared by the work
of their hands.[r]   Higgaion.[t]
                                            Selah

[17]The wicked return to the grave,[u] [s]
all the nations that forget God.[t]

[18]But the needy will not always be
forgotten,
nor the hope[u] of the afflicted[v] ever
perish.

[19]Arise,[w] O LORD, let not man triumph;[x]
let the nations be judged[y] in your
presence.

[20]Strike them with terror,[z] O LORD;
let the nations know they are but
men.[a]   Selah

Psalm 10[v]

[1]Why, O LORD, do you stand far off?[b]
Why do you hide yourself[c] in times
of trouble?

[2]In his arrogance the wicked man hunts
down the weak,[d]
who are caught in the schemes he
devises.

[3]He boasts[e] of the cravings of his heart;
he blesses the greedy and reviles the
LORD.[f]

[4]In his pride the wicked does not seek
him;
in all his thoughts there is no room
for God.[g]

[5]His ways are always prosperous;
he is haughty[h] and your laws are far
from him;
he sneers at all his enemies.

[6]He says to himself, "Nothing will shake
me;
I'll always be happy[i] and never have
trouble."

[7]His mouth is full of curses[j] and lies and
threats;[k]
trouble and evil are under his
tongue.[l]

[8]He lies in wait[m] near the villages;
from ambush he murders the
innocent,[n]
watching in secret for his victims.

[9]He lies in wait like a lion in cover;
he lies in wait to catch the helpless;[o]
he catches the helpless and drags
them off in his net.[p]

[10]His victims are crushed,[q] they collapse;
they fall under his strength.

[11]He says to himself, "God has
forgotten;[r]
he covers his face and never sees."[s]

9:14 [n]2Ki 19:21; Isa 1:8; 10:32; 37:22; 62:11; Jer 4:31; 6:2; La 1:6; Mic 1:13; Zep 3:14; Zec 2:10; Mt 21:5; Jn 12:15 [o]Ps 13:5; 35:9; 50:23; 51:12
9:15 [p]S Job 4:8; Ps 35:7 [q]Ps 35:8; 57:6
9:16 [r]Pr 5:22
9:17 [s]S Nu 16:30; Pr 5:5 [s]S Job 8:13
9:18 [u]Ps 25:3; 39:7; 71:5; Pr 23:18; Jer 14:8 [v]ver 12; Ps 74:19
9:19 [w]Ps 3:7 [x]2Ch 14:11 [y]Ps 110:6; Isa 2:4; Joel 3:12
9:20 [z]S Ge 35:5; Ps 31:13; Isa 13:8; Lk 21:26 [a]Ps 62:9;
Isa 31:3; Eze 28:2
10:1 [b]Ps 22:1,11; 35:22; 38:21; 71:12 [c]Ps 13:1
10:2 [d]ver 9; S Job 20:19
10:3 [e]Ps 49:6; 94:4; Jer 48:30 [f]S Job 1:5

10:4 [g]Ps 36:1
10:5 [h]Ps 18:27; 101:5; Pr 6:17; Isa 13:11; Jer 48:29
10:6 [i]Rev 18:7
10:7 [j]Ro 3:14* [k]Ps 73:8; 119:134; Ecc 4:1; Isa 30:12 [l]S Job 20:12
10:8 [m]Ps 37:32; 59:3; 71:10; Pr 1:11; Jer 5:26; Mic 7:2 [n]Hos 6:9
10:9 [o]S ver 2 [p]S Job 18:8

10:10 [q]S Job 9:17 **10:11** [r]Job 22:13; Ps 42:9; 77:9 [s]S Job 22:14

[t]16 Or Meditation; possibly a musical notation
[u]17 Hebrew Sheol [v]Psalms 9 and 10 may have been originally a single acrostic poem, the stanzas of which begin with the successive letters of the Hebrew alphabet. In the Septuagint they constitute one psalm.

celebrate his deliverance (see note on v. 1) in "the gates of ... Zion." *Daughter of Zion.* A personification of Jerusalem and its inhabitants.
9:15–18 Under the Lord's just rule, those who wickedly attack others bring destruction on themselves (see 7:14–16 and note) and their end will be the grave. But those who are attacked ("the needy," v. 18) will not trust in the Lord in vain.
9:17 *forget.* Take no account of.
9:18 *needy ... afflicted.* In this psalm David and Israel are counted among them because of the threat from the enemies. *not ... forgotten.* Those who forget God will come to nothing, but the needy and afflicted will not be forgotten by God (see v. 12).
9:19–20 A prayer at the conclusion of praise, asking that the Lord may ever rule over the nations as he has done in the event here celebrated—that those who "forget God" (v. 17) may know that they are only men, not gods, and cannot withstand the God of Israel (see 10:18).
9:19 *Arise.* See note on 3:7.
Ps 10 A prayer for rescue from the attacks of unscrupulous men—containing a classic OT portrayal of "the wicked." See introduction to Ps 9.
10:1 See note on 6:3; see also Introduction: Theology.
10:2–11 Accusation lodged against the oppressors (see note on 5:9–10). In the Hebrew the interchange of singular and plural indicates that these accusations are being lodged against wicked oppressors in general. Their deeds betray the

arrogance (see vv. 2–5—so long as they prosper, v. 5) with which they defy God (see vv. 3–4,13; see especially their words in vv. 6,11,13). They greedily seek to glut their unrestrained appetites (see v. 3) by victimizing others, taking account of neither God (see v. 4) nor his law (see v. 5).
10:2 *hunts ... caught.* The psalmists often use imagery from the hunt (see vv. 8–9).
10:3 *heart.* See note on 4:7.
10:4 The wicked man does not consider that he has God to contend with (see note on v. 11; see also 14:1; 36:1; 53:1).
10:6 See vv. 11,13 and note on 3:2. *to himself.* Lit. "in his heart" (also in vv. 11,13); see note on 4:7. *shake me.* Disturb my well-being, unsettle my security.
10:7 *curses and lies and threats.* The three most common weapons of the tongue in Israel's experience (see note on 5:9). *curses.* The ancient Near Eastern peoples thought that by pronouncing curses on someone they could bring down the power of the gods (or other mysterious powers) on that person. They had a large conventional stock of such curses. *lies.* Slander and false testimony for malicious purposes (see, e.g., 1Ki 21:8–15).
10:9 See note on 7:2.
10:11 See note on 3:2. The arrogance with which the wicked speak (see 17:10), especially their easy dismissal of God's knowledge of their evil acts and his unfailing prosecution of their malicious deeds, is frequently noted by the psalmists (see v. 13; 12:4; 42:3,10; 59:7; 64:5; 71:11; 73:11; 94:7; 115:2; see also Isa 29:15; Eze 8:12).

¹²Arise,^{t} LORD! Lift up your hand,^{u}
    O God.
Do not forget the helpless.^{v}
¹³Why does the wicked man revile
    God?^{w}
Why does he say to himself,
    "He won't call me to account"?^{x}
¹⁴But you, O God, do see trouble^y and
    grief;
you consider it to take it in hand.
The victim commits himself to you;^{z}
    you are the helper^a of the fatherless.
¹⁵Break the arm of the wicked and evil
    man;^{b}
call him to account for his
    wickedness
that would not be found out.

¹⁶The LORD is King for ever and ever;^{c}
    the nations^d will perish from his
    land.
¹⁷You hear, O LORD, the desire of the
    afflicted;^{e}
you encourage them, and you listen
    to their cry,^{f}
¹⁸defending the fatherless^g and the
    oppressed,^{h}
in order that man, who is of the
    earth, may terrify no more.

10:12 ^{t}Ps 3:7	
^{u}Ps 17:7; 20:6;	
106:26;	
Isa 26:11; Mic 5:9	
^{v}Ps 9:12	
10:13 ^{w}ver 3	
^{x}S Job 31:14	
10:14 ^{y}ver 7;	
Ps 22:11 ^{z}Ps 37:5	
^{a}S Dt 33:29	
10:15	
^{b}S Job 31:22	
10:16	
^{c}S Ex 15:18	
^{d}S Dt 8:20	
10:17 ^{e}S Ps 9:12	
^{f}S Ex 22:23	
10:18	
^{g}S Dt 24:17;	
Ps 146:9	
^{h}S Ps 9:9	

11:1 ^{i}S Ps 7:1	
^{j}S Ge 14:10	
^{k}Ps 50:11	
11:2 ^{l}S 2Sa 22:35	
^{m}S Ps 7:13;	
S 58:7 ^{n}Ps 10:8	
^{o}S Job 33:3;	
Ps 7:10	
11:3 ^{p}Ps 18:15;	
82:5; Isa 24:18	
11:4 ^{q}S 1Ki 8:48;	
Ps 18:6; 27:4;	
Jnh 2:7; Mic 1:2;	
Hab 2:20	
^{r}S 2Ch 6:18;	
S Ps 9:7; Mt 5:34;	
23:22; S Rev 4:2	
^{s}Pr 15:3	
^{t}Ps 33:18; 66:7	
11:5 ^{u}S Dt 7:13;	
S Job 23:10	
^{v}S Job 28:28;	
Ps 5:5; 45:7;	
Isa 1:14	
11:6	
^{w}S Ge 19:24;	
S Rev 9:17	

Psalm 11

For the director of music. Of David.

¹In the LORD I take refuge.^{i}
How then can you say to me:
    "Flee^j like a bird to your mountain.^{k}
²For look, the wicked bend their bows;^{l}
    they set their arrows^m against the
        strings
to shoot from the shadows^n
    at the upright in heart.^{o}
³When the foundations^p are being
        destroyed,
    what can the righteous do^w?"

⁴The LORD is in his holy temple;^{q}
    the LORD is on his heavenly throne.^{r}
He observes the sons of men;^{s}
    his eyes examine^t them.
⁵The LORD examines the righteous,^{u}
    but the wicked^x and those who love
        violence
    his soul hates.^{v}
⁶On the wicked he will rain
    fiery coals and burning sulfur;^{w}
    a scorching wind^x will be their lot.

⁷For the LORD is righteous,^{y}

^{x}S Ge 41:6; S Job 1:19 **11:7** ^{y}S 2Ch 12:6; S Ezr 9:15; 2Ti 4:8

^{w}3 Or *what is the Righteous One doing* ^{x}5 Or *The LORD, the Righteous One, examines the wicked,* /

10:12–15 Prayer that God will call the wicked to account.
10:12 *Arise.* See note on 3:7. *forget.* See 9:18. *helpless.*
Those at the mercy of the oppressors (see v. 9).
10:13 *Why . . . ? Why . . . ?* See note on 6:3.
10:14 Appeal to God's righteous rule (see 5:4–6).
10:15 *Break the arm.* Destroy the power to oppress. *call him to account.* Humble his arrogance (see v. 13) with your righteous judgment.
10:16–18 The psalmist's confidence in the righteous reign of the Lord (see note on 3:8). Reference to the nations (v. 16) and to the humbling of proud man (see v. 18; see also 9:19–20) suggests links with Ps 9. As the conclusion to Ps 10, this stanza expands the vision of God's just rule to its universal scope and sets the purging of the Lord's land of all nations that do not acknowledge him (see v. 16) alongside God's judicial dealing with the wicked oppressors. Both belong to God's assertion of his righteous rule in the face of man's arrogant denial of it.
10:18 *who is of the earth.* Who is not God and so constitutes no ultimate threat (see 49:12,20; 56:4,11; 62:9; 78:39; 103:14–16; 118:6,8–9; 144:4; Isa 31:3; Jer 17:5).
Ps 11 A confession of confident trust in the Lord's righteous rule, at a time when wicked adversaries seem to have the upper hand.
11 title *For the director of music.* See note on Ps 4 title.
11:1–3 David testifies of his unshakable trust in the Lord (his refuge) to apprehensive people around him. These people, seeing the power and underhandedness of the enemy (they "shoot from the shadows," v. 2), fear that the foundations (v. 3) are crumbling and that flight to a mountain refuge is the only recourse. He dismisses their fearful advice with disdain.
11:2 It is not clear whether those who wield the bows and

arrows are archers or whether they are false accusers (see 57:4; 64:4; see also note on 5:9). *heart.* See note on 4:7.
11:3 *foundations.* Of the world order (see 82:5). To those who counsel flight, the powerful upsurge of evil appears to indicate that the righteous can no longer count on a world order in which good triumphs over evil. *righteous.* See note on 1:5.
11:4–7 Reply to the fearful: The Lord is still securely on his heavenly throne. And the righteous Lord (see v. 7) discerns the righteous (see v. 5) to give them a place in his presence (see v. 7), while his judgment will "rain" (v. 6) on the wicked.
11:4 *The LORD is in his holy temple.* Repeated verbatim in Hab 2:20. Here reference is to his heavenly temple.
11:6 Perhaps recalling God's judgment on Sodom and Gomorrah (see Rev 14:10; 20:10; 21:8). *their lot.* Lit. "the portion of their cup" (see 75:8 and note on 16:5).
11:7 *righteous.* See note on 4:1. *upright men.* Those concerning whom the fearful despaired (see v. 2). *see his face.* The Hebrew for "see the king's face" was an expression denoting access to the king (see Ge 43:3,5; 44:23,26; 2Sa 3:13, "come into my presence"; 14:24,28,32). Sometimes it referred to those who served before the king (see 2Ki 25:19, "royal advisers"; Est 1:14, those "who had special access to the king"). Here David speaks of special freedom of access before the heavenly King. Reference is no doubt to his presence at the temple (God's earthly royal house), but that is still the presence of the One who sits on the heavenly throne. Ultimate access to the heavenly temple may also be implied (see 16:11; 17:15; see also 23:6; 140:13). Even the pagan peoples surrounding Israel believed that man continued after death, though only in some kind of shadowy existence in the netherworld (see Isa 14:9–17).

he loves justice;[z]
upright men[a] will see his face.[b]

Psalm 12

For the director of music. According to
sheminith.[y] A psalm of David.

[1]Help, LORD, for the godly are no
  more;[c]
  the faithful have vanished from
      among men.
[2]Everyone lies[d] to his neighbor;
  their flattering lips speak with
      deception.[e]

[3]May the LORD cut off all flattering lips[f]
  and every boastful tongue[g]
[4]that says, "We will triumph with our
      tongues;[h]
  we own our lips[z]—who is our
      master?"

[5]"Because of the oppression[i] of the
      weak
  and the groaning[j] of the needy,
I will now arise,[k]" says the LORD.
  "I will protect them[l] from those
      who malign them."

[6]And the words of the LORD are
      flawless,[m]
  like silver refined[n] in a furnace[o] of
      clay,
  purified seven times.

[7]O LORD, you will keep us safe[p]

and protect us from such people
      forever.[q]
[8]The wicked freely strut[r] about
  when what is vile is honored among
      men.

Psalm 13

For the director of music.
A psalm of David.

[1]How long,[s] O LORD? Will you forget
      me[t] forever?
  How long will you hide your face[u]
      from me?
[2]How long must I wrestle with my
      thoughts[v]
  and every day have sorrow in my
      heart?
  How long will my enemy triumph
      over me?[w]

[3]Look on me[x] and answer,[y] O LORD my
      God.
  Give light to my eyes,[z] or I will sleep
      in death;[a]
[4]my enemy will say, "I have overcome
      him,[b]"
  and my foes will rejoice when I fall.[c]

[5]But I trust in your unfailing love;[d]

Center column references

11:7 [z]S Ps 9:8;
33:5; 99:4;
Isa 28:17; 30:18;
56:1; 61:8;
Jer 9:24
[a]S Job 1:1;
Lk 23:50
[b]Ps 17:15;
140:13
12:1 [c]Isa 57:1;
Mic 7:2
12:2 [d]Ps 5:6;
34:13; 141:3;
Pr 6:19; 12:17;
13:3; Isa 32:7
[e]S Ps 5:9;
Ro 16:18
12:3 [f]Pr 26:28;
28:23 [g]Ps 73:9;
Da 7:8; Jas 3:5;
Rev 13:5
12:4 [h]Pr 18:21;
Jas 3:6
12:5 [i]Ps 44:24;
62:10; 72:14;
73:8; Ecc 4:1;
5:8; Isa 3:15;
5:7; 30:12;
59:13; Ac 7:34
[j]S Ps 6:6 [k]Ps 3:7
[l]Ps 34:6; 35:10
12:6
[m]S 2Sa 22:31;
Ps 18:30
[n]S Job 23:10;
S 28:1; Isa 48:10;
Zec 13:9
[o]Ps 119:140
12:7 [p]Ps 16:1;
27:5

[q]Ps 37:28;
Jn 17:12
12:8
[r]Ps 55:10-11
13:1 [s]Ps 6:3
[t]Ps 42:9; La 5:20
[u]S Dt 31:17;
S Ps 22:24;
S Isa 8:17; S 54:9
13:2 [v]Ps 42:4;
55:2; 139:23;
Isa 33:18;
Da 7:28 [w]Ps 94:3

13:3 [x]Ps 9:12; 25:18; 31:7; 35:23; 59:4; 80:14; 107:41;
119:50,153 [y]S Ps 4:1 [z]S Ezr 9:8 [a]Ps 76:5; 90:5; Jer 51:39
13:4 [b]S 1Ki 19:2; Ps 25:2 [c]Ps 38:16; 118:13 13:5 [d]S Ps 6:4

[y]Title: Probably a musical term   [z]4 Or / our lips are
our plowshares

Ps 12 A prayer for help when it seems that all men are
faithless and every tongue false (see Mic 7:1–7).
12 title *For the director of music.* See note on Ps 4 title.
According to sheminith. See note on Ps 6 title.
12:1–2 Initial appeal, with description of the cause of
distress.
12:1 *godly.* See note on 4:3. *the faithful.* Those who
maintain moral integrity.
12:2 See 5:9 and note.
12:3–4 The prayer.
12:3 *cut off.* Put an end to (physical mutilation is not in
view). *boastful.* See note on 10:2–11.
12:4 See notes on 3:2; 10:11.
12:5–6 A reassuring word from the Lord. Such words of
assurance following prayer in the Psalms were perhaps
spoken by a priest (see 1Sa 1:17) or a prophet (see 51:8 and
note; 2Sa 12:13). It may be that abrupt transitions from
prayer to confidence in the Psalms (see note on 3:8) presuppose such priestly or prophetic words, even when they are
not contained in the psalm. Here it is possible that David
merely recalls this appropriate word from the Lord; notice
that it is a general reassurance concerning the righteous rule
of God (see note on 4:1).
12:5 *I will now arise.* See Isa 33:10.
12:6 *words of the LORD.* Set in sharp contrast with the
boastful words of the adversaries; they are as flawless as
thoroughly refined silver. *furnace of clay.* See note on Dt
4:20. *seven.* Signifies fullness or completeness—here
thoroughness of refining.

12:7–8 Concluding expression of confidence (see note on
3:8).
12:8 David is confident, even though at the present time
the wicked think they have the upper hand (see vv. 1–4).
Ps 13 A cry to the Lord for deliverance from a serious illness
that threatens death (see v. 3), which would give David's
enemies just what they wanted. See introduction to Ps 6.
13 title *For the director of music.* See note on Ps 4 title.
13:1–2 An anguished complaint concerning a prolonged
serious illness.
13:1 *How long . . . ?* See note on 6:3; see also Introduction: Theology. *forget.* Ignore. *hide your face.* For use in
combination with "forget" see 44:24. In moments of need
the psalmists frequently ask God why he hides his face (see
30:7; 44:24; 88:14), or they plead with him not to do so
(see 27:9; 69:17; 102:2; 143:7). When he does hide his
face, those who depend on him can only despair (see 30:7;
104:29). When his face shines on a person, blessing and
deliverance come (see 4:6 and note; 31:16; 67:1; 80:3,7,
19; 119:135).
13:2 *heart.* See note on 4:7.
13:3–4 Appeal for deliverance from death.
13:3 *Give light to my eyes.* Restore me (see note on 6:7).
13:4 See notes on 3:2; 5:9. *fall.* Referring to death (as in
18:38; 82:7; 106:26; Jdg 5:27; 2Sa 1:19; Job 18:12).
13:5–6 Concluding expression of confidence (see note on
3:8).
13:5 *unfailing love.* See note on 6:4. *heart.* See note on
4:7. *rejoices.* It is David who will rejoice, not his enemies.

my heart rejoices in your salvation. *e*

⁶I will sing*f* to the LORD,
for he has been good to me.

Psalm 14

14:1–7pp — Ps 53:1–6

For the director of music. Of David.

¹The fool*a* says in his heart,
"There is no God."*g*
They are corrupt, their deeds are vile;
there is no one who does good.

²The LORD looks down from heaven*h*
on the sons of men
to see if there are any who
understand,*i*
any who seek God.*j*
³All have turned aside,*k*
they have together become corrupt;*l*
there is no one who does good,*m*
not even one.*n*

⁴Will evildoers never learn—*o*
those who devour my people*p* as
men eat bread
and who do not call on the LORD?*q*
⁵There they are, overwhelmed with
dread,
for God is present in the company of
the righteous.
⁶You evildoers frustrate the plans of the
poor,
but the LORD is their refuge.*r*

13:5
*e*S Job 33:26;
Ps 9:14; Isa 25:9;
33:2
13:6 *f*S Ex 15:1;
Ps 7:17
14:1 *g*Ps 10:4
14:2 *h*Job 41:34;
Ps 85:11; 102:19;
La 3:50 *i*Ps 92:6
*j*S Ezr 6:21
14:3 *k*S 1Sa 8:3;
1Ti 5:15 *l*2Pe 2:7
*m*1Ki 8:46;
Ps 143:2;
Ecc 7:20
*n*Ro 3:10-12*
14:4 *o*Ps 82:5;
Jer 4:22 *p*Ps 27:2;
Mic 3:3 *q*Ps 79:6;
Isa 64:7; 65:1;
Jer 10:25; Hos 7:7
14:6 *r*S 2Sa 22:3

14:7 *s*Ps 2:6
*t*S Dt 30:3;
S Jer 48:47
15:1 *u*Ex 29:46;
Ps 23:6; 27:4;
61:4 *v*Ex 25:8;
1Ch 22:19;
Ps 20:2; 78:69;
150:1
*w*S Ps 15:17
15:2 *x*S Ge 6:9;
S Ps 18:32;
Eph 1:4;
S 1Th 3:13;
Tit 1:6 *y*Pr 16:13;
Isa 45:19;
Jer 7:28; 9:5;
Zec 8:3,16;
Ro 9:1;
S Eph 4:25
15:3
*z*S Lev 19:16
15:4 *a*S Job 19:9;
Ac 28:10
*b*S Dt 23:21;
S Jos 9:18;
Mt 5:33
15:5 *c*S Ex 22:25
*d*S Ex 18:21;

---

⁷Oh, that salvation for Israel would come
out of Zion!*s*
When the LORD restores the
fortunes*t* of his people,
let Jacob rejoice and Israel be glad!

Psalm 15

A psalm of David.

¹LORD, who may dwell*u* in your
sanctuary?*v*
Who may live on your holy hill?*w*

²He whose walk is blameless*x*
and who does what is righteous,
who speaks the truth*y* from his heart
³ and has no slander*z* on his tongue,
who does his neighbor no wrong
and casts no slur on his fellowman,
⁴who despises a vile man
but honors*a* those who fear the
LORD,
who keeps his oath*b*
even when it hurts,
⁵who lends his money without usury*c*
and does not accept a bribe*d* against
the innocent.

He who does these things
will never be shaken.*e*

S 1Sa 8:3; Ac 24:26 *e*S Job 29:18; Ps 21:7; 112:6; Ac 2:25;
Heb 12:28; 2Pe 1:10

a 1 The Hebrew words rendered *fool* in Psalms denote
one who is morally deficient.

13:6 See note on 7:17.
Ps 14 A testimony concerning the folly of evil men. This
psalm has many links with Ps 10; 12. It shares the view of Ps
11 that the righteous Lord is on the throne, and it stands in
contrast with Ps 15, which describes those who are acceptable to God. Ps 53 is a somewhat revised duplicate of this
psalm.
14 title *For the director of music.* See note on Ps 4 title.
14:1–3 Characterization of the wicked. For Paul's use of
these verses in a different context see Ro 3:10–12.
14:1 Not intended as a definition of the "fool"; see previous note and NIV text note. *says.* See note on 3:2. *heart.* See
note on 4:7. *no God.* A practical atheism (see 10:4,6,11,13;
36:1; see also note on 10:4). *no one who does good.*
Mankind in general is corrupt. Here the reference is to those
who take no account of God and do not hesitate to show
their malice toward "the company of the righteous" (see vv.
4–5)—as in 9:19–20; 10:2–11,13,18; 12:1–4,7–8 (this is
also the situation that Ps 11 describes). Elsewhere the psalmists included themselves among those who are not righteous in God's eyes (see 130:3; 143:2; see also 1Ki 8:46; Job
9:2; Ecc 7:20).
14:2 *The LORD.* Emphatically contrasted with "the fool" (v.
1). *who seek God.* Those who truly seek God are described
in Ps 15.
14:3 *turned aside.* From God and goodness.
14:4–6 The folly of the wicked exposed.
14:4 *devour . . . do not call on the LORD.* Renewed characterization of the wicked: They live by the violence of their
own hands and do not rely on the Lord (see 10:2–4).

14:5 Even God's mighty defense of the righteous teaches
them nothing. *righteous.* See note on 1:5.
14:6 *poor.* God's people as the victims of injustice. *refuge.*
See note on 4:1.
14:7 The psalmist longs for Israel's complete deliverance
from her enemies—which will come when God deals with
the wicked in defense of their victims. For a similar expansion of scope see 10:16–18 and note. *Zion.* See note on
9:11. *Jacob . . . Israel.* Synonyms (see Ge 32:28).
Ps 15 Instruction to those who wish to have access to God
at his temple (see 24:3–6; Isa 33:14–16). See also introduction to Ps 14.
15:1 *dwell . . . live on.* Not as a priest but as God's guest in
his holy, royal house, the temple (see 23:6; 27:4–6; 61:4;
84:10; 2Sa 12:20). *holy hill.* See note on 2:6.
15:2–5 Not sacrifices or ritual purity (as among the religions of the ancient Near East) but moral righteousness gives
access to the Lord, the God of Israel (see the basic covenantal
law: Ex 20:1–17; see also Isa 1:10–17; 33:14–16;
58:6–10; Jer 7:2–7; Eze 18:5–9; Hos 6:6; Am 5:14–15,
21–24; Mic 6:6–8; Zec 7:9–10; 8:16–17).
15:2 *blameless.* See Ge 17:1 and note. *righteous.* See note
on 1:5. *heart.* See note on 4:7.
15:3 *tongue.* See note on 5:9.
15:4 *those who fear the LORD.* Those who honor God and
order their lives in accordance with his will (see note on Ge
20:11) because of their reverence for him.
15:5 *usury.* See note on Ex 22:25–27. *be shaken.* See note
on 10:6.

Psalm 16

A *miktam*b of David.

[1] Keep me safe,f O God,
for in you I take refuge.g

[2] I said to the LORD, "You are my Lord;h
apart from you I have no good
thing."i

[3] As for the saintsj who are in the land,k
they are the glorious ones in whom is
all my delight.c

[4] The sorrowsl of those will increase
who run after other gods.m
I will not pour out their libations of
blood
or take up their namesn on my lips.

[5] LORD, you have assigned me my
portiono and my cup;p
you have made my lotq secure.

[6] The boundary linesr have fallen for me
in pleasant places;
surely I have a delightful
inheritance.s

[7] I will praise the LORD, who counsels
me;t
even at nightu my heart instructs me.

[8] I have set the LORD always before me.
Because he is at my right hand,v

16:1 /S Ps 12:7
gPs 2:12
16:2 hPs 31:14;
118:28; 140:6
iPs 73:25
16:3 /Dt 33:3;
Ps 30:4; 85:8;
Da 7:18; Ac 9:13;
Ro 1:7 kPs 101:6
16:4 lPs 32:10;
Pr 23:29
mEx 18:11; 20:3;
S Dt 8:19;
S 31:20
nS Ex 23:13
16:5 oS Lev 2:2
pPs 23:5; 75:8;
116:13;
Isa 51:17;
La 4:21;
Eze 23:32-34;
Hab 2:16
qS Job 31:2
16:6 rS Dt 19:14;
Ps 104:9; Pr 8:29;
Jer 5:22
sS Job 22:26
16:7 tPs 73:24;
Pr 15:22; Isa 11:2
uJob 35:10;
Ps 42:8; 77:6
16:8 v1Ki 2:19;
1Ch 6:39;
Ps 73:23

wPs 15:5
16:9 xPs 4:7;
13:5; 28:7; 30:11
yS Dt 33:28
16:10
zS Nu 16:30;
Ps 30:3; 31:17;
86:13; Hos 13:14
aS 2Ki 19:22
**bS Job 17:14;
Ac 2:31; 13:35*

I will not be shaken.w

[9] Therefore my heart is gladx and my
tongue rejoices;
my body also will rest secure,y

[10] because you will not abandon me to the
grave,d z
nor will you let your Holy Onee a see
decay.b

[11] You have madef known to me the path
of life;c
you will fill me with joy in your
presence,d
with eternal pleasurese at your right
hand.f

Psalm 17

A prayer of David.

[1] Hear,g O LORD, my righteous plea;
listen to my cry.h
Give eari to my prayer—
it does not rise from deceitful lips.j

16:11 cPs 139:24; Mt 7:14 dAc 2:25-28* ePs 21:6 fPs 80:17
17:1 gPs 30:10; 64:1; 80:1; 140:6 hPs 5:2; 39:12; 142:6;
143:1 iS Ps 5:1 /Isa 29:13

bTitle: Probably a literary or musical term   c3 Or As
for the pagan priests who are in the land / and the
nobles in whom all delight, I said: d10 Hebrew Sheol
e10 Or your faithful one   f11 Or You will make

Ps 16 A prayer for safekeeping (the petition element in
prayer psalms is often relatively short; see 3:7; 22:19–21;
44:23–26), pleading for the Lord's protection against the
threat of death. It could also be called a psalm of trust.
16 title *miktam*. The term remains unexplained, though it
always stands in the superscription of Davidic prayers occasioned by great danger (see Ps 56–60).
16:1 The petition and the basis for it. The rest of the psalm
elaborates on the latter element.
16:2–4 The Lord is David's one and only good thing (see
73:25,28); David will have nothing to do with the counterfeit gods to whom others pour out their libations (see 4:2).
16:3 See Ps 101.
16:4 *sorrows . . . will increase*. In contrast with David's
good "portion" (v. 5; see note on 11:6), which affords him
much joy (see 73:18–20). *libations of blood*. Blood of sacrifices poured on altars. *take up their names*. Appeal to or
worship them (see Jos 23:7).
16:5–6 Joy over the inheritance received from the Lord.
David refers to what the Lord bestowed on his people in the
promised land, either to the gift of fields there (see Nu 16:14)
or to the Lord himself (as in 73:26; 119:57; 142:5; La
3:24), who was the inheritance of the priests (see Nu 18:20)
and the Levites (see Dt 10:9).
16:5 *cup*. A metaphor referring to what the host offers his
guests to drink. To the godly the Lord offers a cup of blessings
(see 23:5) or salvation (see 116:13); he makes the wicked
drink from a cup of wrath (see Jer 25:15; Rev 14:10; 16:19).
secure. Just as each Israelite's family inheritance in the
promised land was to be secure (see Lev 25; Nu 36:7).
16:7–8 Praise of the Lord who counsels and keeps.
16:7 *counsels*. Shows the way that leads to life (see v. 11).
heart. Lit. "kidneys" (see note on 7:9).
16:8 *he is at my right hand*. As sustainer and protector (see
73:23; 109:31; 110:5; 121:5); complemented by the refer-

---

ence to the Lord's right hand in v. 11. *not be shaken*. See
note on 10:6.
16:9–11 Describes the joy of total security. David speaks
here, as in the rest of his psalms, first of all of himself and of
the life he now enjoys by the gracious provision and care of
God. The Lord, in whom the psalmist takes refuge, wills life
for him (hence he made known to him the path of life, v. 11)
and will not abandon him to the grave, even though "flesh
and . . . heart . . . fail" (73:26). But implicit in these words of
assurance (if not actually explicit) is the confidence that, with
the Lord as his refuge, even the grave cannot rob him of life
(see 17:15; 73:24; see also note on 11:7). If this could be
said of David, how much more of David's promised Son! So
Peter quotes vv. 8–11 and declares that with these words
David prophesied of Christ and his resurrection (Ac
2:25–28; see Paul's similar use of v. 10b in Ac 13:35). See
also note on 6:5.
16:9 *heart*. See note on 4:7. *tongue*. Lit. "glory" (see note
on 7:5).
16:10 *Holy One*. Hebrew *hasid* (see note on 4:3). Reference is first of all to David (hence the NIV text note; see
also note on 2:2), but the psalm is ultimately fulfilled in
Christ.
16:11 *path of life*. See Pr 15:24. *your right hand*. See note
on v. 8.
Ps 17 The psalmist appeals to the Lord as Judge, when
under attack by ungodly foes. The psalm reflects many of the
Hebrew conventions of lodging a judicial appeal before the
king.
17 title *A prayer*. See titles of Ps 86; 90; 102; 142; see also
72:20.
17:1–2 The initial appeal for justice.
17:1 *my righteous plea*. His case is truly just, not a clever
misrepresentation by deceitful lips (for a similar situation see
1Sa 24:15).

²May my vindication^k come from you;
   may your eyes see what is right. ^l

³Though you probe my heart^m and
      examine me at night,
   though you test me,ⁿ you will find
      nothing;^o
   I have resolved that my mouth will
      not sin.^p
⁴As for the deeds of men—
   by the word of your lips
   I have kept myself
      from the ways of the violent.
⁵My steps have held to your paths;^q
   my feet have not slipped.^r

⁶I call on you, O God, for you will
      answer me;^s
   give ear to me^t and hear my
      prayer.^u
⁷Show the wonder of your great love,^v
   you who save by your right hand^w
   those who take refuge^x in you from
      their foes.

⁸Keep me^y as the apple of your eye;^z
   hide me^a in the shadow of your
      wings^b
⁹from the wicked who assail me,
   from my mortal enemies who
      surround me.^c

¹⁰They close up their callous hearts,^d
   and their mouths speak with
      arrogance.^e
¹¹They have tracked me down, they now
      surround me,^f
   with eyes alert, to throw me to the
      ground.

¹²They are like a lion^g hungry for prey,^h
   like a great lion crouching in cover.

¹³Rise up,ⁱ O Lord, confront them, bring
      them down;^j
   rescue me from the wicked by your
      sword.
¹⁴O Lord, by your hand save me from
      such men,
   from men of this world^k whose
      reward is in this life. ^l

You still the hunger of those you
      cherish;
   their sons have plenty,
   and they store up wealth^m for their
      children.
¹⁵And I—in righteousness I will see your
      face;
   when I awake,ⁿ I will be satisfied
      with seeing your likeness.^o

Psalm 18

18:Title–50pp — 2Sa 22:1–51

For the director of music. Of David the
servant of the Lord. He sang to the Lord
the words of this song when the Lord
delivered him from the hand of all his
enemies and from the hand of Saul.
He said:

¹I love you, O Lord, my strength.^p
²The Lord is my rock,^q my fortress^r
   and my deliverer;^s

Cross references (center column)

17:2 ^kPs 24:5;
26:1; Isa 46:13;
50:8-9; 54:17
^lPs 99:4
17:3 ^mPs 139:1;
Jer 12:3
ⁿS Job 7:18
^oJob 23:10;
Jer 50:20
^pPs 39:1
17:5 ^qJob 23:11;
Ps 44:18;
119:133
^rDt 32:35;
Ps 73:2; 121:3
17:6 ^sPs 86:7
^tPs 116:2
^uS Ps 4:1
17:7 ^vPs 31:21;
69:13; 106:45;
107:43; 117:2
^wPs 10:12
^xPs 2:12
17:8 ^yS Nu 6:24
^zS Dt 32:10;
Pr 7:2 ^aPs 27:5;
31:20; 32:7
^bRu 2:12;
Ps 36:7; 63:7;
Isa 34:15
17:9 ^cPs 109:3
17:10 ^dPs 73:7;
119:70; Isa 6:10
^eS 1Sa 2:3
17:11 ^fPs 88:17

17:12 ^gPs 7:2;
Jer 5:6; 12:8;
La 3:10
^hS Ge 49:9
17:13
ⁱS Nu 10:35
^jPs 35:8; 55:23;
73:18
17:14 ^kLk 16:8
^lPs 49:17;
Lk 16:25
^mIsa 2:7; 57:17
17:15 ⁿS Ps 3:5
^oS Nu 12:8;
S Mt 5:8; 1Jn 3:2
18:1 ^pS Ex 15:2;
S Dt 33:29;
S 1Sa 2:10;
Ps 22:19; 28:7;
59:9; 81:1;
Isa 12:2; 49:5;

Jer 16:19 18:2 ^qS Ex 33:22 ^rPs 28:8; 31:2,3; Isa 17:10;
Jer 16:19 ^sPs 40:17

17:3–5 David's claim of innocence in support of the right-ness of his case. He is not guilty of the ungodly ways of his attackers—let God examine him (cf. 139:23–24).
17:3 *heart.* See note on 4:7.
17:4 *word of your lips.* God's revealed will, by which he has made known the "paths" (v. 5) that people are to walk.
17:6–9 The petition: what the Lord is to do for him—motivated by David's trust in him ("for you will an-swer me," v. 6) and the Lord's unfailing righteousness (see v. 7).
17:7 *wonder.* See note on 9:1. *great love.* See note on 6:4.
17:8 *apple of your eye.* See note on Dt 32:10. *shadow.* A conventional Hebrew metaphor for protection against op-pression—as shade protects from the oppressive heat of the hot desert sun. Kings were spoken of as the "shade" of those dependent on them for protection (as in Nu 14:9, "protec-tion"—lit. "shade"; La 4:20; Eze 31:6,12,17). Similarly, the Lord is the protective "shade" of his people (see 91:1; 121:5; Isa 25:4; 49:2; 51:16). *wings.* Metaphor for the protective outreach of God's power (see 36:7; 57:1; 61:4; 63:7; 91:4; Ru 2:12; see also Mt 23:37).
17:10–12 The accusation lodged against the vicious ad-versaries (see note on 5:9–10).
17:10 *mouths.* See note on 5:9. *speak with arrogance.* See note on 10:11.
17:12 *lion.* See note on 7:2.
17:13–14a Petition: how the Lord is to deal with the two

parties in the conflict.
17:13 *Rise up.* See note on 3:7. *bring them down.* See note on 5:10.
17:14 *such men.* See 9:19–20; 10:18; 12:1–4,8; 14:1–3.
17:14b–15 Concluding confession of confidence (see note on 3:8).
17:15 *in righteousness.* The righteous Judge (see note on 4:1) will acknowledge and vindicate the innocence (right-eousness) of the petitioner. *see your face.* See note on 11:7. *when I awake.* From the night of death (see note on 11:7)—in radical contrast to the destiny of the "men of this world" (v. 14; see notes on 6:5; 16:9–11). *seeing your likeness.* As Moses the servant of the Lord had seen it (see Nu 12:8).
Ps 18 This song of David occurs also (with minor varia-tions) in 2Sa 22 (see notes there). In its structure, apart from the introduction (vv. 1–3) and the conclusion (vv. 46–50), the song is composed of three major divisions: (1) the Lord's deliverance of David from his mortal enemies (vv. 4–19); (2) the moral grounds for the Lord's saving help (vv. 20–29); (3) the Lord's help recounted (vv. 30–45).
18 title *For the director of music.* See note on Ps 4 title. *servant of the Lord.* See 78:70; 89:3,20,39; 132:10; 144:10. The title designates David in his royal office as, in effect, an official in the Lord's own kingly rule over his people (see 2Sa 7:5)—as were Moses (see Ex 14:31 and note), Joshua (see Jos 24:29) and the prophets (Elijah, 2Ki 9:36;

my God is my rock, in whom I take
    refuge.ᵗ
He is my shieldᵘ and the hornᵍ of
    my salvation,ᵛ my stronghold.
³I call to the LORD, who is worthy of
    praise,ʷ
and I am saved from my enemies.ˣ

⁴The cords of deathʸ entangled me;
    the torrentsᶻ of destruction
        overwhelmed me.
⁵The cords of the graveʰ coiled around
    me;
    the snares of deathᵃ confronted me.
⁶In my distressᵇ I called to the LORD;ᶜ
    I cried to my God for help.
From his temple he heard my voice;ᵈ
    my cry cameᵉ before him, into his
        ears.

⁷The earth trembledᶠ and quaked,ᵍ
    and the foundations of the mountains
        shook;ʰ
    they trembled because he was
        angry.ⁱ
⁸Smoke rose from his nostrils;ʲ
    consuming fireᵏ came from his
        mouth,
    burning coalsˡ blazed out of it.
⁹He parted the heavens and came
    down;ᵐ
    dark cloudsⁿ were under his feet.
¹⁰He mounted the cherubimᵒ and flew;
    he soaredᵖ on the wings of the
        wind.ᑫ
¹¹He made darkness his covering,ʳ his
    canopyˢ around him—
    the dark rain clouds of the sky.

¹²Out of the brightness of his presenceᵗ
    clouds advanced,
    with hailstonesᵘ and bolts of
        lightning.ᵛ
¹³The LORD thunderedʷ from heaven;
    the voice of the Most High
        resounded.ⁱ
¹⁴He shot his arrowsˣ and scattered ˍthe
    enemies,
    great bolts of lightningʸ and routed
        them.ᶻ
¹⁵The valleys of the sea were exposed
    and the foundationsᵃ of the earth laid
        bare
    at your rebuke,ᵇ O LORD,
    at the blast of breath from your
        nostrils.ᶜ

¹⁶He reached down from on high and
    took hold of me;
    he drew me out of deep waters.ᵈ
¹⁷He rescued me from my powerful
    enemy,ᵉ
    from my foes, who were too strong
        for me.ᶠ
¹⁸They confronted me in the day of my
    disaster,ᵍ
    but the LORD was my support.ʰ
¹⁹He brought me out into a spacious
    place;ⁱ

Cross references (center column):

18:2 ʳPs 2:12; 9:9; 94:22
ᵘS Ge 15:1; Ps 28:7; 84:9; 119:114; 144:2
ᵛS 1Sa 2:1; S Lk 1:69
18:3 ʷS 1Ch 16:25
ˣS Ps 9:13
18:4 ʸPs 116:3
ᶻPs 93:4; 124:4; Isa 5:30; 17:12; Jer 6:23; 51:42, 55; Eze 43:2
18:5 ᵃPr 13:14
18:6 ᵇS Dt 4:30
ᶜPs 30:2; 99:6; 102:2; 120:1
ᵈPs 66:19; 116:1
ᵉS Job 16:18
18:7 ᶠPs 97:4; Isa 5:25; 64:3
ᵍS Jdg 5:4
ʰS Jdg 5:5
ⁱS Job 9:5; Jer 10:10
18:8 ʲS Job 41:20
ᵏS Ex 15:7; S 19:18; S Job 41:21; Ps 50:3; 97:3; Da 7:10
ˡPr 25:22; Ro 12:20
18:9 ᵐS Ge 11:5; S Ps 57:3
ⁿS Ex 20:21; S Dt 33:26; S Ps 104:3
18:10 ᵒS Ge 3:24; Eze 10:18
ᵖS Dt 33:26
ᑫPs 104:3
18:11 ʳS Ex 19:9; S Dt 4:11
ˢS Job 22:14; Isa 4:5; Jer 43:10
18:12 ᵗPs 104:2
ᵘS Jos 10:11
ᵛS Job 36:30
18:13 ʷS Ex 9:23; S 1Sa 2:10
18:14 ˣS Dt 32:23
ʸS Job 36:30;
Rev 4:5 ᶻS Jdg 4:15 18:15 ᵃS Ps 11:3 ᵇPs 76:6; 104:7; 106:9; Isa 50:2 ᶜS Ex 15:8 18:16 ᵈEx 15:5; Ps 69:2; Pr 18:4; 20:5 18:17 ᵉver 48; Ps 38:19; 59:1; 143:9 ᶠS Jdg 18:26 18:18 ᵍPr 1:27; 16:4; Jer 17:17; 40:2; Ob 1:13 ʰPs 20:2; Isa 3:1 18:19 ⁱPr 31:8

g.2 *Horn* here symbolizes strength.   **h.5** Hebrew *Sheol*
i.13 Some Hebrew manuscripts and Septuagint (see also 2
Samuel 22:14); most Hebrew manuscripts *resounded, /
amid hailstones and bolts of lightning*

Jonah, 2Ki 14:25; Isaiah, Isa 20:3; Daniel, Da 6:20). *song.*
See note on Ps 30 title. *when the LORD delivered him.* It is
possible that David composed his song shortly after his victories over his foreign enemies (2Sa 8:1–14), but it may have
been later in his life.
18:1–3 A prelude of praise.
18:1 Does not occur in 2Sa 22. *I love you.* From an unusual
Hebrew expression that emphasizes the fervor of David's
love.
18:2 *rock . . . rock.* The translation of two different Hebrew
words. "Rock" is a common poetic figure for God (or the
gods: Dt 32:31,37; Isa 44:8), symbolizing his unfailing (see
Isa 26:4) strength as a fortress refuge (see vv. 31,46;
31:2–3; 42:9; 62:7; 71:3; 94:22; Isa 17:10) or as deliverer
(see 19:14; 62:2; 78:35; 89:26; 95:1; Dt 32:15). It is a
figure particularly appropriate for David's experience (see
1Sa 23:14,25; 24:2,22; 26:20), for the Lord was his true
security. *fortress.* See note on 2Sa 22:2. *shield.* See note on
3:3. *horn.* See NIV text note; Dt 33:17; Jer 48:25.
18:4–6 God heard his cry for help.
18:4–5 David depicts his experiences in poetic figures of
mortal danger.
18:4 *cords.* 2Sa 22:5 has "waves." *torrents of destruction.*
See note on 30:1.
18:5 *cords of the grave . . . snares of death.* See 116:3. He
had, as it were, been snared by death (personified) and

bound as a prisoner of the grave (see Job 36:8).
18:6 *temple.* God's heavenly abode, where he sits enthroned (see 11:4; 113:5; Isa 6:1; 40:22).
18:7–15 The Lord came to the aid of his servant
—depicted as a fearful theophany (divine manifestation)
of the heavenly Warrior descending in wrathful attack upon
David's enemies (see 5:4–5; 68:1–8; 77:16–19; Mic
1:3–4; Na 1:2–6; Hab 3:3–15). He sweeps down upon
them like a fierce thunderstorm (see Jos 10:11; Jdg
5:20–22; 1Sa 2:10; 7:10; 2Sa 5:24; Isa 29:6).
18:8 God's fierce majesty is portrayed in terms similar to
those applied to the awesome leviathan (Job 41:19–21).
18:9 *parted the heavens and came down.* See Isa 64:1 and
note.
18:10 *cherubim.* Symbols of royalty (see 80:1; 99:1; see
also notes on Ge 3:24; Ex 25:18). In Eze 1; 10, cherubim
appear as the bearers of the throne-chariot of God.
18:13 *voice.* For thunder as the voice of God see Ps 29; Job
37:2–5. *Most High.* See note on Ge 14:19.
18:14 *arrows.* For shafts of lightning as the arrows of God
see 77:17; 144:6; Hab 3:11.
18:15 Perhaps recalls the great deed of the heavenly Warrior when he defeated Israel's enemy at the Red Sea (see Ex
15:1–12).
18:16–19 The deliverance.
18:16 *deep waters.* See note on 32:6.

he rescued me because he delighted in me.ⁱ

²⁰The LORD has dealt with me according to my righteousness;^k
according to the cleanness of my hands^l he has rewarded me.^m
²¹For I have kept the ways of the LORD;ⁿ
I have not done evil by turning^o from my God.
²²All his laws are before me;^p
I have not turned away from his decrees.
²³I have been blameless^q before him and have kept myself from sin.
²⁴The LORD has rewarded me according to my righteousness,^r
according to the cleanness of my hands in his sight.

²⁵To the faithful^s you show yourself faithful,^t
to the blameless you show yourself blameless,
²⁶to the pure^u you show yourself pure,
but to the crooked you show yourself shrewd.^v
²⁷You save the humble^w
but bring low those whose eyes are haughty.^x
²⁸You, O LORD, keep my lamp^y burning;
my God turns my darkness into light.^z
²⁹With your help^a I can advance against a troop^j;
with my God I can scale a wall.

³⁰As for God, his way is perfect;^b
the word of the LORD is flawless.^c
He is a shield^d
for all who take refuge^e in him.
³¹For who is God besides the LORD?^f

And who is the Rock^g except our God?
³²It is God who arms me with strength^h
and makes my way perfect.ⁱ
³³He makes my feet like the feet of a deer;^j
he enables me to stand on the heights.^k
³⁴He trains my hands for battle;^l
my arms can bend a bow of bronze.
³⁵You give me your shield of victory,
and your right hand sustains^m me;
you stoop down to make me great.
³⁶You broaden the pathⁿ beneath me,
so that my ankles do not turn.^o
³⁷I pursued my enemies^p and overtook them;
I did not turn back till they were destroyed.
³⁸I crushed them^q so that they could not rise;^r
they fell beneath my feet.^s
³⁹You armed me with strength^t for battle;
you made my adversaries bow^u at my feet.
⁴⁰You made my enemies turn their backs^v in flight,
and I destroyed^w my foes.
⁴¹They cried for help, but there was no one to save them^x—
to the LORD, but he did not answer.^y

Cross references (center column):

18:19 /S Nu 14:8
18:20 ^kS 1Sa 26:23 /Job 22:30; Ps 24:4 ^mS Ru 2:12; S 2Ch 15:7; 1Co 3:8
18:21 ⁿ2Ch 34:33; Ps 37:34; 119:2; Pr 8:32; 23:26 ^oPs 119:102
18:22 ^pPs 119:30
18:23 ^qS Ge 6:9
18:24 ^rS 1Sa 26:23
18:25 ^sPs 31:23; 37:28; 50:5; Pr 2:8 ^tPs 25:10; 40:11; 89:24; 146:6
18:26 ^uPr 15:26; Mt 5:8; Php 1:10; 1Ti 5:22; Tit 1:15; 1Jn 3:3 ^vPr 3:34; Mt 10:16; Lk 16:8
18:27 ^wS 2Ch 33:23; S Mt 23:12 ^xS Job 41:34; S Ps 10:5; Pr 3:33-34
18:28 ^y1Ki 11:36; Ps 132:17 ^zJob 29:3; Ps 97:11; 112:4; Jn 1:5; S Ac 26:18; 2Co 4:6; 2Pe 1:19
18:29 ^aver 32, 39; Isa 45:5; Heb 11:34
18:30 ^bS Dt 32:4 ^cS Ps 12:6; Pr 30:5 ^dPs 3:3 ^ePs 2:12
18:31 ^fS Dt 4:35; 32:39; Ps 35:10; 86:8; 89:6; Isa 44:6,8; 45:5, 6,14,18,21; 46:9
18:32 ^gS Ge 49:24 ^hS ver 29; 1Pe 5:10
18:33 ⁱS Ps 15:2; 19:13; Heb 10:14; Jas 3:2 ^jPs 42:1; Pr 5:19; Isa 35:6

Hab 3:19 ^kS Dt 32:13 18:34 ^lPs 144:1 18:35 ^mPs 3:5; 37:5, 17; 41:3; 51:12; 54:4; 55:22; 119:116; Isa 41:4,10,13; 43:2; 46:4 18:36 ⁿPs 31:8 ^oS Job 18:7; Ps 66:9 18:37 ^pS Lev 26:7 18:38 ^qPs 68:21; 110:6 ^rPs 36:12; 140:10; Isa 26:14 ^sPs 47:3 18:39 ^tver 32; Isa 45:5,24 ^uver 47; Ps 47:3; 144:2 18:40 ^vS Jos 7:12 ^wver 37 18:41 ^xS 2Ki 14:26; Ps 50:22 ^yS 1Sa 8:18; S 14:37; Jer 11:11

j29 Or can run through a barricade

18:19 *spacious place.* See 4:1 and note; where he is free to roam unconfined by the threats and dangers that had hemmed him in (vv. 4-6,16-18). To be afflicted or oppressed is like being bound by fetters (Job 36:8,13). To be delivered is to be set free (Job 36:16). *delighted in me.* God was pleased with David as "a man after his own heart" (1Sa 13:14; see also 1Sa 15:28; 1Ki 14:8; 15:5), a man with whom he had made a covenant assuring him of an enduring dynasty (2Sa 7). The thought is further elaborated in vv. 20-29.
18:20-24 David's righteousness rewarded. David's assertion of his righteousness (like that of Samuel, 1Sa 12:3; Hezekiah, 2Ki 20:3; Job, Job 13:23; 27:6; 31; see also Ps 17:3-5; 26; 44:17-18; 101) is not a pretentious boast of sinless perfection (see 51:5). Rather, it is a claim that, in contrast to his enemies, he has devoted himself heart and life to the service of the Lord, that his has been a godliness with integrity—itself the fruit of God's gracious working in his heart (see 51:10-12).
18:20,24 *my righteousness.* See note on 1:5. *rewarded me.* As a king benevolently rewards those who loyally serve him.

18:21 *ways of the LORD.* See 25:4 and note.
18:25-29 Because God responds to man in kind (see Job 34:1; Pr 3:34), David has experienced the Lord's favor.
18:26 *crooked.* Deviating from the straight path of truth and righteousness. *shrewd.* God responds to his perverse dealings thrust for thrust, like a wrestler countering his opponent.
18:27 The thought of this verse fits well with David's and Saul's reversals of status. It also echoes the central theme of Hannah's song, which the author of Samuel uses to highlight a major thesis of his account of the ways of God as he brings about his kingdom.
18:28 *keep my lamp burning.* God causes his life and undertakings to flourish (see especially Job 18:5-6; 21:17). *light.* See note on 27:1.
18:30-36 By God's blessing David the king has thrived.
18:30 *is perfect.* Does not fail—and so, because of his blessing, David's way has not failed (see v. 32). *word of the LORD.* While the reference is general, it applies especially to God's promise to David (see 2Sa 7:8-11). *flawless.* See note on 12:6. *shield.* See note on 3:3.
18:37-42 With God's help David has crushed all his foes.

⁴²I beat them as fine as dust *z* borne on
the wind;
I poured them out like mud in the
streets.

⁴³You have delivered me from the attacks
of the people;
you have made me the head of
nations; *a*
people I did not know *b* are subject to
me.
⁴⁴As soon as they hear me, they obey me;
foreigners *c* cringe before me.
⁴⁵They all lose heart; *d*
they come trembling *e* from their
strongholds. *f*

⁴⁶The LORD lives! *g* Praise be to my
Rock! *h*
Exalted be God *i* my Savior! *j*
⁴⁷He is the God who avenges *k* me,
who subdues nations *l* under me,
⁴⁸ who saves *m* me from my enemies. *n*
You exalted me above my foes;
from violent men *o* you rescued me.
⁴⁹Therefore I will praise you among the
nations, *p* O LORD;
I will sing *q* praises to your name. *r*
⁵⁰He gives his king great victories;
he shows unfailing kindness to his
anointed, *s*
to David *t* and his descendants
forever. *u*

Psalm 19

For the director of music.
A psalm of David.

¹The heavens *v* declare *w* the glory of
God; *x*
the skies *y* proclaim the work of his
hands. *z*
²Day after day they pour forth speech;
night after night they display
knowledge. *a*
³There is no speech or language
where their voice is not heard. *k*
⁴Their voice *l* goes out into all the earth,
their words to the ends of the
world. *b*

In the heavens he has pitched a tent *c*
for the sun, *d*
⁵ which is like a bridegroom *e* coming
forth from his pavilion, *f*
like a champion *g* rejoicing to run his
course.
⁶It rises at one end of the heavens *h*
and makes its circuit to the other; *i*
nothing is hidden from its heat.

⁷The law of the LORD *j* is perfect, *k*
reviving the soul. *l*

18:42 *z* S Dt 9:21;
S Isa 2:22
18:43
a 2Sa 8:1-14
b Isa 55:5
18:44 *c* Ps 54:3;
144:7,11;
Isa 25:5
18:45
d S 1Sa 17:32;
2Co 4:1;
Heb 12:3
e Isa 66:2;
Hos 3:5; 11:10
f Ps 9:9; Mic 7:17
18:46
g S Jos 3:10;
S 1Sa 14:39;
2Co 13:4 *h* ver
31; Ex 33:22
i Ps 21:13; 35:27;
40:16; 108:5
j S 1Ch 16:35;
S Lk 1:47
18:47 *k* S Ge 4:24
l S ver 39;
S Jdg 4:23
18:48 *m* Ps 7:10;
37:40; Da 3:17
n S ver 17
o Ps 140:1
18:49 *p* S Ps 9:11
q Ps 7:17; 9:2;
101:1; 108:1;
146:2 *r* Ro 15:9*
18:50
s S 2Sa 23:1
t Ps 144:10
u Ps 89:4

19:1 *v* Ps 89:5;
Isa 40:22
w Ps 50:6; 148:3;
Ro 1:19 *x* Ps 4:2;
8:1; 97:6; Isa 6:3
y S Ge 1:8
z S Ps 8:6;
S 103:22
19:2 *a* Ps 74:16
19:4 *b* Ro 10:18*
c S Job 36:29;
Ps 104:2
d S Jdg 5:31
19:5 *e* Joel 2:16
f S Job 36:29
g 1Sa 17:4

19:6 *h* Dt 30:4 *i* Ps 113:3; Ecc 1:5 **19:7** *j* S Ps 1:2
k Ps 119:142; Jas 1:25 *l* Ps 23:3

k 3 Or *They have no speech, there are no words;* / *no
sound is heard from them*   *l* 4 Septuagint, Jerome and
Syriac; Hebrew *line*

18:43–45 God has made David the head of nations (see
2Sa 5; 8; 10)—he who had been, it seemed, on the brink of
death (see vv. 4–5), sinking into the depths (see v. 16).
18:43 *attacks of the people.* All the threats he had endured
from his own people in the days of Saul, and perhaps also in
the time of Absalom's rebellion. *people I did not know.*
Those with whom he had had no previous relations.
18:46–50 Concluding doxology.
18:46 *The LORD lives!* God's interventions and blessings in
David's behalf have shown him to be the living God (see Dt
5:26).
18:47 *avenges me.* Redresses the wrongs committed
against me (see Dt 32:41).
18:49 David vows to praise the Lord among the nations
(see note on 9:1). *name.* See note on 5:11.
18:50 *his king . . . his anointed.* David views himself as the
Lord's chosen and anointed king (see 1Sa 16:13; see also
notes on 1Sa 10:25; 12:14–15). *shows unfailing kindness.*
David's final words recall the Lord's covenant with him (see
2Sa 7:8–16). The whole song is to be understood in the
context of David's official capacity and the Lord's covenant
with him. What David claims in this grand conclusion—as,
indeed, in the whole psalm—has been and is being fulfilled
in Jesus Christ, David's great descendant.
Ps 19 A hymn extolling "the glory of God" (v. 1) as
revealed to all by the starry heavens (see vv. 1–6) and "the
law of the LORD" (v. 7), which has been given to Israel (see
vv. 7–13). Placed next to Ps 18, it completes the cycle of

praise—for the Lord's saving acts, for his glory reflected in
creation and for his law.
19 title *For the director of music.* See note on Ps 4 title.
19:1–4a The silent heavens speak, declaring the glory of
their Maker to all who are on the earth (see 148:3). The
heavenly lights are not divine (see Dt 4:19; 17:3), nor do
they control or disclose man's destiny (see Isa 47:13; Jer
10:2; Da 4:7). Their glory testifies to the righteousness and
faithfulness of the Lord who created them (see 50:6;
89:5–8; 97:6; see also Ro 1:19–20).
19:4 Interpreting this heavenly proclamation eschatologi-
cally in the light of Christ, Paul applies this verse to the
proclamation of the gospel in his own day (see Ro 10:18). He
thus associates these two universal proclamations.
19:4b–6 The heavens are the divinely pitched "tent" for
the lordly sun—widely worshiped in the ancient Near East
(cf. Dt 4:19; 17:3; 2Ki 23:5,11; Jer 8:2; Eze 8:16), but
here, as in 136:7–8; Ge 1:16, a mere creature of God. Of the
created realm, the sun is the supreme metaphor of the glory
of God (see 84:11; Isa 60:19–20), as it makes its daily
triumphant sweep across the whole extent of the heavens
and pours out its heat (felt presence) on every creature.
19:7–9 Stately, rhythmic celebration of the life-nurturing
effects of the Lord's revealed law (see Ps 119).
19:7 *the simple.* The childlike, those whose understanding
and judgment have not yet matured (see Pr 1:4). See also
119:98–100; 2Ti 3:15.

The statutes of the LORD are
      trustworthy, *m*
  making wise the simple. *n*
8The precepts of the LORD are right, *o*
  giving joy *p* to the heart.
The commands of the LORD are radiant,
  giving light to the eyes. *q*
9The fear of the LORD *r* is pure,
  enduring forever.
The ordinances of the LORD are sure
  and altogether righteous. *s*
10They are more precious than gold, *t*
  than much pure gold;
they are sweeter than honey, *u*
  than honey from the comb. *v*
11By them is your servant warned;
  in keeping them there is great
      reward.

12Who can discern his errors?
  Forgive my hidden faults. *w*
13Keep your servant also from willful
      sins; *x*
  may they not rule over me. *y*
Then will I be blameless, *z*
  innocent of great transgression.

14May the words of my mouth and the
      meditation of my heart
  be pleasing *a* in your sight,
O LORD, my Rock *b* and my
      Redeemer. *c*

Psalm 20

For the director of music.
A psalm of David.

1May the LORD answer you when you
      are in distress; *d*
  may the name of the God of Jacob *e*
      protect you. *f*

2May he send you help *g* from the
      sanctuary *h*
  and grant you support *i* from Zion. *j*
3May he remember *k* all your sacrifices
  and accept your burnt offerings. *l*
                                      Selah
4May he give you the desire of your
      heart *m*
  and make all your plans succeed. *n*
5We will shout for joy *o* when you are
      victorious
  and will lift up our banners *p* in the
      name of our God.
May the LORD grant all your requests. *q*

6Now I know that the LORD saves his
      anointed; *r*
  he answers him from his holy heaven
  with the saving power of his right
      hand. *s*
7Some trust in chariots *t* and some in
      horses, *u*
  but we trust in the name of the LORD
      our God. *v*
8They are brought to their knees and
      fall, *w*
  but we rise up *x* and stand firm. *y*

9O LORD, save the king!
  Answer *m* us *z* when we call!

Psalm 21

For the director of music.
A psalm of David.

1O LORD, the king rejoices in your
      strength. *a*

19:7 *m* Ps 93:5; 111:7; 119:138, 144 *n* S Dt 4:6; Ps 119:130
19:8 *o* Ps 33:4; 119:128 *p* Ps 119:14 *q* S Ezr 9:8; Ps 38:10
19:9 *r* Ps 34:11; 111:10; Pr 1:7; Ecc 12:13; Isa 33:6 *s* Ps 119:138
19:10 *t* S Job 22:24; Ps 119:72; Pr 8:10 *u* Ps 119:103; SS 4:11; Eze 3:3 *v* S 1Sa 14:27
19:12 *w* Ps 51:2; 90:8; Ecc 12:14
19:13 *x* S Nu 15:30 *y* Ps 119:133 *z* S Ge 6:9; S Ps 18:32
19:14 *a* Ps 104:34 *b* Ps 18:31 *c* S Ex 6:6; S Job 19:25
20:1 *d* Ps 4:1 *e* Ex 3:6; Ps 46:7, 11 *f* Ps 59:1; 69:29; 91:14
20:2 *g* Ps 30:10; 33:20; 37:40; 40:17; 54:4; 118:7 *h* S Nu 3:28 *i* S Ps 18:18 *j* Ps 2:6; 128:5; 134:3; 135:21
20:3 *k* Ac 10:4 *l* S Dt 33:11
20:4 *m* Ps 21:2; 37:4; 145:16,19; Isa 26:8; Eze 24:25; Ro 10:1 *n* Ps 140:8; Pr 16:3; Da 11:17
20:5 *o* S Job 3:7 *p* S Nu 1:52; Ps 60:4; Isa 5:26; 11:10,12; 13:2; 30:17; 49:22; 62:10; Jer 50:2; 51:12,27 *q* 1Sa 1:17
20:6 *r* S 2Sa 23:1; Ps 28:8 *s* S Job 40:14; Hab 3:13
20:7 *t* S 2Ki 19:23 *u* S Dt 17:16; Ps 33:17; 147:10; Pr 21:31; Isa 31:1; 36:8,9 *v* S 2Ch 32:8 **20:8** *w* Ps 27:2; Isa 40:30; Jer 46:6; 50:32 *x* Mic 7:8 *y* S Job 11:15; Ps 37:23; Pr 10:25; Isa 7:9 **20:9** *z* Ps 17:6 **21:1** *a* S 1Sa 2:10
m 9 Or *save!* / *O King, answer*

19:8 *heart.* See note on 4:7.
19:9 *fear of the LORD.* The sum of what the law requires (see note on 15:4).
19:10 *sweeter than honey.* By contrast, those who abandon the law turn justice into bitterness (see Am 5:7; 6:12).
19:11–13 The law marks the way that leads to life (see Dt 5:33). But man's moral consciousness remains flawed and imperfect; hence he errs without realizing it and has reason to seek pardon for hidden faults (v. 12; see Lev 5:2–4). Willful sins (v. 13), however, are open rebellion; they are the great transgression (v. 13) that leads to being cut off from God's people (see Nu 15:30–31).
19:11,13 *your servant.* The psalmist himself.
19:14 The psalmist presents this hymn as a praise offering to the Lord. *heart.* See note on 4:7. *Rock . . . Redeemer.* See 78:35. *Rock.* See notes on 18:2; Ge 49:24. *Redeemer.* See note on Ex 6:6.
Ps 20 A liturgy of prayer for the king just before he goes out to battle against a threatening force (see 2Ch 20:1–30).
20 title *For the director of music.* See note on Ps 4 title.
20:1–5 The people (perhaps his assembled army) address

the king, adding their prayers to his prayer for victory.
20:1 *answer you.* Hear your prayers, offered in the present distress, accompanied by "sacrifices" (v. 3); see v. 9. *name.* See vv. 5,7; see also note on 5:11. *Jacob.* See note on 14:7. *protect you.* Lit. "raise you to a high, secure place."
20:2 *Zion.* See note on 9:11.
20:4 *heart.* See note on 4:7.
20:5 *We will shout . . . name of our God.* See note on 7:17. *banners.* Probably the troop standards around which the units rallied.
20:6 A participant in the liturgy (perhaps a Levite; see 2Ch 20:14) announces assurance that the king's prayer will be heard. *his anointed.* The king appointed by the Lord to rule in his name (see 2:2 and note).
20:7–8 The army's confession of trust in the Lord rather than in a chariot corps (cf. 33:16–17)—the enemy perhaps came reinforced by such a prized corps. See David's similar confession of confidence when he faced Goliath (1Sa 17:45–47).
20:9 The army's concluding petition. *Answer . . . when.* See note on v. 1. The psalm ends as it began.

How great is his joy in the victories
you give! *b*

²You have granted him the desire of his
heart *c*

and have not withheld the request of
his lips.   *Selah*

³You welcomed him with rich blessings
and placed a crown of pure gold *d* on
his head. *e*

⁴He asked you for life, and you gave it to
him—

length of days, for ever and ever. *f*

⁵Through the victories *g* you gave, his
glory is great;

you have bestowed on him splendor
and majesty. *h*

⁶Surely you have granted him eternal
blessings

and made him glad with the joy *i* of
your presence. *j*

⁷For the king trusts in the LORD; *k*

through the unfailing love *l* of the
Most High *m*

he will not be shaken. *n*

⁸Your hand will lay hold *o* on all your
enemies;

your right hand will seize your foes.

⁹At the time of your appearing
you will make them like a fiery
furnace.

In his wrath the LORD will swallow
them up,

and his fire will consume them. *p*

¹⁰You will destroy their descendants from
the earth,

their posterity from mankind. *q*

¹¹Though they plot evil *r* against you
and devise wicked schemes, *s* they
cannot succeed;

¹²for you will make them turn their
backs *t*

when you aim at them with drawn
bow.

¹³Be exalted, *u* O LORD, in your
strength; *v*

we will sing and praise your might.

Psalm 22

For the director of music. To the tune of
"The Doe of the Morning."
A psalm of David.

¹My God, my God, why have you
forsaken me? *w*

Why are you so far *x* from saving me,
so far from the words of my
groaning? *y*

²O my God, I cry out by day, but you do
not answer, *z*

by night, *a* and am not silent.

Cross references (center column):

21:1 *b*S 2Sa 22:51
21:2 *c*S Ps 20:4
21:3 *d*S 2Sa 12:30; Rev 14:14 *e*Zec 6:11
21:4 *f*Ps 10:16; 45:17; 48:14; 133:3
21:5 *g*ver 1; Ps 18:50; 44:4 *h*S Ps 8:5; 45:3; 93:1; 96:6; 104:1
21:6 *i*Ps 43:4; 126:3 *j*S 1Ch 17:27
21:7 *k*S 2Ki 18:5 *l*Ps 6:4 *m*Ge 14:18 *n*S Ps 15:5; S 55:22
21:8 *o*Isa 10:10

21:9 *p*S Dt 32:22; Ps 50:3; Jer 15:14
21:10 *q*Dt 28:18
21:11 *r*Ps 2:1 *s*Job 10:3; Ps 10:2; 26:10; 37:7
21:12 *t*S Ex 23:27
21:13 *u*S Ps 18:46 *v*Ps 18:1
22:1 *w*S Job 6:15; S Ps 9:10; Mt 27:46*; Mk 15:34* *x*Ps 10:1 *y*S Job 3:24
22:2 *z*S Job 19:7 *a*Ps 42:3; 88:1

Ps 21 A psalm of praise for victories granted to the king. It is thus linked with Ps 20, but whether both were occasioned by the same events is unknown. Here the people's praise follows that of the king (see v. 1); there (Ps 20) the people's prayer was added to the king's. In its structure, the psalm is framed by vv. 1,13 ("O LORD, in your strength" is in both verses) and is centered around v. 7, which proclaims the king's trust in the Lord and the security afforded him by God's unfailing love (see Introduction: Literary Features).
21 title *For the director of music.* See note on Ps 4 title.
21:2–6 The people celebrate the Lord's many favors to the king: all "the desire of his heart" (v. 2). Verse 2 announces the theme; vv. 3–5 develop the theme; v. 6 climactically summarizes the theme.
21:2 *heart.* See note on 4:7.
21:3 *welcomed him.* Back from the battles. *placed a crown . . . on his head.* Exchanged the warrior's helmet for the ceremonial emblem of royalty—possibly the captured crown of the defeated king (see 2Sa 12:30).
21:4 The king's life has been spared—to live for ever and ever (see 1Ki 1:31; Da 2:4; 3:9; see also 1Sa 10:24; 1Ki 1:25,34,39).
21:5 *glory . . . splendor and majesty.* See 45:3; like that of his heavenly Overlord (see 96:6).
21:6 *eternal blessings.* Either (1) blessings of enduring value or (2) an unending flow of blessings. *your presence.* Your favor, which is the supreme cause of joy because it is the greatest blessing and the wellspring of all other blessings.
21:7 The center of the psalm (see note on 6:6). A participant in the liturgy (perhaps a priest or Levite) proclaims the reasons for the king's security. *LORD . . . Most High.* That is, LORD Most High (see 7:17; see also note on 3:7). *unfailing*

love. See note on 6:4. *Most High.* See note on Ge 14:19.
shaken. See note on 10:6.
21:8–12 The people hail the future victories of their triumphant king. Verse 8 announces the theme; vv. 9–11 develop the theme; v. 12 summarizes the theme.
21:9 *In his wrath the LORD.* Credits the king's victories to the Lord's wrath (see note on 2:5).
21:10 The king's royal enemies will be left no descendants to rise against him again.
21:13 Conclusion—and return to the beginning: Lord, assert your strength, in which "the king rejoices" (v. 1; see also v. 7), and we will ever praise your might.
Ps 22 The anguished prayer of David as a godly sufferer victimized by the vicious and prolonged attacks of enemies whom he has not provoked and from whom the Lord has not (yet) delivered him. It has many similarities with Ps 69, but contains no calls for redress (see note on 5:10) such as are found in 69:22–28. No other psalm fitted quite so aptly the circumstances of Jesus at his crucifixion. Hence on the cross he took it to his lips (see Mt 27:46 and parallels), and the Gospel writers, especially Matthew and John, frequently alluded to it (as they did to Ps 69) in their accounts of Christ's passion (Mt 27:35,39,43; Jn 19:23–24,28). They saw in the passion of Jesus the fulfillment of this cry of the righteous sufferer. The author of Hebrews placed the words of v. 22 on Jesus' lips (see Heb 2:12 and note). No psalm is quoted more frequently in the NT.
22 title See notes on Ps 4; 9 titles.
22:1 *why . . . ? Why . . . ?* See note on 6:3; see also Introduction: Theology.
22:1a Quoted by Jesus in Mt 27:46; Mk 15:34.

³Yet you are enthroned as the Holy
One; *b*
you are the praise *c* of Israel. *n*
⁴In you our fathers put their trust;
they trusted and you delivered
them. *d*
⁵They cried to you *e* and were saved;
in you they trusted *f* and were not
disappointed. *g*
⁶But I am a worm *h* and not a man,
scorned by men *i* and despised *j* by
the people.
⁷All who see me mock me; *k*
they hurl insults, *l* shaking their
heads: *m*
⁸"He trusts in the LORD;
let the LORD rescue him. *n*
Let him deliver him, *o*
since he delights *p* in him."
⁹Yet you brought me out of the womb; *q*
you made me trust *r* in you
even at my mother's breast.
¹⁰From birth *s* I was cast upon you;
from my mother's womb you have
been my God.
¹¹Do not be far from me, *t*
for trouble is near *u*
and there is no one to help. *v*
¹²Many bulls *w* surround me; *x*
strong bulls of Bashan *y* encircle me.
¹³Roaring lions *z* tearing their prey *a*
open their mouths wide *b* against me.
¹⁴I am poured out like water,
and all my bones are out of joint. *c*
My heart has turned to wax; *d*
it has melted away *e* within me.

¹⁵My strength is dried up like a
potsherd, *f*
and my tongue sticks to the roof of
my mouth; *g*
you lay me *o* in the dust *h* of death.
¹⁶Dogs *i* have surrounded me;
a band of evil men has encircled me,
they have pierced *p i* my hands and
my feet.
¹⁷I can count all my bones;
people stare *k* and gloat over me. *l*
¹⁸They divide my garments among them
and cast lots *m* for my clothing. *n*

¹⁹But you, O LORD, be not far off; *o*
O my Strength, *p* come quickly *q* to
help me. *r*
²⁰Deliver my life from the sword, *s*
my precious life *t* from the power of
the dogs. *u*
²¹Rescue me from the mouth of the
lions; *v*
save *q* me from the horns of the wild
oxen. *w*

²²I will declare your name to my
brothers;

22:3
b S 2Ki 19:22;
Ps 71:22;
S Mk 1:24
c S Ex 15:2;
Ps 148:14
22:4 *d* Ps 78:53;
107:6
22:5 *e* S 1Ch 5:20
/Isa 8:17; 25:9;
26:3; 30:18
g S 2Ch 13:18;
Ps 25:3; 31:17;
71:1; Isa 49:23;
Ro 9:33
22:6 *h* S Job 4:19
i S 2Sa 12:14;
Ps 31:11; 64:8;
69:19; 109:25
/Ps 119:141;
Isa 49:7; 53:3;
60:14; Mal 2:9;
Mt 16:21
22:7 *k* S Job 17:2;
Ps 35:16; 69:12;
74:18; Mt 27:41;
Mk 15:31;
Lk 23:36
/Mt 27:39,44;
Mk 15:32;
Lk 23:39
m Mk 15:29
22:8 *n* Ps 91:14
o S Ps 3:2
p S 2Sa 22:20;
S Mt 3:17; 27:43
22:9 *q* Job 10:18;
Ps 71:6 *r* Ps 78:7;
Na 1:7
22:10 *s* Ps 71:6;
Isa 46:3; 49:1
22:11 *t* ver 19;
S Ps 10:1
u S Ps 10:14
v S 2Ki 14:26;
S Isa 41:28
22:12 *w* Ps 68:30
x Ps 17:9; 27:6;
49:5; 109:3;
140:9 *y* Dt 32:14;
Isa 2:13;
Eze 27:6; 39:18;
Am 4:1
22:13 *z* ver 21;
Eze 22:25;
Zep 3:3
a S Ge 49:9
b La 3:46

22:14 *c* S Ps 6:2 *d* Job 23:16; Ps 68:2; 97:5; Mic 1:4 *e* Jos 7:5;
Ps 107:26; Da 5:6 **22:15** /Isa 45:9 *g* Ps 137:6; La 4:4;
Eze 3:26; Jn 19:28 *h* S Job 7:21; Ps 104:29 **22:16** *i* Php 3:2
/Isa 51:9; 53:5; Zec 12:10; Jn 20:25 **22:17** *k* Lk 23:35
/Ps 25:2; 30:1; 35:19; 38:16; La 2:17; Mic 7:8 **22:18**
m S Lev 16:8; Mt 27:35*; Mk 15:24; Lk 23:34; Jn 19:24*
n Mk 9:12 **22:19** *o* S ver 11 *p* S Ps 18:1 *q* Ps 38:22; 70:5;
141:1 *r* Ps 40:13 **22:20** *s* S Job 5:20; Ps 37:14 *t* Ps 35:17
u Php 3:2 **22:21** *v* S ver 13; S Job 4:10 *w* ver 12; S Nu 23:22

n 3 Or *Yet you are holy, / enthroned on the praises of
Israel.* *o* 15 Or */ I am laid* *p* 16 Some Hebrew
manuscripts, Septuagint and Syriac; most Hebrew
manuscripts */ like the lion,* *q* 21 Or */ you have heard*

22:3–5 Recollection of what the Lord has been for Israel
(see note on vv. 9–10).
22:3 *enthroned.* See note on 9:11. *praise of Israel.* The
one Israel praises for his saving acts in her behalf (see
148:14; Dt 10:21; Jer 17:14).
22:6 *a worm and not a man.* See Job 25:6; Isa 41:14.
22:7 *hurl insults, shaking their heads.* See Mt 27:39; Mk
15:29; see also note on 5:9.
22:8 Quoted in part in Mt 27:43; see note on 3:2.
22:9–10 Recollection of what the Lord has been for him
(see note on vv. 3–5).
22:12–18 The psalmist's deep distress. In vv. 12–13,
16–18 he uses four figures to portray the attacks of his
enemies; in vv. 14–15 he describes his inner sense of powerlessness under their fierce attacks.
22:12–13,16 *bulls . . . lions . . . Dogs.* Metaphors for the
enemies (see note on 7:2).
22:12 *Bashan.* Noted for its good pasturage, and hence for
the size and vigor of its animals (see Dt 32:14, Eze 39:18 and
note; Am 4:1).
22:14 *bones . . . heart.* See note on 102:4. *heart.* See note
on 4:7.
22:15 See Jn 19:28 and note. *dust of death.* See v. 29; see
also Job 7:21 and note.
22:16 *pierced my hands and my feet.* The dogs and/or evil
men wound his limbs as he seeks to ward off their attacks.

But see also Isa 53:5; Zec 12:10; Jn 19:34.
22:17 *I can count all my bones.* Perhaps better, "I must
display all my bones." The figure may be of one attacked by
highway robbers or enemy soldiers, who strip him of his
garments (see v. 18; see also note on vv. 20–21).
22:18 See NIV text note on Mt 27:35.
22:20–21 The psalmist's prayer recalls in reverse order the
four figures by which he portrayed his attackers in vv.
12–13,16–18: "sword," "dogs," "lions," "wild oxen."
Here "sword" may evoke the scene described in vv. 16b–18,
and thus many interpret it as an attack by robbers or enemy
soldiers, though "sword" is often used figuratively of any
violent death.
22:21 *save me.* The NIV text note gives the alternative
translation "you have heard me," which would mean that
the psalmist experiences the assurance of having been heard.
The sense would be: You have heard my petition and will
answer me by delivering me from death at the hands of my
enemies (see note on 3:8). *wild oxen.* Aurochs, wild ancestors of domestic cattle; or possibly oryxes, large straight-
horned antelopes.
22:22–31 Vows to praise the Lord when the Lord's sure
deliverance comes (see note on 7:17). The vows proper
appear in vv. 22,25. Verses 23–24 anticipate the calls to
praise that will accompany the psalmist's praise (see note on
9:1). Verses 26–31 describe the expanding company of

in the congregation[x] I will praise
  you.[y]

23You who fear the LORD, praise him![z]
  All you descendants of Jacob, honor
    him![a]
  Revere him,[b] all you descendants of
    Israel!

24For he has not despised[c] or disdained
  the suffering of the afflicted one;[d]
he has not hidden his face[e] from him
  but has listened to his cry for help.[f]

25From you comes the theme of my praise
    in the great assembly;[g]
  before those who fear you[r] will I
    fulfill my vows.[h]

26The poor will eat[i] and be satisfied;
  they who seek the LORD will praise
    him—[j]
  may your hearts live forever!

27All the ends of the earth[k]
  will remember and turn to the LORD,
and all the families of the nations
  will bow down before him,[l]

28for dominion belongs to the LORD[m]
  and he rules over the nations.

29All the rich[n] of the earth will feast and
    worship;[o]

all who go down to the dust[p] will
    kneel before him—
  those who cannot keep themselves
    alive.[q]

30Posterity[r] will serve him;
  future generations[s] will be told about
    the Lord.

31They will proclaim his righteousness[t]
  to a people yet unborn[u]—
  for he has done it.[v]

Psalm 23

A psalm of David.

1The LORD is my shepherd,[w] I shall not
    be in want.[x]

2 He makes me lie down in green
      pastures,
  he leads me beside quiet waters,[y]

3 he restores my soul.[z]
He guides me[a] in paths of
    righteousness[b]
  for his name's sake.[c]

4Even though I walk

22:22 xPs 26:12;
40:9,10; 68:26
yPs 35:18;
Heb 2:12*
22:23 zPs 33:2;
66:8; 86:12;
103:1; 106:1;
113:1; 117:1;
135:19
aPs 50:15;
Isa 24:15; 25:3;
49:23; 60:9;
Jer 3:17
bS Dt 14:23;
Ps 33:8
22:24 cPs 102:17
dS Ps 9:12
ePs 13:1; 27:9;
69:17; 102:2;
143:7
fS Job 24:12;
S 36:5; Heb 5:7
22:25 gPs 26:12;
35:18; 40:9; 82:1
hS Nu 30:2
22:26 iPs 107:9
jPs 40:16
22:27 kS Ps 2:8
lPs 86:9; 102:22;
Da 7:27; Mic 4:1
22:28 mPs 47:7;
Zec 14:9
22:29 nPs 45:12
oPs 95:6; 96:9;
99:5; Isa 27:13;
49:7; 66:23;
Zec 14:16

pIsa 26:19
qPs 89:48
22:30 rIsa 53:10;
54:3; 61:9; 66:22
sPs 102:18
22:31 tS Ps 5:8;
40:9 uPs 71:18;
78:6; 102:18
vLk 18:31; 24:44

23:1 wS Ge 48:15; S Ps 28:9; S Jn 10:11 xPs 34:9,10; 84:11;
107:9; Php 4:19 23:2 yPs 36:8; 46:4; Rev 7:17 23:3
zPs 19:7 aPs 25:9; 73:24; Isa 42:16 bS Ps 5:8 cPs 25:11;
31:3; 79:9; 106:8; 109:21; 143:11

r25 Hebrew him

those who will take up the praise—a worldwide company of persons from every station in life and continuing through the generations. No psalm or prophecy contains a grander vision of the scope of the throng of worshipers who will join in the praise of God's saving acts.
22:22 See Heb 2:12 and note. *name.* See note on 5:11.
22:23 *fear the LORD.* See v. 25; see also note on 15:4.
22:25 *assembly.* See note on 1:5.
22:26 *will eat and be satisfied.* As they share in the ceremonial festival of praise (see Lev 7:11–27).
22:27 *All the ends of the earth.* They too will be told of God's saving acts (see 18:49 and note on 9:1). The good news that the God of Israel hears the prayers of his people and saves them will move others to turn from their idols to the true God.
22:28 The rule of the God of Israel is universal, and the nations will come to recognize that fact through what he does in behalf of his people (see Ps 47; Ge 12:2–3; see also Dt 32:21; Ro 10:19; 11:13–14).
22:29 *All the rich . . . all who go down.* The most prosperous and those on the brink of death, and all those whose life situation falls in between these two extremes. *dust.* See v. 15; see also Job 7:21 and note.
22:31 *righteousness.* See note on 4:1.
Ps 23 A profession of joyful trust in the Lord as the good Shepherd-King. The psalm may have accompanied a festival of praise at "the house of the LORD" (v. 6) following a deliverance, such as is contemplated in 22:25–31 (see note on 7:17). The psalm can be divided into two balanced stanzas, each having four couplets (a couplet is one line of Hebrew poetry): (1) stanza one: vv. 1–2a,2b–3a, 3b-c,4a-c (v. 4a-b is metrically a half-couplet); (2) stanza two: vv. 5a-b,5c-d,6a-b,6c-d. The triplet in the middle (v. 4d-f) is then a centering line (see note on 6:6), focusing on the Shepherd-King's reassuring presence with his people. It

serves as a transition between the two stanzas, concluding the shepherd-sheep motif of the first and introducing the direct address ("you") of the second. The psalm is framed by the first and last couplets, each of which refers to "the LORD."
23:1 *shepherd.* A widely used metaphor for kings in the ancient Near East, and also in Israel (see 78:71–72; 2Sa 5:2; Isa 44:28; Jer 3:15; 23:1–4; Mic 5:4). For the Lord as the shepherd of Israel see 28:9; 79:13; 80:1; 95:7; 100:3; Ge 48:15; Isa 40:11; Jer 17:16; 31:10; 50:19; Eze 34:11–16. Here David the king acknowledges that the Lord is his Shepherd-King. For Jesus as the shepherd of his people see Jn 10:11,14; Heb 13:20; 1Pe 5:4; Rev 7:17. *not be in want.* On the contrary, he will enjoy "goodness" all his life (v. 6).
23:2 *lie down.* For flocks lying down in contented and secure rest see Isa 14:30; 17:2; Jer 33:12; Eze 34:14–15; Zep 2:7; 3:13. *green pastures.* Metaphor for all that makes life to flourish (see Eze 34:14; Jn 10:9). *leads me.* Like a shepherd (see Isa 40:11). *quiet waters.* Lit. "waters of resting places," i.e., restful waters—waters that provide refreshment and well-being (see Isa 49:10).
23:3 *restores my soul.* Revives me, refreshes my spirit (see 19:7; Ru 4:15; Pr 25:13; La 1:16). *guides me in paths of righteousness.* As a shepherd leads his sheep (see 77:20; 78:72) in paths that offer safety and well-being, so David's Shepherd-King guides him in ways that cause him to be secure and prosperous. For this meaning of "righteousness" see Pr 8:18 ("prosperity"); 21:21 ("prosperity"); Isa 48:18; see also Pr 8:20–21. It is also possible that "paths of righteousness" refers to the paths that conform to God's moral will. *for his name's sake.* The prosperity of the Lord's servant brings honor to the Lord's name (see 1Ki 8:41–42; Isa 48:9; Jer 14:21; Eze 20:9,14,22).
23:4 *for you . . . comfort me.* The very center of the psalm; see introductory note above. *with me.* See 16:8 and note;

through the valley of the shadow of
  death,^{s} ^{d}
I will fear no evil,^{e}
  for you are with me;^{f}
your rod and your staff,
  they comfort me.

^{5}You prepare a table^g before me
  in the presence of my enemies.
You anoint my head with oil;^{h}
  my cup^i overflows.
^{6}Surely goodness and love^j will follow
  me
all the days of my life,
and I will dwell in the house of the
  Lord
  forever.

Psalm 24

Of David. A psalm.

^{1}The earth is the Lord's,^{k} and
  everything in it,
the world, and all who live in it;^{l}

^{2}for he founded it upon the seas
  and established it upon the waters. ^{m}

^{3}Who may ascend the hill^n of the Lord?
  Who may stand in his holy place? ^{o}
^{4}He who has clean hands^p and a pure
  heart, ^{q}
who does not lift up his soul to an
  idol^r
or swear by what is false.^{t}
^{5}He will receive blessing^s from the Lord
  and vindication^t from God his
  Savior.
^{6}Such is the generation of those who
  seek him,
who seek your face, ^{u} O God of
  Jacob.^{u} Selah

^{7}Lift up your heads, O you gates; ^{v}
  be lifted up, you ancient doors,
that the King^w of glory^x may come
  in.^{y}

Cross references (center column)

23:4 ^{d}S Job 3:5;
Ps 107:14
^{e}Ps 3:6; 27:1
/Ps 16:8; Isa 43:2
23:5 ^{g}S Job 36:16
^{h}Ps 45:7; 92:10;
Lk 7:46 ^{i}S Ps 16:5
23:6 /S Ne 9:25
24:1 ^{k}S Ex 9:29;
Job 41:11
/1Co 10:26*

24:2 ^{m}S Ge 1:6;
Ps 104:3; 2Pe 3:5
24:3 ^{n}Ps 2:6
^{o}Ps 15:1; 65:4
24:4
^{p}S 2Sa 22:21
^{q}Ps 51:10; 73:1;
Mt 5:8
^{r}Eze 18:15
24:5 ^{s}Dt 11:26
^{t}Ps 17:2
24:6 ^{u}Ps 27:8;
105:4; 119:58;
Hos 5:15
24:7 ^{v}Ps 118:19,
20; Isa 26:2;
60:11,18; 62:10
^{w}Ps 44:4; 74:12
^{x}Ps 29:3; Ac 7:2;
1Co 2:8 ^{y}Zec 9:9;
Mt 21:5

s 4 Or *through the darkest valley*   t 4 Or *swear falsely*
u 6 Two Hebrew manuscripts and Syriac (see also
Septuagint); most Hebrew manuscripts *face, Jacob*

---

see also Dt 31:6,8; Mt 28:20. rod. Instrument of authority
(as in 2:9; 45:6; Ex 21:20; 2Sa 7:14; Job 9:34); used also by
shepherds for counting, guiding, rescuing and protecting
sheep (see Lev 27:32; Eze 20:37). staff. Instrument of support (as in Ex 21:19; Jdg 6:21; 2Ki 4:29; Zec 8:4). comfort
me. Reassure me (as in 71:21; 86:17; Ru 2:13; Isa 12:1;
40:1; 49:13).
23:5 The heavenly Shepherd-King receives David at his
table as his vassal king and takes him under his protection. In
the ancient Near East, covenants were often concluded with
a meal expressive of the bond of friendship (see 41:9; Ge
31:54; Ob 7); in the case of vassal treaties or covenants, the
vassal was present as the guest of the overlord (see Ex
24:8–12). anoint my head with oil. Customary treatment of
an honored guest at a banquet (see Lk 7:46; see also 2Sa
12:20; Ecc 9:8; Da 10:3). cup. Of the Lord's banquet (see
note on 16:5).
23:6 goodness and love. Both frequently refer to covenant
benefits (see note on 6:4); here they are personified (see
25:21; 43:3; 79:8; 89:14). follow. Lit. "pursue." dwell in
the house of the Lord. See note on 15:1. forever. The
Hebrew for this word suggests "throughout the years." But
see also notes on 11:7; 16:9–11.
Ps 24 A processional liturgy (see Ps 47; 68; 118; 132)
celebrating the Lord's entrance into Zion—composed either
for the occasion when David brought the ark to Jerusalem
(see 2Sa 6) or for a festival commemorating the event. It was
probably placed next to Ps 23 because it prescribes who may
enter the sanctuary (see 23:6). The church has long used this
psalm in celebration of Christ's ascension into the heavenly
Jerusalem—and into the sanctuary on high (see introduction
to Ps 47).
24:1–2 The prelude (perhaps spoken by a Levite), proclaiming the Lord as the Creator, Sustainer and Possessor of
the whole world, and therefore worthy of worship and reverent loyalty as "the King of glory" (vv. 7–10; see Ps 29;
33:6–11; 89:5–18; 93; 95:3–5; 104).
24:1 The earth . . . everything in it. For Paul's use of this
declaration see 1Co 10:25–26.
24:2 An echo of Ge 1:1–10. founded . . . established. A
metaphor taken from the founding of a city (see Jos 6:26; 1Ki

16:24; Isa 14:32) or of a temple (see 1Ki 5:17; 6:37; Ezr
3:6–12; Isa 44:28; Hag 2:18; Zec 4:9; 8:9). Like a temple,
the earth was depicted as having foundations (see 18:15;
82:5; 1Sa 2:8; Pr 8:29; Isa 24:18) and pillars (see 75:3; Job
9:6). In the ancient Near East, temples were thought of as
microcosms of the created world, so language applicable to a
temple could readily be applied to the earth. upon. Or
"above" (see 104:5–9; Ge 1:9; 49:25; Ex 20:4; Dt 33:13).
24:3–6 Instruction concerning those who may enter the
sanctuary (probably spoken by a priest); see Ps 15 and introduction.
24:3 hill of the Lord. See 2:6 and note.
24:4 clean hands. Guiltless actions. pure heart. Right attitudes and motives. Jesus said that the "pure in heart . . . will
see God" (Mt 5:8). heart. See note on 4:7. lift up his soul to.
Worship or put his trust in (see 25:1–2). soul. See note on
6:3. by what is false. Or "falsely" (see NIV text note). Thus
it includes perjury (for the same concern see Ex 20:16; Lev
19:12; Jer 5:2; 7:9; Zec 5:4; Mal 3:5).
24:5 vindication. That is, the fruits of vindication, such as
righteous treatment from a faithful God; hence, here a synonym of "blessing" (see 23:3 and note).
24:6 generation. See note on 78:8. Jacob. See note on
14:7.
24:7–10 Heralding the approach of the King of glory (perhaps spoken by the king at the head of the assembled Israelites, with responses by the keepers of the gates). The Lord's
arrival at his sanctuary in Zion completes his march from
Egypt. "The Lord Almighty" (v. 10), "the Lord mighty in
battle" (v. 8; see Ex 15:1–18), has triumphed over all his
enemies and comes now in victory to his own city (see Ps 46;
48; 76; 87), his "resting place" (132:8,14; see 68:7–8; Jdg
5:4–5; Hab 3:3–7). Henceforth Jerusalem is the royal city of
the kingdom of God (see note on 9:11).
24:7 Lift up your heads . . . be lifted up. In jubilant reception of the victorious King of glory (see 3:3; 27:6; 110:7).
gates. Reference could be to the gates of either the city or the
sanctuary. doors. A synonym for "gates," not in this case the
doors of the gates (as in Jdg 16:3; 1Sa 21:13). The gates are
personified for dramatic effect, as in Isa 14:31.

8Who is this King of glory?
   The LORD strong and mighty,[z]
   the LORD mighty in battle. [a]
9Lift up your heads, O you gates;
   lift them up, you ancient doors,
   that the King of glory may come in.
10Who is he, this King of glory?
   The LORD Almighty[b] —
   he is the King of glory.   *Selah*

Psalm 25[v]

Of David.

1To you, O LORD, I lift up my soul;[c]
2   in you I trust,[d] O my God.
Do not let me be put to shame,
   nor let my enemies triumph over me.
3No one whose hope is in you
   will ever be put to shame,[e]
but they will be put to shame
   who are treacherous[f] without
   excuse.

4Show me your ways, O LORD,
   teach me your paths;[g]
5guide me in your truth[h] and teach me,
   for you are God my Savior,[i]
   and my hope is in you[j] all day long.
6Remember, O LORD, your great mercy
   and love,[k]
   for they are from of old.
7Remember not the sins of my youth[l]
   and my rebellious ways;[m]
   according to your love[n] remember me,

for you are good,[o] O LORD.

8Good and upright[p] is the LORD;
   therefore he instructs[q] sinners in his
   ways.
9He guides[r] the humble in what is right
   and teaches them[s] his way.
10All the ways of the LORD are loving and
   faithful[t]
   for those who keep the demands of
   his covenant.[u]
11For the sake of your name,[v] O LORD,
   forgive[w] my iniquity,[x] though it is
   great.
12Who, then, is the man that fears the
   LORD?[y]
   He will instruct him in the way[z]
   chosen for him.
13He will spend his days in prosperity,[a]
   and his descendants will inherit the
   land.[b]
14The LORD confides[c] in those who fear
   him;
   he makes his covenant known[d] to
   them.
15My eyes are ever on the LORD,[e]
   for only he will release my feet from
   the snare.[f]

24:8
[z]S 1Ch 29:11;
Ps 89:13;
Jer 50:34;
Eph 6:10
[a]Ex 15:3,6;
Dt 4:34
24:10
[b]S 1Sa 1:11
25:1 [c]Ps 86:4;
143:8
25:2 [d]Ps 31:6;
143:8
25:3 [e]S Ps 22:5;
S Isa 29:22
[f]Isa 24:16;
Hab 1:13;
Zep 3:4; 2Ti 3:4
25:4 [g]S Job 34:32
25:5 [h]Ps 31:3;
43:3; Jn 16:13
[i]Ps 24:5 [j]ver 3;
Ps 33:20; 39:7;
42:5; 71:5;
130:7; 131:3
25:6 [k]Ps 5:7;
98:3; Isa 63:7,15;
Jer 31:20;
Hos 11:8
25:7 [l]Job 13:26;
Isa 54:4; Jer 3:25;
31:19; 32:30;
Eze 16:22,60;
23:3; 2Ti 2:22
[m]S Ex 23:21;
Ps 107:17
[n]Ps 6:4; 51:1;
69:16; 109:26;
119:124

[o]S 1Ch 16:34;
Ps 34:8; 73:1
25:8 [p]Ps 92:15;
Isa 26:7 [q]Ps 32:8;
Isa 28:26
25:9 [r]S Ps 23:3
[s]ver 4; Ps 27:11
25:10 [t]S Ps 18:25
[u]Ps 103:18;
132:12
25:11
[v]S Ex 9:16;
Ps 31:3; 79:9;

Jer 14:7 [w]S Ex 34:9 [x]S Ex 32:30; S Ps 78:38 **25:12** [y]S Job 1:8
[z]ver 8 **25:13** [a]S Dt 30:15; S 1Ki 3:14; S Job 8:7 [b]S Nu 14:24;
Mt 5:5 **25:14** [c]Pr 3:32 [d]Ge 17:2; Jn 7:17 **25:15**
[e]S 2Ch 20:12; Ps 123:2; Heb 12:2 [f]S Job 34:30; S Ps 119:110

[v]This psalm is an acrostic poem, the verses of which begin
with the successive letters of the Hebrew alphabet.

24:10 LORD *Almighty.* See note on 1Sa 1:3. Here it stands in climactic position.
Ps 25 The psalmist prays for God's covenant mercies when suffering affliction for sins and when enemies seize the occasion to attack, perhaps by trying to discredit the king through false accusations (see note on 5:9). Appealing to God's covenant benevolence (his mercy, love, goodness, uprightness, faithfulness and grace; see vv. 6–8,10,16) and to his own reliance on the Lord (see vv. 1,5,15,20–21), he prays for deliverance from his enemies (see vv. 2,19), for guidance in God's will (see vv. 4–5,21; see also vv. 8–10,12), for the forgiveness of his sins (see vv. 7,11,18) and for relief from his affliction (see vv. 2,16–18,20). These are related: God's forgiveness will express itself in removing his affliction, and then his enemies will no longer have occasion to slander him. And with God guiding him in "his way" (v. 9)—i.e., in "the demands of his covenant" (v. 10)—he will no longer wander into "rebellious ways" (v. 7). This psalm is linked with Ps 24 by its reference to "lifting up the soul" in reliance on God (see v. 1; 24:4). Structurally, the psalm is an alphabetic acrostic (somewhat irregular, with an additional, concluding verse that extends the lines beyond the alphabet). It is composed of four unequal stanzas (of three, four, eight and six verses). The first and fourth stanzas are thematically related, as are the second and third (an *abba* pattern).
25:1–3 Prayer for relief from distress or illness and the slander of his enemies that it occasions.
25:3 *without excuse.* David has given no cause for the hostility of his adversaries.
25:4–7 Prayer for guidance and pardon.

25:4 *your ways . . . your paths.* Metaphors for "the demands of his covenant" (v. 10; see Dt 8:6; 10:12–13; 26:17; 30:16; Jos 22:5; see also vv. 8–9; 18:21; 51:13; 81:13; 95:10; 119:3,15; 128:1).
25:5 *your truth.* A life of faithfulness to the Lord.
25:6–7 *Remember . . . Remember not.* Remember your long-standing ("from of old") "mercy and love," but do not remember my long-standing sins (those "of my youth"). *love.* See v. 10 and note on 6:4.
25:8–15 Confidence in the Lord's covenant favors. In this context of prayer for pardon, David implicitly identifies himself with sinners (v. 8) as well as with the humble (v. 9)—those who keep God's covenant (see vv. 10,14) and those who fear the Lord (see vv. 12,14). As sinner he is in need of forgiveness; as humble servant of the Lord he hopefully awaits God's pardon and guidance in covenant faithfulness.
25:9 *humble.* Those who acknowledge that they are without resources.
25:10 *ways of the LORD.* The Lord's benevolent dealings (see 103:7; 138:5) with those who are true to his ways (see note on v. 4).
25:11 *For the sake of your name.* See note on 23:3; see also 1Jn 2:12. *name.* See note on 5:11.
25:12 *the way chosen for him.* Or "the way he ought to choose."
25:13 *inherit the land.* Retain their family portion in the promised land (see 37:9,11,18,22,29,34; 69:36; Isa 60:21).
25:14 *confides.* Takes them into his confidence, as friends (see Ge 18:17–19; Job 29:4). *fear.* See note on 15:4.

¹⁶Turn to me^g and be gracious to me,^h
　　for I am lonelyⁱ and afflicted.
¹⁷The troubles^j of my heart have
　　multiplied;
　　free me from my anguish.^k
¹⁸Look upon my affliction^l and my
　　distress^m
　　and take away all my sins.ⁿ
¹⁹See how my enemies^o have increased
　　and how fiercely they hate me!^p
²⁰Guard my life^q and rescue me;^r
　　let me not be put to shame,^s
　　for I take refuge^t in you.
²¹May integrity^u and uprightness^v protect
　　me,
　　because my hope is in you.^w

²²Redeem Israel,^x O God,
　　from all their troubles!

Psalm 26

Of David.

¹Vindicate me,^y O LORD,
　　for I have led a blameless life;^z
　I have trusted^a in the LORD
　　without wavering.^b
²Test me,^c O LORD, and try me,
　　examine my heart and my mind;^d

³for your love^e is ever before me,
　　and I walk continually^f in your
　　truth.^g
⁴I do not sit^h with deceitful men,
　　nor do I consort with hypocrites;ⁱ
⁵I abhor^j the assembly of evildoers
　　and refuse to sit with the wicked.
⁶I wash my hands in innocence,^k
　　and go about your altar, O LORD,
⁷proclaiming aloud your praise^l
　　and telling of all your wonderful
　　deeds.^m
⁸I loveⁿ the house where you live,
　　O LORD,
　　the place where your glory dwells.^o

⁹Do not take away my soul along with
　　sinners,
　　my life with bloodthirsty men,^p
¹⁰in whose hands are wicked schemes,^q
　　whose right hands are full of bribes.^r
¹¹But I lead a blameless life;
　　redeem me^s and be merciful to me.

¹²My feet stand on level ground;^t

Cross references

25:16 gS Ps 6:4
  hS Nu 6:25
  iPs 68:6
25:17 jIKi 1:29;
  Ps 34:6,17;
  40:12; 54:7;
  116:3 kPs 6:3;
  39:2
25:18 lS Ps 13:3;
  Ro 12:12
  mS 2Sa 16:12
  nPs 103:3
25:19 oPs 3:1;
  9:13 pPs 35:19;
  38:19; 69:4
25:20 qPs 86:2
  rPs 17:13; 22:21;
  43:1; 71:2;
  116:4; 140:1;
  142:6; 144:11
  sver 3 tPs 2:12
25:21
  uS Ge 20:5;
  Pr 10:9 vIKi 9:4;
  Ps 85:10; 111:8;
  Isa 60:17; Mal 2:6
  wver 3
25:22 xPs 130:8;
  Lk 24:21
26:1
  yS 1Sa 24:15
  zPs 15:2; Pr 20:7
  aPs 22:4; 40:4;
  Isa 12:2; 25:9;
  Jer 17:7; Da 3:28
  b2Ki 20:3;
  Heb 10:23
26:2 cPs 66:10
  dS Dt 6:6;
  S Ps 7:9;
  Jer 11:20; 20:12;
  Eze 11:5
26:3 ePs 6:4
  fS 1Ki 2:4
  gPs 40:11; 43:3;
  86:11; 119:30
26:4 hPs 1:1 iPs 28:3; Mt 6:2 26:5 jPs 139:21 26:6
  kPs 73:13; Mt 27:24 26:7 lIsa 42:12; 60:6 mS Jos 3:5; Ps 9:1
26:8 nPs 122:6; Isa 66:10 oS Ex 29:43; 2Ch 7:1; Ps 96:6
26:9 pPs 5:6; 28:3; 55:23; 139:19; Pr 29:10 26:10
  qS Ps 21:11 rS Job 36:18; S Isa 1:23; S Eze 22:12 26:11
  sPs 31:5; 69:18; 119:134; Tit 2:14 26:12 tPs 27:11; 40:2;
  143:10; Isa 26:7; 40:3-4; 45:13; Zec 4:7; Lk 6:17

Notes

25:16–21 Prayer for relief from distress or illness and the attacks of his enemies.
25:17 *heart.* See note on 4:7.
25:21 *integrity and uprightness.* Personified virtues (see 23:6 and note). Pardon is not enough; David prays that God will enable him to live a life of unmarred moral rectitude—even as God is "good and upright" (v. 8; see 51:10–12).
25:22 A concluding prayer in behalf of all God's people (see 3:8 and note). *Redeem.* Here, as often, a synonym for "deliver."
Ps 26 A prayer for God's discerning mercies—to spare his faithful and godly servant from the death that overtakes the wicked and ungodly. The prayer for vindication (see v. 1) suggests that the king is threatened by the "deceitful" (v. 4) and "bloodthirsty" (v. 9) men to whom he refers (as in Ps 23; 25; 27–28). This psalm is linked with Ps 27–28 (see also Ps 23–24) by the theme of the Lord's house: Here David's "love" (v. 8) for the temple (or tabernacle) testifies to the authenticity of his piety; in Ps 27 the Lord's temple is David's sanctuary from his enemies; in Ps 28 David directs his cry for help to the Lord's throne room ("your Most Holy Place," 28:2) in the temple.
26:1–8 An appeal for God to take account of David's moral integrity, his unwavering trust and his genuine delight in the Lord—not a boast of self-righteousness, such as that of the Pharisee (see Lk 18:9–14).
26:1 *blameless life.* See v. 11 and note; a claim of moral integrity (see vv. 2–5), not sinless perfection (see 7:8; 41:12; 101:2; and especially 1Ki 9:4). *trusted.* Obedience and trust are the twin sides of godliness, as the Abraham story exemplifies (see Ge 12:4 and note; 22:12; see also Ps 34:8–14 and note).
26:2 *heart . . . mind.* See note on 7:9.
26:3 *your love . . . your truth.* That is, your love-and-truth

(see 40:10). David keeps his eye steadfastly on the Lord's love (see note on 6:4) and truth (faithfulness; see 25:10), which are pledged to those "who keep the demands of his covenant" (25:10). *walk continually.* In order to receive the covenant benefits.
26:4–5 *sit with.* David refuses to settle in or associate himself with that company he describes as "deceitful men," "hypocrites," "evildoers," "the wicked" (see 1:1 and note; see also Ps 101).
26:4 *hypocrites.* Context may suggest those who deal fraudulently—or people like those described in Pr 6:12–14.
26:6 *wash my hands in innocence.* Reference appears to be to a ritual claiming innocence. "Clean hands and a pure heart" are requisite for those who come to God (see 24:4 and note). *go about your altar.* To vocally celebrate God's saving acts beside his altar was a public act of devotion in which one also invited all the assembled worshipers to praise (see 43:4).
26:7 *your praise.* See note on 9:1.
26:8 *where your glory dwells.* The presence of God's glory signaled the presence of God himself (see Ex 24:16; 33:22). His glory dwelling in the tabernacle (see Ex 40:35), and later the temple (see 1Ki 8:11), assured Israel of the Lord's holy, yet gracious, presence among them. Jn 1:14 announces that same presence in the Word become flesh who "made his dwelling among us."
26:9–11 An appeal that God will not bring on David the end (death) that awaits the wicked.
26:9 *soul.* See note on 6:3.
26:11 *lead a blameless life.* A return to the appeal with which David began (see v. 1). *redeem.* See note on 25:22.
26:12 A concluding confession of confidence (see note on 3:8) and a vow to praise (see note on 7:17). *level ground.* Where the going is smooth and free from the danger of falling (see 143:10; Isa 40:4; 42:16). *assembly.* See note on 1:5.

in the great assembly[u] I will praise the LORD.

Psalm 27

Of David.

[1]The LORD is my light[v] and my
   salvation[w]—
whom shall I fear?
The LORD is the stronghold[x] of my
   life—
of whom shall I be afraid?[y]
[2]When evil men advance against me
   to devour my flesh,[w]
when my enemies and my foes attack
   me,
they will stumble and fall.[z]
[3]Though an army besiege me,
   my heart will not fear;[a]
though war break out against me,
   even then will I be confident.[b]

[4]One thing[c] I ask of the LORD,
   this is what I seek:
that I may dwell in the house of the
   LORD
all the days of my life,[d]
to gaze upon the beauty of the LORD
   and to seek him in his temple.
[5]For in the day of trouble[e]
   he will keep me safe[f] in his
   dwelling;
he will hide me[g] in the shelter of his
   tabernacle
   and set me high upon a rock.[h]
[6]Then my head will be exalted[i]
   above the enemies who surround
   me;[j]

at his tabernacle will I sacrifice[k] with
   shouts of joy;[l]
I will sing[m] and make music[n] to the
   LORD.

[7]Hear my voice[o] when I call, O LORD;
   be merciful to me and answer me.[p]
[8]My heart says of you, "Seek his[x]
   face![q]"
Your face, LORD, I will seek.
[9]Do not hide your face[r] from me,
   do not turn your servant away in
   anger;[s]
you have been my helper.[t]
Do not reject me or forsake[u] me,
   O God my Savior.[v]
[10]Though my father and mother forsake
   me,
   the LORD will receive me.
[11]Teach me your way,[w] O LORD;
   lead me in a straight path[x]
   because of my oppressors.[y]
[12]Do not turn me over to the desire of my
   foes,
for false witnesses[z] rise up against
   me,
breathing out violence.

[13]I am still confident of this:
   I will see the goodness of the LORD[a]
   in the land of the living.[b]
[14]Wait[c] for the LORD;
   be strong[d] and take heart
   and wait for the LORD.

26:12
[u]S Ps 22:25
27:1
[v]S 2Sa 22:29
[w]S Ex 15:2;
S Ps 3:8 [x]Ps 9:9
[y]S Job 13:15;
Ps 56:4,11; 118:6
27:2 [z]Ps 9:3;
S 20:8; 37:24;
Da 11:19;
Ro 11:11
27:3 [a]S Ge 4:7;
S Ps 3:6
[b]S Job 4:6
27:4 [c]Lk 10:42
[d]Ps 23:6; 61:4
27:5 [e]S Job 38:23
[f]S Ps 12:7
[g]S Ps 17:8
[h]Ps 40:2
27:6 [i]2Sa 22:49;
Ps 3:3; 18:48
[j]S Ps 22:12

[k]Ps 50:14; 54:6;
107:22; 116:17
[l]S Ezr 3:13;
S Job 22:26
[m]S Ex 15:1
[n]Ps 33:2; 92:1;
147:7; S Eph 5:19
27:7 [o]Ps 5:3;
18:6; 55:17;
119:149; 130:2;
Isa 28:23
[p]S Ps 4:1
27:8
[q]S 1Ch 16:11
27:9 [r]S Dt 31:17;
S Ps 22:24
[s]S Ps 2:5
[t]S Ge 49:25;
S Dt 33:29
[u]S Dt 4:31;
Ps 37:28; 119:8;
Isa 41:17; 62:12;
Jer 14:9 [v]Ps 18:46
27:11
[w]S Ex 33:13
[x]S Ezr 8:21;
Ps 5:8 [y]Ps 72:4;
78:42; 106:10;
Jer 21:12
27:12
[z]S Dt 19:16;
S Mt 26:60;
Ac 6:13;
1Co 15:15

27:13 [a]Ex 33:19; S 2Ch 6:41; Ps 23:6; 31:19; 145:7
[b]S Job 28:13 **27:14** [c]Ps 33:20; 130:5,6; Isa 8:17; 30:18;
Hab 2:3; Zep 3:8; Ac 1:4 [d]S Dt 1:21; S Jdg 5:21; S Eph 6:10

[w]2 Or to slander me [x]8 Or To you, O my heart, he
has said, "Seek my

---

praise. See note on 9:1.
Ps 27 David's triumphantly confident prayer to God to deliver him from all those who conspire to bring him down. The prayer presupposes the Lord's covenant with David (see 2Sa 7). Faith's soliloquy (in two stanzas: vv. 1–3, 4–6), which publicly testifies to the king's confident reliance on the Lord, introduces the prayer of vv. 7–12. The conclusion (vv. 13–14) echoes the confidence of vv. 1–6 and adds faith's dialogue with itself—faith exhorting faith to wait patiently for that which is sure, though not yet seen (see Ps 42–43; Heb 11:1). See further the introduction to Ps 26.
27:1–3 The king's security in the Lord in the face of all that his enemies can do (see Ps 2).
27:1 light. Often symbolizes well-being (see 97:11; Job 18:5–6; 22:28; 29:3; Pr 13:9; La 3:2) or life and salvation (see 18:28; Isa 9:2; 49:6; 58:8; 59:9; Jer 13:16; Am 5:18–20). To say "The LORD is my light" is to confess confidence in him as the source of these benefits (see Isa 10:17; 60:1–2,19–20; Mic 7:8–9). my salvation. My Savior (see v. 9).
27:2 devour my flesh. See 7:2 and note.
27:3 heart. See note on 4:7.
27:4–6 The Lord's temple (or tabernacle) is the king's stronghold—because the Lord himself is his stronghold (see v. 1; see notes on 9:11; 18:2).

27:4 dwell in. See note on 15:1. beauty of the LORD. His unfailing benevolence (see 90:17: "favor of the Lord").
27:5 shelter of his tabernacle. See 31:20; 32:7; 61:4; 91:1.
27:6 will I sacrifice. See note on 7:17. I will sing. See note on 9:1.
27:7–12 Prayer for deliverance from treacherous enemies. These remain unspecified, whether from inside or outside the kingdom or both. Their chief weapon is false charges intent on discrediting the king (see note on 5:9).
27:9 hide your face. See note on 13:1. anger. See note on 2:5. you have been my helper. Or "be my helper."
27:10 the LORD will receive me. Or "may the LORD receive me."
27:11 Teach me your way. Only those who know and do the Lord's will can expect to receive favorable response to their prayers (see Ps 24–26; see also 2Sa 7:14). lead me in a straight path. See 5:8 and note.
27:13–14 Concluding note of confidence (see note on 3:8).
27:13 goodness of the LORD. The "good" things promised in the Lord's covenant with David (see 2Sa 7:28; see also 31:19 and note). land of the living. This life.
27:14 Wait for the LORD. Faith encouraging faith (see 42:5,11; 43:5; 62:5).

Psalm 28

Of David.

¹To you I call, O LORD my Rock;
  do not turn a deaf ear[e] to me.
For if you remain silent,[f]
  I will be like those who have gone
    down to the pit.[g]
²Hear my cry for mercy[h]
  as I call to you for help,
as I lift up my hands[i]
  toward your Most Holy Place.[j]

³Do not drag me away with the wicked,
  with those who do evil,
who speak cordially with their
    neighbors
  but harbor malice in their hearts.[k]
⁴Repay them for their deeds
  and for their evil work;
repay them for what their hands have
    done[l]
  and bring back upon them what they
    deserve.[m]
⁵Since they show no regard for the
    works of the LORD
  and what his hands have done,[n]
he will tear them down

and never build them up again.

⁶Praise be to the LORD,[o]
  for he has heard my cry for mercy.[p]
⁷The LORD is my strength[q] and my
    shield;
  my heart trusts[r] in him, and I am
    helped.
My heart leaps for joy[s]
  and I will give thanks to him in
    song.[t]

⁸The LORD is the strength[u] of his people,
  a fortress of salvation[v] for his
    anointed one.[w]
⁹Save your people[x] and bless your
    inheritance;[y]
  be their shepherd[z] and carry them[a]
    forever.

Psalm 29

A psalm of David.

¹Ascribe to the LORD,[b] O mighty ones,[c]
  ascribe to the LORD glory[d] and
    strength.

Cross references (center column)

28:1 eS Dt 1:45
/S Est 4:14
gS Job 33:18
28:2 hPs 17:1;
61:1; 116:1;
130:2; 142:1;
143:1 /S Ezr 9:5;
Ps 63:4; 141:2;
La 2:19; 1Ti 2:8
/Ps 5:7; 11:4
28:3 kPs 12:2;
S 26:4; 55:21;
Jer 9:8
28:4 lPs 62:12;
2Ti 4:14;
Rev 22:12
mLa 3:64;
Rev 18:6
28:5 nIsa 5:12

28:6
oS Ge 24:27;
2Co 1:3; Eph 1:3;
1Pe 1:3 pver 2
28:7 qS Ps 18:1
rPs 13:5; 112:7;
Isa 26:3
sS Dt 16:15;
S Ps 16:9
tPs 33:3; 40:3;
69:30; 144:9;
149:1
28:8 uPs 18:1
vS Ex 15:2;
Ps 27:1; Hab 3:13
wS Ps 20:6
28:9 x1Ch 16:35;
Ps 106:47;
118:25
yS Ex 34:9
z1Ch 11:2;
S Ps 23:1; 78:52,
71; 80:1;
Isa 40:11;

Jer 31:10; Eze 34:12-16,23,31; Mic 7:14 aS Dt 1:31; 32:11;
Isa 46:3; 63:9 29:1 bver 2; 1Ch 16:28 cS 2Sa 1:19;
Ps 103:20; Isa 10:13 dPs 8:1

Ps 28 A prayer for deliverance from deadly peril at the hands of malicious and God-defying enemies. As with Ps 25, the prayer ends with intercession for all the people of the Lord (see 3:8 and note). Reference in the last verse to the Lord as the shepherd of his people connects this psalm with Ps 23 and probably marks off Ps 23–28 as a collection linked by many common themes. See introductions to Ps 26; 29.
28:1–2 Initial appeal to be heard.
28:1 *Rock.* See note on 18:2. *remain silent.* Do not act in my behalf. *pit.* Metaphor for the grave (see note on 30:1).
28:2 *lift up my hands.* In worship and prayer (see 63:4; 134:2; 141:2). *Most Holy Place.* The inner sanctuary of the temple (see 1Ki 6:5), where the ark of the covenant stood (see 1Ki 8:6–8); it was God's throne room on earth.
28:3–5 Prayer for the Lord, enthroned in the temple, to deliver his servant and deal in judgment with those who harbor malice toward the king and God's people and defy God himself.
28:3 *harbor malice.* See note on 5:9. *hearts.* See note on 4:7.
28:4 *Repay them.* See note on 5:10; see also Mt 16:27; 2Ti 4:14; Rev 20:12–13; 22:12.
28:5 *works of the LORD.* His redemption of Israel, the establishment of Israel as his kingdom (by covenant, Ex 19–24), and the appointment of the house of David (also by covenant, 2Sa 7) as his earthly regent over his people. *what his hands have done.* By "what their hands have done" (v. 4), "the wicked" (v. 3) show that they do not acknowledge Israel and David's regency as the work of God's hands. *he will tear.* Or "may he tear."
28:6–7 Joyful praise, in confidence of being heard (see note on 3:8).
28:7 *shield.* See note on 3:3. *heart.* See note on 4:7. *I will give thanks.* See note on 7:17.
28:8–9 The Lord and his people (see note on 3:8).
28:8 *people . . . anointed one.* These constitute a unity (see note on 2:2).

28:9 *Save . . . bless.* God's two primary acts by which he effects his people's well-being: He saves from time to time as circumstances require; he blesses day by day to make their lives and labors fruitful. *your inheritance.* See Dt 9:29. *shepherd.* See introduction; see also 80:1; Isa 40:11; Jer 31:10; Eze 34; Mic 5:4. The answer to this prayer—the last, full answer—has come in the ministry of the "good shepherd" (Jn 10:11,14).
Ps 29 A hymn in praise of the King of creation, whose majesty and power are trumpeted by the thunderbolts of the rainstorm—as the storm rose above the Mediterranean ("the mighty waters," v. 3), swept across the Lebanon range (see vv. 5–6) and rolled over the wilds of Kadesh (northern Kadesh, on the upper reaches of the Orontes River, v. 8). The glory of the Lord is not only visible in the creation (19:1–6; 104 and often elsewhere); it is also audible in creation's most awesome voice. This hymn to Yahweh ("the LORD") served also as a testimony and protest against the worship of the Canaanite god Baal, who was thought to be the divine power present in the thunderstorm. Its climactic word (that "in his temple all cry, 'Glory!' ") suggests that in its present location it was intended to serve as a conclusion to the small collection, Ps 23–28 (see introductions to Ps 26; 28). In its structure, a two-verse introduction and a two-verse conclusion enclose a seven-verse stanza. In both the introduction and the conclusion the name Yahweh ("the LORD") is sounded four times; in the body of the psalm it is heard ten times. "The voice of the LORD" is repeated seven times—the seven thunders of God. (The numbers four, seven and ten often signified completeness in OT number symbolism.)
29:1–2 A summons to all beings in the divine realm (see note on v. 1) to worship the Lord—adapted from a conventional call to praise in the liturgy of the temple (see 96:7–9; 1Ch 16:28–29).
29:1 *mighty ones.* Lit. "sons of god(s)." Perhaps reference is to the angelic host (see 103:20; 148:2; Job 1:6 and NIV text note; 2:1 and NIV text note; Isa 6:2), or possibly to all

²Ascribe to the LORD the glory due his
    name;
  worship the LORD in the splendor of
    his ʸ holiness. ᵉ

³The voice ᶠ of the LORD is over the
    waters;
  the God of glory ᵍ thunders, ʰ
  the LORD thunders over the mighty
    waters. ⁱ
⁴The voice of the LORD is powerful; ʲ
  the voice of the LORD is majestic.
⁵The voice of the LORD breaks the
    cedars;
  the LORD breaks in pieces the cedars
    of Lebanon. ᵏ
⁶He makes Lebanon skip ˡ like a calf,
  Sirion ᶻ ᵐ like a young wild ox. ⁿ
⁷The voice of the LORD strikes
  with flashes of lightning. ᵒ
⁸The voice of the LORD shakes the
    desert;
  the LORD shakes the Desert of
    Kadesh. ᵖ
⁹The voice of the LORD twists the
    oaks ᵃ ᑫ
  and strips the forests bare.
  And in his temple all cry, "Glory!" ʳ

29:2
eS 1Ch 16:29;
Ps 96:7-9
29:3 ᶠJob 37:5
ᵍS Ps 24:7; Ac 7:2
ʰS 1Sa 2:10;
Ps 18:13; 46:6;
68:33; 77:17;
Jer 10:13; 25:30;
Joel 2:11; Am 1:2
ⁱS Ex 15:10
29:4 ʲPs 68:33
29:5 ᵏS Jdg 9:15
29:6 ˡPs 114:4
ᵐDt 3:9
ⁿS Nu 23:22;
Job 39:9;
Ps 92:10
29:7 ᵒEze 1:14;
Rev 8:5
29:8 ᵖNu 13:26;
S 20:1
29:9 ᑫ Isa 2:13;
Eze 27:6; Am 2:9
ʳPs 26:8

29:10 ˢGe 6:17
ᵗS Ex 15:18
29:11 ᵘS Ps 18:1;
28:8; 68:35
ᵛS Lev 26:6;
S Nu 6:26
30:1 ʷS Ex 15:2
ˣJob 11:8;
Ps 63:9; 107:26;
Pr 9:18; Isa 14:15
ʸS Ps 22:17
30:2 ᶻPs 5:2;
88:13
ᵃS Nu 12:13
30:3 ᵇS Ps 16:10;
S 56:13 ᶜPs 28:1;
55:23; 69:15;

¹⁰The LORD sits ᵇ enthroned over the
    flood; ˢ
  the LORD is enthroned as King
    forever. ᵗ
¹¹The LORD gives strength to his people; ᵘ
  the LORD blesses his people with
    peace. ᵛ

Psalm 30

A psalm. A song. For the dedication of the
    temple. ᶜ Of David.

¹I will exalt ʷ you, O LORD,
  for you lifted me out of the depths ˣ
  and did not let my enemies gloat over
    me. ʸ
²O LORD my God, I called to you for
    help ᶻ
  and you healed me. ᵃ
³O LORD, you brought me up from the
    grave ᵈ; ᵇ
  you spared me from going down into
    the pit. ᶜ

86:13; 143:7; Pr 1:12; Isa 38:17; Jnh 2:6

ʸ2 Or LORD with the splendor of   ᶻ6 That is, Mount
Hermon   ᵃ9 Or LORD makes the deer give birth
ᵇ10 Or sat   ᶜTitle: Or palace   ᵈ3 Hebrew Sheol

those foolishly thought to be gods—as in Ps 97 (see v. 7), which has several thematic links with this psalm. The Lord alone must be acknowledged as the divine King.
29:2 *name.* See note on 5:11. *in the splendor of his holiness.* A rather literal translation of a difficult Hebrew phrase (see NIV text note). It is uncertain if it describes God himself or the sanctuary or the (priestly) garb the worshipers are to wear when they approach God. The use of an almost identical Hebrew phrase in 110:3 (translated "in holy majesty") gives support for the last alternative; thus "in holy garments of splendor."
29:3–9 Praise of the Lord, whose voice the crashing thunder is (see 68:4,33). The sound and fury of creation's awesome displays of power proclaim the glory of Israel's God.
29:5 *cedars of Lebanon.* The mightiest of trees (see Isa 2:13 and note).
29:6 *skip.* See 114:4 and note.
29:9 *temple.* A primary thematic link with Ps 23–28. Reference may be to the temple in Jerusalem or to God's heavenly temple, where he sits enthroned (see 2:4; 11:4; 113:5; Isa 6:1; 40:22) as the Lord of all creation. But perhaps it is the creation itself that here is named God's temple (see note on 24:2). Then the "all" (those who cry "Glory!") is absolutely all—all creation shouts his praise (cf. 150:6). *Glory!* See note on 26:8.
29:10–11 The Lord's absolute and everlasting rule is committed to his people's complete salvation and unmixed blessedness—the crowning comfort in a world where threatening tides seem to make everything uncertain.
29:10 *enthroned over the flood.* As the One who by his word brought the ordered creation out of the formless "deep" (Ge 1:2,6–10); or the reference may be to the Noahic flood (see Ge 6:17).
Ps 30 A song of praise publicly celebrating the Lord's deliverance from the threat of death, probably brought on by illness ("you healed me," v. 2; see note on 7:17). The psalm is framed by commitments to praise (see vv. 1,12).

30 title *A song.* See titles of Ps 18; 45–46; 48; 65–68; 75–76; 83; 87–88; 92; 108—all psalms of praise except 83; 88. In addition there are the songs "of ascents" (Ps 120–134). *For the dedication of the temple. Of David.* If "Of David" indicates authorship, the most probable occasion for the psalm is recorded in 1Ch 21:1–22:6. In 1Ch 22:1–6 David dedicated both property and building materials for the temple, and he may well have intended that Ps 30 be used at the dedication of the temple itself. If this is the case, vv. 2–3 would refer to David's predicament in 1Ch 21:17–30. The "favor" of v. 5 would be an echo of the "mercy" of 1Ch 21:13, and v. 6 would refer to his sin of misplaced trust in a large, superior army (see 1Ch 21:1–8). Later, the psalm came to be applied to the exile experience of Israel. In Jewish liturgical practice dating from Talmudic times it is chanted at Hanukkah, the feast that celebrates the rededication of the temple by Judas Maccabeus (165 B.C.) after its desecration by Antiochus Epiphanes (168). In such communal use, the "I" of the psalm becomes the corporate "person" of Israel—a common mode of speaking in the OT.
30:1–3 Introductory announcement of the occasion for praise.
30:1 *out of the depths.* The vivid imagery that associates distress with "the depths"—so expressive of universal human experience—is common in OT poetry (see 69:2,15; 71:20; 88:6; 130:1; La 3:55; Jnh 2:2). The depths are often linked, as here, with Sheol ("the grave," v. 3) and "the pit" (v. 3), together with a cluster of related associations: silence (see 31:17; 94:17; 115:17; 1Sa 2:9), darkness (see 88:6, 12; 143:3; Job 10:21–22; 17:13; Ecc 6:4; La 3:6), destruction (see v. 9; 18:4; 55:23, "corruption"; 88:11; Isa 38:17; Hos 13:14), dust (see v. 9; 7:5; 22:15,29; Job 17:16; 40:13; Isa 26:19; 29:4), mire (see 40:2; 69:2,14), slime (see 40:2) and mud (see 40:2; Job 30:19). See also note on 49:14. *my enemies gloat over me.* See introduction to Ps 6.
30:3 *grave.* Figurative of a "brink-of-death" experience, as in 18:5; Jnh 2:2. *pit.* See note on 28:1.

Psalm 30 (continued)

⁴Sing^d to the LORD, you saints^e of his;
　praise his holy name.^f
⁵For his anger^g lasts only a moment,^h
　but his favor lasts a lifetime;ⁱ
weeping^j may remain for a night,
　but rejoicing comes in the morning.^k

⁶When I felt secure, I said,
　"I will never be shaken."^l
⁷O LORD, when you favored me,
　you made my mountain^e stand firm;
but when you hid your face,^m
　I was dismayed.

⁸To you, O LORD, I called;
　to the Lord I cried for mercy:
⁹"What gain is there in my destruction,^f
　in my going down into the pit?ⁿ
Will the dust praise you?
　Will it proclaim your faithfulness?^o
¹⁰Hear,^p O LORD, and be merciful to
　me;^q
　O LORD, be my help.^r "

¹¹You turned my wailing^s into dancing;^t
　you removed my sackcloth^u and
　　clothed me with joy,^v
¹²that my heart may sing to you and not
　be silent.
O LORD my God, I will give you
　thanks^w forever.^x

Cross references (center column)

30:4 ^dPs 33:1; 47:7; 68:4
^eS Ps 16:3
^fEx 3:15; Ps 33:21; 103:1; 145:21
30:5 ^gPs 103:9
^hS Job 14:13
ⁱS Ezr 3:11
^j2Sa 15:30; Ps 6:6; 126:6; Jer 31:16
^k2Co 4:17
30:6 ^lS Job 29:18
30:7 ^mS Dt 31:17
30:9 ⁿS Job 33:18; Isa 38:18
^oS Ps 6:5; 88:11
30:10 ^pS Ps 17:1
^qPs 4:1 ^rS Ps 20:2
30:11 ^sS Est 4:1
^tS Ex 15:20
^uS 2Sa 3:31; S Ps 35:13
^vS Dt 16:15; S Ps 16:9
30:12 ^wPs 35:18; 75:1; 118:21; Rev 11:17
^xPs 44:8; 52:9

31:1 ^yS Ps 7:1
^zPs 5:8
31:2 ^aS Ps 6:4
^bS Ex 2:17
^cS 2Sa 22:3; S Ps 18:2
31:3 ^dS Ps 18:2
^eS Ps 23:3
31:4 ^fS 1Sa 28:9; S Job 18:10
^gPs 9:9
31:5 ^hLk 23:46; Ac 7:59
ⁱIsa 45:19; 65:16
31:6 ^jS Dt 32:21
^kS Ps 4:5

31:7 ^lS Ps 13:3

Psalm 31

31:1-4pp — Ps 71:1-3

For the director of music.
A psalm of David.

¹In you, O LORD, I have taken refuge;^y
　let me never be put to shame;
　deliver me in your righteousness.^z
²Turn your ear to me,^a
　come quickly to my rescue;^b
be my rock of refuge,^c
　a strong fortress to save me.
³Since you are my rock and my
　fortress,^d
for the sake of your name^e lead and
　guide me.
⁴Free me from the trap^f that is set for
　me,
　for you are my refuge.^g
⁵Into your hands I commit my spirit;^h
　redeem me, O LORD, the God of
　　truth.ⁱ

⁶I hate those who cling to worthless
　idols;^j
　I trust in the LORD.^k
⁷I will be glad and rejoice in your love,
　for you saw my affliction^l

^e7 Or hill country　　^f9 Or there if I am silenced

30:4—5 Call to the gathered worshipers to take up the praise of God (see note on 9:1).
30:4 *saints.* See note on 4:3. *name.* Lit. "memorial" (see Isa 26:8; Hos 12:5).
30:5 *anger.* See note on 2:5. *lasts only a moment.* See Isa 54:7. *remain for a night.* Lit. "come in at evening to lodge." The figure is that of a guest lodging for only one night.
30:6—10 Expanded recollection of the Lord's gracious deliverance.
30:6—7 In security he had grown arrogant, forgetful of who had made his "mountain stand firm," but the Lord reminded him.
30:6 *never be shaken.* He spoke as do the wicked (see 10:6), hence lost the blessing of the righteous (see 15:5). *shaken.* See note on 10:6.
30:7 *made my mountain stand firm.* Reference may be to David's security in his mountain fortress, Zion; or that mountain fortress may here serve as a metaphor for David's state as a vigorous and victorious king, the "mountain" on which he sat with such secure confidence in God. *hid your face.* See note on 13:1.
30:8—10 Shattered strength swept away all self-reliance; at the brink of death his cries for God's mercy rose.
30:9 See note on 6:5. *your faithfulness.* To your covenant.
30:11—12 God answered—and David vows to prolong his praise forever (see note on 7:17). Dancing and joy replace wailing and sackcloth so that songs of praise, not silence, may attend the acts of God.
30:11 *sackcloth.* A symbol of mourning (see 35:13; Ge 37:34).
30:12 *heart.* Lit. "glory" (see note on 7:5).
Ps 31 A prayer for deliverance when confronted by a conspiracy so powerful and open that all David's friends

abandoned him. According to Lk 23:46, Jesus on the cross applied Ps 31:5 to his own circumstances; thus those who share in his sufferings at the hands of anti-Christian forces are encouraged to hear and use this psalm in a new light (see Ac 7:59; 1Pe 4:19). No psalm expresses a more sturdy trust in the Lord when powerful human forces threaten. The heart of the prayer itself is found in vv. 9—18, which is both preceded and followed by eight Hebrew poetic lines—stanzas that resound with the theme of trust (see v. 14). Verse 13, at the center of the psalm, expresses most clearly the prayer's occasion.
31 title *For the director of music.* See note on Ps 4 title.
31:1—5 Initial appeal to the Lord, the faithful refuge.
31:1 *righteousness.* See note on 4:1.
31:2 *rock.* See note on 18:2.
31:3 *for the sake of your name.* God's honor is at stake in the safety of his servant now under attack (see note on 23:3). *name.* See note on 5:11. *lead and guide.* As a shepherd (see 23:2—3 and notes).
31:4 *trap that is set for me.* By his enemies (see v. 11).
31:5 *Into your hands I commit my spirit.* The climactic expression of trust in the Lord—quoted by Jesus in Lk 23:46. *commit.* Lit. "deposit" (as in Jer 36:20, "put"), here in the very hands of God, thus entrusting to God's care (see Lev 6:4; 1Ki 14:27). *my spirit.* His very life. *redeem.* See note on 25:22. *God of truth.* The faithful, trustworthy God (see note on 30:9).
31:6—8 Confession of loyal trust in the Lord, whose past mercies to David when enemies threatened are joyfully recalled.
31:6 *hate.* Refuse to be associated with.
31:7 *love.* See vv. 16,21; see also note on 6:4. *soul.* See note on 6:3.

and knew the anguish *m* of my soul.
[8]You have not handed me over *n* to the
enemy
but have set my feet in a spacious
place. *o*

[9]Be merciful to me, O Lord, for I am in
distress; *p*
my eyes grow weak with sorrow, *q*
my soul and my body *r* with grief.
[10]My life is consumed by anguish *s*
and my years by groaning; *t*
my strength fails *u* because of my
affliction, *g v*
and my bones grow weak. *w*
[11]Because of all my enemies, *x*
I am the utter contempt *y* of my
neighbors; *z*
I am a dread to my friends—
those who see me on the street flee
from me.
[12]I am forgotten by them as though I
were dead; *a*
I have become like broken pottery.
[13]For I hear the slander *b* of many;
there is terror on every side; *c*
they conspire against me *d*
and plot to take my life. *e*

[14]But I trust *f* in you, O Lord;
I say, "You are my God."
[15]My times *g* are in your hands;
deliver me from my enemies
and from those who pursue me.
[16]Let your face shine *h* on your servant;
save me in your unfailing love. *i*

[17]Let me not be put to shame, *j* O Lord,
for I have cried out to you;
but let the wicked be put to shame
and lie silent *k* in the grave. *h*
[18]Let their lying lips *l* be silenced,
for with pride and contempt
they speak arrogantly *m* against the
righteous.

[19]How great is your goodness, *n*
which you have stored up for those
who fear you,
which you bestow in the sight of men *o*
on those who take refuge *p* in you.
[20]In the shelter *q* of your presence you
hide *r* them
from the intrigues of men; *s*
in your dwelling you keep them safe
from accusing tongues.

[21]Praise be to the Lord, *t*
for he showed his wonderful love *u* to
me
when I was in a besieged city. *v*
[22]In my alarm *w* I said,
"I am cut off *x* from your sight!"
Yet you heard my cry *y* for mercy
when I called to you for help.

[23]Love the Lord, all his saints! *z*
The Lord preserves the faithful, *a*
but the proud he pays back *b* in full.
[24]Be strong and take heart, *c*

31:7
*m*S Ps 25:17;
Lk 22:44
31:8 *n*S Dt 32:30
*o*S 2Sa 22:20
31:9 *p*Ps 4:1
*q*Ps 6:7 *r*Ps 63:1
31:10 *s*ver 7
*t*Ps 6:6
*u*Ps 22:15; 32:4;
38:10; 73:26
*v*Ps 25:18
*w*S Ps 6:2
31:11 *x*Dt 30:7;
Ps 3:7; 25:19;
102:8 *y*S Ps 22:6
*z*Ps 38:11
31:12 *a*Ps 28:1;
88:4
31:13
*b*S Lev 19:16;
Ps 50:20
*c*S Job 18:11;
Isa 13:8; Jer 6:25;
20:3,10; 46:5;
49:5; La 2:22
*d*Ps 41:7; 56:6;
71:10; 83:3
*e*S Ge 37:18;
S Mt 12:14
31:14 *f*Ps 4:5
31:15 *g*S Job 14:5
31:16 *h*S Nu 6:25
*i*S Ps 6:4

31:17 *j*S Ps 22:5
*k*1Sa 2:9;
Ps 94:17; 115:17
31:18 *l*Ps 120:2;
Pr 10:18; 26:24
*m*S 1Sa 2:3;
Jude 1:15
31:19
*n*S Ps 27:13;
Ro 11:22
*o*Ps 23:5 *p*Ps 2:12
31:20 *q*Ps 55:8
*r*S Ps 17:8
*s*S Ge 37:18
31:21 *t*Ps 28:6
*u*S Ps 17:7
*v*1Sa 23:7
31:22
*w*Ps 116:11
*x*Job 6:9; 17:1;
Ps 37:9; 88:5;

Isa 38:12 *y*Ps 6:9; 66:19; 116:1; 145:19 **31:23** *z*S Ps 4:3
*a*S Ps 18:25; Rev 2:10 *b*Dt 32:41; Ps 94:2 **31:24** *c*Ps 27:14

*g*10 Or *guilt*   *h*17 Hebrew *Sheol*

31:8 *spacious place.* See note on 18:19.
31:9–13 The distress described: He is utterly drained physically and emotionally (see vv. 9–10; see also 22:14–15); all his friends have abandoned him like a piece of broken pottery (see vv. 11–12); and all this because the conspiracy against him is so strong (v. 13).
31:9 *eyes grow weak.* See note on 13:3. *soul.* See note on 6:3.
31:10 *bones.* See note on 6:2.
31:11–12 Abandonment by friends was a common experience at a time when God seemed to have withdrawn his favor (see 38:11; 41:9; 69:8; 88:8,18; Job 19:13–19; Jer 12:6; 15:17).
31:13 *slander.* See note on 5:9. *terror on every side.* See notes on Jer 6:25; 20:3.
31:14–18 His trust in the Lord is unwavering; his defense against his powerful enemies is his reliance on God's faithfulness and discerning judgment.
31:14 Cf. v. 22.
31:15 *My times are in your hands.* All the events and circumstances of life are in the hands of the Lord, "my God" (v. 14).
31:16 *face shine.* See note on 13:1.
31:17–18 *but let the wicked . . . be silenced.* See note on 5:10.
31:18 *lying lips.* See note on 5:9. *righteous.* See note on 1:5.
31:19–20 Confident anticipation of God's saving help (see

note on 3:8).
31:19 *stored up.* David deposits his life in the hands of God to share in the covenant benefits that God has stored up for his faithful servants ("goodness"; see Ex 18:9; Nu 10:29, 32; Dt 26:11; Jos 21:45; 23:14–15; 2Ch 6:41; Ne 9:25, 35; Isa 63:7; Jer 33:9; see also Jer 31:12,14, "bounty"). *fear.* See note on 15:4. *bestow in the sight of men.* Thus showing the Lord's approval of and his standing with his faithful servants in contrast to the accusations of their adversaries (see 86:17).
31:20 *shelter of your presence.* See note on 27:5. *accusing tongues.* See "slander" (v. 13) and "lying lips" (v. 18).
31:21–22 Praise anticipating deliverance (see note on 12:5–6).
31:21 *besieged city.* Metaphor for the threat he had experienced.
31:22 *cut off from your sight.* See note on 13:1.
31:23–24 Praise advances to encouragement of the saints (see 62:8).
31:23 *saints.* See note on 4:3. *the faithful.* Those who maintain moral integrity. *the proud.* Those who refuse to live in humble reliance on the Lord. They arrogantly try to make their way in the world either as a law to themselves (see, e.g., v. 18; 10:2–11; 73:6; 94:2–7; Dt 8:14; Isa 2:17; Eze 28:2,5; Hos 13:6) or by relying on false gods (see Jer 13:9–10). Hence "the proud" is often equivalent to "the wicked."

all you who hope in the LORD.

Psalm 32

Of David. A *maskil.* [i]

[1]Blessed is he
  whose transgressions are forgiven,
  whose sins are covered. [d]
[2]Blessed is the man
  whose sin the LORD does not count
    against him [e]
  and in whose spirit is no deceit. [f]

[3]When I kept silent, [g]
  my bones wasted away [h]
  through my groaning [i] all day long.
[4]For day and night
  your hand was heavy [j] upon me;
  my strength was sapped [k]
    as in the heat of summer.   *Selah*
[5]Then I acknowledged my sin to you
  and did not cover up my iniquity. [l]
I said, "I will confess [m]

my transgressions [n] to the LORD"—
  and you forgave
  the guilt of my sin. [o]   *Selah*

[6]Therefore let everyone who is godly
  pray to you
  while you may be found; [p]
  surely when the mighty waters [q] rise, [r]
  they will not reach him. [s]
[7]You are my hiding place; [t]
  you will protect me from trouble [u]
  and surround me with songs of
    deliverance. [v]   *Selah*

[8]I will instruct [w] you and teach you [x] in
  the way you should go;
  I will counsel you and watch over [y]
  you.
[9]Do not be like the horse or the mule,
  which have no understanding
  but must be controlled by bit and
    bridle [z]

Cross references

32:1 [d]Ps 85:2; 103:3
32:2 [e]S Ro 4:7-8* [f]Jn 1:47; Rev 14:5
32:3 [g]S Job 31:34 [h]Ps 31:10 [i]S Job 3:24; Ps 6:6
32:4 [j]1Sa 5:6; S Job 9:34; Ps 38:2; 39:10 [k]Ps 22:15
32:5 [l]Job 31:33 [m]Pr 28:13
[n]Ps 103:12 [o]S Lev 26:40; 1Jn 1:9
32:6 [p]Ps 69:13; Isa 55:6 [q]S Ex 15:10 [r]Ps 69:1 [s]Isa 43:2
32:7 [t]S Jdg 9:35 [u]S Ps 9:9 [v]S Jdg 5:1
32:8 [w]S Ps 25:8 [x]Ps 34:11 [y]Ps 33:18
32:9 [z]S Job 30:11; S 39:10; Jas 3:3

[i]Title: Probably a literary or musical term

Ps 32 A grateful testimony of joy for God's gift of forgiveness toward those who with integrity confess their sins and are receptive to God's rule in their lives. The psalm appears to be a liturgical dialogue between David and God in the presence of the worshipers at the sanctuary. In vv. 1–2 and again in v. 11 David speaks to the assembly; in vv. 3–7 he speaks to God (in their hearing); in vv. 8–10 he is addressed by one of the Lord's priests (but see note on vv. 8–10). In traditional Christian usage the psalm has been numbered among the penitential psalms (see introduction to Ps 6). **32 title** *maskil.* Occurs also in the titles of Ps 42; 44–45; 52–55; 74; 78; 88–89; 142. The Hebrew word perhaps indicates that these psalms contain instruction in godliness (see 14:2; 53:2, "any who understand"; 41:1, "he who has regard"; but see also 47:7 and NIV text note). **32:1–2** Exuberant proclamation of the happy state of those who experience God's forgiveness. *Blessed . . . Blessed.* See note on 1:1. Repetition underscores. *are forgiven . . . are covered . . . does not count against him.* Repetition with variation emphasizes and illumines. For Paul's use of these verses see Ro 4:6–8. **32:2** *in whose spirit is no deceit.* Only those honest with God receive pardon. **32:3–5** Testimony to a personal experience of God's pardon. God's heavy hand, brought down "day and night" on the stubborn silence of unacknowledged sin, filled life with groaning, but full confession brought blessed relief. Neither the sin nor the form of suffering is identified, other than that the latter was physically and psychologically devastating. But it would be uncharacteristic of the Psalms to speak of mere emotional disturbance brought on by suppressed guilt. Some affliction, perhaps illness, was the instrument of God's chastisement (see Ps 38). **32:4** *strength was sapped.* Under God's heavy hand he wilted like a plant in the heat of summer. **32:5** Again repetition is used (see note on vv. 1–2). *sin . . . iniquity . . . transgressions.* See 51:1–2; the three most common OT words for evil thoughts and actions (see Isa 59:12 and note). *confess.* See Ps 51; 2Sa 12:13. **32:6–7** A chastened confession that life is secure only with God. **32:6** Though addressed to God as confession, it is also intended for the ears of the fellow worshipers. He ad-

monishes them to "seek the LORD while he may be found . . . while he is near" (Isa 55:6) and not to foolishly provoke his withdrawal—and the coming near of his heavy hand—as David had done. A God who forgives is a God to whom one can entrust and devote his life (see 130:4). *godly.* See note on 4:3. *mighty waters.* Powerful imagery for threatening forces or circumstances. This and related imagery was borrowed from ancient Near Eastern creation myths. In many of these a primal mass of chaotic waters (their threatening and destructive forces were often depicted as a many-headed monster of the deep; see 74:13–14 and note) had to be subdued by the creator-god before he could fashion the world and/or rule as the divine king over the earth. Though in these myths the chaotic waters were subdued when the present world was created, they remained a constant threat to the security and well-being of the present order in the earth (the world in which man lives). Hence by association they were linked with anything that in human experience endangered or troubled that order. They were also associated with the sea, whose angry waves seemed determined at times to engulf the land. Since in Canaanite mythology Sea and Death were the two great enemies of Baal ("lord" of earth), imagery drawn from both realms was used by OT poets, sometimes side by side, to depict threats and distress (see 18:4–5,16; 42:7; 65:7; 74:12–14; 77:16,19; 89:9–10; 93:3–4; 124:4–5; 144:7–8; Job 7:12; 26:12; 38:8–11; Isa 5:30; 8:7–8; 17:12–14; 51:9–10; Jer 5:22; 47:2; 51:55; Hab 3:8–10; see also note on SS 8:7). For imagery associated with the realm of death see notes on 30:1; 49:14. **32:7** *surround me with songs of deliverance.* Because of your help, I will be surrounded by people celebrating your acts of deliverance, as I bring my thank offerings to you (see notes on 7:17; 9:1; see also 35:27; 51:8). **32:8–10** A priestly word of godly instruction, either to David (do not be foolish toward God again) or to those who have just been exhorted to trust in the Lord (to trust add obedience). Some believe that the psalmist himself here turns to others to warn them against the ways into which he had fallen (see 51:13). **32:9** God's servant must be wiser than beasts, more open to God's will than horses and mules are to the will of their masters (see Isa 1:3).

or they will not come to you.
[10]Many are the woes of the wicked,[a]
  but the LORD's unfailing love
  surrounds the man who trusts[b] in
    him.

[11]Rejoice in the LORD[c] and be glad, you
    righteous;
  sing, all you who are upright in heart!

Psalm 33

[1]Sing joyfully[d] to the LORD, you
    righteous;
  it is fitting[e] for the upright[f] to praise
    him.
[2]Praise the LORD with the harp;[g]
  make music to him on the
    ten-stringed lyre.[h]
[3]Sing to him a new song;[i]
  play skillfully, and shout for joy.[j]

[4]For the word of the LORD is right[k] and
    true;[l]
  he is faithful[m] in all he does.
[5]The LORD loves righteousness and
    justice;[n]
  the earth is full of his unfailing love.[o]

[6]By the word[p] of the LORD were the
    heavens made,[q]
  their starry host[r] by the breath of his
    mouth.
[7]He gathers the waters[s] of the sea into
    jars[i] ;[t]
  he puts the deep into storehouses.

[8]Let all the earth fear the LORD;[u]
  let all the people of the world[v]
    revere him.[w]
[9]For he spoke, and it came to be;
  he commanded,[x] and it stood firm.
[10]The LORD foils[y] the plans[z] of the
    nations;[a]
  he thwarts the purposes of the
    peoples.
[11]But the plans of the LORD stand firm[b]
    forever,
  the purposes[c] of his heart through all
    generations.

[12]Blessed is the nation whose God is the
    LORD,[d]
  the people he chose[e] for his
    inheritance.[f]
[13]From heaven the LORD looks down[g]
  and sees all mankind;[h]
[14]from his dwelling place[i] he watches
  all who live on earth—
[15]he who forms[j] the hearts of all,
  who considers everything they do.[k]
[16]No king is saved by the size of his
    army;[l]
  no warrior escapes by his great
    strength.
[17]A horse[m] is a vain hope for deliverance;
  despite all its great strength it cannot
    save.

32:10 aRo 2:9
  bPs 4:5; Pr 16:20
32:11 cPs 64:10
33:1 dS Ps 5:11;
  S 101:1 ePs 147:1
fPs 11:7
33:2 gS Ge 4:21;
  1Co 14:7; Rev 5:8
hPs 92:3; 144:9
33:3 iPs 40:3;
  Isa 42:10;
  S Rev 5:9
jS Job 3:7;
  Ps 35:27; 47:1
33:4 kS Ps 19:8
lPs 119:142;
  Rev 19:9; 22:6
mPs 18:25; 25:10
33:5 nPs 11:7
oPs 6:4
33:6 pS Ge 1:3;
  Heb 11:3
qS Ex 8:19;
  S 2Ch 2:12
rS Ge 1:16
33:7 sS Ge 1:10
tS Jos 3:16

33:8 uS Dt 6:13;
  Ps 2:11 vPs 49:1;
  Isa 18:3; Mic 1:2
wS Dt 14:23
33:9 xPs 148:5
33:10 yIsa 44:25
zS Job 5:12
aPs 2:1
33:11
  bS Nu 23:19
  cJer 51:12,29
33:12 dPs 144:15
  eS Ex 8:22;
  Dt 7:6; Ps 4:3;
  65:4; 84:4
fS Ex 34:9
33:13 gPs 53:2;
  102:19
hJob 28:24;
  Ps 11:4; 14:2;
  S Heb 4:13
33:14
  iS Lev 15:31;
  1Ki 8:39

33:15 jJob 10:8; Ps 119:73 kS Job 10:4; Jer 32:19 33:16
l1Sa 14:6 33:17 mS Ps 20:7

j7 Or sea as into a heap

32:10 *unfailing love.* See note on 6:4.
32:11 A final word to the assembled worshipers—let the praise of God resound (see note on 9:1). See also note on 1:5. *heart.* See note on 4:7.
Ps 33 A liturgy in praise of the Lord, the sovereign God of Israel. In the Psalms, calls to praise (as in vv. 1–3) and motivations for praise (as in vv. 4–19) belong to the language of praise (see note on 9:1). Most likely the voices of the Levitical choir (see 1Ch 16:7–36; 25:1) are heard in this psalm. Perhaps the choir leader spoke vv. 1–3, the choir vv. 4–19, and the people responded with the words of vv. 20–22. The original occasion is unknown, but reference to a "new song" (see note on v. 3) suggests a national deliverance, such as Judah experienced in the time of Jehoshaphat (see 2Ch 20) or Hezekiah (see 2Ki 19); see vv. 10–11, 16–17. Along with Ps 1–2; 10 (but see introduction to Ps 9), this is one of the only four psalms in Book I without a superscription. Although structurally not an alphabetic acrostic like the psalm that follows it, the length of the psalm (22 verses) has been determined by the length of the Hebrew alphabet (22 letters); see Ps 38; 103; La 5. The body of the psalm is framed by a three-verse introduction (call to praise) and a three-verse conclusion (response to praise). In vv. 4–19 are heard the praise of the Lord, developed in two parts of eight verses each (vv. 4–11, 12–19).
33:1–3 The call to praise. Cf. Eph 5:19.
33:1 *righteous.* The assembly of worshipers (see note on 1:5).
33:3 *new song.* Celebrating God's saving act, as in 40:3; 96:1; 98:1; 144:9; 149:1; see Isa 42:10; Rev 5:9; 14:3; see

also note on 7:17.
33:4–19 The praise, in two eight-verse parts.
33:4–11 Because the Lord is the Creator, who by his power imposed his order on the creation (see Ge 1), no power or combination of powers can thwart his plan and purpose to save his people. (Hence his chosen people are the blessed nation; see vv. 12–19.)
33:4 *word.* God's royal word by which he governs all things (see 107:20; 147:15,18). *right and true.* Not chaotic, devious or erratic. Under the Lord's rule in the creation there is goodness, order and dependability.
33:5 *loves.* Delights in doing. *righteousness and justice.* See note on 4:1. *his unfailing love.* Here, his goodness to all his creatures (see 36:5–9; 104:27–28; see also note on 6:4).
33:6 *word.* God's creating word (see v. 9; 104:7; 119:89; Ge 1; Job 38:8–11; Heb 11:3).
33:7 *into jars . . . storehouses.* Like a householder storing up his olive oil and grain (see 104:9; Ge 1:9–10; Job 38:8–11; Pr 8:29; Jer 5:22).
33:8 *all the earth . . . all the people.* Not only Israel, but all mankind, for all experience the goodness of his sovereign rule (see note on 9:1)—but he foils all their contrary designs (vv. 10–11). *fear the LORD.* See v. 18; see also note on 15:4.
33:11 *heart.* See note on 4:7.
33:12–19 Israel is safe and secure under God's protective rule.
33:12 *Blessed.* See note on 1:1. *people he chose for his inheritance.* Israel (see Dt 9:29).
33:16 *king.* Nation (see v. 12) and king constitute an organic social unit (see 28:8 and note).

18But the eyes[n] of the LORD are on those
who fear him,
on those whose hope is in his
unfailing love,[o]
19to deliver them from death[p]
and keep them alive in famine.[q]

20We wait[r] in hope for the LORD;
he is our help and our shield.
21In him our hearts rejoice,[s]
for we trust in his holy name.[t]
22May your unfailing love[u] rest upon us,
O LORD,
even as we put our hope in you.

Psalm 34[k]

Of David. When he pretended to be
insane[v] before Abimelech, who drove
him away, and he left.

1I will extol the LORD at all times;[w]
his praise will always be on my lips.
2My soul will boast[x] in the LORD;
let the afflicted hear and rejoice.[y]
3Glorify the LORD[z] with me;
let us exalt[a] his name together.

4I sought the LORD,[b] and he answered
me;
he delivered[c] me from all my fears.

5Those who look to him are radiant;[d]
their faces are never covered with
shame.[e]
6This poor man called, and the LORD
heard him;
he saved him out of all his troubles.[f]
7The angel of the LORD[g] encamps
around those who fear him,
and he delivers[h] them.

8Taste and see that the LORD is good;[i]
blessed is the man who takes refuge[j]
in him.
9Fear the LORD,[k] you his saints,
for those who fear him lack
nothing.[l]
10The lions may grow weak and hungry,
but those who seek the LORD lack no
good thing.[m]

11Come, my children, listen[n] to me;
I will teach you[o] the fear of the
LORD.[p]
12Whoever of you loves life[q]
and desires to see many good days,
13keep your tongue[r] from evil

Cross references

33:18
n S Ex 3:16;
S Ps 11:4;
1Pe 3:12
o S Ps 6:4
33:19 p Ps 56:13;
Ac 12:11
q S Job 5:20
33:20 r Ps 27:14
33:21 s S 1Sa 2:1;
S Joel 2:23
t S Ps 30:4; S 99:3
33:22 u Ps 6:4
34 Title
v 1Sa 21:13
34:1 w Ps 71:6;
S Eph 5:20;
1Th 5:18
34:2 x Ps 44:8;
Jer 9:24;
1Co 1:31
y Ps 69:32;
107:42; 119:74
34:3 z Ps 63:3;
86:12; Da 4:37;
Jn 17:1; Ro 15:6
a S Ex 15:2
34:4
b S Ex 32:11;
Ps 77:2 c ver 17;
Ps 18:43; 22:4;
56:13; 86:13

34:5 d S Ex 34:29
e Ps 25:3; 44:15;
69:7; 83:16
34:6 f S Ps 25:17
34:7 g S Ge 32:1;
S Da 3:28;
S Mt 18:10
h Ps 22:4; 37:40;
41:1; 97:10;
Isa 31:5;
Ac 12:11
34:8 i Heb 6:5;
1Pe 2:3 j S Ps 2:12

34:9 k S Dt 6:13; Rev 14:7 l S Ps 23:1 **34:10** m S Ps 23:1
34:11 n Ps 66:16 o S Ps 32:8 p S Ps 19:9 **34:12** q Ecc 3:13
34:13 r Ps 39:1; 141:3; Pr 13:3; 21:23; Jas 1:26

k This psalm is an acrostic poem, the verses of which begin
with the successive letters of the Hebrew alphabet.

33:18–19 The concluding couplet of the second eight-verse stanza of praise contrasts with the concluding couplet of the first (vv. 10–11); both are climactic and together they voice the heart of the praise.
33:18,22 *unfailing love.* Here, his covenant favor toward Israel (see note on 6:4).
33:20–22 The people's response: faith's commitment expressed in confession (vv. 20–21) and petition (v. 22).
33:20 *shield.* See note on 3:3.
33:21 *hearts.* See note on 4:7. *name.* See note on 5:11.
Ps 34 Praise of the Lord for deliverance in answer to prayer, and instruction in godliness. In the Psalms, praise commonly leads to a call to praise, as in v. 3 (see note on 9:1). Here, uniquely (but see also Ps 92), praise (vv. 1–7) leads into godly instruction (vv. 8–22) in the manner of the wisdom teachers (see Introduction to Proverbs: Wisdom Literature). Structurally, the psalm is a somewhat irregular alphabetic acrostic (it lacks a verse for one Hebrew letter and adds a verse at the end). Its eight stanzas develop four major themes, with two stanzas devoted to each (see following notes).
34 title The superscription assigns this psalm to the occasion in David's life (see note on Ps 3 title) narrated in 1Sa 21:10–15—but note "Abimelech" rather than "Achish" (perhaps Abimelech was a traditional dynastic name or title for Philistine kings; see Ge 20; 21:22–34; 26). Not all agree with this tradition, however; they feel that it is more likely that early Hebrew editors of the Psalms linked 1Sa 21 with Ps 34 on the basis of word association (the Hebrew for "pretended to be insane," 1Sa 21:13, comes from the same root as the Hebrew used here for "taste," v. 8).
34:1–7 Praise for the Lord's deliverance in answer to prayer.
34:1–3 Commitment to continual praise—to the encouragement of the godly who are afflicted (v. 2; see the instruc-

tion in vv. 8–22).
34:2 *soul.* See note on 6:3.
34:3 *name.* See note on 5:11.
34:4–7 The occasion: God's saving answer to prayer.
34:5 *radiant.* With joy (see Isa 60:5).
34:6 *poor.* Here, as often in the Psalms, "poor" characterizes not necessarily one who has no possessions, but one who is (and recognizes that he is) without resources to effect his own deliverance (or secure his own life, safety or well-being)—and so is dependent on God.
34:7 *angel of the LORD.* God's heavenly representative, his "messenger," sent to effect his will on earth (see 35:5–6; see also note on Ge 16:7). *encamps around.* The line speaks of the security with which the Lord surrounds his people, individually and collectively; it does not teach a doctrine of individual "guardian angels." *those who fear him.* Those described in vv. 8–14.
34:8–14 Instruction in "the fear of the LORD." The two stanzas really belong together, with the title line (v. 11) at the center—Hebrew authors often centered key lines (see note on 6:6). Note the pattern of the imperatives: "Taste" (v. 8), "Fear" (v. 9), "Come" (v. 11), "keep" (v. 13), "Turn" (v. 14). A symmetrical development of the theme "good" dominates the stanza: Because the Lord is good (v. 8), those who trust in him will lack nothing good (v. 10); but in order to experience good days (v. 12), they must shun evil and do good (v. 14). To trust and obey—that is "the fear of the LORD." On the instruction of this stanza see Ps 37. For Peter's use of vv. 12–16 see 1Pe 3:8–12.
34:8 *blessed.* See note on 1:1.
34:9 *Fear the LORD.* See v. 11; see also note on 15:4. *saints.* See note on 4:3.
34:11 *Come, my children.* Conventional language of the wisdom teachers (see Introduction to Proverbs: Purpose and Teaching).

and your lips from speaking lies. *s*
¹⁴Turn from evil and do good; *t*
   seek peace *u* and pursue it.

¹⁵The eyes of the LORD *v* are on the
   righteous *w*
  and his ears are attentive *x* to their
   cry;
¹⁶the face of the LORD is against *y* those
   who do evil, *z*
  to cut off the memory *a* of them from
   the earth.

¹⁷The righteous cry out, and the LORD
   hears *b* them;
  he delivers them from all their
   troubles.
¹⁸The LORD is close *c* to the
   brokenhearted *d*
  and saves those who are crushed in
   spirit.

¹⁹A righteous man may have many
   troubles, *e*
  but the LORD delivers him from them
   all; *f*
²⁰he protects all his bones,
  not one of them will be broken. *g*

²¹Evil will slay the wicked; *h*
  the foes of the righteous will be
   condemned.
²²The LORD redeems *i* his servants;
  no one will be condemned who takes
   refuge *j* in him.

Psalm 35

Of David.

¹Contend, *k* O LORD, with those who
   contend with me;
  fight *l* against those who fight against
   me.
²Take up shield *m* and buckler;
  arise *n* and come to my aid. *o*
³Brandish spear *p* and javelin¹ *q*
  against those who pursue me.
Say to my soul,
  "I am your salvation. *r* "

⁴May those who seek my life *s*
  be disgraced *t* and put to shame; *u*
  may those who plot my ruin
  be turned back *v* in dismay.
⁵May they be like chaff *w* before the
   wind,
  with the angel of the LORD *x* driving
   them away;
⁶may their path be dark and slippery,
  with the angel of the LORD pursuing
   them.
⁷Since they hid their net *y* for me
   without cause *z*
  and without cause dug a pit *a* for me,
⁸may ruin overtake them by surprise— *b*
  may the net they hid entangle them,
  may they fall into the pit, *c* to their
   ruin.
⁹Then my soul will rejoice *d* in the LORD
  and delight in his salvation. *e*

34:13 *s*S Ps 12:2; 1Pe 2:22 **34:14** *t*Ps 37:27; Isa 1:17; 3Jn 1:11 *u*S Ro 14:19 **34:15** *v*Ps 33:18 *w*S Job 23:10; S 36:7 *x*Mal 3:16; S Jn 9:31 **34:16** *y*Lev 17:10; Jer 23:30 *z*1Pe 3:10-12* *a*S Ex 17:14; Ps 9:6 **34:17** *b*Ps 145:19 **34:18** *c*Dt 4:7; Ps 119:151; 145:18; Isa 50:8 *d*Ps 51:17; 109:16; 147:3; Isa 61:1 **34:19** *e*ver 17; Ps 25:17 *f*S Job 5:19; 2Ti 3:11 **34:20** *g*Jn 19:36* **34:21** *h*Ps 7:9; 9:16; 11:5; 37:20; 73:27; 94:23; 106:43; 112:10; 140:11; Pr 14:32; 24:16 **34:22** *i*S Ex 6:6; S 15:13; Lk 1:68; Rev 14:3 *j*Ps 2:12 **35:1** *k*S 1Sa 24:15 *l*S Ex 14:14 **35:2** *m*Ps 3:3 *n*Ps 3:7 *o*S Ge 50:24; S Job 17:3 **35:3** *p*S Nu 25:7 *q*S Jos 8:18 *r*Ps 27:1 **35:4** *s*Ps 38:12; 40:14; Jer 4:30 *t*Ps 69:6,19; 70:2; 83:17; Isa 45:16; Mal 2:9 *u*Ps 25:3 *v*Ps 129:5 **35:5** *w*S Job 13:25; Ps 1:4 *x*Ps 34:7 **35:7** *y*S Job 18:8 *z*S Ps 7:4 *a*S Job 9:31; **35:8** *b*Isa 47:11; 1Th 5:3 *c*S Ps 7:15 **35:9** *d*S Ps 2:11; S Lk 1:47 *e*Ps 9:14; 13:5; 27:1

13 Or *and block the way*

34:13 See 15:2–3; Jas 3:5–10. For the tongue as a weapon see note on 5:9.
34:14 *seek peace.* See 37:37; 120:7; Pr 12:20; Zec 8:19 (also Zec 8:16–17); Mt 5:9; Ro 12:18; 1Co 7:15; 2Co 13:11; 1Th 5:13; Heb 12:14; Jas 3:17–18.
34:15–18 Assurance that the Lord hears the prayers of the righteous. He so thoroughly thwarts those who do evil that they are forgotten (v. 16).
34:15 *righteous.* See vv. 8–14; see also note on 1:5.
34:16 *face of the LORD.* See note on 13:1.
34:17–18 See especially 51:17.
34:19–22 Assurance that the Lord is the unfailing deliverer of the righteous—and condemns the wicked for their hostility toward the righteous (see v. 21).
34:20 *all his bones.* His whole being (see note on 6:2). *not one of them will be broken.* Perhaps John's Gospel applies this word to Jesus (see NIV text note on Jn 19:36)—as the one above all others who could be called a "righteous man" (v. 19).
34:21–22 *condemned.* Dealt with as guilty.
34:22 *redeems.* See note on 25:22.
Ps 35 An appeal to the heavenly King, as divine Warrior and Judge, to come to the defense of "his servant" (v. 27) who is being maliciously slandered by those toward whom he had shown only the most tender friendship. The attack

seems to have been occasioned by some "distress" (v. 26) that had overtaken the king (see vv. 15,19,21,25), perhaps an illness (see v. 13; see also introduction to Ps 6). Ps 35 exemplifies such a "cry" to the Lord in expectation of vindication as that spoken of in 34:15–22—except that here the author does not expressly identify himself as one of the "righteous" (34:21); he appeals to the Lord rather as innocent victim of an unmotivated attack. Regarding structure, after an initial appeal to the Lord as divine Warrior (vv. 1–3) there follows a threefold elaboration of David's petition to the divine Judge, each concluding with a vow to praise (vv. 4–10, 11–18, 19–28); see note on 7:17.
35:1–3 Appeal to the Lord as Warrior-King (see Ex 15:1–18), David's Overlord.
35:2 *arise.* See note on 3:7.
35:3 *soul.* See note on 6:3.
35:4–10 Appeal to the Lord to deal with the attackers, matching judgment with their violent intent (see note on 5:10).
35:4 *plot my ruin.* See note on 5:9.
35:5–6 *angel of the LORD.* See 34:7 and note.
35:5 *like chaff.* See note on 1:4.
35:9–10 See note on 7:17.
35:9 *soul.* See note on 6:3.

10My whole being will exclaim,
  "Who is like you,*f* O LORD?
You rescue the poor from those too
    strong*g* for them,
  the poor and needy*h* from those who
    rob them."

11Ruthless witnesses*i* come forward;
  they question me on things I know
    nothing about.
12They repay me evil for good*j*
  and leave my soul forlorn.
13Yet when they were ill, I put on
    sackcloth*k*
  and humbled myself with fasting.*l*
When my prayers returned to me
    unanswered,
14 I went about mourning*m*
    as though for my friend or brother.
  I bowed my head in grief
    as though weeping for my mother.
15But when I stumbled, they gathered in
    glee;*n*
  attackers gathered against me when I
    was unaware.
  They slandered*o* me without ceasing.
16Like the ungodly they maliciously
    mocked*m; p*
  they gnashed their teeth*q* at me.
17O Lord, how long*r* will you look on?
  Rescue my life from their ravages,
  my precious life*s* from these lions.*t*
18I will give you thanks in the great
    assembly;*u*
  among throngs*v* of people I will
    praise you.*w*

19Let not those gloat over me
  who are my enemies*x* without cause;
  let not those who hate me without
    reason*y*
  maliciously wink the eye.*z*
20They do not speak peaceably,
  but devise false accusations*a*
  against those who live quietly in the
    land.

21They gape*b* at me and say, "Aha!
    Aha!*c*
  With our own eyes we have seen it."

22O LORD, you have seen*d* this; be not
    silent.
  Do not be far*e* from me, O Lord.
23Awake,*f* and rise*g* to my defense!
  Contend*h* for me, my God and Lord.
24Vindicate me in your righteousness,
    O LORD my God;
  do not let them gloat*i* over me.
25Do not let them think, "Aha,*i* just
    what we wanted!"
  or say, "We have swallowed him
    up."*k*

26May all who gloat*l* over my distress*m*
  be put to shame*n* and confusion;
  may all who exalt themselves over me*o*
  be clothed with shame and disgrace.
27May those who delight in my
    vindication*p*
  shout for joy*q* and gladness;
  may they always say, "The LORD be
    exalted,
  who delights*r* in the well-being of
    his servant."*s*
28My tongue will speak of your
    righteousness*t*
  and of your praises all day long.*u*

Psalm 36

For the director of music. Of David the
servant of the LORD.

1An oracle is within my heart
    concerning the sinfulness of the
    wicked:*n v*
  There is no fear*w* of God

35:10 /S Ex 9:14;
S Ps 18:31; 113:5
*g*Ps 18:17
*h*Ps 12:5; 37:14;
74:21; 86:1;
109:16; 140:12;
Isa 41:17
35:11 /S Ex 23:1;
S Mt 26:60
35:12 /Ps 38:20;
109:5; Pr 17:13;
Jer 18:20
35:13
*k*S 2Sa 3:31;
1Ki 20:31;
Ps 30:11; 69:11
/Job 30:25;
Ps 69:10; 109:24
35:14 *m*Ps 38:6;
42:9; 43:2
35:15
*n*S Job 31:23
*o*S Job 16:10
35:16 *p*S Ps 22:7;
Mk 10:34
*q*S Job 16:9;
Mk 9:18; Ac 7:54
35:17 *r*Ps 6:3
*s*Ps 22:20
*t*Ps 22:21; 57:4;
58:6
35:18
*u*S Ps 22:25
*v*Ps 42:4; 109:30
*w*S Ps 22:22
35:19 *x*Ps 9:13
*y*ver 7; Ps 38:19;
69:4; Jn 15:25*
*z*Pr 6:13; 10:10
35:20 *a*Ps 38:12;
55:21; Jer 9:8;
Mic 6:12

35:21
*b*S Job 16:10
*c*Ps 40:15; 70:3;
Eze 25:3
35:22 *d*Ex 3:7;
Ps 10:14
*e*S Ps 10:1
35:23 /S Ps 7:6;
80:2 *g*Ps 17:13
*h*S 1Sa 24:15
35:24 /Ps 22:17
35:25 /ver 21
*k*Ps 124:3;
Pr 1:12; La 2:16
35:26 /Ps 22:17
*m*Ps 4:1
*n*S Job 8:22;
Ps 109:29;
Mic 7:10
*o*Job 19:5;
Ps 38:16
35:27 *p*Ps 9:4
*q*Ps 20:5; S 33:3
*r*Ps 147:11; 149:4
*s*S Job 17:3
35:28 *t*Ps 5:8;
51:14 *u*Ps 71:15,
24; 72:15

36:1 *v*S Job 21:16 *w*Jer 2:19; 36:16,24

m 16 Septuagint; Hebrew may mean *ungodly circle of
mockers.* *n 1* Or *heart: / Sin proceeds from the
wicked.*

35:10 *poor and needy.* See 34:6 and note.
35:11–18 The accusation—they repaid my friendship
with malicious slander—with a renewed petition (v. 17) and
a vow to praise (v. 18).
35:12 *soul.* See note on 6:3.
35:13 *sackcloth.* A symbol of mourning (see 30:11; Ge
37:34). *fasting.* An act of mourning (see 69:10).
35:15 *stumbled.* Not morally. He was brought low by
circumstances (see 9:3; 27:2; 37:24; 56:13; 119:165).
35:16 *gnashed their teeth.* In malice (see 37:12; La 2:16).
35:17 *how long . . . ?* See note on 6:3 (see also Introduction: Theology). *lions.* See note on 7:2.
35:18 *assembly.* See note on 1:5.
35:19–28 Renewed appeal for judgment, with a concluding vow to praise (v. 28).
35:19 *enemies without cause.* See vv. 11–17; an experience frequently reflected also elsewhere in the Psalter (see

38:19; 69:4; 109:3; 119:78,86,161). See also La 3:52. *hate
me without reason.* See 69:4. It is not known which of these
passages is referred to in Jn 15:25. Both psalms reflect circumstances applicable also to Jesus' experience (but see
introduction to Ps 69).
35:21 *Aha! Aha!* See v. 25; see also note on 3:2.
35:22 *be not silent.* Do not remain inactive (see 28:1 and
note; 83:1; 109:1).
35:23 *Awake.* See note on 7:6. *rise.* See note on 3:7.
35:24 *righteousness.* See note on 4:1.
35:25 *swallowed.* See 124:3.
35:26 Once again: May their judgment match their evil
intent (see vv. 4–10).
35:27 May all who are faithful supporters of the Lord's
"servant" (here no doubt equivalent to his "anointed"; see
note on 2:2) have reason to rejoice and praise the Lord.
35:28 *righteousness.* See note on 4:1.

before his eyes. *x*

²For in his own eyes he flatters himself
too much to detect or hate his sin. *y*

³The words of his mouth *z* are wicked
and deceitful; *a*
he has ceased to be wise *b* and to do
good. *c*

⁴Even on his bed he plots evil; *d*
he commits himself to a sinful
course *e*
and does not reject what is wrong. *f*

⁵Your love, O Lᴏʀᴅ, reaches to the
heavens,
your faithfulness *g* to the skies. *h*

⁶Your righteousness *i* is like the mighty
mountains, *j*
your justice like the great deep. *k*
O Lᴏʀᴅ, you preserve both man and
beast. *l*

⁷ How priceless is your unfailing
love! *m*
Both high and low among men
find *o* refuge in the shadow of your
wings. *n*

⁸They feast on the abundance of your
house; *o*
you give them drink from your river *p*
of delights. *q*

⁹For with you is the fountain of life; *r*
in your light *s* we see light.

¹⁰Continue your love *t* to those who
know you, *u*
your righteousness to the upright in
heart. *v*

¹¹May the foot of the proud not come
against me,
nor the hand of the wicked *w* drive
me away.

¹²See how the evildoers lie fallen—
thrown down, not able to rise! *x*

36:1
*x*S Job 23:15;
Ro 3:18*
36:2 *y*Dt 29:19
36:3 *z*Ps 10:7
*a*S Job 5:13;
Ps 5:6,9; 43:1;
144:8,11;
Isa 44:20
*b*Ps 94:8
*c*Jer 4:22; 13:23;
Am 3:10
36:4 *d*Pr 4:16
*e*Isa 65:2
*f*Ps 52:3; Ro 12:9
36:5 *g*Ps 89:1;
119:90
*h*Ps 57:10; 71:19;
89:2; 103:11;
108:4
36:6 *i*Ps 5:8
*j*Ps 68:15
*k*S Ge 1:2; S 7:11
*l*Ne 9:6;
Ps 104:14;
145:16
36:7 *m*Ps 6:4
*n*S Ru 2:12;
S Ps 17:8; 57:1;
91:4

36:8 *o*Ps 65:4;
Isa 25:6;
Jer 31:12,14
*p*Job 20:17;
Rev 22:1
*q*S Ps 23:2; 63:5
36:9 *r*Ps 87:7;
Pr 10:11; 16:22;
Jer 2:13 *s*Ps 4:6;
27:1; 76:4;

104:2; Isa 2:5; 9:2; 60:1,19; Jn 1:4; 1Pe 2:9 **36:10** *t*Jer 31:3
*u*Jer 9:24; 22:16 *v*Ps 7:10; 11:2; 94:15; 125:4 **36:11**
*w*Ps 71:4; 140:4 **36:12** *x*S Ps 18:38

*o*7 Or *love, O God! / Men find*; or *love! / Both heavenly
beings and men / find*

Ps 36 A prayer for God's unfailing protection, as the psalmist reflects on the godlessness of the wicked and the goodness
of God. In Jewish practice, vv. 7–10 form part of the morning
prayer.
36 title *For the director of music.* See note on Ps 4 title.
servant of the Lᴏʀᴅ. His royal servant (see notes on Ps 18
title; 35:27; see also 2Sa 7:20).
36:1–4 The foolish and haughty godlessness of the wicked.
36:1 *oracle.* Usually reserved for words of revelation from
God, such as those spoken by the prophets (see, e.g., Nu
23:7; Isa 13:1; Jer 23:33–38; Eze 12:10; see also note on
Nu 23:7). Here reference is to an insight, perhaps coming
like a flash, into the true character of the wicked. *heart.* See
note on 4:7. *no fear of God.* See 55:19. They take no
account of his all-seeing eye, his righteous judgment and his
power to deal with them (see note on 10:11). For Paul's use
of this verse see Ro 3:18.
36:2 *flatters himself.* Not in self-righteousness but out of
the smug, conceited notion that he is accountable to no one.
36:3 *words of his mouth.* See note on 5:9. *ceased to be
wise.* See 94:8–11; Pr 2:9–11. *do good.* See 34:8–14 and
note.
36:4 *on his bed.* When one's thoughts are free to range,
and to set the course for the activities of the day. The wicked
do not meditate on God's law "day and night" (1:2; see
119:55), or let a godly heart instruct them at night (see
16:7), or at night commune with God (see 42:8), think of
him (see 63:6) and reflect on his promises (see 119:148).
36:5–9 The goodness of the Lord—his benevolence
toward all his creatures (see 33:4–5).
36:5 *love . . . faithfulness.* That is, love-and-faithfulness (as
in 57:3; 61:7; 85:10; 86:15; 89:14; 115:1; 138:2; Pr 3:3;
14:22; 16:6; 20:28; see note on 3:7). *reaches to the heavens . . . to the skies.* Encompasses all the realms of creaturely
existence (see 57:10; 108:4).
36:6 *righteousness . . . justice.* That is, righteousness-and-
justice (as in 33:5; 89:14; 97:2; Hos 2:19; see also Isa 9:7;
33:5; Jer 9:24). *righteousness.* See note on 4:1. *mighty
mountains . . . great deep.* As high as the mountains, as deep

as the sea.
36:7 *unfailing love.* See v. 5; see also note on 6:4. *high and
low.* All conditions of men. *shadow of your wings.* See 17:8
and note.
36:8 *feast . . . drink.* Life-giving food and water. *house.*
Here, God's whole estate or realm—i.e., the earth, from
which springs the abundance of food for all living things (see
note on 24:2). *river.* The "channel" (Job 38:25) by which
God brings forth the rain out of his "storehouses" (33:7; see
Job 38:8–11,22,37; Jer 10:13) in his "upper chambers"
(104:13; see 65:9; Isa 30:25 and the references to "blessings" from heaven in Ge 49:25; Dt 33:23). This vivid imagery, depicting God's control over, and gift of, the waters from
heaven, which feed the rivers and streams of earth to give life
and health wherever they flow, is the source of the symbol of
"the river of the water of life" that flows from the temple of
God (Rev 22:1–2; see also Eze 47:1–12). *of delights.* Fur-
nishing many sources of joy.
36:9 The climax and summation of vv. 5–9. *fountain of
life.* See Jer 2:13; 17:13. Ultimately, for sinners, God provides the water of life through Jesus Christ (Jn 4:10,14). *your
light.* See 27:1 and note. *see.* Experience, have, enjoy, as in
16:10; 27:13; 34:8,12; 49:9,19; 89:48; 90:15; 106:5
("enjoy"); Job 9:25 ("glimpse"); 42:5; Ecc 1:16 ("experienced"); 3:13 ("find"); 6:6 ("enjoy"); 8:16; Isa 53:10; La
3:1. *light.* Life in its fullness as it was created to be. For the
association of light with life see 49:19; 56:13; Job 3:20;
33:30; Isa 53:11.
36:10–11 The prayer: Your "love" (v. 5) and "righteousness" (v. 6), which you display in all creation—show these
to all who know (acknowledge) you and are upright (the
people of God). But keep the wicked, "foot" and "hand,"
from success against me (the king; see note on 33:16).
36:10 *love.* See note on 6:4. *righteousness.* See note on
4:1.
36:11 *proud.* See note on 31:23.
36:12 Confidence (see note on 3:8). *lie fallen.* Perhaps in
death (see note on 13:4).

Psalm 37[p]

Of David.

[1]Do not fret because of evil men
  or be envious[y] of those who do
    wrong;[z]
[2]for like the grass they will soon
    wither,[a]
  like green plants they will soon die
    away.[b]

[3]Trust in the LORD and do good;
  dwell in the land[c] and enjoy safe
    pasture.[d]
[4]Delight[e] yourself in the LORD
  and he will give you the desires of
    your heart.[f]

[5]Commit your way to the LORD;
  trust in him[g] and he will do this:
[6]He will make your righteousness[h] shine
    like the dawn,[i]
  the justice of your cause like the
    noonday sun.

[7]Be still[j] before the LORD and wait
    patiently[k] for him;
  do not fret[l] when men succeed in
    their ways,[m]
  when they carry out their wicked
    schemes.[n]

[8]Refrain from anger[o] and turn from
    wrath;
  do not fret[p]—it leads only to evil.
[9]For evil men will be cut off,[q]
  but those who hope[r] in the LORD
    will inherit the land.[s]

[10]A little while, and the wicked will be no
    more;[t]
  though you look for them, they will
    not be found.
[11]But the meek will inherit the land[u]
  and enjoy great peace.[v]

[12]The wicked plot[w] against the righteous
  and gnash their teeth[x] at them;
[13]but the Lord laughs at the wicked,
  for he knows their day is coming.[y]

[14]The wicked draw the sword[z]
  and bend the bow[a]
  to bring down the poor and needy,[b]
  to slay those whose ways are upright.
[15]But their swords will pierce their own
    hearts,[c]
  and their bows will be broken.[d]

[16]Better the little that the righteous have

Cross references (center column)

37:1 yPr 3:31; 23:17-18
zPs 73:3; Pr 24:19
37:2 aS 2Ki 19:26; Job 14:2;
Ps 102:4; Isa 40:7
bver 38; Ps 90:6; 92:7; Jas 1:10
37:3 cDt 30:20
dEze 34:14; Jn 10:9
37:4 eS Job 27:10
fS Job 7:6; Ps 21:2; 145:19; Mt 6:33
37:5 gPs 4:5
37:6 hPs 18:24; 103:17; 112:3
iS Job 11:17
37:7 jS Ex 14:14; S Isa 41:1
kS Ps 27:14; 40:1; 130:5; Isa 38:13; Hab 3:16; Ro 8:25
lver 1
mJer 12:1
nPs 21:11; 26:10; 119:150

37:8 oEph 4:31; Col 3:8
pver 1
37:9 qS Ps 31:22; 101:8; 118:10; Pr 2:22
rIsa 25:9; 26:8; 40:31; 49:23; 51:5
sver 22; Ps 25:13; Isa 49:8; 57:13; Mt 5:5
37:10 tS Job 7:10; Eze 27:36
37:11 uS Nu 14:24; Mt 5:5
vS Lev 26:6;

S Nu 6:26 **37:12** wPs 2:1; 31:13 xS Job 16:9; Ps 35:16; 112:10 **37:13** yISa 26:10; Eze 12:23 **37:14** zS Ps 22:20 aPs 11:2 bS Ps 35:10 **37:15** cS Ps 9:16 dS 1Sa 2:4; Ps 46:9; Jer 49:35

[p]This psalm is an acrostic poem, the stanzas of which begin with the successive letters of the Hebrew alphabet.

Ps 37 Instruction in godly wisdom. (For other "wisdom" psalms see 34:8–22; 49; 112; others closely related are Ps 1; 73; 91; 92:6–9,12–15; 111; 119; 127–128; 133; see Introduction to Proverbs: Wisdom Literature.) This psalm's dominant theme is related to the contrast between the wicked and the righteous reflected in Ps 36. The central issue addressed is: Who will "inherit the land" (vv. 9,11,22,29), i.e., live on to enjoy the blessings of the Lord in the promised land? Will the wicked, who plot (v. 12), scheme (vv. 7,32), default on debts (v. 21), use raw power to gain advantage (v. 14) and seem thereby to flourish (vv. 7,16,35)? Or will the righteous, who trust in the Lord (vv. 3,5,7,34) and are humble (v. 11), blameless (vv. 18,37), generous (vv. 21,26), upright (v. 37) and peaceable (v. 37), and from whose mouth is heard the moral wisdom that reflects meditation on God's law (vv. 30–31)? For a similar characterization of the wicked see 10:2–11; 73:4–12. For a similar characterization of the righteous see Ps 112. For a similar statement concerning the transitoriness of the wicked see Ps 49; 73:18–20. Structurally, in this alphabetic acrostic, two verses are devoted to each letter of the alphabet, though with some irregularity. The main theme is developed in vv. 1–11, then further elaborated in the rest of the psalm. The whole is framed by statements contrasting the brief career of the wicked (vv. 1–2) and the Lord's sustaining help of the righteous (vv. 39–40).

37:1–2 See v. 7; Ps 73.
37:2 See note on v. 20.
37:3 See 34:8–14 and note.
37:4 *heart.* See note on 4:7.
37:5 *Commit.* See 1Pe 5:7.
37:6 *righteousness . . . justice.* That is, righteousness-and-justice (see note on 36:6). *righteousness.* See note on 1:5.

37:8 *anger . . . wrath.* Evidence of fretting over the wicked's prosperity, gained to the disadvantage of and even at the expense of the righteous.

37:9 *inherit the land.* Receive from the Lord secure entitlement (for them and their children) to the promised land as the created and redeemed sphere and bountiful source of provision for the life of God's people. Those who hope in the Lord—i.e., trustfully look to him to bestow life and its blessings as a gift—will inherit the land, not those who apart from God and by evil means try to take possession of it and its wealth (see vv. 11,22,29; cf. Jos 7).

37:10 *A little while.* Shortness of time is here a figure for certainty of event (see 58:9; Job 20:5–11; Hag 2:6).

37:11 See Mt 5:5. *meek.* Those who humbly acknowledge their dependence on the goodness and grace of God and betray no arrogance toward their fellowman. *great peace.* Unmixed blessedness.

37:12 *righteous.* See note on 1:5. *gnash their teeth.* See 35:16 and note.

37:13 *Lord laughs.* See 2:4. *knows their day is coming.* Strikingly, the psalmist nowhere speaks of God's active involvement in bringing the wicked down—though he hints at it in v. 22. The certainty that the life of the wicked "will be cut off" is frequently asserted (vv. 9,22,28,34,38; cf. vv. 2,8,10,15,17,20,36,38)—and the Lord also knows it—but God's positive action is here reserved for his care for and protection of the righteous. *their day.* The time for each of them, when he will be "cut off," as in 1Sa 26:10 ("his time," lit. "his day"); Job 18:20 ("his fate").

37:14 *poor and needy.* See 34:6 and note.
37:15 *pierce . . . hearts.* See 45:5.
37:16–17 *righteous.* See note on 1:5.

than the wealth[e] of many wicked;
[17]for the power of the wicked will be broken,[f]
but the LORD upholds[g] the righteous.

[18]The days of the blameless are known to the LORD,[h]
and their inheritance will endure forever.[i]

[19]In times of disaster they will not wither;
in days of famine they will enjoy plenty.

[20]But the wicked will perish:[j]
The LORD's enemies will be like the beauty of the fields,
they will vanish—vanish like smoke.[k]

[21]The wicked borrow and do not repay,
but the righteous give generously;[l]
[22]those the LORD blesses will inherit the land,
but those he curses[m] will be cut off.[n]

[23]If the LORD delights[o] in a man's way,
he makes his steps firm;[p]
[24]though he stumble, he will not fall,[q]
for the LORD upholds[r] him with his hand.

[25]I was young and now I am old,
yet I have never seen the righteous forsaken[s]
or their children begging[t] bread.
[26]They are always generous and lend freely;[u]
their children will be blessed.[v]

[27]Turn from evil and do good;[w]
then you will dwell in the land forever.[x]
[28]For the LORD loves the just
and will not forsake his faithful ones.[y]

They will be protected forever,
but the offspring of the wicked will be cut off;[z]
[29]the righteous will inherit the land[a]
and dwell in it forever.[b]

[30]The mouth of the righteous man utters wisdom,[c]
and his tongue speaks what is just.
[31]The law of his God is in his heart;[d]
his feet do not slip.[e]

[32]The wicked lie in wait[f] for the righteous,[g]
seeking their very lives;
[33]but the LORD will not leave them in their power
or let them be condemned[h] when brought to trial.[i]

[34]Wait for the LORD
and keep his way.[k]
He will exalt you to inherit the land;
when the wicked are cut off,[l] you will see[m] it.

[35]I have seen a wicked and ruthless man flourishing[n] like a green tree in its native soil,
[36]but he soon passed away and was no more;
though I looked for him, he could not be found.[o]

[37]Consider the blameless,[p] observe the upright;[q]
there is a future[q] for the man of peace.[r]
[38]But all sinners[s] will be destroyed;[t]
the future[r] of the wicked will be cut off.[u]

[39]The salvation[v] of the righteous comes from the LORD;
he is their stronghold in time of trouble.[w]
[40]The LORD helps[x] them and delivers[y] them;
he delivers them from the wicked and saves[z] them,
because they take refuge[a] in him.

37:16 [e]Pr 15:16; 16:8
37:17 [f]Job 38:15; Ps 10:15
[g]Ps 41:12; 140:12; 145:14; 146:7
37:18 [h]S Job 23:10; Ps 44:21 [i]ver 27, 29
37:20 [j]S Ps 34:21 [k]Ps 68:2; 102:3; Isa 51:6
37:21 [l]S Lev 25:35; Ps 112:5
37:22 [m]S Job 5:3 [n]ver 9
37:23 [o]S Nu 14:8; Ps 147:11 [p]S Job 11:5; S Ps 7:9; 66:9
37:24 [q]S Ps 13:4; 27:2; 38:17; 55:22; 119:165; Pr 3:23; 10:9 [r]2Ch 9:8; Ps 41:12; 145:14
37:25 [s]ver 28; S Ge 15:1; Heb 13:5 [t]Ps 111:5; 145:15; Mk 10:46
37:26 [u]S Lev 25:35 [v]Dt 28:4; Ps 112:2
37:27 [w]Ps 34:14; 3Jn 1:11 [x]S Nu 24:21
37:28 [y]S Dt 7:6; S Ps 18:25; S 97:10 [z]S Ge 17:14; S Dt 32:26; Pr 2:22
37:29 [a]ver 9; Pr 2:21 [b]Isa 34:17
37:30 [c]Ps 49:3; Pr 10:13
37:31 [d]S Dt 6:6; S Job 22:22 [e]S Dt 32:35
37:32 [f]S Ps 10:8 [g]Ps 11:5
37:33 [h]Job 32:3; Ps 34:22; 79:11 [i]2Pe 2:9
37:34 [j]Ps 27:14 [k]S Ps 18:21 [l]ver 9 [m]Ps 52:6
37:35 [n]S Job 5:3
37:36 [o]ver 10; Pr 12:7; Isa 41:12; Da 11:19
37:37 [p]ver 18; S Ge 6:9; Ps 18:25 [q]Ps 11:7 [r]Isa 57:1-2
37:38 [s]S Ps 1:1 [t]S ver 2; Ps 73:19 [u]ver 9 37:39 [v]S Ps 3:8 [w]S Ps 9:9 37:40 [x]S 1Ch 5:20; S Ps 20:2 [y]S Ps 34:7 [z]S Ps 18:48 [a]Ps 2:12

[q]37 Or there will be posterity   [r]38 Or posterity

37:18 blameless. See v. 37; 15:2; see also note on 26:1.
37:20 beauty. The grass and flowers (cf. v. 2; 90:5–6; 102:11; 103:15–16; Job 14:2; Isa 40:6–8; see Jas 1:10–11).
37:21 Or "The wicked must borrow and cannot repay,/but the righteous are able to give generously" (see Dt 15:6; 28:12,44).
37:24 See Pr 24:16.
37:26 See note on v. 21.
37:28 faithful ones. See note on 4:3.
37:29 forever. They and their children and children's children, in contrast to the wicked (see v. 28).
37:30 wisdom. See 119:98,130; Dt 4:6.
37:31 heart. See note on 4:7. do not slip. From the right path (see 17:5).
37:32 lie in wait. See 10:8–9; see also note on 7:2. seeking their very lives. Attempting to seize by false charges at court (see v. 33) the very livelihood of their intended victims.
37:35–36 Cf. vv. 25–26.
37:37–38 The great contrast: hope for the one, no hope for the other.
37:37 blameless. See note on v. 18.
37:39–40 the righteous ... them. They are not at the mercy of the wicked: The Lord is their refuge, and in spite of all that the wicked do, the Lord makes secure their inheritance in the promised land.

Psalm 38

A psalm of David. A petition.

[1] O Lord, do not rebuke me in your anger
or discipline me in your wrath. [b]
[2] For your arrows [c] have pierced me,
and your hand has come down upon me.
[3] Because of your wrath there is no health [d] in my body;
my bones [e] have no soundness because of my sin.
[4] My guilt has overwhelmed [f] me
like a burden too heavy to bear. [g]

[5] My wounds [h] fester and are loathsome [i]
because of my sinful folly. [j]
[6] I am bowed down [k] and brought very low;
all day long I go about mourning. [l]
[7] My back is filled with searing pain; [m]
there is no health [n] in my body.
[8] I am feeble and utterly crushed; [o]
I groan [p] in anguish of heart. [q]

[9] All my longings [r] lie open before you, O Lord;
my sighing [s] is not hidden from you.
[10] My heart pounds, [t] my strength fails [u] me;
even the light has gone from my eyes. [v]
[11] My friends and companions avoid me
because of my wounds; [w]
my neighbors stay far away.

[12] Those who seek my life set their traps, [x]
those who would harm me talk of my ruin; [y]
all day long they plot deception. [z]

[13] I am like a deaf man, who cannot hear, [a]
like a mute, who cannot open his mouth;
[14] I have become like a man who does not hear,
whose mouth can offer no reply.
[15] I wait [b] for you, O Lord;
you will answer, [c] O Lord my God.
[16] For I said, "Do not let them gloat [d]
or exalt themselves over me when my foot slips." [e]

[17] For I am about to fall, [f]
and my pain [g] is ever with me.
[18] I confess my iniquity; [h]
I am troubled by my sin.
[19] Many are those who are my vigorous enemies; [i]
those who hate me [j] without reason [k] are numerous.
[20] Those who repay my good with evil [l]
slander [m] me when I pursue what is good.

[21] O Lord, do not forsake me; [n]
be not far [o] from me, O my God.
[22] Come quickly [p] to help me, [q]
O Lord my Savior. [r]

Cross references

38:1 [b] Ps 6:1
38:2 [c] S Job 6:4
38:3 [d] Pr 3:8; 4:22
[e] S Job 33:19
38:4 [f] Ps 40:12; 65:3
[g] S Nu 11:14; S Ezr 9:6; Lk 11:46
38:5 [h] ver 11; Ps 147:3
[i] Job 19:17
[j] Ps 69:5; Pr 5:23; 12:23; 13:16; Ecc 10:3
38:6 [k] Ps 57:6; 145:14; 146:8
[l] Ps 35:14
38:7 [m] S Job 14:22 [n] ver 3
38:8 [o] Ps 34:18; Pr 17:22
[p] Ps 6:6; 22:1; Pr 5:11 [q] S Ps 6:3
38:9 [r] Ps 119:20; 143:7 [s] S Job 3:24
38:10 [t] S Job 37:1
[u] Ps 31:10
[v] Ps 6:7; S 19:8; 88:9
38:11 [w] S ver 5

38:12 [x] Ps 31:4; 140:5; 141:9
[y] Ps 35:4; 41:5
[z] S Ps 35:20
38:13 [a] Ps 115:6; 135:17; Isa 43:8; Mk 7:37
38:15 [b] Ps 27:14
[c] Ps 17:6
38:16
[d] S Ps 22:17
[e] S Dt 32:35
38:17 [f] S Ps 37:24
[g] ver 7; S Job 6:10
38:18
[h] S Lev 26:40
38:19 [i] S Ps 18:17
[j] S Ps 25:19
[k] S Ps 35:19
38:20 [l] S Ge 44:4; 1Jn 3:12
[m] Ps 54:5; 59:10; 119:23
38:21 [n] Ps 27:9; 71:18; 119:8
38:22 [p] S Ps 22:19

[o] S Ps 10:1; S 22:11; 35:22; 71:12 38:22 [p] S Ps 22:19
[q] Ps 40:13 [r] S 1Ch 16:35

Ps 38 An urgent appeal for relief from a severe and painful illness, God's "rebuke" for a sin David has committed. Neither the specific occasion nor the illness can be identified. David's suffering is aggravated by the withdrawal of his friends (see v. 11) and the unwarranted efforts of his enemies to seize this opportunity to bring him down (vv. 12,16, 19–20). See introductions to Ps 39–41. In traditional Christian usage, this is one of seven penitential psalms (see introduction to Ps 6). Like Ps 33 (see introductory note on its structure), its length (22 verses) is based on the number of letters in the Hebrew alphabet. The psalm is composed of five stanzas of four verses each, with a two-verse conclusion. **38 title** *A petition.* Occurs elsewhere only in the title of Ps 70.
38:1–4 Plea for relief from the Lord's rebuke.
38:1 *rebuke . . . discipline.* That is, rebuke-and-discipline (see 39:11; see also note on 3:7). *anger . . . wrath.* See note on 2:5.
38:2 *arrows.* A vivid metaphor for God's blows (see Job 6:4; 34:6; La 3:12; Eze 5:16). *your hand has come down upon me.* See 32:4 and note on 32:3–5.
38:3 *bones.* See note on 6:2.
38:4 *burden.* Not only a psychological "burden of guilt," but the heavy burden of suffering described in vv. 5–8.
38:5–8 The devastating physical and psychological effects of his illness.

38:8 *heart.* See note on 4:7.
38:9–12 Renewed appeal, with further elaboration of his troubles: his illness (v. 10), abandonment by his friends (v. 11) and the hostility of his enemies (v. 12).
38:10 *light has gone from my eyes.* See note on 13:3.
38:11 See note on 31:11–12.
38:12 See note on 5:9.
38:13–16 Let the Lord answer (v. 15) my enemies. Like a deaf-mute, David will not reply to his enemies (vv. 13–14); he waits for the Lord to act in his behalf (vv. 15–16). See 1Sa 25:32–39; 2Sa 16:10,12.
38:16 *when my foot slips.* When he experiences a personal blow to health or circumstance—here referring to his illness (see 66:9; 94:18; 121:3).
38:17–20 As health declines, the vigor of his many enemies increases.
38:17 *about to fall.* Death seems near (see note on 13:4).
38:18 See vv. 3–4; Ps 32.
38:19–20 He has sinned against the Lord, but is innocent of any wrong against those attacking him (see note on 35:19).
38:20 *slander.* Accuse (falsely), as in 71:13; 109:4,20,29; Zec 3:1. *when.* Or "though." *good.* Morally good (see 34:14).
38:21–22 In conclusion, a renewed appeal.

Psalm 39

For the director of music. For Jeduthun.
A psalm of David.

[1] I said, "I will watch my ways[s]
and keep my tongue from sin;[t]
I will put a muzzle on my mouth[u]
as long as the wicked are in my
presence."
[2] But when I was silent[v] and still,
not even saying anything good,
my anguish[w] increased.
[3] My heart grew hot[x] within me,
and as I meditated,[y] the fire[z]
burned;
then I spoke with my tongue:

[4] "Show me, O LORD, my life's end
and the number of my days;[a]
let me know how fleeting[b] is my
life.[c]
[5] You have made my days[d] a mere
handbreadth;
the span of my years is as nothing
before you.
Each man's life is but a breath.[e]
                                    Selah
[6] Man is a mere phantom[f] as he goes to
and fro:[g]
He bustles about, but only in vain;[h]
he heaps up wealth,[i] not knowing
who will get it.[j]

[7] "But now, Lord, what do I look for?
My hope is in you.[k]
[8] Save me[l] from all my transgressions;[m]

do not make me the scorn[n] of fools.
[9] I was silent;[o] I would not open my
mouth,[p]
for you are the one who has done
this.[q]
[10] Remove your scourge from me;
I am overcome by the blow[r] of your
hand.[s]
[11] You rebuke[t] and discipline[u] men for
their sin;
you consume[v] their wealth like a
moth[w]—
each man is but a breath.[x]   *Selah*

[12] "Hear my prayer, O LORD,
listen to my cry for help;[y]
be not deaf[z] to my weeping.[a]
For I dwell with you as an alien,[b]
a stranger,[c] as all my fathers were.[d]
[13] Look away from me, that I may rejoice
again
before I depart and am no more."[e]

Psalm 40

40:13–17pp — Ps 70:1–5

For the director of music. Of David.
A psalm.

[1] I waited patiently[f] for the LORD;
he turned to me and heard my cry.[g]
[2] He lifted me out of the slimy pit,[h]

Cross references (center column):

39:1 [s]1Ki 2:4; Ps 119:9,59; Pr 20:11 [t]S Job 1:22; Ps 34:13; Jas 3:2 [u]S Job 6:24; Jas 1:26
39:2 [v]ver 9; S Job 31:34; Ps 77:4 [w]Ps 6:3; S 25:17; 31:10
39:3 [x]Lk 24:32 [y]Ps 1:2; 48:9; 77:12; 119:15 [z]Jer 5:14; 20:9; 23:29
39:4 [a]S Job 14:5 [b]S Job 14:2 [c]S Ge 47:9; S Job 7:7
39:5 [d]S Job 10:20; Ps 89:45; 102:23 [e]S Job 7:7; Ps 62:9
39:6 [f]Job 8:9; Ps 102:11; Ecc 6:12; S Jas 4:14 [g]Jas 1:11 [h]Ps 127:2 [i]S Job 27:17 /Lk 12:20
39:7 [k]S Ps 9:18; S 25:5
39:8 [l]Ps 6:4; 51:14 [m]Ps 32:1; 51:1; Isa 53:5,8, 10
[n]S Dt 28:37; Ps 69:7; 79:4; Isa 43:28; Da 9:16
39:9 [o]S ver 2
[p]Ps 38:13
[q]Isa 38:15
39:10
[r]2Ch 21:14; Eze 7:9; 24:16 [s]S Ex 9:3
39:11
[t]S Dt 28:20; Isa 66:15; Eze 5:15; 2Pe 2:16

[u]Ps 94:10; Isa 26:16 [v]Ps 90:7 [w]S Job 13:28; S Isa 51:8; Lk 12:33; S Jas 5:2 [x]S Job 7:7 **39:12** [y]S Ps 17:1 [z]S Dt 1:45 [a]S 2Ki 20:5 [b]Lev 25:23 [c]S Ge 23:4; S Heb 11:13 [d]S Ge 47:9; S 1Ch 29:15 **39:13** [e]S Job 10:21 **40:1** /S Ps 37:7 [g]Ps 6:9; S 31:22; 34:15; 116:1; 145:19 **40:2** [h]S Job 9:31; S Ps 7:15

Ps 39 The poignant prayer of a soul deeply troubled by the fragility of human life. He is reminded of this by the present illness through which God is rebuking him (vv. 10–11) for his "transgressions" (v. 8). Ps 38 speaks of silence before the enemy, Ps 39 of silence before God. Both are prayers in times of illness (God's "rebuke," v. 11; 38:1); both acknowledge sin, and both express deep trust in God. See introduction to Ps 40. In addition, this psalm has many links with Ps 90; see also Ps 49.

39 title *For the director of music.* See note on Ps 4 title. *Jeduthun.* One of David's three choir leaders (1Ch 16:41–42; 25:1,6; 2Ch 5:12; called his "seer" in 2Ch 35:15). Jeduthun is probably also the Ethan of 1Ch 6:44; 15:19; if so, he represented the family of Merari, even as Asaph did the family of Gershon and Heman the family of Kohath, the three sons of Levi (see 1Ch 6:16,33,39,43–44). See titles of Ps 62; 77; 89.

39:1–3 Introduction: Having determined to keep silent, he could finally no longer suppress his anguish.
39:1 He had kept a muzzle on his mouth for fear that rebellious words would escape in the hearing of the wicked (see Ps 73).
39:2–3 Suppressed anguish only intensified the agony (see Jer 20:9).
39:4–6 A prayer for understanding and patient acceptance of the brief span of human life.
39:4 *how fleeting is my life.* See 78:39 and note on 37:20.
39:5 *as nothing before you.* See 90:4. *but a breath.* See v.

11; 144:4; Job 14:2; Ecc 6:12.
39:6 Could almost serve as a summary of Ecclesiastes.
39:7–11 A modest prayer: Only grant me relief from your present rebuke.
39:8 *Save me.* As from an enemy. *scorn of fools.* If the Lord does not restore him, he will be mocked (see 22:7–8; 69:6–12) by godless fools (see 14:1).
39:10 *blow of your hand.* See 32:4; 38:2.
39:11 *rebuke and discipline.* See 6:1; 38:1. *but a breath.* See note on v. 5.
39:12–13 The modest prayer repeated even more modestly.
39:12 *an alien, a stranger.* He lives this life before God only as a pilgrim passing through.
39:13 *Look away from me.* See Job 7:17–19; 10:20–21; 14:6. *rejoice again.* See Job 9:27; 10:20. *am no more.* Here there is no glimpse of what lies beyond the horizon of death (see note on 6:5).
Ps 40 A prayer for help when troubles abound. The causes of distress are not specified, but David acknowledges that they are occasioned by his sin (see v. 12), as in Ps 38–39; 41 (see introductions to Ps 39; 41). They are aggravated by the gloating of his enemies, a theme also present in Ps 38–39; 41 (see introduction to Ps 6). The prayer begins with praise of God for his past mercies (vv. 1–5) and a testimony to the king's own faithfulness to the Lord (vv. 6–10). These form the grounds for his present appeal for help (vv. 11–17). See also the lengthy prefaces to prayer in Ps 44; 89. Ps 70 is a

out of the mud*i* and mire;*j*
he set my feet*k* on a rock*l*
and gave me a firm place to stand.
³He put a new song*m* in my mouth,
a hymn of praise to our God.
Many will see and fear*n*
and put their trust*o* in the LORD.

⁴Blessed is the man*p*
who makes the LORD his trust,*q*
who does not look to the proud,*r*
to those who turn aside to false
gods.*s* *s*
⁵Many, O LORD my God,
are the wonders*t* you have done.
The things you planned for us
no one can recount*u* to you;
were I to speak and tell of them,
they would be too many*v* to declare.

⁶Sacrifice and offering you did not
desire,*w*
but my ears you have pierced*t,u;x*
burnt offerings*y* and sin offerings
you did not require.
⁷Then I said, "Here I am, I have come—
it is written about me in the scroll.*v z*
⁸I desire to do your will,*a* O my God;*b*
your law is within my heart."*c*

⁹I proclaim righteousness*d* in the great
assembly;*e*
I do not seal my lips,

as you know,*f* O LORD.
¹⁰I do not hide your righteousness in my
heart;
I speak of your faithfulness*g* and
salvation.
I do not conceal your love and your
truth
from the great assembly.*h*

¹¹Do not withhold your mercy*i* from me,
O LORD;
may your love*j* and your truth*k*
always protect*l* me.
¹²For troubles*m* without number surround
me;
my sins have overtaken me, and I
cannot see.*n*
They are more than the hairs of my
head,*o*
and my heart fails*p* within me.

¹³Be pleased, O LORD, to save me;
O LORD, come quickly to help me.*q*
¹⁴May all who seek to take my life*r*
be put to shame and confusion;*s*
may all who desire my ruin*t*

40:2 *i*S Job 30:19 /Ps 69:14 *k*Ps 31:8 *l*Ps 27:5 40:3 *m*S Ps 28:7; S 96:1; Rev 5:9 *n*Ps 52:6; 64:9 *o*S Ex 14:31 40:4 *p*Ps 34:8 *q*Ps 84:12 *r*Ps 101:5; 138:6; Pr 3:34; 16:5; Isa 65:5; 1Pe 5:5 *s*S Dt 31:20; S Ps 4:2; S 26:11 40:5 *t*S Dt 4:34; Ps 75:1; 105:5; 136:4 *u*Ps 139:18 *v*Ps 71:15; 139:17 40:6 *w*S 1Sa 15:22; Jer 6:20; Am 5:22 *x*Ex 21:6 *y*Ps 50:8; 51:16; Isa 1:11; Hos 6:6 40:7 *z*Job 19:23; Jer 36:2; 45:1; Eze 2:9; Zec 5:1 40:8 *a*S Mt 26:39 *b*Heb 10:5-7* *c*S Dt 6:6; S Job 22:22; Ro 7:22 40:9 *d*S Ps 22:31 *e*S Ps 22:25

/S Jos 22:22 40:10 *g*Ps 89:1 *h*S Ps 22:22 40:11 *i*Zec 1:12 /Pr 20:28 *k*S Ps 26:3 *l*Ps 61:7 40:12 *m*S Ps 25:17 *n*Ps 38:4; 65:3 *o*Ps 69:4 *p*Ps 73:26

40:13 *q*Ps 22:19; 38:22 40:14 *r*S 1Sa 20:1 *s*S Est 9:2; Ps 35:26 *t*S Ps 35:4

*s*4 Or *to falsehood* *t*6 Hebrew; Septuagint *but a body you have prepared for me* (see also Symmachus and Theodotion) *u*6 Or *opened* *v*7 Or *come / with the scroll written for me*

somewhat revised duplicate of vv. 13–17 of this psalm.
40 title *For the director of music.* See note on Ps 4 title.
40:1–5 Praise of the Lord for past mercies (see introduction to Ps 9).
40:1–3 David's experience of God's past help in time of trouble, which moved him to praise and others to faith (see notes on 7:17; 9:1).
40:2 See 30:1 and note.
40:3 *new song.* See note on 33:3. *Many will see.* As a result of David's praise (see 18:49; 22:22–31; see also note on 9:1). *fear.* See note on 34:8–14.
40:4–5 The Lord's benevolence to others: to all who trust in the Lord (v. 4), to his people Israel (v. 5).
40:4 See Jer 17:7; praise of the Lord for the blessedness of those who trust in him (see 32:1–2; 146:5). *Blessed.* See note on 1:1. *proud.* See note on 31:23.
40:5 *wonders.* See note on 9:1. *planned.* God's actions in behalf of Israel are according to his predetermined purpose (see Isa 25:1; 46:10–11).
40:6–8 David's commitment to God's will. Heb 10:5–10 applies these verses to Christ (see notes there).
40:6 *did not desire . . . not require.* More important is obedience (see 1Sa 15:22), especially to God's moral law (see Isa 1:10–17; Am 5:21–24; Mic 6:6–8)—i.e., the ten basic commandments of his covenant (see Ex 20:3–17; Dt 5:7–21). *pierced.* Lit. "dug." Translated "pierced," it probably refers to the sign by which a servant pledged lifelong service to his beloved master (see Ex 21:6; Dt 15:17). If, however, it is translated "opened" (see NIV text note), it refers to ears made able and eager to hear God's law (see Pr 28:9; Isa 48:8; 50:4–5).
40:7 *Here I am, I have come.* Probably refers to David's commitment to the Lord at the time of his enthronement. *it*

is written about me in the scroll. Some take this to be a reference to a prophecy, perhaps Dt 17:14–15. The context, however, strongly suggests that the "scroll" refers to the personal copy of the law that the king is to take at the time of his enthronement to serve as the covenant charter of his administration (see Dt 17:18–20; 2Ki 11:12; cf. 1Ki 2:3; see also NIV text note).
40:8 *I desire.* Whatever is in full accord with God's "desire" (v. 6)—a claim that frames the stanza.
40:9–10 David's life is filled with praise, proclaiming God's faithful and loving acts in behalf of his people. This, too, God desires more than animal sacrifices (see 50:7–15, 23).
40:9 *proclaim.* See 68:11; 96:2; as good tidings (see 1Ki 1:42; Isa 40:9; 41:27; 52:7; 61:1). *righteousness.* See note on 4:1. *in the great assembly.* See notes on 1:5; 9:1. *not seal my lips.* He is not silent about God's praise (see 38:13–16; 39:1 and notes).
40:10 *heart.* See note on 4:7. *your love and your truth.* See note on 26:3.
40:11–17 The prayer for help.
40:11 *your love and your truth.* Which he has been proclaiming to all at the temple (see v. 10 and note).
40:12 *sins have overtaken me.* In the form of the "troubles without number" that burden him (see Ps 38–39 and their introductions). *cannot see.* See note on 13:3. *more than the hairs of my head.* See Mt 10:30; Lk 12:7. *heart.* See note on 4:7.
40:14–15 In the midst of his troubles his enemies harass him, as in 38:12; 39:8; 41:5,7 and often in the Psalms (see note on 5:9). May those who wish to put him to shame themselves be put to shame (see note on 5:10).

be turned back in disgrace.
¹⁵May those who say to me, "Aha!
Aha!" *u*
be appalled at their own shame.
¹⁶But may all who seek you *v*
rejoice and be glad *w* in you;
may those who love your salvation
always say,
"The LORD be exalted!" *x*

¹⁷Yet I am poor and needy; *y*
may the Lord think *z* of me.
You are my help *a* and my deliverer; *b*
O my God, do not delay. *c*

Psalm 41

For the director of music.
A psalm of David.

¹Blessed *d* is he who has regard for the
weak; *e*
the LORD delivers him in times of
trouble. *f*
²The LORD will protect *g* him and
preserve his life; *h*
he will bless him in the land *i*
and not surrender him to the desire
of his foes. *j*
³The LORD will sustain him on his
sickbed *k*
and restore him from his bed of
illness. *l*

⁴I said, "O LORD, have mercy *m* on me;
heal *n* me, for I have sinned *o* against
you."

⁵My enemies say of me in malice,
"When will he die and his name
perish? *p*"
⁶Whenever one comes to see me,
he speaks falsely, *q* while his heart
gathers slander; *r*
then he goes out and spreads *s* it
abroad.

⁷All my enemies whisper together *t*
against me;
they imagine the worst for me,
saying,
⁸"A vile disease has beset him;
he will never get up *u* from the place
where he lies."
⁹Even my close friend, *v* whom I trusted,
he who shared my bread,
has lifted up his heel against me. *w*

¹⁰But you, O LORD, have mercy *x* on me;
raise me up, *y* that I may repay *z*
them.
¹¹I know that you are pleased with me, *a*
for my enemy does not triumph over
me. *b*
¹²In my integrity *c* you uphold me *d*
and set me in your presence
forever. *e*

¹³Praise *f* be to the LORD, the God of
Israel, *g*
from everlasting to everlasting.
Amen and Amen. *h*

40:15
u Ps 35:21
40:16 *v* Dt 4:29;
1Ch 28:9;
Ps 9:10; 119:2
w Ps 9:2
x Ps 35:27
40:17 *y* Ps 86:1;
109:22 *z* Ps 144:3
a S Ps 20:2
b S Ps 18:2
c Ps 119:60
41:1 *d* S Dt 14:29
e S Job 24:4
/Ps 25:17
41:2 *g* Ps 12:5;
32:7 *h* Ezr 9:9;
Ps 71:20; 119:88,
159; 138:7;
143:11 /Ps 37:22
/S Dt 6:24
41:3 *k* Ps 6:6
l 2Sa 13:5; 2Ki 1:4
41:4 *m* Ps 6:2;
S 9:13
n S Dt 32:39
o Ps 51:4

41:5 *p* S Ps 38:12
41:6 *q* Ps 12:2;
101:7; Mt 5:11
r Pr 26:24
s Lev 19:16
41:7 *t* Ps 71:10
41:8 *u* S 2Ki 1:4
41:9
v S 2Sa 15:12;
S Job 19:14
w Nu 30:2;
Job 19:19;
Ps 55:20; 89:34;
Mt 26:23;
Lk 22:21;
Jn 13:18*
41:10 *x* ver 4
y Ps 3:3; 9:13
z 2Sa 3:39
41:11 *a* S Nu 14:8
b Ps 25:2
41:12
c S Ps 25:21
d Ps 18:35;
S 37:17; 63:8
e S Job 4:7;
Ps 21:6; 61:7
41:13
f S Ge 24:27
g Ps 72:18
h Ps 72:19; 89:52;
106:48

40:15 *Aha! Aha!* See note on 3:2.
40:17 *poor and needy.* In need of God's help (see note on 34:6).
Ps 41 David's prayer for mercy when seriously ill. He acknowledges that his illness is related to his sin (v. 4). See the introductions to Ps 38–40. His enemies greet the prospect of his death with malicious glee (see note on 5:9), and even his "close friend" (v. 9) betrays his friendship (see note on 31:11–12). This psalm concludes a collection of four psalms connected by common themes, and also forms the conclusion to Book I. (Book I begins and ends with a "Blessed" psalm.) In its structure, the psalm is very symmetrical, composed of four stanzas of three verses each. The first and fourth stanzas frame the prayer with a note of confidence; stanzas two and three elaborate the prayer. Verse 13 is actually not part of the psalm but the doxology that closes Book I (see note on v. 13).
41 title *For the director of music.* See note on Ps 4 title.
41:1–3 Confidence that the Lord will restore.
41:1 *Blessed is he who has regard for the weak.* Especially if he is king, whose duty it is to defend the powerless (see 72:2,4,12–14; 82:3–4; Pr 29:14; 31:8–9; Isa 11:4; Jer 22:16). *Blessed.* See note on 1:1.
41:4–6 Prayer for God to show mercy and to heal.
41:4 *sinned.* See note on 32:3–5.

41:5 *When will he die . . . ?* See note on 3:2. *his name perish.* See note on 9:5.
41:6 *see me.* Visit him in his sickness. *speaks falsely.* Speaks as if he were a friend. *heart.* See note on 4:7.
41:7–9 His enemies and his friend.
41:9 *close friend . . . who shared my bread.* One who shared the king's table—i.e., was an honored, as well as trusted, friend (see note on 31:11–12). Reference may be to one who had sealed his friendship by a covenant (see note on 23:5). For Jesus' use of this verse in application to himself see Jn 13:18. In fulfilling the role of his royal ancestor as God's anointed king over Israel, the great Son of David also experienced the hostility of men and the betrayal of a trusted associate, and thus fulfilled his forefather's lament.
41:10–12 Prayer, with confidence.
41:10 *that I may repay them.* That I (as king) may call them to account.
41:12 *set.* Establish. *in your presence.* As the royal servant of Israel's heavenly King. (For the idiom see 101:7; 1Sa 16:22, "in my service"; 1Ki 10:8, "before you"; 17:1, "whom I serve.") *forever.* Never to be rejected (see 2Sa 7:15–16).
41:13 The doxology with which the worshiping community is to respond to the contents of Book I (see 72:18–19; 89:52; 106:48; 150).

BOOK II

Psalms 42–72

Psalm 42[w]

For the director of music. A *maskil*[x] of the Sons of Korah.

1As the deer[i] pants for streams of water,[j]
so my soul pants[k] for you, O God.
2My soul thirsts[l] for God, for the living God.[m]
When can I go[n] and meet with God?
3My tears[o] have been my food
day and night,
while men say to me all day long,
"Where is your God?"[p]
4These things I remember
as I pour out my soul:[q]
how I used to go with the multitude,
leading the procession to the house of God,[r]
with shouts of joy[s] and thanksgiving[t]
among the festive throng.[u]

5Why are you downcast,[v] O my soul?
Why so disturbed[w] within me?
Put your hope in God,[x]
for I will yet praise[y] him,
my Savior[z] and 6my God.[a]

My[y] soul is downcast within me;
therefore I will remember[b] you
from the land of the Jordan,[c]
the heights of Hermon[d]—from Mount Mizar.
7Deep calls to deep[e]
in the roar of your waterfalls;
all your waves and breakers

42:1 [i]S Ps 18:33 [j]S Dt 10:7 [k]S Job 19:27; Ps 119:131; Joel 1:20 **42:2** [l]Ps 63:1; 143:6 [m]S Jos 3:10; S 1Sa 14:39; S Mt 16:16; Ro 9:26 [n]Ps 43:4; 84:7 **42:3** [o]S Job 3:24 [p]ver 10; Ps 79:10; 115:2; Joel 2:17; Mic 7:10 **42:4** [q]S 1Sa 1:15 [r]Ps 55:14; 122:1; Isa 2:2; 30:29 [s]S Ezr 3:13 [t]S Jos 6:5; Ps 95:2; 100:4; 147:7; Jnh 2:9 [u]Ps 35:18; 109:30 **42:5** [v]Ps 38:6; 77:3; La 3:20; Mt 26:38 [w]S Job 20:2 [x]S Ps 25:5; S 71:14 [y]Ps 9:1 [z]Ps 18:46 **42:6** [a]ver 11; Ps 43:5 [b]Ps 63:6; 77:11 [c]Ge 13:10; S Nu 13:29 [d]S Dt 3:8; S 4:48 **42:7** [e]S Ge 1:2; S 7:11

[w]In many Hebrew manuscripts Psalms 42 and 43 constitute one psalm. [x]Title: Probably a literary or musical term [y]*5,6* A few Hebrew manuscripts, Septuagint and Syriac; most Hebrew manuscripts *praise him for his saving help. / 6O my God, my*

Ps 42–43 A prayer for deliverance from being "oppressed by the enemy" (42:9; 43:2) and for restoration to the presence of God at his temple. That these two psalms form a single prayer (though they are counted as two psalms also in the Septuagint) is evident from its unique structure (see below) and the development of common themes. Ps 43 may have come to be separated from Ps 42 for a particular liturgical purpose (see introduction to Ps 9). The speaker may have been a leading member of the Korahites whose normal duties involved him in the liturgical activities of the temple (see especially 42:4 and note on Ps 42 title). It may be that the "ungodly nation" (43:1) referred to was the Arameans of Damascus and that the author had been taken captive by the Arameans during one of their incursions into Judah, such as that of Hazael (see 2Ki 12:17–18). (This attack by Hazael affected especially the area in which the Korahites, descendants of Kohath, had been assigned cities; see Jos 21:4,9–19.) See also notes below. This psalm begins Book II of the Psalter, a collection that is distinguished from Book I primarily by the fact that the Hebrew word for "God" (*Elohim*) predominates, whereas in the first book the Hebrew word for "the LORD" (*Yahweh*) predominates.

Structurally, the three stanzas of this psalm are symmetrical (each contains four verses), and each is followed by the same refrain (42:5,11; 43:5). The middle stanza, however, has at its center (see note on 6:6) an additional verse (42:8) that interrupts the developing thought and injects a note of confidence, such as comes to expression also in the threefold refrain. Apart from the refrains, the prayer is framed by an expression of longing for God's presence (42:1) and a vow to praise God at his altar (43:4). For other psalms with recurring refrains see Ps 46; 49; 59; 80; 107.

42 title *For the director of music.* See note on Ps 4 title. *maskil.* See note on Ps 32 title. *of the Sons of Korah.* Or "for the Sons of Korah"; see "For Jeduthun" in Ps 39 title. "Sons of Korah" refers to the Levitical choir made up of the descendants of Korah appointed by David to serve in the temple liturgy. The Korahites represented the Levitical family of Kohath son of Levi. Their leader in the days of David was Heman (see Ps 88 title)—just as Asaph led the choir of the Gershonites and Jeduthun (Ethan) the choir of the Merarites (see 1Ch 6:31–47 and note on Ps 39 title). This is the first of a collection of seven psalms ascribed to the "Sons of Korah" (Ps 42–49); four more occur in Book III (Ps 84–85; 87–88).

42:1–4 Longing to be with God at the temple.

42:1 *deer pants for . . . water.* Because its life depends on water—especially when being pressed by hunters, as the psalmist was by his oppressors. *soul.* See note on 6:3.

42:2 *living God.* See Dt 5:26. *When . . . ?* Circumstances (see v. 9; 43:1–2) now prevent him from being at the temple. *meet with God.* Enter his presence to commune with him (see Ex 19:17; 29:42–43; 30:6,36).

42:3 *day and night.* See vv. 8,10. *Where is your God?* See note on 10:11.

42:4 *soul.* See note on 6:3. *leading the procession.* Suggests that the author normally had a leading role in the liturgy of the temple.

42:5 The refrain: faith encouraging faith (see 27:13–14 and introduction to Ps 27). *praise him.* For his saving help (see notes on 7:17; 9:1; see also 43:4).

42:6–10 The cause and depth of the trouble of his soul.

42:6 *soul is downcast.* See vv. 5,11; 43:5. *therefore I will remember you.* As he remembers (v. 4) in his exile the joy of his past intimacy with God, so now in his exile he remembers God and painfully wonders (vv. 7,9–10), yet not without hope (v. 8). (But some believe that the clause should be rendered "because I remember you.") *from the land . . . from Mount Mizar.* Probably indicating that the author speaks from exile outside the contemporary boundaries of Israel and Judah. Some think the author locates himself at Mount Mizar (a small peak or village, not otherwise known) on the flanks of Mount Hermon somewhere near the headwaters of the Jordan. Others translate the Hebrew for "from" as "far from" and understand "the land of the Jordan" to refer to the promised land (which lies along the Jordan and from which the author was separated). The mention of "the heights of Hermon" may then be a reference to the high peak that marked the northern border of the land (see Dt 3:8; Jos 11:17; 13:11; 1Ch 5:23) and looked down upon it (see 133:3; SS 4:8). Some have suggested that "Mount Mizar" is an additional reference to "the heights of Hermon," calling that high peak the "little mountain" (literal translation) in comparison with Mount Zion (see 68:15–16).

42:7 *deep calls . . . your waterfalls.* Often taken to be an allusion to the cascading waters of the upper Jordan as they rush down from Mount Hermon. It is more likely, however,

have swept over me. *f*

[8] By day the LORD directs his love, *g*
    at night *h* his song *i* is with me—
    a prayer to the God of my life. *j*

[9] I say to God my Rock, *k*
    "Why have you forgotten *l* me?
Why must I go about mourning, *m*
    oppressed *n* by the enemy?" *o*

[10] My bones suffer mortal agony *p*
    as my foes taunt *q* me,
saying to me all day long,
    "Where is your God?" *r*

[11] Why are you downcast, O my soul?
    Why so disturbed within me?
Put your hope in God,
    for I will yet praise him,
    my Savior and my God. *s*

Psalm 43 *z*

[1] Vindicate me, O God,
    and plead my cause *t* against an
        ungodly nation;
    rescue me *u* from deceitful and
        wicked men. *v*

[2] You are God my stronghold.
    Why have you rejected *w* me?
Why must I go about mourning, *x*
    oppressed by the enemy? *y*

[3] Send forth your light *z* and your truth, *a*
    let them guide me; *b*

let them bring me to your holy
        mountain, *c*
    to the place where you dwell. *d*
[4] Then will I go *e* to the altar *f* of God,
    to God, my joy *g* and my delight. *h*
I will praise you with the harp, *i*
    O God, my God.

[5] Why are you downcast, O my soul?
    Why so disturbed within me?
Put your hope in God,
    for I will yet praise him,
    my Savior and my God. *j*

Psalm 44

For the director of music. Of the Sons of
Korah. A *maskil.* *a*

[1] We have heard with our ears, *k* O God;
    our fathers have told us *l*
what you did in their days,
    in days long ago. *m*
[2] With your hand you drove out *n* the
        nations
    and planted *o* our fathers;
you crushed *p* the peoples
    and made our fathers flourish. *q*
[3] It was not by their sword *r* that they
        won the land,

42:7 *f* Ps 69:2;
Jnh 2:3
42:8 *g* Ps 57:3
h S Ps 16:7
i Ps 77:6
j Ps 133:3;
Ecc 5:18; 8:15
42:9 *k* Ps 18:31
l S Ps 10:11
m S Ps 35:14
n Job 20:19;
Ps 43:2; 106:42
o Ps 9:13; 43:2
42:10 *p* S Ps 6:2
q Dt 32:27;
Ps 44:16; 89:51;
102:8; 119:42
r S ver 3
42:11 *s* ver 5;
Ps 43:5
43:1 *t* S Jdg 6:31
u S Ps 25:20
v S Ps 36:3; 109:2
43:2 *w* Ps 44:9;
74:1; 88:14;
89:38 *x* S Ps 35:14
y S Ps 42:9
43:3 *z* Ps 27:1
a S Ps 26:3
b S Ps 25:5

c Ps 2:6
d S 2Sa 15:25
43:4 *e* S Ps 42:2
f Ps 26:6; 84:3
g S Ps 21:6
h Ps 16:3
i S Ge 4:21
43:5 *j* S Ps 42:6
44:1 *k* 2Sa 7:22;
1Ch 17:20;
Jer 26:11
l S Jdg 6:13
m S Dt 32:7;
S Job 37:23
44:2 *n* S Jos 3:10;
Ac 7:45
o S Ex 15:17;
S Isa 60:21
p S Jdg 4:23;
S 2Ch 14:13
q Ps 80:9;

Jer 32:23 **44:3** *r* Jos 24:12

---

z In many Hebrew manuscripts Psalms 42 and 43
constitute one psalm.   *a* Title: Probably a literary or
musical term

---

that this is a literary allusion to the "waterfalls" by which the
waters from God's storehouse of water above (see note on
36:8)—the "deep" above—pour down into the streams and
rivers that empty into the seas—the "deep" below. It pictures the great distress the author suffers, and the imagery is
continued in the following reference to God's "waves and
breakers" sweeping over him (see 69:1–2; 88:7; Jnh 2:3,5;
see also note on 32:6). God's hand is involved in the psalmist's suffering, at least to the extent that he has allowed this
catastrophe. He seems to the psalmist to have "forgotten" (v.
9)—to have "rejected" (43:2)—him. But he makes no link
between this and any sin in his life (see Ps 44; 77).
42:8 The center: confession of hope in all the trouble. That
is, "Day-and-night [cf. v. 3] the LORD directs his love, and his
song is with me" (see note on 3:7). *the LORD.* Only here at
the center in this psalm (see introduction). *directs his love.*
Sends forth his love, like a messenger to do his will (see
43:3). *love.* See note on 6:4. *his song.* A song concerning
him. *prayer.* Praise and prayer belong together in the thought
of the psalmist.
42:9 Echoed in 43:2. *Rock.* See note on 18:2. *Why ... ?
Why ... ?* See note on 6:3 (see also Introduction: Theology).
42:10 See v. 3. *bones.* See note on 6:2.
43:1–4 Prayer for deliverance from the enemy and for
restoration to God's presence.
43:1 A plea in the language of the court (see introduction to
Ps 17).
43:2 Echoes 42:9.
43:3 *your light and your truth.* Personified as God's messengers who work out (1) his salvation (light; see note on
27:1) and (2) his faithful care in behalf of his own (truth; see

26:3; 30:9; 40:10). May these guide me back to your temple. *holy mountain.* See note on 2:6.
43:4 See note on 7:17. *to the altar.* See 26:6 and note.
Ps 44 Israel's cry for help after suffering a devastating defeat
at the hand of an enemy. In the light of vv. 17–22, it is
difficult to associate this psalm with any of those defeats
announced by the prophets as judgments on Israel's covenant unfaithfulness. It probably relates to an experience of
the kingdom of Judah (which as a nation did not break
covenant with the Lord until late in her history), perhaps
during the reign of Jehoshaphat or Hezekiah. Structurally,
three thematic developments rise one upon the other as the
psalm advances to the prayer in the closing verses. Its structure is like the stages of a ziggurat (a stepped pyramid
structure that the Babylonians built as a mountain-like base
for some of their temples; see Ge 11:4 and note) leading to
the temple that crowns it. First there is praise of the Lord for
past victories (vv. 1–8), second a description of the present
defeat and its consequences (vv. 9–16), third a plea of innocence (vv. 17–22), then finally the prayer (vv. 23–26). Each
of the themes (recalling of past mercies, description of the
present distress, and claim of covenant loyalty) in its own
way functions as a ground for the appeal for help (see Ps 40
and its introduction; see also the lengthy prefaces to prayer in
Ps 40; 89).
44 title See note on Ps 42 title.
44:1–8 Praise to God for past victories: (1) those by which
Israel became established in the land (vv. 1–3); (2) those by
which Israel has been kept secure in the land (vv. 4–8).
44:1 See 78:3.
44:3 *light of your face.* See notes on 4:6; 13:1.

nor did their arm bring them victory;
it was your right hand,^{s} your arm,^{t}
and the light^u of your face, for you
loved^v them.
⁴You are my King^w and my God,^{x}
who decrees^b victories^y for Jacob.
⁵Through you we push back^z our
enemies;
through your name we trample^a our
foes.
⁶I do not trust in my bow,^{b}
my sword does not bring me victory;
⁷but you give us victory^c over our
enemies,
you put our adversaries to shame.^{d}
⁸In God we make our boast^e all day
long,^{f}
and we will praise your name
forever.^{g} *Selah*

⁹But now you have rejected^h and
humbled us;^{i}
you no longer go out with our
armies.^{j}
¹⁰You made us retreat^k before the enemy,
and our adversaries have plundered^l
us.
¹¹You gave us up to be devoured like
sheep^m
and have scattered us among the
nations.^{n}
¹²You sold your people for a pittance,^{o}
gaining nothing from their sale.
¹³You have made us a reproach^p to our
neighbors,^{q}
the scorn^r and derision^s of those
around us.
¹⁴You have made us a byword^t among
the nations;
the peoples shake their heads^u at us.
¹⁵My disgrace^v is before me all day long,
and my face is covered with shame^w

¹⁶at the taunts^x of those who reproach
and revile^y me,
because of the enemy, who is bent
on revenge.^{z}

¹⁷All this happened to us,
though we had not forgotten^a you
or been false to your covenant.
¹⁸Our hearts had not turned^b back;
our feet had not strayed from your
path.
¹⁹But you crushed^c us and made us a
haunt for jackals^d
and covered us over with deep
darkness.^{e}

²⁰If we had forgotten^f the name of our
God
or spread out our hands to a foreign
god,^{g}
²¹would not God have discovered it,
since he knows the secrets of the
heart?^{h}
²²Yet for your sake we face death all day
long;
we are considered as sheep^i to be
slaughtered.^{j}

²³Awake,^{k} O Lord! Why do you sleep?^{l}
Rouse yourself!^{m} Do not reject us
forever.^{n}
²⁴Why do you hide your face^o
and forget^p our misery and
oppression?^{q}
²⁵We are brought down to the dust;^{r}
our bodies cling to the ground.

44:3 ^{s}Ps 78:54
^{t}Ex 15:16;
Ps 77:15; 79:11;
89:10; 98:1;
Isa 40:10; 52:10;
63:5 ^{u}Ps 89:15
^{v}S Dt 4:37
44:4 ^{w}S Ps 24:7
^{x}Ps 5:2 ^{y}Ps 21:5
44:5 ^{z}S Jos 23:5
^{a}Ps 60:12;
108:13
44:6 ^{b}Ge 48:22;
Hos 1:7
44:7 ^{c}S Dt 20:4
^{d}S Job 8:22
44:8 ^{e}S Ps 34:2;
1Co 1:31;
2Co 10:17
^{f}Ps 52:1
^{g}S Ps 30:12
44:9 ^{h}S Ps 43:2
^{i}S Dt 8:3;
S 31:17;
Ps 107:39;
Isa 5:15
^{j}S Jos 7:12;
Ps 108:11
44:10
^{k}S Lev 26:17
^{l}S Jdg 2:14
44:11 ^{m}ver 22;
Jer 12:3
^{n}S Lev 26:33;
S Ps 9:11;
Eze 6:8; Zec 2:6
44:12
^{o}S Dt 32:30;
Isa 50:1; 52:3;
Jer 15:13
44:13
^{p}S 2Ch 29:8;
Isa 30:3; Jer 25:9;
42:18; 44:8
^{q}Ps 79:4; 80:6;
89:41
^{r}S Dt 28:37;
S Mic 2:6
^{s}Eze 23:32
44:14 ^{t}S 1Ki 9:7
^{u}S 2Ki 19:21
44:15 ^{v}Ge 30:23;
2Ch 32:21;
Ps 35:26
^{w}S Ps 34:5

44:16
^{x}S Ps 42:10
^{y}Ps 10:13; 55:3;
74:10
^{z}S 1Sa 18:25;
S Jer 11:19;
Ro 12:19
44:17 ^{a}S Dt 6:12;
S 32:18;
Ps 119:16,61,153,
176; Pr 3:1

44:18 ^{b}Ps 119:51,157 44:19 ^{c}S 2Ch 14:13; Ps 51:8
^{d}S Job 30:29; S Isa 34:13 ^{e}S Job 3:5 44:20 ^{f}S Dt 32:18;
S Jdg 3:7 ^{g}S Ex 20:3; Isa 43:12; Jer 5:19 44:21 ^{h}S 1Sa 16:7;
^{i}Pr 15:11; Jer 12:3; 17:10 44:22 ^{i}S ver 11
^{j}Isa 53:7; Jer 11:19; 12:3; Ro 8:36* 44:23 ^{k}S Ps 7:6
^{l}Ps 78:65 ^{m}Ps 59:5 ^{n}Ps 74:1; 77:7 44:24 ^{o}S Dt 32:20;
Ps 13:1 ^{p}La 5:20 ^{q}S Dt 26:7 44:25 ^{r}Ps 119:25

^{b}4 Septuagint, Aquila and Syriac; Hebrew *King, O God; /
command*

44:4 *my.* Here and elsewhere in this psalm the first-person
singular pronoun refers to the nation corporately (see note on
Ps 30 title). *Jacob.* See note on 14:7.
44:5,8 *your name.* See v. 20; see also note on 5:11.
44:9–16 But now you have forsaken us: (1) You have
caused us to suffer defeat (vv. 9–12); (2) you have shamed us
before our enemies (vv. 13–16).
44:11 *gave us up to be devoured like sheep.* Have not
protected us as our Shepherd-King (see v. 4 and note on
23:1).
44:12 *sold your people.* Like chattel no longer valued (see
Dt 32:30; Jdg 2:14). *for a pittance.* For nothing of value (see
Isa 52:3; Jer 15:13; cf. Isa 43:3–4).
44:14 *shake their heads.* In scorn (see 64:8).
44:16 *bent on revenge.* See 8:2 and note.
44:17–22 And we have not been disloyal to you: (1) We
have not been untrue to your covenant (vv. 17–19); (2) you
are our witness that we have not turned to another god (vv.
20–22).
44:17 *your covenant.* See Ex 19–24.

44:18 *hearts.* See note on 4:7. *your path.* The way marked
out in God's covenant (see note on 5:8).
44:19 *you crushed us.* But that cannot be used as evidence
that we have been disloyal. *haunt for jackals.* A desolate
place, uninhabited by man (see Isa 13:22; Jer 9:11). *deep
darkness.* The absence of all that was associated with the
metaphor "light" (see notes on 30:1; 36:9).
44:20 *spread out our hands.* Prayed (see Ex 9:29).
44:22 *Yet.* Or "As a matter of fact" or "As you, O God,
know." From the time of her stay in Egypt (see Ex 1), Israel
has suffered the hostility of the nations because of her relationship with the Lord (see Mt 10:34). For Paul's application
of this verse to the Christian community in the light of
Christ's death and resurrection see Ro 8:36.
44:23–26 The appeal for help: (1) Awake to our need (vv.
23–24); (2) arise to our help (vv. 25–26; see introduction to
Ps 16).
44:23 *Awake.* See note on 7:6. *Why . . . ?* See note on 6:3
(see also Introduction: Theology).
44:24 *hide your face.* See note on 13:1.

^{26}Rise up^s and help us;
   redeem^t us because of your unfailing
      love. ^{u}

Psalm 45

For the director of music. To the tune of
"Lilies." Of the Sons of Korah. A *maskil.*^{c}
A wedding song. ^{v}

^{1}My heart is stirred by a noble theme
   as I recite my verses for the king;
   my tongue is the pen of a skillful
      writer.

^{2}You are the most excellent of men
   and your lips have been anointed
      with grace, ^{w}
   since God has blessed you forever. ^{x}
^{3}Gird your sword^y upon your side,
   O mighty one;^{z}
clothe yourself with splendor and
   majesty. ^{a}

^{4}In your majesty ride forth victoriously^b
   in behalf of truth, humility and
      righteousness; ^{c}
   let your right hand^d display awesome
      deeds. ^{e}
^{5}Let your sharp arrows^f pierce the
      hearts^g of the king's enemies; ^{h}
   let the nations fall beneath your feet.
^{6}Your throne, O God, will last for ever
      and ever; ^{i}
   a scepter of justice will be the scepter
      of your kingdom.
^{7}You love righteousness^j and hate
      wickedness; ^{k}
   therefore God, your God, has set you
      above your companions
   by anointing^l you with the oil of
      joy. ^{m}
^{8}All your robes are fragrant^n with

44:26
^{s}S Nu 10:35;
S Ps 12:5; 102:13
^{t}Ps 26:11 ^{u}Ps 6:4
45 Title ^{v}SS 1:1
45:2 ^{w}Lk 4:22
^{x}Ps 21:6
45:3 ^{y}S Dt 32:41;
Ps 149:6;
Rev 1:16
^{z}S 2Sa 1:19
^{a}S Job 40:10;
S Ps 21:5

45:4 ^{b}Rev 6:2
^{c}Zep 2:3 ^{d}Ps 21:8
^{e}S Dt 4:34;
Ps 65:5; 66:3
45:5 ^{f}S Dt 32:23
^{g}S Nu 24:8
^{h}Ps 9:13; 92:9
45:6 ^{i}S Ge 21:33;
La 5:19
45:7 ^{j}Ps 33:5
^{k}S Ps 11:5
^{l}Ps 2:2; Isa 45:1;
61:1; Zec 4:14
^{m}S Ps 23:5;
Heb 1:8-9*
45:8 ^{n}Pr 27:9;
SS 1:3; 4:10

^{c}Title: Probably a literary or musical term

44:25 *brought down to the dust.* About to sink into death (see 22:29 and note; see also note on 30:1).
44:26 *Rise up.* See note on 3:7. *redeem.* See note on 25:22. *unfailing love.* See note on 6:4.
Ps 45 A song in praise of the king on his wedding day (see title). He undoubtedly belonged to David's dynasty, and the song was probably used at more than one royal wedding. Since the bride is a foreign princess (see vv. 10,12), the wedding reflects the king's standing as a figure of international significance (see note on v. 9). Accordingly he is addressed as one whose reign is to be characterized by victories over the nations (vv. 3–5; cf. Ps 2; 110). As a royal son of David, he is a type (foreshadowing) of Christ. After the exile this psalm was applied to the Messiah, the promised Son of David who would sit on David's throne (for the application of vv. 6–7 see Heb 1:8–9). The superscription implies that it was composed and sung by a member of the Levitical temple choir, a fact not surprising in view of the close link between the temple (housing the earthly throne room of Israel's heavenly King) and the Davidic dynasty (the Lord's appointed regents over his people, described throughout the books of Samuel, Kings and Chronicles). As a word from one of the temple personnel, the song was no doubt received as a word from the temple—and from the One who sat enthroned there. In its structure, the song is framed by vv. 1,17 while vv. 2,16 constitute a secondary frame within them—all addressed to the king. The body of the song falls into two parts: (1) words addressed to the king (vv. 3–9) and (2) words addressed to the royal bride (vv. 10–15). These in turn each contain two parts, reflecting a similar pattern: (1) (a) exhortations to the king (vv. 3–5), (b) the glory of the king (vv. 6–9); (2) (a) exhortations to the bride (vv. 10–11), (b) the glory of the bride (vv. 12–15).
45 title *For the director of music.* See note on Ps 4 title. *To the tune of.* See note on Ps 9 title. *Lilies.* See Ps 69 title. "Lilies" may be an abbreviated form of "The Lily (Lilies) of the Covenant" found in the titles of Ps 60; 80. *Of the Sons of Korah.* See note on Ps 42 title. *maskil.* See note on Ps 32 title. *song.* See note on Ps 30 title.
45:1 See v. 17, where the speaker pledges (perhaps by means of this song) to perpetuate the king's memory throughout the generations and awaken the praise of the nations. *heart.* See note on 4:7.
45:2 *most excellent of men.* One who excels in manly

traits and beauty, as a king should (see 1Sa 9:2; 16:18)—but he is so beyond ordinary men as to be almost Godlike (see note on v. 6). *lips . . . anointed with grace.* See Pr 22:11; Ecc 10:12; cf. Isa 50:4; Lk 4:22; see also v. 16, where it is suggested that such a king will be perpetuated in his sons. *forever.* See note on v. 6.
45:3–5 Go forth with your sword victoriously in the service of all that is right, and clothe yourself thereby with glory—make your reign adorn you more truly than the wedding garb with which you are now arrayed (v. 8).
45:3 *splendor and majesty.* See 21:5 and note.
45:4 *righteousness.* See note on 1:5. *awesome deeds.* See 66:5; 106:22; 145:6.
45:5 *nations fall beneath your feet.* See 2:8–9; 110:1–2, 5–6.
45:6–9 The glory of the king's reign: justice and righteousness (see Ps 72).
45:6 *O God.* Possibly the king's throne is called God's throne because he is God's appointed regent. But it is also possible that the king himself is addressed as "god." The Davidic king (the "Lord's anointed," 2Sa 19:21), because of his special relationship with God, was called at his enthronement the "son" of God (see 2:7; 2Sa 7:14; 1Ch 28:6; cf. 89:27). In this psalm, which praises the king and especially extols his "splendor and majesty" (v. 3), it is not unthinkable that he was called "god" as a title of honor (cf. Isa 9:6). Such a description of the Davidic king attains its fullest meaning when applied to Christ, as the author of Hebrews does (Heb 1:8–9). (The pharaohs of Egypt were sometimes addressed as "my god" by their vassal kings in Palestine, as evidenced by the Amarna letters; see chart on "Ancient Texts Relating to the OT," p. 5.) *for ever and ever.* See vv. 2,17. Such was the language used with respect to kings (see note on 21:4). It here gains added significance in the light of God's covenant with David (see 89:4,29,36; 132:12; 2Sa 7:16). In Christ, the Son of David, it is fulfilled.
45:7 *companions.* The noble guests of the king, perhaps from other lands. *oil of joy.* God has anointed him with a more delightful oil than the aromatic oils with which his head and body were anointed on his wedding day—namely, with joy (see 23:5; Isa 61:3).
45:8–9 The glory of the king's wedding.
45:8 *myrrh.* See notes on Ge 37:25; SS 1:13. *aloes.* See note on SS 4:14. *cassia.* See note on Ex 25:6. *palaces*

myrrh[o] and aloes[p] and
cassia;[q]
from palaces adorned with ivory[r]
the music of the strings[s] makes you
glad.
[9]Daughters of kings[t] are among your
honored women;
at your right hand[u] is the royal
bride[v] in gold of Ophir.[w]

[10]Listen, O daughter,[x] consider[y] and give
ear:
Forget your people[z] and your father's
house.
[11]The king is enthralled by your beauty;[a]
honor[b] him, for he is your lord.[c]
[12]The Daughter of Tyre[d] will come with
a gift,[d][e]
men of wealth will seek your favor.

[13]All glorious[f] is the princess within her
chamber;
her gown is interwoven with gold.[g]
[14]In embroidered garments[h] she is led to
the king;[i]
her virgin companions[j] follow her
and are brought to you.
[15]They are led in with joy and gladness;[k]
they enter the palace of the king.

[16]Your sons will take the place of your
fathers;

you will make them princes[l]
throughout the land.
[17]I will perpetuate your memory through
all generations;[m]
therefore the nations will praise you[n]
for ever and ever.[o]

Psalm 46

For the director of music. Of the Sons of
Korah. According to *alamoth*.[e] A song.

[1]God is our refuge[p] and strength,[q]
an ever-present[r] help[s] in trouble.[t]
[2]Therefore we will not fear,[u] though the
earth give way[w]
and the mountains fall[w] into the
heart of the sea,[x]
[3]though its waters roar[y] and foam[z]
and the mountains quake[a] with their
surging.   *Selah*

[4]There is a river[b] whose streams[c] make
glad the city of God,[d]

45:8 oS Ge 37:25;
pS Nu 24:6;
Jn 19:39
qS Ex 30:24
rS 1Ki 22:39
sPs 144:9; 150:4;
Isa 38:20
45:9 tSS 6:8
u1Ki 2:19
vIsa 62:5
wS Ge 10:29
45:10 xRu 1:11
yJer 5:1 zRu 1:16
45:11 aS Est 1:11;
S La 2:15
bEph 5:33
c1Pe 3:6
45:12 dS Jos 19:29
eS 1Ki 9:16;
S 2Ch 9:24
45:13 fS Isa 61:10
gEx 39:3
45:14 hS Jdg 5:30
iEst 2:15 /SS 1:3
45:15 kS Est 8:17
45:16 lSa 2:8;
Ps 68:27; 113:8
45:17 mS Ex 3:15;
Ps 33:11; 119:90;
135:13 nPs 138:4
oS Ps 21:4;
Rev 22:5
46:1 pPs 9:9;
37:39; 61:3;
73:26; 91:2,9;
142:5; Isa 33:16;
Jer 16:19; 17:17;
Joel 3:16; Na 1:7
qPs 18:1
rPs 34:18;
La 3:57 sPs 18:6;
Lk 1:54
tS Dt 4:30;
Ps 25:17
46:2 uS Ge 4:7; Ps 3:6 vPs 82:5; Isa 13:13; 24:1,19,20;
Jer 4:23; Da 11:19; Am 8:14; S Rev 6:14 wver 6; Ps 18:7;
97:5; Isa 54:10; Am 9:5; Mic 1:4; Na 1:5; Hab 3:6 xEx 15:8
46:3 yPs 93:3; Isa 17:13; Jer 5:22; Eze 1:24; Rev 19:6
zS Job 9:26 aS Jdg 5:5 **46:4** bS Ge 2:10; Rev 22:1 cS Ps 1:3
dPs 48:1,8; 87:3; 101:8; Rev 3:12

d*12* Or *A Tyrian robe is among the gifts*   e*Title:*
Probably a musical term

---

adorned with ivory. See 1Ki 22:39; Am 3:15; 6:4.
45:9 *Daughters of kings.* Whether members of his royal
harem (see 1Ki 11:1–3) or guests at his wedding, they
represent international recognition of the king. *in gold of
Ophir.* Adorned with jewels of finest gold (see notes on Ge
10:29; 1Ki 9:28) and all the finery associated with it.
45:10–15 The word to the royal bride.
45:10–11 Be totally loyal to your adoring king.
45:12–15 The royal bride's glory.
45:12 *Daughter of Tyre.* A personification of the city of
Tyre and its inhabitants (see note on 2Ki 19:21). The king of
Tyre was the first foreign ruler to recognize the Davidic
dynasty (see 2Sa 5:11), and Solomon maintained close relations with that city-state (see 1Ki 5; 9:10–14,26–28). As a
great trading center on the Mediterranean coast, Tyre was
world-renowned for its wealth (see Isa 23; Eze
26:1–28:19). *men of wealth.* Such as those from your
homeland. *seek your favor.* Desire to be in your good graces
as the wife of this king.
45:14 *virgin companions.* She too has "companions" (see
v. 7), perhaps her permanent attendants. *to you.* To the king.
45:16 *Your.* The king's. *take the place of your fathers.* In
the family line continues (dynastic succession). Perhaps it is
also hinted that they will surpass the fathers in honor (see
note on v. 2). *land.* Or "earth."
45:17 See note on v. 1. *for ever and ever.* See note on v. 6.
Ps 46 A celebration of the security of Jerusalem as the city
of God (the inspiration of Martin Luther's great hymn, "A
Mighty Fortress Is Our God"). Thematically this psalm is
closely related to Ps 48 (see also Ps 76; 87), while Ps 47
celebrates God's victorious reign over all the earth. It probably predates the exile. However, as a song concerning the
"city of God" (v. 4), the royal city of his kingdom on earth
(see Ps 48), it remained for Israel a song of hope celebrating

the certain triumph of God's kingdom. It was originally
liturgical and sung at the temple: The citizens of Jerusalem
(or the Levitical choir in their stead) apparently sang the
opening stanza (vv. 1–3) and the responses (vv. 7,11), while
the Levitical leader of the liturgy probably sang the second
and third stanzas (vv. 4–6,8–10). In its structure, apart from
the refrains (vv. 7,11), the psalm is composed of three symmetrical stanzas, each containing three verses. For other
psalms with recurring refrains see introduction to Ps 42–43.
46 title *For the director of music.* See note on Ps 4 title. *Of
the Sons of Korah.* See note on Ps 42 title. *According to.* See
note on Ps 6 title. *alamoth.* See NIV text note. Since the
Hebrew word appears to mean "maidens," the phrase "according to *alamoth*" may refer to the "maidens playing
tambourines" who accompanied the singers as the liturgical
procession made its way to the temple (68:25). *A song.* See
note on Ps 30 title.
46:1–3 A triumphant confession of fearless trust in God,
though the continents break up and sink beneath the resurg-
ing waters of the seas—i.e., though the creation itself may
seem to become uncreated (see 104:6–9; Ge 1:9–10) and
all may appear to be going down before the onslaught of the
primeval deep. The described upheaval is probably imagery
for great threats to Israel's existence (see note on 32:6),
especially from her enemies (see vv. 6,8–10; 65:5–8).
46:4–6 A description of blessed Zion—a comforting declaration of God's mighty, sustaining presence in his city.
46:4 *river.* Jerusalem had no river, unlike Thebes (Na 3:8),
Damascus (2Ki 5:12), Nineveh (Na 2:6,8) or Babylon
(137:1), yet she had a "river." Here the "river" of 36:8 (see
note there) serves as a metaphor for the continual outpouring
of the sustaining and refreshing blessings of God, which
make the city of God like the Garden of Eden (see Ge 2:10;
Isa 33:21; 51:3; cf. also Eze 31:4–9). *city of God.* See v. 5;

the holy place where the Most High^e dwells.^f

⁵God is within her,^g she will not fall;^h
   God will helpⁱ her at break of day.
⁶Nations^j are in uproar,^k kingdoms^l fall;
   he lifts his voice,^m the earth melts.ⁿ

⁷The LORD Almighty^o is with us;^p
   the God of Jacob^q is our fortress.^r
                                    Selah

⁸Come and see the works of the LORD,^s
   the desolations^t he has brought on
      the earth.
⁹He makes wars^u cease to the ends of
      the earth;
   he breaks the bow^v and shatters the
      spear,
   he burns the shields^f with fire.^w
¹⁰"Be still, and know that I am God;^x
   I will be exalted^y among the nations,
   I will be exalted in the earth."

¹¹The LORD Almighty is with us;

the God of Jacob^z is our fortress.^a
                                    Selah

Psalm 47

For the director of music. Of the Sons of
Korah. A psalm.

¹Clap your hands,^b all you nations;
   shout to God with cries of joy.^c
²How awesome^d is the LORD Most
      High,^e
   the great King^f over all the earth!
³He subdued^g nations under us,
   peoples under our feet.
⁴He chose our inheritance^h for us,
   the pride of Jacob,ⁱ whom he loved.
                                    Selah

⁵God has ascended^j amid shouts of
      joy,^k

46:4 ^eGe 14:18
/S 2Sa 15:25
46:5 ^gDt 23:14;
S Ps 26:8;
Isa 12:6; Zec 2:5
^hPs 125:1
ⁱS 1Ch 5:20
46:6 /S Job 12:23
^kPs 74:23;
Isa 5:30; 17:12
/Ps 68:32;
102:22; Isa 13:4,
13; 23:11;
Eze 26:18; Mt 4:8
^mS Ps 29:3;
Isa 33:3 ⁿS ver 2
46:7 ^oS 1Sa 1:11
^pS Ge 21:22
^qS Ps 20:1 ^rver
11; Ps 18:2
46:8 ^sPs 66:5
^tIsa 17:9; 64:10;
Da 9:26; Lk 21:20
46:9 ^uIsa 2:4
^vS Ps 37:15;
S Isa 22:6
^wIsa 9:5;
Eze 39:9;
Hos 2:18
46:10 ^xDt 4:35;
1Ki 18:36,39;
Ps 100:3;
Isa 37:16,20;
43:11; 45:21;
Eze 36:23
^yPs 18:46;
Isa 2:11
46:11 ^zS Ps 20:1

[†]9 Or chariots

^aS ver 7 47:1 ^bS 2Ki 11:12 ^cS Ps 33:3 47:2 ^dS Dt 7:21
^eGe 14:18 /Ps 2:6; 48:2; 95:3; Mt 5:35 47:3 ^gPs 18:39,47;
Isa 14:6 47:4 ^hPs 2:8; 16:6; 78:55; 1Pe 1:4 ⁱAm 6:8; 8:7
47:5 /Ps 68:18; Eph 4:8 ^kS Job 8:21; S Ps 106:5

---

see especially Ps 48. *God . . . Most High.* That is, God Most
High (see 57:2; see also note on 3:7). *Most High.* See note
on Ge 14:19. *dwells.* See note on 9:11.
46:5 *at break of day.* Or "as dawn approaches"—i.e.,
when attacks against cities were likely to be launched. His
help brings on the dawn of deliverance, dispelling the night
of danger (see 44:19 and note; cf. Isa 37:36 for an example).
46:6 *Nations . . . fall.* Because of God's victory (see vv.
8–9; 48:4–7). *in uproar.* See v. 3 and note on vv. 1–3; see
also 2:1–3; Rev 11:18. *lifts his voice.* See 2:5; 9:5; Jer
25:30; Am 1:2; see also 104:7. God's thunder is evoked (see
introduction to Ps 29), the thunder of his wrath (see 18:13;
Isa 2:10). *earth melts.* As though struck by lightning (see
97:4–5).
46:7 The people's glad response (also v. 11). *LORD Almighty.* See note on 1Sa 1:3. *Jacob.* See note on 14:7.
46:8–10 A declaration of the blessed effects of God's
triumph over the nations.
46:8 *Come and see.* An invitation to see God's victories in
the world (see 48:8 and note). *the LORD.* Emphatic because of
its rare use in Book II of the Psalter. *on the earth.* Among the
hostile nations.
46:9 No more attacks against his city. The verse probably
speaks of universal peace (see note on 65:6–7). *breaks . . .
shatters . . . burns.* See 76:3; see also 1Sa 2:4. For the
Messiah's universal victory over Israel's enemies see Isa
9:2–7.
46:10 God's voice breaks through, as he addresses the
nations (see v. 6)—the climax. *Be still.* Here, the Hebrew for
this phrase probably means "Enough!" as in 1Sa 15:16
("Stop!"). *know.* Acknowledge. *I will be exalted . . . in the
earth.* God's mighty acts in behalf of his people will bring him
universal recognition, a major theme in the Psalter (see
22:27; 47:9; 57:5,11; 64:9; 65:8; 66:1–7; 67:2–5; 86:9;
98:2–3; 99:2–3; 102:15) and elsewhere in the OT (see Ex
7:5; 14:4,18; Lev 26:45; Nu 14:15; 1Sa 17:46; 1Ki
8:41–43; 2Ki 19:19; Eze 20:41; 28:25; 36:23; Hab 2:14).
This has proven to be supremely true of God's climactic
saving act in the birth, life, death, resurrection and glorification of Jesus Christ— yet to be brought to complete fruition
at his return.

46:11 See note on v. 7.
Ps 47 Celebration of the universal reign of Israel's God: a
testimony to the nations. This psalm belongs to a group of
hymns to the Great King found elsewhere clustered in Ps
92–100. Here it serves to link Ps 46 and 48, identifying the
God who reigns in Zion as "the great King over all the earth"
(v. 2; see v. 7; 48:2). It dates from the period of the monarchy and was composed for use in the temple liturgy on one
of the high festival days. The specific setting is perhaps the
Feast of Tabernacles (see Lev 23:34), which was also the
festival for which Solomon waited to dedicate the temple
(see 1Ki 8:2). A liturgical procession is presupposed (v. 5),
similar to that indicated in Ps 24; 68. Later Jewish usage
employed this psalm in the synagogue liturgy for *Rosh Hashanah* (the New Year festival). The Christian church has
appropriately employed it in the celebration of Christ's ascension (see v. 5). Structurally, vv. 5–6 form a centered (see
note on 6:6) couplet between two four-line stanzas (in Hebrew). This center may represent a different voice in the
liturgy.
47 title See note on Ps 42 title.
47:1–4 The nations are called to rejoice in the God of
Israel, the Lord over all the earth—OT anticipation of the
evangelization of the nations (see note on 9:1).
47:1 *Clap your hands.* As at the enthronement of a king
(see 2Ki 11:12; see also 98:8) or at other times of rejoicing
(see Isa 55:12). *cries of joy.* See 1Ki 1:40; 2Ki 11:14.
47:2–3 The Lord of all the earth has shaped the destiny of
his people Israel (see 105:6; 135:4; Ex 9:29; 15:1–18;
19:5–6; Dt 7:6; 14:2; Isa 41:8).
47:2 *How awesome . . . !* See 68:35; 89:7; 99:3; 111:9;
see also note on 45:4. *Most High.* See note on Ge 14:19.
great King. A title often used by the imperial rulers of Assyria
(see note on 2Ki 18:19).
47:3 See 2Sa 5:17–25; 8:1–14; 10.
47:4 *inheritance.* The promised land (see Ge 12:7; 17:8;
Ex 3:8; Dt 1:8; Jer 3:18). *pride.* That in which he took
supreme delight. *Jacob.* See note on 14:7.
47:5–6 The center of the poem (see note on 6:6). These
verses portray the liturgical ascension of God to the temple—perhaps represented by the processional bearing of the

the LORD amid the sounding of
   trumpets. *l*
6Sing praises *m* to God, sing praises;
   sing praises to our King, sing praises.

7For God is the King of all the earth; *n*
   sing to him a psalm*g o* of praise.
8God reigns*p* over the nations;
   God is seated on his holy throne. *q*
9The nobles of the nations assemble
   as the people of the God of Abraham,
for the kings*h* of the earth belong to
   God;*r*
he is greatly exalted. *s*

Psalm 48

A song. A psalm of the Sons of Korah.

1Great is the LORD, *t* and most worthy of
   praise, *u*
in the city of our God, *v* his holy
   mountain. *w*
2It is beautiful *x* in its loftiness,
   the joy of the whole earth.
Like the utmost heights of Zaphon*i y* is
   Mount Zion, *z*
the*j* city of the Great King. *a*

3God is in her citadels; *b*
   he has shown himself to be her
      fortress. *c*

4When the kings joined forces,
   when they advanced together, *d*
5they saw *her* and were astounded;
   they fled in terror. *e*
6Trembling seized*f* them there,
   pain like that of a woman in labor. *g*
7You destroyed them like ships of
      Tarshish *h*
   shattered by an east wind. *i*

8As we have heard,
   so have we seen
in the city of the LORD Almighty,
   in the city of our God:
God makes her secure forever.*j*
                                    Selah

9Within your temple, O God,

47:5 *l*S Nu 10:2;
S 2Sa 6:15
47:6
*m*S 2Sa 22:50
47:7 *n*Zec 14:9
*o*1Ch 16:7;
Col 3:16
47:8
*p*S 1Ch 16:31
*q*S 1Ki 22:19;
S Ps 9:4; Rev 4:9
47:9 *r*S Job 25:2
*s*Ps 46:10; 97:9
48:1 *t*Ps 86:10;
96:4; 99:2;
135:5; 147:5;
Jer 10:6
*u*S 2Sa 22:4;
S 1Ch 16:25;
Ps 18:3 *v*S Ps 46:4
*w*S Dt 33:19;
Ps 2:6; 87:1;
Isa 11:9; 32:16;
Jer 31:23;
Da 9:16; Mic 4:1;
Zec 8:3
48:2 *x*Ps 50:2;
La 2:15;
Eze 16:14
*y*S Jos 13:27
*z*S Ps 2:6
*a*Mt 5:35

48:3 *b*ver 13;
Ps 122:7 *c*Ps 18:2
48:4
*d*2Sa 10:1-19
48:5 *e*Ex 15:16;
Isa 13:8; Jer 46:5;
Da 5:9
48:6 *f*S Job 4:14
*g*S Ge 3:16

48:7 *h*S Ge 10:4; S 1Ki 10:22; 22:48 *i*S Ge 41:6 **48:8**
*j*Jer 23:6; Zec 8:13; 14:11

*g*7 Or *a maskil* (probably a literary or musical term)
*h*9 Or *shields*   *i*2 *Zaphon* can refer to a sacred
mountain or the direction north.   *j*2 Or *earth, /*
Mount Zion, on the northern side / of the

---

ark into the temple. The ark is symbolic of God's throne; the temple is the earthly symbol of his heavenly palace (see Ps 24; 68).
47:5 *shouts of joy . . . sounding of trumpets.* See note on v. 1. *trumpets.* The ram's horn, here announcing the presence of God as King (see 98:6; Ex 19:16,19; Jos 6:4).
47:7–9 The liturgical enthronement of God as world ruler.
47:7 *God is the King of all the earth.* See 2Sa 15:10; 2Ki 9:13; Isa 52:7. *psalm.* See NIV text note; see also note on Ps 32 title.
47:8 *seated on his holy throne.* In the Most Holy Place of the temple, where he takes the reins of world rule into his hands (see Jer 17:12). This verse is frequently echoed in Revelation (see Rev 4:9,10; 5:1,7,13; 6:16; 7:10,15; 19:4).
47:9 The nations acknowledge the God of Israel to be the Great King—anticipated as the final effect of God's rule (see note on 46:10). *as the people of the God of Abraham.* Thus the promises to Abraham will be fulfilled (see Ge 12:2–3; 17:4–6; 22:17–18). *kings.* See NIV text note; see also note on 3:3; cf. Isa 2:2; 56:7.
Ps 48 A celebration of the security of Zion (as viewed with the eyes of faith) in that it is the city of the Great King (see introductions to Ps 46–47). It may have been sung by the Levitical choir on behalf of the assembled worshipers at the temple. Structure and theme are beautifully matched. The first and last verses combine to frame the whole with a comforting confession concerning Zion's God. The center, v. 8 (see note on 6:6), summarizes the main theme of the body of the psalm. Four stanzas (having a symmetrical pattern in Hebrew: three lines, four lines, four lines, three lines) develop the theme: (1) the beauty of Zion as God's impregnable citadel (vv. 2–3); (2) the futility of all enemy attacks (vv. 4–7); (3) Zion's joy over God's saving acts (vv. 9–11)—related to the second stanza; (4) Zion as impregnable citadel (vv. 12–13)—related to the first stanza. Regularly distributed between the four main stanzas are allusions to the four primary directions (see notes on vv. 2,7,10,13)—suggesting that the city is secure from all points of attack.

48 title *song.* See note on Ps 30 title. *of the Sons of Korah.* See note on Ps 42 title.
48:1 *in the city of our God, his holy mountain.* See 46:4. *our God.* Occurs in this psalm only here, in the center (v. 8) and at the end (v. 14). *holy mountain.* See 43:3; see also note on 2:6.
48:2–3 Describes the lofty impregnability of Mount Zion.
48:2 *beautiful.* Its loftiness and secure position are its beauty (see note on 27:4). *loftiness.* Although not the highest ridge in its environment, in its significance as the mountain of God it is the "highest" mountain in the world (see 68:15–16 and note; Isa 2:2). *joy of the whole earth.* Perhaps referring to admiration from other nations, like that expressed by the queen of Sheba (see 1Ki 10:1–13). *Zaphon.* See NIV text note. Mount Zaphon in the far north was for the Phoenicians the sacred residence of El, the chief of their gods—as Mount Olympus was the mountain citadel of Zeus for the Greeks. *Great King.* See note on 47:2.
48:3 God himself, not her walls, was Zion's defense, a fact on which the next stanza elaborates (see note on vv. 12–13). *her citadels.* See v. 13.
48:4–7 The futile attacks of hostile nations—they fled in panic when they saw that the Great King was in Zion. Such events as the destruction of the confederacy in the days of Jehoshaphat (see 2Ch 20) or the slaughter of the Assyrians in the time of Hezekiah (see 2Ki 19:35–36) may have been in the psalmist's mind.
48:7 *ships of Tarshish.* Great merchant ships of the Mediterranean (see 1Ki 10:22 and NIV text note). *shattered by an east wind.* See Ac 27:14; see also 1Ki 22:48. *east.* See introduction above.
48:8 The central verse and theme (see note on 6:6). *heard . . . seen.* "Seen" is climactic, as in Job 42:5. They had heard because "our fathers have told us what you did in their days" (44:1; see 78:3), but now in the liturgical experience of God at his temple they have "seen" how secure the city of God is. *LORD Almighty.* See note on 1Sa 1:3. *our God.* See note on v. 1.

we meditate[k] on your unfailing
    love.[l]
¹⁰Like your name,[m] O God,
    your praise reaches to the ends of the
        earth;[n]
    your right hand is filled with
        righteousness.
¹¹Mount Zion rejoices,
    the villages of Judah are glad
    because of your judgments.[o]

¹²Walk about Zion, go around her,
    count her towers,[p]
¹³consider well her ramparts,[q]
    view her citadels,[r]
    that you may tell of them to the next
        generation.[s]
¹⁴For this God is our God for ever and
        ever;
    he will be our guide[t] even to the
        end.

Psalm 49

For the director of music. Of the Sons of
Korah. A psalm.

¹Hear[u] this, all you peoples;[v]
    listen, all who live in this world,[w]
²both low and high,[x]
    rich and poor alike:

³My mouth will speak words of
        wisdom;[y]
    the utterance from my heart will give
        understanding.[z]
⁴I will turn my ear to a proverb;[a]
    with the harp[b] I will expound my
        riddle:[c]

⁵Why should I fear[d] when evil days
        come,
    when wicked deceivers surround
        me—
⁶those who trust in their wealth[e]
    and boast[f] of their great riches?[g]
⁷No man can redeem the life of another
    or give to God a ransom for him—
⁸the ransom[h] for a life is costly,
    no payment is ever enough—[i]
⁹that he should live on[j] forever
    and not see decay.[k]

¹⁰For all can see that wise men die;[l]
    the foolish and the senseless[m] alike
        perish
    and leave their wealth[n] to others.[o]
¹¹Their tombs[p] will remain their houses[k]
        forever,
    their dwellings for endless
        generations,[q]

Cross references

48:9 [k]S Ps 39:3; [l]Ps 6:4
48:10 [m]S Ex 6:3; S Jos 7:9; [n]1Sa 2:10; Ps 22:27; 65:5; 98:3; 100:1; Isa 11:12; 24:16; 42:10; 49:6
48:11 [o]Ps 97:8
48:12 [p]S Ne 3:1
48:13 [q]2Sa 20:15; Isa 26:1; La 2:8; Hab 2:1 [r]S ver 3 [s]Ps 71:18; 78:6; 109:13
48:14 [t]Ps 25:5; 73:24; Pr 6:22; Isa 49:10; 57:18; 58:11
49:1 [u]Isa 1:2 [v]Ps 78:1 [w]S Ps 33:8
49:2 [x]Ps 62:9
49:3 [y]S Ps 37:30 [z]Ps 119:130
49:4 [a]Ps 78:2; Pr 1:6; Eze 12:22; 16:44; 18:2-3; Lk 4:23
[b]S 1Sa 16:16; Ps 33:2 [c]S Nu 12:8
49:5 [d]Ps 23:4; 27:1
49:6 [e]S Job 22:25; Ps 73:12; Jer 48:7 [f]S Ps 10:3 [g]S Job 36:19
49:8 [h]S Nu 35:31 [i]Mt 16:26
49:9 [j]Ps 22:29; 89:48 [k]Ps 16:10
49:10 [l]Ecc 2:16 [m]Ps 92:6; 94:8 [n]S Job 27:17
[o]Ecc 2:18,21; Lk 12:20 49:11 [p]Mk 5:3; Lk 8:27 [q]Ps 106:31

[k]*11* Septuagint and Syriac; Hebrew *In their thoughts
their houses will remain*

48:9–11 The worshipers meditate at the temple with joy
because of God's mighty acts in Zion's behalf.
48:9 *Within your temple.* In the temple courts. *unfailing
love.* See note on 6:4. As is clear from vv. 10–11, reference
here is to God's saving acts by which he has expressed his
covenant love for his people (see 31:21; 40:9–10).
48:10 *name.* See note on 5:11. *reaches.* From the temple
to the ends of the earth (see 9:11; 22:27). *right hand.* In
Hebrew idiom a subtle reference to the south. *righteousness.*
Righteous acts (see 40:9–10 and note; see also note on 4:1).
48:11 *judgments.* God's righteous judgments by which he
has acted in defense of Zion.
48:12–13 The people contemplate Zion's defense, viewed
from the perspective of what they have "seen" (v. 8) at the
temple. The strength of Zion's "towers," "ramparts" and
"citadels" is the presence of God.
48:13 *next generation.* Lit. "the generation behind"; in
Hebrew idiom "behind" is a subtle reference to the west.
48:14 *our God.* See note on v. 1. *guide.* The great Shepherd-King (see note on 23:1). *the end.* Lit. "death."
Ps 49 A word of instruction from the temple following
upon Ps 46–48 (see introductions to those psalms). It concerns rich fools who proudly rely on their great wealth and
on themselves to assure their security in the world (see Ps
52). The Levitical author knows what it is to be without
wealth (see Nu 18:21–24; Dt 14:27–29) and has observed
the attitudes of many of the rich (see vv. 5–6). He has seen
through their folly, however, and offers his wisdom for all to
hear (vv. 1–2), so that those who are awed by the rich may
be freed from their spell. Inescapable death is their undoing
and their destiny, and in the end the "upright will rule over
them" (v. 14). The date of this psalm may well be postexilic.
See introduction to Ps 37.

49 title See note on Ps 42 title.
49:1–4 Introduction.
49:1–2 More like the address of the prophets (see 1Ki
22:28; Isa 34:1; Mic 1:2) than that of the wisdom teachers
(see 34:11; Pr 1:8,10; 2:1).
49:3 See Mt 12:34. *wisdom.* See Introduction to Proverbs:
Wisdom Literature. *heart.* See note on 4:7.
49:4 *turn my ear.* The wisdom he is about to speak first had
to be "heard" by him—all true wisdom is from God (see Job
28). *with the harp.* Another hint of the author's sense of
inspiration (see 1Sa 10:5–6; 2Ki 3:15).
49:5–11 Those of little means or power need not be
unsettled when surrounded by rich fools who threaten and
strut; death is their destiny.
49:7–9 Wealth cannot buy escape from death—not even
one's "redeemer" can accomplish it (cf. Ex 21:30; Lev
25:47–49). Only God himself can redeem a life from the
grave (see v. 15 and note).
49:10 Anyone with "eyes in his head" (Ecc 2:14) can see
that even the wise die (see Ecc 7:2; 9:5) and leave their
wealth to others (see Ecc 2:18,21). How much more the fool
(see 73:18–20; 92:6–7)! See also 89:48; Job 30:23; Ecc
2:14–16. *wise men . . . foolish.* Essentially the "righteous"
and the "wicked" of Ps 37. *wealth.* Often gotten by devious
means that their foolish "wisdom" has contrived (v. 5). *to
others.* But not to their children (see note on 37:29; see also
39:6; Lk 12:20–21).
49:11 Though they lavish wealth on their tombs and try at
least to perpetuate their memory by putting their names to
their large landholdings (see Nu 32:41) as an enduring
memorial, they only suffer the bitter irony of having their
graves as their "eternal home" (Ecc 12:5).

though they had[1] named[r] lands after themselves.

[12]But man, despite his riches, does not endure;[s]
he is[m] like the beasts that perish.[t]

[13]This is the fate of those who trust in themselves,[u]
and of their followers, who approve their sayings. *Selah*

[14]Like sheep they are destined[v] for the grave,[n][w]
and death will feed on them.
The upright will rule[x] over them in the morning;
their forms will decay in the grave,[n]
far from their princely mansions.

[15]But God will redeem my life[o] from the grave;[y]
he will surely take me to himself.[z]
Selah

[16]Do not be overawed when a man grows rich,
when the splendor of his house increases;

[17]for he will take nothing[a] with him when he dies,
his splendor will not descend with him.[b]

[18]Though while he lived he counted himself blessed—[c]
and men praise you when you prosper—

[19]he will join the generation of his fathers,[d]
who will never see the light[e] of life.

[20]A man who has riches without understanding[f]
is like the beasts that perish.[g]

Psalm 50

A psalm of Asaph.

[1]The Mighty One, God, the LORD,[h]
speaks and summons the earth
from the rising of the sun to the place where it sets.[i]

Cross references (center column):

49:11 [r]S Dt 3:14
49:12 [s]S Job 14:2
[t]ver 20; 2Pe 2:12
49:13 [u]Lk 12:20
49:14 [v]Jer 43:11; Eze 31:14
[w]Nu 16:30; S Job 21:13; Ps 9:17; 55:15
[x]Isa 14:2; Da 7:18; 1Co 6:2
49:15 [y]Ps 56:13; Hos 13:14
[z]S Ge 5:24

49:17 [a]1Ti 6:7
[b]S Ps 17:14
49:18 [c]Ps 10:6; Lk 12:19
49:19 [d]S Ge 15:15
[e]S Job 33:30
49:20 [f]Pr 16:16
[g]S ver 12
50:1 [h]Jos 22:22
[i]Ps 113:3

Text notes:

[1]11 Or / for they have   [m]12 Hebrew; Septuagint and Syriac read verse 12 the same as verse 20.
[n]14 Hebrew *Sheol*; also in verse 15   [o]15 Or *soul*

49:12 Their epitaph (see note on 10:18; see also Ecc 3:19; 7:2) and the psalm's refrain (see NIV text note; see also introduction to Ps 42–43).
49:13–15 Their fate and mine—so "why should I fear?" (v. 5).
49:13 *in themselves.* As those who have "succeeded" (see v. 6).
49:14 *Like sheep.* Death is already their shepherd, "guiding" them to the grave. *death will feed on them.* For the imagery of death (or the grave) as an insatiable monster feeding on its victims see 69:15; 141:7; Pr 1:12; 27:20; 30:15–16; Isa 5:14; Jnh 2:2 ("depths"; lit. "belly"); Hab 2:5. The imagery is borrowed from Canaanite mythology, which so depicts the god Mot (death). As one Canaanite document reads, "Do not approach divine Mot, lest he put you like a lamb into his mouth." *rule over.* See Lev 26:17; Isa 14:2; perhaps "prevail over" in contrast to the situation referred to in v. 5. *in the morning.* See vv. 15,19 and notes on 6:5; 11:7; 16:9–11; 17:15. But see also introduction to Ps 57.
49:15 See note on vv. 7–9. *redeem . . . from the grave.* While this may refer to saving (for a while) from the universal prospect of death (as in Job 5:20; see 116:8), the context strongly suggests that the author, as one of the upright, speaks of his final destiny. Perhaps the thought is of being conveyed into the presence of God in his heavenly temple, analogous to the later Jewish thought of being conveyed to "Abraham's side" (Lk 16:22; see notes on 6:5; 11:7; 16:9–11; 17:15). *my life.* Lit. "my soul" (see NIV text note; see also note on 6:3). *take me to himself.* See 73:24; see also Ge 5:24 and note.
49:16–19 So do not let the present state of the wealthy captivate you.
49:16 *his house.* His whole estate (see Ex 20:17).
49:19 *light of life.* See notes on 27:1; Isa 53:11.
49:20 The last word. See note on v. 12.
Ps 50 The Lord calls his covenant people to account as they meet before him in worship at the temple. (Thus the psalm has links with Ps 46–49; see introductions to those psalms.)

The psalm appears to have been composed for a temple liturgy in which Israel reaffirms her commitment to God's covenant. A leader of the Levitical choir addresses Israel on behalf of the Lord (see Ps 15; 24, either of which may have been spoken earlier in the same liturgy). This liturgy was possibly related to the Feast of Tabernacles (see Dt 31:9–13; see also introduction to Ps 47). In its rebuke of a false understanding of sacrifice the psalm has affinity with the prophecies of Amos, Micah and Isaiah and so may date from the late eighth and/or early seventh centuries B.C. Others find a closer relationship with the reformation of Josiah (2Ki 22:1–23:25) and the ministry of Jeremiah. Structurally, the psalm has three parts: (1) the announcement of the "coming" of Israel's covenant Lord to call his people to account (vv. 1–6); (2) the Lord's words of correction for those of honest intent (vv. 7–15); (3) his sharp rebuke of "the wicked" among them (vv. 16–23).
50 title A traditional ascription of the psalm to Asaph; or it may mean "for Asaph" (see "For Jeduthun" in Ps 39 title) or for the descendants of Asaph who functioned in his place. This psalm may have been separated from the other psalms of Asaph (73–83) because of its thematic links with Ps 46–49. Asaph was one of David's three choir leaders (see note on Ps 39 title).
50:1–6 The Lord comes (v. 3) in the temple worship to correct and rebuke his people: Israel must know that the God of Zion is the God of Sinai (see Ex 19:16–20).
50:1 *The Mighty One, God, the LORD.* A sequence found elsewhere only in Jos 22:22 (see note there). Ps 50 is noteworthy for its use of numerous names and titles for God (seven in all: three in v. 1, four in the rest of the psalm; see notes on vv. 6,14,21–22). *the earth.* See "the heavens . . . the earth" (v. 4) and "the heavens" (v. 6). When Moses renewed the covenant between the Lord and Israel on the plains of Moab, he called upon heaven and earth to serve as third-party witnesses to the covenant (Dt 30:19; 31:28). The Lord now summons these to testify that his present word to his people is in complete accord with that covenant (see Isa 1:2).

[2]From Zion,[j] perfect in beauty,[k]
  God shines forth. [l]
[3]Our God comes[m] and will not be
    silent;[n]
  a fire devours[o] before him,[p]
  and around him a tempest[q] rages.
[4]He summons the heavens above,
  and the earth,[r] that he may judge his
    people:[s]
[5]"Gather to me my consecrated ones,[t]
  who made a covenant[u] with me by
    sacrifice."
[6]And the heavens proclaim[v] his
    righteousness,
  for God himself is judge. [w]   Selah

[7]"Hear, O my people, and I will speak,
  O Israel, and I will testify[x] against
    you:
  I am God, your God.[y]
[8]I do not rebuke[z] you for your sacrifices
  or your burnt offerings,[a] which are
    ever before me.
[9]I have no need of a bull[b] from your
    stall
  or of goats[c] from your pens,[d]
[10]for every animal of the forest[e] is mine,
  and the cattle on a thousand hills.[f]
[11]I know every bird[g] in the mountains,
  and the creatures of the field[h] are
    mine.
[12]If I were hungry I would not tell you,

for the world[i] is mine, and all that is
    in it.[j]
[13]Do I eat the flesh of bulls
  or drink the blood of goats?
[14]Sacrifice thank offerings[k] to God,
  fulfill your vows[l] to the Most High,[m]
[15]and call[n] upon me in the day of
    trouble;[o]
  I will deliver[p] you, and you will
    honor[q] me."

[16]But to the wicked, God says:

"What right have you to recite my laws
  or take my covenant[r] on your lips?[s]
[17]You hate[t] my instruction
  and cast my words behind[u] you.
[18]When you see a thief, you join[v] with
    him;
  you throw in your lot with
    adulterers.[w]
[19]You use your mouth for evil
  and harness your tongue to deceit.[x]
[20]You speak continually against your
    brother[y]
  and slander your own mother's son.
[21]These things you have done and I kept
    silent;[z]

50:2 /Ps 2:6
k S Ps 48:2;
S La 2:15
/S Dt 33:2
50:3 m Ps 96:13
n ver 21;
Isa 42:14; 64:12;
65:6 o S Lev 10:2
p S Ps 18:8
q Job 37:9;
Ps 83:15; 107:25;
147:18; Isa 29:6;
30:28; Jnh 1:4;
Na 1:3
50:4 r Dt 4:26;
31:28; Isa 1:2
s Heb 10:30
50:5 t S Dt 7:6;
S Ps 18:25
u Ex 24:7;
S 2Ch 6:11
50:6 v S Ps 19:1
w S Ge 16:5;
S Job 9:15
50:7 x Heb 2:4
y Ex 20:2;
Ps 48:14
50:8 z S 2Sa 22:16
a S Ps 40:6
50:9 b S Lev 1:5
c S Lev 16:5
d S Nu 32:16
50:10 e Ps 104:20;
Isa 56:9; Mic 5:8
f Ps 104:24
50:11 g Mt 6:26
h Ps 8:7; 80:13

50:12 i Ex 19:5
j Dt 10:14;
S Jos 3:11;
Ps 24:1;
1Co 10:26
50:14 k S Ezr 1:4;
S Ps 27:6
l S Nu 30:2;
S Ps 66:13; 76:11
m Ps 7:8

50:15 n Ps 4:1; 81:7; Isa 55:6; 58:9; Zec 13:9 o Ps 69:17;
86:7; 107:6; 142:2; Jas 5:13 p Ps 3:7 q S Ps 22:23 50:16
r Ps 25:10 s Isa 29:13 50:17 t Pr 1:22 u S 1Ki 14:9 50:18
v Ro 1:32; 1Ti 5:22 w S Job 22:15 50:19 x Ps 10:7; 36:3;
52:2; 101:7 50:20 y Mt 10:21 50:21 z Isa 42:14; 57:11;
62:1; 64:12

50:2 *perfect in beauty.* Because God resides there (cf. Eze 27:3–4,11; 28:12). *shines forth.* Manifests his glory as he comes to act (see 80:1; 94:1; Dt 33:2; cf. Eze 28:7,17), now confronting his people, but not yet announcing judgment as in Isa 1 or Mic 1.
50:3 *comes.* From his enthronement between the cherubim (see 80:1; 99:1; see also 1Sa 4:4; 2Sa 6:2; 2Ki 19:15) in the Most Holy Place of the temple (see note on 28:2; see also Isa 26:21; Mic 1:3). *will not be silent.* No longer (see v. 21) will he let their sins go unrebuked. *fire . . . tempest.* See Ex 19:16,18.
50:4 *judge.* Call them to account in accordance with his covenant.
50:5 *consecrated ones.* See note on 4:3. *by sacrifice.* Sacrifices were a part of the ritual that sealed the covenant (see Ex 24:4–8) and continued to be an integral part of Israel's expression of covenant commitment to the Lord.
50:6 *proclaim.* See note on v. 1. *righteousness.* See note on 4:1. *judge.* Lord over his people (the Hebrew for "judge" and that for "king" are sometimes used synonymously; see, e.g., Isa 33:22). "Judge" occurs as a title for God (see note on v. 1) in, e.g., 94:2; Ge 18:25; Jdg 11:27.
50:7–15 The Lord corrects his people.
50:7 *my people.* "Our God" (v. 3) and "your God" (here) reflect the covenant bond. *I am God, your God.* See Ex 19:3–6; Lev 19:2–4,10,25,31,34,36; 20:7,24; 22:33; 23:22.
50:8–13 Israel had not failed to bring enough sacrifices (v. 8), but she was ever tempted to think that sacrifices were of first importance to God, as though he was dependent on them. This notion was widespread among Israel's pagan neighbors. See note on 40:6.

50:10 *thousand.* Used here figuratively for a very large number.
50:12 *the world . . . in it.* See 24:1 and note.
50:14–15 God wants Israel to acknowledge her dependence on him, by giving thank offerings for his mercies (v. 14) and by praying to him in times of need (v. 15; see 116:17–19). Those who do so may expect God's gracious answer to their prayers (stated more directly in v. 23). God also desires obedience to his moral law (see vv. 16–21 and note on 40:6).
50:14 *thank offerings.* See Lev 7:12–13. *God . . . Most High.* That is, God Most High (see 57:2 and note on 3:7). *your vows.* Vows that accompanied prayer in times of need, usually involving thank offerings (see 66:13–15), always involving praise of the Lord for his answer to prayer (see note on 7:17). See also Heb 13:15. *Most High.* See note on v. 1; see also note on Ge 14:19.
50:15 *honor me.* With praise in the fulfillment of the vows (see v. 23)—and, implicitly, with obedience to his covenant law (see following verses).
50:16–23 The Lord's rebuke of the wicked.
50:16 *recite my laws.* Apparently a part of the liturgy of covenant commitment.
50:17 *You hate my instruction.* They formally participate in the holy ritual but reject God's law as the rule for life outside the ritual.
50:19 *use your mouth for evil.* See note on 5:9.
50:21 God's merciful and patient "silence" is distorted by the wicked into bad and self-serving theology (see Ecc 8:11; Isa 42:14; 57:11). *thought I was altogether.* See NIV text note; Ex 3:14 and note (see also note on v. 1). *accuse you to your face.* Set forth the particulars of my indictment before

you thought I was altogether[p] like
you.
But I will rebuke[a] you
and accuse[b] you to your face.

22"Consider this, you who forget God,[c]
or I will tear you to pieces, with none
to rescue:[d]
23He who sacrifices thank offerings honors
me,
and he prepares the way[e]
so that I may show him[q] the
salvation of God.[f]"

Psalm 51

For the director of music. A psalm of
David. When the prophet Nathan came to
him after David had committed adultery
with Bathsheba.[g]

1Have mercy[h] on me, O God,
according to your unfailing love;[i]
according to your great compassion[j]
blot out[k] my transgressions.[l]
2Wash away[m] all my iniquity
and cleanse[n] me from my sin.

3For I know my transgressions,
and my sin is always before me.[o]
4Against you, you only, have I sinned[p]

and done what is evil in your sight,[q]
so that you are proved right when you
speak
and justified when you judge.[r]
5Surely I was sinful[s] at birth,[t]
sinful from the time my mother
conceived me.
6Surely you desire truth in the inner
parts[r];
you teach[s] me wisdom[u] in the
inmost place.[v]

7Cleanse[w] me with hyssop,[x] and I will
be clean;
wash me, and I will be whiter than
snow.[y]
8Let me hear joy and gladness;[z]
let the bones[a] you have crushed
rejoice.
9Hide your face from my sins[b]
and blot out[c] all my iniquity.

10Create in me a pure heart,[d] O God,

Cross references (center column)

50:21 [a]Ps 6:1; S 18:15; 76:6; 104:7; Isa 50:2
[b]Ps 85:5; Isa 57:16
50:22 [c]S Job 8:13; S Isa 17:10
[d]S Dt 32:39; Mic 5:8
50:23 [e]Ps 85:13
[f]S Ps 9:14; 91:16; 98:3; Isa 52:10
51 Title [g]2Sa 11:4; 12:1
51:1 [h]S 2Sa 24:14; S Ps 9:13
[i]S Ps 25:7; S 119:88
[j]S Ne 9:27; Ps 86:15; Isa 63:7
[k]S 2Sa 12:13; S 2Ch 6:21; S Ne 4:5; Ac 3:19
[l]S Ps 39:8
51:2 [m]S Ru 3:3; Jer 2:22; 13:27; Ac 22:16; 1Jn 1:9
[n]Pr 20:30; Isa 4:4; Eze 36:25; Zec 13:1; Mt 23:25-26; Heb 9:14
51:3 [o]Isa 59:12
51:4 [p]S 1Sa 15:24
[q]S Ge 20:6; Lk 15:21 [r]Ro 3:4*
51:5 [s]S Lev 5:2
[t]S Job 5:7
51:6 [u]Ps 119:66; 143:10
[v]S Job 9:4; S 34:32

51:7 [w]Isa 4:4; Eze 36:25; Zec 13:1 [x]S Ex 12:22; S Nu 19:6; Heb 9:19 [y]Isa 1:18; 43:25; 44:22 51:8 [z]Isa 35:10; Jer 33:11; Joel 1:16 [a]S Ex 12:46 51:9 [b]Jer 16:17; Zec 4:10 [c]S 2Sa 12:13
51:10 [d]S Ps 24:4; 78:37; Mt 5:8; Ac 15:9

[p]21 Or *thought the 'I AM' was / who considers his way / I will show*   [q]23 Or *and to him*   [r]6 The meaning of the Hebrew for this phrase is uncertain.   [s]6 Or *you desired . . . ; / you taught*

Study notes

your eyes.
50:22 *God.* A relatively rare word for "God" (Hebrew *Eloah*), though common in Job. See note on v. 1.
50:23 See note on vv. 14–15.
Ps 51 David's humble prayer for forgiveness and cleansing. As the prayer of a contrite sinner, it represents a proper response to the Lord's confrontation of his people in Ps 50 (compare v. 16 with 50:8–15). This psalm has many points of contact with Ps 25. In traditional Christian usage it is one of seven penitential psalms (see introduction to Ps 6). The psalm is constructed symmetrically: A two-verse introduction balances a two-verse conclusion, and the enclosed four stanzas in Hebrew consist of five lines, three lines, three lines and five lines respectively. The whole is framed by David's prayer for himself (vv. 1–2) and for Zion (vv. 18–19). The well-being of the king and the city stand and fall together (see 28:8 and note on 3:8).
51 title *For the director of music.* See note on Ps 4 title. *When.* For the event referred to see 2Sa 11:1–12:25; see also note on Ps 3 title.
51:1–2 In mercy grant pardon (see Lk 18:13). Note the piling up of synonyms: mercy, unfailing love, great compassion; blot out, wash, cleanse; transgressions, iniquity, sin (for this last triad see note on 32:5).
51:1 *unfailing love.* See note on 6:4. *blot out.* See v. 9. The image is that of a papyrus scroll (see note on 9:5) on which God had recorded David's deeds. The "blotting out" of sins pictures forgiveness (Jer 18:23; see Isa 43:25). For the imagery of God's keeping records of the events in his realm in the way that earthly kings do, see 56:8; 87:6; 130:3; 139:16; Ne 13:14; Da 7:10; see also Ex 32:32–33.
51:2 See v. 7. *Wash.* As a filthy garment. *cleanse me.* Make me clean in your sight (see Lev 11:32).
51:3–6 Confession of sin (cf. Pr 28:13; 1Jn 1:9).
51:3 *before me.* On my mind.

51:4 *Against you . . . only.* David acknowledges that his sin was preeminently against God (see 2Sa 12:13; cf. Ge 20:6; 39:9; Lk 15:18). He had violated specific covenant stipulations (Ex 20:13–14,17). *when you speak . . . when you judge.* As the Lord did through Nathan the prophet (2Sa 12:7–12). For a NT application see Ro 3:4.
51:5 He cannot plead that this sin was a rare aberration in his life; it sprang from what he is and has been (in his "inner parts," v. 6) from birth (see 58:3; Ge 8:21; cf. Jn 9:34; Eph 2:3). The apparently similar statements in Job 14:4; 15:14; 25:4–6 rise from a different motivation.
51:6 The great contrast: He has acted absolutely contrary to what God desires and to what God has been teaching him in the inmost place. But it is just this "desire" of God and this "teaching" of God that are his hope—what he pleads for in vv. 7,10. *truth.* Moral integrity. *inner parts.* See 139:13–16; Job 38:36. *wisdom.* Whoever gives himself over to sin is a fool; he who has God's law in his heart is wise (see 37:30–31). *inmost place.* The most secret place within.
51:7–9 Renewed prayer for pardon.
51:7 *Cleanse me.* Lit. "Un-sin me." *hyssop.* Used in ritual cleansing; see note on Ex 12:22. *be clean.* The Hebrew root for this phrase is the same as that for "cleanse" in v. 2. *whiter than snow.* Like a filthy garment, he needs washing (see note on v. 2); but if God washes him, he will be so pure that there is no figurative word that can describe him (see Isa 1:18; Da 7:9; Rev 7:14; 19:14).
51:8 *Let me hear joy.* Let me be surrounded by joy (see 32:7 and note; see also 35:27), or let me hear a prophetic oracle of forgiveness that will result in joy—from the assurance of sins forgiven (see 2Sa 12:13). *bones.* See note on 6:2.
51:9 *Hide your face.* From what is "always before me" (v. 3). *blot out.* See note on v. 1.
51:10–12 Prayer for purity—for a pure heart, a steadfast

and renew a steadfast spirit within
me. [e]
[11]Do not cast me[f] from your presence[g]
or take your Holy Spirit[h] from me.
[12]Restore to me the joy of your salvation[i]
and grant me a willing spirit,[j] to
sustain me. [k]

[13]Then I will teach transgressors your
ways, [l]
and sinners[m] will turn back to you. [n]
[14]Save me[o] from bloodguilt, [p] O God,
the God who saves me, [q]
and my tongue will sing of your
righteousness. [r]
[15]O Lord, open my lips, [s]
and my mouth will declare your
praise.
[16]You do not delight in sacrifice, [t] or I
would bring it;
you do not take pleasure in burnt
offerings.
[17]The sacrifices[u] of God are[t] a broken
spirit;
a broken and contrite heart, [v]
O God, you will not despise.

[18]In your good pleasure make Zion[w]
prosper;
build up the walls of Jerusalem. [x]
[19]Then there will be righteous sacrifices, [y]

whole burnt offerings[z] to delight
you;
then bulls[a] will be offered on your
altar.

Psalm 52

For the director of music. A *maskil*[u] of
David. When Doeg the Edomite [b] had
gone to Saul and told him: "David has
gone to the house of Ahimelech."

[1]Why do you boast of evil, you mighty
man?
Why do you boast[c] all day long, [d]
you who are a disgrace in the eyes of
God?
[2]Your tongue plots destruction; [e]
it is like a sharpened razor, [f]
you who practice deceit.[g]
[3]You love evil[h] rather than good,
falsehood[i] rather than speaking the
truth.   *Selah*
[4]You love every harmful word,
O you deceitful tongue![j]
[5]Surely God will bring you down to
everlasting ruin:

51:10
[e]Eze 18:31;
36:26
51:11 [f]Ps 27:9;
71:9; 138:8
[g]S Ge 4:14;
S Ex 33:15
[h]Ps 106:33;
Isa 63:10;
Eph 4:30
51:12
[i]S Job 33:26
[j]Ps 110:3
[k]S Ps 18:35
51:13
[l]S Ex 33:13;
Ac 9:21-22
[m]S Ps 1:1
[n]S Job 33:27
51:14 [o]S Ps 39:8
[p]S 2Sa 12:9
[q]Ps 25:5; 68:20;
88:1 [r]S Ps 5:8;
35:28; 71:15
51:15 [s]Ex 4:15
51:16
[t]S 1Sa 15:22
51:17 [u]Pr 15:8;
Hag 2:14
[v]Mt 11:29
51:18
[w]Ps 102:16;
147:2; Isa 14:32;
51:3; Zec 1:16-17
[x]Ps 69:35;
Isa 44:26
51:19 [y]Dt 33:19

[z]Ps 66:13; 96:8;
Jer 17:26
[a]Ps 66:15
52 Title
[b]1Sa 21:7; 22:9
52:1 [c]Ps 10:3;
94:4 [d]Ps 44:8
52:2 [e]Ps 5:9
[f]S Nu 6:5
[g]S Ps 50:19

52:3 [h]Ex 10:10; 1Sa 12:25; Am 5:14-15; Jn 3:20 [i]Ps 58:3;
Jer 9:5; Rev 21:8 **52:4** [j]Ps 5:9; 10:7; 109:2; 120:2,3;
Pr 10:31; 12:19

[t]*17* Or *My sacrifice, O God, is*   [u]Title: Probably a
literary or musical term

---

spirit of faithfulness and a willing spirit of service. These can
be his only if God does not reject him and take his Holy Spirit
from him. If granted, the joy of God's salvation will return to
gladden his troubled soul.
51:10 *Create.* As something new, which cannot emerge
from what now is (see v. 5), and which only God can fashion
(see Ge 1:1; Isa 65:17; Jer 31:22). *heart.* See note on 4:7.
51:11 The two requests are essentially one (see 139:7; Eze
39:29). David's prayer recalls the rejection of Saul (see 1Sa
16:1,14; 2Sa 7:15) and pleads for God not to take away his
Spirit, by which he had equipped and qualified him for his
royal office (see 16:13; cf. 2Sa 23:1-2). *Holy Spirit.* The
phrase is found elsewhere in the OT only in Isa 63:10-11.
By his Spirit, God effected his purposes in creation (see
104:30; Ge 1:2; Job 33:4) and redemption (see Isa 32:15;
44:3; 63:11,14; Hag 2:5), equipped his servants for their
appointed tasks (see Ex 31:3; Nu 11:29; Jdg 3:10; 1Sa
10:6; 16:13; Isa 11:2; 42:1), inspired his prophets (see Nu
24:2-3; 2Sa 23:2; Ne 9:30; Isa 59:21; 61:1; Eze 11:5; Mic
3:8; Zec 7:12) and directed their ministries (see 1Ki 18:12;
2Ki 2:16; Isa 48:16; Eze 2:2; 3:14). And it is by his Spirit
that God gives his people a "new heart and . . . a new spirit"
to live by his will (see Eze 36:26-27; see also Jer 24:7;
32:39; Eze 11:19; 18:31).
51:13–17 The vow to praise (see note on 7:17).
51:13 His praise for God's forgiveness and purification will
be accompanied by instruction for sinners (see Ps 34 and
note on 32:8-10). *your ways.* See 25:4 and note.
51:14 If God will only forgive, praise will follow. *righteousness.* See note on 4:1.
51:15 *open my lips.* By granting the forgiveness and
cleansing I seek.
51:16 See note on 40:6.

51:17 *broken spirit; a broken and contrite heart.* What
pleases God more than sacrifices is a humble heart that looks
to him when troubles crush and penitently pleads for mercy
when sin has been committed (see 50:7–15 and notes; see
also 34:17–18).
51:18–19 Prayer for Zion (see note on 3:8).
51:19 *righteous sacrifices.* Such as are pleasing to God;
here, sacrifices accompanied by praise for God's mercies (see
50:14–15 and notes).
Ps 52 Fearless confidence in God when under attack by an
arrogant and evil enemy. David stands in the presence of God
and from the high tower of that refuge hurls his denunciation
(much like the prophetic denunciation in Isa 22:15–19) into
the face of his attacker. Though not a wisdom psalm, it has
much in common with Ps 49. The extended depiction of
David's enemy forms a sharp contrast with the spirit of Ps 51.
See also David's denunciation of Goliath (1Sa 17:45–47).
52 title *For the director of music.* See note on Ps 4 title.
maskil. See note on Ps 32 title. *When.* See note on Ps 3 title.
For the event referred to see 1Sa 22:9–10.
52:1–4 The enemy castigated.
52:1 *Why . . . ?* By what right? See 50:16; Isa 3:15. *boast.*
By act as well as by word (see 75:4–5). *mighty man.* In his
own estimation (see Isa 22:17).
52:2 *Your tongue.* See v. 4; see also note on 5:9.
52:3 Your whole moral sense is perverted. *love.* Prefer.
52:4 *tongue.* See note on v. 2.
52:5–7 The enemy's end announced (implicitly a prayer):
God will slay you, and the righteous will mock you.
52:5 Note the triple imagery: "bring you down," "snatch
you up," "uproot you." The arrogant enemy will meet the
same end as the rich fools of Ps 49. *from your tent.* See Job
18:14. *uproot you.* Contrast v. 8.

He will snatch you up and tear[k] you
from your tent;
he will uproot[l] you from the land of
the living.[m]   *Selah*
[6]The righteous will see and fear;
they will laugh[n] at him, saying,
[7]"Here now is the man
who did not make God his
stronghold[o]
but trusted in his great wealth[p]
and grew strong by destroying
others!"

[8]But I am like an olive tree[q]
flourishing in the house of God;
I trust[r] in God's unfailing love
for ever and ever.
[9]I will praise you forever[s] for what you
have done;
in your name I will hope,[t] for your
name is good.[u]
I will praise you in the presence of
your saints.[v]

Psalm 53

53:1–6pp — Ps 14:1–7

For the director of music. According to
mahalath.[v] A *maskil*[w] of David.

[1]The fool[w] says in his heart,
"There is no God."[x]
They are corrupt, and their ways are
vile;
there is no one who does good.

[2]God looks down from heaven[y]
on the sons of men

to see if there are any who
understand,[z]
any who seek God.[a]
[3]Everyone has turned away,
they have together become corrupt;
there is no one who does good,
not even one.[b]

[4]Will the evildoers never learn—
those who devour my people as men
eat bread
and who do not call on God?
[5]There they were, overwhelmed with
dread,
where there was nothing to dread.[c]
God scattered the bones[d] of those who
attacked you;[e]
you put them to shame,[f] for God
despised them.[g]

[6]Oh, that salvation for Israel would come
out of Zion!
When God restores the fortunes of
his people,
let Jacob rejoice and Israel be glad!

Psalm 54

For the director of music. With stringed
instruments. A *maskil*[w] of David. When
the Ziphites[h] had gone to Saul and said,
"Is not David hiding among us?"

[1]Save me[i], O God, by your name;[j]
vindicate me by your might.[k]
[2]Hear my prayer, O God;[l]

Cross references (center column):

52:5 [k]S Dt 29:28;
S Job 40:12;
Isa 22:19;
Eze 17:24
[l]S Dt 28:63
[m]S Job 28:13
52:6 [n]S Job 22:19
52:7 [o]S 2Sa 22:3
[p]S Ps 49:6;
S Pr 11:28;
Mk 10:23
52:8 [q]S Ps 1:3;
S Rev 11:4
[r]Ps 6:4; 13:5
52:9 [s]S Ps 30:12
[t]S Job 7:6;
Ps 25:3 [u]S Ps 54:6
[v]S Dt 7:6; Ps 16:3
53:1 [w]Ps 74:22;
107:17; Pr 10:23
[x]Ps 10:4
53:2 [y]S Ps 33:13

[z]Ps 82:5;
Jer 4:22; 8:8
[a]2Ch 15:2
53:3
[b]Ro 3:10-12*
53:5
[c]S Lev 26:17
[d]2Ki 23:14;
Ps 141:7; Jer 8:1;
Eze 6:5
[e]2Ki 17:20
[f]S Job 8:22
[g]Jer 6:30; 14:19;
La 5:22
54 Title
[h]1Sa 23:19; 26:1
54:1 [i]S 1Sa 24:15
[j]Ps 20:1
[k]2Ch 20:6
54:2 [l]S Ps 4:1;
5:1; 55:1

[v]Title: Probably a musical term   [w]Title: Probably a
literary or musical term

52:6 *righteous.* See note on 1:5. *fear.* Learn from your
downfall (see 40:3 and note on 34:8–14).
52:7 See Ps 49.
52:8–9 David's security is God.
52:8 *like an olive tree.* Which lives for hundreds of years.
flourishing. See 1:3. It will not be uprooted (see v. 5). *in the
house of God.* Olive trees were not planted in the temple
courts, but David had access to God's temple as his refuge
(see 15:1; 23:6; 27:4; 61:4 and note), where he was kept
safe (see 27:5 and note). *unfailing love.* See note on 6:4.
52:9 A vow to praise (see note on 7:17). *name.* See note on
5:11. *saints.* See note on 4:3.
Ps 53 A testimony concerning the folly of evil men, a
somewhat revised duplicate of Ps 14; see introduction there.
(The main difference between the two psalms is that here the
word "God" is used instead of "the LORD"; see also note on
v. 5.) The original psalm may have been revised in the light
of an event such as is narrated in 2Ch 20. Here it also serves
as a further commentary on the kind of arrogant fool denounced in Ps 52.
53 title *For the director of music.* See note on Ps 4 title.
According to. See note on Ps 6 title. *mahalath.* Possibly the
name of a tune (see note on Ps 9 title). The Hebrew appears
to be the word for "suffering" or "sickness" (see Ps 88 title
and NIV text note there). Perhaps the Hebrew phrase indicates here that the psalm is to be used in a time of affliction,
when the godless mock (see Ps 102; see also note on 5:9).

maskil. See note on Ps 32 title.
53:1–4 See notes on 14:1–4.
53:5 Differs considerably from 14:5–6, though the basic
thought remains the same: God overwhelms the godless
who attack his people. Here the verbs are in the past tense
(perhaps to express the certainty of their downfall). *where
there was nothing to dread.* They fell victim to fear when,
humanly speaking, they were not even threatened. God's
curse fell on them rather than on Israel (see Lev 26:36–37;
see also Jdg 7:21; 2Ki 3:22–23; 7:6–7; Pr 28:1). *scattered
the bones.* Over the battlefield of their defeat, their bodies
left unburied like something loathsome (see Isa 14:18–20;
Jer 8:2 and note). *God despised them.* As they had despised
him.
53:6 See note on 14:7.
Ps 54 A prayer for deliverance from enemies who want to
have David killed. The prayer is short, like that of Ps 3; 4; 13;
yet it is one of the most typical prayers of the Psalter. Completely symmetrical, the prayer is framed by David's cry for
vindication (v. 1) and his statement of assurance that he will
look in triumph on his foes (v. 7). A confession of confidence
(v. 4) centers the prayer (see 42:8 and note on 6:6). The
opening stanza has two verses, like the conclusion, while vv.
3,5 each form a separate element in the prayer.
54 title *For the director of music.* See note on Ps 4 title.
With stringed instruments. See note on Ps 4 title. *maskil.* See
note on Ps 32 title. *When.* For the event referred to see 1Sa

listen to the words of my mouth.

[3]Strangers are attacking me; [m]
ruthless men [n] seek my life [o]—
men without regard for God. [p] *Selah*

[4]Surely God is my help; [q]
the Lord is the one who sustains
me. [r]

[5]Let evil recoil [s] on those who slander
me;
in your faithfulness [t] destroy them.

[6]I will sacrifice a freewill offering [u] to
you;
I will praise [v] your name, O Lord,
for it is good. [w]

[7]For he has delivered me [x] from all my
troubles,
and my eyes have looked in triumph
on my foes. [y]

Psalm 55

For the director of music. With stringed
instruments. A *maskil*[x] of David.

[1]Listen to my prayer, O God,
do not ignore my plea; [z]
[2] hear me and answer me. [a]
My thoughts trouble me and I am
distraught [b]
[3] at the voice of the enemy,
at the stares of the wicked;
for they bring down suffering upon me [c]
and revile [d] me in their anger. [e]

[4]My heart is in anguish [f] within me;
the terrors [g] of death assail me.

(center reference column)

54:3 [m]Ps 86:14
[n]Ps 18:48; 140:1,
4,11 [o]S 1Sa 20:1
[p]Ps 36:1
54:4
[q]S 1Ch 5:20;
S Ps 20:2
[r]S Ps 18:35
54:5 [s]S Dt 32:35;
Ps 94:23;
Pr 24:12
[t]Ps 89:49;
Isa 42:3
54:6 [u]S Lev 7:12,
16; S Ezr 1:4;
S Ps 27:6
[v]Ps 44:8; 69:30;
138:2; 142:7;
145:1 [w]Ps 52:9
54:7 [x]Ps 34:6
[y]Ps 59:10; 92:11;
112:8; 118:7
55:1 [z]Ps 27:9;
La 3:56
55:2 [a]Ps 4:1
[b]1Sa 1:15-16;
Ps 77:3; 86:6-7;
142:2
55:3
[c]S 2Sa 16:6-8;
Ps 17:9; 143:3
[d]S Ps 44:16
[e]Ps 71:11
55:4 [f]S Ps 6:3
[g]S Job 18:11

55:5 [h]S Job 4:14;
S 2Co 7:15
[i]Dt 28:67;
Isa 21:4; Jer 46:5;
49:5; Eze 7:18
55:7 [j]1Sa 23:14
55:8 [k]Ps 31:20
[l]Ps 77:18; Isa 4:6;
25:4; 28:2; 29:6;
32:2
55:9 [m]Ge 11:9;
Ac 2:4 [n]Ps 11:5;
Isa 59:6; Jer 6:7;
Eze 7:11; Hab 1:3
[o]Ge 4:17
55:10 [p]1Pe 5:8
55:11 [q]Ps 5:9
[r]Ps 10:7
55:13
[s]S 2Sa 15:12
55:14
[t]Ac 1:16-17
[u]Ps 42:4

[5]Fear and trembling [h] have beset me;
horror [i] has overwhelmed me.
[6]I said, "Oh, that I had the wings of a
dove!
I would fly away and be at rest—
[7]I would flee far away
and stay in the desert; [j] *Selah*
[8]I would hurry to my place of shelter, [k]
far from the tempest and storm. [l] "

[9]Confuse the wicked, O Lord, confound
their speech, [m]
for I see violence and strife [n] in the
city. [o]
[10]Day and night they prowl [p] about on its
walls;
malice and abuse are within it.
[11]Destructive forces [q] are at work in the
city;
threats and lies [r] never leave its
streets.

[12]If an enemy were insulting me,
I could endure it;
if a foe were raising himself against me,
I could hide from him.
[13]But it is you, a man like myself,
my companion, my close friend, [s]
[14]with whom I once enjoyed sweet
fellowship [t]
as we walked with the throng at the
house of God. [u]

[15]Let death take my enemies by
surprise; [v]

55:15 [v]Ps 64:7; Pr 6:15; Isa 29:5; 47:9,11; 1Th 5:3

[x]Title: Probably a literary or musical term

23:19; see also note on Ps 3 title.
54:1–2 Prayer for God to judge his case (see Ps 17).
54:1 *name.* See v. 6; see also note on 5:11.
54:3 The case against his enemies. *without regard for God.*
Like those of Ps 53.
54:4 The confession of confidence and the center of the
poem (see 42:8 and note).
54:5 The call for redress (see note on 5:10).
54:6 The vow to praise (see note on 7:17). *name.* See v. 1;
see also note on 5:11.
54:7 Assurance of being heard (see note on 3:8).
Ps 55 A prayer for God's help when threatened by a
powerful conspiracy in Jerusalem under the leadership of a
former friend. The situation described is like that of Absalom's conspiracy against the king (see 2Sa 15–17): The city
is in turmoil; danger is everywhere; there is uncertainty as to
who can be trusted; rumors, false reports and slander are
circulating freely. Under such circumstances David longs for
a quiet retreat to escape it all (vv. 6–8). That being out of the
question, he casts his cares on the Lord, whom he knows he
can trust. In its structure, the prayer is framed by a plea for
help (v. 1) and a simple confession of faith: "I trust in you"
(v. 23).
55 title *For the director of music.* See note on Ps 4 title.
With stringed instruments. See note on Ps 4 title. *maskil.* See
note on Ps 32 title.

55:1–3 Initial appeal for God to hear.
55:4–8 His heart's anguish.
55:4–5 Danger is everywhere (see 31:13), a danger so
great that it is as if death itself were stalking him (see 18:4–5;
116:3).
55:4 *heart.* See note on 4:7. *terrors of death.* See 1Sa 5:11;
15:32; 28:5; Job 18:14.
55:6–8 He longs for a quiet retreat, away from treacherous
and conniving people (see similarly Jer 9:2–6).
55:9–11 Prayer for God to foil the plots of his enemies.
55:9 *Confuse . . . confound their speech.* Paralyze the
conspirators with conflicting designs, as at Babel (Ge
11:5–9; see 2Sa 17:1–14). *the city.* See v. 11; Jerusalem.
55:10 *malice and abuse.* Like watchmen on the walls (see
127:1; 130:6; SS 5:7).
55:11 *threats and lies.* Like watchmen who patrol the city
streets (see SS 3:3).
55:12–14 The insults and plots of an enemy can be endured—but those of a treacherous friend?
55:13 *my companion, my close friend.* See v. 20; see also
41:9 and note.
55:14 *at the house of God.* Their ties of friendship had
been a bond hallowed by common commitment to the Lord
and sealed by its public display in the presence of God and
the worshipers at the temple.
55:15 Prayer for redress (see note on 5:10). *Let death take*

let them go down alive to the
grave,[y] [w]
for evil finds lodging among them.

16 But I call to God,
and the LORD saves me.
17 Evening,[x] morning[y] and noon[z]
I cry out in distress,
and he hears my voice.
18 He ransoms me unharmed
from the battle waged against me,
even though many oppose me.
19 God, who is enthroned forever,[a]
will hear[b] them and afflict them—
Selah
men who never change their ways
and have no fear of God.[c]

20 My companion attacks his friends;[d]
he violates his covenant.[e]
21 His speech is smooth as butter,[f]
yet war is in his heart;
his words are more soothing than oil,[g]
yet they are drawn swords.[h]

22 Cast your cares on the LORD
and he will sustain you;[i]
he will never let the righteous fall.[j]
23 But you, O God, will bring down the
wicked
into the pit[k] of corruption;
bloodthirsty and deceitful men[l]
will not live out half their days.[m]

But as for me, I trust in you.[n]

55:15 [w]S Ps 49:14 **55:17** [x]Ps 141:2; Ac 3:1; 10:3,30 [y]Ps 5:3; 88:13; 92:2 [z]Ac 10:9 **55:19** [a]S Ex 15:18; Dt 33:27; Ps 29:10 [b]Ps 78:59 [c]Ps 36:1; 64:4 **55:20** [d]Ps 7:4 [e]S Ps 41:9 **55:21** [f]Ps 12:2 [g]Pr 5:3; 6:24 [h]Ps 57:4; 59:7; 64:3; Pr 12:18; Rev 1:16 **55:22** [i]S Ps 18:35; Mt 6:25-34; 1Pe 5:7 [j]Ps 15:5; 21:7; 37:24; 112:6 **55:23** [k]Ps 9:15; S 30:3; 73:18; 94:13; Isa 14:15; Eze 28:8; S Lk 8:31 [l]Ps 5:6 [m]S Job 15:32 [n]Ps 11:1; 25:2; 56:3

56:1 [o]Ps 6:2 [p]Ps 57:1-3 [q]Ps 17:9 **56:2** [r]Ps 35:25; 124:3 [s]Ps 35:1 **56:3** [t]Ps 55:4-5 [u]S Ps 55:23 **56:4** [v]ver 10 [w]S Ps 27:1 [x]Ps 118:6; Mt 10:28; Heb 13:6 **56:5** [y]Ps 41:7; 2Pe 3:16 **56:6** [z]Ps 59:3; 94:21; Mk 3:6 [a]Ps 17:11 [b]Ps 71:10 **56:7** [c]Pr 19:5; Eze 17:15; Ro 2:3; Heb 12:25

Psalm 56

For the director of music. To ⌞the tune of⌟ "A Dove on Distant Oaks." Of David. A *miktam.*[z] When the Philistines had seized him in Gath.

1 Be merciful to me,[o] O God, for men
hotly pursue me;[p]
all day long they press their attack.[q]
2 My slanderers pursue me all day long;[r]
many are attacking me in their
pride.[s]

3 When I am afraid,[t]
I will trust in you.[u]
4 In God, whose word I praise,[v]
in God I trust; I will not be afraid.[w]
What can mortal man do to me?[x]

5 All day long they twist my words;[y]
they are always plotting to harm me.
6 They conspire,[z] they lurk,
they watch my steps,[a]
eager to take my life.[b]
7 On no account let them escape;[c]
in your anger, O God, bring down
the nations.[d]
8 Record my lament;
list my tears on your scroll[a] [e]—
are they not in your record?[f]

9 Then my enemies will turn back[g]

[d]Ps 36:12; 55:23 **56:8** [e]S 2Ki 20:5 [f]Isa 4:3; Da 7:10; 12:1; Mal 3:16 **56:9** [g]Ps 9:3

[y]*15* Hebrew *Sheol* [z]Title: Probably a literary or musical term [a]*8* Or */ put my tears in your wineskin*

---

my enemies. The conspirators were seeking his death. *alive to the grave.* May they go to the grave before life has run its normal course (see v. 23; Nu 16:29–33; Pr 1:12; Isa 5:14).
55:16–19 Assurance of being heard (see note on 3:8).
55:17 *Evening, morning and noon I cry out.* Cf. Da 6:10.
55:18 *ransoms.* Here a vivid synonym for "rescues" (see Isa 50:2; Jer 31:11).
55:19 He who is the eternal King will deal with those who "never change" in their ways and show "no fear of God" (see 36:1 and note; see also Ps 14; 53).
55:20–21 Further sorrowful (or angry) reflection over the treachery of his former friend.
55:20 *his friends.* Lit. "those at peace with him" (see 7:4).
55:21 See 28:3; Pr 5:3–4; see also note on 5:9. *heart.* See note on 4:7.
55:22–23 Once more, assurance of being heard.
55:22 A testimony to all who are assembled at the temple. 1Pe 5:7 echoes this assurance. *righteous.* See note on 1:5.
55:23 *pit of corruption.* The grave (see note on 30:1). *not live out half their days.* See note on v. 15.
Ps 56 A prayer for help when the psalmist is attacked by enemies and his very life is threatened. It is marked by consoling trust in the face of unsettling fear. Structurally, the prayer is framed by an urgent appeal to God (vv. 1–2) and a word of confident assurance (vv. 12–13). An inner frame, vv. 3–4 and vv. 10–11, confesses a sure trust in God in a form that is almost a refrain. The prayer itself is developed in the intervening verses (vv. 5–9).
56 title *For the director of music.* See note on Ps 4 title. *To ⌞the tune of⌟.* See note on Ps 9 title. *miktam.* See note on Ps 16 title. *When.* See note on Ps 3 title. For the event referred to see 1Sa 21:10–15; see also Ps 34 title and note. *had seized.* Or "were about to seize."
56:1–2 Initial appeal for God's help.
56:2 *My slanderers.* The enemies' chief weapon is the tongue (see note on 5:9). *their pride.* Confident in their position of strength, they take no account of David's God (see notes on 3:2; 5:9; 10:11).
56:3–4 See vv. 10–11; confession of trust in the face of fear.
56:4 *word.* God's reassuring promise that he will be the God of his people and will come to their aid when they appeal to him (see 50:15; 91:15; see also 119:74,81; 130:5). *mortal man.* Lit. "flesh"—i.e., man's feebleness compared with God's power (see note on 10:18).
56:5–7 Accusation and call for redress (see note on 5:9–10).
56:5 *twist my words.* See v. 2.
56:7 See note on 5:10. *anger.* See note on 2:5.
56:8–9 Appeal for God to take special note of the psalmist's troubles.
56:8 *Record . . . list . . . on your scroll.* Record my troubles in your heavenly royal records as matters calling for your action (see note on 51:1).
56:9 If God takes such note of his tears that he records them in his book, he will surely respond to David's call for

when I call for help. *h*
By this I will know that God is for
me. *i*
¹⁰In God, whose word I praise,
in the Lᴏʀᴅ, whose word I praise—
¹¹in God I trust; I will not be afraid.
What can man do to me?

¹²I am under vows*j* to you, O God;
I will present my thank offerings to
you.
¹³For you have delivered me*b* from
death*k*
and my feet from stumbling,
that I may walk before God
in the light of life. *c l*

Psalm 57

57:7-11pp — Ps 108:1-5

For the director of music. ˌTo the tune of˳
"Do Not Destroy." Of David. A *miktam.* *d*
When he had fled from Saul
into the cave. *m*

¹Have mercy on me, O God, have mercy
on me,
for in you my soul takes refuge. *n*
I will take refuge in the shadow of your
wings*o*
until the disaster has passed. *p*

²I cry out to God Most High,

56:9 *h*Ps 102:2
*i*S Nu 14:8;
S Dt 31:6;
Ro 8:31
56:12 *j*Ps 50:14
56:13 *k*Ps 30:3;
33:19; 49:15;
86:13; 107:20;
116:8
*l*S Job 33:30
57 Title
*m*1Sa 22:1; 24:3;
Ps 142 Title
57:1 *n*Ps 2:12;
9:9; 34:22
*o*S Ru 2:12;
S Mt 23:37
*p*Isa 26:20

57:2 *q*Ps 138:8
57:3 *r*Ps 18:9,16;
69:14; 142:6;
144:5,7 *s*Ps 56:1
*t*Ps 25:10; 40:11;
115:1
57:4 *u*Ps 35:17
*v*S Ps 55:21;
Pr 30:14
57:5 *w*ver 11;
Ps 108:5
57:6 *x*Ps 10:9;
31:4; 140:5
*y*S Ps 38:6;
145:14 *z*S Ps 9:15
*a*S Est 6:13;
Ps 7:15; Pr 28:10;
Ecc 10:8
57:7 *b*Ps 112:7
57:8 *c*Ps 33:2;
149:3; 150:3

---

to God, who fulfills ˌhis purpose˳ for
me. *q*
³He sends from heaven and saves me, *r*
rebuking those who hotly pursue
me; *s*   *Selah*
God sends his love and his
faithfulness. *t*

⁴I am in the midst of lions; *u*
I lie among ravenous beasts—
men whose teeth are spears and arrows,
whose tongues are sharp swords. *v*

⁵Be exalted, O God, above the heavens;
let your glory be over all the earth. *w*

⁶They spread a net for my feet*x* —
I was bowed down*y* in distress.
They dug a pit*z* in my path—
but they have fallen into it
themselves. *a*   *Selah*

⁷My heart is steadfast, O God,
my heart is steadfast; *b*
I will sing and make music.
⁸Awake, my soul!
Awake, harp and lyre! *c*
I will awaken the dawn.

⁹I will praise you, O Lord, among the
nations;
I will sing of you among the peoples.

b13 Or my soul   *c13 Or the land of the living*
dTitle: Probably a literary or musical term

---

help.
56:10-11 Renewed confession of trust in the face of fear
(see vv. 3-4).
56:12-13 Assurance of being heard (see note on 3:8).
56:12 *I am under vows.* Speaking as if his prayer has
already been heard, David acknowledges that now he must
keep the vows he made to God when he was in trouble (see
66:14 and note on 7:17).
56:13 *me.* See NIV text note; see also note on 6:3. *stumbling.* See note on 35:15. *before God.* See note on 11:7. *light
of life.* The full blessedness of life (see note on 36:9).
Ps 57 A prayer for deliverance when threatened by fierce
enemies (it has many links with Ps 56). The psalm appears to
reflect the imagery of the night of danger (v. 4: "I lie
[down]") followed by the morning of salvation (v. 8: "I will
awaken the dawn"). For other instances of these associations
see 30:5; 46:5; 59:6,14,16; 63:1,6; 90:14. Verses 7-11
are used again in 108:1-5. The psalm is composed of two
parts, equal in length (vv. 1-5 and vv. 6-11) and alike in
structure—both contain three Hebrew couplets and end
with an identical refrain. (For the use of refrains elsewhere
see introduction to Ps 42-43.)
57 title See note on Ps 56 title. *Do Not Destroy.* See Ps 58;
59; 75 titles. *When.* For the event referred to see 1Sa
24:1-3; see also Ps 142 title.
57:1-5 The prayer.
57:1 Initial cry for God's merciful help. *my soul.* Or "I," as
in v. 4, where the first "I" is lit. "My soul" (see note on 6:3).
shadow of your wings. See note on 17:8.
57:2-3 Confidence of being heard.
57:2 *Most High.* See note on Ge 14:19. *who fulfills ˌhis
purpose˳ for me.* See 138:8. God will not let David's enemies
thwart his divine purposes for anointing him king (see 1Sa

16:1,12; 2Sa 7). But the Hebrew can also be translated
"who makes an end ˌof troubles˳ for me" (see 7:9).
57:3 *He sends.* God sends his love and faithfulness (here
personified; see note on 23:6) as his messengers from
heaven to save his servant (see note on 43:3). *his love and
his faithfulness.* See note on 26:3. *love.* See note on 6:4.
57:4 The threatening situation. *I lie.* As a sheep among
lions. *ravenous beasts.* The psalmists often compare their
enemies to ferocious beasts (see note on 7:2). (The use of the
metaphor here has no connection with the description of
Saul and Jonathan in 2Sa 1:23.) *tongues.* See note on 5:9.
57:5 A prayer for God to show his exalted power and glory
throughout his creation by coming to his servant's rescue
(see 7:6-7; 21:13; 46:10; 59:5,8; 113:4-9; cf. Ex 14:4;
Isa 26:15; 44:23; 59:19; see also note on Ps 46:10).
57:6-11 Praise for God's saving help—confidently anticipating the desired deliverance. For such a sudden transition from prayer to assurance see note on 3:8.
57:6 The threat and its outcome: The enemies suffer the
calamity they plotted. *not . . . pit.* They hunted him as if he
were a wild beast, but the "lions" themselves were caught.
57:7 All cause for fear has been removed. *heart.* See note
on 4:7. *is steadfast.* Feels secure (see 112:7).
57:8 *Awake . . . Awake.* Greet with joy the dawn of the day
of deliverance (see Isa 51:9,17; 52:1). *soul.* Lit. "glory" (see
note on 7:5). *harp and lyre.* Instruments (here personified) to
accompany the praise of the Lord at his temple in celebration
of deliverance (see 71:22; 81:2; and note on Ps 4 title).
awaken the dawn. With joyful cries proclaiming God's saving act. (Dawn, too, is here personified—the Canaanites
even deified it.)
57:9-10 The vow to praise (see notes on 7:17; 9:1).

¹⁰For great is your love, reaching to the
   heavens;
   your faithfulness reaches to the
   skies. *d*

¹¹Be exalted, O God, above the
   heavens; *e*
   let your glory be over all the earth. *f*

Psalm 58

For the director of music. To the tune of
"Do Not Destroy." Of David.
A *miktam*.*e*

¹Do you rulers indeed speak justly? *g*
   Do you judge uprightly among men? *h*
²No, in your heart you devise injustice, *h*
   and your hands mete out violence on
   the earth. *i*
³Even from birth the wicked go astray;
   from the womb they are wayward
   and speak lies.
⁴Their venom is like the venom of a
   snake, *j*
   like that of a cobra that has stopped
   its ears,

⁵that will not heed *k* the tune of the
   charmer, *l*
   however skillful the enchanter may
   be.

⁶Break the teeth in their mouths,
   O God; *m*
   tear out, O LORD, the fangs of the
   lions! *n*
⁷Let them vanish like water that flows
   away; *o*
   when they draw the bow, let their
   arrows be blunted. *p*
⁸Like a slug melting away as it moves
   along, *q*
   like a stillborn child, *r* may they not
   see the sun.

⁹Before your pots can feel the heat of
   the thorns *s* —
   whether they be green or dry—the
   wicked will be swept away. *t*
¹⁰The righteous will be glad *u* when they
   are avenged, *v*

57:10 *d*S Ps 36:5
57:11 *e*S Ps 8:1;
113:4 *f*S ver 5
58:1 *g*Ps 82:2
58:2 *h*Mt 15:19
*i*Ps 94:20;
Isa 10:1; Lk 6:38
58:4 *j*S Nu 21:6

58:5 *k*Ps 81:11
*l*Ecc 10:11;
Jer 8:17
58:6 *m*Ps 3:7
*n*S Job 4:10
58:7
*o*S Lev 26:36;
S Job 11:16
*p*Ps 11:2; 57:4;
64:3
58:8 *q*Isa 13:7
*r*S Job 3:16
58:9 *s*Ps 118:12;
Ecc 7:6
*t*S Job 7:10;
S 21:18
58:10
*u*S Job 22:19
*v*Dt 32:35;
Ps 7:9; 91:8;
Jer 11:20;
Ro 12:17-21

*e*Title: Probably a literary or musical term   *f*9 The
meaning of the Hebrew for this verse is uncertain.

57:10 *love.* See note on 6:4. *love . . . faithfulness.* That is, love-and-faithfulness (see v. 3; note on 36:5; see also note on 3:7). *reaching to the heavens . . . to the skies.* See note on 36:5.
57:11 The refrain (see v. 5), but now as praise (see 18:46; 30:1; 34:3; 35:27; 40:16; 70:4; 92:8; 97:9; 99:2; 113:4; 148:13).
Ps 58 A prayer for God, the supreme Judge, to set right the affairs of men, judging those rulers who corrupt justice, and championing the cause of the righteous. (The psalm was applied by the early church to Jesus' trial before the Sanhedrin; see Mt 26:57–68 and parallels.) Concern for the just use of judicial power is pervasive throughout the OT. This was the primary agency in the administrative structures of the ancient Near East for the protection of the innocent, usually the poor and powerless, against the assaults of unscrupulous men, usually the rich and powerful. Israelite society was troubled with the corruption of this judicial power from the days of Samuel to the end of the monarchy (see, e.g., 1Sa 8:3; Isa 1:23; 5:23; 10:1–2; Eze 22:6,12; Am 5:7,10–13; Mic 3:1–3,9–11; 7:2). Even in David's time all was not well (see 2Sa 15:1–4). For the central concern of this psalm see Ps 82. Structurally, the psalm is framed by a rhetorical address to the wicked judges in their absence (vv. 1–2) and by a reassuring word to "the righteous" (vv. 9–11). The frame also emphasizes the fact that those who do not judge uprightly (v. 1) will be judged by God (v. 11).
58 title *For the director of music.* See note on Ps 4 title. *To the tune of.* See note on Ps 9 title. *Do Not Destroy.* See Ps 57; 59; 75 titles. *miktam.* See note on Ps 16 title.
58:1–5 Accusation against the wicked judges whose mouths, hearts and hands (vv. 1–2) are united in the pursuit of injustice.
58:1 *rulers.* Lit. "gods," a title applied to those whose administrative positions called upon them to act as earthly representatives of God's heavenly court (see NIV text notes on Ex 21:6; 22:8–9; see also Dt 1:17; 2Ch 19:6). *speak justly.* Make just judicial pronouncements.

58:2 *heart.* See note on 4:7. *mete out violence.* Issue decisions that result in cruel injustice.
58:3 *from birth . . . from the womb.* Their corrupt ways are not sporadic; they act in accordance with their nature (see 51:5). Here reference is to the wicked; the author does not make a general statement about all people, as is the case in Ge 6:5; 8:21; Job 14:4; 15:14–16; 25:4–6. *the wicked.* See their description in Ps 10. *speak lies.* They have never been concerned for the truth (see Jn 8:44).
58:4 *venom.* What issues from their mouths is as cruel and deadly as the venom of snakes (see 140:3; Mt 23:33; Jas 3:8). *stopped its ears.* They are incorrigible; nothing—neither appeals nor threats—will move them.
58:6–8 Prayer for God to purge the land of such perverse judges. The author uses imagery drawn from conventional curses of the ancient Near East (see note on 5:10).
58:6 Let the weapons of their mouths (see 57:4) be broken and torn out. *lions.* See note on 7:2.
58:7 *water that flows away.* And is absorbed by the ground. *arrows.* Malicious pronouncements (see 57:4 and note on 5:9).
58:8 *slug.* That appears to dry up to nothing as it moves over a stone in the hot sun.
58:9–11 Assurance that God will surely judge them (see note on 3:8).
58:9 See NIV text note. The verse may be speaking picturesquely of the speed of God's judgment—speed probably signifying here the inescapable certainty of his judgment (see note on 37:10; see also Lk 18:7–8). *thorns.* Twigs from wild thornbushes were used as fuel for quick heat (see 118:12; Ecc 7:6). *swept away.* As by a storm—God's storm (see Job 27:21).
58:10 *righteous.* Here a judicial term for those who are in the right but who have been wronged (see note on 1:5). *when they are avenged.* When the wrongs committed against them are redressed. *bathe their feet in the blood.* Vivid imagery borrowed from the literary conventions of the ancient Near East (see 68:23). Its origins are the exaggerated language of triumphant reports of victory on the battlefield.

when they bathe their feet in the
blood of the wicked. *w*

[11] Then men will say,
"Surely the righteous still are
rewarded; *x*
surely there is a God who judges the
earth." *y*

Psalm 59

For the director of music. To the tune of
"Do Not Destroy." Of David. A *miktam.* g
When Saul had sent men to watch
David's house *z* in order to kill him.

[1] Deliver me from my enemies, O God; *a*
protect me from those who rise up
against me. *b*
[2] Deliver me from evildoers *c*
and save me from bloodthirsty men. *d*

[3] See how they lie in wait for me!
Fierce men conspire *e* against me
for no offense or sin of mine,
O LORD.
[4] I have done no wrong, *f* yet they are
ready to attack me. *g*
Arise to help me; look on my plight! *h*
[5] O LORD God Almighty, the God of
Israel, *i*
rouse yourself *j* to punish all the
nations; *k*

show no mercy to wicked traitors. *l*
Selah

[6] They return at evening,
snarling like dogs, *m*
and prowl about the city.
[7] See what they spew from their
mouths *n* —
they spew out swords *o* from their
lips,
and they say, "Who can hear us?" *p*
[8] But you, O LORD, laugh at them; *q*
you scoff at all those nations. *r*

[9] O my Strength, *s* I watch for you;
you, O God, are my fortress, *t* [10] my
loving God.

God will go before me
and will let me gloat over those who
slander me.
[11] But do not kill them, O Lord our
shield, h *u*
or my people will forget. *v*
In your might make them wander
about,
and bring them down. *w*
[12] For the sins of their mouths, *x*

Center column references:

58:10 wPs 68:23
58:11 xS Ge 15:1;
S Ps 128:2;
Lk 6:23
yS Ge 18:25
59 Title zISa 19:11
59:1 aPs 143:9
bS Ps 20:1
59:2 cPs 14:4;
36:12; 53:4;
92:7; 94:16
dS Ps 26:9;
139:19; Pr 29:10
59:3 eS Ps 56:6
59:4 fPs 119:3
gMt 5:11
hS Ps 13:3
59:5 iPs 69:6;
80:4; 84:8
jS Ps 44:23
kS Ps 9:5;
S Isa 10:3

jJer 18:23
59:6 mver 14;
Ps 22:16
59:7 nPs 94:4;
Pr 10:32; 12:23;
15:2,28
oPs 55:21
pS Job 22:13
59:8 qPs 37:13;
Pr 1:26 rPs 2:4
59:9 sS Ps 18:1
tPs 9:9; 18:2;
62:2; 71:3
59:11 uPs 3:3;
84:9 vDt 4:9;
6:12 wPs 89:10;
106:27; 146:6;
Isa 33:3
59:12 xPs 10:7

gTitle: Probably a literary or musical term   h[11] Or
sovereign

58:11 The climax: When God has judged the unjust
"gods" (see note on v. 1), all people will see that right
ultimately triumphs under God's just rule (see note on
46:10). No more will people despair, like those in Mal 3:15.
Ps 59 A prayer for deliverance when endangered by enemy
attacks. If originally composed by David under the circumstances noted in the superscription, it must have been revised for use by one of David's royal sons when Jerusalem
was under siege by a hostile force made up of troops from
many nations—as when Hezekiah was besieged by the Assyrians (see 2Ki 18:19). (Some, however, ascribe it to Nehemiah; see Ne 4.) The enemy weapon most prominent is the
tongue, attacking with slander and curses. In this psalm, too,
the imagery of the night of danger (vv. 6,14), followed by the
morning of deliverance (v. 16), is evoked (see introduction to
Ps 57). Regarding the structure, the two halves of the psalm
(vv. 1–9,10–17) each conclude with an almost identical
refrain (vv. 9,17), preceded by a stanza that begins with a
like characterization of the enemies (vv. 6,14). The first half
of the psalm is predominantly prayer, the second half
predominantly assurance of deliverance. The whole is
framed by a cry for protection (v. 1) and a joyful confession
that God is the psalmist's "fortress" (v. 17, in Hebrew the
same root as that for "protect" in v. 1).
59 title See note on Ps 56 title. *Do Not Destroy.* See Ps 57;
58; 75 titles. *When.* For the event referred to see 1Sa 19:11.
59:1–2 The cry for deliverance.
59:1 *protect me.* Lit. "raise me to a high, secure place."
59:2 *evildoers . . . bloodthirsty men.* Common characterizations of those who attack the psalmists out of malice.
59:3–5 By slander (v. 10) and lies (v. 12) the enemies seek
to justify their attacks, but the psalmist protests his innocence
and pleads with God to judge those who wrong him (see
58:11).

59:3 *lie in wait.* See 10:8–9 and note on 7:2.
59:4 *Arise.* See note on 3:7.
59:5 *LORD God Almighty.* See note on 1Sa 1:3. *God of
Israel.* This appeal to the Lord as the God of Israel to punish
the nations makes clear that the attack on the psalmist
involves an attack by the nations on Israel. *rouse yourself.*
See note on 7:6. *punish . . . show no mercy.* See note on
5:10. *traitors.* Whether Israelites had joined in the attack is
not clear; the Hebrew indicates only that the enemies were
treacherous.
59:6–8 Confidence: Surely God mocks such a pack of dogs
(see 22:16–17).
59:6 *about the city.* The enemies besiege the city like dogs
at night on the prowl for food (see vv. 14–15).
59:7 *swords from their lips.* Their "curses and lies" (v. 12).
For the imagery see 57:4; see also note on 5:9. *they say.* See
note on 3:2.
59:9 *watch.* Hebrew *shamar* (see note on v. 17). The
psalmist watches as one who longingly waits for the morning
(of salvation); see 130:6.
59:10–13 The prayer renewed. Confident that the Lord
will hear his prayer (v. 10) and will punish the nations (v. 5),
the psalmist prays that God will not sweep them away
suddenly but will prolong their punishment so that Israel
("my people," v. 11) will not forget God's acts of salvation,
as they had done so often before (see 78:11; 106:13).
Nevertheless, the psalmist asks God not to allow the enemies
to escape the full consequences of their malice (vv. 12–13).
59:10 *loving.* See note on 6:4.
59:11 *shield.* See note on 3:3. *wander about.* Like vaga-
bonds, with no place to settle (see Ge 4:12; 2Sa 15:20; La
4:15) and having to hunt for food (like dogs, v. 15; see
109:10; Am 4:8).
59:12 See note on v. 7. *caught in their pride.* Let the pride

for the words of their lips, *y*
    let them be caught in their pride. *z*
For the curses and lies they utter,
13 consume them in wrath,
    consume them till they are no
        more. *a*
Then it will be known to the ends of
    the earth
    that God rules over Jacob. *b*   *Selah*

14They return at evening,
    snarling like dogs,
    and prowl about the city.
15They wander about for food *c*
    and howl if not satisfied.
16But I will sing *d* of your strength, *e*
    in the morning *f* I will sing of your
        love; *g*
for you are my fortress, *h*
    my refuge in times of trouble. *i*

17O my Strength, I sing praise to you;
    you, O God, are my fortress, my
        loving God. *j*

59:12
y Ps 64:8;
Pr 10:14; 12:13
z Isa 2:12; 5:15;
Zep 3:11
59:13 *a* Ps 104:35
b Ps 83:18
59:15 *c* Job 15:23
59:16 *d* Ps 108:1
e S 1Sa 2:10
f Ps 5:3; 88:13
g Ps 101:1
h S 2Sa 22:3
i S Dt 4:30
59:17 *j* ver 10

60 Title
k 2Sa 8:13
60:1 *l* 2Sa 5:20;
Ps 44:9 *m* Ps 79:5
n Ps 80:3
60:2 *o* Ps 18:7
p S 2Ch 7:14
60:3 *q* Ps 71:20
r Ps 75:8;
Isa 29:9; 51:17;
63:6; Jer 25:16;
Zec 12:2;
Rev 14:10
60:4 *s* Isa 5:26;
11:10,12; 18:3

Psalm 60

60:5–12pp — Ps 108:6–13

For the director of music. To the tune of
"The Lily of the Covenant." A *miktam*[i]
of David. For teaching. When he fought
Aram Naharaim[j] and Aram Zobah,[k] and
when Joab returned and struck down
twelve thousand Edomites in the Valley of
Salt. [k]

1You have rejected us, *l* O God, and
        burst forth upon us;
    you have been angry *m*—now restore
        us! *n*
2You have shaken the land *o* and torn it
        open;
    mend its fractures, *p* for it is quaking.
3You have shown your people desperate
        times; *q*
    you have given us wine that makes
        us stagger. *r*

4But for those who fear you, you have
    raised a banner *s*
    to be unfurled against the bow. *Selah*

[i]Title: Probably a literary or musical term   [j]Title: That
is, Arameans of Northwest Mesopotamia   [k]Title: That
is, Arameans of central Syria

---

with which they treacherously attack the Lord's servant and
his people be the trap that catches them. *curses and lies.* See
10:7 and note.
59:13 *Then it will be known.* When God has thus dealt
with Israel's enemies, all the world will acknowledge that
the Judge of all the earth (see 58:11) is the God of Israel.
Jacob. See note on 14:7.
59:14–16 Assurance of being heard (see note on 3:8). Just
as God mocks the defiant pack of dogs (vv. 6–8), so the
psalmist will sing for joy at God's triumph over them.
59:16 *strength . . . love . . . fortress.* See the refrain (vv.
9,17). *morning.* See introduction.
59:17 The vow to praise (see note on 7:17). *sing.* Hebrew
zamar (see note on v. 9). The play on words in the refrain
marks an advance from watching during the night of danger
to singing in the morning of salvation.
Ps 60 A national prayer for God's help after suffering a
severe blow by a foreign nation, presumably Edom (see v. 9).
The prayer leader may have been the king (the "me" in v. 9),
as in 2Ch 20. The lament that God has "rejected" (v. 1) his
people and no longer accompanies their armies links the
psalm with Ps 44. Verses 5–12 appear again in 108:6–13. As
for its structure, the prayer is framed by three verses lament-
ing God's rejection of his people (vv. 1–3) and three verses
expressing confidence that the God who has rejected them
will yet give them victory (vv. 10–12). This transition from
lament to confidence constitutes the overarching movement
of the prayer. Verses 4–8 contain the plea for help (v. 5) and
the grounds for confidence (vv. 4,6–8).
60 title See note on Ps 56 title. *The Lily of the Covenant.*
See Ps 80 title and note on Ps 45 title. *For teaching.* Only
here in the psalm titles. For other songs that Israel was to
learn see Dt 31:19,21; 2Sa 1:18. That it was intended for a
variety of uses, especially to convey confidence in times of
national threat, is illustrated by its use in Ps 108. *When.* For
the events referred to see 2Sa 8; 1Ch 18 (perhaps also 2Sa
10). If the tradition that assigns the prayer to these events is

correct, it must be supposed that our knowledge of the
events is incomplete, since these accounts do not mention
Edom. The Israelite war against Edom at this time of great
northern battles may have been occasioned by an attack on
the part of Edom trying to take advantage of Israel's preoccupation elsewhere, an attack in which Edom succeeded in
overrunning the garrisons that guarded Judah's southern
borders.
60:1–3 Lament over God's rejection of his people (see
44:9–16; 89:38–45) and prayer for restoration.
60:1 *rejected us.* At least momentarily (see 30:5). Defeat
by the enemy is interpreted as a sign of God's anger (though
no reason for that anger is noted, and the bond between
Israel and God is not broken). *burst forth.* Like a flood (see
2Sa 5:20).
60:2 *shaken the land.* As by a devastating earthquake—such as was occasionally experienced in ancient
Canaan.
60:3 *wine that makes us stagger.* God has made them
drink from the cup of his wrath rather than from his cup of
blessing and salvation (see note on 16:5).
60:4–8 A plea for help, grounded in reasons for confidence.
60:4 *those who fear you.* Your people, in distinction from
the nations (see 61:5; see also note on Ge 20:11). *have
raised.* Or "raise"—in which case v. 4 already begins the
plea voiced in v. 5, rather than being an expression of
confidence. *banner.* Banners were used as rallying points for
troops in preparation for battle and for leading them in
action. This practice is often alluded to in Isaiah (5:26;
11:10,12; 13:2; 18:3; 30:17; 49:22; 62:10) and Jeremiah
(4:21, "standard"; 50:2; 51:12,27). It is possible to read v.
4 as a petition, in which case it pleads for God to rally the
troops of Israel and lead them against the foe. If, however, it
is an expression of confidence (as the NIV renders it), the
"banner" must be the reassuring word from God recited in
vv. 6–8 (see Ex 17:15). *bow.* The enemy armed with bows.

⁵Save us and help us with your right
    hand, ᵗ
  that those you love ᵘ may be
    delivered.
⁶God has spoken from his sanctuary:
  "In triumph I will parcel out
    Shechem ᵛ
  and measure off the Valley of
    Succoth. ʷ
⁷Gilead ˣ is mine, and Manasseh is mine;
  Ephraim ʸ is my helmet,
  Judah ᶻ my scepter. ᵃ
⁸Moab is my washbasin,
  upon Edom I toss my sandal;
  over Philistia I shout in triumph. ᵇ"

⁹Who will bring me to the fortified city?
  Who will lead me to Edom?
¹⁰Is it not you, O God, you who have
    rejected us
  and no longer go out with our
    armies? ᶜ

¹¹Give us aid against the enemy,
  for the help of man is worthless. ᵈ
¹²With God we will gain the victory,
  and he will trample down our
    enemies. ᵉ

Psalm 61

For the director of music. With stringed
instruments. Of David.

¹Hear my cry, O God; ᶠ
  listen to my prayer. ᵍ

²From the ends of the earth I call to you,
  I call as my heart grows faint; ʰ
  lead me to the rock ⁱ that is higher
    than I.
³For you have been my refuge, ʲ
  a strong tower against the foe. ᵏ

⁴I long to dwell ˡ in your tent forever
  and take refuge in the shelter of your
    wings. ᵐ   *Selah*

Cross references (center column)

60:5 ʳS Job 40:14
uS Dt 33:12
60:6 ᵛS Ge 12:6
ʷS Ge 33:17
60:7 ˣJos 13:31
ʸS Ge 41:52
ᶻS Nu 34:19
60:8 ᵃS Ge 49:10
ᵇS 2Sa 8:1
60:10 ᶜS Jos 7:12
60:11 ᵈPs 146:3;
Pr 3:5
60:12
ᵉS Job 40:12;
Ps 44:5
61:1 ᶠPs 64:1
61:2 ʰS Ps 6:2
ⁱPs 18:2; 31:2;
94:22
61:3 ʲPs 9:9;
S 46:1; 62:7
ᵏPs 59:9;
Pr 18:10
61:4 ˡS Ps 15:1
ᵐS Dt 32:11;
S Mt 23:37

60:5 *those you love.* The Hebrew for this expression is here a word of special endearment, as in 127:2; 2Sa 12:25; Jer 11:15.

60:6–8 A comforting oracle from the Lord, perhaps recalling an already ancient word from the time of the conquest. If so, it may have been preserved in the "Book of the Wars of the Lord" (Nu 21:14). In any event, the Lord is depicted as Israel's triumphant Warrior-King (see Ex 15:3,13–18).

60:6 *parcel out . . . measure off.* Divide his conquered territory among his servant people who were with him in the battles. *Shechem . . . Succoth.* Places representative of the territory west and east of the Jordan taken over by the Lord and Israel (see Ge 33:17–18; 1Ki 12:25).

60:7 Israel is the Lord's kingdom—the land conquered and his people established within it. *Gilead . . . Manasseh.* Half of Manasseh was established in Gilead, east of the Jordan, and half of it west of the Jordan, just north of Ephraim (see Jos 13:29–31; 17:5–11). This once again showed that the Lord's kingdom included territory both east and west of the Jordan. *Ephraim . . . Judah.* The two leading tribes of Israel, the one representative of the Rachel tribes (Ephraim) in the north, the other of the Leah tribes (Judah) in the south; see Ge 48:13–20; 49:8–12; Nu 2:3,18; Jos 15–16. Together they represented all Israel (Isa 11:13; Zec 9:13). *helmet.* As a powerful and aggressive tribe (Dt 33:17; Jdg 7:24–8:3; 12:1), Ephraim figuratively represents the Lord's helmet. *scepter.* Called such because from Judah would come (Ge 49:10)—and had now come (1Sa 16:1–13)—the Lord's chosen earthly regent over his people (see 2Sa 7).

60:8 *Moab . . . Edom . . . Philistia.* Perpetual enemies on Israel's eastern, southern and western borders respectively (see Ex 15:14–15; see also Ex 13:17; Nu 20:14–21; 22–24). *is my washbasin.* Is reduced to a household vessel in which the Lord washes his feet (Ge 18:4). The metaphor is perhaps suggested by the fact that Moab lay along the east shore of the Dead Sea. *toss my sandal.* Perhaps refers to the conventional symbolic act by which one claimed possession of land (cf. Ru 4:7).

60:9 A rhetorical question following the reassuring oracle and leading to the confidence expressed in vv. 10–12. *me . . . me.* Possibly referring to the king (see introduction), though the praying community may be referring to itself collectively (see note on Ps 30 title). *lead me.* As God went before his people into battle in the desert (Ex 13:21) and

during the conquest (Ex 23:27–28; 33:2; Dt 9:3; 31:8).
60:10–12 Confidence of victory (see note on 3:8).
60:10 *rejected.* See v. 1.
60:11 *help.* Lit. "salvation" (see v. 5, "Save"). *of man.* See 33:17.
60:12 *gain the victory.* Lit. "do mighty things." With God's help Israel will achieve in a manner similar to that of the Lord himself (see 118:15–16) and will triumph over Edom (see Nu 24:18, "grow strong"). *trample down.* Like a victorious warrior (see Isa 14:19, 25; Jer 12:10; Zec 10:5).
Ps 61 A prayer for restoration to God's presence. The circumstances appear to be similar to those referred to in Ps 42–43. Here, however, a king is involved (v. 6), and if the author was David, he may have composed this prayer at the time of his flight from Absalom (see 2Sa 17:21–29). For another possibility see note on v. 2. Ps 61–64 form a series linked together by the common theme of trust in God when under threat. Structurally, the prayer is framed by a cry to God (v. 1) and a vow to praise (v. 8). The body of the psalm is composed of three couplets: vv. 2–3, 4–5, 6–7.
61 title See note on Ps 4 title.
61:1 Initial plea for God to hear.
61:2–3 The prayer.
61:2 *ends of the earth.* So it seemed (see 42:6). Possibly the phrase here refers to the brink of the netherworld, i.e., the grave (see 63:9); the psalmist feels himself near death. *heart.* See note on 4:7. *lead me.* See 23:2. *rock.* Secure place (see 27:5; 40:2). *higher than I.* The place of security that he seeks is beyond his reach; only God can bring him to it. Since God is often confessed by the psalmists to be their "rock of refuge" (31:2; 71:3; see also 18:2; 62:2,6–7; 94:22), it may be that God himself is that higher "rock" (the secure refuge) that the psalmist pleads for (see v. 3). Or it may be the secure refuge of God's sanctuary (see v. 4; see also 27:5).
61:3 The reason he appeals to God: God has never failed him as a refuge. *foe.* If this is a prayer when faced with death, death is the present foe (see 68:20; 141:8; Job 33:22; Isa 25:8; 28:15; Jer 9:21; Hos 13:14; see also 1Co 15:26). See note on 49:14.
61:4–5 Longing for the security of God's sanctuary (see 27:5 and note).
61:4 *dwell in.* See note on 15:1. *tent.* Residence (see 2Sa 6:17; 7:2; 1Ki 1:39; 2:28–30). *shelter of your wings.* See note on 17:8.

5For you have heard my vows, n O God;
you have given me the heritage of
those who fear your name. o

6Increase the days of the king's life, p
his years for many generations. q
7May he be enthroned in God's presence
forever; r
appoint your love and faithfulness to
protect him. s

8Then will I ever sing praise to your
name t
and fulfill my vows day after day. u

Psalm 62

For the director of music. For Jeduthun.
A psalm of David.

1My soul finds rest v in God alone; w
my salvation comes from him.
2He alone is my rock x and my
salvation; y
he is my fortress, z I will never be
shaken. a

3How long will you assault a man?
Would all of you throw him down—
this leaning wall, b this tottering
fence?

Cross references (center column)

61:5 nS Nu 30:2;
Ps 56:12
oS Ex 6:3;
S Dt 33:9;
Ne 1:11;
Ps 102:15;
Isa 59:19; Mt 6:9
61:6 pI Ki 3:14
qS Ps 21:4
61:7 rS Ps 41:12;
Lk 22:69;
Eph 1:20; Col 3:1
sPs 40:11
61:8 tS Ex 15:1;
Ps 7:17; 30:4
uS Nu 30:2;
S Dt 23:21
62:1 vS Ps 5:3
wver 5
62:2 xPs 18:31;
89:26 yS Ex 15:2
zS Ps 59:9
aS Job 29:18
62:3 bIsa 30:13

62:4 cPs 28:3;
55:21
62:5 dver 1
62:7 eS Ps 61:3
62:8 fPs 37:5;
Isa 26:4
gI Sa 1:15;
Ps 42:4;
Mt 26:36-46
62:9 hPs 49:2
iS Job 7:7
jIsa 40:15
62:10 kS Ps 12:5;
1Ti 6:17
lIsa 61:8;
Eze 22:29; Na 3:1
mS Job 31:25;
Mt 19:23-24;
1Ti 6:6-10

4They fully intend to topple him
from his lofty place;
they take delight in lies.
With their mouths they bless,
but in their hearts they curse. c   Selah

5Find rest, O my soul, in God alone; d
my hope comes from him.
6He alone is my rock and my salvation;
he is my fortress, I will not be
shaken.
7My salvation and my honor depend on
God1 ;
he is my mighty rock, my refuge. e
8Trust in him at all times, O people; f
pour out your hearts to him, g
for God is our refuge.   Selah

9Lowborn men h are but a breath, i
the highborn are but a lie;
if weighed on a balance, j they are
nothing;
together they are only a breath.
10Do not trust in extortion k
or take pride in stolen goods; l
though your riches increase,
do not set your heart on them. m

11One thing God has spoken,

17 Or / God Most High is my salvation and my honor

61:5 The reason for his longing: Either (1) because God has been so responsive to him in the past, or (2) confidence that his longing is about to be satisfied. *my vows.* The vows that accompanied his prayers (see 50:14; 66:14; see also note on 7:17). *heritage.* A place with God's people in the promised land, together with all that the Lord had promised to give and to be to his people (see 16:6; 37:18; 135:12; 136:21–22). *those who fear.* See 60:4 and note. *your name.* See note on 5:11.

61:6–7 Prayer for the king's long life. The king himself may have made this prayer—such transitions to the third person are known from the literature of the ancient Near East—or it may be the prayer of the people, perhaps voiced by a priest or Levite. Later Jewish interpretations applied these verses to the Messiah. They are fulfilled in Christ, David's great Son.

61:6 May the king live forever (see note on 45:6).

61:7 *enthroned in God's presence.* See note on 41:12. *love and faithfulness.* Personified as God's messengers (see notes on 23:6; 43:3; see also note on 26:3).

61:8 The vow to praise (see note on 7:17).

Ps 62 The psalmist commits himself to God when threatened by the assaults of conspirators who wish to dethrone him. The author surely was a king and, if it was David, the circumstances could well have been the efforts of the family of Saul to topple him. Verse 3 suggests a time of weakness and may indicate advanced age. Implicitly the psalm is an appeal to God to uphold him. No psalm surpasses it in its expression of simple trust in God (see Ps 31 and introduction to Ps 61). The psalm is composed of three parts: vv. 1–4, 5–8, 9–12. The middle stanza (vv. 5–8), which begins by echoing vv. 1–2, constitutes the central expression of trust and hope. The whole is framed by a confession of tranquil resting in God (vv. 1–2) and the reason for such trust (vv. 11–12). The remaining verses (vv. 3–4,9–10) speak of those who threaten.

62 title See note on Ps 39 title.

62:1–4 Confidence in God in the face of conspiracy.

62:1 *My soul.* See note on 6:3. *finds rest.* Lit. "is silence," i.e., is in repose.

62:2,6 *shaken.* See note on 10:6.

62:3 Question to the assailants: Will you never give up? *leaning wall . . . tottering fence.* A metaphor for David's fragile condition: either (1) a confession that he has no strength in himself, or (2) an acknowledgment that he is in a weakened condition—or, perhaps, (3) a reflection on how his enemies perceive him, a "pushover."

62:4 *lofty place.* Throne. *lies . . . curse.* See note on 10:7. *bless.* For example, "Long live the king" (1Sa 10:24; 2Sa 16:16; see also 1Ki 1:25,34,39).

62:5–8 Trust in God: an exhortation to himself (v. 5) and to the people (v. 8).

62:5 *Find rest.* See note on v. 1; faith encouraging faith (see 27:13–14; 42:5,11; 43:5).

62:8 Exhortation to God's people (see 31:23–24). *pour out your hearts.* In earnest prayer (see La 2:19). *hearts.* See note on 4:7.

62:9–12 Frail, misguided man; mighty, trustworthy God.

62:9–10 Man, as a threat, is nothing (see note on 10:18).

62:9 *Lowborn . . . highborn.* Persons of every condition. *breath . . . lie.* People appear to be much more than a puff of wind, especially the rich and powerful.

62:10 A warning to those (including those conspiring against him) who trust in their own devices to get what they want (by fair means or foul) rather than trusting in God to sustain them—a virtual summary of Ps 49. *heart.* See note on 4:7.

62:11–12 The climax: recollection of God's reassuring word to his people. *strong . . . loving.* Able to do all that he has promised; committed to his people's salvation and blessedness.

62:11 *One thing . . . two things.* See note on Am 1:3.

two things have I heard:
that you, O God, are strong, [n]
[12] and that you, O Lord, are loving. [o]
Surely you will reward each person
  according to what he has done. [p]

Psalm 63

A psalm of David. When he was in the
Desert of Judah.

[1] O God, you are my God,
  earnestly I seek you;
my soul thirsts for you, [q]
  my body longs for you,
in a dry and weary land
  where there is no water. [r]

[2] I have seen you in the sanctuary [s]
  and beheld your power and your
    glory. [t]
[3] Because your love is better than life, [u]
  my lips will glorify you.
[4] I will praise you as long as I live, [v]
  and in your name I will lift up my
    hands. [w]
[5] My soul will be satisfied as with the
    richest of foods; [x]
  with singing lips my mouth will
    praise you.

[6] On my bed I remember you;
  I think of you through the watches of
    the night. [y]
[7] Because you are my help, [z]
  I sing in the shadow of your wings. [a]
[8] My soul clings to you; [b]
  your right hand upholds me. [c]

[9] They who seek my life will be
    destroyed; [d]
  they will go down to the depths of
    the earth. [e]
[10] They will be given over to the sword [f]
  and become food for jackals. [g]

[11] But the king will rejoice in God;
  all who swear by God's name will
    praise him, [h]
  while the mouths of liars will be
    silenced. [i]

Psalm 64

For the director of music.
A psalm of David.

[1] Hear me, O God, as I voice my
    complaint; [j]
  protect my life from the threat of the
    enemy. [k]

62:11
[n] S 1Ch 29:11;
Rev 19:1
62:12 [o] Ps 86:5;
103:8; 130:7
[p] S Job 21:31;
S 28:4;
S Mt 16:27;
Ro 2:6*; 1Co 3:8;
Col 3:25
63:1 [q] Ps 42:2;
84:2 [r] Ps 143:6
63:2 [s] S Ps 15:1;
27:4; 68:24
[t] S Ex 16:7
63:3 [u] Ps 36:7;
69:16; 106:45;
109:21
63:4 [v] Ps 104:33;
146:2; Isa 38:20
[w] S Ps 28:2;
1Ti 2:8
63:5 [x] S Ps 36:8;
Mt 5:6

63:6 [y] Dt 6:4-9;
Ps 16:7; 119:148;
Mt 14:25
63:7 [z] Ps 27:9;
118:7 [a] S Ru 2:12
63:8
[b] S Nu 32:12;
Hos 6:3
[c] S Ps 41:12
63:9 [d] Ps 40:14
[e] Ps 55:15; 71:20;
95:4; 139:15
63:10 [f] Jer 18:21;
Eze 35:5;
Am 1:11 [g] La 5:18
63:11 [h] Isa 19:18;
45:23; 65:16
[i] S Job 5:16;
Ro 3:19
64:1 [j] Ps 142:2
[k] Ps 140:1

62:12 *loving.* See note on 6:4. *Surely.* Ultimately every
person will experience God's righteousness (see note on
4:1). *reward ... according to.* See notes on Jer 17:10;
32:19.
Ps 63 A confession of longing for God and for the security
his presence offers when deadly enemies threaten. That
longing is vividly described by the metaphor of thirst (v. 1)
and hunger (v. 5; see 42:1-2). Like Ps 62 this psalm is an
implicit prayer. It is linked to that psalm also by the advancement from hearing (62:11) to seeing (v. 2; see 48:8 and
note). The imagery of the night of danger (v. 6) and the
morning of salvation (see note on v. 1) once more occurs (see
introduction to Ps 57). This psalm was prescribed for daily
public prayers of the early church. In its structure, the initial
expression of longing (v. 1) gives way at the end to the
expectation of joy (v. 11)—the literary frame of the psalm.
What he has seen in the sanctuary (v. 2) he remembers on his
bed at night (v. 6), and that reassures him that his enemies
will suffer the end they plot for him (vv. 9-10).
63 title See note on Ps 3 title. *When.* If this tradition is
correct, the reference is probably to 2Sa 15:23-28; 16:2,14;
17:16,29 since the psalmist is referred to as king (see v.
11).
63:1 Intense longing for God in a time of need. *earnestly.*
Lit. "at dawn," "in the morning." *my soul ... my body.* I,
with my whole being (see note on 6:3). *dry and weary land.*
A metaphor for his situation of need, in which he does not
taste "the richest of foods" (v. 5) supplied by the "river
whose streams make glad the city of God" (see 46:4 and
note).
63:2-5 Comforting reflection on what he had seen in the
sanctuary; it awakens joyful expectations.
63:2 See 27:4; 48:8 and notes.
63:3 *love.* See note on 6:4.
63:4 *name.* See note on 5:11. *lift up my hands.* In praise.

63:5 *soul.* See note on 6:3. *the richest of foods.* Lit.
"marrow and fat."
63:6-8 Night reflections, remembering what he had seen
"in the sanctuary" (v. 2).
63:6 *On my bed.* At night as he expectantly awaits the
dawning of the morning of deliverance. *watches of the night.*
See note on Jdg 7:19; see also 119:148; La 2:19.
63:7 *shadow of your wings.* See note on 17:8.
63:9-10 His enemies will get what they deserve; in seeking his life they forfeit their own (see Ge 9:5; Ex 21:23; Dt
19:21; see also note on Ps 5:10).
63:9 *depths.* See note on 30:1. *earth.* Here, the netherworld or grave (see note on 61:2).
63:10 *food for jackals.* Like bodies of enemies left unburied
on the battlefield to add to their disgrace (see note on 53:5).
63:11 *all who swear by God's name.* Those who revere
and trust God (see Dt 6:13). *mouths of liars.* Those who live
by falsehood.
Ps 64 Prayer to God for protection when threatened by a
conspiracy. The circumstances may be similar to those reflected in Ps 62 (see introduction to that psalm), but here
there is no allusion to the king's weakened condition, and it
is not clear whether the conspirators come from within or
outside Israel (see note on v. 2). As so often in the prayers of
the Psalter, the enemy's tongue is his main weapon (see note
on 5:9). The prayer is framed by a plea for protection (vv.
1-2) and a confident word concerning the effects of God's
saving action (vv. 9-10). At the center, vv. 5-6 describe the
disdainful confidence of the conspirators. Verses 3-4 relate
how the enemies attack with their tongues, while vv. 7-8
proclaim how God will turn their tongues against them.
64 title See note on Ps 4 title.
64:1-2 The prayer for protection.
64:1 *Hear.* In Hebrew a wordplay on the word for "rejoice" in v. 10 (see note there).

²Hide me from the conspiracy l of the
wicked, m
from that noisy crowd of evildoers.

³They sharpen their tongues like
swords n
and aim their words like deadly
arrows. o

⁴They shoot from ambush at the
innocent man; p
they shoot at him suddenly, without
fear. q

⁵They encourage each other in evil plans,
they talk about hiding their snares; r
they say, "Who will see them m?" s

⁶They plot injustice and say,
"We have devised a perfect plan!"
Surely the mind and heart of man are
cunning.

⁷But God will shoot them with arrows;
suddenly they will be struck down.

⁸He will turn their own tongues against
them t
and bring them to ruin;
all who see them will shake their
heads u in scorn. v

⁹All mankind will fear; w
they will proclaim the works of God
and ponder what he has done. x

¹⁰Let the righteous rejoice in the Lord y
and take refuge in him; z
let all the upright in heart praise
him! a

Psalm 65

For the director of music.
A psalm of David. A song.

¹Praise awaits n you, O God, in Zion; b
to you our vows will be fulfilled. c
²O you who hear prayer,
to you all men will come. d
³When we were overwhelmed by sins, e
you forgave o our transgressions. f
⁴Blessed are those you choose g
and bring near h to live in your
courts!
We are filled with the good things of
your house, i
of your holy temple.

⁵You answer us with awesome deeds of
righteousness, j
O God our Savior, k
the hope of all the ends of the earth l
and of the farthest seas, m

64:2 lS Ex 1:10
mPs 56:6; 59:2
64:3 nS Ps 55:21;
Isa 49:2
oS Ps 7:13; S 58:7
64:4 pS Job 9:23;
Ps 10:8; 11:2
qS Ps 55:19
64:5 rPs 91:3;
119:110; 140:5;
141:9
sS Job 22:13
64:8 tS Ps 59:12;
Pr 18:7
uS 2Ki 19:21;
Ps 109:25
vS Dt 28:37
64:9 wS Ps 40:3
xJer 51:10

64:10
yS Job 22:19
zPs 11:1; 25:20;
31:2 aPs 32:11
65:1 bPs 2:6
cS Dt 23:21;
Ps 116:18
65:2 dPs 86:9;
Isa 66:23
65:3 eS Ps 40:12
fPs 79:9; Ro 3:25;
Heb 9:14
65:4 gS Ps 33:12
hS Nu 16:5
iS Ps 36:8
65:5 jS Dt 4:34;
S Ps 45:4;
106:22; Isa 64:3
kPs 18:46; 68:19;
85:4 lS Ps 48:10
mPs 107:23

---

m 5 Or us n 1 Or befits; the meaning of the Hebrew
for this word is uncertain. o 3 Or made atonement for

64:2 *noisy crowd.* The Hebrew root underlying this
expression is the same as that for "conspire" in 2:1.
64:3–4 The enemy attacks.
64:3 *tongues.* See note on 5:9. *swords . . . deadly arrows.*
See 59:7.
64:4 *without fear.* They feel themselves secure from exposure and retaliation, but see vv. 7–8.
64:5–6 The enemies' contemptuous self-confidence.
64:5 *they say.* See notes on 3:2; 10:11.
64:6 *heart.* See note on 4:7. *cunning.* Lit. "deep" (see Pr
18:4; 20:5).
64:7–8 Confidence in God's righteous judgment: He will
do to them what they had intended to do to David (see
63:9–10 and note). *shoot . . . arrows; suddenly . . . tongues.*
See vv. 3–4.
64:8 *shake their heads.* See 44:14.
64:9–10 The happy effects of God's judgment: All mankind will fear, proclaim, ponder (see note on 46:10); the
righteous will rejoice, take refuge, praise.
64:9 See 58:11; see also 40:3; 52:6; 65:8.
64:10 *righteous.* See note on 1:5. *rejoice.* In Hebrew this
is the first word of the line, and it is a wordplay on the
Hebrew for "Hear," which is the first word of the first line.
Ps 65 A hymn in praise of God's great goodness to his
people. In answer to their prayers (1) he pardons their sins so
that they continue to enjoy the "good things" of fellowship
with him at his temple (vv. 3–4); (2) he orders the affairs of
the world so that international turbulence is put to rest and
Israel is secure in her land (vv. 5–8); and (3) he turns the
promised land into a veritable Garden of Eden (vv. 9–13).
This hymn begins a series of four that are linked by many
common themes.
65 title See notes on Ps 4; 30 titles.
65:1–2 Introductory commitment to praise.

65:1 *awaits.* Or "is silent before" (see note on 62:1; see
also NIV text note here). Perhaps the imagery is that of praise
personified as a permanent resident of the temple, lying
quietly at rest, whom the people will awaken when they
come to make good their vows (see 57:8). *our vows.* Those
made in conjunction with their prayers in time of need (see
66:14 and note on 7:17).
65:2 *all men.* Lit. "all flesh," perhaps referring to all God's
people, as in Joel 2:28 ("all people"). Most interpreters
believe (in light of vv. 5,8) that the reference is more universal, as in 64:9; 66:1,4,8; 67:3–5 and elsewhere. *will come.*
To praise God as the (only) God who hears and graciously
answers prayers.
65:3–4 The first and primary blessing.
65:3 *forgave our transgressions.* Accepted the atonement
sacrifices you appointed and so forgave our sins (see NIV text
note; see also 32:1–2; 78:38; 79:9 and notes on Lev
16:20–22; 17:11; Heb 2:17; 9:5,7).
65:4 *Blessed.* See note on 1:1. *those you choose and bring
near.* Everyone belonging to Israel as God's chosen people
(see, e.g., 33:12; Dt 4:37) and whom God accepts at his
temple. *live in your courts.* See note on 15:1; see also 23:6.
good things of your house. All the blessings that flow from
God's presence (see 36:8 and note).
65:5–8 God stills the nations and makes Israel secure in
answer to her prayers.
65:5 *awesome deeds.* Acts of God such as were associated
with his deliverance of Israel from Egypt and the conquest of
Canaan, acts of power that made Israel's enemies cringe (see
66:3; see also 106:22; 145:6; Dt 10:21; 2Sa 7:23; Isa
64:3). *righteousness.* Saving acts by which God kept his
covenanted promises to Israel (see note on 4:1). *hope of all.*
Even though the nations of the world did not yet know
it.

[6]who formed the mountains[n] by your
power,
having armed yourself with
strength,[o]
[7]who stilled the roaring of the seas,[p]
the roaring of their waves,
and the turmoil of the nations.[q]
[8]Those living far away fear your
wonders;
where morning dawns and evening
fades
you call forth songs of joy.[r]

[9]You care for the land and water it;[s]
you enrich it abundantly.[t]
The streams of God are filled with
water
to provide the people with grain,[u]
for so you have ordained it.[P]
[10]You drench its furrows
and level its ridges;
you soften it with showers[v]
and bless its crops.
[11]You crown the year with your bounty,[w]
and your carts overflow with
abundance.[x]
[12]The grasslands of the desert overflow;[y]
the hills are clothed with gladness.[z]

[13]The meadows are covered with flocks[a]
and the valleys are mantled with
grain;[b]
they shout for joy and sing.[c]

Psalm 66

For the director of music. A song.
A psalm.

[1]Shout with joy to God, all the earth![d]
[2] Sing the glory of his name;[e]
make his praise glorious![f]
[3]Say to God, "How awesome are your
deeds![g]
So great is your power
that your enemies cringe[h] before
you.
[4]All the earth bows down[i] to you;
they sing praise[j] to you,
they sing praise to your name." Selah

[5]Come and see what God has done,

Cross references

65:6 [n]Am 4:13; [o]S Ps 18:1; 93:1; Isa 51:9
65:7 [p]Ps 89:9; 93:3-4; 107:29; S Mt 8:26
[q]Dt 32:41; Ps 2:1; 74:23; 139:20; Isa 17:12-13
65:8 [r]Ps 100:2; 107:22; 126:2; Isa 24:16; 52:9
65:9 [s]S Lev 26:4; Ps 68:9-10
[t]Ps 104:24
[u]S Ge 27:28; S Dt 32:14; Ps 104:14
65:10 [v]S Dt 32:2; S 2Sa 1:21; S Job 36:28; Ac 14:17
65:11 [w]S Dt 28:12; Ps 104:28; Jn 10:10
[x]Job 36:28; Ps 147:14; Lk 6:38
65:12 [y]S Job 28:26; Joel 2:22 [z]Ps 98:8
65:13 [a]Ps 144:13; Isa 30:23; Zec 8:12
[b]Ps 72:16
[c]Ps 98:8; Isa 14:8; 44:23; 49:13; 55:12
66:1 [d]Ps 81:1; 84:8; 95:1; 98:4;

100:1 66:2 [e]Ps 79:9; 86:9 [f]Isa 42:8,12; 43:21 66:3 [g]S Dt 7:21; S 10:21; Ps 65:5; 106:22; 111:6; 145:6 [h]S 2Sa 22:45 66:4 [i]Ps 22:27 [j]Ps 7:17; 67:3

[P]9 Or for that is how you prepare the land

65:6—7 The God of creation who by his power brought order to the world out of the earlier chaos (see Ge 1) similarly in the redemption of his people establishes a peaceful order among nations (see Isa 2:4; 11:6–9; Mic 4:3–4) so that Israel may be at rest in the promised land (see Ps 33; 46). God's mighty acts in redemption are often compared by OT poets with his mighty acts in creation (see 74:12–17; 89:9–18; Isa 27:1; 40:6–14,21–31; 51:9–11), since his power as Creator guaranteed his power as Redeemer. *formed the mountains . . . stilled . . . the seas.* Gave order to the whole creation (see 95:4–5).

65:7 *turmoil of the nations.* God's stilling the turbulence of the nations—which often threatened Israel—is compared to his taming the turbulence of the primeval waters of chaos (see notes on 32:6; 33:7).

65:8 All peoples will (ultimately) see God's saving acts in behalf of his people and will be moved to fear (see note on 46:10). And all creation will rejoice (see v. 13). *wonders.* Or "signs," referring to God's great saving acts, such as those he performed when he delivered Israel out of Egypt (Dt 4:34; see Ps 78:43; 105:27; 135:9). As "signs" they indicated that God was at work (see Jn 2:11 and note).

65:9—13 God blesses the promised land with all good things in answer to Israel's prayers.

65:9 *streams of God.* See note on 36:8.

65:11 *bounty.* Lit. "goodness" (see 68:10; see also 31:19 and note).

65:13 *they shout for joy and sing.* In the exuberant language of the psalmists, all creation—even its inanimate elements—joins the human chorus to celebrate the goodness of God in creation, blessing and redemption (see 89:12; 96:11–13; 98:8–9; 103:22; 145:10; 148:3–4,7–10; see also Job 38:7; Isa 44:23; 49:13; 55:12).

Ps 66 A psalm of praise for God's answer to prayer. It seems that God has saved the author, probably a king, from an enemy threat, and his deliverance has involved also that of

the whole nation. It has often been suggested that the psalm speaks of Judah's remarkable deliverance from the Assyrians (see 2Ki 19). The praise is offered at the temple in fulfillment of a vow (vv. 13–14; see note on 7:17). Such praise was often climaxed by a call for others to take up the praise (see note on 9:1). Here the psalmist exuberantly begins with that call and, as often elsewhere (e.g., 67:3–5; 68:32; 98:4; 99:3; 100:1; 117:1), addresses it even to the far corners of the earth. This psalm is the second in a series of four (see introduction to Ps 65). The psalm is framed by a call to praise (vv. 1–2) and a declaration of the present occasion for praise (vv. 19–20, in Hebrew involving a play on words—the Hebrew for "praise" and "prayer" sound very much alike). The opening stanza is followed by two thematic sequences having the same structure: a three-verse stanza followed by a five-verse stanza. The first line of the first stanza of the first sequence (v. 5) begins with "Come and see"; the first line of the second stanza of the second sequence (v. 16) begins with "Come and listen."

66 title See notes on Ps 4; 30 titles.

66:1—4 Calling all the earth to joyful praise.

66:1 *all the earth.* See note on 65:2.

66:2 *name.* See note on 5:11.

66:3 *awesome.* See v. 5; see also note on 65:5. *cringe.* See Jos 5:1; 2Ch 20:29.

66:4 See note on 46:10.

66:5—7 Recollection of God's deliverance of Israel at the Red Sea as a sign of his power to rule over the nations. The psalmist portrays his deliverance (see introduction above) both as similar to this Red Sea rescue in its manifestation of God's saving power (see 65:5–7 for a comparison of God's mighty saving acts with his mighty acts of creation) and as a continuation of God's same saving purposes.

66:5 *Come and see.* God's saving acts of old can still be "seen" at his temple, where they are continually celebrated (see 46:8; 48:8–9 and notes). *in man's behalf.* Specifically in behalf of his people.

how awesome his works[k] in man's
behalf!

⁶He turned the sea into dry land,[l]
they passed through[m] the waters on
foot—
come, let us rejoice[n] in him.

⁷He rules forever[o] by his power,
his eyes watch[p] the nations—
let not the rebellious[q] rise up against
him.   *Selah*

⁸Praise[r] our God, O peoples,
let the sound of his praise be heard;

⁹he has preserved our lives
and kept our feet from slipping.[t]

¹⁰For you, O God, tested[u] us;
you refined us like silver.[v]

¹¹You brought us into prison[w]
and laid burdens[x] on our backs.

¹²You let men ride over our heads;[y]
we went through fire and water,
but you brought us to a place of
abundance.[z]

¹³I will come to your temple with burnt
offerings[a]
and fulfill my vows[b] to you—

¹⁴vows my lips promised and my mouth
spoke
when I was in trouble.

¹⁵I will sacrifice fat animals to you
and an offering of rams;

I will offer bulls and goats.[c]   *Selah*

¹⁶Come and listen,[d] all you who fear
God;
let me tell[e] you what he has done for
me.

¹⁷I cried out to him with my mouth;
his praise was on my tongue.

¹⁸If I had cherished sin in my heart,
the Lord would not have listened;[f]

¹⁹but God has surely listened
and heard my voice[g] in prayer.

²⁰Praise be to God,
who has not rejected[h] my prayer
or withheld his love from me!

Psalm 67

For the director of music. With stringed
instruments. A psalm. A song.

¹May God be gracious to us and bless us
and make his face shine upon us,[i]
Selah

²that your ways may be known on earth,
your salvation[j] among all nations.[k]

³May the peoples praise you, O God;
may all the peoples praise you.[l]

⁴May the nations be glad and sing for
joy,[m]

Cross references

66:5 [k]ver 3; Ps 106:22
66:6 [l]S Ge 8:1; S Ex 14:22 [m]1Co 10:1 [n]S Lev 23:40
66:7 [o]S Ex 15:18; Ps 145:13 [p]S Ex 3:16; S Ps 11:4 [q]S Nu 17:10; Ps 112:10; 140:8
66:8 [r]S Ps 22:23
66:9 [s]Ps 30:3 [t]S Dt 32:35; S Job 12:5
66:10 [u]S Ex 15:25 [v]S Job 6:29; S 28:1; S Ps 12:6
66:11 [w]Ps 142:7; 146:7; Isa 42:7, 22; 61:1 [x]S Ge 3:17; S Ex 1:14; Ps 38:4; Isa 10:27
66:12 [y]Isa 51:23 [z]Ps 18:19
66:13 [a]S Ps 51:19 [b]Ps 22:25; 50:14; 116:14; Ecc 5:4; Jnh 2:9
66:15 [c]S Lev 16:5; Ps 51:19
66:16 [d]Ps 34:11 [e]Ps 71:15,24
66:18 [f]S Dt 1:45; S 1Sa 8:18; Jas 4:3
66:19 [g]S Ps 18:6
66:20 [h]Ps 22:24
67:1 [i]Nu 6:24-26
67:2 [j]Isa 40:5; 52:10; 62:1 [k]Ps 98:2; Isa 62:2; Ac 10:35; Tit 2:11
67:3 ver 5
67:4 [m]Ps 100:1-2

Study notes

66:6 *waters.* Possibly the Jordan, but more likely a parallel reference to the Red Sea.

66:7 *rebellious.* Nations that are in revolt against God's rule (see 68:6).

66:8-12 Proclamation in praise of God's new deliverance of his people.

66:8 *peoples.* Here probably the grateful throng of worshipers (see 2Ch 20:27-28).

66:9 *from slipping.* See note on 38:16.

66:10 *tested . . . refined.* From one point of view, times of distress constitute a testing of God's people as to their trust in and loyalty to God. The metaphor is borrowed from the technology of refining precious metals, which included heating the metals in a crucible to see if all impurities had been removed (see 12:6; 17:3).

66:11-12 *You . . . You.* God's rule is all-pervasive; even when enemies for malicious purposes attack his people, God is not a mere passive observer but has his own holy purposes in it (see Isa 45:7; Am 3:6). *prison . . . burdens . . . ride over.* Three metaphors describe their suffering: captives thrown into prison, prisoners of war turned into slaves, defeated troops overrun by a chariot force.

66:12 *fire and water.* Conventional metaphors for severe trials (see Isa 43:2). *to a place of abundance.* Lit. "to an overflowing" (see 23:5). They were brought out of a situation of distress into a situation of overflowing well-being.

66:13-15 Announcement of fulfillment of vows: addressed to God (see note on 7:17; see also 50:14; 116:17-19).

66:13 *I.* The king.

66:16-20 Proclamation of what God has done: in praise of God, addressed to the worshiping congregation.

66:16 *fear God.* See note on Ge 20:11.

66:17 *his praise.* Prayer and praise belonged together in the OT (see also Php 4:6; 1Ti 2:1).

66:20 *Praise be to God.* See v. 8. *love.* See note on 6:4.

Ps 67 A communal prayer for God's blessing. Its content, form and brevity suggest that it served as a liturgical prayer of the people at the conclusion of worship, perhaps just prior to (or immediately after) the priestly benediction (see note on v. 1). God's blessing of his people (as well as his saving acts in their behalf) will catch the attention of the nations and move them to praise (see 65:2). This psalm is the third in a series of four (see introduction to Ps 65). It has a completely symmetrical structure: Two verses at the beginning contain the prayer, while the two verses of the concluding stanza speak of the effects of God's answer. In the intervening stanza, framed by a refrain (vv. 3,5), the people seek to motivate God's answer by referring to the worldwide praise that his mercies to his people will awaken.

67 title See notes on Ps 4; 30 titles.

67:1-2 The prayer.

67:1 The heart of the prayer, anticipating (or echoing) the priestly benediction (see Nu 6:24-26). *make his face shine.* See notes on 4:6; 13:1.

67:2 May God's favors to his people be so obvious that all the world takes notice (see note on 46:10).

67:3-5 The motivation. Elaborating on v. 2, the people speak of the worldwide praise that will resound to God when he graciously blesses his people. Their wish is twofold: (1) that God's blessings may be so abundant that the people will be moved to praise, and (2) that the nations may indeed add their praise to that of Israel—an appropriate expression at this climax of the liturgy of worship.

67:4 May the nations rejoice in the Lord when they see how benevolent the rule of God is (see 98:4-6; 100:1).

for you rule the peoples justly [n]
and guide the nations of the earth. [o]

Selah

[5]May the peoples praise you, O God;
may all the peoples praise you.

[6]Then the land will yield its harvest, [p]
and God, our God, will bless us. [q]
[7]God will bless us,
and all the ends of the earth [r] will
fear him. [s]

Psalm 68

For the director of music. Of David.
A psalm. A song.

[1]May God arise, [t] may his enemies be
scattered; [u]
may his foes flee [v] before him.
[2]As smoke [w] is blown away by the wind,
may you blow them away;
as wax melts [x] before the fire,
may the wicked perish [y] before God.
[3]But may the righteous be glad
and rejoice [z] before God;
may they be happy and joyful.

[4]Sing to God, sing praise to his name, [a]

extol him who rides on the
clouds [q] [b] —
his name is the LORD [c] —
and rejoice before him.
[5]A father to the fatherless, [d] a defender
of widows, [e]
is God in his holy dwelling. [f]
[6]God sets the lonely [g] in families, [r] [h]
he leads forth the prisoners [i] with
singing;
but the rebellious live in a
sun-scorched land. [j]

[7]When you went out [k] before your
people, O God,
when you marched through the
wasteland, [l]   *Selah*
[8]the earth shook, [m]
the heavens poured down rain, [n]
before God, the One of Sinai, [o]
before God, the God of Israel. [p]
[9]You gave abundant showers, [q] O God;
you refreshed your weary inheritance.
[10]Your people settled in it,

Cross references (center column):

67:4 [n]S Ps 9:4; 96:10-13 [o]Ps 68:32
67:6 [p]S Ge 8:22; S Lev 26:4; Ps 85:12; Isa 55:10; Eze 34:27; Zec 8:12 [q]S Ge 12:2
67:7 [r]S Ps 2:8 [s]Ps 33:8
68:1 [t]Ps 12:5; 132:8 [u]Ps 18:14; 89:10; 92:9; 144:6 [v]Nu 10:35; Isa 17:13; 21:15; 33:3
68:2 [w]S Ps 37:20 [x]S Ps 22:14 [y]S Nu 10:35; Ps 9:3; 80:16
68:3 [z]Ps 64:10; 97:12
68:4 [a]S 2Sa 22:50; Ps 7:17; S 30:4; 66:2; 96:2; 100:4; 135:3
[b]ver 33; S Ex 20:21; S Dt 33:26 [c]S Ex 6:3; Ps 83:18
68:5 [d]Ps 10:14 [e]S Ex 22:22; S Dt 10:18
[f]S Dt 26:15; Jer 25:30
68:6 [g]Ps 25:16 [h]Ps 113:9 [i]Ps 79:11; 102:20; 146:7; Isa 61:1; Lk 4:18
[j]Isa 35:7; 49:10; 58:11 68:7 [k]S Ex 13:21 [l]Ps 78:40; 106:14
68:8 [m]S 2Sa 22:8 [n]S Jdg 5:4; 2Sa 21:10; Ecc 11:3 [o]S Dt 33:2 [p]S Jdg 5:5 68:9 [q]S Dt 32:2; S Job 36:28; S Eze 34:26

[q]4 Or / *prepare the way for him who rides through the deserts*   [r]6 Or *the desolate in a homeland*

67:6—7 The effects of God's blessing his people.
67:6 The promised land will yield its abundance (see 65:9–13).
Ps 68 A processional liturgy celebrating the glorious and triumphant rule of Israel's God (see introductions to Ps 24; 47; 118; 132). Verses 1–18 contain many clear references to God's triumphal march from Mount Sinai (in the days of Moses) to Mount Zion (in the days of David). The events at Mount Sinai marked the birth of the kingdom of God among his people; the establishing of the ark of the covenant, symbol of God's throne, in Jerusalem marked the establishment of God's redemptive kingdom in the earth, with Jerusalem as its royal city. The early church, taking its cue from Eph 4:8–13, understood this psalm to foreshadow the resurrection, ascension and present rule of Christ and the final triumph of his church over the hostile world. Ps 68 is the last in a series of four (see introduction to Ps 65).
The psalm is composed of nine stanzas (vv. 19–20 should probably be joined with vv. 21–23), with a concluding doxology. The first stanza indicates the beginning of the liturgical procession, and the last refers to its conclusion—God enthroned in his sanctuary. The seventh (vv. 24–27) speaks expressly of the procession coming into view and entering the sanctuary. In light of these clear references, the third stanza (vv. 7–10) suggests a stage in the procession recalling the desert journey from Sinai to the promised land, while the fifth (vv. 15–18) marks that stage in which the Lord ascends Mount Zion. On the other hand, the second stanza (vv. 4–6) reflects on the benevolence of God's rule; the fourth (vv. 11–14) recalls his victories over the kings of Canaan; the sixth (vv. 19–23) speaks reassuringly of God's future victories; and the eighth (vv. 28–31) contains prayers that God may muster his power to subdue the enemy as he had done before.
68 title See notes on Ps 4; 30 titles.
68:1–3 The start of the procession, liturgically recalling the

beginning of God's march with his people in army formation from Sinai (see Nu 10:33–35).
68:1 *enemies be scattered.* See note on v. 30.
68:3 *righteous.* Israel as the committed people of God in distinction from those opposed to the coming of God's kingdom (the "wicked" of v. 2).
68:4–6 A call to praise God for the benevolence of his rule.
68:4 *name.* See note on 5:11. *who rides on the clouds.* An epithet of Baal found in Canaanite literature is used to make the point that the Lord (Yahweh, not Baal) is the exalted One who truly makes the storm cloud his chariot (see v. 33; 18:9; 104:3; Isa 19:1; Mt 26:64).
68:5–6 God is the defender of the powerless (see 10:14; 146:7–9; 147:6; Dt 10:18).
68:6 *sets the lonely in families.* See Ex 1:21; Ru 4:14–17; 1Sa 2:5. *leads forth the prisoners.* As he led Israel out of Egypt (see 69:33; 107:10,14). *rebellious.* See notes on v. 18; 66:7. *sun-scorched land.* A place utterly barren, lacking even soil for vegetation (see Eze 26:4,14).
68:7–10 Recollection of God's march through the desert from Sinai into the promised land (see Jdg 5:4–5; Hab 3:3–6).
68:8 *earth shook.* A reference to the quaking of Mount Sinai (Ex 19:18). *heavens poured down rain.* The Pentateuch preserves no tradition of rain during the desert wanderings, but here (and in Jdg 5:4) rain is closely associated with the quaking of the earth as a manifestation of the majesty of God. Perhaps the "thunder and lightning, with a thick cloud" over Mount Sinai (Ex 19:16) were accompanied by rain. But see also v. 9, which suggests rains that refreshed the people on their journey.
68:9 *your ... inheritance.* The people of Israel (see Dt 9:29).
68:10 *it.* Probably refers to the promised land. *bounty.* Lit. "goodness" (see 65:11 and note). *provided.* From the produce of Canaan (see Jos 5:11–12). *poor.* Israel as a people

and from your bounty,[r] O God, you
    provided[s] for the poor.

[11]The Lord announced the word,
    and great was the company[t] of those
        who proclaimed it:
[12]"Kings and armies flee[u] in haste;
    in the camps men divide the
        plunder.[v]
[13]Even while you sleep among the
        campfires,[s] [w]
    the wings of my, dove are sheathed
        with silver,
    its feathers with shining gold."
[14]When the Almighty[t] scattered[x] the
        kings in the land,
    it was like snow fallen on Zalmon.[y]

[15]The mountains of Bashan[z] are majestic
        mountains;[a]
    rugged are the mountains of Bashan.
[16]Why gaze in envy, O rugged mountains,
    at the mountain where God chooses[b]
        to reign,
    where the LORD himself will dwell
        forever?[c]
[17]The chariots[d] of God are tens of
        thousands
    and thousands of thousands;[e]

the Lord has come, from Sinai into
    his sanctuary.
[18]When you ascended[f] on high,[g]
    you led captives[h] in your train;
    you received gifts from men,[i]
    even from[u] the rebellious[j] —
        that you,[v] O LORD God, might dwell
            there.

[19]Praise be to the Lord, to God our
        Savior,[k]
    who daily bears our burdens.[l]   Selah
[20]Our God is a God who saves;[m]
    from the Sovereign LORD comes
        escape from death.[n]

[21]Surely God will crush the heads[o] of his
        enemies,
    the hairy crowns of those who go on
        in their sins.
[22]The Lord says, "I will bring them from
        Bashan;
    I will bring them from the depths of
        the sea,[p]
[23]that you may plunge your feet in the
        blood of your foes,[q]
    while the tongues of your dogs[r] have
        their share."

Cross references

68:10
[r]S Dt 28:12
[s]Ps 65:9
68:11 [t]Lk 2:13
68:12 [u]Jos 10:16
[v]S Jdg 5:30
68:13
[w]S Ge 49:14
68:14 [x]2Sa 22:15
[y]Jdg 9:48
68:15 [z]ver 22;
Nu 21:33;
Jer 22:20
[a]S Ps 36:6
68:16 [b]Dt 12:5;
S Ps 2:6; 132:13
[c]Ps 132:14
68:17
[d]S 2Ki 2:11;
Isa 66:15;
Hab 3:8 [e]Da 7:10

68:18 [f]S Ps 47:5
[g]Ps 7:7 [h]Jdg 5:12
[i]Eph 4:8*
[j]S Nu 17:10
68:19 [k]S Ps 65:5
[l]Ps 81:6
68:20
[m]S 1Sa 10:19
[n]Ps 56:13;
Jer 45:5; Eze 6:8
68:21 [o]Ps 74:14;
110:5; Hab 3:13
68:22
[p]S Job 36:30;
Mt 18:6
68:23 [q]Ps 58:10
[r]S 1Ki 21:19;
S 2Ki 9:36

[s]13 Or saddlebags   [t]14 Hebrew Shaddai   [u]18 Or
gifts for men, / even   [v]18 Or they

---

dependent on God.
68:11–14 Recollection of God's victories over the kings of
Canaan.
68:11 *announced the word.* God declared beforehand that
he would be victorious over the Canaanite kings (see Ex
23:22–23,27–28,31; Dt 7:10–24; 11:23–25; Jos 1:2–6).
proclaimed it. Celebrated God's victories (see Ex 15:1–21;
1Sa 18:6–7; 2Ch 20:26–28). *proclaimed.* See 40:9 and
note.
68:13 *sleep among the campfires.* Rest in camp (see Jdg
5:16; see also NIV text note on Ge 49:14). *wings of my,
dove are sheathed.* Israel, God's "dove" (see 74:19 and
note; cf. Hos 7:11), is enriched with the silver and gold of
plunder from the kings of Canaan even though she still
remains in camp. This poetic hyperbole (a figure of speech
that uses exaggeration for emphasis) celebrates the fact that
God had defeated the kings even before Israel met them in
battle (see Jos 2:8–11; 5:1; 6:16; see also 2Sa 5:24; 2Ki
7:5–7; 19:35; 2Ch 20:22–30).
68:14 *Almighty.* See NIV text note; see also note on Ge
17:1. *like snow fallen on Zalmon.* Zalmon was a mountain
near Shechem (see Jdg 9:46–48), but others identify it here
as Jebel Druze, a dark volcanic mountain east of Bashan. Its
name appears to mean "the dark one"—in distinction from
the Lebanon ("the white one") range, composed of limestone—and the figure may involve the contrast of white
snow scattered on "Dark Mountain." The reference may
then be to abandoned weapons littering the field from which
the kings have fled headlong (see 2Ki 7:15).
68:15–18 Celebration of God's ascent to Mount Zion.
68:15–16 The mountains surrounding Bashan, including
the towering Mount Hermon, are portrayed as being jealous
because God has chosen Mount Zion as the seat of his rule,
making it the "highest" of mountains (see 48:2 and note).
68:17 *chariots of God.* God's great heavenly host, here

likened to a vast chariot force (see 2Ki 6:17; Hab 3:8,15). In
the time of the Roman empire Jesus referred to God's host in
terms of "legions" (Mt 26:53).
68:18 *ascended on high.* Went up to your place of enthronement on Mount Zion (see 47:5–6 and note; see also
7:7). *led captives . . . received gifts.* Like a victorious king
after triumphs on the field of battle. *rebellious.* Those who
had opposed the kingdom of God (see v. 6 and note on 66:7)
are compelled to submit to him and bring tribute. *that you
. . . might dwell there.* Grammatically completes the clause,
"When you ascended on high." Paul applies this verse (as
translated in the Septuagint) to the ascended Christ (Eph
4:8–13), thereby implying that Christ's ascension was a
continuation of, and a fulfillment of, God's establishment of
his kingdom in his royal city Jerusalem (see introduction).
68:19–23 Joyous confession of hope that God's victorious
campaigns will continue until the salvation of his people is
complete.
68:19 *bears our burdens.* Releases us from bearing the
burdens that enslavement to our enemies would impose on
us (see 81:6; Isa 9:4; 10:27). But some associate this line
with such passages as 55:22; Isa 46:4.
68:20 *escape from death.* At the hand of our enemies—implicitly, perhaps, also from death itself as the last
great enemy (see notes on 6:5; 11:7; 16:9–11; 17:15;
49:14–15).
68:21 As God assures the life of his people (see v. 20), so he
will crush those who oppose him. *crush the heads.* See Nu
24:17.
68:22 *them.* The enemies who fled at the victorious onward march of God and his host (see vv. 12,17). *Bashan . . .
depths of the sea.* The former (see also v. 15) was the high
plateau east of the Jordan, the latter the Mediterranean
Sea—none of the enemies will escape (see Am 9:1–4).
68:23 See note on 58:10.

²⁴Your procession has come into view,
O God,
the procession of my God and King
into the sanctuary. ˢ
²⁵In front are the singers, ᵗ after them the
musicians; ᵘ
with them are the maidens playing
tambourines. ᵛ
²⁶Praise God in the great congregation; ʷ
praise the LORD in the assembly of
Israel. ˣ
²⁷There is the little tribe ʸ of Benjamin, ᶻ
leading them,
there the great throng of Judah's
princes,
and there the princes of Zebulun and
of Naphtali. ᵃ

²⁸Summon your power, ᵇ O God ʷ;
show us your strength, ᶜ O God, as
you have done ᵈ before.
²⁹Because of your temple at Jerusalem
kings will bring you gifts. ᵉ
³⁰Rebuke the beast ᶠ among the reeds, ᵍ
the herd of bulls ʰ among the calves
of the nations.
Humbled, may it bring bars of silver.
Scatter the nations ⁱ who delight in
war. ʲ
³¹Envoys will come from Egypt; ᵏ
Cush ˣ ˡ will submit herself to God.

³²Sing to God, O kingdoms of the earth, ᵐ

sing praise ⁿ to the Lord,   *Selah*
³³to him who rides ᵒ the ancient skies
above,
who thunders ᵖ with mighty voice. ۹
³⁴Proclaim the power ʳ of God,
whose majesty ˢ is over Israel,
whose power is in the skies.
³⁵You are awesome, ᵗ O God, in your
sanctuary; ᵘ
the God of Israel gives power and
strength ᵛ to his people. ʷ

Praise be to God! ˣ

Psalm 69

For the director of music. To the tune of
"Lilies." Of David.

¹Save me, O God,
for the waters ʸ have come up to my
neck. ᶻ
²I sink in the miry depths, ᵃ
where there is no foothold.
I have come into the deep waters;
the floods engulf me.
³I am worn out calling for help; ᵇ
my throat is parched.

Cross references (center column):

68:24 ˢPs 63:2
68:25
ʳS 1Ch 15:16
ᵘS 1Ch 6:31;
S 2Ch 5:12;
Rev 18:22
ᵛS Ge 31:27;
S Isa 5:12
68:26
ʷS Ps 22:22;
Heb 2:12
ˣS Lev 19:2
68:27
ʸS 1Sa 9:21
ᶻS Nu 34:21
ᵃS Jdg 5:18
68:28 ᵇS Ex 9:16
ᶜPs 29:11
ᵈIsa 26:12;
29:23; 45:11;
60:21; 64:8
68:29
ᵉS 2Ch 9:24;
S 32:23
68:30 ᶠIsa 27:1;
51:9; Eze 29:3
ᵍS Job 40:21
ʰPs 22:12;
Isa 34:7;
Jer 50:27
ⁱPs 18:14; 89:10
ʲPs 120:7; 140:2
68:31 ᵏIsa 19:19;
43:3; 45:14
ˡIsa 11:11; 18:1;
Zep 3:10
68:32
ᵐS Ps 46:6; 67:4
ⁿPs 7:17
68:33
ᵒS Dt 33:26
ᵖS Ex 9:23;
S Ps 29:3
۹Ps 29:4;
Isa 30:30; 33:3;
66:6
68:34 ʳver 28
ˢPs 45:3
68:35 ᵗS Dt 7:21
ᵘS Ge 28:17

ʸPs 18:1; Isa 40:29; 41:10; 50:2 ʷS Ps 29:11 ˣPs 28:6;
66:20; 2Co 1:3 69:1 ʸS Ps 42:7 ᶻPs 32:6; Jnh 2:5 69:2
ᵃS Job 30:19 69:3 ᵇPs 6:6

ʷ*28* Many Hebrew manuscripts, Septuagint and Syriac;
most Hebrew manuscripts *Your God has summoned
power for you*   ˣ*31* That is, the upper Nile region

68:24–27 The liturgical procession approaches the temple (see Ps 24; 47).
68:25 *maidens playing tambourines.* See note on Jer 31:4.
68:27 All Israel is represented, from little Benjamin to powerful Judah, and tribes from the north as well as the south. *Benjamin, leading.* Perhaps reflecting the fact that from the tribe of Benjamin came the first king (Saul), who began the royal victories over Israel's enemies (see 1Sa 11:11; 14:20–23).
68:28–31 Prayer for God to continue his conquest of the threatening powers.
68:28 *Summon your power.* Or, perhaps, "Command your power to act."
68:29 *Because of your temple.* Because your earthly royal house has been established in Jerusalem. *bring you gifts.* Acknowledge you by bringing tribute, as subjected kings brought tribute to their conquerers (see 2Sa 8:2,6,10; 2Ki 3:4).
68:30 *Rebuke.* See note on 76:6. *beast among the reeds.* Pharaoh (see Eze 29:3). *herd of bulls among the calves.* Powerful princes supporting the pharaoh, and the lesser princes of other nations. Egypt is singled out here as representative of the hostile nations—because of Israel's past experiences with that world power and because at the time the psalm was composed it was the one great empire on Israel's immediate horizons. *Scatter the nations.* See v. 1; so that Israel may have peace (see 46:9; 48:4–7; 65:7; 76:3).
68:32–35 Climax of the liturgical procession: a call for all kingdoms to hail with praise the God of Israel as the God who reigns in heaven and has established his earthly throne in the temple in Jerusalem (see Ps 47).
68:33 See v. 4 and note. *thunders with mighty voice.* See

note on 29:3–9.
68:35 *awesome.* See 45:4 and note. *gives power and strength to his people.* The Lord of all has made Israel his people (his "kingdom"; see Ex 19:5–6), and his rule among them makes them participants in his victorious power (see 29:10–11).
Ps 69 A plea for God to have mercy and to save from a host of enemies: the prayer of a godly king when under vicious attack by a widespread conspiracy at a time when God had "wounded" him (see v. 26) for some sin in his life (see v. 5). If, as tradition claims, David authored the original psalm (see the superscription), the occasion is unknown. In its present form the prayer suggests a later son of David who ruled over the southern kingdom of Judah (see v. 35). That king may have been Hezekiah (see 2Ki 18–20; 2Ch 29–32). In themes and language this psalm has many links with Ps 32; 35; 38; 40; 109 (all psalms "of David"; see also Ps 18). It begins a series of three prayers for deliverance when threatened by enemies. The authors of the NT viewed this cry of a godly sufferer as foreshadowing the sufferings of Christ; no psalm, except Ps 22, is quoted more frequently in the NT.
69 title *For the director of music.* See note on Ps 4 title. *To the tune of.* See note on Ps 9 title. *Lilies.* See note on Ps 45 title.
69:1–4 Initial plea for God to save.
69:1–2 *waters . . . miry depths . . . deep waters . . . floods.* Conventional imagery for great distress (see notes on 30:1; 32:6)—here the results of God's "wounding" (see v. 26), but especially of the attacks of the enemies (see vv. 14–15, 29).
69:3 *throat is parched.* See 22:15. *eyes fail.* See 6:7 and note.

My eyes fail, *c*
  looking for my God.
⁴Those who hate me *d* without reason *e*
  outnumber the hairs of my head;
many are my enemies without cause, *f*
  those who seek to destroy me. *g*
I am forced to restore
  what I did not steal.

⁵You know my folly, *h* O God;
  my guilt is not hidden from you. *i*

⁶May those who hope in you
  not be disgraced because of me,
  O Lord, the LORD Almighty;
may those who seek you
  not be put to shame because of me,
  O God of Israel.

⁷For I endure scorn *j* for your sake, *k*
  and shame covers my face. *l*
⁸I am a stranger to my brothers,
  an alien to my own mother's sons; *m*
⁹for zeal for your house consumes me, *n*
  and the insults of those who insult
  you fall on me. *o*
¹⁰When I weep and fast, *p*
  I must endure scorn;
¹¹when I put on sackcloth, *q*
  people make sport of me.
¹²Those who sit at the gate *r* mock me,
  and I am the song of the drunkards. *s*

¹³But I pray to you, O LORD,
  in the time of your favor; *t*

in your great love, *u* O God,
  answer me with your sure salvation.
¹⁴Rescue me from the mire,
  do not let me sink;
deliver me from those who hate me,
  from the deep waters. *v*
¹⁵Do not let the floodwaters *w* engulf me
  or the depths swallow me up *x*
  or the pit close its mouth over
  me. *y*

¹⁶Answer me, O LORD, out of the
  goodness of your love; *z*
  in your great mercy turn to me.
¹⁷Do not hide your face *a* from your
  servant;
  answer me quickly, *b* for I am in
  trouble. *c*
¹⁸Come near and rescue me;
  redeem *d* me because of my foes.

¹⁹You know how I am scorned, *e*
  disgraced and shamed;
  all my enemies are before you.
²⁰Scorn has broken my heart
  and has left me helpless;
I looked for sympathy, but there was
  none,
  for comforters, *f* but I found none. *g*
²¹They put gall in my food
  and gave me vinegar *h* for my thirst. *i*

²²May the table set before them become a
  snare;

Cross references

69:3 *c*Ps 119:82
69:4 *d*S Ps 25:19
  *e*Jn 15:25*
  /S Ps 35:19;
  38:19 *g*Ps 40:14;
  119:95; Isa 32:7
69:5 *h*Ps 38:5
  /S Ps 44:21
69:7 /S Ps 39:8
  *k*Jer 15:15
  *l*Ps 44:15
69:8
  *m*Job 19:13-15;
  Ps 31:11; 38:11;
  Isa 53:3; Jn 7:5
69:9 *n*Jn 2:17*
  *o*Ps 89:50-51;
  Ro 15:3
69:10
  *p*S Ps 35:13
69:11
  *q*S 2Sa 3:31;
  S Ps 35:13
69:12
  *r*S Ge 18:1;
  S 23:10 *s*Job 30:9
69:13 *t*Isa 49:8;
  2Co 6:2
  *u*S Ps 17:7; 51:1
69:14 *v*ver 2;
  Ps 144:7
69:15
  *w*Ps 124:4-5
  *x*Nu 16:33
  *y*Ps 28:1
69:16 *z*S Ps 63:3
69:17
  *a*S Ps 22:24
  *b*Ps 143:7
  *c*S Ps 50:15;
  66:14
69:18 *d*Ps 49:15
69:19 *e*S Ps 22:6
69:20 /Job 16:2
  *g*Ps 142:4;
  Isa 63:5
69:21 *h*S Nu 6:3;
  Mt 27:48;
  Mk 15:36;
  Lk 23:36
  *i*Mt 27:34;
  Mk 15:23;
  Jn 19:28-30

69:4 *without reason ... without cause.* Those whom he has not wronged are pitted against him (see 35:19 and note). *outnumber the hairs of my head.* See note on 40:12. *I am forced.* An illustrative way of saying that his enemies are spreading false accusations about him (see 5:9 and note).
69:5–12 Prayer that God's discipline of his godly servant may not bring disgrace on all those who trustingly look to the Lord. The author acknowledges (v. 5) that God's "wounding" of him (see v. 26) has been occasioned by some sin in his life (but he has not sinned against those who have become his enemies). Because of his present suffering, his enemies mock his deep commitment to the Lord (see 22:6–8; 42:3; 79:10; 115:2; Job 2:9). Implicitly he prays that God will restore him again and vindicate his trust in him.
69:5 *folly.* See NIV text note on 14:1.
69:8 Even those nearest him dissociate themselves from him (see 31:11–12 and note).
69:9 *zeal for your house.* What was true of the author was even more true of Jesus (see Jn 2:17). *insults of those who insult you.* Those who mock God also mock his servant who trusts in him (see 74:18,22–23; 2Ki 18:31–35)—as Christ also experienced (see Ro 15:3).
69:10–11 *weep and fast ... put on sackcloth.* As tokens of humbling himself before the Lord in repentance as he prays for God to have mercy and restore him (see 35:13 and note; see also Ge 37:34; 2Sa 12:16–17; Joel 1:13–14; 2:15–17; Jnh 3:5).
69:12 *Those who sit at the gate ... drunkards.* Everyone, from the elders of the city to the town drunks.
69:13–18 Though they mock, I pray to you.

69:13 *time of your favor.* When God is near to save (see 32:6 and note; see also Isa 49:8; 61:2; 2Co 6:2). *great love.* See note on 6:4.
69:14–15 *mire ... deep waters ... floodwaters ... depths.* See note on vv. 1–2.
69:15 *swallow me.* See note on 49:14. *pit.* See note on 30:1.
69:16 *love.* See note on 6:4.
69:17 *hide your face.* See note on 13:1.
69:18 *redeem.* See note on 25:22.
69:19–21 In my trouble they heaped on scorn instead of bringing comfort (see 35:11–16; see also 142:4; Job 13:4; 16:2; 21:34).
69:20 *heart.* See note on 4:7.
69:21 *gall in my food ... vinegar for my thirst.* Vivid metaphors for the bitter scorn they made him eat and drink when his whole being craved for the nourishment and refreshment of comfort. The authors of the Gospels, especially Matthew, suggest that the suffering expressed in this verse foreshadowed Christ's suffering on the cross (see Mt 27:34, 48; Mk 15:23,36; Lk 23:36; Jn 19:29).
69:22–28 Prayer for God to redress the wrongs committed (see note on 5:10).
69:22–23 For Paul's application of these verses to the Jews who rejected the Christ see Ro 11:9–10.
69:22 They had set his table with "gall" and "vinegar" (v. 21). *table set before them.* Reference may be to the meal accompanying the sealing of a covenant (see note on 23:5). In that case, this verse alludes to a pact uniting the enemies and calls on God to turn it against them.

may it become retribution and[y] a
　　trap.[i]
[23]May their eyes be darkened so they
　　cannot see,
　　and their backs be bent forever.[k]
[24]Pour out your wrath[l] on them;
　　let your fierce anger overtake them.
[25]May their place be deserted;[m]
　　let there be no one to dwell in their
　　tents.[n]
[26]For they persecute those you wound
　　and talk about the pain of those you
　　hurt.[o]
[27]Charge them with crime upon crime;[p]
　　do not let them share in your
　　salvation.[q]
[28]May they be blotted out of the book of
　　life[r]
　　and not be listed with the righteous.[s]

[29]I am in pain and distress;
　　may your salvation, O God, protect
　　me.[t]

[30]I will praise God's name in song[u]
　　and glorify him[v] with thanksgiving.
[31]This will please the LORD more than an
　　ox,
　　more than a bull with its horns and
　　hoofs.[w]
[32]The poor will see and be glad[x] —
　　you who seek God, may your hearts
　　live![y]
[33]The LORD hears the needy[z]

69:22
[i]S 1Sa 28:9;
S Job 18:10
69:23
[k]Ro 11:9-10*
69:24 [l]Ps 79:6;
Jer 10:25
69:25
[m]S Lev 26:43;
Mt 23:38
[n]Ac 1:20*
69:26
[o]S Job 19:22;
Zec 1:15
69:27 [p]Ne 4:5
[q]Ps 109:14
69:28
[r]Ex 32:32-33;
S Lk 10:20
[s]Eze 13:9
69:29 [t]S Ps 20:1
69:30 [u]Ps 28:7
[v]Ps 34:3
69:31
[w]Ps 50:9-13;
51:16
69:32 [x]S Ps 34:2
[y]Ps 22:26
69:33 [z]Ps 12:5

69:34 [a]Ps 96:11;
98:7; Isa 44:23
69:35 [b]Ob 1:17
[c]S Ezr 9:9;
S Ps 51:18
69:36 [d]Ps 25:13
[e]S Ps 37:29
70:1 [f]Ps 22:19;
71:12
70:2 [g]Ps 35:4
[h]Ps 6:10; 35:26;
71:13; 109:29;
129:5
70:3 [i]S Ps 35:21
70:4 [j]Ps 9:10
[k]Ps 31:6-7;
32:11; 118:24
[l]Ps 35:27

---

and does not despise his captive
　　people.

[34]Let heaven and earth praise him,
　　the seas and all that move in them,[a]
[35]for God will save Zion[b]
　　and rebuild the cities of Judah.[c]
　Then people will settle there and
　　possess it;
[36]　the children of his servants will
　　inherit it,[d]
　and those who love his name will
　　dwell there.[e]

Psalm 70

70:1–5pp — Ps 40:13–17

For the director of music. Of David.
A petition.

[1]Hasten, O God, to save me;
　　O LORD, come quickly to help me.[f]
[2]May those who seek my life[g]
　　be put to shame and confusion;
　may all who desire my ruin
　　be turned back in disgrace.[h]
[3]May those who say to me, "Aha!
　　Aha!"[i]
　turn back because of their shame.
[4]But may all who seek you[j]
　　rejoice and be glad[k] in you;
　may those who love your salvation
　　always say,
　　"Let God be exalted!"[l]

[y]22 Or snare / and their fellowship become

69:23 They mocked him for his "wound" (v. 26); now may they experience the same failing of the eyes (see v. 3 and note on 6:7) and bending of the back (from weakness and pain; see 38:5–8). *May . . . their backs be bent.* Lit. "May . . . their loins give way." "Loins" refers to the belly and lower part of the back; they were viewed as the back's center of strength (see 66:11; see also Job 40:16).
69:24 *wrath . . . anger.* See note on 2:5. *overtake them.* Like a flash flood.
69:25 They sought to remove him from his place; may they be removed. Cf. Peter's application of this judgment to Judas (Ac 1:20).
69:26 The great wrong committed by his enemies against him and to which reference has repeatedly been made.
69:27 They have falsely charged him with crimes (v. 4); may their real crimes all be charged against them.
69:28 They had plotted his death; may death be their destiny. *book of life.* God's royal list of the righteous, whom God blesses with life (see 1:3; 7:9; 11:7; 34:12; 37:17,29; 55:22; 75:10; 92:12–14; 140:13). For other references to God's books see notes on 9:5; 51:1. In the NT the "book of life" refers to God's list of those destined for eternal life (see Php 4:3; Rev 3:5; 13:8; 17:8; 20:12,15; 21:27).
69:29 Renewal of the prayer just prior to the vow to praise. *protect me.* Lit. "raise me to a high, secure place."
69:30–33 A vow to praise (see note on 7:17) out of assurance that the prayer will be heard (see note on 3:8).
69:30 *God's name.* See v. 36 and note on 5:11.
69:32 *poor.* See note on 34:6. *see and be glad.* See 22:26

and note. *hearts.* See note on 4:7. *live.* Bubble over with the joy of life, because the Lord does hear the prayers of his people in need—contrary to the mocking of scoffers.
69:34–36 A call to praise (see note on 9:1) in the assurance that God will restore Judah and assure his people's inheritance in the promised land. This stanza appears to indicate that in its final form this royal prayer was used at a time when not only the king was in trouble but the kingdom of Judah had also suffered devastating defeat.
69:34 Let all creation praise him (see 148:1–13; Isa 49:13).
69:35–36 *people . . . children.* God's people and their children through the generations, specifically those who love his name.
69:35 *Zion.* See note on 9:11.
Ps 70 An urgent prayer for God's help when threatened by enemies—a somewhat revised duplicate of 40:13–17 (see notes there). This is the second in a series of three such prayers; its language has many links with that of Ps 71. The prayer is framed by pleas for God to "come quickly" with his help (vv. 1,5). The rest of the prayer focuses on the effects of God's saving help: (1) upon those "who seek my life" (vv. 2–3) and (2) for those "who seek you" (v. 4).
70 title See note on Ps 4 title. *A petition.* See note on Ps 38 title.
70:4 God's deliverance of his servant will give joy to all who trust in the Lord, because they see in it the assurance of their own salvation. *Let God be exalted!* Because his saving help is sure and effective (contrast v. 3).

⁵Yet I am poor and needy; *m*
　come quickly to me, *n* O God.
You are my help *o* and my deliverer; *p*
　O LORD, do not delay. *q*

Psalm 71

71:1–3pp — Ps 31:1–4

¹In you, O LORD, I have taken refuge; *r*
　let me never be put to shame. *s*
²Rescue me and deliver me in your
　　righteousness;
　turn your ear *t* to me and save me.
³Be my rock of refuge,
　to which I can always go;
give the command to save me,
　for you are my rock and my
　　fortress. *u*
⁴Deliver *v* me, O my God, from the hand
　　of the wicked, *w*
　from the grasp of evil and cruel
　　men. *x*

⁵For you have been my hope, *y*
　　O Sovereign LORD,
　my confidence *z* since my youth.
⁶From birth *a* I have relied on you;
　you brought me forth from my
　　mother's womb. *b*
　I will ever praise *c* you.
⁷I have become like a portent *d* to many,
　but you are my strong refuge. *e*
⁸My mouth *f* is filled with your praise,
　declaring your splendor *g* all day long.

⁹Do not cast *h* me away when I am old; *i*
　do not forsake *j* me when my
　　strength is gone.
¹⁰For my enemies *k* speak against me;

those who wait to kill *l* me conspire *m*
　　together.
¹¹They say, "God has forsaken *n* him;
　pursue him and seize him,
　for no one will rescue *o* him."
¹²Be not far *p* from me, O God;
　come quickly, O my God, to help *q*
　　me.
¹³May my accusers *r* perish in shame; *s*
　may those who want to harm me
　be covered with scorn and disgrace. *t*

¹⁴But as for me, I will always have
　　hope; *u*
　I will praise you more and more.
¹⁵My mouth will tell *v* of your
　　righteousness, *w*
　of your salvation all day long,
　though I know not its measure.
¹⁶I will come and proclaim your mighty
　　acts, *x* O Sovereign LORD;
　I will proclaim your righteousness,
　　yours alone.
¹⁷Since my youth, O God, you have
　　taught *y* me,
　and to this day I declare your
　　marvelous deeds. *z*
¹⁸Even when I am old and gray, *a*
　do not forsake me, O God,
　till I declare your power *b* to the next
　　generation,
　your might to all who are to come. *c*

¹⁹Your righteousness reaches to the
　　skies, *d* O God,
　you who have done great things. *e*

70:5 *m*Ps 86:1;
109:22 *n*Ps 141:1
*o*Ps 30:10; 33:20
*p*Ps 18:2
*q*Ps 119:60
71:1 *r*S Dt 23:15;
Ru 2:12
*s*S Ps 22:5
71:2 *t*S 2Ki 19:16
71:3 *u*Ps 18:2
71:4 *v*S 2Ki 19:19
*w*Ps 140:4
*x*S Ge 48:16
71:5 *y*S Ps 9:18;
S 25:5 *z*S Job 4:6;
Jer 17:7
71:6 *a*S Ps 22:10
*b*S Job 3:16;
S Ps 22:9 *c*Ps 9:1;
34:1; 52:9;
119:164; 145:2
71:7
*d*S Dt 28:46;
Isa 8:18; 1Co 4:9
*e*S 2Sa 22:3;
Ps 61:3
71:8 *f*ver 15;
Ps 51:15; 63:5
*g*Ps 96:6; 104:1
71:9 *h*S Ps 51:11
*i*Ps 92:14;
Isa 46:4
*j*S Dt 4:31; S 31:6
71:10 *k*Ps 3:7

*l*S Ps 10:8; 59:3;
Pr 1:18
*m*S Ex 1:10;
S Ps 31:13;
S Mt 12:14
71:11 *n*S Ps 9:10;
Isa 40:27; 54:7;
La 5:20; Mt 27:46
*o*S Ps 7:2
71:12
*p*S Ps 38:21
*q*Ps 22:19; 38:22
71:13 *r*Jer 18:19
*s*S Job 8:22;
Ps 25:3 *t*S Ps 70:2
71:14 *u*Ps 25:3;
42:5; 130:7;
131:3
71:15 *v*S ver 8;
S Ps 66:16
*w*S Ps 51:14
71:16 *x*Ps 9:1;
77:12; 106:2;
118:15; 145:4

71:17 *y*S Dt 4:5; S Jer 7:13 *z*S Job 5:9; Ps 26:7; 86:10; 96:3
71:18 *a*Isa 46:4 *b*S Ex 9:16 *c*Job 8:8; Ps 22:30,31; 78:4;
145:4; Joel 1:3 **71:19** *d*S Ps 36:5 *e*Ps 126:2; Lk 1:49

Ps 71 A prayer for God's help in old age when enemies threaten because they see that the king's strength is waning (see note on 5:9). The psalm bears no superscription, but it may well be that Ps 70 was viewed by the editors of the Psalms as the introduction to Ps 71, in which case the psalm is ascribed to David (in his old age; see vv. 9,18). This suggestion gains support from the fact that Ps 72 is identified as a prayer by and/or for King Solomon (see introduction to that psalm). This is the third in a series of three prayers; its dominant theme is hope (see v. 14). Formally symmetrical, the psalm is composed of six stanzas, having a five-four-five, five-four-five (in Hebrew) line pattern: vv. 1–4 (five lines), vv. 5–8 (four lines), vv. 9–13 (five lines), vv. 15–18 (five lines), vv. 19–21 (four lines). At the center (v. 14; see note on 6:6) stands a confident confession of hope. The whole is framed by an appeal for help (vv. 1–4) and a vow to praise in anticipation of deliverance (vv. 22–24). The second and fifth stanzas are linked by references to the troubles the king has experienced; stanzas three and four are linked by references to old age.

71:1–4 The initial appeal for God's help.
71:2 *your righteousness.* See vv. 15–16,19,24; see also note on 4:1.
71:5–8 A confession that the Lord has always been his hope (see vv. 14,19–21).

71:5 *since my youth.* See 22:9.
71:7 *like a portent.* The troubles of his life (see v. 20) have been viewed by others as holding some special significance—especially since the Lord has been his "strong refuge" through them all.
71:9–13 A prayer for God's continuing help in the waning years of his life.
71:10 *enemies speak against me.* See notes on 3:2; 5:9.
71:13 A plea for redress (see note on 5:10).
71:14 The centered confession of unfaltering hope (see 42:8; see also notes on 6:6; 42:8).
71:15–18 A vow to praise, accompanying the renewal of his prayer (v. 18); see note on 7:17.
71:16–17 *mighty acts . . . righteousness . . . marvelous deeds.* God's "mighty (marvelous) acts" in behalf of his people are expressions of his righteousness; thus they can also be called his "righteous acts" (v. 24).
71:16 *come.* To the temple, where God's people assemble for worship.
71:19–21 A confession that the Lord is still his hope, in the face of all his troubles (see vv. 5–8,14).
71:19 *reaches to the skies.* Is as expansive as all space above the earth (see also 36:5 and note). *Who, O God, is like you?* See Mic 7:18.

Who, O God, is like you?[f]
20Though you have made me see
troubles,[g] many and bitter,
you will restore[h] my life again;
from the depths of the earth[i]
you will again bring me up.
21You will increase my honor[j]
and comfort[k] me once again.

22I will praise you with the harp[l]
for your faithfulness, O my God;
I will sing praise to you with the lyre,[m]
O Holy One of Israel.[n]
23My lips will shout for joy[o]
when I sing praise to you—
I, whom you have redeemed.[p]
24My tongue will tell of your righteous
acts
all day long,[q]
for those who wanted to harm me[r]
have been put to shame and
confusion.[s]

Psalm 72

Of Solomon.

1Endow the king with your justice,[t]
O God,
the royal son with your
righteousness.
2He will[z] judge your people in
righteousness,[u]
your afflicted ones with justice.
3The mountains will bring prosperity to
the people,
the hills the fruit of righteousness.
4He will defend the afflicted[v] among the
people
and save the children of the needy;[w]
he will crush the oppressor.[x]

5He will endure[a][y] as long as the sun,
as long as the moon, through all
generations.[z]
6He will be like rain[a] falling on a mown
field,
like showers watering the earth.
7In his days the righteous will flourish;[b]
prosperity will abound till the moon
is no more.

8He will rule from sea to sea
and from the River[b][c] to the ends of
the earth.[c][d]
9The desert tribes will bow before him
and his enemies will lick the dust.
10The kings of Tarshish[e] and of distant
shores[f]
will bring tribute to him;

71:19 [f]Ps 35:10; 77:13; 89:8 **71:20** [g]Ps 25:17 [h]Ps 80:3,19; 85:4; Hos 6:2 [i]S Ps 63:9 **71:21** [j]Ps 18:35 [k]Ps 23:4; 86:17; Isa 12:1; 40:1-2; 49:13; 54:10 **71:22** [l]Ps 33:2 [m]S Job 21:12; Ps 92:3; 144:9 [n]S 2Ki 19:22 **71:23** [o]Ps 20:5 [p]S Ex 15:13 **71:24** [q]S Ps 35:28 [r]ver 13 [s]S Est 9:2 **72:1** [t]S Dt 1:16; S Ps 9:8 **72:2** [u]Isa 9:7; 11:4-5; 16:5; 32:1; 59:17; 63:1; Jer 23:5; 33:15 **72:4** [v]S Ps 9:12; 76:9; Isa 49:13 [w]ver 13; Isa 11:4; 29:19; 32:7 [x]S Ps 27:11 **72:5** [y]1Sa 13:13 [z]Ps 33:11 **72:6** [a]S Dt 32:2 **72:7** [b]Ps 92:12; Pr 14:11 **72:8** [c]S Ex 23:31; S 1Ki 4:21 [d]Zec 9:10 **72:10** [e]S Ge 10:4 [f]S Est 10:1

z2 Or *May he*; similarly in verses 3-11 and 17 **a**5 Septuagint; Hebrew *You will be feared* **b**8 That is, the Euphrates **c**8 Or *the end of the land*

71:20 *restore my life again.* He who gave him life (see v. 6) will renew his life. *depths of the earth.* The realm of the dead, of which the grave is the portal (see note on 30:1).
71:22–24 A vow to praise in confident anticipation of God's saving help (see notes on 3:8; 7:17).
71:22 *harp . . . lyre.* See note on 57:8. *Holy One of Israel.* See 78:41; 89:18; see also note on Isa 1:4.
71:23 *redeemed.* Here, as often, a synonym for "deliver."
71:24 *righteous acts.* God's saving acts in behalf of his people according to his covenant promises.
Ps 72 A prayer for the king, a son of David who rules on David's throne as God's earthly regent over his people. It may have been used at the time of the king's coronation (as were Ps 2; 110). Possibly vv. 2–11,17 are expressly a petition (see NIV text note on v. 2), but even if the NIV text rendering is taken, these verses are implicit prayers. They express the desire of the nation that the king's reign will, as a consequence of God's endowment of his servant, be characterized by justice and righteousness, the supreme virtues of kingship. The prayer reflects the ideal concept of the king and the glorious effects of his reign. See Jeremiah's indictment of some of the last Davidic kings (e.g., Jer 22:2–3,13, 15) and the prophetic announcement of the Messiah's righteous rule (see Isa 9:7; 11:4–5; Jer 23:5–6; 33:15–16; Zec 9:9). Later Jewish tradition saw in this psalm a description of the Messiah, as did the early church. The last three verses do not belong to the prayer (see notes there).
72 title *Of Solomon.* Either by him or for him—of course, both may be true. Undoubtedly it was also used by Israel (Judah) as a prayer for later Davidic kings.
72:1 The basic prayer. *justice . . . righteousness.* May the king be endowed with the gift for and the love of justice and righteousness so that his reign reflects the rule of God himself. Solomon asked for wisdom (see 1Ki 3:9,11–12; see also Pr 16:12). *righteousness.* See note on 4:1.
72:2–7 The quality of his reign: May it be righteous, prosperous and enduring.
72:3 Righteousness in the realm will be like fertilizing rain on the land, for then the Lord will bless his people with abundance (see vv. 6–7; 5:12; 65:9–13; 133:3; Lev 25:19; Dt 28:8).
72:5 *endure as long as the sun.* See 21:4 and note.
72:6 See v. 3 and note; see also v. 7. For another vivid metaphor expressive of the significance of the Lord's anointed for the realm see La 4:20.
72:7 *righteous.* See note on 1:5. *will flourish.* Because the king supports and protects them, but uses all his royal power to suppress the wicked (see Ps 101).
72:8–14 The extent of his domain (vv. 8–11) as the result of his righteous rule (vv. 12–14).
72:8 His kingdom will reach to the full extent of the promised land, but his authority will extend to all the world (see vv. 9–11). Ideally and potentially, as God's earthly regent, he possesses royal authority that extends on earth as far as God's—an expectation fulfilled in Christ.
72:9 The tribes of the Arabian Desert to the east will yield to him. *lick the dust.* See Mic 7:17.
72:10 The kings whose lands border the Mediterranean Sea to the west will acknowledge him as overlord, as will those who rule in south Arabia and along the eastern African coast. *Tarshish.* A distant Mediterranean seaport, perhaps as far west as modern Spain. *Sheba.* See notes on Ge 10:28; 1Ki 10:1; Joel 3:8. *Seba.* Elsewhere in the OT associated with Cush (Ge 10:7; Isa 43:3); it may refer to a region in modern Sudan, south of Egypt.

the kings of Sheba[g] and Seba
  will present him gifts.[h]
[11]All kings will bow down[i] to him
  and all nations will serve[j] him.

[12]For he will deliver the needy who cry
    out,
  the afflicted who have no one to
    help.
[13]He will take pity[k] on the weak and the
    needy
  and save the needy from death.
[14]He will rescue[l] them from oppression
    and violence,
  for precious[m] is their blood in his
    sight.

[15]Long may he live!
  May gold from Sheba[n] be given him.
May people ever pray for him
  and bless him all day long.[o]
[16]Let grain[p] abound throughout the land;
  on the tops of the hills may it sway.
Let its fruit[q] flourish like Lebanon;[r]
  let it thrive like the grass of the
    field.[s]
[17]May his name endure forever;[t]
  may it continue as long as the sun.[u]

All nations will be blessed through him,
  and they will call him blessed.[v]

[18]Praise be to the LORD God, the God of
    Israel,[w]
  who alone does marvelous deeds.[x]

72:10 [g]S Ge 10:7
[h]S 1Ki 9:16;
S 2Ch 9:24
72:11
[i]S Ge 27:29
[j]S Ezr 1:2
72:13 [k]Isa 60:10;
Joel 2:18;
Lk 10:33
72:14 [l]Ps 69:18;
Eze 13:23; 34:10
[m]1Sa 26:21
72:15 [n]S Ge 10:7
[o]S Ps 35:28
72:16
[p]S Ge 27:28;
Ps 4:7 [q]Isa 4:2;
27:6; Eze 34:27
[r]Ps 92:12; 104:16
[s]S Nu 22:4;
Isa 44:4; 58:11;
66:14
72:17 [t]S Ex 3:15
[u]Ps 89:36
[v]S Ge 12:3;
Lk 1:48
72:18
[w]1Ch 29:10;
Ps 41:13; 106:48;
Lk 1:68 [x]S Job 5:9

72:19
[y]S 2Sa 7:26
[z]Nu 14:21
[a]S Ps 41:13
72:20 [b]S Ru 4:17
73:1 [c]S Ps 24:4;
Mt 5:8
73:2 [d]S Dt 32:35
[e]Ps 69:2;
Eph 4:27
73:3 [f]Pr 3:31;
23:17; 24:1-2
[g]S Job 9:24;
S 21:7; Jer 12:1;
Mal 3:15
73:5 [h]ver 12;
Eze 23:42
73:6 [i]S Lev 26:19
[j]S Ge 41:42;
SS 4:9; Eze 16:11

[19]Praise be to his glorious name[y] forever;
  may the whole earth be filled with
    his glory.[z]
      Amen and Amen.[a]

[20]This concludes the prayers of David son
    of Jesse.[b]

BOOK III

Psalms 73–89

Psalm 73

A psalm of Asaph.

[1]Surely God is good to Israel,
  to those who are pure in heart.[c]

[2]But as for me, my feet had almost
    slipped;[d]
  I had nearly lost my foothold.[e]
[3]For I envied[f] the arrogant
  when I saw the prosperity of the
    wicked.[g]

[4]They have no struggles;
  their bodies are healthy and strong.[d]
[5]They are free[h] from the burdens
    common to man;
  they are not plagued by human ills.
[6]Therefore pride[i] is their necklace;[j]

[d] 4 With a different word division of the Hebrew;
Masoretic Text *struggles at their death; / their bodies are
healthy*

72:15–17 Concluding summation: May the king enjoy a long, prosperous, world-renowned reign—one that blesses all the nations.
72:17 *All nations.* The language recalls the promise to Abraham (see Ge 12:3; 22:18) and suggests that it will be fulfilled through the royal son of David—ultimately the Messiah.
72:18–19 A doxology at the conclusion of Book II of the Psalter (see 41:13 and note). It is the people's response, their "Amen," to the contents of Book II (see note on Ps 4 title).
72:19 *filled with his glory.* See note on 85:9.
72:20 An editorial notation probably carried over from an earlier collection of psalms ascribed exclusively to David. *prayers of David.* See titles of Ps 86; 142.
Ps 73 A word of godly wisdom concerning the destinies of the righteous and the wicked. The editors of the Psalter placed it at the beginning of Book III, as they did Ps 1 at the beginning of the whole collection (see introduction to Ps 1). Here is addressed one of the most disturbing problems of the OT saints: How is it that the wicked so often prosper while the godly suffer so much? Thematically the psalm has many links with Ps 49 (see introduction to that psalm; see also Ps 37). Its date may be as late as the postexilic era. Thematic development divides the psalm's structure into two halves of 14 verses each. The whole is framed by the sharply etched contrast of v. 1 and v. 27.
73 title The psalm is ascribed to Asaph, leader of one of David's Levitical choirs (see notes on Ps 39; 42; 50 titles). It begins a collection of 11 Asaphite psalms (Ps 73–83), to which Ps 50 at one time probably belonged. In view of the

fact that the collection clearly contains prayers from a later date (e.g., Ps 74; 79; 83), references to Asaph in these titles must sometimes include descendants of Asaph who functioned in his place (see note on Ps 50 title). The Asaphite psalms are dominated by the theme of God's rule over his people and the nations. Apart from an introductory word of instruction (Ps 73) the collection is bracketed by prayers for God to rescue his people from foreign oppression (Ps 74; 83). The rest of the collection (Ps 75–82) appears to reflect thematic pairing: 1. The God who brings down the wicked and exalts the righteous (Ps 75) is the God and Savior of Israel (Ps 76). 2. God's saving acts in behalf of his people are remembered (Ps 77–78). 3. God is petitioned for help against the devastating attacks of Israel's enemies (Ps 79–80). 4. God is portrayed as presiding in judgment over his people (Ps 81) and over the world powers (Ps 82).
73:1–14 An almost fatal trial of faith: In the midst of his many troubles a godly man lets his eyes become fixed on the prosperity of the wicked.
73:1 *pure in heart.* See v. 13; see also note on 24:4. *heart.* See note on 4:7.
73:2 *feet had almost slipped.* From the path of truth and godliness (see 37:31 and note).
73:4–12 A description of the prosperous state of the wicked and the haughty self-reliance it engenders—hardly an objective account; it is rather the exaggerated picture that envious and troubled eyes perceived (see the description of the wicked in 10:2–11; cf. Job's anguished portrayal of the prosperity of the wicked in Job 21).
73:6 *pride is their necklace.* Contrast Pr 1:9; 3:3,22.

they clothe themselves with
   violence. [k]
[7]From their callous hearts [l] comes
   iniquity [e];
   the evil conceits of their minds know
   no limits.
[8]They scoff, and speak with malice; [m]
   in their arrogance [n] they threaten
   oppression. [o]
[9]Their mouths lay claim to heaven,
   and their tongues take possession of
   the earth.
[10]Therefore their people turn to them
   and drink up waters in abundance. [f]
[11]They say, "How can God know?
   Does the Most High have
   knowledge?"
[12]This is what the wicked are like—
   always carefree, [p] they increase in
   wealth. [q]
[13]Surely in vain [r] have I kept my heart
   pure;
   in vain have I washed my hands in
   innocence. [s]
[14]All day long I have been plagued; [t]
   I have been punished every morning.
[15]If I had said, "I will speak thus,"
   I would have betrayed your children.
[16]When I tried to understand [u] all this,
   it was oppressive to me
[17]till I entered the sanctuary [v] of God;
   then I understood their final
   destiny. [w]
[18]Surely you place them on slippery
   ground; [x]
   you cast them down to ruin. [y]
[19]How suddenly [z] are they destroyed,

completely swept away [a] by terrors!
[20]As a dream [b] when one awakes, [c]
   so when you arise, O Lord,
   you will despise them as fantasies. [d]
[21]When my heart was grieved
   and my spirit embittered,
[22]I was senseless [e] and ignorant;
   I was a brute beast [f] before you.
[23]Yet I am always with you;
   you hold me by my right hand. [g]
[24]You guide [h] me with your counsel, [i]
   and afterward you will take me into
   glory.
[25]Whom have I in heaven but you? [j]
   And earth has nothing I desire
   besides you. [k]
[26]My flesh and my heart [l] may fail, [m]
   but God is the strength [n] of my heart
   and my portion [o] forever.
[27]Those who are far from you will
   perish; [p]
   you destroy all who are unfaithful [q] to
   you.
[28]But as for me, it is good to be near
   God. [r]
   I have made the Sovereign LORD my
   refuge; [s]
   I will tell of all your deeds. [t]

Psalm 74

A *maskil* [g] of Asaph.

[1]Why have you rejected [u] us forever, [v]
   O God?

Cross references

73:6 [k]S Ge 6:11;
S Pr 4:17
73:7 [l]S Ps 17:10
73:8 [m]Ps 41:5;
Eze 25:15;
Col 3:8 [n]Ps 17:10
[o]S Ps 10:7; S 12:5
73:12 [p]S ver 5
[q]S Ps 49:6
73:13
[r]S Job 9:29-31;
S 21:15
[s]S Ge 44:16
73:14 [t]ver 5
73:16 [u]Ecc 8:17
73:17 [v]Ex 15:17;
Ps 15:1
[w]S Job 8:13;
Php 3:19
73:18
[x]S Dt 32:35;
Ps 35:6
[y]S Ps 17:13
73:19 [z]Dt 28:20;
Pr 24:22;
Isa 47:11

[a]S Ge 19:15
73:20 [b]S Job 20:8
[c]Ps 78:65;
Isa 29:8
[d]Pr 12:11; 28:19
73:22 [e]Ps 49:10;
92:6; 94:8
[f]Ps 49:12,20;
Ecc 3:18; 9:12
73:23
[g]S Ge 48:13
73:24
[h]S Ps 48:14
[i]S 1Ki 22:5
73:25 [j]Ps 16:2
[k]Php 3:8
73:26 [l]Ps 84:2
[m]S Ps 31:10;
40:12 [n]Ps 18:1
[o]S Dt 32:9
73:27
[p]S Ps 34:21
[q]S Lev 6:2;
Jer 5:11;
Hos 4:12; 9:1
73:28 [r]Zep 3:2;
Heb 10:22;
Jas 4:8 [s]Ps 9:9
[t]Ps 26:7; 40:5
74:1 [u]S Ps 43:2
[v]S Ps 44:23

[e]7 Syriac (see also Septuagint); Hebrew *Their eyes bulge
with fat*   [f]10 The meaning of the Hebrew for this verse
is uncertain.   [g]Title: Probably a literary or musical term

---

73:11 *God . . . Most High.* That is, God Most High (see
57:2; see also note on 3:7). *Most High.* See note on Ge
14:19.
73:13–14 The thoughts that plagued him when he compared the state of the wicked with his own troubled lot.
73:13 *heart pure.* See note on v. 1.
73:14 *punished.* As a child by his father to keep him in the
right way (see Pr 3:12; 23:13–14).
73:15–28 The renewal of faith: In the temple the godly
man sees the destiny God has appointed for the wicked.
73:15 *If I had said.* If he had given public expression to his
thoughts as embodying true insight. *your children.* Those
characterized by a humble reliance on and commitment to
God.
73:18–20 Though the wicked seem to prosper, God has
made their position precarious, and without warning they
are swept away. The psalmist does not reflect on their state
after death but leaves it as his final word that the wicked fall
utterly and inevitably from their state of proud prosperity (see
Ps 49; cf. the final state of the godly in v. 24).
73:20 When God arouses himself as from sleep (see note
on 7:6) and deals with the wicked, they vanish like the
shadowy characters of a dream.
73:21 *heart.* See note on 4:7. *spirit.* Lit. "kidneys" (see

note on 7:9).
73:22 *a brute beast.* As stupid as a beast (see Job 18:3).
73:23–26 Although he had (almost) fallen to the level of
beastly stupidity, God has not, will not, let him go—ever!
73:24 God's counsel has overcome his folly and will guide
him through all the pitfalls of life (see 16:7; 32:8; 48:14).
take me into glory. At the end of the believer's pilgrimage
(see 49:15 and note).
73:25 Though he has envied the prosperity of the wicked,
he now confesses that nothing in heaven or earth is more
desirable than God.
73:26 *My flesh . . . heart.* My whole being (see 84:2).
heart. See note on 4:7. *portion.* Since the psalmist was a
Levite, the Lord was his portion in the promised land in that
he lived by the people's tithes dedicated to the Lord (see Nu
18:21–24; Dt 10:9; 18:1–2). Here he confesses more: The
Lord himself is his sustainer, his preserver—his very life.
73:28 *I will tell of all your deeds.* A concluding vow to
praise God for all his mercies to him (see note on 7:17).
Ps 74 A prayer for God to come to the aid of his people and
defend his cause in the face of the mocking of the enemies—the Lord's relation to his people is like that of a king to
his nation. The psalm dates from the time of the exile when
Israel had been destroyed as a nation, the promised land

Why does your anger smolder against
the sheep of your pasture? *w*
2Remember the people you purchased *x*
of old, *y*
the tribe of your inheritance, *z* whom
you redeemed *a* —
Mount Zion, *b* where you dwelt. *c*
3Turn your steps toward these
everlasting ruins, *d*
all this destruction the enemy has
brought on the sanctuary.

4Your foes roared *e* in the place where
you met with us;
they set up their standards *f* as signs.
5They behaved like men wielding axes
to cut through a thicket of trees. *g*
6They smashed all the carved *h* paneling
with their axes and hatchets.
7They burned your sanctuary to the
ground;
they defiled *i* the dwelling place *j* of
your Name. *k*
8They said in their hearts, "We will
crush *l* them completely!"

They burned *m* every place where
God was worshiped in the
land.
9We are given no miraculous signs; *n*
no prophets *o* are left,
and none of us knows how long this
will be.

10How long *p* will the enemy mock *q* you,
O God?
Will the foe revile *r* your name
forever?
11Why do you hold back your hand, your
right hand? *s*
Take it from the folds of your
garment *t* and destroy them!

12But you, O God, are my king *u* from of
old;
you bring salvation *v* upon the earth.
13It was you who split open the sea *w* by
your power;
you broke the heads of the monster *x*
in the waters.

74:1 wPs 79:13;
95:7; 100:3
74:2
xS Ex 15:16;
S 1Co 6:20
yS Dt 32:7
zS Ex 34:9
aS Ex 15:13;
S Isa 48:20
bPs 2:6 cPs 43:3;
68:16; Isa 46:13;
Joel 3:17,21;
Ob 1:17
74:3 dIsa 44:26;
52:9
74:4 eLa 2:7
fS Nu 2:2;
S Jer 4:6
74:5 gJer 46:22
74:6 hS 1Ki 6:18
74:7 iS Lev 20:3;
Ac 21:28
jS Lev 15:31
kPs 75:1
74:8 lPs 94:5

m2Ki 25:9;
2Ch 36:19;
Jer 21:10; 34:22;
52:13
74:9 nS Ex 4:17;
S 10:1 oS 1Sa 3:1
74:10 pPs 6:3;
79:5; 80:4 qver
22 rS Ps 44:16
74:11 sS Ex 15:6
tNe 5:13; Eze 5:3
74:12 uPs 2:6;
S 24:7; 68:24

vPs 27:1 74:13 wS Ex 14:21 xIsa 27:1; 51:9; Eze 29:3; 32:2

devastated and the temple reduced to ruins (see Ps 79; La 2).
Its relationship to the ministries of Jeremiah and Ezekiel is
uncertain (see note on v. 9). Thematically the psalm divides
into two halves of 11 verses each, with v. 12 (the center line;
see note there) highlighting the primary thematic element
that unifies the prayer. Verses 1–11 are framed by the
"Why's" of the people's complaint (vv. 1,11); the whole
psalm is framed by pleas for God to "remember"(vv. 2,22).
Note also that the "they's" of vv. 4–8 have their counterpoint in the "you's" of vv. 13–17 (highlighted in the Hebrew
by seven emphatic pronouns)—the mighty acts of God are
appealed to against the destructive and haughty deeds of the
enemies.
74 title *maskil.* See note on Ps 32 title. *Asaph.* See note on
Ps 73 title.
74:1–2 Initial complaint and appeal.
74:1 *Why . . . ? Why . . . ?* Cf. "How long . . . ?" (v. 10) and
"Why . . . ?" (v. 11). See note on 6:3; see also Introduction:
Theology. *forever.* So it seemed, since no relief was in sight.
anger. See note on 2:5. *sheep of your pasture.* See note on
23:1.
74:2 *purchased.* Or "acquired"; or "created." *tribe.* Here
referring to all Israel. *your inheritance.* See Dt 9:29. *redeemed.* Here, as often, a synonym for "deliver." *Mount
Zion.* See note on 9:11. This verse recalls the victory song of
Ex 15 (see especially vv. 13–17, and compare the center
verse of this psalm, v. 12, with the last verse of the song, Ex
15:18) and thus sets the stage for the other exodus recollections that follow. The Babylonian destruction of Zion seems
to be the undoing of God's great victory over Egypt when he
redeemed his people.
74:3–8 The Babylonians' high-handed destruction of the
Lord's temple.
74:3 *Turn your steps toward.* Hurry to restore.
74:4 *standards.* Probably troop standards (see Nu 1:52; Isa
31:9; Jer 4:21). *as signs.* Signifying their triumph.
74:6 *carved paneling.* See 1Ki 6:15.
74:7 *your Name.* See note on 5:11. The NIV capitalizes
"Name" when it stands for God's presence at the sanctuary
(see Dt 12:5).
74:8 *They said.* See note on 10:11. *every place where God*

was worshiped. Lit. "all the meeting places of God" (see v.
4). The reference is uncertain. At the time of the Babylonian
attacks there may have been a number of (illegitimate) places
in Judah where people went to worship God (see notes on
1Ki 3:2; 2Ki 18:4).
74:9–11 The complaint and prayer renewed (see vv. 1–2).
74:9 *no miraculous signs.* As there were at the time of the
exodus (see vv. 13–15; 78:43). *no prophets.* Jeremiah had
been taken to Egypt (see Jer 43:6–7), but whether Ezekiel
was no longer prophesying is unknown. Perhaps this psalm
was composed by an Asaphite who remained in Israel, part of
a small group overlooked by Johanan when that army officer
led the remnant to Egypt (see Jer 43:4–7).
74:10 *mock you . . . revile your name.* See v. 18; see also
v. 22; 2Ki 18:32–35; Isa 37:6,23.
74:12 The center verse (center line in the Hebrew text; see
note on 6:6). The whole psalm presupposes the truth confessed here: God is Israel's King, her hope and Savior; Israel
is God's people (kingdom). This accounts for both the complaint and the prayer, and why the destruction of Israel
brings with it the mocking of God. *my.* Communal use of the
singular pronoun (see note on Ps 30 title). *from of old.* From
the days of the exodus (see Ex 3:7; 19:5–6).
74:13–17 The Lord is the mighty God of salvation and
creation (see 65:6–7 and note).
74:13–14 Recollection of God's mighty acts when he
delivered his people from Egypt. The imagery is borrowed
from ancient Near Eastern creation myths, in which the
primeval chaotic waters were depicted as a many-headed
monster that the creator-god overcame, after which he
established the world order (see note on 32:6). The poet
here interweaves creation and salvation themes to celebrate
the fact that the God of Israel has shown by his saving acts
(his opening of the Red Sea for his people and his destruction
of the Egyptians) that he is able to overcome all hostile
powers to redeem his people and establish his new order in
the world. For poetic use of this imagery (1) to celebrate
God's creation works see 89:10; Job 9:13; 26:12–13; (2) to
celebrate the deliverance from Egypt see Isa 51:9; (3) to
announce a future deliverance of Israel see Isa 27:1. Echoes
of the same imagery are present in the judgment announced

14It was you who crushed the heads of
Leviathan[y]
and gave him as food to the creatures
of the desert.[z]
15It was you who opened up springs[a] and
streams;
you dried up[b] the ever flowing
rivers.
16The day is yours, and yours also the
night;
you established the sun and moon.[c]
17It was you who set all the boundaries[d]
of the earth;
you made both summer and winter.[e]

18Remember how the enemy has mocked
you, O LORD,
how foolish people[f] have reviled
your name.
19Do not hand over the life of your dove[g]
to wild beasts;
do not forget the lives of your
afflicted[h] people forever.
20Have regard for your covenant,[i]
because haunts of violence fill the
dark places[j] of the land.
21Do not let the oppressed[k] retreat in
disgrace;
may the poor and needy[l] praise your
name.
22Rise up,[m] O God, and defend your
cause;
remember how fools[n] mock you all
day long.
23Do not ignore the clamor[o] of your
adversaries,[p]
the uproar[q] of your enemies,[r] which
rises continually.

74:14 [y]S Job 3:8 [z]Isa 13:21; 23:13; 34:14; Jer 50:39 **74:15** [a]S Ex 17:6; S Nu 20:11 [b]S Ex 14:29; S Jos 2:10 **74:16** [c]S Ge 1:16; Ps 136:7-9 **74:17** [d]Dt 32:8; Ac 17:26 [e]S Ge 8:22 **74:18** [f]Dt 32:6 **74:19** [g]S Ge 8:8; S Isa 59:11 [h]S Ps 9:18 **74:20** [i]S Ge 6:18 [j]Job 34:22 **74:21** [k]Ps 9:9; 10:18; 103:6; Isa 58:10 [l]S Ps 35:10 **74:22** [m]Ps 17:13 [n]S Ps 53:1 **74:23** [o]Isa 31:4 [p]S Ps 65:7 [q]S Ps 46:6 [r]S Nu 25:17 **75:1** [s]Ps 145:18 [t]S Jos 3:5; Ps 44:1; S 71:16; 77:12; 105:2; 107:8,15; 145:5, 12 **75:2** [u]S Ex 13:10 [v]S Ps 7:11 **75:3** [w]Isa 24:19 [x]1Sa 2:8; S 2Sa 22:8 **75:4** [y]S Ps 5:5 [z]S 1Sa 2:3 [a]Zec 1:21 **75:5** [b]S Job 15:25

Psalm 75

For the director of music. ⌞To the tune of⌟ "Do Not Destroy." A psalm of Asaph. A song.

1We give thanks to you, O God,
we give thanks, for your Name is
near;[s]
men tell of your wonderful deeds.[t]

2You say, "I choose the appointed
time;[u]
it is I who judge uprightly.[v]
3When the earth and all its people
quake,[w]
it is I who hold its pillars[x] firm. *Selah*
4To the arrogant[y] I say, 'Boast no
more,'[z]
and to the wicked, 'Do not lift up
your horns.[a]
5Do not lift your horns against heaven;
do not speak with outstretched
neck.[b]' "
6No one from the east or the west
or from the desert can exalt a man.

against Egypt in Eze 29:3–5; 32:2–6.
74:15 Recollection of God's water miracles at the Red Sea, in the desert and at the Jordan.
74:16–17 God is the One who established the orders of creation; he (alone) is able to effect redemption and establish his kingdom in the world against all creaturely opposition.
74:18–23 A prayer for God to defend his cause and restore his people.
74:18 See vv. 2,10. *foolish people.* The "foes" of v. 10 are here called fools for their contempt of God (see v. 22; see also NIV text note on 14:1).
74:19 *your dove.* Israel—probably a figure of endearment (see SS 2:14; 5:2; 6:9; see also Ps 68:13 and note). *wild beasts.* See note on 7:2.
74:20 *your covenant.* God's covenant to be the God of Israel, who makes them secure and richly blessed in the promised land (see Ex 19:5–6; 23:27–31; 34:10–11; Lev 26:11–12,42,44–45; Dt 28:1–14; see also Ps 105:8–11; 106:45; 111:5,9; Isa 54:10; Jer 14:21; Eze 16:60).
74:21 *poor and needy.* See note on 34:6. *praise your name.* May they have cause to do so.
74:22 *Rise up.* See note on 3:7.
74:23 *clamor . . . uproar.* See 64:2.
Ps 75 A song of reassurance when arrogant worldly powers threaten Israel's security. The psalm may date from the time of the Assyrian menace (see 2Ki 18:13–19:37). See also Ps 11; 76. Thematic parallels to the song of Hannah (1Sa 2:1–10) are numerous. The worshiping congregation speaks (v. 1), perhaps led in its praise by one of the descendants of Asaph (v. 9). The psalm is framed by thanksgiving (v. 1) and praise (vv. 9–10). Two stanzas of four (Hebrew) lines each form the body of the psalm, and each stanza is composed of two couplets. The first stanza contains a reassuring word from heaven; the second contains a triumphant response from earth.
75 title *For the director of music.* See note on Ps 4 title. ⌞*To the tune of*⌟. See note on Ps 9 title. *Do Not Destroy.* See Ps 57; 58; 59 titles. *Asaph.* See note on Ps 73 title. *song.* See note on Ps 30 title.
75:1 The congregation begins with thanksgiving in the form of praise (see 7:17; 28:7; 30:12; 35:18). *Name.* See notes on 5:11; 74:7. *wonderful deeds.* See note on 9:1.
75:2–5 A reassuring word from above: God will not fail to call the arrogant to account. It is not clear whether a new word from the Lord is heard or whether these verses recall (and perhaps summarize) earlier prophetic words (such as those of Isaiah in 2Ki 19:21–34).
75:2 God will not fail to judge—but in his own time.
75:3 When, because of the upsurge of evil powers, the whole moral order of the world seems to have crumbled, God still guarantees its stability (see note on 11:3). *pillars.* A figure for that which stabilizes the world order (see note on 24:2).
75:4 *arrogant . . . wicked.* To the psalmists the wicked are both arrogant (see especially Ps 10; 73:4–12; 94:4; see also note on 31:23) and foolish (see 14:1; 74:18,22; 92:6; 94:8). *lift up your horns.* A figure for defiant opposition, based on the action of attacking bulls. "Horn" (see also v. 10) is a common Biblical metaphor for vigor or strength (see NIV text note on 18:2).
75:5 *outstretched neck.* A sign of defiance.
75:6–8 Triumphant echo from earth: perhaps spoken by the Levitical song leader in elaboration of the comforting word from God.

⁷But it is God who judges: ^c
He brings one down, he exalts
another. ^d
⁸In the hand of the LORD is a cup
full of foaming wine mixed ^e with
spices;
he pours it out, and all the wicked of
the earth
drink it down to its very dregs. ^f

⁹As for me, I will declare ^g this forever;
I will sing ^h praise to the God of
Jacob. ⁱ
¹⁰I will cut off the horns of all the
wicked,
but the horns of the righteous will be
lifted up. ^j

Psalm 76

For the director of music. With stringed
instruments. A psalm of Asaph. A song.

¹In Judah God is known;
his name is great ^k in Israel.
²His tent is in Salem, ^l
his dwelling place in Zion. ^m

³There he broke the flashing arrows, ⁿ
the shields and the swords, the
weapons of war. ^o *Selah*

⁴You are resplendent with light, ^p
more majestic than mountains rich
with game.
⁵Valiant men ^q lie plundered,
they sleep their last sleep; ^r
not one of the warriors
can lift his hands.
⁶At your rebuke, ^s O God of Jacob,
both horse and chariot ^t lie still.
⁷You alone are to be feared. ^u
Who can stand ^v before you when
you are angry? ^w
⁸From heaven you pronounced
judgment,
and the land feared ^x and was
quiet—
⁹when you, O God, rose up to judge, ^y
to save all the afflicted ^z of the land.
Selah
¹⁰Surely your wrath against men brings
you praise, ^a

75:7 ^cS Ge 16:5;
Ps 50:6; 58:11;
Rev 18:8
^d1Sa 2:7;
S Job 5:11;
Ps 147:6;
Eze 21:26;
Da 2:21
75:8 ^ePr 23:30
^fIsa 51:17;
Jer 25:15;
Zec 12:2
75:9 ^gPs 40:10
^hPs 108:1
ⁱS Ge 24:12;
Ps 76:6
75:10 ^jPs 89:17;
92:10; 112:9;
148:14
76:1 ^kPs 99:3
76:2 ^lS Ge 14:18;
Heb 7:1
^mS 2Sa 5:7;
Ps 2:6

76:3 ⁿEze 39:9
^oPs 46:9
76:4 ^pS Ps 36:9
76:5 ^qS Jdg 20:44
^rS Ps 13:3;
S Mt 9:24
76:6 ^sS Ps 50:21
^tS Ex 15:1
76:7
^u1Ch 16:25
^vS Ezr 9:15;
Rev 6:17 ^wPs 2:5;
Na 1:6
76:8
^xS 1Ch 16:30;
Eze 38:20
76:9 ^yS Ps 9:8;
58:11; 74:22;
82:8; 96:13

^zS Ps 72:4 76:10 ^aEx 9:16; Ro 9:17

75:8 *cup.* See note on 16:5. *mixed with spices.* The spices
used increased the intoxicating effect (see Pr 9:2,5;
23:29–30; SS 8:2; Isa 65:11). *drink it down.* Because God
pours it out, they have no choice.
75:9 Concluding vow to praise God forever (see note on
7:17) for his righteous judgments. *me.* Probably the Levitical
song leader speaking representatively for the people, but the
pronoun may be a communal use of the singular, as in 74:12
(see note on Ps 30 title). *Jacob.* A synonym for Israel (see Ge
32:28).
75:10 It is unclear who is speaking. The action pledged
appears unlikely for a Levite but appropriate for a king (see Ps
101). This is not, however, a royal psalm. It seems best, then,
to suppose that the speaker(s) of v. 9 recall(s) another word
from the Lord. The connection would be: " . . . the God of
Jacob/(who declares), 'I will . . .' " *righteous.* See note on
1:5. *lifted up.* See v. 7; see also note on v. 4.
Ps 76 A celebration of the Lord's invincible power in
defense of Jerusalem, his royal city. The psalm is thematically
related to Ps 46; 48; 87 (see introduction to Ps 46). The
ancient tradition may well be correct that the psalm was
composed after the Lord's destruction of Sennacherib's army
when it threatened Jerusalem (see 2Ki 19:35). Structurally,
the opening (vv. 1–3) and closing (vv. 11–12) stanzas contain the main thematic development. Between them, a seven-
en-verse stanza of praise addressed to God (vv. 4–10) celebrates his awesome act of judgment. The internal structure is
notable: Verses 4,7,10 present general reflections, while the
intervening verses recall the judgment itself. Verse 7, the
center line (see note on 6:6), states the main theme of this
stanza.
76 title *For the director of music.* See note on Ps 4 title.
With stringed instruments. See note on Ps 4 title. *Asaph.* See
note on Ps 73 title. *song.* See note on Ps 30 title.
76:1–3 God's crushing defeat of the enemy in defense of
Zion.
76:1 *is known.* Now especially—as a result of his marvel-

ous act. *Israel.* The poet probably does not intend to distinguish between the two kingdoms (Judah and Israel) but only,
by joining their names together, to refer to the whole of
God's covenant people. Moreover, as a result of the Assyrian
invasions, many displaced Israelites from the northern kingdom now resided in and around Jerusalem.
76:2 *tent.* Lit. "booth," referring to the temple. Since the
Lord has just achieved a great victory over a menacing army,
the poet may have wished to speak of the temple as the
Lord's campaign tent (see 2Sa 11:11; 1Ki 20:12,16). But see
also 18:11 ("canopy"); 31:20 ("dwelling"). *Salem.* Jerusalem, as the parallelism makes clear (see note on Ge 14:18).
Zion. See note on 9:11.
76:4–10 Praise of God's awesome majesty, whose mighty
judgment evokes fearful reverence (see introduction).
76:5–6 Perhaps echoes also God's victory over the Egyptians at the Red Sea (see Ex 14:28,30; 15:4–5,10).
76:6 *rebuke.* This word, when predicated of God, usually
refers to either (1) the thunder of his fierce majesty by which
he wields his sovereign control over cosmic entities (see
18:15; 104:7; 106:9; Job 26:11; Isa 50:2; Na 1:4) or
repulses his enemies (as here; see also 9:5; 68:30; Isa
17:13), or (2) the thunder of his wrath (see 80:16; Isa
51:20; 54:9; 66:15; Mal 2:3). *God of Jacob.* A link with Ps
75 (see 75:9 and note).
76:7 The thematic center of vv. 4–10 (see note on 6:6).
76:8 *From heaven.* Though God is present in Zion (see v.
2), he sovereignly rules from heaven.
76:10 *wrath.* See note on 2:5. *brings you praise.* When his
judgments bring deliverance, those rescued praise him. If the
alternative translation in the NIV text note is taken, "the
wrath of men brings you praise" would mean that when men
rise against God's kingdom, he crushes them in wrath to his
own praise as Victor and Deliverer. And "the remainder of
wrath" would indicate that particular judgments do not
exhaust his wrath; a remainder is left to deal with other
hostile powers.

and the survivors of your wrath are
   restrained. h

11Make vows to the LORD your God and
      fulfill them; b
   let all the neighboring lands
   bring gifts c to the One to be feared.
12He breaks the spirit of rulers;
   he is feared by the kings of the earth.

Psalm 77

For the director of music. For Jeduthun.
Of Asaph. A psalm.

1I cried out to God d for help;
   I cried out to God to hear me.
2When I was in distress, e I sought the
      Lord;
   at night f I stretched out untiring
      hands g
   and my soul refused to be
      comforted. h

3I remembered i you, O God, and I
      groaned; j
   I mused, and my spirit grew faint. k
                                    Selah
4You kept my eyes from closing;
   I was too troubled to speak. l
5I thought about the former days, m
   the years of long ago;
6I remembered my songs in the night.

My heart mused and my spirit
   inquired:

7"Will the Lord reject forever? n
   Will he never show his favor o again?
8Has his unfailing love p vanished
      forever?
   Has his promise q failed for all time?
9Has God forgotten to be merciful? r
   Has he in anger withheld his
      compassion? s "   Selah

10Then I thought, "To this I will appeal:
   the years of the right hand t of the
      Most High."
11I will remember the deeds of the LORD;
   yes, I will remember your miracles u
      of long ago.
12I will meditate v on all your works
   and consider all your mighty deeds. w

13Your ways, O God, are holy.
   What god is so great as our God? x
14You are the God who performs
      miracles; y
   you display your power among the
      peoples.
15With your mighty arm you redeemed
      your people, z
   the descendants of Jacob and Joseph.
                                    Selah

16The waters a saw you, O God,

Cross references

76:11 hS Lev 22:18; S Ps 50:14; Ecc 5:4-5
cS 2Ch 32:23
77:1 dS 1Ki 8:52
77:2 eS Ge 32:7; S 2Sa 22:7; S Ps 118:5
fPs 6:6; 22:2; 88:1 gS Ex 9:29; S Job 11:13
hS Ge 37:35; Mt 2:18
77:3 iPs 78:35 jEx 2:23; S Ps 6:6; Jer 45:3
kS Ps 6:2
77:4 lS Ps 39:2
77:5 mDt 32:7; Ps 44:1; 143:5; Ecc 7:10

77:7 nS 1Ch 28:9 oPs 85:1; 102:13; 106:4
77:8 pS Ps 6:4; 90:14 q2Pe 3:9
77:9 rPs 25:6; 40:11; 51:1 sIsa 49:15
77:10 tS Ex 15:6
77:11 uS Ne 9:17
77:12 vS Ge 24:63 wPs 143:5
77:13 xS Ex 15:11; S Ps 71:19; 86:8
77:14 yS Ex 3:20; S 34:10
77:15 zS Ex 6:6
77:16 aEx 14:21, 28; Isa 50:2; Hab 3:8

h 10 Or Surely the wrath of men brings you praise, / and
with the remainder of wrath you arm yourself

76:11–12 Let Israel acknowledge God's help with grateful vows; let the nations acknowledge his sovereign rule with tribute.
76:11 Make vows. See note on 50:14.
76:12 spirit of rulers. Their bold rebelliousness.
Ps 77 Comforting reflections in a time of great distress. The interplay of verb forms in vv. 1–6 makes it uncertain whether the psalm is a prayer (in which case the verbs of these verses would have to be rendered in the present tense) or the recollection of a past experience (as the NIV understands it). The distress appears to be personal rather than national. Comparison of vv. 16–19 with Hab 3:8–10 suggests, but does not prove, a time late in the monarchy. The poetic development advances from anguished bewilderment (vv. 1–9) to comforting recollection (vv. 10–20). A striking and dramatic feature is the insertion of a four-verse stanza (vv. 16–19) between the third and fourth verses of another four-verse stanza (vv. 13–15,20).
77 title For the director of music. See note on Ps 4 title. Jeduthun. See note on Ps 39 title. Asaph. See note on Ps 73 title.
77:1–9 Anguished perplexity over God's inaction, when he fails to respond to unceasing and urgent prayers.
77:2 soul. See note on 6:3.
77:3–6 Remembrance of God's past mercies intensifies the present perplexity (as also in 22:1–11). God's failure to act now is so troubling that he cannot sleep (cf. 3:5; 4:8) and words fail (but see vv. 10–20).
77:6 heart. See note on 4:7.
77:7–9 Though words fail (v. 4), troubled thoughts will not go away.

77:8 unfailing love. See note on 6:4.
77:9 anger. See note on 2:5.
77:10–20 Reassuring recollection of God's mighty acts in behalf of Israel in the exodus.
77:10–12 Faith's decision to look beyond the present troubles—and God's bewildering inactivity—to draw hope anew from God's saving acts of old.
77:10 Most High. See note on Ge 14:19.
77:11,14 miracles. See note on 9:1 ("wonders").
77:13–20 God's mighty acts in the exodus recalled.
77:13 Appears to echo Ex 15:11. are holy. Or "are seen in the sanctuary" (see 63:2).
77:15 redeemed. Here, as often, a synonym for "deliver" (see 74:2). Joseph. OT authors sometimes refer to the northern kingdom as "Joseph" (or "Ephraim," Joseph's son) in distinction from the southern kingdom of Judah (see 78:67; 2Sa 19:20; 1Ki 11:28; Eze 37:16,19; Am 5:6,15; 6:6; Zec 10:6). However, here and elsewhere (see 80:1; 81:5; Ob 18) Joseph—the one elevated to the position of firstborn (see Ge 48:5 and note; Jos 16:1–4; 1Ch 5:2; Eze 47:13)—represents the whole of his generation and thus also all the descendants of Jacob.
77:16–19 A poetically heightened description of the majesty of God displayed when he opened a way through the Red Sea. Verses 16,19 speak expressly of that event; the intervening verses (vv. 17–18) evoke the majesty of God displayed in the thunderstorm and earthquake. Ex 14:19 speaks only of God's cloud, not of a thunderstorm or earthquake, but the Hebrew poets often associated either or both with the Lord's coming to effect redemption or judgment—no doubt because these were the two most fearsome

the waters saw you and writhed; [b]
the very depths were convulsed.
[17]The clouds poured water, [c]
the skies resounded with thunder; [d]
your arrows [e] flashed back and forth.
[18]Your thunder was heard in the
whirlwind, [f]
your lightning [g] lit up the world;
the earth trembled and quaked. [h]
[19]Your path [i] led through the sea, [j]
your way through the mighty waters,
though your footprints were not seen.
[20]You led your people [k] like a flock [l]
by the hand of Moses and Aaron. [m]

Psalm 78

A maskil[1] of Asaph.

[1]O my people, hear my teaching; [n]
listen to the words of my mouth.
[2]I will open my mouth in parables, [o]
I will utter hidden things, things from
of old—

[3]what we have heard and known,
what our fathers have told us. [p]
[4]We will not hide them from their
children; [q]
we will tell the next generation [r]
the praiseworthy deeds [s] of the LORD,
his power, and the wonders [t] he has
done.
[5]He decreed statutes [u] for Jacob [v]
and established the law in Israel,
which he commanded our forefathers
to teach their children,
[6]so the next generation would know
them,
even the children yet to be born, [w]
and they in turn would tell their
children.
[7]Then they would put their trust in God
and would not forget [x] his deeds
but would keep his commands. [y]
[8]They would not be like their
forefathers [z] —

77:16	[b]Ps 114:4; Hab 3:10
77:17	[c]S Jdg 5:4
	[d]S Ex 9:23; S Ps 29:3
	[e]S Dt 32:23
77:18	[f]S Ps 55:8
	[g]S 2Sa 22:13
	[h]S Jdg 5:4
77:19	[i]S Ex 14:22
	[j]S Job 9:8
77:20	[k]S Ex 13:21
	[l]Ps 78:52; Isa 63:11
	[m]S Ex 4:16; S Nu 33:1
78:1	[n]Isa 51:4; 55:3
78:2	[o]S Ps 49:4; S Mt 13:35*
78:3	[p]S Jdg 6:13
78:4	[q]S Dt 11:19
	[r]S Dt 32:7; S Ps 71:18
	[s]Ps 26:7; 71:17
	[t]S Job 5:9
78:5	[u]Ps 19:7; 81:5 [v]Ps 147:19
78:6	[w]S Ps 22:31
78:7	[x]S Dt 6:12
	[y]S Dt 5:29
78:8	[z]S 2Ch 30:7

[1]Title: Probably a literary or musical term

displays of power known to them (see 18:12–14; 68:8; Jdg 5:4–5; Hab 3:6,10). Here the psalmist declares: It was the God of thunderstorm and earthquake who made his majestic way through the mighty waters of the sea to bring his people out of bondage. For Christians the display of God's power in behalf of his people now includes the resurrection of Jesus Christ from the dead (see Mt 28:2; cf. Eph 1:18–23).

77:17 *arrows.* Lightning bolts.

77:20 Completes the thought of v. 15 (see introduction). *led your people.* Through the Desert of Sinai.

Ps 78 A psalm of instruction—of warnings not to repeat Israel's sins of the past but to remember God's saving acts and marvelously persistent grace and, remembering, to keep faith with him and his covenant. Here as elsewhere (pervasively in the OT), trust in and loyalty to God on the part of God's people are covenant matters. They do not spring from abstract principles (such as the formal structure of the God-man relationship) or from general human consciousness (such as feelings of dependence on "God" or a sense of awe in the presence of the "holy"), but they result from remembering God's mighty saving acts. Correspondingly, unfaithfulness is the more blameworthy because it contemptuously disregards all God's wonderful acts in his people's behalf (see Ps 105–106).

The psalm probably dates from the period of the divided monarchy and may have been composed about the time of the prophet Hosea (both Hosea and Isaiah speak frequently of the northern kingdom as Ephraim since it was the dominant tribe of that realm). Israel's unfaithfulness is here epitomized in the sin of Ephraim (v. 9); the psalm concludes by recalling the rejection of "Israel" (v. 59) and the abandonment of Shiloh (v. 60), but the election of Judah and Mount Zion (v. 68). Coming, as may be assumed, from the pen of an Asaphite, the psalm was no doubt a warning to worshipers at Jerusalem not to fall away after the manner of their brothers to the north.

By placing this psalm next to Ps 77, the editors of the Psalter ranged David alongside Moses (and Aaron) as the Lord's shepherd over his people (see vv. 70–72; 77:20) who brought the exodus to its (provisionally) climactic fruition by completing the conquest of the promised land—a perspective apparently shared by the author of the psalm.

The psalm is composed of 77 (Hebrew) lines (72 numbered verses) and seven stanzas—with an 11-line introduction. After the introduction, the structure of the stanzas is symmetrical: 8 lines, 16 lines, 9 lines, 16 lines, 9 lines, 8 lines. The two sequences of 16 lines–9 lines constitute a thematic cycle, while the two 8-line stanzas frame the double cycle and underscore the contrast between the sin of Israel ("Ephraim," vv. 9–16) and the unending mercy of God to his people—mercy that is evidenced in his victory over his enemies and his election of Zion (in Judah) and David (vv. 65–72).

78 title *maskil.* See note on Ps 32 title. *Asaph.* See note on Ps 73 title.

78:1–8 Our children must hear what our fathers have told us, so that they may be faithful to the Lord.

78:1–2 This introduction is written in the style of a wisdom writer (see Introduction to Proverbs: Wisdom Literature; see also Ps 49:1–4).

78:2 *parables . . . hidden things.* The Hebrew underlying these two expressions occurs in 49:4 ("proverb," "riddle") and Eze 17:2 ("parable," "allegory")—which raises the question of whether the author is here influenced by prophetic use of wisdom language. While both terms had specialized uses—those reflected in 49:4—they apparently also became conventionalized more generally for instruction in a wide variety of forms. *things from of old.* Things for instruction from the past. Mt 13:35 refers to this verse as a prophecy of Jesus' parabolic teaching. Matthew apparently perceived in this psalm a prophetic voice anticipating that of the great Prophet. The "parables" of the psalm are, however, more like the teaching of Stephen (Ac 7) than that of Jesus.

78:4–5 The Lord's saving acts and covenant statutes—both must be taught, and in relationship, for together they remain the focal point for faith and obedience down through the generations (see vv. 7–8).

78:4 *not hide them.* See Job 15:18.

78:5 *teach their children.* See, e.g., Ex 10:2; 12:26–27; 13:8,14; Dt 4:9; 6:20–21.

78:8 *stubborn and rebellious.* Like a rebellious son (see Dt 9:6–7, 24; 31:27). *generation.* A people with certain characteristics (see 24:6; Dt 32:5,20), thus not limited to the exodus generation (see vv. 9–11,56–64). *hearts.* See note

a stubborn[a] and rebellious[b]
  generation,
whose hearts were not loyal to God,
whose spirits were not faithful to
  him.

[9]The men of Ephraim, though armed
  with bows,[c]
  turned back on the day of battle;[d]
[10]they did not keep God's covenant[e]
  and refused to live by his law.[f]
[11]They forgot what he had done,[g]
  the wonders he had shown them.
[12]He did miracles[h] in the sight of their
  fathers
  in the land of Egypt,[i] in the region of
  Zoan.[j]
[13]He divided the sea[k] and led them
  through;
  he made the water stand firm like a
  wall.[l]
[14]He guided them with the cloud by day
  and with light from the fire all
  night.[m]
[15]He split the rocks[n] in the desert
  and gave them water as abundant as
  the seas;
[16]he brought streams out of a rocky crag
  and made water flow down like
  rivers.
[17]But they continued to sin[o] against him,
  rebelling in the desert against the
  Most High.
[18]They willfully put God to the test[p]
  by demanding the food they craved.[q]
[19]They spoke against God,[r] saying,

"Can God spread a table in the
  desert?
[20]When he struck the rock, water gushed
  out,[s]
  and streams flowed abundantly.
But can he also give us food?
  Can he supply meat[t] for his people?"
[21]When the LORD heard them, he was
  very angry;
  his fire broke out[u] against Jacob,
  and his wrath rose against Israel,
[22]for they did not believe in God
  or trust[v] in his deliverance.
[23]Yet he gave a command to the skies
  above
  and opened the doors of the
  heavens;[w]
[24]he rained down manna[x] for the people
  to eat,
  he gave them the grain of heaven.
[25]Men ate the bread of angels;
  he sent them all the food they could
  eat.
[26]He let loose the east wind[y] from the
  heavens
  and led forth the south wind by his
  power.
[27]He rained meat down on them like
  dust,
  flying birds[z] like sand on the
  seashore.
[28]He made them come down inside their
  camp,
  all around their tents.
[29]They ate till they had more than
  enough,[a]

Cross references

78:8 [a]S Ex 32:9
[b]S Ex 23:21;
S Dt 21:18;
Isa 30:9; 65:2
78:9 [c]ver 57;
1Ch 12:2;
Hos 7:16
[d]S Jdg 20:39
78:10 [e]S Jos 7:11;
S 2Ki 17:15
[f]S Ex 16:28;
S Jer 11:8
78:11 [g]Ps 106:13
78:12 [h]S Ne 9:17;
Ps 106:22
[i]Ex 11:9
[j]S Nu 13:22
78:13 [k]S Ex 14:21;
Ps 66:6; 136:13
[l]S Ex 14:22;
S 15:8
78:14 [m]Ex 13:21;
Ps 105:39
78:15 [n]S Nu 20:11;
1Co 10:4
78:17 [o]ver 32,
40; Dt 9:22;
Isa 30:1; 63:10;
Heb 3:16
78:18 [p]S Ex 17:2;
1Co 10:9
[q]S Ex 15:24;
Nu 11:4
78:19 [r]Nu 21:5
78:20 [s]S Nu 20:11;
S Isa 35:6
[t]Nu 11:18
78:21 [u]S Nu 11:1
78:22 [v]S Dt 1:32;
Heb 3:19
78:23 [w]Ge 7:11;
S 2Ki 7:2
78:24 [x]S Ex 16:4;
Jn 6:31*
78:26 [y]S Nu 11:31
78:27 [z]S Ex 16:13;
Nu 11:31
78:29 [a]S Nu 11:20

Study notes

on 4:7.
78:9–16 The northern kingdom has violated God's covenant, not remembering his saving acts (a message emphasized by the prophets Amos and Hosea). Israel's history with God has been a long series of rebellions on her part (vv. 9–16,32–39,56–64), beginning already in the desert (vv. 17–31,40–55).
78:9 *men of Ephraim.* The northern kingdom, dominated by the tribe of Ephraim (see introduction). *turned back.* Neither the tribe of Ephraim nor the northern kingdom had a reputation for cowardice or ineffectiveness in battle (see, e.g., Dt 33:17). This verse is best understood as a metaphor for Israel's betrayal of God's covenant (see v. 10), related to the figure of the "faulty bow" (v. 57).
78:12–16 A summary reference to the plagues in Egypt and to the water miracles at the Red Sea and in the desert. In the two cycles that follow (vv. 17–39,40–64), further elaboration intensifies the indictment.
78:12 See Ex 7–12. *Zoan.* A city in the northeast part of the Nile delta (see v. 43; see also Nu 13:22 and note).
78:13 See Ex 14:1–15:21.
78:15–16 See v. 20; Ex 17:6; Nu 20:8,10–11.
78:17–31 Israel's rebelliousness in the desert; God's marvelous provision of food—and his anger.
78:17 *continued.* Although no sin in the desert has yet been mentioned, the poet probably expected his readers to

recall (in conjunction with the miraculous provisions of water just mentioned) how the people grumbled at Marah because of lack of water (see Ex 15:24). *Most High.* See vv. 35,56; see also note on Ge 14:19.
78:18 See Ex 16:2–3. *put God to the test.* See vv. 41,56; see also note on Ex 17:2.
78:19 *Can God spread a table . . . ?* For a different use of the same imagery see 23:5.
78:20 *food . . . meat.* The poet is probably combining and compressing two episodes (Ex 16:2–3; Nu 11:4).
78:21 *wrath.* See vv. 31,49–50,58–59,62; see also note on 2:5.
78:23 *opened the doors of the heavens.* For this imagery see Ge 7:11; 2Ki 7:11; Mal 3:10.
78:25 *bread of angels.* So called because it came down from heaven. *angels.* Lit. "mighty ones." The Hebrew word is used only here of the angels, but reference is clearly to heavenly beings (see 103:20).
78:26–28 See Ex 16:13; Nu 11:31.
78:26 *east wind . . . south wind.* Since the quail were migrating from Egypt at this time, the south wind may have carried them north and the east wind may have diverted them to the desert area occupied by the Israelites (the book of Numbers does not provide wind directions).
78:27 *like dust . . . like sand.* Similes for a huge number (see note on Ge 13:16).

for he had given them what they
craved.
30But before they turned from the food
they craved,
even while it was still in their
mouths,[b]
31God's anger rose against them;
he put to death the sturdiest[c] among
them,
cutting down the young men of
Israel.

32In spite of all this, they kept on
sinning;[d]
in spite of his wonders,[e] they did not
believe.[f]
33So he ended their days in futility[g]
and their years in terror.
34Whenever God slew them, they would
seek[h] him;
they eagerly turned to him again.
35They remembered that God was their
Rock,[i]
that God Most High was their
Redeemer.[j]
36But then they would flatter him with
their mouths,[k]
lying to him with their tongues;
37their hearts were not loyal[l] to him,
they were not faithful to his
covenant.
38Yet he was merciful;[m]
he forgave[n] their iniquities[o]
and did not destroy them.
Time after time he restrained his anger[p]
and did not stir up his full wrath.
39He remembered that they were but
flesh,[q]
a passing breeze[r] that does not
return.

40How often they rebelled[s] against him
in the desert[t]
and grieved him[u] in the wasteland!
41Again and again they put God to the
test;[v]
they vexed the Holy One of Israel.[w]
42They did not remember[x] his power—
the day he redeemed them from the
oppressor,[y]
43the day he displayed his miraculous
signs[z] in Egypt,
his wonders[a] in the region of Zoan.
44He turned their rivers to blood;[b]
they could not drink from their
streams.
45He sent swarms of flies[c] that devoured
them,
and frogs[d] that devastated them.
46He gave their crops to the
grasshopper,[e]
their produce to the locust.[f]
47He destroyed their vines with hail[g]
and their sycamore-figs with sleet.
48He gave over their cattle to the hail,
their livestock[h] to bolts of lightning.
49He unleashed against them his hot
anger,[i]
his wrath, indignation and hostility—
a band of destroying angels.[j]
50He prepared a path for his anger;
he did not spare them from death
but gave them over to the plague.
51He struck down all the firstborn of
Egypt,[k]
the firstfruits of manhood in the tents
of Ham.[l]
52But he brought his people out like a
flock;[m]
he led them like sheep through the
desert.
53He guided them safely, so they were
unafraid;
but the sea engulfed[n] their
enemies.[o]
54Thus he brought them to the border of
his holy land,
to the hill country his right hand[p]
had taken.
55He drove out nations[q] before them

78:30 [b]S Nu 11:33 **78:31** [c]Isa 10:16 **78:32** [d]S ver 17 [e]ver 11 [f]ver 22 **78:33** [g]Nu 14:29,35 **78:34** [h]S Dt 4:29; Hos 5:15 **78:35** [i]S Ge 49:24 [j]S Dt 9:26 **78:36** [k]Eze 33:31 **78:37** [l]ver 8; Ac 8:21 **78:38** [m]S Ex 34:6 [n]Isa 1:25; 27:9; 48:10; Da 11:35 [o]Ps 25:11; 85:2 [p]S Job 9:13; S Isa 30:18 **78:39** [q]S Ge 6:3; S Isa 29:5 [r]S Job 7:7; Jas 4:14 **78:40** [s]S Ex 23:21 [t]Ps 95:8; 106:14 [u]Eph 4:30 **78:41** [v]S Ex 17:2 [w]S 2Ki 19:22; Ps 71:22; 89:18 **78:42** [x]S Jdg 3:7; S Ne 9:17 [y]S Ps 27:11 **78:43** [z]Ex 10:1 [a]S Ex 3:20 **78:44** [b]Ex 7:20,21; Ps 105:29 **78:45** [c]Ex 8:24; Ps 105:31 [d]S Ex 8:2,6 **78:46** [e]Na 3:15 [f]S Ex 10:13 **78:47** [g]Ex 9:23; Ps 105:32; 147:17 **78:48** [h]Ex 9:25 **78:49** [i]Ex 15:7 [j]S Ge 19:13; 1Co 10:10 **78:51** [k]S Ex 12:12; Ps 135:8 [l]Ps 105:23; 106:22 **78:52** [m]S Job 21:11; S Ps 28:9; 77:20 **78:53** [n]S Ex 14:28 [o]Ex 15:7; Ps 106:10 **78:54** [p]Ps 44:3 **78:55** [q]Ps 44:2

78:30–31 See Nu 11:33.
78:32–39 Rebelliousness, which became Israel's way of life, showed itself early in the desert wandering (vv. 17–31) and continued throughout that journey.
78:32 *did not believe.* That God could give them victory over the Canaanites (see Nu 14:11).
78:33 The exodus generation was condemned to die in the desert (see Nu 14:22–23,28–35).
78:34–37 A cycle repeated frequently during the period of the judges.
78:35 *Rock.* See note on 18:2. *Redeemer.* Deliverer (see note on Ex 6:6).
78:36 See Isa 29:13.
78:37 *hearts.* See note on 4:7.
78:38 See Ex 32:14; Nu 14:20. *forgave.* See note on 65:3.
78:39 See 103:14; see also note on 10:18.
78:40–64 The second cycle (the first is vv. 17–39).
78:40–55 Israel's rebelliousness began in the desert; she did not remember how she had been delivered from oppression by God's plagues upon Egypt (see v. 12). Yet he brought them through the sea and the desert and established them in the promised land.
78:41 *Holy One of Israel.* See 71:22; 89:18; see also note on Isa 1:4.
78:44–51 The plagues upon Egypt (see Ex 7–12): The sequence in Exodus is followed only in the first and last; the third, fifth, sixth and ninth plagues are not mentioned.
78:47 *sycamore-figs.* See note on Am 7:14.
78:49 *destroying angels.* The poet personifies God's wrath, indignation and hostility as agents of his anger.
78:51 *tents.* Dwellings. *Ham.* For the association of Ham with Egypt see 105:23,27; 106:21–22; Ge 10:6 and note.
78:53 *sea.* Red Sea.
78:55 Summarizes the story told in Joshua.

and allotted their lands to them as an
        inheritance; [r]
he settled the tribes of Israel in their
        homes.

[56]But they put God to the test
        and rebelled against the Most High;
        they did not keep his statutes.
[57]Like their fathers [s] they were disloyal
        and faithless,
        as unreliable as a faulty bow. [t]
[58]They angered him [u] with their high
        places; [v]
        they aroused his jealousy with their
        idols. [w]
[59]When God heard [x] them, he was very
        angry; [y]
        he rejected Israel [z] completely.
[60]He abandoned the tabernacle of
        Shiloh, [a]
        the tent he had set up among men. [b]
[61]He sent ˌthe ark ofˌ his might [c] into
        captivity, [d]
        his splendor into the hands of the
        enemy.
[62]He gave his people over to the sword; [e]
        he was very angry with his
        inheritance. [f]
[63]Fire consumed [g] their young men,

and their maidens had no wedding
        songs; [h]
[64]their priests were put to the sword, [i]
        and their widows could not weep.

[65]Then the Lord awoke as from sleep, [j]
        as a man wakes from the stupor of
        wine.
[66]He beat back his enemies;
        he put them to everlasting shame. [k]
[67]Then he rejected the tents of Joseph,
        he did not choose the tribe of
        Ephraim; [l]
[68]but he chose the tribe of Judah, [m]
        Mount Zion, [n] which he loved.
[69]He built his sanctuary [o] like the heights,
        like the earth that he established
        forever.
[70]He chose David [p] his servant
        and took him from the sheep pens;
[71]from tending the sheep [q] he brought
        him
        to be the shepherd [r] of his people
        Jacob,
        of Israel his inheritance.
[72]And David shepherded them with
        integrity of heart; [s]
        with skillful hands he led them.

78:55 [r]S Dt 1:38; S Jos 13:7; Ac 13:19
78:57 [s]S 2Ch 30:7; Eze 20:27 [t]S ver 9
78:58 [u]S Jdg 2:12 [v]S Lev 26:30 [w]Ex 20:4; S Dt 5:8; 32:21
78:59 [x]Ps 55:19 [y]S Lev 26:28; S Nu 32:14 [z]S Dt 32:19
78:60 [a]S Jos 18:1 [b]Eze 8:6
78:61 [c]Ps 132:8 [d]S 1Sa 4:17
78:62 [e]S Dt 28:25 [f]S 1Sa 10:1
78:63 [g]S Nu 11:1
78:63 [h]S 1Ki 4:32; Jer 7:34; 16:9; 25:10
78:64 [i]1Sa 4:17
78:65 [j]Ps 44:23
78:66 [k]1Sa 5:6
78:67 [l]Jer 7:15; Hos 9:13; 12:1
78:68 [m]S Nu 1:7; Ps 108:8 [n]S Ex 15:17; S Ps 68:16
78:69 [o]S Ps 15:1
78:70 [p]S 1Sa 16:1
78:71 [q]S Ge 37:2 [r]S Ps 28:9
78:72 [s]S Ge 17:1

78:56—64 Rebelliousness continued to be Israel's way of life in the promised land (a recurring theme of Judges; see also 1Sa 2:12–7:2), so God rejected Israel (v. 59; see Jer 7:15).
78:57 *faulty bow.* See note on v. 9.
78:58 *high places.* See note on 1Sa 9:12. *jealousy.* God's intense reaction to disloyalty to him (see note on Ex 20:5).
78:59 *rejected Israel completely.* Abandoned her to her enemies. The psalmist does not speak of a permanent casting off of Israel, not even of the ten northern tribes.
78:60 *Shiloh.* The center of worship since the time of Joshua (see Jos 18:1,8; 21:1–2; Jdg 18:31; 1Sa 1:3; Jer 7:12), it was located in Ephraim between Bethel and Shechem (see Jdg 21:19). Apparently it was destroyed by the Philistines when they captured the ark or shortly afterward (see note on Jer 7:12).
78:61 *his might . . . his splendor.* The ark is here so called because it was the sign of God's kingship in Israel and the focal point for the display of his power and glory (see 26:8; 63:2; 1Sa 4:3,21–22).
78:62,71 *his inheritance.* See Dt 9:29.
78:63 *Fire.* Often associated with the sword (see vv. 62, 64) as the two primary instruments of destruction in ancient warfare. *no wedding songs.* So great was the catastrophe that both the wedding songs of the brides and the wailing of the widows (see v. 64) were silenced in the land.
78:64 *priests were put to the sword.* See 1Sa 4:11.
78:65—72 The Lord's election of Judah (instead of Ephraim) as the leading tribe in Israel (anticipated in Jacob's deathbed blessing of his sons, Ge 49:8–12), of Mount Zion (instead of Shiloh) as the place of his sanctuary (royal seat), and of David as his regent to shepherd his people. By these acts the Lord established his people securely as his kingdom in the promised land, following the long period of Israel's troubles from the death of Joshua to the death of Saul—by then God's salvation of Israel begun in the exodus reached its

climactic (if provisional) fulfillment (see introduction to Ps 68 and the combination of echoes of God's saving act in the exodus and through David in Isaiah's prophecy of Israel's future deliverance, Isa 11:11–16).
78:65 *awoke as from sleep.* Poetic hyperbole to highlight the contrast between God's action in behalf of his people in the days of David and the preceding time of Israel's troubles (see note on 7:6).
78:66—72 The saving events noted have two focal points: (1) God's decisive victory over his enemies (thus securing his realm) and the establishment of Zion as his royal city, and (2) the appointment of David to be the shepherd of his people.
78:67 *tents of Joseph.* A figure for the tribe of Ephraim (for the figurative use of "tents" see v. 51; see also 69:25; 83:6; 84:10; 120:5; Ge 9:27; Dt 33:18; 1Ki 12:16; Job 8:22; 12:6; Hab 3:7; Mal 2:12).
78:68,70 *he chose . . . Mount Zion . . . He chose David.* See Ps 132.
78:69 *heights . . . earth.* The verse is subject to two interpretations: (1) The Lord built his sanctuary as impregnable as a mountain fortress and as enduring and unmovable as the age-old earth, or (2) the Lord built his sanctuary as secure and enduring as the heavens and the earth (see note on 24:2) and there manifests himself as the Lord of glory (see 24:7–10; 26:8; 63:2; 96:6), even as he does in the creation (see 19:1; 29:9; 97:6).
78:70—71 See 1Sa 16:11–13; 2Sa 7:8.
78:70 *his servant.* Here an official title marking David as a member of God's royal administration (see notes on Ex 14:31; Ps 18 title; Isa 41:8–9; 42:1).
78:71 *shepherd.* See note on 23:1.
78:72 Israel under the care of the Lord's royal shepherd from the house of David was for the prophets the hope of God's people (see Eze 34:23; 37:24; Mic 5:4—fulfilled in Jesus Christ, Mt 2:6; Jn 10:11; Rev 7:17).

Psalm 79

A psalm of Asaph.

1 O God, the nations have invaded your
inheritance;[t]
they have defiled[u] your holy temple,
they have reduced Jerusalem to
rubble.[v]
2 They have given the dead bodies of
your servants
as food to the birds of the air,[w]
the flesh of your saints to the beasts
of the earth.[x]
3 They have poured out blood like water
all around Jerusalem,
and there is no one to bury[y] the
dead.[z]
4 We are objects of reproach to our
neighbors,
of scorn[a] and derision to those
around us.[b]
5 How long,[c] O LORD? Will you be
angry[d] forever?
How long will your jealousy burn like
fire?[e]
6 Pour out your wrath[f] on the nations
that do not acknowledge[g] you,
on the kingdoms
that do not call on your name;[h]
7 for they have devoured[i] Jacob
and destroyed his homeland.
8 Do not hold against us the sins of the
fathers;[j]
may your mercy come quickly to
meet us,
for we are in desperate need.[k]
9 Help us,[l] O God our Savior,
for the glory of your name;
deliver us and forgive our sins
for your name's sake.[m]
10 Why should the nations say,
"Where is their God?"[n]
Before our eyes, make known among
the nations
that you avenge[o] the outpoured
blood[p] of your servants.
11 May the groans of the prisoners come
before you;
by the strength of your arm
preserve those condemned to die.
12 Pay back into the laps[q] of our neighbors
seven times[r]
the reproach they have hurled at you,
O Lord.
13 Then we your people, the sheep of your
pasture,[s]

79:1 [t]S Ex 34:9 [u]S Lev 20:3 [v]S 2Ki 25:9; S Ne 4:2; S Isa 6:11 **79:2** [w]Rev 19:17-18 [x]S Dt 28:26; Jer 7:33 **79:3** [y]Jer 25:33; Rev 11:9 [z]Jer 16:4 **79:4** [a]S Ps 39:8; S Eze 5:14 [b]Ps 44:13; 80:6 **79:5** [c]S Ps 74:10 [d]Ps 74:1; 85:5 [e]S Dt 29:20; Ps 89:46; Zep 3:8 **79:6** [f]S Ps 2:5; 69:24; 110:5; Rev 16:1 [g]Ps 147:20; Jer 10:25 [h]S Ps 14:4 **79:7** [i]Isa 9:12; Jer 10:25 **79:8** [j]S Ge 9:25; Jer 44:21 [k]Ps 116:6; 142:6 **79:9** [l]S 2Ch 14:11 [m]Ps 25:11; 31:3; Jer 14:7 **79:10** [n]S Ps 42:3 [o]Ps 94:1; S Rev 6:10 [p]ver 3 **79:12** [q]Isa 65:6; Jer 32:18 [r]S Ge 4:15 **79:13** [s]S Ps 74:1

Ps 79 Israel's prayer for God's forgiveness and help and for his judgment on the nations that have so cruelly destroyed her, showing utter contempt for both the Lord and his people. Like Ps 74, with which it has many thematic links, it dates from the time of the exile. The poignancy of its appeal is heightened by its juxtaposition to Ps 77 (recalling God's saving acts under Moses) and Ps 78 (recalling God's saving acts under David), two psalms with which it is significantly linked by the shepherd-sheep figure and other thematic elements. Israel acknowledges that the Lord has used the nations to punish her for her sins, so she pleads for pardon. But she knows too that the nations have acted out of their hostility to and disdain for God and his people; that warrants her plea for God's judgment on them (see Isa 10:5–11; 47:6–7). Daniel's prayer (Da 9:4–19) contains much that is similar to the elements of penitence in this psalm.
79 title *Asaph.* See note on Ps 73 title.
79:1–4 What the nations have done: They have attacked God's own special domain, violated his temple, destroyed his royal city, slaughtered his people, degraded them in death (by withholding burial—see note on 53:5—and leaving their bodies as carrion for birds and beasts) and reduced them to the scorn of the world.
79:1 *your inheritance.* Cf. 78:62,71. Here reference is to Israel's homeland as the Lord's domain (see note on 2:8). *holy temple.* See note on 78:69.
79:2 *your servants.* Though banished from the Lord's land for sins that cannot be denied, the exiles plead their special covenant relationship with God (see "your saints," here, and "your people, the sheep of your pasture," v. 13). *saints.* See note on 4:3.
79:3 *poured out blood . . . all around Jerusalem.* Cf. 2Ki 21:16.
79:5–8 A prayer for God to relent and deal with the nations who do not acknowledge him.
79:5 *How long . . . ?* See note on 6:3 (see also Introduction: Theology). *angry.* See v. 6 ("wrath"); see also note on 2:5. *jealousy.* See note on 78:58. *burn like fire.* See Dt 4:24; 6:15; Zep 1:18; 3:8.
79:6–7 See Jer 10:25 and note. Perhaps the psalmist is quoting Jeremiah here.
79:6 *Pour out your wrath.* As they "poured out" (v. 3) the blood of your people. The exiles plead with God to redress the wrongs committed against them (see note on 5:10).
79:7 *devoured.* Like wild beasts (see 44:11; 74:19 and note on 7:2). *Jacob.* A synonym for Israel (see Ge 32:28).
79:8 *sins of the fathers.* Israel suffered exile because of the accumulated sins of the nation (see 2Ki 17:7–23; 23:26–27; 24:3–4; Da 9:4–14), from which she did not repent until the judgment of God had fallen on her. The exiles here pray that God will take notice of their penitence and not continue to hold the sins of past generations against his now repentant people. *mercy.* Here personified as God's agent sent to bring relief (see notes on 23:6; 43:3).
79:9–11 A prayer for God to help and forgive his people and to redress the violent acts of the enemies.
79:9 *for the glory of your name.* As the desolation of God's people brings reproach to God (see v. 10), so their salvation and prosperity bring him glory (see note on 23:3). *forgive.* See note on 65:3.
79:10 *Where is their God?* See note on 3:2. *avenge.* Redress (see Dt 32:35,43).
79:11 *prisoners . . . those condemned to die.* The exiles, as imperial captives in Babylonia (see 102:20)—not actually in prisons, but under threat of death should they seek to return to their homeland.
79:12–13 Concluding prayer and vow to praise.
79:12 *Pay back into the laps.* See note on Jer 32:18. *seven times.* In full measure; the number seven symbolized completeness. *reproach . . . at you.* The enemies' violent action against Israel was above all a high-handed reviling of God (see vv. 1,10; 2Ki 19:10–12,22–23; Isa 52:5).

will praise you forever; *t*
from generation to generation
  we will recount your praise.

Psalm 80

For the director of music. To the tune of,
"The Lilies of the Covenant." Of Asaph.
A psalm.

¹Hear us, O Shepherd of Israel,
  you who lead Joseph like a flock; *u*
you who sit enthroned between the
      cherubim, *v* shine forth
²   before Ephraim, Benjamin and
      Manasseh. *w*
Awaken *x* your might;
  come and save us. *y*

³Restore *z* us, *a* O God;
  make your face shine upon us,
  that we may be saved. *b*

⁴O Lord God Almighty,
  how long *c* will your anger smolder *d*
  against the prayers of your people?

⁵You have fed them with the bread of
      tears; *e*
  you have made them drink tears by
      the bowlful. *f*

⁶You have made us a source of
      contention to our neighbors,
  and our enemies mock us. *g*

⁷Restore us, O God Almighty;
  make your face shine upon us,
  that we may be saved. *h*

⁸You brought a vine *i* out of Egypt;
  you drove out *j* the nations and
      planted *k* it.
⁹You cleared the ground for it,
  and it took root and filled the land.
¹⁰The mountains were covered with its
      shade,
  the mighty cedars with its branches.
¹¹It sent out its boughs to the Sea, *j*
  its shoots as far as the River. *k* *l*

¹²Why have you broken down its walls *m*

79:13 *t* Ps 44:8
80:1 *u* Ps 77:20
      v S Ex 25:22
80:2
      w Nu 2:18-24
      x S Ps 35:23
      y Ps 54:1; 69:1;
      71:2; 109:26;
      116:4; 119:94
80:3 *z* S Ps 71:20;
      85:4; Jer 31:18;
      La 5:21
      a S Nu 6:25 *b* ver
      7,19
80:4 *c* S Ps 74:10
      d S Dt 29:20

80:5 *e* S Job 3:24
      f Isa 30:20
80:6 *g* S Ps 79:4
80:7 *h* ver 3
80:8 *i* Isa 5:1-2;
Jer 2:21;
Mt 21:33-41
/Ex 23:28-30;
S Jos 13:6;
Ac 7:45
k S Ex 15:17
80:11 *l* Ps 72:8
80:12 *m* Ps 89:40;
Isa 5:5; 30:13;
Jer 39:8

j 11 Probably the Mediterranean   *k 11* That is, the
Euphrates

79:13 See note on 7:17. *sheep of your pasture.* See 74:1;
77:20; 78:72. *from generation to generation.* See 78:4.
Ps 80 Israel's prayer for restoration when she had been
ravaged by a foreign power. It seems likely that "Ephraim,
Benjamin and Manasseh" (v. 2) here represent the northern
kingdom. If Jeroboam was indeed given ten tribes (see 1Ki
11:29–36), leaving only one to Rehoboam—Judah (see 1Ki
12:20), which was actually two tribes because Simeon was
located within Judah (see Jos 19:1–9)—then Benjamin belonged to the northern kingdom. However, part of Benjamin
must always have remained with the southern kingdom
since its territory actually bordered on Jerusalem itself, and
the southern kingdom continued to control Jerusalem's environs (see 1Ki 12:21). This suggests that the disaster suffered
was the Assyrian campaign that swept the northern kingdom
away (see 2Ki 17:1–6). Recent archaeological surveys of
Palestine have shown that Jerusalem and the surrounding
countryside experienced at this time a dramatic increase of
population, no doubt the result of a massive influx of displaced persons from the north fleeing the Assyrian beast. This
could account for the presence of "Ephraim, Benjamin and
Manasseh" at the Jerusalem sanctuary, and for a national
prayer for restoration with special focus on these tribes (see
notes below).
  The prayer has five stanzas of four (Hebrew) lines each. A
recurring petition climaxes the first, second and last (for
other refrains see introduction to Ps 42–43), with a progressing urgency of appeal: "O God" (v. 3); "O God Almighty"
(v. 7); "O Lord God Almighty" (v. 19).
80 title *For the director of music.* See note on Ps 4 title. *To
the tune of.* See note on Ps 9 title. *Lilies.* See note on Ps 45
title. *Asaph.* See note on Ps 73 title.
80:1–3 An appeal for God to arouse himself and go before
his people again with all his glory and might as he did of old
in the desert.
80:1 See the shepherd-flock motif in 74:1; 77:20; 78:52;
71–72; 79:13. *Joseph.* See note on 77:15. *enthroned between the cherubim.* See note on Ex 25:18. *shine forth.* Let
your glory be seen again, as in the desert journey (see Ex
24:16–17; 40:34–35), but now especially through your

new saving act (see 102:15–16; Ex 14:4,17–18; Nu 14:22;
Isa 40:5; 44:23; 60:1–2).
80:2 *before Ephraim, Benjamin and Manasseh.* March
against the nations as you marched in the midst of your army
from Sinai into the promised land (in that march the ark of
the covenant advanced in front of the troops of these three
tribes; see Nu 10:21–24; see also introduction to Ps 68).
Awaken. See note on 7:6.
80:3 *make your face shine.* See vv. 7,19; an echo of the
priestly benediction (see Nu 6:25; see also notes on 4:6;
13:1).
80:4–7 A lament over the Lord's severe punishment of his
people.
80:4 *Lord . . . Almighty.* See vv. 7,14,19; see also note on
1Sa 1:3. *how long . . . ?* See note on 6:3 (see also Introduction: Theology). *anger.* See note on 2:5.
80:5 God has now given them tears to eat and tears to
drink rather than "the bread of angels" and water from the
rock (see 78:20,25).
80:8–16 This use of the vine-vineyard metaphor (here to
describe Israel's changed condition) is found also in the
prophets (see Isa 3:14; 5:1–7; 27:2; Jer 2:21; 12:10; Eze
17:6–8; 19:10–14; Hos 10:1; 14:7; Mic 7:1; see also Ge
49:22; Mt 20:1–16; Mk 12:1–9; Lk 20:9–16; Jn 15:1–5).
80:8–11 Israel was once God's flourishing transplanted
vine.
80:8 *brought.* See 78:52; here the Hebrew for this verb has
the sense of "uprooted" (as in Job 19:10). *drove out the
nations and planted.* See 44:2. *planted.* Transplanted.
80:9 *cleared the ground.* See Isa 5:2.
80:10 *mighty cedars.* Lit. "cedars of God" (the Hebrew
word for "God" is sometimes used in the sense of "mighty";
see, e.g., note on 29:1).
80:11 *Sea . . . River.* See NIV text notes; see also Ex 23:31
and note.
80:12–15 A prayer for God to renew his care for his
ravaged vine.
80:12 *Why . . . ?* Israel's anguished perplexity over God's
abandonment (see note on 6:3). *broken down its walls.*
Taken away its defenses.

so that all who pass by pick its
    grapes?
[13]Boars from the forest ravage[n] it
    and the creatures of the field feed on
    it.
[14]Return to us, O God Almighty!
    Look down from heaven and see![o]
    Watch over this vine,
[15] the root your right hand has planted,
    the son[1] you have raised up for
    yourself.

[16]Your vine is cut down, it is burned with
    fire;[p]
    at your rebuke[q] your people perish.
[17]Let your hand rest on the man at your
    right hand,
    the son of man[r] you have raised up
    for yourself.
[18]Then we will not turn away from you;
    revive[s] us, and we will call on your
    name.

80:13 [n]Jer 5:6
80:14
[o]S Dt 26:15
80:16 [p]Ps 79:1
[q]S Dt 28:20
80:17 [r]S Job 25:6
80:18 [s]Ps 85:6;
Isa 57:15; Hos 6:2

81:1 [t]S Ps 66:1
81:2 [u]S Ex 15:20
[v]Ps 92:3
[w]S Job 21:12
81:3 [x]S Ex 19:13
[y]S Ne 10:33
81:4 [z]ver 1

[19]Restore us, O Lᴏʀᴅ God Almighty;
    make your face shine upon us,
    that we may be saved.

Psalm 81

For the director of music. According to
gittith.[m] Of Asaph.

[1]Sing for joy to God our strength;
    shout aloud to the God of Jacob![t]
[2]Begin the music, strike the
    tambourine,[u]
    play the melodious harp[v] and lyre.[w]

[3]Sound the ram's horn[x] at the New
    Moon,[y]
    and when the moon is full, on the
    day of our Feast;
[4]this is a decree for Israel,
    an ordinance of the God of Jacob.[z]
[5]He established it as a statute for Joseph

[1]15 Or branch   [m]Title: Probably a musical term

80:14 *Watch over.* See Ex 3:16. But the Hebrew for this
phrase may have the sense here that it has in Ru 1:6: "come
to the aid of."
80:15 *son.* Israel (see Ex 4:22–23; Hos 11:1). But "son"
may sometimes be used also to refer to a vine branch (see
NIV text note; see also note on Ge 49:22). That may be the
case here, thus yielding the conventional pair "root and
branch," a figure for the whole vine (see Job 18:16; 29:19;
Eze 17:7; Mal 4:1; see also Isa 5:24; 27:6; 37:31; Eze
17:9; 31:7; Hos 9:16; Am 2:9; Ro 11:16). *raised up.* See v.
17; lit. "made vigorous."
80:16–19 Concluding prayer for restoration.
80:16 *rebuke.* See 9:5 and note on 76:6.
80:17 *Let your hand rest on.* Show your favor to (see Ezr
7:6,9,28; 8:18,22,31; Ne 2:8,18). *at.* Lit. "of." *your right
hand.* Reference may be to the Davidic king as the Lord's
anointed, seated in the place of honor in God's presence (see
110:1) and the one in whom the hope of the nation rested
(see 2:7–9; 72:8–11; 89:21–25). But v. 15 strongly suggests another sense: that "the man" is Jacob/Israel and that
he is "of " God's "right hand" in that he has been "planted"
and "raised up" by him.
80:18 A vow to be loyal to God and to trust in him alone.
It occurs in a place where it would be more common to find
a vow to praise (see note on 7:17).
Ps 81 A festival song. But it is unclear whether the festival
is Passover/Unleavened Bread (v. 5; see Ex 12:14–17) or
the Jewish New Year (v. 3; see Lev 23:24; Nu 29:1) or the
Feast of Tabernacles (v. 3; see Lev 23:34; Nu 29:12). It may
have been used at all three. But more likely it was composed
for use at both New Year (the first day of the month, "New
Moon") and the beginning of Tabernacles (the 15th day of
the month, full moon); see notes below. Whether the psalm
is preexilic or postexilic cannot be determined, but it clearly
shows the grand significance of Israel's annual religious festivals (see chart on "OT Feasts and Other Sacred Days," p.
176). As memorials of God's saving acts they called Israel to
celebration, remembrance and recommitment (see Ps 95). In
this psalm Israel is addressed by a Levite, speaking (prophetically) on behalf of God.
    Though the psalm falls into two parts (vv. 1–5, 6–16),
thematic development follows a symmetrical pattern: two
verses, three verses; two verses, three verses; two verses,
four verses. Note also the contrast between vv. 6–7 and vv.

11–12, and the thematic link between v. 10c and v. 16.
81 title *For the director of music.* See note on Ps 4 title.
According to. See note on Ps 6 title. *gittith.* See note on Ps 8
title. *Asaph.* See note on Ps 73 title.
81:1–5 A summons to celebrate the appointed sacred
feast.
81:1 *Jacob.* A synonym for Israel (see Ge 32:28).
81:2 *tambourine.* See note on Jer 31:4. *harp and lyre.* See
on 57:8.
81:3 *ram's horn.* The ram's horn trumpet (see Ex 19:13).
our Feast. Probably the Feast of Tabernacles, often called
simply "the feast/festival" (see 1Ki 8:2,65; 12:32; 2Ch 5:3;
7:8; Ne 8:14,18; Eze 45:25; see also Dt 16:14). As the great
seven-day autumn festival, beginning on the 15th of the
month (full moon), it followed shortly after the Day of Atonement (observed on the tenth of the month, Lev 16:29),
recalled God's care for his people during the desert journey
(see Lev 23:43), served as a feast of thanksgiving for the
harvest (see Lev 23:39–40; Dt 16:13–15) and marked the
conclusion of the annual cycle of religious festivals that began
with Passover and Unleavened Bread six months earlier (see
Ex 23:14–17; Lev 23; Dt 16:16). Every seventh year at this
festival the covenant law was to be read to all the people (see
Dt 31:9–13; Ne 8:2,15). The first day of this month (New
Moon) was commemorated with trumpets (see Lev 23:24).
It later came to be known as New Year since the seventh
month marked the end of harvest and the beginning of the
rainy season, when the new crops were planted.
81:4–5 *decree . . . ordinance . . . statute.* See the passages
referred to in note on v. 3.
81:5 *Joseph.* See note on 77:15. *when he went out against
Egypt.* Some believe this indicates that the festival referred to
is Passover and Unleavened Bread (see Ex 12:14,42). More
likely it serves as a reference to the whole exodus period,
while highlighting especially God's triumph over Egypt by
which he had set his people free (see vv. 6–7). *heard a
language we did not understand.* Were aliens in a foreign
land (see 114:1; see also Dt 28:49; Isa 33:19; Jer
5:15; Eze 3:5–6). If the alternative translation in the NIV
text note is taken, the "voice" is the "thunder" of God's
judgment against Egypt (see v. 7), which the Levitical author
then proceeds to interpret as to its present reference for the
celebrating congregation (vv. 6–16).

when he went out against Egypt,[a]
where we heard a language we did
not understand.[n] [b]

[6]He says, "I removed the burden[c] from
their shoulders;[d]
their hands were set free from the
basket.
[7]In your distress you called[e] and I
rescued you,
I answered[f] you out of a
thundercloud;
I tested you at the waters of
Meribah.[g]   Selah

[8]"Hear, O my people,[h] and I will warn
you—
if you would but listen to me,
O Israel!
[9]You shall have no foreign god[i] among
you;
you shall not bow down to an alien
god.
[10]I am the LORD your God,
who brought you up out of Egypt.[j]
Open[k] wide your mouth and I will
fill[l] it.

[11]"But my people would not listen to me;[m]
Israel would not submit to me.[m]
[12]So I gave them over[n] to their stubborn
hearts
to follow their own devices.

Reference column
81:5 [a]S Ex 11:4
[b]Ps 114:1
81:6 [c]S Ex 1:14
[d]Isa 9:4; 52:2
81:7 [e]S Ex 2:23
[f]Ex 19:19
[g]S Ex 17:7;
S Dt 33:8
81:8 [h]Ps 50:7;
78:1
81:9 [i]S Ex 20:3
81:10 [j]S Ex 6:6;
S 13:3; S 29:46
[k]Eze 2:8
[l]Ps 107:9
81:11 [m]Ex 32:1-6
81:12 [n]Eze 20:25;
Ac 7:42; Ro 1:24
81:13 [o]S Dt 5:29
81:14 [p]Ps 47:3
[q]Am 1:8
81:15 [r]S 2Sa 22:45
81:16 [s]S Dt 32:14
82:1 [t]Ps 7:8;
58:11; Isa 3:13;
66:16; Joel 3:12
[u]S Job 21:22
82:2 [v]Dt 1:17
[w]Ps 58:1-2;
Pr 18:5
82:3 [x]S Dt 24:17
[y]Ps 140:12;
Jer 5:28; 22:16

[13]"If my people would but listen to me,[o]
if Israel would follow my ways,
[14]how quickly would I subdue[p] their
enemies
and turn my hand against[q] their foes!
[15]Those who hate the LORD would
cringe[r] before him,
and their punishment would last
forever.
[16]But you would be fed with the finest of
wheat;[s]
with honey from the rock I would
satisfy you."

Psalm 82

A psalm of Asaph.

[1]God presides in the great assembly;
he gives judgment[t] among the
"gods":[u]

[2]"How long will you[o] defend the unjust
and show partiality[v] to the wicked?[w]
                                               Selah
[3]Defend the cause of the weak and
fatherless;[x]
maintain the rights of the poor[y] and
oppressed.
[4]Rescue the weak and needy;

[n]5 Or / and we heard a voice we had not known
[o]2 The Hebrew is plural.

81:6–10 God heard and delivered and now summons his
people to loyalty.
81:6 *burden ... basket.* The forced labor to which the
Israelites were subjected in Egypt (see Ex 1:11–14).
81:7 *you called and I rescued.* See Ex 3:7–10. *out of a
thundercloud.* See 106:9; Ex 14:21,24; 15:8,10; see also
note on 76:6. *I tested you.* See Ex 17:1–7.
81:8–10 God heard his people in their distress (vv. 6–7);
now they must listen to him.
81:9–10 See Ex 19:4–5; 20:2–4; Dt 4:15–20.
81:10 *Open wide your mouth.* Trust in the Lord alone for
all of life's needs. *I will fill it.* See v. 16; as he did in the desert
(see 78:23–29; see also 37:3–4; Dt 11:13–15; 28:1–14).
81:11–16 Israel has not listened—if only they would! See
Eze 18:23,32; 33:11.
81:11 See 78:10,17,32,40,56; Dt 9:7,24; Jer 7:24–26.
81:12 It is God who "circumcises" the heart (see Dt 30:6;
see also 1Ki 8:58; Jer 31:33; Eze 11:19; 36:26). Thus for
God to abandon his people to their sins is the most fearful of
punishments (see 78:29; Isa 6:9–10; 29:10; 63:17; cf. Ro
1:24,26,28).
81:13–16 See the promised covenant blessings outlined in
Ex 23:22–27; Lev 26:3–13; Dt 7:12–26; 28:1–14.
81:13 *my ways.* See 25:4 and note.
81:16 *honey from the rock.* See note on Dt 32:13.
Ps 82 A word of judgment on unjust rulers and judges. The
Levitical author of this psalm evokes a vision of God presiding over his heavenly court—analogous to the experiences of
the prophets (see 1Ki 22:19–22; Isa 6:1–7; Jer 23:18,22;
see also Job 15:8). As the Great King (see introduction to Ps
47) and the Judge of all the earth (see 94:2; Ge 18:25; 1Sa
2:10) who "loves justice" (99:4) and judges the nations in

righteousness (see 9:8; 96:13; 98:9), he is seen calling to
account those responsible for defending the weak and oppressed on earth. An early rabbinic interpretation (see Jn
10:34–35) understood the "gods" (vv. 1,6) to be unjust
rulers and judges in Israel, of whom there were many (see
1Sa 8:3; Isa 1:16–17; 3:13–15; Jer 21:12; 22:3; Eze 34:4,
21; Mic 3:1–3; 7:3). Today many identify the "gods" as the
kings of surrounding nations who encouraged the conceit
that they were actually or virtually divine beings but who
ruled with lofty disregard for justice—though honoring it as
a royal ideal. Others hold that the "gods" are the divine
beings in whose names the kings claimed to rule (see 95:3).
In any event, rulers and judges here are confronted by their
King and Judge (see Ps 58). Structurally, the words of the
Levite (vv. 1,6) frame the words of God. At the very center
(v. 5a; see note on 6:6) stands the most devastating judgment of all.
82 title See note on Ps 73 title.
82:1 *great assembly.* The assembly in the great Hall of
Justice (cf. 1Ki 7:7) in heaven (see 89:5; 1Ki 22:19; Job 1:6;
2:1; Isa 6:1–4). As if in a vision, the psalmist sees the rulers
and judges gathered before the Great King to give account of
their administration of justice. *gods.* See v. 6. In the language
of the OT—and in accordance with the conceptual world of
the ancient Near East—rulers and judges, as deputies of the
heavenly King, could be given the honorific title "god" (see
note on 45:6; see also note on Ex 21:6; 22:8) or
be called "son of God" (see 2:7 and note).
82:3–4 In the OT a first-order task of kings and judges was
to protect the powerless against all who would exploit or
oppress them (see 72:2,4,12–14; Pr 31:8–9; Isa 11:4; Jer
22:3,16).

deliver them from the hand of the
wicked.

5"They know nothing, they understand
nothing. *z*

They walk about in darkness; *a*
all the foundations *b* of the earth are
shaken.

6"I said, 'You are "gods"; *c*
you are all sons of the Most High.'

7But you will die *d* like mere men;
you will fall like every other ruler."

8Rise up, *e* O God, judge *f* the earth,
for all the nations are your
inheritance. *g*

Psalm 83

A song. A psalm of Asaph.

1O God, do not keep silent; *h*
be not quiet, O God, be not still.

2See how your enemies are astir, *i*
how your foes rear their heads. *j*

3With cunning they conspire *k* against
your people;
they plot against those you cherish. *l*

4"Come," they say, "let us destroy *m*
them as a nation, *n*

that the name of Israel be
remembered *o* no more."

5With one mind they plot together; *p*
they form an alliance against you—

6the tents of Edom *q* and the Ishmaelites,
of Moab *r* and the Hagrites, *s*

7Gebal, *p t* Ammon *u* and Amalek, *v*
Philistia, *w* with the people of Tyre. *x*

8Even Assyria *y* has joined them
to lend strength to the descendants of
Lot. *z*   *Selah*

9Do to them as you did to Midian, *a*
as you did to Sisera *b* and Jabin *c* at
the river Kishon, *d*

10who perished at Endor *e*
and became like refuse *f* on the
ground.

11Make their nobles like Oreb and Zeeb, *g*
all their princes like Zebah and
Zalmunna, *h*

12who said, "Let us take possession *i*
of the pasturelands of God."

82:5 *z*S Ps 14:4;
S 53:2
*a*Job 30:26;
Isa 5:30; 8:21-22;
Jer 13:16; 23:12;
La 3:2 *b*S Jdg 5:4;
S Ps 11:3
82:6 *c*Jn 10:34*
82:7 *d*Ps 49:12;
Eze 31:14
82:8 *e*Ps 12:5
*f*S Ps 76:9 *g*Ps 2:8
83:1 *h*Ps 28:1;
35:22; Isa 42:14;
57:11; 62:1;
64:12
83:2 *i*Ps 2:1;
Isa 17:12
*j*Jdg 8:28
83:3 *k*S Ex 1:10;
S Ps 31:13
*l*Ps 17:14
83:4 *m*S Est 3:6
*n*Jer 33:24

*o*Jer 11:19
83:5 *p*Ps 2:2
83:6 *q*Ps 137:7;
Isa 34:5; Jer 49:7;
Am 1:11
*r*2Ch 20:1
*s*S Ge 25:16
83:7 *t*S Jos 13:5
*u*Ge 19:38
*v*S Ge 14:7;
S Ex 17:14
*w*S Ex 15:14
*x*Isa 23:3;
Eze 27:3
83:8 *y*S Ge 10:11
*z*S Dt 2:9
83:9 *a*S Ge 25:2;
Jdg 7:1-23
*b*S Jdg 4:2

*c*S Jos 11:1 *d*S Jdg 4:23-24 **83:10** *e*S 1Sa 28:7 *f*S 2Ki 9:37;
Isa 5:25; Jer 8:2; 9:22; 16:4; 25:33; Zep 1:17 **83:11**
*g*Jdg 7:25 *h*S Jdg 8:5 **83:12** *i*2Ch 20:11; Eze 35:10

*p*7 That is, Byblos

82:5 *They know ... nothing.* The center of the poem (see note on 6:6). They ought to have shared in the wisdom of God (see 1Ki 3:9; Pr 8:14–16; Isa 11:2), but they are utterly devoid of true understanding of moral issues or of the moral order that God's rule sustains (see Isa 44:19). *foundations ... are shaken.* When such men are the wardens of justice, the whole world order crumbles (see 11:3; 75:3 and notes). **82:6** *I said.* Those who rule (or judge) do so by God's appointment (see 2:7; Isa 44:28) and thus they are his representatives—whether they acknowledge him or not (see Ex 9:16; Jer 27:6; Da 2:21; 4:17,32; 5:18; Jn 19:11; Ro 13:1). *gods.* See note on v. 1. *sons of.* See note on v. 1. *Most High.* See note on Ge 14:19. **82:7** However exalted their position, these corrupt "gods" will be brought low by the same judgment as other men. *fall.* See note on 13:4. **82:8** Having seen the prospect in store, the psalmist prays for God's judgment to hasten and for the perfect reign of God to come quickly to the whole world. *Rise up.* See note on 3:7. *inheritance.* Domain (see note on 79:1). **Ps 83** Israel's prayer for God to crush his enemies when the whole world—or so it seemed—was arrayed against his people. Neither Kings nor Chronicles tells of a confederacy as extensive as that described here. Perhaps only some of the nations mentioned were actually attacking, while the rest of Israel's historic enemies were more passively supporting the campaign. If so, the occasion may have been that reported in 2Ch 20, when Moab, Ammon, Edom and their allies were invading Judah. In any event, the psalm must date from sometime after the reign of Solomon and before the great thrust of Assyria in the time of King Menahem (see 2Ki 15:19).

Each of the two main divisions (vv. 1–8, 9–18) consists of two four-verse stanzas, with the latter division being extended by a two-verse stanza that brings the prayer to its climactic conclusion.

83 title *song.* See note on Ps 30 title. *Asaph.* See note on Ps 73 title. **83:1–4** An appeal to God to act in the face of Israel's imminent danger. **83:1** *do not keep silent.* Do not remain inactive (see 35:22; 109:1). **83:4** *they say.* See note on 3:2. *let us destroy them.* Israel's very existence is at stake (see v. 12). **83:5–8** The array of nations allied against Israel—threat from every quarter. **83:6** *Hagrites.* Either Ishmaelites (descendants of Hagar) or a group mentioned in Assyrian inscriptions as an Aramean confederacy (see 1Ch 5:10,18–22; 27:31). **83:7** *Gebal.* See 1Ki 5:18; Eze 27:9. Gebal was an important Phoenician city (see NIV text note). **83:8** *Assyria.* Since it is mentioned only as an ally of Moab and Ammon (the descendants of Lot; see note on Ge 19:36–38), Assyria, though distantly active in the region, must not yet have become a major threat in its own right. **83:9–12** A plea for God to destroy his enemies as he did of old in the time of the judges. Those who hurl themselves against the kingdom of God to destroy it from the earth—so that the godless powers are left to shape the destiny of the world as they will—must be crushed if God's kingdom of righteousness and peace is to come and be at rest (see note on 5:10). **83:9** *as you did to Midian.* In Gideon's great victory (see Jdg 7). *as you did to Sisera and Jabin.* In Barak's defeat of the Canaanite coalition (see Jdg 4). **83:10** *Endor.* See Jos 17:11 and note; northeast of where the main battle was fought—apparently where much of the fleeing army was overtaken and decimated. **83:11** *Oreb and Zeeb ... Zebah and Zalmunna.* Leaders of the Midianite host destroyed by Gideon. **83:12** See v. 4.

[13]Make them like tumbleweed, O my
God,
like chaff[j] before the wind.
[14]As fire consumes the forest
or a flame sets the mountains
ablaze,[k]
[15]so pursue them with your tempest[l]
and terrify them with your storm.[m]
[16]Cover their faces with shame[n]
so that men will seek your name,
O LORD.

[17]May they ever be ashamed and
dismayed;[o]
may they perish in disgrace.[p]
[18]Let them know that you, whose name is
the LORD[q]—
that you alone are the Most High[r]
over all the earth.[s]

Psalm 84

For the director of music. According to *gittith*.[q] Of the Sons of Korah. A psalm.

[1]How lovely is your dwelling place,[t]
O LORD Almighty!
[2]My soul yearns,[u] even faints,
for the courts of the LORD;
my heart and my flesh cry out
for the living God.[v]

[3]Even the sparrow has found a home,
and the swallow a nest for herself,
where she may have her young—
a place near your altar,[w]
O LORD Almighty,[x] my King[y] and
my God.[z]
[4]Blessed are those who dwell in your
house;
they are ever praising you. *Selah*

[5]Blessed are those whose strength[a] is in
you,
who have set their hearts on
pilgrimage.[b]
[6]As they pass through the Valley of Baca,
they make it a place of springs;[c]
the autumn[d] rains also cover it with
pools.[r]
[7]They go from strength to strength,[e]
till each appears[f] before God in
Zion.[g]

83:13 [j]S Job 13:25 **83:14** [k]Dt 32:22; Isa 9:18 **83:15** [l]S Ps 50:3 [m]S Job 9:17 **83:16** [n]S Ps 34:5; 109:29; 132:18 **83:17** [o]S 2Ki 19:26 [p]S Ps 35:4 **83:18** [q]S Ps 68:4 [r]Ps 7:8; 18:13 [s]S Job 34:29 **84:1** [t]S Dt 33:27; Ps 27:4; 43:3; 90:1; 132:5 **84:2** [u]S Job 19:27 [v]S Jos 3:10 **84:3** [w]S Ps 43:4 [x]Jer 44:11 [y]Ps 2:6 [z]Ps 5:2 **84:5** [a]Ps 81:1 [b]Jer 31:6 **84:6** [c]S Job 38:26 [d]Joel 2:23 **84:7** [e]S Job 17:9 [f]S Dt 16:16 [g]1Ki 8:1

[q]Title: Probably a musical term [r]6 Or *blessings*

83:13–16 The plea renewed, with vivid imagery of fleeing armies and of God's fearsome power.
83:15 Imagery of the heavenly Warrior attacking his enemies out of the thunderstorm (see 18:7–15; 68:33; 77:17–18; Ex 15:7–10; Jos 10:11; Jdg 5:4,20–21; 1Sa 2:10; 7:10; Isa 29:5–6; 33:3). For the storm cloud as God's chariot see 68:4 and note.
83:16 *will seek.* See note on v. 18. *name.* See note on 5:11.
83:17–18 The prayer's climactic conclusion.
83:18 The ultimate goal of God's warfare is not merely the security of Israel and the destruction of Israel's (and God's) enemies but the worldwide acknowledgment of the true God and of his rule, even to the point of seeking him as his people do (see v. 16; see also 40:9; 47:9; 58:11; 59:13 and notes). *Most High.* See note on Ge 14:19.
Ps 84 A prayer of longing for the house of the Lord. In tone and perspective it stands close to Ps 42 and may reflect similar circumstances. If so, the author (presumably a Levite who normally functioned in the temple service), now barred from access to God's house (perhaps when Sennacherib was ravaging Judah; see 2Ki 18:13–16), gives voice to his longing for the sweet nearness to God in his temple that he had known in the past. Reference to God and his temple and to the "blessedness" (see vv. 4–5,12) of those having free access to both dominates the psalm and highlights its central themes.
The psalm has three main divisions (vv. 1–4, 5–7, 8–11) and a conclusion (v. 12). In the Hebrew text, a six-line unit precedes and follows a three-line reflection on the blessedness of those free to make pilgrimage to Zion. Each of these six-line divisions contains three references to the "LORD," while the seventh reference (symbolizing completeness or perfection) appears in the conclusion.
84 title *For the director of music.* See note on Ps 4 title. *According to.* See note on Ps 6 title. *gittith.* See note on Ps 8 title. *Of the Sons of Korah.* See note on Ps 42 title.
84:1–4 A confession of deep longing for the house of the Lord.
84:1 *lovely.* The traditional rendering of the Hebrew here, but perhaps better translated "beloved" or "loved." *LORD Almighty.* See vv. 3,8,12; see also note on 1Sa 1:3.
84:2 *My soul.* I (see note on 6:3). *courts.* Of the temple (see v. 10; 2Ki 21:5; 23:11–12). *my heart . . . flesh.* My whole being (see 73:26). *heart.* See note on 4:7. *living God.* See Dt 5:26.
84:3 The psalmist is jealous of the small birds that have such unhindered access to the temple and the altar. They are able even to build their nests there for their young—the place where Israel was to have communion with God.
84:4–5,12 *Blessed.* See note on 1:1.
84:4 *who dwell in your house.* See note on 15:1.
84:5–7 The joyful blessedness of those who are free to make pilgrimage to Zion—them too the psalmist envies.
84:5 *those whose strength is in you.* Those who have come to know the Lord as their deliverer and the sustainer of their lives. *who have set their hearts on pilgrimage.* Lit. "in whose hearts are (the) highways," i.e., the highways the Israelites took to observe the religious festivals at Jerusalem (Zion, v. 7). *hearts.* See note on 4:7.
84:6 *As they pass.* On their way to the temple. *Baca.* Means either "weeping" or "balsam trees" (common in arid valleys). The place is unknown and may be figurative (see 23:4) for arid stretches the pilgrims had to traverse. *place of springs.* The joyful expectations of the pilgrims transform the difficult ways into places of refreshment. *autumn rains.* The gentle early showers that are harbingers of the later spring rains (see Joel 2:23). *pools.* Whether the Hebrew for this word refers to "blessings" or whether it refers to "pools" (see NIV text note), it is likely that both are intended. By God's benevolent care over his pilgrims, the vale of weeping (or balsam trees), already transformed by the glad hearts of the expectant wayfarers, is turned into a valley of praise (see 2Ch 20:26). God's saints on their hopeful way to Zion experience anew the bountiful hand of God as their ancestors did on their way through the Desert of Sinai to the promised land (see 78:15–16; 105:41; 114:8)—and as their descendants would on their return to Zion from Babylo-

⁸Hear my prayer,ʰ O Lᴏʀᴅ God Almighty;
　listen to me, O God of Jacob.　　*Selah*
⁹Look upon our shield,ˢ ⁱ O God;
　look with favor on your anointed one.ʲ

¹⁰Better is one day in your courts
　than a thousand elsewhere;
　I would rather be a doorkeeperᵏ in the house of my God
　than dwell in the tents of the wicked.
¹¹For the Lᴏʀᴅ God is a sunˡ and shield;ᵐ
　the Lᴏʀᴅ bestows favor and honor;
　no good thing does he withholdⁿ
　from those whose walk is blameless.

¹²O Lᴏʀᴅ Almighty,
　blessedᵒ is the man who trusts in you.

Psalm 85

For the director of music. Of the Sons of Korah. A psalm.

¹You showed favor to your land, O Lᴏʀᴅ;
　you restored the fortunesᵖ of Jacob.

²You forgaveᑫ the iniquityʳ of your people
　and covered all their sins.　　*Selah*
³You set aside all your wrathˢ
　and turned from your fierce anger.ᵗ

⁴Restoreᵘ us again, O God our Savior,ᵛ
　and put away your displeasure toward us.
⁵Will you be angry with us forever?ʷ
　Will you prolong your anger through all generations?
⁶Will you not reviveˣ us again,
　that your people may rejoiceʸ in you?
⁷Show us your unfailing love,ᶻ O Lᴏʀᴅ,
　and grant us your salvation.ᵃ

⁸I will listen to what God the Lᴏʀᴅ will say;
　he promises peaceᵇ to his people, his saints—
　but let them not return to folly.ᶜ
⁹Surely his salvationᵈ is near those who fear him,
　that his gloryᵉ may dwell in our land.

¹⁰Love and faithfulnessᶠ meet together;

84:8 ʰPs 4:1
84:9 ⁱS Ps 59:11
/1Sa 16:6; Ps 2:2;
18:50; 132:17
84:10 ᵏ1Ch 23:5
84:11 ˡIsa 60:19;
Jer 43:13;
Rev 21:23
ᵐS Ge 15:1
ⁿPs 34:10
84:12 ᵒPs 2:12
85:1 ᵖS Dt 30:3;
Ps 14:7

85:2 ᑫS Nu 14:19
ʳS Ex 32:30;
S Ps 78:38
85:3 ˢPs 106:23;
Da 9:16
ᵗEx 32:12;
Dt 13:17;
Ps 78:38; Jnh 3:9
85:4 ᵘS Ps 71:20
ᵛS Ps 65:5
85:5 ʷS Ps 50:21
85:6 ˣS Ps 80:18
ʸPhp 3:1
85:7 ᶻS Ps 6:4
ᵃPs 27:1
85:8 ᵇS Lev 26:6;
S Isa 60:17;
S Jn 14:27;
2Th 3:16
ᶜPr 26:11; 27:22
85:9 ᵈPs 27:1;
Isa 43:3; 45:8;
46:13; 51:5;
56:1; 62:11
ᵉS Ex 29:43;
Isa 60:19;
Hag 2:9; Zec 2:5
85:10 ᶠPs 89:14;
115:1; Pr 3:3

ˢ9 Or *sovereign*

---

nian exile (see Isa 41:17–20; 43:19–20; 49:10).
84:7 *from strength to strength.* Whatever the toils and hardships of the journey (see Isa 40:31). *Zion.* See 9:11 and note.
84:8–11 A prayer for the king, and its motivation: Only as God blesses the king in Jerusalem will the psalmist once more realize his great desire to return to his accustomed service in the temple (see introduction).
84:8 *Lᴏʀᴅ God Almighty . . . God of Jacob.* That is, Lᴏʀᴅ God Almighty, the God of Jacob (see 59:5; see also note on 3:7). *Jacob.* A synonym for Israel (see Ge 32:28).
84:9 *our shield.* The king in Jerusalem (see NIV text note; see also note on 3:3). *anointed one.* God's earthly regent over his people (from David's line); see note on 2:2.
84:10 *doorkeeper.* Probably the psalmist's normal (and humble) service at the temple (see 2Ki 22:4). *dwell in the tents of the wicked.* Share in the life of those who do not honor the God of Zion.
84:11 *sun.* The glorious source of the light of life (see note on 27:1). *shield.* See note on 3:3. *blameless.* See 15:2 and note on Ge 17:1.
84:12 *The sum of it all* (see 40:4).
Ps 85 A communal prayer for the renewal of God's mercies to his people at a time when they are once more suffering distress. Many believe that vv. 1–3 refer to the return from exile and that the troubles experienced are those alluded to by Nehemiah and Malachi. Verse 12 suggests that a drought has ravaged the land and may reflect the drought with which the Lord chastened his people in the time of Haggai (see Hag 1:5–11). Christian liturgical usage has often employed this psalm in the Christmas season.
　The psalm has two main divisions of seven (Hebrew) lines each: (1) the prayer (vv. 1–7); (2) a reassuring word (vv. 8–13). Each division contains a three-line stanza followed by a four-line stanza, with the corresponding stanzas of the second half answering to those of the first: Verses 1–3 speak

of mercies granted, while vv. 8–9 speak of mercies soon to come; vv. 4–7 voice the prayer, and vv. 10–13 offer the blessed reassurance that the prayer will be heard. Each of the four stanzas contains one reference to the "Lᴏʀᴅ."
85 title *For the director of music.* See note on Ps 4 title. *Of the Sons of Korah.* See note on Ps 42 title.
85:1–7 Prayer for the renewal of God's favor.
85:1–3 Israel begins her prayer by appealing to the Lord's past mercies, recalling how he has forgiven and restored them before (perhaps a reference to the restoration from exile).
85:1 *restored the fortunes of Jacob.* Or "brought Jacob back from exile" (see Jer 29:14 and NIV text note). *Jacob.* A synonym for Israel (see Ge 32:28).
85:3 *wrath . . . anger.* See v. 5; see also note on 2:5.
85:4–7 The prayer acknowledges that the present troubles are indicative of God's displeasure. No confession of sin is expressed, but in the light of v. 3 (and possibly v. 8; see below) it is probably implicit.
85:7 *unfailing love.* See v. 10; see also note on 6:4.
85:8–13 God's reassuring answer to the prayer, conveyed through a priest or Levite, perhaps one of the Korahites (see note on 12:5–6; see also 2Ch 20:14).
85:8–9 The assurance that God will again bless his people.
85:8 *I will listen.* The speaker awaits the word from the Lord. *promises peace.* The word from the Lord perhaps takes the form of the priestly benediction (see Nu 6:22–26). *saints.* See note on 4:3. *but let them not return to folly.* And so provoke God's displeasure again. But it is also possible to translate the clause: "and to those who turn from folly." *folly.* See NIV text note on 14:1.
85:9 *glory.* Wherever God's saving power is displayed, his glory is revealed (see 57:5,11; 72:18–19; Ex 14:4,17–18; Nu 14:22; Isa 40:5; 44:23; 66:19; Eze 39:21).
85:10–13 God's sure mercies to his people spring from his covenant love, to which in his faithfulness and righteousness

righteousness^g and peace kiss each other.
¹¹Faithfulness springs forth from the earth,
and righteousness^h looks down from heaven.
¹²The LORD will indeed give what is good, ⁱ
and our land will yield^j its harvest.
¹³Righteousness goes before him
and prepares the way for his steps.

Psalm 86

A prayer of David.

¹Hear, O LORD, and answer^k me,
for I am poor and needy.
²Guard my life, for I am devoted to you.
You are my God; save your servant
who trusts in you. ^l
³Have mercy^m on me, O Lord,
for I callⁿ to you all day long.
⁴Bring joy to your servant,
for to you, O Lord,
I lift^o up my soul.

⁵You are forgiving and good, O Lord,
abounding in love^p to all who call to you.
⁶Hear my prayer, O LORD;
listen to my cry^q for mercy.
⁷In the day of my trouble^r I will call^s to you,
for you will answer^t me.

⁸Among the gods^u there is none like you, ^v O Lord;
no deeds can compare with yours.
⁹All the nations you have made
will come^w and worship^x before you, O Lord;
they will bring glory^y to your name.
¹⁰For you are great^z and do marvelous deeds; ^a
you alone^b are God.

¹¹Teach me your way, ^c O LORD,
and I will walk in your truth; ^d
give me an undivided^e heart,
that I may fear^f your name.

85:10
^gPs 72:2-3;
Isa 32:17
85:11 ^hIsa 45:8
85:12 ⁱPs 84:11;
Jas 1:17
^jLev 26:4;
S Ps 67:6;
Zec 8:12
86:1 ^kPs 17:6
86:2 ^lPs 25:2;
31:14
86:3 ^mPs 4:1;
S 9:13; 57:1
ⁿPs 88:9
86:4 ^oPs 46:5;
143:8

86:5 ^pEx 34:6;
Ne 9:17;
Ps 103:8; 145:8;
Joel 2:13; Jnh 4:2
86:6 ^qPs 5:2;
17:1
86:7 ^rPs 27:5;
S 50:15; 94:13;
Hab 3:16
^sJob 22:27;
Ps 4:3; 80:18;
91:15; Isa 30:19;
58:9; 65:24;
Zec 13:9 ^tPs 3:4
86:8 ^uS Ex 8:10;
S Job 21:22
^vS Ps 18:31
86:9 ^wS Ps 65:2
^xPs 66:4;
Isa 19:21; 27:13;
49:7;
Zec 8:20-22;
14:16; Rev 15:4

86:10 ^zS 2Sa 7:22; S Ps 48:1 ^aS Ex 3:20;
S Ps 71:17; 72:18 ^bS Dt 6:4; S Isa 43:10; Mk 12:29; 1Co 8:4
86:11 ^cS Ex 33:13; S 1Sa 12:23; Ps 25:5 ^dS Ps 26:3
^eJer 24:7; 32:39; Eze 11:19; 1Co 7:35 ^fS Dt 6:24

he remains true, and that assures his people's welfare (peace).
85:10 *Love and faithfulness . . . righteousness and peace.* These expressions of God's favor toward his people are here personified (see note on 23:6), and the vivid portrayal of their meeting and embracing offers one of the most beautiful images in all Scripture of God's gracious dealings with his covenant people. *righteousness.* See vv. 11,13; see also note on 4:1. *peace.* See note on Nu 6:26.
85:11 *Faithfulness springs forth.* As new growth springs from the earth to bless mankind with plenty. *righteousness looks down.* It shines down benevolently. (With "disaster" as subject, the Hebrew for "looks down" indicates the opposite effect: Jer 6:1, "looms.") From heaven and from earth, God's covenant blessings will abound till Israel's cup overflows.
85:12 *what is good.* See 31:19 and note.
85:13 *Righteousness goes before.* Again the psalmist personifies. Acting either as herald or guide, righteousness leads the way and marks the course for God's engagement in his people's behalf—and righteousness is God's perfect faithfulness to all his covenant commitments (see note on 4:1).
Ps 86 A prayer for God's help when attacked by enemies, whose fierce onslaughts betray their disdain for the Lord. Whether or not David was the author (see Introduction: Authorship and Titles), the psalmist's identification of himself as God's "servant" (v. 2) suggests his royal status and thus his special relationship with the Lord (see 2Sa 7:5,8 and note on Ps 18 title). The enemies may then be either those within the kingdom who refuse to acknowledge him as the Lord's anointed, or foreign powers that are attempting to remove him from the international scene.
    The psalm is composed of five stanzas, having a symmetrical verse pattern (four, three, three, three, four). The author identifies himself as the Lord's servant in the first and last stanzas, which also contain the prayer for God's mercy and deliverance from the enemy threat. The center stanza (vv. 8-10) hails the Lord as the incomparable, the only God, whom all the nations will someday worship. Verse 9 is the

center verse (see note on 6:6).
86 title *prayer.* See note on Ps 17 title; see also note on 72:20. *of David.* This is the only psalm in Book III (Ps 73–89) that is ascribed to David. Perhaps its placement among the Korahite psalms is because those who arranged the Psalter perceived a thematic link between v. 9 and 87:4.
86:1–4 Initial prayer for God to have mercy and protect the life of his servant.
86:1 *poor and needy.* See 35:10; see also 34:6 and note.
86:2 *devoted to you.* The Hebrew for this phrase is *hasid* (see note on 4:3). *You are my God.* Not that David has chosen him, but that he has chosen David to be his servant (see 1Sa 13:14; 15:28; 16:12; 2Sa 7:8). David's devotion to God and God's commitment to him are deliberately juxtaposed. *your servant.* See vv. 4,16; see also introduction.
86:4 *my soul.* See note on 6:3.
86:5–7 In his need David prays to the Lord because, out of his kindness and love, God answers prayer.
86:5 *love.* See vv. 13,15; see also note on 6:4.
86:8–10 The God to whom David appeals is the only true God. No other "god" acts with such sovereign power (see 115:3–7; 135:13–17)—that is why David appeals to him and why all the nations will someday worship him.
86:9 *All the nations.* See note on 46:10. This is the center verse of the psalm (see note on 6:6) and contains the psalm's most exalted confession of faith concerning God's sovereign and universal rule. *they will bring glory.* As David vows to do (v. 12). *your name.* See vv. 11–12; see also note on 5:11.
86:10 *marvelous deeds.* See note on 9:1.
86:11–13 A prayer for godliness and a vow to praise.
86:11 *Teach me . . . give me.* What would be the benefit if God saved him from his enemies but abandoned him to his own waywardness? David's dependence on God is complete, and so is his devotion to God—save me from the enemy outside but also from my frailty within (see 25:5; 51:7,10). Only one who is thus devoted to God may expect God's help and will truly fulfill the vow (v. 12). *undivided heart.* See Eze 11:19; see also 1Ch 12:33; 1Co 7:35. *heart.* See note on 4:7.

12I will praise you, O Lord my God, with
  all my heart;*g*
  I will glorify your name forever.
13For great is your love toward me;
  you have delivered me*h* from the
  depths of the grave.*t* *i*

14The arrogant are attacking me, O God;
  a band of ruthless men seeks my
  life—
  men without regard for you.*j*
15But you, O Lord, are a compassionate
  and gracious*k* God,
  slow to anger,*l* abounding*m* in love
  and faithfulness.*n*
16Turn to me*o* and have mercy*p* on me;
  grant your strength*q* to your servant
  and save the son of your
  maidservant.*u* *r*
17Give me a sign*s* of your goodness,
  that my enemies may see it and be
  put to shame,
  for you, O Lord, have helped me and
  comforted me.

Psalm 87

Of the Sons of Korah. A psalm. A song.

1He has set his foundation on the holy
  mountain;*t*
2 the Lord loves the gates of Zion*u*
  more than all the dwellings of Jacob.
3Glorious things are said of you,
  O city of God:*v*   *Selah*
4"I will record Rahab*v* *w* and Babylon
  among those who acknowledge me—
  Philistia*x* too, and Tyre*y*, along with
  Cush*w*—
  and will say, 'This*x* one was born in
  Zion.*z* '"

5Indeed, of Zion it will be said,
  "This one and that one were born in
  her,
  and the Most High himself will
  establish her."
6The Lord will write in the register*a* of
  the peoples:

Cross reference column:

86:12 *g*S Ps 9:1
86:13 *h*S Ps 34:4;
49:15; 116:8
*i*S Ps 16:10;
S 56:13
86:14 *j*Ps 54:3
86:15 *k*S Ps 51:1;
103:8; 111:4;
116:5; 145:8
*l*Nu 14:18 *m*ver 5
*n*S Ex 34:6;
S Ne 9:17;
Joel 2:13
86:16 *o*S Ps 6:4
*p*S Ps 9:13
*q*Ps 18:1
*r*Ps 116:16
86:17 *s*S Ex 3:12;
Mt 24:3;
S Jn 2:11

87:1 *t*S Ps 48:1
87:2 *u*Ps 2:6
87:3 *v*S Ps 46:4
87:4 *w*S Job 9:13
*x*S 2Sa 8:1;
Ps 83:7
*y*Ps 45:12;
Joel 3:4
*z*Isa 19:25
87:6 *a*Ex 32:32;
Ps 69:28; Isa 4:3;
Mal 3:16

NIV text notes:

*t*13 Hebrew *Sheol*   *u*16 Or *save your faithful son*
*v*4 A poetic name for Egypt   *w*4 That is, the upper
Nile region   *x*4 Or *"O Rahab and Babylon, / Philistia,
Tyre and Cush, / I will record concerning those who
acknowledge me: / 'This*

86:12 Vow to praise (see note on 7:17).
86:13 David anticipates the answer to his prayer (see note on 3:8). *depths*. See note on 30:1.
86:14–17 Conclusion: the prayer renewed.
86:14 *ruthless*. The Hebrew for this word suggests also ferocity. *men without regard for you*. In their arrogance they dismiss the heavenly Warrior, who is David's defender (see note on 10:11; see also Jer 20:11).
86:15 Echoes v. 5, but is even more similar to Ex 34:6 (see note on Ex 34:6–7).
86:16 *grant your strength*. Exert your power in my behalf. *son of your maidservant*. See NIV text note; see also 116:16 and NIV text note.
86:17 *goodness*. Covenanted favors (see 27:13 and note). *may see it*. May see that you stand with me and help me (see 31:19 and note).
Ps 87 A celebration of Zion as the "city of God" (v. 3), the special object of his love and the royal city of his kingdom (see introductions to Ps 46; 48; 76). According to the ancient and consistent interpretation of Jewish and Christian scholars alike, this psalm stands in lonely isolation in the Psalter (but see 47:9) in that it foresees the ingathering of the nations into Zion as fellow citizens with Israel in the kingdom of God—after the manner of such prophetic visions as Isa 2:2–4; 19:19–25; 25:6; 45:14,22–24; 56:6–8; 60:3; 66:23; Da 7:14; Mic 4:1–3; Zec 8:23; 14:16. (Accordingly, some have assigned it to the time of Isaiah and Micah, while others have thought it to be postexilic.) So interpreted, this psalm stands in sharpest possible contrast with the other Zion songs of the Psalter (see Ps 46; 48; 76; 125; 129; 137). The key to its main thrust lies in v. 4. It may be that its historic interpretation has sprung from the failure of tradition to preserve memory of the Hebrew poetic device of interrupted syntax (which occurs elsewhere) and that the references to foreign nations should be read as vocatives (see NIV text note on v. 4). With this reading, the psalm stands in thematic accord with the other Zion songs, celebrating God's special love for Zion—which is thrown into the teeth of Zion's

historic enemies (see note on v. 4).
87 title *Of the Sons of Korah*. See note on Ps 42 title. *song*. See note on Ps 30 title.
87:1 *his foundation*. The Lord himself has laid the foundations of Zion (see Isa 14:32) and of the temple as his royal house. *mountain*. The Hebrew for this word is plural, emphasizing the majesty of the holy mountain on which God's throne has been set (see 48:2 and note).
87:2 *loves . . . more than*. As the city of his founding, his chosen seat of rule over his people, Zion is the Lord's most cherished city, even among the towns of Israel (see 9:11; 78:68; 132:12–14). *Jacob*. A synonym for Israel (see Ge 32:28).
87:4 *I will record . . . This one was born in Zion*. God will list them in his royal register (see notes on 9:5; 51:1; 69:28) as those who are native (born) citizens of his royal city, having all the privileges and enjoying all the benefits and security of such citizenship. *Rahab*. Whereas elsewhere this name is applied to the mythical monster of the deep (see 89:10; see also notes on 32:6; Job 9:13), here the reference is to Egypt (see NIV text note), as in Isa 30:7 (see note there); 51:9. The nations listed are representative of all Gentile peoples. As usually interpreted, the psalm here foresees a widespread conversion to the Lord from the peoples who from time immemorial had been hostile to him and to his kingdom (see Isa 19:21). More likely (see NIV text note and v. 5), the Lord is here portrayed as carefully recording the names of all his people, those who acknowledge him as their covenant Lord (Hos 6:3), so as to take them under his protection as the citizens of his royal city. Ominously he warns the nations (as in Isa 14:28–32) that he has carefully registered his people one and all and will hold the nations accountable for the harm they do to any one of them (see 105:15).
87:5 *This one and that one*. Wherever they may be dispersed among the nations. *Most High*. See note on Ge 14:19.

"This one was born in Zion." *Selah*
[7]As they make music[b] they will sing,
"All my fountains[c] are in you."

Psalm 88

A song. A psalm of the Sons of Korah. For
the director of music. According to
mahalath leannoth.[y] A *maskil*[z] of
Heman the Ezrahite.

[1]O LORD, the God who saves me,[d]
  day and night I cry out[e] before you.
[2]May my prayer come before you;
  turn your ear to my cry.

[3]For my soul is full of trouble[f]
  and my life draws near the grave.[a][g]
[4]I am counted among those who go
  down to the pit;[h]
  I am like a man without strength.[i]
[5]I am set apart with the dead,
  like the slain who lie in the grave,
  whom you remember no more,
  who are cut off[j] from your care.

[6]You have put me in the lowest pit,
  in the darkest depths.[k]
[7]Your wrath[l] lies heavily upon me;

you have overwhelmed me with all
  your waves.[m]   *Selah*
[8]You have taken from me my closest
  friends[n]
  and have made me repulsive to them.
I am confined[o] and cannot escape;[p]
[9] my eyes[q] are dim with grief.

I call[r] to you, O LORD, every day;
  I spread out my hands[s] to you.
[10]Do you show your wonders to the
  dead?
  Do those who are dead rise up and
  praise you?[t]   *Selah*
[11]Is your love declared in the grave,
  your faithfulness[u] in Destruction[b]?
[12]Are your wonders known in the place
  of darkness,
  or your righteous deeds in the land of
  oblivion?

[13]But I cry to you for help,[v] O LORD;
  in the morning[w] my prayer comes
  before you.[x]
[14]Why, O LORD, do you reject[y] me
  and hide your face[z] from me?

Cross references

87:7 [b]Ps 149:3
[c]S Ps 36:9
88:1 [d]S Ps 51:14
[e]Ps 3:4; 22:2;
Lk 18:7
88:3 [f]Ps 6:3;
25:17
[g]S Job 33:22
88:4 [h]S Ps 31:12
[i]Ps 18:1
88:5 [j]S Ps 31:22
88:6 [k]Ps 30:1;
S 69:15; La 3:55;
Jnh 2:3
88:7 [l]Ps 7:11

88:8 [m]S Ps 42:7
[n]S Job 19:13;
Ps 31:11
[o]Jer 32:2; 33:1
[p]S Job 3:23
88:9 [q]S Ps 38:10
[r]Ps 5:2
[s]Job 11:13;
Ps 143:6
88:10 [t]S Ps 6:5
88:11 [u]S Ps 30:9
88:13 [v]S Ps 30:2
[w]Ps 5:3; S 55:17
[x]Ps 119:147
88:14 [y]S Ps 43:2
[z]Ps 13:1

[y]Title: Possibly a tune, "The Suffering of Affliction"
[z]Title: Probably a literary or musical term   [a]3 Hebrew
Sheol   [b]11 Hebrew *Abaddon*

87:7 *All my fountains.* All that refreshes them is found in
the city of God, a possible allusion to God's "river of delights" (36:8) "whose streams make glad the city of God"
(46:4); see notes on those passages. Alternatively, "fountains" may be a metaphor for sources; the sense of the line
would then be: We all spring from you. *my.* Communal use
of the singular pronoun (see introduction to Ps 30).
Ps 88 A cry out of the depths, the prayer of one on the edge
of death, whose whole life has been lived, as it were, in the
near vicinity of the grave. So troubled have been his years
that he seems to have known only the back of God's hand
(God's "wrath," v. 7), and even those nearest him have
withdrawn themselves as from one with an infectious skin
disease (see v. 8). No expressions of hopeful expectation (as
in most prayers of the Psalter) burst from these lips; the last
word speaks of darkness as "my closest friend." And yet the
prayer begins, "O LORD, the God who saves me." The psalm
recalls the fact that although sometimes godly persons live
lives of unremitting trouble (see 73:14), they can still grasp
the hope that God is Savior. In its Hebrew structure, three
four-line stanzas (vv. 3–5, 6–9a, 9b–12) are framed by two
two-line prayers; to this is appended an additional four-line
stanza in which the psalmist complains that his present
distress is but characteristic of his whole troubled life.
88 title The psalm bears a double title, perhaps representing two different traditions. *song.* See note on Ps 30 title. *of
the Sons of Korah.* See note on Ps 42 title. *For the director of
music.* See note on Ps 4 title. *According to.* See note on Ps 6
title. *maskil.* See note on Ps 32 title. *Heman.* See note on Ps
39 title. *Ezrahite.* The reference appears to be to Zerah, one
of Judah's sons, who is recorded as having a Heman and an
Ethan (see Ps 89 title) among his sons (see 1Ch 2:6). If so,
the title here represents a confusion in the tradition, arising
from the similarity between these two Judahite names and
those of two famous Korahite choir leaders, Heman and
Ethan (Jeduthun; see note on Ps 39 title).

88:1–2 Opening appeal to the Lord as "the God who saves
me."
88:3–5 Living on the brink of death. Whether the psalmist
lies mortally ill or experiences some analogous trouble or
peril cannot be known.
88:3 *my soul.* See note on 6:3.
88:4 *pit.* See note on 30:1.
88:5 *remember no more.* From the perspective of this life,
death cuts off from God's care; there is no remembering by
God of the needy sufferer to rescue and restore (see 25:7;
74:2; 106:4). In his dark mood the author portrays his
situation in bleakest colors (see note on 6:5).
88:6–9a *You, O God, have done this!* The psalmist knows
no reason for it (see v. 14), but he knows God's hand is in it
(see Ru 1:20–21; Am 3:6). That his Savior-God shows him
the face of wrath deepens his anguish and helplessness. But
he does not try to resolve the dark enigma; he simply pleads
his case—and it is to his Savior-God that he can appeal.
88:6 *lowest pit . . . darkest depths.* See note on 30:1.
88:7 *wrath.* See v. 16; see also note on 2:5. *all your waves.*
See note on 32:6.
88:8 *my closest friends.* See v. 18 and note on 31:11–12.
88:9 *eyes are dim.* See note on 6:7.
88:9b–12 Appeal to God to help before the psalmist sinks
into "the land of oblivion" (see note on v. 5).
88:10,12 *wonders.* God's saving acts in behalf of his
people (see note on 9:1).
88:10 *rise up.* In the realm of the dead (not in the resurrection); see Isa 14:9.
88:11 *love . . . faithfulness.* That is, love-and-faithfulness
(see note on 36:5; see also note on 3:7). *love.* See note on
6:4.
88:12 *righteous deeds.* See note on 71:24.
88:13–14 Concluding prayer.
88:14 *Why . . . ?* See note on 6:3; see also Introduction:
Theology. *hide your face.* See note on 13:1.

15From my youth[a] I have been afflicted[b] and close to death;
  I have suffered your terrors[c] and am in despair.[d]
16Your wrath[e] has swept over me;
  your terrors[f] have destroyed me.
17All day long they surround me like a flood;[g]
  they have completely engulfed me.
18You have taken my companions[h] and loved ones from me;
  the darkness is my closest friend.

Psalm 89

A *maskil*[c] of Ethan the Ezrahite.

1I will sing[i] of the LORD's great love forever;
  with my mouth I will make your faithfulness known[j] through all generations.
2I will declare that your love stands firm forever,
  that you established your faithfulness in heaven itself.[k]

3You said, "I have made a covenant with my chosen one,
  I have sworn to David my servant,
4'I will establish your line forever

and make your throne firm through all generations.' "[l]   *Selah*

5The heavens[m] praise your wonders, O LORD,
  your faithfulness too, in the assembly[n] of the holy ones.
6For who in the skies above can compare with the LORD?
  Who is like the LORD among the heavenly beings?[o]
7In the council[p] of the holy ones[q] God is greatly feared;
  he is more awesome than all who surround him.[r]
8O LORD God Almighty,[s] who is like you?[t]
  You are mighty, O LORD, and your faithfulness surrounds you.

9You rule over the surging sea;
  when its waves mount up, you still them.[u]
10You crushed Rahab[v] like one of the slain;
  with your strong arm you scattered[w] your enemies.
11The heavens are yours,[x] and yours also the earth;[y]

88:15 [a]Ps 129:1; Jer 22:21; Eze 16:22; Hos 2:15 [b]Ps 9:12 [c]Job 6:4; S 18:11 [d]2Co 4:8
88:16 [e]Ps 7:11 [f]Job 6:4
88:17 [g]Ps 124:4
88:18 [h]ver 8; Ps 38:11
89:1 [i]Ps 59:16 [j]S Ps 36:5; 40:10
89:2 [k]S Ps 36:5

89:4 [l]2Sa 7:12-16; 1Ki 8:16; Ps 132:11-12; Isa 9:7; Eze 37:24-25; S Mt 1:1; S Lk 1:33
89:5 [m]S Ps 19:1 [n]S Ps 1:5
89:6 [o]S Ge 1:26; S Ex 9:14; S Ps 18:31; 113:5
89:7 [p]Ps 111:1 [q]Job 5:1 [r]Ps 47:2
89:8 [s]Isa 6:3 [t]S Ps 71:19
89:9 [u]S Ps 65:7
89:10 [v]Job 9:13 [w]S Ps 59:11; S 68:1; 92:9
89:11 [x]S Dt 10:14; Ps 115:16 [y]1Ch 29:11; S Ps 24:1

[c]Title: Probably a literary or musical term

88:15–18 The psalmist has been no stranger to trouble; all his life he has suffered the terrors of God.
88:17 *like a flood.* See v. 7; see also note on 32:6.
Ps 89 A prayer that mourns the downfall of the Davidic dynasty and pleads for its restoration. The bitter shock of that event (reflected partially in the sudden transition of v. 38) is almost unbearable—that God, the faithful and almighty One, has abandoned his anointed and made him the mockery of the nations, in seeming violation of his firm covenant with David—and it evokes from the psalmist a lament that borders on reproach (vv. 38–45). The event may have been the attack on Jerusalem by Nebuchadnezzar and the exile of King Jehoiachin in 597 B.C. (see 2Ki 24:8–17).
  As with Ps 44 (see introduction to that psalm), a massive foundation is laid for the prayer with which the psalm concludes. An introduction (vv. 1–4) sings of God's love and faithfulness (vv. 1–2) and his covenant with David (vv. 3–4). These two themes are then jubilantly expanded in order: vv. 5–18, God's love and faithfulness; vv. 19–37, his covenant with David. Suddenly jubilation turns to lament, and the psalmist recounts in detail how God has rejected his anointed (vv. 38–45). Thus he comes to his prayer, impatient and urgent, that God will remember once more his covenant with David (vv. 46–51). (Verse 52 concludes not the psalm but Book III of the Psalter.)
89 title *maskil.* See note on Ps 32 title. *Ethan.* Jeduthun (see note on Ps 39 title). The author was no doubt a Levite (perhaps a descendant of Jeduthun) who voiced this agonizing prayer as spokesman for the nation. *Ezrahite.* See note on Ps 88 title.
89:1–2 God's love and faithfulness celebrated.
89:1 *love . . . faithfulness.* See vv. 2,33,49; that is, love-and-faithfulness (see v. 14); see note on 36:5. *love.* See vv. 2,14,24,28,33,49; see also note on 6:4. It is God's love and

faithfulness that appear to have failed in his rejection (see vv. 38–45) of the Davidic king. The author repeats each of these words precisely seven times (in v. 14 the Hebrew uses a different—but related—word for "faithfulness").
89:2 *in heaven itself.* God's love and faithfulness have been made sure in the highest seat of power and authority (see vv. 5–8).
89:3–4 God's covenant with David celebrated (see 2Sa 7:8–16).
89:3 *servant.* See vv. 20,39,50; here an official title (see note on 78:70).
89:5–8 The Lord's faithfulness and awesome power set him apart among all the powers in the heavenly realm, and they acknowledge him with praise and reverence.
89:5 *The heavens.* All beings belonging to the divine realm in the heavens. *wonders.* God's mighty acts in creation and redemption (see note on 9:1). *assembly of the holy ones.* The divine council in heaven (see v. 7; see also note on 82:1).
89:6 *heavenly beings.* Lit. "sons of god(s)" (see 29:1 and note).
89:8 *LORD . . . Almighty.* See note on 1Sa 1:3. *your faithfulness surrounds you.* It also surrounds this stanza (see v. 5).
89:9–13 The Lord's power as Creator—and creation's joy in him.
89:9–10 Poetic imagery borrowed from ancient Near Eastern myths of creation, here celebrating God's power in ordering the primeval chaotic waters so that the creation order could be established (see Ge 1:6–10; see also notes on 65:6–7; 74:13–14).
89:10 *Rahab.* Mythical monster of the deep (see notes on 32:6; 87:4), probably another name for Leviathan (see 74:14; 104:26). The last half of this verse is probably echoed in Lk 1:51.

you founded the world and all that is in it.ᶻ

¹²You created the north and the south; Taborᵃ and Hermonᵇ sing for joyᶜ at your name.

¹³Your arm is endued with power; your hand is strong, your right hand exalted.ᵈ

¹⁴Righteousness and justice are the foundation of your throne;ᵉ love and faithfulness go before you.ᶠ

¹⁵Blessed are those who have learned to acclaim you, who walkᵍ in the lightʰ of your presence, O LORD.

¹⁶They rejoice in your nameⁱ all day long; they exult in your righteousness.

¹⁷For you are their glory and strength,ʲ and by your favor you exalt our horn.ᵈ ᵏ

¹⁸Indeed, our shieldᵉ ˡ belongs to the LORD, our kingᵐ to the Holy One of Israel.

¹⁹Once you spoke in a vision, to your faithful people you said: "I have bestowed strength on a warrior; I have exalted a young man from among the people.

²⁰I have found Davidⁿ my servant;ᵒ with my sacred oilᵖ I have anointedᑫ him.

²¹My hand will sustain him; surely my arm will strengthen him.ʳ

²²No enemy will subject him to tribute;ˢ no wicked man will oppressᵗ him.

²³I will crush his foes before himᵘ and strike down his adversaries.ᵛ

²⁴My faithful love will be with him,ʷ

and through my name his hornᶠ will be exalted.

²⁵I will set his hand over the sea, his right hand over the rivers.ˣ

²⁶He will call out to me, 'You are my Father,ʸ my God, the Rockᶻ my Savior.'ᵃ

²⁷I will also appoint him my firstborn,ᵇ the most exaltedᶜ of the kingsᵈ of the earth.

²⁸I will maintain my love to him forever, and my covenant with him will never fail.ᵉ

²⁹I will establish his line forever, his throne as long as the heavens endure.ᶠ

³⁰"If his sons forsake my law and do not follow my statutes,

³¹if they violate my decrees and fail to keep my commands,

³²I will punish their sin with the rod, their iniquity with flogging;ᵍ

³³but I will not take my love from him,ʰ nor will I ever betray my faithfulness.

³⁴I will not violate my covenant or alter what my lips have uttered.ⁱ

³⁵Once for all, I have sworn by my holiness— and I will not lie to David—

³⁶that his line will continue forever and his throne endure before me like the sun;ʲ

³⁷it will be established forever like the moon, the faithful witness in the sky."ᵏ

Selah

³⁸But you have rejected,ˡ you have spurned,

Cross references (center column):

89:11 ᶻS Ge 1:1
89:12
ᵃS Jos 19:22
ᵇS Dt 3:8; S 4:48
ᶜPs 98:8
89:13 ᵈS Jos 4:24
89:14 ᵉPs 97:2
ᶠPs 85:10-11
89:15 ᵍPs 1:1
ʰPs 44:3
89:16 ⁱPs 30:4; 105:3
89:17 ʲPs 18:1
ᵏver 24; Ps 75:10; 92:10; 112:9; 148:14
89:18 ˡPs 18:2
ᵐPs 47:9; Isa 16:5; 33:17, 22
89:20 ⁿAc 13:22
ᵒPs 78:70
ᵖS Ex 29:7; S 1Ki 1:39
ᑫS 1Sa 2:35; S 2Sa 22:51
89:21 ʳver 13; Ps 18:35
89:22 ˢS Jdg 3:15
ᵗ2Sa 7:10
89:23 ᵘPs 18:40
ᵛ2Sa 7:9
89:24 ʷS 2Sa 7:15
89:25 ˣPs 72:8
89:26 ʸS 2Sa 7:14; S Jer 3:4; Heb 1:5
ᶻS Ps 62:2
ᵃS 2Sa 22:47
89:27 ᵇS Col 1:18
ᶜS Nu 24:7
ᵈPs 2:6; Rev 1:5; 19:16
89:28 ᵉver 33-34; Isa 55:3
89:29 ᶠver 4,36
89:32 ᵍ2Sa 7:14
89:33 ʰS 2Sa 7:15
89:34 ⁱS Nu 23:19
89:36 ʲver 4
89:37 ᵏJer 33:20-21
89:38 ˡ1Ch 28:9; Ps 44:9; 78:59

Footnotes:

ᵈ *17 Horn* here symbolizes strong one.   ᵉ *18* Or *sovereign*   ᶠ *24 Horn* here symbolizes strength.

89:12 *the north and the south.* Reference may be to two mountains, here parallel to Tabor and Hermon: "Mount North" (Zaphon; see 48:2 and note) and Mount Amana (see SS 4:8). *Tabor.* See note on Jdg 4:6. *Hermon.* See note on Dt 3:8. *sing for joy.* See note on 65:13. *name.* See vv. 16,24; see also note on 5:11.

89:14-18 The Lord's righteousness and faithfulness in his rule in behalf of his people—and their joy in him.

89:14 Righteousness and justice are the foundation stones of God's throne; love and faithfulness are personified as angelic attendants that herald his royal movements (see note on 23:6). *Righteousness.* See v. 16; see also note on 4:1.

89:17 *horn.* King (see NIV text note; see also v. 18).

89:18 *Holy One of Israel.* See note on Isa 1:4.

89:19-29 The Lord's election of David to be his regent over his people, and his everlasting covenant with him. The thought is developed by couplets: (1) introduction (v. 19); (2) I have anointed David as my servant and will sustain him (vv. 20-21); (3) I will crush all his foes (vv. 22-23); (4) I will extend his realm (vv. 24-25); (5) I will make him first among the kings (vv. 26-27); (6) I will cause his dynasty to

endure forever (vv. 28-29)—a promise fulfilled in the eternal reign of Jesus Christ (see Jn 12:34).

89:19 *vision.* Reference is to the revelation to Samuel (see 1Sa 16:12) and/or to Nathan (see 2Sa 7:4-16). *faithful people.* See note on 4:3.

89:25 *sea . . . rivers.* David's rule will reach from the Mediterranean Sea to the Euphrates River (see 72:8; 80:11 and note on Ex 23:31). But the author uses imagery that underscores the fact that, as his royal "son" (see v. 26) and regent, David's rule will be a reflection of God's (see vv. 9-10 and notes; also compare v. 23 with v. 10).

89:27 *firstborn.* The royal son of highest privilege and position in the kingdom of God (see 2:7-12; 45:6-9; 72:8-11; 110), thus the most exalted of the kings of the earth (see Rev 1:5).

89:29 *as long as the heavens endure.* See vv. 36-37.

89:30-37 The Lord's covenant with David and his dynasty (see chart on "Major Covenants in the OT," p. 19) is everlasting (see v. 28) and unconditional—though if any of his royal descendants is unfaithful he will individually suffer under God's rod (to the detriment of the entire nation).

you have been very angry with your
anointed one.

39You have renounced the covenant with
your servant
and have defiled his crown in the
dust. *m*

40You have broken through all his walls *n*
and reduced his strongholds *o* to
ruins.

41All who pass by have plundered *p* him;
he has become the scorn of his
neighbors. *q*

42You have exalted the right hand of his
foes;
you have made all his enemies
rejoice. *r*

43You have turned back the edge of his
sword
and have not supported him in
battle. *s*

44You have put an end to his splendor
and cast his throne to the ground.

45You have cut short *t* the days of his
youth;
you have covered him with a mantle
of shame. *u*   *Selah*

46How long, O LORD? Will you hide
yourself forever?
How long will your wrath burn like
fire? *v*

47Remember how fleeting is my life. *w*
For what futility you have created all
men!

48What man can live and not see death,
or save himself from the power of the
grave *g* ? *x*   *Selah*

49O Lord, where is your former great
love,
which in your faithfulness you swore
to David?

50Remember, Lord, how your servant
has *h* been mocked, *y*
how I bear in my heart the taunts of
all the nations,

51the taunts with which your enemies
have mocked, O LORD,
with which they have mocked every
step of your anointed one. *z*

52Praise be to the LORD forever!
Amen and Amen. *a*

BOOK IV

Psalms 90–106

Psalm 90

A prayer of Moses the man of God.

1Lord, you have been our dwelling
place *b*
throughout all generations.

2Before the mountains were born *c*
or you brought forth the earth and
the world,
from everlasting to everlasting *d* you
are God. *e*

3You turn men back to dust,
saying, "Return to dust, O sons of
men." *f*

4For a thousand years in your sight
are like a day that has just gone by,

g48 Hebrew *Sheol*   *h50* Or *your servants have*

---

or like a watch in the night. *g*

⁵You sweep men away *h* in the sleep of
        death;
    they are like the new grass of the
        morning—
⁶though in the morning it springs up
        new,
    by evening it is dry and withered. *i*

⁷We are consumed by your anger
    and terrified by your indignation.
⁸You have set our iniquities before you,
    our secret sins *j* in the light of your
        presence. *k*
⁹All our days pass away under your
        wrath;
    we finish our years with a moan. *l*
¹⁰The length of our days is seventy
        years *m*—
    or eighty, *n* if we have the strength;
    yet their span *i* is but trouble and
        sorrow, *o*
    for they quickly pass, and we fly
        away. *p*

¹¹Who knows the power of your anger?
    For your wrath *q* is as great as the
        fear that is due you. *r*
¹²Teach us to number our days *s* aright,
    that we may gain a heart of
        wisdom. *t*

¹³Relent, O LORD! How long *u* will it be?
    Have compassion on your servants. *v*

¹⁴Satisfy *w* us in the morning with your
        unfailing love, *x*
    that we may sing for joy *y* and be glad
        all our days. *z*
¹⁵Make us glad for as many days as you
        have afflicted us,
    for as many years as we have seen
        trouble.
¹⁶May your deeds be shown to your
        servants,
    your splendor to their children. *a*
¹⁷May the favor *j* of the Lord our God
        rest upon us;
    establish the work of our hands for
        us—
    yes, establish the work of our
        hands. *b*

Psalm 91

¹He who dwells in the shelter *c* of the
        Most High
    will rest in the shadow *d* of the
        Almighty. *k*
²I will say *l* of the LORD, "He is my
        refuge *e* and my fortress, *f*
    my God, in whom I trust."

³Surely he will save you from the
        fowler's snare *g*
    and from the deadly pestilence. *h*
⁴He will cover you with his feathers,

90:4 *g*S Job 10:5;
2Pe 3:8
90:5 *h*S Ge 19:15
90:6 *i*Isa 40:6-8;
Mt 6:30; Jas 1:10
90:8 *j*S Ps 19:12;
2Co 4:2;
Eph 5:12
*k*S Heb 4:13
90:9 *l*Ps 78:33
90:10
*m*Isa 23:15,17;
Jer 25:11
*n*2Sa 19:35
*o*S Job 5:7
*p*S Job 20:8;
S 34:15
90:11 *q*Ps 7:11
*r*Ps 76:7
90:12 *s*Ps 39:4;
139:16; Pr 16:9;
20:24 *t*Dt 32:29
90:13 *u*Ps 6:3
*v*S Dt 32:36

90:14 *w*Ps 103:5;
107:9; 145:16,19
*x*S Ps 77:8; 143:8
*y*S Ps 5:11
*z*Ps 31:7
90:16 *a*Ps 44:1;
Hab 3:2
90:17 *b*Isa 26:12
91:1 *c*S Ex 33:22
*d*Ps 63:7;
Isa 49:2; La 4:20
91:2 *e*ver 9;
S 2Sa 22:3; Ps 9:9
*f*S 2Sa 22:2
91:3 *g*Ps 124:7;
Pr 6:5 *h*1Ki 8:37

*i*10 Or *yet the best of them*   *j*17 Or *beauty*
*k*1 Hebrew *Shaddai*   *l*2 Or *He says*

90:7–10 Even life's short span is filled with trouble, as God
ferrets out man's every sin and makes him feel his righteous
anger.
90:7 *anger . . . indignation.* See vv. 9,11; see also note on
2:5.
90:8 *light of your presence.* The holy light of God that
illumines the hidden corners of the heart and exposes its dark
secrets.
90:10 *eighty.* Hebrew poetic convention called for 80
following 70 in parallel construction (see note on Am 1:3).
their span. Lit. "their pride" (see NIV text note), i.e., what
men prize in their years. The thought could be: All their
health, joys, riches and honor are soured by trouble and
sorrow. *sorrow.* Or "emptiness."
90:11–12 *Who knows . . . ? . . . Teach us.* No one has
taken the measure of God's anger. But everyone ought to
know the measure of his (few) days or he will play the
arrogant fool, with no thought of his mortality or of his
accountability to God (see Ps 49; 73:4–12).
90:11 *fear that is due you.* See note on Ge 20:11.
90:12 *gain.* Or "harvest." *heart.* See note on 4:7.
90:13–17 Prayer for God's compassion—from him comes
also joy and gladness.
90:13 *Relent.* Lit. "Turn" (cf. v. 3). *How long . . . ?* See
note on 6:3 (see also Introduction: Theology).
90:14 *in the morning.* Let there be for us a dawning of your
love to relieve this long, dark night of your anger. Perhaps
Moses (see title) pleads for the promised rest of the promised
land (see Ex 33:14; Dt 12:9). The final answer to his prayer
comes with the resurrection (see Ro 5:2–5; 8:18; 2Co

4:16–18). *unfailing love.* See note on 6:4.
90:16 *deeds . . . splendor.* That is, deeds-of-splendor (see
111:3; see also note on 3:7). For a fuller description of such
deeds see the whole of Ps 111. *to their children.* As to past
generations (v. 1).
90:17 *favor.* See NIV text note; see also 27:4 and note.
establish. As you only have been our security in the world
(see v. 1), so also make our labors to be effective and enduring—though we are so transient.
Ps 91 A glowing testimony to the security of those who
trust in God. It was probably written by one of the temple
personnel (a priest or Levite) as a word of assurance to godly
worshipers. Because the "you" of vv. 3–13 applies to any of
the godly who "make the Most High your dwelling" (v. 9;
see 90:1), the devil applied vv. 11–12 to Jesus (see Mt 4:6;
Lk 4:10–11). Structurally, the psalm is divided into two
halves of eight verses each, with the opening couplet of the
second half (vv. 9–10) echoing the theme of vv. 1–2. In the
first half, the godly are assured of security from four threats
(vv. 5–6)—though thousands fall (v. 7). In the second half,
they are assured of triumphing over four menacing beasts (v.
13). The oracle of vv. 14–16 offers climactic assurance.
91:1 *shelter.* The temple (as in 27:5; 31:20; see also 23:6;
27:4), where the godly find safety under the protective
wings of the Lord (see v. 4; 61:4). *Most High.* See v. 9; see
also note on Ge 14:19. *shadow.* See note on 17:8. *Almighty.*
See NIV text note and note on Ge 17:1.
91:3 *fowler's snare.* Metaphor for danger from an enemy
(see 124:7). *pestilence.* These two threats are further elaborated in vv. 5–6.

and under his wings you will find
refuge; *i*
his faithfulness will be your shield *j*
and rampart.
⁵You will not fear *k* the terror of night,
nor the arrow that flies by day,
⁶nor the pestilence that stalks in the
darkness,
nor the plague that destroys at
midday.
⁷A thousand may fall at your side,
ten thousand at your right hand,
but it will not come near you.
⁸You will only observe with your eyes
and see the punishment of the
wicked. *l*
⁹If you make the Most High your
dwelling—
even the LORD, who is my refuge—
¹⁰then no harm *m* will befall you,
no disaster will come near your tent.
¹¹For he will command his angels *n*
concerning you
to guard you in all your ways; *o*
¹²they will lift you up in their hands,
so that you will not strike your foot
against a stone. *p*
¹³You will tread upon the lion and the
cobra;

you will trample the great lion and
the serpent. *q*
¹⁴"Because he loves me," says the LORD,
"I will rescue him;
I will protect him, for he
acknowledges my name.
¹⁵He will call upon me, and I will answer
him;
I will be with him in trouble,
I will deliver him and honor him. *r*
¹⁶With long life *s* will I satisfy him
and show him my salvation. *t* "

Psalm 92

A psalm. A song. For the Sabbath day.

¹It is good to praise the LORD
and make music *u* to your name, *v*
O Most High, *w*
²to proclaim your love in the morning *x*
and your faithfulness at night,
³to the music of the ten-stringed lyre *y*
and the melody of the harp. *z*

⁴For you make me glad by your deeds,
O LORD;
I sing for joy *a* at the works of your
hands. *b*
⁵How great are your works, *c* O LORD,
how profound your thoughts! *d*
⁶The senseless man *e* does not know,

91:4 *i*S Ru 2:12;
Ps 17:8
*j*S Dt 32:10;
Ps 35:2; Isa 27:3;
31:5; Zec 12:8
91:5 *k*S Job 5:21
91:8 *l*Ps 37:34;
S 58:10
91:10 *m*Pr 12:21
91:11
*n*S Ge 32:1;
Heb 1:14
*o*Ps 34:7
91:12 *p*Mt 4:6*;
Lk 4:10-11*

91:13 *q*Da 6:22;
Lk 10:19
91:15
*r*S 1Sa 2:30;
Jn 12:26
91:16 *s*Dt 6:2;
S Ps 21:4
*t*S Ps 50:23
92:1 *u*S Ps 27:6
*v*S Ps 9:2; 147:1
*w*Ps 135:3
92:2 *x*S Ps 55:17
92:3 *y*S Ps 71:22
*z*S 1Sa 10:5;
S Ne 12:27;
S Ps 33:2; 81:2
92:4 *a*S Ps 5:11;
27:6 *b*S Ps 8:6;
111:7; 143:5
92:5
*c*S Job 36:24;
Rev 15:3
*d*Ps 40:5; 139:17;
Isa 28:29; 31:2;
Ro 11:33
92:6 *e*S Ps 73:22

91:4 *with his feathers.* See note on 17:8.
91:5 *terror.* As in 64:1 ("threat"), reference is to attack by enemies; thus it is paired with "arrow." These two references to threats from war are arrayed alongside "pestilence" and "plague" (v. 6), two references to mortal diseases that often reached epidemic proportions. *night . . . day.* At whatever time of day or night the threat may come, you will be kept safe—the time references are not specific to their respective phrases (see also v. 6).
91:7 *ten thousand.* Hebrew poetic convention called for 10,000 following 1,000 in parallel construction (see notes on 90:10; Am 1:3). Cf. 1Sa 18:7.
91:9 *dwelling.* See 90:1 and note.
91:11-12 Quoted by Satan in Mt 4:6; Lk 4:10-11.
91:11 *his angels.* See note on 34:7.
91:12 *against a stone.* On the stony trails of Canaan (see Pr 3:23).
91:13 *lion . . . cobra . . . great lion . . . serpent.* These double references to lions and to poisonous snakes balance the double references of vv. 5-6, and complete the illustrative roster of mortal threats (see Am 5:19).
91:14-16 Employing the form of a prophetic oracle, the author (see introduction) supports his testimony by assuring the godly that it is confirmed by all the promises of God to those who truly love and trust him.
91:14 *protect him.* Lit. "raise him to a high, secure place." *my name.* See note on 5:11.
Ps 92 A joyful celebration of the righteous rule of God. Its testimony to the prosperity of the righteous, "planted in the house of the LORD" (v. 13), links it thematically with Ps 91, while its joy over God's righteous reign relates it to the cluster of psalms that follow (Ps 93-100; see especially Ps 94). In fact, celebration of God's love and faithfulness as

characteristic of his reign (see v. 2; 100:5) may have served for the editors of the Psalter as a frame enclosing the collection. The psalmist here may have been the king (see vv. 10-11). Following the introduction on praise (vv. 1-3), vv. 4-5 offer the motivation for the praise ("me," "I"), which is picked up again in vv. 10-11 ("my," "me," "My," "my," "my," "my"). Verses 6-9 expound the folly and destiny of evildoers, while vv. 12-15 expound the prosperity of the righteous. Notice also the link between v. 7 and v. 13. The NIV text offers a different analysis of the psalm's structure. If the analysis presented here is followed, v. 8 should be read as concluding the thought of v. 7.
92 title *A song.* See note on Ps 30 title. *For the Sabbath day.* In the postexilic liturgy of the temple, this psalm came to be sung at the time of the morning sacrifice on the Sabbath. (The rest of the weekly schedule was: first day, Ps 24; second day, Ps 48; third day, Ps 82; fourth day, Ps 94; fifth day, Ps 81; sixth day, Ps 93.)
92:1-3 Hymnic introduction.
92:1 *LORD . . . Most High.* That is, LORD Most High (see 7:17; see also note on 3:7). *name.* See note on 5:11. *Most High.* See note on Ge 14:19.
92:2 *love . . . faithfulness.* That is, love-and-faithfulness (see note on 36:5; see also note on 3:7). *love.* See note on 6:4. *morning . . . night.* Continuously.
92:3 *lyre . . . harp.* See note on 57:8. *harp.* See note on Ge 31:27.
92:4-5 Joy over God's saving acts (see vv. 10-11).
92:5 *profound.* Lit. "deep." *your thoughts.* As shown by your deeds.
92:6-9 The fatal folly of evildoers (contrast vv. 12-15).
92:6 *senseless . . . fools.* See NIV text note on 14:1; see also 49:10; 94:8-11. They do not know that the Lord rules

fools do not understand,
7that though the wicked spring up like
　grass
　and all evildoers flourish,
　they will be forever destroyed. f

8But you, O LORD, are exalted forever.

9For surely your enemies g, O LORD,
　surely your enemies will perish;
　all evildoers will be scattered. h

10You have exalted my horn m i like that
　of a wild ox; j
　fine oils k have been poured upon
　me.
11My eyes have seen the defeat of my
　adversaries;
　my ears have heard the rout of my
　wicked foes. l

12The righteous will flourish m like a palm
　tree,
　they will grow like a cedar of
　Lebanon; n
13planted in the house of the LORD,
　they will flourish in the courts of our
　God. o
14They will still bear fruit p in old age,
　they will stay fresh and green,
15proclaiming, "The LORD is upright;
　he is my Rock, and there is no
　wickedness in him. q "

Psalm 93

1The LORD reigns, r he is robed in
　majesty; s
　the LORD is robed in majesty
　and is armed with strength. t
The world is firmly established; u
　it cannot be moved. v
2Your throne was established w long ago;
　you are from all eternity. x

3The seas y have lifted up, O LORD,
　the seas have lifted up their voice; z
　the seas have lifted up their pounding
　waves. a
4Mightier than the thunder b of the great
　waters,
　mightier than the breakers c of the
　sea—
　the LORD on high is mighty. d

5Your statutes stand firm;
　holiness e adorns your house f
　for endless days, O LORD.

Psalm 94

1O LORD, the God who avenges, g
　O God who avenges, shine forth. h

92:7 /S Ps 37:2
92:9 gS Ps 45:5
hS Ps 68:1;
S 89:10
92:10 /S Ps 89:17
/S Ps 29:6
kS Ps 23:5
92:11 /S Ps 54:7;
91:8
92:12 mS Ps 72:7
nS Ps 1:3; 52:8;
Jer 17:8; Hos 14:6
92:13 oPs 135:2
92:14 pS Ps 1:3;
S Jn 15:2
92:15
qS Job 34:10

93:1
rS 1Ch 16:31;
S Ps 97:1
sS Job 40:10;
S Ps 21:5
tS Ps 65:6
uPs 24:2; 78:69;
119:90
v1Ch 16:30;
Ps 96:10
93:2 wS 2Sa 7:16
xS Ge 21:33
93:3 yPs 96:11;
98:7; Isa 5:30;
17:12-13;
Jer 6:23
zS Ps 46:3
aJob 9:8;
Ps 107:25,29;
Isa 51:15;
Jer 31:35;
Hab 3:10
93:4 bPs 65:7;
Jer 6:23
cS Ps 18:4;
Jnh 1:15
dS Ne 9:32;
S Job 9:4
93:5 ePs 29:2;
96:9 /Ps 5:7;

23:6 94:1 gS Ge 4:24; Ro 12:19 hS Dt 33:2; Ps 80:1

m 10 Horn here symbolizes strength.

---

righteously. They see the wicked flourishing, but do not see
the Lord or foresee the end he has appointed for them. The
author thus characterizes his "wicked foes" (v. 11), whom
the Lord has routed.
92:7 A condensed statement of what is expounded more
fully in Ps 73 (see note on 90:4–5).
92:8 *exalted forever.* God's eternal exaltation assures the
destruction of his enemies.
92:9 *enemies.* Here the evildoers, referred to also in v. 7.
92:10–11 Joy over God's favors (see vv. 4–5): God has
made him triumphant (see 89:24) and anointed him with
"the oil of joy" (45:7; see also 23:5) by giving him victory
over all his enemies.
92:12–15 The secure prosperity of the righteous (contrast
vv. 6–9).
92:13 *planted in the house of the LORD.* Though the
wicked may "spring up like grass," their end is sure (see v.
7). But the righteous are planted in a secure place (see Ps 91)
and so retain the vigor of youth into old age, rejoicing in
God's just discrimination (see v. 15). *courts.* Of the temple
(see 84:2,10; 2Ki 21:5; 23:11–12).
Ps 93 A hymn to the eternal, universal and invincible reign
of the Lord, a theme it shares with Ps 47; 94–100. Together
they offer a majestic confession of faith in and hope for the
kingdom of God on earth. These hymns were composed for
the liturgy of a high religious festival in which the kingship of
the Lord—over the cosmic order, over the nations and in a
special sense over Israel—was annually celebrated (see introduction to Ps 47). And implicitly, where not explicitly, the
Lord's kingship is hailed in contrast to the claims of all other
gods; he is "the great King above all gods" (95:3). Ps
93–100 may all have been composed by temple personnel
and spoken by them in the liturgy. They probably date from
the preexilic era. Structurally, the psalm has two short stan-

zas (vv. 1–2, 3–4) and a conclusion (v. 5).
93:1–2 The Lord's reign, by which the creation order has
been and will be secure throughout the ages, is from eternity
(see Ge 1:1). Though Israel as a nation has come late on the
scene, her God has been King since before the creation of the
world.
93:1 *The LORD reigns.* The ultimate truth, and first article,
in Israel's creed (see 96:10; 97:1; 99:1; see also Zec 14:9
and note).
93:3–4 Since his founding of the world, the Lord has
shown himself to be mightier than all the forces of disorder
that threaten his kingdom.
93:3 *seas.* Reference is to the primeval chaotic waters,
tamed and assigned a place by the Lord's creative word (see
33:7; 104:7–9; Ge 1:6–10; Job 38:8–11). Implicitly they
symbolize all that opposes the coming of the Lord's kingdom
(see 65:6–7; 74:13–14 and notes).
93:4 The thunder of the chaotic waters is no match for the
thunder of the Lord's ordering word (see 104:7).
93:5 *statutes.* He whose indisputable rule has made the
world secure has given his people life directives that are
stable and reliable (see 19:7)—and that they must honor (see
95:8–11). *your house.* His earthly temple—but also the
heavenly. *for endless days.* Qualifies both clauses.
Ps 94 An appeal to the Lord, as "Judge of the earth" (v. 2),
to redress the wrongs perpetrated against the weak by arrogant and wicked men who occupy seats of power. The psalm
has links with Ps 92, but is the voice of the oppressed within
Israel (thus not the king), seeking redress at God's throne for
injustices done them by those smugly established in the
power structures of the nation. Thus it is unique within the
Ps 92–100 collection. (See introduction to Ps 93.) Following
a three-verse introduction, the thought advances regularly in
five stanzas of four verses each.

²Rise up,ⁱ O Judgeʲ of the earth;
pay backᵏ to the proud what they
deserve.
³How long will the wicked, O LORD,
how long will the wicked be
jubilant?ˡ

⁴They pour out arrogantᵐ words;
all the evildoers are full of boasting.ⁿ
⁵They crush your people,ᵒ O LORD;
they oppress your inheritance.ᵖ
⁶They slay the widowᑫ and the alien;
they murder the fatherless.ʳ
⁷They say, "The LORD does not see;ˢ
the God of Jacobᵗ pays no heed."

⁸Take heed, you senseless onesᵘ among
the people;
you fools, when will you become
wise?
⁹Does he who implanted the ear not
hear?
Does he who formed the eye not
see?ᵛ
¹⁰Does he who disciplinesʷ nations not
punish?
Does he who teachesˣ man lack
knowledge?
¹¹The LORD knows the thoughtsʸ of man;
he knows that they are futile.ᶻ

¹²Blessed is the man you discipline,ᵃ
O LORD;
the man you teachᵇ from your law;
¹³you grant him relief from days of
trouble,ᶜ
till a pitᵈ is dug for the wicked.
¹⁴For the LORD will not reject his
people;ᵉ

he will never forsake his inheritance.
¹⁵Judgment will again be founded on
righteousness,ᶠ
and all the upright in heartᵍ will
follow it.

¹⁶Who will rise upʰ for me against the
wicked?
Who will take a stand for me against
evildoers?ⁱ
¹⁷Unless the LORD had given me help,ʲ
I would soon have dwelt in the
silence of death.ᵏ
¹⁸When I said, "My foot is slipping,ˡ"
your love, O LORD, supported me.
¹⁹When anxietyᵐ was great within me,
your consolationⁿ brought joy to my
soul.

²⁰Can a corrupt throneᵒ be allied with
you—
one that brings on misery by its
decrees?ᵖ
²¹They band togetherᑫ against the
righteous
and condemn the innocentʳ to
death.ˢ
²²But the LORD has become my fortress,
and my God the rockᵗ in whom I
take refuge.ᵘ
²³He will repayᵛ them for their sins
and destroyʷ them for their
wickedness;
the LORD our God will destroy
them.

94:2 ⁱS Nu 10:35;
ʲS Ge 18:25;
Heb 12:23;
S Jas 5:9
ᵏS Ps 31:23
94:3 ˡPs 13:2
94:4 ᵐJer 43:2
ⁿS Ps 52:1
94:5 ᵒPs 44:2;
74:8; Isa 3:15;
Jer 8:21 ᵖPs 28:9
94:6
ᑫS Dt 10:18;
S Isa 1:17
ʳDt 24:19
94:7 ˢS Job 22:14
ᵗS Ge 24:12
94:8 ᵘS Dt 32:6;
S Ps 73:22
94:9 ᵛEx 4:11;
Pr 20:12
94:10
ʷS Ps 39:11
ˣS Ex 35:34;
Job 35:11;
Isa 28:26
94:11 ʸPs 139:2;
Pr 15:26;
S Mt 9:4
ᶻ1Co 3:20*
94:12
ᵃS Job 5:17;
1Co 11:32;
Heb 12:5
ᵇS Dt 8:3;
S 1Sa 12:23
94:13 ᶜS Ps 86:7
ᵈS Ps 7:15;
S 55:23
94:14
ᵉS Dt 31:6;
Ps 37:28; Ro 11:2

94:15 ᶠPs 97:2
ᵍPs 7:10; 11:2;
S 36:10
94:16
ʰNu 10:35;
Ps 17:13;
Isa 14:22
ⁱS Ps 59:2
94:17 ʲPs 124:2
ᵏS Ps 31:17
94:18
ˡS Dt 32:35;
S Job 12:5
94:19
ᵐEcc 11:10
ⁿS Job 6:10
94:20 ᵒJer 22:30;
36:30 ᵖS Ps 58:2

94:21 ᑫS Ps 56:6 ʳPs 106:38; Pr 17:15,26; 28:21; Isa 5:20,
23; Mt 27:4 ˢS Ge 18:23 94:22 ᵗS Ps 61:2 ᵘS 2Sa 22:3;
S Ps 18:2 94:23 ᵛS Ex 32:34; S Ps 54:5 ʷPs 9:5; 37:38;
145:20

94:1–3 Initial appeal to God, the Judge.
94:1 *avenges.* Redresses wrongs (see Dt 32:35,41 and note on Dt 32:35).
94:2 *the proud.* See vv. 4–7.
94:3 *How long . . . ?* See note on 6:3; see also Introduction: Theology.
94:4–7 Indictment of the wicked.
94:4 *arrogant words . . . boasting.* For the arrogance of the wicked see 10:2–11 and notes.
94:5 *your people . . . your inheritance.* Those among them who are vulnerable (see v. 6).
94:7 *They say.* See notes on 3:2; 10:11. *Jacob.* A synonym for Israel (see Ge 32:28).
94:8–11 Warning to the wicked—those "senseless . . . fools" (see 92:6–9; see also NIV text note on 14:1).
94:10 *disciplines.* Keeps them in line by means of punishment (see Lev 26:18; Jer 31:18). *teaches.* Gives him some knowledge of the creation order (see Isa 28:26).
94:11 *The LORD knows.* Contrary to their foolish supposition (see v. 7).
94:12–15 Those whose lives are directed by God's law are the blessed ones (see Ps 1)—contrary to the arrogant expectations of the wicked and in spite of their oppressions.
94:12 *Blessed.* See note on 1:1. *discipline . . . teach.* See

v. 10. Here the author speaks of God's correcting and teaching his people in the ways of his law.
94:14 *people . . . inheritance.* See v. 5. The Lord will not abandon the powerless among his people to the injustice of their oppressors. Paul may be echoing this verse in Ro 11:1–2.
94:15 *be founded on.* Or "restore." *heart.* See note on 4:7. *will follow it.* Or "with it." In any event, the author appears to say that God's judgment will restore justice for the upright in heart.
94:16–19 The Lord is the only sure court of appeal.
94:17 *silence of death.* See note on 30:1. Without God's help the wicked would have silenced the psalmist in the grave, but now it is the wicked for whom the pit will be dug (see v. 13).
94:18 *When I said.* When he felt he was about to be overwhelmed by the wicked (see note on 38:16). *love.* See note on 6:4.
94:19 *soul.* See note on 6:3.
94:20–23 Confidence that the Lord's justice will prevail.
94:20 *corrupt throne.* A seat of authority that works mischief. The author speaks of injustice at the center of power.
94:21 *righteous.* See note on 1:5.

Psalm 95

1Come,[x] let us sing for joy[y] to the
LORD;
let us shout aloud[z] to the Rock[a] of
our salvation.
2Let us come before him[b] with
thanksgiving[c]
and extol him with music[d] and song.

3For the LORD is the great God,[e]
the great King[f] above all gods.[g]
4In his hand are the depths of the
earth,[h]
and the mountain peaks belong to
him.
5The sea is his, for he made it,
and his hands formed the dry land.[i]

6Come, let us bow down[j] in worship,[k]
let us kneel[l] before the LORD our
Maker;[m]
7for he is our God
and we are the people of his
pasture,[n]
the flock under his care.

Today, if you hear his voice,
8do not harden your hearts[o] as you
did at Meribah,[n] [p]
as you did that day at Massah[o] in the
desert,[q]
9where your fathers tested[r] and tried
me,
though they had seen what I did.
10For forty years[s] I was angry with that
generation;
I said, "They are a people whose
hearts go astray,[t]
and they have not known my
ways."[u]
11So I declared on oath[v] in my anger,
"They shall never enter my rest."[w]

Psalm 96

96:1–13pp — 1Ch 16:23–33

1Sing to the LORD[x] a new song;[y]
sing to the LORD, all the earth.

95:1 [x]Ps 34:11; 80:2 [y]S Ps 5:11 [z]Ps 81:1; Isa 44:23; Zep 3:14 [a]S 2Sa 22:47 **95:2** [b]Ps 100:2; Mic 6:6 [c]S Ps 42:4 [d]Ps 81:2; S Eph 5:19 **95:3** [e]Ps 48:1; 86:10; 145:3; 147:5 [f]S Ps 47:2 [g]Ps 96:4; 97:9 **95:4** [h]S Ps 63:9 **95:5** [i]S Ge 1:9; Ps 146:6 **95:6** [j]S 2Sa 12:16; Php 2:10 [k]S Ps 22:29 [l]2Ch 6:13 [m]Ps 100:3; 149:2; Isa 17:7; 54:5; Da 6:10-11; Hos 8:14 **95:7** [n]S Ps 74:1 **95:8** [o]Mk 10:5; Heb 3:8 [p]S Ex 17:7; S Dt 33:8; Heb 3:15*; 4:7 [q]S Ps 78:40 **95:9** [r]S Nu 14:22; 1Co 10:9 **95:10** [s]S Ex 16:35; S Nu 14:34; Ac 7:36; Heb 3:17 [t]Ps 58:3; 119:67,176; Pr 12:26; 16:29; Isa 53:6; Jer 31:19; 50:6; Eze 34:6 [u]S Dt 8:6 **95:11** [v]S Nu 14:23 [w]Dt 1:35; Heb 3:7-11*; 4:3,5* **96:1** [x]Ps 30:4 [y]Ps 33:3; S 40:3; 98:1; 144:9; 149:1; Isa 42:10; S Rev 5:9

[n] *8 Meribah* means *quarreling.* [o] *8 Massah* means *testing.*

Ps 95 A call to worship the Lord, spoken by a priest or Levite to the assembled Israelites at the temple. (See introduction to Ps 93.) The psalm is composed of two parts: (1) a call to praise the Lord of all the earth (vv. 1–5); (2) a call to acknowledge by submissive attitude and obedient heart the Lord's kingship over his people (vv. 6–11). Each part also has two subdivisions, the latter of which forms the climax. Cf. the structure of Ps 96.
95:1–2 The call to praise.
95:1 *Rock of our salvation.* See note on 18:2.
95:3–5 Why Israel is to praise the Lord—because he is above all gods, and there is no corner of the universe that is not in his hand. The ancient pagan world had different gods for different peoples, different geographical areas, different cosmic regions (heaven, earth, netherworld) and different aspects of life (e.g., war, fertility, crafts).
95:4–5 *depths . . . mountain peaks . . . sea . . . dry land.* All the world—the extremes and all that lies between and all that is in them.
95:6–11 The exhortation to submit to the Lord with obedient hearts—a bent knee is not enough. For a NT reflection on these verses in the light of the advent of Christ see Heb 3:7–4:13.
95:6–7 The call to confess submission to the Lord by kneeling before him.
95:6 *our Maker.* Both as Creator of all things (see Ge 1) and as Israel's Redeemer, he has "made" her what she is: the people of the Lord in the earth (see Isa 45:9–13; 51:12–16).
95:7 *people of his pasture.* See 100:3; Jer 23:1; Eze 34:21. Since kings were commonly called the "shepherds" of their people (see note on 23:1), their realms could be referred to as their "pastures" (see Jer 25:36; 49:20; 50:45). *if you hear his voice.* In the liturgy of the religious festival, possibly in some such manner as Ps 50 and/or 78.
95:8 *Meribah . . . Massah.* See NIV text notes. The leader of the liturgy reminds Israel of times of her rebellion in the desert (see Ex 17:7; Nu 20:13).
95:9 *me.* Official representatives of the Lord, when speaking for him, could shift to first person (see 50:5,7–15; see also note on Ge 16:7). *had seen what I did.* In Egypt and at the Red Sea—and his provision of food in the desert (see Ex 16; see also Nu 14:11).
95:10 *forty years.* The climax of Israel's rebellion came when she faithlessly refused to undertake the conquest of Canaan and considered returning to Egypt (see Nu 14:1–4). It was then that God condemned her to a 40-year stay in the desert (see Nu 14:34). *angry.* See note on 2:5. *that generation.* The (adult) Israelites who came out of Egypt and covenanted with God at Sinai (see Nu 32:13). *They are a people . . . my ways.* A restatement of the Lord's word in Nu 14:11. *hearts.* See note on 4:7. *my ways.* See 25:4 and note.
95:11 *on oath.* See Nu 14:28. *never enter my rest.* The language of Nu 14:30 is "not one of you will enter the land," but since the promised land was also called the place where God will give his people "rest" (Jos 1:13,15; see Ex 33:14; Dt 12:10; 25:19), the two statements are equivalent. *rest.* Here a fertile concept indicating Israel's possession of a place with God in the earth where she is secure from all external threats and internal calamities (see 1Ki 5:4).
Ps 96 A call to all nations to praise the Lord as the only God and to proclaim the glory of his reign throughout the world—an OT anticipation of the world mission of the NT people of God (see Mt 28:16–20). (See introductions to Ps 93; 95.) This psalm appears in slightly altered form in 1Ch 16:23–33. The psalm is composed of two parts: (1) a call to all nations to sing the praise of the Lord (vv. 1–6); (2) a call to all nations to worship the Lord and to hail throughout the world the glory of his righteous rule (vv. 7–13). Each part has two subdivisions, the last of which forms the climax to the whole psalm. Cf. the structure of Ps 95.
96:1–3 The call to all the earth to sing the praise of the Lord among the nations. Triple repetition ("Sing . . . sing . . . Sing") was a common feature in OT liturgical calls to worship (see vv. 7–9 and note; see also 103:20–22; 118:2–4; 135:1; 136:1–3).
96:1 *new song.* See note on 33:3. *all the earth.* See v. 9; or "all the land," in which case the call is addressed to all Israel. However, the worldwide perspective of this psalm (see espe-

2Sing to the LORD, praise his name;[z]
proclaim his salvation[a] day after day.
3Declare his glory[b] among the nations,
his marvelous deeds[c] among all
peoples.

4For great is the LORD and most worthy
of praise;[d]
he is to be feared[e] above all gods.[f]
5For all the gods of the nations are
idols,[g]
but the LORD made the heavens.[h]
6Splendor and majesty[i] are before him;
strength and glory[j] are in his
sanctuary.

7Ascribe to the LORD,[k] O families of
nations,[l]
ascribe to the LORD glory and
strength.
8Ascribe to the LORD the glory due his
name;
bring an offering[m] and come into his
courts.[n]
9Worship the LORD[o] in the splendor of
his[p] holiness;[p]
tremble[q] before him, all the earth.[r]

10Say among the nations, "The LORD
reigns.[s]"
The world is firmly established,[t] it
cannot be moved;[u]
he will judge[v] the peoples with
equity.[w]
11Let the heavens rejoice,[x] let the earth
be glad;[y]
let the sea resound, and all that is in
it;
12 let the fields be jubilant, and
everything in them.
Then all the trees of the forest[z] will
sing for joy;[a]
13 they will sing before the LORD, for he
comes,
he comes to judge[b] the earth.
He will judge the world in
righteousness[c]
and the peoples in his truth.[d]

Psalm 97

1The LORD reigns,[e] let the earth be
glad;[f]

96:2 [z]S Ps 68:4 [a]Ps 27:1; 71:15 **96:3** [b]Ps 8:1 [c]S Ps 71:17; Rev 15:3 **96:4** [d]S Ps 48:1 [e]S Dt 28:58; S 1Ch 16:25; Ps 89:7 [f]S Ps 95:3 **96:5** [g]S Lev 19:4 [h]S Ge 1:1; S 2Ch 2:12 **96:6** [i]S Ps 21:5 [j]Ps 29:1; 89:17 **96:7** [k]Ps 29:1 [l]Ps 22:27 **96:8** [m]Ps 45:12; S 51:19; 72:10 [n]Ps 65:4; 84:10; 92:13; 100:4 **96:9** [o]Ex 23:25; Jnh 1:9 [p]S Ps 93:5 [q]S Ex 15:14; Ps 114:7 [r]Ps 33:8 **96:10** [s]Ps 97:1 [t]Ps 24:2; 78:69; 119:90 [u]S Ps 93:1 [v]Ps 58:11 [w]Ps 67:4; 98:9 **96:11** [x]S Rev 12:12 [y]Ps 97:1; Isa 49:13 **96:12** [z]Isa 44:23; 55:12; Eze 17:24 [a]Ps 65:13 **96:13** [b]Rev 19:11 [c]S Ps 7:11; Ac 17:31 [d]Ps 86:11 **97:1** [e]Ex 15:18; Ps 93:1; 96:10; 99:1; Isa 24:23; 52:7 [f]S Ps 96:11

p 9 Or *LORD with the splendor of*

cially v. 7) suggests that here the psalmist has in view broader horizons (see 97:1; 100:1 and note; 117:1; see also note on 9:1).

96:2 *name.* See v. 8; see also note on 5:11. *proclaim his salvation.* Proclaim (see 40:9 and note) that deliverance comes from the Lord (see 3:8; see also 85:9).

96:3 *glory.* See note on 85:9. *marvelous deeds.* See note on 71:16–17.

96:4–6 Why "all the earth" is to praise the Lord: He alone is God (see Ps 115).

96:4 *feared.* See note on Ge 20:11.

96:5 *made the heavens.* As the Maker of the heavenly realm, in pagan eyes the abode of the gods, the Lord is greater than all the gods (see 97:7).

96:6 *Splendor and majesty . . . strength and glory.* Two pairs of divine attributes personified as throne attendants whose presence before the Lord heralds the exalted nature of the one, universal King. For similar personifications see 23:6 and note. *glory.* The Hebrew for this word here connotes radiant beauty.

96:7–9 The call to all nations to worship the Lord (see 29:1–2 and note). The two half-sentences of 29:2 have been expanded in this psalm. The threefold "ascribe" here balances the threefold "sing" of vv. 1–2.

96:8 *courts.* Of the temple (see 84:2,10; 2Ki 21:5; 23:11–12).

96:9 *tremble.* In reverent awe, equivalent to "fear" (see v. 4).

96:10–13 The call to all nations to proclaim among the nations the righteous reign of the Lord.

96:10 *The Lord reigns.* See 93:1 and note. *The world . . . with equity.* In OT perspective, the world order is one, embracing both its physical and moral aspects because both have been established by God as aspects of his one kingdom and both are upheld by his one rule. Therefore God's rule over creation and over the affairs of men (also his acts of creation and redemption) is often spoken of in one breath, and "righteousness," "faithfulness" and "love" are equally ascribable to both. And since the creation order is secure in its "goodness" (see Ge 1), it often serves in OT poetry (as it does here) as a manifest assurance that God's rule over the affairs of men will also be "with equity," "in righteousness" and "in . . . truth" (v. 13; see 11:3; 33:4–11; 36:5–9; 57:10; 65:6–7; 71:19; 74:13–14,16–17; 75:3; 82:5; 93:3–4; 119:89–91 and notes). *will judge.* See v. 13 and note.

96:11–12 Because God's kingdom is one (see v. 10 and note), all his creatures will rejoice when God's rule over mankind brings righteousness to full expression in his cosmic kingdom (see note on 65:13; see also 97:7–9). For the present state of the creation as it awaits the fullness of redemption see Ro 8:21–22 and notes.

96:13 *comes . . . comes . . . will judge.* Because God reigns over all things and is the Lord of history, Israel lived in hope (as the prophets announced) of the "coming" of God—his future acts by which he would decisively deal with all wickedness and establish his righteousness in the earth. *righteousness.* See note on 4:1.

Ps 97 A joyful celebration of the Lord's righteous reign over all the earth. (See introductions to Ps 93; 95.) The psalm's two main divisions (vv. 1–6, 8–12) are joined by a centered verse (v. 7; see note on 6:6) that serves as a counterpoint to the main theme. The opening verses of the two main divisions are thematically linked: v. 1, "be glad . . . rejoice"; v. 8, "rejoices . . . are glad"—in reverse order, a frequent stylistic device in OT poetry.

97:1–6 A testimony to the nations—that they too have seen God's majesty displayed (vv. 2–6) and ought to rejoice with Israel that the Lord reigns supreme.

97:1 *The Lord reigns.* See 93:1 and note. *earth.* See 96:1; 99:1; 117:1; see also note on 9:1. *distant shores.* Even distant lands reached by the far-ranging ships that sail the seas (see 1Ki 9:26–28; 10:22; Isa 60:9; Jnh 1:3).

let the distant shores *g* rejoice.

²Clouds *h* and thick darkness *i* surround
   him;
   righteousness and justice are the
      foundation of his throne. *j*
³Fire *k* goes before *l* him
   and consumes *m* his foes on every
      side.
⁴His lightning *n* lights up the world;
   the earth *o* sees and trembles. *p*
⁵The mountains melt *q* like wax *r* before
      the LORD,
   before the Lord of all the earth. *s*
⁶The heavens proclaim his
      righteousness, *t*
   and all the peoples see his glory. *u*

⁷All who worship images *v* are put to
      shame, *w*
   those who boast in idols *x* —
   worship him, *y* all you gods! *z*

⁸Zion hears and rejoices
   and the villages of Judah are glad *a*
   because of your judgments, *b* O LORD.
⁹For you, O LORD, are the Most High *c*
      over all the earth; *d*
   you are exalted *e* far above all gods.

¹⁰Let those who love the LORD hate evil, *f*
   for he guards *g* the lives of his faithful
      ones *h*

and delivers *i* them from the hand of
   the wicked. *j*
¹¹Light is shed *k* upon the righteous *l*
   and joy on the upright in heart. *m*
¹²Rejoice in the LORD, *n* you who are
      righteous,
   and praise his holy name. *o*

Psalm 98

A psalm.

¹Sing to the LORD *p* a new song, *q*
   for he has done marvelous
      things; *r*
   his right hand *s* and his holy arm *t*
   have worked salvation *u* for him.
²The LORD has made his salvation
      known *v*
   and revealed his righteousness *w* to
      the nations. *x*
³He has remembered *y* his love
   and his faithfulness to the house of
      Israel;
   all the ends of the earth *z* have seen
      the salvation of our God. *a*

97:1 *g*S Est 10:1
97:2 *h*S Job 22:14
*i*S Ex 19:9
*j*Ps 89:14
97:3 *k*Isa 9:19;
Da 7:10;
Joel 1:19; 2:3
*l*Hab 3:5
*m*S 2Sa 22:9
97:4 *n*S Job 36:30
*o*S 2Sa 22:8
*p*S Ps 18:7;
104:32;
S Rev 6:12
97:5 *q*S Ps 46:2,6
*r*S Ps 22:14
*s*S Jos 3:11
97:6 *t*Ps 50:6;
98:2 *u*S Ps 19:1
97:7 *v*S Lev 26:1
*w*Isa 42:17;
Jer 10:14
*x*S Dt 5:8
*y*Heb 1:6
*z*Ex 12:12;
Ps 16:4
97:8 *a*S Ps 9:2
*b*Ps 48:11
97:9 *c*Ps 7:8
*d*S Job 34:29
*e*S Ps 47:9
97:10
*f*S Job 28:28;
Am 5:15; Ro 12:9
*g*Ps 145:20
*h*Ps 31:23; 37:28;
Pr 2:8

*i*S Ps 34:7;
Da 3:28; 6:16
*j*Ps 37:40;
Jer 15:21; 20:13
97:11
*k*S Job 22:28
*l*Ps 11:5 *m*Ps 7:10
97:12
*n*S Job 22:19;
Ps 104:34;
Isa 41:16; Php 4:4

*o*S Ex 3:15; S Ps 99:3 **98:1** *p*Ps 30:4 *q*S Ps 96:1 *r*Ex 15:1;
Ps 96:3; Isa 12:5; Lk 1:51 *s*S Ex 15:6 *t*S Jos 4:24; Job 40:9;
Isa 51:9; 52:10; 53:1; 63:5 *u*S Ps 44:3; Isa 59:16 **98:2**
*v*Isa 52:10; Lk 3:6 *w*S Ps 97:6 *x*S Ps 67:2 **98:3** *y*S 1Ch 16:15
*z*S Ge 49:10; S Ps 48:10 *a*S Ps 50:23

97:2–6 The Lord's majestic glory revealed in the sky's awesome displays, especially in the thunderstorm (see 18:7–15 and note; see also introduction to Ps 29).
97:2 *Clouds and thick darkness.* The dark storm clouds that hide the sun and cast a veil across the sky are dramatic visual reminders that the fierce heat and brilliance (also metaphors) of God's naked glory must be veiled from creaturely eyes (see Ex 19:9; 1Ki 8:12). Thus also a curtain closed off the Most Holy Place in the tabernacle and temple (see Ex 26:33; 2Ch 3:14), veiling it in darkness. *righteousness.* See v. 6; see also note on 4:1. *foundation of his throne.* God rules by his power (see 66:7), but his reign is founded on righteousness and justice, which also the heavens proclaim (see v. 6 and note).
97:3 *Fire.* Manifested in the storm cloud's lightning bolts (see v. 4), fire often signified God's judicial wrath (see, e.g., 21:9; 50:3; 83:14; Dt 4:24; 9:3; 32:22; 1Ki 19:12; Isa 10:17; 30:27,30).
97:4 *earth.* Here probably the physical earth personified.
97:6 *proclaim his righteousness.* The stable order of the heaven's vast array "speaks" (see 19:1–4); it declares that God's reign similarly upholds the moral order (see note on 96:10). *all the peoples see.* Verses 2–6 have spoken of general revelation.
97:7 The center verse (see note on 6:6) and counterpoint of the psalm: joy to all who acknowledge the Lord; shame and disgrace to those who trust in the false gods. *worship him.* With biting irony the psalm calls on all the gods that people foolishly worship to bow in worship before the Lord (see v. 9; see also 29:1 and note).
97:8–12 A declaration of Zion's joy that the Lord reigns (vv. 8–9), and a reminder that only those who hate evil have real cause to rejoice in his righteous rule (vv. 10–12).

97:8 *Zion hears.* That "the LORD reigns" (v. 1) in "righteousness" (v. 6). *judgments.* God's righteous acts in the affairs of mankind (see 105:7; Isa 26:9), especially his saving acts in Israel's behalf (see 48:11; 105:5; Dt 33:21).
97:9 *Most High.* See note on Ge 14:19.
97:10 *faithful ones.* See note on 4:3.
97:11 *Light.* See 27:1 and note; see also 36:9. *righteous.* See v. 12; see also note on 1:5. *heart.* See note on 4:7.
97:12 *name.* See note on 30:4.
Ps 98 A call to celebrate with joy the righteous reign of the Lord. Its beginning and end echo Ps 96. (See introductions to Ps 93; 95.) The three stanzas progressively extend the call to ever wider circles: (1) the worshiping congregation at the temple; (2) all the peoples of the earth; (3) the whole creation. The first stanza recalls God's revelation of his righteousness (v. 2) in the past; the last stanza speaks confidently of his coming rule "in righteousness" (v. 9); the middle stanza is enclosed by the jubilant cry, "Shout for joy" (vv. 4,6).
98:1–3 The call to celebrate in song God's saving acts in behalf of his people.
98:1 *new song.* See note on 33:3. *marvelous things.* See note on 9:1 ("wonders").
98:2 *made . . . known . . . revealed . . . to the nations.* God's saving acts in behalf of his people are also his self-revelation to the nations; in this sense God is his own evangelist (see note on 46:10; see also Isa 52:10). *salvation . . . righteousness.* God's saving acts reveal his righteousness (see notes on 4:1; 71:24).
98:3 *love . . . faithfulness.* That is, love-and-faithfulness (see note on 36:5; see also note on 3:7). This compound expression often sums up God's covenant commitment to his people (see note on 6:4).

⁴Shout for joy *b* to the LORD, all the
earth,
burst into jubilant song with music;
⁵make music to the LORD with the
harp, *c*
with the harp and the sound of
singing, *d*
⁶with trumpets *e* and the blast of the
ram's horn *f* —
shout for joy *g* before the LORD, the
King. *h*

⁷Let the sea *i* resound, and everything in
it,
the world, and all who live in it. *j*
⁸Let the rivers clap their hands, *k*
let the mountains *l* sing together for
joy;
⁹let them sing before the LORD,
for he comes to judge the earth.
He will judge the world in righteousness
and the peoples with equity. *m*

Psalm 99

¹The LORD reigns, *n*
let the nations tremble; *o*

he sits enthroned *p* between the
cherubim, *q*
let the earth shake.
²Great is the LORD *r* in Zion; *s*
he is exalted *t* over all the nations.
³Let them praise *u* your great and
awesome name *v* —
he is holy. *w*

⁴The King *x* is mighty, he loves
justice *y* —
you have established equity; *z*
in Jacob you have done
what is just and right. *a*
⁵Exalt *b* the LORD our God
and worship at his footstool;
he is holy.

⁶Moses *c* and Aaron *d* were among his
priests,
Samuel *e* was among those who
called on his name;
they called on the LORD
and he answered *f* them.
⁷He spoke to them from the pillar of
cloud; *g*

98:4 *b*Ps 20:5;
Isa 12:6; 44:23;
52:9; 54:1; 55:12
98:5 *c*Ps 33:2;
92:3; 147:7
*d*Isa 51:3
98:6 *e*S Nu 10:2;
2Sa 6:15
*f*S Ex 19:13
*g*Ps 20:5; 100:1;
Isa 12:6 *h*Ps 2:6;
47:7
98:7 *i*S Ps 93:3
*j*S Ps 24:1
98:8 *k*S 2Ki 11:12
*l*Ps 148:9;
Isa 44:23; 55:12
98:9 *m*S Ps 96:10
99:1
*n*S 1Ch 16:31;
S Ps 97:1
*o*S Ex 15:14;
S 1Ch 16:30

*p*S 2Sa 6:2
*q*S Ex 25:22
99:2 *r*S Ps 48:1
*s*Ps 2:6 *t*Ex 15:1;
Ps 46:10; 97:9;
113:4; 148:13
99:3 *u*Ps 30:4;
33:21; 97:12;
103:1; 106:47;
111:9; 145:21;
148:5 *v*Ps 76:1
*w*S Ex 15:11;
S Lev 11:44;
Rev 4:8
99:4 *x*Ps 2:6
*y*S 1Ki 10:9
*z*Ps 98:9
*a*S Ge 18:19;
Rev 15:3

99:5 *b*S Ex 15:2 99:6 *c*S Ex 24:6 *d*S Ex 28:1 *e*1Sa 7:5
*f*Ps 4:3; 91:15 99:7 *g*S Ex 13:21; S 19:9; S Nu 11:25

98:4–6 The call to all the earth to join in the celebration.
98:4 See 100:1. *all the earth.* The peoples of the earth (see 96:1 and note; see also 99:1).
98:5 *harp.* See note on Ge 31:27.
98:6 *trumpets.* The special long, straight trumpets of the sanctuary (referred to only here in Psalms; see notes on Nu 10:2–3,10). *ram's horn.* The more common trumpet (referred to also in 47:5; 81:3; 150:3; see note on Joel 2:1).
98:7–9 The call to the whole creation to celebrate (see note on 96:11–12).
98:7 *sea . . . world.* The two great regions of creaturely life.
98:8 *rivers . . . mountains.* From the rivers to the mountains, let every feature of the whole earth clap and sing (see note on 65:13).
98:9 *comes to judge.* See 96:13 and note. Israel in faith lived between the past (see vv. 1–3) and the future righteous (saving) acts of God.
Ps 99 A hymn celebrating the Lord as the great and holy King in Zion. In developing his theme, the poet makes striking use of the symbolic significance (completeness) of the number seven: Seven times he speaks of the "LORD," and seven times he refers to him by means of independent personal pronouns (Hebrew). (See introduction to Ps 93.) The form is symmetrical, with four stanzas of three (Hebrew) poetic lines and with each of the two main divisions concluded by the major refrain (vv. 5,9). The lesser refrain, "he is holy" (vv. 3,5, and expanded in v. 9), probably reflects a traditional threefold liturgical rubric (see Isa 6:3; Rev 4:8; see also Ps 96:1–3,7–9 and notes for further evidence of a liturgical penchant for triple repetition). The second half of the psalm develops the theme introduced in the second stanza.
99:1–3 The God enthroned in Zion is ruler over all the nations—let them acknowledge him.
99:1 *The LORD reigns.* See 93:1 and note. *tremble . . . shake.* In reverent awe before God. *cherubim.* See 80:1; see also note on Ex 25:18.
99:3 *Let them praise.* As the Great King, he ought to be

shown the fear (v. 1) and honor that are his due. *name.* See v. 6; see also note on 5:11. *holy.* See vv. 5,9; see also Introduction to Leviticus: Themes; note on Lev 11:44.
99:4–5 The Lord has shown the quality of his rule by what he has done for Israel.
99:4 See 103:6–12. *is mighty . . . loves justice.* Two chief characteristics of God's reign. *established equity.* As a (his) throne (see 9:7–8; 97:2; 2Sa 7:13). *Jacob.* A synonym for Israel (see Ge 32:28). *just and right.* Justice and righteousness, as in 97:2. Though even the heavens proclaim God's righteousness (see 97:6 and note), it is in the whole complex of his saving acts in and for Israel that the "righteousness" of God's reign is especially disclosed (see 98:2 and note).
99:5 See also v. 9. For other refrains in the Psalms see introduction to Ps 42–43. *footstool.* God's royal footstool (see 2Ch 9:18), here a metaphor linking the heavenly throne with the earthly; when God sits on his heavenly throne, his earthly throne is his footstool (here "his holy mountain," v. 9; see 132:7; 1Ch 28:2; La 2:1).
99:6–7 In Israel the Lord provided priestly intermediaries, who (1) were appointed to intercede with him on behalf of his faltering people (v. 6), and (2) were given knowledge of his will so they could instruct Israel.
99:6 *Moses . . . Aaron . . . Samuel.* These three no doubt serve here as representatives of all those the Lord used as intermediaries with his people in times of great crises. *priests . . . who called on his name.* The priestly function of intercession is highlighted (see Ex 17:11 and note; 32:11–13, 31–32; Nu 14:13–19; 21:7; 1Sa 7:5,8–9; 12:19,23; Jer 15:1). *answered them.* See v. 8; see also the Lord's responses to the intercessions referred to in note on vv. 6–7.
99:7 *spoke to them from the pillar of cloud.* Though reference may be to all Israel ("them"), more likely the hymn recalls God's speaking with Moses (see Ex 33:9) and Aaron (see Nu 12:5–6). But that special mode of revelation in the desert may also be generalized here to include God's revelations to Samuel, who was called to his prophetic ministry at the sanctuary, "where the ark of God was" (1Sa 3:3; see also

they kept his statutes and the decrees
    he gave them.

[8]O LORD our God,
    you answered them;
you were to Israel[q] a forgiving God,[h]
    though you punished[i] their
        misdeeds.[r]
[9]Exalt the LORD our God
    and worship at his holy mountain,
    for the LORD our God is holy.

Psalm 100

A psalm. For giving thanks.

[1]Shout for joy[j] to the LORD, all the
    earth.
[2] Worship the LORD[k] with gladness;
    come before him[l] with joyful songs.
[3]Know that the LORD is God.[m]
    It is he who made us,[n] and we are
        his[s];

we are his people,[o] the sheep of his
    pasture.[p]

[4]Enter his gates with thanksgiving[q]
    and his courts[r] with praise;
    give thanks to him and praise his
        name.[s]
[5]For the LORD is good[t] and his love
    endures forever;[u]
    his faithfulness[v] continues through
        all generations.

Psalm 101

Of David. A psalm.

[1]I will sing of your love[w] and justice;
    to you, O LORD, I will sing praise.
[2]I will be careful to lead a blameless
        life[x] —
    when will you come to me?

Cross-reference column:

99:8
[h]S Ex 22:27;
S Nu 14:20
[i]S Lev 26:18
100:1 /S Ps 98:6
100:2
[k]S Dt 10:12
/S Ps 95:2
100:3
[m]S 1Ki 18:21;
S Ps 46:10
[n]S Job 10:3

[o]Ps 79:13;
Isa 19:25; 63:8,
17-19; 64:9
[p]S 2Sa 24:17;
S Ps 74:1
100:4 [q]S Ps 42:4
[r]S Ps 96:8
[s]Ps 116:17
100:5
[t]S 1Ch 16:34
[u]S Ezr 3:11;
Ps 106:1
[v]Ps 108:4;
119:90
101:1 [w]Ps 33:1;
51:14; 89:1;
145:7
101:2
[x]S Ge 17:1;
Php 1:10

[q]8 Hebrew them   [r]8 Or / an avenger of the wrongs
done to them   [s]3 Or and not we ourselves

1Sa 12:23). *they kept.* However imperfectly, it was in Israel
that God's righteous statutes and decrees were kept because
only in Israel had they been made known (see 147:19–20;
Dt 4:5–8).
99:8–9 The justice and righteousness of God's rule in
Israel (see v. 4) have been especially shown in the manner in
which he has dealt with their sins (see Ex 34:6–7; see also
note on 4:1).
99:9 *holy mountain.* See v. 5 and note. *the LORD our God is
holy.* Climactic expansion of the secondary refrain.
Ps 100 A call to praise the Lord. Whether or not it was
composed for that purpose, the final editors of the Psalter
here used it to close the series that begins with Ps 93. It has
special affinity with 95:1–2,6–7; see also Ps 117. (See introduction to Ps 93.) The second main division (vv. 4–5) parallels the structure of the first (vv. 1–3), namely, a call to praise
followed by a declaration of why the Lord is worthy of
praise—the corresponding elements of the two divisions are
complementary.
100 title *thanks.* Grateful praise (see v. 4; see also note on
75:1). Perhaps it indicates that the psalm was to accompany
a thank offering (see Lev 7:12).
100:1 *all the earth.* Though vv. 3,5 clearly speak of God's
special relationship with Israel, the call to worship goes out
to the whole world, which ought to acknowledge the Lord
because of what he has done for his people (see also Ps
98–99; 117).
100:3 *Know.* Acknowledge. *made us.* See 95:6 and note.
sheep of his pasture. See 95:7 and note.
100:4 *his gates.* The gates of the temple (see 24:7 and
note). *courts.* Of the temple (see 84:2,10; 2Ki 21:5;
23:11–12).
100:5 *the LORD is good.* In that his love-and-faithfulness
(see note on 36:5) are unfailing through all time (see 98:3
and note). *love.* See note on 6:4.
Ps 101 A king's pledge to reign righteously (see 2Ki 23:3).
If authored by David (see title), it may have been composed
for Solomon's use at his coronation (see 1Ki 2:2–4; see also
2Sa 23:1–7 and introduction to Ps 72). Only Christ, the
great Son of David, has perfectly fulfilled these commitments. In the final arrangement of the Psalter this psalm,
together with Ps 110 (both relating to the king), frames the
collection of ten psalms located between the preceding thematic group (Ps 92–100; see introduction to Ps 92) and that

which follows (Ps 111–118; see introduction to Ps 111).
This little psalter-within-the-Psalter is concentrically arranged: Ps 102 and 109 are individual prayers; Ps 103 and
108 praise the Lord for his "great . . . love" (103:11; 108:4)
that reaches to the heavens; Ps 104, which celebrates God's
many wise and benevolent acts in creation, and Ps 107,
which celebrates God's "wonderful deeds" (107:8,15,21,
24,31) for man through his lordship over creation, are complements; and so also are Ps 105, which recites the history of
Israel's redemption, and Ps 106, which recites the same
history as a history of Israel's rebellion. As a mini-Psalter, it
includes most of the forms and themes found in the rest of
the Psalter. Its outer frame is devoted to royal psalms and its
center pair is devoted to recitals of Israel's history with
God—with its themes ranging from creation and God's eternal enthronement to the covenant with Abraham, Isaac and
Jacob, the exodus from Egypt and entrance into Canaan, the
exile and restoration, and finally the ultimate triumph of the
Lord's anointed. The collection bears a distinctive redemp-
tion-history stamp and evokes recollection of all the salient
elements of the OT message. (For the problem of the Book
division at Ps 107 see introduction to that psalm.)
    Composed of seven couplets (the number of complete-
ness), the psalm begins with a twofold introduction (vv.
1–3a; see notes below), followed by a five-stanza (vv. 3b–8)
elaboration of the theme of the second stanza. Of these five
stanzas, the middle one (v. 6) speaks of the king's commitment to the "faithful" and "blameless," while the other four
(vv. 3b–4, 5, 7, 8) declare his repudiation of all the "faithless" and "wicked" in the land. (For the parallel relationship
of stanzas six and seven with three and four see notes
below.) The middle stanza is linked with stanzas one and
two also by the catchword "blameless." (For centering in the
Psalms see note on 6:6.)
101:1–2a Celebration of the pattern of God's reign, which
the king makes the model for his own.
101:1 *love and justice.* Two of the chief qualities of God's
rule (see 6:4; 99:4 and notes).
101:2a *blameless.* See vv. 2b,6; see also note on Ge 17:1.
when . . . ? An urgent prayer for God to come and sustain in
him his pledge (see 1Ki 3:7–9; see also Ps 72).
101:2b–3a The essential commitment. *heart . . . eyes.* In
OT understanding, a person follows the dictates of the
heart—the inner man (see note on 4:7)—and/or the attrac-

I will walk[y] in my house
with blameless heart.
[3]I will set before my eyes
no vile thing.[z]

The deeds of faithless men I hate;[a]
they will not cling to me.
[4]Men of perverse heart[b] shall be far
from me;
I will have nothing to do with evil.

[5]Whoever slanders his neighbor[c] in
secret,
him will I put to silence;
whoever has haughty eyes[d] and a
proud heart,
him will I not endure.

[6]My eyes will be on the faithful in the
land,
that they may dwell with me;
he whose walk is blameless[e]
will minister to me.

[7]No one who practices deceit
will dwell in my house;
no one who speaks falsely

will stand in my presence.

[8]Every morning[f] I will put to silence
all the wicked[g] in the land;
I will cut off every evildoer[h]
from the city of the LORD.[i]

Psalm 102

A prayer of an afflicted man. When he is
faint and pours out his lament before the
LORD.

[1]Hear my prayer,[j] O LORD;
let my cry for help[k] come to you.
[2]Do not hide your face[l] from me
when I am in distress.
Turn your ear[m] to me;
when I call, answer me quickly.

[3]For my days vanish like smoke;[n]
my bones[o] burn like glowing embers.
[4]My heart is blighted and withered like
grass;[p]
I forget to eat my food.[q]
[5]Because of my loud groaning[r]
I am reduced to skin and bones.

Cross-reference column

101:2
[y]S 1Ki 3:14
101:3 [z]Jer 16:18;
Eze 11:21;
Hos 9:10
[a]S Ps 5:5
101:4 [b]Pr 3:32;
6:16-19; 11:20
101:5
[c]S Ex 20:16;
S Lev 19:16
[d]S Ps 10:5
101:6 [e]ver 2;
Ps 119:1

101:8 [f]Ps 5:3;
Jer 21:12
[g]Ps 75:10
[h]S 2Sa 3:39;
Ps 118:10-12
[i]S Ps 46:4
102:1 [j]Ps 4:1
[k]S Ex 2:23
102:2 [l]S Ps 22:24
[m]S 2Ki 19:16;
Ps 31:2; 88:2
102:3
[n]S Ps 37:20;
S Jas 4:14
[o]La 1:13
102:4 [p]S Ps 37:2;
90:5-6
[q]S 1Sa 1:7;
S Ezr 10:6;
S Job 33:20
102:5 [r]S Ps 6:6

Study notes

tions of the eye—external influences (see 119:37; Jdg 14:1–2; 2Sa 11:2; 2Ki 16:10; Job 31:1; Pr 4:25; 17:24). For the combination heart-eyes see v. 5; Nu 15:39; Job 31:7; Pr 21:4; Ecc 2:10; Jer 22:17.
101:2 *house.* Royal administration (also in v. 7).
101:3a *vile.* Belial (see 2Co 6:15) is derived from the Hebrew for this word (see note on Dt 13:13).
101:3b–4 A repudiation of evil deeds and those who promote them (see v. 7).
101:3b *faithless.* Those who rebel against the right (see Hos 5:2, "rebels").
101:4 *perverse.* The opposite of "blameless" (see 18:26, "crooked"; see also Pr 11:20; 19:1; 28:6). A perverse heart and a deceitful tongue (see v. 7) are root and fruit (see Pr 17:20).
101:5 A pledge to remove from his presence all slanderous and all arrogant persons (see v. 8). *put to silence.* Destroy (as in 54:5; 94:23). See v. 8. *haughty eyes . . . proud heart.* See vv. 2b–3a and note; see also 131:1; Pr 21:4; Isa 10:12. The arrogant tend to be ruthless (see Isa 10:12) and are a law to themselves (see note on 31:23).
101:6 A pledge to surround himself in his reign with the faithful and blameless. *My eyes will be on.* I will look with favor on (see 33:18; 34:15). *the faithful.* Those who maintain moral integrity. *minister to me.* Serve as my aide (see Ex 24:13), attendant (see Ge 39:4; 1Ki 19:21), personal servant (see 2Ki 4:43), commander and official (see 1 Ch 27:1; 2Ch 17:19; Pr 29:12).
101:7 A repudiation of all those who make their way by double-dealing (see vv. 3b–4).
101:8 A pledge to remove all the wicked from the Lord's kingdom (see v. 5). *Every morning.* With diligence and persistence (see Jer 21:12; Zep 3:5). It may have been traditional for kings to hear cases in the morning. *city of the LORD.* See Ps 46; 48; 87; see also note on 3:4.
Ps 102 The prayer of an individual in a time of great distress. It is also one of the traditional penitential psalms (see introduction to Ps 6). Some interpreters believe that the "I" of vv. 1–11,23–24 was originally communal (see note on Ps 30 title; see also note on title below). (See introduction

to Ps 101.) The main body of the psalm (vv. 1–22) is developed in four stanzas (initial appeal for God to hear, vv. 1–2; description of distress, vv. 3–11; assurance that the Lord will surely hear, vv. 12–17; call for the Lord's certain deliverance to be recorded for his enduring praise, vv. 18–22), followed by a concluding recapitulation (vv. 23–28).
102 title Unique in the Psalter (no author named and no liturgical or historical notes), the title identifies only the life situation in which the prayer is to be used, and in accordance with vv. 1–11,23–24 it designates the prayer as that of an individual. But vv. 12–22,28 clearly indicate national involvement in the calamity. It may be that the distress suffered by the individual, while its description suggests physical illness, is the result of his sharing in a national disaster such as the exile—a suggestion supported by references to the restoration of Zion. Because of the close relationship of the fortunes of king and nation and because of the many themes shared by this and some of the royal psalms, it has been plausibly suggested that the prayer was originally that of a Davidic king, or of a member of the Davidic royal house, while in Babylonian exile. *prayer.* See vv. 1,17. *faint.* See 61:2; 77:3; 142:3; 143:4; see also 107:5; Jnh 2:7. *lament.* The Hebrew for this word is translated "complaint" in 64:1; 142:2; Job 7:13; 9:27; 10:1; 21:4.
102:1–2 Initial appeal for God to hear.
102:2 *hide your face.* See note on 13:1.
102:3–11 The description of distress—a suffering so great that it withers body and spirit—brought on by a visitation of God's wrath (v. 10) and making him the mockery of his enemies (v. 8).
102:3 *my days.* His life wastes away—a lament that frames the whole stanza (see v. 11). *bones burn.* As if a fire is consuming his physical frame (see 31:10; 32:3; 42:10).
102:4 *heart.* See note on 4:7. Here "heart" is used in combination with "bones" (v. 3) to refer to the whole man (body and spirit); see 22:14; Pr 14:30; 15:30; Isa 66:14 ("and you" represents the Hebrew for "and your bones"); Jer 20:9; 23:9. *blighted.* Or "scorched" (by the hot sun); see 121:6. *withered like grass.* See v. 11; see also note on 90:4–5.

⁶I am like a desert owl,^s
   like an owl among the ruins.
⁷I lie awake;^t I have become
   like a bird alone^u on a roof.
⁸All day long my enemies^v taunt me;^w
   those who rail against me use my
      name as a curse.^x
⁹For I eat ashes^y as my food
   and mingle my drink with tears^z
¹⁰because of your great wrath,^a
   for you have taken me up and
      thrown me aside.
¹¹My days are like the evening shadow;^b
   I wither^c away like grass.

¹²But you, O LORD, sit enthroned
   forever;^d
   your renown endures^e through all
      generations.^f
¹³You will arise^g and have compassion^h
   on Zion,
   for it is timeⁱ to show favor^j to her;
      the appointed time^k has come.
¹⁴For her stones are dear to your servants;
   her very dust moves them to pity.
¹⁵The nations will fear^l the name of the
   LORD,
   all the kings^m of the earth will revere
      your glory.
¹⁶For the LORD will rebuild Zionⁿ
   and appear in his glory.^o
¹⁷He will respond to the prayer^p of the
   destitute;
   he will not despise their plea.

¹⁸Let this be written^q for a future
   generation,
   that a people not yet created^r may
      praise the LORD:
¹⁹"The LORD looked down^s from his
   sanctuary on high,
   from heaven he viewed the earth,
²⁰to hear the groans of the prisoners^t
   and release those condemned to
      death."
²¹So the name of the LORD will be
   declared^u in Zion
   and his praise^v in Jerusalem
²²when the peoples and the kingdoms
   assemble to worship^w the LORD.

²³In the course of my life^t he broke my
   strength;
   he cut short my days.^x
²⁴So I said:
   "Do not take me away, O my God,
      in the midst of my days;
   your years go on^y through all
      generations.
²⁵In the beginning^z you laid the
   foundations of the earth,
   and the heavens^a are the work of
      your hands.^b
²⁶They will perish,^c but you remain;

102:6
^sS Dt 14:15-17;
Job 30:29;
Isa 34:11;
Zep 2:14
102:7 ^tPs 77:4
^uPs 38:11
102:8
^vS Ps 31:11
^wS Ps 42:10;
Lk 22:63-65;
23:35-37
^xS Ex 22:28;
Isa 65:15;
Jer 24:9; 25:18;
42:18; 44:12;
Eze 14:8;
Zec 8:13
102:9 ^yIsa 44:20
^zPs 6:6; 42:3;
80:5
102:10 ^aPs 7:11;
38:3
102:11
^bS 1Ch 29:15;
S Job 14:2;
S Ps 39:6
^cS Job 8:12;
Jas 1:10
102:12
^dS Ex 15:18
^ePs 135:13;
Isa 55:13; 63:12
^fS Ex 3:15
102:13
^gS Ps 44:26
^hS Dt 32:36;
S 1Ki 3:26;
Isa 54:8; 60:10;
Zec 10:6
ⁱPs 119:126
^jS Ps 77:7
^kS Ex 13:10;
Da 8:19; Ac 1:7
102:15
^l1Ki 8:43;
Ps 67:7; Isa 2:2
^mPs 76:12;
138:4; 148:11
102:16
ⁿS Ps 51:18
^oPs 8:1;
Isa 60:1-2
102:17
^pS 1Ki 8:29;
Ps 4:1; 6:9

102:18 ^qS Ro 4:24 ^rS Ps 22:31 102:19 ^sPs 53:2 102:20
^tS Ps 68:6; S Lk 4:19 102:21 ^uPs 22:22 ^vPs 9:14 102:22
^wS Ps 22:27; Isa 49:22-23; Zec 8:20-23 102:23 ^xS Ps 39:5
102:24 ^yS Ge 21:33; Job 36:26; Ps 90:2 102:25 ^zS Ge 1:1;
Heb 1:10-12* ^aS 2Ch 2:12 ^bS Ps 8:3 102:26 ^cIsa 13:10,13;
34:4; 51:6; Eze 32:8; Joel 2:10; Mt 24:35; 2Pe 3:7-10;
Rev 20:11

^t23 Or By his power

102:6   owl . . . owl. Translations of two different Hebrew
words (cf. Lev 11:16–18). The owl was associated with
ruins and desert areas (see Isa 34:11,15; Jer 50:39; Zep
2:14).
102:8   enemies taunt me. See 109:25; see also notes on
5:9; 39:8. use my name as a curse. They say, "May you
become like that one (the one named) is."
102:9   drink . . . tears. For tears as food and drink see 42:3;
80:5.
102:10   wrath. See note on 2:5.
102:11   A concluding summation of vv. 3–4.
102:12–17   Assurance that the King eternal will surely
hear the prayer of the destitute (v. 17) and restore Zion (see
note on 3:8).
102:12   sit enthroned forever. A central theme of the
preceding collection (Ps 92–100). Because God reigns forever and remains the same (see v. 27), his mercies to those
who look to him for salvation will not fail. renown. See note
on 30:4 ("name"). For elaborate celebrations of the Lord's
renown see Ps 111; 135; 145.
102:13   This verse and v. 16 form an inner frame around
the stanza. The two verses (see v. 14) suggest that the
psalmist's distress was occasioned by the Babylonian exile.
arise. See note on 3:7. appointed time. The time set by God
for judgment and deliverance (see 75:2; Ex 9:5; 2Sa 24:15;
Da 11:27,35). Perhaps the psalmist is referring to a time
announced by a prophet.
102:14   dear to your servants. If Zion, the city of God (see

46:4; 48:1–2,8; 87:3; 101:8; 132:13), is so loved by the
Lord's servants (see Ps 126; 137), how much more is she
cherished by God!
102:15   See note on 46:10. name. See note on 5:11.
102:16   and appear in his glory. Or "and thus appear in his
glory" (see v. 15 and note on 46:10; see also Isa 40:1–5).
This hope will find its fullest expression in the "new Jerusalem" (see Rev 21).
102:18–22   Let God's certain deliverance of his people be
recorded for his continual praise.
102:18   written. Only here does a psalmist call for memory
to be sustained by a written record of God's saving act;
usually oral transmission suffices (see 22:30; 44:1; 78:1–4).
created. Brought into being by God's sovereign act (see
51:10; 104:30; 139:13).
102:20   prisoners . . . those condemned to death. Perhaps
prisoners of war, but more likely the exiles in Babylon (see
79:11 and note).
102:21   praise. See note on 9:1.
102:22   See note on 46:10; see also 47:9 and note; 96; 98;
100. The expectation here expressed may also be influenced
by such prophecies as Isa 2:2–4; Mic 4:1–3.
102:23–28   Concluding recapitulation.
102:23–24a   See vv. 3–11.
102:24b–27   See v. 12 and note. For a NT application of
vv. 25–27 to Christ see Heb 1:10–12 and note on Heb 1:10.
102:26   Like clothing. With his first creation God clothed
himself with the manifestation of his glory (see 8:1,3–4;

they will all wear out like a garment.
Like clothing you will change them
　　and they will be discarded.
27But you remain the same, d
　　and your years will never end. e
28The children of your servants f will live
　　in your presence;
　　their descendants g will be established
　　　before you."

Psalm 103

Of David.

1Praise the LORD, h O my soul; i
　　all my inmost being, praise his holy
　　　name. j
2Praise the LORD, k O my soul,
　　and forget not l all his benefits—
3who forgives all your sins m
　　and heals n all your diseases,
4who redeems your life o from the pit
　　and crowns you with love and
　　　compassion, p
5who satisfies q your desires with good
　　things
　　so that your youth is renewed r like
　　　the eagle's. s

6The LORD works righteousness t
　　and justice for all the oppressed. u

7He made known v his ways w to Moses,
　　his deeds x to the people of Israel:
8The LORD is compassionate and
　　gracious, y

slow to anger, abounding in love.
9He will not always accuse,
　　nor will he harbor his anger forever; z
10he does not treat us as our sins
　　　deserve a
　　or repay us according to our
　　　iniquities.
11For as high as the heavens are above
　　the earth,
　　so great is his love b for those who
　　　fear him; c
12as far as the east is from the west,
　　so far has he removed our
　　　transgressions d from us.
13As a father has compassion e on his
　　children,
　　so the LORD has compassion on those
　　　who fear him;
14for he knows how we are formed, f
　　he remembers that we are dust. g
15As for man, his days are like grass, h
　　he flourishes like a flower i of the
　　　field;
16the wind blows j over it and it is gone,
　　and its place k remembers it no more.
17But from everlasting to everlasting
　　the LORD's love is with those who
　　　fear him,
　　and his righteousness with their
　　　children's children l —

102:27
d S Nu 23:19;
Heb 13:8;
Jas 1:17 e Ps 9:7
102:28 f Ps 69:36
g Ps 25:13; 89:4
103:1 h Ps 28:6
i Ps 104:1
j S Ps 30:4
103:2 k Ps 106:1;
117:1 l S Dt 6:12;
Ps 77:11
103:3 m S Ex 34:7
n S Ex 15:26;
Col 3:13;
1Pe 2:24; 1Jn 1:9
103:4 o Ps 34:22;
56:13; Isa 43:1
p S Ps 8:5; 23:6
103:5
q S Ps 90:14;
S 104:28
r Job 33:25;
Ps 119:25,93;
2Co 4:16
s S Ex 19:4
103:6 t Ps 9:8;
65:5; Isa 9:7
u S Ps 74:21;
S Lk 4:19
103:7 v Ps 99:7;
147:19
w S Ex 33:13
x Ps 106:22
103:8
y S Ex 22:27;
S Ps 86:15;
Mic 7:18-19;
Jas 5:11

103:9 z Ps 30:5;
79:5; Isa 57:16;
Jer 3:5,12;
Mic 7:18
103:10
a S Ezr 9:13;
Ro 6:23
103:11 b Ps 13:5;
57:10; 100:5;
106:45; 117:2;
La 3:22; Eph 3:18
c S 2Ch 6:31
103:12
d S 2Sa 12:13;
Ro 4:7; Eph 2:5

103:13 e Mal 3:17; 1Jn 3:1 **103:14** f Ps 119:73; 139:13-15;
Isa 29:16 g S Ge 2:7; S Ps 146:4 **103:15** h Ps 37:2; 90:5;
102:11; Isa 40:6 i S Job 14:2; Jas 1:10 **103:16** j Isa 40:7;
Hag 1:9 k S Job 7:8 **103:17** l S Ge 48:11; S Ezr 9:12

19:1; 29:3–9; 104:1,31; Isa 6:3; see also Job 38–41, especially 40:10). But he is more enduring than what he has made—and the first creation will give way to a new creation (see Isa 65:17; 66:22).
102:28 Because the Lord does not change (see v. 27), Israel's future is secure (see Mal 3:6). *live in your presence.* Or "dwell in the (promised) land" (see 69:36; see also 37:3,29; Isa 65:9). *established before you.* See 2Sa 7:24.
Ps 103 A hymn to God's love and compassion toward his people. (See introduction to Ps 101.) Calls to praise frame the body of the hymn (vv. 1–2, 20–22) and set its tone. The recital of praise falls into two unequal parts: (1) a three-verse celebration of personal benefits received (vv. 3–5) and (2) a 14-verse recollection of God's mercies to his people Israel (vv. 6–19). The major division (vv. 6–19) is composed of six couplets framed by vv. 6 and 19, which describe the general character of God's reign. Thematic development divides the six couplets into two equal parts (vv. 7–12, 13–18), of which the first celebrates God's compassion on his people as sinners while the second sings of his compassion on them as frail mortals. The two concluding couplets proclaim the vastness of his love (vv. 11–12) and its unending perseverance (vv. 17–18). As with the hymn found in Ps 33, the length of the psalm has been determined by the number of letters in the Hebrew alphabet (see introduction to Ps 33).
103:1–2 Call to praise, directed inward (cf. vv. 20–22).
103:1–2,22 *O my soul.* A conventional Hebrew way of addressing oneself (see 104:1,35; 116:7). *soul.* See note on 6:3.

103:3–5 Recital of personal blessings received.
103:4 *redeems.* A synonym for "delivers." *pit.* A metaphor for the grave (see note on 30:1). *love and compassion.* The key words of the hymn (see vv. 8,11,13,17). *love.* See vv. 8,11,17; see also note on 6:4.
103:5 *like the eagle's.* The vigor of youth is restored to match the proverbial unflagging strength of the eagle (see Isa 40:31).
103:6–19 God's love and compassion toward his people.
103:6 Together with v. 19 (the other side of the literary frame) it characterizes the reign of God under which Israel has been so graciously blessed. *righteousness.* See v. 17; see also note on 4:1.
103:7–12 God's compassion on his people as sinners.
103:7–8 See 99:7; Ex 33:13; see also note on Ex 34:6–7.
103:7 *his ways.* See 25:10 and note.
103:9 *anger.* See note on 2:5.
103:11–12 The vastness of God's love is supremely shown in his forgiving Israel's sins.
103:11 See 36:5–9. *so great is.* So prevails. *those who fear him.* See vv. 13,17–18; see also 34:8–14 and note.
103:12 See Isa 1:18; 38:17; 43:25; Jer 31:34; 50:20; Mic 7:18–19.
103:13–18 God's compassion on his people as frail mortals; perhaps echoed in Lk 1:50.
103:14 *we are dust.* See note on 78:39.
103:17 The infinite span of God's love overarches man's little time (see v. 11). *with their children's children.* See note on 109:12.

18with those who keep his covenant[m]
　and remember[n] to obey his
　　precepts.[o]

19The LORD has established his throne[p] in
　heaven,
　and his kingdom rules[q] over all.

20Praise the LORD,[r] you his angels,[s]
　you mighty ones[t] who do his
　　bidding,[u]
　who obey his word.
21Praise the LORD, all his heavenly hosts,[v]
　you his servants[w] who do his will.
22Praise the LORD, all his works[x]
　everywhere in his dominion.

　Praise the LORD, O my soul.[y]

Psalm 104

1Praise the LORD, O my soul.[z]

O LORD my God, you are very great;
　you are clothed with splendor and
　　majesty.[a]
2He wraps[b] himself in light[c] as with a
　garment;

he stretches[d] out the heavens[e] like a
　tent[f]
3　and lays the beams[g] of his upper
　　chambers on their waters.[h]
He makes the clouds[i] his chariot[j]
　and rides on the wings of the wind.[k]
4He makes winds his messengers,[u][l]
　flames of fire[m] his servants.

5He set the earth[n] on its foundations;[o]
　it can never be moved.
6You covered it[p] with the deep[q] as with
　a garment;
　the waters stood[r] above the
　　mountains.
7But at your rebuke[s] the waters fled,
　at the sound of your thunder[t] they
　　took to flight;
8they flowed over the mountains,
　they went down into the valleys,
　to the place you assigned[u] for them.
9You set a boundary[v] they cannot cross;
　never again will they cover the earth.

Cross-references (center column):

103:18
mS Dt 29:9
nPs 119:52
oS Nu 15:40;
Jn 14:15
103:19 pPs 47:8;
80:1; 113:5
qPs 22:28; 66:7;
Da 4:17
103:20 rPs 28:6
sS Ne 9:6;
Lk 2:13; Heb 1:14
tS Ps 29:1
uPs 107:25;
135:7; 148:8
103:21
vS 1Ki 22:19
wS Ne 7:73
103:22 xPs 19:1;
67:3; 145:10;
150:6 yver 1;
Ps 104:1
104:1
zS Ps 103:22
aS Job 40:10
104:2 bIsa 49:18;
Jer 43:12
cPs 18:12;
1Ti 6:16

dJob 9:8;
Jer 51:15
eJob 37:18;
Isa 40:22; 42:5;
44:24; Zec 12:1
fS Ps 19:4
104:3 gAm 9:6
hS Ps 24:2
iS Dt 33:26;
Isa 19:1; Na 1:3
jS 2Ki 2:11
kPs 18:10
104:4 lPs 148:8;
Heb 1:7*

mGe 3:24; 2Ki 2:11 104:5 nEx 31:17; Job 26:7; Ps 24:1-2;
102:25; 121:2 oS 1Sa 2:8 104:6 pGe 7:19 qS Ge 1:2
r2Pe 3:6 104:7 sS Ps 18:15 tS Ex 9:23; Ps 29:3 104:8
uPs 33:7 104:9 vS Ge 1:9; S Ps 16:6

u4 Or angels

103:19 See v. 6 and note; see also 9:4,7; 11:4; 47:2,7–8;
123:1.
103:20–22 Concluding call to praise, directed to all creatures (cf. vv. 1–2). A call to praise is often the climax of praise in the Psalter (as also of 9:1. *Praise . . . Praise . . . Praise.* See note on 96:1–3 (the final line was probably added by the editors of the Psalter; see 104:1,35).
103:20 *who do his bidding.* See 91:11; Heb 1:14.
103:21 *heavenly hosts.* Uniquely here and in 148:2 the Hebrew for "hosts" is masculine, and in both places the "hosts" are associated with "angels." *servants.* Translates the participle of the Hebrew verb for "minister" in 101:6 (see note there; see also note on 104:4).
103:22 *all his works.* See 65:13; 96:11–12 and notes.
Ps 104 A hymn to the Creator. Obviously influenced by Ge 1, the preexilic author has adapted that account to his different purpose and has subordinated its sequence somewhat to his own design (see next paragraph). Whereas Ge 1 recounts creation as God's first work at the beginning, the poet views the creation displayed before his eyes and sings the glory of its Maker and Sustainer. Surprisingly, he only hints at the angelic world (v. 4) and mentions man only in passing (vv. 14,23); his theme is the visible creation around him, which he views as the radiant and stately robe with which the invisible Creator has clothed himself to display his glory. (See introduction to Ps 101.)
Following his one-verse introduction, the poet designed the main body of his poem concentrically, with stanzas of three-nine-five-nine-five-three verses. The first stanza speaks of the celestial realm (vv. 2–4) and the fifth of the nautical (vv. 24–26)—the two realms that bracket the "earth" of his experience. The second stanza speaks of the earth's solid foundations and secure boundaries (vv. 5–9) and the fourth of the orderly cycles of life on earth governed by sun and moon (vv. 19–23). At the center a nine-verse stanza (composed of three triplets) celebrates the luxuriation of life in the earth

(vv. 10–18). To the poem's main body he added a four-verse stanza that recites how God maintains life on earth (vv. 27–30), a two-verse conclusion (vv. 31–32—which together with v. 1 frames the whole), and a three-verse epilogue (vv. 33–35). The outer frame ("Praise the LORD, O my soul") was probably added by the editors of the Psalter when they inserted the Book division after Ps 106—thus concluding Book IV with doxologies (see the liturgical frames added to Ps 105–106 and the similar conclusion to Book V: Ps 146–150).
104:1 Introduction: the theme of the hymn. *clothed.* See note on 102:26.
104:2–4 The celestial realm.
104:2 *light.* Cf. the first day of creation in Ge 1. *heavens.* Cf. the second day of creation in Ge 1. *like a tent.* Over the earth and the luminaries that give it light.
104:3 *upper chambers.* Vivid imagery for the heavenly abode of God (see v. 13). In the singular, the Hebrew for this phrase usually refers to the upper-level room of a house (as in 1Ki 17:19; 2Ki 1:2). *their waters.* The waters above the "tent" (v. 2; see Ge 1:7), from which, in the imagery of the OT, God gives the rain (see v. 13; see also 36:8 and note). *clouds his chariot.* See 18:7–15; 68:4; 77:16–19 and notes.
104:4 *winds . . . flames of fire.* The winds and lightning bolts of the thunderstorm, here personified as the agents of God's purposes (see 148:8; cf. 103:21).
104:5–9 The earth realm made secure (vv. 5,9 frame the stanza, highlighting its two main themes).
104:5 *earth.* Land in distinction from sky and seas, not the earth as a planet (see Ge 1:10). *foundations.* See 24:2 and note. *can never be moved.* Firmly founded (see 93:1; 96:10), it will not give way (cf. v. 9).
104:7 *rebuke.* See note on 76:6. *waters fled.* Cf. the third day of creation in Ge 1.
104:9 *set a boundary.* So that the land ("earth") will never be overwhelmed by the sea (cf. v. 5; see 33:7 and note; see also Ge 9:15).

[10]He makes springs[w] pour water into the
ravines;
it flows between the mountains.
[11]They give water[x] to all the beasts of the
field;
the wild donkeys[y] quench their
thirst.
[12]The birds of the air[z] nest by the
waters;
they sing among the branches.[a]
[13]He waters the mountains[b] from his
upper chambers;[c]
the earth is satisfied by the fruit of his
work.[d]
[14]He makes grass grow[e] for the cattle,
and plants for man to cultivate—
bringing forth food[f] from the earth:
[15]wine[g] that gladdens the heart of man,
oil[h] to make his face shine,
and bread that sustains[i] his heart.
[16]The trees of the LORD[j] are well
watered,
the cedars of Lebanon[k] that he
planted.
[17]There the birds[l] make their nests;
the stork has its home in the pine
trees.
[18]The high mountains belong to the wild
goats;[m]
the crags are a refuge for the
coneys.[v] [n]
[19]The moon marks off the seasons,[o]
and the sun[p] knows when to go
down.
[20]You bring darkness,[q] it becomes
night,[r]
and all the beasts of the forest[s]
prowl.
[21]The lions roar for their prey[t]
and seek their food from God.[u]
[22]The sun rises, and they steal away;
they return and lie down in their
dens.[v]
[23]Then man goes out to his work,[w]
to his labor until evening.[x]
[24]How many are your works,[y] O LORD!
In wisdom you made[z] them all;
the earth is full of your creatures.[a]
[25]There is the sea,[b] vast and spacious,
teeming with creatures beyond
number—
living things both large and small.[c]
[26]There the ships[d] go to and fro,
and the leviathan,[e] which you
formed to frolic[f] there.[g]
[27]These all look to you
to give them their food[h] at the
proper time.
[28]When you give it to them,
they gather it up;
when you open your hand,
they are satisfied[i] with good things.
[29]When you hide your face,[j]
they are terrified;
when you take away their breath,
they die and return to the dust.[k]
[30]When you send your Spirit,[l]
they are created,
and you renew the face of the earth.
[31]May the glory of the LORD[m] endure
forever;
may the LORD rejoice in his
works[n]—
[32]he who looks at the earth, and it
trembles,[o]
who touches the mountains,[p] and
they smoke.[q]
[33]I will sing[r] to the LORD all my life;

104:10 [w]Ps 107:33; Isa 41:18 **104:11** [x]ver 13 [y]S Ge 16:12; Isa 32:14; Jer 14:6 **104:12** [z]ver 17; Mt 8:20 [a]Mt 13:32 **104:13** [b]Ps 135:7; 147:8; Jer 10:13; Zec 10:1 [c]S Lev 26:4 [d]Am 9:6 **104:14** [e]S Job 38:27; Ps 147:8 [f]S Ge 1:30; S Job 28:5 **104:15** [g]S Ge 14:18; S Jdg 9:13 [h]Ps 23:5; 92:10; Lk 7:46 [i]S Dt 8:3; Mt 6:11 **104:16** [j]Ge 1:11 [k]S Ps 72:16 **104:17** [l]ver 12 **104:18** [m]S Dt 14:5 [n]Pr 30:26 **104:19** [o]S Ge 1:14 [p]Ps 19:6 **104:20** [q]Isa 45:7; Am 5:8 [r]Ps 74:16 [s]S Ps 50:10 **104:21** [t]Am 3:4 [u]Ps 145:15; Joel 1:20; S Mt 6:26 **104:22** [v]S Job 37:8 **104:23** [w]S Ge 3:19 [x]Jdg 19:16 **104:24** [y]Ps 40:5 [z]S Ge 1:31 [a]Ps 24:1; 50:10-11 **104:25** [b]Ps 69:34 [c]Eze 47:10 **104:26** [d]Ps 107:23; Eze 27:9; Jnh 1:3 [e]S Job 3:8; 41:1 [f]Job 40:20 [g]S Ge 1:21 **104:27** [h]Job 36:31; Ps 145:15; 147:9 **104:28** [i]Ps 103:5; 145:16; Isa 58:11 **104:29** [j]S Dt 31:17 [k]S Job 7:21 **104:30** [l]S Ge 1:2 **104:31** [m]Ex 40:35; Ps 8:1; S Ro 11:36 [n]S Ge 1:4 **104:32** [o]S Ps 97:4 [p]S Ex 19:18 [q]Ps 144:5 **104:33** [r]S Ex 15:1; Ps 108:1

[v]*18* That is, the hyrax or rock badger

104:10–18 The earth a flourishing garden of life—the center of the psalm and the focal point of the author's contemplation of the creation (the earth, bounded by sky, vv. 2–4, and sea, vv. 24–26). Cf. the third and sixth days of creation in Ge 1.
104:10–12 The gift of water from below—watering the ravines of the Negev.
104:13–15 The gift of water from above—watering the uplands of Israel with their cultivated fields.
104:13 *upper chambers.* See v. 3 and note.
104:15 *heart . . . heart.* See note on 4:7. *oil.* Olive oil. *make his face shine.* As food (see 1Ki 17:12), causing man's face to glow with health, and/or as cosmetic (see Est 2:12).
104:16–18 Well-watered Lebanon, with its great trees, its hordes of birds and its alpine animals, the very epitome of God's earthly parkland (see 72:16; 2Ki 14:9; 19:23; Isa 10:34; 35:2; 40:16; 60:13; Jer 22:6; Hos 14:7).
104:19–23 The orderly cycles of life on earth, governed by the moon and sun. Cf. the fourth day of creation in Ge 1.
104:21,23 *lions . . . man.* The one (representing the animal world), lord of the night; the other, lord of the day.
104:24–26 The nautical realm. Cf. the fifth day of creation in Ge 1. The realm of the sea is structurally balanced with the celestial realm (vv. 2–4) as the other boundary to the realm of earth.
104:24 A pause to recapitulate before treating the sea.
104:25 *teeming.* See Ge 1:20–21.
104:26 *leviathan.* That fearsome mythological monster of the deep (see Job 3:8 and note) is merely God's harmless pet playing in the ocean.
104:27–30 By God's benevolent care this zoological garden flourishes. Cf. the sixth day of creation in Ge 1.
104:29 *hide your face.* See note on 13:1.
104:30 *created.* See note on 102:18.
104:31 *glory of the LORD.* Such as is displayed in his creation.
104:32 He is so much greater than his creation that with a look or a touch he could undo it.

I will sing praise to my God as long
    as I live.
³⁴May my meditation be pleasing to him,
    as I rejoice^s in the LORD.
³⁵But may sinners vanish^t from the earth
    and the wicked be no more. ^u

Praise the LORD, O my soul.

Praise the LORD.^{w v}

Psalm 105

105:1–15pp — 1Ch 16:8–22

¹Give thanks to the LORD,^w call on his
    name;^x
    make known among the nations what
    he has done.
²Sing to him,^y sing praise^z to him;
    tell of all his wonderful acts. ^a
³Glory in his holy name;^b
    let the hearts of those who seek the
    LORD rejoice.
⁴Look to the LORD and his strength;
    seek his face^c always.
⁵Remember the wonders^d he has done,
    his miracles, and the judgments he
    pronounced, ^e
⁶O descendants of Abraham his servant,^f
    O sons of Jacob, his chosen^g ones.
⁷He is the LORD our God;
    his judgments are in all the earth.

⁸He remembers his covenant^h forever,
    the word he commanded, for a
    thousand generations,
⁹the covenant he made with Abraham, ⁱ
    the oath he swore to Isaac.
¹⁰He confirmed it^j to Jacob as a decree,
    to Israel as an everlasting covenant: ^k
¹¹"To you I will give the land of Canaan^l
    as the portion you will inherit." ^m
¹²When they were but few in number, ⁿ
    few indeed, and strangers in it, ^o
¹³they wandered from nation to nation, ^p
    from one kingdom to another.
¹⁴He allowed no one to oppress^q them;
    for their sake he rebuked kings: ^r
¹⁵"Do not touch^s my anointed ones;
    do my prophets^t no harm."

¹⁶He called down famine^u on the land
    and destroyed all their supplies of
    food;
¹⁷and he sent a man before them—
    Joseph, sold as a slave. ^v
¹⁸They bruised his feet with shackles, ^w
    his neck was put in irons,

Cross references

104:34
^sS Ps 2:11; 9:2;
32:11
104:35 ^tPs 37:38
^uS Job 7:10
^vPs 28:6; 105:45;
106:48
105:1
^wS 1Ch 16:34
^xPs 80:18; 99:6;
116:13; Joel 2:32;
Ac 2:21
105:2 ^yPs 30:4;
33:3; 96:1
^zPs 7:17; 18:49;
27:6; 59:17;
71:22; 146:2
^aS Ps 75:1
105:3
^bS Ps 89:16
105:4 ^cS Ps 24:6
105:5 ^dS Ps 40:5
^eS Dt 7:18
105:6 ^fver 42
^gS Dt 10:15;
Ps 106:5
105:8
^hS Ge 9:15;
Ps 106:45; 111:5;
Eze 16:60;
S Lk 1:72
105:9 ⁱGe 12:7;
S 15:18;
S 22:16-18;
Lk 1:73;
Gal 3:15-18
105:10
^jGe 28:13-15
^kIsa 55:3
105:11
^lS Ge 12:7
^mS Nu 34:2
105:12 ⁿDt 7:7
^oGe 23:4;
Heb 11:9
105:13
^pGe 15:13-16;
Nu 32:13;

33:3-49 105:14 ^qGe 35:5 ^rGe 12:17-20; S 20:3; S Ps 9:5
105:15 ^sS Ge 26:11; S 1Sa 12:3 ^tS Ge 20:7 105:16
^uS Ge 12:10; S Lev 26:26; Isa 3:1; Eze 4:16 105:17
^vS Ge 37:28; Ac 7:9 105:18 ^wS Ge 40:15

^w35 Hebrew *Hallelu Yah*; in the Septuagint this line
stands at the beginning of Psalm 105.

104:33–35 Pious epilogue.
104:33 A vow to praise—here attached to a hymn of praise
(see note on 7:17).
104:34 *my meditation.* The preceding hymn (see 19:14
and note).
104:35 May the earth be purged of that which alone mars
it (cf. Rev 21:27). *Praise the LORD* (last occurrence). Probably
belongs to Ps 105 (see NIV text note and 105:45; 106:1,48).
Ps 105 An exhortation to Israel to worship and trust in the
Lord because of all his saving acts in fulfillment of his covenant with Abraham to give his descendants the land of
Canaan. It was composed to be addressed to Israel by a
Levite (see 1Ch 16:7 and compare vv. 1–15 with 1Ch
16:8–22) on one of her annual religious festivals (see chart
on "OT Feasts and Other Sacred Days," p. 176), possibly the
Feast of Tabernacles (see Lev 23:34) but more likely the
Feast of Weeks (see Ex 23:16; Lev 23:15–21; Nu 28:26; Dt
16:9–12; see also Dt 26:1–11). For other recitals of the
same history (but for different purposes) see Ps 78; 106; Jos
24:2–13; Ne 9:7–25.
    The introduction is composed of seven verses in two parts:
(1) an exhortation (with ten imperatives) to worship the Lord
(vv. 1–4); (2) a call to remember what the Lord has done (vv.
5–7). The main body that follows is framed by two four-verse
stanzas (vv. 8–11, 42–45) that summarize—as introduction
and conclusion—its main theme: The Lord has remembered
his covenant with Abraham. The editors of the Psalter have
added an outer frame of "Hallelujahs" (see introduction to Ps
104; see also note on 104:35).
105:1–4 The exhortation to worship and trust.
105:1 *Give thanks.* Through praise (see note on Ps 100
title). *call on.* In prayer (see v. 4). The first two imperatives
highlight the two themes of the ten imperatives of the exhor-

tation: praise and prayer as expressions of devotion to the
Lord (celebration of his past saving acts; trust in him for
future deliverance and blessing). *his name.* See v. 3; see also
note on 5:11. *make known among the nations.* As an integral part of praise (see note on 9:1).
105:2 *wonderful acts.* See v. 5 ("wonders"); see also note
on 9:1.
105:3,25 *hearts.* See note on 4:7.
105:5–7 Exhortation to remember God's saving acts.
105:5 *Remember.* As a motivation for and focus of worship
and the basis for trust—remember how the Lord has remembered (see vv. 8–11). *judgments.* See v. 7; see also notes on
48:11; 97:8. *pronounced.* As Lord, he commands and it is
done.
105:8–11 The Lord remembers his covenant with Abraham (see vv. 42–45).
105:8 *covenant.* The promissory covenant of Ge 15:9–21.
This verse and v. 9 may be echoed in Lk 1:72–73. *thousand
generations.* See Ex 20:6; Dt 7:9; 1Ch 16:15.
105:10 *as a decree.* As a fixed policy governing his future
actions (see note on v. 45).
105:12–41 A recital of God's saving acts in Israel's behalf
from the granting of the covenant (see v. 11; Ge 15:9–20) to
its fulfillment (see v. 44; Jos 21:43). Cf. the recital prescribed
by Moses in conjunction with the offering of firstfruits (Dt
26:1–11).
105:14–15 See Ge 20:2–7; see also note on Ge 20:7.
105:18 *shackles . . . irons.* That is, shackles of iron (see
149:8; see also note on 3:7). The poet takes the freedom to
use a later conventional description of prisoners (see Job
13:27; 33:11). (Shackles are not spoken of in Ge 39:20–23,
and iron came into common use for them at a later
time—earlier shackles were made of bronze; see Jdg 16:21.)

19till what he foretold[x] came to pass,
till the word[y] of the LORD proved
him true.
20The king sent and released him,
the ruler of peoples set him free.[z]
21He made him master of his household,
ruler over all he possessed,
22to instruct his princes[a] as he pleased
and teach his elders wisdom.[b]

23Then Israel entered Egypt;[c]
Jacob lived[d] as an alien in the land of
Ham.[e]
24The LORD made his people very fruitful;
he made them too numerous[f] for
their foes,
25whose hearts he turned[g] to hate his
people,
to conspire[h] against his servants.
26He sent Moses[i] his servant,
and Aaron,[j] whom he had chosen.[k]
27They performed[l] his miraculous signs[m]
among them,
his wonders[n] in the land of Ham.
28He sent darkness[o] and made the land
dark—
for had they not rebelled against[p] his
words?
29He turned their waters into blood,[q]
causing their fish to die.[r]
30Their land teemed with frogs,[s]
which went up into the bedrooms of
their rulers.
31He spoke,[t] and there came swarms of
flies,[u]
and gnats[v] throughout their country.
32He turned their rain into hail,[w]
with lightning throughout their land;
33he struck down their vines[x] and fig
trees[y]

105:19 [x]S Ge 12:10; 40:20-22 [y]Ge 41:40 **105:20** [z]Ge 41:14 **105:22** [a]Ge 41:43-44 [b]S Ge 41:40 **105:23** [c]Ge 46:6; Ac 7:15; 13:17 [d]Ge 47:28 [e]S Ps 78:51 **105:24** [f]Ex 1:7, 9; Ac 7:17 **105:25** [g]S Ex 4:21 [h]Ex 1:6-10; Ac 7:19 **105:26** [i]S Ex 3:10 [j]S Ex 4:16; S Nu 33:1 [k]S Nu 16:5; 17:5-8 **105:27** [l]ver 28-37; Ex 7:8-12:51 [m]S Ex 4:17; S 10:1 [n]S Ex 3:20; Da 4:3 **105:28** [o]S Ge 1:4; S Ex 10:22 [p]S Ex 7:22 **105:29** [q]S Ps 78:44 [r]Ex 7:21 **105:30** [s]S Ex 8:2, 6 **105:31** [t]Ps 107:25; 148:8 [u]Ex 8:21-24; S Ps 78:45 [v]Ex 8:16-18 **105:32** [w]Ex 9:22-25; S Job 38:22; S Ps 78:47 **105:33** [x]Ps 78:47 [y]Ex 10:5,12 **105:34** [z]Ps 107:25 [a]S Ex 10:4,12-15 [b]S 1Ki 8:37 [c]Joel 1:6 **105:36** [d]S Ex 4:23; S 12:12 **105:37** [e]S Ex 3:21,22

and shattered the trees of their
country.
34He spoke,[z] and the locusts came,[a]
grasshoppers[b] without number;[c]
35they ate up every green thing in their
land,
ate up the produce of their soil.
36Then he struck down all the firstborn[d]
in their land,
the firstfruits of all their manhood.

37He brought out Israel, laden with silver
and gold,[e]
and from among their tribes no one
faltered.
38Egypt was glad when they left,
because dread of Israel[f] had fallen on
them.
39He spread out a cloud[g] as a covering,
and a fire to give light at night.[h]
40They asked,[i] and he brought them
quail[j]
and satisfied them with the bread of
heaven.[k]
41He opened the rock,[l] and water gushed
out;
like a river it flowed in the desert.

42For he remembered his holy promise[m]
given to his servant Abraham.
43He brought out his people with
rejoicing,[n]
his chosen ones with shouts of joy;
44he gave them the lands of the nations,[o]
and they fell heir to what others had
toiled[p] for—
45that they might keep his precepts

105:38 [f]Ex 15:16 **105:39** [g]S Ex 13:21; 1Co 10:1 [h]S Ps 78:14 **105:40** [i]Ps 78:18 [j]S Ex 16:13 [k]S Ex 16:4; Jn 6:31 **105:41** [l]S Nu 20:11; 1Co 10:4 **105:42** [m]Ge 12:1-3; 13:14-17; 15:13-16 **105:43** [n]Ex 15:1-18; Ps 106:12 **105:44** [o]Ex 32:13; Jos 11:16-23; 12:8; 13:6-7; Ps 111:6 [p]Dt 6:10-11; Ps 78:55

105:22 *instruct.* Lit. "bind," i.e., govern or control. He whose "neck" (v. 18; Hebrew *nephesh*) had been shackled was given authority to "bind" Pharaoh's princes "as he pleased" (Hebrew "with his *nephesh*"—here meaning his will). *elders.* Pharaoh's counselors, conventionally older men of wide experience and learning (see note on Ex 3:16).
105:23,27 *land of Ham.* See 78:51 and note.
105:25 *turned.* In OT perspective God's sovereign control over Israel's destiny is so complete that it governs—mysteriously—even the evil that men commit against her; hence the bold language used here (see Ex 4:21; 7:3; Jos 11:20; 2Sa 24:1; Isa 10:5–7; 37:26–27; Jer 34:22).
105:26,42 *servant.* See 78:70 and note.
105:28–36 Recital of the plagues against Egypt. In this poetic recollection seven plagues (symbolizing completeness) represent the ten plagues of Ex 7–11. Apart from omissions (the plagues of livestock disease and boils) the poet follows the order of Exodus except that he combines the third and fourth plagues (gnats and flies)—in reverse order—to stay within the number seven. He also places the ninth plague (darkness) first in order to frame his recital with mention of the two plagues that climaxed the series.
105:39 *as a covering.* Elsewhere it is said that the cloud (symbolic of God's presence) served (1) as a guide for Israel in her desert journeys (see 78:14; Ex 13:21; Nu 9:17; Ne 9:12,19), (2) as a shield of darkness to protect Israel from the pursuing Egyptians (see Ex 14:19–20) and (3) as a covering for the fiery manifestations of God's glorious presence (see Ex 16:10; 24:16; 34:5; 40:34–35,38; Nu 11:25; 12:5; 16:42; Dt 31:15; 1Ki 8:11). The psalmist appears to highlight yet another function: God's protective cover over his people in the desert, perhaps as his shading "wings" (17:8; see note there), so that the sun would not harm them by day (see 121:5–6).
105:40 *bread of heaven.* See 78:24–25 and notes.
105:41 *like a river.* Poetically heightened imagery to evoke due wonder for the event. This miracle of the desert wanderings concludes the recital and has been placed in climactic position as one of the most striking manifestations of God's redeeming power and benevolence (see 114:8; Isa 43:19–20; cf. Isa 50:2).
105:42–45 Concluding summary (balancing the introduction to the recital: vv. 8–11).
105:44 *gave them the lands.* See v. 11.

and observe his laws. *q*

Praise the LORD. *x r*

Psalm 106

106:1,47–48pp — 1Ch 16:34–36

¹Praise the LORD. *y s*

Give thanks to the LORD, for he is
good; *t*
his love endures forever. *u*
²Who can proclaim the mighty acts *v* of
the LORD
or fully declare his praise?
³Blessed are they who maintain justice, *w*
who constantly do what is right. *x*
⁴Remember me, *y* O LORD, when you
show favor *z* to your people,
come to my aid *a* when you save
them,
⁵that I may enjoy the prosperity *b* of your
chosen ones, *c*
that I may share in the joy *d* of your
nation
and join your inheritance *e* in giving
praise.
⁶We have sinned, *f* even as our fathers *g*
did;
we have done wrong and acted
wickedly. *h*
⁷When our fathers were in Egypt,
they gave no thought *i* to your
miracles;

they did not remember *j* your many
kindnesses,
and they rebelled by the sea, *k* the
Red Sea. *z*
⁸Yet he saved them *l* for his name's
sake, *m*
to make his mighty power *n* known.
⁹He rebuked *o* the Red Sea, and it dried
up; *p*
he led them through *q* the depths as
through a desert.
¹⁰He saved them *r* from the hand of the
foe; *s*
from the hand of the enemy he
redeemed them. *t*
¹¹The waters covered *u* their adversaries;
not one of them survived.
¹²Then they believed his promises
and sang his praise. *v*
¹³But they soon forgot *w* what he had
done
and did not wait for his counsel. *x*
¹⁴In the desert *y* they gave in to their
craving;
in the wasteland *z* they put God to
the test. *a*

105:45
*q*S Dt 4:40;
6:21-24;
Ps 78:5-7
*r*S Ps 104:35
106:1
*s*S Ps 22:23;
S 103:2
*t*S Ps 119:68
*u*S Ezr 3:11;
Ps 136:1-26;
Jer 33:11
106:2
*v*S Ps 71:16
106:3 *w*Ps 112:5;
Hos 12:6 *x*Ps 15:2
106:4 *y*Ps 25:6,7
*z*S Ps 77:7
*a*S Ge 50:24
106:5
*b*S Dt 30:15;
Ps 1:3 *c*S Ps 105:6
*d*Ps 20:5; 27:6;
47:5; 118:15
*e*S Ex 34:9
106:6
*f*S 1Ki 8:47;
S Ro 3:9
*g*S 2Ch 30:7
*h*Ne 1:7
106:7 *i*S Jdg 3:7

*j*Ps 78:42
*k*Ex 14:11-12
106:8 *l*Ex 14:30;
S Ps 80:3;
107:13; Isa 25:9;
Joel 2:32
*m*S Ps 9:16;
S Ps 23:3
*n*S Ex 14:31
106:9 *o*Ps 18:15;
Isa 50:2
*p*S Ex 14:21;
Na 1:4 *q*Ps 78:13;
Isa 63:11-14
106:10
*r*Ex 14:30;
Ps 107:13
*s*S Ps 78:53
*t*Ps 78:42; 107:2;
Isa 35:9; 62:12

106:11 *u*S Ex 14:28 106:12 *v*Ex 15:1-21; S Ps 105:43
106:13 *w*S Ex 15:24 *x*S Ex 16:28; S Nu 27:21 106:14
*y*S Ps 78:40 *z*S Ps 68:7 *a*S Ex 17:2; 1Co 10:9

*x*45 Hebrew *Hallelu Yah* *y*1 Hebrew *Hallelu Yah*; also
in verse 48 *z*7 Hebrew *Yam Suph*; that is, Sea of
Reeds; also in verses 9 and 22

105:45 *precepts.* God has kept his "decree" (v. 10) so that
Israel might keep his "precepts"—the Hebrew word is the
same (see note on v. 5: "remember"). God's redemptive
working in fulfillment of his covenant promise has as its goal
the creating of a people in the earth who conform their lives
to his holy will. Thus the list of appropriate responses begun
in v. 1—praise and prayer (trust)—is completed by the third:
obedience (see Ge 18:19).

Ps 106 A confession of Israel's long history of rebellion and
a prayer for God to once again save his people. In length,
poetic style and shared themes it has much affinity with Ps
105 even while it contrasts with it by reciting the past as a
history of rebellion (see Ps 78; Ne 9:5–37). It was most likely
authored by a Levite in Jerusalem sometime after the return
of some of the exiles. The first verse and the last two verses
seem to have been taken over from an earlier composition
(see 1Ch 16:34–36). These may have been added (along
with the "Hallelujah"; see NIV text note) by the editors of
the Psalter (borrowing from an earlier Davidic psalter) when
they set the Book divisions between Ps 106 and 107. (See
introduction to Ps 101.)

Apart from the fact that the psalm has an introduction (vv.
1–5) and a (composite) conclusion (vv. 44–48), the recital
character of its main theme (as in Ps 105) controls its basic
outline. Beginning with the events at the Red Sea (vv. 6–12),
the psalm next narrates at length Israel's many rebellions
during the desert wanderings (vv. 13–33), follows with a
summary description of Israel's apostasy in the promised land
(vv. 34–39) and completes its recital with a general
statement of God's stern measures in the promised land (vv.
40–43).

106:1–5 Introduction.
106:1 *Give thanks.* With praise (see note on Ps 100 title);
a conventional liturgical call to praise (see 107:1; 118:1,29;
136:1–3). *love.* See note on 6:4.
106:2 *Who can . . . ?* With integrity. *his praise.* Praise for
his mighty acts (see v. 47; see also note on 9:1).
106:3 *Blessed.* See note on 1:1. *justice . . . what is right.*
That is, justice-and-righteousness (see 36:6 and note; see
also note on 3:7). This verse answers the question posed in v.
2.
106:4 *Remember me.* As one committed to the way of life
described in v. 3. *when you show favor.* Or "with the favor
you show" (see vv. 44–46). *when you save them.* Or "with
your salvation." The psalmist prays that God will include
him in all the mercies of his "great love" (v. 45), which he
shows to his people. Thus the inner logic of the prayer seems
to be completed at v. 46. The editors of the Psalter appear to
have converted an individual prayer into a communal one by
their additions (see introduction).
106:5 *prosperity . . . joy . . . praise.* A progressive sequence
of cause and effect. *your inheritance.* See v. 40.
106:6–43 Israel's history of rebellion.
106:6 A general confession of sin introducing the recital.
We. The author identifies himself with Israel in her rebellion
even as he prays for inclusion in God's mercies toward his
people (see Ezr 9:6–7).
106:7,22 *miracles.* For example, the plagues against Egypt
(see note on 9:1, "wonders").
106:10 *redeemed.* Here, as often, a synonym for "delivered."
106:13 *his counsel.* The working out of his plan.

¹⁵So he gave them[b] what they asked for,
but sent a wasting disease[c] upon
them.

¹⁶In the camp they grew envious[d] of
Moses
and of Aaron, who was consecrated
to the LORD.
¹⁷The earth opened[e] up and swallowed
Dathan;[f]
it buried the company of Abiram.[g]
¹⁸Fire blazed[h] among their followers;
a flame consumed the wicked.

¹⁹At Horeb they made a calf[i]
and worshiped an idol cast from
metal.
²⁰They exchanged their Glory[j]
for an image of a bull, which eats
grass.
²¹They forgot the God[k] who saved them,
who had done great things[l] in Egypt,
²²miracles in the land of Ham[m]
and awesome deeds[n] by the Red Sea.
²³So he said he would destroy[o] them—
had not Moses, his chosen one,
stood in the breach[p] before him
to keep his wrath from destroying
them.

²⁴Then they despised[q] the pleasant
land;[r]
they did not believe[s] his promise.
²⁵They grumbled[t] in their tents
and did not obey the LORD.
²⁶So he swore[u] to them with uplifted
hand
that he would make them fall in the
desert,[v]
²⁷make their descendants fall among the
nations

and scatter[w] them throughout the
lands.

²⁸They yoked themselves to the Baal of
Peor[x]
and ate sacrifices offered to lifeless
gods;
²⁹they provoked the LORD to anger[y] by
their wicked deeds,[z]
and a plague[a] broke out among
them.
³⁰But Phinehas[b] stood up and intervened,
and the plague was checked.[c]
³¹This was credited to him[d] as
righteousness
for endless generations[e] to come.

³²By the waters of Meribah[f] they angered
the LORD,
and trouble came to Moses because
of them;
³³for they rebelled[g] against the Spirit[h] of
God,
and rash words came from Moses'
lips.[a][i]

³⁴They did not destroy[j] the peoples
as the LORD had commanded[k] them,
³⁵but they mingled[l] with the nations
and adopted their customs.
³⁶They worshiped their idols,[m]
which became a snare[n] to them.
³⁷They sacrificed their sons[o]
and their daughters to demons.[p]
³⁸They shed innocent blood,

106:15
[b]S Ex 16:13;
Ps 78:29
[c]S Nu 11:33
106:16
[d]Nu 16:1-3
106:17 [e]Dt 11:6
[f]S Ex 15:12
[g]S Nu 16:1
106:18
[h]S Lev 10:2
106:19
[i]S Ex 32:4;
Ac 7:41
106:20 [j]Jer 2:11;
Ro 1:23
106:21 [k]Ps 78:11
[l]Dt 10:21;
Ps 75:1
106:22
[m]S Ps 78:51
[n]S Ex 3:20;
S Dt 4:34
106:23
[o]S Ex 32:10
[p]Ex 32:11-14;
S Nu 11:2;
S Dt 9:19
106:24
[q]Nu 14:30-31
[r]S Dt 8:7;
S Jer 3:19
[s]S Nu 14:11;
Heb 3:18-19
106:25
[t]S Ex 15:24;
Dt 1:27;
1Co 10:10
106:26
[u]S Nu 14:23;
Heb 4:3
[v]S Dt 2:14;
Heb 3:17
106:27
[w]S Lev 26:33
106:28
[x]S Nu 23:28
106:29 [y]Nu 25:3
[z]Ps 64:2; 141:4
[a]S Nu 16:46;
25:8
106:30
[b]S Ex 6:25
[c]Nu 25:8
106:31
[d]S Ge 15:6;
S Nu 25:11-13
[e]Ps 49:11
106:32
[f]S Ex 17:7;
Nu 20:2-13
106:33
[g]S Ex 23:21;

Ps 107:11 [h]S Ps 51:11; Isa 63:10 [i]Ex 17:4-7; Nu 20:8-12
106:34 [j]S Jos 9:15; Jdg 1:27-36 [k]Ex 23:24; S Dt 2:34; 7:16;
20:17 **106:35** [l]Jdg 3:5-6; Ezr 9:1-2 **106:36** [m]S Dt 7:16
[n]S Ex 10:7 **106:37** [o]S Lev 18:21; S Dt 12:31; Eze 16:20-21
[p]S Ex 22:20; S Dt 32:17; 1Co 10:20

[a]33 Or *against his spirit,* / *and rash words came from
his lips*

106:16–18 See Nu 16:1–35.
106:19 *Horeb.* See note on Ex 3:1.
106:20 *Glory.* Glorious One (see 1Sa 15:29; Jer 2:11).
106:22 *land of Ham.* See 78:51 and note.
106:23 *stood in the breach.* See Ex 32:11–14,31–32.
wrath. See note on 2:5.
106:24 *pleasant land.* So described in Jer 3:19; 12:10; Zec
7:14; see also Dt 8:7–9; Eze 20:6.
106:26–27 *fall.* See note on 13:4.
106:28–31 See Nu 25.
106:31 *credited to him as righteousness.* As Abram's faith
was "credited to him as righteousness" (Ge 15:6), so, says
the psalmist, was Phinehas's priestly zeal for the Lord (see
Nu 25:7–8). *for endless generations.* The psalmist refers to
the "covenant of a lasting priesthood" (Nu 25:13) that the
Lord granted Phinehas as a gracious reward for his zealous
act. It was the granting of this promissory covenant that
warranted the statement about crediting righteousness, for
God's granting of a promissory covenant to Abram had followed upon his crediting Abram's faith to him as righteousness (see Ge 15:9–21). Similarly, God's promissory covenants with Noah (see Ge 9:9–17) and with David (see 2Sa

7:5–16) followed upon God's testimony to their righteousness (see Ge 7:1; 1Sa 13:14). See chart on "Major Covenants in the OT," p. 19.
106:32 *Meribah.* See note on Ex 17:7.
106:33 *against the Spirit of God.* For a literal rendering of
the Hebrew see NIV text note. The interpretation embodied
in the NIV text appears warranted by Isa 63:10 (see also Ps
78:40). For the Spirit of God present and at work in the
desert wanderings see Ex 31:3; Nu 11:17; 24:2; Ne 9:20;
Isa 63:10–14.
106:34–39 A general description of the worst of rebellious
Israel's sins, applicable from the time of the judges to the
Babylonian exile.
106:37 *demons.* The Hebrew for this word occurs
elsewhere in the OT only in Dt 32:17, where it refers to false
gods. It is related to a Babylonian word referring to (pagan)
protective spirits.
106:38 Cf. Jer 19:4–5. *innocent blood.* The blood of
anyone not guilty of a capital crime. *desecrated.* The very
land itself is defiled by the slaughter of innocents (see Nu
35:33; Jer 3:2,9).

the blood of their sons *q* and
daughters,
whom they sacrificed to the idols of
Canaan,
and the land was desecrated by their
blood.
³⁹They defiled themselves *r* by what they
did;
by their deeds they prostituted *s*
themselves.

⁴⁰Therefore the LORD was angry *t* with
his people
and abhorred his inheritance. *u*
⁴¹He handed them over *v* to the nations,
and their foes ruled over them.
⁴²Their enemies oppressed *w* them
and subjected them to their power.
⁴³Many times he delivered them, *x*
but they were bent on rebellion *y*
and they wasted away in their sin.

⁴⁴But he took note of their distress
when he heard their cry; *z*
⁴⁵for their sake he remembered his
covenant *a*
and out of his great love *b* he
relented. *c*

⁴⁶He caused them to be pitied *d*
by all who held them captive.

⁴⁷Save us, *e* O LORD our God,
and gather us *f* from the nations,
that we may give thanks *g* to your holy
name *h*
and glory in your praise.

⁴⁸Praise be to the LORD, the God of Israel,
from everlasting to everlasting.
Let all the people say, "Amen!" *i*

Praise the LORD.

BOOK V

Psalms 107–150

Psalm 107

¹Give thanks to the LORD, *j* for he is
good; *k*
his love endures forever.
²Let the redeemed *l* of the LORD say
this—

106:38
*q*S Lev 18:21;
S Dt 18:10;
S 2Ki 3:27
106:39
*r*S Ge 3:17;
Lev 18:24;
Eze 20:18
*s*S Nu 15:39
106:40
*t*S Lev 26:28
*u*S Ex 34:9;
S Dt 9:29
106:41
*v*S Jdg 2:14
106:42
*w*S Jdg 4:3
106:43
*x*S Jos 10:14;
Jdg 7:1-25;
S Ne 9:28;
Ps 81:13-14
*y*S Jdg 2:16-19;
6:1-7
106:44 *z*S Jdg 3:9
106:45
*a*S Ge 9:15;
Ps 105:8;
S Lk 1:72
*b*S Ps 17:7;
S 103:11
*c*S Ex 32:14
106:46
*d*S Ex 3:21;
S 1Ki 8:50
106:47
*e*S Ps 28:9
*f*Ps 107:3; 147:2;
Isa 11:12; 27:13;
56:8; 66:20;
Jer 31:8;
Eze 20:34;
106:48 *g*Ps 105:1 *h*Ps 30:4; S 99:3 **106:48** *i*S Ps 41:13;
S 72:19 **107:1** *j*S 1Ch 16:8; S 2Ch 5:13 *k*S 2Ch 7:3 **107:2**
*l*S Ps 106:10; S Isa 35:9

106:39 *defiled.* See Lev 18:24; Jer 2:23; Eze 20:30–31; 22:3–4. *prostituted themselves.* Committed prostitution by joining themselves with false gods (see Eze 23:3,5–8; Hos 5:3; 6:10; see also note on Jdg 2:17).
106:40–43 God's stern measures against his rebellious people—a general description applicable from the days of the judges to the Babylonian exile and focusing particularly on God's most severe form of covenant sanctions (see Lev 26:25–26,33,38–39; Dt 28:25,36–37,48–57,64–68).
106:40 *angry.* See note on 2:5. *abhorred.* See 5:6.
106:44–46 God's gracious remembering of his covenant—a general description applicable from the days of the judges to the Babylonian exile.
106:44 *heard their cry.* See Ex 2:23; 3:7–9; Nu 20:16; Jdg 3:9,15; 4:3; 6:6–7; 10:10; 1Sa 9:16; 2Ch 20:6–12; Ne 9:27–28.
106:45 *remembered his covenant.* See 105:8,42; Ex 2:24; Lev 26:42,45. *love.* See note on 6:4.
106:46 *pitied by all who held them captive.* Makes clear that the author's recital includes the Babylonian captivity (see 1Ki 8:50; 2Ch 30:9; Ezr 9:9; Jer 42:12). Although there were earlier captivities of Israelite communities, no other captor group was said to have been shown pity.
106:47 A communal prayer for deliverance and restoration from dispersion (see introduction and note on v. 4). *name.* See note on 5:11. *glory in.* Triumphantly celebrate. The Hebrew for this phrase is found elsewhere only in the parallel in 1Ch 16:35. *praise.* See note on 9:1.
106:48 The doxology for Book IV (see 41:13 and note). *Amen!* See note on Dt 27:15.
Ps 107 An exhortation to praise the Lord for his unfailing love in that he hears the prayers of those in need and saves them (see next paragraph—on structure). It was composed for liturgical use at one of Israel's annual religious festivals. Interpretations vary widely, but the following is most likely: Having experienced anew God's mercies in her return from Babylonian exile (v. 3; see Jer 33:11), Israel is led by a Levite in celebrating God's unfailing benevolence toward those

who have cried to him in the crises of their lives. In its recitational style the psalm is closely related to Ps 104–106, and in its language to Ps 105–106. For that reason it has been seriously proposed that with these last two psalms it forms a trilogy from the same author. Whether or not this is so, its affinity with the preceding psalms strongly suggests that it was associated with them before the insertion of a Book division between Ps 106 and 107 and that it was intended to conclude the little series, Ps 104–107. Its recital of God's "wonderful deeds for men" (v. 8)—which climaxes Ps 105–106—balances the recital of his many wise works in creation (see 104:2–26) and his benevolent care over the animal world (see 104:27–30). The editors may have inserted a Book division between Ps 106 and 107 with a view to a fivefold division of the Psalter (see Introduction: Collection, Arrangement and Date). (See introduction to Ps 101.)
The introduction (vv. 1–3) and conclusion (v. 43) enclose six stanzas, of which the last two (vv. 33–38, 39–42) stand apart as an instructive supplement focusing in a more general way on reversals in fortunes—which, however, end up with God restoring the "hungry" (v. 36) and the "needy" (v. 41). Of the four remaining stanzas (marked by recurring refrains: vv. 6,13,19,28; vv. 8,15,21,31), the first and last refer to God's deliverance of those lost in the trackless desert (vv. 4–9) and those imperiled on the boisterous sea (vv. 23–32). The two central stanzas celebrate deliverance from the punishment of foreign bondage (vv. 10–16) and from the punishment of disease (vv. 17–22). Of the concluding lines to these four stanzas, the first two (vv. 9,16) and the last two (vv. 22,32) are similar. The verse pattern of these four stanzas (six-seven-six-ten) makes deliberate use of the significant numbers seven and ten.
107:1–3 Introductory call to praise.
107:1 A conventional liturgical call to praise (see 106:1; 118:1,29; 136:1; Jer 33:11). *Give thanks.* See vv. 8,15,21, 31; see also note on Ps 100 title. *love.* See vv. 8,15,21,31, 43; see also note on 6:4.
107:2 *redeemed.* Here, as often, a synonym for "de-

those he redeemed from the hand of
the foe,
3those he gathered[m] from the lands,
from east and west, from north and
south.[b]
4Some wandered in desert[n] wastelands,
finding no way to a city[o] where they
could settle.
5They were hungry[p] and thirsty,[q]
and their lives ebbed away.
6Then they cried out[r] to the LORD in
their trouble,
and he delivered them from their
distress.
7He led them by a straight way[s]
to a city[t] where they could settle.
8Let them give thanks[u] to the LORD for
his unfailing love[v]
and his wonderful deeds[w] for men,
9for he satisfies[x] the thirsty
and fills the hungry with good
things.[y]

10Some sat in darkness[z] and the deepest
gloom,
prisoners suffering[a] in iron chains,[b]
11for they had rebelled[c] against the words
of God
and despised[d] the counsel[e] of the
Most High.
12So he subjected them to bitter labor;
they stumbled, and there was no one
to help.[f]
13Then they cried to the LORD in their
trouble,
and he saved them[g] from their
distress.
14He brought them out of darkness[h] and
the deepest gloom[i]
and broke away their chains.[j]
15Let them give thanks[k] to the LORD for
his unfailing love[l]
and his wonderful deeds[m] for men,
16for he breaks down gates of bronze
and cuts through bars of iron.
17Some became fools[n] through their
rebellious ways[o]
and suffered affliction[p] because of
their iniquities.
18They loathed all food[q]

107:3 [m]S Ne 1:9 **107:4** [n]S Jos 5:6 [o]ver 36 **107:5** [p]Ex 16:3 [q]S Ex 15:22; S 17:2 **107:6** [r]S Ex 14:10 **107:7** [s]S Ezr 8:21 [t]ver 36 **107:8** [u]Ps 105:1 [v]Ps 6:4 [w]S Ps 75:1 **107:9** [x]Ps 22:26; 63:5; Isa 58:11; Mt 5:6; Lk 1:53 [y]S Ps 23:1; Jer 31:25 **107:10** [z]ver 14; Ps 88:6; 143:3; Isa 9:2; 42:7,16; 49:9; Mic 7:9 [a]Ps 102:20; Isa 61:1 [b]S Job 36:8 **107:11** [c]S Ps 5:10 [d]S Nu 14:11 [e]S 1Ki 22:5; 2Ch 36:16 **107:12** [f]S 2Ki 14:26; Ps 72:12 **107:13** [g]S Ps 106:8 **107:14** [h]S ver 10; Isa 9:2; 42:7; 50:10; 59:9; 60:2; S Lk 1:79 [i]Ps 86:13; Isa 29:18 [j]S Job 36:8; Ps 116:16; Ac 12:7 **107:15** [k]ver 8,21,31; Ps 105:1 [l]Ps 6:4 [m]S Ps 75:1 **107:17** [n]S Ps 53:1 [o]S Ps 25:7 [p]S Lev 26:16; Isa 65:6-7; Jer 30:14-15; Gal 6:7-8 **107:18** [q]S Job 3:24; S 6:6

[b]3 Hebrew *north and the sea*

livered."
107:3 *from the lands.* From the dispersion resulting from the Assyrian (see 2Ki 17:6) and Babylonian captivities (see 2Ki 24:14,16; 25:11,26; Jer 52:28–30; see also Ne 1:8; Est 8:5,9,13; Isa 11:12; 43:5–6; Eze 11:17; 20:34). *south.* Lit. "(the) sea" (see NIV text note), i.e., the west, as in Isa 49:12. But perhaps the final letter of the Hebrew word has been lost, which if supplied yields "south."
107:4–9 Deliverance for those lost in the trackless desert. No reference is made to rebellion (as in the third and fourth stanzas), but since Israel had journeyed through the desert on her way to Canaan she had firsthand experience of the terrors of the desert. She was, moreover, bounded on the east by the great Arabian Desert (as on the west by the Mediterranean Sea; see vv. 23–32), across which her merchant caravans traveled.
107:4,7,36 *city where they could settle.* Lit. "city of habitation," i.e., where people live and where a steady supply of food and water makes human life secure.
107:6 *they cried out.* The author uses the same Hebrew verb in v. 28, thus linking the fifth stanza with the second. In vv. 13,19 he uses a different (but similar-sounding) Hebrew verb, linking the third and fourth stanzas. Just as Israel's history was a history of divine deliverance (see Ps 105) and a history of rebellion (see Ps 106), so also it was a history of crying out to the Lord in distress (see references in note on 106:44).
107:7 *straight way.* Direct route, clear of dangerous and difficult obstacles.
107:8 For other refrains see introduction to Ps 42–43. *wonderful deeds.* See vv. 15,21,24,31; see also note on 9:1 ("wonders").
107:9 *satisfies the thirsty . . . fills the hungry.* See v. 5; see also 105:40–41.
107:10–16 Deliverance from the punishment of foreign bondage. God even delivers those who cry to him when their distress is a result of his discipline for their sins (see vv. 17–20,33–41).
107:10 *sat in darkness . . . deepest gloom.* Vivid imagery for distress (see 18:28; Isa 5:30; 8:22; 59:9; see also note on 44:19). *prisoners.* While reference is no doubt to foreign bondage, the imagery of being bound was also used by OT poets to refer to other forms of distress (see Job 36:8; Isa 28:22; La 3:7); so the reference may be deliberately ambiguous.
107:11 *God . . . Most High.* That is, God Most High (see Ge 14:19 and note; see also note on 3:7). *counsel.* God's wise directives embodied in his words.
107:12 *subjected them to bitter labor.* Lit. "brought down their heart with labor," i.e., a labor so burdensome it broke their spirit. *stumbled.* Their strength failed (see 31:10; 109:24; Ne 4:10; Isa 40:30; Zec 12:8).
107:13 *cried to.* See note on v. 6.
107:16 Either this verse is quoted from Isa 45:2, or both verses quote an established saying. *gates of bronze.* City gates—normally of wood; here proverbially of bronze, the strongest gates then imaginable (see Jer 1:18). *bars of iron.* Bars that secured city gates (see Dt 3:5; Jer 51:30), usually made of wood (see Na 3:13) but sometimes of bronze (see 1Ki 4:13). "Can a man break iron . . . or bronze?" was a proverb of the time (see Jer 15:12).
107:17–22 Deliverance from the punishment of wasting disease (see note on vv. 10–16).
107:17 *fools.* See Jer 4:22; see also NIV text note on 14:1. "Fools despise wisdom and discipline" (Pr 1:7; see v. 43). *affliction because of their iniquities.* See Lev 26:16,25; Dt 28:20–22,35,58–61.
107:18 *gates of death.* The realm of the dead was sometimes depicted as a netherworld city with a series of concentric walls and gates (seven, each inside the other, according to ancient Near Eastern mythology) to keep those descending there from returning to the land of the living (see 9:13 and note on Job 38:17; see also Mt 16:18).

and drew near the gates of death. [r]

[19]Then they cried[s] to the LORD in their trouble,
and he saved them[t] from their distress.

[20]He sent forth his word[u] and healed them; [v]
he rescued[w] them from the grave. [x]

[21]Let them give thanks[y] to the LORD for his unfailing love[z]
and his wonderful deeds[a] for men.

[22]Let them sacrifice thank offerings[b]
and tell of his works[c] with songs of joy. [d]

[23]Others went out on the sea[e] in ships; [f]
they were merchants on the mighty waters.

[24]They saw the works of the LORD, [g]
his wonderful deeds in the deep.

[25]For he spoke[h] and stirred up a tempest[i]
that lifted high the waves. [j]

[26]They mounted up to the heavens and went down to the depths;
in their peril[k] their courage melted[l] away.

[27]They reeled[m] and staggered like drunken men;
they were at their wits' end.

[28]Then they cried[n] out to the LORD in their trouble,
and he brought them out of their distress. [o]

[29]He stilled the storm[p] to a whisper;
the waves[q] of the sea were hushed. [r]

[30]They were glad when it grew calm,
and he guided them[s] to their desired haven.

[31]Let them give thanks[t] to the LORD for his unfailing love[u]

and his wonderful deeds[v] for men.

[32]Let them exalt[w] him in the assembly[x] of the people
and praise him in the council of the elders.

[33]He turned rivers into a desert, [y]
flowing springs[z] into thirsty ground,

[34]and fruitful land into a salt waste, [a]
because of the wickedness of those who lived there.

[35]He turned the desert into pools of water[b]
and the parched ground into flowing springs; [c]

[36]there he brought the hungry to live,
and they founded a city where they could settle.

[37]They sowed fields and planted vineyards[d]
that yielded a fruitful harvest;

[38]he blessed them, and their numbers greatly increased, [e]
and he did not let their herds diminish. [f]

[39]Then their numbers decreased, [g] and they were humbled[h]
by oppression, calamity and sorrow;

[40]he who pours contempt on nobles[i]
made them wander in a trackless waste. [j]

[41]But he lifted the needy[k] out of their affliction
and increased their families like flocks. [l]

[42]The upright see and rejoice, [m]

107:18
[r]S Job 17:16;
S 33:22
107:19 [s]ver 28;
Ps 5:2 [t]ver 13;
Ps 34:4
107:20
[u]S Dt 32:2;
Ps 147:15;
Mt 8:8; Lk 7:7
[v]S Ex 15:26
[w]S Job 33:28
[x]Ps 16:10; 30:3;
S 56:13
107:21 [y]S ver 15
[z]Ps 6:4 [a]Ps 75:1
107:22
[b]S Lev 7:12
[c]Ps 9:11; 73:28;
118:17
[d]S Job 8:21;
S Ps 65:8
107:23
[e]Isa 42:10
[f]S Ps 104:26
107:24 [g]Ps 64:9;
111:2; 143:5
107:25
[h]S Ps 105:31
[i]S Ps 50:3
[j]S Ps 93:3
107:26 [k]Lk 8:23
[l]S Jos 2:11
107:27
[m]Isa 19:14;
24:20; 28:7
107:28 [n]S ver 19
[o]Ps 4:1; Jnh 1:6
107:29 [p]Lk 8:24
[q]S Ps 93:3
[r]S Ps 65:7;
Jnh 1:15
107:30 [s]ver 7
107:31 [t]S ver 15
[u]Ps 6:4

[v]Ps 75:1; 106:2
107:32 [w]Ps 30:1;
34:3; 99:5
[x]S Ps 1:5; 22:22;
26:12; 35:18
107:33
[y]1Ki 17:1;
Ps 74:15;
Isa 41:15; 42:15;
50:2 [z]S Ps 104:10
107:34
[a]S Ge 13:10
107:35
[b]S 2Ki 3:17;
Ps 105:41; 126:4;
Isa 43:19; 51:3
[c]S Job 38:26;
S Isa 35:7

107:37 [d]S 2Ki 19:29; S Isa 37:30 **107:38** [e]S Ge 12:2;
S Dt 7:13 /S Ge 49:25 **107:39** [g]S 2Ki 10:32; Eze 5:12
[h]S Ps 44:9 **107:40** [i]S Job 12:18 /S Dt 32:10 **107:41**
[k]S 1Sa 2:8; Ps 113:7-9 [l]S Job 21:11 **107:42** [m]S Job 22:19;
Ps 97:10-12

107:19 *cried to.* See note on v. 6. *saved.* See v. 13 (another link between the second and third stanzas); cf. vv. 6,28.
107:20 *his word.* His command, here personified as the agent of his purpose (see 147:15,18; see also note on 23:6).
107:22 *thank offerings.* See Lev 7:12–15; 22:29–30. *tell of his works.* See note on 7:17. In their concluding lines, stanzas four and five are linked, as are stanzas two and three. *songs of joy.* See, e.g., Ps 116.
107:23–32 Deliverance from the perils of the sea (see note on vv. 4–9). Israel's merchants also braved the sea in pursuit of trade (see Ge 49:13; Jdg 5:17; 1Ki 9:26–28; 10:22).
107:23 *mighty waters.* See 29:3.
107:24 *wonderful deeds in the deep.* Since the peoples of the eastern Mediterranean coastlands associated the "mighty waters" (v. 23) of the sea with the primeval chaotic waters (see note on 32:6), the Lord's total control of them was always for Israel a cause of wonder and of a sense of security. Therefore the terrifying storms that sometimes swept the Mediterranean (see Jnh 1; Ac 27) are here included among his wonderful deeds.
107:30 *haven.* Perhaps trading center.
107:32 See v. 22. *elders.* See note on Ex 3:16.

107:33–42 A twofold instructive supplement recalling how the Lord sometimes disciplined his people by turning the fruitful land (v. 34) into a virtual desert (see 1Ki 17:1–7; 2Ki 8:1) but then restored the land again (see Ru 1:6; 1Ki 18:44–45), so that the hungry (v. 36) could live there and prosper in the midst of plenty. But then he sent powerful armies against them (such as the Assyrians, 2Ki 17:3–6, and the Babylonians, 2Ki 24:20–17; 25:1–26) that devastated the land once more and deported its people; yet afterward he restored the needy (v. 41). But the poet generalizes upon these experiences in the manner of the wisdom teachers.
107:33–35 The imagery is similar to that found in Isa 35:6–7; 41:18; 42:15; 43:19–20; 50:2 and may indicate that the author has been influenced by Isaiah.
107:40 Perhaps quoted from Job 12:21,24. In their prosperity the people, led by their nobles, grow proud and turn their backs on the God who has blessed them (see Dt 31:20; 32:15), so he returns them to the desert (see Dt 32:10; Hos 2:3,14).
107:41 *needy.* Those in need of help (see v. 39; see also 9:18 and note).
107:42 Conclusion to the instruction (vv. 33–41); perhaps

but all the wicked shut their
mouths. [n]

43Whoever is wise, [o] let him heed these
things
and consider the great love [p] of the
LORD.

Psalm 108

108:1-5pp — Ps 57:7-11
108:6-13pp — Ps 60:5-12

A song. A psalm of David.

1My heart is steadfast, [q] O God;
I will sing [r] and make music with all
my soul.
2Awake, harp and lyre! [s]
I will awaken the dawn.
3I will praise you, O LORD, among the
nations;
I will sing of you among the peoples.
4For great is your love, [t] higher than the
heavens;
your faithfulness [u] reaches to the
skies. [v]
5Be exalted, O God, above the heavens, [w]
and let your glory be over all the
earth. [x]
6Save us and help us with your right
hand, [y]
that those you love may be delivered.
7God has spoken [z] from his sanctuary: [a]
"In triumph I will parcel out
Shechem [b]
and measure off the Valley of
Succoth. [c]

8Gilead is mine, Manasseh is mine;
Ephraim is my helmet,
Judah [d] my scepter.
9Moab [e] is my washbasin,
upon Edom [f] I toss my sandal;
over Philistia [g] I shout in triumph."
10Who will bring me to the fortified city?
Who will lead me to Edom?
11Is it not you, O God, you who have
rejected us
and no longer go out with our
armies? [h]
12Give us aid against the enemy,
for the help of man is worthless. [i]
13With God we will gain the victory,
and he will trample down [j] our
enemies.

Psalm 109

For the director of music. Of David.
A psalm.

1O God, whom I praise, [k]
do not remain silent, [l]
2for wicked and deceitful men [m]
have opened their mouths against
me;
they have spoken against me with
lying tongues. [n]
3With words of hatred [o] they surround
me;
they attack me without cause. [p]
4In return for my friendship they accuse
me,
but I am a man of prayer. [q]

Cross references (center column)

107:42
[n]S Job 5:16;
Ro 3:19
107:43 [o]Jer 9:12;
Hos 14:9
[p]Ps 103:11
108:1 [q]Ps 112:7;
119:30,112
[r]S Ps 18:49
108:2
[s]S Job 21:12
108:4 [t]Nu 14:18;
Ps 106:45
[u]S Ex 34:6
[v]S Ps 36:5
108:5 [w]S Ps 8:1
[x]S Ps 57:5
108:6
[y]S Job 40:14
108:7 [z]Ps 89:35
[a]Ps 68:35;
102:19
[b]S Ge 12:6
[c]S Ge 33:17

108:8
[d]S Ps 78:68
108:9
[e]S Ge 19:37
[f]S 2Sa 8:13-14
[g]S 2Sa 8:1
108:11
[h]S Ps 44:9
108:12
[i]Ps 118:8; 146:3;
Isa 10:3; 30:5;
31:3; Jer 2:36;
17:5
108:13 [j]Ps 44:5;
Isa 22:5; 63:3,6
109:1
[k]S Ex 15:2;
Jer 17:14
109:2 [m]S Ps 43:1
[n]S Ps 52:4
109:3 [o]Ps 69:4
[p]Ps 35:7;
Jn 15:25
109:4 [q]Ps 69:13;
141:5

---

an echo of Job 5:16. *upright . . . wicked.* A frequent contrast
in OT wisdom literature (see Pr 2:21–22; 11:6–7; 12:6;
14:11; 15:8; 21:18,29; 29:27—but the Hebrew for
"wicked" here is shared more often with Job).
107:43 Conclusion to the psalm. *Whoever is wise.* See Dt
32:29; Hos 14:9. *these things.* The instruction in vv.
33–42. *consider the great love of the LORD.* The theme of vv.
4–32.
Ps 108 Praise of God's love, and prayer for his help against
the enemies—a combination (with very slight modifications)
of 57:7–11 and 60:5–12. For a similar composition of a new
psalm by combination of portions from several psalms see
1Ch 16:8–36. The celebration of the greatness of God's love
(v. 4) links this psalm thematically with Ps 103 (see 103:11).
See introduction to Ps 101.
108 title *song.* See note on Ps 30 title. *of David.* Both
sources (Ps 57; 60) were credited to him.
108:1–5 Praise of God's love, possibly intended to function here as an expression of trust in God (the God of vv.
7–9,11), to whom appeal is to be made (vv. 6,12); see 109:1
and note. For this stanza see notes on 57:7–11.
108:1 *soul.* Lit. "glory" (see note on 7:5).
108:6–13 Prayer for God's help against enemies (see notes
on 60:5–12).
Ps 109 A prayer for God to judge a case of false accusation.
The author speaks of his enemies in the singular in vv. 6–19
but in the plural elsewhere. Some therefore suppose that vv.

6–19 contain the enemies' curses pronounced against the
author (see NIV text note on v. 6). But it is more likely that
either (1) the author shifts here to a collective mode of
speaking, or (2) the enemies are united under a leader whose
personal animosity toward the psalmist has fired the antagonism of others and so is singled out for special attention.
Traditional attempts to isolate a distinct class of psalms called
"imprecatory" (and then identify Ps 109 as the climax of the
series) are mistaken (see note on vv. 6–15). This prayer has
much affinity with Ps 35. See introduction to Ps 101.
    Two (Hebrew) four-line stanzas of petition frame the
whole (vv. 1–5, 26–29), followed by a two-line conclusion
(vv. 30–31). The remaining 20 lines fall into two main
divisions of ten lines each (vv. 6–15, 16–25). Of these, the
second is thematically divided into two parts of five lines
each, the first of which (vv. 16–20) catalogues what "he"
has done while the second (vv. 21–25) describes how "I"
am suffering.
109 title See note on Ps 4 title.
109:1–5 Appeal to God to deliver him from false accusers.
109:1 *whom I praise.* The one he publicly praises as his
trustworthy deliverer and defender (see 22:3 and note; see
also 35:18; 74:21; 76:10; 79:13; 102:18). *silent.* (Judicial-
ly) inactive (see 28:1; 35:22; 50:3,21; 83:1).
109:2–5 The particulars of his case, which he presents
before the heavenly bar of justice (see 35:11–16).
109:2 *opened their mouths against me.* See note on 5:9.

⁵They repay me evil for good,^r
and hatred for my friendship.

⁶Appoint^c an evil man^d to oppose him;
let an accuser^{e s} stand at his right
hand.

⁷When he is tried, let him be found
guilty,^t
and may his prayers condemn^u him.

⁸May his days be few;^v
may another take his place^w of
leadership.

⁹May his children be fatherless
and his wife a widow.^x

¹⁰May his children be wandering
beggars;^y
may they be driven^f from their
ruined homes.

¹¹May a creditor^z seize all he has;
may strangers plunder^a the fruits of
his labor.^b

¹²May no one extend kindness to him
or take pity^c on his fatherless
children.

¹³May his descendants be cut off,^d
their names blotted out^e from the
next generation.

¹⁴May the iniquity of his fathers^f be
remembered before the LORD;
may the sin of his mother never be
blotted out.

¹⁵May their sins always remain before^g
the LORD,

that he may cut off the memory^h of
them from the earth.

¹⁶For he never thought of doing a
kindness,
but hounded to death the poor
and the needyⁱ and the
brokenhearted.^j

¹⁷He loved to pronounce a curse—
may it^g come on him;^k
he found no pleasure in blessing—
may it be^h far from him.

¹⁸He wore cursing^l as his garment;
it entered into his body like water,^m
into his bones like oil.

¹⁹May it be like a cloak wrappedⁿ about
him,
like a belt tied forever around him.

²⁰May this be the LORD's payment^o to my
accusers,
to those who speak evil^p of me.

²¹But you, O Sovereign LORD,
deal well with me for your name's
sake;^q
out of the goodness of your love,^r
deliver me.^s

²²For I am poor and needy,
and my heart is wounded within me.

²³I fade away like an evening shadow;^t

109:5 ʳS Ge 44:4
109:6 ˢ1Ch 21:1; Job 1:6; Zec 3:1
109:7 ᵗPs 1:5
ᵘPr 28:9; Isa 41:24
109:8 ᵛS Job 15:32
ʷAc 1:20*
109:9 ˣEx 22:24; Jer 18:21
109:10 ʸS Ge 4:12
109:11 ᶻNe 5:3
ᵃS Nu 14:3; Isa 1:7; 6:11; 36:1; La 5:2
ᵇJob 20:18
109:12 ᶜS Job 5:4
109:13 ᵈJob 18:19; Ps 21:10
ᵉS Nu 14:12; Ps 9:5; Pr 10:7
109:14 ᶠEx 20:5; Nu 14:18; Isa 65:6-7; Jer 32:18
109:15 ᵍPs 90:8
ʰS Ex 17:14; S Dt 32:26
109:16 ⁱS Job 20:19; S Ps 35:10; S Ps 34:18
109:17 ᵏPr 28:27; S Mt 7:2
109:18 ˡPs 10:7
ᵐNu 5:22
109:19 ⁿver 29; Ps 73:6; Eze 7:27
109:20 ᵒS Ex 32:34; Ps 54:5; 94:23; Isa 3:11; 2Ti 4:14
ᵖPs 71:10
109:21 ᵠS Ex 9:16; S Ps 23:3
ʳPs 69:16
ˢPs 3:7
109:23 ᵗS Job 14:2

^c6 Or *They say;* "Appoint (with quotation marks at the end of verse 19)"   ^d6 Or *the Evil One*   ^e6 Or *let Satan*   ^f10 Septuagint; Hebrew *sought*   ^g17 Or *curse, / and it has*   ^h17 Or *blessing, / and it is*

109:4 *but I am a man of prayer.* In contrast to the enemy (see vv. 16–18). The intent may be: But I have prayed for them (as in 35:13–14).

109:6–15 Appeal for judicial redress—that the Lord will deal with them in accordance with their malicious intent against him, matching punishment with crime (see note on 5:10; see also 35:4–10 and note).

109:6 *evil man . . . accuser.* It may well be that the alternative translations in the NIV text notes are to be preferred (see note on Job 1:6). The psalmist's enemy falsely accused him in order to bring him down; now let the enemy be confronted by an accuser.

109:7 *his prayers.* The petitions he offers in his defense.

109:8 *days be few.* The false accuser was no doubt seeking to effect David's death (see 1Ki 21:8–15). *another take his place of leadership.* The enemy held some official position and was perhaps plotting a coup. For a NT application of these words to Judas see Ac 1:20.

109:10–11 May he also be deprived of all his property so that he has no inheritance to pass on to his children.

109:12 *no one extend kindness.* See v. 16. *his . . . children.* The close identity of a man with his children and of children with their parents, resulting from the tightly bonded unity of the three- or four-generation households of that ancient society, is alien to the modern reader, whose sense of self is highly individualistic. But that deep, profoundly human bond accounts for the ancient legal principle of "punishing the children for the sin of the fathers to the third and fourth generation" (see Ex 20:5; but see also 103:17; Ge 18:19).

109:13 Since a man lived on in his children (see previous note), the focus of judgment remains on the false accuser (see 21:10; 37:28). *names blotted out.* See note on 9:5.

109:14–15 *iniquity of his fathers . . . sin of his mother . . . their sins.* These verses return to the theme of vv. 7–8 (and thus form a frame around the stanza): May the indictment the accuser lodges against him include the sins of his parents (see note on v. 12).

109:15 *cut off the memory of them.* May this slanderer be the last of their family line.

109:16–20 The ruthless character of the enemy—may he be made to suffer the due consequences (see 10:2–15; 59:12–13). Accusation of the adversary is a common feature in psalms that are appeals to the heavenly Judge (see, e.g., 5:9–10; 10:2–11; 17:10–12).

109:17 *curse.* The enemy added curses to lies (see note on 10:7).

109:18 *into his body like water, into his bones like oil.* Cursing was his food and drink as well as his clothing; he lived by cursing (see Pr 4:17).

109:21–25 The intensity of "my" suffering—Lord, deliver me!

109:21 *for your name's sake.* See notes on 5:11; 23:3. *love.* See v. 26; see also note on 6:4.

109:22 The psalmist's description of his situation echoes the words of v. 16. *poor and needy.* Dependent on the Lord (see note on 34:6). *heart.* See note on 4:7. *is wounded.* The Hebrew for this phrase sounds like the Hebrew for "curse" in vv. 17–18, a deliberate wordplay—while he lives by cursing, I live with deep inward pain.

I am shaken off like a locust.
²⁴My knees give ᵘ way from fasting; ᵛ
my body is thin and gaunt. ʷ
²⁵I am an object of scorn ˣ to my
accusers;
when they see me, they shake their
heads. ʸ

²⁶Help me, ᶻ O LORD my God;
save me in accordance with your
love.
²⁷Let them know ᵃ that it is your hand,
that you, O LORD, have done it.
²⁸They may curse, ᵇ but you will bless;
when they attack they will be put to
shame,
but your servant will rejoice. ᶜ
²⁹My accusers will be clothed with
disgrace
and wrapped in shame ᵈ as in a cloak.

³⁰With my mouth I will greatly extol the
LORD;
in the great throng ᵉ I will praise him.
³¹For he stands at the right hand ᶠ of the
needy one,

---

to save his life from those who
condemn him.

Psalm 110

Of David. A psalm.

¹The LORD says ᵍ to my Lord:
"Sit at my right hand ʰ
until I make your enemies
a footstool for your feet." ⁱ

²The LORD will extend your mighty
scepter ʲ from Zion; ᵏ
you will rule ˡ in the midst of your
enemies.
³Your troops will be willing
on your day of battle.
Arrayed in holy majesty, ᵐ
from the womb of the dawn
you will receive the dew of your
youth. ⁱ ⁿ

⁴The LORD has sworn

Cross references (center column):

109:24
ᵘHeb 12:12
ᵛS Ps 35:13
ʷS Job 16:8
109:25
ˣS Ps 22:6
ʸS Job 16:4;
S Mt 27:39;
Mk 15:29
109:26 ᶻPs 12:1;
119:86
109:27
ᵃS Job 37:7
109:28
ᵇS 2Sa 16:12
ᶜPs 66:4;
Isa 35:10; 51:11;
54:1; 65:14
109:29
ᵈS Ps 35:26
109:30
ᵉS Ps 35:18
109:31 ᶠPs 16:8;
108:6

110:1
ᵍMt 22:44*;
Mk 12:36*;
Lk 20:42*;
Ac 2:34*
ʰS Mk 16:19;
Heb 1:13*; 12:2
ⁱS Jos 10:24;
S 1Ki 5:3;
1Co 15:25
110:2
ʲS Ge 49:10;
Ps 45:6; Isa 14:5;
Jer 48:17
ᵏS Ps 2:6 ˡPs 72:8

110:3 ᵐS Ex 15:11 ⁿMic 5:7

ⁱ3 Or / your young men will come to you like the dew

109:23 *I fade away.* Apparently the psalmist suffers a life-sapping affliction, which is the occasion for his enemies to turn on him (see vv. 24–25; see also note on 5:9). *like an evening shadow.* See 102:11. *shaken off.* See Ne 5:13; Job 38:13.
109:26–29 Concluding petition, with many echoes of preceding themes.
109:28 *servant.* Perhaps identifies the psalmist as the Lord's anointed (see title; see also 78:70 and note).
109:30–31 A vow to praise the Lord for his deliverance (see note on 7:17).
Ps 110 Oracles concerning the Messianic King-Priest. This psalm (specifically its two brief oracles, vv. 1,4) is frequently referred to in the NT testimony to Christ. Like Ps 2, it has the marks of a coronation psalm, composed for use at the enthronement of a new Davidic king. Before the Christian era Jews already viewed it as Messianic. Because of the manner in which it has been interpreted in the NT—especially by Jesus (see Mt 22:43–45; Mk 12:36–37; Lk 20:42–44), but also by Peter (see Ac 2:34–36) and the author of Hebrews (see especially Heb 1:13; 5:6–10; 7:11–28)—Christians have generally held that this is the most directly "prophetic" of all the psalms. If so, David, speaking prophetically (see 2Sa 23:2), composed a coronation psalm for his great future Son, of whom the prophets did not speak until later. It may be, however, that David composed the psalm for the coronation of his son Solomon, that he called him "my Lord" (v. 1) in view of his new status, which placed him above the aged David, and that in so doing he spoke a word that had far larger meaning than he knew. This would seem to be in more accord with what we know of David from Samuel, Kings and Chronicles. See introduction to Ps 101.
The psalm falls into two precisely balanced halves (vv. 1–3, 4–7). Each of the two brief oracles (vv. 1,4) is followed by thematically similar elaboration.
110:1–3 The Lord's decree, establishing his anointed as his regent in the face of all opposition (see 2:7–12).
110:1 The first oracle (see note on v. 4). *my Lord.* My sovereign, therefore superior to David (see Mt 22:44–45; Mk 12:36–37; Lk 20:42–44; Ac 2:34–35; Heb 1:13 and

their contexts). *Sit.* Sit enthroned. *right hand.* The place of honor beside a king (see 45:9; 1Ki 2:19); thus he is made second in authority to God himself. NT references to Jesus' exaltation to this position are many (see Mt 26:64; Mk 14:62; 16:19; Lk 22:69; Ac 2:33; 5:31; 7:55–56; Ro 8:34; Eph 1:20; Col 3:1; Heb 1:3; 8:1; 10:12; 12:2). *enemies.* See note on 2:1–3. *footstool for your feet.* See Heb 10:12–13. Ancient kings often had themselves portrayed as placing their feet on vanquished enemies (see Jos 10:24). For a royal footstool as part of the throne see 2Ch 9:18. For the thought here see 1Ki 5:3. Paul applies this word to Christ in 1Co 15:25; Eph 1:22.
110:2 *extend your mighty scepter.* Expand your reign in ever widening circles until no foe remains to oppose your rule. *Zion.* David's royal city (see 2Sa 5:7,9), but also God's (see 9:11 and note), where he rules as the Great King (see Ps 46; 48; 132:13–18). The Lord's anointed is his regent over his emerging kingdom in the world.
110:3 *willing.* Lit. "freewill offerings," i.e., they will offer themselves as dedicated warriors to support you on the battlefield (see Jdg 5:2)—as the Israelites offered of their treasures for the building of the tabernacle in the desert (see Ex 35:29; 36:3; see also Ezr 1:4; 2:68). Accordingly, Paul speaks of Christ's followers offering their bodies "as living sacrifices" (Ro 12:1) and of himself as a "drink offering" (Php 2:17); see also 2Co 8:5. *Arrayed . . . your youth.* If the text is descriptive of the Lord's anointed, as seems likely, it depicts him as clothed in royal majesty and glory and perpetually preserving the bloom of youth even as the "womb of the dawn" gives birth each morning to the dew (for a different use of this imagery see Isa 26:19). If it speaks of the young warriors who flock to him (see NIV text note), it apparently describes them as dressed in priestly garb, ready for participation in a holy war (see 1Sa 21:4–5; 25:28; 2Ch 13:8,12; 20:15,21; Isa 13:3–4; Jer 6:4; 51:27), and pouring into his camp morning by morning as copious as the dew (see 2Sa 17:11–12). *holy majesty.* See note on 29:2.
110:4–7 The Lord's oath establishing his anointed as king-priest in Zion and assuring him victory over all powers that oppose him.

and will not change his mind: *o*
"You are a priest forever,*p*
    in the order of Melchizedek. *q*"

⁵The Lord is at your right hand; *r*
    he will crush kings*s* on the day of his
        wrath. *t*
⁶He will judge the nations, *u* heaping up
        the dead*v*
    and crushing the rulers*w* of the whole
        earth.
⁷He will drink from a brook beside the
        way*j*;
    therefore he will lift up his head. *x*

Psalm 111*k*

¹Praise the Lord.*l*

I will extol the Lord*y* with all my
        heart*z*
    in the council*a* of the upright and in
        the assembly. *b*

²Great are the works*c* of the Lord;

---

they are pondered by all*d* who
        delight in them.
³Glorious and majestic are his deeds,
    and his righteousness endures*e*
        forever.
⁴He has caused his wonders to be
        remembered;
    the Lord is gracious and
        compassionate.*f*
⁵He provides food*g* for those who fear
        him;*h*
    he remembers his covenant*i* forever.
⁶He has shown his people the power of
        his works,*j*
    giving them the lands of other
        nations. *k*
⁷The works of his hands*l* are faithful
        and just;
    all his precepts are trustworthy. *m*

110:4
*o*S Nu 23:19
*p*Zec 6:13;
Heb 5:6*; 7:21*
*q*S Ge 14:18;
Heb 5:10;
7:15-17*
110:5 *r*Ps 16:8
*s*S Dt 7:24;
Ps 2:12; 68:21;
76:12; Isa 60:12;
Da 2:44 *t*S Ps 2:5;
Ro 2:5; Rev 6:17;
11:18
110:6 *u*S Ps 9:19
*v*Isa 5:25; 34:3;
66:24
*w*S Ps 18:38
110:7 *x*Ps 3:3;
27:6
111:1 *y*Ps 34:1;
109:30; 115:18;
145:10 *z*S Ps 9:1
*a*Ps 89:7
*b*S Ps 1:5
111:2
*c*S Job 36:24;
Ps 143:5;
Rev 15:3

*d*Ps 64:9
111:3 *e*Ps 112:3,
9; 119:142
111:4 *f*S Dt 4:31;
S Ps 86:15
111:5
*g*S Ge 1:30;
S Ps 37:25;
Mt 6:31-33

*h*Ps 103:11 *i*S 1Ch 16:15; S Ps 105:8 111:6 *j*Ps 64:9; S 66:3,
5 *k*S Ps 105:44 111:7 *l*S Ps 92:4 *m*Ps 19:7; 119:128

*j*7 Or *l* / *The One who grants succession will set him in
authority* *k*This psalm is an acrostic poem, the lines of
which begin with the successive letters of the Hebrew
alphabet. *l*1/ Hebrew *Hallelu Yah*

110:4 The second oracle (see note on v. 1). *has sworn.* In accordance also with his sworn covenant to maintain David's royal line forever (see 89:35–37). The force of this oath is elaborated by the author of Hebrews (Heb 6:16–18; 7:20–22). *priest . . . in the order of Melchizedek.* David and his royal sons, as chief representatives of the rule of God, performed many worship-focused activities, such as overseeing the ark of the covenant (see 2Sa 6:1–15, especially v. 14; 1Ki 8:1), building and overseeing the temple (see 1Ki 5–7; 2Ki 12:4–7; 22:3–7; 23:4–7; 2Ch 15:8; 24:4–12; 29:3–11; 34:8) and overseeing the work of the priests and Levites and the temple liturgy (see 1Ch 6:31; 15:11–16; 16:4–42; 23:3–31; 25:1; 2Ch 17:7–9; 19:8–11; 29:25, 30; 31:2; 35:15–16; Ezr 3:10; 8:20; Ne 12:24,36,45). In all these duties they exercised authority over even the high priest. But they could not engage in those specifically priestly functions that had been assigned to the Aaronic priesthood (see 2Ch 26:16–18). In the present oracle the son of David is installed by God as king-priest in Zion after the manner of Melchizedek, the king-priest of God Most High at Jerusalem in the days of Abraham (see Ge 14:18). As such a king-priest, he was appointed to a higher order of priesthood than that of Aaron and his sons. (For the union of king and priest in one person see Zec 6:13.) What this means for Christ's priesthood is the main theme of Heb 7. *forever.* Permanently and irrevocably; perhaps alluded to in Jn 12:34.

110:5 *The Lord is at your right hand.* God is near to assist you in your warfare (see v. 2; 109:31). Some take these words as an address to God: The Lord (David's superior son) is at your (God's) right hand (as in v. 1). *on the day of his wrath.* See 2:5 and note.

110:6 *He.* The Lord's anointed. *heaping up the dead.* Battlefield imagery (borrowed from David's victories) that depicts the victory of the Lord's anointed over all powers that oppose the kingdom of God (see 2:9; Rev 19:11–21).

110:7 *drink from a brook.* Even in the heat of battle he will find refreshment and lift up his head with undiminished vigor (see note on v. 3). For another possible but less likely rendering of this line see NIV text note.

Ps 111 Praise of God for his unfailing righteousness. The

psalm combines hymnic praise with wisdom instruction, as its first and last verses indicate. Close comparison with Ps 112 shows that these two psalms are twins, probably written by the same author and intended to be kept together. The two psalms are most likely postexilic. They introduce a series of Hallelujah psalms (Ps 111–118), but stand apart from them in traditional Jewish liturgical use (see introduction to Ps 113). Structurally, both Ps 111 and Ps 112 are alphabetic acrostics (see NIV text note), but unique in that each (Hebrew) half-line advances the alphabet. Both psalms are framed by first and last verses that highlight their primary themes, and in both psalms the main body develops the theme introduced by the first verse, while the closing verse adds a counterpart. In both psalms the main body of eight verses falls thematically into two halves of four verses each, with the corresponding verses of each half containing parallel thematic links (compare, e.g., 111:2 and 111:6; also vv. 5 and 9). Corresponding verses of the two psalms also tend to share common themes (compare, e.g., 111:3–5 with 112:3–5).

111:1 *I will extol.* Introductory to the praise that follows in vv. 2–9. *council of the upright.* Probably a more intimate circle than the assembly (see 107:32 for a similar distinction) and referring to those who are truly godly—such as the "upright" of 112:2,4 (see 11:7; 33:1; 49:14; 97:11; 107:42; 140:13). *in the assembly.* See note on 9:1.

111:2 *works of the Lord.* The hymn focuses especially on what God has done for his people. Verses 2,9 sum it up. *pondered.* Reflectively examined (see Ezr 10:16, "investigate"; Ecc 1:13, "study").

111:3 *righteousness.* As embodied in his deeds (see note on 4:1).

111:4 *wonders.* See note on 9:1. *gracious and compassionate.* See Ex 34:6–7 and note.

111:5 *provides food.* Illustrative of his bountiful provisions for the daily needs of his people (as in the Lord's prayer: "Give us today our daily bread," Mt 6:11). *fear.* See v. 10 and note. *his covenant.* See v. 9; see also 105:8–11.

111:6 Cf. v. 2.

111:7 *faithful and just.* Cf. "Glorious and majestic" (v. 3). *precepts are trustworthy.* See note on 93:5.

[8]They are steadfast for ever[n] and ever,
　done in faithfulness and uprightness.
[9]He provided redemption[o] for his
　people;
　he ordained his covenant forever—
　holy and awesome[p] is his name.

[10]The fear of the LORD[q] is the beginning
　of wisdom;[r]
　all who follow his precepts have good
　understanding.[s]
　To him belongs eternal praise.[t]

Psalm 112[m]

[1]Praise the LORD.[n] [u]

Blessed is the man[v] who fears the
　LORD,[w]
　who finds great delight[x] in his
　commands.

[2]His children[y] will be mighty in the
　land;
　the generation of the upright will be
　blessed.
[3]Wealth and riches[z] are in his house,
　and his righteousness endures[a]
　forever.
[4]Even in darkness light dawns[b] for the
　upright,
　for the gracious and compassionate
　and righteous[c] man.[o]
[5]Good will come to him who is generous
　and lends freely,[d]
　who conducts his affairs with justice.

[6]Surely he will never be shaken;[e]
　a righteous man will be
　remembered[f] forever.
[7]He will have no fear of bad news;
　his heart is steadfast,[g] trusting in the
　LORD.[h]
[8]His heart is secure, he will have no
　fear;[i]
　in the end he will look in triumph on
　his foes.[j]
[9]He has scattered abroad his gifts to the
　poor,[k]
　his righteousness endures[l] forever;
　his horn[p] will be lifted[m] high in
　honor.

[10]The wicked man will see[n] and be
　vexed,
　he will gnash his teeth[o] and waste
　away;[p]
　the longings of the wicked will come
　to nothing.[q]

Psalm 113

[1]Praise the LORD.[q] [r]

Praise, O servants of the LORD,[s]

111:8
[n]Ps 119:89,152,
160; Isa 40:8;
S Mt 5:18
111:9 [o]Ps 34:22;
S 103:4; 130:7;
Lk 1:68 [p]Ps 30:4;
99:3; Lk 1:49
111:10
[q]S Job 23:15;
S Ps 19:9 [r]Dt 4:6
[s]S Dt 4:6;
Ps 119:98,104,
130 [t]Ps 28:6;
89:52
112:1 [u]Ps 33:2;
103:1; 150:1
[v]Ps 1:1-2
[w]S Job 1:8;
Ps 103:11;
115:13; 128:1
[x]S Ps 1:2; 119:14,
16,47,92
112:2 [y]Ps 25:13;
37:26; 128:2-4
112:3 [z]S Dt 8:18
[a]S Ps 37:6;
S 111:3
112:4
[b]S Ps 18:28
[c]Ps 5:12
112:5
[d]S Ps 37:21,26;
Lk 6:35

112:6 [e]S Ps 15:5;
S 55:22 [f]Pr 10:7;
Ecc 2:16
112:7 [g]Ps 57:7;
108:1 [h]S Ps 28:7;
56:3-4; S Isa 12:2
112:8 [i]Ps 3:6;
27:1; 56:11;
Pr 1:33; Isa 12:2
[j]S Ps 54:7
112:9 [k]Lk 19:8;
Ac 9:36;
2Co 9:9*
[l]S Ps 111:3
[m]S Ps 75:10
112:10 [n]Ps 86:17
[o]S Ps 37:12;
S Mt 8:12

[p]S Ps 34:21 [q]S Job 8:13 **113:1** [r]S Ps 22:23 [s]Ps 34:22;
S 103:21; 134:1

[m]This psalm is an acrostic poem, the lines of which begin
with the successive letters of the Hebrew alphabet.
[n]1 Hebrew *Hallelu Yah* [o]4 Or / *for the LORD is
gracious and compassionate and righteous* [p]9 *Horn*
here symbolizes dignity. [q]1 Hebrew *Hallelu Yah*; also
in verse 9

111:8 *They.* "The works of his hands" (v. 7). *faithfulness
and uprightness.* Cf. "gracious and compassionate" (v. 4).
111:9 *provided redemption.* The other great benefit of
God's deeds in behalf of his people (cf. "provides food," v. 5).
holy and awesome. As shown by his works. *name.* See note
on 5:11.
111:10 Concluding word of godly wisdom. *The fear of the
LORD is the beginning of wisdom.* The classic OT statement
concerning the religious basis of what it means to be wise
(see Job 28:28; Pr 1:7; 9:10; see also note on Ge 20:11).
who follow his precepts. Lit. "who do them." The plural
Hebrew pronoun refers back to "precepts" in v. 7 (see
19:7-9, where "The fear of the LORD" stands parallel to
"statutes," "precepts," "commands," "ordinances"; see
also 112:1).
Ps 112 A eulogy to the godly man—in the spirit of Ps 1 but
formed after the pattern of Ps 111 and likely intended as its
complement (see introduction to Ps 111).
112:1 The basic theme, developed more fully in vv. 2-9.
Verse 10 states its converse. See 1:1-2; 128:1. *Blessed.* See
note on 1:1. *fears the LORD.* See 34:8-14 and note.
112:2 *children.* The godly man brings blessing to his children and is himself blessed through them (cf. v. 6; see 37:26;
127:3-5; 128:3; see also note on 109:12). *will be mighty.*
Will be persons of influence and reputation.
112:3 *Wealth and riches.* See 1:3; 128:2. *righteousness.*
See v. 9; see also note on 1:5. *endures.* It is not an occasional
characteristic of his actions (see "steadfast," v. 7).
112:4 *darkness.* A metaphor for calamitous times (see
107:10 and note). *light.* See note on 27:1. *gracious and*

compassionate. See Ex 34:6-7 and note.
112:5 *Good.* Well-being and prosperity (see 34:8-14 and
note). *is generous and lends freely.* See v. 9; see also 111:5.
112:6 *shaken.* See note on 10:6. *remembered forever.* His
righteousness will have erected an enduring memorial of
honor in the memory of both God and man (see v. 2 and
note).
112:7 *heart.* See v. 8; see also note on 4:7. *trusting.* His
trust in God will be as steadfast as his righteousness is
enduring (see v. 3). For trust and obedience to God's righteous will as the sum of true godliness see 34:8-14 and note.
112:8 *will look in triumph.* "Even in darkness light
dawns" (v. 4).
112:9 *gifts to the poor.* See v. 5. *lifted high in honor.* As
God's name is held in holy awe (see 111:9), so the godly man
will be held in honor.
112:10 The counterpart. *see and be vexed.* That godliness
is the way to blessedness is the reverse of the expectations of
the wicked (see 10:2-11; 107:42). *come to nothing.* See
1:4-6; see also Ps 37; cf. 111:10.
Ps 113 A hymn to the Lord celebrating his high majesty and
his mercies to the lowly (see 138:6). It was probably composed originally for the temple liturgy. This psalm begins the
"Egyptian Hallel" (Ps 113-118), which came to be used in
Jewish liturgy at the great religious festivals (Passover,
Weeks, Tabernacles, Dedication, New Moon; see Lev 23;
Nu 10:10; Jn 10:22; see also chart on "OT Feasts and Other
Sacred Days," p. 176). At Passover, Ps 113 and 114 were
sung before the meal and Ps 115-118 after the meal. (See
introduction to Ps 111.)

praise the name of the LORD.
²Let the name of the LORD be praised,ᵗ
  both now and forevermore.ᵘ
³From the rising of the sunᵛ to the place
    where it sets,
  the name of the LORD is to be
    praised.

⁴The LORD is exaltedʷ over all the
    nations,
  his glory above the heavens.ˣ
⁵Who is like the LORD our God,ʸ
  the One who sits enthronedᶻ on
    high,ᵃ
⁶who stoops down to lookᵇ
  on the heavens and the earth?

⁷He raises the poorᶜ from the dust
  and lifts the needyᵈ from the ash
    heap;
⁸he seats themᵉ with princes,
  with the princes of their people.
⁹He settles the barrenᶠ woman in her
    home
  as a happy mother of children.

Praise the LORD.

Psalm 114

¹When Israel came out of Egypt,ᵍ
  the house of Jacob from a people of
    foreign tongue,
²Judahʰ became God's sanctuary,ⁱ
  Israel his dominion.

³The sea looked and fled,ʲ
  the Jordan turned back;ᵏ
⁴the mountains skippedˡ like rams,
  the hills like lambs.

⁵Why was it, O sea, that you fled,ᵐ
  O Jordan, that you turned back,
⁶you mountains, that you skipped like
    rams,
  you hills, like lambs?

⁷Tremble, O earth,ⁿ at the presence of
    the Lord,
  at the presence of the God of Jacob,
⁸who turned the rock into a pool,

113:2 ᵗS Ps 30:4; 48:10; 145:21; 148:13; 149:3; Isa 12:4
ᵘPs 115:18; 131:3; Da 2:20
113:3 ᵛIsa 24:15; 45:6; 59:19; Mal 1:11
113:4 ʷS Ps 99:2 ˣS Ps 8:1; S 57:11
113:5 ʸS Ex 8:10; S Ps 35:10 ᶻS Ps 103:19 ᵃS Job 16:19
113:6 ᵇPs 11:4; 138:6; Isa 57:15
113:7 ᶜ1Sa 2:8; Ps 35:10; 68:10; 140:12 ᵈPs 107:41
113:8 ᵉS 2Sa 9:11
113:9 ᶠS 1Sa 2:5

114:1 ᵍS Ex 13:3; S 29:46
114:2 ʰPs 76:1 ⁱS Ex 15:17; Ps 78:68-69
114:3 ʲEx 14:21; Ps 77:16 ᵏS Ex 15:8; S Jos 3:16
114:4 ˡS Jdg 5:5
114:5
ᵐS Ex 14:21

114:7 ⁿS Ex 15:14; S 1Ch 16:30

Three precisely balanced stanzas (each having three verses) give the psalm a pleasing symmetry. With seven (the number of completeness) verbs the author celebrates God's praise in stanzas two and three ("is exalted," "sits . . . on high," "stoops down," "raises," "lifts," "seats," "settles")—and note the fourfold praise in the first stanza. At the center (v. 5; see note on 6:6) a rhetorical question focuses and heightens the hymnic theme.
113:1b–3 The fourfold call to praise.
113:1 name of the LORD. See vv. 2–3. Triple repetition was a common liturgical convention (see note on 96:1–3). name. See note on 5:11.
113:2 now and forevermore. The praise of those who truly praise the Lord cannot rest content until it fills all time—and space (v. 3).
113:4–6 The Lord is enthroned on high, exalted over all creation.
113:4 See the refrain in 57:5,11. over all the nations. And implicitly over all their gods (see 95:3; 96:4–5; 97:9; see also 47:2,7–8). above the heavens. Above even the most exalted aspect of the creation (see v. 6).
113:5 The rhetorical center (see note on 6:6). our God. What grace, that he has covenanted to be "our" God (see Ge 17:7; Ex 19:5–6; 20:2)!
113:7–9 The Lord exalts the lowly—the God of highest majesty does not ally himself with the high and mighty of the earth but stands with and raises up the poor and needy (see 1Sa 2:3–8; Lk 1:46–55).
113:7–8 Repeated almost verbatim from 1Sa 2:8.
113:7 poor . . . needy. See 9:18; 34:6 and notes. dust . . . ash heap. Symbolic of a humble status (see Ge 18:27; 1Ki 16:2), but here probably also of extreme distress and need (see Job 30:19; 42:6; Isa 47:1; Jer 25:34).
113:9 barren woman. In that ancient society barrenness was for a woman the greatest disgrace and the deepest tragedy (see Ge 30:1; 1Sa 1:6–7,10); in her old age she would be as desolate as Naomi because she would have no one to sustain her (see Ru 1:11–13; see also 2Ki 4:14). home. Family circle. happy mother. Because of God's gracious provision, as in the case of Sarah (see Ge 21:2), Rebekah (see Ge 25:21), Rachel (see Ge 30:23), Hannah (see

1Sa 1:20), the Shunammite (see 2Ki 4:17) and others. Praise the LORD. Probably once stood at the beginning of Ps 114, which now lacks a Hallelujah.
Ps 114 A hymnic celebration of the exodus—one of the most exquisitely fashioned songs of the Psalter. It probably dates from the period of the monarchy sometime after the division of the kingdom (see v. 2). No doubt it was composed for liturgical use at the temple during one of the annual religious festivals (see introduction to Ps 113). The theme is progressively developed through four balanced stanzas, reaching its climax in the fourth. The first two stanzas (vv. 1–4) recall the great events of the exodus; the last two (vv. 5–8) celebrate their continuing significance.
114:1–2 The great OT redemptive event.
114:1 Israel . . . house of Jacob. Synonyms (see Ex 19:3). came out of Egypt. Recalls the exodus and all the great events of the desert journey.
114:2 Judah . . . Israel. The southern and northern kingdoms, viewed here as the one people of God. became. The crucial event was the establishment of the covenant at Sinai, where Israel became bound to the Lord as a "kingdom of priests and a holy nation" (Ex 19:3–6). God's. Lit. "his." The "antecedent" is not expressed until the climax (v. 7). sanctuary. His temple in which he took up his residence in the world—symbolized by the tabernacle, later the temple. In Ex 15:17 the promised land is similarly called God's sanctuary. dominion. The special realm over which he ruled as King. This, rather than the exodus itself, was the great wonder of God's grace.
114:3–4 The author evokes a fearsome scene such as that portrayed by other poets (see 18:7–15; 68:7–8; 77:16–19; Jdg 5:4–5; Hab 3:3–10).
114:3 sea . . . Jordan. The Red Sea and the Jordan River, through which the Lord brought his people—here they are personified. looked and fled. Saw the mighty God approach in his awesome pillar of cloud and fled.
114:4 skipped. Or "leaped"; the mountains and hills quaked at God's approach (see 29:6).
114:7–8 The Lord of yesterday (vv. 5–6)—the God of Jacob—is still with us.
114:7 Tremble. In awesome recognition. earth. All crea-

the hard rock into springs of water. o

Psalm 115

115:4–11pp — Ps 135:15–20

[1] Not to us, O LORD, not to us
  but to your name be the glory, p
  because of your love and
    faithfulness. q

[2] Why do the nations say,
  "Where is their God?" r
[3] Our God is in heaven; s
  he does whatever pleases him. t
[4] But their idols are silver and gold, u
  made by the hands of men. v
[5] They have mouths, but cannot speak, w
  eyes, but they cannot see;
[6] they have ears, but cannot hear,
  noses, but they cannot smell;
[7] they have hands, but cannot feel,
  feet, but they cannot walk;
  nor can they utter a sound with their
    throats.
[8] Those who make them will be like
    them,
  and so will all who trust in them.

[9] O house of Israel, trust x in the LORD—
  he is their help and shield.
[10] O house of Aaron, y trust in the LORD—
  he is their help and shield.

[11] You who fear him, z trust in the
    LORD—
  he is their help and shield.

[12] The LORD remembers a us and will bless
    us: b
  He will bless the house of Israel,
  he will bless the house of Aaron,
[13] he will bless those who fear c the
    LORD—
  small and great alike.

[14] May the LORD make you increase, d
  both you and your children.
[15] May you be blessed by the LORD,
  the Maker of heaven e and earth.

[16] The highest heavens belong to the
    LORD, f
  but the earth he has given g to man.
[17] It is not the dead h who praise the
    LORD,
  those who go down to silence;
[18] it is we who extol the LORD, i
  both now and forevermore. j

  Praise the LORD. r k

Psalm 116

[1] I love the LORD, l for he heard my
  voice;

r *18* Hebrew *Hallelu Yah*

Cross references

114:8
oS Ex 17:6;
S Nu 20:11
115:1 PPs 29:2;
66:2; 96:8
qS Ex 34:6
115:2 rS Ps 42:3
115:3 sEzr 5:11;
Ne 1:4;
Ps 103:19;
136:26; Mt 6:9
tPs 135:6
115:4 uRev 9:20
vS 2Ki 19:18;
S 2Ch 32:19;
Jer 10:3-5;
Ac 19:26
115:5 wJer 10:5
115:9 xPs 37:3;
62:8
115:10
yEx 30:30;
Ps 118:3
115:11
zPs 22:23;
103:11; 118:4
115:12
aS 1Ch 16:15
bS Ge 12:2
115:13
cS Ps 112:1
115:14 dDt 1:11
115:15
eS Ge 1:1;
Ac 14:15;
S Rev 10:6
115:16
fS Ps 89:11
gS Ge 1:28;
Ps 8:6-8
115:17
hPs 88:10-12
115:18
iS Ps 111:1
jS Ps 113:2
kPs 28:6; 33:2;
103:1
116:1 lPs 18:1

---

tion. *Jacob.* A synonym for Israel (see Ge 32:28).
114:8 *turned the rock into a pool.* Thus sustaining and refreshing life (see Ex 17:6; Nu 20:11).
Ps 115 Praise of the Lord, the one true God, for his love and faithfulness toward his people. It was composed as a liturgy of praise for the temple worship. It may have been written for use at the dedication of the second temple (see Ezr 6:16) when Israel was beginning to revive after the disruption of the exile. See introduction to Ps 113. Structurally, the song advances in five movements involving a liturgical exchange between the people and temple personnel: (1) vv. 1–8: the people; (2) vv. 9–11: Levitical choir leader (the refrain perhaps spoken by the Levitical choir); (3) vv. 12–13: the people; (4) vv. 14–15: the priests; (5) vv. 16–18: the people.
115:1–8 Praise of God's love and faithfulness toward his people, which silences the taunts of the nations.
115:1 *Not to us . . . not to us.* Israel's existence, and now her revival, is not her own achievement. *name.* See note on 5:11. *love and faithfulness.* The most common OT expression for God's covenant benefits (see note on 26:3). *love.* See note on 6:4.
115:2 *Where is their God?* The taunt of the nations when Israel is decimated by natural disasters (see Joel 2:17) or crushed by enemies, especially when Judah is destroyed and the temple of God razed (see 79:10; Mic 7:10).
115:3 *is in heaven.* Sits enthroned (see 113:5) in the "highest heavens" (v. 16). *whatever pleases him.* If Israel is decimated or destroyed, it is God's doing; it is not his failure or inability to act, nor is it the achievement of the idols the nations worship. And when Israel is revived, that is also God's doing, and no other god can oppose him.

115:4–7 Whatever glory and power the false gods are thought to have (as symbolized in the images made to represent them), they are mere figments of human imagination and utterly worthless (see 135:15–18; Isa 46:1–7).
115:8 *Those who make them.* The taunting nations (cf. v. 2). *like them.* Powerless and ineffectual. For a graphic elaboration of this truth see Isa 44:9–20.
115:9–11 The call to trust in the Lord, not in idols (see v. 8). For triple repetition as a liturgical convention see note on 96:1–3. For the same groupings see 118:2–4; see also 135:19–20.
115:11 *You who fear him.* Perhaps proselytes (see 1Ki 8:41–43; Ezr 6:21; Ne 10:28).
115:12–13 The people's confession of trust.
115:14–15 The priestly blessing.
115:14 *make you increase.* In numbers, wealth and strength (cf. Ecc 2:9: "became greater by far than"—lit. "increased more than").
115:16–18 The people's concluding doxology.
115:16 *highest heavens . . . earth.* The one the exclusive realm of the exalted, all-sovereign God; the other the divinely appointed place for man, where he lives under God's rule and care, enjoys his abundant blessings (vv. 12–13) and celebrates his praise (v. 18).
115:17 *not the dead.* The dead no longer live in "the earth" (v. 16) but have descended to the silent realm below, where blessings are no longer enjoyed and hence praise is absent (see notes on 6:5; 30:1).
Ps 116 Praise of the Lord for deliverance from death. It may have been written by a king (see v. 16 and note; cf. also Hezekiah's thanksgiving, Isa 38:10–20); its language echoes many of the psalms of David. As used in Jewish liturgy (see

he heard my cry[m] for mercy.[n]

[2]Because he turned his ear[o] to me,
I will call on him as long as I live.

[3]The cords of death[p] entangled me,
the anguish of the grave[s] came upon
me;
I was overcome by trouble and
sorrow.

[4]Then I called on the name[q] of the
LORD:
"O LORD, save me!["]"

[5]The LORD is gracious and righteous;[s]
our God is full of compassion.[t]

[6]The LORD protects the simplehearted;
when I was in great need,[u] he saved
me.[v]

[7]Be at rest[w] once more, O my soul,
for the LORD has been good[x] to you.

[8]For you, O LORD, have delivered my
soul[y] from death,
my eyes from tears,
my feet from stumbling,

[9]that I may walk before the LORD[z]
in the land of the living.[a]

[10]I believed;[b] therefore[t] I said,
"I am greatly afflicted."[c]

[11]And in my dismay I said,

"All men are liars."[d]

[12]How can I repay the LORD
for all his goodness[e] to me?

[13]I will lift up the cup of salvation
and call on the name[f] of the LORD.

[14]I will fulfill my vows[g] to the LORD
in the presence of all his people.

[15]Precious in the sight[h] of the LORD
is the death of his saints.[i]

[16]O LORD, truly I am your servant;[j]
I am your servant, the son of your
maidservant[u];[k]
you have freed me from my chains.[l]

[17]I will sacrifice a thank offering[m] to you
and call on the name of the LORD.

[18]I will fulfill my vows[n] to the LORD
in the presence of all his people,

[19]in the courts[o] of the house of the
LORD—
in your midst, O Jerusalem.[p]

116:1
[m]S Ps 31:22;
S 40:1 [n]S Ps 6:9;
S 28:2
116:2 [o]S Ps 5:1
116:3
[p]S 2Sa 22:6;
Ps 18:4-5
116:4 [q]Ps 80:18;
118:5 [r]S Ps 80:2
116:5
[s]S Ex 9:27;
S 2Ch 12:6;
S Ezr 9:15
[t]S Ex 22:27;
S Ps 86:15
116:6 [u]S Ps 79:8
[v]Ps 18:3; 22:5;
107:13
116:7 [w]Ps 46:10;
62:1; 131:2;
Mt 11:29
[x]Ps 13:6; 106:1;
142:7
116:8
[y]S Ps 86:13
116:9
[z]S Ge 5:22;
Ps 56:13; 89:15
[a]S Job 28:13;
Ps 27:13;
Isa 38:11;
Jer 11:19
116:10
[b]2Co 4:13*
[c]Ps 9:18; 72:2;
S 107:17; 119:67,
71,75

116:11
[d]Jer 9:3-5;
Hos 7:13;
Mic 6:12; Ro 3:4
116:12
[e]Ps 103:2; 106:1

116:13 [f]S Ps 105:1 **116:14** [g]S Nu 30:2; S Ps 66:13 **116:15**
[h]Ps 72:14 [i]S Nu 23:10 **116:16** [j]Ps 119:125; 143:12
[k]S Ps 86:16 [l]S Job 12:18 **116:17** [m]S Lev 7:12; S Ezr 1:4
116:18 [n]ver 14; S Lev 22:18 **116:19** [o]Ps 92:13; 96:8;
100:4; 135:2 [p]Ps 102:21

---

[s]3 Hebrew *Sheol* [t]10 Or *believed even when*
[u]16 Or *servant, your faithful son*

---

introduction to Ps 113), the singular personal pronoun must
have been used corporately (see note on Ps 30 title), and the
references to "death" may have been understood as alluding
to the Egyptian bondage and/or the exile. This thanksgiving
song of seven stanzas (reading v. 7 with the following verses;
see note on v. 7) falls into three main divisions (vv. 1-6,
7-14, 15-19), each of which contains a unified thematic
development.
116:1-6 I love the Lord because he has heard and saved
me.
116:2 *I will call on him.* In him I will trust and my prayers
will ever be to him—a declaration repeated in each of the
main divisions (see vv. 13,17).
116:3-4 See 18:4-6.
116:3 *cords of death.* See note on 18:5.
116:5 *our God.* The author is conscious of those about
him; he is praising the Lord "in the presence of all his
people" (vv. 14,18).
116:6 *simplehearted.* The person who is childlike in his
sense of dependence on and trust in the Lord (see note on
19:7).
116:7-14 The Lord's goodness to me and how I will repay
him.
116:7 *rest.* A state of unthreatened well-being (cf. Jer
6:16; see 1Ki 5:4, "peace"; see also note on 23:2, "quiet
waters"). *O my soul.* See note on 103:1-2,22. *has been
good.* The Hebrew underlying this phrase is the same as that
underlying "goodness" in v. 12 (see note there) and so marks
v. 7 as introductory to vv. 7-14.
116:8 *my soul.* Me (see note on 6:3).
116:10 *I believed.* The author speaks of his faith that
moved him to call on the Lord when he was threatened. *I am
greatly afflicted.* This and the quotation in v. 11 should
perhaps be taken, together with the one in v. 4, as a brief
recollection of the prayer offered when the psalmist was in
distress. The threat of death from which he had been de-

livered was brought on by the false accusations of enemies,
as in Ps 109 (see notes on 5:9; 10:7). (For another interpretation see following note.)
116:11 *All men are liars.* The heart of the accusation he
had lodged against his false accusers (for examples of similar
accusations see 5:9-10; 35:11,15; 109:2-4). Others interpret these words as a declaration that all men offer but a false
hope for deliverance (see 60:11; 118:8-9)—therefore the
psalmist called on the Lord.
116:12 *How can I repay . . . ?* By offering to the Lord those
expressions of devotion he desires (compare vv. 13-14,
17-18 with 50:14-15,23). *goodness.* The Hebrew for this
word occurs only here in the OT, but represents the same
basic root as "has been good" in v. 7 (see note there).
116:13 *cup of salvation.* Often thought to be related to the
cup of the Passover meal referred to in Mt 26:27 and parallels, but far more likely the cup of wine drunk at the festal
meal that climaxed a thank offering (see 22:26,29; Lev
7:11-21)—called the "cup of salvation" because the thank
offering and its meal celebrated deliverance by the Lord. See
the parallel with "sacrifice a thank offering" in the corresponding series in vv. 17-18.
116:14 *vows.* To praise the Lord (see note on 7:17).
116:15-19 Because God has counted my life precious, I
offer him the expressions of my devotion.
116:15 *Precious . . . is the death.* Not in the sense of highly
valued but of that which is carefully watched over; cf. the
analogous expression, "precious is their blood in his sight"
(72:14). *saints.* See note on 4:3.
116:16 *your servant.* This may identify the psalmist as the
Lord's anointed (see 78:70), but in any event as one devoted
to the Lord (see 19:11,13). *son of your maidservant.* See
NIV text note; see also 86:16 and NIV text note.
116:19 *courts.* Of the temple (see 84:2,10; 2Ki 21:5;
23:11-12).

Praise the LORD.[v]

Psalm 117

1Praise the LORD,[q] all you nations;[r]
extol him, all you peoples.
2For great is his love[s] toward us,
and the faithfulness of the LORD[t]
endures forever.

Praise the LORD.[v]

Psalm 118

1Give thanks to the LORD,[u] for he is
good;[v]
his love endures forever.[w]
2Let Israel say:[x]
"His love endures forever."[y]
3Let the house of Aaron say:[z]
"His love endures forever."
4Let those who fear the LORD[a] say:
"His love endures forever."

5In my anguish[b] I cried to the LORD,
and he answered[c] by setting me free.
6The LORD is with me;[d] I will not be
afraid.
What can man do to me?[e]
7The LORD is with me; he is my helper.[f]
I will look in triumph on my
enemies.[g]

8It is better to take refuge in the LORD[h]
than to trust in man.[i]
9It is better to take refuge in the LORD
than to trust in princes.[j]

10All the nations surrounded me,
but in the name of the LORD I cut
them off.[k]
11They surrounded me[l] on every side,[m]
but in the name of the LORD I cut
them off.
12They swarmed around me like bees,[n]
but they died out as quickly as
burning thorns;[o]
in the name of the LORD I cut them
off.[p]

13I was pushed back and about to fall,
but the LORD helped me.[q]
14The LORD is my strength[r] and my song;
he has become my salvation.[s]

117:1 [q]S Ps 22:23; S 103:2 [r]Ro 15:11* **117:2** [s]S Ps 17:7; S 103:11 [t]Ps 119:90; 146:6 **118:1** [u]S 1Ch 16:8 [v]S 2Ch 5:13; S 7:3 [w]S Ezr 3:11 **118:2** [x]Ps 115:9 [y]Ps 106:1; 136:1-26 **118:3** [z]Ex 30:30; Ps 115:10 **118:4** [a]S Ps 115:11 **118:5** [b]Ps 18:6; 31:7; 77:2; 120:1 [c]ver 21; Ps 34:4; 86:7; 116:1; 138:3 **118:6** [d]S Dt 31:6; Heb 13:5 [e]S Ps 56:4 **118:7** [f]S Dt 33:29; Heb 13:6* [g]S Ps 54:7 **118:8** [h]Ps 2:12; 5:11; 9:9; 37:3; 40:4; Isa 25:4; 57:13 [i]2Ch 32:7-8; S Ps 108:12; S Isa 2:22 **118:9** [j]Ps 146:3 **118:10** [k]S Ps 37:9 **118:11** [l]Ps 88:17 [m]Ps 3:6 **118:12** [n]Dt 1:44 [o]S Ps 58:9 [p]Ps 37:9 **118:13** [q]ver 7; 2Ch 18:31; Ps 86:17 **118:14** [r]S Ex 15:2 [s]S Ps 62:2

[v] *19,2* Hebrew *Hallelu Yah*

Ps 117 The shortest psalm in the Psalter—and the shortest chapter in the Bible—Ps 117 is an expanded Hallelujah (sometimes joined with Ps 118). It may originally have served as the conclusion to the preceding collection of Hallelujah psalms (Ps 111–116)—of which it is the seventh. All nations and peoples are called on to praise the Lord (as in 47:1; 67:3–5; 96:7; 98:4; 100:1; see note on 9:1) for his great love and enduring faithfulness toward Israel (see Isa 12:4–6). Thus the Hallelujahs of the OT Psalter, when fully expounded, express that great truth, so often emphasized in the OT, that the destiny of all peoples is involved in what God was doing in and for his people Israel (see, e.g., 2:8–12; 47:9; 67:2; 72:17; 102:15; 110; Ge 12:3; Dt 32:43; 1Ki 8:41–43; Isa 2:2–4; 11:10; 14:2; 25:6–7; 52:15; 56:7; 60:3; 66:18–24; Jer 3:17; 16:19–21; 33:9; Am 9:11–12; Mic 5:7–9; Zep 3:8–9; Hag 2:7; Zec 2:10–11; 8:20–23; 9:9–10; 14:2–3; Mal 3:12). See introduction to Ps 113.
117:1 Quoted in Ro 15:11 as proof that the salvation of Gentiles and the glorifying of God by Gentiles was not a divine afterthought.
117:2 The reason for the praise. *love . . . faithfulness.* That is, love-and-faithfulness (see 36:5 and note; see also note on 3:7). *love.* See note on 6:4.
Ps 118 A hymn of thanksgiving for deliverance from enemies. Of the many interpretations of this psalm, three have gained the most adherents (but with much variation in detail): 1. A Davidic king leads the nation in a liturgy of thanksgiving for deliverance and victory after a hard-fought battle with a powerful confederacy of nations (cf. 2Ch 20:27–28; see note on v. 19). 2. Israel celebrates—probably at the Feast of Tabernacles—her deliverance from Egypt and victory over the Canaanites. 3. The postexilic Jews celebrate deliverance from their enemies, either at the dedication of the second temple (see Ezr 6:16) or at the dedication of the rebuilt walls of Jerusalem (see Ne 12:37–43). According to the first interpretation, the speaker in vv. 5–21 is the king; according to the second and third, the speaker is the Levitical (or priestly) leader of the liturgy, speaking (representatively) on behalf of the people. The notes that follow assume the first interpretation. In the postexilic liturgy developed for the annual festivals (see introduction to Ps 113), the song was used as a thanksgiving for national deliverance. As the last song of that liturgy, it may have been the hymn sung by Jesus and his disciples at the conclusion of the Last Supper (see Mt 26:30).
Following a liturgical call to praise (vv. 1–4), the king offers a song of thanksgiving for deliverance and victory in battle (vv. 5–21). In vv. 22–27 the people rejoice over what the Lord has done. Thereafter, the king speaks his final word of praise (v. 28), and a liturgical conclusion (v. 29) repeats the opening call to praise, thus framing the whole service.
118:1–4 The liturgical call to praise.
118:1 A conventional call to praise (shared in whole or in part with Ps 105–107; 136; 1Ch 16:8,34; 2Ch 20:21). *Give thanks.* See note on Ps 100 title. This, together with vv. 2–4 (except for the refrain) and 29, may have been by the same voice that speaks in vv. 5–21. *love.* See vv. 2–4,29; see also note on 6:4.
118:2–4 *Israel . . . house of Aaron . . . those who fear the LORD.* See 115:9–11 and note. Triple repetition is a common feature in this psalm (see note on 96:1–3).
118:5–21 The king's song of thanksgiving for deliverance and victory.
118:5 *free.* Lit. "in a broad place"; see 18:19 and note ("spacious place").
118:7 *I will look.* Or "I look."
118:8–9 See 33:16–19; see also Ps 62; 146.
118:10 *in the name of the LORD.* See 1Sa 17:45. *name.* See vv. 11–12,26; see also note on 5:11.
118:12 *as burning thorns.* See 58:9 and note.
118:13 *fall.* Be killed (see vv. 17–18; see also note on 13:4).
118:14 Perhaps recalls the triumph song of Ex 15, but more likely the verse had become a widely used testimony of

¹⁵Shouts of joy^{*t*} and victory
   resound in the tents of the righteous:
   "The LORD's right hand^{*u*} has done
     mighty things!^{*v*}
¹⁶ The LORD's right hand is lifted high;
   the LORD's right hand has done
     mighty things!"

¹⁷I will not die^{*w*} but live,
   and will proclaim^{*x*} what the LORD
   has done.
¹⁸The LORD has chastened^{*y*} me severely,
   but he has not given me over to
   death.^{*z*}

¹⁹Open for me the gates^{*a*} of
   righteousness;
   I will enter^{*b*} and give thanks to the
   LORD.
²⁰This is the gate of the LORD^{*c*}
   through which the righteous may
   enter.^{*d*}
²¹I will give you thanks, for you answered
   me;^{*e*}
   you have become my salvation.^{*f*}

²²The stone^{*g*} the builders rejected
   has become the capstone;^{*h*}
²³the LORD has done this,
   and it is marvelous^{*i*} in our eyes.

²⁴This is the day the LORD has made;
   let us rejoice and be glad^{*j*} in it.

²⁵O LORD, save us;^{*k*}
   O LORD, grant us success.
²⁶Blessed is he who comes^{*l*} in the name
   of the LORD.
   From the house of the LORD we bless
   you.^{*w*}^{*m*}
²⁷The LORD is God,^{*n*}
   and he has made his light shine^{*o*}
   upon us.
   With boughs in hand,^{*p*} join in the festal
   procession
   up^{*x*} to the horns of the altar.^{*q*}

²⁸You are my God, and I will give you
   thanks;
   you are my God,^{*r*} and I will exalt^{*s*}
   you.

²⁹Give thanks to the LORD, for he is
   good;
   his love endures forever.

118:15 ^{*t*}S Job 8:21;
S Ps 106:5
^{*u*}S Ex 15:6;
Ps 89:13; 108:6
^{*v*}Lk 1:51
118:17
^{*w*}Hab 1:12
^{*x*}S Dt 32:3;
Ps 64:9; 71:16;
73:28
118:18
^{*y*}Jer 31:18;
1Co 11:32;
Heb 12:5
^{*z*}Ps 86:13
118:19
^{*a*}S Ps 24:7
^{*b*}Ps 100:4
118:20
^{*c*}Ps 122:1-2
^{*d*}Ps 15:1-2;
24:3-4; Rev 22:14
118:21 ^{*e*}S ver 5
^{*f*}Ps 27:1
118:22 ^{*g*}Isa 8:14
^{*h*}Isa 17:10;
19:13; 28:16;
Zec 4:7; 10:4;
Mt 21:42;
Mk 12:10;
Lk 20:17*;
S Ac 4:11*;
1Pe 2:7
118:23
^{*i*}Mt 21:42*;
Mk 12:11*
118:24 ^{*j*}S Ps 70:4

118:25
^{*k*}S Ps 28:9; 116:4
118:26
^{*l*}S Mt 11:3;
21:9*; 23:39;
Mk 11:9*;
Lk 13:35*;
19:38; Jn 12:13*
^{*m*}Ps 129:8

118:27 ^{*n*}S 1Ki 18:21 ^{*o*}Ps 27:1; Isa 58:10; 60:1,19,20;
Mal 4:2; 1Pe 2:9 ^{*p*}S Lev 23:40 ^{*q*}Ex 27:2 **118:28**
^{*r*}S Ge 28:21; S Ps 16:2; 63:1; Isa 25:1 ^{*s*}S Ex 15:2

^{*w*}26 The Hebrew is plural.   ^{*x*}27 Or *Bind the festal
sacrifice with ropes / and take it*

---

praise (see Isa 12:2).
118:15 *tents.* Dwellings. *righteous.* Israel as the people
(ideally) committed in heart and life to the Lord (see v. 20;
see also 68:3 and note). Cf. "the tents of the wicked"
(84:10).
118:17 *live, and . . . proclaim.* See 115:17–18; see also
note on 6:5.
118:18 *chastened me.* The king acknowledges that the
grave threat through which he has passed has also served
God's purpose—to discipline him and teach him humble
godliness (see 6:1; 38:1; 94:12; Dt 4:36; 8:5).
118:19 *Open for me.* This line suggests a liturgical procession (see v. 27) in which the king approaches the inner court
of the temple at the head of the jubilant worshipers (see Ps
24; 68). *gates.* Those leading to the inner temple court. *of
righteousness.* Often thought to be the name of a particular
gateway, but more likely only descriptive here of the gate
"through which the righteous may enter" (v. 20). It is
possible that the procession began outside the city and that
"the gates of righteousness" are the gates of Jerusalem, the
city of God (see note on 24:7; see also Isa 26:2).
118:21 This closing verse of the thanksgiving song echoes
the "Give thanks" of v. 1, the "answered . . . me" of v. 5 and
the testimony of v. 14.
118:22–27 The people's exultation.
118:22 *The stone the builders rejected.* Most likely a
reference to the king (whose deliverance and victory are
being celebrated), who had been looked on with disdain by
the kings invading his realm—the builders of worldly empires. Others suppose that the stone refers to Israel, a nation
held in contempt by the world powers. *capstone.* Lit. "head
of the corner"—either a capstone over a door (a large stone
used as a lintel), or a large stone used to anchor and align the
corner of a wall, or the keystone of an arch (see Zec 4:7;

10:4). By a wordplay (pun) the author hints at "chief ruler"
(the Hebrew word for "corner" is sometimes used as a
metaphor for leader/ruler; see Isa 19:13; see also Jdg 20:2;
1Sa 14:38). This stone, disdained by the worldly powers, has
become the most important stone in the structure of the new
world order that God is bringing about through Israel. Jesus
applied this verse (and v. 23) to himself (see Mt 21:42; Mk
12:10–11; Lk 20:17; see also Ac 4:11; Eph 2:20; 1Pe 2:
7).
118:24 *day the LORD has made . . . rejoice.* This day of
rejoicing was made possible by God's deliverance in the
victory being celebrated. Others suppose a reference to Passover or the Feast of Tabernacles. *has made.* Or "has done it"
(see vv. 15–17,23)—has made the "stone" the "capstone"
(v. 22).
118:25 Prayer for the Lord to continue to save and sustain
his people.
118:26 *who comes in the name of the LORD.* The one who
with God's help had defeated the enemies "in the name of
the LORD" (see vv. 10–12). *From the house of the LORD.*
From God's very presence (see 134:3). *you.* The plural (see
NIV text note) may have been used to exalt the king (the
plural was often used with reference to God), whom God
had so singularly blessed (see NIV text note on 1Ki 9:6).
Alternatively, it may refer to those who have come with the
king victoriously from the battle. The crowds who greeted
Jesus at his Triumphal Entry into Jerusalem used the words of
vv. 25–26 (see Jn 12:13).
118:27 *made his light shine upon us.* An echo of the
priestly benediction (see Nu 6:25). *With boughs . . . up.*
Apparently a call to complete the climax of the liturgy of a
thank offering (see Lev 7:11–21), though others suggest the
liturgy of the Feast of Tabernacles.
118:28–29 See introduction.

Psalm 119 ʸ

א Aleph

¹Blessed are they whose ways are
  blameless, ᵗ
  who walk ᵘ according to the law of
  the LORD. ᵛ
²Blessed ʷ are they who keep his
  statutes ˣ
  and seek him ʸ with all their heart. ᶻ
³They do nothing wrong; ᵃ
  they walk in his ways. ᵇ
⁴You have laid down precepts ᶜ
  that are to be fully obeyed. ᵈ
⁵Oh, that my ways were steadfast
  in obeying your decrees! ᵉ
⁶Then I would not be put to shame ᶠ
  when I consider all your commands. ᵍ
⁷I will praise you with an upright heart
  as I learn your righteous laws. ʰ
⁸I will obey your decrees;

ב Beth

⁹How can a young man keep his way
  pure? ⁱ
  By living according to your word. ᵏ
¹⁰I seek you with all my heart; ˡ
  do not let me stray from your
  commands. ᵐ
¹¹I have hidden your word in my heart ⁿ
  that I might not sin ᵒ against you.
¹²Praise be ᵖ to you, O LORD;
  teach me ᑫ your decrees. ʳ
¹³With my lips I recount
  all the laws that come from your
  mouth. ˢ

119:1
ʳS Ge 17:1;
S Dt 18:13;
Pr 11:20
ᵘPs 128:1
ᵛS Ps 1:2
119:2 ʷPs 112:1;
Isa 56:2 ˣver 146;
Ps 99:7
ʸS 1Ch 16:11;
S Ps 40:16
ᶻS Dt 10:12
119:3 ᵃS Ps 59:4;
1Jn 3:9; 5:18
ᵇPs 128:1;
Jer 6:16; 7:23
119:4 ᶜPs 103:18
ᵈS ver 56;
S Dt 6:17
119:5
ᵉS Lev 19:37
119:6 ᶠver 46,80
ᵍver 117
119:7 ʰS Dt 4:8

119:8 ⁱS Ps 38:21
119:9 ʲS Ps 39:1
ᵏver 65,169
119:10 ˡS Ps 9:1
ᵐver 21,118
119:11
ⁿS Dt 6:6;
S Job 22:22 ᵒver

do not utterly forsake me. ⁱ

133,165; Ps 18:22-23; 19:13; Pr 3:23; Isa 63:13 **119:12**
ᵖPs 28:6 ᑫPs 143:8,10 ʳS Ex 18:20 **119:13** ˢver 72

ʸThis psalm is an acrostic poem; the verses of each stanza
begin with the same letter of the Hebrew alphabet.

Ps 119 A devotional on the word of God. The author was an Israelite of exemplary piety (probably postexilic) who (1) was passionately devoted to the word of God as the word of life; (2) humbly acknowledged, nevertheless, the errant ways of his heart and life; (3) knew the pain—but also the fruits—of God's corrective discipline; and (4) had suffered much at the hands of those who arrogantly disregarded God's word and made him the target of their hostility, ridicule and slander. It is possible that he was a priest (see notes on vv. 23,57)—and the psalm might well be a vehicle for priestly instruction in godliness. He elaborated on the themes of 19:7–13 and interwove with them many prayers for deliverance, composing a massive alphabetic acrostic (see NIV text note) that demands patient, meditative reading. In regard to length, form and type it stands alone in the Psalter. And of all the psalms, this one is the most likely to have been composed originally in writing and intended to be read rather than sung or recited. Most of its lines are addressed to God, mingling prayers with professions of devotion to God's law. Yet, as the opening verses (and perhaps also its elaborate acrostic form) make clear, it was intended for godly instruction (in the manner of Ps 1; see v. 9 and note). It was included in the Psalter no doubt as a model of piety.

Whereas elsewhere in the Psalter the focus falls primarily on God's mighty acts of creation and redemption and his rule over all the world, here devotion to the word of God (and the God of the word) is the dominant theme. The author highlights two aspects of that word: (1) God's directives for life and (2) God's promises—the one calling for obedience, the other for faith (the two elements of true godliness; see 34:8–14 and note). In referring to these, he makes use of eight Hebrew terms supplied him by OT traditions: *torah*, "law"; *'edot*, "statutes"; *piqqudim*, "precepts"; *miṣwot*, "commands, commandments"; *mishpaṭim*, "laws" (all shared with 19:7–9; *mishpaṭim* is translated "ordinances" in 19:9); *ḥuqqim*, "decrees"; *dabar*, "word" (sometimes in the sense of "law," sometimes in the sense of "promise"); *'imrah*, "word," but more often "promise." These terms he distributes throughout the 22 stanzas (using all eight in *He, Waw, Heth, Yodh, Kaph, Pe*—never using less than six), employing a different order in each stanza. It may be that the availability of these eight terms determined (in large part) for the author the decision to devote eight verses to each letter of the alphabet. The alphabetic acrostic form, especially one as elaborate as this, may appear arbitrary and artificial to a

modern reader (as if the author merely selected a traditional form from the poet's workshop and then labored to fill it with pious sentences), but a sympathetic and reflective reading of this devotional will compel a more favorable judgment. The author had a theme that filled his soul, a theme as big as life, that ranged the length and breadth and height and depth of a person's walk with God. Nothing less than the use of the full power of language would suffice, and of that the alphabet was a most apt symbol.

Apart from the obvious formal structure dictated by the chosen acrostic form, little need (or can) be said. It must be noted, however, that the first three and the last three verses were designed as introduction and conclusion to the whole. The former sets the tone of instruction in godly wisdom; the latter succinctly restates and summarizes the main themes. It may also be observed that the middle of the psalm has been marked by a similar three-verse introduction to the second half (see note on vv. 89–91). For the rest, the thought meanders, turns back upon itself and repeats (with varied nuances). The following notes point out continuities of thought and possible structure within stanzas.

119:1–3 General introduction.
119:1–2 *Blessed.* See note on 1:1.
119:1 *whose ways are blameless.* This opening general description is further elaborated in the rest of the introduction, which concludes with an equally general statement: "they walk in his ways" (v. 3). See Ge 17:1; cf. Ge 26:5. *law.* Hebrew *torah*, a collective term for God's covenant directives for his people (see Dt 4:44). "Law" often came, especially later, to have a broader reference—the whole Pentateuch (see Lk 24:44) or even the whole OT (see Jn 15:25; 1Co 14:21)—but here it is limited by the synonyms with which it is used interchangeably.
119:2 *statutes.* Hebrew *'edot*, a specifically covenantal term referring to stipulations laid down by the covenant Lord (see 25:10, "demands"; Dt 4:45, "stipulations"). *heart.* See v. 7; see also note on 4:7.
119:3 *ways.* The Hebrew for this word occurs only rarely in this psalm, but is common in Deuteronomy and elsewhere as a general reference to God's covenant requirements (see note on 25:4)—used here to balance "ways" in v. 1.
119:4–8 Those who obey God's law (see vv. 4–5,8) can hope for God's help (see vv. 6–8).
119:4 *precepts.* Hebrew *piqqudim*, covenant regulations laid down by the Lord (see 19:8; 111:7).

¹⁴I rejoice in following your statutes ᵗ
  as one rejoices in great riches.
¹⁵I meditate on your precepts ᵘ
  and consider your ways.
¹⁶I delight ᵛ in your decrees;
  I will not neglect your word.

‎ג Gimel

¹⁷Do good to your servant, ʷ and I will
  live;
  I will obey your word. ˣ
¹⁸Open my eyes that I may see
  wonderful things in your law.
¹⁹I am a stranger on earth; ʸ
  do not hide your commands from
  me.
²⁰My soul is consumed ᶻ with longing
  for your laws ᵃ at all times.
²¹You rebuke the arrogant, ᵇ who are
  cursed ᶜ

and who stray ᵈ from your
  commands.
²²Remove from me scorn ᵉ and contempt,
  for I keep your statutes. ᶠ
²³Though rulers sit together and slander
  me,
  your servant will meditate on your
  decrees.
²⁴Your statutes are my delight;
  they are my counselors.

‎ד Daleth

²⁵I am laid low in the dust; ᵍ
  preserve my life ʰ according to your
  word. ⁱ
²⁶I recounted my ways and you answered
  me;
  teach me your decrees. ʲ
²⁷Let me understand the teaching of your
  precepts;

119:14 ᵗver 111
119:15 ᵘver 97, 148; Ps 1:2
119:16 ᵛS Ps 112:1
119:17 ʷPs 13:6; 116:7 ˣver 67; Ps 103:20
119:19 ʸS Ge 23:4; Heb 11:13
119:20 ᶻPs 42:2; 84:2 ᵃver 131; S Ps 63:1; Isa 26:9
119:21 ᵇver 51; Job 30:1; Ps 5:5; Jer 20:7; 50:32; Da 4:37; Mal 3:15 ᶜDt 27:26
ᵈS ver 10
119:22 ᵉPs 39:8 ᶠver 2
119:25 ᵍPs 44:25 ʰver 50,107; Ps 143:11 ⁱver 9
119:26 ʲPs 25:4; 27:11; 86:11

119:5 *decrees*. Hebrew *ḥuqqîm*, covenant directives (see Dt 6:2; 28:15,45; 30:10,16; 1Ki 11:11), emphasizing their fixed character.

119:6 *not be put to shame*. The psalmist would not suffer poverty or sickness, or humiliation at the hands of his enemies, and so become the object of sneers (see vv. 31,46,80; 25:2–3,20), but he would have reason to praise the Lord (see v. 7) for blessings received and deliverances granted because the Lord does not forsake him (see v. 8). *consider*. Respect, have regard for (see v. 15; 74:20). *commands*. Hebrew *miṣwot*, covenant directives (see Ex 20:6; 24:12; Dt 4:2), designated specifically as that which God has commanded.

119:7 *righteous*. One of the author's favorite characterizations of God's law (see vv. 62,75,106,123,138,144,160, 164,172; see also 19:9). *laws*. Hebrew *mishpāṭîm*, covenant directives (see Ex 21:1; 24:3; Dt 4:1), as the laws laid down by a ruler (king).

119:8 *not . . . forsake me*. Not abandon me to poverty, sickness or my enemies.

119:9 *young man*. Some have thought this a characterization of the author, but more likely it indicates instruction addressed to the young after the manner of the wisdom teachers (see 34:11; Pr 1:4; Ecc 11:9; 12:1). *pure*. Free from all moral taint (see 73:13). *word*. Hebrew *dabar*, a general designation for God's (word) revelation, but here used with special reference to his law (sometimes promises).

119:10 *I seek you*. The author's devotion is first of all to the God of the law and the promises; they have meaning for him only because they are God's word of life for him. *heart*. See v. 11; see also note on 4:7.

119:11 *word*. Hebrew *'imrah*, a synonym of *dabar* ("word"; see note on v. 9; see also Dt 33:9; Pr 30:5). Except where noted, as here, "word" in this psalm is *dabar*; *'imrah* is usually translated "promise."

119:13 *recount*. Either in meditation or in liturgies of covenant commitment to the Lord (see 50:16, "recite").

119:14 *as one rejoices in great riches*. See vv. 72,111, 162.

119:15 *ways*. The Hebrew for this word is a synonym of the Hebrew for "ways" in v. 3 (the two Hebrew words parallel each other in 25:4).

119:17–24 Devotion to God's law marks the Lord's servant, but alienates him from the arrogant (v. 21) of the world.

119:17 *I will obey*. Out of gratitude for God's care and blessing.

119:18 *wonderful things*. Usually ascribed to God's redeeming acts (see 9:1 and note)—but God's law contains matters just as wonderful (see v. 27).

119:19 *stranger on earth*. As a servant of the Lord, i.e., a citizen of his kingdom, he is not at home in any of the kingdoms of the world (see 39:12 and note; see also note on v. 54).

119:20 *My soul is*. I am (see vv. 28,81; see also note on 6:3).

119:21 *the arrogant*. Those who are a law to themselves, most fully described in 10:2–11 (see vv. 51,69,78,85,122; see also note on 31:23). The author has suffered much from their hostility because of his zeal for God and his law, as the next two verses and many others indicate. *cursed*. Ripe for God's judgment.

119:22 *scorn and contempt*. Of the arrogant.

119:23 *rulers*. Because the author mentions also speaking "before kings" (v. 46) and being persecuted by "rulers" (v. 161), it may be that he held some official position, such as priest (one of whose functions it would have been to teach God's law; see Lev 10:11; Ezr 7:6; Ne 8:2–8; Jer 2:8; 18:18; Mal 2:7; see also note on v. 57). (These kings and rulers are probably either Israelite from the time of the monarchy or Persian in the postexilic period.) *sit*. As those securely settled in the world—not as strangers (cf. v. 19). *together and slander*. As they share their worldly counsels, they speak derisively of the one who stands apart because he delights in God's statutes and makes them his "counselors" (v. 24).

119:25–32 Whether "laid low" (v. 25) or "set . . . free" (v. 32), he is determined to "hold fast" (v. 31) to God's word.

119:25 *laid low*. The author speaks much of his sorrow, suffering and affliction (see vv. 28,50,67,71,75,83,92,107, 143,153). It is likely that the ridicule, slander and persecution from his adversaries are usually occasioned by this suffering of God's devoted servant, who makes God's word (his law and promises) the hope of his life (see vv. 42,51,65,69,78,85,95,110,134,141,150,154,157,161; see also notes on v. 6; 31:11–12). *in the dust*. See 44:25 and note. *word*. Especially its promises, as also in vv. 28,37,42,49,65,74,81,107,114,147.

119:27 *wonders*. See note on v. 18.

then I will meditate on your
  wonders. *k*
28My soul is weary with sorrow; *l*
  strengthen me *m* according to your
  word. *n*
29Keep me from deceitful ways; *o*
  be gracious to me *p* through your law.
30I have chosen *q* the way of truth; *r*
  I have set my heart *s* on your laws.
31I hold fast *t* to your statutes, O LORD;
  do not let me be put to shame.
32I run in the path of your commands,
  for you have set my heart free.

ה He

33Teach me, *u* O LORD, to follow your
  decrees;
  then I will keep them to the end.
34Give me understanding, *v* and I will
  keep your law *w*
  and obey it with all my heart. *x*
35Direct me *y* in the path of your
  commands, *z*
  for there I find delight. *a*
36Turn my heart *b* toward your statutes
  and not toward selfish gain. *c*
37Turn my eyes away from worthless
  things;
  preserve my life *d* according to your
  word. *z* *e*
38Fulfill your promise *f* to your servant,
  so that you may be feared.
39Take away the disgrace *g* I dread,
  for your laws are good.
40How I long *h* for your precepts!
  Preserve my life *i* in your
  righteousness.

ו Waw

41May your unfailing love *j* come to me,
  O LORD,
  your salvation according to your
  promise; *k*
42then I will answer *l* the one who taunts
  me, *m*
  for I trust in your word.
43Do not snatch the word of truth from
  my mouth, *n*
  for I have put my hope *o* in your
  laws.
44I will always obey your law, *p*
  for ever and ever.
45I will walk about in freedom,
  for I have sought out your precepts. *q*
46I will speak of your statutes before
  kings *r*
  and will not be put to shame, *s*
47for I delight *t* in your commands
  because I love them. *u*
48I lift up my hands to *a* your commands,
  which I love,
  and I meditate *v* on your decrees.

ז Zayin

49Remember your word *w* to your servant,
  for you have given me hope. *x*
50My comfort in my suffering is this:
  Your promise preserves my life. *y*
51The arrogant mock me *z* without
  restraint,
  but I do not turn *a* from your law.
52I remember *b* your ancient laws,
  O LORD,

119:27
*k*Ps 105:2; 145:5
119:28 *l*Ps 6:7;
116:3; Isa 51:11;
Jer 45:3
*m*Ps 18:1;
Isa 40:29; 41:10
*n*ver 9
119:29 *o*Ps 26:4
*p*S Nu 6:25
119:30
*q*S Jos 24:22
*r*S Ps 26:3
*s*S Ps 108:1
119:31
*t*S Dt 10:20
119:33 *u*ver 12
119:34 *v*ver 27,
73,144,169;
S Job 32:8;
Pr 2:6; Da 2:21;
Jas 1:5
*w*S Dt 6:25 *x*ver
69
119:35
*y*Ps 25:4-5 *z*ver
32 *a*S Ps 1:2
119:36
*b*S Jos 24:23
*c*Eze 33:31
119:37 *d*ver 25;
Ps 71:20 *e*ver 9
119:38
*f*S Nu 23:19
119:39 *g*ver 22;
Ps 69:9; 89:51;
Isa 25:8; 51:7;
54:4
119:40 *h*ver 20
*i*ver 25,149,154

119:41 *j*S Ps 6:4
*k*ver 76,116,154,
170
119:42 *l*Pr 27:11
*m*S Ps 42:10
119:43
*n*S 1Ki 17:24 *o*ver
74,81,114,147
119:44 *p*ver 33,
34,55; S Dt 6:25
119:45 *q*ver 94,
155
119:46
*r*Mt 10:18;
Ac 26:1-2 *s*S ver 6
119:47 *t*ver 77,
143; S Ps 112:1
*u*ver 97,127,159,
163,165
119:48
*v*Ge 24:63
119:49 *w*ver 9
*x*ver 43

119:50 *y*S ver 25 **119:51** *z*S ver 21; S Job 16:10; S 17:2
*a*S Job 23:11 **119:52** *b*Ps 103:18

*z*37 Two manuscripts of the Masoretic Text and Dead Sea
Scrolls; most manuscripts of the Masoretic Text *life in
your way* *a*48 Or *for*

119:29 *deceitful ways.* Ways that seem right but lead to
death (see Pr 14:12)—in contrast to the ways prescribed by
God's law, which are trustworthy (see vv. 86,138) and true
(see vv. 142,151,160). *through your law.* By keeping me
true to your law, let me enjoy your blessings.
119:30 *way of truth.* See note on v. 29.
119:31 *put to shame.* See note on v. 6.
119:32 *set my heart free.* Lit. "enlarged my heart," i.e.,
expanded it with joy (see Isa 60:5, "swell with joy"). Others
translate it "increased my understanding" (see 1Ki 4:29,
"breadth of understanding"). *heart.* See note on 4:7.
119:33–40 Prayer for instruction in God's will as he longs
for his precepts.
119:34 *heart.* See v. 36; see also note on 4:7.
119:36–37 *heart . . . eyes.* See 101:2b–3a and note.
119:38 *that you may be feared.* The Lord's saving acts in
fulfillment of his promises contribute to the recognition that
he is the true God (see 130:4; 2Sa 7:25–26; 1Ki 8:39–40;
Jer 33:8–9).
119:39 *disgrace I dread.* See notes on vv. 6,25.
119:40 *righteousness.* See note on 4:1.
119:41–48 May the Lord deliver me and not take his truth

from my mouth; then I will honor his law in my life and
speak of it before kings, for I love his commands.
119:41 *love.* See vv. 64,76,88,124,149,159; see also note
on 6:4.
119:42 *one who taunts me.* See note on v. 25 ("laid low").
word. See note on v. 25.
119:43 *word of truth from my mouth.* See v. 13 and note;
see also v. 46.
119:45 *freedom.* Lit. "a wide space," i.e., unconfined by
affliction or oppression (see 18:19 and note).
119:46 *before kings.* Such will be his boldness (see note on
v. 23).
119:48 *I lift up my hands to.* An act accompanying praise
(as in 63:4; 134:2); so the sense may be: I praise.
119:49–56 God's word is my comfort and my guide whatever my circumstances.
119:49 *word.* See note on v. 25.
119:50–51 *in my suffering . . . The arrogant mock.* See
note on v. 25 ("laid low").
119:51 *arrogant.* See note on v. 21.
119:52 *ancient.* God's law is not fickle, but it is grounded
firmly in his unchanging moral character. This is a major

and I find comfort in them.
⁵³Indignation grips me ^c because of the
wicked,
who have forsaken your law. ^d
⁵⁴Your decrees are the theme of my
song ^e
wherever I lodge.
⁵⁵In the night I remember ^f your name,
O Lord,
and I will keep your law. ^g
⁵⁶This has been my practice:
I obey your precepts. ^h

ⁿ Heth

⁵⁷You are my portion, ⁱ O Lord;
I have promised to obey your
words. ^j
⁵⁸I have sought ^k your face with all my
heart;
be gracious to me ^l according to your
promise. ^m
⁵⁹I have considered my ways ⁿ
and have turned my steps to your
statutes.
⁶⁰I will hasten and not delay
to obey your commands. ^o
⁶¹Though the wicked bind me with ropes,
I will not forget ^p your law.
⁶²At midnight ^q I rise to give you thanks
for your righteous laws. ^r
⁶³I am a friend to all who fear you, ^s
to all who follow your precepts. ^t
⁶⁴The earth is filled with your love, ^u
O Lord;
teach me your decrees. ^v

ט Teth

⁶⁵Do good ^w to your servant
according to your word, ^x O Lord.
⁶⁶Teach me knowledge ^y and good
judgment,
for I believe in your commands.
⁶⁷Before I was afflicted ^z I went astray, ^a
but now I obey your word. ^b
⁶⁸You are good, ^c and what you do is
good;
teach me your decrees. ^d
⁶⁹Though the arrogant have smeared me
with lies, ^e
I keep your precepts with all my
heart.
⁷⁰Their hearts are callous ^f and unfeeling,
but I delight in your law.
⁷¹It was good for me to be afflicted ^g
so that I might learn your decrees.
⁷²The law from your mouth is more
precious to me
than thousands of pieces of silver and
gold. ^h

י Yodh

⁷³Your hands made me ⁱ and formed me;
give me understanding to learn your
commands.
⁷⁴May those who fear you rejoice ^j when
they see me,
for I have put my hope in your
word. ^k
⁷⁵I know, O Lord, that your laws are
righteous, ^l

119:53
^cS Ex 32:19;
S 33:4 ^dPs 89:30
119:54 ^ever 172;
Ps 101:1; 138:5
119:55 ^fver 62,
72; Ps 1:2; 42:8;
S 63:6; 77:2;
Isa 26:9;
Ac 16:25 ^gS ver
44
119:56 ^hver 4,
100,134,168;
S Nu 15:40
119:57
ⁱS Dt 32:9;
Jer 51:19; La 3:24
^jver 17,67,101
119:58
^kS Dt 4:29;
S 1Ch 16:11;
Ps 34:4
^lS Ge 43:29;
S Ezr 9:8 ^mver 41
119:59
ⁿJos 24:14-15;
S Ps 39:1
119:60 ^over 115
119:61 ^pver 83,
109,153,176
119:62 ^qS ver
55; Ac 16:25
^rver 7
119:63 ^sPs 15:4;
101:6-7; 103:11
^tver 56;
Ps 111:10
119:64 ^uPs 33:5
^vver 12,108

119:65 ^wver 17;
Ps 125:4;
Isa 50:2; 59:1;
Mic 2:7 ^xS ver 9
119:66
^yS Ps 51:6
119:67
^zS Ps 116:10
^aS Ps 95:10;
S Jer 8:4 ^bS ver 17
119:68
^cPs 100:5; 106:1;
107:1; 135:3
^dS Ex 18:20
119:69
^eJob 13:4;
Ps 109:2
119:70
^fS Ps 17:10;
Isa 29:13;

Ac 28:27 **119:71** ^gver 67,75 **119:72** ^hS Job 28:17;
S Ps 19:10 **119:73** ⁱS Ge 1:27; S Job 4:17; 10:8; Ps 138:8;
139:13-16 **119:74** ^jS Ps 34:2 ^kver 9; Ps 130:5 **119:75** ^lver
7,138,172

---

source of the author's comfort and one of the main reasons
he cherishes the law so highly (see vv. 89,144,152,160).
119:53 *Indignation grips me.* Zeal for God's law (see vv.
136,139) awakens righteous anger against those who reject
it (see vv. 113,115,158), and it brings abhorrence of all that
is contrary to it (see vv. 104,128,163); but it draws together
those who honor it (see v. 63).
119:54 *wherever I lodge.* Lit. "in my temporary house."
The sense may be that of v. 19 (see note there).
119:55 *name.* See note on 5:11.
119:57–64 The Lord is the psalmist's true homestead
because it is God's law that fills the earth with all that makes
life secure and joyous. So God's promises are his hope, and
God's righteous laws his delight.
119:57 *portion.* May identify the author as a priest or
Levite (see 73:26 and note).
119:58 *heart.* See note on 4:7.
119:61 *bind me with ropes.* Oppress me.
119:62 *give you thanks.* See note on Ps 100 title. *righteous.* See note on v. 7.
119:63 *friend.* See note on v. 53.
119:65–72 Do good to me in accordance with your goodness, even if that means affliction, because your affliction is
good for me; it teaches me knowledge and good judgment
from your law.

119:65 *Do good.* Cf. v. 68; see 31:19; 86:17 and notes.
word. See note on v. 25.
119:66 *believe in.* Have confidence in; God's commands
are not deceitful (see note on v. 29) or fickle (see note on v.
52).
119:67 *afflicted.* At the hands of God (see v. 71; see also
note on v. 25, "laid low"). *word.* See note on v. 11.
119:69 *arrogant.* See note on v. 21.
119:70 *callous and unfeeling.* Lit. "fat as grease." Similar
expressions occur also in Isa 6:10; Jer 5:28 (see also 17:10).
119:72 *than thousands . . . of silver and gold.* See vv.
14,57,111,162.
119:73–80 Complete your forming of me by helping me to
conform to your righteous laws so that the arrogant may be
put to shame and those who fear you may rejoice with me.
(The stanza has a concentric structure; compare vv. 73 and
80, 74 and 79, 75 and 78, 76 and 77.)
119:73 *give me understanding.* What I need to perfect the
work you began when you formed me.
119:74 *fear you.* See v. 79; see also note on 34:8–14.
when they see me. When I am perfectly formed and enjoying
the blessings of the godly. *word.* See note on v. 25.
119:75 *laws.* Here the Hebrew for this word (*mishpatim*)
may refer to God's just decisions in dealing with his servant,
as the rest of the verse implies (see v. 84 and note). *you have*

and in faithfulness ^{m} you have afflicted
  me.
76May your unfailing love ^{n} be my
    comfort,
  according to your promise ^{o} to your
    servant.
77Let your compassion ^{p} come to me that
    I may live,
  for your law is my delight. ^{q}
78May the arrogant ^{r} be put to shame for
    wronging me without cause; ^{s}
  but I will meditate on your precepts.
79May those who fear you turn to me,
    those who understand your statutes. ^{t}
80May my heart be blameless ^{u} toward
    your decrees, ^{v}
  that I may not be put to shame. ^{w}

כ Kaph

81My soul faints ^{x} with longing for your
    salvation, ^{y}
  but I have put my hope ^{z} in your
    word.
82My eyes fail, ^{a} looking for your
    promise; ^{b}
  I say, "When will you comfort me?"
83Though I am like a wineskin in the
    smoke,
  I do not forget ^{c} your decrees.
84How long ^{d} must your servant wait?
  When will you punish my
    persecutors? ^{e}
85The arrogant ^{f} dig pitfalls ^{g} for me,
    contrary to your law.

86All your commands are trustworthy; ^{h}
  help me, ^{i} for men persecute me ^{j}
    without cause. ^{k}
87They almost wiped me from the earth,
    but I have not forsaken ^{l} your
    precepts.
88Preserve my life ^{m} according to your
    love, ^{n}
  and I will obey the statutes ^{o} of your
    mouth.

ל Lamedh

89Your word, O LORD, is eternal; ^{p}
  it stands firm in the heavens.
90Your faithfulness ^{q} continues through all
    generations; ^{r}
  you established the earth, and it
    endures. ^{s}
91Your laws endure ^{t} to this day,
  for all things serve you. ^{u}
92If your law had not been my delight, ^{v}
  I would have perished in my
    affliction. ^{w}
93I will never forget ^{x} your precepts,
  for by them you have preserved my
    life. ^{y}
94Save me, ^{z} for I am yours;
  I have sought out your precepts. ^{a}
95The wicked are waiting to destroy me, ^{b}
  but I will ponder your statutes. ^{c}
96To all perfection I see a limit;

119:75
mHeb 12:5-11
119:76 nPs 6:4
oS ver 41
119:77
pPs 90:13;
103:13 qS ver 47
119:78 rver 51;
Jer 50:32 sver 86,
161; Ps 35:19
119:79 tver 27,
125
119:80 uver 1;
S 1Ki 8:61
vS Ge 26:5 wS ver
6
119:81 xver 20;
Ps 84:2 yver 123
zS ver 43
119:82 aS Ps 6:7;
69:3; La 2:11
bver 41,123
119:83 cS ver 61
119:84 dPs 6:3;
Rev 6:10 ever 51;
Jer 12:3; 15:15;
20:11
119:85 fver 51
gPs 35:7; 57:6;
Jer 18:20,22
119:86 hver 138
iS Ps 109:26
jS Ps 7:1 kS ver
78
119:87 lver 150;
Isa 1:4,28; 58:2;
59:13
119:88
mS Ps 41:2 nver
124; Ps 51:1;
109:26 over 2,
100,129,134,168
119:89 pver 111,
144; S Ps 111:8;
Isa 51:6;
S Mt 5:18;
1Pe 1:25
119:90
qS Ps 36:5
rS Ps 45:17
sS Job 8:19;
Ps 148:6
119:91
tJer 33:25

uPs 104:2-4; Jer 31:35 119:92 vPs 37:4; S 112:1 wver 50,67
119:93 xver 83 yS Ps 103:5 119:94 zver 146; Ps 54:1;
116:4; Jer 17:14; 31:18; 42:11 aS ver 45 119:95 bS Ps 69:4
cver 99

---

afflicted me. See vv. 67,71.
119:76 unfailing love. See note on 6:4. my comfort. In my
affliction.
119:77 that I may live. And not perish in my affliction.
119:78 the arrogant. See note on v. 21. be put to shame.
As they have subjected me to shame (see note on 5:10). for
wronging me. See note on v. 25 ("laid low").
119:79 turn to me. See v. 63 and note on v. 53.
119:80 heart. See note on 4:7. not be put to shame. See
note on v. 6.
119:81–88 Save me from my affliction and my persecutors, according to your promises, and I will obey your statutes. This last stanza of the first half of the psalm, like the
closing stanza, is dominated by prayer for God's help (see
note on v. 25).
119:81 soul. See note on 6:3.
119:82 My eyes fail. See note on 6:7.
119:83 like a wineskin in the smoke. As a wineskin hanging in the smoke and heat above a fire becomes smudged and
shriveled, so the psalmist bears the marks of his affliction.
119:84 How long . . . wait? Lit. "How (many are) the days
of your servant?" That is, do not delay the punishment of my
persecutors, because my life is short. punish. Lit. "effect
justice upon" (the Hebrew for "justice" is mishpat; see note
on v. 7, "laws"; see also note on 5:10).
119:85 The arrogant. See note on v. 21. dig pitfalls.
Probably referring to slander—public accusations that the
psalmist must be guilty of vile sins or he would not be
suffering such affliction. contrary to your law. See Ex 20:16.

119:86 trustworthy. See note on v. 29 ("deceitful ways").
119:88 love. See note on 6:4.
119:89–91 God's sovereign and unchanging word governs and maintains all creation. (These first three verses of
the second half of the psalm teach a general truth; cf. vv.
1–3.)
119:89 Your word. Here God's word by which he created,
maintains and governs all things (see 33:4,6; 107:20;
147:15,18). stands firm in the heavens. The secure order of
the heavens and the earth (v. 90) declares (19:1–4) the
reassuring truth that God's word (his "laws," v. 91), by
which he upholds and governs all things, is enduring (eternal) and trustworthy ("Your faithfulness," v. 90). And that is
the larger truth that confirms the godly man's confidence in
the trustworthiness of God's word (his laws and promises) of
special revelation (see notes on 93:5; 96:10; see also note on
v. 29, "deceitful ways").
119:90 Your faithfulness. An indirect reference to God's
word (see v. 89 and note).
119:92 would have perished in my affliction. Would not
have learned the way of life (see v. 93) from your law (see vv.
67,71 and note on vv. 65–72).
119:95 The wicked. See note on v. 21 ("the arrogant").
waiting to destroy me. See note on v. 25 ("laid low").
119:96 perfection. Probably that which has been perfected
in the sense of completed, given fixed bounds so that it is no
longer open-ended. boundless. Lit. "very broad," i.e., an
inexhaustible source of wise counsel for life (see vv.
97–100).

but your commands are boundless. *d*

מ Mem

⁹⁷Oh, how I love your law! *e*
  I meditate *f* on it all day long.
⁹⁸Your commands make me wiser *g* than
    my enemies,
  for they are ever with me.
⁹⁹I have more insight than all my
    teachers,
  for I meditate on your statutes. *h*
¹⁰⁰I have more understanding than the
    elders,
  for I obey your precepts. *i*
¹⁰¹I have kept my feet *j* from every evil
    path
  so that I might obey your word. *k*
¹⁰²I have not departed from your laws, *l*
  for you yourself have taught *m* me.
¹⁰³How sweet are your words to my taste,
  sweeter than honey *n* to my mouth! *o*
¹⁰⁴I gain understanding *p* from your
    precepts;
  therefore I hate every wrong path. *q*

נ Nun

¹⁰⁵Your word is a lamp *r* to my feet
  and a light *s* for my path.
¹⁰⁶I have taken an oath *t* and confirmed
    it,
  that I will follow your righteous
    laws. *u*
¹⁰⁷I have suffered much;
  preserve my life, *v* O LORD, according
    to your word.
¹⁰⁸Accept, O LORD, the willing praise of
    my mouth, *w*
  and teach me your laws. *x*
¹⁰⁹Though I constantly take my life in my
    hands, *y*
  I will not forget *z* your law.

¹¹⁰The wicked have set a snare *a* for me,
  but I have not strayed *b* from your
    precepts.
¹¹¹Your statutes are my heritage forever;
  they are the joy of my heart. *c*
¹¹²My heart is set *d* on keeping your
    decrees
  to the very end. *e*

ס Samekh

¹¹³I hate double-minded men, *f*
  but I love your law. *g*
¹¹⁴You are my refuge and my shield; *h*
  I have put my hope *i* in your word.
¹¹⁵Away from me, *j* you evildoers,
  that I may keep the commands of my
    God!
¹¹⁶Sustain me *k* according to your
    promise, *l* and I will live;
  do not let my hopes be dashed. *m*
¹¹⁷Uphold me, *n* and I will be delivered; *o*
  I will always have regard for your
    decrees. *p*
¹¹⁸You reject all who stray *q* from your
    decrees,
  for their deceitfulness is in vain.
¹¹⁹All the wicked of the earth you discard
    like dross; *r*
  therefore I love your statutes. *s*
¹²⁰My flesh trembles *t* in fear of you; *u*
  I stand in awe *v* of your laws.

ע Ayin

¹²¹I have done what is righteous and
    just; *w*
  do not leave me to my oppressors.
¹²²Ensure your servant's well-being; *x*
  let not the arrogant oppress me. *y*

119:96 *d*Ps 19:7 **119:97** *e*S ver 47 /S ver 15 **119:98** *g*ver 130; S Dt 4:6; Ps 19:7; 2Ti 3:15 **119:99** *h*ver 15 **119:100** *i*S ver 56; S Dt 6:17 **119:101** *j*Pr 1:15 *k*S ver 57 **119:102** /S Dt 17:20 *m*S Dt 4:5 **119:103** *n*S Ps 19:10 *o*Pr 24:13-14 **119:104** *p*S Ps 111:10 *q*ver 128 **119:105** *r*Pr 20:27; 2Pe 1:19 *s*ver 130; Pr 6:23 **119:106** *t*S Ne 10:29 *u*ver 7 **119:107** *v*S ver 25 **119:108** *w*Ps 51:15; 63:5; 71:8; 109:30 *x*S ver 64 **119:109** *y*S Jdg 12:3 *z*S ver 61 **119:110** *a*Ps 25:15; S 64:5; Isa 8:14; Am 3:5 *b*ver 10 **119:111** *c*ver 14, 162 **119:112** *d*S Ps 108:1 *e*ver 33 **119:113** /S 1Ki 18:21; Jas 1:8; 4:8 *g*ver 47 **119:114** *h*S Ge 15:1; S Ps 18:2 *i*S ver 43 **119:115** /S Ps 6:8 **119:116** *k*S Ps 18:35; 41:3; 55:22; Isa 46:4 /S ver 41 *m*Ro 5:5 **119:117** *n*Isa 41:10; 46:4 *o*Ps 34:4 *p*ver 6 **119:118** *q*S ver 10 **119:119** *r*Isa 1:22,25; Eze 22:18,19 *s*ver 47 **119:120** *t*S Job 4:14; S Isa 66:2 *u*S Jos 24:14 *v*Jer 10:7; Hab 3:2 **119:121** *w*S 2Sa 8:15; S Job 27:6 **119:122** *x*S Job 17:3 *y*ver 21,121,134; Ps 106:42

119:97–104 Meditation on God's law yields the highest wisdom.
119:98 *my enemies.* Those arrogant ones (see note on v. 21) who place confidence in worldly wisdom. *they.* Your commands.
119:99 *teachers.* Merely human teachers.
119:100 *elders.* Old men, taught by experience (see note on Ex 3:16).
119:102 *you . . . have taught me.* Through your laws.
119:103 *words.* Perhaps better understood here as "laws" (see vv. 67,133,158,172 and note on v. 11).
119:104 *hate every wrong path.* See note on v. 53.
119:105 *lamp . . . light.* Apart from which I could only grope about in the darkness.
119:106 *have taken an oath and confirmed it.* Have covenanted (see Ne 10:29).
119:107 See v. 25 and note.
119:109 *take my life in my hands.* By publicly honoring God's law even in the face of threats and hostility (see especially vv. 23,46,161).
119:110 *set a snare.* See v. 85 and note.

119:111–112 *heart.* See note on 4:7.
119:111 *my heritage.* The possession I have received from God as my homestead and that from which I draw the provisions for my life (see note on vv. 57–64).
119:113 *hate double-minded men.* See v. 115; see also note on v. 53. A double-minded man is "unstable in all he does" (Jas 1:8).
119:114 *word.* See note on v. 25.
119:118 *reject.* Or "shake off" or "make light of." *their deceitfulness.* Probably their ways, which are deceitful (see note on v. 29).
119:119 *dross.* Scum removed from molten ore or metal. The Hebrew for this word is a pun on the word for "stray" in v. 118: Those who stray are treated like dross.
119:120 *My flesh trembles.* He quivers out of his deep reverence for God.
119:121–128 As your faithful servant I pray for deliverance from my oppressors—another stanza in which prayer for deliverance is dominant (see vv. 81–88 and note; see also note on v. 25, "laid low").
119:121 *what is righteous and just.* God's law.

123My eyes fail,[z] looking for your
salvation,[a]
looking for your righteous promise.[b]
124Deal with your servant according to
your love[c]
and teach me your decrees.[d]
125I am your servant;[e] give me
discernment
that I may understand your statutes.[f]
126It is time for you to act, O LORD;
your law is being broken.[g]
127Because I love your commands[h]
more than gold,[i] more than pure
gold,[j]
128and because I consider all your precepts
right,[k]
I hate every wrong path.[l]

פ Pe

129Your statutes are wonderful;[m]
therefore I obey them.[n]
130The unfolding of your words gives
light;[o]
it gives understanding to the simple.[p]
131I open my mouth and pant,[q]
longing for your commands.[r]
132Turn to me[s] and have mercy[t] on me,
as you always do to those who love
your name.[u]
133Direct my footsteps according to your
word;[v]
let no sin rule[w] over me.
134Redeem me from the oppression of
men,[x]
that I may obey your precepts.[y]
135Make your face shine[z] upon your
servant
and teach me your decrees.[a]
136Streams of tears[b] flow from my eyes,
for your law is not obeyed.[c]

119:123 [z]Isa 38:14 [a]ver 81 [b]S ver 82 **119:124** [c]S ver 88; S Ps 25:7 [d]ver 12 **119:125** [e]S Ps 116:16 [f]S ver 79 **119:126** [g]S Nu 15:31 **119:127** [h]S ver 47 [i]Ps 19:10 [j]S Job 3:21 **119:128** [k]S Ps 19:8 [l]ver 104,163; Ps 31:6; Pr 13:5 **119:129** [m]ver 18 [n]ver 22,S 88 **119:130** [o]S ver 105 [p]S Ps 19:7 **119:131** [q]Ps 42:1 [r]S ver 20 **119:132** [s]S Ps 6:4 [t]S 2Sa 24:14; S Ps 9:13 [u]S Ps 5:11 **119:133** [v]ver 9 [w]S ver 11; S Ro 6:16 **119:134** [x]S ver 122 [y]S ver 56, S 88 **119:135** [z]S Nu 6:25; Ps 4:6; 67:1; 80:3 [a]ver 12 **119:136** [b]Ps 6:6; Isa 22:4; Jer 9:1, 18; 13:17; 14:17; La 1:16; 3:48 [c]ver 158; Ps 106:25; Isa 42:24; Eze 9:4

119:137 [d]S Ex 9:27; S Ezr 9:15 [e]S Ne 9:13 **119:138** [f]S ver 75; S Ps 19:7 [g]ver 86 **119:139** [h]Ps 69:9; Jn 2:17 **119:140** [i]S Jos 23:14 [j]Ps 12:6 [k]ver 47 **119:141** [l]S Ps 22:6 [m]ver 61,134

צ Tsadhe

137Righteous are you,[d] O LORD,
and your laws are right.[e]
138The statutes you have laid down are
righteous;[f]
they are fully trustworthy.[g]
139My zeal wears me out,[h]
for my enemies ignore your words.
140Your promises[i] have been thoroughly
tested,[j]
and your servant loves them.[k]
141Though I am lowly and despised,[l]
I do not forget your precepts.[m]
142Your righteousness is everlasting
and your law is true.[n]
143Trouble and distress have come upon
me,
but your commands are my delight.[o]
144Your statutes are forever right;
give me understanding[p] that I may
live.

ק Qoph

145I call with all my heart;[q] answer me,
O LORD,
and I will obey your decrees.[r]
146I call out to you; save me[s]
and I will keep your statutes.
147I rise before dawn[t] and cry for help;
I have put my hope in your word.
148My eyes stay open through the watches
of the night,[u]
that I may meditate on your
promises.
149Hear my voice[v] in accordance with
your love;[w]

119:142 [n]ver 151,160; Ps 19:7 **119:143** [o]ver 24,S 47 **119:144** [p]S ver 34 **119:145** [q]ver 10 [r]ver 22,55 **119:146** [s]S ver 94 **119:147** [t]Ps 5:3; 57:8; 108:2 **119:148** [u]S Ps 63:6 **119:149** [v]S Ps 27:7 [w]ver 124

119:122 The only verse in this psalm that does not have either a direct or an indirect (as in vv. 90,121,132; see note on v. 75) reference to God's word. *the arrogant.* See note on v. 21.
119:123 *My eyes fail.* See note on 6:7.
119:124 *love.* See note on 6:4.
119:126 *act.* Either in defense of his servant, or in judgment on the lawbreakers, or both.
119:127 *more than gold.* See vv. 14,57,72,111.
119:128 *I hate every wrong path.* See note on v. 53.
119:129 *wonderful.* See v. 18 and note.
119:130 *unfolding.* Lit. "opening," here meaning (1) the revelation of your words, (2) the interpretation (see "expound," 49:4) of your words, or (3) the entering of your words into the heart. *the simple.* See 19:7 and note.
119:132 *as you always do.* Lit. "as is (your) manner" (the Hebrew for "manner" is *mishpaṭ*); hence an indirect reference (see note on v. 122) to God's law (see note on v. 7).
119:134,154 *Redeem.* Here, as often, a synonym for "deliver."
119:134 *oppression.* See note on v. 25 ("laid low").
119:135 *your face shine.* See note on 13:1 ("hide your face").
119:136 See v. 53 and note.
119:137–144 The Lord and his laws are righteous.
119:137 *Righteous.* See note on 4:1.
119:138 *trustworthy.* See v. 142; see also note on v. 29 ("deceitful ways").
119:139 *My zeal.* See note on v. 53.
119:140 *promises.* Hebrew *'imrah*; perhaps better rendered "word" here (see note on v. 11). *tested.* Lit. "refined," i.e., God's word contains nothing worthless or useless.
119:141 *lowly and despised.* Cf. v. 143; see also note on v. 25.
119:145–152 Save me, O Lord, and I will keep your law. As the psalm draws to a close, prayer for deliverance becomes more dominant (see note on v. 25, "laid low").
119:148 *watches of the night.* See note on Jdg 7:19; see also La 2:19.
119:149 *love.* See note on 6:4. *your laws.* Or "your justice" (complementing "your love"); Hebrew *mishpaṭ* (see note on v. 75).

preserve my life,[x] O LORD, according
to your laws.
150Those who devise wicked schemes[y]
are near,
but they are far from your law.
151Yet you are near,[z] O LORD,
and all your commands are true.[a]
152Long ago I learned from your statutes[b]
that you established them to last
forever.[c]

ר Resh

153Look upon my suffering[d] and deliver
me,[e]
for I have not forgotten[f] your law.
154Defend my cause[g] and redeem me;[h]
preserve my life[i] according to your
promise.[j]
155Salvation is far from the wicked,
for they do not seek out[k] your
decrees.
156Your compassion is great,[l] O LORD;
preserve my life[m] according to your
laws.[n]
157Many are the foes who persecute me,[o]
but I have not turned[p] from your
statutes.
158I look on the faithless with loathing,[q]
for they do not obey your word.[r]
159See how I love your precepts;
preserve my life,[s] O LORD, according
to your love.
160All your words are true;
all your righteous laws are eternal.[t]

ש Sin and Shin

161Rulers persecute me[u] without cause,
but my heart trembles[v] at your word.
162I rejoice[w] in your promise
like one who finds great spoil.[x]
163I hate and abhor[y] falsehood
but I love your law.[z]
164Seven times a day I praise you
for your righteous laws.[a]
165Great peace[b] have they who love your
law,

119:149 [x]S ver 40 **119:150** [y]S Ps 37:7 **119:151** [z]S Ps 34:18; Php 4:5 [a]S ver 142 **119:152** [b]ver 7, 73 [c]S ver 89; S Ps 111:8; Lk 21:33 **119:153** [d]S Ps 13:3 [e]S Ps 3:7 [f]S Ps 44:17 **119:154** [g]Ps 35:1; Jer 50:34; Mic 7:9 [h]S 1Sa 24:15 [i]ver 25 [j]S ver 41 **119:155** [k]ver 94, 118 **119:156** [l]S Ne 9:27; Jas 5:11 [m]ver 25 [n]ver 149 **119:157** [o]S Ps 7:1 [p]S Ps 44:18 **119:158** [q]ver 104; S Ex 32:19 [r]S ver 136 **119:159** [s]ver 25; S Ps 41:2 **119:160** [t]S ver 89; S Ps 111:8 **119:161** [u]ver 23, 122,157; 1Sa 24:14-15 [v]ver 120 **119:162** [w]S ver 111 [x]1Sa 30:16; Isa 9:3; 53:12 **119:163** [y]S ver 128 [z]ver 47 **119:164** [a]ver 7, 160 **119:165** [b]Ps 37:11; Isa 26:3,12; 27:5; 32:17; 57:19; 66:12 [c]S ver 11; S Ps 37:24; 1Jn 2:10 **119:166** [d]ver 81 **119:167** [e]ver 47 **119:168** [f]S ver 56,S 88 [g]ver 2,22 [h]S Job 10:4; S 23:10; Ps 139:3; Pr 5:21 **119:169** [i]S Job 16:18 [j]S ver 34 [k]S ver 9 **119:170** [l]1Ki 8:30; 2Ch 6:24; Ps 28:2; 140:6; 143:1 [m]Ps 3:7; 22:20; 59:1

and nothing can make them
stumble.[c]
166I wait for your salvation,[d] O LORD,
and I follow your commands.
167I obey your statutes,
for I love them[e] greatly.
168I obey your precepts[f] and your
statutes,[g]
for all my ways are known[h] to you.

ת Taw

169May my cry come[i] before you,
O LORD;
give me understanding[j] according to
your word.[k]
170May my supplication come[l] before
you;
deliver me[m] according to your
promise.[n]
171May my lips overflow with praise,[o]
for you teach me[p] your decrees.
172May my tongue sing[q] of your word,
for all your commands are
righteous.[r]
173May your hand be ready to help[s] me,
for I have chosen[t] your precepts.
174I long for your salvation,[u] O LORD,
and your law is my delight.[v]
175Let me live[w] that I may praise you,
and may your laws sustain me.
176I have strayed like a lost sheep.[x]
Seek your servant,
for I have not forgotten[y] your
commands.

Psalm 120

A song of ascents.

1I call on the LORD[z] in my distress,[a]
and he answers me.
2Save me, O LORD, from lying lips[b]

[n]S ver 41 **119:171** [o]Ps 51:15; 63:3 [p]Ps 94:12; Isa 2:3; Mic 4:2 **119:172** [q]Ps 51:14 [r]ver 7,S 75 **119:173** [s]Ps 37:24; 73:23; Isa 41:10 [t]S Jos 24:22 **119:174** [u]ver 166 [v]ver 16,24 **119:175** [w]ver 116,159; Isa 55:3 **119:176** [x]ver 10; S Ps 95:10; Jer 50:17; Eze 34:11; S Lk 15:4 [y]S Ps 44:17 **120:1** [z]S Ps 18:6 [a]S 2Sa 22:7; S Ps 118:5 **120:2** [b]S Ps 31:18

119:150 *far from your law.* See vv. 21,53,85,118,126, 139,155,158.
119:151 *are true.* See note on v. 29 ("deceitful ways").
119:152 *last forever.* See note on v. 52.
119:153–160 See note on vv. 145–152.
119:155 *the wicked.* See note on v. 21 ("the arrogant").
119:156 *your laws.* See v. 149 and note.
119:158 *word.* Hebrew *'imrah* (see note on v. 11).
119:160 *All.* Lit. "The sum of" (as in 139:17). *true.* See note on v. 29 ("deceitful ways"). *eternal.* See note on v. 52.
119:161–168 See note on vv. 145–152.
119:161 *Rulers.* See note on v. 23. *heart.* See note on 4:7.
119:162 *great spoil.* See vv. 14,72,111.
119:163 *I hate.* See note on v. 53. *falsehood.* Or "that which is (ways that are) deceitful" (see v. 29 and note).
119:164 *Seven.* A number signifying completeness—he praises God throughout the day.
119:165 *Great peace.* Complete security and well-being.
119:169–176 See note on vv. 145–152.
119:171 *overflow with praise.* Because you have delivered me.
119:172 *righteous.* See note on v. 7.
119:174–176 The conclusion to the psalm.
119:176 *I have strayed.* See Isa 53:6; the clearest expression of the author's acknowledgment that, for all his devotion to God's law, he has again and again wandered into other (deceitful) ways and, like a lost sheep, must be brought back by his heavenly Shepherd. For one who has made God's law the guide and dearest treasure of his life, the last word can only be such a confession—and such a prayer.

and from deceitful tongues. *c*

³What will he do to you,
  and what more besides, O deceitful
    tongue?
⁴He will punish you with a warrior's
    sharp arrows, *d*
  with burning coals of the broom tree.

⁵Woe to me that I dwell in Meshech,
  that I live among the tents of Kedar! *e*
⁶Too long have I lived
  among those who hate peace.
⁷I am a man of peace;
  but when I speak, they are for war.

Psalm 121

A song of ascents.

¹I lift up my eyes to the hills—
  where does my help come from?

120:2 *c*S Ps 52:4
120:4
*d*S Dt 32:23
120:5
*e*S Ge 25:13;
Jer 2:10

121:2 *f*S Ge 1:1
*g*S Ps 104:5
121:4 *h*Ps 127:1
121:5 *i*S Ps 1:6
121:6 *j*Isa 49:10
121:7 *k*S Ps 9:9
121:8 *l*Dt 28:6

²My help comes from the LORD,
  the Maker of heaven *f* and earth. *g*

³He will not let your foot slip—
  he who watches over you will not
    slumber;
⁴indeed, he who watches *h* over Israel
  will neither slumber nor sleep.

⁵The LORD watches over *i* you—
  the LORD is your shade at your right
    hand;
⁶the sun *j* will not harm you by day,
  nor the moon by night.

⁷The LORD will keep you from all
    harm *k*—
  he will watch over your life;
⁸the LORD will watch over your coming
    and going
  both now and forevermore. *l*

Ps 120 A prayer for deliverance from false accusers. Verse 7 suggests that the speaker is a king, in which case the accusers seek either to discredit him before his people or, more likely, to awaken suspicion concerning him in foreign courts. But if "war" is understood metaphorically, the psalm could be used also by a private individual beset by slanderers.
120 title *ascents.* Some have thought that the Hebrew for this word refers to stairs leading to the temple, hence "a song of the stairs," to be used in the temple liturgy (probably at the Feast of Tabernacles). Most believe it refers to the annual religious pilgrimages to Jerusalem (see 84:5–7; Ex 23:14–17; Dt 16:16; Mic 4:2; Zec 14:16), which brought the worshipers singing to Mount Zion (Isa 30:29)—a view that does not exclude the psalm's use also in the temple liturgy. This title, found also at the head of Ps 121–134, no doubt reflects postexilic usage rather than the original purpose of composition and also marks Ps 120–134 as a collection that was taken up as a unit into the final postexilic arrangement of the Psalter. Together with Ps 135–136, it came to be known in Jewish liturgy as the "Great Hallel" (in distinction from the "Egyptian Hallel"; see introduction to Ps 113). The spirit of Ps 84 pervades it (see also Ps 42–43). Whether a thematic (or some other) scheme controls the arrangement of Ps 120–134 is unclear, though it is probably not coincidental that they begin with a prayer that evokes the experience of one far from home and beset by barbarians and end with a call to praise in the sanctuary. See introduction to Ps 122.
120:2 *lying lips . . . deceitful tongues.* See note on 5:9.
120:3–4 Assurance that God will act (see 6:8–10 and note on 3:8).
120:3 *he.* The Lord. *what more besides.* An echo of a common oath formula (see 1Sa 3:17 and note), thus suggesting the certainty of God's judgment on the enemies.
120:4 *sharp arrows . . . burning coals.* As a weapon, the tongue is a sharp arrow (see Pr 25:18; Jer 9:8; see also 57:4; 64:3) and a searing fire (see Pr 16:27; Jas 3:6), and God's judgment will answer in kind (see 7:11–13; 11:6; 64:7). For judgment in kind see 63:9–10; 64:7–8 and notes. *broom tree.* A desert shrub, sometimes large enough to provide shade.
120:5–7 Complaint over prolonged harassment.
120:5 *Meshech . . . Kedar.* The former was in central Asia

Minor (see note on Ge 10:2), the latter in Arabia (see note on Isa 21:16). Besieged by slanderers, the psalmist feels as if far from home, surrounded by barbarians.
Ps 121 A dialogue (perhaps liturgical) of confession and assurance. Its use as a pilgrimage song provides the key to its understanding. Whether the dialogue takes place in a single heart (cf. the refrain in Ps 42–43) or between individuals in the caravan is of no great consequence since all would share the same convictions. The comforting assurance expressed (see Ps 33) is equally appropriate for the pilgrimage to Jerusalem and for the pilgrimage of life to the "glory" into which the faithful will be received (see notes on 49:15; 73:24). The psalm is composed of four couplets, each having an introductory line, which the rest of the couplet develops. Key terms are "the LORD" and "watch over," each occurring five times.
121 title See note on Ps 120 title.
121:1–2 Confession of trust in the Lord.
121:1 *hills.* Those in the vicinity of Jerusalem, of which Mount Zion is one (125:2), or, if the plural indicates majesty (as in the Hebrew in 87:1; 133:3), Mount Zion itself.
121:2 *Maker of heaven and earth.* The one true God, the King of all creation (see 124:8; 134:3; see also 33:6; 89:11–13; 96:4–5; 104:2–9; 136:4–9).
121:3–4 Assurance concerning the unsleeping guardian over Israel.
121:3 *not let your foot slip.* Not even where the way is treacherous. *not slumber.* Like the pagan god Baal (see 1Ki 18:27).
121:4 *he who watches over Israel.* The Lord of all creation and the guardian over Israel—the One in whom the faithful may put unfaltering trust.
121:5–6 Assurance concerning unfailing protection.
121:5 *shade.* See 91:1 ("shadow") and note on 17:8. *at your right hand.* See 16:8 and note.
121:6 *sun . . . moon.* Here, in agreement with the "shade" metaphor, these serve as figures for all that distresses or threatens, day or night (see Isa 4:6; 25:4–5; 49:10; Jnh 4:8).
121:7–8 Assurance concerning all of life.
121:8 *your coming and going.* Lit. "your going and coming." Although the Hebrew order is like that in such military contexts as 1Sa 29:6 ("to have you serve"); 2Sa 3:25 ("your movements"), the sense here is similar to that in Dt 28:6.

Psalm 122

A song of ascents. Of David.

[1]I rejoiced with those who said to me,
"Let us go to the house of the
Lord."
[2]Our feet are standing
in your gates, O Jerusalem.

[3]Jerusalem is built like a city
that is closely compacted together.
[4]That is where the tribes go up,
the tribes of the Lord,
to praise the name of the Lord
according to the statute given to
Israel.
[5]There the thrones for judgment stand,
the thrones of the house of David.

[6]Pray for the peace of Jerusalem:
"May those who love[m] you be
secure.
[7]May there be peace[n] within your walls
and security within your citadels.[o]"
[8]For the sake of my brothers and friends,
I will say, "Peace be within you."
[9]For the sake of the house of the Lord
our God,

I will seek your prosperity.[p]

Psalm 123

A song of ascents.

[1]I lift up my eyes to you,
to you whose throne[q] is in heaven.
[2]As the eyes of slaves look to the hand of
their master,
as the eyes of a maid look to the
hand of her mistress,
so our eyes look to the Lord[r] our God,
till he shows us his mercy.

[3]Have mercy on us, O Lord, have mercy
on us,
for we have endured much contempt.
[4]We have endured much ridicule from
the proud,
much contempt from the arrogant.

Psalm 124

A song of ascents. Of David.

[1]If the Lord had not been on our side—
let Israel say[s]—
[2]if the Lord had not been on our side

122:6 mS Ps 26:8
122:7
nS 1Sa 25:6
oS Ps 48:3

122:9 pPs 128:5
123:1 qS Ps 68:5;
Isa 6:1; 63:15
123:2 rS Ps 25:15
124:1 sPs 129:1

Ps 122 A hymn of joy over Jerusalem (see Ps 42–43; 46; 48; 84; 87; 137 and the introductions to those psalms). Sung by a pilgrim in Jerusalem (very likely at one of the three annual festivals, Dt 16:16), it expresses his deep joy over the city and his prayer for its welfare. As the third of the pilgrim-age psalms (see introduction to Ps 120), it shares many dominant themes with Ps 132, the third from the end of this collection—possibly a deliberate arrangement. Structurally, a two-verse introduction locates the worshiper with the festival throng in the city of his joy, and the major themes are developed in two stanzas of four (Hebrew) lines each. References to "the house of the Lord" (vv. 1,9) frame the song. **122 title** ascents. See note on Ps 120 title. Of David. This element is not present in all ancient witnesses to the text, and the content suggests a later date (see note on v. 1). **122:1–2** Joy for having joined the pilgrimage to Jerusalem. **122:1** the house of the Lord. The temple (2Sa 7:5,13; 1Ki 5:3,5, "temple"; 8:10, "temple"). That Jerusalem became the city of pilgrimage before the dedication of the temple is doubtful in light of 1Ki 3:4; 8:1–11. **122:2** gates. Gateways. **122:3–5** Jerusalem's significance for the faithful. **122:3** closely compacted together. Perhaps refers to the city's well-knit construction (see Ps 48) and probably recalls the construction of the tabernacle (cf. Ex 26:11, "fasten . . . together as a unit"). If so, Jerusalem is being celebrated as the earthly residence of God (see note on 9:11; see also Isa 4:5). **122:4** to praise. For God's saving acts in behalf of Israel and his blessings on the nation. name. See note on 5:11. statute given to Israel. See 81:3–5; Dt 16:1–17. **122:5** There . . . the thrones of the house of David. Jerusa-lem is both the city of the Lord and the royal city of his chosen dynasty, through which he (ideally) protects and governs the nation (see 2:2,6–7; 89:3–4,19–37; 110; 2Sa 7:8–16 and notes). In postexilic times it remained, though now in Messianic hope, the city of David. **122:6–9** Prayers for Jerusalem's peace.

122:6 In Hebrew a beautiful wordplay tightly binds to-gether "pray," "peace," "Jerusalem" and "be secure." peace. See vv. 7–8; includes both security and prosperity. those who love you. The psalmist, those referred to in vv. 1,8 and all who love Jerusalem because they are devoted to the Lord and his chosen king. These constitute a loving broth-erhood, who worship together, pray together and seek each other's welfare as the people of God (see Ps 133). **122:7** walls . . . citadels. See 48:13 ("ramparts . . . cita-dels"). **122:8–9** For the sake of . . . For the sake of. Because Jerusalem is the place supreme where God and his people meet together in fruitful union, the psalmist vows to seek the city's peace. **Ps 123** A prayer of God's humble people for him to show mercy and so foil the contempt of the proud. See introduc-tion to Ps 124. As to its structure, a one-verse introduction is followed by two couplets, each developing its own theme. **123 title** See note on Ps 120 title. **123:1** whose throne is in heaven. The same God whose earthly throne is in the temple on Mount Zion (see 122:5 and note; see also 2:4; 9:11; 11:4; 80:1; 99:1; 113:5; 132:14). **123:2** slaves . . . maid. Similes by which the faithful (men and women alike) present themselves as humbly dependent on God. **123:4** the proud . . . the arrogant. Those who live by their own wits and strength (see notes on 10:2–11; 31:23) pour contempt on those who humbly rely on God, especially when those who rely on God suffer or do not prosper. **Ps 124** Israel's praise of the Lord for deliverance from powerful enemies—an appropriate sequel to Ps 123. Very likely a Levite speaks in vv. 1–5, while the worshipers answer in vv. 6–8. Like Ps 129 it divides into two well-balanced stanzas. **124 title** ascents. See note on Ps 120 title. Of David. Not all ancient witnesses to the text contain this element, and both language and theme suggest a postexilic date (see note

when men attacked us,
³when their anger flared against us,
they would have swallowed us alive;
⁴the flood ᵗ would have engulfed us,
the torrent ᵘ would have swept over us,
⁵the raging waters
would have swept us away.

⁶Praise be to the LORD,
who has not let us be torn by their teeth.
⁷We have escaped like a bird
out of the fowler's snare; ᵛ
the snare has been broken, ʷ
and we have escaped.
⁸Our help is in the name ˣ of the LORD,
the Maker of heaven ʸ and earth.

Psalm 125

A song of ascents.

¹Those who trust in the LORD are like Mount Zion, ᶻ
which cannot be shaken ᵃ but endures forever.
²As the mountains surround Jerusalem, ᵇ
so the LORD surrounds ᶜ his people
both now and forevermore.

³The scepter ᵈ of the wicked will not remain ᵉ

over the land allotted to the righteous,
for then the righteous might use their hands to do evil. ᶠ

⁴Do good, O LORD, ᵍ to those who are good,
to those who are upright in heart. ʰ
⁵But those who turn ⁱ to crooked ways ʲ
the LORD will banish ᵏ with the evildoers.

Peace be upon Israel. ˡ

Psalm 126

A song of ascents.

¹When the LORD brought back ᵐ the captives to ᵇ Zion,
we were like men who dreamed. ᶜ
²Our mouths were filled with laughter, ⁿ
our tongues with songs of joy. ᵒ
Then it was said among the nations,
"The LORD has done great things ᵖ for them."
³The LORD has done great things ᵠ for us,
and we are filled with joy. ʳ

⁴Restore our fortunes, ᵈ ˢ O LORD,
like streams in the Negev. ᵗ

124:4 ᵗPs 88:17
ᵘS Ps 18:4
124:7 ᵛS Ps 91:3
ʷPs 25:15
124:8
ˣS 1Sa 17:45
ʸGe 1:1;
Ps 115:15; 121:2; 134:3
125:1 ᶻPs 48:12;
Isa 33:20
ᵃPs 46:5; 48:2-5
125:2
ᵇS 1Ch 21:15
ᶜPs 32:10; Zec 2:4-5
125:3 ᵈS Est 4:11
ᵉPs 89:22;
Pr 22:8;
Isa 13:11; 14:5

ᶠ1Sa 24:10
125:4
ᵍS Ps 119:65
ʰS Ps 36:10
125:5
ⁱS Job 23:11
ʲPr 2:15; Isa 59:8
ᵏPs 92:7
ˡPs 128:6;
Pr 17:6; Gal 6:16
126:1
ᵐEzr 1:1-3;
Ps 85:1; Hos 6:11
126:2 ⁿS Ge 21:6
ᵒS Job 8:21;
S Ps 65:8
ᵖS Dt 10:21;
Ps 71:19; Lk 1:49
126:3
ᵠPs 106:21;
Joel 2:21,26
ʳS Ps 9:2; 16:11
126:4 ˢS Dt 30:3
ᵗS Ps 107:35;
Isa 43:19; 51:3

ᵇ1 Or LORD restored the fortunes of   ᶜ1 Or men restored to health   ᵈ4 Or Bring back our captives

---

on Ps 122 title). It may have been assigned to David because of supposed echoes of Ps 18; 69.
124:1–5 Let Israel acknowledge that the Lord alone has saved her from extinction (see 20:7; 94:17).
124:2 *men attacked.* Proud and arrogant men (123:4) may attack, but the Lord is Israel's help (v. 8).
124:3 *swallowed us.* Like death (see note on 49:14). But see 69:15.
124:4–5 *flood . . . torrent . . . raging waters.* See 18:16; see also 32:6; 69:1–2 and notes.
124:6–8 Response of praise for deliverance—with a vivid enrichment of the imagery.
124:6 *torn by their teeth.* As by wild beasts (see note on 7:2).
124:7 *escaped like a bird out of the fowler's snare.* A most apt figure for Israel's release from Babylonian captivity.
124:8 In climax, the great confession (see 121:2 and note).
Ps 125 Israel's peace: in testimony, prayer and benediction. The psalm is most likely postexilic and was probably spoken in the temple liturgy by a Levite.
125 title See note on Ps 120 title.
125:1–2 The solid security of God's people.
125:1 *Those who trust in the LORD.* God's "people" (v. 2) are also characterized as "the righteous" (v. 3) and "those who are good," "who are upright in heart" (v. 4). For a similar description of the "righteous" see 34:8–14 and note. *like Mount Zion.* In their security (see Ps 46; 48).
125:2 *mountains surround Jerusalem.* Though Jerusalem is not surrounded by a ring of peaks, the city is located in what OT writers called a mountainous region. *so the LORD surrounds his people.* As surely, as substantially and as immovably (see 2Ki 6:17; Zec 2:5).
125:3 Wicked rulers, whether by example or by oppres-

sion, tend to corrupt even the righteous, but the Lord will preserve his people also from this corrosive threat. *scepter of the wicked.* Probably referring to Persian rule (see Ne 9:36–37) and its invidious underlings, such as those Nehemiah had to contend with (see Ne 2:19; 4:1–3,7–8; 6:1–14,17–19; 13:7–8,28). *land allotted to the righteous.* The promised land (see 78:55).
125:4–5 To each according as he is and does—that is God's way (see 18:25–27); thus the confident prayer (v. 4) and the equally confident assertion (v. 5).
125:4 *heart.* See note on 4:7.
125:5 *Peace be upon Israel.* Perhaps a concise form of the priestly benediction (Nu 6:24–26).
Ps 126 A song of joy for restoration to Zion. If not composed for those who returned from Babylonian exile (see Ezra and Nehemiah)—the place of exile is not named—it surely served to voice the joy of that restored community (cf. Ps 42–43; 84; 137). The psalm divides into two stanzas of four (Hebrew) lines each, with their initial lines sharing a common theme. Thematic unity is further served by repetition (cf. vv. 2–3) and other key words ("the LORD," "songs of joy," "carrying"). References to God's action (vv. 1,3) frame the first stanza, while v. 2 offers exposition.
126 title See note on Ps 120 title.
126:1–3 Joy over restoration experienced.
126:1 *brought back the captives.* This translation and its alternative (see NIV text note here and on v. 4) have essentially the same result. *dreamed.* The wonder and joy of the reality were so marvelous that they hardly dared believe it. It seemed more like the dreams with which they had so long been tantalized.
126:2 The twofold effect: joy for those who returned and honor for God among the nations (see note on 46:10).

5Those who sow in tears[u]
 will reap[v] with songs of joy.[w]
6He who goes out weeping,[x]
 carrying seed to sow,
will return with songs of joy,
 carrying sheaves with him.

Psalm 127

A song of ascents. Of Solomon.

1Unless the LORD builds[y] the house,
 its builders labor in vain.
Unless the LORD watches[z] over the city,
 the watchmen stand guard in vain.
2In vain you rise early
 and stay up late,
toiling for food[a] to eat—
 for he grants sleep[b] to[e] those he loves.[c]

3Sons are a heritage from the LORD,
 children a reward[d] from him.
4Like arrows[e] in the hands of a warrior
 are sons born in one's youth.
5Blessed is the man
 whose quiver is full of them.[f]
They will not be put to shame
 when they contend with their enemies[g] in the gate.[h]

Psalm 128

A song of ascents.

1Blessed are all who fear the LORD,[i]
 who walk in his ways.[j]
2You will eat the fruit of your labor;[k]
 blessings and prosperity[l] will be yours.
3Your wife will be like a fruitful vine[m]
 within your house;
your sons[n] will be like olive shoots[o]
 around your table.
4Thus is the man blessed[p]
 who fears the LORD.[q]

5May the LORD bless you from Zion[r]
 all the days of your life;

126:5 [u]Ps 6:6; 80:5; Jer 50:4 [v]Gal 6:9 [w]Ps 16:11; 20:5; 23:6; Isa 35:10; 51:11; 60:15; 61:7; Jer 31:6-7, 12 **126:6** [x]S Nu 25:6; S Ps 30:5 **127:1** [y]Ps 78:69 [z]Ps 121:4 **127:2** [a]S Ge 3:17 [b]S Nu 6:26; S Job 11:18 [c]S Dt 33:12; Ecc 2:25 **127:3** [d]S Ge 1:28 **127:4** [e]Ps 112:2 **127:5** [f]Ps 128:2-3 [g]S Ge 24:60 [h]S Ge 23:10 **128:1** [i]Ps 103:11; S 112:1 [j]Ps 119:1-3 **128:2** [k]S Ps 58:11; 109:11; Isa 3:10 [l]S Ge 39:3; Pr 10:22 **128:3** [m]S Ge 49:22 [n]S Job 29:5 [o]Ps 52:8; 144:12 **128:4** [p]S Ps 1:1 [q]Ps 112:1 **128:5** [r]S Ps 20:2

[e]2 Or *eat— / for while they sleep he provides for*

126:4–6 Prayer for restoration to be completed.
126:4 *Restore our fortunes.* Either complete the repatriation of exiles or fully restore the security and prosperity of former times. *like streams in the Negev.* Which are bone-dry in summer, until the winter rains renew their flow.
126:5–6 An apt metaphorical portrayal of the joy already experienced and the joy anticipated. *in tears . . . weeping.* Even when sowing is accompanied by trouble or sorrow, harvest brings joy. For a related figure see 20:5.
Ps 127 Godly wisdom concerning home and hearth. Its theme is timeless; it reminded the pilgrims on their way to Jerusalem that all of life's securities and blessings are gifts from God rather than their own achievements (see Dt 28:1–14). Two balanced stanzas develop, respectively, two distinct but related themes.
127 title *ascents.* See note on Ps 120 title. *Of Solomon.* If Solomon was not the author (not all witnesses to the text ascribe it to him), it is easy to see why some thought him so.
127:1–2 It is the Lord who provides shelter, security and food.
127:1 *house.* Domestic shelter. *builders.* The Hebrew for this word is a pun on that for "Sons" in v. 3. *watches over.* See 121:3–8. *city.* The center of power, the refuge when enemies invade the land. *watchmen.* See 2Sa 13:34; 18:24–27; SS 3:3; 5:7.
127:2 *he grants sleep.* A good harvest is not the achievement of endless toil, but it is the result of God's blessing (see Pr 10:22; Mt 6:25–34; 1Pe 5:7). *those he loves.* See especially Dt 33:12; Jer 11:15.
127:3–5 Children are God's gift and a sign of his favor.
127:3 *Sons.* See note on v. 1. Children too are a gift—not the mere product of virility and fertility (see 113:9 and note; Ge 30:2). *heritage.* Emphasis here is on gift rather than possession. But perhaps more is implied. In the OT economy, an Israelite's "inheritance" from the Lord was first of all property in the promised land (Nu 26:53; Jos 11:23; Jdg 2:6), which provided a sure place in the life and "rest" (Jos 1:13) of the Lord's kingdom. But without children the inheritance in the land would be lost (Nu 27:8–11), so that offspring were a heritage in a double sense. *reward from him.* Bestowed by God on one who stands in his favor because he has been faithful.
127:5 *when they contend with their enemies.* Fathers with many sons have many defenders when falsely accused in court. Moreover, the very fact that they have many sons as God's "reward" (v. 3) testifies to God's favor toward them (in effect, they are God-provided character witnesses; see 128:3–4). *in the gate.* For "(city) gate" as court see Dt 17:5; 21:19; 22:15,24; 25:7; Isa 29:21 ("court"); Am 5:12 ("courts").
Ps 128 The blessedness of the godly man; another word of wisdom concerning hearth and home (see Ps 127). The concluding benediction suggests that the psalm originally served as a Levitical (or priestly) word of instruction to those assembled from their homes to worship in Jerusalem. Its date may well be preexilic. Structurally, the frame ("who fear[s] the LORD") around vv. 1–4 sets off those verses as the main body of the psalm.
128 title See note on Ps 120 title.
128:1–4 Blessedness affirmed.
128:1 *Blessed.* See note on 1:1. *fear the LORD.* See note on 34:8–14. *his ways.* See note on 25:4.
128:2 Blessings upon labor.
128:3 A faithful and fruitful wife. *vine.* Symbol of fruitfulness (Ge 49:22)—and perhaps also of sexual charms (SS 7:8–12) and festivity (Jdg 9:13). *within your house.* She is not like the faithless wife whose "feet never stay at home" (Pr 7:11). *olive shoots.* Ever green and with the promises of both long life and productivity (of staples: wood, fruit, oil). The vine and the olive tree are frequently paired in the OT (as, e.g., in Ex 23:11). Both were especially long-lived, and they produced the wine and the oil that played such a central role in the lives of the people. *around your table.* Converting each family meal into a banquet of domestic joys.
128:5–6 The benediction pronounced—completing the scope of true blessedness: unbroken prosperity, secure relationship with God and secure national existence (the prosperity of Jerusalem entailed both), and long life.
128:5 *from Zion.* See 9:11 and note; 20:2; 135:21.

may you see the prosperity of
  Jerusalem, *s*
6 and may you live to see your
  children's children. *t*

Peace be upon Israel. *u*

Psalm 129

A song of ascents.

[1] They have greatly oppressed *v* me from
  my youth *w*—
  let Israel say *x*—
[2] they have greatly oppressed me from
  my youth,
  but they have not gained the victory *y*
  over me.
[3] Plowmen have plowed my back
  and made their furrows long.
[4] But the LORD is righteous; *z*
  he has cut me free *a* from the cords
  of the wicked. *b*

[5] May all who hate Zion *c*
  be turned back in shame. *d*
[6] May they be like grass on the roof, *e*
  which withers *f* before it can grow;
[7] with it the reaper cannot fill his hands, *g*
  nor the one who gathers fill his arms.
[8] May those who pass by not say,
  "The blessing of the LORD be upon
  you;
  we bless you *h* in the name of the
  LORD."

Reference column

128:5 *s*Ps 122:9
128:6 *t*S Ge 48:11
  *u*S Ps 125:5
129:1 *v*S Ex 1:13
  *w*S Ps 88:15
  *x*Ps 124:1
129:2 *y*Jer 1:19;
  15:20; 20:11;
  Mt 16:18
129:4 *z*S Ex 9:27
  *a*Ps 37:9
  *b*Ps 140:5
129:5 *c*Mic 4:11
  *d*S Ps 70:2
129:6 *e*Isa 37:27
  *f*S 2Ki 19:26;
  Ps 102:11
129:7 *g*S Dt 28:38;
  Ps 79:12
129:8 *h*Ps 118:26

130:1 *i*S Job 30:19;
  Ps 42:7; La 3:55
  *j*Ps 22:2; 55:17;
  142:5
130:2 *k*S Ps 27:7;
  28:2 *l*S 2Ch 6:40
  *m*S Ps 28:6;
  31:22; 86:6;
  140:6
130:3 *n*S 1Sa 6:20;
  S Ezr 9:15;
  Ps 143:2; Na 1:6;
  Rev 6:17
130:4 *o*S Ex 34:7;
  S 2Sa 24:14;
  S Jer 31:34
  *p*S 1Ki 8:40
130:5 *q*S Ps 27:14;
  Isa 8:17; 26:8;
  30:18; 49:23
  *r*S Ps 5:3
  *s*S Ps 119:74
130:6 *t*Ps 63:6
  *u*S 2Sa 23:4
130:7 *v*S Ps 25:5;
  S 71:14
  *w*S 1Ch 21:13
  *x*S Ps 111:9;
S Ro 3:24 130:8 *y*Lk 1:68 *z*S Ex 34:7; S Mt 1:21 131:1
*a*Ps 101:5; Isa 2:12; Ro 12:16 *b*S 2Sa 22:28; S Job 41:34

Psalm 130

A song of ascents.

[1] Out of the depths *i* I cry to you, *j*
  O LORD;
[2] O Lord, hear my voice. *k*
  Let your ears be attentive *l*
  to my cry for mercy. *m*

[3] If you, O LORD, kept a record of sins,
  O Lord, who could stand? *n*
[4] But with you there is forgiveness; *o*
  therefore you are feared. *p*

[5] I wait for the LORD, *q* my soul waits, *r*
  and in his word *s* I put my hope.
[6] My soul waits for the Lord
  more than watchmen *t* wait for the
  morning,
  more than watchmen wait for the
  morning. *u*

[7] O Israel, put your hope *v* in the LORD,
  for with the LORD is unfailing love *w*
  and with him is full redemption. *x*
[8] He himself will redeem *y* Israel
  from all their sins. *z*

Psalm 131

A song of ascents. Of David.

[1] My heart is not proud, *a* O LORD,
  my eyes are not haughty; *b*

128:6 *Peace be upon Israel.* See 125:5 and note.
Ps 129 Israel's prayer for the continued withering of all her powerful enemies. The rescue celebrated (v. 4) is probably from Babylonian exile. Against the background of Ps 124–128, this prayer for the withholding of God's blessing is set in sharp relief. Like Ps 124 (with which Ps 129 shares other affinities), the psalm is composed of two nicely balanced stanzas.
129 title See note on Ps 120 title.
129:1–4 The wicked oppressors have not prevailed.
129:1 *from my youth.* From the time Israel was enslaved in Egypt, she has suffered much at the hands of hostile powers.
129:2 *have not gained the victory.* Have not succeeded in their efforts to destroy Israel totally or to hold her permanently in bondage.
129:4 *righteous.* See note on 4:1.
129:5–8 May all who hate Zion wither.
129:5 See note on 5:10.
129:6 *like grass on the roof.* May those who would "plow" the backs of Israel (see v. 3) wither like grass that sprouts on the flat, sunbaked housetops, where no plow can prepare a nurturing soil to sustain the young shoots—and so there is no harvest (v. 7).
129:8 *those who pass by.* Whoever may pass by the harvesters in the fields will exchange no joyful greetings (Ru 2:4) because the hands of the harvesters will be empty.
Ps 130 A testimony of trust in the Lord—by one who knows that even though he is a sinner, the Lord hears his cry out of the depths. The language of the psalm suggests a

postexilic date. This is the sixth of seven penitential psalms (see introduction to Ps 6). Composed of four couplets, the psalm further divides into two halves of two couplets each.
130 title See note on Ps 120 title.
130:1–4 A prayer for mercy, and grounds for assurance.
130:1 *the depths.* As in 69:2 (see notes on 30:1; 32:6).
130:4 *there is forgiveness.* No doubt recalling such reassuring words as Ex 34:6–7. *feared.* Honored, worshiped, trusted and served as the one true God. If God were not forgiving, people could only flee from him in terror.
130:5–8 Trust in the Lord: a personal testimony, expanding into a reassuring invitation (see 131:3).
130:5 *I wait.* In hopeful expectation. *my soul.* See note on 6:3. *his word.* Especially his covenant promises (see 119:25,28,37,42,49,65,74,81,107,114,147).
130:6 *watchmen.* See 127:1; 2Sa 13:34; 18:24–27; SS 3:3; 5:7. *the morning.* See introduction to Ps 57; see also note on 59:9.
130:7 *unfailing love.* See note on 6:4.
130:8 *from all their sins.* From the root of trouble—but also from all its consequences. This greatest of all hopes has been fulfilled in Christ.
Ps 131 A confession of humble trust in the Lord —appropriately placed next to Ps 130.
131 title *ascents.* See note on Ps 120 title.
131:1 *heart.* See note on 4:7. *proud . . . haughty.* More than all else, it is human pride that pits man against God (see note on 31:23; cf. 2Sa 6:21–22). *concern myself with.* (Presume to) walk among, live among, be party to. *great*

I do not concern myself with great
    matters c
or things too wonderful for me. d
2But I have stilled and quieted my soul; e
    like a weaned child with its mother,
    like a weaned child is my soul f
    within me.

3O Israel, put your hope g in the LORD
    both now and forevermore. h

Psalm 132

132:8-10pp — 2Ch 6:41-42

A song of ascents.

1O LORD, remember David
    and all the hardships he endured. i

2He swore an oath to the LORD
    and made a vow to the Mighty One
    of Jacob: j
3"I will not enter my house k
    or go to my bed—

131:1 c Jer 45:5
d S Job 5:9;
Ps 139:6
131:2 e S Ps 116:7
f Mt 18:3;
1Co 13:11; 14:20
131:3 g S Ps 25:5;
119:43; 130:7
h S Ps 113:2
132:1 i 1Sa 18:11;
S 2Sa 15:14
132:2 j S Ge 49:24;
Isa 49:26; 60:16
132:3 k S 2Sa 7:2,
27
132:5 l S 1Ki 8:17;
Ac 7:46
132:6 m S 1Sa 17:12
n S Jos 9:17;
S 1Sa 7:2
132:7 o S 2Sa 15:25;
Ps 5:7; 122:1
p S 1Ch 28:2
132:8 q S Nu 10:35
132:9 r S Job 27:6;
Isa 61:3,10;
Zec 3:4; Mal 3:3;

4I will allow no sleep to my eyes,
    no slumber to my eyelids,
5till I find a place l for the LORD,
    a dwelling for the Mighty One of
    Jacob."

6We heard it in Ephrathah, m
    we came upon it in the fields of
    Jaar f: g n
7"Let us go to his dwelling place; o
    let us worship at his footstool p—
8arise, O LORD, q and come to your
    resting place,
    you and the ark of your might.
9May your priests be clothed with
    righteousness; r
    may your saints s sing for joy."

10For the sake of David your servant,

Eph 6:14 s Ps 16:3; 30:4; 149:5

f 6 That is, Kiriath Jearim   g 6 Or *heard of it in
Ephrathah, / we found it in the fields of Jaar.* (And no
quotes around verses 7-9)

---

matters ... too wonderful for me. Heroic exploits or
achievements to rival, if not substitute for, the mighty works
of God. The focus seems to be on not claiming Godlike
powers (thus trusting in God for deliverance and blessing)
rather than on seeking (or claiming) Godlike understanding.
131:2 *soul.* See note on 6:3. *weaned child.* A child of four
or five who walks trustingly beside his mother.
131:3 As he has done, so ought all Israel—for all time.
Ps 132 A prayer for God's favor on the son of David who
reigns on David's throne—as the structure makes clear (and
see note on v. 10). Its language suggests a date early in the
monarchy. The venerable belief that it was composed for the
dedication of the temple may be correct (compare vv. 8-10
with 2Ch 6:41-42), but the possibility cannot be ruled out
that it was used in the coronation ritual (cf. Ps 2; 72; 110).
The author of Chronicles places the prayer (or a portion of it)
on the lips of the king himself. In the postexilic liturgy it had
Messianic implications.
    Two verses of petition (vv. 1,10) are each followed (in
Hebrew) by two four-line stanzas, all having an identical
form: an introductory line followed by a three-line quotation
(see the structure of these quotations). A final couplet brings
the prayer to its climactic conclusion. The four stanzas,
together with the final couplet, ground the prayer made in
vv. 1,10. Verses 2-9 appeal to David's oath to the Lord to
find a "place" for the Lord and to his bringing the ark to its
"resting place," while vv. 11-18 appeal to the Lord's oath to
David and to his election of Zion as his "resting place" (but
see note on v. 10).
132 title See note on Ps 120 title.
132:1 *remember.* See 20:3; see also 1Ki 11:12-13;
15:4-5. *hardships.* Those he took on himself in his vow (vv.
2-5; see Nu 30:13, where the same technical term for a
self-denying oath is used).
132:2 *He swore an oath.* This prayer for David's son is
grounded in the special relationship between David and the
Lord, as epitomized in their mutual oaths (see vv. 11-12). In
2Sa 6-7, which narrates the events here recalled, David's
oath is not mentioned. *LORD ... Mighty One of Jacob.* See v.
5; Isa 1:24; see also note on 3:7. *Jacob.* A synonym for Israel
(see Ge 32:28).
132:6 *it. ... it.* Often thought to refer to the ark (see second
NIV text note), but more likely it refers to the call to worship

that follows (in Hebrew the pronoun is feminine, but the
Hebrew for "ark" is masculine). *Ephrathah.* The region
around Bethlehem, David's hometown (see Ru 4:11; Mic
5:2). *fields of Jaar.* See first NIV text note; see also 2Sa 6:2
and first NIV text note there. The call to worship is depicted
as emanating from David's city and the city where the ark
had been since the days of Samuel (see 1Sa 7:1). The call
appears to come from a time after the temple had been
built—thus involving a poetic compression of events.
132:7 *footstool.* See 99:5 and note.
132:8 *arise.* Although the Hebrew omits (a common feature in Hebrew poetry) an introductory word, such as "saying," vv. 8-9 are probably words on the lips of the worshipers. See introduction to Ps 24. *resting place.* As the promised
land was Israel's place of rest at the end of her wanderings
(see Nu 10:33; Jos 1:13; Mic 2:10), so the temple was the
Lord's resting place after he had been moving about in a tent
(see 2Sa 7:6; see also 1Ch 28:2). The expression may suggest that the temple was the place of God's throne (v. 14).
ark of your might. See note on 78:61.
132:9 *clothed with.* Beyond their normal priestly
garb—may their ministry bear the character of (see Job
29:14; Pr 31:25), i.e., result in. *righteousness.* Since the
corresponding word in v. 16 is "salvation," the same word
used by the author of Chronicles when quoting this verse
(2Ch 6:41), and since "righteousness" and "salvation" are
often paralleled (40:10; 51:14; 71:15; 98:2; Isa 45:8;
46:13; 51:5-6; 56:1; 59:17; 60:17-18; 61:10; 62:1), the
reference is clearly to God's righteousness that effects the
salvation of his people (see note on 4:1). *saints.* See note on
4:3.
132:10 See v. 1. *your servant.* See note on Ps 18 title. *do
not reject.* Do not refuse his petitions (as in 1Ki 2:16-17,20;
see 1Ki 8:59; 2Ch 6:41-42). If, as some have proposed, the
petitions in vv. 1,10 form a frame around the first half of the
psalm, the second half offers assurance that the prayer will be
heard (perhaps spoken by a priest or Levite). In any event,
David's vow to provide the Lord a dwelling place, which
would be for his royal sons and for Israel a house of prayer
(see 1Ki 8:27-53; 9:3; 2Ch 7:15-16; Isa 56:7), is made the
basis for the appeal that God will hear his anointed's prayer.
your anointed one. See note on 2:2.

do not reject your anointed one.

11The LORD swore an oath to David,[t]
a sure oath that he will not revoke:
"One of your own descendants[u]
I will place on your throne—
12if your sons keep my covenant[v]
and the statutes I teach them,
then their sons will sit
on your throne[w] for ever and ever."

13For the LORD has chosen Zion,[x]
he has desired it for his dwelling:[y]
14"This is my resting place for ever and ever;[z]
here I will sit enthroned,[a] for I have desired it—
15I will bless her with abundant provisions;
her poor will I satisfy with food.[b]
16I will clothe her priests[c] with salvation,
and her saints will ever sing for joy.[d]

17"Here I will make a horn[h] grow[e] for David
and set up a lamp[f] for my anointed one.[g]
18I will clothe his enemies with shame,[h]
but the crown on his head[i] will be resplendent."

132:11 [t]S Ps 89:3-4,35 [u]S 1Ch 17:11-14; S Mt 1:1; Lk 3:31 **132:12** [v]2Ch 6:16; S Ps 25:10 [w]Lk 1:32; Ac 2:30 **132:13** [x]S Ex 15:17; Ps 48:1-2; S 68:16 [y]S 1Ki 8:13 **132:14** [z]ver 8; Ps 68:16 [a]S 2Sa 6:2; Ps 80:1 **132:15** [b]Ps 107:9; 147:14 **132:16** [c]S 2Ch 6:41 [d]S Job 8:21; Ps 149:5 **132:17** [e]S 1Sa 2:10; Ps 92:10; Eze 29:21; S Lk 1:69 [f]1Ki 11:36; 2Ki 8:19; 2Ch 21:7; Ps 18:28 [g]S Ps 84:9 **132:18** [h]S Job 8:22 [i]S 2Sa 12:30

133:1 [j]S Ge 13:8; S Ro 12:10 [k]Jn 17:11 **133:2** [l]S Ex 29:7 **133:3** [m]Job 29:19; Pr 19:12; Isa 18:4; 26:19; 45:8; Hos 14:5; Mic 5:7

Psalm 133

A song of ascents. Of David.

1How good and pleasant it is
when brothers live together[j] in unity![k]
2It is like precious oil poured on the head,[l]
running down on the beard,
running down on Aaron's beard,
down upon the collar of his robes.
3It is as if the dew[m] of Hermon[n]
were falling on Mount Zion.[o]
For there the LORD bestows his blessing,[p]
even life forevermore.[q]

Psalm 134

A song of ascents.

1Praise the LORD, all you servants[r] of the LORD
who minister[s] by night[t] in the house of the LORD.
2Lift up your hands[u] in the sanctuary[v]

[n]S Dt 3:8; S 4:48 [o]S Ex 15:17; S Ps 2:6; 74:2 [p]S Lev 25:21 [q]S Ps 21:4 **134:1** [r]S Ps 113:1; 135:1-2; Rev 19:5 [s]S Nu 16:9; S 1Ch 15:2 [t]S 1Ch 23:30 **134:2** [u]S Ps 28:2; 1Ti 2:8 [v]Ps 15:1

h *17 Horn* here symbolizes strong one, that is, king.

132:11–12 The Lord's covenant with David is recalled, as grounds for the prayer. These and vv. 13–18 are a poetic recollection of 1Ki 9:1–5 (see 2Ch 7:11–18).
132:11 *swore an oath.* See v. 2 and note. 2Sa 7 does not mention an oath, but elsewhere God's promise to David is called a covenant (89:3,28,34,39; 2Sa 23:5; Isa 55:3), and covenants were made on oath. *will not revoke.* See 110:4.
132:12 *covenant . . . statutes.* The stipulations of the Sinai covenant, which all Israelites were to keep (see 1Sa 10:25 and note; see also 1Ki 2:3–4).
132:13–16 The Lord's election of Zion recalled, as grounds for the prayer.
132:13 *desired it for his dwelling.* David's and the Lord's desires harmonize (see Dt 12:5–14).
132:15 The Lord enthroned in his resting place (see vv. 8,14) will bless the land, making it a place of rest for his people (see Dt 12:9; Jos 1:13; 1Ki 5:4).
132:16 See note on v. 9.
132:17–18 Concluding word of assurance, which addresses the petition (vv. 1,10) directly and climactically.
132:17 *horn.* The Lord's anointed (see NIV text note). *grow.* Like a plant or branch. *set up a lamp for.* See note on 1Ki 11:36.
132:18 *clothe . . . with shame.* In contrast with v. 16. *be resplendent.* Lit. "blossom"—subtly evoking the imagery: grow (v. 17) and blossom.
Ps 133 A song in praise of brotherly unity among the people of God. If David was the author (see title), he may have been moved to write it by some such occasion as when, after many years of conflict, all Israel came to Hebron to make him king (2Sa 5:1–3). The first and last (Hebrew) lines (vv. 1,3b) frame the whole with the song's main theme. Next to these an inner frame (lines 2,4) elaborates with two striking complementary similes (vv. 2a,3a). The center line (v. 2b) extends the first simile.
133 title *ascents.* See note on Ps 120 title. *Of David.* Not all textual sources ascribe the psalm to him.
133:1 *good and pleasant.* See 135:3; 147:1.
133:2 *like precious oil . . . on Aaron's beard . . . upon the collar of his robes.* The oil of Aaron's anointing (Ex 29:7; Lev 21:10) saturated all the hair of his beard and ran down on his priestly robes, signifying his total consecration to holy service. Similarly, brotherly harmony sanctifies God's people.
133:3 *dew of Hermon . . . on Mount Zion.* A dew as profuse as that of Mount Hermon would make Mount Zion (or the mountains of Zion) richly fruitful (see Ge 27:28; Hag 1:10; Zec 8:12). So would brotherly unity make Israel richly fruitful. The two similes (vv. 2–3) are well chosen: God's blessings flowed to Israel through the priestly ministrations at the sanctuary (Ex 29:44–46; Lev 9:22–24; Nu 6:24–26)—epitomizing God's redemptive mercies—and through heaven's dew that sustained life in the fields—epitomizing God's providential mercies in the creation order. *life.* The great covenant blessing (see Dt 30:15, 19–20; 32:47).
Ps 134 A liturgy of praise—a brief exchange between the worshipers, as they are about to leave the temple after the evening service, and the Levites, who kept the temple watch through the night. In the Psalter it concludes the "songs of ascent," as Ps 117 concludes a collection of Hallelujah psalms (Ps 111–117). Its date is probably postexilic.
134 title See note on Ps 120 title.
134:1–2 The departing worshipers call on the Levites to continue the praise of the Lord through the night (see 1Ch 9:33).
134:2 *Lift up your hands.* See 63:4.

and praise the LORD. w

³May the LORD, the Maker of heaven x
and earth,
bless you from Zion. y

Psalm 135

135:15–20pp — Ps 115:4–11

¹Praise the LORD. i

Praise the name of the LORD;
praise him, you servants z of the
LORD,
²you who minister in the house a of the
LORD,
in the courts b of the house of our
God.

³Praise the LORD, for the LORD is good; c
sing praise to his name, d for that is
pleasant. e
⁴For the LORD has chosen Jacob f to be
his own,
Israel to be his treasured possession. g

⁵I know that the LORD is great, h
that our Lord is greater than all
gods. i
⁶The LORD does whatever pleases him, j
in the heavens and on the earth, k
in the seas and all their depths.
⁷He makes clouds rise from the ends of
the earth;
he sends lightning with the rain l
and brings out the wind m from his
storehouses. n

⁸He struck down the firstborn o of Egypt,
the firstborn of men and animals.

⁹He sent his signs p and wonders into
your midst, O Egypt,
against Pharaoh and all his servants. q
¹⁰He struck down many r nations
and killed mighty kings—
¹¹Sihon s king of the Amorites, t
Og king of Bashan u
and all the kings of Canaan v —
¹²and he gave their land as an
inheritance, w
an inheritance to his people Israel.

¹³Your name, O LORD, endures forever, x
your renown, y O LORD, through all
generations.
¹⁴For the LORD will vindicate his people z
and have compassion on his
servants. a

¹⁵The idols of the nations b are silver and
gold,
made by the hands of men. c
¹⁶They have mouths, but cannot speak, d
eyes, but they cannot see;
¹⁷they have ears, but cannot hear,
nor is there breath e in their mouths.
¹⁸Those who make them will be like
them,
and so will all who trust in them.

¹⁹O house of Israel, praise the LORD; f
O house of Aaron, praise the LORD;
²⁰O house of Levi, praise the LORD;
you who fear him, praise the LORD.
²¹Praise be to the LORD from Zion, g

134:2 wPs 33:2; 103:1
134:3 xS Ps 124:8 yS Lev 25:21; S Ps 20:2
135:1 zNe 7:73
135:2 aS 1Ch 15:2; Lk 2:37 bS Ps 116:19
135:3 cS 1Ch 16:34; S Ps 119:68 dS Ps 68:4 eS Ps 92:1; 147:1
135:4 fS Dt 10:15 gEx 19:5; Dt 7:6; Mal 3:17; S Tit 2:14
135:5 hS Ps 48:1; 145:3 iS Ex 12:12; S 1Ch 16:25; S Job 21:22
135:6 jPs 115:3; Da 4:35 kMt 6:10
135:7 lS Job 5:10; Ps 68:9; Isa 30:23; Jer 10:13; 51:16; Joel 2:23; Zec 10:1 mAm 4:13 nS Dt 28:12
135:8 oS Ex 4:23; S 12:12
135:9 pS Ex 7:9 qPs 136:10-15
135:10 rNu 21:21-25; Jos 24:8-11; Ps 44:2; 78:55; 136:17-21
135:11 sS Nu 21:21 tS Nu 21:26 uS Nu 21:33 vS Jos 12:7-24; 24:12
135:12 wS Dt 29:8
135:13 xS Ex 3:15 yS Ps 102:12
135:14 zS 1Sa 24:15; Heb 10:30* aS Dt 32:36 **135:15** bPs 96:5; Rev 9:20 cIsa 2:8; 31:7; 37:19; 40:19; Jer 1:16; 10:5 **135:16** dS 1Ki 18:26 **135:17** eJer 10:14; Hab 2:19 **135:19** fS Ps 22:23 **135:21** gPs 128:5; 134:3

i1 Hebrew *Hallelu Yah*; also in verses 3 and 21

134:3 One of the Levites responds with a benediction on the worshipers (see note on 121:2; see also 124:8; 128:5).
Ps 135 A call to praise the Lord—the one true God: Lord of all creation, Lord over all the nations, Israel's Redeemer. No doubt postexilic, it echoes many lines found elsewhere in the OT. It was clearly composed for the temple liturgy. For its place in the Great Hallel see note on Ps 120 title. Framed with "Hallelujahs" (as are also Ps 146–150), its first and last stanzas are also calls to praise. Recital of God's saving acts for Israel in Egypt and Canaan (vv. 8–12) makes up the middle of seven stanzas, while the remaining four constitute two pairs related to each other by theme and language (vv. 3–4, 13–14; vv. 5–7, 15–18).
135:1–2 Initial call to praise, addressed to priests and Levites (see 134:1–2).
135:1,3,13 *name*. See note on 5:11.
135:3–4 A central reason for Israel to praise the Lord (see vv. 13–14).
135:3 *that is pleasant*. See 133:1. Or "he (the Lord) is beautiful" (see 27:4 and note).
135:4 *Jacob*. A synonym for Israel (see Ge 32:28). *his treasured possession*. See Ex 19:5 and note.
135:5–7 The Lord is great as well as good (v. 3); he is the absolute Lord in all creation (cf. the word about idols in vv. 15–18; see Jer 10:11–16; see also 115:3 and 96:5; 97:7

and notes).
135:6 *does whatever pleases him*. The idols can do nothing (vv. 16–17); they are themselves "done" (made) by their worshipers (v. 18). *heavens . . . earth . . . seas*. The three great domains of the visible creation, as the ancients viewed it (see Ge 1:8–10 and introduction to Ps 104).
135:7 *He makes clouds*. The Lord, not Baal or any other god, brings the life-giving rains (see Ps 29). *wind*. See 104:4; 148:8. The idols do not even have any "wind" (breath) in their mouths (v. 17). *storehouses*. See 33:7 and note; Job 38:22.
135:8–12 The Lord's triumph over Egypt and over the kings whose lands became Israel's inheritance, a concise recollection of Ex 7–14; Nu 21:21–35; Joshua.
135:13–14 See vv. 3–4 and note.
135:14 *vindicate*. Uphold against all attacks by the world powers both Israel's cause and her claim that the Lord is the only true God. *have compassion on*. See Ex 34:6–7. *his servants*. His covenant people.
135:15–18 The powerlessness of the false gods and of those who trust in them (see vv. 5–7 and note; see also 115:4–8 and notes).
135:19–21 Concluding call to praise, addressed to all who are assembled at the temple (see 115:9–11; 118:2–4).

to him who dwells in Jerusalem. *h*

Praise the LORD.

Psalm 136

¹Give thanks *i* to the LORD, for he is
good. *j*
     His love endures forever. *k*
²Give thanks *l* to the God of gods. *m*
     His love endures forever.
³Give thanks *n* to the Lord of lords: *o*
     His love endures forever.
⁴to him who alone does great wonders, *p*
     His love endures forever.
⁵who by his understanding *q* made the
heavens, *r*
     His love endures forever.
⁶who spread out the earth *s* upon the
waters, *t*
     His love endures forever.
⁷who made the great lights *u* —
     His love endures forever.
⁸the sun to govern *v* the day,
     His love endures forever.
⁹the moon and stars to govern the night;
     His love endures forever.
¹⁰to him who struck down the firstborn *w*
,of Egypt
     His love endures forever.
¹¹and brought Israel out *x* from among
them
     His love endures forever.
¹²with a mighty hand *y* and outstretched
arm; *z*
     His love endures forever.
¹³to him who divided the Red Sea *a*
asunder
     His love endures forever.
¹⁴and brought Israel through *b* the midst
of it,
     His love endures forever.

¹⁵but swept Pharaoh and his army into
the Red Sea; *c*
     His love endures forever.
¹⁶to him who led his people through the
desert, *d*
     His love endures forever.
¹⁷who struck down great kings, *e*
     His love endures forever.
¹⁸and killed mighty kings *f* —
     His love endures forever.
¹⁹Sihon king of the Amorites *g*
     His love endures forever.
²⁰and Og king of Bashan *h* —
     His love endures forever.
²¹and gave their land *i* as an
inheritance, *j*
     His love endures forever.
²²an inheritance *k* to his servant Israel; *l*
     His love endures forever.
²³to the One who remembered us *m* in our
low estate
     His love endures forever.
²⁴and freed us *n* from our enemies, *o*
     His love endures forever.
²⁵and who gives food *p* to every creature.
     His love endures forever.

²⁶Give thanks *q* to the God of heaven. *r*
     His love endures forever. *s*

Psalm 137

¹By the rivers of Babylon *t* we sat and
wept *u*
when we remembered Zion. *v*
²There on the poplars *w*

135:21
*h*S 1Ki 8:13;
S 2Ch 6:2
136:1 *i*Ps 105:1
/Ps 100:5; 106:1;
145:9; Jer 33:11;
Na 1:7 *k*ver 2-26;
S 2Ch 5:13;
S Ezr 3:11;
Ps 118:1-4
136:2 *l*Ps 105:1
*m*S Dt 10:17
136:3 *n*Ps 105:1
*o*S Dt 10:17;
S 1Ti 6:15
136:4
*p*S Ex 3:20;
S Job 9:10
136:5 *q*Pr 3:19;
Jer 51:15
136:6 *s*S Ge 1:1;
Isa 42:5;
Jer 10:12; 33:2
*t*S Ge 1:6
136:7 *u*Ge 1:14,
16; Ps 74:16;
Jas 1:17
136:8 *v*S Ge 1:16
136:10
*w*S Ex 4:23;
S 12:12
136:11
*x*S Ex 6:6; 13:3;
Ps 105:43
136:12
*y*S Ex 3:20;
S Dt 5:15
*z*S Dt 9:29
136:13
*a*S Ps 78:13
136:14
*b*Ex 14:22;
Ps 106:9
136:15
*c*S Ex 14:27
136:16
*d*S Ex 13:18;
Ps 78:52
136:17
*e*Nu 21:23-25;
Jos 24:8-11;
Ps 78:55;
135:9-12
136:18 /Dt 29:7;
S Jos 12:7-24
136:19
*g*Nu 21:21-25
136:20
*h*Nu 21:33-35
136:21 /Jos 12:1
/S Dt 1:38;
S Jos 14:1
136:22
*k*S Dt 29:8;
Ps 78:55

136:23
*m*Ps 78:39; 103:14; 115:12 136:24 *n*S Jos 10:14; S Ne 9:28
*o*S Dt 6:19 136:25 *p*S Ge 1:30; S Mt 6:26 136:26 *q*Ps 105:1
*r*S Ps 115:3 *s*S Ezr 3:11 137:1 *t*Eze 1:1,3; 3:15; 10:15
*u*Ne 1:4 *v*Isa 3:26; La 1:4 137:2 *w*S Lev 23:40

/Isa 20:3; 41:8; 42:19; 43:10; 44:1,21; 45:4; 49:5-7 136:23
*i*13 Hebrew *Yam Suph*; that is, Sea of Reeds; also in verse
15

Ps 136 A liturgy of praise to the Lord as Creator and as
Israel's Redeemer. Its theme and many of its verses parallel
much of Ps 135. Most likely a Levitical song leader led the
recital, while the Levitical choir (1Ch 16:41; 2Ch 5:13; Ezr
3:11) or the worshipers (2Ch 7:3,6; 20:21) responded with
the refrain (see 106:1; 107:1; 118:1–4,29). This liturgy
concludes the Great Hallel (see note on Ps 120 title). Following the initial call to praise (vv. 1–3), the recital devotes six
verses to God's creation acts (vv. 4–9), six to his deliverance
of Israel out of Egypt (vv. 10–15), one to the desert journey
(v. 16) and six to the conquest (vv. 17–22). The four concluding verses return to the same basic themes in reverse
order: God's action in history in behalf of his people (vv.
23–24), God's action in the creation order (v. 25) and a
closing call to praise (v. 26).
136:1–3,26 *Give thanks to.* Or "Praise" (see 7:17 and
note).
136:2 *the God of gods.* See Dt 10:17; see also 135:5.
136:5 *by his understanding.* See Pr 3:19; Jer 10:12.
136:6 *upon the waters.* See 24:2 and note.

136:7–9 Direct echoes of Ge 1:16.
136:23–24 Probably a concluding summary of the deliverance recalled above, but may allude also to the deliverances
experienced during the period of the judges and the reign of
David.
136:26 *the God of heaven.* A Persian title for God (see note
on Da 2:18) found frequently in Ezra, Nehemiah and Daniel.
Its intent is similar to that of the language of vv. 2–3.
Ps 137 A plaintive song of the exile—of one who has
recently returned from Babylon but in whose soul there
lingers the bitter memory of the years in a foreign land and of
the cruel events that led to that enforced stay. Here speaks
the same deep love of Zion as that found in Ps 42–43; 46;
48; 84; 122; 126. The 12 poetic lines of the Hebrew song
divide symmetrically into three stanzas of four lines each: the
remembered sorrow and torment (vv. 1–3), an oath of total
commitment to Jerusalem (vv. 4–6), a call for retribution on
Edom and Babylon (vv. 7–9).
137:1 *rivers.* The Tigris and Euphrates and the many canals
associated with them. *we sat.* Again and again the thought of

we hung our harps,[x]

[3]for there our captors[y] asked us for
  songs,
  our tormentors demanded[z] songs of
    joy;
  they said, "Sing us one of the songs
    of Zion!" [a]

[4]How can we sing the songs of the
  Lord[b]
  while in a foreign land?
[5]If I forget you,[c] O Jerusalem,
  may my right hand forget its skill.
[6]May my tongue cling to the roof[d] of my
  mouth
  if I do not remember[e] you,
  if I do not consider Jerusalem[f]
  my highest joy.

[7]Remember, O Lord, what the
  Edomites[g] did
  on the day Jerusalem fell.[h]
  "Tear it down," they cried,
  "tear it down to its foundations!" [i]

[8]O Daughter of Babylon, doomed to
  destruction,[j]
  happy is he who repays you
  for what you have done to us—
[9]he who seizes your infants
  and dashes them[k] against the rocks.

137:2
[x]Job 30:31;
Isa 24:8;
Eze 26:13;
Am 6:5
137:3
[y]Ps 79:1-4; La 1:5
[z]S Job 30:9;
Ps 80:6
[a]Eze 16:57; 22:4;
34:29
137:4
[b]S Ne 12:46
137:5 [c]Isa 2:3;
56:7; 65:11;
66:20
137:6
[d]S Ps 22:15
[e]Ne 2:3
[f]S Dt 4:29;
Jer 51:50; Eze 6:9
137:7
[g]S Ge 25:30;
S 2Ch 28:17;
S Ps 83:6;
La 4:21-22
[h]2Ki 25:1-10;
Ob 1:11 /Ps 74:8
137:8 /Isa 13:1,
19; 47:1-15;
Jer 25:12,26;
50:1; 50:2-51:58
137:9
[k]S 2Ki 8:12;
S Isa 13:16;
Lk 19:44

138:1 /Ps 95:3;
96:4 [m]Ps 27:6;
108:1
138:2
[n]S 1Ki 8:29;
S Ps 5:7
[o]Ps 74:21; 97:12;
140:13
[p]Ps 108:4; 115:1
[q]Ps 119:9

Psalm 138

Of David.

[1]I will praise you, O Lord, with all my
  heart;
  before the "gods" [l] I will sing[m] your
  praise.
[2]I will bow down toward your holy
  temple[n]
  and will praise your name[o]
  for your love and your faithfulness,[p]
  for you have exalted above all things
  your name and your word. [q]
[3]When I called,[r] you answered me;[s]
  you made me bold[t] and
  stouthearted. [u]

[4]May all the kings of the earth[v] praise
  you, O Lord,
  when they hear the words of your
  mouth.
[5]May they sing[w] of the ways of the
  Lord,
  for the glory of the Lord[x] is great.

[6]Though the Lord is on high, he looks
  upon the lowly,[y]

138:3 [r]Ps 18:6; 30:2; 99:6; 116:4 [s]S Ps 118:5 [t]Pr 28:1;
S Ac 4:29 [u]Ps 28:7 **138:4** [v]Ps 72:11; 102:15 **138:5**
[w]S Ps 51:14; 71:16; 145:7 [x]Ps 21:5 **138:6** [y]S Ps 113:6

---

their forced separation from Zion brought them down to the
posture of mourning (see Job 2:8,13; La 2:10).
137:2 *we hung our harps.* "The joyful harp is silent" (Isa
24:8) because the callous Babylonians demanded exotic entertainment with the joyful songs of distant Zion, while the
exiles' instruments were only "tuned to mourning" (Job
30:31).
137:4–6 Only he whose heart had disowned the Lord and
his holy city Jerusalem could play the puppet on a Babylonian
stage. But may I never play the harp again or sing another
syllable if I am untrue to that beloved city!
137:7–9 Lord, remember Edom; and as for you, Babylon,
I bless whoever does to you what you did to Jerusalem: a
passionate call for redress from a loyal son of the ravaged city
(see note on 5:10).
137:7 *Edomites.* The agelong animosity of
Edom—descendants of Esau, Jacob's brother—showed its
most dastardly face in Jerusalem's darkest hour. No doubt
the author knew the Lord's judgments against that nation
announced by the prophets (Isa 63:1–4; Jer 49:7–22; Eze
25:8,12–14; 35; Obadiah). *Tear it down.* Lit. "Strip
her"—cities were conventionally portrayed as women. La
4:21 anticipates that Edom will be punished by suffering the
same humiliation.
137:8 *Daughter.* A personification of Babylon and its inhabitants. *doomed to destruction.* The author may have
known the Lord's announced judgments on this cruel destroyer (Isa 13; 21:1–10; 47; Jer 50–51; Hab 2:4–20).
137:9 *your infants.* War was as cruel then as now; women
and children were not spared (see 2Ki 8:12; 15:16; Isa
13:16,18; Hos 10:14; 13:16; Am 1:13; Na 3:10). For the
final announcement of the destruction of the "Babylon" that
persists in its warfare against the City of God, and the joy
with which that announcement is greeted, see Rev
18:1–19:4.

Ps 138 A royal song of praise for God's saving help against
threatening foes. In many respects it is like Ps 18, though it is
more concise and direct. Two (Hebrew) four-line stanzas
(vv. 1–3, 6–8) develop the main theme; at the center a
two-line stanza (vv. 4–5) expands the praise of the Lord to a
universal company of earth's royalty.
138 title This begins a collection of eight "Davidic" psalms
(Ps 138–145): six prayers framed by two psalms of praise.
138:1–3 Praise for God's faithful love shown in answer to
prayers for help.
138:1 *heart.* See note on 4:7. *gods.* Either pagan kings (see
vv. 4–5) or the gods they claimed to represent (see introduction to Ps 82; see also note on 82:1).
138:2 *your holy temple.* If David is in fact the author,
reference is to the tent he set up for the ark (2Sa
6:17)—many psalms ascribed to David refer to the "temple"
(see, e.g., 5:7; 11:4; 18:6; 27:4; see also Ps 30 title). *name.*
See note on 5:11. *love and . . . faithfulness.* See note on
36:5. *love.* See v. 8; see also note on 6:4. *your word.*
Especially God's promises. God's display of his love and
faithfulness in his answers to prayer (v. 3) has made his name
and promises more precious than all else that even a king
may possess.
138:4–5 The center of the poem (see note on 6:6): a wish
and hope that all the kings of earth may come to join him in
his praise of the Lord (see note on 9:1).
138:4 *words of your mouth.* God's grand commitments to
his people.
138:5 *ways of the Lord.* See 25:10 and note. God's words
and his ways are in harmony, and together they display his
great glory (see Ps 145).
138:6–8 A testimony to God's condescending and faithful
love, concluded with a prayer.
138:6 See 113:4–9 and notes. *looks.* With favor. *the
proud.* See notes on 31:23; 101:5; 131:1. *knows from afar.*

but the proud[z] he knows from afar.
7Though I walk[a] in the midst of trouble,
you preserve my life;[b]
you stretch out your hand[c] against the anger of my foes,[d]
with your right hand[e] you save me.[f]
8The LORD will fulfill ⌞his purpose⌟[g] for me;
your love, O LORD, endures forever[h]—
do not abandon[i] the works of your hands.[j]

Psalm 139

For the director of music. Of David.
A psalm.

1O LORD, you have searched me[k]
and you know[l] me.
2You know when I sit and when I rise;[m]
you perceive my thoughts[n] from afar.
3You discern my going out[o] and my lying down;
you are familiar with all my ways.[p]
4Before a word is on my tongue
you know it completely,[q] O LORD.

5You hem me in[r]—behind and before;
you have laid your hand upon me.
6Such knowledge is too wonderful for me,[s]
too lofty[t] for me to attain.

7Where can I go from your Spirit?
Where can I flee[u] from your presence?
8If I go up to the heavens,[v] you are there;
if I make my bed[w] in the depths,[k]
you are there.
9If I rise on the wings of the dawn,
if I settle on the far side of the sea,
10even there your hand will guide me,[x]
your right hand[y] will hold me fast.
11If I say, "Surely the darkness will hide me
and the light become night around me,"
12even the darkness will not be dark[z] to you;
the night will shine like the day,
for darkness is as light to you.

13For you created my inmost being;[a]
you knit me together[b] in my mother's womb.[c]
14I praise you[d] because I am fearfully and wonderfully made;
your works are wonderful,[e]
I know that full well.

138:6 [z]S Ps 40:4; S Mt 23:12 **138:7** [a]Ps 23:4 [b]S Ps 41:2 [c]S Ex 7:5 [d]Ps 7:6 [e]Ps 20:6; 60:5; 108:6 [f]Ps 17:7,14 **138:8** [g]Php 1:6 [h]S Ezr 3:11; Ps 100:5 [i]S Ps 51:11 [j]S Job 10:3,8 **139:1** [k]S Ps 17:3; Ro 8:27 [l]Ps 44:21 **139:2** [m]2Ki 19:27 [n]Ps 94:11; Pr 24:12; Jer 12:3 **139:3** [o]2Ki 19:27 [p]S Job 31:4 **139:4** [q]S Heb 4:13 **139:5** [r]S 1Sa 25:16; Ps 32:10; 34:7; 125:2 **139:6** [s]S Ps 131:1 [t]Ro 11:33 **139:7** [u]Jer 23:24; Jnh 1:3 **139:8** [v]Dt 30:12-15; Am 9:2-3 [w]Job 17:13 **139:10** [x]Ps 23:3 [y]Ps 108:6; Isa 41:10 **139:12** [z]Job 34:22; Da 2:22 **139:13** [a]Ps 119:73 [b]S Job 10:11 [c]Isa 44:2,24; 46:3; 49:5; Jer 1:5

139:14 [d]Ps 119:164; 145:10 [e]S Job 40:19

[k]*8* Hebrew *Sheol*

Already from a great distance recognizes them for what they are and so does not let them "see his face" (see note on 11:7).

138:8 *will fulfill ⌞his purpose⌟.* See note on 57:2. *works of your hands.* The king himself, whom the Lord had made. The Hebrew often uses plurals to refer to God or the king.

Ps 139 A prayer for God to examine the heart and see its true devotion. Like Job, the author firmly claims his loyalty to the Lord. Nowhere (outside Job) does one find expressed such profound awareness of how awesome it is to ask God to examine not only one's life but also his soul—God, who knows every thought, word and deed, from whom there is no hiding, who has been privy even to one's formation in the dark concealment of the womb. The thought progresses steadily in four poetic paragraphs of six verses each (vv. 1–6, 7–12, 13–18, 19–24), and each paragraph is concluded with a couplet that elaborates on the unit's central theme. References to God's searching and knowing begin and end the prayer.

139 title *For the director of music.* See note on Ps 4 title. *Of David.* See note on Ps 138 title.

139:1–6 God, you know me perfectly, far beyond my knowledge of myself: my every action (v. 2a), my every undertaking (v. 3a) and the manner in which I pursue it (v. 3b), even my thoughts before they are fully crystallized (v. 2b) and my words before they are uttered (v. 4).

139:5 *You hem me in.* To keep me under scrutiny. *laid your hand upon me.* So that I do not escape you. The figures are different in Job 13:27, but the thought is much the same. *hand.* Or "hands."

139:6 *too wonderful for me.* Yours is a "wonder" knowledge, beyond my human capacity—the Hebrew term regularly applies to God's wondrous acts (see 77:11,14, "miracles"; Ex 15:11).

139:7–12 There is no hiding from you—here no abstract doctrine of divine omnipresence but an awed confession that God cannot be escaped (see Jer 23:23–24).

139:7 *your Spirit . . . your presence.* See 51:11; Isa 63:9–10; Eze 39:29 ("face . . . Spirit").

139:8 *the heavens . . . the depths.* The two vertical extremes (see NIV text note).

139:9 *wings of the dawn . . . far side of the sea.* The two horizontal extremes: east and west (the sea is the Mediterranean). Using a literary figure in which the totality is denoted by referring to its two extremes (merism), vv. 8–9 specify all spatial reality, the whole creation.

139:10 *guide me . . . hold me fast.* Though this language occurs in 73:23–24 to indicate God's solicitous care, it here denotes God's inescapable supervision, not unlike the thought of v. 5.

139:11–12 Just as the whole creation offers no hiding place (vv. 8–9), neither does even the darkness.

139:13–16 You yourself put me together in the womb and ordained the span of my life before I was born.

139:13 *created.* The Hebrew for this verb is the same as in Ge 14:19,22; Pr 8:22 ("brought . . . forth"), not as in Ge 1:1,21,27. *inmost being.* Lit. "kidneys"—in Hebrew idiom, the innermost center of emotions and of moral sensitivity—that which God tests and examines when he "searches" a person (see note on 7:9).

139:14 *fearfully . . . wonderfully . . . wonderful.* You know me as the One who formed me (see vv. 15–16), but I cannot begin to comprehend this creature you have fashioned. I can only look upon him with awe and wonder (see note on v. 6)—and praise you (see Ecc 11:5).

[15]My frame was not hidden from you
    when I was made[f] in the secret
        place.
When I was woven together[g] in the
    depths of the earth,[h]
[16]   your eyes saw my unformed body.
All the days ordained[i] for me
    were written in your book
    before one of them came to be.

[17]How precious to[1] me are your
    thoughts,[j] O God![k]
    How vast is the sum of them!
[18]Were I to count them,[l]
    they would outnumber the grains of
        sand.[m]
When I awake,[n]
    I am still with you.

[19]If only you would slay the wicked,[o]
    O God!
Away from me,[p] you bloodthirsty
    men![q]
[20]They speak of you with evil intent;
    your adversaries[r] misuse your
        name.[s]
[21]Do I not hate those[t] who hate you,
    O Lord,
    and abhor[u] those who rise up against
        you?
[22]I have nothing but hatred for them;
    I count them my enemies.[v]

[23]Search me,[w] O God, and know my
    heart;[x]
    test me and know my anxious
        thoughts.

[24]See if there is any offensive way[y] in
    me,
    and lead me[z] in the way everlasting.

Psalm 140

For the director of music.
A psalm of David.

[1]Rescue me,[a] O Lord, from evil men;
    protect me from men of violence,[b]
[2]who devise evil plans[c] in their hearts
    and stir up war[d] every day.
[3]They make their tongues as sharp as[e] a
        serpent's;
    the poison of vipers[f] is on their lips.
                                        Selah

[4]Keep me,[g] O Lord, from the hands of
        the wicked;[h]
    protect me from men of violence
    who plan to trip my feet.
[5]Proud men have hidden a snare[i] for
        me;
    they have spread out the cords of
        their net[j]
    and have set traps[k] for me along my
        path.   Selah

[6]O Lord, I say to you, "You are my
        God."[l]
    Hear, O Lord, my cry for mercy.[m]
[7]O Sovereign Lord,[n] my strong
        deliverer,

139:15 /Ecc 11:5
gS Job 10:11
hS Ps 63:9
139:16
iS Job 33:29;
S Ps 90:12
139:17 /S Ps 92:5
kS Job 5:9
139:18 /Ps 40:5
mS Job 29:18
nS Ps 3:5
139:19 oPs 5:6;
Isa 11:4 pS Ps 6:8
qS Ps 59:2
139:20
rS Ps 65:7
sS Dt 5:11
139:21
t2Ch 19:2;
Ps 31:6; 119:113
uS Ps 26:5
139:22 vMt 5:43
139:23
wJob 31:6
xS 1Sa 16:7;
S 1Ch 29:17;
S Ps 7:9; Pr 17:3;
Jer 11:20;
S Rev 2:23

139:24 yJer 25:5;
36:3 zPs 5:8;
23:2; 143:10
140:1 aPs 17:13;
S 25:20; 59:2;
71:4; 142:6;
143:9 bver 11;
Ps 86:14
140:2 cPs 36:4;
52:2; Pr 6:14;
16:27; Isa 59:4;
Hos 7:15
dS Ps 68:30
140:3 ePs 57:4
/Ps 58:4;
Ro 3:13*; Jas 3:8
140:4 gPs 141:9
hS Ps 36:11
140:5
iS Job 34:30;
S Ps 119:110
/S Job 18:8
kJob 18:9;
Ps 31:4; S 38:12
140:6 /S Ps 16:2
mS Ps 28:2,6

140:7 nPs 68:20

117 Or *concerning*

139:15 *secret place . . . depths of the earth.* Reference is
to the womb: called "the secret place" because it normally
conceals (see 2Sa 12:12), and it shares with "the depths of
the earth" (see note on 30:1) associations with darkness,
dampness and separation from the visible realm of life. Moreover, both phrases refer to the place of the dead (63:9; Job
14:13; Isa 44:23; 45:19), with which on one level the
womb appears to have been associated: Man comes from the
dust and returns to the dust (90:3; Ge 3:19; Ecc 3:20;
12:7), and the womb is the "depth"-like place where he is
formed (see Isa 44:2,24; 49:5; Jer 1:5).
139:16 *All the days ordained.* The span of life sovereignly
determined. *your book.* The heavenly royal register of God's
decisions (see note on 56:8).
139:17 *your thoughts.* As expressed in his works—and in
contrast with "my thoughts" (v. 2).
139:18 *When I awake.* The sleep of exhaustion overcomes
every attempt to count God's thoughts/works (see 63:6;
119:148), and waking only floods my soul once more with
the sense of the presence of this God.
139:19-22 My zeal for you sets me against all your adversaries.
139:19 *If only.* Jealous impatience with God's patience
toward the wicked—whose end will come (Isa 11:4). But
the psalmist leaves it to God.
139:20 *misuse your name.* Perhaps by calling down curses
on those trying to be the faithful servants of God.
139:21-22 A declaration of loyalty that echoes the pledge

required by ancient Near Eastern kings of their vassals (e.g.,
"With my friend you shall be friend, and with my enemy you
shall be enemy," from a treaty between Mursilis II, a Hittite
king, and Tette of Nuhassi, 14th century B.C.).
139:23-24 Examine me, see the integrity of my devotion
and keep me true (see 17:3-5 and note).
139:23 *heart.* See note on 4:7. *anxious thoughts.* See
94:19. It is no light matter to be examined by God.
139:24 *the way everlasting.* See note on 16:9-11.
Ps 140 A prayer for deliverance from the plots and slander
of unscrupulous enemies. It recalls Ps 58; 64 but employs a
number of words found nowhere else in the OT. Four well-
balanced stanzas are followed by a two-verse conclusion.
The prayer is strikingly rich in physiological allusions: heart,
head, tongue, lips, hands, feet—also ears (lit. "Give ear to,"
v. 6) and teeth (by a wordplay on the Hebrew for "make
sharp," v. 3). See Ps 141.
140 title *For the director of music.* See note on Ps 4 title.
of David. See note on Ps 138 title.
140:1-3 Rescue me from those "vipers."
140:2 *hearts.* See note on 4:7.
140:3 *tongues.* See note on 5:9. *poison of vipers.* See 58:4
and note.
140:4-5 Protect me from those proud and wicked hunters
(see 10:2-11 and notes).
140:5 *Proud men.* See note on 31:23.
140:6-8 Do not let these wicked men attain their evil
designs against me.

who shields my head in the day of
    battle—
[8]do not grant the wicked[o] their desires,
    O LORD;
do not let their plans succeed,
    or they will become proud.   *Selah*

[9]Let the heads of those who surround
    me
be covered with the trouble their lips
    have caused.[p]
[10]Let burning coals fall upon them;
    may they be thrown into the fire,[q]
    into miry pits, never to rise.
[11]Let slanderers not be established in the
    land;
    may disaster hunt down men of
    violence.[r]

[12]I know that the LORD secures justice for
    the poor[s]
and upholds the cause[t] of the
    needy.[u]
[13]Surely the righteous will praise your
    name[v]
    and the upright will live[w] before
    you.[x]

Psalm 141

A psalm of David.

[1]O LORD, I call to you; come quickly[y] to
    me.
    Hear my voice[z] when I call to you.
[2]May my prayer be set before you like
    incense;[a]

140:8
[o]Ps 10:2-3;
S 66:7
140:9 [p]Pr 18:7
140:10 [q]Ps 11:6;
21:9; S Mt 3:10;
Lk 12:49;
Rev 20:15
140:11
[r]S Ps 34:21
140:12
[s]S Ps 82:3
[t]S 1Ki 8:45
[u]S Ps 35:10
140:13
[v]S Ps 138:2
[w]S Ps 11:7
[x]Ps 16:11
141:1
[y]S Ps 22:19
[z]S Ps 4:1; 5:1-2;
27:7; 143:1
141:2 [a]S Lk 1:9;
Rev 5:8; 8:3

[b]S Ps 28:2; 63:4;
1Ti 2:8
[c]S Ex 29:39,41;
30:8
141:3
[d]S Ps 34:13;
Jas 1:26; 3:8
[e]S Ps 12:2
141:4
[f]S Jos 24:23
[g]S Ps 106:29
[h]Pr 23:1-3
141:5 [i]Pr 9:8;
19:25; 25:12;
Ecc 7:5
[j]S Ex 29:7;
Ps 23:5
141:6
[k]S 2Ch 25:12
141:7 [l]Ps 129:3
[m]Nu 16:32-33
[n]S Nu 16:30
141:8 [o]Ps 123:2
[p]Ps 2:12; 11:1
141:9 [q]Ps 140:4
[r]S Ps 64:5
[s]S Ps 38:12

may the lifting up of my hands[b] be
    like the evening sacrifice.[c]

[3]Set a guard over my mouth,[d] O LORD;
    keep watch over the door of my
    lips.[e]
[4]Let not my heart[f] be drawn to what is
    evil,
    to take part in wicked deeds[g]
with men who are evildoers;
    let me not eat of their delicacies.[h]

[5]Let a righteous man[m] strike me—it is a
    kindness;
    let him rebuke me[i]—it is oil on my
    head.[j]
My head will not refuse it.

Yet my prayer is ever against the deeds
    of evildoers;
[6] their rulers will be thrown down
        from the cliffs,[k]
    and the wicked will learn that my
        words were well spoken.
[7]They will say,[l] "As one plows[l] and
        breaks up the earth,[m]
    so our bones have been scattered at
        the mouth[n] of the grave.[n]"

[8]But my eyes are fixed[o] on you,
        O Sovereign LORD;
    in you I take refuge[p]—do not give
        me over to death.
[9]Keep me[q] from the snares they have
        laid[r] for me,
    from the traps set[s] by evildoers.

m5 Or *Let the Righteous One*   **n**7 Hebrew *Sheol*

140:9–11 Let the harm they plot against them recoil on their heads (see note on 5:10).
140:10 *burning coals.* See note on 11:6. *fire . . . miry pits.* This combination, together with the conjunction of fire and darkness in Job 15:30; 20:26, suggests the idea that the fire of God's judgment (see, e.g., 21:9; 97:3; Isa 1:31; 26:11; 33:14) reaches even into the realm of the dead (see Job 31:12 and note on Ps 30:1). *never to rise.* See 36:12; Isa 26:14.
140:11 *hunt down.* May these hunters (vv. 4–5) themselves be hunted by the ruin they intended to bring on me.
140:12–13 Confidence in God's just judgment (see note on 3:8).
140:12 *poor . . . needy.* See notes on 9:18; 34:6.
140:13 *the righteous.* See note on 1:5. *will praise.* Having experienced God's help (see notes on 7:17; 9:1). *will live before you.* In contrast to the wicked (v. 10; see notes on 11:7; 16:9–11).
Ps 141 A prayer for deliverance from the wicked and their evil ways. The stanza structure of the first half (two Hebrew lines plus three lines) is repeated in the second half, while at the center a couplet develops a complementary theme (see note on v. 5). Like Ps 140, the prayer is profuse in its physiological allusions: hands, mouth, lips, heart, head, bones, eyes.
141 title See note on Ps 138 title.
141:1–2 Initial appeal for God to hear.
141:3–4 A plea that God will keep him from speaking,

desiring or doing what is evil.
141:4 *Let not my heart.* Keep me from yielding to the example and urgings of the wicked (see Pr 1:10–16). *heart.* See note on 4:7. *their delicacies.* The luxuriant tables the wicked set from their unjust gains—keep me from acquiring an appetite for such unholy dainties.
141:5 The center of the poem (see note on 6:6). *Let a righteous man strike me.* The disciplining blows and rebukes of the righteous are the true "kindness" (Hebrew *hesed,* meaning "love" or "acts of authentic friendship"; see Pr 27:6; see also note on 6:4). *oil on my head.* See note on 23:5. *My head . . . deeds of evildoers.* Perhaps better: "Let my head not refuse it (this 'oil' from the righteous),/for my prayer is still against their (the wicked's) evil deeds."
141:6–7 The destiny of the wicked. *their rulers will be thrown down . . . the wicked will learn . . . They will say.* Perhaps better: "let their rulers be thrown down . . . let the wicked learn . . . Let them say,."
141:6 *my words.* Of commitment to righteousness, as in vv. 3–5. *well spoken.* Good and right.
141:8–10 A plea that God will deliver from the designs of the wicked.
141:8 *do not give me over to death.* As you do the wicked (see v. 7; see also 73:18–20,23–26 and notes).
141:9 *snares . . . traps.* Perhaps, as usual, the plots of men to bring him down (as in 38:12; 64:5; 91:3; 140:5; 142:3)—but here reference may be to the enticements to evil that the wicked lay before him (see Ex 23:33; Dt 7:16;

¹⁰Let the wicked fall ᵗ into their own
    nets,
  while I pass by in safety. ᵘ

Psalm 142

A *maskil*ᵒ of David. When he was in the
cave. ᵛ A prayer.

¹I cry aloud ʷ to the LORD;
  I lift up my voice to the LORD for
    mercy. ˣ
²I pour out my complaint ʸ before him;
  before him I tell my trouble. ᶻ

³When my spirit grows faint ᵃ within me,
  it is you who know my way.
  In the path where I walk
    men have hidden a snare for me.
⁴Look to my right and see;
  no one is concerned for me.
  I have no refuge; ᵇ
    no one cares ᶜ for my life.

⁵I cry to you, O LORD;
  I say, "You are my refuge, ᵈ
  my portion ᵉ in the land of the
    living." ᶠ
⁶Listen to my cry, ᵍ
  for I am in desperate need; ʰ
  rescue me ⁱ from those who pursue me,
    for they are too strong ʲ for me.
⁷Set me free from my prison, ᵏ
  that I may praise your name. ˡ

Then the righteous will gather about me
  because of your goodness to me. ᵐ

Psalm 143

A psalm of David.

¹O LORD, hear my prayer, ⁿ
  listen to my cry for mercy; ᵒ
  in your faithfulness ᵖ and righteousness ᵠ
    come to my relief.
²Do not bring your servant into
    judgment,
  for no one living is righteous ʳ before
    you.

³The enemy pursues me,
  he crushes me to the ground;
  he makes me dwell in darkness ˢ
    like those long dead. ᵗ
⁴So my spirit grows faint within me;
  my heart within me is dismayed. ᵘ

⁵I remember ᵛ the days of long ago;
  I meditate ʷ on all your works
  and consider what your hands have
    done.
⁶I spread out my hands ˣ to you;
  my soul thirsts for you like a parched
    land.   *Selah*

⁷Answer me quickly, ʸ O LORD;
  my spirit fails. ᶻ

141:10 ᵗPs 7:15; 35:8; 57:6
ᵘPs 124:7
142 Title
ᵛ1Sa 22:1; 24:3; Ps 57 Title
142:1
ʷS 1Ki 8:52; Ps 3:4 ˣPs 30:8
142:2 ʸPs 64:1
ᶻS Ps 50:15
142:3 ᵃPs 6:2; 77:3; 84:2; 88:4; 143:4,7; Jer 8:18; La 1:22
142:4 ᵇJer 25:35 ᶜJer 30:17
142:5 ᵈS Ps 46:1 ᵉS Dt 32:9; Ps 16:5 ᶠS Job 28:13; Ps 27:13
142:6 ᵍS Ps 17:1 ʰS Ps 79:8 ⁱS Ps 25:20 ʲJer 31:11
142:7 ᵏS Ps 66:11 ˡPs 7:17; 9:2

ᵐS 2Ch 6:41
143:1 ⁿS Ps 141:1 ᵒS Ps 28:2; 130:2 ᵖS Ex 34:6; Ps 89:1-2 ᵠPs 71:2
143:2 ʳS Ps 14:3; Ro 3:10
143:3 ˢS Ps 107:10 ᵗLa 3:6
143:4 ᵘPs 30:7
143:5 ᵛPs 77:6 ʷS Ge 24:63
143:6 ˣS Ex 9:29; S Job 11:13
143:7 ʸS Ps 69:17 ᶻS Ps 142:3

ᵒTitle: Probably a literary or musical term

Jos 23:13; Jdg 2:3).
141:10 *Let the wicked fall.* See note on 5:10.
Ps 142 A plaintive prayer for deliverance from powerful enemies—when powerless, alone and without refuge. Apart from the introduction (vv. 1–2) and conclusion (v. 7b), the prayer (in Hebrew) is composed of two four-line stanzas (vv. 3–7a).
142 title *maskil.* See note on Ps 32 title. *of David.* See note on Ps 138 title. *When . . . cave.* See note on Ps 57 title. *A prayer.* See note on Ps 17 title.
142:1–2 Initial appeal—using the formal third person (as was often done when addressing kings), equivalent to: "I cry aloud to you, O LORD."
142:3–4 Description of his "desperate need" (v. 6).
142:3 *When my spirit grows faint.* Because he is overwhelmed by his situation (see 22:14–15). *you who know.* And are concerned about (cf. v. 4).
142:4 *to my right.* To my right hand, where one's helper or defender stands (see 16:8 and note). *is concerned.* In Hebrew a less common synonym of "know" (v. 3); see Ru 2:10,19 ("notice").
142:5–7 Prayer for rescue.
142:5 *portion.* The sustainer and preserver of his life (see 73:26 and note).
142:7 *prison.* Metaphor for the sense of being fettered by affliction (see note on 18:19; see also Job 36:8). *that I may praise.* In celebration of God's saving help (see note on 7:17). *name.* See note on 5:11. *righteous.* See note on 1:5. *will gather about me.* He will no longer be alone. The conclusion expresses an expectant word of confidence (see note on 3:8).
Ps 143 A prayer for deliverance from enemies and for

divine leading. This is the seventh and final penitential psalm (see introduction to Ps 6). In the first half (vv. 1–6) the psalmist makes his appeal and describes his situation; in the second half (vv. 7–12) he presents his prayer. Appeal to God's righteousness (vv. 1,11) and the author's self-identification as "your servant" (vv. 2,12) enclose the prayer. See also his appeal to God's faithfulness (v. 1) and unfailing love (v. 12), which together form a frequent pair (see note on 36:5). For another enclosure see note on v. 7.
143 title See note on Ps 138 title.
143:1–2 Initial appeal.
143:1 *righteousness.* See note on 4:1.
143:2 As he begins his prayer, he pleads that God not sit in judgment over his servant (he knows his own failings) but that he focus his judicial attention on the enemy's harsh and unwarranted attacks.
143:3–4 The distress he suffers.
143:3 The last half of this verse appears almost verbatim in La 3:6. *in darkness.* As one cut off from the enjoyments of life (see v. 7; see also notes on 27:1; 30:1).
143:4 *my spirit grows faint.* See note on 142:3. *heart.* See note on 4:7.
143:5–6 Remembrance of God's past acts of deliverance encourages him in his appeal.
143:6 *spread out my hands.* In prayer (see 44:20; 88:9; Ex 9:29). *soul.* See v. 8; see also note on 6:3. *thirsts for you.* See note on 63:1.
143:7–10 The prayer.
143:7 *my spirit faints with longing.* Or perhaps: "my spirit fails." The translation parallels that in 119:81, but in view of the next line the thought appears closer to that of 104:29 (where "breath" translates the same Hebrew word as that

Do not hide your face[a] from me
　or I will be like those who go down
　　to the pit.
[8]Let the morning bring me word of your
　　unfailing love,[b]
for I have put my trust in you.
Show me the way[c] I should go,
　for to you I lift up my soul.[d]
[9]Rescue me[e] from my enemies,[f]
　O Lord,
　for I hide myself in you.
[10]Teach me[g] to do your will,
　for you are my God;[h]
may your good Spirit
　lead[i] me on level ground.[j]

[11]For your name's sake,[k] O Lord,
　preserve my life;[l]
in your righteousness,[m] bring me out
　of trouble.
[12]In your unfailing love, silence my
　enemies;[n]
destroy all my foes,[o]
　for I am your servant.[p]

Psalm 144

Of David.

[1]Praise be to the Lord my Rock,[q]
　who trains my hands for war,
　my fingers for battle.
[2]He is my loving God and my fortress,[r]
　my stronghold[s] and my deliverer,
my shield,[t] in whom I take refuge,
　who subdues peoples[p][u] under me.

[3]O Lord, what is man[v] that you care for
　him,
　the son of man that you think of
　　him?
[4]Man is like a breath;[w]
　his days are like a fleeting shadow.[x]

[5]Part your heavens,[y] O Lord, and come
　down;[z]
touch the mountains, so that they
　smoke.[a]
[6]Send forth lightning[b] and scatter[c] the
　enemies,;
shoot your arrows[d] and rout them.
[7]Reach down your hand from on high;[e]
　deliver me and rescue me[f]
from the mighty waters,[g]
　from the hands of foreigners[h]
[8]whose mouths are full of lies,[i]
　whose right hands[j] are deceitful.[k]

[9]I will sing a new song[l] to you, O God;
　on the ten-stringed lyre[m] I will make
　　music to you,
[10]to the One who gives victory to kings,[n]
　who delivers his servant David[o] from
　　the deadly sword.[p]

[11]Deliver me and rescue me[q]
　from the hands of foreigners[r]
whose mouths are full of lies,[s]

Cross references (center column)

143:7
[a]S Ps 22:24; 27:9; 30:7
143:8 [b]Ps 6:4; 90:14
[c]S Ex 33:13; S Job 34:32; Ps 27:11; 32:8
[d]Ps 25:1-2; S 86:4
143:9
[e]S Ps 140:1
[f]S Ps 18:17; 31:15
143:10
[g]S Ps 119:12
[h]Ps 31:14
[i]S Ne 9:20; Ps 25:4-5
[j]Ps 26:12
143:11 [k]Ps 25:11
[l]S Ps 41:2
[m]Ps 31:1; 71:2
143:12 [n]Ps 8:2
[o]Ps 54:5
[p]S Ps 116:16
144:1
[q]S Ge 49:24
144:2 [r]Ps 59:9; 91:2 [s]Ps 27:1; 37:39; 43:2
[t]S Ge 15:1;
S Ps 18:2
[u]S Jdg 4:23;
S Ps 18:39

144:3 [v]Heb 2:6
144:4 [w]S Job 7:7; 27:3; Isa 2:22
[x]S 1Ch 29:15; S Job 14:2; S Jas 4:14
144:5 [y]Ps 18:9; Isa 64:1
[z]S Ge 11:5; S Ps 57:3
[a]Ps 104:32
144:6 [b]Hab 3:11; Zec 9:14
[c]S Ps 59:11; S 68:1
[d]Ps 7:12-13; 18:14
144:7
[e]S 2Sa 22:17
[f]Ps 3:7; S 57:3
[g]Ps 69:2

[h]S Ps 18:44 **144:8** [i]Ps 12:2; 41:6 [j]Ge 14:22; Dt 32:40
[k]S Ps 18:44 **144:9** [l]S Ps 28:7; S 96:1 [m]Ps 33:2-3; S 71:22
144:10 [n]S 2Sa 8:14 [o]Ps 18:50 [p]S Job 5:20 **144:11** [q]Ps 3:7; S 25:20 [r]S Ps 18:44 [s]Ps 41:6-7

P2 Many manuscripts of the Masoretic Text, Dead Sea Scrolls, Aquila, Jerome and Syriac; most manuscripts of the Masoretic Text *subdues my people*

---

for "spirit" here). Ultimately, the failing of "my spirit" will be healed by the leading of "your good Spirit" (v. 10)—the two references enclose the prayer. *hide your face.* See note on 13:1. *the pit.* See v. 3 and note on 30:1.

143:8 *the morning.* Of salvation from the present "darkness" (v. 3; see introduction to Ps 57). *unfailing love.* See v. 12; see also note on 6:4. *Show me the way.* See v. 10. Deliverance from the enemy is not enough—either for God's "servant" (vv. 2,12) or for entrance into life.

143:10 *level ground.* See note on 26:12.

143:11-12 Concluding summary of the prayer (see introduction).

143:11 *For your name's sake.* See note on 23:3.

143:12 *destroy all my foes.* See note on 5:10.

Ps 144 A royal prayer for victory over treacherous enemies (but see note on vv. 12-15). Verses 1-10 show much affinity with Ps 18; this section begins and ends like that psalm, and vv. 5-7 all appear to be variations on corresponding lines found there (see notes below). The remaining lines of this section contain similar echoes of other psalms, and the author may have drawn directly on them. The main body (vv. 1-10) is fairly typical of the prayers of the Psalter, but the conclusion (vv. 12-15) is unique. Verse 11 appears to be transitional.

144 title See note on Ps 138 title.

144:1-2 Praise of the Lord. As the opening words of a prayer, it seems to function both as an initial appeal (see 143:1-2) and as a confession of confidence that the prayer will be heard. Notice the unusual piling up of epithets for God—all having their counterparts in Ps 18.

144:2 *my loving God.* Lit. "my unfailing love" (see note on 6:4); so called because God is the source of benevolent acts of love that David can count on—just as God can be called "my salvation" because he is the source of salvation (see 27:1; 35:3; 62:2).

144:3-4 Confession of man's insignificance and of his dependence on God's help.

144:3 A variation of 8:4.

144:4 See 39:4-6 and notes.

144:5-8 Prayer for deliverance.

144:5 See 18:9 and note on 18:7-15.

144:6 See 18:14 and note.

144:7 See 18:16-17 and note on 32:6. *foreigners.* Bordering kingdoms.

144:8 *mouths.* See note on 5:9. *right hands.* Hands raised to swear covenant oaths of allegiance or submission (see 106:26; Ex 6:8; Dt 32:40).

144:9-10 Vow to praise (see note on 7:17).

144:9 *new song.* See note on 33:3.

144:10 *his servant David.* See note on Ps 18 title.

144:11 Repetition of the prayer in vv. 7-8, apparently to serve as transition to what follows: If God will deliver his servant David, the realm will prosper and be secure.

whose right hands are deceitful. [t]

[12]Then our sons in their youth
will be like well-nurtured plants, [u]
and our daughters will be like pillars [v]
carved to adorn a palace.
[13]Our barns will be filled [w]
with every kind of provision.
Our sheep will increase by thousands,
by tens of thousands in our fields;
[14] our oxen [x] will draw heavy loads. [q]
There will be no breaching of walls, [y]
no going into captivity,
no cry of distress in our streets. [z]

[15]Blessed are the people [a] of whom this is
true;
blessed are the people whose God is
the LORD.

Psalm 145 [r]

A psalm of praise. Of David.

[1]I will exalt you, [b] my God the King; [c]
I will praise your name [d] for ever and
ever.
[2]Every day I will praise [e] you
and extol your name [f] for ever and
ever.

[3]Great is the LORD [g] and most worthy of
praise; [h]
his greatness no one can fathom. [i]
[4]One generation [j] will commend your
works to another;
they will tell [k] of your mighty acts. [l]
[5]They will speak of the glorious
splendor [m] of your majesty,
and I will meditate on your
wonderful works. [s] [n]
[6]They will tell [o] of the power of your
awesome works, [p]

and I will proclaim [q] your great
deeds. [r]
[7]They will celebrate your abundant
goodness [s]
and joyfully sing [t] of your
righteousness. [u]

[8]The LORD is gracious and
compassionate, [v]
slow to anger and rich in love. [w]
[9]The LORD is good [x] to all;
he has compassion [y] on all he has
made.

[10]All you have made will praise you, [z]
O LORD;
your saints will extol [a] you. [b]
[11]They will tell of the glory of your
kingdom [c]
and speak of your might, [d]
[12]so that all men may know of your
mighty acts [e]
and the glorious splendor of your
kingdom. [f]
[13]Your kingdom is an everlasting
kingdom, [g]
and your dominion endures through
all generations.

The LORD is faithful [h] to all his
promises [i]
and loving toward all he has made. [t]
[14]The LORD upholds [j] all those who fall

144:11 [t]Ps 12:2;
S 36:3; 106:26;
Isa 44:20
144:12
[u]Ps 92:12-14;
S 128:3 [v]SS 4:4;
7:4
144:13 [w]Pr 3:10
144:14 [x]Pr 14:4
[y]2Ki 25:11
[z]Isa 24:11;
Jer 14:2-3
144:15 [a]Dt 28:3
145:1 [b]Ps 30:1;
34:1 [c]Ps 2:6; 5:2
[d]S Ps 54:6
145:2 [e]S Ps 71:6
[f]Ps 34:1;
Isa 25:1; 26:8
145:3 [g]S Ps 95:3
[h]S 2Sa 22:4;
Ps 96:4 [i]S Job 5:9
145:4 [j]Ps 22:30
[k]S Dt 11:19
[l]S Ps 71:16
145:5 [m]Ps 96:6;
148:13 [n]S Ps 75:1
145:6 [o]Ps 78:4
[p]S Ps 66:3

[q]S Dt 32:3
[r]Ps 75:1; 106:22
145:7
[s]S Ex 18:9;
S Ps 27:13
[t]S Ps 5:11;
S 101:1
[u]S Ps 138:5
145:8
[v]S Ps 86:15;
103:8 [w]S Ps 86:5
145:9
[x]S 1Ch 16:34;
S Ps 136:1;
Mt 19:17;
Mk 10:18
[y]Ps 103:13-14
145:10 [z]S Ps 8:6;
S 103:22;
S 139:14
[a]Ps 30:4; 148:14;
149:9
[b]Ps 115:17-18
145:11 [c]ver
12-13; S Ex 15:2;
Mt 6:33
[d]Ps 21:13
145:12
[e]S Ps 75:1; 105:1
[f]ver 11;
Ps 103:19;
Isa 2:10,19,21
145:13
[g]S Ex 15:18;
1Ti 1:17;

2Pe 1:11; Rev 11:15 [h]S Dt 7:9; S 1Co 1:9 [i]S Jos 23:14
145:14 [j]S Ps 37:17

[q]14 Or our chieftains will be firmly established   [r]This
psalm is an acrostic poem, the verses of which (including
verse 13b) begin with the successive letters of the Hebrew
alphabet.   [s]5 Dead Sea Scrolls and Syriac (see also
Septuagint); Masoretic Text On the glorious splendor of
your majesty / and on your wonderful works I will
meditate   [t]13 One manuscript of the Masoretic Text,
Dead Sea Scrolls and Syriac (see also Septuagint); most
manuscripts of the Masoretic Text do not have the last
two lines of verse 13.

144:12–15 Many believe this to be a separate prayer
("May our sons . . ."), unrelated to vv. 1–11, but the
apparently transitional function of v. 11 supports the NIV
rendering.
144:12 daughters . . . like pillars carved. Temple columns
in the shape of women were not uncommon (e.g., on the
Acropolis in Athens).
144:14 our oxen will draw heavy loads. Or "our oxen will
be heavy with flesh" or "our oxen will be heavy with young"
(see also NIV text note).
144:15 Blessed. See note on 1:1.
Ps 145 A hymn to the Lord, the Great King, for his mighty
acts and benevolent virtues, which are the glory of his kingly
rule. It exploits to the full the traditional language of praise
and, as an alphabetic acrostic, reflects the care of studied
composition. Between the two-line introduction (vv. 1–2)
and one-line conclusion (v. 21), four poetic paragraphs develop as many themes, each introduced with a thematic line
(see vv. 3,8,13b,17).
145 title praise. Hebrew tehillah, occurring only here in

the psalm titles, but from a plural form (tehillim) has come
the traditional Hebrew name of the Psalter. Of David. See
note on Ps 138 title.
145:1–2 Initial commitment to praise. name. See v. 21,
thus framing the psalm (see note on 5:11).
145:3–7 Praise of God's mighty acts, which display his
greatness (v. 3) and his goodness (v. 7)—as the author
underscores by enclosing the paragraph with these two references. For the same combination see 86:10,17; 135:3,5.
145:4 will commend . . . will tell. See vv. 5–7,10–12,21;
see also note on 9:1. your works. In creation, providence and
redemption.
145:7 righteousness. See v. 17; see also note on 4:1.
145:8–13a Praise of God's benevolent virtues, which
move all creatures to celebrate the glory of his kingdom.
145:8 See Ex 34:6–7 and note.
145:10 All you have made will praise you. See v. 21; see
also note on 65:13. saints. See also note on 4:3.
145:13b–16 Praise God's faithfulness.
145:13b,17 loving. See note on 6:4. For the combination
"faithful . . . and loving" see note on 36:5.

and lifts up all[k] who are bowed down.[l]

[15]The eyes of all look to you,
and you give them their food[m] at the proper time.

[16]You open your hand
and satisfy the desires[n] of every living thing.

[17]The LORD is righteous[o] in all his ways
and loving toward all he has made.[p]

[18]The LORD is near[q] to all who call on him,[r]
to all who call on him in truth.

[19]He fulfills the desires[s] of those who fear him;[t]
he hears their cry[u] and saves them.[v]

[20]The LORD watches over[w] all who love him,[x]
but all the wicked he will destroy.[y]

[21]My mouth will speak[z] in praise of the LORD.
Let every creature[a] praise his holy name[b]
for ever and ever.

Psalm 146

[1]Praise the LORD.[u]

Praise the LORD,[c] O my soul.
[2]   I will praise the LORD all my life;[d]
I will sing praise[e] to my God as long as I live.[f]

[3]Do not put your trust in princes,[g]
in mortal men,[h] who cannot save.
[4]When their spirit departs, they return to the ground;[i]
on that very day their plans come to nothing.[j]

[5]Blessed is he[k] whose help[l] is the God of Jacob,

whose hope is in the LORD his God,
[6]the Maker of heaven[m] and earth,
the sea, and everything in them—
the LORD, who remains faithful[n] forever.

[7]He upholds[o] the cause of the oppressed[p]
and gives food to the hungry.[q]
The LORD sets prisoners free,[r]
[8]   the LORD gives sight[s] to the blind,[t]
the LORD lifts up those who are bowed down,[u]
the LORD loves the righteous.[v]
[9]The LORD watches over the alien[w]
and sustains the fatherless[x] and the widow,[y]
but he frustrates the ways of the wicked.

[10]The LORD reigns[z] forever,
your God, O Zion, for all generations.

Praise the LORD.

Psalm 147

[1]Praise the LORD.[v]

How good it is to sing praises to our God,
how pleasant[a] and fitting to praise him![b]

[2]The LORD builds up Jerusalem;[c]
he gathers the exiles[d] of Israel.
[3]He heals the brokenhearted[e]
and binds up their wounds.[f]

145:14
[k]S 1Sa 2:8;
Ps 146:8
[l]S Ps 38:6
145:15
[m]S Ge 1:30;
S Job 28:5;
S Ps 37:25;
S Mt 6:26
145:16
[n]S Ps 90:14;
S 104:28
145:17
[o]S Ex 9:27;
S Ezr 9:15 [p]ver 13
145:18
[q]S Nu 23:21;
S Ps 46:1; Php 4:5
[r]Ps 18:6; 80:18
145:19
[s]S Ps 20:4
[t]S Job 22:28
[u]S Ps 31:22;
S 40:1
[v]S 1Sa 10:19;
Ps 7:10; 34:18
145:20 [w]S Ps 1:6
[x]Ps 31:23; 91:14;
97:10 [y]S Ps 94:23
145:21 [z]Ps 71:8
[a]Ps 65:2; 150:6
[b]S Ex 3:15;
S Ps 30:4; S 99:3
146:1 [c]Ps 103:1;
104:1
146:2 [d]Ps 104:33
[e]S Ps 105:2
[f]S Ps 63:4
146:3 [g]Ps 118:9
[h]Ps 60:11;
S 108:12; Isa 2:22
146:4 [i]S Ge 3:19;
S Job 7:21;
Ps 103:14;
Ecc 12:7
[j]Ps 33:10;
1Co 2:6
146:5 [k]Ps 33:18;
37:9; 119:43;
144:15; Jer 17:7
[l]Ps 70:5; 71:5;
121:2
146:6
[m]S 2Ch 2:12;
Ps 115:15;
Ac 14:15;
S Rev 10:6
[n]S Dt 7:9;
S Ps 18:25;
108:4; 117:2
146:7
[o]S Ps 37:17
[p]Ps 103:6
[q]Ps 107:9;
145:15

[r]S Ps 66:11; S 68:6 **146:8** [s]Pr 20:12; Isa 29:18; 32:3; 35:5;
42:7,18-19; 43:8; Mt 11:5 [t]S Ex 4:11 [u]S Ps 38:6 [v]S Dt 7:13;
S Job 23:10 **146:9** [w]S Lev 19:34 [x]S Ps 10:18 [y]S Ex 22:22;
Jas 1:27 **146:10** [z]S Ge 21:33; S 1Ch 16:31; Ps 93:1; 99:1;
Rev 11:15 **147:1** [a]S Ps 135:3 [b]Ps 33:1 **147:2** [c]S Ps 51:18
[d]S Ps 106:47 **147:3** [e]S Ps 34:18 [f]S Nu 12:13; S Job 5:18;
Isa 1:6; Eze 34:16

[u]1 Hebrew *Hallelu Yah*; also in verse 10   [v]1 Hebrew
Hallelu Yah; also in verse 20

145:17–20 Praise of God's righteousness.
145:18 *in truth.* With godly integrity.
145:21 The praise of God must continue, and every creature take it up—forever. *every creature.* Or perhaps "every human" (lit. "all flesh"; see 65:2, "all men"; but see also 150:6).
Ps 146 An exhortation to trust in the Lord, Zion's King. The first of five Hallelujah psalms with which the Psalter closes, its date is probably postexilic. This and the remaining four psalms are all framed with Hallelujahs, which may have been added by the final editors (see Ps 105–106; 111–117).
146:1–2 Initial vow to praise—as long as life continues (see 145:21).
146:1 *Praise the LORD, O my soul.* See the frames around Ps 103–104. *soul.* See note on 6:3.
146:3–4 The call to trust in the Lord (see vv. 5–9) is heightened by contrast.
146:5–9 Exhortation to trust in the covenant God of Jacob (see note on 14:7), who as Creator is Lord over all, as the Faithful One defends the defenseless and provides for the

needy, and as the Righteous One shows favor to the righteous but checks the wicked in their pursuits.
146:6 *Maker of heaven and earth.* See note on 121:2.
146:8 *righteous.* See note on 1:5.
146:10 Concluding exultant testimony to the citizens of God's royal city. *Zion.* See note on 9:11.
Ps 147 Praise of God, the Creator, for his special mercies to Israel—possibly composed for the Levitical choirs on the joyous occasion of the dedication of the rebuilt walls of Jerusalem (see Ne 12:27–43). The Septuagint (the Greek translation of the OT) divides the work into two separate psalms (vv. 1–11, 12–20), but it is actually a three-part song (vv. 1–6, 7–11, 12–20), bound together by the frame (vv. 2–3, 19–20), in which the Lord's unique favors to Israel are celebrated. See introduction to Ps 146.
147:1 See note on 135:3.
147:2 *builds up . . . gathers.* Refers to the postexilic restoration of Jerusalem and Israel.
147:3 *brokenhearted.* Such as the exiles (see Ps 137; cf. Ps 126) and those who struggled in the face of great opposition

⁴He determines the number of the stars^g
  and calls them each by name.
⁵Great is our Lord^h and mighty in
    power;ⁱ
  his understanding has no limit.^j
⁶The Lord sustains the humble^k
  but casts the wicked^l to the ground.

⁷Sing to the Lord^m with thanksgiving;ⁿ
  make music^o to our God on the
    harp.^p
⁸He covers the sky with clouds;^q
  he supplies the earth with rain^r
  and makes grass grow^s on the hills.
⁹He provides food^t for the cattle
  and for the young ravens^u when they
    call.

¹⁰His pleasure is not in the strength^v of
    the horse,^w
  nor his delight in the legs of a man;
¹¹the Lord delights^x in those who fear
    him,^y
  who put their hope^z in his unfailing
    love.^a

¹²Extol the Lord, O Jerusalem;^b
  praise your God, O Zion,
¹³for he strengthens the bars of your
    gates^c
  and blesses your people^d within you.
¹⁴He grants peace^e to your borders
  and satisfies you^f with the finest of
    wheat.^g

¹⁵He sends his command^h to the earth;
  his word runsⁱ swiftly.
¹⁶He spreads the snow^j like wool
  and scatters the frost^k like ashes.

¹⁷He hurls down his hail^l like pebbles.
  Who can withstand his icy blast?
¹⁸He sends his word^m and melts them;
  he stirs up his breezes,ⁿ and the
    waters flow.

¹⁹He has revealed his word^o to Jacob,^p
  his laws and decrees^q to Israel.
²⁰He has done this for no other nation;^r
  they do not know^s his laws.

  Praise the Lord.^t

Psalm 148

¹Praise the Lord.^{w u}

  Praise the Lord from the heavens,^v
    praise him in the heights above.
²Praise him, all his angels,^w
  praise him, all his heavenly hosts.^x
³Praise him, sun^y and moon,
  praise him, all you shining stars.
⁴Praise him, you highest heavens^z
  and you waters above the skies.^a
⁵Let them praise the name^b of the Lord,
  for he commanded^c and they were
    created.
⁶He set them in place for ever and ever;
  he gave a decree^d that will never
    pass away.

⁷Praise the Lord^e from the earth,

147:4 ^gS Ge 15:5
147:5 ^hS Ps 48:1
ⁱS Ex 14:31
^jPs 145:3;
Isa 40:28
147:6
^kS 2Ch 33:23;
Ps 146:8-9
^lPs 37:9-10;
145:20
147:7 ^mPs 30:4;
33:3 ⁿS Ps 42:4
^oS Ps 27:6
^pS Ps 98:5
147:8 ^qS Job 26:8
^rS Dt 11:14;
S 32:2;
S 2Sa 1:21;
S Job 5:10
^sS Job 28:26;
S Ps 104:14
147:9
^tS Ge 1:30;
Ps 104:27-28;
S Mt 6:26
^uS Ge 8:7
147:10
^vS 1Sa 16:7
^wS Job 39:11;
Ps 33:16-17
147:11
^xS Ps 35:27
^yPs 33:18;
103:11
^zPs 119:43
^aPs 6:4
147:12 ^bPs 48:1
147:13
^cS Dt 33:25
^dS Lev 25:21;
Ps 128:5; 134:3
147:14
^eS Lev 26:6;
S 2Sa 7:10;
S Isa 48:18
^fS Ps 132:15
^gS Dt 32:14
147:15
^hJob 37:12;
Ps 33:9; 148:5
ⁱIsa 55:11
147:16 ^jPs 148:8
^kS Job 37:12;
38:29
147:17
^lEx 9:22-23;
S Job 38:22;
S Ps 78:47

147:18 ^mver 15; Ps 33:9; 107:20 ⁿS Ps 50:3 **147:19**
^oS Ex 20:1; Ro 3:2 ^pPs 78:5 ^qS Dt 33:4; Jos 1:8; 2Ki 22:8;
Mal 4:4; Ro 9:4 **147:20** ^rDt 4:7-8,32-34 ^sS Ps 79:6 ^tPs 33:2;
103:1 **148:1** ^uPs 33:2; 103:1 ^vPs 19:1; 69:34; 150:1 **148:2**
^wPs 103:20 ^xS 1Ki 22:19 **148:3** ^yS Ps 19:1 **148:4**
^zS Dt 10:14 ^aS Ge 1:7 **148:5** ^bPs 145:21 ^cS Ps 147:15 **148:6**
^dJer 31:35-36; 33:25 **148:7** ^ePs 33:2

^w 1 Hebrew *Hallelu Yah*; also in verse 14

---

to rebuild Jerusalem's walls (Ne 2:17–20; 4:1–23).
147:4–6 He whose power and understanding are such that he fixes the number of (or counts) the stars and names them is able to sustain his humble ones and bring the wicked down (see 20:8; 146:9; see also Isa 40:26–29).
147:6 *humble.* Those who acknowledge that they are without resources (see 149:4). *ground.* Probably the grave (see note on 61:2).
147:7–11 The God who governs the rain and thus provides food for beast and bird is not pleased by man's reliance on his own capabilities or those of the animals he has domesticated (or the technologies he has developed); he is pleased when people serve him and trust his loving care.
147:11 *fear.* See note on 34:8–14. *unfailing love.* See note on 6:4.
147:12–18 The Lord of all creation, Zion's God, secures his people's defenses and prosperity, their peace and abundant provision. The verses mention clouds and rain (v. 8); snow, frost and hail (vv. 16–17); icy winds and warm breezes (vv. 17–18)—the whole range of weather.
147:15 *his command . . . his word.* Personified as messengers commissioned to carry out a divine order (see notes on 23:6; 33:4; 104:4).
147:19–20 God's most unique gift to Israel: his other word, his redemptive word, by which he makes known his program of salvation and his holy will.

Ps 148 A call to all things in all creation to praise the Lord. Whatever its original liturgical purpose, its placement here serves to complete the scope of the calls to praise with which the Psalter concludes. Two balanced stanzas of six verses each are followed by a two-verse conclusion. In the first stanza (vv. 1–6) the call goes to all creatures in the heavens, in the second (vv. 7–12) to all beneath the heavens (see 103:20–22). The conclusion (vv. 13–14) focuses on motivation for praise. See introduction to Ps 146.
148:1–6 Let all creatures in the heavens praise the Lord.
148:3 *sun and moon . . . shining stars.* See note on 65:13.
148:4 *waters above the skies.* The "deep" above (see Ge 1:7; cf. "ocean depths" in v. 7; see also note on 42:7).
148:5 *name of the Lord.* See v. 13; see also note on 5:11. They are to praise the Lord because he has created them and made their existence secure.
148:7–12 Let all creatures of earth praise the Lord. ("Heaven and earth" are the sum of all creation; see v. 13; see also 89:11; 113:6; 136:5–6; Ge 2:1,4.)
148:7 *sea creatures and all ocean depths.* Likely with Ge 1 in mind (see Ge 1:7,10,21), the call begins with these and moves toward the human components. This and the pairs that follow employ a figure of speech (merism) that refers to all reality pertaining to the sphere to which they belong—here, all creatures great and small that belong to the realm of lakes and seas.

you great sea creatures[f] and all
　　ocean depths,[g]
[8]lightning and hail,[h] snow and clouds,
　　stormy winds that do his bidding,[i]
[9]you mountains and all hills,[j]
　　fruit trees and all cedars,
[10]wild animals[k] and all cattle,
　　small creatures and flying birds,
[11]kings[l] of the earth and all nations,
　　you princes and all rulers on earth,
[12]young men and maidens,
　　old men and children.

[13]Let them praise the name of the Lord,[m]
　　for his name alone is exalted;
　　his splendor[n] is above the earth and
　　　the heavens.[o]
[14]He has raised up for his people a
　　horn,[x][p]
　　the praise[q] of all his saints,[r]
　　of Israel, the people close to his
　　　heart.[s]

Praise the Lord.

Psalm 149

[1]Praise the Lord.[y][t]

Sing to the Lord a new song,[u]
　　his praise in the assembly[v] of the
　　saints.

[2]Let Israel rejoice[w] in their Maker;[x]
　　let the people of Zion be glad in their
　　King.[y]

[3]Let them praise his name with dancing[z]
　　and make music to him with
　　　tambourine and harp.[a]
[4]For the Lord takes delight[b] in his
　　people;
　　he crowns the humble with
　　　salvation.[c]
[5]Let the saints rejoice[d] in this honor
　　and sing for joy on their beds.[e]

[6]May the praise of God be in their
　　mouths[f]
　　and a double-edged[g] sword in their
　　hands,[h]
[7]to inflict vengeance[i] on the nations
　　and punishment[j] on the peoples,
[8]to bind their kings with fetters,[k]
　　their nobles with shackles of iron,[l]
[9]to carry out the sentence written against
　　them.[m]
　　This is the glory of all his saints.[n]

Praise the Lord.

Psalm 150

[1]Praise the Lord.[z][o]

　Praise God in his sanctuary;[p]

148:7 /S Ge 1:21;
Ps 74:13-14
gS Dt 33:13
148:8
hS Ex 9:18;
S Jos 10:11
/Job 37:11-12;
S Ps 103:20;
147:15-18
148:9 /Isa 44:23;
49:13; 55:12
148:10
kIsa 43:20;
Hos 2:18
148:11
/S Ps 102:15
148:13
mS Ps 113:2;
138:4 nS Ps 145:5
oS Ps 8:1
148:14
pS 1Sa 2:1
qS Ex 15:2;
Ps 22:3
rS Ps 145:10
sS Dt 26:19
149:1 rPs 33:2;
103:1 uS Ps 28:7;
S 96:1; Rev 5:9
vS Ps 1:5
149:2 wIsa 13:3;
Jer 51:48
xS Job 10:3;
Ps 95:6; Isa 44:2;
45:11; 54:5
yPs 10:16; 47:6;
Isa 32:1; Zec 9:9

149:3
zS Ex 15:20
aS Ps 57:8
149:4 bPs 35:27;
147:11
cPs 132:16
149:5
dS Ps 132:16
eJob 35:10;
Ps 42:8
149:6 /Ps 66:17
gHeb 4:12;
Rev 1:16
hNe 4:17

149:7 /S Nu 31:3; S Dt 32:41 /Ps 81:15 kS 2Sa 3:34;
S Isa 14:1-2 /2Ch 33:11 **149:9** mDt 7:1; Eze 28:26
nS Ps 145:10 **150:1** oS Ps 112:1 pPs 68:24-26; 73:17;
102:19

x[14] *Horn* here symbolizes strong one, that is, king.
y[1] Hebrew *Hallelu Yah*; also in verse 9　　z[1] Hebrew
Hallelu Yah; also in verse 6

148:8 *his bidding.* Lit. "his word" (see 147:15 and note).
148:13–14 Conclusion, with focus on motivation for
praise.
148:13 *his name . . . his splendor.* As shown in the glory of
his creation. *is above.* The glory of the Creator is greater than
the glory of the creation.
148:14 *horn.* The Lord's anointed (see NIV text note; see
also notes on 2:2; Ps 18 title). It may be, however, that
"horn" here represents the strength and vigor of God's
people (see 92:10; 1Sa 2:1; Jer 48:25; La 2:17). In any
event, reference is to God's saving acts for Israel—God is to
be praised for his works in creation and redemption (see note
on 65:6–7). *praise.* See 22:3 and note.
Ps 149 Praise of God for the high honor bestowed on his
people. It is no doubt postexilic. Israel's unique honor has
two sides: She has been granted salvation (in fact and in
promise), and she has been armed to execute God's sentence
of judgment on the world powers that have launched their
attacks against the kingdom of God—she is the earthly contingent of the armies of the King of heaven (see 68:17 and
note; see also Jos 5:14; 2Sa 5:23–24; 2Ch 20:15–17,22;
Hab 3:3–15). This next-to-last psalm clearly marks the Psalter as the prayer book (liturgical book of prayer and praise) of
OT Israel.
　Following an introductory verse, the two main themes are
developed in two balanced stanzas of four verses each. References to God's "saints" enclose the song (see also v. 5). The
common pair of synonyms, "honor" (v. 5) and "glory" (v. 9),
effectively link the two stanzas (see 8:5; 21:5, "glory . . .
majesty"; 104:1,31, "majesty . . . glory"; 145:5,12, "glori-

ous splendor"; Isa 35:2, "glory . . . splendor").
149:1 *new song.* See note on 33:3. *in the assembly.* See
note on 9:1. *saints.* See vv. 5,9; see also note on 4:3.
149:2–5 Let Israel rejoice in their King, who has crowned
them with the honor of salvation.
149:3 *his name.* See note on 5:11.
149:4 *crowns.* Endows with splendor (see Isa 55:5; 60:9;
61:3). *humble.* Those who acknowledge that they are without resources (see 147:6).
149:5 *on their beds.* The salvation (v. 4) so tangible in the
daytime evokes songs in the night (see 42:8; 63:6; 77:6).
149:6–9 Let Israel praise their God, who has given them
the glory of bearing the sword as his army in service.
149:7 *vengeance.* God's just retribution on those who
have attacked his kingdom. Of this divine retribution the OT
speaks often: 58:10; 79:10; 94:1; Nu 31:2; Dt 32:35,41,
43; 2Ki 9:7; Isa 34:8; 35:4; 47:3; 59:17; 61:2; 63:4; Jer
46:10; 50:15,28; 51:6,11,36; Eze 25:14,17; Mic 5:15; Na
1:2. In the NT age, however, God's people are armed with
the "sword of the Spirit" for overcoming the powers arrayed
against God's kingdom (see 2Co 6:7; 10:4; Eph 6:12,17;
Heb 4:12); their participation in God's retribution on the
world awaits the final judgment (see 1Co 6:2–3).
149:9 *sentence written.* God's firmly determined judgment (see 139:16 and note).
Ps 150 The final great Hallelujah—perhaps composed
specifically to close the Psalter. See the conclusions to the
first four Books: 41:13; 72:18–19; 89:52; 106:48. This
final call to praise moves powerfully by stages from place to
themes to orchestra to choir, framed with Hallelujahs. See

praise him in his mighty heavens. ^{q}
^{2}Praise him for his acts of power; ^{r}
praise him for his surpassing
greatness. ^{s}
^{3}Praise him with the sounding of the
trumpet, ^{t}
praise him with the harp and lyre, ^{u}
^{4}praise him with tambourine and
dancing, ^{v}

150:1
^{q}S Ps 148:1
150:2 ^{r}S Dt 3:24
^{s}S Ex 15:7
150:3 ^{t}S Nu 10:2
^{u}S Ps 57:8
150:4
^{v}S Ex 15:20

^{w}S Ps 45:8
^{x}S Ge 4:21
150:5 ^{y}S 2Sa 6:5
150:6
^{z}S Ps 103:22

praise him with the strings ^{w} and
flute, ^{x}
^{5}praise him with the clash of cymbals, ^{y}
praise him with resounding cymbals.
^{6}Let everything ^{z} that has breath praise
the LORD.

Praise the LORD.

---

introduction to Ps 146.
150:1 Where God should be praised. *his sanctuary.* At Jerusalem. *his mighty heavens.* Lit. "the expanse of his power" (see 19:1, "skies"; Ge 1:6), i.e., the expanse that displays or symbolizes his power or in which his power resides. Usually thought to refer to God's heavenly temple (see 11:4), it may signify the vaulted ceiling of the visible universe viewed as a cosmic temple.

150:2 Why God should be praised. *his acts of power.* In creation and redemption.
150:3–5 How God should be praised—with the whole orchestra (eight instruments: wind, string, percussion), with dancing aptly placed at the middle.
150:6 Who should praise God. Finally the choir, with articulate expression, celebrates God's mighty acts and surpassing greatness.

PROVERBS

Authors

Although the book begins with a title ascribing the proverbs to Solomon, it is clear from later chapters that he was not the only author of the book. Pr 22:17 refers to the "sayings of the wise," and 24:23 mentions additional "sayings of the wise." The presence of an introduction in 22:17-21 further indicates that these sections stem from a circle of wise men, not from Solomon himself. Ch. 30 is attributed to Agur son of Jakeh and 31:1-9 to King Lemuel, neither of whom is mentioned elsewhere. Lemuel's sayings contain several Aramaic spellings that point to a non-Israelite background.

Most of the book, however, is closely linked with Solomon. The headings in 10:1 and 25:1 again include his name, though 25:1 states that these proverbs were copied by the men of Hezekiah. This indicates that a group of wise men or scribes compiled these proverbs as editors and added chs. 25-29 to the earlier collections. Solomon's ability to produce proverbs is specified in 1Ki 4:32, where 3,000 proverbs are attributed to him. Coupled with the statements about his unparalleled wisdom (1Ki 4:29-31), it is quite likely that he was the source of most of Proverbs. The book contains a short prologue (1:1-7) and a longer epilogue (31:10-31), which may have been added to the other materials. It is possible that the discourses in the large opening section (1:8-9:18) were the work of a compiler or editor, but the similarities of this section with other chapters (compare 6:1 with 11:15; 17:18; 20:16; 27:13; compare 6:19 with 14:5,25; 19:5) fit a Solomonic origin equally well. The emphasis on the "fear of the LORD" (1:7) throughout the book ties the various segments together.

Date

If Solomon is granted a prominent role in the book, most of Proverbs would stem from the tenth century B.C. during the time of Israel's united kingdom. The peace and prosperity that characterized that era accord well with the development of reflective wisdom and the production of literary works. Moreover, several scholars have noted that the 30 sayings of the wise in 22:17-24:22 contain similarities to the 30 sections of the Egyptian "Wisdom of Amenemope," an instructional piece that is roughly contemporary with the time of Solomon. Likewise, the personification of wisdom so prominent in chs. 1-9 (see 1:20 and note; 3:15-18; 8:1-36) can be compared with the personification of abstract ideas in both Mesopotamian and Egyptian writings of the second millennium B.C.

The role of Hezekiah's men (see 25:1) indicates that important sections of Proverbs were compiled and edited from 715 to 686 B.C. This was a time of spiritual renewal led by the king, who also showed great interest in the writings of David and Asaph (see 2Ch 29:30). Perhaps it was also at this time that the sayings of Agur (ch. 30) and Lemuel (31:1-9) and the other "sayings of the wise" (22:17-24:22; 24:23-34) were added to the Solomonic collections, though it is possible that the task of compilation was not completed until after the reign of Hezekiah.

Wisdom Literature

The Jews sometimes speak of the OT as the Law, the Prophets and the Writings. Included within the third division are Psalms and wisdom materials such as Job, Proverbs and Ecclesiastes. These wisdom books are associated with a class of people called "wise men" or "sages" who are listed with priests and prophets as an important force in Israelite society (Jer 18:18). Wise men were called on to give advice to kings and to instruct the young. Whereas the priests and prophets dealt more with the religious side of life, wise men were concerned about practical and philosophical matters. Some of their writings, like Proverbs, were optimistic, as they showed the young how to behave in order to live prosperous and happy lives. Other materials, such as Job and Ecclesiastes, were more pessimistic as they wrestled with difficult philosophical and theological questions such as the problem of evil and the prosperity of the wicked (see also Ps 37; 73). Both viewpoints—the optimistic and the pessimistic— are also found in the literature of other nations in the ancient Near East.

Because of the nature of Proverbs, we must not interpret it as prophecy or its statements about certain effects and results as promises. For instance, 10:27 says that the years of the wicked are cut short, while the righteous live long and prosperous lives (see 3:2 and note). The righteous have abundant food (10:3), but the wicked will go hungry (13:25). While such verses are generally true, there are enough exceptions to indicate that sometimes the righteous suffer and the wicked prosper. Normally the righteous and wicked "receive their due on earth" (11:31), but at other times reward and punishment lie beyond the grave.

The Nature of a Proverb

The Hebrew word translated "proverb" is also translated "taunt" (Isa 14:4), "oracle" (Nu 23:7,18) and "parable" (Eze 17:2); so its meaning is considerably broader than the English term. This may help explain the presence of the longer discourse sections in chs. 1-9. Most proverbs are short, compact statements that express truths about human behavior. Often there is some repetition of a word or sound that aids memorization. In 30:33, e.g., the same Hebrew verb is translated "churning," "twisting" and "stirring up."

In the largest section of the book (10:1-22:16) most of the proverbs are two lines long, and those in chs. 10-15 almost always express a contrast. Sometimes the writer simply makes a general observation, such as "a bribe is a charm to the one who gives it" (17:8; cf. 14:20), but usually he evaluates conduct: "but he who hates bribes will live" (15:27). Many proverbs, in fact, describe the consequences of a particular action or character trait: "A wise son brings joy to his father" (10:1). Since the proverbs were written primarily for instruction, often they are given in the form of commands: "Do not love sleep or you will grow poor" (20:13). Even where the imperative form is not used, the desired action is quite clear (see 14:5).

A common feature of the proverbs is the use of figurative language: "Like cold water to a weary soul / is good news from a distant land" (25:25). In ch. 25 alone there are 11 verses that begin with "like" or "as." These similes make the proverbs more vivid and powerful. Occasionally the simile is used in a humorous or sarcastic way: "Like a gold ring in a pig's snout / is a beautiful woman who shows no discretion" (11:22; cf. 26:9), or, "As a door turns on its hinges, / so a sluggard turns on his bed" (26:14). Equally effective is the use of metaphors: "The teaching of the wise is a fountain of life" (13:14), and "the tongue that brings healing is a tree of life" (15:4). According to 16:24 "pleasant words are a honeycomb." The figure of sowing and reaping is used in both a positive and a negative way (cf. 11:18; 22:8).

In order to develop a proper set of values, a number of proverbs use direct comparisons: "Better a poor man whose walk is blameless / than a rich man whose ways are perverse" (28:6). This "better . . . than" pattern can be seen also in 15:16-17; 16:19,32; 17:1,12; a modified form occurs in 22:1. Another pattern found in the book is the so-called numerical proverb. Used for the first time in 6:16 (see note there), this type of saying normally has the number three in the first line and four in the second (cf. 30:15,18,21,29).

The repetition of entire proverbs (compare 6:10-11 with 24:33-34; 14:12 with 16:25; 20:16 with 27:13) or parts of proverbs may serve a poetic purpose. A slight variation allows the writer(s) to use the same image to make a related point (as in 17:3; 27:21) or to substitute a word to achieve greater clarity or a different emphasis (cf. 19:1; 28:6). In 26:4-5 the same line is repeated in a seemingly contradictory way, but this was designed to make two different points (see notes there).

At times the book of Proverbs is very direct and earthy (cf. 6:6; 21:9; 25:16; 26:3,11). This is the nature of wisdom literature as it seeks to drive home truth and to turn sinners from their wicked ways.

Purpose and Teaching

According to the prologue, Proverbs was written to give "prudence to the simple, knowledge and discretion to the young" (1:4), and to make wise men wiser (1:5). The frequent references to "my son" (1:8,10; 2:1; 3:1; 4:1; 5:1) emphasize instructing the young and guiding them into a happy and prosperous life. Acquiring wisdom and knowing how to avoid the pitfalls of folly will lead to health and success. Although Proverbs is a practical book dealing with the art of living, it bases wisdom solidly on the fear of the Lord (1:7). Throughout the book this reverence for God is set forth as the path to life and security (cf. 3:5; 9:10; 22:4). People must trust in the Lord (3:5) and not in themselves (28:26). The references to the "tree of life" (3:18; 11:30; 13:12) recall the joyful bliss of the Garden of Eden and figuratively say that the one who finds wisdom will be greatly blessed.

In chs. 1-9 the writer contrasts the way of wisdom with the path of violence (1:11-18) and immorality (2:16-18). The adulteress with her seductive words tries to lure a young man to her house and ultimately to death (cf. ch. 5; 6:24-35; 7; 9:13-18). Sexual immorality is thus an example of and a symbol for the antithesis of wisdom (cf. 22:14; 23:27; 30:20).

At the same time, Proverbs condemns the quarrelsome wife and her unbearable ways (19:13; 21:9,19). The home is supposed to be a place of love, not dissension (cf. 15:17; 17:1). Quarrelsome, quick-tempered men are also denounced (cf. 14:29; 26:21), and gossiping is viewed as a source of great trouble (11:13; 18:8; 26:22). If anyone is able to control his tongue, he is a man of knowledge (cf. 10:19; 17:27). At the same time, the tongue must be used to instruct one's children (cf. 1:8; 22:6; 31:26), and discipline is necessary for their well-being (see 13:24 and note).

Proverbs strongly encourages diligence and hard work (see 10:4 and note; 31:17-19) and holds the sluggard up to contempt for his laziness (see 6:6 and note). A son "who sleeps during harvest is a disgraceful son" (10:5), and those who love sleep are sure to grow poor (cf. 20:13). Generally, wealth is connected to righteousness (cf. 3:16) and poverty to wickedness (cf. 22:16), but some verses link riches with the wicked (15:16; 28:6). Honesty and justice are praised repeatedly, and it is expected that a king will defend the rights of the poor and needy (cf. 31:5). Those who are kind to the needy will be richly blessed (see 14:21 and note), but there are several warnings against putting up security for a neighbor (see 6:1 and note).

The proud and the arrogant are sure to be destroyed (cf. 11:2; 16:18), especially the mocker with his "overweening pride" (see 21:24 and note on 1:22). Drunkards are depicted as the epitome of the fool (cf. 20:1), and their woes and miseries are described in graphic terms in 23:29-35.

Although Proverbs is more practical than theological, God's work as Creator is especially highlighted. The role of wisdom in creation is the subject of 8:22-31 (see notes there), where wisdom as an attribute of God is personified. Twice God is called the Maker of the poor (14:31; 17:5). He also directs the steps of a man (cf. 16:9; 20:24), and his eyes observe all his actions (cf. 5:21; 15:3). God is sovereign over the kings of the earth (21:1), and all history moves forward under his control (see notes on 16:4,33).

Literary Structure

The sectional headings found in the NIV text itself divide the book into well-defined units. A short prologue (stating the purpose and theme, 1:1-7) opens the book, and a longer epilogue (identifiable by its subject matter and its alphabetic form, 31:10-31) closes it. The first nine chapters contain a series of discourses that contrast the way and benefits of wisdom with the way of the fool. Except for the sections where personified wisdom speaks (1:20; 8:1,22; 9:1), each discourse begins with "my son" or "my sons." These units are similar to the discourses found in Job and Ecclesiastes, which also contain speeches given in poetic form.

A key feature in the introductory discourses of Proverbs is the personification of both wisdom and folly (as women), each of whom (by appeals and warnings on the part of Lady Wisdom, by enticements on the part of Lady Folly) seeks to persuade "simple" youths to follow her ways. These discourses are strikingly organized. Beginning (1:8-33) and ending (chs. 8-9) with direct enticements and appeals, the main body of the discourses is made up of two nicely balanced sections, one devoted to the commendation of wisdom (chs. 2-4) and the other to warnings against folly (chs. 5-7). In these discourses the young man is depicted as being enticed to folly by men who try to get ahead in the world by exploiting others (1:10-19) and by women who seek sexual pleasure outside the bond of marriage (ch. 5; 6:20-25; 7). In the social structures of that day, these were the two great temptations for young men. The second especially functions here as illustrative and emblematic of the appeal of Lady Folly.

The main collection of Solomon's proverbs in 10:1-22:16 consists of individual couplets, many of which express a contrast. On the surface, there does not seem to be any discernible arrangement, though occasionally two or three proverbs deal with the same subject. For example, 11:24-25 deals with generosity, 16:12-15 mentions a king, and 19:4,6-7 talks about friendship. However, there is growing evidence that arrangements of larger units were deliberate. Further study of this possibility is necessary. The second Solomonic collection (chs. 25-29) continues the pattern of two-line verses, but there are also examples of proverbs with three (25:13; 27:10,22) or four (25:4-5,21-22; 26:18-19) lines. The last five verses of ch. 27 (vv. 23-27) present a short discourse on the benefits of raising flocks and herds.

In the "thirty sayings" of the wise (22:17-24:22) and the "further sayings" of 24:23-34, there is a prevalence of two- or three-verse units and something of a return to the style of chs. 1-9 (see 23:29-35

especially). These sections function as an appendix to 10:1-22:16 and contain some similar proverbs (compare 24:6 with 11:14; 24:16 with 11:5). Even stronger are the links with chs. 1-9 (compare 23:27 with 2:16; 24:33-34 with 6:10-11).

The last two chapters serve as an appendix to chs. 25-29. The words of Agur are dominated by the numerical proverb (30:15,18,21,24,29) and include a close parallel to Ps 18:30 in 30:5 (also compare 30:6 with Dt 4:2). After the nine verses attributed to King Lemuel (31:1-9), Proverbs concludes with an epilogue, an impressive acrostic poem honoring the wife of noble character. She demonstrates, and thus epitomizes, many of the qualities and values identified with wisdom throughout the book. In view of the fact that Proverbs is primarily addressed to young men on the threshold of mature life, this focus on the wife of noble character appears surprising. But its purpose may be twofold: (1) to offer counsel on the kind of wife a young man ought to seek, and (2) in a subtle way to advise the young man (again) to marry Lady Wisdom, thus returning to the theme of chs. 1-9 (as climaxed in ch. 9; compare the description of Lady Wisdom in 9:1-2 with the virtues of the wife of noble character). In any event, the concluding epitomizing of wisdom in the wife of noble character forms a literary frame with the opening discourses, where wisdom is personified as a woman.

Outline

Prologue: Purpose and Theme

1 The proverbs[a] of Solomon[b] son of David, king of Israel:[c]

2for attaining wisdom and discipline;
    for understanding words of insight;
3for acquiring a disciplined and prudent
        life,
    doing what is right and just and fair;
4for giving prudence to the simple,[d]
    knowledge and discretion[e] to the
        young—
5let the wise listen and add to their
        learning,[f]
    and let the discerning get guidance—
6for understanding proverbs and
        parables,[g]
    the sayings and riddles[h] of the
        wise.[i]

7The fear of the LORD[j] is the beginning
        of knowledge,
    but fools[a] despise wisdom[k] and
        discipline.[l]

Exhortations to Embrace Wisdom

Warning Against Enticement

8Listen, my son,[m] to your father's[n]
        instruction

and do not forsake your mother's
        teaching.[o]
9They will be a garland to grace your
        head
    and a chain to adorn your neck.[p]

10My son, if sinners entice[q] you,
    do not give in[r] to them.[s]
11If they say, "Come along with us;
    let's lie in wait[t] for someone's blood,
    let's waylay some harmless soul;
12let's swallow[u] them alive, like the
        grave,[b]
    and whole, like those who go down
        to the pit;[v]
13we will get all sorts of valuable things
    and fill our houses with plunder;
14throw in your lot with us,
    and we will share a common
        purse[w]"—
15my son, do not go along with them,
    do not set foot[x] on their paths;[y]
16for their feet rush into sin,[z]
    they are swift to shed blood.[a]
17How useless to spread a net
    in full view of all the birds!
18These men lie in wait[b] for their own
        blood;
    they waylay only themselves![c]

1:1 aMt 13:3
b 1Ki 4:29-34
cPr 10:1; 25:1;
Ecc 1:1
1:4 dPr 8:5
ePr 8:12
1:5 fPr 9:9
1:6 gS Ps 49:4;
Mt 13:10-17
hS Nu 12:8;
S Jdg 14:12
iPr 22:17; 24:23
1:7 jS Ex 20:20;
S Job 23:15;
Ps 34:4-22;
S 112:1; Pr 9:10;
15:33; Isa 33:6;
50:10; 59:19
kS Dt 4:6; Jer 8:9
lPr 8:33-36;
9:7-9; 12:1;
13:18; 15:32
1:8 mver 8-9;
Pr 2:1; 3:1; 4:1;
5:1; 6:1; 7:1;
19:27; 22:17;
23:26-28
nJer 35:8

oS Dt 21:18;
Pr 6:20
1:9 pPr 3:21-22;
4:1-9
1:10 qS Job 24:15
rDt 13:8 sver 15;
Ps 1:1; Pr 16:29
1:11 tS Ps 10:8
1:12 uS Ps 35:25
vver 16-18;
S Job 33:18;
S Ps 30:3
1:14 wver 19
1:15
xS Ps 119:101
yS Ge 49:6;
Pr 4:14
1:16 zS Job 15:31
aPr 6:18; Isa 59:7
1:18 bS Ps 71:10
cS ver 11-12

a 7 The Hebrew words rendered *fool* in Proverbs, and often elsewhere in the Old Testament, denote one who is morally deficient.   b 12 Hebrew *Sheol*

1:1 *Solomon.* His wisdom and prolific production of proverbs and songs are mentioned in 1Ki 4:32. His name occurs again in the headings of 10:1 and 25:1. Cf. Ecc 1:1; SS 1:1.
1:2–4 Verses 2–3 apply to the son (or student); v. 4 refers to the father (or teacher).
1:2 *wisdom.* This key term occurs 41 times in the book. It includes skill in living—following God's design and thus avoiding moral pitfalls. A craftsman can be called a wise (skillful) man (Ex 31:3). Proverbs urges people to get wisdom (4:5), for it is worth more than silver or gold (3:13–14). The NT refers to Christ as "wisdom from God" (1Co 1:30; cf. Col 2:3).
1:3 *right and just and fair.* See 2:9.
1:4 *prudence.* Good judgment or good sense (see 15:5; 19:25). Outside Proverbs the Hebrew word is used in the negative sense of "shrewd" or "crafty" (Ge 3:1; Job 5:13). *simple.* Another key word in Proverbs, occurring some 15 times. It denotes those who are easily persuaded and who "lack judgment" (9:4,16), who are immature, inexperienced and naive (cf. Ps 19:7. See NIV text note on v. 22.
1:6 *riddles.* The Hebrew for this word can sometimes refer to allegories (cf. Eze 17:2).
1:7 The theme of the book (see 9:10; 31:30; cf. Job 28:28; Ps 111:10). *fear of the LORD.* A loving reverence for God that includes submission to his lordship and to the commands of his word (Ecc 12:13). God is our king (Mal 1:14), but even as we stand in awe of him we can rejoice (see Ps 2:11; Isa 12:6). *fools.* Those who hate knowledge (v. 22) and correction of any kind (12:1), who are "quick to quarrel" (20:3) and "give full vent" to their anger (29:11), who are complacent (v. 32) and who trust in themselves (28:26) rather than in God (Ps 14:1). *despise wisdom and discipline.* See 5:12

and note.
1:8 A typical introduction to an instruction speech in Proverbs, evoking a domestic situation of a father preparing his son for life in the world. Here and in 6:20 the mother is also depicted as teacher.
1:9 *to grace . . . to adorn.* Those who follow wisdom add beauty and honor to their lives.
1:11 *lie in wait for . . . blood.* Their goal is personal enrichment by theft or oppression (vv. 13,19), even if they have to commit murder. The author uses two major enticements that confronted the young man (in that culture) as examples of the way of folly: (1) to get rich by exploiting others (here) and (2) to be drawn into illicit sexual pleasure by immoral women who fail to honor their marriage vows (5:1–6; 6:24; 7:5; cf. 2:12–19).
1:12 *swallow . . . like the grave.* Vivid poetic imagery for shamelessly victimizing others.
1:13 *valuable things.* By contrast, the book of Proverbs teaches that wisdom brings the greatest riches man could ever gain (3:14–16; 16:16; see also Job 28:12–19).
1:15 *paths.* Cf. the destructive paths of the adulteress in 2:18; 7:25.
1:16 The same as the first two lines of Isa 59:7 and partially quoted in Ro 3:15. Cf. Pr 6:17–18.
1:17 *net.* Nets were used to catch birds and animals (see 6:5; 7:23; Ecc 9:12; Isa 51:20; Jer 5:26).
1:18 *waylay only themselves.* The wicked unintentionally spread a net for their own feet (29:6; Ps 35:8), so they are less intelligent than birds (see 7:22–23). According to Isa 17:14, the lot of those who plunder God's people is destruction.

¹⁹Such is the end of all who go after
ill-gotten gain;
it takes away the lives of those who
get it. ^d

Warning Against Rejecting Wisdom

²⁰Wisdom calls aloud ^e in the street,
she raises her voice in the public
squares;
²¹at the head of the noisy streets ^c she
cries out,
in the gateways of the city she makes
her speech:

²²"How long will you simple ones ^{d f} love
your simple ways?
How long will mockers delight in
mockery
and fools hate ^g knowledge?
²³If you had responded to my rebuke,
I would have poured out my heart to
you
and made my thoughts known to
you.
²⁴But since you rejected ^h me when I
called ⁱ
and no one gave heed ^j when I
stretched out my hand,
²⁵since you ignored all my advice
and would not accept my rebuke,
²⁶I in turn will laugh ^k at your disaster; ^l

I will mock ^m when calamity
overtakes you ⁿ—
²⁷when calamity overtakes you like a
storm,
when disaster ^o sweeps over you like
a whirlwind,
when distress and trouble overwhelm
you.

²⁸"Then they will call to me but I will not
answer; ^p
they will look for me but will not find
me. ^q
²⁹Since they hated knowledge
and did not choose to fear the
LORD, ^r
³⁰since they would not accept my advice
and spurned my rebuke, ^s
³¹they will eat the fruit of their ways
and be filled with the fruit of their
schemes. ^t
³²For the waywardness of the simple will
kill them,
and the complacency of fools will
destroy them; ^u
³³but whoever listens to me will live in
safety ^v
and be at ease, without fear of
harm." ^w

1:19 ^dS ver
13-14;
Pr 4:14-17; 11:19
1:20
^eS Job 28:12;
Pr 7:10-13; 9:1-3,
13-15
1:22 ^fPr 6:32;
7:7; 8:5; 9:4,16
^gPs 50:17
1:24 ^hJer 26:5;
35:17; 36:31
ⁱIsa 65:12; 66:4;
Jer 7:13
^jS 1Sa 8:19
1:26 ^kS Ps 2:4
^lver 33; S Ps 59:8

1:27 ^mS 2Ki 19:21
ⁿDt 28:63
^oS Ps 18:18;
Ps 5:12-14
1:28 ^pS Dt 1:45;
S 1Sa 8:18;
S Jer 11:11
^qS Job 27:9;
Pr 8:17; Eze 8:18;
Hos 5:6; Zec 7:13
1:29 ^rS Job 21:14
1:30 ^sver 25
1:31
^tS 2Ch 36:16;
Pr 14:14;
Jer 6:19; 14:16;
21:14; 30:15
1:32 ^uPr 5:22;
15:10; Isa 66:4
1:33
^vS Nu 24:21;
S Dt 33:28;
Pr 3:23 ^wS ver
21-26; S Ps 112:8

^c21 Hebrew; Septuagint / on the tops of the walls
^d22 The Hebrew word rendered *simple* in Proverbs
generally denotes one without moral direction and
inclined to evil.

1:19 Cf. Isa 17:14. Contrast the long life enjoyed by the one who hates ill-gotten gain (28:16).

1:20 *Wisdom calls aloud.* Here and in 3:15–18; 8; 9:1–12 wisdom is personified. This is a poetic device common also in Isaiah (cf. 55:12; 59:14). *public squares.* Open areas inside the gate of a fortified city.

1:21 *gateways.* Where the leaders of the city met to hold court (see 31:23; Ru 4:11; Job 29:7) and where the marketplace was located (2Ki 7:1). As a young man confronts life in its social context, two voices lure him, appeal for his allegiance, and seek to shape his life: (1) the voice of wisdom (as exemplified in the instructions of the teachers of wisdom) and (2) the voice of folly (as exemplified in the sinners of vv. 10–14 and in the adulteress of 5:3; 6:24; 7:5). Thus in the midst of life the youth must learn to exercise discretion. Here and in chs. 8–9 wisdom makes her appeal. She speaks neither out of heaven (by special revelation, as do the prophets) nor out of the earth (through voices from the dead—necromancy; see Lev 19:31; Dt 18:11; 1Sa 28:7–19), but out of the center of the life of the city, where man's communal experience of the creation order (established by God's wisdom, 8:22–31) is concentrated (see, e.g., 11:10 and note). And it is there also that the godly, the truly wise, test human experience in the crucible of faith and afterward give divine wisdom a human voice in their wise instructions—as in Proverbs.

1:22 *mockers.* Those who are proud and arrogant (21:24), who are full of insults, hatred and strife (9:7–8; 22:10; 29:8), who resist correction (13:1; 15:12) even though they

deserve flogging (19:25; 21:11).

1:23 *poured out my heart.* Wisdom is like a fountain. Her words would constantly refresh and strengthen (see 18:4).

1:24 *rejected me.* As God was rejected by Israel (see Isa 1:4; 5:24) and Jesus by the people of Jerusalem (Mt 23:37). *stretched out my hand.* Cf. Isa 65:2, where God held out his hands all day long to a stubborn people.

1:25 *ignored . . . advice.* Cf. 8:33.

1:26 *laugh at your disaster.* Not an expression of heartlessness but a reaction to the absurdity of fools, who laugh at wisdom and bring disaster on themselves. Cf. the Lord's response to kings whom they think they can rebel against him (Ps 2:4). *calamity overtakes you.* Also the fate of "a scoundrel and villain" (6:12–15).

1:27 *like a storm.* See 10:25. *like a whirlwind.* When Job's family was killed by a mighty wind (Job 1:19), his comforters concluded that his wickedness was the cause of the disaster (Job 18:5,12). *distress and trouble.* See Isa 8:22.

1:28 *I will not answer.* Just as God refused to listen to Israel when the people sinned (Dt 1:45; Isa 1:15). *find me.* Those who find wisdom find life and blessing (see v. 32; 3:13; 8:17,35).

1:29 *fear the LORD.* See note on v. 7.

1:31 *eat . . . be filled with the fruit.* The consequences depend on their actions (18:20; 31:31; Isa 3:10). "A man reaps what he sows" (Gal 6:7).

1:32 *complacency.* A false sense of security (see Isa 32:9; Am 6:1; Zep 1:12).

1:33 *in safety . . . at ease.* Words used of places that enjoy God's protection (see Isa 32:18; Eze 34:27).

Moral Benefits of Wisdom

2 My son,[x] if you accept my words
and store up my commands within
you,
[2]turning your ear to wisdom
and applying your heart to
understanding,[y]
[3]and if you call out for insight[z]
and cry aloud for understanding,
[4]and if you look for it as for silver
and search for it as for hidden
treasure,[a]
[5]then you will understand the fear of the
Lord
and find the knowledge of God.[b]
[6]For the Lord gives wisdom,[c]
and from his mouth come knowledge
and understanding.[d]
[7]He holds victory in store for the upright,
he is a shield[e] to those whose walk
is blameless,[f]
[8]for he guards the course of the just
and protects the way of his faithful
ones.[g]
[9]Then you will understand[h] what is
right and just
and fair—every good path.
[10]For wisdom will enter your heart,[i]
and knowledge will be pleasant to
your soul.
[11]Discretion will protect you,

and understanding will guard you.[j]

[12]Wisdom will save[k] you from the ways
of wicked men,
from men whose words are perverse,
[13]who leave the straight paths
to walk in dark ways,[l]
[14]who delight in doing wrong
and rejoice in the perverseness of
evil,[m]
[15]whose paths are crooked[n]
and who are devious in their ways.[o]

[16]It will save you also from the
adulteress,[p]
from the wayward wife with her
seductive words,
[17]who has left the partner of her youth
and ignored the covenant she made
before God.[e][q]
[18]For her house leads down to death
and her paths to the spirits of the
dead.[r]
[19]None who go to her return
or attain the paths of life.[s]

[20]Thus you will walk in the ways of good
men
and keep to the paths of the
righteous.
[21]For the upright will live in the land,[t]
and the blameless will remain in it;

2:1 *x*S Pr 1:8
2:2 *y*Pr 22:17;
23:12
2:3 *z*Jas 1:5
2:4 *a*S Job 3:21;
Mt 13:44
2:5 *b*S Dt 4:6
2:6 *c*S Job 12:13;
S Ps 119:34
*d*S Job 9:4;
S 22:22
2:7 *e*S Ge 15:1;
Pr 30:5-6
*f*S Ge 6:9;
Ps 84:11
2:8 *g*1Sa 2:9;
S Ps 18:25;
S 97:10
2:9 *h*S Dt 1:16
2:10 *i*Pr 14:33

2:11 *j*Pr 4:6
2:12 *k*ver 16;
Pr 3:13-18; 4:5
2:13 *l*Pr 4:19
2:14 *m*Pr 10:23;
15:21
2:15 *n*S Ps 125:5
*o*Pr 21:8
2:16 *p*Pr 5:1-6;
6:20-29; 7:5-27
2:17 *q*Mal 2:14
2:18 *r*Pr 5:5;
7:27; 9:18
2:19 *s*Pr 3:16-18;
5:8; Ecc 7:26
2:21 *t*S Ps 37:29

*e*17 Or *covenant of her God*

2:1 *store up ... within you.* Just as the psalmist urged young men to avoid sin by hiding God's word in their hearts (Ps 119:11).
2:2 *turning your ear.* Listening implies obedience (Isa 55:3; Jer 13:15). *heart.* The Hebrew word translated "heart" here (and in 4:21; 1Ki 3:9) can sometimes be translated "mind" (see Job 12:3).
2:4 *silver ... hidden treasure.* Job 28:1–11 describes ancient mining techniques, comparing mining with the search for wisdom (see Job 28:12).
2:5 *fear of the Lord.* See note on 1:7. *knowledge of God.* Involves knowing God as a person (Php 3:10) and knowing what he is teaching us (v. 6). *God.* Hebrew *Elohim* (see note on Ge 2:4); occurs elsewhere in Proverbs only in v. 17; 3:4; 25:2; 30:9.
2:7 *holds ... in store.* For those who "store up" his commands (v. 1). *shield.* Associated with victory also in Ps 18:2,35; cf. Pr 30:5. *blameless.* Those with spiritual and moral integrity. This does not imply sinlessness (see 19:1; see also note on Job 1:1).
2:8 *guards ... protects.* See Ps 91:3–7,11–12.
2:9–11 Those who know the Lord and the wisdom he gives will know what course of action to follow (cf. Heb 5:11–14).
2:9 *right and just and fair.* See 1:3; Php 4:8. *good path.* See "the paths of righteousness" of Ps 23:3.
2:10 *pleasant to your soul.* Just as the words of a wise man are "sweet to the soul" of another (16:24; cf. 3:17).
2:11 *protect ... guard.* As God guards the faithful (v. 8).
2:12–19 Wisdom will save from the enticements of men to follow perverse ways (vv. 12–15) and from the enticements of the adulteress (vv. 16–19). See note on 1:11.

2:12 *words are perverse.* Cf. v. 14. The deceitfulness of men's speech is also mentioned in 8:13; 10:31–32; 17:20.
2:13 *straight paths.* See 3:6; 9:15–16. *dark ways.* Men love darkness instead of light (see Jn 3:19–21; see also Job 24:15–16; Isa 29:15; Ro 13:12).
2:14 *delight ... rejoice in ... evil.* Like the sinners of 1:10–16.
2:15 *paths are crooked.* See Isa 59:7–8.
2:16 *adulteress ... wayward wife.* The Hebrew for these terms occurs again in 5:20 and 7:5. The terms mean lit. "stranger" and "foreigner" (cf. 5:10) because anyone other than one's own wife was to be considered off limits, like a foreigner who worshiped another god (cf. 1Ki 11:1). "Wayward wife" is parallel to "immoral woman" in 6:24 and "prostitute" in 23:27. *seductive words.* Equal to the "smooth tongue" of 6:24 and the "smooth talk" of 7:21. Cf. 5:3.
2:17 *partner of her youth.* Her husband, whom she married when she was a young woman (cf. Isa 54:6). *covenant ... before God.* Probably the marriage covenant, spoken in God's presence (see Eze 16:8; Mal 2:14). Alternatively, the breaking of the seventh commandment (Ex 20:14) may be indicated (see NIV text note).
2:18 *leads down to death.* According to 7:27, "her house is a highway to the grave." A life of immorality leads to the destruction and death of all who are involved (cf. 5:5; 9:18). *spirits of the dead.* See Job 26:5; Isa 14:9; 26:14 and notes. The deceased are in the grave (or Sheol), "the chambers of death" (7:27).
2:21 *live in the land.* Israel had been promised the land of Canaan (Ge 17:8; Dt 4:1), and Ps 37:29 says that "the righteous will inherit the land" (see Ps 37:9,11; Mt 5:5).

22but the wicked[u] will be cut off from the land,[v]
and the unfaithful will be torn from it.[w]

Further Benefits of Wisdom

3 My son,[x] do not forget my teaching,[y]
but keep my commands in your heart,
2for they will prolong your life many years[z]
and bring you prosperity.[a]
3Let love and faithfulness[b] never leave you;
bind them around your neck,
write them on the tablet of your heart.[c]
4Then you will win favor and a good name
in the sight of God and man.[d]
5Trust in the LORD[e] with all your heart
and lean not on your own understanding;
6in all your ways acknowledge him,
and he will make your paths[f] straight.[f] [g]
7Do not be wise in your own eyes;[h]
fear the LORD[i] and shun evil.[j]
8This will bring health to your body[k]
and nourishment to your bones.[l]
9Honor the LORD with your wealth,
with the firstfruits[m] of all your crops;
10then your barns will be filled[n] to overflowing,
and your vats will brim over with new wine.[o]
11My son,[p] do not despise the LORD's discipline[q]
and do not resent his rebuke,
12because the LORD disciplines those he loves,[r]
as a father[g] the son he delights in.[s]
13Blessed is the man who finds wisdom,
the man who gains understanding,
14for she is more profitable than silver
and yields better returns than gold.[t]
15She is more precious than rubies;[u]
nothing you desire can compare with her.[v]
16Long life is in her right hand;[w]
in her left hand are riches and honor.[x]
17Her ways are pleasant ways,
and all her paths are peace.[y]

2:22 [u]S Ps 5:4 [v]S Job 18:17 [w]Dt 28:63; S 29:28; Ps 37:9, 28-29; Pr 10:30 **3:1** [x]S Pr 1:8 [y]S Ps 44:17 **3:2** [z]S Dt 11:21 [a]S Dt 5:16; S 30:15,16; S 1Ki 3:13,14; Pr 9:6,10-11 **3:3** [b]S Ps 85:10 [c]S Ex 13:9; S Dt 6:6; Pr 6:21; 7:3; S 2Co 3:3 **3:4** [d]S 1Sa 2:26; Lk 2:52 **3:5** [e]S Ps 4:5 **3:6** [f]S Job 33:11; S Isa 30:11 [g]Ps 5:8; Pr 16:3; Isa 40:3; Jer 42:3 **3:7** [h]Pr 26:5,12; Isa 5:21 [i]Ps 111:10 [j]S Ex 20:20; S Dt 4:6; S Job 1:1 **3:8** [k]S Ps 38:3; Pr 4:22 [l]Job 21:24 **3:9** [m]S Ex 22:29; Dt 26:1-15 **3:10** [n]Ps 144:13 [o]S Job 22:21; Joel 2:24; Mal 3:10-12 **3:11** [p]Pr 1:8-9 [q]S Job 5:17 **3:12** [r]Pr 13:24; Rev 3:19 [s]S Dt 8:5; S Job 5:17; Heb 12:5-6* **3:14** [t]S Job 28:15; Pr 8:19; 16:16 **3:15** [u]S Job 28:18 [v]S Job 28:17-19 **3:16** [w]S Ge 15:15 [x]S 1Ki 3:13,14 **3:17** [y]Mt 11:28-30

[f]6 Or *will direct your paths* [g]12 Hebrew; Septuagint */ and he punishes*

blameless. See note on v. 7.
2:22 *cut off from the land . . . torn from it.* In Dt 28:63 God warned that if the people refuse to obey him, they "will be uprooted from the land." Evil men and their offspring will be cut off (Ps 37:9,28).
3:2 *prolong your life.* Fear of the Lord (10:27; 19:23) brings health to the body (v. 8) and "adds length to life" (10:27; see also 9:10–11). *prosperity.* When Solomon prayed for wisdom, God promised him riches as well as long life if he obeyed God's commands (1Ki 3:13–14). Normally the righteous are prosperous and happy (12:21), but sometimes it is the wicked who are strong and prosperous (Ps 73:3,12), temporary though that may be (Ps 73:17–19). Job 1–2 also shows how disaster and death can strike a godly person.
3:3 *bind . . . neck.* Like a beautiful necklace (cf. 1:9; 3:22). *write them on the tablet of your heart.* See Jer 31:33.
3:4 *favor.* See 8:35; Ge 6:8. *God and man.* See Lk 2:52; Ro 12:17; 2Co 8:21.
3:5 *Trust in the LORD.* Commit your way to the Lord (Ps 37:5), like Israel's forefathers, who trusted in God and were rescued (Ps 22:4–5). *with all your heart.* Like Caleb (Nu 14:24; Dt 1:36) or the godly King Hezekiah (Isa 38:3). David challenged Solomon to serve God with wholehearted devotion (1Ch 28:9).
3:6 *acknowledge him.* Be ever mindful of God and serve him with a willing and faithful heart (see 1Ch 28:9; Hos 4:1; 6:6). *make your paths straight.* He will remove the obstacles from your pathway and bring you to your appointed goal (see 11:5; Isa 45:13).
3:7 *fear the LORD and shun evil.* Cf. Job, who was a "blameless and upright" man (Job 1:1). See note on 1:7.
3:8 *bones.* The whole body. Elsewhere, good news and pleasant words bring health to the bones (15:30; 16:24; cf. 17:22).
3:9 *firstfruits.* The Israelites were required to give to the priests the first part of the olive oil, wine and grain produced each year (see Lev 23:10; Nu 18:12–13).
3:10 *filled to overflowing.* For those who bring to the Lord his tithes and offerings, God promises to pour out more blessing than they have room for (see Mal 3:10; see also Dt 28:8,12; 2Co 9:8).
3:11–12 A warning that the righteous are not always prosperous (see v. 2 and note). Through times of testing and affliction, God is teaching them (see 12:1; Job 5:17; 36:22; Ps 119:71). Heb 12:5–6 quotes both of these verses to encourage believers to endure hardship (Heb 12:7). "God disciplines us for our good" (Heb 12:10).
3:12 *as a father.* God disciplined his son Israel by testing the nation in the desert 40 years (Dt 8:2–5).
3:13–18 A poem praising wisdom that begins and ends with the word "blessed" (cf. Job 5:17).
3:14 *more profitable than silver . . . gold.* The psalmist makes the same claim for the commands and precepts of the Lord (Ps 19:10; 119:72,127).
3:15–18 Wisdom is personified (see note on 1:20).
3:15 *rubies.* Considered of less value than wisdom also in Job 28:18. The "wife of noble character" is worth more than rubies (31:10).
3:16 *Long life.* See note on v. 2. *riches and honor.* See 8:18; 22:4.
3:17 *pleasant ways.* See note on 2:10. *peace.* Hebrew *shalom,* translated "prosperity" in v. 2 (see 16:7; Ps 119:165).

18She is a tree of life *z* to those who
    embrace her;
    those who lay hold of her will be
    blessed. *a*

19By wisdom *b* the LORD laid the earth's
    foundations, *c*
    by understanding he set the heavens *d*
    in place;
20by his knowledge the deeps were
    divided,
    and the clouds let drop the dew.

21My son, *e* preserve sound judgment and
    discernment,
    do not let them out of your sight; *f*
22they will be life for you, *g*
    an ornament to grace your neck. *h*
23Then you will go on your way in
    safety, *i*
    and your foot will not stumble; *j*
24when you lie down, *k* you will not be
    afraid; *l*
    when you lie down, your sleep *m* will
    be sweet.
25Have no fear of sudden disaster
    or of the ruin that overtakes the
    wicked,
26for the LORD will be your confidence *n*
    and will keep your foot *o* from being
    snared. *p*
27Do not withhold good from those who
    deserve it,
    when it is in your power to act.
28Do not say to your neighbor,
    "Come back later; I'll give it
    tomorrow"—

when you now have it with you. *q*
29Do not plot harm against your neighbor,
    who lives trustfully near you. *r*
30Do not accuse a man for no reason—
    when he has done you no harm.

31Do not envy *s* a violent man
    or choose any of his ways,
32for the LORD detests a perverse man *t*
    but takes the upright into his
    confidence. *u*

33The LORD's curse *v* is on the house of
    the wicked, *w*
    but he blesses the home of the
    righteous. *x*

34He mocks *y* proud mockers *z*
    but gives grace to the humble. *a*
35The wise inherit honor,
    but fools he holds up to shame.

Wisdom Is Supreme

4 Listen, my sons, *b* to a father's
    instruction; *c*
    pay attention and gain
    understanding. *d*
2I give you sound learning,
    so do not forsake my teaching.
3When I was a boy in my father's house,
    still tender, and an only child of my
    mother,
4he taught me and said,
    "Lay hold *e* of my words with all
    your heart;
    keep my commands and you will
    live. *f*
5Get wisdom, *g* get understanding;

Cross references (center column)

3:18 *z*S Ge 2:9;
S Pr 10:11;
S Rev 2:7
*a*S Pr 2:12; 4:3-9,
8; 8:17-21
3:19 *b*S Ge 1:31;
Ps 136:5-9
*c*S Job 28:25-27
*d*Pr 8:27-29
3:21 *e*Pr 1:8-9;
6:20 *f*Pr 4:20-22
3:22 *g*S Dt 30:20;
Pr 4:13
*h*S Pr 1:8-9
3:23 *i*S Pr 1:33
*j*S Ps 37:24;
S 119:11; Pr 4:12
3:24 *k*S Lev 26:6
*l*Ps 91:5; 112:8
*m*S Job 11:18;
Jer 31:26
3:26 *n*S 2Ki 18:5;
S Job 4:6
*o*S 1Sa 2:9
*p*S Job 5:19

3:28 *q*Lev 19:13;
Dt 24:15;
Lk 10:25-37
3:29 *r*Zec 8:17
3:31 *s*S Ps 37:1;
Pr 24:1-2
3:32 *t*S Ps 101:4
*u*S Job 29:4
3:33 *v*S Job 5:3
*w*Zec 5:4
*x*Ps 37:22;
Pr 14:11
3:34 *y*S 2Ki 19:21
*z*S Ps 40:4
*a*S Ps 18:25-27;
S Mt 23:12;
Jas 4:6*; 1Pe 5:5*
4:1 *b*S Pr 1:8
*c*Pr 19:20
*d*S Job 8:10
4:4 *e*S 1Ki 9:4
*f*Pr 7:2
4:5 *g*S Pr 2:12;
3:13-18

3:18 *tree of life.* Source of life. This figure of speech may allude to the tree in the Garden of Eden (see Ge 2:9 and note; cf. Pr 11:30; 13:12; 15:4).
3:19–20 The role of wisdom in creation is described more fully in 8:22–31. Divine wisdom guided the Creator and now permeates the whole creation. To live by wisdom is to imitate the Lord and conform to the divinely appointed creation order.
3:19 *earth's foundations.* God's work in creation is compared to the construction of a building (see 1Ki 5:17; 6:37; see also 8:29; Job 38:4–6; Ps 104:5; Zec 12:1). *set the heavens in place.* See Isa 42:5; 51:16.
3:20 *divided.* Or "broken open." God opened up springs and streams (see Ge 7:11; 49:25; Ps 74:15). Alternatively, though perhaps less likely, reference is to the dividing of the waters above from the waters below (see Ge 1:7; Ps 42:7 and note). *dew.* Probably also includes rain (see Dt 33:13; 2Sa 1:21).
3:22 *ornament to grace your neck.* See note on v. 3.
3:23 *in safety, and your foot will not stumble.* Cf. 10:9.
3:24 *when you lie down, you will not be afraid.* Also listed among the covenant blessings (see Lev 26:6; Job 11:18–19; Mic 4:4; Zep 3:13; see also Pr 1:33 and note). *your sleep will be sweet.* See 6:22; Ps 4:8.
3:25 *disaster . . . ruin.* The Lord shields the godly from deadly arrows and plagues (see 10:25; Ps 91:3–8; Job 5:21). *the wicked.* See 1:26–27 and notes.

3:26 *will keep your foot from being snared.* Contrast the fate of the fool in 1:18; 7:22–23.
3:27 *withhold good.* See Ac 9:36; Gal 6:10; 1Jn 3:17–18. *those who deserve it.* Especially the poor and needy.
3:28 See Lk 11:5–8; Jas 2:15–16.
3:30 *Do not accuse . . . for no reason.* See Job 2:3.
3:31 *Do not envy.* See 24:19; Ps 37:1,7. *violent man.* Like the sinners of 1:10–16 (cf. 16:29).
3:32 *detests.* A word that elsewhere expresses abhorrence of pagan practices (see Dt 18:9,12) and moral abuses. It is common in Proverbs (e.g., 6:16; 8:7; 11:20). *takes the upright into his confidence.* See Ge 18:17–19; Job 29:4; Ps 25:14; Jn 15:15.
3:33 This contrast is seen also in Dt 11:26–28. *The LORD's curse is on the house of the wicked.* See Jos 7:24–25; Zec 5:3–4. *blesses the home of the righteous.* See Job 42:12–14.
3:34 *mocks proud mockers.* See note on 1:26. *gives grace.* Shows favor (see v. 4).
4:3 *still tender.* Cf. David's words about Solomon, who was "young and inexperienced" (1Ch 22:5; 29:1). This is part of an autobiographical statement, such as was sometimes used by the wisdom teachers (see 24:30–34; see also the book of Ecclesiastes). *only child.* Therefore deeply loved (cf. Ge 37:3; Zec 12:10).
4:4 *with all your heart.* See note on 3:5.

do not forget my words or swerve
from them.
6Do not forsake wisdom, and she will
protect you;[h]
love her, and she will watch over
you.[i]
7Wisdom is supreme; therefore get
wisdom.
Though it cost all[j] you have,[h] get
understanding.[k]
8Esteem her, and she will exalt you;
embrace her, and she will honor
you.[l]
9She will set a garland of grace on your
head
and present you with a crown of
splendor.[m]"

10Listen, my son,[n] accept what I say,
and the years of your life will be
many.[o]
11I guide[p] you in the way of wisdom
and lead you along straight paths.[q]
12When you walk, your steps will not be
hampered;
when you run, you will not
stumble.[r]
13Hold on to instruction, do not let it go;
guard it well, for it is your life.[s]
14Do not set foot on the path of the
wicked
or walk in the way of evil men.[t]
15Avoid it, do not travel on it;
turn from it and go on your way.
16For they cannot sleep till they do evil;[u]
they are robbed of slumber till they
make someone fall.
17They eat the bread of wickedness
and drink the wine of violence.[v]

18The path of the righteous[w] is like the
first gleam of dawn,[x]
shining ever brighter till the full light
of day.[y]
19But the way of the wicked is like deep
darkness;[z]
they do not know what makes them
stumble.[a]

20My son,[b] pay attention to what I say;
listen closely to my words.[c]
21Do not let them out of your sight,[d]
keep them within your heart;
22for they are life to those who find them
and health to a man's whole body.[e]
23Above all else, guard[f] your heart,
for it is the wellspring of life.[g]
24Put away perversity from your mouth;
keep corrupt talk far from your lips.
25Let your eyes[h] look straight ahead,
fix your gaze directly before you.
26Make level[i] paths for your feet[i]
and take only ways that are firm.
27Do not swerve to the right or the left;[j]
keep your foot from evil.

Warning Against Adultery

5 My son,[k] pay attention to my
wisdom,
listen well to my words[l] of insight,
2that you may maintain discretion
and your lips may preserve
knowledge.
3For the lips of an adulteress drip honey,

4:6 [h]2Th 2:10 [i]S Pr 2:11 **4:7** [j]Mt 13:44-46 [k]Pr 23:23 **4:8** [l]S Pr 3:18 **4:9** [m]S Pr 1:8-9 **4:10** [n]Ps 34:11-16; Pr 1:8-9 [o]S Dt 11:21 **4:11** [p]S 1Sa 12:23 [q]2Sa 22:37; Ps 5:8 **4:12** [r]S Job 18:7; Pr 3:23 **4:13** [s]S Pr 3:22 **4:14** [t]Ps 1:1; S Pr 1:15 **4:16** [u]Ps 36:4; Mic 7:3 **4:17** [v]Ge 49:5; Ps 73:6; Pr 1:10-19; 14:22; Isa 59:6; Jer 22:3; Hab 1:2; Mal 2:16 **4:18** [w]Job 17:9 [x]S Job 22:28 [y]S 2Sa 23:4; Da 12:3; Mt 5:14; Jn 8:12; Php 2:15 **4:19** [z]S Pr 2:13 [a]S Dt 32:35; S Job 3:23; Pr 13:9; S Isa 8:15 **4:20** [b]Ps 34:11-16; Pr 1:8-9 [c]Pr 5:1 **4:21** [d]Pr 3:21 **4:22** [e]S Pr 3:8 **4:23** [f]S 2Ki 10:31 [g]Pr 10:11; Lk 6:45 **4:25** [h]S Job 31:1 **4:26** [i]Heb 12:13* **4:27** [j]S Lev 10:11; S Dt 5:32 **5:1** [k]S Pr 1:8 [l]Pr 4:20

h *7* Or *Whatever else you get* **i** *26* Or *Consider the*

4:6 *protect . . . watch over.* The Hebrew for these two verbs is used together also in 2:8,11. *love her.* To love wisdom is to prosper (8:21); to hate wisdom is to "love death" (8:36).
4:7 *is supreme.* Or "ranks first"; translated "is the beginning" in 1:7. *Though it cost all you have.* Cf. the merchant who sold everything to buy a pearl of great value (Mt 13:45–46).
4:9 *crown of splendor.* Wreaths or crowns were worn at joyous occasions, such as weddings or feasts (see Eze 16:12; 23:42).
4:10 *years . . . will be many.* See note on 3:2.
4:11 *straight paths.* Right paths (see notes on 3:6; Ps 23:3).
4:12 *you will not stumble.* Because of some obstacle or lack of light (see v. 19; 3:23; 10:9; Ps 18:36; Isa 40:30–31).
4:14 *path of the wicked.* See 1:15 and note; Ps 1:1; 17:4–5.
4:16 *cannot sleep till they do evil.* See Ps 36:4; Mic 2:1. Contrast the attitude of David, who would not sleep until he found a permanent place for God's house (Ps 132:3–5).
4:17 *eat the bread . . . drink the wine.* They thrive on wickedness and violence (see 13:2; Job 15:16).
4:18 *path of the righteous is . . . shining ever brighter.* The godly have all the guidance and protection they need (see vv. 11–12) and are able to lead others to righteousness (Da 12:3).
4:19 *deep darkness.* A dangerous path that leads to destruction (see note on 2:13; see also Isa 59:9–10; Jer 23:12; Jn 11:10; 12:35).
4:21 *heart.* See 3:1,3.
4:22 *health.* Physical, psychological and spiritual (see 3:8 and note).
4:23 *wellspring of life.* If we store up good things (2:1) in our hearts, our words and actions will be good. "Out of the overflow of the heart the mouth speaks" (Mt 12:34; cf. Mk 7:21).
4:24 *Put away perversity from your mouth.* See note on 2:12; see also 19:1. *corrupt talk.* See 6:12; 19:28; Eph 4:29; Jas 3:6.
4:25 *look straight ahead.* Not at worthless things (Ps 119:37).
4:26 *Make level paths.* Remove every moral hindrance (see vv. 11–12; Isa 26:7).
4:27 *Do not swerve to the right or the left.* A warning found also in Dt 5:32–33; 28:14; Jos 1:7. *foot from evil.* See 1:15.
5:2 *lips may preserve knowledge.* Applied to a priest in Mal 2:7.
5:3 *lips . . . drip honey.* Probably a reference to the pleas-

and her speech is smoother than
    oil; [m]
[4]but in the end she is bitter as gall, [n]
    sharp as a double-edged sword.
[5]Her feet go down to death;
    her steps lead straight to the
        grave.[j] [o]
[6]She gives no thought to the way of life;
    her paths are crooked, but she knows
        it not. [p]

[7]Now then, my sons, listen [q] to me;
    do not turn aside from what I say.
[8]Keep to a path far from her, [r]
    do not go near the door of her house,
[9]lest you give your best strength to
        others
    and your years to one who is cruel,
[10]lest strangers feast on your wealth
    and your toil enrich another man's
        house. [s]
[11]At the end of your life you will groan,
    when your flesh and body are spent.
[12]You will say, "How I hated discipline!
    How my heart spurned correction! [t]
[13]I would not obey my teachers
    or listen to my instructors.
[14]I have come to the brink of utter ruin [u]
    in the midst of the whole
        assembly." [v]

[15]Drink water from your own cistern,
    running water from your own well.

[16]Should your springs overflow in the
        streets,
    your streams of water in the public
        squares?
[17]Let them be yours alone,
    never to be shared with strangers.
[18]May your fountain [w] be blessed,
    and may you rejoice in the wife of
        your youth. [x]
[19]A loving doe, a graceful deer[y] —
    may her breasts satisfy you always,
    may you ever be captivated by her
        love.
[20]Why be captivated, my son, by an
        adulteress?
    Why embrace the bosom of another
        man's wife?

[21]For a man's ways are in full view[z] of
        the LORD,
    and he examines[a] all his paths. [b]
[22]The evil deeds of a wicked man ensnare
        him; [c]
    the cords of his sin hold him fast. [d]
[23]He will die for lack of discipline, [e]
    led astray by his own great folly.[f]

Warnings Against Folly

6 My son,[g] if you have put up
    security[h] for your neighbor, [i]

15 Hebrew *Sheol*

Cross references

5:3 [m]S Ps 55:21;
Pr 7:5
5:4 [n]Ecc 7:26
5:5 [o]S Ps 9:17;
S Pr 2:18;
7:26-27
5:6 [p]Pr 9:13;
30:20
5:7 [q]Pr 1:8-9
5:8
[r]S Pr 2:16-19;
6:20-29; 7:1-27
5:10 [s]Pr 29:3
5:12 [t]Pr 12:1
5:14
[u]Pr 1:24-27; 6:33
[v]Pr 31:3

5:18 [w]SS 4:12-15
[x]S Dt 20:7;
Pr 2:17; Ecc 9:9;
Mal 2:14
5:19 [y]SS 4:5;
8:14
5:21
[z]S Ps 119:168
[a]Jer 29:23
[b]S Job 10:4;
S 14:16; Pr 15:3;
Jer 32:19;
S Heb 4:13
5:22 [c]Ps 9:16
[d]Nu 32:23;
S Job 18:9;
Ps 7:15-16;
S Pr 1:31-32
5:23 [e]S Job 4:21;
Pr 10:21
[f]Job 34:21-25;
Pr 11:5
6:1 [g]S Pr 1:8
[h]Job 17:3
[i]Pr 17:18

---

ant-sounding talk (cf. 16:24) of the adulteress, though some
explain it as kisses (cf. SS 4:11; 5:13; 7:9). *adulteress.* See
note on 2:16. *smoother than oil.* See 2:16. Her words are
soothing (see Ps 55:21) but full of flattery (Pr 29:5) and
hypocrisy (Ps 5:9).
5:4 *gall.* A bitter herb (see Dt 29:18; La 3:15,19; Am
6:12). *double-edged sword.* A lethal weapon (see Jdg 3:16;
see also Ps 55:21; 149:6; Heb 4:12; Rev 1:16).
5:5 *down to death.* Her immorality hastens her end (see
note on 2:18).
5:6 *paths are crooked.* See 2:15; 10:9. *knows it not.* Or
"does not acknowledge it."
5:7–14 The father (teacher) warns the son (student) about
the price of immorality.
5:8 *far from her.* See Ge 39:12; 2Ti 2:22. *door of her
house.* Cf. 7:25; 9:14.
5:9 *one who is cruel.* Possibly the vengeful husband (see
6:34–35).
5:10 *strangers feast on your wealth.* Contrast the riches
and honor that come to the man who embraces wisdom
(3:16–18). Immorality eventually reduces one "to a loaf of
bread" (6:26).
5:11 *flesh and body are spent.* Possibly because of the
debilitating effects of immorality (see 1Co 6:18; cf. Pr 3:8;
4:22), but more likely referring to the loss of vigor that
accompanies old age.
5:12 *hated discipline . . . spurned correction.* In old age he
will look back and sadly acknowledge that he has played the
fool (see 1:7,22,29–30).
5:13 *would not obey.* In spite of the repeated urging to
"listen" or "pay attention" to their instruction (1:8; 3:1;
4:1; 5:1).

5:14 *utter ruin.* Physical, financial and social. *in the midst
of the whole assembly.* The offender was subject to "blows
and disgrace" (6:33) or even death (see Dt 22:22).
5:15 *your own cistern . . . your own well.* Your own wife
(see SS 4:12,15). Let your own wife be your source of
pleasure, as water refreshes a thirsty man. Wells and cisterns
were privately owned and of great value (2Ki 18:31; Jer
38:6).
5:16 *springs . . . streams of water.* Like "cistern" and
"well" in v. 15 and "fountain" in v. 18, these also refer to
the wife (see SS 4:12,15). *in the public squares.* The wife
may become promiscuous if the husband is unfaithful.
5:18 *fountain.* See note on v. 16. *wife of your youth.*
Chosen by you when you were young (see note on 2:17).
5:19 *doe . . . deer.* Descriptive of the wife, perhaps because
of the delicate beauty of the doe's limbs (see SS 2:9). *may her
breasts satisfy you always.* See SS 7:7–8. *captivated.* Or
"exhilarated," "intoxicated." Marital love is portrayed as
better than wine in SS 4:10 (cf. SS 7:9).
5:20 *Why . . . ?* In light of the sheer joy found within the
bonds of marriage and the "utter ruin" (v. 14) outside it, why
commit adultery? *adulteress.* See v. 3; 2:16 and note.
5:21 *in full view of the LORD.* See 15:3; Job 31:4; 34:21;
Jer 16:17. *examines all his paths.* See Job 7:18; 34:23; Ps
11:4; 26:2; 139:23; Jer 17:10.
5:22 *ensnare him.* See 1:18 and note; Dt 7:25; 12:30. In
Ecc 7:26 the sinner is ensnared by a woman "whose heart is
a trap." *cords of his sin.* See Job 36:8; Ecc 4:12; Isa 5:18.
5:23 The death of the fool is described in similar terms in
1:29–32; 7:21–25; cf. Job 36:12. *discipline.* See v. 12.
6:1 *put up security . . . struck hands in pledge.* Refers to
responsibility for someone else's debt (cf. 22:26) or for some

if you have struck hands in pledge /
　　for another,
[2] if you have been trapped by what you
　　said,
　　ensnared by the words of your
　　　mouth,
[3] then do this, my son, to free yourself,
　　since you have fallen into your
　　　neighbor's hands:
　Go and humble yourself;
　　press your plea with your neighbor!
[4] Allow no sleep to your eyes,
　　no slumber to your eyelids. k
[5] Free yourself, like a gazelle l from the
　　hand of the hunter, m
　　like a bird from the snare of the
　　　fowler. n

[6] Go to the ant, you sluggard; o
　　consider its ways and be wise!
[7] It has no commander,
　　no overseer or ruler,
[8] yet it stores its provisions in summer p
　　and gathers its food at harvest. q

[9] How long will you lie there, you
　　sluggard? r
　When will you get up from your
　　sleep?
[10] A little sleep, a little slumber,
　　a little folding of the hands to rest s —

[11] and poverty t will come on you like a
　　bandit
　　and scarcity like an armed man. k

[12] A scoundrel and villain,
　　who goes about with a corrupt
　　　mouth,
[13] who winks with his eye, u
　　signals with his feet
　　and motions with his fingers, v
[14] who plots evil w with deceit in his
　　heart—
　　he always stirs up dissension. x
[15] Therefore disaster will overtake him in
　　an instant; y
　　he will suddenly z be
　　　destroyed—without remedy. a

[16] There are six things the LORD hates, b
　　seven that are detestable to him:
[17]　haughty eyes, c
　　　a lying tongue, d
　　　hands that shed innocent blood, e
[18]　a heart that devises wicked
　　　　schemes,
　　　feet that are quick to rush into
　　　　evil, f
[19]　a false witness g who pours out
　　　　lies h
　　　and a man who stirs up dissension
　　　　among brothers. i

Cross references (center column):

6:1 *j* Pr 11:15;
22:26-27
6:4 *k* Ps 132:4
6:5 *l* S 2Sa 2:18
m Isa 13:14
n S Ps 91:3
6:6 *o* ver 6-11;
Pr 20:4
6:8 *p* Pr 30:24-25
q Pr 10:4
6:9 *r* Pr 24:30-34;
26:13-16
6:10 *s* Pr 24:33;
Ecc 4:5

6:11 *t* ver 10-11;
Pr 20:13;
24:30-34
6:13 *u* S Ps 35:19;
Pr 16:30 *v* Isa 58:9
6:14 *w* S Ps 140:2
x ver 16-19
6:15 *y* S Ps 55:15
z Job 5:3
a Pr 14:32; 29:1
6:16 *b* ver 16-19;
Pr 3:32; 8:13;
15:8,9,26; 16:5
6:17
c S Job 41:34;
S Ps 10:5
d Pr 12:22
e S Dt 19:10;
Pr 1:16; Isa 1:21;
59:7; Jer 2:34;
Mic 7:2
6:18 *f* S Job 15:31
6:19 *g* S Dt 19:16
h S Ps 12:2 *i* ver
12-15; Pr 15:18;
Zec 8:17

k 11 Or *like a vagrant / and scarcity like a beggar*

---

other obligation. It can end in abject poverty (cf. 22:27) or
even slavery if you cannot pay. For example, Judah volunteered to personally guarantee the safe return of Benjamin to
Jacob (Ge 43:9), and when this seemed impossible, he had to
offer himself to Joseph as a slave (Ge 44:32–33). Such an
arrangement was sealed by "striking hands," equivalent to
our handshake (see 11:15; 17:18; 20:16; 22:26; cf. Job
17:3).
6:2 *trapped . . . ensnared.* Cf. v. 5; 5:22.
6:3 *to free yourself.* To gain release from the obligation.
fallen into your neighbor's hands. Assumed responsibility for
his obligation. *press your plea.* Be as persistent as the man in
Lk 11:8.
6:4 *no sleep . . . no slumber.* Like David in Ps 132:4.
6:5 *snare of the fowler.* See Ps 124:7.
6:6 *sluggard.* A lazy individual who refuses to work and
whose desires are not met (see 10:26; 13:4; 15:19; 19:24;
22:13; 24:30; 26:13–16).
6:7 *no commander.* Cf. the locust in 30:27.
6:9 *How long will you lie there, you sluggard?* His love for
sleep is described also in 26:14.
6:10–11 Repeated in 24:33–34.
6:11 *poverty . . . scarcity.* Connected with too much sleep
also in 10:5; 19:15; 20:13. Hard work is an antidote to
poverty (see 12:11; 14:23; 28:19). *like a bandit . . . an
armed man.* Poverty will come when it is too late to do
anything about it (cf. Mt 24:43).
6:12–14 A vivid description of one who uses mouth, eyes,
feet and fingers (all a person's means of communication) in
devious ways to achieve the deceitful plots of his
heart—here especially to spread slander about someone to
destroy him.

6:12 *scoundrel.* A worthless, wicked man (Jdg 19:22; 1Sa
25:25; Job 34:18). See note on Dt 13:13. *corrupt mouth.*
See 19:28; 2:12 and note.
6:13 *winks with his eye.* To make insinuations (see 10:10;
16:30).
6:14 *plots evil.* See v. 18; 3:29; Mic 2:1. *stirs up dissension.* Through slander he creates distrust that culminates in
alienation and conflict.
6:15 *disaster will overtake him in an instant.* Usually a sign
of God's judgment (see 1:26; 24:22; Job 34:20). *suddenly
be destroyed—without remedy.* He will suffer the same fate
he thought to bring upon another—his punishment will fit
his crime.
6:16–19 A further elaboration on the theme of vv. 12–15,
explaining why "disaster will overtake" (v. 15) the scoundrel described here.
6:16 *six . . . seven.* A way of handling numbers in synonymous parallelism in Hebrew poetry (see Introduction: The
Nature of a Proverb). Such catalogues of items are frequent in
the wisdom literature of the OT (see 30:15,18,21,29; see
also Job 5:19). *detestable.* See 3:32 and note.
6:17 *haughty eyes.* They reflect a proud heart, and God
will judge them (see 21:4; 30:13; Ps·18:27; 101:5). *lying
tongue.* See 2:12 and note; 12:19; 17:7; 21:6. *hands that
shed innocent blood.* See 1:11,16 and notes; 28:17.
6:18 *heart that devises wicked schemes.* See 1:31; 24:2;
Ge 6:5. *feet that . . . rush into evil.* See 1:16 and note.
6:19 *false witness.* Proverbs emphasizes the damage done
by the false witness (12:17–18; 25:18; see note on Ps 5:9)
and the punishment he receives (see note on v. 15; see also
19:5,9; 21:28). *pours out lies.* See 14:5,25. *stirs up dissension.* See note on v. 14.

Warning Against Adultery

20My son,^{j} keep your father's commands
   and do not forsake your mother's
      teaching.^{k}
21Bind them upon your heart forever;
   fasten them around your neck.^{l}
22When you walk, they will guide you;
   when you sleep, they will watch over
      you;
   when you awake, they will speak to
      you.
23For these commands are a lamp,
   this teaching is a light,^{m}
   and the corrections of discipline
      are the way to life,^{n}
24keeping you from the immoral woman,
   from the smooth tongue of the
      wayward wife.^{o}
25Do not lust in your heart after her
      beauty
   or let her captivate you with her
      eyes,
26for the prostitute reduces you to a loaf
      of bread,
   and the adulteress preys upon your
      very life.^{p}
27Can a man scoop fire into his lap
   without his clothes being burned?
28Can a man walk on hot coals
   without his feet being scorched?
29So is he who sleeps^q with another
      man's wife;^{r}
   no one who touches her will go
      unpunished.

30Men do not despise a thief if he steals
   to satisfy his hunger when he is
      starving.
31Yet if he is caught, he must pay
      sevenfold,^{s}
   though it costs him all the wealth of
      his house.

32But a man who commits adultery^t
      lacks judgment;^{u}
   whoever does so destroys himself.
33Blows and disgrace are his lot,
   and his shame will never^v be wiped
      away;
34for jealousy^w arouses a husband's fury,^{x}
   and he will show no mercy when he
      takes revenge.
35He will not accept any compensation;
   he will refuse the bribe, however
      great it is.^{y}

Warning Against the Adulteress

7 My son,^{z} keep my words
   and store up my commands within
      you.
2Keep my commands and you will live;^{a}
   guard my teachings as the apple of
      your eye.
3Bind them on your fingers;
   write them on the tablet of your
      heart.^{b}
4Say to wisdom, "You are my sister,"
   and call understanding your kinsman;
5they will keep you from the adulteress,
   from the wayward wife with her
      seductive words.^{c}

6At the window of my house
   I looked out through the lattice.
7I saw among the simple,
   I noticed among the young men,
   a youth who lacked judgment.^{d}
8He was going down the street near her
      corner,
   walking along in the direction of her
      house
9at twilight,^{e} as the day was fading,
   as the dark of night set in.

10Then out came a woman to meet him,

Cross references (center column):

6:20 /S Pr 3:21
^{k}Pr 1:8
6:21 /Dt 6:8;
S Pr 3:3; 7:1-3
6:23
^{m}S Ps 119:105
^{n}Pr 10:17
6:24 ^{o}Ge 39:8;
S Ps 55:21;
Pr 2:16; 7:5
6:26 ^{p}Pr 7:22-23
6:29 ^{q}S Ex 20:14
^{r}Pr 2:16-19; S 5:8
6:31 ^{s}Ex 22:1-14

6:32 ^{t}S Ex 20:14
^{u}Pr 7:7; 9:4,16
6:33 ^{v}Pr 5:9-14
6:34 ^{w}S Nu 5:14
^{x}S Ge 34:7
6:35
^{y}Job 31:9-11;
SS 8:7
7:1 ^{z}S Pr 1:8
7:2 ^{a}Pr 4:4
7:3 ^{b}S Pr 3:3
7:5 ^{c}ver 21;
S Job 31:9;
S Pr 2:16; 6:24
7:7 ^{d}S Pr 1:22;
S 6:32
7:9 ^{e}Job 24:15

Footnotes (bottom):

6:20 See 1:8.
6:21 See 1:9; 3:3 and notes.
6:22 *walk.* Cf. 4:11. *when you sleep.* See note on 3:24. *watch over you.* See 4:6.
6:23 *lamp ... light.* Just as the word of God "is a lamp to my feet and a light for my path" (Ps 119:105; cf. Ps 19:8). *way to life.* See 3:22; 4:22. Contrast the way to death for the one who hates discipline (5:23).
6:24 See notes on 2:16; 5:3.
6:25 *Do not lust.* Jesus shows the close connection between lust and adultery (Mt 5:28; cf. Ex 20:17). *captivate you.* See 5:20.
6:26 *reduces you to a loaf of bread.* Both the prostitute (29:3) and the adulteress (5:10) reduce a man to poverty (see 1Sa 2:36).
6:29 *no one ... will go unpunished.* See vv. 33-34; see also note on 5:14.
6:31 *sevenfold.* Hebrew law demanded no more than fivefold payment as a penalty for any theft (Ex 22:1-9). The number seven is here symbolic—he will pay in full.

6:32 *destroys himself.* See 5:14 and note; 7:22-23.
6:33 *disgrace.* Disgrace followed Amnon's raping of Tamar (2Sa 13:13,22).
6:34 *jealousy.* Its strength is also illustrated in 27:4; SS 8:6.
7:1 See 2:1 and note.
7:2 *the apple of your eye.* The pupil, which is cared for and protected because of its great value (see Dt 32:10 and note).
7:3 *Bind them on your fingers.* As a reminder (see 6:21; Dt 6:8). *tablet of your heart.* See Jer 31:33.
7:4 *wisdom.* As embodied in the instructions of the wisdom teacher (vv. 1-3). *my sister ... kinsman.* Make wisdom your most intimate companion. "Sister" may be used here in the sense of "bride" (see SS 4:9-10,12; 5:1-2).
7:5 See note on 2:16.
7:7 *simple.* See note on 1:4. *who lacked judgment.* See 6:32; 9:4,16.
7:8 *in the direction of her house.* See 5:8.
7:9 *dark of night.* He was hoping no one would see him (see 2:13 and note).
7:10 *dressed like a prostitute.* Perhaps in a gaudy manner

dressed like a prostitute and with
  crafty intent.
[11](She is loud[f] and defiant,
  her feet never stay at home;
[12]now in the street, now in the squares,
  at every corner she lurks.)[g]
[13]She took hold of him[h] and kissed him
  and with a brazen face she said:[i]

[14]"I have fellowship offerings[j] at home;
  today I fulfilled my vows.
[15]So I came out to meet you;
  I looked for you and have found you!
[16]I have covered my bed
  with colored linens from Egypt.
[17]I have perfumed my bed[k]
  with myrrh,[l] aloes and cinnamon.
[18]Come, let's drink deep of love till
  morning;
  let's enjoy ourselves with love![m]
[19]My husband is not at home;
  he has gone on a long journey.
[20]He took his purse filled with money
  and will not be home till full moon."

[21]With persuasive words she led him
  astray;
  she seduced him with her smooth
  talk.[n]
[22]All at once he followed her
  like an ox going to the slaughter,
  like a deer[m] stepping into a noose[n] [o]
[23] till an arrow pierces[p] his liver,
  like a bird darting into a snare,
  little knowing it will cost him his
  life.[q]

[24]Now then, my sons, listen[r] to me;
  pay attention to what I say.

[25]Do not let your heart turn to her ways
  or stray into her paths.[s]
[26]Many are the victims she has brought
  down;
  her slain are a mighty throng.
[27]Her house is a highway to the grave,[o]
  leading down to the chambers of
  death.[t]

Wisdom's Call

8 Does not wisdom call out?[u]
  Does not understanding raise her
  voice?
[2]On the heights along the way,
  where the paths meet, she takes her
  stand;
[3]beside the gates leading into the city,
  at the entrances, she cries aloud:[v]
[4]"To you, O men, I call out;[w]
  I raise my voice to all mankind.
[5]You who are simple,[x] gain prudence;[y]
  you who are foolish, gain
  understanding.
[6]Listen, for I have worthy things to say;
  I open my lips to speak what is right.
[7]My mouth speaks what is true,[z]
  for my lips detest wickedness.
[8]All the words of my mouth are just;
  none of them is crooked or perverse.
[9]To the discerning all of them are right;
  they are faultless to those who have
  knowledge.
[10]Choose my instruction instead of silver,
  knowledge rather than choice gold,[a]

7:11 /Pr 9:13
7:12 gPr 8:1-36;
23:26-28
7:13 hS Ge 39:12
/S Pr 1:20
7:14
/S Lev 7:11-18
7:17 kS Est 1:6;
Isa 57:7;
Eze 23:41;
Am 6:4
/S Ge 37:25
7:18 mS Ge 39:7
7:21 nS ver 5
7:22 oS Job 18:10
7:23
pS Job 15:22;
S 16:13
qS Pr 6:26;
Ecc 7:26
7:24 rPr 1:8-9;
8:32

7:25 sPr 5:7-8
7:27 /Jdg 16:19;
S Pr 2:18;
Rev 22:15
8:1 uS Job 28:12
8:3 vPr 7:6-13
8:4 wIsa 42:2
8:5 xS Pr 1:22
yPr 1:4
8:7 zJn 8:14
8:10
aS Job 28:17;
S Ps 19:10

[1]14 Traditionally *peace offerings*
Septuagint); Hebrew *fool*   [n]22 The meaning of the
Hebrew for this line is uncertain.   [o]27 Hebrew *Sheol*

(see Eze 16:16) and heavily veiled (see Ge 38:14–15).
7:11 *loud.* Applied to the "woman Folly" in 9:13.
7:12 *she lurks.* Ready to catch her prey (see v. 22).
7:13 *kissed him.* A bold greeting (see Ge 29:11).
7:14 *fellowship offerings.* Part of the meat could be eaten
by the one who brought the offering and by his (or her)
family (Lev 7:12–15). *today I fulfilled my vows.* An offering
made as the result of a vow was one of the fellowship
offerings, and the meat had to be eaten on the first or second
day (see Lev 7:15–16). So the young man had an opportunity to enjoy a real feast, one that ironically had a religious
significance (cf. Am 5:21–22).
7:16 *colored linens from Egypt.* Linen is associated with
the wealthy in 31:22. Egyptian linen was of great value (see
Isa 19:9; Eze 27:7).
7:17 *myrrh, aloes and cinnamon.* Fragrant perfumes that
are linked with making love also in Ps 45:8; SS 4:14; 5:5.
7:18 *drink deep of love.* Making love is compared to eating
and drinking also in 9:17; 30:20; SS 4:16; 5:1. *enjoy ourselves.* See SS 4:10.
7:19 *not at home.* So he will never know (cf. 6:34–35).
long journey. Perhaps he was a wealthy merchant.
7:20 *money.* Pieces of silver of various weights were a
common medium of exchange, but not in the form of coins
until a later period (see note on Ge 20:16).
7:21 *persuasive words . . . smooth talk.* See notes on 2:16;

5:3; see also 6:24; 7:5. *led him astray.* Cf. 5:23.
7:22 *like an ox going to the slaughter.* Totally oblivious of
the fate that awaits him. *noose.* See Isa 51:20.
7:23 *pierces his liver.* The terrible fate of the wicked is
similarly described in Job 20:24–25. *darting into a snare.*
See notes on 1:17–18; 5:22.
7:24 See 5:7.
7:25 *her paths.* See 1:15.
7:26 *Many are the victims.* See 9:18; Isa 5:14.
7:27 *highway to the grave.* See notes on 2:18; 5:5; see also
14:12; 16:25; Mt 7:13; cf. 1Co 6:9–10.
8:1–36 Wisdom is personified (see note on 1:20) as she
addresses mankind in preparation for the final plea from both
"Wisdom" and "Folly" in ch. 9.
8:1 *call . . . raise her voice.* See 1:20.
8:2–3 See notes on 1:20–21.
8:4 *mankind.* See v. 31.
8:5 *simple . . . foolish.* Both are addressed in wisdom's
speech in 1:22,32. *simple, gain prudence.* See note on 1:4.
8:6 *worthy things . . . what is right.* See Php 4:8.
8:7 *my lips detest wickedness.* See 3:32; 12:22.
8:8 *crooked or perverse.* See Php 2:15; cf. Pr 2:15.
8:9 *To the discerning.* The wiser a person is, the more he
appreciates words of wisdom. *who have knowledge.* Especially the knowledge of God (see note on 2:5).
8:10 *silver . . . gold.* See v. 19; 2:4; 3:14 and note.

11for wisdom is more precious[b] than
    rubies,
  and nothing you desire can compare
    with her. [c]

12"I, wisdom, dwell together with
    prudence;
  I possess knowledge and discretion. [d]
13To fear the LORD[e] is to hate evil;[f]
  I hate[g] pride and arrogance,
    evil behavior and perverse speech.
14Counsel and sound judgment are mine;
  I have understanding and power. [h]
15By me kings reign
  and rulers[i] make laws that are just;
16by me princes govern,[j]
  and all nobles who rule on earth.[P]
17I love those who love me,[k]
  and those who seek me find me. [l]
18With me are riches and honor, [m]
  enduring wealth and prosperity. [n]
19My fruit is better than fine gold;[o]
  what I yield surpasses choice silver.[p]
20I walk in the way of righteousness, [q]
  along the paths of justice,
21bestowing wealth on those who love
    me
  and making their treasuries full. [r]

22"The LORD brought me forth[q] as the
    first of his works,[r]
  before his deeds of old;
23I was appointed[s] from eternity,
  from the beginning, before the world
    began.

24When there were no oceans, I was
    given birth,
  when there were no springs
    abounding with water;[s]
25before the mountains were settled in
    place,[t]
  before the hills, I was given birth,[u]
26before he made the earth or its fields
  or any of the dust of the world. [v]
27I was there when he set the heavens in
    place,[w]
  when he marked out the horizon[x] on
    the face of the deep,
28when he established the clouds above[y]
  and fixed securely the fountains of
    the deep,[z]
29when he gave the sea its boundary[a]
  so the waters would not overstep his
    command, [b]
  and when he marked out the
    foundations of the earth. [c]
30 Then I was the craftsman at his
    side. [d]
I was filled with delight day after day,
  rejoicing always in his presence,
31rejoicing in his whole world
  and delighting in mankind. [e]

32"Now then, my sons, listen[f] to me;

Cross-references column:

8:11 [b]ver 19; S Job 28:17-19 [c]Pr 3:13-15
8:12 [d]Pr 1:4
8:13 [e]S Ge 22:12 [f]S Ex 20:20; S Job 28:28 [g]Jer 44:4
8:14 [h]S Job 9:4; Pr 21:22; Ecc 7:19
8:15 [i]S Ps 2:10
8:16 [j]S 2Ch 1:10; Pr 29:4
8:17 [k]S 1Sa 2:30; Jn 14:21-24 [l]S 1Ch 16:11; S Pr 1:28; 3:13-18; Mt 7:7-11
8:18 [m]S 1Ki 3:13 [n]S Dt 8:18
8:19 [o]S Job 28:17-19 [p]S Pr 3:13-14
8:20 [q]S Ps 5:8
8:21 [r]Pr 15:6; 24:4
8:24 [s]S Ge 7:11
8:25 [t]S Job 38:6 [u]S Job 15:7
8:26 [v]S Ps 90:2
8:27 [w]S Job 26:7 [x]S Job 22:14
8:28 [y]S Job 36:29 [z]S Ge 1:7; S Job 9:8; S 26:10
8:29 [a]S Ge 1:9; S Ps 16:6 [b]S Job 38:8 [c]S 1Sa 2:8; S Job 38:5
8:30 [d]Pr 3:19-20; Rev 3:14
8:31 [e]S Job 28:25-27; 38:4-38; Ps 104:1-30; Pr 30:4; Jn 1:1-4; Col 1:15-20
8:32 [f]S Pr 7:24

[P]16 Many Hebrew manuscripts and Septuagint; most Hebrew manuscripts and nobles—all righteous rulers   [q]22 Or The LORD possessed me   [r]22 Or way, or dominion   [s]23 Or fashioned

Notes (bottom section):

8:11 Almost identical with 3:15 (see note there).
8:12 *dwell together with prudence.* Cf. Job 28:20. *prudence . . . knowledge and discretion.* See 1:4 and note.
8:13 *To fear the LORD is to hate evil.* See 1:7; 3:7 and notes; see also 9:10; 16:6. *I hate pride and arrogance.* See 16:18; 1Sa 2:3; Isa 13:11; see also Ps 10:2–11 and note. *evil behavior and perverse speech.* See note on 2:12; see also 6:12,16–19.
8:14 *Counsel and sound judgment . . . understanding and power.* These characterize the Lord (2:6–7; Job 12:13,16; Isa 40:13–14; Ro 16:27) and the Spirit of the Lord (Isa 11:2). *Counsel.* See 1:25; 19:20. *power.* Cf. Ecc 9:16.
8:15 *By me kings reign.* See 29:4. Solomon prayed for wisdom to govern Israel (see 1Ki 3:9; 2Ch 1:10).
8:17 *I love.* I pour out my benefits on (see 4:6 and note; see also Jn 14:21). *those who seek me find me.* See 2:4–5; Isa 55:6; Jas 1:5.
8:18 *riches and honor.* See 3:16; 22:4. *prosperity.* See note on 3:2; see also 21:21.
8:19 *My fruit.* Wisdom is called a "tree of life" in 3:18 (see note there). *fine gold . . . choice silver.* See v. 10; Job 28:15; see also 3:14 and note.
8:20 *way . . . paths.* See 3:17. *justice.* See v. 15.
8:21 *bestowing wealth.* See v. 18; Zec 8:12. *making their treasuries full.* See note on 3:10; see also 24:4.
8:22–31 A hymn describing wisdom's role in creation. Wisdom is here personified, as in 1:20–33; 3:15–18; 9:1–12. Therefore these verses should not be interpreted as a direct description of Christ. Yet they provide part of the background for the NT portrayal of Christ as the divine Word

(Jn 1:1–3) and as the wisdom of God (1Co 1:24,30; Col 2:3). Here, wisdom is an attribute of God involved with him in creation.
8:22 *brought . . . forth.* The Hebrew for this verb is also used in Ge 4:1; 14:19,22 ("Creator"). *me.* Wisdom (see 3:19; Ps 104:24). *as the first of his works.* Cf. Job's statement about the behemoth (Job 40:19).
8:23 *from eternity.* Descriptive also of Christ (see Jn 1:1; cf. Mic 5:2). *before the world began.* Wisdom was already there before God began to create the world (cf. Christ's statement in Jn 17:5).
8:24 *I was given birth.* Elsewhere it is the sea (Job 38:8–9) and the mountains and earth that are "brought forth" (Ps 90:2; Job 15:7). *springs abounding with water.* See Ps 104:10.
8:25 *mountains.* See Ps 90:2.
8:27 *set the heavens in place.* See 3:19. *when he marked out the horizon on the face of the deep.* See Job 26:10.
8:28 *fountains of the deep.* Earth's springs and streams (see note on 3:20; cf. Ge 7:11).
8:29 *the sea its boundary.* See Ge 1:9; Job 38:10–11; Ps 104:9. *foundations of the earth.* See note on 3:19.
8:30 *craftsman.* A craftsman was sometimes called a wise man. See, e.g., Bezalel, who designed and built the tabernacle (Ex 31:3). Here the term stresses the skill demonstrated in creation. *filled with delight . . . rejoicing.* Cf. the joyful shouts of the angels at the time of creation (Job 38:7).
8:31 *delighting in mankind.* Cf. v. 4. Man, made in the image of God, represented the climax of creation (see Ge 1:26–28).

blessed are[g] those who keep my
ways.[h]
[33]Listen to my instruction and be wise;
do not ignore it.
[34]Blessed is the man who listens[i] to me,
watching daily at my doors,
waiting at my doorway.
[35]For whoever finds me[j] finds life[k]
and receives favor from the LORD.[l]
[36]But whoever fails to find me harms
himself;[m]
all who hate me love death."[n]

Invitations of Wisdom and of Folly

9 Wisdom has built[o] her house;
she has hewn out its seven pillars.
[2]She has prepared her meat and mixed
her wine;[p]
she has also set her table.[q]
[3]She has sent out her maids, and she
calls[r]
from the highest point of the city.[s]
[4]"Let all who are simple[t] come in
here!"
she says to those who lack
judgment.[u]
[5]"Come,[v] eat my food
and drink the wine I have mixed.[w]
[6]Leave your simple ways and you will
live;[x]
walk in the way of understanding.[y]

[7]"Whoever corrects a mocker invites
insult;

whoever rebukes a wicked man
incurs abuse.[z]
[8]Do not rebuke a mocker[a] or he will
hate you;
rebuke a wise man and he will love
you.[b]
[9]Instruct a wise man and he will be
wiser still;
teach a righteous man and he will
add to his learning.[c]
[10]"The fear of the LORD[d] is the beginning
of wisdom,
and knowledge of the Holy One[e] is
understanding.[f]
[11]For through me your days will be many,
and years will be added to your life.[g]
[12]If you are wise, your wisdom will
reward you;
if you are a mocker, you alone will
suffer."
[13]The woman Folly is loud;[h]
she is undisciplined and without
knowledge.[i]
[14]She sits at the door of her house,
on a seat at the highest point of the
city,[j]
[15]calling out[k] to those who pass by,
who go straight on their way.
[16]"Let all who are simple come in here!"
she says to those who lack
judgment.[l]
[17]"Stolen water is sweet;
food eaten in secret is delicious![m]"

8:32 gLk 11:28
hS 2Sa 22:22;
S Ps 18:21
8:34 iI Ki 10:8
kPr 9:6;
Jn 5:39-40
jS Job 33:26
8:36 mPr 15:32;
Isa 3:9; Jer 40:2
nS Job 28:22
9:1 oEph 2:20-22;
1Pe 2:5
9:2 pIsa 25:6;
62:8
qLk 14:16-23
9:3 rS Pr 1:20;
8:1-3 sver 14
9:4 tS Pr 1:22
uver 16; S Pr 6:32
9:5 vJn 7:37-38
wS Ps 42:2; 63:1;
143:6; Isa 44:3;
55:1
9:6 xS Pr 8:35
yS Pr 3:1-2
9:7 zPr 23:9;
Mt 7:6
9:8 aPr 15:12
bPs 141:5
9:9 cPr 1:5,7;
12:15; 13:10;
14:6; 15:31;
19:25
9:10 dS Pr 1:7
ePs 22:3; Pr 30:3
fS Dt 4:6
9:11 gS Ge 15:15;
S Dt 11:21;
S Pr 3:1-102;
10:27
9:13 hPr 7:11
iS Pr 5:6
9:14 jver 3;
Eze 16:25
9:15 kS Pr 1:20
9:16 lS Pr 1:22
9:17 mPr 20:17

8:32 *blessed.* The blessings associated with gaining wisdom are also given in 3:13–18; see also Ps 119:1–2; 128:1.
8:34 *watching daily at my doors.* Contrast the warning not to go near the door of the adulteress's house (5:8).
8:35 *finds life.* See 3:2; 4:22 and notes. *favor.* See 3:4; 12:2; 18:22.
8:36 *all who hate me love death.* See 1:28–33; 5:12,23; 7:27 and notes.
9:1 *has built her house.* Both wisdom and folly have a house to which mankind is invited (see v. 14; 7:8; 8:34), but wisdom has built her house (see note on 14:1)—for her there is no "sitting" (v. 14). Cf. the virtues of the wife of noble character (31:10–27). *seven pillars.* Indicating a large house. Perhaps "seven" refers to seven major aspects of wisdom.
9:2 See v. 17 and note. The banquet prepared by wisdom contrasts with the "perfumed bed" made ready by the adulteress in 7:17. *mixed her wine.* With spices, to make it tastier (see SS 8:2).
9:3 *she calls from the highest point of the city.* See the description of Folly in v. 14; see also 8:1–3.
9:4 The same invitation is given by Folly in v. 16. *simple.* See 1:4 and note on 8:5. *lack judgment.* See v. 16; 7:7.
9:5 As in v. 2, wisdom's gifts to mankind are described symbolically as a great banquet (see Isa 55:1–2 and note; cf. Jn 6:27,35).
9:6 *Leave your simple ways.* See 1:22. *you will live.* See v. 11; 8:35; see also note on 3:2.
9:7 *Whoever corrects a mocker invites insult.* See 1:22 and note; cf. 1:30. *incurs abuse.* Cf. 1Pe 4:4.

9:8 *he will hate you.* See 15:12,32. *rebuke a wise man and he will love you.* See 10:8; 17:10.
9:9 *he will be wiser still.* See 18:15; 21:11.
9:10–12 Wisdom's final words summarize the heart of the message in chs. 1–9.
9:10 *The fear of the LORD is the beginning of wisdom.* See 1:7 and note. *knowledge of the Holy One.* See note on 2:5. "Holy One" occurs elsewhere in Proverbs only in 30:3.
9:11 *years will be added to your life.* See note on 3:2; see also 3:16; 10:27; 14:27; 19:23.
9:12 *your wisdom will reward you.* Some of wisdom's rewards are given in 3:16–18; 4:22; 8:35; 14:14. *mocker.* See v. 7; see note on 1:22. *will suffer.* See 1:26 and note; 19:29.
9:13 *The woman Folly is loud.* "Loud" links the personified "Folly" with the adulteress, the wayward wife of 2:16 and 7:11. *undisciplined and without knowledge.* She lacks good judgment, prudence and the fear of the Lord (see 1:3–4,22,29; 5:6).
9:14 *sits.* Cf. wisdom's building her house (v. 1). *at the door of her house.* See 5:8; 8:34. *at the highest point of the city.* Cf. the position of wisdom in v. 3; 8:2.
9:15 *calling out.* Cf. the appeal of wisdom in v. 3; 8:1,4.
9:16 Her invitation is identical to wisdom's (v. 4; see note on 1:21).
9:17 *Stolen water . . . food eaten in secret.* The "banquet" prepared by "Folly" seems poorer than the wine and meat of wisdom (v. 2). And it was stolen at that! This "meal" refers to stolen pleasures, exemplified by the illicit sex offered by the adulteress (see 7:18 and note; cf. 5:15–16). *sweet.* But

18But little do they know that the dead
    are there,
  that her guests are in the depths of
    the grave.t n

Proverbs of Solomon

10 The proverbso of Solomon: p

  A wise son brings joy to his
    father, q
  but a foolish son grief to his mother.

2Ill-gotten treasures are of no value, r
  but righteousness delivers from
    death. s

3The LORD does not let the righteous go
    hungryt
  but he thwarts the craving of the
    wicked. u

4Lazy hands make a man poor, v
  but diligent hands bring wealth. w

5He who gathers crops in summer is a
    wise son,
  but he who sleeps during harvest is a
    disgraceful son. x

6Blessings crown the head of the
    righteous,
  but violence overwhelms the mouth
    of the wicked. u y

7The memory of the righteousz will be a
    blessing,
  but the name of the wickeda will
    rot. b

8The wise in heart accept commands,
  but a chattering fool comes to ruin. c

9The man of integrityd walks securely, e
  but he who takes crooked paths will
    be found out.f

10He who winks maliciouslyg causes
    grief,
  and a chattering fool comes to ruin.

11The mouth of the righteous is a fountain
    of life, h
  but violence overwhelms the mouth
    of the wicked. i

12Hatred stirs up dissension,
  but love covers over all wrongs.j

13Wisdom is found on the lips of the
    discerning, k
  but a rod is for the back of him who
    lacks judgment. l

14Wise men store up knowledge, m
  but the mouth of a fool invites ruin. n

15The wealth of the rich is their fortified
    city, o
  but poverty is the ruin of the poor. p

9:18 nS Pr 2:18;
7:26-27
10:1 oS 1Ki 4:32
pS Pr 1:1
qPr 15:20; 17:21;
19:13; 23:22-25;
27:11; 29:3
10:2 rPr 13:11;
21:6 sver 16;
Pr 11:4,19; 12:28
10:3 tMt 6:25-34
uPr 13:25
10:4 vPr 6:6-8;
19:15; 24:30-34
wPr 12:24; 21:5
10:5
xPr 24:30-34
10:6 yver 8,11,
14; Pr 12:13;
13:3; Ecc 10:12

10:7 zS Ps 112:6
aS Job 18:17;
S Ps 109:13
bS Job 18:17;
Ps 9:6
10:8 cver 14;
S Job 33:33;
Mt 7:24-27
10:9 dS Ps 25:21
eS Ps 37:24
fPr 28:18
10:10
gS Ps 35:19
10:11 hver 27;
S Pr 3:18; S 4:23;
11:30; 13:12,14,
19; 14:27; 15:4;
16:22 iS ver 6
10:12 jPr 17:9;
1Co 13:4-7;
1Pe 4:8
10:13 kver 31;
S Ps 37:30;
Pr 15:7
lS Dt 25:2;
Pr 14:3; 26:3
10:14 mPr 11:13;
12:23 nS ver 6;
S Ps 59:12;
S Pr 14:3; 18:6,7;
S Mt 12:37

10:15 oPr 18:11 pPr 19:7

t18 Hebrew Sheol   u6 Or but the mouth of the
wicked conceals violence; also in verse 11

---

see Job 20:12-14.
9:18 *the dead are there . . . her guests are in the depths of
the grave.* Similar to 2:18; 5:5; 7:27 (see notes).
10:1 *The proverbs of Solomon.* The title of a collection of
individual proverbs that extends through 22:16. The
numerical values of the consonants in the Hebrew word for
"Solomon" total 375—the exact number of verses in
10:1–22:16; 375 of Solomon's proverbs were selected from
a much larger number (cf. 1Ki 4:32). *wise son.* See v. 5;
15:20; 17:21,25; 29:3,15. In later collections he is described as a "righteous man" (23:24–25) and as one "who
keeps the law" (28:7).
10:2 *Ill-gotten treasures are of no value.* They are fleeting
(21:6) and result in God's judgment (see 1:19 and note;
10:16; Eze 7:19). *righteousness delivers from death.* See
2:16–18; 3:2; 13:21.
10:3 *not let the righteous go hungry.* See 13:25; 28:25; Ps
34:9–10; 37:19,25. But see note on Pr 3:2. *thwarts the
craving of the wicked.* See Nu 11:34; Ps 112:10.
10:4 Many proverbs praise diligence and the profit it
brings, and they condemn laziness as a cause of hunger and
poverty (see 6:6–11 and notes; 12:11,24,27; 13:4; 14:23;
18:9; 27:23–27; 28:19).
10:5 *sleeps during harvest.* Sleeping when there is work to
be done is condemned also in 6:9–11; 19:15; 20:13. *disgraceful son.* See 17:2; 19:26; 28:7; 29:15.
10:6 *Blessings.* God's gifts and favors (see 3:13–18;
28:20; Ge 49:26; Dt 33:16). *crown.* See 11:26. *violence
overwhelms the mouth of the wicked.* The trouble caused by

their lips will eventually ruin them (see Ps 140:9; Hab 2:17;
but cf. Pr 2:11).
10:7 *memory of the righteous.* Remembering the righteous
(see 22:1).
10:8 *The wise . . . accept commands.* See 9:8–9 and
notes. *chattering fool comes to ruin.* See vv. 10,14,18,19.
10:9 *man of integrity walks securely.* See 2:7 and note; see
also 3:23; 13:6; Ps 23:4; Isa 33:15–16. *he who takes
crooked paths will be found out.* See 26:26; Lk 8:17; 1Ti
5:24–25; 2Ti 3:9.
10:10 *winks maliciously.* See note on 6:13. *chattering
fool.* See v. 8 and note.
10:11 *fountain of life.* A source of life-giving wisdom (see
13:14; 14:27; 16:22; see also Ps 37:30). *violence overwhelms.* Perhaps the meaning is that violence controls his
mouth, but see note on v. 6.
10:12 *stirs up dissension.* See note on 6:14. *covers over all
wrongs.* Promotes forgiveness (see 17:9). This line is quoted
in Jas 5:20; 1Pe 4:8.
10:13 *rod is for the back.* See 14:3; 19:29.
10:14 *store up knowledge.* Rather than babbling folly—and so the wise prosper. See 2:1 and note. *invites ruin.*
Quick with his mouth, the fool only brings ruin on himself
(see vv. 8,10; 13:3).
10:15 An observation about wealth and poverty. *wealth
. . . is their fortified city.* Wealth brings friends (14:20; 19:4)
and power (18:23; 22:7)—but ultimate security is found
only in God (Ps 52:7). *poverty is the ruin of the poor.*
Poverty has no influence (18:23), no friends (19:4,7), no
security. See v. 4 and note.

[16]The wages of the righteous bring them life, [q]

but the income of the wicked brings them punishment. [r]

[17]He who heeds discipline shows the way to life, [s]

but whoever ignores correction leads others astray.

[18]He who conceals his hatred has lying lips, [t]

and whoever spreads slander is a fool.

[19]When words are many, sin is not absent,

but he who holds his tongue is wise. [u]

[20]The tongue of the righteous is choice silver,

but the heart of the wicked is of little value.

[21]The lips of the righteous nourish many,

but fools die for lack of judgment. [v]

[22]The blessing of the LORD [w] brings wealth, [x]

and he adds no trouble to it. [y]

[23]A fool finds pleasure in evil conduct, [z]

but a man of understanding delights in wisdom.

[24]What the wicked dreads [a] will overtake him; [b]

what the righteous desire will be granted. [c]

[25]When the storm has swept by, the wicked are gone,

but the righteous stand firm [d] forever. [e]

[26]As vinegar to the teeth and smoke [f] to the eyes,

so is a sluggard to those who send him. [g]

[27]The fear of the LORD adds length to life, [h]

but the years of the wicked are cut short. [i]

[28]The prospect of the righteous is joy,

but the hopes of the wicked come to nothing. [j]

[29]The way of the LORD is a refuge for the righteous,

but it is the ruin of those who do evil. [k]

[30]The righteous will never be uprooted,

but the wicked will not remain in the land. [l]

[31]The mouth of the righteous brings forth wisdom, [m]

but a perverse tongue [n] will be cut out.

[32]The lips of the righteous know what is fitting, [o]

but the mouth of the wicked only what is perverse. [p]

11 The LORD abhors dishonest scales, [q]

but accurate weights are his delight. [r]

10:16
[q]S Dt 30:15
[r]Pr 11:18-19;
15:6; S Ro 6:23
10:17 [s]Pr 6:23;
15:5
10:18 [t]S Ps 31:18
10:19
[u]S Job 1:22;
S 6:24; Pr 17:28;
S 20:25; 21:23;
Jas 1:19; 3:2-12
10:21
[v]Pr 5:22-23;
Isa 5:13; Jer 5:4;
Hos 4:1,6,14
10:22
[w]S Ps 128:2
[x]S Ge 13:2;
S 49:25;
S Dt 8:18
[y]S 2Ch 25:9
10:23 [z]S Pr 2:14
10:24 [a]Isa 65:7;
66:4 [b]S Ge 42:36
[c]S Ps 37:4;
145:17-19;
Eze 11:8

10:25 [d]S Ps 20:8
[e]Pr 12:3,7;
Mt 7:24-27
10:26 [f]Isa 65:5
[g]Pr 13:17; 25:13;
26:6
10:27 [h]S ver 11;
Dt 11:9;
Pr 9:10-11;
19:23; 22:4
[i]S Job 15:32
10:28 [j]Est 7:10;
S Job 8:13;
Ps 112:10;
Pr 11:7
10:29 [k]Pr 21:15;
Hos 14:9
10:30 [l]Ps 37:9,
28-29;
S Pr 2:20-22
10:31 [m]S ver 13;
S Pr 15:2; 31:26
[n]S Ps 52:4
10:32 [o]Ecc 10:12
[p]S Ps 59:7
11:1
[q]S Lev 19:36;
Dt 25:13-16;
S Job 6:2;
Pr 20:10,23
[r]Pr 16:11; Eze 45:10

10:16 *wages of the righteous bring them life.* Not wealth (v. 15) but righteousness assures life (see note on 3:2; see also 3:16; 4:22). *income of the wicked brings them punishment.* See 1:13,31 and notes. "The wages of sin is death" (Ro 6:23).
10:17 *way to life.* See note on 6:23. *whoever ignores correction.* See 5:12; 15:10.
10:18 *conceals his hatred.* By pretending friendliness (see 26:24,26,28).
10:20 *choice silver.* What the righteous say has great value (see 3:14; 8:10; 25:11). *heart of the wicked.* Their thoughts and schemes (see 6:14,18).
10:21 *nourish many.* See v. 11 and note. *die for lack of judgment.* See 5:23 and note; see also 7:7; 9:16.
10:22 *blessing of the LORD brings wealth.* Wealth is a gift from God, not a product of human attainment (see notes on v. 6; 3:10; see also 8:21; Ge 24:35; 26:12). *adds no trouble to it.* Unlike the "ill-gotten treasures" of v. 2 (see note); cf. 15:6.
10:23 *finds pleasure in evil conduct.* See 2:14; 15:21; 26:19.
10:24 *What the wicked dreads.* Calamity and distress (see 1:27 and note; 3:25; Job 15:21; Isa 66:4). *what the righteous desire.* See Ps 37:4; 145:19; Mt 5:6; 1Jn 5:14–15.
10:25 Cf. the wise man who built his house on a rock, and the foolish man who built his on the sand (Mt 7:24–27). *the*

wicked are gone. See Ps 37:10; Isa 28:18. *the righteous stand firm.* Unshakable, unmovable (see 3:25 and note; see also 12:3,7; 14:11; Ps 15:5; 1Co 15:58).
10:26 *vinegar.* See 25:20; Ps 69:21. *sluggard.* See note on 6:6. *who send him.* As a messenger (cf. 25:13; 26:6) or worker.
10:27 *fear of the LORD.* See note on 1:7. *adds length to life.* See note on 3:2. *years . . . are cut short.* See Job 22:16; Ps 37:36; 55:23.
10:28 *prospect of the righteous.* See v. 24 and note; Ps 9:18. *joy.* Of fulfillment (cf. 11:23). *hopes of the wicked come to nothing.* See 11:7,23.
10:29 *way of the LORD.* The way he prescribes, the life of wisdom (see Ps 27:11; 143:8; Mt 22:16; Ac 18:25). *ruin of those who do evil.* Since judgment comes to those who refuse God's way (see 21:15; 2Co 2:15–16; 2Pe 2:21).
10:30 *never be uprooted.* See 2:21 and note; 10:25; 12:3; Ps 125:1. *not remain in the land.* See note on 2:22.
10:31 *perverse tongue.* See note on 2:12. *cut out.* See Ps 12:3; cf. Mt 5:30.
11:1 *abhors dishonest scales.* Similar denunciation is found in the law (see Lev 19:35 and note) and the prophets (Am 8:5; Mic 6:11). See also 16:11; 20:10,23. *accurate weights.* Silver was weighed on scales balanced against a stone weight. Weights with dishonest labels were used for cheating.

2When pride comes, then comes
disgrace,[s]
but with humility comes wisdom.[t]

3The integrity of the upright guides
them,
but the unfaithful are destroyed by
their duplicity.[u]

4Wealth[v] is worthless in the day of
wrath,[w]
but righteousness delivers from
death.[x]

5The righteousness of the blameless
makes a straight way[y] for
them,
but the wicked are brought down by
their own wickedness.[z]

6The righteousness of the upright
delivers them,
but the unfaithful are trapped by evil
desires.[a]

7When a wicked man dies, his hope
perishes;[b]
all he expected from his power comes
to nothing.[c]

8The righteous man is rescued from
trouble,
and it comes on the wicked instead.[d]

9With his mouth the godless destroys his
neighbor,
but through knowledge the righteous
escape.[e]

10When the righteous prosper, the city
rejoices;[f]
when the wicked perish, there are
shouts of joy.[g]

11Through the blessing of the upright a
city is exalted,[h]
but by the mouth of the wicked it is
destroyed.[i]

12A man who lacks judgment derides his
neighbor,[j]
but a man of understanding holds his
tongue.[k]

13A gossip betrays a confidence,[l]
but a trustworthy man keeps a
secret.[m]

14For lack of guidance a nation falls,[n]
but many advisers make victory
sure.[o]

15He who puts up security[p] for another
will surely suffer,
but whoever refuses to strike hands
in pledge is safe.[q]

16A kindhearted woman gains respect,[r]
but ruthless men gain only wealth.

17A kind man benefits himself,
but a cruel man brings trouble on
himself.

18The wicked man earns deceptive wages,
but he who sows righteousness reaps
a sure reward.[s]

19The truly righteous man attains life,[t]
but he who pursues evil goes to his
death.[u]

20The LORD detests men of perverse
heart[v]

11:2 [s]Pr 16:18 [t]Pr 18:12; 29:23 **11:3** [u]ver 5; Pr 13:6 **11:4** [v]Eze 27:27 [w]S Job 20:20; S Eze 7:19 [x]S Pr 10:2 **11:5** [y]S 1Ki 8:36 [z]S ver 3; Pr 5:21-23; 13:6; 21:7 **11:6** [a]S Est 7:9 **11:7** [b]S Job 8:13 [c]S Pr 10:28 **11:8** [d]Pr 21:18 **11:9** [e]Pr 12:6; Jer 45:5 **11:10** [f]S 2Ki 11:20 [g]S Est 8:17 **11:11** [h]Pr 14:34 [i]Pr 29:8 **11:12** [j]Pr 14:21 [k]S Job 6:24 **11:13** [l]Pr 20:19 [m]S Pr 10:14 **11:14** [n]Pr 20:18 [o]S 2Sa 15:34; Pr 15:22; 24:6 **11:15** [p]S Pr 6:1 [q]Pr 17:18; 22:26-27 **11:16** [r]Pr 31:31 **11:18** [s]S Ex 1:20; S Job 4:8; Hos 10:12-13 **11:19** [t]S Dt 30:15; S Pr 10:2 [u]1Sa 2:6; Ps 89:48; Pr 1:18-19; Ecc 7:2; Jer 43:11 **11:20** [v]Pr 3:32

11:2 *When pride comes, then comes disgrace.* Along with destruction (see 16:18; cf. the humbling of proud Assyria in Isa 10:12; cf. also Isa 14:13–15). *with humility comes wisdom.* Along with honor (see note on 15:33).
11:3 *integrity . . . guides them.* Cf. the actions of Joseph in Ge 39:6–12. *unfaithful are destroyed.* See 2:22 and note; see also 19:3. *duplicity.* Cf. Lk 20:23.
11:4 *day of wrath.* The day of judgment (see Isa 10:3; Zep 1:18). *righteousness delivers from death.* See 2:16–18; 3:2; 10:2; 13:21.
11:5 *blameless.* See note on 2:7. *makes a straight way for them.* Enables them to reach their goals (see note on 3:6; see also v. 3; 10:9). *wicked are brought down.* See 5:22 and note.
11:6 *righteousness . . . delivers them.* See vv. 3–4. *trapped.* See 5:22 and note.
11:7 *his hope perishes.* See v. 23; 10:28.
11:8 Cf. the rescue of Mordecai and the execution of Haman in Est 5:14; 7:10.
11:9 *destroys his neighbor.* By spreading slander (cf. 10:18). *through knowledge.* Perhaps the knowledge of the schemes and distortions of the godless (cf. Jn 2:25).
11:10 *city rejoices.* See 28:12; 29:2. Thus life in the city is itself a teacher of wisdom (see note on 1:21). *shouts of joy.* Cf. the joy at the fall of Assyria (Isa 30:32; Na 3:19; cf. 2Ch 21:20).
11:11 *blessing of the upright.* Their good influence and desire for justice as well as their prosperity (v. 10) bring honor to the city. *mouth of the wicked.* Their deceit, dishonesty and sowing of discord (see v. 9; 6:12–14).
11:12 *derides his neighbor.* Shows his contempt openly (see 10:18; 14:21). *holds his tongue.* See 10:19.
11:14 See the close parallels in 15:22; 20:18; 24:6. *advisers.* See 2Sa 16:23; Isa 1:26.
11:15 See note on 6:1.
11:16 Assumes that "a good name is more desirable than great riches" (22:1) and insightfully observes that a woman, if she is kindhearted, will be accorded more respect than wealthy men if they are ruthless. *kindhearted woman.* See 31:28,30.
11:17 *benefits himself.* See Mt 5:7. *brings trouble on himself.* See Ge 34:25–30; 49:7.
11:18 *deceptive wages.* Because they do not last (see notes on 10:2,16; see also Hag 1:6). *reaps a sure reward.* See 10:24; Gal 6:8–9; Jas 3:18.
11:19 *attains life.* See note on 10:16; see also 12:28; 19:23. *goes to his death.* See 5:23; 21:16; Ro 6:23; Jas 1:15.
11:20 *detests men of perverse heart.* See 3:32 and note; 16:5. *blameless.* See note on 2:7.

but he delights[w] in those whose ways
    are blameless.[x]

21Be sure of this: The wicked will not go
    unpunished,
    but those who are righteous will go
    free.[y]

22Like a gold ring in a pig's snout
    is a beautiful woman who shows no
    discretion.

23The desire of the righteous ends only in
    good,
    but the hope of the wicked only in
    wrath.

24One man gives freely, yet gains even
    more;
    another withholds unduly, but comes
    to poverty.

25A generous[z] man will prosper;
    he who refreshes others will himself
    be refreshed.[a]

26People curse the man who hoards grain,
    but blessing crowns him who is
    willing to sell.

27He who seeks good finds goodwill,
    but evil comes to him who searches
    for it.[b]

28Whoever trusts in his riches will fall,[c]
    but the righteous will thrive like a
    green leaf.[d]

29He who brings trouble on his family will
    inherit only wind,

and the fool will be servant to the
    wise.[e]

30The fruit of the righteous is a tree of
    life,[f]
    and he who wins souls is wise.

31If the righteous receive their due[g] on
    earth,
    how much more the ungodly and the
    sinner!

12

Whoever loves discipline loves
    knowledge,
    but he who hates correction is
    stupid.[h]

2A good man obtains favor from the
    LORD,[i]
    but the LORD condemns a crafty
    man.[j]

3A man cannot be established through
    wickedness,
    but the righteous cannot be
    uprooted.[k]

4A wife of noble character[l] is her
    husband's crown,
    but a disgraceful wife is like decay in
    his bones.[m]

5The plans of the righteous are just,
    but the advice of the wicked is
    deceitful.

6The words of the wicked lie in wait for
    blood,
    but the speech of the upright rescues
    them.[n]

11:20
wS Nu 14:8
xS 1Ch 29:17;
S Ps 15:2;
101:1-4; S 119:1;
Pr 12:2,22; 15:9
11:21 yPr 16:5
11:25
z1Ch 29:17;
Isa 32:8 aPr 22:9;
2Co 9:6-9
11:27
bPs 7:15-16
11:28
cJob 31:24-28;
S Ps 49:6; S 52:7;
62:10; Jer 9:23;
48:7 dPs 52:8;
92:12-14

11:29 ePr 14:19
11:30 fS Ge 2:9;
S Pr 10:11
11:31 gJer 25:29;
49:12; 1Pe 4:18
12:1
hPr 5:11-14;
S 9:7-9; 13:1,18;
15:5,10,12,32
12:2
iS Job 33:26;
Ps 84:11
j2Sa 15:3;
S Pr 11:20
12:3 kS Pr 10:25
12:4 lS Ru 3:11;
Pr 31:10-11
mPr 18:22
12:6 nS Pr 11:9;
14:3

11:21 *will not go unpunished.* See 6:29. *will go free.* See
Ps 118:5.
11:22 *gold ring.* Commonly worn by women on their
noses (see Ge 24:47; Eze 16:12). *shows no discretion.*
Abigail was praised by David for her display of "good judgment" (1Sa 25:33).
11:23 See 10:24,28 and notes. *wrath.* Judgment (see v. 4;
Isa 10:3; Zep 1:18; Ro 2:8–9).
11:24 Generosity is the path to blessing and further prosperity (see 3:9–10 and notes; Ecc 11:1–2 and notes; Ps
112:9; 2Co 9:6–9). By contrast, the stingy person does not
make any friends and hurts himself in the long run (21:13).
11:25 *generous man will prosper.* "For he shares his food
with the poor" (22:9). "Whoever sows generously will also
reap generously" (2Co 9:6; cf. Lk 6:38). *be refreshed.* See
Ro 15:32.
11:26 *hoards grain.* Probably in times of scarcity to raise
the price. *blessing crowns.* See 10:6. *who is willing to sell.*
Like Joseph during the famine in Eygpt (Ge 41:53–57).
11:27 *He who seeks good finds goodwill.* Like the man in
v. 25 (cf. Mt 7:12). *evil comes to him who searches for it.*
His wicked schemes will backfire (see v. 8 and note; 1:18).
11:28 *Whoever trusts in his riches.* Usually said of the
wicked (Ps 49:6; 62:10; but see Mk 10:25; 1Ti 6:17). *like
a green leaf.* See Ps 1:3.
11:29 *He who brings trouble on his family will inherit only
wind.* The inheritance of Levi and Simeon was affected

because of their cruelty against Shechem (Ge 34:25–30;
49:7). See 15:27 and note. *servant to the wise.* As the evil
man serves the good (14:19; cf. 17:2).
11:30 *fruit of the righteous.* What a wise man produces
(8:18–19). *tree of life.* See note on 3:18. *wins souls.* Wins
people over to wisdom and righteousness (see Da 12:3; 1Co
9:19–22; Jas 5:20). However, the Hebrew for this expression is unusual so that its translation is somewhat uncertain.
11:31 *the righteous receive their due.* Even Moses and
David were punished for their sins (see Nu 20:11–12; 2Sa
12:10). *how much more the ungodly and the sinner!* See
1:18,31 and notes; Ps 11:6; 73:18–19.
12:1 *loves discipline loves knowledge.* See 1:7; 10:17; see
also 6:23 and note. *hates correction is stupid.* See 1:22;
5:12 and note.
12:2 *obtains favor.* See 3:4; 8:35. *condemns a crafty man.*
Cf. Job 5:12–13; 1Co 3:19.
12:3 *cannot be established.* See 11:5. *righteous cannot be
uprooted.* See 2:21; see also notes on 10:25,30.
12:4 *wife of noble character.* Someone like Ruth (Ru
3:11). Such a woman is fully described in 31:10–31. *her
husband's crown.* She brings him honor and joy (see 4:9 and
note). *decay.* See Hab 3:16. *his bones.* See note on 3:8.
12:5 *advice of the wicked is deceitful.* See Ps 1:1.
12:6 *lie in wait for blood.* See note on 1:11; see also 1:16.
speech of the upright rescues them. See 11:3–4,6,9.

7Wicked men are overthrown and are no
more, ^{o}
but the house of the righteous stands
firm. ^{p}

8A man is praised according to his
wisdom,
but men with warped ^{q} minds are
despised.

9Better to be a nobody and yet have a
servant
than pretend to be somebody and
have no food.

10A righteous man cares for the needs of
his animal, ^{r}
but the kindest acts of the wicked are
cruel.

11He who works his land will have
abundant food,
but he who chases fantasies lacks
judgment. ^{s}

12The wicked desire the plunder of evil
men,
but the root of the righteous
flourishes.

13An evil man is trapped by his sinful
talk, ^{t}
but a righteous man escapes
trouble. ^{u}

14From the fruit of his lips a man is filled
with good things ^{v}
as surely as the work of his hands
rewards him. ^{w}

15The way of a fool seems right to him, ^{x}
but a wise man listens to advice. ^{y}

16A fool ^{z} shows his annoyance at once, ^{a}
but a prudent man overlooks an
insult. ^{b}

17A truthful witness gives honest
testimony,
but a false witness tells lies. ^{c}

18Reckless words pierce like a sword, ^{d}
but the tongue of the wise brings
healing. ^{e}

19Truthful lips endure forever,
but a lying tongue lasts only a
moment.

20There is deceit in the hearts of those
who plot evil,
but joy for those who promote
peace. ^{f}

21No harm befalls the righteous, ^{g}
but the wicked have their fill of
trouble.

22The LORD detests lying lips, ^{h}
but he delights ^{i} in men who are
truthful. ^{j}

23A prudent man keeps his knowledge to
himself, ^{k}
but the heart of fools blurts out
folly. ^{l}

24Diligent hands will rule,
but laziness ends in slave labor. ^{m}

25An anxious heart weighs a man down, ^{n}
but a kind word cheers him up.

26A righteous man is cautious in
friendship, ^{v}

^{v}26 Or *man is a guide to his neighbor*

12:7 ^{o}S Ps 37:36
^{p}S Pr 10:25;
14:11; 15:25
12:8 ^{q}Isa 19:14;
29:24
12:10
^{r}S Nu 22:29
12:11 ^{s}Pr 28:19
12:13
^{t}S Ps 59:12;
S Pr 10:6; 18:7
^{u}Pr 21:23
12:14 ^{v}Pr 13:2;
15:23; 18:20
^{w}Pr 14:14
12:15 ^{x}Pr 14:12;
16:2,25
^{y}S Pr 9:7-9;
19:20

12:16
^{z}S 1Sa 25:25
^{a}S Job 5:2
^{b}Pr 29:11
12:17 ^{c}S Ps 12:2;
Pr 14:5,25
12:18
^{d}S Ps 55:21;
Pr 25:18 ^{e}Pr 15:4
12:20
^{f}S Ro 14:19
12:21 ^{g}S Job 4:7
12:22
^{h}1Ki 13:18;
Pr 6:17 ^{i}Ps 18:19
^{j}S Pr 11:20
12:23
^{k}S Pr 10:14
^{l}S Ps 38:5;
S 59:7; Pr 18:2
12:24 ^{m}S Pr 10:4
12:25 ^{n}Pr 15:13

12:7 See 10:25 and note.
12:8 *praised according to his wisdom.* See 3:4 and note.
men with warped minds are despised. See Dt 32:5; Tit
3:11.
12:9 *yet have a servant.* Even people of moderate means
had servants (see Jdg 6:15,27). *pretend to be somebody.* Cf.
13:7.
12:10 *cares for the needs of his animal.* See 27:23; Dt
25:4. *kindest acts of the wicked are cruel.* Probably to both
man and beast.
12:11 Repeated with slight variation in 28:19. *chases
fantasies.* Schemes for making easy money.
12:12 *desire the plunder of evil men.* See 1:13 and note;
21:10. *root of the righteous flourishes.* They bear fruit, like
firmly rooted trees (see vv. 3,7; 11:30; Ps 1:3; see also
10:25 and note).
12:13 *trapped by his sinful talk.* See 1:18 and note; 29:6.
righteous man escapes trouble. See 11:8-9 and notes;
21:23; 2Pe 2:9.
12:14 A man who speaks with wisdom will reap a harvest
from his words, just as a farmer enjoys the crops he planted
(see 1:31 and note; Job 34:11).
12:15 *seems right.* But ends in death (see 1:25,30).
12:16 *overlooks an insult.* Has good self-control (see
29:11; 2Sa 16:11-12).

12:17 *false witness tells lies.* See note on 6:19.
12:18 *Reckless words.* Cf. Ps 106:33. *pierce like a sword.*
See note on Ps 5:9. *tongue of the wise brings healing.* By
soothing, comforting words (see 4:22; 15:4).
12:19 *lasts only a moment.* The lies will be refuted and the
liar punished (see 19:9; Ps 52:4-5).
12:20 *deceit in the hearts.* See 6:14 and note; see also
1:31; 24:2; Ge 6:5. *joy for those who promote peace.*
"Blessed are the peacemakers" (Mt 5:9).
12:21 *No harm.* See 1:33 and note; 2:8; Ps 91:10-12;
121:7. *their fill of trouble.* See 1:31 and note; 11:5,8; 22:8;
Job 4:8.
12:22 Compare the structure of this verse with that of
11:1,20. *detests.* See note on 3:32. *men who are truthful.*
See 16:13.
12:23 *keeps his knowledge to himself.* Stores up knowledge (see 10:14). *blurts out folly.* See v. 16; 13:16; 15:2;
29:11.
12:24 *Diligent hands . . . laziness.* Contrasted also in 10:4
(see note there). *will rule.* Cf. 17:2. *slave labor.* See Jdg 1:28;
see also note on 2Sa 20:24.
12:25 *anxious heart.* See Ps 94:19. *kind word cheers him
up.* See 15:23.
12:26 *cautious in friendship.* He chooses his friends with
care (see 18:24; 22:24). *leads them astray.* See 5:23; 14:22.

but the way of the wicked leads them astray. *o*

27The lazy man does not roast w his game,
but the diligent man prizes his possessions.

28In the way of righteousness there is life; *p*
along that path is immortality.

13 A wise son heeds his father's instruction,
but a mocker does not listen to rebuke. *q*

2From the fruit of his lips a man enjoys good things, *r*
but the unfaithful have a craving for violence.

3He who guards his lips *s* guards his life, *t*
but he who speaks rashly will come to ruin. *u*

4The sluggard craves and gets nothing, *v*
but the desires of the diligent are fully satisfied.

5The righteous hate what is false, *w*
but the wicked bring shame and disgrace.

6Righteousness guards the man of integrity,
but wickedness overthrows the sinner. *x*

7One man pretends to be rich, yet has nothing; *y*
another pretends to be poor, yet has great wealth. *z*

8A man's riches may ransom his life,
but a poor man hears no threat. *a*

9The light of the righteous shines brightly,
but the lamp of the wicked is snuffed out. *b*

10Pride only breeds quarrels,
but wisdom is found in those who take advice. *c*

11Dishonest money dwindles away, *d*
but he who gathers money little by little makes it grow.

12Hope deferred makes the heart sick,
but a longing fulfilled is a tree of life. *e*

13He who scorns instruction will pay for it, *f*
but he who respects *g* a command is rewarded. *h*

14The teaching of the wise is a fountain of life, *i*
turning a man from the snares of death. *j*

15Good understanding wins favor,
but the way of the unfaithful is hard. *x*

16Every prudent man acts out of knowledge,
but a fool exposes *k* his folly. *l*

17A wicked messenger falls into trouble, *m*
but a trustworthy envoy brings healing. *n*

Cross references:

12:26 *o*S Ps 95:10
12:28 *p*S Dt 30:15; S Pr 10:2
13:1 *q*S Pr 12:1; 15:5
13:2 *r*S Pr 12:14
13:3 *s*S Ps 12:2; S 34:13
*t*S Pr 10:6; 21:23
*u*S Job 1:22; Pr 18:7,20-21
13:4 *v*Pr 21:25-26
13:5 *w*S Ps 119:128
13:6 *x*S Pr 11:3,5; Jer 44:5
13:7 *y*Rev 3:17
*z*2Co 6:10
13:8 *a*Pr 15:16
13:9 *b*S Job 18:5; S Pr 4:18-19
13:10 *c*S Jdg 19:30; S Pr 9:9
13:11 *d*S Pr 10:2
13:12 *e*S Pr 10:11
13:13 *f*S Nu 15:31
*g*Ex 9:20
*h*Pr 16:20
13:14 *i*S Pr 10:11
*j*Pr 14:27
13:16 *k*Ecc 10:3
*l*Est 5:11; S Ps 38:5
13:17 *m*S Pr 10:26
*n*Pr 25:13

w27 The meaning of the Hebrew for this word is uncertain.   x15 Or *unfaithful does not endure*

12:27 *does not roast his game.* And is too lazy to lift the food from the dish to his mouth (19:24). *prizes his possessions.* Cf. Ecc 5:19.
12:28 *there is life.* Cf. 3:2; 11:4. *immortality.* Lit. "no death." The way or path of righteousness does not lead to death. Cf. the identification of wisdom with the "tree of life" (3:18 and note; cf. 14:32).
13:1 *heeds his father's instruction.* See 1:8; 4:1. *mocker does not listen to rebuke.* See 1:22; 9:7-8 and notes.
13:2 See 12:14 and note. *have a craving for violence.* See 4:17 and note.
13:3 *guards his lips guards his life.* The ability to control the tongue is one of the clearest marks of wisdom. "The tongue has the power of life and death" (18:21; see 10:19; 21:23; Jas 3:2). *he who speaks rashly will come to ruin.* See 12:18 and note; see also 10:14; 18:7; 2Ti 3:3-4.
13:4 *sluggard.* See 6:6 and note. *craves and gets nothing.* Is never satisfied, yet refuses to work (see 21:25-26). *desires of the diligent are fully satisfied.* Diligence yields a profit (see 6:6; see also notes on 10:4,24).
13:5 *bring shame and disgrace.* Like a lazy or ungrateful son (10:5; 19:26).
13:6 This contrast repeats the thought of 2:21-22; 10:9; 11:3,5 (see notes); cf. 21:12; Ps 25:21.
13:7 Both pretenses are folly and lead to folly (see 14:8 and

note; see also 11:24; 12:9).
13:8 *may ransom his life.* Has the means to pay off robbers or enemies (see 10:15 and note; Jer 41:8). *poor man hears no threat.* Even poverty has its advantages.
13:9 *light . . . lamp.* Symbols of life (cf. Job 3:20). *shines brightly.* There is joy and prosperity (see note on 4:18). *lamp of the wicked is snuffed out.* His life will end (see 20:20; 24:20; Job 18:5; 21:17).
13:10 *Pride.* See 11:2 and note.
13:11 *Dishonest money dwindles away.* Such as wealth gained by extortion (Ps 62:10) or deceit (Pr 21:6). See note on 10:2; see also Jer 17:11. *makes it grow.* See note on 10:4.
13:12 *Hope deferred makes the heart sick.* Cf. Ge 30:1. *longing fulfilled is a tree of life.* It revives and strengthens (see note on 3:18; see also 10:28; 13:19).
13:13 *He who scorns instruction will pay for it.* See 1:29-31; see also 5:12 and note. *who respects a command is rewarded.* With the benefits wisdom gives (see 3:2 and note; 3:16-18; 13:21).
13:14 *fountain of life.* See note on 10:11. *from the snares of death.* See notes on 1:17; 5:22; see also 7:23; 22:5.
13:15 *wins favor.* See 3:4; 8:35. *is hard.* See note on v. 13.
13:16 See 12:23 and note.
13:17 *falls into trouble.* Perhaps by misrepresenting those

¹⁸He who ignores discipline comes to
poverty and shame, ^o
but whoever heeds correction is
honored. ^p

¹⁹A longing fulfilled is sweet to the soul, ^q
but fools detest turning from evil.

²⁰He who walks with the wise grows
wise,
but a companion of fools suffers
harm. ^r

²¹Misfortune pursues the sinner, ^s
but prosperity ^t is the reward of the
righteous. ^u

²²A good man leaves an inheritance for
his children's children,
but a sinner's wealth is stored up for
the righteous. ^v

²³A poor man's field may produce
abundant food,
but injustice sweeps it away.

²⁴He who spares the rod ^w hates his son,
but he who loves him is careful to
discipline ^x him. ^y

²⁵The righteous eat to their hearts'
content,
but the stomach of the wicked goes
hungry. ^z

14 The wise woman builds her
house, ^a
but with her own hands the foolish
one tears hers down.

²He whose walk is upright fears the
LORD,
but he whose ways are devious
despises him.

³A fool's talk brings a rod to his back, ^b
but the lips of the wise protect
them. ^c

⁴Where there are no oxen, the manger is
empty,
but from the strength of an ox ^d
comes an abundant harvest.

⁵A truthful witness does not deceive,
but a false witness pours out lies. ^e

⁶The mocker seeks wisdom and finds
none,
but knowledge comes easily to the
discerning. ^f

⁷Stay away from a foolish man,
for you will not find knowledge on
his lips.

⁸The wisdom of the prudent is to give
thought to their ways, ^g
but the folly of fools is deception. ^h

⁹Fools mock at making amends for sin,
but goodwill is found among the
upright.

¹⁰Each heart knows its own bitterness,
and no one else can share its joy.

¹¹The house of the wicked will be
destroyed, ⁱ
but the tent of the upright will
flourish. ^j

¹²There is a way that seems right to a
man, ^k
but in the end it leads to death. ^l

¹³Even in laughter ^m the heart may ache,
and joy may end in grief.

13:18 ^oS Pr 1:7;
S 12:1 ^pPs 141:5;
Pr 25:12; Ecc 7:5
13:19
^qS Pr 10:11
13:20 ^r2Ch 10:8
13:21 ^s2Sa 3:39;
Jer 40:3; 50:7;
Eze 14:13; 18:4
^tPs 25:13
^uPs 32:10
13:22 ^vS Est 8:2;
S Job 27:17;
Ecc 2:26
13:24
^wS 2Sa 7:14
^xS Pr 3:12
^yPr 19:18; 22:15;
23:13-14; 29:15,
17; Eph 6:4;
Heb 12:7
13:25 ^zPr 10:3
14:1 ^aS Ru 3:11;
Pr 24:3

14:3 ^bS Pr 10:14;
Ecc 10:12
^cS Pr 10:13;
S 12:6
14:4 ^dPs 144:14
14:5 ^eS Ps 12:2;
S Pr 12:17
14:6 ^fS Pr 9:9
14:8 ^gver 15;
Pr 15:28; 21:29
^hver 24
14:11
ⁱS Job 8:22;
Pr 21:12
^jS Ps 72:7;
S Pr 3:33; S 12:7
14:12
^kS Pr 12:15
^lPr 16:25
14:13 ^mEcc 2:2;
7:3,6

---

who sent him. *brings healing.* His tactful, honest approach
benefits both parties (see 25:13; cf. 12:18; 15:4).
13:18 *comes to poverty and shame.* See 5:10–12 and
notes. *whoever heeds correction is honored.* See v. 1;
3:16–18; 8:35; 10:17.
13:19 *longing fulfilled.* See v. 12. *fools detest turning from
evil.* Cf. their hatred of correction in 5:12.
13:20 *who walks with the wise grows wise.* Choose your
friends with care (see 2:20; 12:26). *companion of fools
suffers harm.* See 1:10,18; 2:12; 16:29; 22:24–25.
13:21 See v. 13 and note.
13:22 *is stored up for the righteous.* Job agrees that this is
often what happens to a wicked man's possessions (Job
27:16–17; cf. Pr 28:8).
13:23 *injustice sweeps it away.* Probably a case of the rich
and powerful oppressing the poor (cf. Ps 35:10).
13:24 *who spares the rod hates his son.* Parents are
encouraged to apply the rod of punishment to drive out folly
(22:15) so that the child will not follow a path of destruction
(19:18; 23:13–14). The rod "imparts wisdom" (29:15) and
promotes a healthy and happy family (29:17). Discipline is
rooted in love (see 3:11–12 and note). *rod.* Probably a figure
of speech for discipline of any kind.
13:25 States more specifically the teaching of vv. 13,18,

21; see 10:3 and note.
14:1 *wise woman builds her house.* She is a source of
strength and an example of diligence for her family (see
31:10–31). Cf. the house built by wisdom in 9:1.
14:2 *fears the LORD.* See note on 1:7.
14:3 *rod to his back.* See 10:13; 19:29; 26:3.
14:4 Perhaps the thought is that men need to take good
care of their oxen (the means of production) if they expect an
abundant harvest (see 12:10).
14:5 See note on 6:19.
14:6 *mocker.* See 1:22 and note. *seeks wisdom and finds
none.* Because he refuses to fear the Lord or accept any
correction.
14:8 *folly of fools is deception.* What a fool believes to be
prudent (but is really folly) does not bring success; instead, it
tends toward his ruin.
14:9 *mock at making amends for sin.* Cf. 19:28. *goodwill
. . . among the upright.* See 11:27 and note.
14:10 *knows its own bitterness.* See 1Ki 8:38. Cf. the
experience of Hannah (1Sa 1:10) and Peter (Mt 26:75). *can
share its joy.* Cf. Mt 13:44; 1Pe 1:8.
14:11 See 10:25 and note.
14:12 *in the end it leads to death.* See 5:4,23; 7:21–27;
Mt 7:13–14.

14The faithless will be fully repaid for
their ways, n
and the good man rewarded for his. o

15A simple man believes anything,
but a prudent man gives thought to
his steps. p

16A wise man fears the LORD and shuns
evil, q
but a fool r is hotheaded and reckless.

17A quick-tempered s man does foolish
things, t
and a crafty man is hated. u

18The simple inherit folly,
but the prudent are crowned with
knowledge.

19Evil men will bow down in the
presence of the good,
and the wicked at the gates of the
righteous. v

20The poor are shunned even by their
neighbors,
but the rich have many friends. w

21He who despises his neighbor sins, x
but blessed is he who is kind to the
needy. y

22Do not those who plot evil go astray? z
But those who plan what is good
find y love and faithfulness.

23All hard work brings a profit,
but mere talk leads only to poverty.

24The wealth of the wise is their crown,

but the folly of fools yields folly. a

25A truthful witness saves lives,
but a false witness is deceitful. b

26He who fears the LORD has a secure
fortress, c
and for his children it will be a
refuge. d

27The fear of the LORD is a fountain of
life, e
turning a man from the snares of
death. f

28A large population is a king's glory,
but without subjects a prince is
ruined. g

29A patient man has great
understanding, h
but a quick-tempered man displays
folly. i

30A heart at peace gives life to the body,
but envy rots the bones. j

31He who oppresses the poor shows
contempt for their Maker, k
but whoever is kind to the needy
honors God. l

32When calamity comes, the wicked are
brought down, m
but even in death the righteous have
a refuge. n

33Wisdom reposes in the heart of the
discerning o

14:14 nS Pr 1:31
oS 2Ch 15:7;
Pr 12:14
14:15 PS ver 8
14:16
qS Ex 20:20;
Pr 22:3
rS 1Sa 25:25
14:17 sS 2Ki 5:12
tver 29; Pr 15:18;
16:28; 26:21;
28:25; 29:22
uS Est 5:9
14:19 vPr 11:29
14:20 wPr 19:4,7
14:21 xPr 11:12
yPr 19:17
14:22
zPr 4:16-17

14:24 aver 8
14:25
bS Pr 12:17
14:26 cPr 18:10
dPs 9:9
14:27
eS Pr 10:11
fPs 18:5; Pr 13:14
14:28
gS 2Sa 19:7
14:29
hS 2Ki 5:12;
Pr 17:27 iS ver
17; Ecc 7:8-9
14:30 jPr 17:22
14:31 kPr 17:5
lS Dt 24:14;
S Job 20:19;
S Mt 10:42
14:32
mS Ps 34:21;
S Pr 6:15
nS Job 13:15
14:33 oPr 2:6-10 | y22 Or show

14:13 in laughter the heart may ache. Cf. Ezr 3:11–12. joy
may end in grief. As the death of Rachel in childbirth (Ge
35:17–18).
14:14 See 1:31; 12:14 and notes; see also 11:5,8; 18:20;
22:8; Job 4:8.
14:15 simple man. See note on 1:4. gives thought to his
steps. See 4:26 and note; 21:29.
14:16 fears the LORD and shuns evil. See notes on 1:7; 3:7.
hotheaded. Cf. 21:24. reckless. In words (12:18; 13:3) and
actions (Jdg 9:4).
14:17 quick-tempered. See Tit 1:7. crafty. Cf. 12:2; Job
5:12–13; 1Co 3:19.
14:18 crowned with knowledge. Adorned and blessed
with knowledge (see note on 4:9; see also v. 24; 12:4; Ps
103:4).
14:19 Evil men will bow down. Cf. 17:2. at the gates of
the righteous. Perhaps to beg for some favor (cf. 1Sa 2:36).
14:20 shunned even by their neighbors. And sometimes
by their relatives (see 19:7).
14:21 blessed is he who is kind to the needy. Sharing food
(22:9), lending money (28:8) and defending rights (31:9) are
ways one can show kindness. Such a person "honors God"
(v. 31; cf. 17:5) and will lack nothing (28:27). Cf. 21:13; Ps
41:1.
14:22 plot evil. See 3:29; 6:14,18; Mic 2:1. go astray. See
5:23; 12:26. find love and faithfulness. Receive the support
and care of faithful friends (cf. 3:3; 16:6; 20:28)—perhaps
God's support and care are also implied here.

14:23 hard work brings a profit. See note on 10:4; see also
21:5.
14:24 wealth . . . is their crown. The wise obtain wealth,
and it adorns them like a crown (see 10:22). yields folly. An
empty inheritance (see v. 18; 3:35).
14:25 See v. 5; 12:17; see also note on 6:19.
14:26 fears the LORD. See 1:7; 3:7 and notes. secure
fortress . . . refuge. Means either that the father's godliness
will result in blessing for himself and his children (see 20:7)
or that the "fear of the LORD" will be a strong tower where
the children also can find refuge (see 18:10; Ps 71:7; Isa
33:6).
14:27 See note on 10:11; see also 13:14.
14:29 patient man. See 15:18; 16:32; 19:11; Jas 1:19.
14:30 gives life to the body. Cf. the healthy effects of
fearing the Lord and walking in wisdom in 3:7–8,16–18.
envy rots the bones. See note on 3:8; see also 12:4; Ps
37:7–8.
14:31 shows contempt for their Maker. Because God
created both the rich and the poor in his image (see 22:2; Job
31:15; Jas 3:9). kind to the needy. See note on v. 21. honors
God. Does God's will, and in a sense gives to God himself
(see 19:17; Mt 25:40).
14:32 wicked are brought down. See 1:26–27 and note;
11:5; 24:16. even in death the righteous have a refuge.
Their faith in God gives them hope beyond the grave (see
note on 12:28; see also Ps 49:14–15; 73:24).
14:33 even among fools she lets herself be known. Per-

and even among fools she lets herself be known. z

34Righteousness exalts a nation, p
but sin is a disgrace to any people.

35A king delights in a wise servant,
but a shameful servant incurs his wrath. q

15 A gentle answer r turns away wrath, s
but a harsh word stirs up anger.

2The tongue of the wise commends knowledge, t
but the mouth of the fool gushes folly. u

3The eyes v of the LORD are everywhere, w
keeping watch on the wicked and the good. x

4The tongue y that brings healing is a tree of life, z
but a deceitful tongue crushes the spirit. a

5A fool spurns his father's discipline,
but whoever heeds correction shows prudence. b

6The house of the righteous contains great treasure, c
but the income of the wicked brings them trouble. d

7The lips of the wise spread knowledge; e
not so the hearts of fools.

8The LORD detests the sacrifice f of the wicked, g
but the prayer of the upright pleases him. h

9The LORD detests the way of the wicked i
but he loves those who pursue righteousness. j

10Stern discipline awaits him who leaves the path;
he who hates correction will die. k

11Death and Destruction a lie open before the LORD l —
how much more the hearts of men! m

12A mocker resents correction; n
he will not consult the wise.

13A happy heart makes the face cheerful, o
but heartache crushes the spirit. p

14The discerning heart seeks knowledge, q
but the mouth of a fool feeds on folly.

15All the days of the oppressed are wretched,
but the cheerful heart has a continual feast. r

16Better a little with the fear of the LORD than great wealth with turmoil. s

17Better a meal of vegetables where there is love
than a fattened calf with hatred. t

18A hot-tempered man stirs up dissension, u

z.33 Hebrew; Septuagint and Syriac / but in the heart of fools she is not known   a 11 Hebrew Sheol and Abaddon

14:34 pPr 11:11
14:35 qS Est 8:2;
Mt 24:45-51;
25:14-30
15:1 rI Ki 12:7;
2Ch 10:7
sPr 25:15
15:2 tver 7;
S Pr 10:31
uS Ps 59:7;
Ecc 10:12
15:3 vS 2Ch 16:9
wS Job 10:4;
S 31:4;
S Heb 4:13
xS Job 34:21;
Pr 5:21; Jer 16:17
15:4 yS Ps 5:9
zS Pr 10:11
aPr 12:18
15:5 bS Pr 10:17;
S 12:1; S 13:1
15:6 cS Pr 8:21
dS Pr 10:16
15:7 eS ver 2;
S Pr 10:13
15:8 fS Ps 51:17;
S Isa 1:13
gS Pr 6:16; 21:27
hver 29;
Job 35:13;
Pr 28:9; S Jn 9:31
15:9 iS Pr 6:16
jS Dt 7:13;
S Pr 11:20
15:10
kS Pr 1:31-32;
S 12:1
15:11 lS Job 26:6
mS 1Sa 2:3;
S 2Ch 6:30;
S Ps 44:21;
S Rev 2:23
15:12 nS Pr 9:8;
S 12:1
15:13 over 15
pS Pr 12:25;
17:22; 18:14
15:14 qPr 18:15
15:15 rver 13
15:16 sver 17;
Ps 37:16-17;
Pr 13:8; 16:8;
17:1
15:17 tS ver 16;
Pr 17:1; Ecc 4:6
15:18
uS Pr 6:16-19;
S 14:17

---

haps means that even fools occasionally display a bit of wisdom (cf. Ac 17:27–28; Ro 1:19–20), but see NIV text note.

14:34 *Righteousness exalts a nation.* See note on 11:11. Israel was promised prosperity and prestige if she obeyed God's laws (see Dt 28:1–14). *sin is a disgrace to any people.* The Canaanites were driven out because of their terrible sin (Lev 18:24–25), and Israel later received the same curse (Dt 28:15–68; cf. 2Sa 12:10).

14:35 *incurs his wrath.* See 16:14; 19:12; Da 2:12.

15:1 *gentle answer turns away wrath.* Cf. the way Gideon calmed the anger of the men of Ephraim in Jdg 8:1–3 (cf. also Pr 15:18; Ecc 10:4). *harsh word stirs up anger.* Nabal's sarcastic response put David in a fighting mood (1Sa 25:10–13).

15:2 *gushes folly.* See vv. 7, 28; 12:23; 13:16.

15:3 *eyes of the LORD are everywhere.* See 5:21; Job 31:4; 34:21; Jer 16:17.

15:4 *tongue that brings healing.* See note on 12:18. *tree of life.* See note on 3:18. *deceitful tongue crushes the spirit.* Especially false testimony in court (see 6:19; 22:22), or slander in the community.

15:6 See 10:2,16,22 and notes. *great treasure.* See 8:18, 21; 24:4; Zec 8:12; see also note on 3:10.

15:8 *detests the sacrifice of the wicked.* Those whose hearts are not right with God gain nothing by offering sacrifices (see 21:3,27; Ecc 5:1; Isa 1:11–15; Jer 6:20). *prayer of the upright.* See 3:32.

15:9 *who pursue righteousness.* See 21:21; 1Ti 6:11.

15:10 *the path.* The right (or "straight") path (see 2:13). *who hates correction will die.* See notes.

15:11 *Death and Destruction lie open before the LORD.* Not even the grave, the netherworld, is inaccessible to God (see Job 26:6; Ps 139:8). Therefore he knows the secrets of man's innermost being (cf. 1Sa 16:7).

15:12 See 1:30; 10:8; 13:1; 17:10. *mocker.* See note on 1:22.

15:13 *happy heart makes the face cheerful.* Cf. 14:30. *heartache crushes the spirit.* Cf. the great sorrow of Job (Job 3) and David (Ps 51:8,10).

15:15 *cheerful heart has a continual feast.* Life is as joyful and satisfying as the days of a festival (see v. 13; 14:30; cf. Lev 23:39–41).

15:16 *great wealth with turmoil.* The "ill-gotten treasures" of 10:2.

15:17 *fattened calf.* Such meat was something of a luxury, reserved for special occasions (cf. 7:14; Mt 22:4; Lk 15:23).

15:18 *stirs up dissension.* See note on 6:14. *patient man.* See 14:29; 16:32; 19:11; Jas 1:19.

but a patient man calms a quarrel. *v*

¹⁹The way of the sluggard is blocked with
thorns, *w*
but the path of the upright is a
highway.

²⁰A wise son brings joy to his father, *x*
but a foolish man despises his
mother.

²¹Folly delights a man who lacks
judgment, *y*
but a man of understanding keeps a
straight course.

²²Plans fail for lack of counsel, *z*
but with many advisers *a* they
succeed. *b*

²³A man finds joy in giving an apt
reply *c* —
and how good is a timely word! *d*

²⁴The path of life leads upward for the
wise
to keep him from going down to the
grave. *b*

²⁵The LORD tears down the proud man's
house *e*
but he keeps the widow's boundaries
intact. *f*

²⁶The LORD detests the thoughts *g* of the
wicked, *h*
but those of the pure *i* are pleasing to
him.

²⁷A greedy man brings trouble to his
family,
but he who hates bribes will live. *j*

²⁸The heart of the righteous weighs its
answers, *k*
but the mouth of the wicked gushes
evil. *l*

²⁹The LORD is far from the wicked
but he hears the prayer of the
righteous. *m*

³⁰A cheerful look brings joy to the heart,
and good news gives health to the
bones. *n*

³¹He who listens to a life-giving rebuke
will be at home among the wise. *o*

³²He who ignores discipline despises
himself, *p*
but whoever heeds correction gains
understanding. *q*

³³The fear of the LORD *r* teaches a man
wisdom, *c*
and humility comes before honor. *s*

16 To man belong the plans of the
heart,
but from the LORD comes the reply of
the tongue. *t*

²All a man's ways seem innocent to
him, *u*
but motives are weighed *v* by the
LORD. *w*

³Commit to the LORD whatever you do,
and your plans will succeed. *x*

⁴The LORD works out everything for his
own ends *y* —

Cross references (center column)

15:18 *r*S Ge 13:8
15:19 *w*Pr 22:5
15:20 *x*S Pr 10:1
15:21 *y*S Pr 2:14
15:22 *z*S Ps 16:7
  *a*1Ki 1:12;
  Pr 24:6
  *b*S Pr 11:14
15:23
  *c*S Pr 12:14
  *d*Pr 25:11
15:25 *e*S Pr 12:7
  *f*S Dt 19:14;
  Pr 23:10-11
15:26
  *g*S Ps 94:11
  *h*S Pr 6:16
  *i*S Ps 18:26
15:27 *j*S Ex 23:8;
  S Ps 15:5;
  Isa 1:23; 33:15
15:28 *k*S Pr 14:8
  *l*S Ps 59:7
15:29 *m*S ver 8;
  S Job 15:31;
  Ps 145:18-19;
  Isa 59:2; S Jn 9:31
15:30 *n*Pr 25:25
15:31
  *o*S Pr 9:7-9;
  S 12:1
15:32 *p*S Pr 1:7;
  S 12:1
  *q*S Pr 9:7-9;
  S 12:1; Ecc 7:5
15:33 *r*S Pr 1:7
  *s*Pr 16:18; 18:12;
  22:4; 29:23;
  Isa 66:2
16:1 *t*ver 9;
  Pr 19:21
16:2 *u*S Pr 12:15;
  30:12 *v*S 1Sa 2:3
  *w*S 2Ch 6:30;
  Pr 20:27; 21:2;
  Lk 16:15
16:3
  *x*S 2Ch 20:20;
  S Ps 20:4; 37:5-6;
  S Pr 3:5-6
16:4 *y*Ex 9:16

---

*b*24 Hebrew *Sheol*   *c*33 Or *Wisdom teaches the fear
of the LORD*

15:19 *sluggard.* See note on 6:6. *blocked with thorns.*
Mainly because he was too lazy to remove them (see
24:30-31; Hos 2:6). *highway.* The upright can make
progress and reach their goals (see note on 3:6).
15:20 See 10:1 and note.
15:21 A variation of 10:23.
15:22 See the close parallels in 11:14; 20:18; 24:6.
15:23 *apt reply.* Cf. Isa 50:4. *how good is a timely word!*
Cf. 24:26.
15:24 *leads upward.* Along the highway (v. 19), the
straight course (v. 21) that leads to life. *to keep him from
going down to the grave.* See note on 2:18.
15:25 *tears down the proud man's house.* See 2:22;
14:11; see also 10:25 and note. *keeps the widow's boundaries intact.* In ancient times boundary stones marked a
person's property. Anyone who moved such a stone was, in
effect, stealing land (see 22:28; Job 24:2; Ps 68:5; see also
Dt 19:14 and note).
15:26 *detests the thoughts of the wicked.* Cf. vv. 8-9.
those of the pure. See 22:11; Ps 24:4.
15:27 *greedy man brings trouble to his family.* See 1:19;
11:29; 28:25. Achan's whole family perished because of his
greed at Jericho (Jos 7:24-26). *he who hates bribes will live.*
See 17:8; 28:16; Dt 16:19; 1Sa 12:3; Ecc 7:7; 1Ti 6:10.
15:28 *weighs its answers.* Cf. 10:32; 1Pe 3:15. *gushes
evil.* See v. 2; see also v. 7; 12:23.

15:29 *far from the wicked.* See 1:28 and note.
15:30 *cheerful look brings joy.* Cf. v. 13; 16:15; Job
29:24. *good news gives health to the bones.* See 3:8 and
note; see also Php 2:19.
15:31 *who listens to a life-giving rebuke.* See 1:23; 6:23
and note.
15:32 *who ignores discipline despises himself.* See note
on 5:12; see also 1:7; 5:23; 8:36. *whoever heeds correction.* Cf. vv. 5,31.
15:33 *fear of the LORD.* See note on 1:7. *humility comes
before honor.* See 22:24; 25:6-7; Mt 23:12; Lk 14:11;
18:14; 1Pe 5:6. Wisdom also comes with humility (11:2;
13:10).
16:1 *from the LORD comes the reply of the tongue.* God
must give the ability to articulate and accomplish those plans
(cf. 19:21).
16:2 *seem innocent.* See 14:12. *motives are weighed by
the LORD.* See 24:12; Ps 139:23; 1Co 4:4-5; Heb 4:12.
16:3 *Commit.* See 1Pe 5:7. *plans will succeed.* Goals will
be reached (see 3:5-6 and notes; Ps 1:3; 55:22; 90:
17).
16:4 *works out everything for his own ends.* God is sovereign in every life and in all of history (see Ecc 7:14; Ro 8:28).
the wicked for a day of disaster. Even through wicked men
God displays his power (cf. Ex 9:16), and all evil will be
judged (cf. Eze 38:22-23; Ro 2:5-11).

even the wicked for a day of
disaster. *z*

5The LORD detests all the proud of
heart. *a*
Be sure of this: They will not go
unpunished. *b*

6Through love and faithfulness sin is
atoned for;
through the fear of the LORD *c* a man
avoids evil. *d*

7When a man's ways are pleasing to the
LORD,
he makes even his enemies live at
peace *e* with him. *f*

8Better a little with righteousness
than much gain *g* with injustice. *h*

9In his heart a man plans his course,
but the LORD determines his steps. *i*

10The lips of a king speak as an oracle,
and his mouth should not betray
justice. *j*

11Honest scales and balances are from the
LORD;
all the weights in the bag are of his
making. *k*

12Kings detest wrongdoing,
for a throne is established through
righteousness. *l*

13Kings take pleasure in honest lips;

they value a man who speaks the
truth. *m*

14A king's wrath is a messenger of
death, *n*
but a wise man will appease it. *o*

15When a king's face brightens, it means
life; *p*
his favor is like a rain cloud in
spring. *q*

16How much better to get wisdom than
gold,
to choose understanding *r* rather than
silver! *s*

17The highway of the upright avoids evil;
he who guards his way guards his
life. *t*

18Pride *u* goes before destruction,
a haughty spirit *v* before a fall. *w*

19Better to be lowly in spirit and among
the oppressed
than to share plunder with the proud.

20Whoever gives heed to instruction
prospers, *x*
and blessed is he who trusts in the
LORD. *y*

21The wise in heart are called discerning,
and pleasant words promote
instruction. *d z*

16:4
z S Ch 34:24;
S Ps 18:18;
Ro 9:22
16:5 *a* S Ps 40:4;
S Pr 6:16
b Pr 11:20-21
16:6
c S Ge 20:11;
S Ex 1:17
d S Ex 20:20
16:7 *e* S Ge 39:21
f Ps 105:15;
Jer 39:12; 40:1;
42:12; Da 1:9
16:8 *g* S Ps 37:16
h S Pr 15:16;
17:1; Ecc 4:6
16:9 *i* S ver 1;
S Job 33:29;
S Ps 90:12
16:10 *j* Pr 24:23
16:11 *k* S Pr 11:1;
Eze 45:10
16:12 *l* Pr 26:28;
25:5; 29:14; 31:5

16:13 *m* Pr 22:11
16:14
n S Ge 40:2;
S Job 29:24;
Pr 20:2
o Pr 25:15; 29:8;
Ecc 10:4
16:15
p S Ge 40:2;
S Job 29:24
q Pr 19:12; 25:2-7
16:16 *r* Ps 49:20
s S Job 28:15;
S Pr 3:13-14
16:17 *t* Pr 19:16
16:18
u S 1Sa 17:42
v Ps 18:27;
Isa 13:11;
Jer 48:29
w S Est 5:12;
Pr 11:2; S 15:33;
18:12; 29:23
16:20 *x* Pr 13:13
y S Ps 32:10;
40:4; Pr 19:8;
29:25; Jer 17:7

16:21 *z* ver 23

d 21 Or words make a man persuasive

16:5 See 11:20–21 and notes.
16:6 *Through love and faithfulness sin is atoned for.* The
moral quality of conduct that God desires is sometimes
summed up as "love and faithfulness" (3:3; Hos 4:1). When
his people repent of sin and bring their lives into accord with
his will, God forgives and withdraws his judgment (see Isa
1:18–19; 55:7; Jer 3:22; Eze 18:23,30–32; 33:11–12,
14–16; Hos 14:1–2,4). Thus it can be said that love and
faithfulness, in a manner of speaking, "atone for" sin, i.e.,
they turn away God's wrath against it. *fear of the LORD.* See
note on 1:7.
16:7 *makes even his enemies live at peace with him.* As in
the reigns of godly Asa and Jehoshaphat (2Ch 14:6–7;
17:10). *peace.* See 3:17 and note; Ro 12:18; Heb 12:14.
16:8 See note on 10:2 and note.
16:9 *the LORD determines his steps.* Verses 1,3–4 (see
notes) also emphasize God's control of men's lives (see
19:21; 20:24; Ps 37:23; Jer 10:23).
16:10 *speak as an oracle.* In judging cases brought before
him, a king functioned as God's representative (see Dt 1:17).
Therefore he needed the divine gift of wisdom to discern
between right and wrong in order to render God's judgment
(see 1Ki 3:9). When he did so, his judgment was tantamount
to a divine oracle for the people (see 1Ki 3:28; see also 2Sa
14:17,20; 19:27).
16:11 See note on 11:1. *Honest scales . . . from the LORD.*
Cf. 21:2; 24:12; Job 6:2; 31:6. *all the weights in the bag.*
Merchants carried stones of different sizes with them to

weigh and measure quantities of silver for payment (cf. Mic
6:11).
16:12 *throne is established through righteousness.* When
the king "judges the poor with fairness" (29:14), refuses to
take bribes (29:4) and removes any wicked advisers (25:5).
See 14:34; Dt 17:19–20; Isa 16:5; Ro 13:3.
16:13 *in honest lips.* Rather than in flattering lips (cf.
20:28).
16:14 *messenger of death.* Any angry king can pronounce
death quickly and effectively (see 19:12; Est 7:7–10; Mt
22:7; Lk 19:27). *wise man will appease it.* Cf. Daniel's
response to the rage of Nebuchadnezzar (Da 2:12–16).
16:15 *face brightens.* Cf. Nu 6:25. *his favor is like a rain
cloud in spring.* The spring rain was essential for the full
development of barley and wheat; it was therefore a sign of
good things to come. Cf. the "dew" of 19:12; see Ps 72:6.
16:16 See 3:14 and note; 8:10,19.
16:17 *highway of the upright.* See note on 15:19. *avoids
evil.* Cf. the thorns and snares in the paths of the wicked
(22:5).
16:18 See note on 11:2.
16:19 *Better to be lowly in spirit.* See 3:34; Isa 57:15; Mt
5:3. *share plunder with the proud.* See 1:13–14; Jdg 5:30.
16:20 *prospers.* See 13:13 and note. *blessed is he who
trusts in the LORD.* See v. 3; 3:5–6; 28:25; Ps 34:8; 37:4–5.
16:21 *pleasant words promote instruction.* The last line
of v. 23. "Pleasant" (lit. "sweet") is expanded in v. 24. Cf.
the persuasive but destructive words of the adulteress in
7:21.

²²Understanding is a fountain of life to
　　those who have it,ª
　but folly brings punishment to fools.

²³A wise man's heart guides his mouth,ᵇ
　and his lips promote instruction.ᵉ ᶜ

²⁴Pleasant words are a honeycomb,ᵈ
　sweet to the soul and healing to the
　　bones.ᵉ

²⁵There is a way that seems right to a
　　man,ᶠ
　but in the end it leads to death.ᵍ

²⁶The laborer's appetite works for him;
　his hunger drives him on.

²⁷A scoundrelʰ plots evil,
　and his speech is like a scorching
　　fire.ⁱ

²⁸A perverse man stirs up dissension,ʲ
　and a gossip separates close friends.ᵏ

²⁹A violent man entices his neighbor
　and leads him down a path that is
　　not good.ˡ

³⁰He who winksᵐ with his eye is plotting
　　perversity;
　he who purses his lips is bent on evil.

³¹Gray hair is a crown of splendor;ⁿ
　it is attained by a righteous life.

³²Better a patient man than a warrior,
　a man who controls his temper than
　　one who takes a city.

³³The lot is castᵒ into the lap,

but its every decisionᵖ is from the
　LORD.�q

17 Better a dry crust with peace and
　　quiet
　than a house full of feasting,ᶠ with
　　strife.ʳ

²A wise servant will rule over a
　　disgraceful son,
　and will share the inheritance as one
　　of the brothers.

³The crucible for silver and the furnace
　　for gold,ˢ
　but the LORD tests the heart.ᵗ

⁴A wicked man listens to evil lips;
　a liar pays attention to a malicious
　　tongue.

⁵He who mocks the poorᵘ shows
　　contempt for their Maker;ᵛ
　whoever gloats over disasterʷ will
　　not go unpunished.ˣ

⁶Children's childrenʸ are a crown to the
　　aged,
　and parents are the pride of their
　　children.

⁷Arrogantᵍ lips are unsuited to a fool—
　how much worse lying lips to a
　　ruler!ᶻ

⁸A bribe is a charm to the one who gives
　　it;
　wherever he turns, he succeeds.ª

Cross references (center column):

16:22
ªS Pr 10:11
16:23 ᵇJob 15:5
ᶜver 21
16:24
ᵈS 1Sa 14:27
ᵉPr 24:13-14
16:25 ᶠS Pr 12:15
ᵍEst 3:6; Pr 14:12
16:27
ʰS Ps 140:2
ⁱJas 3:6
16:28 ʲS Pr 14:17
ᵏPr 17:9
16:29 ˡS Pr 1:10;
12:26
16:30 ᵐS Pr 6:13
16:31 ⁿPr 20:29
16:33
ᵒS Lev 16:8;
S 1Sa 10:21;
Eze 21:21

ᵖ1Sa 14:41
qJos 7:14;
Pr 18:18; 29:26;
Jnh 1:7
17:1 ʳS Pr 15:16,
17; S 16:8
17:3 ˢPr 27:21
ᵗ1Ch 29:17;
Ps 26:2;
S 139:23; 1Pe 1:7
17:5 ᵘS Job 5:16
ᵛPr 14:31
ʷS Job 31:29
ˣEze 25:3;
Ob 1:12
17:6 ʸS Ps 125:5
17:7 ᶻPr 16:10
17:8 ªS Ex 23:8;
Pr 19:6

ᵉ23 Or mouth / and makes his lips persuasive
ᶠ1 Hebrew sacrifices   ᵍ7 Or Eloquent

16:22 fountain of life. See note on 10:11. punishment to
fools. See 13:13 and note; see also 7:22; 13:15; 15:10.
16:23 guides his mouth. See 22:17–18.
16:24 Pleasant words are a honeycomb. They are good for
you (see 24:13–14), and they taste good (cf. 2:10; Ps
19:10). healing to the bones. See notes on 4:22; 12:18;
15:30. bones. See note on 3:8.
16:25 in the end it leads to death. See 5:4,23; 7:21–27;
Mt 7:13–14.
16:26 Cf. 2Th 3:10: "If a man will not work, he shall not
eat"; see also Ecc 6:7; Eph 4:28.
16:27 scoundrel. See 6:12 and note; see also note on Dt
13:13. plots evil. See 3:29; 6:14; Mic 2:1. scorching fire.
His speech is inflammatory and destructive (see Jas 3:6).
16:28 stirs up dissension. See note on 6:14. gossip. See
11:13.
16:30 winks with his eye. See note on 6:13. purses his
lips. Thereby making insinuations (see note on 6:12–14).
16:31 Gray hair is a crown of splendor. The elderly were
to receive deep respect (see Lev 19:32). by a righteous life.
See 3:1–2,16.
16:32 patient man . . . warrior. See 14:29; 15:18; 19:11;
Jas 1:19. "Wisdom is better than weapons of war" (Ecc
9:18). man who controls his temper than one who takes a
city. Although one who practices patience and self-control
receives far less attention and acclaim than a warrior who
takes a city, he accomplishes better things.
16:33 The lot is cast into the lap. Here the lot may have

been several pebbles held in the fold of a garment and then
drawn out or shaken to the ground. It was commonly used to
make decisions (see notes on Ex 28:30; Nu 26:53; Ne 11:1;
Jnh 1:7; Ac 1:26; see also Ps 22:18). every decision is from
the LORD. God, not chance, is in control (see vv. 1,3–4,9).
17:2 A wise servant will rule over a disgraceful son. See
11:29 and note. disgraceful son. See 10:5; 19:26; 28:7;
29:15.
17:3 The crucible . . . the furnace. Silver and gold were
refined to remove their impurities (cf. Isa 1:25; Mal 3:3).
tests the heart. See 15:11; 16:2 and notes; Jer 17:10.
17:5 who mocks the poor shows contempt for their Maker. See 14:31 and note. whoever gloats over disaster will not
go unpunished. The people of Edom in particular were
condemned for gloating over the collapse of "brother" Israel
(Ob 10; see Eze 35:12,15; see also Pr 24:17).
17:6 crown to the aged. Cf. the "gray hair" of 16:31. To
live to see one's grandchildren was considered a great
blessing (see Ge 48:11; Ps 128:5–6). parents are the pride
of their children. See Ge 47:7.
17:7 For the structure of this verse cf. 19:10; 26:1. Arrogant. See NIV text note. lying lips to a ruler. His right to rule
depends on honesty and justice (see 12:22; 16:12–13)
17:8 A bribe is a charm. A sad commentary on human
behavior (see 18:16; 21:14; Ecc 10:19). Elsewhere, bribes
are condemned (see v. 23; 15:27; 28:16; Dt 16:19; 1Sa
12:3; Ecc 7:7; Isa 1:23; Am 5:12; 1Ti 6:10).

9He who covers over an offense
promotes love,[b]
but whoever repeats the matter
separates close friends.[c]

10A rebuke impresses a man of
discernment
more than a hundred lashes a fool.

11An evil man is bent only on rebellion;
a merciless official will be sent against
him.

12Better to meet a bear robbed of her
cubs
than a fool in his folly.[d]

13If a man pays back evil[e] for good,[f]
evil will never leave his house.

14Starting a quarrel is like breaching a
dam;
so drop the matter before a dispute
breaks out.[g]

15Acquitting the guilty and condemning
the innocent[h]—
the LORD detests them both.[i]

16Of what use is money in the hand of a
fool,
since he has no desire to get
wisdom?[j]

17A friend loves at all times,
and a brother is born for adversity.[k]

18A man lacking in judgment strikes
hands in pledge
and puts up security for his
neighbor.[l]

19He who loves a quarrel loves sin;
he who builds a high gate invites
destruction.

17:9 [b]S Pr 10:12
[c]Pr 16:28
17:12
[d]S 1Sa 25:25
17:13
[e]S 1Sa 19:4
[f]S Ge 44:4;
S Ps 35:12
17:14
[g]Mt 5:25-26
17:15
[h]S Ps 94:21;
S Pr 18:5
[i]Ex 23:6-7;
Isa 5:23;
La 3:34-36
17:16 [j]Pr 23:23
17:17
[k]S 2Sa 15:21;
Pr 27:10
17:18 [l]Pr 6:1-5;
S 11:15;
22:26-27

17:21 [m]S Pr 10:1
17:22 [n]S Ps 38:8
[o]S Ex 12:46;
Pr 14:30;
S 15:13; 18:14
17:23
[p]S Ex 18:21;
S 23:8; S 1Sa 8:3
[q]S Job 34:33
17:24 [r]S Job 31:1
17:25 [s]S Pr 10:1
17:26 [t]S Ps 94:21
17:27 [u]S Job 6:24
[v]S Pr 14:29
17:28
[w]S Job 2:13;
13:5; S Pr 10:19

20A man of perverse heart does not
prosper;
he whose tongue is deceitful falls into
trouble.

21To have a fool for a son brings grief;
there is no joy for the father of a
fool.[m]

22A cheerful heart is good medicine,
but a crushed[n] spirit dries up the
bones.[o]

23A wicked man accepts a bribe[p] in
secret
to pervert the course of justice.[q]

24A discerning man keeps wisdom in
view,
but a fool's eyes[r] wander to the ends
of the earth.

25A foolish son brings grief to his father
and bitterness to the one who bore
him.[s]

26It is not good to punish an innocent
man,[t]
or to flog officials for their integrity.

27A man of knowledge uses words with
restraint,[u]
and a man of understanding is
even-tempered.[v]

28Even a fool is thought wise if he keeps
silent,
and discerning if he holds his
tongue.[w]

18 An unfriendly man pursues selfish
ends;
he defies all sound judgment.

17:9 *He who covers over an offense promotes love.* See 10:12 and note.
17:10 *rebuke impresses a man of discernment.* See 9:8–9. *a hundred lashes a fool.* Fools deserved and received flogging (cf. 10:13; 19:25,29; 26:3; Dt 25:3).
17:11 *merciless official.* Cf. the dispatching of Abishai and Joab to end Sheba's rebellion against David (2Sa 20:1–22; see 1Ki 2:25,29,46; Pr 16:14).
17:12 *bear robbed of her cubs.* Sure to attack you and rip you open (see 2Sa 17:8; Hos 13:8; cf. the raging of the fool in 29:9).
17:13 *pays back evil for good.* Like Nabal, who refused to pay David's men (1Sa 25:21; see Ps 109:5; Ro 12:17–21). *evil will never leave his house.* The fate of David's family after his affair with Bathsheba and the murder of Uriah (2Sa 12:10; cf. Jer. 18:20–23).
17:15 *Acquitting the guilty.* Perhaps because of a bribe (see v. 8; 24:24).
17:16 *money in the hand of a fool.* Perhaps to pay the fee for his schooling.
17:17 *friend loves at all times.* Cf. David's friendship with Jonathan (2Sa 1:26; see 18:24; Ru 1:16; 1Co 13:4–7).
17:18 See note on 6:1.
17:19 *who loves a quarrel loves sin.* A hot-tempered man commits many sins (29:22). *builds a high gate.* Out of pride (cf. 16:18; 29:23).
17:20 *does not prosper.* Contrast 16:20. *whose tongue is deceitful.* See note on 2:12. *falls into trouble.* See note on 6:15.
17:21 *grief . . . no joy.* See v. 25; 19:13.
17:22 *cheerful heart.* See 14:30; 15:13,30; 16:15; Job 29:24. *crushed spirit dries up the bones.* See note on 3:8; see also 12:4; 14:30; Ps 32:3; 37:7–8.
17:23 *accepts a bribe.* See note on v. 8.
17:24 *wander to the ends of the earth.* He chases fantasies and is interested in everything except wisdom (see 12:11; cf. Dt 30:11–14).
17:25 See v. 21. *bitterness.* See 14:10 and note.
17:26 *punish an innocent man.* See v. 15 and note. *flog officials.* Cf. the beating and disgrace endured by Jeremiah (Jer 20:2; see v. 10 and note).
17:27 *uses words with restraint.* See 10:19. *even-tempered.* See 16:32.
17:28 *a fool is thought wise if he keeps silent.* Cf. Job's sarcastic comment in Job 13:5.
18:1 *pursues selfish ends.* He is quarrelsome and hot-tem-

2A fool finds no pleasure in understanding
but delights in airing his own opinions.[x]
3When wickedness comes, so does contempt,
and with shame comes disgrace.
4The words of a man's mouth are deep waters,[y]
but the fountain of wisdom is a bubbling brook.
5It is not good to be partial to the wicked[z]
or to deprive the innocent of justice.[a]
6A fool's lips bring him strife,
and his mouth invites a beating.[b]
7A fool's mouth is his undoing,
and his lips are a snare[c] to his soul.[d]
8The words of a gossip are like choice morsels;
they go down to a man's inmost parts.[e]
9One who is slack in his work
is brother to one who destroys.[f]
10The name of the LORD is a strong tower;[g]
the righteous run to it and are safe.[h]
11The wealth of the rich is their fortified city;[i]
they imagine it an unscalable wall.
12Before his downfall a man's heart is proud,
but humility comes before honor.[j]
13He who answers before listening—
that is his folly and his shame.[k]
14A man's spirit sustains him in sickness,
but a crushed spirit who can bear?[l]
15The heart of the discerning acquires knowledge;[m]
the ears of the wise seek it out.
16A gift[n] opens the way for the giver
and ushers him into the presence of the great.
17The first to present his case seems right,
till another comes forward and questions him.
18Casting the lot settles disputes[o]
and keeps strong opponents apart.
19An offended[p] brother is more unyielding than a fortified city,
and disputes are like the barred gates of a citadel.
20From the fruit of his mouth a man's stomach is filled;
with the harvest from his lips he is satisfied.[q]
21The tongue has the power of life and death,[r]
and those who love it will eat its fruit.[s]
22He who finds a wife finds what is good[t]
and receives favor from the LORD.[u]
23A poor man pleads for mercy,
but a rich man answers harshly.
24A man of many companions may come to ruin,

18:2 [x]S Pr 12:23 **18:4** [y]S Ps 18:16 **18:5** [z]Pr 24:23-25; 28:21 [a]S Ps 82:2; S Pr 17:15 **18:6** [b]S Pr 10:14 **18:7** [c]Ps 140:9 [d]S Ps 64:8; S Pr 10:14; S 12:13; S 13:3; Ecc 10:12 **18:8** [e]Pr 26:22 **18:9** [f]Pr 28:24 **18:10** [g]S Ps 61:3 [h]S Ps 20:1; Pr 14:26 **18:11** [i]Pr 10:15 **18:12** [j]S Pr 11:2; 15:33; S 16:18 **18:13** [k]Pr 20:25 **18:14** [l]S Pr 15:13; S 17:22 **18:15** [m]S Pr 15:14 **18:16** [n]S Ge 32:13; S 1Sa 10:4; Pr 19:6 **18:18** [o]S Pr 16:33 **18:19** [p]S 1Sa 17:28 **18:20** [q]S Pr 12:14 **18:21** [r]S Ps 12:4 [s]Pr 13:2-3; S Mt 12:37 **18:22** [t]S Pr 12:4 [u]S Job 33:26; Pr 19:14; 31:10

pered (cf. 17:14; Gal 5:20).
18:2 *airing his own opinions.* Cf. Ecc 10:3.
18:3 *contempt . . . shame . . . disgrace.* Cf. 3:35; 6:33; 10:5; 11:2; Ps 31:19; Isa 22:18.
18:4 *deep waters.* Profound or obscure (cf. 20:5). *fountain of wisdom is a bubbling brook.* A wise man's words are refreshing and a source of life (see 1:23; 13:14; see also 10:11 and note).
18:5 *partial to the wicked.* See 17:15 and note. Favoritism of any kind was condemned in the law (see Lev 19:15; Dt 1:17; 16:19). *to deprive the innocent of justice.* See 17:26; 31:5; Mal 3:5.
18:6 *bring him strife.* A fool is quick to quarrel (see 17:14, 19; 20:3). *invites a beating.* By a rod on his back (see 10:13; 19:29).
18:7 See 10:14 and note.
18:8 *words of a gossip are like choice morsels.* They are as pleasant as a wise man's words (cf. 16:21,23), but they promote dissension (see 11:13; 26:20,22). *they go down to a man's inmost parts.* Where they are thoroughly digested and so are carried about and live on and on.
18:9 *who is slack in his work.* See 10:4 and note.
18:10 *name of the LORD.* The "name" equals the person, since it expresses his nature and qualities (see Ex 3:14–15 and notes). *strong tower.* See Ps 18:2; 91:2; 144:2. *safe.* See 29:25; Ps 27:5.
18:11 *wealth . . . is their fortified city.* Identical to 10:15 (see note there). *unscalable wall.* But God can bring it down (see Isa 25:12).
18:12 See 15:33 and note.
18:14 See 15:13; 17:22 and notes.
18:16 *A gift opens the way.* A reference to the effectiveness of a bribe (see note on 17:8).
18:17 A warning to judges to hear both sides of a case (cf. Dt 1:16), but applicable to many situations.
18:18 *Casting the lot settles disputes.* See note on 16:33. Cf. Mt 27:35.
18:19 *An offended brother.* Cf. Esau's anger because of the blessing Jacob received from Isaac (Ge 27:41).
18:20 See 12:14 and note.
18:21 *tongue has the power of life and death.* See note on 13:3. *its fruit.* See v. 20.
18:22 *who finds a wife finds what is good.* See 12:4 and note; 19:14. *receives favor from the LORD.* Identical to 8:35, where finding wisdom brought such favor.
18:24 *man of many companions may come to ruin.* One must choose friends carefully (see 12:26 and note; 17:17).

but there is a friend who sticks closer
than a brother. *v*

19 Better a poor man whose walk is
blameless
than a fool whose lips are perverse. *w*

²It is not good to have zeal without
knowledge,
nor to be hasty and miss the way. *x*

³A man's own folly *y* ruins his life,
yet his heart rages against the LORD. *z*

⁴Wealth brings many friends,
but a poor man's friend deserts him. *a*

⁵A false witness *b* will not go
unpunished, *c*
and he who pours out lies will not go
free. *d*

⁶Many curry favor with a ruler, *e*
and everyone is the friend of a man
who gives gifts. *f*

⁷A poor man is shunned by all his
relatives—
how much more do his friends avoid
him! *g*
Though he pursues them with pleading,
they are nowhere to be found. *h h*

⁸He who gets wisdom loves his own
soul;
he who cherishes understanding
prospers. *i*

⁹A false witness will not go unpunished,
and he who pours out lies will
perish. *j*

¹⁰It is not fitting for a fool *k* to live in
luxury—
how much worse for a slave to rule
over princes! *l*

¹¹A man's wisdom gives him patience; *m*

it is to his glory to overlook an
offense.

¹²A king's rage is like the roar of a lion, *n*
but his favor is like dew *o* on the
grass. *p*

¹³A foolish son is his father's ruin, *q*
and a quarrelsome wife is like a
constant dripping. *r*

¹⁴Houses and wealth are inherited from
parents, *s*
but a prudent wife is from the
LORD. *t*

¹⁵Laziness brings on deep sleep,
and the shiftless man goes hungry. *u*

¹⁶He who obeys instructions guards his
life,
but he who is contemptuous of his
ways will die. *v*

¹⁷He who is kind to the poor lends to the
LORD, *w*
and he will reward him for what he
has done. *x*

¹⁸Discipline your son, for in that there is
hope;
do not be a willing party to his
death. *y*

¹⁹A hot-tempered man must pay the
penalty;
if you rescue him, you will have to
do it again.

²⁰Listen to advice and accept
instruction, *z*
and in the end you will be wise. *a*

²¹Many are the plans in a man's heart,
but it is the LORD's purpose that
prevails. *b*

Center column cross references:

18:24
*v*S 1Sa 20:42;
Jn 15:13-15
19:1 *w*Pr 28:6
19:2 *x*Pr 29:20
19:3 *y*Ps 14:1;
Pr 9:13; 24:9;
Isa 32:6
*z*Jas 1:13-15
19:4 *a*ver 7;
Pr 14:20
19:5 *b*S Ex 23:1
*c*S Ps 56:7 *d*ver 9;
S Dt 19:19;
Pr 21:28
19:6 *e*Pr 29:26
*f*S Pr 17:8;
S 18:16
19:7 *g*Pr 10:15
*h*S ver 4
19:8 *i*S Pr 16:20
19:9 *j*S ver 5;
S Dt 19:19
19:10 *k*Pr 26:1
*l*Pr 30:21-23;
Ecc 10:5-7
19:11
*m*S 2Ki 5:12

19:12 *n*Pr 20:2
*o*S Ps 133:3
*p*S Est 1:12;
S 7:7; Ps 72:5-6;
Pr 16:14-15
19:13 *q*S Pr 10:1
*r*S Est 1:18;
Pr 21:9
19:14
*s*2Co 12:14
*t*S Pr 18:22
19:15 *u*S Pr 10:4;
20:13
19:16
*v*S Pr 16:17;
S Ro 10:5
19:17
*w*S Dt 24:14
*x*S Dt 24:19;
Pr 14:21; 22:9;
S Mt 10:42
19:18
*y*S Pr 13:24;
23:13-14
19:20 *z*Pr 4:1
*a*S Pr 12:15
19:21 *b*Ps 33:11;
Pr 16:9; 20:24;
Isa 8:10; 14:24,
27; 31:2; 40:8;
46:10; 48:14;
55:11; Jer 44:29;
La 3:37

h 7 The meaning of the Hebrew for this sentence is
uncertain.

19:1 *blameless.* See note on 2:7. *than a fool.* Even if he
becomes rich (see 28:6).
19:2 *zeal without knowledge.* Cf. Ro 10:2. *be hasty.* Haste
can lead to poverty (21:5) or folly (29:20). *miss the way.* The
Hebrew for this expression often refers to sin.
19:3 *his heart rages against the LORD.* He blames God for
his troubles (see Ge 4:5; Isa 8:21; cf. La 3:39).
19:4 See v. 7; 14:20.
19:5 See note on 6:19.
19:6 *curry favor.* Cf. Job 11:19. *friend of a man who gives
gifts.* Generosity (v. 4) or bribery (18:16) could be in view.
19:7 *poor man is shunned.* See v. 4; 14:20; Job 19:19; Ps
38:11.
19:8 *loves his own soul.* Cf. 8:35–36. *prospers.* See 13:13
and note.
19:10 *not fitting for a fool to live in luxury.* Or have honor
(26:1). *for a slave to rule over princes.* Because of his lack of
wisdom and tendency to become a tyrant (see 17:2; 29:2;
Isa 3:4).

19:11 *patience.* See 14:29; 15:18; 16:32; Ecc 7:9; Jas
1:19. *overlook an offense.* Has good self-control (see 12:16;
29:11; 2Sa 16:11–12).
19:12 *A king's rage is like the roar of a lion.* See 16:14 and
note. *his favor is like dew.* See 16:15 and note.
19:13 *foolish son.* See 17:21,25. *quarrelsome wife.* Also
denounced in 21:9,19; 25:24; 27:15. Stirring up dissension is condemned throughout Proverbs (see 6:14 and
note).
19:14 *prudent wife.* See 12:4 and note; see also 18:22.
19:15 See 6:11; 10:4 and notes.
19:16 See 13:13; 15:10; 16:17 and notes.
19:17 *who is kind to the poor.* See note on 14:21; see also
14:31. *lends to the LORD.* The Lord regards it as a gift to him
(cf. Mt 25:40).
19:18 *Discipline your son . . . not . . . to his death.* See
note on 13:24.
19:19 *hot-tempered man.* Cf. 14:16–17,29; 15:18.
19:21 See 16:1,9 and notes.

22What a man desires is unfailing love[i];
  better to be poor than a liar.

23The fear of the LORD leads to life:
  Then one rests content, untouched
    by trouble.[c]

24The sluggard buries his hand in the
    dish;
  he will not even bring it back to his
    mouth![d]

25Flog a mocker, and the simple will learn
    prudence;
  rebuke a discerning man,[e] and he
    will gain knowledge.[f]

26He who robs his father and drives out
    his mother[g]
  is a son who brings shame and
    disgrace.

27Stop listening to instruction, my son,[h]
  and you will stray from the words of
    knowledge.

28A corrupt witness mocks at justice,
  and the mouth of the wicked gulps
    down evil.[i]

29Penalties are prepared for mockers,
  and beatings for the backs of fools.[j]

20 Wine[k] is a mocker[l] and beer a
    brawler;
  whoever is led astray[m] by them is not
    wise.[n]

2A king's wrath is like the roar of a
    lion;[o]
  he who angers him forfeits his life.[p]

3It is to a man's honor to avoid strife,
  but every fool[q] is quick to quarrel.[r]

4A sluggard[s] does not plow in season;

so at harvest time he looks but finds
    nothing.[t]

5The purposes of a man's heart are deep
    waters,[u]
  but a man of understanding draws
    them out.

6Many a man claims to have unfailing
    love,
  but a faithful man who can find?[v]

7The righteous man leads a blameless
    life;[w]
  blessed are his children after him.[x]

8When a king sits on his throne to
    judge,[y]
  he winnows out all evil with his
    eyes.[z]

9Who can say, "I have kept my heart
    pure;[a]
  I am clean and without sin"?[b]

10Differing weights and differing
    measures—
  the LORD detests them both.[c]

11Even a child is known by his actions,
  by whether his conduct is pure[d] and
    right.

12Ears that hear and eyes that see—
  the LORD has made them both.[e]

13Do not love sleep or you will grow
    poor;[f]
  stay awake and you will have food to
    spare.

14"It's no good, it's no good!" says the
    buyer;

Cross references (center column):

19:23 c S Job 4:7; S Pr 10:27
19:24 d Pr 26:15
19:25 e S Ps 141:5 /S Pr 9:9; 21:11
19:26 g Pr 28:24
19:27 h S Pr 1:8
19:28 l S Job 15:16
19:29 j S Dt 25:2
20:1 k S Lev 10:9; Hab 2:5 l S 1Sa 25:36 m 1Ki 20:16 n Pr 31:4
20:2 o S Pr 19:12 p S Est 7:7; S Pr 16:14
20:3 q S 1Sa 25:25 r S Ge 13:8
20:4 s S Pr 6:6
t Ecc 10:18
20:5 u S Ps 18:16
20:6 v Ps 12:1
20:7 w S Ps 26:1 x Ps 37:25-26; 112:2
20:8 y S 1Ki 7:7 z ver 26; Pr 25:4-5
20:9 a S Job 15:14 b 1Ki 8:46; Ecc 7:20; 1Jn 1:8
20:10 c ver 23; S Pr 11:1
20:11 d S Ps 39:1
20:12 e S Ps 94:9
20:13 f S Pr 6:11; S 19:15

19:22 *desires... unfailing love.* But such loyalty is difficult to find (cf. 20:6; 14:22). *better to be poor than a liar.* See vv. 1,28; 6:12.
19:23 *fear of the LORD.* See note on 1:7. *leads to life.* See note on 10:11. *untouched by trouble.* See 3:2; 14:26 and notes.
19:24 *sluggard.* See note on 6:6.
19:25 *Flog a mocker.* See v. 29; 14:3; see also notes on 1:22; 17:10. *simple.* Not to be confused with the mocker (see note on 1:4).
19:26 *robs his father and drives out his mother.* Children were expected to take care of their parents when they were sick or elderly (cf. Isa 51:18). Robbing them (cf. Jdg 17:1–2) and attacking them (Ex 21:15,17) were serious crimes. *shame and disgrace.* See note on 10:5; 13:5.
19:27 See 5:1–2.
19:28 *corrupt witness.* See v. 5; see also note on 6:19. *gulps down evil.* Cf. the description of man as one "who drinks up evil like water" (Job 15:16; see Job 34:7).
19:29 *Penalties... for mockers.* See v. 25. *beatings for the backs of fools.* See 10:13; 14:3; 26:3.
20:1 *Wine is a mocker and beer a brawler.* Those who overindulge become mockers and brawlers (see Hos 7:5).

Proverbs associates drunkenness with poverty (23:20–21), strife (23:29–30) and injustice (31:4–5). *led astray.* See Ge 9:21; Isa 28:7.
20:2 See 16:14 and note.
20:3 *quick to quarrel.* See 6:14; 17:14,19; 18:6.
20:4 *sluggard.* See note on 6:6. *but finds nothing.* See 13:4; 21:25–26.
20:5 *purposes.* Or "motives" (cf. 16:1–2). *deep waters.* Cf. 18:4. *draws them out.* As if from a well.
20:6 *unfailing love.* See note on 19:22. *a faithful man who can find?* Cf. Ecc 7:28–29.
20:7 *blameless life.* See note on 2:7. *blessed are his children.* See 13:22; see also note on 14:26.
20:8 *winnows out all evil.* See 16:10; Ps 11:4.
20:9 *pure... clean... without sin.* No one is without sin (cf. Job 14:4; Ro 3:23)—but those whose sins have been forgiven have "clean hands and a pure heart" (Ps 24:4; see also 51:1–2,9–10).
20:10 See note on 11:1; cf. 16:11.
20:13 *sleep... grow poor.* See 24:33–34.
20:14 *It's no good, it's no good!* Prices were often agreed upon by bargaining, so the buyer is questioning the quality of the article in order to buy it more cheaply.

i22 Or *A man's greed is his shame*

then off he goes and boasts about his purchase.

15Gold there is, and rubies in abundance, but lips that speak knowledge are a rare jewel.

16Take the garment of one who puts up security for a stranger; hold it in pledge g if he does it for a wayward woman. h

17Food gained by fraud tastes sweet to a man, i but he ends up with a mouth full of gravel. j

18Make plans by seeking advice; if you wage war, obtain guidance. k

19A gossip betrays a confidence; l so avoid a man who talks too much.

20If a man curses his father or mother, m his lamp will be snuffed out in pitch darkness. n

21An inheritance quickly gained at the beginning will not be blessed at the end.

22Do not say, "I'll pay you back for this wrong!" o Wait for the LORD, and he will deliver you. p

23The LORD detests differing weights, and dishonest scales do not please him. q

24A man's steps are directed r by the LORD. s How then can anyone understand his own way? t

25It is a trap for a man to dedicate something rashly and only later to consider his vows. u

26A wise king winnows out the wicked; he drives the threshing wheel over them. v

27The lamp of the LORD w searches the spirit of a man j ; it searches out his inmost being. x

28Love and faithfulness keep a king safe; through love y his throne is made secure. z

29The glory of young men is their strength, gray hair the splendor of the old. a

30Blows and wounds cleanse b away evil, and beatings c purge the inmost being.

21 The king's heart is in the hand of the LORD; he directs it like a watercourse wherever he pleases. d

2All a man's ways seem right to him, but the LORD weighs the heart. e

3To do what is right and just

Cross references (center column):

20:16
gS Ex 22:26
hPr 27:13
20:17 iPr 9:17
jJob 20:14;
La 3:16
20:18 kPr 11:14;
24:6
20:19 lPr 11:13
20:20 mPr 30:11
nEx 21:17;
S Job 18:5
20:22 oPr 24:29
pIsa 37:20;
Jer 1:19; 42:11;
Ro 12:19
20:23 qS ver 10;
S Dt 25:13

20:24 rS Ps 90:12
sS Job 33:29
tS Pr 19:21;
Jer 10:23
20:25
uS Pr 10:19;
18:13; Ecc 5:2,
4-5; Jer 44:25
20:26 vS ver 8
20:27
wS Ps 119:105
xS Pr 16:2
20:28 yPs 40:11
zS Pr 16:12;
Isa 16:5
20:29 aPr 16:31
20:30 bS Ps 51:2;
Pr 22:15 cIsa 1:5
21:1 dEst 5:1;
Jer 39:11-12
21:2 eS Pr 16:2

j 27 Or The spirit of man is the LORD's lamp

20:15 *Gold . . . rubies.* Earlier, wisdom itself was valued more highly than gold or rubies (3:14–15; 8:10–11).
20:16 See note on 6:1. *Take the garment.* A garment could be taken as security for a debt (Dt 24:10–13). Anyone who foolishly assumes responsibility for the debt of a stranger, whose reliability is unknown, or of a wayward woman, whose unreliability is known, ought to be held accountable, even to the degree of taking his garment as a pledge.
20:17 *tastes sweet to a man.* Cf. the sweet "food" prepared by the adulteress in 9:17. Zophar observes that evil is sweet in the mouth of a wicked man, but it turns sour in his stomach (Job 20:12–18). See note on 10:2.
20:18 *advice . . . guidance.* See 15:22; Lk 14:31.
20:20 *curses his father or mother.* Punishable by death (see Lev 20:9; cf. Pr 30:11,17). *lamp . . . snuffed out.* He will die (see note on 13:9).
20:21 *inheritance quickly gained . . . will not be blessed.* Cf. 19:26; cf. also the sad experience of the son who "squandered his wealth in wild living" (Lk 15:12–13).
20:22 *I'll pay you back.* Vengeance was God's prerogative. He would repay the wicked for their actions (see Dt 32:35; Ps 94:1). *Wait for the LORD.* See Ps 27:14; 37:34.
20:23 See v. 10; see also note on 11:1.
20:24 See notes on 3:5–6; 16:9.
20:25 *dedicate something rashly.* Promise to make a special gift to the Lord if he answers an earnest request (see Lev 27:1–25; Dt 23:21; Jdg 11:30–31,34–35; 1Sa 1:11). Sometimes such a vow was made hastily and was not carried

out (cf. Ecc 5:4–6).
20:26 *threshing wheel.* The wheel of the threshing cart that separated the grain from the husk (cf. Isa 28:27–28). The wicked will be separated from the righteous and duly punished.
20:27 *lamp of the LORD.* Perhaps his eyes (cf. 5:21; 15:3). *searches the spirit . . . his inmost being.* See note on 15:11.
20:28 *Love and faithfulness keep a king safe . . . secure.* Benevolence and kindness endear a king to his people and encourage them to be loyal subjects (cf. 3:3; 14:22; 16:12; 29:14).
20:29 *their strength.* Cf. Jer 9:23. *gray hair the splendor of the old.* See note on 16:31.
20:30 *Blows and wounds cleanse away evil.* Stern punishment is necessary to restrain evil. Several verses refer to fools whose backs are beaten (10:13; 14:3; 19:29), but even then, because they are fools, they may not change their ways (cf. 17:10; 27:22).
21:1 *king's heart is in the hand of the LORD.* God controls the lives and actions even of kings, such as Nebuchadnezzar (Da 4:31–32,35) and Cyrus (Isa 45:1–3; cf. Ezr 6:22). *directs it . . . wherever he pleases.* See 16:9; see also 16:1; 19:21; 20:24.
21:2 *seem right.* See 14:12; 16:2. *weighs the heart.* See 24:12; Job 31:6; Ps 139:23; 1Co 4:4–5; Heb 4:12.
21:3 *more acceptable . . . than sacrifice.* A theme also found in the prophets (Hos 6:6; Mic 6:7–8). See v. 27; see also note on 15:8.

is more acceptable to the LORD than sacrifice.ᶠ

⁴Haughty eyesᵍ and a proud heart,
the lamp of the wicked, are sin!

⁵The plans of the diligent lead to profitʰ
as surely as haste leads to poverty.

⁶A fortune made by a lying tongue
is a fleeting vapor and a deadly
snare.ᵏ ⁱ

⁷The violence of the wicked will drag
them away,ʲ
for they refuse to do what is right.

⁸The way of the guilty is devious,ᵏ
but the conduct of the innocent is
upright.

⁹Better to live on a corner of the roof
than share a house with a
quarrelsome wife.ˡ

¹⁰The wicked man craves evil;
his neighbor gets no mercy from him.

¹¹When a mocker is punished, the simple
gain wisdom;
when a wise man is instructed, he
gets knowledge.ᵐ

¹²The Righteous Oneˡ takes note of the
house of the wicked
and brings the wicked to ruin.ⁿ

¹³If a man shuts his ears to the cry of the
poor,
he too will cry outᵒ and not be
answered.ᵖ

¹⁴A gift given in secret soothes anger,
and a bribe concealed in the cloak
pacifies great wrath.ᑫ

¹⁵When justice is done, it brings joy to
the righteous
but terror to evildoers.ʳ

¹⁶A man who strays from the path of
understanding
comes to rest in the company of the
dead.ˢ

¹⁷He who loves pleasure will become
poor;
whoever loves wine and oil will
never be rich.ᵗ

¹⁸The wicked become a ransomᵘ for the
righteous,
and the unfaithful for the upright.

¹⁹Better to live in a desert
than with a quarrelsome and
ill-tempered wife.ᵛ

²⁰In the house of the wise are stores of
choice food and oil,
but a foolish man devours all he has.

²¹He who pursues righteousness and love
finds life, prosperityᵐ ʷ and honor.ˣ

²²A wise man attacks the city of the
mightyʸ
and pulls down the stronghold in
which they trust.

²³He who guards his mouthᶻ and his
tongue
keeps himself from calamity.ᵃ

²⁴The proud and arrogantᵇ
man—"Mocker" is his name;
he behaves with overweening pride.

21:3
ᶠS 1Sa 15:22;
Isa 1:11;
Mic 6:6-8
21:4 ᵍS Job 41:34
21:5 ʰS Pr 10:4
21:6 ⁱS Pr 10:2
21:7 ʲS Pr 11:5
21:8 ᵏS Pr 2:15
21:9 ˡver 19;
Pr 19:13; 25:24
21:11
ᵐS Pr 19:25
21:12
ⁿS Pr 14:11
21:13 ᵒS Ex 11:6
ᵖS Job 29:12
21:14
ᑫS Ge 32:20

21:15 ʳS Pr 10:29
21:16 ˢEze 18:24
21:17
ᵗPr 23:20-21,
29-35
21:18 ᵘPr 11:8;
Isa 43:3
21:19 ᵛS ver 9
21:21 ʷPs 25:13
ˣMt 5:6
21:22 ʸS Pr 8:14
21:23
ᶻS Ps 34:13
ᵃS Pr 10:19;
12:13; S 13:3
21:24 ᵇJer 43:2

ᵏ6 Some Hebrew manuscripts, Septuagint and Vulgate;
most Hebrew manuscripts vapor for those who seek death
ˡ12 Or The righteous man   ᵐ21 Or righteousness

21:4 *Haughty eyes.* See note on 6:17; see also 16:5,18. *lamp.* Eyes (see 20:27; Lk 11:34).
21:5 *The plans of the diligent lead to profit.* See note on 10:4. *haste.* Either rash actions (19:2) or a desire to get rich quick (see 13:11 and note; 20:21; 28:20).
21:6 *fortune made by a lying tongue.* See note on 10:2; cf. 19:1. *fleeting vapor.* See 13:11 and note; Ecc 1:14. *deadly snare.* Cf. 5:22; 7:23.
21:7 *violence of the wicked will drag them away.* See 1:18–19 and notes.
21:9 *corner of the roof.* Roofs were flat, and small rooms could be built there (see Dt 22:8; 2Ki 4:10). *quarrelsome wife.* See note on 19:13.
21:10 *craves evil.* See 4:16; 10:23. *his neighbor gets no mercy.* Cf. 14:21.
21:11 See 19:25 and note.
21:12 *Righteous One.* Cf. Job 34:17. *house of the wicked ... to ruin.* See 10:25 and note; 14:11.
21:13 *cry of the poor.* See note on 14:21; see also 28:27. *he too will ... not be answered.* See note on 1:28. Cf. the fate of the rich man (Lk 16:19–31) and the unmerciful servant (Mt 18:23–34).
21:14 *gift ... bribe.* See note on 17:8; see also 18:16; 19:6. *soothes anger ... wrath.* Perhaps that of an offended

party (see 6:34–35).
21:15 *joy to the righteous.* See 11:10 and note. *terror to evildoers.* See 10:29 and note; Ro 13:3.
21:16 Graphically illustrated by the man who succumbed to the adulteress (see 2:18; 5:23; 7:22–23; 9:18).
21:17 *wine and oil.* Both were associated with lavish feasting (see 23:20–21; Am 6:6). Oil was used in various lotions or perfumes, some of which were very expensive (Jn 12:5).
21:18 *The wicked become a ransom for the righteous.* Close to the thought of 11:8. In Isa 43:3–4 God gave three nations to Persia in exchange for Persia's willingness to release the exiles of Judah (see note on Isa 43:4).
21:19 See note on 19:13.
21:20 *stores of choice food.* See 3:10 and note; 8:21. *oil.* Olive oil (see v. 17; see also Dt 7:13).
21:21 *pursues righteousness.* See 15:9. *life, prosperity and honor.* Benefits for those who seek wisdom (see note on 3:2; see also 3:16; 8:18; cf. 22:4).
21:22 *wise man ... pulls down the stronghold.* Probably another way of saying, "Wisdom is better than strength" (Ecc 9:16). Cf. 24:5; 2Co 10:4, where spiritual weapons "have divine power to demolish strongholds."
21:23 See 13:3 and note; 18:21.

²⁵The sluggard's craving will be the death
of him, c
because his hands refuse to work.
²⁶All day long he craves for more,
but the righteous d give without
sparing. e
²⁷The sacrifice of the wicked is
detestable f —
how much more so when brought
with evil intent! g
²⁸A false witness h will perish, i
and whoever listens to him will be
destroyed forever. n
²⁹A wicked man puts up a bold front,
but an upright man gives thought to
his ways. j
³⁰There is no wisdom, k no insight, no
plan
that can succeed against the LORD. l
³¹The horse is made ready for the day of
battle,
but victory rests with the LORD. m

22 A good name is more desirable
than great riches;
to be esteemed is better than silver or
gold. n
²Rich and poor have this in common:
The LORD is the Maker of them all. o
³A prudent man sees danger and takes
refuge, p
but the simple keep going and suffer
for it. q
⁴Humility and the fear of the LORD

bring wealth and honor r and life. s

⁵In the paths of the wicked lie thorns
and snares, t
but he who guards his soul stays far
from them.
⁶Train o u a child in the way he should
go, v
and when he is old he will not turn
from it. w
⁷The rich rule over the poor,
and the borrower is servant to the
lender.
⁸He who sows wickedness reaps
trouble, x
and the rod of his fury will be
destroyed. y
⁹A generous man will himself be
blessed, z
for he shares his food with the poor. a
¹⁰Drive out the mocker, and out goes
strife;
quarrels and insults are ended. b
¹¹He who loves a pure heart and whose
speech is gracious
will have the king for his friend. c
¹²The eyes of the LORD keep watch over
knowledge,
but he frustrates the words of the
unfaithful.
¹³The sluggard says, "There is a lion
outside!" d

21:25 cPr 13:4
21:26
dS 2Sa 17:27
eS Lev 25:35
21:27
fS 1Ki 14:24
gS Pr 15:8
21:28 hIsa 29:21
iS Pr 19:5
21:29 jS Pr 14:8
21:30
kS Job 12:13;
S 15:25
lS 2Ch 13:12;
S Job 5:13;
Isa 8:10
21:31
mPs 33:12-19;
Isa 31:1
22:1 nEcc 7:1
22:2
oS Job 31:15;
Pr 29:13; Mt 5:45
22:3 pS Pr 14:16
qPr 27:12

22:4 rS Pr 15:33
sS Pr 10:27;
Da 4:36
22:5 tPr 15:19
22:6 uS Ge 14:14
vEph 6:4
wS Dt 6:7
22:8 xS Ex 1:20;
S Job 4:8;
Gal 6:7-8
yHos 8:7
22:9 zS Dt 14:29
aS Pr 11:25;
S 19:17; 28:27
22:10 bPr 26:20
22:11 cPr 16:13;
Mt 5:8
22:13 dPr 26:13

n28 Or / but the words of an obedient man will live on
o6 Or Start

21:24 "Mocker" is his name. See note on 1:22. God
mocks and punishes him for his "overweening pride" (cf.
3:34; 19:25,29; 21:11).
21:25 sluggard's craving. See notes on 6:6; 13:4.
21:26 give without sparing. The righteous are prosperous,
so they can share with those in need (see Ps 37:26; 112:9;
cf. Eph 4:28).
21:27 The sacrifice of the wicked is detestable. See notes
on v. 3; 15:8.
21:28 false witness will perish. See 19:5,9; see also note
on 6:19.
21:29 bold front. Cf. the behavior of the adulteress in 7:13.
21:30 no plan that can succeed against the LORD. Because
he is sovereign and controls people and nations (see 16:4,9
and notes; 19:21; 21:1; 1Co 3:19–20).
21:31 horse. Many times God cautions against trusting in
horses and chariots for victory (e.g., Ps 20:7; Hos 1:7; cf. Dt
17:16). victory rests with the LORD. See 1Sa 17:47; Ps 3:8.
22:1 good name. Its value is recognized also in 3:4; 10:7;
Ecc 7:1. better than silver or gold. Like the possession of
wisdom (see 3:14; 16:16).
22:2 Maker of them all. See 14:31 and note.
22:3 prudent man . . . takes refuge. Cf. 14:8. the simple.
See note on 1:4; see also 9:16.
22:4 See 18:12. Humility and the fear of the LORD. Associated also in 15:33 (see note on 1:7). wealth and honor and

life. Benefits for those who seek wisdom (see note on 3:2;
see also 3:16; 8:18; cf. 21:21).
22:5 thorns and snares. Evil (cf. 15:19). stays far from
them. By taking the "highway of the upright" (16:17).
22:6 Train. Or "Dedicate," as in 1Ki 8:63; see also NIV
text note; cf. Ge 18:19. Instruction (1:8) and discipline
(22:15) are primarily involved. way he should go. The right
way, the way of wisdom (see 4:11 and note). old. Or
"grown."
22:7 The rich. See note on 10:15. the borrower is servant
to the lender. One of the reasons why putting up security for
someone else (v. 26) was frowned upon (cf. Ne 5:4–5).
22:8 sows wickedness reaps trouble. See 12:21. rod of his
fury. His ability to oppress others (see Ps 125:3; Isa 14:5–6).
22:9 generous man will . . . be blessed. See note on 11:25.
shares his food. See note on 14:21; see also Pr 15:8–11.
22:10 Drive out the mocker. See note on 1:22; cf. Ge
21:9–10. out goes strife . . . insults. Cf. 17:14; 18:3; 20:3.
22:11 pure heart. Cf. Ps 24:4. whose speech is gracious.
Characteristic of the wise man in Ecc 10:12. king for his
friend. Cf. v. 29.
22:12 The eyes of the LORD keep watch. See 5:21; 15:3;
Job 31:4; 34:21; Jer 16:17; Heb 4:13. over knowledge. God
protects those who have knowledge (cf. Ps 1:6; 34:15).
frustrates . . . the unfaithful. Overrules their plans and desires (see 16:9; see also note on 21:30).

or, "I will be murdered in the
     streets!"

¹⁴The mouth of an adulteress is a deep
          pit; ^e
     he who is under the LORD's wrath
          will fall into it. ^f

¹⁵Folly is bound up in the heart of a child,
     but the rod of discipline will drive it
          far from him. ^g

¹⁶He who oppresses the poor to increase
          his wealth
     and he who gives gifts to the
          rich—both come to poverty.

Sayings of the Wise

¹⁷Pay attention ^h and listen to the sayings
          of the wise; ⁱ
     apply your heart to what I teach, ^j
¹⁸for it is pleasing when you keep them in
          your heart
     and have all of them ready on your
          lips.
¹⁹So that your trust may be in the LORD,
     I teach you today, even you.
²⁰Have I not written thirty^p sayings for
          you,
     sayings of counsel and knowledge,
²¹teaching you true and reliable words, ^k
     so that you can give sound answers
          to him who sent you?

²²Do not exploit the poor ^l because they
          are poor

and do not crush the needy in
          court, ^m
²³for the LORD will take up their case ⁿ
     and will plunder those who plunder
          them. ^o

²⁴Do not make friends with a
          hot-tempered man,
     do not associate with one easily
          angered,
²⁵or you may learn his ways
     and get yourself ensnared. ^p

²⁶Do not be a man who strikes hands in
          pledge ^q
     or puts up security for debts;
²⁷if you lack the means to pay,
     your very bed will be snatched from
          under you. ^r

²⁸Do not move an ancient boundary
          stone ^s
     set up by your forefathers.

²⁹Do you see a man skilled ^t in his work?
     He will serve ^u before kings; ^v
     he will not serve before obscure men.

23 When you sit to dine with a ruler,
     note well what ^q is before you,
²and put a knife to your throat
     if you are given to gluttony.
³Do not crave his delicacies, ^w
     for that food is deceptive.

⁴Do not wear yourself out to get rich;
     have the wisdom to show restraint.

Cross references

22:14
^eS Pr 5:3-5;
23:27 ^fEcc 7:26
22:15
^gS Pr 13:24;
S 20:30
22:17 ^hS Pr 1:8
ⁱS Pr 1:6; 30:1;
31:1 ^jS Pr 2:2
22:21 ^kEcc 12:10
22:22
^lS Lev 25:17;
S Job 5:16

^mS Ex 23:6
22:23
ⁿS Job 29:16;
Ps 140:12
^oEst 8:1; S 9:1;
Pr 23:10-11
22:25
^p1Co 15:33
22:26 ^qPr 6:1-5
22:27
^rS Pr 11:15;
S 17:18
22:28
^sS Dt 19:14
22:29
^tS 1Ki 11:28
^uS Ge 41:46
^vS Ge 39:4
23:3 ^wver 6-8;
Ps 141:4

^p20 Or not formerly written; or not written excellent
^q1 Or who

22:13 The sluggard (see note on 6:6) creates excuses to avoid work.
22:14 mouth of an adulteress. Her seductive words (see note on 5:3; see also 2:16; 7:5). deep pit. Perhaps a well or a hunter's trap (see 5:22 and note; 7:22).
22:15 rod of discipline. See note on 13:24.
22:16 who oppresses the poor. Condemned also in 14:31; 28:3. gives gifts to the rich. Perhaps bribes (see 17:8; 18:16; 19:6). poverty. See 21:5; 28:22.
22:17—24:22 A new section that returns more to the style of chs. 1–9. Verses 17–21 form the introduction to these 30 sayings.
22:17 Pay attention and listen. See 4:20; 5:1. sayings of the wise. A title, like "proverbs of Solomon" in 10:1.
22:18 it is pleasing. See 2:10; 16:24.
22:19 that your trust may be in the LORD. See note on 3:5.
22:20 thirty sayings. There are 30 units in 22:22–24:22. Most of them are two or three verses long, but see 23:29–35. The Egyptian "Wisdom of Amenemope" (see Introduction: Date) also contains 30 sections.
22:21 give sound answers. See 1Pe 3:15. him who sent you. Possibly a parent or guardian.
22:22 Do not exploit the poor. See v. 16; 14:31. do not crush the needy in court. See Isa 1:17.
22:23 the LORD will take up their case. See 23:11; Ps 12:5; 140:12; Isa 3:13–15; Mal 3:5. will plunder those who

plunder them. See Ex 22:22–24.
22:24 Do not make friends. Cf. 12:26. hot-tempered man. His characteristics are given in 14:16–17; 15:18; 29:22.
22:25 may learn his ways. "Bad company corrupts good character" (1Co 15:33). ensnared. See note on 5:22; see also 12:13; 13:14; 29:6.
22:26 See note on 6:1.
22:27 your very bed will be snatched. You will be reduced to poverty.
22:28 ancient boundary stone. See note on 15:25; see also 23:10.
22:29 skilled in his work. Craftsmen were considered to be wise (see note on 8:30; see also Ex 35:30–35). serve before kings. Like Joseph, an administrator (Ge 41:46); David, a musician (1Sa 16:21–23); and Huram, a worker in bronze (1Ki 7:14).
23:2 gluttony. Cf. the similar warning in vv. 20–21.
23:3 Do not crave his delicacies. Repeated in a different context in v. 6. deceptive. Perhaps the meaning is that the ruler wants to obligate you in some way, even to influence you to support a wicked scheme (cf. Ps 141:4).
23:4 Do not wear yourself out to get rich. The desire to get rich can ruin a person physically and spiritually. "For the love of money is a root of all kinds of evil" (1Ti 6:10; cf. 15:27; 28:20; Heb 13:5).

[5]Cast but a glance at riches, and they are
gone,[x]
for they will surely sprout wings
and fly off to the sky like an eagle.[y]

[6]Do not eat the food of a stingy man,
do not crave his delicacies;[z]
[7]for he is the kind of man
who is always thinking about the
cost.[r]
"Eat and drink," he says to you,
but his heart is not with you.
[8]You will vomit up the little you have
eaten
and will have wasted your
compliments.

[9]Do not speak to a fool,
for he will scorn the wisdom of your
words.[a]

[10]Do not move an ancient boundary
stone[b]
or encroach on the fields of the
fatherless,
[11]for their Defender[c] is strong;[d]
he will take up their case against
you.[e]

[12]Apply your heart to instruction[f]
and your ears to words of knowledge.

[13]Do not withhold discipline from a child;
if you punish him with the rod, he
will not die.
[14]Punish him with the rod
and save his soul from death.[s] [g]

[15]My son, if your heart is wise,
then my heart will be glad;
[16]my inmost being will rejoice
when your lips speak what is right.[h]

[17]Do not let your heart envy[i] sinners,
but always be zealous for the fear of
the LORD.
[18]There is surely a future hope for you,
and your hope will not be cut off.[j]

[19]Listen, my son,[k] and be wise,
and keep your heart on the right
path.
[20]Do not join those who drink too much
wine[l]
or gorge themselves on meat,
[21]for drunkards and gluttons become
poor,[m]
and drowsiness clothes them in rags.

[22]Listen to your father, who gave you life,
and do not despise your mother
when she is old.[n]
[23]Buy the truth and do not sell it;
get wisdom, discipline and
understanding.[o]
[24]The father of a righteous man has great
joy;
he who has a wise son delights in
him.[p]
[25]May your father and mother be glad;
may she who gave you birth rejoice![q]

[26]My son,[r] give me your heart
and let your eyes keep to my ways,[s]
[27]for a prostitute is a deep pit[t]
and a wayward wife is a narrow well.
[28]Like a bandit she lies in wait,[u]
and multiplies the unfaithful among
men.

[29]Who has woe? Who has sorrow?
Who has strife? Who has complaints?
Who has needless bruises? Who has
bloodshot eyes?

23:5 [x]S Mt 6:19 [y]Pr 27:24 **23:6** [z]ver 1-3; Ps 141:4 **23:9** [a]S Pr 9:7 **23:10** [b]S Dt 19:14 **23:11** [c]S Job 19:25 [d]Ps 24:8 [e]Ex 22:22-24; Pr 15:25; 22:22-23 **23:12** [f]S Pr 2:2 **23:14** [g]S Pr 13:24; S 19:18 **23:16** [h]ver 24; Pr 27:11; 29:3 **23:17** [i]S Ps 37:1; S 73:3 **23:18** [j]S Ps 9:18; 37:1-4; Pr 24:14, 19-20 **23:19** [k]Dt 4:9; Pr 28:7 **23:20** [l]Isa 5:11, 22; 56:12; Hab 2:15 **23:21** [m]S Pr 21:17 **23:22** [n]S Lev 19:32 **23:23** [o]Pr 4:7; 17:16 **23:24** [p]S ver 15-16 **23:25** [q]S Pr 10:1 **23:26** [r]Pr 5:1-6 [s]S Ps 18:21 **23:27** [t]S Pr 22:14 **23:28** [u]Pr 7:11-12

[r]7 Or *for as he thinks within himself, / so he is*; or *for as he puts on a feast, / so he is* [s]14 Hebrew *Sheol*

23:5 *riches . . . are gone.* Our trust must be in God, not in riches (see Jer 17:11; Lk 12:21; 1Ti 6:17).
23:6 *stingy man.* One eager to get rich (see 28:22).
23:7 *his heart is not with you.* Cf. 26:24–25.
23:8 *vomit.* Out of disgust at the attitude of the host.
23:9 *scorn the wisdom of your words.* Fools despise wisdom (1:7) and hate knowledge and correction (1:22; 12:1). They heap abuse on one who rebukes them (9:7).
23:10 *ancient boundary stone.* See note on 15:25; see also 22:28. *fatherless.* Oppressing the widow and the fatherless is strongly denounced (see Isa 10:2; Jer 22:3; Zec 7:10).
23:11 *Defender.* Kinsman-Redeemer, someone who helped a close relative regain land (see Lev 25:25 and note) or who avenged his death (Nu 35:12,19). God is a "father to the fatherless, a defender of widows" (Ps 68:5). See notes on Ru 2:20; Jer 31:11; see also Jer 50:34. *will take up their case.* See Ps 12:5; 140:12; Isa 3:13–15; Mal 3:5.
23:13–14 See note on 13:24.
23:15 See 10:1 and note; see also v. 24; 27:11; 29:3. *My son.* See 1:8,10.
23:17 *Do not . . . envy sinners.* See 3:31; 24:1,19. *fear of the LORD.* See notes on 1:7; 3:7.
23:18 *future hope.* See Ps 37:37; Jer 29:11.
23:19 *right path.* Cf. 4:25–26.
23:20 *Do not join.* See 1:15; 12:26. *those who drink too much wine.* Drunkenness is also condemned in vv. 29–35; 20:1 (see note there); cf. Dt 21:20; Mt 24:49; Lk 21:34; Ro 13:13; Eph 5:18; 1Ti 3:3.
23:21 *gluttons.* See v. 2; 28:7; cf. Mt 11:19. *become poor.* See 21:17. *drowsiness.* Cf. the poverty that overtakes the sluggard in 6:9–11.
23:22 *do not despise your mother.* Cf. 15:20; 30:17.
23:23 *Buy the truth . . . get wisdom . . . understanding.* See 4:5; see also 4:7 and note.
23:24–25 See v. 15; 27:11; see also 10:1 and note.
23:27 *deep pit.* See note on 22:14. *wayward wife.* See note on 2:16; see also 5:20; 7:17–23.
23:28 *lies in wait.* See 6:26; 7:12; Ecc 7:26. *multiplies the unfaithful.* Cf. 7:26.
23:29–35 A vivid description of the physical and psychological effects of drunkenness.
23:29 *Who has woe?* Cf. the woes pronounced on drunkards in Isa 5:11,22. *strife.* See 20:1. *bruises.* Cf. the "beatings for the backs of fools" in 19:29.

30Those who linger over wine,ᵛ
  who go to sample bowls of mixed
    wine.
31Do not gaze at wine when it is red,
  when it sparkles in the cup,
  when it goes down smoothly!
32In the end it bites like a snake
  and poisons like a viper.
33Your eyes will see strange sights
  and your mind imagine confusing
    things.
34You will be like one sleeping on the
    high seas,
  lying on top of the rigging.
35"They hit me," you will say, "but I'm
    not hurt!
  They beat me, but I don't feel it!
  When will I wake up
  so I can find another drink?"ʷ

24 Do not envyˣ wicked men,
  do not desire their company;
2for their hearts plot violence,ʸ
  and their lips talk about making
    trouble.ᶻ

3By wisdom a house is built,ᵃ
  and through understanding it is
    established;
4through knowledge its rooms are filled
  with rare and beautiful treasures.ᵇ

5A wise man has great power,
  and a man of knowledge increases
    strength;
6for waging war you need guidance,
  and for victory many advisers.ᶜ

7Wisdom is too high for a fool;
  in the assembly at the gate he has
    nothing to say.

8He who plots evil
  will be known as a schemer.
9The schemes of folly are sin,
  and men detest a mocker.

10If you falter in times of trouble,
  how small is your strength!ᵈ

11Rescue those being led away to death;
  hold back those staggering toward
    slaughter.ᵉ
12If you say, "But we knew nothing about
    this,"
  does not he who weighsᶠᵍ the heart
    perceive it?
  Does not he who guards your life know
    it?
  Will he not repayʰ each person
    according to what he has
    done?ⁱ

13Eat honey, my son, for it is good;
  honey from the comb is sweet to
    your taste.
14Know also that wisdom is sweet to your
    soul;
  if you find it, there is a future hope
    for you,
  and your hope will not be cut off.ʲ ᵏ

15Do not lie in wait like an outlaw against
    a righteous man's house,
  do not raid his dwelling place;
16for though a righteous man falls seven
    times, he rises again,
  but the wicked are brought down by
    calamity.ˡ

17Do not gloatᵐ when your enemy falls;
  when he stumbles, do not let your
    heart rejoice,ⁿ
18or the LORD will see and disapprove

Cross references (center column):

23:30 ᵛver
20-21; Isa 5:11
23:35 ʷPr 20:1
24:1 ˣPr 3:31-32;
23:17-18
24:2 ʸS Ps 2:1;
Isa 32:6; 55:7-8;
59:7; 65:2;
66:18; Hos 4:1
ᶻPs 10:7
24:3 ᵃS Pr 14:1
24:4 ᵇS Pr 8:21
24:6 ᶜS Pr 11:14;
S 20:18; Lk 14:31

24:10 ᵈS Job 4:5
24:11 ᵉPs 82:4
24:12 ᶠS Ps 139:2
ᵍS 1Sa 2:3
ʰS Ps 54:5
ⁱJob 34:11;
Ps 62:12;
S Mt 16:27;
Ro 2:6*
24:14
ʲPs 119:103;
Pr 16:24
ᵏPr 23:18
24:16
ˡS Job 5:19;
S Ps 34:21
24:17 ᵐOb 1:12
ⁿS 2Sa 3:32;
Mic 7:8

23:30 *linger over wine.* See 1Sa 25:36. *mixed wine.* Probably with spices (see 9:2; Ps 75:8).
23:32 *bites like a snake.* Death will be the result (cf. Nu 21:6).
23:33 *see strange sights . . . imagine confusing things.* Perhaps a reference to the delirium that afflicts the alcoholic.
23:34 *You will be like one sleeping on the high seas.* Your head will be spinning.
23:35 *They beat me, but I don't feel it!* Cf. the condition of Israel in Jer 5:3. *so I can find another drink.* The woe and misery do not prevent him from repeating his folly (cf. 26:11; 27:22; Isa 56:12).
24:1 *Do not envy.* See v. 19; Ps 37:1. *do not desire their company.* See 1:15; 12:26; 23:20.
24:2 *plot violence.* See 1:10–11; 6:14; Job 15:35; Ps 38:12.
24:3 *house.* Symbolic of the life of an individual or a family. *is built.* Cf. the similar expression in 9:1.
24:4 *rare and beautiful treasures.* Wisdom promises to bestow wealth on those who love her (8:21).
24:5 *has great power.* See note on 21:22.
24:7 *at the gate.* The normal meeting place for official business (see note on 1:21).

24:8 *plots evil.* See v. 2; see also 1:10–11; 6:14; Job 15:35; Ps 38:12. *schemer.* Called a "crafty man" in 12:2.
24:9 *schemes of folly are sin.* Cf. 1:11–16; 9:13–18. *men detest a mocker.* Because he is proud, insulting (9:7) and quarrelsome (22:10). See note on 1:22.
24:10 Cf. Jer 12:5; Gal 6:9.
24:11 *those being led away to death.* Perhaps innocent men condemned to die (cf. 17:15; Isa 58:6–7).
24:12 *does not he who weighs the heart perceive it?* God knows even our thoughts and motives (see 16:2; 21:2; Ps 94:9–11).
24:14 *wisdom is sweet to your soul.* It nourishes and brings healing (see 16:24 and note). *future hope.* See Ps 9:18; 37:37; Jer 29:11.
24:15 *lie in wait.* Cf. 1:11; 12:6; Ps 10:9–10.
24:16 *seven times.* Many times (see 6:16; Job 5:19 and note). *rises again.* God promises to uphold and rescue the righteous (cf. Ps 34:19; 37:24; Mic 7:8). *wicked are brought down.* See v. 22; 4:19; 6:15; 11:3,5.
24:17 *Do not gloat.* See note on 17:5.
24:18 *turn his wrath away from him.* Edom was made desolate because she rejoiced over Israel's destruction (see

and turn his wrath away from him. *o*

19Do not fret *p* because of evil men
　or be envious of the wicked,
20for the evil man has no future hope,
　and the lamp of the wicked will be
　　snuffed out. *q*

21Fear the LORD and the king, *r* my son,
　and do not join with the rebellious,
22for those two will send sudden
　　destruction *s* upon them,
　and who knows what calamities they
　　can bring?

Further Sayings of the Wise

23These also are sayings of the wise: *t*

To show partiality *u* in judging is not
　good: *v*
24Whoever says to the guilty, "You are
　　innocent" *w*—
　peoples will curse him and nations
　　denounce him.
25But it will go well with those who
　　convict the guilty,
　and rich blessing will come upon
　　them.

26An honest answer
　is like a kiss on the lips.

27Finish your outdoor work
　and get your fields ready;
　after that, build your house.

28Do not testify against your neighbor
　　without cause, *x*

or use your lips to deceive.

29Do not say, "I'll do to him as he has
　　done to me;
　I'll pay that man back for what he
　　did." *y*

30I went past the field of the sluggard, *z*
　past the vineyard of the man who
　　lacks judgment;
31thorns had come up everywhere,
　the ground was covered with weeds,
　and the stone wall was in ruins.
32I applied my heart to what I observed
　and learned a lesson from what I
　　saw:
33A little sleep, a little slumber,
　a little folding of the hands to rest *a* —
34and poverty will come on you like a
　　bandit
　and scarcity like an armed man. *t* *b*

More Proverbs of Solomon

25 These are more proverbs *c* of Solomon, copied by the men of Heze-
kiah king of Judah: *d*

2It is the glory of God to conceal a
　　matter;
　to search out a matter is the glory of
　　kings. *e*

3As the heavens are high and the earth is
　　deep,
　so the hearts of kings are
　　unsearchable.

Cross-references (center column)

24:18
*o*S Job 31:29
24:19 *p*Ps 37:1
24:20
*q*S Job 18:5;
S Pr 23:17-18
24:21 *r*Ro 13:1-5
24:22
*s*S Ps 73:19
24:23 *t*S Pr 1:6
*u*S Ex 18:16;
S Lev 19:15
*v*Ps 72:2;
Pr 28:21; 31:8-9;
Jer 22:16
24:24
*w*S Pr 17:15
24:28 *x*S Ps 7:4
24:29 *y*Pr 20:22;
Mt 5:38-41
24:30
*z*Pr 6:6-11;
26:13-16
24:33 *a*S Pr 6:10
24:34 *b*S Pr 10:4;
Ecc 10:18
25:1 *c*S 1Ki 4:32
*d*S Pr 1:1
25:2
*e*Pr 16:10-15

t 34 Or like a vagrant / and scarcity like a beggar

Eze 35:15).
24:19 Almost identical to Ps 37:1; see v. 1; 23:17.
24:20 *no future hope.* For himself or his posterity (see Ps 37:2,28,38; contrast v. 14; 23:18). *lamp . . . will be snuffed out.* See note on 13:9.
24:21 *Fear the LORD and the king.* Submission to civil authority is also commanded in Ecc 8:2-5. 1Pe 2:17 says, "fear God, honor the king," and Ro 13:1-7 urges the same obedience. These passages all view the king as a terror to the wicked (cf. 20:8,26).
24:22 *those two.* God and the king. *sudden destruction . . . calamities.* God's judgment is more common (see 6:15; 11:3,5), but the power of the king is seen in 20:26.
24:23-34 An appendix to 22:17-24:22, giving a few additional sayings of the wise.
24:23 *partiality in judging is not good.* See 18:5 and note.
24:24 *You are innocent.* See 17:15. *peoples will curse him.* Just as they "curse the man who hoards grain" (11:26).
24:25 *rich blessing.*
24:26 *honest answer.* Cf. 16:13. *like a kiss.* Cf. the "pleasant words" that are "sweet to the soul" in 16:24.
24:27 *get your fields ready.* Plan carefully and acquire the means as you build your house. *house.* See note on v. 3.
24:28 *testify . . . without cause.* See 3:30. *use your lips to deceive.* See 6:19 and note; 12:17; 25:18.
24:29 *I'll pay that man back.* A spirit of revenge is dis-

couraged also in 20:22 (see note there); cf. 25:21-22; Mt 5:43-45; Ro 12:17.
24:30 *sluggard.* See note on 6:6; see also 20:4.
24:31 *thorns . . . weeds.* Cf. 15:19; Isa 34:13.
24:33-34 See 6:10-11 and note on 6:11.
25:1-29:27 Another collection of Solomon's proverbs similar to 10:1-22:16.
25:1 *proverbs of Solomon.* See notes on 1:1; 10:1. *copied by the men of Hezekiah.* There was a great revival in the reign of Hezekiah (c. 715-686 B.C.), and the king restored the singing of hymns to its proper place (2Ch 29:30). His interest in the words of David corresponds to his support of a compilation of Solomon's proverbs. Solomon was the last king to rule over all Israel during the united monarchy; Hezekiah was the first king to rule over all Israel (now restricted to the southern kingdom) after the destruction of the divided monarchy's northern kingdom.
25:2 *to conceal a matter.* God gets glory because man cannot understand his universe or the way he rules it (see Dt 29:29; Job 26:14 and note; Isa 40:12-24; Ro 11:33-36). *to search out a matter.* A king gets glory if he can uncover the truth and administer justice (see 1Ki 3:9; 4:34).
25:3 *are unsearchable.* Cannot be understood; like the four things in 30:18-19. Yet God controls the hearts of kings (see note on 21:1).

⁴Remove the dross from the silver,
and out comes material for^u the
silversmith;
⁵remove the wicked from the king's
presence,^f
and his throne will be established^g
through righteousness. ^h

⁶Do not exalt yourself in the king's
presence,
and do not claim a place among great
men;
⁷it is better for him to say to you, "Come
up here," ⁱ
than for him to humiliate you before
a nobleman.

What you have seen with your eyes
⁸ do not bring^v hastily to court,
for what will you do in the end
if your neighbor puts you to shame?^j

⁹If you argue your case with a neighbor,
do not betray another man's
confidence,
¹⁰or he who hears it may shame you
and you will never lose your bad
reputation.

¹¹A word aptly spoken
is like apples of gold in settings of
silver. ^k

¹²Like an earring of gold or an ornament
of fine gold
is a wise man's rebuke to a listening
ear. ^l

¹³Like the coolness of snow at harvest
time
is a trustworthy messenger to those
who send him;

he refreshes the spirit of his
masters. ^m

¹⁴Like clouds and wind without rain
is a man who boasts of gifts he does
not give.

¹⁵Through patience a ruler can be
persuaded, ⁿ
and a gentle tongue can break a
bone. ^o

¹⁶If you find honey, eat just enough—
too much of it, and you will vomit. ^p
¹⁷Seldom set foot in your neighbor's
house—
too much of you, and he will hate
you.

¹⁸Like a club or a sword or a sharp arrow
is the man who gives false testimony
against his neighbor. ^q

¹⁹Like a bad tooth or a lame foot
is reliance on the unfaithful in times
of trouble.

²⁰Like one who takes away a garment on
a cold day,
or like vinegar poured on soda,
is one who sings songs to a heavy
heart.

²¹If your enemy is hungry, give him food
to eat;
if he is thirsty, give him water to
drink.
²²In doing this, you will heap burning
coals^r on his head,
and the LORD will reward you. ^s

Cross references (center column):

25:5 /S Pr 20:8
^gS 2Sa 7:13
^hS Pr 16:12;
29:14
25:7 ⁱLk 14:7-10
25:8 /Mt 5:25-26
25:11 ^kver 12;
Pr 15:23
25:12 /S ver 11;
Ps 141:5;
S Pr 13:18

25:13
^mS Pr 10:26;
13:17
25:15 ⁿEcc 10:4
^oPr 15:1
25:16 ^pver 27
25:18
^qS Pr 12:18
25:22 ^rS Ps 18:8
^sS 2Ch 28:15;
Mt 5:44;
Ro 12:20*

^u4 Or *comes a vessel from*   ^v7,8 Or *nobleman / on
whom you had set your eyes. / ⁸Do not go*

25:4 *Remove the dross from the silver.* A process compared to the purification of society in general and rulers in particular in Isa 1:22–25; Eze 22:18; Mal 3:2–3.
25:5 *his throne will be established through righteousness.* See note on 16:12; see also 20:26.
25:6 *in the king's presence.* Probably at a feast (cf. 23:1). Jesus spoke about the place of honor at a wedding feast (Lk 14:7–11).
25:7 *Come up here.* Cf. "Friend, move up to a better place" (Lk 14:10); contrast Isa 22:15–19.
25:8 *do not bring hastily to court.* A warning about the seriousness of disputes (see 17:14) and the need to exercise caution (see 24:28).
25:9 *do not betray another man's confidence.* If you do, you are a gossip (see 11:13; 20:19).
25:10 *bad reputation.* A good name is one of life's most valuable possessions (see 22:1 and note).
25:11 *gold . . . silver.* Cf. the fruit of wisdom in 8:19.
25:12 *earring of gold.* Comparable to the beautiful wreath and necklace that represent the adornment of wisdom and sound teaching (see 1:9; 3:22; 4:9). *wise man's rebuke.* Cf. the "life-giving rebuke" of 15:31.
25:13 *coolness of snow.* Probably a drink cooled by snow from the mountains; it did not snow at harvest time. See

26:1; contrast 10:26. *trustworthy messenger.* See 13:17 and note.
25:14 *Like clouds . . . without rain.* An image applied to unproductive men in Jude 12.
25:15 *Through patience a ruler can be persuaded.* Cf. 14:29. *gentle tongue.* See note on 15:1.
25:18 *club . . . sword . . . arrow.* Cf. Ps 57:4; Jer 9:8. *false testimony.* See note on 6:19; see also 24:28; Ex 20:16.
25:19 *bad tooth . . . lame foot.* Relying on Egypt was like leaning on a splintered reed (Isa 36:6).
25:20 *soda.* Probably sodium carbonate, "natron" (see Jer 2:22). There is a vigorous reaction when vinegar is poured on it. *sings songs to a heavy heart.* The exiles were reluctant to sing the songs of Zion (Ps 137:3–4).
25:21–22 Quoted in Ro 12:20 as a way to overcome evil with good.
25:21 Kindness to one's enemy is encouraged in 20:22; Ex 23:4–5. *give him food . . . water.* At Elisha's request, a trapped Aramean army was given a great feast and then sent home (2Ki 6:21–23; cf. 2Ch 28:15).
25:22 *heap burning coals on his head.* Horrible punishment reserved for the wicked (see Ps 140:10). Here, however, it is kindness that will hurt the enemy (cf. the broken bone of v. 15) but perhaps win him over. Alternatively, the

23As a north wind brings rain,
so a sly tongue brings angry looks.

24Better to live on a corner of the roof
than share a house with a
quarrelsome wife. *t*

25Like cold water to a weary soul
is good news from a distant land. *u*

26Like a muddied spring or a polluted
well
is a righteous man who gives way to
the wicked.

27It is not good to eat too much honey, *v*
nor is it honorable to seek one's own
honor. *w*

28Like a city whose walls are broken
down
is a man who lacks self-control.

26 Like snow in summer or rain *x* in
harvest,
honor is not fitting for a fool. *y*

2Like a fluttering sparrow or a darting
swallow,
an undeserved curse does not come
to rest. *z*

3A whip for the horse, a halter for the
donkey, *a*
and a rod for the backs of fools! *b*

4Do not answer a fool according to his
folly,
or you will be like him yourself. *c*

5Answer a fool according to his folly,
or he will be wise in his own eyes. *d*

6Like cutting off one's feet or drinking
violence
is the sending of a message by the
hand of a fool. *e*

7Like a lame man's legs that hang limp
is a proverb in the mouth of a fool. *f*

8Like tying a stone in a sling
is the giving of honor to a fool. *g*

9Like a thornbush in a drunkard's hand
is a proverb in the mouth of a fool. *h*

10Like an archer who wounds at random
is he who hires a fool or any
passer-by.

11As a dog returns to its vomit, *i*
so a fool repeats his folly. *j*

12Do you see a man wise in his own
eyes? *k*
There is more hope for a fool than for
him. *l*

13The sluggard says, *m* "There is a lion in
the road,
a fierce lion roaming the streets!" *n*

14As a door turns on its hinges,
so a sluggard turns on his bed. *o*

15The sluggard buries his hand in the
dish;
he is too lazy to bring it back to his
mouth. *p*

16The sluggard is wiser in his own eyes
than seven men who answer
discreetly.

17Like one who seizes a dog by the ears

Cross-references (center column):
25:24 *t*S Pr 21:9
25:25 *u*Pr 15:30
25:27 *v*ver 16
*w*Pr 27:2;
S Mt 23:12
26:1
*x*S 1Sa 12:17 *y*ver
8; Pr 19:10
26:2 *z*S Dt 23:5
26:3 *a*Ps 32:9
*b*S Pr 10:13
26:4 *c*ver 5;
Isa 36:21
26:5 *d*ver 4;
S Pr 3:7

26:6 *e*S Pr 10:26
26:7 *f*ver 9
26:8 *g*S ver 1
26:9 *h*ver 7
26:11 *i*2Pe 2:22*
*j*S Ps 85:8
26:12 *k*S Pr 3:7
*l*Pr 29:20
26:13
*m*Pr 6:6-11;
24:30-34
*n*Pr 22:13
26:14 *o*S Pr 6:9
26:15 *p*Pr 19:24

---

expression may reflect an Egyptian expiation ritual, in which a guilty person, as a sign of his repentance, carried a basin of glowing coals on his head. The meaning here, then, would be that in returning good for evil and so being kind to your enemy, you may cause him to repent or change. LORD *will reward you*. Even if the enemy remains hostile (cf. 11:18; 19:17).
25:23 *north*. Perhaps northwest (cf. Lk 12:54). *sly tongue*. One that spreads slander (cf. 10:18).
25:25 *good news from a distant land*. See Ge 45:25–28.
25:26 *muddied spring*. Cf. Eze 34:18–19. *righteous man who gives way*. Perhaps through bribery (cf. 17:8; 29:4; Isa 1:21–23).
25:27 *to seek one's own honor*. See vv. 6–7 and notes.
25:28 *city whose walls are broken down*. Defenseless and disgraced (cf. Ne 1:3). *man who lacks self-control*. See 16:32 and note.
26:1 *rain in harvest*. It rarely rains in Palestine from June through September, but see 1Sa 12:17–18. *honor is not fitting for a fool*. See v. 8; 30:22.
26:2 *undeserved curse does not come to rest*. When David was cursed by Shimei, he realized that the curse would not take effect because he was innocent of the charge of murdering members of Saul's family (2Sa 16:8,12).
26:3 *rod for the backs of fools*. See 14:3; 19:29.
26:4 *Do not answer a fool according to his folly*. Do not

stoop to his level (see 23:9; Mt 7:6).
26:5 *Answer a fool according to his folly*. Sometimes folly must be plainly exposed and denounced.
26:6 *drinking violence*. See 4:17; Job 34:7. *sending of a message by the hand of a fool*. He will likely misrepresent the one who sends him, or in some other manner frustrate the sender's purpose (see 13:17).
26:8 *Like tying a stone in a sling*. A fool with authority wields a formidable weapon, but it is useless in his hands—as useless as a stone that is tied, not placed, in the sling.
26:9 A fool reciting a proverb will do as much damage to himself and others as a drunkard wielding a thornbush.
26:10 *he who hires a fool or any passer-by*. Abimelech hired "reckless adventurers" to help him murder his half brothers and set up a brief and ill-fated rule (Jdg 9:4–6).
26:11 *As a dog returns to its vomit*. Quoted in 2Pe 2:22 with reference to false teachers. *fool repeats his folly*. The drunkard returns to his drink (23:35).
26:12 *wise in his own eyes*. This conceit is applied to the sluggard in v. 16 and the rich in 28:11; cf. 26:5.
26:13 See 22:13 and note.
26:14 The sluggard loves to sleep and seems to be attached to his bed as a door to its hinges.
26:16 *wiser in his own eyes*. See v. 12 and note.
26:17 *seizes a dog by the ears*. To do so is to immediately create a disturbance.

is a passer-by who meddles in a
   quarrel not his own.

¹⁸Like a madman shooting
   firebrands or deadly arrows
¹⁹is a man who deceives his neighbor
   and says, "I was only joking!"

²⁰Without wood a fire goes out;
   without gossip a quarrel dies down. ^q

²¹As charcoal to embers and as wood to
   fire,
   so is a quarrelsome man for kindling
   strife. ^r

²²The words of a gossip are like choice
   morsels;
   they go down to a man's inmost
   parts. ^s

²³Like a coating of glaze^w over
   earthenware
   are fervent lips with an evil heart.

²⁴A malicious man disguises himself with
   his lips, ^t
   but in his heart he harbors deceit. ^u
²⁵Though his speech is charming, ^v do not
   believe him,
   for seven abominations fill his heart. ^w
²⁶His malice may be concealed by
   deception,
   but his wickedness will be exposed in
   the assembly.

²⁷If a man digs a pit, ^x he will fall into
   it; ^y
   if a man rolls a stone, it will roll back
   on him. ^z

²⁸A lying tongue hates those it hurts,
   and a flattering mouth^a works ruin.

27 Do not boast^b about tomorrow,
   for you do not know what a day
   may bring forth. ^c

²Let another praise you, and not your
   own mouth;
   someone else, and not your own
   lips. ^d

³Stone is heavy and sand^e a burden,
   but provocation by a fool is heavier
   than both.

⁴Anger is cruel and fury overwhelming,
   but who can stand before jealousy?^f

⁵Better is open rebuke
   than hidden love.

⁶Wounds from a friend can be trusted,
   but an enemy multiplies kisses. ^g

⁷He who is full loathes honey,
   but to the hungry even what is bitter
   tastes sweet.

⁸Like a bird that strays from its nest^h
   is a man who strays from his home.

⁹Perfumeⁱ and incense bring joy to the
   heart,
   and the pleasantness of one's friend
   springs from his earnest
   counsel.

¹⁰Do not forsake your friend and the
   friend of your father,
   and do not go to your brother's house
   when disaster^j strikes you—
   better a neighbor nearby than a
   brother far away.

¹¹Be wise, my son, and bring joy to my
   heart; ^k

Cross references (center column):

26:20 ^qPr 22:10
26:21 ^rS Pr 14:17
26:22 ^sPr 18:8
26:24 ^tS Ps 31:18
  ^uPs 41:6
26:25 ^vPs 28:3
  ^wJer 9:4
26:27 ^xS Ps 7:15
  ^yS Est 6:13
  ^zS Est 2:23;
S 7:9; Ps 35:8;
141:10; Pr 28:10;
29:6; Isa 50:11
26:28 ^aS Ps 12:3;
Pr 29:5

27:1
^bS 1Ki 20:11
^cMt 6:34;
Jas 4:13-16
27:2 ^dS Pr 25:27
27:3 ^eS Job 6:3
27:4 ^fS Nu 5:14
27:6 ^gPs 141:5;
Pr 28:23
27:8 ^hIsa 16:2
27:9 ⁱS Est 2:12;
S Ps 45:8
27:10 ^jS Pr 17:17
27:11 ^kS Pr 10:1;
S 23:15-16

^w23 With a different word division of the Hebrew;
Masoretic Text *of silver dross*

26:18 *Like a madman shooting.* Cf. the archer in v. 10.
firebrands. Could easily ignite sheaves of grain (cf. Zec 12:6).
26:19 *I was only joking!* Explaining it as a prank is a poor
excuse.
26:21 *kindling strife.* See note on 6:14.
26:22 See note on 18:8.
26:23 *coating of glaze over earthenware.* Cf. the clean
outside of the cup and dish (Lk 11:39; cf. Mt 23:27). *fervent
lips with an evil heart.* The speech of the adulteress is
seductive (2:16; 5:3).
26:24 *in heart he harbors deceit.* See 12:20.
26:25 *his speech is charming.* See Jer 9:8. *seven.* Many
(see note on Job 5:19). For seven things the Lord detests
see 6:16–19.
26:26 *will be exposed in the assembly.* See 5:14; Lk 8:17.
26:27 *If a man digs a pit, he will fall into it.* "The trouble
he causes recoils on himself" (Ps 7:16). See 1:18 and note;
28:10; 29:6; Est 7:10; Ps 7:15; Ecc 10:8–9.
26:28 *lying tongue hates those it hurts.* See 10:18. *flattering mouth works ruin.* See 29:5; cf. 16:13.
27:1 Cf. the words of the rich fool in Lk 12:19–20; see Pr
16:9; Isa 56:12.

27:2 *Let another praise you.* See 2Co 10:12,18.
27:4 *who can stand before jealousy?* See 6:34; SS 8:6.
27:5 *open rebuke.* Called "life-giving rebuke" in 15:31;
cf. Gal 2:14.
27:6 *Wounds from a friend can be trusted.* Called a "kindness" in Ps 141:5. *enemy multiplies kisses.* See 5:3–4; Mt
26:49.
27:7 *loathes honey.* Cf. 25:16,27.
27:8 *man who strays from his home.* He has lost his
security and may be vulnerable to temptation (cf. 7:21–23).
27:9 *Perfume.* See note on 21:17 ("oil"). *incense.* Cf. the
one "perfumed with myrrh and incense" (SS 3:6). *pleasantness of one's friend.* Cf. 16:21,24.
27:10 *Do not fail a friend in need; when in need rely on
friendship rather than on mere family relationships. *brother
far away.* Either physically or emotionally.
27:11 *Be wise, my son.* See 10:1 and note. *then I can
answer anyone who treats me with contempt.* A wise son
(or student) serves as a powerful testimony that the father (or
teacher) who has shaped him has shown himself to be a man
of worth.

then I can answer anyone who treats me with contempt. *l*

12The prudent see danger and take refuge,
but the simple keep going and suffer
for it. *m*

13Take the garment of one who puts up
security for a stranger;
hold it in pledge if he does it for a
wayward woman. *n*

14If a man loudly blesses his neighbor
early in the morning,
it will be taken as a curse.

15A quarrelsome wife is like
a constant dripping*o* on a rainy day;
16restraining her is like restraining the
wind
or grasping oil with the hand.

17As iron sharpens iron,
so one man sharpens another.

18He who tends a fig tree will eat its
fruit,*p*
and he who looks after his master
will be honored. *q*

19As water reflects a face,
so a man's heart reflects the man.

20Death and Destruction*x* are never
satisfied,*r*
and neither are the eyes of man. *s*

21The crucible for silver and the furnace
for gold,*t*
but man is tested by the praise he
receives.

22Though you grind a fool in a mortar,

grinding him like grain with a pestle,
you will not remove his folly from
him.

23Be sure you know the condition of your
flocks,*u*
give careful attention to your herds;
24for riches do not endure forever,*v*
and a crown is not secure for all
generations.
25When the hay is removed and new
growth appears
and the grass from the hills is
gathered in,
26the lambs will provide you with
clothing,
and the goats with the price of a
field.
27You will have plenty of goats' milk
to feed you and your family
and to nourish your servant girls.

28 The wicked man flees *w* though no
one pursues,*x*
but the righteous are as bold as a
lion.*y*

2When a country is rebellious, it has
many rulers,
but a man of understanding and
knowledge maintains order.

3A ruler*y* who oppresses the poor
is like a driving rain that leaves no
crops.

4Those who forsake the law praise the
wicked,

27:11
*l*S Ge 24:60
27:12 *m*Pr 22:3
27:13 *n*Pr 20:16
27:15 *o*S Est 1:18
27:18 *p*1Co 9:7
*q*Lk 19:12-27
27:20
*r*Pr 30:15-16;
Hab 2:5 *s*Ecc 1:8;
6:7
27:21 *t*S Pr 17:3

27:23 *u*Pr 12:10
27:24 *v*Pr 23:5
28:1 *w*S 2Ki 7:7
*x*S Lev 26:17
*y*S Ps 138:3

*x*20 Hebrew *Sheol and Abaddon*   *y*3 Or *A poor man*

27:12 *the simple.* See note on 1:4. *keep going and suffer for it.* See 7:22–23; 9:16–18.
27:13 A repetition of 20:16 (see note there).
27:14 *blesses his neighbor.* Perhaps to win his favor (cf. Ps 12:2).
27:15 See note on 19:13.
27:17 *sharpens another.* Develops and molds his character.
27:18 *will eat its fruit.* Cf. 2Ti 2:6. *will be honored.* Cf. Ge 39:4; see also Mt 25:21; Lk 12:42–44; Jn 12:26.
27:19 *a man's heart reflects the man.* The condition of a man's heart indicates his true character (see Mt 5:8).
27:20 *Death and Destruction.* See note on Job 26:6; see also 15:11. *are never satisfied.* Their appetite is insatiable (see Isa 5:14). *neither are the eyes of man.* See Ecc 4:8.
27:21 *crucible . . . gold.* Silver and gold were refined to remove their impurities (cf. Isa 1:25; Mal 3:3). *man is tested by the praise he receives.* He must not become proud, and he must be wary of flattery (cf. 12:8; Lk 6:26).
27:22 *mortar.* A bowl (see Nu 11:8). *pestle.* A club-like tool for pounding grain in a mortar. *you will not remove his folly.* In spite of severe punishment, fools refuse to change (see note on 20:30; see also 26:11; Jer 5:3).
27:23–27 A section praising the basic security afforded by agricultural pursuits—reflecting the agricultural base of the ancient economy.

27:23 *give careful attention to your herds.* Like Jacob, with Laban's flocks (Ge 31:38–40).
27:24 *riches do not endure.* See note on 23:5. *crown is not secure.* Even kings may lose their wealth and power (see Job 19:9; La 5:16).
27:25 *hay is removed.* This began in March or April.
27:26 *price of a field.* See 31:16. Sheep and goats sometimes also served as tribute payments (see 2Ki 3:4).
27:27 *goats' milk.* Commonly drunk along with cows' milk (see Dt 32:13–14; Isa 7:21–22). *servant girls.* See 31:15.
28:1 *wicked man flees.* See Lev 26:17,36; Ps 53:5. *bold as a lion.* Like David in 1Sa 17:46; cf. Ps 18:33–38.
28:2 *it has many rulers.* Israel's rebellion often brought rapid change in leadership (see 1Ki 16:8–28; 2Ki 15:8–15). *man of understanding . . . maintains order.* A wise ruler will be successful (see 8:15–16; 24:5; 29:4).
28:3 *who oppresses the poor.* See 14:31. *driving rain.* Describes the destructive power of Assyria's army in Isa 28:2. The gentle rain is compared to a righteous king in Ps 72:6–7.
28:4 *law.* Either the teachings of wisdom (3:1; 7:2) or the law of Moses (Ps 119:53). *praise the wicked.* Cf. Ro 1:32. *who keep the law.* See v. 7; 29:18; cf. v. 9. *resist them.* See Eph 5:11; cf. Ro 1:32.

but those who keep the law resist them.

⁵Evil men do not understand justice,
but those who seek the LORD
understand it fully.

⁶Better a poor man whose walk is
blameless
than a rich man whose ways are
perverse. *z*

⁷He who keeps the law is a discerning
son,
but a companion of gluttons disgraces
his father. *a*

⁸He who increases his wealth by
exorbitant interest *b*
amasses it for another, *c* who will be
kind to the poor. *d*

⁹If anyone turns a deaf ear to the law,
even his prayers are detestable. *e*

¹⁰He who leads the upright along an evil
path
will fall into his own trap, *f*
but the blameless will receive a good
inheritance.

¹¹A rich man may be wise in his own
eyes,
but a poor man who has discernment
sees through him.

¹²When the righteous triumph, there is
great elation; *g*
but when the wicked rise to power,
men go into hiding. *h*

¹³He who conceals his sins *i* does not
prosper,
but whoever confesses *j* and
renounces them finds mercy. *k*

¹⁴Blessed is the man who always fears the
LORD,
but he who hardens his heart falls
into trouble.

¹⁵Like a roaring lion or a charging bear
is a wicked man ruling over a
helpless people.

¹⁶A tyrannical ruler lacks judgment,
but he who hates ill-gotten gain will
enjoy a long life.

¹⁷A man tormented by the guilt of murder
will be a fugitive *l* till death;
let no one support him.

¹⁸He whose walk is blameless is kept
safe, *m*
but he whose ways are perverse will
suddenly fall. *n*

¹⁹He who works his land will have
abundant food,
but the one who chases fantasies will
have his fill of poverty. *o*

²⁰A faithful man will be richly blessed,
but one eager to get rich will not go
unpunished. *p*

²¹To show partiality *q* is not good *r* —
yet a man will do wrong for a piece
of bread. *s*

²²A stingy man is eager to get rich

Cross-references

28:6 *z*Pr 19:1
28:7 *a*Pr 23:19-21
28:8 *b*S Ex 18:21;
Eze 18:8
*c*S Job 27:17
*d*S Job 3:15;
Ps 112:9;
Lk 14:12-14
28:9 *e*S Ps 109:7;
S Pr 15:8;
S Isa 1:13
28:10 *f*S Ps 57:6;
S Pr 26:27
28:12 *g*S 2Ki 11:20 *h*ver
28; Job 24:4;
Pr 29:2
28:13 *i*S 2Sa 12:13;
S Job 31:33
*j*S Lev 5:5
*k*Ps 32:1-5;
Da 4:27; 1Jn 1:9
28:17 *l*1Sa 30:17;
1Ki 20:20;
Jer 41:15; 44:14
28:18 *m*Jer 39:18
*n*S Est 6:13;
Pr 10:9
28:19 *o*Pr 12:11
28:20 *p*ver 22
28:21 *q*S Lev 19:15
*r*S Ps 94:21;
S Pr 18:5
*s*Eze 13:19

28:5 *who seek the LORD.* Who fear him (see note on 1:7). *understand it fully.* They know "what is right and just and fair" (2:9).
28:6 *blameless.* See note on 2:7.
28:7 *who keeps the law.* See note on v. 4. *companion of gluttons.* See notes on 23:20–21.
28:8 *exorbitant interest.* Prohibited in Ex 22:25; Lev 25:35–37; Dt 23:19–20; Eze 22:12. *amasses it for another.* See 13:22 and note. *kind to the poor.* See 14:31; see also note on 14:21.
28:9 *law.* See note on v. 4. *his prayers are detestable.* Like the sacrifice of the wicked in 15:8 (see note on 3:32; see also Ps 66:18; Isa 1:15; 59:1–2).
28:10 *into his own trap.* See note on 26:27. *blameless.* See note on 2:7. *good inheritance.* See 3:35; Heb 6:12; 1Pe 3:9.
28:11 *rich man may be wise in his own eyes.* Like the fool (26:5) or the sluggard (26:16).
28:12 *there is great elation.* See 11:10 and note. *men go into hiding.* Obadiah hid 100 prophets during the reign of Ahab (1Ki 18:13), and Joash was hidden for six years while the wicked Athaliah ruled (2Ki 11:2–3).
28:13 *He who conceals his sins does not prosper.* Note the physical and psychological pain referred to in 3:7–8; Ps 32:3. *whoever confesses and renounces them finds mercy.* Note the joy of forgiveness in Ps 32:5,10–11.

28:14 *fears the LORD.* See note on 1:7; see also 23:17. *who hardens his heart.* Like Pharaoh (Ex 7:13), and the Israelites who tested the Lord at Horeb (Ex 17:7; cf. Ps 95:8; Ro 2:5).
28:15 *roaring lion.* Full of rage and murderous intent (cf. 19:12; Mt 2:16; 1Pe 5:8). *charging bear.* See note on 17:12. *wicked man ruling.* See v. 12.
28:16 *he who hates ill-gotten gain will enjoy a long life.* Unlike those who love such gain (see 1:19).
28:17 *will be a fugitive till death.* Cain was a "restless wanderer" in fear of his life (Ge 4:14). Murder was punishable by death (see Ge 9:6; Ex 21:14).
28:18 *blameless ... perverse.* Contrasted also in v. 6; 19:1. *will suddenly fall.* Cf. 11:5.
28:19 *chases fantasies.* Schemes for making easy money.
28:20 *richly blessed.* With God's gifts and favors (see 3:13–18; 10:6; Ge 49:26; Dt 33:16). *one eager to get rich will not go unpunished.* Cf. similar warnings in 20:21; 23:4 (see notes).
28:21 *To show partiality is not good.* See 18:5 and note; 24:23. *will do wrong for a piece of bread.* Perhaps a reference to a bribe, however small (cf. Eze 13:19).
28:22 *stingy man.* See 23:6. *eager to get rich.* A warning to him is given in v. 20 (cf. similar warnings in 20:21; 23:4). *poverty awaits him.* Because it is the generous man who prospers (see note on 11:25).

and is unaware that poverty awaits
  him. *t*

23He who rebukes a man will in the end
  gain more favor
than he who has a flattering tongue. *u*

24He who robs his father or mother *v*
  and says, "It's not wrong"—
he is partner to him who destroys. *w*

25A greedy man stirs up dissension, *x*
  but he who trusts in the LORD *y* will
  prosper.

26He who trusts in himself is a fool, *z*
  but he who walks in wisdom is kept
  safe. *a*

27He who gives to the poor will lack
  nothing, *b*
but he who closes his eyes to them
  receives many curses. *c*

28When the wicked rise to power, people
  go into hiding; *d*
but when the wicked perish, the
  righteous thrive.

29 A man who remains stiff-necked *e*
  after many rebukes
will suddenly be destroyed *f*
  —without remedy. *g*

2When the righteous thrive, the people
  rejoice; *h*
when the wicked rule, *i* the people
  groan. *j*

3A man who loves wisdom brings joy to
  his father, *k*
but a companion of prostitutes
  squanders his wealth. *l*

4By justice a king gives a country
  stability, *m*

but one who is greedy for bribes tears
  it down.

5Whoever flatters his neighbor
  is spreading a net for his feet. *n*

6An evil man is snared by his own sin, *o*
but a righteous one can sing and be
  glad.

7The righteous care about justice for the
  poor, *p*
but the wicked have no such
  concern.

8Mockers stir up a city,
  but wise men turn away anger. *q*

9If a wise man goes to court with a fool,
  the fool rages and scoffs, and there is
  no peace.

10Bloodthirsty men hate a man of integrity
  and seek to kill the upright. *r*

11A fool gives full vent to his anger, *s*
but a wise man keeps himself under
  control. *t*

12If a ruler *u* listens to lies,
  all his officials become wicked. *v*

13The poor man and the oppressor have
  this in common:
The LORD gives sight to the eyes of
  both. *w*

14If a king judges the poor with fairness,
  his throne will always be secure. *x*

15The rod of correction imparts wisdom,
  but a child left to himself disgraces
  his mother. *y*

16When the wicked thrive, so does sin,
  but the righteous will see their
  downfall. *z*

28:22 *t*ver 20
28:23
*u*S Pr 27:5-6
28:24 *v*Pr 19:26
*w*S Pr 18:9
28:25
*x*S Pr 14:17
*y*Pr 29:25
28:26 *z*S Ps 4:5
*a*1Co 3:18
28:27
*b*S Dt 24:19;
S Pr 22:9
*c*S Ps 109:17
28:28 *d*S ver 12;
S Job 20:19
29:1 *e*S Ex 32:9;
S Dt 9:27
*f*Jer 19:15; 36:31;
Hab 2:7
*g*S 2Ch 36:16;
Pr 6:15
29:2
*h*S 2Ki 11:20
*i*Pr 30:22;
Ecc 10:6
*j*S Pr 28:12
29:3 *k*S Pr 10:1;
S 23:15-16
*l*Pr 5:8-10;
Lk 15:11-32
29:4 *m*ver 14;
S Pr 8:15-16

29:5
*n*S Job 32:21;
S Pr 26:28
29:6 *o*S Job 5:13;
S Pr 26:27;
Ecc 9:12
29:7 *p*Pr 31:8-9
29:8 *q*Pr 11:11;
S 16:14
29:10 *r*ver 27;
1Jn 3:12
29:11
*s*S Job 15:13
*t*Pr 12:16
29:12 *u*2Ki 21:9
*v*S Job 34:30
29:13
*w*S Pr 22:2;
Mt 5:45
29:14 *x*S ver 4;
Ps 72:1-5;
S Pr 16:12
29:15 *y*ver 17;
S Pr 13:24
29:16 *z*S Ps 91:8;
S 92:11

28:23 *He who rebukes a man.* See Gal 2:14; cf. 15:31;
25:12. *who has a flattering tongue.* Cf. 16:13; 26:28; 29:5.
28:24 *who robs his father or mother.* See note on 19:26;
cf. Mt 15:4–6; Mk 7:10–12.
28:25 *stirs up dissension.* See note on 6:14. *will prosper.*
As does also the generous person (11:25) and the one who is
diligent (13:4, lit. "the desires of the diligent prosper").
28:26 *who walks in wisdom.* Equals "who trusts in the
LORD" in 29:25; cf. 3:5.
28:27 *gives to the poor.* See note on 14:21. *will lack
nothing.* Generosity is the path to blessing (see 11:24 and
note; 14:21; 19:17). *closes his eyes to them.* See 21:13.
28:28 *people go into hiding.* See v. 12 and note. *righteous
thrive.* See v. 2; 29:2.
29:1 *stiff-necked after many rebukes.* Eli's sons died because of their stubbornness (see 1Sa 2:25; cf. Dt 9:6,13). *will
suddenly be destroyed—without remedy.* Identical to 6:15.
Cf. the fate of the mockers in 1:22–27.
29:2 *When the righteous thrive, the people rejoice.* See
11:10 and note. *when the wicked rule, the people groan.*
See 28:12 and note; see also Jdg 2:18. The Israelites groaned
in Egypt (Ex 2:23–24).

29:3 *man who loves wisdom brings joy to his father.* See
10:1 and note. *companion of prostitutes squanders his
wealth.* See 5:10; 6:26 and notes.
29:4 *By justice a king gives a country stability.* See note on
16:12. *bribes.* See note on 17:8.
29:6 *snared by his own sin.* See 1:18 and note; 22:5.
29:7 *The righteous care about justice for the poor.* Like Job
(Job 29:16); cf. v. 14; 19:17; 22:22.
29:8 *Mockers stir up a city.* See notes on 6:14; 11:11; see
also 26:21. *Mockers.* See 1:22 and note. *wise men turn
away anger.* See Jas 3:17–18.
29:9 *the fool rages and scoffs.* Like an angry bear (17:12)
or the tossing sea (Isa 57:20–21).
29:10 *Bloodthirsty men hate a man of integrity.* Their
schemes are described in 1:11–16; cf. Ps 5:6.
29:11 *gives full vent to his anger.* See v. 9; 14:16–17.
keeps himself under control. See note on 16:32.
29:12 *all his officials become wicked.* Cf. Isa 1:23.
29:14 See note on 16:12; see also v. 4; Isa 9:7.
29:15 *rod of correction.* See note on 13:24.
29:16 *When the wicked thrive.* See v. 2; 11:11; 28:12,28.
righteous will see their downfall. See 10:25 and note;

17Discipline your son, and he will give
you peace;
he will bring delight to your soul.[a]
18Where there is no revelation, the people
cast off restraint;
but blessed is he who keeps the
law.[b]
19A servant cannot be corrected by mere
words;
though he understands, he will not
respond.
20Do you see a man who speaks in haste?
There is more hope for a fool than for
him.[c]
21If a man pampers his servant from
youth,
he will bring grief[z] in the end.
22An angry man stirs up dissension,
and a hot-tempered one commits
many sins.[d]
23A man's pride brings him low,[e]
but a man of lowly spirit gains
honor.[f]
24The accomplice of a thief is his own
enemy;
he is put under oath and dare not
testify.[g]
25Fear[h] of man will prove to be a snare,
but whoever trusts in the LORD[i] is
kept safe.[j]
26Many seek an audience with a ruler,[k]
but it is from the LORD that man gets
justice.[l]
27The righteous detest the dishonest;
the wicked detest the upright.[m]

Sayings of Agur

30 The sayings[n] of Agur son of Jakeh—an oracle[a]:

This man declared to Ithiel,
to Ithiel and to Ucal:[b]

2"I am the most ignorant of men;
I do not have a man's understanding.
3I have not learned wisdom,
nor have I knowledge of the Holy
One.[o]
4Who has gone up[p] to heaven and come
down?
Who has gathered up the wind in the
hollow[q] of his hands?
Who has wrapped up the waters[r] in his
cloak?[s]
Who has established all the ends of
the earth?
What is his name,[t] and the name of his
son?
Tell me if you know!

5"Every word of God is flawless;[u]
he is a shield[v] to those who take
refuge in him.
6Do not add[w] to his words,
or he will rebuke you and prove you
a liar.

29:17 [a]S ver 15 **29:18** [b]Ps 1:1-2; 19:11; 119:1-2 **29:20** [c]Pr 19:2; 26:12 **29:22** [d]S Pr 14:17 **29:23** [e]S Est 5:12 [f]S Pr 11:2; S 15:33; S 16:18 **29:24** [g]S Lev 5:1 **29:25** [h]S 1Sa 15:24 [i]Pr 28:25 [j]S Pr 16:20 **29:26** [k]Pr 19:6 [l]S Pr 16:33 **29:27** [m]S ver 10 **30:1** [n]S Pr 22:17 **30:3** [o]S Pr 9:10 **30:4** [p]Dt 30:12; Ps 24:1-2; S Pr 8:22-31; Jn 3:13; Eph 4:7-10 [q]Isa 40:12 [r]Job 26:8 [s]S Ge 1:2 [t]Rev 19:12 **30:5** [u]S Ps 12:6; S 18:30 [v]S Ge 15:1 **30:6** [w]S Dt 4:2

[z]*21* The meaning of the Hebrew for this word is uncertain. [a]*1* Or *Jakeh of Massa* [b]*1* Masoretic Text; with a different word division of the Hebrew *declared, "I am weary, O God; / I am weary, O God, and faint.*

14:11; 21:12.
29:17 *Discipline your son.* Teach him and train him (see 13:24 and note; 22:6).
29:18 *revelation.* A message from God given through a prophet; a prophetic vision (see 1Sa 3:1; Isa 1:1; Am 8:11–12). *people cast off restraint.* Possibly an allusion to the sinful actions of the Israelites while Moses was on Mount Sinai (see Ex 32:25 and note). *blessed is he who keeps the law.* See 28:4 and note; see also 8:32; 28:14.
29:19 *cannot be corrected by mere words.* Servants, like sons (vv. 15,17), must be disciplined (see note on 22:6).
29:20 *who speaks in haste.* See 10:19; 17:27–28; Jas 1:19. *There is more hope for a fool than for him.* Identical to 26:12.
29:21 *pampers his servant.* See v. 19.
29:22 *angry man stirs up dissension.* See note on 6:14; see also 15:18.
29:23 See 15:33 and note; see also 18:12.
29:24 *he is put under oath.* He will be held responsible for failing to testify (cf. Lev 5:1).
29:25 *Fear of man.* Cf. 1Sa 15:24; Isa 51:12; Jn 12:42–43. *whoever trusts in the LORD is kept safe.* See 18:10 and note; cf. 3:5–6.
29:26 *Many seek an audience.* See 1Ki 10:24. *it is from the LORD that man gets justice.* God controls a king's actions (see note on 21:1) and defends the cause of the poor and the just (cf. Job 36:6).
30:1–33 The first of two chapters that serve as an appendix to Proverbs.
30:1 *Agur son of Jakeh.* Probably a wise man like Ethan and Heman (1Ki 4:31). *oracle.* Usually the message of a prophet (see note on Isa 13:1). If "oracle" is taken as the place name "Massa" (see NIV text note), Agur would then be associated with an Ishmaelite people (cf. Ge 25:13–14). *Ithiel . . . Ucal.* Perhaps students of Agur, but see NIV text note.
30:2 *I am the most ignorant of men.* Paul described himself as the "worst of sinners" (1Ti 1:16).
30:3 *knowledge of the Holy One.* See note on 2:5. "Holy One" occurs elsewhere in Proverbs only in 9:10.
30:4 The use of rhetorical questions to express God's greatness as Creator occurs also in Job 38:4–11; Isa 40:12. *gathered up the wind.* Cf. Ps 135:7. *wrapped up the waters in his cloak.* See Job 26:8; 38:8–9. *Tell me if you know!* God similarly challenged Job (Job 38:4).
30:5 Almost identical to Ps 18:30. *shield.* See note on 2:7. *to those who take refuge in him.* See 14:32; 18:10.
30:6 *Do not add to his words.* Cf. Moses' warning to the Israelites in Dt 4:2.

7"Two things I ask of you, O LORD;
  do not refuse me before I die:
8Keep falsehood and lies far from me;
  give me neither poverty nor riches,
  but give me only my daily bread. *x*
9Otherwise, I may have too much and
    disown*y* you
  and say, 'Who is the LORD?' *z*
  Or I may become poor and steal,
  and so dishonor the name of my
    God. *a*

10"Do not slander a servant to his master,
  or he will curse you, and you will pay
    for it.

11"There are those who curse their
    fathers
  and do not bless their mothers; *b*
12those who are pure in their own eyes *c*
  and yet are not cleansed of their
    filth; *d*
13those whose eyes are ever so haughty, *e*
  whose glances are so disdainful;
14those whose teeth*f* are swords
  and whose jaws are set with knives*g*
  to devour*h* the poor*i* from the earth,
  the needy from among mankind. *j*

15"The leech has two daughters.
  'Give! Give!' they cry.

"There are three things that are never
    satisfied, *k*
  four that never say, 'Enough!':
16the grave, *c l* the barren womb,
  land, which is never satisfied with
    water,

and fire, which never says, 'Enough!'

17"The eye that mocks*m* a father,
  that scorns obedience to a mother,
  will be pecked out by the ravens of the
    valley,
  will be eaten by the vultures. *n*

18"There are three things that are too
    amazing for me,
  four that I do not understand:
19the way of an eagle in the sky,
  the way of a snake on a rock,
  the way of a ship on the high seas,
  and the way of a man with a maiden.

20"This is the way of an adulteress:
  She eats and wipes her mouth
  and says, 'I've done nothing wrong.' *o*

21"Under three things the earth trembles,
  under four it cannot bear up:
22a servant who becomes king, *p*
  a fool who is full of food,
23an unloved woman who is married,
  and a maidservant who displaces her
    mistress.

24"Four things on earth are small,
  yet they are extremely wise:
25Ants are creatures of little strength,
  yet they store up their food in the
    summer; *q*
26coneys*d r* are creatures of little power,
  yet they make their home in the
    crags;
27locusts *s* have no king,

Cross references (center column):

30:8 *x*Mt 6:11
30:9 *y*Jos 24:27; Isa 1:4; 59:13
  *z*Dt 6:12; 8:10-14; Hos 13:6
  *a*S Dt 8:12
30:11 *b*S Pr 20:20
30:12 *c*S Pr 16:2 *d*Jer 2:23,35
30:13 *e*S 2Sa 22:28; S Job 41:34
30:14 *f*S Job 4:11; S Ps 3:7 *g*Ps 57:4 *h*S Job 24:9 *i*Am 8:4; Mic 2:2 *j*S Job 19:22
30:15 *k*Pr 27:20
30:16 *l*Isa 5:14; 14:9,11; Hab 2:5
30:17 *m*Dt 21:18-21 *n*S Job 15:23
30:20 *o*Pr 5:6
30:22 *p*S Pr 19:10; S 29:2
30:25 *q*Pr 6:6-8
30:26 *r*S Ps 104:18
30:27 *s*S Ex 10:4

c 16 Hebrew *Sheol*   *d 26* That is, the hyrax or rock badger

---

30:7 *Two things.* The use of lists characterizes Agur's sayings (see vv. 15,18,21,24,29).
30:8 *my daily bread.* Cf. Job 23:12 and the Lord's Prayer (Mt 6:11).
30:9 *I may have too much and disown you.* Moses predicted that Israel would forget God when their food was plentiful and their herds large (Dt 8:12-17; 31:20). *Who is the LORD?* Or, Why should I serve him (see Job 21:14-16)? *become poor and steal.* Cf. 6:30.
30:10 *you will pay for it.* Since the accusation is false, the servant's curse will be effective (cf. 26:2)—so do not suppose you can take advantage of a servant's lowly position.
30:11 *curse their fathers.* Punishable by death (see Ex 21:17; Lev 20:9; cf. v. 17).
30:12 *those who are pure in their own eyes.* Like the Pharisee (Lk 18:11; cf. Isa 65:5).
30:13 *whose eyes are . . . haughty.* See note on 6:17; see also Isa 3:16.
30:14 *whose teeth are swords . . . whose jaws are . . . knives.* The wicked are like ravenous beasts that devour the prey (see Job 29:17). *to devour the poor . . . the needy.* Cf. Ps 14:4; Mic 3:2-3.
30:15,18,21,29 *three . . . four.* See note on 6:16.
30:16 *grave.* Its appetite is never satisfied (Isa 5:14; Hab 2:5). *barren womb.* In ancient Israel, a wife without children was desolate, even desperate (cf. Ge 16:2; 30:1; Ru 1:11-13,20-21; 1Sa 1:6,10-11; 2Ki 4:14).

30:17 *The eye.* Haughty and disdainful (see v. 13). *mocks a father . . . a mother.* See v. 11 and note; 15:20. *will be pecked out by the ravens . . . the vultures.* The loss of an eye was a terrible curse (see the story of Samson in Jdg 16:21). Since vultures normally devoured the dead (see Jer 16:4; Mt 24:28), the meaning may be that the body of a disgraceful son will lie unburied and exposed.
30:18-19 It is difficult to understand the four "ways" because there are no tracks that can be readily followed.
30:19 *way of an eagle.* Soaring and swooping majestically (cf. Job 39:27; Jer 48:40; 49:22). *way of a man with a maiden.* Probably a reference to the mystery of courting and how it leads to consummation.
30:20 *adulteress.* See 2:16 and note. *She eats and wipes her mouth.* Making love is compared to eating food also in 9:17 (see note there; see also 7:18 and note).
30:22 *servant who becomes king.* See note on 19:10.
30:23 *unloved woman who is married.* Probably one of several wives, who is miserable because her husband does not love her (cf. Leah in Ge 29:31-32). *maidservant who displaces her mistress.* Perhaps because she was able to bear a child, whereas the wife was barren (cf. Hagar and Sarah in Ge 16:1-6).
30:26 *in the crags.* Which provide a refuge for them (see Ps 104:18).
30:27 *locusts have no king.* Cf. 6:7. *advance together in ranks.* Locusts are portrayed as a mighty army in Joel 2:3-9.

yet they advance together in ranks;
²⁸a lizard can be caught with the hand,
     yet it is found in kings' palaces.

²⁹"There are three things that are stately
          in their stride,
     four that move with stately bearing:
³⁰a lion, mighty among beasts,
     who retreats before nothing;
³¹a strutting rooster, a he-goat,
     and a king with his army around
          him. e

³²"If you have played the fool and exalted
          yourself,
     or if you have planned evil,
     clap your hand over your mouth! f
³³For as churning the milk produces
          butter,
     and as twisting the nose produces
          blood,
     so stirring up anger produces strife."

Sayings of King Lemuel

31 The sayings u of King Lemuel—an
     oracle f his mother taught him:

²"O my son, O son of my womb,
     O son of my vows, g v
³do not spend your strength on women,
     your vigor on those who ruin kings. w

⁴"It is not for kings, O Lemuel—
     not for kings to drink wine, x
     not for rulers to crave beer,
⁵lest they drink y and forget what the
          law decrees, z

and deprive all the oppressed of their
          rights.
⁶Give beer to those who are perishing,
     wine a to those who are in anguish;
⁷let them drink b and forget their poverty
     and remember their misery no more.

⁸"Speak c up for those who cannot speak
          for themselves,
     for the rights of all who are destitute.
⁹Speak up and judge fairly;
     defend the rights of the poor and
          needy." d

Epilogue: The Wife of Noble Character

10 h A wife of noble character e who can
          find? f
     She is worth far more than rubies.
¹¹Her husband g has full confidence in her
     and lacks nothing of value. h
¹²She brings him good, not harm,
     all the days of her life.
¹³She selects wool and flax
     and works with eager hands. i
¹⁴She is like the merchant ships,
     bringing her food from afar.
¹⁵She gets up while it is still dark;
     she provides food for her family
     and portions for her servant girls.
¹⁶She considers a field and buys it;

Cross references

30:32 rS Job 29:9
31:1 uS Pr 22:17
31:2 vS Jdg 11:30
31:3 wS Dt 17:17;
S 1Ki 11:3;
Pr 5:1-14
31:4 xS Pr 20:1;
Ecc 10:16-17;
Isa 5:22
31:5 yS 1Ki 16:9
zS Pr 16:12

31:6 aS Ge 14:18
31:7 bS Est 1:10
31:8 cS 1Sa 19:4
31:9 dS Pr 24:23;
29:7
31:10
eS Ru 3:11;
S Pr 18:22
fPr 8:35
31:11 gS Ge 2:18
hS Pr 12:4
31:13 i1Ti 2:9-10

e 31 Or king secure against revolt   f 1 Or of Lemuel
king of Massa, which   g 2 Or / the answer to my
prayers   h 10 Verses 10-31 are an acrostic, each verse
beginning with a successive letter of the Hebrew alphabet.

30:28 *found in kings' palaces.* Lizards climb stone walls easily.
30:30 *lion, mighty among beasts.* See 2Sa 1:23; Mic 5:8.
30:31 *he-goat.* Goats were used to lead flocks of sheep (see Jer 50:8; Da 8:5).
30:32 *exalted yourself.* Pride is condemned in 8:13; 11:2; 16:18. *planned evil.* Cf. 6:14; 16:27. *clap your hand over your mouth.* Stop your plotting immediately (cf. Job 21:5; 40:4).
30:33 *stirring up anger produces strife.* See notes on 6:14; 15:1; see also 29:22.
31:1-9 This brief section is also of non-Israelite origin. King Lemuel is otherwise unknown.
31:1 *oracle.* See note on 30:1. *his mother.* This entire chapter emphasizes the role and significance of wise women. The queen mother was an influential figure (see 1Ki 1:11-13; 15:13).
31:2 *son of my vows.* Hannah made a vow as she prayed for a son (1Sa 1:11). *vows.* See 20:25 and note.
31:3 *your strength on women.* A warning against a large harem and sexual immorality (see 5:9-11 and notes; 1Ki 11:1; Ne 13:26).
31:4 *It is not for kings . . . to drink wine.* Woe to the land whose rulers are drunkards (Ecc 10:16-17; see 20:1 and note; Hos 7:5).
31:5 *deprive all the oppressed of their rights.* See 30:14

and note; see also 17:15; Isa 5:23; 10:2.
31:7 *let them drink and forget.* Contrast v. 5: "lest they drink."
31:8-9 The king represents God as the defender of the poor and needy (see 16:10; Ps 82:3; cf. Lev 19:15; Job 29:12-17; Isa 1:17).
31:10-31 The epilogue: an acrostic poem (see NIV text note) praising the "wife of noble character" (v. 10). It corresponds to 1:1-7 (the prologue) as it describes a "woman who fears the LORD" (v. 30; see note on 1:7). Such a wife is almost a personification of wisdom. Like wisdom, she is "worth far more than rubies" (v. 10; 3:15; 8:11), and he who finds her "receives favor from the LORD" (8:35; 18:22). See Introduction: Literary Structure.
31:10 *wife of noble character.* Like Ruth (Ru 3:11). She is "her husband's crown" (12:4).
31:12 *She brings him good.* See 18:22; 19:14.
31:13 *flax.* Its fibers were made into linen (see vv. 19,22, 24; cf. Isa 19:9).
31:14 *like the merchant ships.* She is an enterprising person (see v. 18).
31:15 *She gets up while it is still dark.* She is the opposite of the sluggard (see 6:9-10; 20:13). *portions for her servant girls.* See 27:27; Lk 12:42.
31:16 *considers a field . . . plants a vineyard.* She shows good judgment—unlike the sluggard, whose vineyard is

out of her earnings she plants a
vineyard.
¹⁷She sets about her work vigorously;
her arms are strong for her tasks.
¹⁸She sees that her trading is profitable,
and her lamp does not go out at
night.
¹⁹In her hand she holds the distaff
and grasps the spindle with her
fingers.
²⁰She opens her arms to the poor
and extends her hands to the
needy.^j
²¹When it snows, she has no fear for her
household;
for all of them are clothed in scarlet.
²²She makes coverings for her bed;
she is clothed in fine linen and
purple.
²³Her husband is respected at the city
gate,
where he takes his seat among the
elders^k of the land.
²⁴She makes linen garments and sells
them,

31:20 /Dt 15:11
31:23 ^kS Ex 3:16

31:26 /S Pr 10:31
31:31 ^mPr 11:16

and supplies the merchants with
sashes.
²⁵She is clothed with strength and
dignity;
she can laugh at the days to come.
²⁶She speaks with wisdom,
and faithful instruction is on her
tongue./
²⁷She watches over the affairs of her
household
and does not eat the bread of
idleness.
²⁸Her children arise and call her blessed;
her husband also, and he praises her:
²⁹"Many women do noble things,
but you surpass them all."
³⁰Charm is deceptive, and beauty is
fleeting;
but a woman who fears the LORD is
to be praised.
³¹Give her the reward she has earned,
and let her works bring her praise^m at
the city gate.

---

overgrown with thorns and weeds (24:30–31).
31:17 *sets about her work vigorously.* See 10:4 and note.
31:18 *her trading is profitable.* Like wisdom, she is "worth far more than rubies" (v. 10; 3:15; 8:11). Wisdom "is more profitable than silver" (3:14).
31:19 *distaff . . . spindle.* Spinning thread was women's work.
31:20 *opens her arms to the poor.* See note on 14:21; see also 22:9; Job 31:16–20.
31:21 *clothed in scarlet.* Of high quality, probably made of wool (cf. 2Sa 1:24; Rev 18:16).
31:22 *fine linen.* Associated with nobility (see note on 7:16; see also Ge 41:42). *purple.* Linked with kings (Jdg 8:26; SS 3:10) or the rich (Lk 16:19; Rev 18:16).
31:23 *at the city gate.* The court (see note on 1:21). **31:24** *linen garments.* See Jdg 14:12–13; Isa 3:23. *merchants.* Cf. v. 18.

31:25 *clothed with strength and dignity.* See Isa 52:1; 1Ti 2:9–10. The opposite is to be "clothed with shame and disgrace" (Ps 35:26). *she can laugh at the days to come.* She is free of anxiety and worry (cf. Job 39:7).
31:26 *faithful instruction.* Given to her children and friends. She is a wise and loving counselor (see 1:8; 6:20).
31:28 *blessed.* That is, one who enjoys happy circumstances and from whom joy radiates to others. See Ge 30:13; Ps 72:17; SS 6:9; Mal 3:12; cf. Ru 4:14–15.
31:29 *do noble things.* See Isa 32:8.
31:30 *Charm is deceptive.* Cf. 5:3. *beauty is fleeting.* Cf. Job 14:2; 1Pe 3:3–5. *who fears the LORD.* See note on 1:7.
31:31 *reward she has earned.* See 12:14 and note. *bring her praise.* Honor comes through "humility and the fear of the LORD" (22:4). *at the city gate.* See v. 23; see also note on 1:21.

ECCLESIASTES

Author and Date

No time period or writer's name is mentioned in the book, but several passages strongly suggest that King Solomon is the author (1:1,12,16; 2:4-9; 7:26-29; 12:9; cf. 1Ki 2:9; 3:12; 4:29-34; 5:12; 10:1-8). On the other hand, the writer's title ("Teacher," Hebrew *qoheleth;* see note on 1:1), his unique style of Hebrew and his attitude toward rulers (suggesting that of a subject rather than a monarch—see, e.g., 4:1-2; 5:8-9; 8:2-4; 10:20) may point to another person and a later period.

Purpose and Method

With his life largely behind him, the author takes stock of the world as he has experienced it between the horizons of birth and death—the latter a horizon beyond which man cannot see. The world is seen as being full of enigmas, the greatest of which is man himself.

From the perspective of his own understanding, the Teacher takes measure of man, examining his capabilities. He discovers that human wisdom, even that of a godly person, has limits (1:13,16-18; 7:24; 8:16-17). It cannot find out the larger purposes of God or the ultimate meaning of man's existence.

As the author looks about at the human enterprise, he sees man in mad pursuit of one thing and then another—laboring as if he could master the world, lay bare its secrets, change its fundamental structures, break through the bounds of human limitations and master his own destiny. He sees man vainly pursuing hopes and expectations that in reality are "meaningless, a chasing after the wind" (1:14; 2:11,17,26; 4:4,16; 6:9; cf. 1:17; 4:6).

But faith teaches him that God has ordered all things according to his own purposes (3:1-15; 5:19; 6:1-2; 9:1) and that man's role is to accept these, including his own limitations, as God's appointments. Man, therefore, should be patient and enjoy life as God gives it. He should know his own limitations and not vex himself with unrealistic expectations. He should be prudent in everything, living carefully before God and the king and, above all, fearing God and keeping his commandments (12:13).

Teaching

Life not centered on God is purposeless and meaningless. Without him, nothing else can satisfy (2:25). With him, all of life and his other good gifts are to be gratefully received (see Jas 1:17) and used and enjoyed to the full (2:26; 11:8). The book contains the philosophical and theological reflections of an old man (12:1-7), most of whose life was meaningless because he had not himself relied on God.

Outline

I. Author (1:1)
II. Theme: The meaninglessness of man's efforts on earth apart from God (1:2)
III. Introduction: The profitlessness of working to accumulate things to achieve happiness (1:3-11)
IV. Discourse, Part 1: In spite of life's apparent enigmas and meaninglessness, it is to be enjoyed as a gift from God (1:12-11:6)
V. Discourse, Part 2: Since old age and death will soon come, man should enjoy life in his youth, remembering that God will judge (11:7-12:7)
VI. Theme Repeated (12:8)
VII. Conclusion: Reverently trust in and obey God (12:9-14)

Everything Is Meaningless

1 The words of the Teacher,[a][a] son of
David, king in Jerusalem:[b]

[2]"Meaningless! Meaningless!"
    says the Teacher.
"Utterly meaningless!
    Everything is meaningless."[c]

[3]What does man gain from all his labor
    at which he toils under the sun?[d]
[4]Generations come and generations go,
    but the earth remains forever.[e]
[5]The sun rises and the sun sets,
    and hurries back to where it rises.[f]
[6]The wind blows to the south
    and turns to the north;
round and round it goes,
    ever returning on its course.
[7]All streams flow into the sea,
    yet the sea is never full.
To the place the streams come from,
    there they return again.[g]
[8]All things are wearisome,
    more than one can say.
The eye never has enough of seeing,[h]
    nor the ear its fill of hearing.
[9]What has been will be again,
    what has been done will be done
        again;[i]
    there is nothing new under the sun.
[10]Is there anything of which one can say,

"Look! This is something new"?
It was here already, long ago;
    it was here before our time.
[11]There is no remembrance of men of
        old,[j]
    and even those who are yet to come
will not be remembered
    by those who follow.[k]

Wisdom Is Meaningless

[12]I, the Teacher,[l] was king over Israel
in Jerusalem.[m] [13]I devoted myself to study
and to explore by wisdom all that is done
under heaven.[n] What a heavy burden God
has laid on men![o] [14]I have seen all the
things that are done under the sun; all of
them are meaningless, a chasing after the
wind.[p]

[15]What is twisted cannot be
        straightened;[q]
    what is lacking cannot be counted.

[16]I thought to myself, "Look, I have
grown and increased in wisdom more than
anyone who has ruled over Jerusalem before me;[r] I have experienced much of
wisdom and knowledge." [17]Then I applied
myself to the understanding of wisdom,[s]
and also of madness and folly,[t] but I

Cross references (center column):

1:1 [a]ver 12;
Ecc 7:27; 12:10
[b]S Pr 1:1
1:2 [c]Ps 39:5-6;
62:9; Ecc 12:8;
Ro 8:20-21
1:3 [d]Ecc 2:11,22;
3:9; 5:15-16
1:4 [e]S Job 8:19
1:5 [f]Ps 19:5-6
1:7 [g]Job 36:28
1:8 [h]Pr 27:20
1:9 [i]Ecc 2:12;
3:15

1:11 [j]Ge 40:23;
Ecc 9:15
[k]Ps 88:12;
Ecc 2:16; 8:10;
9:5
1:12 [l]S ver 1
[m]Ecc 2:9
1:13 [n]S Job 28:3
[o]S Ge 3:17;
Ecc 3:10
1:14 [p]Ecc 2:11,
17; 4:4; 6:9
1:15 [q]Ecc 7:13
1:16 [r]S 1Ki 3:12
1:17 [s]Ecc 7:23;
8:16 [t]Ecc 2:3,12;
7:25

[a]1 Or *leader of the assembly*; also in verses 2 and 12

1:1 *Teacher.* The teacher of wisdom (12:9). The Hebrew
term for "Teacher" (*qoheleth*) is related to that for "assembly" (see NIV text note; Ex 16:3; Nu 16:3). Perhaps the
Teacher, whose work is described in 12:9–10, also held an
office in the assembly. The Septuagint (the Greek translation
of the OT) word for "Teacher" is *ekklesiastes*, from which
most English titles of the book are taken, and from which
such English words as "ecclesiastical" are derived. *son of
David.* Suggests Solomon, though his name occurs nowhere
in the book. The Hebrew word for "son" can refer to a
descendant (even many generations removed)—or even to
someone who follows in the footsteps of another (see Ge
4:21; see also Introduction: Author and Date).
1:2 Briefly states the author's theme (see 12:8). *Meaningless!* This key term occurs about 35 times in the book and
only once elsewhere (Job 27:12). The Hebrew for it originally meant "breath" (see Ps 39:5,11; 62:9; 144:4). The
basic thrust of Ecclesiastes is that all of life is meaningless,
useless, hollow, futile and vain if it is not rightly related to
God. Only when based on God and his word is life worthwhile. *Everything.* See v. 8; whatever man undertakes apart
from God.
1:3–11 In this section the author elaborates his theme that
human effort appears to be without benefit or purpose.
1:3 Jesus expands on this question in Mk 8:36–38. *under
the sun.* Another key expression (used 29 times), which
refers to this present world and the limits of what it offers.
"Under heaven," though it occurs less frequently (v. 13;
2:3; 3:1), is used synonymously.
1:4 *earth remains forever.* By contrast, man's life is fleeting.
1:8 *All things.* Everything mentioned in vv. 4–7 (see note

on v. 2).
1:10 *something new.* Many things seem to be new simply
because the past is easily and quickly forgotten. The old ways
reappear in new guises.
1:12–18 Having set forth his theme that all human striving
seems futile (see especially vv. 3,11, which frame the section), the Teacher shows that both human endeavor (vv.
12–15; cf. 2:1–11) and the pursuit of human wisdom (vv.
16–18; cf. 2:12–17) are futile and meaningless.
1:12 *I.* The author shifts to the first person, returning to the
third person only in the conclusion (12:9–14).
1:13 *God.* The only Hebrew word the writer uses for God
is *Elohim* (used almost 30 times), which emphasizes his
absolute sovereignty. He does not use the covenant name,
Yahweh (translated "LORD"; see note on Ex 3:15).
1:14 *chasing after the wind.* A graphic illustration of futility and meaninglessness (see Introduction: Purpose and
Method). These words are used nine times in the first half of
the discourse (here; v. 17; 2:11,17,26; 4:4,6,16; 6:9; see
also 5:16).
1:15 See 7:13 and note. Because of the unalterableness of
events, human effort is meaningless and hopeless. We should
therefore learn to happily accept things the way they are and
to accept our divinely appointed lot in life, as the Teacher
later counsels.
1:16 *anyone who has ruled over Jerusalem before me.* See
2:7,9. This does not necessarily exclude Solomon as the
Teacher. The reference could include kings prior to David,
such as Melchizedek (Ge 14:18), Adoni-Zedek (Jos 10:1)
and Abdi-Khepa (mentioned in the Amarna letters from
Egypt; see chart on "Ancient Texts Relating to the OT,"
p. 5).

learned that this, too, is a chasing after the wind.

¹⁸For with much wisdom comes much sorrow; *u*
the more knowledge, the more grief. *v*

Pleasures Are Meaningless

2 I thought in my heart, "Come now, I will test you with pleasure *w* to find out what is good." But that also proved to be meaningless. ²"Laughter," *x* I said, "is foolish. And what does pleasure accomplish?" ³I tried cheering myself with wine, *y* and embracing folly *z*—my mind still guiding me with wisdom. I wanted to see what was worthwhile for men to do under heaven during the few days of their lives.

⁴I undertook great projects: I built houses for myself *a* and planted vineyards. *b* ⁵I made gardens and parks and planted all kinds of fruit trees in them. ⁶I made reservoirs to water groves of flourishing trees. ⁷I bought male and female slaves and had other slaves *c* who were born in my house. I also owned more herds and flocks than anyone in Jerusalem before me. ⁸I amassed silver and gold *d* for myself, and the treasure of kings and provinces. *e* I acquired men and women singers, *f* and a harem *b* as well—the delights of the heart of man. ⁹I became greater by far than anyone in Jerusalem *g* before me. *h* In all this my wisdom stayed with me.

¹⁰I denied myself nothing my eyes desired;
I refused my heart no pleasure.
My heart took delight in all my work,
and this was the reward for all my labor.

¹¹Yet when I surveyed all that my hands had done

and what I had toiled to achieve,
everything was meaningless, a chasing after the wind; *i*
nothing was gained under the sun. *j*

Wisdom and Folly Are Meaningless

¹²Then I turned my thoughts to consider wisdom,
and also madness and folly. *k*
What more can the king's successor do than what has already been done? *l*
¹³I saw that wisdom *m* is better than folly, *n*
just as light is better than darkness.
¹⁴The wise man has eyes in his head,
while the fool walks in the darkness;
but I came to realize
that the same fate overtakes them both. *o*

¹⁵Then I thought in my heart,

"The fate of the fool will overtake me also.
What then do I gain by being wise?" *p*
I said in my heart,
"This too is meaningless."
¹⁶For the wise man, like the fool, will not be long remembered; *q*
in days to come both will be forgotten. *r*
Like the fool, the wise man too must die! *s*

Toil Is Meaningless

¹⁷So I hated life, because the work that is done under the sun was grievous to me. All of it is meaningless, a chasing after the wind. *t* ¹⁸I hated all the things I had toiled for under the sun, because I must leave them to the one who comes after me. *u* ¹⁹And who knows whether he will be a

Cross references (center column)

1:18 *u*Jer 45:3
*v*Ecc 2:23; 12:12
2:1 *w*ver 24;
Ecc 7:4; 8:15
2:2 *x*S Pr 14:13
2:3 *y*ver 24-25;
S Jdg 9:13;
Ru 3:3;
Ecc 3:12-13;
5:18; 8:15
*z*S Ecc 1:17
2:4 *a*2Ch 2:1;
8:1-6 *b*SS 8:11
2:7 *c*2Ch 8:7-8
2:8 *d*S 1Ki 9:28
*e*S Jdg 3:15
*f*S 2Sa 19:35
2:9 *g*Ecc 1:12
*h*1Ch 29:25

2:11 *i*S Ecc 1:14
*j*S Ecc 1:3
2:12 *k*S Ecc 1:17
*l*S Ecc 1:9
2:13 *m*Ecc 7:19;
9:18
*n*Ecc 7:11-12
2:14 *o*Ps 49:10;
Ecc 3:19; 6:6;
7:2; 9:3,11-12
2:15 *p*ver 19;
Ecc 6:8
2:16 *q*S Ps 112:6
*r*S Ecc 1:11
*s*Ps 49:10
2:17 *t*S Ecc 1:14
2:18 *u*Ps 39:6;
49:10

b 8 The meaning of the Hebrew for this phrase is uncertain.

1:18 Humanistic wisdom—wisdom without God—leads to grief and sorrow.

2:1–11 The Teacher now shows that mere pleasure cannot give meaning or satisfaction (see 1:12–15; see also note on 1:12–18).

2:1 *I thought in my heart.* See v. 15; 1:16.

2:3 *my mind still guiding me with wisdom.* From first to last (v. 9) the author used wisdom to discover the good (v. 1) and the worthwhile (v. 3).

2:4–9 See 1Ki 4–11, which tells of Solomon's splendor and of his wives.

2:8 *harem.* The Hebrew for this word occurs only here in Scripture (see NIV text note). The meaning seems to be indicated in an early Egyptian letter that uses a similar Canaanite term for concubines. It fits the situation of Solomon, who had 300 concubines in addition to 700 wives (1Ki 11:3).

2:10 *work . . . labor.* A key thought in Ecclesiastes is the meaninglessness (v. 11), apart from God, of toil, labor, work—words that occur more than 25 times.

2:12–17 The Teacher returns to the folly of trying to find satisfaction in merely human wisdom (see 1:16–18; see also note on 1:12–18).

2:13 *wisdom is better than folly.* Even secular wisdom is better than folly, but in the end it is of no value, since "the same fate overtakes them both" (i.e., overtakes both the wise believer and the foolish unbeliever, v. 14; see Ps 49:10).

2:14 *eyes.* Understanding.

2:16 People tend to soon forget even the greatest leaders and heroes (see 1:11).

2:18 *leave them to the one who comes after me.* See v. 21; Ps 39:6; Lk 12:20.

2:19 *who knows . . . ?* For a more searching "Who knows . . . ?" for secular man see 3:21.

wise man or a fool?^{v} Yet he will have control over all the work into which I have poured my effort and skill under the sun. This too is meaningless. ^{20}So my heart began to despair over all my toilsome labor under the sun. ^{21}For a man may do his work with wisdom, knowledge and skill, and then he must leave all he owns to someone who has not worked for it. This too is meaningless and a great misfortune. ^{22}What does a man get for all the toil and anxious striving with which he labors under the sun?^{w} ^{23}All his days his work is pain and grief;^{x} even at night his mind does not rest.^{y} This too is meaningless.

^{24}A man can do nothing better than to eat and drink^z and find satisfaction in his work.^{a} This too, I see, is from the hand of God,^{b} ^{25}for without him, who can eat or find enjoyment?^{c} ^{26}To the man who pleases him, God gives wisdom,^{d} knowledge and happiness, but to the sinner he gives the task of gathering and storing up wealth^e to hand it over to the one who pleases God.^{f} This too is meaningless, a chasing after the wind.

A Time for Everything

3 There is a time^g for everything,
and a season for every activity under
heaven:

^{2} a time to be born and a time to die,
a time to plant and a time to
uproot,^{h}
^{3} a time to kill^i and a time to heal,
a time to tear down and a time to
build,
^{4} a time to weep and a time to laugh,
a time to mourn and a time to dance,
^{5} a time to scatter stones and a time to
gather them,
a time to embrace and a time to
refrain,
^{6} a time to search and a time to give
up,

2:19 ^{v}S ver 15
2:22 ^{w}S Ecc 1:3
2:23 ^{x}S Ecc 1:18
^{y}S Ge 3:17;
S Job 7:2
2:24 ^{z}ver 3;
1Co 15:32 ^{a}S ver
1; Ecc 3:22
^{b}S Job 2:10;
Ecc 3:12-13;
5:17-19; 7:14;
9:7-10; 11:7-10
2:25 ^{c}S Ps 127:2
2:26 ^{d}S Job 9:4
^{e}S Job 27:17
^{f}S Pr 13:22
3:1 ^{g}ver 11,17;
Ecc 8:6
3:2 ^{h}Isa 28:24
3:3 ^{i}S Dt 5:17

3:7 ^{j}S Est 4:14
3:9 ^{k}S Ecc 1:3
3:10 ^{l}S Ecc 1:13
3:11 ^{m}S ver 1
^{n}S Job 11:7
^{o}S Job 28:23;
Ro 11:33
3:13 ^{p}Ecc 2:3
^{q}Ps 34:12
^{r}S Dt 12:7,18;
S Ecc 2:24
3:14
^{s}S Job 23:15;
Ecc 5:7; 7:18;
8:12-13
3:15 ^{t}Ecc 6:10
^{u}S Ecc 1:9
3:17
^{v}S Job 19:29;
Ecc 11:9; 12:14
^{w}ver 1

---

a time to keep and a time to throw
away,
^{7} a time to tear and a time to mend,
a time to be silent^j and a time to
speak,
^{8} a time to love and a time to hate,
a time for war and a time for peace.

^{9}What does the worker gain from his toil?^{k} ^{10}I have seen the burden God has laid on men.^{l} ^{11}He has made everything beautiful in its time.^{m} He has also set eternity in the hearts of men; yet they cannot fathom^n what God has done from beginning to end.^{o} ^{12}I know that there is nothing better for men than to be happy and do good while they live. ^{13}That everyone may eat and drink,^{p} and find satisfaction^q in all his toil—this is the gift of God.^{r} ^{14}I know that everything God does will endure forever; nothing can be added to it and nothing taken from it. God does it so that men will revere him.^{s}

^{15}Whatever is has already been,^{t}
and what will be has been before;^{u}
and God will call the past to
account.^{c}

^{16}And I saw something else under the sun:

In the place of judgment—wickedness
was there,
in the place of justice—wickedness
was there.

^{17}I thought in my heart,

"God will bring to judgment^v
both the righteous and the wicked,
for there will be a time for every
activity,
a time for every deed."^{w}

^{18}I also thought, "As for men, God tests them so that they may see that they are

^{c}15 Or *God calls back the past*

2:24–25 The heart of Ecclesiastes, a theme repeated in 3:12–13,22; 5:18–20; 8:15; 9:7 and climaxed in 12:13. Only in God does life have meaning and true pleasure. Without him nothing satisfies, but with him we find satisfaction and enjoyment. True pleasure comes only when we acknowledge and revere God (12:13).
2:26 *but to the sinner.* For exceptions to this general principle see 8:14; Ps 73:1–12.
3:1–22 The Teacher shows that we are subject to times and changes over which we have little or no control, and contrasts this state with God's eternity and sovereignty. God sovereignly predetermines all of life's activities (e.g., the 14 opposites of vv. 2–8).
3:1 Cf. 8:6.
3:2 *a time.* Divinely appointed (see Ps 31:15; Pr 16:1–9).
3:11 The chapter summarized: God's beautiful but tantal-

izing world is too big for us, yet its satisfactions are too small. Since we were made for eternity, the things of time cannot fully and permanently satisfy.
3:12–13 A pointer to the book's conclusion. God's people find meaning in life when they cheerfully accept it from the hand of God.
3:14 *forever.* In this word the "eternity" of v. 11 becomes clearer. *revere.* Sums up the message of the book (cf. 12:13).
3:15 See 1:9.
3:17 *judgment.* God's true judgments are the answer to human cynicism about man's injustices. "The past" (v. 15) is not meaningless (as people dismiss it as being, 1:11), and God will override the perverse judgments (v. 16) of men (see 12:14).
3:18 *like the animals.* Man "under the sun" (man on his own) is as mortal as any animal; but, unlike them, he must be

like the animals.ˣ ¹⁹Man's fateʸ is like that of the animals; the same fate awaits them both: As one dies, so dies the other. All have the same breathᵈ; man has no advantage over the animal. Everything is meaningless. ²⁰All go to the same place; all come from dust, and to dust all return.ᶻ ²¹Who knows if the spirit of man rises upwardᵃ and if the spirit of the animalᵉ goes down into the earth?"

²²So I saw that there is nothing better for a man than to enjoy his work,ᵇ because that is his lot.ᶜ For who can bring him to see what will happen after him?

Oppression, Toil, Friendlessness

4 Again I looked and saw all the oppressionᵈ that was taking place under the sun:

I saw the tears of the oppressed—
and they have no comforter;
power was on the side of their
oppressors—
and they have no comforter.ᵉ
²And I declared that the dead,ᶠ
who had already died,
are happier than the living,
who are still alive.ᵍ
³But better than both
is he who has not yet been,ʰ
who has not seen the evil
that is done under the sun.ⁱ

⁴And I saw that all labor and all achievement spring from man's envy of his neighbor. This too is meaningless, a chasing after the wind.ʲ

⁵The fool folds his handsᵏ
and ruins himself.
⁶Better one handful with tranquillity
than two handfuls with toilˡ
and chasing after the wind.

3:18 ˣS Ps 73:22
3:19 ʸS Ecc 2:14
3:20 ᶻS Ge 2:7;
S Job 34:15
3:21 ᵃEcc 12:7
3:22 ᵇS Ecc 2:24
ᶜS Job 31:2
4:1 ᵈS Ps 12:5
ᵉLa 1:16
4:2
ᶠJer 20:17-18;
22:10
ᵍS Job 3:17;
S 10:18
4:3 ʰS Job 3:16
ⁱS Job 3:22
4:4 ʲS Ecc 1:14
4:5 ᵏS Pr 6:10
4:6 ˡPr 15:16-17;
S 16:8

4:8 ᵐPr 27:20

⁷Again I saw something meaningless under the sun:

⁸There was a man all alone;
he had neither son nor brother.
There was no end to his toil,
yet his eyes were not contentᵐ with
his wealth.
"For whom am I toiling," he asked,
"and why am I depriving myself of
enjoyment?"
This too is meaningless—
a miserable business!

⁹Two are better than one,
because they have a good return for
their work:
¹⁰If one falls down,
his friend can help him up.
But pity the man who falls
and has no one to help him up!
¹¹Also, if two lie down together, they will
keep warm.
But how can one keep warm alone?
¹²Though one may be overpowered,
two can defend themselves.
A cord of three strands is not quickly
broken.

Advancement Is Meaningless

¹³Better a poor but wise youth than an old but foolish king who no longer knows how to take warning. ¹⁴The youth may have come from prison to the kingship, or he may have been born in poverty within his kingdom. ¹⁵I saw that all who lived and walked under the sun followed the youth, the king's successor. ¹⁶There was no end to all the people who were before them. But those who came later were not pleased with the successor. This too is meaningless, a chasing after the wind.

ᵈ19 Or spirit   ᵉ21 Or Who knows the spirit of man, which rises upward, or the spirit of the animal, which

---

made to see this condition and, through his dim awareness of eternity (v. 11), be distressed.

3:19 same breath. See Ps 104:27–30.

3:20 to the same place. Not heaven or hell but man's observable destination, which is a return to dust, just like the animals. Death is the great leveler of all living things (see Ge 3:19; Ps 103:14).

3:21 Who knows . . . ? See 2:19 and note; cf. 12:7. Man on his own cannot know; he can only guess. The answer, revealed at first in glimpses (e.g., Ps 16:9–11; 49:15; 73:23–26; Isa 26:19; Da 12:2–3), was brought fully "to light through the gospel" (2Ti 1:10).

3:22 nothing better. As an end in itself, work too is meaningless (see 4:4; 9:9). Only receiving it as a gift from God (v. 13) gives it enduring worth (v. 14).

4:1 oppression. A theme already touched on (3:16) and another ingredient in the human tragedy. To find life mean-

ingless is sad enough, but to taste its cruelty is bitter beyond words.

4:2 happier than the living. See Job 3; Jer 20:14–18. For faith that sees a bigger picture see Ro 8:35–39.

4:4–6 Neither hard work (motivated by envy) nor idleness brings happiness.

4:4 all labor and all achievement. This too is meaningless unless done with God's blessing (see 3:13; cf. the selfless success of Joseph, Ge 39).

4:5 The ruin of the idle person is vividly pictured in 10:18; Pr 6:6–11; 24:30–34.

4:6 tranquillity. See Pr 30:7–9. Paul says the last word on this subject (Php 4:11–13).

4:7–12 The loner, too, has a meaningless and difficult life if he is an unbeliever.

4:12 two . . . three. A climactic construction.

4:13–16 Advancement without God is another example of the meaninglessness of secularism.

Stand in Awe of God

5 Guard your steps when you go to the house of God. Go near to listen rather than to offer the sacrifice of fools, who do not know that they do wrong.

[2] Do not be quick with your mouth,
do not be hasty in your heart
to utter anything before God. [n]
God is in heaven
and you are on earth,
so let your words be few. [o]
[3] As a dream [p] comes when there are
many cares,
so the speech of a fool when there
are many words. [q]

[4] When you make a vow to God, do not delay in fulfilling it. [r] He has no pleasure in fools; fulfill your vow. [s] [5] It is better not to vow than to make a vow and not fulfill it. [t] [6] Do not let your mouth lead you into sin. And do not protest to the temple messenger, "My vow was a mistake." Why should God be angry at what you say and destroy the work of your hands? [7] Much dreaming and many words are meaningless. Therefore stand in awe of God. [u]

Riches Are Meaningless

[8] If you see the poor oppressed [v] in a district, and justice and rights denied, do not be surprised at such things; for one official is eyed by a higher one, and over them both are others higher still. [9] The increase from the land is taken by all; the king himself profits from the fields.

[10] Whoever loves money never has money
enough;
whoever loves wealth is never
satisfied with his income.
This too is meaningless.

[11] As goods increase,
so do those who consume them.
And what benefit are they to the owner

except to feast his eyes on them?

[12] The sleep of a laborer is sweet,
whether he eats little or much,
but the abundance of a rich man
permits him no sleep. [w]

[13] I have seen a grievous evil under the sun: [x]

wealth hoarded to the harm of its
owner,
[14] or wealth lost through some
misfortune,
so that when he has a son
there is nothing left for him.
[15] Naked a man comes from his mother's
womb,
and as he comes, so he departs. [y]
He takes nothing from his labor [z]
that he can carry in his hand. [a]

[16] This too is a grievous evil:

As a man comes, so he departs,
and what does he gain,
since he toils for the wind? [b]
[17] All his days he eats in darkness,
with great frustration, affliction and
anger.

[18] Then I realized that it is good and proper for a man to eat and drink, [c] and to find satisfaction in his toilsome labor [d] under the sun during the few days of life God has given him—for this is his lot. [19] Moreover, when God gives any man wealth and possessions, [e] and enables him to enjoy them, [f] to accept his lot [g] and be happy in his work—this is a gift of God. [h] [20] He seldom reflects on the days of his life, because God keeps him occupied with gladness of heart. [i]

6 I have seen another evil under the sun, and it weighs heavily on men: [2] God gives a man wealth, possessions and honor, so that he lacks nothing his heart desires, but God does not enable him to

---

Cross references (center column):

5:2 [n]S Jdg 11:35
[o]S Job 6:24;
S Pr 20:25
5:3 [p]S Job 20:8
[q]Ecc 10:14
5:4 [r]S Dt 23:21;
S Jdg 11:35;
Ps 119:60
[s]S Nu 30:2;
Ps 66:13-14
5:5 [t]Nu 30:2-4;
Jnh 2:9
5:7 [u]Ecc 3:14
5:8 [v]S Ps 12:5

5:12 [w]Job 20:20
5:13 [x]Ecc 6:1-2
5:15 [y]S Job 1:21
[z]Ps 49:17;
1Ti 6:7 [a]Ecc 1:3
5:16 [b]S Ecc 1:3
5:18 [c]S Ecc 2:3
[d]Ecc 2:24
5:19
[e]S 1Ch 29:12
[f]Ecc 6:2
[g]S Job 31:2
[h]S Ecc 2:24
5:20 [i]S Dt 12:7, 18

5:1–7 The theme of this section is the meaninglessness of superficial religion, as reflected in making rash vows.
5:1 *Guard your steps.* Think about what you ought to say and do. *listen.* Obey. 1Sa 15:22 uses the same Hebrew verb and makes the same contrast between real and superficial worship. *sacrifice.* Probably connected with the vow of vv. 4–6.
5:2 *quick with your mouth.* As in a rash vow.
5:3 A proverb. In the context it suggests that in the midst of cares a person dreams of bliss (as a starving man dreams of a banquet), and in anticipation may offer rash vows ("many words") to God (see v. 7).
5:4 *vow.* See Dt 23:21–23; 1Sa 1:11, 24–28. *no pleasure in fools.* In Scripture the fool is not one who cannot learn, but one who refuses to learn (see Pr 1:20–27; see also NIV text note on Pr 1:7).

5:6 *messenger.* See Mal 2:7.
5:8 *do not be surprised.* For other frank appraisals of human society see 4:1–3. This teacher, like Jesus, who "knew what was in a man" (Jn 2:25), had no illusions or utopian schemes.
5:9 *king . . . profits from the fields.* See note on Am 7:1.
5:10 Greater wealth does not bring satisfaction (see 1Ti 6:9–10).
5:11–12 Greater wealth brings greater anxiety.
5:13 *harm.* Including worry about his possessions.
5:15 *He takes nothing.* See Lk 12:14–21.
5:18–20 See note on 2:24–25.
6:2–3,6 *enjoy.* Comparing v. 2 with 5:19 demonstrates that the ability to enjoy God's blessings is a bonus—a gift of God, not a right or guarantee. God calls the person who forgets this truth a fool (Lk 12:20).

enjoy them,^{j} and a stranger enjoys them instead. This is meaningless, a grievous evil.^{k}

^{3}A man may have a hundred children and live many years; yet no matter how long he lives, if he cannot enjoy his prosperity and does not receive proper burial, I say that a stillborn^l child is better off than he.^{m} ^{4}It comes without meaning, it departs in darkness, and in darkness its name is shrouded. ^{5}Though it never saw the sun or knew meaning, it has more rest than does that man— ^{6}even if he lives a thousand years twice over but fails to enjoy his prosperity. Do not all go to the same place?^{n}

^{7}All man's efforts are for his mouth,
yet his appetite is never satisfied.^{o}
^{8}What advantage has a wise man
over a fool?^{p}
What does a poor man gain
by knowing how to conduct himself
before others?
^{9}Better what the eye sees
than the roving of the appetite.
This too is meaningless,
a chasing after the wind.^{q}

^{10}Whatever exists has already been
named,^{r}
and what man is has been known;
no man can contend
with one who is stronger than he.
^{11}The more the words,
the less the meaning,
and how does that profit anyone?

^{12}For who knows what is good for a man in life, during the few and meaningless days^s he passes through like a shadow?^{t} Who can tell him what will happen under the sun after he is gone?

Wisdom

7 A good name is better than fine
perfume,^{u}
and the day of death better than the
day of birth.^{v}

^{2}It is better to go to a house of mourning
than to go to a house of feasting,
for death^w is the destiny^x of every
man;
the living should take this to heart.
^{3}Sorrow is better than laughter,^{y}
because a sad face is good for the
heart.
^{4}The heart of the wise is in the house of
mourning,
but the heart of fools is in the house
of pleasure.^{z}
^{5}It is better to heed a wise man's
rebuke^a
than to listen to the song of fools.
^{6}Like the crackling of thorns^b under the
pot,
so is the laughter^c of fools.
This too is meaningless.

^{7}Extortion turns a wise man into a fool,
and a bribe^d corrupts the heart.

^{8}The end of a matter is better than its
beginning,
and patience^e is better than pride.
^{9}Do not be quickly provoked^f in your
spirit,
for anger resides in the lap of fools.^{g}

^{10}Do not say, "Why were the old days^h
better than these?"
For it is not wise to ask such
questions.

^{11}Wisdom, like an inheritance, is a good
thing^i
and benefits those who see the sun.^{j}
^{12}Wisdom is a shelter
as money is a shelter,
but the advantage of knowledge is this:
that wisdom preserves the life of its
possessor.

^{13}Consider what God has done:^{k}

Who can straighten
what he has made crooked?^{l}
^{14}When times are good, be happy;
but when times are bad, consider:

Cross references (center column):

6:2 /Ecc 5:19
^{k}Ecc 5:13
6:3 /S Job 3:16
^{m}S Job 3:3
6:6 ^{n}Ecc 2:14
6:7 ^{o}S Pr 27:20
6:8 ^{p}S Ecc 2:15
6:9 ^{q}S Ecc 1:14
6:10 ^{r}Ecc 3:15
6:12
^{s}S Job 10:20;
S 20:8
^{t}S 1Ch 29:15;
S Job 14:2;
S Ps 39:6
7:1 ^{u}Pr 22:1;
SS 1:3
^{v}S Job 10:18

7:2 ^{w}S Pr 11:19
^{x}S Ecc 2:14
7:3 ^{y}S Pr 14:13
7:4 ^{z}S Ecc 2:1;
Jer 16:8
7:5 ^{a}S Pr 13:18;
15:31-32
7:6 ^{b}S Ps 58:9
^{c}S Pr 14:13
7:7 ^{d}S Ex 18:21;
S 23:8
7:8 ^{e}Pr 14:29
7:9 /S Mt 5:22
^{g}S Pr 14:29
7:10 ^{h}S Ps 77:5
7:11 /Ecc 2:13
/Ecc 11:7
7:13 ^{k}Ecc 2:24
/Ecc 1:15

6:3 *does not receive proper burial.* Dies unlamented or dishonored, like King Jehoiakim (Jer 22:18–19). *stillborn child.* For the secularist, life is a pointless journey to extinction, to which being stillborn is the quickest and easiest route (cf. Job 3:16; Ps 58:8).
6:6 *to the same place.* Still talking in terms of what we can observe (that all men die), not of what lies beyond death (see v. 12; 3:21).
6:7–12 In confronting complacency, the Teacher gives several causes for concern: the short-lived (v. 7), debatable (v. 8) and elusive (v. 9) rewards of life; the limits of our creativity, power and wisdom (vv. 10–11); and the unreliability of merely human values and predictions (v. 12).
6:10 *named.* Predetermined by God. *known.* Foreknown

by God. *one who is stronger.* God.
6:12 *like a shadow.* See 1Ch 29:15.
7:1 *day of death better.* The Christian has ample reason to say this (2Co 5:1–10; Php 1:21–23). But the Teacher's point is valid, as explained in vv. 2–6, namely, that happy times generally teach us less than hard times.
7:7 *bribe.* See Mt 28:11–15; Lk 22:4–6.
7:9 *anger.* See, e.g., Pr 16:32; 17:14; 1Co 13:4–5.
7:12 *preserves the life.* The Hebrew for this expression can also mean "gives life" or "renews life" (see Pr 3:13–18; 13:14).
7:13 *Who can straighten . . . ?* Not fatalism, but a reminder of who is God. Man cannot change what God determines (see note on 1:15).

God has made the one
as well as the other. *m*
Therefore, a man cannot discover
anything about his future.

[15] In this meaningless life *n* of mine I
have seen both of these:

a righteous man perishing in his
righteousness,
and a wicked man living long in his
wickedness. *o*

[16] Do not be overrighteous,
neither be overwise—
why destroy yourself?

[17] Do not be overwicked,
and do not be a fool—
why die before your time? *p*

[18] It is good to grasp the one
and not let go of the other.
The man who fears God *q* will avoid
all extremes. *f*

[19] Wisdom *r* makes one wise man more
powerful *s*
than ten rulers in a city.

[20] There is not a righteous man *t* on earth
who does what is right and never
sins. *u*

[21] Do not pay attention to every word
people say,
or you *v* may hear your servant
cursing you—

[22] for you know in your heart
that many times you yourself have
cursed others.

[23] All this I tested by wisdom and I said,

"I am determined to be wise" *w*—
but this was beyond me.

[24] Whatever wisdom may be,
it is far off and most profound—
who can discover it? *x*

[25] So I turned my mind to understand,
to investigate and to search out
wisdom and the scheme of
things *y*

and to understand the stupidity of
wickedness
and the madness of folly. *z*

[26] I find more bitter than death
the woman who is a snare, *a*
whose heart is a trap
and whose hands are chains.
The man who pleases God will escape
her,
but the sinner she will ensnare. *b*

[27] "Look," says the Teacher, *&c* "this is
what I have discovered:

"Adding one thing to another to
discover the scheme of
things—
[28]   while I was still searching
but not finding—
I found one upright man among a
thousand,
but not one upright woman *d* among
them all.
[29] This only have I found:
God made mankind upright,
but men have gone in search of many
schemes."

8 Who is like the wise man?
Who knows the explanation of
things?
Wisdom brightens a man's face
and changes its hard appearance.

Obey the King

[2] Obey the king's command, I say, because you took an oath before God. [3] Do
not be in a hurry to leave the king's presence. *e* Do not stand up for a bad cause, for
he will do whatever he pleases. [4] Since a
king's word is supreme, who can say to
him, "What are you doing? *f* "

[5] Whoever obeys his command will come
to no harm,

f18 Or *will follow them both*   *&27* Or *leader of the
assembly*

Cross references (center column):

7:14 *m*S Job 1:21;
S Ecc 2:24
7:15 *n*S Job 7:7
*o*S Job 21:7;
Ecc 8:12-14;
Jer 12:1
7:17 *p*Job 15:32
7:18 *q*S Ecc 3:14
7:19 *r*S Ecc 2:13
*s*S Pr 8:14
7:20 *t*S Ps 14:3
*u*2Ch 6:36;
Ro 3:12;
S Job 4:17;
S Pr 20:9
7:21 *v*Pr 30:10
7:23 *w*S Ecc 1:17
7:24 *x*S Job 28:12
7:25 *y*S Job 28:3

7:26 *z*S Ecc 1:17
*a*S Ex 10:7;
S Jdg 14:15
*b*S Pr 2:16-19;
5:3-5; S 7:23;
22:14
7:27 *c*S Ecc 1:1
7:28 *d*1Ki 11:3
8:3 *e*Ecc 10:4
8:4 *f*Est 1:19

7:14 *God has made the one* [bad times] *as well as the other*
[good times]. Cf. Ro 8:28-29.
7:15 *righteous man perishing*. Righteousness is no sure
protection against hard times or an early death.
7:16 *not ... overrighteous ... overwise*. If true righteousness and wisdom do not necessarily prevent ruin, then extreme, legalistic righteousness and wisdom will surely not
help.
7:17 *not ... overwicked*. Extreme wickedness is even
more foolhardy.
7:18 *the one ... the other*. The God-fearing person will
avoid both extremes (legalism and libertinism) and lead a
balanced—truly righteous and wise—life.
7:20 *not a righteous man on earth*. A sober Biblical truth
(see Ro 3:10-20).

7:24 See Job 28:12-28; 1Co 2:9-16.
7:26 See Pr 7:6-27.
7:27 *Teacher*. See note on 1:1. *Adding one thing to another to discover the scheme of things*. This inductive
method can never be complete, nor can we reliably interpret
all that we manage to observe (3:11b). Human wisdom and
understanding must always yield to revealed truth.
7:29 *God made mankind upright, but*. See Ge 3:1-6; Ro
5:12.
8:2 *king's command*. Both principle (v. 2) and prudence
(vv. 3-6) set limits on our freedom. *took an oath*. Of loyalty
to the king (as seen, e.g., in 1Ch 29:24).
8:4 *who can say ... , "What are you doing?"* Cf. Isa 45:9;
Ro 9:20.

and the wise heart will know the
proper time and procedure.
⁶For there is a proper time and
procedure for every matter,ᵍ
though a man's misery weighs
heavily upon him.

⁷Since no man knows the future,
who can tell him what is to come?
⁸No man has power over the wind to
contain itʰ;
so no one has power over the day of
his death.
As no one is discharged in time of war,
so wickedness will not release those
who practice it.

⁹All this I saw, as I applied my mind to
everything done under the sun. There is a
time when a man lords it over others to his
ownⁱ hurt. ¹⁰Then too, I saw the wicked
buriedʰ—those who used to come and go
from the holy place and receive praiseʲ in
the city where they did this. This too is
meaningless.
¹¹When the sentence for a crime is not
quickly carried out, the hearts of the
people are filled with schemes to do
wrong. ¹²Although a wicked man commits
a hundred crimes and still lives a long
time, I know that it will go betterⁱ with
God-fearing men,ʲ who are reverent before God.ᵏ ¹³Yet because the wicked do
not fear God,ˡ it will not go well with
them, and their daysᵐ will not lengthen
like a shadow.
¹⁴There is something else meaningless
that occurs on earth: righteous men who
get what the wicked deserve, and wicked
men who get what the righteous deserve.ⁿ
This too, I say, is meaningless.ᵒ ¹⁵So I
commend the enjoyment of lifeᵖ, because
nothing is better for a man under the sun
than to eat and drinkᵠ and be glad.ʳ Then
joy will accompany him in his work all the

days of the life God has given him under
the sun.
¹⁶When I applied my mind to know wis-
domˢ and to observe man's labor on
earthᵗ—his eyes not seeing sleep day or
night— ¹⁷then I saw all that God has
done.ᵘ No one can comprehend what goes
on under the sun. Despite all his efforts to
search it out, man cannot discover its
meaning. Even if a wise man claims he
knows, he cannot really comprehend it.ᵛ

A Common Destiny for All

9 So I reflected on all this and concluded
that the righteous and the wise and
what they do are in God's hands, but no
man knows whether love or hate awaits
him.ʷ ²All share a common destiny—the
righteous and the wicked, the good and
the bad,ᵏ the clean and the unclean, those
who offer sacrifices and those who do not.

As it is with the good man,
so with the sinner;
as it is with those who take oaths,
so with those who are afraid to take
them.ˣ

³This is the evil in everything that happens under the sun: The same destiny
overtakes all.ʸ The hearts of men, moreover, are full of evil and there is madness
in their hearts while they live,ᶻ and afterward they join the dead.ᵃ ⁴Anyone who is
among the living has hopeˡ—even a live
dog is better off than a dead lion!

⁵For the living know that they will die,
but the dead know nothing;ᵇ
they have no further reward,
and even the memory of themᶜ is
forgotten.ᵈ

8:6 ᵍEcc 3:1
8:10 ʰS Ecc 1:11
8:12 ⁱS Dt 12:28
ʲS Ex 1:20
ᵏEcc 3:14
8:13 ˡEcc 3:14
ᵐDt 4:40;
Job 5:26;
Ps 34:12;
Isa 65:20
8:14 ⁿS Job 21:7
ᵒS Ecc 7:15
8:15 ᵖS Ps 42:8
ᵠS Ex 32:6;
S Ecc 2:3
ʳS Ecc 2:1

8:16 ˢS Ecc 1:17
ᵗEcc 1:13
8:17 ᵘS Job 28:3
ᵛS Job 28:23;
Ro 11:33
9:1 ʷEcc 10:14
9:2 ˣJob 9:22;
Ecc 2:14
9:3 ʸS Job 9:22;
S Ecc 2:14
ᶻJer 11:8; 13:10;
16:12; 17:9
ᵃS Job 21:26
9:5 ᵇS Job 14:21
ᶜS Ps 9:6
ᵈS Ecc 1:11

ʰ8 Or over his spirit to retain it   ⁱ9 Or to their
ˡ10 Some Hebrew manuscripts and Septuagint (Aquila);
most Hebrew manuscripts and are forgotten
ᵏ2 Septuagint (Aquila), Vulgate and Syriac; Hebrew does
not have and the bad.   ˡ4 Or What then is to be
chosen? With all who live, there is hope

8:6 a man's misery. One should put the king's command
above his own misery.
8:7–8 no man knows .... No man has power. See Ps
31:15; 2Cor 5:1–10; Jas 4:13–16.
8:10 the wicked buried. In this context it implies undeserved respect (see note on 6:3; cf. Job 21:28–33; Lk
16:22).
8:11 Delayed punishment tends to induce more wrongdoing.
8:12 I know. Here the Teacher speaks from mature faith,
not as one "still searching but not finding" (7:28). For similar
declarations see 3:17; 11:9; 12:14.
8:14 Job 21–24 enlarges on this; Ps 73 draws the sting of
it; and Jn 5:28–29 gives the final explanation.
8:15 eat ... drink ... be glad. Spoken gratefully (see 5:19;
9:7; Dt 8). For such words spoken arrogantly see Lk

12:19–20; 1Co 15:32.
8:17 No one can comprehend. Dt 29:29 sums up what we
are allowed and not allowed to know.
9:1 whether love or hate. The future is under God's control, and no one knows whether that future will be good or
bad.
9:2 common destiny. Not only the wise and foolish (2:14),
but also the good and the bad are seen leveled, in the sense
noted at 3:20. For the Teacher's conviction (beyond mere
observation) that God ultimately will see justice done see
note on 8:12.
9:3 evil ... evil. The apparently common destiny (both the
righteous and the wicked die) encourages some people to
sin.
9:5 no further reward. The dead have lost all opportunity in
this life for enjoyment and reward from labor (see v. 6).

6Their love, their hate
   and their jealousy have long since
      vanished;
  never again will they have a part
   in anything that happens under the
      sun. *e*

7Go, eat your food with gladness, and
drink your wine*f* with a joyful heart,*g* for
it is now that God favors what you do.
8Always be clothed in white,*h* and always
anoint your head with oil. 9Enjoy life with
your wife,*i* whom you love, all the days of
this meaningless life that God has given
you under the sun— all your meaningless
days. For this is your lot*j* in life and in
your toilsome labor under the sun.
10Whatever*k* your hand finds to do, do it
with all your might,*l* for in the grave,*mm*
where you are going, there is neither
working nor planning nor knowledge nor
wisdom. *n*

11I have seen something else under the
sun:

The race is not to the swift
  or the battle to the strong,*o*
nor does food come to the wise*p*
  or wealth to the brilliant
  or favor to the learned;
but time and chance*q* happen to them
   all.*r*

12Moreover, no man knows when his
hour will come:

As fish are caught in a cruel net,
  or birds are taken in a snare,
so men are trapped by evil times*s*
  that fall unexpectedly upon them. *t*

Wisdom Better Than Folly

13I also saw under the sun this example
of wisdom*u* that greatly impressed me:
14There was once a small city with only a
few people in it. And a powerful king came
against it, surrounded it and built huge
siegeworks against it. 15Now there lived in
that city a man poor but wise, and he
saved the city by his wisdom. But nobody

remembered that poor man. *v* 16So I said,
"Wisdom is better than strength." But the
poor man's wisdom is despised, and his
words are no longer heeded. *w*

17The quiet words of the wise are more to
   be heeded
  than the shouts of a ruler of fools.
18Wisdom*x* is better than weapons of
   war,
  but one sinner destroys much good.

10 As dead flies give perfume a bad
   smell,
  so a little folly*y* outweighs wisdom
   and honor.
2The heart of the wise inclines to the
   right,
  but the heart of the fool to the left.
3Even as he walks along the road,
  the fool lacks sense
  and shows everyone*z* how stupid he
   is.
4If a ruler's anger rises against you,
  do not leave your post;*a*
  calmness can lay great errors to rest.*b*

5There is an evil I have seen under the
   sun,
  the sort of error that arises from a
   ruler:
6Fools are put in many high positions,*c*
  while the rich occupy the low ones.
7I have seen slaves on horseback,
  while princes go on foot like slaves.*d*

8Whoever digs a pit may fall into it;*e*
  whoever breaks through a wall may
   be bitten by a snake.*f*
9Whoever quarries stones may be injured
   by them;
  whoever splits logs may be
   endangered by them.*g*
10If the ax is dull
  and its edge unsharpened,
more strength is needed
  but skill will bring success.
11If a snake bites before it is charmed,
  there is no profit for the charmer. *h*

9:6 *e*S Job 21:21
9:7 *f*S Nu 6:20
*g*S Ecc 2:24
9:8 *h*S Rev 3:4
9:9 *i*S Pr 5:18
*j*S Job 31:2
9:10 *k*S 1Sa 10:7
*l*Ecc 11:6
*m*Nu 16:33;
S Ps 6:5;
Isa 38:18
*n*S Ecc 2:24
9:11
*o*Am 2:14-15
*p*Job 32:13;
Isa 47:10;
Jer 9:23
*q*Ecc 2:14
*r*S Dt 8:18
9:12 *s*S Pr 29:6
*t*S Ps 73:22;
S Ecc 2:14
9:13
*u*2Sa 20:22

9:15
*v*S Ge 40:14;
S Ecc 1:11
9:16 *w*Est 6:3
9:18 *x*S Ecc 2:13
10:1 *y*Pr 13:16;
18:2
10:3 *z*Pr 13:16
10:4 *a*Ecc 8:3
*b*S Pr 16:14
10:6 *c*S Pr 29:2
10:7 *d*Pr 19:10
10:8 *e*S Ps 57:6
*f*S Est 2:23;
Ps 9:16; Am 5:19
10:9 *g*S Pr 26:27
10:11 *h*S Ps 58:5;
S Isa 3:3

m 10 Hebrew *Sheol*

9:7–9 The Babylonian *Epic of Gilgamesh* contains a section (10.3.6–14) remarkably similar to this passage, illustrating the international flavor of ancient wisdom literature (see chart on "Ancient Texts Relating to the OT," p. 5).

9:7 See note on 8:15.

9:10 Cf. Col 3:23.

9:11 *time and chance.* Success is uncertain—more evidence that man does not ultimately control events.

9:12 *hour.* Of disaster. *men are trapped.* Success is unpredictable, because man is not wise enough to know when misfortune may overtake him.

9:15 *But nobody remembered.* Further warning against placing too high hopes on one's wisdom. Its reputation fades, its good is soon undone (v. 18b), and it has no answer to death (2:15–16).

10:1 *a little folly outweighs.* 2Ki 20:12–19 presents a striking example.

10:2 *to the right . . . to the left.* These can stand for the greater and the lesser good (cf. Ge 48:13–20); or perhaps here, as in some later Jewish writings, for good and evil.

10:5 *error . . . from a ruler.* For the Teacher's observations on human regimes see vv. 4,6–7,16–17,20; 3:16; 4:1–3, 13–16; 5:8–9; 8:2–6,10–11; 9:17.

[12]Words from a wise man's mouth are
　　gracious, [i]
but a fool is consumed by his own
　　lips. [j]
[13]At the beginning his words are folly;
　　at the end they are wicked
　　madness—
[14]　and the fool multiplies words. [k]

No one knows what is coming—
　who can tell him what will happen
　　after him? [l]

[15]A fool's work wearies him;
　he does not know the way to town.

[16]Woe to you, O land whose king was a
　　servant [n] [m]
and whose princes feast in the
　　morning.
[17]Blessed are you, O land whose king is of
　　noble birth
and whose princes eat at a proper
　　time—
for strength and not for
　　drunkenness. [n]

[18]If a man is lazy, the rafters sag;
　if his hands are idle, the house
　　leaks. [o]

[19]A feast is made for laughter,
　and wine [p] makes life merry,
but money is the answer for
　everything.

[20]Do not revile the king [q] even in your
　　thoughts,
or curse the rich in your bedroom,
because a bird of the air may carry your
　words,
and a bird on the wing may report
　what you say.

Bread Upon the Waters

11 Cast [r] your bread upon the waters,
for after many days you will find it
again. [s]

[2]Give portions to seven, yes to eight,
　for you do not know what disaster
　　may come upon the land.

[3]If clouds are full of water,
　they pour rain upon the earth.
Whether a tree falls to the south or to
　　the north,
in the place where it falls, there will
　　it lie.
[4]Whoever watches the wind will not
　　plant;
whoever looks at the clouds will not
　　reap.

[5]As you do not know the path of the
　　wind, [t]
or how the body is formed [o] in a
　　mother's womb, [u]
so you cannot understand the work of
　　God,
the Maker of all things.

[6]Sow your seed in the morning,
　and at evening let not your hands be
　　idle, [v]
for you do not know which will
　　succeed,
whether this or that,
or whether both will do equally well.

Remember Your Creator While Young

[7]Light is sweet,
　and it pleases the eyes to see the
　　sun. [w]
[8]However many years a man may live,
　let him enjoy them all.
But let him remember [x] the days of
　　darkness,
for they will be many.
Everything to come is meaningless.

[9]Be happy, young man, while you are
　　young,

Cross references (center column)

10:12 [i]Pr 10:32
/S Pr 10:6;
S 14:3; S 15:2;
S 18:7
10:14 [k]Ecc 5:3
[l]Ecc 9:1
10:16 [m]Isa 3:4-5,
12
10:17
[n]S Dt 14:26;
S 1Sa 25:36;
S Pr 31:4
10:18 [o]Pr 20:4;
S 24:30-34
10:19
[p]S Ge 14:18;
S Jdg 9:13
10:20
[q]S Ex 22:28
11:1 [r]ver 6;
Isa 32:20;
Hos 10:12
[s]S Dt 24:19

11:5 [t]Jn 3:8-10
[u]Ps 139:14-16
11:6 [v]S Ecc 9:10
11:7 [w]Ecc 7:11
11:8 [x]Ecc 12:1

[n]16 Or *king is a child*　　[o]5 Or *know how life* (or *the*
spirit) / *enters the body being formed*

10:12 *Words.* A favorite topic in wisdom literature (see,
e.g., Pr 15).
10:15 *does not know the way to town.* Since in Scripture
a fool is one who refuses God's teaching (see note on 5:4),
this caustic saying (probably proverbial) refers to more than
mere stupidity.
10:16 *whose king was a servant.* A small-minded upstart,
not a "poor but wise youth" as in 4:13. See 2Ki 15:8–25;
Hos 7:3–7, which portray some of the short-lived usurpers
and vicious courtiers who hastened the downfall of Israel.
10:18 *lazy . . . idle.* See note on 4:5.
10:19 *money is the answer for everything.* Can be read at
various levels—as a wry comment on human values, as
sober advice to earn a good living rather than have a good
time (see the first two lines) or as stating the great versatility
of money (cf. Lk 16:9).
11:1 *Cast your bread upon the waters.* Be adventurous,

like those who accept the risks and reap the benefits of
seaborne trade. Do not always play it safe (see Pr 11:24).
11:2 *Give portions to seven.* Be generous while you have
plenty; unforeseen disasters may make you dependent on
the generosity of others.
11:3–6 *clouds . . . tree . . . wind . . . seed.* Do not toy with
maybes and might-have-beens. Start where you can, and
recognize how limited your role (or knowledge) is.
11:5 *wind.* See NIV text note; cf. Jn 3:8 ("wind" and
"spirit" are the same word in the original in both verses).
11:7–10 Live life to the fullest.
11:8,10 *meaningless.* Warns against letting the wonderful
gifts mentioned in vv. 7–10 dazzle and distract us. Verse
9 sets us on the true course.
11:9 *judgment.* See 12:14 and note. The prospect of divine
praise or blame makes every detail of life significant rather
than meaningless. To know this gives direction to our heart

and let your heart give you joy in the
days of your youth.
Follow the ways of your heart
and whatever your eyes see,
but know that for all these things
God will bring you to judgment. *y*
¹⁰So then, banish anxiety *z* from your
heart
and cast off the troubles of your body,
for youth and vigor are meaningless. *a*

12 Remember *b* your Creator
in the days of your youth,
before the days of trouble *c* come
and the years approach when you
will say,
"I find no pleasure in them"—
²before the sun and the light
and the moon and the stars grow
dark,
and the clouds return after the rain;
³when the keepers of the house tremble,
and the strong men stoop,
when the grinders cease because they
are few,
and those looking through the
windows grow dim;
⁴when the doors to the street are closed
and the sound of grinding fades;
when men rise up at the sound of birds,
but all their songs grow faint; *d*
⁵when men are afraid of heights
and of dangers in the streets;
when the almond tree blossoms
and the grasshopper drags himself
along
and desire no longer is stirred.
Then man goes to his eternal home *e*
and mourners *f* go about the streets.

⁶Remember him—before the silver cord
is severed,
or the golden bowl is broken;
before the pitcher is shattered at the
spring,
or the wheel broken at the well,
⁷and the dust returns *g* to the ground it
came from,
and the spirit returns to God *h* who
gave it. *i*

⁸"Meaningless! Meaningless!" says the
Teacher. *p j*
"Everything is meaningless! *k* "

The Conclusion of the Matter

⁹Not only was the Teacher wise, but
also he imparted knowledge to the people.
He pondered and searched out and set in
order many proverbs. *l* ¹⁰The Teacher *m*
searched to find just the right words, and
what he wrote was upright and true. *n*

¹¹The words of the wise are like goads,
their collected sayings like firmly embedded nails *o*—given by one Shepherd. ¹²Be
warned, my son, of anything in addition to
them.
Of making many books there is no end,
and much study wearies the body. *p*

¹³Now all has been heard;
here is the conclusion of the matter:
Fear God *q* and keep his
commandments, *r*
for this is the whole ⌊duty⌋ of man. *s*
¹⁴For God will bring every deed into
judgment, *t*
including every hidden thing, *u*
whether it is good or evil.

11:9
*y*S Job 19:29;
S Ecc 2:24; S 3:17
11:10 *z*Ps 94:19
*a*S Ecc 2:24
12:1 *b*Ecc 11:8
*c*S 2Sa 19:35
12:4 *d*Jer 25:10
12:5 *e*S Job 10:21
*f*Jer 9:17;
Am 5:16

12:7 *g*S Ge 2:7;
S Ps 146:4
*h*Ecc 3:21
*i*S Job 20:8
12:8 *j*Ecc 1:1
*k*S Ecc 1:2
12:9 *l*1Ki 4:32
12:10 *m*S Ecc 1:1
*n*Pr 22:20-21
12:11 *o*S Ezr 9:8;
S Job 6:25
12:12
*p*S Ecc 1:18
12:13
*q*S Ex 20:20;
S 1Sa 12:24;
S Job 23:15;
S Ps 19:9
*r*S Dt 4:2
*s*S Dt 4:6;
S Job 37:24
12:14
*t*S Job 19:29;
S Ecc 3:17
*u*S Job 34:21;
S Ps 19:12;
Jer 16:17; 23:24

p8 Or the leader of the assembly; also in verses 9 and 10

---

and discrimination to our eyes. The stage is set for ch. 12.
12:2–5 A graphic description of man's progressive deterioration; an allegory of aging.
12:3 *keepers of the house.* This and the other metaphors
may refer to parts of the body (hands, legs, etc.). But the
imagery should not be pressed to the extent that it destroys
the poetry, which moves freely between figures such as
darkness, storm, a house in decline and a deserted well, and
such literal descriptions as in v. 5a.
12:5 *almond tree.* Its pale blossom possibly suggests the
white hair of age. *grasshopper.* Normally agile, its slow
movements on a cold morning (cf. Na 3:17) recall the stiff-
ness of old age. *eternal home.* In context, probably points
simply to the grave, not beyond it.
12:6 *silver cord . . . golden bowl.* A hanging lamp suspended by a silver chain. If only one link snaps, this light and
beauty will perish, suggesting how fragile life is.
12:8 *Meaningless!* Such is life "under the sun" (on earth,
apart from God), ending in brokenness. But with a relation-

ship to our Creator already demanded (v. 1), and with the
fact of his judgment affirmed (11:9), meaninglessness is not
the last word. *Teacher.* See note on 1:1.
12:9 *pondered and searched.* The rigorous process on
man's side, with no pains spared in seeking truth and comprehension.
12:11 *given by one Shepherd.* The other side of the matter,
recognizing that Scripture is in a class of its own, as v. 12
insists.
12:13–14 The chief end of man.
12:13 *Fear God.* Loving reverence is the foundation of
wisdom (Ps 111:10; Pr 1:7; 9:10), as well as its content (Job
28:28) and its goal and conclusion. *the whole ⌊duty⌋ of man.*
Here is our fulfillment, our all—a far cry from "meaninglessness."
12:14 *every deed into judgment.* Glimpses of this truth are
given at intervals in the book: 3:17; 8:12–13; 11:9 and
note; see Mt 12:36; 1Co 3:12–15; 2Co 5:9–10; Heb
4:12–13. *every hidden thing.* See Ro 2:16.

SONG OF SONGS

Title

The title in the Hebrew text is "Solomon's Song of Songs," meaning a song by, for, or about Solomon. The phrase "Song of Songs" means the greatest of songs (cf. Dt 10:17, "God of gods and Lord of lords"; 1Ti 6:15, "King of kings").

Author and Date

Verse 1 appears to ascribe authorship to Solomon (see note on 1:1; but see also Title above). Solomon is referred to seven times (1:1,5; 3:7,9,11; 8:11-12), and several verses speak of the "king" (1:4,12; 7:5), but whether he was the author remains an open question.

To date the Song in the tenth century B.C. during Solomon's reign is not impossible. In fact, mention of Tirzah and Jerusalem in one breath (6:4) has been used to prove a date prior to King Omri (885-874 B.C.; see 1Ki 16:23-24), though the reason for Tirzah's mention is not clear. On the other hand, many have appealed to the language of the Song as proof of a much later date, but on present evidence the linguistic data are ambiguous.

Consistency of language, style, tone, perspective and recurring refrains seems to argue for a single author. However, many who have doubted that the Song came from one pen, or even from one time or place, explain this consistency by ascribing all the Song's parts to a single literary tradition, since Near Eastern traditions were very careful to maintain stylistic uniformity.

Interpretation

To find the key for unlocking the Song, interpreters have looked to prophetic, wisdom and apocalyptic passages of Scripture, as well as to ancient Egyptian and Babylonian love songs, traditional Semitic wedding songs and songs related to ancient Mesopotamian fertility cults. The closest parallels appear to be those found in Proverbs (see Pr 5:15-20; 6:24-29; 7:6-23). The description of love in 8:6-7 (cf. the descriptions of wisdom found in Pr 1-9 and Job 28) seems to confirm that the Song belongs to Biblical wisdom literature and that it is wisdom's description of an amorous relationship. The Bible speaks of both wisdom and love as gifts of God, to be received with gratitude and celebration.

This understanding of the Song contrasts with the long-held view that the Song is an allegory of the love relationship between God and Israel, or between Christ and the church, or between Christ and the soul (though the NT nowhere quotes from or even alludes to the Song). It is also distinct from more modern interpretations of the Song, such as that which sees it as a poetic drama celebrating the triumph of a maiden's pure, spontaneous love for her rustic shepherd lover over the courtly blandishments of Solomon, who sought to win her for his royal harem. Rather, it views the Song as a linked chain of lyrics depicting love in all its spontaneity, beauty, power and exclusiveness—experienced in its varied moments of separation and intimacy, anguish and ecstasy, tension and contentment. The Song shares with the love poetry of many cultures its extensive use of highly sensuous and suggestive imagery drawn from nature.

Theme and Theology

In ancient Israel everything human came to expression in words: reverence, gratitude, anger, sorrow, suffering, trust, friendship, commitment, loyalty, hope, wisdom, moral outrage, repentance. In the Song, it is love that finds words—inspired words that disclose its exquisite charm and beauty as one of God's choicest gifts. The voice of love in the Song, like that of wisdom in Pr 8:1-9:12, is a woman's voice, suggesting that love and wisdom draw men powerfully with the subtlety and mystery of a woman's allurements.

This feminine voice speaks profoundly of love. She portrays its beauty and delights. She claims its exclusiveness ("My lover is mine and I am his," 2:16) and insists on the necessity of its pure spontaneity

("Do not arouse or awaken love until it so desires," 2:7). She also proclaims its overwhelming power—it rivals that of the fearsome enemy, death; it burns with the intensity of a blazing fire; it is unquenchable even by the ocean depths (8:6-7a). She affirms its preciousness: All a man's possessions cannot purchase it, nor (alternatively) should they be exchanged for it (8:7b). She hints, without saying so explicitly (see the last NIV text note on 8:6), that it is a gift of the Lord to man.

God intends that such love—grossly distorted and abused by both ancient and modern people—be a normal part of marital life in his good creation (see Ge 1:26-31; 2:24).

Literary Features

No one who reads the Song with care can question the artistry of the poet. The subtle delicacy with which he evokes intense sensuous awareness while avoiding crude titillation is one of the chief marks of his achievement. This he accomplishes largely by indirection, by analogy and by bringing to the foreground the sensuous in the world of nature (or in food, drink, cosmetics and jewelry). To liken a lover's enjoyment of his beloved to a gazelle "browsing among lilies" (2:16), or her breasts to "twin fawns of a gazelle that browse among the lilies" (4:5), or the beloved herself to a garden filled with choice fruits inviting the lover to feast (4:12-16)—these combine exquisite artistry and fine sensitivity.

Whether the Song has the unity of a single dramatic line linking all the subunits into a continuing story is a matter of ongoing debate among interpreters. There do appear to be connected scenes in the love relationship (see Outline).

Virtually all agree that the literary climax of the Song is found in 8:6-7, where the unsurpassed power and value of love—the love that draws man and woman together—are finally expressly asserted. Literary relaxation follows the intenseness of that declaration. A final expression of mutual desire between the lovers brings the Song to an end, suggesting that love goes on. This last segment (8:8-14) is in some sense also a return to the beginning, as references to the beloved's brothers, to her vineyard and to Solomon (the king) link 8:8-12 with 1:2-6.

In this song of love the voice of the beloved is dominant. It is her experience of love, both as the one who loves and as the one who is loved, that is most clearly expressed. The Song begins with her wish for the lover's kiss and ends with her urgent invitation to him for love's intimacy.

Outline

I. Title (1:1)
II. The First Meeting (1:2-2:7)
III. The Second Meeting (2:8-3:5)
IV. The Third Meeting (3:6-5:1)
V. The Fourth Meeting (5:2-6:3)
VI. The Fifth Meeting (6:4-8:4)
VII. The Literary Climax (8:5-7)
VIII. The Conclusion (8:8-14)

1

Solomon's Song of Songs. [a]

Beloved[a]

[2]Let him kiss me with the kisses of his
   mouth—
   for your love[b] is more delightful than
      wine.[c]
[3]Pleasing is the fragrance of your
      perfumes;[d]
   your name[e] is like perfume poured
      out.
   No wonder the maidens[f] love you!
[4]Take me away with you—let us hurry!
   Let the king bring me into his
      chambers.[g]

Friends

We rejoice and delight[h] in you[b];
   we will praise your love[i] more than
      wine.

Beloved

How right they are to adore you!

[5]Dark am I, yet lovely,[j]
   O daughters of Jerusalem,[k]
   dark like the tents of Kedar,[l]
   like the tent curtains of Solomon.[c]
[6]Do not stare at me because I am dark,
   because I am darkened by the sun.
My mother's sons were angry with me
   and made me take care of the
      vineyards;[m]
   my own vineyard I have neglected.

[7]Tell me, you whom I love, where you
      graze your flock
   and where you rest your sheep[n] at
      midday.
   Why should I be like a veiled[o] woman
   beside the flocks of your friends?

Friends

[8]If you do not know, most beautiful of
      women,[p]
   follow the tracks of the sheep
and graze your young goats
   by the tents of the shepherds.

Lover

[9]I liken you, my darling, to a mare
   harnessed to one of the chariots[q] of
      Pharaoh.
[10]Your cheeks[r] are beautiful with
      earrings,
   your neck with strings of jewels.[s]
[11]We will make you earrings of gold,
   studded with silver.

Beloved

[12]While the king was at his table,
   my perfume spread its fragrance.[t]
[13]My lover is to me a sachet of myrrh[u]

1:1 [a]S 1Ki 4:32;
Ps 45 Title
1:2 [b]ver 4;
SS 4:10; 8:6
[c]S Ge 14:18;
S Jdg 9:13
1:3 [d]S Est 2:12;
S Ps 45:8
[e]S Ecc 7:1
[f]Ps 45:14
1:4 [g]Ps 45:15
[h]SS 2:3 [i]S ver 2
1:5 [j]SS 2:14; 4:3
[k]SS 5:16
[l]S Ge 25:13
1:6 [m]SS 2:15;
7:12; 8:12

1:7 [n]Isa 13:20
[o]S Ge 24:65
1:8 [p]SS 5:9; 6:1
1:9 [q]2Ch 1:17
1:10 [r]SS 5:13
[s]Isa 61:10
1:12 [t]SS 4:11-14
1:13 [u]S Ge 37:25

[a]Primarily on the basis of the gender of the Hebrew
pronouns used, male and female speakers are indicated in
the margins by the captions *Lover* and *Beloved*
respectively. The words of others are marked *Friends*. In
some instances the divisions and their captions are
debatable.   [b]4 The Hebrew is masculine singular.
[c]5 Or *Salma*

1:1 *Solomon's.* See Introduction: Title; Author and Date.
Song of Songs. Greatest of songs (see Introduction: Title).
1Ki 4:32 says that Solomon wrote 1,005 songs.
1:2–3 *kisses ... your love ... your perfumes.* Cf.
4:10–11, "your love ... your perfume ... Your lips."
1:2 *him ... his ... your.* These pronouns all refer to the
same person, the lover (Solomon). *love.* Expressions of
love—caresses, embraces and consummation (see v. 4;
4:10; 7:12; see also Pr 7:18; Eze 16:8; 23:17). *more delightful than wine.* See v. 4. In 4:10 the lover speaks similarly
of the beloved's love.
1:3 *perfumes.* Aromatic spices and gums blended in cosmetic oil. *your name.* The very mention of the lover's name
fills the air with a pleasant aroma. The Hebrew words for
"name" and "perfume" sound alike. *maidens.* Probably girls
of the court or of the royal city (see 6:8–9).
1:4 *king.* Solomon. *his chambers.* The king's private quarters. *We.* Probably the maidens of v. 3. *praise your love more
than wine.* For the reason given in v. 2.
1:5 *Dark.* Deeply browned by the sun (see v. 6); not
considered desirable. *daughters of Jerusalem.* Probably the
maidens of v. 3 and usually the "Friends" in the sectional
headings. *tents ... tent curtains.* Handwoven from black
goat hair. *Kedar.* See note on Isa 21:16.
1:6 *my own vineyard.* Her body, as in 8:12 (see 2:15).
Vineyard is an apt metaphor since it yields wine, and the
excitements of love are compared with those produced by
wine (see note on v. 2). The beloved is also compared to a
garden, yielding precious fruits for the lover (see note on

4:12).
1:7 *whom I love.* See 3:1. *where you graze your flock.* The
lover is portrayed as a shepherd. In v. 8 the beloved is
depicted as a shepherdess. *midday.* A time of rest in warm
climates. *veiled woman.* Prostitute (see Ge 38:14–15). The
beloved does not wish to look for her lover among the
shepherds, appearing as though she were a prostitute.
1:8 *beautiful.* The beloved; also in v. 15; 2:10,13; 4:1,7;
5:9; 6:1,4,10 ("fair"). The lover is called "handsome" in v.
16 (in Hebrew the same word as that for "beautiful"). *your
young goats.* The beloved is pictured as a shepherdess (see v.
7). *by the tents of the shepherds.* The beloved is instructed
to learn where the lover is by joining the shepherds in the
fields.
1:9 *my darling.* Used only of the beloved (see note on v.
13). *mare.* A flattering comparison, similar to Theocritus's
praise of the beautiful Helen of Troy (*Idyl,* 18.30–31). *harnessed to one of the chariots of Pharaoh.* Her beauty attracts
attention the way a mare would among the Egyptian chariot
stallions. According to 1Ki 10:28, Solomon imported horses
from Egypt (but see NIV text note there).
1:11 *We.* Perhaps the "daughters of Jerusalem."
1:12 *king.* Solomon. *at his table.* Reclining on his couch at
the table. *my perfume.* Nard, an aromatic oil extracted from
the roots of a perennial herb that grows in India (see
4:13–14; Mk 14:3; Jn 12:3).
1:13 *My lover.* Used only of the lover (see note on v. 9).
myrrh. An aromatic gum exuding from the bark of a balsam
tree that grows in Arabia, Ethiopia and India. It was com-

resting between my breasts.
¹⁴My lover ᵛ is to me a cluster of henna ʷ
blossoms
from the vineyards of En Gedi. ˣ

Lover

¹⁵How beautiful ʸ you are, my darling!
Oh, how beautiful!
Your eyes are doves. ᶻ

Beloved

¹⁶How handsome you are, my lover! ᵃ
Oh, how charming!
And our bed is verdant.

Lover

¹⁷The beams of our house are cedars; ᵇ
our rafters are firs.

*Beloved*ᵈ

2 I am a rose ᵉ ᶜ of Sharon, ᵈ
a lily ᵉ of the valleys.

Lover

²Like a lily among thorns
is my darling among the maidens.

Beloved

³Like an apple tree among the trees of
the forest
is my lover ᶠ among the young men.
I delight ᵍ to sit in his shade,
and his fruit is sweet to my taste. ʰ
⁴He has taken me to the banquet hall, ⁱ
and his banner ʲ over me is love. ⁱ
⁵Strengthen me with raisins,
refresh me with apples, ᵏ
for I am faint with love. ˡ

⁶His left arm is under my head,
and his right arm embraces me. ᵐ
⁷Daughters of Jerusalem, I charge you ⁿ
by the gazelles and by the does of the
field:
Do not arouse or awaken love
until it so desires. ᵒ

⁸Listen! My lover!
Look! Here he comes,
leaping across the mountains,
bounding over the hills. ᵖ
⁹My lover is like a gazelle ᵍ or a young
stag. ʳ
Look! There he stands behind our
wall,
gazing through the windows,
peering through the lattice.
¹⁰My lover spoke and said to me,
"Arise, my darling,
my beautiful one, and come with me.
¹¹See! The winter is past;
the rains are over and gone.
¹²Flowers appear on the earth;
the season of singing has come,
the cooing of doves
is heard in our land.
¹³The fig tree forms its early fruit; ˢ
the blossoming ᵗ vines spread their
fragrance.
Arise, come, my darling;
my beautiful one, come with me."

Lover

¹⁴My dove ᵘ in the clefts of the rock,
in the hiding places on the
mountainside,
show me your face,

1:14 ᵛver 16;
SS 2:3,17; 5:8
ʷSS 4:13
ˣS 1Sa 23:29;
S 2Ch 20:2
1:15 ʸSS 4:7; 7:6
ᶻPs 74:19;
SS 2:14; 4:1; 5:2,
12; 6:9; Jer 48:28
1:16 ᵃS ver 14
1:17 ᵇ1Ki 6:9
2:1 ᶜIsa 35:1
ᵈS 1Ch 27:29
ᵉSS 5:13;
Hos 14:5
2:3 ᶠS SS 1:14
ᵍSS 1:4 ʰSS 4:16
2:4 ⁱEst 1:11
ʲS Nu 1:52
2:5 ᵏSS 7:8
ˡSS 5:8

2:6 ᵐSS 8:3
2:7 ⁿSS 5:8
ᵒSS 3:5; 8:4
2:8 ᵖver 17;
SS 8:14
2:9 ᵍS 2Sa 2:18
ʳver 17; SS 8:14
2:13 ˢIsa 28:4;
Jer 24:2;
Hos 9:10;
Mic 7:1; Na 3:12
ᵗSS 7:12
2:14 ᵘS Ge 8:8;
S SS 1:15

ᵈ *l* Or *Lover*   ᵉ *l* Possibly a member of the crocus
family

---

monly used as an alluring feminine perfume (Est 2:12; Pr
7:17). It was also used to perfume royal nuptial robes (Ps
45:8). The Magi brought myrrh to the young Jesus as a gift fit
for a king (Mt 2:2,11). Myrrh was an ingredient in the holy
anointing oil (Ex 30:23).
1:14 *henna.* A shrub of Palestine (perhaps the cypress)
with tightly clustered, aromatic blossoms. *En Gedi.* An oasis
watered by a spring, located on the west side of the Dead
Sea. David sought refuge there from King Saul (1Sa 24:1).
1:15 *How beautiful...darling!* See 4:1; 6:4; cf. v. 16. *my
darling.* See note on v. 9. *doves.* See 4:1.
1:16 *handsome.* See note on v. 8 ("beautiful"). *verdant.*
The lovers lie together in the field under the trees.
2:1 *rose.* See NIV text note and Isa 35:1–2. *Sharon.* The
fertile coastal plain south of Mount Carmel (see map No. 2
at the end of the Study Bible). *lily.* Probably either lotus or
anemone.
2:2 *my darling.* See note on 1:9. *maidens.* See note on 1:3.
2:3 *apple tree.* The precise nature of this fruit tree is
uncertain.
2:4 *banner.* See 6:4; Nu 2:2; Ps 20:5. The king's love for
her is displayed for all to see, like a large military banner.
2:5 *raisins...apples.* Probably metaphors for love's ca-

resses and embraces.
2:7 A recurring refrain in the Song (see 3:5; 8:4; cf. 5:8).
It is always spoken by the beloved and always in a context of
physical intimacy with her lover. *Daughters of Jerusalem.*
See note on 1:5. *charge.* Place under oath. *gazelles...does.*
Perhaps in the imaginative language of love the gazelles and
does are portrayed as witnesses to the oath. This would be in
harmony with the author's frequent reference to nature.
until it so desires. Out of the beloved's experience of love
comes wise admonition that love is not to be artificially
stimulated; utter spontaneity is essential to its genuine truth
and beauty.
2:9 *gazelle.* Celebrated for its form and beauty. *young stag.*
An apt simile for youthful vigor (cf. Isa 35:6). *gazing...
lattice.* The eager lover tries to catch sight of the beloved
while she is still preparing herself for their meeting.
2:10 *Arise...with me.* See v. 13; cf. 7:11–13. *my beautiful one.* See note on 1:8.
2:11–13 The first signs of spring appear (see 6:11;
7:12)—the time of love.
2:14 *dove...on the mountainside.* Cf. Ps 55:6–8; Jer
48:28.

let me hear your voice;
for your voice is sweet,
and your face is lovely. *v*
¹⁵Catch for us the foxes, *w*
the little foxes
that ruin the vineyards, *x*
our vineyards that are in bloom. *y*

Beloved

¹⁶My lover is mine and I am his; *z*
he browses among the lilies. *a*
¹⁷Until the day breaks
and the shadows flee, *b*
turn, my lover, *c*
and be like a gazelle
or like a young stag *d*
on the rugged hills. *f* *e*

3 All night long on my bed
I looked *f* for the one my heart loves;
I looked for him but did not find him.
²I will get up now and go about the city,
through its streets and squares;
I will search for the one my heart loves.
So I looked for him but did not find
him.
³The watchmen found me
as they made their rounds in the
city. *g*
"Have you seen the one my heart
loves?"
⁴Scarcely had I passed them
when I found the one my heart loves.
I held him and would not let him go
till I had brought him to my mother's
house, *h*
to the room of the one who
conceived me. *i*
⁵Daughters of Jerusalem, I charge you *j*

by the gazelles and by the does of the
field:
Do not arouse or awaken love
until it so desires. *k*

⁶Who is this coming up from the desert *l*
like a column of smoke,
perfumed with myrrh *m* and incense
made from all the spices *n* of the
merchant?
⁷Look! It is Solomon's carriage,
escorted by sixty warriors, *o*
the noblest of Israel,
⁸all of them wearing the sword,
all experienced in battle,
each with his sword at his side,
prepared for the terrors of the night. *p*
⁹King Solomon made for himself the
carriage;
he made it of wood from Lebanon.
¹⁰Its posts he made of silver,
its base of gold.
Its seat was upholstered with purple,
its interior lovingly inlaid
by *g* the daughters of Jerusalem.
¹¹Come out, you daughters of Zion, *q*
and look at King Solomon wearing
the crown,
the crown with which his mother
crowned him
on the day of his wedding,
the day his heart rejoiced. *r*

Lover

4 How beautiful you are, my darling!
Oh, how beautiful!

Cross references (center column):

2:14 *v* S SS 1:5
2:15 *w* Jdg 15:4
x S SS 1:6
y SS 7:12
2:16 *z* SS 7:10
a SS 4:5; 6:3
2:17 *b* SS 4:6
c S SS 1:14 *d* S ver
9 *e* S ver 8
3:1 *f* SS 5:6
3:3 *g* SS 5:7
3:4 *h* SS 8:2
i SS 6:9; 8:5
3:5 *j* S SS 2:7

k SS 8:4
3:6 *l* SS 8:5
m SS 4:6,14
n Ex 30:34
3:7 *o* 1Sa 8:11
3:8 *p* SS Job 15:22;
Ps 91:5
3:11 *q* Isa 3:16;
4:4; 32:9-13
r Isa 54:5; 62:5;
Jer 3:14

Footnotes:

f17 Or *the hills of Bether*   *g10* Or *its inlaid interior a
gift of love / from*

2:15 Perhaps spoken by the beloved. *vineyards.* As in 1:6 ("my own vineyard"), probably a metaphor for the lovers' physical beauty. Thus the desire is expressed that the lovers be kept safe from whatever ("foxes") might mar their mutual attractiveness. *in bloom.* Their attractiveness is in its prime.
2:16 *My lover is mine and I am his.* See 6:3; 7:10. They belong to each other exclusively in a relationship that allows no intrusion. *browses among the lilies.* The lover is compared to a gazelle (see v. 17). The browsing is a metaphor for the lover's intimate enjoyment of her charms (see 6:2-3).
3:1 This verse begins a new moment in love's experience. *All night long.* Night, with its freedom from the distractions of the day, allows the heart to be filled with its own preoccupations.
3:3 *watchmen.* Were stationed at the city gates (see Ne 3:29; 11:19; 13:22) and on the walls (see 5:7; 2Sa 13:34; 18:24-27; 2Ki 9:17-20; Ps 127:1; Isa 52:8; 62:6). Apparently they also patrolled the streets at night (see 5:7).
3:4 *mother's.* Mothers are referred to frequently in the Song; fathers are never mentioned.
3:5 See note on 2:7. Once again the charge occurs at the moment of intimacy.
3:6-11 Perhaps spoken by the friends (see 8:5). If so, this section probably portrays the wedding procession of Solo-

mon and his bride approaching the city.
3:6 This verse begins a new moment in the relationship. *Who . . . desert.* See 8:5, where the reference is to the beloved. *desert.* Uncultivated seasonal grasslands. *smoke.* Incense (see note on Ex 30:34). *of the merchant.* Imported.
3:7 *carriage.* A richly adorned royal conveyance, a palanquin (see vv. 9-10).
3:8 *terrors of the night.* See Ps 91:5.
3:10 *posts.* Supporting the canopy. *silver . . . gold.* Probably metals that overlay the Lebanon wood. *purple.* See notes on 7:5; Ex 25:4.
3:11 *daughters of Zion.* Elsewhere "daughters of Jerusalem" (see note on 1:5). *crown.* A wedding wreath (see Isa 61:10). *mother.* See note on v. 4. Here the reference is to Bathsheba.
4:1-7 For other exuberant descriptions of the beloved's beauty see 6:4-9; 7:1-7.
4:1b-2 See 6:5b-6.
4:1 *How beautiful . . . darling!* See 1:15 and note. *eyes behind your veil.* With the rest of her face concealed, the lover's attention is focused on the beloved's eyes. *doves.* See 1:15 and note. *flock of goats.* The goats of Canaan were usually black (see note on 1:5). The lover's hair was also black (5:11). *descending from Mount Gilead.* The beloved's

Your eyes behind your veil[s] are
　doves.[t]
Your hair is like a flock of goats
　descending from Mount Gilead.[u]
[2]Your teeth are like a flock of sheep just
　shorn,
　coming up from the washing.
Each has its twin;
　not one of them is alone.[v]
[3]Your lips are like a scarlet ribbon;
　your mouth[w] is lovely.[x]
Your temples behind your veil
　are like the halves of a
　pomegranate.[y]
[4]Your neck is like the tower[z] of David,
　built with elegance[h];
on it hang a thousand shields,[a]
　all of them shields of warriors.
[5]Your two breasts[b] are like two fawns,
　like twin fawns of a gazelle[c]
　that browse among the lilies.[d]
[6]Until the day breaks
　and the shadows flee,[e]
I will go to the mountain of myrrh[f]
　and to the hill of incense.
[7]All beautiful[g] you are, my darling;
　there is no flaw[h] in you.

[8]Come with me from Lebanon, my
　bride,[i]
　come with me from Lebanon.
Descend from the crest of Amana,

from the top of Senir,[j] the summit of
　Hermon,[k]
from the lions' dens
　and the mountain haunts of the
　leopards.
[9]You have stolen my heart, my sister, my
　bride;[l]
you have stolen my heart
　with one glance of your eyes,
　with one jewel of your necklace.[m]
[10]How delightful[n] is your love[o], my
　sister, my bride!
How much more pleasing is your love
　than wine,[p]
and the fragrance of your perfume[q]
　than any spice!
[11]Your lips drop sweetness as the
　honeycomb, my bride;
milk and honey are under your
　tongue.[r]
The fragrance of your garments is like
　that of Lebanon.[s]
[12]You are a garden[t] locked up, my sister,
　my bride;[u]
you are a spring enclosed, a sealed
　fountain.[v]
[13]Your plants are an orchard of
　pomegranates[w]
with choice fruits,
　with henna[x] and nard,
[14]　nard and saffron,

4:1 [s]S Ge 24:65;
[t]S SS 1:15;
[u]Ge 37:25;
Nu 32:1; SS 6:5;
Jer 22:6; Mic 7:14
4:2 [v]SS 6:6
4:3 [w]SS 5:16
[x]S SS 1:5 [y]SS 6:7
4:4 [z]S Ps 144:12
[a]Eze 27:10
4:5 [b]SS 7:3
[c]S Pr 5:19
[d]SS 2:16
4:6 [e]SS 2:17
[f]S SS 3:6
4:7 [g]S SS 1:15
[h]SS 5:2
4:8 [i]ver 9,12;
SS 5:1
[j]S Dt 3:9
[k]S 1Ch 5:23
4:9 [l]S ver 8
[m]S Ge 41:42;
S Ps 73:6
4:10 [n]SS 7:6
[o]S SS 1:2
[p]S Jdg 9:13 [q]ver
16; S Ps 45:8;
Isa 57:9
4:11 [r]S Ps 19:10;
SS 5:1 [s]Hos 14:6
4:12 [t]ver 16;
SS 5:1; 6:2;
Isa 5:7 [u]S ver 8
[v]Pr 5:15-18
4:13 [w]SS 7:12
[x]SS 1:14

[h]4 The meaning of the Hebrew for this word is uncertain.

---

black tresses flowing from her head remind the lover of a flock of sleek black goats streaming down one of the hills of Gilead (noted for its good pasturage).
4:2 *just shorn.* Clean and white. *coming up from the washing.* Still wet, like moistened teeth.
4:3 *Your lips . . . scarlet.* Perhaps the beloved painted her lips, like Egyptian women. *temples behind . . . veil.* See note on v. 1. *halves of a pomegranate.* Round and blushed with red.
4:4 The beloved's erect, bespangled neck is like a tower on the city wall adorned with warriors' shields (cf. 7:4).
4:5 See 7:3. *fawns.* Representing tender, delicate beauty, and promise rather than full growth (cf. 8:8). *gazelle.* See note on 2:9. Elsewhere the simile is used of the lover. *browse among the lilies.* For a different use of this phrase see 2:16 and note.
4:6 *Until . . . shadows flee.* See 2:17. *mountain of myrrh . . . hill of incense.* Metaphors for lovers' intimacy.
4:8 To the lover the beloved seems to have withdrawn as if to a remote mountain. *Lebanon . . . Amana . . . Hermon.* Mountain peaks on the northern horizon. *Senir.* Amorite name for Mount Hermon (Dt 3:9).
4:9 *my sister.* For lovers to address each other as "brother" and "sister" was common in the love poetry of the ancient Near East (see vv. 10,12; 5:1). *one glance of your eyes.* See 6:5 and note.
4:10 *more pleasing . . . than wine.* See note on 1:2. *fragrance of your perfume.* See 1:3. *spice.* See v. 14; 5:1,13; 6:2; 8:14. Spice was an imported luxury item (see 1Ki 10:2,10,25; Eze 27:22). Spices were used for fragrance in the holy anointing oil (Ex 25:6; 30:23-25; 35:8) and for

fragrant incense (Ex 25:6; 35:8) as well as for perfume.
4:11 *Your lips drop sweetness.* The beloved speaks to him of love (cf. Pr 5:3; 16:24). People in the ancient Near East associated sweetness with the delights of love. *milk and honey.* Perhaps reminiscent of the description of the promised land (see note on Ex 3:8). *under your tongue.* See Job 20:12; Ps 10:7.
4:12 *garden.* A place of sensual delights (see v. 16; 5:1; 6:2; see also note on 1:6). *locked up . . . enclosed . . . sealed.* Metaphors for the beloved's virginity—or perhaps for the fact that she keeps herself exclusively for her husband. *spring . . . fountain.* Sources of refreshment; metaphors for the beloved as a sexual partner, as in Pr 5:15-20.
4:13-15 Verses 13-14 elaborate on the garden metaphor of v. 12a, and v. 15 on the fountain metaphor of v. 12b. The trees and spices in vv. 13-14 are mostly exotic, referring to the beloved's charms.
4:13 *Your plants.* All the beloved's features that delight the lover. *orchard.* Hebrew *pardes* (from which the English word "paradise" comes), a loanword from Old Persian meaning "enclosure" or "park." In Ne 2:8 and Ecc 2:5 it refers to royal parks and forests. *henna.* See note on 1:14. *nard.* See note on 1:12.
4:14 *saffron.* A plant of the crocus family bearing purple or white flowers, parts of which, when dried, were used as a cooking spice. *calamus.* An imported (see Jer 6:20), aromatic spice cane, used also in the holy anointing oil (Ex 30:23,25, "cane") and in incense (Isa 43:23-24). *cinnamon.* Used in the holy anointing oil (Ex 30:23,25). *myrrh.* See note on 1:13. *aloes.* Aromatic aloes, used to perfume royal nuptial robes (Ps 45:8). Pr 7:17 says that the adulteress perfumed

calamus and cinnamon, *y*
with every kind of incense tree,
with myrrh *z* and aloes *a*
and all the finest spices. *b*
¹⁵You are *i* a garden *c* fountain, *d*
a well of flowing water
streaming down from Lebanon.

Beloved

¹⁶Awake, north wind,
and come, south wind!
Blow on my garden, *e*
that its fragrance *f* may spread
abroad.
Let my lover *g* come into his garden
and taste its choice fruits. *h*

Lover

5 I have come into my garden, *i* my
sister, my bride; *j*
I have gathered my myrrh with my
spice.
I have eaten my honeycomb and my
honey;
I have drunk my wine and my milk. *k*

Friends

Eat, O friends, and drink;
drink your fill, O lovers.

Beloved

²I slept but my heart was awake.
Listen! My lover is knocking:
"Open to me, my sister, my darling,
my dove, *l* my flawless *m* one. *n*
My head is drenched with dew,
my hair with the dampness of the
night."
³I have taken off my robe—
must I put it on again?
I have washed my feet—
must I soil them again?
⁴My lover thrust his hand through the
latch-opening;

my heart began to pound for him.
⁵I arose to open for my lover,
and my hands dripped with myrrh, *o*
my fingers with flowing myrrh,
on the handles of the lock.
⁶I opened for my lover, *p*
but my lover had left; he was gone. *q*
My heart sank at his departure. *i*
I looked *r* for him but did not find him.
I called him but he did not answer.
⁷The watchmen found me
as they made their rounds in the
city. *s*
They beat me, they bruised me;
they took away my cloak,
those watchmen of the walls!
⁸O daughters of Jerusalem, I charge
you *t* —
if you find my lover, *u*
what will you tell him?
Tell him I am faint with love. *v*

Friends

⁹How is your beloved better than others,
most beautiful of women? *w*
How is your beloved better than others,
that you charge us so?

Beloved

¹⁰My lover is radiant and ruddy,
outstanding among ten thousand. *x*
¹¹His head is purest gold;
his hair is wavy
and black as a raven.
¹²His eyes are like doves *y*
by the water streams,
washed in milk, *z*
mounted like jewels.
¹³His cheeks *a* are like beds of spice *b*
yielding perfume.
His lips are like lilies *c*
dripping with myrrh. *d*

4:14 *y*S Ex 30:23
*z*S SS 3:6
*a*S Nu 24:6
*b*SS 1:12
4:15 *c*Isa 27:2;
58:11; Jer 31:12
*d*Pr 5:18
4:16 *e*S ver 12
*f*S ver 10 *g*SS 7:13
*h*SS 2:3
5:1 *i*S SS 4:12
*j*S SS 4:8
*k*S SS 4:11;
Isa 55:1; Joel 3:18
5:2 *l*S SS 1:15
*m*SS 4:7 *n*SS 6:9

5:5 *o*ver 13
5:6 *p*SS 6:1
*q*SS 6:2 *r*SS 3:1
5:7 *s*SS 3:3
5:8 *t*SS 2:7
*u*SS 1:14
*v*SS 2:5
5:9 *w*SS 1:8
5:10 *x*Ps 45:2
5:12 *y*S SS 1:15
*z*Ge 49:12
5:13 *a*SS 1:10
*b*SS 6:2 *c*S SS 2:1
*d*ver 5

i 15 Or *I am* (spoken by the *Beloved*)   *16* Or *heart had gone out to him when he spoke*

4:15 *flowing.* Fresh, not stagnant. *streaming ... from Lebanon.* Fresh, cool, sparkling water from the snowfields on the Lebanon mountains.
4:16 May the fragrance of my charms be wafted about to draw my lover to me so that we may enjoy love's intimacies. *his garden.* She belongs to him and she yields herself to her lover (see 6:2).
5:1 The lover claims the beloved as his garden and enjoys all her delights. *my sister.* See note on 4:9. *Eat ... O lovers.* The friends of the lovers applaud their enjoyment of love.
5:2–8 See 3:1–5 and note on 3:1.
5:2 *I slept ... was awake.* Love holds sway even in sleep—just as a new mother sleeps with an ear open to her baby's slightest whimper.
5:3 Instinctive reaction raises a foolish complaint before the language of love takes over.

5:5 *my hands ... flowing myrrh.* Love's eager imagination extravagantly lotioned the beloved's hands with perfume.
5:9 The friends' question provides an opportunity for the beloved to describe the beauty of her lover—which she does only here.
5:10 *ruddy.* See 1Sa 16:12.
5:11 *black.* The beloved's hair was also black (see note on 4:1).
5:12 *doves.* See note on 1:15. *by the water streams.* The lover's eyes sparkle. *washed in milk.* Describing the white of the eye.
5:13 *spice ... lilies.* These similes probably compare sensuous effects rather than appearances, as do the following similes and metaphors, at least in part. *lilies.* See note on 2:1. *dripping with myrrh.* Love's pleasant excitements are aroused by the lover's lips.

¹⁴His arms are rods of gold
    set with chrysolite.
His body is like polished ivory
    decorated with sapphires.ᵏ ᵉ
¹⁵His legs are pillars of marble
    set on bases of pure gold.
His appearance is like Lebanon,ᶠ
    choice as its cedars.
¹⁶His mouthᵍ is sweetness itself;
    he is altogether lovely.
This is my lover,ʰ this my friend,
    O daughters of Jerusalem.ⁱ

Friends

6 Where has your loverʲ gone,
    most beautiful of women?ᵏ
Which way did your lover turn,
    that we may look for him with you?

Beloved

²My lover has goneˡ down to his
        garden,ᵐ
    to the beds of spices,ⁿ
to browse in the gardens
    and to gather lilies.
³I am my lover's and my lover is mine;ᵒ
    he browses among the lilies.ᵖ

Lover

⁴You are beautiful, my darling, as
        Tirzah,�q
lovely as Jerusalem,ʳ
    majestic as troops with banners.ˢ
⁵Turn your eyes from me;
    they overwhelm me.
Your hair is like a flock of goats
    descending from Gilead.ᵗ

⁶Your teeth are like a flock of sheep
    coming up from the washing.
Each has its twin,
    not one of them is alone.ᵘ
⁷Your temples behind your veilᵛ
    are like the halves of a
        pomegranate.ʷ
⁸Sixty queensˣ there may be,
    and eighty concubines,ʸ
    and virgins beyond number;
⁹but my dove,ᶻ my perfect one,ᵃ is
        unique,
    the only daughter of her mother,
    the favorite of the one who bore
        her.ᵇ
The maidens saw her and called her
        blessed;
    the queens and concubines praised
        her.

Friends

¹⁰Who is this that appears like the dawn,
    fair as the moon, bright as the sun,
    majestic as the stars in procession?

Lover

¹¹I went down to the grove of nut trees
    to look at the new growth in the
        valley,
to see if the vines had budded
    or the pomegranates were in bloom.ᶜ
¹²Before I realized it,
    my desire set me among the royal
        chariots of my people.ˡ

5:14 ᵉS Job 28:6
5:15 ᶠ1Ki 4:33;
SS 7:4
5:16 ᵍSS 4:3
ʰSS 7:9 ⁱSS 1:5
6:1 ʲSS 5:6
ᵏSS 1:8
6:2 ˡSS 5:6
ᵐSS 4:12
ⁿSS 5:13
6:3 ᵒSS 7:10
ᵖSS 2:16
6:4 qS Jos 12:24;
S 1Ki 15:33
ʳPs 48:2; 50:2
ˢS Nu 1:52
6:5 ᵗS SS 4:1

6:6 ᵘSS 4:2
6:7 ᵛS Ge 24:65
ʷSS 4:3
6:8 ˣPs 45:9
ʸS Ge 22:24;
S Est 2:14
6:9 ᶻSS 1:15
ᵃSS 5:2 ᵇS SS 3:4
6:11 ᶜSS 7:12

ᵏ*14* Or *lapis lazuli*   ˡ*12* Or *among the chariots of
Amminadab;* or *among the chariots of the people of the
prince*

5:14 *chrysolite.* See note on Eze 1:16. *sapphires.* Hebrew
sappir (from which the English word "sapphire" comes).
5:15 *appearance is like Lebanon.* Awesome and majestic.
choice as its cedars. The cedars of Lebanon were renowned
throughout the ancient Near East, and their wood was desired for adorning temples and palaces.
5:16 *mouth.* The lover's kisses and loving speech. *daughters of Jerusalem.* See note on 1:5.
6:1 The question asked by the friends forms a transition
from the beloved's description of the lover to her delighted
acknowledgment of his intimacy with her and the exclusiveness of their relationship.
6:2 *his garden.* The beloved. *beds of spices.* Her sensuous
attractions (cf. 5:13). *browse.* Enjoy (see note on 2:16).
gather lilies. See note on 2:1. The lover, enjoying intimacies
with the beloved, is compared to a graceful gazelle (see notes
on 2:7,9), nibbling from lily to lily in undisturbed enjoyment
of exotic delicacies.
6:3 *I . . . mine.* See note on 2:16. Notice the reversal; here
her yielding to her lover is emphasized.
6:4 *Tirzah.* An old Canaanite city in the middle of the land
(see Jos 12:24). It was chosen by Jeroboam I (930–909 B.C.)
as the first royal city of the northern kingdom (see 1Ki 14:17;
see also 1Ki 15:21; 16:23–24). The meaning of its name
("pleasure, beauty") suggests that it was a beautiful site,

perhaps explaining why the author here sets it alongside
Jerusalem (though what constituted the beauty of Tirzah is
not known). Comparison of the beloved's beauty to that of
cities was perhaps not so unusual in the ancient Near East,
since cities were regularly depicted as women (see note on
2Ki 19:21). *majestic.* See v. 10. *as troops with banners.* The
beloved's noble beauty evoked in the lover emotions like
those aroused by a troop marching under its banners.
6:5–7 See 4:1–3 and notes.
6:5 *your eyes . . . overwhelm me.* The beloved's eyes
awaken in the lover such intensity of love that he is held
captive (see 4:9).
6:8 *queens . . . concubines . . . virgins.* The reference is
either to Solomon's harem or to all the beautiful women of
the realm.
6:9 *perfect one.* Cf. "flawless one" in 5:2. *only daughter.*
Not literally, but the one uniquely loved (cf. Ge 22:2; Jdg
11:34; Pr 4:3). *maidens . . . praised her.* All the other
women praised her beauty (see 1:8; 5:9; 6:1).
6:10 See 5:9; 6:1.
6:11 *nut.* Perhaps walnut. *look . . . in the valley.* For the
first signs of spring (see note on 2:11–13).
6:12 The most obscure verse in the Song. See NIV text
note for other possible translations. *chariots.* Solomon was
famous for his chariots (1Ki 10:26).

Friends

¹³Come back, come back, O Shulammite;
    come back, come back, that we may
        gaze on you!

Lover

Why would you gaze on the
        Shulammite
    as on the dance *d* of Mahanaim?

7 How beautiful your sandaled feet,
        O prince's *e* daughter!
    Your graceful legs are like jewels,
        the work of a craftsman's hands.
²Your navel is a rounded goblet
        that never lacks blended wine.
    Your waist is a mound of wheat
        encircled by lilies.
³Your breasts *f* are like two fawns,
        twins of a gazelle.
⁴Your neck is like an ivory tower. *g*
    Your eyes are the pools of Heshbon *h*
        by the gate of Bath Rabbim.
    Your nose is like the tower of Lebanon *i*
        looking toward Damascus.
⁵Your head crowns you like Mount
        Carmel. *j*
    Your hair is like royal tapestry;
        the king is held captive by its tresses.
⁶How beautiful *k* you are and how
        pleasing,
    O love, with your delights! *l*
⁷Your stature is like that of the palm,
        and your breasts *m* like clusters of
            fruit.
⁸I said, "I will climb the palm tree;
    I will take hold of its fruit."

6:13	*d*S Ex 15:20
7:1	*e*Ps 45:13
7:3	*f*SS 4:5
7:4	*g*S Ps 144:12
	*h*Nu 21:26
7:5	*i*SS 5:15
7:5	*j*Isa 35:2
7:6	*k*S SS 1:15
	*l*SS 4:10
7:7	*m*SS 4:5

7:8	*n*SS 2:5
7:9	*o*SS 5:16
7:10	*p*Ps 45:11
	*q*SS 2:16; 6:3
7:12	*r*S SS 1:6
	*s*SS 2:15 *t*SS 2:13
	*u*SS 4:13
	*v*SS 6:11
7:13	*w*S Ge 30:14
	*x*SS 4:16

May your breasts be like the clusters of
        the vine,
    the fragrance of your breath like
        apples, *n*
⁹   and your mouth like the best wine.

Beloved

May the wine go straight to my lover, *o*
    flowing gently over lips and teeth. *m*
¹⁰I belong to my lover,
    and his desire *p* is for me. *q*
¹¹Come, my lover, let us go to the
        countryside,
    let us spend the night in the
        villages. *n*
¹²Let us go early to the vineyards *r*
    to see if the vines have budded, *s*
    if their blossoms *t* have opened,
    and if the pomegranates *u* are in
        bloom *v* —
    there I will give you my love.
¹³The mandrakes *w* send out their
        fragrance,
    and at our door is every delicacy,
both new and old,
    that I have stored up for you, my
        lover. *x*

8 If only you were to me like a brother,
        who was nursed at my mother's
            breasts!
    Then, if I found you outside,
        I would kiss you,
        and no one would despise me.

m 9 Septuagint, Aquila, Vulgate and Syriac; Hebrew *lips of
sleepers*   *n 11* Or *henna bushes*

6:13 *Shulammite.* The beloved. It is either a variant of
"Shunammite" (see 1Ki 1:3), i.e., a girl from Shunem (see
Jos 19:18), or a feminine form of the word "Solomon,"
meaning "Solomon's girl." In ancient Semitic languages the
letters *l* and *n* were sometimes interchanged.

7:1–7 Here the description moves up from the feet rather
than down from the head (cf. 5:11–15).

7:1 Cf. v. 6. *prince's daughter.* Alludes to the nobility of
her beauty (see Ps 45:13). *graceful.* The Hebrew for this
word suggests "curvaceous."

7:2 *goblet.* A large, two-handled, ring-based bowl (see Ex
24:6; Isa 22:24; see also Am 6:6). *encircled by lilies.* The
beloved perhaps wore a loose garland of flowers around her
waist.

7:3 See note on 4:5.

7:4 *ivory tower.* Mixed imagery, referring to shape as well
as to color and texture. *pools.* The beloved's eyes reflect like
the surface of a pool; or the imagery may depict serenity and
gentleness. *Heshbon.* Once the royal city of King Sihon (Nu
21:26), it was blessed with an abundant supply of spring
water. *Bath Rabbim.* Means "daughter of many"; perhaps a
popular name for Heshbon. *tower of Lebanon.* Perhaps a
military tower on the northern frontier of Solomon's kingdom, but more likely the beautiful, towering Lebanon mountain range.

7:5 *Mount Carmel.* A promontory midway along the western coast of the kingdom, with a wooded top and known for
its beauty. *royal tapestry.* A reference to purple, royal cloth,
as in 3:10 (see note on Ex 25:4). *king.* Solomon. *tresses.* The
Hebrew for this word suggests a similarity to flowing water
(cf. 4:1; 6:5).

7:7 *palm.* The stately date palm.

7:8 *I said.* To myself. *I will climb.* The beloved's beauty
draws him irresistibly. *vine.* Grape. *apples.* Perhaps the fragrance of apple blossoms (but see note on 2:3).

7:9 *May the wine . . . to my lover.* The beloved offers the
wine (see 5:1) of her love to her lover.

7:10 *I belong.* See notes on 2:16; 6:3. *desire.* Cf. Ge 3:
16.

7:11–12 In 2:10–13 the beloved reports a similar invitation from her lover.

7:12 *I will give you my love.* She offers herself completely
to her lover.

7:13 *mandrakes.* Short-stemmed herbs associated with
fertility (see note on Ge 30:14). The odor of its blossom is
pungent. *at our door.* Where the lovers meet. *every delicacy.*
Metaphor for the delights the beloved has for her lover from
her "garden" (cf. 4:13–14). *both new and old.* Those already shared and those still to be enjoyed.

8:1 *no one would despise me.* The beloved could openly
show affection without any public disgrace.

²I would lead you
  and bring you to my mother's
    house*y* —
she who has taught me.
I would give you spiced wine to drink,
  the nectar of my pomegranates.
³His left arm is under my head
  and his right arm embraces me.*z*
⁴Daughters of Jerusalem, I charge you:
  Do not arouse or awaken love
    until it so desires.*a*

Friends

⁵Who is this coming up from the desert*b*
  leaning on her lover?

Beloved

Under the apple tree I roused you;
  there your mother conceived*c* you,
  there she who was in labor gave you
    birth.
⁶Place me like a seal over your heart,
  like a seal on your arm;
for love*d* is as strong as death,
  its jealousy°*e* unyielding as the
    grave.*P*
It burns like blazing fire,
  like a mighty flame.*q*
⁷Many waters cannot quench love;
  rivers cannot wash it away.
If one were to give

all the wealth of his house for love,
  it*r* would be utterly scorned.*f*

Friends

⁸We have a young sister,
  and her breasts are not yet grown.
What shall we do for our sister
  for the day she is spoken for?
⁹If she is a wall,
  we will build towers of silver on her.
If she is a door,
  we will enclose her with panels of
    cedar.

Beloved

¹⁰I am a wall,
  and my breasts are like towers.
Thus I have become in his eyes
  like one bringing contentment.
¹¹Solomon had a vineyard*g* in Baal
    Hamon;
  he let out his vineyard to tenants.
  Each was to bring for its fruit
    a thousand shekels*s* *h* of silver.
¹²But my own vineyard*i* is mine to give;
  the thousand shekels are for you,
    O Solomon,
  and two hundred*t* are for those who
    tend its fruit.

8:2 *y* SS 3:4
8:3 *z* SS 2:6
8:4 *a* SS 2:7; S 3:5
8:5 *b* SS 3:6
  c SS 3:4
8:6 *d* SS 1:2
  e S Nu 5:14
8:7 *f* S Pr 6:35

8:11 *g* Ecc 2:4
  h Isa 7:23
8:12 *i* SS 1:6

°6 Or *ardor* *P*6 Hebrew *Sheol* *q*6 Or / *like the
very flame of the* Lord *r*7 Or *he* *s*11 That is,
about 25 pounds (about 11.5 kilograms); also in verse 12
*t*12 That is, about 5 pounds (about 2.3 kilograms)

8:2 *I would give you.* She would offer her lover the delights
of her love. *nectar.* The Hebrew for this word refers to
intoxicating juices.
8:4 See 2:7 and note.
8:5 *Who . . . desert.* See 3:6. *Under the apple tree.* In the
ancient world, sexual union and birth were often associated
with fruit trees.
8:6–7 *love is . . . grave. It burns . . . flame. Many waters
. . . away.* These three wisdom statements (see Introduction
to Proverbs: Wisdom Literature) characterize marital love as
the strongest, most unyielding and invincible force in human
experience. With these statements the Song reaches its literary climax and discloses its purpose.
8:6 *seal.* Seals were precious to their owners, as personal as
their names (see note on Ge 38:18). *arm.* Probably a poetic
synonym for "hand." *unyielding as the grave.* As the grave
will not give up the dead, so love will not surrender the loved
one. *mighty flame.* The Hebrew expression conveys the idea
of a most intense flame, hinting that it has been kindled by
the Lord (see NIV text note).
8:7 *Many waters.* Words that suggest not only the ocean
depths (see Ps 107:23) but also the primeval waters that the
people of the ancient Near East regarded as a permanent
threat to the world (see note on Ps 32:6). The waters were
also associated with the realm of the dead (see note on Ps
30:1). *If one . . . scorned.* A fourth wisdom statement (see
note on vv. 6–7), declaring love's unsurpassed worth.
8:8–14 In the closing lines of the Song, the words of the
brothers (vv. 8–9), the beloved's reference to her own vine-

yard (v. 12) and her final reference to Solomon (vv. 11–12)
suggest a return to the beginning of the Song (see 1:2–7).
The lines may recall the beloved's development into the age
for love and marriage and the blossoming of her relationship
with her lover.
8:8 In the ancient Near East, brothers often were guardians
of their sisters, especially in matters pertaining to marriage
(see Ge 24:50–60; 34:13–27). *the day she is spoken for.*
Marriage was often contracted at an early age.
8:9 This imaginative verse probably expresses the brothers'
determination to defend their young sister (the beloved) until
her proper time for love and marriage has come. Or it may
mean that the brothers are concerned to see that she is
properly adorned for marriage before she is spoken for.
8:10 *I . . . like towers.* In contrast to the time when she was
watched over by her brothers, the beloved rejoices in her
maturity (see Eze 16:7–8). *his.* The lover's.
8:11–12 *thousand shekels . . . two hundred.* Whether
these figures are to be taken literally (see Isa 7:23) is uncertain.
8:11 *Baal Hamon.* Location unknown. The Hebrew *hamon* sometimes means "wealth" or "abundance"; hence
Baal (i.e., "lord") Hamon could mean "lord of abundance,"
bringing to mind Solomon's great wealth.
8:12 *my own vineyard.* Her body (see note on 1:6). *mine to
give.* As Solomon is master of his vineyard, so the beloved is
mistress of her attractions to dispense them as she will. She
offers Solomon the owner's portion of her vineyard.

Lover

¹³You who dwell in the gardens
    with friends in attendance,
    let me hear your voice!

Beloved

¹⁴Come away, my lover,
    and be like a gazelle ʲ
or like a young stag ᵏ
    on the spice-laden mountains. ˡ

8:14 /S Pr 5:19
ᵏS SS 2:9
/S SS 2:8

8:13 *in the gardens.* In 7:11–12 the beloved invites her lover to accompany her to the countryside and the vineyards. Here the imagery places her appropriately in a garden. *friends.* Male; perhaps the companions of the lover (see 1:7).

let me hear your voice. See 2:14.
8:14 *be like a gazelle or . . . stag.* Display your virile strength and agility for my delight (see note on 2:9). *on the spice-laden mountains.* Cf. 2:17.

ISAIAH

Author

Isaiah son of Amoz is often thought of as the greatest of the writing prophets. His name means "The LORD saves." He was a contemporary of Amos, Hosea and Micah, beginning his ministry in 740 B.C., the year King Uzziah died (see note on 6:1). According to an unsubstantiated Jewish tradition (*The Ascension of Isaiah*), he was sawed in half during the reign of Manasseh (cf. Heb 11:37). Isaiah was married and had at least two sons, Shear-Jashub (7:3) and Maher-Shalal-Hash-Baz (8:3). He probably spent most of his life in Jerusalem, enjoying his greatest influence under King Hezekiah (see 37:1-2). Isaiah is also credited with writing a history of the reign of King Uzziah (2Ch 26:22).

Many scholars today challenge the claim that Isaiah wrote the entire book that bears his name. Yet his is the only name attached to it (see 1:1; 2:1; 13:1). The strongest argument for the unity of Isaiah is the expression "the Holy One of Israel," a title for God that occurs 12 times in chs. 1-39 and 14 times in chs. 40-66. Outside Isaiah it appears in the OT only 6 times. There are other striking verbal parallels between chs. 1-39 and chs. 40-66. Compare the following verses:

1:2	66:24
1:5-6	53:4-5
5:27	40:30
6:1	52:13; 57:15
6:11-12	62:4
11:1	53:2
11:6-9	65:25
11:12	49:22
35:10	51:11

Altogether, there are at least 25 Hebrew words or forms found in Isaiah (i.e., in both major divisions of the book) that occur in no other prophetic writing.

Isaiah's use of fire as a figure of punishment (see 1:31; 10:17; 26:11; 33:11-14; 34:9-10; 66:24), his references to the "holy mountain" of Jerusalem (see note on 2:2-4) and his mention of the highway to Jerusalem (see note on 11:16) are themes that recur throughout the book.

The structure of Isaiah also argues for its unity. Chs. 36-39 constitute a historical interlude, which concludes chs. 1-35 and introduces chs. 40-66 (see note on 36:1).

Several NT verses refer to the prophet Isaiah in connection with various parts of the book: Mt 12:17-21 (Isa 42:1-4); Mt 3:3 and Lk 3:4 (Isa 40:3); Ro 10:16,20 (Isa 53:1; 65:1); see especially Jn 12:38-41 (Isa 53:1; 6:10).

Date

Most of the events discussed in chs. 1-39 occurred during Isaiah's ministry (see 6:1; 14:28; 36:1), so it is likely that these chapters were completed not long after 701 B.C., the year the Assyrian army was destroyed (see note on 10:16). The prophet lived until at least 681 (see note on 37:38) and may have written chs. 40-66 during his later years. In his message to the exiles of the sixth century B.C., Isaiah was projected into the future, just as the apostle John was in Rev 4–22.

Background

Isaiah wrote during the stormy period marking the expansion of the Assyrian empire and the decline of Israel. Under King Tiglath-Pileser III (745-727 B.C.) the Assyrians swept westward into Aram (Syria) and Canaan. About 733 the kings of Aram and Israel tried to pressure Ahaz king of Judah into joining a coalition against Assyria. Ahaz chose instead to ask Tiglath-Pileser for help, a decision condemned by Isaiah (see note on 7:1). Assyria did assist Judah and conquered the northern kingdom in 722-721.

This made Judah even more vulnerable, and in 701 King Sennacherib of Assyria threatened Jerusalem itself (see 36:1 and note). The godly King Hezekiah prayed earnestly, and Isaiah predicted that God would force the Assyrians to withdraw from the city (37:6-7).

Nevertheless Isaiah warned Judah that her sin would bring captivity at the hands of Babylon. The visit of the Babylonian king's envoys to Hezekiah set the stage for this prediction (see 39:1,6 and notes). Although the fall of Jerusalem would not take place until 586 B.C., Isaiah assumes the demise of Judah and proceeds to predict the restoration of the people from captivity (see 40:2-3 and notes). God would redeem his people from Babylon just as he rescued them from Egypt (see notes on 35:9; 41:14). Isaiah predicts the rise of Cyrus the Persian, who would unite the Medes and Persians and conquer Babylon in 539 (see 41:2 and note). The decree of Cyrus would allow the Jews to return home in 538, a deliverance that prefigured the greater salvation from sin through Christ (see 52:7 and note).

Themes and Theology

Isaiah is a book that unveils the full dimensions of God's judgment and salvation. God is "the Holy One of Israel" (see 1:4; 6:1 and notes) who must punish his rebellious people (1:2) but will afterward redeem them (41:14,16). Israel is a nation blind and deaf (6:9-10; 42:7), a vineyard that will be trampled (5:1-7), a people devoid of justice or righteousness (5:7; 10:1-2). The awful judgment that will be unleashed upon Israel and all the nations that defy God is called "the day of the LORD." Although Israel has a foretaste of that day (5:30; 42:25), the nations bear its full power (see 2:11,17,20 and note). It is a day associated in the NT with Christ's second coming and the accompanying judgment (see 24:1,21; 34:1-2 and notes). Throughout the book, God's judgment is referred to as "fire" (see 1:31; 30:33 and notes). He is the "Sovereign LORD" (see note on 25:8), far above all nations and rulers (40:15-24).

Yet God will have compassion on his people (14:1-2) and will rescue them from both political and spiritual oppression. Their restoration is like a new exodus (43:2,16-19; 52:10-12) as God redeems them (see 35:9; 41:14 and notes) and saves them (see 43:3; 49:8 and notes). Israel's mighty Creator (40:21-22; 48:13) will make streams spring up in the desert (32:2) as he graciously leads them home. The theme of a highway for the return of exiles is a prominent one (see 11:16; 40:3 and notes) in both major parts of the book. The Lord raises a banner to summon the nations to bring Israel home (see 5:26 and note).

Peace and safety mark this new Messianic age (11:6-9). A king descended from David will reign in righteousness (9:7; 32:1), and all nations will stream to the holy mountain of Jerusalem (see 2:2-4 and note). God's people will no longer be oppressed by wicked rulers (11:14; 45:14), and Jerusalem will truly be the "City of the LORD" (60:14).

The Lord calls the Messianic King "my servant" in chs. 42-53, a term also applied to Israel as a nation (see 41:8-9; 42:1 and notes). It is through the suffering of the servant that salvation in its fullest sense is achieved. Cyrus was God's instrument to deliver Israel from Babylon (41:2), but Christ delivered mankind from the prison of sin (52:13-53:12). He became a "light for the Gentiles" (42:6), so that those nations that faced judgment (chs. 13-23) could find salvation (55:4-5). These Gentiles also became "servants of the LORD" (see 54:17 and note).

The Lord's kingdom on earth, with its righteous Ruler and his righteous subjects, is the goal toward which the book of Isaiah steadily moves. The restored earth and the restored people will then conform to the divine ideal, and all will result in the praise and glory of the Holy One of Israel for what he has accomplished.

Literary Features

Isaiah contains both prose and poetry; the beauty of its poetry is unsurpassed in the OT. The main prose material is found in chs. 36-39, the historical interlude that unites the two parts of the book (see Author). The poetic material includes a series of oracles in chs. 13-23. A taunting song against the king of Babylon is found in 14:4-23. Chs. 24-27 comprise an apocalyptic section stressing the last days (see note on 24:1). A wisdom poem is found in 28:23-29 (also cf. 32:5-8). The song of the vineyard (5:1-7) begins as a love song as Isaiah describes God's relationship with Israel. Hymns of praise are given in 12:1-6 and 38:10-20, and a national lament occurs in 63:7-64:12. The poetry is indeed rich and varied, as is the prophet's vocabulary (e.g., he uses nearly 2,200 different Hebrew words—more than any other OT writer).

One of Isaiah's favorite techniques is personification. The sun and moon are ashamed (24:23), while the desert and parched land rejoice (see 35:1 and note) and the mountains and forests burst into song

(44:23). The trees "clap their hands" (55:12). A favorite figure is the vineyard, which represents Israel (5:7). Treading the winepress is a picture of judgment (see 63:3 and note), and to drink God's "cup of wrath" is to stagger under his punishment (see 51:17 and note). Isaiah uses the name "Rock" to describe God (17:10), and animals such as Leviathan and Rahab represent nations (see 27:1; 30:7; 51:9).

The power of Isaiah's imagery is seen in 30:27-33, and he makes full use of sarcasm in his denunciation of idols in 44:9-20. A forceful example of wordplay appears in 5:7 (see note there), and one finds chiasm (inversion) in 6:10 (see note there; see also note on 16:7) and alliteration and assonance in 24:17 (see note there). The "overwhelming scourge" of 28:15,18 is an illustration of mixed metaphor.

Isaiah often alludes to earlier events in Israel's history, especially the exodus from Egypt. The crossing of the Red Sea forms the background for 11:15 and 43:2,16-17, and other allusions occur in 4:5-6; 31:5; 37:36 (see notes on these verses). The overthrow of Sodom and Gomorrah is referred to in 1:9, and Gideon's victory over Midian is mentioned in 9:4; 10:26 (see also 28:21). Several times Isaiah draws upon the song of Moses in Dt 32 (cf. 1:2 and Dt 32:1; 30:17 and Dt 32:30; 43:11,13 and Dt 32:39). Isaiah, like Moses, called the nation to repentance and to faith in a holy, all-powerful God. See also note on 49:8.

Outline

1 The vision[a] concerning Judah and Jerusalem[b] that Isaiah son of Amoz saw[c] during the reigns of Uzziah,[d] Jotham,[e] Ahaz[f] and Hezekiah,[g] kings of Judah.

A Rebellious Nation

2Hear, O heavens! Listen, O earth![h]
For the LORD has spoken:[i]
"I reared children[j] and brought them up,
but they have rebelled[k] against me.
3The ox knows[l] his master,
the donkey his owner's manger,[m]
but Israel does not know,[n]
my people do not understand.[o]"

4Ah, sinful nation,
a people loaded with guilt,[p]
a brood of evildoers,[q]
children given to corruption![r]
They have forsaken[s] the LORD;
they have spurned the Holy One[t] of Israel
and turned their backs[u] on him.

5Why should you be beaten[v] anymore?
Why do you persist[w] in rebellion?[x]
Your whole head is injured,
your whole heart[y] afflicted.[z]
6From the sole of your foot to the top of your head[a]
there is no soundness[b] —
only wounds and welts[c]
and open sores,
not cleansed or bandaged[d]

or soothed with oil.[e]

7Your country is desolate,[f]
your cities burned with fire;[g]
your fields are being stripped by foreigners[h]
right before you,
laid waste as when overthrown by strangers.[i]
8The Daughter of Zion[i] is left[k]
like a shelter in a vineyard,
like a hut[l] in a field of melons,
like a city under siege.
9Unless the LORD Almighty
had left us some survivors,[m]
we would have become like Sodom,
we would have been like Gomorrah.[n]

10Hear the word of the LORD,[o]
you rulers of Sodom;[p]
listen to the law[q] of our God,
you people of Gomorrah![r]
11"The multitude of your sacrifices—
what are they to me?" says the LORD.
"I have more than enough of burnt offerings,
of rams and the fat of fattened animals;[s]
I have no pleasure[t]

1:1 [a]1Sa 3:1; Isa 22:1,5; Ob 1:1; Na 1:1 [b]Isa 40:9; 44:26 [c]Isa 2:1; 13:1 [d]S 2Ki 14:21; S 2Ch 26:22 [e]S 2Ki 16:1 [f]S 1Ch 3:12 [g]S 1Ch 3:13 **1:2** [h]S Dt 4:26 [i]Jdg 11:10; Jer 42:5; Mic 1:2 [j]Isa 23:4; 63:16 [k]ver 4,23; Isa 24:5,20; 30:1, 9; 46:8; 48:8; 57:4; 65:2; 66:24; Eze 24:3; Hag 1:12; Mal 1:6; 3:5 **1:3** [l]Job 39:9 [m]S Ge 42:27 [n]Jer 4:22; 5:4; 9:3,6; Hos 2:8; 4:1 [o]S Dt 32:28; Isa 42:25; 48:8; Hos 4:6; 7:9 **1:4** [p]Isa 5:18 [q]S ver 2; Isa 9:17; 14:20; 31:2; Jer 23:14 [r]Ps 14:3 [s]S Dt 32:15; S Ps 119:87 [t]S 2Ki 19:22; Isa 5:19,24; 31:1; 37:23; 41:14; 43:14; 45:11; 47:4; Eze 39:7 [u]S Pr 30:9; Isa 59:13 **1:5** [v]Pr 20:30 [w]Jer 2:30; 5:3; 8:5 [x]S ver 2; Isa 31:6; Jer 44:16-17; Heb 3:16 [y]La 2:11; 5:17 [z]Isa 30:26; 33:6, 24; 58:8; Jer 30:17 **1:6** [a]S Dt 28:35 [b]Ps 38:3 [c]Isa 53:5 [d]S Ps 147:3; Isa 30:26; Jer 8:22; 14:19;

30:17; La 2:13; Eze 34:4 [e]2Sa 14:2; Ps 23:5; 45:7; 104:15; Isa 61:3; Lk 10:34 **1:7** [f]S Lev 26:34 [g]S Dt 29:23 [h]Lev 26:16; Jdg 6:3-6; Isa 62:8; Jer 5:17 [i]S 2Ki 18:13; Isa 13:16 **1:8** [j]S Ps 9:14; S Isa 10:32 [k]Isa 30:17; 49:21 [l]S Job 27:18 **1:9** [m]S Ge 45:7; S 2Ki 21:14; Isa 4:2; 6:13; 27:12; 28:5; 37:4,31-32; 45:25; 56:8; Jer 23:3; Joel 2:32 [n]S Ge 19:24; Ro 9:29* **1:10** [o]Isa 28:14 [p]S Ge 13:13; S 18:20; Eze 16:49; Ro 9:29; Rev 11:8 [q]Isa 5:24; 8:20; 30:9 [r]Isa 13:19 **1:11** [s]Ps 50:8; Am 6:4 [t]S Job 22:3

1:1–31 Compare the indictment of ch. 1 with that of ch. 5; the two enclose the first series of oracles. Ch. 1 also serves as an introduction to the whole book.
1:1 The title of the book. Other headings occur in 2:1; 13:1; 14:28; 15:1; 17:1; 19:1; 21:1,11,13; 22:1; 23:1. *vision.* In the sense of "revelation" or "prophecy" (see 1Sa 3:1; Pr 29:18; Ob 1). *Amoz.* Not to be confused with the prophet Amos. *Uzziah, Jotham, Ahaz and Hezekiah.* These kings reigned from 792 to 686 B.C. None of the kings of Israel is mentioned since Isaiah ministered primarily to the southern kingdom (Judah).
1:2 Isaiah begins and ends (66:24) with a condemnation of those who rebel against God. The prophet calls on heaven and earth to testify to the truth of God's accusation against Israel and the rightness of his judgment—since they were witnesses of his covenant (see Dt 30:19; 31:28; 32:1).
1:3 *manger.* Feeding trough. *does not know.* Refusal to know and understand God later resulted in Judah's exile from her land (5:13).
1:4 *Holy One of Israel.* Occurs 26 times in Isaiah (see especially 5:24) and only 6 times elsewhere in the OT (see Introduction: Author).
1:5–6 The pitiable moral and spiritual condition of Israel is transferred to the suffering servant in 53:4–5. The Hebrew words for "beaten," "injured" and "welts" correspond to those for "smitten," "infirmities" and "wounds."
1:6 The disease ravages the entire body, as with Job (2:7).

oil. Commonly used for treating wounds (see Lk 10:34).
1:7–9 The desolation of the land of Judah is the result of foreign invasion: e.g., by Aram, the northern kingdom of Israel, Edom and Philistia (2Ch 28:5–18); later (701 B.C.), by King Sennacherib and the Assyrian army (36:1–2); still later (605–586), by King Nebuchadnezzar and the Neo-Babylonian army.
1:8 *Daughter of Zion.* A personification of Jerusalem and its inhabitants. *shelter . . . hut.* Temporary structures used by watchmen (Job 27:18), who were on the lookout for thieves and intruders. Thus Jerusalem was not very defensible. *melons.* Or possibly "cucumbers."
1:9–10 *Sodom . . . Gomorrah.* Classic examples of sinful cities that were completely destroyed (see 3:9; Ge 13:13; 18:20–21; 19:5,24–25). Just as Jesus addressed Peter as though he were Satan (Mt 16:23), so Isaiah addresses his countrymen as though they were the rulers of Sodom and the people of Gomorrah.
1:9 Quoted in Ro 9:29, where it is linked with Isa 10:22–23. Isaiah often refers to the remnant that will survive God's judgment on the nation and take possession of the land (see 4:3; 10:20–23; 11:11,16; 46:3).
1:11–15 The sincerity of the worshiper, not the number of his religious activities, is most important (see 66:3; Jer 7:21–26; Hos 6:6; Am 5:21–24; Mic 6:6–8).
1:11 *fattened animals.* Those kept in confinement for special feeding.

in the blood of bulls^u and lambs and
goats. ^{v}

¹²When you come to appear before me,
who has asked this of you, ^{w}
this trampling of my courts?

¹³Stop bringing meaningless offerings! ^{x}
Your incense^y is detestable^z to me.
New Moons, ^{a} Sabbaths and
convocations^b —
I cannot bear your evil assemblies.

¹⁴Your New Moon^c festivals and your
appointed feasts^d
my soul hates. ^{e}
They have become a burden to me;^{f}
I am weary^g of bearing them.

¹⁵When you spread out your hands^h in
prayer,
I will hide^i my eyes from you;
even if you offer many prayers,
I will not listen.^{j}
Your hands^k are full of blood;^{l}

¹⁶ wash^m and make yourselves clean.
Take your evil deeds
out of my sight!^{n}
Stop doing wrong, ^{o}

¹⁷ learn to do right!^{p}
Seek justice, ^{q}
encourage the oppressed.$^{a\ r}$
Defend the cause of the fatherless, ^{s}
plead the case of the widow. ^{t}

¹⁸"Come now, let us reason together," ^{u}
says the Lord.
"Though your sins are like scarlet,
they shall be as white as snow;^{v}
though they are red as crimson,
they shall be like wool. ^{w}

¹⁹If you are willing and obedient, ^{x}
you will eat the best from the
land;^{y}

²⁰but if you resist and rebel, ^{z}
you will be devoured by the
sword." ^{a}
For the mouth of the Lord
has spoken.^{b}

²¹See how the faithful city
has become a harlot! ^{c}
She once was full of justice;
righteousness ^{d} used to dwell in
her—
but now murderers! ^{e}

²²Your silver has become dross,^{f}
your choice wine is diluted with
water.

²³Your rulers are rebels, ^{g}
companions of thieves; ^{h}
they all love bribes^i
and chase after gifts.
They do not defend the cause of the
fatherless,
the widow's case does not come
before them.^{j}

²⁴Therefore the Lord, the Lord Almighty,
the Mighty One^k of Israel, declares:
"Ah, I will get relief from my foes
and avenge^l myself on my enemies. ^{m}

²⁵I will turn my hand against you; ^{n}
I will thoroughly purge^o away your
dross^p
and remove all your impurities. ^{q}

²⁶I will restore your judges as in days of
old, ^{r}
your counselors as at the beginning.
Afterward you will be called^s
the City of Righteousness, ^{t}
the Faithful City. $^{u\,"}$

²⁷Zion will be redeemed with justice,

Cross-references (center column)

1:11 ^{u}Isa 66:3;
Jer 6:20
^{v}Isa 15:22;
S Ps 40:6;
Mal 1:10;
Heb 10:4
1:12 ^{w}Ex 23:17;
Dt 31:11
1:13 ^{x}Pr 15:8;
Isa 66:3;
Hag 2:14 ^{y}Jer 7:9;
18:15; 44:8
^{z}S 1Ki 14:24;
Ps 115:8; Pr 28:9;
Isa 41:24;
Mal 2:11
^{a}S Nu 10:10
^{b}1Ch 23:31
1:14 ^{c}S Ne 10:33
^{d}Ex 12:16;
Lev 23:1-44;
Nu 28:11-29:39;
Dt 16:1-17;
Isa 5:12; 29:1;
Hos 2:11
^{e}S Ps 11:5
^{f}S Job 7:12
^{g}Ps 69:3;
Isa 7:13; 43:22,
24; Jer 44:22;
Mal 2:17; 3:14
1:15 ^{h}S Ex 9:29
^{i}S Dt 31:17;
Isa 57:17; 59:2
^{j}S Dt 1:45;
S 1Sa 8:18;
S Job 15:31;
S Jn 9:31
^{k}S Job 9:30
^{l}Isa 4:4; 59:3;
Jer 2:34;
Eze 7:23;
Hos 4:2; Joel 3:21
1:16 ^{m}S Ru 3:3;
Mt 27:24; Jas 4:8
^{n}Nu 19:11,16;
Isa 52:11
^{o}Isa 55:7;
Jer 25:5
1:17 ^{p}S Ps 34:14
^{q}S Ps 72:1;
Isa 11:4; 33:5;
56:1; 61:8;
Am 5:14-15;
Mic 6:8; Zep 2:3
^{r}S Dt 14:29 ^{s}ver
23; Job 22:9;
Ps 82:3; 94:6;
Isa 10:2
^{t}S Ex 22:22;
Eze 18:31; 22:7;
Lk 18:3; Jas 1:27
1:18 ^{u}S 1Sa 2:25;
Isa 41:1; 43:9,26
^{v}S Ps 51:7;
Rev 7:14
^{w}Isa 55:7
1:19
^{x}S Job 36:11;
S Isa 50:10
^{y}Dt 30:15-16;

1:20 ^{z}S 1Sa 12:15 ^{a}S Job 15:22; Isa 3:25; 27:1;
65:12; 66:16; Jer 17:27 ^{b}Nu 23:19; Isa 21:17; 34:16; 40:5;
58:14; Jer 49:13; Mic 4:4; Zec 1:6; Rev 1:16 1:21
^{c}Isa 57:3-9; Jer 2:20; 3:2,9; 13:27; Eze 23:3; Hos 2:1-13
^{d}Isa 5:7; 46:13; 59:14; Am 6:12 ^{e}S Pr 6:17 1:22
^{f}S Ps 119:119 1:23 ^{g}S ver 2 ^{h}S Dt 19:14; Mic 2:1-2; 6:12
^{i}S Ex 23:8; Am 5:12 ^{j}Isa 10:2; Jer 5:28; Eze 22:6-7; Mic 3:9;
Hab 1:4 1:24 ^{k}S Ge 49:24 ^{l}Isa 34:2,8; 35:4; 47:3; 59:17;
61:2; 63:4; Jer 51:6; Eze 5:13 ^{m}S Dt 32:43; S Isa 10:3 1:25
^{n}Dt 28:63 ^{o}S Ps 78:38 ^{p}S Ps 119:119 2Ch 29:15; Isa 48:10;
Jer 6:29; 9:7; Eze 22:22; Mal 3:3 1:26 ^{r}Jer 33:7,11; Mic 4:8
^{s}S Ge 32:28 ^{t}Isa 32:16; 33:5; 46:13; 48:18; 61:11; 62:1;
Jer 31:23; Zec 8:3 ^{u}Isa 4:3; 48:2; 52:1; 60:14; 62:2; 64:10;
Da 9:24

1:27 Ezr 9:12; Ps 34:10; Isa 30:23; 55:2; 58:14; 62:9; 65:13,
21-22

^{a}17 Or / rebuke the oppressor

1:14 *New Moon festivals.* Celebrated on the first day of each month. Special sacrifices and feasts were part of the observance (see Nu 28:11–15). *appointed feasts.* Included the annual feasts, such as Passover, Weeks (Pentecost) and Tabernacles (Ex 23:14–17; 34:18–25; Lev 23; Dt 16:1–17).
1:15 *hide my eyes.* In 8:17; 59:2 God hides his face from Israel (see also Mic 3:4).
1:17 See Jer 22:16; Jas 1:27. *fatherless . . . widow.* Represented the weak and often oppressed part of society. Rulers were warned not to take advantage of them (see v. 23; 10:2; Jer 22:3).
1:18 *scarlet . . . crimson.* Refers to the blood that has stained the hands of murderers (see vv. 15,21). *white as snow.* A powerful figurative description of the result of forgiveness (see Ps 51:7). This offer of forgiveness is conditioned on the reformation of life called for in v. 19.

1:19–20 *eat . . . be devoured.* The vivid contrast is stressed by the use of the same Hebrew verb.
1:21 *Jerusalem* (representing all Judah) has been an unfaithful wife to the Lord. By following idols and foreign gods she has become a harlot in a spiritual sense (see v. 4; Jer 3:6–14; Eze 16:25–26).
1:24 *The Lord, the Lord Almighty, the Mighty One of Israel.* Stressing God's authority as Judge.
1:25–26 *turn . . . restore.* The use of the same Hebrew verb emphasizes the contrast (see note on vv. 19–20).
1:25 *purge away your dross.* Purifying fire is also mentioned in 4:4; 48:10.
1:26 *Faithful City.* See v. 21. Using a related Hebrew noun, Zec 8:3 similarly refers to the future Jerusalem as the "City of Truth."
1:27–28 This contrast between the redemption of Zion (Jerusalem) as a whole and the perishing of individuals who

her penitent[v] ones with
righteousness. [w]
28But rebels and sinners[x] will both be
broken,
and those who forsake[y] the LORD
will perish. [z]

29"You will be ashamed[a] because of the
sacred oaks[b]
in which you have delighted;
you will be disgraced because of the
gardens[c]
that you have chosen.
30You will be like an oak with fading
leaves, [d]
like a garden without water.
31The mighty man will become tinder
and his work a spark;
both will burn together,
with no one to quench the fire. [e]"

The Mountain of the LORD

2:1–4pp — Mic 4:1–3

2 This is what Isaiah son of Amoz saw
concerning Judah and Jerusalem:[f]

2In the last days[g]

the mountain[h] of the LORD's temple
will be established
as chief among the mountains; [i]
it will be raised[j] above the hills,
and all nations will stream to it. [k]

3Many peoples[l] will come and say,

"Come, let us go[m] up to the mountain[n]
of the LORD,
to the house of the God of Jacob.
He will teach us his ways,
so that we may walk in his paths."
The law[o] will go out from Zion,
the word of the LORD from
Jerusalem. [p]

4He will judge[q] between the nations
and will settle disputes[r] for many
peoples.
They will beat their swords into
plowshares
and their spears into pruning hooks. [s]
Nation will not take up sword against
nation, [t]
nor will they train for war anymore.

5Come, O house of Jacob, [u]
let us walk in the light[v] of the LORD.

The Day of the LORD

6You have abandoned[w] your people,
the house of Jacob. [x]
They are full of superstitions from the
East;
they practice divination[y] like the
Philistines[z]
and clasp hands[a] with pagans. [b]
7Their land is full of silver and gold; [c]
there is no end to their treasures. [d]
Their land is full of horses; [e]
there is no end to their chariots.[f]
8Their land is full of idols; [g]
they bow down[h] to the work of their
hands, [i]
to what their fingers[j] have made.
9So man will be brought low[k]
and mankind humbled[l] —
do not forgive them.[b] [m]

10Go into the rocks,
hide[n] in the ground

1:27 vIsa 30:15; 31:6; 59:20;
Eze 18:30
wIsa 35:10; 41:14; 43:1; 52:3; 62:12; 63:4; Hos 2:19
1:28 xIsa 33:14; 43:27; 48:8; 50:1; 59:2; Jer 4:18
yS Dt 32:15
zPs 9:5; Isa 24:20; 66:24; Jer 16:4; 42:22; 44:12; 2Th 1:8-9
1:29 aPs 97:7; Isa 42:17; 44:9, 11; 45:16; Jer 10:14
bIsa 57:5; Eze 6:13; Hos 4:13
cIsa 65:3; 66:17
1:30 dS Ps 1:3
1:31 eIsa 4:4; 5:24; 9:18-19; 10:17; 24:6; 26:11; 30:27,33; 33:14; 34:10; 66:15-16,24; Jer 5:14; 7:20; 21:12; Ob 1:18; Mal 3:2; 4:1; S Mt 25:41
2:1 fIsa 1:1
2:2 gAc 2:17; Heb 1:2
hIsa 11:9; 24:23; 25:6,10; 27:13; 56:7; 57:13; 65:25; 66:20; Jer 31:23; Da 11:45; Joel 3:17; Mic 4:7
iIsa 65:9
jZec 14:10
kPs 102:15; Jer 16:19
2:3 lIsa 45:23; 49:1; 60:3-6,14; 66:18; Jer 3:17; Joel 3:2; Zep 3:8; Zec 14:2
mIsa 45:14; 49:12,23; 55:5
nS Dt 33:19; S Ps 137:5
oIsa 1:10; 33:22; 51:4,7
pLk 24:47; S Jn 4:22

2:4 qPs 7:6; S 9:19; 96:13; 98:9; Isa 1:27; 3:13; 9:7; 42:4;

51:4; Joel 3:14 rS Ge 49:10 sJoel 3:10 tPs 46:9; Isa 9:5; 11:6-9; 32:18; 57:19; 65:25; Jer 30:10; Da 11:45; Hos 2:18; Mic 4:3; Zec 9:10 **2:5** uIsa 58:1 vIsa 60:1,19-20; 1Jn 1:5,7
2:6 wS Dt 31:17 xJer 12:7 yS Dt 18:10; S Isa 44:25
zS 2Ki 1:2; S 2Ch 26:6 aPr 6:1 bS 2Ki 16:7; Mic 5:12 **2:7** cS Dt 17:17 dS Ps 17:14 eS Dt 17:16 fS Ge 41:43; Isa 31:1; Mic 5:10 **2:8** gIsa 10:9-11; Rev 9:20 hIsa 44:17
iS 2Ch 32:19; S Ps 135:15; Mic 5:13 jIsa 17:8 **2:9** kPs 62:9
lver 11,17; Isa 5:15; 13:11 mS Ne 4:5 **2:10** nver 19; Na 3:11

b9 Or *not raise them up*

refuse to repent is developed in 65:8–16.
1:29 *sacred oaks . . . gardens.* Pagan sacrifices were offered and sexual immorality occurred at such places (see
65:3; 66:17).
1:31 *fire.* A figure of punishment (see 33:11–14;
34:9–10).
2:1 A second introduction, probably relating to chs. 2–4 or
to chs. 2–12 (see 13:1).
2:2–5 See note on 4:2–6.
2:2–4 Almost identical to Mic 4:1–3. The theme of the
"mountain of the LORD" (Mount Zion) is common in Isaiah;
it occurs in passages that depict the coming of both Jews and
Gentiles to Jerusalem (Zion) in the last days (see 19:19;
27:13; 56:7; 57:13; 65:25; 66:20; see also 60:3–5; Zec
14:16). Some believe that the peace described in this passage
has been inaugurated through the coming of Christ and the
preaching of the gospel, and will be consummated at the
return of Christ. Others maintain that it is a prophecy of
conditions during a future reign of Christ on the earth.
2:2 *the last days.* Can refer to the future generally (see Ge

49:1), but usually it seems to have in view the Messianic era.
In a real sense the last days began with the first coming of
Christ (see Ac 2:17; Heb 1:2) and will be fulfilled at his
second coming.
2:4 *swords into plowshares.* The reverse process occurs in
Joel 3:10. What is here called a plowshare was actually an
iron point mounted on a wooden beam. Ancient plows did
not have a plowshare proper.
2:6 *East.* Probably means Aram (Syria) and Mesopotamia.
divination like the Philistines. See 1Sa 6:2; see also Dt
18:10–11 for a description of such practices.
2:7 *silver and gold . . . horses.* Accumulating large quantities of these was forbidden to the king (Dt 17:16–17). They
usually led to a failure to trust in God (see 31:1).
2:10,19,21 These verses form a refrain that builds to a
climax in v. 21. Lines 3–4 of each verse are identical.
2:10 *rocks . . . ground.* During times of severe oppression
the Israelites took refuge in caves and holes in the ground
(see Jdg 6:1–2; 1Sa 13:6). *majesty.* The Hebrew for this
word is translated "pride" when used of man. Pride is an

from dread of the LORD
and the splendor of his majesty! *o*

[11]The eyes of the arrogant *p* man will be
humbled *q*
and the pride *r* of men brought low; *s*
the LORD alone will be exalted *t* in that
day. *u*

[12]The LORD Almighty has a day *v* in store
for all the proud *w* and lofty, *x*
for all that is exalted *y*
(and they will be humbled), *z*
[13]for all the cedars of Lebanon, *a* tall and
lofty, *b*
and all the oaks of Bashan, *c*
[14]for all the towering mountains
and all the high hills, *d*
[15]for every lofty tower *e*
and every fortified wall, *f*
[16]for every trading ship *c g*
and every stately vessel.
[17]The arrogance of man will be brought
low *h*
and the pride of men humbled; *i*
the LORD alone will be exalted in that
day, *j*
[18] and the idols *k* will totally disappear. *l*

[19]Men will flee to caves *m* in the rocks
and to holes in the ground *n*
from dread *o* of the LORD
and the splendor of his majesty, *p*
when he rises to shake the earth. *q*
[20]In that day *r* men will throw away
to the rodents and bats *s*
their idols of silver and idols of gold, *t*
which they made to worship. *u*
[21]They will flee to caverns in the rocks *v*
and to the overhanging crags
from dread of the LORD
and the splendor of his majesty, *w*
when he rises *x* to shake the earth. *y*

[22]Stop trusting in man, *z*
who has but a breath *a* in his nostrils.
Of what account is he? *b*

Judgment on Jerusalem and Judah

3 See now, the Lord,
the LORD Almighty,
is about to take from Jerusalem and
Judah
both supply and support: *c*
all supplies of food *d* and all supplies of
water, *e*
[2] the hero and warrior, *f*
the judge and prophet,
the soothsayer *g* and elder, *h*
[3]the captain of fifty *i* and man of rank, *j*
the counselor, skilled craftsman *k* and
clever enchanter. *l*

[4]I will make boys their officials;
mere children will govern them. *m*
[5]People will oppress each other—
man against man, neighbor against
neighbor. *n*
The young will rise up against the old,
the base against the honorable.

[6]A man will seize one of his brothers
at his father's home, and say,
"You have a cloak, you be our leader;
take charge of this heap of ruins!"
[7]But in that day *o* he will cry out,
"I have no remedy. *p*

2:10 *o*S Ps 145:12; 2Th 1:9; Rev 6:15-16 2:11 *p*S Ne 9:29; Hab 2:5 *q*S ver 9 *r*Isa 5:15; 10:12; 37:23; Eze 31:10 *s*S Job 40:11 *t*S Ps 46:10 *u*ver 17,20; Isa 3:7,18; 4:1,2; 5:30; 7:18; 17:4,7; 24:21; 25:9; 26:1; 27:1 2:12 *v*Isa 13:6,9; 22:5,8,12; 34:8; 61:2; Jer 30:7; La 1:12; Eze 7:7; 30:3; Joel 1:15; 2:11; Am 5:18; Zep 1:14 *w*S Ps 59:12 *x*S 2Sa 22:28 *y*Ps 76:12; Isa 24:4,21; 60:11; Mal 4:1 *z*S Job 40:11 2:13 *a*S Jdg 9:15; Isa 10:34; 29:17; Eze 27:5 *b*Isa 10:33 *c*S Ps 22:12; Zec 11:2 2:14 *d*Isa 30:25; 40:4 2:15 *e*Isa 30:25; 32:14; 33:18 *f*Isa 25:2,12; Zep 1:16 2:16 *g*S Ge 10:4; S 1Ki 9:26 2:17 *h*S 2Sa 22:28; S Job 40:11 *i*S ver 9 /S ver 11 2:18 *k*S 1Sa 5:2; Eze 36:25 *l*S Dt 9:21; Isa 21:9; Jer 10:11; Mic 5:13 2:19 *m*S Jdg 6:2; Isa 7:19 *n*S Jdg 6:2; S Job 30:6; Lk 23:30; Rev 6:15 *o*S Dt 2:25 *p*S Ps 145:12 *q*ver 21; S Job 9:6; S Isa 14:16; Heb 12:26

2:20 *r*S ver 11 *s*Lev 11:19 *t*S Job 22:24; Eze 36:25; Rev 9:20 *u*Eze 7:19-20; 14:6 2:21 *v*S Ex 33:22 *w*S Ps 145:12 *x*Isa 33:10 *y*S ver 19 2:22 *z*Ps 118:6,8; 146:3; Isa 51:12; Jer 17:5 *a*S Ge 2:7; S Ps 144:4 *b*S Job 12:19; Ps 8:4; 18:42; 144:3; Isa 17:13; 29:5; 40:15; S Jas 4:14 3:1 *c*S Ps 18:18 *d*S Lev 26:26; Am 4:6 *e*Isa 5:13; 65:13; Eze 4:16 3:2 *f*Eze 17:13 *g*Dt 18:10 *h*Isa 9:14-15 3:3 *i*S 2Ki 1:9 /S Job 22:8 *k*2Ki 24:14 /S Ecc 10:11; Jer 8:17 3:4 *m*ver 12; Ecc 10:16 *fn* 3:5 *n*Ps 28:3; Isa 9:19; Jer 9:8; Mic 7:2,6 3:7 *o*S Isa 2:11 *p*Jer 30:12; Eze 34:4; Hos 5:13

c 16 Hebrew *every ship of Tarshish*

attempt by man to be his own god (see 14:13–14).
2:11,17,20 *in that day.* The phrase occurs seven times in chs. 2–4 (see 3:7,18; 4:1–2). The day of the Lord (see also v. 12) is a time of judgment and/or blessing as God intervenes decisively in the affairs of the nations (see Zep 1:14–2:3). Assyria and Babylon would bring the terror of judgment upon Judah in Isaiah's day (5:30).
2:13 *cedars of Lebanon.* Even inanimate things that people stand in awe of will be humbled so that "the LORD alone will be exalted" (v. 11). *Bashan.* A region east of the Jordan River and north of Gilead. It was famous for its oaks (Eze 27:6) and its animals (Eze 39:18).
2:16 *trading ship.* These "ships of Tarshish" (see NIV text note) were large vessels such as those used by Solomon (1Ki 10:22) and the Phoenicians (Isa 23:1,14) to ply the sea in far-flung commercial ventures.
2:20 The futility of worshiping idols is repeatedly noted by Isaiah (see, e.g., 30:22; 31:7; 40:19–20; 44:9–20). See also note on 40:18–20.
2:22 *Stop trusting in man.* Lit. "Cease from man" or "Give up on man." The term describes the rejection of the Messiah

in 53:3. Ironically, the one Man who should have been trusted and "esteemed" (equals "of what account" here) was "rejected," "given up on" by men. He alone was worthy of the esteem wrongly given to frail leaders.
3:1–3 Leaders would be taken away by either death or deportation (see 2Ki 24:14; 25:18–21).
3:2–3 *soothsayer . . . enchanter.* Occult practitioners and snake charmers (see Dt 18:10; Jer 8:17), whose activities were condemned. Both legitimate and illegitimate kinds of assistance would be removed or deported (see 2Ki 24:14–16; Hos 3:4).
3:3 *captain of fifty.* A company of 50 was a common military unit (see 2Ki 1:9). It was also used for civil groupings (Ex 18:25).
3:6 Normally it was unnecessary to force anyone to be a leader. In 4:1 the same social upheaval is seen as seven women "take hold of" one man. *You have a cloak.* Perhaps the one brother was not as poor as the others. *heap of ruins.* Probably Jerusalem (v. 8).
3:7,18 *in that day.* See note on 2:11,17,20.

I have no food[q] or clothing in my
house;
do not make me the leader of the
people."[r]

[8]Jerusalem staggers,
Judah is falling;[s]
their words[t] and deeds[u] are against the
LORD,
defying[v] his glorious presence.
[9]The look on their faces testifies[w] against
them;
they parade their sin like Sodom;[x]
they do not hide it.
Woe to them!
They have brought disaster[y] upon
themselves.

[10]Tell the righteous it will be well[z] with
them,
for they will enjoy the fruit of their
deeds.[a]
[11]Woe to the wicked![b] Disaster[c] is upon
them!
They will be paid back[d] for what their
hands have done.[e]

[12]Youths[f] oppress my people,
women rule over them.
O my people, your guides lead you
astray;[g]
they turn you from the path.

[13]The LORD takes his place in court;[h]
he rises to judge[i] the people.
[14]The LORD enters into judgment[j]
against the elders and leaders of his
people:
"It is you who have ruined my
vineyard;
the plunder[k] from the poor[l] is in
your houses.
[15]What do you mean by crushing my
people[m]
and grinding[n] the faces of the
poor?"[o]
declares the Lord,
the LORD Almighty.[p]

[16]The LORD says,
"The women of Zion[q] are haughty,
walking along with outstretched
necks,[r]
flirting with their eyes,
tripping along with mincing steps,
with ornaments jingling on their
ankles.
[17]Therefore the Lord will bring sores on
the heads of the women of
Zion;
the LORD will make their scalps
bald.[s]"

[18]In that day[t] the Lord will snatch away
their finery: the bangles and headbands
and crescent necklaces,[u] [19]the earrings
and bracelets[v] and veils,[w] [20]the headdresses[x] and ankle chains and sashes, the
perfume bottles and charms, [21]the signet
rings and nose rings,[y] [22]the fine robes and
the capes and cloaks,[z] the purses [23]and
mirrors, and the linen garments[a] and
tiaras[b] and shawls.

[24]Instead of fragrance[c] there will be a
stench;[d]
instead of a sash,[e] a rope;
instead of well-dressed hair, baldness;[f]
instead of fine clothing, sackcloth;[g]
instead of beauty,[h] branding.[i]
[25]Your men will fall by the sword,[j]
your warriors in battle.[k]
[26]The gates[l] of Zion will lament and
mourn;[m]
destitute,[n] she will sit on the
ground.[o]

4 In that day[p] seven women
will take hold of one man[q]
and say, "We will eat our own food[r]
and provide our own clothes;

Cross references (center column):

3:7 [q]Joel 1:16;
[r]Isa 24:2
3:8 [s]Isa 1:7
[t]Isa 9:15,17;
28:15; 30:9;
59:3,13
[u]2Ch 33:6
[v]S Job 1:11;
Ps 73:9,11;
Isa 65:7
3:9 [w]Nu 32:23;
Isa 59:12;
Jer 14:7; Hos 5:5
[x]S Ge 13:13
[y]S 2Ch 34:24;
S Pr 8:36; Ro 6:23
3:10 [z]S Dt 5:33;
S 12:28; 28:1-14;
Ps 37:17;
Jer 22:15
[a]S Ge 15:1;
S Ps 128:2
3:11 [b]S Job 9:13;
Isa 57:20
[c]Dt 28:15-68
[d]S 2Ch 6:23
[e]Jer 21:14;
La 5:16;
Eze 24:14
3:12 [f]S ver 4
[g]Isa 9:16; 19:14;
28:7; 29:9;
Jer 23:13; 25:16;
Mic 3:5
3:13 [h]S Job 10:2
[i]S Ps 82:1;
S Isa 2:4
3:14 [j]S 1Sa 12:7;
S Job 22:4
[k]S Job 24:9;
Jas 2:6 [l]Isa 11:4;
25:4
3:15 [m]S Ps 94:5
[n]S Job 24:14
[o]Isa 10:6; 11:4;
26:6; 29:19;
32:6; 51:23
[p]Isa 5:7

3:16 [q]S SS 3:11
[r]S Job 15:25
3:17 [s]ver 24;
Eze 27:31;
Am 8:10
3:18 [t]S Isa 2:11
[u]S Ge 41:42;
S Jdg 8:21
3:19 [v]S Ge 24:47
[w]Eze 16:11-12
3:20 [x]Ex 39:28;
Eze 24:17,23;
44:18
3:21 [y]S Ge 24:22
3:22 [z]Ru 3:15
3:23 [a]Eze 16:10;
23:26 [b]S Ge 29:6;
SS 3:11; Isa 61:3;
62:3
3:24 [c]S Est 2:12
[d]Isa 4:4
[e]Pr 31:24 [s]S ver
17; S Lev 13:40;

S Job 1:20 [g]S Ge 37:34; Job 16:15; Isa 20:2; Jer 4:8; La 2:10;
Eze 27:30-31; Jnh 3:5-8 [h]1Pe 3:3 [i]S 2Sa 10:4; Isa 20:4 3:25
[j]S Isa 1:20 [k]Jer 15:8 3:26 [l]Isa 14:31; 24:12; 45:2
[m]S Ps 137:1; Isa 24:4,7; 29:2; 33:9; Jer 4:28; 14:2
[n]S Lev 26:31 [o]S Job 2:13; La 4:5 4:1 [p]S Isa 2:11 [q]Isa 13:12;
32:9 [r]2Th 3:12

Notes:

3:8 *Judah is falling.* Consummated almost 150 years later.
3:9 *Sodom.* See note on 1:9–10.
3:12 In the Near East, neither the rule of the young nor that
of women was looked on with favor.
3:14 *vineyard.* Represents Israel (see 5:1).
3:15 The leaders were grinding the poor, as men grind
grain between two millstones.
3:16–24 For a NT warning against overemphasis on outward adornment see 1Pe 3:3–4.
3:16 *walking . . . tripping along.* In the Near East the way
one walked communicated specific attitudes. Ornaments on
ankles made short steps necessary.
3:17 *bald.* Baldness was associated with mourning over
catastrophe (see v. 24; 15:2).
3:18 *crescent necklaces.* Probably moon-shaped; they implied veneration of the popular moon-god.

3:20 *headdresses.* Perhaps a kind of turban (see Eze
24:17,23).
3:21 *signet rings.* Contained a seal and were a mark of
authority (see Ge 41:42 and note). *nose rings.* Sometimes
made of gold and worn by brides.
3:24 *rope . . . branding.* Captives were treated like cattle.
They were led away by ropes and sometimes branded.
3:26 *gates of Zion.* The gates are personified, as in Ps
24:7,9. They will lament because the crowds that used to
assemble there are gone.
4:1–2 *In that day.* See notes on 2:2 and 2:11,17,20. After
judgment comes salvation.
4:1 See note on 3:6. War will decimate the male population (3:25; see 13:12), leaving many women with the double disgrace of being widows and childless. See 54:4.

only let us be called by your name.
Take away our disgrace!" [s]

The Branch of the LORD

[2] In that day [t] the Branch of the LORD [u] will be beautiful [v] and glorious, and the fruit [w] of the land will be the pride and glory [x] of the survivors [y] in Israel. [3] Those who are left in Zion, [z] who remain [a] in Jerusalem, will be called holy, [b] all who are recorded [c] among the living in Jerusalem. [4] The Lord will wash away the filth [d] of the women of Zion; [e] he will cleanse [f] the bloodstains [g] from Jerusalem by a spirit [d] of judgment [h] and a spirit [d] of fire. [i] [5] Then the LORD will create [j] over all of Mount Zion [k] and over those who assemble there a cloud of smoke by day and a glow of flaming fire by night; [l] over all the glory [m] will be a canopy. [n] [6] It will be a shelter [o] and shade from the heat of the day, and a refuge [p] and hiding place from the storm [q] and rain.

The Song of the Vineyard

5 I will sing for the one I love
a song about his vineyard: [r]
My loved one had a vineyard
on a fertile hillside.
[2] He dug it up and cleared it of stones
and planted it with the choicest vines. [s]
He built a watchtower [t] in it
and cut out a winepress [u] as well.
Then he looked for a crop of good grapes,
but it yielded only bad fruit. [v]

[3] "Now you dwellers in Jerusalem and
men of Judah,
judge between me and my vineyard. [w]
[4] What more could have been done for
my vineyard
than I have done for it? [x]
When I looked for good grapes,
why did it yield only bad? [y]
[5] Now I will tell you
what I am going to do to my
vineyard:
I will take away its hedge,
and it will be destroyed; [z]
I will break down its wall, [a]
and it will be trampled. [b]
[6] I will make it a wasteland, [c]
neither pruned nor cultivated,
and briers and thorns [d] will grow
there.
I will command the clouds
not to rain [e] on it."

[7] The vineyard [f] of the LORD Almighty
is the house of Israel,
and the men of Judah
are the garden of his delight.
And he looked for justice, [g] but saw
bloodshed;
for righteousness, [h] but heard cries of
distress. [i]

4:1 [s]S Ge 30:23	
4:2 [t]S Isa 2:11	
[u]Isa 11:1-5; 52:13; 53:2; 33:15-16; Eze 17:22; Zec 3:8; 6:12	
[v]Isa 33:17; 53:2	
[w]S Ps 72:16; Eze 36:8	
[x]Isa 60:15; Eze 34:29	
[y]S Isa 1:9	
4:3 [z]S Isa 1:26	
[a]Isa 1:9; Ro 11:5	
[b]S Ex 19:6; Isa 26:2; 45:25; 52:1; 60:21; Joel 3:17; Ob 1:17; Zep 3:13	
[c]S Ps 56:8; S 87:6; S Lk 10:20	
4:4 [d]Isa 3:24	
[e]S S 3:11	
[f]S Ps 51:2	
[g]S Isa 1:15	
[h]Isa 28:6	
[i]S Isa 1:31; S 30:30; S Zec 13:9; Mt 3:11; Lk 3:17	
4:5 [j]Isa 41:20; 65:18 [k]Rev 14:1	
[l]S Ex 13:21	
[m]Isa 35:2; 58:8; 60:1 [n]S Ps 18:11; Rev 7:15	
4:6	
[o]Lev 23:34-43; Ps 27:5; Isa 8:14; 25:4; Eze 11:16	
[p]Isa 14:32; 25:4; 30:2; 57:13	
[q]S Ps 55:8	
5:1 [r]Ps 80:8-9; Isa 27:2; Jn 15:1	
5:2 [s]S Ex 15:17; Isa 16:8 [t]Isa 2:9; Isa 27:3; 31:5; 49:8; Mt 21:33	
[u]S Job 24:11	
[v]Mt 21:19; Mk 11:13; Lk 13:6	
5:3 [w]Mt 21:40	
5:4	
[x]S 2Ch 36:15;	

Jer 2:5-7; Mic 6:3-4; Mt 23:37 [y]Jer 2:21; 24:2; 29:17 **5:5** [z]2Ch 36:21; Isa 6:12; 27:10 [a]S Ps 80:12; S Isa 22:5 [b]Isa 10:6; 26:6; 28:3,18; 41:25; 63:3; Jer 12:10; 34:22; La 1:15; Hos 2:12; Mic 7:10; Mal 4:3; S Lk 21:24 **5:6** [c]S Ge 6:13; S Lev 26:32; Isa 6:13; 49:17,19; 51:3; Joel 1:10 [d]ver 10,17; S 2Sa 23:6; Isa 7:23,24; 32:13; 34:13; 55:13; Eze 28:24; Hos 2:12; Heb 6:8 [e]S Dt 28:24; S 2Sa 1:21; Am 4:7 **5:7** [f]Ps 80:8; Isa 17:10; 18:5; 37:30 [g]Isa 10:2; 29:21; 32:7; 59:15; 61:8; Eze 9:9; 22:29 [h]S Isa 1:21 [i]S Ps 12:5

4:2–6 An oracle of redemption just before the long message of indictment and judgment in ch. 5. It balances that found in 2:2–5, which immediately follows the long message of indictment and judgment in ch. 1 (see note on 1:1–31). These two oracles of redemption were intended to complement each other.
4:2–3 *survivors . . . are left.* See note on 1:9.
4:2 *Branch.* A Messianic title related to the "shoot" and "Branch" (11:1; 53:2) descended from David—but some believe that here "branch" refers to Judah. *pride.* A legitimate pride in the fruitfulness of the land that will characterize the Messiah's reign (see Ps 72:3,6,16). Contrast the pride of 2:11,17. *glory.* Here the fruitfulness of the land will be Israel's glory; in 46:13 God's salvation will be her glory ("splendor"); in 60:19 God himself will be her glory.
4:3 *holy.* Means "set apart" to God. See 1:26; 6:13; see also Zec 14:20.
4:4 *judgment . . . fire.* Purifying fire is also mentioned in 1:25; 48:10.
4:5–6 *cloud . . . fire . . . shelter.* These words recall Israel's desert wanderings, when the pillar of cloud and fire guided and protected the people (Ex 13:21–22; 14:21–22). Isaiah often refers to the time of the exodus (see 11:15–16; 31:5; 51:10).

4:5 *the glory.* The manifestation of God's presence represented by a glow of flaming fire (see Ex 16:10; 24:17; 40:34–35). *canopy.* The cloud of smoke.
4:6 God's presence in cloud and fire will protect and preserve redeemed Zion (cf. Ps 121:5–6).
5:1–30 See note on 1:1–31.
5:1 *loved one.* God. *vineyard.* Israel (see v. 7; 3:14; Ps 80:8–16). Jesus' parable of the tenants (Mt 21:33–44; Mk 12:1–11; Lk 20:9–18) is probably based on this song. See Jn 15:1–17.
5:2 *watchtower.* Contrast the more modest "shelter" of 1:8. God's vineyard had every advantage (see Mt 21:33). *winepress.* Or "wine vat," a trough into which the grape juice flowed (see 16:10). *he looked for . . . but.* The interpretation (v. 7) uses the same expression.
5:6 *briers and thorns.* This pair occurs five more times (7:23–25; 9:18; 27:4). *not to rain.* The withholding of rain constituted a curse on the land. See Dt 28:23–24; 2Sa 1:21; 1Ki 17:1.
5:7 The song of the vineyard (vv. 1–6) is now interpreted. A powerful play on words makes the point: The words for "justice" and "bloodshed" (*mishpat* and *mispah*) sound alike, as do those for "righteousness" (*sedaqah*) and "distress" (*se'aqah*).

Woes and Judgments

[8]Woe[j] to you who add house to house
   and join field to field[k]
till no space is left
   and you live alone in the land.

[9]The LORD Almighty[l] has declared in
my hearing:[m]

"Surely the great houses will become
      desolate,[n]
   the fine mansions left without
      occupants.
[10]A ten-acre[e] vineyard will produce only
      a bath[f] of wine,
   a homer[g] of seed only an ephah[h] of
      grain."[o]

[11]Woe[p] to those who rise early in the
      morning
   to run after their drinks,
who stay up late at night
   till they are inflamed with wine.[q]
[12]They have harps and lyres at their
      banquets,
   tambourines[r] and flutes[s] and wine,
but they have no regard[t] for the deeds
      of the LORD,
   no respect for the work of his
      hands.[u]

[13]Therefore my people will go into exile[v]
   for lack of understanding;[w]
their men of rank[x] will die of hunger
   and their masses will be parched with
      thirst.[y]
[14]Therefore the grave[i][z] enlarges its
      appetite
   and opens its mouth[a] without limit;
into it will descend their nobles and
      masses
   with all their brawlers and revelers.[b]
[15]So man will be brought low[c]
   and mankind humbled,[d]
   the eyes of the arrogant[e] humbled.
[16]But the LORD Almighty will be exalted[f]
   by his justice,[g]

and the holy God will show himself
      holy[h] by his righteousness.
[17]Then sheep will graze as in their own
      pasture;[i]
   lambs will feed[j] among the ruins of
      the rich.

[18]Woe[j] to those who draw sin along
      with cords[k] of deceit,
   and wickedness[l] as with cart ropes,
[19]to those who say, "Let God hurry,
   let him hasten[m] his work
      so we may see it.
Let it approach,
   let the plan of the Holy One[n] of
      Israel come,
   so we may know it."[o]

[20]Woe[p] to those who call evil good[q]
      and good evil,[r]
who put darkness for light
   and light for darkness,[s]
who put bitter for sweet
   and sweet for bitter.[t]

[21]Woe to those who are wise in their
      own eyes[u]
   and clever in their own sight.

[22]Woe to those who are heroes at
      drinking wine[v]
   and champions at mixing drinks,[w]
[23]who acquit the guilty for a bribe,[x]
   but deny justice[y] to the innocent.[z]

[24]Therefore, as tongues of fire[a] lick up
      straw[b]
   and as dry grass sinks down in the
      flames,
   so their roots will decay[c]

Cross references (center column)

5:8 [j]ver 11,18, 20; Isa 6:5; 10:1; 24:16; Jer 22:13 [k]Job 20:19; Mic 2:2; Hab 2:9-12
5:9 [l]Jer 44:11 [m]Isa 22:14 [n]Isa 6:11-12; Mt 23:38
5:10 [o]S ver 6; Lev 26:26; S Dt 28:38; Zec 8:10
5:11 [p]S ver 8 [q]S 1Sa 25:36; S Pr 23:29-30
5:12 [r]Ps 68:25; Isa 24:8 [s]S Job 21:12 [t]S 1Sa 12:24 [u]Ps 28:5; Eze 26:13
5:13 [v]Isa 49:21 [w]S Pr 10:21; S Isa 1:3 [x]S Job 22:8 [y]S Isa 3:1
5:14 [z]S Pr 30:16 [a]S Nu 16:30 [b]Isa 22:2,13; 23:7; 24:8
5:15 [c]Isa 10:33 [d]S Isa 2:9 [e]S Isa 2:11
5:16 [f]Ps 97:9; Isa 33:10 [g]Isa 28:17; 30:18; 33:5; 61:8
[h]S Lev 10:3; Isa 29:23; Eze 36:23
5:17 [i]Isa 7:25; 17:2; 32:14; Zep 2:6,14
5:18 [j]S ver 8 [k]Hos 11:4 [l]Isa 59:4-8; Jer 23:14
5:19 [m]Isa 60:22 [n]S Isa 1:4; 29:23; 30:11,12 [o]Jer 17:15; Eze 12:22; 2Pe 3:4
5:20 [p]S ver 8 [q]S Ge 18:25; S 1Ki 22:8 [r]S Ps 94:21 [s]S Job 24:13; Mt 6:22-23; Lk 11:34-35 [t]Am 5:7
5:21 [u]S Pr 3:7; Isa 47:10; Ro 12:16; 1Co 3:18-20
5:22 [v]S 1Sa 25:36; S Pr 23:20; S Isa 22:13
[w]S Pr 31:4; Isa 65:11; Jer 7:18 5:23 [x]S Ex 23:8; S Eze 22:12 [y]ver 7; S Isa 1:17; 10:2; 29:21; 59:4,13-15 [z]S Ps 94:21; Am 5:12; Jas 5:6 5:24 [a]S Isa 1:31 [b]Isa 47:14; Na 1:10 [c]S 2Ki 19:30; S Job 18:16

[e]10 Hebrew ten-yoke, that is, the land plowed by 10 yoke of oxen in one day   [f]10 That is, probably about 6 gallons (about 22 liters)   [g]10 That is, probably about 6 bushels (about 220 liters)   [h]10 That is, probably about 3/5 bushel (about 22 liters)   [i]14 Hebrew Sheol
[i]17 Septuagint; Hebrew / strangers will eat

5:8–23 A series of six woes are pronounced (vv. 8, 11–12, 18–19, 20, 21, 22–23), followed by three judgment sections (vv. 9–10, 13–15, 24–25).
5:8 house to house . . . field to field. Land in Israel could only be leased, never sold, because parcels had been permanently assigned to individual families (see Nu 27:7–11; 1Ki 21:1–3).
5:10 ephah. A tenth of a homer. Meager crops often accompanied national sin (Dt 28:38–39; Hag 2:16–17). The amount of wine and grain is only a tiny fraction of what a ten-acre vineyard and a homer of seed would normally produce.
5:11–13 See Am 4:1–3; 6:6–7, where a style of life characterized by drunkenness and revelry is likewise condemned.
5:14 grave. See note on Ge 37:35. The grave has an

insatiable appetite (see Hab 2:5).
5:18 Contrast Hos 11:4, where God leads his people with "cords of human kindness."
5:19 The Hebrew for the words "hurry" and "hasten" corresponds to that of the first and third elements of the name "Maher-Shalal-Hash-Baz" (see NIV text note on 8:1). When Isaiah named his son (8:3), he may have been responding to the sarcastic taunts of these sinners. God did bring swift judgment, according to v. 26. Holy One of Israel. See 1:4 and note.
5:22 mixing drinks. Spices were added to beer and wine (see Pr 23:30).
5:23 See 1:23; 10:1–2.
5:24 spurned . . . the Holy One of Israel. See v. 19; see also 1:4 and note.

and their flowers blow away like
  dust; [d]
for they have rejected the law of the
  LORD Almighty
and spurned the word [e] of the Holy
  One [f] of Israel.
25Therefore the LORD's anger [g] burns
  against his people;
his hand is raised and he strikes them
  down.
The mountains shake, [h]
and the dead bodies [i] are like refuse [j]
  in the streets. [k]

Yet for all this, his anger is not turned
  away, [l]
his hand is still upraised. [m]

26He lifts up a banner [n] for the distant
  nations,
he whistles [o] for those at the ends of
  the earth. [p]
Here they come,
  swiftly and speedily!
27Not one of them grows tired [q] or
  stumbles,
not one slumbers or sleeps;
not a belt [r] is loosened at the waist, [s]
not a sandal thong is broken. [t]
28Their arrows are sharp, [u]
all their bows [v] are strung;
their horses' hoofs [w] seem like flint,
their chariot wheels like a
  whirlwind. [x]
29Their roar is like that of the lion, [y]
  they roar like young lions;

they growl as they seize [z] their prey
and carry it off with no one to
  rescue. [a]
30In that day [b] they will roar over it
  like the roaring of the sea. [c]
And if one looks at the land,
he will see darkness [d] and distress; [e]
even the light will be darkened [f] by
  the clouds.

Isaiah's Commission

6 In the year that King Uzziah [g] died, [h] I
  saw the Lord [i] seated on a throne, [j]
high and exalted, [k] and the train of his
robe [l] filled the temple. 2Above him were
seraphs, [m] each with six wings: With two
wings they covered their faces, with two
they covered their feet, [n] and with two
they were flying. 3And they were calling to
one another:

"Holy, holy [o], holy is the LORD
  Almighty; [p]
the whole earth [q] is full of his
  glory." [r]

4At the sound of their voices the doorposts
and thresholds shook and the temple was
filled with smoke. [s]

5"Woe [t] to me!" I cried. "I am ruined! [u]

5:24
[d]S Job 24:24;
Isa 40:8
[e]Ps 107:11;
Isa 8:6; 30:9,12
[f]Job 6:10; Isa 1:4;
10:20; 12:6
5:25
[g]S 2Ki 22:13;
S Job 40:11;
Isa 10:17; 26:11;
31:9; 66:15;
S Jer 6:12
[h]S Ex 19:18
[i]S Ps 110:6
[j]S 2Ki 9:37
[k]S 2Sa 22:43
[l]Jer 4:8; Da 9:16
[m]Isa 9:12,17,21;
10:4
5:26 [n]S Ps 20:5
[o]Isa 7:18;
Zec 10:8
[p]Dt 28:49;
Isa 13:5; 18:3
5:27 [q]Isa 14:31;
40:29-31
[r]Isa 22:21;
Eze 23:15
[s]S Job 12:18
[t]Joel 2:7-8
5:28
[u]S Job 39:23;
Ps 45:5 [v]S Ps 7:12
[w]Eze 26:11
[x]S 2Ki 2:1;
S Job 1:19
5:29
[y]S 2Ki 17:25;
Jer 51:38;
Zep 3:3; Zec 11:3

[z]Isa 10:6;
49:24-25
[a]Isa 42:22;
Mic 5:8
5:30 [b]S Isa 2:11
[c]S Ps 93:3;
Jer 50:42;
Lk 21:25
[d]S 1Sa 2:9;
S Job 21:30;
Ps 18:28; 44:19;
S 82:5 [e]S Jdg 6:2;
Isa 22:5; 33:2;
Jer 4:23-28

[f]Isa 13:10; 50:3; Joel 2:10 **6:1** [g]S 2Ch 26:22,23 [h]S 2Ki 15:7
[i]S Ex 24:10; S Nu 12:8; Jn 12:41 [j]S 1Ki 22:19; S Ps 9:4;
S 123:1; S Rev 4:2 [k]Isa 52:13; 53:12 [l]Rev 1:13 **6:2**
[m]Eze 1:5; 10:15; Rev 4:8 [n]Eze 1:11 **6:3** [o]S Ex 15:11
[p]Ps 89:8 [q]Isa 11:9; 54:5; Mal 1:11 [r]S Ex 16:7; Nu 14:21;
Ps 72:19; Rev 4:8 **6:4** [s]S Ex 19:18; S 40:34; Eze 43:5; 44:4;
Rev 15:8 **6:5** [t]S Isa 5:8 [u]S Nu 17:12; S Dt 5:26

5:25 *The mountains shake.* When God takes action, even
the mountains tremble (see 64:3; Jer 4:24–26). This is the
language of theophany (a manifestation or appearance of
God). *Yet . . . upraised.* A refrain repeated in 9:12,17,21;
10:4.
5:26 *lifts up a banner.* A pole with a banner was often
placed on a hill as a signal for gathering troops (13:2) or for
summoning the nations to bring Israel back home (11:10,12;
49:22; 62:10). *distant nations.* Such as Assyria, whose armies struck Israel and Judah in 722 and 701 B.C., and
Babylon, which began its invasions in 605. *those at the ends
of the earth.* Nations like Egypt and Assyria.
5:27 *Not one . . . grows tired or stumbles.* Cf. the use of
these terms in 40:29–31.
5:30 *In that day.* See note on 2:11,17,20. *darkness and
distress.* Similar words describe the horrors of war in 8:22.
6:1 *the year that King Uzziah died.* 740 B.C. Isaiah's commission probably preceded his preaching ministry; the account was postponed to serve as a climax to the opening
series of oracles and to provide warrant for the shocking
announcements of judgment they contain. The people had
mocked the "Holy One of Israel" (5:19), and now he has
commissioned Isaiah to call them to account. Uzziah reigned
from 792 to 740 and was a godly and powerful king. When
he insisted on burning incense in the temple, however, he
was struck with leprosy and remained leprous until his death
(2Ch 26:16–21). He was also called Azariah (2Ki 14:21;
2Ch 26:1). *I saw.* Probably in a vision in the temple. *the*

Lord. The true King (see v. 5). *high and exalted.* The same
Hebrew words are applied to God in 57:15, and similar
terms are used of the suffering servant in 52:13. *train of his
robe.* A long, flowing garment. Cf. the robe of the "son of
man" in Rev 1:13. *temple.* Probably the heavenly temple,
with which the earthly temple was closely associated. John's
vision of God on his throne is similar (Rev 4:1–8).
6:2 *seraphs.* See v. 6; angelic beings not mentioned
elsewhere. The Hebrew root underlying this word means
"burn," perhaps to indicate their purity as God's ministers.
(It refers to venomous snakes in 14:29; 30:6; see Nu 21:6.)
They correspond to the "living creatures" of Rev 4:6–9,
each of whom also had six wings. *covered their faces.* Apparently they could not gaze directly at the glory of God.
6:3 *Holy, holy, holy.* The repetition underscores God's
infinite holiness. Note the triple use of "the temple of the
LORD" in Jer 7:4 to stress the people's confidence in the
security of Jerusalem because of the presence of that sanctuary. *full of his glory.* In Nu 14:21–22; Ps 72:18–19 the
worldwide glory of God is linked with his miraculous
signs.
6:4 *doorposts . . . shook . . . filled with smoke.* Similarly
the power of God's voice terrified the Israelites at Mount
Sinai, and the mountain was covered with smoke (see Ex
19:18–19; 20:18–19).
6:5 *eyes have seen the King.* Isaiah was dismayed because
anyone who saw God expected to die immediately (see Ge
16:13; 32:30 and notes; Ex 33:20).

For I am a man of unclean lips, [v][w] and I live among a people of unclean lips, [x] and my eyes have seen [y] the King, [z] the LORD Almighty." [a]

[6]Then one of the seraphs flew to me with a live coal [b] in his hand, which he had taken with tongs from the altar. [7]With it he touched my mouth and said, "See, this has touched your lips; [c] your guilt is taken away and your sin atoned for. [d]"

[8]Then I heard the voice [e] of the Lord saying, "Whom shall I send? [f] And who will go for us? [g]"

And I said, "Here am I. [h] Send me!"

[9]He said, "Go [i] and tell this people:

" 'Be ever hearing, but never
understanding;
be ever seeing, but never
perceiving.' [j]
[10]Make the heart of this people
callloused; [k]
make their ears dull
and close their eyes. [k] [l]
Otherwise they might see with their
eyes,
hear with their ears, [m]
understand with their hearts,
and turn and be healed." [n]

[11]Then I said, "For how long,
O Lord?" [o]

And he answered:

"Until the cities lie ruined [p]
and without inhabitant,
until the houses are left deserted [q]
and the fields ruined and ravaged, [r]

[12]until the LORD has sent everyone far
away [s]
and the land is utterly forsaken. [t]
[13]And though a tenth remains [u] in the
land,
it will again be laid waste. [v]
But as the terebinth and oak
leave stumps [w] when they are cut
down,
so the holy [x] seed will be the stump
in the land." [y]

The Sign of Immanuel

7 When Ahaz [z] son of Jotham, the son of Uzziah, was king of Judah, King Rezin [a] of Aram [b] and Pekah [c] son of Remaliah [d] king of Israel marched up to fight against Jerusalem, but they could not overpower it.

[2]Now the house of David [e] was told, "Aram has allied itself with [1] Ephraim [f]"; so the hearts of Ahaz and his people were shaken, [g] as the trees of the forest are shaken by the wind.

[3]Then the LORD said to Isaiah, "Go out, you and your son Shear-Jashub, [m] [h] to meet Ahaz at the end of the aqueduct of the Upper Pool, on the road to the Washerman's Field. [i] [4]Say to him, 'Be careful,

---

6:5 [v]Lk 5:8
[w]Ex 6:12
[x]Isa 59:3;
Jer 9:3-8
[y]S Ex 24:10
[z]Ps 45:3;
Isa 24:23; 32:1;
33:17; Jer 51:57
[a]S Job 42:5
6:6 [b]S Lev 10:1;
Eze 10:2
6:7 [c]Jer 1:9;
Da 10:16
[d]S Lev 26:41;
Isa 45:25;
Da 12:3; 1Jn 1:7
6:8 [e]S Job 40:9;
Ac 9:4 [f]Jer 26:12,
15 [g]S Ge 1:26
[h]S Ge 22:1;
S Ex 3:4
6:9 [i]Eze 3:11;
Am 7:15;
Mt 28:19
[j]Jer 5:21;
S Mt 13:15*;
Lk 8:10*
6:10 [k]S Ex 4:21;
Dt 32:15;
Ps 119:70
[l]Isa 29:9;
42:18-20; 43:8;
44:18
[m]S Dt 29:4;
Eze 12:2;
Mk 8:18
[n]S Dt 32:39;
Mt 13:13-15;
Mk 4:12*;
Jn 12:40*;
Ac 28:26-27*
6:11 [o]Ps 79:5
[p]S Lev 26:31;
S Jer 4:13
[q]S Lev 26:43;
Isa 24:10
[r]Ps 79:1;
S 109:11;
Jer 35:17

6:12 [s]S Dt 28:64
[t]Isa 5:5,9;
60:15; 62:4;
Jer 4:29; 30:17
6:13 [u]S Isa 1:9;
10:22 [v]S Isa 5:6
[w]S Job 14:8
[x]S Lev 27:30;
S Dt 14:2
[y]S Job 14:7

7:1 [z]S 1Ch 3:13 [a]S ver 8; S 2Ki 15:37 [b]2Ch 28:5
[c]S 2Ki 15:25 [d]ver 5,9; Isa 8:6 7:2 [e]ver 13; S 2Sa 7:11;
Isa 16:5; 22:22; Jer 21:12; Am 9:11 [f]Isa 9:9; Hos 5:3
[g]Isa 6:4; Da 5:6 7:3 [h]Isa 10:21-22 [i]2Ki 18:17; Isa 36:2

[k]9,10 Hebrew; Septuagint *You will be ever hearing, but never understanding; / you will be ever seeing, but never perceiving.* / [10]This people's heart has become calloused; / they hardly hear with their ears, / and they have closed their eyes [12] Or has set up camp in [m]3 Shear-Jashub means *a remnant will return.*

6:6 *live coal.* Coals of fire were taken inside the Most Holy Place on the Day of Atonement (Lev 16:12), when sacrifice was made to atone for sin. See note on 1:25.
6:7 *touched my mouth.* When God commissioned Jeremiah, his hand touched the prophet's mouth (Jer 1:9).
6:8–10 Isaiah's prophetic commission will have the ironic but justly deserved effect of hardening the callous hearts of rebellious Israel—and so rendering the warnings of judgment sure (see vv. 11–13). See also Jer 1:8,19; Eze 2:3–4.
6:8 *for us.* The heavenly King speaks in the divine council. As a true prophet, Isaiah is made privy to that council, as were Micaiah (1Ki 22:19–20) and Jeremiah (23:18,22). Cf. Ge 1:26; 11:7; Am 3:7. *Here am I.* See note on Ge 22:1.
6:9–10 Quoted by Jesus in the parable of the sower (Mt 13:14–15; Mk 4:12; Lk 8:10). See also Ro 11:7–10,25.
6:10 *heart ... ears ... eyes ... eyes ... ears ... hearts.* The *abc/cba* inversion is called a "chiastic" arrangement, a common literary device in the OT. *ears dull ... close their eyes.* Israel's deafness and blindness are also mentioned in 29:9; 42:18; 43:8. One day, however, the nation will be able to see and hear (29:18; 35:5).
6:12 *far away.* See 5:13.
6:13 *a tenth.* A remnant—even it will be laid waste. *holy seed.* The few that are faithful in Israel (cf. 1Ki 19:18; see note on 1:9). *stump.* Out of which the nation will grow

again. For a similar use of this imagery see 11:1.
7:1–12:6 The second section of Isaiah's prophecies, climaxing in the songs of praise found in ch. 12.
7:1 The invasion of Rezin and Pekah (probably in 735/734 B.C.) is known as the Syro-Ephraimite War. Aram (Syria) and Israel (Ephraim; see note on v. 2) were trying unsuccessfully to persuade Ahaz to join a coalition against Assyria, which had strong designs on lands to the west. Isaiah was trying to keep Ahaz from forming a counteralliance with Assyria (see 2Ki 16:5–18; 2Ch 28:16–21). *Pekah.* Ruled 752–732 B.C. (see 2Ki 15:27–31).
7:2 *house of David.* A reference to Ahaz, who belonged to David's dynasty (see 2Sa 7:8–11). *Ephraim.* Another name for Israel, the northern kingdom. *hearts ... were shaken.* Ahaz had been defeated by Aram and Israel earlier (2Ch 28:5–8).
7:3 *Shear-Jashub.* See NIV text note; see also 10:21–22. Isaiah gave each of his sons symbolic names (see 8:1,3,18). *aqueduct of the Upper Pool.* Location unknown. Ahaz was probably inspecting the city's water supply. *Washerman's Field.* Clothes were cleaned by trampling on them in cold water and using a kind of soap (soda) or bleach (Mal 3:2; Mk 9:3).
7:4 *two smoldering stubs.* Damascus (Aram's capital; see v. 8) was crushed by Tiglath-Pileser III in 732 B.C., and Israel

keep calm[j] and don't be afraid.[k] Do not lose heart[l] because of these two smoldering stubs[m] of firewood—because of the fierce anger[n] of Rezin and Aram and of the son of Remaliah.[o] 5Aram, Ephraim and Remaliah's[p] son have plotted[q] your ruin, saying, 6"Let us invade Judah; let us tear it apart and divide it among ourselves, and make the son of Tabeel king over it." 7Yet this is what the Sovereign LORD says: [r]

" 'It will not take place,
     it will not happen,[s]
8for the head of Aram is Damascus,[t]
     and the head of Damascus is only
        Rezin.[u]
Within sixty-five years
     Ephraim will be too shattered[v] to be
        a people.
9The head of Ephraim is Samaria,[w]
     and the head of Samaria is only
        Remaliah's son.
If you do not stand[x] firm in your faith,[y]
     you will not stand at all.' "[z]

10Again the LORD spoke to Ahaz, 11"Ask the LORD your God for a sign,[a] whether in the deepest depths or in the highest heights.[b]"

12But Ahaz said, "I will not ask; I will not put the LORD to the test.[c]"

13Then Isaiah said, "Hear now, you house of David![d] Is it not enough[e] to try the patience of men? Will you try the patience[f] of my God[g] also? 14Therefore the Lord himself will give you[n] a sign:[h] The virgin[i] will be with child and will give birth to a son,[j] and[o] will call him Immanuel.[p][k] 15He will eat curds[l] and honey[m] when he knows enough to reject the wrong and choose the right. 16But before the boy knows[n] enough to reject the wrong and choose the right,[o] the land of the two kings you dread will be laid waste.[p] 17The LORD will bring on you and on your people and on the house of your father a time unlike any since Ephraim broke away[q] from Judah—he will bring the king of Assyria.[r]"

18In that day[s] the LORD will whistle[t] for flies from the distant streams of Egypt and for bees from the land of Assyria.[u] 19They will all come and settle in the steep ravines and in the crevices[v] in the rocks, on all the thornbushes[w] and at all the water holes. 20In that day[x] the Lord will use[y] a razor hired from beyond the Riv-

7:4 /Isa 30:15; La 3:26
kS Ge 15:1;
S Dt 3:2; Isa 8:12; 12:2; 35:4; 37:6; Mt 24:6
/S Dt 20:3;
S Isa 21:4
mAm 4:11;
Zec 3:2
nIsa 10:24;
51:13; 54:14
oS 2Ki 15:27
7:5 pS ver 1 qver 2
7:7 rIsa 24:3; 25:8; 28:16
sPs 2:1; Isa 8:10; 14:24; 28:18; 40:8; 46:10; Ac 4:25
7:8 tS Ge 14:15
uver 1; Isa 9:11
v 2Ki 17:24;
Isa 8:4; 17:1-3
7:9 wS 2Ki 15:29;
Isa 9:9; 28:1,3
xS Ps 20:8;
Isa 8:10; 40:8
y2Ch 20:20
zIsa 8:6-8;
30:12-14
7:11 aS Ex 7:9;
S Dt 13:2
bPs 139:8
7:12 cDt 4:34
7:13 dS ver 2
eS Ge 30:15

/S Isa 1:14
gPs 63:1; 118:28;
Isa 25:1; 49:4;
61:10
7:14 hS Ex 3:12;
S Lk 2:12
/S Ge 24:43
/S Ge 3:15;
Lk 1:31
kS Ge 21:22;
Isa 8:8,10;
Mt 1:23*

7:15 /S Ge 18:8 mver 22 7:16 nIsa 8:4 oDt 1:39
pS Dt 13:16; Isa 17:3; Jer 7:15; Hos 5:9,13; Am 1:3-5 7:17
q1Ki 12:16 rS ver 20; S 2Ch 28:20 7:18 sver 20,21;
S Isa 2:11 tS Isa 5:26 uIsa 13:5 7:19 vS Isa 2:19 wver 25;
Isa 17:9; 34:13; 55:13 7:20 xS ver 18 yIsa 10:15; 29:16

n14 The Hebrew is plural.   o14 Masoretic Text; Dead Sea Scrolls and he or and they   p14 Immanuel means God with us.

was soundly defeated the same year.

7:6 *Tabeel.* An Aramaic name sometimes associated with the "land of Tob" east of the Jordan River (see Jdg 11:3).

7:8 *Within sixty-five years.* By c. 670 B.C. Esarhaddon (and, shortly after him, Ashurbanipal) king of Assyria settled foreign colonists in Israel. Their intermarriage with the few Israelites who had not been deported resulted in the "Samaritans" (see 2Ki 17:24–34 and note on 2Ki 17:29) and marked the end of Ephraim as a separate nation.

7:9 *only Remaliah's son.* Pekah was a usurper and hardly worthy to challenge Ahaz, a son of David. Aram (v. 8) and Israel (v. 9) had human heads. Judah had a divine head; God was with them (v. 14; 8:8,10). *stand firm . . . stand.* The use of the same Hebrew verb emphasizes the seriousness of the Lord's warning (see 1:19–20,25–26 and notes).

7:11 *a sign.* God was willing to strengthen the faith of Ahaz through a sign (see Ex 3:12).

7:13 *house of David.* See note on v. 2.

7:14 *sign.* A sign was normally fulfilled within a few years (see 20:3; 37:30; cf. 8:18). *virgin.* May refer to a young woman betrothed to Isaiah (8:3), who was to become his second wife (his first wife presumably having died after Shear-Jashub was born). In Ge 24:43 the same Hebrew word ('almah) refers to a woman about to be married (see also Pr 30:19). Mt 1:23 apparently understood the woman mentioned here to be a type (a foreshadowing) of the Virgin Mary. *Immanuel.* The name "God is with us" was meant to convince Ahaz that God could rescue him from his enemies. See Nu 14:9; 2Ch 13:12; Ps 46:7. "Immanuel" is used again in 8:8,10, and it may be another name for Maher-Shal-al-Hash-Baz (8:3). If so, the boy's names had complementary significance (see note on 8:3). Jesus was the final fulfillment

of this prophecy, for he was "God with us" in the fullest sense (Mt 1:23; cf. Isa 9:6–7).

7:15 *curds and honey.* Curds (a kind of yogurt) and honey meant a return to the simple diet of those who lived off the land. The Assyrian invasion would devastate the countryside and make farming impossible. (See vv. 22–25 for the significance of the expression.) *when he knows . . . wrong . . . right.* Suggests the age of moral determination and responsibility under the law—most likely 12 or 13 years of age. Thus, "when" this boy is 12 or 13 (722/721 B.C.), he will be eating curds and honey instead of agricultural products—due to the devastation of Israel by Assyria. Some believe that this expression involves a shorter period of time, identical to that in v. 16 and 8:4.

7:16 *before the boy knows . . . land . . . laid waste.* See note on v. 4; cf. 8:4. "Before" the boy is 12 or 13 years old, Aram and Israel will be plundered. This happened in 732 B.C., when the boy was about two years old.

7:17 *Ephraim broke away from Judah.* Almost two centuries earlier (see 1Ki 12:19–20). *king of Assyria.* Ahaz's appeal to Assyria would bring temporary relief (2Ki 16:8–9), but eventually Assyria would attack Judah (see 8:7–8; 36:1).

7:18,20,23 *In that day.* Their difficulties will be a foretaste of the "day of the LORD." See note on 2:11,17,20.

7:18 *flies . . . bees.* See Ex 23:28 and note.

7:19 *crevices in the rocks.* See note on 2:10. It will be impossible to escape from the invaders.

7:20 *shave . . . head . . . beards.* The forcible shaving of the beard was considered a great insult (2Sa 10:4–5). In times of mourning, a man would shave his own head and beard (see 15:2; see also note on 3:17).

er[q] [z]—the king of Assyria[a]—to shave
your head and the hair of your legs, and to
take off your beards[b] also.[c] 21In that
day,[d] a man will keep alive a young cow
and two goats.[e] 22And because of the
abundance of the milk they give, he will
have curds to eat. All who remain in the
land will eat curds[f] and honey.[g] 23In that
day,[h] in every place where there were a
thousand vines worth a thousand silver
shekels,[r] [i] there will be only briers and
thorns.[j] 24Men will go there with bow
and arrow, for the land will be covered
with briers[k] and thorns. 25As for all the
hills[l] once cultivated by the hoe, you will
no longer go there for fear of the briers and
thorns;[m] they will become places where
cattle are turned loose and where sheep
run.[n]

Assyria, the LORD's Instrument

8 The LORD said to me, "Take a large
scroll[o] and write on it with an ordinary
pen: Maher-Shalal-Hash-Baz.[s] [p]
2And I will call in Uriah[q] the priest and
Zechariah son of Jeberekiah as reliable witnesses[r]
for me."

3Then I went to the prophetess,[s] and
she conceived and gave birth to a son.[t]
And the LORD said to me, "Name him
Maher-Shalal-Hash-Baz.[u] 4Before the boy
knows[v] how to say 'My father' or 'My
mother,' the wealth of Damascus[w] and the
plunder of Samaria will be carried off by
the king of Assyria.[x]"

5The LORD spoke to me again:

6"Because this people has rejected[y]
the gently flowing waters of Shiloah[z]
and rejoices over Rezin
and the son of Remaliah,[a]
7therefore the Lord is about to bring
against them
the mighty floodwaters[b] of the
River[q]—
the king of Assyria[c] with all his
pomp.[d]
It will overflow all its channels,
run over all its banks[e]
8and sweep on into Judah, swirling over
it,[f]
passing through it and reaching up to
the neck.
Its outspread wings[g] will cover the
breadth of your land,
O Immanuel[t]!"[h]

9Raise the war cry,[u] [i] you nations, and
be shattered![j]
Listen, all you distant lands.
Prepare[k] for battle, and be shattered!
Prepare for battle, and be shattered!
10Devise your strategy, but it will be
thwarted;[l]
propose your plan, but it will not
stand,[m]
for God is with us.[v] [n]

Fear God

11The LORD spoke to me with his strong
hand upon me,[o] warning me not to follow[p]
the way of this people. He said:

7:20 [z]Isa 11:15; Jer 2:18 [a]ver 17; 2Ki 18:16; Isa 8:7; 10:5 [b]S 2Sa 10:4 [c]S Dt 28:49 **7:21** [d]ver 23; Isa 2:17 [e]Jer 39:10 **7:22** [f]S Ge 18:8 [g]ver 15; Isa 14:30 **7:23** [h]ver 21 [i]SS 8:11 [j]S Isa 5:6; Hos 2:12 **7:24** [k]S Isa 5:6 **7:25** [l]Hag 1:11 [m]S ver 19 [n]S Isa 5:17 **8:1** [o]S Dt 27:8; Job 19:23; Isa 30:8; Jer 51:60 [p]ver 3; Jer 20:3; Hos 1:4 **8:2** [q]S 2Ki 16:10 [r]ver 16; S Jos 24:22; S Ru 4:9; Jer 32:10,12,25, 44 **8:3** [s]S Ex 15:20 [t]S Ge 3:15 [u]S ver 1 **8:4** [v]Isa 7:16 [w]S Ge 14:15 [x]S Isa 7:8 **8:6** [y]S Isa 5:24 [z]S Ne 3:15; Jn 9:7 [a]S Isa 7:1 **8:7** [b]Isa 17:12-13; 28:2,17; 30:28; 43:2; Da 11:40; Na 1:8 [c]S 2Ch 28:20; S Isa 7:20 [d]Isa 10:16 [e]S Jos 3:15 **8:8** [f]Isa 28:15 [g]Isa 18:6; 46:11; Jer 4:13; 48:40 [h]S Isa 7:14 **8:9** [i]S Jos 6:5; Isa 17:12-13 [j]S Job 34:24 [k]Jer 6:4; 46:3; 51:12,27-28; Eze 38:7; Joel 3:9; Zec 14:2-3 **8:10** [l]S Job 5:12 [m]S Pr 19:21; S 21:30; S Isa 7:7 [n]S Isa 7:14; Mt 1:23; Ro 8:31 **8:11** [o]Eze 1:3; 3:14 [p]Eze 2:8

[q]*20,7* That is, the Euphrates [r]*23* That is, about 25 pounds (about 11.5 kilograms)
[s]*1* *Maher-Shalal-Hash-Baz* means *quick to the plunder, swift to the spoil*; also in verse 3. [t]*8* *Immanuel* means *God with us.* [u]*9* Or *Do your worst* [v]*10* Hebrew *Immanuel*

7:23 *briers and thorns.* See note on 5:6. The destruction of the vineyards and the farmlands would fulfill 5:5–6.

8:1–2 *scroll . . . witnesses.* The witnesses would attest to a legal transaction, either the marriage of Isaiah (see note on 7:14) or a symbolic deed connected with Maher-Shalal-Hash-Baz. The Hebrew word for "scroll" is related to the word for "unsealed copy" in Jer 32:11.

8:2 *Uriah the priest.* Served under King Ahaz (see 2Ki 16:10–11).

8:3–4 See 7:14–17.

8:3 *prophetess . . . son.* Probably the initial fulfillment of 7:14. This is the only known case of a prophetess (see note on Ex 15:20) marrying a prophet. But the young woman may be called a prophetess here because she had become the wife of a prophet. *Maher-Shalal-Hash-Baz.* This symbolic name (see NIV text note on v. 1) meant that Ahaz's enemies would be plundered (see v. 4 and note on 7:4), but it also implied that Judah would suffer (see vv. 7–8).

8:4 *knows how to say.* At about age two. The time period is identical to that in 7:16 (see notes on 7:4,16). *plunder of Samaria will be carried off.* The first stage of the destruction of the northern kingdom (see note on 7:4), which was not completed until 722–721 B.C. (see note on 7:15).

8:6 *waters of Shiloah.* The waters in Jerusalem that flow from the Gihon spring (see 2Ch 32:30) to the Pool of Siloam (see Jn 9:7) may be intended (see Ne 3:15). Here they symbolize the sustaining power of the Lord. *Rezin and the son of Remaliah.* Rezin and Pekah both died in 732 B.C. (see 2Ki 16:9; see note on Isa 7:1).

8:7–8 *floodwaters . . . sweep on.* Mighty rivers were often used to symbolize a powerful invading army (see 28:17–19).

8:8 *up to the neck.* Sennacherib's invasion in 701 B.C. overwhelmed all the cities of Judah except Jerusalem (see 1:7–9). *outspread wings.* The figure changes to a bird of prey, perhaps the eagle, renowned for its speed. *Immanuel.* All seems lost, but "God is with us" (v. 10) and defeats the enemy (see note on 7:14).

8:9 *nations . . . be shattered.* Just as Aram and Israel would be shattered (7:7–9), so Assyria and Babylon would eventually fall.

8:10 *it will not stand.* Only God's plans and purposes will last.

8:11 *his strong hand upon me.* See Eze 1:3; 37:1; 40:1. The prophets were conscious of God's presence in and control over their lives.

12"Do not call conspiracy q
    everything that these people call
        conspiracy w;
    do not fear what they fear, r
    and do not dread it. s
13The LORD Almighty is the one you are
        to regard as holy, t
    he is the one you are to fear, u
    he is the one you are to dread, v
14and he will be a sanctuary; w
    but for both houses of Israel he will
        be
    a stone x that causes men to stumble y
    and a rock that makes them fall. z
    And for the people of Jerusalem he will
        be
    a trap and a snare. a
15Many of them will stumble; b
    they will fall and be broken,
    they will be snared and captured."

16Bind up the testimony c
    and seal d up the law among my
        disciples.
17I will wait e for the LORD,
    who is hiding f his face from the
        house of Jacob.
    I will put my trust in him. g

18Here am I, and the children the LORD
has given me. h We are signs i and symbols j in Israel from the LORD Almighty,
who dwells on Mount Zion. k

19When men tell you to consult l mediums and spiritists, m who whisper and mutter, n should not a people inquire o of their
God? Why consult the dead on behalf of
the living? 20To the law p and to the testimony! q If they do not speak according to

this word, they have no light r of dawn.
21Distressed and hungry, s they will roam
through the land; t when they are famished, they will become enraged and, looking upward, will curse u their king and
their God. 22Then they will look toward
the earth and see only distress and darkness and fearful gloom, v and they will be
thrust into utter darkness. w

To Us a Child Is Born

9 Nevertheless, there will be no more
    gloom x for those who were in dis-
tress. In the past he humbled the land of
Zebulun and the land of Naphtali, y but in
the future he will honor Galilee of the
Gentiles, by the way of the sea, along the
Jordan—

2The people walking in darkness z
    have seen a great light; a
    on those living in the land of the
            shadow of death x b
    a light has dawned. c
3You have enlarged the nation d
    and increased their joy; e
    they rejoice before you
    as people rejoice at the harvest,
    as men rejoice
        when dividing the plunder. f
4For as in the day of Midian's defeat, g
    you have shattered h

8:12 qIsa 7:2;
20:5; 30:1; 36:6
rS Isa 7:4;
Mt 10:28
s1Pe 3:14*
8:13 tS Nu 20:12
uS Ex 20:20
vIsa 29:23
8:14 wS Isa 4:6
xS Ps 118:22
yJer 6:21;
Eze 3:20; 14:3,7;
Lk 20:18
zS Lk 2:34;
Ro 9:33*;
1Pe 2:8*
aS Ps 119:110;
Isa 24:17-18
8:15 bPr 4:19;
Isa 28:13; 59:10;
Ro 9:32
8:16 cS Ru 4:7
dIsa 29:11-12;
Jer 32:14;
Da 8:26; 12:4
8:17 eS Ps 27:14
fS Dt 31:17
gS Ps 22:5;
Heb 2:13*
8:18 hS Ge 33:5;
Heb 2:13*
iS Ex 3:12;
Eze 4:3; 12:6;
24:24; Lk 2:34
jS Dt 28:46;
S Eze 12:11
kPs 9:11
8:19 lS 1Sa 28:8
mS Lev 19:31
nIsa 29:4
oS Nu 27:21
8:20 pS Isa 1:10;
Lk 16:29
qS Ru 4:7

rver 22; Isa 9:2;
59:9; 60:2;
Mic 3:6
8:21 sS Job 18:12
tJob 30:3
uS Ex 22:28;
Rev 16:11
8:22 vS Job 15:24
wS ver 20;
S Job 3:13;
S Isa 5:30;
S Joel 2:2;
Mt 25:30;
Rev 16:10

9:1 xS Job 15:24 yS 2Ki 15:29 9:2 zS Ps 82:5; S 107:10,14;
S Isa 8:20 aS Ps 36:9; Isa 42:6; 49:6; 60:19; Mal 4:2;
Eph 5:8 bS Lk 1:79 cIsa 58:8; Mt 4:15-16* 9:3 dS Job 12:23
eS Ps 4:7; S Isa 25:9 fS Ex 15:9; S Jos 22:8; S Ps 119:162 9:4
gS Jdg 7:25 hS Job 34:24; Isa 37:36-38

w12 Or Do not call for a treaty / every time these people
call for a treaty   x2 Or land of darkness

8:12 conspiracy. Isaiah's warning against relying on Assyria was considered treason (see note on 7:1; cf. Jer
37:13–14).
8:13 the one you are to fear. See 7:2; Pr 1:7.
8:14 sanctuary . . . stone . . . fall. Either the Lord is the
cornerstone of our lives (see 28:16) or he is a rock over
which we fall. See Ro 9:33; 1Pe 2:6–8 for an application to
Christ. both houses. The northern and southern kingdoms,
Israel and Judah.
8:16 Perhaps a reference to the legal transaction connected
with vv. 1–2 (see note there). testimony. See v. 20. By
preserving Isaiah's teaching ("the law"), his disciples could
later prove that his predictions had come true. This term
occurs elsewhere only in Ru 4:7 ("method of legalizing
transactions"). law. The Hebrew for this word can also mean
"teaching" or "instruction." The legal document containing
Isaiah's teaching about Assyria's invasion was tied and sealed
and then given to the prophet's followers, who were to
preserve it until the time of its fulfillment, when God would
authenticate it by the events of history (see Jer 32:12–14,
44).
8:17–18 In Heb 2:13 these verses are applied to Christ.
8:17 hiding his face. See 1:15; 59:2; Mic 3:4.
8:18 signs and symbols. See notes on 7:3,14; cf. 20:3.
8:19 mediums and spiritists. In the present crisis, people

were turning to the spirits of the dead (necromancy), as King
Saul did when he went to a medium to contact the spirit of
Samuel (1Sa 28:8–11) and learn about the future. See note
on 3:2–3.
8:20 the law . . . the testimony. See v. 16 and note. Only
by heeding the Lord's word through Isaiah—reinforced by
the "signs and symbols" (v. 18) that Isaiah and his sons
represented—would the light dawn for Israel.
8:21–22 The Assyrian invasion would bring deep distress
on all Israel.
8:21 curse . . . king and . . . God. Because of their terrible
suffering (cf. Pr 19:3)—but severe punishment awaited anyone who cursed God or a ruler (Ex 22:28; Lev 24:15–16).
9:1 Naphtali. This tribe in northern Israel suffered greatly
when the Assyrian Tiglath-Pileser III attacked in 734 and
732 B.C. (2Ki 15:29). will honor Galilee. Fulfilled when Jesus
ministered in Capernaum—near the major highway from
Egypt to Damascus, called the "way of the sea" (Mt
4:13–15).
9:2 great light. Jesus and his salvation would be a "light for
the Gentiles" (42:6; 49:6).
9:4 Midian's defeat. Gideon defeated the hordes of Midian
and broke their domination over Israel (Jdg 7:22–25). yoke
. . . bar. In 10:26–27 Isaiah predicts that God will destroy
the Assyrian army and their oppressive yoke. This was ful-

the yoke[i] that burdens them,
the bar across their shoulders,[j]
the rod of their oppressor.[k]

[5]Every warrior's boot used in battle
and every garment rolled in blood
will be destined for burning,[l]
will be fuel for the fire.

[6]For to us a child is born,[m]
to us a son is given,[n]
and the government[o] will be on his
shoulders.[p]
And he will be called
Wonderful Counselor,[y][q] Mighty
God,[r]
Everlasting[s] Father,[t] Prince of
Peace.[u]

[7]Of the increase of his government[v] and
peace[w]
there will be no end.[x]
He will reign[y] on David's throne
and over his kingdom,
establishing and upholding it
with justice[z] and righteousness[a]
from that time on and forever.[b]
The zeal[c] of the LORD Almighty
will accomplish this.

The LORD's Anger Against Israel

[8]The Lord has sent a message[d] against
Jacob;
it will fall on Israel.

[9]All the people will know it—
Ephraim[e] and the inhabitants of
Samaria[f]—
who say with pride
and arrogance[g] of heart,

[10]"The bricks have fallen down,
but we will rebuild with dressed
stone;[h]
the fig[i] trees have been felled,

but we will replace them with
cedars.[j] "

[11]But the LORD has strengthened Rezin's[k]
foes against them
and has spurred their enemies on.

[12]Arameans[l] from the east and
Philistines[m] from the west
have devoured[n] Israel with open
mouth.

Yet for all this, his anger[o] is not turned
away,
his hand is still upraised.[p]

[13]But the people have not returned[q] to
him who struck[r] them,
nor have they sought[s] the LORD
Almighty.

[14]So the LORD will cut off from Israel both
head and tail,
both palm branch and reed[t] in a
single day;[u]

[15]the elders[v] and prominent men[w] are
the head,
the prophets[x] who teach lies[y] are
the tail.

[16]Those who guide[z] this people mislead
them,
and those who are guided are led
astray.[a]

[17]Therefore the Lord will take no pleasure
in the young men,[b]
nor will he pity[c] the fatherless and
widows,
for everyone is ungodly[d] and wicked,[e]

9:4 [i]Isa 14:25; 58:6,9; Jer 2:20; 30:8; Eze 30:18; Na 1:13; Mt 11:30 [j]S Ps 81:6; S Isa 10:27 [k]Isa 14:4; 16:4; 29:5,20; 49:26; 51:13; 54:14; 60:18 9:5 [l]S Isa 2:4 9:6 [m]S Ge 3:15; Isa 53:2; Lk 2:11 [n]Jn 3:16 [o]S Mt 28:18 [p]Isa 22:22 [q]S Job 15:8; Isa 28:29 [r]S Dt 7:21; Ps 24:8; Isa 10:21; 11:2; 42:13 [s]S Ps 90:2 [t]S Ex 4:22; Isa 64:8; Jn 14:9-10 [u]Isa 26:3,12; 53:5; 66:12; Jer 33:6; Mic 5:5; S Lk 2:14 9:7 [v]S Isa 2:4 [w]S Ps 85:8; 119:165; Isa 11:9; 26:3,12; 32:17; 48:18 [x]Da 2:44; 4:3; S Lk 1:33; Jn 12:34 [y]Isa 1:26; 32:1; 60:17; 1Co 15:25 [z]Isa 11:4; 16:5; 32:1,16; 33:5; 42:1; Jer 23:5; 33:14 [a]S Ps 72:2 [b]S 2Sa 7:13 [c]2Ki 19:31; Isa 26:11; 37:32; 42:13; 59:17; 63:15 9:8 [d]S Dt 32:2 9:9 [e]S Isa 7:2 [f]S Isa 7:9 [g]Isa 46:12; 48:4; Eze 2:4; Zec 7:11 9:10 [h]S Ge 11:3 [i]Am 7:14; Lk 19:4

[1Ki 7:2-3 9:11 [k]S Isa 7:8 9:12 [l]2Ki 16:6 [m]S 2Ch 28:18 [n]S Ps 79:7 [o]S Job 40:11 [p]S Isa 5:25

9:13 [q]S 2Ch 28:22; Am 4:9; Zep 3:7; Hag 2:17 [r]Jer 5:3; Eze 7:9 [s]Isa 2:3; 17:7; 31:1; 55:6; Jer 50:4; Da 9:13; Hos 3:5; 7:7,10; Am 4:6,10; Zep 1:6 9:14 [t]ver 14-15; Isa 19:15 [u]Rev 18:8 9:15 [v]Isa 3:2-3 [w]S Isa 5:13 [x]Isa 28:7; Eze 13:2 [y]S Job 13:4; S Isa 3:8; 44:20; Eze 13:22; Mt 24:24 9:16 [z]Mt 15:14; 23:16,24 [a]S Isa 3:12 9:17 [b]Jer 9:21; 11:22; 18:21; 48:15; 49:26; Am 4:10; 8:13 [c]S Job 5:4; Isa 27:11; Jer 13:14 [d]Isa 10:6; 32:6; Mic 7:2 [e]S Isa 1:4

[y]6 Or Wonderful, Counselor

filled in 701 B.C. (see 37:36–38).
9:5 *boot . . . garment.* Military equipment will no longer be needed. See notes on 2:2–4.
9:6 *son.* A royal son, a son of David (see v. 7; see also 2Sa 7:14; Ps 2:7; Mt 1:1; 3:17; Lk 1:32). *Wonderful Counselor.* Each of the four throne names of the Messiah consists of two elements. Unlike Immanuel (see note on 7:14), these titles were not like normal OT personal names. "Counselor" points to the Messiah as a king (see Mic 4:9) who determines upon and carries out a program of action (see 14:27, "purposed"; Ps 20:4, "plans"). As Wonderful Counselor, the coming Son of David will carry out a royal program that will cause all the world to marvel. What that program will be is spelled out in ch. 11, and more fully in chs. 24–27 (see 25:1—"marvelous things, things planned [counseled] long ago"). *Mighty God.* See 10:21. His divine power as a warrior is stressed. *Everlasting Father.* He will be an enduring, compassionate provider and protector (cf. 40:9–11). *Prince of Peace.* His rule will bring wholeness and well-being to individuals and to society (see 11:6–9).
9:7 *David's throne . . . righteousness . . . forever.* In spite

of the sins of kings like Ahaz, Christ will be a descendant of David who will rule in righteousness forever (see 11:3–5; 2Sa 7:12–13,16; Jer 33:15,20–22). *The zeal . . . this.* God is like a jealous lover who will not abandon his people.
9:9 *Ephraim.* See note on 7:2.
9:10 *bricks have fallen down.* Bricks made of clay and dried by the sun crumbled easily. *dressed stone.* Amos denounces the stone mansions of the wicked (Am 5:11). *cedars.* The cedars of Lebanon provided the most valuable wood in the ancient Near East (see 1Ki 7:2–3).
9:11 *Rezin's foes.* The Assyrians (see note on 7:1).
9:12,17,21 *Yet . . . upraised.* See 5:25. This refrain is repeated in 10:4, where the anger of the Lord reaches a climax in the captivity of his people.
9:14 *head and tail . . . palm branch and reed.* The leaders of Israel (see also 3:1–3). These two pairs refer to Egyptian leaders in 19:15.
9:17 *fatherless and widows.* They often suffered at the hands of the powerful (see note on 1:17), but now even they are wicked.

every mouth speaks vileness. *f*

Yet for all this, his anger is not turned
        away,
    his hand is still upraised. *g*

[18]Surely wickedness burns like a fire; *h*
    it consumes briers and thorns, *i*
    it sets the forest thickets ablaze, *j*
        so that it rolls upward in a column of
            smoke.
[19]By the wrath *k* of the LORD Almighty
        the land will be scorched *l*
    and the people will be fuel for the fire; *m*
        no one will spare his brother. *n*
[20]On the right they will devour,
        but still be hungry; *o*
    on the left they will eat, *p*
        but not be satisfied.
    Each will feed on the flesh of his own
        offspring *z* :
[21]   Manasseh will feed on Ephraim, and
            Ephraim on Manasseh; *q*
        together they will turn against
            Judah. *r*

Yet for all this, his anger is not turned
        away,
    his hand is still upraised. *s*

10 Woe *t* to those who make unjust
            laws,
        to those who issue oppressive
            decrees, *u*
[2]to deprive *v* the poor of their rights
        and withhold justice from the
            oppressed of my people, *w*
    making widows their prey
        and robbing the fatherless. *x*
[3]What will you do on the day of
        reckoning, *y*
    when disaster *z* comes from afar?
    To whom will you run for help? *a*
        Where will you leave your riches?
[4]Nothing will remain but to cringe
        among the captives *b*

or fall among the slain. *c*

Yet for all this, his anger is not turned
        away, *d*
    his hand is still upraised.

God's Judgment on Assyria

[5]"Woe *e* to the Assyrian, *f* the rod *g* of
        my anger,
    in whose hand is the club *h* of my
        wrath! *i*
[6]I send him against a godless *j* nation,
    I dispatch *k* him against a people who
        anger me, *l*
    to seize loot and snatch plunder, *m*
        and to trample *n* them down like mud
            in the streets.
[7]But this is not what he intends, *o*
    this is not what he has in mind;
    his purpose is to destroy,
        to put an end to many nations.
[8]'Are not my commanders *p* all kings?'
        he says.
[9]   'Has not Calno *q* fared like
            Carchemish? *r*
    Is not Hamath *s* like Arpad, *t*
        and Samaria *u* like Damascus? *v*
[10]As my hand seized the kingdoms of the
        idols, *w*
    kingdoms whose images excelled
        those of Jerusalem and
            Samaria—
[11]shall I not deal with Jerusalem and her
        images
    as I dealt with Samaria and her
        idols?' " *x*

[12]When the Lord has finished all his

Cross-references (center column):

9:17 *f* S Isa 3:8;
Mt 12:34;
Ro 3:13-14
g S Isa 5:25
9:18
h S Dt 29:23;
S Isa 1:31
i S Isa 5:6
j S Ps 83:14
9:19
k S Job 40:11;
Isa 13:9,13
l Jer 17:27
m S Ps 97:3;
S Isa 1:31
n S Isa 3:5
9:20
o S Lev 26:26;
S Job 18:12
p Isa 49:26;
Zec 11:9
9:21 *q* S Jdg 7:22;
S 12:4
r S 2Ch 28:6
s S Isa 5:25
10:1 *t* S Isa 5:8
u S Ps 58:2
10:2 *v* Isa 3:14
w S Isa 5:23
x S Dt 10:18;
S Job 6:27;
S Isa 1:17
10:3 *y* S Job 31:14
z ver 25; Ps 59:5;
Isa 1:24; 13:6;
14:23; 24:6;
26:14; 47:11;
Jer 5:9; 9:9;
50:15; Lk 19:44
a S Ps 108:12;
Isa 20:6; 30:7;
31:3
10:4 *b* Isa 24:22;
Zec 9:11

c Isa 22:2; 34:3;
66:16; Jer 39:6;
Na 3:3
d S Isa 5:25; 12:1;
63:10; 64:5;
Jer 4:8; 30:24;
La 1:12
10:5
e S 2Ki 19:21;
S Isa 28:1 *f* ver 12,
18; S Isa 7:20;
14:25; 31:8;
37:7; Zep 2:13
g Isa 14:5; 54:16
h ver 15,24;
Isa 30:31; 41:15;
45:1; Jer 50:23;
51:20 *i* Isa 9:4;
13:3,5,13; 26:20;
30:30; 34:2;
63:6; 66:14;
Eze 30:24-25
10:6 *j* S Isa 9:17
k Hab 1:12
l S 2Ch 28:9;
Isa 9:19

m S Jdg 6:4; S Isa 5:29; 8:1 *n* S 2Sa 22:43; S Ps 7:5; S Isa 5:5;
37:26-27 10:7 *o* S Ge 50:20; Ac 4:23-28 10:8 *p* 2Ki 18:24
10:9 *q* S Ge 10:10 *r* S 2Ch 35:20 *s* Nu 34:8; 2Ch 8:4;
Isa 11:11 *t* 2Ki 18:34 *u* 2Ki 17:6 *v* S Ge 14:15; 2Ki 16:9;
Jer 49:24 10:10 *w* 2Ki 19:18 10:11 *x* S 2Ki 19:13; S Isa 2:8;
36:18-20; 37:10-13

z 20 Or arm

Footnotes (bottom):

9:18 *briers and thorns.* See note on 5:6.
9:19 *fuel for the fire.* Contrast v. 5.
9:21 *Manasseh ... Ephraim.* These two prominent tribes
in the northern kingdom were descended from the two sons
of Joseph (see Ge 46:20; see also Ge 48:5–6 and notes).
They had fought each other centuries earlier (Jdg 12:4).
10:1 *Woe.* Cf. the series of woes in 5:8–23.
10:2 *widows ... fatherless.* See notes on 1:17; 9:17.
10:4 *captives ... slain.* Jer 39:6–7 similarly describes the
plight of Judah's rulers when Nebuchadnezzar captured
Jerusalem in 586 B.C. *Yet ... uprais ed.* See note on 9:12,
17,21.
10:5 *rod ... club.* See 9:4 and note. Babylon also was a
hammer or club used by God to punish other nations (Jer
50:23; 51:20; Hab 1:6).
10:6 *godless nation.* Judah (see v. 10). *loot ... plunder.*
The last part of the fulfillment symbolized by Maher-Shalal-

Hash-Baz ("loot" here is the translation of Hebrew *shalal*,
and "plunder" is the translation of *baz*). See 8:1–4 and note
on 8:3.

10:9 *Calno.* A region in northern Aram (Syria). See Calneh
in Am 6:2. *Carchemish.* The great fortress on the
Euphrates River east of Calno (see Jer 46:2). *Hamath.* A city
on the Orontes River that marked the northern extent of
Solomon's rule (2Ch 8:4). See note on 2Ki 17:24. *Arpad.* A
city near Hamath and just south of Calno. All these areas
submitted to Assyria by c. 717 B.C. (see 36:19).

10:10 *images ... of Jerusalem and Samaria.* No Israelite
was supposed to worship idols, but the land was full of them
(2:8). Samaria fell to Shalmaneser V (2Ki 17:3–6) and Sargon II in 722–721 B.C.

10:12 *pride.* Judgment against the proud was announced
in 2:11,17.

work[y] against Mount Zion[z] and Jerusalem, he will say, "I will punish the king of Assyria[a] for the willful pride[b] of his heart and the haughty look[c] in his eyes. [13]For he says:

" 'By the strength of my hand[d] I have
    done this,[e]
and by my wisdom, because I have
    understanding.
I removed the boundaries of nations,
    I plundered their treasures;[f]
like a mighty one I subdued[a] their
    kings.[g]
[14]As one reaches into a nest,[h]
    so my hand reached for the wealth[i]
        of the nations;
as men gather abandoned eggs,
    so I gathered all the countries;[j]
not one flapped a wing,
    or opened its mouth to chirp.[k] ' "

[15]Does the ax raise itself above him who
    swings it,
    or the saw boast against him who
        uses it?[l]
As if a rod were to wield him who lifts
    it up,
    or a club[m] brandish him who is not
        wood!
[16]Therefore, the Lord, the LORD Almighty,
    will send a wasting disease[n] upon his
        sturdy warriors;[o]
under his pomp[p] a fire[q] will be kindled
    like a blazing flame.
[17]The Light of Israel will become a fire,[r]
    their Holy One[s] a flame;
in a single day it will burn and consume
    his thorns[t] and his briers.[u]
[18]The splendor of his forests[v] and fertile
    fields
it will completely destroy,[w]
    as when a sick man wastes away.
[19]And the remaining trees of his forests[x]
    will be so few[y]

10:12
[y]Isa 28:21-22;
65:7; 66:4;
Jer 5:29
[z]2Ki 19:31 [a]S ver
5; S 2Ki 19:7;
Isa 30:31-33;
37:36-38;
Isa 50:18
[b]S Isa 2:11;
S Eze 28:17
[c]Ps 18:27
10:13 [d]S Dt 8:17
[e]S Dt 32:26-27;
Isa 47:7; Da 4:30
[f]Eze 28:4
[g]Isa 14:13-14
10:14 [h]Jer 49:16;
Ob 1:4;
Hab 2:6-11
[i]S Job 31:25
[j]Isa 14:6
[k]2Ki 19:22-24;
Isa 37:24-25
10:15 [l]S Isa 7:20;
45:9; Ro 9:20-21
[m]S ver 5
10:16 [n]ver 18;
S Nu 11:33;
Isa 17:4
[o]Ps 78:31
[p]S Isa 8:7
[q]Jer 21:14
10:17
[r]S Job 41:21;
S Isa 1:31; 31:9;
Zec 2:5 [s]Isa 37:23
[t]S Nu 11:1-3;
S 2Sa 23:6
[u]S Isa 9:18
10:18
[v]S 2Ki 19:23
[w]S ver 5
10:19 [x]ver
33-34; Isa 32:19
[y]Isa 17:6; 21:17;
27:13; Jer 44:28

10:20 [z]ver 27;
Isa 11:10,11;
12:1,4; 19:18,19;
24:21; 28:5;
52:6; Zec 9:16
[a]S Isa 1:9;
Eze 7:16
[b]S 2Ki 16:7
[c]2Ch 28:20
[d]2Ch 14:11;
Isa 17:7; 48:2;
50:10; Jer 21:2;
Hos 3:5; 6:1;
Mic 3:11; 7:7
[e]S Isa 5:24
10:21 [f]S Ge 45:7;
Isa 6:13; Zep 3:13
[g]Isa 7:3 [h]S Isa 9:6
10:22 [i]S Ge 12:2;
Isa 48:19;
Jer 33:22

that a child could write them down.

The Remnant of Israel

[20]In that day[z] the remnant of Israel,
    the survivors[a] of the house of Jacob,
will no longer rely[b] on him
    who struck them down[c]
but will truly rely[d] on the LORD,
    the Holy One of Israel. [e]
[21]A remnant[f] will return,[b][g] a remnant
    of Jacob
    will return to the Mighty God. [h]
[22]Though your people, O Israel, be like
    the sand[i] by the sea,
    only a remnant will return.[j]
Destruction has been decreed,[k]
    overwhelming and righteous.
[23]The Lord, the LORD Almighty, will carry
    out
    the destruction decreed[l] upon the
        whole land. [m]

[24]Therefore, this is what the Lord, the
LORD Almighty, says:

"O my people who live in Zion, [n]
    do not be afraid[o] of the Assyrians,
who beat[p] you with a rod[q]
    and lift up a club against you, as
        Egypt did.
[25]Very soon[r] my anger against you will
    end
    and my wrath[s] will be directed to
        their destruction. [t] "

[26]The LORD Almighty will lash[u] them
    with a whip,

[Ezr 1:4; Isa 11:11; 46:3 [k]ver 23; Isa 28:22; Jer 40:2;
Da 9:27 10:23 [l]S ver 22 [m]Isa 6:12; 28:22; Ro 9:27-28*
10:24 [n]Ps 87:5-6 [o]S Isa 7:4 [p]S Ex 5:14 [q]S ver 5 10:25
[r]Isa 17:14; 29:17; Hag 2:6 [s]ver 5; Ps 30:5; Isa 13:5; 24:21;
26:20; 30:30; 34:2; 66:14; Da 8:19; 11:36 [t]S ver 3; Mic 5:6
10:26 [u]Isa 37:36-38

[a]13 Or / I subdued the mighty,   [b]21 Hebrew
shear-jashub; also in verse 22

10:13-14   my . . . I. The king of Assyria boastfully refers to himself nine times. Cf. 14:13-14; Eze 28:2-5.
10:15   ax . . . saw . . . rod . . . club. See v. 5; 9:4 and notes.
10:16   the Lord, the LORD Almighty. See 1:24 and note. wasting disease. When the angel put to death 185,000 soldiers of the Assyrian king Sennacherib in 701 B.C., he may have used a rapidly spreading plague (see note on 37:36; see also 2Sa 24:15-16; 1Ch 21:22,27).
10:17,20   Holy One. See note on 1:4.
10:18-19   forests. A reference to the Assyrian army. See vv. 33-34.
10:19   Probably fulfilled between 612 B.C. (fall of Nineveh) and 605 (battle of Carchemish).
10:20,27   In that day. The day of victory and joy, the positive aspect of the "day of the LORD" (see notes on 2:11,17,20; 9:4). Israel is restored and the people praise God. Ch. 11 connects this "day" with the Messianic age (see 11:10-11; see also 12:1,4).

10:20-22   remnant. See note on 1:9. "A remnant will return" was the name of Isaiah's first son (see NIV text note on 7:3). A faithful remnant led by Hezekiah survived the Assyrian invasion of 701 B.C. (see 37:4). Later, a remnant returned from Babylonian exile.
10:20   him who struck them. The king of Assyria (see note on 7:17).
10:21   Mighty God. See note on 9:6.
10:22   the sand by the sea. See notes on Ge 13:16; 22:17. Destruction . . . decreed. Because of Israel's sin, God would punish the nation through foreign invaders.
10:23-24   The Lord, the LORD Almighty. See 1:24 and note.
10:24   rod . . . club. See v. 5; 9:4 and notes.
10:26-27   Midian . . . burden . . . yoke. See note on 9:4.
10:26   Oreb. One of the Midianite leaders (Jdg 7:25). the waters . . . in Egypt. When Moses stretched out his hand over the Red Sea, the waters engulfed the chariots of Pharaoh

as when he struck down Midian[v] at
   the rock of Oreb;
and he will raise his staff[w] over the
   waters,[x]
as he did in Egypt.
[27]In that day[y] their burden[z] will be lifted
   from your shoulders,
   their yoke[a] from your neck;[b]
the yoke[c] will be broken
   because you have grown so fat.[c]

[28]They enter Aiath;
   they pass through Migron;[d]
   they store supplies[e] at Micmash.[f]
[29]They go over the pass, and say,
   "We will camp overnight at Geba.[g]"
Ramah[h] trembles;
   Gibeah[i] of Saul flees.[j]
[30]Cry out, O Daughter of Gallim![k]
   Listen, O Laishah!
   Poor Anathoth![l]
[31]Madmenah is in flight;
   the people of Gebim take cover.
[32]This day they will halt at Nob;[m]
   they will shake their fist[n]
at the mount of the Daughter of
   Zion,[o]
at the hill of Jerusalem.

[33]See, the Lord, the LORD Almighty,
   will lop off[p] the boughs with great
   power.
The lofty trees will be felled,[q]
   the tall[r] ones will be brought low.[s]
[34]He will cut down[t] the forest thickets
   with an ax;
Lebanon[u] will fall before the Mighty
   One.[v]

The Branch From Jesse

11 A shoot[w] will come up from the
   stump[x] of Jesse;[y]
   from his roots a Branch[z] will bear
   fruit.[a]
[2]The Spirit[b] of the LORD will rest on
   him—
   the Spirit of wisdom[c] and of
   understanding,
   the Spirit of counsel and of power,[d]
   the Spirit of knowledge and of the
   fear of the LORD—
[3]and he will delight in the fear[e] of the
   LORD.

He will not judge by what he sees with
   his eyes,[f]
or decide by what he hears with his
   ears;[g]
[4]but with righteousness[h] he will judge
   the needy,[i]
   with justice[j] he will give decisions
   for the poor[k] of the earth.
He will strike[l] the earth with the rod of
   his mouth;[m]
with the breath[n] of his lips he will
   slay the wicked.[o]
[5]Righteousness will be his belt[p]
   and faithfulness[q] the sash around his
   waist.[r]

[6]The wolf will live with the lamb,[s]

10:26 [v]S Isa 9:4; [w]Isa 30:32; [x]S Ex 14:16 **10:27** [y]S ver 20; [z]S Ps 66:11; [a]S Lev 26:13; S Isa 9:4; [b]Isa 14:25; 47:6; 52:2 [c]Jer 30:8 **10:28** [d]S 1Sa 14:2; [e]S Jos 1:11; [f]1Sa 13:2 **10:29** [g]S Jos 18:24; S Ne 11:31; [h]S Jos 18:25; [i]S Jdg 19:14; [j]Isa 15:5 **10:30** [k]1Sa 25:44; [l]S Ne 11:32 **10:32** [m]S 1Sa 21:1; [n]S Job 15:25; [o]S Ps 9:14; Isa 16:1; Jer 6:23 **10:33** [p]Isa 18:5; 27:11; Eze 17:4; [q]S Ex 12:12; [r]Isa 2:13; Am 2:9; [s]Isa 5:15 **10:34** [t]Na 1:12; Zec 11:2; [u]S 2Ki 19:23; [v]S Ge 49:24; Ps 93:4; Isa 33:21

11:1 [w]S 2Ki 19:26; S Job 14:7; [x]S Job 14:8 [y]ver 10; Isa 9:7; S Mt 1:1; S Rev 5:5; [z]S Isa 4:2; [a]S 2Ki 19:30; S Isa 27:6 **11:2** [b]S Jdg 3:10; Isa 32:15; 42:1; 44:3; 48:16; 59:21; 61:1; Eze 37:14; 39:29; Joel 2:28; Mt 3:16; Jn 1:32-33; 16:13 [c]S Ex 28:3; S Eph 1:17; S Col 2:3; [d]S Isa 9:6; 2Ti 1:7

11:3 [e]Isa 33:6 [f]Jn 7:24 [g]Jn 2:25 **11:4** [h]S Ps 72:2; [i]S Ps 72:4; S Isa 14:30 [j]S Isa 9:7; Rev 19:11 [k]S Job 5:16; S Isa 3:14; [l]Isa 27:7; 30:31; Zec 14:12; Mal 4:6; [m]S Job 40:18; S Ps 2:9; Rev 19:15 [n]S Job 4:9; Ps 18:8; Isa 30:28,33; 40:24; 59:19; Eze 21:31; 2Th 2:8 [o]S Ps 139:19 **11:5** [p]Ex 12:11; 1Ki 18:46; [q]Isa 25:1 [r]Eph 6:14 **11:6** [s]Isa 65:25

[c]27 Hebrew; Septuagint *broken / from your shoulders*

(see Ex 14:26–28).
10:27 *fat.* Like a sturdy animal, Israel is able to break the yoke.
10:28–32 As if seeing a vision, Isaiah describes the approach of the Assyrian army to Jerusalem from about ten miles north of the city.
10:28 *Micmash.* Located about seven miles north of Jerusalem.
10:29 *Ramah.* The home of Samuel. It was about five miles from Jerusalem (1Sa 7:17). *Gibeah of Saul.* About three miles from Jerusalem. It had been the capital of Israel's first king (see 1Sa 10:26).
10:30 *Poor Anathoth.* Jeremiah's hometown (see Jer 1:1). The Hebrew for "poor" sounds like the word "Anathoth," thus a wordplay.
10:32 *Nob.* Perhaps on Mount Scopus, on the outskirts of Jerusalem. *Daughter of Zion.* A personification of Jerusalem and its inhabitants.
10:33 *the Lord, the LORD Almighty.* See 1:24 and note. *boughs . . . trees.* Sennacherib and his armies will fall (see vv. 16–19 and notes).
10:34 *Lebanon.* Refers to the famed cedars of Lebanon (see note on 2:13).
11:1 *shoot . . . stump.* The Assyrians all but destroyed

Judah, but it was the Babylonian exile that brought the kingdom of Judah to an end in 586 B.C. The Messiah will grow as a shoot from that stump of David's dynasty. See 6:13 and note. *Jesse.* David's father (see 1Sa 16:10–13). *Branch.* See notes on 4:2; Mt 2:23.
11:2 *The Spirit . . . will rest on him.* The Messiah, like David (1Sa 16:13), will be empowered by the Holy Spirit. *counsel . . . power.* The Spirit will endow him with the wisdom to undertake wise purposes and with the power to carry them out (see note on 9:6). *fear of the LORD.* See Pr 1:7.
11:3 *delight in the fear of the LORD.* See Jn 8:29.
11:4 *righteousness . . . justice.* The rulers of Isaiah's day lacked these qualities (see 1:17; 5:7; see also note on 9:7). *rod of his mouth.* Assyria was God's rod in 10:5,24, but the Messiah will rule the nations with an iron scepter (Ps 2:9; Rev 19:15).
11:5 *belt.* When a man prepared for vigorous action, he tied up his loose, flowing garments with a belt (see 5:27).
11:6–9 The peace and safety of the Messianic age are reflected in the fact that little children will be unharmed as they play with formerly ferocious animals. Such conditions are a description of the future consummation of the Messianic kingdom. See 2:2–4 and notes; 35:9; 65:20–25; Eze 34:25–29.

the leopard will lie down with the
　　goat,
the calf and the lion and the yearling[d]
　　together;
and a little child will lead them.
[7]The cow will feed with the bear,
　　their young will lie down together,
　　and the lion will eat straw like the
　　　　ox.[t]
[8]The infant[u] will play near the hole of
　　the cobra,
and the young child put his hand into
　　the viper's[v] nest.
[9]They will neither harm nor destroy[w]
　　on all my holy mountain,[x]
for the earth[y] will be full of the
　　knowledge[z] of the LORD
　　as the waters cover the sea.

[10]In that day[a] the Root of Jesse[b] will
stand as a banner[c] for the peoples; the
nations[d] will rally to him,[e] and his place
of rest[f] will be glorious.[g] [11]In that day[h]
the Lord will reach out his hand a second
time to reclaim the remnant[i] that is left of
his people from Assyria,[j] from Lower
Egypt, from Upper Egypt,[e][k] from
Cush,[f][l] from Elam,[m] from Babylonia,[g]
from Hamath[n] and from the islands[o] of
the sea.[p]

[12]He will raise a banner[q] for the nations
　　and gather[r] the exiles of Israel;[s]
he will assemble the scattered people[t]
　　of Judah
from the four quarters of the earth.[u]
[13]Ephraim's jealousy will vanish,
　　and Judah's enemies[h] will be cut off;
Ephraim will not be jealous of Judah,

nor Judah hostile toward Ephraim.[v]
[14]They will swoop down on the slopes of
　　Philistia[w] to the west;
together they will plunder the people
　　to the east.[x]
They will lay hands on Edom[y] and
　　Moab,[z]
and the Ammonites[a] will be subject
　　to them.[b]
[15]The LORD will dry up[c]
　　the gulf of the Egyptian sea;
with a scorching wind[d] he will sweep
　　his hand[e]
　　over the Euphrates River.[i] [f]
He will break it up into seven streams
　　so that men can cross over in
　　sandals.[g]
[16]There will be a highway[h] for the
　　remnant[i] of his people
that is left from Assyria,[j]
as there was for Israel
　　when they came up from Egypt.[k]

Songs of Praise

12 In that day[l] you will say:
"I will praise[m] you, O LORD.

Center column references

11:7 [t]S Job 40:15
11:8 [u]Isa 65:20
[v]Isa 14:29; 30:6;
59:5
11:9
[w]S Nu 25:12;
S Isa 2:4; S 9:7
[x]S Ps 48:1;
S Isa 2:2
[y]Isa 17:46;
Ps 98:2-3;
Isa 45:22; 48:20;
52:10 [z]Ex 7:5;
Isa 19:21; 45:6,
14; 49:26;
Jer 24:7; 31:34;
Hab 2:14
11:10
[a]S Isa 10:20
[b]S ver 1
[c]S Ps 20:5;
Isa 18:3; Jer 4:6;
Jn 12:32 [d]Isa 2:4;
14:1; 49:23;
56:3,6; 60:5,10;
Lk 2:32; Ac 11:18
[e]Ro 15:12*
[f]S Ps 116:7;
Isa 14:3; 28:12;
32:17-18; 40:2;
Jer 6:16; 30:10;
46:27 [g]Hag 2:9;
Zec 2:5
11:11
[h]S Isa 10:20
[i]S Dt 30:4;
S Isa 1:9
[j]Isa 19:24;
Hos 11:11;
Mic 7:12;
Zec 10:10
[k]Jer 44:1,15;
Eze 29:14; 30:14
[l]S Ge 10:6;
Ac 8:27
[m]S Ge 10:22
[n]S Isa 10:9
[o]Isa 24:15; 41:1,
5; 42:4,10,12;
49:1; 51:5;
59:18; 60:9;
66:19 [p]Isa 49:12;
Jer 16:15; 46:27;
Eze 38:8; Zec 8:7
11:12 [q]S Ps 20:5
[r]Isa 14:2; 43:5;
49:22; 54:7;
Jer 16:15; 31:10;
32:37 [s]S Ne 1:9;
S Ps 106:47;
Isa 14:1; 41:14;

49:5 [t]Eze 28:25; Zep 3:10 [u]S Ps 48:10; 67:7; Isa 41:5;
Rev 7:1 **11:13** [v]S 2Ch 28:6; Jer 3:18; Eze 37:16-17,22;
Hos 1:11 **11:14** [w]S 2Ch 26:6; S 28:18 [x]S Jdg 6:3
[y]S Nu 24:18; S Ps 137:7; Isa 34:5-6; 63:1; Jer 49:22;
Eze 25:12; Da 11:41; Joel 3:19; Ob 1:1; Mal 1:4 [z]Isa 15:1;
16:14; 25:10; Jer 48:40; Zep 2:8-11 [a]Jdg 11:14-18 [b]Isa 25:3;
60:12 **11:15** [c]S Ex 14:22; S Dt 11:10; Isa 37:25; 42:15;
Jer 50:38; 51:36 [d]S Ge 41:6 [e]Isa 19:16; 30:32 [f]S Isa 7:20
[g]S Ex 14:29 **11:16** [h]Isa 19:23; 35:8; 40:3; 49:11; 51:10;
57:14; 62:10; Jer 50:5 [i]S Ge 45:7 [j]S ver 11 [k]Ex 14:26-31
12:1 [l]S Isa 10:20 [m]Ps 9:1; Isa 25:1

[d]6 Hebrew; Septuagint *lion will feed* e 11 Hebrew
from Pathros　f 11 That is, the upper Nile region
g 11 Hebrew *Shinar*　h 13 Or *hostility*　i 15 Hebrew
the River

11:9 *my holy mountain.* See 2:2–4 and note. *full of the knowledge.* See 2:3, where the word of the Lord is taught in Jerusalem.
11:10 *In that day.* See note on 10:20,27. *Root of Jesse.* A Messianic title closely connected with v. 1 (see also 53:2; Ro 15:12; Rev 5:5; 22:16). *banner.* See 5:26 and note.
11:11 *second time.* The first time was the exodus from Egypt (see v. 16). The second is probably the return from Assyrian and Babylonian exile, though some interpreters, who believe that the passage refers to the dispersion after the destruction of Jerusalem in A.D. 70, place the regathering at Christ's second coming. *remnant.* See notes on 1:9; 10:20–22. *Lower Egypt.* The delta region of the Nile, in the north. *Upper Egypt.* Southern Egypt, upstream from the delta. *Elam.* The land northeast of the lower Tigris Valley (see 21:2; Jer 49:34–39; Da 8:2). *Hamath.* See note on 10:9. *islands of the sea.* The coastlands and islands of the Mediterranean are probably intended (see 41:1,5; 42:4; Ge 10:5).
11:12 *gather the exiles.* See 27:13; 49:22; 56:8; 62:10; 66:20. *four quarters.* Lit. "four wings." "Four quarters of the earth" is equivalent to "ends of the earth" (see 24:16; Job 37:3).
11:13 *Ephraim's jealousy.* See note on 7:2. Prior to the

exile, Ephraim and Judah were frequently fighting each other (see 9:21).
11:14 *people to the east.* Perhaps the Midianites, who plundered Israel, along with other eastern peoples (see 9:4). *Edom . . . Moab . . . Ammonites.* After the exodus, Israel did not attack these nations (see Jdg 11:14–18). Israel's future political domination is also referred to in 14:2; 49:23; 60:12 (see also 25:10; 34:5).
11:15 *dry up . . . the Egyptian sea.* An allusion to the drying up of the Red Sea during the exodus (see Ex 14:21–22). *gulf.* Lit. "tongue" (see "bay" in Jos 15:2,5). *Euphrates.* Rev 16:12 refers to the drying up of the Euphrates, perhaps symbolizing the removal of barriers preventing the coming of "the kings from the East."
11:16 *highway.* The removal of obstacles and the building of a highway leading to Jerusalem are also described in 57:14; 62:10 (cf. 40:3–4).
12:1–6 Two short psalms of praise for deliverance (vv. 1–3, 4–6) climax chs. 7–11 (see note on 7:1–12:6; see also note on 6:1).
12:1,4 *In that day.* See note on 10:20,27.
12:1 *I will praise you.* The "I" is probably the nation, praising the Lord for the deliverance he is sure to bring. *your anger has turned away.* See note on 9:12,17,21. After God

Although you were angry with me,
your anger has turned away[n]
and you have comforted[o] me.
[2]Surely God is my salvation;[p]
I will trust[q] and not be afraid.
The LORD, the LORD,[r] is my strength[s]
and my song;
he has become my salvation.[t] "

[3]With joy you will draw water[u]
from the wells[v] of salvation.

[4]In that day[w] you will say:

"Give thanks to the LORD, call on his
name;[x]
make known among the nations[y]
what he has done,
and proclaim that his name is
exalted.[z]
[5]Sing[a] to the LORD, for he has done
glorious things;[b]
let this be known to all the world.
[6]Shout aloud and sing for joy,[c] people of
Zion,
for great[d] is the Holy One of Israel[e]
among you.[f] "

A Prophecy Against Babylon

13 An oracle[g] concerning Babylon[h]
that Isaiah son of Amoz[i] saw:[j]

[2]Raise a banner[k] on a bare hilltop,

shout to them;
beckon to them
to enter the gates[l] of the nobles.
[3]I have commanded my holy ones;
I have summoned my warriors[m] to
carry out my wrath[n]—
those who rejoice[o] in my triumph.

[4]Listen, a noise on the mountains,
like that of a great multitude![p]
Listen, an uproar[q] among the
kingdoms,
like nations massing together!
The LORD Almighty[r] is mustering[s]
an army for war.
[5]They come from faraway lands,
from the ends of the heavens[t]—
the LORD and the weapons[u] of his
wrath[v]—
to destroy[w] the whole country.

[6]Wail,[x] for the day[y] of the LORD is near;
it will come like destruction[z] from
the Almighty.[j] [a]

12:1 [n]S Job 13:16; [o]S Ps 71:21 **12:2** [p]Isa 17:10; 25:9; 33:6; 45:17; 51:5,6; 54:8; 59:16; 61:10; 62:11 [q]S Job 13:15; S Ps 26:1; S 112:7; Isa 26:3; Da 6:23 [r]Isa 26:4; 38:11 [s]S Ps 18:1 [t]S Ex 15:2 **12:3** [u]S 2Ki 3:17; Ps 36:9; Jer 2:13; 17:13; Jn 4:10,14 [v]Ex 15:25 **12:4** [w]S Isa 10:20 [x]Ex 3:15; Ps 80:18; 105:1; Isa 24:15; 25:1; 26:8,13; Hos 12:5 [y]Isa 54:5; 60:3; Jer 10:7; Zep 2:11; Mal 1:11 [z]S Ps 113:2 **12:5** [a]S Ex 15:1 [b]S Ps 98:1 **12:6** [c]S Ge 21:6; S Ps 98:4; Isa 24:14; 48:20; 52:8; Jer 20:13; 31:7; Zec 2:10 [d]Ps 48:1 [e]S Ps 78:41; 99:2; Isa 1:24; 10:20; 17:7; 29:19; 37:23; 43:3,14; 45:11; 49:26; 55:5; Eze 39:7 [f]S Ps 46:5; Zep 3:14-17 **13:1** [g]Isa 14:28; 15:1; 21:1; Na 1:1; Hab 1:1; Zec 9:1; 12:1; Mal 1:1 [h]ver 19;

S Ge 10:10; Isa 14:4; 21:9; 46:1-2; 48:14; Jer 24:1; 25:12; Rev 14:8 [i]Isa 20:2; 37:2 [j]S Isa 1:1 **13:2** [k]S Ps 20:5; Jer 50:2; 51:27 [l]Isa 24:12; 45:2; Jer 51:58 **13:3** [m]ver 17; Isa 21:2; Jer 51:11; Da 5:28,31; Joel 3:11 [n]S Job 40:11; S Isa 10:5 [o]S Ps 149:2 **13:4** [p]Joel 3:14 [q]S Ps 46:6 [r]Isa 47:4; 51:15 [s]Isa 42:13; Jer 50:41 **13:5** [t]S Isa 5:26 [u]Isa 45:1; 54:16; Jer 50:25 [v]S Isa 10:25 [w]S Jos 6:17; Isa 24:1; 30:25; 34:2 **13:6** [x]Isa 14:31; 15:2; 16:7; 23:1; Eze 30:2; Jas 5:1 [y]S Isa 2:12 [z]S Isa 10:3; S 14:15 [a]S Ge 17:1

[j]6 Hebrew *Shaddai*

---

punishes Israel, his anger will be directed against nations like Assyria and Babylon.
12:2 *The LORD, the LORD.* Two forms for the personal name of God are given: The first is "Yah"; the second was probably pronounced "Yahweh." See note on Ex 3:15. *The LORD... salvation.* These lines quote Ex 15:2, a verse commemorating the defeat of the Egyptians at the Red Sea. See also Ps 118:14.
12:3 *wells.* Perhaps an allusion to God's abundant provision of water for Israel during the desert wanderings (cf. Ex 15:25,27). But here God's future saving act is itself the "well" from which Israel will draw life-giving water (see Ps 36:9; Jer 2:13; Jn 4:10).
12:6 *Shout aloud and sing for joy.* These two imperatives occur again in 54:1, where Zion rejoices over the restoration of her people. *Holy One of Israel.* See notes on 1:4; 6:1.
13:1—23:18 A series of prophecies against the nations (see also Jer 46-51; Eze 25-32; Am 1-2; Zep 2:4-15). They begin with Babylon (13:1—14:23) and Assyria (14:24—27) before moving on to smaller nations. God's judgment on his people does not mean that the pagan nations will be spared (see Jer 25:29). In fact, God's judgments on the nations are often a part of his salvation of his people (see, e.g., 10:12).
13:1—14:27 This prophecy concerns Babylon during the Assyrian empire rather than during the Neo-Babylonian empire. Thus the prophecy is actually against the Assyrian empire, Babylon being its most important city. From 729 B.C. on, the kings of Assyria also assumed the title "king of Babylon." Note that there is no new "oracle" heading at 14:24, even though 14:24—27 clearly pertains to Assyria; so 13:1—14:27 forms a unit.
13:1 See note on 1:1. *oracle.* The Hebrew for this word is related to a Hebrew verb meaning "to lift up, carry" and is

possibly to be understood as either lifting up one's voice or carrying a burden. Such an "oracle" often contains a message of doom. *Babylon.* See 21:1-9; 46:1-2; 47:1-15; Jer 50-51. Its judgment is announced first because of the present Assyrian threat and because Babylon would later bring about the downfall of Judah and Jerusalem between 605 and 586 B.C. Babylon was conquered by Cyrus the Persian (see 45:1; 47:1) in 539. Subsequently it came to symbolize the world powers arrayed against God's kingdom (cf. 1Pe 5:13), and its final destruction is announced in Rev 14:8; 16:19; 17-18. Here, however, Babylon is still part of the Assyrian empire (see 14:24-27; see also note on 13:1-14:27).
13:2 *Raise a banner.* See note on 5:26.
13:3 *my holy ones.* Or "my consecrated ones," those set apart to carry out God's will. Cf. 10:5, where the Lord calls Assyria "the rod of my anger"; see also 45:1. *wrath.* God's anger is no longer turned against Israel (see 5:25; 9:12,17, 21; 10:4) but rather against his enemies (see vv. 5,9,13; cf. 30:27). God must punish sin, particularly arrogance (see v. 11).
13:4 *The LORD Almighty is mustering an army.* The Hebrew for "army" is the singular form of the word for "Almighty." God is the head of the armies of Israel (1Sa 17:45), of angelic powers (1Ki 22:19; Lk 2:13) and, here, of the armies that will destroy Babylon.
13:5 *weapons of his wrath.* Assyria was the club in God's hand during Isaiah's day, and Babylon itself would later serve as God's weapon (see 10:5 and note).
13:6,9 *day of the LORD.* See note on 2:11,17,20.
13:6 *destruction.* Hebrew *shod,* forming a wordplay on "Almighty" (Hebrew *Shaddai*)—as also in Joel 1:15. See note on 5:7. For *Shaddai* see note on Ge 17:1.

[7]Because of this, all hands will go limp,[b]
every man's heart will melt.[c]

[8]Terror[d] will seize them,
pain and anguish will grip[e] them;
they will writhe like a woman in
labor.[f]
They will look aghast at each other,
their faces aflame.[g]

[9]See, the day[h] of the LORD is coming
—a cruel[i] day, with wrath[j] and
fierce anger[k]—
to make the land desolate
and destroy the sinners within it.

[10]The stars of heaven and their
constellations
will not show their light.[l]
The rising sun[m] will be darkened[n]
and the moon will not give its light.[o]

[11]I will punish[p] the world for its evil,
the wicked[q] for their sins.
I will put an end to the arrogance of the
haughty[r]
and will humble[s] the pride of the
ruthless.[t]

[12]I will make man[u] scarcer than pure
gold,
more rare than the gold of Ophir.[v]

[13]Therefore I will make the heavens
tremble;[w]
and the earth will shake[x] from its
place
at the wrath[y] of the LORD Almighty,
in the day of his burning anger.[z]

[14]Like a hunted[a] gazelle,
like sheep without a shepherd,[b]
each will return to his own people,
each will flee[c] to his native land.[d]

[15]Whoever is captured will be thrust
through;
all who are caught will fall[e] by the
sword.[f]

[16]Their infants[g] will be dashed to pieces
before their eyes;
their houses will be looted and their
wives ravished.[h]

[17]See, I will stir up[i] against them the
Medes,[j]
who do not care for silver
and have no delight in gold.[k]

[18]Their bows[l] will strike down the young
men;[m]
they will have no mercy[n] on infants
nor will they look with compassion
on children.[o]

[19]Babylon,[p] the jewel of kingdoms,[q]
the glory[r] of the Babylonians'[k] pride,
will be overthrown[s] by God
like Sodom and Gomorrah.[t]

[20]She will never be inhabited[u]
or lived in through all generations;
no Arab[v] will pitch his tent there,
no shepherd will rest his flocks there.

[21]But desert creatures[w] will lie there,
jackals[x] will fill her houses;

13:7
[b]S 2Ki 19:26;
S Job 4:3;
S Jer 47:3
[c]S Jos 2:11;
Eze 21:7
13:8 [d]S Ps 31:13;
S 48:5; S Isa 21:4
[e]Ex 15:14
[f]S Ge 3:16;
S Jn 16:21
[g]Joel 2:6; Na 2:10
13:9 [h]S Isa 2:12;
Jer 51:2 [i]Jer 6:23
[j]S Isa 9:19
[k]Isa 26:21;
66:16; Jer 25:31;
Joel 3:2
13:10 [l]S Job 9:7
[m]Isa 24:23;
Zec 14:7
[n]S Ex 10:22;
S Isa 5:30;
Rev 8:12
[o]Eze 32:7;
Am 5:20; 8:9;
S Mt 24:29*;
Mk 13:24*
13:11 [p]Isa 3:11;
11:4; 26:21;
65:6-7; 66:16
[q]S Ps 125:3
[r]S Ps 10:5;
S Pr 16:18;
Da 5:23
[s]S Isa 2:9; 23:9;
Eze 28:2; Da 4:37
[t]Isa 25:3,5; 29:5,
20; 49:25,26
13:12 [u]S Isa 4:1
[v]S Ge 10:29
13:13
[w]S Ps 102:26;
Isa 34:4; 51:6
[x]S Job 9:6;
S Isa 14:16;
Mt 24:7; Mk 13:8
[y]S Isa 9:19
[z]S Job 9:5
13:14 [a]Pr 6:5
[b]S 1Ki 22:17;
S Mt 9:36;
S Jn 10:11

[c]S Ge 11:9;
Isa 17:13; 21:15;
22:3; 33:3;
Jer 4:9
[d]Jer 46:16;

50:16; 51:9; Na 3:7 **13:15** [e]Jer 51:4 [f]Isa 14:19; Jer 50:25
13:16 [g]ver 18; S Nu 16:27; S 2Ki 8:12 [h]S Ge 34:29;
S Hos 13:16 **13:17** [i]Jer 50:9,41; 51:1 [j]S ver 3 [k]2Ki 18:14-16;
Pr 6:34-35 **13:18** [l]S Ps 7:12; Isa 41:2; Jer 50:9,14,29
[m]S Dt 32:25; Jer 49:26; 50:30; 51:4 [n]Isa 47:6; Jer 6:23;
50:42 [o]S ver 16; Isa 14:22; 47:9 **13:19** [p]S ver 1 [q]Isa 47:5;
Da 2:37-38 [r]Da 4:30 [s]S Ps 137:8; S Rev 14:8 [t]S Ge 19:25;
Isa 1:9-10; Ro 9:29 **13:20** [u]Isa 14:23; 34:10-15; Jer 51:29,
37-43,62 [v]2Ch 17:11 **13:21** [w]S Ps 74:14; Rev 18:2 [x]Jer 14:6

[k]*19 Or Chaldeans'*

13:7 *hands will go limp.* Courage will fail. See Jer 6:24.
13:8 *Terror.* Holy war usually brings panic to the enemy
(see Ex 15:14-16; Jdg 7:21-22). *pain . . . labor.* The prophets often compare the suffering of judgment and war with the
pain and anguish that frequently accompany childbirth (see
26:17; Jer 4:31; 6:24).
13:10 *stars . . . sun . . . moon.* Cosmic darkness is associated with the day of the Lord also in Joel 2:10,31; Rev
6:12-13. Cf. Jdg 5:20.
13:11 *arrogance . . . pride.* Cf. 2:9,11,17; 5:15.
13:12 *scarcer . . . rare.* War will reduce the male population drastically (see 4:1 and note). *gold of Ophir.* Solomon
imported large quantities of gold from this place (see 1Ki
9:28; 10:11 and notes).
13:13 *heavens tremble . . . earth . . . shake.* Thunderstorms and earthquakes often accompany the powerful presence of the Lord (see notes on v. 10; 34:4; Ex 19:16). Hail
may also be involved (cf. 30:30; Jos 10:11).
13:14 *flee.* From parts of the Assyrian empire.
13:16 *infants . . . dashed to pieces.* Invading armies often
slaughtered infants and children; thus there would be no
future warriors, nor would there be a remnant through
which the city (or nation or people) might be revived (see Ps
137:8-9; Hos 10:14; Na 3:10). *wives ravished.* Women
also suffered greatly in war. With their husbands killed, they
were often used as prostitutes (see note on Am 7:17).

13:17 *the Medes.* Located in what is today northwestern
Iran. There was conflict between the enemy Assyria and Media during
the eighth century B.C. Some, however, relate the fulfillment
of this verse to the period when the Medes joined the
Babylonians in defeating Assyria in 612-609 but later united
with Cyrus to conquer Babylon in 539. See Jer 51:11,28; Da
5:31; 6:28.
13:19 *glory . . . pride.* Babylon with its temples and palaces
became a very beautiful city (see Da 4:29-30). The hanging
gardens of Nebuchadnezzar were one of the seven wonders
of the ancient world. In 4:2 the Hebrew words for "glory"
and "pride" were used to describe the "Branch of the
LORD." *Babylonians.* The Neo-Babylonian empire of
612-539 B.C. was led by the Chaldean people of southern
Babylonia. Nabopolassar welded the tribes together c. 626,
and his son Nebuchadnezzar became their most powerful
ruler (605-562). *Sodom and Gomorrah.* Previously Isaiah
compared Judah to these cities (see 1:9-10 and note).
13:20-22 See the similar description of the desolation of
Edom in 34:10-15. Cf. Rev 18:2.
13:20 *never be inhabited.* Babylon was completely deserted by the seventh century A.D.
13:21 *wild goats.* This term is connected with demons
("goat idols") in Lev 17:7; 2Ch 11:15. In Rev 18:2 fallen
Babylon is described as a home for demons and evil spirits.

there the owls[y] will dwell,
and there the wild goats[z] will leap
about.
[22]Hyenas[a] will howl in her strongholds,[b]
jackals[c] in her luxurious palaces.
Her time is at hand,[d]
and her days will not be prolonged.[e]

14 The LORD will have compassion[f]
on Jacob;
once again he will choose[g] Israel
and will settle them in their own
land.[h]
Aliens[i] will join them
and unite with the house of Jacob.
[2]Nations will take them
and bring[j] them to their own place.
And the house of Israel will possess the
nations[k]
as menservants and maidservants in
the LORD's land.
They will make captives[l] of their
captors
and rule over their oppressors.[m]

[3]On the day the LORD gives you relief[n]
from suffering and turmoil[o] and cruel
bondage,[p] [4]you will take up this taunt[q]
against the king of Babylon:[r]

How the oppressor[s] has come to an
end!
How his fury[1] has ended!
[5]The LORD has broken the rod[t] of the
wicked,[u]
the scepter[v] of the rulers,
[6]which in anger struck down peoples[w]
with unceasing blows,
and in fury subdued[x] nations
with relentless aggression.[y]
[7]All the lands are at rest and at peace;[z]

they break into singing.[a]
[8]Even the pine trees[b] and the cedars of
Lebanon
exult over you and say,
"Now that you have been laid low,
no woodsman comes to cut us
down."[c]

[9]The grave[m][d] below is all astir
to meet you at your coming;
it rouses the spirits of the departed[e] to
greet you—
all those who were leaders[f] in the
world;
it makes them rise from their thrones—
all those who were kings over the
nations.[g]
[10]They will all respond,
they will say to you,
"You also have become weak, as we
are;
you have become like us."[h]
[11]All your pomp has been brought down
to the grave,[i]
along with the noise of your harps;[j]
maggots are spread out beneath you
and worms[k] cover you.[l]

[12]How you have fallen[m] from heaven,
O morning star,[n] son of the dawn!
You have been cast down to the earth,
you who once laid low the nations![o]
[13]You said in your heart,

Cross-references (center column):

13:21 [y]S Lev 11:16-18; S Dt 14:15-17 [z]Lev 17:7; 2Ch 11:15 13:22 [a]Isa 34:14 [b]Isa 25:2; 32:14 [c]Isa 34:13; 35:7; 43:20; Jer 9:11; 49:33; 51:37; Mal 1:3 [d]Dt 32:35; Jer 48:16; 51:33 [e]Jer 50:39 14:1 [f]Ps 102:13; Isa 49:10,13; 54:7-8,10; Jer 33:26; Zec 10:6 [g]Ge 18:19; 2Ch 6:6; Isa 41:8; 42:1; 44:1; 45:4; 49:7; 65:9,22; Zec 1:17; 2:11; 3:2 [h]Jer 3:18; 16:15; 23:8 [i]S Ex 12:43; S Isa 11:10; Eze 47:22; Zec 8:22-23; Eph 2:12-19 14:2 [j]S Isa 11:12; 60:9 [k]S Ps 49:14; Isa 26:15; 43:14; 49:7,23; 54:3 [l]Ps 149:8; Isa 45:14; 49:25; 60:12; Jer 40:1 [m]Isa 60:14; 61:5; Jer 30:16; 49:2; Eze 39:10; Zep 3:19; Zec 2:9 14:3 [n]S Isa 11:10 [o]S Job 3:17 [p]S Ex 1:14 14:4 [q]Mic 2:4; Hab 2:6 [r]S Isa 13:1 [s]S Isa 9:4 14:5 [t]S Isa 10:15 [u]S Ps 125:3 [v]S Ps 110:2 14:6 [w]Isa 10:14 [x]S Ps 47:3 [y]S 2Ki 15:29; Isa 47:6; Hab 1:17 14:7 [z]S Nu 6:26; Jer 50:34; Zec 1:11

14:8 [b]S 1Ch 16:33; S Ps 65:13; Eze 31:16 [c]S 2Ki 19:23; Isa 37:24 14:9 [d]S Pr 30:16; Eze 32:21 [e]S Job 26:5 [f]Zec 10:3 [g]S Job 3:14 14:10 [h]Eze 26:20; 32:21 14:11 [i]S Nu 16:30; S Pr 30:16 [j]Isa 5:12; Eze 26:13; Am 6:5 [k]S Job 7:5; 24:20; Isa 51:8; 66:24 [l]S Job 21:26 14:12 [m]Lk 10:18 [n]2Pe 1:19; Rev 2:28; 8:10; 9:1 [o]Eze 26:17

14 Dead Sea Scrolls, Septuagint and Syriac; the meaning of the word in the Masoretic Text is uncertain.
[m]9 Hebrew Sheol; also in verses 11 and 15

[a]Ps 98:1; 126:1-3; Isa 12:6

14:1 *will have compassion . . . will settle them.* Babylon's fall will be linked with Israel's restoration. God's compassion on his people is the theme of chs. 40–66 (see 40:1–2). *in their own land.* See 2:2–4; 11:10–12 and notes. *Aliens will join them.* See 11:10; 56:6–7; 60:3.
14:2 *Nations . . . place.* See note on 5:26. *will possess the nations.* See note on 11:14.
14:3–21 However exalted (and almost divine) the king of Babylon may have thought himself (see vv. 12–14), he will go the way of all world rulers—down to the grave.
14:3 *suffering . . . cruel bondage.* The Babylonian captivity was much like Israel's experience in Egypt (cf. Ex 1:14).
14:4 *taunt.* Cf. the taunts against Babylon in Rev 18. *king of Babylon.* Another title used by the king of Assyria at this time.
14:5 *rod . . . scepter.* See 10:5 and note; see also 10:24.
14:7 *break into singing.* See 12:6 and note.
14:8 *pine trees . . . cedars.* Isaiah often personified nature. The trees along with the mountains burst into song in 44:23 (cf. 55:12). *cedars of Lebanon.* These highly prized timbers were hauled away by the kings of Assyria and Babylon for centuries.

14:9 *leaders.* Lit. "goats"; a goat often led a flock of sheep (see Jer 50:8). In Zec 10:3 the term is parallel to "shepherds." *rise from their thrones.* Conditions among the dead are described in terms of their roles on earth.

14:11 *pomp . . . grave.* Cf. 5:14. *noise of your harps.* Music is sometimes a sign of luxury and pleasure (see Am 6:5–6).

14:12–15 Some believe that Isaiah is giving a description of the fall of Satan (cf. Lk 10:18—where, however, Jesus seems to be referring to an event contemporary with himself). But the passage clearly applies to the king of Babylon, who is later used as a type (prefiguration) of the "beast" who will lead the Babylon of the last days (see Rev 13:4; 17:3). Cf. the description of the ruler of Tyre in Eze 28.

14:12 *morning star.* The Hebrew for this expression is translated "Lucifer" in the Latin Vulgate.

14:13 *sacred mountain.* Mount Zaphon (see Ps 48:1–2), also called Mount Casius, was about 25 miles northeast of Ugarit in Syria. The Canaanites considered it the home and meeting place of the gods, much like Mount Olympus for the Greeks (see Ps 48:2 and note). Cf. Ps 82:1.

"I will ascend[p] to heaven;
I will raise my throne[q]
    above the stars of God;
I will sit enthroned on the mount of
    assembly,[r]
    on the utmost heights[s] of the sacred
    mountain.[n]
14I will ascend above the tops of the
    clouds;[t]
I will make myself like the Most
    High."[u]

15But you are brought down[v] to the
    grave,[w]
    to the depths[x] of the pit.[y]

16Those who see you stare at you,
    they ponder your fate:[z]
"Is this the man who shook[a] the earth
    and made kingdoms tremble,
17the man who made the world a
    desert,[b]
    who overthrew[c] its cities
    and would not let his captives go
    home?"[d]

18All the kings of the nations lie in state,
    each in his own tomb.[e]
19But you are cast out[f] of your tomb
    like a rejected branch;
you are covered with the slain,[g]
    with those pierced by the sword,[h]
    those who descend to the stones of
    the pit.[i]
Like a corpse trampled underfoot,
20   you will not join them in burial,[j]
for you have destroyed your land
    and killed your people.

The offspring[k] of the wicked[l]
    will never be mentioned[m] again.
21Prepare a place to slaughter his sons[n]
    for the sins of their forefathers;[o]
they are not to rise to inherit the land
    and cover the earth with their cities.

22"I will rise up[p] against them,"
    declares the LORD Almighty.
"I will cut off from Babylon her name[q]
    and survivors,
    her offspring and descendants,[r]"
    declares the LORD.
23"I will turn her into a place for owls[s]
    and into swampland;
I will sweep her with the broom of
    destruction,[t]"
    declares the LORD Almighty.[u]

A Prophecy Against Assyria

24The LORD Almighty has sworn,[v]

"Surely, as I have planned,[w] so it will
    be,
    and as I have purposed, so it will
    stand.[x]
25I will crush the Assyrian[y] in my land;
    on my mountains I will trample him
    down.
His yoke[z] will be taken from my
    people,
    and his burden removed from their
    shoulders.[a]"

26This is the plan[b] determined for the
    whole world;
    this is the hand[c] stretched out over
    all nations.
27For the LORD Almighty has purposed,[d]
    and who can thwart him?
His hand[e] is stretched out, and who
    can turn it back?[f]

A Prophecy Against the Philistines

28This oracle[g] came in the year[h] King
    Ahaz[i] died:

14:13 pDa 5:23;
8:10; Ob 1:4;
Mt 11:23
qEze 28:2;
2Th 2:4 rPs 82:1
sIsa 37:24
14:14 tS Job 20:6
uS Ge 3:5;
S Nu 24:16;
Isa 10:13; 47:8;
Jer 50:29; 51:53;
Da 11:36;
2Th 2:4
14:15 vIsa 13:6;
45:7; 47:11;
Jer 51:8,43
wS Job 21:13
xMt 11:23;
Lk 10:15
yS Ps 55:23;
Eze 31:16; 32:23
14:16 zJer 50:23;
Rev 18:9
aS Isa 2:19;
13:13; Joel 3:16;
Hag 2:6,21
14:17 bIsa 15:6;
Joel 2:3 cPs 52:7
dEx 7:14;
S 2Ki 15:29;
Jer 50:33;
Rev 18:18
14:18 eJob 21:32
14:19
fIsa 22:16-18;
Jer 8:1; 36:30
gIsa 34:3
hS Isa 13:15
iJer 41:7-9
14:20
jS 1Ki 21:19
kS Job 18:19
lS Isa 1:4
mS Dt 32:26
14:21
nS Nu 16:27
oS Ge 9:25;
S Lev 26:39
14:22
pS Ps 94:16
qS Job 18:17;
Ps 109:13;
Na 1:14
r2Sa 18:18;
1Ki 14:10;
Job 18:19;
S Ps 9:6;
S Isa 13:18
14:23
sS Lev 11:16-18;
Isa 34:11-15;
Zep 2:14
tS Isa 10:3;
Jer 25:12
uJer 50:3; 51:62
14:24 vIsa 45:23;
49:18; 54:9; 62:8
wIsa 19:12,17;
23:8-9; 25:1; Da 4:35 xS Job 9:3; S Isa 7:7; 46:10-11;
Eze 12:25; Ac 4:28 14:25 yS Isa 10:5,12; 37:36-38 zS Isa 9:4
aS Isa 10:27 14:26 bIsa 23:9 cEx 15:12; S Job 30:21 14:27
dJer 49:20 eS Ex 14:21 fS 2Ch 20:6; Isa 43:13; Da 4:35
14:28 gS Isa 13:1 hS 2Ki 15:7 iS 2Ki 16:1

n 13 Or the north; Hebrew Zaphon

14:16—20a These verses seem to take place on earth, not in the realm of the dead (Sheol)—probably also vv. 9–10.

14:17 captives go home. Babylon, like Assyria, deported large segments of defeated populations to subdue the rebellious among them (see 2Ki 24:14–16).

14:19 cast out of your tomb. A proper burial was considered important for an ordinary individual, and especially so for a king. To have one's body simply discarded was a terrible fate. corpse trampled. See 5:25.

14:21 slaughter his sons. A man's children, as well as his tombstone, were his memorial (cf. 2Sa 18:18). The king of Babylon would have neither (cf. 47:9).

14:22–23 The taunt is extended to include Babylon itself (see note on vv. 3–21); fulfilled, at least partially, through Sennacherib's destruction of Babylon in 689 B.C.—ultimately by the Medes and Persians after they took Babylon in 539.

14:22 survivors. A remnant; Israel will survive through a remnant (see 10:20–22; 11:11,16), but Babylon will not.

14:23 See 13:20–22 and notes. swampland. Southern Babylonia, where the Chaldean tribes once lived, was a region of marshlands.

14:24–27 See Zep 2:13–15; see also note on 13:1–14:27.
14:24 it will stand. See 8:10 and note. God's sovereign purposes regarding Assyria and Babylon will be carried out.
14:25 yoke . . . burden. See 9:4 and note.
14:26–27 hand stretched out. See 9:12; 12:1 and notes. God's hand was stretched out against Egypt at the Red Sea (see Ex 15:12).
14:28–32 See Jer 47; Eze 25:15–17; Am 1:6–8; Zep 2:4–7.
14:28 oracle. See note on 13:1. the year. Perhaps 715 B.C. The occasion appears to be the Philistine revolt against Assyria while King Sargon (see 20:1) was too preoccupied with serious revolts elsewhere to give much attention to Canaan.

²⁹Do not rejoice, all you Philistines, /
that the rod that struck you is
broken;
from the root of that snake will spring
up a viper, ᵏ
its fruit will be a darting, venomous
serpent. ˡ
³⁰The poorest of the poor will find
pasture,
and the needy ᵐ will lie down in
safety. ⁿ
But your root I will destroy by famine; ᵒ
it will slay ᵖ your survivors. ᑫ

³¹Wail, ʳ O gate! ˢ Howl, O city!
Melt away, all you Philistines! ᵗ
A cloud of smoke comes from the
north, ᵘ
and there is not a straggler in its
ranks. ᵛ
³²What answer shall be given
to the envoys ʷ of that nation?
"The LORD has established Zion, ˣ
and in her his afflicted people will
find refuge. ʸ "

A Prophecy Against Moab

16:6–12pp — Jer 48:29–36

15 An oracle ᶻ concerning Moab: ᵃ
Ar ᵇ in Moab is ruined, ᶜ
destroyed in a night!
Kir ᵈ in Moab is ruined,
destroyed in a night!
²Dibon ᵉ goes up to its temple,

to its high places ᶠ to weep;
Moab wails ᵍ over Nebo ʰ and
Medeba.
Every head is shaved ⁱ
and every beard cut off. ʲ
³In the streets they wear sackcloth; ᵏ
on the roofs ˡ and in the public
squares ᵐ
they all wail, ⁿ
prostrate with weeping. ᵒ
⁴Heshbon ᵖ and Elealeh ᑫ cry out,
their voices are heard all the way to
Jahaz. ʳ
Therefore the armed men of Moab cry
out,
and their hearts are faint.

⁵My heart cries out ˢ over Moab; ᵗ
her fugitives ᵘ flee as far as Zoar, ᵛ
as far as Eglath Shelishiyah.
They go up the way to Luhith,
weeping as they go;
on the road to Horonaim ʷ
they lament their destruction. ˣ
⁶The waters of Nimrim are dried up ʸ
and the grass is withered; ᶻ
the vegetation is gone ᵃ
and nothing green is left. ᵇ
⁷So the wealth they have acquired ᶜ and
stored up

Cross references

14:29 /S Jos 13:3;
S 2Ki 1:2;
S 2Ch 26:6
ᵏS Isa 11:8
ˡS Dt 8:15
14:30 ᵐIsa 3:15;
25:4
ⁿS Isa 7:21-22
ᵒIsa 8:21; 9:20;
51:19 ᵖJer 25:16;
Zec 9:5-6
ᑫEze 25:15-17;
Zep 2:5
14:31 ʳS Isa 13:6
ˢS Isa 3:26
ᵗS Ge 10:14
ᵘIsa 41:25;
Jer 1:14; 4:6; 6:1,
22; 10:22; 13:20;
25:9; 46:20,24;
47:2; 50:41;
Eze 32:30
ᵛS Isa 5:27
14:32 ʷIsa 37:9
ˣS Ps 51:18; 87:2,
5; Isa 2:2; 26:1;
28:16; 31:5;
33:5,20; 44:28;
51:21; 54:11
ʸS Isa 4:6; Jas 2:5
15:1 ᶻS Isa 13:1
ᵃNu 22:3-6;
S Dt 23:6;
S Isa 11:14
ᵇS Nu 21:15
ᶜS Nu 17:12;
Isa 25:12; 26:5;
Jer 48:24,41;
51:58 ᵈS 2Ki 3:25
15:2 ᵉS Nu 21:30
/1Ki 11:7;
Isa 16:12;
Jer 48:35
ᵍS Isa 13:6; 65:14
ʰS Nu 32:38
ⁱS Lev 13:40;
S Job 1:20
/S 2Sa 10:4
15:3 ᵏS Isa 3:24
ˡS Jos 2:8
ᵐJer 48:38
ⁿIsa 14:31;
Jer 47:2 ᵒver 5;
Isa 16:9; 22:4;
15:4 ᵖS Nu 21:25; S Jos 13:26
ᑫS Nu 32:3 ʳS Nu 21:23 15:5 ˢS ver 3 ᵗIsa 16:11; Jer 48:31
ᵘS Nu 21:29 ᵛS Ge 13:10 ʷJer 48:3,34 ˣJer 4:20; 48:5 15:6
ʸIsa 19:5-7; Jer 48:34 ᶻPs 37:2; Isa 16:8; 24:4,7,11; 33:9;
34:4; 37:27; 40:7; 51:6,12; Hos 4:3; Joel 1:12 ᵃS Isa 14:17
ᵇJer 14:5 15:7 ᶜIsa 30:6; Jer 48:36

14:29 *Philistines.* See note on Ge 10:14. Philistine territory was vulnerable to attack by the great empires (Egypt and Assyria) since it lay along the main route from Egypt to Mesopotamia. *the rod.* Probably Sargon of Assyria. *is broken.* If the rod was Sargon, reference is to the threats to his empire by a series of revolts in Babylonia and Asia Minor. *root . . . fruit.* A figure of speech that refers to the whole (tree) by speaking of its two extremes. After Sargon will come other Assyrian kings: Sennacherib, Esarhaddon, Ashurbanipal.
14:30 *poor . . . needy.* Israelites (see v. 32).
14:31 *Wail.* Cf. the similar reaction in 13:6; 15:2; 16:7; 23:1. *cloud of smoke.* The dust raised by the marching feet and the chariots of the Assyrians—who always invaded Palestine from the north. *not a straggler.* A longer description is found in 5:26–29.
14:32 *has established Zion.* God will protect Jerusalem from the Assyrians (compare 31:4–5 with 2:2).
15:1–16:14 See Jer 48; Eze 25:8–11; Am 2:1–3; Zep 2:8–11.
15:1 *oracle.* See note on 13:1. *Moab.* A country east of the Dead Sea that was a perpetual enemy of Israel (see 25:10; 2Ki 13:20). *Ar.* The location of this city is unknown. *ruined.* The same word describes Isaiah's feelings about himself in 6:5. The destruction of Moab was probably connected with an invasion by Sargon of Assyria in 715/713 B.C. Cf. Jer 48:1–17. *Kir.* Probably Kir Hareseth, 15 miles south of the Arnon River and perhaps the capital of Moab at this time. Kir means "city."
15:2 *Dibon.* Located four miles north of the Arnon River

and given to the tribe of Gad at one time (see Nu 32:34). *high places.* Shrines originally built on hilltops and usually associated with pagan worship. *Nebo.* North of the Arnon River, perhaps near Mount Nebo (Dt 34:1). *Medeba.* About six miles south of Heshbon (see v. 4) and once captured by Israel from Sihon (see Nu 21:26,30). *head is shaved . . . beard cut off.* Characteristic of intense mourning (Jer 48:37).
15:3 *sackcloth.* The coarse garb of mourners (see Job 16:15; Jer 48:37; La 2:10), made of goat hair. *roofs.* Perhaps chosen because incense was sometimes offered there (see Jer 19:13).
15:4 *Heshbon.* Located about 18 miles east of the northern tip of the Dead Sea. See also Jer 48:34. It was King Sihon's capital before Israel captured it (see Nu 21:23–26). *Elealeh.* About a mile north of Heshbon and always mentioned with it. *Jahaz.* Just north of the Arnon River and about 20 miles from Heshbon (Nu 21:23; Jer 48:34).
15:5 *Zoar.* Probably located near the southern end of the Dead Sea. Lot fled there from Sodom (see Ge 14:2; 19:23, 30). *Eglath Shelishiyah.* Location unknown (see also Jer 48:34). The words may mean "a three-year-old heifer" (cf. 1Sa 1:24). *Luhith.* Location unknown (see also Jer 48:5). *Horonaim.* Location unknown (see also Jer 48:3,5,34).
15:6 *waters of Nimrim.* Perhaps to be identified with the Wadi en-Numeirah, ten miles from the southern end of the Dead Sea (cf. Jer 48:34). *grass is withered.* The advancing enemy may have stopped up the major springs of Moab.
15:7 *Ravine of the Poplars.* Probably at the border between Moab and Edom (see v. 8).

they carry away over the Ravine of
the Poplars.
[8]Their outcry echoes along the border of
Moab;
their wailing reaches as far as Eglaim,
their lamentation as far as Beer[d]
Elim.
[9]Dimon's[o] waters are full of blood,
but I will bring still more upon
Dimon[o]—
a lion[e] upon the fugitives of Moab[f]
and upon those who remain in the
land.

16

Send lambs[g] as tribute[h]
to the ruler of the land,
from Sela,[i] across the desert,
to the mount of the Daughter of
Zion.[j]
[2]Like fluttering birds
pushed from the nest,[k]
so are the women of Moab[l]
at the fords[m] of the Arnon.[n]

[3]"Give us counsel,
render a decision.
Make your shadow like night—
at high noon.
Hide the fugitives,[o]
do not betray the refugees.
[4]Let the Moabite fugitives stay with you;
be their shelter[p] from the destroyer."

The oppressor[q] will come to an end,
and destruction will cease;[r]
the aggressor will vanish from the
land.
[5]In love a throne[s] will be established;[t]

in faithfulness a man will sit on it—
one from the house[p] of David[u]—
one who in judging seeks justice[v]
and speeds the cause of
righteousness.

[6]We have heard of Moab's[w] pride[x]—
her overweening pride and conceit,
her pride and her insolence—
but her boasts are empty.
[7]Therefore the Moabites wail,[y]
they wail together for Moab.
Lament and grieve
for the men[q][z] of Kir Hareseth.[a]
[8]The fields of Heshbon[b] wither,[c]
the vines of Sibmah[d] also.
The rulers of the nations
have trampled down the choicest
vines,[e]
which once reached Jazer[f]
and spread toward the desert.
Their shoots spread out[g]
and went as far as the sea.[h]
[9]So I weep,[i] as Jazer weeps,
for the vines of Sibmah.
O Heshbon, O Elealeh,[j]
I drench you with tears![k]
The shouts of joy[l] over your ripened
fruit
and over your harvests[m] have been
stilled.
[10]Joy and gladness are taken away from
the orchards;[n]
no one sings or shouts[o] in the
vineyards;

Cross references

15:8 [d]S Nu 21:16
15:9
[e]S 2Ki 17:25
[f]Eze 25:8-11
16:1 [g]S 2Ch 3:4
[h]S 2Ch 32:23
[i]S Jdg 1:36;
Ob 3 [j]n
[j]S Isa 10:32
16:2 [k]Pr 27:8
[l]Nu 21:29
[m]Jdg 12:5
[n]Nu 21:13-14;
Jer 48:20
16:3 [o]S 1Ki 18:4
16:4 [p]Isa 58:7
[q]S Isa 9:4
[r]Isa 2:2-4
16:5
[s]S 1Sa 13:14;
Da 7:14; Mic 4:7
[t]S Pr 20:28

[u]S Isa 7:2;
Lk 1:32 [v]S Isa 9:7
16:6 [w]Jer 25:21;
Eze 25:8;
Am 2:1; Zep 2:8
[x]S Lev 26:19;
S Job 20:6;
Jer 49:16; Ob 1:3;
Zep 2:10
16:7 [y]S Isa 13:6;
Jer 48:20; 49:3
[z]S 1Ch 16:3
[a]S 2Ki 3:25
16:8 [b]S Nu 21:25
[c]S Isa 15:6
[d]S Nu 32:3
[e]S Isa 5:2
[f]S Nu 21:32
[g]S Job 8:16
[h]Ps 80:11
16:9 [i]S Isa 15:3;
Eze 27:31
[j]S Nu 32:3
[k]S Job 7:3
[l]S Ezr 3:13
[m]Jer 40:12
16:10 [n]Isa 24:7-8
[o]Jer 25:30

Text notes

[o]9 Masoretic Text; Dead Sea Scrolls, some Septuagint
manuscripts and Vulgate *Dibon*   [p]5 Hebrew *tent*
[q]7 Or "*raisin cakes,*" a wordplay

15:8 *Eglaim.* Perhaps near the northern border of Moab.
Beer Elim. Beer means "well" (cf. Nu 21:16). This site may
have been close to the southern border.
15:9 *Dimon's waters . . . blood.* The Hebrew for "blood"
(dam) sounds like "Dimon." This is probably also a wordplay
on the name "Dibon" (v. 2), close to the Arnon River. Many
Moabites will die in the conflict. *a lion.* A reference to either
the Assyrian army (cf. 5:29; Jer 50:17) or actual lions (cf.
13:21–22).
16:1 *lambs as tribute.* As King Mesha sent 100,000 lambs
to King Ahab of Israel each year (see 2Ki 3:4), so now proud
Moab, which has often oppressed Israel, is advised in her
crisis to submit to the king in Jerusalem. *Sela.* The naturally
fortified capital of the Edomites south of the Dead Sea,
situated on a rocky plateau that towers 1,000 feet above the
nearby Petra (cf. 42:11). The name means "cliff." The tribute would be sent around the southern end of the Dead Sea.
Daughter of Zion. A personification of Jerusalem and its
inhabitants.
16:2 *fords of the Arnon.* The women were fleeing south,
away from the northern invader.
16:3 *Hide the fugitives.* The Moabites are asking Judah for
refuge (contrast Ru 1:1; 1Sa 22:3–4).
16:4 *destroyer.* Probably Assyria (see notes on 15:1; 33:1).
oppressor. Moab.

16:5 *house of David.* See 9:7; Am 9:11 and notes.
"House" equals "dynasty" (see note on 7:2). *in judging
seeks justice.* See 11:2–4 and notes. The Messiah is again in
view.
16:6 *Moab's pride.* Though a small nation, Moab is proud
and defiant like Assyria and Babylon. Cf. 10:12; 14:13;
25:11; Jer 48:42.
16:7 *men.* See NIV text note. *Kir Hareseth.* See note on
15:1. The four cities in vv. 7–8 appear in inverted (chiastic)
order in vv. 9–11.
16:8 *Heshbon.* See note on 15:4. *Sibmah.* Perhaps three
miles west of Heshbon. See Jer 48:32. *choicest vines.* The
poet shifts to a metaphor, comparing Moab to a vineyard (see
5:1–7). He returns to a literal description again in v. 10.
Jazer. Possibly located about 15 miles north of the Dead Sea.
desert. On the eastern edge of Moab. *shoots spread out.* This
is hyperbole, as in Ps 80:11, where Israel is the vineyard. *sea.*
Probably the Dead Sea.
16:9–11 *I . . . I . . . I . . . My . . . my.* The Lord weeps and
laments over the destruction he has had to bring on proud
Moab to humble her.
16:9 *Elealeh.* See note on 15:4.
16:10 *treads out wine.* The grapes were trampled on, and
the juice flowed into the wine vat (see note on 5:2; cf. Jer
48:33; Am 9:13).

no one treads[p] out wine at the
　presses,[q]
　for I have put an end to the shouting.
[11]My heart laments for Moab[r] like a
　harp,[s]
　my inmost being[t] for Kir Hareseth.
[12]When Moab appears at her high place,[u]
　she only wears herself out;
　when she goes to her shrine[v] to pray,
　it is to no avail.[w]

[13]This is the word the Lord has already
spoken concerning Moab. [14]But now the
Lord says: "Within three years,[x] as a servant bound by contract[y] would count
them,[z] Moab's splendor and all her many
people will be despised,[a] and her survivors
will be very few and feeble."[b]

An Oracle Against Damascus

17 An oracle[c] concerning Damascus:[d]

　"See, Damascus will no longer be a city
　but will become a heap of ruins.[e]
[2]The cities of Aroer[f] will be deserted
　and left to flocks,[g] which will lie
　down,[h]
　with no one to make them afraid.[i]
[3]The fortified[j] city will disappear from
　Ephraim,
　and royal power from Damascus;
　the remnant of Aram will be
　like the glory[k] of the Israelites,"[l]
　　declares the Lord Almighty.

[4]"In that day[m] the glory[n] of Jacob will
　fade;
　the fat of his body will waste[o] away.
[5]It will be as when a reaper gathers the
　standing grain

and harvests[p] the grain with his
　arm—
　as when a man gleans heads of grain[q]
　in the Valley of Rephaim.[r]
[6]Yet some gleanings will remain,[s]
　as when an olive tree is beaten,[t]
leaving two or three olives on the
　topmost branches,
　four or five on the fruitful boughs,"
　　declares the Lord,
　　　the God of Israel.

[7]In that day[u] men will look[v] to their
　Maker[w]
　and turn their eyes to the Holy One[x]
　of Israel.
[8]They will not look to the altars,[y]
　the work of their hands,[z]
　and they will have no regard for the
　Asherah poles[r] [a]
　and the incense altars their fingers[b]
　have made.

[9]In that day their strong cities, which
they left because of the Israelites, will be
like places abandoned to thickets and undergrowth.[c] And all will be desolation.

[10]You have forgotten[d] God your Savior;[e]
　you have not remembered the
　Rock,[f] your fortress.[g]
Therefore, though you set out the finest
　plants
　and plant imported vines,[h]
[11]though on the day you set them out,
　you make them grow,

16:10 [p]S Jdg 9:27;
[q]S Job 24:11;
S Isa 5:2
16:11 [r]S Isa 15:5
[s]S Job 30:31
[t]Isa 63:15;
Hos 11:8; Php 2:1
16:12 [u]1Ki 11:7
[v]S Isa 15:2
[w]S 1Ki 18:29;
Ps 115:4-7;
Isa 44:17-18;
1Co 8:4
16:14 [x]Isa 20:3;
37:30
[y]S Lev 25:50
[z]S Lev 19:13
[a]Isa 25:10;
Jer 48:42
[b]Isa 21:17
17:1 [c]Isa 13:1
[d]S Ge 14:15;
Ac 9:2
[e]S Dt 13:16;
S Isa 25:2
17:2 [f]S 2Ki 10:33
[g]S Isa 5:17; 7:21;
Eze 25:5
[h]Isa 27:10
[i]S Lev 26:6;
Jer 7:33; Mic 4:4
17:3 [j]Isa 25:2,12;
Hos 10:14 [k]ver 4;
Isa 21:16;
Hos 9:11 [l]Isa 7:8,
16; 8:4
17:4 [m]S Isa 2:11
[n]S ver 3
[o]S Isa 10:16

17:5 [p]ver 11;
Isa 33:4;
Jer 51:33;
Joel 3:13;
Mt 13:30
[q]Job 24:24
[r]S Jos 17:15;
S 1Ch 11:15
17:6 [s]S Dt 4:27;
S Isa 10:19;
S 24:13 [t]ver 11;
Isa 27:12
17:7 [u]S Isa 2:11
[v]S Isa 9:13;
S 10:20
[w]S Ps 95:6
[x]S Isa 12:6
17:8
[y]S Lev 26:30
[z]S 2Ch 32:19;
Isa 2:18,20;
30:22; 46:6;
Rev 9:20

[a]S Jdg 3:7; S 2Ki 17:10 [b]Isa 2:8 **17:9** [c]S Isa 7:19 **17:10**
[d]S Dt 6:12; 8:11; Ps 50:22; 106:21; Isa 51:13; 57:11;
Jer 2:32; 3:21; 13:25; 18:15; Eze 22:12; 23:35; Hos 8:14;
13:6 [e]S Isa 12:2; S Lk 1:47 [f]S Ge 49:24 [g]S Ps 18:2 [h]S Isa 5:7

[r]8 That is, symbols of the goddess Asherah

16:11 Cf. Jer 48:36.
16:12 *high place.* See 15:2 and note. *pray . . . to no avail.*
Moab's god, Chemosh, was a mere idol (see 44:17-20; 1Ki
11:7).
16:13-14 An epilogue to 15:1-16:12.
16:14 *Within three years.* Other signs that have a three-
year limit are given in 20:3; 37:30; see also notes on 7:14,
16. Moab's three years were over by c. 715 B.C. (see note on
15:1). *servant bound by contract.* Cf. 21:16-17, where the
prophecy against Kedar follows the pattern of this verse.
17:1-14 See Jer 49:23-27; Am 1:3-5.
17:1 *oracle.* See note on 13:1. *Damascus.* The capital of
Aram (Syria), located northeast of Mount Hermon on strategic trade routes between Mesopotamia, Egypt and Arabia.
Since the time of David, the Arameans of Damascus were
frequent enemies of Israel (see 2Sa 8:5; 1Ki 22:31).
17:2 *Aroer.* About 14 miles east of the Dead Sea on the
Arnon River. It marked the southern boundary of Aram's
sphere of control (see 2Ki 10:32-33).
17:3 *Ephraim.* The northern kingdom (see note on 7:2) is
mentioned here because of its alliance with Damascus
against Assyria (see note on 7:1). *royal power.* In 732 B.C.
Tiglath-Pileser III captured Damascus and made it an Assyr-

ian province. Many of the cities of Israel were also captured
(see note on 9:1).
17:4-11 The prophet shifts from Damascus to Israel (likely
the northern kingdom)—a shift prepared for at the end of v.
3. This association of judgment on Damascus and Israel
reflects the same linkage as that in ch. 7.
17:4,7,9 *In that day.* See notes on 2:11,17,20; 10:20,27.
17:5 *harvests the grain.* Harvest can signify a time of
judgment (see Joel 3:13). *Valley of Rephaim.* A fertile area
west of Jerusalem (Jos 15:8) and the scene of Philistine raids
(1Ch 14:9).
17:7-8 Cf. 2:20; 10:20.
17:7 *Holy One of Israel.* See note on 1:4.
17:8 *altars.* Probably altars for Baal (cf. 1Ki 16:32).
Asherah poles. See notes on Ex 34:13; Jdg 2:13; see also
NIV text note here. *incense altars.* Associated with high
places in Lev 26:30 and with altars for Baal in 2Ch 34:4.
17:9 *they.* Perhaps the Canaanites, whose religious practices are referred to in v. 8. *thickets and undergrowth.* Cf.
7:23-25.
17:10 *the Rock.* See 26:4; 30:29; 44:8; Dt 32:4,15,18; Ps
19:14. *vines.* Probably representing the people of Israel (see
5:7; 18:5; 37:30-31).

and on the morning[i] when you plant
　　them, you bring them to bud,
yet the harvest[j] will be as nothing[k]
　in the day of disease and incurable[l]
　　pain.[m]

[12]Oh, the raging[n] of many nations—
　　they rage like the raging sea![o]
Oh, the uproar[p] of the peoples—
　　they roar like the roaring of great
　　　waters![q]

[13]Although the peoples roar[r] like the roar
　　of surging waters,
when he rebukes[s] them they flee[t]
　　far away,
driven before the wind like chaff[u] on
　　the hills,
like tumbleweed before a gale.[v]

[14]In the evening, sudden[w] terror![x]
　Before the morning, they are gone![y]
This is the portion of those who loot us,
　the lot of those who plunder us.

A Prophecy Against Cush

18 Woe[z] to the land of whirring
　　　　wings[s]
　along the rivers of Cush,[t] [a]
[2]which sends envoys[b] by sea
　in papyrus[c] boats over the water.

Go, swift messengers,
to a people tall and smooth-skinned,[d]
　to a people feared far and wide,
an aggressive[e] nation of strange speech,
　whose land is divided by rivers.[f]

[3]All you people of the world,[g]
　you who live on the earth,
when a banner[h] is raised on the
　　mountains,
　you will see it,
and when a trumpet[i] sounds,
　you will hear it.

[4]This is what the LORD says to me:
　"I will remain quiet[j] and will look
　　on from my dwelling place,[k]
like shimmering heat in the sunshine,[l]
　like a cloud of dew[m] in the heat of
　　harvest."

[5]For, before the harvest, when the
　　blossom is gone
　and the flower becomes a ripening
　　grape,
he will cut off[n] the shoots with pruning
　　knives,
　and cut down and take away the
　　spreading branches.[o]

[6]They will all be left to the mountain
　　birds of prey[p]
and to the wild animals;[q]
the birds will feed on them all summer,
　the wild animals all winter.

[7]At that time gifts[r] will be brought to
the LORD Almighty

from a people tall and
　　smooth-skinned,[s]
　from a people feared[t] far and wide,
an aggressive nation of strange speech,
　whose land is divided by rivers[u]—

the gifts will be brought to Mount Zion,
the place of the Name of the LORD Almighty.[v]

A Prophecy About Egypt

19 An oracle[w] concerning Egypt:[x] [y]

　　　See, the LORD rides on a swift
　　　　cloud[z]
　　　and is coming to Egypt.

Cross references (center column)

17:11 [i]Ps 90:6
/S ver 5
[k]S Lev 26:20;
Hos 8:7;
Joel 1:11; Hag 1:6
[l]Jer 10:19; 30:12
[m]S Dt 28:39;
S Job 4:8
17:12 [n]ver 13;
Isa 41:11
[o]S Ps 18:4;
Lk 21:25
[p]S Ps 46:6;
Isa 8:9 [q]Isa 8:7
17:13 [r]S Ps 46:3
[s]S Dt 28:20;
S Ps 9:5
[t]S Ps 68:1;
S Isa 13:14
[u]S Job 13:25;
S Isa 2:22; 41:2,
15-16; Da 2:35
[v]Job 21:18;
S Ps 65:7
17:14 [w]Isa 29:5;
30:13; 47:11;
48:3 [x]Isa 33:18;
54:14
[y]S 2Ki 19:35
18:1 [z]Isa 5:8
[a]S Ge 10:6;
S Ps 68:31;
S Eze 29:10
18:2 [b]Ob 1:1
[c]Ex 2:3; Job 9:26
[d]S Ge 41:14
[e]S Ge 10:8-9;
S 2Ch 12:3 [f]ver 7
18:3 [g]S Ps 33:8
[h]S Ps 60:4;
Isa 5:26; 11:10;
13:2; 31:9;
Jer 4:21
[i]S Jos 6:20;
S Jdg 3:27

18:4 [j]Isa 62:1;
64:12 [k]Isa 26:21;
Hos 5:15; Mic 1:3
[l]S Jdg 5:31;
S Ps 18:12;
Hab 3:4
[m]2Sa 1:21;
S Ps 133:3;
Isa 26:19;
Hos 14:5
18:5 [n]S Isa 10:33
[o]Isa 17:10-11;
Eze 17:6
18:6 [p]S Isa 8:8
[q]Isa 37:36; 56:9;
Jer 7:33;
Eze 32:4; 39:17
18:7
[r]S 2Ch 9:24;

S Isa 60:7 [s]S Ge 41:14 [t]Hab 1:7 [u]ver 2 [v]Ps 68:31 19:1
[w]Isa 13:1 [x]Isa 20:3; Joel 3:19 [y]S Ex 12:12; S Jer 44:3
[z]S Dt 10:14; S 2Sa 22:10; S Rev 1:7

[s]/ Or of locusts　　[t]/ That is, the upper Nile region

Notes (bottom)

17:11 *disease and incurable pain.* Brought by the Assyrian invasions.

17:12-14 The same sequence of a powerful invader that is quickly cut down occurs in 10:28-34. Both passages may refer to Sennacherib's invasion of 701 B.C. (see 37:36-37). But it is more likely that the prophet here speaks more generally of Israel's experience of the world of nations as a perpetual threat to their existence.

17:12 *raging sea.* Assyria is called "floodwaters" in 8:7.

17:13 *chaff . . . tumbleweed.* Symbolic of the enemy also in 29:5; 41:15-16; Ps 83:13.

18:1-7 See Zep 2:12.

18:1 *whirring wings.* Either a reference to insects (perhaps locusts) or a figurative description of the armies of Cush (see 7:18-19). *Cush.* Nubia or ancient Ethiopia (not to be confused with modern Ethiopia, which is located farther to the southeast), south of Egypt. In 715 B.C. a Cushite named Shabako gained control of Egypt and founded the 25th dynasty.

18:2 *sea.* Perhaps the Nile River (cf. 19:5; Na 3:8, where the same Hebrew word is translated "river"). *papyrus boats.*

See note on Ex 2:3. *Go, swift messengers.* With the message contained in vv. 3–6. *people tall and smooth-skinned.* Probably the peoples of Cush and Egypt. Unlike Semites, they were clean-shaven (see note on Ge 41:14). *rivers.* The Nile and its tributaries.

18:3 *All you people of the world.* All the nations arrayed against God's people Israel (see 17:12-14 and note). *banner.* See 5:26 and note. *trumpet.* Used to summon troops.

18:4 *remain quiet.* In the face of the hostility of the nations, the Lord will not act immediately; but when they are in the full growth of summer (v. 5), he will cut them down.

18:6 *birds of prey . . . wild animals.* Cf. 56:9; Jer 7:33; Eze 32:4; 39:17-20.

18:7 See v. 2. *gifts.* According to 2Ch 32:23 gifts were brought to Hezekiah after Sennacherib's death. The Moabites were asked to send tribute to Mount Zion in 16:1 (cf. 45:14; Zep 3:10). *place of the Name.* See Dt 12:5 and note. See Jer 46; Eze 29–32.

19:1-20:6 See Jer 46; Eze 29–32.

19:1 *oracle.* See note on 13:1. *rides on a swift cloud.* A metaphor used also in Ps 68:4; 104:3; cf. Mt 26:64. *idols . . . tremble.* See Jer 50:2. God had also previously judged

The idols of Egypt tremble before him,
and the hearts of the Egyptians melt[a]
within them.

2"I will stir up Egyptian against
Egyptian—
brother will fight against brother,[b]
neighbor against neighbor,
city against city,
kingdom against kingdom.[c]
3The Egyptians will lose heart,[d]
and I will bring their plans[e] to
nothing;[f]
they will consult the idols and the
spirits of the dead,
the mediums and the spiritists.[g]
4I will hand the Egyptians over
to the power of a cruel master,
and a fierce king[h] will rule over them,"
declares the Lord, the LORD
Almighty.

5The waters of the river will dry up,[i]
and the riverbed will be parched and
dry.[j]
6The canals will stink;[k]
the streams of Egypt will dwindle and
dry up.[l]
The reeds[m] and rushes will wither,[n]
7 also the plants[o] along the Nile,
at the mouth of the river.
Every sown field[p] along the Nile
will become parched, will blow away
and be no more.[q]
8The fishermen[r] will groan and lament,
all who cast hooks[s] into the Nile;
those who throw nets on the water
will pine away.

9Those who work with combed flax[t]
will despair,
the weavers of fine linen[u] will lose
hope.
10The workers in cloth will be dejected,
and all the wage earners will be sick
at heart.

11The officials of Zoan[v] are nothing but
fools;
the wise counselors[w] of Pharaoh give
senseless advice.[x]
How can you say to Pharaoh,
"I am one of the wise men,[y]
a disciple of the ancient kings"?

12Where are your wise men[z] now?
Let them show you and make known
what the LORD Almighty
has planned[a] against Egypt.
13The officials of Zoan[b] have become
fools,
the leaders of Memphis[u][c] are
deceived;
the cornerstones[d] of her peoples
have led Egypt astray.
14The LORD has poured into them
a spirit of dizziness;[e]
they make Egypt stagger in all that she
does,
as a drunkard staggers[f] around in his
vomit.
15There is nothing Egypt can do—
head or tail, palm branch or reed.[g]

16In that day[h] the Egyptians will be like

Cross references (center column):

19:1 [a]S Jos 2:11
19:2 [b]S Jdg 7:22;
S 12:4; Mt 10:21,
36 [c]S 2Ch 15:6;
20:23; Mt 24:7;
Mk 13:8;
Lk 21:10
19:3 [d]Ps 18:45
[e]ver 11;
S Job 5:12
[f]2Ch 10:13
[g]S Lev 19:31;
Isa 47:13; Da 2:2,
10; 3:8; 5:7
19:4 [h]Isa 20:4;
Jer 46:26;
Eze 29:19; 32:11
19:5 [i]Isa 44:27;
50:2; Jer 50:38;
51:36
[j]S 2Sa 14:14
19:6 [k]Ex 7:18
[l]Isa 37:25;
Eze 30:12
[m]S Ge 41:2;
S Job 8:11
[n]Isa 15:6
19:7 [o]Nu 11:5
[p]Dt 29:23;
Isa 23:3
[q]Zec 10:11
19:8 [r]Nu 11:5;
Eze 47:10
[s]Am 4:2;
Hab 1:15

19:9 [t]S Jos 2:6
[u]Pr 7:16;
Eze 16:10; 27:7
19:11
[v]S Nu 13:22
[w]S Ge 41:37
[x]S ver 3
[y]S 1Ki 4:30;
Ac 7:22
19:12 [z]1Co 1:20
[a]S Isa 14:24;
Ro 9:17
19:13
[b]S Nu 13:22
[c]Jer 2:16; 44:1;
46:14,19;
Eze 30:13,16;
Hos 9:6
[d]S Ps 118:22
19:14 [e]S Pr 12:8;
Mt 17:17
[f]S Ps 107:27

19:15 [g]S Isa 9:14 19:16 [h]Isa 2:17; 11:10

[u]13 Hebrew Noph

Footnotes:

Egypt's idols during the ten plagues (see Ex 12:12 and note). *hearts . . . melt.* See 13:7.
19:2 *Egyptian against Egyptian.* Cf. 9:21. The Libyan dynasty clashed with the "Ethiopians" (Cushites; see note on 18:1) and with the Saites of Dynasty 24.
19:3 *consult . . . spiritists.* Israel also did so in desperate times (see 8:19 and note).
19:4 *cruel master.* The king of Assyria (see 20:4). Esarhaddon conquered Egypt in 670 B.C.
19:5 *river will dry up.* The Nile was the lifeline of Egypt; its annual flooding provided essential water and produced the only fertile soil there.
19:6 *canals.* For irrigation.
19:7 *sown field.* Egypt's crops were normally abundant, and some were exported.
19:8 *fishermen.* Fish were usually plentiful (see Nu 11:5).
19:9 *work with . . . flax.* Large amounts of water were needed to process flax. *fine linen.* Another well-known Egyptian export.
19:11 *Zoan.* A city (possibly Tanis) in the northeastern part of the Nile delta, familiar to the Israelites during their years in Egypt (see Nu 13:22; Ps 78:12,43). It was the northern capital for the 25th dynasty (see note on 18:1). *wise men.* See v. 12. Egypt was famous for its wise men (see 1Ki 4:30).
19:13 *Memphis.* An important city 15 miles south of the

delta that was the capital during the Old Kingdom (c. 2686–2160 B.C.). *cornerstones.* Prophets and priests, as well as political leaders (see 9:15–16).
19:14 *drunkard staggers.* Israel's leaders stagger in 28:7–8.
19:15 *head or tail, palm branch or reed.* Egypt's leaders. The same two pairs are used of Israel's leaders in 9:14–15.
19:16–25 A chain of four announcements of coming events associated with "that day": 1. An act of divine judgment will cause Egypt to "shudder with fear" (v. 16) and be in terror of Judah (vv. 16–17). 2. "Five cities" in Egypt will "swear allegiance" to the Lord (v. 18). 3. Because of a divine act of deliverance and healing in Egypt, an altar will be erected in Egypt where Egyptians will offer sacrifices to the Lord (vv. 19–22). 4. Egypt, Assyria and Israel will be linked into one people of the Lord (vv. 23–25). The prophet looks well beyond the present realities in which the world powers do not acknowledge the true God and proudly pursue their own destinies, running roughshod over the people of the Lord. He foresees a series of divine acts that will bring about the conversion of the nations.
19:16,18–19,23–24 *In that day.* The coming day of the Lord (see 10:20,27 and note; cf. 11:10–11).
19:16 *shudder with fear.* Like the people of Jericho (Jos 2:9,11). *hand . . . the LORD . . . raises.* See 14:26–27 and note.

women.^{i} They will shudder with fear^j at the uplifted hand^k that the LORD Almighty raises against them. ^{17}And the land of Judah will bring terror to the Egyptians; everyone to whom Judah is mentioned will be terrified,^{l} because of what the LORD Almighty is planning^m against them.

^{18}In that day^n five cities^o in Egypt will speak the language of Canaan and swear allegiance^p to the LORD Almighty. One of them will be called the City of Destruction.$^{v\ q}$

^{19}In that day^r there will be an altar^s to the LORD in the heart of Egypt,^{t} and a monument^u to the LORD at its border. ^{20}It will be a sign and witness^v to the LORD Almighty in the land of Egypt. When they cry out to the LORD because of their oppressors, he will send them a savior^w and defender, and he will rescue^x them. ^{21}So the LORD will make himself known to the Egyptians, and in that day they will acknowledge^y the LORD. They will worship^z with sacrifices and grain offerings; they will make vows to the LORD and keep them.^{a} ^{22}The LORD will strike^b Egypt with a plague;^{c} he will strike them and heal them. They will turn^d to the LORD, and he will respond to their pleas and heal^e them.

^{23}In that day^f there will be a highway^g from Egypt to Assyria.^{h} The Assyrians will go to Egypt and the Egyptians to Assyria.

The Egyptians and Assyrians will worship^i together. ^{24}In that day^j Israel will be the third, along with Egypt and Assyria,^{k} a blessing^l on the earth. ^{25}The LORD Almighty will bless^m them, saying, "Blessed be Egypt my people,^{n} Assyria my handiwork,^{o} and Israel my inheritance.^{p}"

A Prophecy Against Egypt and Cush

20 In the year that the supreme commander,^{q} sent by Sargon king of Assyria, came to Ashdod^r and attacked and captured it— ^{2}at that time the LORD spoke through Isaiah son of Amoz.^{s} He said to him, "Take off the sackcloth^t from your body and the sandals^u from your feet." And he did so, going around stripped^v and barefoot. ^{w}

^{3}Then the LORD said, "Just as my servant^x Isaiah has gone stripped and barefoot for three years,^{y} as a sign^z and por-

19:16 ^{i}Jer 50:37; 51:30; Na 3:13
^{j}S Dt 2:25; Heb 10:31
^{k}S Isa 11:15
19:17 ^{l}S Ge 35:5
^{m}S Isa 14:24
19:18
^{n}S Isa 10:20
^{o}Jer 44:1
^{p}Ps 22:27;
S 63:11; Isa 48:1;
Jer 4:2; Zep 3:9
^{q}Isa 17:1; 24:12; 32:19;
^{fn}Jer 43:13
19:19
^{r}S Isa 10:20
^{s}S Jos 22:10
^{t}S Ps 68:31
^{u}S Ge 28:18
19:20
^{v}S Ge 21:30
^{w}S Dt 28:29;
S Jdg 2:18;
S Isa 25:9
^{x}Isa 49:24-26
19:21
^{y}S Isa 11:9;
S 43:10 ^{z}ver 19;
S Ge 27:29;
S Ps 86:9;
Isa 56:7; 60:7;
Mal 1:11
^{a}S Nu 30:2;
S Dt 23:21
19:22 ^{b}Ex 12:23;
Heb 12:11
^{c}Ex 11:10
^{d}Isa 45:14;
Eze 33:11;
Hos 6:1; 10:12;
12:6; 14:1;
Joel 2:13
^{e}S Dt 32:39
19:23 ^{f}S ver 16, 24; Isa 20:6
^{g}S Isa 11:16
^{h}Mic 7:12

^{i}S Ge 27:29;

Isa 2:3; 27:13; 66:23 **19:24** ^{j}S ver 23 ^{k}S Isa 11:11 ^{l}S Ge 12:2
19:25 ^{m}S Ge 12:3; Eph 2:11-14 ^{n}Ps 87:4; S 100:3
^{o}Isa 29:23; 43:7; 45:11; 60:21; 64:8; Eph 2:10 ^{p}S Ex 34:9;
Jer 30:22; Hos 2:23 **20:1** ^{q}2Ki 18:17 ^{r}S Jos 11:22; S 13:3
20:2 ^{s}S Isa 13:1 ^{t}2Ki 1:8; S Isa 3:24; Zec 13:4; Mt 3:4
^{u}Eze 24:17,23 ^{v}S 1Sa 19:24 ^{w}Eze 4:1-12; Mic 1:8 **20:3**
^{x}Isa 22:20; 41:8-9; 42:1; 43:10; 49:3,5-7; 50:10; 52:13;
53:11; Jer 7:25; Hag 2:23; Zec 4:14 ^{y}S Isa 16:14 ^{z}S Ex 3:12;
S Isa 8:18; 37:30; 38:7; Ac 21:11

^{v}18 Most manuscripts of the Masoretic Text; some manuscripts of the Masoretic Text, Dead Sea Scrolls and Vulgate *City of the Sun* (that is, Heliopolis)

19:17 *land of Judah.* The Egyptians will somehow recognize (perhaps through court contacts with Hezekiah) that it is the God of Judah who has brought judgment upon them.
19:18 *five.* Perhaps in the sense of "many." *speak the language of Canaan.* Either a symbolic reference to Egypt's allegiance to the Lord (see vv. 21–22,25) or a literal reference to Jews living in Egypt. After the fall of Jerusalem in 586 B.C., many Jews fled to Egypt (Jer 44:1). *City of Destruction.* Probably a reference to Heliopolis, city of the sun-god; it was destroyed by Nebuchadnezzar (see Jer 43:12–13). The Hebrew for "destruction" is almost identical to the Hebrew for "sun."
19:19 *altar.* Some relate this to the temple built in Egypt by the Jewish high priest Onias IV, who fled to Egypt in the second century B.C., but the reference appears to be to a conversion to the Lord of a significant number of Egyptians.
19:20 *sign and witness.* Cf. the purpose of the altar built near the Jordan River by the Transjordan tribes in Jos 22:26–27. *oppressors . . . savior.* The language of the book of Judges (see Jdg 2:18). It is uncertain who this savior and defender is, but the prophet may well have in mind the promised Son of the house of David (see 11:1–10).
19:21 *make himself known.* Cf. Ex 7:5. *worship with sacrifices.* Offerings of foreigners are also mentioned in 56:7; 60:7 (cf. Zec 14:16–19).
19:22 *strike Egypt with a plague.* Oppression (see v. 20) and plague were two common forms of divine affliction. Contrast the results of the plague on the firstborn in Ex 12:23. *turn . . . heal.* Cf. 6:10; here parallel to sending Egypt a "savior and defender" (v. 20). Earlier a hardhearted pharaoh had not turned to the Lord (Ex 9:34–35).

19:23 *highway.* Cf. the highway to Jerusalem in 11:16 (see note there). For centuries Egyptians and Assyrians had fought each other (see 20:4), but in the future they would be linked in a bond of friendship sealed by their common allegiance to the Lord (cf. 25:3). *worship together.* This description of peace and of unity in worship is similar to 2:2–4 (see note there; see also note on v. 21).
19:25 *will bless them.* A fulfillment of Ge 12:3. *Egypt my people.* Such a universal vision seems possible for Isaiah only in the light of what has been said about the "shoot . . . from the stump of Jesse" (11:1; see 11:1–10). Cf. 45:14; Eph 2:11–13.
20:1–6 An epilogue to chs. 18–19, as 16:13–14 is to 15:1–16:12.
20:1 *the year.* Probably 711 B.C. *Sargon.* Sargon II, who reigned 721–705 B.C. He is mentioned by name only here in the OT. *Ashdod.* One of the five Philistine cities (see 1Sa 6:17), Ashdod was located near the Mediterranean Sea about 18 miles northeast of Gaza. The city had rebelled against Assyria in 713 under King Azuri. In 1963 three fragments of an Assyrian monument commemorating Sargon's victory and mentioning Sargon by name were discovered at Ashdod.
20:2 *sackcloth.* Normally the garment of mourners (see map, p. 330), but perhaps also the usual garb of prophets (see 2Ki 1:8; Zec 13:4).
20:3 *my servant.* A title for prophets and others used by God in a special way. *three years.* See 16:14 and note. *sign and portent.* See 8:18; see also 7:3,14 and notes. The prophet Ezekiel's behavior also had symbolic significance (Eze 24:24,27; cf. Zec 3:8). *Egypt and Cush.* See 18:1; 19:1.

tent[a] against Egypt[b] and Cush,[w c] [4]so the king[d] of Assyria will lead away stripped[e] and barefoot the Egyptian captives[f] and Cushite[g] exiles, young and old, with buttocks bared[h]—to Egypt's shame.[i] [5]Those who trusted[j] in Cush[k] and boasted in Egypt[l] will be afraid and put to shame.[m] [6]In that day[n] the people who live on this coast will say, 'See what has happened[o] to those we relied on,[p] those we fled to for help[q] and deliverance from the king of Assyria! How then can we escape?[r]' "

A Prophecy Against Babylon

21 An oracle[s] concerning the Desert[t] by the Sea:

Like whirlwinds[u] sweeping through the
   southland,[v]
an invader comes from the desert,
   from a land of terror.

[2]A dire[w] vision has been shown to me:
   The traitor betrays,[x] the looter takes
      loot.
Elam,[y] attack! Media,[z] lay siege!
   I will bring to an end all the groaning
      she caused.

[3]At this my body is racked with pain,[a]
   pangs seize me, like those of a
      woman in labor;[b]
I am staggered by what I hear,
   I am bewildered[c] by what I see.
[4]My heart[d] falters,
   fear makes me tremble;[e]
the twilight I longed for
   has become a horror[f] to me.

[5]They set the tables,
   they spread the rugs,
   they eat, they drink![g]

Get up, you officers,
   oil the shields![h]

[6]This is what the Lord says to me:

"Go, post a lookout[i]
   and have him report what he sees.
[7]When he sees chariots[j]
   with teams of horses,
riders on donkeys
   or riders on camels,[k]
let him be alert,
   fully alert."

[8]And the lookout[x l] shouted,

"Day after day, my lord, I stand on the
      watchtower;
   every night I stay at my post.
[9]Look, here comes a man in a chariot[m]
   with a team of horses.
And he gives back the answer:
   'Babylon[n] has fallen,[o] has fallen!
All the images of its gods[p]
   lie shattered[q] on the ground!' "

[10]O my people, crushed on the threshing
      floor,[r]
   I tell you what I have heard
from the LORD Almighty,
   from the God of Israel.

A Prophecy Against Edom

[11]An oracle concerning Dumah[y : s]

20:3 [a]S Dt 28:46 [b]S Isa 19:1 [c]ver 5; S Ge 10:6; Isa 37:9; 43:3 **20:4** [d]S Isa 19:4 [e]S Job 12:17 [f]Jer 46:19; Na 3:10 [g]Isa 18:1; Zep 2:12 [h]S Isa 3:24 [i]Isa 47:3; Jer 13:22,26; Na 3:5 **20:5** [j]S Isa 8:12 [k]S ver 3 [l]S 2Ki 18:21; S Isa 30:5 [m]Eze 29:16 **20:6** [n]Isa 2:11; S 19:23 [o]S 2Ki 18:21 [p]Jer 46:25 [q]S Isa 10:3 [r]Jer 30:15-17; 31:2; Mt 23:33; 1Th 5:3; Heb 2:3 **21:1** [s]S Isa 13:1 [t]Isa 13:21; Jer 50:12; 51:43 [u]S Job 1:19 [v]Da 11:40; Zec 9:14 **21:2** [w]Ps 60:3 [x]Isa 24:16; 33:1 [y]S Ge 10:22; Isa 22:6 [z]S Isa 13:3; Jer 25:25; 51:28 **21:3** [a]S Job 14:22 [b]S Ge 3:16; Ps 48:6; Isa 26:17; 37:3; Jer 30:6; 48:41; 49:22; Jn 16:21 [c]Da 7:28; 8:27; 10:16 **21:4** [d]Isa 7:4; 35:4 [e]S Isa 13:8; Da 5:9 /S Ps 55:5 **21:5** [g]Isa 5:12; 22:2,13; 23:7; 24:8; 32:13; Jer 25:16,27; 51:39,57; Da 5:2 [h]2Sa 1:21; 1Ki 10:16-17; Jer 46:3; 51:11 **21:6** [i]S 2Ki 9:17 **21:7** [j]ver 9 [k]S Jdg 6:5

21:8 [l]Mic 7:7; Hab 2:1 **21:9** [m]ver 7 [n]S Isa 13:1; 47:1,5; S Rev 14:8 [o]Isa 47:11; Jer 51:8; Da 5:30 [p]S Lev 26:30; Isa 46:1; Jer 50:2; 51:44 [q]S Isa 2:18 **21:10** [r]Isa 27:12; 28:27,28; 41:15; Jer 51:33; Mic 4:13; Hab 3:12; Mt 3:12 **21:11** [s]S Ge 25:14; S Isa 34:11

[w]3 That is, the upper Nile region; also in verse 5
[x]8 Dead Sea Scrolls and Syriac; Masoretic Text *A lion*
[y]11 *Dumah* means *silence* or *stillness*, a wordplay on *Edom*.

20:4 *stripped and barefoot.* Cf. 2Ch 28:15; Mic 1:8.
20:5 *trusted in Cush . . . Egypt.* After Assyria conquered the northern kingdom of Israel in 722–721 B.C., King Hezekiah of Judah was under great pressure to make an alliance with Egypt. Isaiah urgently warned against such a policy (cf. 30:1–2; 31:1).
21:1 *oracle.* See note on 13:1. *Desert.* The coming judgment would eventually turn Babylon (see v. 9) into a wasteland (cf. 13:20–22). *the Sea.* Refers either to the Persian Gulf, which was just south of Babylon, or to the alluvial plain deposited by the Euphrates and Tigris rivers and their tributaries. *whirlwinds . . . desert.* The desert sometimes spawns powerful winds (see Hos 13:15). *an invader.* Lit. "it"; it is not clear whether "comes from the desert, from a land of terror" is ascribed to an invader or continues the description of the whirlwinds.
21:2 *Elam.* See note on 11:11. The Elamites were a perpetual enemy of Assyria and Babylon. Much later, they were part of the Persian army that conquered Babylon under Cyrus in 539 B.C. *Media.* See note on 13:17. *she.* Babylon.
21:3 *racked with pain, pangs seize me.* See Daniel's reaction to visions in Da 8:27; 10:16–17; but see also note on 29:9–11.

21:4 *twilight.* Perhaps the end of the Babylonian empire (see note on v. 12). *a horror to me.* The devastation is beyond even what he had desired.
21:5 *eat . . . drink.* With the kind of confident assurance reflected in Belshazzar's feast (see Da 5:1). *Get up . . . !* Rhetorically the prophet, who has seen in a vision the coming attack on Babylon, calls on the officers of Babylon to prepare. *oil the shields.* To make supple the leather that covers the shields so that blows from swords or arrows would glance off.
21:6 *Go, post a lookout.* Probably on the walls of Jerusalem.
21:7 *chariots . . . donkeys . . . camels.* Bearing messengers from afar.
21:9 *Babylon has fallen.* See 13:19. Babylon fell in 689 B.C. and again in 539. These words were adapted by John in Rev 14:8; 18:2. *its gods lie shattered.* The fall of a kingdom meant the disgrace of its gods (cf. 46:1–2).
21:10 *crushed.* Judah would be punished by the Babylonians and taken into captivity (see 39:5–7). *on the threshing floor.* Threshing was a common metaphor for judgment or destruction from war (see Am 1:3).
21:11–12 See Jer 49:7–22; Eze 25:12–14; Am 1:11–12.

Someone calls to me from Seir, [t]
"Watchman, what is left of the night?
Watchman, what is left of the night?"
[12]The watchman replies,
"Morning is coming, but also the
night.
If you would ask, then ask;
and come back yet again."

A Prophecy Against Arabia

[13]An oracle [u] concerning Arabia: [v]

You caravans of Dedanites, [w]
who camp in the thickets of Arabia,
[14] bring water for the thirsty;
you who live in Tema, [x]
bring food for the fugitives.
[15]They flee [y] from the sword, [z]
from the drawn sword,
from the bent bow
and from the heat of battle.

[16]This is what the Lord says to me:
"Within one year, as a servant bound by
contract [a] would count it, all the pomp [b] of
Kedar [c] will come to an end. [17]The survivors of the bowmen, the warriors of Kedar,
will be few. [d]" The LORD, the God of Israel, has spoken. [e]

A Prophecy About Jerusalem

22 An oracle [f] concerning the Valley [g]
of Vision: [h]

What troubles you now,
that you have all gone up on the
roofs, [i]
[2]O town full of commotion,

O city of tumult [j] and revelry? [k]
Your slain [l] were not killed by the
sword, [m]
nor did they die in battle.
[3]All your leaders have fled [n] together;
they have been captured [o] without
using the bow.
All you who were caught were taken
prisoner together,
having fled while the enemy was still
far away.
[4]Therefore I said, "Turn away from me;
let me weep [p] bitterly.
Do not try to console me
over the destruction of my people." [q]

[5]The Lord, the LORD Almighty, has a
day [r]
of tumult and trampling [s] and terror [t]
in the Valley of Vision, [u]
a day of battering down walls [v]
and of crying out to the mountains.
[6]Elam [w] takes up the quiver, [x]
with her charioteers and horses;
Kir [y] uncovers the shield.
[7]Your choicest valleys [z] are full of
chariots,
and horsemen are posted at the city
gates; [a]
[8] the defenses of Judah are stripped
away.

And you looked in that day [b]
to the weapons [c] in the Palace of the
Forest; [d]
[9]you saw that the City of David
had many breaches [e] in its defenses;

Cross references (center column):

21:11 [t]Ge 32:3
21:13 [u]Isa 13:1
[v]S 2Ch 9:14
[w]S Ge 10:7;
S 25:3
21:14 [x]S Ge 25:15
21:15 [y]S Isa 13:14
[z]Isa 31:8
21:16 [a]S Lev 25:50
[b]S Isa 17:3
[c]S Ge 25:13
21:17 [d]S Dt 4:27;
S Isa 10:19
[e]S Isa 1:20; 16:14
22:1 [f]Isa 13:1
[g]Ps 125:2;
Jer 21:13;
Joel 3:2,12,14
[h]S Isa 1:1
[i]S Jos 2:8;
Jer 48:38

22:2 [j]Eze 22:5
[k]S Isa 5:14;
S 21:5 [l]S Isa 10:4
[m]S 2Ki 25:3
22:3 [n]S Isa 13:14
[o]S 2Ki 25:6
22:4 [p]S Isa 15:3;
S La 1:16;
Eze 21:6;
Lk 19:41 [q]Jer 9:1
22:5 [r]S Isa 2:12
[s]S Job 40:12;
S Ps 108:13
[t]S 2Sa 22:43;
Isa 13:3; Jer 30:7;
La 1:5;
Eze 8:17-18;
9:9-10; Joel 2:31;
Am 5:18-20;
Zep 1:15
[u]S Isa 1:1
[v]Ne 6:15;
S Ps 89:40;
Isa 5:5; Jer 39:8;
Eze 13:14
22:6 [w]S Isa 21:2
[x]Ps 46:9;
Jer 49:35; 51:56
[y]S 2Ki 16:9
22:7 [z]Jos 15:8
[a]S 2Ch 32:1-2
22:8 [b]S Isa 2:12
[c]S 2Ch 32:5
[d]S 1Ki 7:2 22:9 [e]S Ne 1:3

21:11 *oracle.* See note on 13:1. *Seir.* A synonym for Edom (Ge 32:3), homeland of Esau's descendants, south of the Dead Sea. Edom is dealt with more extensively in 34:5–15 (cf. 63:1).
21:12 *Morning . . . but also the night.* Perhaps meaning that the long night of Assyrian oppression is almost over, but only a short "morning" will precede Babylonian domination.
21:13–17 See Jer 49:28–33.
21:13 *oracle.* See note on 13:1. *Dedanites.* An Arabian tribe whose merchant activities are mentioned also in Eze 27:20; 38:13. *thickets.* The caravans had to hide from the invader (cf. Jdg 5:6). The Assyrians began to attack the Arabs in 732 B.C., and the Babylonians did the same under Nebuchadnezzar (see Jer 25:17,23–24).
21:14 *Tema.* An oasis in northern Arabia about 400 miles southwest of Babylon (cf. Job 6:19; Jer 25:23).
21:15 *sword . . . bow.* The simple bows of the Arabs were ineffective against the swords and composite bows of Assyria.
21:16 *servant bound by contract.* See 16:14 and note. *pomp.* See 14:11; 16:14. *Kedar.* The home of Bedouin tribes in the Arabian Desert. Kedar was known for its flocks (60:7; Eze 27:21). Nebuchadnezzar defeated the people of Kedar (Jer 49:28–29; cf. Jer 2:10).
21:17 *survivors . . . will be few.* Cf. 10:19; 16:14; 17:6.
22:1–13 The notes on this prophecy assume that it refers

primarily to the final Babylonian siege of Jerusalem in 588–586 B.C. But it is also possible that the primary reference is to the siege by the Assyrian king Sennacherib in 701.
22:1 *oracle.* See note on 13:1. *Valley of Vision.* A valley where God revealed himself in visions, probably one of the valleys near Jerusalem (see note on v. 7). See also v. 5. *roofs.* See 15:3 and note.
22:2 *tumult and revelry.* See v. 13; 5:11–12; 32:13. Jerusalem is behaving just like Babylon (see 21:5; cf. 23:7). *not killed by the sword.* Perhaps a reference to death from disease and famine when the Babylonians besieged Jerusalem in 586 B.C.
22:3 *leaders have fled.* King Zedekiah and his army fled Jerusalem but were captured near Jericho (see 2Ki 25:4–6).
22:5 *has a day.* See 2:12 and note on 2:11,17,20. Also cf. "in that day" in v. 8 and "on that day" in v. 12. *tumult.* A fulfillment of the curse of Dt 28:20.
22:6 *Elam.* See note on 11:11. Elamites probably fought in the Babylonian army. *Kir.* Perhaps another name for Media (see 21:2).
22:7 *choicest valleys.* The Kidron Valley lay east of Jerusalem (see Jn 18:1), the Hinnom Valley to the south and west (see Jos 15:8).
22:8 *Palace of the Forest.* Built by King Solomon out of cedars from Lebanon (see 1Ki 7:2–6; 10:17,21).
22:9 *City of David.* See 2Sa 5:6–7,9. *Lower Pool.* Probably

you stored up water
  in the Lower Pool. f
[10]You counted the buildings in Jerusalem
  and tore down houses g to strengthen
    the wall. h
[11]You built a reservoir between the two
    walls i
  for the water of the Old Pool, j
but you did not look to the One who
    made it,
  or have regard k for the One who
    planned l it long ago.

[12]The Lord, the LORD Almighty,
    called you on that day m
to weep n and to wail,
  to tear out your hair o and put on
    sackcloth. p
[13]But see, there is joy and revelry, q
  slaughtering of cattle and killing of
    sheep,
  eating of meat and drinking of
    wine! r
"Let us eat and drink," you say,
  "for tomorrow we die!" s

[14]The LORD Almighty has revealed this
in my hearing: t "Till your dying day this
sin will not be atoned u for," says the Lord,
the LORD Almighty.

[15]This is what the Lord, the LORD Almighty, says:

"Go, say to this steward,
  to Shebna, v who is in charge w of the
    palace: x
[16]What are you doing here and who gave
    you permission
  to cut out a grave y for yourself z
    here,

hewing your grave on the height
  and chiseling your resting place in the
    rock?

[17]"Beware, the LORD is about to take firm
    hold of you
  and hurl a you away, O you mighty
    man.
[18]He will roll you up tightly like a ball
  and throw b you into a large country.
There you will die
  and there your splendid chariots c
    will remain—
  you disgrace to your master's house!
[19]I will depose you from your office,
  and you will be ousted d from your
    position. e

[20]"In that day f I will summon my servant, g Eliakim h son of Hilkiah. [21]I will
clothe him with your robe and fasten your
sash i around him and hand your authority j over to him. He will be a father to
those who live in Jerusalem and to the
house of Judah. [22]I will place on his shoulder k the key l to the house of David; m
what he opens no one can shut, and what
he shuts no one can open. n [23]I will drive
him like a peg o into a firm place; p he will
be a seat z of honor q for the house of his
father. [24]All the glory of his family will
hang on him: its offspring and off-
shoots—all its lesser vessels, from the
bowls to all the jars.

[25]"In that day," declares the LORD Almighty, "the peg s driven into the firm
place will give way; it will be sheared off

22:9
f S 2Ki 18:17;
S 2Ch 32:4
22:10 g Jer 33:4
h S 2Ch 32:5
22:11 i 2Ki 25:4;
2Ch 32:5;
Jer 39:4
j S 2Ch 32:4
k S 1Sa 12:24
l 2Ki 19:25
22:12
m S Isa 2:12
n Joel 1:9; 2:17
o S Lev 13:40;
Mic 1:16
p S Isa 3:24
22:13 q S Isa 21:5
r S 1Sa 25:36;
Ecc 8:15;
Isa 5:22; 28:7-8;
56:12;
Lk 17:26-29
s 1Co 15:32*
22:14 t Isa 5:9
u S Isa 2:25;
Isa 13:11; 26:21;
30:13-14;
Eze 24:13
22:15
v S 2Ki 6:30;
S 18:18 w ver 21
x S Ge 41:40
22:16 y Mt 27:60
z S Ge 50:5;
S Nu 32:42

22:17 a Jer 10:18;
13:18; 22:26
22:18
b S Job 18:11;
Isa 14:19; 17:13
c S Ge 41:43
22:19 d S 1Sa 2:7;
S Ps 52:5
e Lk 16:3
22:20 f ver 25
g S Isa 20:3
h S 2Ki 18:18;
S Isa 36:3
22:21 i S Isa 5:27
j ver 15
22:22 k Isa 9:6
l 1Ch 9:27;
Mt 16:19;
Rev 3:7
m S Isa 7:2
n S Job 12:14
22:23 o ver 25;
Eze 15:3;
Zec 10:4
p S Ezr 9:8;
S Job 6:25

q S 1Sa 2:7-8; S Job 36:7 **22:25** r ver 20 s S ver 23

z 23 Or throne

---

the same as the "Old Pool" of v. 11. Hezekiah made a pool
and a tunnel as a precaution against Sennacherib's invasion
(see 2Ki 20:20). The "Upper Pool" is mentioned in 7:3;
36:2.
22:10 strengthen the wall. Cf. Hezekiah's preparations in
2Ch 32:5.
22:11 did not look to the One. In 31:1 those who look to
horses and chariots rather than to God are similarly condemned.
22:12 tear out your hair. The hair was either torn out or
shaved off (cf. Jer 16:6; Eze 27:31).
22:13 joy and revelry. The same Hebrew phrase is translated "gladness and joy" in 35:10; 51:11, passages depicting
great hope in connection with restoration. But this was a
time to mourn (Ecc 3:4). See note on v. 2.
22:15 Shebna. Apparently a foreigner, possibly Egyptian; a
contemporary of King Hezekiah. in charge of the palace. A
position second only to the king (see note on v. 21; cf. 36:3;
1Ki 4:6; 2Ki 15:5).
22:16 cut out a grave. One's place of burial was considered
very important, and Shebna coveted a tomb worthy of a king
(cf. 2Ch 16:14).
22:17 hurl you away. Cf. Jer 22:24-26.

22:18 There you will die. Apparently without an honorable
burial (see note on 14:19). chariots. A sign of luxury and
high office (see 2:7; Ge 41:43).
22:20 In that day. When the Lord acts in judgment (see vv.
17-19). my servant. See note on 20:3. Eliakim. See 36:3,
11,22; 37:2.
22:21 hand your authority over to him. By 701 B.C. (see
36:3) Eliakim had replaced Shebna, who was demoted to
"secretary."
22:22 Quoted in part in Rev 3:7. The mention of "father"
(v. 21) and of the responsibility "on his shoulder" recalls the
words about the Messiah in 9:6. key to the house of David.
The authority delegated to him by the king, who belongs to
David's dynasty—perhaps controlling entrance into the royal
palace. Cf. the "keys of the kingdom" given to Peter (Mt
16:19).
22:23 peg. Normally the Hebrew for this word refers to a
tent peg, but here to a peg driven into wood (see Eze 15:3).
seat of honor. Cf. 1Sa 2:8.
22:25 In that day. Another (unspecified) day when the
Lord will come in judgment. peg . . . will give way. Eliakim,
like Shebna, will eventually fall from power.

and will fall, and the load hanging on it will be cut down." The LORD has spoken. [t]

A Prophecy About Tyre

23 An oracle concerning Tyre: [u]

Wail, [v] O ships [w] of Tarshish! [x]
For Tyre is destroyed [y]
and left without house or harbor.
From the land of Cyprus [a]
word has come to them.

[2] Be silent, [z] you people of the island
and you merchants [a] of Sidon, [b]
whom the seafarers have enriched.

[3] On the great waters
came the grain of the Shihor; [c]
the harvest of the Nile [b] [d] was the
revenue of Tyre, [e]
and she became the marketplace of
the nations.

[4] Be ashamed, O Sidon, [f] and you,
O fortress of the sea,
for the sea has spoken:
"I have neither been in labor nor given
birth; [g]
I have neither reared sons nor
brought up daughters."

[5] When word comes to Egypt,
they will be in anguish [h] at the report
from Tyre. [i]

[6] Cross over to Tarshish; [j]
wail, you people of the island.

[7] Is this your city of revelry, [k]
the old, old city,
whose feet have taken her
to settle in far-off lands?

[8] Who planned this against Tyre,
the bestower of crowns,
whose merchants [l] are princes,

whose traders [m] are renowned in the
earth?

[9] The LORD Almighty planned [n] it,
to bring low [o] the pride of all glory
and to humble [p] all who are
renowned [q] on the earth.

[10] Till [c] your land as along the Nile,
O Daughter of Tarshish,
for you no longer have a harbor.

[11] The LORD has stretched out his hand [r]
over the sea
and made its kingdoms tremble. [s]
He has given an order concerning
Phoenicia [d]
that her fortresses be destroyed. [t]

[12] He said, "No more of your reveling, [u]
O Virgin Daughter [v] of Sidon, now
crushed!

"Up, cross over to Cyprus [a] ; [w]
even there you will find no rest."

[13] Look at the land of the Babylonians, [e] [x]
this people that is now of no account!
The Assyrians [y] have made it
a place for desert creatures; [z]
they raised up their siege towers, [a]
they stripped its fortresses bare
and turned it into a ruin. [b]

[14] Wail, you ships [c] of Tarshish; [d]
your fortress is destroyed! [e]

[15] At that time Tyre [f] will be forgotten
for seventy years, [g] the span of a king's life.

Cross references

22:25 [t] Isa 46:11;
Mic 4:4
23:1 [u] Jos 19:29;
1Ki 5:1; Jer 47:4;
Joel 3:4-8;
Am 1:9-10;
Zec 9:2-4
[v] S Isa 13:6
[w] S 1Ki 10:22
[x] S Ge 10:4;
Isa 2:16 [fn]
[y] S Ge 1:2;
Eze 26:4
23:2 [z] S Job 2:13
[a] Eze 27:5-24
[b] Jdg 1:31
23:3 [c] S Ge 41:5
[d] S Isa 19:7
[e] S Ps 83:7
23:4 [f] S Ge 10:15,
19 [g] Isa 54:1
23:5 [h] Eze 30:9
[i] Eze 26:17-18
23:6 [j] S Ge 10:4
23:7 [k] ver 12;
S Isa 5:14; S 21:5;
32:13; Eze 26:13
23:8 [l] Na 3:16

[m] Eze 28:5;
Rev 18:23
23:9 [n] S Isa 14:24
[o] S Job 40:11
[p] S Isa 13:11
[q] Isa 5:13; 9:15;
Eze 27:3
23:11 [r] S Ex 14:21
[s] S Ps 46:6 (ver
14; Isa 25:2;
Eze 26:4;
Zec 9:3-4
23:12 [u] S ver 7;
Rev 18:22
[v] Isa 37:22; 47:1;
Jer 14:17; 46:11;
La 2:13;
Zep 3:14;
Zec 2:10
[w] S Ge 10:4
23:13 [x] Isa 43:14;
Jer 51:12
[y] Isa 10:5
[z] S Ps 74:14;
Isa 18:6
[a] S 2Ki 25:1
[b] Isa 10:7
23:14
[c] S 1Ki 10:22
[d] S Ge 10:4;
Isa 2:16 [fn] [e] S ver
11
23:15 [f] Jer 25:22 [g] S Ps 90:10

[a] 1,12 Hebrew *Kittim*   [b] 2,3 Masoretic Text; one Dead Sea Scroll *Sidon, / who cross over the sea; / your envoys* [3] *are on the great waters. / The grain of the Shihor, / the harvest of the Nile,*   [c] 10 Dead Sea Scrolls and some Septuagint manuscripts; Masoretic Text *Go through* [d] 11 Hebrew *Canaan*   [e] 13 Or *Chaldeans*

Study notes

23:1–18 See Eze 26:1–28:19; Am 1:9–10.

23:1 *oracle.* See note on 13:1. *Tyre.* The main seaport along the Phoenician coast, about 35 miles north of Mount Carmel. Part of the city was built on two rocky islands about half a mile from the shore. King Hiram of Tyre supplied cedars and craftsmen for the temple (see 1Ki 5:8–9) and sailors for Solomon's commercial fleet (1Ki 9:27). *Wail, O ships.* See v. 14. *ships of Tarshish.* Trading ships (see note on 2:16). *destroyed.* Fulfilled through Assyria, Nebuchadnezzar and Alexander. Nebuchadnezzar captured the mainland city in 572 B.C. (see Eze 26:7–11), but the island fortress was not taken until Alexander the Great destroyed it in 332 (cf. Eze 26:3–5). *Cyprus.* An island that had close ties with Tyre (see Eze 27:6).

23:2,4,12 *Sidon.* See Eze 28:20–26; the other prominent Phoenician city, about 25 miles north of Tyre.

23:2 *merchants . . . seafarers.* Tyre's commercial ventures affected the entire Mediterranean world (see vv. 3,8).

23:3 *Shihor.* Probably the easternmost branch of the Nile (see Jer 2:18). *harvest of the Nile.* See 19:7 and note.

23:4 *fortress of the sea.* Tyre (see note on v. 1). *labor . . . birth.* Contrast 54:1.

23:6 *Tarshish.* Perhaps Tartessus in Spain (see Jnh 1:3 and

note), or an island in the western Mediterranean, or a site on the coast of North Africa.

23:7 *revelry.* See note on 22:2. *old, old city.* Tyre was founded before 2000 B.C. *settle in far-off lands.* Carthage in north Africa was a colony of Tyre. Tarshish may have been another.

23:8–9 *planned.* See 14:24,26–27; 25:1.

23:8 *bestower of crowns.* Tyre crowned kings in her colonies. *traders are renowned.* See Eze 28:4–5.

23:9 *pride of all glory.* See Eze 27:3–4.

23:10 *Daughter of Tarshish.* A personification of Tarshish and its inhabitants.

23:11 *stretched out his hand.* See note on 14:26–27. *Phoenicia.* Roughly the same as modern Lebanon.

23:12 *Virgin Daughter of Sidon.* See note on v. 10. *now crushed.* Sidon was captured by Esarhaddon in the seventh century B.C. and later by Nebuchadnezzar c. 587 (cf. Jer 25:22).

23:13 *Assyrians.* Sennacherib destroyed the city of Babylon in 689 B.C. Phoenicia would look like the Babylon of that time. *desert creatures.* Cf. 13:21. *siege towers.* See note on 2Ki 25:1.

23:14 See v. 1 and note.

But at the end of these seventy years, it will happen to Tyre as in the song of the prostitute:

¹⁶"Take up a harp, walk through the city,
O prostitute^h forgotten;
play the harp well, sing many a song,
so that you will be remembered."

¹⁷At the end of seventy years,ⁱ the LORD will deal with Tyre. She will return to her hire as a prostitute^j and will ply her trade with all the kingdoms on the face of the earth.^k ¹⁸Yet her profit and her earnings will be set apart for the LORD;^l they will not be stored up or hoarded. Her profits will go to those who live before the LORD,^m for abundant food and fine clothes.ⁿ

The LORD's Devastation of the Earth

24 See, the LORD is going to lay waste
the earth^o
and devastate^p it;
he will ruin its face
and scatter^q its inhabitants—
²it will be the same
for priest as for people,^r
for master as for servant,
for mistress as for maid,
for seller as for buyer,^s
for borrower as for lender,
for debtor as for creditor.^t
³The earth will be completely laid
waste^u
and totally plundered.^v
The LORD has spoken^w
this word.

⁴The earth dries up^x and withers,^y
the world languishes and withers,

the exalted^z of the earth languish.^a
⁵The earth is defiled^b by its people;
they have disobeyed^c the laws,
violated the statutes
and broken the everlasting
covenant.^d
⁶Therefore a curse^e consumes the earth;
its people must bear their guilt.
Therefore earth's inhabitants are burned
up,^f
and very few are left.
⁷The new wine dries up^g and the vine
withers;^h
all the merrymakers groan.ⁱ
⁸The gaiety of the tambourines^j is
stilled,
the noise^k of the revelers^l has
stopped,
the joyful harp^m is silent.ⁿ
⁹No longer do they drink wine^o with a
song;
the beer is bitter^p to its drinkers.
¹⁰The ruined city^q lies desolate;^r
the entrance to every house is barred.
¹¹In the streets they cry out^s for wine;^t
all joy turns to gloom,^u
all gaiety is banished from the earth.
¹²The city is left in ruins,^v
its gate^w is battered to pieces.
¹³So will it be on the earth
and among the nations,
as when an olive tree is beaten,^x
or as when gleanings are left after the
grape harvest.^y

¹⁴They raise their voices, they shout for
joy;^z

Cross references (center column)

23:16 ^hPr 7:10
23:17 ⁱS Ps 90:10
^jDt 23:17-18;
Eze 16:26;
Na 3:4; Rev 17:1;
18:3,9 ^kJer 25:26
23:18 ^lEx 28:36;
S 39:30;
Jos 6:17-19;
Ps 72:10
^mIsa 18:7;
60:5-9; 61:6;
Mic 4:13
ⁿAm 1:9-10;
Zec 14:1,14
24:1 ^over 20;
Isa 2:19-21; 33:9;
Jer 25:29
^pS Jos 6:17;
S Isa 13:5
^qS Ge 11:9
24:2 ^rHos 4:9
^sEze 7:12;
1Co 7:29-31
^tS Lev 25:35-37;
Dt 23:19-20;
Isa 3:1-7
24:3 ^uS Ge 6:13
^vIsa 6:11-12;
10:6 ^wS Isa 7:7
24:4 ^xJer 12:11;
14:4; Joel 1:10
^yS Isa 15:6
^zS Isa 2:12

^aS Isa 3:26
24:5 ^bS Ge 3:17
^cS Isa 1:2; 9:17;
10:6; 59:12;
Jer 7:28
^dS Ge 9:11;
S Jer 11:10
24:6 ^eS Jos 23:15
^fS Isa 1:31
24:7 ^gJer 48:33;
Joel 1:5 ^hIsa 7:23;
S 15:6; 32:10
ⁱS Isa 3:26;
16:8-10
24:8 ^jS Ge 31:27;
S Isa 5:12
^kJer 7:34; 16:9;
25:10; 33:11;
Hos 2:11
^lS Isa 5:14; S 21:5
^mS Ps 137:2;
Rev 18:22
ⁿLa 5:14;
Eze 26:13
24:9 ^oIsa 5:11,22
^pIsa 5:20
24:10 ^qIsa 25:2;
26:5 ^rS Ge 1:2;
S Isa 6:11

24:11 ^sS Ps 144:14 ^tLa 2:12 ^uS Isa 15:6; 16:10; 32:13;
Jer 14:3 24:12 ^vS Isa 19:18 ^wS Isa 3:26; S 13:2 24:13
^xS Dt 30:4; S Isa 17:6 ^yOb 1:5; Mic 7:1 24:14 ^zS Isa 12:6

Study notes (bottom)

23:15 *seventy years.* Also the length of the Babylonian captivity (see Jer 25:11; 29:10), and the length of time Sennacherib decreed that Babylon should remain devastated.
23:16 Cf. Pr 7:10-15.
23:17 *her hire as a prostitute.* A "prostitute" nation was one that sought to make the highest profits, regardless of the means. Self-gratification was the key (cf. Rev 17:5).
23:18 *set apart for the LORD.* The earnings of a prostitute could not be given to the Lord (Dt 23:18), but the silver and gold of a city "devoted to destruction" (see note on Dt 2:34) were placed in the Lord's treasury (see Jos 6:17,19; cf. Mic 4:13). *to those.* Israel will one day receive the wealth of the nations (see note on 18:7; cf. 60:5-11; 61:6).
24:1-27:13 Chs. 24-27 deal with judgment and blessing in the last days, the time of God's final victory over the forces of evil. These chapters form a conclusion to chs. 13-23 just as chs. 34-35 form a conclusion to chs. 28-33.
24:1 *lay waste the earth.* Cf. 2:10,19,21; see also 13:13 and note. *scatter its inhabitants.* See Ge 11:9.
24:2 Social distinctions will provide no escape from the judgment (cf. 3:1-3).
24:4 *dries up and withers.* Words applied to Moab in 15:6;

16:8. Cf. 34:4.
24:5 *broken the everlasting covenant.* Reference is probably to the covenant of Ge 9:8-17 (see Ge 9:11 and note). See also v. 18 and note. Although everlasting from the divine viewpoint, God's covenants can be broken by sinful mankind.
24:6 *curse.* Because of the intensification of evil in the world, God's devastating curse will burn up the earth's inhabitants (cf. Ge 8:21-22; cf. also the covenant of Ge 9:8-17).
24:7 *vine withers.* See v. 4 and note.
24:8 *gaiety . . . is stilled.* Cf. 22:2,13; 23:7.
24:9 *wine with a song.* Characteristic of Judah in 5:11-13 (see note there).
24:10 *ruined city.* The same idea appears in 25:2; 26:5; 27:10 (cf. 17:1; 19:18). It is probably a composite of all the cities opposed to God—such as Babylon, Tyre, Jerusalem and Rome.
24:13 Only a few olives and grapes will be left (see v. 6; 17:6,11).
24:14 *They.* The godly remnant that survives the judgment.

from the west[a] they acclaim the
Lord's majesty.
[15]Therefore in the east[b] give glory[c] to
the Lord;
exalt[d] the name[e] of the Lord, the
God of Israel,
in the islands[f] of the sea.
[16]From the ends of the earth[g] we hear
singing:[h]
"Glory[i] to the Righteous One."[j]

But I said, "I waste away, I waste
away![k]
Woe[l] to me!
The treacherous[m] betray!
With treachery the treacherous
betray![n]"
[17]Terror[o] and pit and snare[p] await you,
O people of the earth.[q]
[18]Whoever flees[r] at the sound of terror
will fall into a pit;[s]
whoever climbs out of the pit
will be caught in a snare.[t]

The floodgates of the heavens[u] are
opened,
the foundations of the earth shake.[v]
[19]The earth is broken up,[w]
the earth is split asunder,[x]
the earth is thoroughly shaken.
[20]The earth reels like a drunkard,[y]
it sways like a hut[z] in the wind;
so heavy upon it is the guilt of its
rebellion[a]
that it falls[b]—never to rise again.[c]

[21]In that day[d] the Lord will punish[e]
the powers[f] in the heavens above
and the kings[g] on the earth below.
[22]They will be herded together
like prisoners[h] bound in a dungeon;[i]
they will be shut up in prison
and be punished[f] after many days.[j]

[23]The moon will be abashed, the sun[k]
ashamed;
for the Lord Almighty will reign[l]
on Mount Zion[m] and in Jerusalem,
and before its elders, gloriously.[n]

Praise to the Lord

25 O Lord, you are my God;[o]
I will exalt you and praise your
name,[p]
for in perfect faithfulness[q]
you have done marvelous things,[r]
things planned[s] long ago.
[2]You have made the city a heap of
rubble,[t]
the fortified[u] town a ruin,[v]
the foreigners' stronghold[w] a city no
more;
it will never be rebuilt.[x]
[3]Therefore strong peoples will honor
you;[y]
cities of ruthless[z] nations will revere
you.
[4]You have been a refuge[a] for the poor,[b]
a refuge for the needy[c] in his
distress,
a shelter from the storm[d]
and a shade from the heat.
For the breath of the ruthless[e]
is like a storm driving against a wall
5   and like the heat of the desert.
You silence[f] the uproar of foreigners;[g]

24:14 [a]Isa 43:5; 49:12
24:15
[b]S Ps 113:3
[c]Isa 42:12; 66:19; 2Th 1:12
[d]S Ex 15:2; Isa 25:3; 59:19; Mal 1:11
[e]S Isa 12:4
[f]S Isa 11:11
24:16
[g]S Ps 48:10
[h]S Ps 65:8
[i]Isa 28:5; 60:1,19
[j]S Ezr 9:15
[k]S Lev 26:39
[l]Isa 4:8; S Isa 5:8; Jer 10:19; 45:3
[m]S Ps 25:3
[n]Isa 21:2; 33:1; Jer 3:6,20; 5:11; 9:2; Hos 5:7; 9:1
24:17
[o]Isa 8:14;
Jer 48:43
[q]Lk 21:35
24:18
[r]S Job 20:24
[s]Isa 42:22
[t]S Job 18:9;
S Isa 8:14;
La 3:47;
Eze 12:13
[u]S Ge 7:11
[v]S Jdg 5:4;
S Job 9:6;
S Ps 11:3;
S Eze 38:19
24:19 [w]S Ps 46:2
[x]S Dt 11:6
24:20
[y]S Job 12:25
[z]S Job 27:18
[a]S Isa 1:2,28;
43:27; 58:1
[b]S Ps 46:2
[c]S Job 12:14
24:21
[d]S Isa 2:11;
S 10:20;
Rev 16:14
[e]Isa 10:12;
13:11; Jer 25:29
[f]1Co 6:3;
Eph 6:11-12
[g]S Isa 2:12
24:22 [h]S Isa 10:4
[i]Isa 42:7,22;
Lk 8:31;
Rev 20:7-10
/Eze 38:8

24:23
[k]S Isa 13:10

[l]S Ps 97:1; Rev 22:5 [m]S Isa 2:2; Heb 12:22 [n]Isa 28:5; 41:16; 45:25; 60:19; Eze 48:35; Zec 2:5; Rev 21:23 25:1 [o]S Isa 7:13 [p]S Ps 145:2; S Isa 12:1,4 [q]Isa 11:5 [r]Ps 40:5; 98:1; Joel 2:21,26 [s]Nu 23:19; S Isa 14:24; 37:26; 46:11; Eph 1:11 25:2 [t]Isa 17:1; 26:5; 37:26 [u]S Isa 17:3 [v]S Dt 13:16 [w]S Isa 13:22 [x]S Job 12:14 25:3 [y]S Ex 6:2; S Ps 22:23; S Isa 11:14 [z]S Isa 13:11 25:4 [a]S 2Sa 22:3; S Ps 118:8; S Isa 4:6; 17:10; 27:5; 33:16; Joel 3:16 [b]S Isa 3:14 [c]S Isa 14:30; 29:19 [d]S Ps 55:8 [e]Isa 29:5; 49:25 25:5 [f]Jer 51:55 [g]S Ps 18:44

[f]22 Or *released*

24:15 *islands.* See note on 11:11.
24:16 *ends of the earth.* See note on 11:12. *I.* Probably collective for the godly community that wastes away because of the villainy of the treacherous nations that seek to crush the people of God. *I waste away . . . betray!* In the Hebrew text these last four lines of the verse *(Razi li, razi li! 'Oy li! Bogedim bagadu! Ubeged bogedim bagadu!)* contain a powerful example of alliteration and assonance. *Woe to me!* Isaiah had the same reaction in 6:5. *The treacherous.* The enemies of God's people.
24:17–18 Cf. Am 5:19.
24:17 *Terror and pit and snare.* Another example (see note on v. 16) of alliteration and assonance (see note on Jer 48:43). The Hebrew words are *pahad, pahat* and *pah.*
24:18 *floodgates of the heavens.* An echo of Noah's flood (Ge 7:11; 8:2). *foundations . . . shake.* Earthquakes and thunder (see note on 13:13; cf. Joel 3:16).
24:20 *like a drunkard.* Cf. 19:14. *like a hut.* See 1:8 and note.
24:21 *In that day.* The day of the Lord (see notes on

2:11,17,20; 10:20,27; cf. 25:9; 26:1; 27:1–2,12–13). *powers in the heavens.* Satan and the fallen angels (see Eph 6:11–12).
24:22 *shut up in prison.* Cf. Rev 20:2. *punished after many days.* See NIV text note; cf. Rev 20:7–10.
24:23 *moon . . . abashed, the sun ashamed.* The sun and moon do not shine during judgment (see note on 13:10) or when the Lord is the "everlasting light" (60:19–20; cf. Rev 21:23; 22:5). *reign on Mount Zion.* See 2:2–4 and note.
25:1–5 A song of praise celebrating the deliverance brought about by the judgments of ch. 24 (see 24:14–16; see also ch. 12).
25:1 *planned long ago.* See 14:24,26–27; 23:8–9.
25:2 *the city . . . a ruin.* See 24:10 and note. *never be rebuilt.* Cf. 24:20.
25:3 *strong peoples . . . ruthless nations.* Such as Egypt and Assyria (see 19:18–25 and notes). *honor you . . . revere you.* See 24:15.
25:4–5 *refuge . . . shelter . . . shade . . . cloud.* See 4:5–6 and note; cf. 32:2.

as heat is reduced by the shadow of a
      cloud,
so the song of the ruthless *h* is stilled.

⁶On this mountain *i* the LORD Almighty
      will prepare
   a feast *j* of rich food for all peoples,
a banquet of aged wine—
   the best of meats and the finest of
      wines. *k*
⁷On this mountain he will destroy
   the shroud *l* that enfolds all peoples, *m*
   the sheet that covers all nations;
⁸   he will swallow up death *n* forever.
The Sovereign LORD will wipe away the
      tears *o*
   from all faces;
he will remove the disgrace *p* of his
      people
   from all the earth.
                  The LORD has spoken. *q*

⁹In that day *r* they will say,

"Surely this is our God; *s*
   we trusted *t* in him, and he saved *u*
      us.
This is the LORD, we trusted in him;
   let us rejoice *v* and be glad in his
      salvation." *w*

¹⁰The hand of the LORD will rest on this
      mountain; *x*
   but Moab *y* will be trampled under
      him
   as straw is trampled down in the
      manure.
¹¹They will spread out their hands in it,
   as a swimmer spreads out his hands
      to swim.
God will bring down *z* their pride *a*
   despite the cleverness *g* of their
      hands.

¹²He will bring down your high fortified
      walls *b*
   and lay them low; *c*
he will bring them down to the ground,
   to the very dust.

A Song of Praise

26 In that day *d* this song will be
      sung *e* in the land of Judah:

We have a strong city; *f*
   God makes salvation
      its walls *g* and ramparts. *h*
²Open the gates *i*
   that the righteous *j* nation may enter,
      the nation that keeps faith.
³You will keep in perfect peace *k*
   him whose mind is steadfast,
      because he trusts *l* in you.
⁴Trust *m* in the LORD forever, *n*
   for the LORD, the LORD, is the Rock *o*
      eternal.
⁵He humbles those who dwell on high,
   he lays the lofty city low;
he levels it to the ground *p*
   and casts it down to the dust. *q*
⁶Feet trample *r* it down—
   the feet of the oppressed, *s*
   the footsteps of the poor. *t*

⁷The path of the righteous is level; *u*
   O upright One, *v* you make the way
      of the righteous smooth. *w*
⁸Yes, LORD, walking in the way of your
      laws, *h x*

Cross references

25:5 *h*S Isa 13:11
25:6 *i*S Isa 2:2 /S Ge 29:22; 1Ki 1:25; Isa 1:19; 55:1-2; 66:11; Joel 3:18; Mt 8:11; 22:4; Rev 19:9 *k*S Ps 36:8; S Pr 9:2
25:7 *l*2Co 3:15-16; Eph 4:18 *m*S Job 4:9
25:8 *n*Isa 26:19; Hos 13:14; 1Co 15:54-55* *o*Isa 15:3; 30:19; 35:10; 51:11; 65:19; Jer 31:16; Rev 7:17; 21:4 *p*S Ge 30:23; S Ps 119:39; Mt 5:11; 1Pe 4:14; Rev 7:14 *q*S Isa 7:7
25:9 *r*S Isa 2:11; S 10:20 *s*Isa 40:9 *t*S Ps 22:5; S Isa 12:2 *u*Ps 145:19; Isa 19:20; 33:22; 35:4; 43:3,11; 45:15,21; 49:25-26,26; 60:16; 63:8; Jer 14:8 *v*S Dt 32:43; S Ps 9:2; Isa 9:3; 35:2,10; 41:16; 51:3; 61:7,10; 66:14 *w*S Ps 13:5; S Isa 12:2
25:10 *x*S Isa 2:2 *y*S Ge 19:37; S Nu 21:29; S Dt 23:6; S Isa 11:14; Am 2:1-3
25:11 *z*Isa 5:25; 14:26; 16:14 *a*S Lev 26:19; S Job 40:12
25:12 *b*S Isa 2:15 *c*S Job 40:11; S Isa 15:1; S Jer 51:44
26:1 *d*S Isa 10:20 *e*Isa 30:29 /S Isa 14:32 *g*Isa 32:18; 60:18; Zec 2:5; 9:8 *h*S Ps 48:13
26:2 *i*S Ps 24:7 /Ps 24:3-4;
85:13; S Isa 1:26; S 4:3; 9:7; 50:8; 53:11; 54:14; 58:8; 62:2
26:3 *k*S Job 22:21; S Isa 9:6,7; Php 4:7 *l*S 1Ch 5:20; S Ps 22:5; S 28:7; S Isa 12:2 26:4 *m*S Isa 12:2; 50:10 *n*S Ps 62:8 *o*S Ge 49:24 26:5 *p*S Isa 25:12; Eze 26:11 *q*S Isa 25:2 26:6 *r*S Isa 5:5 *s*Isa 49:26 *t*S Isa 3:15; S 14:30 26:7 *u*S Ps 26:12 *v*S Ps 25:8 *w*S Ex 14:19; Isa 40:4; 42:16 26:8 *x*S Dt 18:18; Ps 1:2; Isa 56:1; 64:5

*g*11 The meaning of the Hebrew for this word is uncertain.   *h*8 Or *judgments*

Notes

25:6–8 The eschatological feast of God.
25:6–7,10 *this mountain.* Mount Zion. See 2:2–4 and note; cf. 24:23.
25:6 *feast . . . banquet.* Associated with a coronation (1Ki 1:25) or wedding (Jdg 14:10); cf. the "wedding supper of the Lamb" (Rev 19:9). *rich food.* Symbolic of great spiritual blessings (see 55:2). *aged wine.* The best wine—aged by being left on its dregs (see Jer 48:11; Zep 1:12).
25:7 *shroud . . . sheet.* Or "covering . . . veil," with which faces were covered in mourning—in any event, the associations are with death.
25:8 Quoted in part in 1Co 15:54. *swallow up death.* Death, the great swallower (see Ps 49:14 and note), will be swallowed up. *Sovereign LORD.* See 7:7; 28:16; 30:15; 40:10; 49:22; 52:4; 61:11; 65:13. *remove the disgrace.* See 54:4.
25:9 Another brief song of praise. *In that day.* See 12:1,4; 24:21; see also 10:20,27 and note. *we trusted . . . he saved.* Cf. Ps 22:4–5. *rejoice and be glad.* Cf. 35:10; 51:11; 66:10.

25:10–12 An elaboration on the theme of judgment.
25:10 *Moab.* Symbolic of all the enemies of God, like Edom in 34:5–17. See note on 15:1.
25:11 *pride.* See note on 16:6.
25:12 *high fortified walls.* See v. 2; 2:15; 2Ki 3:27; Jer 51:58.
26:1–15 Another song of praise for God's deliverance.
26:1 *In that day.* See 12:1,4; 24:21; 25:9; see also note on 10:20,27. *ramparts.* Sloping fortifications of earth or stone (cf. 2Sa 20:15).
26:3 See 30:15. *mind is steadfast.* Cf. Ps 112:6–8. *trusts.* Cf. 25:9.
26:4 *Rock.* See 17:10 and note.
26:5 *lofty city.* See note on 24:10. *levels it . . . to the dust.* Cf. 25:2,12.
26:6 *feet of the oppressed.* The oppressors are humiliated also in 49:24–26; 51:22–23 (contrast 3:14–15).
26:7 *path . . . level; . . . way . . . smooth.* A theme found also in 40:3–4; 42:16; 45:13.
26:8 A desire for God to reveal his power in their behalf

we wait[y] for you;
your name[z] and renown
  are the desire of our hearts.
[9]My soul yearns for you in the night;[a]
  in the morning my spirit longs[b] for
    you.
When your judgments[c] come upon the
    earth,
  the people of the world learn
    righteousness. [d]
[10]Though grace is shown to the wicked,[e]
  they do not learn righteousness;
even in a land of uprightness they go on
    doing evil[f]
  and regard[g] not the majesty of the
    LORD.
[11]O LORD, your hand is lifted high, [h]
  but they do not see[i] it.
Let them see your zeal[j] for your people
    and be put to shame;[k]
  let the fire[l] reserved for your
    enemies consume them.

[12]LORD, you establish peace[m] for us;
  all that we have accomplished you
    have done[n] for us.
[13]O LORD, our God, other lords[o] besides
    you have ruled over us,
  but your name[p] alone do we honor. [q]
[14]They are now dead,[r] they live no
    more;
  those departed spirits[s] do not rise.
You punished them and brought them
    to ruin;[t]
  you wiped out all memory of them. [u]
[15]You have enlarged the nation, O LORD;
  you have enlarged the nation. [v]
You have gained glory for yourself;
  you have extended all the borders[w]
    of the land.

[16]LORD, they came to you in their
    distress;[x]
  when you disciplined[y] them,
    they could barely whisper[z] a
      prayer.[i]
[17]As a woman with child and about to
    give birth[a]
  writhes and cries out in her pain,
  so were we in your presence,
    O LORD.
[18]We were with child, we writhed in
    pain,
  but we gave birth[b] to wind.
We have not brought salvation[c] to the
    earth;
  we have not given birth to people of
    the world. [d]

[19]But your dead[e] will live;
  their bodies will rise.
You who dwell in the dust,[f]
  wake up and shout for joy.
Your dew[g] is like the dew of the
    morning;
  the earth will give birth to her dead.[h]

[20]Go, my people, enter your rooms
    and shut the doors[i] behind you;
  hide[j] yourselves for a little while
    until his wrath[k] has passed by. [l]
[21]See, the LORD is coming[m] out of his
    dwelling[n]
  to punish[o] the people of the earth for
    their sins.
The earth will disclose the blood[p] shed
    upon her;
  she will conceal her slain no longer.

26:8 [y]S Ps 37:9;
S 130:5
[z]S Ps 145:2;
S Isa 12:4
26:9
[a]S Ps 119:55
[b]Ps 42:1-3; 63:1;
78:34; Isa 55:6
[c]S 1Ch 16:14
[d]Mt 6:33
26:10 [e]Mt 5:45
[f]Isa 32:6; 59:7,13
[g]S 1Sa 12:24;
Isa 22:12-13;
Jer 2:19;
Hos 11:7;
Jn 5:37-38;
Ro 2:4
26:11
[h]S Ps 10:12
[i]Isa 18:3; 44:9,18
[j]S Isa 9:7;
Joel 2:18;
Zec 1:14
[k]Mic 7:16
[l]S Isa 1:31;
Heb 10:27
26:12
[m]S Ps 119:165;
S Isa 9:6
[n]S Ps 68:28
26:13 [o]Isa 2:8;
10:5,11
[p]S Isa 12:4
[q]Isa 42:8; 63:7
26:14 [r]S Dt 4:28
[s]S Job 26:5
[t]S Ps 9:5;
S Isa 10:3
[u]S Ps 9:6
26:15
[v]S Job 12:23;
S Isa 14:2
[w]Isa 33:17

26:16 [x]S Jdg 6:2;
S Isa 5:30
[y]S Ps 39:11
[z]Isa 29:4
26:17
[a]S Isa 21:3;
S Jn 16:21;
Rev 12:2
26:18 [b]Isa 33:11;
59:4 [c]S Ge 49:10;
Ps 17:14
[d]Isa 42:6; 49:6;
51:4; Jer 12:16
26:19
[e]S Isa 25:8;
Eph 5:14
[f]Ps 22:29
[g]S Ge 27:28;
S Isa 18:4
[h]Isa 66:24;

Eze 37:1-14; Da 12:2 26:20 [i]Ex 12:23 [j]Ps 91:1,4
[k]S Isa 10:25; S 30:27 [l]S Job 14:13 26:21 [m]Isa 29:6;
Jude 1:14 [n]S Isa 18:4 [o]S Isa 13:9,11; 30:12-14 [p]S Job 16:18;
Lk 11:50-51

[i]16 The meaning of the Hebrew for this clause is
uncertain.

(see Hos 12:5–6). *name and renown.* See v. 13; 24:15;
25:1.
26:9 *judgments.* Punishment (cf. 4:4).
26:10 *grace.* Perhaps the blessings of harvest and general
prosperity (cf. Mt. 5:45).
26:11 *hand is lifted high.* A sign of power. See 9:12,17,21
and note; Ps 89:13. *zeal.* See 9:7 and note; cf. 37:32;
63:15. *fire.* See note on 1:31.
26:12 *peace.* See v. 3.
26:13 *other lords.* Foreign rulers, such as those of Egypt or
Assyria.
26:14 *dead . . . departed spirits.* Cf. the fate of the king of
Babylon in 14:9–10.
26:15 *enlarged the nation.* Applied to the return from
Babylonian exile in 54:2–3; also cf. 9:3.
26:16–18 The prophet speaks to the Lord on behalf of
God's people.
26:16 *distress.* Perhaps the Assyrian oppression, described
in 5:30; 8:21–22. The period of the judges is also possible
(see Jdg 6:2,6).
26:17–18 *give birth writhes . . . in pain.* See 13:8 and note

(cf. 37:3).
26:18 *salvation to the earth.* Israel was designed to be "a
light for the Gentiles" (see 42:6; 49:6 and notes; see also
9:2 and note).
26:19–21 The prophet speaks a word of reassurance to
God's people.
26:19 *dead will live . . . bodies will rise.* A reference to the
restoration of Israel (see Eze 37:11–12)—perhaps including
the resurrection of the body (Da 12:2). Cf. 25:8; contrast
26:14. *dew.* A symbol of fruitfulness (see 2Sa 1:21; Hos
14:5).
26:20–21 See 24:21–22 and note on 2:11,17,20.
26:20 *a little while . . . wrath.* Cf. 10:25; 54:7–8. Assyrian
tyranny and Babylonian exile, as well as all other oppressions, will end.
26:21 *punish.* See 66:14–16. *will disclose . . . will conceal . . . no longer.* The blood and bodies of the inno-
cent/righteous who have been slaughtered by the oppressive
powers will no longer be hidden in the ground, but will be
brought forth to testify against their murderers, so that God
may in judgment avenge their deaths (see Ge 4:10).

Deliverance of Israel

27 In that day,[q]

the LORD will punish with his
sword,[r]
his fierce, great and powerful sword,
Leviathan[s] the gliding serpent,[t]
Leviathan the coiling serpent;
he will slay the monster[u] of the sea.

[2]In that day[v] —

"Sing[w] about a fruitful vineyard:[x]
[3] I, the LORD, watch over it;
I water[y] it continually.
I guard[z] it day and night
so that no one may harm[a] it.
[4] I am not angry.
If only there were briers and thorns
confronting me!
I would march against them in battle;
I would set them all on fire.[b]
[5]Or else let them come to me for
refuge;[c]
let them make peace[d] with me,
yes, let them make peace with me."

[6]In days to come Jacob will take root,[e]
Israel will bud and blossom[f]
and fill all the world with fruit.[g]

[7]Has the LORD struck her
as he struck[h] down those who struck
her?
Has she been killed
as those were killed who killed her?
[8]By warfare[i] and exile[i] you contend
with her—
with his fierce blast he drives her out,
as on a day the east wind[j] blows.
[9]By this, then, will Jacob's guilt be
atoned[k] for,
and this will be the full fruitage of the
removal of his sin: [l]

When he makes all the altar stones[m]
to be like chalk stones crushed to
pieces,
no Asherah poles[k][n] or incense altars[o]
will be left standing.
[10]The fortified city stands desolate,[p]
an abandoned settlement, forsaken[q]
like the desert;
there the calves graze,[r]
there they lie down;[s]
they strip its branches bare.
[11]When its twigs are dry, they are broken
off[t]
and women come and make fires[u]
with them.
For this is a people without
understanding;[v]
so their Maker has no compassion on
them,
and their Creator[w] shows them no
favor.[x]

[12]In that day the LORD will thresh[y] from
the flowing Euphrates[1] to the Wadi of
Egypt,[z] and you, O Israelites, will be gathered[a] up one by one. [13]And in that day[b] a
great trumpet[c] will sound. Those who
were perishing in Assyria and those who
were exiled[d] in Egypt[e] will come and
worship[f] the LORD on the holy mountain[g]
in Jerusalem.

Woe to Ephraim

28 Woe[h] to that wreath, the pride of
Ephraim's[i] drunkards,

Cross references (center column)

27:1 [q]ver 13;
S Isa 2:11; 28:5
[r]S Ge 3:24;
S Dt 32:41;
Isa 31:8; 34:6;
65:12; 66:16;
Eze 21:3; Na 3:15
[s]S Job 3:8
[t]Job 26:13
[u]S Ps 68:30;
S 74:13; Rev 12:9
27:2 [v]Isa 24:21
[w]S Isa 5:1
[x]Jer 2:21
27:3 [y]Isa 58:11
[z]S Ps 91:4;
S Isa 5:2
[a]S Jn 6:39
27:4 [b]S ver 11;
S Isa 10:17;
Mt 3:12; Heb 6:8
27:5 [c]S Isa 25:4
[d]S Job 22:21;
S Ps 119:165;
Ro 5:1; 2Co 5:20
27:6
[e]S 2Ki 19:30;
Isa 11:10
[f]S Ge 40:10
[g]S Ps 72:16;
Isa 11:1; 37:31;
Eze 17:23; 36:8;
Hos 14:8
27:7 [h]Isa 10:26;
S 11:4; 37:36-38
27:8 [i]Isa 49:14;
50:1; 54:7
[j]S Ge 41:6
27:9 [k]S Ps 78:38
[l]Ro 11:27*

[m]S Ex 23:24
[n]S Ex 34:13
[o]S Lev 26:30;
S 2Ch 14:5
27:10 [p]S Ge 1:2;
S Dt 13:16;
Isa 5:6; 32:14;
Jer 10:22; 26:6;
La 1:4; 5:18
[q]S Isa 5:5
[r]S Isa 5:17
[s]Isa 17:2
27:11
[t]S Isa 10:33
[u]S ver 4;
Isa 33:12
[v]S Dt 32:28;
S Isa 1:3
[w]S Dt 32:18;
Isa 41:8; 43:1,7,
15; 44:1-2,21,24
[x]S Isa 9:17;
Jer 11:16
27:12
[y]S Isa 21:10;
Mt 3:12

[z]S Ge 15:18 [a]S Dt 30:4; S Isa 1:9; S 11:12; S 17:6 27:13
[b]S ver 1 [c]S Lev 25:9; S Jdg 3:27; S Mt 24:31 [d]S Ps 106:47
[e]S Isa 10:19; 19:21,25 [f]S Ge 27:29; S Ps 22:29; S 86:9
[g]S Isa 2:2 28:1 [h]Isa 10:5; 29:1; 30:1; 31:1; 33:1 [i]ver 3;
Isa 7:2; 9:9

[1]8 See Septuagint; the meaning of the Hebrew for this
word is uncertain.   [k]9 That is, symbols of the goddess
Asherah   [1]12 Hebrew River

Study notes (bottom)

27:1–2,12–13 *In that day.* See 10:20,27 and note; see
also 12:1,4; 24:21; 25:9; 26:1.
27:1 The climactic word of judgment. *Leviathan . . . monster.* A symbol (drawn from Canaanite myths) of wicked
nations, such as Egypt (see 30:7 and note; 51:9; Eze 29:3;
32:2). *gliding . . . coiling serpent.* Cf. Job 3:8; 41:1; Ps
74:14. Such descriptions of Leviathan occur outside the
Bible as well.
27:2–6 A second vineyard song (see 5:1–7 and notes).
27:2 *vineyard.* Israel.
27:4–5 A picture of Israel's lukewarmness toward the
Lord—not "briers and thorns" (v. 4) like the other nations,
but not fully trusting in the Lord either (see 29:13).
27:4 *briers and thorns.* See 5:6 and note.
27:6 *take root.* See 11:1,10 and notes. *bud and blossom.*
See 4:2 and note. *fill all the world.* The Messianic age is in view. *fill all the
world.* Contrast 26:18.
27:7–11 What the Lord is going to do with Israel in the
judgments that are about to overtake her in Isaiah's day.
27:7 *struck her.* Cf. 10:24–26.

27:8 *exile.* Probably the Babylonian captivity. *east wind.* A
hot wind from the desert (see Jer 4:11; Eze 19:12).
27:9 *atoned for.* Israel (Jacob) will have to atone for her
guilt through the coming judgment. *altar . . . Asherah poles
. . . incense altars.* See 17:8 and note. *crushed to pieces.* See
Ex 34:13.
27:10 *fortified city.* Jerusalem. *desolate . . . forsaken.* Cf.
6:11–12. *calves graze.* Cf. 5:5; 7:25.
27:12–13 The redemption that lies beyond the coming
judgment.
27:12 *will thresh.* Judgment on the nations into which
Israel has been dispersed (see note on 21:10). The threshing
will separate Israelites from Gentiles. *Wadi of Egypt.* Probably the Wadi el-Arish, the southern border of the promised
land (the Euphrates is the northern border). See Ge 15:18
and note; 1Ki 4:21; 8:65.
27:13 *great trumpet.* Used especially to summon troops
(see 1Sa 13:3). *Assyria . . . Egypt.* See 11:11–12 and notes.
holy mountain. Mount Zion (see 2:2–4 and note; see also
24:23; 25:6–7,10 and note).

to the fading flower, his glorious
beauty,
set on the head of a fertile valley[j] —
to that city, the pride of those laid
low by wine![k]
²See, the LORD has one who is powerful[l]
and strong.
Like a hailstorm[m] and a destructive
wind,[n]
like a driving rain and a flooding[o]
downpour,
he will throw it forcefully to the
ground.
³That wreath, the pride of Ephraim's[p]
drunkards,
will be trampled[q] underfoot.
⁴That fading flower, his glorious beauty,
set on the head of a fertile valley,[r]
will be like a fig[s] ripe before harvest—
as soon as someone sees it and takes
it in his hand,
he swallows it.

⁵In that day[t] the LORD Almighty
will be a glorious[u] crown,[v]
a beautiful wreath
for the remnant[w] of his people.
⁶He will be a spirit of justice[x]
to him who sits in judgment,[y]
a source of strength
to those who turn back the battle[z] at
the gate.

⁷And these also stagger[a] from wine[b]
and reel[c] from beer:
Priests[d] and prophets[e] stagger from
beer
and are befuddled with wine;
they reel from beer,
they stagger when seeing visions,[f]
they stumble when rendering
decisions.

⁸All the tables are covered with vomit[g]
and there is not a spot without filth.

⁹"Who is it he is trying to teach?[h]
To whom is he explaining his
message?[i]
To children weaned[j] from their milk,[k]
to those just taken from the breast?
¹⁰For it is:
Do and do, do and do,
rule on rule, rule on rule[m];
a little here, a little there.[l] "

¹¹Very well then, with foreign lips and
strange tongues[m]
God will speak to this people,[n]
¹²to whom he said,
"This is the resting place, let the
weary rest";[o]
and, "This is the place of repose"—
but they would not listen.

¹³So then, the word of the LORD to them
will become:
Do and do, do and do,
rule on rule, rule on rule;
a little here, a little there[p]—
so that they will go and fall backward,
be injured[q] and snared and
captured.[r]

¹⁴Therefore hear the word of the LORD,[s]
you scoffers[t]
who rule this people in Jerusalem.
¹⁵You boast, "We have entered into a
covenant with death,[u]
with the grave[n] we have made an
agreement.

Cross references

28:1 /ver 4
[k]S Lev 10:9;
Isa 5:11; Hos 7:5;
Am 6:6
28:2 /Isa 40:10
[m]S Jos 10:11
[n]Isa 29:6
[o]S Isa 8:7;
S Da 9:26
28:3 [p]S ver 1
[q]S Job 40:12;
S Isa 5:5
28:4 [r]ver 1
[s]S SS 2:13;
Hos 9:10;
Na 3:12
28:5 [t]S Isa 10:20;
S 27:1; 29:18;
30:23
[u]S Isa 24:16,23
[v]Isa 62:3;
Jer 13:18;
Eze 16:12; 21:26;
Zec 9:16
[w]S Isa 1:9
28:6
[x]S 2Sa 14:20;
Isa 11:2-4; 32:1,
16; 33:5 [y]Isa 4:4;
Jn 5:30
[z]Jdg 9:44-45;
S 2Ch 32:8
28:7 [a]S Isa 3:12
[b]S Lev 10:9;
S Isa 22:13;
S Eph 5:18
[c]S Ps 107:27
[d]Isa 24:2
[e]S Isa 9:15
[f]S Isa 1:1; 29:11

28:8 [g]Jer 48:26
28:9 [h]ver 26;
Ps 32:8; Isa 2:3;
30:20; 48:17;
50:4; 54:13;
Jer 31:34; 32:33
[i]Isa 52:7; 53:1
[j]Ps 131:2
[k]Heb 5:12-13;
1Pe 2:2
28:10 [l]ver 13
28:11
[m]S Ge 11:7;
Isa 33:19;
Jer 5:15 [n]Eze 3:5;
1Co 14:21*
28:12
[o]S Ex 14:14;
S Jos 1:13;
S Job 11:18;
S Isa 11:10;
Mt 11:28-29
28:13 [p]ver 10
[q]Mt 21:44

[r]S Isa 8:15 28:14 [s]Isa 1:10 [t]2Ch 36:16 28:15 [u]S Job 5:23;
Isa 8:19

[m]10 Hebrew / sav lasav sav lasav / kav lakav kav lakav
(possibly meaningless sounds); perhaps a mimicking of the
prophet's words); also in verse 13   [n]15 Hebrew Sheol;
also in verse 18

Study notes

28:1—35:10 A series of six woes (28:1; 29:1; 29:15;
30:1; 31:1; 33:1), concluded with an announcement of
judgment on the nations (ch. 34) and a song celebrating the
joy of the redeemed (ch. 35). Cf. the six woes in ch. 5 (see
note on 5:8–23).
28:1 *wreath.* Samaria, the capital of the northern kingdom,
was a beautiful city on a prominent hill. *pride.* See v. 3 and
note on 16:6. *Ephraim's.* See note on 7:2. *drunkards.* In the
eighth century B.C. Samaria was a city of luxury and indulgence. See 5:11–13 and note; Am 6:4–7. *fertile valley.* Cf.
5:1.
28:2 *one who is powerful.* The king of Assyria. *hailstorm*
... *flooding downpour.* See v. 17; 8:7–8 and note; 17:12
and note. Cf. 30:30; 32:19.
28:5 *In that day.* See 4:1–2; 10:20,27 and note; 12:1,4;
24:21; 25:9; 26:1; 27:1–2,12–13. *glorious ... beautiful.*
See 4:2. *remnant.* See note on 1:9.
28:6 *spirit of justice.* See 11:2–4 and notes. *gate.* The most
vulnerable part of a city.
28:7 *wine ... beer.* The religious leaders should have been
filled with the Spirit, not with wine. See Lev 10:9; Nu

11:29; Eph 5:18.
28:8 *vomit.* Cf. Jer 25:16,27.
28:9–10 The mocking response of Isaiah's hearers (see
NIV text note on v. 10). Cf. the mocking tones of 5:19.
28:11–12 Quoted in part in 1Co 14:21.
28:11 *foreign lips.* The language of the Assyrians.
28:12 *resting place.* The land given to them by the Lord, in
whom they were to trust (see 26:3; 30:15; 40:31; Jos 1:13).
would not listen. Cf. Jer 6:16.
28:13 *will become.* They say the prophet is speaking nonsense, so the word of the Lord that he speaks will remain
nonsense to them (see 6:9–10 and notes).
28:15,18 *covenant with death.* Possibly an allusion to
necromancy and worship of idols (see 8:19). By using a vivid
figure of speech, Isaiah mocks their sense of assurance
against national calamity, placing on their lips a claim to have
a covenant with death that it will not harm them (see Hos
2:18). *overwhelming scourge.* A mixed metaphor referring
to the armies of Assyria and Babylonia. "Overwhelming"
pictures an army as a flooding river (see 8:7); a "scourge" is
a whip (10:26).

When an overwhelming scourge sweeps
by,[v]
it cannot touch us,
for we have made a lie[w] our refuge
and falsehood[o] our hiding place.[x]"

[16]So this is what the Sovereign LORD
says:

"See, I lay a stone in Zion,[y]
a tested stone,[z]
a precious cornerstone for a sure
foundation;[a]
the one who trusts will never be
dismayed.[b]
[17]I will make justice[c] the measuring line
and righteousness the plumb line;[d]
hail[e] will sweep away your refuge, the
lie,
and water will overflow[f] your hiding
place.
[18]Your covenant with death will be
annulled;
your agreement with the grave will
not stand.[g]
When the overwhelming scourge
sweeps by,[h]
you will be beaten down[i] by it.
[19]As often as it comes it will carry you
away;[j]
morning after morning,[k] by day and
by night,
it will sweep through."

The understanding of this message
will bring sheer terror.[l]
[20]The bed is too short to stretch out on,
the blanket too narrow to wrap
around you.[m]
[21]The LORD will rise up as he did at
Mount Perazim,[n]
he will rouse himself as in the Valley
of Gibeon[o] —
to do his work,[p] his strange work,
and perform his task, his alien task.
[22]Now stop your mocking,[q]
or your chains will become heavier;

the Lord, the LORD Almighty, has told
me
of the destruction decreed[r] against
the whole land.[s]

[23]Listen[t] and hear my voice;
pay attention and hear what I say.
[24]When a farmer plows for planting,[u]
does he plow continually?
Does he keep on breaking up and
harrowing the soil?
[25]When he has leveled the surface,
does he not sow caraway and scatter
cummin?[v]
Does he not plant wheat in its place,[p]
barley[w] in its plot,[p]
and spelt[x] in its field?
[26]His God instructs him
and teaches[y] him the right way.

[27]Caraway is not threshed[z] with a
sledge,[a]
nor is a cartwheel rolled over
cummin;
caraway is beaten out with a rod,[b]
and cummin with a stick.
[28]Grain must be ground to make bread;
so one does not go on threshing it
forever.
Though he drives the wheels of his
threshing cart[c] over it,
his horses do not grind it.
[29]All this also comes from the LORD
Almighty,
wonderful in counsel[d] and
magnificent in wisdom.[e]

Woe to David's City

29 Woe[f] to you, Ariel, Ariel,[g]
the city[h] where David settled!
Add year to year
and let your cycle of festivals[i] go on.
[2]Yet I will besiege Ariel;[j]
she will mourn and lament,[k]

Cross references (center column)

28:15 [v]ver 2,18;
Isa 8:7-8; 10:26;
29:6; 30:28;
Da 11:22
[w]S Isa 9:15
[x]S Jdg 9:35;
Isa 29:15;
Jer 23:24
28:16
[y]S Isa 14:32
[z]Ps 118:22;
Isa 8:14-15;
Da 2:34-35,45;
Zec 12:3;
[a]S Ac 4:11
[a]Jer 51:26;
1Co 3:11;
2Ti 2:19
[b]Isa 29:22;
45:17; 50:7;
54:4; Ro 9:33*;
10:11*; 1Pe 2:6*
28:17 [c]S Ps 11:7;
S Isa 5:16
[d]S 2Ki 21:13
[e]S Jos 10:11
[f]S Isa 8:7
28:18 [g]S Isa 7:7
[h]S ver 15
[i]S Isa 5:5; 63:18;
Da 8:13
28:19 [j]2Ki 24:2
[k]S Ps 5:3
[l]S Job 18:11
28:20 [m]Isa 59:6
28:21
[n]S Ge 38:29;
S 1Ch 14:11
[o]S Jos 9:3
[p]Isa 10:12; 65:7;
Lk 19:41-44
28:22
[q]S 2Ch 36:16;
Jer 29:18;
La 2:15; Zep 2:15

[r]S Isa 10:22
[s]S Isa 10:23
28:23 [t]Isa 32:9
28:24 [u]Ecc 3:2
28:25 [v]Mt 23:23
[w]S Ex 9:31
[x]Ex 9:32; Eze 4:9
28:26
[y]S Ps 94:10
28:27
[z]S Isa 21:10
[a]S Isa 41:30
[b]Isa 10:5
28:28
[c]S Isa 21:10
28:29 [d]S Isa 9:6
[e]S Ps 92:5;
Ro 11:33
29:1
[f]Isa 22:12-13;
S 28:1 [g]ver 2,7
[h]S 2Sa 5:7
[i]S Isa 1:14
29:2 [j]S ver 1
[k]S Isa 3:26;
La 2:5

[o]15 Or *false gods*   [p]25 The meaning of the Hebrew
for this word is uncertain.

28:16 *stone.* The Lord (see 8:14; 17:10 and notes). *cornerstone.* Cf. the "capstone" of Ps 118:22. *sure foundation.* See 1Co 3:11; cf. 1Pe 2:4-7.
28:17 *measuring line ... plumb line.* The standards and tests the Lord will apply are his justice and righteousness. *hail.* See v. 2; 30:30; 32:19.
28:20 *too short ... too narrow.* Israel was unprepared both militarily and spiritually.
28:21 *Mount Perazim.* Where God "broke out" against the Philistines (2Sa 5:20). *Valley of Gibeon.* Where God sent hail to demolish the Amorites (Jos 10:10-12). *strange work ... alien task.* This time God would fight against Israel.
28:22 *destruction decreed.* See 10:22-23 and note on 10:22.
28:23-29 A wisdom poem (a poetic parable) in two stan-

zas, each ending in a verse that praises the wisdom of God. In the context, and since "threshing" is emphasized (vv. 27-28), the point may be that though God must punish Israel, his actions will be as measured and as well-timed as a farmer's. See 27:12 and note.
28:25 *cummin.* An herb for seasoning. *spelt.* A kind of wheat (see note on Ex 9:32).
28:27 *rod.* See 10:5 and note.
28:29 *wonderful in counsel.* See 9:6 and note.
29:1,2,7 *Ariel.* Jerusalem. Fighting and bloodshed will turn Jerusalem into a virtual "altar hearth" (Hebrew *'ari'el*; see NIV text note on v. 2). Similar Hebrew words for the same term are used in Eze 43:15-16.
29:1 *Woe.* See note on 28:1. *city where David settled.* See 2Sa 5:6-9. *cycle of festivals.* See 1:13-14 and note on 1:14.

she will be to me like an altar
hearth.[q] [l]
3 I will encamp against you all around;
I will encircle[m] you with towers
and set up my siege works[n] against
you.
4 Brought low, you will speak from the
ground;
your speech will mumble[o] out of the
dust.[p]
Your voice will come ghostlike[q] from
the earth;
out of the dust your speech will
whisper.[r]
5 But your many enemies will become
like fine dust,[s]
the ruthless[t] hordes like blown
chaff.[u]
Suddenly,[v] in an instant,
6 the LORD Almighty will come[w]
with thunder[x] and earthquake[y] and
great noise,
with windstorm and tempest[z] and
flames of a devouring fire.[a]
7 Then the hordes of all the nations[b] that
fight against Ariel,[c]
that attack her and her fortress and
besiege her,
will be as it is with a dream,[d]
with a vision in the night—
8 as when a hungry man dreams that he
is eating,
but he awakens,[e] and his hunger
remains;
as when a thirsty man dreams that he is
drinking,
but he awakens faint, with his thirst
unquenched.[f]
So will it be with the hordes of all the
nations
that fight against Mount Zion.[g]
9 Be stunned and amazed,[h]
blind yourselves and be sightless;[i]
be drunk,[j] but not from wine,[k]

29:2 [l]Eze 43:15 **29:3** [m]Lk 19:43-44 [n]S 2Ki 25:1 **29:4** [o]Isa 8:19 [p]Isa 47:1; 52:2 [q]S Lev 19:31 [r]Isa 26:16 **29:5** [s]S Dt 9:21; Ps 78:39; 103:15; S Isa 2:22; 37:27; 40:6; 51:12 [t]S Isa 13:11 [u]S Isa 17:13 [v]S Ps 55:15; S Isa 17:14; 1Th 5:3 **29:6** [w]S Isa 26:21; Zec 14:1-5 [x]S Ex 19:16 [y]Mt 24:7; Mk 13:8; Lk 21:11; S Rev 6:12; 11:19 [z]S Ps 50:3; S 55:8; S Isa 28:15 [a]S Lev 10:2; Ps 83:13-15 **29:7** [b]Mic 4:11-12; Zec 12:9 [c]S ver 1 [d]S Job 20:8 **29:8** [e]S Ps 73:20 [f]ver 5,7; Isa 41:11,15; Jer 30:16; Zec 12:3 [g]Isa 17:12-14; 54:17 **29:9** [h]ver 14; Jer 4:9; Hab 1:5 [i]S Isa 6:10 [j]Isa 51:17; 63:6; Jer 13:13; 25:27 [k]S Lev 10:9; Isa 28:1; 51:21-22 [l]S Ps 60:3; S Isa 3:12 **29:10** [m]S Jdg 4:21; Jnh 1:5 [n]Ps 69:23; S Isa 6:9-10; 44:18; Ro 11:8*; 2Th 2:9-11 [o]Mic 3:6 [p]S 1Sa 9:9 **29:11** [q]S Isa 28:7 [r]S Isa 8:16; Da 8:26; 12:9; Mt 13:11; Rev 5:1-2 **29:13** [s]Jer 14:11; Hag 1:2; 2:14 [t]S Ps 50:16 [u]S Ps 119:70; Isa 58:2; Jer 12:2; Eze 33:31 [v]Mt 15:8-9*; Mk 7:6-7*; Col 2:22 **29:14** [w]S Job 10:16 [x]S Job 5:13; Jer 8:9; 49:7 [y]Isa 6:9-10; 1Co 1:19* **29:15** [z]S Ge 3:8; S Isa 28:15 [a]S Job 8:3; Ps 10:11-13; 94:7; Isa 47:10; 57:12; Eze 8:12; 9:9 [b]S 2Ki 21:16; S Job 22:13

stagger,[l] but not from beer.
10 The LORD has brought over you a deep
sleep:[m]
He has sealed your eyes[n] (the
prophets);[o]
he has covered your heads (the
seers).[p]

11 For you this whole vision[q] is nothing
but words sealed[r] in a scroll. And if you
give the scroll to someone who can read,
and say to him, "Read this, please," he will
answer, "I can't; it is sealed." 12 Or if you
give the scroll to someone who cannot
read, and say, "Read this, please," he will
answer, "I don't know how to read."

13 The Lord says:
"These people[s] come near to me with
their mouth
and honor me with their lips,[t]
but their hearts are far from me.[u]
Their worship of me
is made up only of rules taught by
men.[r] [v]
14 Therefore once more I will astound
these people
with wonder upon wonder;[w]
the wisdom of the wise[x] will perish,
the intelligence of the intelligent will
vanish.[y]"
15 Woe to those who go to great depths
to hide[z] their plans from the LORD,
who do their work in darkness and
think,
"Who sees us?[a] Who will know?"[b]
16 You turn things upside down,

[q]2 The Hebrew for *altar hearth* sounds like the Hebrew for *Ariel.* [r]13 Hebrew; Septuagint *They worship me in vain; / their teachings are but rules taught by men*

29:3 *towers.* Pushed up to the city wall by attackers so they could fight the defenders on the same level.
29:4 *whisper.* Used of mediums and spiritists in 8:19. Judah speaks as from the realm of the dead—so much for their covenant with death (see 28:15,18).
29:5–8 In God's time, those nations that devastate Jerusalem will be devastated (see 10:5–19; 27:1). The sudden destruction of the enemy resembles that of Assyria's army in 701 B.C. (see 10:16 and note).
29:5 *chaff.* See 17:13; Ps 1:4 and notes.
29:6 *thunder and earthquake . . . windstorm and tempest.* As in Jdg 5:4–5; Ps 18:7–15; Hab 3:3–7; see also 28:2; Ps 83:13–15 and notes.
29:9–14 Isaiah speaks again of Israel's spiritual state and warns of the Lord's impending judgment.
29:9 *blind yourselves . . . be drunk.* Refers to spiritual stupor (see 6:10 and note; cf. 28:1,7).
29:10 Quoted in part in Ro 11:8. *seers.* See 1Sa 9:9 and note; 2Ki 17:13.
29:11 *vision.* See 1:1 and note. *I can't.* God's word is a closed book even to the educated.
29:13 Quoted in part by Jesus to show the hypocrisy of the Pharisees (Mt 15:8–9). *These people.* Not "my people" (cf. 8:6,11–12; Jer 14:10–11; Hag 1:2).
29:14 Quoted in part in 1Co 1:19. *wonder upon wonder.* He who showed them wonders in the exodus (see Ex 15:11; Ps 78:12) will now show them wonders in judgment. *wisdom . . . will perish.* Cf. 44:25; Jer 8:9.
29:15 *Woe.* A new woe begins (see note on 28:1–35:10). *their plans.* Perhaps the alliance between Ahaz and Assyria or between Hezekiah and Egypt (see 30:1–2). *Who sees us?* See note on Ps 10:11.
29:16 Quoted in part in Ro 9:20. Cf. the creation of Adam in Ge 2:7; also cf. Isa 10:15.

as if the potter were thought to be
    like the clay! *c*
Shall what is formed say to him who
    formed *d* it,
    "He did not make me"?
Can the pot say of the potter, *e*
    "He knows nothing"? *f*

¹⁷In a very short time, *g* will not
    Lebanon *h* be turned into a
    fertile field *i*
    and the fertile field seem like a
    forest? *j*
¹⁸In that day *k* the deaf *l* will hear the
    words of the scroll,
    and out of gloom and darkness *m*
    the eyes of the blind will see. *n*
¹⁹Once more the humble *o* will rejoice in
    the LORD;
    the needy *p* will rejoice in the Holy
    One *q* of Israel.
²⁰The ruthless *r* will vanish, *s*
    the mockers *t* will disappear,
    and all who have an eye for evil *u*
    will be cut down—
²¹those who with a word make a man out
    to be guilty,
    who ensnare the defender in court *v*
    and with false testimony *w* deprive the
    innocent of justice. *x*

²²Therefore this is what the LORD, who
redeemed *y* Abraham, *z* says to the house
of Jacob:

    "No longer will Jacob be ashamed; *a*
    no longer will their faces grow pale. *b*
²³When they see among them their
    children, *c*
    the work of my hands, *d*
    they will keep my name holy; *e*

they will acknowledge the holiness of
    the Holy One *f* of Jacob,
    and will stand in awe of the God of
    Israel.
²⁴Those who are wayward *g* in spirit will
    gain understanding; *h*
    those who complain will accept
    instruction." *i*

Woe to the Obstinate Nation

30 "Woe *j* to the obstinate
    children," *k*
    declares the LORD,
"to those who carry out plans that are
    not mine,
    forming an alliance, *l* but not by my
    Spirit,
    heaping sin upon sin;
²who go down to Egypt *m*
    without consulting *n* me;
    who look for help to Pharaoh's
    protection, *o*
    to Egypt's shade for refuge. *p*
³But Pharaoh's protection will be to your
    shame,
    Egypt's shade *q* will bring you
    disgrace. *r*
⁴Though they have officials in Zoan *s*
    and their envoys have arrived in
    Hanes,
⁵everyone will be put to shame
    because of a people *t* useless *u* to
    them,
    who bring neither help *v* nor advantage,

29:16
c S Job 10:9;
S Isa 10:15
d S Ge 2:7
e Isa 45:9; 64:8;
Jer 18:6;
Ro 9:20-21*
f S Job 9:12
29:17
g S Isa 10:25
h S Isa 2:13
i Ps 84:6; 107:33
j Isa 32:15
29:18 *k* S Isa 28:5
l Mk 7:37
m S Ps 107:14
n S Ps 146:8;
S Isa 32:3;
Mt 11:5; Lk 7:22
29:19 *o* Ps 25:9;
37:11; Isa 61:1;
Mt 5:5; 11:29
p S Ps 72:4;
S Isa 3:15;
S 14:30; Mt 11:5;
Lk 7:22; Jas 1:9;
2:5 *q* ver 23;
Isa 1:4; S 5:19;
S 12:6; 30:11
29:20 *r* S Isa 9:4;
S 13:11
s Isa 34:12
t S 2Ch 36:16;
Isa 28:22
u S Job 15:35;
Ps 7:14; Isa 32:7;
33:11; 59:4;
Eze 11:2;
Mic 2:1; Na 1:11
29:21 *v* Am 5:10,
15 *w* Pr 21:28
x S Isa 5:23; 32:7;
Hab 1:4
29:22 *y* S Ex 6:6
z Ge 17:16;
Isa 41:8; 51:2;
63:16 *a* Ps 22:5;
25:3; S Isa 28:16;
49:23; 61:7;
Joel 2:26;
Zep 3:11
b Jer 30:6,10;
Joel 2:6,21;
Na 2:10
29:23
c Isa 49:20-26;
53:10; 54:1-3
d S Ps 8:6;
S Isa 19:25
e Mt 6:9

29:24 *g* Ps 95:10; S Pr 12:8; Isa 28:7; Heb 5:2 *h* Isa 1:3; 32:4;
41:20; 60:16 *i* Isa 30:21; 42:16 30:1 *j* S Isa 28:1 *k* S Dt 21:18;
S Isa 1:2 *l* S 2Ki 17:4; S Isa 8:12 30:2 *m* 2Ki 25:26; Isa 31:1;
36:6; Jer 2:18,36; 42:14; Eze 17:15; 29:16 *n* S Ge 25:22;
S Nu 27:21 *o* Isa 36:9 *p* S Isa 4:6 30:3 *q* Jdg 9:8-15 *r* ver 5;
S Ps 44:13; Isa 20:4-5; 36:6 30:4 *s* S Nu 13:22 30:5 *t* ver 7;
Isa 20:5; 31:1; 36:6 *u* S 2Ki 18:21 *v* S Ps 108:12; Jer 37:3-5

29:17–24 Another sudden shift to the theme of redemption, as in 28:5–8.
29:17 *Lebanon.* Perhaps symbolic of Assyria (see 10:34). The forests of Lebanon were unequaled (see 2:13), so "fertile field" represents a lesser status (see 32:15).
29:18 *In that day.* See notes on 10:20,27; 26:1. Beyond the day of Assyria's destruction lies the day of Israel's restoration. *deaf will hear . . . blind will see.* Linked with the Messianic age in 35:5.
29:19 *needy.* See 11:4. *Holy One of Israel.* See note on 1:4.
29:20 *ruthless.* See v. 21. *mockers.* Cf. 28:14,22.
29:21 *deprive . . . of justice.* See 1:17; 9:17 and notes; see also 10:2; Am 5:10,12.
29:22 *redeemed.* Normally used of the deliverance of Israel from Egypt (see Ex 6:6; 15:13). Cf. 43:1,3,14. But Abraham also had an "exodus" out of a pagan world (see Ge 12:1; Jos 24:2–3,14–15). *be ashamed.* Cf. 45:17; 50:7; 54:4. *grow pale.* From fear of the enemy.
29:23 *see . . . their children.* Cf. 49:20–21; 54:1–2. Restoration from exile may be in view. See also 53:10. *children, the work of my hands.* See 45:11 (cf. Eph 2:10). *acknowl-*

edge the holiness . . . stand in awe. See 8:13. Isaiah's contemporaries showed little respect for the Lord. *Holy One of Jacob.* Cf. v. 19; see note on 1:4.
29:24 *wayward in spirit.* See 19:14. *gain understanding.* Contrast 1:3.
30:1 *Woe.* See note on 28:1–35:10. *obstinate children.* See 1:2 and note. *plans . . . not mine.* See 29:15 and note. *alliance.* After Shabako became pharaoh in 715 B.C., the smaller nations in Aram (Syria) and Canaan sought his help against Assyria. Judah apparently joined them (see 20:5 and note). *my Spirit.* Who spoke through his prophet.
30:2 Hezekiah did this (see 2Ki 18:21). *shade.* A metaphor for a king as one who provides protection (see Jdg 9:15; La 4:20). The Lord should have been Israel's "shade" (cf. 49:2; 51:16; see Ps 91:1; 121:5).
30:3,5 *shame . . . disgrace.* Cf. 20:4–5; see Jdg 9:14–15 and notes.
30:4 *Zoan.* Ironically, where the Israelites once served as slaves; see 19:11 and note. *Hanes.* Possibly Heracleopolis Magna, about 50 miles south of Cairo, or perhaps a city in the Nile delta, close to Zoan.

but only shame and disgrace. [w]"

[6]An oracle[x] concerning the animals of the Negev:[y]

Through a land of hardship and
    distress,[z]
of lions[a] and lionesses,
of adders and darting snakes,[b]
the envoys carry their riches on
    donkeys'[c] backs,
    their treasures[d] on the humps of
    camels,
to that unprofitable nation,
[7] to Egypt, whose help is utterly
    useless. [e]
Therefore I call her
    Rahab[f] the Do-Nothing.

[8]Go now, write it on a tablet[g] for them,
    inscribe it on a scroll,[h]
that for the days to come
    it may be an everlasting witness. [i]
[9]These are rebellious[j] people, deceitful[k]
    children,
    children unwilling to listen to the
    LORD's instruction. [l]
[10]They say to the seers, [m]
    "See no more visions[n]!"
and to the prophets,
    "Give us no more visions of what is
    right!
Tell us pleasant things, [o]
    prophesy illusions. [p]
[11]Leave this way, [q]
    get off this path,
and stop confronting[r] us
    with the Holy One[s] of Israel!"

[12]Therefore, this is what the Holy One[t]
of Israel says:

"Because you have rejected this
    message, [u]
    relied on oppression[v]
    and depended on deceit,
[13]this sin will become for you

like a high wall, [w] cracked and
    bulging,
that collapses[x] suddenly, [y] in an
    instant.
[14]It will break in pieces like pottery, [z]
    shattered so mercilessly
that among its pieces not a fragment
    will be found
    for taking coals from a hearth
    or scooping water out of a cistern.''

[15]This is what the Sovereign[a] LORD, the
Holy One[b] of Israel, says:

"In repentance and rest[c] is your
    salvation,
in quietness and trust[d] is your
    strength,
but you would have none of it. [e]
[16]You said, 'No, we will flee[f] on
    horses.'[g]
Therefore you will flee!
You said, 'We will ride off on swift
    horses.'
Therefore your pursuers will be swift!
[17]A thousand will flee
    at the threat of one;
at the threat of five[h]
    you will all flee[i] away,
till you are left[j]
    like a flagstaff on a mountaintop,
    like a banner[k] on a hill.''

[18]Yet the LORD longs[l] to be gracious to
    you;
he rises to show you compassion. [m]
For the LORD is a God of justice. [n]
    Blessed are all who wait for him![o]

[19]O people of Zion, who live in Jerusalem, you will weep no more. [p] How gracious he will be when you cry for help![q] As soon as he hears, he will answer[r] you.

30:5 [w]S ver 3; S 2Ki 18:21; Eze 17:15
30:6 [x]Isa 13:1 [y]S Jdg 1:9 [z]S Ex 1:13; 5:10, 21; Isa 5:30; 8:22; Jer 11:4 [a]S Isa 5:29; 35:9 [b]S Dt 8:15 [c]S Ge 42:26; S 1Sa 25:18 [d]S Isa 15:7
30:7 [e]S 2Ki 18:21; S Jer 2:36 [f]S Job 9:13
30:8 [g]S Dt 27:8 [h]S Ex 17:14; S Isa 8:1; Jer 25:13; 30:2; 36:28; Hab 2:2 [i]Jos 24:26-27
30:9 [j]S Ps 78:8; S Isa 1:2; S Eze 2:6 [k]Isa 28:15; 59:3-4 [l]S Isa 1:10
30:10 [m]S 1Sa 9:9 [n]Jer 11:21; 32:3; Am 7:13 [o]S 1Ki 22:8; S Jer 4:10 [p]Jer 23:26; 25:9; 26:9; 36:29; Eze 13:7; Ro 16:18; 2Ti 4:3-4
30:11 [q]ver 21; Pr 3:6; Isa 35:8-9; 48:17 [r]S Job 21:14 [s]S Isa 29:19
30:12 [t]ver 15; S Isa 5:19; 31:1 [u]S Isa 5:24 [v]S Ps 10:7; S 12:5; S Isa 5:7

30:13 [w]S Ne 2:17; Ps 62:3; S 80:12 [x]S 1Ki 20:30 [y]S Isa 17:14
30:14 [z]S Ps 2:9
30:15 [a]Jer 7:20; Eze 3:11 [b]S ver 12 [c]S Ex 14:14; S Jos 1:13 [d]S 2Ch 20:12; Isa 32:17 [e]Isa 8:6; 42:24; 57:17
30:16 [f]Jer 46:6 [g]S Dt 17:16; 1Ki 10:28-29; S Ps 20:7; Isa 31:1,3; 36:8
30:17 [h]S Lev 26:8 [i]Lev 26:36; Dt 28:25;

[j]S 2Ki 7:7 [j]S Isa 1:8 [k]S Ps 20:5 **30:18** [l]S Ge 43:31; Isa 42:14; 2Pe 3:9,15 [m]Ps 78:38; Isa 48:9; Jnh 3:10 [n]S Ps 11:7; S Isa 5:16 [o]S Ps 27:14; Isa 25:9; 33:2; 40:31; 64:4; La 3:25; Da 12:12 **30:19** [p]S Isa 25:8; 60:20; 61:3 [q]S Job 24:12 Job 22:27; Ps 50:15; S 86:7; Isa 41:17; 58:9; 65:24; Zec 13:9; Mt 7:7-11

30:6 *oracle.* See 13:1 and note. *Negev.* The dry region in the southern part of Palestine (see Ge 12:9 and note; cf. Jdg 1:9). *hardship and distress.* Perhaps it was necessary to use back roads because the Assyrians had control of the main coastal road (see Dt 8:15; Jdg 5:6). *darting snakes.* See 14:29.
30:7 *Rahab.* A mythical sea monster, here symbolic of Egypt. The name itself means "storm," and also "arrogance." See 27:1 and note.
30:8 *write it.* Probably the name "Rahab the Do-Nothing."
30:9 *rebellious people.* See v. 1; see also 1:2 and note.
30:10 *seers.* See 1Sa 9:9 and note; 2Ki 17:13. *See no more visions.* Cf. Am 2:12. *Tell us pleasant things.* As false prophets do (1Ki 22:13; Jer 6:14; 8:11; 23:17,26).
30:11–12,15 *Holy One of Israel.* See 1:4 and note.
30:12 *oppression.* Especially in their domestic policy (see

1:15–17,23; 5:7; 29:21; 58:3–4; 59:3,6–8,13). *deceit.* Especially in their foreign policy (see vv. 1–2; 29:15).
30:13 *like a high wall.* Oppression and deceit (v. 12) had been the "wall" they built to assure their safety and prosperity, but it will be shattered to pieces.
30:15 See 26:3. *repentance and rest.* The true way to salvation and security.
30:16 *horses.* See Ps 33:17.
30:17 *A thousand will flee.* A fulfillment of the curse of Dt 32:30. *flagstaff . . . banner.* See 5:26 and note (see also 1:8 and note).
30:18 *longs to be gracious.* After punishing Israel, God will once again bless them (cf. 40:2).
30:19 *weep no more.* See 25:8 and note. God's response is similar to his zeal for the vineyard (Israel) in 27:2–6.

²⁰Although the Lord gives you the bread^s of adversity and the water of affliction, your teachers^t will be hidden^u no more; with your own eyes you will see them. ²¹Whether you turn to the right or to the left, your ears will hear a voice^v behind you, saying, "This is the way;^w walk in it." ²²Then you will defile your idols^x overlaid with silver and your images covered with gold;^y you will throw them away like a menstrual^z cloth and say to them, "Away with you!^a"

²³He will also send you rain^b for the seed you sow in the ground, and the food that comes from the land will be rich^c and plentiful.^d In that day^e your cattle will graze in broad meadows.^f ²⁴The oxen^g and donkeys that work the soil will eat fodder^h and mash, spread out with forkⁱ and shovel. ²⁵In the day of great slaughter,^j when the towers^k fall, streams of water will flow^l on every high mountain and every lofty hill. ²⁶The moon will shine like the sun,^m and the sunlight will be seven times brighter, like the light of seven full days, when the Lord binds up the bruises of his people and healsⁿ the wounds he inflicted.

²⁷See, the Name^o of the Lord comes
   from afar,
  with burning anger^p and dense
   clouds of smoke;
his lips are full of wrath,^q
  and his tongue is a consuming fire.^r
²⁸His breath^s is like a rushing torrent,^t
  rising up to the neck.^u
He shakes the nations in the sieve^v of
   destruction;
he places in the jaws of the peoples

  a bit^w that leads them astray.
²⁹And you will sing
  as on the night you celebrate a holy
   festival;^x
your hearts will rejoice^y
  as when people go up with flutes^z
to the mountain^a of the Lord,
  to the Rock^b of Israel.
³⁰The Lord will cause men to hear his
   majestic voice^c
and will make them see his arm^d
   coming down
with raging anger^e and consuming
   fire,^f
  with cloudburst, thunderstorm^g and
   hail.^h
³¹The voice of the Lord will shatter
   Assyria;ⁱ
  with his scepter he will strike^j them
   down.
³²Every stroke the Lord lays on them
  with his punishing rod^k
will be to the music of tambourines^l
   and harps,
  as he fights them in battle with the
   blows of his arm.^m
³³Tophethⁿ has long been prepared;
  it has been made ready for the king.
Its fire pit has been made deep and
   wide,
  with an abundance of fire and wood;
the breath^o of the Lord,
  like a stream of burning sulfur,^p
   sets it ablaze.^q

30:20 s1Ki 22:27; tS Isa 28:9; uPs 74:9; Am 8:11 **30:21** vS Isa 29:24; wS ver 11; S Job 33:11 **30:22** xS Ex 32:4; S Isa 17:8; yS Job 22:24; Isa 31:7; zLev 15:19-23; aEze 7:19-20 **30:23** bS Dt 28:12; Isa 65:21-22; cIsa 25:6; 55:2; Jer 31:14; dS Job 36:31; Isa 62:8; eS Isa 28:5; fS Ps 65:13 **30:24** gIsa 32:14, 20; hS Job 6:5; iMt 3:12; Lk 3:17 **30:25** jS Isa 13:5; 34:6; 65:12; Jer 25:32; 50:27; kS Isa 2:15; lS Ex 17:6; Isa 32:2; 41:18; Joel 3:18; Zec 14:8 **30:26** mIsa 24:23; 60:19-20; Zec 14:7; Rev 21:23; 22:5; nS Dt 32:39; S 2Ch 7:14; Ps 107:20; S Isa 1:5; Jer 3:22; 17:14; Hos 14:4 **30:27** oKi 18:24; Ps 20:1; Isa 59:19; 64:2; pIsa 26:20; 66:14; Eze 22:31; qIsa 10:5; 13:5; rS ver 30; S Job 41:21 **30:28** sS Isa 11:4; tS Ps 50:3; S Isa 28:15; uS Isa 8:8; vAm 9:9; w2Ki 19:28

30:29 xIsa 25:6; yIsa 12:1; zS 1Sa 10:5; aS Ps 42:4; Mt 26:30; bS Ge 49:24 **30:30** cS Ps 68:33; dIsa 9:12; 40:10; 51:9; 52:10; 53:1; 59:16; 62:8; 63:12; eS ver 27; S Isa 10:25; fS Isa 4:4; 47:14; gEx 20:18; Ps 29:3; hS Ex 9:18 **30:31** iS Isa 10:5,12; jS Isa 11:4 **30:32** kIsa 10:26; lS Ex 15:20; mS Isa 11:15; Eze 32:10 **30:33** nS 2Ki 23:10; oS Ex 15:10; S 2Sa 22:16; pS Ge 19:24; S Rev 9:17; qS Isa 1:31

30:20 *bread of adversity . . . water of affliction.* Prisoners' food (see 1Ki 22:27). *teachers.* Prophets, like Isaiah.
30:21 *This is the way.* Contrast the attitude shown in vv. 10–11 (cf. 29:24).
30:22 *defile your idols.* In repentance, not in despair as in 2:20 (see note there).
30:23 *rain . . . food . . . rich and plentiful.* Part of the covenant blessings promised in Dt 28:11–12. See 5:6 and note. *In that day.* Cf. 29:18; see notes on 10:20,27; 26:1. *cattle will graze.* Cf. 32:20.
30:24 *mash.* Seasoned, tasty fodder.
30:25 *day of great slaughter.* Cf. 24:1; 34:2,6. Assyria's fall (v. 31) is one illustration. *streams . . . on every high mountain.* Paradise-like conditions will return to the land (see 41:18; Ps 104:13–15).
30:26 *moon . . . brighter.* The darkness will be past: Night will be like the day, and day will be illumined with sevenfold light. *binds up the bruises . . . heals the wounds.* Israel was bruised politically because of the sins of the people (see 1:6; 61:1; Jer 33:6).
30:27 *the Name.* The revelation of God, especially his power and glory. *anger . . . clouds of smoke.* The language of theophany (a manifestation or appearance of God). God is

portrayed as coming in a storm (see v. 30; see also 28:2; 29:6; Ps 18:7–15 and notes). *consuming fire.* Perhaps lightning.
30:28 *rising up to the neck.* The army of Assyria was similarly described in 8:8 (see note there). *bit.* Cf. 37:29.
30:29 *sing . . . holy festival.* Perhaps the Passover, alluded to in 31:5 (cf. Mt 26:30). *mountain of the Lord.* Zion, where the temple was (see 2:2–4 and note). *Rock.* God himself (see 17:10 and note).
30:30–31 *voice.* Associated with thunder in Ex 20:18–19; Ps 29:3–4. **30:30** *arm coming down.* See 9:12,17,21; 51:9 and notes. *cloudburst . . . hail.* See 28:2.
30:31 *voice of the Lord will shatter.* Cf. Ps 29:5–9.
30:32 *his punishing rod.* See 11:4 and note. *music of tambourines.* After a great victory the women rejoiced with singing and dancing (see Ex 15:20–21; 1Sa 18:6).
30:33 *Topheth.* A region outside Jerusalem where children were sacrificed to Molech (see 2Ki 23:10; Jer 7:31–32; 19:6,11–14), the god of the Ammonites (see 1Ki 11:7). Thus it was a place of burning. *king.* Of Assyria. *burning sulfur.* See 1:31; Ge 19:24 and notes.

Woe to Those Who Rely on Egypt

31 Woe[r] to those who go down to
Egypt[s] for help,
who rely on horses,[t]
who trust in the multitude of their
chariots[u]
and in the great strength of their
horsemen,
but do not look to the Holy One[v] of
Israel,
or seek help from the LORD.[w]
[2]Yet he too is wise[x] and can bring
disaster;[y]
he does not take back his words.[z]
He will rise up against the house of the
wicked,[a]
against those who help evildoers.
[3]But the Egyptians[b] are men and not
God;[c]
their horses[d] are flesh and not spirit.
When the LORD stretches out his
hand,[e]
he who helps will stumble,
he who is helped[f] will fall;
both will perish together.[g]

[4]This is what the LORD says to me:

"As a lion[h] growls,
a great lion over his prey—
and though a whole band of shepherds[i]
is called together against him,
he is not frightened by their shouts
or disturbed by their clamor[j] —
so the LORD Almighty will come down[k]
to do battle on Mount Zion and on its
heights.
[5]Like birds hovering[l] overhead,
the LORD Almighty will shield[m]
Jerusalem;
he will shield it and deliver[n] it,

he will 'pass over'[o] it and will rescue
it."

[6]Return[p] to him you have so greatly revolted[q] against, O Israelites. [7]For in that
day[r] every one of you will reject the idols
of silver and gold[s] your sinful hands have
made.[t]

[8]"Assyria[u] will fall by a sword that is not
of man;
a sword, not of mortals, will devour[v]
them.
They will flee before the sword
and their young men will be put to
forced labor.[w]
[9]Their stronghold[x] will fall because of
terror;
at sight of the battle standard[y] their
commanders will panic,[z] "
declares the LORD;
whose fire[a] is in Zion,
whose furnace[b] is in Jerusalem.

The Kingdom of Righteousness

32 See, a king[c] will reign in
righteousness
and rulers will rule with justice.[d]
[2]Each man will be like a shelter[e] from
the wind
and a refuge from the storm,[f]
like streams of water[g] in the desert[h]
and the shadow of a great rock in a
thirsty land.

[3]Then the eyes of those who see will no
longer be closed,[i]
and the ears[j] of those who hear will
listen.

31:1 [r]S Isa 28:1
[s]S Dt 17:16;
S Isa 30:2,5;
S Jer 37:5
[t]S Isa 30:16
[u]S Isa 2:7
[v]Job 6:10;
S Isa 1:4; S 30:12
[w]S Dt 20:1;
S Pr 21:31;
S Isa 9:13;
Jer 46:9;
Eze 29:16
31:2 [x]S Ps 92:5;
Ro 16:27
[y]Isa 45:7; 47:11;
Am 3:6
[z]Nu 23:19;
S Pr 19:21
[a]S Isa 1:4; 29:15;
32:6
31:3 [b]Isa 20:5;
36:9 [c]S Ps 9:20;
Eze 28:9; 2Th 2:4
[d]S Isa 30:16
[e]Ne 1:10;
S Job 30:21;
Isa 9:17,21;
Jer 51:25;
Eze 20:34
[f]Isa 10:3; 30:5-7
[g]S Isa 20:6;
Jer 17:5
31:4 [h]Nu 24:9;
S 1Sa 17:34;
Hos 11:10;
Am 3:8 [i]Jer 3:15;
23:4; Eze 34:23;
Na 3:18 [j]Ps 74:23
[k]Isa 42:13
31:5 [l]S Ge 1:2;
S Mt 23:37
[m]S Ps 91:4;
S Isa 5:2;
S Zec 9:15
[n]S Ps 34:7;
Isa 37:35; 38:6

[o]S Ex 12:23
31:6
[p]S Job 22:23;
S Isa 1:27
[q]S Isa 1:5
31:7 [r]Isa 29:18
[s]S Isa 30:22
[t]S Ps 135:15
31:8 [u]S Isa 10:12
[v]S Ex 12:12;
Isa 10:12; 14:25;
S 27:1; 33:1;
37:7; Jer 25:12;
Hab 2:8
[w]S Ge 49:15;
S Dt 20:11
31:9 [x]Dt 32:31,
37 [y]S Isa 18:3;
S Jer 4:6

[z]Jer 51:9; Na 3:7 [a]S Isa 10:17 [b]Ps 21:9; Mal 4:1 **32:1**
[c]S Ps 149:2; S Isa 6:5; 55:4; Eze 37:24 [d]Ps 72:1-4; S Isa 9:7;
S 28:6 **32:2** [e]S 1Ki 18:4 [f]S Ps 55:8 [g]S 23:2; S Isa 30:25;
49:10; Jer 31:9 [h]S Ps 107:35; Isa 44:3 **32:3** [i]S Isa 29:18;
35:5; 42:7,16 [j]S Dt 29:4

31:1 See 30:1 and note. Ch. 31 recapitulates ch. 30. *go down to Egypt.* See Ge 26:2. *horses . . . chariots.* Egypt had large numbers of horses and chariots (see 1Ki 10:28–29). *Holy One of Israel.* See 1:4 and note.

31:2 *he too is wise.* People had questioned God's wisdom in 29:14–16.

31:3 *stretches out his hand.* Cf. the refrain in 5:25; 9:12, 17,21; 10:4. *helps will stumble.* Cf. 30:3,5.

31:4 *lion.* A simile, but perhaps also an allusion to the Assyrian king (see note on 15:9). *shepherds.* Perhaps an allusion to the rulers of the nations (see NIV text note on Na 3:18).

31:5 *birds . . . will shield.* Cf. Dt 32:10–11. *pass over.* The technical word used of the destroying angel who "passed over" every house in Egypt that had blood on the doorposts (see Ex 12:13,23). Cf. Isa 37:35.

31:6 *greatly revolted.* See 1:2 and note.

31:7 *reject the idols.* See 2:20 and note.

31:8 *sword, not of mortals.* The angel of the Lord struck

down 185,000 soldiers (see 37:36). *put to forced labor.* As prisoners of war.

31:9 *stronghold.* Nineveh was destroyed by the Medes and Babylonians in 612 B.C. (see Na 3:7). *commanders will panic.* Cf. Na 2:10. *fire . . . furnace.* The Lord's glory resides in Zion, and from that center of his people his fire of judgment breaks out upon the wicked (see 10:17; 30:33; cf. Lev 10:2; Joel 3:16; Am 1:2).

32:1 *king . . . in righteousness.* The Messianic age is again in view (see 9:7; 11:4; 16:5 and notes). Cf. vv. 16–17; 33:17.

32:2 *Each man.* The Lord's redeemed, as sources of protection and blessing, will reflect him (see the rest of this note; see also vv. 3–8). *shelter . . . refuge . . . shadow.* Similar terms are applied to the Lord in 25:4 (see 4:5–6 and note). *streams . . . in the desert.* See 35:6–7; 41:18; 49:10.

32:3 *eyes . . . no longer be closed . . . ears . . . listen.* See 35:5 and note (contrast 6:9–10).

⁴The mind of the rash will know and
understand, ^k
and the stammering tongue ^l will be
fluent and clear.
⁵No longer will the fool ^m be called noble
nor the scoundrel be highly
respected.
⁶For the fool speaks folly, ⁿ
his mind is busy with evil: ^o
He practices ungodliness ^p
and spreads error ^q concerning the
LORD;
the hungry he leaves empty ^r
and from the thirsty he withholds
water.
⁷The scoundrel's methods are wicked, ^s
he makes up evil schemes ^t
to destroy the poor with lies,
even when the plea of the needy ^u is
just. ^v
⁸But the noble man makes noble plans,
and by noble deeds ^w he stands. ^x

The Women of Jerusalem

⁹You women ^y who are so complacent,
rise up and listen ^z to me;
you daughters who feel secure, ^a
hear what I have to say!
¹⁰In little more than a year ^b
you who feel secure will tremble;
the grape harvest will fail, ^c
and the harvest of fruit will not
come.
¹¹Tremble, ^d you complacent women;
shudder, you daughters who feel
secure! ^e
Strip off your clothes, ^f
put sackcloth ^g around your waists.
¹²Beat your breasts ^h for the pleasant
fields,
for the fruitful vines ⁱ
¹³and for the land of my people,

a land overgrown with thorns and
briers ^j —
yes, mourn ^k for all houses of merriment
and for this city of revelry. ^l
¹⁴The fortress ^m will be abandoned,
the noisy city deserted; ⁿ
citadel and watchtower ^o will become a
wasteland forever,
the delight of donkeys, ^p a pasture for
flocks, ^q
¹⁵till the Spirit ^r is poured upon us from
on high,
and the desert becomes a fertile
field, ^s
and the fertile field seems like a
forest. ^t
¹⁶Justice ^u will dwell in the desert ^v
and righteousness ^w live in the fertile
field.
¹⁷The fruit of righteousness ^x will be
peace; ^y
the effect of righteousness will be
quietness and confidence ^z
forever.
¹⁸My people will live in peaceful ^a
dwelling places,
in secure homes, ^b
in undisturbed places of rest. ^c
¹⁹Though hail ^d flattens the forest ^e
and the city is leveled ^f completely,
²⁰how blessed you will be,
sowing ^g your seed by every stream, ^h
and letting your cattle and donkeys
range free. ⁱ

Distress and Help

33 Woe ^j to you, O destroyer,
you who have not been destroyed!

32:4 ^kIsa 6:10;
S 29:24 ^lIsa 35:6
32:5
^mS 1Sa 25:25
32:6 ⁿS Pr 19:3
^oS Pr 24:2;
S Isa 26:10
^pS Isa 9:17
^qIsa 3:12; 9:16
^rS Isa 3:15
32:7
^sJer 5:26-28;
Da 12:10
^tS Isa 29:20;
Mic 7:3
^uS Ps 72:4;
Isa 29:19; 61:1
^vS Isa 29:21
32:8 ^w1Ch 29:9;
S Pr 11:25
^xIsa 14:24
32:9 ^yS Isa 4:1
^zIsa 28:23 ^aver
11; Isa 47:8;
Da 4:4; Am 6:1;
Zep 2:15
32:10 ^bIsa 37:30
^cIsa 5:5-6; S 24:7
32:11 ^dIsa 33:14
^eS ver 9 ^fIsa 47:2;
Mic 1:8; Na 3:5
^gS Isa 3:24
32:12 ^hNa 2:7
ⁱIsa 16:9

32:13 ^jS Isa 5:6;
Hos 10:8
^kS Isa 24:11
^lS Isa 23:7
32:14
^mS Isa 13:22
ⁿS Isa 6:11;
S 27:10
^oS Isa 2:15; 34:13
^pS Ps 104:11
^qS Isa 5:17
32:15 ^rS Isa 11:2;
S Eze 37:9
^sPs 107:35;
Isa 35:1-2
^tIsa 29:17
32:16 ^uS Isa 9:7;
S 28:6 ^vIsa 35:1,
6; 42:11
^wS Ps 48:1;
S Isa 1:26
32:17
^xS Ps 85:10
^yS Ps 119:165;
S Isa 9:7;
Ro 14:17;
Heb 12:11;
Jas 3:18
^zS Isa 30:15
32:18 ^aS Isa 2:4
^bS Isa 26:1;
33:20; 37:33;
65:21; 66:14; Am 9:14 ^cS Jos 1:13; S Job 11:18; Hos 2:18-23
32:19 ^dIsa 28:17 ^eS Isa 10:19; Zec 11:2 ^fS Job 40:11;
S Isa 19:18; 24:10; 27:10 32:20 ^gS Ecc 11:1 ^hS Dt 28:12
ⁱJob 39:8; S Isa 30:24 33:1 ^jS 2Ki 19:21; S Isa 28:1

32:5–8 The redeemed will no longer be among the fools.
The contrast between the fool and the wise or noble man is
characteristic of wisdom literature (compare Pr 9:1–6 with
Pr 9:13–18).
32:6 *fool speaks folly.* Cf. 9:16–17; Ps 14:1; 53:1.
32:7 *plea of the needy.* See 1:17 and note.
32:8 *plans . . . stands.* See 8:10 and note.
32:9 *women.* Cf. 3:16–4:1. *complacent . . . feel secure.*
See v. 11; Am 6:1. These words are used in a good sense in
v. 18 (the Hebrew for "undisturbed" is the same as that for
"complacent").
32:10 *a year.* Perhaps the invasion of Sennacherib (701
B.C.) is in view. *grape harvest will fail.* Cf. 37:30. The armies
of Assyria would bring widespread destruction, ruining the
summer fruit.
32:11 *Strip.* Cf. 47:2–3. *sackcloth.* Cf. 3:24; 22:12; see
note on Ge 37:34.
32:12 *Beat your breasts.* Like the slave girls of Nineveh (Na
2:7). *for the fruitful vines.* Cf. the Lord's weeping in 16:9.
32:13 *thorns and briers.* See 5:6; 7:23 and notes. *merri-*

ment . . . revelry. See 22:2 and note; cf. Jer 16:8–9.
32:14 *fortress . . . noisy city.* Assyria's invasion is a warning that Jerusalem (see 24:10 and note) will one day be
destroyed. *donkeys . . . flocks.* Cf. 7:25; 13:21–22; 34:13.
32:15 *till the Spirit.* The outpouring of the Spirit is linked
with abundance also in 44:3 (see v. 2; 11:2, and notes; see
also Joel 2:28–32). *fertile field . . . forest.* The forest probably stands for Lebanon (see 29:17 and note; cf. 35:1–2).
32:16 *Justice . . . righteousness.* See v. 1 and note.
32:17 *peace.* Cf. 9:7; 11:6–9. *quietness and confidence.*
Contrast 30:15.
32:18 *secure . . . undisturbed.* See note on v. 9. *places of
rest.* See 28:12 and note.
32:19 *hail.* Cf. 28:2. *forest.* Probably Assyria. See
10:33–34 and notes. *city.* See 24:10 and note.
32:20 The abundance of the day of the Lord is described
(see 30:23–24 and notes).
33:1 *Woe.* See note on 28:1–35:10. *destroyer . . . traitor.*
Probably Assyria—depicted as treacherous (see 10:5–6;
16:4; 21:2; 24:16 and notes).

Woe to you, O traitor,
  you who have not been betrayed!
When you stop destroying,
  you will be destroyed; [k]
when you stop betraying,
  you will be betrayed. [l]

[2]O Lord, be gracious [m] to us;
  we long for you.
Be our strength [n] every morning,
  our salvation [o] in time of distress. [p]
[3]At the thunder of your voice, [q] the
    peoples flee; [r]
  when you rise up, [s] the nations
    scatter.
[4]Your plunder, [t] O nations, is harvested [u]
    as by young locusts; [v]
  like a swarm of locusts men pounce
    on it.

[5]The Lord is exalted, [w] for he dwells on
    high; [x]
  he will fill Zion with justice [y] and
    righteousness. [z]
[6]He will be the sure foundation for your
    times,
  a rich store of salvation [a] and wisdom
    and knowledge;
  the fear [b] of the Lord is the key to
    this treasure. [s] [c]

[7]Look, their brave men [d] cry aloud in the
    streets;
  the envoys [e] of peace weep bitterly.
[8]The highways are deserted,
  no travelers [f] are on the roads. [g]
The treaty is broken, [h]
  its witnesses [t] are despised,
  no one is respected.
[9]The land mourns [u] [i] and wastes away,
  Lebanon [j] is ashamed and withers; [k]
Sharon [l] is like the Arabah,

and Bashan [m] and Carmel [n] drop their
    leaves.

[10]"Now will I arise, [o]" says the Lord.
  "Now will I be exalted; [p]
  now will I be lifted up.
[11]You conceive [q] chaff,
  you give birth [r] to straw;
  your breath is a fire [s] that consumes
    you.
[12]The peoples will be burned as if to
    lime; [t]
  like cut thornbushes [u] they will be set
    ablaze. [v]"

[13]You who are far away, [w] hear [x] what I
    have done;
  you who are near, acknowledge my
    power!
[14]The sinners [y] in Zion are terrified;
  trembling [z] grips the godless:
"Who of us can dwell with the
    consuming fire? [a]
Who of us can dwell with everlasting
    burning?"
[15]He who walks righteously [b]
  and speaks what is right, [c]
who rejects gain from extortion [d]
  and keeps his hand from accepting
    bribes, [e]
who stops his ears against plots of
    murder
  and shuts his eyes [f] against
    contemplating evil—
[16]this is the man who will dwell on the
    heights, [g]

33:1 [k]S Isa 31:8;
S Mt 7:2
[l]S Isa 21:2;
Jer 30:16;
Eze 39:10
33:2
[m]S Ge 43:29;
S Ezr 9:8
[n]Isa 40:10; 51:9;
59:16; 63:5
[o]S Ps 13:5;
S Isa 12:2
[p]S Isa 5:30
33:3 [q]S Ps 46:6;
S 68:33
[r]S Ps 68:1;
S Isa 13:14 [s]ver
10; Nu 10:35;
Ps 12:5;
Isa 59:16-18
33:4 [t]S Nu 14:3;
S 2Ki 7:16
[u]S Isa 17:5;
Joel 3:13 [v]Joel 1:4
33:5 [w]S Isa 5:16
[x]S Job 16:19
[y]S Isa 9:7; S 28:6
[z]S Isa 1:26
33:6 [a]S Isa 12:2;
26:1; 51:6; 60:18
[b]S Pr 1:7;
Isa 11:2-3;
Mt 6:33
[c]S Ge 39:3;
S Job 22:25
33:7 [d]Isa 10:34
[e]S 2Ki 18:37
33:8 [f]Isa 60:15;
Zec 7:14
[g]S Jdg 5:6;
Isa 30:21; 35:8
[h]S 2Ki 18:14
33:9 [i]S Isa 3:26
[j]S 2Ki 19:23;
Isa 2:13; 35:2;
37:24; Jer 22:6
[k]S Isa 15:6
[l]S 1Ch 27:29

[m]Mic 7:14
[n]1Ki 18:19;
Isa 35:2; Na 1:4
33:10 [o]S ver 3;
Isa 2:21
[p]S Isa 5:16
33:11 [q]Ps 7:14;
Isa 59:4; Jas 1:15
[r]S Isa 26:18
[s]Isa 1:31
33:12 [t]Am 2:1
[u]S Isa 5:6
[v]S Isa 10:17;
S 27:11

33:13 [w]Ps 48:10; 49:1 [x]Isa 34:1; 48:16; 49:1 **33:14**
[y]S Isa 1:28 [z]S Isa 32:11 [a]S Isa 1:31; S 30:30; S Zec 13:9;
Heb 12:29 **33:15** [b]Isa 58:8 [c]Ps 15:2; 24:4 [d]Eze 22:13;
33:31 [e]S Pr 15:27 [f]Ps 119:37 **33:16** [g]S Dt 32:13

[s] 6 Or *is a treasure from him*   [t] 8 Dead Sea Scrolls;
Masoretic Text / *the cities*   [u] 9 Or *dries up*

33:2–9 A prayer asking the Lord to bring about the promised destruction of Assyria.
33:2 *be gracious.* See 30:18 and note. *strength . . . salvation.* See 12:2 and note; cf. 59:16. *distress.* See 37:3.
33:3 *thunder of your voice.* See 30:30–31 and note. *rise up . . . scatter.* An allusion to Nu 10:35; cf. Ps 68:1.
33:5 *fill . . . righteousness.* See 1:26; 32:1 and note.
33:6 *wisdom . . . knowledge . . . fear of the Lord.* Terms linked with the Messiah in 11:2. See 9:6; Pr 1:7 and notes.
33:7 *their brave men.* The men of Judah, during Sennacherib's invasion of 701 B.C. (see 10:28–34). *envoys of peace.* Perhaps the three officials who conferred with the Assyrian field commander (see 36:3,22).
33:8 *highways are deserted.* Travel and trade were impossible, creating economic hardship (see Jdg 5:6). *treaty.* Perhaps the agreement made when Hezekiah paid large sums to Sennacherib (2Ki 18:14).
33:9 *land . . . wastes away.* Farmland and pastures were ruined by the invaders. See 24:4 and note. *Lebanon.* Renowned for its cedars (2:13) and animals (40:16). *Sharon.* A plain along the Mediterranean coast north of Joppa, known

for its beautiful foliage and superb grazing land (see 35:2; 65:10; 1Ch 27:29). *Arabah.* Desert land associated with the Jordan River and the Dead Sea (see Dt 1:1; 2:8). *Bashan.* See 2:13 and note. *Carmel.* See note on 1Ki 18:19; means "fertile field" (as in 29:17; 32:15) or "orchards" (as in 16:10) and is also associated with lush pasturelands (see 35:2; Mic 7:14 and NIV text note; Na 1:4).
33:10 *be exalted.* Through the judgment he brings on his rebellious people (see v. 13).
33:11 *conceive . . . give birth.* Cf. 26:18. *breath is a fire.* They only produce what results in their destruction.
33:12 *to lime.* The burning will be complete (see Am 2:1). *thornbushes.* They burn very quickly (see 27:4; 2Sa 23:6–7).
33:13 *hear . . . acknowledge.* Cf. 34:1.
33:14 *sinners in Zion.* See 1:27–28; 4:4. *consuming fire.* The presence of the God of judgment (see 29:6; 30:27,30; Ex 24:17; Dt 4:24; 9:3; 2Sa 22:9; Ps 18:8; Heb 12:29).
33:15 Similar requirements are found in Ps 15:2–5; 24:4. *bribes.* See 1:23.
33:16 *heights . . . fortress.* Symbolic of the security found in God (cf. Ps 18:1–3). *bread . . . water.* Cf. 49:10.

whose refuge[h] will be the mountain
    fortress.[i]
His bread will be supplied,
    and water will not fail[j] him.

[17]Your eyes will see the king[k] in his
    beauty[l]
    and view a land that stretches afar.[m]
[18]In your thoughts you will ponder the
    former terror:[n]
    "Where is that chief officer?
    Where is the one who took the
        revenue?
    Where is the officer in charge of the
        towers?[o]"
[19]You will see those arrogant people[p] no
    more,
    those people of an obscure speech,
    with their strange, incomprehensible
        tongue.[q]

[20]Look upon Zion,[r] the city of our
    festivals;
    your eyes will see Jerusalem,
    a peaceful abode,[s] a tent[t] that will
        not be moved;[u]
its stakes will never be pulled up,
    nor any of its ropes broken.
[21]There the LORD will be our Mighty[v]
    One.
    It will be like a place of broad rivers
        and streams.[w]
No galley with oars will ride them,
    no mighty ship[x] will sail them.
[22]For the LORD is our judge,[y]
    the LORD is our lawgiver,[z]
    the LORD is our king;[a]
    it is he who will save[b] us.

[23]Your rigging hangs loose:
    The mast is not held secure,
    the sail is not spread.
Then an abundance of spoils will be
        divided
    and even the lame[c] will carry off
        plunder.[d]
[24]No one living in Zion will say, "I am
    ill";[e]
    and the sins of those who dwell there
        will be forgiven.[f]

Judgment Against the Nations

34 Come near, you nations, and
    listen;[g]
    pay attention, you peoples![h]
Let the earth[i] hear, and all that is in it,
    the world, and all that comes out of
        it![j]
[2]The LORD is angry with all nations;
    his wrath[k] is upon all their armies.
He will totally destroy[v][l] them,
    he will give them over to slaughter.[m]
[3]Their slain[n] will be thrown out,
    their dead bodies[o] will send up a
        stench;[p]
    the mountains will be soaked with
        their blood.[q]
[4]All the stars of the heavens will be
        dissolved[r]
    and the sky rolled up[s] like a scroll;
all the starry host will fall[t]
    like withered[u] leaves from the vine,
    like shriveled figs from the fig tree.

33:16 [h]S Ps 46:1;
S Isa 25:4
[i]Ps 18:1-2;
Isa 26:1
[j]Isa 48:21; 49:10;
65:13
33:17 [k]S Isa 6:5
[l]S Isa 4:2
[m]S Isa 26:15
33:18
[n]S Isa 17:14
[o]S Isa 2:15
33:19 [p]S Ps 5:5
[q]S Ge 11:7;
S Isa 28:11
33:20 [r]S Ps 125:1
[s]S Isa 32:18
[t]S Ge 26:22 [u]ver
6; Ps 46:5
33:21
[v]S Isa 10:34
[w]S Ex 17:6;
S Ps 1:3; Isa 32:2;
41:18; 48:18;
49:10; 66:12;
Na 3:8 [x]Isa 23:1
33:22 [y]Isa 11:4
[z]S Isa 2:3;
Jas 4:12
[a]S Ps 89:18
[b]S Isa 25:9

33:23 [c]S 2Ki 7:8
[d]S 2Ki 7:16
33:24
[e]S Isa 30:26
[f]S Nu 23:21;
S 2Ch 6:21;
Isa 43:1; 48:20;
Jer 31:34; 33:8;
1Jn 1:7-9
34:1 [g]S Isa 33:13
[h]Isa 41:1; 43:9
[i]S Dt 4:26;
Ps 49:1 /Ps 24:1
34:2 [k]S Isa 10:25
[l]S Isa 13:5;
S Zec 5:3
[m]S Isa 30:25
34:3 [n]S Isa 5:25;
S 10:4
[o]S Ps 110:6;
Eze 39:11
[p]Joel 2:20;
Am 4:10 [q]ver 7;
S 2Sa 1:22;
Isa 63:6;
Eze 5:17; 14:19;
32:6; 35:6; 38:22
34:4 [r]S Job 9:7;
S Isa 13:13;
2Pe 3:10
[s]Isa 38:12;

Heb 1:12 [t]S Mt 24:29*; Mk 13:25* [u]S Job 8:12;
S Isa 15:6; Mt 21:19

v2 The Hebrew term refers to the irrevocable giving over
of things or persons to the LORD, often by totally
destroying them; also in verse 5.

33:17 *king.* See 32:1 and note; cf. 6:5. *in his beauty.*
Reflecting on the splendor and majesty of a Davidic king;
probably a foreshadowing of the Messianic kingdom (cf. 4:2;
Ps 45:3-4; contrast Isa 53:2). *land . . . afar.* See 26:15 and
note.
33:18 *former terror.* The Assyrian invasion (see 17:12-14
and note). *revenue.* Forced tribute (see note on v. 8). *towers.*
Judah's fortifications were probably under strict Assyrian
control (see 2:15).
33:19 *arrogant.* Cf. 10:12. *obscure speech.* The Assyrian
language was related to Hebrew but was different enough to
sound strange to Israelite ears. See 28:11; Dt 28:49.
33:20 *Look upon Zion.* The redeemed city, in contrast to
the city described in vv. 7-9. *festivals.* See 1:14 and note.
peaceful abode. See 32:17-18 and notes. *tent . . . not . . .
moved.* Her exile will be over. *stakes . . . ropes.* Cf. the
similar description of Jerusalem in 54:2.
33:21 *Mighty One.* See 10:34 (cf. Ps 93:4). *broad rivers.*
To prevent easy access to her borders—thus like Tyre (23:1)
or Thebes (see Na 3:8).
33:22 *our judge.* See 2:4; 11:4 and note. *our lawgiver.* See
2:3; 51:4; Ge 49:10. *our king.* See v. 17; 32:1 and note; see
also Ps 46; 48. *save.* See Jdg 2:16.

33:23 *rigging.* Jerusalem is pictured as a ship, unprepared
to sail into battle against Assyria. *Then.* When God strikes
down the Assyrian army (see 10:33-34; 37:36). *plunder.*
See v. 4.
33:24 Looking beyond Isaiah's own day to the physically
and spiritually whole Jerusalem of vv. 17,20-22.
34:1—35:10 Chs. 34-35 conclude chs. 28-33 and comprise an eschatological section corresponding to chs. 24-27,
which conclude chs. 13-23 (see note on 24:1-27:13).
34:2 *angry . . . wrath.* In the day of the Lord (see 2:11,17,
20; 26:20-21 and notes). See also 13:3 and note; 13:13.
totally destroy. The kind of destruction the Canaanites had
deserved. See NIV text note; see also v. 5; Jos 6:17. *slaughter.* See 30:25 and note.
34:3 *thrown out.* Not to have a proper burial was considered a disgrace (see 14:19 and note).
34:4 *stars . . . dissolved.* Disturbances in the heavens characterize the day of the Lord (see 13:10,13 and notes; cf. Eze
32:7-8). *sky . . . scroll . . . starry host will fall.* Referred to in
Mt 24:29; Rev 6:13-14 in connection with the "great
distress" (Mt 24:21) and the second coming of Christ. *withered leaves.* Cf. 24:4; 40:7-8.

⁵My sword ᵛ has drunk its fill in the
    heavens;
  see, it descends in judgment on
    Edom, ʷ
  the people I have totally destroyed. ˣ
⁶The sword ʸ of the LORD is bathed in
    blood,
  it is covered with fat—
  the blood of lambs and goats,
    fat from the kidneys of rams.
  For the LORD has a sacrifice ᶻ in
    Bozrah ᵃ
  and a great slaughter ᵇ in Edom.
⁷And the wild oxen ᶜ will fall with them,
  the bull calves and the great bulls. ᵈ
  Their land will be drenched with
    blood, ᵉ
  and the dust will be soaked with fat.

⁸For the LORD has a day ᶠ of
    vengeance, ᵍ
  a year of retribution, ʰ to uphold
    Zion's cause.
⁹Edom's streams will be turned into
    pitch,
  her dust into burning sulfur; ⁱ
  her land will become blazing pitch!
¹⁰It will not be quenched ʲ night and day;
  its smoke will rise forever. ᵏ
  From generation to generation ˡ it will
    lie desolate; ᵐ
  no one will ever pass through it
    again.
¹¹The desert owl ʷ ⁿ and screech owl ʷ
    will possess it;
  the great owl ʷ and the raven ᵒ will
    nest there.
  God will stretch out over Edom ᵖ
    the measuring line of chaos ᑫ
    and the plumb line ʳ of desolation.

¹²Her nobles will have nothing there to
    be called a kingdom,
  all her princes ˢ will vanish ᵗ away.
¹³Thorns ᵘ will overrun her citadels,
  nettles and brambles her
    strongholds. ᵛ
  She will become a haunt for jackals, ʷ
    a home for owls. ˣ
¹⁴Desert creatures ʸ will meet with
    hyenas, ᶻ
  and wild goats will bleat to each
    other;
  there the night creatures ᵃ will also
    repose
  and find for themselves places of
    rest.
¹⁵The owl will nest there and lay eggs,
  she will hatch them, and care for her
    young under the shadow of her
    wings; ᵇ
  there also the falcons ᶜ will gather,
    each with its mate.

¹⁶Look in the scroll ᵈ of the LORD and
    read:

  None of these will be missing, ᵉ
    not one will lack her mate.
  For it is his mouth ᶠ that has given the
    order, ᵍ
  and his Spirit will gather them
    together.
¹⁷He allots their portions; ʰ
  his hand distributes them by
    measure.
  They will possess it forever

34:5
ᵛDt 32:41-42;
Jer 47:6;
Eze 21:5;
Zec 13:7
ʷS 2Sa 8:13-14;
S 2Ch 28:17;
Am 1:11-12
ˣS Dt 13:15;
S Jos 6:17;
Isa 24:6;
Am 3:14-15;
6:11; Mal 1:4
34:6 ʸS Dt 32:41;
S Isa 27:1
ᶻS Lev 3:9
ᵃS Ge 36:33
ᵇS Isa 30:25;
S Jer 25:34;
Rev 19:17
34:7 ᶜS Nu 23:22
ᵈS Ps 68:30
ᵉS 2Sa 1:22
34:8 ᶠS Isa 2:12
ᵍS Isa 1:24; 35:4;
47:3; 63:4
ʰIsa 59:18;
Eze 25:12-17;
Joel 3:4;
Am 1:6-8,9-10
34:9 ⁱS Ge 19:24
34:10 ʲS Isa 1:31
ᵏRev 14:10-11;
19:3 ˡver 17
ᵐIsa 13:20; 24:1;
Jer 49:18;
Eze 29:12; 35:3;
Mal 1:3
34:11
ⁿS Lev 11:16-18;
S Dt 14:15-17;
Rev 18:2
ᵒS Ge 8:7
ᵖS Isa 21:11;
Eze 35:15;
Joel 3:19; Ob 1:1;
Mal 1:4 ᑫS Ge 1:2
ʳS 2Ki 21:13;
Am 7:8

34:12
ˢJob 12:21;
Ps 107:40;
Isa 40:23;
Jer 21:7; 27:20;
39:6; Eze 24:5
ᵗIsa 29:20;
41:11-12
34:13 ᵘS Isa 5:6;
S 7:19
ᵛS Isa 13:22
ʷPs 44:19;
S Isa 13:22;
Jer 9:11; 10:22

ˣS Lev 11:16-18 **34:14** ʸS Ps 74:14 ᶻIsa 13:22 ᵃRev 18:2
34:15 ᵇS Ps 17:8 ᶜDt 14:13 **34:16** ᵈIsa 30:8 ᵉIsa 40:26;
48:13 ᶠIsa 1:20; 58:14 ᵍS Isa 1:20 **34:17** ʰIsa 17:14;
Jer 13:25

ʷ11 The precise identification of these birds is uncertain.

34:5 *drunk its fill.* Cf. Eze 39:18–20. *Edom.* Symbolic of
all the enemies of God and his people, like Moab in
25:10–12. See note on 21:11. The Edomites were driven
from their homeland by the Nabatean Arabs, perhaps as early
as 500 B.C.
34:6 *fat.* Considered the best part of the meat, and therefore offered to the Lord in the sacrifices (see Lev 3:9–11).
lambs and goats. Symbolizing the people. *sacrifice.* Battles
are often compared to sacrifices (see Jer 46:10; 50:27; Eze
39:17–19). *Bozrah.* An important city of Edom and a sheep-
herding center, it was located about 25 miles southeast of the
southern end of the Dead Sea. The name means "grape-gath-
ering" (cf. 63:1–3).
34:7 *wild oxen . . . great bulls.* Symbolizing the troops
and/or leaders of the nations. *drenched with blood.* See v. 3.
34:8 *day of vengeance.* See 35:4; 61:2. The Edomites
opposed Israel at every opportunity (see 2Sa 8:13–14) and
rejoiced when Jerusalem was destroyed (La 4:21; Ps 137:7).
But Edom's day would come (see 63:4).
34:9 *burning sulfur.* Edom's destruction is compared with
the overthrow of Sodom and Gomorrah (see Jer 49:17–18).
See also 1:31 and note; Ge 19:24 and note.

34:10 *smoke . . . forever.* Applied to Babylon in Rev 19:3
(see also Rev 14:10–11). *lie desolate.* See 13:20–22 and
note; Mal 1:3–4.
34:11 *desert owl . . . screech owl . . . great owl . . . raven.*
"Unclean" birds (see Dt 14:14–17). Such birds would also
live in the ruins of Babylon (13:21) and Nineveh (Zep 2:14).
measuring line . . . plumb line. See 28:17 and note. *chaos
. . . desolation.* The Hebrew for these words is used in Ge
1:2 (see note there) to describe the earth in its "formless"
and "empty" state (see also Jer 4:23 and note).
34:13 *Thorns . . . nettles.* Cf. 7:24–25.
34:14 *Desert creatures . . . hyenas.* See 13:21–22. *wild
goats.* Sometimes connected with demons (see note on
13:21). *night creatures.* Outside the Bible a related Semitic
word refers to a "night demon."
34:15 *owl . . . falcons.* Ceremonially unclean (see v. 11
and note; Dt 14:13,15–17).
34:16 *scroll.* After the destruction of Edom, people will
read this prophecy given by Isaiah. *these.* The creatures just
listed.
34:17 *allots their portions.* God will give the creatures of
vv. 11,13–15 clear title to the land of Edom.

and dwell there from generation to generation. [i]

Joy of the Redeemed

35 The desert[j] and the parched land will be glad;
the wilderness will rejoice and blossom. [k]
Like the crocus,[l] [2]it will burst into bloom;
it will rejoice greatly and shout for joy. [m]
The glory of Lebanon[n] will be given to it,
the splendor of Carmel[o] and Sharon;[p]
they will see the glory[q] of the LORD, the splendor of our God. [r]

[3]Strengthen the feeble hands, steady the knees[s] that give way;
[4]say[t] to those with fearful hearts,[u] "Be strong, do not fear;[v]
your God will come,[w]
he will come with vengeance;[x]
with divine retribution
he will come to save[y] you."

[5]Then will the eyes of the blind be opened[z]
and the ears of the deaf[a] unstopped.
[6]Then will the lame[b] leap like a deer,[c]
and the mute tongue[d] shout for joy. [e]
Water will gush forth in the wilderness
and streams[f] in the desert.
[7]The burning sand will become a pool,
the thirsty ground[g] bubbling springs. [h]
In the haunts where jackals[i] once lay,

grass and reeds[j] and papyrus will grow.

[8]And a highway[k] will be there;
it will be called the Way of Holiness. [l]
The unclean[m] will not journey on it;
it will be for those who walk in that Way;
wicked fools will not go about on it. [x]
[9]No lion[n] will be there,
nor will any ferocious beast[o] get up on it;
they will not be found there.
But only the redeemed[p] will walk there,
[10] and the ransomed[q] of the LORD will return.
They will enter Zion with singing;[r]
everlasting joy[s] will crown their heads.
Gladness[t] and joy will overtake them,
and sorrow and sighing will flee away. [u]

Sennacherib Threatens Jerusalem

36:1–22pp — 2Ki 18:13,17–37; 2Ch 32:9-19

36 In the fourteenth year of King Hezekiah's[v] reign, Sennacherib[w] king of Assyria attacked all the fortified cities of Judah and captured them. [x] [2]Then the king of Assyria sent his field com-

34:17 [i]ver 10
35:1 [j]Isa 27:10; 32:15,16; 41:18-19
[k]Isa 27:6; 51:3
[l]SS 2:1
35:2 [m]S Ge 21:6; Ps 105:43; Isa 12:6; S 25:9; 44:23; 51:11; 52:9; 55:12
[n]S Ezr 3:7; S Isa 33:9 [o]SS 7:5
[p]S 1Ch 27:29; Isa 65:10
[q]S Ex 16:7; S Isa 4:5; S 59:19
[r]S Isa 25:9
35:3 [s]S Job 4:4; Heb 12:12
35:4 [t]2Ch 32:6; Isa 40:2; Zec 1:13
[u]S Dt 20:3; S Isa 21:4
[v]S Jos 1:9; S Isa 7:4; Da 10:19
[w]Isa 40:9,10-11; 51:5; 62:11; Rev 22:12
[x]S Isa 1:24; S 34:8 [y]S Isa 25:9
35:5 [z]S Ps 146:8; Jn 9:6-7; Ac 26:18
[a]Isa 29:18; 42:18; 50:4
35:6 [b]Mt 15:30; Lk 7:22; Jn 5:8-9; Ac 3:8
[c]S 2Sa 22:34
[d]Isa 32:4; Mt 9:32-33; 12:22; Mk 7:35; Lk 11:14 [e]Ps 20:5
[f]S Ex 17:6; Jn 7:38
35:7 [g]S Ps 68:6; Isa 41:17; 44:3; 55:1 [h]Ps 107:35; Isa 49:10; 58:11
[i]S Isa 13:22

[j]S Job 8:11; S 40:21
35:8 [k]S Isa 11:16; S 33:8; S Jer 31:21; Mt 7:13-14

[l]Isa 4:3; 1Pe 1:15 [m]Isa 52:1 **35:9** [n]S Isa 30:6 [o]Isa 11:6; 13:22; 34:14 [p]S Ex 6:6; Lev 25:47-55; Isa 51:11; 62:12; 63:4 **35:10** [q]S Job 19:25; S Isa 1:27 [r]Isa 30:29 [s]S Ps 4:7; S 126:5; S Isa 25:9 [t]S Ps 51:8; S Isa 51:3 [u]S Isa 30:19; Rev 7:17; 21:4 **36:1** [v]S 2Ki 18:9 [w]S 2Ch 32:1 [x]S Ps 109:11

[x]8 Or / the simple will not stray from it

35:1 *desert . . . will be glad.* The personification of nature is common in Isaiah (see 33:9; 44:23; 55:12). *wilderness.* The Arabah (see note on 33:9). *crocus.* See NIV text note on SS 2:1.
35:2 *rejoice . . . shout for joy.* See 54:1. *Lebanon . . . Carmel . . . Sharon.* Fertile areas renowned for their beautiful trees and foliage (see note on 33:9). *glory of the LORD.* In the great transformation just announced. See 6:3 and note.
35:4 *Be strong, do not fear.* Cf. God's words of encouragement to Joshua (see Jos 1:6–7,9,18. *God will come.* Similar language is used of the coming of the Messiah (see 62:11; cf. Rev 22:12). *vengeance . . . retribution.* See note on 34:8.
35:5 *eyes . . . ears.* See 29:18; 32:3; 42:7 and notes. Spiritual and physical healing are also linked together in Christ's ministry (see Mt 11:5).
35:6 *lame leap . . . mute tongue shout.* Signs of the Messianic age (see Mt 12:22; Ac 3:7–8). *Water . . . streams.* See 32:2 and note. Cf. God's provision of water in Ex 17:6; 2Ki 3:15–20.
35:7 *springs.* Cf. 41:18. *reeds and papyrus.* Plants that grow in marshes and lakes (cf. 19:6–7).
35:8 *highway.* A road built up to make travel easier (see 11:16; 40:3 and notes). *the Way of Holiness.* The way set apart for those who are holy; only the redeemed (v. 9) could use it. In ancient times, certain roads between temples were

open only to those who were ceremonially pure.
35:9 *lion . . . beast.* Sometimes wild animals made travel dangerous (see Dt 8:15; Jdg 14:5). *redeemed.* Those the Lord has delivered from bondage (cf. 1:27; 51:10; 62:12; Lev 25:47–48; Dt 7:8).
35:10 Repeated verbatim in 51:11. *enter Zion with singing.* As the Israelites did when they returned from Babylonian exile (see Ps 126). *overtake them.* They will be pursued, not by wild animals (v. 9) but by gladness and joy (cf. Ps 23:6). *sorrow . . . will flee.* Cf. 25:8; 65:19.
36:1–39:8 Much of chs. 36–39 is paralleled, sometimes verbatim, in 2Ki 18:13–20:19. The compiler of 2 Kings may have used Isa 36–39 as one of his sources, or both may have drawn on a common source. Chs. 36–37 describe the fulfillment of many predictions about Assyria's collapse, while chs. 38–39 point toward the Babylonian context of chs. 40–66.
36:1 *fourteenth year of . . . Hezekiah's reign.* The 14th year of his sole reign. Hezekiah ruled as sole king from 715 to 686 but was a co-regent from c. 729 (see note on 2Ki 18:1). *Sennacherib.* Reigned over Assyria from 705 to 681. *all the . . . cities.* In his annals Sennacherib lists 46 such cities (see note on 2Ki 18:13).
36:2 *large army.* Cf. 37:36. *Lachish.* An important city about 30 miles southwest of Jerusalem that guarded the main approach to Judah's capital from that quarter (see Jer 34:7).

mander with a large army from Lachish[y] to King Hezekiah at Jerusalem. When the commander stopped at the aqueduct of the Upper Pool, on the road to the Washerman's Field,[z] [3]Eliakim[a] son of Hilkiah the palace administrator,[b] Shebna[c] the secretary,[d] and Joah[e] son of Asaph the recorder[f] went out to him.

[4]The field commander said to them, "Tell Hezekiah,

" 'This is what the great king, the king of Assyria, says: On what are you basing this confidence of yours? [5]You say you have strategy and military strength—but you speak only empty words. On whom do you speak depending, that you rebel[g] against me? [6]Look now, you are depending[h] on Egypt,[i][j] that splintered reed[k] of a staff, which pierces a man's hand and wounds him if he leans on it! Such is Pharaoh king of Egypt to all who depend on him. [7]And if you say to me, "We are depending[l] on the LORD our God"—isn't he the one whose high places and altars Hezekiah removed,[m] saying to Judah and Jerusalem, "You must worship before this altar"? [n]

[8]" 'Come now, make a bargain with my master, the king of Assyria: I will give you two thousand horses[o]—if you can put riders on them! [9]How then can you repulse one officer of the least of my master's officials, even though you are depending on Egypt[p] for chariots[q] and horsemen?[r] [10]Furthermore, have I come to

attack and destroy this land without the LORD? The LORD himself told[s] me to march against this country and destroy it.' "

[11]Then Eliakim, Shebna and Joah[t] said to the field commander, "Please speak to your servants in Aramaic,[u] since we understand it. Don't speak to us in Hebrew in the hearing of the people on the wall."

[12]But the commander replied, "Was it only to your master and you that my master sent me to say these things, and not to the men sitting on the wall—who, like you, will have to eat their own filth and drink their own urine?[v] "

[13]Then the commander stood and called out in Hebrew,[w] "Hear the words of the great king, the king of Assyria![x] [14]This is what the king says: Do not let Hezekiah deceive[y] you. He cannot deliver you! [15]Do not let Hezekiah persuade you to trust in the LORD when he says, 'The LORD will surely deliver[z] us; this city will not be given into the hand of the king of Assyria.'[a]

[16]"Do not listen to Hezekiah. This is what the king of Assyria says: Make peace with me and come out to me. Then every one of you will eat from his own vine and fig tree[b] and drink water from his own cistern,[c] [17]until I come and take you to a land like your own[d]—a land of grain and new wine,[e] a land of bread and vineyards.

[18]"Do not let Hezekiah mislead you when he says, 'The LORD will deliver us.' Has the god of any nation ever delivered his land from the hand of the king of Assyria? [19]Where are the gods of Hamath and

36:2 [y]S Jos 10:3; [z]S Isa 7:3
36:3 [a]Isa 22:20, 20-21; 37:2 [b]S Ge 41:40 [c]S 2Ki 18:18 [d]S 2Sa 8:17 [e]ver 11 [f]S 2Sa 8:16
36:5 [g]S 2Ki 18:7
36:6 [h]S 2Ki 17:4; S Isa 8:12 [i]Eze 17:17 [j]S Isa 30:2,5 [k]Isa 42:3; 58:5; Eze 29:6-7
36:7 [l]Ps 22:8; Mt 27:43 [m]S 2Ki 18:4 [n]Dt 12:2-5; S 2Ch 31:1
36:8 [o]S Ps 20:7; S Isa 30:16
36:9 [p]S Isa 31:3 [q]Isa 37:24 [r]S Ps 20:7; Isa 30:2-5
36:10 [s]S 1Ki 13:18; Isa 10:5-7
36:11 [t]ver 3 [u]S Ezr 4:7
36:12 [v]2Ki 6:25; Eze 4:12
36:13 [w]S 2Ch 32:18 [x]Isa 37:4
36:14 [y]S 2Ch 32:15
36:15 [z]S Ps 3:2,7 [a]Isa 37:10
36:16 [b]S 1Ki 4:25 [c]Pr 5:15
36:17 [d]S 2Ki 15:29 [e]S Ge 27:28; S Dt 28:51

aqueduct . . . Field. See 7:3 and note; see also note on 2Ki 18:17.
36:3 *Eliakim.* See 22:20-21 and notes. *palace administrator.* In charge of the palace (see 22:15 and note). *Shebna.* See 22:15 and note. *secretary.* Perhaps equivalent to secretary of state (see Jer 36:12; see also note on 2Sa 8:17). *recorder.* An official position also associated elsewhere with "secretary" (see 1Ki 4:3). See also note on 2Sa 8:16.
36:4,13 *great king.* See note on 2Ki 18:19.
36:5 *rebel.* By refusing to pay the expected tribute (see 2Ki 17:4; 18:7).
36:6 *Egypt.* Hezekiah had been under pressure to make an alliance with Egypt since 715 B.C. or earlier (see 20:5; 30:1 and notes). *splintered reed.* Egypt is compared to a reed again in Eze 29:6-7. *Such is Pharaoh.* Cf. 30:3,7.
36:7 *high places and altars.* Hezekiah had destroyed these popular shrines often dedicated to Baal worship (see note on 2Ki 18:4; see also 2Ch 31:1). *this altar.* In Solomon's temple.
36:8 *two thousand horses.* A sizable number for any army. Horses and chariots were highly prized (see note on 30:16). *if you can put riders on them!* See note on 2Ki 18:23. *riders.* Probably charioteers, since cavalry was not employed by these nations this early (see v. 9).
36:10 *The LORD . . . told me.* The Lord had used Assyria to

punish Israel (see 10:5-6), but now it was Assyria's turn to be judged. Pharaoh Neco claimed God's approval on his mission according to 2Ch 35:21.
36:11 *Eliakim . . . Joah.* See v. 3 and note. *Aramaic.* The diplomatic language of that day (see note on 2Ki 18:26). *Don't speak . . . in Hebrew.* The officials feared that the commander's speech might damage the people's morale.
36:12 *eat . . . filth . . . drink . . . urine.* A crude way of describing the horrors of famine if Jerusalem was to be besieged (cf. 2Ki 6:25). Contrast v. 16.
36:14 *deceive you.* Cf. 37:10.
36:16 *own vine and fig tree.* Symbols of security and prosperity in the best of times (see 1Ki 4:25; Mic 4:4).
36:17 *come and take you.* The Assyrians deported rebellious peoples to reduce their will to revolt (see 2Ki 15:29; 17:6). *grain and new wine.* Two of the staples of Israel (cf. Dt 28:51; Hag 1:11).
36:18-20 The commander's words echo the boasts of the proud Assyrians in 10:8-11. See note on 2Ki 18:33-35.
36:19 *Hamath and Arpad.* See 10:9 and note. *Sepharvaim.* Probably located in northern Aram (Syria) not far from Hamath. Residents of Sepharvaim were deported to Samaria, though they still worshiped the gods Adrammelech and Anammelech. See 2Ki 17:24,31. *Samaria.* The Assyrians assumed that each people had its own gods and so did not

Arpad?[f] Where are the gods of Sepharvaim?[g] Have they rescued Samaria[h] from my hand? [20]Who of all the gods[i] of these countries has been able to save his land from me? How then can the LORD deliver Jerusalem from my hand?"[j]

[21]But the people remained silent and said nothing in reply, because the king had commanded, "Do not answer him."[k]

[22]Then Eliakim[l] son of Hilkiah the palace administrator, Shebna the secretary, and Joah son of Asaph the recorder[m] went to Hezekiah, with their clothes torn,[n] and told him what the field commander had said.

Jerusalem's Deliverance Foretold

37:1–13pp — 2Ki 19:1–13

37 When King Hezekiah heard this, he tore his clothes[o] and put on sackcloth[p] and went into the temple[q] of the LORD. [2]He sent Eliakim[r] the palace administrator, Shebna[s] the secretary, and the leading priests, all wearing sackcloth, to the prophet Isaiah son of Amoz.[t] [3]They told him, "This is what Hezekiah says: This day is a day of distress[u] and rebuke and disgrace, as when children come to the point of birth[v] and there is no strength to deliver them. [4]It may be that the LORD your God will hear the words of the field commander, whom his master, the king of Assyria, has sent to ridicule[w] the living God,[x] and that he will rebuke him for the words the LORD your God has heard.[y] Therefore pray[z] for the remnant[a] that still survives."

[5]When King Hezekiah's officials came to Isaiah, [6]Isaiah said to them, "Tell your master, 'This is what the LORD says: Do not be afraid[b] of what you have heard—those words with which the underlings of the king of Assyria have blasphemed[c] me. [7]Listen! I am going to put a spirit[d] in him so that when he hears a certain report,[e] he will return to his own country, and there I will have him cut down[f] with the sword.' "

[8]When the field commander heard that the king of Assyria had left Lachish,[g] he withdrew and found the king fighting against Libnah.[h]

[9]Now Sennacherib[i] received a report[j] that Tirhakah, the Cushite[y][k] king of Egypt, was marching out to fight against him. When he heard it, he sent messengers to Hezekiah with this word: [10]"Say to Hezekiah king of Judah: Do not let the god you depend on deceive[l] you when he says, 'Jerusalem will not be handed over to the king of Assyria.' [m] [11]Surely you have heard what the kings of Assyria have done to all the countries, destroying them completely. And will you be delivered?[n] [12]Did the gods of the nations that were destroyed by my forefathers[o] deliver them—the gods of Gozan, Haran,[p] Rezeph and the people of Eden[q] who were in Tel Assar? [13]Where is the king of Hamath, the king of Arpad,[r] the king of the city of Sepharvaim,[s] or of Hena or Ivvah?"[t]

Hezekiah's Prayer

37:14–20pp — 2Ki 19:14–19

[14]Hezekiah received the letter[u] from the messengers and read it. Then he went

Cross references

36:19
/S 2Ki 18:34
gS 2Ki 17:24
hS 2Ki 15:29
36:20
/S 1Ki 20:23
/Ex 5:2;
2Ch 25:15;
Isa 10:8-11;
37:10-13,18-20;
40:18; Da 3:15
36:21 kPr 9:7-8;
S 26:4
36:22
/S 2Ki 18:18
mS 2Sa 8:16
nS Ge 37:29;
S 2Ch 34:19
37:1
oS Ge 37:29;
S 2Ch 34:19
pS Ge 37:34
qS ver 14;
S 1Ki 8:33;
Mt 21:13
37:2
rS 2Ki 18:18;
S Isa 36:3
sS 2Ki 18:18 tver
21; Isa 1:1;
S 13:1; 38:1
37:3 uS Jdg 6:2;
S Isa 5:30
vIsa 26:18; 66:9;
Hos 13:13
37:4 wver 23-24;
S 2Ch 32:17
xS Jos 3:10
yIsa 36:13,18-20
zS 1Sa 7:8
aS Isa 1:9;
Am 7:2

37:6 bS Jos 1:9;
S Isa 7:4
cS Nu 15:30
37:7 d1Ch 5:26
ever 9 /S Isa 31:8
37:8 gS Jos 10:3
hS Nu 33:20
37:9 iS 2Ch 32:1
/ver 7 kS Isa 20:3
37:10
/2Ch 32:11,15
mIsa 36:15
37:11
nIsa 36:18-20
37:12 oS 2Ki 18:11
pGe 11:31;
12:1-4; Ac 7:2
qEze 27:23;
Am 1:5

37:13 rIsa 10:9 sS 2Ki 17:24 tS Isa 36:20 37:14 u2Ch 32:17

y 9 That is, from the upper Nile region

Study notes

associate the God of Judah with that of Samaria.
36:21 *people remained silent.* The Assyrians had hoped that the masterful psychology of vv. 4–20 would produce panic.
36:22 See v. 3 and note. *clothes torn.* See note on 2Ki 18:37.
37:1 *clothes . . . sackcloth.* See Ge 37:34 and note; see also note on 2Ki 18:37. *temple.* Designated as a place of prayer by Solomon (see 1Ki 8:33). The Assyrian references to Hezekiah's dependence on the Lord (36:7,15,18) were true.
37:2 *Eliakim . . . Shebna.* See note on 36:3. *leading priests.* See note on 2Ki 19:2. *Isaiah son of Amoz.* See note on 1:1. Prophet, priests and king join in supplication.
37:3 *day of distress.* See 5:30; 26:16; 33:2 and notes. *point of birth.* An even more vivid description than that of childbirth (see 13:8 and note).
37:4 *ridicule.* The Hebrew is translated "insult" in vv. 17,23–24. *pray.* See note on 2Ki 19:4. *remnant.* Jerusalem was left almost alone (see 36:1 and notes on 1:9; 2Ki 19:4; see also 10:20–22).
37:6 *Do not be afraid.* Cf. 7:4; see 35:4 and note.
37:7 *spirit.* Perhaps a compulsion or a disposition (cf. 1Ch 5:26). *report.* See note on 2Ki 19:7. *return . . . cut down*

with the sword. See vv. 37–38.
37:8 *Lachish.* See note on 36:2. *Libnah.* See note on 2Ki 8:22; see also Jos 10:31.
37:9 *Tirhakah, the Cushite king.* In 701 B.C. he was actually a prince (the brother of the new pharaoh Shebitku, who sent him with an army to help Hezekiah withstand the Assyrian invasion); he did not become king until 690. But this part of Isaiah was not written before 681 (see note on v. 38), so it was natural to speak of Tirhakah as king. See 18:1 and note.
37:10 *god . . . deceive.* See 36:14–15,18. The message of vv. 10–13 is similar to that of 36:18–20 (see note there).
37:12 *Gozan.* A city in northern Mesopotamia to which some of the Israelites had been deported by the Assyrians (see 2Ki 17:6). *Haran.* A city west of Gozan where Abraham lived for a number of years (see Ge 11:31 and note). *Rezeph.* A city between Haran and the Euphrates River. *Eden.* The state of Bit Adini, located between the Euphrates and Balikh rivers (see note on 2Ki 19:12).
37:13 *Hamath . . . Arpad.* See 10:9 and note. *Sepharvaim.* See 36:19 and note.
37:14 *temple.* See v. 1 and note. *spread it out.* Contrast the hypocritical spreading out of hands to pray in 1:15.

up to the temple^v of the LORD and spread it out before the LORD. ^{15}And Hezekiah prayed^w to the LORD: ^{16}"O LORD Almighty, God of Israel, enthroned^x between the cherubim,^{y} you alone are God^z over all the kingdoms^a of the earth. You have made heaven and earth. ^{b} ^{17}Give ear, O LORD, and hear; ^{c} open your eyes, O LORD, and see; ^{d} listen to all the words Sennacherib^e has sent to insult^f the living God.^{g}

^{18}"It is true, O LORD, that the Assyrian kings have laid waste all these peoples and their lands. ^{h} ^{19}They have thrown their gods into the fire^i and destroyed them,^{j} for they were not gods^k but only wood and stone, fashioned by human hands.^{l} ^{20}Now, O LORD our God, deliver^m us from his hand, so that all kingdoms on earth^n may know that you alone, O LORD, are God.^{z} ^{o}"

Sennacherib's Fall

37:21–38pp — 2Ki 19:20–37; 2Ch 32:20–21

^{21}Then Isaiah son of Amoz^p sent a message to Hezekiah: "This is what the LORD, the God of Israel, says: Because you have prayed to me concerning Sennacherib king of Assyria, ^{22}this is the word the LORD has spoken against him:

"The Virgin Daughter^q of Zion^r
　　despises and mocks you.
The Daughter of Jerusalem
　　tosses her head^s as you flee.
^{23}Who is it you have insulted and
　　blasphemed?^{t}
　Against whom have you raised your
　　voice^u
and lifted your eyes in pride?^{v}
　Against the Holy One^w of Israel!
^{24}By your messengers
　you have heaped insults on the Lord.
And you have said,
　'With my many chariots^x

I have ascended the heights of the
　　mountains,
　the utmost heights^y of Lebanon. ^{z}
I have cut down its tallest cedars,
　the choicest of its pines. ^{a}
I have reached its remotest heights,
　the finest of its forests.
^{25}I have dug wells in foreign lands^a
　and drunk the water there.
With the soles of my feet
　I have dried up^b all the streams of
　　Egypt. ^{c}'

^{26}"Have you not heard?
　Long ago I ordained^d it.
In days of old I planned^e it;
　now I have brought it to pass,
that you have turned fortified cities
　into piles of stone.^{f}
^{27}Their people, drained of power,
　are dismayed and put to shame.
They are like plants in the field,
　like tender green shoots,
like grass^g sprouting on the roof, ^{h}
　scorched^b before it grows up.

^{28}"But I know where you stay
　and when you come and go^i
　and how you rage^j against me.
^{29}Because you rage against me
　and because your insolence^k has
　　reached my ears,
I will put my hook^l in your nose^m
　and my bit in your mouth,
and I will make you return
　by the way you came. ^{n}

Cross references

37:14 ^{v}ver 1,38; S 1Ki 8:33
37:15 ^{w}S 2Ch 32:20
37:16 ^{x}S Ps 2:4; ^{y}S Ge 3:24; ^{z}Dt 10:17; S Ps 46:10; 80:10; 136:2-3; ^{a}Da 4:34; ^{b}S Ge 1:1;
37:17 S Isa 11:12; 41:9; 43:6; Ac 4:24; ^{c}S 1Ki 8:29; S 2Ch 6:40; ^{d}Jer 25:29; Da 9:18; ^{e}S 2Ch 32:1; ^{f}S 2Ch 32:17; ^{g}S Jos 3:10
37:18 ^{h}S 2Ki 15:29; Na 2:11-12
37:19 ^{i}S Jos 7:15 /Isa 26:14; 36:20; ^{k}2Ch 13:9; Isa 40:17; 41:24, 29; Jer 2:11; 5:7; 16:20; Gal 4:8; ^{l}S 2Ch 32:19; S Ps 135:15; Isa 40:18-20; 44:9-11
37:20 ^{m}S Ps 3:2, 7; S Pr 20:22 ^{n}S Jos 4:24 ^{o}S 1Sa 17:46; S Ps 46:10
37:21 ^{p}S ver 2
37:22 ^{q}S Isa 23:12 ^{r}S Isa 10:32 ^{s}S Job 16:4
37:23 ^{t}ver 4; S Nu 15:30; Isa 52:5; Eze 36:20,23; Da 7:25 ^{u}S Job 15:25 ^{v}S Isa 2:11 ^{w}S Isa 1:4; S 12:6
37:24 ^{x}Isa 36:9

^{y}Isa 14:13 ^{z}S 1Ki 7:2; S Isa 14:8; S 33:9 ^{a}1Ki 5:8-10; Isa 41:19; 55:13; 60:13; Hos 14:8
37:25 ^{b}S Isa 19:6; 44:27 ^{c}S Dt 11:10; S Isa 10:14; Da 4:30
37:26 ^{d}Ac 2:23; 4:27-28; 1Pe 2:8 ^{e}Isa 10:6; S 25:1 ^{f}S Dt 13:16; S Isa 25:2
37:27 ^{g}S Isa 15:6 ^{h}Ps 129:6 37:28 ^{i}Ps 139:1-3 ^{j}Ps 2:1
37:29 ^{k}Isa 10:12 ^{l}S 2Ch 33:11 ^{m}S Job 40:24 ^{n}ver 34

^{z}20 Dead Sea Scrolls (see also 2 Kings 19:19); Masoretic Text alone are the LORD ^{a}25 Dead Sea Scrolls (see also 2 Kings 19:24); Masoretic Text does not have in foreign lands. ^{b}27 Some manuscripts of the Masoretic Text, Dead Sea Scrolls and some Septuagint manuscripts (see also 2 Kings 19:26); most manuscripts of the Masoretic Text roofs / and terraced fields

---

37:16 LORD Almighty. See 13:4 and note. enthroned . . . cherubim. See note on 1Sa 4:4. all the kingdoms. Cf. 40:17. made heaven and earth. The role of God as Creator is emphasized also in 40:26,28; 42:5; 45:12.

37:17 Give ear . . . open your eyes. Cf. Solomon's prayer in 1Ki 8:52; 2Ch 6:40. insult the living God. See v. 4 and note.

37:19 not gods. See 36:19 and note. wood and stone. Cf. 2:8; 44:9–20.

37:20 you alone . . . are God. Cf. 43:11; 45:18,21–22.

37:22 Virgin Daughter of Zion. A personification of Jerusalem and its inhabitants. tosses her head. A gesture of mocking (see Ps 22:7; 44:14).

37:23 lifted . . . in pride. Assyria's great pride had been condemned earlier (see 10:12 and note). Holy One of Israel. A designation of the God of Israel characteristic of Isaiah (see 1:4 and note).

37:24 many chariots. See 36:8 and note. ascended the heights. Cf. the words of the king of Babylon in 14:13–14. Lebanon. See 33:9; 35:2 and notes. cut down . . . cedars. For many centuries the kings of Mesopotamia had used the cedars of Lebanon in their royal buildings (cf. 1Ki 5:8–10).

37:25 dug wells. Desert lands could not stop him. dried up all the streams. The branches of the Nile were no obstacle either. This boast was almost a claim to deity. See 11:15; 44:27 and notes.

37:26 Cf. 40:21. cities into piles of stone. Assyria had been God's tool of judgment against the nations (see 10:5–6).

37:27 See 40:6–8; Ps 37:1–2. grass . . . on the roof. Roofs in the Near East were flat.

37:29 hook in your nose. The Assyrians often led away captives by tying ropes to rings placed in their noses (see note on 2Ki 19:28). bit. Cf. 30:28.

30"This will be the sign[o] for you, O Hezekiah:

"This year[p] you will eat what grows by itself,
and the second year what springs from that.
But in the third year[q] sow and reap,
plant vineyards[r] and eat their fruit.[s]
31Once more a remnant of the house of Judah
will take root[t] below and bear fruit[u] above.
32For out of Jerusalem will come a remnant,[v]
and out of Mount Zion a band of survivors.[w]
The zeal[x] of the LORD Almighty will accomplish this.

33"Therefore this is what the LORD says concerning the king of Assyria:

"He will not enter this city[y]
or shoot an arrow here.
He will not come before it with shield
or build a siege ramp[z] against it.
34By the way that he came he will return;[a]
he will not enter this city,"
declares the LORD.
35"I will defend[b] this city and save it,
for my sake[c] and for the sake of David[d] my servant!'"

36Then the angel[e] of the LORD went out and put to death[f] a hundred and eighty-five thousand men in the Assyrian[g] camp. When the people got up the next morning—there were all the dead bodies! 37So Sennacherib[h] king of Assyria broke camp and withdrew. He returned to Nineveh[i] and stayed there.

38One day, while he was worshiping in the temple[j] of his god Nisroch, his sons Adrammelech and Sharezer cut him down with the sword, and they escaped to the land of Ararat.[k] And Esarhaddon[l] his son succeeded him as king.[m]

Hezekiah's Illness

38:1–8pp — 2Ki 20:1–11; 2Ch 32:24–26

38 In those days Hezekiah became ill and was at the point of death. The prophet Isaiah son of Amoz[n] went to him and said, "This is what the LORD says: Put your house in order,[o] because you are going to die; you will not recover."[p]

2Hezekiah turned his face to the wall and prayed to the LORD, 3"Remember, O LORD, how I have walked[q] before you faithfully and with wholehearted devotion[r] and have done what is good in your eyes.[s]" And Hezekiah wept[t] bitterly.

4Then the word[u] of the LORD came to Isaiah: 5"Go and tell Hezekiah, 'This is what the LORD, the God of your father David,[v] says: I have heard your prayer and seen your tears;[w] I will add fifteen years[x] to your life. 6And I will deliver you and this city from the hand of the king of Assyria. I will defend[y] this city.

7"'This is the LORD's sign[z] to you that the LORD will do what he has promised: 8I will make the shadow cast by the sun go back the ten steps it has gone down on the stairway of Ahaz.'" So the sunlight went back the ten steps it had gone down.[a]

9A writing of Hezekiah king of Judah after his illness and recovery:

10I said, "In the prime of my life[b]

37:30 oS Isa 20:3
pIsa 32:10
qS Isa 16:14
rS Lev 25:4
sPs 107:37;
Isa 30:23; 65:21;
Jer 31:5
37:31 tIsa 11:10
uS Isa 27:6
37:32
vS Isa 11:11
wS Isa 1:9
xS Isa 9:7
37:33
yS Isa 32:18
zS 2Sa 20:15
37:34 aver 29
37:35 bS Isa 31:5
cIsa 43:25; 48:9,
11; Eze 36:21-22
dS 1Ch 17:19
37:36
eS Ex 12:23
fS Ex 12:12
gS Isa 10:12
37:37
hS 2Ch 32:1
iS Ge 10:11;
S Na 1:1

37:38 jS ver 14
kGe 8:4;
Jer 51:27
lS 2Ki 17:24
mS Isa 9:4;
10:26; S 14:25
38:1 nS Isa 37:2
o2Sa 17:23
p2Ki 8:10
38:3 qPs 26:3
rS 1Ki 8:61;
S 1Ch 29:19
sS Dt 6:18;
S 10:20 tPs 6:8
38:4 uS 1Sa 13:13;
Isa 39:5
38:5 v2Ki 18:3
wPs 6:6
xS 2Ki 18:2
38:6 yS Isa 31:5
38:7
zS Ge 24:14;
S 2Ch 32:31;
Isa 7:11,14;
S 20:3
38:8 aJos 10:13
38:10 bPs 102:24

37:30 *sign.* See 7:11,14 and notes. *what grows by itself.* See note on 2Ki 19:29. *second . . . third year.* See note on 2Ki 19:29. Probably the second year was to begin shortly, so the total time was less than 36 months. Another three-year sign was given in 20:3. *plant vineyards and eat.* The response to Assyria's proposal in 36:16 (see note there).
37:31–32 *remnant.* See notes on v. 4; 1:9; 2Ki 19:4, 30–31.
37:31 *take root . . . bear fruit.* See 4:2; 11:1,10; 27:6 and notes.
37:32 *The zeal . . . this.* See 9:7 and note.
37:33 *siege ramp.* To help the invaders bring up battering rams and scale the walls (see 2Sa 20:15).
37:35 *sake of David.* God had promised David an enduring throne in Jerusalem (see 9:7; 55:3; 2Sa 7:16).
37:36 *angel of the LORD . . . put to death.* Cf. the striking down of the firstborn in Egypt (Ex 12:12) and the angel's sword poised against Jerusalem (2Sa 24:16). The Greek historian Herodotus attributed this destruction to a bubonic plague. The death of these soldiers fulfills the prophecies of 10:33–34; 30:31; 31:8.

37:37 *Nineveh.* The capital of Assyria. See Jnh 1:2.
37:38 *in the temple.* Hezekiah had gone to the Lord's temple and gained strength (vv. 1,14). Twenty years later (681 B.C.) Sennacherib went to the temple of his god and was killed. *Ararat.* Urartu, north of Assyria in Armenia (see note on Ge 8:4). *Esarhaddon.* Reigned 681–669. See Ezr 4:2.
38:1 *In those days.* Sometime before Sennacherib's invasion of 701 B.C. (see v. 6). *Isaiah.* He is prominent in this historical interlude (chs. 36–39). *Put your house in order.* See note on 2Ki 20:1. *you are going to die.* Elisha similarly predicted the death of Ben-Hadad (2Ki 8:9–10). See note on 2Ki 20:1.
38:2 *wall.* Perhaps of the nearby temple. *prayed.* Hezekiah apparently had no son and successor to the throne yet (cf. 39:7; 2Ki 21:1).
38:3 *wholehearted devotion.* Like David (1Ki 11:4), Hezekiah was truly faithful (see 36:7; 2Ki 18:3–5).
38:6 *deliver . . . this city.* See 31:5; 37:35.
38:7 *sign.* See 7:11,14 and notes.
38:8 *sunlight went back.* Perhaps the miracle involved the refraction of light. See 2Ki 20:9–11; Jos 10:12–14.

must I go through the gates of
death[c c]
and be robbed of the rest of my
years?[d]"
[11]I said, "I will not again see the LORD,
the LORD,[e] in the land of the living;[f]
no longer will I look on mankind,
or be with those who now dwell in
this world.[d]
[12]Like a shepherd's tent[g] my house
has been pulled down[h] and taken
from me.
Like a weaver I have rolled[i] up my life,
and he has cut me off from the
loom;[j]
day and night[k] you made an end of
me.
[13]I waited patiently[l] till dawn,
but like a lion he broke[m] all my
bones;[n]
day and night[o] you made an end of
me.
[14]I cried like a swift or thrush,
I moaned like a mourning dove.[p]
My eyes grew weak[q] as I looked to the
heavens.
I am troubled; O Lord, come to my
aid!"[r]

[15]But what can I say?[s]
He has spoken to me, and he himself
has done this.[t]
I will walk humbly[u] all my years
because of this anguish of my soul.[v]
[16]Lord, by such things men live;
and my spirit finds life in them too.
You restored me to health
and let me live.[w]
[17]Surely it was for my benefit[x]

that I suffered such anguish.[y]
In your love you kept me
from the pit[z] of destruction;
you have put all my sins[a]
behind your back.[b]
[18]For the grave[c c] cannot praise you,
death cannot sing your praise;[d]
those who go down to the pit[e]
cannot hope for your faithfulness.
[19]The living, the living—they praise[f]
you,
as I am doing today;
fathers tell their children[g]
about your faithfulness.

[20]The LORD will save me,
and we will sing[h] with stringed
instruments[i]
all the days of our lives[j]
in the temple[k] of the LORD.

[21]Isaiah had said, "Prepare a poultice of
figs and apply it to the boil, and he will
recover."
[22]Hezekiah had asked, "What will be
the sign[l] that I will go up to the temple of
the LORD?"

Envoys From Babylon

39:1–8pp — 2Ki 20:12–19

39 At that time Merodach-Baladan
son of Baladan king of Babylon[m]
sent Hezekiah letters and a gift, because he
had heard of his illness and recovery.
[2]Hezekiah received the envoys[n] gladly and

Cross-references

38:10
cS Job 17:16;
Ps 107:18;
2Co 1:9
dS Job 17:11
38:11 eS Isa 12:2
fS Job 28:13;
S Ps 116:9
38:12 gIsa 33:20;
2Co 5:1,4;
2Pe 1:13-14
hS Job 4:21
iS Isa 34:4;
Heb 1:12
jS Nu 11:15;
S Job 7:6;
S Ps 31:22 kver
13; Ps 32:4;
73:14
38:13 lS Ps 37:7
mS Job 9:17;
Ps 51:8
nS Job 10:16;
Jer 34:17; La 3:4;
Da 6:24 oS ver 12
38:14 pS Ge 8:8;
S Isa 59:11
qS Ps 6:7
rS Ge 50:24;
S Job 17:3
38:15 s2Sa 7:20
tS Ps 39:9
u1Ki 21:27
vS Job 7:11
38:16
wPs 119:25;
Heb 12:9
38:17 xRo 8:28;
Heb 12:11

yS Job 7:11;
Ps 119:71,75
zS Job 17:16;
S Ps 30:3
aPs 103:3;
Jer 31:34
bS Ps 103:12;
Isa 43:25;
Mic 7:19
38:18
cS Nu 16:30;
S Ecc 9:10
dPs 6:5;
88:10-11; 115:17
eS Ps 30:9
38:19
fPs 118:17;
119:175
gS Dt 11:19
38:20 hPs 68:25
iS Ps 33:2; S 45:8

jPs 23:6; S 63:4; 116:2 kPs 116:17-19 **38:22** lS 2Ch 32:31
39:1 mS 2Ch 32:31 **39:2** n2Ch 32:31

c10,18 Hebrew *Sheol*   d11 A few Hebrew
manuscripts; most Hebrew manuscripts *in the place of
cessation*

38:10–20 A hymn of thanksgiving in two stanzas, similar
to many of the psalms. Hezekiah was deeply interested in the
psalms of David and Asaph (see 2Ch 29:30).
38:10–14 Hezekiah voices his complaint.
38:11 *the LORD, the LORD.* See 26:4. *land of the living.* Cf.
Ps 27:13.
38:12 *rolled up my life.* Cf. the rolling up of the sky like a
scroll in 34:4 (see also Heb 1:12).
38:13 *broke all my bones.* Physical or spiritual distress is
often described in terms of aching or broken bones (see Ps
6:2; 32:3).
38:15–20 Hezekiah offers praise for God's healing.
38:15 *what can I say?* See 2Sa 7:20. Hezekiah wonders
how he can praise God.
38:16 *by such things.* Perhaps referring to God's promises
and gracious acts, though his gracious acts can include such
experiences as sickness and peril.
38:17 *pit of destruction.* The grave (see Ps 55:23). *all my
sins.* Physical and spiritual healing are sometimes linked
together (see 53:4–5). *sins behind your back.* God not only
puts our sins out of sight; he also puts them out of reach (Mic
7:19; Ps 103:12), out of mind (Jer 31:34) and out of existence (Isa 43:25; 44:22; Ps 51:1,9; Ac 3:19).
38:18 *cannot hope.* Knowledge about the afterlife was

limited in the OT period, but the gospel of Christ has
"brought . . . immortality to light" (2Ti 1:10).
38:20 *sing with stringed instruments.* Instrumental music
and hymns of praise were closely linked in worship (cf. Ps
33:1–3). *all . . . our lives in the temple.* Hezekiah, like David
(Ps 23:6), loved God's house.
38:21 *Prepare . . . apply.* The verbs are plural (probably
addressed to the court physicians). *poultice of figs.* Figs were
used for medicinal purposes in ancient Ugarit. *he will recover.* Contrast v. 1. God answered Hezekiah's prayer for healing (see v. 5).
38:22 *sign.* Perhaps the healing of the boil (see v. 21).
39:1 *Merodach-Baladan.* Reigned 721–710 B.C. and again
later (see note on 2Ki 20:12). *Babylon.* See note on 13:1.
sent . . . letters and a gift. Merodach-Baladan probably
wanted Hezekiah's support in a campaign against Assyria.
During his career, he organized several revolts against his
hated neighbors. See note on 2Ki 20:12.
39:2 *silver . . . gold . . . treasures.* See 2Ch 32:27–29,31.
Probably Hezekiah was seeking help from the Babylonians
against the Assyrian threat (see note on 2Ki 20:13). But the
information gained during this ill-advised tour escorted by
Hezekiah would be valuable to Merodach-Baladan's powerful successors (vv. 5–7).

showed them what was in his store-houses—the silver, the gold, *o* the spices, the fine oil, his entire armory and everything found among his treasures. *p* There was nothing in his palace or in all his kingdom that Hezekiah did not show them.

3Then Isaiah the prophet went to King Hezekiah and asked, "What did those men say, and where did they come from?"

"From a distant land, *q*" Hezekiah replied. "They came to me from Babylon."

4The prophet asked, "What did they see in your palace?"

"They saw everything in my palace," Hezekiah said. "There is nothing among my treasures that I did not show them."

5Then Isaiah said to Hezekiah, "Hear the word *r* of the LORD Almighty: 6The time will surely come when everything in your palace, and all that your fathers have stored up until this day, will be carried off to Babylon. *s* Nothing will be left, says the LORD. 7And some of your descendants, your own flesh and blood who will be born to you, will be taken away, and they will become eunuchs in the palace of the king of Babylon. *t* "

8"The word of the LORD you have spoken is good, *u*" Hezekiah replied. For he thought, "There will be peace and security in my lifetime. *v* "

Comfort for God's People

40 Comfort, comfort *w* my people, says your God.
2Speak tenderly *x* to Jerusalem,
    and proclaim to her
    that her hard service *y* has been
            completed, *z*
    that her sin has been paid for, *a*
    that she has received from the LORD's
            hand
    double *b* for all her sins.

3A voice of one calling:
    "In the desert prepare
        the way *c* for the LORD *e* ;
    make straight *d* in the wilderness
        a highway for our God. *f e*
4Every valley shall be raised up, *f*
    every mountain and hill *g* made low;
    the rough ground shall become level, *h*
        the rugged places a plain.
5And the glory *i* of the LORD will be
            revealed,
    and all mankind together will see it. *j*
        For the mouth of the LORD
                    has spoken." *k*

6A voice says, "Cry out."
    And I said, "What shall I cry?"

"All men are like grass, *l*
    and all their glory is like the flowers
        of the field.

Cross-references column:

39:2
*o*S 2Ki 18:15
*p*2Ch 32:27-29
39:3 *q*S Dt 28:49
39:5 *r*S Isa 38:4
39:6 *s*S Jdg 6:4;
S 2Ki 24:13
39:7
*t*S 2Ki 24:15;
Da 1:1-7
39:8
*u*S Jdg 10:15;
Job 1:21; Ps 39:9
*v*S 2Ch 32:26

40:1 *w*Isa 12:1;
49:13; 51:3,12;
52:9; 57:18;
61:2; 66:13;
Jer 31:13;
Zep 3:14-17;
Zec 1:17; 2Co 1:3
40:2 *x*S Ge 34:3;
S Isa 35:4
*y*S Job 7:1
*z*Isa 41:11-13;
49:25
*a*S Lev 26:41
*b*Isa 51:19; 61:7;
Jer 16:18; 17:18;
Zec 9:12;
Rev 18:6
40:3
*c*S Isa 11:16;
43:19; Mal 3:1
*d*S Pr 3:5-6
*e*Mt 3:3*;
Mk 1:3*;
Jn 1:23*
40:4 *f*Isa 49:11
*g*S Isa 2:14
*h*S Ps 26:12;
S Isa 26:7; 45:2,
13; Jer 31:9
40:5 *i*S Ex 16:7;
S Isa 59:19
*j*Isa 52:10; 62:2;
Lk 2:30; 3:4-6*
*k*S Isa 1:20; 58:14
40:6 *l*S Ge 6:3;
S Isa 29:5

*e*3 Or *A voice of one calling in the desert: / "Prepare the way for the LORD*   *f*3 Hebrew; Septuagint *make straight the paths of our God*

39:3 *Isaiah the prophet.* Earlier God had sent Isaiah to confront Ahaz (7:3); cf. also Nathan's rebuke of David (2Sa 12:1,7).
39:5 *word of the LORD.* Contrast the word of hope in 38:4-6.
39:6 *carried off to Babylon.* The first mention of Babylon as Jerusalem's conqueror, though 14:3-4 implied the Babylonian captivity. The wickedness of Hezekiah's son Manasseh was a major cause of the captivity (see 2Ki 21:11-15). See also note on 2Ki 20:17.
39:7 *your descendants.* Such as King Jehoiachin (2Ki 24:15). *eunuchs.* Cf. Da 1:3-6, where the Hebrew for "court officials" (Da 1:3) can also be translated "eunuchs." *king of Babylon.* Nebuchadnezzar.
39:8 *word . . . is good.* See note on 2Ki 20:19. *peace . . . in my lifetime.* See 2Ki 22:20. "Peace" recurs in a refrain in 48:22; 57:21, dividing the last 27 chapters into 3 sections of 9 chapters each (40-48; 49-57; 58-66).
40:1—66:24 In chs. 1-35 Isaiah prophesied against the backdrop of the Assyrian threat against Judah and Jerusalem, in chs. 36-39 he recorded Assyria's failure and warned about the future rise of Babylon, and in chs. 40-66 he wrote as if the Babylonian exile of Judah was almost over.
40:1 *Comfort, comfort.* Repeated for emphasis ("Comfort greatly"). The double imperative is found also in 51:9,17; 52:1,11; 57:14; 62:10.
40:2 *Speak tenderly.* The Hebrew for this phrase is used also in 2Ch 32:6, where Hezekiah "encouraged" Judah to trust in God in spite of the Assyrian invasion. *hard service.*

The exile in Babylon (cf. Ps 137:1-6; La 1:1-2,9,16-17, 21). *sin . . . paid for.* By enduring the punishment of captivity (see Lev 26:41). *double.* Full (or enough) punishment. Cf. the "double calamities" of 51:19.
40:3 *voice.* Three voices are mentioned (vv. 3,6,9), each showing how the comfort of v. 1 will come about. The NT links the voice of v. 3 with John the Baptist in Mt 3:3; Mk 1:3; Lk 3:4; Jn 1:23. *prepare the way.* Clear obstacles out of the road (cf. 57:14; 62:10). The language of vv. 3-4 has in view the ancient Near Eastern custom of sending representatives ahead to prepare the way for the visit of a monarch. The picture is that of preparing a processional highway for the Lord's coming to Jerusalem. In Mt 3:1-8 John declares that repentance is necessary to prepare the way for Christ. *make straight . . . a highway.* See 11:16; 35:8 and notes.
40:4 *rough ground . . . level.* See 26:7 and note.
40:5 *glory . . . revealed.* God would redeem Israel from Babylon (see 35:2 and note; 44:23), and all the nations would see the deliverance (52:10; cf. Lk 3:6). Ultimately the glory of the redeeming God would be seen in Jesus Christ (Jn 1:14; 11:4,40; 17:4; Heb 1:3), especially at his return (Mt 16:27; 24:30; 25:31; Rev 1:7)—but also in the redeemed (see 1Co 10:31; 2Co 3:18; Eph 3:21). See also Isa 6:3 and note.
40:6,8 Quoted in part in 1Pe 1:24-25.
40:6 *like grass.* See 37:27 and note; 51:12. *all their glory . . . field.* Even the power of Assyria and Babylon would soon vanish.

7The grass withers[m] and the flowers fall,
  because the breath[n] of the LORD
    blows[o] on them.
  Surely the people are grass.
8The grass withers and the flowers[p] fall,
  but the word[q] of our God stands[r]
    forever.[s]"

9You who bring good tidings[t] to Zion,
  go up on a high mountain.
You who bring good tidings to
    Jerusalem,[g][u]
  lift up your voice with a shout,
lift it up, do not be afraid;
  say to the towns of Judah,
    "Here is your God!"[v]
10See, the Sovereign LORD comes[w] with
    power,[x]
  and his arm[y] rules[z] for him.
See, his reward[a] is with him,
  and his recompense accompanies
    him.
11He tends his flock like a shepherd:[b]
  He gathers the lambs in his arms[c]
and carries them close to his heart;[d]
  he gently leads[e] those that have
    young.[f]

12Who has measured the waters[g] in the
    hollow of his hand,[h]
  or with the breadth of his hand
    marked off the heavens?[i]
Who has held the dust of the earth in a
    basket,
  or weighed the mountains on the
    scales
  and the hills in a balance?[j]
13Who has understood the mind[h][k] of the
    LORD,
  or instructed him as his counselor?[l]
14Whom did the LORD consult to
    enlighten him,

and who taught him the right way?
Who was it that taught him
    knowledge[m]
  or showed him the path of
    understanding?[n]

15Surely the nations are like a drop in a
    bucket;
  they are regarded as dust on the
    scales;[o]
he weighs the islands as though they
    were fine dust.[p]
16Lebanon[q] is not sufficient for altar fires,
  nor its animals[r] enough for burnt
    offerings.
17Before him all the nations[s] are as
    nothing;[t]
  they are regarded by him as worthless
    and less than nothing.[u]

18To whom, then, will you compare
    God?[v]
  What image[w] will you compare him
    to?
19As for an idol,[x] a craftsman casts it,
  and a goldsmith[y] overlays it with
    gold[z]
  and fashions silver chains for it.
20A man too poor to present such an
    offering
  selects wood[a] that will not rot.
  He looks for a skilled craftsman
    to set up an idol[b] that will not
    topple.[c]

Cross-references (center column):

40:7 mS Job 8:12;
S Isa 15:6
nS Ex 15:10;
S Job 41:21
oS Ps 103:16;
S Eze 22:21
40:8 pS Isa 5:24;
Jas 1:10
qIsa 55:11; 59:21
rS Pr 19:21;
S Isa 7:7,9;
S Jer 39:16
sS Ps 119:89;
S Mt 5:18;
1Pe 1:24-25*
40:9 tIsa 41:27;
44:28; 52:7-10;
61:1; Na 1:15;
S Ac 13:32;
Ro 10:15;
1Co 15:1-4
uS Isa 1:1
vIsa 25:9
40:10 wIsa 35:4;
59:20; Mt 21:5;
Rev 22:7
xIsa 28:2
yS Ps 44:3;
S Isa 30:30;
S 33:2 zIsa 9:6-7
aS Isa 35:4;
Rev 22:12
40:11 bS Ge 48:15;
S Ps 28:9;
S Mic 5:4;
S Jn 10:11
cS Nu 11:12
dS Dt 26:19
eIsa 49:10
fS Ge 33:13;
S Dt 30:4
40:12 gS Job 12:15;
S 38:10 hPr 30:4
iS Job 38:5;
Heb 1:10-12
jS Job 38:18;
Pr 16:11
40:13 kIsa 11:2;
42:1 lS Job 15:8;
Ro 11:34*;
1Co 2:16*

40:14
mJob 21:22;
Col 2:3
40:15 nS Job 12:13;
S 34:13; Isa 55:9
40:15 oS Ps 62:9
pS Dt 9:21;
Isa 2:22
40:16 qIsa 33:9;
37:24
rPs 50:9-11;

Mic 6:7; Heb 10:5-9 40:17 sIsa 30:28 tS Job 12:19; Isa 29:7
uS Isa 37:19; Da 4:35 40:18 vS Ex 8:10; S 1Sa 2:2
wS Dt 4:15; Ac 17:29 40:19 xS Ex 20:4; Ps 115:4;
S Isa 37:19; 42:17; Jer 2:8,28; 10:8; 16:19; Hab 2:18;
Zec 10:2 yIsa 41:7; 46:6; Jer 10:3 zIsa 2:20; 31:7 40:20
aIsa 44:19 bS 1Sa 12:21 cS 1Sa 5:3

g9 Or O Zion, bringer of good tidings, / go up on a high
mountain. / O Jerusalem, bringer of good tidings
h13 Or Spirit; or spirit

40:8 *word of our God stands.* The plans and purposes of
the nations will not prevail (see 8:10 and note).

40:9 *good tidings.* The news that God is leading his people
back to Judah (vv. 10–11). He cares for his people and will
redeem them (52:7–10; 61:1). The NT expands this "good
news" or "gospel" to refer to the salvation that Christ brings
to all people (1Co 15:1–4). See NIV text note for an alternative translation. *Here is your God!* The Lord is returning to
Jerusalem. These words apply to the return from exile
(52:7–9), the first coming of Christ (Mt 21:5) and the second coming of Christ (62:11; Rev 22:12). See 35:4 and
note.

40:10 *arm rules.* Cf. 51:9; 59:16. He is characterized by
both strength and gentleness (v. 11). *reward . . . recompense.* His delivered people, the flock of v. 11 (see
62:11–12).

40:11 *tends his flock.* Cf. Jer 31:10; Eze 34:11–16.

40:12–31 Rhetorical questions are used to persuade the
people to trust in the Lord, who has the ability to deliver,
strengthen and restore his people.

40:12 *measured the waters.* See Job 28:25; 38:8. In Job
38–41 the Lord overwhelms Job with a description of his
greatness. *marked off the heavens.* See 48:13.

40:13 Quoted in Ro 11:34; 1Co 2:16. *counselor.* See 9:6
and note.

40:15 *nations . . . a drop in a bucket.* See note on v. 6.
dust. See 17:13 and note; 29:5.

40:16 *Lebanon.* The wood of its cedar trees. *its animals.*
Cf. Ps 104:16–18. Sacrifices, however numerous, could
never do justice to the greatness of God.

40:17 *nothing . . . worthless.* In spite of the temporary
splendor they might possess (see 13:19 and note).

40:18–20 More than any other prophet, Isaiah shows the
folly of worshiping idols. His sarcastic caricature, satire and
denunciation of these false gods reach a peak in 44:9–20 (see
41:7,22–24; 42:17; 46:5–7; 48:5).

40:18 *To whom . . . compare God?* See v. 25; 46:5.

40:19 *craftsman . . . goldsmith.* See 41:7; 44:10–12. *gold
. . . silver.* See 2:20; Hab 2:18–19 and notes.

40:20 *wood.* See 44:14–16,19. *that will not topple.* See
41:7; 46:7.

21Do you not know?
Have you not heard?[d]
Has it not been told[e] you from the beginning?[f]
Have you not understood[g] since the earth was founded?[h]
22He sits enthroned[i] above the circle of the earth,
and its people are like grasshoppers.[j]
He stretches out the heavens[k] like a canopy,[l]
and spreads them out like a tent[m] to live in.[n]
23He brings princes[o] to naught
and reduces the rulers of this world to nothing.[p]
24No sooner are they planted,
no sooner are they sown,
no sooner do they take root[q] in the ground,
than he blows[r] on them and they wither,[s]
and a whirlwind sweeps them away like chaff.[t]

25"To whom will you compare me?[u]
Or who is my equal?" says the Holy One.[v]
26Lift your eyes and look to the heavens:[w]
Who created[x] all these?
He who brings out the starry host[y] one by one,
and calls them each by name.
Because of his great power and mighty strength,[z]
not one of them is missing.[a]

27Why do you say, O Jacob,
and complain, O Israel,
"My way is hidden from the LORD;
my cause is disregarded by my God"?[b]
28Do you not know?
Have you not heard?[c]
The LORD is the everlasting[d] God,
the Creator[e] of the ends of the earth.[f]
He will not grow tired or weary,[g]
and his understanding no one can fathom.[h]
29He gives strength[i] to the weary[j]
and increases the power of the weak.
30Even youths grow tired and weary,
and young men[k] stumble and fall;[l]
31but those who hope[m] in the LORD
will renew their strength.[n]
They will soar on wings like eagles;[o]
they will run and not grow weary,
they will walk and not be faint.[p]

The Helper of Israel

41 "Be silent[q] before me, you islands![r]
Let the nations renew their strength![s]
Let them come forward[t] and speak;
let us meet together[u] at the place of judgment.

2"Who has stirred[v] up one from the east,[w]

40:21 [d]ver 28; 2Ki 19:25; Isa 41:22; 42:9; 44:8; 48:3,5 [e]Ps 19:1; 50:6; Ac 14:17 [f]S Ge 1:1 [g]Ro 1:19 [h]Isa 48:13; 51:13 **40:22** [i]S 2Ch 6:18; S Ps 2:4 [j]S Nu 13:33 [k]S Ge 1:1; S Isa 48:13 [l]S Ge 1:8; S Job 22:14 [m]S Job 36:29 [n]S Job 26:7 **40:23** [o]S Job 12:18; S Isa 34:12 [p]S Job 12:19; Am 2:3 **40:24** [q]S Job 5:3 [r]S 2Sa 22:16; S Isa 11:4; 41:16 [s]S Job 8:12; S 18:16 [t]S Job 24:24; S Isa 41:2 **40:25** [u]S 1Sa 2:2; S 1Ch 16:25 [v]Isa 1:4; 37:23 **40:26** [w]Isa 51:6 [x]ver 28; Ps 89:11-13; Isa 42:5; 66:2 [y]S 2Ki 17:16; S Ne 9:6; S Job 38:32 [z]S Job 9:4; S Isa 45:24; Eph 1:19 [a]S Isa 34:16 **40:27** [b]S Job 6:29; S 27:2; Lk 18:7-8 **40:28** [c]S ver 21 [d]S Dt 33:27; S Ps 90:2 [e]S ver 26 [f]S Isa 37:16 [g]Isa 44:12 [h]S Ps 147:5; Ro 11:33 **40:29** [i]S Ge 18:14; S Ps 68:35; S 119:28 [j]Isa 50:4; 57:19; Jer 31:25 **40:30** [k]Isa 9:17; Jer 6:11; 9:21 [l]S Ps 20:8; Isa 5:27 **40:31** [m]S Ps 37:9; 40:1; S Isa 30:18; Lk 18:1 [n]S 1Sa 2:4; S 2Ki 6:33; S 2Co 4:16 [o]S Ex 19:4 [p]2Co 4:1; Heb 12:1-3 **41:1** [q]Ps 37:7; Hab 2:20; Zep 1:7; Zec 2:13 [r]S Isa 11:11 [s]S 1Sa 2:4 [t]Isa 48:16; 57:3 [u]S Isa 1:18; 34:1; 50:8 **41:2** [v]S Ezr 1:2 [w]ver 25; Isa 13:4,17; 44:28; 45:1,13; 48:14; Jer 50:3; 51:11

40:21 *from the beginning.* God's work as Creator is emphasized in the rest of the chapter (cf. 37:26; 41:4,26). **40:22** *sits enthroned.* Cf. 66:1; see 37:16 and note. *circle.* Or "horizon." See Job 22:14; Pr 8:27. *stretches out the heavens . . . like a tent.* See 42:5; 44:24; 51:13; Ps 19:4; 104:2.
40:23 *princes . . . rulers . . . to nothing.* See v. 17; 2:22 and notes; cf. Jer 25:17–26; Da 2:21.
40:24 *whirlwind . . . like chaff.* See 17:13 and note; 41:15–16.
40:25 See v. 18. Apparently some Israelite doubters were comparing their God with the gods of their captors, and they believed that the Lord was failing the test. *Holy One.* See 1:4 and note.
40:26 *created.* See vv. 21–22 and notes. *brings out.* The Hebrew for this expression is used for bringing forth the constellations in Job 38:32. *starry host.* Also worshiped by the people (see 47:13; Jer 19:13). *each by name.* See Ps 147:4. *not one . . . missing.* See 34:16 and note.
40:27–31 As in many psalms of praise, Isaiah now stresses the goodness of God after describing his majesty (vv. 12–26). Such a God is able to deliver and restore his distressed people if they will wait in faith for him to act. They are to trust in him and draw strength from him.
40:27 *way.* Condition. *hidden . . . disregarded.* Cf. 49:14; 54:8.
40:28 *everlasting God.* See 9:6. *Creator.* See vv. 21–22 and notes. *ends of the earth.* See 11:12 and note; cf. 5:26; 41:9; 43:6. *not grow tired.* Contrast 44:12.
40:30 *grow tired . . . stumble.* See note on 5:27.
40:31 *hope in.* Trust in or look expectantly to (see 5:2; 49:23). *renew.* Lit. "exchange." Their weakness will give way to God's strength (v. 29). The Hebrew for this verb is used of changes of clothes (Ge 35:2; Jdg 14:12), which can symbolize strength and beauty (Isa 52:1). Paul tells believers to clothe themselves with Christ (Ro 13:14; cf. Eph 4:24; Col 3:10). *eagles.* Known for their vigor (Ps 103:5) and speed (Jer 4:13; 48:40).
41:1,5 *islands.* Or "coastlands" (see 11:11 and note).
41:1 *renew their strength.* See 40:31. The nations and their gods are challenged to display the same power and wisdom as Israel's God (see vv. 21–24).
41:2 *one from the east.* Cyrus the Great, king of Persia (559–530 B.C.), who conquered Babylon in 539 (see 13:17 and note) and issued the decree allowing the Jews to return to Jerusalem (see Ezr 1:1–4; 6:3–5). Cyrus is referred to also in v. 25; 44:28–45:5,13; 46:11. *calling him in righteousness.* Like the servant of the Lord in 42:6, Cyrus was chosen to carry out God's righteous purposes. *subdues kings.* Such as Croesus king of Lydia in Asia Minor. *windblown chaff.* See

calling him in righteousness[x] to his
   service[i] ?[y]
He hands nations over to him
   and subdues kings before him.
He turns them to dust[z] with his sword,
   to windblown chaff[a] with his bow.[b]
[3]He pursues them and moves on
      unscathed,[c]
   by a path his feet have not traveled
      before.
[4]Who has done this and carried it
      through,
   calling[d] forth the generations from
      the beginning?[e]
I, the LORD—with the first of them
   and with the last[f]—I am he.[g]"

[5]The islands[h] have seen it and fear;
   the ends of the earth[i] tremble.
They approach and come forward;
[6]   each helps the other
   and says to his brother, "Be
      strong![j]"
[7]The craftsman[k] encourages the
      goldsmith,[l]
   and he who smooths with the
      hammer
spurs on him who strikes the anvil.
He says of the welding, "It is good."
   He nails down the idol so it will not
      topple.[m]

[8]"But you, O Israel, my servant,[n]
   Jacob, whom I have chosen,[o]
   you descendants of Abraham[p] my
      friend,[q]

[9]I took you from the ends of the earth,[r]
   from its farthest corners I called[s]
      you.
I said, 'You are my servant';[t]
   I have chosen[u] you and have not
      rejected you.
[10]So do not fear,[v] for I am with you;[w]
   do not be dismayed, for I am your
      God.
I will strengthen[x] you and help[y] you;
   I will uphold you[z] with my righteous
      right hand.[a]

[11]"All who rage[b] against you
   will surely be ashamed and
      disgraced;[c]
those who oppose[d] you
   will be as nothing and perish.[e]
[12]Though you search for your enemies,
   you will not find them.[f]
Those who wage war against you
   will be as nothing[g] at all.
[13]For I am the LORD, your God,
   who takes hold of your right hand[h]
   and says to you, Do not fear;
   I will help[i] you.
[14]Do not be afraid,[j] O worm[k] Jacob,
   O little Israel,
   for I myself will help[l] you," declares
      the LORD,

41:2 [x]Isa 45:8,13
[y]Isa 44:28;
Jer 25:9
[z]S 2Sa 22:43
[a]Ps 1:4; Isa 40:24
[b]S Isa 13:18
41:3 [c]Da 8:4
41:4 [d]ver 9;
Isa 43:7 [e]ver 26;
S Ge 1:1;
Isa 46:10
[f]Isa 44:6; 48:12;
Rev 1:8,17
[g]S Dt 32:39
41:5 [h]S Isa 11:11;
Eze 26:17-18
[i]S Dt 30:4;
S Isa 11:12
41:6 [j]S Jos 1:6
41:7 [k]Isa 44:13;
Jer 10:3-5
[l]S Isa 40:19
[m]S 1Sa 5:3;
Isa 46:7
41:8 [n]S Ps 136:22;
S Isa 27:11
[o]S Isa 14:1
[p]S Isa 29:22;
51:2; 63:16
[q]2Ch 20:7;
Jas 2:23

41:9 [r]Isa 11:12;
S 37:16 [s]S ver 4
[t]S Isa 20:3
[u]S Dt 7:6
41:10 [v]S Ge 15:1
[w]S Dt 3:22;
Jos 1:9; Isa 43:2,
5; Jer 30:10;
46:27-28;
Ro 8:31
[x]S Ps 68:35;
S 119:28 [y]ver
13-14; Isa 44:2;
49:8; 50:7,9
[z]S Ps 18:35;
S 119:117
[a]S Ex 3:20;
S Job 40:14
41:11 [b]S Isa 17:12
[c]Isa 29:22;
45:24; 54:17

[d]S Ex 23:22 [e]S Isa 29:8; S Jer 2:3 41:12 [f]Ps 37:35-36;
S Isa 34:12 [g]S Job 7:8; Isa 17:14; 29:20 41:13 [h]Ps 73:23;
Isa 42:6; 45:1; 51:18 [i]ver 10 41:14 [j]S Ge 15:1 [k]S Job 4:19;
S Ps 22:6 [l]S ver 10

[i]2 Or / whom victory meets at every step

17:13 and note. *his bow.* The Persians were renowned for
their ability as archers.
41:4 *from the beginning.* See 40:21 and note. *with the
first . . . with the last.* Since the Lord was present with the
first of the generations and will still be there with the last of
them, he is the eternal Lord of history and nations (see Heb
13:8; Rev 1:8,17; 2:8; 21:6; 22:13).
41:5–7 By 546 B.C. Cyrus had fought his way victoriously
to the west coast of Asia Minor, where his leading opponent
was Croesus king of Lydia. Sarcasm and satire are used in the
description of the frantic efforts in vv. 6–7—all of them futile
(cf. 40:19–20).
41:5 *ends of the earth.* See 11:12 and note.
41:6 *Be strong!* See 35:4 and note.
41:7 *hammer.* Cf. 44:12. *so it will not topple.* See
40:18–20 and notes.
41:8–9 *my servant.* A significant term in chs. 41–53,
referring sometimes to the nation of Israel and other times to
an individual. In these passages the title refers to one who
occupies a special position in God's royal administration of
his kingdom, as in "my servant Moses" (Ex 14:31; Nu
12:7), "my servant David" (2Sa 3:18; 7:5,8), "my servants
the prophets" (2Ki 17:13; Jer 7:25). See note on 42:1; see
also 20:3; 22:20; 42:1,19; 43:10; 44:1–2,21; 45:4; 49:3,
5–7; 50:10; 52:13; 53:11.
41:8 *But.* In contrast to the nations of vv. 5–7, Israel does
not need to be afraid (v. 10). *my friend.* See Ge 18; 2Ch
20:7; Jas 2:23. Some believe, however, that here "my

friend" refers to "descendants" (Israel), thus paralleling "my
servant" and "whom I have chosen."
41:9 *ends of the earth.* See v. 5; probably a reference to
Mesopotamia and Egypt (see Ge 11:31; 12:1; 15:7; Ps
114:1–2; Jer 31:32).
41:10 *do not fear . . . be dismayed.* See vv. 13–14; 43:1,
5; see also 35:4 and note. *strengthen . . . help you.* As one
called to God's service (see vv. 9,15–16). See also v. 14;
40:29; 44:2; 49:8. *right hand.* A hand of power and salvation (see Ex 15:6,12; Ps 20:6; 48:10; 89:13; 98:1).
41:11 *be ashamed and disgraced.* Cf. 45:17; 50:7; 54:4.
will be as nothing. See vv. 15–16 and notes.
41:13 *takes hold . . . right hand.* To strengthen them and
keep them from stumbling. *Do not fear.* See v. 10 and note.
41:14 *worm.* A reference to their feeble and despised
condition in exile (cf. Job 25:6). *Redeemer.* Deliverer from
Babylonian exile (in a new exodus). The Hebrew for this
word refers to an obligated family protector and thus portrays
the Lord as the Family Protector of Israel. He is related to
Israel as Father (63:16; 64:8) and Husband (54:5). As Redeemer (or Family Protector), he redeems their property (for
he regathers them to their land, 54:1–8), guarantees their
freedom (35:9; 43:1–4; 48:20; 52:11–12), avenges them
against their tormentors (47:3; 49:25–26; 64:4) and secures their posterity for the future (61:8–9). See note on Ru
2:20. *Holy One of Israel.* See vv. 16,20; see also 1:4 and
note. The title occurs with "Redeemer" also in 43:14; 47:4;
48:17; 49:7; 54:5.

your Redeemer, [m] the Holy One [n] of
Israel.
15"See, I will make you into a threshing
sledge, [o]
new and sharp, with many teeth.
You will thresh the mountains [p] and
crush them,
and reduce the hills to chaff. [q]
16You will winnow [r] them, the wind will
pick them up,
and a gale [s] will blow them away. [t]
But you will rejoice [u] in the LORD
and glory [v] in the Holy One [w] of
Israel.

17"The poor and needy search for water, [x]
but there is none;
their tongues are parched with
thirst. [y]
But I the LORD will answer [z] them;
I, the God of Israel, will not forsake [a]
them.
18I will make rivers flow [b] on barren
heights,
and springs within the valleys.
I will turn the desert [c] into pools of
water, [d]
and the parched ground into
springs. [e]
19I will put in the desert [f]
the cedar and the acacia, [g] the myrtle
and the olive.
I will set pines [h] in the wasteland,
the fir and the cypress [i] together, [j]
20so that people may see and know, [k]
may consider and understand, [l]
that the hand [m] of the LORD has done
this,
that the Holy One [n] of Israel has
created [o] it.

21"Present your case, [p]" says the LORD.

"Set forth your arguments," says
Jacob's King. [q]
22"Bring in your idols, to tell us
what is going to happen. [r]
Tell us what the former things [s] were,
so that we may consider them
and know their final outcome.
Or declare to us the things to come, [t]
23   tell us what the future holds,
so we may know [u] that you are gods.
Do something, whether good or bad, [v]
so that we will be dismayed [w] and
filled with fear.
24But you are less than nothing [x]
and your works are utterly
worthless; [y]
he who chooses you is detestable. [z]

25"I have stirred [a] up one from the
north, [b] and he comes—
one from the rising sun who calls on
my name.
He treads [c] on rulers as if they were
mortar,
as if he were a potter treading the
clay.
26Who told of this from the beginning, [d]
so we could know,
or beforehand, so we could say, 'He
was right'?
No one told of this,
no one foretold [e] it,
no one heard any words [f] from you.
27I was the first to tell [g] Zion, 'Look, here
they are!'
I gave to Jerusalem a messenger of
good tidings. [h]
28I look but there is no one [i] —

41:14
[m]S Ex 15:13;
S Job 19:25;
S Isa 1:27 [n]ver
16,20; S Isa 1:4
41:15
[o]S Job 41:30;
S Isa 10:5;
S 21:10
[p]S Ex 19:18;
S Ps 107:33;
Jer 9:10;
Eze 33:28 [q]S ver
2
41:16 [r]Jer 15:7;
51:2 [s]Isa 40:24
[t]Da 2:35
[u]S Isa 25:9
[v]Isa 45:25; 60:19
[w]S ver 14;
S Mk 1:24
41:17 [x]Isa 43:20
[y]S Isa 35:7
[z]S Isa 30:19
[a]S Dt 31:6;
S Ps 27:9
41:18
[b]S Isa 30:25
[c]Isa 43:19
[d]S 2Ki 3:17
[e]S Job 38:26;
S Isa 35:7
41:19 [f]S Isa 35:1;
51:3 [g]Isa 25:5,10,
13 [h]S Isa 37:24
[i]Isa 44:14
[j]Isa 60:13
41:20 [k]S Ex 6:7
[l]S Isa 29:24
[m]Ezr 7:6; 8:31;
Isa 50:2; 51:9;
59:1; 66:14;
Jer 32:17 [n]S ver
14; Isa 43:3,14
[o]S Isa 4:5
41:21 [p]S ver 1

[q]Isa 43:15; 44:6
41:22 [r]ver 26;
Isa 43:9; 44:7;
45:21; 48:14
[s]Isa 43:18,26;
46:9; 48:3
[t]Isa 42:9; 43:19;
46:10; 48:6;
65:17; Jn 13:19
41:23 [u]Isa 45:3
[v]Jer 10:5
[w]S 2Ki 19:26
41:24
[x]S Isa 37:19;
1Co 8:4
[y]S 1Sa 12:21;
Jer 8:19; 10:5,8,
15 [z]S Ps 109:7;

S Isa 1:13; S 48:8 **41:25** [a]S Ezr 1:2 [b]S ver 2; Jer 50:9,41;
51:48 [c]S 2Sa 22:43; S Isa 5:5; Na 3:14 **41:26** [d]S ver 4 [e]S ver
22; Isa 52:6 [f]S 1Ki 18:26; Hab 2:18-19 **41:27** [g]Isa 48:3,16
[h]S Isa 40:9 **41:28** [i]Ps 22:11; Isa 50:2; 59:16; 63:5; 64:7;
Eze 22:30

41:15 *threshing sledge.* Cf. 28:27; Mic 4:13; Hab 3:12.
mountains . . . hills. Probably represents the nations. See
2:14. *reduce . . . to chaff.* See v. 2; 17:13 and note; 29:5–6.
41:16 *winnow.* A figure of judgment used also in Jer 51:2.
rejoice. Cf. 25:9; 35:10; 51:11.
41:17 *poor and needy.* Israel in exile or on the way home
(cf. v. 14; 32:7). *will answer.* See 30:19 and note.
41:18 *rivers . . . on barren heights.* See 30:25 and note.
desert into pools . . . springs. See 32:2; 35:6–7 and notes.
41:19 These trees will beautify the desert (cf. 35:1–2).
Several are named in 60:13 in connection with adorning the
place of God's sanctuary. Acacia wood was used for the
tabernacle (Ex 25:5,10,13). The pine tree and myrtle replace
thorns and briers in 55:13.
41:20 *created it.* These fruitful conditions are part of God's
new creation in behalf of his people (see 48:7; 57:19;
65:17–18).
41:21–22 God takes the nations and their idols to court
(see v. 1 and note).
41:22 *former things.* Earlier predictions or accomplishments (see 42:9; 43:9,18; 46:9; 48:3).

41:23 *Do something . . . good or bad.* See note on
40:18–20.
41:24 *less than nothing . . . worthless.* Like the nations
that worship them. See 40:17; 44:9; Hos 9:10. *detestable.*
Like those who marry idolaters (see Mal 2:11).
41:25 *stirred up.* See v. 2 and note. *from the north.* Cyrus
came from the east (v. 2) but conquered a number of kingdoms north of Babylon early in his reign. From the perspective of a Palestinian writer, invasions came primarily from the
north (see 14:31; Jer 1:14; 6:1,22; 10:22; 46:20; 50:3,9,
41; 51:48). *calls on my name.* Cyrus used the Lord's name
in his decree (Ezr 1:2) but did not acknowledge him (see
45:4–5). *treads on . . . mortar . . . clay.* Similar to Assyria in
10:6. Cf. Na 3:14; Mic 7:10.
41:26 *from the beginning.* Before these events began to
unfold (cf. v. 4). *you.* Idols or their worshipers.
41:27 *here they are.* Words about the deliverance from
Babylon. *messenger of good tidings.* Isaiah. See 40:9; 52:7
and notes.
41:28 *no one to give answer.* See 46:7.

no one among them to give
counsel,[j]
no one to give answer[k] when I ask
them.
[29]See, they are all false!
Their deeds amount to nothing;[l]
their images[m] are but wind[n] and
confusion.

The Servant of the LORD

42 "Here is my servant,[o] whom I
uphold,
my chosen one[p] in whom I delight;[q]
I will put my Spirit[r] on him
and he will bring justice[s] to the
nations.[t]
[2]He will not shout or cry out,[u]
or raise his voice in the streets.
[3]A bruised reed[v] he will not break,[w]
and a smoldering wick he will not
snuff out.[x]
In faithfulness he will bring forth
justice;[y]
[4] he will not falter or be discouraged
till he establishes justice[z] on earth.
In his law[a] the islands[b] will put their
hope."[c]

[5]This is what God the LORD says—
he who created the heavens[d] and
stretched them out,
who spread out the earth[e] and all
that comes out of it,[f]
who gives breath[g] to its people,
and life to those who walk on it:
[6]"I, the LORD, have called[h] you in
righteousness;[i]
I will take hold of your hand.[j]
I will keep[k] you and will make you
to be a covenant[l] for the people

and a light[m] for the Gentiles,[n]
[7]to open eyes that are blind,[o]
to free[p] captives from prison[q]
and to release from the dungeon
those who sit in darkness.[r]

[8]"I am the LORD;[s] that is my name![t]
I will not give my glory to another[u]
or my praise to idols.[v]
[9]See, the former things[w] have taken
place,
and new things I declare;
before they spring into being
I announce[x] them to you."

Song of Praise to the LORD

[10]Sing[y] to the LORD a new song,[z]
his praise[a] from the ends of the
earth,[b]
you who go down to the sea, and all
that is in it,[c]
you islands,[d] and all who live in
them.
[11]Let the desert[e] and its towns raise their
voices;
let the settlements where Kedar[f]
lives rejoice.
Let the people of Sela[g] sing for joy;
let them shout from the
mountaintops.[h]
[12]Let them give glory[i] to the LORD
and proclaim his praise[j] in the
islands.[k]

41:28
/Isa 40:13-14
kS 1Ki 18:26;
Isa 65:12; 66:4;
Jer 25:4
41:29
/S 1Sa 12:21
mS Isa 37:19
nJer 5:13
42:1 oS Isa 20:3;
S Mt 20:28
pS Isa 14:1;
Lk 9:35; 23:35;
1Pe 2:4,6
qMt 3:17
rS Isa 11:2;
S 44:3;
Mt 3:16-17;
S Jn 3:34
sS Isa 9:7
tS Ge 49:10
42:2 uPr 8:1-4
42:3 vS Isa 36:6
wS Job 30:24
xS Job 13:25
yPs 72:2; 96:13
42:4 zS Isa 2:4
aver 21;
Ex 34:29;
Isa 51:4
bS Isa 11:11
cS Ge 49:10;
Mt 12:18-21*
42:5 dS Ge 1:6;
Ps 102:25;
Isa 48:13
eS Ge 1:1
fPs 24:2;
Ac 17:24
gS Ge 2:7;
Ac 17:25
42:6 hEx 31:2;
S Jdg 4:10;
Isa 41:9-10; 43:1
iIsa 45:24;
Jer 23:6; Da 9:7
jIsa 41:13; 45:1
kIsa 26:3; 27:3
lIsa 49:8; 54:10;
59:21; 61:8;
Jer 31:31; 32:40;
Mal 3:1;
S Lk 22:20

mS Isa 9:2
nS Isa 26:18;
S Lk 2:32
42:7 oS Ps 146:8;
S Isa 32:3;
Mt 11:5
pIsa 49:9; 51:14;
52:2; Zec 2:7
qS Ps 66:11;

S Isa 24:22; 48:20; Zec 9:11; S Lk 4:19; 2Ti 2:26;
Heb 2:14-15 rS Ps 107:10,14; Ac 26:18 42:8 sPs 81:10;
Isa 43:3,11,15; 46:9; 49:23 tS Ex 3:15; S 6:3 uIsa 48:11
vS Ex 8:10; S 20:4 42:9 wS Isa 41:22 xS Isa 40:21; Eze 2:4
42:10 yS Ex 15:1 zS Ps 96:1 a1Ki 10:9; Isa 60:6 bS Dt 30:4;
S Ps 48:10; 65:5; Isa 49:6 cS 1Ch 16:32; Ps 96:11
dS Isa 11:11 42:11 eS Isa 32:16 fS Ge 25:13; Isa 60:7
gS Jdg 1:36 hIsa 52:7; Na 1:15 42:12 iS 1Ch 16:24;
S Isa 24:15 jS Ps 26:7; S 66:2; 1Pe 2:9 kS Isa 11:11

41:29 *amount to nothing.* See v. 24.
42:1–4 Quoted in part in Mt 12:18–21 with reference to
Christ. There are four "servant songs" in which the servant
is the Messiah: 42:1-4 (or 42:1-7 or 42:1-9); 49:1-6 (or
49:1-7 or 49:1-13); 50:4-9 (or 50:4-11); 52:13-53:12.
He is "Israel" in its ideal form (49:3). The nation was a
kingdom of priests (Ex 19:6), but the Messiah would be the
high priest who would atone for the sins of the world
(53:4-12). Cyrus was introduced in ch. 41 as a deliverer
from Babylon, but the servant would deliver the world from
the prison of sin (see v. 7).
42:1 *my servant.* See 41:8-9 and note; Zec 3:8. In the
royal terminology of the ancient Near East "servant" meant
something like "trusted envoy" or "confidential representative." *chosen one.* See 41:8-9 and note. *delight.* Cf. Lk
3:22. *my Spirit on him.* Like the "Branch" of 11:2 (see note
there); cf. 61:1. *justice.* A righteous world order (see v. 4);
see also 9:7 and note; 11:4 and note.
42:2 *not shout or cry out.* He will bring peace (see 9:6).
42:3 *bruised reed.* Someone who is weak (see Ps 72:2,4).
The servant will mend broken lives.
42:4 *falter.* Cf. 40:28. *justice.* Perfect order (see v. 1 and
note). *In his law ... hope.* As do the nations in 2:2-4. The

servant will be a new Moses (see Dt 18:15–18; Ac
3:21–23,26). *islands.* See note on 11:11.
42:5 *created the heavens ... stretched.* See 40:22 and
note. *gives breath ... life.* Cf. 57:15.
42:6 *called ... righteousness.* Similar to the call of Cyrus
(see 41:2 and note). *take hold of your hand.* See 41:13 and
note. *covenant.* See 49:8. The Messiah will fulfill the Davidic covenant as king (9:7) and will institute the new covenant
by his death (Jer 31:31–34; Heb 8:6–13; 9:15). *people.*
Probably the Israelites (see 49:8; Ac 26:17–18). *light.* Parallel to "salvation" in 49:6 (cf. 51:4).
42:7 *open eyes.* See 29:18; 32:3; 35:5 and notes. *free ...
from prison.* From the prison of Babylon and also from
spiritual and moral bondage (compare 61:1 with Lk 4:18).
42:8 *my glory.* See 40:5 and note.
42:9 *former things.* See 41:22 and note. *new things.* The
restoration of Israel (43:19). Cf. 48:6.
42:10 *new song.* To celebrate the "new things" of v. 9.
ends of the earth. See 11:12 and note; 41:5. *islands.* See v.
12; 11:11 and note.
42:11 *desert.* See 35:1 and note. *Kedar.* See note on
21:16. *Sela.* See note on 16:1.
42:12 *give glory ... praise.* See 24:14–16.

¹³The Lᴏʀᴅ will march out like a mighty*ˡ*
man,
like a warrior *ᵐ* he will stir up his
zeal; *ⁿ*
with a shout *ᵒ* he will raise the battle
cry
and will triumph over his enemies. *ᵖ*

¹⁴"For a long time I have kept silent, *q*
I have been quiet and held myself
back. *ʳ*
But now, like a woman in childbirth,
I cry out, I gasp and pant. *ˢ*
¹⁵I will lay waste *ᵗ* the mountains *ᵘ* and
hills
and dry up all their vegetation;
I will turn rivers into islands
and dry up *ᵛ* the pools.
¹⁶I will lead *ʷ* the blind *ˣ* by ways they
have not known,
along unfamiliar paths I will guide
them;
I will turn the darkness into light *ʸ*
before them
and make the rough places smooth. *ᶻ*
These are the things I will do;
I will not forsake *ᵃ* them.
¹⁷But those who trust in idols,
who say to images, 'You are our
gods,' *ᵇ*
will be turned back in utter shame. *ᶜ*

Israel Blind and Deaf

¹⁸"Hear, you deaf; *ᵈ*
look, you blind, and see!
¹⁹Who is blind *ᵉ* but my servant, *ᶠ*
and deaf like the messenger *ᵍ* I send?
Who is blind like the one committed *ʰ*
to me,
blind like the servant of the Lᴏʀᴅ?
²⁰You have seen many things, but have
paid no attention;

your ears are open, but you hear
nothing." *ⁱ*
²¹It pleased the Lᴏʀᴅ
for the sake *ʲ* of his righteousness
to make his law *ᵏ* great and glorious.
²²But this is a people plundered *ˡ* and
looted,
all of them trapped in pits *ᵐ*
or hidden away in prisons. *ⁿ*
They have become plunder,
with no one to rescue them; *ᵒ*
they have been made loot,
with no one to say, "Send them
back."

²³Which of you will listen to this
or pay close attention *ᵖ* in time to
come?
²⁴Who handed Jacob over to become loot,
and Israel to the plunderers? *q*
Was it not the Lᴏʀᴅ, *ʳ*
against whom we have sinned?
For they would not follow *ˢ* his ways;
they did not obey his law. *ᵗ*
²⁵So he poured out on them his burning
anger, *ᵘ*
the violence of war.
It enveloped them in flames, *ᵛ* yet they
did not understand; *ʷ*
it consumed them, but they did not
take it to heart. *ˣ*

Israel's Only Savior

43 But now, this is what the Lᴏʀᴅ
says—
he who created *ʸ* you, O Jacob,
he who formed *ᶻ* you, O Israel: *ᵃ*
"Fear not, for I have redeemed *ᵇ* you;

42:13 *ˡ*S Isa 9:6
*ᵐ*S Ex 14:14
*ⁿ*S Isa 26:11
*ᵒ*S Jos 6:5;
Jer 25:30;
Hos 11:10;
Joel 3:16;
Am 1:2; 3:4,8
*ᵖ*Isa 66:14
42:14
*q*S Est 4:14;
S Ps 50:21
*ʳ*S Ge 43:31;
Lk 18:7; 2Pe 3:9
*ˢ*Jer 4:31
42:15 *ʳ*Eze 38:20
*ᵘ*S Ps 107:33
*ᵛ*S Isa 11:15;
50:2; Na 1:4-6
42:16
*ʷ*S Isa 29:24;
40:11; 57:18;
58:11; Jer 31:8-9;
Lk 1:78-79
*ˣ*S Isa 32:3
*ʸ*S Ps 18:28;
Isa 58:8,10;
S Ac 26:18
*ᶻ*S Isa 26:7;
Lk 3:5
*ᵃ*S Dt 4:31;
Heb 13:5
42:17 *ᵇ*S Ex 32:4
*ᶜ*S Ps 97:7;
S Isa 1:29
42:18 *ᵈ*S Isa 35:5
42:19 *ᵉ*Isa 43:8;
Eze 12:2
*ᶠ*Isa 41:8-9
*ᵍ*Isa 44:26;
Hag 1:13
*ʰ*Isa 26:3

42:20
*ⁱ*Isa 6:9-10; 43:8;
Jer 5:21; 6:10
42:21 *ʲ*Isa 43:25
*ᵏ*S ver 4; 2Co 3:7
42:22 *ˡ*S Jdg 6:4;
S 2Ki 24:13
*ᵐ*S Isa 24:18
*ⁿ*S Ps 66:11;
S Isa 24:22
*ᵒ*S Isa 5:29
42:23 *ᵖ*Dt 32:29;
Ps 81:13;
Isa 47:7; 48:18;
57:11
42:24
*q*S 2Ki 17:6;
Isa 43:28; 47:6
*ʳ*Isa 10:5-6
*ˢ*S Isa 30:15
*ᵗ*S Jos 1:7;
S Ps 119:136;
Isa 5:24;
Jer 44:10

42:25 *ᵘ*S 2Ki 22:13; S Job 40:11; S Isa 51:17; S Eze 7:19
*ᵛ*2Ki 25:9; Isa 66:15; Jer 4:4; 21:12; La 2:3; Na 1:6
*ʷ*S Isa 1:3 *ˣ*Isa 29:13; 47:7; 57:1,11; Hos 7:9 **43:1**
*ʸ*S Isa 27:11 *ᶻ*S ver 7; S Ge 2:7 *ᵃ*Ge 32:28; Isa 44:21
*ᵇ*S Ex 6:6; S Job 19:25

42:13 *mighty man.* God will fight as he did at the Red Sea
(Ex 15:3); see 9:6 and note. *zeal.* Cf. 9:7; 37:32; 59:17;
63:15. *raise the battle cry.* To cause panic among the enemy
(see 1Sa 4:5–8).
42:14 *For a long time.* During Israel's humiliation and
exile. *held myself back.* See 63:15; 64:12. The Hebrew verb
is also used of Joseph, who controlled his emotions while he
tested his brothers (Ge 43:31; 45:1). See 30:18 and note.
42:15 *lay waste . . . dry up.* The opposite of 35:1–2;
41:18. *rivers into islands.* Perhaps to make travel easier. See
37:25; 44:27.
42:16 *blind.* Israel (vv. 19–20). *rough places smooth.* See
40:4. *not forsake.* Cf. 40:27; 49:14; 54:8.
42:18 *deaf . . . blind.* See 6:10 and note.
42:19 *my servant.* Israel. See note on 41:8–9. *messenger
I send.* A term associated with prophets (see Hag 1:13; cf. Isa
44:26; Mal 3:1).
42:21 *law great and glorious.* Especially the law of Moses,
given in the awesome setting of Mount Sinai (see Ex 34:29).

42:22 *plundered and looted.* By the Assyrians (see 10:6
and note) and the Babylonians (see 39:6). *trapped in pits . . .
prisons.* See v. 7 and note. Cf. Jdg 6:2–4.

42:24 *Who handed Jacob over . . . ?* Babylon conquered
Israel, not because their gods were stronger than the Lord
(see 40:17–18; 1Ki 20:23), but because the Lord was punishing his people.

42:25 *poured out . . . anger.* Israel had a foretaste of the
day of the Lord (see 5:25; 9:12,17,21; 13:3; 34:2 and
notes; cf. Jer 10:25).

43:1 *created . . . formed.* God made the nation Israel as
surely as he made the first man (see Ge 1:27; see also Isa
43:7,15,21; 44:2,24). *Fear not.* See 41:10 and note. *redeemed you.* See notes on 35:9; 41:14. The verb is also used
in 29:22; 44:22–23; 48:20 (cf. Ex 15:13). *summoned . . .
by name.* God chose Israel to serve him in a special way. See
45:3–4 (Cyrus). In Ex 31:2; 35:30 the Hebrew underlying
this expression is translated "chosen."

I have summoned you by name; [c]
you are mine. [d]
2When you pass through the waters, [e]
I will be with you; [f]
and when you pass through the rivers,
they will not sweep over you.
When you walk through the fire, [g]
you will not be burned;
the flames will not set you ablaze. [h]
3For I am the LORD, your God, [i]
the Holy One [j] of Israel, your
Savior; [k]
I give Egypt [l] for your ransom,
Cush [m] and Seba [n] in your stead. [o]
4Since you are precious and honored [p] in
my sight,
and because I love [q] you,
I will give men in exchange for you,
and people in exchange for your life.
5Do not be afraid, [r] for I am with you; [s]
I will bring your children [t] from the
east
and gather [u] you from the west. [v]
6I will say to the north, 'Give them up!'
and to the south, [w] 'Do not hold them
back.'
Bring my sons from afar
and my daughters [x] from the ends of
the earth [y] —
7everyone who is called by my name, [z]
whom I created [a] for my glory, [b]
whom I formed and made. [c]"

8Lead out those who have eyes but are
blind, [d]
who have ears but are deaf. [e]
9All the nations gather together [f]
and the peoples assemble.

Which of them foretold [g] this
and proclaimed to us the former
things?
Let them bring in their witnesses to
prove they were right,
so that others may hear and say, "It
is true."
10"You are my witnesses, [h]" declares the
LORD,
"and my servant [i] whom I have
chosen,
so that you may know [j] and believe me
and understand that I am he.
Before me no god [k] was formed,
nor will there be one after me. [l]
11I, even I, am the LORD, [m]
and apart from me there is no
savior. [n]
12I have revealed and saved and
proclaimed—
I, and not some foreign god [o] among
you.
You are my witnesses, [p]" declares the
LORD, "that I am God.
13 Yes, and from ancient days [q] I am
he. [r]
No one can deliver out of my hand.
When I act, who can reverse it?" [s]

God's Mercy and Israel's Unfaithfulness

14This is what the LORD says—

43:1 cS Isa 42:6; 45:3-4; 49:1
dS Dt 7:6; Mal 3:17
43:2 eS Isa 8:7 fS Ge 26:3; S Ex 14:22
gIsa 29:6; 30:27 hPs 66:12; Da 3:25-27
43:3 iS Ex 20:2 jS Isa 41:20
kS Ex 14:30; S Jdg 2:18; S Ps 3:8;
S Isa 25:9 lS Ps 68:31; Isa 19:1;
Eze 29:20 mS Isa 20:3; nS Ge 10:7
oS Pr 21:18 **43:4** pEx 19:5; Isa 49:5
qIsa 63:9; Rev 3:9 **43:5** rS Ge 15:1;
Isa 44:2 sS Ge 21:22; S Ex 14:22;
Jer 30:10-11 tIsa 41:8; 54:3; 61:9; 66:22
uS Isa 11:12; S 49:18 vS Isa 24:14;
Zec 8:7; S Mt 8:11 **43:6** wPs 107:3
xIsa 60:4; Eze 16:61; 2Co 6:18
yS Dt 30:4; S Isa 11:12; Jer 23:8;
Eze 36:24 **43:7** zIsa 48:1; 56:5; 62:2;
63:19; 65:1; Jer 15:16; Jas 2:7
aS Isa 27:11 bS Ps 86:9 cver 1,
21; Ps 100:3; S Isa 19:25
43:8 dS Isa 6:9-10 eS Isa 42:20;
Eze 12:2 **43:9** fS Isa 41:1;
45:20; 48:14

gS Isa 41:26

43:10 hver 12; S Jos 24:22 iS Isa 20:3; 41:8-9 jS Ex 6:7 kver
11; S Ps 86:10; Isa 19:21; 44:6,8; 45:5-6,14 lS Dt 4:35;
S 32:39; Jer 14:22 **43:11** mS Ex 6:2; S Isa 42:8 nS ver 10;
S Ps 3:8; S 18:31; S Isa 25:9; 64:4 **43:12** oS Dt 32:12 pS ver
10 **43:13** qPs 90:2 rS Dt 32:39; Isa 46:4; 48:12 sS Nu 23:8;
S Job 9:12

13 That is, the upper Nile region

43:2 *waters . . . rivers.* Probably an allusion to crossing the Red Sea (Ex 14:21–22) and the Jordan River (Jos 3:14–17). Cf. Ps 66:6,12. *walk through the fire.* Fulfilled literally in the experience of Shadrach, Meshach and Abednego (Da 3:25–27). Contrast 42:25.
43:3 *Holy One of Israel.* See notes on 1:4; 41:14. *Savior.* Who delivers from the oppression of Egypt or Babylon and from the spiritual oppression of sin (see 19:20 and note; 25:9 and note; 33:22; 35:4 and note; 43:11–12; 45:15,21–22; 49:25; 60:16; 63:8–9). The name "Isaiah" means "The LORD saves." *ransom.* The Persians conquered Egypt, Cush and Seba, and perhaps this was a reward or ransom for Persia's kindness to Israel (see note on 41:2; cf. Eze 29:19–20). *Cush.* See note on 18:1. *Seba.* A land near Cush (cf. 45:14) or Sheba (Ps 72:10). It was probably either in south Arabia (see Ge 10:7 and note; see also Eze 27:21–22) or across the Red Sea in Africa.
43:5 *Do not be afraid.* See 41:10 and note. *east.* Especially Assyria and Babylonia. See 11:11–12 and notes; cf. Ps 107:3. *west.* For example, the "islands" of 11:11 (see also 24:14–15; 49:12).
43:6 *north.* For example, Hamath (see 10:9 and note; 11:11). *south.* Egypt. *ends of the earth.* See note on 11:12 (cf. 41:5; 42:10).

43:7 *called by my name.* People belonging to God. *created . . . formed.* See v. 1 and note.
43:8 *blind . . . deaf.* Probably referring to Israel (see 6:10 and note; 42:18–20).
43:9–13 A court scene; see also 41:21–22.
43:9 *nations . . . peoples assemble.* See 41:1 and note. *foretold.* See 41:26 and note. *former things.* See 41:22 and note. *witnesses.* To verify the accuracy of earlier predictions by idols or their worshipers (see 41:26).
43:10 *You are my witnesses.* See also v. 12; 44:8. God's work in behalf of Israel is proof of his saving power. *my servant.* See 41:8–9 and note.
43:11 The main thrust is repeated in 44:6,8; 45:5–6,18, 21–22; 46:9 (see also Dt 32:39). *savior.* See v. 3 and note.
43:12 *foreign god.* Cf. Dt 32:12,16. Israel repeatedly worshiped other gods (see Jdg 2:12–13). *witnesses.* See v. 10 and note.
43:13 See v. 11. *No one can deliver . . . hand.* Quoted verbatim from Dt 32:39.
43:14 *Redeemer.* See 41:14 and note. *Holy One of Israel.* See 1:4; 41:14 and notes. *Babylon.* See note on 13:1. *fugitives . . . in the ships.* The Babylonians used the Persian Gulf, as well as the Tigris and Euphrates rivers, for trading purposes. But their splendid ships (cf. 2:16) would one day

your Redeemer, [t] the Holy One [u] of Israel:

"For your sake I will send to Babylon
and bring down as fugitives [v] all the Babylonians, [k] [w]
in the ships in which they took pride.

[15] I am the LORD, [x] your Holy One,
Israel's Creator, [y] your King. [z] "

[16] This is what the LORD says—
he who made a way through the sea,
a path through the mighty waters, [a]
[17] who drew out [b] the chariots and horses, [c]
the army and reinforcements together, [d]
and they lay [e] there, never to rise again,
extinguished, snuffed out like a wick: [f]
[18] "Forget the former things; [g]
do not dwell on the past.
[19] See, I am doing a new thing! [h]
Now it springs up; do you not perceive it?
I am making a way in the desert [i]
and streams in the wasteland. [j]
[20] The wild animals [k] honor me,
the jackals [l] and the owls,
because I provide water [m] in the desert
and streams in the wasteland,
to give drink to my people, my chosen,
[21] the people I formed [n] for myself [o]
that they may proclaim my praise. [p]

[22] "Yet you have not called upon me,
O Jacob,
you have not wearied [q] yourselves for me, O Israel. [r]
[23] You have not brought me sheep for burnt offerings, [s]
nor honored [t] me with your sacrifices. [u]

I have not burdened [v] you with grain offerings
nor wearied you with demands [w] for incense. [x]
[24] You have not bought any fragrant calamus [y] for me,
or lavished on me the fat [z] of your sacrifices.
But you have burdened me with your sins
and wearied [a] me with your offenses. [b]

[25] "I, even I, am he who blots out your transgressions, [c] for my own sake, [d]
and remembers your sins [e] no more. [f]
[26] Review the past for me,
let us argue the matter together; [g]
state the case [h] for your innocence.
[27] Your first father [i] sinned;
your spokesmen [j] rebelled [k] against me.
[28] So I will disgrace the dignitaries of your temple,
and I will consign Jacob to destruction [l] [l]
and Israel to scorn. [m]

Israel the Chosen

44 "But now listen, O Jacob, my servant, [n]
Israel, whom I have chosen. [o]
[2] This is what the LORD says—

43:14
[t] S Ex 15:13;
S Job 19:25
[u] S Isa 1:4;
S 41:20
[v] Isa 13:14-15
[w] S Isa 23:13
43:15 [x] S Isa 42:8
[y] S Isa 27:11;
45:11
[z] S Isa 41:21
43:16
[a] S Ex 14:29;
S 15:8;
S Isa 11:15
43:17
[b] Ps 118:12;
Isa 1:31
[c] S Ex 14:22
[d] S Ex 14:9
[e] Ps 76:5-6
[f] S Job 13:25;
Jer 51:21;
Eze 38:4
43:18
[g] S Isa 41:22
43:19
[h] S Isa 41:22;
Jer 16:14-15;
23:7-8; 2Co 5:17;
Rev 21:5
[i] S Isa 40:3
[j] S Ps 126:4;
S Isa 33:21;
S 35:7
43:20
[k] S Ps 148:10
[l] S Isa 13:22
[m] S Nu 20:8
43:21 [n] S ver 7;
S Ge 2:7
[o] Mal 3:17
[p] S Ps 66:2;
102:18; 1Pe 2:9
43:22
[q] S Jos 22:5;
S Isa 1:14
[r] Isa 30:11
43:23
[s] S Ex 29:41
[t] Zec 7:5-6;
Mal 1:6-8
[u] Am 5:25

[v] Mic 6:3;
Mal 1:12-13
[w] Jer 7:22
[x] Ex 30:35;
S Lev 2:1
43:24
[y] S Ex 30:23
[z] Lev 3:9
[a] S Isa 1:14;
S 7:13; S Jer 8:21
[b] Jer 44:22;
Mal 2:17

43:25 [c] S 2Sa 12:13; S 2Ch 6:21; Mk 2:7; Lk 5:21; Ac 3:19
[d] S Isa 37:35; S Eze 20:44 [e] Isa 64:9; Mic 7:18 [f] S Job 7:21;
S Isa 38:17 **43:26** [g] S Isa 1:18 [h] S Isa 41:1; 49:25; 50:8 **43:27**
[i] S Ge 12:18 [j] Isa 9:15; 28:7; Jer 5:31 [k] S Isa 24:20; S 48:8
43:28 [l] S Nu 5:27; S Dt 13:15; S Isa 42:24; S Zec 5:3
[m] S Ps 39:8; Jer 24:9; Eze 5:15 **44:1** [n] ver 21 [o] S Ge 6:11;
S Isa 14:1

---

become their means of flight (cf. Jer 51:13).

43:15 *Creator.* See v. 1 and note. *King.* God was called "king over Jeshurun" (Israel) in Dt 33:5 (contrast 1Sa 8:7).

43:16–17 A reference to crossing the Red Sea (see v. 2 and note). Pharaoh's chariots and horsemen were destroyed as Israel's God fought against them (see 51:10; Ex 14:28; 15:4).

43:17 *snuffed out like a wick.* Contrast 42:3.

43:19 *new thing.* See 42:9 and note. *way in the desert.* See 35:8; 40:3 and notes. *streams in the wasteland.* See v. 20; 32:2 and note. Contrast 42:15 and note.

43:20 *jackals . . . owls.* Creatures of the desert (see 13:21–22; 34:13–15; 35:7).

43:21 *people . . . proclaim my praise.* Cf. 42:12.

43:22–24 The Israelites may have brought sacrifices (see 1:11–15 and note), but their hearts were not right with God.

43:22 *not called . . . not wearied.* Apparently their prayers were halfhearted (contrast Ps 69:3).

43:23 *not burdened . . . nor wearied.* God did not make excessive demands on his people.

43:24 *calamus.* Linked with incense (see v. 23) also in SS 4:14; Jer 6:20. *fat.* See note on 34:6. *burdened . . . wearied.* See 1:14.

43:25 *blots out . . . transgressions.* In spite of the punishment Israel must suffer (v. 28), God is eager to forgive his people (see 1:18; 44:22; see also 40:2 and note).

43:26 *state the case.* The Lord takes Israel to court, as he did the nations in 41:21–22.

43:27 *first father.* See 51:2. Even Abraham was a sinner (see Ge 12:18; 20:9). *spokesmen.* Probably the priests and prophets.

43:28 *consign . . . to destruction.* See NIV text note; see also note on 34:2. Any town of Israel that harbored idolatry was to receive this fate (Dt 13:12–15). Jerusalem suffered destruction at the hands of the Babylonians (2Ki 25:8–9) because of idolatry (see Eze 7:15–22).

44:1–2 *my servant.* See 41:8–9 and note.

44:2 *formed you.* See 43:1 and note. *in the womb.* See v. 24. The tenderness of the Creator is shown (see also 49:5; Jer 1:5). *Do not be afraid.* See v. 8; 41:10 and note. *Jeshu-*

he who made^p you, who formed you
  in the womb, ^q
and who will help^r you:
Do not be afraid, ^s O Jacob, my
  servant, ^t
Jeshurun, ^u whom I have chosen.
³For I will pour water^v on the thirsty
  land,
and streams on the dry ground; ^w
I will pour out my Spirit^x on your
  offspring,
and my blessing^y on your
  descendants. ^z
⁴They will spring up like grass^a in a
  meadow,
like poplar trees^b by flowing
  streams. ^c
⁵One will say, 'I belong^d to the LORD';
another will call himself by the name
  of Jacob;
still another will write on his hand, ^e
  'The LORD's,'^f
and will take the name Israel.

The LORD, Not Idols

⁶"This is what the LORD says—
Israel's King^g and Redeemer, ^h the
  LORD Almighty:
I am the first and I am the last; ⁱ
  apart from me there is no God. ^j
⁷Who then is like me? ^k Let him
  proclaim it.
Let him declare and lay out before
  me
what has happened since I established
  my ancient people,
and what is yet to come—
  yes, let him foretell^l what will come.
⁸Do not tremble, do not be afraid.
Did I not proclaim^m this and foretell
  it long ago?
You are my witnesses. Is there any
  Godⁿ besides me?

No, there is no other Rock; ^o I know
  not one."

⁹All who make idols^p are nothing,
and the things they treasure are
  worthless. ^q
Those who would speak up for them
  are blind; ^r
they are ignorant, to their own
  shame. ^s
¹⁰Who shapes a god and casts an idol, ^t
which can profit him nothing? ^u
¹¹He and his kind will be put to shame; ^v
craftsmen are nothing but men.
Let them all come together and take
  their stand;
they will be brought down to terror
  and infamy. ^w

¹²The blacksmith^x takes a tool
and works with it in the coals;
he shapes an idol with hammers,
he forges it with the might of his
  arm. ^y
He gets hungry and loses his strength;
he drinks no water and grows faint. ^z
¹³The carpenter^a measures with a line
and makes an outline with a marker;
he roughs it out with chisels
and marks it with compasses.
He shapes it in the form of man, ^b
of man in all his glory,
that it may dwell in a shrine. ^c
¹⁴He cut down cedars,
or perhaps took a cypress or oak.
He let it grow among the trees of the
  forest,
or planted a pine, ^d and the rain
  made it grow.
¹⁵It is man's fuel^e for burning;
some of it he takes and warms
  himself,

44:2 ^pver 21; S Ps 149:2
^qS Ge 2:7; S Ps 139:13;
^rS Isa 27:11
^sS Isa 41:10
^tS Isa 43:5
^tJer 30:10; 46:27
^uS Nu 23:21; S Dt 32:15
44:3 ^vJoel 3:18; Jn 4:10 ^wS Pr 9:5; S Isa 32:2; S 35:7
^xS Isa 11:2; Eze 36:27;
S Mk 1:8; S Ac 2:17
^yMal 3:10
^zIsa 61:9; 65:23
44:4 ^aS Job 5:25; S Ps 72:16
^bS Lev 23:40
^cS Job 40:22
44:5 ^dPs 116:16; Isa 19:21; Jer 50:5 ^eEx 13:9
^fIsa 60:3; 66:23; Zec 8:20-22; 13:9; 14:16
44:6 ^gS Isa 41:21
^hS Job 19:25; Isa 43:1
ⁱS Isa 41:4; Rev 1:8,17
^jS Dt 6:4; S 1Ch 17:20; S Ps 18:31; S Isa 43:10
44:7 ^kS Dt 32:39
^lS Isa 41:22,26
44:8 ^mS Isa 40:21; S 42:9
ⁿS Isa 43:10

^oS Ge 49:24
44:9 ^pS Ex 20:4; S Lev 19:4; Isa 40:19
^qS Isa 41:24
^rS Isa 26:11
^sS Isa 1:29; 65:13; 66:5; Jer 22:22
44:10 ^tS Isa 40:19
^uIsa 41:29; Jer 10:5; Ac 19:26
44:11 ^vS ver 9; S Isa 1:29
^wS 2Ki 19:18; S Isa 37:19
44:12 ^xS Isa 40:19; 41:6-7; 54:16
^yAc 17:29
^zIsa 40:28

44:13 ^aS Isa 41:7 ^bPs 115:4-7 ^cJdg 17:4-5 **44:14**
^dS Isa 41:19 **44:15** ^ever 19

---

run. Israel (see v. 1); found elsewhere only in Dt 32:15 (see
NIV text note there); 33:5,26.
44:3 *pour water . . . streams.* See 30:25; 32:2; 35:6–7
and notes; see also 41:18. *pour out my Spirit.* Associated
with the Messianic age in 32:15 (see note there) and Joel
2:28.
44:4 *grass.* A symbol of luxuriant growth also in 35:7
(contrast 37:27; 40:6–8).
44:5 *call . . . by the name.* A willingness to identify with
Jacob, the Lord's people. See 43:7 and note. *write on his
hand.* Perhaps a mark of ownership (cf. 49:16; Rev 13:16) or
a reminder of one's allegiance (cf. Ex 13:9,16).
44:6 *King.* See 43:15 and note. *Redeemer.* See v. 24;
41:14 and note. *first . . . last.* See 41:4 and note. *apart . . .
God.* See 43:11 and note.
44:7 *foretell.* See 41:22,26 and notes.
44:8 *You are my witnesses.* See 43:10 and note. *Rock.* See
17:10 and note. As in v. 2; 43:11–13, Isaiah may be drawing on the song of Moses, which describes God as "the

Rock" (Dt 32:4,15,30–31), but the metaphor is also common in the Psalms (see note on Ps 18:2).
44:9–20 A satire on the folly of idolatry (see 40:18–20 and
note).
44:9 *nothing . . . worthless.* Like the nations and their idols
(see 40:17; 41:24 and notes). *shame.* Cf. v. 11; 42:17;
45:16.
44:11 *craftsmen.* See 40:19 and note.
44:12–20 Two idols are described: a metal one in v. 12
and a wooden one in vv. 13–20. The latter was more common (see 40:20).
44:12 *grows faint.* But God never gets tired (40:28).
44:13 *in the form of man.* Man was made in the image of
God (see Ge 1:26–27 and notes), but an idol is made in the
image of man (Dt 4:16; Ro 1:23).
44:14 *cedars . . . cypress . . . oak.* The most valuable kinds
of wood then known. See 9:10; 41:19 and notes.
44:15 *worships . . . bows down.* Repeated in vv. 17,19;
see 2:8,20.

he kindles a fire and bakes bread.
But he also fashions a god and
    worships[f] it;
he makes an idol and bows[g] down to
    it.
[16]Half of the wood he burns in the fire;
    over it he prepares his meal,
he roasts his meat and eats his fill.
He also warms himself and says,
    "Ah! I am warm; I see the fire. [h]"
[17]From the rest he makes a god, his idol;
    he bows down to it and worships. [i]
He prays[j] to it and says,
    "Save[k] me; you are my god."
[18]They know nothing, they understand[l]
    their eyes[m] are plastered over so they
        cannot see,
and their minds closed so they cannot
    understand.
[19]No one stops to think,
    no one has the knowledge or
        understanding[n] to say,
"Half of it I used for fuel;[o]
    I even baked bread over its coals,
I roasted meat and I ate.
Shall I make a detestable[p] thing from
    what is left?
Shall I bow down to a block of
    wood?"[q]
[20]He feeds on ashes,[r] a deluded[s] heart
    misleads him;
he cannot save himself, or say,
    "Is not this thing in my right hand a
        lie?[t] [u]"

[21]"Remember[v] these things, O Jacob,
    for you are my servant, O Israel. [w]
I have made you, you are my servant;[x]
    O Israel, I will not forget you.[y]
[22]I have swept away[z] your offenses like a
    cloud,

your sins like the morning mist.
Return[a] to me,
    for I have redeemed[b] you."

[23]Sing for joy,[c] O heavens, for the Lord
    has done this;
    shout aloud, O earth[d] beneath.
Burst into song, you mountains,[e]
    you forests and all your trees,[f]
for the Lord has redeemed[g] Jacob,
    he displays his glory[h] in Israel.

Jerusalem to Be Inhabited

[24]"This is what the Lord says—
    your Redeemer,[i] who formed[j] you
        in the womb:[k]

I am the Lord,
    who has made all things,
who alone stretched out the heavens,[l]
    who spread out the earth[m] by myself,

[25]who foils[n] the signs of false prophets
    and makes fools of diviners,[o]
who overthrows the learning of the
    wise[p]
    and turns it into nonsense,[q]
[26]who carries out the words[r] of his
    servants
and fulfills[s] the predictions of his
    messengers,

who says of Jerusalem,[t] 'It shall be
    inhabited,'
    of the towns of Judah, 'They shall be
        built,'

44:15 /S Ex 20:5;
Rev 9:20
gS 2Ch 25:14
44:16 hIsa 47:14
44:17 /S Ex 20:5;
Isa 2:8; Jer 1:16
/S 1Ki 18:26
kS Jdg 10:14;
Isa 45:20; 46:7;
47:15
44:18 /Isa 1:3;
S 16:12; Jer 4:22;
10:8,14,15-15
mS Isa 6:9-10;
S 29:10
44:19 nver
18-19; Isa 5:13;
27:11; 45:20
over 15
pS Dt 27:15
qIsa 40:20
44:20 rPs 102:9
sS Job 15:31;
Ro 1:21-23,28;
2Th 2:11;
2Ti 3:13
tS Dt 4:28;
Hos 10:5; 13:2
uIsa 59:3,4,13;
Jer 9:3; 10:14;
51:17; Ro 1:25
44:21 vIsa 46:8;
Zec 10:9
wS Isa 43:1
xS Ps 136:22;
S Isa 27:11
yPs 27:10;
Isa 49:15;
Jer 31:20
44:22
zS 2Sa 12:13;
S 2Ch 6:21;
Ac 3:19

aS Job 22:23;
Isa 45:22; 55:7;
Jer 36:3; Mal 3:7
bS Isa 33:24;
S Mt 20:28;
1Co 6:20
44:23 cS Ps 98:4;
Isa 52:6
dS 1Ch 16:31;
Ps 148:7
eS Ps 98:8
/S Ps 65:13
gS Ex 6:6;
hS Ex 16:7;
S Lev 10:3;
S Isa 4:2; 43:7;
46:13; 49:3;
52:1; 55:5; 60:9,
21; 61:3;
Jer 30:19

44:24 iS Job 19:25; Isa 43:14 /S Isa 27:11 kS Ps 139:13
/S Ge 2:1; S Isa 42:5 mS Ge 1:1 **44:25** nPs 33:10 oLev 19:26;
1Sa 6:2; Isa 2:6; 8:19; 47:13; Jer 27:9; Da 2:2,10; 4:7;
Mic 3:7; Zec 10:2 pS Job 5:13; 1Co 1:27 q2Sa 15:31;
1Co 1:19-20 **44:26** rIsa 59:21; Zec 1:6 sIsa 46:10; 55:11;
Jer 23:20; 39:16; La 2:17; Da 9:12; S Mt 5:18 tS Isa 1:1

44:16 *roasts his meat . . . warms himself.* Although wood serves common purposes, it is also made into an idol (see v. 19).
44:17 *Save me.* King Amaziah was condemned for worshiping the gods of Seir, a nation he had defeated in battle (2Ch 25:14–15). Isaiah denounces such idolatry as totally irrational (see 45:20). Whereas those who worshiped idols associated the god with the idol, for Isaiah there was no god for the idol to represent, so he depicts idolatry as worship of a mere "block of wood" (v. 19).
44:18 *eyes are plastered . . . minds closed.* Israel's condition in 6:9–10 (see note there). The description ironically characterizes both the idols and those who worship them. See also Ps 82:5.
44:19 *detestable thing.* The Lord detests idols (see Dt 27:15). In 1Ki 11:5,7; 2Ki 23:13 Molech and Chemosh are called detestable gods. Those who worship idols are also called detestable (see 41:24 and note).
44:20 *feeds on ashes.* Even devoted worship does not benefit the idolater. Cf. Hos 12:1. *lie.* Or "fraud." See 2Th 2:11.

44:21 *my servant.* See vv. 1–2; 41:8–9 and note.
44:22 *swept away your offenses.* As in 40:2 (see note there), the suffering of Israel has paved the way for forgiveness and the restoration of the nation (see 43:25 and note). *Return to me.* Cf. Jer 31:18. *redeemed.* Cf. v. 23; see notes on 35:9; 41:14; 43:1.
44:23 *Sing for joy . . . shout aloud.* Nature is called on to join in praise (see also 35:1; 49:13). *Burst into song, you mountains.* See 49:13; 55:12. *displays his glory.* See 35:2 and note; 40:5 and note.
44:24 *Redeemer.* See 41:14 and note. *stretched out . . . spread out.* See 40:22 and note; cf. 51:13.
44:25 *signs of false prophets.* See Dt 13:1–3. *diviners.* The Hebrew for this word is used of Balaam (Jos 13:22), the witch of Endor (1Sa 28:8) and false prophets (Jer 27:9). It is linked with soothsaying and sorcery (see 3:2–3 and note; Dt 18:10–11). *overthrows . . . the wise.* See 29:14 and note.
44:26 *servants . . . messengers.* The true prophets (see 42:19 and note; Jer 7:25). *inhabited . . . built.* See Jer 32:15; cf. Isa 58:12; 61:4. *ruins . . . restore.* Contrast 6:11.

and of their ruins, [u] 'I will restore them,' [v]

27who says to the watery deep, 'Be dry, and I will dry up [w] your streams,'

28who says of Cyrus, [x] 'He is my shepherd and will accomplish all that I please; he will say of Jerusalem, [y] "Let it be rebuilt," and of the temple, [z] "Let its foundations [a] be laid." '

45 "This is what the LORD says to his anointed, [b] to Cyrus, [c] whose right hand I take hold [d] of to subdue nations [e] before him and to strip kings of their armor, to open doors before him so that gates will not be shut:
2I will go before you [f] and will level [g] the mountains [m]; I will break down gates [h] of bronze and cut through bars of iron. [i]
3I will give you the treasures [j] of darkness, riches stored in secret places, [k] so that you may know [l] that I am the LORD, the God of Israel, who summons you by name. [m]
4For the sake of Jacob my servant, [n] of Israel my chosen, I summon you by name and bestow on you a title of honor, though you do not acknowledge [o] me.
5I am the LORD, and there is no other; [p] apart from me there is no God. [q] I will strengthen you, [r]

though you have not acknowledged me,
6so that from the rising of the sun to the place of its setting [s] men may know [t] there is none besides me. [u] I am the LORD, and there is no other.
7I form the light and create darkness, [v] I bring prosperity and create disaster; [w] I, the LORD, do all these things.

8"You heavens above, rain [x] down righteousness; [y] let the clouds shower it down. Let the earth open wide, let salvation [z] spring up, let righteousness grow with it; I, the LORD, have created it.

9"Woe to him who quarrels [a] with his Maker, [b] to him who is but a potsherd [c] among the potsherds on the ground. Does the clay say to the potter, [d] 'What are you making?' [e] Does your work say, 'He has no hands'? [f]
10Woe to him who says to his father, 'What have you begotten?' or to his mother, 'What have you brought to birth?'

11"This is what the LORD says— the Holy One [g] of Israel, and its Maker: [h]

44:26 [u]S Ps 74:3; S Isa 51:3
[v]S Ezr 9:9; S Ps 51:18;
Isa 49:8-21; S 61:4
44:27 [w]S Isa 11:15; S 19:5; Rev 16:12
44:28 [x]S 2Ch 36:22; S Isa 41:2
[y]S Isa 14:32
[z]Ezr 1:2-4
[a]S Isa 28:16; 58:12
45:1 [b]S Ps 45:7
[c]S 2Ch 36:22; S Isa 41:2
[d]Ps 73:23;
Isa 41:13; 42:6
[e]Isa 48:14; Jer 50:35; 51:20, 24; Mic 4:13
45:2 [f]Ex 23:20
[g]S Isa 40:4
[h]S Isa 13:2
[i]Ps 107:16; 147:13; Jer 51:30; La 2:9; Na 3:13
45:3 [j]S 2Ki 24:13; Jer 50:37; 51:13
[k]Jer 41:8
[l]Isa 41:23
[m]S Ex 33:12; S Isa 43:1
45:4 [n]S Isa 14:1; 41:8-9 [o]Ac 17:23
45:5 [p]S Isa 44:8
[q]S Dt 32:12; S Ps 18:31; S Isa 43:10
[r]S Ps 18:39; Eze 30:24-25

45:6 [s]S Ps 113:3; Isa 43:5
[t]S Isa 11:9 [u]ver 5, 18; Isa 14:13-14; 47:8,10; Zep 2:15
45:7 [v]S Ge 1:4; S Ex 10:22
[w]S Isa 14:15; S 31:2; La 3:38
45:8 [x]Ps 72:6; S 133:3; Joel 3:18
[y]ver 24; Ps 85:11; S Isa 41:2; 46:13; 48:18; 60:21; 61:10,11; 62:1; Hos 10:12;

Joel 2:23; Am 5:24; Mal 4:2 [z]S Ps 85:9; Isa 12:3 45:9 [a]S Job 12:13; S 15:25; S 27:2; 1Co 10:22 [b]S Job 33:13 [c]Ps 22:15 [d]S Isa 29:16; Ro 9:20-21* [e]S Job 9:12; Da 4:35 [f]S Isa 10:15 45:11 [g]S Isa 1:4 [h]S Ps 149:2; S Isa 51:13

[m]2 Dead Sea Scrolls and Septuagint; the meaning of the word in the Masoretic Text is uncertain.

44:27 *Be dry.* A reference to the crossing of the Red Sea (see 11:15; 37:25; 43:16–17 and notes; cf. 50:2; 51:10).
44:28 *Cyrus.* See 41:2 and note. *shepherd.* Often applied to rulers (see 2Sa 5:2; Jer 23:2). *Jerusalem . . . temple.* The decree of Cyrus (Ezr 1:2-4; 6:3-5) authorized the rebuilding of the temple, which would lead to a restored Jerusalem (see 45:13).
45:1 *anointed.* "Messiah" comes from the Hebrew for this word. Cyrus, a foreign emperor, is called "his anointed" just as he is called "my shepherd" (44:28), because God has appointed him to carry out a divine commission in his role as king. Nebuchadnezzar is similarly called "my servant" (Jer 25:9; 27:6; 43:10). The servant—Christ (see note on 42:1–4)—is called "the Anointed One" in Da 9:25–26 (see NIV text note on Mt 1:17). See also Ps 2:2 and note. *right hand I . . . hold.* See 41:13 and note.
45:2 *gates of bronze . . . bars of iron.* Normally the doors of city gates were made of wood, and the bars were metal (see Jdg 16:3 and note).
45:3 *that you may know.* God's actions reveal his power (cf. Eze 6:7; 7:27). *summons you by name.* To indicate God's control of Cyrus's activities. See v. 4; see also note on

43:1.
45:4 *my servant.* See 41:8–9 and note. *title of honor.* Perhaps "anointed" (v. 1). *though . . . not acknowledge me.* See v. 5. Cyrus apparently worshiped the chief Babylonian deity, Marduk, whom he praised in his inscriptions.
45:5 *I . . . there is no other.* See vv. 6,14,18,21–22; 43:11 and note.
45:6 *rising . . . to . . . setting.* The whole earth (see Mal 1:11 and note).
45:7 *darkness . . . disaster.* Such as the darkness that plagued the Egyptians (see Ex 10:21–23; Ps 105:28; cf. Isa 47:11; Am 3:6).
45:8 *rain down . . . shower.* A picture of abundance (see Hos 10:12). *righteousness.* In v. 13; 41:2 Cyrus is mentioned in connection with God's righteousness. God is "making things right" through the Persian king. *salvation spring up.* God will deliver his people. *righteousness grow.* Peace and justice will prevail (see 11:4 and note).
45:9 *clay say to the potter.* See 29:16 and note; cf. 64:8; Jer 18:6.
45:11 *Holy One of Israel.* See 1:4 and note. *children . . . work of my hands.* See 29:23 and note.

Concerning things to come,
do you question me about my
children,
or give me orders about the work of
my hands? *i*
12It is I who made the earth*j*
and created mankind upon it.
My own hands stretched out the
heavens; *k*
I marshaled their starry hosts. *l*
13I will raise up Cyrus*n* *m* in my
righteousness:
I will make all his ways straight. *n*
He will rebuild my city*o*
and set my exiles free,
but not for a price or reward, *p*
says the LORD Almighty."

14This is what the LORD says:

"The products*q* of Egypt and the
merchandise of Cush, *o*
and those tall Sabeans*r* —
they will come over to you*s*
and will be yours;
they will trudge behind you, *t*
coming over to you in chains. *u*
They will bow down before you
and plead*v* with you, saying,
'Surely God is with you, *w* and there is
no other;
there is no other god. *x* '"

15Truly you are a God who hides*y*
himself,
O God and Savior*z* of Israel.
16All the makers of idols will be put to
shame and disgraced; *a*
they will go off into disgrace together.
17But Israel will be saved*b* by the LORD
with an everlasting salvation; *c*
you will never be put to shame or
disgraced, *d*

to ages everlasting.

18For this is what the LORD says—
he who created the heavens,
he is God;
he who fashioned and made the earth, *e*
he founded it;
he did not create it to be empty, *f*
but formed it to be inhabited*g*—
he says:
"I am the LORD,
and there is no other. *h*
19I have not spoken in secret, *i*
from somewhere in a land of
darkness; *j*
I have not said to Jacob's descendants, *k*
'Seek*l* me in vain.'
I, the LORD, speak the truth;
I declare what is right. *m*

20"Gather together*n* and come;
assemble, you fugitives from the
nations.
Ignorant*o* are those who carry*p* about
idols of wood,
who pray to gods that cannot save. *q*
21Declare what is to be, present it—
let them take counsel together.
Who foretold*r* this long ago,
who declared it from the distant
past? *s*
Was it not I, the LORD?
And there is no God apart from me, *t*
a righteous God*u* and a Savior; *v*
there is none but me.

22"Turn*w* to me and be saved, *x*
all you ends of the earth; *y*
for I am God, and there is no other. *z*
23By myself I have sworn, *a*

45:11 *l*S Ps 8:6;
S Isa 19:25
45:12 *j*S Ge 1:1
*k*S Ge 2:1;
S Isa 48:13
*l*S Ne 9:6;
S Job 38:32
45:13
*m*S 2Ch 36:22;
S Isa 41:2
*n*S 1Ki 8:36;
S Ps 26:12;
S Isa 40:4
*o*S Ezr 1:2
*p*Isa 52:3
45:14 *q*2Sa 8:2;
Isa 18:7; 60:5
*r*S Isa 2:3; 60:11;
62:2; Zec 8:20-22
*s*S Isa 2:3
*t*S Ge 27:29
*u*S 2Sa 3:34;
S Isa 14:1-2
*v*Jer 16:19;
Zec 8:20-23
*w*1Co 14:25
*x*S Ps 18:31;
S Isa 11:9;
S 43:10
45:15
*y*S Dt 31:17;
Ps 44:24;
S Isa 1:15
*z*S Isa 25:9
45:16 *a*S Ps 35:4;
S Isa 1:29
45:17 *b*Jer 23:6;
33:16; Ro 11:26
*c*S Isa 12:2
*d*S Ge 30:23;
S Isa 29:22;
S 41:11
45:18 *e*S Ge 1:1
*f*S Ge 1:2
*g*S Ge 1:26 *h*ver
5; Dt 4:35
45:19 *i*Isa 48:16;
65:4 *j*Jer 2:31
*k*ver 25; Isa 41:8;
65:9; Jer 31:36
*l*S Dt 4:29;
S 2Ch 15:2
*m*S Dt 30:11
45:20 *n*S Isa 43:9
*o*S Isa 44:19
*p*Ps 115:7;
Isa 46:1; Jer 10:5
*q*Dt 32:37;
S Isa 44:17;
Jer 1:16; 2:28
45:21
*r*S Isa 41:22
*s*Isa 46:10 *t*ver 5;
S Ps 46:10;
Isa 46:9;
Mk 12:32
*u*Ps 11:7 *v*S Ps 3:8; S Isa 25:9 45:22 *w*S Isa 44:22; Zec 12:10
*x*Nu 21:8-9; S 2Ch 20:12 *y*S Ge 49:10; S Isa 11:9,12; 49:6,12
*z*Hos 13:4 45:23 *a*S Ge 22:16; S Isa 14:24

*n*13 Hebrew *him*   *o*14 That is, the upper Nile region

45:12 *stretched ... heavens.* See 40:22 and note. *marshaled ... starry hosts.* See 40:26 and note.
45:13 *Cyrus in my righteousness.* See note on 41:2. *make ... ways straight.* Enabling him to reach his goals (see v. 2; see also 40:3 and note; cf. Pr 3:6). *rebuild my city.* See on 44:28. *not for a price.* Since God had not received a payment when he sold them (see 52:3 and note; contrast note on 43:3).
45:14 *products ... merchandise.* See 18:7 and note. *Egypt ... Cush ... Sabeans.* See notes on 18:1; 43:3. *coming over to you ... bow down.* Israel's future domination over her former enemies has been mentioned in 11:14; 14:1-2 (see note on 14:1); it is also the theme of 49:23; 54:3; 60:11-14. *Surely God is with you.* One day the nations will acknowledge Israel's God (see v. 23; 19:23-25; Zec 8:20-23).
45:15 *hides himself.* God's plans and actions are a mystery to man (cf. 54:8; 55:8-9). *Savior.* See v. 21 and note on 43:3.
45:16 *put to shame.* See 42:17; 44:9.

45:17 *everlasting salvation.* Cf. the "everlasting kindness" of 54:8. *never be put to shame.* See 29:22 and note.
45:18 *created ... fashioned.* See 40:21-22 and notes. *empty.* Or "formless" or "chaotic" (see Ge 1:2 and note). *to be inhabited.* Palestine was now empty (see 6:11; Jer 4:23-26) and chaotic but would soon have inhabitants (see 44:26,28) and be orderly again.
45:19 *in secret ... darkness.* Probably an allusion to the clandestine ways of mediums and spiritists (see 8:19; 29:4). *Seek me in vain.* Cf. Jer 29:13-14.
45:20 *Ignorant ... save.* See 44:17-18 and notes.
45:21 *Declare ... present.* See 41:21-22 and note. *foretold ... distant past.* See 41:26 and note.
45:22 *Turn ... be saved.* Cf. 49:6 and the invitation of 55:7. *ends of the earth.* See 11:12 and note; 42:10.
45:23 *By myself I have sworn.* Explained in Heb 6:13. See also 62:8. *word ... not ... revoked.* See 55:10-11. *every knee ... every tongue.* See v. 14 and note. Paul quotes this portion of Isaiah in Ro 14:11 and Php 2:10-11 to describe Christ's exalted position.

my mouth has uttered in all
integrity[b]
a word that will not be revoked:[c]
Before me every knee will bow;[d]
by me every tongue will swear.[e]
24They will say of me, 'In the LORD alone
are righteousness[f] and strength.[g]' "
All who have raged against him
will come to him and be put to
shame.[h]
25But in the LORD all the descendants[i] of
Israel
will be found righteous[j] and will
exult.[k]

Gods of Babylon

46 Bel[l] bows down, Nebo stoops
low;
their idols[m] are borne by beasts of
burden.[p]
The images that are carried[n] about are
burdensome,
a burden for the weary.
2They stoop and bow down together;
unable to rescue the burden,
they themselves go off into
captivity.[o]

3"Listen[p] to me, O house of Jacob,
all you who remain[q] of the house of
Israel,
you whom I have upheld since you
were conceived,[r]
and have carried[s] since your birth.[t]
4Even to your old age and gray hairs[u]
I am he,[v] I am he who will sustain
you.
I have made you and I will carry you;
I will sustain[w] you and I will rescue
you.

5"To whom will you compare me or
count me equal?
To whom will you liken me that we
may be compared?[x]

6Some pour out gold from their bags
and weigh out silver on the scales;
they hire a goldsmith[y] to make it into a
god,
and they bow down and worship it.[z]
7They lift it to their shoulders and carry[a]
it;
they set it up in its place, and there it
stands.
From that spot it cannot move.[b]
Though one cries out to it, it does not
answer;[c]
it cannot save[d] him from his
troubles.

8"Remember[e] this, fix it in mind,
take it to heart, you rebels.[f]
9Remember the former things,[g] those of
long ago;[h]
I am God, and there is no other;
I am God, and there is none like
me.[i]
10I make known the end from the
beginning,[j]
from ancient times,[k] what is still to
come.[l]
I say: My purpose will stand,[m]
and I will do all that I please.
11From the east I summon[n] a bird of
prey;[o]
from a far-off land, a man to fulfill my
purpose.
What I have said, that will I bring
about;
what I have planned,[p] that will I
do.[q]
12Listen[r] to me, you stubborn-hearted,[s]
you who are far from righteousness.[t]
13I am bringing my righteousness[u] near,

Cross references

45:23 [b]S Dt 30:11; Heb 6:13 [c]Isa 55:11 [d]S ver 14 [e]S Ps 63:11; S Isa 19:18; Ro 14:11*; Php 2:10-11
45:24 [f]S ver 8; Jer 33:16 [g]S Dt 33:29; S Ps 18:39; S Isa 40:26; 63:1 [h]S Isa 41:11
45:25 [i]S ver 19 [j]S Isa 4:3; S 49:4 [k]S Isa 24:23; S 41:16
46:1 [l]S Isa 21:9; Jer 50:2; 51:44 [m]S 1Sa 5:2 [n]ver 7; S Isa 45:20
46:2 [o]S Jdg 18:17-18; S 2Sa 5:21; Jer 51:47
46:3 [p]ver 12; Isa 48:12; 51:1 [q]S Isa 1:9 [r]S Ps 139:13; Isa 44:2 [s]S Dt 1:31; S Ps 28:9 [t]S Ps 22:10
46:4 [u]Ps 71:18 [v]S Dt 32:39; S Isa 43:13 [w]S Ps 18:35; S 119:117
46:5 [x]S Ex 15:11; Job 41:10; Isa 40:18,25; Jer 49:19
46:6 [y]S Isa 40:19 [z]S Ex 20:5; Isa 44:17; Hos 13:2
46:7 [a]S ver 1 [b]S 1Sa 5:3; S Isa 41:7 [c]S 1Ki 18:26 [d]S Isa 44:17; S 47:13
46:8 [e]S Isa 44:21 [f]S Isa 1:2
46:9 [g]S Isa 41:22 [h]S Dt 32:7 [i]S Ex 8:10; S Isa 45:21; Mk 12:32
46:10 [j]S Isa 41:4 [k]S Isa 45:21 [l]S Isa 41:22 [m]S Pr 19:21; S Isa 7:9,9; S 44:26; Ac 5:39; Eph 1:11

46:11 [n]S Jdg 4:10; S Ezr 1:2 [o]S Isa 8:8 [p]S Isa 25:1 [q]S Ge 41:25; Jer 44:28 46:12 [r]S ver 3 [s]S Ex 32:9; S Isa 9:9 [t]Ps 119:150; Isa 48:1; Jer 2:5 46:13 [u]S Isa 1:26; S 45:8; Ro 3:21

[p] 1 Or are but beasts and cattle

45:24 *In the* LORD *alone . . . strength.* See v. 5 and note. This is the climax of the refrain that runs through the chapter. *All . . . put to shame.* Very similar to 41:11 except for "against you" (Israel).

45:25 *exult.* The Hebrew for this verb is translated "glory" in 41:16.

46:1 *Bel.* Another name for Marduk, the chief deity of Babylon. The name "Bel" is equivalent to Canaanite "Baal" and means "lord." *bows down . . . stoops.* In disgrace (see v. 2; 21:9 and note). *Nebo.* Nabu, the god of learning and writing who was the son of Marduk.

46:2 *go off into captivity.* The idols join their worshipers in exile (see Jer 48:7; 49:3; Hos 10:5; Am 1:15).

46:3 *who remain.* The remnant (see 1:9 and note). *since . . . conceived . . . since . . . birth.* See 44:2 and note.

46:4 *old age and gray hairs.* Cf. Ps 37:25. *sustain . . . made . . . rescue.* Unlike the helpless idols of vv. 1–2. See 41:10, 13; 43:1–2 and notes.

46:5–7 See 40:18–20 and note.

46:6 *bow down and worship.* See 44:15,17,19.

46:7 *carry.* See v. 1. *cannot save.* See 44:17 and note.

46:8 *rebels.* Israel. See 1:2 and note; cf. 1:20,23,28; 30:1; 57:4.

46:9 *former things.* See 41:22 and note. *there is no other.* See 43:11 and note.

46:10–11 *My purpose.* Especially God's purposes and plans regarding Babylon and Israel (see 8:9–10; 14:24; 48:14 and notes). Cf. Ps 33:11.

46:10 *from the beginning.* See 41:26 and note.

46:11 *east . . . bird of prey.* Cyrus king of Persia (see 41:2 and note). The swiftness and power of a bird of prey in view (see 8:8 and note; Jer 49:22; cf. Da 8:4).

46:12 *stubborn-hearted.* See v. 8; 48:4; Eze 2:4.

46:13 *righteousness.* Here equivalent to salvation. See 41:2 and note; 45:8 and note. *salvation.* See note on 43:3. *splendor.* See 35:2 and note; 40:5 and note; see also 44:23;

it is not far away;
and my salvation ^{v} will not be
delayed.
I will grant salvation to Zion, ^{w}
my splendor ^{x} to Israel.

The Fall of Babylon

47 "Go down, sit in the dust, ^{y}
Virgin Daughter ^{z} of Babylon;
sit on the ground without a throne,
Daughter of the Babylonians. $^{q\ a}$
No more will you be called
tender or delicate. ^{b}

^{2}Take millstones ^{c} and grind ^{d} flour;
take off your veil. ^{e}
Lift up your skirts, ^{f} bare your legs,
and wade through the streams.

^{3}Your nakedness ^{g} will be exposed
and your shame ^{h} uncovered.
I will take vengeance; ^{i}
I will spare no one. ^{j} "

^{4}Our Redeemer ^{k}—the Lord Almighty ^{l}
is his name ^{m}—
is the Holy One ^{n} of Israel.

^{5}"Sit in silence, ^{o} go into darkness, ^{p}
Daughter of the Babylonians; ^{q}
no more will you be called
queen ^{r} of kingdoms. ^{s}
^{6}I was angry ^{t} with my people
and desecrated my inheritance; ^{u}
I gave them into your hand, ^{v}
and you showed them no mercy. ^{w}
Even on the aged
you laid a very heavy yoke.
^{7}You said, 'I will continue forever ^{x}—
the eternal queen!' ^{y}
But you did not consider these things
or reflect ^{z} on what might happen. ^{a}

^{8}"Now then, listen, you wanton
creature,
lounging in your security ^{b}

and saying to yourself,
'I am, and there is none besides me. ^{c}
I will never be a widow ^{d}
or suffer the loss of children.'
^{9}Both of these will overtake you
in a moment, ^{e} on a single day:
loss of children ^{f} and widowhood. ^{g}
They will come upon you in full
measure,
in spite of your many sorceries ^{h}
and all your potent spells. ^{i}

^{10}You have trusted ^{i} in your wickedness
and have said, 'No one sees me.' ^{k}
Your wisdom ^{l} and knowledge mislead ^{m}
you
when you say to yourself,
'I am, and there is none besides me.'
^{11}Disaster ^{n} will come upon you,
and you will not know how to
conjure it away.
A calamity will fall upon you
that you cannot ward off with a
ransom;
a catastrophe you cannot foresee
will suddenly ^{o} come upon you.

^{12}"Keep on, then, with your magic spells
and with your many sorceries, ^{p}
which you have labored at since
childhood.
Perhaps you will succeed,
perhaps you will cause terror.
^{13}All the counsel you have received has
only worn you out! ^{q}
Let your astrologers ^{r} come forward,
those stargazers who make predictions
month by month,
let them save ^{s} you from what is
coming upon you.

46:13 ^{v}S Ps 85:9
^{w}S Ps 74:2;
Joel 2:32
^{x}S Isa 44:23
47:1 ^{y}S Job 2:13;
S Isa 29:4
^{z}S Isa 21:9;
S 23:12
^{a}Ps 137:8;
Jer 50:42; 51:33;
Zec 2:7 ^{b}Dt 28:56
47:2 ^{c}Ex 11:5;
Mt 24:41
^{d}S Jdg 16:21
^{e}S Ge 24:65
^{f}S Isa 32:11
47:3 ^{g}S Ge 2:25;
Eze 16:37; Na 3:5
^{h}S Isa 20:4
^{i}S Isa 1:24; S 34:8
Isa 13:18-19
47:4 ^{k}S Job 19:25
^{l}S Isa 13:4
^{m}Isa 48:2;
Jer 50:34;
Am 4:13
^{n}S Isa 1:4; 48:17
47:5 ^{o}S Job 2:13
^{p}Isa 9:2; 13:10
^{q}S Isa 21:9 ^{r}ver
7; La 1:1;
Rev 18:7
^{s}S Isa 13:19;
Rev 17:18
47:6 ^{t}S 2Ch 28:9
^{u}S Dt 13:15;
S Isa 42:24;
Jer 2:7; 50:11
^{v}Isa 10:13
^{w}S Isa 14:6
47:7
^{x}S Isa 10:13;
Da 4:30 ^{y}S ver 5;
Rev 18:7
^{z}S Isa 42:23,25
^{a}S Dt 32:29
47:8 ^{b}S Isa 32:9

^{c}S Isa 45:6
^{d}Isa 49:21; 54:4;
La 1:1; Rev 18:7
47:9 ^{e}S Ps 55:15;
73:19; 1Th 5:3;
Rev 18:8-10
^{f}S Isa 13:18
^{g}Isa 4:1; Jer 15:8;
18:21 ^{h}ver 12;
Na 3:4; Mal 3:5
^{i}Dt 18:10-11;
Rev 9:21; 18:23
47:10
^{j}S Job 15:31;
Ps 52:7; 62:10
^{k}S 2Ki 21:16;
S Isa 29:15
^{l}S Isa 5:21
^{m}Isa 44:20

47:11 ^{n}S Isa 10:3; S 14:15; S 21:9; S 31:2; Lk 17:27
^{o}S Ps 55:15; S Isa 17:14; 1Th 5:3 **47:12** ^{p}S ver 9; S Ex 7:11
47:13 ^{q}Isa 57:10; Jer 51:58; Hab 2:13 ^{r}S Isa 19:3; S 44:25
^{s}ver 15; S Isa 5:29; 43:13; 46:7

^{q} 1 Or Chaldeans; also in verse 5

49:3.
47:1 *sit in the dust . . . on the ground.* A sign of mourning
(see 3:26). *Virgin Daughter of Babylon.* A personification of
Babylon and its inhabitants.
47:2 *millstones and grind.* A menial task performed by
women (see Ex 11:5 and note; Jdg 9:53 and note). *through
the streams.* Probably on the way to exile.
47:3 *nakedness will be exposed.* See Eze 16:36. Babylon is
no longer a queen (see vv. 5,7); she is reduced to a servant
girl or a prostitute (see v. 8). *take vengeance.* See 34:8 and
note. *spare no one.* See 13:18-20.
47:4 *Redeemer.* See note on 41:14. *Lord Almighty.* See
13:4 and note. *Holy One of Israel.* See 1:4; 41:14 and notes.
47:5 *queen of kingdoms.* Babylon was a very beautiful city
(see 13:19 and note).
47:6 *angry . . . desecrated my inheritance.* See 10:5-6
(where Assyria is God's tool); 42:24 and note; 43:28 and
note; La 2:2. *Even on the aged.* Their suffering fulfilled
Moses' curse for covenant disobedience (Dt 28:49-50).

47:7 *I will continue forever.* Cf. the arrogant words of
Nebuchadnezzar in Da 4:30.
47:8,10 *I am . . . none besides me.* Almost a claim of deity
(cf. the Lord's words in 43:11; 45:5-6,18,22). See also
14:12-15 and note.
47:8 *lounging in your security.* Similar language is used of
the complacent women of Jerusalem in 32:9,11. *widow.*
Deserted and distressed. *loss of children.* See v. 9; 13:16,
18; 14:22.
47:9,12 *sorceries . . . spells.* Magical practices to avoid
danger and to inflict harm on the enemy (see 3:2-3 and
note).
47:10 *No one sees me.* See 29:15 and note.
47:11 *with a ransom.* The Medes and Persians would not
accept any settlement short of surrender (see 13:17).
47:13 *astrologers . . . stargazers.* Babylon probably uti-
lized their services more than any other nation (see Da 2:2,
10).

14Surely they are like stubble;[t]
the fire[u] will burn them up.
They cannot even save themselves
from the power of the flame.[v]
Here are no coals to warm anyone;
here is no fire to sit by.
15That is all they can do for you—
these you have labored with
and trafficked[w] with since childhood.
Each of them goes on in his error;
there is not one that can save[x] you.

Stubborn Israel

48 "Listen to this, O house of Jacob,
you who are called by the name of
Israel[y]
and come from the line of Judah,[z]
you who take oaths[a] in the name of the
LORD[b]
and invoke[c] the God of Israel—
but not in truth[d] or righteousness—
2you who call yourselves citizens of the
holy city[e]
and rely[f] on the God of Israel—
the LORD Almighty is his name:[g]
3I foretold the former things[h] long ago,
my mouth announced[i] them and I
made them known;
then suddenly[j] I acted, and they
came to pass.
4For I knew how stubborn[k] you were;
the sinews of your neck[l] were iron,
your forehead[m] was bronze.
5Therefore I told you these things long
ago;
before they happened I announced[n]
them to you
so that you could not say,
'My idols did them;[o]
my wooden image and metal god
ordained them.'
6You have heard these things; look at
them all.
Will you not admit them?

"From now on I will tell you of new
things,[p]
of hidden things unknown to you.
7They are created[q] now, and not long
ago;[r]
you have not heard of them before
today.
So you cannot say,
'Yes, I knew[s] of them.'
8You have neither heard nor
understood;[t]
from of old your ear[u] has not been
open.
Well do I know how treacherous[v] you
are;
you were called a rebel[w] from birth.
9For my own name's sake[x] I delay my
wrath;[y]
for the sake of my praise I hold it
back from you,
so as not to cut you off.[z]
10See, I have refined[a] you, though not as
silver;
I have tested[b] you in the furnace[c] of
affliction.
11For my own sake,[d] for my own sake, I
do this.
How can I let myself be defamed?[e]
I will not yield my glory to another.[f]

Israel Freed

12"Listen[g] to me, O Jacob,

47:14 [t]S Isa 5:24 [u]S Isa 30:30 [v]Isa 10:17; Jer 51:30,32,58 **47:15** [w]Rev 18:11 [x]S ver 13; S Isa 44:17 **48:1** [y]S Ge 17:5 [z]S Ge 29:35 [a]S Isa 19:18 [b]S 1Sa 20:42; S Isa 43:7 [c]Ex 23:13; 2Sa 14:11; Ps 50:16; Isa 58:2; Jer 7:9-10; 44:26 [d]Isa 59:14; Jer 4:2; 5:2; Da 8:12; Zec 8:3 **48:2** [e]S Ne 11:1; S Isa 1:26; S Mt 4:5 [f]S Isa 10:20; Ro 2:17 [g]S Isa 47:4 **48:3** [h]S Isa 41:22 [i]S Isa 40:21; 45:21 [j]S Isa 17:14; 30:13 **48:4** [k]S Isa 9:9 [l]S Ex 32:9; S Dt 9:27; Ac 7:51 [m]Eze 3:9 **48:5** [n]S Isa 40:21; S 42:9 [o]Jer 44:15-18 **48:6** [p]S Isa 41:22; S Ro 16:25 **48:7** [q]Isa 65:18 [r]Isa 45:21 [s]S Ex 6:7 **48:8** [t]S Isa 1:3 [u]S Dt 29:4 [v]Isa 41:24; Mal 2:11,14 [w]Dt 9:7,24; Ps 58:3; S Isa 1:2; 43:27; 58:1 **48:9** [x]S 1Sa 12:22; S Isa 37:35 [y]S Job 9:13; S Isa 30:18 [z]S Ne 9:31 **48:10** [a]S Isa 1:25; Zec 13:9; Mal 3:3; 1Pe 1:7 [b]S Ex 15:25 [c]S Ex 1:13; S 1Ki 8:51 **48:11** [d]S 1Sa 12:22; S Isa 37:35 [e]S Lev 18:21; Dt 32:27; Jer 14:7,21; Eze 20:9,14,22,44 [f]Isa 42:8 **48:12** [g]S Isa 46:3

47:14 *stubble.* This will be a rapid, powerful fire. See note on 1:31; cf. Mal 4:1. *cannot . . . save themselves.* In contrast to the mighty Savior of Israel (see 43:3 and note), astrologers and sorcerers are as helpless as idols (see 44:17 and note). *no coals to warm anyone.* A subtle reference to firewood, a material from which pagans sometimes made idols (see 44:15).
48:1 *called by the name.* They belong to Israel (see 43:7 and note). *Israel.* See Ge 32:28 and note. *Judah.* The main tribe of the southern kingdom. See Ge 49:8 and note. *not in truth.* Contrast the oaths of 65:16.
48:2 *holy city.* Jerusalem, where the temple was located (see 2:2–4 and note; 52:1; 56:7; 57:13; 64:10–11; 65:11). See also 1:26 and note; 4:3 and note; Da 9:24. *rely on . . . God.* Theoretically at least (10:20). Contrast 31:1; 36:6,9; Eze 29:6–7. *LORD Almighty.* See 13:4 and note.
48:3 *former things.* See 41:22 and note. *they came to pass.* See 42:9.
48:4 *stubborn . . . bronze.* See Jer 6:28; cf. Eze 3:7.
48:5 *My idols did them.* See Isaiah's harsh words about idolatry in 44:17–20 (see also notes there). *wooden image and metal god.* See note on 44:12–20.
48:6 *new things.* For example, Israel's restoration (see 42:9 and note). The Messianic age and the new heavens and new earth may also be in view (cf. 65:17). *hidden things.* Cf. Ro 16:25–26.
48:7 *created now.* Now given substance in the prophetic announcement of their coming.
48:8 *neither heard nor understood.* See 1:3. *ear . . . not . . . open.* See 6:10 and note. *rebel.* See 1:2; 46:8 and notes.
48:9 *delay my wrath.* Cf. Ps 78:38. *my praise.* The praise God is worthy of.
48:10 *refined . . . tested.* Images of judgment (see Jer 9:7; Eze 22:18–22). Purifying fire is also mentioned in 1:25; 4:4. *furnace of affliction.* For Israel, Egypt had been an "iron-smelting furnace" (Dt 4:20; 1Ki 8:51; Jer 11:4). The fall of Jerusalem and the Babylonian exile were a similar furnace.
48:11 *For . . . defamed.* Jerusalem's fall and God's scattered people had brought dishonor to God's name (see Eze 36:20–23). *my glory.* See 40:5 and note.
48:12 *called.* To be God's servant, his chosen people. See 42:6; see also 41:2; 43:1 and notes. *first and . . . last.* See 41:4 and note.

Israel, whom I have called: [h]
I am he; [i]
I am the first and I am the last. [j]
[13]My own hand laid the foundations of
the earth, [k]
and my right hand spread out the
heavens; [l]
when I summon them,
they all stand up together. [m]

[14]"Come together, [n] all of you, and listen:
Which of ˌthe idols˴ has foretold [o]
these things?
The LORD's chosen ally [p]
will carry out his purpose [q] against
Babylon; [r]
his arm will be against the
Babylonians. [r]
[15]I, even I, have spoken;
yes, I have called [s] him.
I will bring him,
and he will succeed [t] in his mission.

[16]"Come near [u] me and listen [v] to this:

"From the first announcement I have
not spoken in secret; [w]
at the time it happens, I am there."

And now the Sovereign LORD [x] has
sent [y] me,
with his Spirit. [z]

[17]This is what the LORD says—
your Redeemer, [a] the Holy One [b] of
Israel:
"I am the LORD your God,
who teaches [c] you what is best for
you,
who directs [d] you in the way [e] you
should go.

[18]If only you had paid attention [f] to my
commands,
your peace [g] would have been like a
river, [h]
your righteousness [i] like the waves of
the sea.
[19]Your descendants [j] would have been
like the sand, [k]
your children like its numberless
grains; [l]
their name would never be cut off [m]
nor destroyed from before me."

[20]Leave Babylon,
flee [n] from the Babylonians!
Announce this with shouts of joy [o]
and proclaim it.
Send it out to the ends of the earth; [p]
say, "The LORD has redeemed [q] his
servant Jacob."
[21]They did not thirst [r] when he led them
through the deserts;
he made water flow [s] for them from
the rock;
he split the rock
and water gushed out. [t]

[22]"There is no peace," [u] says the LORD,
"for the wicked." [v]

The Servant of the LORD

49 Listen [w] to me, you islands; [x]
hear this, you distant nations:

48:12 [h]Isa 41:8;
42:6; 43:1
[i]S Isa 43:13
[j]S Isa 41:4;
S Rev 1:17
48:13
[k]Heb 1:10-12
[l]S Ge 2:1;
Ex 20:11;
Job 9:8;
Isa 40:22; S 42:5;
45:18; 51:16;
65:17
[m]S Isa 34:16
48:14 [n]S Isa 43:9
[o]S Isa 41:22
[p]S Isa 41:2
[q]Isa 46:10-11
[r]S Isa 21:9;
S 45:1; Jer 50:45
48:15
[s]S Jdg 4:10;
Isa 45:1
[t]Isa 44:28-45:4
48:16 [u]S Isa 41:1
[v]S Isa 33:13
[w]S Isa 45:19
[x]Isa 50:5,7,9
[y]Zec 2:9,11
[z]S Isa 11:2
48:17
[a]S Job 19:25;
Isa 49:7; 54:8
[b]S Isa 47:4
[c]S Isa 28:9;
S Jer 7:13
[d]Isa 49:10;
57:18; 58:11
[e]S Isa 30:11

48:18
[f]S Isa 42:23
[g]Ps 147:14;
S Isa 9:7; 54:13;
66:12
[h]S Isa 33:21
[i]S Isa 1:26; S 45:8
48:19 [j]Isa 43:5;
44:3; 61:9
[k]S Ge 12:2
[l]S Job 5:25
[m]Isa 56:5; 65:23;
66:22; Jer 35:19
48:20 [n]Isa 52:11;
Jer 48:6; 50:8;
51:6,45;
Zec 2:6-7;
Rev 18:4
[o]S Isa 12:6;
49:13; 51:11
[p]S Ps 49:10;

S Dt 30:4; S Jer 25:22 [q]S Ex 6:6; S Isa 33:24; 52:9; 63:9;
Mic 4:10 48:21 [r]S Isa 33:16 [s]S Isa 30:25 [t]S Nu 20:11;
S Isa 35:6 48:22 [u]S Job 3:26 [v]S Isa 3:11; 57:21 49:1
[w]S Isa 33:13 [x]S Isa 11:11

[t]14 Or Chaldeans; also in verse 20

48:13 *laid the foundations . . . spread out the heavens.*
Isaiah often refers to God as Creator (see 40:21–22; 42:5;
51:13 and notes). Cf. Ps 102:25. *when I summon . . . all
stand up.* All creation does God's bidding (see 40:26 and
note; Ps 103:22).
48:14 *idols . . . foretold.* See 41:21–23,26; 43:9 and
notes. *chosen ally.* Cyrus the Great (see 41:2 and note). *his
purpose.* See 46:10–11 and note. *Babylon.* See 13:1 and
note.
48:15 *called him.* Cyrus (see 41:2 and note). *will succeed.*
See 44:28; 45:1–4 and notes.
48:16 *first announcement.* The prediction about Cyrus
and his mission (see 41:25–27 and notes). *not spoken in
secret.* See 45:19 and note. *has sent me, with his Spirit.* A
reference to either Isaiah or the servant of the Lord. The
Spirit of the Lord comes upon the servant in 42:1 (see note
there) and upon the Messianic prophet of 61:1 (see note
there).
48:17 *Redeemer, the Holy One of Israel.* See 41:14 and
note. *teaches you . . . the way you should go.* Through the
prophets (see 30:20–21 and notes; Ps 32:8).
48:18 *peace . . . like a river, righteousness like the waves.*
Abundant and overflowing peace and righteousness (see
45:8 and note; Am 5:24 and note). Peace and righteousness

are also linked in 9:7; 32:17; 54:13–14; 60:17; Ps 85:10;
Heb 7:2.
48:19 *descendants . . . like the sand.* See 10:22; see also
Ge 13:16 and note; Ge 22:17; Jer 33:22 and note. *name . . .
never be cut off.* Israel's name would not be completely
obliterated (see v. 9; 54:3).
48:20 *Leave Babylon, flee.* Although the Jews did not have
to flee (see 52:12), they were encouraged to depart quickly
because of the judgment coming on Babylon (cf. Rev 18:4).
This is the last mention of Babylon by name in Isaiah. *shouts
of joy.* See 44:23; 49:13; 52:9 and notes. *ends of the earth.*
See 11:12; 42:10 and notes. *redeemed.* See 43:1 and note.
his servant. See 41:8–9 and note.
48:21 *did not thirst . . . water . . . from the rock.* A reference to God's provision after the exodus (see Ex 17:6 and
note; Nu 20:11; see also Isa 32:2; 35:6; 43:19; 49:10 and
notes). God's people would have water on the way home
from Babylonian exile also.
48:22 Repeated almost verbatim in 57:21. *peace.* See 39:8
and note. *wicked.* Those who rebel against the Lord (see note
on 1:2).

49:1–6 (or *1–7* or *1–13*) The second of the four servant
songs (see note on 42:1–4).

Before I was born^y the LORD called^z
  me;
from my birth he has made mention
  of my name. ^a
²He made my mouth^b like a sharpened
  sword, ^c
in the shadow of his hand^d he hid
  me;
he made me into a polished arrow^e
  and concealed me in his quiver.
³He said to me, "You are my servant,^f
  Israel, in whom I will display my
  splendor.^g"
⁴But I said, "I have labored to no
  purpose;
I have spent my strength in vain^h
  and for nothing.
Yet what is due me is in the LORD's
  hand,ⁱ
and my reward^j is with my God." ^k

⁵And now the LORD says—
  he who formed me in the womb^l to
  be his servant
to bring Jacob back to him
  and gather Israel^m to himself,
for I am honoredⁿ in the eyes of the
  LORD
and my God has been my
  strength^o—
⁶he says:

"It is too small a thing for you to be my
  servant^p
to restore the tribes of Jacob
  and bring back those of Israel I have
  kept. ^q
I will also make you a light^r for the
  Gentiles, ^s
that you may bring my salvation to
  the ends of the earth." ^t

⁷This is what the LORD says—
  the Redeemer and Holy One of
  Israel^u—
to him who was despised^v and
  abhorred by the nation,
to the servant of rulers:
"Kings^w will see you and rise up,
  princes will see and bow down, ^x
because of the LORD, who is faithful,^y
  the Holy One of Israel, who has
  chosen^z you."

Restoration of Israel

⁸This is what the LORD says:

"In the time of my favor^a I will answer
  you,
and in the day of salvation I will help
  you;^b
I will keep^c you and will make you

49:1 *y*Isa 44:24;
46:3; Mt 1:20
*z*Isa 7:14; 9:6;
44:2; Jer 1:5;
Gal 1:15
*a*S Ex 33:12;
S Isa 43:1
49:2 *b*S Job 40:18
*c*S Ps 64:3;
Eph 6:17;
S Rev 1:16
*d*S Ex 33:22;
S Ps 91:1
*e*S Dt 32:23;
Zec 9:13
49:3 *f*S Isa 20:3;
Zec 3:8
*g*S Lev 10:3;
S Isa 44:23
49:4
*h*S Lev 26:20;
Isa 55:2; 65:23
*i*Isa 45:25; 50:8;
53:10; 54:17
*j*S Isa 35:4
*k*S Job 27:2
49:5
*l*S Ps 139:13;
Gal 1:15
*m*S Dt 30:4;
S Isa 11:12
*n*S Isa 43:4
*o*S Ps 18:1

49:6 *p*S ver 3
*q*Isa 1:9
*r*S Isa 9:2; Jn 1:9
*s*S Isa 26:18;
55:5; Zec 8:22;
S Lk 2:32
*t*S Dt 30:4;
S Ps 48:10;
S Mt 28:19;
Jn 11:52;
Ac 13:47*
49:7 *u*S Isa 48:17
*v*S Ps 22:6;
69:7-9
*w*S Ezr 1:2;
Isa 52:15
*x*S Ge 27:29;

S Ps 22:29; S 86:9 *y*S Dt 7:9; S 1Co 1:9 *z*S Isa 14:1 **49:8**
*a*Ps 69:13; Isa 60:10; 61:2 *b*S Isa 41:10; 2Co 6:2* *c*S Isa 5:2;
26:3

49:1 *islands.* Or "coastlands." In 42:4 the islands "put
their hope" in the servant's law. *Before I was born . . . called
me.* Cf. v. 5. The language is similar to that of the call of the
prophet Jeremiah (Jer 1:5) and of the apostle Paul (Gal 1:15).
Cf. 41:9. *made mention of my name.* See 43:1 and
note.
49:2 *my mouth . . . sharpened sword.* See Eph 6:17; Heb
4:12; Rev 1:16; 2:12,16. In 11:4 a powerful rod comes
from the mouth of the Messiah. *shadow of his hand.* Descriptive of protection (see 30:2–3; 51:16). *polished arrow.*
Arrows are used of God's judgment in Dt 32:23,42, of the
deadly words of the wicked in Ps 64:3–4 and of Satan's
schemes and temptations in Eph 6:11,16.
49:3 *my servant, Israel.* See notes on 41:8–9; 42:1–4;
42:1. "Servant" here cannot mean literally national Israel,
since in v. 5 this servant has a mission to Israel. Rather, the
Messianic servant is the ideal Israel through whom the Lord
will be glorified. He will succeed where national Israel failed.
display my splendor. Through the redemption he will accomplish (see notes on 35:2; 40:5).
49:4 *labored to no purpose . . . in vain.* Just as the nation
Israel had toiled in vain (see 65:23), so Christ would encounter strong opposition during his ministry and would temporarily suffer apparent failure. The "suffering servant"
theme is developed in the third and fourth of the four servant
songs (50:4–9 or 50:4–11; 52:13–53:12). *what is due me
. . . my reward.* Perhaps referring to the spiritual offspring of
the servant (see 53:10)—Jews and Gentiles alike who believe in him (vv. 5–6); see 40:10 and note. In any case, he
will be vindicated and rewarded (50:8; 53:10–12; 1Ti
3:16).
49:5 *formed me in the womb.* See v. 1; 44:2 and notes.

bring Jacob back . . . gather Israel. A prophecy of release from
captivity in Babylon (see vv. 9–12,22; 41:2 and note) and
from the greater captivity of sin (see 42:7 and note). *my
strength.* See 12:2.
49:6 Together with Ge 12:1–3; Ex 19:5–6, this verse is
sometimes called the "great commission of the OT" and is
quoted in part by Paul and Barnabas in Ac 13:47. *those . . .
I have kept.* Probably referring to the remnant (see 1:9 and
note). *light for the Gentiles.* See 42:6 and note; Ac 26:23.
Christ is the light of the world (Lk 2:30–32; Jn 8:12; 9:5),
and Christians reflect his light (Mt 5:14). *ends of the earth.*
See 11:12 and note; see also 41:5; 42:10; 48:20.
49:7 *Redeemer and Holy One of Israel.* See 41:14 and
note. *despised.* Applied twice to the suffering servant in
53:3. In 60:14 Zion is despised by her enemies. *nation.*
Refers to either Israel (1:4) or Gentiles. *Kings will see . . .
bow down.* See v. 23. This reaction to the servant is similar
to that of 52:15. Former oppressors bow before a restored
Jerusalem in 60:14 (cf. 45:14; 60:11–12; 66:23). *chosen
you.* See 41:8–9; 42:1 and notes.
49:8 Quoted in part in 2Co 6:2. *time of my favor . . . day of
salvation.* The background of this verse is probably the Year
of Jubilee (see 61:1–2; Lev 25:10). The return from exile
will bring the same restoration of land for the people as that
year of liberty did. *keep you . . . to be a covenant.* See 42:6
and note. *reassign its desolate inheritances.* See 44:26. It
was under Joshua that the land was divided among
individual tribes and families (Jos 14:1–5). The Messianic
servant will be a new Joshua—as well as a new Moses (see
vv. 9–10, which echo Israel's deliverance from Egypt and
her desert experiences under Moses during the period of the
exodus).

to be a covenant for the people, [d]
to restore the land [e]
and to reassign its desolate
inheritances, [f]
[9]to say to the captives, [g] 'Come out,'
and to those in darkness, [h] 'Be free!'

"They will feed beside the roads
and find pasture on every barren
hill. [i]
[10]They will neither hunger nor thirst, [j]
nor will the desert heat or the sun
beat upon them. [k]
He who has compassion [l] on them will
guide [m] them
and lead them beside springs [n] of
water.
[11]I will turn all my mountains into roads,
and my highways [o] will be raised
up. [p]
[12]See, they will come from afar [q]—
some from the north, some from the
west, [r]
some from the region of Aswan. [s] "

[13]Shout for joy, [s] O heavens;
rejoice, O earth; [t]
burst into song, O mountains! [u]
For the LORD comforts [v] his people
and will have compassion [w] on his
afflicted ones. [x]

[14]But Zion [y] said, "The LORD has
forsaken [z] me,
the Lord has forgotten me."

[15]"Can a mother forget the baby at her
breast
and have no compassion on the
child [a] she has borne?
Though she may forget,
I will not forget you! [b]

[16]See, I have engraved [c] you on the palms
of my hands;
your walls [d] are ever before me.
[17]Your sons hasten back,
and those who laid you waste [e]
depart from you.
[18]Lift up your eyes and look around;
all your sons gather [f] and come to
you.
As surely as I live, [g] " declares the LORD,
"you will wear [h] them all as
ornaments;
you will put them on, like a bride.

[19]"Though you were ruined and made
desolate [i]
and your land laid waste, [j]
now you will be too small for your
people, [k]
and those who devoured [l] you will
be far away.
[20]The children born during your
bereavement
will yet say in your hearing,
'This place is too small for us;
give us more space to live in.' [m]
[21]Then you will say in your heart,
'Who bore me these? [n]
I was bereaved [o] and barren;
I was exiled and rejected. [p]
Who brought these [q] up?
I was left [r] all alone, [s]
but these—where have they come
from?' "

[22]This is what the Sovereign LORD [t]
says:

Cross references (center column)

49:8 [d]S Isa 42:6
[e]Lev 25:10;
S Ps 37:9;
Isa 44:26; 58:12;
61:4; Eze 36:10,
33; Am 9:11,14
[f]S Nu 34:13;
S Isa 60:21
49:9 [g]Isa 42:7;
61:1; S Lk 4:19
[h]S Ps 107:10
[i]Isa 41:18
49:10
[j]S Isa 33:16
[k]Ps 121:6;
Rev 7:16
[l]S Isa 14:1
[m]Ps 48:14;
S Isa 42:16;
S 48:17
[n]S Isa 33:21;
S 35:7
49:11
[o]S Isa 11:16
[p]Isa 40:4;
Jer 31:9
49:12 [q]S Isa 2:3;
S 11:11; 43:5-6
[r]Isa 59:19;
S Mt 8:11
49:13
[s]S Isa 48:20
[t]S Ps 96:11
[u]S Ps 65:12-13;
98:4; Isa 44:23
[v]S Ps 71:21;
S Isa 40:1;
S 2Co 1:4
[w]S Isa 14:1
[x]S Ps 9:12
49:14 [y]Isa 40:9
[z]S Ps 9:10;
S 71:11;
S Isa 27:8
49:15
[a]S 1Ki 3:26;
Isa 66:13
[b]S Isa 44:21

49:16
[c]S Ge 38:18;
S Ex 28:9
[d]Ps 48:12-13;
Isa 62:6
49:17 [e]S Isa 5:6;
10:6; 37:18
49:18
[f]S Isa 11:12;
14:1; 43:5; 51:3;
54:7
[g]S Nu 14:21;
Isa 45:23; 54:9;
62:8; Ro 14:11*
[h]Isa 52:1; 61:10;
Jer 2:32
49:19
[i]S Lev 26:33;

Isa 54:1,3; 60:18; 62:4 [j]S Isa 5:6 [k]Eze 36:10-11; Zec 10:10
[l]S Isa 1:20 49:20 [m]Isa 54:1-3; Zec 2:4; 10:10 49:21
[n]Isa 29:23; 66:7-8 [o]S Isa 47:8; 54:1 [p]Isa 5:13; 54:6
[q]Isa 60:8 [r]S Isa 1:8 [s]S Ps 142:4; Isa 51:18; Jer 10:20 49:22
[t]S Ge 15:2

[s] 12 Dead Sea Scrolls; Masoretic Text Sinim

Study notes

49:9 *captives.* The exiles. See 42:7 and note. *barren hill.* See 41:18 and note.

49:10 *neither hunger nor thirst.* See 48:21 and note. *has compassion.* See 14:1 and note. *will guide them.* As a shepherd (see 40:11 and note). This whole verse is also a picture of heaven according to Rev 7:16–17.

49:11 *mountains into roads.* See 26:7 and note. *highways ... raised up.* See 11:16; 35:8; 40:3; 62:10 and notes.

49:12 *come from afar.* See 11:11 and note; 60:4. *north ... west.* See 43:5–6 and notes. *Aswan.* See Eze 29:10; 30:6; located in the most southern part of Egypt.

49:13 *Shout for joy ... mountains.* Nature is personified often in Isaiah. See 44:23 and note. *comforts his people.* As he redeems and saves them. Cf. 2Co 1:3–4. *will have compassion.* See v. 10 and note; 54:7–10.

49:14 *forsaken ... forgotten.* See 40:27; 54:7; La 5:20–22.

49:15 *Can a mother forget ... ?* Cf. Ps 27:10.

49:16 *engraved you on ... my hands.* As the names of the tribes of Israel were engraved on stones and fastened to the ephod of the high priest as a memorial before the Lord (Ex 28:9–12; cf. SS 8:6). *ever before me.* Cf. Ps 137:5–6.

49:17 *sons.* Or "builders," following the reading of the Dead Sea Scrolls and some ancient versions (see note on 62:5).

49:18 *sons gather.* See vv. 5,12 and notes. *ornaments.* Beautiful clothes and jewels symbolize strength and joy.

49:19–20 *too small.* The restoration of Israel will be astonishing and complete. The prophecy was partially fulfilled in the return from Babylon (see note on 11:11) and may include spiritual offspring among both Jews and Gentiles (see 54:17 and note).

49:19 *ruined ... desolate.* Cf. v. 8; see 44:26 and note.

49:21 *bereaved and barren.* The concept of Israel as a barren woman is stressed in 54:1.

49:22 *lift up my banner.* See 5:26 and note; 13:2. *bring your sons ... daughters.* See 11:12 and note. The nations bring Israel back also in 14:2; 43:6; 60:9. *in their arms.* Cf. 60:4; see 40:11 and note.

"See, I will beckon to the Gentiles,
  I will lift up my banner[u] to the
    peoples;
they will bring[v] your sons in their arms
  and carry your daughters on their
    shoulders.[w]
23Kings[x] will be your foster fathers,
  and their queens your nursing
    mothers.[y]
They will bow down[z] before you with
    their faces to the ground;
  they will lick the dust[a] at your feet.
Then you will know that I am the
    LORD;[b]
  those who hope[c] in me will not be
    disappointed.[d]"

24Can plunder be taken from warriors,[e]
  or captives rescued from the fierce[t]?

25But this is what the LORD says:

"Yes, captives[f] will be taken from
    warriors,[g]
  and plunder retrieved from the
    fierce;[h]
I will contend with those who contend
    with you,[i][j]
  and your children I will save.[k]
26I will make your oppressors[l] eat[m] their
    own flesh;
  they will be drunk on their own
    blood,[n] as with wine.
Then all mankind will know[o]
  that I, the LORD, am your Savior,[p]
  your Redeemer,[q] the Mighty One of
    Jacob.[r]"

49:22
[u]S Isa 11:10
[v]S Isa 11:12;
S 14:2 [w]Lk 15:5
49:23 [x]Isa 60:3,
10-11
[y]S Nu 11:12;
S Isa 60:16
[z]S Ge 27:29;
Rev 3:9
[a]S Ge 3:14;
Ps 72:9
[b]S Ex 6:2;
S Ps 22:23;
S Isa 42:8
[c]S Ps 37:9;
S 130:5
[d]S Ps 22:5;
S Isa 29:22;
S 41:11
49:24
[e]Mt 12:29;
Mk 3:27;
Lk 11:21
49:25 [f]S Isa 14:2
[g]Jer 50:33-34;
Mk 3:27
[h]S Isa 13:11;
S 25:4 [i]Isa 25:5;
S 43:26; 51:22;
Jer 50:34
[j]S Isa 24:15
[k]Isa 25:9; 33:22;
35:4
49:26 [l]S Isa 9:4;
S 13:11
[m]S Isa 9:20
[n]Nu 23:24;
Jer 25:27;
Na 1:10; 3:11;
Rev 16:6 [o]Ex 6:7;
S Isa 11:9;
Eze 39:7
[p]S Isa 25:9
[q]S Job 19:25;
S Isa 48:17
[r]S Ge 49:24;
S Ps 132:2

50:1 [s]S Dt 24:1;
Hos 2:2; Mt 19:7;
Mk 10:4
[t]S Ne 5:5;
S Mt 18:25
[u]S Isa 1:28
[v]S Dt 32:30;
S Jdg 3:8
50:2
[w]S 1Sa 8:19;
S Isa 41:28
[x]Nu 11:23;
Isa 59:1
[y]S Ge 18:14;

Israel's Sin and the Servant's Obedience

50 This is what the LORD says:

"Where is your mother's
    certificate of divorce[s]
  with which I sent her away?
Or to which of my creditors
  did I sell[t] you?
Because of your sins[u] you were sold;[v]
  because of your transgressions your
    mother was sent away.
2When I came, why was there no one?
  When I called, why was there no one
    to answer?[w]
Was my arm too short[x] to ransom you?
  Do I lack the strength[y] to rescue
    you?
By a mere rebuke[z] I dry up the sea,[a]
  I turn rivers into a desert;[b]
their fish rot for lack of water
  and die of thirst.
3I clothe the sky with darkness[c]
  and make sackcloth[d] its covering."

4The Sovereign LORD[e] has given me an
    instructed tongue,[f]
  to know the word that sustains the
    weary.[g]
He wakens me morning by morning,[h]
  wakens my ear to listen like one
    being taught.[i]
5The Sovereign LORD[j] has opened my
    ears,[k]

S Ps 68:35; Jer 14:9 [z]S Ps 18:15 [a]S Ex 14:22 [b]S Ps 107:33
50:3 [c]S Ex 10:22; S Isa 5:30 [d]Rev 6:12 **50:4** [e]ver 5; Isa 61:1
[f]S Ex 4:12 [g]S Isa 40:29; Mt 11:28 [h]Ps 5:3; 88:13; 119:147;
143:8 [i]S Isa 28:9 **50:5** [j]S Isa 48:16 [k]Isa 35:5

[t]24 Dead Sea Scrolls, Vulgate and Syriac (see also
Septuagint and verse 25); Masoretic Text *righteous*

49:23 *Kings . . . will bow down.* See v. 7; 11:14 and notes.
know that I am the LORD. See v. 26; 60:16; Eze 12:20; 13:9;
36:38. *hope in me.* See 40:31 and note. *not be disappointed.* See 29:22 and note.
49:24 *warriors . . . fierce.* The Babylonians (see 51:13).
49:25 *captives will be taken.* See Ezr 2:1,64–65; Jer
50:33–34; 52:27–30. *I will contend.* God takes up the case
of his people. He will "defend their cause" (Jer 50:34). *I will
save.* See 35:4 and note.
49:26 *oppressors.* See 14:4; 16:4; 51:13. *eat their own
flesh.* During the siege of Jerusalem its people were reduced
to cannibalism (La 4:10). *drunk on their own blood.* Cf.
51:22–23. *mankind will know.* See v. 23 and note. *Savior.*
See 43:3 and note; 60:16. *Redeemer.* See 41:14 and note.
Mighty One of Jacob. See 1:24 and note; 60:16.
50:1 *certificate of divorce.* A husband was required to give
this to a wife he wished to divorce (see Dt 24:1,3; Mt 19:7;
Mk 10:4). According to Jer 3:8 God gave the northern
kingdom of Israel her certificate of divorce, and Isa 54:6–7
indicates that God had left Judah (see 62:4). Perhaps Isaiah's
point is that God did not initiate the divorce; Judah broke her
relationship with him. The exile, then, was actually a temporary period of separation (see 54:7) rather than a divorce. *my*

creditors. If a man's debts were not paid, his children could
be sold into slavery (see 2Ki 4:1). But God has no creditors.
you were sold. Cf. 45:13; 52:3.
50:2 *I came . . . called.* Through his servants the prophets
(see Jer 25:4). *no one to answer.* Israel was deaf toward God
(see 6:10 and note; 66:4). *arm too short.* The arm represented power. *dry up the sea.* A reference to crossing the Red Sea
(see 43:16–17 and notes; Ps 106:9). *rivers into a desert.* See
42:15 and note. *fish rot.* Perhaps a reference to one of the
plagues in Egypt (see 19:5–6,8; Ex 7:18).
50:3 *sky with darkness.* Perhaps an allusion to the plague
of darkness (Ex 10:21); but see 13:10 and note.
50:4–9 (or **4–11**) The third of the four servant songs (see
note on 42:1–4).
50:4–5,7,9 *Sovereign LORD.* The only uses of this title in
the servant songs.
50:4 *word that sustains the weary.* In 42:3 the servant
assisted the weak (contrast 49:2). Cf. Jer 31:25. *wakens my
ear.* Unlike Israel (see v. 2), the servant was responsive to
God.
50:5 *opened my ears.* A sign of obedience (see 1:19; Ps
40:6 and second NIV text note there). *not been rebellious.*
Unlike Israel (see 1:2 and note; 1:20).

and I have not been rebellious;[l]
I have not drawn back.
[6]I offered my back to those who beat[m]
me,
my cheeks to those who pulled out
my beard;[n]
I did not hide my face
from mocking and spitting.[o]
[7]Because the Sovereign LORD[p] helps[q]
me,
I will not be disgraced.
Therefore have I set my face like flint,[r]
and I know I will not be put to
shame.[s]
[8]He who vindicates[t] me is near.[u]
Who then will bring charges against
me?[v]
Let us face each other![w]
Who is my accuser?
Let him confront me!
[9]It is the Sovereign LORD[x] who helps[y]
me.
Who is he that will condemn[z] me?
They will all wear out like a garment;
the moths[a] will eat them up.

[10]Who among you fears[b] the LORD
and obeys[c] the word of his servant?[d]
Let him who walks in the dark,
who has no light,[e]
trust[f] in the name of the LORD
and rely on his God.
[11]But now, all you who light fires
and provide yourselves with flaming
torches,[g]
go, walk in the light of your fires[h]
and of the torches you have set
ablaze.

This is what you shall receive from my
hand:[i]
You will lie down in torment.[j]

Everlasting Salvation for Zion

51 "Listen[k] to me, you who pursue
righteousness[l]
and who seek[m] the LORD:
Look to the rock[n] from which you were
cut
and to the quarry from which you
were hewn;
[2]look to Abraham,[o] your father,
and to Sarah, who gave you birth.
When I called him he was but one,
and I blessed him and made him
many.[p]
[3]The LORD will surely comfort[q] Zion[r]
and will look with compassion on all
her ruins;[s]
he will make her deserts like Eden,[t]
her wastelands[u] like the garden of
the LORD.
Joy and gladness[v] will be found in her,
thanksgiving[w] and the sound of
singing.

[4]"Listen to me, my people;[x]
hear me,[y] my nation:
The law[z] will go out from me;
my justice[a] will become a light to
the nations.[b]
[5]My righteousness draws near speedily,

Cross references (center column):

50:5 [l]Eze 2:8; 24:3; S Mt 26:39; Jn 8:29; 14:31; 15:10; Ac 26:19; Heb 5:8
50:6 [m]Isa 53:5; Mt 27:30; Mk 14:65; 15:19; Lk 22:63; Jn 19:1
[n]S 2Sa 10:4
[o]S Nu 12:14; La 3:30; Mt 26:67; Mk 10:34
50:7 [p]S Isa 48:16
[q]S Isa 41:10; 42:1
[r]Jer 1:18; 15:20; Eze 3:8-9
[s]S Isa 28:16; S 29:22
50:8 [t]S Isa 26:2; S 49:4
[u]S Ps 34:18
[v]S Job 13:19; S Isa 43:26; Ro 8:32-34
[w]S Isa 41:1
50:9 [x]S Isa 48:16
[y]S Isa 41:10
[z]Ro 8:1,34
[a]S Job 13:28; S Isa 51:8
50:10 [b]S Pr 1:7
[c]Isa 1:19; Hag 1:12
[d]S Isa 49:3
[e]S Ps 107:14; Ac 26:18
[f]S Isa 10:20; S 26:4
50:11 [g]Pr 26:18
[h]Isa 1:31; Jas 3:6

[i]S Dt 21:22-23; S Pr 26:27
[j]S Job 15:20; Isa 65:13-15
51:1 [k]S Isa 46:3
[l]ver 7; S Dt 7:13; 16:20; Ps 94:15; Isa 63:8; Ro 9:30-31
[m]Isa 55:6; 65:10
[n]Isa 17:10
51:2 [o]S Ge 17:6; S Isa 29:22; Ro 4:16; Heb 11:11
[p]S Ge 12:2

51:3 [q]S Isa 40:1 [r]S Ps 51:18; S Isa 44:26; 52:9; 61:4 [s]S Isa 25:9; 35:10; 65:18; 66:10; Jer 16:9 [w]Jer 17:26; 30:19; 33:11 51:4 [x]Ex 6:7; Ps 50:7; Isa 3:15; 63:8; 64:9 [y]S Ps 78:1 [z]S Dt 18:18 [a]S Isa 2:4 [b]S Isa 26:18; S 49:6

50:6 *my back to those who beat me.* Beatings were for criminals or fools (see Pr 10:13; 19:29; 26:3; Mt 27:26; Jn 19:1). *pulled out my beard.* A sign of disrespect and contempt (see 2Sa 10:4–5; Ne 13:25). *mocking and spitting.* To show hatred (Job 30:10) or to insult or disgrace (Dt 25:9; Job 17:6; Mt 27:30). This treatment of the servant anticipates his ultimate suffering in 52:13–53:12.
50:7 *helps me.* See v. 9; 49:8. *not be disgraced . . . put to shame.* See 29:22 and note. Ultimately the servant will be honored (see 49:7; 52:13; 53:10–12). *my face like flint.* Like the prophets, the servant will endure with great determination. Cf. Lk 9:51, where Jesus "resolutely set out for Jerusalem" (lit. "resolutely set his face to go to Jerusalem").
50:8 *vindicates me.* The Lord will find him righteous (see 45:25; for its ultimate fulfillment see 1Ti 3:16). *bring charges.* See 49:25 and note. Because Christ was sinless, he also nullifies the charges brought against any who believe in him (see Ro 8:31–34). *my accuser.* Cf. 54:17.
50:9 *wear out like a garment; the moths.* Those who falsely accuse the righteous succumb to moths in 51:8 (i.e., they will be destroyed).
50:10 *fears the LORD.* See Ge 20:11; Pr 1:7 and notes. Cf. 25:3; 59:19. *in the dark.* Perhaps trouble or distress, similar to the experience of the servant (cf. 8:22). *trust . . . rely.* The Lord encouraged such trust in 12:2; 31:1.

50:11 *light fires . . . flaming torches.* Perhaps a reference to wicked practices that will ultimately destroy those who engage in them. Fire is a frequent figure of punishment (see 1:31 and note; cf. 9:18; 47:14; Ps 7:13). *torment.* Cf. 66:24.
51:1 *who pursue righteousness.* Cf. v. 7; Dt 16:20; Pr 15:9. *rock.* Abraham (v. 2). Elsewhere God is called "the Rock" (see 17:10 and note).
51:2 *was but one.* See Ge 12:1; Eze 33:24. *blessed him and made him many.* See Ge 12:2–3; 13:16; 15:5; 17:5; 22:17.
51:3 *comfort . . . compassion.* See 49:13 and note. *deserts like Eden.* See 35:1–2. The contrast between the lush splendor of Eden and the barrenness of the desert is found also in Joel 2:3. Cf. Ge 2:8,10. *Joy and gladness.* See v. 11; 25:9 and note.
51:4 *law . . . my justice.* The rule of the servant would bring justice also (see 2:2–4; 42:4 and notes). *light to the nations.* The servant is the light in 42:6; 49:6.
51:5 *righteousness draws near.* In the deliverance from exile. Ultimately, salvation through Christ will come to all nations. See 46:13 and note. *arm.* Symbolizes power. *islands.* See 11:11 and note. *look to me . . . hope.* See 40:31 and note; 42:4 and note.

my salvation[c] is on the way,[d]
and my arm[e] will bring justice to the
nations.
The islands[f] will look to me
and wait in hope[g] for my arm.
⁶Lift up your eyes to the heavens,
look at the earth beneath;
the heavens will vanish like smoke,[h]
the earth will wear out like a
garment[i]
and its inhabitants die like flies.
But my salvation[j] will last forever,[k]
my righteousness will never fail.[l]

⁷"Hear me, you who know what is
right,[m]
you people who have my law in your
hearts:[n]
Do not fear the reproach of men
or be terrified by their insults.[o]
⁸For the moth will eat them up like a
garment;[p]
the worm[q] will devour them like
wool.
But my righteousness will last forever,[r]
my salvation through all
generations."

⁹Awake, awake![s] Clothe yourself with
strength,[t]
O arm[u] of the LORD;
awake, as in days gone by,
as in generations of old.[v]
Was it not you who cut Rahab[w] to
pieces,
who pierced that monster[x] through?
¹⁰Was it not you who dried up the sea,[y]
the waters of the great deep,[z]
who made a road in the depths of the
sea[a]
so that the redeemed[b] might cross
over?
¹¹The ransomed[c] of the LORD will return.
They will enter Zion with singing;[d]
everlasting joy will crown their
heads.

Gladness and joy[e] will overtake them,
and sorrow and sighing will flee
away.[f]

¹²"I, even I, am he who comforts[g] you.
Who are you that you fear[h] mortal
men,[i]
the sons of men, who are but grass,[j]
¹³that you forget[k] the LORD your
Maker,[l]
who stretched out the heavens[m]
and laid the foundations of the earth,
that you live in constant terror[n] every
day
because of the wrath of the
oppressor,
who is bent on destruction?
For where is the wrath of the
oppressor?[o]
14   The cowering prisoners will soon be
set free;[p]
they will not die in their dungeon,
nor will they lack bread.[q]
¹⁵For I am the LORD your God,
who churns up the sea[r] so that its
waves roar[s] —
the LORD Almighty[t] is his name.
¹⁶I have put my words in your mouth[u]
and covered you with the shadow of
my hand[v] —
I who set the heavens in place,
who laid the foundations of the
earth,[w]
and who say to Zion, 'You are my
people.[x] ' "

The Cup of the LORD's Wrath

¹⁷Awake, awake![y]
Rise up, O Jerusalem,

Cross references

51:5 cS Ps 85:9; S Isa 12:2 dS Isa 35:4 ePs 98:1; Isa 40:10; 50:2; 52:10; 59:16; 63:1,5 fS Isa 11:11 gS Ge 49:10; S Ps 37:9 51:6 hS Ps 37:20; S 102:26; Mt 24:35; Lk 21:33; 2Pe 3:10 iPs 102:25-26; Heb 1:10-12 jS Isa 12:2 kver 8; S Ps 119:89 lPs 89:33; Isa 54:10 51:7 mS ver 1 nS Dt 6:6; Ps 119:11 oS Ps 119:39; Isa 50:7; 54:4; Mt 5:11; Lk 6:22; Ac 5:41 51:8 pS Job 13:28; Jas 5:2 qS Isa 14:11 rS ver 6 51:9 sS Jdg 5:12 tS Ge 18:14; S Ps 65:6; Isa 40:31; 52:1 uS Ps 98:1; S Isa 30:30; S 33:2 vEx 6:3; Dt 4:34; S 32:7 wS Job 9:13 xS Ps 68:30; S 74:13 51:10 yS Ex 14:22; Zec 10:11; Rev 16:12 zEx 15:5,8 aS Job 36:30 bS Ex 15:13 51:11 cS Isa 35:9; S 44:23 dS Ps 109:28; Isa 65:14; Jer 30:19; Zep 3:14 eS Isa 48:20; Jer 33:11 fS Isa 30:19; Jer 31:13; S Rev 7:17 51:12 gS Isa 40:1; S 2Co 1:4 hS 2Ki 1:15 iS Isa 2:22 jS Isa 15:6; 40:6-7; 1Pe 1:24 51:13 kS Job 8:13; S Isa 17:10 lS Job 4:17; Isa 17:7; 45:11; 54:5 mS Ge 1:1; S Isa 48:13 nS Isa 7:4 oS Isa 9:4 51:14 pS Isa 42:7 qIsa 49:10 51:15 rS Ex 14:21 sS Ps 93:3 tS Isa 13:4 51:16 uS Ex 4:12,15 vS Ex 33:22 wS Isa 48:13 xJer 7:23; 11:4; 24:7; Eze 14:11; Zec 8:8 51:17 yS Jdg 5:12; Isa 52:1

Study notes

51:6 *Lift . . . to the heavens.* See 40:26. *heavens will vanish.* See 34:4 and note. *earth will wear out like a garment.* See 24:4; Heb 1:10–11; cf. Isa 50:9. *last forever.* See v. 8; 45:17. The word of God will also endure forever (see 40:8 and note; Mt 24:35; Lk 21:33).
51:7 *who know what is right.* See v. 1 and note. *who have my law in your hearts.* See Ps 37:31; Jer 31:33. *reproach . . . insults.* Such as those borne by the servant in 50:6–7.
51:8 *moth . . . like a garment.* See 50:9 and note; cf. 51:6.
51:9,17 *Awake, awake!* See 52:1 for the same double command (see also 40:1 and note).
51:9 *Clothe . . . with strength.* Cf. 50:2; see note on 40:31. *arm of the LORD.* Symbol of God's power (cf. v. 5). See 30:30; 50:2 and notes; 52:10; 53:1; 63:12. *Rahab . . . monster.* Egypt. See 27:1 and note; 30:7 and note.
51:10 *sea.* The Red Sea (see 50:2 and note). *the redeemed.* See 35:9 and note.

51:11 This verse is the same as 35:10 (see note there).
51:12 *who comforts.* See v. 3; 49:13 and note. *grass.* See 37:27; 40:6 and notes.
51:13 *stretched out the heavens and . . . earth.* See v. 16; 48:13 and note. *wrath of the oppressor.* See 49:26 and note. Babylon's wrath was insignificant beside the mighty wrath of God (cf. 13:3,5; 30:27).
51:14 *prisoners . . . set free.* The exiles in Babylon (see 42:7 and note; 49:9). *in their dungeon.* Cf. 42:7; Jer 37:16.
51:15 *churns up the sea.* Cf. Job 26:12; Ps 107:25; Jer 31:35. *LORD Almighty.* See 13:4 and note.
51:16 *my words.* Primarily the law of Moses, mentioned in v. 7. Like the servant of 49:2, the people are responding to God's word (cf. 59:21; Jos 1:8). *shadow of my hand.* See 49:2 and note. *set the heavens . . . earth.* See v. 13 and note.
51:17 *cup of his wrath.* See vv. 20–22; 13:3 and note. Experiencing God's judgment is often compared to becom-

you who have drunk from the hand of
the LORD
the cup z of his wrath, a
you who have drained to its dregs b
the goblet that makes men stagger. c
18Of all the sons d she bore
there was none to guide her; e
of all the sons she reared
there was none to take her by the
hand. f
19These double calamities g have come
upon you—
who can comfort you? h—
ruin and destruction, i famine j and
sword k—
who can u console you?
20Your sons have fainted;
they lie at the head of every street, l
like antelope caught in a net. m
They are filled with the wrath n of the
LORD
and the rebuke o of your God.

21Therefore hear this, you afflicted p one,
made drunk, q but not with wine.
22This is what your Sovereign LORD says,
your God, who defends r his people:
"See, I have taken out of your hand
the cup s that made you stagger;
from that cup, the goblet of my wrath,
you will never drink again.
23I will put it into the hands of your
tormentors, t
who said to you,
'Fall prostrate u that we may walk v
over you.'
And you made your back like the
ground,
like a street to be walked over." w

52 Awake, awake, x O Zion,
clothe yourself with strength. y
Put on your garments of splendor, z

O Jerusalem, the holy city. a
The uncircumcised b and defiled c
will not enter you again. d
2Shake off your dust; e
rise up, f sit enthroned, O Jerusalem.
Free yourself from the chains on your
neck, g
O captive Daughter of Zion. h

3For this is what the LORD says:

"You were sold for nothing, i
and without money j you will be
redeemed. k "

4For this is what the Sovereign LORD
says:

"At first my people went down to
Egypt l to live;
lately, Assyria m has oppressed them.

5"And now what do I have here?" declares the LORD.

"For my people have been taken away
for nothing,
and those who rule them mock, v "
declares the LORD.

"And all day long
my name is constantly blasphemed. n
6Therefore my people will know o my
name; p
therefore in that day q they will know
that it is I who foretold r it.
Yes, it is I."

7How beautiful on the mountains s

51:17 zS ver 22;
S Ps 16:5;
S Mt 20:22 aver
20; Job 21:20;
Isa 42:25; 66:15;
Rev 14:10; 16:19
bS Ps 75:8 cS ver
23; S Ps 60:3
51:18 dPs 88:18
eS Job 31:18;
S Isa 49:21
fS Isa 41:13
51:19
gS Isa 40:2; 47:9
hIsa 49:13;
54:11; Jer 15:5;
Na 3:7 iIsa 60:18;
62:4; Jer 48:3;
La 3:47
jS Isa 14:30
kJer 14:12; 24:10
51:20 lIsa 5:25;
Jer 14:16; La 2:19
mS Job 18:10
nS ver 17;
S Job 40:11;
Jer 44:6
oS Dt 28:20
51:21
pS Isa 14:32 qver
17; S Isa 29:9
51:22
rS Isa 49:25
sS ver 17;
Jer 25:15; 51:7;
Hab 2:16;
S Mt 20:22
51:23 tIsa 14:4;
49:26;
Jer 25:15-17,26,
28; 49:12 uver
17; Zec 12:2
vS Jos 10:24
wPs 66:12;
Mic 7:10
52:1 xS Isa 51:17
yS 1Sa 2:4;
S Isa 51:9
zEzk 28:2,40;
Est 6:8; Ps 110:3;
Isa 49:18; 61:10;
Zec 3:4

aS Ne 11:1;
S Isa 1:26;
Mt 4:5;
S Rev 21:2
bS Ge 34:14
cS Isa 35:8
dJoel 3:17;
Na 1:15; Zec 9:8;
Rev 21:27
52:2 eS Isa 29:4
fIsa 60:1
gS Ps 81:6;
S Isa 10:27
hPs 9:14

52:3 iS Ps 44:12 jIsa 45:13 kS Isa 1:27; 1Pe 1:18 52:4
lS Ge 46:6 mIsa 10:24 52:5 nS Isa 37:23; Ro 2:24* 52:6
oS Isa 49:23 pS Ex 6:3 qS Isa 10:20 rS Isa 41:26 52:7
sS Isa 42:11

u 19 Dead Sea Scrolls, Septuagint, Vulgate and Syriac;
Masoretic Text / how can I   v 5 Dead Sea Scrolls and
Vulgate; Masoretic Text wail

---

ing drunk on strong wine. It is the fate of wicked nations in
particular. See 29:9; 63:6; Ps 60:3; 75:8; Jer 25:15–16; La
4:21; Eze 23:32–34; Hab 2:16; Zec 12:2; cf. Jn 18:11.
51:18 Children were expected to take care of parents who
were sick or unsteady.
51:19 who can comfort you? A question also asked in Jer
15:5. Contrast v. 3.
51:20 caught in a net. Cf. Pr 7:22. rebuke. See 17:13;
54:9; 66:15.
51:21 afflicted one. Jerusalem (see 54:11). made drunk.
On God's wrath (see v. 17 and note).
51:22 defends his people. See 49:25 and note. cup . . . of
my wrath. See v. 17 and note.
51:23 your tormentors. The Babylonians. See vv. 13–14;
14:4. your back like the ground. Perhaps figurative, but cf.
Jos 10:24.
52:1 Awake, awake . . . clothe . . . with strength. See
51:9,17 and notes. garments of splendor. Perhaps the robes
of the priests, which belong to Jerusalem as a "holy city." See
49:18 and note. holy city. See 48:2 and note. uncircumcised

and defiled. Foreign invaders. See 35:8 and note; Jdg 14:3
and note.
52:2 Shake off your dust. Contrast the fate of Babylon in
47:1 (see note there). Free yourself. See 42:7 and note;
49:9; 51:14. Daughter of Zion. A personification of Jerusalem and its inhabitants.
52:3 sold for nothing. The enemy paid the Lord nothing for
acquiring Jerusalem. See 45:13; 50:1 and notes. without
money . . . redeemed. See 41:14 and note; 43:1; 45:13.
52:4 Assyria . . . oppressed them. See 9:4 and note.
52:5 Quoted in part in Ro 2:24. for nothing. See v. 3 and
note. my name is . . . blasphemed. The captivity brought
disrespect to the God of helpless Jerusalem (see Eze
36:20–23). Cf. Assyria's blasphemy in 37:23–24.
52:6 know my name. See 49:26 and note. in that day. The
day of deliverance from Babylon. See 10:20,27 and note.
foretold it. The return from exile.
52:7 feet of those who bring good news. A reference to
messengers who ran from the scene of a battle to bring news
of the outcome to a waiting king and people (see 2Sa 18:26).

are the feet of those who bring good
news, [t]
who proclaim peace, [u]
who bring good tidings,
who proclaim salvation,
who say to Zion,
"Your God reigns!" [v]
[8]Listen! Your watchmen [w] lift up their
voices; [x]
together they shout for joy. [y]
When the LORD returns [z] to Zion, [a]
they will see it with their own eyes.
[9]Burst into songs of joy [b] together,
you ruins [c] of Jerusalem,
for the LORD has comforted [d] his people,
he has redeemed Jerusalem. [e]
[10]The LORD will lay bare his holy arm [f]
in the sight of all the nations, [g]
and all the ends of the earth [h] will see
the salvation [i] of our God.

[11]Depart, [j] depart, go out from there!
Touch no unclean thing! [k]
Come out from it and be pure, [l]
you who carry the vessels [m] of the
LORD.
[12]But you will not leave in haste [n]
or go in flight;
for the LORD will go before you, [o]
the God of Israel will be your rear
guard. [p]

52:7
[t]S 2Sa 18:26;
S Isa 40:9;
Ro 10:15*
[u]Na 1:15;
Lk 2:14; Eph 6:15
[v]S 1Ch 16:31;
S Ps 97:1;
1Co 15:24-25
52:8
[w]S 1Sa 14:16;
Isa 56:10; 62:6;
Jer 6:17; 31:6;
Eze 3:17; 33:7
[x]Isa 40:9
[y]S Isa 12:6
[z]S Nu 10:36
[a]Isa 59:20;
Zec 8:3
52:9 [b]S Ps 98:4;
S Isa 35:2
[c]S Ps 74:3;
S Isa 51:3
[d]S Isa 40:1;
Lk 2:25
[e]S Ezr 9:9;
S Isa 48:20
52:10
[f]S 2Ch 32:8;
S Ps 44:3;
S Isa 30:30
[g]Isa 66:18
[h]S Jos 4:24;
S Isa 11:9
[i]S Ps 67:2;
Lk 2:30; 3:6
52:11
[j]S Isa 48:20
[k]S Isa 1:16;
2Co 6:17*
[l]S Nu 8:6;
2Ti 2:19
[m]S 2Ch 36:10
52:12
[n]S Ex 12:11
[o]Mic 2:13;
Jn 10:4
[p]S Ex 14:19

52:13 [q]S Jos 1:8;
S Isa 4:2; S 20:3

The Suffering and Glory of the Servant

[13]See, my servant [q] will act wisely [w];
he will be raised and lifted up and
highly exalted. [r]
[14]Just as there were many who were
appalled [s] at him [x]—
his appearance was so disfigured [t]
beyond that of any man
and his form marred beyond human
likeness [u]—
[15]so will he sprinkle [v] many nations, [y]
and kings [w] will shut their mouths [x]
because of him.
For what they were not told, they will
see,
and what they have not heard, they
will understand. [y]

53
Who has believed our message [z]
and to whom has the arm [a] of the
LORD been revealed? [b]
[2]He grew up before him like a tender
shoot, [c]

[r]S Isa 6:1; 57:15; Ac 3:13; S Php 2:9 **52:14** [s]S Lev 26:32;
S Job 18:20 [t]S 2Sa 10:4 [u]S Job 2:12; S 16:16 **52:15**
[v]S Lev 14:7; S 16:14-15 [w]S Isa 49:7 [x]S Jdg 18:19; Ps 107:42
[y]Ro 15:21*; Eph 3:4-5 **53:1** [z]S Isa 28:9; Ro 10:16*
[a]S Ps 98:1; S Isa 30:30 [b]Jn 12:38* **53:2** [c]S 2Ki 19:26;
S Job 14:7; S Isa 4:2

w 13 Or *will prosper*   **x** 14 Hebrew *you*
y 15 Hebrew; Septuagint *so will many nations marvel at him*

Here the news refers to the return from exile (vv. 11–12; see
40:9 and note; 41:27), a deliverance that prefigures Christ's
deliverance from sin. See Ro 10:15; Eph 6:15. *salvation.* See
49:8 and note. *Your God reigns!* See Ps 96:10. The return of
God's people to Jerusalem emphasizes his sovereign rule
over the world (see 40:9 and note). God's kingdom will
come more fully at the second coming of Christ (see Rev
19:6).
52:8 *watchmen.* Those in Jerusalem watching for the arrival of the messengers (cf. 62:6–7; 2Sa 18:24–27).
52:9 *Burst into songs.* See 44:23 and note. *comforted.* See
49:13 and note. *redeemed.* See v. 3 and note.
52:10 *holy arm.* See 51:9 and note. God's arm is often
associated with redemption and salvation (see Ex 6:6). *all
the ends of the earth.* Equivalent to "all mankind" in 40:5
(see note there). Cf. 45:22.
52:11 *Depart, depart . . . !* See note on 40:1. *unclean
thing.* Perhaps referring to pagan religious objects (cf. Ge
31:19; 35:2). *you who carry the vessels.* Cyrus allowed the
people to take back the articles of the temple seized by
Nebuchadnezzar (Ezr 1:7–11). The priests and Levites were
responsible for them (see Nu 3:6–8; 2Ch 5:4–7).
52:12 *not leave in haste.* See 48:20 and note. *go before
you . . . be your rear guard.* As he did for the Israelites when
they were freed from Egypt (see Ex 13:21; 14:19–20; cf. Isa
42:16; 49:10; 58:8).
52:13–53:12 The fourth and longest of the four servant
songs (see note on 42:1–4). It constitutes the central and
most important unit in chs. 40–66 as well as in chs. 49–57
(see note on 39:8). The song contains five stanzas of three
numbered verses each. It is quoted more frequently in the
NT than any other OT passage and is often referred to as the

"gospel in the OT."
52:13 *my servant.* See note on 42:1. *act wisely.* A mark of
God's blessing (see 1Sa 18:14) and of obedience to God's
word (see Jos 1:8). The Messianic King will "reign wisely"
(Jer 23:5). Cf. 53:10. *raised and lifted up.* Words that describe the Lord in Isaiah's vision (see 6:1 and note; 57:15).
Christ's exaltation is referred to in Ac 2:33; 3:13; Eph
1:20–23; Php 2:9–11 (see also 1Pe 1:10–11).
52:14 *appalled at him.* When they saw Christ's suffering
on the cross. Cf. the reaction to the ruined city of Tyre (Eze
27:35). *disfigured.* A term used of a "blemished animal,"
which should not be offered to the Lord (Mal 1:14). Cf. the
disgraceful treatment of the servant (see 50:6 and note).
beyond that of any man. Cf. Ps 22:6. His treatment was
inhuman.
52:15 *sprinkle many nations.* With the sprinkling of
cleansing (see Lev 14:7; Nu 8:7; 19:18–19) and/or of
consecration (see Ex 29:21; Lev 8:11,30). But see NIV text
note. *kings will shut their mouths.* In astonishment at the
suffering and exaltation of the servant (see 49:6–7 and
notes). Cf. Job 21:5. *For what . . . understand.* Quoted in Ro
15:21. Even though they have not heard the prophetic word,
kings will understand the mission of the servant when they
see his humiliation and exaltation (contrast 6:9–10).
53:1 Quoted in whole or in part in Jn 12:38; Ro 10:16. *our
message.* The good news about salvation, given by the
prophets to Israel and the nations (see 52:7,10). *arm of the
LORD.* See 51:9 and note.
53:2 *tender shoot.* The Messiah would grow from the
"stump of Jesse." See 4:2; 11:1 and notes. His beginnings
would be humble. *root.* See 11:10 and note. *beauty.* The
Hebrew for this word is used of David in 1Sa 16:18, where

and like a root[d] out of dry ground.
He had no beauty or majesty to attract
us to him,
nothing in his appearance[e] that we
should desire him.
[3]He was despised and rejected by men,
a man of sorrows,[f] and familiar with
suffering.[g]
Like one from whom men hide[h] their
faces
he was despised,[i] and we esteemed
him not.

[4]Surely he took up our infirmities
and carried our sorrows,[j]
yet we considered him stricken by
God,[k]
smitten by him, and afflicted.[l]
[5]But he was pierced[m] for our
transgressions,[n]
he was crushed[o] for our iniquities;
the punishment[p] that brought us
peace[q] was upon him,
and by his wounds[r] we are healed.[s]
[6]We all, like sheep, have gone astray,[t]
each of us has turned to his own
way;[u]
and the LORD has laid on him
the iniquity[v] of us all.

[7]He was oppressed[w] and afflicted,
yet he did not open his mouth;[x]
he was led like a lamb[y] to the
slaughter,[z]

and as a sheep before her shearers is
silent,
so he did not open his mouth.
[8]By oppression[z] and judgment[a] he was
taken away.
And who can speak of his
descendants?
For he was cut off from the land of the
living;[b]
for the transgression[c] of my people
he was stricken.[a]
[9]He was assigned a grave with the
wicked,[d]
and with the rich[e] in his death,
though he had done no violence,[f]
nor was any deceit in his mouth.[g]

[10]Yet it was the LORD's will[h] to crush[i]
him and cause him to suffer,[j]
and though the LORD makes[b] his life
a guilt offering,[k]
he will see his offspring[l] and prolong
his days,
and the will of the LORD will
prosper[m] in his hand.

53:2 [d]S Isa 11:10;
[e]Isa 52:14 **53:3** [f]Ps 69:29
[g]ver 4,10;
S Ex 1:10;
S Mt 16:21;
Lk 18:31-33;
Heb 5:8
[h]S Dt 31:17;
Isa 1:15
[i]S 1Sa 2:30;
S Ps 22:6;
Mt 27:29;
Jn 1:10-11
53:4 [j]Mt 8:17*
[k]S Dt 5:24;
S Job 4:5;
Jer 23:5-6; 25:34;
Eze 34:23-24;
Mic 5:2-4;
Zec 13:7; Jn 19:7
[l]S ver 3;
S Ge 12:17;
S Ru 1:21
53:5 [m]S Ps 22:16
[n]S Ex 28:38;
S Ps 39:8;
S Jn 3:17;
Ro 4:25;
1Co 15:3;
Heb 9:28
[o]Ps 34:18
[p]S Isa 50:6
[q]S Isa 9:6; Ro 5:1
[r]Isa 1:6;
Mt 27:26; Jn 19:1
[s]S Dt 32:39;
S 2Ch 7:14;
1Pe 2:24-25
53:6 [t]S Ps 95:10;
1Pe 2:24-25
[u]S 1Sa 8:3;
Isa 56:11; 57:17;
Mic 3:5 [v]ver 12;
S Ex 28:38;
Ro 4:25
53:7 [w]Isa 49:26
[x]S Mk 14:61;
1Pe 2:23
[y]Mt 27:31;
S Jn 1:29
[z]S Ps 44:22

53:8 [a]Mk 14:49 [b]Ps 88:5; Da 9:26; Ac 8:32-33* [c]ver 12;
S Ps 39:8 **53:9** [d]Mt 27:38; Mk 15:27; Lk 23:32; Jn 19:18
[e]Mt 27:57-60; Mk 15:43-46; Lk 23:50-53; Jn 19:38-41
[f]Isa 42:1-3 [g]S Job 16:17; 1Pe 2:22*; 1Jn 3:5; Rev 14:5 **53:10**
[h]Isa 46:10; 55:11; Ac 2:23 [i]ver 5 /S ver 3; S Ge 12:17
[k]S Lev 5:15; Jn 3:17 [l]S Ps 22:30 [m]S Jos 1:8; S Isa 49:4

[z]8 Or From arrest   [a]8 Or away. / Yet who of his
generation considered / that he was cut off from the
land of the living / for the transgression of my people, /
to whom the blow was due?   [b]10 Hebrew though you
make

---

it is translated "fine-looking." Christ had nothing of the
bearing or trappings of royalty.
53:3 *despised.* See 49:7 and note; Ps 22:6. *rejected . . .
esteemed.* The Hebrew words used here occur together also
in 2:22 (see note there). Cf. Jn 1:10–11. *sorrows.* The
Hebrew for this word is used of both physical and mental
pain (see v. 4; Ex 3:7). *hide their faces.* See 1:15 and note;
8:17.
53:4 Quoted in part in Mt 8:17 with reference to Jesus'
healing ministry. *infirmities.* Diseases often result from sinful
living and are ultimately the consequences of original
(Adamic) sin. See 1:5–6 and note. *stricken by God.* With a
terrible disease (see Ge 12:17; 2Ki 15:5). People (Israel in
particular) thought the servant was suffering for his own sins.
afflicted. Or "humbled," or "oppressed" (see v. 7; 58:10).
53:5 *pierced.* See Ps 22:16; Zec 12:10; Jn 19:34. *crushed.*
In spirit (see Ps 34:18; cf. Isa 57:15). The sins of the world
weighed heavily upon him. *healed.* Here probably equivalent
to "forgiven" (see 6:10; Jer 30:17; see also note on 1Pe
2:24).
53:6 *have gone astray.* Cf. Ps 119:176; Jer 50:6; Eze
34:4–6,16; 1Pe 2:25. *laid on him the iniquity of us all.* Just
as the priest laid his hands on the scapegoat and symbolically
put Israel's sins on it (Lev 16:21). See 1Pe 2:24.
53:7–8 Verses read by the Ethiopian eunuch in the presence of Philip (Ac 8:32–33).
53:7 *oppressed.* Like Israel. See 49:26 and note. The
Hebrew for this word is translated "slave drivers" in Ex 5:6.
lamb to the slaughter. Cf. Ps 44:22; Rev 5:6. John the
Baptist called Jesus "the Lamb of God" (Jn 1:29,35). *did not*

open his mouth. Jesus remained silent before the chief
priests and Pilate (Mt 27:12–14; Mk 14:60–61; 15:4–5; Jn
19:8–9) and before Herod (Lk 23:8–9).
53:8 *By oppression and judgment.* Jesus was given an
unfair trial. *his descendants.* To die without children was
considered a tragedy (2Sa 18:18). Cf. also v. 10. But see
second NIV text note here.
53:9 *the wicked.* The manner of his death would indicate
that, as far as those who condemned him were concerned,
he was to be buried with executed criminals. *the rich.* Not as
a burial with honor. The parallelism (with its effective wordplay in Hebrew) makes clear that Isaiah here associates the
rich with the wicked, as do many OT writers—because they
acquired their wealth by wicked means and/or trusted in
their wealth rather than in God (see, e.g., Ps 37:16,35; Pr
18:23; 28:30; Jer 5:26–27; Mic 6:10,12). According to the
Gospels (Mt 27:57–60 and parallels), the wealthy Joseph of
Arimathea gave Jesus an honorable burial by placing his body
in his own tomb. But this was undoubtedly an act of love
growing out of his awareness that he had been forgiven
much (see Lk 7:47). Thus the fulfillment fitted but also
transcended the prophecy. *he had done no violence, nor . . .
deceit in his mouth.* Peter quotes these lines as he encourages believers to endure unjust suffering (1Pe 2:22).
53:10 *crush him.* See v. 5 and note. *guilt offering.* An
offering where restitution was usually required (Lev 5:16;
6:5) and the offender sacrificed a ram (Lev 5:15). *his offspring.* Spiritual descendants. *prolong his days.* Christ would
live forever (see 9:7 and note). *prosper.* See 52:13 and NIV
text note there.

11After the suffering[n] of his soul,
    he will see the light[o] of life[c] and be
        satisfied[d];
by his knowledge[e] my righteous
        servant[p] will justify[q] many,
    and he will bear their iniquities.[r]
12Therefore I will give him a portion
        among the great,[f][s]
    and he will divide the spoils[t] with
        the strong,[g]
because he poured out his life unto
        death,[u]
    and was numbered with the
        transgressors.[v]
For he bore[w] the sin of many,[x]
    and made intercession[y] for the
        transgressors.

The Future Glory of Zion

54 "Sing, O barren woman,[z]
    you who never bore a child;
burst into song, shout for joy,[a]
    you who were never in labor;[b]
because more are the children[c] of the
        desolate[d] woman
    than of her who has a husband,[e]"
        says the LORD.
2"Enlarge the place of your tent,[f]
    stretch your tent curtains wide,
        do not hold back;
lengthen your cords,
    strengthen your stakes.[g]
3For you will spread out to the right and
        to the left;
    your descendants[h] will dispossess
        nations[i]
    and settle in their desolate[j] cities.

4"Do not be afraid;[k] you will not suffer
        shame.[l]
    Do not fear disgrace;[m] you will not
        be humiliated.
You will forget the shame of your
        youth[n]
    and remember no more the
        reproach[o] of your
        widowhood.[p]
5For your Maker[q] is your husband[r] —
    the LORD Almighty is his name—
the Holy One[s] of Israel is your
        Redeemer;[t]
    he is called the God of all the earth.[u]
6The LORD will call you back[v]
    as if you were a wife deserted[w] and
        distressed in spirit—
a wife who married young,[x]
    only to be rejected," says your God.
7"For a brief moment[y] I abandoned[z]
        you,
    but with deep compassion[a] I will
        bring you back.[b]
8In a surge of anger[d]
    I hid[d] my face from you for a
        moment,
    but with everlasting kindness[e]

53:11
n Jn 10:14-18
o S Job 33:30
p S Isa 20:3;
  Ac 7:52
q S Isa 6:7;
  Jn 1:29;
  Ac 10:43;
  S Ro 4:25
r S Ex 28:38
53:12 s S Isa 6:1;
  S Php 2:9
t S Ex 15:9;
  S Ps 119:162;
  Lk 11:22
u Mt 26:28,38,39,
  42 v Mt 27:38;
  Mk 15:27*;
  Lk 22:37*; 23:32
w S ver 6;
  1Pe 2:24
x Heb 9:28
y Isa 59:16;
  S Ro 8:34
54:1 z S Ge 30:1
a S Ge 21:6;
  S Ps 98:4
b Isa 66:7
c Isa 49:20
d S Isa 49:19
e S 1Sa 2:5;
  Gal 4:27*
54:2 f S Ge 26:22;
  Isa 26:15;
  49:19-20
g Ex 35:18; 39:40
54:3
h S Ge 13:14;
  S Isa 48:19
i S Job 12:23;
  S Isa 14:2;
  60:4-11
j S Isa 49:19

54:4 k Jer 30:10;
  Joel 2:21
l S Isa 28:16;
  S 29:22
m S Ge 30:23;
  S Ps 119:39;
  S Isa 41:11
n S Ps 25:7;
  S Jer 2:2; S 22:21
o S Isa 51:7
p S Isa 47:8
54:5 q S Ps 95:6;
  S 149:2;
  S Isa 51:13
r S SS 3:11;

Jer 3:14; 31:32; Hos 2:7,16 s S Isa 1:4; 49:7; 55:5; 60:9
t S Isa 48:17 u S Isa 6:3; S 12:4 **54:6** v Isa 49:14-21 w ver 6-7;
Isa 1:4; 50:1-2; 60:15; 62:4,12; Jer 44:2; Hos 1:10
x S Ex 20:14; Mal 2:15 **54:7** y S Job 14:13; Isa 26:20
z S Ps 71:11; S Isa 27:8 a S Ps 51:1 b S Isa 49:18 **54:8**
c Isa 9:12; 26:20; 60:10 d S Isa 1:15 e ver 10; S Ps 25:6; 92:2;
Isa 55:3; 63:7

c 11 Dead Sea Scrolls (see also Septuagint); Masoretic Text
does not have *the light of life*.   d 11 Or (with
Masoretic Text) 11*He will see the result of the suffering of
his soul / and be satisfied*   e 11 Or *by knowledge of
him*   f 12 Or *many*   g 12 Or *numerous*

53:11 *light of life*. A reference to the resurrection of
Christ; see 1Co 15:4 (but see also the first two NIV text
notes here). For "of life" see also Job 33:28,30; Ps 49:19;
56:13. *be satisfied*. In 1:11, where the same Hebrew word
appears, God had "more than enough" of innumerable sacrifices that accomplished nothing. Here the one sacrifice of
Christ brings perfect satisfaction. *his knowledge*. His true
knowledge of the true God (see 1:3; 6:9; 43:10; 45:4-5;
52:6; 56:10). The Spirit of knowledge (11:2) rested on the
Messiah (but see the third NIV text note here). Cf. 52:13. *my
... servant*. See 41:8-9; 42:1 and notes. *justify*. Cause
many to be declared righteous. See 5:23 ("acquit"); Ro 5:19
and note. *many*. See NIV text notes on v. 12; see also 52:15;
Da 12:3.
53:12 *among the great ... with the strong*. God will
reward his servant as if he was a king sharing in the spoils of
a great victory (see 52:15). *divide the spoils*. God's gift to his
suffering servant (cf. 9:3). *poured out his life*. As a sacrifice
(see v. 10). *unto death*. See Php 2:8. *and was numbered
with the transgressors*. Quoted in Lk 22:37 with reference
to Jesus. *bore*. The Hebrew for this verb is translated "took
up" in v. 4. *made intercession*. See Jer 7:16 ("pray"); 27:18
("plead"). Cf. 59:16; Heb 7:25.
54:1 This verse is applied by Paul to Sarah and the covenant of promise, representing "the Jerusalem that is above"
(Gal 4:26-27). *Sing ... burst into song*. See 12:6; 44:23;

52:9 and notes. *barren woman*. Jerusalem (representing
Israel), especially during the exile (see 49:21). In the Near
East, barrenness was considered a disgrace (see 4:1 and
note). *more are the children of the desolate woman*. See
49:19-20 and note. Israel will be restored both physically
and spiritually (cf. 62:4). *husband*. See 50:1 and note.
54:2 See 26:15; 33:20 and notes. *your tent*. Jerusalem is
viewed as a woman living in her own tent.
54:3 *spread out*. See 49:19-20 and note; cf. Ge 28:14.
dispossess nations. See 11:14; 49:7 and notes.
54:4 *not suffer shame ... disgrace*. See 29:22 and note;
45:17. *shame of your youth*. Probably the period of slavery in
Egypt. Cf. Jer 31:19; Eze 16:60. *reproach of your widowhood*. Probably referring to the exile, when Israel was alone,
like a widow (vv. 6-7).
54:5 *husband*. See 62:4-5. *Holy One of Israel ... Redeemer*. See 1:4, 41:14 and notes.
54:6-7 *wife deserted ... abandoned*. Israel's experience
in exile (see 49:14; 50:1 and note; 62:4).
54:7-8,10 *compassion*. See 14:1; 49:10,13; 51:3.
54:7 *brief moment*. The Babylonian exile was relatively
brief (see 26:20; 50:1 and notes).
54:8 *surge of anger*. See 9:12,17,21 and note; 60:10. *hid
my face*. See 1:15 and note. *everlasting kindness*. See v. 10;
55:3 and note. Cf. 45:17. *Redeemer*. See v. 5.

I will have compassion[f] on you,"
says the LORD your Redeemer.[g]

9"To me this is like the days of Noah,
when I swore that the waters of
Noah would never again cover
the earth.[h]
So now I have sworn[i] not to be angry[j]
with you,
never to rebuke[k] you again.
10Though the mountains be shaken[l] [m]
and the hills be removed,
yet my unfailing love[n] for you will not
be shaken[o]
nor my covenant[p] of peace[q] be
removed,"
says the LORD, who has compassion[r]
on you.

11"O afflicted[s] city, lashed by storms[t]
and not comforted,[u]
I will build you with stones of
turquoise,[h] [v]
your foundations[w] with sapphires.[i] [x]
12I will make your battlements of rubies,
your gates[y] of sparkling jewels,
and all your walls of precious stones.
13All your sons will be taught by the
LORD,[z]
and great will be your children's
peace.[a]
14In righteousness[b] you will be
established:[c]
Tyranny[d] will be far from you;
you will have nothing to fear.[e]
Terror[f] will be far removed;
it will not come near you.
15If anyone does attack you, it will not be
my doing;

whoever attacks you will surrender[g]
to you.

16"See, it is I who created the
blacksmith[h]
who fans the coals into flame
and forges a weapon[i] fit for its work.
And it is I who have created the
destroyer[j] to work havoc;
17 no weapon forged against you will
prevail,[k]
and you will refute[l] every tongue
that accuses you.
This is the heritage of the servants[m] of
the LORD,
and this is their vindication[n] from
me,"

declares the LORD.

Invitation to the Thirsty

55 "Come, all you who are thirsty,[o]
come to the waters;[p]
and you who have no money,
come, buy[q] and eat!
Come, buy wine and milk[r]
without money and without cost.[s]
2Why spend money on what is not
bread,
and your labor on what does not
satisfy?[t]
Listen, listen to me, and eat what is
good,[u]

54:8
[f]S Ps 102:13;
[g]S Isa 14:1;
Hos 2:19
[g]S Isa 48:17
54:9 [h]S Ge 8:21
[i]S Isa 14:24;
S 49:18 /Ps 13:1;
103:9; Isa 12:1;
57:16; Jer 3:5,12;
Eze 39:29;
Mic 7:18
[k]S Dt 28:20
54:10 [l]Rev 6:14
[m]S Ps 46:2
[n]S Ps 6:4
[o]S Isa 51:6;
Heb 12:27
[p]S Ge 9:16;
Ex 34:10;
Ps 89:34;
S Isa 42:6
[q]S Nu 25:12 [r]ver
8; S Isa 14:1;
55:7
54:11
[s]S Isa 14:32
[t]Isa 28:2; 29:6
[u]S Isa 51:19
[v]1Ch 29:2;
Rev 21:18
[w]S Isa 28:16;
Rev 21:19-20
[x]S Ex 24:10;
S Job 28:6
54:12 [y]Rev 21:21
54:13
[z]S Isa 28:9;
Mic 4:2;
Jn 6:45*;
Heb 8:11
[a]S Lev 26:6;
S Isa 48:18
54:14 [b]S Isa 26:2
[c]Jer 30:20
[d]S 2Sa 7:10;
S Isa 9:4
[e]Zep 3:15;
Zec 9:8
[f]S Isa 17:14

54:15
[g]Isa 41:11-16
54:16
[h]S Isa 44:12
[i]S Isa 10:5
[j]S Isa 13:5
54:17 [k]S Isa 29:8
[l]S Isa 41:11
[m]Isa 56:6-8;
63:17; 65:8,9,

13-15; 66:14 [n]S Ps 17:2; Zec 1:20-21 **55:1** [o]S Pr 9:5;
S Isa 35:7; Mt 5:6; Lk 6:21; Jn 4:14; 7:37 [p]Jer 2:13;
Eze 47:1,12; Zec 14:8 [q]La 5:4; Mt 13:44; Rev 3:18 [r]S SS 5:1;
1Pe 2:2 [s]Hos 14:4; Mt 10:8; Rev 21:6; 22:17 **55:2**
[t]Ps 22:26; Ecc 6:2; Isa 49:4; Jer 12:13; Hos 4:10; 8:7;
Mic 6:14; Hag 1:6 [u]S Isa 1:19

---

[h]11 The meaning of the Hebrew for this word is
uncertain. [i]11 Or *lapis lazuli*

54:9 *never again cover the earth.* See Ge 9:11 and note. *not to be angry.* See 12:1 and note.
54:10 *mountains . . . be removed.* Cf. 51:6; Ps 46:2; 102:26–27. *unfailing love . . . covenant of peace.* A reference to either the covenant with Israel or the Davidic covenant, described in similar terms in 55:3 (see note there). Cf. Jer 33:20–21; for the language see Nu 25:11–13.
54:11–12 A figurative description of restored Jerusalem, echoed in the description of the new Jerusalem in Rev 21:10,18–21.
54:11 *afflicted city.* Jerusalem. See 51:21. *lashed by storms.* See 28:2 and note. *turquoise.* Perhaps a bluish-green stone. It was used in Solomon's temple (1Ch 29:2). *sapphires.* Cf. the "pavement made of sapphire" (a blue stone) in Ex 24:10 (see also Eze 1:26; 10:1).
54:12 *battlements.* Parapets on the top of walls. *walls.* Cf. 26:1.
54:13–14 *peace . . . righteousness.* See 48:18 and note.
54:13 *taught by the LORD.* Like the servant of the Lord in 50:4. Cf. Jer 31:34.
54:14 *Tyranny . . . Terror . . . far removed.* Cf. 14:4; 33:18–19.
54:15 *surrender to you.* See v. 3.
54:16 *created the destroyer.* God raised up nations such as

Assyria and Babylonia to punish Israel (see 10:5 and note; 33:1 and note).

54:17 *refute every tongue.* Just as no legitimate charges could be brought against the servant of 50:8–9. *servants of the LORD.* After ch. 53 the singular "servant" no longer occurs in Isaiah. The "servants" (see 63:17; 65:8–9,13–15; 66:14) are true believers—both Jew and Gentile (see 56:6–8)—who are faithful to the Lord. They are in a sense the "offspring" of the servant (53:10). See 49:19–20 and note.

55:1 The exiles are summoned to return and be restored. *thirsty.* Spiritual thirst is primary (see 41:17; 44:3; Ps 42:1–2; 63:1). *waters.* Figurative for spiritual refreshment. Cf. Wisdom's invitation in Pr 9:5. Christ similarly invited people to drink the water of life (Jn 4:14; 7:37). *no money.* In hard times even water had to be purchased (see La 5:4). *wine and milk.* Symbols of abundance, enjoyment and nourishment. *without money.* The death of the servant (53:5–9) paid for the free gift of life (see Ro 6:23).

55:2 *what is not bread.* Perhaps the husks of pagan religious practices. Cf. Dt 8:3. *richest of fare.* Great spiritual blessings are compared to a banquet (see 25:6 and note; Ps 22:26; 34:8; Jer 31:14).

and your soul will delight in the
   richest[v] of fare.

[3]Give ear and come to me;
   hear[w] me, that your soul may live.[x]
I will make an everlasting covenant[y]
   with you,
   my faithful love[z] promised to
     David.[a]
[4]See, I have made him a witness[b] to the
   peoples,
   a leader and commander[c] of the
   peoples.
[5]Surely you will summon nations[d] you
   know not,
   and nations that do not know you
    will hasten to you,[e]
because of the LORD your God,
   the Holy One[f] of Israel,
   for he has endowed you with
    splendor."[g]

[6]Seek[h] the LORD while he may be
   found;[i]
   call[j] on him while he is near.
[7]Let the wicked forsake[k] his way
   and the evil man his thoughts.[l]
Let him turn[m] to the LORD, and he will
   have mercy[n] on him,
   and to our God, for he will freely
    pardon.[o]

[8]"For my thoughts[p] are not your
   thoughts,
neither are your ways my ways,"[q]
         declares the LORD.
[9]"As the heavens are higher than the
   earth,[r]
so are my ways higher than your
   ways
and my thoughts than your
   thoughts.[s]

[10]As the rain[t] and the snow
   come down from heaven,
and do not return to it
   without watering the earth
and making it bud and flourish,[u]
   so that it yields seed[v] for the sower
    and bread for the eater,[w]
[11]so is my word[x] that goes out from my
   mouth:
It will not return to me empty,[y]
   but will accomplish what I desire
and achieve the purpose[z] for which I
    sent it.
[12]You will go out in joy[a]
   and be led forth in peace;[b]
the mountains and hills
   will burst into song[c] before you,
and all the trees[d] of the field
   will clap their hands.[e]
[13]Instead of the thornbush will grow the
   pine tree,
   and instead of briers[f] the myrtle[g]
    will grow.
This will be for the LORD's renown,[h]
   for an everlasting sign,
   which will not be destroyed."

Salvation for Others

56 This is what the LORD says:

   "Maintain justice[i]
   and do what is right,[j]
for my salvation[k] is close at hand
   and my righteousness[l] will soon be
    revealed.
[2]Blessed[m] is the man who does this,
   the man who holds it fast,

55:2 [v]S Isa 30:23
55:3 [w]S Ps 78:1
[x]S Lev 18:5;
S Jn 6:27; Ro 10:5
[y]S Ge 9:16;
S Isa 54:10;
S Heb 13:20
[z]S Isa 54:8
[a]Ac 13:34*
55:4 [b]Rev 1:5
[c]S 1Sa 13:14;
S 2Ch 7:18;
S Isa 32:1
55:5 [d]S Isa 49:6
[e]S Isa 2:3
[f]S Isa 12:6; S 54:5
[g]S Isa 44:23
55:6 [h]S Dt 4:29;
S 2Ch 15:2;
S Isa 9:13
[i]Ps 32:6; Isa 49:8;
Ac 17:27;
2Co 6:1-2
[j]S Ps 50:15;
Isa 65:24;
Jer 29:12; 33:3
55:7 [k]S 2Ch 7:14;
S 30:9;
Eze 18:27-28
[l]Isa 32:7; 59:7
[m]S Isa 44:22;
S Jer 26:3;
S Eze 18:32
[n]S Isa 54:10
[o]S 2Ch 6:21;
Isa 1:18; 40:2
55:8 [p]Php 2:5;
4:8 [q]Isa 53:6;
Mic 4:12
55:9 [r]S Job 11:8;
Ps 103:11
[s]S Nu 23:19;
S Isa 40:13-14
55:10 [t]Isa 30:23
[u]S Lev 25:19;
S Job 14:9;
S Ps 67:6
[v]S Ge 47:23
[w]2Co 9:10
55:11 [x]S Dt 32:2;
Jn 1:1 [y]Isa 40:8;
45:23; S Mt 5:18;
Heb 4:12
[z]S Pr 19:21;
S Isa 44:26;
Eze 12:25
55:12 [a]S Ps 98:4;
S Isa 35:2
[b]Isa 54:10,13
[c]S Ps 65:12-13;
S 96:12-13
[d]S 1Ch 16:33

[e]Ps 98:8 **55:13** [f]S Nu 33:55; S Isa 5:6 [g]Isa 41:19
[h]S Ps 102:12; Isa 63:12; Jer 32:20; 33:9 **56:1** [i]S Ps 11:7;
S Isa 1:17; S Jer 22:3 [j]S Isa 26:8 [k]S Ps 85:9 [l]Jer 23:6; Da 9:24
56:2 [m]S Ps 119:2

55:3 *everlasting covenant.* David had been promised an unending dynasty, one that would culminate in the Messiah (see 9:7; 54:10; 61:8; 2Sa 7:14–16 and notes). *faithful love.* Assuring the continuation of the nation. See 54:8 and note. Christ's resurrection was further proof of God's faithfulness to David (see Ac 13:34, which quotes from this verse).
55:4 *witness to the peoples.* A reference either to David, who exalted the Lord among the nations (Ps 18:43,49–50), or to David's Son, the Messiah, who was a light to the nations (see 42:6; 49:6 and notes). *leader . . . of the peoples.* Similar titles are used of David (1Sa 13:14; 25:30) and the Messiah (Da 9:25).
55:5 *you will summon nations.* The attraction of nations to Zion and to the God of Israel is a major Biblical theme (see, e.g., 2:2–4; 45:14; Zec 8:22 and notes). *that do not know you.* The reverse of the exile, when Israel was sent to a nation unknown to them (see Dt 28:36). Ruth left Moab to live with a people she "did not know before" (Ru 2:11). *Holy One of Israel.* See 1:4; 41:14 and notes. *endowed . . . with splendor.* See 4:2; 60:9. The nation will be restored physically and spiritually.

55:6 *Seek the LORD.* See Jer 29:13–14; Hos 3:5; Am 5:4,6,14 (contrast the hypocritical seeking of 58:2).
55:7 *wicked forsake.* See 1:16. *turn to the LORD . . . freely pardon.* See 43:25 and note; 44:22 and note.
55:9 *my ways higher.* See Ps 145:3.
55:11 *my word.* Especially the promises of vv. 3,5,12. The word is viewed as a messenger also in 9:8; Ps 107:20. Cf. Jn 1:1. *achieve the purpose.* See 46:10–11 and note; cf. 40:8; Heb 4:12.
55:12 *go out in joy.* The departure from Babylon provides the background (see 35:10 and note; 52:9–12 and notes). *mountains . . . will burst into song.* See 44:23 and note. *hands.* Branches. The language is figurative (cf. 1Ch 16:33; Ps 98:8; 114:3–6).
55:13 *thornbush . . . pine tree . . . briers . . . myrtle.* The reverse of the desolation Isaiah had prophesied about earlier (5:6; 32:13). For the significance of trees see 35:2; see also 41:19 and note. *LORD's renown.* Similar to God's fame in the exodus (see 63:12,14). God's deliverance would never be forgotten. Cf. 19:20; 56:5.
56:1 *salvation . . . righteousness.* See 45:8; 46:13; 51:5 and notes.

who keeps the Sabbath[n] without
    desecrating it,
and keeps his hand from doing any
    evil."

[3]Let no foreigner[o] who has bound
    himself to the LORD say,
    "The LORD will surely exclude me
        from his people."[p]
And let not any eunuch[q] complain,
    "I am only a dry tree."

[4]For this is what the LORD says:

"To the eunuchs[r] who keep my
    Sabbaths,
who choose what pleases me
    and hold fast to my covenant[s] —
[5]to them I will give within my temple
    and its walls[t]
a memorial[u] and a name
    better than sons and daughters;
I will give them an everlasting name[v]
    that will not be cut off.[w]
[6]And foreigners[x] who bind themselves
        to the LORD
    to serve[y] him,
to love the name[z] of the LORD,
    and to worship him,
all who keep the Sabbath[a] without
    desecrating it
and who hold fast to my covenant—
[7]these I will bring to my holy mountain[b]
    and give them joy in my house of
        prayer.
Their burnt offerings and sacrifices[c]
    will be accepted on my altar;
for my house will be called
    a house of prayer for all nations.[d]"[e]

[8]The Sovereign LORD declares—
    he who gathers the exiles of Israel:
"I will gather[f] still others to them
    besides those already gathered."

God's Accusation Against the Wicked

[9]Come, all you beasts of the field,[g]
    come and devour, all you beasts of
        the forest!
[10]Israel's watchmen[h] are blind,
    they all lack knowledge;[i]
they are all mute dogs,
    they cannot bark;
they lie around and dream,
    they love to sleep.[j]
[11]They are dogs with mighty appetites,
    they never have enough.
They are shepherds[k] who lack
    understanding;[l]
    they all turn to their own way,[m]
    each seeks his own gain.[n]
[12]"Come," each one cries, "let me get
    wine![o]
Let us drink our fill of beer!
And tomorrow will be like today,
    or even far better."[p]

57 The righteous perish,[q]
    and no one ponders it in his
        heart;[r]
devout men are taken away,
    and no one understands
that the righteous are taken away
    to be spared from evil.[s]
[2]Those who walk uprightly[t]

Cross references (center column)

56:2 [n]S Ex 20:8, 10
56:3 [o]S Ex 12:43; S 1Ki 8:41; S Isa 11:10; Zec 8:20-23 [p]Dt 23:3 [q]S Lev 21:20; Jer 38:7 [fm]; Ac 8:27
56:4 [r]Jer 38:7 [fn] [s]S Ex 31:13
56:5 [t]Isa 26:1; 60:18 [u]S Nu 32:42; 1Sa 15:12 [v]S Isa 43:7 [w]S Isa 48:19; 55:13
56:6 [x]S Ex 12:43; S 1Ki 8:41 [y]S 1Ch 22:2; Isa 60:7,10; 61:5 [z]Mal 1:11 [a]ver 2, 4
56:7 [b]S Isa 2:2; Eze 20:40 [c]S Isa 19:21; Ro 12:1; Php 4:18; Heb 13:15 [d]Mt 21:13*; Lk 19:46* [e]Mk 11:17*
56:8 [f]S Dt 30:4; S Isa 1:9; S 11:12; 60:3-11; Eze 34:12; Jn 10:16
56:9 [g]Isa 18:6; Jer 12:9; Eze 34:5,8; 39:17-20
56:10 [h]S Isa 52:8; 62:6; Jer 6:17; 31:6; Eze 3:17; 33:7 [i]Jer 2:8; 10:21; 14:13-14 [j]Na 3:18
56:11 [k]Jer 23:1; Eze 34:2 [l]Isa 1:3 [m]S Isa 53:6; Hos 4:7-8 [n]Isa 57:17; Jer 6:13; 8:10; 22:17; Eze 13:19;
56:12 [o]S Lev 10:9; S Pr 23:20; S Isa 22:13 [p]Ps 10:6; Lk 12:18-19 57:1 [q]S Ps 12:1; Eze 21:3 [r]S Isa 42:25 [s]S 2Ki 22:20 57:2 [t]Isa 26:7

56:2 *keeps the Sabbath.* See vv. 4,6. Just as the Sabbath had been instituted after the exodus from Egypt (see Ex 20:8–11) as a sign of the Mosaic covenant (see Ex 31:13–17), so God's new deliverance (55:12) afforded an opportunity to obey him fully, an obedience summed up in "keeping the Sabbath" (see 58:13; 66:23; Jer 17:21–27; Eze 20:20–21).

56:3 *foreigner.* See v. 6. Members of certain nations who came to live among the Israelites had been excluded from worship, at least for several generations (see Ex 12:43; Dt 23:3,7–8). But the work of the servant of the Lord would change this (see 49:19–20; 54:17; 60:10 and notes). Cf. 14:1. *eunuch.* See v. 4. Eunuchs were also excluded from the assembly of the Lord (Dt 23:1), but they could still be part of God's offspring (see Ac 8:27,38–40).

56:4,6 *hold fast to my covenant.* Keeping the Sabbath was a sign of the covenant (see Ex 31:13–17; Eze 20:12,20), as was circumcision (see Ge 17:11).

56:5 *memorial.* Absalom built a "Monument" (same Hebrew word) as a memorial since he had no surviving sons (2Sa 18:18). *name.* The Hebrew for this word is translated "renown" in 55:13. The Hebrew for "a memorial and a name" *(yad vashem)* was chosen from v. 5 as the name of the main Holocaust monument in Jerusalem in modern Is-

rael. *that will not be cut off.* An idiom sometimes referring to the preserving of a name through one's descendants.
56:6 *serve.* Cf. 60:7,10.
56:7 *my holy mountain.* See 2:2–4 and note. *offerings . . . accepted on my altar.* Cf. 60:7; contrast 1:11–13. *house of prayer for all nations.* Solomon may have anticipated this in his prayer of dedication for the temple (1Ki 8:41–43).
56:8 *gathers the exiles.* See 11:11–12 and notes. *gather still others.* Including Gentiles (see v. 3 and note; cf. Jn 10:16).
56:9–59:15 Many verses in these sections could apply to conditions before or during the Babylonian exile.
56:9 *beasts.* Foreign invaders (see 18:6 and note).
56:10 *watchmen.* The prophets (see Hab 2:1). *blind . . . love to sleep.* Cf. 29:9–10. *mute dogs.* Watchdogs who guarded the sheep (cf. Job 30:1).
56:11 *mighty appetites.* They devour the sheep. See Eze 34:3. *shepherds.* Rulers may be included. See Eze 34:1–6.
56:12 *wine . . . beer.* Cf. the behavior of priests and prophets in 28:7. *tomorrow will be . . . far better.* Cf. the words of the rich fool in Lk 12:19.
57:1 *spared from evil.* Huldah explained that righteous King Josiah would die before disaster struck (2Ki 22:19–20).
57:2 *peace.* Contrast v. 21. *find rest.* Cf. Paul's words in Php 1:21,23.

enter into peace;
they find rest [u] as they lie in death.

3"But you—come here, you sons of a
sorceress, [v]
you offspring of adulterers [w] and
prostitutes! [x]
4Whom are you mocking?
At whom do you sneer
and stick out your tongue?
Are you not a brood of rebels, [y]
the offspring of liars?
5You burn with lust among the oaks [z]
and under every spreading tree; [a]
you sacrifice your children [b] in the
ravines
and under the overhanging crags.
6The idols [c] among the smooth stones of
the ravines are your portion;
they, they are your lot.
Yes, to them you have poured out drink
offerings [d]
and offered grain offerings.
In the light of these things, should I
relent? [e]
7You have made your bed on a high and
lofty hill; [f]
there you went up to offer your
sacrifices. [g]
8Behind your doors and your doorposts
you have put your pagan symbols.
Forsaking me, you uncovered your bed,
you climbed into it and opened it
wide;
you made a pact with those whose beds
you love, [h]
and you looked on their nakedness. [i]
9You went to Molech[j] with olive oil
and increased your perfumes. [k]
You sent your ambassadors[k l] far away;
you descended to the grave[l m] itself!
10You were wearied [n] by all your ways,
but you would not say, 'It is
hopeless.' [o]

You found renewal of your strength, [p]
and so you did not faint.

11"Whom have you so dreaded and
feared [q]
that you have been false to me,
and have neither remembered [r] me
nor pondered [s] this in your hearts?
Is it not because I have long been
silent [t]
that you do not fear me?
12I will expose your righteousness and
your works, [u]
and they will not benefit you.
13When you cry out [v] for help,
let your collection of idols save [w]
you!
The wind will carry all of them off,
a mere breath will blow [x] them away.
But the man who makes me his refuge [y]
will inherit the land [z]
and possess my holy mountain." [a]

Comfort for the Contrite

14And it will be said:

"Build up, build up, prepare the road! [b]
Remove the obstacles out of the way
of my people." [c]
15For this is what the high and lofty [d] One
says—
he who lives forever, [e] whose name
is holy:
"I live in a high[f] and holy place,
but also with him who is contrite[g]
and lowly in spirit, [h]
to revive the spirit of the lowly
and to revive the heart of the
contrite. [i]
16I will not accuse[j] forever,

57:2 [u]Da 12:13
57:3 [v]S Ex 22:18;
Mal 3:5 [w]ver 7-8;
Mt 16:4; Jas 4:4
[x]Isa 1:21;
Jer 2:20
57:4 [y]S Isa 1:2
57:5 [z]S Isa 1:29
[a]S Dt 12:2;
2Ki 16:4
[b]S Lev 18:21;
S Dt 18:10;
Ps 106:37-38;
Eze 16:20
57:6
[c]S 2Ki 17:10;
Jer 3:9; Hab 2:19
[d]Jer 7:18; 19:13;
44:18 [e]Jer 5:9,
29; 9:9
57:7 [f]Jer 3:6;
Eze 6:3; 16:16;
20:29 [g]Isa 65:7;
Jer 13:27;
Eze 6:13;
20:27-28
57:8 [h]Eze 16:26;
23:7 [i]Eze 16:15,
36; 23:18
57:9
[j]S Lev 18:21;
S 1Ki 11:5
[k]S SS 4:10
[l]Eze 23:16,40
[m]S Isa 8:19
57:10
[n]S Isa 47:13
[o]Jer 2:25; 18:12;
Mal 3:14

[p]S 1Sa 2:4
57:11
[q]S 2Ki 1:15;
Pr 29:25; Isa 7:2
[r]S Isa 17:10;
Jer 2:32; 3:21;
13:25; 18:15;
Eze 22:12
[s]S Isa 42:23
[t]S Est 4:14;
S Ps 50:21; S 83:1
57:12 [u]Isa 29:15;
58:1; 59:6,12;
65:7; 66:18;
Eze 16:2;
Mic 3:2-4,8
57:13 [v]Jer 22:20;
30:15
[w]S Jdg 10:14
[x]Isa 40:7,24
[y]S Ps 118:8
[z]S Ps 37:9
[a]Isa 2:2-3; 56:7;
65:9-11
57:14
[b]S Isa 11:16
[c]Isa 62:10;
Jer 18:15

57:15 [d]S Isa 52:13 [e]S Dt 33:27; S Ps 90:2 [f]S Job 16:19
[g]Ps 147:3 [h]Ps 34:18; 51:17; Isa 66:2; Mic 6:8; Mt 5:3
[i]S 2Ki 22:19; S Job 5:18; S Mt 23:12 **57:16** [j]S Ps 50:21;
Isa 3:13-14

[9] Or *to the king*   [k] 9 Or *idols*   [l] 9 Hebrew *Sheol*

57:3 *sorceress.* One who practices soothsaying or magic
(see 3:2; 47:12; Dt 18:10). *adulterers and prostitutes.* Spiritual adultery (idolatry) is in view (see vv. 5–8).
57:4 *mocking . . . sneer.* The people mocked Isaiah in
28:9,14. *brood of rebels.* See 1:4; 46:8 and note.
57:5 *oaks.* Sacred trees (see 1:29 and note). *spreading
tree.* Associated with high places of pagan worship in 1Ki
14:23. Cf. Jer 2:20; 3:13. *sacrifice your children.* Often
associated with the worship of Molech (cf. v. 9; see note on
30:33, "Topheth") or Baal (Jer 19:5). Ps 106:37–38 says
that children were sacrificed to idols and demons.
57:6 *ravines.* Possibly the Hinnom Valley, southwest of
Jerusalem, where Molech was worshiped. *drink offerings.*
These pagan libations were especially popular.
57:7 *high and lofty hill.* "High places" or "mountain
shrines" (see Jer 3:6; Eze 16:16; 22:9).
57:8 *those . . . you love.* Pagan deities or idols.
57:9 *Molech.* The main god of the Ammonites (see v. 5 and

note; 1Ki 11:7). *olive oil.* Used as an ointment for perfume.
See SS 4:10, where the Hebrew word for "oil" is translated
"perfume." *to the grave.* Cf. 8:19.
57:10 *It is hopeless.* Ironically, the people said that turning
away from their own plans or from foreign gods was hopeless. *renewal of your strength.* Contrast 40:30–31.
57:11 *so dreaded and feared.* They feared men (see
51:12). *neither remembered me.* See 51:13. *long been
silent.* God had not acted in judgment (see 42:14 and note).
57:12 *righteousness.* See 58:2–3; 64:6.
57:13 *idols save you.* See 44:17 and note. *wind will carry
. . . breath will blow.* Idols are no stronger than men. *me his
refuge.* See 25:4. *inherit the land.* See 49:8 and note. *my
holy mountain.* See 2:2–4 and note.
57:14 *Build up, build up.* See note on 40:1. *prepare the
road.* See 40:3 and note.
57:15 *high and lofty One.* See 6:1; 52:13 and notes; cf.
33:5. *contrite.* Or "crushed" (see 53:5).

nor will I always be angry, [k]
for then the spirit of man would grow
faint before me—
the breath [l] of man that I have
created.
17I was enraged by his sinful greed; [m]
I punished him, and hid [n] my face in
anger,
yet he kept on in his willful ways. [o]
18I have seen his ways, but I will heal [p]
him;
I will guide [q] him and restore
comfort [r] to him,
19 creating praise on the lips [s] of the
mourners in Israel.
Peace, peace, [t] to those far and near," [u]
says the LORD. "And I will heal
them."
20But the wicked [v] are like the tossing
sea, [w]
which cannot rest,
whose waves cast up mire [x] and
mud.
21"There is no peace," [y] says my God,
"for the wicked." [z]

True Fasting

58 "Shout it aloud, [a] do not hold
back.
Raise your voice like a trumpet. [b]
Declare to my people their rebellion [c]
and to the house of Jacob their sins. [d]
2For day after day they seek [e] me out;
they seem eager to know my ways,
as if they were a nation that does what
is right
and has not forsaken [f] the commands
of its God.
They ask me for just decisions

and seem eager for God to come
near [g] them.
3'Why have we fasted,' [h] they say,
'and you have not seen it?
Why have we humbled [i] ourselves,
and you have not noticed?' [j]

"Yet on the day of your fasting, you do
as you please [k]
and exploit all your workers.
4Your fasting ends in quarreling and
strife, [l]
and in striking each other with
wicked fists.
You cannot fast as you do today
and expect your voice to be heard [m]
on high.
5Is this the kind of fast [n] I have chosen,
only a day for a man to humble [o]
himself?
Is it only for bowing one's head like a
reed [p]
and for lying on sackcloth and
ashes? [q]
Is that what you call a fast,
a day acceptable to the LORD?
6"Is not this the kind of fasting [r] I have
chosen:
to loose the chains of injustice [s]
and untie the cords of the yoke,
to set the oppressed [t] free
and break every yoke? [u]
7Is it not to share your food with the
hungry [v]
and to provide the poor wanderer
with shelter [w]—

Cross references

57:16
[k]S Ps 103:9;
S Isa 54:9
[l]S Ge 2:7;
Zec 12:1
57:17
[m]S Isa 56:11;
Jer 8:10
[n]S Isa 1:15
[o]Isa 1:4; S 30:15;
S 53:6; 66:3
57:18
[p]S Dt 32:39;
S 2Ch 7:14;
S Isa 30:26
[q]S Ps 48:14;
S Isa 42:16;
S 48:17
[r]Isa 49:13; 61:1-3
57:19 [s]Isa 6:7;
51:16; 59:21;
Heb 13:15
[t]S Isa 2:4; 26:3,
12; 32:17;
S Lk 2:14
[u]Ac 2:39
57:20
[v]Job 18:5-21
[w]S Ge 49:4;
Eph 4:14;
Jude 1:13
[x]Ps 69:14
57:21
[y]S Isa 26:3; 59:8;
Eze 13:16
[z]S Isa 48:22
58:1 [a]Isa 40:6
[b]S Ex 20:18
[c]S Isa 24:20;
S 48:8
[d]S Isa 57:12;
Eze 3:17
58:2 [e]S Isa 48:1;
Tit 1:16; Jas 4:8
[f]S Dt 32:15;
S Ps 119:87

[g]Isa 29:13
58:3
[h]S Lev 16:29
[i]S Ex 10:3;
S 2Ch 6:37;
Jer 44:10
[j]Mal 3:14
[k]Isa 22:13;
Zec 7:5-6
58:4
[l]1Ki 21:9-13;
Isa 59:6; Jer 6:7;
Eze 7:11;
Mal 2:16
[m]S 1Sa 8:18;
Isa 59:2; La 3:44;
Eze 8:18; Mic 3:4

58:5 [n]Zec 7:5 [o]1Ki 21:27; Mt 6:16 [p]S Isa 36:6 [q]S Job 2:8
58:6 [r]Joel 2:12-14 [s]Ne 5:10-11 [t]S Dt 14:29; Isa 61:1;
Jer 34:9; Am 4:1; S Lk 4:19 [u]S Isa 9:4 58:7 [v]S Job 22:7;
Eze 18:16; Lk 3:11 [w]Isa 16:4; Mt 13:2

Study notes

57:16 not accuse forever. He had taken Israel to court repeatedly (see 3:13–14). nor . . . be angry. See 54:9 and note; Jer 3:12.
57:17 hid my face in anger. See 54:8; see also 1:15 and note.
57:18 heal him. See v. 19; 6:10; 30:26; Jer 3:22. God will forgive and restore his people. guide. Cf. 40:11; 42:16; 49:10. restore comfort. See 49:13 and note.
57:19 mourners. Those mourning the judgment on Jerusalem (see 66:10). Peace, peace. Contrast Jer 6:13–14; 8:10–11. those far. Either Gentiles or exiled Jews. Paul probably had this verse in mind in Eph 2:17.
57:20 like the tossing sea. See Jer 49:23. cannot rest. Contrast v. 2.
57:21 See 39:8; 48:22 and notes.
58:1 voice like a trumpet. God's powerful voice is compared to a trumpet blast at Mount Sinai (see Ex 19:19; 20:18–19). rebellion. See 1:2 and note. sins. See 1:4; 59:12–13.
58:2 seek me out. See 55:6 and note. Cf. the frequent sacrifices of 1:11. eager for God to come near. The same hypocrisy is mentioned in 29:13 (see note there).

58:3 fasted . . . fasting. See v. 6; a time of self-denial and repentance for sin. After the fall of Jerusalem, the number of fast days increased (see Lev 16:29 and NIV text note; see also Zec 7:5). humbled ourselves. Cf. 2Ch 7:14; 1Ki 21:29. you have not noticed. Note the same attitude in Mal 3:14; cf. Lk 18:12. exploit all your workers. See 3:14–15; 10:2.
58:4 to be heard on high. Hypocritical religious activity is a hindrance to prayer (see 1:15; 59:2).
58:5 like a reed. A sign of weakness and humility (see 42:3 and note). sackcloth and ashes. Cf. 1Ki 21:27; Jnh 3:5–8. acceptable. A term often applied to sacrifices (see 56:7; 60:7; Lev 1:3).
58:6 chains of injustice. During the siege of Jerusalem, Hebrew slaves were rightly released—only to be reclaimed by their masters (see Jer 34:8–11). yoke. See v. 9; 9:4; 10:27, where the yoke imposed by Assyria is mentioned. oppressed. See 1:17.
58:7 share your food . . . provide . . . shelter . . . clothe. The outward evidence of genuine righteousness. See Job 31:17–20; Eze 18:7,16 and Jesus' identification with the hungry and naked in Mt 25:35–36. flesh and blood. Probably refers to close relatives (Ge 37:27), but see 2Sa 5:1.

when you see the naked, to clothe[x]
 him,
and not to turn away from your own
 flesh and blood?[y]
[8]Then your light will break forth like the
 dawn,[z]
and your healing[a] will quickly
 appear;
then your righteousness[m][b] will go
 before you,
and the glory of the LORD will be
 your rear guard.[c]
[9]Then you will call,[d] and the LORD will
 answer;[e]
you will cry for help, and he will say:
 Here am I.

"If you do away with the yoke of
 oppression,
with the pointing finger[f] and
 malicious talk,[g]
[10]and if you spend yourselves in behalf of
 the hungry
and satisfy the needs of the
 oppressed,[h]
then your light[i] will rise in the
 darkness,
and your night will become like the
 noonday.[j]
[11]The LORD will guide[k] you always;
he will satisfy your needs[l] in a
 sun-scorched land[m]
and will strengthen[n] your frame.
You will be like a well-watered
 garden,[o]
like a spring[p] whose waters never
 fail.
[12]Your people will rebuild the ancient
 ruins[q]
and will raise up the age-old
 foundations;[r]

you will be called Repairer of Broken
 Walls,[s]
Restorer of Streets with Dwellings.

[13]"If you keep your feet from breaking
 the Sabbath[t]
and from doing as you please on my
 holy day,
if you call the Sabbath a delight[u]
and the LORD's holy day honorable,
and if you honor it by not going your
 own way
and not doing as you please or
 speaking idle words,[v]
[14]then you will find your joy[w] in the
 LORD,
and I will cause you to ride on the
 heights[x] of the land
and to feast on the inheritance[y] of
 your father Jacob."
The mouth of the LORD
 has spoken.[z]

Sin, Confession and Redemption

59 Surely the arm[a] of the LORD is not
 too short[b] to save,
nor his ear too dull to hear.[c]
[2]But your iniquities have separated[d]
 you from your God;
your sins have hidden his face from you,
 so that he will not hear.[e]
[3]For your hands are stained with blood,[f]
 your fingers with guilt.[g]
Your lips have spoken lies,[h]
 and your tongue mutters wicked
 things.
[4]No one calls for justice;[i]
 no one pleads his case with integrity.
They rely[j] on empty arguments and
 speak lies;[k]

58:7
[x]Job 31:19-20;
S Mt 25:36
[y]S Ge 29:14;
Lk 10:31-32
58:8
[z]S Job 11:17;
S Isa 9:2
[a]S Isa 1:5;
S 30:26
[b]S Isa 26:2
[c]S Ex 14:19
58:9 [d]S Ps 50:15
[e]S Job 8:6;
S Isa 30:19;
Da 9:20;
S Zec 10:6
/S Pr 6:13
[g]Ps 12:2;
Isa 59:13
58:10 [h]Dt 15:7-8
/S Isa 42:16;
/S Job 11:17
58:11
[k]S Ps 48:14;
S Isa 42:16;
S 48:17
/S Ps 104:28;
S 107:9
[m]S Ps 68:6
[n]S Ps 72:16
[o]S SS 4:15
[p]S Isa 35:7;
Jn 4:14
58:12 [q]S Isa 49:8
[r]S Isa 44:28

[s]Ne 2:17
58:13 [t]S Ex 20:8
[u]Ps 37:4; 42:4;
84:2,10 [v]Isa 59:3
58:14
[w]S Job 22:26
[x]S Dt 32:13
[y]Ps 105:10-11
[z]S Isa 1:20
59:1 [a]S Isa 41:20
[b]S Isa 50:2
[c]Isa 30:19; 58:9;
65:24
59:2 [d]Jer 5:25;
Eze 39:23
[e]S Ps 18:41;
S Isa 58:4;
S Jer 11:11;
S Jn 9:31
59:3
/S 2Ki 21:16;
S Isa 1:15;
S Eze 22:9
[g]Ps 7:3 [h]S Isa 3:8
59:4 /S Isa 5:23
/S Job 15:31
[k]S Isa 44:20

[m]8 Or your righteous One

58:8 *light.* The joy, prosperity and salvation brought by the Lord (see 9:2; 60:1–3). *healing.* See 57:18 and note. *go before you . . . be your rear guard.* See 52:12 and note. The Lord will protect them and guide them. *glory of the LORD.* Probably a reference to the pillar of cloud and fire in the desert (see 4:5–6; Ex 13:21; 14:20 and notes).

58:9 *LORD will answer.* See 30:19 and note. *Here am I.* See 65:1. *pointing finger.* A gesture of either contempt (see Pr 6:13) or accusation. *malicious talk.* See Pr 6:12–14.

58:10 *hungry . . . oppressed.* See vv. 6–7 and notes. *light.* See v. 8 and note.

58:11 *guide you.* See 57:18 and note. *needs.* Both material and spiritual (see note on 32:2). *sun-scorched land.* See 35:7; 49:10. *well-watered garden.* In 1:30 Jerusalem was a garden without water. *spring . . . never fail.* Cf. the "living water" Jesus gives in Jn 4:10,14.

58:12 *ancient ruins . . . age-old foundations.* See 44:26, 28 and notes; 61:4; Eze 36:10; Am 9:11,14. *Repairer of Broken Walls.* Cf. the work of Nehemiah in Ne 2:17.

58:13 *Sabbath.* See 56:2 and note. *my holy day.* A day set apart to God (see Ex 3:5 and note). *delight.* They were also to delight themselves in the Lord (Ps 37:4) and in his law (Ps 1:2). *going your own way.* Perhaps to engage in business (see Am 8:5).

58:14 *joy in the LORD.* See 61:10. *ride on the heights.* Thus controlling the land. See 33:16 and note; see also Hab 3:19. *feast on the inheritance.* Enjoying plentiful food in the promised land (see Dt 32:13–14). *mouth . . . has spoken.* See 40:5 and note.

59:1 *arm . . . too short.* See 51:9 and note. *too dull to hear.* See 30:19 and note.

59:2 *hidden his face . . . he will not hear.* See 1:15 and note.

59:3–4 *lies.* See v. 13; 28:15; Hos 4:2.

59:3 *stained with blood.* See v. 7; 1:15,21; Eze 7:23.

59:4 *justice . . . pleads his case.* The poor and helpless could not receive fair trials (see v. 14; 1:17–23; 5:7,23). *they conceive . . . evil.* This statement appears verbatim in Job 15:35. Cf. Isa 33:11; Ps 7:14.

they conceive trouble and give birth
to evil. [l]
[5]They hatch the eggs of vipers [m]
and spin a spider's web. [n]
Whoever eats their eggs will die,
and when one is broken, an adder is
hatched.
[6]Their cobwebs are useless for clothing;
they cannot cover themselves with
what they make. [o]
Their deeds are evil deeds,
and acts of violence [p] are in their
hands.
[7]Their feet rush into sin;
they are swift to shed innocent
blood. [q]
Their thoughts are evil thoughts; [r]
ruin and destruction mark their
ways. [s]
[8]The way of peace they do not know; [t]
there is no justice in their paths.
They have turned them into crooked
roads; [u]
no one who walks in them will know
peace. [v]

[9]So justice is far from us,
and righteousness does not reach us.
We look for light, but all is darkness; [w]
for brightness, but we walk in deep
shadows.
[10]Like the blind [x] we grope along the
wall,
feeling our way like men without
eyes.
At midday we stumble [y] as if it were
twilight;
among the strong, we are like the
dead. [z]

[11]We all growl like bears;
we moan mournfully like doves. [a]
We look for justice, but find none;
for deliverance, but it is far away.

[12]For our offenses [b] are many in your
sight,
and our sins testify [c] against us.
Our offenses are ever with us,
and we acknowledge our iniquities: [d]
[13]rebellion [e] and treachery against the
LORD,
turning our backs [f] on our God,
fomenting oppression [g] and revolt,
uttering lies [h] our hearts have
conceived.
[14]So justice [i] is driven back,
and righteousness [j] stands at a
distance;
truth [k] has stumbled in the streets,
honesty cannot enter.
[15]Truth [l] is nowhere to be found,
and whoever shuns evil becomes a
prey.

The LORD looked and was displeased
that there was no justice. [m]
[16]He saw that there was no one, [n]
he was appalled that there was no
one to intervene; [o]
so his own arm worked salvation [p] for
him,
and his own righteousness [q] sustained
him.
[17]He put on righteousness as his
breastplate, [r]

Cross references (center column):

59:4 [l]S Job 4:8; S Isa 29:20; Jas 1:15
59:5 [m]S Isa 11:8; Mt 3:7; [n]S Job 8:14
59:6 [o]Isa 28:20; [p]S Ps 55:9; S Pr 4:17; S Isa 58:4
59:7 [q]S 2Ki 21:16; S Pr 6:17; S Mic 3:10; [r]S Pr 24:2; S Isa 26:10; Mk 7:21-22; [s]Ro 3:15-17*
59:8 [t]Ro 3:15-17*; [u]S Jdg 5:6; [v]S Isa 57:21; Lk 1:79
59:9 [w]S Job 19:8; S Ps 107:14; S Isa 5:30; S 8:20; S Lk 1:79
59:10 [x]Dt 28:29; S Isa 6:9-10; 56:10; La 4:14; Zep 1:17; [y]S Job 3:23; S Isa 8:15; Jn 11:9-10; [z]La 3:6
59:11 [a]S Ge 8:8; Ps 74:19; Isa 38:14; Jer 48:28; Eze 7:16; Na 2:7
59:12 [b]S Ezr 9:6; S Isa 57:12; [c]S Ge 4:7; S Isa 3:9; S Jer 2:19; [d]Ps 51:3
59:13 [e]Isa 46:8; 48:8; [f]S Nu 11:20; S Pr 30:9; Mt 10:33; Tit 1:16; [g]S Ps 12:5; S Isa 5:7; [h]S Isa 3:8; S 44:20; Mk 7:21-22
59:14 [i]S Isa 29:21; [j]S Isa 1:21; [k]S Isa 48:1;
S Jer 33:16 **59:15** [l]Jer 7:28; 9:5; Da 8:12 [m]S Isa 5:7 **59:16** [n]S Isa 41:28 [o]S Isa 53:12 [p]S Isa 51:5 [q]S Isa 45:8,13; 46:13 **59:17** [r]Eph 6:14; 1Th 5:8

59:5 *spider's web.* Verse 6 and Job 8:14–15 stress how fragile it is.

59:6 *acts of violence.* See v. 3; Jer 6:7; Eze 7:11.

59:7–8 Quoted in part in Ro 3:15–17 by Paul to show the universality of sin.

59:7 *Their feet rush . . . to shed innocent blood.* This sentence appears in Pr 1:16. *evil thoughts.* God's thoughts are different (see 55:7–9). *ruin and destruction.* Contrast 60:18.

59:8 *way of peace.* Cf. 26:3,12; 57:20–21; Lk 1:79. *crooked roads.* Unsafe (see Jdg 5:6 and note).

59:9 *us . . . We.* The prophet includes himself with the people. *justice . . . righteousness.* Personified here and in v. 14. See v. 4 and note; 1:21. *darkness . . . deep shadows.* Similar language describes conditions when Assyria invaded Israel (see 5:30; 8:21–22; 9:1–2). Contrast 58:8.

59:10 *Like the blind we grope . . . At midday.* The fulfillment of the curse for disobedience in Dt 28:29. Cf. Job 5:14. *strong.* Perhaps enemies or oppressors.

59:11 *growl like bears.* Impatient and frustrated.

59:12 *offenses are many.* See 58:1. *we acknowledge our iniquities.* Like Ezra (9:6–7), Isaiah confesses the sins of the nation. In this verse he uses the three most common Hebrew words for evil thoughts and deeds.

59:13 *rebellion and treachery.* See 46:8; 48:8 and notes. *turning our backs.* See 1:4. *oppression.* See 30:12. *lies.* See vv. 3–4.

59:14 *justice . . . truth.* Cf. the personification of wisdom in Pr 8:1–9:12. *righteousness stands at a distance.* Cf. v. 9; contrast 46:13 and note.

59:15 *Truth.* Restored Jerusalem is called the "City of Truth" in Zec 8:3 (see 1:21 and note). *becomes a prey.* See 32:7.

59:16 *there was no one.* To help (see 63:5, a parallel to the whole verse). Cf. Eze 22:30. *appalled.* Cf. the reaction to the servant in 52:14. *intervene.* Cf. the intercession of the servant in 53:12 (see note there). *his own arm worked salvation.* See 51:9; 52:10. For the meaning of salvation see 43:3; 49:8; 52:7 and notes. *righteousness.* For the relationship between righteousness and salvation see 45:8; 46:13 and notes.

59:17 *righteousness as his breastplate.* The Lord's armor is compared to the believer's armor in the battle against Satan in Eph 6:14. *garments of vengeance.* Cf. the blood-spattered garments of 63:1–3. God's vengeance is described also in 34:8 (see note there); 63:4. It is part of the day of the Lord (see 34:2 and note). *zeal.* God's jealous love (see 9:7 and note; 37:32; 42:13).

and the helmet[s] of salvation on his
head;
he put on the garments[t] of vengeance[u]
and wrapped himself in zeal[v] as in a
cloak.
[18]According to what they have done,
so will he repay[w]
wrath to his enemies
and retribution to his foes;
he will repay the islands[x] their due.
[19]From the west,[y] men will fear the
name of the LORD,
and from the rising of the sun,[z] they
will revere his glory.[a]
For he will come like a pent-up flood
that the breath[b] of the LORD drives
along.[n]

[20]"The Redeemer[c] will come to Zion,[d]
to those in Jacob who repent of their
sins,"[e]
declares the LORD.

[21]"As for me, this is my covenant[f] with
them," says the LORD. "My Spirit,[g] who is
on you, and my words that I have put in
your mouth[h] will not depart from your
mouth,[i] or from the mouths of your children, or from the mouths of their descendants from this time on and forever," says
the LORD.

The Glory of Zion

60 "Arise,[j] shine, for your light[k] has
come,

and the glory[l] of the LORD rises
upon you.
[2]See, darkness[m] covers the earth
and thick darkness[n] is over the
peoples,
but the LORD rises upon you
and his glory appears over you.
[3]Nations[o] will come to your light,[p]
and kings[q] to the brightness of your
dawn.

[4]"Lift up your eyes and look about you:
All assemble[r] and come to you;
your sons come from afar,[s]
and your daughters[t] are carried on
the arm.[u]
[5]Then you will look and be radiant,[v]
your heart will throb and swell with
joy;[w]
the wealth[x] on the seas will be brought
to you,
to you the riches of the nations will
come.
[6]Herds of camels[y] will cover your land,
young camels of Midian[z] and
Ephah.[a]
And all from Sheba[b] will come,
bearing gold and incense[c]
and proclaiming the praise[d] of the
LORD.

59:17 [s]Eph 6:17;
1Th 5:8
[t]S Job 27:6;
Isa 63:3
[u]S Isa 1:24
[v]S Isa 9:7;
Eze 5:13
59:18
[w]S Lev 26:28;
S Nu 10:35;
S Isa 34:8;
S Mt 16:27
[x]Isa 11:11; 41:5
59:19
[y]S Isa 49:12;
S Mt 8:11
[z]S Ps 113:3
[a]Ps 97:6;
S Isa 24:15; 35:2;
40:5; 52:10;
66:18 [b]S Isa 11:4
59:20
[c]S Job 19:25;
Isa 60:16; 63:16
[d]S Isa 52:8;
S Joel 3:21
[e]S Job 22:23;
S Isa 1:27;
S Jer 35:15;
Ac 2:38-39;
Ro 11:26-27*
59:21 [f]S Ge 9:16;
S Dt 29:14;
S Isa 42:6
[g]S Isa 11:2;
S 44:3 [h]S Ex 4:15
[i]S Jos 1:8
60:1 [j]Isa 52:2
[k]S Ps 36:9;
S 118:27;
S Isa 9:2; Jn 8:12;
Eph 5:14
[l]S Ex 16:7;
S Isa 4:5;
Rev 21:11
60:2 [m]S Isa 2:9;
S Ps 82:5;
S 107:14;
S Isa 8:20
[n]Jer 13:16;
Col 1:13
60:3 [o]S Isa 44:5;
S 45:14;
Mt 2:1-11;
Rev 21:24

[p]S Isa 9:2; 42:6; 49:23 [q]S Isa 49:23 **60:4** [r]S Isa 11:12 [s]S Isa 2:3;
Jer 30:10 [t]S Isa 43:6 [u]Isa 49:20-22 **60:5** [v]S Ex 34:29
[w]Isa 35:2; 65:13; 66:14; Zec 10:7 [x]S Dt 33:19; S Jdg 3:15;
Rev 21:26 **60:6** [y]S Jdg 6:5 [z]S Ge 25:2 [a]Ge 25:4 [b]S Ge 10:7,
28 [c]Isa 43:23; Jer 6:20; Mt 2:11 [d]S 1Ki 5:7; S Isa 42:10

[n] *19* Or *When the enemy comes in like a flood, /*
Spirit of the LORD will put him to flight

59:18 *enemies...foes.* God will judge the nations, but he
must also punish wicked Israelites (see 65:6–7; 66:6; Jer
25:29). Only the remnant will be blessed (see v. 20; see
also 1:9 and note). *islands.* See note on 11:11.
59:19 *From the west...rising of the sun.* All nations will
see God's saving work in behalf of his people (see 40:5;
45:6; 52:10 and notes). *name.* See 30:27 and note. *pent-up
flood.* The coming of the Lord will be irresistible, like a
"rushing torrent" that overwhelms the enemy (see 30:28).
59:20 *Redeemer.* See 41:14 and note. *come to Zion.* In
the return from exile, but more fully in the person of Christ.
See 35:4; 40:9; 52:7 and notes. Cf. Zec 8:3. *those...who
repent.* See 1:27–28 and note; 30:15; 31:6; Eze 18:30–32.
59:21 *covenant.* The description fits the "new covenant"
best (see 42:6 and note; Jer 31:31–34). *My Spirit.* See 11:2
and note; 32:15; Eze 36:27; Jn 16:13. *you...your...
your...your.* In Hebrew the pronouns are singular but are
probably intended in a collective sense—the citizens of Zion.
my words...in your mouth. Then Israel will truly be God's
people (see 51:16 and note; Jer 31:33). *not depart from your
mouth.* See Jos 1:8.
60:1–2 *glory.* Probably an allusion to the pillar of cloud,
but announcing a new manifestation of God's redeeming
glory (see 58:8 and note). See also 35:2 and note.
60:1 *light.* See 58:8 and note. Here the Lord himself is
viewed as the light (see vv. 19–20).
60:2 *darkness.* A symbol of gloom, oppression and sin (see
8:22; 9:2; 59:9).

60:3 *Nations will come.* See vv. 5,10–12 and notes. This
theme was first mentioned in 2:2–4 (see note there). *light.*
See 42:6; 49:6 and notes.
60:4 The first two lines are almost identical to the beginning of 49:18, the last two to the end of 49:22 (see note
there). The setting there was the return from exile, but here
much broader implications are involved. *afar.* See v. 9;
49:12 and note.
60:5 *wealth on the seas.* Jerusalem will be enriched by the
nations (see v. 11; 61:6; 66:12; see also 18:7; 23:18; 45:14
and notes). The contribution of King Darius to Zerubbabel's
temple may be a partial fulfillment (Ezr 6:8–9). Some interpret this verse as referring to conditions during the future
phase of the Messianic kingdom, while others apply it to the
influx of Gentiles into the church (see note on 2:2–4). See
Rev 21:26 (the new Jerusalem); see also Hag 2:7; Zec 14:14
and notes.
60:6 *camels will cover your land.* As caravans bringing
goods. Ironically it was on camels that the Midianites once
devastated Israel (see 9:4; Jdg 6:1–6). *Midian.* Abraham's
son through Keturah (Ge 25:2). The Midianites roamed the
deserts of Transjordan. *Ephah.* A son of Midian (Ge 25:4).
Sheba. A wealthy land in southern Arabia, perhaps roughly
equal to modern Yemen (see Ge 25:3; 1Ki 10:1–2). *gold
and incense.* The queen of Sheba brought gold and spices to
Solomon (1Ki 10:2). Jer 6:20 mentions the incense of Sheba.
Cf. Ps 72:10; Mt 2:11. *proclaiming the praise.* Cf. the
queen's words in 1Ki 10:9.

[7]All Kedar's[e] flocks will be gathered to you,
the rams of Nebaioth will serve you;
they will be accepted as offerings[f] on my altar,[g]
and I will adorn my glorious temple.[h]

[8]"Who are these[i] that fly along like clouds,[j]
like doves to their nests?
[9]Surely the islands[k] look to me;
in the lead are the ships of Tarshish,[o][l]
bringing[m] your sons from afar,
with their silver and gold,[n]
to the honor[o] of the LORD your God,
the Holy One[p] of Israel,
for he has endowed you with splendor. [q]

[10]"Foreigners[r] will rebuild your walls,
and their kings[s] will serve you.
Though in anger I struck you,
in favor[t] I will show you compassion. [u]

[11]Your gates[v] will always stand open,
they will never be shut, day or night,
so that men may bring you the wealth of the nations[w]—
their kings[x] led in triumphal procession.
[12]For the nation or kingdom that will not serve[y] you will perish;
it will be utterly ruined. [z]

[13]"The glory of Lebanon[a] will come to you,
the pine, the fir and the cypress together, [b]
to adorn the place of my sanctuary; [c]

and I will glorify the place of my feet. [d]

[14]The sons of your oppressors[e] will come bowing before you;
all who despise you will bow down[f] at your feet
and will call you the City[g] of the LORD,
Zion[h] of the Holy One[i] of Israel.

[15]"Although you have been forsaken[j] and hated,
with no one traveling[k] through,
I will make you the everlasting pride[l]
and the joy[m] of all generations.
[16]You will drink the milk of nations
and be nursed[n] at royal breasts.
Then you will know[o] that I, the LORD,
am your Savior,[p]
your Redeemer, [q] the Mighty One of Jacob. [r]
[17]Instead of bronze I will bring you gold, [s]
and silver in place of iron.
Instead of wood I will bring you bronze,
and iron in place of stones.
I will make peace[t] your governor
and righteousness your ruler. [u]
[18]No longer will violence[v] be heard in your land,
nor ruin or destruction[w] within your borders,
but you will call your walls Salvation[x]
and your gates Praise.[y]
[19]The sun will no more be your light by day,

Cross references

60:7 [e]S Ge 25:13
/Isa 18:7;
Eze 20:40; 43:27;
Zep 3:10
[g]S Isa 19:21 [h]ver 13; Hag 2:3,7,9
60:8 /Isa 49:21
/Isa 19:1
60:9 [k]S Isa 11:11
/S Ge 10:4;
Isa 2:16 [m]n
[m]S Isa 14:2;
S 43:6
[n]S 1Ki 10:22
[o]S Ps 22:23 [p]ver 14; Isa 1:4;
S 54:5
[q]S Isa 44:23;
55:5; Jer 30:19
60:10 [r]S Ex 1:11;
S Isa 14:1-2;
S 56:6 [s]S Ezr 1:2;
Rev 21:24
[t]S Isa 49:8
[u]S Ps 102:13
60:11 [v]ver 18;
S Ps 24:7;
Isa 62:10;
Mic 2:13;
Rev 21:25 [w]S ver 5; Isa 61:6;
Rev 21:26
[x]Ps 149:8;
S Isa 2:12
60:12
[y]S Isa 11:14;
S 14:2
[z]S Ge 27:29;
S Ps 110:5;
Da 2:34
60:13 [a]S Ezr 3:7
[b]Isa 41:19 [c]S ver 7

[d]S 1Ch 28:2
60:14 [e]S Isa 14:2
/S Ge 27:29;
S Isa 2:3; Rev 3:9
[g]S Ge 32:28;
S Isa 1:26
[h]Heb 12:22 [i]S ver 9
60:15 /Isa 1:7-9;
S 6:12; S 54:6
[k]S Isa 33:8
/S Isa 4:2
[m]S Ps 126:5;
Isa 65:18
60:16 [n]S Ex 6:2;
Isa 49:23; 66:11,
12 [o]S Ex 6:7

[p]S Ex 14:30; S Isa 25:9 [q]S Job 19:25; S Isa 59:20
[r]S Ge 49:24; S Ps 132:2 60:17 [s]1Ki 10:21 [t]S Ps 85:8;
Isa 66:12; Hag 2:9 [u]S Isa 9:7 60:18 [v]S Lev 26:6; S 2Sa 7:10;
S Isa 9:4 [w]S Isa 49:19; S 51:19 [x]S Isa 33:6 [y]Isa 61:11; 62:7;
Jer 33:9; Zep 3:20

[o]9 Or *the trading ships*

Study notes

60:7 *Kedar's flocks.* See note on 21:16. *Nebaioth.* The firstborn son of Ishmael (Ge 25:13). The name is probably preserved in that of the later Nabatean kingdom. *serve.* See v. 10; 56:6. *accepted as offerings.* See 56:7; 58:5 and notes.
60:9 *islands look to me.* See 11:11 and note. *ships of Tarshish.* See note on 2:16. *bringing your sons.* See 49:22 and note. *silver and gold.* Ships of Tarshish had brought these to Solomon every three years (1Ki 10:22). *Holy One of Israel.* See v. 14; 1:4 and note. *endowed... with splendor.* See 55:5 and note.
60:10 *Foreigners... kings.* See vv. 12,14; 49:7,23; 61:5. *will rebuild your walls.* In 445 B.C. King Artaxerxes issued the decree allowing Nehemiah to rebuild the walls of Jerusalem (Ne 2:8). Some also apply the rebuilt walls to the building up of the church through Gentile believers (Ac 15:14–16) and notes. *Though in anger... compassion.* See 54:7–8 and notes.
60:11 *gates... always... open.* As are the gates of the new Jerusalem (Rev 21:25). *wealth.* See v. 5.
60:12 *nation... will perish.* Israel's future political domination is referred to also in 11:14; 14:2; 49:23 (cf. vv. 10,14).
60:13 *glory of Lebanon.* Its magnificent cedar trees, which

were used in the construction of Solomon's temple, along with pine trees (1Ki 5:10,18). See also 35:2. The glory of Solomon's era would return. *pine... fir... cypress.* See 41:19 and note. Perhaps the trees would be ornamental rather than building material. *adorn... sanctuary.* See v. 7. *place of my feet.* The temple, and especially the ark of the covenant, God's "footstool."
60:14 *oppressors... bow down.* See 49:7,23 and notes. Cf. vv. 10,12. *the City of the LORD.* Cf. the names for the future Jerusalem in 1:26; 62:4; Eze 48:35; Zec 8:3; Heb 12:22.
60:15 *forsaken and hated.* See 6:11–12; 62:4; Jer 30:17. *pride... joy.* See 4:2 and note.
60:16 *nursed at royal breasts.* Jerusalem will receive the very best nourishment, the "riches of the nations" (v. 5). *Then... Jacob.* For this sentence see 49:26 and note.
60:17 *gold... silver.* As in Solomon's day gold and silver were plentiful (1Ki 10:21,27), so the future Jerusalem will have the most valuable metals as well as the strongest (iron). Cf. 9:10. *peace... righteousness.* Both are also present in the rule of the Messianic king in 9:7. See note on 48:18.
60:18 *No longer... violence.* Cf. 54:14. *ruin or destruction.* See 51:19 and note. *walls Salvation.* See 26:1.
60:19 *sun... moon.* According to Rev 21:23; 22:5 their

nor will the brightness of the moon
    shine on you,
for the LORD will be your everlasting
    light, *z*
and your God will be your glory. *a*

20Your sun *b* will never set again,
    and your moon will wane no more;
the LORD will be your everlasting light,
    and your days of sorrow *c* will end.

21Then will all your people be righteous *d*
    and they will possess *e* the land
    forever.
They are the shoot I have planted, *f*
    the work of my hands, *g*
for the display of my splendor. *h*

22The least of you will become a
    thousand,
    the smallest a mighty nation. *i*
I am the LORD;
    in its time I will do this swiftly." *j*

The Year of the LORD's Favor

61 The Spirit *k* of the Sovereign
    LORD *l* is on me,
because the LORD has anointed *m* me
    to preach good news *n* to the poor. *o*
He has sent me to bind up *p* the
    brokenhearted,
to proclaim freedom *q* for the
    captives *r*
and release from darkness for the
    prisoners, *p*

2to proclaim the year of the LORD's
    favor *s*

and the day of vengeance *t* of our
    God,
to comfort *u* all who mourn, *v*
3 and provide for those who grieve in
    Zion—
to bestow on them a crown *w* of beauty
    instead of ashes, *x*
the oil *y* of gladness
    instead of mourning, *z*
and a garment of praise
    instead of a spirit of despair.
They will be called oaks of
    righteousness,
a planting *a* of the LORD
    for the display of his splendor. *b*

4They will rebuild the ancient ruins *c*
    and restore the places long
    devastated;
they will renew the ruined cities
    that have been devastated for
    generations.
5Aliens *d* will shepherd your flocks;
    foreigners will work your fields and
    vineyards.
6And you will be called priests *e* of the
    LORD,
you will be named ministers of our
    God.
You will feed on the wealth *f* of nations,

60:19 *z*S Ps 36:9;
S 118:27;
Rev 22:5
*a*S Ps 85:9;
S Isa 24:16,23;
Rev 21:23
60:20 *b*Isa 30:26
*c*S Isa 30:19;
S 35:10;
S Rev 7:17
60:21 *d*S Isa 4:3;
S 26:2; Rev 21:27
*e*Ps 37:11,22;
Isa 49:8; 57:13;
61:7; 65:9;
Zec 8:12
*f*S Ex 15:17;
Ps 44:2; 80:8-11;
Jer 32:41;
Am 9:15;
Mt 15:13
*g*S Job 10:3;
S Ps 8:6;
S Isa 19:25;
Eph 2:10
*h*S Lev 10:3;
S Isa 44:23
60:22 *i*S Ge 12:2;
S Dt 1:10
*j*Isa 5:19
61:1 *k*S Isa 11:2;
2Co 3:17
*l*S Isa 50:4
*m*S Ps 45:7;
S Da 9:24-26;
S Ac 4:26
*n*S 2Sa 18:26;
S Isa 40:9
*o*S Job 5:16;
S Mt 11:5;
Lk 7:22
*p*S 2Ki 22:19;
S Job 5:18
*q*S Lev 25:10
*r*S Ps 68:6;
S Isa 49:9
61:2 *s*S Isa 49:8;
S Lk 4:18-19*

*t*S Isa 1:24
*u*S Isa 40:1;
Mt 5:4
*v*S Job 5:11;
Lk 6:21
61:3 *w*S Isa 3:23
*x*S Job 2:8

*y*S Ru 3:3; S Isa 1:6; Heb 1:9 *z*Jer 31:13; Mt 5:4 *a*Ps 1:3;
92:12-13; Mt 15:13; 1Co 3:9 *b*S Isa 44:23 **61:4** *c*S Isa 44:26;
51:3; 65:21; Eze 36:33; Am 9:14; Zec 1:16-17 **61:5**
*d*S Isa 14:1-2; S 56:6 **61:6** *e*S Ex 19:6; 1Pe 2:5 *f*Dt 33:19;
S Isa 60:11

p *l* Hebrew; Septuagint *the blind*

---

light will no longer be needed in the new Jerusalem, since
God and the Lamb will be the "everlasting light." *glory.* See
vv. 1–2 and note; Zec 2:5.
60:20 *sun will never set.* There will be no night there (cf.
Rev 22:5) but only the light of joy and salvation (see 58:8
and note). *sorrow will end.* See 25:8; 35:10; 51:11; 65:19;
Rev 21:4.
60:21 *people be righteous.* Only the redeemed will be
there (see 4:3; 35:8; Rev 21:27). *possess the land forever.*
Enter into full blessing (see 49:8 and note; see also 57:13;
61:7; Ps 37:11,22). *shoot I have planted.* Cf. the vineyard of
5:2,7 (see also 11:1). *work of my hands.* God made them as
a potter forms clay (see 64:8; see also 29:23; 45:11). *display
of my splendor.* They are the evidence of God's redemptive
work. See 49:3; 61:3; see also notes on 35:2; 40:5.
60:22 *least . . . will become a thousand.* See 51:2; 54:3
and notes. The blessing of Lev 26:8 is similar. *do this swiftly.*
Cf. 5:19, where the same Hebrew verb is translated "hasten."
61:1–2 Jesus applied these verses to himself in the synagogue at Nazareth (see Lk 4:16–21; cf. Mt 11:5).
61:1 *Spirit . . . is on me.* The statement may refer to Isaiah
in a limited sense, but the Messianic servant is the main
figure intended (cf. what is said of him in 42:1; see 11:2;
48:16 and notes). *Sovereign LORD.* See 50:4–5,7,9 and note.
anointed me. See 45:1 and note. *good news.* See 40:9 and
note. *poor.* Cf. 11:4; 29:19. *bind up the brokenhearted.* See
30:26 and note. *freedom for the captives.* Freedom is used of

the Year of Jubilee in Lev 25:10 (see 49:8 and note). *Release*
from sin has as its background release from Babylon (see
42:7 and note).
61:2 *year of the LORD's favor.* Corresponds to the "day of
salvation" in 49:8 (see note there) and the "year of my
redemption" in 63:4. Christ ended his quotation at this point
(Lk 4:19–20), probably because the "day of vengeance" will
not occur until his second coming. *day of vengeance.* See
34:2,8 and notes. *comfort all who mourn.* See 49:13; 57:19
and notes; 66:10; Jer 31:13; Mt 5:4.
61:3 *crown of beauty.* A "turban" (as the Hebrew for this
phrase is translated in Eze 24:17) or headdress. In 3:20 the
women of Jerusalem were to lose their beautiful headdresses.
oil of gladness. Anointing with olive oil was common on
joyous occasions (see Ps 23:5; 45:7; 104:15; 133:1–2; cf.
2Sa 14:2). See also 1:6 and note. *garment of praise.* Contrast
the "garments of vengeance" in 59:17. *oaks of righteousness.* Contrast the oaks of 1:30. *planting . . . for the display.*
See 60:21 and note.
61:4 *rebuild the ancient ruins . . . ruined cities.* See 58:12
and note.
61:5 *Aliens . . . foreigners.* See 14:1–2; 56:3; 60:10 and
notes.
61:6 *priests of the LORD.* See 66:21. True Israel will be a
"kingdom of priests" among the Gentiles (see Ex 19:6 and
note). *ministers.* Priests. See 1Ki 8:11, where the Hebrew
word for "minister" is translated "perform their service."
wealth of nations. See 60:5 and note.

and in their riches you will boast.

[7]Instead of their shame[g]
my people will receive a double[h]
portion,
and instead of disgrace
they will rejoice in their inheritance;
and so they will inherit[i] a double
portion in their land,
and everlasting joy[j] will be theirs.

[8]"For I, the LORD, love justice;[k]
I hate robbery and iniquity.
In my faithfulness I will reward them
and make an everlasting covenant[l]
with them.
[9]Their descendants[m] will be known
among the nations
and their offspring among the
peoples.
All who see them will acknowledge
that they are a people the LORD has
blessed."[n]

[10]I delight greatly in the LORD;
my soul rejoices[o] in my God.
For he has clothed me with garments of
salvation
and arrayed me in a robe of
righteousness,[p]
as a bridegroom adorns his head[q] like a
priest,
and as a bride[r] adorns herself with
her jewels.
[11]For as the soil makes the sprout come
up
and a garden[s] causes seeds to grow,
so the Sovereign LORD will make
righteousness[t] and praise
spring up before all nations.

Zion's New Name

62 For Zion's sake I will not keep
silent,[u]
for Jerusalem's sake I will not remain
quiet,
till her righteousness[v] shines out like
the dawn,[w]
her salvation[x] like a blazing torch.
[2]The nations[y] will see your
righteousness,
and all kings your glory;
you will be called by a new name[z]
that the mouth of the LORD will
bestow.
[3]You will be a crown[a] of splendor in the
LORD's hand,
a royal diadem in the hand of your
God.
[4]No longer will they call you Deserted,[b]
or name your land Desolate.[c]
But you will be called Hephzibah,[q][d]
and your land Beulah[r];
for the LORD will take delight[e] in you,
and your land will be married.[f]
[5]As a young man marries a maiden,
so will your sons[s] marry you;
as a bridegroom[g] rejoices over his
bride,
so will your God rejoice[h] over you.
[6]I have posted watchmen[i] on your
walls, O Jerusalem;
they will never be silent day or night.
You who call on the LORD,
give yourselves no rest,[j]
[7]and give him no rest[k] till he establishes
Jerusalem

61:7
gS Isa 29:22;
S 41:11
hS Dt 21:17;
S Isa 40:2
iS Isa 60:21
jS Ps 126:5;
S Isa 25:9
61:8 kS Ps 11:7;
S Isa 1:17; S 5:16
lS Ge 9:16;
S Isa 42:6;
S Heb 13:20
61:9 mS Isa 43:5;
S 48:19
nS Ge 12:2;
S Dt 28:3-12
61:10 oPs 2:11;
S Isa 7:13; S 25:9;
Hab 3:18;
S Lk 1:47
pS Job 27:6;
S Ps 132:9;
S Isa 52:1;
Rev 19:8
qS Ex 39:28
rS Isa 49:18;
Rev 21:2
61:11
sS Ge 47:23;
Isa 58:11
tS Isa 45:8

62:1 uS Est 4:14;
S Ps 50:21; S 83:1
vS Isa 1:26;
S 45:8
wS Job 11:17
xS Ps 67:2
62:2 yS Ps 67:2;
S Isa 40:5;
S 45:14; 52:10
zS Ge 32:28;
S Isa 1:26;
Rev 2:17; 3:12
62:3 aS Isa 28:5;
1Th 2:19
62:4
bS Lev 26:43;
S Isa 6:12; S 54:6
cS Isa 49:19;
S 51:19 dS 2Ki 21:1
eIsa 65:19;
Jer 32:41;
Zep 3:17;
Mal 3:12
fIsa 54:5;
Jer 3:14; Hos 2:19
62:5 gS SS 3:11
hS Dt 28:63;
Isa 65:19;
Jer 31:12;
Zep 3:17
62:6 iS Isa 52:8;
Heb 13:17

jPs 132:4 **62:7** kMt 15:21-28; Lk 18:1-8

q4 *Hephzibah* means *my delight is in her.*   r4 *Beulah*
means *married.*   s5 Or *Builder*

61:7 *shame . . . disgrace.* See 45:17; 54:4. *double portion.* The firstborn son received a double share of the inheritance (see Dt 21:17; Zec 9:12). Contrast the "double"
punishment Israel received (40:2). *everlasting joy.* See
35:10; 51:11; cf. Ps 16:11.
61:8 *love justice.* Cf. 30:18; 59:15. *robbery and iniquity.*
Israel had been mistreated by her conquerors. Cf. 42:24;
59:18. *everlasting covenant.* Probably the new covenant
(see 55:3; 59:21 and notes; cf. Jer 31:35–37; 32:40).
61:9 *people the LORD has blessed.* See 44:3; 65:23 and the
promises to Abraham in Ge 12:1–3.
61:10 Zion is probably the speaker. *garments of salvation.*
See v. 3; 52:1 and note. *head like a priest.* Putting on a
turban or headband (see note on v. 3). *bride . . . with her
jewels.* See 49:18 and note.
61:11 *sprout . . . grow.* Cf. 55:10. *righteousness and
praise spring up.* See 45:8 and note.
62:1,6 *I.* The Lord.
62:1 *not keep silent . . . quiet.* See v. 6; 42:14; 57:11 and
note; 64:12; 65:6; see also Ps 28:1. *righteousness . . .
salvation.* See 46:13 and note. *dawn.* Cf. 58:8.

62:2 *nations will see . . . glory.* See 52:10; see also 40:5;
60:3 and notes. *your.* Jerusalem's (see vv. 1,6). *new name.*
To reflect a new status (see vv. 4,12; see also 1:26; 60:14;
Ge 32:28 and notes).
62:3 *crown of splendor.* In 28:5 the Lord is a "glorious
crown" for his people (cf. Zec 9:16).
62:4 *Deserted . . . Desolate.* See 54:6–7; 60:15 and note.
Hephzibah. Also the name of Hezekiah's wife (2Ki 21:1).
married. Israel's relationship with the Lord will be restored.
See 50:1 and note.
62:5 *sons marry you.* The Israelites will again possess the
land once deserted. Cf. 54:1. Or the Hebrew for "sons"
could be read as "Builder," referring to God (see note on
49:17).
62:6 *watchmen.* Probably those (the prophets especially;
see 56:10) waiting for the messenger with good news (see
52:8 and note). *never be silent.* They will be praying that
God will not be silent (see v. 1) but will restore Jerusalem.
give yourselves no rest. Cf. David's intense prayer as he
searched for a home for the ark (Ps 132:1–5).
62:7 *praise of the earth.* Cf. Jer 33:9; Zep 3:19–20; see

and makes her the praise[l] of the earth.

[8]The LORD has sworn[m] by his right hand
    and by his mighty arm:
"Never again will I give your grain[n]
    as food for your enemies,
and never again will foreigners drink
        the new wine
    for which you have toiled;
[9]but those who harvest it will eat[o] it
    and praise the LORD,[p]
and those who gather the grapes will
        drink it
    in the courts of my sanctuary."[q]

[10]Pass through, pass through the gates![r]
    Prepare the way for the people.
Build up, build up the highway![s] [t]
    Remove the stones.
Raise a banner[u] for the nations.

[11]The LORD has made proclamation
    to the ends of the earth:[v]
"Say to the Daughter of Zion,[w]
    'See, your Savior comes![x]
See, his reward is with him,
    and his recompense accompanies
        him.' "[y]
[12]They will be called[z] the Holy People,[a]
    the Redeemed[b] of the LORD;
and you will be called Sought After,
    the City No Longer Deserted.[c]

God's Day of Vengeance and Redemption

63 Who is this coming from Edom,[d]
    from Bozrah,[e] with his garments
    stained crimson?[f]

Who is this, robed in splendor,
    striding forward in the greatness of
        his strength?[g]
"It is I, speaking in righteousness,
    mighty to save."[h]

[2]Why are your garments red,
    like those of one treading the
        winepress?[i]

[3]"I have trodden the winepress[j] alone;
    from the nations no one was with
        me.
I trampled[k] them in my anger
    and trod them down in my wrath;[l]
their blood spattered my garments,[m]
    and I stained all my clothing.
[4]For the day of vengeance[n] was in my
        heart,
    and the year of my redemption has
        come.
[5]I looked, but there was no one[o] to
        help,
    I was appalled that no one gave
        support;
so my own arm[p] worked salvation for
        me,
    and my own wrath sustained me.[q]
[6]I trampled[r] the nations in my anger;
    in my wrath I made them drunk[s]
    and poured their blood[t] on the
        ground."

Praise and Prayer

[7]I will tell of the kindnesses[u] of the
        LORD,

Cross references (center column)

62:7 [l]S Dt 26:19;
S Isa 60:18
62:8
[m]S Ge 22:16;
S Isa 14:24;
S 49:18
[n]Dt 28:30-33;
S Isa 1:7
62:9 [o]S Isa 1:19;
Am 9:14
[p]S Dt 12:7;
Joel 2:26
[q]Lev 23:39
62:10 [r]S Ps 24:7;
S Isa 60:11
[s]Isa 57:14
[t]S Isa 11:16
[u]S Isa 11:10
62:11 [v]S Dt 30:4
[w]S Ps 9:14;
Zec 9:9; Mt 21:5
[x]S Isa 35:4;
Rev 22:12
[y]S Isa 40:10
62:12
[z]S Ge 32:28
[a]S Ex 19:6;
1Pe 2:9
[b]S Ps 106:10;
S Isa 35:9;
S 44:23
[c]S Ps 27:9;
Isa 42:16; S 54:6
63:1
[d]S 2Ch 28:17;
S Isa 11:14
[e]S Ge 36:33;
Am 1:12
[f]Rev 19:13

[g]S Job 9:4;
S Isa 45:24 [h]Ver
5; S Isa 46:13;
S 51:5; Jer 42:11;
Zep 3:17
63:2 [i]S Ge 49:11
63:3 [j]S Jdg 6:11;
S Rev 14:20
[k]S Job 40:12;
S Ps 108:13;
S Isa 5:5
[l]S Isa 22:5
[m]Rev 19:13
63:4 [n]S Isa 1:24;
S Jer 50:15
63:5
[o]S 2Ki 14:26;
S Isa 41:28
[p]S Ps 44:3;
S 98:1; S Isa 33:2

[q]Isa 59:16 63:6 [r]S Job 40:12; S Ps 108:13 [s]S Isa 29:5;
La 4:21 [t]S Isa 34:3 63:7 [u]S Isa 54:8

Study notes (bottom)

60:3 and note.
62:8 *has sworn.* Cf. 45:23; 54:9. *mighty arm.* See 51:9 and note. *grain . . . for your enemies . . . foreigners drink the new wine.* Punishment Moses warned about in Lev 26:16; Dt 28:33. See also 52:1 and note; Jer 5:17.
62:9 *eat it . . . drink it.* See 65:13,21–23. *in the courts of my sanctuary.* During a festival, or when they brought the tithe to the Lord (Lev 23:39–40; Dt 14:22–26).
62:10 *Pass through, pass through.* See note on 40:1. *gates.* Probably of Babylon (cf. 48:20; Mic 2:12–13). *Prepare the way . . . build up the highway.* See 40:3; 49:11 and notes. *Remove the stones.* See 57:14. *banner.* See 5:26 and note.
62:11 *ends of the earth.* See 11:12; 49:6 and notes. *Daughter of Zion.* A personification of Jerusalem and its inhabitants. *your Savior comes!* See 40:9 and note; Zec 9:9; Mt 21:5; see also 43:3 and note. *reward . . . recompense.* See 40:10 and note.
62:12 *Holy People.* See 4:3; Ex 19:6 and notes. *Redeemed.* See 35:9 and note. *Sought After . . . No Longer Deserted.* See v. 4.
63:1 *Edom.* See 21:11; 34:5 and notes. Edom here symbolizes a world that hates God's people. *Bozrah.* See 34:6 and note. *stained crimson.* Cf. Christ's robe "dipped in blood" (Rev 19:13) as he wages war at his second coming.

righteousness, mighty to save. See 45:8; 46:13; 59:16 and notes.
63:2 *Why . . . ?* Isaiah responds with a question. *treading the winepress.* See 16:10 and note.
63:3 *trodden the winepress.* A figure of judgment also in La 1:15; Joel 3:13; Rev 14:17–20; 19:15. *in my anger . . . wrath.* The day of the Lord. See v. 6; 13:3; 34:2 and notes.
63:4 *day of vengeance . . . year of my redemption.* See 61:2 and note. The day of judging the enemy meant at the same time redemption for God's people. See 35:9; 41:14 and notes.
63:5 See 59:16 (a parallel to the whole verse) and note. *wrath.* In 59:16 "righteousness" is used. God's righteousness and holiness resulted in his wrath.
63:6 *made them drunk.* They drank the "cup of his wrath" (see 51:17 and note). *poured their blood.* Here the battle is compared to a sacrifice, as in 34:6.
63:7–64:12 A prayer of Isaiah, asking the Lord to bring about the redemption he has promised—as one of the "watchmen" the Lord has posted on the walls of Jerusalem (see 62:6 and note). It is similar to a national lament (see, e.g., Ps 44).
63:7 *kindnesses.* A demonstration of God's unfailing love as he stood true to his covenant with Israel. *many good things.* Cf. Jos 21:45; 1Ki 8:66. *compassion.* See 54:7–8,10

the deeds for which he is to be
 praised,
according to all the Lord has done
 for us—
yes, the many good things _v_ he has done
 for the house of Israel,
according to his compassion _w_ and
 many kindnesses.
⁸He said, "Surely they are my people, _x_
 sons who will not be false to me";
and so he became their Savior. _y_
⁹In all their distress he too was
 distressed,
and the angel _z_ of his presence _a_
 saved them.
In his love and mercy he redeemed _b_
 them;
he lifted them up and carried _c_ them
 all the days of old. _d_
¹⁰Yet they rebelled _e_
 and grieved his Holy Spirit. _f_
So he turned and became their enemy _g_
 and he himself fought _h_ against them.
¹¹Then his people recalled _t_ the days of
 old,
the days of Moses and his people—
where is he who brought them through
 the sea, _i_
with the shepherd of his flock? _j_
Where is he who set
 his Holy Spirit _k_ among them,
¹²who sent his glorious arm _l_ of power
 to be at Moses' right hand,
who divided the waters _m_ before them,
 to gain for himself everlasting
  renown, _n_
¹³who led _o_ them through the depths? _p_
Like a horse in open country,
 they did not stumble; _q_
¹⁴like cattle that go down to the plain,

they were given rest _r_ by the Spirit of
 the Lord.
This is how you guided your people
 to make for yourself a glorious name.
¹⁵Look down from heaven _s_ and see
 from your lofty throne, _t_ holy and
  glorious.
Where are your zeal _u_ and your might?
 Your tenderness and compassion _v_ are
  withheld _w_ from us.
¹⁶But you are our Father, _x_
 though Abraham does not know us
 or Israel acknowledge _y_ us;
you, O Lord, are our Father,
 our Redeemer _z_ from of old is your
  name.
¹⁷Why, O Lord, do you make us
 wander _a_ from your ways
 and harden our hearts _b_ so we do not
  revere _c_ you?
Return _d_ for the sake of your servants,
 the tribes that are your inheritance. _e_
¹⁸For a little while _f_ your people
 possessed your holy place,
but now our enemies have trampled _g_
 down your sanctuary. _h_
¹⁹We are yours from of old;
 but you have not ruled over them,
 they have not been called by your
  name. _u i_

64 Oh, that you would rend the
heavens _j_ and come down, _k_

Cross-references (center column)

63:7 _v_S Ex 18:9
_w_S Ps 51:1;
Eph 2:4
63:8 _x_S Ps 100:3;
S Isa 51:4
_y_S Ex 14:30;
S Isa 25:9
63:9 _z_S Ex 14:19
_a_S Ex 33:14
_b_Dt 7:7-8;
S Ezr 9:9;
S Isa 48:20
_c_S Dt 1:31;
S Ps 28:9
_d_S Dt 32:7;
S Job 37:23
63:10
_e_S Ps 78:17;
Eze 20:8;
Ac 7:39-42
_f_S Ps 51:11;
Ac 7:51; Eph 4:30
_g_Ps 106:40;
S Isa 10:4
_h_S Jos 10:14
63:11
_i_S Ex 14:22,30
_j_S Ps 77:20
_k_S Nu 11:17
63:12
_l_S Ge 49:24;
S Ex 3:20
_m_Ex 14:21-22;
Isa 11:15
_n_S Ps 102:12;
S Isa 55:13;
S Jer 13:11
63:13
_o_S Dt 32:12
_p_S Ex 14:22
_q_S Ps 119:11;
Jer 31:9

63:14
_r_S Ex 33:14;
S Dt 12:9
63:15
_s_S Dt 26:15;
La 3:50
_t_S 1Ki 22:19;
S Ps 123:1
_u_S Isa 9:7;
S 26:11
_v_S 1Ki 3:26;
S Ps 25:6
_w_S Ge 43:31;
Isa 64:12
63:16
_x_S Ex 4:22;
S Jer 3:4; Jn 8:41
_y_S Job 14:21
_z_Isa 41:14; 44:6;
S 59:20

63:17 _a_S Ge 20:13; La 3:9 _b_S Ex 4:21 _c_Isa 29:13
_d_S Nu 10:36 _e_S Ex 34:9 63:18 _f_Dt 4:26; 11:17 _g_S Isa 28:18;
Da 8:13; S Lk 21:24 _h_S Lev 26:31; S 2Ki 25:9 63:19
_i_S Isa 43:7; S Jer 14:9 64:1 _j_Ps 18:9; 144:5 _k_ver 3; Mic 1:3

_t 11_ Or _But may he recall_ _u 19_ Or _We are like those
you have never ruled, / like those never called by your
name_

---

and note.
63:8 _my people, sons who will not be false._ But see 1:2–4.
Savior. See 43:3 and note.
63:9 _In all their distress . . . distressed._ The suffering in
Egypt and during the period of the judges is probably in view
(see Jdg 10:16). _angel of his presence._ See Ex 23:20–23;
33:14–15. _redeemed._ See 41:14; 43:1 and notes. _lifted . . .
carried._ Like a father (see Dt 1:31; 32:10–12).
63:10 _rebelled._ In the desert (see 1:2 and note; 30:1; Nu
20:10; Ps 78:40). _grieved his Holy Spirit._ See Ps 106:33; cf.
Isa 11:1–2; 42:1. _became their enemy._ See 43:28 and note.
63:11 _sea._ The Red Sea (see 50:2 and note; 51:10). _shep-
herd._ Moses. _Holy Spirit._ See note on Ps 51:11. The Spirit
rested on Moses and 70 elders (Nu 11:17,25). See also v. 14.
63:12 _arm of power._ See 51:9 and note; Ex 15:16. _divided
the waters._ See Ex 14:21; cf. 11:15; 51:10. _everlasting
renown._ See 55:13 and note.
63:13 _depths._ Of the Red Sea (see Ex 15:5,8; Ps 106:9).
But the crossing of the Jordan may be intended as well (see v.
14 and note).
63:14 _to the plain._ To find pasture and water. _given rest._
They found a home in Canaan, the promised land (see Dt

12:9; Jos 1:13; 21:44).
63:15 _lofty throne._ See 6:1. _zeal._ See 9:7; 42:13 and
notes. _tenderness and compassion._ Cf. Hos 11:8. _withheld._
See 42:14 and note.
63:16 _Father._ See 64:8; Dt 32:6. _Abraham does not
know._ Even if their human fathers abandon them, God will
not (see 49:14–15 and notes). _Redeemer._ See 41:14 and
note.
63:17 _make us wander._ When Israel went astray (see
53:6), God let them wander. _harden our hearts._ The
people's hearts were hard (see 6:10; Ps 95:8), and the Lord
confirmed that condition (see 6:10; Ex 4:21 and notes).
servants. True believers (see 54:17 and note).
63:18 _enemies._ The Babylonians. _trampled down your
sanctuary._ Graphically described in Ps 74:3–7; cf. Isa 64:11.
Since it was God's sanctuary, his honor was at stake (cf.
48:11).
63:19 _called by your name._ See 43:7 and note.
64:1 _rend the heavens._ The sky is compared to a tent
curtain. For this and the further description of the cosmic
effects of God's coming in judgment and redemption see Jdg
5:4–5; Ps 18:7–15; 144:5; Na 1:5; Hab 3:3–7.

that the mountains[l] would tremble
    before you!
[2]As when fire sets twigs ablaze
    and causes water to boil,
come down to make your name[m]
    known to your enemies
and cause the nations to quake[n]
    before you!
[3]For when you did awesome[o] things
    that we did not expect,
you came down, and the mountains
    trembled[p] before you.
[4]Since ancient times no one has heard,
    no ear has perceived,
no eye has seen any God besides you,[q]
    who acts on behalf of those who wait
    for him.[r]
[5]You come to the help of those who
    gladly do right,[s]
who remember your ways.
But when we continued to sin against
    them,
    you were angry.[t]
    How then can we be saved?
[6]All of us have become like one who is
    unclean,[u]
and all our righteous[v] acts are like
    filthy rags;
we all shrivel up like a leaf,[w]
    and like the wind our sins sweep us
    away.[x]
[7]No one[y] calls on your name[z]
    or strives to lay hold of you;
for you have hidden[a] your face from us
    and made us waste away[b] because of
    our sins.

[8]Yet, O LORD, you are our Father.[c]
    We are the clay, you are the potter;[d]
    we are all the work of your hand.[e]

[9]Do not be angry[f] beyond measure,
    O LORD;
    do not remember our sins[g] forever.
Oh, look upon us, we pray,
    for we are all your people.[h]
[10]Your sacred cities[i] have become a
    desert;
    even Zion is a desert, Jerusalem a
    desolation.[j]
[11]Our holy and glorious temple,[k] where
    our fathers praised you,
has been burned with fire,
    and all that we treasured[l] lies in
    ruins.
[12]After all this, O LORD, will you hold
    yourself back?[m]
Will you keep silent[n] and punish us
    beyond measure?

Judgment and Salvation

65 "I revealed myself to those who
    did not ask for me;
    I was found by those who did not
    seek me.[o]
To a nation[p] that did not call on my
    name,[q]
I said, 'Here am I, here am I.'
[2]All day long I have held out my hands
    to an obstinate people,[r]
who walk in ways not good,
    pursuing their own imaginations[s] —
[3]a people who continually provoke me
    to my very face,[t]
offering sacrifices in gardens[u]
    and burning incense[v] on altars of
    brick;

Cross-references (center column)

64:1 [l]S Ex 19:18
64:2 [m]S Isa 30:27
[n]Ps 99:1;
119:120;
Jer 5:22; 33:9
64:3 [o]S Ps 65:5
[p]S Ps 18:7
64:4
[q]S Isa 43:10-11
[r]S Isa 30:18;
1Co 2:9*
64:5 [s]S Isa 26:8
[t]S Isa 10:4
64:6 [u]S Lev 5:2;
S 12:2 [v]Isa 46:12;
48:1 [w]S Ps 1:3;
90:5-6 [x]Ps 1:4;
Jer 4:12
64:7
[y]S Isa 41:28;
59:4; 63:5;
Jer 8:6; Eze 22:30
[z]S Isa 14:4
[a]Dt 31:18;
Isa 1:15; 54:8
[b]S Isa 9:18;
Eze 22:18-22
64:8 [c]S Ex 4:22;
S Jer 3:4
[d]S Isa 29:16;
Ro 9:20-21
[e]S Job 10:3;
S Isa 19:25

64:9 [f]Isa 54:8;
57:17; 60:10;
La 5:22
[g]S Isa 43:25
[h]S Ps 100:3;
S Isa 51:4
64:10 [i]Ps 78:54;
S Isa 1:26
[j]S Dt 29:23
64:11
[k]S Lev 26:31;
S 2Ki 25:9;
Ps 74:3-7; La 2:7
[l]ver 10-11;
La 1:7,10
64:12
[m]S Ge 43:31;
Ps 74:10-11
[n]S Est 4:14;
S Ps 50:21; S 83:1
65:1 [o]Hos 1:10;
Ro 9:24-26;
10:20* [p]Ro 9:30;
Eph 2:12
[q]S Ps 14:4;
S Isa 43:7
65:2 [r]S Ps 78:8;
S Isa 1:2,23;
Ro 10:21*

[s]Ps 81:11-12; S Pr 24:2; Isa 66:18 65:3 [t]S Job 1:11
[u]S Isa 1:29 [v]S Lev 2:2; Jer 41:5; 44:17; Eze 23:41

Study notes

64:2 *make your name known.* See 30:27 and note.
64:3 *awesome things.* See Ps 66:3,5–6.
64:4 *no . . . God besides you.* See 43:11 and note. *wait for him.* See 30:18; see also 40:31 and note.
64:5 *do right.* See 56:1. *you were angry.* See 9:12,17,21 and note. God's anger culminated in the exile. *saved.* Or "delivered" (see 43:3 and note).
64:6 *unclean.* Ceremonially unclean, like a person with a terrible disease (see 6:5; Lev 5:2; 13:45). *righteous acts.* See 57:12 and note. *filthy rags.* The cloths a woman uses during her period, a time when she is "unclean" (see Lev 15:19–24; Eze 36:17). *shrivel up like a leaf.* A figure used also in 1:30. *like the wind.* Which blows away the chaff (see 17:13; 40:24 and note).
64:7 *No one calls on your name.* The Lord urges earnest prayer in times of distress (see, e.g., 2Ch 7:14). *hidden your face.* See 1:15 and note.
64:8 *Father.* See 63:16 and note. *clay . . . potter.* See 45:9 and note. *work of your hand.* See 60:21 and note.
64:9 *Do not be angry.* Cf. the promise to end that anger in 54:7–8 (see notes there). *do not remember our sins.* See 43:25 and note; Jer 31:34; Mic 7:18. *your people.* See 63:17–19; Ps 79:13.

64:10 *sacred cities.* Sacred because Israel was the "holy land" (Ps 78:54). Jerusalem is often called the "holy city" (see 48:2 and note). *Zion is a desert . . . desolation.* See 1:7–9 and note; 6:11; Jer 12:11.
64:11 *holy and glorious temple.* See 60:7 and note; 63:15. *burned with fire.* Isaiah here reaches the climax of his lament. See 63:18 and note.
64:12 *hold yourself back . . . keep silent.* See 42:14; 57:11; 62:1,6–7 and notes.
65:1—66:24 The grand conclusion to chs. 58–66, as well as to chs. 40–66 and to the whole book.
65:1 *did not ask . . . did not seek.* The Lord now proceeds to answer Isaiah's prayer. Israel failed to stay close to the Lord, though they sought him in a superficial way (see 55:6; 58:2 and notes). *did not call on my name.* See 64:7. *Here am I.* See 58:9.
65:2 *obstinate people.* See 1:2; 30:1,9 and notes. *imaginations.* See 59:7 and note.
65:3 *provoke me.* By worshiping idols (see Jdg 2:12–13). *to my very face.* Defiantly (cf. 3:8–9). *gardens.* See 1:29 and note. *burning incense.* As when worshiping the Queen of Heaven (see Jer 44:17–19).

4who sit among the graves *w*
and spend their nights keeping secret
vigil;
who eat the flesh of pigs, *x*
and whose pots hold broth of unclean
meat;
5who say, 'Keep away; don't come near
me,
for I am too sacred *y* for you!'
Such people are smoke *z* in my nostrils,
a fire that keeps burning all day.

6"See, it stands written before me:
I will not keep silent *a* but will pay
back *b* in full;
I will pay it back into their laps *c* —
7both your sins *d* and the sins of your
fathers," *e*
says the LORD.
"Because they burned sacrifices on the
mountains
and defied me on the hills, *f*
I will measure into their laps
the full payment *g* for their former
deeds."

8This is what the LORD says:

"As when juice is still found in a cluster
of grapes *h*
and men say, 'Don't destroy it,
there is yet some good in it,'
so will I do in behalf of my servants; *i*
I will not destroy them all.
9I will bring forth descendants *j* from
Jacob,
and from Judah those who will
possess *k* my mountains;
my chosen *l* people will inherit them,
and there will my servants live. *m*

10Sharon *n* will become a pasture for
flocks, *o*
and the Valley of Achor *p* a resting
place for herds,
for my people who seek *q* me.

11"But as for you who forsake *r* the LORD
and forget my holy mountain, *s*
who spread a table for Fortune
and fill bowls of mixed wine *t* for
Destiny,
12I will destine you for the sword, *u*
and you will all bend down for the
slaughter; *v*
for I called but you did not answer, *w*
I spoke but you did not listen. *x*
You did evil in my sight
and chose what displeases me." *y*

13Therefore this is what the Sovereign
LORD says:

"My servants will eat, *z*
but you will go hungry; *a*
my servants will drink, *b*
but you will go thirsty; *c*
my servants will rejoice, *d*
but you will be put to shame. *e*
14My servants will sing *f*
out of the joy of their hearts,
but you will cry out *g*
from anguish of heart
and wail in brokenness of spirit.
15You will leave your name
to my chosen ones as a curse; *h*
the Sovereign LORD will put you to
death,

65:4
*w*S Lev 19:31;
S Isa 8:19
*x*S Lev 11:7
65:5 *y*S Ps 40:4;
Mt 9:11; Lk 7:39;
18:9-12
*z*Pr 10:26
65:6 *a*S Ps 50:3
*b*S 2Ch 6:23;
Isa 59:18;
Jer 16:18
*c*S Ps 79:12;
Eze 9:10; Lk 6:38
65:7 *d*S Isa 22:14
*e*Ex 20:5;
Jer 32:18
*f*S Isa 57:7
*g*S Pr 10:24;
S Isa 10:12
65:8 *h*Isa 5:2
*i*S Isa 54:17
65:9 *j*S Isa 45:19
*k*S Nu 34:13;
S Isa 60:21;
Jer 50:19;
Am 9:11-15
*l*S Isa 14:1
*m*Isa 32:18

65:10
*n*S 1Ch 27:29;
S Isa 35:2;
Ac 9:35
*o*Jer 31:12;
33:12;
Eze 34:13-14
*p*S Jos 7:26
*q*S Isa 51:1
65:11 *r*Dt 28:20;
29:24-25;
S 32:15; Isa 1:28;
Jer 2:13; 19:4
*s*S Dt 33:19;
S Ps 137:5
*t*S Isa 5:22
65:12
*u*S Isa 1:20;
S 27:1
*v*S Isa 30:25
*w*S Pr 1:24-25;
S Isa 41:28; 66:4;
Jer 7:27
*x*2Ch 36:15-16;
Jer 7:13; 13:11;
25:3; 26:5
*y*Ps 149:7;
Isa 1:24; 66:4;
Mic 5:15
65:13 *z*S Isa 1:19
*a*S Job 18:12;
Lk 6:25 *b*S Isa 33:16 *c*S Isa 3:1; 41:17 *d*S Isa 60:5; 61:7
*e*S Isa 44:9 **65:14** *f*S Ps 109:28; Zep 3:14-20; Jas 5:13
*g*S Isa 15:2; Mt 8:12; Lk 13:28 **65:15** *h*S Nu 5:27; S Ps 102:8

65:4 *sit among the graves.* Perhaps to consult the dead (see 8:19 and note; 57:9; Dt 18:11). *flesh of pigs.* Considered ceremonially unclean (see 66:3,17; Lev 11:7–8).
65:5 *I am too sacred for you.* Those who engage in pagan rituals believe they are superior to others (cf. the attitude of the Pharisees in Mt 9:11; Lk 7:39; 18:9–12).
65:6 *not keep silent.* The answer to 64:12. *pay back.* See 59:18 and note.
65:7 *burned sacrifices on the mountains.* Offered to Baal on the high places (see 57:7; Hos 2:13). *defied me.* See Eze 20:27–28.
65:8 *cluster of grapes.* Israel was a vineyard that had produced bad grapes (5:2,4,7). *servants.* See vv. 9,13–15; 54:17 and note. Here the Lord's servants are equivalent to the remnant (see 1:9 and note).
65:9 *descendants.* See Jer 31:36. *Jacob . . . Judah.* The northern and southern kingdoms respectively. *possess my mountains.* See 49:8; 60:21 and notes. "Mountains" refers to the whole land, since so much of it was hilly (see Jdg 1:9; Eze 6:2–3). *chosen people.* See 41:8–9 and note. *inherit.* See 57:13 and note.
65:10 *Sharon.* See 33:9 and note. *Valley of Achor.* A valley near Jericho (see Jos 7:24,26; Hos 2:15). Since Sharon and Achor are on the western and eastern edges of the land

respectively, they probably represent the whole country. *seek me.* See v. 1; 51:1 and notes.
65:11 *forsake the LORD.* See 1:4. *holy mountain.* See 2:2–4 and note. *spread a table . . . mixed wine.* A meal and drink offering presented to deities. See note on 5:22; cf. v. 3; Jer 7:18. *Fortune . . . Destiny.* The pagan gods of good fortune and fate. See Jos 11:17, where "Gad" may mean "Fortune."
65:12 *sword.* Designed for God's enemies, such as Edom (34:5–6), but the wicked of Israel would also suffer (see 1:20; 59:18 and note; 66:16). *called . . . not answer.* See 50:2 and note; 2Ch 36:15–16. *chose what displeases me.* Contrast the faithfulness of the eunuchs in 56:4. The last four lines of v. 12 are almost identical to those of 66:4.
65:13 *eat . . . drink.* See 41:17–18; 49:10. *go hungry . . . thirsty.* See 5:13; 8:21. *rejoice.* See 61:7 and note; 66:14. *put to shame.* See 42:17; 44:9,11.
65:14 *sing out of . . . joy.* See 35:10; 54:1 and notes. *brokenness of spirit.* They had refused God's healing. See 61:1 and note.
65:15 *chosen ones.* See v. 9 and note. *as a curse.* The rebellious Israelites will be used as an example when curses are uttered (see Jer 29:22). *another name.* Perhaps the "new name" of 62:2 (see note there).

but to his servants he will give
    another name. *i*
16Whoever invokes a blessing*j* in the
    land
    will do so by the God of truth; *k*
he who takes an oath in the land
    will swear *l* by the God of truth.
For the past troubles *m* will be forgotten
    and hidden from my eyes.

New Heavens and a New Earth

17"Behold, I will create
    new heavens and a new earth. *n*
The former things will not be
    remembered, *o*
    nor will they come to mind.
18But be glad and rejoice*p* forever
    in what I will create,
for I will create Jerusalem *q* to be a
    delight
    and its people a joy.
19I will rejoice *r* over Jerusalem
    and take delight *s* in my people;
the sound of weeping and of crying *t*
    will be heard in it no more.

20"Never again will there be in it
    an infant *u* who lives but a few days,
    or an old man who does not live out
    his years; *v*
he who dies at a hundred
    will be thought a mere youth;
he who fails to reach*v* a hundred
    will be considered accursed.
21They will build houses*w* and dwell in
    them;
    they will plant vineyards and eat their
    fruit. *x*
22No longer will they build houses and
    others live in them, *y*
    or plant and others eat.

For as the days of a tree, *z*
    so will be the days*a* of my people;
my chosen *b* ones will long enjoy
    the works of their hands.
23They will not toil in vain *c*
    or bear children doomed to
      misfortune; *d*
for they will be a people blessed *e* by
    the LORD,
they and their descendants *f* with
    them.
24Before they call*g* I will answer; *h*
    while they are still speaking *i* I will
    hear.
25The wolf and the lamb*j* will feed
    together,
    and the lion will eat straw like the
    ox, *k*
but dust will be the serpent's *l* food.
They will neither harm nor destroy
    on all my holy mountain," *m*
                says the LORD.

Judgment and Hope

66 This is what the LORD says:

"Heaven is my throne, *n*
    and the earth is my footstool. *o*
Where is the house*p* you will build for
    me?
    Where will my resting place be?
2Has not my hand made all these
    things, *q*
    and so they came into being?"
           declares the LORD.

"This is the one I esteem:

Cross references

65:15
i S Ge 32:28;
Rev 2:17
65:16
j S Dt 29:19
k Ps 31:5;
Rev 3:14
l S Ps 63:11;
S Isa 19:18
m S Job 11:16
65:17
n S Isa 41:22;
66:22; 2Co 5:17;
S 2Pe 3:13
o Isa 43:18;
Jer 3:16;
S Rev 7:17
65:18
p S Dt 32:43;
Ps 98:1-9;
S Isa 25:9
q Rev 21:2
65:19
r S Isa 35:10;
S 62:5 *s* S Dt 30:9
t S Isa 25:8;
Rev 7:17
65:20 *u* Isa 11:8
v Ge 5:1-32;
S 15:15;
S Ecc 8:13;
Zec 8:4
65:21
w S Isa 32:18;
S 61:4
x S 2Ki 19:29;
S Isa 37:30;
Eze 28:26;
Am 9:14
65:22
y S Dt 28:30

z Ps 1:3; 92:12-14
a Ps 21:4; 91:16
b S Isa 14:1
65:23
c S Isa 49:4;
1Co 15:58
d Dt 28:32,41;
Jer 16:3-4
e S Ge 12:2;
S Dt 28:3-12
f S Isa 44:3;
Ac 2:39
65:24
g S Isa 55:6;
Mt 6:8
h S Job 8:6;
S Isa 30:19;
S Zec 10:6
i Da 9:20-23;
10:12
65:25 *j* Isa 11:6
k S Job 40:15
l Ge 3:14;

Mic 7:17 *m* S Job 5:23; S Isa 2:4 **66:1** *n* S 2Ch 6:18; S Ps 2:4;
S 9:7; Mt 23:22 *o* S 1Ki 8:27; Mt 5:34-35 *p* S 2Sa 7:7;
Jn 4:20-21; Ac 7:49*; 17:24 **66:2** *q* S Isa 40:26; Ac 7:50*;
17:24

v 20 Or / *the sinner who reaches*

65:16 *invokes a blessing.* See 48:1; Dt 29:19. *God of truth.* God is true to his promises. The Hebrew word for "truth" here is *amen* (see 2Co 1:20; cf. Rev 3:14). *swear by.* See 45:23. Perhaps a contrast is intended with those who took oaths in the name of Baal (see Jer 12:16).
65:17 *new heavens and a new earth.* The climax of the "new things" Isaiah has been promising (see 42:9; 48:6 and notes). *former things.* The "old order of things" (Rev 21:4), including pain and sorrow.
65:18 *be glad and rejoice.* See 66:10; see also 51:3 and note. *create Jerusalem.* John links the notion of a new heaven and a new earth with the "new Jerusalem" (Rev 21:1–2). A restored Jerusalem after the exile and in the Messianic kingdom pointed toward this greater Jerusalem. See note on 54:11–12.
65:19 *rejoice . . . take delight.* See 62:4–5 and notes. *weeping . . . crying.* See 25:8 and note; 35:10.
65:20–25 See 11:6–9 and note.
65:20 *hundred . . . mere youth.* Comparable to the longevity of Adam and his early descendants. See the genealogy of Ge 5 (but see note on Ge 5:5).

65:21–22 Contrast Moses' curse for disobedience in Dt 28:30.
65:21 *plant vineyards.* See 62:8–9.
65:22 *days of a tree.* Compared to the righteous also in Ps 1:3; 92:12–14. *chosen ones.* See 41:8–9 and note. *long enjoy.* Cf. Ps 91:16.
65:23 *toil in vain.* See 49:4 and note. *misfortune.* Such as death or captivity. *people blessed by the LORD.* See 61:9 and note.
65:24 *Before they call I will answer.* See 30:19; 58:9; Mt 6:8.
65:25 *wolf . . . lamb . . . lion.* See 11:6–9 and notes. *dust . . . serpent's food.* See Ge 3:14 and note. The serpent will be harmless (see 11:8). *They . . . mountain.* Identical to the first two lines of 11:9.
66:1 *throne . . . footstool.* See 40:22 and note. *Where is the house . . . ?* Solomon realized that God could not be localized in a man-made temple, magnificent though it may be (1Ki 8:27).
66:2 *made all these things.* See 40:26 and note. *humble and contrite.* See 57:15 and note.

he who is humble and contrite in
 spirit,[r]
and trembles at my word. [s]
[3]But whoever sacrifices a bull[t]
 is like one who kills a man,
and whoever offers a lamb,
 like one who breaks a dog's neck;
whoever makes a grain offering
 is like one who presents pig's[u] blood,
and whoever burns memorial incense, [v]
 like one who worships an idol.
They have chosen their own ways, [w]
 and their souls delight in their
  abominations;[x]
[4]so I also will choose harsh treatment for
 them
 and will bring upon them what they
  dread.[y]
For when I called, no one answered,[z]
 when I spoke, no one listened.
They did evil[a] in my sight
 and chose what displeases me." [b]

[5]Hear the word of the LORD,
 you who tremble at his word: [c]
"Your brothers who hate[d] you,
 and exclude you because of my
 name, have said,
'Let the LORD be glorified,
 that we may see your joy!'
Yet they will be put to shame. [e]
[6]Hear that uproar from the city,
 hear that noise from the temple!
It is the sound[f] of the LORD
 repaying[g] his enemies all they
  deserve.

[7]"Before she goes into labor, [h]
 she gives birth;
before the pains come upon her,
 she delivers a son. [i]
[8]Who has ever heard of such a thing?
 Who has ever seen[j] such things?
Can a country be born in a day[k]

or a nation be brought forth in a
 moment?
Yet no sooner is Zion in labor
 than she gives birth to her children. [l]
[9]Do I bring to the moment of birth[m]
 and not give delivery?" says the
 LORD.
"Do I close up the womb
 when I bring to delivery?" says your
 God.

[10]"Rejoice[n] with Jerusalem and be glad
 for her,
 all you who love[o] her;
rejoice greatly with her,
 all you who mourn[p] over her.
[11]For you will nurse[q] and be satisfied
 at her comforting breasts; [r]
you will drink deeply
 and delight in her overflowing
  abundance." [s]

[12]For this is what the LORD says:

"I will extend peace[t] to her like a
 river, [u]
and the wealth[v] of nations like a
 flooding stream;
you will nurse and be carried[w] on her
 arm
 and dandled on her knees.
[13]As a mother comforts her child, [x]
 so will I comfort[y] you;
and you will be comforted over
 Jerusalem."

[14]When you see this, your heart will
 rejoice[z]
and you will flourish[a] like grass;
the hand[b] of the LORD will be made
 known to his servants, [c]
but his fury[d] will be shown to his
 foes.
[15]See, the LORD is coming with fire, [e]

66:2 [r]S Isa 57:15;
Mt 5:3-4;
Lk 18:13-14
[s]S Ezr 9:4
66:3 [t]S Isa 1:11
[u]S Lev 11:7
[v]S Lev 2:2
[w]S Isa 57:17 [x]ver
17; S Dt 27:15;
Eze 8:9-13
66:4 [y]S Pr 10:24;
S Isa 10:12
[z]S 1Sa 8:19;
S Isa 41:28
[a]2Ki 21:2,4,6;
Isa 59:12
[b]S Isa 65:12
66:5 [c]S Ezr 9:4
[d]Ps 38:20;
Isa 60:15;
Jn 15:21
[e]S Isa 44:9;
Lk 13:17
66:6 [f]S 1Sa 2:10;
S Ps 68:33
[g]S Lev 26:28;
Isa 65:6; Joel 3:7
66:7 [h]S Isa 54:1
[i]Rev 12:5
66:8 [j]Isa 64:4;
Jer 18:13
[k]S Isa 49:20

[l]S Isa 49:21
66:9 [m]S Isa 37:3
66:10
[n]S Dt 32:43;
S Isa 25:9;
Ro 15:10
[o]S Ps 26:8
[p]Isa 57:19; 61:2
66:11
[q]S Nu 11:12;
S Isa 60:16
[r]Ge 49:25
[s]S Nu 25:1;
S Isa 25:6
66:12
[t]S Ps 119:165;
S Isa 9:6
[u]S Isa 33:21
[v]Ps 72:3;
Isa 60:5; 61:6
[w]S Nu 11:12;
Isa 60:4
66:13
[x]S Isa 49:15;
1Th 2:7
[y]S Isa 40:1;
S 2Co 1:4
66:14
[z]S Isa 25:9;
S 60:5;
S Joel 2:23
[a]S Ps 72:16
[b]S Ezr 5:5;
S Isa 41:20
[c]S Isa 54:17

[d]S Isa 10:5; S 30:27 **66:15** [e]S Isa 1:31; S 42:25

66:3 Cf. Isaiah's harsh words about ineffective sacrifices in
1:11–14. *breaks a dog's neck.* The dog was "unclean" and
not used in offerings. Cf. the law about breaking a donkey's
neck in Ex 13:13. *pig's blood.* See 65:4 and note. The dog
and pig are mentioned together also in Mt 7:6; 2Pe 2:22.
worships an idol. See 44:19 and note. *abominations.* Probably idols (see Jer 4:1).
66:4 *choose harsh treatment.* Cf. 65:7. *For when . . .
displeases me.* For these last four lines see 65:12 and note.
66:5 *tremble.* See v. 2. *Your brothers.* Fellow Israelites (see
Ac 22:1). *Let . . . joy.* Apparently spoken sarcastically, much
like 5:19; Ps 22:8.
66:6 *city.* Probably Jerusalem. *repaying his enemies.* See
59:18 and note; 65:6–7.
66:7 *Before . . . labor.* See 54:1 (and note), where Zion was
barren.
66:8 *country . . . born in a day.* See 49:19–20 and note.
66:9 *moment of birth.* See 37:3 and note.
66:10 *Rejoice . . . be glad.* See 65:18 and note. *all . . . who*

love her. Cf. Ps 137:6. *who mourn.* See 57:19; 61:2 and
notes.
66:11 *nurse and be satisfied.* In 60:16 (see note there)
Jerusalem was drinking the milk of nations. Here she is the
mother (cf. v. 12; 49:23).
66:12 *peace . . . like a river.* See 48:18 and note. *wealth of
nations.* See 60:5 and note. *flooding stream.* Contrast the
destructive flood of 8:7–8 (see note there). *on her arm.* See
40:11.
66:13 *comforted over Jerusalem.* See 49:13 and note. Cf.
2Co 1:3–4.
66:14 *heart will rejoice.* See 60:5. *grass.* Usually a symbol
of weakness. See 37:27 and note; 51:12; but contrast 44:4.
hand of the LORD. Cf. Ezr 7:9; 8:31. *servants.* See 54:17 and
note. *fury.* See v. 15; 13:3 and note.
66:15–16 *fire.* A figure of judgment (see 1:31 and note;
30:27).
66:15 *chariots . . . like a whirlwind.* See 5:28; 2Ki 2:11;
6:17; Ps 68:17. *anger.* See 34:2; 42:25 and notes. *rebuke.*

and his chariots*f* are like a
  whirlwind;*g*
he will bring down his anger with fury,
  and his rebuke*h* with flames of fire.
¹⁶For with fire*i* and with his sword*j*
  the LORD will execute judgment*k*
  upon all men,
and many will be those slain*l* by the
  LORD.

¹⁷"Those who consecrate and purify
themselves to go into the gardens, *m* following the one in the midst of*w* those who
eat the flesh of pigs*n* and rats*o* and other
abominable things—they will meet their
end*p* together," declares the LORD.

¹⁸"And I, because of their actions and
their imaginations,*q* am about to come*x*
and gather all nations*r* and tongues, and
they will come and see my glory.*s*

¹⁹"I will set a sign*t* among them, and I
will send some of those who survive*u* to
the nations—to Tarshish, *v* to the Libyans*y*
and Lydians*w* (famous as archers), to Tubal*x* and Greece,*y* and to the distant islands*z* that have not heard of my fame or
seen my glory.*a* They will proclaim my
glory among the nations. ²⁰And they will
bring*b* all your brothers, from all the nations, to my holy mountain*c* in Jerusalem

as an offering to the LORD—on horses, in
chariots and wagons, and on mules and
camels," *d* says the LORD. "They will bring
them, as the Israelites bring their grain offerings, to the temple of the LORD in ceremonially clean vessels. *e* ²¹And I will select
some of them also to be priests*f* and Le-
vites," says the LORD.

²²"As the new heavens and the new
earth*g* that I make will endure before
me," declares the LORD, "so will your
name and descendants endure.*h* ²³From
one New Moon to another and from one
Sabbath*i* to another, all mankind will
come and bow down*j* before me," says
the LORD. ²⁴"And they will go out and look
upon the dead bodies*k* of those who rebelled*l* against me; their worm*m* will not
die, nor will their fire be quenched, *n* and
they will be loathsome to all mankind."

66:15
/S 2Ki 2:11;
S Ps 68:17
gS 2Ki 2:1
hS Dt 28:20;
S Ps 9:5; S 39:11
66:16 /iIsa 30:30;
Am 7:4; Mal 4:1
/S Isa 1:20;
S 27:1;
S Eze 14:21
kS Isa 13:9,11;
S Jer 2:35;
S Eze 36:5
/S Isa 10:4
66:17
mS Isa 1:29
nS Lev 11:7
oLev 11:29
pPs 37:20;
Isa 1:28
66:18 qS Pr 24:2;
S Isa 65:2
rS Isa 2:3;
S Zec 12:3
sS Ex 16:7;
S Isa 59:19
66:19 tIsa 11:10;
49:22; Mt 24:30
uS 2Ki 19:31
vS Isa 2:16
wJer 46:9;
Eze 27:10
xS Ge 10:2
yJer 31:10;
Da 11:18
zIsa 11:11
aS 1Ch 16:24;
S Isa 24:15
66:20
bS Isa 11:12;
S Jer 25:22;
Eze 34:13
cS Dt 33:19;
S Isa 2:2;
Jer 31:23

dS Ezr 2:66 eIsa 52:11 66:21 /S Ex 19:6; 1Pe 2:5,9 66:22
gS Isa 65:17; Heb 12:26-27; S 2Pe 3:13 hS Isa 48:19;
Jn 10:27-29; 1Pe 1:4-5 66:23 /Eze 46:1-3 /S Ps 22:29;
S Isa 19:21; S 44:5; Rev 15:4 66:24 kS Ps 110:6 /S Isa 1:2
mS Isa 14:11 nS Isa 1:31; S Mt 25:41; Mk 9:48*

w 17 Or *gardens behind one of your temples, and*
x 18 The meaning of the Hebrew for this clause is
uncertain.   **y** 19 Some Septuagint manuscripts *Put*
(Libyans); Hebrew *Pul*

See 51:20 and note.
66:16 *sword.* See 27:1; 34:6 and note. *execute judgment.*
The day of the Lord (see note on 2:11,17,20; cf. Eze
38:21–22).
66:17 *consecrate and purify themselves.* By special rituals
required by their pagan religion. Cf. 2Ch 30:17. *gardens.*
See 1:29 and note. *flesh of pigs.* See 65:4 and note.
66:18 *their imaginations.* See 65:2 and note. Wicked
Israelites may be the antecedent. *gather all nations.* Cf. Joel
3:2; Zep 3:8; Zec 14:2. *see my glory.* Usually linked with
God's deliverance of his people (see 35:2–4; 40:5 and
notes).
66:19 *sign.* Possibly the banner of 11:10,12 (see note on
5:26; cf. Ps 74:4). Cf. the "sign of the Son of Man" (Mt
24:30) at the second coming. *those who survive.* After the
judgment of v. 16. Cf. Zec 14:16. *Tarshish.* See 23:6 and
note. *Libyans.* People who lived west of Egypt. See Na 3:9.
Lydians. People from either west-central Asia Minor (see Ge
10:13 and note) or Africa. *archers.* See Jer 46:9. *Tubal.*
Usually mentioned with Meshech (see Ge 10:2 and note;
Eze 27:13; 38:2–3; 39:1). It was probably a region southeast of the Black Sea. *islands.* See 11:11 and note. *proclaim*

my glory. See 42:12; 1Ch 16:24.
66:20 *bring all your brothers.* Gentiles will bring back the
remnant (see 11:11–12; 49:22; 60:4 and notes). *holy
mountain.* See 2:2–4 and note. *as an offering . . . to the
temple.* As the Israelites were to bring their tithes and offerings (see Dt 12:5–7).
66:21 *some of them.* A reference either to believing Jews
(see 61:6 and note) or to Gentiles as part of the church or
Messianic kingdom (see 1Pe 2:5,9 and notes).
66:22 *new heavens . . . new earth.* See 65:17 and note.
name and descendants endure. See 48:19 and note.
66:23 *New Moon.* See 1:14 and note. *all mankind . . .
bow down.* See 19:21; Zec 14:16 and notes.
66:24 Quoted in part in Mk 9:48. *go out and look.* The
Valley of Hinnom (Hebrew *ge' hinnom*, from which the
word "Gehenna" comes) was located southwest of
Jerusalem and became a picture of hell. See Ne 11:30; Jer
7:32. *dead bodies.* See 5:25; 34:3. *rebelled.* See 1:2 and
note; 24:20. *worm will not die.* There will be everlasting
torment. See 14:11; 48:22; 50:11; 57:21. *fire . . .
quenched.* See 1:31 and note; Mt 3:12. *loathsome.* The
Hebrew for this word is translated "contempt" in Da 12:2.

JEREMIAH

Author and Date

The book preserves an account of the prophetic ministry of Jeremiah, whose personal life and struggles are known to us in greater depth and detail than those of any other OT prophet. The meaning of his name is uncertain. Suggestions include "The LORD exalts" and "The LORD establishes," but a more likely proposal is "The LORD throws," either in the sense of "hurling" the prophet into a hostile world or of "throwing down" the nations in divine judgment for their sins. Jeremiah's prophetic ministry began in 626 B.C. and ended sometime after 586 (see notes on 1:2-3). His ministry was immediately preceded by that of Zephaniah. Habakkuk was a contemporary, and Obadiah may have been also. Since Ezekiel began his ministry in Babylon in 593 he too was a late contemporary of the great prophet in Jerusalem. How and when Jeremiah died is not known; Jewish tradition, however, asserts that while living in Egypt he was put to death by being stoned (cf. Heb 11:37).

Jeremiah was a priest, a member of the household of Hilkiah. His hometown was Anathoth (1:1), so he may have been a descendant of Abiathar (1Ki 2:26), a priest during the days of King Solomon. The Lord commanded Jeremiah not to marry and raise children because the impending divine judgment on Judah would sweep away the next generation (16:1-4). Primarily a prophet of doom, he attracted only a few friends, among whom were Ahikam (26:24), Gedaliah (Ahikam's son, 39:14) and Ebed-Melech (38:7-13; cf. 39:15-18). Jeremiah's closest companion was his faithful secretary, Baruch, who wrote down Jeremiah's words as the prophet dictated them (36:4-32). He was advised by Jeremiah not to succumb to the temptations of ambition but to be content with his lot (ch. 45). He also received from Jeremiah and deposited for safekeeping a deed of purchase (32:11-16), and accompanied the prophet on the long road to exile in Egypt (43:6-7). It is possible that Baruch was also responsible for the final compilation of the book of Jeremiah itself, since no event recorded in chs. 1-51 occurred after 580 B.C. (ch. 52 is an appendix added by a later hand).

Given to self-analysis and self-criticism (10:24), Jeremiah has revealed a great deal about his character and personality. Although timid by nature (1:6), he received the Lord's assurance that he would become strong and courageous (1:18; 6:27; 15:20). In his "confessions" (11:18-23; 12:1-4; 15:10-21; 17:12-18; 18:18-23; 20:7-18) he laid bare the deep struggles of his inmost being, sometimes making startlingly honest statements about his feelings toward God (12:1; 15:18). On occasion, he engaged in calling for redress against his personal enemies (12:1-3; 15:15; 17:18; 18:19-23)—a practice that explains the origin of the English word "jeremiad," referring to a denunciatory tirade or complaint. Jeremiah, so often characterized by anguish of spirit (4:19; 9:1; 10:19-20; 23:9), has justly been called the "weeping prophet." But it is also true that the memory of his divine call (1:17) and the Lord's frequent reaffirmations of his commissioning as a prophet (see, e.g., 3:12; 7:2,27-28; 11:2,6; 13:12-13; 17:19-20) made Jeremiah fearless in the service of his God (cf. 15:20).

Background

Jeremiah began prophesying in Judah halfway through the reign of Josiah (640-609 B.C.) and continued throughout the reigns of Jehoahaz (609), Jehoiakim (609-598), Jehoiachin (598-597) and Zedekiah (597-586). It was a period of storm and stress when the doom of entire nations—including Judah itself—was being sealed. The smaller states of western Asia were often pawns in the power plays of such imperial giants as Egypt, Assyria and Babylon, and the time of Jeremiah's ministry was no exception. Ashurbanipal, last of the great Assyrian rulers, died in 627. His successors were no match for Nabopolassar, the founder of the Neo-Babylonian empire, who began his rule in 626 (the year of Jeremiah's call to prophesy). Soon after Assyria's capital city Nineveh fell under the onslaught of a coalition of Babylonians and Medes in 612, Egypt (no friend of Babylon) marched northward in an attempt to rescue Assyria, which was near destruction. King Josiah of Judah made the mistake of trying to stop the Egyptian advance, and his untimely death near Megiddo in 609 at the hands of Pharaoh

Neco II was the sad result (2Ch 35:20-24). Jeremiah, who had found a kindred spirit in the godly Josiah and had perhaps proclaimed the messages recorded in 11:1-8; 17:19-27 during the king's reformation movement, lamented Josiah's death (2Ch 35:25).

Josiah's son Jehoahaz (see NIV text note on 22:11), also known as Shallum, is mentioned only briefly in the book of Jeremiah (22:10b-12), and then in an unfavorable way. Neco put Jehoahaz in chains and made Eliakim, another of Josiah's sons, king in his place, renaming him Jehoiakim. Jehoahaz had ruled for a scant three months (2Ch 36:2), and his reign marks the turning point in the court's attitude toward Jeremiah. Once the king's friend and confidant, the prophet now entered a dreary round of persecution and imprisonment, alternating with only brief periods of freedom (20:1-2; 26:8-9; 32:2-3; 33:1; 36:26; 37:12-21; 38:6-13,28).

Jehoiakim was relentlessly hostile toward Jeremiah. On one occasion, when an early draft of the prophet's writings was being read to Jehoiakim (36:21), the king used a scribe's knife to cut the scroll apart, three or four columns at a time, and threw it piece by piece into the firepot in his winter apartment (vv. 22-23). At the Lord's command, however, Jeremiah simply dictated his prophecies to Baruch a second time, adding "many similar words" to them (v. 32).

Just prior to this episode in Jeremiah's life, an event of extraordinary importance took place that changed the course of history: In 605 B.C., the Egyptians were crushed at Carchemish on the Euphrates by Nebuchadnezzar (46:2), the gifted general who succeeded his father Nabopolassar as ruler of Babylon that same year. Neco returned to Egypt with heavy losses, and Babylon was given a virtually free hand in western Asia for the next 70 years. Nebuchadnezzar besieged Jerusalem in 605, humiliating Jehoiakim (Da 1:1-2) and carrying off Daniel and his three companions to Babylon (Da 1:3-6). Later, in 598-597, Nebuchadnezzar attacked Jerusalem again, and the rebellious Jehoiakim was heard of no more. His son Jehoiachin ruled Judah for only three months (2Ch 36:9). Jeremiah foretold the captivity of Jehoiachin and his followers (22:24-30), a prediction that was later fulfilled (24:1; 29:1-2).

Mattaniah, Jehoiachin's uncle and a son of Josiah, was renamed Zedekiah and placed on Judah's throne by Nebuchadnezzar in 597 B.C. (37:1; 2Ch 35:11-14). Zedekiah, a weak and vacillating ruler, sometimes befriended Jeremiah and sought his advice but at other times allowed the prophet's enemies to mistreat and imprison him. Near the end of Zedekiah's reign, Jeremiah entered into an agreement with him to reveal God's will to him in exchange for his own personal safety (38:15-27). Even then the prophet was under virtual house arrest until Jerusalem was captured in 586 (38:28).

While trying to flee the city, Zedekiah was overtaken by the pursuing Babylonians. In his presence his sons were executed, after which he himself was blinded by Nebuchadnezzar (39:1-7). Nebuzaradan, commander of the imperial guard, advised Jeremiah to live with Gedaliah, whom Nebuchadnezzar had made governor over Judah (40:1-6). After a brief reign, Gedaliah was murdered by his opponents (ch. 41). Others in Judah feared Babylonian reprisal and fled to Egypt, taking Jeremiah and Baruch with them (43:4-7). By that time the prophet was probably over 70 years old. His last recorded words are found in 44:24-30, the last verse of which is the only explicit reference in the Bible to Pharaoh Hophra, who ruled Egypt from 589 to 570 B.C.

Themes and Message

Referred to frequently as "Jeremiah the prophet" in the book that bears his name (20:2; 25:2; 28:5,10-12,15; 29:1,29; 32:2; 34:6; 36:8,26; 37:2,3,6; 38:9-10,14; 42:2,4; 43:6; 45:1; 46:1,13; 47:1; 49:34; 50:1) and elsewhere (2Ch 36:12; Da 9:2; Mt 2:17; 27:9; see Mt 16:14), Jeremiah was ever conscious of his call from the Lord (1:5; 15:19) to be a prophet. As such, he proclaimed words that were spoken first by God himself (19:2) and were therefore certain of fulfillment (28:9; 32:24). Jeremiah had only contempt for false prophets (14:13-18; 23:13-40; 27:14-18) like Hananiah (ch. 28) and Shemaiah (29:24-32). Many of his own predictions were fulfilled in the short term (e.g., 16:15; 20:4; 25:11-14; 27:19-22; 29:10; 34:4-5; 43:10-11; 44:30; 46:13), and others were—or will yet be—fulfilled in the long term (e.g., 23:5-6; 30:8-9; 31:31-34; 33:15-16).

As hinted earlier, an aura of conflict surrounded Jeremiah almost from the beginning. He lashed out against the sins of his countrymen (44:23), scoring them severely for their idolatry (16:10-13,20; 22:9; 32:29; 44:2-3,8,17-19,25)—which sometimes even involved sacrificing their children to foreign gods (7:30-34). But Jeremiah loved the people of Judah in spite of their sins, and he prayed for them (14:7,20) even when the Lord told him not to (7:16; 11:14; 14:11).

Judgment is one of the all-pervasive themes in Jeremiah's writings, though he was careful to point out that repentance, if sincere, would postpone the inevitable. His counsel of submission to Babylon and his message of "life as usual" for the exiles of the early deportations branded him as a traitor in

the eyes of many. Actually, of course, his advice against rebellion marked him as a true patriot, a man who loved his countrymen too much to stand by silently and watch them destroy themselves. By warning them to submit and not rebel, Jeremiah was revealing God's will to them—always the most sensible prospect under any circumstances.

For Jeremiah, God was ultimate. The prophet's theology conceived of the Lord as the Creator of all that exists (10:12-16; 51:15-19), as all-powerful (32:27; 48:15; 51:57), as everywhere present (23:24). Jeremiah ascribed the most elevated attributes to the God whom he served (32:17-25), viewing him as the Lord not only of Judah but also of the nations (5:15; 18:7-10; 25:17-28; chs. 46-51).

At the same time, God is very much concerned about individual people and their accountability to him. Jeremiah's emphasis in this regard (see, e.g., 31:29-30) is similar to that of Ezekiel (see Eze 18:2-4), and the two men have become known as the "prophets of individual responsibility." The undeniable relationship between sin and its consequences, so visible to Jeremiah as he watched his beloved Judah in her death throes, made him—in the pursuit of his divine vocation—a fiery preacher (5:14; 20:9; 23:29) of righteousness, and his oracles have lost none of their power with the passing of the centuries.

Called to the unhappy task of announcing the destruction of the kingdom of Judah (thoroughly corrupted by the long and evil reign of Manasseh and only superficially affected by Josiah's efforts at reform), it was Jeremiah's commission to lodge God's indictment against his people and proclaim the end of an era. At long last, the Lord was about to inflict on the remnant of his people the ultimate covenant curse (see Lev 26:31-33; Dt 28:49-68). He would undo all that he had done for them since the day he brought them out of Egypt. It would then seem that the end had come, that Israel's stubborn and uncircumcised (unconsecrated) heart had sealed her final destiny, that God's chosen people had been cast off, that all the ancient promises and covenants had come to nothing.

But God's judgment of his people (and the nations), though terrible, was not to be the last word, the final work of God in history. Mercy and covenant faithfulness would triumph over wrath. Beyond the judgment would come restoration and renewal. Israel would be restored, the nations that crushed her would be crushed, and the old covenants (with Israel, David and the Levites) would be honored. God would make a new covenant with his people in which he would write his law on their hearts (31:31-34) and thus consecrate them to his service. The house of David would rule them in righteousness, and faithful priests would serve. God's commitment to Israel's redemption was as unfailing as the secure order of creation (ch. 33).

Jeremiah's message illumined the distant as well as the near horizon. It was false prophets who proclaimed peace to a rebellious nation, as though the God of Israel's peace was indifferent to her unfaithfulness. But the very God who compelled Jeremiah to denounce sin and pronounce judgment was the God who authorized him to announce that the divine wrath had its bounds, its 70 years. Afterward forgiveness and cleansing would come—and a new day, in which all the old expectations, aroused by God's past acts and his promises and covenants, would yet be fulfilled in a manner transcending all God's mercies of old.

Literary Features

Jeremiah is the longest book in the Bible, containing more words than any other book. Although a number of chapters were written mainly in prose (chs. 7; 11; 16; 19; 21; 24-29; 32-45), including the appendix (ch. 52), most sections are predominantly poetic in form. Jeremiah's poetry is as lofty and lyrical as any found elsewhere in Scripture. A creator of beautiful phrases, he has given us an abundance of memorable passages (e.g., 2:13,26-28; 7:4,11,34; 8:20,22; 9:23-24; 10:6-7,10,12-13; 13:23; 15:20; 17:5-9; 20:13; 29:13; 30:7,22; 31:3,15,29-30,31-34; 33:3; 51:10).

Poetic repetition was used by Jeremiah with particular skill (see, e.g., 4:23-26; 51:20-23). He understood the effectiveness of repeating a striking phrase over and over. An example is "sword, famine and plague," found in 15 separate verses (14:12; 21:7,9; 24:10; 27:8,13; 29:17-18; 32:24,36; 34:17; 38:2; 42:17,22; 44:13). He made use of cryptograms (see NIV text notes on 25:26; 51:1,41) on appropriate occasions. Alliteration and assonance were also a part of his literary style, examples being *zarim wezeruha* ("foreigners . . . to winnow her," 51:2) and *pahad wapahat wapah* ("Terror and pit and snare," 48:43; see note on Isa 24:17).

Like Ezekiel, Jeremiah was often instructed to use symbolism to highlight his message: a ruined and useless belt (13:1-11), a smashed clay jar (19:1-12), a yoke of straps and crossbars (ch. 27), large stones in a brick pavement (43:8-13). Symbolic value is also seen in the Lord's commands to Jeremiah not

to marry and raise children (16:1-4), not to enter a house where there is a funeral meal or where there is feasting (16:5-9), and to buy a field in his hometown, Anathoth (32:6-15). Similarly, the Lord used visual aids in conveying his message to Jeremiah: potter's clay (18:1-10), two baskets of figs (ch. 24).

Outline

Unlike Ezekiel, the oracles in Jeremiah are not arranged in chronological order. Had they been so arranged, the sequence of sections within the book would have been approximately as follows: 1:1-7:15; ch. 26; 7:16-20:18; ch. 25; chs. 46-51; 36:1-8; ch. 45; 36:9-32; ch. 35; chs. 21-24; chs. 27-31; 34:1-7; 37:1-10; 34:8-22; 37:11-38:13; 39:15-18; chs. 32-33; 38:14-39:14; 52:1-30; chs. 40-44; 52:31-34. The outline below represents an analysis of the book of Jeremiah in its present canonical order.

1 The words of Jeremiah son of Hilkiah, one of the priests at Anathoth *a* in the territory of Benjamin. ²The word of the Lord came *b* to him in the thirteenth year of the reign of Josiah *c* son of Amon king of Judah, ³and through the reign of Jehoiakim *d* son of Josiah king of Judah, down to the fifth month of the eleventh year of Zedekiah *e* son of Josiah king of Judah, when the people of Jerusalem went into exile. *f*

The Call of Jeremiah

⁴The word of the Lord came to me, saying,

⁵"Before I formed you in the womb *g* I
　　knew *a h* you,
　before you were born *i* I set you
　　apart; *j*

I appointed you as a prophet to the
　　nations. *k* "

⁶"Ah, Sovereign Lord," I said, "I do not know how to speak; *l* I am only a child." *m* ⁷But the Lord said to me, "Do not say, 'I am only a child.' You must go to everyone I send you to and say whatever I command you. ⁸Do not be afraid *n* of them, for I am with you *o* and will rescue *p* you," declares the Lord. *q*

⁹Then the Lord reached out his hand and touched *r* my mouth and said to me, "Now, I have put my words in your mouth. *s* ¹⁰See, today I appoint you over nations *t* and kingdoms to uproot *u* and tear down, to destroy and overthrow, to build and to plant." *v*

¹¹The word of the Lord came to me: "What do you see, Jeremiah?" *w*

Cross references (center column):

1:1 *a*S Jos 21:18
1:2 *b*Eze 1:3;
Hos 1:1; Joel 1:1
*c*S 2Ki 22:1
1:3 *d*S 2Ki 23:34
*e*S 2Ki 24:17
*f*Ezr 5:12;
Jer 52:15
1:5 *g*S Ps 139:13
*h*Ps 139:16
*i*S Isa 49:1
*j*Jn 10:36
*k*ver 10;
Jer 25:15-26
1:6 *l*S Ex 3:11;
S 6:12 *m*1Ki 3:7
1:8 *n*S Ge 15:1;
S Jos 8:1
*o*S Ge 26:3;
S Jos 1:5;
Jer 15:20 *p*ver 19;
Jer 15:21; 26:24;
36:26; 42:11
1:9 *r*S Isa 6:7
*s*S Ex 4:12
1:10 *t*Jer 25:17;
46:1 *u*Jer 12:17
*v*Jer 18:7-10;
24:6; 31:4,28
1:11 *w*Jer 24:3;
Am 7:8

*a*5 Or *chose*

1:1—3 The background and setting of Jeremiah's call are stated concisely but comprehensively.
1:1 *The words of.* See 36:10; see also Ne 1:1; Ecc 1:1; Am 1:1; cf. Dt 1:1. *Jeremiah.* For the meaning of the name see Introduction: Author and Date. Nine other OT men had the same name (see 1Ch 5:24; 12:4,10,13; Ne 10:2; 12:1,34), two of whom were the prophet's contemporaries (Jer 35:3; 52:1). *Hilkiah.* Means "The Lord is my portion." For Hilkiah's possible relationship to a priestly house dating back to King Solomon see Introduction: Author and Date. Two other men named Hilkiah (a common OT name) were also Jeremiah's contemporaries (see 29:3; Ezr 7:1 and note). *priests.* Like Ezekiel (Eze 1:3) and Zechariah (see Introduction to Zechariah: Author), Jeremiah was both prophet and priest. *Anathoth.* See 11:21—23; 32:6—9. The Hebrew word is the plural form of the name of the Canaanite deity Anat(h), goddess of war. Anathoth had had priestly connections in Israel as early as the times of Joshua (Jos 21:18) and Solomon (1Ki 2:26), and its pagan origins had presumably been almost forgotten by Jeremiah's time. Present-day Anata, three miles northeast of Jerusalem, preserves the ancient name, though the ancient site was about half a mile southwest of Anata. *Benjamin.* Anathoth was one of the four Levitical towns in the tribal territory of Benjamin (Jos 21:17—18), and after the exile Benjamites settled there again (Ne 11:31—32).
1:2 *The word of the Lord came.* The most common way of introducing a divine oracle at the beginning of a prophetic book (see Eze 1:3; Jnh 1:1; Hag 1:1; Zec 1:1; cf. Hos 1:1; Joel 1:1; Mic 1:1; Zep 1:1). *to him.* Beginning in v. 4, Jeremiah speaks in the first person (see, e.g., vv. 11,13; 2:1). *thirteenth year.* 626 b.c. (see 25:3). *Josiah.* See 3:6; 36:2. He was the last good and godly king of Judah. Jeremiah sympathized with and supported his attempts at spiritual reformation and renewal (see 22:15b—16), which began in earnest in 621 (see 2Ki 22:3—23:25; 2Ch 34:8—35:19; cf. 2Ch 34:3—7).
1:3 *Jehoiakim.* His predecessor (Jehoahaz) and successor (Jehoiachin) are not mentioned, since they each reigned only three months. In contrast to his father Josiah, Jehoiakim was a wicked ruler (see 2Ki 23:36—37; 2Ch 36:5)—as Jeremiah discovered almost immediately (see Introduction: Background; see also 22:13—15a,17—19; 26:20—23). *fifth month of the eleventh year.* Ab (July-August), 586 b.c. (see 52:12). *Zedekiah.* The last king of Judah (see Introduction: Background), as wicked in his own way as Jehoiakim (see

52:1—2; 2Ch 36:11—14; see also Jer 24:8; 37:1—2). *exile.* The main captivity of Judah's people coincided with the destruction of Jerusalem and Solomon's temple by Nebuchadnezzar in 586 (see 2Ki 25:8—11).
1:4—19 The account of Jeremiah's call includes two prophetic visions (vv. 10—16) and some closing words of exhortation and encouragement (vv. 17—19).
1:4 See note on v. 2.
1:5 See Jdg 13:5; Gal 1:15. *I formed you.* See Isa 49:5. God's creative act (see Ge 2:7; Ps 119:73) is the basis of his sovereign right (see 18:4—6; Isa 43:21) to call Jeremiah into his service. *I knew you.* In the sense of making Jeremiah the object of his choice (see NIV text note). The Hebrew verb used here is translated "chosen" in Ge 18:19; Am 3:2. *I appointed you.* The Hebrew for this verb is not the same as that in v. 10, but both refer to the commissioning of a prophet. *prophet.* Lit. "one who has been called" to be God's spokesman (see Ex 7:1—2; 1Sa 9:9 and notes). *nations.* Although Judah's neighbors are probably the primary focus (see 25:8—38; chs. 46—51), Judah herself is not excluded.
1:6 *not know how to speak.* Like Moses (Ex 4:10), Jeremiah claimed inability to be a prophet; God nevertheless made him his spokesman (15:19). *only a child.* See 1Ki 3:7. Jeremiah's objection is denied immediately by the Lord (v. 7).
1:7 Youth and inexperience do not disqualify when God calls (see 1Ti 4:12); he equips and sustains those he commissions.
1:8 *Do not be afraid.* See 10:5; 30:10; 40:9; 42:11; 46:27—28; 51:46; see also Isa 35:4 and note; 41:10. *I am with you.* See v. 19; 15:20. God's promise of his continuing presence should calm the fears of the most reluctant of prophets (see Ex 3:12; see also note on Ge 26:3). *rescue.* See v. 19; 15:20; 39:17. The Lord does not promise that Jeremiah will not be persecuted or imprisoned, but that no serious physical harm will come to him.
1:9 *touched my mouth.* Either in prophetic vision (see note on v. 11) or figuratively—or both (cf. Isa 6:7). *I have put my words in your mouth.* Continues the figure of speech begun earlier in the verse and provides a classic description of the relationship between the Lord and his prophet (see 5:14; Ex 4:15; Nu 22:38; 23:5,12,16; Dt 18:18; Isa 51:16; cf. 2Pe 1:21).
1:10 *appoint.* See note on v. 5. *uproot and tear down . . .*

"I see the branch of an almond tree," I replied.

¹²The LORD said to me, "You have seen correctly, for I am watching[b][x] to see that my word is fulfilled."

¹³The word of the LORD came to me again: "What do you see?"[y]

"I see a boiling pot, tilting away from the north," I answered.

¹⁴The LORD said to me, "From the north[z] disaster will be poured out on all who live in the land. ¹⁵I am about to summon all the peoples of the northern kingdoms," declares the LORD.

"Their kings will come and set up their
    thrones
  in the entrance of the gates of
    Jerusalem;
they will come against all her
    surrounding walls
  and against all the towns of Judah.[a]
¹⁶I will pronounce my judgments[b] on my
    people
  because of their wickedness[c] in
    forsaking me,[d]
in burning incense to other gods[e]

and in worshiping[f] what their hands
    have made.[g]

¹⁷"Get yourself ready! Stand up and say[h] to them whatever I command you. Do not be terrified[i] by them, or I will terrify you before them. ¹⁸Today I have made you[j] a fortified city, an iron pillar and a bronze wall to stand against the whole land—against the kings of Judah, its officials, its priests and the people of the land. ¹⁹They will fight against you but will not overcome[k] you, for I am with you[l] and will rescue[m] you," declares the LORD.

Israel Forsakes God

2 The word[n] of the LORD came to me: ²"Go and proclaim in the hearing of Jerusalem:

" 'I remember the devotion of your
    youth,[o]
  how as a bride you loved me
and followed me through the desert,[p]
  through a land not sown.
³Israel was holy[q] to the LORD,[r]

Cross references (center column):

1:12 xS Job 29:2;
Jer 44:27
1:13 yJer 24:3;
Zec 4:2; 5:2
1:14 zS Isa 14:31
1:15 aJer 4:16;
9:11; 10:22
1:16 bJer 4:12
cS Ge 6:5;
Jer 44:5
dJer 2:13; 17:13
eS Ex 20:3;
Jer 7:9; 19:4;
44:3

fS Nu 25:3
gPs 115:4-8;
S 135:15
1:17 hver 7;
Jer 7:27; 26:2,15;
42:4 iS Dt 31:6;
S 2Ki 1:15
1:18 jS Isa 50:7
1:19 kS Ps 129:2
lS Ge 26:3;
Isa 43:2;
Jer 20:11 mS ver
8; S Pr 20:22;
Ac 26:17
2:1 nIsa 38:4;
Eze 1:3; Mic 1:1
2:2 oPs 71:17;
Isa 54:4; Jer 3:4;
Eze 16:8-14,60;
Hos 2:15; 11:1;
Rev 2:4
pS Ex 13:21;
S Dt 1:19
2:3 qS Dt 7:6
rS Ex 19:6;
S Dt 7:6

b 12 The Hebrew for *watching* sounds like the Hebrew for *almond tree.*

---

destroy and overthrow . . . build and . . . plant. See 12:14–15,17; 18:7–10; 24:6; 31:28; 42:10; 45:4. The first two pairs of verbs are negative, stressing the fact that Jeremiah is to be primarily a prophet of doom, while the last pair is positive, indicating that he is also to be a prophet of restoration—even if only secondarily. The first verb ("uproot") is the opposite of the last ("plant"), and fully half of the verbs ("tear down," "destroy," "overthrow") are the opposite of "build."

1:11 *What do you see . . . ?* Often spoken by the Lord (or his representative) to introduce a prophetic vision (see v. 13; Am 7:8; 8:2; Zec 4:2; 5:2).

1:12 *watching.* See NIV text note. Just as the almond tree (v. 11) blooms first in the year (and therefore "wakes up" early—the Hebrew word for "watching" means to be wakeful), so the Lord is ever watchful to make sure that his word is fulfilled.

1:13 *pot.* The Hebrew for this word is translated "caldron" in Job 41:31 and stresses its large size (see Eze 24:3–5).

1:14 *From the north disaster.* See note on Isa 41:25. *will be poured out.* The Hebrew for this word has a similar sound to that for "boiling" in v. 13. Although the verb usually means "be opened," in Isa 14:17 it is translated "let . . . go," a meaning similar to that in this verse. *land.* Judah (see v. 15).

1:15 *northern kingdoms.* Since Assyria posed a minimal threat to Judah after the death of Ashurbanipal in 627 B.C., reference is most likely to Babylon and her allies. *set up their thrones in . . . the gates of Jerusalem.* For the fulfillment see 39:3. Since the gateway of a city was the place where its ruling council sat (see notes on Ge 19:1; Ru 4:1), the Babylonians replaced Judah's royal authority with their own (cf. 43:10; 49:38).

1:16 *my judgments on my people.* God, sovereign over his own, judges his own for their sins, using the Babylonians as his agents of judgment. *burning incense to other gods.* A common feature of pagan worship (e.g., 7:9; 11:12–13,17; 18:15; 19:13; 32:29; 44:17). *what their hands have made.*

Idols (see 16:19–20; 25:6; 2Ki 22:17; 2Ch 33:22; Isa 46:6).

1:17 *Get yourself ready!* Lit. "Tighten your belt around your waist!" For related expressions see Ex 12:11; 1Ki 18:46; 2Ki 4:29; 9:1; Job 38:3; 40:7.

1:18 *fortified city.* A symbol of security and impregnability (see 5:17; Pr 18:11,19). *iron pillar.* Unique in the OT, the expression signifies dignity and strength. *bronze wall.* See 15:20. Jeremiah would be able to withstand the abuse and persecution that his divine commission would evoke, even though his enemies themselves would be "bronze and iron" (6:28). *kings . . . officials . . . priests . . . people.* The whole nation would defy the prophet and his God (see, e.g., 2:26; 23:8; 32:32).

1:19 See note on v. 8; see also 15:20.

2:1—6:30 It is generally agreed that these chapters are among Jeremiah's earliest discourses, delivered during the reign of Josiah (3:6). The basic theme is the virtually total apostasy of Judah (chs. 2–5), leading inevitably to divine retribution through foreign invasion (ch. 6).

2:1–3:5 The wickedness and backsliding of God's people are vividly portrayed in numerous colorful figures of speech.

2:1 See note on 1:2.

2:2 *devotion.* The Hebrew for this word refers to the most intimate degree of loyalty, love and faithfulness that can exist between two people or between an individual and the Lord. *youth . . . as a bride.* Early in her history, Israel had enjoyed a close and cordial relationship with the Lord, who is often described figuratively as Israel's husband (3:14; 31:32; Isa 54:5; Hos 2:16). *you loved me.* But later God's people forsook him and loved "foreign gods" (v. 25), tragically abandoning their first love (cf. Rev 2:4). *followed me.* But later they followed "worthless idols" (vv. 5,8), "the Baals" (v. 23). *desert.* Sinai (see v. 6).

2:3 *holy to the LORD.* Set apart to him and his service (see notes on Ex 3:5; Lev 11:44; Dt 7:6). *firstfruits.* Just as the "best of the firstfruits" of Israel's crops were to be brought to the Lord (Ex 23:19; see Nu 18:12; 2Ch 31:5; Eze 44:30),

the firstfruits^s of his harvest;
all who devoured^t her were held
guilty,^u
and disaster overtook them,'"
declares the Lord.

⁴Hear the word of the Lord, O house of
Jacob,
all you clans of the house of Israel.

⁵This is what the Lord says:

"What fault did your fathers find in me,
that they strayed so far from me?
They followed worthless idols^v
and became worthless^w themselves.
⁶They did not ask, 'Where is the Lord,
who brought us up out of Egypt^x
and led us through the barren
wilderness,
through a land of deserts^y and rifts,^z
a land of drought and darkness,^c
a land where no one travels^a and no
one lives?'
⁷I brought you into a fertile land
to eat its fruit and rich produce.^b
But you came and defiled my land
and made my inheritance
detestable.^c
⁸The priests did not ask,
'Where is the Lord?'

Those who deal with the law did not
know me;^d
the leaders^e rebelled against me.
The prophets prophesied by Baal,^f
following worthless idols.^g

⁹"Therefore I bring charges^h against you
again,"
declares the Lord.
"And I will bring charges against
your children's children.
¹⁰Cross over to the coasts of Kittim^{d i}
and look,
send to Kedar^{e j} and observe closely;
see if there has ever been anything
like this:
¹¹Has a nation ever changed its gods?
(Yet they are not gods^k at all.)
But my people have exchanged their^f
Glory^l
for worthless idols.
¹²Be appalled at this, O heavens,
and shudder with great horror,"
declares the Lord.
¹³"My people have committed two sins:
They have forsaken^m me,
the spring of living water,ⁿ

2:3 ^sLev 23:9-14; Jas 1:18; Rev 14:4 | ^tIsa 41:11; Jer 10:25; 30:16 | ^uJer 50:7
2:5 ^vS Dt 32:21; S 1Sa 12:21; Ps 31:6; ^w2Ki 17:15
2:6 ^xS Ex 6:6; Hos 13:4 | ^yS Dt 1:19 | ^zS Dt 32:10 | ^aJer 51:43
2:7 ^bS Nu 13:27; Dt 8:7-9; 11:10-12 | ^cPs 106:34-39; Jer 3:9; 7:30; 16:18; Eze 11:21; 36:17
2:8 ^dS 1Sa 2:12; Jer 4:22 | ^eJer 3:15; 23:1; 25:34; 50:6 | ^fS 1Ki 18:22 | ^gver 25; S Isa 40:19; S 56:10; Jer 5:19; 9:14; 16:19; 22:9
2:9 ^hJer 25:31; Hos 4:1; Mic 6:2
2:10 ⁱS Ge 10:4 | ^jS Ge 25:13
2:11 ^kS Isa 37:19; Jer 16:20; Gal 4:8 | ^lS 1Sa 4:21; Ro 1:23
2:13 ^mS Dt 31:16; S Isa 65:11 | ⁿS Isa 12:3; Jn 4:14

^c6 Or *and the shadow of death* ^d10 That is, Cyprus and western coastlands ^e10 The home of Bedouin tribes in the Syro-Arabian desert ^f11 Masoretic Text; an ancient Hebrew scribal tradition *my*

---

so also the people themselves were his first and choicest treasure (cf. Jas 1:18; Rev 14:4). *disaster overtook them.* See, e.g., Ex 17:8–16.

2:4 *Hear.* A common divine imperative in prophetic writings, summoning God's people—as well as the nations—into his courts to remind them of their legal obligations to him and, when necessary, to pass judgment on them (see, e.g., 7:2; 17:20; 19:3; 21:11; 22:2,29; 31:10; 42:15; 44:24,26; Isa 1:10; Eze 13:2; Hos 4:1; Am 7:16).

2:5 *This is what the Lord says.* The so-called messenger formula, introducing God's word through the prophet. Though frequent in overall occurrence, its use is restricted to Jeremiah, Isaiah (e.g., 7:7), Ezekiel (e.g., 2:4), Amos (e.g., 1:3), Obadiah (1), Micah (3:5), Nahum (1:12), Haggai (e.g., 1:2), Zechariah (e.g., 1:3) and Malachi (1:4). *strayed.* See 4:1; 23:13,32; 31:19; 50:6; Isa 53:6; Eze 34:4–6,16; 1Pe 2:25. *followed worthless idols.* See also note on v. 2. "Worthless" is Jeremiah's favorite way of describing idols (8:19; 10:8,15; 14:22; 16:19; 51:18). *became worthless themselves.* See 2Ki 17:15. Idolaters are no better than the idols they worship (see Ps 115:8).

2:6 *Lord ... brought us up out of Egypt.* The Lord, Israel's Redeemer (see notes on Ge 2:4; Ex 3:15), freed his people from Egyptian bondage so that they might serve him alone (Ex 20:2–6). *led us.* As a shepherd leads his sheep (see v. 17; Dt 8:15; Ps 23:2–3). *land of deserts ... land of ... darkness.* The desert often symbolized darkness with its attendant dangers, including death (v. 31; 9:10; 12:12; 17:6; 23:10; Ps 44:19).

2:7 *fertile.* The Hebrew for this word is *karmel,* translated "orchards" in 48:33 and also used as the name of a place (see Isa 33:9 and note). Rendered "fruitful land" in 4:26, it is the opposite of a desert. *defiled my land.* Made it ceremo-

nially unclean (see 3:1–2,9; 16:18; see also note on Lev 4:12). The promised land, given by God to Israel as a legacy and often intimately associated with the people themselves (see especially 12:7–9,14–15). *detestable.* See note on Lev 7:21.

2:8 No one consulted the Lord (see v. 6). *priests ... leaders ... prophets.* See note on 1:18. *Those who deal with the law.* Priests (see Dt 31:11 and note). *leaders.* Lit. "shepherds," a term used elsewhere to denote rulers (23:1–4; 49:19; 50:44; see especially Eze 34:1–10, 23–24). *by Baal.* In the name of Baal (cf. 11:21; 14:15; 23:25; 26:9). *worthless.* Lit. "unprofitable" (see v. 11; the Hebrew for this word is not the same as that in v. 5, though the meaning is similar).

2:9 *bring charges against.* See note on v. 4; see also 25:31; Hos 4:1; 12:2; Mic 6:2.

2:10 *Kittim.* Represents the western nations and regions. *Kedar.* Represents the eastern nations and regions (see NIV text note; see also 49:28; Isa 21:16 and note).

2:11 *Has ... gods?* A rhetorical question, clearly expecting a negative answer and emphasizing how incredible is Judah's practice of substituting idolatry for the worship of the Lord. *their Glory.* God (see Ps 106:20; Hos 4:7; see also 1Sa 15:29). *worthless.* See note on v. 8.

2:12 *Be appalled ... O heavens.* See note on Isa 1:2; see also Mic 6:1–2 and note. The Hebrew for these phrases offers a striking play on words: *shommu shamayim.*

2:13 See 1:16. *me, the spring of living water.* See 17:13. God himself provides life-giving power to his people (see Ps 36:9; see also note on Jn 4:10; Isa 55:1 and note; Rev 21:6). *broken cisterns.* Watertight plaster was used to keep cisterns from losing water. Idols, like broken cisterns, will always fail their worshipers; by contrast, God provides life abundant and unfailing.

and have dug their own cisterns,
        broken cisterns that cannot hold
        water.
[14]Is Israel a servant, a slave[o] by birth?
        Why then has he become plunder?
[15]Lions[p] have roared;
        they have growled at him.
They have laid waste[q] his land;
        his towns are burned[r] and
        deserted.[s]
[16]Also, the men of Memphis[g][t] and
        Tahpanhes[u]
    have shaved the crown of your
        head.[h]
[17]Have you not brought this on
        yourselves[v]
    by forsaking[w] the LORD your God
        when he led you in the way?
[18]Now why go to Egypt[x]
        to drink water from the Shihor[i]?[y]
And why go to Assyria[z]
        to drink water from the River[j]?[a]
[19]Your wickedness will punish you;
        your backsliding[b] will rebuke[c] you.
Consider then and realize
        how evil and bitter[d] it is for you
when you forsake[e] the LORD your God
        and have no awe[f] of me,"
                declares the Lord,
                the LORD Almighty.

[20]"Long ago you broke off your yoke[g]
        and tore off your bonds;[h]

you said, 'I will not serve you!'[i]
Indeed, on every high hill[j]
        and under every spreading tree[k]
    you lay down as a prostitute.[l]
[21]I had planted[m] you like a choice vine[n]
        of sound and reliable stock.
How then did you turn against me
        into a corrupt,[o] wild vine?
[22]Although you wash[p] yourself with
        soda[q]
        and use an abundance of soap,
    the stain of your guilt is still before
        me,"
                declares the Sovereign LORD.[r]
[23]"How can you say, 'I am not defiled;[s]
        I have not run after the Baals'?[t]
See how you behaved in the valley;[u]
        consider what you have done.
You are a swift she-camel
        running[v] here and there,
[24]a wild donkey[w] accustomed to the
        desert,[x]
    sniffing the wind in her craving—
        in her heat who can restrain her?
    Any males that pursue her need not tire
        themselves;
        at mating time they will find her.
[25]Do not run until your feet are bare

Cross references (center column):

2:14 oEx 4:22; Jer 31:9
2:15 pJer 4:7; 50:17 qS Isa 1:7 rS 2Ki 25:9 sS Lev 26:43
2:16 tS Isa 19:13 uJer 43:7-9
2:17 vJer 4:18 wS Isa 1:28; Jer 17:13; 19:4
2:18 xS Isa 30:2 yS Jos 13:3 zS 2Ki 16:7; Hos 5:13; 7:11; 8:9 aS Isa 7:20
2:19 bJer 3:11, 22; 7:24; 11:10; 14:7; Hos 14:4 cIsa 3:9; 59:12; Hos 5:5 dS Job 20:14; Am 8:10 eJer 19:4 fS Ps 36:1
2:20 gS Lev 26:13 hPs 2:3; Jer 5:5
iS Job 21:14 jIsa 57:7; Jer 3:23; 17:2 kS Dt 12:2 lS Isa 1:21; Eze 16:15
2:21 mS Ex 15:17 nS Ps 80:8 oS Isa 5:4
2:22 pS Ps 51:2; La 1:8,17 qS Job 9:30 rJer 17:1
2:23 sS Pr 30:12 tver 25; Jer 9:14; 23:27 uS 2Ki 23:10; Jer 7:31; 19:2; 31:40 vver 33; Jer 31:22
2:24 wS Ge 16:12; Jer 14:6

xS Job 39:6

g16 Hebrew Noph   h16 Or have cracked your skull
i18 That is, a branch of the Nile   j18 That is, the Euphrates

---

2:14 *Is . . . birth?* Another rhetorical question (see note on v. 11), again expecting a negative answer in the light of God's redemptive acts during the period of the exodus (see Ex 6:6; 20:2). *plunder.* To Assyria and Egypt (see vv. 15–16).

2:15 *Lions.* Possibly literal (see 2Ki 17:25–26), though probably here symbolizing Assyria (see v. 18; 50:17; see also notes on 4:7; Isa 15:9). *roared . . . growled.* See Am 3:4. *laid waste his land.* See 4:7; 18:16; 50:3. *towns are burned and deserted.* The Hebrew for this phrase is very similar to that in 4:7, rendered there "towns will lie in ruins without inhabitant" (cf. 22:6).

2:16 *Memphis.* See 44:1; 46:14,19; see also note on Isa 19:13. *Tahpanhes.* Probably the city later called Daphnai by the Greeks, located just south of Lake Menzaleh in the eastern delta region of Egypt and known today as Tell Defneh (see 43:7–9; 44:1; 46:14; Eze 30:18). *shaved the crown of your head.* Figurative for bringing disgrace and devastation (see 47:5; 48:37; see also notes on Isa 3:17; 7:20).

2:17 *he led you.* See note on v. 6. *the way.* See Ex 18:8; 23:20; Dt 1:33.

2:18 See v. 36. The tendency of Israel or Judah to seek help alternately from Egypt and Assyria was not restricted to Jeremiah's time (see, e.g., Hos 7:11; 12:2). *drink water.* Provided by enemies, whether national or spiritual, rather than by God (see v. 13; Isa 8:6–8 and notes).

2:19 *backsliding.* See 3:22; 5:6; 14:7. The word implies repeated apostasy.

2:20—3:5 The rebellion of Judah against God is vividly portrayed by Jeremiah with the use of numerous figures of speech.

2:20 Like a stubborn draft animal (see Hos 4:16), Judah refuses to obey the Lord's commands. *broke off your yoke and tore off your bonds.* See 5:5; see also 31:18; cf. Ps 2:3. Judah has broken God's law and violated his covenant. *on every high hill and under every spreading tree.* Locales of pagan worship (see 1Ki 14:23; 2Ki 17:10; Eze 6:13). *as a prostitute.* Ritual prostitution was a particularly detestable practice (see, e.g., Hos 4:10–14).

2:21 See Isa 5:1–7; see also Ps 80:8–16; Eze 17:1–10; Hos 10:1–2; cf. Jn 15:1–8. *choice vine.* See Isa 5:2. The Hebrew for this word refers to a grape of exceptional quality. *wild.* Lit. "foreign." A vine symbolizing Israel should not be like a vine symbolizing Israel's enemies (see Dt 32:32).

2:22 *soda . . . soap.* Mineral alkali and vegetable alkali respectively. Sins can be removed and forgiven (see Ps 51:2, 7; Isa 1:18), but only when the sinner repents and confesses (see Pr 28:13; cf. 1Jn 1:7,9).

2:23 *defiled.* Ceremonially unclean (see 19:13; see also note on Lev 4:12). *run after.* See note on v. 2; see also v. 25. *Baals.* See 9:14; see also note on Jdg 2:11. *the valley.* Probably the Hinnom Valley (see note on Jos 15:5), known also as the Valley of Ben Hinnom (7:31–32; 19:2,6; 32:35). *running here and there.* Instead, the people of Judah should have been obeying the Lord, not turning aside either "to the right or to the left" (Dt 28:14).

2:24 *wild donkey.* An unruly (see Ge 16:12) and intractable (see Job 39:5–8) animal. *accustomed to the desert.* See 14:6; Job 24:5. *sniffing the wind.* The picture is one of active searching, not passive waiting (see Hos 2:7,13).

2:25 *your feet are bare.* You wear out your sandals. *It's no use!* See 18:12; see also note on Isa 57:10. *I love foreign*

and your throat is dry.
But you said, 'It's no use!*y*
    I love foreign gods,*z*
    and I must go after them.'*a*

26"As a thief is disgraced*b* when he is
        caught,
    so the house of Israel is disgraced—
    they, their kings and their officials,
        their priests*c* and their prophets.*d*
27They say to wood,*e* 'You are my
        father,'
    and to stone,*f* 'You gave me birth.'
They have turned their backs*g* to me
        and not their faces;*h*
    yet when they are in trouble,*i* they say,
        'Come and save*j* us!'
28Where then are the gods*k* you made for
        yourselves?
    Let them come if they can save you
        when you are in trouble!*l*
For you have as many gods
    as you have towns,*m* O Judah.

29"Why do you bring charges against me?
    You have all*n* rebelled against me,"
                            declares the LORD.
30"In vain I punished your people;
    they did not respond to correction.*o*
Your sword has devoured your
        prophets*p*
    like a ravening lion.

31"You of this generation, consider the
word of the LORD:

    "Have I been a desert to Israel
        or a land of great darkness?*q*

Why do my people say, 'We are free to
        roam;
    we will come to you no more'?*r*
32Does a maiden forget her jewelry,
    a bride her wedding ornaments?
Yet my people have forgotten*s* me,
    days without number.
33How skilled you are at pursuing*t* love!
    Even the worst of women can learn
        from your ways.
34On your clothes men find
    the lifeblood*u* of the innocent poor,
    though you did not catch them
        breaking in.*v*
Yet in spite of all this
35   you say, 'I am innocent;*w*
    he is not angry with me.'
But I will pass judgment*x* on you
    because you say, 'I have not
        sinned.'*y*
36Why do you go about so much,
    changing*z* your ways?
You will be disappointed by Egypt*a*
    as you were by Assyria.
37You will also leave that place
    with your hands on your head,*b*
    for the LORD has rejected those you
        trust;
    you will not be helped*c* by them.

3   "If a man divorces*d* his wife
        and she leaves him and marries
            another man,
    should he return to her again?
    Would not the land be completely
        defiled?*e*

Center cross-references:

2:25 *y*S Isa 57:10
*z*Dt 32:16;
Jer 3:13; 14:10
*a*S ver 8,S 23
2:26 *b*Jer 48:27;
La 1:7;
Eze 16:54; 36:4
*c*Eze 22:26
*d*Jer 32:32;
44:17,21
2:27 *e*Jer 10:8
*f*Jer 3:9
*g*S 1Ki 14:9;
S 2Ch 29:6;
Ps 14:3; Eze 8:16
*h*Jer 18:17;
32:33; Eze 7:22
*i*Jdg 10:10;
Isa 26:16
*j*Isa 37:20;
Hos 5:15
2:28 *k*S Isa 45:20
*l*S Dt 32:37;
S Isa 40:19
*m*S 2Ki 17:29
2:29 *n*Jer 5:1;
6:13; Da 9:11;
Mic 3:11; 7:2
2:30
*o*S Lev 26:23
*p*S Ne 9:26;
S Jer 11:21;
Ac 7:52;
1Th 2:15
2:31 *q*Isa 45:19

*r*S Job 21:14
2:32 *s*S Dt 32:18;
S Isa 57:11
2:33 *t*S ver 23
2:34
*u*S 2Ki 21:16;
S Pr 6:17
*v*S Ex 22:2
2:35 *w*S Pr 30:12
*x*Isa 66:16;
Jer 25:31; 39:7;
45:5; Eze 17:20;
20:35; Joel 3:2
*y*S 2Sa 12:13;
1Jn 1:8,10
2:36 *z*Jer 31:22
*a*S Ps 108:12;
S Isa 30:2,3,7;
Jer 37:7
2:37 *b*2Sa 13:19
*c*Jer 37:7
3:1 *d*Dt 24:1-4
*e*S Ge 3:17

---

gods. As opposed to the love Judah was expected to express toward God under the terms of their covenant relationship (see, e.g., Dt 6:6; 7:7–13; Hos 2:14–3:1). *go after them.* See v. 23; see also note on v. 2.

2:26 *disgraced when he is caught.* See, e.g., Ex 22:3–4. The Hebrew word underlying "disgraced" means lit. "shame," a term often used as a pejorative synonym for the name of Baal, the chief god of Canaan (see 11:13 and note; Hos 9:10; see also note on Jdg 6:32). *kings ... officials ... priests ... prophets.* See note on 1:18.

2:27 See Isa 44:13–17; contrast Dt 32:6,18; Isa 64:8; Mal 2:10. *Come ... save.* See v. 28.

2:28 *as many gods as ... towns.* See 11:13; cf. 1Co 8:5. Every ancient Near Eastern town of any importance had its own patron deity (cf. Ac 19:28,34–35), and many towns were named after deities (see, e.g., note on 1:1).

2:29 *bring charges against.* Cf. v. 9; see 12:1; Job 33:13.

2:30 *I punished your people.* Cf. Heb 12:6. *did not respond to correction.* See 5:3. *sword has devoured your prophets.* See, e.g., 26:20–23; 2Ki 21:16; 24:4; see also Ne 9:26.

2:31 *generation.* Often has negative connotations (see, e.g., Dt 32:5). *Have I been a desert ... a land of great darkness?* On the contrary, the Lord led his people through the desert and its darkness (v. 6). The phrase "great darkness" translates the Hebrew for "darkness of the LORD" (i.e.,

darkness sent by the Lord; cf. 1Sa 26:12), just as "mighty flame" in SS 8:6 translates "flame of the LORD" (see NIV text note there).

2:32 See Isa 49:15,18 and notes. *bride.* Cf. v. 2. *my people have forgotten me.* See 18:15; see also 3:21; 13:25; Isa 17:10; Eze 22:12; 23:35; Hos 8:14. Israel was always to "remember" the Lord and all that he had done for her (Dt 7:18; 8:18) and so trust and worship him alone, but she often "forgot" him—put him out of mind (see Jdg 2:10; Hos 2:13).

2:33 *love.* Here, worship of pagan gods (see note on v. 20).

2:34 See Am 2:6–8; 4:1; 5:11–12. *catch them breaking in.* See Ex 22:2 and note.

2:36 *disappointed by Egypt ... by Assyria.* See vv. 15–18 and notes. The days of Ahaz (see 2Ch 28:21), and perhaps the days of Zedekiah (see 37:7), are in view here.

2:37 *with your hands on your head.* Ancient reliefs depict captives with wrists tied together above their heads. *those you trust.* Egypt and Assyria.

3:1 *If ... defiled?* Cf. Dt 24:1–4. Divorce and remarriage on a widespread scale defiles not only the participants but also the land in which they live (cf. v. 2; Lev 18:25–28). *lived as a prostitute.* See note on 2:20. *many.* See note on 2:28. *return to me.* Repent of your sins against me (see vv. 12–14,22; 4:1).

But you have lived as a prostitute with
　　many lovers[f] —
　　would you now return to me?"[g]
　　　　　　　　　declares the LORD.
[2]"Look up to the barren heights[h] and
　　see.
　Is there any place where you have
　　not been ravished?
By the roadside[i] you sat waiting for
　　lovers,
　sat like a nomad[k] in the desert.
You have defiled the land[j]
　　with your prostitution[k] and
　　wickedness.
[3]Therefore the showers have been
　　withheld,[l]
　and no spring rains[m] have fallen.
Yet you have the brazen[n] look of a
　　prostitute;
　you refuse to blush with shame.[o]
[4]Have you not just called to me:
　'My Father,[p] my friend from my
　　youth,[q]
[5]will you always be angry?[r]
　Will your wrath continue forever?'
This is how you talk,
　but you do all the evil you can."

Unfaithful Israel

[6]During the reign of King Josiah,[s] the
LORD said to me, "Have you seen what
faithless[t] Israel has done? She has gone up
on every high hill and under every spreading tree[u] and has committed adultery[v]
there. [7]I thought that after she had done all
this she would return to me but she did
not, and her unfaithful sister[w] Judah saw

it.[x] [8]I gave faithless Israel[y] her certificate
of divorce[z] and sent her away because of
all her adulteries. Yet I saw that her unfaithful sister Judah had no fear;[a] she also
went out and committed adultery. [9]Be-
cause Israel's immorality mattered so little
to her, she defiled the land[b] and committed adultery[c] with stone[d] and wood.[e]
[10]In spite of all this, her unfaithful sister
Judah did not return[f] to me with all her
heart, but only in pretense,[g]" declares the
LORD.[h]

[11]The LORD said to me, "Faithless Israel
is more righteous[i] than unfaithful[j]
Judah.[k] [12]Go, proclaim this message
toward the north:[l]

" 'Return,[m] faithless[n] Israel,' declares
　　　　the LORD,
　'I will frown on you no longer,
for I am merciful,'[o] declares the LORD,
　'I will not be angry[p] forever.
[13]Only acknowledge[q] your guilt—
　you have rebelled against the LORD
　　　your God,
you have scattered your favors to
　　　foreign gods[r]
　under every spreading tree,[s]
　and have not obeyed[t] me,' "
　　　　　　　　　declares the LORD.

[14]"Return,[u] faithless people," declares
the LORD, "for I am your husband.[v] I will

3:1 /S 2Ki 16:7;
S Isa 1:21;
Jer 2:25; 4:30;
La 1:2; Eze 16:26,
29; Hos 2:5,12;
3:1 gHos 2:7
3:2 hver 21
/Ge 38:14;
Eze 16:25 /ver 9
kS Nu 15:39;
S Isa 1:21
3:3 /Lev 26:19;
Jer 5:25; Am 4:7
mS Dt 11:14;
Jer 14:4; Joel 1:10
nEze 3:7; 16:30
oJer 6:15; 8:12;
Zep 2:1; 3:5
3:4 pver 19;
S Dt 32:6;
S Ps 89:26;
Isa 63:16; 64:8;
Jer 31:9 qS Jer 2:2
3:5 rS Ps 103:9;
S Isa 54:9
3:6 sS 1Ch 3:14
tver 12,22;
S Isa 24:16;
Jer 31:22; 49:4
uS Dt 12:2;
Jer 17:2;
Eze 20:28;
Hos 4:13
vS Lev 17:7;
Jer 2:20
3:7 wEze 16:46;
23:2,11

xAm 4:8
3:8 yJer 11:10
zS Dt 4:27;
S 24:1
aEze 16:47;
23:11
3:9 bver 2
cS Lev 17:7;
S Isa 1:21
dS Isa 57:6
eJer 2:27
3:10 fIsa 31:6;
Am 4:9; Hag 2:17
gJer 12:2;
Eze 33:31
hS 2Ki 17:19
3:11 iEze 16:52;
23:11 /ver 7
kS Jer 2:19
3:12 l2Ki 17:3-6
mver 14;

S Dt 4:30; Jer 31:21,22; Eze 14:6; 33:11; Hos 14:1 nS ver 6
oS 1Ki 3:26; S Ps 6:2 pS Ps 103:9; S Isa 54:9 **3:13**
qDt 30:1-3; Jer 14:20; 1Jn 1:9 rS Jer 2:25 sS Dt 12:2 rver 25;
Jer 22:21 **3:14** uS ver 12; S Job 22:23; Jer 4:1 vS Isa 54:5

k2 Or an Arab

3:2 *barren heights.* Places where pagan gods were consulted and worshiped (see v. 21; 12:12; Nu 23:3). *ravished.* Cf.
Dt 28:30. *By the roadside you sat.* See Ge 38:14 and note;
Pr 7:10,12. The connection of this imagery with ritual prostitution is made explicit in Eze 16:25. *like a nomad in the
desert.* Waiting in ambush to waylay a traveler (see Lk
10:30). *defiled the land.* See v. 9.
3:3 *showers have been withheld.* See 14:1-6; Am 4:7-8.
This is the reverse of God's gracious response to his people in
Hos 2:21; 6:3. *spring rains.* See note on Dt 11:14. *brazen
look.* See Pr 7:13.
3:4 *My Father.* See v. 19; contrast 2:27 and see note there.
Compared to the NT, the title "Father" for God is relatively
rare in the OT. However, it often occurs in personal
names—compound names that begin with Abi- (e.g., Abinadab and Abiram) refer to God as "(my) Father." *my friend.*
Claiming intimate association (see Ps 55:13; Pr 16:28; 17:9;
Mic 7:5); perhaps even claiming to be the Lord's faithful wife
(cf. Pr 2:17). *from my youth.* See note on 2:2.
3:5 *Will your wrath continue forever?* Not if God's people
repent (vv. 12-13).
3:6—6:30 The unfaithfulness of Judah (3:6–5:31) will ultimately bring the Babylonians as God's instrument of judgment (ch. 6).
3:6 *King Josiah.* See Introduction: Background; see also
note on 1:2. *faithless Israel.* The northern kingdom, de-

stroyed in 722–721 B.C. (see vv. 8,11–12). *on every high hill
and under every spreading tree . . . committed adultery.* See
note on 2:20.
3:7 *her unfaithful sister Judah.* The southern kingdom (see
vv. 8,10–11). Samaria (Israel's capital) and Jerusalem
(Judah's capital) are similarly compared as adulterous sisters
in Eze 23. *it.* Israel's adultery.
3:8 *certificate of divorce.* See v. 1 and note; see also Dt
24:1–14; Isa 50:1 and notes. *sent her away.* Into exile in
721 B.C. *Judah had no fear.* She refused to learn from Israel's
tragic experience.
3:9 *committed adultery with stone and wood.* Worshiped
pagan deities (see 2:27).
3:10 *in pretense.* Judah's response to Josiah's reform measures (see note on 1:2) was superficial and hypocritical.
3:11 *Israel is more righteous than . . . Judah.* See note on
v. 8; see also Eze 16:51–52; 23:11.
3:12 *Go, proclaim.* See 2:2. *north.* Assyria's northern
provinces, to which many Israelites had been exiled. *Return.*
Repent (see v. 13). *merciful.* The Hebrew for this word is
used of God elsewhere only in Ps 145:13,17, where it is
translated "loving." *not be angry forever.* See note on v. 5.
3:13 *scattered your favors.* See Eze 16:15,33–34. *foreign
gods.* See note on 2:25. *under every spreading tree.* See note
on 2:20.
3:14 *husband.* See 31:32; Hos 2:16–17. The Hebrew root

choose you—one from a town and two from a clan—and bring you to Zion. [15]Then I will give you shepherds [w] after my own heart, [x] who will lead you with knowledge and understanding. [16]In those days, when your numbers have increased greatly in the land," declares the LORD, "men will no longer say, 'The ark [y] of the covenant of the LORD.' It will never enter their minds or be remembered; [z] it will not be missed, nor will another one be made. [17]At that time they will call Jerusalem The Throne [a] of the LORD, and all nations [b] will gather in Jerusalem to honor [c] the name of the LORD. No longer will they follow the stubbornness of their evil hearts. [d] [18]In those days the house of Judah will join the house of Israel, [e] and together [f] they will come from a northern [g] land to the land [h] I gave your forefathers as an inheritance.

[19]"I myself said,

" 'How gladly would I treat you like sons
and give you a desirable land, [i]
the most beautiful inheritance [j] of any nation.'
I thought you would call me 'Father' [k]
and not turn away from following me.
[20]But like a woman unfaithful to her husband,
so you have been unfaithful [l] to me, O house of Israel,"
declares the LORD.

[21]A cry is heard on the barren heights, [m]

the weeping [n] and pleading of the people of Israel,
because they have perverted their ways
and have forgotten [o] the LORD their God.

[22]"Return, [p] faithless people;
I will cure [q] you of backsliding." [r]

"Yes, we will come to you,
for you are the LORD our God.
[23]Surely the idolatrous commotion on the hills [s]
and mountains is a deception;
surely in the LORD our God
is the salvation [t] of Israel.
[24]From our youth shameful [u] gods have consumed
the fruits of our fathers' labor—
their flocks and herds,
their sons and daughters.
[25]Let us lie down in our shame, [v]
and let our disgrace cover us.
We have sinned [w] against the LORD our God,
both we and our fathers; [x]
from our youth [y] till this day
we have not obeyed [z] the LORD our God."

4 "If you will return [a], O Israel, return to me,"
declares the LORD.
"If you put your detestable idols [b] out of my sight
and no longer go astray,
[2]and if in a truthful, just and righteous way

Cross references (center column):

3:15 [w]S Isa 31:4
[x]Ac 13:22
3:16 [y]S Nu 3:31; S 1Ch 15:25
[z]S Isa 65:17
3:17 [a]S Ps 47:8; Jer 17:12; 33:16; Eze 1:26; 43:7; 48:35 [b]S Isa 2:3; Mic 4:1
[c]S Ps 22:23; Jer 13:11; 33:9
[d]Ps 81:12; Jer 7:24; 9:14; 11:8; 13:10; 16:12; 18:12
3:18 [e]Jer 30:3; Eze 37:19
[f]S Isa 11:13; Jer 50:4
[g]Jer 16:15; 31:8
[h]Dt 31:7; S Isa 14:1; Eze 11:17; 37:22; Am 9:15
3:19 [i]S Dt 8:7
[j]Ps 106:24; Eze 20:6 [k]S ver 4; S Ex 4:22; S 2Sa 7:14
3:20 [l]S Isa 24:16
3:21 [m]ver 2

[n]Jer 31:18
[o]S Isa 57:11
3:22 [p]S ver 12; S Job 22:23
[q]S Isa 30:26; 57:18; Jer 33:6; Hos 6:1
[r]S Jer 2:19
3:23 [s]S Jer 2:20
[t]Ps 3:8; Jer 17:14
3:24 [u]Jer 11:13; Hos 9:10
3:25 [v]S Ezr 9:6; Jer 31:19; Da 9:7
[w]S Jdg 10:10; S 1Ki 8:47
[x]Jer 14:20
[y]S Ps 25:7; S Jer 22:21 [z]S ver 13; Eze 2:3
4:1 [a]S Dt 4:30; S 2Ki 17:13; S Hos 12:6
[b]S 2Ki 21:4; Jer 16:18; 35:15; Eze 8:5

---

underlying this word is *ba'al*. Instead of allowing God to be their husband, his people followed "the Baals" (2:23; see note on Jdg 2:11). *one . . . two*. A remnant will return (see note on Isa 10:20–22). *Zion*. Jerusalem.
3:15 See 23:4. *shepherds*. Rulers (see note on 2:8). *after my own heart*. Like David (see 1Sa 13:14; see also Eze 34:23; Hos 3:5).
3:16 *In those days*. The Messianic age (see v. 18; 31:29). *numbers have increased*. See 23:3; Eze 36:11. For the fuller meaning of the Hebrew underlying this phrase see note on Ge 1:28. *nor will another one be made*. The ark of the covenant, formerly symbolizing God's royal presence (see 1Sa 4:3 and NIV text note), will be irrelevant when the Messiah comes.
3:17 *Throne*. The Lord had been "enthroned between the cherubim" above the ark (see 1Sa 4:4 and note), but Jerusalem itself would someday be his throne. *all nations will gather*. See Zec 2:11; see also note on Isa 2:2–4. *they*. Israel. *follow the stubbornness of their evil hearts*. A stock phrase referring to Israel's disobedience and often involving the worship of pagan gods (see 9:14; 11:8; 13:10; 16:12; 18:12; 23:17).
3:18 *Judah will join . . . Israel*. In the Messianic age God's divided people will again be united (see, e.g., Isa 11:12; Eze 37:15–23; Hos 1:11). *northern land*. Where they had been exiles (see note on v. 12; see also 31:8). *land I gave . . . as an*

inheritance. See note on 2:7.
3:19 *sons*. Israel was the Lord's firstborn (see Ex 4:22; cf. Hos 11:1). *desirable land*. The Hebrew for this phrase is translated "pleasant land" in Ps 106:24; Zec 7:14. *beautiful inheritance*. Judah, Jerusalem, the people themselves—ideally, all were beautiful in God's eyes (see 6:2; 11:16). *Father*. See note on v. 4.
3:20 A concise summary of the story told in Hos 1–3.
3:21 *barren heights*. See note on v. 2. *weeping and pleading*. A description of repentance, verbalized in vv. 22b–25. *forgotten*. See note on 2:32.
3:22 See v. 14. *Return, faithless . . . backsliding*. Each of these three words is derived from the same Hebrew root, producing a striking series of puns. *I will cure you*. See 30:17; 33:6; Hos 6:1; 14:1,4. *Yes*. The people's repentance begins.
3:23 *commotion*. See, e.g., 1Ki 18:25–29. *in the LORD . . . is . . . salvation*. See Ge 49:18; Ps 3:8; Jnh 2:9 and note.
3:24 *our youth*. The period of the judges. *shameful gods*. See notes on 2:26; 11:13. *consumed the fruits*. False worship is costly, both financially and spiritually. *sons and daughters*. Often sacrificed to pagan gods (see note on 7:31).
3:25 *shame*. The Hebrew for this word is translated "shameful gods" in v. 24.
4:1 *go astray*. The Hebrew for this word implies wandering, as in Ge 4:12,14 (see NIV text note on Ge 4:16).

you swear,^{c} 'As surely as the LORD
  lives,'^{d}
then the nations will be blessed^e by
  him
and in him they will glory.^{f} "

^{3}This is what the LORD says to the men
of Judah and to Jerusalem:

"Break up your unplowed ground^g
  and do not sow among thorns.^{h}
^{4}Circumcise yourselves to the LORD,
  circumcise your hearts,^{i}
  you men of Judah and people of
    Jerusalem,
or my wrath^j will break out and burn
  like fire^k
because of the evil^l you have
  done—
  burn with no one to quench^m it.

Disaster From the North

^{5}"Announce in Judah and proclaim^n in
  Jerusalem and say:
  'Sound the trumpet^o throughout the
    land!'
Cry aloud and say:
  'Gather together!
Let us flee to the fortified cities!'^{p}
^{6}Raise the signal^q to go to Zion!
  Flee for safety without delay!
For I am bringing disaster^r from the
  north,^{s}
  even terrible destruction."

^{7}A lion^t has come out of his lair;^{u}
  a destroyer^v of nations has set out.

He has left his place
  to lay waste^w your land.
Your towns will lie in ruins^x
  without inhabitant.
^{8}So put on sackcloth,^{y}
  lament^z and wail,
for the fierce anger^a of the LORD
  has not turned away from us.

^{9}"In that day," declares the LORD,
  "the king and the officials will lose
    heart,^{b}
the priests will be horrified,
  and the prophets will be appalled."^{c}

^{10}Then I said, "Ah, Sovereign LORD,
how completely you have deceived^d this
people and Jerusalem by saying, 'You will
have peace,'^{e} when the sword is at our
throats."

^{11}At that time this people and Jerusalem
will be told, "A scorching wind^f from the
barren heights in the desert blows toward
my people, but not to winnow or cleanse;
^{12}a wind^g too strong for that comes from
me.^{l} Now I pronounce my judgments^h
against them."

^{13}Look! He advances like the clouds,^{i}
  his chariots^j come like a
    whirlwind,^{k}
his horses^l are swifter than eagles.^{m}

Cross references column:

4:2 ^{c}Dt 10:20;
S Isa 19:18; 65:16
^{d}S Nu 14:21;
Jer 5:2; 12:16;
44:26; Hos 4:15
^{e}S Ge 12:2;
Gal 3:8 /Jer 9:24
4:3 ^{g}Hos 10:12
^{h}Mk 4:18
4:4 ^{i}S Lev 26:41
/Zep 1:18; 2:2
^{k}S Job 41:21
^{l}S Ex 32:22
^{m}Isa 1:31;
Am 5:6
4:5 ^{n}Jer 5:20;
11:2,6 ^{o}S ver 21;
S Nu 10:2,7;
S Job 39:24
^{p}S Jos 10:20
4:6 ^{q}ver 21;
Ps 74:4;
S Isa 11:10; 31:9;
Jer 50:2
^{r}Jer 11:11; 18:11
^{s}S Isa 14:31;
Jer 50:3
4:7 ^{t}S 2Ki 24:1;
S Jer 2:15
^{u}Jer 25:38;
Hos 5:14; 13:7;
Na 2:12
^{v}Jer 6:26; 15:8;
22:7; 48:8; 51:1,
53; Eze 21:31;
25:7

^{w}S Isa 1:7;
Eze 12:20 ^{x}ver
29; S Lev 26:31;
S Isa 6:11
4:8 ^{y}1Ki 21:27;
S Isa 3:24;
Jer 6:26;
Eze 7:18; Joel 1:8
^{z}Jer 7:29; 9:20;
Am 5:1
^{a}S Isa 10:4;
S Jer 30:24
4:9 ^{b}S 1Sa 17:32
^{c}S Isa 29:9
4:10 ^{d}S Ex 5:23;
2Th 2:11
^{e}Isa 30:10;
Jer 6:14; 8:11;
14:13; 23:17;

Eze 13:10; Mic 3:5; 1Th 5:3 4:11 ^{f}S Ge 41:6; S Lev 26:33;
S Job 1:19 4:12 ^{g}S Isa 64:6 ^{h}Jer 1:16 4:13 ^{i}S 2Sa 22:10;
Isa 19:1 /Isa 66:15; Eze 26:10; Na 2:4 ^{k}S 2Ki 2:1 ^{l}Hab 3:8
^{m}S Dt 28:49; Hab 1:8

^{l}12 Or comes at my command

4:2 *truthful, just and righteous.* The piling up of qualifying
words underscores the need for repentance that is sincere
and not perfunctory. *As surely as the LORD lives.* See note on
Ge 42:15. *nations will be blessed by him.* Reflects the
language of the seventh of God's great promises to Abram
(see Ge 12:2–3 and note). Israel's repentance is a necessary
precondition for the ultimate blessing of the nations.
4:3 *Break up your unplowed ground.* Probably quoted
from Hos 10:12. *do not sow among thorns.* See Mt 13:7,22.
Openness to the Lord's overtures is necessary, as is total
commitment to him (see Eze 18:31).
4:4 *circumcise your hearts.* Consecrate your hearts (see
6:10 and NIV text note; 9:26; see also Ge 17:10 and note;
Dt 10:16; 30:6). *wrath will . . . burn with no one to quench.*
See 21:12; see also Isa 1:31; Am 5:6. *because of the evil you
have done.* Probably quoted from Dt 28:20.
4:5–31 The invaders from the north will bring God's
judgment against his unrepentant people (see ch. 6).
4:5 *Sound the trumpet.* To warn of impending doom (see
6:1; see also note on Joel 2:1). *flee to the fortified cities.* See
v. 6. To avoid capture by hostile troops, people living in the
countryside would take refuge in the nearest walled town
(see 5:17; 8:14; 34:7; 48:18).
4:6 See 6:1. *Raise the signal.* See note on Isa 5:26. *disaster
from the north.* The Babylonians (see 1:14; see also note on
Isa 41:25). *terrible destruction.* See 6:1; cf. 48:3; 50:22;
51:54.
4:7 *lion.* A symbol of Babylon (see note on 2:15). *destroy-*

er. Usually refers to Babylon (6:26; 15:8; 48:8,32), but in
51:1,56 it refers to Persia and her allies (see 51:48,53).
towns . . . without inhabitant. See note on 2:15; see also v.
25; 46:19.
4:8 *sackcloth.* See note on Ge 37:34. *anger . . . has not
turned away.* Contrast 2:35.
4:9 *In that day.* See note on Isa 2:11,17,20. *king . . .
officials . . . priests . . . prophets.* See note on 1:18.
4:10 *you have deceived.* Not directly, but through false
prophets (see, e.g., 1Ki 22:20–23 and note on 1Ki 22:23).
You will have peace. Here the words of false prophets, not of
God (see 14:13; 23:17; see also 6:13–14; 8:10–11).
throats. The Hebrew for this word is usually translated
"soul" or "life," but originally it had the meaning "throat,
neck" (see, e.g., Ps 69:1).
4:11 *scorching wind.* The sirocco or khamsin, a hot, dry
wind that brings sand and dust (see Ps 11:6; Isa 11:15; Jnh
4:8). *winnow.* See note on Ru 1:22.
4:12 *too strong for that.* Neither winnowing (separating
grain from chaff) nor cleansing (blowing dust from the grain),
God's judgments will sweep away good and bad alike.
4:13 *advances like the clouds.* Cf. Eze 38:16. *chariots . . .
like a whirlwind.* See 2Ki 2:11; 6:17; Ps 68:17; Isa 66:15.
horses are swifter than eagles. See Hab 1:8, where the
Babylonians (Hab 1:6) use horses that are "swifter than
leopards" and employ cavalry that "fly like a vulture" (the
Hebrew word for "vulture" is translated "eagle" in 4:13; see
Dt 28:49). *ruined.* See v. 20; 9:19; 48:1.

Woe to us! We are ruined! [n]

14O Jerusalem, wash [o] the evil from your
heart and be saved. [p]
How long [q] will you harbor wicked
thoughts?
15A voice is announcing from Dan, [r]
proclaiming disaster from the hills of
Ephraim. [s]
16"Tell this to the nations,
proclaim it to Jerusalem:
'A besieging army is coming from a
distant land, [t]
raising a war cry [u] against the cities of
Judah. [v]
17They surround [w] her like men guarding
a field,
because she has rebelled [x] against
me,' "
declares the LORD.
18"Your own conduct and actions [y]
have brought this upon you. [z]
This is your punishment.
How bitter [a] it is!
How it pierces to the heart!"

19Oh, my anguish, my anguish! [b]
I writhe in pain. [c]
Oh, the agony of my heart!
My heart pounds [d] within me,
I cannot keep silent. [e]
For I have heard the sound of the
trumpet; [f]
I have heard the battle cry. [g]
20Disaster follows disaster; [h]
the whole land lies in ruins. [i]
In an instant my tents [j] are destroyed,
my shelter in a moment.
21How long must I see the battle
standard [k]

and hear the sound of the trumpet? [l]

22"My people are fools; [m]
they do not know me. [n]
They are senseless children;
they have no understanding. [o]
They are skilled in doing evil; [p]
they know not how to do good." [q]

23I looked at the earth,
and it was formless and empty; [r]
and at the heavens,
and their light [s] was gone.
24I looked at the mountains,
and they were quaking; [t]
all the hills were swaying.
25I looked, and there were no people;
every bird in the sky had flown
away. [u]
26I looked, and the fruitful land was a
desert; [v]
all its towns lay in ruins [w]
before the LORD, before his fierce
anger. [x]

27This is what the LORD says:

"The whole land will be ruined, [y]
though I will not destroy [z] it
completely.
28Therefore the earth will mourn [a]
and the heavens above grow dark, [b]
because I have spoken and will not
relent, [c]
I have decided and will not turn
back. [d]"

Cross references (center column):

4:13 [n]ver 20,27;
Isa 6:11; 24:3;
Jer 7:34; 9:11,19;
12:11; 25:11;
44:6; Mic 2:4
4:14 [o]S Ru 3:3;
S Ps 51:2; Jas 4:8
[p]Isa 45:22
[q]S Ps 6:3
4:15 [r]S Ge 30:6
[s]Jer 31:6
4:16 [t]S Dt 28:49
[u]ver 19;
Eze 21:22
[v]S Jer 1:15
4:17 [w]S 2Ki 25:1,
4 [x]S 1Sa 12:15;
Jer 5:23
4:18 [y]Ps 107:17;
S Isa 1:28;
Jer 5:25 [z]Jer 2:17
[a]Jer 2:19
4:19 [b]Isa 22:4;
Jer 6:24; 9:10;
La 1:20
[c]S Job 6:10;
S 14:22; Jer 10:19
[d]S Job 37:1;
Jer 23:9
[e]S Job 4:2;
Jer 20:9 [f]S ver 21;
S Nu 10:2;
S Job 39:24 [g]S ver
16; Nu 10:9;
Jer 49:2; Zep 1:16
4:20 [h]S Dt 31:17
[i]S ver 13
[j]S Nu 24:5;
Jer 10:20; La 2:4
4:21 [k]S ver 6;
S Nu 2:2;
S Isa 18:3

[l]ver 5,19;
S Jos 6:20;
Jer 6:1; Hos 5:8;
Am 3:6; Zep 1:16
4:22 [m]Jer 5:21;
10:8 [n]S Isa 1:3;
27:11; Jer 2:8;
8:7; Hos 5:4; 6:6
[o]S Ps 14:4; S 53:2
[p]Jer 13:23;
S 1Co 14:20
[q]S Ps 36:3
4:23 [r]S Ge 1:2
[s]ver 28;
S Job 9:7; 30:26;
S Isa 5:30; 59:9;
La 3:2

4:24 [t]S Ex 19:18; S Job 9:6 4:25 [u]Jer 7:20; 9:10; 12:4;
Hos 4:3; Zep 1:3 4:26 [v]S Ge 13:10; Jer 12:4; 23:10
[w]S Isa 6:11 [x]Jer 12:13; 25:38 4:27 [y]S ver 13 [z]S Jer 26:44;
Jer 5:10,18; 12:12; 30:11; 46:28; Eze 20:17; Am 9:8 4:28
[a]Jer 12:4,11; 14:2; Hos 4:3 [b]S ver 23 [c]S Nu 23:19 [d]ver 8;
Jer 23:20; 30:24

4:14 *wash.* See 2:22 and note. *wicked thoughts.* Against
other people (see Pr 6:18; Isa 59:7).
4:15 *Dan.* Far away, close to the northern border of Israel
(see 8:16). *Ephraim.* A few miles north of Jerusalem. The
enemy, in the mind's eye of the prophet, is making fearfully
rapid progress toward the holy city.
4:16 *besieging army.* See Isa 1:8. *distant land.* Babylon.
raising a war cry. The Hebrew underlying this phrase is
translated "growled" in 2:15.
4:17 *surround her.* See 1:15.
4:19—26 A brief personal interlude, broken only by the
divine complaint in v. 22. Jeremiah voices his agony at the
approaching destruction of his beloved land and its people.
4:19 See 10:19—20. *anguish.* Often associated with labor
pangs, as here (see 6:24; 49:24; 50:43). *heart pounds.* See
Job 37:1; Ps 38:10; Hab 3:16. *sound of the trumpet.* See
note on v. 5.
4:20 *lies in ruins.* See v. 13; 9:19; 48:1. *shelter.* Lit. "tent
curtains" (as in Isa 54:2), usually made of goat hair (see Ex
26:7) and therefore strong enough to protect from cold and
rain (see 10:20).
4:21 *battle standard . . . sound of the trumpet.* See notes
on vv. 5–6.
4:22 The Lord speaks. *fools.* See NIV text note on Pr 1:7.

do not know me. See 2:8. Leaders and people alike had
committed the ultimate sin (see Isa 1:3; Hos 4:1). *senseless.*
See 5:21; 10:8,14,21; 51:17. *skilled in doing evil.* See Mic
7:3.
4:23—26 The striking repetition of "I looked" at the beginning of each verse ties this poem together and underscores its
visionary character, as the prophet sees his beloved land in
ruins after the Babylonian onslaught. Creation, as it were,
has been reversed.
4:23 *formless and empty.* The phrase occurs elsewhere
only in Ge 1:2 (see note there). In Jeremiah's vision, the
primeval chaos has returned. *light was gone.* Contrast Ge
1:3.
4:24 See Na 1:5.
4:25 *there were no people.* The Hebrew underlying this
phrase occurs elsewhere only in Ge 2:5, where it is translated "there was no man." Again, uncreation has replaced
creation.
4:26 *fruitful land.* See note on 2:7. *fierce anger.* See v. 8;
Isa 13:13; Na 1:6.
4:27 *not destroy it completely.* See 5:10,18; 30:11;
46:28. God's mercy tempers the total judgment envisioned
by Jeremiah in vv. 23–26.
4:28 *will not relent.* Unless his people repent (see 18:7–8).

29At the sound of horsemen and archers *e*
   every town takes to flight. *f*
Some go into the thickets;
   some climb up among the rocks. *g*
All the towns are deserted; *h*
   no one lives in them.

30What are you doing, *i* O devastated
   one?
Why dress yourself in scarlet
   and put on jewels *j* of gold?
Why shade your eyes with paint? *k*
   You adorn yourself in vain.
Your lovers *l* despise you;
   they seek your life. *m*

31I hear a cry as of a woman in labor, *n*
   a groan as of one bearing her first
      child—
the cry of the Daughter of Zion *o*
   gasping for breath, *p*
stretching out her hands *q* and saying,
   "Alas! I am fainting;
   my life is given over to murderers." *r*

Not One Is Upright

5 "Go up and down *s* the streets of
      Jerusalem,
look around and consider, *t*
   search through her squares.
If you can find but one person *u*
   who deals honestly *v* and seeks the
      truth,
   I will forgive *w* this city.
2Although they say, 'As surely as the
      LORD lives,' *x*
   still they are swearing falsely. *y* "

3O LORD, do not your eyes *z* look for
   truth?

You struck *a* them, but they felt no
   pain;
you crushed them, but they refused
   correction. *b*
They made their faces harder than
   stone *c*
   and refused to repent. *d*
4I thought, "These are only the poor;
   they are foolish, *e*
for they do not know *f* the way of the
   LORD,
   the requirements of their God.
5So I will go to the leaders *g*
   and speak to them;
surely they know the way of the LORD,
   the requirements of their God."
But with one accord they too had
   broken off the yoke
   and torn off the bonds. *h*
6Therefore a lion from the forest *i* will
   attack them,
a wolf from the desert will ravage *j*
   them,
a leopard *k* will lie in wait near their
   towns
to tear to pieces any who venture
   out,
for their rebellion is great
   and their backslidings many. *l*

7"Why should I forgive you?
   Your children have forsaken me
and sworn *m* by gods that are not
   gods. *n*
I supplied all their needs,
   yet they committed adultery *o*
   and thronged to the houses of
      prostitutes. *p*
8They are well-fed, lusty stallions,

Cross references (center column):

4:29 *e*S ver 13;
   Jer 6:23; 8:16
*f*2Ki 25:4
*g*S Ex 33:22;
   S 1Sa 26:20
*h*S ver 7;
   S Isa 6:12
4:30 *i*Isa 10:3-4
*j*Eze 16:11; 23:40
*k*S 2Ki 9:30
*l*Job 19:14;
   La 1:2; Eze 23:9,
   22 *m*S Ps 35:4
4:31 *n*S Ge 3:16;
   Jer 6:24; 13:21;
   22:23; 30:6;
   Mic 4:10
*o*S Ps 9:14
*p*Isa 42:14
*q*Isa 1:15; La 1:17
*r*S Dt 32:25;
   La 2:21
5:1 *s*2Ch 16:9;
   Eze 22:30
*t*Ps 45:10
*u*Ge 18:32;
   S Jer 2:29 *v*ver
   31; Jer 14:14;
   Eze 13:6
*w*S Ge 18:24
5:2 *x*S Jer 4:2
*y*S Lev 19:12
5:3 *z*2Ch 16:9
*a*S Isa 9:13
*b*S Lev 26:23
*c*Jer 7:26; 19:15;
   Eze 3:8-9; 36:26;
   Zec 7:12
*d*S 2Ch 28:22;
   S Isa 1:5;
   Eze 2:4-5;
   Am 4:6; Zec 7:11
5:4 *e*S ver 21;
   S Jer 4:22
*f*S Pr 10:21;
   S Isa 1:3
5:5 *g*Mic 3:1,9
*h*S Jer 2:20
5:6 *i*S Ps 17:12
*j*S Lev 26:22
*k*Hos 13:7
*l*Jer 14:7; 30:14
5:7 *m*S Jos 23:7
*n*Dt 32:21;
   Jer 2:11; 16:20;
   Gal 4:8
*o*S Nu 25:1
*p*Jer 13:27

4:29 *archers.* Babylon's evil deeds against Judah will some-day recoil on her (see 50:29). *Some go.* See Jdg 6:2; 1Sa 13:6; Isa 2:19,21. Even people living in fortified towns feel unsafe. *deserted.* Contrast Isa 62:4.
4:30 *paint.* Antimony, a black powder used to enlarge the eyes and make them more attractive (see 2Ki 9:30; Eze 23:40). *lovers.* The Hebrew root underlying this word is found elsewhere only in Eze 23:5,7,9,12,16,20, where it is used of Samaria and Jerusalem, the adulterous sisters (see notes on 2:20; 3:7) who "lusted" after foreign nations and their gods. *seek your life.* They are intent only on murdering you (see v. 31).
4:31 *Daughter of Zion.* A personification of Jerusalem and its inhabitants (see 6:2,23). *stretching out her hands.* In prayer for help (see Job 11:13).
5:1—31 Jeremiah resumes his vivid description of the wickedness of the people of Judah and Jerusalem.
5:1 See Zep 1:12. The Lord challenges anyone to find just one righteous person in Israel—a rhetorical way of charging that corruption pervaded the city (see Ps 14:1-3; Isa 64:6-7; Hos 4:1-2; Mic 7:2). *If you can find . . . I will forgive.* See Ge 18:26-32.
5:2 *As surely as the LORD lives.* See 4:2; see also Ge 42:15 and note. *they are swearing falsely.* In violation of Lev 19:12

(see note on Ex 20:7). The Hebrew underlying this phrase is translated "commit . . . perjury" in 7:9 (see NIV text note there).
5:3 *refused correction.* See 2:30. *made their faces harder than stone.* A striking portrayal of rebellion (see Eze 3:7-9).
5:4 *poor.* Concerned about basic physical needs (cf. 39:10; 40:7), they are uninformed of God's word and way. *foolish.* See 4:22; see also Nu 12:11 and NIV text note on Pr 1:7. *do not know . . . requirements of their God.* They are more ignorant than the birds of the heavens (see 8:7).
5:5 *leaders.* Lit. "great ones." Although possessing every advantage, they were no more righteous than the poorest of the common people. *broken . . . bonds.* See note on 2:20.
5:6 *lion . . . wolf . . . leopard.* See Lev 26:22; Eze 14:15; cf. 2Ki 17:25-26. *lie in wait.* The Hebrew for this phrase is translated "watching" in 1:12. *backslidings.* See 2:19; 3:22; 14:7. The word implies repeated apostasy.
5:7 *Why should I forgive you?* See v. 1. *gods that are not gods.* Idols (see 2:11). *I supplied . . . yet they.* See Dt 32:15-16; Hos 2:8. *committed adultery.* See note on 2:20.
5:8 Religious prostitution (v. 7; see Am 2:7) leads quite naturally to literal adultery, the breaking of God's law (see Ex 20:14,17). *lusty stallions.* See 13:27; 50:11; Eze 23:20.

each neighing for another man's
wife. *q*

⁹Should I not punish them for this?" *r*
declares the LORD.
"Should I not avenge *s* myself
on such a nation as this?

¹⁰"Go through her vineyards and ravage
them,
but do not destroy them completely. *t*
Strip off her branches,
for these people do not belong to the
LORD.
¹¹The house of Israel and the house of
Judah
have been utterly unfaithful *u* to me,"
declares the LORD.

¹²They have lied *v* about the LORD;
they said, "He will do nothing!
No harm will come to us; *w*
we will never see sword or famine. *x*
¹³The prophets *y* are but wind *z*
and the word is not in them;
so let what they say be done to
them."

¹⁴Therefore this is what the LORD God
Almighty says:

"Because the people have spoken these
words,
I will make my words in your
mouth *a* a fire *b*
and these people the wood it
consumes. *c*
¹⁵O house of Israel," declares the LORD,
"I am bringing a distant nation *d*
against you—
an ancient and enduring nation,
a people whose language *e* you do not
know,
whose speech you do not understand.
¹⁶Their quivers *f* are like an open grave;

all of them are mighty warriors.
¹⁷They will devour *g h* your harvests and
food,
devour *i j* your sons and daughters;
they will devour *k* your flocks and
herds,
devour your vines and fig trees. *l*
With the sword *m* they will destroy
the fortified cities *n* in which you
trust. *o*

¹⁸"Yet even in those days," declares the
LORD, "I will not destroy *p* you completely.
¹⁹And when the people ask, *q* 'Why has the
LORD our God done all this to us?' you will
tell them, 'As you have forsaken me and
served foreign gods *r* in your own land, so
now you will serve foreigners *s* in a land
not your own.'

²⁰"Announce this to the house of Jacob
and proclaim *t* it in Judah:
²¹Hear this, you foolish and senseless
people, *u*
who have eyes *v* but do not see,
who have ears but do not hear: *w*
²²Should you not fear *x* me?" declares the
LORD.
"Should you not tremble *y* in my
presence?
I made the sand a boundary for the
sea, *z*
an everlasting barrier it cannot cross.
The waves may roll, but they cannot
prevail;
they may roar, *a* but they cannot
cross it.
²³But these people have stubborn and
rebellious *b* hearts;
they have turned aside *c* and gone
away.
²⁴They do not say to themselves,
'Let us fear *d* the LORD our God,

5:8 *q*Jer 29:23;
Eze 22:11; 33:26
5:9 *r*ver 29;
Jer 9:9 *s*S Isa 57:6
5:10 *t*S Jer 4:27;
Am 9:8
5:11
*u*S 1Ki 19:10;
S Ps 73:27;
S Isa 24:16
5:12 *v*Isa 28:15
*w*Jer 23:17
*x*Jer 14:13; 27:8
5:13 *y*Jer 14:15
*z*S 2Ch 36:16;
S Job 6:26
5:14 *a*Hos 6:5
*b*S Ps 39:3;
Jer 23:29
*c*S Isa 1:31
5:15
*d*S Dt 28:49;
S 2Ki 24:2
*e*S Ge 11:7;
S Isa 28:11
5:16 /S Job 39:23

5:17 *g*S Isa 1:7;
Jer 8:16; 30:16
*h*Lev 26:16
*i*Jer 50:7,17
*j*Dt 28:32
*k*Dt 28:31
*l*S Nu 16:14;
Jer 8:13; Hos 2:12
*m*S Lev 26:25
*n*S Jos 10:20
*o*Dt 28:33
5:18 *p*S Jer 4:27
5:19 *q*S Dt 4:28;
S 1Ki 9:9
*r*S Jer 2:8; 15:14;
16:13; 17:4
*s*Dt 28:48
5:20 *t*S Jer 4:5
5:21 *u*ver 4;
S Dt 32:6;
S Jer 4:22;
Hab 2:18
*v*Isa 6:10;
Eze 12:2
*w*S Dt 29:4;
S Isa 42:20;
S Mt 13:15;
Mk 8:18
5:22 *x*S Dt 28:58
*y*S Job 4:14;
S Isa 64:2
*z*S Ge 1:9
*a*S Ps 46:3
5:23 *b*S Dt 21:18
*c*Ps 14:3
5:24 *d*Dt 6:24

5:10 *Go.* Addressed to Israel's enemies (see v. 15). *vineyards.* Vines and vineyards are often symbolic of Israel (see notes on 2:21; Isa 5:1). *not destroy them completely.* See v. 18; see also note on 4:27. *Strip off her branches.* See Isa 18:5; Jn 15:2,6. *people do not belong to the LORD.* See Hos 1:9.
5:11 See note on 3:7.
5:12 *He will do nothing.* Either good or bad (see Zep 1:12). *sword or famine.* Jeremiah introduces us to the first two elements of his characteristic triad: "sword, famine and plague" (see note on 14:12).
5:13 *prophets are but wind.* Like images of false gods (see Isa 41:29). *let what they say be done to them.* See note on 4:29; see also Ps 7:16; 54:5.
5:14 *my words in your mouth a fire.* In contrast to the total lack of God's word in the mouths of false prophets (v. 13). *consumes.* See note on Isa 1:31.
5:15 *distant nation.* See note on 4:16. *ancient and enduring nation.* Babylon, whose history reached back 2,000 years and more. *whose language you do not know.* See Dt 28:49

and note.
5:16 *open grave.* Symbolizing insatiability, destruction and death (see Ps 5:9; Pr 30:15–16).
5:17 *devour your sons and daughters.* Either as sacrifices to pagan gods (see note on 3:24), or as casualties of war (see 10:25). *fortified cities in which you trust.* See note on 4:5; see also Dt 28:52.
5:18 See v. 10; see also note on 4:27.
5:21 *Hear this.* See note on 2:4. *foolish and senseless.* See 4:22; see also NIV text note on Pr 1:7. *who have eyes . . . do not hear.* See note on Isa 6:10; see also Dt 29:4; Ps 115:4–8; 135:15–18.
5:22 *fear me.* See note on Ge 20:11. *boundary for the sea.* See Job 38:8–11; Ps 104:6–9.
5:23 Though the sea never crosses its divinely appointed boundaries, God's people have violated the limits he has set for them.
5:24 *God, who gives.* See v. 7 and note. *autumn and spring rains.* See 3:3; see also note on Dt 11:14. *regular weeks of harvest.* Perhaps the seven weeks between Pass-

who gives autumn and spring rains[e] in
    season,
who assures us of the regular weeks
    of harvest.'[f]
25Your wrongdoings have kept these
    away;
    your sins have deprived you of
      good.[g]

26"Among my people are wicked[h] men
    who lie in wait[i] like men who snare
      birds
    and like those who set traps[j] to
      catch men.
27Like cages full of birds,
    their houses are full of deceit;[k]
they have become rich[l] and powerful
28   and have grown fat[m] and sleek.
Their evil deeds have no limit;
    they do not plead the case of the
      fatherless[n] to win it,
    they do not defend the rights of the
      poor.[o]
29Should I not punish them for this?"
    declares the LORD.
"Should I not avenge[p] myself
    on such a nation as this?

30"A horrible[q] and shocking thing
    has happened in the land:
31The prophets prophesy lies,[r]
    the priests[s] rule by their own
      authority,
and my people love it this way.
    But what will you do in the end?[t]

Reference column

5:24 [e]S Lev 26:4; S 2Sa 1:21; Jas 5:7
[f]S Ge 8:22; Ac 14:17
5:25 [g]Ps 84:11
5:26 [h]S Mt 7:15
[i]S Ps 10:8
[j]Ecc 9:12; Jer 9:8; Hos 5:1; Mic 7:2
5:27 [k]Jer 8:5; 9:6
[l]Jer 12:1
5:28 [m]S Dt 32:15
[n]Zec 7:10
[o]Ex 22:21-24; S Ps 82:3; S Isa 1:23; Jer 7:6; Eze 16:49; Am 5:12
5:29 [p]S Isa 57:6
5:30 [q]ver 30-31; Jer 18:13; 23:14; Hos 6:10
5:31 [r]S ver 1; Mic 2:11 [s]La 4:13
[t]Hos 9:5

6:1 [u]S Nu 10:7; S Jer 4:21
[v]2Ch 14:2; Am 1:1 [w]Ne 3:14
[x]S Jer 4:6
6:2 [y]S Ps 9:14
[z]La 4:5
6:3 [a]Jer 12:10
[b]S 2Ki 25:4; Lk 19:43
6:4 [c]Jer 15:8; 22:7
6:6 [d]Dt 20:19-20
[e]S 2Sa 20:15; Jer 32:24; 52:4; Eze 26:8
[f]S Dt 28:33; Jer 25:38; Zep 3:1

Jerusalem Under Siege

6 "Flee for safety, people of Benjamin!
    Flee from Jerusalem!
Sound the trumpet[u] in Tekoa![v]
    Raise the signal over Beth
      Hakkerem![w]
For disaster looms out of the north,[x]
    even terrible destruction.
2I will destroy the Daughter of Zion,[y]
    so beautiful and delicate.[z]
3Shepherds[a] with their flocks will come
    against her;
    they will pitch their tents around[b]
      her,
    each tending his own portion."

4"Prepare for battle against her!
    Arise, let us attack at noon![c]
But, alas, the daylight is fading,
    and the shadows of evening grow
      long.
5So arise, let us attack at night
    and destroy her fortresses!"

6This is what the LORD Almighty says:

"Cut down the trees[d]
    and build siege ramps[e] against
      Jerusalem.
This city must be punished;
    it is filled with oppression.[f]
7As a well pours out its water,
    so she pours out her wickedness.

---

over and the Feast of Weeks (see Lev 23:15–16).
5:26 *traps.* Lit. "destroyer" (see, e.g., Ex 12:23) or "destruction" (see, e.g., Eze 21:31). *men.* Innocent (see Isa 29:21), godly, upright people (see Mic 7:2).
5:27 *cages.* Traps woven of wicker. The Hebrew for this word is translated "basket" in Am 8:1–2. *deceit.* Riches gained through extortion and deception (see Hab 2:6).
5:28 *grown fat and sleek.* Symbolic of prosperity (see Dt 32:15). *evil deeds have no limit.* See Ps 73:7. *they do not plead the case.* What the wicked will not do, God must do (see Dt 10:18)—and so must those who truly know and serve him (see 22:16; Jas 1:27).
5:29 Repeated from v. 9.
5:31 See 1:18 and note. *prophesy lies.* See 20:6 (often, and arrogantly, in God's name; see 23:25; 27:15; 29:9). *people love it this way.* See note on Am 4:5.
6:1–30 The prophet envisions the future Babylonian attack on Jerusalem.
6:1 The Lord speaks in vv. 1–3. Verse 1 is strongly reminiscent of 4:6 (see note there). But whereas in 4:6 the command was to seek protection in Jerusalem, in 6:1 the people are to flee from Jerusalem, because no place—not even the holy city itself—will be safe from the invader. *Benjamin.* The tribal territory bordering Judah north of Jerusalem. Jeremiah himself was from Benjamite territory (see 1:1). *Sound . . . Tekoa.* In the Hebrew there is a play on these words. Tekoa was the hometown of Amos (see Introduction to Amos: Author). *Raise . . . signal.* In the Hebrew there is a play on words, made possible by using a different Hebrew word (found also in Lachish Letter 4:10) for "signal" (caused by

the smoke of a fire; see Jdg 20:38,40) than the one used in 4:6. *Beth Hakkerem.* Mentioned elsewhere only in Ne 3:14 (see note there). *disaster . . . out of the north.* See 1:14 and note.
6:2 *destroy.* The Hebrew for this verb is found with the meaning "destroy" also in Hos 4:5. *Daughter of Zion.* See v. 23; see also note on 4:31. *delicate.* Used to describe the city of Babylon in Isa 47:1.
6:3 See 1:15. *Shepherds with their flocks.* Rulers (see note on 2:8) with their troops. *pitch.* The Hebrew for this verb continues the pun on "Tekoa" in v. 1 (see note on v. 8). *each . . . his own portion.* The Hebrew for this phrase is used similarly ("each . . . his own place") in Nu 2:17. *tending.* Grazing or depasturing, and thus destroying.
6:4 The invaders speak in vv. 4–5. *Prepare for.* Lit. "Consecrate" (also in Joel 3:9; Mic 3:5). Since ancient battles had religious connotations, soldiers had to prepare themselves ritually as well as militarily (see Dt 20:2–4; 1Sa 25:28). *at noon.* To take advantage of the element of surprise, since the usual time of attack was early in the morning.
6:5 *at night.* Since attacking soldiers normally retired for the night and resumed siege the following morning, the phrase underscores their eagerness and determination.
6:6 The Lord addresses the Babylonian troops. *siege ramps.* To help them bring up battering rams and scale Jerusalem's walls (see 33:4). *oppression.* Against its own people (see note on Isa 30:12).
6:7 *sickness and wounds.* Jerusalem suffers from spiritual decay and disease (see v. 14), and is not aware of it.

Violence[g] and destruction[h] resound in
  her;
her sickness and wounds are ever
  before me.
⁸Take warning, O Jerusalem,
  or I will turn away[i] from you
and make your land desolate
  so no one can live in it."

⁹This is what the LORD Almighty says:

"Let them glean the remnant[j] of Israel
  as thoroughly as a vine;
pass your hand over the branches again,
  like one gathering grapes."

¹⁰To whom can I speak and give
    warning?
  Who will listen[k] to me?
Their ears are closed[m][l]
  so they cannot hear.[m]
The word[n] of the LORD is offensive to
    them;
  they find no pleasure in it.
¹¹But I am full of the wrath[o] of the LORD,
  and I cannot hold it in.[p]

"Pour it out on the children in the
    street
  and on the young men[q] gathered
    together;
both husband and wife will be caught in
    it,
  and the old, those weighed down
    with years.[r]
¹²Their houses will be turned over to
    others,[s]
  together with their fields and their
    wives,[t]
when I stretch out my hand[u]
  against those who live in the land,"
    declares the LORD.

¹³"From the least to the greatest,
  all[v] are greedy for gain;[w]
prophets and priests alike,
  all practice deceit.[x]
¹⁴They dress the wound of my people
  as though it were not serious.
'Peace, peace,' they say,
  when there is no peace.[y]
¹⁵Are they ashamed of their loathsome
    conduct?
  No, they have no shame at all;
  they do not even know how to
    blush.[z]
So they will fall among the fallen;
  they will be brought down when I
    punish[a] them,"
      says the LORD.

¹⁶This is what the LORD says:

"Stand at the crossroads and look;
  ask for the ancient paths,[b]
ask where the good way[c] is, and walk
    in it,
  and you will find rest[d] for your souls.
But you said, 'We will not walk in it.'
¹⁷I appointed watchmen[e] over you and
    said,
  'Listen to the sound of the trumpet!'[f]
But you said, 'We will not listen.'[g]
¹⁸Therefore hear, O nations;
  observe, O witnesses,
  what will happen to them.
¹⁹Hear, O earth:[h]
  I am bringing disaster[i] on this people,
  the fruit of their schemes,[j]
because they have not listened to my
    words[k]
  and have rejected my law.[l]
²⁰What do I care about incense from
  Sheba[m]

6:7 gS Ps 55:9;
S Isa 58:4
hJer 20:8
6:8 iEze 23:18
6:9 jS Ge 45:7
6:10 kJer 7:13,
24; 35:15
lJer 4:4; Ac 7:51
mS Isa 42:20
nJer 15:10,15;
20:8
6:11 oJer 7:20;
15:17
pJob 32:20;
Jer 20:9
qS 2Ch 36:17;
S Isa 40:30
rLa 2:21
6:12 sS Dt 28:30;
Mic 2:4
t1Ki 11:4;
Jer 8:10; 29:23;
38:22; 43:6;
44:9,15
uLa 5:25;
Jer 21:5; 32:21;
Eze 6:14; 35:3;
Zep 1:4

6:13 vS Jer 2:29
wS Isa 56:11
xLa 4:13
6:14
yS Isa 30:10;
S Jer 4:10
6:15 zJer 3:3;
8:10-12; Mic 3:7;
Zec 13:4
a2Ch 25:16;
Jer 27:15
6:16 bJer 18:15
cS 1Ki 8:36;
S Ps 119:3
dS Jos 1:13;
S Isa 11:10;
Mt 11:29
6:17 eS Isa 52:8
/S Ex 20:18
gJer 11:7-8;
Eze 33:4; Zec 1:4
6:19 hS Dt 4:26;
Jer 22:29; Mic 1:2
iS Jos 23:15;
Jer 11:11; 19:3
/Pr 1:31
kJer 29:19
/Jer 8:9;
Eze 20:13;
Am 2:4
6:20 mS Ge 10:7

m 10 Hebrew *uncircumcised*

6:8 *Take warning.* The better part of wisdom (see v. 10; Ps 2:10). *turn away.* In sorrow, but also in disgust. The Hebrew for this phrase continues the pun on "Tekoa" in v. 1 (see note on v. 3). *desolate so no one can live in it.* See 22:6.
6:9 *glean.* See notes on Ru 2:2; Isa 17:5. *remnant.* See 11:23; 23:3; 31:7; 40:11,15; 42:2,15,19; 43:5; 44:7,12, 14,28; 50:20; see also note on Isa 10:20–22. *thoroughly.* Stopping just short of complete destruction (see 4:27; 5:10, 18; 30:11; 46:28). *vine.* Symbolic of Israel (see 2:21 and note; 5:10).
6:10 Jeremiah speaks. *give warning.* See note on v. 8. *ears are closed.* See NIV text note; see also 4:4 and note. The imagery of uncircumcised ears is found elsewhere only in Ac 7:51.
6:11 The prophet speaks, then the Lord resumes his speech (through v. 23). *full of the wrath.* See 25:15. *children . . . young men . . . husband and wife . . . old.* All will be judged, from youngest to oldest (see v. 13). *in the street.* Where children play (see 9:21; Zec 8:5).
6:12–15 Repeated almost verbatim in 8:10–12.
6:12 *houses . . . fields . . . wives.* See Ex 20:17; Dt 5:21.

turned over to others. As Dt 28:30 warned—one of the covenant curses. *stretch out my hand against.* To destroy (see 15:6).
6:13 See 1:18 and note.
6:14 *wound.* See note on v. 7. *Peace . . . when there is no peace.* A common message of false and greedy prophets (see Eze 13:10; Mic 3:5). The wicked, in any case, cannot expect to enjoy peace (see Isa 48:22; 57:21).
6:16 *ancient paths.* The tried and true ways of Judah's godly ancestors (see 18:15; Dt 32:7). *walk in it.* See Isa 30:21. *you will find rest for your souls.* Quoted by Jesus in Mt 11:29 (see Isa 28:12; cf. Ps 119:165).
6:17 *watchmen.* True prophets (see Eze 3:17; 33:7; Hab 2:1). *sound of the trumpet.* To warn of approaching danger (see v. 1; see also note on Joel 2:1).
6:18 *hear, O nations.* See Mic 1:2.
6:19 *rejected my law.* Disobeyed the law of Moses (see 8:8–9).
6:20 *Sheba.* Located in southwestern Arabia, it was the center of the spice trade (see Isa 60:6 and note). *calamus.* See SS 4:14; Isa 43:24 and notes. The Hebrew for this word

or sweet calamus [n] from a distant
land?
Your burnt offerings are not
acceptable; [o]
your sacrifices [p] do not please me." [q]

21Therefore this is what the LORD says:

"I will put obstacles before this people.
Fathers and sons alike will stumble [r]
over them;
neighbors and friends will perish."

22This is what the LORD says:

"Look, an army is coming
from the land of the north; [s]
a great nation is being stirred up
from the ends of the earth. [t]
23They are armed with bow and spear;
they are cruel and show no mercy. [u]
They sound like the roaring sea [v]
as they ride on their horses; [w]
they come like men in battle formation
to attack you, O Daughter of Zion. [x] "

24We have heard reports about them,
and our hands hang limp. [y]
Anguish [z] has gripped us,
pain like that of a woman in labor. [a]
25Do not go out to the fields
or walk on the roads,
for the enemy has a sword,

and there is terror on every side. [b]
26O my people, put on sackcloth [c]
and roll in ashes; [d]
mourn with bitter wailing [e]
as for an only son, [f]
for suddenly the destroyer [g]
will come upon us.

27"I have made you a tester [h] of metals
and my people the ore,
that you may observe
and test their ways.
28They are all hardened rebels, [i]
going about to slander. [j]
They are bronze and iron; [k]
they all act corruptly.
29The bellows blow fiercely
to burn away the lead with fire,
but the refining [l] goes on in vain;
the wicked are not purged out.
30They are called rejected silver, [m]
because the LORD has rejected
them." [n]

False Religion Worthless

7 This is the word that came to Jeremiah
from the LORD: 2"Stand [o] at the gate
of the LORD's house and there proclaim
this message:
"'Hear the word of the LORD, all you

Cross references

6:20 [n]S Ex 30:23
[o]Am 5:22;
Mal 1:9
[p]Ps 50:8-10;
Jer 7:21;
Mic 6:7-8
[q]S Isa 1:11;
Jer 14:12;
Hos 8:13; 9:4
6:21
[r]S Lev 26:37;
S Isa 8:14
6:22 [s]S Jer 4:6
[t]S Dt 28:49
6:23 [u]S Isa 13:18
[v]S Ps 18:4; S 93:3
[w]S Jer 4:29
[x]S Isa 10:32
6:24 [y]Isa 13:7
[z]S Jer 4:19
[a]S Jer 4:31;
50:41-43
6:25
[b]S Job 15:21;
S Ps 31:13;
Jer 49:29
6:26 [c]S Jer 4:8
[d]S Job 2:8;
Jer 25:34;
Eze 27:30;
Jnh 3:6 [e]Jer 9:1;
18:22; 20:16;
25:36
[f]S Ge 21:16
[g]S Ex 12:23;
S Jer 4:7
6:27 [h]Jer 9:7;
Zec 13:9
6:28 [i]Jer 5:23
[j]S Lev 19:16
[k]Eze 22:18
6:29 [l]Mal 3:3
Eze 22:18
6:30 [m]Pr 17:3;
[n]Ps 53:5;
119:119;
Jer 7:29; La 5:22;
Hos 9:17
7:2 [o]Jer 17:19

Footnotes

is translated "cane" in Ex 30:23; calamus, which probably
came from India, was an ingredient in the sacred anointing
oil (Ex 30:25). *burnt offerings are not acceptable.* The attitude of one's heart and the manner of one's life are far more
important than the ritual of sacrifice (see note on Isa
1:11–15).
6:21 *obstacles.* The Babylonian invaders (see v. 22).
6:22–24 Repeated almost verbatim in 50:41–43.
6:22 *land of the north.* Babylonia (see 4:6; Isa 41:25 and
notes). *from the ends of the earth.* See 25:32; 31:8.
6:23 *spear.* The Hebrew for this word is translated "javelin" in 1Sa 17:6. Another possibility is "sword," as attested
in *The War of the Sons of Light against the Sons of Darkness,* one of the Dead Sea Scrolls (see "The Time between
the Testaments," p. 1431). *like the roaring sea.* See Isa 5:30;
see also Isa 17:12 and note. *horses.* See note on 4:13; see
also 8:16. *Daughter of Zion.* A personification of Jerusalem
and its inhabitants (see v. 2; 4:31).
6:24–26 The prophet speaks to, and on behalf of, the
people of Judah.
6:24 *hands hang limp.* Courage will fail (see Isa 13:7).
anguish. See note on 4:19.
6:25 *terror on every side.* A favorite expression of Jeremiah
(20:10; 46:5; 49:29). The Hebrew for this phrase is used
once as a proper name, "Magor-Missabib" (20:3; see NIV
text note there).
6:26 *put on sackcloth.* See 4:8; see also note on Ge 37:34.
roll in ashes; mourn. See Eze 27:30–31; cf. Mic 1:10. *only
son.* A father's most precious possession (see Ge 22:12,16;
Am 8:10; Zec 12:10; Ro 8:32). *destroyer.* Babylon (see note
on 4:7).
6:27–30 The Lord speaks to Jeremiah and appoints him to
test the people of Judah as a refiner tests metals (see 9:7; Isa

1:25; Mal 3:2–3).
6:27 *tester of metals.* See Job 23:10.
6:28 *going about to slander.* Contrary to Lev 19:16.
bronze and iron. Base metals when compared to gold and
silver. *act corruptly.* See Dt 31:29; Isa 1:4.
6:29 In ancient times, lead was added to silver ore in the
refining process. When the crucible was heated, the lead
oxidized and acted as a flux to remove the alloys. Here the
process fails because the ore is not pure enough (cf. Eze
24:11–13).
6:30 *They are . . . rejected.* The "hardened rebels" (v. 28),
the "wicked" (v. 29), have failed to pass the Lord's test.
Nothing worthwhile can be made of them.
7:1–10:25 A series of temple messages delivered by Jeremiah, perhaps over a period of several years. Since 26:2–6,
12–15 is very similar in content to ch. 7, it is possible that
chs. 7–10 (or at least ch. 7) date to the reign of Jehoiakim
(see 26:1). On the other hand, Jeremiah may have repeated
various themes on several occasions during his lengthy ministry. In any event, nothing in chs. 7–10 is inappropriate to
the time of King Josiah.
7:1–8:3 The straightforward narrative of this section asserts that Solomon's temple in Jerusalem will not escape the
fate of the earlier sanctuary at Shiloh if the people of Judah
persist in worshiping false gods.
7:1 *the word that came.* See 1:2 and note; 1:4,11,13; 2:1.
7:2 *gate.* In the wall between the inner and outer courts of
the temple, perhaps the so-called New Gate (26:10; 36:10).
Hear. See note on 2:4. *all you people . . . who come . . . to
worship.* Perhaps during one of the three annual pilgrimage
festivals (see Dt 16:16 and note). *gates.* Leading into the
outer court.

people of Judah who come through these
gates to worship the LORD. 3This is what
the LORD Almighty, the God of Israel, says:
Reform your ways[p] and your actions, and I
will let you live[q] in this place. 4Do not
trust[r] in deceptive[s] words and say, "This
is the temple of the LORD, the temple of
the LORD, the temple of the LORD!" 5If you
really change[t] your ways and your actions
and deal with each other justly,[u] 6if you do
not oppress[v] the alien, the fatherless or
the widow and do not shed innocent
blood[w] in this place, and if you do not
follow other gods[x] to your own harm,
7then I will let you live in this place, in the
land[y] I gave your forefathers[z] for ever and
ever. 8But look, you are trusting[a] in
deceptive[b] words that are worthless.

9" 'Will you steal[c] and murder,[d] commit adultery[e] and perjury,[n][f] burn incense
to Baal[g][h] and follow other gods[i] you
have not known, 10and then come and
stand[j] before me in this house,[k] which
bears my Name, and say, "We are
safe"—safe to do all these detestable
things?[l] 11Has this house,[m] which bears
my Name, become a den of robbers[n] to
you? But I have been watching![o] declares
the LORD.

12" 'Go now to the place in Shiloh[p]
where I first made a dwelling[q] for my
Name,[r] and see what I did[s] to it because
of the wickedness of my people Israel.
13While you were doing all these things,
declares the LORD, I spoke[t] to you again
and again,[u] but you did not listen;[v] I
called[w] you, but you did not answer.[x]
14Therefore, what I did to Shiloh[y] I will
now do to the house that bears my
Name,[z] the temple[a] you trust in, the
place I gave to you and your fathers. 15I
will thrust you from my presence,[b] just as
I did all your brothers, the people of
Ephraim.'[c]

16"So do not pray for this people nor
offer any plea[d] or petition for them; do not
plead with me, for I will not listen[e] to you.
17Do you not see what they are doing in
the towns of Judah and in the streets of
Jerusalem? 18The children gather wood,
the fathers light the fire, and the women

7:3 [p]Jer 18:11; 26:13; 35:15 [q]ver 7 **7:4** [r]S Job 15:31 [s]ver 8; Jer 28:15; Mic 3:11 **7:5** [t]ver 3; Jer 18:11; 26:13; 35:15 [u]S Ex 22:22; S Lev 25:17; S Isa 1:17 **7:6** [v]S Jer 5:28; Eze 22:7 [w]S 2Ki 21:16; Jer 2:34; 19:4; 22:3 [x]S Ex 20:3; S Dt 8:19 **7:7** [y]S Dt 4:40 [z]S Jos 1:6 **7:8** [a]S Job 15:31 [b]S ver 4 **7:9** [c]Ex 20:15 [d]Ex 20:13 [e]Ex 20:14; S Nu 25:1 [f]Ex 20:16; S Lev 19:12; Zec 8:17; Mal 3:5 [g]S Isa 1:13 [h]Jer 11:13,17; 32:29 [i]S Ex 20:3; Hos 2:13 **7:10** [j]S Isa 48:1 [k]ver 30; 2Ki 21:4-5; Jer 23:11; 32:34; Eze 23:38-39 [l]Eze 33:25 **7:11** [m]Isa 56:7 [n]Mt 21:13*; Mk 11:17*; Lk 19:46 [o]Ge 31:50; Jdg 11:10; Jer 29:23; 42:5

7:12 [p]S Jos 18:1; S 1Sa 2:32 [q]S Ex 40:2; S Jos 18:10 [r]Da 9:18 [s]S 1Sa 4:10-11,22; Ps 78:60-64 **7:13** [t]Ps 71:17; Isa 48:17; Jer 32:33 [u]S 2Ch 36:15 [v]S ver 26; S Isa 65:12 [w]S Pr 1:24 [x]Jer 35:17 **7:14** [y]S Jdg 18:31; S 1Sa 2:32 [z]S 1Ki 9:7 [a]ver 4; Eze 24:21 **7:15** [b]S Ge 4:14; S Ex 33:15; S 2Ki 17:20; Jer 23:39 [c]S Ps 78:67 **7:16** [d]S Ex 32:10; Dt 9:14; Jer 15:1 [e]S Nu 23:19

[n]9 Or *and swear by false gods*

7:3 *this place.* The land God had given them (see v. 7; 14:13,15; 24:5–6).
7:4 *deceptive words.* Spoken by false prophets. The idea that God would not destroy Jerusalem simply because his dwelling, the temple, was located there was a delusion, fostered in part by the miraculous deliverance of the city during the reign of Hezekiah (see 2Ki 19:32–36; cf. 2Sa 7:11b–13; Ps 132:13–14). In the light of Judah's sinful rebellion against the Lord such an idea was "worthless" (v. 8; see Mic 3:11). *This is.* Lit. "They are," referring to the buildings that constituted the entire temple complex. *temple . . . temple . . . temple.* Vain and repetitious babbling (cf. Mt 6:7). Often such a threefold repeating of a word or phrase is for emphasis (see 22:29; see also note on Isa 6:3).
7:6 Rulers and people alike needed to hear and act on these prophetic words (see 22:2–3). *alien . . . fatherless . . . widow.* See Dt 16:11,14; 24:19–21; 26:12–13; 27:19. *innocent blood.* See 19:4; 22:17; 26:15; see also the frightening example of King Manasseh (2Ki 21:16).
7:7 *land . . . for ever and ever.* See Ge 17:8 and note.
7:8 *deceptive words.* See note on v. 4.
7:9 This one verse mentions the violation of fully half of the Ten Commandments (cf. Hos 4:2). *burn incense to Baal.* See note on 1:16. *follow other gods you have not known.* See 19:4. Tragically, such sins would be the cause of their exile to lands they had not known (see 9:14,16; 16:11,13).
7:10 *house, which bears my Name.* See vv. 11,14,30; 25:29; 32:34; 34:15; 1Ki 8:43; 2Ch 6:33; 20:9; Da 9:18. The "Name" of God is equivalent to his gracious presence in such passages (see vv. 12,15). *We are safe.* See 12:12. *detestable.* See 2:7; see also note on Lev 7:21.
7:11 Together with the last half of Isa 56:7, part of this verse is quoted by Jesus in Mt 21:13; Mk 11:17; Lk 19:46. *den of robbers.* As thieves hide in caves and think they are safe, so the people of Judah falsely trust in the temple to protect them in spite of their sins.
7:12 See note on 7:1–8:3. *place in Shiloh . . . see what I did to it.* See v. 14; 26:6,9; Ps 78:60–61. The tabernacle had been set up in Shiloh after the conquest of Canaan (Jos 18:1) and was still there at the end of the period of the judges (see 1Sa 1:9 and NIV text note). Modern Seilun, near a main highway about 18 miles north of Jerusalem, preserves the name of the ancient site. Archaeological excavations there indicate that it was destroyed by the Philistines c. 1050 B.C. The tabernacle itself was not included in that destruction, since it was still in existence at Gibeon during David's reign (see 1Ch 21:29). One or more auxiliary buildings had apparently been erected at Shiloh near the tabernacle in connection with various aspects of public worship there (cf. the reference to the "doors of the house of the LORD" in 1Sa 3:15). Such structures would have been destroyed with the city itself, perhaps sometime after the events of 1Sa 4.
7:13 *again and again.* The Hebrew idiom underlying this phrase is found frequently in Jeremiah (v. 25; 11:7; 25:3–4; 26:5; 29:19; 32:33; 35:14–15; 44:4), but appears nowhere else in the OT.
7:15 *thrust you from my presence.* Into exile (see Dt 29:28). *just as I did all your brothers.* God sent Israel, the northern kingdom, into captivity in 721 B.C. (see 2Ki 17:20). *Ephraim.* Another name for Israel (see, e.g., 31:9)—and, ironically, the tribal territory in which Shiloh was located.
7:16 Perhaps the events of ch. 26 belong chronologically between vv. 15 and 16 (see Introduction: Outline). *do not pray for this people.* As a true prophet would (see 27:18; Ex 32:31–32; 1Sa 12:23). See 11:14; 14:11. There is virtually no hope for them. On various occasions, however, Jeremiah prayed for his countrymen (see, e.g., 18:20).
7:18 *children . . . fathers . . . women.* Entire families participate in idolatrous worship. *cakes of bread.* See 44:19. *Queen of Heaven.* A Babylonian title for Ishtar, an important

knead the dough and make cakes of bread for the Queen of Heaven./ They pour out drink offerings*g* to other gods to provoke*h* me to anger. ¹⁹But am I the one they are provoking?*i* declares the LORD. Are they not rather harming themselves, to their own shame?*j*

²⁰"'Therefore this is what the Sovereign*k* LORD says: My anger*l* and my wrath will be poured*m* out on this place, on man and beast, on the trees of the field and on the fruit of the ground, and it will burn and not be quenched.*n*

²¹"'This is what the LORD Almighty, the God of Israel, says: Go ahead, add your burnt offerings to your other sacrifices*o* and eat*p* the meat yourselves! ²²For when I brought your forefathers out of Egypt and spoke to them, I did not just give them commands*q* about burnt offerings and sacrifices,*r* ²³but I gave them this command:*s* Obey*t* me, and I will be your God and you will be my people.*u* Walk in all the ways*v* I command you, that it may go well*w* with you. ²⁴But they did not listen*x* or pay attention;*y* instead, they followed the stubborn inclinations of their evil hearts.*z* They went backward*a* and not forward. ²⁵From the time your forefathers

left Egypt until now, day after day, again and again*b* I sent you my servants*c* the prophets.*d* ²⁶But they did not listen to me or pay attention.*e* They were stiff-necked*f* and did more evil than their forefathers.'*g*

²⁷"When you tell*h* them all this, they will not listen*i* to you; when you call to them, they will not answer.*j* ²⁸Therefore say to them, 'This is the nation that has not obeyed the LORD its God or responded to correction.*k* Truth*l* has perished; it has vanished from their lips. ²⁹Cut off*m* your hair and throw it away; take up a lament*n* on the barren heights, for the LORD has rejected and abandoned*o* this generation that is under his wrath.

The Valley of Slaughter

³⁰"'The people of Judah have done evil*p* in my eyes, declares the LORD. They have set up their detestable idols*q* in the house that bears my Name and have defiled*r* it. ³¹They have built the high places of Topheth*s* in the Valley of Ben

---

7:18
/Jer 44:17-19
gS Isa 57:6
hS Dt 31:17;
S 1Ki 14:9
7:19 /Dt 32:21;
Jer 44:3
/S Job 7:20;
Jer 9:19; 20:11;
22:22
7:20 kS Isa 30:15
/S Job 40:11;
Jer 42:18;
La 2:3-5
mJer 6:11-12;
La 4:11
nS Isa 1:31;
Jer 11:16; 13:14;
15:6,14; 17:4,27;
Eze 20:47-48
7:21 oS Jer 6:20;
Am 5:21-22
pS 1Sa 2:12-17;
Hos 8:13
7:22 qIsa 43:23
/S 1Sa 15:22
7:23 sJn 3:23
tS Ex 19:5
uS Lev 26:12;
S Isa 51:16
vS 1Ki 8:36;
S Ps 119:3
wS Dt 5:33
7:24 xS Jer 6:10
yJer 11:8; 17:23;
34:14 zS Jer 3:17
aS Jer 2:19;
Eze 37:23

7:25
bS 2Ch 36:15
cS Isa 20:3
dS Nu 11:29;
Jer 25:4; 35:15
7:26 ever 13,24;
S 2Ch 36:16;
Ps 81:11;

Jer 13:11; 22:21; 25:3; 35:15; Eze 20:8,21 /S Ex 32:9;
Ac 7:51 gJer 16:12; Mal 3:7; Lk 11:47 7:27 hEze 2:7 iver 13; Eze 3:7; Zec 7:13 /S Isa 65:12 7:28 kS Lev 26:23; Zep 3:7 /S Ps 15:2; S Isa 59:15 7:29 mS Lev 21:5; S Job 1:20 nS Jer 4:8; S Eze 19:1 oS Jer 6:30; 12:7; Hos 11:8; Mic 5:3 7:30 pS ver 10; S Lev 18:21 qS Jer 2:7; S 4:1; Eze 7:20-22 /S Lev 20:3; Jer 32:34 7:31 sS 2Ki 23:10

---

goddess in the Babylonian pantheon (see 44:17–19,25). *drink offerings to other gods.* And sometimes to the Queen of Heaven herself (see 44:19,25). *provoke me to anger.* See Dt 31:29.
7:19 *their own shame.* See 3:25.
7:20 All nature suffers when God judges sinners (see 5:17; Ro 8:20–22). *burn and not be quenched.* See 4:4; 21:12; see also Isa 1:31; Am 5:6.
7:21 Because of your sinful deeds your sacrifices are worthless, so you might as well eat them yourselves.
7:22–23 Sacrifices are valid only when accompanied by sincere repentance and joyful obedience (see 6:20; Isa 1:11–15 and note).
7:23 *I will be . . . my people.* The most basic summary of the relationship between God and Israel implied in the covenant at Sinai (see Ex 6:7; Lev 26:12 and notes; Dt 26:17–18).
7:24 *followed . . . evil hearts.* See note on 3:17; see also Ge 6:5 and note.
7:25 *again and again.* See note on v. 13. *my servants the prophets.* See 25:4; 26:5; 29:19; 35:15; 44:4; see also Zec 1:6 and note. God had promised that Moses would be the first in a long line of prophets who would speak in the Lord's name and serve him faithfully (see Dt 18:15–22 and notes).
7:26 *stiff-necked.* See 17:23; 19:15; see also notes on Ex 32:9; Ne 3:5.
7:28 *not . . . responded to correction.* See 2:30; 5:3. *Truth . . . has vanished from their lips.* No one seeks the truth (see 5:1 and note).
7:29 Addressed to Jerusalem. *Cut off your hair.* A sign of mourning (see Job 1:20; Mic 1:16). The Hebrew for the word "hair" is related to the word "Nazirite" (see Nu 6:2) and referred originally to the diadem worn by the high priest (see Ex 29:6). The Nazirite's hair was the symbol of his separation or consecration (Nu 6:7). As the Nazirite was

commanded to cut off his hair when he became ceremonially unclean (Nu 6:9), so also Jerusalem must cut off her hair because of her sins. *lament on the barren heights.* See 3:21; see also note on 3:2.
7:30 *set up their . . . idols in the house.* Manasseh had put a carved Asherah pole (see NIV text note on 2Ki 13:6) in the temple (2Ki 21:7). Jeremiah's contemporary, the good King Josiah, removed the pole and other accessories to idol worship (2Ki 23:4–7). But less than 20 years after Josiah's death, Ezekiel reported that there were numerous idols in the temple courts (see Eze 8:3,5–6,10,12). *defiled it.* See note on 2:7.
7:31 *high places.* Pagan cult centers, usually (but not here) located on natural heights (see 1Sa 9:13–14; 10:5; 1Ki 11:7). *Topheth.* See v. 32; 19:6,11–14; see also note on Isa 30:33. The word may be of Aramaic origin with the meaning "fireplace," though in cultures outside Israel it was used as a common noun meaning "place of child sacrifice." Its vocalization was perhaps intentionally conformed to that of Hebrew *bosheth,* "shameful thing" (see note on Jdg 6:32), often used in connection with idol worship (see notes on 2:26; 3:25). The OT Topheth had a fire pit (see Isa 30:33), into which the hapless children were apparently thrown. *Valley of Ben Hinnom.* See v. 32; 19:2,6; 32:35; see also note on Jos 15:5. It was used as a trash dump and also as a place for sacrificing children to pagan gods. From the abbreviated name "Valley of Hinnom" (see Ne 11:30), Hebrew *ge' hinnom,* came "Gehenna" (Greek *geenna*), consistently translated in the NT as "hell," the place of eternal, fiery punishment for all who die without having trusted Christ as Savior (see, e.g., Mt 18:9; Mk 9:47–48). *burn their sons and daughters in the fire.* A horrible ritual, prohibited in the law of Moses (see Lev 18:21 and note; Dt 18:10) but practiced by Ahaz (see 2Ki 16:2–3) and Manasseh (2Ki 21:1,6).

Hinnom[t] to burn their sons and daughters[u] in the fire—something I did not command, nor did it enter my mind. [v] 32So beware, the days are coming, declares the LORD, when people will no longer call it Topheth or the Valley of Ben Hinnom, but the Valley of Slaughter,[w] for they will bury[x] the dead in Topheth until there is no more room. 33Then the carcasses[y] of this people will become food[z] for the birds of the air and the beasts of the earth, and there will be no one to frighten them away.[a] 34I will bring an end to the sounds[b] of joy and gladness and to the voices of bride and bridegroom[c] in the towns of Judah and the streets of Jerusalem, [d] for the land will become desolate. [e]

8 " 'At that time, declares the LORD, the bones of the kings and officials of Judah, the bones of the priests and prophets, and the bones[f] of the people of Jerusalem will be removed[g] from their graves. 2They will be exposed to the sun and the moon and all the stars of the heavens, which they have loved and served[h] and which they have followed and consulted and worshiped.[i] They will not be gathered up or buried,[j] but will be like refuse lying on the ground.[k] 3Wherever I banish them,[l] all the survivors of this evil nation will prefer death to life,[m] declares the LORD Almighty.'

Sin and Punishment

4"Say to them, 'This is what the LORD says:

Cross-references column:

7:31 [r]S Jos 15:8; 2Ch 33:6
[u]S Lev 18:21; Eze 16:20
[v]Jer 19:5; 32:35; Eze 20:31; Mic 6:7
7:32 [w]Jer 19:6
[x]Jer 19:11
7:33 [y]S Ge 15:11
[z]S Dt 28:26; Eze 29:5
[a]Jer 6:11; 14:16
7:34 [b]S Isa 24:8
[c]Rev 18:23
[d]Isa 24:7-12; Jer 33:10
[e]S Lev 26:34; Zec 7:14; Mt 23:38
8:1 [f]S Ps 53:5
[g]S Isa 14:19
8:2 [h]S 2Ki 23:5; Jer 19:13;
Zep 1:5; Ac 7:42
[i]S Job 31:27
[j]Jer 14:16;
Eze 29:5; 37:1
[k]S 2Ki 9:37;
Jer 31:40; 36:30
8:3 [l]Dt 29:28
[m]S Job 3:22;
Rev 9:6

8:4 [n]Pr 24:16;
Mic 7:8
[o]Ps 119:67;
Jer 31:19
8:5 [p]S Jer 5:27
[q]Zec 7:11
8:6 [r]Mal 3:16
[s]Rev 9:20
[t]Ps 14:1-3
8:7 [u]S Dt 32:28;
S Jer 4:22
8:8 [v]Ro 2:17
8:9 [w]S Isa 29:14
[x]S 2Ki 19:26
[y]S Job 5:13
[z]S Jer 6:19
[a]Pr 1:7; 1Co 1:20
8:10 [b]S Jer 6:12

" 'When men fall down, do they not get up? [n]
When a man turns away,[o] does he not return?
5Why then have these people turned away?
Why does Jerusalem always turn away?
They cling to deceit;[p]
they refuse to return. [q]
6I have listened[r] attentively,
but they do not say what is right.
No one repents[s] of his wickedness,
saying, "What have I done?"
Each pursues his own course[t]
like a horse charging into battle.
7Even the stork in the sky
knows her appointed seasons,
and the dove, the swift and the thrush
observe the time of their migration.
But my people do not know[u]
the requirements of the LORD.

8" 'How can you say, "We are wise,
for we have the law[v] of the LORD,"
when actually the lying pen of the scribes
has handled it falsely?
9The wise[w] will be put to shame;
they will be dismayed[x] and trapped.[y]
Since they have rejected the word[z] of the LORD,
what kind of wisdom[a] do they have?
10Therefore I will give their wives to other men
and their fields to new owners. [b]

Notes section (bottom):

7:32 *So beware . . . Valley of Slaughter.* Repeated almost verbatim in 19:6. Their place of sacrifice would become their cemetery when the people of Judah were slaughtered by the Babylonian invaders.

7:33 The punishment announced here is one of the curses for covenant disobedience (see Dt 28:26). *food for the birds . . . of the earth.* See 16:4; 19:7; see also 34:20, where the same judgment is the result of violating God's covenant (34:18–19). To remain unburied was an unspeakable abomination in ancient times.

7:34 See 16:9; 25:10; contrast 33:10–11. *land will become desolate.* Another covenant curse (Lev 26:31,33).

8:1 *bones . . . removed from their graves.* A gross indignity and sacrilege (see 2Ki 23:16,18; Am 2:1 and note). *kings . . . officials . . . priests . . . prophets.* See 2:26; see also note on 1:18.

8:2 *exposed to the sun . . . moon . . . stars.* To hasten their disintegration, and perhaps also to demonstrate that the heavenly bodies, which had been worshiped by some of Judah's kings (see 2Ki 21:3,5; 23:11), among others, were powerless to help. *loved and served and . . . followed and consulted and worshiped.* Acts of homage and adoration that should have been given to God alone. *They.* The bones. *not be gathered up or buried.* Contrast 2Sa 21:13–14. *refuse.* Lit. "dung" (see 9:22; 16:4; 25:33).

8:3 *survivors.* See note on 6:9.

8:4–9:26 In contrast to 7:1–8:3, this section is almost

completely in poetic form. Jeremiah resumes his extended commentary on the inevitability of divine judgment against sinners.

8:4 *Say to them.* Connects this section with the previous (see 7:28). *turns away . . . return.* The Hebrew for these two verbs is identical, forming a play on words.

8:5 The general truths stated in v. 4 are routinely and perversely violated by the people of Jerusalem. *turned away . . . turn away . . . return.* Continuing the wordplay of v. 4.

8:6 *l. The Lord. pursues.* The Hebrew for this word continues the wordplay of vv. 4–5. *his own course.* And therefore evil (see 23:10).

8:7 See Isa 1:3. Although migratory birds obey their God-given instincts, God's rebellious people refuse to obey his laws. *swift . . . thrush.* Linked also in Isa 38:14. *do not know . . . requirements of the LORD.* See note on 5:4.

8:8–9 *law of the LORD . . . word of the LORD.* Misinterpreting and manipulating the first (the written law of Moses) leads to rejection of the second (God's truth as found in the law and proclaimed by his servants the prophets).

8:8 *lying pen.* Symbolizes mistreatment of the written law. *scribes.* The earliest mention of them as a recognizable group. They were apparently organized on the basis of families (see 1Ch 2:55; 2Ch 34:13). *handled it falsely.* Contrast 2Ti 2:15.

8:9 *rejected . . . wisdom.* Contrast Dt 4:5–6.

8:10–12 See 6:12–15 and notes.

From the least to the greatest,
all are greedy for gain; [c]
prophets [d] and priests alike,
all practice deceit. [e]
11They dress the wound of my people
as though it were not serious.
"Peace, peace," they say,
when there is no peace. [f]
12Are they ashamed of their loathsome
conduct?
No, they have no shame [g] at all;
they do not even know how to blush.
So they will fall among the fallen;
they will be brought down when they
are punished, [h]
says the LORD. [i]

13" 'I will take away their harvest,
declares the LORD.
There will be no grapes on the vine. [j]
There will be no figs [k] on the tree,
and their leaves will wither. [l]
What I have given them
will be taken [m] from them. [o]' "

14"Why are we sitting here?
Gather together!
Let us flee to the fortified cities [n]
and perish there!
For the LORD our God has doomed us
to perish
and given us poisoned water [o] to
drink,
because we have sinned [p] against
him.
15We hoped for peace [q]
but no good has come,
for a time of healing
but there was only terror. [r]
16The snorting of the enemy's horses [s]

is heard from Dan; [t]
at the neighing of their stallions
the whole land trembles. [u]
They have come to devour [v]
the land and everything in it,
the city and all who live there."

17"See, I will send venomous snakes [w]
among you,
vipers that cannot be charmed, [x]
and they will bite you,"
declares the LORD.

18O my Comforter [P] in sorrow,
my heart is faint [y] within me.
19Listen to the cry of my people
from a land far away: [z]
"Is the LORD not in Zion?
Is her King [a] no longer there?"

"Why have they provoked [b] me to
anger with their images,
with their worthless [c] foreign
idols?" [d]

20"The harvest is past,
the summer has ended,
and we are not saved."

21Since my people are crushed, [e] I am
crushed;
I mourn, [f] and horror grips me.
22Is there no balm in Gilead? [g]
Is there no physician [h] there?
Why then is there no healing [i]
for the wound of my people?

9 1Oh, that my head were a spring of
water
and my eyes a fountain of tears! [j]

o 13 The meaning of the Hebrew for this sentence is
uncertain. P 18 The meaning of the Hebrew for this
word is uncertain.

Cross references (center column)

8:10 [c]S Isa 56:11
[d]Jer 14:14;
La 2:14
[e]Jer 23:11,15
8:11 [f]ver 15;
S Jer 4:10;
Eze 7:25
8:12 [g]S Jer 3:3
[h]Ps 52:5-7;
Isa 3:9 /S Jer 6:15
8:13 [l]Hos 2:12;
Joel 1:7 [k]Lk 13:6
[l]Mt 21:19
[m]S Jer 5:17
8:14
[n]S Jos 10:20;
Jer 35:11
[o]Dt 29:18;
Jer 9:15; 23:15
[p]Jer 14:7,20;
Da 9:5
8:15 [q]S ver 11
[r]S Job 19:8;
Jer 14:19
8:16 [s]S Jer 4:29

[t]S Ge 30:6
[u]Jer 51:29
[v]S Jer 5:17
8:17 [w]Nu 21:6;
S Dt 32:24
[x]S Ps 58:5;
S Isa 3:3
8:18 [y]La 5:17
8:19 [z]Dt 28:64;
Jer 9:16 [a]Mic 4:9
[b]Jer 44:3
[c]S Isa 41:24
[d]S Dt 32:21
8:21 [e]S Ps 94:5
/Ps 78:40;
Isa 43:24;
Jer 4:19; 10:19;
14:17; 30:14;
La 2:13; Eze 6:9
8:22 [g]S Ge 37:25
[h]Job 13:4
/S Isa 1:6;
Jer 30:12
9:1 /S Ps 119:136

8:13—9:24 This section is read aloud in synagogues every year on the ninth of Ab (see chart on "Hebrew Calendar," p. 102), the day the temple in Jerusalem was destroyed by the Babylonians in 586 B.C. and by the Romans in A.D. 70.
8:13 *vine.* Israel (see 2:21 and note). *grapes . . . figs.* Symbolic of individual people also in Mic 7:1; see ch. 24. *leaves will wither.* Contrast 17:8; Ps 1:3.
8:14—16 On behalf of the people the prophet speaks, envisioning the Babylonian invasion.
8:14 *Gather together!* See 4:5. The Hebrew for this phrase forms a wordplay with the Hebrew for "take away" and "harvest" in v. 13. *flee to the fortified cities.* See note on 4:5. *poisoned water.* The phrase is unique to the prophet Jeremiah (see 9:15; 23:15; cf. 25:15).
8:15 Repeated almost verbatim in 14:19. *peace.* Under the circumstances, a false hope (see notes on 4:10; 6:14). *healing.* See note on 6:7.
8:16 *the enemy's horses.* See note on 4:13. *Dan.* Far away, close to the northern border of Israel. *stallions.* Lit. "mighty ones"; the Hebrew word is translated "stallions" again in 50:11, "steeds" in 47:3.
8:17 *vipers that cannot be charmed.* Such are the wicked always (see Ps 58:4–5).
8:18 The prophet speaks. *my heart is faint.* See La 1:22;

5:17.
8:19 The prophet speaks in the first part of the verse, the Lord in the last part. *my people from a land far away.* Judah in Babylonian exile (see Ps 137:1–4) as Jeremiah envisions the future. *Is the LORD not in Zion?* Cf. Mic 3:11. The people are perplexed at their fate, still wondering how God could have permitted the destruction of his land and temple (see note on 7:4). *King.* God (see Isa 33:22). *provoked me to anger.* See 7:18; Dt 31:29. *worthless . . . idols.* See note on 2:5.
8:20 The people speak from the hopelessness of their exile. *we are not saved.* We have been captured by the enemy.
8:21 Jeremiah identifies himself with his exiled countrymen. *grips me.* See 6:24.
8:22 *balm in Gilead.* See 46:11; 51:8. The territory of Gilead was an important source of spices and medicinal herbs (see note on Ge 37:25). *no healing for the wound.* See 30:17.
9:1–2 The prophet's frustration is highlighted as he speaks of his countrymen with tender sympathy in v. 1 and with indignant disgust in v. 2.
9:1 Jeremiah is often called the "weeping prophet"—a well-deserved title (see v. 10; the book of Lamentations; cf. 2Sa 18:33; Mt 23:37; Ro 9:2–4; 10:1).

I would weep[k] day and night
  for the slain of my people. [l]
[2]Oh, that I had in the desert[m]
  a lodging place for travelers,
so that I might leave my people
  and go away from them;
for they are all adulterers, [n]
  a crowd of unfaithful[o] people.

[3]"They make ready their tongue
  like a bow, to shoot lies; [p]
it is not by truth
  that they triumph[q] in the land.
They go from one sin to another;
  they do not acknowledge[q] me,"
            declares the LORD.

[4]"Beware of your friends; [r]
  do not trust your brothers. [s]
For every brother is a deceiver,[r] [t]
  and every friend a slanderer. [u]
[5]Friend deceives friend, [v]
  and no one speaks the truth. [w]
They have taught their tongues to lie; [x]
  they weary themselves with sinning.
[6]You[s] live in the midst of deception;[y]
  in their deceit they refuse to
  acknowledge me,"
            declares the LORD.

[7]Therefore this is what the LORD Almighty says:

"See, I will refine[z] and test[a] them,
  for what else can I do
because of the sin of my people?
[8]Their tongue[b] is a deadly arrow;
  it speaks with deceit.
With his mouth each speaks cordially to
  his neighbor, [c]

but in his heart he sets a trap[d] for
  him. [e]
[9]Should I not punish them for this?"
  declares the LORD.
"Should I not avenge[f] myself
  on such a nation as this?"

[10]I will weep and wail for the mountains
  and take up a lament concerning the
    desert pastures. [g]
They are desolate and untraveled,
  and the lowing of cattle is not heard.
The birds of the air[h] have fled
  and the animals are gone.

[11]"I will make Jerusalem a heap[i] of
    ruins,
  a haunt of jackals; [j]
and I will lay waste the towns of
    Judah[k]
  so no one can live there." [l]

[12]What man is wise[m] enough to understand this? Who has been instructed by the LORD and can explain it? Why has the land been ruined and laid waste like a desert that no one can cross?

[13]The LORD said, "It is because they have forsaken my law, which I set before them; they have not obeyed me or followed my law. [n] [14]Instead, they have followed[o] the stubbornness of their hearts; [p] they have followed the Baals, as their fathers taught them." [15]Therefore, this is what the LORD Almighty, the God of Israel, says: "See, I will make this people eat bitter food[q] and drink poisoned water. [r] [16]I

Cross references (center column):

9:1 [k]Jer 13:17; 14:17; La 2:11, 18; 3:48 [l]Isa 22:4
9:2 [m]Ps 55:7 [n]S Nu 25:1; Jer 23:10; Hos 4:2; 7:4 [o]S 1Ki 19:10; S Isa 24:16
9:3 [p]ver 8; S Ex 20:16; Ps 64:3; S Isa 44:20; Jer 18:18; Mic 6:12 [q]S Isa 1:3
9:4 [r]S 2Sa 15:12 [s]Mic 7:5-6 [t]S Ge 27:35 [u]S Ex 20:16; S Lev 19:16
9:5 [v]S Lev 6:2 [w]S Ps 15:2; S Isa 59:15 [x]S Ps 52:3
9:6 [y]S Jer 5:27
9:7 [z]S Job 28:1; S Isa 1:25 [a]S Jer 6:27
9:8 [b]S ver 3; S Ps 35:20 [c]S Isa 3:5

9:9 [d]S Jer 5:26 [e]ver 4 [f]S Dt 32:43; S Isa 10:3
9:10 [g]Jer 23:10; Joel 1:19 [h]S Jer 4:25; 12:4; Hos 4:3; Joel 1:18
9:11 [i]Jer 26:18 [j]S Job 30:29; S Isa 34:13 [k]S Jer 1:15 [l]S Lev 26:31; Isa 25:2; S Jer 4:13; 26:9; 33:10; 50:3,13; 51:62; La 1:4
9:12 [m]S Ps 107:43
9:13 [n]S 2Ch 7:19; S Ps 89:30-32
9:14 [o]S Jer 2:8, 23; Am 2:4 [p]S Jer 3:17; S 7:24
9:15 [q]La 3:15 [r]S Jer 8:14

---

[q]3 Or *lies; / they are not valiant for truth*   [r]4 Or *a deceiving Jacob*   [s]6 That is, Jeremiah (the Hebrew is singular)

9:2 The prophet wants to get as far away from his wicked countrymen as possible (cf. Ps 55:6-8). *adulterers*. See note on 2:20. *crowd*. The Hebrew for this word is always used elsewhere in the OT in the sense of a solemn religious assembly (see, e.g., Dt 16:8), sometimes perverted by the worshipers and therefore falling under divine judgment (see Isa 1:13; Am 5:21). *unfaithful*. Toward God (see note on 3:7).
9:3-9 The Lord speaks.
9:3 *tongue like a bow*. See vv. 5,8; see also Ps 64:3-4; Jas 3:5-12. *do not acknowledge me*. See v. 6; Jdg 2:10; 1Sa 2:12; Job 18:21; Hos 4:1; Ro 1:28; contrast Hos 6:3.
9:4 *deceiver*. See NIV text note; Ge 25:26 and note; NIV text note on Ge 27:36; Hos 12:2-3 and NIV text note on Hos 12:2.
9:6 *refuse to acknowledge me*. The situation has deteriorated even further (v. 3 says simply "do not acknowledge me").
9:7 *refine and test*. See 6:27-30 and notes. The Lord will test his people "in the furnace of affliction" (see Isa 48:10 and note).
9:8 *tongue . . . deceit*. See v. 3 and note. *With his mouth . . . but in his heart*. See Ps 55:21. *cordially*. The Hebrew for this word is translated "peace" in 6:14 (see note there).

9:9 Repeated from 5:9,29.
9:10 The prophet speaks. See 4:23-26 and notes. *weep and wail*. See v. 18; see also note on v. 1. *desert pastures*. Good for poor grazing at best (see 1Sa 17:28; cf. Ex 3:1). *desolate*. Lit. "burned" (as in 2:15); here parched by the blazing sun. *untraveled*. See v. 12; Eze 33:28.
9:11 The Lord speaks. *haunt of jackals*. See 10:22; 49:33; 51:37; Ps 44:19; Isa 13:21-22; La 5:18; Eze 13:4; Mal 1:3; contrast Isa 35:7. *no one can live there*. See 2:15; 4:7 and notes.
9:12 The prophet asks a series of questions. *What man is wise . . .?* See Hos 14:9.
9:13 The Lord answers the prophet and then continues to speak through v. 19. *law, which I set before them*. In the days of Moses (see Dt 4:8).
9:14 *stubbornness*. See note on 3:17. *Baals*. See 2:23; see also note on Jdg 2:11.
9:15 *eat bitter food and drink poisoned water*. Repeated in 23:15; see note on 8:14. Centuries earlier, Moses had warned the Israelites concerning just such a fate (see Dt 29:18).
9:16 *I will scatter them*. See 13:24; 18:17; 30:11; 46:28. This warning was given in Dt 28:64 as one of the covenant curses. *pursue them with the sword*. See 42:16. *destroyed*

will scatter them among nations[s] that neither they nor their fathers have known,[t] and I will pursue them with the sword[u] until I have destroyed them."[v]

[17]This is what the LORD Almighty says:

"Consider now! Call for the wailing
women[w] to come;
send for the most skillful of them.
[18]Let them come quickly
and wail over us
till our eyes overflow with tears
and water streams from our eyelids.[x]
[19]The sound of wailing is heard from
Zion:
'How ruined[y] we are!
How great is our shame!
We must leave our land
because our houses are in ruins.'"

[20]Now, O women, hear the word of the
LORD;
open your ears to the words of his
mouth.[z]
Teach your daughters how to wail;
teach one another a lament.[a]
[21]Death has climbed in through our
windows[b]
and has entered our fortresses;
it has cut off the children from the
streets
and the young men[c] from the public
squares.

[22]Say, "This is what the LORD declares:

"'The dead bodies of men will lie

like refuse[d] on the open field,
like cut grain behind the reaper,
with no one to gather them.'"

[23]This is what the LORD says:

"Let not the wise man boast of his
wisdom[e]
or the strong man boast of his
strength[f]
or the rich man boast of his riches,[g]
[24]but let him who boasts boast[h] about
this:
that he understands and knows[i] me,
that I am the LORD,[j] who exercises
kindness,[k]
justice and righteousness[l] on earth,
for in these I delight,"
declares the LORD.

[25]"The days are coming," declares the
LORD, "when I will punish all who are circumcised only in the flesh[m]— [26]Egypt,
Judah, Edom, Ammon, Moab and all who
live in the desert in distant places.[t][n] For
all these nations are really uncircumcised,[o] and even the whole house of Israel
is uncircumcised in heart.[p]"

God and Idols

10:12–16pp — Jer 51:15–19

10 Hear what the LORD says to you, O
house of Israel. [2]This is what the
LORD says:

"Do not learn the ways of the nations[q]

Cross references (center column):

9:16
[s]S Lev 26:33
[t]S Dt 4:32;
S Jer 8:19
[u]Jer 14:12;
24:10; Eze 5:2
[v]Jer 44:27;
Eze 5:12
9:17 [w]S Ecc 12:5
9:18
[x]S Ps 119:136;
La 3:48
9:19 [y]S Jer 4:13
9:20 [z]Jer 23:16
[a]Isa 32:9-13
9:21 [b]Joel 2:9
[c]S 2Ch 36:17;
S Isa 40:30;
S Jer 16:6

9:22 [d]S 2Ki 9:37
9:23 [e]S Job 4:12;
S Ecc 9:11
[f]S 1Ki 20:11
[g]Ps 62:10;
S Pr 11:28;
Jer 48:7; 49:4;
Eze 28:4-5
9:24 [h]S Ps 34:2;
1Co 1:31*;
Gal 6:14
[i]S Ps 36:10
[j]2Co 10:17*
[k]Ps 51:1 [l]Ps 36:6
9:25
[m]S Lev 26:41;
Ro 2:25
9:26 [n]Jer 25:23;
49:32
[o]S 1Sa 14:6;
Eze 31:18
[p]Ac 7:51
10:2
[q]S Ex 23:24;
S Lev 20:23

[t]26 Or *desert and who clip the hair by their foreheads*

---

them. But not to the last man (see note on 4:27; see especially 44:27–28).
9:17 *wailing women*. Professionals, paid to mourn at funerals and other sorrowful occasions (see 2Ch 35:25; Ecc
12:5; Am 5:16).
9:18 The purpose of the professional mourners was to
arouse the bereaved to weep and lament. *wail*. See v. 10.
eyes overflow with tears. See v. 1.
9:19 *How ruined we are!* See 4:13,20; 48:1.
9:20–21 The prophet speaks.
9:20 The wailing women will have to teach their daughters
how to lament, so great will be the need for their services.
9:21 *Death*. Personified here (as in Hab 2:5). Canaanite
mythology included a deity named Mot (a word related to
the Hebrew word for "death"), the god of infertility and the
netherworld. *climbed in through our windows*. Said of enemy soldiers in Joel 2:9. *children . . . young men*. See 6:11.
9:22 *dead bodies*. See 7:33 and note. *like refuse*. See note
on 8:2. *reaper*. The concept of death as the "grim reaper"
comes largely from this verse.
9:23 *Let not . . . the rich man boast of his riches*. An
almost exact parallel occurs in the Aramaic *Words of Ahiqar*,
written about a century after Jeremiah's time: "Let not the
rich man say, 'In my riches I am glorious.'"
9:24 1Co 1:31 summarizes: "Let him who boasts boast in
the Lord." *this . . . these*. Ultimately, only God and our
knowledge of and love for him are worthwhile. *understands
and knows*. See 3:15; see also note on 4:22. *I am the LORD*.

Ex 6:2–8, a key passage on the doctrine of redemption,
begins and ends with this statement of divine self-disclosure.
kindness. The Hebrew for this word is translated "devotion"
in 2:2 (see note there). *in these I delight*. See Ps 11:7; 33:5;
99:4; 103:6; Mic 6:8; 7:18.
9:25–26 See Ro 2:25–29; see also note on Ge 17:10.
9:26 *who live . . . in distant places*. Arab tribes (see 25:23;
49:32), later to be attacked by the Babylonians under Nebuchadnezzar (see 49:28–33). With the NIV text note contrast
Lev 19:27. *uncircumcised in heart*. See 4:4 and note.
10:1–25 Jeremiah concludes his series of temple messages
with a poetic section that focuses primarily on the vast
difference between idols and the Lord (vv. 2–16). Idols and
their worshipers are condemned in vv. 2–5,8–9,11,14–15,
while the one true God is praised in the alternate passages
(vv. 6–7,10,12–13,16). See Isa 40:18–20; 41:7; 44:9–20;
46:5–7.
10:1 *Hear*. See note on 2:4.
10:2 *Do not . . . be terrified*. See 1:17. *ways*. The Hebrew
for this word is singular and refers to the religious practices of
the nations. The early Christians often called their distinctive
beliefs "the Way" (see Ac 9:2; 19:9,23; 22:4; 24:14,22).
signs in the sky. The heavenly bodies were created by the
Lord for purposes other than idolatrous worship (see Ge
1:14–18 and notes). *nations are terrified*. Not only by the
heavenly bodies themselves but also by unusual phenomena
associated with them (such as comets, meteors and eclipses).

or be terrified by signs *r* in the sky,
though the nations are terrified by
  them.
³For the customs of the peoples are
    worthless;
  they cut a tree out of the forest,
  and a craftsman *s* shapes it with his
    chisel. *t*
⁴They adorn it with silver *u* and gold;
  they fasten it with hammer and nails
  so it will not totter. *v*
⁵Like a scarecrow in a melon patch,
    their idols cannot speak; *w*
  they must be carried
    because they cannot walk. *x*
  Do not fear them;
    they can do no harm *y*
  nor can they do any good." *z*
⁶No one is like you, *a* O LORD;
    you are great, *b*
  and your name is mighty in power.
⁷Who should not revere *c* you,
  O King of the nations? *d*
    This is your due.
  Among all the wise men of the nations
    and in all their kingdoms,
  there is no one like you.
⁸They are all senseless *e* and foolish; *f*
  they are taught by worthless wooden
    idols. *g*
⁹Hammered silver is brought from
    Tarshish *h*
  and gold from Uphaz.
  What the craftsman and goldsmith have
    made *i*
  is then dressed in blue and purple—

all made by skilled workers.
¹⁰But the LORD is the true God;
  he is the living God, *j* the eternal
    King. *k*
  When he is angry, *l* the earth
    trembles; *m*
  the nations cannot endure his
    wrath. *n*

¹¹"Tell them this: 'These gods, who did
not make the heavens and the earth, will
perish *o* from the earth and from under the
heavens.' " *u*

¹²But God made *p* the earth *q* by his
    power;
  he founded the world by his
    wisdom *r*
  and stretched out the heavens *s* by
    his understanding.
¹³When he thunders, *t* the waters in the
    heavens roar;
  he makes clouds rise from the ends of
    the earth.
  He sends lightning *u* with the rain *v*
  and brings out the wind from his
    storehouses. *w*
¹⁴Everyone is senseless and without
    knowledge;
  every goldsmith is shamed *x* by his
    idols.
  His images are a fraud; *y*
    they have no breath in them.
¹⁵They are worthless, *z* the objects of
    mockery;

Cross references (center column)

10:2 *r*S Ge 1:14
10:3 *s*S Isa 40:19
  *t*Dt 9:21;
  S 1Ki 8:36;
  Jer 44:8; Eze 7:20
10:4 *u*Ps 135:15;
  Hos 13:2;
  Hab 2:19
  *v*S 1Sa 5:3;
  Isa 41:7
10:5 *w*S 1Ki 18:26;
  1Co 12:2
  *x*S Isa 45:20
  *y*Isa 41:23
  *z*S Isa 41:24;
  44:9-20; 46:7;
  Ac 19:26
10:6 *a*S Ex 8:10
  *b*S 2Sa 7:22;
  S Ps 48:1
10:7 *c*Jer 5:22
  *d*Ps 22:28;
  S Isa 12:4;
  Rev 15:4
10:8 *e*S Isa 44:18
  *f*S Isa 40:19;
  S Jer 4:22
  *g*S Dt 32:21
10:9 *h*S Ge 10:4
  *i*Ps 115:4;
  S Isa 40:19
10:10 *j*S Jos 3:10;
  S Mt 16:16
  *k*S Ge 21:33;
  Da 6:26
  *l*S Ps 18:7
  *m*S Jdg 5:4;
  S Job 9:6; Ps 29:8
  *n*Ps 76:7;
  Jer 21:12; Na 1:6
10:11 *o*S Isa 2:18
10:12 *p*S 1Sa 2:8
  *q*S ver 16
  *r*S Ge 1:31
  *s*S Ge 1:1,8
10:13 *t*S Job 36:29
  *u*S Job 36:30
  *v*S Ps 104:13;
  S 135:7
  *w*S Dt 28:12
10:14 *x*S Ps 97:7;
  S Isa 1:29
  *y*S Isa 44:20
10:15 *z*S Isa 41:24;
  S Jer 14:22

u 11 The text of this verse is in Aramaic.

10:3 *worthless.* A term that Jeremiah often applies to idols
(see vv. 8,15; see also note on 2:5). *cut a tree.* See Isa
44:14–15. *craftsman.* The word is often used of idol-makers
who work usually—but not always (see Isa 40:19)—with
wood (see Isa 41:7). *chisel.* Cf. Isa 44:13.
10:4 *silver and gold.* Wooden idols were plated with precious metals to beautify them (see Isa 30:22; 40:19). *fasten
it . . . so it will not totter.* See Isa 40:20; 41:7; cf. 46:7;
contrast 1Sa 5:2–4.
10:5 The impotence of idols is described in classic form in
Ps 115:4–7; 135:15–18. *scarecrow.* Verse 70 in the Apocryphal *Letter of Jeremiah* uses the same imagery. *melon
patch.* See Isa 1:8 and note. *must be carried.* Usually on the
backs of animals. See Isa 46:1. *harm nor . . . good.* Idols can
do nothing at all (see Isa 41:23).
10:6 *No one.* Among the gods (see Ps 86:8). *your name is
mighty in power.* See 16:21.
10:7 *King of the nations.* See Ps 47:8–9; 96:10. Unlike the
tribal deities, limited to their own territories, the Lord is King
over all. *This.* Reverence. *Among all the wise men . . . no
one like you.* See Isa 19:12; 29:14; 1Co 1:20.
10:8 *senseless and foolish.* See vv. 14,21; 5:21; see also
NIV text note on Pr 1:7. *taught by . . . idols.* Instead of by the
Lord (see Dt 11:2; Job 5:17; Pr 3:11, where the Hebrew
word for "taught by" is translated "discipline"). *worthless.*
See note on v. 3.

10:9 *silver . . . from Tarshish.* See Eze 27:12; see also
notes on Isa 23:6; Jnh 1:3. *Uphaz.* Mentioned only here;
location unknown. *craftsman and goldsmith.* See Isa 40:19;
41:7. *dressed in blue and purple.* To make it look regal. *all.*
The idols.
10:10 Everything that idols are not, the Lord is. *true.* See
1Th 1:9. *living.* See Dt 5:26. *eternal.* See Ex 15:18; Ps
10:16; 29:10. *When . . . wrath.* See Ps 97:5; Na 1:5.
10:11 See NIV text note. The other major Aramaic passages in the OT are Ezr 4:8–6:18; 7:12–26; Da 2:4–7:28.
This verse is in prose. *them.* Pagan idolaters, who would
have been more likely to understand Aramaic (the language
of diplomacy during this period) than Hebrew.
10:12–16 Repeated almost verbatim in 51:15–19.
10:12 *But God.* In contrast to the false gods of v. 11.
stretched out the heavens. Like a tent or canopy (see Ps
104:2; Isa 40:22 and note).
10:13 *he makes clouds . . . his storehouses.* Repeated in Ps
135:7, where the one true God is contrasted to false gods
(see Ps 135:5,15–17); cf. Job 38:22.
10:14 *senseless.* See vv. 8,21; see also note on 4:22.
images. Cast in metal; the Hebrew for this word is translated
"metal god" in Isa 48:5 and "metal images" in Da 11:8. *no
breath.* See Ps 135:17.
10:15 *worthless.* See note on v. 3.

when their judgment comes, they
will perish.
[16]He who is the Portion[a] of Jacob is not
like these,
for he is the Maker of all things, [b]
including Israel, the tribe of his
inheritance[c] —
the LORD Almighty is his name. [d]

Coming Destruction

[17]Gather up your belongings[e] to leave the
land,
you who live under siege.
[18]For this is what the LORD says:
"At this time I will hurl[f] out
those who live in this land;
I will bring distress[g] on them
so that they may be captured."

[19]Woe to me because of my injury!
My wound[h] is incurable!
Yet I said to myself,
"This is my sickness, and I must
endure[i] it."
[20]My tent[j] is destroyed;
all its ropes are snapped.
My sons are gone from me and are no
more;[k]
no one is left now to pitch my tent
or to set up my shelter.
[21]The shepherds[l] are senseless[m]
and do not inquire of the LORD;[n]
so they do not prosper[o]
and all their flock is scattered. [p]
[22]Listen! The report is coming—
a great commotion from the land of
the north![q]

It will make the towns of Judah
desolate,[r]
a haunt of jackals. [s]

Jeremiah's Prayer

[23]I know, O LORD, that a man's life is not
his own;
it is not for man to direct his steps. [t]
[24]Correct me, LORD, but only with
justice—
not in your anger, [u]
lest you reduce me to nothing. [v] [w]
[25]Pour out your wrath on the nations[x]
that do not acknowledge you,
on the peoples who do not call on
your name. [y]
For they have devoured[z] Jacob;
they have devoured him completely
and destroyed his homeland. [a]

The Covenant Is Broken

11 This is the word that came to Jeremiah from the LORD: [2]"Listen to
the terms of this covenant[b] and tell them
to the people of Judah and to those who
live in Jerusalem. [3]Tell them that this is
what the LORD, the God of Israel, says:
'Cursed[c] is the man who does not obey
the terms of this covenant— [4]the terms I
commanded your forefathers when I
brought them out of Egypt, [d] out of the
iron-smelting furnace. [e]' I said, 'Obey[f] me
and do everything I command you, and
you will be my people, [g] and I will be your
God. [5]Then I will fulfill the oath I swore[h]
to your forefathers, to give them a land

Cross-references (center column)

10:16 [a]S Dt 32:9;
S Ps 119:57 [b]ver
12; Jer 32:17;
33:2 [c]S Ex 34:9;
Ps 74:2
[d]Jer 31:35; 32:18
10:17
[e]Eze 12:3-12
10:18
[f]S 1Sa 25:29;
S Isa 22:17
[g]S Dt 28:52
10:19 [h]Job 34:6;
Jer 14:17; 15:18;
30:12,15;
La 2:13; Mic 1:9;
Na 3:19 [i]Mic 7:9
10:20 [j]S Jer 4:20
[k]Jer 31:15; La 1:5
10:21 [l]Jer 22:22;
23:1; 25:34; 50:6
[m]ver 8
[n]S Isa 56:10
[o]Jer 22:30
[p]Jer 23:2;
Eze 34:6
10:22 [q]Jer 6:22;
27:6; 49:28,30

[r]Eze 12:19
[s]S Isa 34:13
10:23
[t]S Job 33:29;
S Pr 3:5-6; 20:24
10:24 [u]Ps 6:1;
38:1; S Jer 7:20;
18:23 [v]Jer 46:28
[w]Jer 30:11
10:25
[x]S Ps 69:24;
Zep 2:2; 3:8
[y]S Ps 14:4
[z]S Ps 79:7;
S Jer 2:3
[a]Ps 79:6-7
11:2 [b]S Dt 5:2
11:3
[c]Dt 11:26-28;
27:26; 28:15-68;
Gal 3:10
11:4 [d]ver 7
[e]S 1Ki 8:51
[f]S Ex 24:3;
Jer 7:23
[g]Jer 7:23; 31:33;
Eze 11:20
11:5 [h]S Ex 6:8;
13:5; Dt 7:12;
Ps 105:8-11

Study notes (bottom)

10:16 Portion of Jacob. A title for God, used again only in 51:19 (see Ps 73:26; 119:57; 142:5; La 3:24). tribe of his inheritance. See Isa 63:17. the LORD Almighty is his name. See Isa 54:5; Am 4:13.
10:17–22 Destruction and exile are imminent.
10:18 hurl out. As from a sling.
10:19–20 On behalf of his countrymen, the prophet bemoans their fate and his own (see 4:19–21).
10:20 sons. The people of Judah and Jerusalem (Jeremiah never married or had children; see 16:2). shelter. See note on 4:20.
10:21 shepherds . . . flock. Rulers and people (see note on 2:8). senseless. See vv. 8,14; see also note on 4:22. do not inquire of the LORD. Instead, they consult the heavenly bodies (see 8:2). scattered. See note on 9:16.
10:22 great commotion. The sound of the invaders (see 6:23; 8:16). land of the north. Babylonia (see 4:6; 6:22; see also note on Isa 41:25). haunt of jackals. See 9:11 and note.
10:23–25 On the people's behalf, the prophet prays for divine justice.
10:23 Only the Lord can direct a man's steps (see Ps 37:23; Pr 16:9).
10:25 Repeated almost verbatim in Ps 79:6–7, where the context (see Ps 79:1–5) shows that the prayer is not vengeful but is an appeal for God's justice. The verse is recited annually by Jews during their Passover service.

11:1–13:27 Because of Judah's violations of its covenant obligations, the people will be exiled to Babylonia. The section is perhaps to be dated to the reign of Josiah (but see note on 13:18).
11:1–17 God's people have broken his covenant with them.
11:2 Listen. See note on 2:4. terms. Lit. "words," a technical term for covenant stipulations (see vv. 3–4,6; 34:18; see also note on Ex 20:1). this covenant. See vv. 3,6,8,10; Dt 29:9. Reference is to the covenant established by God with Israel through Moses at Mount Sinai (see v. 4; Ex 19–24). tell them. Periodic public reading of covenants was a common and necessary practice (see Dt 31:10–13; Jos 8:34–35).
11:3 Cursed is the man. The phrase appears at the beginning of every verse in Dt 27:15–26 (and "Amen" appears at the end; see note on v. 5). Blessings resulted from obedience to the covenant (see Dt 28:1–14); curses resulted from disobedience (see Dt 28:15–68; see also Dt 11:26–28; 29:20–21).
11:4 out of Egypt . . . the iron-smelting furnace. See note on Dt 4:20. Obey me. See v. 7; 7:23; Ex 19:5. you will be my people . . . your God. See note on 7:23.
11:5 land flowing with milk and honey. See 32:22; see also note on Ex 3:8. Amen. Appears at the end of every verse in Dt 27:15–26 (and "Cursed is the man" appears at the

flowing with milk and honey' *i*—the land you possess today.' "

I answered, "Amen,*j* LORD."

⁶The LORD said to me, "Proclaim*k* all these words in the towns of Judah and in the streets of Jerusalem: 'Listen to the terms of this covenant and follow*l* them. ⁷From the time I brought your forefathers up from Egypt until today, I warned them again and again, *m* saying, "Obey me." ⁸But they did not listen or pay attention; *n* instead, they followed the stubbornness of their evil hearts. *o* So I brought on them all the curses*p* of the covenant I had commanded them to follow but that they did not keep. *q* ' "

⁹Then the LORD said to me, "There is a conspiracy*r* among the people of Judah and those who live in Jerusalem. ¹⁰They have returned to the sins of their forefathers, *s* who refused to listen to my words. *t* They have followed other gods*u* to serve them. *v* Both the house of Israel and the house of Judah have broken the covenant*w* I made with their forefathers. ¹¹Therefore this is what the LORD says: 'I will bring on them a disaster*x* they cannot escape. *y* Although they cry*z* out to me, I will not listen*a* to them. ¹²The towns of Judah and the people of Jerusalem will go and cry out to the gods to whom they burn incense, *b* but they will not help them at all when disaster*c* strikes. ¹³You have as many gods*d* as you have towns, *e* O Judah; and the altars you have set up to burn incense*f* to that shameful*g* god Baal are as many as the streets of Jerusalem.'

¹⁴"Do not pray*h* for this people nor offer any plea or petition for them, because I will not listen*i* when they call to me in the time of their distress.

---

¹⁵"What is my beloved doing in my temple
　as she works out her evil schemes with many?
Can consecrated meat*j* avert ˌyour punishmentˌ? *k*
When you engage in your wickedness, then you rejoice. *v* "

¹⁶The LORD called you a thriving olive tree*l*
　with fruit beautiful in form.
But with the roar of a mighty storm he will set it on fire, *m*
　and its branches will be broken. *n*

¹⁷The LORD Almighty, who planted*o* you, has decreed disaster*p* for you, because the house of Israel and the house of Judah have done evil and provoked*q* me to anger by burning incense to Baal. *r*

Plot Against Jeremiah

¹⁸Because the LORD revealed their plot to me, I knew it, for at that time he showed me what they were doing. ¹⁹I had been like a gentle lamb led to the slaughter; *s* I did not realize that they had plotted*t* against me, saying,

"Let us destroy the tree and its fruit;
　let us cut him off from the land of the living, *u*
that his name be remembered*v* no more."

²⁰But, O LORD Almighty, you who judge righteously*w*

11:5 *f*S Ex 3:8 /S Dt 27:26
11:6 *k*S Jer 4:5 /S Ex 15:26; S Dt 15:5; Jas 1:22
11:7 *m*S 2Ch 36:15
11:8 *n*S Jer 7:26 *o*S Ecc 9:3; S Jer 3:17 *p*Lev 26:14-43; Dt 28:15-68; S Jos 23:15 *q*S 2Ch 7:19; Ps 78:10; Jer 26:4; 32:23; 44:10
11:9 *r*Eze 22:25
11:10 *s*Dt 9:7; S 2Ch 30:7 *t*Zec 7:11 *u*S Jdg 2:12-13; S 10:13 *v*Jer 16:11; Eze 20:8 *w*Isa 24:5; Jer 34:18; Hos 6:7; 8:1
11:11 *x*S 2Ki 22:16; S Jer 4:6 *y*S Job 11:20; La 2:22 *z*S Job 27:9; Jer 14:12; Eze 8:18; Mal 2:13 *a*ver 14; S Ps 66:18; Pr 1:28; S Isa 1:15; 59:2; Eze 8:8; Zec 7:13
11:12 *b*S Dt 32:38; S Jer 44:17 *c*S Dt 32:37; S Jdg 10:14
11:13 *d*S Ex 20:3; Jer 19:4 *e*S 2Ki 17:29 S Jer 7:9; 44:21 *g*S Jer 3:24
11:14 *h*S Ex 32:10 /S ver 11

11:15 /Hag 2:12 *k*S Jer 7:9-10
11:16 /S Ps 1:3; Hos 14:6 *m*S Jer 7:20; 21:14 *n*S Isa 27:11; Ro 11:17-24

11:17 *o*S Ex 15:17; Isa 5:2; Jer 12:2; 45:4 *p*ver 11 *q*Jer 7:18 *r*S Jer 7:9 **11:19** *s*S Ps 44:22 *t*ver 21; S Ps 44:16; 54:3; 71:10; Jer 18:18; 20:10 *u*S Job 28:13; S Ps 116:9; Isa 53:8 *v*Ps 83:4 **11:20** *w*Ps 7:11

v 15 Or *Could consecrated meat avert your punishment?*
/ *Then you would rejoice*

---

beginning; see note on v. 3). *fulfill the oath I swore.* See Ge 15:17–18 and notes; Dt 7:8.
11:6 *Proclaim.* See 2:2; 3:12.
11:7 *again and again.* See note on 7:13.
11:8 See 7:24. *stubbornness of their evil hearts.* See note on 3:17. *curses of the covenant.* See note on v. 3. *So I brought on them.* See 2Ki 17:18–23.
11:9 *conspiracy.* Against the intended reforms of Josiah (see Introduction: Background; see also note on 1:2).
11:10 *refused.* Their sin was deliberate (see note on 9:6). *the covenant.* Lit. "my covenant," emphasizing its origin in God himself.
11:11 *I will bring on them.* Judah will be judged, just as Israel had been judged earlier (see vv. 10; see also 2Ki 17:18–23).
11:12 *burn incense.* See vv. 13,17; see also note on 1:16.
11:13 *as many gods as . . . towns.* See 2:28. *altars . . . as many as the streets.* See 2Ch 28:24. *to that shameful god Baal.* Lit. "to the shame(ful god) . . . to Baal." See 3:24; see also notes on 2:26; Jdg 6:32.
11:14 *Do not pray for this people.* See note on 7:16; cf.

1Jn 5:16.
11:15 See 7:10–11,21–24. *my beloved.* Judah (see 12:7; cf. Dt 33:12, where Benjamin is called the "beloved of the LORD").
11:16 *called you . . . olive tree.* See Ps 52:8; 128:3. *storm.* The Hebrew for this word appears elsewhere only in Eze 1:24, where it is translated "tumult" in reference to the noise made by an army (see Isa 13:4). *branches will be broken.* See Eze 31:12.
11:17 Fulfilled when Judah was destroyed in 586 B.C. (see 44:2–3). *provoked me to anger.* See 8:19; Dt 31:29.
11:18–23 The first of Jeremiah's "confessions" (see Introduction: Author and Date).
11:18 *their . . . they.* Jeremiah's personal enemies, the "men of Anathoth" (vv. 21,23), his hometown.
11:19 *lamb led to the slaughter.* See 51:40; see also Isa 53:7 and note. *destroy the tree and its fruit.* Contrast 12:2. *cut him off from the land of the living.* See Isa 53:8; contrast Ps 27:13. *name.* Since Jeremiah had no children (see 16:2), his name would die with him. *be remembered no more.* As though he were evil (see Job 24:20; Eze 21:32).

and test the heart[x] and mind,[y]
let me see your vengeance[z] upon them,
for to you I have committed my
cause.

21"Therefore this is what the LORD says
about the men of Anathoth[a] who are
seeking your life[b] and saying, 'Do not
prophesy[c] in the name of the LORD or you
will die[d] by our hands'— 22therefore this
is what the LORD Almighty says: 'I will
punish them. Their young men[e] will die
by the sword, their sons and daughters by
famine. 23Not even a remnant[f] will be left
to them, because I will bring disaster on
the men of Anathoth in the year of their
punishment.[g]'"

Jeremiah's Complaint

12 You are always righteous,[h]
O LORD,
when I bring a case[i] before you.
Yet I would speak with you about your
justice:[j]
Why does the way of the wicked
prosper?[k]
Why do all the faithless live at ease?
2You have planted[l] them, and they have
taken root;
they grow and bear fruit.[m]
You are always on their lips
but far from their hearts.[n]
3Yet you know me, O LORD;
you see me and test[o] my thoughts
about you.

Drag them off like sheep[p] to be
butchered!
Set them apart for the day of
slaughter![q]
4How long will the land lie parched[w][r]
and the grass in every field be
withered?[s]
Because those who live in it are wicked,
the animals and birds have perished.[t]
Moreover, the people are saying,
"He will not see what happens to
us."

God's Answer

5"If you have raced with men on foot
and they have worn you out,
how can you compete with horses?
If you stumble in safe country,[x]
how will you manage in the
thickets[u] by[y] the Jordan?
6Your brothers, your own family—
even they have betrayed you;
they have raised a loud cry against
you.[v]
Do not trust them,
though they speak well of you.[w]
7"I will forsake[x] my house,
abandon[y] my inheritance;
I will give the one I love[z]
into the hands of her enemies.[a]
8My inheritance has become to me
like a lion[b] in the forest.

11:20 [x]S 1Sa 2:3;
S 1Ch 29:17
[y]S Ps 26:2
[z]S Ps 58:10;
La 3:60
11:21
[a]S Isa 21:18
[b]S ver 19;
Jer 12:6; 21:7;
34:20
[c]S Isa 30:10
[d]Jer 2:30; 18:23;
26:8,11; 38:4
11:22
[e]S Isa 9:17;
Jer 18:21
11:23 [f]Jer 6:9
[g]Jer 23:12
12:1 [h]S Ezr 9:15;
Job 8:3; Da 9:14
[i]S Job 5:8
[j]Eze 18:25
[k]S Job 21:7,13;
Ps 37:7;
Jer 5:27-28
12:2 [l]S Jer 11:17
[m]S Job 5:3
[n]S Isa 29:13;
S Jer 3:10;
S Eze 22:27;
Mt 15:8; Mk 7:6;
Tit 1:16
12:3 [o]Ps 7:9;
11:5; 139:1-4

[p]S Ps 44:11
[q]Jer 16:18;
17:18; 20:11
12:4 [r]S Jer 4:28
[s]S ver 11;
S Jer 4:26;
Joel 1:10-12;
Am 1:2
[t]Dt 28:15-18;
S Jer 4:25; S 9:10
12:5 [u]Jer 49:19;
50:44
12:6
[v]S Pr 26:24-25;
Jer 9:4 [w]Ps 12:2
12:7 [x]S 2Ki 21:14
[y]S Jer 7:29
[z]Isa 5:1 [a]Jer 17:4
12:8 [b]S Ps 17:12

---

[w]4 Or land mourn   [x]5 Or If you put your trust in a
land of safety   [y]5 Or the flooding of

11:20 Repeated almost verbatim in 20:12; see also 17:10. *you who judge righteously.* See note on Ge 18:25.
11:21 *men of Anathoth who are seeking your life.* See 12:6. "A man's enemies are the members of his own household" (Mic 7:6, quoted by Jesus in Mt 10:36).
11:22 *sword...famine.* See note on 5:12.
11:23 *remnant.* See 6:9; Isa 10:20-22 and notes. *them.* The conspirators in Anathoth, not its entire population, since 128 men of Anathoth returned to their hometown after the exile (see Ezr 2:23).
12:1-6 The second of Jeremiah's "confessions," continuing (and closely related to) the first (11:18-23). Jeremiah speaks in vv. 1-4, and God responds in vv. 5-6.
12:1 *You are...righteous.* See note on Ge 18:25; see also 11:20; Ps 51:4; Ro 3:4. Because God is righteous, he is a dependable arbiter and judge. *Yet.* He is nevertheless ready to listen to our questions and complaints. *Why does...the wicked prosper?* The question is not unique to Jeremiah (see, e.g., Job 21:7-15; Mal 3:15). The Lord replies that ultimately the wicked in Judah will perish (vv. 7-13) and that the wicked invaders who destroy them will themselves be destroyed (vv. 14-17).
12:2 *You have planted them.* But a sovereign God can always reconsider his intentions if conditions warrant a change (18:9-10). *bear fruit.* The wicked flourish, while Jeremiah's fellow citizens plot to destroy his own "fruit" (see 11:19). *on their lips...far from their hearts.* Quoted in part by Jesus in Mt 15:8-9.
12:3 *test my thoughts.* See 11:20. *like sheep to be butch-*

ered. Jeremiah asks that his wicked countrymen receive the fate mentioned for himself in 11:19. His request arises not so much out of a desire for revenge as for the vindication of God's righteousness.
12:4 *parched...withered.* See 23:10; see also 3:3; 14:1. Apparently there was a series of droughts in Judah during Jeremiah's ministry. *He will not see.* The prophet's enemies do not believe that his predictions will be fulfilled.
12:5 The Lord warns Jeremiah that in the future his troubles will increase (see, e.g., 38:4-6). *stumble.* The Hebrew for this word, which usually means "trust" (see NIV text note), has a negative meaning in a few passages (see, e.g., Pr 14:16, where it is translated "reckless"). *thickets.* Providing cover for lions (see 49:19; 50:44; Zec 11:3). If the Hebrew for this word means "flooding" (see NIV text note) here, an ancient example is described in Jos 3:15.
12:6 *family.* Lit. "house," linking this verse verbally with the following context (see v. 7). Apparently, members of Jeremiah's own family were included in the "men of Anathoth" (11:21,23) who wanted to kill him.
12:7-17 The Lord will judge Judah (vv. 7-13) as well as the wicked neighboring nations (vv. 14-17).
12:7 *house.* Judah (see, e.g., 11:17). *inheritance.* God's land and people (see vv. 8-9,14-15; see also Ex 15:17 and note; Dt 4:20; Isa 19:25; 47:6). *the one I love.* See note on 11:15.
12:8 *I hate her.* I will withdraw my love from her by giving her "into the hands of her enemies" (v. 7; see Mal 1:3).

She roars at me;
  therefore I hate her. ^c

⁹Has not my inheritance become to me
    like a speckled bird of prey
    that other birds of prey surround and
      attack?
  Go and gather all the wild beasts;
    bring them to devour. ^d
¹⁰Many shepherds ^e will ruin my vineyard
    and trample down my field;
  they will turn my pleasant field
    into a desolate wasteland. ^f
¹¹It will be made a wasteland, ^g
    parched and desolate before me; ^h
  the whole land will be laid waste
    because there is no one who cares.
¹²Over all the barren heights in the desert
    destroyers will swarm,
  for the sword ⁱ of the LORD ^j will
    devour ^k
  from one end of the land to the
    other; ^l
  no one will be safe. ^m
¹³They will sow wheat but reap thorns;
  they will wear themselves out but
    gain nothing. ⁿ
So bear the shame of your harvest
  because of the LORD's fierce anger." ^o

¹⁴This is what the LORD says: "As for all
my wicked neighbors who seize the inheritance ^p I gave my people Israel, I will
uproot ^q them from their lands and I will
uproot ^r the house of Judah from among
them. ¹⁵But after I uproot them, I will

again have compassion ^s and will bring ^t
each of them back to his own inheritance
and his own country. ¹⁶And if they learn ^u
well the ways of my people and swear by
my name, saying, 'As surely as the LORD
lives' ^v—even as they once taught my
people to swear by Baal ^w—then they will
be established among my people. ^x ¹⁷But if
any nation does not listen, I will complete-
ly uproot and destroy ^y it," declares the
LORD.

A Linen Belt

13 This is what the LORD said to me:
"Go and buy a linen belt and put it
around your waist, but do not let it touch
water." ²So I bought a belt, as the LORD
directed, and put it around my waist.

³Then the word of the LORD came to me
a second time: ^z ⁴"Take the belt you
bought and are wearing around your waist,
and go now to Perath ^{z a} and hide it there
in a crevice in the rocks." ⁵So I went and
hid it at Perath, as the LORD told me. ^b

⁶Many days later the LORD said to me,
"Go now to Perath and get the belt I told
you to hide there." ⁷So I went to Perath
and dug up the belt and took it from the
place where I had hidden it, but now it
was ruined and completely useless.

⁸Then the word of the LORD came to
me: ⁹"This is what the LORD says: 'In the
same way I will ruin the pride of Judah and

^{z4} Or possibly *the Euphrates*; also in verses 5-7

Cross references column:

12:8 ^cPs 5:5;
Hos 9:15; Am 6:8
12:9
^dS Dt 28:26;
Isa 56:9; Jer 15:3;
Eze 23:25;
39:17-20
12:10 ^eJer 23:1;
25:34;
Eze 34:2-10
^fIsa 5:1-7;
Jer 9:10; 25:11
12:11 ^gS Isa 5:6;
S 24:4 ^hver 4;
Jer 9:12; 14:4;
23:10
12:12
ⁱEze 21:3-4
^jS Dt 32:41;
Isa 31:8;
Jer 46:10; 47:6;
Eze 14:17; 21:28;
33:2 ^kS Dt 32:42
^lJer 3:2 ^mJer 7:10
12:13
ⁿS Lev 26:20;
S Dt 28:38
^oS Ex 15:7;
S Jer 4:26
12:14
^pS Dt 29:28;
S 2Ch 7:20
^qS Ps 9:6;
Zec 2:7-9
^rS Dt 28:63

12:15 ^sS Ps 6:2
^tS Dt 30:3;
Am 9:14-15
12:16 ^uJer 18:8
^vS Jer 4:2
^wS Jos 23:7
^xS Isa 26:18;
49:6; Jer 3:17
12:17
^yS Ge 27:29
13:3 ^zJer 33:1
13:4 ^aS Ge 2:14
13:5 ^bEx 40:16

Notes:

12:9 *other birds of prey ... wild beasts.* Judah's enemies
(see Isa 56:9 and note).
12:10 *shepherds.* Rulers (see note on 2:8). *my vineyard.*
Judah (see 2:21 and note). *pleasant field.* See 3:19 and note.
12:11 *parched.* See v. 4 and note. A total of seven *s*-sounds
and seven *m*-sounds in the Hebrew of this brief verse provides a striking example of Jeremiah's literary gifts.
12:12 *barren heights.* Places of idolatrous worship (see
3:2; Nu 23:3). *destroyers.* The Babylonians (see note on
4:7). *sword of the LORD.* Symbolizing God's instruments of
judgment (see 25:29; 47:6). *from one end ... to the other.*
See 25:33. *no one will be safe.* Lit. "there will be no peace
for anyone" (see 6:14 and note).
12:13 See 14:2-4.
12:14 *wicked neighbors.* See, e.g., 2Ki 24:2. *seize.* Lit.
"touch," used in the context of attack and plunder in Zec
2:8. *uproot.* Carry off into exile (see, e.g., 1Ki 14:15).
12:15 The exiles from Judah, and those from the neighboring nations, will eventually be brought back to their respective lands (see v. 16; 32:37,44; 33:26; 48:47; 49:6).
12:16 See Isa 56:6-7. The Messianic age is in view (see Isa
2:2-4). *ways.* See note on 10:2. *be established.* The Hebrew
for this phrase is translated "prosper" in Mal 3:15.
13:1-27 A series of five warnings, the first two (vv. 1-11,
12-14) written in prose and the last three (vv. 15-17,
18-19, 20-27) in poetry.
13:1-11 The story of the ruined, useless belt is the first
major example of the Lord's commanding Jeremiah to perform symbolic acts to illustrate his message (see Introduc-

tion: Literary Features).
13:1-2,4-7 *Go and buy ... So I bought ... Take the belt
... and hide it ... So I went and hid it ... Go now to Perath
and get the belt ... So I went to Perath and dug up the belt.*
Like his spiritual ancestor Abraham (see note on Ge 12:4),
Jeremiah was characterized by prompt obedience.
13:1 *linen.* The material of which the priests' garments
were made (see Eze 44:17-18), symbolic of Israel's holiness
as a "kingdom of priests" (see Ex 19:6 and note). The linen
belt is a symbol of the formerly intimate relationship between
God and Judah (see v. 11). *do not let it touch water.* Do not
wash it—symbolic of Judah's sinful pride (see v. 9).
13:3 *Then.* Some time later.
13:4 *Perath.* Perhaps the same as Parah (Jos 18:23), near
the modern Wadi Farah, three miles northeast of Anathoth.
Since in other contexts the Hebrew for Perath refers to the
river Euphrates (see NIV text note), it serves as an appropriate symbol of the corrupting Assyrian and Babylonian influence on Judah that began during the reign of Ahaz (see 2Ki
16).
13:6 *Many days later.* Perhaps a reference to the lengthy
Babylonian exile.
13:7 *dug up.* The belt had either been buried by the
prophet or silted over by the water of the wadi. *it was ruined.*
As foreseen in Lev 26:39, God's people in exile would waste
away because of their sins and the sins of their ancestors.
13:9 *pride ... great pride.* Contrast 9:23-24. Judah's
vaunted pride would be a cause of her downfall and exile
(see vv. 15,17), as foreshadowed in Lev 26:19.

the great pride[c] of Jerusalem. [10]These wicked people, who refuse to listen[d] to my words, who follow the stubbornness of their hearts[e] and go after other gods[f] to serve and worship them,[g] will be like this belt—completely useless![h] [11]For as a belt is bound around a man's waist, so I bound the whole house of Israel and the whole house of Judah to me,' declares the LORD, 'to be my people for my renown[i] and praise and honor.[j] But they have not listened.'[k]

Wineskins

[12]"Say to them: 'This is what the LORD, the God of Israel, says: Every wineskin should be filled with wine.' And if they say to you, 'Don't we know that every wineskin should be filled with wine?' [13]then tell them, 'This is what the LORD says: I am going to fill with drunkenness[l] all who live in this land, including the kings who sit on David's throne, the priests, the prophets and all those living in Jerusalem. [14]I will smash them one against the other, fathers and sons alike, declares the LORD. I will allow no pity[m] or mercy or compassion[n] to keep me from destroying[o] them.' "

Threat of Captivity

[15]Hear and pay attention,
do not be arrogant,
for the LORD has spoken.[p]
[16]Give glory[q] to the LORD your God
before he brings the darkness,
before your feet stumble[r]
on the darkening hills.

You hope for light,
but he will turn it to thick darkness
and change it to deep gloom.[s]
[17]But if you do not listen,[t]
I will weep in secret
because of your pride;
my eyes will weep bitterly,
overflowing with tears,[u]
because the LORD's flock[v] will be
taken captive.[w]

[18]Say to the king[x] and to the queen
mother,[y]
"Come down from your thrones,
for your glorious crowns[z]
will fall from your heads."
[19]The cities in the Negev will be shut up,
and there will be no one to open
them.
All Judah[a] will be carried into exile,
carried completely away.

[20]Lift up your eyes and see
those who are coming from the
north.[b]
Where is the flock[c] that was entrusted
to you,
the sheep of which you boasted?
[21]What will you say when the LORD sets
over you
those you cultivated as your special
allies?[d]
Will not pain grip you
like that of a woman in labor?[e]
[22]And if you ask yourself,
"Why has this happened to me?"[f] —
it is because of your many sins[g]
that your skirts have been torn off[h]

Cross references:

13:9 [c]S Lev 26:19; [S] Mt 23:12; [S] Lk 1:51
13:10 [d]Jer 22:21 [e]S Ecc 9:3; [S] Jer 3:17 [f]S Dt 8:19; Jer 9:14 [g]S Jdg 10:13 [h]Eze 15:3
13:11 [i]Isa 63:12; Jer 32:20 [j]Ex 19:5-6; Isa 43:21; [S] Jer 3:17 [k]S Isa 65:12; [S] Jer 7:26
13:13 [l]Ps 60:3; 75:8; [S] Isa 29:9; Jer 25:18; 51:57
13:14 [m]Eze 7:4; 8:18; 9:5,10; 24:14; Zec 11:6 [n]S Isa 9:17;
Jer 16:5 [o]Dt 29:20; Isa 9:19-21; [S] Jer 7:20; 49:32, 36; La 2:21; Eze 5:10
13:15 [p]S Ex 23:21; Ps 95:7-8
13:16 [q]S Jos 7:19 [r]S Lev 26:37; [S] Job 3:23; Isa 51:17; Jer 23:12

[s]S 1Sa 2:9; [S] Job 3:5; [S] Ps 82:5
13:17 [t]Mal 2:2 [u]S Jer 9:1 [v]Ps 80:1; Jer 23:1 [w]Jer 14:18; 29:1
13:18 [x]Jer 21:11; 22:1 [y]S 1Ki 2:19; [S] 2Ki 24:8; [S] Isa 22:17 [z]S 2Sa 12:30; La 5:16; Eze 16:12; 21:26
13:19 [a]Jer 20:4; 52:30; La 1:3
13:20 [b]Jer 6:22; Hab 1:6 [c]Jer 23:2
13:21 [d]S Ps 41:9; Jer 4:30; 20:10; 38:22; Ob 1:7

[e]S Jer 4:31 13:22 [f]S 1Ki 9:9 [g]Jer 9:2-6; 16:10-12 [h]S Isa 20:4

13:10 *refuse to listen.* See note on 9:6. *stubbornness of their hearts.* See note on 3:17. *completely useless.* See 24:8.
13:11 *But they have not listened.* And therefore the promise of Dt 26:19 can no longer be fulfilled in them.
13:12–14 The Lord uses the imagery of filled wineskins to point toward the eventual destruction of Judah's leaders and people.
13:13 *drunkenness.* In a literal sense (see, e.g., Isa 28:7), but also symbolizing the effects of the wine of God's wrath (see 25:15–29; Ps 60:3; Isa 51:17–20; Eze 23:32–34). *kings . . . priests . . . prophets . . . all those living in Jerusalem.* See 26:16; see also note on 1:18.
13:14 *smash them one against the other.* The various factions in Judah produced only confusion and chaos in the face of determined outside enemies. *no pity or mercy or compassion.* See 21:7; see also Eze 5:11.
13:15–17 Sinful pride carries the seeds of its own destruction, says the prophet.
13:15 *Hear.* See note on 2:4. *do not be arrogant.* See v. 17; see also note on v. 9.
13:16 *Give glory to . . . God.* Confess your sins (see Jos 7:19; Jn 9:24 and NIV text notes). *You hope for light, but.* Cf. the description of the day of the Lord in Am 5:18–20; 8:9.

13:17 *I will weep.* See note on 9:1. *pride.* See v. 15; see also note on v. 9. *flock.* People (see v. 20; Zec 10:3; see also notes on 2:8; 10:21). *taken captive.* Into exile (see v. 19).
13:18–19 The prophet speaks: Exile is imminent.
13:18 *king and . . . queen mother.* Probably Jehoiachin and Nehushta (2Ki 24:8). If so, the date is 597 B.C., about 12 years after Josiah's death (see note on 11:1–13:27). *your . . . crowns will fall.* See 22:24–26; 29:2; 2Ki 24:15.
13:19 *Negev.* The dry southland (see note on Ge 12:9). *shut up.* Blocked by debris (see Isa 24:10). *carried completely away.* See Am 1:6,9.
13:20–27 First the prophet speaks (vv. 20–23), then the Lord (vv. 24–27). Judah's willful rebellion has made exile inevitable.
13:20 *your . . . you . . . you.* Jerusalem, personified as a woman (see vv. 21–22,26–27), is being addressed. *the north.* Babylonia (see 4:6; see also note on Isa 41:25). *flock . . . sheep.* See note on v. 17.
13:21 *special allies.* Perhaps Egypt and Babylon, who alternated in dominating Judah (see Introduction: Background). *like . . . a woman in labor.* See 6:24; 49:24; 50:43.
13:22 *skirts . . . torn off.* Disgraced publicly, like a common prostitute (see vv. 26–27; Isa 47:3; Hos 2:3,10).

and your body mistreated. *i*
23Can the Ethiopian[a] change his skin
or the leopard its spots?
Neither can you do good
who are accustomed to doing evil. *j*

24"I will scatter you like chaff[k]
driven by the desert wind. *l*
25This is your lot,
the portion[m] I have decreed for you,"
declares the LORD,
"because you have forgotten[n] me
and trusted in false gods. *o*
26I will pull up your skirts over your face
that your shame may be seen[p]—
27your adulteries and lustful neighings,
your shameless prostitution![q]
I have seen your detestable acts
on the hills and in the fields. *r*
Woe to you, O Jerusalem!
How long will you be unclean?"[s]

Drought, Famine, Sword

14 This is the word of the LORD to
Jeremiah concerning the drought:[t]

2"Judah mourns,[u]
her cities languish;
they wail for the land,
and a cry goes up from Jerusalem.
3The nobles send their servants for
water;
they go to the cisterns
but find no water. *v*
They return with their jars unfilled;
dismayed and despairing,
they cover their heads. *w*
4The ground is cracked
because there is no rain in the land;[x]
the farmers are dismayed

and cover their heads.
5Even the doe in the field
deserts her newborn fawn
because there is no grass.[y]
6Wild donkeys stand on the barren
heights[z]
and pant like jackals;
their eyesight fails
for lack of pasture."[a]

7Although our sins testify[b] against us,
O LORD, do something for the sake of
your name.[c]
For our backsliding[d] is great;
we have sinned[e] against you.
8O Hope[f] of Israel,
its Savior[g] in times of distress,[h]
why are you like a stranger in the land,
like a traveler who stays only a night?
9Why are you like a man taken by
surprise,
like a warrior powerless to save?[i]
You are among[j] us, O LORD,
and we bear your name;[k]
do not forsake[l] us!

10This is what the LORD says about this
people:

"They greatly love to wander;
they do not restrain their feet.[m]
So the LORD does not accept[n] them;
he will now remember[o] their
wickedness
and punish them for their sins."[p]

11Then the LORD said to me, "Do not

13:22 *l*La 1:8; Eze 16:37; 23:26; Na 3:5-6
13:23 /S 2Ch 6:36
13:24 *k*S Ps 1:4 /S Lev 26:33; S Job 1:19; S 27:21
13:25 *m*S Job 20:29; Mt 24:51 *n*S Isa 17:10 *o*S Dt 31:20; S Ps 4:2; 106:19-21
13:26 *p*La 1:8; Eze 16:37; Na 3:5
13:27 *q*Eze 23:29 *r*S Isa 57:7; Eze 6:13 *s*Hos 8:5
14:1 *t*S Dt 28:22; S Isa 5:6
14:2 *u*S Isa 3:26
14:3 *v*S Dt 28:48; S 2Ki 18:31; Job 6:19-20 *w*S Est 6:12
14:4 *x*S Jer 3:3; S 12:11; Am 4:8; Zec 14:17
14:5 *y*Isa 15:6
14:6 *z*S Job 39:5-6; S Ps 104:11; S Jer 2:24 *a*S Ge 47:4
14:7 *b*S Isa 3:9; Hos 5:5 *c*S 1Sa 12:22; S Ps 79:9 *d*S Jer 2:19; 5:6 *e*S Jer 8:14
14:8 /S Ps 9:18; Jer 17:13; 50:7 *g*Ps 18:46; S Isa 25:9 *h*Ps 46:1
14:9 /S Isa 50:2 /S Ge 17:7; Jer 8:19 *k*Isa 63:19; Jer 15:16 /S Ps 27:9
14:10 *m*Ps 119:101; Jer 2:25 *n*Jer 6:20; Am 5:22 *o*Hos 7:2; 9:9; Am 8:7 *p*Jer 44:21-23; Hos 8:13; Am 3:2

[a]23 Hebrew *Cushite* (probably a person from the upper Nile region)

13:23 A rhetorical question, expecting a negative answer (see 17:9).
13:24 *like chaff driven.* The fate of the wicked (see, e.g., Ps 1:4). *desert wind.* See note on 4:11.
13:25 *forgotten me.* See note on 2:32.
13:26 See v. 22 and note.
13:27 *adulteries and lustful neighings.* See note on 5:8. *shameless prostitution.* See Eze 16:27. *How long ... ?* There is yet hope, however slender, to postpone the divine wrath (cf., e.g., 12:14-16).
14:1—15:21 Messages delivered by Jeremiah during an especially severe drought, the date of which is unknown.
14:1—15:9 After an initial vivid description of the drought (14:2-6), Jeremiah alternately prays (14:7-9,13,19-22) and God responds (14:10-12,14-18; 15:1-9).
14:1 *drought.* See 17:8. Unlike that in 3:3; 12:4, the suffering is increased because an enemy has invaded the land (see v. 18). Drought was one of the curses threatened (see 23:10) for disobedience to the covenant (see Lev 26:19-20; Dt 28:22-24).
14:2 *cities.* Lit. "gates" (see note on Ge 22:17); see 15:7.
14:3 *nobles.* A drought is no respecter of class distinctions. *cover their heads.* In mourning (see v. 4; 2Sa 15:30; cf. 2Sa 19:4).

14:4 *because there is no rain.* See 1Ki 17:7. Unlike Egypt, where the mighty Nile waters the ground, Palestine depends on adequate rainfall.
14:6 *pant.* The Hebrew underlying this word is translated "sniffing the wind" in 2:24. There a female wild donkey (Jerusalem) was in the heat of desire, while here the male wild donkeys are panting because of a drought brought on by Judah's sin.
14:7—9 The prophet prays on behalf of the people (see v. 11).
14:7 *for the sake of your name.* See v. 21; Jos 7:9; Isa 48:9-11. *backsliding.* See 2:19; 3:22; 5:6. The word implies apostasy.
14:8 *O Hope of Israel.* See v. 22; 17:13; 50:7; Ac 28:20.
14:9 *we bear your name.* We belong to you, our ever-present Savior (see note on 7:10).
14:10—12 The Lord responds.
14:10—11 *this people.* God does not acknowledge them as his own (see Isa 6:9-10; 8:6,11-12).
14:10 *wander.* After false gods (see 2:23,31). *the LORD does not ... their sins.* The Hebrew for these three lines is quoted verbatim from Hos 8:13 (cf. Hos 9:9).
14:11 *Do not pray.* See note on 7:16; cf. 1Sa 7:8; 12:19.

pray[q] for the well-being of this people. [12]Although they fast, I will not listen to their cry;[r] though they offer burnt offerings[s] and grain offerings,[t] I will not accept[u] them. Instead, I will destroy them with the sword,[v] famine[w] and plague."[x]

[13]But I said, "Ah, Sovereign LORD, the prophets[y] keep telling them, 'You will not see the sword or suffer famine.[z] Indeed, I will give you lasting peace[a] in this place.'"

[14]Then the LORD said to me, "The prophets are prophesying lies[b] in my name. I have not sent[c] them or appointed them or spoken to them. They are prophesying to you false visions,[d] divinations,[e] idolatries[b] and the delusions of their own minds. [15]Therefore, this is what the LORD says about the prophets who are prophesying in my name: I did not send them, yet they are saying, 'No sword or famine will touch this land.' Those same prophets will perish[f] by sword and famine.[g] [16]And the people they are prophesying to will be thrown out into the streets of Jerusalem because of the famine and sword. There will be no one to bury[h] them or their wives, their sons or their daughters.[i] I will pour out on them the calamity they deserve.[j]

[17]"Speak this word to them:

" 'Let my eyes overflow with tears[k]
    night and day without ceasing;
for my virgin[l] daughter—my people—
    has suffered a grievous wound,
    a crushing blow.[m]
[18]If I go into the country,
    I see those slain by the sword;
if I go into the city,

I see the ravages of famine.[n]
Both prophet and priest
    have gone to a land they know
      not.[o] '"

[19]Have you rejected Judah completely?[p]
    Do you despise Zion?
Why have you afflicted us
    so that we cannot be healed?[q]
We hoped for peace
    but no good has come,
for a time of healing
    but there is only terror.[r]
[20]O LORD, we acknowledge[s] our
    wickedness
    and the guilt of our fathers;[t]
    we have indeed sinned[u] against you.
[21]For the sake of your name[v] do not
    despise us;
    do not dishonor your glorious
      throne.[w]
Remember your covenant[x] with us
    and do not break it.
[22]Do any of the worthless idols[y] of the
    nations bring rain?[z]
Do the skies themselves send down
    showers?
No, it is you, O LORD our God.
    Therefore our hope is in you,
for you are the one who does all
    this.[a]

15 Then the LORD said to me: "Even if Moses[b] and Samuel[c] were to stand before me, my heart would not go out to this people.[d] Send them away from my presence![e] Let them go! [2]And if they

---

Cross references (center column):

14:11 qS Ex 32:10; S 1Sa 2:25
14:12 rS Dt 1:45; S 1Sa 8:18; S Jer 11:11; sLev 1:1-17; Jer 7:21; tS Lev 2:1-16; uAm 5:22; vS Isa 51:19; S Jer 9:16; wJer 15:2; 16:4; xJer 21:6; 27:8, 13; 32:24; 34:17; Eze 14:21
14:13 yDt 18:22; Jer 27:14; 37:19; zS Jer 5:12; aS Isa 30:10; S Jer 4:10
14:14 bS Jer 5:1; 23:25; 27:14; Eze 13:2; cJer 23:21,32; 29:31; Eze 13:6; dJer 23:16; La 2:9; eEze 12:24
14:15 fJer 20:6; Eze 14:9; gJer 5:12-13; 16:4; La 1:19
14:16 hPs 79:3; iS Jer 7:33; jS Pr 1:31; S Jer 17:10
14:17 kPs 119:136; lS 2Ki 19:21; S Isa 23:12; mS Jer 8:21
14:18 nEze 7:15; oS 2Ch 36:10; S Jer 13:17
14:19 pJer 7:29; qS Isa 1:6; Jer 30:12-13; rS Job 19:8; S Jer 8:15
14:20 sS Jer 3:13; tS Lev 26:40; S 1Ki 8:47; S Ezr 9:6; uS Jdg 10:10; Da 9:7-8
14:21 vver 7; S Jos 7:9; wIsa 62:7; Jer 3:17; xS Ex 2:24
14:22 yS Isa 41:24; S 44:10;

Jer 10:15; 16:19; Hab 2:18 zS 1Ki 8:36; S Ps 135:7
15:1 aS Isa 43:10 bS Ex 32:11; Nu 14:13-20 cS 1Sa 1:20; S 7:8 dS 1Sa 2:25; S Jer 7:16 eS 2Ki 17:20; Jer 16:13

b14 Or visions, worthless divinations

Footnotes (bottom):

14:12 *not accept them.* See v. 10. Sacrifice is to no avail when unaccompanied by repentance (see note on 6:20). *sword, famine and plague.* Curses for violating God's covenant (see Lev 26:25-26); the first occurrence of this triad, which occurs 15 times in Jeremiah (see Introduction: Literary Features).
14:13 Jeremiah reminds the Lord of what the false prophets are saying. *not . . . sword or . . . famine.* See 5:12. *lasting peace.* Jeremiah's elaboration of the false prophets' "Peace, peace" (see 6:14; 8:11).
14:14-18 The Lord responds.
14:14 *lies.* See 5:12. *in my name.* See Dt 18:20,22. *delusions of their own minds.* See 23:26.
14:15 *Those . . . prophets will perish.* See 28:15-17; Dt 18:20.
14:16 *no one to bury them.* See note on 7:33. *wives . . . sons . . . daughters.* All would perish, because all had worshiped false gods (see note on 7:18).
14:17 *my eyes overflow with tears.* See 9:18; 13:17. *virgin daughter.* Used of Jerusalem in Isa 37:22 (see note there; see also Isa 23:12 and note); see 18:13.
14:19-22 The prophet prays on behalf of the people.

14:20 *guilt of our fathers.* See 2:5-6; 7:25-26. *we have . . . sinned.* Repentance brings restoration (see Dt 30:2-3).
14:21 *your glorious throne.* The Jerusalem temple (see 17:12; 2Ki 19:14-15; Ps 99:1-2). *Remember your covenant . . . do not break it.* Jeremiah pleads the ancient promise of God in Lev 26:44-45.
14:22 See Hos 2:8,21-22. *worthless idols.* See note on 2:5. *it is you.* Only the Lord (not Baal) can send the showers to end the drought (see v. 1). *our hope is in you.* See note on v. 8.
15:1-9 The Lord responds, concluding this section (see note on 14:1-15:9).
15:1 *Moses and Samuel.* Famed for their intercession for sinful Israel (see Ex 32:11-14,30-34; Nu 14:13-23; Dt 9:18-20,25-29; 1Sa 7:5-9; 12:19-25; Ps 99:6-8). *stand before me.* The posture of God's servants as they are about to pray to him (see Ge 18:22). *Send them away.* The people are so wicked that God refuses to hear prayers offered on their behalf. They are beyond divine help (see notes on 7:16; 14:11-12).
15:2 See Eze 14:21; 33:27. *death.* Probably by plague; see 14:12 (and note), where "sword, famine and plague" are

ask you, 'Where shall we go?' tell them,
'This is what the LORD says:

" 'Those destined for death, to death;
those for the sword, to the sword;*f*
those for starvation, to starvation;*g*
those for captivity, to captivity.'*h*

³"I will send four kinds of destroyers*i*
against them," declares the LORD, "the
sword*j* to kill and the dogs*k* to drag away
and the birds*l* of the air and the beasts of
the earth to devour and destroy.*m* ⁴I will
make them abhorrent*n* to all the kingdoms
of the earth*o* because of what Manasseh*p*
son of Hezekiah king of Judah did in
Jerusalem.

⁵"Who will have pity*q* on you,
  O Jerusalem?
Who will mourn for you?
Who will stop to ask how you are?
⁶You have rejected*r* me," declares the
  LORD.
"You keep on backsliding.
So I will lay hands*s* on you and destroy
  you;
I can no longer show compassion.*t*
⁷I will winnow*u* them with a winnowing
  fork
  at the city gates of the land.
I will bring bereavement*v* and
  destruction on my people,*w*
for they have not changed their
  ways.*x*

⁸I will make their widows*y* more
  numerous
  than the sand of the sea.
At midday I will bring a destroyer*z*
  against the mothers of their young
  men;
suddenly I will bring down on them
  anguish and terror.*a*
⁹The mother of seven will grow faint*b*
  and breathe her last.*c*
Her sun will set while it is still day;
  she will be disgraced*d* and
  humiliated.
I will put the survivors to the sword*e*
  before their enemies,"*f*
                            declares the LORD.

¹⁰Alas, my mother, that you gave me
  birth,*g*
  a man with whom the whole land
    strives and contends!*h*
I have neither lent*i* nor borrowed,
  yet everyone curses*j* me.

¹¹The LORD said,

"Surely I will deliver you*k* for a good
  purpose;
surely I will make your enemies
  plead*l* with you
in times of disaster and times of
  distress.

¹²"Can a man break iron—

15:2 *f*Jer 42:22;
43:11; 44:13
*g*S Dt 28:26;
S Jer 14:12;
La 4:9
*h*Eze 12:11;
Rev 13:10
15:3 *i*S Nu 33:4
*j*S Lev 26:25
*k*S 1Ki 21:19;
S 2Ki 9:36
*l*S Dt 28:26
*m*S Lev 26:22;
Eze 14:21; 33:27
15:4 *n*Jer 24:9;
29:18; 34:17
*o*S Dt 28:25;
S Job 17:6
*p*S 2Ki 21:2;
23:26-27
15:5 *q*Isa 27:11;
51:19;
S Jer 13:14;
16:13; 21:7;
Na 3:7
15:6 *r*S Dt 32:15;
Jer 6:19 *s*Isa 31:3;
Zep 1:4
*t*S Jer 7:20;
Am 7:8
15:7 *u*S Isa 41:16
*v*Isa 3:26
*w*Jer 18:21
*x*S 2Ch 28:22

15:8 *y*S Isa 47:9
*z*S Jer 4:7; S 6:4
*a*S Job 18:11
15:9 *b*1Sa 2:5
*c*S Job 8:13
*d*Jer 7:19
*e*Jer 21:7; 25:31
*f*2Ki 25:7;
Jer 19:7
15:10 *g*S Job 3:1;
S 10:18-19
*h*Jer 1:19
*i*S Lev 25:36;
Ne 5:1-12
*j*S Jer 6:10
15:11 *k*ver 21;
Jer 40:4

*l*Jer 21:1-2; 37:3; 42:1-3

God's three agents of destruction, paralleling the first three here is the Hebrew word for "starvation" here is the same as that for "famine" in 14:12).
15:3–4 Foreseen in Dt 28:25–26.
15:3 *four kinds.* Not the same four as in v. 2, but an elaboration of three of the fates awaiting the corpses of those killed by the sword. The seventh-century B.C. vassal treaties of Esarhaddon present similar curses: "May Ninurta, leader of the gods, fell you with his fierce arrow, fill the plain with your corpses, and give your flesh to the eagles and vultures to feed on . . . May dogs and pigs eat your flesh." *dogs.* See 1Ki 21:23. *beasts of the earth.* See Rev 6:8.
15:4 *abhorrent.* The Hebrew for this word is translated "a thing of horror" in the parallel in Dt 28:25. *what Manasseh . . . did in Jerusalem.* Manasseh, good King Josiah's grandfather, was the most wicked king in Judah's long history (see 2Ki 21:1–11,16). His sins were a primary cause of Judah's eventual destruction (see 2Ki 21:12–15; 23:26–27; 24:3–4).
15:5–9 A poem concerning the forthcoming destruction of Jerusalem in 586 B.C (see La 1:1,12,21; 2:13,20).
15:5 Cf. Mt 23:37.
15:6 *You keep on backsliding.* Lit. "You go backward" (cf. 7:24; see note on 2:19).
15:7 *winnow.* See note on Ru 1:22. Winnowing as a figure of judgment is found also in 51:2; Pr 20:8,26; Isa 41:16. *city gates of the land.* Or, more simply, "gates of the land" (as in Na 3:13), i.e., the approaches to the land. *bereavement . . . on my people.* The young men will fall in battle, and Judah and Jerusalem will be left childless (see Eze 5:17). *not*

changed. Lit. "not repented of," reminiscent of the refrain in Am 4:6,8–11: "yet you have not returned to me," where the same Hebrew verb is used (see note on 3:1).
15:8 *widows more numerous than the sand of the sea.* A tragic reversal of the covenant promise of innumerable offspring (see Ge 22:17 and note). *At midday . . . suddenly.* Military attacks at noon were unexpected (see note on 6:4). *destroyer.* Babylon (see note on 4:7). *anguish.* See note on 4:19.
15:9 *seven.* The complete, ideal number of sons (see Ru 4:15 and note)—soon to be destroyed. *sun will set while it is still day.* See Am 8:9; cf. Mt 27:45. *survivors.* Lit. "remnant" (see note on 6:9). Even they will be put to the sword (see Mic 6:14).
15:10–21 The third of Jeremiah's "confessions" (see Introduction: Author and Date), including in this case two responses by the Lord (vv. 11–14, 19–21).
15:10 See 20:14–15; Job 3:3–10. *mother.* See v. 8. In the OT, adjacent paragraphs are often linked by key words. *have neither lent nor borrowed.* Have not become involved in matters likely to evoke dispute or difference of opinion.
15:11–14 The Lord speaks, first to Jeremiah (v. 11), then to the people of Judah (vv. 12–14).
15:11 God encourages Jeremiah. *I will make your enemies plead with you.* Fulfilled, e.g., in 21:1–2; 37:3; 38:14–26; 42:1–3.
15:12 A rhetorical question assuming a negative answer. *iron.* Symbolic of great strength (see 28:13). *from the north.* From Babylonia (see note on Isa 41:25).

iron from the north *m*—or bronze?
13Your wealth *n* and your treasures
  I will give as plunder, *o* without
    charge, *p*
because of all your sins
  throughout your country. *q*
14I will enslave you to your enemies
  in *c* a land you do not know, *r*
for my anger will kindle a fire *s*
  that will burn against you."

15You understand, O LORD;
  remember me and care for me.
  Avenge me on my persecutors. *t*
You are long-suffering *u*—do not take
    me away;
  think of how I suffer reproach for
    your sake. *v*
16When your words came, I ate *w* them;
  they were my joy and my heart's
    delight, *x*
for I bear your name, *y*
  O LORD God Almighty.
17I never sat *z* in the company of revelers,
  never made merry with them;
I sat alone because your hand *a* was on
    me
  and you had filled me with
    indignation.
18Why is my pain unending
  and my wound grievous and
    incurable? *b*
Will you be to me like a deceptive
    brook,

like a spring that fails? *c*

19Therefore this is what the LORD says:

"If you repent, I will restore you
  that you may serve *d* me;
if you utter worthy, not worthless,
    words,
  you will be my spokesman. *e*
Let this people turn to you,
  but you must not turn to them.
20I will make you a wall *f* to this people,
  a fortified wall of bronze;
they will fight against you
  but will not overcome *g* you,
for I am with you
  to rescue and save you," *h*
              declares the LORD.
21"I will save *i* you from the hands of the
    wicked *j*
  and redeem *k* you from the grasp of
    the cruel." *l*

Day of Disaster

16 Then the word of the LORD came
to me: 2"You must not marry *m* and
have sons or daughters in this place." 3For
this is what the LORD says about the sons
and daughters born in this land and about
the women who are their mothers and the
men who are their fathers: *n* 4"They will
die of deadly diseases. They will not be

15:12
*m*S Dt 28:48;
Jer 28:14;
La 1:14;
Hos 10:11
15:13
*n*S 2Ki 25:15
*o*S 2Ki 24:13;
Eze 38:12-13
*p*S Ps 44:12
*q*Jer 17:3
15:14
*r*S Dt 28:36;
S Jer 5:19
*s*S Ps 21:9
15:15 *t*Jdg 16:28;
S Ps 119:84
*u*S Ex 34:6
*v*Ps 44:22;
69:7-9; S Jer 6:10
15:16 *w*Eze 2:8;
3:3; Rev 10:10
*x*S Job 15:11;
Ps 119:72,103
*y*S Isa 43:7;
S Jer 14:9
15:17 *z*Ru 3:3;
Ps 1:1; 26:4-5;
Jer 16:8
*a*S 2Ki 3:15
15:18 *b*S Job 6:4;
S Jer 10:19;
30:12; Mic 1:9

*c*S Job 6:15;
S Ps 9:10
15:19 *d*Zec 3:7
*e*S Ex 4:16
15:20 *f*S Isa 50:7
*g*S Ps 129:2
*h*S Jer 1:8; 20:11;
42:11; Eze 3:8
15:21 *i*S Jer 1:8
*j*S Ps 97:10
*k*Jer 50:34
*l*S Ge 48:16
16:2 *m*Mt 19:12;
1Co 7:26-27
16:3 *n*Jer 6:21

c 14 Some Hebrew manuscripts, Septuagint and Syriac
(see also Jer. 17:4); most Hebrew manuscripts *I will cause
your enemies to bring you / into*

15:13–14 Repeated in large part in 17:3–4.
15:13 Fulfilled in 52:17–23. *without charge.* Cf. Isa 55:1.
People and plunder alike would be free for the taking (see
note on Isa 52:3).
15:14 *for my anger will kindle a fire.* Quoted verbatim
from Dt 32:22, where the Hebrew is translated "For a fire
has been kindled by my wrath."
15:15 *You understand.* The Lord is aware of what Jeremiah has suffered (see v. 10). *remember.* Express concern for
(see note on Ge 8:1).
15:16 *your words . . . I ate them.* I digested them, I assimilated them, I made them a part of me (see Eze 2:8–3:3;
Rev 10:9–10). *came.* Lit. "were found"—perhaps referring
to the discovery of the Book of the Law in the temple during
the reign of Josiah in 621 B.C. (see 2Ki 22:13; 23:2; see also
note on 1:2). *they were . . . my heart's delight.* See Ps 1:2. *I
bear your name.* See 14:9. I belong to you (see note on
7:10).
15:17 *sat alone.* Jeremiah never married (see 16:1), and he
attracted only a few friends (see Introduction: Author and
Date). *your hand.* Divine constraint (see 2Ki 3:15; Isa 8:11
and note; Eze 1:3; 3:14,22; 37:1; 40:1). *indignation.* At
the sins of Judah (see 6:11).
15:18 Two rhetorical questions used by Jeremiah to
express his nagging doubts about himself, his mission and
God's faithfulness. *pain unending . . . wound grievous and
incurable.* Jerusalem is similarly described in 30:12–15, together with God's promise of healing in 30:17. *Will you be to
me . . . ?* See Ps 22:1; Mt 27:46. *deceptive brook.* See Mic
1:14, where also "deceptive" probably refers to the kind of

intermittent streams described in Job 6:15–20. Jeremiah
here accuses God of being undependable, in contrast to the
Lord's own earlier description of himself as a "spring of living
water" (see 2:13 and note).
15:19–21 The Lord commands Jeremiah to repent, then
encourages him and renews his call.
15:19 *repent . . . restore . . . turn . . . turn.* The Hebrew
root is the same for all four words (see notes on 3:1; Isa
1:25–26). *serve.* Lit. "stand before"—the appropriate posture for the obedient servant (see Nu 16:9; Dt 10:8). *spokesman.* Lit. "mouth" (see 1:9 and note; Ex 4:15–16; see also
note on Ex 7:1–2).
15:20 See 1:8,18–19 and notes.
15:21 *save you from . . . the wicked.* See, e.g., 36:26;
38:6–13.
16:1–17:18 Messages of disaster and comfort, with the
note of disaster predominating (16:1–13,16–18;
16:21–17:6; 17:9–13,18). The first half of the section is
prose (16:1–18), the second half poetry (16:19–17:18).
16:2 Jeremiah's ministry was such that he had to face life
alone (see note on 15:17), without the comfort and support
a family can provide. *You must not.* The Hebrew underlying
this phrase is used for the most forceful of negative commands, as, e.g., in the Ten Commandments (see Ex 20:3–4,
7,13–17). *this place.* Judah and Jerusalem, especially the
latter (see, e.g., Zep 1:4).
16:4 *diseases.* The Hebrew for this word is translated
"ravages" in 14:18. *not be mourned or buried.* See v. 6;
7:33 and note; 8:2; 14:16; 25:33. *refuse.* Lit. "dung" (see
8:2; 9:22; 25:33). *perish by sword and famine.* See

mourned or buried [o] but will be like refuse lying on the ground. [p] They will perish by sword and famine, [q] and their dead bodies will become food for the birds of the air and the beasts of the earth." [r]

[5]For this is what the LORD says: "Do not enter a house where there is a funeral meal; do not go to mourn or show sympathy, because I have withdrawn my blessing, my love and my pity [s] from this people," declares the LORD. [6]"Both high and low will die in this land. [t] They will not be buried or mourned, [u] and no one will cut [v] himself or shave [w] his head for them. [7]No one will offer food [x] to comfort those who mourn [y] for the dead—not even for a father or a mother—nor will anyone give them a drink to console [z] them.

[8]"And do not enter a house where there is feasting and sit down to eat and drink. [a] [9]For this is what the LORD Almighty, the God of Israel, says: Before your eyes and in your days I will bring an end to the sounds [b] of joy and gladness and to the voices of bride [c] and bridegroom in this place. [d]

[10]"When you tell these people all this and they ask you, 'Why has the LORD decreed such a great disaster against us? What wrong have we done? What sin have we committed against the LORD our God?' [e] [11]then say to them, 'It is because your fathers forsook me,' declares the LORD, 'and followed other gods and served and worshiped [f] them. They forsook me and did not keep my law. [g] [12]But you have

behaved more wickedly than your fathers. [h] See how each of you is following the stubbornness of his evil heart [i] instead of obeying me. [13]So I will throw you out of this land [j] into a land neither you nor your fathers have known, [k] and there you will serve other gods [l] day and night, for I will show you no favor.' [m]

[14]"However, the days are coming," [n] declares the LORD, "when men will no longer say, 'As surely as the LORD lives, who brought the Israelites up out of Egypt,' [o] [15]but they will say, 'As surely as the LORD lives, who brought the Israelites up out of the land of the north [p] and out of all the countries where he had banished them.' [q] For I will restore [r] them to the land I gave their forefathers. [s]

[16]"But now I will send for many fishermen," declares the LORD, "and they will catch them. [t] After that I will send for many hunters, and they will hunt [u] them down on every mountain and hill and from the crevices of the rocks. [v] [17]My eyes are on all their ways; they are not hidden [w] from me, nor is their sin concealed from my eyes. [x] [18]I will repay [y] them double [z] for their wickedness and their sin, because they have defiled my land [a] with the lifeless forms of their vile images [b] and have filled my inheritance with their detestable idols. [c] " [d]

16:4 [o] ver 6; Jer 25:33
[p] S Jer 9:22
[q] S Jer 14:15
[r] S Dt 28:26; Ps 79:1-3; S Jer 14:12; 19:7
16:5 [s] S Jer 15:5
16:6 [t] Jer 9:21; Eze 9:5-6 [u] S ver 4
[v] S Lev 19:28
[w] S Lev 21:5; S Job 1:20
16:7 [x] S 2Sa 3:35
[y] Jer 22:10; Eze 24:17; Hos 9:4 [z] La 1:9, 16
16:8 [a] S Ex 32:6; S Ecc 7:2-4; S Jer 15:17
16:9 [b] S Isa 24:8; S 51:3; Eze 26:13; Am 6:4-7
[c] S Ps 78:63
[d] Isa 22:12-14; Rev 18:23
16:10 [e] S Dt 29:24; Jer 5:19
16:11 [f] S Job 31:27 [g] Dt 29:25-26; S 1Ki 9:9; Ps 106:35-43
16:12 [h] S Ex 32:8; S Jer 7:26; Eze 20:30; Am 2:4 [i] S Ecc 9:3; S Jer 3:17
16:13 [j] S 2Ch 7:20 [k] S Dt 28:36; S Jer 5:19 [l] S Dt 4:28; S 1Ki 9:9 [m] S Jer 15:5
16:14 [n] Jer 29:10; 30:3; 31:27,38 [o] S Dt 15:15
16:15 [p] S Jer 3:18 [q] S Isa 11:11; Jer 23:8 [r] Ps 53:6; S Isa 11:12; Jer 30:3; 32:44;

Eze 38:14; Joel 3:1 [s] S Dt 30:3; S Isa 14:1 16:16 [t] Am 4:2; Hab 1:14-15 [u] Am 9:3; Mic 7:2 [v] S Isa 26:20 16:17 [w] S Ge 3:8; S Ecc 12:14; S Mk 4:22; 1Co 4:5; S Heb 4:13 [x] S Ps 51:9; Pr 15:3; Zep 1:12 16:18 [y] S Isa 65:6 [z] S Isa 40:2; S Jer 12:3; Rev 18:6 [a] Nu 35:34; Jer 2:7 [b] S Ps 101:3 [c] S 1Ki 14:24 [d] S Jer 2:7; S 4:1; Eze 5:11; 8:10

14:15-16; see also note on 5:12. *food for the birds ... and the beasts.* See note on 7:33.

16:5 *do not go to mourn.* See the similar command of God in Eze 24:16-17,22-23.

16:6 *cut himself ... shave his head.* Actions forbidden in the law (see Lev 19:28; 21:5 and note; Dt 14:1 and note), but sometimes practiced by Israelites (see 41:5; Eze 7:18; Mic 1:16).

16:7 Food was customarily offered to mourners (see 2Sa 3:35; 12:16-17; Eze 24:17,22; Hos 9:4). *drink to console them.* Lit. "cup of consolation," in later Judaism a special cup of wine for the chief mourner.

16:8 *do not enter a house where there is.* The present crisis is a time for neither feasting nor mourning (see v. 5).

16:9 See 7:34; 25:10; contrast 33:10-11.

16:10-13 The same question but a more elaborate answer than in 5:19 (see 9:12-16; 22:8-9; Dt 29:24-28; 1Ki 9:8-9).

16:10 Cf. the similar questions in Mal 1:6-7; 2:17; 3:7-8,13.

16:11 See 11:10, where committing sins like those mentioned here is called breaking the Lord's covenant.

16:12 *behaved more wickedly than your fathers.* See 1Ki 14:9. The coming judgment cannot be blamed on the sins of previous generations (see 31:29-30; Eze 18:2-4). *following the stubbornness of his evil heart.* See note on 3:17; see also

7:24.

16:13 See Dt 28:36,64. *I will throw you out.* Into exile (see 7:15; 22:26; Dt 29:28). *land neither you nor your fathers have known.* Babylonia (see 9:16).

16:14-15 Repeated almost verbatim in 23:7-8, the passage outlines nearly 1,000 years of Israelite history: exodus (c. 1446 B.C.), exile (586), restoration (538). See Isa 43:16-21; 48:20-21; 51:9-11. *As surely as the LORD lives.* See note on Ge 42:15.

16:15 *land of the north.* Babylonia (see note on Isa 41:25).

16:16 *fishermen ... hunters.* Symbolic of conquerors (see Eze 12:13; 29:4; Am 4:2 and note). *mountain and hill.* To which the people would flee in vain (see 4:29 and note). *crevices of the rocks.* The phrase occurs outside Jeremiah only in Isa 7:19. The Lord may be recalling here the episode of the ruined linen belt, hidden in a "crevice in the rocks" (13:4).

16:17 *My eyes are on all their ways.* See 32:19. *they are not hidden from me.* See 23:24.

16:18 *repay them double.* See 17:18; Isa 40:2 and note. *defiled my land.* Made it ceremonially unclean (see 2:7; 3:1-2; see also note on Lev 4:12). *lifeless forms of their vile images.* See Lev 26:30. Idols have no life in them (see Ps 115:4-7; 135:15-17). *my inheritance.* God's land (see 17:4; see also note on 2:7). *detestable.* Abominable in the Lord's eyes (see 2:7; see also note on Lev 7:21).

[19]O Lord, my strength and my fortress,
    my refuge[e] in time of distress,
to you the nations will come[f]
    from the ends of the earth and say,
"Our fathers possessed nothing but false
        gods,[g]
    worthless idols[h] that did them no
        good.[i]
[20]Do men make their own gods?
    Yes, but they are not gods!"[j]

[21]"Therefore I will teach them—
    this time I will teach them
    my power and might.
Then they will know
    that my name[k] is the Lord.

17 "Judah's sin is engraved with an
        iron tool,[l]
    inscribed with a flint point,
on the tablets of their hearts[m]
    and on the horns[n] of their altars.
[2]Even their children remember
    their altars and Asherah poles[d][o]
beside the spreading trees
    and on the high hills.[p]
[3]My mountain in the land
    and your[e] wealth and all your
        treasures
I will give away as plunder,[q]
    together with your high places,[r]
    because of sin throughout your
        country.[s]
[4]Through your own fault you will lose
    the inheritance[t] I gave you.

I will enslave you to your enemies[u]
    in a land[v] you do not know,
for you have kindled my anger,
    and it will burn[w] forever."

[5]This is what the Lord says:

"Cursed is the one who trusts in man,[x]
    who depends on flesh for his strength
    and whose heart turns away from the
        Lord.[y]
[6]He will be like a bush in the
        wastelands;
    he will not see prosperity when it
        comes.
He will dwell in the parched places[z] of
        the desert,
    in a salt[a] land where no one lives.
[7]But blessed[b] is the man who trusts[c]
    in the Lord,
    whose confidence is in him.
[8]He will be like a tree planted by the
        water
    that sends out its roots by the
        stream.[d]
It does not fear when heat comes;
    its leaves are always green.
It has no worries in a year of drought[e]
    and never fails to bear fruit."[f]

[9]The heart[g] is deceitful above all things
    and beyond cure.

Cross references

16:19
eS 2Sa 22:3;
S Ps 46:1
fS Isa 2:2;
Jer 3:17 gS Ps 4:2
hS Dt 32:21;
S 1Sa 12:21
iS Isa 40:19;
S Jer 14:22
16:20
jPs 115:4-7;
S Jer 2:11;
Ro 1:23
16:21 kS Ex 3:15
17:1 lJob 19:24
mS Dt 6:6;
S 2Co 3:3
nS Ex 27:2
17:2
oS 2Ch 24:18
pS Jer 2:20
17:3
qS 2Ki 24:13
rJer 26:18;
Mic 3:12
sJer 15:13
17:4 tLa 5:2

uDt 28:48;
S Jer 12:7
vJer 16:13; 22:28
wS Jer 7:20
17:5
xS Ps 108:12;
S Isa 2:22
y2Co 1:9
17:6 zJob 30:3
aDt 29:23;
S Job 39:6;
Ps 107:34;
Jer 48:9
17:7 bS Ps 146:5
cS Ps 26:1; 34:8;
40:4; Pr 16:20;
Jer 39:18
17:8 dS Job 14:9
eJer 14:1-6
fPs 1:3;
92:12-14;
Eze 19:10; 47:12
17:9 gS Ecc 9:3;
Mt 13:15;
Mk 7:21-22

d2 That is, symbols of the goddess Asherah   e2,3 Or
hills / 3and the mountains of the land. / Your

16:19–20 The prophet interjects a few brief words of
hope.
16:19 *strength . . . fortress . . . refuge in time of distress.*
Such descriptions of God's dependability and protecting
power are common in the Psalms (see, e.g., Ps 18:1–2;
28:7–8; 59:9,16–17). *to you the nations will come.* See 4:2
and note; see also Isa 2:2–4; 42:4; 45:14; 49:6; Zec
8:20–23; 14:16. *worthless idols.* See note on 2:5. *did them
no good.* Were unprofitable to them (see note on 2:8).
16:20 *not gods.* See 5:7.
16:21–17:4 The Lord responds to Jeremiah and continues
his solemn warnings that began in v. 1.
16:21 *teach . . . teach . . . know.* The same Hebrew root
underlies each of these words. God would "cause them to
know," and then they would surely "know." *them . . . they.*
Probably includes Judah as well as the nations (see Eze
36:23; 37:14). *know that my name is the Lord.* "Name"
often means "person" or "being" in the OT (see note on Ps
5:11). Ezekiel's equivalent of Jeremiah's phrase is "know
that I am the Lord," found in his prophecy about 70 times
(see note on Eze 6:7).
17:1 *engraved with an iron tool.* The method used to
inscribe the most permanent of records (see Job 19:24). *flint.*
One of the hardest of stones known to ancient man (see Eze
3:9; Zec 7:12). *tablets of their hearts.* For the same imagery
see Pr 3:3; 7:3. *horns of their altars.* The people of Judah
have backslid so badly that their sins are engraved not only
on their hearts but also on their altars—to be remembered by
God rather than to be atoned for (see Lev 16:18).
17:2 *altars and Asherah poles.* See notes on Ex 34:13; Dt

7:5. *spreading trees . . . high hills.* See note on 2:20.
17:3–4 Repeated in large part from 15:13–14 (see notes
there).
17:3 *My mountain.* Mount Zion, the location of the temple
in Jerusalem (see Ps 24:3; Isa 2:3; Zec 8:3). *high places.*
Locales of idolatrous worship.
17:4 *inheritance.* The land of Canaan (see 16:18; see also
note on 2:7).
17:5–8 See Ps 1 and notes.
17:5 *Cursed.* See note on 11:3. *flesh.* The opposite of
"spirit" (see Isa 31:3; see also Job 10:4).
17:6 *bush.* See 48:6 and NIV text note. Apart from these
two places in Jeremiah, the Hebrew for this word appears
elsewhere in the OT only in Ps 102:17, where it is translated
"destitute." *prosperity.* Lit. "good." The Hebrew for this
word is translated "bounty" in Dt 28:12, where it refers to
rain. *salt land.* An evidence of God's curse also in Dt 29:
23.
17:7 *trusts . . . confidence.* The same Hebrew root underlies both words.
17:8 *planted.* Or "transplanted." *stream.* See Isa 44:4,
where the same Hebrew root is used again to illustrate the
source of the righteous man's strength. *drought.* See note on
14:1. *bear fruit.* The Lord's answer to Jeremiah's complaint
in 12:1–2 (see notes there).
17:9 The prophet makes an observation, then asks a
rhetorical question. *The heart.* The "wellspring of life," in
which wickedness must not be allowed to take root (Pr
4:23). *deceitful.* The Hebrew root for this word is the basis of
the name Jacob (see NIV text note on Ge 27:36).

Who can understand it?

[10]"I the LORD search the heart[h]
and examine the mind,[i]
to reward[j] a man according to his
conduct,
according to what his deeds
deserve."[k]

[11]Like a partridge that hatches eggs it did
not lay
is the man who gains riches by unjust
means.
When his life is half gone, they will
desert him,
and in the end he will prove to be a
fool.[l]

[12]A glorious throne,[m] exalted from the
beginning,
is the place of our sanctuary.

[13]O LORD, the hope[n] of Israel,
all who forsake[o] you will be put to
shame.
Those who turn away from you will be
written in the dust[p]
because they have forsaken the LORD,
the spring of living water.[q]

[14]Heal me, O LORD, and I will be
healed;[r]
save[s] me and I will be saved,
for you are the one I praise.[t]

[15]They keep saying to me,

"Where is the word of the LORD?
Let it now be fulfilled!"[u]

[16]I have not run away from being your
shepherd;
you know I have not desired the day
of despair.
What passes my lips[v] is open before
you.

[17]Do not be a terror[w] to me;
you are my refuge[x] in the day of
disaster.[y]

[18]Let my persecutors be put to shame,
but keep me from shame;
let them be terrified,
but keep me from terror.
Bring on them the day of disaster;
destroy them with double
destruction.[z]

Keeping the Sabbath Holy

[19]This is what the LORD said to me: "Go
and stand at the gate of the people,
through which the kings of Judah go in
and out; stand also at all the other gates of
Jerusalem.[a] [20]Say to them, 'Hear the word
of the LORD, O kings of Judah and all
people of Judah and everyone living in
Jerusalem[b] who come through these
gates.[c] [21]This is what the LORD says: Be
careful not to carry a load on the Sabbath[d]

17:10
[h]S Jos 22:22;
S 2Ch 6:30;
S Rev 2:23
[i]Ps 17:3; 139:23;
Jer 11:20; 20:12;
Eze 11:5; 38:10
[j]S Lev 26:28;
Ps 62:12;
Jer 32:19;
S Mt 16:27
[k]Jer 12:13;
14:16; 21:14;
32:19
17:11 [l]Lk 12:20
17:12
[m]S Jer 3:17
17:13 [n]Ps 71:5;
Jer 14:8
[o]S Jer 2:17
[p]S Ps 69:28;
87:6; Eze 13:9;
Da 12:1
[q]S Isa 12:3;
Jn 4:10
17:14
[r]S Isa 30:26;
Jer 15:18
[s]S Ps 119:94
[t]S Ex 15:2;
S Ps 109:1

17:15
[u]S Isa 5:19;
2Pe 3:4
17:16 [v]Ps 139:4
17:17
[w]Ps 88:15-16
[x]S Ps 46:1;
Jer 16:19; Na 1:7
[y]S Ps 18:18
17:18
[z]Ps 35:1-8;
S Isa 40:2;
S Jer 12:3
17:19 [a]Jer 7:2;
26:2
17:20 [b]Jer 19:3
[c]Jer 22:2
17:21
[d]Nu 15:32-36;
S Dt 5:14; Ne 13:15-21; Jn 5:10

17:10 The Lord responds to Jeremiah's question. *search
... examine.* See 11:20; 12:3. *mind.* Lit. "kidneys" (see
11:20). The Hebrew for this word is translated "heart(s)" in
12:2. *what his deeds deserve.* Lit. "the fruit of his deeds"
(cf. 6:19).

17:11 The prophet uses a proverb to make his point (as in
v. 9); see especially Pr 23:5. *partridge.* Mentioned
elsewhere in the OT only in 1Sa 26:20. *hatches eggs.* The
Hebrew root underlying this phrase is found again only in Isa
34:15. Its Aramaic cognate, however, is used to explain Job
39:14 in the Targum (ancient Aramaic paraphrase). *When
his life is half gone.* Lit. "In the midst of his days" (as in Ps
102:24). *fool.* Morally and spiritually reprobate (see note on
Pr 1:7).

17:12—18 The fourth of Jeremiah's "confessions" (see
Introduction: Author and Date).

17:12 *glorious throne.* See note on 14:21; see also Isa 6:1.
The Lord is often represented as sitting on a throne between
the cherubim on the ark of the covenant in the temple (see,
e.g., Ps 80:1; 99:1). *exalted.* Mount Zion is the "high mountain of Israel" (Eze 20:40). *from the beginning.* From time
immemorial, Zion had been chosen by God as the place of his
sanctuary (see Ex 15:17).

17:13 *hope of Israel.* See note on 14:8. *dust.* Lit. "earth,"
sometimes referring to the netherworld (see note on Ps 61:2;
see also note on Job 7:21), as also in Canaanite and Mesopotamian literature. "Written in the dust" would then mean
"destined for death," the opposite of "written in the book"
of life (see Ex 32:32; Da 12:1; see also Ps 69:28 and note;
Lk 10:20; Rev 20:12; 21:27). *forsaken . . . spring of living
water.* Contrast 15:18; see note on 2:13.

17:14 *Heal me.* See 15:18; Ps 6:2. *you are the one I
praise.* Lit. "you are my praise" (see Dt 10:21).

17:15 See 20:8. Jeremiah's enemies accuse him of being a
false prophet (see Dt 18:21–22). The accusation must have
been voiced before the first invasion of Judah by the Babylonians in 605 B.C. after the battle of Carchemish (see 46:2;
see also Introduction: Background).

17:16 *shepherd.* Symbolic of leadership (see note on 2:8),
and therefore of Jeremiah's role as a prophet.

17:17 *my refuge.* See note on 16:19. *day of disaster.* See v.
18; 15:11.

17:18 *my persecutors.* See 15:15. *double.* see 16:18; Isa
40:2 and note.

17:19—27 An extended commentary on the Sabbath-day
commandment (the covenant sign of God's relationship with
Israel; see Ex 31:13–17; Eze 20:12), probably the version
recorded in Dt 5:12–15 (see especially note on v. 22).

17:19 *people.* Lit. "sons of the people." The Hebrew for
this word is translated "common people" in 26:23; 2Ki 23:6
and "lay people" in 2Ch 35:5,7. The latter meaning seems
intended here, and therefore the "gate of the people" is most
likely the east gate of the temple, where the people assembled in large numbers and which the kings would be expected to use frequently.

17:20 *kings of Judah.* The current king and all subsequent
ruling members of David's dynasty (see, e.g., v. 25; 1:18;
2:26; 13:13; 19:3).

17:21 *Be careful.* See Jos 23:11. The Hebrew underlying
this phrase is translated "watch yourselves . . . carefully" in
Dt 4:15, and a similar expression is translated "guard yourself in your spirit" in Mal 2:15, stressing the urgency and
solemnity of the Lord's command.

day or bring it through the gates of Jerusalem. 22Do not bring a load out of your houses or do any work on the Sabbath, but keep the Sabbath day holy, as I commanded your forefathers.*e* 23Yet they did not listen or pay attention;*f* they were stiff-necked*g* and would not listen or respond to discipline.*h* 24But if you are careful to obey me, declares the Lord, and bring no load through the gates of this city on the Sabbath, but keep the Sabbath day holy*i* by not doing any work on it, 25then kings who sit on David's throne*j* will come through the gates of this city with their officials. They and their officials will come riding in chariots and on horses, accompanied by the men of Judah and those living in Jerusalem, and this city will be inhabited forever.*k* 26People will come from the towns of Judah and the villages around Jerusalem, from the territory of Benjamin and the western foothills, from the hill country and the Negev,*l* bringing burnt offerings and sacrifices, grain offerings, incense and thank offerings to the house of the Lord. 27But if you do not obey*m* me to keep the Sabbath*n* day holy by not carrying any load as you come through the gates of Jerusalem on the Sabbath day, then I will kindle an unquench-

17:22 *e*S Ge 2:3; S Ex 20:8; Isa 56:2-6
17:23 *f*Jer 7:26 *g*Jer 19:15 *h*S 2Ch 28:22; S Jer 7:28; Zec 7:11
17:24 *i*ver 22
17:25 *j*S 2Sa 7:13; Isa 9:7; Jer 22:2, 4; Lk 1:32 *k*Jer 30:10; 33:16; Eze 28:26
17:26 *l*Jer 32:44; 33:13; Zec 7:7
17:27 *m*S 1Ki 9:6; Jer 22:5 *n*S Ne 10:31

18:6 *o*S Jer 7:20 *p*2Ki 25:9; Hos 8:14; Am 2:5
18:6 *q*S Isa 29:16; 45:9; Ro 9:20-21 *r*S Ge 2:7
18:7 *s*Jer 1:10
18:8 *t*S Ex 32:14; Ps 25:11; Jer 26:13; 36:3; Jnh 3:8-10 *u*Jer 31:28; 42:10; Da 9:14; Hos 11:8-9; Joel 2:13; Jnh 4:2
18:9 *v*Jer 1:10; 31:28
18:10 *w*Eze 33:18 *x*1Sa 2:29-30; 13:13 *y*S Jer 1:10

able fire*o* in the gates of Jerusalem that will consume her fortresses.' "*p*

At the Potter's House

18 This is the word that came to Jeremiah from the Lord: 2"Go down to the potter's house, and there I will give you my message." 3So I went down to the potter's house, and I saw him working at the wheel. 4But the pot he was shaping from the clay was marred in his hands; so the potter formed it into another pot, shaping it as seemed best to him.

5Then the word of the Lord came to me: 6"O house of Israel, can I not do with you as this potter does?" declares the Lord. "Like clay*q* in the hand of the potter, so are you in my hand,*r* O house of Israel. 7If at any time I announce that a nation or kingdom is to be uprooted,*s* torn down and destroyed, 8and if that nation I warned repents of its evil, then I will relent*t* and not inflict on it the disaster*u* I had planned. 9And if at another time I announce that a nation or kingdom is to be built*v* up and planted, 10and if it does evil*w* in my sight and does not obey me, then I will reconsider*x* the good I had intended to do for it.*y*

11"Now therefore say to the people of

17:22 *Do not.* See note on 16:2. The Hebrew for this negative expression is stronger than that in v. 21. *not . . . do any work . . . keep the Sabbath day holy.* Specific references to the Sabbath-day commandment of Ex 20:8,10; Dt 5:12, 14. *as I commanded.* The Hebrew underlying this phrase is unique to the Ten Commandments as recorded in Deuteronomy (see Dt 5:12,15–16; see note on vv. 19–27).
17:23 *did not listen . . . were stiff-necked.* Repeated from 7:26 (see note there; see also 11:10). *not . . . respond to discipline.* See 2:30; 5:3.
17:25 Repeated in part in 22:4. King David's dynasty will last forever (see 23:5–6; 30:9; 33:15; 2Sa 7:12–17), and Jerusalem will be inhabited for all time (Zec 2:2–12; 8:3; 14:11), if the people of Judah obey the Lord (see v. 27)—and they will, according to 31:33–34.
17:26 *territory of Benjamin.* Jeremiah's hometown was located there (see 1:1). *western foothills . . . hill country.* See note on Dt 1:7. *Negev.* See note on Ge 12:9. *thank offerings.* Lit. "bringing thank offerings." The repetition here of "bringing" from earlier in the verse separates the thank offerings from the other specific sacrifices mentioned and gives them the more general designation of offerings of thanksgiving (as intended also in 33:11).
17:27 Disobedience will bring disaster and will negate—at least temporarily—the promises of vv. 24–26. *gates of Jerusalem.* The symbols of Sabbath violation would be the first structures destroyed. *kindle . . . fire . . . consume her fortresses.* Common prophetic language for divine judgment against rebellious cities (see 49:27; 50:32; Am 1:4,7,10, 12,14; 2:2,5; cf. Jer 21:14).
18:1—20:18 Three chapters focusing on lessons the Lord taught Jeremiah at the potter's workshop, probably before 605 B.C. (see note on 17:15).
18:1–17 As the potter controls what he does with the clay,

so the Lord is sovereign over the people of Judah.
18:2 *Go down.* The potter's workshop was probably located on the slopes of the Valley of Ben Hinnom near the Potsherd Gate (see 19:2 and note).
18:3 *wheel.* Lit. "two stones." Both wheels were attached to a single upright shaft, one end of which was sunk permanently in the ground. The potter would spin the lower wheel with his foot and would work the clay on the upper wheel; the process is described in the Apocryphal book of Ecclesiasticus (38:29–30).
18:4 *marred.* The Hebrew for this word is translated "ruined" in 13:7 with respect to the linen belt that Jeremiah had hidden (see note there). *as seemed best to him.* The flaw was in the clay itself, not in the potter's skill.
18:6 *Like clay . . . so are you.* Biblical imagery often pictures mankind as made of clay by a potter (see Job 4:19 and note). *potter.* The Hebrew for this word is translated "Maker" in 10:16 with reference to God.
18:7—10 The Lord retains the right of limiting his own absolute sovereignty on the basis of human response to his offers of pardon and restoration and his threats of judgment and destruction. *If . . . if . . . if . . . if.* God's promises and threats are conditioned on man's actions. God, who himself does not change (see Nu 23:19; Mal 3:6; Jas 1:17), nevertheless will change his preannounced response to man, depending on what the latter does (see note on 4:28; see also Joel 2:13; Jnh 3:9 and note; Jnh 3:8–4:2; 4:11).
18:7 *uprooted, torn down and destroyed.* See 1:10 and note.
18:8 See 26:3. *evil . . . disaster.* The Hebrew is the same for both words (also in v. 11).
18:9 *built up and planted.* See 1:10 and note.
18:11 *devising a plan.* See Est 8:3; 9:25; Eze 38:10. *turn from.* The Hebrew underlying this phrase is translated "re-

Judah and those living in Jerusalem, 'This is what the LORD says: Look! I am preparing a disaster[z] for you and devising a plan[a] against you. So turn[b] from your evil ways,[c] each one of you, and reform your ways and your actions.'[d] 12But they will reply, 'It's no use.[e] We will continue with our own plans; each of us will follow the stubbornness of his evil heart.[f] ' "

13Therefore this is what the LORD says:

"Inquire among the nations:
  Who has ever heard anything like
    this?[g]
A most horrible[h] thing has been done
    by Virgin[i] Israel.
14Does the snow of Lebanon
    ever vanish from its rocky slopes?
Do its cool waters from distant sources
    ever cease to flow?[f]
15Yet my people have forgotten[j] me;
    they burn incense[k] to worthless
      idols,[l]
which made them stumble[m] in their
    ways
  and in the ancient paths.[n]
They made them walk in bypaths
    and on roads not built up.[o]
16Their land will be laid waste,[p]
    an object of lasting scorn;[q]
all who pass by will be appalled[r]
    and will shake their heads.[s]
17Like a wind[t] from the east,
    I will scatter them before their
      enemies;
  I will show them my back and not my
    face[u]

in the day of their disaster."

18They said, "Come, let's make plans[v] against Jeremiah; for the teaching of the law by the priest[w] will not be lost, nor will counsel from the wise,[x] nor the word from the prophets.[y] So come, let's attack him with our tongues[z] and pay no attention to anything he says."

19Listen to me, O LORD;
    hear what my accusers[a] are saying!
20Should good be repaid with evil?[b]
    Yet they have dug a pit[c] for me.
Remember that I stood[d] before you
    and spoke in their behalf[e]
  to turn your wrath away from them.
21So give their children over to famine;[f]
    hand them over to the power of the
      sword.[g]
Let their wives be made childless and
    widows;[h]
  let their men be put to death,
    their young men[i] slain by the sword
      in battle.
22Let a cry[j] be heard from their houses
    when you suddenly bring invaders
      against them,
for they have dug a pit[k] to capture me
    and have hidden snares[l] for my feet.
23But you know, O LORD,
    all their plots to kill[m] me.
  Do not forgive[n] their crimes

18:11 zS 2Ki 22:16; S Jer 4:6 aver 18 bS Dt 4:30; S 2Ki 17:13; Isa 1:16-19 cS Jer 7:3 dS Job 16:17
18:12 eS Isa 57:10 fS Jer 3:17
18:13 gS Isa 66:8 hS Jer 5:30 iS 2Ki 19:21
18:15 jS Isa 17:10 kS Isa 1:13; Jer 44:15,19 lJer 10:15; 51:18; Hos 11:2 mEze 44:12; Mal 2:8 nJer 6:16 oS Isa 57:14; 62:10
18:16 pS Dt 28:37; Jer 25:9; Eze 33:28-29 qJer 19:8; 42:18 rS Lev 26:32 sS 2Ki 19:21; S Job 16:4; Ps 22:7; La 1:12
18:17 tS Job 7:10; Jer 13:24 uS 2Ch 29:6; S Jer 2:27
18:18 vver 11; Jer 11:19 wJer 2:8; Hag 2:11; Mal 2:7 xS Job 5:13; Eze 7:26 yJer 5:13 zPs 52:2; 64:2-8; S Jer 9:3
18:19 aPs 71:13
18:20 bS Ge 44:4 cPs 35:7; 57:6; S 119:85 dJer 15:1 eS Ge 20:7; S Dt 9:19; Ps 106:23; Jer 14:7-9
18:21 fJer 11:22; 14:16 gS Ps 63:10
hS 1Sa 15:33; Ps 109:9; S Isa 47:9; La 5:3 iS Isa 9:17 18:22 jS Jer 6:26 kS Ps 119:85 lPs 35:15; 140:5; Jer 5:26; 20:10
18:23 mS Jer 11:21; 37:15 nS Ne 4:5

f14 The meaning of the Hebrew for this sentence is uncertain.

pents of" in v. 8.
18:12 It's no use. See 2:25; see also note on Isa 57:10. follow the stubbornness of his evil heart. See note on 3:17.
18:13–17 See 2:10–13.
18:13 horrible thing. See 5:30; 23:14; Hos 6:10. Virgin Israel. See 14:17 and note.
18:14–15 Although nature is reliable (v. 14), Judah is fickle and unfaithful (v. 15).
18:14 Lebanon. One of the highest of the northern mountains (see 22:6), reaching an altitude of over 10,000 feet.
18:15 my people have forgotten me. Repeated from 2:32 (see note there). burn incense. See note on 1:16. worthless idols. Lit. "nothing" (see Ps 31:6). The Hebrew for this phrase is different from that in either 2:5 or 2:8 (see note on 2:8). which made them stumble. See 2Ch 28:23. ancient paths. See note on 6:16. roads not built up. See note on Isa 35:8.
18:16 waste . . . appalled. The same Hebrew root underlies both words. object of . . . scorn. See 19:8; 25:9,18; 29:18; 51:37. The phrase implies hissing or whistling to express shock, ridicule and contempt. all . . . appalled. See 19:8; 1Ki 9:8. shake their heads. See 48:27; Job 16:4 and note; see also Ps 44:14; 109:25.
18:17 wind from the east. See note on 4:11; see also Ps 48:7. show them my back and not my face. As the people themselves had done to God (see 2:27). His face symbolizes

his gracious blessing and favor (see Nu 6:24–26).
18:18–23 The fifth of Jeremiah's "confessions" (see Introduction: Author and Date).
18:18 They. Jeremiah's enemies (see note on 17:15). plans against Jeremiah. See v. 12; 11:18–23; 12:6; 15:10–11, 15–21. teaching of the law. Delegated to the priests (see note on Dt 31:11). priest . . . wise . . . prophets. See 8:8–10; see also Eze 7:26, where the wise are replaced by the elders. attack him with our tongues. See note on 9:3.
18:20 good . . . repaid with evil. See Ps 35:12. dug a pit. Symbolic of his enemies' plots against him (see v. 22; Ps 57:6 and note; Pr 22:14; 23:27). stood before you. See note on 15:1. spoke in their behalf. See 14:7–9,21.
18:21 hand them over to the power of the sword. The Hebrew underlying this phrase occurs also in Ps 63:10; Eze 35:5. be put to death. Lit. "be slain by death," probably referring to plague, as in 15:2 (see note there).
18:22–23 See Ps 141:8–10.
18:22 hidden snares. See Ps 140:5; 142:3.
18:23 you know, O LORD. See 12:3; 15:15. Do not forgive their crimes . . . Let them be overthrown before you. A prayer not for human vengeance but for divine vindication. blot out. The Phoenician cognate of the Hebrew for this phrase appears in a ninth-century B.C. inscription on a gateway: "If . . . a man . . . blots out the name of Azitawadda from this gate . . . may (the gods) wipe out . . . that man!"

or blot out their sins from your sight.
Let them be overthrown before you;
   deal with them in the time of your
     anger. *o*

19 This is what the LORD says: "Go and buy a clay jar from a potter. *p* Take along some of the elders *q* of the people and of the priests 2and go out to the Valley of Ben Hinnom, *r* near the entrance of the Potsherd Gate. There proclaim the words I tell you, 3and say, 'Hear the word of the LORD, O kings *s* of Judah and people of Jerusalem. This is what the LORD Almighty, the God of Israel, says: Listen! I am going to bring a disaster *t* on this place that will make the ears of everyone who hears of it tingle. *u* 4For they have forsaken *v* me and made this a place of foreign gods *w*; they have burned sacrifices *x* in it to gods that neither they nor their fathers nor the kings of Judah ever knew, and they have filled this place with the blood of the innocent. *y* 5They have built the high places of Baal to burn their sons *z* in the fire as offerings to Baal—something I did not command or mention, nor did it enter my mind. *a* 6So beware, the days are coming, declares the LORD, when people will no longer call this place Topheth *b* or the

Valley of Ben Hinnom, *c* but the Valley of Slaughter. *d*

7" 'In this place I will ruin *g* the plans *e* of Judah and Jerusalem. I will make them fall by the sword before their enemies, *f* at the hands of those who seek their lives, and I will give their carcasses *g* as food *h* to the birds of the air and the beasts of the earth. 8I will devastate this city and make it an object of scorn; *i* all who pass by will be appalled *j* and will scoff because of all its wounds. *k* 9I will make them eat *l* the flesh of their sons and daughters, and they will eat one another's flesh during the stress of the siege imposed on them by the enemies *m* who seek their lives.'

10"Then break the jar *n* while those who go with you are watching, 11and say to them, 'This is what the LORD Almighty says: I will smash *o* this nation and this city just as this potter's jar is smashed and cannot be repaired. They will bury *p* the dead in Topheth until there is no more room. 12This is what I will do to this place and to those who live here, declares the LORD. I will make this city like Topheth. 13The houses *q* in Jerusalem and those of the

Reference column:
18:23 *o*Ps 59:5; S Jer 10:24
19:1 *p*Jer 18:2 *q*S Nu 11:17; 1Ki 8:1
19:2 *r*S Jos 15:8
19:3 *s*Jer 17:20 *t*S Jer 6:19 *u*S 1Sa 3:11
19:4 *v*S Dt 31:16; S Isa 65:11 *w*S Ex 20:3; S Jer 1:16 *x*S Lev 18:21 *y*S 2Ki 21:16
19:5 *z*S Lev 18:21; S 2Ki 3:27; Ps 106:37-38 *a*S Jer 7:31; Eze 16:36
19:6 *b*S 2Ki 23:10
*c*S Jos 15:8 *d*Jer 7:32
19:7 *e*Ps 33:10-11 S Lev 26:17; S Dt 28:25 *g*S Jer 16:4; 34:20 *h*S Dt 28:26
19:8 *i*S Dt 28:37; S Jer 18:16; 25:9 *j*S Lev 26:32; La 2:15-16 *k*S Dt 29:22
19:9 *l*S Lev 26:29; Dt 28:49-57; La 4:10 *m*S ver 7; Jer 21:7; 34:20
19:10 *n*ver 1; S Ps 2:9; Jer 13:14
19:11 *o*Ps 2:9; Isa 30:14

*p*Jer 7:32 19:13 *q*Jer 32:29; 52:13; Eze 16:41

g 7 The Hebrew for *ruin* sounds like the Hebrew for *jar* (see verses 1 and 10).

19:1–15 A jar deliberately broken by Jeremiah (vv. 1–10) symbolizes the forthcoming destruction of Judah and Jerusalem (vv. 11–15). In ch. 18, the potter's clay was still moist and pliable, making it possible to reshape and rework it (see 18:1–11). In ch. 19, however, the clay jar is hard and, if unsuitable for the owner's use, can only be destroyed (see v. 11).

19:1 *jar.* The Hebrew for this word implies a vessel with a narrow neck, perhaps the water decanter frequently found in excavations and ranging from 5 to 12 inches high. *elders.* See note on Ex 3:16. *of the people.* See 1Ki 8:1–3. *of the priests.* See 2Ki 19:2, "leading priests" (lit. "elders of the priests"). Elders in Israel were of two kinds, one performing primarily civil functions and the other primarily religious functions.

19:2 *Valley of Ben Hinnom.* See note on 7:31. *Potshard Gate.* The Hebrew underlying the word "Potsherd" is the same as that translated "clay" in v. 1. The Jerusalem Targum identified the Potsherd Gate (so called because it overlooked the main dump for broken pottery) with the Dung Gate of Ne 2:13 (see note there); 3:13–14; 12:31.

19:3 *kings.* See note on 17:20. *disaster . . . make the ears . . . tingle.* Echoed from 2Ki 21:12 (see 1Sa 3:11). The phrase refers to the shock of hearing an announcement of threatened punishment.

19:4 *they.* All who tried to combine the worship of idols with the worship of the one true God. *this . . . place.* Jerusalem. *burned sacrifices.* The Hebrew for this word is always translated "burned incense" elsewhere in Jeremiah (see note on 1:16). *filled this place with the blood of the innocent.* The blood of godly people (see 2:34; 7:6; 22:3,17; 26:15), specifically as shed by wicked King Manasseh (see 15:4 and note; see also especially 2Ki 21:16).

19:5–6 Repeated in large part from 7:31–32 (see notes

there).

19:7 *ruin.* Lit. "pour out"; see NIV text note (see also note on v. 1). As Jeremiah was saying this, he may have been pouring water from the jar to the ground (cf. 2Sa 14:14). *fall by the sword before their enemies.* The Babylonians are the instruments of the divine threat (see 20:6). *carcasses as food . . . beasts of the earth.* See 7:33 and note.

19:8 Echoes the language of 18:16 (see note there; see also Eze 27:35; Zep 2:15). *devastate . . . appalled.* The same Hebrew root underlies both words. *scorn . . . scoff.* The same Hebrew root underlies both words.

19:9 One of the covenant curses (see Lev 26:29; Dt 28:53–57). *eat the flesh of their sons and daughters . . . eat one another's flesh.* When Jerusalem's food supply ran out during the Babylonian siege in 586 B.C., cannibalism resulted (see La 2:20; 4:10; Eze 5:10). Such shocking activity was not unprecedented in Israel (see 2Ki 6:28–29), and it would occur again in A.D. 70 during the Roman siege of Jerusalem (see Zec 11:9 and note): "A woman . . . who . . . had fled to Jerusalem . . . killed her son, roasted him, and ate one half, concealing and saving the rest" (Josephus, *Jewish War,* 6.3.4).

19:11 *smash this nation . . . as this potter's jar is smashed.* Egyptians of the 12th Dynasty (1991–1786 B.C.) inscribed the names of their enemies on pottery bowls and then smashed them, hoping to break the power of their enemies by so doing. *cannot be repaired.* See note on vv. 1–15.

19:13 *will be defiled like . . . Topheth.* King Josiah had earlier "desecrated Topheth" (2Ki 23:10). *burned incense.* See note on 1:16. *on the roofs.* See 32:29; see also note on Isa 15:3. The kings of Judah had built pagan altars on the roof of the palace in Jerusalem (see 2Ki 23:12). The Ugaritic Keret epic of the 14th century B.C. (see chart on "Ancient Texts Relating to the OT," p. 5) describes a similar practice: "Go to

kings of Judah will be defiled*r* like this place, Topheth—all the houses where they burned incense on the roofs*s* to all the starry hosts*t* and poured out drink offerings*u* to other gods.' "

¹⁴Jeremiah then returned from Topheth, where the LORD had sent him to prophesy, and stood in the court*v* of the LORD's temple and said to all the people, ¹⁵"This is what the LORD Almighty, the God of Israel, says: 'Listen! I am going to bring on this city and the villages around it every disaster*w* I pronounced against them, because they were stiff-necked*x* and would not listen*y* to my words.' "

Jeremiah and Pashhur

20 When the priest Pashhur son of Immer,*z* the chief officer*a* in the temple of the LORD, heard Jeremiah prophesying these things, ²he had Jeremiah the prophet beaten*b* and put in the stocks*c* at the Upper Gate of Benjamin*d* at the LORD's temple. ³The next day, when Pashhur released him from the stocks, Jeremiah said to him, "The LORD's name*e* for you is not Pashhur, but Magor-Missabib.*h f* ⁴For this is what the LORD says: 'I will make you a terror to yourself and to all your friends; with your own eyes*g* you will see them fall by the sword of their enemies. I will hand*h* all Judah over to the king of Babylon, who will carry*i* them away to Babylon or put them to the sword. ⁵I will hand over to their enemies all the wealth*j* of this city—all its products, all its valuables and all the treasures of the kings of Judah. They will take it away*k* as plunder and carry it off to Babylon. ⁶And you, Pashhur, and all who live in your house will go into exile to Babylon. There you will die and be buried, you and all your friends to whom you have prophesied*l* lies.' "

Jeremiah's Complaint

⁷O LORD, you deceived*i m* me, and I was
    deceived*i*;
  you overpowered*n* me and prevailed.
I am ridiculed*o* all day long;
  everyone mocks*p* me.
⁸Whenever I speak, I cry out
  proclaiming violence and
    destruction.*q*
So the word of the LORD has brought
  me
  insult and reproach*r* all day long.
⁹But if I say, "I will not mention him

19:13 *r* Ps 74:7
s 2Ki 23:12
t Dt 4:19;
S 2Ki 17:16;
S Job 38:32;
Jer 8:2; Ac 7:42
u S Isa 57:6;
Eze 20:28
19:14 *v* 2Ch 20:5;
S Jer 7:2; 26:2
19:15 *w* ver 3;
Jer 11:11
x S Ne 9:16;
Ac 7:51
y Jer 22:21
20:1
z S 1Ch 24:14
a 2Ki 25:18;
Lk 22:52
20:2 *b* Dt 25:2-3;
S Jer 1:19; 15:15;
37:15; 2Co 11:24
c S Job 13:27;
Jer 29:26;
Ac 16:24;
Heb 11:36
d S Job 29:7;
Jer 37:13; 38:7;
Zec 14:10
20:3 *e* Hos 1:4
f S ver 10;
S Ps 31:13
20:4 *g* Jer 29:21

h Jer 21:10; 25:9
i Jer 13:19; 39:9;
52:27
20:5
j S 2Ki 25:15;
Jer 17:3
k S 2Ki 20:17
20:6 *l* S Jer 14:15;
La 2:14
20:7 *m* S Ex 5:23;
22:16 *n* Isa 8:11;
Am 3:8; 1Co 9:16
o Job 12:4
p S Job 17:2;
S Ps 119:21

20:8 *q* Jer 6:7; 28:8 *r* S 2Ch 36:16; S Jer 6:10

h3 Magor-Missabib means *terror on every side.*   *i 7* Or *persuaded*

---

the top of a tower, bestride the top of the wall . . . Honor Baal with your sacrifice . . . Then descend . . . from the housetops." **starry hosts.** Worship of the sun, moon and stars was common in Judah throughout much of the later history of the monarchy (see, e.g., 2Ki 17:16; 21:3,5; 23:4–5; Zep 1:5). **drink offerings to other gods.** See note on 7:18.
19:14 *all the people.* A much larger audience than the elders of v. 1.
19:15 *the villages around it.* The towns of Judah that were dependent on Jerusalem (see 1:15; 9:11). *were stiff-necked and would not listen.* Repeated from 7:26 (see note there; see also 11:10).
20:1–6 Pashhur's response to Jeremiah's symbolic act (vv. 1–2), and Jeremiah's rejoinder (vv. 3–6).
20:1 *Pashhur.* One or more different men with the same name appear in 21:1; 38:1. *Immer.* Perhaps a descendant of the head of the 16th division of priests in the Jerusalem temple (see 1Ch 24:14). *chief officer.* The priest in charge of punishing troublemakers, real or imagined, in the temple courts (see v. 2; 29:26). The position was second only to that of the chief priest himself (compare 29:25–26 with 52:24).
20:2 The first of many recorded acts of physical violence against Jeremiah. *the prophet.* The first time Jeremiah is so called in the book (see Introduction: Themes and Message; here to stress the enormity of Pashhur's actions. *beaten.* Probably in accordance with the Mosaic law of Dt 25:2–3 (see note on Dt 25:3). *stocks.* Lit. "restraint, confinement" (the Hebrew for this word is translated "prison" in 2Ch 16:10). *Upper Gate of Benjamin.* Probably the same as the "north gate of the inner court" (Eze 8:3; see 2Ki 15:35; see also Eze 9:2). *at the LORD's temple.* The qualifying phrase distinguishes the temple's Gate of Benjamin from the "Benjamin Gate" in the city wall (37:13; 38:7). Both gates were

in the northern part of the city, facing the territory of Benjamin.
20:3 *Magor-Missabib.* See NIV text note; see also note on 6:25. The phrase "terror on every side" (see v. 10) is found in the plural in La 2:22.
20:4 Pashhur's new name symbolizes terror to all Judah, whose people will be exiled to Babylonia or put to death. *friends.* Associates and allies in the sense of covenant partners (see v. 6). *king of Babylon.* Nebuchadnezzar, who acceded to the Babylonian throne in 605 B.C. (see notes on 17:15; 18:1–20:18).
20:5 Fulfilled in 597 B.C. (see 2Ki 24:13) and in 586 (see 52:17–23; 2Ki 25:13–17).
20:6 *you, Pashhur, . . . will go into exile.* Probably in 597 B.C., because shortly after that year (see 29:2) two other men in succession had replaced Pashhur as chief officer in the temple (see 29:25–26). *you have prophesied lies.* The priest Pashhur had pretended to be a prophet.
20:7–18 The sixth, last and longest of Jeremiah's "confessions" (see Introduction: Author and Date). In some respects, it is the most daring and bitter of them all.
20:7 Cf. 15:18. *deceived.* Lit. "seduced" (Ex 22:16) or "enticed" (1Ki 22:20–22); see v. 10. Jeremiah feels that when the Lord originally called him to be a prophet, he had overly persuaded him (see NIV text note; see also 1:7–8, 17–19; cf. Eze 14:9).
20:8 Jeremiah attributes his suffering to the Lord's demands on his life. *violence and destruction.* The prophet's message echoes the Lord's word (see 6:7). *reproach.* See Ps 44:13; 79:4.
20:9 A classic description of prophetic reluctance overcome by divine compulsion (see 1:6–8; Am 3:8; Ac 4:20; 1Co 9:16). *his word is . . . like a fire.* See 5:14; 23:29. The

or speak any more in his name," s
his word is in my heart like a fire, t
  a fire shut up in my bones.
I am weary of holding it in; u
  indeed, I cannot.
10I hear many whispering,
  "Terror v on every side!
  Report w him! Let's report him!"
All my friends x
  are waiting for me to slip, y saying,
"Perhaps he will be deceived;
  then we will prevail z over him
  and take our revenge a on him."

11But the Lord b is with me like a mighty
  warrior;
so my persecutors c will stumble and
  not prevail. d
They will fail and be thoroughly
  disgraced; e
  their dishonor will never be
  forgotten.
12O Lord Almighty, you who examine
  the righteous
and probe the heart and mind, f
let me see your vengeance g upon them,
  for to you I have committed h my
  cause.

13Sing i to the Lord!

Give praise to the Lord!
He rescues j the life of the needy
  from the hands of the wicked. k

14Cursed be the day I was born! l
  May the day my mother bore me not
    be blessed!
15Cursed be the man who brought my
    father the news,
who made him very glad, saying,
  "A child is born to you—a son!"
16May that man be like the towns m
  the Lord overthrew without pity.
May he hear wailing n in the morning,
  a battle cry at noon.
17For he did not kill me in the womb, o
  with my mother as my grave,
  her womb enlarged forever.
18Why did I ever come out of the womb p
  to see trouble q and sorrow
  and to end my days in shame? r

God Rejects Zedekiah's Request

21 The word came to Jeremiah from
the Lord when King Zedekiah s
sent to him Pashhur t son of Malkijah and
the priest Zephaniah u son of Maaseiah.
They said: 2"Inquire v now of the Lord for

Cross references

20:9 sJer 44:16
tS Ps 39:3;
S Jer 4:19
uS Job 4:2;
S Jer 6:11;
Am 3:8; Ac 4:20
20:10 vJer 6:25
wNe 6:6-13;
Isa 29:21
xS Job 19:14;
S Jer 13:21
yS Ps 57:4;
S Jer 18:22;
Lk 11:53-54
zS 1Ki 19:2
aS 1Sa 18:25;
S Jer 11:19
20:11 bJer 1:8;
Ro 8:31
cJer 15:15; 17:18
dS Ps 129:2
eS Jer 7:19; 23:40
20:12 fS Ps 7:9;
S Jer 17:10
gDt 32:35;
S Ro 12:19
hPs 62:8;
Jer 11:20
20:13 iS Isa 12:6
jPs 34:6; 35:10
kS Ps 97:10
20:14 lS Job 3:8,
16; Jer 15:10
20:16 mS Ge 19:25
nS Jer 6:26
20:17 oS Job 3:16;
S 10:18-19
20:18 pS Job 3:10-11;
S Ecc 4:2
qS Ge 3:17;
S Job 5:7
rS 1Ki 19:4;
Ps 90:9; 102:3
21:1 s 2Ki 24:18; Jer 52:1 tS 1Ch 9:12 uS 2Ki 25:18 21:2
vS Ge 25:22; S 2Ki 22:18

---

figure is unique to the prophet Jeremiah (see also La 1:13).
20:10 The Hebrew of the first two lines is identical with
that of the first two lines of Ps 31:13. *Terror on every side!*
See note on 6:25. The phrase is here used as a nickname for
Jeremiah in the light of his doleful message. *friends.* Lit.
"men of my peace/welfare" (a similar Hebrew phrase appears in Ps 41:9, where it is translated "close friend").
waiting for me to slip. See Ps 35:15; 38:16. *deceived.* See v.
7 and note. *we will prevail over him.* Or so they think (see v.
11). *take our revenge on him.* His enemies will not give up,
no matter what it takes (see 11:19; 12:6; 26:11; cf. Ps
56:5-6; 71:10).
20:11 *the Lord is with me.* See 1:8 and note. *mighty.* The
Hebrew for this word is translated "cruel" in 15:21, where
it describes Jeremiah's enemies. Here it has a different nuance and is applied to God, whose "might" overcomes all
"cruelty." *warrior.* See notes on Ex 14:14; 15:3.
20:12 Repeated almost verbatim from 11:20.
20:13 *Sing . . . Give praise.* See 31:7; see also introduction
to Ps 9. *rescues . . . from the hands of the wicked.* See
15:21; 21:12. *needy.* See 22:16. By Jeremiah's time,
"poor/needy" had become virtually synonymous with
"righteous" (see Am 2:6; see also notes on Ps 9:18; 34:6).
20:14-18 See Job 3:3-19. From the heights of exultation
(v. 13), Jeremiah now sinks to the depths of despair. The
irreversibility of his divine call (v. 9), the betrayal of his
friends (v. 10), the relentless pursuit of his enemies (vv.
7,11), the negative and condemnatory nature of his message
(v. 8)—all have combined to bring to his lips a startling
expression of despondency and hopelessness. The passage
serves also as a transition to the next major section of the
book. Judah and Jerusalem, Jeremiah will soon say, are now
irrevocably doomed (see 21:1-10).
20:14 *Cursed be the day I was born!* See note on Job 3:3.
The prophet questions the very basis of his divine commis-

sion (see 1:5).
20:15 News of the birth of a son, normally a blessing in
ancient times (see, e.g., Ge 29:31-35), Jeremiah sees as a
curse in his own case. *Cursed be the man.* A rhetorical curse,
not directed against the man personally.
20:16 *towns the Lord overthrew.* Sodom and Gomorrah
(see Ge 19:24-25,29). By Jeremiah's time, their wickedness
had long been proverbial (see 23:14; Dt 29:23; see also note
on Isa 1:9-10). *battle cry.* See 4:19. *at noon.* See note on
6:4.
20:17 *enlarged.* Lit. "pregnant." In his anguish, Jeremiah
wishes that his mother's womb, which gave him birth, had
been instead his eternal tomb.
21:1-24:10 The prophet denounces Judah's rulers
(21:1-23:7), false prophets (23:8-40) and sinful people (ch.
24). Although for the most part chs. 1-20 relate events in
chronological order, chs. 21-52 are arranged on the basis of
subject matter rather than chronology (see 24:1; 25:1;
26:1; 27:1; 29:2; 32:1; 35:1; 36:1; 37:1; 45:1; 49:34;
51:59; 52:4).
21:1-23:7 The rulers of Judah, who bear the primary
responsibility for the nation's economic, social and spiritual
ills, are the first to be denounced by Jeremiah.
21:1 *The word came.* The phrase does not appear again
until 25:1, suggesting that chs. 21-24 constitute an integral
section in the book. *Zedekiah.* Means "The Lord is my
righteousness." See Introduction: Background. *Pashhur son
of Malkijah.* Not the same as the Pashhur of 20:1-6 (see
38:1). *the priest Zephaniah son of Maaseiah.* Not the same
as the prophet Zephaniah (see 29:25,29; 37:3; 52:24; see
also Zep 1:1).
21:2 *Inquire . . . of the Lord.* A request for knowledge or
information (see Ge 25:22; 2Ki 22:13), not necessarily for
help. *Nebuchadnezzar.* See NIV text note. The name means
"O Nabu [a god], protect my son/boundary!" He was the

us because Nebuchadnezzar[j][w] king of Babylon[x] is attacking us. Perhaps the LORD will perform wonders[y] for us as in times past so that he will withdraw from us."

[3]But Jeremiah answered them, "Tell Zedekiah, [4]"This is what the LORD, the God of Israel, says: I am about to turn[z] against you the weapons of war that are in your hands, which you are using to fight the king of Babylon and the Babylonians[k] who are outside the wall besieging[a] you. And I will gather them inside this city. [5]I myself will fight[b] against you with an outstretched hand[c] and a mighty arm[d] in anger and fury and great wrath. [6]I will strike[e] down those who live in this city—both men and animals—and they will die of a terrible plague.[f] [7]After that, declares the LORD, I will hand over Zedekiah[g] king of Judah, his officials and the people in this city who survive the plague,[h] sword and famine, to Nebuchadnezzar king of Babylon[i] and to their enemies[j] who seek their lives.[k] He will put them to the sword;[l] he will show them no mercy or pity or compassion.'[m]

[8]"Furthermore, tell the people, 'This is what the LORD says: See, I am setting before you the way of life[n] and the way of death. [9]Whoever stays in this city will die by the sword, famine or plague.[o] But whoever goes out and surrenders[p] to the Babylonians who are besieging you will live;

he will escape with his life.[q] [10]I have determined to do this city harm[r] and not good, declares the LORD. It will be given into the hands[s] of the king of Babylon, and he will destroy it with fire.'[t]

[11]"Moreover, say to the royal house[u] of Judah, 'Hear the word of the LORD; [12]O house of David, this is what the LORD says:

" 'Administer justice[v] every morning;
    rescue from the hand of his
        oppressor[w]
    the one who has been robbed,
or my wrath will break out and burn
        like fire[x]
    because of the evil[y] you have
        done—
    burn with no one to quench[z] it.
[13]I am against[a] you, Jerusalem,
    you who live above this valley[b]
    on the rocky plateau,
                declares the LORD—
you who say, "Who can come against
    us?
Who can enter our refuge?"[c]
[14]I will punish you as your deeds[d]
    deserve,
                declares the LORD.

21:2 [w]S 2Ki 25:1
[x]S Ge 10:10
[y]Ps 44:1-4;
Jer 32:17
21:4 [z]Jer 32:5
[a]Jer 37:8-10
21:5
[b]S Jos 10:14;
Eze 5:8
[c]S 2Ki 22:13;
S Jer 6:12
[d]S Ex 3:20
21:6 [e]S Jer 7:20
[f]S Jer 14:12
21:7 [g]S 2Ki 25:7;
Jer 52:9;
Eze 12:14
[h]Jer 14:12; 27:8
[i]S 2Ch 36:10;
Jer 27:6; 32:4;
34:3; 37:17;
38:18; 39:5;
Eze 29:19
[j]S Lev 26:17;
S Jer 19:9
[k]S Jer 11:21
[l]S Jer 15:9
[m]S 2Ch 36:17;
S Jer 15:5;
Eze 7:9; Hab 1:6
21:8 [n]S Dt 30:15
21:9 [o]Jer 14:12;
Eze 5:12
[p]Jer 27:11; 40:9

[q]Jer 27:12; 38:2,
17; 39:18; 45:5
21:10 [r]Jer 44:27;
Am 9:4
[s]S Jer 20:4;
32:28; 38:2-3
[t]S 2Ki 25:9;
S 2Ch 36:19
21:11
[u]S Jer 13:18
21:12
[v]S Ex 22:22;
S Lev 25:17
[w]S Ps 27:11
[x]S Isa 42:25;
S Jer 10:10
[y]Jer 23:2

[z]S Isa 1:31 21:13 [a]Jer 23:30; 50:31; 51:25; Eze 5:8; 13:8;
21:3; 29:10; 34:10; Na 2:13; 3:5 [b]Ps 125:2 [c]2Sa 5:6-7;
Jer 49:4; La 4:12; Ob 1:3-4 21:14 [d]S Pr 1:31; S Isa 3:10-11;
S Jer 17:10

[j]2 Hebrew Nebuchadrezzar, of which Nebuchadnezzar is
a variant; here and often in Jeremiah and Ezekiel
[k]4 Or Chaldeans; also in verse 9

most famous ruler (605–562 B.C.) of the Neo-Babylonian empire (612–539). *is attacking.* About 588, because the brash Zedekiah had rebelled against Babylon (see 52:3). *us.* Jerusalem. *perform wonders . . . as in times past.* For example, in the days of Hezekiah (see Isa 37:36). *he will withdraw.* See Isa 37:37.

21:4 *turn against you the weapons.* Your defense of Jerusalem will fail. *Babylonians.* See NIV text note; see also note on Job 1:17. *gather them inside this city.* Either (1) the weapons, meaning that Judah's troops would be totally unable to defend the approaches to the city, or (2) the Babylonians, meaning that Jerusalem's defeat is imminent and inevitable.

21:5 *I myself will fight against you.* The Lord, usually his people's defender, will now destroy them and seal their doom. *with an outstretched hand and a mighty arm.* See 27:5; 32:17. A similar phrase is used to describe God's powerful redemption of Israel at the exodus (see 32:21; Dt 4:34; 5:15; 7:19; 26:8), but here God turns his wrath against his own people. *in anger and fury and great wrath.* Probably quoted from Dt 29:28, where the Hebrew for this phrase is translated "in furious anger and in great wrath."

21:7 *I will hand over Zedekiah . . . his officials and the people.* Fulfilled in 52:8–11,24–27 (see Eze 12:13–14). *plague, sword and famine.* See v. 9. For this triad see note on 14:12. *no mercy or pity or compassion.* For this triad see 13:14; see also Eze 5:11. The three triads here heighten the literary effect of the passage.

21:8–10 See 27:12–13. Similar advice is offered in 38:2–3,17–28 (see Dt 30:15–20).

21:8 *See, I am setting before you.* See Dt 11:26. The people are offered a choice, but few of them will make the

right decision. *the way of life and the way of death.* See Dt 30:15,19; see also Pr 6:23.

21:9 Repeated almost verbatim in 38:2. Jeremiah's counsel of surrender branded him as a traitor in the eyes of many (see 37:13), but he was in fact a true patriot who wanted to stay in Judah even after Jerusalem was destroyed (see 37:14; 40:6; 42:7–22). *whoever . . . surrenders to the Babylonians . . . will live.* Fulfilled in 39:9; 52:15. *he will escape with his life.* Lit. "his life will be his (only) booty." The victorious in battle can expect to share plunder; the defeated are fortunate indeed if their lives are spared.

21:10 *determined.* Lit. "set my face" (see 44:11). *harm and not good.* See Am 9:4; contrast 24:6. *It will be given . . . destroy it with fire.* See 34:2.

21:12 *Administer justice.* See 5:28; 22:16; 1Ki 3:28; La 3:59. The king was obliged and expected to do so, as was the future Messiah (see 23:5; 33:15). *every morning.* When the mind is clear and the day is cool (court sessions were held outside, at the city gate; see notes on Ge 19:1; Ru 4:1). *rescue . . . robbed.* Repeated in 22:3. *or my wrath . . . no one to quench it.* Repeated verbatim from 4:4 (see Am 5:6). *wrath will . . . burn.* See 15:14; 17:4,27.

21:13 *valley.* Jerusalem, surrounded on three sides by valleys (see note on Isa 22:7), is called the "Valley of Vision" in Isa 22:1,5. *rocky plateau.* Mount Zion. *you who say.* The pronouns are plural in the second half of the verse (referring to Jerusalem's inhabitants), singular in the first half (referring to Jerusalem personified). *Who can come against us?* The people think that no one can successfully besiege them (see notes on 7:4; 8:19).

21:14 *as your deeds deserve.* See note on 17:10. *kindle a*

I will kindle a fire^e in your forests^f
  that will consume everything around
    you.' "

Judgment Against Evil Kings

22 This is what the LORD says: "Go
down to the palace of the king^g of
Judah and proclaim this message there:
²'Hear^h the word of the LORD, O king of
Judah, you who sit on David's
throneⁱ—you, your officials and your
people who come through these gates.^j
³This is what the LORD says: Do what is
just^k and right. Rescue from the hand of
his oppressor^l the one who has been
robbed. Do no wrong or violence to the
alien, the fatherless or the widow,^m and do
not shed innocent bloodⁿ in this place.
⁴For if you are careful to carry out these
commands, then kings^o who sit on David's throne will come through the gates of
this palace, riding in chariots and on
horses, accompanied by their officials and
their people. ⁵But if you do not obey^p
these commands, declares the LORD, I
swear^q by myself that this palace will
become a ruin.' "

⁶For this is what the LORD says about
the palace of the king of Judah:

"Though you are like Gilead^r to me,
  like the summit of Lebanon,^s
I will surely make you like a desert,^t

like towns not inhabited.
⁷I will send destroyers^u against you,
  each man with his weapons,
and they will cut^v up your fine cedar
    beams
  and throw them into the fire.^w

⁸"People from many nations will pass by
this city and will ask one another, 'Why
has the LORD done such a thing to this
great city?'^x ⁹And the answer will be: 'Because they have forsaken the covenant of
the LORD their God and have worshiped
and served other gods.^y ' "

¹⁰Do not weep for the dead^z ₍king₎ or
  mourn^a his loss;
rather, weep bitterly for him who is
  exiled,
because he will never return^b
  nor see his native land again.

¹¹For this is what the LORD says about
Shallum^{1c} son of Josiah, who succeeded
his father as king of Judah but has gone
from this place: "He will never return.
¹²He will die^d in the place where they
have led him captive; he will not see this
land again."

¹³"Woe^e to him who builds^f his palace
  by unrighteousness,
  his upper rooms by injustice,

21:14
^eS 2Ch 36:19;
La 2:3
^fS 2Ki 19:23;
Eze 20:47
22:1
^gS Jer 13:18; 34:2
22:2 ^hAm 7:16
ⁱS Jer 17:25;
Lk 1:32 ^jJer 17:20
22:3
^kS Lev 25:17;
Isa 56:1; Jer 5:1;
Eze 33:14; 45:9;
Hos 12:6;
Am 5:24;
Mic 6:8; Zec 7:9
^lPs 72:4;
Jer 21:12
^mS Ex 22:22;
S Isa 1:17;
Jer 5:28 ⁿS Jer 7:6
22:4 ^oS Jer 17:25
22:5 ^pS Jer 17:27
^qS Ge 22:16;
Heb 6:13
22:6
^rS Ge 31:21;
S SS 4:1
^sS 1Ki 7:2;
S Isa 33:9
^tMic 3:12

22:7 ^uS Jer 4:7;
S 6:4 ^vPs 74:5;
Isa 10:34
^wS 2Ch 36:19;
Zec 11:1
22:8
^xDt 29:25-26;
1Ki 9:8-9;
Jer 16:10-11
22:9 ^yS 1Ki 9:9;
Jer 16:11;
Eze 39:23
22:10 ^zS Ecc 4:2
^aver 18;
Eze 24:16 ^bver
27; Jer 24:9;
29:18; 42:18
22:11
^cS 2Ki 23:31
22:12 ^d2Ki 23:34

22:13 ^eS Isa 5:8 ^fMic 3:10; Hab 2:9

¹11 Also called *Jehoahaz*

---

fire . . . consume. See note on 17:27. *forests.* The Hebrew
for this word is singular and perhaps refers figuratively to
Jerusalem's royal palace, called the "Palace of the Forest of
Lebanon" (1Ki 7:2; 10:17,21; see Isa 22:8) because of the
cedar (see 22:7,14,15,23) used in its construction. The palace (see 22:1) is compared to the "summit of Lebanon" in
22:6 (see 22:23 and NIV text note).
22:1 *Go down.* The palace was at a lower elevation than
the temple (see 26:10; 36:10-12).
22:2 *king of Judah.* Probably Zedekiah (see 21:3,7; compare v. 3 with 21:12), whose predecessors are mentioned in
sequence later in the chapter (Josiah, vv. 10a,15b-16;
Jehoahaz/Shallum, vv. 10b-12; Jehoiakim, vv. 13-15a,
17-19; Jehoiachin/Coniah, vv. 24-30). *David's throne.*
Though all the kings of the Davidic dynasty failed to a greater
or lesser degree, the victorious Messiah would someday
appear as the culmination of David's royal line (see 23:5 and
NIV text note; 33:15; Eze 34:23-24; Mt 1:1). *who come
through these gates.* See 17:25 and note.
22:3 Contrast Isa 11:3-5 with Eze 22:6-7.
22:4 Repeated in part from 17:25.
22:5 See 17:27 and note. *swear by myself.* See notes on Ge
22:16; Isa 45:23; see also 49:13; 51:14; cf. 44:26. *become
a ruin.* Fulfilled in 52:13 (see 27:17).
22:6 *Gilead . . . Lebanon.* Renowned for their forests.
Lebanon in particular supplied cedar for the royal palace (see
note on 21:14; see also 1Ki 5:6,8-10; 7:2-3; 10:27).
22:7 *send.* Lit. "consecrate" (see note on 6:4). *destroyers.*
The Babylonians (see note on 4:7; see also 12:12). *each man*

with his weapons. See Eze 9:2. *cut up your . . . cedar.* Cf. Isa
10:33-34; cf. especially the vivid description of the Babylonian troops smashing the carved paneling of the Jerusalem
temple with their axes and hatchets (Ps 74:3-6).
22:8-9 Echoed in 1Ki 9:8-9; see Dt 29:24-26.
22:9 *forsaken the covenant . . . and served other gods.* A
gross violation of the first and second stipulations of the
Mosaic covenant (see Ex 20:3-5 and notes).
22:10 *weep for the dead king.* Josiah, who was mourned
long after his death (see 2Ch 35:24-25). *him who is exiled.*
Jehoahaz/Shallum. In 609 B.C., Pharaoh Neco "carried him
off to Egypt, and there he died" (2Ki 23:34).
22:11 *Shallum.* The fourth son of Josiah (see 1Ch 3:15).
"Shallum" was his personal name, "Jehoahaz" his throne
name (the latter means "The LORD seizes").
22:12 *the place where they have led him captive.* Egypt
(see note on v. 10).
22:13-19 A scathing denunciation of King Jehoiakim, who
is described in the third person (vv. 13-14), then rhetorically
addressed in the second person (vv. 15,17), then identified
by name (v. 18), meaning "The LORD raises up." Good King
Josiah is referred to in vv. 15b-16 by way of contrast.
22:13 *Woe to him who builds.* See Hab 2:9,12. *by unrighteousness . . . by injustice.* Contrast v. 3; 21:12. *upper
rooms.* See note on Jdg 3:20. *making his countrymen work
for nothing.* Contrary to the law (see Lev 25:39; Dt
24:14-15). Jehoiakim's refusal to pay them may have been
due partly to inability, since Judah was under heavy tribute to
Egypt during the early part of his reign (see 2Ki 23:35).

making his countrymen work for
    nothing,
  not paying*g* them for their labor.
[14]He says, 'I will build myself a great
    palace*h*
  with spacious upper rooms.'
So he makes large windows in it,
  panels it with cedar*i*
  and decorates it in red.*j*

[15]"Does it make you a king
  to have more and more cedar?
Did not your father have food and
    drink?
He did what was right and just,*k*
  so all went well*l* with him.
[16]He defended the cause of the poor and
    needy,*m*
  and so all went well.
Is that not what it means to know*n*
    me?"
    declares the LORD.
[17]"But your eyes and your heart
  are set only on dishonest gain,*o*
  on shedding innocent blood*p*
  and on oppression and extortion."*q*

[18]Therefore this is what the LORD says
about Jehoiakim son of Josiah king of
Judah:

"They will not mourn*r* for him:
  'Alas, my brother! Alas, my sister!'
They will not mourn for him:
  'Alas, my master! Alas, his splendor!'

[19]He will have the burial*s* of a donkey—
  dragged away and thrown*t*
  outside the gates of Jerusalem."

[20]"Go up to Lebanon and cry out,*u*
  let your voice be heard in Bashan,*v*
  cry out from Abarim,*w*
  for all your allies*x* are crushed.
[21]I warned you when you felt secure,*y*
  but you said, 'I will not listen!'
This has been your way from your
    youth;*z*
  you have not obeyed*a* me.
[22]The wind*b* will drive all your
    shepherds*c* away,
  and your allies*d* will go into exile.
Then you will be ashamed and
    disgraced*e*
  because of all your wickedness.
[23]You who live in 'Lebanon,*mf* '
  who are nestled in cedar buildings,
how you will groan when pangs come
    upon you,
  pain*g* like that of a woman in labor!

[24]"As surely as I live," declares the
LORD, "even if you, Jehoiachin*nh* son of
Jehoiakim king of Judah, were a signet
ring*i* on my right hand, I would still pull
you off. [25]I will hand you over*j* to those
who seek your life, those you fear—to
Nebuchadnezzar king of Babylon and to

Cross references

22:13 *g*Lev 19:13; Jas 5:4
22:14 *h*Isa 5:8-9 *i*S 2Sa 7:2 *j*Eze 23:14
22:15 *k*2Ki 23:25 *l*Ps 128:2; S Isa 3:10
22:16 *m*Ps 72:1-4, 12-13; S 82:3; S Pr 24:23 *n*S Ps 36:10
22:17 *o*S Isa 56:11 *p*S 2Ki 24:4 *q*S Dt 28:33; Eze 18:12; Mic 2:2
22:18 *r*S 2Sa 1:26
22:19 *s*2Ki 24:6 *t*Jer 8:2; 36:30
22:20 *u*S Isa 57:13 *v*S Ps 68:15 *w*S Nu 27:12 *x*ver 22; Jer 30:14; La 1:19; Eze 16:33-34; Hos 8:9
22:21 *y*Zec 7:7 *z*Dt 9:7; Ps 25:7; Isa 54:4; Jer 3:25; 31:19; 32:30 *a*S Jer 3:13; 7:23-28; Zep 3:2
22:22 *b*Dt 28:64; S Job 27:21 *c*S Jer 10:21 *d*ver 20 *e*S Jer 7:19
22:23 *f*S 1Ki 7:2; Eze 17:3 *g*S Jer 4:31
22:24 *h*S 2Ki 24:6,8 *i*S Ge 38:18
22:25 *j*S 2Ki 24:16; S 2Ch 36:10

*m*23 That is, the palace in Jerusalem (see 1 Kings 7:2)
*n*24 Hebrew *Coniah,* a variant of *Jehoiachin*; also in verse 28

22:14 *large windows.* The windows described here may well be the same as those found in the ruins of Beth Hakkerem (see 6:1; see also note on Ne 3:14) by archaeologists in the early 1960s. *panels.* Haggai similarly deplores the use of paneling as an extravagant and unneeded luxury in certain situations (see Hag 1:4).

22:15 *your father.* Josiah. *have food and drink.* Enjoy life (see Ecc 2:24–25; 3:12–13). *did what was right and just.* Like his ancestor David (see 2Sa 8:15); contrast v. 13 (see note there).

22:16 James defines a proper relationship to God in similar terms (see Jas 1:27); contrast 5:28 (see note there). *poor and needy.* See note on 20:13. *to know me.* To love God fully, which results in living a pious life and serving those in need (see Dt 10:12–13; Hos 6:6; Mic 6:8).

22:17 *your.* Jehoiakim's (see v. 18). *dishonest gain.* See 6:13; 8:10. *shedding innocent blood.* See note on 19:4; for an illustration of Jehoiakim's cruelty in this regard see 26:20–23. *oppression.* See v. 3; 6:6; 21:12.

22:18 Contrast 2Ch 35:24–25. *They will not mourn for him: "Alas, my brother!"* Contrast 1Ki 13:30.

22:19 *burial of a donkey.* Tantamount to no burial at all (see 36:30); fulfilled in 2Ki 24:6, where no burial is described and where it says that Jehoiakim "rested with his fathers," a euphemism for dying (see notes on Ge 25:8; 1Ki 1:21). *dragged away.* See 15:3.

22:20–23 The Lord speaks to Jerusalem, which is personified as a woman (see v. 23).

22:20 *Lebanon . . . Bashan . . . Abarim.* Mountainous regions (see v. 6; Nu 27:12; 33:47–48; Dt 32:49; Jdg 3:3; Ps

68:15), the first two in the north and the third in the south, suitable heights from which the whole land of Israel could be rhetorically addressed. *allies.* Lit. "lovers" (see 4:30 and note), here referring to nations joined together by treaty. Judah's onetime allies included Egypt, Assyria (see 2:36), Edom, Moab, Ammon and Phoenicia (see 27:3), all of whom had been—or soon would be—conquered by Babylonia (see 27:6–7; 28:14). *crushed.* See 14:17.

22:21 *not listen . . . not obeyed me.* See 7:22–26; 11:7–8. *your youth.* The days of Israel's early history in Egypt (see 2:2 and note; Hos 2:15).

22:22 *drive . . . shepherds . . . wickedness.* The Hebrew root is the same for the first two words, and that of the third is very similar. For "shepherds" see 2:8 and note; 10:21; 23:1–4. The initial fulfillment of this verse took place in 597 B.C. (see 2Ki 24:12–16). *wind will drive . . . away.* See 13:24; Job 27:21; Isa 27:8.

22:23 *Lebanon . . . cedar.* See NIV text note; see also 21:14 and note; Eze 17:3–4,12. *pain like that of a woman in labor.* See 4:31; 6:24; 13:21; see also note on 4:19.

22:24–30 A prophecy against King Jehoiachin (fulfilled in 24:1; 29:2), who was also known as Coniah (see NIV text note on v. 24), a shortened form of Jeconiah (see NIV text note on 24:1); see Introduction: Background. All three forms of the name mean "The Lord establishes."

22:24 *As surely as I live.* See note on Ge 42:15. *even if you . . . were a signet ring.* The curse on Jehoiachin is apparently reversed in Hag 2:23 (see note there).

22:25 *hand you over to . . . those you fear.* Contrast 39:17.

the Babylonians.⁰ ²⁶I will hurl^k you and the mother^l who gave you birth into another country, where neither of you was born, and there you both will die. ²⁷You will never come back to the land you long to return^m to."

²⁸Is this man Jehoiachinⁿ a despised,
  broken pot,^o
    an object no one wants?
  Why will he and his children be
    hurled^p out,
      cast into a land^q they do not know?
²⁹O land,^r land, land,
  hear the word of the LORD!
³⁰This is what the LORD says:
  "Record this man as if childless,^s
    a man who will not prosper^t in his
      lifetime,
  for none of his offspring^u will prosper,
    none will sit on the throne^v of David
      or rule anymore in Judah."

The Righteous Branch

23 "Woe to the shepherds^w who are destroying and scattering^x the sheep of my pasture!"^y declares the LORD. ²Therefore this is what the LORD, the God of Israel, says to the shepherds^z who tend my people: "Because you have scattered my flock^a and driven them away and have

not bestowed care on them, I will bestow punishment on you for the evil^b you have done," declares the LORD. ³"I myself will gather the remnant^c of my flock out of all the countries where I have driven them and will bring them back to their pasture, ^d where they will be fruitful and increase in number. ⁴I will place shepherds^e over them who will tend them, and they will no longer be afraid^f or terrified, nor will any be missing,^g" declares the LORD.

⁵"The days are coming," declares the
  LORD,
  "when I will raise up to David^p a
    righteous Branch,^h
  a Kingⁱ who will reign^j wisely
    and do what is just and right^k in the
      land.
⁶In his days Judah will be saved
  and Israel will live in safety.^l
This is the name^m by which he will be
  called:
    The LORD Our Righteousness.ⁿ

⁷"So then, the days are coming," ^o de-

Cross references (center column)

22:26
^kS 1Sa 25:29;
S 2Ki 24:8;
2Ch 36:10;
S Isa 22:17;
^lS 1Ki 2:19
22:27 ^mS ver 10
22:28
ⁿS 2Ki 24:6
^oPs 31:12;
S Jer 19:10;
25:34; 48:38
^pJer 15:1
^qS Jer 17:4
22:29 ^rS Jer 6:19
22:30 ^s1Ch 3:18;
Jer 38:23; 52:10;
Mt 1:12
^tJer 10:21
^uS Job 18:19
^vS Ps 94:20
23:1 ^wJer 10:21;
12:10; 25:36;
Eze 34:1-10;
Zec 10:2;
11:15-17
^xS Isa 56:11
^yPs 100:3;
S Jer 13:17;
Eze 34:31
23:2 ^zJn 10:8
^aS Jer 10:21;
13:20

^bJer 21:12;
Eze 34:8-10
23:3
^cIsa 11:10-12;
Jer 32:37;
Eze 34:11-16
^dS 1Ki 8:48
23:4
^eS Ge 48:15;
S Isa 31:4;
Jer 31:10
^fJer 30:10;
46:27-28

^gS Jn 6:39 **23:5** ^hS 2Ki 19:26; S Isa 4:2; Eze 17:22 ⁱS Mt 2:2; ^jIsa 9:7; S Mt 1:1 ^kS Ge 18:19 **23:6** ^lS Lev 25:18; S Dt 32:8; Hos 2:18 ^mEx 23:21; Jer 33:16; Mt 1:21-23 ⁿS Ezr 9:15; S Isa 42:6; Ro 3:21-22; S 1Co 1:30 **23:7** ^oJer 30:3

^o*25* Or *Chaldeans*   ^p*5* Or *up from David's line*

22:26 Fulfilled in 597 B.C. (see 29:2; 2Ki 24:15). *hurl . . . into another country.* Send into exile in Babylonia (see 7:15; 16:13; Dt 29:28). *you and the mother who gave you birth.* Jehoiachin and Nehushta (see note on 13:18).
22:28 A rhetorical question, answered in v. 30. *broken pot . . . hurled out.* Jehoiachin and his descendants, like Judah itself (see 19:10–11), are under God's judgment. *he and his children.* Though Jehoiachin was only 18 years old at the time of his exile (see 2Ki 24:8), he already had more than one wife (see 2Ki 24:15) and therefore probably one or more children.
22:29 *land, land, land.* The repetition implies the strongest possible emphasis and intensity (see 7:4; 23:30–32; Eze 21:27; see also note on Isa 6:3).
22:30 *as if childless.* Not in the sense of Jehoiachin's having no children at all (he had at least seven; see 1Ch 3:17–18), but of having none to sit on the throne of David in Judah. Jehoiachin's grandson Zerubbabel (1Ch 3:17–19; Mt 1:12) became governor of Judah (see Hag 1:1), but not king. Zedekiah was a son of Josiah (see 37:1), not of Jehoiachin, and he and his sons died before the latter (see 52:10–11). Jehoiachin therefore was Judah's last surviving Davidic king—until Christ.
23:1–8 A summary statement (probably dating to Zedekiah's reign; see note on v. 6) that includes God's intention to judge the wicked rulers and leaders of Judah (vv. 1–2), to ultimately bring his people back from exile (vv. 3–4,7–8), and to raise up an ideal Davidic King (vv. 5–6).
23:1 See 10:21 and note. *sheep.* The people of Judah (see v. 2).
23:2 *bestowed care . . . bestow punishment.* The same Hebrew root underlies both phrases (see v. 4 and note). What Judah's rulers had failed to do is summarized in Eze 34:4.

23:3 *remnant.* See notes on 6:9; Isa 10:20–22. *I have driven.* Although Judah's sins and the sins of their leaders had caused them to be "driven . . . away" (v. 2) into exile, the Lord himself ultimately carried out the results of his people's repeated violations of their covenant commitments. *be fruitful and increase.* See note on Ge 1:28.
23:4 *be afraid . . . terrified.* The absence of a concerned shepherd invites attacks by wild animals (see Eze 34:8). *be missing.* See Nu 31:49. The Hebrew root underlying this phrase is the same as that for "bestowed care" and "bestow punishment" in v. 2 (see note there).
23:5–6 One of the most important Messianic passages in Jeremiah, echoed in 33:15–16.
23:5 *raise up.* See 2Sa 7:12; see also 30:9; Eze 34:23–24; 37:24. The Hebrew for this phrase is translated "place" in v. 4. *to David.* See NIV text note; see also Mt 1:1 and NIV text note on Mt 1:17. The Messiah, unlike any previous descendant of David, would be the ideal King. He would sum up in himself all the finest qualities of the best rulers, and infinitely more. *Branch.* A Messianic title (see note on Isa 4:2). The Targum (ancient Aramaic paraphrase) reads "Messiah" here. *reign wisely.* See note on Isa 52:13. *do what is just and right.* See 22:3,15; said also of King David (see 2Sa 8:15).
23:6 *Judah . . . and Israel.* God's reunited people will be restored (see Eze 37:15–22). *be saved . . . live in safety.* The deliverance will be both spiritual and physical (see Dt 33:28–29). *The LORD Our Righteousness.* Although Zedekiah did not live up to the meaning of his name, "The LORD is my righteousness," Jesus the Messiah would bestow on his people the abundant blessings (see Eze 34:25–31) that come from the hands of a King who does "what is just and right" (v. 5).
23:7–8 Repeated almost verbatim from 16:14–15 (see notes there).

clares the LORD, "when people will no
longer say, 'As surely as the LORD lives,
who brought the Israelites up out of
Egypt,'[p] 8but they will say, 'As surely as
the LORD lives, who brought the descendants of Israel up out of the land of the
north and out of all the countries where he
had banished them.' Then they will live in
their own land."[q]

Lying Prophets

9Concerning the prophets:

My heart[r] is broken within me;
all my bones tremble.[s]
I am like a drunken man,
like a man overcome by wine,
because of the LORD
and his holy words.[t]
10The land is full of adulterers;[u]
because of the curse[q][v] the land lies
parched[r]
and the pastures[w] in the desert are
withered.[x]
The ⌊prophets⌋ follow an evil course
and use their power unjustly.

11"Both prophet and priest are godless;[y]
even in my temple[z] I find their
wickedness,"
declares the LORD.
12"Therefore their path will become
slippery;[a]
they will be banished to darkness
and there they will fall.
I will bring disaster on them
in the year they are punished,[b]"
declares the LORD.

13"Among the prophets of Samaria
I saw this repulsive thing:
They prophesied by Baal[c]
and led my people Israel astray.[d]
14And among the prophets of Jerusalem
I have seen something horrible:[e]
They commit adultery and live a lie.[f]
They strengthen the hands of
evildoers,[g]
so that no one turns from his
wickedness.[h]
They are all like Sodom[i] to me;
the people of Jerusalem are like
Gomorrah."[j]

15Therefore, this is what the LORD Almighty says concerning the prophets:

"I will make them eat bitter food
and drink poisoned water,[k]
because from the prophets of Jerusalem
ungodliness[l] has spread throughout
the land."

16This is what the LORD Almighty says:

"Do not listen[m] to what the prophets
are prophesying to you;
they fill you with false hopes.
They speak visions[n] from their own
minds,
not from the mouth[o] of the LORD.
17They keep saying[p] to those who despise
me,
'The LORD says: You will have
peace.'[q]
And to all who follow the
stubbornness[r] of their hearts
they say, 'No harm[s] will come to
you.'
18But which of them has stood in the
council[t] of the LORD
to see or to hear his word?
Who has listened and heard his
word?
19See, the storm[u] of the LORD

[q]10 Or *because of these things* [r]10 Or *land mourns*

23:7 [p]S Dt 15:15 **23:8** [q]S Isa 14:1; S 43:5-6; Jer 30:10; Eze 20:42; 34:13; Am 9:14-15 **23:9** [r]S Jer 4:19 [s]S Job 4:14 [t]Jer 20:8-9 **23:10** [u]S Jer 9:2 [v]Dt 28:23-24 [w]Ps 107:34; S Jer 9:10 [x]S Jer 4:26; S 12:11 **23:11** [y]Jer 6:13; S 8:10; Zep 3:4 [z]S 2Ki 21:4; S Jer 7:10 **23:12** [a]S Dt 32:35; S Job 3:23; Jer 13:16 [b]Jer 11:23 **23:13** [c]S 1Ki 18:22 [d]ver 32; S Isa 3:12; Eze 13:10 **23:14** [e]S Jer 5:30; Hos 6:10 [f]Jer 29:23 [g]ver 22 [h]S Isa 5:18 [i]S Ge 18:20; Mt 11:24 [j]Jer 20:16; Am 4:11 **23:15** [k]S Jer 8:14; 9:15 [l]S Jer 8:10 **23:16** [m]Jer 27:9-10,14; S Mt 7:15 [n]S Jer 14:14; Eze 13:3 [o]Jer 9:20 **23:17** [p]ver 31 [q]S 1Ki 22:8; S Jer 4:10 [r]S Jer 13:10 [s]Jer 5:12; Am 9:10; Mic 3:11 **23:18** [t]S 1Ki 22:19; S Ro 11:34 **23:19** [u]Isa 30:30; Jer 25:32; 30:23

23:9–40 False prophets denounced (see 2:8; 4:9; 5:30–31; 6:13–15; 8:10–12; 14:13–15; 18:18–23; 26:8, 11,16; 27–28; Isa 28:7–13; Eze 13; Mic 3:5–12).
23:9 *Concerning.* Introduces headings also in 46:2; 48:1; 49:1,7,23,28. *his holy words.* Contrast the unholy words of the false prophets (see vv. 16–18).
23:10 See Isa 24:4–6. *adulterers.* See 5:7–8; 9:2; see also note on 2:20. *curse.* Brought on by violating the Lord's covenant (see 11:3 and note; 11:8). *parched . . . withered.* See 12:4 and note. To worship other gods is to deny to the land the fertility that only the Lord can bring (see Hos 2:5–8,21–22; Am 4:4–9). *pastures in the desert.* See note on 9:10. *evil course.* Evil because it is their own and not God's (see 8:6).
23:11 *even in my temple . . . wickedness.* For examples see 32:34; 2Ki 16:10–14; 21:5; Eze 8:5,10,14,16.
23:12 *their path will become slippery . . . banished to darkness.* See Ps 35:5–6; see also Ps 73:18.
23:13 *prophesied by Baal.* See 2:8 and note; see also 1Ki 18:19–40.
23:14 *They . . . live a lie.* See 14:13. *strengthen the hands of.* The Hebrew underlying this phrase is translated "encouraged" in Eze 13:22. *no one turns from his wickedness.* See Eze 13:22. *like Sodom . . . like Gomorrah.* See note on 20:16.
23:15 *I will make . . . poisoned water.* Repeated almost verbatim from 9:15 (see note there). *ungodliness.* See v. 11.
23:16 *visions.* "Revelations" or "prophecies" (see 1Sa 3:1; Pr 29:18; Isa 1:1; Ob 1). *from their own minds.* See v. 26; 14:14. False prophets are like preachers of a "different gospel" (Gal 1:6–9).
23:17 *You will have peace.* The essential message of the false prophets (see 6:14 and note; 8:11; 14:13 and note; cf. 28:8–9). *stubbornness of their hearts.* See note on 3:17.
23:18 *council of the LORD.* God's heavenly confidants (see v. 22; Job 15:7–10 and note; see also 1Ki 22:19–22; Job 1:6; 2:1; 29:4 and note; Ps 89:7). In Am 3:7 the Hebrew for "council" is translated "plan," the purposes that God has promised to reveal to his chosen servants (see v. 20).
23:19–20 Repeated almost verbatim in 30:23–24.
23:19 *storm . . . whirlwind.* A vivid image of God's wrath.

will burst out in wrath,
a whirlwind^v swirling down
on the heads of the wicked.
20The anger^w of the LORD will not turn
back^x
until he fully accomplishes
the purposes of his heart.
In days to come
you will understand it clearly.
21I did not send^y these prophets,
yet they have run with their message;
I did not speak to them,
yet they have prophesied.
22But if they had stood in my council,^{z}
they would have proclaimed^a my
words to my people
and would have turned^b them from
their evil ways
and from their evil deeds.^{c}

23"Am I only a God nearby,^{d}"
declares the LORD,
"and not a God far away?
24Can anyone hide^e in secret places
so that I cannot see him?"
declares the LORD.
"Do not I fill heaven and earth?"^{f}
declares the LORD.

25"I have heard what the prophets say
who prophesy lies^g in my name. They say,
'I had a dream!'^{h} I had a dream!' 26How
long will this continue in the hearts of
these lying prophets, who prophesy the
delusions^i of their own minds? 27They
think the dreams they tell one another will
make my people forget^k my name, just as
their fathers forgot^l my name through
Baal worship. ^{m} 28Let the prophet who has
a dream^n tell his dream, but let the one

who has my word^o speak it faithfully. For
what has straw to do with grain?" declares
the LORD. 29"Is not my word like fire,"^{p}
declares the LORD, "and like a hammer^q
that breaks a rock in pieces?

30"Therefore," declares the LORD, "I am
against^r the prophets^s who steal from one
another words supposedly from me.
31Yes," declares the LORD, "I am against
the prophets who wag their own tongues
and yet declare, 'The LORD declares.'^{t}
32Indeed, I am against those who prophesy
false dreams,^{u}" declares the LORD. "They
tell them and lead my people astray^v with
their reckless lies,^{w} yet I did not send^x or
appoint them. They do not benefit^y these
people in the least," declares the LORD.

False Oracles and False Prophets

33"When these people, or a prophet or a
priest, ask you, 'What is the oracle$^{s\,z}$ of
the LORD?' say to them, 'What oracle?^{t} I
will forsake^a you, declares the LORD.' 34If
a prophet or a priest or anyone else claims,
'This is the oracle^b of the LORD,' I will
punish^c that man and his household.
35This is what each of you keeps on saying
to his friend or relative: 'What is the
LORD's answer?'^{d} or 'What has the LORD
spoken?' 36But you must not mention 'the
oracle of the LORD' again, because every
man's own word becomes his oracle and
so you distort^e the words of the living
God,^{f} the LORD Almighty, our God. 37This
is what you keep saying to a prophet:

23:19 ^{v}Zec 7:14
23:20
^{w}S 2Ki 23:26
^{x}S Jer 4:28
23:21
^{y}S Jer 14:14;
27:15
23:22
^{z}S 1Ki 22:19
^{a}S Dt 33:10
^{b}S 2Ki 17:13;
Jer 25:5; Zec 1:4
^{c}ver 14; Am 3:7
23:23
^{d}Ps 139:1-10
23:24 ^{e}S Ge 3:8;
S Job 11:20;
22:12-14;
S Ecc 12:14;
S Isa 28:15;
1Co 4:5
^{f}S 1Ki 8:27
23:25 ^{g}ver 16;
Jer 14:14; 27:10
^{h}ver 28,32;
S Dt 13:1;
Jer 27:9; 29:8
23:26
^{i}S Isa 30:10;
1Ti 4:1-2
^{j}Jer 14:14;
Eze 13:2
23:27
^{k}Dt 13:1-3;
Jer 29:8
^{l}S Jdg 3:7;
S 8:33-34
^{m}S Jer 2:23
23:28 ^{n}S ver 25

^{o}S 1Sa 3:17
23:29 ^{p}S Ps 39:3;
Jer 5:14;
S 1Co 3:13
^{q}Heb 4:12
23:30 ^{r}S Ps 34:16
^{s}ver 2; Dt 18:20;
Jer 14:15; S 21:13
23:31 ^{t}ver 17
23:32 ^{u}S ver 25
^{v}S ver 13;
S Jer 50:6
^{w}S Jer 13:4;
Eze 13:3; 22:28
^{x}S Jer 14:14
^{y}Jer 7:8; La 2:14
23:33 ^{z}Mal 1:1
^{a}S 2Ki 21:14
23:34 ^{b}La 2:14
^{c}Zec 13:3
23:35 ^{d}Jer 33:3;
42:4

23:36 ^{e}Gal 1:7-8; 2Pe 3:16 ^{f}S Jos 3:10

^{s}33 Or *burden* (see Septuagint and Vulgate)
^{t}33 Hebrew; Septuagint and Vulgate *'You are the burden.*
(The Hebrew for *oracle* and *burden* is the same.)

23:20 *you will understand it clearly.* Unlike the false
prophets, who continued to mislead their hearers even in
Babylonia after the exile of 597 B.C. (see 29:20–23).
23:21 *I did not send.* See v. 32; 29:9; contrast 1:7; Isa
6:8; Eze 3:5. *did not speak to them.* See 29:23.
23:22 *my council.* See note on v. 18.
23:23 *God nearby . . . God far away.* God is both transcendent and immanent; he lives "in a high and holy place, but
also with him who is . . . lowly in spirit" (Isa 57:15).
23:24 *hide . . . so that I cannot see him.* See Job 26:6; Ps
139:7–12; Am 9:2–4. *I fill heaven and earth.* See Isa 66:1.
23:25 *lies.* See 5:12. *in my name.* See Dt 18:20,22.
dream. Usually not a means of divine revelation to a true
prophet (see 27:9; Dt 13:1–3; 1Sa 28:6; Zec 10:2; but cf.
Nu 12:6; Joel 2:28).
23:26 *hearts . . . minds.* The Hebrew is the same for both
words. *their own minds.* See note on v. 16.
23:27 *my name.* To forget the Lord's name is tantamount
to forgetting him. *forgot . . . through Baal worship.* When
Judah's ancestors forgot God, they began to serve Baal (see
Jdg 3:7; 1Sa 12:9–10).
23:28–29 The true word of God is symbolized in three
figures of speech (grain, fire, hammer).

23:28 *straw . . . grain.* Of the two, only grain can feed and
nourish (see note on 15:16).
23:29 *like fire.* See note on 20:9. The fire of the divine
word ultimately tests "the quality of each man's work" (1Co
3:13). *like a hammer.* Similarly, the divine word works
relentlessly, like a sword or hammer, to judge "the thoughts
and attitudes of the heart" (Heb 4:12).
23:30–32 *I am against.* The threefold statement is for
emphasis (see note on 22:29).
23:31 *prophets who . . . declare.* False prophets are claiming that their own prophecies are the oracles of God. The
Hebrew for this verb is used only here with someone other
than God as the subject. The phrase "declares the LORD" or
its equivalent occurs hundreds of times in the OT, more
frequently in Jeremiah (over 175 times) than in any other
book.
23:32 *did not send.* See v. 21 and note.
23:33 *oracle.* The Hebrew for this word can also mean
"burden" (see NIV text note), a term that may refer to a
burdensome message from the Lord (see, e.g., Na 1:1).
23:36 The three divine titles at the end of the verse enhance the solemnity of what is being said. *living God.* See
10:10; Dt 5:26.

'What is the LORD's answer to you?' or 'What has the LORD spoken?' [38]Although you claim, 'This is the oracle of the LORD,' this is what the LORD says: You used the words, 'This is the oracle of the LORD,' even though I told you that you must not claim, 'This is the oracle of the LORD.' [39]Therefore, I will surely forget you and cast[g] you out of my presence along with the city I gave to you and your fathers. [40]I will bring upon you everlasting disgrace[h]—everlasting shame that will not be forgotten."

Two Baskets of Figs

24 After Jehoiachin[u][i] son of Jehoiakim king of Judah and the officials, the craftsmen and the artisans of Judah were carried into exile from Jerusalem to Babylon by Nebuchadnezzar king of Babylon, the LORD showed me two baskets of figs[j] placed in front of the temple of the LORD. [2]One basket had very good figs, like those that ripen early;[k] the other basket had very poor[l] figs, so bad they could not be eaten.

[3]Then the LORD asked me, "What do you see,[m] Jeremiah?"

"Figs," I answered. "The good ones are very good, but the poor ones are so bad they cannot be eaten."

[4]Then the word of the LORD came to me: [5]"This is what the LORD, the God of Israel, says: 'Like these good figs, I regard as good the exiles from Judah, whom I sent[n] away from this place to the land of the Babylonians.[v] [6]My eyes will watch over them for their good, and I will bring them back[o] to this land. I will build[p] them up and not tear them down; I will plant[q] them and not uproot them. [7]I will give them a heart to know[r] me, that I am the LORD. They will be my people,[s] and I will be their God, for they will return[t] to me with all their heart.[u]

[8]" 'But like the poor[v] figs, which are so bad they cannot be eaten,' says the LORD, 'so will I deal with Zedekiah[w] king of Judah, his officials[x] and the survivors[y] from Jerusalem, whether they remain in this land or live in Egypt.[z] [9]I will make them abhorrent[a] and an offense to all the kingdoms of the earth, a reproach and a byword,[b] an object of ridicule and cursing,[c] wherever I banish[d] them. [10]I will send the sword,[e] famine[f] and plague[g] against them until they are destroyed from the land I gave to them and their fathers.[h] '"

Seventy Years of Captivity

25 The word came to Jeremiah concerning all the people of Judah in the fourth year of Jehoiakim[i] son of Josiah king of Judah, which was the first year of Nebuchadnezzar[j] king of Babylon. [2]So Jeremiah the prophet said to all the people of Judah[k] and to all those living in Jerusalem: [3]For twenty-three years—from the thirteenth year of Josiah[l] son of Amon

---

Cross-reference column:

23:39 [g]S Jer 7:15
23:40 [h]S Jer 20:11; Eze 5:14-15
24:1 [i]S 2Ki 24:16; S 2Ch 36:9 /Ex 23:19; Dt 26:2; Am 8:1-2
24:2 [k]S SS 2:13 [l]S Isa 5:4
24:3 [m]Jer 1:11; Am 8:2
24:5 [n]Jer 29:4,20

24:6 [o]S Dt 30:3; Jer 27:22; 29:10; 30:3; Eze 11:17 [p]Jer 33:7; 42:10 [q]S Dt 30:9; S Jer 1:10; Am 9:14-15
24:7 [r]S Isa 11:9 [s]S Lev 26:12; S Isa 51:16; S Zec 2:11; Heb 8:10 [t]Jer 32:40 [u]S 2Ch 6:37; Eze 11:19
24:8 [v]Jer 29:17 [w]Jer 32:4-5; 38:18,23; 39:5; 44:30 [x]Jer 39:6 [y]Jer 39:9 [z]Jer 44:1,26; 46:14
24:9 [a]S Jer 15:4; 25:18 [b]S Dt 28:25; S 1Ki 9:7 [c]S 2Ki 22:19; S Jer 29:18 [d]S Dt 28:37; Da 9:7
24:10 [e]S Isa 51:19; S Jer 9:16; Rev 6:8 [f]Jer 15:2 [g]Jer 27:8 [h]S Dt 28:21
25:1 [i]S 2Ki 24:2 [j]S 2Ki 24:1
25:2 [k]Jer 18:11
25:3 [l]S 1Ch 3:14

---

[u][i] Hebrew *Jeconiah,* a variant of *Jehoiachin*   [v][5] Or *Chaldeans*

23:39 *forget.* The Hebrew for this word is a pun on the Hebrew for the word "oracle" in vv. 33–34,36,38. *the city.* Jerusalem.

23:40 Echoed from 20:11.

24:1–10 See Am 8:1–3. Having denounced Judah's leaders (21:1–23:8) and false prophets (23:9–40), Jeremiah now describes the division of Judah's people into good and bad (24:1–3) and summarizes the Lord's determination to restore the good (vv. 4–7) but destroy the bad (vv. 8–10).

24:1 *Jehoiachin . . . and the officials . . . were carried into exile.* In 597 B.C. *craftsmen and . . . artisans.* See 29:2; 2Ki 24:14,16. Only the poorest and weakest people were left behind in Judah (see 2Ki 24:14). *the LORD showed me.* A common way of introducing prophetic visions (see Am 7:1, 4,7). *figs.* See note on 8:13. *placed.* The Hebrew root underlying this word is translated "meet" in Ex 29:42–43. As the Lord desired to "meet" with the Israelites at the entrance to the tabernacle, so the figs (symbolizing the people of Judah) would be "met" by him in front of the Jerusalem temple.

24:2 *very good figs . . . that ripen early.* The first figs in June are especially juicy and delicious (see Isa 28:4; Hos 9:10; Mic 7:1; Na 3:12).

24:3 *What do you see . . . ?* See note on 1:11.

24:5–6 Just as good figs should be protected and preserved by their owner, so also the exiles of 597 B.C., who were the best of Judah's leaders and craftsmen (see 2Ki 24:14–16), would be watched over and cared for by the Lord (see

29:4–14).

24:6 *My eyes will watch over them for their good.* Contrast Am 9:4. *bring them back.* In 538 B.C. *build them up . . . tear them down . . . plant . . . uproot.* See 1:10 and note.

24:7 *a heart to know me.* For a more comprehensive prediction including the same promise see 31:31–34. *my people . . . their God.* The classic statement of covenant relationship (see 31:33; 32:38; see also notes on Ge 17:7; Zec 8:8). *with all their heart.* See 29:13.

24:8 *live in Egypt.* Perhaps those deported with Jehoahaz in 609 B.C. (see 22:10b–12 and notes; 2Ki 23:31–34) and/or those who fled to Egypt after the Babylonians defeated the Egyptians in the battle of Carchemish in 605 (see 46:2).

24:9 *abhorrent . . . to all the kingdoms.* See 34:17. *reproach . . . object of ridicule.* See Dt 28:37. *byword.* See notes on 1Ki 9:7; Job 17:6.

24:10 *sword, famine and plague.* See note on 14:12. *destroyed from the land.* In 586 B.C. (see 52:4–27).

25:1–29:32 The dominant theme in chs. 25–29 is the forthcoming destruction of Jerusalem and exile to Babylonia in 586 B.C. (hinted at briefly in 24:10).

25:1–38 Divine judgment will descend not only on Judah but on "all the surrounding nations" (v. 9) as well.

25:1 *fourth year of Jehoiakim . . . first year of Nebuchadnezzar.* The synchronism yields the date 605 B.C. (see note on Da 1:1).

king of Judah until this very day—the word of the LORD has come to me and I have spoken to you again and again, *m* but you have not listened. *n*

⁴And though the LORD has sent all his servants the prophets *o* to you again and again, you have not listened or paid any attention. *p* ⁵They said, "Turn *q* now, each of you, from your evil ways and your evil practices, and you can stay in the land *r* the LORD gave to you and your fathers for ever and ever. ⁶Do not follow other gods *s* to serve and worship them; do not provoke me to anger with what your hands have made. Then I will not harm you."

⁷"But you did not listen to me," declares the LORD, "and you have provoked *t* me with what your hands have made, *u* and you have brought harm *v* to yourselves."

⁸Therefore the LORD Almighty says this: "Because you have not listened to my words, ⁹I will summon *w* all the peoples of the north *x* and my servant *y* Nebuchadnezzar *z* king of Babylon," declares the LORD, "and I will bring them against this land and its inhabitants and against all the surrounding nations. I will completely destroy *w* *a* them and make them an object of horror and scorn, *b* and an everlasting ruin. *c* ¹⁰I will banish from them the sounds *d* of joy and gladness, the voices of bride and bridegroom, *e* the sound of millstones *f* and the light of the lamp. *g* ¹¹This

whole country will become a desolate wasteland, *h* and these nations will serve *i* the king of Babylon seventy years. *j*

¹²"But when the seventy years *k* are fulfilled, I will punish the king of Babylon *l* and his nation, the land of the Babylonians, *x* for their guilt," declares the LORD, "and will make it desolate *m* forever. ¹³I will bring upon that land all the things I have spoken against it, all that are written *n* in this book and prophesied by Jeremiah against all the nations. ¹⁴They themselves will be enslaved *o* by many nations *p* and great kings; I will repay *q* them according to their deeds and the work of their hands."

The Cup of God's Wrath

¹⁵This is what the LORD, the God of Israel, said to me: "Take from my hand this cup *r* filled with the wine of my wrath and make all the nations to whom I send *s* you drink it. ¹⁶When they drink *t* it, they will stagger *u* and go mad *v* because of the sword *w* I will send among them."

¹⁷So I took the cup from the LORD's hand and made all the nations to whom he sent *x* me drink it: ¹⁸Jerusalem *y* and the

25:3 *m*Jer 11:7; 26:5
*n*S Isa 65:12; S Jer 7:26
25:4 *o*Jer 6:17; S 7:25; 29:19
*p*S Jer 7:26; 34:14; 44:5
25:5 *q*S Jdg 6:8; S 2Ch 7:14; S 30:9; S Jer 23:22
*r*S Ge 12:7; S Dt 4:40
25:6 *s*S Ex 20:3; S Dt 8:19
25:7 *t*Jer 30:14; 32:35; 44:5
*u*Dt 32:21
*v*2Ki 17:20; 21:15
25:9 *w*Isa 13:3-5
*x*S Isa 14:31
*y*S Isa 41:2; Jer 27:6
*z*S 2Ch 36:6
*a*S Nu 21:2
*b*S 2Ch 29:8
*c*S Jer 19:8; S 20:4; Eze 12:20
25:10 *d*S Isa 24:8; Eze 26:13
*e*Jer 7:34; 33:11
*f*Ecc 12:3-4
*g*S Job 18:5; La 5:15; Rev 18:22-23
25:11 *h*S Lev 26:31,32; Jer 4:26-27; 12:11-12
*i*Jer 28:14
/S 2Ch 36:21
25:12 *k*Jer 27:7; 29:10
/S Ge 10:10; S Ps 137:8
*m*S Isa 13:19-22; 14:22-23
25:13 *n*S Isa 30:8
25:14 *o*Isa 14:6; Jer 27:7
*p*Jer 50:9;
51:27-28 *q*S Dt 32:41; S Job 21:19; S Jer 51:6 25:15 *r*S Isa 51:17; Jer 49:12; La 4:21; Eze 23:31; Rev 14:10
*s*Jer 1:5 25:16 *t*ver 26 *u*S Ps 60:3 *v*Jer 51:7 *w*ver 27-29
25:17 *x*Jer 1:10; 27:3 25:18 *y*S Jer 13:13

w 9 The Hebrew term refers to the irrevocable giving over of things or persons to the LORD, often by totally destroying them. *x 12* Or *Chaldeans*

25:3 *twenty-three years.* Nineteen under Josiah and four under Jehoiakim (see v. 1). *thirteenth year of Josiah.* 626 B.C. (or possibly as early as 627); see 1:2. *again and again.* See v. 4; see also note on 7:13. *you have not listened.* Jeremiah, now halfway through his prophetic ministry, had been warned at the time of his call that the people of Judah would oppose him (see 1:17–19).

25:4 Echoed from 7:25–26; see also 35:15. *his servants the prophets.* See note on 7:25.

25:5 *stay in the land the LORD gave . . . your fathers for ever and ever.* Echoed from 7:7; see Ge 17:8 and note.

25:6 *provoke me to anger.* See 7:18; Dt 31:29. *what your hands have made.* Idols (see note on 1:16).

25:7 *brought harm to yourselves.* See 7:6.

25:9 *peoples of the north.* Babylonia and her allies (see 1:15 and note). *my servant Nebuchadnezzar.* See 27:6; 43:10. "Servant" is used here not in the sense of "worshiper" but of "vassal" or "agent of judgment," just as the pagan ruler Cyrus is called the Lord's "shepherd" in Isa 44:28 and his "anointed" in Isa 45:1. *this land.* Judah. *surrounding nations.* Named in vv. 19–26. *completely destroy.* See NIV text note; 50:21,26; 51:3; see also note on Dt 2:34. *object of horror and scorn.* See note on 18:16. *everlasting ruin.* See 49:13; Ps 74:3; Isa 58:12 and note.

25:11–12 *seventy years.* See 29:10. This round number (as in Ps 90:10; Isa 23:15) probably represents the period from 605 (see notes on v. 1; Da 1:1) to 538 B.C., which marked the beginning of Judah's return from exile (see 2Ch 36:20–23; see also notes on Da 9:1–2). The 70 years of Zec

1:12 are not necessarily the same as those here and in 29:10. They probably represent the period from 586 (when Solomon's temple was destroyed) to 516 (when Zerubbabel's temple was completed). See note on Zec 7:5.

25:11 *This . . . country . . . and these nations.* Judah and the nations named in vv. 19–26.

25:12 *punish the king . . . and his nation.* See 50:18. The city of Babylon was captured by the Medes and Persians in 539 B.C. (near the end of Jeremiah's 70 years; see note on vv. 11–12). *for their guilt.* See 50:11,31–32; 51:6,49,53,56; Isa 13:19. *make it desolate forever.* See 50:12–13; 51:26; see also note on Isa 13:20.

25:13 *book.* After this word, the Septuagint (the Greek translation of the OT) inserts the material found in chs. 46–51, though rearranged.

25:14 *many nations.* Media, Persia and their allies. *great kings.* Cyrus and his associates. *repay them according to their deeds.* See 50:29; 51:24.

25:15 *cup filled with the wine of my wrath.* Symbolic of divine judgment, especially against wicked nations (see Isa 51:17 and note; see also 51:7; Rev 18:6). *nations to whom I send you.* See 1:5 and note.

25:16 *stagger and go mad.* See 13:12–14 and notes; Rev 14:8. *because of the sword.* As the sting of wine causes people to stagger, so the stroke of the sword causes them to fall, never to rise again (see v. 27).

25:17 A symbolic description of Jeremiah's announcement of divine judgment against the nations.

25:18 *Jerusalem and . . . Judah.* God's own people are to

towns of Judah, its kings and officials, to make them a ruin[z] and an object of horror and scorn[a] and cursing,[b] as they are to-day;[c] [19]Pharaoh king[d] of Egypt,[e] his attendants, his officials and all his people, [20]and all the foreign people there; all the kings of Uz;[f] all the kings of the Philistines[g] (those of Ashkelon,[h] Gaza,[i] Ekron, and the people left at Ashdod); [21]Edom,[j] Moab[k] and Ammon;[l] [22]all the kings of Tyre[m] and Sidon;[n] the kings of the coastlands[o] across the sea; [23]Dedan,[p] Tema,[q] Buz[r] and all who are in distant places[y];[s] [24]all the kings of Arabia[t] and all the kings of the foreign people[u] who live in the desert; [25]all the kings of Zimri,[v] Elam[w] and Media;[x] [26]and all the kings of the north,[y] near and far, one after the other—all the kingdoms[z] on the face of the earth. And after all of them, the king of Sheshach[z][a] will drink it too.

[27]"Then tell them, 'This is what the LORD Almighty, the God of Israel, says: Drink, get drunk[b] and vomit, and fall to rise no more because of the sword[c] I will send among you.' [28]But if they refuse to take the cup from your hand and drink[d], tell them, 'This is what the LORD Almighty says: You must drink it! [29]See, I am beginning to bring disaster[e] on the city that bears my Name,[f] and will you indeed go unpunished?[g] You will not go unpunished, for I am calling down a sword[h]

upon all[i] who live on the earth,[j] declares the LORD Almighty.'

[30]"Now prophesy all these words against them and say to them:

" 'The LORD will roar[k] from on high;
　he will thunder[l] from his holy
　　dwelling[m]
and roar mightily against his land.
He will shout like those who tread[n] the
　grapes,
　shout against all who live on the
　　earth.
[31]The tumult[o] will resound to the ends of
　the earth,
for the LORD will bring charges[p]
　against the nations;
he will bring judgment[q] on all[r]
　mankind
and put the wicked to the sword,[s] ' "
　　　　　' declares the LORD.

[32]This is what the LORD Almighty says:

"Look! Disaster[t] is spreading
　from nation to nation;[u]

25:18
[z]S Job 12:19
[a]S 2Ch 29:8
[b]S Jer 24:9
[c]S Ge 19:13;
Jer 44:22
25:19
[d]S 2Ki 18:21
[e]Isa 19:1; 20:3;
Jer 44:30;
Eze 29:2
25:20
[f]S Ge 10:23
[g]S Jos 13:3;
S 2Ch 26:6;
S 28:18;
Zep 2:4-7
[h]Jer 47:5;
Am 1:7-8
[i]S Ge 10:19
25:21
[j]S Ge 25:30
[k]S Ge 19:37;
S Dt 23:6
[l]S Ge 19:38;
Jer 27:3; 49:1
25:22
[m]S Jos 19:29
[n]S Ge 10:15
[o]Isa 11:11;
48:20; 66:20;
Jer 31:10;
Eze 27:15; 39:6;
Da 11:18
25:23 [p]S Ge 25:3
[q]S Ge 25:15
[r]S Ge 22:21
[s]Jer 9:26; 49:32
25:24
[t]S 2Ch 9:14 [u]ver
20
25:25 [v]Ge 25:2
[w]S Ge 10:22
[x]S Isa 21:2
25:26 [y]ver 9;
Jer 50:3,9; 51:11,
48 [z]Isa 23:17
[a]Jer 51:41
25:27 [b]ver 16,
28; S Isa 29:9;
S 49:26;
Jer 51:57;

Eze 23:32-34; Na 3:18; Hab 2:16 [c]S Jer 12:12; Eze 14:17;
21:4 **25:28** [d]S Isa 51:23 **25:29** [e]S 2Sa 5:7; Isa 10:12;
Jer 13:12-14; 39:1 [f]S Dt 28:10; S Isa 37:17 [g]S Pr 11:31 [h]ver
27 [i]ver 30-31; Isa 34:2 [j]S Isa 24:1 **25:30** [k]Isa 16:10; S 42:13
[l]S Ps 46:6 [m]S Ps 68:5 [n]Isa 63:3; Joel 3:13; Rev 14:19-20
25:31 [o]Jer 23:19 [p]S Jer 2:9 [q]S Isa 12:7; S Jer 2:35;
S Eze 36:5 [r]S ver 29 [s]S Jer 15:9 **25:32** [t]S Isa 30:25 [u]Isa 34:2

[y]23 Or *who clip the hair by their foreheads*
[z]26 *Sheshach* is a cryptogram for Babylon.

---

be judged first (see v. 29; see also Eze 9:6; 1Pe 4:17). *its kings.* See note on 17:20. *ruin . . . horror . . . scorn . . . cursing.* See vv. 9,11; 18:16; 19:8.
25:19–26 The roster of nations begins with Egypt and ends with Babylon, as in chs. 46–51; but Damascus (see 49:23–27) is omitted, and a few other regions are added.
25:19 *Egypt.* See 46:2–28.
25:20 *foreign people.* See v. 24; Ne 13:3. *Uz.* See note on Job 1:1. *Philistines.* See ch. 47; see also note on Ge 10:14. *Ashkelon, Gaza, Ekron.* See note on Jdg 1:18. *people left at Ashdod.* According to the Greek historian Herodotus (2.157), the Egyptian pharaoh Psammetichus I (664–610 B.C.) destroyed Ashdod after a long siege. By Nehemiah's time, it was inhabited again (see note on Ne 4:7). The fifth main Philistine city, Gath (see Jos 13:3), though important earlier (see, e.g., 1Sa 21:10–12), was destroyed and apparently not rebuilt (in later centuries it is not mentioned with the other four cities; see Am 1:6–8; Zep 2:4; Zec 9:5–6).
25:21–22 See 27:3–5.
25:21 *Edom.* See 49:7–22; see also note on Ge 36:1. *Moab and Ammon.* See 48:1–49:6; see also note on Ge 19:36–38.
25:22 *Tyre and Sidon.* See 47:4; see also notes on Isa 23:1–2,4,12. *coastlands across the sea.* Island and maritime regions, some of them Phoenician colonies, located to the west and northwest of Tyre and Sidon (see notes on Eze 27:15; Da 11:18).
25:23 *Dedan.* See 49:8; see also notes on Isa 21:13; Eze 25:13. *Tema.* See note on Isa 21:14. *Buz.* A desert region in the east. *who are in distant places.* See note on 9:26.

25:24 *Arabia.* See 49:28–33; see also 3:2 and NIV text note. *foreign people.* See v. 20; Ne 13:3. The same Hebrew root underlies "Arabia" and "foreign people."
25:25 *Zimri.* Not to be confused with the Israelite king of that name, Zimri is perhaps the same as Zimran, whom Keturah bore to Abraham (see Ge 25:1–2). The region known as Zimri (location unknown) would then have been named after him. *Elam.* See 49:34–39; see also note on Ge 10:22. *Media.* Later to join the Persians in conquering Babylon (see 51:11,28; see also note on Isa 13:17).
25:26 *Sheshach.* See NIV text note. The cryptogram is formed by substituting the first consonant of the Hebrew alphabet for the last, the second for the next-to-last, etc. Its purpose is not fully understood, though in some cases the cryptogram itself bears a suitable meaning (see note on 51:1). *will drink it too.* The Lord's agents of judgment are not themselves exempt from his judgment (see 51:48–49).
25:27 *fall . . . because of the sword.* See note on v. 16.
25:29 *beginning.* See note on v. 18. *city that bears my Name.* Jerusalem (see note on 7:10).
25:30 *The LORD will roar . . . thunder.* An echo of Joel 3:16; Am 1:2 (see note there; see also Hos 11:10; Am 3:8). *his land.* Judah. *shout like those who tread the grapes.* See Isa 9:3; 16:9–10; 63:3 and note; see also Isa 16:10 and note.
25:31 *tumult.* The sounds of war (see Am 2:2). *bring charges . . . bring judgment.* See note on 2:9; see also 2:35; 12:1.
25:32 *mighty storm . . . from the ends of the earth.* The wrath of God (see 23:19), mediated through the coming invasion of the Babylonians (see note on Isa 41:25).

a mighty storm[v] is rising
  from the ends of the earth." [w]

[33] At that time those slain[x] by the LORD
will be everywhere—from one end of the
earth to the other. They will not be
mourned or gathered[y] up or buried,[z] but
will be like refuse lying on the ground.

[34] Weep and wail, you shepherds; [a]
  roll[b] in the dust, you leaders of the
    flock.
For your time to be slaughtered[c] has
    come;
  you will fall and be shattered like fine
    pottery. [d]
[35] The shepherds will have nowhere to
    flee,
  the leaders of the flock no place to
    escape. [e]
[36] Hear the cry[f] of the shepherds,[g]
  the wailing of the leaders of the flock,
  for the LORD is destroying their
    pasture.
[37] The peaceful meadows will be laid
    waste
  because of the fierce anger of the
    LORD.
[38] Like a lion[h] he will leave his lair,
  and their land will become desolate[i]
because of the sword[a] of the
    oppressor[j]
  and because of the LORD's fierce
    anger. [k]

Jeremiah Threatened With Death

26 Early in the reign of Jehoiakim[l]
son of Josiah king of Judah, this
word came from the LORD: [2] "This is what
the LORD says: Stand in the courtyard[m] of
the LORD's house and speak to all the
people of the towns of Judah who come to
worship in the house of the LORD. [n] Tell[o]
them everything I command you; do not
omit[p] a word. [3] Perhaps they will listen
and each will turn[q] from his evil way.
Then I will relent[r] and not bring on them
the disaster I was planning because of the
evil they have done. [4] Say to them, 'This is
what the LORD says: If you do not listen[s]
to me and follow my law,[t] which I have
set before you, [5] and if you do not listen to
the words of my servants the prophets,
whom I have sent to you again and again
(though you have not listened[u]), [6] then I
will make this house like Shiloh[v] and this
city an object of cursing[w] among all the
nations of the earth.' "

[7] The priests, the prophets and all the
people heard Jeremiah speak these words
in the house of the LORD. [8] But as soon as
Jeremiah finished telling all the people
everything the LORD had commanded[x]
him to say, the priests, the prophets and
the people seized[y] him and said, "You
must die![z] [9] Why do you prophesy in the
LORD's name that this house will be like
Shiloh and this city will be desolate and
deserted?" [a] And all the people crowded[b]
around Jeremiah in the house of the LORD.

[10] When the officials[c] of Judah heard
about these things, they went up from the
royal palace to the house of the LORD and
took their places at the entrance of the
New Gate[d] of the LORD's house. [11] Then
the priests and the prophets said to the
officials and all the people, "This man

25:32
[v] S Jer 23:19
[w] S Dt 28:49
25:33 [x] Isa 66:16;
Eze 39:17-20
[y] S Jer 8:2
[z] S Ps 79:3
25:34 [a] S Jer 2:8;
Zec 10:3
[b] S Jer 6:26
[c] S Ps 44:22;
S Isa 34:6;
Jer 50:27; 51:40;
Zec 11:4,7
[d] S Jer 22:28
25:35
[e] S Job 11:20
25:36 [f] S Jer 6:26
[g] S Jer 23:1;
Zec 11:3
25:38
[h] S Job 10:16;
S Jer 4:7
[i] Jer 44:22
[j] Jer 46:16; 50:16
[k] S Ex 15:7;
S Jer 4:26
26:1 [l] 2Ki 23:36
26:2 [m] Jer 19:14

[n] S Jer 17:19
[o] S ver 12;
S Jer 1:17;
Mt 28:20;
Ac 20:27 [p] Dt 4:2
26:3 [q] Dt 30:2;
2Ch 33:12-13;
Isa 55:7;
Jer 35:15; 36:7
[r] S Jer 18:8
26:4 [s] Lev 26:14;
Jer 25:3
[t] Ex 20:1-23:33;
S 1Ki 9:6;
S Jer 11:8
26:5 [u] S Pr 1:24;
S Isa 65:12;
Jer 25:4; 44:5
26:6 [v] S Jos 18:1;
S Jdg 18:31
[w] S Dt 28:25;
S 2Ki 22:19
26:8 [x] Jer 43:1
[y] Ac 6:12; 21:27
[z] Lev 24:15-16;
S Ne 9:26;
S Jer 11:21
26:9
[a] S Lev 26:32;
S Jer 9:11
[b] Ac 21:32
26:10 [c] ver 16;
Jer 34:19;
Eze 22:27

[d] S Ge 23:10

[a] 38 Some Hebrew manuscripts and Septuagint (see also
Jer. 46:16 and 50:16); most Hebrew manuscripts *anger*

25:33 *not be mourned . . . like refuse lying on the ground.*
Repeated from 8:2 (see note there); 16:4.
25:34–36 *shepherds . . . leaders of the flock.* See 10:21;
22:22.
25:34 *roll in the dust.* Or "roll in ashes" (as in 6:26). *your
time . . . has come.* See La 4:18. *shattered like fine pottery.*
Cf. the description of Jehoiachin in 22:28.
26:1–24 A summary (vv. 2–6)—and its results (vv.
7–24)—of one of Jeremiah's temple messages in ch. 7 (see
note on 7:1–10:25).
26:1 *Early in the reign.* See 27:1. The Babylonian equivalent of the Hebrew for this phrase implies that the first year of
King Jehoiakim (609–608 B.C.) is probably meant.
26:2 *courtyard of the LORD's house.* Perhaps near the New
Gate (see v. 10; see also note on 7:2). *who come to worship.*
See 7:2 and note. *do not omit a word.* See Dt 4:2 and note.
26:3 See 7:3,5–7. *relent.* See vv. 13,19; see also notes on
4:28; 18:7–10.
26:4 *If you do not listen.* See v. 5; 7:13. *my law.* See 7:6,9
and notes.
26:5 See 7:13,25–26. *my servants the prophets.* See note
on 7:25. *again and again.* See note on 7:13.

26:6 *make this house like Shiloh.* See v. 9; see also note on
7:12. *this city.* Jerusalem. *object of cursing.* See 24:9;
25:18; see also note on Zec 8:13.
26:8 *You must die.* The Hebrew for this phrase is translated
"you will surely die" in Ge 2:17. A similar phrase describes
the ultimate penalty for gross violations of the law of Moses
(see, e.g., Ex 21:15–17; Lev 24:16–17,21; Dt 18:20; cf.
1Ki 21:13).
26:9 *crowded around.* With hostile intent (see Nu 16:3).
26:10 *officials of Judah.* Those responsible for making legal
decisions concerning disputes taking place in the temple
precincts. The priests and (false) prophets, who had a vested
interest in Jerusalem and its temple, felt that Jeremiah should
be sentenced to death because he was predicting the destruction of both the city and the Lord's house (see vv. 8–9,11).
After hearing Jeremiah's defense (vv. 12–15), the officials
decided in his favor (v. 16). The people, fickle and easily
swayed, first opposed Jeremiah (vv. 8–9), then supported
him (v. 16). *New Gate.* See 36:10; possibly the same as the
"Upper Gate of Benjamin" (see 20:2 and note).
26:11 Jeremiah's enemies judge him before he has a
chance to defend himself (see Dt 19:6).

should be sentenced to death[e] because he has prophesied against this city. You have heard it with your own ears!"[f]

[12]Then Jeremiah said to all the officials[g] and all the people: "The LORD sent me to prophesy[h] against this house and this city all the things you have heard.[i] [13]Now reform[j] your ways and your actions and obey[k] the LORD your God. Then the LORD will relent[l] and not bring the disaster he has pronounced against you. [14]As for me, I am in your hands;[m] do with me whatever you think is good and right. [15]Be assured, however, that if you put me to death, you will bring the guilt of innocent blood[n] on yourselves and on this city and on those who live in it, for in truth the LORD has sent me to you to speak all these words[o] in your hearing."

[16]Then the officials[p] and all the people said to the priests and the prophets, "This man should not be sentenced to death![q] He has spoken to us in the name of the LORD our God."

[17]Some of the elders of the land stepped forward and said to the entire assembly of people, [18]"Micah[r] of Moresheth prophesied in the days of Hezekiah king of Judah. He told all the people of Judah, 'This is what the LORD Almighty says:

" 'Zion[s] will be plowed like a field,
    Jerusalem will become a heap of
        rubble,[t]
    the temple hill[u] a mound overgrown
        with thickets.'[b][v]

[19]"Did Hezekiah king of Judah or anyone else in Judah put him to death? Did not Hezekiah[w] fear the LORD and seek[x] his favor? And did not the LORD relent,[y] so that he did not bring the disaster[z] he pronounced against them? We are about to bring a terrible disaster[a] on ourselves!"

[20](Now Uriah son of Shemaiah from Kiriath Jearim[b] was another man who prophesied in the name of the LORD; he prophesied the same things against this city and this land as Jeremiah did. [21]When King Jehoiakim[c] and all his officers and officials[d] heard his words, the king sought to put him to death.[e] But Uriah heard of it and fled[f] in fear to Egypt. [22]King Jehoiakim, however, sent Elnathan[g] son of Acbor to Egypt, along with some other men. [23]They brought Uriah out of Egypt and took him to King Jehoiakim, who had him struck down with a sword[h] and his body thrown into the burial place of the common people.)[i]

[24]Furthermore, Ahikam[j] son of Shaphan supported Jeremiah, and so he was not handed over to the people to be put to death.

Judah to Serve Nebuchadnezzar

27 Early in the reign of Zedekiah[c][k] son of Josiah king of Judah, this word came to Jeremiah from the LORD:

Cross references (center column):

26:11 [e]Dt 18:20; S Jer 11:21; 18:23; Mt 26:66; Ac 6:11 [f]S Ps 44:1
26:12 [g]Jer 1:18 [h]S Isa 6:8; Am 7:15; Ac 4:18-20; 5:29 [i]S ver 2,15
26:13 [j]S Jer 7:5; Joel 2:12-14 [k]Jer 11:4 [l]S Jer 18:8
26:14 [m]Jos 9:25; Jer 38:5
26:15 [n]S Dt 19:10 [o]S ver 12; S Jer 1:17 [p]S ver 10; S Ac 23:9 [q]Ac 23:29
26:18 [r]Mic 1:1 [s]Isa 2:3 [t]S 2Ki 25:9; S Ne 4:2; Jer 9:11 [u]Mic 4:1; Zec 8:3 [v]S Jer 17:3

26:19 [w]S 1Ch 3:13; 2Ch 32:24-26; Isa 37:14-20 [x]S 1Sa 13:12 [y]S Ex 32:14; S Jer 18:8 [z]Jer 44:7 [a]Hab 2:10
26:20 [b]S Jos 9:17
26:21 [c]S 1Ki 19:2 [d]ver 10; [e]Jer 2:30; Mt 23:37 [f]S Ge 31:21; Mt 10:23
26:22 [g]Jer 36:12, 25
26:23 [h]Heb 11:37 [i]2Ki 23:6
26:24 [j]S 2Ki 22:12
27:1 [k]S 2Ch 36:11

[b]18 Micah 3:12   [c]1 A few Hebrew manuscripts and Syriac (see also Jer. 27:3, 12 and 28:1); most Hebrew manuscripts Jehoiakim (Most Septuagint manuscripts do not have this verse.)

Study notes:

26:12 *The LORD sent me.* Contrast 23:21.
26:13 *Reform your ways and your actions.* Repeated from 7:3 (see also 18:11; 35:15). *relent.* See vv. 3,19; see also notes on 4:28; 18:7-10.
26:15 *innocent blood.* See 7:6 and note; see also Mt 27:24-25; Ac 5:28.
26:16 Contrast v. 11; see note on v. 10.
26:17 *elders.* See 19:1; see also note on Ex 3:16.
26:18-19 The elders cite the precedent of Micah, who lived a century earlier and who (together with Isaiah) convinced King Hezekiah to pray for forgiveness on behalf of his people. The Lord answered the prayers of the king and the prophets, and in 701 B.C. Jerusalem and the temple were spared (see Isa 37:33-37).
26:18 *Micah of Moresheth.* See Introduction to Micah: Author. *Zion will be plowed ... overgrown with thickets.* Quoted verbatim from Mic 3:12—the only place in the OT where one prophet quotes another and identifies his source.
26:19 *seek his favor.* Lit. "stroke his face" (cf. Ps 119:58), "pat his cheek" (see Ex 32:11; 1Sa 13:12; 2Ki 13:4). *relent.* See vv. 3,13; see also notes on 4:28; 18:7-10.
26:20-23 A parenthesis, cited as an example of the contrast between how a good king, Hezekiah, treated the Lord's prophets and how a wicked king, Jehoiakim, was known to have treated them.
26:20 *Uriah.* Not mentioned elsewhere in the OT, though it has been claimed (but not substantiated) that he appears in one of the Lachish letters (see note on 34:7; see also chart on

"Ancient Texts Relating to the OT," p. 5).
26:21 *officers.* Lit. "strong men" (perhaps the royal bodyguard). *Uriah ... fled ... to Egypt.* A fatal mistake, for now he could be accused of treason and sedition.
26:22 *Elnathan son of Acbor.* One of King Jehoiakim's highest officials (see 36:12), he was impressed on another occasion by Jeremiah's prophecies (see 36:16), "urged the king not to burn" Jeremiah's scroll (36:25), and warned the prophet to hide (see 36:19). An Elnathan (perhaps the same man) was Jehoiakim's father-in-law (see 2Ki 24:6,8). An Acbor (perhaps the father of this Elnathan) was one of King Josiah's officials (see 2Ki 22:12,14; see also note on v. 24).
26:23 *brought Uriah out of Egypt.* Mutual rights of extradition were a part of the treaty imposed on Judah by Egypt when Jehoiakim became the vassal of Pharaoh Neco II (see 2Ki 23:34-35). *Jehoiakim ... had him struck down.* Apart from divine intervention, Jeremiah probably would have fallen victim to the same fate (see 36:26). *burial place of the common people.* See note on 17:19. Commoners were buried in the Kidron Valley east of Jerusalem (see 2Ki 23:6).
26:24 *Ahikam son of Shaphan.* One of King Josiah's officials (see 2Ki 22:12,14), along with an Acbor who may have been the father of the Elnathan in v. 22 (see note there). Ahikam was also the father of Gedaliah, who would become governor of Judah after Jerusalem was destroyed in 586 B.C. (see 40:5) and who also befriended Jeremiah (see 39:14). *supported Jeremiah.* Ahikam's high position in Jehoiakim's court was doubtless instrumental in saving the prophet's life.

2This is what the LORD said to me: "Make
a yoke[l] out of straps and crossbars and put
it on your neck. 3Then send[m] word to the
kings of Edom, Moab, Ammon,[n] Tyre and
Sidon[o] through the envoys who have
come to Jerusalem to Zedekiah king of
Judah. 4Give them a message for their masters and say, 'This is what the LORD Almighty, the God of Israel, says: "Tell this
to your masters: 5With my great power
and outstretched arm[p] I made[q] the earth
and its people and the animals[r] that are on
it, and I give[s] it to anyone I please. 6Now I
will hand all your countries over to my
servant[t] Nebuchadnezzar[u] king of Babylon; I will make even the wild animals
subject to him.[v] 7All nations will serve[w]
him and his son and his grandson until the
time[x] for his land comes; then many nations and great kings will subjugate[y] him.
8" ' "If, however, any nation or kingdom will not serve Nebuchadnezzar king
of Babylon or bow its neck under his yoke,
I will punish[z] that nation with the
sword,[a] famine[b] and plague,[c] declares
the LORD, until I destroy it by his hand. 9So
do not listen to your prophets,[d] your diviners,[e] your interpreters of dreams,[f]
your mediums[g] or your sorcerers[h] who
tell you, 'You will not serve[i] the king of
Babylon.' 10They prophesy lies[j] to you
that will only serve to remove[k] you far
from your lands; I will banish you and you
will perish. 11But if any nation will bow its
neck under the yoke[l] of the king of Babylon and serve him, I will let that nation
remain in its own land to till it and to live[m]
there, declares the LORD." ' "

12I gave the same message to Zedekiah
king of Judah. I said, "Bow your neck under the yoke[n] of the king of Babylon; serve
him and his people, and you will live.[o]
13Why will you and your people die[p] by
the sword, famine and plague[q] with which
the LORD has threatened any nation that
will not serve the king of Babylon? 14Do
not listen[r] to the words of the prophets[s]
who say to you, 'You will not serve the
king of Babylon,' for they are prophesying
lies[t] to you. 15'I have not sent[u] them,'
declares the LORD. 'They are prophesying
lies in my name.[v] Therefore, I will banish
you and you will perish,[w] both you and the
prophets who prophesy to you.' "

16Then I said to the priests and all these
people, "This is what the LORD says: Do
not listen to the prophets who say, 'Very
soon now the articles[x] from the LORD's
house will be brought back from Babylon.'
They are prophesying lies to you. 17Do not
listen[y] to them. Serve the king of Babylon,
and you will live.[z] Why should this city
become a ruin? 18If they are prophets and

27:2 [l]S Lev 26:13; S 1Ki 22:11 **27:3** [m]S Jer 25:17 [n]S Jer 25:21 [o]S Ge 10:15; S Jer 25:22 **27:5** [p]S Dt 9:29 [q]S Ge 1:1 [r]S Ge 1:25 [s]Ps 115:16; Da 4:17 **27:6** [t]S Jer 25:9 [u]S Jer 21:7 [v]Jer 28:14; Da 2:37-38 **27:7** [w]S 2Ch 36:20; Da 5:18 [x]S Jer 25:12 [y]S Jer 25:14; 51:47; Da 5:28 **27:8** [z]Jer 9:16 [a]Jer 21:9 [b]S Jer 5:12 [c]S Jer 14:12 **27:9** [d]Eze 13:1-23 [e]S Ge 30:27; S Isa 44:25 [f]S Dt 13:1; S Jer 23:25 [g]S Dt 18:11 [h]S Ex 7:11 [i]Jer 6:14 **27:10** [j]S Jer 23:25; S Mk 13:5 [k]S 2Ki 23:27 **27:11** [l]S Jer 21:9 [m]Dt 6:2 **27:12** [n]Jer 17:4 [o]S Jer 21:9 **27:13** [p]Eze 18:31 [q]S Jer 14:12 **27:14** [r]S Jer 23:16 [s]S Jer 14:13 [t]S Jer 14:14; S Mt 7:15 **27:15** [u]S Jer 23:21 [v]Jer 29:9; 44:16 [w]S Jer 6:15; Mt 15:12-14 **27:16** [x]1Ki 7:48-50; S 2Ki 24:13 **27:17** [y]Jer 23:16 [z]Jer 42:11

27:1–29:32 Further attempts by Jeremiah to counteract the teachings of false prophets, who were claiming that Babylon's doom was near and that rebellion against Nebuchadnezzar was therefore warranted and desirable.

27:1–22 Jeremiah tells the nations (see vv. 3–11), King Zedekiah (see vv. 12–15), and the priests and people of Judah (see vv. 16–22) to submit to the Babylonian yoke.

27:1 *Early in the reign.* See note on 26:1. In this case, however, the phrase has been extended in meaning to include Zedekiah's fourth year (593 B.C.; see 28:1).

27:2 *yoke.* Of the kind worn by oxen, it was a symbol of political submission (see vv. 8,11–12; Lev 26:13). That Jeremiah actually wore such a yoke for a time is clear from 28:10,12.

27:3 *send word.* In his role as a "prophet to the nations" (1:5). *Edom, Moab, Ammon.* Lands east and south of Judah (see 25:21 and note). *Tyre and Sidon.* Prominent cities in Phoenicia, north of Judah (see 25:22 and note). *envoys . . . have come . . . to Zedekiah.* Perhaps to discuss rebellion against Babylonia. They may have counted on support from Egypt, where Psammetichus II had become pharaoh a year earlier (594 B.C.). Zedekiah went to Babylon in 593 (see 51:59), perhaps to be interrogated by Nebuchadnezzar. In any case, Zedekiah rebelled against him (see 52:3).

27:5 *great power and outstretched arm.* See note on 21:5.

27:6 *my servant Nebuchadnezzar.* See note on 25:9. *make . . . wild animals subject to him.* Nothing would be beyond the reach of Nebuchadnezzar's dominion (see 28:14; Da 2:38).

27:7 *him . . . his son . . . his grandson.* Three generations of rulers, not necessarily in direct father-son relationships (cf. Dt 6:2). The words "son" and "father" are often used figuratively in the OT (see note on Da 5:1; see also NIV text notes on Ge 10:2,8). *time for his land comes.* Babylonia will be judged (see note on 25:26). *many nations and great kings.* See note on 25:14.

27:8 *yoke.* See note on v. 2. *sword, famine and plague.* See note on 14:12. *until I destroy.* See 9:15; 24:10.

27:9 See 29:8. *your prophets.* False prophets. *diviners . . . mediums . . . sorcerers.* Forbidden in Israel (see Lev 19:26; Dt 18:10–11). The Hebrew for "sorcerers" is a loanword from Akkadian (the language of Assyria and Babylonia). *interpreters of dreams.* Including prophets and diviners (see 23:25–28; 29:8).

27:10 *prophesy lies.* See note on 5:31; cf. 2Ti 4:3–4.

27:11 *yoke.* See note on v. 2. *serve . . . till.* The Hebrew underlying both words is the same ("work" is the common denominator in serving and tilling).

27:12 *your neck . . . serve . . . live.* The Hebrew for all these words is plural, since Jeremiah is speaking to the people of Judah as well as to Zedekiah (see v. 13). *yoke.* See note on v. 2.

27:13 See v. 8. *sword, famine and plague.* See note on 14:12.

27:14 See v. 10.

27:15 See 14:14; 23:21 and note.

27:16 *prophets who say, 'Very soon now . . .'* As the prophet Hananiah was saying (see 28:1–3). *articles from the LORD's house.* Some were carried off to Babylon by Nebuchadnezzar in 605 B.C. (see Da 1:1–2), others in 597 (see 2Ki 24:13). Still others would be carried off in 586 (see vv. 21–22; 52:17–23).

have the word of the LORD, let them plead[a] with the LORD Almighty that the furnishings remaining in the house of the LORD and in the palace of the king of Judah and in Jerusalem not be taken to Babylon. [19]For this is what the LORD Almighty says about the pillars, the Sea,[b] the movable stands and the other furnishings[c] that are left in this city, [20]which Nebuchadnezzar king of Babylon did not take away when he carried[d] Jehoiachin[d e] son of Jehoiakim king of Judah into exile from Jerusalem to Babylon, along with all the nobles of Judah and Jerusalem— [21]yes, this is what the LORD Almighty, the God of Israel, says about the things that are left in the house of the LORD and in the palace of the king of Judah and in Jerusalem: [22]'They will be taken[f] to Babylon and there they will remain until the day[g] I come for them,' declares the LORD. 'Then I will bring[h] them back and restore them to this place.' "

The False Prophet Hananiah

28 In the fifth month of that same year, the fourth year, early in the reign of Zedekiah[i] king of Judah, the prophet Hananiah son of Azzur, who was from Gibeon,[j] said to me in the house of the LORD in the presence of the priests and all the people: [2]"This is what the LORD Almighty, the God of Israel, says: 'I will break the yoke[k] of the king of Babylon. [3]Within two years I will bring back to this place all the articles[l] of the LORD's house that Nebuchadnezzar king of Babylon removed from here and took to Babylon. [4]I will also bring back to this place Jehoia-

chin[d m] son of Jehoiakim king of Judah and all the other exiles from Judah who went to Babylon,' declares the LORD, 'for I will break the yoke of the king of Babylon.' "[n]

[5]Then the prophet Jeremiah replied to the prophet Hananiah before the priests and all the people who were standing in the house of the LORD. [6]He said, "Amen! May the LORD do so! May the LORD fulfill the words you have prophesied by bringing the articles of the LORD's house and all the exiles back to this place from Babylon.[o] [7]Nevertheless, listen to what I have to say in your hearing and in the hearing of all the people: [8]From early times the prophets who preceded you and me have prophesied war, disaster and plague[p] against many countries and great kingdoms. [9]But the prophet who prophesies peace will be recognized as one truly sent by the LORD only if his prediction comes true.[q]"

[10]Then the prophet Hananiah took the yoke[r] off the neck of the prophet Jeremiah and broke it, [11]and he said[s] before all the people, "This is what the LORD says: 'In the same way will I break the yoke of Nebuchadnezzar king of Babylon off the neck of all the nations within two years.' " At this, the prophet Jeremiah went on his way.

[12]Shortly after the prophet Hananiah had broken the yoke off the neck of the prophet Jeremiah, the word of the LORD came to Jeremiah: [13]"Go and tell Hananiah, 'This is what the LORD says: You have broken a wooden yoke, but in its place you will get a yoke of iron. [14]This is

Cross references (center column)

27:18
a S Nu 21:7;
S 1Sa 7:8
27:19
b 1Ki 7:23-26
c S 1Ki 7:51;
Jer 52:17-23
27:20
d S 2Ch 36:10
e Jer 22:24;
Mt 1:11
27:22
f S 2Ki 20:17;
25:13
g S 2Ch 36:21;
S Jer 24:6
h S Ezr 7:19
28:1
i S 2Ch 36:11
j S Jos 9:3
28:2 k Jer 27:12
28:3 l S 2Ki 24:13
28:4
m S 2Ki 25:30;
Jer 22:24-27
n Hos 7:3
28:6 o Zec 6:10
28:8
p Lev 26:14-17;
Isa 5:5-7; Na 1:14
28:9
q S Dt 18:22;
Eze 33:33
28:10
r S Lev 26:13;
S 1Ki 22:11
28:11 s Jer 14:14;
27:10

d 20,4 Hebrew *Jeconiah*, a variant of *Jehoiachin*

27:18 *If they are prophets . . . let them plead.* If they are true prophets and in communion with the Lord, let them intercede for Judah, because the Lord has announced his intention to judge the nation.
27:19 *the pillars, the Sea, the movable stands.* See 52:17; see also 1Ki 7:15-37 and notes.
27:22 *They will be taken to Babylon.* In 586 B.C. (see 52:17-23). *I will bring them back.* In 538 and shortly afterward (see Ezr 1:7-11).
28:1-17 The true prophet Jeremiah confronts the false prophet Hananiah.
28:1 *fourth year . . . of Zedekiah.* 593 B.C. *early in the reign.* See notes on 26:1; 27:1. *prophet.* The word is used for all prophets, whether true (vv. 5,10-12,15) or false (vv. 1,5,10,12,15,17). *Hananiah.* Means "The LORD is gracious," an appropriate name for a prophet who believed strongly (though mistakenly) that the Lord would soon bring back the exiles of Judah and the temple articles (see vv. 3-4,11). *Gibeon.* See 41:12,16; see also note on Jos 9:3.
28:2 *This is what the LORD . . . says.* See v. 11. Though a false prophet, Hananiah claims to have the same authority as Jeremiah (see vv. 13-14,16; see also 23:31). *yoke.* See note on 27:2.
28:3 Hananiah's prediction directly contradicts the words

of Jeremiah (see 27:16-22 and notes). *two years.* See v. 11. Contrast Jeremiah's 70 years (25:11-12; 29:10).
28:4 *bring back.* Contradicting Jeremiah's prophecy (see 22:24-27), which was fulfilled (see 52:34). *Jehoiachin . . . went to Babylon.* In 597 B.C. *yoke.* See note on 27:2.
28:6 See 1Ki 1:36. *Amen.* See 11:5 and note. *may the LORD fulfill.* The sign of a true prophecy (see v. 9).
28:7 *Nevertheless.* Though in sympathy with what Hananiah is predicting, Jeremiah reminds him that their true predecessors were basically prophets of doom (see v. 8).
28:8 *war, disaster and plague.* An appropriate modification of Jeremiah's usual triad (see note on 14:12).
28:9 *peace.* Ordinarily the message of false prophets (see 6:14 and note).
28:10 *yoke off the neck of the prophet.* See note on 27:2. *broke it.* Perhaps symbolically to break the power of Jeremiah's earlier prophecies (see 25:11-12; 27:7), which contradicted his own.
28:11 *two years.* See note on v. 3.
28:13 *yoke of iron.* The wooden yoke of submission (see note on 27:2) would be exchanged for the iron yoke of servitude (see v. 14; 38:17-23).
28:14 *all these nations . . . will serve him.* See 27:7. *control over the wild animals.* See 27:6 and note.

what the LORD Almighty, the God of Israel, says: I will put an iron yoke^t on the necks of all these nations to make them serve^u Nebuchadnezzar^v king of Babylon, and they will serve him. I will even give him control over the wild animals.^{w} ' "

^{15}Then the prophet Jeremiah said to Hananiah the prophet, "Listen, Hananiah! The LORD has not sent^x you, yet you have persuaded this nation to trust in lies.^{y} ^{16}Therefore, this is what the LORD says: 'I am about to remove you from the face of the earth.^{z} This very year you are going to die,^{a} because you have preached rebellion^b against the LORD.' "

^{17}In the seventh month of that same year, Hananiah the prophet died.^{c}

A Letter to the Exiles

29 This is the text of the letter^d that the prophet Jeremiah sent from Jerusalem to the surviving elders among the exiles and to the priests, the prophets and all the other people Nebuchadnezzar had carried into exile from Jerusalem to Babylon.^{e} ^{2}(This was after King Jehoiachin^{ef} and the queen mother,^{g} the court officials and the leaders of Judah and Jerusalem, the craftsmen and the artisans had gone into exile from Jerusalem.) ^{3}He entrusted the letter to Elasah son of Shaphan and to Gemariah son of Hilkiah, whom Zedekiah king of Judah sent to King Nebuchadnezzar in Babylon. It said:

^{4}This is what the LORD Almighty,

the God of Israel, says to all those I carried^h into exile from Jerusalem to Babylon: ^{5}"Build^i houses and settle down; plant gardens and eat what they produce. ^{6}Marry and have sons and daughters; find wives for your sons and give your daughters in marriage, so that they too may have sons and daughters. Increase in number there; do not decrease.^{j} ^{7}Also, seek^k the peace and prosperity of the city to which I have carried you into exile. Pray^l to the LORD for it, because if it prospers, you too will prosper." ^{8}Yes, this is what the LORD Almighty, the God of Israel, says: "Do not let the prophets^m and diviners among you deceive^n you. Do not listen to the dreams^o you encourage them to have.^{p} ^{9}They are prophesying lies^q to you in my name. I have not sent^r them," declares the LORD.

^{10}This is what the LORD says: "When seventy years^s are completed for Babylon, I will come to you^t and fulfill my gracious promise^u to bring you back^v to this place. ^{11}For I know the plans^w I have for you," declares the LORD, "plans to prosper^x you and not to harm you, plans to give you hope and a future.^{y} ^{12}Then you will call^z upon me and come and pray^a to me, and I will listen^b to you. ^{13}You will seek^c me and find me when you

Cross references (center column)

28:14
^{r}Dt 28:48;
S Jer 15:12
^{u}Jer 25:11
^{v}Jer 39:1; Da 1:1;
5:18 ^{w}S Jer 27:6
28:15 ^{x}Jer 29:31
^{y}S Jer 7:4; 20:6;
29:21; La 2:14;
Eze 13:6
28:16 ^{z}S Ge 7:4
^{a}Dt 18:20;
Zec 13:3
^{b}Dt 13:5;
Jer 29:32
28:17
^{c}S 2Ki 1:17
29:1 ^{d}ver 28
^{e}S 2Ch 36:10;
S Jer 13:17
29:2 ^{f}S 2Ki 24:12
^{g}S 2Ki 24:8

29:4 ^{h}S Jer 24:5
29:5 ^{i}ver 28
29:6 ^{j}Jer 30:19
29:7 ^{k}S Est 3:8
^{l}1Ti 2:1-2
29:8 ^{m}1Jn 4:1
^{n}Jer 37:9
^{o}S Dt 13:1;
S Jer 23:25
^{p}S Jer 23:27
29:9
^{q}S Jer 27:15;
La 2:14; Eze 13:6
^{r}Jer 23:21
29:10
^{s}S 2Ch 36:21;
S Da 9:2 ^{t}S Ru 1:6
^{u}1Ki 8:56;
Jer 32:42; 33:14
^{v}S Jer 16:14;
S 24:6
29:11 ^{w}Ps 40:5
^{x}Isa 55:12
^{y}S Job 8:7;
Zec 8:15
29:12 ^{z}Hos 2:23;
Zep 3:2;
Zec 13:9
^{a}S 1Ki 8:30
^{b}Ps 145:19;
S Isa 55:6
29:13 ^{c}Mt 7:7

^{e}2 Hebrew *Jeconiah,* a variant of *Jehoiachin*

28:15 *The LORD has not sent you.* A mark of the false prophet (see 23:21 and note).
28:16 *remove.* The Hebrew root underlying this word is the same as that underlying "sent" in v. 15. The Lord had not "sent" Hananiah to prophesy, and therefore he would soon be "sent away" to his death. *preached rebellion.* Such activity on the part of false prophets was punishable by death (see Dt 13:5; see also Dt 18:20; cf. Eze 11:13; Ac 5:1–11).
28:17 *In the seventh month . . . Hananiah . . . died.* He who had falsely prophesied restoration "within two years" (vv. 3,11) himself died within two months (see v. 1).
29:1–32 Jeremiah's letter to the exiles of 597 B.C. (vv. 4–23) is followed by God's message of judgment against the false prophet Shemaiah (vv. 24–32).
29:2 *queen mother.* Nehushta (2Ki 24:8). *craftsmen and . . . artisans.* See 24:1 and note.
29:3 *entrusted the letter to.* Placed it in the ancient equivalent of the diplomatic pouch to ensure its safe arrival. *Shaphan.* Perhaps the father also of Ahikam (see 26:24 and note) and/or Gemariah (see 36:10), both of whom were sympathetic to Jeremiah and his mission. *Hilkiah.* Perhaps the Hilkiah who was high priest under Josiah (see 2Ki 22:12, where Hilkiah and one or more Shaphans are mentioned together). *Zedekiah . . . sent to King Nebuchadnezzar.* Possibly at or about the same time (593 B.C.) that Zedekiah himself went to Babylon for a brief period (see 51:59). The purpose of the journey(s) is unknown.
29:4 *I.* The Lord (see v. 7). Since it is God who has exiled

his people, they are to submit to their captors and not rebel against them.
29:5 *Build . . . plant.* Reminiscent of Jeremiah's call (see 1:10), but here used in a literal sense. *settle down.* Ezekiel, e.g., lived in his own house in Babylonia (see Eze 8:1).
29:6 *find wives.* But among the exiles themselves, not among the women of Babylonia (cf. Dt 7:3–4; Ezr 9:1–2).
29:7 An unprecedented and unique concept in the ancient world: working toward and praying for the prosperity of one's captors. *peace and prosperity . . . prospers . . . prosper.* The Hebrew word is *shalom* in all three cases. *city.* Every place in which the exiles settle down. *Pray . . . for it.* See Ezr 6:10 and note; Mt 5:44; in the Apocrypha cf. 1 Maccabees 7:33.
29:8 *prophets and diviners . . . dreams.* See 27:9 and notes. *among you.* The exiles in Babylon had their share of false prophets (see vv. 21,31), who had doubtless accompanied them when they were deported in 597 B.C.
29:9 See v. 31; see also notes on 23:16,21.
29:10 *seventy years.* See note on 25:11–12. *bring you back.* See note on 27:22.
29:11 *I know.* See v. 23. Appearances to the contrary notwithstanding, the Lord has not forgotten his people. *prosper.* See note on v. 7. *and not . . . harm.* God is the ultimate source of both prosperity and disaster (see Isa 45:7).
29:12–13 Echoed from Dt 4:29–30. The Lord's gracious gift of prosperity is contingent on his people's willingness to repent.

seek me with all your heart. *d* 14I will be found by you," declares the LORD, "and will bring you back *e* from captivity. *f* I will gather you from all the nations and places where I have banished you," declares the LORD, "and will bring you back to the place from which I carried you into exile." *f*

15You may say, "The LORD has raised up prophets for us in Babylon," 16but this is what the LORD says about the king who sits on David's throne and all the people who remain in this city, your countrymen who did not go with you into exile— 17yes, this is what the LORD Almighty says: "I will send the sword, famine and plague *g* against them and I will make them like poor figs *h* that are so bad they cannot be eaten. 18I will pursue them with the sword, famine and plague and will make them abhorrent *i* to all the kingdoms of the earth and an object of cursing *j* and horror, *k* of scorn *l* and reproach, among all the nations where I drive them. 19For they have not listened to my words," *m* declares the LORD, "words that I sent to them again and again *n* by my servants the prophets. *o* And you exiles have not listened either," declares the LORD.

20Therefore, hear the word of the LORD, all you exiles whom I have sent *p* away from Jerusalem to Babylon. 21This is what the LORD Almighty, the God of Israel, says about Ahab son of Kolaiah and Zedekiah son of Maaseiah, who are prophesying

lies *q* to you in my name: "I will hand them over to Nebuchadnezzar king of Babylon, and he will put them to death before your very eyes. 22Because of them, all the exiles from Judah who are in Babylon will use this curse: 'The LORD treat you like Zedekiah and Ahab, whom the king of Babylon burned *r* in the fire.' 23For they have done outrageous things in Israel; they have committed adultery *s* with their neighbors' wives and in my name have spoken lies, which I did not tell them to do. I know *t* it and am a witness *u* to it," declares the LORD.

Message to Shemaiah

24Tell Shemaiah the Nehelamite, 25"This is what the LORD Almighty, the God of Israel, says: You sent letters in your own name to all the people in Jerusalem, to Zephaniah *v* son of Maaseiah the priest, and to all the other priests. You said to Zephaniah, 26'The LORD has appointed you priest in place of Jehoiada to be in charge of the house of the LORD; you should put any madman *w* who acts like a prophet into the stocks *x* and neck-irons. 27So why have you not reprimanded Jeremiah from Anathoth, who poses as a prophet among you? 28He has sent this message *y* to us in Babylon: It will be a long time. *z* Therefore build *a* houses and settle down; plant gardens and eat what they produce.' "

29Zephaniah *b* the priest, however, read the letter to Jeremiah the prophet. 30Then the word of the LORD came to Jeremiah: 31"Send this message to all the exiles:

Cross references (center column):

29:13
d S Dt 4:29;
S 2Ch 6:37
29:14
e S Dt 30:3;
Jer 30:3;
Eze 39:25;
Am 9:14;
Zep 3:20
f Jer 23:3-4;
30:10; 46:27;
Eze 37:21
29:17 *g* Jer 27:8
h S Isa 5:4
29:18 *i* S Jer 15:4
j S Nu 5:27;
S Jer 18:16;
S 22:10; 44:12
k S Dt 28:25
l S Dt 28:37;
S Isa 28:22;
S Mic 2:6
29:19 *m* Jer 6:19
n Jer 7:25
o S Jer 25:4
29:20 *p* S Jer 24:5

29:21 *q* ver 9;
Jer 14:14
29:22 *r* Da 3:6
29:23
s S Jer 23:14
t S Heb 4:13
u S Ge 31:48;
S Jer 7:11
29:25
v S 2Ki 25:18
29:26
w S 1Sa 10:11;
Hos 9:7;
S Jn 10:20
x Jer 20:2
29:28 *y* ver 1 *z* ver
10 *a* ver 5
29:29 *b* Jer 21:1

*f*14 Or *will restore your fortunes*

29:14 A summary of Dt 30:3–5. *bring you back from captivity.* See NIV text note; see also 30:3,18; 31:23; 32:44; 33:7,11,26; 48:47; 49:6,39; and note on Ps 126:4. The Hebrew for "bring back" sounds very similar to that for "captivity."

29:15 *prophets . . . in Babylon.* See note on v. 8.

29:16 *the king . . . on David's throne.* Zedekiah. *sits . . . remain.* The Hebrew for both words is identical. King and people alike are guilty.

29:17 *sword, famine and plague.* See v. 18; see also note on 14:12. *poor figs . . . so bad they cannot be eaten.* See 24:8.

29:18 See 24:9 and note.

29:19 *again and again.* See note on 7:13. *my servants the prophets.* See note on 7:25. *you exiles have not listened.* See Eze 2:5,7; 3:7,11.

29:21 *Ahab . . . and Zedekiah.* Not the well-known kings (of Israel and Judah respectively); rather, they were false prophets (see note on v. 8).

29:22 *curse . . . burned.* The Hebrew underlying each of these words sounds like Kolaiah, the name of Ahab's father (v. 21). *fire.* Used in Babylonia as a method of execution (see Da 3:6,24; this is also evident in the Code of Hammurapi,

sections 25; 110; 157).

29:23 *done outrageous things in Israel.* See Ge 34:7 and note. *committed adultery . . . and . . . spoken lies.* See note on 23:10. *I know.* See v. 11.

29:24 *Shemaiah.* A false prophet (see v. 31). *Nehelamite.* The Hebrew root underlying this word is the same as that for "dreams" in v. 8 (see note 27:9 and note).

29:25 *Zephaniah.* Not the prophet of that name (see note on 21:1).

29:26 *Jehoiada.* Not the same as the priest during the days of King Joash (see 2Ki 12:7). *in charge of the house of the LORD.* See note on 20:1. *madman.* Prophetic behavior sometimes appeared deranged to the casual observer (see 2Ki 9:11). *stocks.* See note on 20:2.

29:27 *Anathoth.* See note on 1:1.

29:28 See v. 5 and note. *a long time.* Here 70 years (see 25:11–12 and note; see also 2Sa 3:1).

29:29 *Zephaniah . . . however.* He was apparently sympathetic toward Jeremiah (see 21:1–2; 37:3).

29:31–32 The Lord's threat against Shemaiah is similar to that against Hananiah (see 28:15–16).

29:31 *led . . . to believe a lie.* See 28:15.

'This is what the LORD says about Shema-iah[c] the Nehelamite: Because Shemaiah has prophesied to you, even though I did not send[d] him, and has led you to believe a lie, [32]this is what the LORD says: I will surely punish Shemaiah the Nehelamite and his descendants.[e] He will have no one left among this people, nor will he see the good[f] things I will do for my people, declares the LORD, because he has preached rebellion[g] against me.' "

Restoration of Israel

30 This is the word that came to Jeremiah from the LORD: [2]"This is what the LORD, the God of Israel, says: 'Write[h] in a book all the words I have spoken to you. [3]The days[i] are coming,' declares the LORD, 'when I will bring[j] my people Israel and Judah back from captivity[g] and restore[k] them to the land I gave their forefathers to possess,' says the LORD."

[4]These are the words the LORD spoke concerning Israel and Judah: [5]"This is what the LORD says:

" 'Cries of fear[l] are heard—
  terror, not peace.
[6]Ask and see:
  Can a man bear children?
Then why do I see every strong man
  with his hands on his stomach like a
  woman in labor,[m]

every face turned deathly pale?[n]
[7]How awful that day[o] will be!
  None will be like it.
It will be a time of trouble[p] for Jacob,
  but he will be saved[q] out of it.

[8]" 'In that day,' declares the LORD
  Almighty,
'I will break the yoke[r] off their necks
  and will tear off their bonds;[s]
  no longer will foreigners enslave
  them.[t]
[9]Instead, they will serve the LORD their
  God
  and David[u] their king,[v]
  whom I will raise up for them.

[10]" 'So do not fear,[w] O Jacob my
  servant;[x]
  do not be dismayed, O Israel,'
  declares the LORD.
'I will surely save[y] you out of a distant
  place,
  your descendants from the land of
  their exile.
Jacob will again have peace and
  security,[z]
  and no one will make him afraid.[a]
[11]I am with you[b] and will save you,'
  declares the LORD.
'Though I completely destroy all the
  nations

Cross references

29:31 [c]ver 24
[d]S Jer 14:14
29:32 [e]S 1Sa 2:30-33
[f]ver 10
[g]S Jer 28:16
30:2 [h]S Isa 30:8;
S Jer 36:2
30:3 [i]S Jer 16:14;
S 24:6
[j]S Jer 29:14
[k]S Jer 16:15
30:5 [l]Jer 6:25
30:6 [m]S Jer 4:31

[n]S Isa 29:22
30:7 [o]S Isa 2:12
[p]S Isa 22:5;
Zep 1:15 [q]ver 10;
Jer 23:3
30:8 [r]S Isa 9:4
[s]Ps 107:14
[t]Jer 25:14; 27:7;
Eze 34:27
30:9 [u]S Mt 1:1
[v]ver 21;
S 1Sa 13:14;
Jer 33:15;
Eze 34:23-24;
37:24; Hos 1:11;
3:5
30:10 [w]S Isa 41:10
[x]S Isa 44:2 [y]S ver
7; S Jer 29:14
[z]Isa 35:9;
S Jer 17:25
[a]S Isa 29:22;
S 54:4; S Jer 23:4;
Eze 34:25-28
30:11 [b]S Jos 1:5

[g]3 Or *will restore the fortunes of my people Israel and Judah*

29:32 *preached rebellion against.* See 28:16 and note.
30:1–33:26 Often called Jeremiah's "book of consolation," the section depicts the ultimate restoration of both Israel (the northern kingdom) and Judah (the southern kingdom) and is the longest sustained passage in Jeremiah concerned with the future hope of the people of God (for other and briefer passages on restoration see 3:14–18; 16:14–15; 23:3–8; 24:4–7). The information in 32:1 may be used to date the entire section to 587 B.C., the year before Jerusalem was destroyed by Nebuchadnezzar and its people exiled to Babylon.
30:1–31:40 Written almost entirely in poetry, these two chapters are filled with optimism as the prophet looks forward to the time when God would redeem his people.
30:1 The heading for chs. 30–31 (and perhaps chs. 32–33 as well).
30:2 *Write.* In order to preserve for future generations the predictions of restoration. *book.* In scroll form (see, e.g., 36:2,4; 45:1; see also note on Ex 17:14). *all the words I have spoken to you.* Concerning the future redemption of God's people. The phrase is less comprehensive here than in 36:2.
30:3 *bring . . . back from captivity.* See note on 29:14. *Israel and Judah.* The northern and southern kingdoms, the first of which was exiled in 721 B.C. and the second of which would be entering the final stage of its exile in about a year (see note on 30:1–33:26).
30:5 *Cries of fear . . . terror.* The sounds of battle and destruction.
30:6 *woman in labor.* A symbol of anguish and distress (see

note on 4:19).
30:7 A description of the day of the Lord (see notes on Isa 2:11,17,20; Am 5:18; 8:9). Jeremiah's immediate reference is to the foreseeable future (see vv. 8,18), but a more remote time in the Messianic age is also in view. *awful.* Lit. "great" (as in Joel 2:11; Zep 1:14; cf. Joel 1:15). *None will be like it.* See Da 12:1; Joel 2:2; Mt 24:21. *time of trouble.* The Hebrew for this phrase is translated "time of distress" in Da 12:1 (see Mt 24:21 and note; Rev 16:18). *Jacob.* Israel (see v. 10).
30:8 *In that day.* See note on Isa 2:11,17,20. *yoke.* See note on 27:2. *tear off their bonds.* The Hebrew underlying this phrase is translated "break their chains" in Ps 2:3, where the nations plot to free themselves from the Lord and his anointed ruler. Here the Lord promises to free his people from enslavement to the nations. *foreigners.* Including, but not limited to, Babylonia.
30:9 *David their king.* The Messiah (see note on 23:5). The Targum (ancient Aramaic paraphrase) here reads "Messiah, the son of David, their king." *raise up.* See note on 23:5.
30:10–11 Repeated almost verbatim in 46:27–28.
30:10 *Jacob my servant.* See Isa 41:8–9 and note; 44:1–2,21; 45:4; 48:20. *no one will make him afraid.* Contrast v. 5; see Lev 26:6; Job 11:19; Isa 17:2; Eze 34:28; 39:26; Mic 4:4 and note; Zep 3:13.
30:11 *I am with you and will save you.* Words spoken originally to Jeremiah alone (see 1:8,19; 15:20) are now spoken to all God's people. *scatter.* See 9:16 and note; 23:1–2. *not completely destroy.* See 4:27 and note. *not . . . go . . . unpunished.* See 25:29; 49:12.

among which I scatter you,
I will not completely destroy c you.
I will discipline d you but only with
justice;
I will not let you go entirely
unpunished.' e

12"This is what the LORD says:

" 'Your wound f is incurable,
your injury beyond healing. g
13There is no one to plead your cause, h
no remedy for your sore,
no healing i for you.
14All your allies j have forgotten you;
they care nothing for you.
I have struck you as an enemy k would
and punished you as would the
cruel, l
because your guilt is so great
and your sins m so many.
15Why do you cry out over your wound,
your pain that has no cure? n
Because of your great guilt and many
sins
I have done these things to you. o

16" 'But all who devour p you will be
devoured;
all your enemies will go into exile. q
Those who plunder r you will be
plundered;
all who make spoil of you I will
despoil.
17But I will restore you to health
and heal s your wounds,'
declares the LORD,
'because you are called an outcast, t
Zion for whom no one cares.' u

18"This is what the LORD says:

" 'I will restore the fortunes v of Jacob's
tents w
and have compassion x on his
dwellings;
the city will be rebuilt y on her ruins,
and the palace will stand in its proper
place.
19From them will come songs z of
thanksgiving a
and the sound of rejoicing. b
I will add to their numbers, c
and they will not be decreased;
I will bring them honor, d
and they will not be disdained.
20Their children e will be as in days of
old,
and their community will be
established f before me;
I will punish g all who oppress them.
21Their leader h will be one of their own;
their ruler will arise from among
them. i
I will bring him near j and he will come
close to me,
for who is he who will devote himself
to be close to me?'
declares the LORD.
22"So you will be my people, k
and I will be your God. l ' "

23See, the storm m of the LORD
will burst out in wrath,
a driving wind swirling down
on the heads of the wicked.
24The fierce anger n of the LORD will not
turn back o
until he fully accomplishes
the purposes of his heart.
In days to come

30:11
cS Lev 26:44;
S Jer 5:18; 46:28
dS Jer 10:24
eHos 11:9;
Am 9:8
30:12 /S Job 6:4;
S Jer 10:19
gS Jer 8:22
30:13 hS Jdg 6:31
iS Jer 8:22;
14:19; 46:11;
Na 3:19
30:14
jS Jer 22:20;
La 1:2
kS Job 13:24
lS Job 30:21
mS Jer 25:7
30:15
nS Jer 10:19
oS Pr 1:31; La 1:5
30:16
pS Isa 29:8;
S 33:1; S Jer 2:3
qS Isa 14:2;
Joel 3:4-8
rJer 49:2; 50:10
30:17 sS Isa 1:5;
Hos 6:1
tS Isa 6:12;
Jer 33:24
uPs 142:4

30:18 vver 3;
S Dt 30:3;
Jer 31:23; 32:44
wS Nu 24:5
xPs 102:13;
Jer 33:26;
Eze 39:25
yJer 31:4,24,38;
33:7; Eze 36:10,
33; Am 9:14
30:19 zS Ps 9:2;
Isa 35:10; S 51:11
aS Isa 51:3
bPs 126:1-2;
Jer 31:4
cS Ge 15:5;
22:17; Jer 33:22;
Eze 37:26;
Zec 2:4
dS Isa 44:23;
S 60:9
30:20 eIsa 54:13;
Jer 31:17; Zec 8:5
fIsa 54:14
gS Ex 23:22
30:21 hS ver 9;
Jer 23:5-6
iDt 17:15
jNu 16:5

30:22 kS Isa 19:25; Hos 2:23 lS Lev 26:12 **30:23**
mS Jer 23:19 **30:24** nJer 4:8; La 1:12 oS Jer 4:28

30:12–13 See 8:22; Hos 5:13; 6:1; 7:1; 11:3.

30:12 *Your.* Judah's. *wound is incurable.* See 15:18 and note. *injury beyond healing.* See 14:17.

30:13 *plead your cause.* Against your enemies. *no remedy for your sore.* See Hos 5:13.

30:14 *allies.* See note on 22:20. Egypt, e.g., often supported Judah against the Babylonians (see 37:5–7). *because your guilt . . . so many.* See 5:6; 13:22. The Hebrew for this clause is repeated verbatim in v. 15.

30:16 *all who devour you.* See 3:24; 5:17; 8:16; 10:25. *will be devoured.* See note on 25:26; see also 51:48–49. *will be plundered.* See Isa 17:14.

30:17 *restore you to health.* Contrast 8:22; see 33:6; Isa 58:8.

30:18 *restore the fortunes.* See note on 29:14. *the city . . . the palace.* Lit. "a city . . . a palace," perhaps referring to Judah's cities and palaces in general (see Am 9:14). It is possible, however, that only Jerusalem and its palace are intended (see 31:38). *ruins.* The Hebrew for this word is tel(l), referring to a mound of ruins resulting from the accumulation of the debris of many years or centuries of occupation and on which successive series of towns were often

built (see, e.g., Jos 11:13).

30:19 *songs of thanksgiving.* See 33:11. *rejoicing.* See 31:4 and note; contrast 15:17. *add . . . not be decreased.* See 29:6; Eze 36:37–38. *honor . . . not be disdained.* See Isa 9:1.

30:20 *days of old.* Probably the early days of the united kingdom, especially the reign of David. *community.* In 1Ki 12:20 the Hebrew for this word is translated "assembly," the political and religious governing body of the people. *will be established before me.* See Ps 102:28; 2Sa 7:24.

30:21 *leader . . . ruler.* Although the Targum renders "Messiah" here, the terms probably refer in the first place to the rulers of Judah immediately after the exile. But Jesus Christ ultimately fulfills the promise. *one of their own . . . from among them.* Not foreigners (cf. Dt 18:15,18). *bring him near . . . come close.* See Nu 16:5; contrast Ex 24:2. Unauthorized approaches into God's presence were punishable by death (see Ex 19:21; Nu 8:19).

30:22 See 31:1; see also note on 7:23.

30:23–24 Repeated almost verbatim from 23:19–20 (see notes there).

you will understand[p] this.

31 "At that time," declares the LORD,
"I will be the God[q] of all the clans
of Israel, and they will be my people."

²This is what the LORD says:

"The people who survive the sword
　　will find favor[r] in the desert;
　I will come to give rest[s] to Israel."

³The LORD appeared to us in the past,[h]
saying:

"I have loved[t] you with an everlasting
　　love;
　I have drawn[u] you with
　　loving-kindness.
⁴I will build you up again
　and you will be rebuilt,[v] O Virgin[w]
　　Israel.
Again you will take up your
　　tambourines[x]
and go out to dance[y] with the
　　joyful.[z]
⁵Again you will plant[a] vineyards
　on the hills of Samaria;[b]
the farmers will plant them
　and enjoy their fruit.[c]
⁶There will be a day when watchmen[d]
　cry out

on the hills of Ephraim,
'Come, let us go up to Zion,
　to the LORD our God.' "[e]

⁷This is what the LORD says:

"Sing[f] with joy for Jacob;
　shout for the foremost[g] of the
　　nations.
Make your praises heard, and say,
　'O LORD, save[h] your people,
　the remnant[i] of Israel.'
⁸See, I will bring them from the land of
　　the north[j]
　and gather[k] them from the ends of
　　the earth.
Among them will be the blind[l] and the
　　lame,[m]
　expectant mothers and women in
　　labor;
a great throng will return.
⁹They will come with weeping;[n]
　they will pray as I bring them back.
I will lead[o] them beside streams of
　　water[p]
on a level[q] path where they will not
　　stumble,
because I am Israel's father,[r]

30:24
[p]Jer 23:19-20
31:1
[q]S Lev 26:12
31:2 [r]Nu 14:20
[s]S Ex 33:14;
S Dt 12:9
31:3 [t]S Dt 4:37
[u]Hos 11:4;
Jn 6:44
31:4 [v]S Jer 1:10;
S 30:18
[w]S 2Ki 19:21
[x]S Ge 31:27
[y]S Ex 15:20
[z]S Jer 30:19
31:5 [a]S Dt 20:6
[b]Jer 33:13;
50:19; Ob 1:19
[c]Isa 37:30;
Am 9:14
31:6 [d]S Isa 52:8;
S 56:10

[e]ver 12;
S Dt 33:19;
Jer 50:4-5;
Mic 4:2
31:7 [f]S Isa 12:6
[g]Dt 28:13;
Isa 61:9 [h]Ps 14:7;
28:9 [i]S Isa 37:31
31:8 [j]S Jer 3:18
[k]S Ge 33:13;
S Dt 30:4;
S Ps 106:47;
Eze 34:12-14
[l]Isa 42:16
[m]Eze 34:16;
Mic 4:6
31:9 [n]S Ezr 3:12;
Ps 126:5
[o]Isa 63:13
[p]S Nu 20:8;
S Ps 1:3;
S Isa 32:2
[q]S Isa 40:4;

[r]S 49:11　[s]S Ex 4:22; S Jer 3:4

[h]3 Or LORD has appeared to us from afar

31:1-40 Continuing the theme of restoration begun in 30:1, Jeremiah records the words of the Lord to (1) all the people of God, v. 1 (prose); (2) the restored northern kingdom of Israel, vv. 2-22 (poetry); (3) the restored southern kingdom of Judah, vv. 23-26 (prose); and (4) Israel and Judah together, vv. 27-40 (prose prologue, vv. 27-30; poetic body, vv. 31-37; prose epilogue, vv. 38-40—each section beginning with the words "The days are coming").

31:1 See 30:22; see also note on 7:23. *all the clans of Israel.* All 12 tribes.

31:2 *people who survive the sword.* The righteous remnant (see v. 7; see also note on 6:9), who will return from captivity. *desert.* The Arabian Desert, the antitype of the Sinai Desert through which Israel's ancestors marched after the exodus. Return from exile is often pictured as or compared to release from Egyptian slavery at the time of the exodus (see 16:14-15 and note; see also Isa 35:1-11 and notes; 40:3-4; 42:14-16; 43:18-21; 48:20-21; 51:9-11; cf. Hos 2:14-15). *rest.* See 6:16; contrast Dt 28:65. See notes on Dt 3:20; Jos 1:13. *Israel.* The northern kingdom (see also vv. 4,7,9-10,21). Other names for it are Samaria (v. 5), Ephraim (vv. 6,9,18,20), Jacob (vv. 7,11) and Rachel (v. 15).

31:3 *drawn . . . with loving-kindness.* The Hebrew underlying this phrase is translated "Continue . . . love" in Ps 36:10 (see note on Ps 6:4).

31:4 *build.* See 1:10 and note. *Virgin Israel.* See v. 21; 18:13; see also 14:17 and note. *tambourines.* Used on joyful occasions (see Ps 68:25), especially following a military victory (see Ex 15:20 and note; Jdg 11:34)—in contrast to Judah's experience during the exile (see Ps 137:1-3). *dance.* See v. 13; often a religious activity in ancient times (see 2Sa 6:14). *joyful.* The Hebrew for this word is translated "rejoicing" in 30:19.

31:5 *plant.* See 1:10 and note. *Samaria.* Conquered in 722-721 B.C. (see 2Ki 17:24), it would someday be resettled by God's people. *plant them and enjoy their fruit.* See Dt 28:30; Isa 62:8-9; 65:21-22. Since the law stipulated that the fruit of a tree could not be eaten until the fifth year after planting it (see Lev 19:23-25), a return to normalcy is envisioned here.

31:6 *watchmen . . . on the hills.* For example, in later times watchmen were stationed in appropriate locations to observe and give notice of the appearance of various phases of the moon to fix the times of the most important feasts (see Dt 16:16). *Ephraim . . . to Zion.* In the days of Jeroboam I, the people of the northern kingdom had been required to worship at northern shrines (see 1Ki 12:26-30). In the future, however, they would worship the Lord only in Jerusalem (cf. Jn 4:20). *go up.* The verb is often used of journeys to Jerusalem (see, e.g., Ezr 1:3; 7:7; Isa 2:3), whose elevation is above the surrounding countryside.

31:7 *foremost of the nations.* See Dt 26:19; Am 6:1. Israel was the greatest nation not because of intrinsic merit but because of divine grace and appointment (see Dt 7:6-8; 2Sa 7:23-24). *save.* The Hebrew for this word is the basis of "Hosanna," the cry of the people of Jerusalem on Palm Sunday (see Mt 21:9 and NIV text note; see also Ps 20:9; 28:9; 86:2; and especially 118:25). *remnant.* See note on 6:9.

31:8 *land of the north.* See 3:18 and note; 4:6 and note; 6:22; 16:15. *ends of the earth.* See 6:22; 25:32. *blind . . . lame.* See Isa 35:5-6 and notes; 42:16.

31:9 *with weeping.* Contrast Ps 126:5-6; Isa 55:12. *lead them.* See Isa 40:11; 48:21; contrast Isa 20:4. *beside streams of water.* See Isa 49:10; see also 41:18. *level path.* See Isa 40:3-4 and notes; 43:16,19. *I am Israel's father.* See 3:4 and note; see also Dt 32:6; Isa 63:16; 64:8. *firstborn son.* Cf. v. 20; see Ex 4:22 and note; Hos 11:1-4.

and Ephraim is my firstborn son.

[10]"Hear the word of the LORD, O nations;
    proclaim it in distant coastlands:[s]
'He who scattered[t] Israel will gather[u]
    them
and will watch over his flock like a
    shepherd.'[v]
[11]For the LORD will ransom Jacob
    and redeem[w] them from the hand of
    those stronger[x] than they.
[12]They will come and shout for joy[y] on
    the heights[z] of Zion;
    they will rejoice in the bounty[a] of
    the LORD—
the grain, the new wine and the oil,[b]
    the young of the flocks[c] and herds.
They will be like a well-watered
    garden,[d]
    and they will sorrow[e] no more.
[13]Then maidens will dance and be glad,
    young men and old as well.
I will turn their mourning[f] into
    gladness;
I will give them comfort[g] and joy[h]
    instead of sorrow.
[14]I will satisfy[i] the priests[j] with
    abundance,
and my people will be filled with my
    bounty,[k]"
                    declares the LORD.

[15]This is what the LORD says:

"A voice is heard in Ramah,[l]
    mourning and great weeping,
Rachel weeping for her children
    and refusing to be comforted,[m]
    because her children are no more."[n]

[16]This is what the LORD says:

"Restrain your voice from weeping
    and your eyes from tears,[o]
for your work will be rewarded,[p]"
                    declares the LORD.
"They will return[q] from the land of
    the enemy.
[17]So there is hope[r] for your future,"
                    declares the LORD.
"Your children[s] will return to their
    own land.

[18]"I have surely heard Ephraim's
    moaning:
'You disciplined[t] me like an unruly
    calf,[u]
    and I have been disciplined.
Restore[v] me, and I will return,
    because you are the LORD my God.
[19]After I strayed,[w]
    I repented;
after I came to understand,
    I beat[x] my breast.
I was ashamed[y] and humiliated
    because I bore the disgrace of my
    youth.'[z]
[20]Is not Ephraim my dear son,
    the child[a] in whom I delight?
Though I often speak against him,
    I still remember[b] him.
Therefore my heart yearns for him;
    I have great compassion[c] for him,"
                    declares the LORD.

[21]"Set up road signs;
    put up guideposts.[d]

31:10 [s]Isa 49:1; S 66:19; S Jer 25:22
[t]S Lev 26:33
[u]S Dt 30:4; S Isa 11:12; Jer 50:19
[v]Isa 40:11; Eze 34:12
31:11 [w]S Ex 6:6; Zec 9:16
[x]Ps 142:6
31:12 [y]S Ps 126:5
[z]Eze 17:23; 20:40; 40:2; Mic 4:1
[a]S Ps 36:8; Joel 3:18
[b]S Nu 18:12; Hos 2:21-22; Joel 2:19 [c]ver 24; S Isa 65:10
[d]S SS 4:15
[e]S Isa 30:19; S 62:5; Jn 16:22; S Rev 7:17
31:13 [f]S Isa 61:3
[g]S Isa 40:1
[h]Ps 30:11; S Isa 51:11
31:14 [i]ver 25
[j]Lev 7:35-36
[k]S Ps 36:8; S Isa 30:23
31:15 [l]S Jos 18:25
[m]S Ge 37:35
[n]S Jer 10:20; Mt 2:17-18*
31:16 [o]S Ps 30:5; S Isa 25:8; 30:19
[p]S Ru 2:12; S 2Ch 15:7
[q]Jer 30:3; Eze 11:17
31:17 [r]S Job 8:7; La 3:29
[s]S Jer 30:20
31:18 [t]S Job 5:17
[u]Jer 50:11; Hos 4:16; 10:11
[v]S Ps 80:3
31:19 [w]S Ps 95:10; S Jer 8:4; Eze 36:31
[x]Eze 21:12; Lk 18:13 [y]Ezr 9:6
[z]S Ps 25:7; S Jer 22:21 **31:20** [a]La 3:33 [b]S Isa 44:21
[c]S 1Ki 3:26; S Ps 6:2; Isa 55:7; Mic 7:18 **31:21** [d]Eze 21:19

31:10 *distant coastlands.* Remote areas to the west of Israel (see 2:10; 25:22 and note; 47:4; Ps 72:10; Isa 41:1, 5; 42:10,12; 49:1). *scattered Israel... watch over his flock like a shepherd.* See 23:1–3 and notes.
31:11 *redeem.* See note on Ru 2:20. As the Lord had redeemed his people from Egyptian slavery (see Ex 6:6; 15:13; Dt 7:8; 9:26), so now he would redeem their descendants from Babylonian exile (see Isa 41:14 and note; 43:1 and note; 52:9). *from... those stronger than they.* See Ps 35:10.
31:12 *heights of Zion.* See note on 17:12. *bounty of the LORD.* Primarily material blessings (see v. 14; Hos 3:5). *grain... new wine... oil.* See note on Dt 7:13; see also Hos 2:8. *like a well-watered garden.* See Isa 58:11 and note. *sorrow no more.* See note on Isa 25:8.
31:14 *abundance.* Either (1) a synonym for God's bounty (see Ps 36:8; 63:5; Isa 55:2) or (2) a reference to the special portions of the sacrificial animal reserved for the priests (see Lev 7:31–36).
31:15 Quoted in Mt 2:18, where Herod's orders to kill all the male infants "in Bethlehem and its vicinity" (Mt 2:16) are stated to be a fulfillment of this passage. *Ramah.* Located about five miles north of Jerusalem, it was one of the towns through which Jerusalem's people passed on their way to exile in Babylonia (see 40:1; cf. Isa 10:29; Hos 5:8). *Rachel.*

Jacob's favorite wife (see Ge 29:30) and the grandmother of Ephraim and Manasseh (see Ge 30:22–24; 48:1–2), the two most prominent and powerful tribes in the northern kingdom. The name is used here to personify that kingdom (see note on v. 2).
31:16 *for your work will be rewarded.* Echoed in 2Ch 15:7. Here the work is the bearing and raising of children.
31:17 *hope for your future.* See 29:11. *children will return.* Cf. Hos 11:10–11.
31:18–19 *Restore... return... strayed.* The same Hebrew root underlies all three words (see 8:4–5 and notes).
31:18 *like an unruly calf.* The same figure of speech is used in Hos 4:16; 10:11.
31:19 *beat my breast.* A gesture of mourning and grief (see Eze 21:12). Similar expressions are found in other ancient literature, such as the Babylonian *Descent of Ishtar,* verse 21; Homer, *Iliad,* 15.397–398; 16.125; *Odyssey,* 13.198–199. *ashamed and humiliated.* See Isa 45:16. *youth.* Early history (see 2:2; 3:24–25; 22:21; 32:30; Isa 54:4; Eze 16:22).
31:20 *child in whom I delight.* Cf. Isa 5:7. *Though... I have great compassion for him.* See Hos 11:1–4,8–9. *my heart yearns.* See Isa 16:11.
31:21 The departing exiles are advised to set up markers along their path to exile so that in due time they will be able

Take note of the highway,[e]
the road that you take.
Return,[f] O Virgin[g] Israel,
return to your towns.
[22]How long will you wander,[h]
O unfaithful[i] daughter?
The LORD will create a new thing[j] on
earth—
a woman will surround[ik] a man."

[23]This is what the LORD Almighty, the
God of Israel, says: "When I bring them
back from captivity,[jl] the people in the
land of Judah and in its towns will once
again use these words: 'The LORD bless[m]
you, O righteous dwelling,[n] O sacred
mountain.'[o] [24]People will live[p] together
in Judah and all its towns—farmers and
those who move about with their flocks.[q]
[25]I will refresh the weary[r] and satisfy the
faint."[s]

[26]At this I awoke[t] and looked around.
My sleep had been pleasant to me.

[27]"The days are coming,"[u] declares the
LORD, "when I will plant[v] the house of
Israel and the house of Judah with the offspring of men and of animals. [28]Just as I
watched[w] over them to uproot[x] and tear
down, and to overthrow, destroy and bring
disaster,[y] so I will watch over them to
build and to plant,"[z] declares the LORD.

[29]"In those days people will no longer say,

'The fathers[a] have eaten sour grapes,
and the children's teeth are set on
edge.'[b]

[30]Instead, everyone will die for his own
sin;[c] whoever eats sour grapes—his own
teeth will be set on edge.

[31]"The time is coming," declares the
LORD,
"when I will make a new covenant[d]
with the house of Israel
and with the house of Judah.
[32]It will not be like the covenant[e]
I made with their forefathers[f]
when I took them by the hand
to lead them out of Egypt,[g]
because they broke my covenant,
though I was a husband[h] to[k]
them,[l]"
declares the LORD.
[33]"This is the covenant I will make with
the house of Israel
after that time," declares the LORD.

31:21 [e]Isa 35:8;
Jer 50:5
[f]Isa 52:11;
S Jer 3:12 [g]ver 4
31:22 [h]S Jer 2:23
[i]S Jer 3:6
[j]Isa 43:19
[k]S Dt 32:10
31:23
[l]S Jer 30:18
[m]S Ge 28:3;
S Nu 6:24
[n]S Isa 1:26
[o]S Ps 48:1;
S Isa 2:2
31:24
[p]S Jer 30:18;
Zec 8:4-8 [q]S ver
12
31:25
[r]S Isa 40:29
[s]Jn 4:14
31:26 [t]Zec 4:1
31:27
[u]S Jer 16:14
[v]Hos 2:23
31:28
[w]S Job 29:2
[x]S Dt 29:28
[y]S Jer 18:8
[z]S Dt 28:63;
S 30:9; S Jer 1:10;
Eze 36:10-11;
Am 9:14

31:29
[a]S Ge 9:25;
Dt 24:16; La 5:7
[b]Eze 18:2
31:30
[c]S 2Ki 14:6;
S Isa 3:11; Gal 6:7
31:31
[d]S Dt 29:14;
S Isa 42:6;
S 54:10;
S Lk 22:20;
Heb 8:8-12*;

10:16-17 **31:32** [e]S Ex 24:8 /Dt 5:3 [g]Jer 11:4 [h]S Isa 54:5

[i]22 Or will go about seeking,[j] or will protect   [j]23 Or
I restore their fortunes   [k]32 Hebrew; Septuagint and
Syriac / and I turned away from   [l]32 Or was their
master

to find their way back to Judah. *road signs.* Tombstone-
shaped markers (see 2Ki 23:17; Eze 39:15). *Virgin Israel.*
See v. 4; see also 14:17 and note.
31:22 *unfaithful daughter.* The people of Judah are apostate (see 3:14,22). *create a new thing.* See Isa 42:9 and note.
surround. Embrace with tender and unfailing love (see Ps
32:7,10; see also Ps 26:6). Judah would someday return to
the Lord and love him without reservation.
31:23 *bring . . . back from captivity.* See note on 29:14.
The LORD bless you. See Ps 128:5; 134:3. *righteous dwelling.* Jerusalem (cf. Isa 1:21,26). *sacred mountain.* The temple hill (see Ps 2:6; 48:1-2; Isa 2:2-3; 11:9; 27:13; 66:20).
31:26 *I awoke.* Jeremiah had evidently received the previous divine revelation (beginning in 30:3) in a dream (for
similar examples see Da 10:9; Zec 4:1). *sleep . . . pleasant.*
See Pr 3:24.
31:27 *plant . . . offspring.* See Eze 36:8-11. The same
Hebrew root underlies both words. *Israel and . . . Judah.*
North and south would again be united (see 3:18 and note.)
31:28 *watched . . . watch.* See note on 1:12. *uproot . . .
tear down . . . overthrow, destroy . . . build . . . plant.* See
note on 1:10.
31:29 *The fathers . . . set on edge.* Repeated in Eze 18:2.
This was apparently a popular proverb that originated in a
misunderstanding of such passages as Ex 20:5 and Nu
14:18, which teach that a man's sins can have a negative
effect on his descendants. In the time of Jeremiah and Ezekiel, many people felt that God's hand of judgment against
them was due not to their own sins, but to the sins of their
ancestors.
31:30 *everyone will die for his own sin.* See Dt 24:16; Eze
18:3,20; 33:7-18. Although great or collective responsibility is an important concept, Jeremiah and Ezekiel emphasize
individual responsibility as both preparation and explanation

for the imminent destruction of Jerusalem, which the people
might have been tempted to blame on the sins of their
forefathers.
31:31-34 The high point of Jeremiah's prophecies, this
passage is the longest sequence of OT verses to be quoted in
its entirety in the NT (see note on Heb 8:8-12; see also Heb
10:16-17). Verse 31 contains the only OT use of the phrase
"new covenant," which (together with its NT echoes) has
come down to us (via Latin) as "new testament," the name
that would later be applied to the distinctively Christian part
of the Biblical canon.
31:31 *The time is coming.* Lit. "The days are coming" (as
in vv. 27,38), a phrase that often refers to the Messianic era.
make. Lit. "cut" (see notes on 34:18; Ge 15:18). *new
covenant.* See note on vv. 31-34; see also 1Co 11:25; 2Co
3:6; Heb 9:15; 12:24; and NIV text notes on Mt 26:28; Mk
14:24). As the old covenant was solemnized by the blood of
sacrificial animals, so the new would be solemnized by the
blood of Christ. *house of Israel . . . house of Judah.* The
reunited people of God (see 3:18 and note).
31:32 *covenant I made with their forefathers.* See 7:23;
11:1-8; Ex 19:5; 20:22-23:19 and notes. The covenant at
Sinai eventually became known as the "old covenant" (2Co
3:14) or "first covenant" (Heb 8:7; 9:15,18). *took them by
the hand.* See Hos 11:3-4. *they broke my covenant.* See
11:10. The people, not God, were responsible for violating
his covenant (see note on Isa 24:5). *I was a husband.* See
3:14 and note.
31:33 *house of Israel.* Here includes both Israel and Judah
(see v. 31 and note on 3:18). *put my law in their minds.*
Internally (see Dt 6:6; 11:18; 30:14; Eze 11:19; 18:31;
36:26-27), in contrast to setting it before them externally
(see 9:13; Dt 4:8; 11:32). *write it on their hearts.* So that it
effectively governs their lives, in contrast to the ineffective-

"I will put my law in their minds[i]
and write it on their hearts.[j]
I will be their God,
and they will be my people.[k]
[34]No longer will a man teach[l] his
neighbor,
or a man his brother, saying, 'Know
the LORD,'
because they will all know[m] me,
from the least of them to the
greatest,"
declares the LORD.
"For I will forgive[n] their wickedness
and will remember their sins[o] no
more."

[35]This is what the LORD says,

he who appoints[p] the sun
to shine by day,
who decrees the moon and stars
to shine by night,[q]
who stirs up the sea[r]
so that its waves roar[s] —
the LORD Almighty is his name:[t]
[36]"Only if these decrees[u] vanish from my
sight,"
declares the LORD,
"will the descendants[v] of Israel ever
cease
to be a nation before me."

[37]This is what the LORD says:

"Only if the heavens above can be
measured[w]
and the foundations of the earth
below be searched out

will I reject[x] all the descendants of
Israel
because of all they have done,"
declares the LORD.

[38]"The days are coming," declares the
LORD, "when this city will be rebuilt[y] for
me from the Tower of Hananel[z] to the
Corner Gate.[a] [39]The measuring line[b] will
stretch from there straight to the hill of
Gareb and then turn to Goah. [40]The whole
valley[c] where dead bodies[d] and ashes are
thrown, and all the terraces out to the Kidron Valley[e] on the east as far as the corner of the Horse Gate,[f] will be holy[g] to
the LORD. The city will never again be
uprooted or demolished."

Jeremiah Buys a Field

32 This is the word that came to Jeremiah from the LORD in the tenth[h]
year of Zedekiah king of Judah, which was
the eighteenth[i] year of Nebuchadnezzar.
[2]The army of the king of Babylon was then
besieging[j] Jerusalem, and Jeremiah the
prophet was confined[k] in the courtyard of
the guard[l] in the royal palace of Judah.

[3]Now Zedekiah king of Judah had imprisoned him there, saying, "Why do you
prophesy[m] as you do? You say, 'This is
what the LORD says: I am about to hand
this city over to the king of Babylon, and
he will capture[n] it. [4]Zedekiah[o] king of
Judah will not escape[p] out of the hands of
the Babylonians[m][q] but will certainly be

Cross references (center column):

31:33 /S Ex 4:15
/S Dt 6:6;
S 2Co 3:3
kS Jer 11:4;
Heb 10:16
31:34 /I Jn 2:27
mS Isa 11:9;
S Jn 6:45
nPs 85:2; 130:4;
Jer 33:8; 50:20
oS Job 7:21;
S Isa 38:17;
Mic 7:19;
Heb 10:17*
31:35
pPs 136:7-9
qS Ge 1:16
rS Ex 14:21
sS Ps 93:3
tS Jer 10:16
31:36
uS Job 38:33;
Jer 33:20-26
vPs 89:36-37
31:37
wS Job 38:5;
Jer 33:22

xJer 33:24-26;
Ro 11:1-5
31:38
yS Jer 30:18
zS Ne 3:1
aS 2Ki 14:13;
S 2Ch 25:23
31:39
bS 1Ki 7:23
31:40
cS Jer 2:23;
7:31-32
dS Jer 8:2
eS 2Sa 15:23;
Jn 18:1
/S 2Ki 11:16
gS Isa 4:3;
Joel 3:17;
Zec 14:21
32:1 h2Ki 25:1
/Jer 25:1
32:2 /S 2Ki 25:1
kS Ps 88:8
/S Ne 3:25
32:3 mJer 26:8-9
nver 28; Jer 21:4;
34:2-3
32:4 oJer 34:21;
44:30
pS Jer 21:7;
38:18,23; 39:5-7;

52:9 qver 24

m4 Or *Chaldeans;* also in verses 5, 24, 25, 28, 29 and 43

Bottom notes:

ness of merely presenting it in writing, though inscribed on
durable stone (see Ex 24:4; 31:18; 32:15–16; 34:28–29;
Dt 4:13; 5:22; 9:9,11; 10:4). *I will be . . . my people.* See
note on 7:23. The "new" covenant does not abolish the
"old" but supersedes it in the sense that through the new
covenant the old is fulfilled and its purpose achieved.

31:34 *No longer . . . teach his neighbor.* When the Lord
has done his new work, there will no longer be among his
people those who are ignorant of him and his will for human
lives. True knowledge of the Lord will be shared by
all—young and old, the peasant and the powerful (see 5:4–5
and notes; see also 32:38–40; Isa 54:13 and note; Eze
11:19–20; 36:25–27; Eph 3:12; Heb 4:16; 10:19–22).
Know. In the experiential, not the academic, sense (see Ex
6:3 and note). *I will forgive . . . their sins.* The glorious basis
of the new covenant (see Heb 10:14–17).

31:35 *appoints the sun . . . moon . . . stars.* See Ge
1:16–18 and notes. *who stirs up . . . is his name.* The same
line is found in Isa 51:15 (see Ps 46:3; Isa 17:12).

31:36 See 33:20–21,25–26. Just as God's creation order is
established and secure, so also Israel will always have descendants.

31:37 *reject all.* Israel will continue to exist, even though
a terrible judgment is about to sweep the kingdom of Judah
away.

31:38–40 See Zec 14:10–11.
31:38 *this city.* Jerusalem. *Tower of Hananel . . . Corner
Gate.* The eastern and western ends of the northern wall (see
note on Zec 14:10).
31:39 *measuring line.* Mentioned in connection with restored Jerusalem also in Eze 40:3; Zec 1:16; 2:1. *Gareb . . .
Goah.* Exact locations unknown, but probably to the west of
Jerusalem.
31:40 *valley.* Probably the Hinnom Valley (see 2:23 and
note). *Horse Gate.* See note on Ne 3:28. *holy to the LORD.*
See Zec 14:20 and note. *uprooted . . . demolished.* See note
on 1:10.
32:1–44 Though with some reluctance (see v. 25), Jeremiah obeys the Lord's command to buy a field in Anathoth
from his cousin (see vv. 8–9) even as the Babylonians are
besieging Jerusalem (see vv. 2,24).
32:1 *tenth year of Zedekiah . . . eighteenth year of Nebuchadnezzar.* 587 B.C., the year before Jerusalem was destroyed by the Babylonians (see 52:12–13). The siege began
in 588 (see 39:1; 52:4).
32:2 *confined in the courtyard of the guard.* See Ne 3:25
and note. Jeremiah was imprisoned by King Zedekiah (see
37:21) and remained in the courtyard of the guard until
Jerusalem fell (see 38:13,28; 39:14).
32:3–5 See 21:3–7; 34:2–5; 37:17. The fulfillment is
recorded in 52:7–14.

handed over to the king of Babylon, and will speak with him face to face and see him with his own eyes. ⁵He will take ʳ Zedekiah to Babylon, where he will remain until I deal with him, ˢ declares the LORD. If you fight against the Babylonians, you will not succeed.' " ᵗ

⁶Jeremiah said, "The word of the LORD came to me: ⁷Hanamel son of Shallum your uncle is going to come to you and say, 'Buy my field at Anathoth, ᵘ because as nearest relative it is your right and duty ᵛ to buy it.'

⁸"Then, just as the LORD had said, my cousin Hanamel came to me in the courtyard of the guard and said, 'Buy my field ʷ at Anathoth in the territory of Benjamin. Since it is your right to redeem it and possess it, buy it for yourself.'

"I knew that this was the word of the LORD; ⁹so I bought the field ˣ at Anathoth from my cousin Hanamel and weighed out for him seventeen shekelsⁿ of silver. ʸ 10I signed and sealed the deed, ᶻ had it witnessed, ᵃ and weighed out the silver on the scales. ¹¹I took the deed of purchase—the sealed copy containing the terms and conditions, as well as the unsealed copy— ¹²and I gave this deed to Baruch ᵇ son of Neriah, ᶜ the son of Mahseiah, in the presence of my cousin Hanamel and of the witnesses who had signed the deed and of all the Jews sitting in the courtyard of the guard.

¹³"In their presence I gave Baruch these instructions: ¹⁴'This is what the LORD Almighty, the God of Israel, says: Take these documents, both the sealed ᵈ and unsealed copies of the deed of purchase, and put them in a clay jar so they will last a long time. ¹⁵For this is what the LORD Almighty, the God of Israel, says: Houses, fields and vineyards will again be bought in this land.' ᵉ

¹⁶"After I had given the deed of purchase to Baruch ᶠ son of Neriah, I prayed to the LORD:

¹⁷"Ah, Sovereign LORD, ᵍ you have made the heavens and the earth ʰ by your great power and outstretched arm. ⁱ Nothing is too hard ʲ for you. ¹⁸You show love ᵏ to thousands but bring the punishment for the fathers' sins into the laps ˡ of their children ᵐ after them. O great and powerful God, ⁿ whose name is the LORD Almighty, ᵒ ¹⁹great are your purposes and mighty are your deeds. ᵖ Your eyes are open to all the ways of men; ᑫ you reward everyone according to his conduct and as his deeds deserve. ʳ ²⁰You performed miraculous signs and wonders ˢ in Egypt ᵗ and have continued them to this day, both in Israel and among all mankind, and have gained the renown ᵘ that is still yours.

32:5 ʳJer 39:7; Eze 12:13
ˢS 2Ki 25:7
ᵗJer 21:4; La 1:14
32:7 ᵘS Jos 21:18
ᵛLev 25:24-25; S Ru 4:3-4; Mt 27:10*
32:8 ʷver 25
32:9 ˣJer 37:12
ʸS Ge 23:16
32:10 ᶻGe 23:20
ᵃS Ru 4:9; S Isa 8:2
32:12 ᵇver 16; Jer 36:4; 43:3,6; 45:1 ᶜJer 51:59
32:14 ᵈS Isa 8:16
32:15 ᵉver 43-44; Isa 44:26; Jer 30:18; Eze 28:26; Am 9:14-15
32:16 ᶠS ver 12
32:17 ᵍJer 1:6 ʰS Ge 1:1; S Jer 10:16 ⁱS Dt 9:29; 2Ki 19:15; Ps 102:25 ʲS 2Ki 3:18; Jer 51:15; S Mt 19:26
32:18 ᵏS Dt 5:10 ˡS Ps 79:12 ᵐS Ex 20:5; S Ps 109:14 ⁿJer 10:6 ᵒS Jer 10:16
32:19 ᵖS Job 12:13; Da 2:20 ᑫS Job 14:16; S Pr 5:21; Jer 16:17 ʳS Job 34:11; S Mt 16:27
32:20 ˢS Ex 3:20; S Job 9:10 ᵗEx 9:16 ᵘS Isa 55:13; S Jer 13:11

ⁿ9 That is, about 7 ounces (about 200 grams)

32:5 *until I deal with him.* After his capture by the Babylonians, Zedekiah was taken to Babylon, where he eventually died (see 52:11). *you will not succeed.* See note on 29:4.

32:7 *Anathoth.* Jeremiah's hometown (see note on 1:1). *as nearest relative . . . duty to buy it.* In accordance with the ancient law of redemption (see Lev 25:23–25; see also notes on Ru 2:20; 4:3).

32:8 *came to me in the courtyard.* Though imprisoned, Jeremiah was allowed to have visitors. *in the territory of Benjamin.* Some time earlier, Jeremiah had been on his way home "to get his share of the property" in Benjamin (37:12), but he was arrested, falsely accused of treason, and thrown into prison (see 37:13–16).

32:9 *so I bought.* In obedience to the Lord's command (see v. 7). *weighed out.* Coinage had not yet been invented. *seventeen shekels of silver.* See NIV text note. The size of the field is unknown, but the price was probably not exorbitant (contrast Ge 23:15; see note there).

32:10 *sealed.* Not to attest his signature (as, e.g., in Est 3:12; see note on Ge 38:18) but to guarantee the contents of the deed and keep it from being tampered with (see Isa 8:16; 29:11; Da 12:4,9; Rev 15:1–5).

32:11 *unsealed copy.* For ready reference, the authenticity of which would then be guaranteed by the sealed copy if the unsealed deed should be lost, damaged or changed (deliberately or otherwise). Examples of tied and sealed papyrus documents of the fifth and subsequent centuries B.C. have been found at Elephantine in southern Egypt, in the desert of

Judah west of the Dead Sea, and elsewhere (see chart on "Ancient Texts Relating to the OT," p. 5).

32:12 *Baruch.* Means "blessed (by the Lord)." He was Jeremiah's faithful secretary and friend (see Introduction: Author and Date).

32:14 *put them in a clay jar so they will last a long time.* Documents found in clay jars at Elephantine (see note on v. 11) and Qumran (west of the Dead Sea) were preserved almost intact for more than 2,000 years (see "The Time between the Testaments," p. 1431).

32:15 Jeremiah's deed of purchase would enable him (or his heirs) to reclaim the field as soon as normal economic activity resumed after the exile.

32:17 See 27:5. *great power and outstretched arm.* See v. 21; see also note on 21:5. *Nothing is too hard for you.* See note on Ge 18:14. The Lord's reply to Jeremiah echoes these words (see v. 27).

32:18 *show love to thousands but . . . punishment for the fathers' sins.* See Ex 20:5–6; 34:7; see also note on Ex 20:6. *bring . . . into the laps.* A symbol of retribution (see Ps 79:12; Isa 65:6–7; cf. Lk 6:38). *great and powerful God.* See Dt 10:17. *whose name is the LORD Almighty.* See 31:35; Isa 54:5; Am 4:13.

32:19 *great are your purposes and . . . deeds.* See Ps 66:5; Isa 9:6; 28:29. *you reward everyone . . . as his deeds deserve.* Repeated verbatim from 17:10 (see note there; see also 1Co 3:8; Eph 6:8).

32:20 *miraculous signs and wonders.* See v. 21; Ex 7:3; see also notes on Ex 3:12; 4:8. *to this day.* See 11:7.

21You brought your people Israel out
of Egypt with signs and wonders, by a
mighty hand[v] and an outstretched
arm[w] and with great terror.[x] 22You
gave them this land you had sworn to
give their forefathers, a land flowing
with milk and honey.[y] 23They came
in and took possession[z] of it, but they
did not obey you or follow your law;[a]
they did not do what you commanded
them to do. So you brought all this
disaster[b] upon them.
24"See how the siege ramps[c] are
built up to take the city. Because of
the sword, famine and plague,[d] the
city will be handed over to the Babylonians who are attacking it. What you
said[e] has happened,[f] as you now see.
25And though the city will be handed
over to the Babylonians, you, O Sovereign LORD, say to me, 'Buy the field[g]
with silver and have the transaction
witnessed.[h]' "

26Then the word of the LORD came to
Jeremiah: 27"I am the LORD, the God of all
mankind.[i] Is anything too hard for me?[j]
28Therefore, this is what the LORD says: I
am about to hand this city over to the Babylonians and to Nebuchadnezzar[k] king of
Babylon, who will capture it.[l] 29The Babylonians who are attacking this city will
come in and set it on fire; they will burn it
down,[m] along with the houses[n] where the
people provoked me to anger by burning
incense on the roofs to Baal and by pouring
out drink offerings[o] to other gods.[p]
30"The people of Israel and Judah have
done nothing but evil in my sight from
their youth;[q] indeed, the people of Israel
have done nothing but provoke[r] me with
what their hands have made,[s] declares the
LORD. 31From the day it was built until
now, this city[t] has so aroused my anger
and wrath that I must remove[u] it from my
sight. 32The people of Israel and Judah
have provoked[v] me by all the evil[w] they
have done—they, their kings and officials,[x] their priests and prophets, the men
of Judah and the people of Jerusalem.
33They turned their backs[y] to me and not
their faces; though I taught[z] them again
and again, they would not listen or respond to discipline.[a] 34They set up their
abominable idols[b] in the house that bears
my Name[c] and defiled[d] it. 35They built
high places for Baal in the Valley of Ben
Hinnom[e] to sacrifice their sons and
daughters[°] to Molech,[f] though I never
commanded, nor did it enter my mind,[g]
that they should do such a detestable[h]
thing and so make Judah sin.[i]
36"You are saying about this city, 'By the
sword, famine and plague[j] it will be handed over to the king of Babylon'; but this is
what the LORD, the God of Israel, says: 37I
will surely gather[k] them from all the lands
where I banish them in my furious anger[l]
and great wrath; I will bring them back to
this place and let them live in safety.[m]
38They will be my people,[n] and I will be
their God. 39I will give them singleness[o] of
heart and action, so that they will always
fear[p] me for their own good and the good
of their children after them. 40I will make

32:21 [v]S Ex 6:6; Da 9:15 [w]S Dt 5:15; S Jer 6:12 [x]S Dt 26:8 **32:22** [y]S Ex 3:8; Eze 20:6 **32:23** [z]S Ps 44:2; 78:54-55 [a]S Ex 16:28; S Jos 1:7; S 1Ki 9:6; S Jer 11:8 [b]S Dt 28:64; 31:29; Da 9:14 **32:24** [c]S 2Sa 20:15; S Jer 6:6 [d]S Jer 14:12 [e]Dt 4:25-26; Jos 23:15-16 [f]S Dt 28:2 **32:25** [g]S ver 8 [h]S Isa 8:2 **32:27** [i]S Nu 16:22 [j]S Ge 18:14; S 2Ki 3:18 **32:28** [k]S 2Ch 36:17 [l]S ver 3; S Jer 21:10 **32:29** [m]S 2Ch 36:19 [n]S Jer 19:13 [o]Jer 44:18 [p]S Jer 7:9 **32:30** [q]S Ps 25:7; S Jer 22:21 [r]Jer 8:19 [s]Jer 25:7 **32:31** [t]1Ki 11:7-8; 2Ki 21:4-5; Mt 23:37 [u]S 2Ki 23:27 **32:32** [v]S 1Ki 14:9 [w]Da 9:8 [x]S Jer 2:26; S 44:9 **32:33** [y]S 1Ki 14:9; S Ps 14:3; Jer 2:27; Eze 8:16; Zec 7:11 [z]S Dt 4:5; S Isa 28:9; S Jer 7:13 [a]S Jer 7:28 **32:34** [b]S 2Ki 21:4; Eze 8:3-16 [c]Jer 7:10; 34:15 [d]S Jer 7:30 **32:35** [e]Jer 19:2 [f]S Lev 18:21 [g]S Jer 19:5 [h]S 1Ki 14:24 [i]S Jer 25:7 **32:36** [j]ver 24 **32:37** [k]S Isa 11:12 [l]Jer 21:5 [m]S Lev 25:18; Eze 34:28; 39:26 **32:38** [n]Jer 24:7; 2Co 6:16* **32:39** [o]S 2Ch 30:12; S Ps 86:11; Jn 17:21; Ac 4:32 [p]S Dt 6:24; S 10:16

°*35* Or *to make their sons and daughters pass through the fire*

32:21 Repeated almost verbatim from Dt 26:8 (see Dt 4:34). *mighty hand . . . outstretched arm.* See v. 17 and note on 21:5. *great terror.* See Ex 15:14–16.
32:22 *land flowing with milk and honey.* See 11:5; see also note on Ex 3:8.
32:24 *siege ramps.* See 6:6; 33:4; see also note on Isa 37:33. *sword, famine and plague.* See note on 14:12.
32:25 Jeremiah expresses his doubts concerning what must seem to him to be an unwise investment. Nevertheless, he remains the obedient servant (see vv. 8–9).
32:27 *the LORD, the God of all mankind.* Echoes Nu 16:22; 27:16, emphasizing God's universal dominion. *Is anything too hard for me?* Responds to the description in Jeremiah's prayer (see v. 17 and note on Ge 18:14), stressing God's omnipotence. God is worthy of obedience because he is always faithful in fulfilling his promises.
32:29 *burn it down.* See 21:10; 34:2; 37:8. *provoked me to anger.* See 7:18; Dt 31:29. *burning incense . . . to Baal.* See 1:16 and note. *on the roofs.* See note on 19:13. *drink offerings to other gods.* See 7:18 and note; 19:13.
32:30 Echoes Dt 31:29. *youth.* See note on 31:19. *what their hands have made.* A reference to idols.
32:31 *remove it from my sight.* See 52:3; 2Ki 24:3.
32:32 *kings . . . officials . . . priests . . . prophets.* See 1:18 and note.
32:33 *again and again.* See note on 7:13. *not . . . respond to discipline.* See 2:30; 5:3; 7:28; 17:23.
32:34–35 Repeated from 7:30–31 (see notes there).
32:35 *Molech.* The god of the Ammonites (see 49:1,3; see also note on Lev 18:21).
32:36 *You.* The pronoun is plural, referring to the people of Judah as a whole. *sword, famine and plague.* See note on 14:12. *but.* After judgment on the wicked comes restoration for the righteous.
32:37 See Dt 30:1–5. *furious anger and great wrath.* See note on 21:5. *bring them back . . . let them live.* See Eze 36:11,33; Hos 11:11. The Hebrew underlying the first phrase sounds like that underlying the second.
32:38 See 31:33; see also note on 7:23.
32:39 *singleness of heart.* See 24:7; 31:32 and note; Eze 11:19. *their children after them.* See Dt 4:9–10.
32:40 *everlasting covenant.* See Isa 55:3 and note; Eze 16:60; 37:26. Unlike the old covenant (see 31:32; Isa 24:5), the new covenant would never be broken. *inspire*

an everlasting covenant^q with them: I will never stop doing good to them, and I will inspire^r them to fear me, so that they will never turn away from me.^s ⁴¹I will rejoice^t in doing them good^u and will assuredly plant^v them in this land with all my heart and soul.^w

⁴²"This is what the LORD says: As I have brought all this great calamity^x on this people, so I will give them all the prosperity I have promised^y them. ⁴³Once more fields will be bought^z in this land of which you say, 'It is a desolate^a waste, without men or animals, for it has been handed over to the Babylonians.' ⁴⁴Fields will be bought for silver, and deeds^b will be signed, sealed and witnessed^c in the territory of Benjamin, in the villages around Jerusalem, in the towns of Judah and in the towns of the hill country, of the western foothills and of the Negev,^d because I will restore^e their fortunes,^p declares the LORD."

Promise of Restoration

33 While Jeremiah was still confined^f in the courtyard^g of the guard, the word of the LORD came to him a second time:^h ²"This is what the LORD says, he who made the earth,ⁱ the LORD who formed it and established it—the LORD is his name:^j ³'Call^k to me and I will answer you and tell you great and unsearchable^l things you do not know.' ⁴For this is what the LORD, the God of Israel, says

about the houses in this city and the royal palaces of Judah that have been torn down to be used against the siege^m rampsⁿ and the sword ⁵in the fight with the Babylonians^q: 'They will be filled with the dead bodies of the men I will slay in my anger and wrath.^o I will hide my face^p from this city because of all its wickedness.

⁶" 'Nevertheless, I will bring health and healing to it; I will heal^q my people and will let them enjoy abundant peace^r and security. ⁷I will bring Judah^s and Israel back from captivity^{r t} and will rebuild^u them as they were before.^v ⁸I will cleanse^w them from all the sin they have committed against me and will forgive^x all their sins of rebellion against me. ⁹Then this city will bring me renown,^y joy, praise^z and honor^a before all nations on earth that hear of all the good things I do for it; and they will be in awe and will tremble^b at the abundant prosperity and peace I provide for it.'

¹⁰"This is what the LORD says: 'You say about this place, "It is a desolate waste, without men or animals."^c Yet in the towns of Judah and the streets of Jerusalem that are deserted,^d inhabited by neither men nor animals, there will be heard once more ¹¹the sounds of joy and gladness,^e

32:40
^qS Ge 9:16;
S Isa 42:6
^rS Dt 4:10
^sS Jer 24:7
32:41
^tS Dt 28:63;
S Isa 62:4
^uS Dt 28:3-12
^vJer 24:6; 31:28
^wMic 7:18
32:42 ^xLa 3:38
^yS Jer 29:10
32:43 ^zver 15
^aJer 33:12
32:44 ^bver 10
^cS Ru 4:9;
S Isa 8:2
^dS Jer 17:26
^eS Ezr 9:9;
Ps 14:7
33:1 ^fS Ps 88:8
^gJer 37:21; 38:28
^hJer 13:3
33:2 ⁱS Ps 136:6;
S Jer 10:16
^jS Ex 3:15
33:3 ^kS Isa 55:6
^lS Job 28:11

33:4
^mS 2Ki 25:1;
Eze 4:2
ⁿJer 32:24;
Eze 26:8;
Hab 1:10
33:5 ^oJer 21:4-7
^pS Dt 31:17;
S Isa 8:17
33:6
^qS Dt 32:39;
S Isa 30:26
^rS Isa 9:6
33:7 ^sJer 32:44
^tJer 30:3;
Eze 39:25;
Am 9:14
^uS Jer 24:6
^vS Isa 1:26
33:8
^wS Lev 16:30;
Heb 9:13-14
^xS 2Sa 24:14;
S Jer 31:34
33:9 ^yS Isa 55:13
^zS Isa 60:18

^aS Jer 3:17 ^bS Isa 64:2 **33:10** ^cJer 32:43 ^dS Lev 26:32;
S Jer 9:11 **33:11** ^eS Ps 51:8; S Isa 24:8; S 51:3

^p44 Or *will bring them back from captivity*   ^q5 Or *Chaldeans*   ^r7 Or *will restore the fortunes of Judah and Israel*

---

them to fear me. See Dt 6:24; see also note on Ge 20:11.
never turn away from me. See 26:3; Isa 53:6.
32:41 *rejoice in doing them good.* See Dt 30:9; Isa 62:5; 65:19.
32:43-44 *fields will be bought.* The field purchased by Jeremiah (see v. 9) is symbolic of the many fields that will be purchased in Judah after the Babylonian exile, when economic conditions return to normal (see note on v. 15).
32:43 *you.* See note on v. 36. *desolate waste, without men or animals.* See 4:23-26 and notes.
32:44 *territory of Benjamin.* See 1:1. Here Benjamin is mentioned first because it was the region in which Jeremiah's hometown was located (see vv. 7-8 and notes). *hill country . . . western foothills.* See note on Dt 1:7. *Negev.* See note on Ge 12:9. *restore their fortunes.* See note on 29:14.
33:1-26 Concluding Jeremiah's "book of consolation" (see note on 30:1-33:26), the section is divided into two roughly equal parts: (1) vv. 1-13, which continues and builds on ch. 32, and (2) vv. 14-26, which summarizes a wider range of earlier passages in Jeremiah and elsewhere —it is not found in the Septuagint (the Greek translation of the OT).
33:1 *still confined.* In 587 B.C. (see note on 32:1). *courtyard of the guard.* See 32:2 and note. *a second time.* Ch. 32 comprises the first time.
33:2 See 10:12; 32:17; 51:15; see also 31:35 and note.
33:3 *Call . . . and I will answer.* Man's prayer invites—and

assures—God's response (see Ps 3:4; 4:3; 18:6; 27:7; 28:1-2; 30:8; 55:17; Mt 7:7; contrast 11:14). *great and unsearchable.* The Hebrew for this phrase usually refers to the formidable cities of Canaan and is translated "large, with walls up to the sky" (Dt 1:28; see Nu 13:28; Dt 9:1; Jos 14:12). *unsearchable things you do not know.* The Hebrew (with the change of one letter) for this phrase echoes Isa 48:6: "hidden things unknown to you." As the rest of ch. 33 demonstrates, the Lord will first judge his people (vv. 4-5) and then restore them in ways that will be nothing short of incredible (vv. 6-26).
33:4 Jerusalem's houses—including those of the king—were torn down so that their stones could be used to repair the city's battered walls (see Isa 22:10 and note). *siege ramps.* To help the invaders bring up battering rams and scale Jerusalem's walls (see 6:6).
33:5 *fight with the Babylonians.* See 32:5. *dead bodies.* Of Jerusalem's defenders.
33:6 *health and healing.* See 30:17; contrast 8:22.
33:7 *bring . . . back from captivity.* See vv. 11,26; see also note on 29:14. *Judah and Israel.* See note on 3:18.
33:8 *forgive all their sins.* The basis of the institution of the new covenant (see 31:34 and note; see also 50:20; Eze 36:25-26).
33:9 *tremble at the abundant prosperity.* See Hos 3:5.
33:10 See 32:43 and note.
33:11 *joy and gladness . . . bride and bridegroom.* The glorious reversal of the judgment proclaimed in 7:34; 16:9;

the voices of bride and bridegroom, and the voices of those who bring thank offerings[f] to the house of the LORD, saying,

"Give thanks to the LORD Almighty,
    for the LORD is good;[g]
    his love endures forever."[h]

For I will restore the fortunes[i] of the land as they were before,[j] says the LORD.

12"This is what the LORD Almighty says: 'In this place, desolate[k] and without men or animals[l]—in all its towns there will again be pastures for shepherds to rest their flocks.[m] 13In the towns of the hill[n] country, of the western foothills and of the Negev,[o] in the territory of Benjamin, in the villages around Jerusalem and in the towns of Judah, flocks will again pass under the hand[p] of the one who counts them,' says the LORD.

14" 'The days are coming,' declares the LORD, 'when I will fulfill the gracious promise[q] I made to the house of Israel and to the house of Judah.

15" 'In those days and at that time
    I will make a righteous[r] Branch[s]
        sprout from David's line;[t]
    he will do what is just and right in
        the land.
16In those days Judah will be saved[u]
    and Jerusalem will live in safety.[v]
This is the name by which it[s] will be
        called:[w]
    The LORD Our Righteousness.'[x]

17For this is what the LORD says: 'David will never fail[y] to have a man to sit on the throne of the house of Israel, 18nor will the priests,[z] who are Levites,[a] ever fail to have a man to stand before me continually to offer burnt offerings, to burn grain offerings and to present sacrifices.[b] ' "

19The word of the LORD came to Jeremiah: 20"This is what the LORD says: 'If you can break my covenant with the day[c] and my covenant with the night, so that day and night no longer come at their appointed time,[d] 21then my covenant[e] with David my servant—and my covenant with the Levites[f] who are priests ministering before me—can be broken and David will no longer have a descendant to reign on his throne.[g] 22I will make the descendants of David my servant and the Levites who minister before me as countless[h] as the stars of the sky and as measureless as the sand on the seashore.' "

23The word of the LORD came to Jeremiah: 24"Have you not noticed that these people are saying, 'The LORD has rejected the two kingdoms[i] he chose'? So they despise[j] my people and no longer regard them as a nation.[k] 25This is what the LORD says: 'If I have not established my covenant with day and night[l] and the fixed laws[m] of heaven and earth,[n] 26then I will

---

Cross references (center column):

33:11 /S Lev 7:12; gS 2Ch 7:3; Ps 25:8; S 136:1; Na 1:7
hS 1Ch 16:34; 2Ch 5:13; Ps 100:4-5
/Ps 14:7
/S Isa 1:26
33:12 kJer 32:43
/ver 10
mS Isa 65:10; Jer 34:11-15
33:13 nS Jer 31:5
oS Jer 17:26; Ob 1:20
pS Lev 27:32
33:14 qDt 28:1-14; S Jos 23:15; S Jer 29:10
33:15 rS Ps 72:2 sS Isa 4:2 tS 2Sa 7:12
33:16 uS Isa 45:17 vS Jer 17:25; S 32:37 wIsa 59:14; Jer 3:17; Eze 48:35; Zep 3:13; Zec 8:3, 16 xS 1Co 1:30
33:17 yS 2Sa 7:13; S 2Ch 7:18; Ps 89:29-37; S Lk 1:33
33:18 zS Nu 25:11-13; Heb 7:17-22 aS Dt 18:1 bHeb 13:15
33:20 cPs 89:36 dS Ge 1:14
33:21 ePs 89:34 /S Dt 18:1 gS 2Sa 7:13; S 2Ch 7:18
33:22 hS Ge 12:2; S Jer 30:19; Hos 1:10
33:24 /Eze 37:22 /S Ne 4:4 kS Jer 30:17; Eze 36:20 33:25 /S Ge 1:18 mS Ps 148:6 nPs 74:16-17

s16 Or he   t24 Or families

Study notes (bottom):

25:10. those who bring thank offerings. See note on 17:26.
restore the fortunes. See note on 29:14.
33:13 hill country . . . towns of Judah. See 17:26 and note; 32:44. flocks . . . pass under the hand . . . counts them. See Eze 20:37.
33:15–16 Repeated from 23:5–6 (see notes there).
33:16 it will be called. Because of Jerusalem's intimate relationship to the Messiah, it is given the same name by which he is called in 23:6 (for other examples see Jdg 6:24; Eze 48:35). But see NIV text note.
33:17–26 In the face of the impending judgment in which the nation will be swept away and the promised land reduced to a desolate wasteland, all God's past covenants with his people appear to be rendered of no effect—his covenants with Israel, with David and with Phinehas (see chart on "Major Covenants in the OT," p. 19). This series of oracles, however, gives reassurance that the ancient covenants are not being repudiated, that they are as secure as God's covenant concerning the creation order, and that in the future restoration they will all yet be fulfilled.
33:17 See 2Sa 7:12–16; 1Ki 2:4; 8:25; 9:5; 2Ch 6:16; 7:18. This passage is fulfilled ultimately in Jesus (see Lk 1:32–33).
33:18 See Nu 25:13. The priestly covenant with the Levites, like the royal covenant with David, was not a private grant to the priestly family involving only that family and the Lord. It was rather an integral part of the Lord's dealings with his people in which Israel was assured of the ministry of a priesthood that was acceptable to the Lord and through

whose mediation they could enjoy communion with him. That ministry was and is being fulfilled by Jesus, who administers a higher and better priesthood (see Ps 110:4; Heb 5:6–10; 6:19–20; 7:11–25). priests, who are Levites. See Dt 17:9,18.
33:20 covenant with the day and . . . the night. See v. 25; 31:35–36. Although reference may be to God's sovereign establishment of the creation order in the beginning, more likely the covenant of Ge 9:8–17 (see Ge 8:22) is in view.
33:21 covenant with the Levites. See Mal 2:4.
33:22 In words that echo the covenant promises to the patriarchs (Abraham, Ge 22:17; Isaac, Ge 26:4; Jacob, Ge 32:12), the Lord assures the flourishing of the two mediatorial (royal and priestly) families and thus the continuation of this ministry in the spiritual commonwealth he has established with his people. This promise of a numerous progeny to both the royal and priestly families is no doubt fulfilled in that great throng who (will) reign with Christ (see Ro 5:17; 8:17; 1Co 6:3; 2Ti 2:12; Rev 3:21; 5:10; 20:5–6; 22:5; see also Mt 19:28; Lk 22:30) and who in Christ have been consecrated to be priests (see 1Pe 2:5,9; Rev 1:6; 5:10; 20:6; see also Isa 66:21; Ro 6:13; 12:1; 15:16; Eph 5:2; Php 4:18; Heb 13:15–16).
33:24 two kingdoms. Israel and Judah. But since the Hebrew uses a word here that commonly refers to families (see NIV text note), the reference may be to the two mediatorial (royal and priestly) families, or to the families of Jacob and David (see v. 26). he chose. See Am 3:2 and note.
33:25–26 See v. 20 and note.

reject[o] the descendants of Jacob[p] and David my servant and will not choose one of his sons to rule over the descendants of Abraham, Isaac and Jacob. For I will restore their fortunes[u][q] and have compassion[r] on them.' "

Warning to Zedekiah

34 While Nebuchadnezzar king of Babylon and all his army and all the kingdoms and peoples[s] in the empire he ruled were fighting against Jerusalem[t] and all its surrounding towns, this word came to Jeremiah from the LORD: 2"This is what the LORD, the God of Israel, says: Go to Zedekiah[u] king of Judah and tell him, 'This is what the LORD says: I am about to hand this city over to the king of Babylon, and he will burn it down.[v] 3You will not escape from his grasp but will surely be captured and handed over[w] to him. You will see the king of Babylon with your own eyes, and he will speak with you face to face. And you will go to Babylon.

4"'Yet hear the promise of the LORD, O Zedekiah king of Judah. This is what the LORD says concerning you: You will not die by the sword;[x] 5you will die peacefully. As people made a funeral fire[y] in honor of your fathers, the former kings who preceded you, so they will make a fire in your honor and lament, "Alas,[z] O master!" I myself make this promise, declares the LORD.' "

6Then Jeremiah the prophet told all this to Zedekiah king of Judah, in Jerusalem, 7while the army of the king of Babylon was fighting against Jerusalem and the other cities of Judah that were still holding out—Lachish[a] and Azekah.[b] These were the only fortified cities left in Judah.

Freedom for Slaves

8The word came to Jeremiah from the LORD after King Zedekiah had made a covenant with all the people[c] in Jerusalem to proclaim freedom[d] for the slaves. 9Everyone was to free his Hebrew slaves, both male and female; no one was to hold a fellow Jew in bondage.[e] 10So all the officials and people who entered into this covenant agreed that they would free their male and female slaves and no longer hold them in bondage. They agreed, and set them free. 11But afterward they changed their minds[f] and took back the slaves they had freed and enslaved them again.

12Then the word of the LORD came to Jeremiah: 13"This is what the LORD, the God of Israel, says: I made a covenant with your forefathers[g] when I brought them

Cross references (center column)

33:26
oS Lev 26:44
pS Isa 14:1 qver 7; Ps 14:7
rS Jer 30:18
34:1 sJer 27:7
t2Ki 25:1; Jer 39:1
34:2
uS 2Ch 36:11
vver 22; Jer 32:29; 37:8
34:3
wS 2Ki 25:7; S Jer 21:7
34:4 xJer 52:11
34:5
yS 2Ch 16:14

zJer 22:18
34:7 aS Jos 10:3
bJos 10:10; 2Ch 11:9
34:8 cS 2Ki 11:17
dS Ex 21:2; Lev 25:39-41; Ne 5:5-8
34:9
eDt 15:12-18
34:11 fPs 78:37
34:13 gS Ex 24:8

u26 Or *will bring them back from captivity*

33:26 *restore their fortunes and have compassion.* Echoes Dt 30:3; see note on 29:14.

34:1—35:19 The first major division of the book (chs. 2–35) now draws to a close. Jeremiah's warnings and exhortations to Judah are concluded with a historical appendix (chs. 34–35), a technique used to conclude the third major division of the book (chs. 39–45) as well (see note on 45:1–5). Ch. 52, written by someone other than Jeremiah, serves as a fitting historical appendix to the entire book.

34:1—22 The chapter divides naturally into two parts (vv. 1–7 and 8–22), each of which dates to 588 B.C. (see notes on vv. 7,21–22).

34:1—7 Jeremiah's warning to King Zedekiah parallels the prophet's similar admonition in 21:1–10 (see notes there).

34:1 *kingdoms and peoples in the empire he ruled.* Nebuchadnezzar's empire was vast (see Eze 26:7; Da 3:2–4; 4:1; cf. the similar description of the Medes in 51:28). *fighting against Jerusalem.* Subject nations were expected to supply troops to fight alongside those of their overlord (see 2Ki 24:2). In a 14th-century B.C. treaty between the Hittite ruler Mursilis II and Duppi-Tessub king of the Amorites, Mursilis says, "If you do not send your son or brother with your foot soldiers and charioteers to help the Hittite king, you act in disregard of the gods of the oath." *all its surrounding towns.* See 19:15 and note.

34:2—3 See 32:3–5 and note; see also 39:4–7; Eze 12:12–13; 17:11–20.

34:4 *not die by the sword.* See 32:5; 38:17,20; 52:11; Eze 17:16.

34:5 *funeral fire in honor of . . . the former kings.* Not cremation (see 2Ch 16:14; 21:19; see also note on Am 6:10). *Alas, O master!* Words of mourning at the death of a king (see 22:18; cf. 1Ki 13:30).

34:7 *Lachish and Azekah.* Solomon's son Rehoboam had fortified them (see 2Ch 11:5,9), but Lachish was later besieged (701 B.C.) during Hezekiah's reign by the Assyrian king Sennacherib (see 2Ch 32:9). A contemporary relief depicting Sennacherib's conquest states that he "sat on a throne and passed in review the plunder taken from Lachish." In 1935, 18 ostraca (broken pottery fragments used as writing material) were discovered at Lachish, nearly all of them in the ruins of the latest occupation level (588 B.C.) of the Israelite gate-tower. Ostracon 4, written to the commander at Lachish shortly after the events described here, ends as follows: "We are watching for the fire-signals of Lachish . . . for we cannot see Azekah." See note on 6:1.

34:8—22 Contemporary with the events of 37:4–12 (see note on vv. 21–22).

34:8 *proclaim freedom.* See Lev 25:10 and note. *freedom for the slaves.* In accordance with the general provisions of the law of Moses (see Ex 21:2–11 and notes; Lev 25:39–55; Dt 15:12–18).

34:9 *Hebrew.* See Ex 21:2; see also note on Ge 14:13. *no one . . . hold a fellow Jew in bondage.* See Lev 25:39, 42.

34:10 *They . . . set them free.* To gain God's blessing, and/or in the hope that the freed slaves would be more willing to help defend Jerusalem.

34:11 *afterward.* When the Babylonian siege was temporarily lifted due to Egyptian intervention (see vv. 21–22; 37:5,11). *took back the slaves they had freed.* In violation of Dt 15:12. *enslaved them.* Cf. 2Ch 28:10.

34:13 *land of slavery.* Lit. "house of slaves" (see Ex 13:3, 14; 20:2; Dt 5:6; 6:12; 8:14; 13:5; Jos 24:17; Jdg 6:8). The Israelites were to free their slaves because God had earlier freed the Israelites (see Dt 15:15).

out of Egypt, out of the land of slavery.[h] I said, [14]'Every seventh year each of you must free any fellow Hebrew who has sold himself to you. After he has served you six years, you must let him go free.'[v][i] Your fathers, however, did not listen to me or pay attention[j] to me. [15]Recently you repented and did what is right in my sight: Each of you proclaimed freedom to his countrymen.[k] You even made a covenant before me in the house that bears my Name.[l] [16]But now you have turned around[m] and profaned[n] my name; each of you has taken back the male and female slaves you had set free to go where they wished. You have forced them to become your slaves again.

[17]"Therefore, this is what the LORD says: You have not obeyed me; you have not proclaimed freedom for your fellow countrymen. So I now proclaim 'freedom' for you,[o] declares the LORD—'freedom' to fall by the sword, plague[p] and famine.[q] I will make you abhorrent to all the kingdoms of the earth.[r] [18]The men who have violated my covenant[s] and have not fulfilled the terms of the covenant they made before me, I will treat like the calf they cut in two and then walked between its pieces.[t] [19]The leaders of Judah and Jerusalem, the court officials,[u] the priests and all the people of the land who walked be-

tween the pieces of the calf, [20]I will hand over[v] to their enemies who seek their lives.[w] Their dead bodies will become food for the birds of the air and the beasts of the earth.[x]

[21]"I will hand Zedekiah[y] king of Judah and his officials[z] over to their enemies[a] who seek their lives, to the army of the king of Babylon,[b] which has withdrawn[c] from you. [22]I am going to give the order, declares the LORD, and I will bring them back to this city. They will fight against it, take[d] it and burn[e] it down. And I will lay waste[f] the towns of Judah so no one can live there.'"

The Recabites

35 This is the word that came to Jeremiah from the LORD during the reign of Jehoiakim[g] son of Josiah king of Judah: [2]"Go to the Recabite[h] family and invite them to come to one of the side rooms[i] of the house of the LORD and give them wine to drink."

[3]So I went to get Jaazaniah son of Jeremiah, the son of Habazziniah, and his brothers and all his sons—the whole family of the Recabites. [4]I brought them into the house of the LORD, into the room of the sons of Hanan son of Igdaliah the

Cross references

34:13
[h]S Dt 15:15
34:14 [i]S Ex 21:2
/2Ki 17:14;
S Jer 7:26
34:15 [k]ver 8
/S Jer 32:34
34:16
[m]Eze 3:20; 18:24
[n]S Lev 19:12
34:17 [o]S Mt 7:2;
Gal 6:7 [p]Jer 21:7
[q]S Jer 14:12
[r]Jer 15:4; S 24:9;
S 29:18
34:18
[s]S Jer 11:10
[t]S Ge 15:10
34:19
[u]S Jer 26:10;
Zep 3:3-4

34:20 [v]Jer 21:7;
Eze 16:27; 23:28
[w]S Jer 11:21
[x]S Dt 28:26
34:21 [y]S Jer 32:4
[z]2Ki 25:21;
Jer 39:6;
52:24-27
[a]S Jer 21:7
[b]S 2Ch 36:10
[c]Jer 37:5
34:22 [d]Jer 39:1-2
[e]S Ne 2:17;
Jer 38:18; 39:8;
Eze 23:47
/S Lev 26:32;
S Isa 1:7
35:1 [g]S 2Ch 36:5
35:2
[h]S 2Ki 10:15
/S 1Ki 6:5

[v]14 Deut. 15:12

34:14 *Every seventh year . . . let him go free.* A loose quotation of Dt 15:12.

34:15–16 *you repented . . . you have turned around.* The Hebrew for the two phrases is identical, providing an ironic play on words (see note on v. 18).

34:16 *you have . . . profaned my name.* By breaking the Lord's covenant, Zedekiah was a man whose word could not be trusted (see Eze 17:15,18). *go where they wished.* See Dt 21:14.

34:17 *sword, plague and famine.* See note on 14:12. *abhorrent to all the kingdoms of the earth.* See 15:4 and note.

34:18 *violated . . . walked.* The Hebrew root underlying both words is the same, again providing an ironic play on words (see note on vv. 15–16). *made . . . cut.* The Hebrew for the two words is identical. In ancient times, making a covenant involved a self-maledictory oath ("May thus and so be done to me if I do not keep this covenant"), which was often symbolized by cutting an animal in two and walking between the two halves (see Ge 15:18 and note). *between its pieces.* See note on Ge 15:17.

34:20 *food for the birds . . . of the earth.* See 7:33 and note.

34:21–22 Because of the arrival of the Egyptians on the scene, the Babylonians in 588 B.C. temporarily lifted the siege of Jerusalem (see note on v. 11).

34:21 *withdrawn from you.* See the hope expressed in 21:2.

34:22 *I will bring them back.* See 37:8.

35:1–19 The family of the Recabites, who obeyed their forefather's command, are an example and rebuke to the people of Judah, who have disobeyed the Lord (see v. 16).

The mention of "Babylonian and Aramean armies" (v. 11) dates the chapter to no earlier than the eighth year of King Jehoiakim, who began his reign in 609 B.C., whose capital city of Jerusalem was besieged in 605 (see Da 1:1 and note) by Nebuchadnezzar, and who rebelled against Nebuchadnezzar three or four years later—an unwise act that led to raids on his territory by Babylonians, Arameans and others (see 2Ki 24:1–2). (The raids are perhaps reflected in 12:7–13.)

35:1 *during the reign of Jehoiakim.* Chs. 35–36 (see 36:1) are a flashback to the reign of Jehoiakim (609–598 B.C.; see Introduction: Outline).

35:2 *Recabite family.* A nomadic tribal group related to the Kenites (see 1Ch 2:55), some of whom lived among or near the Israelites (see Jdg 1:16; 4:11; 1Sa 27:10) and were on friendly terms with them (see 1Sa 15:6; 30:26,29). *side rooms of the house of the LORD.* Used for storage and/or as living quarters (see 1Ki 6:5; 1Ch 28:12; 2Ch 31:11; Ne 13:4–5).

35:3 *Jaazaniah.* Means "The LORD hears." It was a common name in Jeremiah's time (see 40:8; Eze 8:11; 11:1) and appears on a stamp seal (discovered at Tell en-Nasbeh north of Jerusalem and dating c. 600 B.C.) as well as on one of the Lachish ostraca (see note on 34:7). *Jeremiah.* Not the prophet.

35:4 *sons.* Perhaps here in the sense of "disciples" (see Am 7:14 and note). *man of God.* A synonym for "prophet" (see 1Ki 12:22; see also note on 1Sa 9:9), emphasizing his relationship to the One who has called him. *Maaseiah.* Perhaps the man of the same name mentioned in 21:1; 29:25; 37:3. *doorkeeper.* One of three supervisors (see 52:24) over those who guarded the entrances to the temple (see 2Ki 12:9).

man of God.*j* It was next to the room of the officials, which was over that of Maaseiah son of Shallum*k* the doorkeeper.*l* [5]Then I set bowls full of wine and some cups before the men of the Recabite family and said to them, "Drink some wine."

[6]But they replied, "We do not drink wine, because our forefather Jonadab*m* son of Recab gave us this command: 'Neither you nor your descendants must ever drink wine.*n* [7]Also you must never build houses, sow seed or plant vineyards; you must never have any of these things, but must always live in tents.*o* Then you will live a long time in the land*p* where you are nomads.' [8]We have obeyed everything our forefather*q* Jonadab son of Recab commanded us. Neither we nor our wives nor our sons and daughters have ever drunk wine [9]or built houses to live in or had vineyards, fields or crops.*r* [10]We have lived in tents and have fully obeyed everything our forefather Jonadab commanded us. [11]But when Nebuchadnezzar king of Babylon invaded*s* this land, we said, 'Come, we must go to Jerusalem*t* to escape the Babylonian*w* and Aramean armies.' So we have remained in Jerusalem."

[12]Then the word of the LORD came to Jeremiah, saying: [13]"This is what the LORD Almighty, the God of Israel, says: Go and tell*u* the men of Judah and the people of Jerusalem, 'Will you not learn a lesson*v* and obey my words?' declares the LORD. [14]'Jonadab son of Recab ordered his sons not to drink wine and this command has been kept. To this day they do not drink wine, because they obey their forefather's command.*w* But I have spoken to you again and again,*x* yet you have not

obeyed*y* me. [15]Again and again I sent all my servants the prophets*z* to you. They said, "Each of you must turn*a* from your wicked ways and reform*b* your actions; do not follow other gods*c* to serve them. Then you will live in the land*d* I have given to you and your fathers." But you have not paid attention or listened*e* to me. [16]The descendants of Jonadab son of Recab have carried out the command their forefather*f* gave them, but these people have not obeyed me.'

[17]"Therefore, this is what the LORD God Almighty, the God of Israel, says: 'Listen! I am going to bring on Judah and on everyone living in Jerusalem every disaster*g* I pronounced against them. I spoke to them, but they did not listen;*h* I called to them, but they did not answer.' "*i*

[18]Then Jeremiah said to the family of the Recabites, "This is what the LORD Almighty, the God of Israel, says: 'You have obeyed the command of your forefather*j* Jonadab and have followed all his instructions and have done everything he ordered.' [19]Therefore, this is what the LORD Almighty, the God of Israel, says: 'Jonadab son of Recab will never fail*k* to have a man to serve*l* me.' "

Jehoiakim Burns Jeremiah's Scroll

36 In the fourth year of Jehoiakim*m* son of Josiah king of Judah, this word came to Jeremiah from the LORD: [2]"Take a scroll*n* and write on it all the words*o* I have spoken to you concerning Israel, Judah and all the other nations from the time I began speaking to you in the reign of Josiah*p* till now. [3]Perhaps*q* when

---

Cross reference column:

35:4 /S Dt 33:1
*k*1Ch 9:19
/S 2Ki 12:9;
S 23:4
35:6
*m*S 2Ki 10:15
*n*S Lev 10:9;
Nu 6:2-4;
S Lk 1:15
35:7 *o*Heb 11:9
*p*S Ex 20:12;
Eph 6:2-3
35:8 *q*Pr 1:8;
Col 3:20
35:9 *r*1Ti 6:6
35:11 *s*2Ki 24:1
*t*S Jos 10:20;
Jer 8:14
35:13 *u*Jer 11:6
*v*Jer 6:10; 32:33
35:14 *w*ver 6-10,
16 *x*S Jer 7:13

*y*Isa 30:9
35:15 *z*S Jer 7:25
*a*S 2Ki 17:13;
S Jer 26:3
*b*S Isa 1:16-17;
S 59:20; Jer 4:1;
18:11; Eze 14:6;
18:30 *c*S Ex 20:3
*d*S Dt 4:40;
Jer 25:5
*e*S Jer 6:10;
S 7:26; 44:4-5
35:16
/S Lev 20:9;
Mal 1:6
35:17
*g*S Jos 23:15;
S 1Ki 13:34;
Jer 21:4-7
*h*S Pr 1:24;
Ro 10:21
*i*Jer 7:13
35:18
/S Ge 31:35
35:19
*k*S Isa 48:19;
Jer 33:17
*l*Jer 15:19
36:1
*m*S 2Ch 36:5
36:2 *n*S ver 4;
S Ex 17:14;
S Ps 40:7;
Jer 30:2; Hab 2:2
*o*Eze 2:7 *p*Jer 1:2;
25:3
36:3 *q*ver 7;
Eze 12:3;
Am 5:15

*w*11 Or Chaldean

Footnotes:

35:5 *bowls.* Large vessels, from which smaller cups would be filled.

35:6 *We do not drink wine.* A permanent vow taken by the Recabites; cf. the Nazirites' temporary vow (see Nu 6:2-3, 20; Jdg 13:4-7). Malkijah son of Recab may have been a later renegade exception to the Recabite vow, since he was "ruler of the district of Beth Hakkerem" (Ne 3:14), which means "house of the vineyard." *Jonadab.* Spelled "Jehonadab" in 2Ki 10:15,23. Nearly 250 years before the days of Jeremiah, he helped King Jehu destroy Baal worship (at least temporarily) in the northern kingdom.

35:7 *must always live in tents.* Except during times of national emergency (see v. 11). *Then you will live a long time in the land.* An echo of Ex 20:12, where honoring one's parents is commanded.

35:8 *We have obeyed . . . Jonadab.* Contrast Judah's disobedience toward God (see v. 16).

35:11 See note on vv. 1-19.

35:13 *learn a lesson.* The Hebrew underlying this phrase is translated "respond(ed) to correction" in 2:30; 7:28 (see 5:3; 17:23 and note).

35:14-15 *again and again.* See note on 7:13.

35:15 See 25:4-5 and notes.

35:17 See 11:11.

35:19 *never fail to have a man to serve me.* See 33:18. Various traditions in the Jewish Mishnah claim that the Recabites were later given special duties to perform in connection with the Jerusalem temple built after the return from Babylonian exile.

36:1-38:28 Three chapters united by the common theme of Jeremiah's suffering and persecution.

36:1-32 An account of King Jehoiakim's attempt to destroy Jeremiah's written prophecies.

36:1 *fourth year of Jehoiakim.* 605 B.C.—a critical year in Judah's history (see notes on 25:1; 46:2).

36:2 *scroll.* See notes on 30:2; Ex 17:14. *write on it.* To preserve Jeremiah's messages for future generations. *all the words I have spoken to you.* This "earliest edition" of Jeremiah's prophecies may have included all or most of chs. 1-26; 46-51. *began speaking to you in the reign of Josiah.* See note on 1:2.

36:3 *Perhaps . . . then.* If the people repent, the Lord will relent (see 18:7-10 and note; 26:3).

the people of Judah hear[r] about every disaster I plan to inflict on them, each of them will turn[s] from his wicked way; then I will forgive[t] their wickedness and their sin."

[4]So Jeremiah called Baruch[u] son of Neriah,[v] and while Jeremiah dictated[w] all the words the LORD had spoken to him, Baruch wrote them on the scroll.[x] [5]Then Jeremiah told Baruch, "I am restricted; I cannot go to the LORD's temple. [6]So you go to the house of the LORD on a day of fasting[y] and read to the people from the scroll the words of the LORD that you wrote as I dictated.[z] Read them to all the people of Judah[a] who come in from their towns. [7]Perhaps they will bring their petition[b] before the LORD, and each will turn[c] from his wicked ways, for the anger[d] and wrath pronounced against this people by the LORD are great."

[8]Baruch son of Neriah did everything Jeremiah the prophet told him to do; at the LORD's temple he read the words of the LORD from the scroll. [9]In the ninth month[e] of the fifth year of Jehoiakim son of Josiah king of Judah, a time of fasting[f] before the LORD was proclaimed for all the people in Jerusalem and those who had come from the towns of Judah. [10]From the room of Gemariah[g] son of Shaphan[h] the secretary,[i] which was in the upper courtyard at the entrance of the New Gate[j] of the temple, Baruch read to all the people at the LORD's temple the words of Jeremiah from the scroll.

[11]When Micaiah son of Gemariah, the son of Shaphan, heard all the words of the LORD from the scroll, [12]he went down to the secretary's[k] room in the royal palace, where all the officials were sitting: Elishama the secretary, Delaiah son of Shemaiah,

Elnathan[l] son of Acbor, Gemariah son of Shaphan, Zedekiah son of Hananiah, and all the other officials. [m] [13]After Micaiah told them everything he had heard Baruch read to the people from the scroll, [14]all the officials sent Jehudi[n] son of Nethaniah, the son of Shelemiah, the son of Cushi, to say to Baruch, "Bring the scroll[o] from which you have read to the people and come." So Baruch son of Neriah went to them with the scroll in his hand. [15]They said to him, "Sit down, please, and read it to us."

So Baruch read it to them. [16]When they heard all these words, they looked at each other in fear[p] and said to Baruch, "We must report all these words to the king." [17]Then they asked Baruch, "Tell us, how did you come to write[q] all this? Did Jeremiah dictate it?"

[18]"Yes," Baruch replied, "he dictated[r] all these words to me, and I wrote them in ink on the scroll."

[19]Then the officials[s] said to Baruch, "You and Jeremiah, go and hide.[t] Don't let anyone know where you are."

[20]After they put the scroll in the room of Elishama the secretary, they went to the king in the courtyard and reported everything to him. [21]The king sent Jehudi[u] to get the scroll, and Jehudi brought it from the room of Elishama the secretary and read it to the king[v] and all the officials standing beside him. [22]It was the ninth month and the king was sitting in the winter apartment,[w] with a fire burning in the firepot in front of him. [23]Whenever Jehudi had read three or four columns of the scroll,[x] the king cut them off with a scribe's knife and threw them into the firepot, until the entire scroll was burned in the fire.[y] [24]The king and all his attendants who heard all these words showed no

---

36:3 [r]Isa 6:9; Mk 4:12
[s]S 2Ki 17:13; S Isa 44:22; S Jer 26:3; Ac 3:19
[t]S Jer 18:8
36:4 [u]S Jer 32:12
[v]Jer 51:59 [w]ver 18 [x]ver 2; Eze 2:9; Da 7:1; Zec 5:1
36:6 [y]ver 9
[z]2Ch 20:4
36:7 [b]Jer 37:20; 42:2 [c]S Jer 26:3
[d]S Dt 31:17
36:9 [e]ver 22
[f]S 2Ch 20:3
36:10 [g]ver 12, 25; Jer 29:3
[h]Jer 26:24
[i]Jer 52:25
[j]S Ge 23:10
36:12 [k]S 2Sa 8:17

36: [l]S Jer 26:22
[m]Jer 38:4
36:14 [n]ver 21
[o]ver 4
36:16 [p]S Ps 36:1
36:17 [q]Jer 30:2
36:18 [r]ver 4
36:19 [s]Jer 26:16
[t]S 1Ki 17:3
36:21 [u]ver 14
[v]2Ki 22:10
36:22 [w]Am 3:15
36:23 [x]ver 2
[y]1Ki 22:8

36:4 *Baruch.* See note on 32:12.
36:5 *I am restricted.* Perhaps because of his unpopular temple message(s) (see 7:2–15; 26:2–6), or perhaps because of the events recorded in 19:1–20:6.
36:6 *day of fasting.* Proclaimed because of a national emergency (cf. Joel 2:15), perhaps in this case the Babylonian attack of 605 B.C. (see Da 1:1 and note).
36:7 See v. 3 and note.
36:8 If the book were in chronological order, ch. 45 would appear after this verse (see Introduction: Outline).
36:9 *ninth month of the fifth year.* December, 604 B.C., during a time of cold weather (see v. 22).
36:10 Cf. 2Ki 23:2. *room.* See note on 35:2. *Gemariah.* A common name in Jeremiah's time (see 29:3), found on one of the Lachish ostraca (see note on 34:7) as well as in at least two of the Elephantine papyri (see note on 32:11) a century later. *Shaphan.* Secretary of state under King Josiah (see 2Ki 22:3; see also notes on 26:24; 29:3). *entrance of the New Gate.* See 26:10 and note.
36:12 *Elnathan son of Acbor.* See note on 26:22.

36:18 *ink.* Mentioned only here in the OT (but see also 2Co 3:3; 2Jn 12; 3Jn 13). In ancient times, ink was made from soot or lampblack mixed with gum arabic, oil, or a metallic substance (as in the case of the Lachish ostraca; see note on 34:7).
36:19 The officials were understandably concerned about the safety of Jeremiah and Baruch (cf. 26:20–23).
36:20 *put.* For safekeeping (the Hebrew root for this word is translated "store" in Isa 10:28).
36:22 *ninth month.* See note on v. 9. *winter apartment.* Lit. "winter house" (as in Am 3:15), here probably a large room in the king's palace. *firepot.* A depression or container in the middle of the floor where coals were kept burning to warm the room.
36:23 Contrast King Josiah's desire to know the word of God and obey it (see 2Ki 22:11–23:3; 23:21–24). *columns.* Lit. "doors," so called because of their rectangular shape. *cut.* Lit. "tore." Instead of tearing his clothes (see note on v. 24), the king tore the prophet's scroll.
36:24 *attendants . . . showed no fear.* See v. 31. Contrast

fear,[z] nor did they tear their clothes.[a] [25]Even though Elnathan, Delaiah[b] and Gemariah[c] urged the king not to burn the scroll, he would not listen to them. [26]Instead, the king commanded Jerahmeel, a son of the king, Seraiah son of Azriel and Shelemiah son of Abdeel to arrest[d] Baruch the scribe and Jeremiah the prophet. But the LORD had hidden[e] them.

[27]After the king burned the scroll containing the words that Baruch had written at Jeremiah's dictation,[f] the word of the LORD came to Jeremiah: [28]"Take another scroll[g] and write on it all the words that were on the first scroll, which Jehoiakim king of Judah burned up. [29]Also tell Jehoiakim king of Judah, 'This is what the LORD says: You burned that scroll and said, "Why did you write on it that the king of Babylon would certainly come and come and destroy this land and cut off both men and animals[h] from it?" [30]Therefore, this is what the LORD says about Jehoiakim[i] king of Judah: He will have no one to sit on the throne of David; his body will be thrown out[k] and exposed[l] to the heat by day and the frost by night.[m] [31]I will punish him and his children[n] and his attendants for their wickedness; I will bring on them and those living in Jerusalem and the people of Judah every disaster[o] I pronounced against them, because they have not listened.[p]' "

[32]So Jeremiah took another scroll and gave it to the scribe Baruch son of Neriah, and as Jeremiah dictated,[q] Baruch wrote[r] on it all the words of the scroll that Jehoiakim king of Judah had burned[s] in the fire. And many similar words were added to them.

Jeremiah in Prison

37 Zedekiah[t] son of Josiah was made king[u] of Judah by Nebuchadnezzar king of Babylon; he reigned in place of Jehoiachin[x][v] son of Jehoiakim. [2]Neither he nor his attendants nor the people of the land paid any attention[w] to the words the LORD had spoken through Jeremiah the prophet.

[3]King Zedekiah, however, sent[x] Jehucal[y] son of Shelemiah with the priest Zephaniah[z] son of Maaseiah to Jeremiah the prophet with this message: "Please pray[a] to the LORD our God for us."

[4]Now Jeremiah was free to come and go among the people, for he had not yet been put in prison.[b] [5]Pharaoh's army had marched out of Egypt,[c] and when the Babylonians[y] who were besieging Jerusalem heard the report about them, they withdrew[d] from Jerusalem.[e]

[6]Then the word of the LORD came to Jeremiah the prophet: [7]"This is what the LORD, the God of Israel, says: Tell the king of Judah, who sent you to inquire[f] of me, 'Pharaoh's army, which has marched[g] out to support you, will go back to its own land, to Egypt.[h] [8]Then the Babylonians will return and attack this city; they will capture[i] it and burn[j] it down.'

[9]"This is what the LORD says: Do not deceive[k] yourselves, thinking, 'The Babylonians will surely leave us.' They will not! [10]Even if you were to defeat the entire Babylonian[z] army that is attacking you and only wounded men were left in their

---

x [1] Hebrew *Coniah,* a variant of *Jehoiachin*   **y** 5 Or *Chaldeans;* also in verses 8, 9, 13 and 14   **z** 10 Or *Chaldean;* also in verse 11

Cross references (center column):

36:24 [z]S Ps 36:1 [a]S Ge 37:29;
S Nu 14:6
36:25 [b]ver 12 [c]S ver 10
36:26 [d]Mt 23:34 [e]S 1Ki 17:3;
Ps 11:1; S Jer 1:8; 15:21
36:27 [f]ver 4
36:28 [g]ver 2
36:29 [h]Jer 33:12
[i]S Isa 30:10
36:30 [j]Jer 52:2
[k]S Isa 14:19
[l]S 2Ki 24:6
[m]S Jer 8:2
36:31 [n]Ex 20:5 [o]S Pr 29:1
[p]S Pr 1:24
36:32 [q]ver 4
[r]Ex 34:1; Jer 30:2
[s]ver 23

37:1 [t]S 2Ki 24:17 [u]1Sa 11:1;
Eze 17:13 [v]S 2Ki 24:8,12;
Jer 22:24
37:2 [w]S 2Ki 24:19
37:3 [x]ver 17; Jer 38:14 [y]Jer 38:1
[z]S 2Ki 25:18; Jer 29:25; 52:24
[a]S Ex 8:28; S Nu 21:7;
1Sa 12:19; 1Ki 13:6;
2Ki 19:4; Jer 42:2
37:4 [b]ver 15; Jer 32:2
37:5 [c]S Ge 15:18; Isa 31:1;
Eze 17:15 [d]Jer 34:21 [e]S Isa 30:5;
Jer 34:11
37:7 [f]S Ge 25:22; S 2Ki 22:18 [g]ver 5 [h]S 2Ki 18:21;
S Jer 2:36; La 1:7; 4:17
37:8 [i]Jer 38:3 [j]Jer 21:10; 38:18; 39:8
37:9 [k]Jer 29:8; S Mk 13:5

---

the response of the "officials" (v. 12; see vv. 16,25). *nor did they tear their clothes.* Contrast the response of Jehoiakim's father Josiah (see 2Ki 22:11; cf. 1Ki 21:27).

36:26 *son of the king.* Since Jehoiakim was only about 30 years old (see 2Ki 23:36), the phrase probably is not to be understood literally but means "member of the royal court" (as also in 38:6; 1Ki 22:26; Zep 1:8).

36:30 *Jehoiakim . . . will have no one to sit on the throne.* His son Jehoiachin (see 2Ki 24:6) "ruled" only 3 months (see 2Ki 24:8) and then was captured and carried off to exile in Babylonia (see 2Ki 24:15), where he eventually died (see 52:33–34). *his body will be thrown out.* As punishment for the fact that he "threw" (v. 23) the prophet's scroll into the fire (see 22:18–19 and notes).

36:31 See 11:11; 19:15; 35:17. *attendants.* See note on v. 24.

36:32 *another scroll.* Cf. similarly Ex 34:1.

37:1–38:28 During the last two years of Zedekiah's reign (588–586 B.C.), Jeremiah is imprisoned by the authorities (see 20:2 and note).

37:1 See 2Ki 24:15,17–18. *Zedekiah.* Means "The LORD is my righteousness." See Introduction: Background. *reigned*

in place of Jehoiachin. In 597 B.C. This fulfills the prophecy concerning Jehoiakim in 36:30.

37:3 *Zedekiah . . . sent . . . to Jeremiah.* See 21:1. *Jehucal son of Shelemiah.* Later became Jeremiah's enemy (see 38:1,4). *the priest Zephaniah son of Maaseiah.* See 21:1 and note. *pray . . . for us.* See 21:2 and note; perhaps to ask the Lord to make the temporary withdrawal of the Babylonians in 588 B.C. (see note on 34:21–22) permanent.

37:5 *Pharaoh's army.* The troops of Hophra (see 44:30), called Apries by Greek historians. *marched out of Egypt.* Probably to help Zedekiah at his request; Lachish ostracon 3 (see note on 34:7) mentions a visit to Egypt made by the commander of Judah's army. All such ploys by Zedekiah would fail, however (see Eze 17:15,17). *Babylonians . . . withdrew.* To deal with the Egyptian threat (see 34:21 and note).

37:7 *Pharaoh's army . . . will go back . . . to Egypt.* Hophra would soon be defeated by Nebuchadnezzar (see note on Eze 30:21).

37:10 *wounded.* Lit. "pierced through," "mortally wounded." Though seriously handicapped, the Babylonians would still destroy Jerusalem.

tents, they would come out and burn[l] this city down."

[11]After the Babylonian army had withdrawn[m] from Jerusalem because of Pharaoh's army, [12]Jeremiah started to leave the city to go to the territory of Benjamin to get his share of the property[n] among the people there. [13]But when he reached the Benjamin Gate,[o] the captain of the guard, whose name was Irijah son of Shelemiah, the son of Hananiah, arrested him and said, "You are deserting to the Babylonians!"[p]

[14]"That's not true!" Jeremiah said. "I am not deserting to the Babylonians." But Irijah would not listen to him; instead, he arrested[q] Jeremiah and brought him to the officials. [15]They were angry with Jeremiah and had him beaten[r] and imprisoned[s] in the house[t] of Jonathan the secretary, which they had made into a prison.

[16]Jeremiah was put into a vaulted cell in a dungeon, where he remained a long time. [17]Then King Zedekiah sent[u] for him and had him brought to the palace, where he asked[v] him privately,[w] "Is there any word from the LORD?"

"Yes," Jeremiah replied, "you will be handed over[x] to the king of Babylon."

[18]Then Jeremiah said to King Zedekiah, "What crime[y] have I committed against you or your officials or this people, that you have put me in prison? [19]Where are your prophets[z] who prophesied to you, 'The king of Babylon will not attack you or this land'? [20]But now, my lord the king, please listen. Let me bring my petition be-

fore you: Do not send me back to the house of Jonathan the secretary, or I will die there."[a]

[21]King Zedekiah then gave orders for Jeremiah to be placed in the courtyard of the guard and given bread from the street of the bakers each day until all the bread[b] in the city was gone.[c] So Jeremiah remained in the courtyard of the guard.[d]

Jeremiah Thrown Into a Cistern

38 Shephatiah son of Mattan, Gedaliah son of Pashhur[e], Jehucal[a][f] son of Shelemiah, and Pashhur son of Malkijah heard what Jeremiah was telling all the people when he said, [2]"This is what the LORD says: 'Whoever stays in this city will die by the sword, famine or plague,[g] but whoever goes over to the Babylonians[b] will live. He will escape with his life; he will live.'[h] [3]And this is what the LORD says: 'This city will certainly be handed over to the army of the king of Babylon, who will capture it.'"[i]

[4]Then the officials[j] said to the king, "This man should be put to death.[k] He is discouraging[l] the soldiers who are left in this city, as well as all the people, by the things he is saying to them. This man is not seeking the good of these people but their ruin."

[5]"He is in your hands,"[m] King Zedekiah answered. "The king can do nothing[n] to oppose you."

[6]So they took Jeremiah and put him into

Cross references (center column):

37:10 [l]Jer 21:10
37:11 [m]ver 5
37:12 [n]S Jer 32:9
37:13 [o]S Jer 20:2; [p]Jer 21:9
37:14 [q]Isa 58:6; Jer 40:4
37:15 [r]S Jer 20:2; Heb 11:36 [s]S 1Ki 22:27 [t]ver 20; Jer 38:26
37:17 [u]S ver 3 [v]S Ge 25:22; Jer 15:11 [w]Jer 38:16 [x]S Jer 21:7
37:18 [y]S 1Sa 26:18; Jn 10:32; Ac 25:8
37:19 [z]S Jer 14:13; Eze 13:2

37:20 [a]S ver 15
37:21 [b]S Lev 26:26; Isa 33:16; Jer 38:9; La 1:11 [c]S 2Ki 25:3 [d]Jer 32:2; 38:6, 13,28; 39:13-14
38:1 [e]S 1Ch 9:12 [f]Jer 37:3
38:2 [g]Jer 34:17 [h]ver 17; S Jer 21:9; 39:18; 45:5
38:3 [i]S Jer 21:4, 10
38:4 [j]S Jer 36:12 [k]S Jer 11:21 [l]S 1Sa 17:32
38:5 [m]S Jer 26:14 [n]1Sa 15:24

[a][f] Hebrew *Jucal*, a variant of *Jehucal*   [b]2 Or *Chaldeans*; also in verses 18, 19 and 23

37:12 *territory of Benjamin.* Where Jeremiah's hometown, Anathoth, was located (see note on 1:1). *get his share of the property.* See 1Sa 30:24. While there was a brief lull in the Babylonian invasion, Jeremiah wanted to settle matters of estate with the other members of his family.
37:13 *Benjamin Gate.* See 38:7; see also note on Zec 14:10. *You are deserting to the Babylonians.* Irijah's fear was understandable, since Jeremiah recommended surrendering to the Babylonians (see 21:9; 38:2) and since many Judahites in fact defected (see 38:19; 39:9; 52:15).
37:14 *That's not true!* Lit. "A lie" (see 2Ki 9:12).
37:15 *had him beaten.* See 20:2 and note. *house of Jonathan.* Jeremiah would later look back on this prison as a place of great danger for him (see v. 20; 38:26).
37:16 *dungeon.* Lit. "house of the cistern," probably underground (see Ex 12:29).
37:17 *Zedekiah . . . asked him privately.* Not wanting to do so in the presence of his officials, whom he apparently feared. *you will be handed over to the king of Babylon.* See 32:4; 34:3.
37:19 *your prophets.* False prophets (see Dt 18:22).
37:20 *bring my petition before you.* See 36:7.
37:21 *courtyard of the guard.* A less objectionable prison than the dungeon of v. 16 (see note on 32:2). *street of the bakers.* Perhaps near the Tower of the Ovens (see note on Ne 3:11). *until all the bread . . . was gone.* The Hebrew word

for "bread" is translated "food" in 52:6.
38:1 *Pashhur.* See note on 20:1. *Jehucal son of Shelemiah.* See note on 37:3. *Pashhur son of Malkijah.* See note on 21:1. *Jeremiah was telling all the people.* Though he was confined in the courtyard of the guard (see 37:21), he was allowed to have visitors and to speak freely to them (see 32:8,12).
38:2 Echoes 21:9 (see note there).
38:3 Echoes 32:28 (see 34:2; 37:8).
38:4 *officials.* Those named in v. 1. *discouraging.* See Ezr 4:4; lit. "weakening the hands of," as in a similar situation in Lachish ostracon 6 (see note on 34:7): "The words of the officials are not good; they serve only to weaken our hands." Contrast Isa 35:3. *seeking the good.* The Hebrew underlying this phrase is translated "seek the peace and prosperity" in 29:7 (see note there). *good . . . ruin.* The Hebrew for these words is translated "prosperity . . . disaster" in Isa 45:7.
38:5 *The king can do nothing.* Not because of inability or lack of authority but through failure of nerve. He feared his own officials (see vv. 25–26; see also 37:17 and note).
38:6 *cistern.* Shaped like a bell, with the narrow end at the top (see 37:16 and note). *king's son.* See note on 36:26. *cistern . . . had no water in it.* Zedekiah's officials wanted to kill Jeremiah (see v. 4), but not by taking his life with their own hands (cf. Ge 37:20–24).

the cistern of Malkijah, the king's son, which was in the courtyard of the guard. ^{o} They lowered Jeremiah by ropes ^{p} into the cistern; it had no water in it, ^{q} only mud, and Jeremiah sank down into the mud. ^{r}

^{7}But Ebed-Melech, ^{s} a Cushite, ^{c} an official $^{d\,t}$ in the royal palace, heard that they had put Jeremiah into the cistern. While the king was sitting in the Benjamin Gate, ^{u} ^{8}Ebed-Melech went out of the palace and said to him, ^{9}"My lord the king, these men have acted wickedly in all they have done to Jeremiah the prophet. They have thrown him into a cistern, ^{v} where he will starve to death when there is no longer any bread ^{w} in the city."

^{10}Then the king commanded Ebed-Melech the Cushite, "Take thirty men from here with you and lift Jeremiah the prophet out of the cistern before he dies."

^{11}So Ebed-Melech took the men with him and went to a room under the treasury in the palace. He took some old rags and worn-out clothes from there and let them down with ropes ^{x} to Jeremiah in the cistern. ^{12}Ebed-Melech the Cushite said to Jeremiah, "Put these old rags and worn-out clothes under your arms to pad the ropes." Jeremiah did so, ^{13}and they pulled him up with the ropes and lifted him out of the cistern. And Jeremiah remained in the courtyard of the guard. ^{y}

Zedekiah Questions Jeremiah Again

^{14}Then King Zedekiah sent ^{z} for Jeremiah the prophet and had him brought to the third entrance to the temple of the LORD. "I am going to ask you something," the king said to Jeremiah. "Do not hide ^{a} anything from me."

^{15}Jeremiah said to Zedekiah, "If I give you an answer, will you not kill me? Even if I did give you counsel, you would not listen to me."

^{16}But King Zedekiah swore this oath secretly ^{b} to Jeremiah: "As surely as the LORD lives, who has given us breath, ^{c} I will neither kill you nor hand you over to those who are seeking your life." ^{d}

^{17}Then Jeremiah said to Zedekiah, "This is what the LORD God Almighty, the God of Israel, says: 'If you surrender ^{e} to the officers of the king of Babylon, your life will be spared and this city will not be burned down; you and your family will live. ^{f} ^{18}But if you will not surrender to the officers of the king of Babylon, this city will be handed over ^{g} to the Babylonians and they will burn ^{h} it down; you yourself will not escape ^{i} from their hands.' "

^{19}King Zedekiah said to Jeremiah, "I am afraid ^{j} of the Jews who have gone over ^{k} to the Babylonians, for the Babylonians may hand me over to them and they will mistreat me."

^{20}"They will not hand you over," Jeremiah replied. "Obey ^{l} the LORD by doing what I tell you. Then it will go well ^{m} with you, and your life ^{n} will be spared. ^{21}But if you refuse to surrender, this is what the LORD has revealed to me: ^{22}All the women ^{o} left in the palace of the king of Judah will be brought out to the officials of the king of Babylon. Those women will say to you:

" 'They misled you and overcame
    you—
    those trusted friends ^{p} of yours.
Your feet are sunk in the mud; ^{q}

38:6 ^{o}S Jer 37:21
^{p}S Jos 2:15
^{q}S Ge 37:24
^{r}S Job 30:19;
La 3:53
38:7 ^{s}Jer 39:16
$^t\!fn$ Isa 56:3-5;
Ac 8:27
^{u}S Job 29:7
38:9 ^{v}S Ge 37:20
^{w}S Jer 37:21
38:11 ^{x}S Jos 2:15
38:13
^{y}S Jer 37:21
38:14 ^{z}S Jer 37:3
^{a}S 1Sa 3:17

38:16 ^{b}Jer 37:17
^{c}Isa 42:5; 57:16
^{d}ver 4
38:17 ^{e}Jer 27:8
^{f}S Jer 21:9
38:18 ^{g}ver 3
^{h}S Jer 37:8
^{i}S Jer 24:8; S 32:4
38:19 ^{j}Isa 51:12;
Jn 12:42
^{k}Jer 39:9; 52:15
38:20 ^{l}Jer 11:4
^{m}S Dt 5:33;
Jer 40:9 ^{n}Isa 55:3
38:22 ^{o}S Jer 6:12
^{p}S Job 19:14;
S Jer 13:21
^{q}S Job 30:19;
Ps 69:14

^{c}7 Probably from the upper Nile region ^{d}7 Or a eunuch

38:7 *Ebed-Melech.* Means "king's servant." *king was sitting in the Benjamin Gate.* See 37:13; see also note on Zec 14:10. Since a city gateway was often used as a courtroom or town hall (see notes on Ge 19:1; Ru 4:1), Zedekiah may have been settling various legal complaints on this occasion (see 2Sa 15:2–4) and would therefore be in a position to help Ebed-Melech.

38:9 *no longer any bread in the city.* See 37:21 and note.

38:10 *thirty men.* The large number was probably to keep the officials (see v. 4) and their friends from trying to prevent Jeremiah's rescue.

38:11 *room under the treasury.* Perhaps a wardrobe storeroom (see 2Ki 10:22).

38:12 *Put these old rags ... to pad the ropes.* Ebed-Melech's kindnesses to Jeremiah were evidence that he trusted in the Lord, and the Lord rewarded him (see 39:15–18).

38:13 *remained in the courtyard of the guard.* See note on 32:2.

38:14 *something ... anything.* Lit. "a word ... a word," probably referring to a "word from the LORD" (37:17).

38:16 *As surely as the LORD lives.* See note on Ge 42:15. *those who are seeking your life.* Zedekiah's officials (see v. 4 and note).

38:17–18 See vv. 2–3; 21:9–10; 32:3–4; 34:2–5. *surrender.* Lit. "come out" (see 2Ki 18:31; 24:12). *officers of the king of Babylon.* Those in charge of the siege of Jerusalem (see 39:3,13).

38:19 *I am afraid.* See v. 5 and note. If Zedekiah had trusted in the Lord, he would not have had to fear either officials or deserters (see Pr 29:25). *gone over to the Babylonians.* See 37:13 and note. *mistreat me.* See Jdg 19:25; 1Ch 10:4.

38:22 *women ... in the palace ... brought out to the officials.* Women in a conquered king's harem became the property of the conquerors (cf. 2Sa 16:21–22). *misled you and overcame you—those trusted friends of yours.* Repeated almost verbatim in Ob 7 (see 20:10 and note). Zedekiah's so-called friends were his officials (see v. 4) and false prophets (see 37:19). *feet are sunk in the mud.* Symbolic of great distress (see Ps 69:14).

your friends have deserted you.'

[23]"All your wives and children[r] will be brought out to the Babylonians. You yourself will not escape[s] from their hands but will be captured[t] by the king of Babylon; and this city will[e] be burned down."[u]

[24]Then Zedekiah said to Jeremiah, "Do not let anyone know[v] about this conversation, or you may die. [25]If the officials hear that I talked with you, and they come to you and say, 'Tell us what you said to the king and what the king said to you; do not hide it from us or we will kill you,' [26]then tell[w] them, 'I was pleading with the king not to send me back to Jonathan's house[x] to die there.' "

[27]All the officials did come to Jeremiah and question him, and he told them everything the king had ordered him to say. So they said no more to him, for no one had heard his conversation with the king.

[28]And Jeremiah remained in the courtyard of the guard[y] until the day Jerusalem was captured.

The Fall of Jerusalem

39:1–10pp — 2Ki 25:1–12; Jer 52:4–16

39 This is how Jerusalem[z] was taken: [1]In the ninth year of Zedekiah[a] king of Judah, in the tenth month, Nebuchadnezzar[b] king of Babylon marched against Jerusalem with his whole army and laid siege[c] to it. [2]And on the ninth day of the fourth[d] month of Zedekiah's eleventh year, the city wall[e] was broken through.[f] [3]Then all the officials[g] of the king of Babylon came and took seats in the Middle Gate: Nergal-Sharezer of Samgar, Nebo-Sarsekim[f] a chief officer, Nergal-Sharezer a high official and all the other officials of the king of Babylon. [4]When Zedekiah king of Judah and all the soldiers saw them, they fled; they left the city at night by way of the king's garden, through the gate between the two walls,[h] and headed toward the Arabah.[g] [i]

[5]But the Babylonian[h] army pursued them and overtook Zedekiah[j] in the plains of Jericho. They captured[k] him and took him to Nebuchadnezzar king of Babylon at Riblah[l] in the land of Hamath, where he pronounced sentence on him. [6]There at Riblah the king of Babylon slaughtered the sons of Zedekiah before his eyes and also killed all the nobles[m] of Judah. [7]Then he put out Zedekiah's eyes[n] and bound him with bronze shackles to take him to Babylon.[o]

[8]The Babylonians[i] set fire[p] to the royal palace and the houses of the people and broke down the walls[q] of Jerusalem. [9]Nebuzaradan commander of the imperial guard carried into exile to Babylon the people who remained in the city, along with those who had gone over to him,[r] and the rest of the people.[s] [10]But Nebuzaradan the commander of the guard left behind in the land of Judah some of the poor people, who owned nothing; and at that time he gave them vineyards and fields.

[11]Now Nebuchadnezzar king of Babylon had given these orders about Jeremiah through Nebuzaradan commander of the imperial guard: [12]"Take him and look after him; don't harm[t] him but do for him whatever he asks." [13]So Nebuzaradan the commander of the guard, Nebushazban a chief officer, Nergal-Sharezer a high official and all the other officers[u] of the king of Babylon [14]sent and had Jeremiah taken out of the courtyard of the guard.[v] They

38:23 [r]S 2Ki 25:6 [s]S Jer 32:4; Eze 17:15 [t]S Jer 24:8 [u]Jer 21:10; 37:8 **38:24** [v]Jer 37:17 **38:26** [w]1Sa 16:2 [x]S Jer 37:15 **38:28** [y]S Jer 37:21 **39:1** [z]S Jer 25:29 [a]S 2Ch 36:11 [b]S 2Ki 24:1; S Jer 28:14 [c]S 2Ki 25:1; Jer 52:4; Eze 4:3; 24:2 **39:2** [d]Zec 8:19 [e]S 2Ki 14:13 [f]Eze 33:21 **39:3** [g]ver 13; Jer 21:4 **39:4** [h]S Isa 22:11 [i]Eze 12:12 **39:5** [j]S Jer 24:8; S 32:4 [k]S Jer 21:7 [l]S Nu 34:11 **39:6** [m]S Isa 34:12 **39:7** [n]S Nu 16:14; Eze 12:13 [o]S Jer 2:35 **39:8** [p]S Jer 34:22 [q]S Ne 1:3; S Ps 80:12; S Isa 22:5; La 2:8 **39:9** [r]Jer 21:9 [s]Jer 40:1; La 1:5 **39:12** [t]S Pr 16:7; Jer 15:20-21; 1Pe 3:13 **39:13** [u]S ver 3 **39:14** [v]S Ne 3:25; Jer 37:21

[e]23 Or *and you will cause this city to* [f]3 Or *Nergal-Sharezer, Samgar-Nebo, Sarsekim* [g]4 Or *the Jordan Valley* [h]5 Or *Chaldean* [i]8 Or *Chaldeans*

38:26 See 37:20. *Jonathan's house.* See 37:15 and note.
38:27 *told them everything the king had ordered him to say.* Jeremiah was not obliged to give the officials the other information, which had been shared in confidence.
38:28 *remained in the courtyard of the guard.* See v. 13; see also note on 32:2.
39:1–45:5 The most detailed account in the OT of the Babylonian conquest of Jerusalem and its aftermath. The section concludes with a brief appendix (ch. 45).
39:1–10 A vivid summary of the siege and fall of Jerusalem and of the exile of its inhabitants (see 52:4–27).
39:1–2 Summarizes 52:4–7a.
39:1 *ninth year of Zedekiah . . . tenth month.* The final Babylonian siege of Jerusalem began on the tenth day of the month (see 52:4; 2Ki 25:1; Eze 24:1–2), or Jan. 15, 588 B.C.
39:2 *ninth day . . . fourth month . . . eleventh year.* July 18, 586 B.C. (see 52:5–6; 2Ki 25:2–3). The siege lasted just over two and a half years.
39:3 *took seats in the Middle Gate.* In fulfillment of 1:15. The Middle Gate may have been located in the wall separating the citadel of Mount Zion from the lower city, therefore serving as a strategic vantage point for the invaders. *Nergal-Sharezer.* Means "Nergal [a god; see 2Ki 17:30], protect the king." One of the two men so named here (see v. 13) is probably Neriglissar, who later became a successor of Nebuchadnezzar as ruler of Babylonia (560–556 B.C.). *chief officer.* See v. 13; see also note on 2Ki 18:17. *high official.* See v. 13. The Hebrew for this phrase is cognate to Babylonian *rab mu(n)gi,* a high military official who sometimes served as an envoy to foreign rulers.
39:4–7 See 52:7–11; see also 2Ki 25:4–7 and notes.
39:5 *plains.* The Hebrew for this word is the plural of the word for "Arabah" (v. 4).
39:8–10 See 52:12–16; see also 2Ki 25:8–12 and notes.
39:12 *look after him.* See note on 40:4.
39:13 *Nergal-Sharezer.* See note on v. 3.
39:14 *had Jeremiah taken out.* Either (1) a summary

turned him over to Gedaliah[w] son of Ahi-kam,[x] the son of Shaphan,[y] to take him back to his home. So he remained among his own people.[z]

[15]While Jeremiah had been confined in the courtyard of the guard, the word of the LORD came to him: [16]"Go and tell Ebed-Melech[a] the Cushite, 'This is what the LORD Almighty, the God of Israel, says: I am about to fulfill my words[b] against this city through disaster,[c] not prosperity. At that time they will be fulfilled before your eyes. [17]But I will rescue[d] you on that day, declares the LORD; you will not be handed over to those you fear. [18]I will save[e] you; you will not fall by the sword[f] but will escape with your life,[g] because you trust[h] in me, declares the LORD.' "

Jeremiah Freed

40 The word came to Jeremiah from the LORD after Nebuzaradan commander of the imperial guard had released him at Ramah.[i] He had found Jeremiah bound in chains among all the captives[j] from Jerusalem and Judah who were being carried into exile to Babylon. [2]When the commander[k] of the guard found Jeremiah, he said to him, "The LORD your God decreed[l] this disaster[m] for this place.[n] [3]And now the LORD has brought it about; he has done just as he said he would. All this happened because you people sinned[o] against the LORD and did not obey[p] him. [4]But today I am freeing[q] you from the chains[r] on your wrists. Come with me to Babylon, if you like, and I will look after you; but if you do not want to, then don't come. Look, the whole country lies before you; go wherever you please."[s] [5]However, be-

fore Jeremiah turned to go,[i] Nebuzaradan added, "Go back to Gedaliah[t] son of Ahikam,[u] the son of Shaphan, whom the king of Babylon has appointed[v] over the towns[w] of Judah, and live with him among the people, or go anywhere else you please."[x]

Then the commander gave him provisions and a present[y] and let him go. [6]So Jeremiah went to Gedaliah son of Ahikam at Mizpah[z] and stayed with him among the people who were left behind in the land.

Gedaliah Assassinated

40:7–9; 41:1–3pp — 2Ki 25:22–26

[7]When all the army officers and their men who were still in the open country heard that the king of Babylon had appointed Gedaliah son of Ahikam as governor[a] over the land and had put him in charge of the men, women and children who were the poorest[b] in the land and who had not been carried into exile to Babylon, [8]they came to Gedaliah at Mizpah[c]—Ishmael[d] son of Nethaniah, Johanan[e] and Jonathan the sons of Kareah, Seraiah son of Tanhumeth, the sons of Ephai the Netophathite,[f] and Jaazaniah[k] the son of the Maacathite,[g] and their men. [9]Gedaliah son of Ahikam, the son of Shaphan, took an oath to reassure them and their men. "Do not be afraid to serve[h] the Babylonians,[i]" he said. "Settle down in the land and serve the king of Babylon, and it

39:14
wS 2Ki 25:22
xS 2Ki 22:12
yS 2Ki 22:3
zJer 40:5
39:16 aJer 38:7
bPs 33:11;
Isa 14:27; 40:8;
Jer 44:28;
La 2:17;
SMt 1:22
cS Jos 23:15;
Jer 21:10
39:17 dPs 34:22;
41:1-2
39:18
eS 1Sa 17:47;
Ac 16:31
fS Job 5:20
gS Jer 21:9;
S 38:2
hS Jer 17:7;
Ro 10:11
40:1 iS Jos 18:25;
1Sa 8:4; Mt 2:18
/S Dt 21:10;
S 2Ki 24:1;
S 2Ch 36:10;
Na 3:10
40:2 kRo 13:4
lS Isa 10:22
mS 2Ch 34:24;
S Ps 18:18;
S Pr 8:36;
Gal 6:7-8
nS Jos 23:15
40:3 oS Pr 13:21;
Ro 6:23; Jas 1:15
pS Lev 26:33;
Dt 28:45-52;
29:24-28;
31:17-18;
S 1Ki 9:9;
Jer 22:8-9;
Da 9:14; Ac 7:39;
Ro 2:5-9
40:4
qPs 105:18-20;
S Jer 37:14
rLa 3:7
sS Ge 13:9

40:5 rS 2Ki 25:22
u2Ki 22:12-14
vNe 5:14;
Jer 41:2
wJer 44:2;
Zec 1:12
xJer 39:14
yS Ge 32:20;
S 1Sa 9:7
40:6 zver 10;
Jdg 20:1;
1Sa 7:5-17

40:7 aS Ge 41:41; S Ne 5:14 bS 2Ki 24:14; S Ac 24:17;
Jas 2:5 40:8 cver 13 dver 14; Jer 41:1,2 ever 15; Jer 41:11
/S 2Sa 23:28 gS Dt 3:14 40:9 hJer 5:19; 27:11; Ro 13:1-2;
Eph 6:5-8 /Eze 23:23

15 Or *Jeremiah answered*   k8 Hebrew *Jezaniah,* a
variant of *Jaazaniah*   19 Or *Chaldeans;* also in verse 10

statement of Jeremiah's release from prison, the specific details of which are given in 40:1–6; or (2) a brief description of the first of two releases, the second of which (made necessary because Jeremiah had been arrested again by mistake in the confusion surrounding the capture and transporting of thousands of exiles) is detailed in 40:1–6. *courtyard of the guard.* See note on 32:2. *Gedaliah son of Ahikam, the son of Shaphan.* See note on 26:24. *his home.* The governor's residence. An early sixth-century seal impression found at Lachish reads: "Belonging to Gedaliah [probably the man named in this verse], who is over the house."

39:15–18 See note on 38:12.

39:16 *Go and tell.* Though confined in prison, Jeremiah was permitted to have visitors (see note on 38:1). *I am about to fulfill my words against this city.* See 19:15.

39:17 *those you fear.* The court officials (see 38:1) who, in Ebed-Melech's judgment, had "acted wickedly" (38:9).

39:18 *escape with your life.* See note on 21:9. *you trust in me.* Ebed-Melech had expressed his faith in God by securing Jeremiah's release from the cistern (see 38:7–13; see also note on 38:12).

40:1–44:30 A lively narrative of the aftermath of the fall of Jerusalem. Chronologically, the chapters are the latest in the book (although 52:31–34 is later, it is part of the appendix and not of the book proper).

40:1 *The word came.* A heading introducing the prophecies of Jeremiah after the exile, just as "The word . . . came" (1:2) introduces his prophecies from the time of his call up to the exile (see 1:3). *Nebuzaradan . . . released him.* See note on 39:14. *Ramah.* See note on 31:15. *chains.* Manacles that were fastened to the wrists (see v. 4; see also Job 36:8; Isa 45:14).

40:2–3 Nebuzaradan doubtless knew the basic content of Jeremiah's prophetic message against Jerusalem, and he here repeats it to the prophet in summary fashion.

40:4 *I will look after you.* Nebuzaradan promises to carry out Nebuchadnezzar's wishes concerning Jeremiah (see 39:12). *The whole country lies before you.* Cf. Abram's offer to Lot in Ge 13:9.

40:5–9 See 2Ki 25:22–24 and notes.

40:5 *Gedaliah son of Ahikam.* See note on 26:24. *provisions.* The Hebrew for this word is translated "allowance" in 52:34.

will go well with you.[j] [10]I myself will stay at Mizpah[k] to represent you before the Babylonians who come to us, but you are to harvest the wine,[l] summer fruit and oil, and put them in your storage jars,[m] and live in the towns you have taken over."[n]

[11]When all the Jews in Moab,[o] Ammon, Edom[p] and all the other countries[q] heard that the king of Babylon had left a remnant in Judah and had appointed Gedaliah son of Ahikam, the son of Shaphan, as governor over them, [12]they all came back to the land of Judah, to Gedaliah at Mizpah, from all the countries where they had been scattered.[r] And they harvested an abundance of wine and summer fruit.

[13]Johanan[s] son of Kareah and all the army officers still in the open country came to Gedaliah at Mizpah[t] [14]and said to him, "Don't you know that Baalis king of the Ammonites[u] has sent Ishmael[v] son of Nethaniah to take your life?" But Gedaliah son of Ahikam did not believe them.

[15]Then Johanan[w] son of Kareah said privately to Gedaliah in Mizpah, "Let me go and kill[x] Ishmael son of Nethaniah, and no one will know it. Why should he take your life and cause all the Jews who are gathered around you to be scattered[y] and the remnant[z] of Judah to perish?"

[16]But Gedaliah son of Ahikam said to Johanan[a] son of Kareah, "Don't do such a thing! What you are saying about Ishmael is not true."

41 In the seventh month Ishmael[b] son of Nethaniah, the son of Elishama, who was of royal blood and had been one of the king's officers, came with ten men to Gedaliah son of Ahikam at Mizpah. While they were eating together there, [2]Ishmael[c] son of Nethaniah and the ten men who were with him got up and struck down Gedaliah son of Ahikam, the son of Shaphan, with the sword,[d] killing the one whom the king of Babylon had appointed[e] as governor over the land.[f] [3]Ishmael also killed all the Jews who were with Gedaliah at Mizpah, as well as the Babylonian[m] soldiers who were there.

[4]The day after Gedaliah's assassination, before anyone knew about it, [5]eighty men who had shaved off their beards,[g] torn their clothes[h] and cut[i] themselves came from Shechem,[j] Shiloh[k] and Samaria,[l] bringing grain offerings and incense[m] with them to the house of the LORD.[n] [6]Ishmael son of Nethaniah went out from Mizpah to meet them, weeping[o] as he went. When he met them, he said, "Come to Gedaliah son of Ahikam."[p] [7]When they went into the city, Ishmael son of Nethaniah and the men who were with him slaughtered them and threw them into a cistern.[q] [8]But ten of them said to Ishmael, "Don't kill us! We have wheat and barley, oil and honey, hidden in a field."[r] So he let them alone and did not kill them with the others. [9]Now the cistern where he threw all the bodies of the men he had killed along with Gedaliah was the one King Asa[s] had made as part of his defense[t] against Baasha[u] king

---

Cross references (center column):

40:9 [j]S Jer 38:20; La 1:1
40:10 [k]S ver 6; [l]S Ge 27:28; S Ex 23:16; [m]Ex 7:19; 2Co 4:7 [n]Dt 1:39
40:11 [o]S Nu 21:11; 25:1 [p]S Ge 25:30 [q]Jer 12:14
40:12 [r]Jer 43:5
40:13 [s]Jer 42:1 [t]ver 8
40:14 [u]S Ge 19:38; 2Sa 10:1-19; Jer 25:21; 41:10; 49:1 [v]S ver 8
40:15 [w]S ver 8 [x]S Dt 5:21; Mt 5:21-22 [y]S Ge 11:4; S Lev 26:33; Mt 26:31; Jn 11:52; Jas 1:1 [z]S 2Ki 21:14; S Isa 1:9; Ro 11:5
40:16 [a]Jer 43:2
41:1 [b]S Jer 40:8

41:2 [c]Ps 41:9; 109:5 [d]S Jos 11:10; Jer 40:15; Heb 11:37 [e]S Jer 40:5 [f]2Sa 3:27; 20:9-10; S Jer 40:8
41:5 [g]S Lev 19:27; Jer 47:5; 48:37 [h]S Ge 37:29; S Lev 10:6; S Mk 14:63 [i]S Lev 19:28 /Ge 12:6; 33:18; Jdg 9:1-57; 1Ki 12:1 [k]S Jos 18:1 [l]1Ki 16:24 [m]S Nu 16:40; [n]S Lk 1:9 [n]1Ki 3:2; 6:38; 2Ki 25:9
41:6 [o]2Sa 3:16
[p]Ps 5:9; Hos 7:11; Rev 20:10

41:7 [q]S Ge 37:24; 2Ki 10:14 41:8 [r]Isa 45:3 41:9 [s]S 1Ki 15:22; S 2Ch 16:6 [t]S Jdg 6:2 [u]S 2Ch 16:1

[m]3 Or Chaldean

---

harvest the wine, summer fruit and oil. Nebuzaradan (see 39:9) had arrived in Jerusalem in August of 586 B.C. (see note on 52:12). Grapes, figs and olives are harvested in Palestine during August and September.
40:14 *Baalis.* Either (1) "King Ba'lay," as his name is written on an early sixth-century B.C. bottle discovered in Jordan, or (2) Ba'al-Yasha', an Ammonite king whose name appears on a stamp seal found at Tell el-'Umeiri in Jordan in 1984. *Ammonites.* Ammon was among the nations that earlier had been allies against Babylonia (see 27:3 and note; see also Eze 21:18–32).
40:15 *privately.* See note on 38:16. *remnant.* See note on 6:9.
40:16 *not true.* Lit. "a lie" (see 37:14 and note). Gedaliah's naive faith in Ishmael's integrity would cost him his life.
41:1–3 See 2Ki 25:25 and note.
41:1 *one of the king's officers.* Ishmael's loyalty to Zedekiah might explain his assassination of Gedaliah, whom he considered to be a Babylonian puppet ruler. *they were eating together.* Ancient custom with respect to hospitality probably made Gedaliah assume that his guests would not harm him, much less kill him (see note on Jdg 4:21).
41:5 *shaved off their beards, torn their clothes and cut themselves.* Signs of mourning (see 16:6 and note; see also

note on Ezr 9:3), probably over the destruction of Jerusalem. *came.* In the "seventh month" (v. 1) to celebrate the Feast of Tabernacles (see note on Ex 23:16). *Shechem, Shiloh and Samaria.* Formerly worship centers in the north (see notes on 7:12; Ge 12:6; see also Jos 24:25–26). After the northern kingdom was destroyed in 722–721 B.C., many Israelites made periodic pilgrimages to Jerusalem, especially during the reform movements of Hezekiah (see 2Ch 30:11) and Josiah (see 2Ch 34:9). *grain offerings and incense.* Bloodless offerings, since the altar of the Jerusalem temple had been destroyed. *house of the LORD.* Though the temple itself was in ruins, the site was still considered holy.
41:6 *weeping.* Pretending to share the sorrow of the mourners from the north.
41:7 *the city.* Mizpah. *cistern.* A favorite place to dispose of victims, whether living or dead (see 37:16 and note; 38:6).
41:8 *wheat and barley, oil and honey.* Supplies that Ishmael perhaps would have taken with him when he fled to Ammon (see v. 15).
41:9 *the cistern . . . was the one King Asa had made.* Probably as part of the fortifications Asa had built at Mizpah (see 1Ki 15:22), since cisterns were essential for storing water during times of siege. Archaeologists have discovered numerous cisterns in the ruins of ancient Mizpah (modern Tell en-Nasbeh, seven and a half miles north of Jerusalem).

of Israel. Ishmael son of Nethaniah filled it with the dead.

[10]Ishmael made captives of all the rest of the people[v] who were in Mizpah—the king's daughters[w] along with all the others who were left there, over whom Nebuzaradan commander of the imperial guard had appointed Gedaliah son of Ahikam. Ishmael son of Nethaniah took them captive and set out to cross over to the Ammonites.[x]

[11]When Johanan[y] son of Kareah and all the army officers who were with him heard about all the crimes Ishmael son of Nethaniah had committed, [12]they took all their men and went to fight[z] Ishmael son of Nethaniah. They caught up with him near the great pool[a] in Gibeon. [13]When all the people[b] Ishmael had with him saw Johanan son of Kareah and the army officers who were with him, they were glad. [14]All the people Ishmael had taken captive at Mizpah[c] turned and went over to Johanan son of Kareah. [15]But Ishmael son of Nethaniah and eight of his men escaped[d] from Johanan and fled to the Ammonites.

Flight to Egypt

[16]Then Johanan son of Kareah and all the army officers[e] who were with him led away all the survivors[f] from Mizpah whom he had recovered from Ishmael son of Nethaniah after he had assassinated Gedaliah son of Ahikam: the soldiers, women, children and court officials he had brought from Gibeon. [17]And they went on, stopping at Geruth Kimham[g] near Bethlehem[h] on their way to Egypt[i] [18]to escape the Babylonians.[n] They were afraid[j] of them because Ishmael son of Nethaniah had killed Gedaliah[k] son of Ahikam, whom the king of Babylon had appointed as governor over the land.

42 Then all the army officers, including Johanan[l] son of Kareah and Jezaniah[o] son of Hoshaiah,[m] and all the people from the least to the greatest[n] approached [2]Jeremiah the prophet and said to him, "Please hear our petition and pray[o] to the LORD your God for this entire remnant.[p] For as you now see, though we were once many, now only a few[q] are left. [3]Pray that the LORD your God will tell us where we should go and what we should do."[r]

[4]"I have heard you," replied Jeremiah the prophet. "I will certainly pray[s] to the LORD your God as you have requested; I will tell[t] you everything the LORD says and will keep nothing back from you."[u]

[5]Then they said to Jeremiah, "May the LORD be a true[v] and faithful[w] witness[x] against us if we do not act in accordance with everything the LORD your God sends you to tell us. [6]Whether it is favorable or unfavorable, we will obey the LORD our God, to whom we are sending you, so that it will go well[y] with us, for we will obey[z] the LORD our God."

[7]Ten days later the word of the LORD came to Jeremiah. [8]So he called together Johanan son of Kareah and all the army officers[a] who were with him and all the people from the least to the greatest.[b] [9]He said to them, "This is what the LORD, the God of Israel, to whom you sent me to present your petition,[c] says:[d] [10]'If you stay in this land,[e] I will build[f] you up and not tear you down; I will plant[g] you and not uproot you,[h] for I am grieved over the disaster I have inflicted on you.[i] [11]Do not be afraid of the king of Babylon,[j] whom you now fear.[k] Do not be afraid of him, declares the LORD, for I am with you and will save[l] you and deliver you from his hands.[m] [12]I will show you compassion[n] so

Cross references

41:10 [v]Jer 40:7, 12 [w]Jer 38:23 [x]S Jer 40:14
41:11 [y]S Jer 40:8
41:12 [z]S Ex 14:14; Jn 18:36 [a]S Jos 9:3; Jn 9:7
41:13 [b]ver 10
41:14 [c]Jer 40:6
41:15 [d]Job 21:30; S Pr 28:17
41:16 [e]Jer 42:1; 43:2 [f]Isa 1:9; Jer 43:4; Eze 7:16; 14:22; Zep 2:9
41:17 [g]2Sa 19:37 [h]Ge 35:19; Mic 5:2 [i]Jer 42:14
41:18 [j]S Nu 14:9; Isa 51:12; Jer 42:16; Lk 12:4-5 [k]S 2Ki 25:22
42:1 [l]S Jer 40:13 [m]S Jer 41:16
[n]Jer 6:13; 44:12
42:2 [o]S Ge 20:7; S Jer 36:7; Ac 8:24; Jas 5:16 [p]S Isa 1:9 [q]S Lev 26:22; La 1:1
42:3 [r]ver 20; Ps 86:11; S Pr 3:6; S Jer 15:11
42:4 [s]Ex 8:29; 1Sa 12:23 [t]S Jer 1:17 [u]S Nu 22:18; S 1Sa 3:17
42:5 [v]1Ki 22:16; Ps 119:160; Ro 3:4 [w]S Dt 7:9; Jn 8:26; S 1Co 1:9 [x]S Ge 31:48; S Dt 4:26; S Isa 1:2; S Ro 1:9; Rev 1:5
42:6 [y]Dt 5:29; 6:3; Jer 7:23; 22:15 [z]S ver 19; S Ex 24:7; S Jos 24:24
42:8 [a]ver 1 [b]Jer 41:16; S Mk 9:35; Lk 7:28; Heb 8:11
42:9 [c]ver 2 [d]2Ki 22:15
42:10 [e]Jer 43:4 [f]S Jer 24:6 [g]S Dt 30:9 [h]S Dt 29:28; Ecc 3:2; Jer 45:4; Eze 36:36; Da 11:4
[i]S 2Ch 34:24; Isa 30:26; S Jer 18:8 42:11 [j]Jer 27:11 [k]S Nu 14:9; S 1Sa 15:24; Ps 23:4; Mt 10:28; 2Ti 1:7 [l]Ps 18:27; 69:35; S 119:94; S Isa 63:1; Heb 7:25 [m]S Ps 3:7; S Pr 20:22; S Jer 1:8; Ro 8:31 42:12 [n]S Ex 3:21; S 2Sa 24:14; 2Co 1:3

[n]18 Or Chaldeans   [o]1 Hebrew; Septuagint (see also 43:2) Azariah

---

41:10 *king's daughters.* Women who had been members of King Zedekiah's court, not necessarily daughters of the king himself (see note on 36:26). *Ammonites.* See 40:14 and note.
41:12 *great pool in Gibeon.* Perhaps the same as the one mentioned in 2Sa 2:13.
41:15 *eight of his men escaped.* Ishmael lost only two of his men (see v. 2) in the fight with Johanan.
41:17 *Geruth Kimham.* Location unknown; perhaps means "lodging place of Kimham," a friend of David who returned with him to Jerusalem after Absalom's death (see 2Sa 19:37-40).
42:1 *Jezaniah son of Hoshaiah.* Possibly the same as "Jaazaniah the son of the Maacathite" (40:8; see NIV text note there). Apparently Jezaniah was also known as Azariah

(see NIV text note; see also 43:2), as was King Uzziah (see NIV text notes on 2Ki 14:21; 2Ch 26:1).
42:2 *Jeremiah.* Had probably been among the "survivors from Mizpah" (41:16). *hear our petition.* See v. 9; 37:20.
42:3 The people may be asking the Lord to confirm what they sincerely believe to be their only option: flight to Egypt (see v. 17; 41:17).
42:6 *we will obey the LORD our God.* Though they twice declare here their desire to do God's will, they soon demonstrate that they have already decided to follow their own inclinations (see 43:2).
42:7 *Ten days later.* Jeremiah does not bring God's word to the people until he is sure of it himself (see 28:10-12).
42:10 *build you up . . . tear you down . . . plant . . . uproot.* See 1:10 and note; see also 31:4,28; 33:7.

that he will have compassion on you and restore you to your land.'[o]

13"However, if you say, 'We will not stay in this land,' and so disobey[p] the LORD your God, [14]and if you say, 'No, we will go and live in Egypt,[q] where we will not see war or hear the trumpet[n] or be hungry for bread,'[s] [15]then hear the word of the LORD,[t] O remnant of Judah. This is what the LORD Almighty, the God of Israel, says: 'If you are determined to go to Egypt and you do go to settle there, [16]then the sword[u] you fear[v] will overtake you there, and the famine[w] you dread will follow you into Egypt, and there you will die.[x] [17]Indeed, all who are determined to go to Egypt to settle there will die by the sword, famine and plague;[y] not one of them will survive or escape the disaster I will bring on them.' [18]This is what the LORD Almighty, the God of Israel, says: 'As my anger and wrath[z] have been poured out on those who lived in Jerusalem,[a] so will my wrath be poured out on you when you go to Egypt. You will be an object of cursing[b] and horror,[c] of condemnation and reproach;[d] you will never see this place again.'[e]

19"O remnant[f] of Judah, the LORD has told you, 'Do not go to Egypt.'[g] Be sure of this: I warn you today [20]that you made a fatal mistake[p] when you sent me to the LORD your God and said, 'Pray to the LORD our God for us; tell us everything he says and we will do it.'[h] [21]I have told you today, but you still have not obeyed the LORD your God in all he sent me to tell you.[i] [22]So now, be sure of this: You will die by the sword, famine[j] and plague[k] in the place where you want to go to settle."[l]

43 When Jeremiah finished telling the people all the words of the LORD their God—everything the LORD had sent him to tell them[m]— [2]Azariah son of Ho-

shaiah[n] and Johanan[o] son of Kareah and all the arrogant[p] men said to Jeremiah, "You are lying![q] The LORD our God has not sent you to say, 'You must not go to Egypt to settle there.'[r] [3]But Baruch[s] son of Neriah is inciting you against us to hand us over to the Babylonians,[q] so they may kill us or carry us into exile to Babylon."[t]

[4]So Johanan son of Kareah and all the army officers and all the people[u] disobeyed the LORD's command[v] to stay in the land of Judah. [w] [5]Instead, Johanan son of Kareah and all the army officers led away all the remnant of Judah who had come back to live in the land of Judah from all the nations where they had been scattered.[x] [6]They also led away all the men, women[y] and children and the king's daughters whom Nebuzaradan commander of the imperial guard had left with Gedaliah son of Ahikam, the son of Shaphan, and Jeremiah the prophet and Baruch[z] son of Neriah. [7]So they entered Egypt[a] in disobedience to the LORD and went as far as Tahpanhes.[b]

[8]In Tahpanhes[c] the word of the LORD came to Jeremiah: [9]"While the Jews are watching, take some large stones[d] with you and bury them in clay in the brick[e] pavement at the entrance to Pharaoh's palace[f] in Tahpanhes. [10]Then say to them, 'This is what the LORD Almighty, the God of Israel, says: I will send for my servant[g] Nebuchadnezzar[h] king of Babylon, and I will set his throne[i] over these stones I have buried here; he will spread his royal canopy[j] above them. [11]He will come and attack Egypt,[k] bringing death[l] to those

Cross references

42:12
[o]S Ge 31:3;
S Ne 1:9;
Ps 106:44-46
42:13
[p]S Dt 11:28
42:14
[q]Nu 11:4-5;
S Dt 17:16;
S Isa 30:2
[r]S Jos 6:20;
S Mt 24:31
[s]S Dt 8:3;
1Sa 2:5; Pr 10:3;
Isa 65:13;
Mt 4:2-4
42:15 [t]Jer 44:24
42:16
[u]S Lev 26:33;
Eze 11:8; 14:17
[v]S Jer 41:18
[w]S Ge 41:55
[x]S Ge 2:17;
2Ch 25:4;
S Job 21:20;
Eze 3:19; 18:4
42:17 [y]ver 22;
S Jer 21:7; 44:13
42:18
[z]Dt 29:18-20;
S 2Ch 12:7
[a]S 2Ch 36:19;
Jer 39:1-9
[b]S Nu 5:27;
S Jer 25:18
[c]S Dt 28:25,37
[d]S Ps 44:13
[e]S Jer 22:10
42:19 [f]Jer 40:15
[g]S ver 6;
Dt 17:16;
Isa 30:7; Jer 43:2;
44:16
42:20 [h]ver 2;
Eze 14:7-8
42:21 [i]S Ex 24:7;
Jer 40:3; Eze 2:7;
12:2; Zec 7:11-12
42:22 [j]S Isa 1:28
[k]S ver 17;
Jer 24:10;
Eze 6:11
[l]S Jer 15:2;
Hos 9:6
43:1 [m]Jer 26:8;
42:9-22

43:2 [n]S Jer 41:16
[o]Jer 40:16
[p]S Ne 9:29;
1Co 4:18-21
43:3 [q]S Ge 19:14;
S Dt 13:3; Ro 9:1;
2Co 11:31;
1Ti 2:7
[r]S Ex 24:7;
2Ki 25:24;
Jer 18:19;
S 42:19;
Eze 37:14
43:3 [s]S Jer 32:12
[t]Jer 38:4; 41:18;

52:30 43:4 [u]S Jer 41:16 [v]2Ch 25:16; Jer 42:5-6 [w]Jer 42:10
43:5 [x]Jer 40:12 **43:6** [y]S Ge 6:12 [z]S Jer 32:12 **43:7**
[a]S 2Ki 25:26 [b]Jer 2:16; 44:1; 46:14; Eze 30:18 **43:8**
[c]Ps 139:7; Jer 2:16 **43:9** [d]Ge 31:45-53; Jos 4:1-7;
1Ki 18:31-32 [e]S Ge 11:3 [f]S Ge 47:14 **43:10** [g]Isa 44:28;
45:1; Jer 25:9; 27:6 [h]Jer 46:13 [i]Jer 49:38 [j]S Ps 18:11 **43:11**
[k]Jer 46:13-26; Eze 29:19-20 [l]S Pr 11:19; Ro 6:23

[p]20 Or *you erred in your hearts*   [q]3 Or *Chaldeans*

42:12 *he will have compassion on you.* For similar examples see Ge 43:14; 1Ki 8:50.
42:16 *the sword you fear will overtake you there.* See 43:11 and note.
42:17–18 See 44:11–14.
42:17 *sword, famine and plague.* See note on 14:12.
42:18 *my anger and wrath have been poured out.* See 7:20; 44:6. *object of cursing . . . and reproach.* See notes on 24:9; 25:18; see also 29:18. *this place.* Jerusalem.
42:19 *I warn you.* See 11:7.
43:2 *Azariah.* See note on 42:1. *arrogant men.* They demonstrate themselves to be such by their words.
43:3 *Baruch.* See note on 32:12. Jeremiah's opponents decide to put the blame on someone they consider less spiritually formidable than the prophet himself.
43:6 *king's daughters.* See note on 41:10. *Jeremiah . . .*

and Baruch. No doubt they went to Egypt unwillingly, in the light of 32:6–15; 40:1–6; 42:13–22.
43:7 *Tahpanhes.* See note on 2:16.
43:9 *Pharaoh's palace.* Not necessarily his main residence. One of the Elephantine papyri, e.g., mentions the "king's house," apparently a more modest dwelling for Pharaoh's use when he visited Elephantine in southern Egypt.
43:10 *my servant Nebuchadnezzar.* See note on 25:9. *his throne.* Symbolizing his authority.
43:11 See 15:2 and note. *He will . . . attack Egypt.* A fragmentary text now owned by the British Museum in London states that Nebuchadnezzar carried out a punitive expedition against Egypt in his 37th year (568–567 B.C.) during the reign of Pharaoh Amasis (see Eze 29:17–20 and notes).

destined *m* for death, captivity to those destined for captivity, *n* and the sword to those destined for the sword. *o* 12He *r* will set fire *p* to the temples *q* of the gods *r* of Egypt; he will burn their temples and take their gods captive. *s* As a shepherd wraps *t* his garment around him, so will he wrap Egypt around himself and depart from there unscathed. 13There in the temple of the sun *s u* in Egypt he will demolish the sacred pillars *v* and will burn down the temples of the gods of Egypt.' "

Disaster Because of Idolatry

44 This word came to Jeremiah concerning all the Jews living in Lower Egypt *w*—in Migdol, *x* Tahpanhes *y* and Memphis *t z*—and in Upper Egypt *u: a* 2"This is what the LORD Almighty, the God of Israel, says: You saw the great disaster *b* I brought on Jerusalem and on all the towns of Judah. *c* Today they lie deserted and in ruins *d* 3because of the evil *e* they have done. They provoked me to anger *f* by burning incense *g* and by worshiping other gods *h* that neither they nor you nor your fathers *i* ever knew. 4Again and again *j* I sent my servants the prophets, *k* who said, 'Do not do this detestable *l* thing that I hate!' 5But they did not listen or pay attention; *m n* they did not turn from their wickedness *o* or stop burning incense *p* to other gods. *q* 6Therefore, my fierce anger was poured out; *r* it raged against the towns of Judah and the streets of Jerusalem and made them the desolate ruins *s* they are today.

7"Now this is what the LORD God Almighty, the God of Israel, says: Why bring such great disaster *t* on yourselves by cutting off from Judah the men and women, *u* the children and infants, and so leave yourselves without a remnant? *v* 8Why provoke me to anger with what your hands have

made, *w* burning incense *x* to other gods in Egypt, *y* where you have come to live? *z* You will destroy yourselves and make yourselves an object of cursing and reproach *a* among all the nations on earth. 9Have you forgotten the wickedness committed by your fathers *b* and by the kings *c* and queens *d* of Judah and the wickedness committed by you and your wives *e* in the land of Judah and the streets of Jerusalem? *f* 10To this day they have not humbled *g* themselves or shown reverence, *h* nor have they followed my law *i* and the decrees *j* I set before you and your fathers. *k*

11"Therefore, this is what the LORD Almighty, *l* the God of Israel, says: I am determined to bring disaster *m* on you and to destroy all Judah. 12I will take away the remnant *n* of Judah who were determined to go to Egypt to settle there. They will all perish in Egypt; they will fall by the sword or die from famine. From the least to the greatest, *o* they will die by sword or famine. *p* They will become an object of cursing and horror, of condemnation and reproach. *q* 13I will punish *r* those who live in Egypt with the sword, *s* famine and plague, *t* as I punished Jerusalem. 14None of the remnant of Judah who have gone to live in Egypt will escape or survive to return to the land of Judah, to which they long to return and live; none will return except a few fugitives." *u*

43:11
m S Ps 49:14;
Heb 9:27
n S Dt 28:64;
Rev 13:10
o S Jer 15:2;
Eze 32:11;
Zec 11:9
43:12 *p* S Jos 7:15
q S 1Ki 16:32 *r* ver 13; S Ex 12:12;
S Isa 2:18;
Jer 46:25;
Eze 30:13;
Zec 13:2
s Da 11:8
t S Ps 104:2;
109:18-19
43:13
u S Ge 1:16;
Isa 19:18 *fn*;
S Dt 4:19
v Jer 52:17;
Eze 26:11
44:1
w S Dt 32:42;
S Jer 24:8
x S Ex 14:2
y S Jer 43:7,8
z S Isa 19:13
a S Isa 11:11
44:2
b S 2Ch 34:24
c S Jer 40:5
d S Lev 26:31;
S Dt 29:23;
S Isa 6:11
44:3 *e* S Ex 32:22
f S Nu 11:33
g S Nu 16:40 *h* ver 8; S Nu 25:3;
Dt 13:6-11;
29:26; Isa 19:1
i S Jdg 2:19
44:4 *j* S Jer 7:13
k S Nu 11:29
l S Dt 18:9;
S 1Ki 14:24;
1Pe 4:3
44:5 *m* Da 9:6
n S Jer 25:4
o S Ge 6:5;
Ro 1:18; 2Ti 2:19
p ver 21; Jer 1:16;
Eze 8:11; 16:18;
23:41
q Jer 11:8-10;
S 25:7
44:6 *r* Eze 8:18;
20:34
s S Lev 26:31,34;
S Dt 29:23;
La 1:13; Zec 7:14
44:7 *t* Jer 26:19
u Jer 51:22
v S 2Ki 21:14

44:8
w S Isa 40:18-20;

x Jer 10:3; Ro 1:23 *x* ver 17-25; Jer 41:5 *y* S ver 3; S Ex 12:12 *z* S 1Co 10:22 *a* S Ps 44:13 44:9 *b* S Jdg 2:19 *c* S 2Ki 23:11 *d* 1Ki 21:25 *e* S Pr 31:10; S Jer 6:12 *f* ver 17,21; Jer 11:12; 32:32 44:10 *g* S Dt 8:3; S Mt 23:12; Php 2:8 *h* S Dt 6:13; S Ps 5:7 *i* S Jos 1:7; S Jer 11:8; Mt 5:17-20; Gal 3:19; 1Jn 3:4 *j* S Lev 18:4 *k* 1Ki 9:6-9; 2Ki 17:17 44:11 *l* Rev 4:8 *m* S 2Ch 34:24; Am 9:4 44:12 *n* ver 7; Jer 40:15 *o* S Jer 42:1 *p* S Isa 1:28 *q* S Dt 28:25; S Jer 29:18 44:13 *r* S Ex 32:34; Lev 26:14-17 *s* S Jer 15:2 *t* S Jer 42:17 44:14 *u* Jer 22:24-27; 49:5; La 4:15; Eze 6:8; S Ro 9:27

r 12 Or *I*   *s* 13 Or *in Heliopolis*   *t* *I* Hebrew *Noph*
u *I* Hebrew *in Pathros*

43:12 *As a shepherd wraps ... so will he wrap.* Routinely and confidently.
43:13 *temple of the sun in Egypt.* Lit. "Beth Shemesh in Egypt," with the qualifying phrase being used to distinguish the site from "Beth Shemesh in Judah" (2Ki 14:11). The Egyptian city is probably to be identified with Heliopolis (Greek for "city of the sun"; see NIV text note), called *On* in Hebrew (see note on Ge 41:45). *sacred pillars.* Obelisks, for which ancient Heliopolis was famous.
44:1–30 The last of Jeremiah's recorded prophecies (see note on 40:1–44:30).
44:1 *Jews living in ... Egypt.* As a result of previous deportations (see, e.g., 2Ki 23:34) and/or the Jews mentioned in 43:5–7. In either case, some time must have elapsed between chs. 43 and 44 to bring about the gathering mentioned in v. 15. *Lower Egypt ... Upper Egypt.* See note on Isa 11:11. *Migdol.* Location uncertain; probably in northern Egypt (see 46:14). The name means "watchtower."

Tahpanhes and Memphis. See notes on 2:16; Isa 19:13.
44:3 See note on 1:16; see also 11:17; 19:4; 32:32.
44:4 See note on 7:25. *Do not do this detestable thing.* See Jdg 19:24.
44:6 *my fierce anger was poured out.* See 7:20; 42:18.
44:7 *bring ... disaster on yourselves.* See 26:19. *men and women, the children and infants.* A stock phrase meaning "everyone" (see 1Sa 15:3; 22:19).
44:8 *what your hands have made.* Idols (see 1:16 and note). *object of cursing and reproach.* See 42:18; see also notes on 24:9; 25:18.
44:9 *wickedness committed by ... queens ... and your wives.* The women joined their husbands in worshiping the "Queen of Heaven" (v. 19; see v. 15).
44:10 *nor ... followed my law.* See 9:13; 26:4; see also 7:9 and note.
44:11–14 See 42:17–18 and notes.
44:11 *am determined.* Lit. "set my face" (see 21:10).

[15]Then all the men who knew that their wives[v] were burning incense[w] to other gods, along with all the women[x] who were present—a large assembly—and all the people living in Lower and Upper Egypt,[v]y said to Jeremiah, [16]"We will not listen[z] to the message you have spoken to us in the name of the LORD![a] [17]We will certainly do everything we said we would:[b] We will burn incense[c] to the Queen of Heaven[d] and will pour out drink offerings to her just as we and our fathers, our kings and our officials[e] did in the towns of Judah and in the streets of Jerusalem.[f] At that time we had plenty of food[g] and were well off and suffered no harm.[h] [18]But ever since we stopped burning incense to the Queen of Heaven and pouring out drink offerings[i] to her, we have had nothing and have been perishing by sword and famine.[j] [k]"

[19]The women added, "When we burned incense[l] to the Queen of Heaven[m] and poured out drink offerings to her, did not our husbands[n] know that we were making cakes[o] like her image[p] and pouring out drink offerings to her?"

[20]Then Jeremiah said to all the people, both men and women, who were answering him, [21]"Did not the LORD remember[q] and think about the incense[r] burned in the towns of Judah and the streets of Jerusalem[s] by you and your fathers,[t] your kings and your officials and the people of the land?[u] [22]When the LORD could no longer endure[v] your wicked actions and the detestable things you did, your land became an object of cursing[w] and a desolate waste[x] without inhabitants, as it is today.[y] [23]Because you have burned incense and have sinned against the LORD and have not obeyed him or followed[z] his law or his decrees[a] or his stipulations, this disaster[b] has come upon you, as you now see."[c]

[24]Then Jeremiah said to all the people, including the women,[d] "Hear the word of the LORD, all you people of Judah in Egypt.[e] [25]This is what the LORD Almighty, the God of Israel, says: You and your wives[f] have shown by your actions what you promised when you said, 'We will certainly carry out the vows we made to burn incense and pour out drink offerings to the Queen of Heaven.'[g]

"Go ahead then, do what you promised! Keep your vows![h] [26]But hear the word of the LORD, all Jews living in Egypt:[i] 'I swear[j] by my great name,' says the LORD, 'that no one from Judah living anywhere in Egypt will ever again invoke my name or swear, "As surely as the Sovereign[k] LORD lives."[l] [27]For I am watching[m] over them for harm,[n] not for good; the Jews in Egypt will perish[o] by sword and famine[p] until they are all destroyed.[q] [28]Those who escape the sword[r] and return to the land of Judah from Egypt will be very few.[s] Then the whole remnant[t] of Judah who came to live in Egypt will know whose word will stand[u]—mine or theirs.[v]

[29]"'This will be the sign[w] to you that I will punish[x] you in this place,' declares the LORD, 'so that you will know that my threats of harm against you will surely stand.'[y] [30]This is what the LORD says: 'I am going to hand Pharaoh[z] Hophra king of Egypt over to his enemies who seek his life, just as I handed Zedekiah[a] king of Judah over to Nebuchadnezzar king of Babylon, the enemy who was seeking his life.'"[b]

44:15 [v]S Pr 31:10; S Jer 6:12 [w]S Jer 18:15 [x]S Ge 3:6; 1Ti 2:14 [y]S Isa 11:11
44:16 [z]S 1Sa 8:19; Job 15:25-26; Jer 11:8-10 [a]S Jer 42:19
44:17 [b]ver 28; Dt 23:23; Zec 1:6 [c]S Isa 65:3 [d]ver 25; Jer 11:12 [e]Ne 9:34 /S ver 9; S Jer 2:26 [g]S Ex 16:3; [h]S Job 21:15; Isa 3:9; Hos 2:5-13; 9:1
44:18 [i]Lev 23:18 /Mal 3:13-15 [k]Jer 42:16
44:19 [l]S Jer 18:15 [m]Jer 7:18 [n]S Ge 3:6; Eph 5:22 [o]Lev 7:12 [p]S Lev 26:1; Ac 17:29
44:21 [q]Isa 64:9; S Jer 14:10; Hos 8:13 [r]S Jer 11:13 [s]ver 9 [t]S Ps 79:8 [u]S Jer 2:26
44:22 [v]S Isa 1:14 [w]S Jer 25:18 [x]S Lev 26:31,32 [y]S Ge 19:13; Ps 107:33-34; Eze 33:28-29
44:23 [z]S 1Ki 9:6 [a]S Lev 18:4 [b]Jer 40:2 [c]S Lev 26:33; S 1Ki 9:9; Jer 7:13-15; Eze 39:23; Da 9:11-12
44:24 [d]S Ge 3:6 [e]Jer 43:7
44:25 /S Pr 31:10 [g]S ver 17; S Dt 32:38 [h]S Pr 20:25; Eze 20:39; Jas 1:13-15
44:26 /S Jer 24:8 /S Ge 22:16; S Isa 48:1; Ac 19:13; Heb 6:13-17 [k]S Ge 15:2 [l]Dt 32:40; Ps 50:16; S Jer 4:2
44:27 [m]S Jer 1:12 [n]S Jer 21:10 [o]S Lev 26:38; S Job 15:22; 2Pe 3:9 [p]S Ge 41:55 [q]S Jer 9:16; Da 9:14; Am 9:8 44:28 [r]Jer 45:5; Eze 6:8 [s]ver 13-14; S Isa 10:19 [t]S 2Ki 21:14 [u]S Isa 7:9; S Jer 39:16; 42:15-18 [v]S ver 17,25-26 44:29 [w]S Ge 24:14; S Ex 3:12; S Nu 16:38; S Mt 12:38; 24:3 [x]S Lev 26:34 [y]S Pr 19:21 44:30 [z]S Jer 25:19; 46:26; Eze 30:21; 32:32 [a]2Ki 25:1-7; S Jer 24:8 [b]Jer 43:9-13

[v]15 Hebrew in Egypt and Pathros

44:15 *wives . . . women.* See v. 19; see also note on v. 9. *Lower and Upper Egypt.* See v. 1; see also note on Isa 11:11.

44:17 *Queen of Heaven.* See note on 7:18. *At that time we . . . were well off.* Judah had been relatively prosperous during King Manasseh's lengthy reign.

44:18 *ever since we stopped.* As a result of King Josiah's reform movement, which began in 621 B.C., *we have had nothing.* Beginning with Josiah's death in 609, a series of disasters, including invasion and exile, had struck Judah. The people understandably (though mistakenly) attributed their misfortune to their failure to worship the Queen of Heaven.

44:19 *women.* Since Ishtar (the "Queen of Heaven") was a Babylonian goddess of fertility, women played a major role in her worship. *did not our husbands know . . . ?* To have validity, a religious vow made by a married woman (see v.

25) had to be confirmed by her husband (see Nu 30:10-15). *we were making cakes like her image.* See 7:18 and note.

44:22 *object of cursing.* See v. 12. *desolate waste.* See v. 6.

44:23 *stipulations.* Of the Lord's covenant with his people (see Dt 4:45; 6:17,20).

44:25 *Go ahead then.* Spoken in irony (see 7:21 and note).

44:26 *I swear by my great name.* See notes on 22:5; Ge 22:15. *As surely as the Sovereign LORD lives.* See note on Ge 42:16.

44:27 *watching.* See note on 1:12; see also 31:28.

44:28 *very few.* See v. 14.

44:30 *Hophra.* Ruled Egypt 589-570 B.C. (see 37:5 and note). *his enemies who seek his life.* Hophra was killed by his Egyptian rivals during a power struggle. *I handed Zedekiah . . . over to Nebuchadnezzar.* See 39:5-7.

A Message to Baruch

45 This is what Jeremiah the prophet told Baruch[c] son of Neriah[d] in the fourth year of Jehoiakim[e] son of Josiah king of Judah, after Baruch had written on a scroll[f] the words Jeremiah was then dictating: [2]"This is what the LORD, the God of Israel, says to you, Baruch: [3]You said, 'Woe[g] to me! The LORD has added sorrow[h] to my pain;[i] I am worn out with groaning[j] and find no rest.' "[k]

[4]The LORD said, "Say this to him: 'This is what the LORD says: I will overthrow what I have built and uproot[l] what I have planted,[m] throughout the land.[n] [5]Should you then seek great[o] things for yourself? Seek them not.[p] For I will bring disaster[q] on all people,[r] declares the LORD, but wherever you go I will let you escape[s] with your life.' "[t]

A Message About Egypt

46 This is the word of the LORD that came to Jeremiah the prophet concerning the nations: [u]

[2]Concerning Egypt: [v]

This is the message against the army of Pharaoh Neco[w] king of Egypt, which was defeated at Carchemish[x] on the Euphrates[y] River by Nebuchadnezzar king of Babylon in the fourth year of Jehoiakim[z] son of Josiah king of Judah:

Cross-references

45:1 [c]S Jer 32:12 [d]Jer 51:59 [e]S 2Ch 36:5 [f]S Ex 17:14; [g]S Ps 40:7
45:3 [g]S Isa 24:16; 1Co 9:16 [h]S Ps 119:28; Mk 14:34; Ro 9:2 [i]S Job 6:10 [j]S Job 23:2; Ps 69:3 [k]S Jos 1:13; Mt 11:28; Heb 4:3
45:4 [l]S Jer 42:10 [m]S Jer 11:17 [n]S Dt 28:63; S 30:9; Isa 5:5-7; Jer 18:7-10
45:5 [o]Ps 131:1 [p]Mt 6:25-27,33 [q]Jer 11:11; 40:2 [r]S Jer 2:35 [s]S Ps 68:20; S Jer 44:28 [t]S Jer 21:9
46:1 [u]S Jer 1:10
46:2 [v]S Ex 1:8 [w]S 2Ki 23:29 [x]S 2Ch 35:20 [y]S Ge 2:14 [z]Jer 1:3; 25:1; 35:1; 36:1; 45:1; Da 1:1

46:3 [a]S Isa 21:5
46:4 [b]Eze 21:9-11 [c]1Sa 17:5,38; 2Ch 26:14; Ne 4:16
46:5 [d]ver 21; Jer 48:44 [e]S Ps 31:13; S 48:5
46:6 [f]Isa 30:16 [g]Ge 2:14; 15:18 [h]ver 12,16; S Ps 20:8
46:7 [i]Jer 47:2

[3]"Prepare your shields,[a] both large and small,
   and march out for battle!
[4]Harness the horses,
   mount the steeds!
Take your positions
   with helmets on!
Polish[b] your spears,
   put on your armor![c]
[5]What do I see?
   They are terrified,
they are retreating,
   their warriors are defeated.
They flee[d] in haste
   without looking back,
   and there is terror[e] on every side,"
           declares the LORD.
[6]"The swift cannot flee[f]
   nor the strong escape.
In the north by the River Euphrates[g]
   they stumble and fall. [h]

[7]"Who is this that rises like the Nile,
   like rivers of surging waters? [i]
[8]Egypt rises like the Nile,[j]
   like rivers of surging waters.
She says, 'I will rise and cover the earth;
   I will destroy cities and their people.'[k]
[9]Charge, O horses!
   Drive furiously, O charioteers![l]

46:8 [j]Eze 29:3,9; 30:12; Am 8:8 [k]Da 11:10 **46:9** [l]Jer 47:3; Eze 26:10; Na 3:2

45:1–5 A brief message of encouragement to Baruch, Jeremiah's faithful secretary (see note on 32:12). Though out of chronological order, the section provides a suitable historical appendix to chs. 39–44 as well as a smooth transition to chs. 46–51 (see notes on v. 1; 46:2).
45:1 *fourth year of Jehoiakim.* 605 B.C. Ch. 45 fits chronologically between 36:8 and 36:9 (see note on 36:8). *had written on a scroll.* See 36:4; see also 36:2 and note.
45:3 To some extent Baruch shared Jeremiah's anguish, the result of Jeremiah's prophetic call and ministry (see, e.g., 8:18–9:2; 20:7–18). *worn out with groaning.* See Ps 6:6. *find no rest.* See La 5:5.
45:4 *overthrow . . . built . . . uproot . . . planted.* See note on 1:10; see also 2:21; 31:4–5,28,40; 32:41; 33:7. *land.* Or "earth" (see "all people" in v. 5; see also 25:15,31; 46–51).
45:5 *great things . . . Seek them not.* See Ps 131:1. Baruch's brother Seraiah would occupy an important position under King Zedekiah (see 32:12; 51:59), but Baruch himself was not to be ambitious or self-seeking. *escape with your life.* See note on 21:9.
46:1–51:64 See notes on 25:1–38; 25:13; 25:19–26. Chs. 46–51 consist of a series of prophecies against the nations (see Isa 13–23; Eze 25–32; Am 1–2; Zep 2:4–15). They begin with Egypt (ch. 46) and end with Babylonia (chs. 50–51), the two powers that vied for control of Judah during Jeremiah's ministry. The arrangement of the prophecies is in a generally west-to-east direction.
46:1 *This is the word of the LORD . . . concerning.* See 14:1; 47:1; 49:34; 50:1. *nations.* To whom Jeremiah was

called to prophesy (see 1:5 and note).
46:2 *Concerning Egypt.* See Isa 19–20; Eze 29–32. *Neco.* Ruled Egypt 610–595 B.C. *Carchemish.* See 2Ch 35:20; Isa 10:9. The name means "fortress of Chemosh" (chief god of Moab; see 2Ki 23:13), as clarified by the Ebla tablets (see Introduction to Genesis: Background; see also chart on "Ancient Texts Relating to the OT," p. 5). *by Nebuchadnezzar.* Egypt's defeat by Babylonia at Carchemish was one of the most decisive battles in the ancient world, ending Egypt's agelong claims and pretensions to power in Syro-Palestine. *fourth year of Jehoiakim.* 605 B.C., the first year of Nebuchadnezzar's reign (see 25:1).
46:3 *Prepare.* Spoken to the Egyptians in sarcasm (see, e.g., Na 2:1; 3:14).
46:4 *horses.* Egypt was a prime source for the finest horses (see 1Ki 10:28). *put on your armor.* See 51:3.
46:5 *terror on every side.* The phrase is used in 6:25 (see note there) with reference to the Babylonian army (see 6:22 and note).
46:7–8 *rivers of surging waters.* In the northern Egyptian delta, where the Nile branches out into numerous streams.
46:8 *rise and cover the earth.* The same metaphor is used of Assyria in Isa 8:7–8 (see note there). *cities.* The Hebrew for this word is in the singular but is used as a generic plural ("city" is generic also in 8:16).
46:9 *Charge.* See note on v. 3; see also 8:6; Na 3:3. *Drive furiously, O charioteers!* See Na 2:4. *Put.* See note on Ge 10:6. *Lydia.* See note on Isa 66:19. Men from Cush, Put and Lydia were mercenaries in the Egyptian army.

March on, O warriors—
  men of Cush [w] [m] and Put who carry
    shields,
  men of Lydia [n] who draw the bow.
[10]But that day [o] belongs to the Lord, the
  LORD Almighty—
  a day of vengeance [p], for vengeance
    on his foes.
The sword will devour [q] till it is
    satisfied,
  till it has quenched its thirst with
    blood. [r]
For the Lord, the LORD Almighty, will
    offer sacrifice [s]
  in the land of the north by the River
    Euphrates. [t]

[11]"Go up to Gilead and get balm, [u]
  O Virgin [v] Daughter of Egypt.
But you multiply remedies in vain;
  there is no healing [w] for you.
[12]The nations will hear of your shame;
  your cries will fill the earth.
One warrior will stumble over another;
  both will fall [x] down together."

[13]This is the message the LORD spoke to
Jeremiah the prophet about the coming of
Nebuchadnezzar king of Babylon [y] to at-
tack Egypt: [z]

[14]"Announce this in Egypt, and proclaim
    it in Migdol;
  proclaim it also in Memphis [x] [a] and
    Tahpanhes: [b]
'Take your positions and get ready,
  for the sword devours [c] those around
    you.'

[15]Why will your warriors be laid low?
  They cannot stand, for the LORD will
    push them down. [d]
[16]They will stumble [e] repeatedly;
  they will fall [f] over each other.
They will say, 'Get up, let us go back
  to our own people [g] and our native
    lands,
  away from the sword of the
    oppressor.' [h]
[17]There they will exclaim,
  'Pharaoh king of Egypt is only a loud
    noise; [i]
  he has missed his opportunity. [j] '

[18]"As surely as I live," declares the
    King, [k]
  whose name is the LORD Almighty,
  "one will come who is like Tabor [l]
    among the mountains,
  like Carmel [m] by the sea.
[19]Pack your belongings for exile, [n]
  you who live in Egypt,
  for Memphis [o] will be laid waste [p]
  and lie in ruins without inhabitant.

[20]"Egypt is a beautiful heifer,
  but a gadfly is coming
    against her from the north. [q]
[21]The mercenaries [r] in her ranks
  are like fattened calves. [s]
They too will turn and flee [t] together,
  they will not stand their ground,

Cross references (center column):

46:9 [m]S Ge 10:6
[n]S Isa 66:19
46:10 [o]Eze 32:10; Joel 1:15; Ob 1:15 [p]S Nu 31:3; S Dt 32:41; 2Ki 23:29-30 [q]S Dt 32:42; S 2Sa 2:26; Zep 2:12 [r]S Dt 32:42 [s]S Lev 3:9; Zep 1:7 [t]Ge 2:14; 15:18
46:11 [u]S Ge 37:25 [v]S 2Ki 19:21 [w]S Jer 30:13; S Mic 1:9
46:12 [x]S ver 6; Isa 19:4; Na 3:8-10
46:13 [y]ver 26; Eze 32:11 [z]Isa 19:1; Jer 27:7
46:14 [a]S Isa 19:13 [b]S Jer 43:8 [c]S Dt 32:42; S 2Sa 2:26; S Jer 24:8
46:15 [d]S Jos 23:5; Isa 66:15-16
46:16 [e]S Lev 26:37 [f]S ver 6 [g]S Isa 13:14 [h]S Jer 25:38
46:17 [i]1Ki 20:10-11 /Isa 19:11-16
46:18 [k]Jer 48:15 [l]S Jos 19:22 [m]1Ki 18:42
46:19 [n]S Isa 20:4 [o]S Isa 19:13 [p]Eze 29:10,12; 35:7
46:20 [q]ver 24; S Isa 14:31; Jer 47:2
46:21 [r]S 2Ki 7:6 [s]Lk 15:27 [t]S ver 5; S Job 20:24

[w]9 That is, the upper Nile region   [x]14 Hebrew Noph; also in verse 19

46:10 *day of vengeance.* See Isa 34:8 and note. The Lord will avenge Egypt's cruelties toward Judah (see, e.g., 2Ki 23:29,33–35). *sword will devour.* See v. 14. *quenched its thirst with blood . . . offer sacrifice.* Battles are often compared with sacrifices (see Isa 34:5–7 and notes; Zep 1:7–8).
46:11 *Gilead . . . balm.* See 8:22 and note. *Virgin Daughter of Egypt.* See v. 19; Isa 23:12 and note; Isa 47:1; see also 14:17 and note; 18:13; 31:4,21. *remedies in vain . . . no healing for you.* The statement is ironic in the light of Egypt's reputation for expertise in the healing arts.
46:12 *stumble . . . fall.* See vv. 6,16.
46:13 *Nebuchadnezzar . . . to attack Egypt.* In 568–567 B.C. (see note on 43:11), long after the battle of Carchemish (see note on v. 2).
46:14 *Migdol.* See note on 44:1. *Memphis and Tahpanhes.* See 44:1; see also notes on 2:16; Isa 19:13. *Take your positions.* See v. 4. *sword devours.* See v. 10.
46:15 *warriors.* The Hebrew for this word is not the same as that for "warrior" in vv. 5,9,12. It is lit. "strong ones," often referring to powerful animals ("stallions" in 8:16; 50:11; "steeds" in 47:3; Jdg 5:22). In Ps 22:12; 50:13; 68:30; Isa 34:7 the Hebrew word is translated "bulls" (see note on Ps 68:30). *be laid low.* The Hebrew for this phrase is translated "Apis has fled" in the Septuagint (the Greek translation of the OT). Apis was a bull-god worshiped in Egypt, especially at Memphis (see v. 14). An alternative translation of v. 15 would then read as follows: "Why did Apis flee?

Why did your bull [many manuscripts have the singular form] not stand? Because the LORD pushed him down."
46:16 *They will stumble repeatedly.* See vv. 6,12; lit. "He will make many stumble." *They will say, '. . . let us go.'* The mercenaries in Pharaoh's army (see v. 9 and note) will decide to return to their homelands. *sword of the oppressor.* See 25:38; 50:16.
46:17 *only a loud noise.* In Isa 30:7, Egypt is called "the Do-Nothing." *missed his opportunity.* After the battle of Carchemish (see v. 2), Nebuchadnezzar returned to Babylonia on learning of his father's death. Egypt failed to press its advantage at that time.
46:18 *As surely as I live.* See notes on Ge 22:15; 42:16. *King.* God is called "King" also in 8:19; 10:7,10; 48:15; 51:57. *one.* Nebuchadnezzar. *Tabor . . . Carmel.* Two prominent mountains in Israel (see notes on Jdg 4:6; SS 7:5; Isa 33:9).
46:19 *Pack your belongings for exile.* Echoed in Eze 12:3. *Egypt.* Lit. "Daughter of Egypt" (see v. 11 and note). *laid waste.* Judah is also described in 2:15; 9:12.
46:20 *heifer.* Perhaps an ironic reference to Egyptian bull-worship (see note on v. 15). *gadfly.* Nebuchadnezzar. Insects are often used to symbolize an attacking enemy (see note on Ex 23:28).
46:21 *mercenaries.* See note on v. 9. *calves.* See note on v. 20. *day of disaster.* See 18:17. *time for them to be punished.* See 11:23; 23:12; 50:27.

for the day[u] of disaster is coming upon
  them,
    the time[v] for them to be punished.
22Egypt will hiss like a fleeing serpent
    as the enemy advances in force;
  they will come against her with axes,
    like men who cut down trees.[w]
23They will chop down her forest,"
            declares the LORD,
  "dense though it be.
  They are more numerous than locusts,[x]
    they cannot be counted.
24The Daughter of Egypt will be put to
    shame,
  handed over to the people of the
    north.[y] "

25The LORD Almighty, the God of Israel,
says: "I am about to bring punishment on
Amon god of Thebes,[y][z] on Pharaoh,[a] on
Egypt and her gods[b] and her kings, and on
those who rely[c] on Pharaoh. 26I will hand
them over[d] to those who seek their lives,
to Nebuchadnezzar king[e] of Babylon and
his officers. Later, however, Egypt will be
inhabited[f] as in times past," declares the
LORD.

27"Do not fear,[g] O Jacob[h] my servant;[i]
  do not be dismayed, O Israel.
I will surely save you out of a distant
    place,
  your descendants from the land of
    their exile.[j]
Jacob will again have peace and
    security,
  and no one will make him afraid.
28Do not fear, O Jacob my servant,
  for I am with you," [k] declares the
    LORD.
"Though I completely destroy[l] all the
    nations
  among which I scatter you,

46:21 [u]Ps 18:18;
37:13; Jer 18:17
[v]S Job 18:20
46:22 [w]Ps 74:5
46:23
[x]S Dt 28:42;
S Jdg 7:12
46:24
[y]S 2Ki 24:7
46:25
[z]Eze 30:14;
Na 3:8 [a]2Ki 24:7;
Eze 30:22
[b]S Jer 43:12
[c]Isa 20:6
46:26
[d]S Jer 44:30
[e]S ver.13;
S Isa 19:4
[f]Eze 29:11-16
46:27 [g]Isa 43:5;
Jer 51:46
[h]Isa 41:8; 44:1;
Mal 1:2
[i]S Isa 44:2
[j]S Isa 11:11;
S Jer 29:14; 50:19
46:28
[k]S Ex 14:22;
S Nu 14:9;
Isa 8:9-10
[l]S Jer 4:27

47:1
[m]S Ge 10:14;
S Jdg 3:31
[n]S Ge 10:19;
Zec 9:5-7
47:2 [o]S Isa 14:31
[p]S Isa 15:3
47:3 [q]S Jer 46:9;
S Eze 23:24
[r]Isa 13:7;
Jer 50:43;
Eze 7:17; 21:7
47:4 [s]S Isa 23:1;
Am 1:9-10;
Zec 9:2-4
[t]S Ge 10:15;
S Jer 25:22
[u]S Ge 10:14;
Joel 3:4
[v]S Dt 2:23
47:5 [w]S Jer 41:5
[x]S Jer 25:20

I will not completely destroy you.
I will discipline you but only with
    justice;
  I will not let you go entirely
    unpunished."

A Message About the Philistines

47 This is the word of the LORD that
    came to Jeremiah the prophet con-
cerning the Philistines[m] before Pharaoh attacked Gaza:[n]

2This is what the LORD says:

"See how the waters are rising in the
    north;[o]
  they will become an overflowing
    torrent.
They will overflow the land and
    everything in it,
  the towns and those who live in
    them.
The people will cry out;
  all who dwell in the land will wail[p]
3at the sound of the hoofs of galloping
    steeds,
  at the noise of enemy chariots[q]
  and the rumble of their wheels.
Fathers will not turn to help their
    children;
  their hands will hang limp.[r]
4For the day has come
  to destroy all the Philistines
and to cut off all survivors
  who could help Tyre[s] and Sidon.[t]
The LORD is about to destroy the
    Philistines,[u]
  the remnant from the coasts of
    Caphtor.[z][v]
5Gaza will shave[w] her head in
    mourning;
  Ashkelon[x] will be silenced.

[y]25 Hebrew No   [z]4 That is, Crete

46:22 *serpent.* Often used by Egyptian pharaohs as a symbol of their sovereignty (see note on Ex 4:3). *the enemy . . .
like men who cut down trees.* See 21:14; see also Isa
10:18–19,33–34 and notes.
46:23 *more numerous than locusts.* Here an invading
army is compared to locusts. In Joel 2:11,25 locusts are
compared to an invading army.
46:24 *Daughter of Egypt.* See note on v. 11.
46:25 *Amon.* The chief god of Egypt during much of its
history. Wicked King Manasseh may have named his son
after the Egyptian deity (see 2Ki 21:18; 2Ch 33:22). *Thebes.*
The capital of Upper (southern) Egypt (see Eze 30:14–16).
46:26 *Egypt will be inhabited as in times past.* Cf. 48:47;
49:6,39. Egypt would be restored in the Messianic age (see
Isa 19:23–25).
46:27–28 Repeated almost verbatim from 30:10–11 (see
notes there).
47:1 *concerning the Philistines.* See Isa 14:28–32; Eze
25:15–17; Am 1:6–8; Zep 2:4–7. *Pharaoh.* It is uncertain
whether Neco II (see 46:2; see also note on 2Ki 23:29) or

Hophra (see notes on 37:5; 44:30) is intended. *Gaza.* See v.
5; 25:20; see also note on Jdg 1:18.
47:2 *waters are rising.* See notes on 46:7–8. *the north.*
Babylonia, as in 1:13–14; 46:20. *the land . . . live in them.*
The Hebrew for this phrase is repeated verbatim from 8:16.
land. Phoenicia and Philistia. *towns.* See note on 46:8;
includes Tyre and Sidon (see v. 4) as well as Gaza, Ashkelon
(see v. 5) and other Philistine cities.
47:3 *steeds.* Lit. "strong ones" (see note on 46:15). *hands
will hang limp.* Paralyzed by terror (see 6:24; Isa 13:7).
47:4 *Tyre and Sidon.* See notes on v. 2; 25:22; 27:3.
remnant. See v. 5. *Caphtor.* Crete (see NIV text note; the
Kerethites of Zep 2:5 and elsewhere were probably Cretans),
one of many islands in the Mediterranean believed to be the
original homeland of the Philistines (see Ge 10:14 and note;
see also Dt 2:23).
47:5 *Gaza.* See v. 1; 25:20; see also note on Jdg 1:18.
shave her head in mourning. See note on 16:6; see also
48:37. *Ashkelon.* See v. 7; 25:20; see also note on Jdg 1:18.
be silenced. A sign of mourning (see La 2:10). *remnant.* See

O remnant on the plain,
how long will you cut[y] yourselves?

6 " 'Ah, sword[z] of the LORD,' you cry,[u]
'how long till you rest?
Return to your scabbard;
cease and be still.'[a]
7 But how can it rest
when the LORD has commanded it,
when he has ordered it
to attack Ashkelon and the coast?"[b]

A Message About Moab

48:29–36pp — Isa 16:6–12

48 Concerning Moab:[c]
This is what the LORD Almighty,
the God of Israel, says:

"Woe to Nebo,[d] for it will be ruined.
Kiriathaim[e] will be disgraced and
captured;
the stronghold[a] will be disgraced and
shattered.
2 Moab will be praised[f] no more;
in Heshbon[b][g] men will plot her
downfall:
'Come, let us put an end to that
nation.'[h]
You too, O Madmen,[c] will be silenced;
the sword will pursue you.
3 Listen to the cries from Horonaim,[i]
cries of great havoc and destruction.
4 Moab will be broken;
her little ones will cry out.[d]
5 They go up the way to Luhith,[j]
weeping bitterly as they go;

on the road down to Horonaim[k]
anguished cries over the destruction
are heard.
6 Flee![l] Run for your lives;
become like a bush[e] in the desert.[m]
7 Since you trust in your deeds and
riches,[n]
you too will be taken captive,
and Chemosh[o] will go into exile,[p]
together with his priests and
officials.[q]
8 The destroyer[r] will come against every
town,
and not a town will escape.
The valley will be ruined
and the plateau[s] destroyed,
because the LORD has spoken.
9 Put salt[t] on Moab,
for she will be laid waste[f];[u]
her towns will become desolate,
with no one to live in them.

10 "A curse on him who is lax in doing the
LORD'S work!
A curse on him who keeps his
sword[v] from bloodshed![w]

11 "Moab has been at rest[x] from youth,
like wine left on its dregs,[y]
not poured from one jar to another—
she has not gone into exile.

Cross references

47:5 [y]S Lev 19:28
47:6 [z]S Isa 34:5; Jer 12:12; 48:10; 50:35 [a]Eze 21:30
47:7 [b]Eze 25:15-17
48:1 [c]S Ge 19:37; S Dt 23:6 [d]S Nu 32:38 [e]S Nu 32:37; S Jos 13:19
48:2 [f]Isa 16:14 [g]S Nu 21:25; S Jos 13:26 [h]ver 42
48:3 [i]S Isa 15:5
48:5 [j]Isa 15:5
[k]ver 3
48:6 [l]S Ge 19:17 [m]Jer 17:6
48:7 [n]S Ps 49:6; S Pr 11:28 [o]S Nu 21:29 [p]Isa 46:1-2; Jer 49:3 [q]Am 2:3
48:8 [r]S Ex 12:23; S Jer 4:7 [s]S Jos 13:9
48:9 [t]Jdg 9:45 [u]Jer 51:29
48:10 [v]S Jer 47:6 [w]S 1Sa 15:11; 1Ki 20:42; 2Ki 13:15-19
48:11 [x]Zec 1:15 [y]Zep 1:12

Footnotes

[a]1 Or / Misgab   [b]2 The Hebrew for Heshbon sounds like the Hebrew for plot.   [c]2 The name of the Moabite town Madmen sounds like the Hebrew for be silenced.   [d]4 Hebrew; Septuagint / proclaim it to Zoar   [e]6 Or like Aroer   [f]9 Or Give wings to Moab, / for she will fly away

---

note on v. 4. plain. Roughly equivalent to the modern Gaza Strip, it lay west of the foothills that separated Philistia from Judah. cut yourselves. See note on 16:6; see also 48:37.

47:6 you. The Philistines.

47:7 attack Ashkelon. The immediate fulfillment took place under Nebuchadnezzar in 604 B.C. coast. See Eze 25:16; the Philistine plain (see note on v. 5).

48:1 Concerning Moab. See Isa 15–16; Eze 25:8–11; Am 2:1–3; Zep 2:8–11. Josephus (Antiquities, 10.9.7) implies that Jeremiah's prophecy concerning the future destruction of Moab was fulfilled in the "twenty-third year of Nebuchadnezzar's reign" (582 B.C.; see 52:30). Nebo. See v. 22; a town originally allotted to the tribe of Reuben (see Nu 32:3,37–38; see also Isa 15:2 and note). Kiriathaim. See v. 23. An ancient town (see Ge 14:5), it too was allotted to Reuben (see Jos 13:19 and note). Nebo, Kiriathaim and several other towns referred to in this chapter are mentioned also in an important Moabite inscription written by Mesha king of Moab (see 2Ki 3:4) and discovered in 1868 (see chart on "Ancient Texts Relating to the OT," p. 5).

48:2 Heshbon. See vv. 34,45; 49:3; Nu 21:25. Originally allotted to Reuben (see Nu 32:37; Jos 13:17), it was later reassigned to Gad as a Levitical town (see Jos 21:39). will plot. The Hebrew for this phrase is a pun on "Heshbon." Madmen. Location unknown; perhaps a longer spelling of "Dimon" (Isa 15:9—but see note there). In Isa 25:10, the feminine form of the Hebrew word madmen is trans-

lated "manure." sword will pursue you. See 9:16; 42:16.

48:3 Horonaim. See vv. 5,34; location unknown.

48:4 broken. Like a clay jar (see 19:11).

48:5 Luhith. Location unknown (see Isa 15:5).

48:6 Flee! Run for your lives. See 51:6. like a bush. See note on 17:6.

48:7 Chemosh. See vv. 13,46; the national god of Moab (see 1Ki 11:7,33; 2Ki 23:13). The Hebrew text here implies the alternate spelling Chemish, as in "Carchemish" (see note on 46:2). will go into exile . . . and officials. A stock phrase (see 49:3; Am 1:15). Images of pagan deities were often carried about from place to place (see 43:12; Am 5:26).

48:8 destroyer. See v. 32; probably Nebuchadnezzar. valley . . . plateau. Much of western Moab overlooks the Jordan Valley.

48:9 See 17:6. Put salt on Moab. To make its farmland unproductive and barren (see note on Jdg 9:45).

48:10 lax. Or "lazy" (as in Pr 10:4; 12:24). Those whom the Lord designates to destroy Moab are urged on in their appointed task.

48:11 A copy of the Hebrew text of this verse has been found inscribed on a large clay seal, dating to the early Christian era and apparently used for stamping the bitumen with which the mouths of wine jars were sealed. from youth. From her early history. like wine. An apt figure, since Moab was noted for her vineyards (see vv. 32–33; Isa 16:8–10). left on its dregs. In order to improve with age (see Isa 25:6). she has not gone into exile. Unlike Israel.

So she tastes as she did,
and her aroma is unchanged.
[12]But days are coming,"
declares the LORD,
"when I will send men who pour from
jars,
and they will pour her out;
they will empty her jars
and smash her jugs.
[13]Then Moab will be ashamed[z] of
Chemosh,[a]
as the house of Israel was ashamed
when they trusted in Bethel.[b]

[14]"How can you say, 'We are warriors,[c]
men valiant in battle'?
[15]Moab will be destroyed and her towns
invaded;
her finest young men[d] will go down
in the slaughter,[e]"
declares the King,[f] whose name is
the LORD Almighty.[g]
[16]"The fall of Moab is at hand;[h]
her calamity will come quickly.
[17]Mourn for her, all who live around her,
all who know her fame;[i]
say, 'How broken is the mighty
scepter,[j]
how broken the glorious staff!'

[18]"Come down from your glory
and sit on the parched ground,[k]
O inhabitants of the Daughter of
Dibon,[l]
for he who destroys Moab
will come up against you
and ruin your fortified cities.[m]

[19]Stand by the road and watch,
you who live in Aroer.[n]
Ask the man fleeing and the woman
escaping,
ask them, 'What has happened?'
[20]Moab is disgraced, for she is shattered.
Wail[o] and cry out!
Announce by the Arnon[p]
that Moab is destroyed.
[21]Judgment has come to the plateau[q]—
to Holon,[r] Jahzah[s] and Mephaath,[t]
[22] to Dibon,[u] Nebo[v] and Beth
Diblathaim,
[23] to Kiriathaim,[w] Beth Gamul and Beth
Meon,[x]
[24] to Kerioth[y] and Bozrah[z]—
to all the towns[a] of Moab, far and
near.
[25]Moab's horn[g][b] is cut off;
her arm[c] is broken,"
declares the LORD.

[26]"Make her drunk,[d]
for she has defied[e] the LORD.
Let Moab wallow in her vomit;[f]
let her be an object of ridicule.[g]
[27]Was not Israel the object of your
ridicule?[h]
Was she caught among thieves,[i]
that you shake your head[j] in scorn[k]
whenever you speak of her?
[28]Abandon your towns and dwell among
the rocks,
you who live in Moab.
Be like a dove[l] that makes its nest

48:13 [z]Hos 10:6
[a]ver 7 [b]S Jos 7:2
48:14 [c]Ps 33:16
48:15 [d]S Isa 9:17
[e]Jer 51:40
[f]S Jer 46:18
[g]Jer 51:57
48:16 [h]Isa 13:22
48:17 [i]2Ki 3:4-5
[j]S Ps 110:2
48:18 [k]Isa 47:1
[l]S Nu 21:30;
S Jos 13:9 [m]ver 8

48:19
[n]S Nu 32:34
48:20 [o]S Isa 16:7
[p]S Nu 21:13
48:21
[q]S Jos 13:9,21
[r]S Jos 15:51
[s]S Nu 21:23;
S Isa 15:4
[t]S Jos 13:18
48:22
[u]S Nu 21:30;
S Jos 13:9,17
[v]S Nu 32:38
48:23
[w]S Nu 32:37;
S Jos 13:19
[x]S Jos 13:17
48:24 [y]Am 2:2
[z]Jer 49:13
[a]S Isa 15:1
48:25 [b]Ps 75:10
[c]Ps 10:15; 37:17;
Eze 30:21
48:26 [d]Jer 25:16,
27; 51:39 [e]ver
42; 1Sa 17:26
[f]S Isa 28:8 [g]ver
39
48:27 [h]S Jer 2:26
[i]2Ki 17:3-6
[j]S Job 16:4;
Ps 44:14;
Jer 18:16
[k]S Dt 28:37;
Mic 7:8-10;
Zep 2:8,10
48:28 [l]S Ge 8:8;
S SS 1:15

g 25 *Horn* here symbolizes strength.

48:12 *days are coming.* Moab will be destroyed (see note on v. 1). *pour from jars.* Gently, in order to leave the unwanted sediment in the bottom. But these men will be the agents of divine judgment and will "smash" Moab (see v. 4 and note).

48:13 *Chemosh.* See note on v. 7. *house of Israel.* The northern kingdom, destroyed and exiled in 722–721 B.C. *Bethel.* Either (1) the well-known town where one of Jeroboam's golden calves was placed (see 1Ki 12:28–30) or, (2) in parallelism with Chemosh, the West Semitic deity known from contemporary Babylonian inscriptions as well as from the Elephantine papyri a century later.

48:14 *How can you say . . . ?* See 2:23; 8:8.

48:15 *go down in the slaughter.* See 50:27; for war depicted as the slaughter of sacrificial animals see Isa 34:6 and note. *King.* See note on 46:18. The true King is the Lord, not Chemosh.

48:16 See Dt 32:35.

48:17 *who live around her . . . who know her fame.* Nations near and far respectively. *mighty.* At one time Moab had been powerful and feared (see 27:3; 2Ki 1:1; 3:5; 24:2). *scepter . . . staff.* Symbols of authority and dominion (see Ge 49:10; Ps 2:9; Eze 19:11,14).

48:18 *Come down . . . sit.* See Isa 47:1 and note. *Daughter of.* See note on Isa 23:10. *Dibon.* See v. 22; Nu 21:30; see also note on Isa 15:2.

48:19 *Aroer.* See NIV text note on v. 6; see also Nu 32:34; Dt 2:36.

48:20 *Arnon.* Moab's most important river.

48:21 *plateau.* See note on v. 8. *Holon.* Not the same as the town mentioned in Jos 15:51; 21:15. Its location is unknown. *Jahzah.* See v. 34; elsewhere called Jahaz (see v. 34; also Isa 15:4 and note).

48:22 *Dibon.* See v. 18. *Nebo.* See note on v. 1. *Beth Diblathaim.* Perhaps the same as, or near, Almon Diblathaim (see Nu 33:46).

48:23 *Kiriathaim.* See note on v. 1. *Beth Gamul.* Modern Khirbet Jumeil, five miles east of Aroer. *Beth Meon.* The same as Baal Meon (see Nu 32:38) and Beth Baal Meon (see Jos 13:17).

48:24 *Kerioth.* See note on Am 2:2. Its location is unknown. *Bozrah.* Not the same as Bozrah in Edom (see 49:13,22) but another name for Bezer in Moab (see note on Dt 4:43).

48:26 The Lord speaks to the Babylonian invaders. *Make her drunk.* By drinking down the cup of God's wrath (see 13:13; 25:15–17,28). *wallow in her vomit.* See 25:27; Isa 19:14. *let her be an object of ridicule.* As she had once ridiculed others (see v. 27; Zep 2:8,10).

48:27 *shake your head in scorn.* See 18:16 and note; see also Ps 64:8.

48:28 *like a dove . . . mouth of a cave.* See Ps 55:6–8; SS 2:14.

at the mouth of a cave. *m*

29"We have heard of Moab's pride *n*—
    her overweening pride and conceit,
    her pride and arrogance
    and the haughtiness *o* of her heart.
30I know her insolence but it is futile,"
                        declares the LORD,
    "and her boasts *p* accomplish nothing.
31Therefore I wail *q* over Moab,
    for all Moab I cry out,
    I moan for the men of Kir Hareseth. *r*
32I weep for you, as Jazer *s* weeps,
    O vines of Sibmah. *t*
Your branches spread as far as the sea;
    they reached as far as the sea of
        Jazer.
The destroyer has fallen
    on your ripened fruit and grapes.
33Joy and gladness are gone
    from the orchards and fields of Moab.
I have stopped the flow of wine *u* from
        the presses;
    no one treads them with shouts of
        joy. *v*
Although there are shouts,
    they are not shouts of joy.

34"The sound of their cry rises
    from Heshbon *w* to Elealeh *x* and
        Jahaz, *y*
    from Zoar *z* as far as Horonaim *a* and
        Eglath Shelishiyah,
    for even the waters of Nimrim are
        dried up. *b*
35In Moab I will put an end
    to those who make offerings on the
        high places *c*
    and burn incense *d* to their gods,"
                        declares the LORD.
36"So my heart laments *e* for Moab like a
        flute;
    it laments like a flute for the men of
        Kir Hareseth. *f*
The wealth they acquired *g* is gone.

37Every head is shaved *h*
    and every beard *i* cut off;
every hand is slashed
    and every waist is covered with
        sackcloth. *j*
38On all the roofs in Moab
    and in the public squares *k*
there is nothing but mourning,
    for I have broken Moab
    like a jar *l* that no one wants,"
                        declares the LORD.
39"How shattered *m* she is! How they
        wail!
    How Moab turns her back in shame!
Moab has become an object of
        ridicule, *n*
    an object of horror to all those
        around her."

40This is what the LORD says:

"Look! An eagle is swooping *o* down,
    spreading its wings *p* over Moab.
41Kerioth *h q* will be captured
    and the strongholds taken.
In that day the hearts of Moab's
        warriors *r*
    will be like the heart of a woman in
        labor. *s*
42Moab will be destroyed *t* as a nation *u*
    because she defied *v* the LORD.
43Terror *w* and pit and snare *x* await you,
    O people of Moab,"
                        declares the LORD.
44"Whoever flees *y* from the terror
    will fall into a pit,
whoever climbs out of the pit
    will be caught in a snare;
for I will bring upon Moab
    the year *z* of her punishment,"
                        declares the LORD.

45"In the shadow of Heshbon
    the fugitives stand helpless,

48:28 *m*S Jdg 6:2
48:29
*n*S Lev 26:19;
S Job 40:12
*o*S Ps 10:5;
S Pr 16:18
48:30 *p*S Ps 10:3
48:31 *q*ver 36;
Isa 15:5-8
*r*S 2Ki 3:25
48:32
*s*S Jos 13:25
*t*S Nu 32:3
48:33 *u*S Isa 24:7
*v*Joel 1:12;
Am 5:17
48:34
*w*S Nu 21:25;
S Jos 13:26
*x*S Nu 32:3
*y*S Nu 21:23;
S Isa 15:4
*z*S Ge 13:10
*a*S Isa 15:5
*b*S Isa 15:6
48:35 *c*S Isa 15:2
*d*Jer 11:13
48:36 *e*S ver 31
*f*S 2Ki 3:25
*g*S Isa 15:7

48:37 *h*Isa 15:2;
S Jer 41:5;
Eze 27:31; 29:18
*i*S Lev 19:27;
S 2Sa 10:4
*j*S Ge 37:34;
S Isa 3:24;
Jer 16:6; Am 8:10
48:38 *k*S Isa 15:3
*l*S Jer 22:28
48:39 *m*Jer 50:23
*n*ver 26
48:40
*o*S Dt 28:49;
Hab 1:8 *p*S Isa 8:8
48:41 *q*S Isa 15:1
*r*Am 2:16
*s*S Isa 21:3
48:42
*t*S Isa 16:14 *u*ver
2 *v*S ver 26
48:43 *w*Jer 49:5
*x*S Isa 24:17
48:44
*y*1Ki 19:17;
S Job 20:24;
Isa 24:18;
S Jer 46:5
*z*Jer 11:23; 23:12

*h*41 Or *The cities*

48:29–30 An expanded version of the description of Moab found in Isa 16:6.
48:29 *Moab's pride.* It had long since become proverbial (see Isa 25:10–11; Zep 2:8–10).
48:31–33 See Isa 16:7–10.
48:31–32 *l.* The prophet (as in Isa 16:9; cf. Isa 15:5).
48:31 *moan.* Like a mourning dove (see Isa 38:14; 59:11). *Kir Hareseth.* See Isa 16:7,11; see also note on Isa 15:1.
48:32 *as Jazer.* Or "more than Jazer" (so also in Isa 16:9). *Jazer . . . Sibmah . . . sea.* See note on Isa 16:8. *vines.* See note on v. 11. *destroyer.* See v. 8; probably Nebuchadnezzar.
48:33 *treads.* See note on Isa 16:10. *not shouts of joy.* Instead, shouts of judgment (see 25:30; 51:14).
48:34 See Isa 15:4–6 and notes.
48:36 See Isa 16:11. *flute.* Played by mourners at funerals (see Mt 9:23–24).
48:37 Signs of mourning (see Isa 15:2–3 and notes). *is*

slashed. See note on 16:6.
48:38 *broken . . . like a jar that no one wants.* See v. 4 and note on v. 12; cf. the description of King Jehoiachin in 22:28 (see note there).
48:39 *object of ridicule.* See v. 26 and note.
48:40–41 Echoed in 49:22 with respect to Edom.
48:40 *eagle.* Nebuchadnezzar (as in Eze 17:3); see Dt 28:49 and note.
48:41 *Kerioth.* Location uncertain (see v. 24; see also note on Am 2:2).
48:43 *Terror and pit and snare.* The Hebrew original illustrates Jeremiah's fondness for the well-turned phrase (see Introduction: Literary Features)—though in this case Jeremiah was not its creator (see note on Isa 24:17).
48:44 *Whoever flees . . . will fall . . . whoever climbs . . . will be caught.* Divine judgment, once determined, is unavoidable (see Am 5:19).
48:45–46 Echoed from Nu 21:28–29; 24:17. Balaam's

for a fire has gone out from Heshbon,
a blaze from the midst of Moab;[a]
it burns the foreheads of Moab,
the skulls[b] of the noisy boasters.
[46]Woe to you, O Moab![c]
The people of Chemosh are
destroyed;
your sons are taken into exile
and your daughters into captivity.

[47]"Yet I will restore[d] the fortunes of
Moab
in days to come,"
declares the LORD.

Here ends the judgment on Moab.

A Message About Ammon

49 Concerning the Ammonites:[e]
This is what the LORD says:

"Has Israel no sons?
Has she no heirs?
Why then has Molech[f] taken
possession of Gad?
Why do his people live in its towns?
[2]But the days are coming,"
declares the LORD,
"when I will sound the battle cry[h]
against Rabbah[i] of the Ammonites;
it will become a mound of ruins,[j]
and its surrounding villages will be
set on fire.
Then Israel will drive out
those who drove her out,[k]"
says the LORD.
[3]"Wail, O Heshbon,[l] for Ai[m] is
destroyed!

Cry out, O inhabitants of Rabbah!
Put on sackcloth[n] and mourn;
rush here and there inside the walls,
for Molech[o] will go into exile,[p]
together with his priests and officials.
[4]Why do you boast of your valleys,
boast of your valleys so fruitful?
O unfaithful daughter,[q]
you trust in your riches[r] and say,
'Who will attack me?'[s]
[5]I will bring terror on you
from all those around you,"
declares the Lord,
the LORD Almighty.
"Every one of you will be driven away,
and no one will gather the fugitives.[t]

[6]"Yet afterward, I will restore[u] the
fortunes of the Ammonites,"
declares the LORD.

A Message About Edom

49:9–10pp — Ob 5–6
49:14–16pp — Ob 1–4

[7]Concerning Edom:[v]

This is what the LORD Almighty says:

"Is there no longer wisdom in Teman?[w]
Has counsel perished from the
prudent?
Has their wisdom decayed?
[8]Turn and flee, hide in deep caves,[x]
you who live in Dedan,[y]
for I will bring disaster on Esau
at the time I punish him.
[9]If grape pickers came to you,

Cross references (center column):

48:45
[a]S Nu 21:21,
26-28; S Jos 12:2
[b]Nu 24:17
48:46
[c]S Nu 21:29
48:47 [d]Ps 14:7;
Isa 11:11;
Jer 12:15; 49:6,
39; Eze 16:53;
Da 11:41
49:1
[e]S Ge 19:38;
S 1Sa 11:1-11;
2Sa 10:1-19
[f]S Lev 18:21
[g]Ge 30:11
49:2 [h]S Jer 4:19
[i]S Dt 3:11
[j]S Dt 13:16
[k]S Isa 14:2;
S Jer 30:16;
Eze 21:28-32;
25:2-11
49:3 [l]S Jos 13:26
[m]S Ge 12:8;
S Jos 8:28

[n]S Ge 37:34
[o]Zep 1:5
[p]S Jer 48:7
49:4 [q]S Jer 3:6
[r]S Jer 9:23;
1Ti 6:17
[s]S Jer 21:13
49:5 [t]S Jer 44:14
49:6
[u]Jer 12:14-17;
S 48:47
49:7
[v]S Ge 25:30;
S Ps 83:6
[w]S Ge 36:11,15,
34
49:8 [x]S Jdg 6:2
[y]S Ge 10:7;
S 25:3

[i]1 Or *their king*; Hebrew *malcam*; also in verse 3

---

oracles against Moab are about to be fulfilled.
48:45 *Heshbon.* See note on v. 2. Apparently at this time it
was controlled by the Ammonites (see 49:3). *Sihon.* Refers
to the associates of Sihon king of the Amorites, whose chief
city was Heshbon (see Nu 21:27) during the time of the
exodus. *boasters.* See note on v. 29.
48:46 *Chemosh.* See note on v. 7.
48:47 See 46:26. *restore the fortunes.* See note on 29:14.
in days to come. During the Messianic era. *Here ends.* A
note by the final compiler of the book of Jeremiah (see
51:64).
49:1 *Concerning the Ammonites.* See Eze 25:1–7; Am
1:13–15; Zep 2:8–11. Ammon was east of the Jordan and
north of Moab (see note on Ge 19:36–38). *Molech.* The
chief god of the Ammonites (see 1Ki 11:5,7,33), also known
as Milcom (see NIV text note on 1Ki 11:5). Both titles are
related to the West Semitic word for "king" (see NIV text
note here). *taken possession of Gad.* Probably refers to the
aftermath of Tiglath-Pileser III's conquest of Transjordan in
734–732 B.C. The Ammonites later apparently recovered
from their defeat and overran some of the territory owned by
the Israelite tribe of Gad. *his.* Molech's.
49:2 *battle cry.* See Am 1:14. *Rabbah of the Ammonites.*
See note on Dt 3:11. *mound.* See note on 30:18.
49:3 *Heshbon.* See note on 48:45; see also Jdg 11:26–27.
Ai. Not the Ai of Jos 8. Its location is unknown. *walls.* The

Hebrew for this word refers not to city walls but to walls
separating vineyards from each other (see Nu 21:24). *Molech.* See note on v. 1. *will go into exile . . . and officials.* See
note on 48:7.
49:4 *unfaithful daughter.* Applied to the people of Judah in
31:22. *you trust in your riches.* Spoken to Moab in 48:7.
Who will attack me? According to Josephus (*Antiquities*,
10.9.7) Nebuchadnezzar destroyed Ammon in the 23rd year
of his reign (582 B.C.).
49:6 See 48:47; see also note on 29:14.
49:7–22 Shares many memorable phrases and concepts
with the book of Obadiah.
49:7 *Concerning Edom.* See Isa 21:11–12; Eze
25:12–14; Am 1:11–12; Ob 1–16. *wisdom.* For which
Edom was justly famed (see notes on Job 1:1; 2:11). *Teman.*
An important Edomite town located south of the Dead Sea
(see note on Job 2:11). In v. 20 it is used in parallelism with
Edom itself.
49:8 *Turn and flee.* See v. 24; 46:21. *Dedan.* See 25:23;
see also notes on Isa 21:13; Eze 25:13. *Esau.* The patriarch
Jacob's brother, and another name for Edom (see Ge
25:29–30; 36:1), just as Israel was another name for Jacob
(see Ge 32:28). The fact that Esau was Jacob's brother made
Edom's enmity toward Israel all the more reprehensible (see
Am 1:11; Ob 10).
49:9–10 Paralleled in Ob 5–6.

would they not leave a few grapes?
If thieves came during the night,
　would they not steal only as much as
　　they wanted?
[10]But I will strip Esau bare;
　I will uncover his hiding places, [z]
　so that he cannot conceal himself.
His children, relatives and neighbors
　　will perish,
and he will be no more. [a]
[11]Leave your orphans; [b] I will protect
　　their lives.
　Your widows [c] too can trust in me."

[12]This is what the LORD says: "If those
who do not deserve to drink the cup [d]
must drink it, why should you go unpunished? [e] You will not go unpunished, but
must drink it. [13]I swear [f] by myself," declares the LORD, "that Bozrah [g] will
become a ruin and an object of horror, [h] of
reproach [i] and of cursing; and all its towns
will be in ruins forever." [j]

[14]I have heard a message from the LORD:
　An envoy was sent to the nations to
　　say,
"Assemble yourselves to attack it!
　Rise up for battle!"

[15]"Now I will make you small among the
　　nations,
　despised among men.
[16]The terror you inspire
　and the pride [k] of your heart have
　　deceived you,
you who live in the clefts of the rocks, [l]
　who occupy the heights of the hill.
Though you build your nest [m] as high as
　　the eagle's,
　from there I will bring you down,"
　　　　　　　　　　　　declares the LORD.

[17]"Edom will become an object of
　　horror; [n]
all who pass by will be appalled and
　　will scoff
because of all its wounds. [o]
[18]As Sodom [p] and Gomorrah [q] were
　　overthrown,
　along with their neighboring towns,"
　　　　　　　　　　　　　says the LORD,
"so no one will live there;
　no man will dwell [r] in it.

[19]"Like a lion [s] coming up from Jordan's
　　thickets [t]
　to a rich pastureland,
I will chase Edom from its land in an
　　instant.
Who is the chosen one I will appoint
　　for this?
Who is like [u] me and who can challenge
　　me? [v]
And what shepherd [w] can stand
　　against me?"

[20]Therefore, hear what the LORD has
　　planned against Edom, [x]
　what he has purposed [y] against those
　　who live in Teman: [z]
The young of the flock [a] will be dragged
　　away;
　he will completely destroy [b] their
　　pasture because of them. [c]
[21]At the sound of their fall the earth will
　　tremble; [d]
　their cry [e] will resound to the Red
　　Sea. [i]
[22]Look! An eagle will soar and swoop [f]
　　down,
　spreading its wings over Bozrah. [g]
In that day the hearts of Edom's
　　warriors [h]

Cross references (center column):

49:10 [z]S Ge 3:8
[a]Isa 34:10-12;
S Jer 11:23;
Eze 35:4;
Ob 1:18;
Mal 1:2-5
49:11 [b]Hos 14:3
[c]S Dt 10:18;
Jas 1:27
49:12
[d]S Isa 51:23;
S Jer 25:15;
Mt 20:22
[e]S Pr 11:31
49:13
[f]S Ge 22:16
[g]S Ge 36:33 [h]ver
17 [i]Jer 42:18
[j]S Jer 19:8;
Eze 35:9
49:16
[k]Eze 35:13;
Ob 1:12
[l]S Job 39:28
[m]S Job 39:27

49:17 [n]ver 13
[o]S Dt 29:22;
Eze 35:7
49:18 [p]Jer 23:14
[q]S Ge 19:24 [r]ver
33; S Isa 34:10
49:19
[s]S 1Sa 17:34
[t]S Jer 12:5
[u]S Ex 8:10;
S 2Ch 20:6;
S Isa 46:5
[v]S Job 9:19;
Jer 50:44
[w]S Isa 17:35
49:20 [x]Isa 34:5
[y]Isa 14:27 [z]ver 7;
S Ge 36:11
[a]Jer 50:45 [b]ver
10; Ob 1:10;
Mal 1:3-4
[c]Jer 50:45
49:21 [d]Ps 114:7;
Eze 26:15; 27:28;
31:16 [e]Jer 50:46;
51:29; Eze 26:18
49:22
[f]S Dt 28:49;
Hos 8:1; Hab 1:8
[g]S Ge 36:33
[h]Jer 50:36;
Na 3:13

[i]21 Hebrew *Yam Suph*; that is, Sea of Reeds

49:9 *grape pickers.* See note on v. 13. *leave a few grapes.* For the poor to glean (see note on Ru 2:2).

49:10 *strip . . . bare.* See note on 13:22. *be no more.* See 31:15; Isa 19:7.

49:12 Echoed from 25:28–29. *those who do not deserve . . . must drink it.* Though they are God's chosen ones, the people of Judah will be punished because of their sin (see Am 3:2).

49:13 *swear by myself.* See notes on Ge 22:16; Isa 45:23; see also 22:5; 51:14. *Bozrah.* Not the Bozrah of 48:24 (see note there); the Edomite Bozrah was probably the capital of Edom in the days of Jeremiah (see v. 22; Ge 36:33; see also notes on Isa 34:6; Am 1:12). The Hebrew root underlying Bozrah is the same as that for "grape pickers" in v. 9. *ruin . . . cursing.* See 25:18. *in ruins forever.* See 25:9; Ps 74:3; Isa 58:12 and note.

49:14–16 Paralleled in Ob 1–4.

49:16 *pride.* Edom's besetting sin (see v. 4; Ob 11–13; cf. 48:29–30). *rocks.* Perhaps a reference to Petra (see note on

2Ki 14:7), the most spectacular of the mountain strongholds for which Edom was noted.

49:17 Echoed from 19:8.

49:18 Repeated almost verbatim in 50:40, and echoed in part in v. 33. *Sodom and Gomorrah were overthrown.* See Ge 19:24–25. Later calamities were often compared with the one that befell Sodom and Gomorrah (see note on Am 4:11). *their neighboring towns.* Primarily Admah and Zeboiim (see Ge 14:2,8; Dt 29:23; Hos 11:8).

49:19–21 Repeated almost verbatim in the oracle against Babylon (see 50:44–46).

49:19 *Jordan's thickets.* See 12:5 and note. *shepherd.* Ruler (see note on 2:8).

49:20 *Teman.* See note on v. 7. *flock.* The people of Edom.

49:22 Echoed from 48:40–41. *eagle.* Represents Nebuchadnezzar in 48:40 (see note there), and probably here also. A more complete subjugation of the Edomites, however, was accomplished by Nabatean Arabs (perhaps the "desert jackals" of Mal 1:3) beginning c. 550 B.C. *Bozrah.* See note on v. 13.

will be like the heart of a woman in labor. [i]

A Message About Damascus

23Concerning Damascus: [j]

"Hamath [k] and Arpad [l] are dismayed,
    for they have heard bad news.
They are disheartened,
    troubled like [k] the restless sea. [m]
24Damascus has become feeble,
    she has turned to flee
    and panic has gripped her;
anguish and pain have seized her,
    pain like that of a woman in labor. [n]
25Why has the city of renown not been
        abandoned,
    the town in which I delight?
26Surely, her young men [o] will fall in the
        streets;
    all her soldiers will be silenced [p] in
        that day,"
        declares the LORD Almighty.
27"I will set fire [q] to the walls of
        Damascus; [r]
    it will consume [s] the fortresses of
        Ben-Hadad. [t] "

A Message About Kedar and Hazor

28Concerning Kedar [u] and the kingdoms
of Hazor, [v] which Nebuchadnezzar [w] king
of Babylon attacked:

This is what the LORD says:

"Arise, and attack Kedar
    and destroy the people of the East. [x]
29Their tents and their flocks [y] will be
        taken;
    their shelters will be carried off
    with all their goods and camels.
Men will shout to them,
    'Terror [z] on every side!'

30"Flee quickly away!
    Stay in deep caves, [a] you who live in
        Hazor, [b] "
        declares the LORD.
"Nebuchadnezzar [c] king of Babylon has
        plotted against you;
    he has devised a plan against you.

31"Arise and attack a nation at ease,
    which lives in confidence,"
        declares the LORD,
"a nation that has neither gates nor
        bars; [d]
    its people live alone.
32Their camels [e] will become plunder,
    and their large herds [f] will be booty.
I will scatter to the winds [g] those who
        are in distant places1 [h]
    and will bring disaster on them from
        every side,"
        declares the LORD.
33"Hazor [i] will become a haunt of
        jackals, [j]
    a desolate [k] place forever.
No one will live there;
    no man will dwell [l] in it."

A Message About Elam

34This is the word of the LORD that came
to Jeremiah the prophet concerning
Elam, [m] early in the reign of Zedekiah [n]
king of Judah:

35This is what the LORD Almighty says:

"See, I will break the bow [o] of Elam,
    the mainstay of their might.
36I will bring against Elam the four
        winds [p]
    from the four quarters of the
        heavens; [q]

Cross references (center column)

49:22 [i]Isa 13:8
49:23 [/]S Ge 14:15; 2Ki 14:28; 2Ch 16:2; Ac 9:2 [k]1Ki 8:65; Isa 10:9; Eze 47:16; Am 6:2; Zec 9:2 [/]S 2Ki 18:34; S 19:13 [m]S Ge 49:4
49:24 [n]Jer 13:21
49:26 [o]S Isa 9:17; S 13:18 [p]Isa 17:12-14
49:27 [q]Jer 21:14; 43:12; 50:32; Eze 30:8; 39:6; Am 1:4 [r]S Ge 14:15 [s]Isa 17:1 [t]S 1Ki 15:18
49:28 [u]S Ge 25:13 [v]S Jos 11:1 [w]S Jer 10:22 [x]S Jdg 6:3
49:29 [y]ver 32 [z]S Jer 6:25
49:30 [a]S Jdg 6:2 [b]Jos 11:1 [c]S Jer 10:22
49:31 [d]Eze 38:11
49:32 [e]S Jdg 6:5 [f]ver 29 [g]ver 36; Jer 13:24 [h]S Jer 9:26
49:33 [i]S Jos 11:1 [/]S Isa 13:22 [k]Jer 48:9 [/]S ver 18; Jer 51:37
49:34 [m]S Ge 10:22 [n]2Ki 24:18
49:35 [o]S Ps 37:15; S Isa 22:6
49:36 [p]S ver 32 [q]Da 11:4

[k]23 Hebrew on or by   [l]32 Or who clip the hair by
their foreheads

49:23 Concerning Damascus. See Isa 17; Am 1:3–5 (see
also note on Isa 17:1). Hamath. An important city in the
kingdom of Aram (see Isa 10:9 and note). Arpad. See note on
Isa 10:9. troubled like the restless sea. See Isa 57:20.
49:24 anguish. See note on 4:19.
49:26 Repeated almost verbatim in 50:30.
49:27 A conventional word of judgment (see note on Am
1:4).
49:28 Concerning Kedar. See Isa 21:13–17; see also 2:10
and note. kingdoms of Hazor. See vv. 30,33; not the Hazor
north of the Sea of Galilee (see Jos 11:1). These kingdoms
may have included Dedan, Tema, Buz and other Arab regions (see 25:23–24 and notes), since the Hebrew root of
the proper name Hazor often serves as a common noun
meaning "settlement" (see especially Isa 42:11; see also Ge
25:16). Nebuchadnezzar . . . attacked. In 599–598 B.C.
people of the East. See Job 1:3; Eze 25:4. The Hebrew for
this phrase is translated "eastern peoples" in Jdg 6:3 (see
note there).
49:29 Terror on every side. See note on 6:25.

49:30 Stay in deep caves. See v. 8.
49:31 at ease. Completely secure (see Job 21:23). in confidence. In safety, unsuspecting (see Jdg 18:7; Eze 38:11).
has neither gates nor bars. Lives in unwalled villages (see Dt
3:5; cf. 1Sa 23:7). alone. A condition that elsewhere characterizes Israel (see Nu 23:9; Dt 33:28).
49:32 scatter to the winds. See Eze 5:12; 12:4. who are in
distant places. See note on 9:26. disaster . . . from every
side. Contrast the description of Solomon's realm in 1Ki 5:
4.
49:33 haunt of jackals. See note on 9:11. No one . . . dwell
in it. Repeated verbatim from v. 18.
49:34 This is the word of the LORD . . . concerning. See
note on 46:1. Elam. See note on Isa 11:11. Zedekiah. Ruled
597–586 B.C.
49:35 bow. The Elamites were skilled archers (see Isa
22:6).
49:36 Contrast Isa 11:12. to the four winds. In every
direction (see Eze 37:9; Da 7:2; 8:8; see also NIV text note
on Zec 6:5).

I will scatter them to the four winds,
and there will not be a nation
where Elam's exiles do not go.
37I will shatter Elam before their foes,
before those who seek their lives;
I will bring disaster upon them,
even my fierce anger," *r*
       declares the LORD.
"I will pursue them with the sword *s*
until I have made an end of them.
38I will set my throne in Elam
and destroy her king and officials,"
       declares the LORD.

39"Yet I will restore *t* the fortunes of Elam
in days to come,"
       declares the LORD.

A Message About Babylon

51:15–19pp — Jer 10:12–16

50 This is the word the LORD spoke
through Jeremiah the prophet concerning Babylon *u* and the land of the Babylonians *m*:

2"Announce and proclaim *v* among the
    nations,
lift up a banner *w* and proclaim it;
keep nothing back, but say,
'Babylon will be captured; *x*
Bel *y* will be put to shame, *z*
Marduk *a* filled with terror.
Her images will be put to shame
and her idols *b* filled with terror.'
3A nation from the north *c* will attack
    her
and lay waste her land.
No one will live *d* in it;
both men and animals *e* will flee
    away.

4"In those days, at that time,"
    declares the LORD,
"the people of Israel and the people of
    Judah together *f*
will go in tears *g* to seek *h* the LORD
    their God.
5They will ask the way *i* to Zion
and turn their faces toward it.
They will come *j* and bind themselves
    to the LORD
in an everlasting covenant *k*
that will not be forgotten.

6"My people have been lost sheep; *l*
their shepherds *m* have led them
    astray *n*
and caused them to roam on the
    mountains.
They wandered over mountain and
    hill *o*
and forgot their own resting place. *p*
7Whoever found them devoured *q* them;
their enemies said, 'We are not
    guilty, *r*
for they sinned against the LORD, their
    true pasture,
the LORD, the hope *s* of their fathers.'

8"Flee *t* out of Babylon; *u*
leave the land of the Babylonians,
and be like the goats that lead the
    flock.
9For I will stir *v* up and bring against
    Babylon
an alliance of great nations *w* from the
    land of the north. *x*
They will take up their positions against
    her,

49:37 *r*Jer 30:24
*s*Jer 9:16;
Eze 32:24
49:39
*t*S Jer 48:47
50:1
*u*S Ge 10:10;
S Ps 137:8
50:2 *v*S Dt 30:4;
Jer 4:16
*w*S Ps 20:5;
S Isa 13:2 *x*ver 9;
Jer 51:31
*y*S Isa 21:9;
S 46:1 *z*Ps 97:7;
Jer 51:52 *a*ver 38;
Isa 46:6;
Jer 51:47
*b*S Lev 26:30
50:3 *c*S ver 26;
S Isa 41:25;
S Jer 25:26 *d*S ver
13;
S Isa 14:22-23;
S Jer 9:11
*e*Zep 1:3

50:4 *f*S Jer 3:18;
Eze 37:22
*g*S Ezr 3:12
*h*S Isa 9:13;
Eze 37:17;
Hos 3:5
50:5 *i*S Isa 11:16;
S Jer 31:21
*j*S Isa 29:1;
Jer 33:7
*k*Dt 29:14;
Isa 55:3;
Jer 32:40;
Heb 8:6-10
50:6
*l*S Ps 119:176;
Mt 9:36; 10:6
*m*S Jer 2:8;
S 10:21
*n*S Ps 95:10;
Jer 23:32;
Eze 13:10
*o*Jer 3:6; Eze 34:6
*p*ver 19
50:7 *q*S Jer 5:17;
10:25; Eze 35:12
*r*Jer 2:3
*s*S Jer 14:8
50:8 *t*S Isa 48:20
*u*ver 28
50:9 *v*S Isa 13:17
*w*S Jer 25:14
*x*S Isa 41:25;
S Jer 25:26

m 1 Or *Chaldeans;* also in verses 8, 25, 35 and 45

49:37 *I will pursue . . . made an end of them.* The Hebrew
for this sentence is repeated verbatim from 9:16.
49:38 *set my throne in.* See 1:15 and note.
49:39 See note on 29:14.
50:1–51:64 See Isa 13:1–14:23; 21:1–9. Jeremiah's
prophecy concerning Babylon is by far the longest of his
oracles against foreign nations (chs. 46–51) and expands on
his earlier and briefer statements (see 25:12–14,26). Its
date, in whole or in part, is 593 B.C. (see 51:59 and note).
The two chapters divide into three main sections (50:2–28;
50:29–51:26; 51:27–58), each of which begins with a
summons concerning war against Babylon, Judah's mortal
enemy (see 50:2–3; 50:29–32; 51:27–32).
50:1 *word.* Or "message" (as in 46:13), comprising chs.
50–51. *through.* See 37:2. The message would eventually be
sent by the prophet to Babylon itself (see 51:59–61).
50:2 *Announce and proclaim.* See 4:5; 46:14. *lift up a
banner.* See note on Isa 5:26. The Hebrew for this phrase is
translated "raise the signal" in 4:6. *Babylon will be captured.* Fulfilled in 539 B.C. *Bel.* See 51:44; Isa 46:1 and note.
put to shame . . . filled with terror. The repetition of each of
these phrases emphasizes that the chief god of Babylon and
his images and idols are alike doomed. *Her . . . her.* Bab-

ylon's. *idols.* Lit. "little pellets of dung." Derogatory references concerning idols and idolatry are common in the OT
(see, e.g., Isa 44:9–20).
50:3 *nation from the north.* In Jeremiah, the foe from the
north is almost always Babylon (see, e.g., 1:14–15). Here,
however, the reference is probably to Persia. Babylon's
nemesis is expanded to "an alliance of great nations" in v. 9,
specified by name in 51:27–28. *men and animals will flee.*
See 33:12.
50:4 *Israel and . . . Judah together.* See note on 3:18.
tears. Of repentance (see 3:21–22; 31:9).
50:5 *everlasting covenant.* See 32:40 and note; see also
31:31–34; 33:20–21.
50:6 *lost sheep.* See Jesus' parable in Lk 15:3–7. *shepherds.* Rulers (see note on 2:8). *mountain and hill.* Places
where pagan gods were worshiped (see note on 2:20). *their
own resting place.* See 33:12.
50:7 *hope of their fathers.* See 14:8,22; Ac 28:20.
50:8 *like the goats that lead the flock.* Judah would be
among the first of the captive peoples to be released from
exile in Babylon.
50:9 *alliance of great nations.* See Isa 13:4. They are
named in 51:27–28 (see note on v. 3). *not return empty-handed.* See Isa 55:11.

and from the north she will be
captured.[y]
Their arrows[z] will be like skilled
warriors
who do not return empty-handed.
[10]So Babylonia[n] will be plundered;[a]
all who plunder her will have their
fill,"
declares the LORD.

[11]"Because you rejoice and are glad,
you who pillage my inheritance,[b]
because you frolic like a heifer[c]
threshing grain
and neigh like stallions,
[12]your mother will be greatly ashamed;
she who gave you birth will be
disgraced.[d]
She will be the least of the nations—
a wilderness, a dry land, a desert.[e]
[13]Because of the LORD's anger she will
not be inhabited
but will be completely desolate.[f]
All who pass Babylon will be horrified[g]
and scoff[h]
because of all her wounds.[i]

[14]"Take up your positions around
Babylon,
all you who draw the bow.[j]
Shoot at her! Spare no arrows,[k]
for she has sinned against the LORD.
[15]Shout[l] against her on every side!
She surrenders, her towers fall,
her walls[m] are torn down.
Since this is the vengeance[n] of the
LORD,
take vengeance on her;
do to her[o] as she has done to
others.[p]
[16]Cut off from Babylon the sower,

and the reaper with his sickle at
harvest.
Because of the sword[q] of the oppressor
let everyone return to his own
people,[r]
let everyone flee to his own land.[s]

[17]"Israel is a scattered flock[t]
that lions[u] have chased away.
The first to devour[v] him
was the king[w] of Assyria;
the last to crush his bones[x]
was Nebuchadnezzar[y] king[z] of
Babylon."

[18]Therefore this is what the LORD Almighty, the God of Israel, says:

"I will punish the king of Babylon and
his land
as I punished the king[a] of Assyria.[b]
[19]But I will bring[c] Israel back to his own
pasture
and he will graze on Carmel and
Bashan;
his appetite will be satisfied[d]
on the hills[e] of Ephraim and
Gilead.[f]
[20]In those days, at that time,"
declares the LORD,
"search will be made for Israel's guilt,
but there will be none,[g]
and for the sins[h] of Judah,
but none will be found,
for I will forgive[i] the remnant[j] I
spare.

[21]"Attack the land of Merathaim
and those who live in Pekod.[k]

50:9 yS ver 2
zS Isa 13:18
50:10 aIsa 47:11;
S Jer 30:16
50:11 bS Isa 47:6
cS Jer 31:18
50:12 dJer 51:47
ever 13;
S Isa 21:1;
Jer 25:12; 51:26
50:13 fver 3,
S 12; S Jer 9:11;
48:9; 51:62
gJer 51:41
hS Jer 18:16;
51:37; Eze 27:36;
Hab 2:6
iS Dt 29:22
50:14 jver 29,42
kS Isa 13:18
50:15 lJer 51:14
mS 2Ki 25:4;
S Jer 51:44 nver
28; S Isa 10:3;
63:4; Jer 51:6
over 29;
Ps 137:8;
Rev 18:6
pJer 51:24;
Hab 2:7-8

50:16 qS Jer 25:38
rS Isa 13:14
sJer 51:9
50:17
tS Lev 26:33;
S Ps 119:176
uS 2Ki 24:1;
S Jer 2:15
vS Jer 5:17
wS Dt 4:27;
S 2Ki 15:29
xS Nu 24:8;
La 3:4 yJer 51:34
zS 2Ki 24:17;
S 25:7
50:18
aS Isa 10:12
bEze 31:3;
Zep 2:13
50:19
cS Jer 31:10;
Eze 34:13
dJer 31:14
eS Jer 31:5
fMic 7:14;
Zec 10:10
50:20 gS Ps 17:3
hPs 103:12;
S Isa 38:17;
Eze 33:16;
Mic 7:18,19;
Zec 3:4,9

lS Isa 33:24 lS Ge 45:7; Isa 1:9; 10:20-22; S Ro 9:27 50:21
kEze 23:23

n10 Or Chaldea

50:11 you. Babylon. my inheritance. God's land and
people (see 2:7; 12:7 and notes). frolic like a heifer. See Mal
4:2. stallions. See note on 8:16.
50:12 mother. Either (1) the city or, more likely, (2) the
land (see Isa 50:1; Hos 2:5). least. Lit. "last." As Amalek,
"first among the nations" (Nu 24:20) to attack Israel, was
destroyed, so Babylon, the last to attack Israel (up to Jeremiah's time), would be destroyed.
50:13 not be inhabited. See Isa 13:20 and note. All who
pass ... because of all her wounds. Said of Jerusalem in
19:8 and of Edom in 49:17.
50:14 you who draw the bow. Including the Medes (see Isa
13:17-18).
50:15 Shout. Give the battle cry (see Jos 6:16). vengeance
of the LORD. See v. 28; 51:11. Though originating in his
sovereign holiness, it was often carried out by his people (see
Nu 31:3).
50:16 sword of the oppressor. See 46:16. let everyone ...
to his own land. The Hebrew for this passage has a parallel in
Isa 13:14. The captive peoples are warned to flee Babylon in
order to avoid being cut down by her invaders.
50:17 scattered flock. See Joel 3:2. lions. Symbolic of

Assyria and Babylon (see 4:7; Isa 15:9 and notes). The first
... was the king of Assyria. The Assyrians destroyed Israel
(the northern kingdom) in 722-721 B.C. the last ... was
Nebuchadnezzar. The Babylonians destroyed Judah (the
southern kingdom) in 586 B.C.
50:18 I punished the king of Assyria. Nineveh, the proud
Assyrian capital, fell in 612 B.C., and Assyria herself was
conquered by a coalition of Medes and Babylonians in 609.
50:19 Carmel. See Isa 33:9 and note. Bashan. See note on
Isa 2:13. hills of Ephraim. The lush mountainsides of central
Israel (see Eze 34:13-14). Gilead. See Nu 32:1; Mic 7:14.
50:20 See 33:8 and note; see also 36:3; Mic 7:18-19.
50:21 Merathaim. Means "double rebellion [against the
Lord]," perhaps referring to vv. 24,29 (see Jdg 3:8; Isa 40:2
and notes). It is probably a pun on the Babylonian word
marratu, which sometimes referred to a region in southern
Babylonia that was characterized by briny waters. Pekod. See
Eze 23:23; means "punishment [from the Lord]," a pun on
Puqudu, the Babylonian name for an Aramean tribe living on
the eastern bank of the lower Tigris River. completely destroy. See NIV text note; v. 26; 25:9; 51:3; see also note on
Dt 2:34.

Pursue, kill and completely destroy[o]
them,"

    declares the LORD.
"Do everything I have commanded
    you.
[22]The noise[l] of battle is in the land,
    the noise of great destruction!
[23]How broken and shattered
    is the hammer[m] of the whole earth![n]
How desolate[o] is Babylon
    among the nations!
[24]I set a trap[p] for you, O Babylon,
    and you were caught before you
      knew it;
you were found and captured[q]
    because you opposed[r] the LORD.
[25]The LORD has opened his arsenal
    and brought out the weapons[s] of his
      wrath,
for the Sovereign LORD Almighty has
    work to do
in the land of the Babylonians.[t]
[26]Come against her from afar.[u]
    Break open her granaries;
pile her up like heaps of grain.[v]
Completely destroy[w] her
    and leave her no remnant.
[27]Kill all her young bulls;[x]
    let them go down to the slaughter![y]
Woe to them! For their day[z] has come,
    the time[a] for them to be punished.
[28]Listen to the fugitives[b] and refugees
    from Babylon
declaring in Zion[c]
how the LORD our God has taken
    vengeance,[d]
vengeance for his temple.[e]

[29]"Summon archers against Babylon,
    all those who draw the bow.[f]
Encamp all around her;
    let no one escape.[g]
Repay[h] her for her deeds;[i]

do to her as she has done.
For she has defied[j] the LORD,
    the Holy One[k] of Israel.
[30]Therefore, her young men[l] will fall in
    the streets;
all her soldiers will be silenced in that
    day,"

    declares the LORD.
[31]"See, I am against[m] you, O arrogant
    one,"

    declares the Lord, the LORD
      Almighty,
"for your day[n] has come,
    the time for you to be punished.
[32]The arrogant[o] one will stumble and
    fall[p]
and no one will help her up;[q]
I will kindle a fire[r] in her towns
    that will consume all who are around
      her."

[33]This is what the LORD Almighty says:

"The people of Israel are oppressed,[s]
    and the people of Judah as well.
All their captors hold them fast,
    refusing to let them go.[t]
[34]Yet their Redeemer[u] is strong;
    the LORD Almighty[v] is his name.
He will vigorously defend their cause[w]
    so that he may bring rest[x] to their
      land,
but unrest to those who live in
    Babylon.

[35]"A sword[y] against the Babylonians!"[z]
    declares the LORD—
"against those who live in Babylon
    and against her officials and wise[a]
      men!
[36]A sword against her false prophets!

Cross references (center column):

50:22 [l]Jer 4:19-21; 51:54
50:23 [m]S Isa 10:5
[n]Jer 51:25; [o]S Isa 14:16
50:24 [p]Jer 51:12; [q]Jer 51:31; [r]Job 9:4
50:25 [s]S Isa 13:5
50:26 [u]ver 3,41; Jer 51:11; [v]S Ru 3:7; [w]S Isa 14:22-23
50:27 [x]S Ps 68:30; Jer 48:15; [y]S Isa 30:25; S Jer 25:34; [z]S Job 18:20
[a]Jer 51:6
50:28 [b]ver 8; [c]Isa 48:20; Jer 51:10 [d]S ver 15 [e]2Ki 24:13; Jer 51:11; 52:13
50:29 [f]S ver 14; [g]S Isa 13:18; Jer 51:3; [h]S Dt 32:41; S Job 21:19; S Jer 51:6; Rev 18:6; [i]Eze 35:11; Ob 1:15

[j]S Isa 14:13-14; 47:10; Da 5:23; [k]Ps 78:41; Isa 41:20; Jer 51:5
50:30 [l]S Isa 13:18
50:31 [m]S Jer 21:13; [n]S Job 18:20; Rev 18:7-8
50:32 [o]S Ps 119:21; [p]S Ps 20:8; [q]Am 5:2; [r]S Jer 49:27
50:33 [s]Isa 58:6; [t]S Isa 14:17
50:34 [u]S Ex 6:6; S Job 19:25; [v]Jer 31:35; 51:19; [w]S Ps 119:154; S Isa 49:25; Jer 15:21; 51:36; La 3:58; [x]S Isa 14:7
50:35 [y]S Jer 47:6; [z]S Isa 45:1; [a]Da 5:7

[o]21 The Hebrew term refers to the irrevocable giving
over of things or persons to the LORD, often by totally
destroying them; also in verse 26.

50:22 great destruction. See 4:6; 6:1; cf. 48:3; 51:54.
50:23 hammer of the whole earth. See note on Isa 10:5.
How desolate . . . among the nations! The Hebrew for this
sentence is repeated verbatim in 51:41.
50:24 caught before you knew it. The Persian attack in 539
B.C. would catch the city of Babylon completely by surprise
(see 51:8; Isa 47:11).
50:25 weapons of his wrath. The nations (see 51:27–28)
that the Lord would use to conquer Babylon (see Isa 13:5
and note). the . . . LORD . . . has work to do. See 48:10.
50:26 heaps of grain. The Hebrew for this expression is
used in Ne 4:2 to describe heaps of rubble that had been
burned. Completely destroy her. By burning (see note on v.
21; see also Jos 11:11–13).
50:27 young bulls. The people of Babylon, including especially her fighting men (see Isa 34:6–7 and notes). go down
to the slaughter. See note on 48:15. time for them to be
punished. See 11:23; 23:12; 46:21.
50:28 fugitives and refugees. Jewish exiles who had fled

the destruction overtaking Babylon. vengeance, vengeance
for his temple. See v. 15 and note; 46:10; 51:6. The conquest of Babylon was the Lord's response to Babylon's burning of the Jerusalem temple.
50:29 Repay her for her deeds. Echoed from 25:14 (see
51:24). do to her as she has done. See v. 15. Holy One of
Israel. A title of God found frequently in Isaiah (see note on
Isa 1:4), it occurs in Jeremiah only here and in 51:5.
50:30 Repeated almost verbatim from 49:26.
50:31–32 A distant echo of 21:13–14, spoken there to
Jerusalem but here to Babylon.
50:33 their captors. See Isa 14:2. refusing to let them go.
Reminiscent of Pharaoh's repeated refusals before the
exodus (see, e.g., Ex 7:14; 8:2,32; 9:2,7).
50:34 Redeemer. See note. defend their cause.
See 51:36. bring rest. See 31:2 and note; see also Isa 14:3,7
and notes on Dt 3:20; Jos 1:13.
50:35–38 Cf. Eze 21.
50:36 false prophets . . . will become fools. See Isa 44:25;

They will become fools.
A sword against her warriors! [b]
They will be filled with terror. [c]
37A sword against her horses and
    chariots [d]
and all the foreigners in her ranks!
They will become women. [e]
A sword against her treasures! [f]
They will be plundered.
38A drought on [p] her waters! [g]
They will dry [h] up.
For it is a land of idols, [i]
    idols that will go mad with terror.

39"So desert creatures [j] and hyenas will
    live there,
and there the owl will dwell.
It will never again be inhabited
    or lived in from generation to
    generation. [k]
40As God overthrew Sodom and
    Gomorrah [l]
    along with their neighboring towns,"
        declares the LORD,
"so no one will live there;
    no man will dwell in it. [m]

41"Look! An army is coming from the
    north; [n]
a great nation and many kings
    are being stirred [o] up from the ends
    of the earth. [p]
42They are armed with bows [q] and spears;
    they are cruel [r] and without mercy. [s]
They sound like the roaring sea [t]
    as they ride on their horses;
they come like men in battle formation
    to attack you, O Daughter of
    Babylon. [u]
43The king of Babylon has heard reports
    about them,
    and his hands hang limp. [v]
Anguish has gripped him,
    pain like that of a woman in labor. [w]
44Like a lion coming up from Jordan's
    thickets [x]

to a rich pastureland,
I will chase Babylon from its land in an
    instant.
Who is the chosen [y] one I will
    appoint for this?
Who is like me and who can challenge
    me? [z]
And what shepherd can stand against
    me?"
45Therefore, hear what the LORD has
    planned against Babylon,
    what he has purposed [a] against the
    land of the Babylonians: [b]
The young of the flock will be dragged
    away;
    he will completely destroy their
    pasture because of them.
46At the sound of Babylon's capture the
    earth will tremble; [c]
    its cry [d] will resound among the
    nations.

51 This is what the LORD says:

"See, I will stir [e] up the spirit of a
    destroyer
against Babylon [f] and the people of
    Leb Kamai. [q]
2I will send foreigners [g] to Babylon
    to winnow [h] her and to devastate her
    land;
they will oppose her on every side
    in the day [i] of her disaster.
3Let not the archer string his bow, [j]
    nor let him put on his armor. [k]
Do not spare her young men;
    completely destroy [r] her army.
4They will fall [l] down slain in Babylon, [s]
    fatally wounded in her streets. [m]
5For Israel and Judah have not been
    forsaken [n]
    by their God, the LORD Almighty,

50:36
[b]S Jer 49:22
[c]Jer 51:30,32
50:37
[d]S 2Ki 19:23;
Jer 51:21
[e]S Isa 19:16
[f]S Isa 45:3
50:38 [g]Ps 137:1;
Jer 51:13
[h]S Isa 11:15;
Jer 51:36 /S ver 2
50:39 /S Ps 74:14
[k]Isa 13:19-22;
34:13-15;
Jer 51:37;
Rev 18:2
50:40
[l]S Ge 19:24;
S Mt 10:15
[m]Jer 51:62
50:41 [n]S ver 26;
S Isa 41:25
[o]S Isa 13:17
[p]S Isa 13:4;
Jer 51:22-28
50:42 [q]S ver 14
[r]S Job 30:21
[s]S Isa 13:18
[t]S Isa 5:30
[u]S Isa 47:1
50:43 [v]S Jer 47:3
[w]Jer 6:22-24
50:44 [x]S Jer 12:5

[y]S Nu 16:5
[z]S Job 41:10;
Isa 46:9;
S Jer 49:19
50:45 [a]Ps 33:11;
Jer 51:11
[b]S Isa 48:14
50:46 [c]S Jdg 5:4;
S Jer 49:21
[d]S Job 24:12;
Rev 18:9-10
51:1 [e]S Isa 13:17
/Jer 25:12
51:2 [g]Isa 13:5
[h]S Isa 41:16;
Mt 3:12
[i]S Isa 13:9
51:3 /S Jer 50:29
[k]Jer 46:4
51:4 /Isa 13:15
[m]S Isa 13:18
51:5
[n]S Lev 26:44;
Isa 54:6-8

[p]38 Or A sword against   [q]1 Leb Kamai is a
cryptogram for Chaldea, that is, Babylonia.   [r]3 The
Hebrew term refers to the irrevocable giving over of things
or persons to the LORD, often by totally destroying them.
[s]4 Or Chaldea

---

see also Nu 12:11 and NIV text note on Pr 1:7.
50:37 *against her horses and chariots.* See Isa 43:17; see
also Ps 20:7. *foreigners.* See 25:20,24; Ne 13:3. *will
become women.* See Na 3:13.
50:38 *idols.* See 51:52; see also note on Isa 21:9. *go mad.*
See 25:16 and note.
50:39 See Isa 13:20–22 and notes.
50:40 Repeated almost verbatim from 49:18 (see note
there).
50:41–43 Repeated almost verbatim from 6:22–24 (see
notes there). The earlier oracle, referring to Jerusalem, is
here applied to Babylon.
50:44–46 Repeated almost verbatim from 49:19–21 (see
notes there). The oracle against Edom is here applied to
Babylon.
51:1 *stir up the spirit.* See 1Ch 5:26; Hag 1:14. The

Hebrew underlying this phrase is translated "aroused . . . the
hostility of" in 2Ch 21:16. *destroyer.* See note on 4:7; here
including the "kings of the Medes" (v. 11). *Leb Kamai.* Lit.
"the heart of my attackers" (cf. Rev 17:5, where Babylon is
called "the mother of prostitutes and of the abominations of
the earth"). Concerning the NIV text note see note on
25:26.
51:2 *foreigners . . . to winnow her.* The Hebrew for this
phrase is an excellent example of alliteration and assonance
(see Introduction: Literary Features).
51:3 *completely destroy.* See NIV text note; 25:9; 50:21,
26; see also note on Dt 2:34.
51:4 *fall . . . in her streets.* See 49:26; 50:30.
51:5 *forsaken.* Lit. "widowed"; contrast Isa 54:4,6–7 and
notes. *Holy One of Israel.* See note on 50:29.

though their land[t] is full of guilt[o]
before the Holy One of Israel.

[6]"Flee[p] from Babylon!
Run for your lives!
Do not be destroyed because of her
sins.[q]
It is time[r] for the LORD's vengeance;[s]
he will pay[t] her what she deserves.
[7]Babylon was a gold cup[u] in the LORD's
hand;
she made the whole earth drunk.
The nations drank her wine;
therefore they have now gone mad.
[8]Babylon will suddenly fall[v] and be
broken.
Wail over her!
Get balm[w] for her pain;
perhaps she can be healed.

[9]" 'We would have healed Babylon,
but she cannot be healed;
let us leave[x] her and each go to his
own land,
for her judgment[y] reaches to the
skies,
it rises as high as the clouds.'

[10]" 'The LORD has vindicated[z] us;
come, let us tell in Zion
what the LORD our God has done.'[a]

[11]"Sharpen the arrows,[b]
take up the shields![c]
The LORD has stirred up[c] the kings[d] of
the Medes,[e]
because his purpose[f] is to destroy
Babylon.
The LORD will take vengeance,[g]
vengeance for his temple.[h]
[12]Lift up a banner[i] against the walls of
Babylon!
Reinforce the guard,
station the watchmen,[j]
prepare an ambush![k]
The LORD will carry out his purpose,[l]

his decree against the people of
Babylon.
[13]You who live by many waters[m]
and are rich in treasures,[n]
your end has come,
the time for you to be cut off.[o]
[14]The LORD Almighty has sworn by
himself:[p]
I will surely fill you with men, as
with a swarm of locusts,[q]
and they will shout[r] in triumph over
you.

[15]"He made the earth by his power;
he founded the world by his
wisdom[s]
and stretched[t] out the heavens by
his understanding.[u]
[16]When he thunders,[v] the waters in the
heavens roar;
he makes clouds rise from the ends of
the earth.
He sends lightning with the rain[w]
and brings out the wind from his
storehouses.[x]

[17]"Every man is senseless and without
knowledge;
every goldsmith is shamed by his
idols.
His images are a fraud;[y]
they have no breath in them.
[18]They are worthless,[z] the objects of
mockery;
when their judgment comes, they
will perish.
[19]He who is the Portion[a] of Jacob is not
like these,
for he is the Maker of all things,
including the tribe of his inheritance[b]—
the LORD Almighty is his name.

[20]"You are my war club,[c]

51:5 [o]Hos 4:1
51:6 [p]S Isa 48:20
[q]Nu 16:26;
Rev 18:4
[r]Jer 50:27
[s]S Isa 1:24;
S Jer 50:15 [t]ver
24,56; Dt 32:35;
S Job 21:19;
Jer 25:14; 50:29;
La 3:64
51:7
[u]S Isa 51:22;
Jer 25:15-16;
49:12;
Rev 14:8-10
51:8
[v]S Isa 14:15;
S 21:9;
S Rev 14:8
[w]Jer 8:22; 46:11
51:9
[x]S Isa 13:14;
S 31:9; Jer 50:16
[y]Rev 18:4-5
51:10 [z]Mic 7:9
[a]Ps 64:9;
S Jer 50:28
51:11 [b]Jer 50:9
[c]S Isa 21:5
[d]S Isa 41:2 [e]ver
28; S Isa 13:3;
S 41:25
[f]S Jer 50:45
[g]S Lev 26:25
[h]S Jer 50:28
51:12 [i]ver 27;
S Ps 20:5
[j]2Sa 18:24;
Eze 33:2
[k]Jer 50:24
[l]S Ps 33:11

51:13
[m]S Jer 50:38
[n]S Isa 45:3;
Eze 22:27;
Hab 2:9 [o]Jer 50:3
51:14
[p]S Ge 22:16;
Am 6:8 [q]ver 27;
Am 7:1; Na 3:15
[r]Jer 50:15
51:15 [s]Ps 104:24
[t]S Ge 1:1;
S Ps 104:2
[u]S Ps 136:5
51:16
[v]Ps 18:11-13
[w]S Job 28:26
[x]S Dt 28:12;
S Ps 135:7;
Jnh 1:4
51:17
[y]S Isa 44:20;
Hab 2:18-19
51:18
[z]S Jer 18:15

51:19 [a]S Ps 119:57 [b]S Ex 34:9 **51:20** [c]S Isa 10:5; Zec 9:13

[t]5 Or / and the land of the Babylonians

51:6 *Flee . . . ! Run for your lives!* See v. 45; 48:6. This was
spoken to the people of Judah (as in 50:8). *the LORD's ven-*
geance. See note on 50:15. *pay her what she deserves.* See
Isa 59:18; 66:6.
51:7 See 25:15–16 and notes. *Babylon was . . . gold.* See
note on Da 2:32–43.
51:8 *Babylon will . . . fall.* See Isa 21:9 and note. *balm.* See
note on 8:22.
51:9 The speakers are the nations conquered by Babylon.
each go to his own land. See 50:16 and note. *her judgment.*
Her sin, deserving of judgment. *reaches to the skies . . . high*
as the clouds. Poetic exaggeration (see Dt 1:28; Ps 57:10;
108:4).
51:10 Judah speaks (see 50:28). *The LORD has vindicated*
us. See Ps 37:6.
51:11 *stirred up.* Lit. "stirred up the spirit of" (see note on
v. 1). *Medes.* See v. 28; Isa 13:17 and note; Isa 21:2; Da
5:28,31; 6:8,12,15; 8:20. *vengeance, vengeance for his*

temple. See note on 50:28.
51:12 *prepare an ambush.* To keep defenders from retreating to the safety of their fortifications (see Jos 8:14–22; Jdg
20:29–39).
51:13 *many waters.* The "rivers of Babylon" (Ps 137:1),
including the mighty Euphrates along with a magnificent
system of irrigation canals, were proverbial. *cut off.* Like a
thread from the loom (see Isa 38:12).
51:14 *sworn by himself.* See note on Ge 22:16. *as with . . .*
locusts. See 46:23. *shout in triumph.* See note on 48:33.
51:15–19 Repeated almost verbatim from 10:12–16 (see
notes there).
51:20–23 Illustrates Jeremiah's fondness for the effective
use of repetition (see 4:23–26; see also Introduction: Literary Features).
51:20 *You are my war club.* Cf. Pr 25:18; either (1) Cyrus
of Persia, soon to conquer Babylon, or, more likely, (2)
Babylon, destroyer of nations (see 50:23; see also note on Isa

my weapon for battle—
with you I shatter^d nations,^e
   with you I destroy kingdoms,
21with you I shatter horse and rider,^f
   with you I shatter chariot^g and
     driver,
22with you I shatter man and woman,
   with you I shatter old man and
     youth,
   with you I shatter young man and
     maiden,^h
23with you I shatter shepherd and flock,
   with you I shatter farmer and oxen,
   with you I shatter governors and
     officials.^i

24"Before your eyes I will repay^j Babylon^k and all who live in Babylonia^u for all
the wrong they have done in Zion," declares the LORD.

25"I am against^l you, O destroying
     mountain,
   you who destroy the whole earth,"^m
       declares the LORD.
  "I will stretch out my hand^n against
     you,
   roll you off the cliffs,
   and make you a burned-out
     mountain.^o
26No rock will be taken from you for a
     cornerstone,
   nor any stone for a foundation,
   for you will be desolate^p forever,"
       declares the LORD.

27"Lift up a banner^q in the land!
   Blow the trumpet among the nations!
   Prepare the nations for battle against
     her;
   summon against her these
     kingdoms:^r
   Ararat,^s Minni and Ashkenaz.^t

Appoint a commander against her;
   send up horses like a swarm of
     locusts.^u
28Prepare the nations for battle against
     her—
   the kings of the Medes,^v
   their governors and all their officials,
   and all the countries they rule.^w
29The land trembles^x and writhes,
   for the LORD's purposes^y against
     Babylon stand—
   to lay waste^z the land of Babylon
   so that no one will live there.^a
30Babylon's warriors^b have stopped
     fighting;
   they remain in their strongholds.
   Their strength is exhausted;
   they have become like women.^c
   Her dwellings are set on fire;^d
   the bars^e of her gates are broken.
31One courier^f follows another
   and messenger follows messenger
   to announce to the king of Babylon
   that his entire city is captured,^g
32the river crossings seized,
   the marshes set on fire,^h
   and the soldiers terrified.^i "

33This is what the LORD Almighty, the
God of Israel, says:

  "The Daughter of Babylon^j is like a
     threshing floor^k
   at the time it is trampled;
   the time to harvest^l her will soon
     come.^m"

34"Nebuchadnezzar^n king of Babylon has
     devoured^o us,^p
   he has thrown us into confusion,
   he has made us an empty jar.
   Like a serpent he has swallowed us

51:20
^dS Job 34:24;
Mic 4:13
^eS Isa 45:1
51:21 /S Ex 15:1
^gS Isa 43:17;
S Jer 50:37
51:22
^hS 2Ch 36:17;
Isa 13:17-18
51:23 ^iver 57
51:24 /S ver 6,
35; S Dt 32:41;
S Jer 50:15;
La 3:64
^kS Isa 45:1
51:25
/S Jer 21:13
^mJer 50:23
^nS Ex 3:20
^oZec 4:7
51:26 ^pver 29;
S Isa 13:19-22;
S Jer 50:12
51:27 ^qS Ps 20:5;
S Isa 13:2
^rS Jer 25:14
^sS Ge 8:4
^tGe 10:3

^uS ver 14
51:28 ^vS ver 11
^wver 48
51:29 ^xS Jdg 5:4;
S Jer 49:21
^yS Ps 33:11
^zJer 48:9 ^aver 43;
S Isa 13:20
51:30
^bS Jer 50:36
^cS Isa 19:16
^dS Isa 47:14
^eS Isa 45:2
51:31
/2Sa 18:19-31
^gS Jer 50:2;
Da 5:30
51:32
^hS Isa 47:14
/S Jer 50:36
51:33 /S Isa 47:1
^kS Isa 21:10
/S Isa 17:5
^mS Isa 13:22
51:34
^nS Jer 50:17
^oNa 2:12
^pHos 8:8

^u24 Or *Chaldea;* also in verse 35

10:5). *shatter.* See vv. 21–23. The Hebrew root for this verb
is the same as that for "war club." See also Ex 15:6. The
Hebrew verb is translated "dash (to pieces)" in Ps 2:9;
137:9; Hos 10:14; 13:16.
51:24 *your.* Judah's. *repay . . . for all the wrong they have
done.* See v. 6; 50:15,29.
51:25 *destroying mountain.* Symbolizes a powerful kingdom (see Da 2:35,44–45), here Babylon. *burned-out mountain.* After being judged by the Lord, Babylon will be like an
extinct volcano.
51:26 *desolate forever.* See 25:12; 50:12–13; see also
note on Isa 13:20.
51:27 See 50:29. *Lift up a banner . . . ! Blow the trumpet
. . . !* See 4:5–6; 6:1 and notes. *Prepare . . . for battle.* Lit.
"Consecrate" (see note on 6:4). *these kingdoms.* Allies of
the Medes (see v. 11 and note). *Ararat.* See note on Ge 8:4.
Minni. A region mentioned in Assyrian inscriptions, it was
located somewhere in Armenia. *Ashkenaz.* See note on Ge
10:3. *commander.* The Hebrew for this word appears again
in the OT only in Na 3:17 ("officials"). It is a Babylonian

loanword meaning lit. "scribe." *like . . . locusts.* See note on
46:23.
51:28 *Medes.* See note on v. 11. *all the countries they
rule.* See note on 34:1; see also 1Ki 9:19.
51:29 *land trembles and writhes.* At the fearful prospect of
war.
51:30 *exhausted . . . women.* In the Hebrew there is a play
on words. *become like women.* See 50:37; Na 3:13.
51:31 *One courier follows another.* They run to the palace
from all parts of the city.
51:32 *river crossings.* Fords and ferries (and perhaps
bridges). *marshes set on fire.* To destroy the reeds and
prevent fugitives from hiding among them.
51:33 *Daughter of Babylon.* See 50:42; see also note on Isa
47:1. *threshing floor.* The destruction of a city or nation is
often depicted as a harvest (see Isa 27:12; Joel 3:13; Mic
4:12–13).
51:34 *serpent.* The Hebrew for this word is translated
"monster" in Isa 51:9, where it symbolizes Egypt (see note
on Ge 1:21). *delicacies.* See Ge 49:20.

and filled his stomach with our
　　delicacies,
and then has spewed ^{q} us out.
^{35}May the violence ^{r} done to our flesh ^{v}
　　be upon Babylon,"
say the inhabitants of Zion.
"May our blood be on those who live in
　　Babylonia,"
says Jerusalem. ^{s}

^{36}Therefore, this is what the LORD says:

"See, I will defend your cause ^{t}
　　and avenge ^{u} you;
I will dry up ^{v} her sea
　　and make her springs dry.
^{37}Babylon will be a heap of ruins,
　　a haunt ^{w} of jackals,
an object of horror and scorn, ^{x}
　　a place where no one lives. ^{y}
^{38}Her people all roar like young lions, ^{z}
　　they growl like lion cubs.
^{39}But while they are aroused,
　　I will set out a feast for them
　　and make them drunk, ^{a}
so that they shout with laughter—
　　then sleep forever ^{b} and not awake,"
　　　　declares the LORD. ^{c}
^{40}"I will bring them down
　　like lambs to the slaughter,
　　like rams and goats. ^{d}

^{41}"How Sheshach ^{w} ^{e} will be captured, ^{f}
　　the boast of the whole earth seized!
What a horror ^{g} Babylon will be
　　among the nations!
^{42}The sea will rise over Babylon;
　　its roaring waves ^{h} will cover her.
^{43}Her towns will be desolate,
　　a dry and desert ^{i} land,
a land where no one lives,
　　through which no man travels. ^{j}
^{44}I will punish Bel ^{k} in Babylon

and make him spew out ^{l} what he
　　has swallowed.
The nations will no longer stream to
　　him.
And the wall ^{m} of Babylon will fall.

^{45}"Come out ^{n} of her, my people!
　　Run ^{o} for your lives!
　　Run from the fierce anger ^{p} of the
　　　　LORD.
^{46}Do not lose heart ^{q} or be afraid ^{r}
　　when rumors ^{s} are heard in the land;
one rumor comes this year, another the
　　next,
　　rumors of violence in the land
　　and of ruler against ruler.
^{47}For the time will surely come
　　when I will punish the idols ^{t} of
　　　　Babylon;
her whole land will be disgraced ^{u}
　　and her slain will all lie fallen within
　　　　her. ^{v}
^{48}Then heaven and earth and all that is in
　　them
　　will shout ^{w} for joy over Babylon,
for out of the north ^{x}
　　destroyers ^{y} will attack her,"
　　　　declares the LORD.

^{49}"Babylon must fall because of Israel's
　　slain,
just as the slain in all the earth
　　have fallen because of Babylon. ^{z}
^{50}You who have escaped the sword,
　　leave ^{a} and do not linger!
Remember ^{b} the LORD in a distant
　　land, ^{c}
　　and think on Jerusalem."

^{51}"We are disgraced, ^{d}
　　for we have been insulted
　　and shame covers our faces,

51:34 ^{a}ver 44;
S Lev 18:25
51:35 ^{r}Joel 3:19;
Hab 2:17 ^{s}S ver
24; Ps 137:8
51:36
^{t}Ps 140:12;
Jer 50:34; La 3:58
^{u}ver 6; Jer 20:12;
S Ro 12:19
^{v}S Isa 11:15;
S 19:5; Hos 13:15
51:37
^{w}S Isa 13:22;
Rev 18:2 ^{x}Na 3:6;
Mal 2:9
^{y}S Jer 50:13,39
51:38 ^{z}S Isa 5:29
51:39 ^{a}S Isa 21:5
^{b}S Ps 13:3 ^{c}ver
57; S Jer 50:24
51:40 ^{d}Eze 39:18
51:41
^{e}S Jer 25:26
^{f}Isa 13:19
^{g}Jer 50:13
51:42 ^{h}S Ps 18:4;
Isa 8:7
51:43 ^{i}S Isa 21:1
^{j}S ver 29,62;
S Isa 13:20;
Jer 2:6
51:44
^{k}S Isa 21:9;
S 46:1

^{l}S ver 34 ^{m}ver
58; S 2Ki 25:4;
Isa 25:12;
Jer 50:15
51:45 ^{n}ver 50
^{o}S Isa 48:20
^{p}Ps 76:10; 79:6
51:46 ^{q}Ps 18:45
^{r}S Jer 46:27
^{s}S 2Ki 19:7
51:47
^{t}S Isa 46:1-2;
S Jer 50:2
^{u}Jer 50:12
^{v}S Jer 27:7
51:48 ^{w}S Job 3:7;
S Ps 149:2;
Rev 18:20 ^{x}ver
11; S Isa 41:25;
S Jer 25:26 ^{y}ver
53,56
51:49 ^{z}Ps 137:8;
S Jer 50:29
51:50 ^{a}ver 45
^{b}S Ps 137:6
^{c}Jer 23:23
51:51
^{d}Ps 44:13-16;
79:4

^{v}35 Or done to us and to our children
^{w}41 Sheshach is a cryptogram for Babylon.

51:35 flesh. See Mic 3:2–3.
51:36 avenge you. See vv. 6,11; see also note on 50:15. sea . . . springs. See note on v. 13. Babylonia is called the "Desert by the Sea" in Isa 21:1 (see note there).
51:37 See 9:11; 18:16 and notes.
51:38 roar like young lions. See 2:15 and note.
51:39 aroused. Lit. "heated"; for a similar image see Hos 7:4–7. drunk. See v. 57; see also notes on 25:15–16,26.
51:40 lambs . . . rams and goats. Symbolic of the people (see Isa 34:6; Eze 39:18) of Babylon. slaughter. See Dt 32:34; Isa 13:22.
51:41 Sheshach. See note on 25:26.
51:42 sea . . . its roaring waves. See Isa 17:12 and note; here and in v. 55, Babylon's enemies (see 46:7 and note).
51:43 See 48:9; 49:18,33; 50:12–13.
51:44 Bel. See 50:2; Isa 46:1 and note. what he has swallowed. Captive peoples (including Judah) and plundered goods (including vessels from the temple in Jerusalem; see Da 5:2–3). wall of Babylon. A wall of double construction,

the outer wall (12 feet thick) being separated from the inner wall (21 feet thick) by a dry moat 23 feet wide.
51:45 Run for your lives! See note on v. 6. fierce anger. See 4:8,26; Isa 13:13; Na 1:6.
51:46 Do not . . . be afraid when rumors are heard. While giving his Olivet discourse, Jesus may have had this passage in mind (see Mt 24:6; Mk 13:7; Lk 21:9).
51:47 punish the idols of Babylon. See v. 52; see also note on 50:2.
51:48 heaven and earth . . . will shout for joy. See Isa 44:23; Rev 18:20; 19:1–3. out of the north. See note on 50:3.
51:49 See note on 25:26.
51:50 leave. See note on v. 6.
51:51 foreigners have entered the holy places. Refers to Nebuchadnezzar's defiling the Jerusalem temple in 586 B.C. The same sacrilege would occur under Antiochus Epiphanes in 168 B.C. and under the Romans in A.D. 70.

because foreigners have entered
the holy places of the LORD's
house."[e]

52"But days are coming," declares the
LORD,
"when I will punish her idols,[f]
and throughout her land
the wounded will groan.[g]
53Even if Babylon reaches the sky[h]
and fortifies her lofty stronghold,
I will send destroyers[i] against her,"
declares the LORD.

54"The sound of a cry[j] comes from
Babylon,
the sound of great destruction[k]
from the land of the Babylonians.[x]
55The LORD will destroy Babylon;
he will silence[l] her noisy din.
Waves[m] ⌞of enemies⌟ will rage like great
waters;
the roar of their voices will resound.
56A destroyer[n] will come against Babylon;
her warriors will be captured,
and their bows will be broken.[o]
For the LORD is a God of retribution;
he will repay[p] in full.
57I will make her officials[q] and wise[r]
men drunk,[s]
her governors, officers and warriors
as well;
they will sleep[t] forever and not
awake,"
declares the King,[u] whose name is
the LORD Almighty.

58This is what the LORD Almighty says:

"Babylon's thick wall[v] will be leveled
and her high gates[w] set on fire;
the peoples[x] exhaust[y] themselves for
nothing,
the nations' labor is only fuel for the
flames."[z]

59This is the message Jeremiah gave to
the staff officer Seraiah son of Neriah,[a] the
son of Mahseiah, when he went to Babylon with Zedekiah[b] king of Judah in the
fourth[c] year of his reign. 60Jeremiah had
written on a scroll[d] about all the disasters
that would come upon Babylon—all that
had been recorded concerning Babylon.
61He said to Seraiah, "When you get to
Babylon, see that you read all these words
aloud. 62Then say, 'O LORD, you have said
you will destroy this place, so that neither
man nor animal will live in it; it will be
desolate[e] forever.' 63When you finish
reading this scroll, tie a stone to it and
throw it into the Euphrates.[f] 64Then say,
'So will Babylon sink to rise no more[g] because of the disaster I will bring upon her.
And her people[h] will fall.' "[i]

The words of Jeremiah end[j] here.

The Fall of Jerusalem

52:1–3pp — 2Ki 24:18–20; 2Ch 36:11–16
52:4–16pp — Jer 39:1–10
52:4–21pp — 2Ki 25:1–21; 2Ch 36:17–20

52 Zedekiah[k] was twenty-one years
old when he became king, and he
reigned in Jerusalem eleven years. His
mother's name was Hamutal daughter of
Jeremiah; she was from Libnah.[l] 2He did
evil in the eyes of the LORD, just as Jehoiakim[m] had done. 3It was because of the
LORD's anger that all this happened to

[x]*54* Or *Chaldeans*

51:51 [e]La 1:10
51:52 [f]ver 47
[g]S Job 24:12
51:53
[h]S Ge 11:4;
S Isa 14:13-14
[i]S ver 48;
S Job 15:21
51:54
[j]S Job 24:12
[k]S Jer 50:22
51:55 [l]Isa 25:5
[m]S Ps 18:4
51:56 [n]S ver 48;
S Job 15:21
[o]Ps 46:9 [p]S ver 6;
S Ge 4:24;
S Dt 32:41;
Ps 94:1-2;
Hab 2:8
51:57 [q]S ver 23
[r]S Job 5:13
[s]S Isa 21:5 [t]S ver 39; Ps 76:5;
S Jer 25:27
[u]S Isa 6:5
51:58 [v]S ver 44;
S 2Ki 25:4;
S Isa 15:1
[w]S Isa 13:2
[x]ver 64
[y]S Isa 47:13
[z]S Isa 47:14
51:59 [a]Jer 36:4
[b]Jer 52:1
[c]Jer 28:1
51:60
[d]S Ex 17:14;
Jer 30:2; 36:2
51:62
[e]S Isa 13:20;
S Jer 9:11;
S 50:13
51:63 [f]S Ge 2:14
51:64
[g]Eze 26:21;
28:19 [h]S ver 58
[i]Rev 18:21
[j]S Job 31:40
52:1 [k]S 2Ki 24:17
[l]S Nu 33:20;
Jos 10:29;
2Ki 8:22
52:2 [m]S Jer 36:30

51:52 *punish her idols.* See note on 50:2.
51:53 *reaches the sky.* Cf. Job 20:6; see Ge 11:4 and note; see also Isa 14:13–15. *destroyers.* See vv. 48,56.
51:54 See 50:46. *great destruction.* See note on 4:6.
51:55 *Waves.* See note on v. 42. *like great waters.* See note on Ps 32:6.
51:56 *God of retribution.* See note on v. 24.
51:57 *drunk.* See v. 39; see also notes on 25:15–16,26. *officials and wise men.* See 50:35. *King.* See note on 46:18. The true King is the Lord, not Bel/Marduk (see 50:2 and note).
51:58 *thick wall.* See note on v. 44. *high gates.* The famous Ishtar Gate was almost 40 feet high. *the peoples . . . fuel for the flames.* Very similar to Hab 2:13.
51:59–64 A prose conclusion to the book in general and to the oracle against Babylon in particular.
51:59 *staff officer.* Lit. "resting-place officer" (see Nu 10:33), the official responsible for determining when and where his men on the march should stay overnight. *Seraiah son of Neriah.* An ancient seal has been found that bears the inscription "Belonging to Seraiah son of Neriah," and it no doubt refers to the man mentioned here. He was a brother of Jeremiah's secretary, Baruch (see 32:12). *he.* Seraiah. *Zedekiah . . . fourth year.* 593 B.C. Zedekiah may have been summoned to Babylon by Nebuchadnezzar to be interrogated by him (see note on 27:3).
51:60 *scroll.* See note on Ex 17:14. *all that had been recorded concerning Babylon.* Probably the oracle of 50:2–51:58 (see note on 50:1).
51:62 *you have said.* See v. 26.
51:64 *The words of Jeremiah end here.* A note by the final compiler of the book of Jeremiah (see 48:47).
52:1–27,31–34 Paralleled almost verbatim in 2Ki 24:18–25:21,27–30 (see notes there). (52:4–27 is summarized in 39:1–10; see notes there.) The writer(s) of Kings and the writer of the appendix to Jeremiah (perhaps Baruch) doubtless had access to the same sources. It is unlikely that either of the two accounts copied from the other, since each has peculiarities characteristic of the larger work that it concludes. In a few passages, Jeremiah is fuller than Kings (compare especially vv. 10–11 with 2Ki 25:7; v. 15 with 2Ki 25:11; vv. 19–23 with 2Ki 25:15–17; v. 31 with 2Ki 25:27; v. 34 with 2Ki 25:30).
52:1 *Jeremiah.* Not the prophet.

Jerusalem and Judah,[n] and in the end he thrust them from his presence.[o]

Now Zedekiah rebelled[p] against the king of Babylon.

4 So in the ninth year of Zedekiah's reign, on the tenth[q] day of the tenth month, Nebuchadnezzar king of Babylon marched against Jerusalem[r] with his whole army. They camped outside the city and built siege works[s] all around it.[t] 5 The city was kept under siege until the eleventh year of King Zedekiah.

6 By the ninth day of the fourth month the famine in the city had become so severe that there was no food for the people to eat.[u] 7 Then the city wall was broken through, and the whole army fled.[v] They left the city at night through the gate between the two walls near the king's garden, though the Babylonians[y] were surrounding the city. They fled toward the Arabah,[z] 8 but the Babylonian[a] army pursued King Zedekiah and overtook him in the plains of Jericho. All his soldiers were separated from him and scattered, 9 and he was captured.[w]

He was taken to the king of Babylon at Riblah[x] in the land of Hamath,[y] where he pronounced sentence on him. 10 There at Riblah the king of Babylon slaughtered the sons[z] of Zedekiah before his eyes; he also killed all the officials of Judah. 11 Then he put out Zedekiah's eyes, bound him with bronze shackles and took him to Babylon, where he put him in prison till the day of his death.[a]

12 On the tenth day of the fifth[b] month, in the nineteenth year of Nebuchadnezzar king of Babylon, Nebuzaradan[c] commander of the imperial guard, who served the king of Babylon, came to Jerusalem. 13 He set fire[d] to the temple[e] of the LORD, the royal palace and all the houses[f] of Jerusalem. Every important building he burned down. 14 The whole Babylonian army under the commander of the imperial guard broke down all the walls[g] around Jerusalem. 15 Nebuzaradan the commander of the guard carried into exile[h] some of the poorest people and those who remained in the city, along with the rest of the craftsmen[b] and those who had gone over[i] to the king of Babylon. 16 But Nebuzaradan left behind[j] the rest of the poorest people of the land to work the vineyards and fields.

17 The Babylonians broke up the bronze pillars,[k] the movable stands[l] and the bronze Sea[m] that were at the temple of the LORD and they carried all the bronze to Babylon.[n] 18 They also took away the pots, shovels, wick trimmers, sprinkling bowls,[o] dishes and all the bronze articles used in the temple service.[p] 19 The commander of the imperial guard took away the basins, censers,[q] sprinkling bowls, pots, lampstands,[r] dishes[s] and bowls used for drink offerings[t]—all that were made of pure gold or silver.[u]

20 The bronze from the two pillars, the Sea and the twelve bronze bulls[v] under it, and the movable stands, which King Solomon had made for the temple of the LORD, was more than could be weighed.[w] 21 Each of the pillars was eighteen cubits high and twelve cubits in circumference[c]; each was four fingers thick, and hollow.[x] 22 The bronze capital[y] on top of the one pillar was five cubits[d] high and was decorated with a network and pomegranates[z] of bronze all around. The other pillar, with its pomegranates, was similar. 23 There were ninety-six pomegranates on the sides; the total number of pomegranates[a] above the surrounding network was a hundred.[b]

24 The commander of the guard took as prisoners Seraiah[c] the chief priest, Zephaniah[d] the priest next in rank and the three doorkeepers.[e] 25 Of those still in the city, he took the officer in charge of the fighting men, and seven royal advisers. He also took the secretary[f] who was chief officer in charge of conscripting the people of the land and sixty of his men who were found in the city. 26 Nebuzaradan[g] the commander took them all and brought them to the king of Babylon at Riblah. 27 There at Riblah,[h] in the land of Hamath, the king had them executed.

So Judah went into captivity, away[i] from her land. 28 This is the number of the

52:3 [n]Isa 3:1 [o]S Ge 4:14; S Ex 33:15 [p]Eze 17:12-16
52:4 [q]Zec 8:19 [r]Jer 34:1 [s]S Jer 6:6 [t]Eze 24:1-2
52:6 [u]S Lev 26:26; S Isa 3:1; La 1:11
52:7 [v]La 4:19
52:9 [w]S Jer 21:7; S 32:4 [x]S Nu 34:11 [y]S Nu 13:21
52:10 [z]S Jer 22:30
52:11 [a]Jer 34:4; Eze 12:13; 17:16
52:12 [b]Zec 7:5; 8:19 [c]ver 26
52:13 [d]S 2Ch 36:19; S Ps 74:8; La 2:6 [e]S Dt 29:24; Ps 79:1; Mic 3:12 [f]S Dt 13:16; S Jer 19:13
52:14 [g]S Ne 1:3; La 2:8
52:15 [h]S 2Ki 24:1; S Jer 1:3 [i]S Jer 38:19
52:16 [j]Jer 40:6
52:17 [k]S 1Ki 7:15 [l]1Ki 7:27-37 [m]S 1Ki 7:23 [n]Jer 27:19-22
52:18 [o]S Nu 4:14 [p]S Ex 27:3; 1Ki 7:45
52:19 [q]S Lev 10:1; S 1Ki 7:50 [r]S Nu 3:31 [s]Ex 25:29 [t]S Nu 4:7 [u]S Ezr 1:7; Da 5:2
52:20 [v]1Ki 7:25 [w]S 1Ki 7:47
52:21 [x]S 1Ki 7:15
52:22 [y]S 1Ki 7:16 [z]S Ex 28:33
52:23 [a]1Ki 7:20 [b]S ver 17; S Jer 27:19
52:24 [c]S 2Ki 25:18 [d]S 2Ki 25:18; S Jer 37:3 [e]S 2Ki 12:9
52:25 [f]Jer 36:10
52:26 [g]S ver 12
52:27 [h]S Nu 34:11 [i]S Jer 20:4

[y]*7* Or *Chaldeans*; also in verse 17 [z]*7* Or *the Jordan Valley* [a]*8* Or *Chaldean*; also in verse 14 [b]*15* Or *populace* [c]*21* That is, about 27 feet (about 8.1 meters) high and 18 feet (about 5.4 meters) in circumference [d]*22* That is, about 7 1/2 feet (about 2.3 meters)

52:12 *tenth day.* The parallel in 2Ki 25:8 reads "seventh day"; one of the numbers is a copyist's error, but we cannot tell which (see vv. 22,25,31).
52:18–19 See notes on 1Ki 7:40,45,50.
52:20 *twelve bronze bulls.* See note on 2Ch 4:4.
52:21–23 See notes on 1Ki 7:15–22.
52:22 *five.* The parallel in 2Ki 25:17 reads "three" (see NIV text note there), probably a copyist's error.
52:25 *seven.* The parallel in 2Ki 25:19 reads "five"; see note on v. 12.
52:28 *seventh year.* Of Nebuchadnezzar's reign (see vv. 29–30), which was 597 B.C. *3,023.* Probably includes only adult males, since the corresponding figure(s) in 2Ki 24:14, 16 are significantly higher.

people Nebuchadnezzar carried into exile:[j]

in the seventh year, 3,023 Jews;
[29]in Nebuchadnezzar's eighteenth year,
832 people from Jerusalem;
[30]in his twenty-third year,
745 Jews taken into exile[k] by
Nebuzaradan the commander of
the imperial guard.
There were 4,600 people in all.[l]

Jehoiachin Released

52:31–34pp — 2Ki 25:27-30

[31]In the thirty-seventh year of the exile

of Jehoiachin[m] king of Judah, in the year Evil-Merodach[e] became king of Babylon, he released Jehoiachin king of Judah and freed him from prison on the twenty-fifth day of the twelfth month. [32]He spoke kindly to him and gave him a seat of honor higher than those of the other kings who were with him in Babylon. [33]So Jehoiachin put aside his prison clothes and for the rest of his life ate regularly at the king's table.[n] [34]Day by day the king of Babylon gave Jehoiachin a regular allowance[o] as long as he lived, till the day of his death.

52:28
/S Dt 28:36;
S 2Ch 36:20;
S Ne 1:2
52:30 *k*S Jer 43:3
/S Jer 13:19

52:31
*m*S 2Ch 36:9
52:33 *n*S 2Sa 9:7
52:34 *o*2Sa 9:10

e31 Also called *Amel-Marduk*

52:29 *eighteenth year.* 586 B.C. In v. 12 the same year is called the "nineteenth year"; the difference is due to alternate ways of computing regnal years (for a similar case see note on Da 1:1).

52:30 *twenty-third year.* 581 B.C. *taken into exile by Nebuzaradan.* Either (1) to quell further rebellion (see v. 3), or (2) in belated reprisal for Gedaliah's assassination (see 41:1–3).

52:31–34 Paralleled almost verbatim in 2Ki 25:27–30 (see notes there). Jeremiah and Kings thus conclude with the

same happy ending.
52:31 *twenty-fifth.* The parallel in 2Ki 25:27 reads "twenty-seventh"; see note on v. 12.
52:34 *till the day of his death.* See v. 11. Since the phrase does not appear in the parallel verses in 2 Kings in either case, its intention is probably to highlight the contrast between Zedekiah, who remained in prison till the day he died (see v. 11), and Jehoiachin, who was released from prison and treated well by the Babylonian kings till the day he died.

LAMENTATIONS

Title

The Hebrew title of the book is *'ekah* ("How . . . !"), the first word not only in 1:1 but also in 2:1; 4:1. Because of its subject matter, the book is also referred to in Jewish tradition as *qinot*, "Lamentations" (the title given to it in the Greek Septuagint and Latin Vulgate).

Author and Date

Although Lamentations is anonymous and we cannot be certain who wrote it, ancient Jewish and Christian tradition ascribes it to Jeremiah. This is partly on the basis of 2Ch 35:25 (though the "Laments" are not to be identified with the OT book of Lamentations); partly on the basis of such texts as Jer 7:29; 8:21; 9:1,10,20; and partly because of the similarity of vocabulary and style between the books of Jeremiah and Lamentations. Also, since the prophet Jeremiah was an eyewitness to the divine judgment on Jerusalem in 586 B.C., it is reasonable to assume that he was the author of the book that so vividly portrays the event. Lamentations poignantly shares the overwhelming sense of loss that accompanied the destruction of the city, temple and ritual as well as the exile of Judah's inhabitants.

The earliest possible date for the book is 586 B.C., and the latest is 516 (when the rebuilt Jerusalem temple was dedicated). The graphic immediacy of Lamentations argues for an earlier date, probably before 575.

Literary Features

The entire book is poetic. Each of its five laments contains 22 verses (except the third, which has 66 verses—3 times 22), reflecting the number of letters in the Hebrew alphabet. Moreover, the first four are alphabetic acrostics (see NIV text notes on 1:1; 2:1; 3:1; 4:1). The first three laments are equal in length; in the first and second each verse (except 1:7) has three Hebrew lines, while in the third each of the 66 verses has one Hebrew line. The fourth is shorter (each of its 22 verses has two Hebrew lines), and the fifth is shorter still (each verse has one Hebrew line). Use of the alphabet as a formal structure indicates that, however passionate these laments, they were composed with studied care.

Themes and Theology

Lamentations is not the only OT book that contains individual or community laments. (A large number of the Psalms are lament poems, and every prophetic book except Haggai includes one or more examples of the lament genre.) However, it is the only book that consists solely of laments.

As a series of laments over the destruction of Jerusalem in 586 B.C., it stands in a tradition with such ancient non-Biblical writings as the Sumerian "Lamentation over the Destruction of Ur," "Lamentation over the Destruction of Sumer and Ur," and "Lamentation over the Destruction of Nippur." Orthodox Jews customarily read it aloud in its entirety on the ninth day of Ab, the traditional date of the destruction of Solomon's temple in 586 as well as the date of the destruction of Herod's temple in A.D. 70. Many also read it each week at the Western Wall (known also as the "Wailing Wall") in the Old City of Jerusalem. In addition the book is important in traditional Roman Catholic liturgy, where it is read during the last three days of Holy Week.

This latter tradition reminds us that the book of Lamentations describes Jerusalem's destruction not only for its own sake but also for the profound theological lessons to be learned from it. The horrors of 586 B.C. are not overlooked, of course:

1. Wholesale devastation and slaughter engulf kings (2:6,9; 4:20), princes (1:6; 2:2,9; 4:7-8; 5:12), elders (1:19; 2:10; 4:16; 5:12), priests (1:4,19; 2:6,20; 4:16), prophets (2:9,20) and commoners (2:10-12; 3:48; 4:6) alike.

2. Starving mothers are reduced to cannibalism (2:20; 4:10).
3. The flower of Judah's citizenry is dragged off into ignominious exile (1:3,18).
4. An elaborate system of ceremony and worship comes to an end (1:4,10).

But other matters, ultimately of far greater significance, are probed as well.

The author of Lamentations understands clearly that the Babylonians were merely the human agents of divine retribution and that God himself has destroyed his city and temple (1:12-15; 2:1-8,17,22; 4:11). Nor was the Lord's action arbitrary; blatant, God-defying sin and covenant-breaking rebellion were the root causes of his people's woes (1:5,8-9; 4:13; 5:7,16). Although weeping (1:16; 2:11,18; 3:48-51) is to be expected and cries for redress against the enemy (1:22; 3:59-66) are understandable, the proper response in the wake of judgment is sincere, heartfelt contrition (3:40-42). The book that begins with lament (1:1-2) rightly ends in repentance (5:21-22).

In the middle of the book, the theology of Lamentations reaches its apex as it focuses on the goodness of God. He is the Lord of hope (3:21,24-25), of love (3:22), of faithfulness (3:23), of salvation (3:26). In spite of all evidence to the contrary, "his compassions never fail. They are new every morning; great is your faithfulness" (3:22-23).

Outline

I. Jerusalem's Misery and Desolation (ch. 1)
II. The Lord's Anger against His People (ch. 2)
III. Judah's Complaint—and Basis for Consolation (ch. 3)
IV. The Contrast between Zion's Past and Present (ch. 4)
V. Judah's Appeal for God's Forgiveness (ch. 5)

1 ^a How deserted^a lies the city,
  once so full of people!^b
How like a widow^c is she,
  who once was great^d among the
    nations!
She who was queen among the
    provinces
  has now become a slave. ^e

²Bitterly she weeps^f at night,
  tears are upon her cheeks.
Among all her lovers^g
  there is none to comfort her.
All her friends have betrayed^h her;
  they have become her enemies. ⁱ

³After affliction and harsh labor,
  Judah has gone into exile. ^j
She dwells among the nations;
  she finds no resting place. ^k
All who pursue her have overtaken
    her^l
  in the midst of her distress.

⁴The roads to Zion mourn, ^m
  for no one comes to her appointed
    feasts.
All her gateways are desolate, ⁿ
  her priests groan,
her maidens grieve,
  and she is in bitter anguish. ^o

⁵Her foes have become her masters;
  her enemies are at ease.
The LORD has brought her grief^p
  because of her many sins. ^q
Her children have gone into exile, ^r
  captive before the foe. ^s

⁶All the splendor has departed
  from the Daughter of Zion. ^t
Her princes are like deer

that find no pasture;
  in weakness they have fled ^u
    before the pursuer.

⁷In the days of her affliction and
    wandering
  Jerusalem remembers all the treasures
    that were hers in days of old.
When her people fell into enemy hands,
  there was no one to help her. ^v
Her enemies looked at her
  and laughed ^w at her destruction.

⁸Jerusalem has sinned^x greatly
  and so has become unclean. ^y
All who honored her despise her,
  for they have seen her nakedness; ^z
she herself groans^a
  and turns away.

⁹Her filthiness clung to her skirts;
  she did not consider her future. ^b
Her fall^c was astounding;
  there was none to comfort^d her.
"Look, O LORD, on my affliction, ^e
  for the enemy has triumphed."

¹⁰The enemy laid hands
  on all her treasures;^f
she saw pagan nations
  enter her sanctuary^g—
those you had forbidden^h
  to enter your assembly.

¹¹All her people groanⁱ
  as they search for bread;^j
they barter their treasures for food
  to keep themselves alive.
"Look, O LORD, and consider,
  for I am despised."

^aThis chapter is an acrostic poem, the verses of which begin with the successive letters of the Hebrew alphabet.

Cross references (center column):

1:1 ^aS Lev 26:43
^bS Jer 42:2
^cS Isa 47:8
^dS 1Ki 4:21
^eIsa 3:26;
S Jer 40:9;
Eze 5:5
1:2 ^fPs 6:6
^gS Jer 3:1
^hS Jer 4:30;
Mic 7:5 ⁱver 16;
S Jer 30:14
1:3 ^jS Jer 13:19
^kDt 28:65
1:4 ^mS Ps 137:1
ⁿS Isa 27:10;
S Jer 9:11 ^over 21; Joel 1:8-13
1:5 ^pS Isa 22:5;
S Jer 30:15
^qS Ps 5:10
^rS Jer 10:20;
S 39:9; 52:28-30
^sS Ps 137:3;
La 2:17
1:6 ^tS Ps 9:14;
Jer 13:18

^uS Lev 26:36
1:7 ^vS 2Ki 14:26;
S Jer 37:7;
La 4:17
^wS Jer 2:26
1:8 ^xver 20;
Isa 59:2-13
^yS Jer 2:22
^zS Jer 13:22,26
^aver 21,22;
S Ps 6:6; S 38:8
1:9
^bDt 32:28-29;
Eze 24:13
^cJer 13:18
^dS Ecc 4:1;
S Jer 16:7
^ePs 25:18
1:10 ^fS Isa 64:11
^gPs 74:7-8; 79:1;
Jer 51:51
^hDt 23:3
1:11 ⁱS Ps 6:6;
S 38:8
^jS Jer 37:21;
S 52:6

1:1 *How . . . !* Expresses a mixture of shock and despair (see 2:1; 4:1-2; Isa 1:21; Jer 48:17). *deserted lies. The* Hebrew underlying this phrase is translated "sat alone" in Jer 15:17. There the prophet sat alone; here his beloved city does the same. *city.* Jerusalem. *once so full of people.* See Isa 1:21. *full . . . great.* The Hebrew is the same for both words. *great among the nations.* Contrast Jer 49:15. *slave.* The Hebrew for this word is translated "forced labor" in Ex 1:11; 1Ki 4:6.
1:2 *Bitterly she weeps.* As did Jeremiah, and for much the same reason (see Jer 13:17). *at night.* See 2:18-19. *lovers . . . friends.* Political allies (see, e.g., Jer 2:36-37; 27:3). *none to comfort her.* See vv. 9,16-17,21. *All . . . have betrayed her.* See v. 19; like Edom (see 4:21-22; Ps 137:7) and Ammon (see Jer 40:14; Eze 25:2-3,6). *become her enemies.* See v. 17.
1:3 *among the nations . . . finds no resting place.* As Moses warned in Dt 28:65.
1:4 *mourn.* Are deserted and desolate (see Jdg 5:6; Isa 33:8 and notes). *appointed feasts.* See Ex 23:14-17 and notes; Lev 23:2. *maidens grieve.* A sign of utter defeat (contrast Ex 15:20 and note; Jdg 21:19,21; Ps 68:25; Jer 31:13).

1:5 *masters.* Lit. "head"—in accordance with Dt 28:44 (contrast Dt 28:13). *at ease.* See Jer 12:1.
1:6 *Daughter of Zion.* A personification of Jerusalem and its inhabitants. *Her princes . . . have fled before the pursuer.* See Jer 52:7-8.
1:7 *affliction and wandering.* See 3:19. *treasures.* See vv. 10-11. *days of old.* For example, the days of David and Solomon. *fell into enemy hands.* See 2Sa 24:14. *destruction.* Lit. "cessation." The Hebrew root for this word is the same as that for "Sabbath"—and may be intended as an ironic pun (see Lev 26:34-35).
1:8 *unclean.* See v. 17 and note. It refers to the ceremonial uncleanness of a woman during her monthly period (see Lev 12:2,5; 15:19); Jerusalem is here personified as a woman (see v. 6).
1:9 *filthiness.* Ceremonial uncleanness (see note on Lev 4:12), here caused by willful sin. *did not consider her future.* See Isa 47:7. *Look, O LORD.* See vv. 11,20. *enemy has triumphed.* See v. 16.
1:10 *forbidden to enter your assembly.* See Eze 44:7,9.
1:11 *search for bread.* Food shortages were an ever-present problem during and after the siege of Jerusalem. *keep themselves alive.* See v. 19; 1Sa 30:12.

12"Is it nothing to you, all you who pass
    by? [k]
  Look around and see.
  Is any suffering like my suffering [l]
    that was inflicted on me,
  that the LORD brought on me
    in the day of his fierce anger? [m]

13"From on high he sent fire,
    sent it down into my bones. [n]
  He spread a net [o] for my feet
    and turned me back.
  He made me desolate, [p]
    faint [q] all the day long.

14"My sins have been bound into a
    yoke [b] ; [r]
  by his hands they were woven
    together.
  They have come upon my neck
    and the Lord has sapped my strength.
  He has handed me over [s]
    to those I cannot withstand.

15"The Lord has rejected
    all the warriors in my midst; [t]
  he has summoned an army [u] against me
    to [c] crush my young men. [v]
  In his winepress [w] the Lord has
    trampled [x]
    the Virgin Daughter [y] of Judah.

16"This is why I weep
    and my eyes overflow with tears. [z]
  No one is near to comfort [a] me,
    no one to restore my spirit.
  My children are destitute
    because the enemy has prevailed." [b]

17Zion stretches out her hands, [c]
    but there is no one to comfort her.
  The LORD has decreed for Jacob
    that his neighbors become his foes; [d]
  Jerusalem has become
    an unclean [e] thing [f] among them.

18"The LORD is righteous, [g]
    yet I rebelled [h] against his command.
  Listen, all you peoples;
    look upon my suffering. [i]
  My young men and maidens
    have gone into exile. [j]

19"I called to my allies [k]
    but they betrayed me.
  My priests and my elders
    perished [l] in the city
  while they searched for food
    to keep themselves alive.

20"See, O LORD, how distressed [m] I am!
    I am in torment [n] within,
  and in my heart I am disturbed, [o]
    for I have been most rebellious. [p]
  Outside, the sword bereaves;
    inside, there is only death. [q]

21"People have heard my groaning, [r]
    but there is no one to comfort me. [s]
  All my enemies have heard of my
    distress;
  they rejoice [t] at what you have done.
  May you bring the day [u] you have
    announced
    so they may become like me.

22"Let all their wickedness come before
    you;
    deal with them
  as you have dealt with me
    because of all my sins. [v]
  My groans [w] are many
    and my heart is faint."

2 [d] How the Lord has covered the Daughter of Zion

Cross references (center column):
1:12 [k]S Jer 18:16
[l]ver 18
[m]S Isa 10:4;
13:13; S Jer 30:24
1:13 [n]S Job 30:30;
Ps 102:3
[o]S Job 18:8
[p]S Jer 44:6
[q]Hab 3:16
1:14 [r]S Dt 28:48;
S Isa 47:6;
S Jer 15:12
[s]S Jer 32:5
1:15 [t]Jer 37:10
[u]Isa 41:2
[v]Isa 28:18;
S Jer 18:21
[w]S Jdg 6:11
[x]S Isa 5:5
[y]Jer 14:17
1:16 [z]S Job 7:3;
S Ps 119:136;
S Isa 22:4;
La 2:11,18;
3:48-49
[a]S Ps 69:20;
Ecc 4:1;
S Jer 16:7 [b]S ver
2; Jer 13:17;
14:17
1:17 [c]S Jer 4:31
[d]S Ex 23:21
[e]Jer 2:22
[f]S Lev 18:25-28
1:18 [g]S Ex 9:27;
S Ezr 9:15
[h]S 1Sa 12:14 [i]ver
12 /Dt 28:32,41
1:19 [k]S Jer 22:20
[l]S Jer 14:15;
La 2:20
1:20 [m]S Jer 4:19
[n]La 2:11
[o]S Job 20:2 [p]S ver
8 [q]S Dt 32:25;
Eze 7:15
1:21 [r]S ver 8;
S Ps 6:6; S 38:8
[s]ver 4 [t]La 2:15
[u]Isa 47:11;
Jer 30:16
1:22 [v]Ne 4:5
[w]S ver 8; S Ps 6:6

b14 Most Hebrew manuscripts; Septuagint *He kept watch over my sins*   c15 Or *has set a time for me / when he will*   dThis chapter is an acrostic poem, the verses of which begin with the successive letters of the Hebrew alphabet.

1:12 See v. 18. Up to this point, the author has been the main speaker. Now, at the halfway mark of ch. 1, the main speaker changes to Jerusalem personified. *fierce anger.* See 2:3,6; 4:11. The expression is common in Jeremiah (see Jer 4:8,26; 12:13; 25:37–38; 44:6; 49:37; 51:45).
1:13 *From on high he sent fire.* See 1Ki 18:38; 2Ki 1:10, 12,14; 2Ch 7:1. *my bones.* The bones of Jerusalem (personified as a woman; see note on v. 8). In a strikingly similar image, the word of the Lord was like fire in the bones of the prophet (see Jer 20:9 and note). *spread a net for my feet.* See Ps 57:6; Pr 29:5. *desolate.* Like Absalom's sister Tamar (see 2Sa 13:20).
1:15 *In his winepress . . . trampled.* A common metaphor of divine judgment (see Isa 63:2–3; Joel 3:13; Rev 14:19–20; 19:15). *Virgin Daughter of Judah.* See 2:13; see also notes on 2Ki 19:21; Jer 14:17.
1:16 *eyes overflow with tears.* See 3:48; Jer 9:18; 13:17; 14:17; see also Jer 9:1. *enemy has prevailed.* See v. 9.
1:17 *become his foes.* See v. 2. *unclean thing.* See note on v. 8; for the same imagery elsewhere see Ezr 9:11; Isa

30:22; 64:6; Eze 7:19–20; 36:17.
1:18 *The LORD is righteous.* See Dt 32:4; 2Ch 12:6; Ps 119:137; Jer 12:1; see also note on Ps 4:1. *rebelled against his command.* See Nu 20:24. *Listen, all you peoples.* See 1Ki 22:28; Ps 49:1; Mic 1:2.
1:19 *allies . . . betrayed me.* See v. 2 and note. *keep themselves alive.* See note on v. 11.
1:20 *I am in torment within.* Repeated in 2:11. *Outside . . . inside.* See Jer 14:18. The Sumerian "Lamentation over the Destruction of Ur" contains a striking parallel: "Inside it we die of famine, outside we are killed by weapons" (lines 403–404).
1:21 *day you have announced.* Day of God's judgment on the nations (see Jer 25:15–38).
1:22 *wickedness . . . before you.* See Ps 109:14–15. *my heart is faint.* The same expression is found in Jer 8:18; see La 5:17; Isa 1:5.
2:1 *"How . . . !"* See note on 1:1. *Daughter of Zion.* See 1:6 and note. *hurled down the splendor of Israel.* The imagery is that of a falling star (as in Isa 14:12). *footstool.*

with the cloud of his anger! [e] [x]
He has hurled down the splendor of
Israel
from heaven to earth;
he has not remembered his footstool [y]
in the day of his anger. [z]

[2]Without pity [a] the Lord has swallowed [b]
up
all the dwellings of Jacob;
in his wrath he has torn down
the strongholds [c] of the Daughter of
Judah.
He has brought her kingdom and its
princes
down to the ground [d] in dishonor.

[3]In fierce anger he has cut off
every horn [e] of Israel.
He has withdrawn his right hand [f]
at the approach of the enemy.
He has burned in Jacob like a flaming
fire
that consumes everything around it. [g]

[4]Like an enemy he has strung his bow; [h]
his right hand is ready.
Like a foe he has slain
all who were pleasing to the eye; [i]
he has poured out his wrath [j] like fire [k]
on the tent [l] of the Daughter of Zion.

[5]The Lord is like an enemy; [m]
he has swallowed up Israel.
He has swallowed up all her palaces
and destroyed her strongholds. [n]
He has multiplied mourning and
lamentation [o]
for the Daughter of Judah. [p]

[6]He has laid waste his dwelling like a
garden;
he has destroyed [q] his place of
meeting. [r]
The LORD has made Zion forget

her appointed feasts and her
Sabbaths; [s]
in his fierce anger he has spurned
both king and priest. [t]

[7]The Lord has rejected his altar
and abandoned his sanctuary. [u]
He has handed over to the enemy
the walls of her palaces; [v]
they have raised a shout in the house of
the LORD
as on the day of an appointed feast. [w]

[8]The LORD determined to tear down
the wall around the Daughter of
Zion. [x]
He stretched out a measuring line [y]
and did not withhold his hand from
destroying.
He made ramparts [z] and walls lament;
together they wasted away. [a]

[9]Her gates [b] have sunk into the ground;
their bars [c] he has broken and
destroyed.
Her king and her princes are exiled [d]
among the nations,
the law [e] is no more,
and her prophets [f] no longer find
visions [g] from the LORD.

[10]The elders of the Daughter of Zion
sit on the ground in silence; [h]
they have sprinkled dust [i] on their
heads [j]
and put on sackcloth. [k]
The young women of Jerusalem
have bowed their heads to the
ground. [l]

[11]My eyes fail from weeping, [m]

2:1 [x]La 3:44
[y]Ps 99:5; 132:7
[z]S Jer 12:7
2:2 [a]ver 17;
La 3:43 [b]Ps 21:9
[c]Ps 89:39-40;
Mic 5:11
[d]S Isa 25:12
2:3 [e]Ps 75:5,10
[f]Ps 74:11
[g]S Isa 42:25;
Jer 21:4-5,14
2:4 [h]S Job 3:23;
16:13; La 3:12-13
[i]S Ps 48:2;
Eze 24:16,25
[j]S 2Ch 34:21;
Eze 20:34
[k]Isa 42:25;
S Jer 7:20
[l]S Jer 4:20
2:5 [m]S Job 13:24
[n]ver 2 [o]S Isa 29:2
[p]S Jer 7:20;
9:17-20
2:6 [q]2Ch 36:19
[r]S Jer 52:13

[s]Zep 3:18
[t]Isa 43:28;
S Jer 7:14;
La 4:16; 5:12
2:7 [u]S Lev 26:31;
S Eze 7:24
[v]Ps 74:7-8;
S Isa 64:11;
Jer 33:4-5;
Eze 7:21-22
[w]Jer 21:4; 52:13
2:8 [x]ver 18
[y]S 2Ki 21:13
[z]S Ps 48:13
[a]Isa 3:26;
S Jer 39:8;
S 52:14
2:9 [b]S Ne 1:3
[c]S Isa 45:2;
Hos 11:6
[d]Dt 28:36;
S 2Ki 24:15;
Jer 16:13; Hos 3:4
[e]S 2Ch 15:3
[f]S 1Sa 3:1
[g]S Jer 14:14
2:10 [h]La 3:28
[i]S Jos 7:6
[j]Job 2:12
[k]S Isa 3:24
[l]S Job 2:13;
S Isa 3:26;
Eze 27:30-31
2:11
[m]S Ps 119:82;
S Isa 15:3;
S La 1:16;
3:48-51

[e]1 Or *How the Lord in his anger / has treated the
Daughter of Zion with contempt* [f]3 Or */ all the
strength*; or *every king*; *horn* here symbolizes strength.

Either (1) the ark of the covenant (see 1Ch 28:2) or, more
likely, (2) Mount Zion (see Ps 99:5,9).
2:2 *swallowed up all the dwellings.* See v. 5. *Daughter of
Judah.* See note on 1:15.
2:3 *cut off every horn.* See Jer 48:25. *flaming fire that
consumes.* See Nu 11:3; Job 1:16; Ps 106:18.
2:4 *strung his bow.* See Dt 32:42; Ps 7:12–13; Zec
9:13–14. *poured out his wrath.* See Ps 69:24; 79:6; Jer
6:11; 7:20; 10:25; 42:18; 44:6; Hos 5:10; Zep 3:8.
2:5 *palaces . . . strongholds.* See Hos 8:14. *He has multiplied . . . Daughter of Judah.* The Sumerian "Lamentation
over the Destruction of Sumer and Ur" offers this parallel:
"In the desolate city there was uttered nothing but laments
and dirges" (lines 361–362, 486–487). *Daughter of Judah.*
See note on 1:15.
2:6 *his dwelling.* Originally the tabernacle, later the temple
(see Ps 27:4–5). *like a garden.* Cf. Isa 5:5–6; Jer 5:10;
12:10. *his place of meeting.* The tabernacle/temple, where
God met with his people (see Ex 25:22; 29:42–43; Ps
74:4).

2:7 *rejected . . . abandoned.* These two verbs are found in
Ps 89:38–39 ("rejected . . . renounced") in connection with
the Lord's forsaking of the king from the dynasty of David.
raised a shout in the house of the LORD. See Ps 74:4. *as on
the day of an appointed feast.* See Hos 12:9.
2:8 *determined to tear down.* See Jer 32:31. *Daughter of
Zion.* A personification of Jerusalem and its inhabitants.
stretched out a measuring line. To destroy with the same
standards of precision and propriety used in building (see Isa
28:17 and note; Am 7:7–8 and notes). *ramparts . . . walls.*
See Isa 26:1. The ramparts were the outer fortifications (see
2Sa 20:15).
2:9 *prophets no longer find visions.* The Lord was no
longer communicating to his people through prophets (see Ps
74:9; Am 8:11 and note; Mic 3:7).
2:10 *elders.* See note on Ex 3:16. *sit on the ground in
silence . . . sprinkled dust on their heads and put on sackcloth . . . bowed their heads.* Signs of mourning (see Job
2:12–13; Ps 35:13–14). *young women of Jerusalem.* See
1:4 and note.

I am in torment within, [n]
my heart [o] is poured out [p] on the
ground
because my people are destroyed, [q]
because children and infants faint [r]
in the streets of the city.

[12]They say to their mothers,
"Where is bread and wine?" [s]
as they faint like wounded men
in the streets of the city,
as their lives ebb away [t]
in their mothers' arms. [u]

[13]What can I say for you? [v]
With what can I compare you,
O Daughter [w] of Jerusalem?
To what can I liken you,
that I may comfort you,
O Virgin Daughter of Zion? [x]
Your wound is as deep as the sea. [y]
Who can heal you?

[14]The visions of your prophets
were false [z] and worthless;
they did not expose your sin
to ward off your captivity. [a]
The oracles they gave you
were false and misleading. [b]

[15]All who pass your way
clap their hands at you; [c]
they scoff [d] and shake their heads [e]
at the Daughter of Jerusalem: [f]
"Is this the city that was called
the perfection of beauty, [g]
the joy of the whole earth?" [h]

[16]All your enemies open their mouths
wide against you; [i]
they scoff and gnash their teeth [j]
and say, "We have swallowed her
up. [k]
This is the day we have waited for;
we have lived to see it." [l]

[17]The LORD has done what he planned;
he has fulfilled [m] his word,
which he decreed long ago. [n]
He has overthrown you without pity, [o]
he has let the enemy gloat over
you, [p]
he has exalted the horn [g] of your
foes. [q]

[18]The hearts of the people
cry out to the Lord. [r]
O wall of the Daughter of Zion, [s]
let your tears [t] flow like a river
day and night; [u]
give yourself no relief,
your eyes no rest. [v]

[19]Arise, cry out in the night,
as the watches of the night begin;
pour out your heart [w] like water
in the presence of the Lord. [x]
Lift up your hands [y] to him
for the lives of your children,
who faint [z] from hunger
at the head of every street.

[20]"Look, O LORD, and consider:
Whom have you ever treated like
this?
Should women eat their offspring, [a]
the children they have cared for? [b]
Should priest and prophet be killed [c]
in the sanctuary of the Lord? [d]

[21]"Young and old lie together
in the dust of the streets;
my young men and maidens
have fallen by the sword. [e]
You have slain them in the day of your
anger;

2:11
[n]S Job 30:27;
La 1:20 [o]S Isa 1:5
[p]ver 19; Ps 22:14
[q]S Jer 9:1 [r]La 4:4
2:12 [s]Isa 24:11
[t]S Job 3:24
[u]La 4:4
2:13 [v]S Isa 1:6
[w]S 2Ki 19:21
[x]Isa 37:22
[y]Jer 14:17;
30:12-15; La 1:12
2:14 [z]S Jer 28:15
[a]Jer 8:11
[b]Jer 2:8; S 20:6;
23:25-32,33-40;
S 29:9; Eze 13:3;
22:28
2:15
[c]S Nu 24:10;
Eze 25:6
[d]S Dt 28:37;
S Isa 28:22;
Jer 19:8;
S Na 3:19
[e]S Job 16:4
[f]S La 1:21
[g]Ps 45:11;
S 48:2; 50:2;
Eze 16:14
[h]Ps 48:2
2:16 [i]Ps 22:13;
La 3:46
[j]S Job 16:9
[k]S Ps 35:25
[l]Eze 36:3;
Mic 4:11

2:17 [m]S Jer 39:16
[n]Dt 28:15-45
[o]S ver 2;
Eze 5:11; 7:9;
8:18 [p]S Ps 22:17
[q]Ps 89:42;
S Isa 44:26;
S La 1:5; Zec 1:6
2:18
[r]S Ps 119:145
[s]ver 8 S La 1:16
[t]S Jer 9:1
[u]La 3:49
2:19 [w]1Sa 1:15
[x]S ver 11;
Isa 26:9
[y]S Ps 28:2
[z]S Isa 51:20
2:20 [a]S Dt 28:53;
Jer 19:9; Eze 5:10
[b]La 4:10
[c]Ps 78:64;
S Jer 14:15;
23:11-12
[d]S La 1:19
2:21 [e]S Dt 32:25;
S 2Ch 36:17;

Ps 78:62-63; Jer 6:11

[g]17 *Horn* here symbolizes strength.

2:11 *My eyes fail.* See note on Ps 6:7. *weeping.* See note on 1:16. *I am in torment within.* Repeated from 1:20. *my people.* Lit. "the daughter of my people" (see 3:48; 4:10; see also note on Jer 14:17).
2:12 *lives ebb away.* See Job 30:16; Ps 107:5; Jnh 2:7.
2:13 *say for you.* See Job 29:11. *Daughter of Jerusalem . . . Virgin Daughter of Zion.* See notes on 1:6; Jer 14:17.
2:14 *prophets . . . false.* Jeremiah often denounced false prophets (see Jer 5:12-13; 6:13-15; 8:10-12; 14:13-15; 23:9-40; 27:9-28:17). *worthless.* Or "whitewash(ed)"; for an explanation of this image see Eze 13:10-16; 22:28. *misleading.* The unusual Hebrew word underlying this word comes from the same root as that underlying "banish" in Jer 27:10,15: The lies of false prophets "mislead" the people and thus lead to "banishment" by the Lord—so they are "banishing" in their effect.
2:15 *who pass your way.* See 1:12. *clap their hands.* See Job 27:23. *scoff.* See v. 16; see also note on Jer 19:8. *shake their heads.* See note on Job 16:4; see also Ps 44:14; 109:25; Jer 18:16. *Daughter of Jerusalem.* See notes on 1:6;

Jer 14:17. *was called the perfection of beauty.* As in Ps 50:2 (see note there). *was called . . . the joy of the whole earth.* As in Ps 48:2 (see note there; cf. Jer 51:41).
2:16 *swallowed her up.* See vv. 2,5; Jer 51:34.
2:17 *fulfilled his word.* See Isa 55:11 and note. *long ago.* The days of Moses (see, e.g., the threats of Lev 26:23-39; Dt 28:15-68). *exalted the horn.* Increased the strength (see NIV text note; see also 1Sa 2:1; Ps 75:4).
2:18 See Jer 14:17. *O wall.* A city gate is similarly addressed in Isa 14:31. *Daughter of Zion.* A personification of Jerusalem and its inhabitants.
2:19 *watches of the night begin.* See note on Jdg 7:19; see also Ps 63:6. *pour out your heart.* In earnest prayer (see Ps 62:8). *like water.* A common simile with "pour out" (see Dt 12:16,24; 15:23; Ps 79:3; Hos 5:10). *Lift up your hands.* In prayer and praise (see Ps 28:2; 63:4; 1Ti 2:8). *children, who faint from hunger.* See vv. 11-12.
2:20-22 The prayer called for in v. 19.
2:20 *women eat their offspring.* See note on Jer 19:9.
2:21 See Jer 6:11 and note.

you have slaughtered them without
pity.*f*

22"As you summon to a feast day,
so you summoned against me
terrors*g* on every side.
In the day of the Lord's anger
no one escaped*h* or survived;
those I cared for and reared,*i*
my enemy has destroyed."

3*h* I am the man who has seen
affliction*j*
by the rod of his wrath.*k*
2He has driven me away and made me
walk
in darkness*l* rather than light;
3indeed, he has turned his hand against
me*m*
again and again, all day long.

4He has made my skin and my flesh
grow old*n*
and has broken my bones.*o*
5He has besieged me and surrounded me
with bitterness*p* and hardship.*q*
6He has made me dwell in darkness
like those long dead.*r*

7He has walled me in so I cannot
escape;*s*
he has weighed me down with
chains.*t*
8Even when I call out or cry for help,*u*
he shuts out my prayer.*v*
9He has barred*w* my way with blocks of
stone;
he has made my paths crooked.*x*

10Like a bear lying in wait,

like a lion*y* in hiding,*z*
11he dragged me from the path and
mangled*a* me
and left me without help.
12He drew his bow*b*
and made me the target*c* for his
arrows.*d*

13He pierced*e* my heart
with arrows from his quiver.*f*
14I became the laughingstock*g* of all my
people;*h*
they mock me in song*i* all day long.
15He has filled me with bitter herbs
and sated me with gall.*j*

16He has broken my teeth with gravel;*k*
he has trampled me in the dust.*l*
17I have been deprived of peace;
I have forgotten what prosperity is.
18So I say, "My splendor is gone
and all that I had hoped from the
Lord."*m*

19I remember my affliction and my
wandering,
the bitterness*n* and the gall.*o*
20I well remember them,
and my soul is downcast*p* within
me.*q*
21Yet this I call to mind
and therefore I have hope:

22Because of the Lord's great love*r* we
are not consumed,*s*

2:21 /S Jer 13:14;
La 3:43; Zec 11:6
2:22 *gS Ps 31:13;
S Jer 20:10
*hS Jer 11:11
/Job 27:14;
Hos 9:13
3:1 /Jer 15:17-18
*kS Job 19:21;
Ps 88:7
3:2 /S Job 19:8;
S Ps 82:5;
S Jer 4:23
3:3 *mPs 38:2;
Isa 5:25
3:4 *nS Job 30:30;
La 4:8 *oPs 51:8;
S Isa 38:13;
S Jer 50:17
3:5 *pver 19
*qJer 23:15
3:6 *rPs 88:5-6;
143:3; Isa 59:10
3:7 *sS Job 3:23
*tJer 40:4
3:8 *uPs 5:2 *vver
44; S Dt 1:45;
S Job 30:20;
Ps 22:2
3:9 *wS Job 19:8
*xS Job 9:24;
S Isa 63:17;
Hos 2:6

3:10 *yS Job 10:16
*zHos 13:8;
Am 5:18-19
3:11 *aHos 6:1
3:12 *bS La 2:4
*cJob 7:20
*dS Job 16:12;
Ps 7:12-13; 38:2
3:13 *eS Job 16:13
/Job 6:4
3:14
*gS Ge 38:23;
Ps 22:6-7;
Jer 20:7
*hS Job 17:2
/S Job 30:9
3:15 /ver 19;
Jer 9:15
3:16 *kS Pr 20:17
/S Ps 7:5
3:18 *mS ver 54;
S Job 17:15
3:19 *nver 5
*oS ver 15
3:20 *pS Ps 42:5
*qPs 42:11; 43:5

3:22 *rS Ps 103:11 *sS Job 34:15; S Hos 11:9

*h*This chapter is an acrostic poem; the verses of each
stanza begin with the successive letters of the Hebrew
alphabet, and the verses within each stanza begin with the
same letter.

2:22 *summoned against me.* See 1:15. *terrors on every side.* See note on Jer 6:25. *day of the Lord's anger.* The chapter ends as it began (see v. 1). *no one escaped or survived.* See Jer 42:17; 44:14.

3:1–2 *I . . . me.* Whether the author is Jeremiah or an anonymous mourner, he speaks not only for himself but also for the suffering community of which he is a part (see "we" and "us" in vv. 22, 40–47). The Hebrew text of v. 1 is at the exact center of the book.

3:1 *affliction.* See v. 19. *rod of his wrath.* See Job 9:34; 21:9. The reference is to Babylon (see Isa 10:5 and note). *his.* God's.

3:2 *darkness rather than light.* See Job 12:25; characteristic of the "day of the Lord" (Am 5:18).

3:4 *grow old.* See Job 13:28 ("wastes away"); Ps 49:14 ("decay"). *broken my bones.* See Isa 38:13 and note.

3:5 *bitterness.* Lit. "poison" (see Jer 8:14 and note).

3:6 Reminiscent of Ps 143:3. *darkness.* The grave.

3:7 *walled.* The Hebrew for this word is the same as that for "barred" in v. 9 (see Job 19:8; Hos 2:6). *cannot escape.* See Ps 88:8.

3:8 *shuts out my prayer.* See v. 44; Ps 18:41; Pr 1:28; Jer 7:16 and note.

3:9 *blocks of stone.* Of enormous size, like those used in the foundation of Solomon's temple (see 1Ki 5:17). *made . . .*

crooked. Or "ruined/destroyed" (as in Isa 24:1); for the imagery see Job 30:13.

3:10 *Like a bear . . . like a lion.* See Ps 10:9; 17:12; Jer 4:7; 5:6; 49:19; 50:44.

3:11 See 1:2.

3:12 *drew his bow.* See note on 2:4. *made me the target.* See note on Job 6:4.

3:13 *heart.* Lit. "kidneys" (as in Job 16:13).

3:14 See Jeremiah's complaint in Jer 20:7. *mock me in song.* See v. 63; Ps 69:12.

3:15 *filled me with bitter herbs.* The Hebrew underlying this phrase is translated "overwhelm me with misery" in Job 9:18 (see note on Jer 9:15). For the significance of the bitter herbs eaten during the Passover meal see note on Ex 12:8.

3:18 *the Lord.* The first mention of God in ch. 3.

3:19 The poet remembers all these experiences and verbalizes them once again. *affliction and . . . wandering.* See 1:7.

3:21–26 The theological high point of the book of Lamentations (see Introduction: Themes and Theology).

3:22 *great love.* See v. 32. The Hebrew for this phrase is plural (as also in Ps 107:43) and denotes the Lord's loving faithfulness to his covenant promises (see Ps 89:1). See note on Ps 6:4; see also Isa 63:7 ("kindnesses") and note. *we.* See note on vv. 1–2.

for his compassions never fail. [t]

23They are new every morning;
   great is your faithfulness. [u]

24I say to myself, "The LORD is my
      portion; [v]
   therefore I will wait for him."

25The LORD is good to those whose hope
      is in him,
   to the one who seeks him; [w]
26it is good to wait quietly [x]
   for the salvation of the LORD. [y]
27It is good for a man to bear the yoke
   while he is young.

28Let him sit alone in silence, [z]
   for the LORD has laid it on him.
29Let him bury his face in the dust [a] —
   there may yet be hope. [b]
30Let him offer his cheek to one who
      would strike him, [c]
   and let him be filled with disgrace. [d]

31For men are not cast off
   by the Lord forever. [e]
32Though he brings grief, he will show
      compassion,
   so great is his unfailing love. [f]
33For he does not willingly bring affliction
   or grief to the children of men. [g]

34To crush underfoot
   all prisoners in the land,
35to deny a man his rights
   before the Most High, [h]
36to deprive a man of justice—
   would not the Lord see such things? [i]

37Who can speak and have it happen
   if the Lord has not decreed it? [j]

38Is it not from the mouth of the Most
      High
   that both calamities and good things
      come? [k]
39Why should any living man complain
   when punished for his sins? [l]

40Let us examine our ways and test
      them, [m]
   and let us return to the LORD. [n]
41Let us lift up our hearts and our hands
   to God in heaven, [o] and say:
42"We have sinned and rebelled [p]
   and you have not forgiven. [q]

43"You have covered yourself with anger
      and pursued [r] us;
   you have slain without pity. [s]
44You have covered yourself with a
      cloud [t]
   so that no prayer [u] can get through. [v]
45You have made us scum [w] and refuse
   among the nations.

46"All our enemies have opened their
      mouths
   wide [x] against us. [y]
47We have suffered terror and pitfalls, [z]
   ruin and destruction. [a] "
48Streams of tears [b] flow from my eyes [c]
   because my people are destroyed. [d]

49My eyes will flow unceasingly,
   without relief, [e]
50until the LORD looks down
   from heaven and sees. [f]

3:22 [t]Ps 78:38; 130:7
3:23 [u]S Ex 34:6; Zep 3:5
3:24 [v]S Ps 119:57
3:25 [w]S Ps 33:18; Isa 25:9; S 30:18
3:26 [x]S Isa 7:4 [y]Ps 37:7; 40:1
3:28 [z]Jer 15:17; La 2:10
3:29 [a]S Job 2:8 [b]S Jer 31:17
3:30 [c]S Job 16:10; S Isa 50:6 [d]Mic 5:1
3:31 [e]S Job 94:14; Isa 54:7
3:32 [f]Ps 78:38; 106:43-45; Hos 11:8; Na 1:12
3:33 [g]S Job 37:23; S Jer 31:20; Eze 18:23; 33:11
3:35 [h]Ge 14:18, 19,20,22
3:36 [i]Ps 140:12; S Pr 17:15; S Jer 22:3; Hab 1:13
3:37 [j]Ps 33:9-11; S Pr 19:21; S 21:30
3:38 [k]S Job 2:10; S Isa 45:7; Jer 32:42
3:39 [l]S Jer 30:15; Mic 7:9
3:40 [m]2Co 13:5 [n]Ps 119:59; 139:23-24
3:41 [o]S Ps 25:1; S 28:2
3:42 [p]Jer 14:20; Da 9:5
[q]S 2Ki 24:4; Jer 5:7-9
3:43 [r]ver 66; Ps 35:6 [s]S La 2:2, 17,21
3:44 [t]Ps 97:2; La 2:1 [u]S ver 8; Zec 7:13

[v]S Isa 58:4 **3:45** [w]1Co 4:13 **3:46** [x]Ps 22:13 [y]La 2:16 **3:47** [z]Jer 48:43 [a]S Isa 24:17-18; S 51:19 **3:48** [b]S Ps 119:136 [c]S Jer 9:1,18; La 1:16 [d]La 2:11 **3:49** [e]Jer 14:17; S La 2:18 **3:50** [f]S Ps 14:2; 80:14; S Isa 63:15

3:23 *They.* The "great love" and "compassions" (v. 22) of the Lord. *every morning.* See Isa 33:2. *great is your faithfulness.* It is beyond measure (see note on v. 32; see also Ps 36:5).

3:24 *The LORD is my portion.* See Ps 73:26; 142:5. He was the inheritance share of the priests and Levites (see Nu 18:20; see also note on Ge 15:1). *therefore I will wait.* The Hebrew for this phrase is the same as that for "therefore I have hope" in v. 21 and serves as a refrain.

3:25 *The LORD is good.* See Ps 34:8; 86:5. *whose hope is in him.* See Ps 25:3; 69:7.

3:26 See Isa 26:3; 30:15.

3:27 *a man to bear the yoke.* Echoes the thought of v. 1: "the man who has seen affliction."

3:28 *sit alone.* See note on 1:1. *it.* The yoke (see v. 27).

3:29 *there may yet be hope.* See Job 11:18.

3:30 *offer his cheek.* See Mt 5:39. *filled with disgrace.* See Ps 123:3-4.

3:31 See Jer 3:5 and note.

3:32 The same God who judges also restores (see Job 5:18; Ps 30:5; Isa 54:8). *great is his unfailing love.* See note on v. 22; see also "great is your faithfulness" (v. 23)—faithfulness and unfailing love are often used together to sum up God's covenant mercies toward his people.

3:33 *does not willingly bring affliction.* See Eze 18:23,32; Hos 11:8; 2Pe 3:9.

3:34 *crush underfoot.* As the Babylonians had done in 586 B.C.

3:35 *deny . . . rights.* As the leaders of Judah had done, in direct violation of the law (see Ex 23:6). *before the Most High.* In the presence of those whom the Most High designates to dispense justice (see Ex 22:8-9 and NIV text notes; see also introduction to Ps 82). *Most High.* See note on Ge 14:19.

3:36 *deprive . . . of justice.* Men might, but God never does (see Job 8:3; 34:12).

3:37 *speak and have it happen.* See note on Ge 1:3.

3:38 See Am 3:6.

3:39 *complain.* As the Israelites did in the desert (see Nu 11:1).

3:40 *us.* See note on vv. 1-2. *examine our ways.* See 1Co 11:28.

3:41 *lift up . . . hands.* See note on 2:19. *heaven.* Where God is enthroned (see Ps 2:4).

3:42 *We have sinned and rebelled.* For similar confessions see Ps 106:6; Da 9:5.

3:43 *with anger . . . pursued us.* See v. 66; Jer 29:18. *slain without pity.* See 2:21.

3:46 See note on 2:16.

3:48 *tears flow from my eyes.* See note on 1:16. *my people.* See note on 2:11.

51What I see brings grief to my soul
because of all the women of my city.

52Those who were my enemies without
cause
hunted me like a bird. *g*

53They tried to end my life in a pit *h*
and threw stones at me;

54the waters closed over my head, *i*
and I thought I was about to be cut
off. *j*

55I called on your name, O LORD,
from the depths *k* of the pit. *l*

56You heard my plea: *m* "Do not close
your ears
to my cry for relief."

57You came near *n* when I called you,
and you said, "Do not fear." *o*

58O Lord, you took up my case; *p*
you redeemed my life. *q*

59You have seen, O LORD, the wrong
done to me. *r*
Uphold my cause! *s*

60You have seen the depth of their
vengeance,
all their plots against me. *t*

61O LORD, you have heard their insults, *u*
all their plots against me—

62what my enemies whisper and mutter
against me all day long. *v*

63Look at them! Sitting or standing,
they mock me in their songs. *w*

64Pay them back what they deserve,
O LORD,
for what their hands have done. *x*

65Put a veil over their hearts, *y*
and may your curse be on them!

66Pursue *z* them in anger and destroy
them
from under the heavens of the LORD.

3:52 *g*Ps 35:7
3:53 *h*Jer 37:16;
S 38:6
3:54 *i*Ps 69:2;
Jnh 2:3-5 *j*ver 18;
Ps 88:5;
Eze 37:11
3:55 *k*S Ps 88:6
*l*Ps 130:1; Jnh 2:2
3:56 *m*S Ps 55:1;
116:1-2
3:57 *n*S Ps 46:1
*o*Isa 41:10
3:58 *p*S Jer 51:36
*q*Ps 34:22;
S Jer 50:34
3:59
*r*Jer 18:19-20
*s*Ps 35:23; 43:1
3:60 *t*S Jer 11:20;
18:18
3:61 *u*Ps 89:50;
Zep 2:8
3:62 *v*Eze 36:3
3:63 *w*S Job 30:9
3:64 *x*S Ps 28:4;
S Jer 51:6
3:65 *y*Ex 14:8;
Dt 2:30; Isa 6:10
3:66 *z*S ver 43

4:1 *a*Eze 7:19
4:2 *b*Isa 51:18
4:3 *c*S Job 39:16
4:4 *d*Dt 28:48;
S 2Ki 18:31
*e*S Ps 22:15
*f*La 2:11,12
4:5 *g*Jer 6:2
*h*S Isa 3:26;
Am 6:3-7
4:6 *i*S Ge 19:25
4:8 *j*S Job 30:28
*k*Ps 102:3-5;
S La 3:4
4:9 *l*S 2Ki 25:3

4 [1] How the gold has lost its luster,
the fine gold become dull!
The sacred gems are scattered
at the head of every street. *a*

2How the precious sons of Zion, *b*
once worth their weight in gold,
are now considered as pots of clay,
the work of a potter's hands!

3Even jackals offer their breasts
to nurse their young,
but my people have become heartless
like ostriches in the desert. *c*

4Because of thirst *d* the infant's tongue
sticks to the roof of its mouth; *e*
the children beg for bread,
but no one gives it to them. *f*

5Those who once ate delicacies
are destitute in the streets.
Those nurtured in purple *g*
now lie on ash heaps. *h*

6The punishment of my people
is greater than that of Sodom, *i*
which was overthrown in a moment
without a hand turned to help her.

7Their princes were brighter than snow
and whiter than milk,
their bodies more ruddy than rubies,
their appearance like sapphires. *j*

8But now they are blacker *j* than soot;
they are not recognized in the streets.
Their skin has shriveled on their
bones; *k*
it has become as dry as a stick.

9Those killed by the sword are better off
than those who die of famine; *l*
racked with hunger, they waste away

[1]This chapter is an acrostic poem, the verses of which
begin with the successive letters of the Hebrew alphabet.
1 7 Or *lapis lazuli*

3:51 *women of my city.* See 1:4,18; 2:20–21; 5:11.
3:52 *enemies without cause.* See note on Ps 35:19. *like a bird.* See Ps 11:1.
3:53 *threw stones at.* See Lev 20:2,27; 1Ki 12:18.
3:54 *waters closed over my head.* See note on Ps 42:7. *cut off.* See Ps 31:22; Isa 53:8.
3:55 *depths of the pit.* See note on Ps 30:1.
3:56 *cry for relief.* See Job 32:20; Ps 118:5.
3:57 *near when I called.* See Ps 145:18. *Do not fear.* Reminiscent of Jeremiah's call to prophesy (see Jer 1:8 and note).
3:58 *redeemed my life.* See Ps 103:4; see also note on Ps 25:22.
3:63 *Sitting or standing.* Engaging in any kind of activity (see Dt 6:7; 11:19; Ps 139:2; Isa 37:28). *mock me in their songs.* See note on v. 14.
3:64 Paralleled in Ps 28:4; see note on Ps 5:10.
3:65 *veil over their hearts.* See 2Co 3:15. *may your curse be on them!* Contrast Ps 3:8.
4:1 *How . . . !* See note on 1:1. *gold . . . gems.* Symbolic of

God's chosen people (see v. 2). For the imagery see SS 5:11–12,14–15; Zec 9:16; see also "The Babylonian Theodicy": "O . . . my precious brother, . . . jewel of gold" (lines 56–57). *become dull.* Lit. "changed"; contrast Mal 3:6. *at the head of every street.* See 2:19; Isa 51:20.
4:2 *worth their weight in gold.* See Job 28:15–19. *pots of clay . . . potter's hands.* See Isa 45:9; 60:21 and notes.
4:3 *my people.* See vv. 6,10; see also note on 2:11.
4:5 *delicacies . . . purple.* See Ge 49:20. Purple was the color of royalty (see, e.g., Jdg 8:26; see also note on SS 7:5); cf. the expressions "born to the purple" and "royal blue." *destitute.* See note on 1:13.
4:6 See note on 2:11. *Sodom.* See note on Jer 20:16. *overthrown in a moment.* And therefore spared the suffering of a lengthy siege (like that of Jerusalem).
4:7 *whiter . . . ruddy.* The Hebrew underlying these two words is translated "radiant . . . ruddy" in SS 5:10. *than rubies.* See Job 28:18. *sapphires.* See SS 5:14 and note; Isa 54:11 and note.
4:8 *skin has shriveled on their bones.* See Job 19:20.

for lack of food from the field. *m*

10With their own hands compassionate women
have cooked their own children, *n*
who became their food
when my people were destroyed.

11The LORD has given full vent to his wrath; *o*
he has poured out *p* his fierce anger. *q*
He kindled a fire *r* in Zion
that consumed her foundations. *s*

12The kings of the earth did not believe,
nor did any of the world's people,
that enemies and foes could enter
the gates of Jerusalem. *t*

13But it happened because of the sins of her prophets
and the iniquities of her priests, *u*
who shed within her
the blood *v* of the righteous.

14Now they grope through the streets
like men who are blind. *w*
They are so defiled with blood *x*
that no one dares to touch their garments.

15"Go away! You are unclean!" men cry to them.
"Away! Away! Don't touch us!"
When they flee and wander *y* about,
people among the nations say,
"They can stay here no longer." *z*

16The LORD himself has scattered them;
he no longer watches over them. *a*
The priests are shown no honor,
the elders *b* no favor. *c*

17Moreover, our eyes failed,
looking in vain *d* for help; *e*
from our towers we watched
for a nation *f* that could not save us.

18Men stalked us at every step,
so we could not walk in our streets.

Our end was near, our days were numbered,
for our end had come. *g*

19Our pursuers were swifter
than eagles *h* in the sky;
they chased us *i* over the mountains
and lay in wait for us in the desert. *j*

20The LORD's anointed, *k* our very life breath,
was caught in their traps. *l*
We thought that under his shadow *m*
we would live among the nations.

21Rejoice and be glad, O Daughter of Edom,
you who live in the land of Uz. *n*
But to you also the cup *o* will be passed;
you will be drunk and stripped naked. *p*

22O Daughter of Zion, your punishment will end; *q*
he will not prolong your exile.
But, O Daughter of Edom, he will punish your sin
and expose your wickedness. *r*

5 Remember, O LORD, what has happened to us;
look, and see our disgrace. *s*
2Our inheritance *t* has been turned over to aliens, *u*
our homes *v* to foreigners. *w*
3We have become orphans and fatherless,
our mothers like widows. *x*
4We must buy the water we drink; *y*
our wood can be had only at a price. *z*
5Those who pursue us are at our heels;
we are weary *a* and find no rest. *b*
6We submitted to Egypt and Assyria *c*
to get enough bread.

4:9 mS Jer 15:2; S 16:4; La 5:10
4:10 nS Lev 26:29; Dt 28:53-57; Jer 19:9; La 2:20; Eze 5:10
4:11 oS Job 20:23 pS 2Ch 34:21 qNa 1:6; Zep 2:2; 3:8 rJer 17:27 sS Dt 32:22; S Jer 7:20; Eze 22:31
4:12 tS 1Ki 9:9; S Jer 21:13
4:13 uJer 5:31; 6:13; Eze 22:28; Mic 3:11 vS 2Ki 21:16
4:14 wS Isa 59:10 xJer 19:4
4:15 yS Jer 44:14 zLev 13:46; Mic 2:10
4:16 aIsa 9:14-16 bLa 5:12 cS La 2:6
4:17 dS Ge 15:18; S Isa 20:5; Eze 29:16 eS La 1:7 fJer 37:7
4:18 gEze 7:2-12; Am 8:2
4:19 hS Dt 28:49 iS Lev 26:36; Isa 5:26-28 jJer 52:7
4:20 kS 1Sa 26:9; 2Sa 19:21 lJer 39:5; Eze 12:12-13; 19:4,8 mS Ps 91:1
4:21 nS Ge 10:23 oS Ps 16:5; S Jer 25:15 pIsa 34:6-10; S 63:6; Eze 35:15; Am 1:11-12; Ob 1:16; Hab 2:16
4:22 qIsa 40:2; Jer 33:8 rS Ps 137:7; Eze 25:12-14; Mal 1:4
5:1 sPs 44:13-16; 89:50
5:2 tPs 79:1 uPs 109:11 vZep 1:13 wJer 17:4
5:3 xS Ex 22:24; Jer 15:8; S 18:21
5:4 yS Isa 55:1; Eze 4:16-17
zIsa 3:1 **5:5** aS Ne 9:37; Isa 47:6 bS Jos 1:13 **5:6** cJer 2:36; Hos 5:13; 7:11; 9:3

4:10 See note on Jer 19:9. *my people.* See note on 2:11.
4:11 *fierce anger.* See note on 1:12. *kindled a fire ... consumed.* See note on Jer 17:27.
4:12 *people.* Or "rulers" (parallel to "kings"); the Hebrew form underlying this word is translated "king" in Am 1:5,8.
4:13 *because of the sins of her prophets and ... priests.* See Jer 26:7-11,16; see also Jer 6:13-15; 23:11-12; Eze 22:26,28.
4:14 *grope ... like men who are blind.* See Dt 28:28-29; Isa 29:9 and note; 59:10 and note; Zep 1:17. *defiled with blood.* See Isa 59:3.
4:15 *unclean!* The cry of the person with a skin disease (see Lev 13:45). *people ... no longer.* Threatened in Dt 28:65-66.
4:16 Threatened in Dt 28:49-50.
4:17 *our eyes failed.* See Dt 28:28; Ps 69:3. *nation that could not save us.* For example, Egypt (see Eze 29:16).

4:19 *eagles.* See Jer 4:13; 48:40 and notes. *desert.* The "plains of Jericho" (Jer 39:5; 52:8).
4:20 *The LORD's anointed.* King Zedekiah. *our very life breath.* Lit. "the breath of our nostrils," a title used also of Pharaoh Rameses II in an inscription found at Abydos in Egypt. *was caught.* See Jer 39:4-7; 52:7-11. *shadow.* Protection (see note on Jdg 9:15).
4:21 *Edom.* See note on Jer 49:8. *land of Uz.* See Jer 25:20; see also note on Job 1:1. *cup.* See note on Jer 25:15. *stripped naked.* See 1:8; see also Jer 49:10; Na 3:5.
4:22 *Daughter of Zion.* A personification of Jerusalem and its inhabitants. *expose your wickedness.* Contrast Ps 32:1; 85:2.
5:2 *Our inheritance.* The land of Judah (see Jer 2:7 and note; 3:18).
5:4 *We must buy the water ... wood.* Contrast Dt 29:11; Jos 9:21,23,27. *wood.* Firewood.

⁷Our fathers *d* sinned and are no more,
   and we bear their punishment. *e*
⁸Slaves *f* rule over us,
   and there is none to free us from
      their hands. *g*
⁹We get our bread at the risk of our lives
   because of the sword in the desert.
¹⁰Our skin is hot as an oven,
   feverish from hunger. *h*
¹¹Women have been ravished *i* in Zion,
   and virgins in the towns of Judah.
¹²Princes have been hung up by their
      hands;
   elders *j* are shown no respect. *k*
¹³Young men toil at the millstones;
   boys stagger under loads of wood.
¹⁴The elders are gone from the city gate;
   the young men have stopped their
      music. *l*
¹⁵Joy is gone from our hearts;
   our dancing has turned to
      mourning. *m*

¹⁶The crown *n* has fallen from our head. *o*
   Woe to us, for we have sinned! *p*
¹⁷Because of this our hearts *q* are faint, *r*
   because of these things our eyes *s*
      grow dim *t*
¹⁸for Mount Zion, *u* which lies desolate, *v*
   with jackals prowling over it.

¹⁹You, O Lᴏʀᴅ, reign forever; *w*
   your throne endures *x* from
      generation to generation.
²⁰Why do you always forget us? *y*
   Why do you forsake *z* us so long?
²¹Restore *a* us to yourself, O Lᴏʀᴅ, that
      we may return;
   renew our days as of old
²²unless you have utterly rejected us *b*
   and are angry with us beyond
      measure. *c*

Cross references:

5:7 *d*S Jer 31:29; *e*Jer 14:20; 16:12
5:8 *f*Ne 5:15; *g*Zec 11:6
5:10 *h*S Job 30:30; S La 4:8-9
5:11 *i*S Ge 34:29; Zec 14:2
5:12 *j*S Lev 19:32; *k*S La 2:6; 4:16
5:14 *l*S Isa 24:8; Jer 7:34
5:15 *m*S Jer 25:10; Am 8:10
5:16 *n*Ps 89:39; S Jer 13:18; *o*S Job 19:9; *p*S Isa 3:11; Jer 14:20
5:17 *q*S Isa 1:5; *r*S Jer 8:18; *s*Ps 6:7; *t*S Job 16:8
5:18 *u*Ps 74:2-3; *v*S Isa 27:10; Mic 3:12
5:19 *w*S 1Ch 16:31; *x*S Ps 45:6; 102:12,24-27
5:20 *y*S Ps 13:1; 44:24 *z*S Ps 71:11
5:21 *a*S Ps 80:3; Isa 60:20-22 5:22 *b*S Ps 53:5; 60:1-2; S Jer 6:30 *c*S Isa 64:9

5:6 *submitted.* See 1Ch 29:24; 2Ch 30:8; Jer 50:15; lit. "gave the hand" (as in 2Ki 10:15; Ezr 10:19; Eze 17:18). *Assyria.* Either (1) Assyria literally (see Jer 2:18), or (2) territory formerly occupied by Assyrians (see note on Ezr 6:22).
5:7 Fathers and sons alike are responsible for the calamity that has befallen Jerusalem (see v. 16; Jer 16:11–12; 31:29–30; Eze 18:2–4; cf. Isa 65:7).
5:8 *Slaves.* An ironic reference to the Babylonians, who now rule over Jerusalem (formerly "queen among the provinces," 1:1; see Pr 30:21–22.
5:9 *sword in the desert.* Marauding bandits.
5:12 *hung.* An added indignity following execution (see notes on Dt 21:22–23).
5:13 *toil at the millstones.* Humiliating work (see note on Jdg 9:53; see also Isa 47:2).
5:14 *city gate.* The municipal court (see Jos 20:4), but also

a gathering place for conversation and entertainment (cf. 1:4).
5:15 See Jer 7:34; 16:9; 25:10; contrast Ps 30:11; Jer 31:13.
5:16 *crown.* Symbolizes the glory and honor embodied in the city of Jerusalem (see note on 1:1; 2:15; cf. Isa 28:1,3).
5:17 *hearts are faint.* See note on 1:22. *eyes grow dim.* See 2:11; see also note on Ps 6:7.
5:18 *jackals.* The Hebrew for this word, different from that used in 4:3, can also mean "foxes" (see note on Jdg 15:4).
5:19 Paralleled in Ps 102:12 (see note there).
5:21 *Restore . . . return.* See Jer 31:18; see also note on Jer 31:18–19.
5:22 See Jer 14:19. *unless.* Or "but." A similarly somber ending characterizes not only other laments (e.g., Ps 88) but also other OT books (e.g., Isaiah and Malachi).

EZEKIEL

Background

Ezekiel lived during a time of international upheaval. The Assyrian empire that had once conquered the Syro-Palestinian area and destroyed the northern kingdom of Israel (which fell to the Assyrians in 722-721 B.C.) began to crumble under the blows of a resurgent Babylon. In 612 the great Assyrian city of Nineveh fell to a combined force of Babylonians and Medes. Three years later, Pharaoh Neco II of Egypt marched north to assist the Assyrians and to try to reassert Egypt's age-old influence over Palestine and Aram (Syria). At Megiddo, King Josiah of Judah, who may have been an ally of Babylon as King Hezekiah had been, attempted to intercept the Egyptian forces but was crushed, losing his life in the battle (see 2Ki 23:29-30; 2Ch 35:20-24).

Jehoahaz, a son of Josiah, ruled Judah for only three months, after which Neco installed Jehoiakim, another son of Josiah, as his royal vassal in Jerusalem (609 B.C.). In 605 the Babylonians overwhelmed the Egyptian army at Carchemish (see Jer 46:2), then pressed south as far as the Philistine plain. In the same year, Nebuchadnezzar was elevated to the Babylonian throne and Jehoiakim shifted allegiance to him. When a few years later the Egyptian and Babylonian forces met in a standoff battle in southwestern Palestine, Jehoiakim rebelled against his new overlord.

Nebuchadnezzar soon responded by sending a force against Jerusalem, subduing it in 597 B.C. Jehoiakim's son Jehoiachin and about 10,000 Jews (see 2Ki 24:14), including Ezekiel, were exiled to Babylon, where they joined those who had been exiled in Jehoiakim's "third year" (see Da 1:1 and note). Nebuchadnezzar placed Jehoiachin's uncle, Zedekiah, on the throne in Jerusalem, but within five or six years he too rebelled. The Babylonians laid siege to Jerusalem in 588, and in July, 586, the walls were breached and the city plundered. On Aug. 14, 586, the city and temple were burned.

Under Nebuchadnezzar and his successors, Babylon dominated the international scene until it was crushed by Cyrus the Persian in 539 B.C. Israel's monarchy was ended; the City of David and the Lord's temple no longer existed.

Author

What is known of Ezekiel is derived solely from the book that bears his name. He was among the Jews exiled to Babylon by Nebuchadnezzar in 597 B.C., and there among the exiles he received his call to become a prophet (see 1:1-3). He was married (see 24:15-18), lived in a house of his own (see 3:24; 8:1) and, along with his fellow exiles, had a relatively free existence.

He was of a priestly family (see NIV text note on 1:3) and therefore was eligible to serve as a priest. As a priest-prophet called to minister to the exiles (cut off from the temple of the Lord with its symbolism, sacrifices, priestly ministrations and worship rituals), his message had much to do with the temple (see especially chs. 8-11; 40-48) and its ceremonies.

Ezekiel was obviously a man of broad knowledge, not only of his own national traditions but also of international affairs and history. His acquaintance with general matters of culture, from shipbuilding to literature, is equally amazing. He was gifted with a powerful intellect and was capable of grasping large issues and of dealing with them in grand and compelling images. His style is often detached, but in places it is passionate and earthy (see chs. 16; 23).

More than any other prophet he was directed to involve himself personally in the divine word by acting it out in prophetic symbolism.

Occasion and Purpose

Though Ezekiel lived with his fellow exiles in Babylon, his divine call forced him to suppress any natural expectations he may have had of an early return to an undamaged Jerusalem. For the first seven years of his ministry (593-586 B.C.) he faithfully relayed to his fellow Jews the harsh, heart-rending, hope-crushing word of divine judgment: Jerusalem would fall (see chs. 1-24). Their being God's

covenant people and Jerusalem's being the city of his temple would not bring their early release from exile or prevent Jerusalem from being destroyed (see Jer 29-30). The only hope the prophet was authorized to extend to his hearers was that of living at peace with themselves and with God during their exile.

After being informed by the Lord that Jerusalem was under siege and would surely fall (24:1-14), Ezekiel was told that his beloved wife would soon die. The delight of his eyes would be taken from him just as the temple, the delight of Israel's eyes, would be taken from her. He was not to mourn openly for his wife, as a sign to his people not to mourn openly for Jerusalem (24:15-27). He was then directed to pronounce a series of judgments on the seven nations of Ammon, Moab, Edom, Philistia, Tyre, Sidon and Egypt (chs. 25-32). The day of God's wrath was soon to come, but not on Israel alone.

Once news was received that Jerusalem had fallen, Ezekiel's message turned to the Lord's consoling word of hope for his people—they would experience revival, restoration and a glorious future as the redeemed and perfected kingdom of God in the world (chs. 33-48).

Date

Since the book of Ezekiel contains more dates (see chart below) than any other OT prophetic book, its prophecies can be dated with considerable precision. In addition, modern scholarship, using archaeology (Babylonian annals on cuneiform tablets) and astronomy (accurate dating of eclipses referred to in ancient archives), provides precise modern calendar equivalents.

Twelve of the 13 dates specify times when Ezekiel received a divine message. The other is the date of the arrival of the messenger who reported the fall of Jerusalem (33:21).

Having received his call in July, 593 B.C., Ezekiel was active for 22 years, his last dated oracle being received in April, 571 (see 29:17). If the "thirtieth year" of 1:1 refers to Ezekiel's age at the time of his call, his prophetic career exceeded a normal priestly term of service by two years (see Nu 4:3). His period of activity coincides with Jerusalem's darkest hour, preceding the 586 destruction by 7 years and following it by 15.

Dates in Ezekiel

REFERENCE	YEAR	MONTH	DAY	MODERN RECKONING	EVENT
1. 1:1	30	4	5	July 31, 593 B.C.	Inaugural vision
1:2	5	—	5		
3:16	"At the end of seven days"				
2. 8:1	6	6	5	Sept. 17, 592	Transport to Jerusalem
3. 20:1-2	7	5	10	Aug. 14, 591	Negative view of Israel's history
4. 24:1	9	10	10	Jan. 15, 588	Beginning of siege (see also 2 Ki 25:1)
5. 26:1	11	—	1	Apr. 23, 587 to Apr. 13, 586	Oracle against Tyre
6. 29:1	10	10	12	Jan. 7, 587	Oracle against Egypt
7. 29:17	27	1	1	Apr. 26, 571	Egypt in exchange for Tyre
8. 30:20	11	1	7	Apr. 29, 587	Oracle against Pharaoh
9. 31:1	11	3	1	June 21, 587	Oracle against Pharaoh
10. 32:1	12	12	1	Mar. 3, 585	Lament over Pharaoh
11. 32:17	12	—	15	Apr. 13, 586, to Apr. 1, 585	Egypt dead
12. 33:21	12	10	5	Jan. 8, 585	Arrival of first fugitive
13. 40:1	25	1	10	Apr. 28, 573	Vision of the future
40:1	"fourteenth year after the fall of the city"				

Themes

The OT in general and the prophets in particular presuppose and teach God's sovereignty over all creation, over people and nations and the course of history. And nowhere in the Bible are God's initiative and control expressed more clearly and pervasively than in the book of Ezekiel. From the first chapter, which graphically describes the overwhelming invasion of the divine presence into Ezekiel's world, to the last phrase of Ezekiel's vision ("THE LORD IS THERE") the book sounds and echoes God's sovereignty.

This sovereign God resolved that he would be known and acknowledged. No less than 65 occurrences of the clause (or variations) "Then they will know that I am the LORD" testify to that divine desire and intention. Chs. 1-24 teach that God will be revealed in the fall of Jerusalem and the destruction of the temple; chs. 25-32 teach that the nations likewise will know God through his judgments; and chs. 33-48 promise that God will be known through the restoration and spiritual renewal of Israel.

God's total sovereignty is also evident in his mobility. He is not limited to the temple in Jerusalem. He can respond to his people's sin by leaving his sanctuary in Israel, and he can graciously condescend to visit his exiled children in Babylon.

God is free to judge, and he is equally free to be gracious. His stern judgments on Israel ultimately reflect his grace. He allows the total dismemberment of Israel's political and religious life so that her renewed life and his presence with her will be clearly seen as a gift from the Lord of the universe.

Furthermore, as God's spokesman, Ezekiel's "son of man" status (see note on 2:1) testifies to the sovereign God he was commissioned to serve.

Literary Features

The three major prophets (Isaiah, Jeremiah, Ezekiel) and Zephaniah all have the same basic sequence of messages: (1) oracles against Israel, (2) oracles against the nations, (3) consolation for Israel. In no other book is this pattern as clear as in Ezekiel (see Outline).

Besides clarity of structure, the book of Ezekiel reveals symmetry. The vision of the desecrated temple fit for destruction (chs. 8-11) is balanced by the vision of the restored and purified temple (chs. 40-48). The God presented in agitated wrath (ch. 1) is also shown to be a God of comfort ("THE LORD IS THERE," 48:35). Ezekiel's call to be a watchman of divine judgment (ch. 3) is balanced by his call to be a watchman of the new age (ch. 33). In one place (ch. 6) the mountains of Israel receive a prophetic rebuke, but in another (ch. 36) they are consoled.

Prophetic books are usually largely poetic, the prophets apparently having spoken in imaginative and rhythmic styles. Most of Ezekiel, however, is prose, perhaps due to his priestly background. His repetitions have an unforgettable hammering effect, and his priestly orientation is also reflected in a case-law type of sentence (compare 3:19, "If you do warn the wicked . . . ," with Ex 21:2, "If you buy a Hebrew servant . . .").

The book contains four visions (chs. 1-3; 8-11; 37:1-14; 40-48) and 12 symbolic acts (3:22-26; 4:1-3; 4:4-8; 4:9-11; 4:12-14; 5:1-3; 12:1-16; 12:17-20; 21:6-7; 21:18-24; 24:15-24; 37:15-28). Five messages are in the form of parables (chs. 15; 16; 17; 19; 23).

Theological Significance

Other prophets deal largely with Israel's idolatry, with her moral corruption in public and private affairs, and with her international intrigues and alliances on which she relied instead of the Lord. They announce God's impending judgment on his rebellious nation but speak also of a future redemption: a new exodus, a new covenant, a restored Jerusalem, a revived Davidic dynasty, a worldwide recognition of the Lord and his Messiah and a paradise-like peace.

The contours and sweep of Ezekiel's message are similar, but he focuses uniquely on Israel as the holy people of the holy temple, the holy city and the holy land. By defiling her worship, Israel had rendered herself unclean and had defiled temple, city and land. From such defilement God could only withdraw and judge his people with national destruction.

But God's faithfulness to his covenant and his desire to save were so great that he would revive his people once more, shepherd them with compassion, cleanse them all of their defilement, reconstitute them as a perfect expression of his kingdom in the promised land under the hand of David, overwhelm all the forces and powers arrayed against them, display his glory among the nations and restore the glory of his presence to the holy city.

Ezekiel powerfully depicts the grandeur and glory of God's sovereign rule (see Themes) and his holiness, which he jealously safeguards. The book's theological center is the unfolding of God's saving purposes in the history of the world—from the time in which he must withdraw from the defilement of his covenant people to the culmination of his grand design of redemption. The message of Ezekiel, which is ultimately eschatological, anticipates—even demands—God's future works in history proclaimed by the NT.

Outline

The Living Creatures and the Glory of the LORD

1 In the[a] thirtieth year, in the fourth
month on the fifth day, while I was
among the exiles[a] by the Kebar River,[b]
the heavens were opened[c] and I saw visions[d] of God.
2 On the fifth of the month—it was the
fifth year of the exile of King Jehoiachin[e]— 3 the word of the LORD came to
Ezekiel[f] the priest, the son of Buzi,[b] by
the Kebar River in the land of the Babylonians.[c] There the hand of the LORD was
upon him.[g]
4 I looked, and I saw a windstorm[h] coming out of the north[i]—an immense cloud
with flashing lightning and surrounded by
brilliant light. The center of the fire looked
like glowing metal,[j] 5 and in the fire was
what looked like four living creatures.[k] In
appearance their form was that of a man,[l]
6 but each of them had four faces[m] and four
wings. 7 Their legs were straight; their feet
were like those of a calf and gleamed like
burnished bronze.[n] 8 Under their wings on
their four sides they had the hands of a
man.[o] All four of them had faces and
wings, 9 and their wings touched one another. Each one went straight ahead; they
did not turn as they moved.[p]
10 Their faces looked like this: Each of
the four had the face of a man, and on the
right side each had the face of a lion, and
on the left the face of an ox; each also had
the face of an eagle.[q] 11 Such were their
faces. Their wings[r] were spread out upward; each had two wings, one touching
the wing of another creature on either
side, and two wings covering its body.
12 Each one went straight ahead. Wherever
the spirit would go, they would go, without turning as they went.[s] 13 The appearance of the living creatures was like burning coals[t] of fire or like torches. Fire
moved back and forth among the creatures; it was bright, and lightning[u] flashed
out of it. 14 The creatures sped back and
forth like flashes of lightning.[v]
15 As I looked at the living creatures,[w] I
saw a wheel[x] on the ground beside each
creature with its four faces. 16 This was the
appearance and structure of the wheels:
They sparkled like chrysolite,[y] and all four
looked alike. Each appeared to be made
like a wheel intersecting a wheel. 17 As
they moved, they would go in any one of
the four directions the creatures faced; the
wheels did not turn[z] about[d] as the creatures went. 18 Their rims were high and
awesome, and all four rims were full of
eyes[a] all around.
19 When the living creatures moved, the
wheels beside them moved; and when the
living creatures rose from the ground, the
wheels also rose. 20 Wherever the spirit
would go, they would go,[b] and the wheels
would rise along with them, because the
spirit of the living creatures was in the
wheels. 21 When the creatures moved, they
also moved; when the creatures stood still,
they also stood still; and when the crea-

1:1 [a]S Dt 21:10; Eze 11:24-25 [b]S Ps 137:1 [c]S Mt 3:16 [d]S Ex 24:10 **1:2** [e]S 2Ki 24:15 **1:3** [f]Eze 24:24 [g]S 2Ki 3:15; Isa 8:11; Eze 3:14,22; 8:1; 33:22; 37:1; 40:1 **1:4** [h]S Job 38:1 [i]Jer 1:14 [j]Eze 8:2 **1:5** [k]S Isa 6:2; Rev 4:6 [l]ver 26; Da 7:13 **1:6** [m]Eze 10:14 **1:7** [n]Eze 40:3; Da 10:6; S Rev 1:15 **1:8** [o]Eze 10:8 **1:9** [p]Eze 10:22 **1:10** [q]Eze 10:14; Rev 4:7 **1:11** [r]Isa 6:2 **1:12** [s]Eze 10:16-19 **1:13** [t]S 2Sa 22:9 [u]Rev 4:5 **1:14** [v]S Ps 29:7 **1:15** [w]Eze 3:13 [x]Eze 10:2; Da 7:9 **1:16** [y]S Ex 28:20 **1:17** [z]ver 9 **1:18** [a]Rev 4:6 **1:20** [b]ver 12

[a]*1* Or *my* [b]*3* Or *Ezekiel son of Buzi the priest* [c]*3* Or *Chaldeans* [d]*17* Or *aside*

1:1 *thirtieth year.* Probably Ezekiel's age (see NIV text note). According to Nu 4:3, a person entered the Levitical priesthood in his 30th year. Denied the priesthood in exile, Ezekiel received another commission—that of prophet. *Kebar River.* A canal of the Euphrates near the city of Nippur, south of Babylon, and possibly a place of prayer for the exiles (see Ps 137:1; cf. Ac 16:13). *visions of God.* A special term, always in the plural and always with the word "God" (not with the more personal "LORD"). The expression precedes this and the two other major visions of the prophet (8:3; 40:2).

1:2 *fifth year of the exile.* Verses 2–3, written in the third person (the only third-person narrative in the book), clarify the date in v. 1. *King Jehoiachin.* Led an early group of exiles to Babylon in 597 B.C. (see Introduction: Background). Ezekiel was among them and received his prophetic call in 593.

1:3 *Ezekiel.* See 24:24. Means "God is strong" (cf. 3:14), "God strengthens" (cf. 30:25; 34:16) or "God makes hard" (cf. 3:8). Jehezkel (1Ch 24:16) is the same name in Hebrew but does not refer to the same person. *priest.* Member of a priestly family (see NIV text note). *hand of the LORD.* A phrase repeated six times in the book (3:14,22; 8:1; 33:22; 37:1; 40:1), indicating an overpowering experience of divine revelation.

1:4 *I looked.* Introduces the first part of the vision: storm and living creatures (vv. 4–14). The "I looked" of v. 15 introduces the second part: wheels and the glory of the Lord. *windstorm.* See Ps 18:10–12.

1:5 *four living creatures.* "Four," which stands for completeness (cf. the four directions in Ge 13:14 and the four quarters of the earth in Isa 11:12), is used often in this chapter—and over 40 times in the book. The living creatures, called "cherubim" in ch. 10, are throne attendants, here (see v. 10) representing God's creation: "man," God's ordained ruler of creation (see Ge 1:26–28; Ps 8); "lion," the strongest of the wild beasts; "ox," the most powerful of the domesticated animals; "eagle," the mightiest of the birds. These four creatures appear again in Rev 4:7 and often are seen in the paintings and sculpture of the Middle Ages, where they represent the four Gospels.

1:7 *like those of a calf.* Perhaps indicates agility (cf. Ps 29:6; Mal 4:2).

1:12 *the spirit.* See v. 20.

1:16 *chrysolite.* The precise identification of this stone is uncertain. See Ex 28:20 (and NIV text note), where the stone appears in the priestly breastplate. *a wheel intersecting a wheel.* Probably two wheels intersecting at right angles in order to move in all four directions (see v. 17). The imagery symbolizes the omnipresence of God.

1:18 *full of eyes.* Symbolizes God's all-seeing nature.

tures rose from the ground, the wheels rose along with them, because the spirit of the living creatures was in the wheels. [c]

[22]Spread out above the heads of the living creatures was what looked like an expanse, [d] sparkling like ice, and awesome. [23]Under the expanse their wings were stretched out one toward the other, and each had two wings covering its body. [24]When the creatures moved, I heard the sound of their wings, like the roar of rushing [e] waters, like the voice [f] of the Almighty, [e] like the tumult of an army. [g] When they stood still, they lowered their wings.

[25]Then there came a voice from above the expanse over their heads as they stood with lowered wings. [26]Above the expanse over their heads was what looked like a throne [h] of sapphire, [f][i] and high above on the throne was a figure like that of a man. [j] [27]I saw that from what appeared to be his waist up he looked like glowing metal, as if full of fire, and that from there down he looked like fire; and brilliant light surrounded him. [k] [28]Like the appearance of a rainbow [l] in the clouds on a rainy day, so was the radiance around him. [m]

This was the appearance of the likeness of the glory [n] of the LORD. When I saw it, I fell facedown, [o] and I heard the voice of one speaking.

Ezekiel's Call

2 He said to me, "Son of man, [p] stand [q] up on your feet and I will speak to you." [r] [2]As he spoke, the Spirit came into me and raised me [s] to my feet, and I heard him speaking to me.

[3]He said: "Son of man, I am sending you to the Israelites, to a rebellious nation that has rebelled against me; they and their fathers have been in revolt against me to this very day. [t] [4]The people to whom I am sending you are obstinate and stubborn. [u] Say to them, 'This is what the Sovereign LORD says.' [v] [5]And whether they listen or fail to listen [w]—for they are a rebellious house [x]—they will know that a prophet has been among them. [y] [6]And you, son of man, do not be afraid [z] of them or their words. Do not be afraid, though briers and thorns [a] are all around you and you live among scorpions. Do not be afraid of what they say or terrified by them, though they are a rebellious house. [b] [7]You must speak [c] my words to them, whether they listen or fail to listen, for they are rebellious. [d] [8]But you, son of man, listen to what I say to you. Do not rebel [ef] like that rebellious house; [g] open your mouth and eat [h] what I give you."

[9]Then I looked, and I saw a hand [i] stretched out to me. In it was a scroll, [j] [10]which he unrolled before me. On both sides of it were written words of lament and mourning and woe. [k]

3 And he said to me, "Son of man, eat what is before you, eat this scroll; then go and speak to the house of Israel." [2]So I opened my mouth, and he gave me the scroll to eat.

[3]Then he said to me, "Son of man, eat

Cross references (center column)

1:21 [c]Eze 10:9-12
1:22 [d]Eze 10:1
1:24 [e]S Ps 46:3; Eze 3:13
[f]Eze 10:5; 43:2; Da 10:6;
Rev 1:15; 14:2; 19:6 [g]S 2Ki 7:6
1:26 [h]S 1Ki 22:19; Isa 6:1; S Jer 3:17
[i]S Ex 24:10 /S ver 5; S Eze 2:1;
S Rev 1:13
1:27 [k]Eze 8:2
1:28 [l]S Ge 9:13; Rev 10:1
[m]S Rev 4:2
[n]S 24:16; Lk 2:9
[o]S Ge 17:3;
S Nu 14:5
2:1 [p]S Job 25:6; Ps 8:4;
S Eze 1:28;
Da 7:13; 8:15
[q]Da 10:11;
Ac 14:10; 26:16
[r]Ac 9:6

2:2 [s]Eze 3:24; Da 8:18
2:3 [t]S Jer 3:25; Eze 5:6; 20:8-24; 24:3
2:4 [u]S Ex 32:9; S Isa 9:9; Eze 3:7
[v]Am 7:15
2:5 [w]Eze 3:11
[x]Eze 3:27
[y]S Jer 5:3;
Eze 33:33; Jn 15:22
2:6 [z]S Dt 31:6; S 2Ki 1:15
[a]S Nu 33:55; Isa 9:18; Mic 7:4
[b]S Isa 1:2; 30:9; Eze 24:3; 44:6
2:7 [c]Jer 7:27
[d]Jer 1:7; S 42:21; Eze 3:10-11
2:8 [e]Nu 20:10-13
[f]Isa 8:11
[g]S Isa 50:5
[h]Ps 81:10;
S Jer 15:16;
Rev 10:9
2:9 [i]Eze 8:3
[j]S Ps 40:7;

S Jer 36:4; Rev 5:1-5; 10:8-10 2:10 [k]Isa 3:11; Rev 8:13

---

[e]24 Hebrew *Shaddai*　[f]26 Or *lapis lazuli*

1:22 *expanse.* The same word occurs in Ge 1:6–8, where its function is to separate the waters above from the waters below. Here it separates the creatures from the glory of the Lord.

1:26 *a figure like that of a man.* Ezekiel is reporting his vision of God, but he carefully avoids saying he saw God directly (see Ge 16:13; Ex 3:6; Jdg 13:22).

1:28 *likeness.* See note on v. 26. *glory of the LORD.* When God's glory was symbolically revealed, it took the form of brilliant light (see Ex 40:34; Isa 6:3). What is remarkable about Ezekiel's experience is that God's glory had for centuries been associated with the temple in Jerusalem (see 1Ki 8:11; Ps 26:8; 63:2; 96:6; 102:16). Now God had left his temple and was appearing to his exiled people in Babylon—a major theme in the first half of Ezekiel's message (see 10:4; 11:23). In his vision of the restored Jerusalem the prophet saw the glory of the Lord returning (43:2).

2:1 *Son of man.* A term used 93 times in Ezekiel, emphasizing the prophet's humanity as he was addressed by the transcendent God (see note on Ps 8:4). Da 7:13 and 8:17 are the only other places where the phrase is used as a title in the OT. Jesus' frequent use of the phrase in referring to himself showed that he was the eschatological figure spoken of in Da 7:13 (see, e.g., Mk 8:31 and note).

2:2 *the Spirit came into me and raised me to my feet.* The Spirit of God, who empowered the chariot wheels (1:12,19; 10:16–17) and the creatures (1:20), now entered Ezekiel—symbolizing the Lord's empowering of the prophet's entire ministry.

2:3 *rebellious nation.* A keynote of Ezekiel's preaching: The entire nation throughout its history had been rebellious against God.

2:6 *briers and thorns . . . scorpions.* Vivid images of those who would make life difficult for the prophet.

2:10 *On both sides.* Normally, ancient scrolls were written on one side only. The implication here is that the scroll was thoroughly saturated with words of divine judgment. See Zec 5:3 and Rev 5:1 for the same figure. *lament and mourning and woe.* Although Ezekiel was later commanded to preach hope (see note on 33:1), his initial commission (until the fall of Jerusalem) was to declare God's displeasure and the certainty of his judgment on Jerusalem and all of Judah.

3:3 *sweet as honey in my mouth.* What Jeremiah experienced emotionally (Jer 15:16) was experienced by Ezekiel in a more sensory way: Words from God are sweet to the taste (see Ps 19:10; 119:103)—even when their content is bitter (see Rev 10:9–10).

this scroll I am giving you and fill your stomach with it." So I ate[l] it, and it tasted as sweet as honey[m] in my mouth.

[4]He then said to me: "Son of man, go now to the house of Israel and speak my words to them.[n] [5]You are not being sent to a people of obscure speech and difficult language,[o] but to the house of Israel— [6]not to many peoples of obscure speech and difficult language, whose words you cannot understand. Surely if I had sent you to them, they would have listened to you.[p] [7]But the house of Israel is not willing to listen[q] to you because they are not willing to listen to me, for the whole house of Israel is hardened and obstinate.[r] [8]But I will make you as unyielding and hardened as they are.[s] [9]I will make your forehead[t] like the hardest stone, harder than flint.[u] Do not be afraid of them or terrified by them, though they are a rebellious house.[v]"

[10]And he said to me, "Son of man, listen carefully and take to heart[w] all the words I speak to you. [11]Go[x] now to your countrymen in exile and speak to them. Say to them, 'This is what the Sovereign LORD says,'[y] whether they listen or fail to listen.[z]"

[12]Then the Spirit lifted me up,[a] and I heard behind me a loud rumbling sound—May the glory of the LORD be praised in his dwelling place!— [13]the sound of the wings of the living creatures[b] brushing against each other and the sound of the wheels beside them, a loud rumbling sound.[c] [14]The Spirit[d] then lifted me up[e] and took me away, and I went in bitterness and in the anger of my spirit, with the strong hand of the LORD[f] upon me. [15]I came to the exiles who lived at Tel Abib

near the Kebar River.[g] And there, where they were living, I sat among them for seven days[h]—overwhelmed.

Warning to Israel

[16]At the end of seven days the word of the LORD came to me:[i] [17]"Son of man, I have made you a watchman[j] for the house of Israel; so hear the word I speak and give them warning from me.[k] [18]When I say to a wicked man, 'You will surely die,'[?] and you do not warn him or speak out to dissuade him from his evil ways in order to save his life, that wicked man will die for[g] his sin, and I will hold you accountable for his blood.[m] [19]But if you do warn the wicked man and he does not turn[n] from his wickedness[o] or from his evil ways, he will die[p] for his sin; but you will have saved yourself.[q]

[20]"Again, when a righteous man turns[r] from his righteousness and does evil, and I put a stumbling block[s] before him, he will die. Since you did not warn him, he will die for his sin. The righteous things he did will not be remembered, and I will hold you accountable for his blood.[t] [21]But if you do warn the righteous man not to sin and he does not sin, he will surely live because he took warning, and you will have saved yourself.[u]"

[22]The hand of the LORD[v] was upon me there, and he said to me, "Get up and go[w] out to the plain,[x] and there I will speak to you." [23]So I got up and went out to the plain. And the glory of the LORD was standing there, like the glory I had seen by the Kebar River,[y] and I fell facedown.[z]

3:3 [l]S Jer 15:16
[m]S Ps 19:10;
Rev 10:9-10
3:4 [n]Eze 11:4,25
3:5 [o]S Isa 28:11;
Jnh 1:2
3:6 [p]Jnh 3:5-10;
Mt 11:21-23;
Ac 13:46-48
3:7 [q]S Jer 7:27
[r]Isa 48:4; Jer 3:3;
S Eze 2:4;
Jn 15:20-23
3:8 [s]Jer 1:18;
S 15:20
3:9 [t]S Isa 48:4
[u]S Jer 5:3
[v]Isa 50:7;
Eze 2:6; 44:6;
Mic 3:8
3:10
[w]S Job 22:22
3:11 [x]S Isa 6:9
[y]ver 27
[z]Eze 2:4-5,7;
11:24-25
3:12 [a]ver 14;
Eze 8:3; 43:5
3:13 [b]Eze 1:15
[c]Eze 1:24; 10:5,
16-17
3:14
[d]S 1Ki 18:12
[e]S ver 12 /ver 22;
S Isa 8:11;
Eze 37:1

3:15 [g]S Ps 137:1
[h]S Ge 50:10
3:16 [i]Jer 42:7
3:17 [j]S Isa 52:8
[k]S Isa 58:1;
Jer 1:17;
Eze 11:4; Hab 2:1
3:18 [l]S Ge 2:17;
Jn 8:21,24 [m]ver
20
3:19 [n]S Ps 7:12
[o]S Ge 6:5
[p]S Jer 42:16
[q]S 2Ki 17:13;
Eze 14:14,20;
Ac 18:6; 20:26;
1Ti 4:14-16
3:20 [r]S Jer 34:16
[s]S Lev 26:37;
S Isa 8:14;
S Eze 7:19 [t]ver
18; Ps 125:5;
Eze 18:24; 33:12,
18
3:21 [u]Ac 20:31
3:22 [v]S ver 14;
S Eze 1:3 [w]Ac 9:6
[x]Eze 8:4

3:23 [y]Eze 1:1 [z]S Ge 17:3

[g]18 Or in; also in verses 19 and 20

3:6 *Surely if I had sent you to them.* Jesus spoke similar words to Israel (see Mt 11:21).

3:9 *I will make your forehead like the hardest stone.* Strength and courage were necessary equipment for a prophet, especially when preaching judgment. Jeremiah was similarly equipped (see Jer 1:18).

3:10 *listen carefully and take to heart.* The prophet is to stand in marked contrast to the people, who do not listen.

3:11 *Go now to your countrymen in exile.* Ezekiel's ministry was to the exilic community, most of whom refused to believe that God would abandon Jerusalem and the temple. After the fall of Jerusalem, therefore, they were strongly inclined to despair.

3:14 *in bitterness and in the anger of my spirit.* The prophet, knowing the righteousness of God's anger, personally identified with the divine emotions. *strong hand of the LORD upon me.* See note on 1:3.

3:15 *Tel Abib.* The only mention of the specific place where the exiles lived. In Babylonian the name meant "mound of the flood [i.e., destruction]," apparently referring

to the ruined condition of the site. When used of the modern Israeli city, Tel Aviv, this name (Abib and Aviv are the same word in Hebrew) is understood to mean "hill of grain." *seven days—overwhelmed.* Ezekiel was in the same state of spiritual shock that others in the Bible experienced after an encounter with God (see Ezr 9:4; Job 2:13; 40:4-5; Ac 9:9). Considering Ezekiel's priestly background (see note on 1:3), the seven-day period may have been a parallel to the time required for a priest's ordination (see Lev 8:1-33).

3:16 *I have made you a watchman.* In ancient Israel, watchmen were stationed on the highest parts of the city wall to inform its inhabitants of the progress of a battle (1Sa 14:16) or of approaching messengers (2Sa 18:24-27; 2Ki 9:17-20). The prophets were spiritual watchmen, relaying God's word to the people (see Jer 6:17; Hos 9:8; Hab 2:1). Ezekiel's function as a watchman was not so much to warn the exiles of the impending doom of Jerusalem as to teach that God holds each one responsible for his own behavior. This commission, repeated in 33:7-9, is spelled out in ch. 18.

3:22 *hand of the LORD.* See note on 1:3.

24Then the Spirit came into me and raised me[a] to my feet. He spoke to me and said: "Go, shut yourself inside your house.[b] 25And you, son of man, they will tie with ropes; you will be bound so that you cannot go out among the people.[c] 26I will make your tongue stick to the roof[d] of your mouth so that you will be silent and unable to rebuke them, though they are a rebellious house.[e] 27But when I speak to you, I will open your mouth and you shall say to them, 'This is what the Sovereign LORD says.'[f] Whoever will listen let him listen, and whoever will refuse let him refuse; for they are a rebellious house.[g]

Siege of Jerusalem Symbolized

4 "Now, son of man, take a clay tablet, put it in front of you and draw the city of Jerusalem on it. 2Then lay siege to it: Erect siege works against it, build a ramp[h] up to it, set up camps against it and put battering rams around it.[i] 3Then take an iron pan,[j] place it as an iron wall between you and the city and turn your face toward[k] it. It will be under siege, and you shall besiege it. This will be a sign[l] to the house of Israel.[m]

4"Then lie on your left side and put the sin of the house of Israel upon yourself.[h] You are to bear their sin for the number of days you lie on your side. 5I have assigned you the same number of days as the years of their sin. So for 390 days you will bear the sin of the house of Israel.

6"After you have finished this, lie down again, this time on your right side, and bear the sin[n] of the house of Judah. I have assigned you 40 days, a day for each year.[o] 7Turn your face[p] toward the siege of Jerusalem and with bared arm prophesy

against her. 8I will tie you up with ropes so that you cannot turn from one side to the other until you have finished the days of your siege.[q]

9"Take wheat and barley, beans and lentils, millet and spelt;[r] put them in a storage jar and use them to make bread for yourself. You are to eat it during the 390 days you lie on your side. 10Weigh out twenty shekels[i][s] of food to eat each day and eat it at set times. 11Also measure out a sixth of a hin[j] of water and drink it at set times.[t] 12Eat the food as you would a barley cake; bake it in the sight of the people, using human excrement[u] for fuel." 13The LORD said, "In this way the people of Israel will eat defiled food among the nations where I will drive them."[v]

14Then I said, "Not so, Sovereign LORD![w] I have never defiled myself. From my youth until now I have never eaten anything found dead[x] or torn by wild animals. No unclean meat has ever entered my mouth.[y]"

15"Very well," he said, "I will let you bake your bread over cow manure instead of human excrement."

16He then said to me: "Son of man, I will cut off[z] the supply of food in Jerusalem. The people will eat rationed food in anxiety and drink rationed water in despair,[a] 17for food and water will be scarce.[b] They will be appalled at the sight of each other and will waste away because of[k] their sin.[c]

5 "Now, son of man, take a sharp sword and use it as a barber's razor[d] to shave[e] your head and your beard.[f] Then

Cross references (center column)

3:24 [a]Eze 2:2 [b]Jer 15:17
3:25 [c]Eze 4:8
3:26 [d]S Ps 22:15 [e]Eze 2:5; 24:27; 33:22; Hos 4:4
3:27 [f]ver 11 [g]Eze 2:5; 12:3; 24:27; 29:21; 33:22; Rev 22:11
4:2 [h]S Jer 6:6; Eze 17:17; Da 11:15 [i]S Jer 33:4; Eze 21:22
4:3 [j]S Lev 2:5 [k]ver 7; Eze 20:46; 21:2 [l]S Isa 8:18; S 20:3; Jer 13:1-7; 18:1-4; 19:1-2; Eze 5:1-4; 12:3-6 [m]S Jer 39:1
4:6 [n]S Ex 28:38 [o]Nu 14:34; Da 9:24-26; 12:11-12
4:7 [p]S ver 3; Eze 6:2; S 13:17

4:8 [q]Eze 3:25
4:9 [r]S Isa 28:25
4:10 [s]S Ex 30:13
4:11 [t]ver 16
4:12 [u]S Isa 36:12 [v]Hos 9:3; Am 7:17
4:14 [w]Jer 1:6; Eze 9:8; 20:49 [x]S Lev 11:39 [y]S Ex 22:31; Dt 14:3; 32:37-38; Da 1:8; Hos 9:3-4
4:16 [z]S Ps 105:16 [a]ver 10-11; S Lev 26:26; Isa 3:1; Eze 12:19
4:17 [b]La 5:4; Eze 5:16; 12:18-19; Am 4:8 [c]S Lev 26:39; Eze 24:23; 33:10
5:1 [d]S Nu 6:5 [e]Eze 44:20 [f]S Lev 21:5; S 2Sa 10:4

[h]4 Or your side   [i]10 That is, about 8 ounces (about 0.2 kilogram)   [j]11 That is, about 2/3 quart (about 0.6 liter)   [k]17 Or away in

---

3:26 *you will be silent.* Verses 26–27 indicate that the prophet would be unable to speak except when he had a direct word from the Lord. His enforced silence underscored Israel's stubborn refusal to take God's word seriously. This condition was relieved only after the fall of Jerusalem (24:27; 33:22). From that time on, Ezekiel was given messages of hope, which he continually shared with his fellow exiles.

4:1 *take a clay tablet.* The first of several symbolic acts to be performed by the prophet. After inscribing a likeness of the city of Jerusalem on a moist clay tablet, such as those commonly used in Babylonia, Ezekiel was to place around it models of siege works to represent the city under attack (v. 2). He was then to place an iron pan (perhaps a baking griddle) between himself and the symbolized city (v. 3) to indicate the unbreakable strength of the siege.

4:3 *you shall besiege it.* Ezekiel's own presence in the scene signified that the siege would actually be laid by the Lord himself.

4:4 *You are to bear their sin.* A representative rather than a substitutionary bearing of sin. The prophet's action symbol-

ized Israel's sins; it did not remove them.

4:5 *for 390 days.* The 390 years may represent the period from the time of Solomon's unfaithfulness to the fall of Jerusalem. Correspondingly, the 40 years of v. 6 may represent the long reign of wicked Manasseh before his repentance (see 2Ki 21:11–15; 23:26–27; 24:3–4; 2Ch 33:12–13).

4:6 *on your right side.* Lying on his left side (see v. 5) placed Ezekiel to the north of the symbolic city; lying on his right side placed him to the south—signifying the northern and southern kingdoms respectively.

4:9 *Take wheat and barley, beans and lentils, millet and spelt.* A scant, vegetarian diet representing the meager provisions of a besieged city.

4:15 *cow manure.* Commonly used in the Near East as a fuel for baking, even today. Ezekiel again showed his sensitivity to things ceremonially unclean (see note on 1:3), and God graciously responded to the prophet's objection by allowing this substitute for human excrement.

5:1 *take a sharp sword.* What Isaiah had expressed in a metaphor (Isa 7:20) Ezekiel acted out in prophetic

take a set of scales and divide up the hair. [2]When the days of your siege come to an end, burn a third[g] of the hair with fire[h] inside the city. Take a third and strike it with the sword all around the city. And scatter a third to the winds.[i] For I will pursue them with drawn sword.[j] [3]But take a few strands of hair and tuck them away in the folds of your garment.[k] [4]Again, take a few of these and throw them into the fire[l] and burn them up. A fire will spread from there to the whole house of Israel.

[5]"This is what the Sovereign LORD says: This is Jerusalem, which I have set in the center of the nations, with countries all around her.[m] [6]Yet in her wickedness she has rebelled against my laws and decrees more than the nations and countries around her. She has rejected my laws and has not followed my decrees.[n]

[7]"Therefore this is what the Sovereign LORD says: You have been more unruly than the nations around you and have not followed my decrees or kept my laws. You have not even[1] conformed to the standards of the nations around you.[o]

[8]"Therefore this is what the Sovereign LORD says: I myself am against you, Jerusalem, and I will inflict punishment on you in the sight of the nations.[p] [9]Because of all your detestable idols, I will do to you what I have never done before and will never do again.[q] [10]Therefore in your midst fathers will eat their children, and children will eat their fathers.[r] I will inflict punishment on you and will scatter all your survivors to the winds.[s] [11]Therefore as surely as I live,[t] declares the Sovereign[u] LORD, because you have defiled my sanctuary[v] with all your vile images[w] and detestable practices,[x] I myself will withdraw my favor; I will not look on you with pity or spare you.[y] [12]A third of your people will die of the plague or perish by famine inside you; a third will fall by the sword outside

your walls; and a third I will scatter to the winds[z] and pursue with drawn sword.[a] [13]"Then my anger will cease and my wrath[b] against them will subside, and I will be avenged.[c] And when I have spent my wrath upon them, they will know that I the LORD have spoken in my zeal.[d]

[14]"I will make you a ruin and a reproach among the nations around you, in the sight of all who pass by.[e] [15]You will be a reproach[f] and a taunt, a warning[g] and an object of horror to the nations around you when I inflict punishment on you in anger and in wrath and with stinging rebuke.[h] I the LORD have spoken.[i] [16]When I shoot at you with my deadly and destructive arrows of famine, I will shoot to destroy you. I will bring more and more famine upon you and cut off your supply of food.[j] [17]I will send famine and wild beasts[k] against you, and they will leave you childless. Plague and bloodshed[l] will sweep through you, and I will bring the sword against you. I the LORD have spoken.[m]"

A Prophecy Against the Mountains of Israel

6 The word of the LORD came to me: [2]"Son of man, set your face[n] against the mountains[o] of Israel; prophesy against them[p] [3]and say: 'O mountains of Israel, hear the word of the Sovereign LORD. This is what the Sovereign LORD says to the mountains and hills, to the ravines and valleys:[q] I am about to bring a sword against you, and I will destroy your high places.[r] [4]Your altars will be demolished and your incense altars[s] will be smashed; and I will

5:2 gZec 13:8; hJer 21:10; Eze 15:7 iver 10; Jer 13:24 /ver 12; S Lev 26:33; S Jer 9:16; S 39:1-2
5:3 k2Ki 25:12; S Ps 74:11; Jer 39:10
5:4 lEze 10:7; 15:7
5:5 mS Dt 4:6; S La 1:1; Eze 16:14
5:6 nS 2Ki 17:15; Ne 9:17; Jer 11:10; S Eze 2:3; 16:47-51; Zec 7:11
5:7 oS 2Ki 21:9; S 2Ch 33:9; Jer 2:10-11; Eze 16:47
5:8 pS Jer 21:5, 13; 24:9; Eze 11:9; 15:7; Zec 14:2
5:9 qDa 9:12; S Mt 24:21
5:10 rS Lev 26:29; S La 2:20; sS Lev 26:33; S Ps 44:11; S Jer 13:14; Eze 12:14
5:11 tS Nu 14:21; uS Ge 15:2; vS Lev 15:31; wEze 7:20; 11:18; x2Ch 36:14; Eze 8:6; yS Job 27:22; S Jer 16:18; S La 2:17; Eze 7:4,9; 8:18; 9:5
5:12 zver 10; Jer 13:24 aS ver 2,17; S Ps 107:39; S Jer 15:2; S 21:9; Eze 6:11-12; 7:15; 12:14; Am 9:4; Zec 13:8; Rev 6:8
5:13 bS 2Ch 12:7; S Job 20:23; Eze 21:17; 24:13; cS Isa 1:24; dS Isa 59:17; Eze 16:42; 38:19; Hos 10:10; Zec 6:8
5:14 eS Lev 26:32; Ne 2:17; Ps 74:3-10;

79:1-4; Isa 64:11; Eze 6:6; 22:4; Da 9:16; Mic 3:12 5:15 fS Isa 43:28 gS Dt 28:46 hS Dt 28:20; S 1Ki 9:7; S Jer 22:8-9; 24:9; Eze 14:8 iS Jer 23:40 5:16 jS Lev 26:26; S Dt 32:24 5:17 kEze 14:15 lEze 38:22 mS ver 12; S Lev 26:25; Eze 14:21; 28:23 6:2 nS Eze 4:7 oEze 18:6; Mic 6:1 pver 13 6:3 qEze 36:4 rS Lev 26:30 6:4 sS 2Ch 14:5

1[7] Most Hebrew manuscripts; some Hebrew manuscripts and Syriac You have

symbolism.

5:5 *This is Jerusalem.* After wordlessly acting out the symbols (beginning in 4:1), Ezekiel received and probably related the divine explanations. *center of the nations.* A privileged position, which made Israel's responsibility and judgment all the more severe (see note on 38:12).

5:8 *I myself am against you.* A short and effective phrase of judgment used often by Ezekiel (see 13:8; 21:3; 26:3; 28:22; 29:3,10; 30:22; 34:10; 35:3; 38:3; 39:1; see also Jer 23:30–32; 50:31; 51:25; Na 2:13; 3:5).

5:10 *fathers will eat their children.* Cannibalism, the most gruesome extremity of life under siege, was threatened as a consequence of breaking the covenant (Dt 28:53; see Jer 19:9; La 2:20; Zec 11:9).

5:11 *as surely as I live.* See note on 18:3.

5:13 *spent my wrath upon.* An expression frequently used

by the Lord in this book (see 6:12; 7:8; 13:15; 20:8,21). *they will know that I the LORD have spoken.* The first of 65 occurrences in Ezekiel of this or similar declarations. God's acts of judgment and salvation reveal who he is. Since the people would not listen to God's words, they would be taught by his actions.

5:15 *a reproach and a taunt, a warning and an object of horror.* A fourfold list (see note on 1:5).

6:3 *high places.* Open-air sanctuaries of Canaanite origin, condemned throughout the OT. The high places, together with the "altars," "incense altars" and "idols" (v. 4), make up a list of four objects (see note on 1:5).

6:4 *incense altars.* Made of burnt clay, about two feet high, usually inscribed with animal figures and idols of Canaanite gods. *idols.* The Hebrew for this word is a derisive term (lit. "dung pellets"), used especially by Ezekiel (38 times, as

slay your people in front of your idols.^{t} ^{5}I will lay the dead bodies of the Israelites in front of their idols, and I will scatter your bones^u around your altars.^{v} ^{6}Wherever you live,^{w} the towns will be laid waste and the high places^x demolished, so that your altars will be laid waste and devastated, your idols^y smashed and ruined, your incense altars^z broken down, and what you have made wiped out.^{a} ^{7}Your people will fall slain^b among you, and you will know that I am the LORD.^{c}

^{8}"'But I will spare some, for some of you will escape^d the sword when you are scattered among the lands and nations.^{e} ^{9}Then in the nations where they have been carried captive, those who escape will remember^f me—how I have been grieved^g by their adulterous hearts, which have turned away from me, and by their eyes, which have lusted after their idols.^{h} They will loathe themselves for the evil^i they have done and for all their detestable practices.^{j} ^{10}And they will know that I am the LORD;^{k} I did not threaten in vain to bring this calamity on them.^{l}

^{11}"'This is what the Sovereign LORD says: Strike your hands together and stamp your feet and cry out "Alas!" because of all the wicked and detestable practices of the house of Israel, for they will fall by the sword, famine and plague.^{m} ^{12}He that is far away will die of the plague, and he that is near will fall by the sword, and he that survives and is spared will die of famine. So will I spend my wrath^n upon them.^{o} ^{13}And they will know that I am the LORD, when their people lie slain among their idols^p around their altars, on every high hill and on all the mountaintops, under every spreading tree and every leafy oak^q—places where they offered fragrant incense to all their idols.^{r} ^{14}And I will stretch out my hand^s against them and make the land a desolate waste from the desert to Diblah^m—wherever they live. Then they will know that I am the LORD.^{t}'"

The End Has Come

7 The word of the LORD came to me: ^{2}"Son of man, this is what the Sovereign LORD says to the land of Israel: The end!^{u} The end has come upon the four corners^v of the land. ^{3}The end is now upon you and I will unleash my anger against you. I will judge you according to your conduct^w and repay you for all your detestable practices.^{x} ^{4}I will not look on you with pity^y or spare you; I will surely repay you for your conduct and the detestable practices among you. Then you will know that I am the LORD.^{z}

^{5}"This is what the Sovereign LORD says: Disaster!^{a} An unheard-of^n disaster is coming. ^{6}The end^b has come! The end has come! It has roused itself against you. It has come! ^{7}Doom has come upon you—you who dwell in the land. The time has come, the day^c is near; ^{d} there is panic, not joy, upon the mountains. ^{8}I am about to pour out my wrath^e on you and spend my anger against you; I will judge you according to your conduct and repay you for all your detestable practices.^{f} ^{9}I will not look on you with pity or spare you; ^{g} I will repay you in accordance with your conduct and the detestable practices among you. ^{h} Then you will know that it is I the LORD who strikes the blow.^{i}

^{10}"The day is here! It has come! Doom has burst forth, the rod^j has budded, arrogance has blossomed! ^{11}Violence^k has grown into^o a rod to punish wickedness; none of the people will be left, none of that crowd—no wealth, nothing of value.^{l} ^{12}The time has come, the day has arrived. Let not the buyer^m rejoice nor the seller grieve, for wrath is upon the whole

Cross references (center column)

6:4 ^{t}Eze 9:6; 14:3; 20:16
6:5 ^{u}S Nu 19:16; S Ps 53:5; Jer 8:1-2 ^{v}ver 13; S Lev 26:30
6:6 ^{w}S Ex 12:20 ^{x}Hos 10:8 ^{y}Eze 30:13; Mic 1:7; Zec 13:2 ^{z}S Lev 26:30 ^{a}S 1Sa 5:4; Isa 6:11; S Eze 5:14
6:7 ^{b}Eze 9:7 ^{c}ver 10,13,14; Eze 11:10-12
6:8 ^{d}S Ps 68:20; S Jer 44:28 ^{e}S Ge 11:4; S Ps 44:11; Isa 6:13; S Jer 44:14; Eze 7:16; 12:16; 14:22
6:9 ^{f}S Ps 137:6; Zec 10:9 ^{g}S Isa 7:13; S Jer 8:21 ^{h}S Ex 22:20; Eze 20:7,24; Mic 5:13 ^{i}S Ex 32:22 ^{j}S Job 42:6; Eze 20:43; 23:14-16; 36:31
6:10 ^{k}S ver 7 ^{l}S Dt 28:52; Jer 40:2
6:11 ^{m}S Jer 42:22; Eze 21:14,17; 22:13; 25:6
6:12 ^{n}S Job 20:23 ^{o}S Eze 5:12; 7:15
6:13 ^{p}S Lev 26:30 ^{q}S Isa 1:29 ^{r}S 1Ki 14:23; S Jer 2:20; Eze 18:6; 20:28; Hos 4:13
6:14 ^{s}S Ex 7:5; S Job 30:21; S Jer 6:12; 51:25; Eze 20:34 ^{t}Eze 12:19; 14:13

7:2 ^{u}Am 8:2,10 ^{v}Rev 7:1; 20:8
7:3 ^{w}Eze 18:30 ^{x}S Ge 6:13
7:4 ^{y}S Jer 13:14; S Eze 5:11 ^{z}S Eze 5:11; 23:49
7:5 ^{a}S 2Ki 21:12
7:6 ^{b}Eze 39:8
7:7 ^{c}S Job 18:20; S Isa 2:12; Am 5:18-20 ^{d}Eze 12:23; 30:3; Zep 1:14; Mal 3:2
7:8 ^{e}Isa 42:25; Eze 9:8; 14:19; 22:22; Hos 5:10;

Na 1:6 ^{f}Eze 20:8,21; 36:19 7:9 ^{g}S Jer 21:7; S Eze 5:11 ^{h}Eze 22:31 ^{i}Dt 32:35; S Ps 39:10; S Isa 9:13 7:10 ^{j}Ps 89:32; Isa 10:5 7:11 ^{k}S Ps 55:9; S Isa 58:4 ^{l}Jer 16:6; Zep 1:18 7:12 ^{m}S Isa 24:2

m14 Most Hebrew manuscripts; a few Hebrew manuscripts *Riblah*   n5 Most Hebrew manuscripts; some Hebrew manuscripts and Syriac *Disaster after*   o11 Or *The violent one has become*

Footnotes (bottom)

opposed to only 9 times elsewhere in the OT).

6:9 *those who escape will remember me.* The corrective outcome God intends from the severe judgment to come (see v. 10).

6:11 *Strike your hands together.* A command to Ezekiel, calling for his personal involvement in the tragedy—though Israel's enemies were condemned for the same practice (see 25:6).

6:14 *I will stretch out my hand against.* A common expression in Ezekiel (see 14:9,13; 16:27; 25:7; 35:3). *Diblah.* Perhaps the Beth Diblathaim of Jer 48:22, a city in Moab; or Riblah, a city north of Damascus on the Orontes River (see NIV text note).

7:2 *four corners of the land.* The whole world would be affected by God's judgment on the land of Israel (see note on 1:5).

7:7 *the day.* The day of the Lord. Beginning with Amos (Am 5:18–20), that day is seen by all the prophets as a day of great judgment—and often (though not here) as a judgment that sweeps away all the enemies that threaten God's people, thereby bringing peace. *panic, not joy.* Cf. Am 5:20 ("darkness, not light").

7:8 *pour out my wrath.* A common expression in Ezekiel (see 9:8; 14:19; 20:8,13,21; 22:31; 30:15; 36:18).

7:12 *Let not the buyer rejoice.* End-time advice similar to that of Jesus (see Mt 24:17–18).

crowd.[n] [13]The seller will not recover the land he has sold as long as both of them live, for the vision concerning the whole crowd will not be reversed. Because of their sins, not one of them will preserve his life.[o] [14]Though they blow the trumpet[p] and get everything ready, no one will go into battle, for my wrath[q] is upon the whole crowd.

[15]"Outside is the sword, inside are plague and famine; those in the country will die by the sword, and those in the city will be devoured by famine and plague.[r] [16]All who survive[s] and escape will be in the mountains, moaning like doves[t] of the valleys, each because of his sins. [u] [17]Every hand will go limp,[v] and every knee will become as weak as water. [w] [18]They will put on sackcloth[x] and be clothed with terror.[y] Their faces will be covered with shame and their heads will be shaved.[z] [19]They will throw their silver into the streets,[a] and their gold will be an unclean thing. Their silver and gold will not be able to save them in the day of the LORD's wrath.[b] They will not satisfy[c] their hunger or fill their stomachs with it, for it has made them stumble[d] into sin. [e] [20]They were proud of their beautiful jewelry and used it to make[f] their detestable idols and vile images.[g] Therefore I will turn these into an unclean thing for them. [h] [21]I will hand it all over as plunder[i] to foreigners and as loot to the wicked of the earth, and they will defile it.[j] [22]I will turn my face[k] away from them, and they will desecrate my treasured place; robbers will enter it and desecrate it.[l]

[23]"Prepare chains, because the land is full of bloodshed[m] and the city is full of violence.[n] [24]I will bring the most wicked of the nations to take possession of their houses; I will put an end to the pride of

the mighty, and their sanctuaries[o] will be desecrated.[p] [25]When terror comes, they will seek peace, but there will be none.[q] [26]Calamity upon calamity[r] will come, and rumor upon rumor. They will try to get a vision from the prophet;[s] the teaching of the law by the priest will be lost, as will the counsel of the elders.[t] [27]The king will mourn, the prince will be clothed with despair, [u] and the hands of the people of the land will tremble. I will deal with them according to their conduct, [v] and by their own standards I will judge them. Then they will know that I am the LORD. [w]"

Idolatry in the Temple

8 In the sixth year, in the sixth month on the fifth day, while I was sitting in my house and the elders[x] of Judah were sitting before[y] me, the hand of the Sovereign LORD came upon me there.[z] [2]I looked, and I saw a figure like that of a man.[p] From what appeared to be his waist down he was like fire, and from there up his appearance was as bright as glowing metal.[a] [3]He stretched out what looked like a hand[b] and took me by the hair of my head. The Spirit lifted me up[c] between earth and heaven and in visions[d] of God he took me to Jerusalem, to the entrance to the north gate of the inner court,[e] where the idol that provokes to jealousy[f] stood. [4]And there before me was the glory[g] of the God of Israel, as in the vision I had seen in the plain. [h]

[5]Then he said to me, "Son of man, look toward the north." So I looked, and in the

Cross references (center column)

7:12 [n]ver 7; Isa 5:13-14; Eze 30:3
7:13 [o]Lev 25:24-28
7:14 [p]S Job 39:24 [q]Jer 25:38
7:15 [r]S Dt 32:25; Jer 14:18; S La 1:20; S Eze 5:12; 33:27
7:16 [s]S Isa 10:20; S Jer 41:16; 42:17 [t]S Ge 8:8; S Isa 59:11 [u]S Ezr 9:15; Jer 9:19; S Eze 6:8
7:17 [v]S 2Ki 19:26; S Jer 47:3; Eze 21:7; 22:14 [w]Da 5:6
7:18 [x]S Jer 4:8; 48:37; 49:3 [y]S Ps 55:5 [z]S Isa 15:2-3; Eze 27:31; Am 8:10
7:19 [a]S La 4:1 [b]Isa 42:25; Eze 13:5; 30:3; Joel 1:5; 2:1; Zep 1:7,18; 2:2 [c]Isa 55:2 [d]Eze 3:20; 14:3; Hos 4:5 [e]S Pr 11:4
7:20 [f]S Jer 10:3 [g]S Eze 5:11 [h]S Isa 2:20; 30:22; Eze 16:17
7:21 [i]S Nu 14:3 [j]S 2Ki 24:13
7:22 [k]S Jer 2:27; Eze 39:23-24 [l]Ps 74:7-8; Jer 19:13; S La 2:7
7:23 [m]S 2Ki 21:16; S Isa 1:15; S Eze 22:9 [n]S Ge 6:11; Eze 11:6
7:24 [o]La 2:7; Eze 24:21 [p]2Ch 7:20; Eze 28:7
7:25 [q]Jer 6:14; S 8:11; Eze 13:10,16
7:26 [r]S Dt 29:21; S 31:17 [s]S Isa 3:1 [t]Isa 47:11;

S Jer 18:18; Eze 20:1-3; Am 8:11; Mic 3:6 **7:27** [u]S Ps 109:19; Eze 26:16 [v]S Isa 3:11; Eze 18:20 [w]S ver 4 **8:1** [x]S 2Ki 6:32; Eze 14:1 [y]Eze 33:31 [z]Eze 1:1-3; 24:1; 40:1 **8:2** [a]Eze 1:4,26-27 **8:3** [b]S Eze 2:9 [c]S Eze 3:12; 11:1 [d]S Ex 24:10 [e]ver 16 [f]ver 5; Ex 20:5; Dt 32:16 **8:4** [g]S Ex 24:16 [h]Eze 3:22

[p]2 Or *saw a fiery figure*

Study notes (bottom)

7:19 *They will throw their silver.* See Isa 2:20.

7:20 *beautiful jewelry.* See Ex 32:2–4.

7:22 *my treasured place.* The Jerusalem temple.

7:24 *pride of the mighty.* The Jerusalem temple, described by the word "pride" (as in 24:21; 33:28).

7:26 *prophet ... priest ... elders.* There would be no guidance from God and no direction from the elders (see 1Sa 28:6; Am 8:11–12; Mic 3:6–7).

7:27 *king ... prince.* Here both nouns describe the same person. Ezekiel considered Jehoiachin to be the true king (1:2) and Zedekiah a mere prince (12:12). *people of the land.* Full citizens of Judah who owned land and served in the army (cf. 12:19; 45:16,22; 46:3).

8:1—11:25 The vision contained in these four chapters vividly depicts the departure of the divine glory from the corrupted temple (see 8:4; 9:3; 10:18–19; 11:23).

8:1 *In the sixth year, in the sixth month on the fifth day.* Sept. 17, 592 B.C.—the second of 13 dates in Ezekiel. This one, like those in 1:2 and 40:1, introduces a vision. *sitting in*

my house. The exiles were free to build houses (see Jer 29:5). *elders of Judah were sitting before me.* They also had freedom of movement, assembly and worship. A year and two months after his inaugural vision and preaching, the prophet commanded a hearing. Some have seen in such meetings the beginnings of the synagogue form of worship. *hand of the Sovereign LORD.* See note on 1:3.

8:2 *figure like that of a man.* An angel, similar in appearance to God in 1:26–27. *like fire ... as bright as glowing metal.* A way of describing the blinding brightness of the divine messenger (see Mt 28:3; cf. Ac 9:3).

8:3 *took me to Jerusalem.* Ezekiel had been directed to prophesy stern judgments on Jerusalem (chs. 1–7). Now he was transported to Jerusalem in visions of God (see 11:24) and shown the reason for the judgments. *idol that provokes to jealousy.* Any idol in the temple provoked the Lord to jealousy, but this one seems to be a statue of Asherah, the Canaanite goddess of fertility, which Josiah had removed some 30 years previously (see 2Ki 23:6).

entrance north of the gate of the altar I saw this idol[i] of jealousy.

[6]And he said to me, "Son of man, do you see what they are doing—the utterly detestable[j] things the house of Israel is doing here, things that will drive me far from my sanctuary?[k] But you will see things that are even more detestable."

[7]Then he brought me to the entrance to the court. I looked, and I saw a hole in the wall. [8]He said to me, "Son of man, now dig into the wall." So I dug into the wall and saw a doorway there.

[9]And he said to me, "Go in and see the wicked and detestable things they are doing here." [10]So I went in and looked, and I saw portrayed all over the walls[l] all kinds of crawling things and detestable[m] animals and all the idols of the house of Israel.[n] [11]In front of them stood seventy elders[o] of the house of Israel, and Jaazaniah son of Shaphan was standing among them. Each had a censer[p] in his hand, and a fragrant cloud of incense[q] was rising.[r]

[12]He said to me, "Son of man, have you seen what the elders of the house of Israel are doing in the darkness,[s] each at the shrine of his own idol? They say, 'The LORD does not see[t] us; the LORD has forsaken the land.'" [13]Again, he said, "You will see them doing things that are even more detestable."

[14]Then he brought me to the entrance to the north gate of the house of the LORD, and I saw women sitting there, mourning for Tammuz.[u] [15]He said to me, "Do you see this, son of man? You will see things that are even more detestable than this."

[16]He then brought me into the inner court[v] of the house of the LORD, and there at the entrance to the temple, between the portico and the altar,[w] were about twenty-five men. With their backs toward the temple of the LORD and their faces toward the east, they were bowing down to the sun[x] in the east.[y]

[17]He said to me, "Have you seen this, son of man? Is it a trivial matter for the house of Judah to do the detestable things[z] they are doing here? Must they also fill the land with violence[a] and continually provoke me to anger?[b] Look at them putting the branch to their nose! [18]Therefore I will deal with them in anger;[c] I will not look on them with pity[d] or spare them. Although they shout in my ears, I will not listen[e] to them."

Idolaters Killed

9 Then I heard him call out in a loud voice, "Bring the guards of the city here, each with a weapon in his hand." [2]And I saw six men coming from the direction of the upper gate, which faces north, each with a deadly weapon in his hand. With them was a man clothed in linen[f] who had a writing kit at his side. They came in and stood beside the bronze altar.

[3]Now the glory[g] of the God of Israel went up from above the cherubim,[h] where it had been, and moved to the threshold of the temple. Then the LORD called to the man clothed in linen who had the writing kit at his side [4]and said to him, "Go throughout the city of Jerusalem[i] and put a mark[j] on the foreheads of those who grieve and lament[k] over all the detestable things that are done in it.[l]"

[5]As I listened, he said to the others, "Follow him through the city and kill, without showing pity[m] or compassion.[n] [6]Slaughter[o] old men, young men and maidens, women and children,[p] but do not touch anyone who has the mark.[q] Begin at my sanctuary." So they began with the elders[r] who were in front of the temple.[s]

8:5 [i]Ps 78:58;
S Jer 4:1; 32:34
8:6 [j]Ps 78:60;
S Eze 5:11
[k]Hos 5:6
8:10
[l]S Jdg 17:4-5;
Eze 23:14
[m]Jer 44:4
[n]Ex 20:4;
Dt 4:15-18;
S Jer 16:18;
Eze 11:12
8:11 [o]S Ex 3:16
[p]S Lev 10:1;
Nu 16:17
[q]Nu 16:35;
S Jer 44:5
[r]Eze 11:1-2
8:12 [s]S Job 22:13
[t]S 2Ki 21:16;
Ps 10:11;
S Isa 29:15;
Eze 9:9; Zep 1:12
8:14 [u]Eze 11:12
8:16 [v]ver 3
[w]Joel 2:17

[x]S Ge 1:16
[y]Dt 4:19; S 17:3;
S Job 31:28;
S Jer 2:27;
Eze 9:6; 11:1,12;
40:6; 43:1
8:17 [z]Eze 16:2
[a]S Ge 6:11
[b]S Nu 11:33;
S 1Ki 14:9;
Eze 16:26
8:18 [c]S Jer 44:6
[d]S Jer 13:14;
S Eze 5:11; 9:10;
24:14
[e]S 1Sa 8:18;
S Isa 58:4;
S Jer 11:11
9:2 [f]S Lev 16:4;
Eze 10:2;
Da 10:5; 12:6;
Rev 15:6
9:3 [g]S 1Sa 4:21;
Eze 10:4
[h]Eze 11:22
9:4 [i]Jer 25:29
[j]S Ge 4:15;
Ex 12:7;
2Co 1:22;
S Rev 7:3
[k]Ps 119:136;
Jer 7:29; 13:17;
Eze 21:6; Am 6:6
[l]Ps 119:53
9:5 [m]S Jer 13:14;
S Eze 5:11
[n]S Ex 32:27;
Isa 13:18
9:6 [o]Jer 7:32
[p]S Jer 16:6
[q]S Ge 4:15;
S Ex 12:7
[r]Eze 8:11-13,16

[s]S 2Ch 36:17; Jer 25:29; S Eze 6:4; 1Pe 4:17

8:5 *idol of jealousy.* See note on v. 3.
8:10 *all kinds of crawling things and detestable animals.* Probably reflecting Egyptian influence (see 2Ki 23:31–35).
8:11 *Jaazaniah.* Not the same person as in 11:1. Ironically, the name means "The LORD hears," and the irony is sharpened by the quotation in v. 12.
8:14 *Tammuz.* The only Biblical reference to this Babylonian fertility god. The women of Jerusalem were bewailing his dying, which they felt caused the annual wilting of vegetation. According to some interpreters, he is alluded to in Da 11:37 ("the one desired by women").
8:16 *With their backs toward the temple.* Almost all ancient temples were oriented toward the east. Worshiping the sun as it rose required one to turn his back to the temple.
8:17 *putting the branch to their nose.* A ceremonial gesture in nature worship, not documented elsewhere in the Bible.

9:1 *loud voice.* The thunderous voice of God (see Ex 19:19 and NIV text note; see also Ps 29).
9:2 *six men coming from the direction of the upper gate.* These six guardian angels of the city, plus the seventh clothed in linen (cf. the seven angels of the judgment in Rev 8:2,6), came from the place where the idol that provoked to jealousy stood (see 8:3 and note). *deadly weapon.* Probably a war club or a battle-ax.
9:3 *the glory . . . went up.* God began to vacate the temple, his glory moving to the door (see note on 8:1–11:25).
9:4 *mark.* A *taw,* the last letter of the Hebrew alphabet, which originally looked like an "x" (cf. Rev 7:2–4; 13:16; 14:9,11; 20:4; 22:4). *those who grieve and lament.* The remnant (see Ex 12:23; 1Ki 19:18).
9:6 *Begin at my sanctuary.* Judgment begins with God's people (see 1Pe 4:17).

⁷Then he said to them, "Defile the temple and fill the courts with the slain.ᵗ Go!" So they went out and began killing throughout the city. ⁸While they were killing and I was left alone, I fell facedown,ᵘ crying out, "Ah, Sovereign LORD!ᵛ Are you going to destroy the entire remnant of Israel in this outpouring of your wrathʷ on Jerusalem?ˣ"

⁹He answered me, "The sin of the house of Israel and Judah is exceedingly great; the land is full of bloodshed and the city is full of injustice.ʸ They say, 'The LORD has forsaken the land; the LORD does not see.'ᶻ ¹⁰So I will not look on them with pityᵃ or spare them, but I will bring down on their own heads what they have done.ᵇ"

¹¹Then the man in linen with the writing kit at his side brought back word, saying, "I have done as you commanded."

The Glory Departs From the Temple

10 I looked, and I saw the likeness of a throneᶜ of sapphire q ᵈ above the expanseᵉ that was over the heads of the cherubim.ᶠ ²The LORD said to the man clothed in linen,ᵍ "Go in among the wheelsʰ beneath the cherubim. Fillⁱ your hands with burning coalsʲ from among the cherubim and scatter them over the city." And as I watched, he went in.

³Now the cherubim were standing on the south side of the temple when the man went in, and a cloud filled the inner court. ⁴Then the glory of the LORDᵏ rose from above the cherubim and moved to the threshold of the temple. The cloud filled the temple, and the court was full of the radiance of the glory of the LORD. ⁵The sound of the wings of the cherubim could be heard as far away as the outer court, like the voiceˡ of God Almightyʳ when he speaks. ᵐ

⁶When the LORD commanded the man in linen, "Take fire from among the wheels,ⁿ from among the cherubim," the man went in and stood beside a wheel. ⁷Then one of the cherubim reached out his

hand to the fireᵒ that was among them. He took up some of it and put it into the hands of the man in linen, who took it and went out. ⁸(Under the wings of the cherubim could be seen what looked like the hands of a man.)ᵖ

⁹I looked, and I saw beside the cherubim four wheels, one beside each of the cherubim; the wheels sparkled like chrysolite. q ¹⁰As for their appearance, the four of them looked alike; each was like a wheel intersecting a wheel. ¹¹As they moved, they would go in any one of the four directions the cherubim faced; the wheels did not turn aboutˢ as the cherubim went. The cherubim went in whatever direction the head faced, without turning as they went. ¹²Their entire bodies, including their backs, their hands and their wings, were completely full of eyes,ʳ as were their four wheels. ˢ ¹³I heard the wheels being called "the whirling wheels." ¹⁴Each of the cherubimᵗ had four faces:ᵘ One face was that of a cherub, the second the face of a man, the third the face of a lion,ᵛ and the fourth the face of an eagle. ʷ

¹⁵Then the cherubim rose upward. These were the living creaturesˣ I had seen by the Kebar River.ʸ ¹⁶When the cherubim moved, the wheels beside them moved; and when the cherubim spread their wings to rise from the ground, the wheels did not leave their side. ¹⁷When the cherubim stood still, they also stood still; and when the cherubim rose, they rose with them, because the spirit of the living creatures was in them. ᶻ

¹⁸Then the gloryᵃ of the LORD departed from over the threshold of the temple and stopped above the cherubim. ᵇ ¹⁹While I watched, the cherubim spread their wings and rose from the ground, and as they went, the wheels went with them. ᶜ They stopped at the entrance to the east gate of the LORD's house, and the gloryᵈ of the God of Israel was above them.

9:7 ᵗEze 6:7
9:8 ᵘS Jos 7:6
ᵛS Eze 4:14
ʷS Eze 7:8
ˣEze 11:13;
Am 7:1-6
9:9 ʸS Ps 58:2;
Jer 12:1;
Eze 22:29;
Hab 1:4
ᶻS Job 22:13;
S Eze 8:12; 14:23
9:10 ᵃS Jer 13:14;
S Eze 8:18
ᵇS Isa 22:5;
S 65:6;
Eze 11:21; 23:49
10:1 ᶜS Rev 4:2
ᵈS Ex 24:10
ᵉEze 1:22
ᶠS Ge 3:24
10:2 ᵍS Eze 9:2
ʰS Eze 1:15
ⁱRev 8:5
ʲS 2Sa 22:9
10:4 ᵏS Ex 24:16;
Eze 9:3; 44:4
10:5 ˡS Job 40:9
ᵐS Eze 3:13
10:6 ⁿDa 7:9

10:7 ᵒS Eze 5:4
10:8 ᵖEze 1:8
10:9 ᵠS Ex 28:20;
Rev 21:20
10:12 ʳRev 4:6-8
ˢEze 1:15-21
10:14 ᵗ1Ki 7:36
ᵘEze 1:6
ᵛ1Ki 7:29
ʷEze 1:10;
41:19; Rev 4:7
10:15 ˣS Isa 6:2
ʸS Ps 137:1
10:17 ᶻS Eze 3:13
10:18 ᵃS 1Sa 4:21
ᵇS Ps 18:10
10:19 ᶜEze 11:1,
22 ᵈEze 43:4

q 1 Or *lapis lazuli*   r 5 Hebrew *El-Shaddai*   s 11 Or *aside*

9:8 *Ah, Sovereign LORD!* One of the few times Ezekiel questioned the Lord (see 4:14; 11:13).

10:1 *I looked.* Ch. 10 echoes ch. 1, underscoring the identity of what Ezekiel saw at the Kebar River with what he now sees in his vision (see 8:4). The creatures in ch. 1 are here called cherubim (see note on 1:5).

10:2 *burning coals.* While in 1:13 the living creatures looked like burning coals, here there are real coals. *scatter them over the city.* A judgment by fire (see Ge 19:24; Am 7:4).

10:7 *one of the cherubim reached out his hand.* Though

the "man clothed in linen" was initially commanded to get the coals himself (v. 2), he received them from the hand of one of the creatures (see 1:8). *who took it and went out.* No further report is given, but the destructive spreading of the coals over Jerusalem is assumed.

10:14 *One face was that of a cherub.* While the faces of the man, lion and eagle are identical with those in 1:10, the ox is here called a cherub (see note on Ge 3:24).

10:19 *to the east gate . . . and the glory of the God of Israel was above them.* A second movement of the glory, again in an easterly direction (see v. 4; 9:3; see also note on 8:1–11:25).

²⁰These were the living creatures I had seen beneath the God of Israel by the Kebar River, *e* and I realized that they were cherubim. ²¹Each had four faces *f* and four wings, *g* and under their wings was what looked like the hands of a man. ²²Their faces had the same appearance as those I had seen by the Kebar River. *h* Each one went straight ahead.

Judgment on Israel's Leaders

11 Then the Spirit lifted me up and brought me to the gate of the house of the LORD that faces east. There at the entrance to the gate were twenty-five men, and I saw among them Jaazaniah son of Azzur and Pelatiah *i* son of Benaiah, leaders *j* of the people. *k* ²The LORD said to me, "Son of man, these are the men who are plotting evil *l* and giving wicked advice in this city. *m* ³They say, 'Will it not soon be time to build houses? *t* This city is a cooking pot, *n* and we are the meat.' *o* ⁴Therefore prophesy *p* against them; prophesy, son of man."

⁵Then the Spirit of the LORD came upon me, and he told me to say: "This is what the LORD says: That is what you are saying, O house of Israel, but I know what is going through your mind. *q* ⁶You have killed many people in this city and filled its streets with the dead. *r*

⁷"Therefore this is what the Sovereign LORD says: The bodies you have thrown there are the meat and this city is the pot, *s* but I will drive you out of it. *t* ⁸You fear the sword, *u* and the sword is what I will bring against you, declares the Sovereign LORD. *v* ⁹I will drive you out of the city and hand you over *w* to foreigners and inflict punishment on you. *x* ¹⁰You will fall by the sword, and I will execute judgment on you at the borders of Israel. *y* Then you will know that I am the LORD. ¹¹This city will not be a pot *z* for you, nor will you be the meat in it; I will execute judgment on you at the borders of Israel. ¹²And you will

Cross references

10:20 *e* Eze 1:1
10:21 *f* Eze 41:18
g Eze 1:6
10:22 *h* Eze 1:1
11:1 *i* ver 13
j Jer 5:5
k S Eze 8:16;
S 10:19; 43:4-5
11:2 *l* S Isa 29:20;
Na 1:11
m Eze 8:11
11:3 *n* Jer 1:13;
Eze 24:3 *o* ver 7,
11; Eze 12:22,27;
Mic 3:3
11:4 *p* S Eze 3:4,
17
11:5 *q* S Ps 26:2;
S Jer 17:10
11:6 *r* S Eze 7:23;
22:6
11:7 *s* Jer 1:13
t ver 3;
Eze 24:3-13;
Mic 3:2-3
11:8
u S Lev 26:25;
S Jer 42:16
v S Pr 10:24;
Isa 66:4
11:9 *w* Ps 106:41
x Dt 28:36;
S Eze 5:8
11:10 *y* 2Ki 14:25
11:11 *z* ver 3;
Eze 24:6

11:12 *a* S Eze 6:7
b S Lev 18:4;
Eze 18:9
c Eze 8:10
11:13 *d* ver 1
e S Eze 9:8;
Am 7:2
11:15 *f* Eze 33:24
11:16 *g* Ps 31:20;
90:1; 91:9;
S Isa 4:6
11:17 *h* S Ne 1:9;
S Jer 3:18;
24:5-6; S 31:16;
Eze 20:41; 28:25;
34:13; 36:28
11:18 *i* S Eze 5:11
/Eze 37:23
11:19
k S 2Ch 30:12;
S Ps 86:11
l Zec 7:12; Ro 2:5
m Eze 18:31;
S 2Co 3:3
11:20 *n* S Ps 1:2
o S Jer 11:4; 32:38
p S Ex 6:7;
Eze 14:11; 34:30;
36:26-28;
Hos 1:9; Zec 8:8;
Heb 8:10
11:21 *q* Jer 16:18
r Jer 16:11;
S Eze 9:10; 16:43

know that I am the LORD, *a* for you have not followed my decrees *b* or kept my laws but have conformed to the standards of the nations around you. *c* "

¹³Now as I was prophesying, Pelatiah *d* son of Benaiah died. Then I fell facedown and cried out in a loud voice, "Ah, Sovereign LORD! Will you completely destroy the remnant of Israel? *e* "

¹⁴The word of the LORD came to me: ¹⁵"Son of man, your brothers—your brothers who are your blood relatives *u* and the whole house of Israel—are those of whom the people of Jerusalem have said, 'They are *v* far away from the LORD; this land was given to us as our possession.' *f*

Promised Return of Israel

¹⁶"Therefore say: 'This is what the Sovereign LORD says: Although I sent them far away among the nations and scattered them among the countries, yet for a little while I have been a sanctuary *g* for them in the countries where they have gone.'

¹⁷"Therefore say: 'This is what the Sovereign LORD says: I will gather you from the nations and bring you back from the countries where you have been scattered, and I will give you back the land of Israel again.' *h*

¹⁸"They will return to it and remove all its vile images *i* and detestable idols. *j* ¹⁹I will give them an undivided heart *k* and put a new spirit in them; I will remove from them their heart of stone *l* and give them a heart of flesh. *m* ²⁰Then they will follow my decrees *n* and be careful to keep my laws. *n* They will be my people, *o* and I will be their God. *p* ²¹But as for those whose hearts are devoted to their vile images and detestable idols, *q* I will bring down on their own heads what they have done, declares the Sovereign LORD. *r* "

t 3 Or *This is not the time to build houses.*   *u* 15 Or *are in exile with you* (see Septuagint and Syriac)
v 15 Or *those to whom the people of Jerusalem have said, 'Stay*

11:1 *Jaazaniah.* See note on 8:11. *Pelatiah.* Means "The LORD delivers."
11:3 *soon . . . time to build houses?* The residents of Jerusalem who were not exiled in 597 B.C. felt smugly secure, thinking that nothing worse would befall them. *cooking pot.* As in ch. 24, Jerusalem is compared to a cooking pot. Those left behind boasted that they were the "meat," the choice portions—the inference being that the exiles in Babylon were the discarded bones (see v. 15).
11:7 *The bodies you have thrown there are the meat.* The meat, redefined by the prophet, is not those in power in Jerusalem (who will be driven out) but the innocent people they killed.

11:11 *at the borders of Israel.* At Riblah (see 2Ki 25:20–21).
11:13 *Ah, Sovereign LORD!* See note on 9:8.
11:16 *I have been a sanctuary for them.* A key verse in Ezekiel. Although the exiles had been driven from Jerusalem and its sanctuary (the symbol of God's presence among his people), God himself became their sanctuary, i.e., he was present among them. Later Christ also became a substitute for the temple (see Jn 2:19–21).
11:19 *undivided heart . . . new spirit.* Inner spiritual and moral transformation that results in single-minded commitment to the Lord and to his will (see 36:26).
11:20 *They will be my people, and I will be their God.* The heart of God's covenant promise (see Ex 6:7).

²²Then the cherubim, with the wheels beside them, spread their wings, and the glory^s of the God of Israel was above them.^{t} ²³The glory^u of the LORD went up from within the city and stopped above the mountain^v east of it. ²⁴The Spirit^w lifted me up and brought me to the exiles in Babylonia^w in the vision^x given by the Spirit of God.

Then the vision I had seen went up from me, ²⁵and I told the exiles everything the LORD had shown me.^{y}

The Exile Symbolized

12 The word of the LORD came to me: ²"Son of man, you are living among a rebellious people.^{z} They have eyes to see but do not see and ears to hear but do not hear, for they are a rebellious people.^{a}

³"Therefore, son of man, pack your belongings for exile and in the daytime, as they watch, set out and go from where you are to another place. Perhaps^b they will understand,^{c} though they are a rebellious house.^{d} ⁴During the daytime, while they watch, bring out your belongings packed for exile. Then in the evening, while they are watching, go out like those who go into exile.^{e} ⁵While they watch, dig through the wall^f and take your belongings out through it. ⁶Put them on your shoulder as they are watching and carry them out at dusk. Cover your face so that you cannot see the land, for I have made you a sign^g to the house of Israel."

⁷So I did as I was commanded.^{h} During the day I brought out my things packed for exile. Then in the evening I dug through the wall with my hands. I took my belongings out at dusk, carrying them on my shoulders while they watched.

⁸In the morning the word of the LORD came to me: ⁹"Son of man, did not that rebellious house of Israel ask you, 'What are you doing?'^{i}

¹⁰"Say to them, 'This is what the Sovereign LORD says: This oracle concerns the prince in Jerusalem and the whole house of Israel who are there.' ¹¹Say to them, 'I am a sign^j to you.'

"As I have done, so it will be done to them. They will go into exile as captives.^{k}

¹²"The prince among them will put his things on his shoulder at dusk^l and leave, and a hole will be dug in the wall for him to go through. He will cover his face so that he cannot see the land.^{m} ¹³I will spread my net^n for him, and he will be caught in my snare;^{o} I will bring him to Babylonia, the land of the Chaldeans,^{p} but he will not see^q it, and there he will die.^{r} ¹⁴I will scatter to the winds all those around him—his staff and all his troops—and I will pursue them with drawn sword.^{s}

¹⁵"They will know that I am the LORD, when I disperse them among the nations^t and scatter them through the countries. ¹⁶But I will spare a few of them from the sword, famine and plague, so that in the nations where they go they may acknowledge all their detestable practices. Then they will know that I am the LORD.^{u}"

¹⁷The word of the LORD came to me: ¹⁸"Son of man, tremble as you eat your food,^{v} and shudder in fear as you drink your water. ¹⁹Say to the people of the land: 'This is what the Sovereign LORD says about those living in Jerusalem and in the land of Israel: They will eat their food in anxiety and drink their water in despair, for their land will be stripped of everything^w in it because of the violence of all who live there.^{x} ²⁰The inhabited towns will be laid waste and the land will be desolate. Then you will know that I am the LORD.^{y}'"

²¹The word of the LORD came to me: ²²"Son of man, what is this proverb^z you have in the land of Israel: 'The days go by

^{w}24 Or *Chaldea*

11:22
s S Ex 24:16
t Eze 9:3; S 10:19
11:23 u Eze 1:28;
S 10:4 v Zec 14:4
11:24 w Eze 37:1;
43:5 x 2Co 12:2-4
11:25 y S Eze 3:4,
11
12:2 z Ps 78:40;
S Jer 42:21
a S Isa 6:10;
S Mt 13:15;
Mk 4:12; 8:18
12:3 b S Jer 36:3
c Jer 26:3 d ver 11;
S Eze 3:27;
2Ti 2:25-26
12:4 e ver 12;
2Ki 25:4;
S Jer 39:4
12:5 f Jer 52:7;
Am 4:3
12:7 h Eze 24:18;
37:10
12:9 i Eze 17:12;
20:49; 24:19

12:11 j Isa 8:18;
Zec 3:8
k S 2Ki 25:7;
S Jer 15:2; 52:15
12:12 l S Jer 39:4
m Jer 52:7
12:13
n Eze 17:20; 19:8;
32:3; Hos 7:12
o S Isa 24:17-18
p Eze 1:3
q S Jer 39:7
r S Jer 24:8;
S 52:11;
S La 4:20;
Eze 17:16
12:14
s S 2Ki 25:5;
S Jer 21:7;
S Eze 5:10,12;
17:21
12:15
t S Lev 26:33
12:16
u S Jer 22:8-9;
Eze 6:8-10;
14:22; 36:20
12:18 v La 5:9
12:19
w Jer 10:22;
S Eze 6:6-14;
Mic 7:13;
Zec 7:14
x S Eze 4:16;
23:33
12:20
y Isa 7:23-24;
S Jer 4:7; S 25:9
12:22 z S Ps 49:4

11:23 *The glory of the LORD went up.* The final eastward movement of the glory (as the Lord left his temple), which stopped above the Mount of Olives (see 9:3; 10:4,19; see also note on 8:1–11:25).
11:24 See note on 8:3.
12:2 *eyes to see but do not see.* The hardening about which the Lord had spoken to Isaiah (Isa 6:9–10).
12:3 *pack your belongings.* Another symbolic act, which, like those in chs. 4–5, follows a vision. *Perhaps they will understand.* Some hope remained that they would change.
12:5 *dig through the wall.* Not the city wall, which was made of stone and was many feet thick, but the sun-dried brick wall of his house.
12:6 *sign.* Prophets were often instructed to perform symbolic acts (see, e.g., v. 11; 24:24,27).

12:8 *In the morning.* After Ezekiel "did as . . . commanded" (v. 7). Again the divine explanation follows the prophet's unquestioning obedience (see note on 8:3).
12:9 *What are you doing?* The book's first indication of the people's response to the prophet's symbolic acts.
12:10 *prince in Jerusalem.* Zedekiah (see note on 7:27).
12:13 *he will not see it.* Nebuchadnezzar's men would put out Zedekiah's eyes (see 2Ki 25:7).
12:18 *tremble as you eat.* Another prophetic symbol. Ezekiel's trembling must have been particularly violent, because the Hebrew word for "tremble" is used elsewhere to describe an earthquake (see Am 1:1; 1Ki 19:11).
12:19 *people of the land.* See note on 7:27.
12:22 *proverb.* A mocking proverb (probably coined by false prophets; see ch. 13; Jer 23:9–40; 28), which had

and every vision comes to nothing'?[a] ²³Say to them, 'This is what the Sovereign LORD says: I am going to put an end to this proverb, and they will no longer quote it in Israel.' Say to them, 'The days are near[b] when every vision will be fulfilled.[c] ²⁴For there will be no more false visions or flattering divinations[d] among the people of Israel. ²⁵But I the LORD will speak what I will, and it shall be fulfilled without delay.[e] For in your days, you rebellious house, I will fulfill[f] whatever I say, declares the Sovereign LORD.[g]' "

²⁶The word of the LORD came to me: ²⁷"Son of man, the house of Israel is saying, 'The vision he sees is for many years from now, and he prophesies about the distant future.'[h]

²⁸"Therefore say to them, 'This is what the Sovereign LORD says: None of my words will be delayed any longer; whatever I say will be fulfilled, declares the Sovereign LORD.'"

False Prophets Condemned

13 The word of the LORD came to me: ²"Son of man, prophesy against the prophets[i] of Israel who are now prophesying. Say to those who prophesy out of their own imagination:[j] 'Hear the word of the LORD![k] ³This is what the Sovereign LORD says: Woe to the foolish[x] prophets[l] who follow their own spirit and have seen nothing![m] ⁴Your prophets, O Israel, are like jackals among ruins. ⁵You have not gone up to the breaks in the wall to repair[n] it for the house of Israel so that it will stand firm in the battle on the day of the LORD.[o] ⁶Their visions are false[p] and their divinations a lie. They say, "The LORD declares," when the LORD has not sent[q] them; yet they expect their words to be fulfilled.[r] ⁷Have you not seen false visions[s] and ut-

tered lying divinations when you say, "The LORD declares," though I have not spoken?

⁸" 'Therefore this is what the Sovereign LORD says: Because of your false words and lying visions, I am against you,[t] declares the Sovereign LORD. ⁹My hand will be against the prophets who see false visions and utter lying[u] divinations. They will not belong to the council of my people or be listed in the records[v] of the house of Israel, nor will they enter the land of Israel. Then you will know that I am the Sovereign LORD.[w]

¹⁰" 'Because they lead my people astray,[x] saying, "Peace,"[y] when there is no peace, and because, when a flimsy wall is built, they cover it with whitewash,[z] ¹¹therefore tell those who cover it with whitewash that it is going to fall. Rain will come in torrents, and I will send hailstones[a] hurtling down,[b] and violent winds will burst forth.[c] ¹²When the wall collapses, will people not ask you, "Where is the whitewash you covered it with?"

¹³" 'Therefore this is what the Sovereign LORD says: In my wrath I will unleash a violent wind, and in my anger hailstones[d] and torrents of rain[e] will fall with destructive fury.[f] ¹⁴I will tear down the wall[g] you have covered with whitewash and will level it to the ground so that its foundation[h] will be laid bare. When it[y] falls,[i] you will be destroyed in it; and you will know that I am the LORD. ¹⁵So I will spend my wrath against the wall and against those who covered it with whitewash. I will say to you, "The wall is gone and so are those who whitewashed it, ¹⁶those prophets of Israel who prophesied to Jerusalem and saw visions of peace for her

Cross-references (center column)

12:22
[a]S Isa 5:19;
Eze 11:3;
Am 6:3; 2Pe 3:4
12:23 [b]S Eze 7:7
[c]S Ps 37:13;
Eze 18:3;
Joel 2:1; Zep 1:14
12:24 [d]Jer 14:14;
Eze 13:23;
Mic 3:6;
Zec 13:2-4
12:25 [e]Hab 2:3
[f]S Nu 11:23;
Eze 13:6
[g]Nu 14:28-34;
S Isa 14:24;
S 55:11; Jer 16:9;
Hab 1:5
12:27
[h]S Eze 11:3;
Da 10:14;
Mt 24:48-50;
2Pe 3:4
13:2 [i]S Isa 9:15
[j]Jer 23:26 [k]ver 17; S Jer 23:16;
S 37:19;
Eze 22:28
13:3 [l]S La 2:14;
Hos 9:7
[m]S Jer 23:25-32
13:5 [n]Isa 58:12;
Eze 22:30
[o]S Eze 7:19; 30:3
13:6 [p]S Jer 5:1;
23:16
[q]S Jer 14:14
[r]S Jer 28:15;
S 29:9;
Eze 12:24-25;
22:28
13:7 [s]S Isa 30:10

13:8 [t]S Jer 21:13
13:9 [u]S Dt 13:3
[v]S Ex 32:32;
S Jer 17:13
[w]S Ex 6:2;
Jer 20:3-6;
Eze 20:38
13:10
[x]S Jer 23:13;
S 50:6 [y]S Jer 4:10
[z]S Eze 7:25;
22:28
13:11
[a]S Jos 10:11
[b]S Job 38:23
[c]Ps 11:6;
Eze 38:22
13:13
[d]S Jos 10:11;
Rev 11:19; 16:21
[e]Job 14:19
[f]S Ex 9:25;
S Job 38:23;
Isa 30:30

13:14 [g]S Isa 22:5 [h]Mic 1:6 [i]Jer 6:15

[x]3 Or *wicked*   [y]14 Or *the city*

Study notes (bottom)

become a popular saying. *vision.* The Hebrew for this word is not the same as that used in 1:1 but is the one used in 7:26, referring to a message that could be written down (see Hab 2:2, "revelation")—specifically Ezekiel's oracles of judgment.

12:23 *every vision will be fulfilled.* Divine affirmation of the true prophetic word (cf. Isa 55:11).

12:27 *many years from now.* Whereas the first proverb denies that Ezekiel's words would ever be fulfilled, this one allows that they might be fulfilled in the distant future, beyond the concern of the present generation.

13:2 *out of their own imagination.* Cf. Jer 23:21–22.

13:3 *have seen nothing.* No revelation from God was received.

13:4 *jackals.* Animals that travel in packs and feed on dead flesh—a powerfully negative image (see Ps 63:10; La 5:18).

13:5 *You have not gone up.* The function of true prophets is described (cf. 22:30; Ps 106:23). *day of the LORD.* See note on 7:7.

13:6 *Their visions are false.* Whether the false prophets had actual visions is unknown, but they claimed to have received revelations from God when in reality their messages only proclaimed what their hearers wanted to hear (see Isa 30:10; Jer 23:9–17; 2Ti 4:3).

13:8 *I am against you.* See 5:8 and note.

13:9 *They will not belong.* A threefold punishment, resulting in total exclusion from the community.

13:10 *"Peace," when there is no peace.* See v. 16; Jer 6:14; 8:11. *whitewash.* The Hebrew for this word is used only by Ezekiel (see 22:28). A similar-sounding Hebrew word means "unsatisfying things," and Ezekiel may have chosen the word he did because of its similarity to the other one.

13:11 *Rain will come in torrents.* The violent thunderstorm of God's judgment (imagery frequently used in the OT) was about to sweep them away (see, e.g., Ps 18:7–15; 77:17–18; 83:15; Isa 28:17; 30:30; Jer 23:19; 30:23).

when there was no peace, declares the Sovereign Lord.*'"'

¹⁷"Now, son of man, set your face* against the daughters* of your people who prophesy out of their own imagination. Prophesy against them *m* ¹⁸and say, 'This is what the Sovereign Lord says: Woe to the women who sew magic charms on all their wrists and make veils of various lengths for their heads in order to ensnare people. Will you ensnare the lives of my people but preserve your own? ¹⁹You have profaned* me among my people for a few handfuls of barley and scraps of bread.* By lying to my people, who listen to lies, you have killed those who should not have died and have spared those who should not live.*

²⁰"'Therefore this is what the Sovereign Lord says: I am against your magic charms with which you ensnare people like birds and I will tear them from your arms; I will set free the people that you ensnare like birds.* ²¹I will tear off your veils and save my people from your hands, and they will no longer fall prey to your power. Then you will know that I am the Lord.* ²²Because you disheartened the righteous with your lies,* when I had brought them no grief, and because you encouraged the wicked not to turn from their evil ways and so save their lives,* ²³therefore you will no longer see false visions* or practice divination.* I will save* my people from your hands. And then you will know that I am the Lord.*'"

Idolaters Condemned

14 Some of the elders of Israel came to me and sat down in front of me.* ²Then the word of the Lord came to me: ³"Son of man, these men have set up idols in their hearts* and put wicked stumbling blocks* before their faces. Should I let them inquire of me at all?* ⁴Therefore speak to them and tell them, 'This is what

the Sovereign Lord says: When any Israelite sets up idols in his heart and puts a wicked stumbling block before his face and then goes to a prophet, I the Lord will answer him myself in keeping with his great idolatry. ⁵I will do this to recapture the hearts of the people of Israel, who have all deserted* me for their idols.'*

⁶"Therefore say to the house of Israel, 'This is what the Sovereign Lord says: Repent!* Turn from your idols and renounce all your detestable practices!*

⁷"'When any Israelite or any alien* living in Israel separates himself from me and sets up idols in his heart and puts a wicked stumbling block* before his face and then goes to a prophet to inquire* of me, I the Lord will answer him myself. ⁸I will set my face against* that man and make him an example* and a byword.* I will cut him off from my people. Then you will know that I am the Lord.*

⁹"'And if the prophet* is enticed* to utter a prophecy, I the Lord have enticed that prophet, and I will stretch out my hand against him and destroy him from among my people Israel.* ¹⁰They will bear their guilt—the prophet will be as guilty as the one who consults him. ¹¹Then the people of Israel will no longer stray* from me, nor will they defile themselves anymore with all their sins. They will be my people,* and I will be their God, declares the Sovereign Lord.*'"

Judgment Inescapable

¹²The word of the Lord came to me: ¹³"Son of man, if a country sins* against me by being unfaithful and I stretch out my hand against it to cut off its food supply* and send famine upon it and kill its men and their animals,* ¹⁴even if these three men—Noah,* Daniel*ˣ and

---

Cross references (center column):

13:16
l S Isa 57:21;
Jer 6:14;
S Eze 7:25
13:17 *k* S Eze 4:7;
25:2; 28:21
l S Ex 15:20;
Rev 2:20 *m* S ver 2
13:19 *n* Jer 44:26;
Eze 20:39; 22:26;
36:20; 39:7
o S Isa 56:11
p Pr 28:21;
Mic 3:11
13:20 *q* Ps 124:7
13:21 *r* Ps 91:3
13:22 *s* S Isa 9:15
t Jer 23:14;
Eze 18:21;
33:14-16
13:23 *u* Ne 6:12
v S Eze 12:24
w S Ps 72:14
x Mic 3:6
14:1 *y* S Eze 8:1;
20:1
14:3 *z* S Eze 6:4
a S ver 7;
S Eze 7:19
b Isa 1:15;
Eze 20:31

14:5 *c* S Dt 32:15;
Eze 16:45;
Hos 5:7; Zec 11:8
d Jer 2:11
14:6 *e* Ne 1:9;
S Jer 3:12;
S 35:15
f S Isa 2:20;
S 30:22
14:7 *g* Ex 12:48;
20:10 *h* ver 3;
S Isa 8:14;
Hos 4:5; 5:5
i S Ge 25:22
14:8 *j* Eze 15:7
k S Nu 16:38
l S Ps 102:8;
S Eze 5:15
m S Jer 42:20
14:9 *n* S Jer 14:15
o Isa 63:17;
Jer 4:10
p 1Ki 22:23;
S 2Ch 18:22;
Zec 13:3
14:11 *q* Eze 48:11
r S Isa 51:16
s S Eze 11:19-20;
37:23
14:13 *t* S Pr 13:21
u S Lev 26:26
v S Eze 5:16;
6:14; 15:8
14:14 *w* Ge 6:8
x ver 20;
Eze 28:3; Da 1:6;
6:13

ˣ14 Or Danel; the Hebrew spelling may suggest a person other than the prophet Daniel; also in verse 20.

13:18 *magic charms.* Exactly what the women were doing is not known, but that it was some kind of black magic or voodoo is clear. The Bible consistently avoids explicit description of occult practices.
13:19 *for a few handfuls of barley.* Involvement in religious matters of any kind for mere gain is consistently condemned in the Bible (see, e.g., Jer 6:13; 8:10; Mic 3:5,11; Ac 8:9–24; Tit 1:11). For the proper attitude and motivation see 2Co 11:7; 2Th 3:8; 1Ti 3:3. *you have killed.* The women have used their evil powers to unjust ends, involving even matters of life and death.
14:1 *elders of Israel.* Apparently interchangeable with "elders of Judah" (see note on 8:1).
14:3 *idols.* See note on 6:4. *inquire.* A technical term for seeking an oracle from a prophet (see 2Ki 1:16; 3:11; 8:8).
14:4 *I the Lord will answer him myself.* The punishment

for idolatry was death (Dt 13:6–18).
14:6 *Repent!* First of three calls for repentance from Ezekiel, who elsewhere proclaims inescapable judgment (see 18:30; 33:11).
14:9 *enticed.* Related to the divine hardening (3:20; cf. 1Ki 22:19–23).
14:14,20 *Noah, Daniel and Job.* Three ancient men of renown, selected because of their proverbial righteousness. As the NIV text note indicates, another Daniel may be referred to (Ugaritic literature speaks of an honored "Danel"; see chart on "Ancient Texts Relating to the OT," p. 5), since the Biblical Daniel's righteousness probably had not become proverbial so soon (Daniel and Ezekiel were contemporaries; see Da 1:1). If the Biblical Daniel is meant, what he shared in common with Noah and Job was not only righteousness but also deliverance (part of Ezekiel's emphasis).

Job[y]—were in it, they could save only themselves by their righteousness,[z] declares the Sovereign LORD.

15"Or if I send wild beasts[a] through that country and they leave it childless and it becomes desolate so that no one can pass through it because of the beasts,[b] 16as surely as I live, declares the Sovereign LORD, even if these three men were in it, they could not save their own sons or daughters. They alone would be saved, but the land would be desolate.[c]

17"Or if I bring a sword[d] against that country and say, 'Let the sword pass throughout the land,' and I kill its men and their animals,[e] 18as surely as I live, declares the Sovereign LORD, even if these three men were in it, they could not save their own sons or daughters. They alone would be saved.

19"Or if I send a plague into that land and pour out my wrath[f] upon it through bloodshed,[g] killing its men and their animals,[h] 20as surely as I live, declares the Sovereign LORD, even if Noah, Daniel and Job were in it, they could save neither son nor daughter. They would save only themselves by their righteousness.[i]

21"For this is what the Sovereign LORD says: How much worse will it be when I send against Jerusalem my four dreadful judgments[j]—sword[k] and famine[l] and wild beasts and plague[m]—to kill its men and their animals![n] 22Yet there will be some survivors[o]—sons and daughters who will be brought out of it.[p] They will come to you, and when you see their conduct[q] and their actions, you will be consoled[r] regarding the disaster I have brought upon Jerusalem—every disaster I have brought upon it. 23You will be consoled when you see their conduct and their

actions, for you will know that I have done nothing in it without cause, declares the Sovereign LORD.[s]"

Jerusalem, A Useless Vine

15 The word of the LORD came to me: 2"Son of man, how is the wood of a vine[t] better than that of a branch on any of the trees in the forest? 3Is wood ever taken from it to make anything useful?[u] Do they make pegs[v] from it to hang things on? 4And after it is thrown on the fire as fuel and the fire burns both ends and chars the middle, is it then useful for anything?[w] 5If it was not useful for anything when it was whole, how much less can it be made into something useful when the fire has burned it and it is charred?

6"Therefore this is what the Sovereign LORD says: As I have given the wood of the vine among the trees of the forest as fuel for the fire, so will I treat the people living in Jerusalem. 7I will set my face against[x] them. Although they have come out of the fire[y][z], the fire will yet consume them. And when I set my face against them, you will know that I am the LORD.[a] 8I will make the land desolate[b] because they have been unfaithful,[c] declares the Sovereign LORD."

An Allegory of Unfaithful Jerusalem

16 The word of the LORD came to me: 2"Son of man, confront[d] Jerusalem with her detestable practices[e] 3and say, 'This is what the Sovereign LORD says to Jerusalem: Your ancestry[f] and birth were in the land of the Canaanites; your father[g] was an Amorite[h] and your mother a Hittite.[i] 4On the day you were born[j] your

Cross references (center column)

14:14 [y]S Job 1:1
[z]S Ge 6:9;
S Job 42:9;
Jer 15:1;
S Eze 3:19; 18:20
14:15 [a]Eze 5:17
[b]S Lev 26:22
14:16 [c]S Ge 19:29;
Eze 18:20
14:17 [d]S Lev 26:25;
S Jer 25:27;
S 42:16
[e]Eze 25:13;
Zep 1:3
14:19 [f]S Eze 7:8
[g]S Isa 34:3
[h]Jer 14:12;
Eze 38:22
14:20 [i]S ver 14
14:21 [j]S Nu 33:4
[k]Isa 31:8; 34:6;
66:16; Eze 21:3,
19 [l]S 2Sa 24:13
[m]S Jer 14:12;
27:8 [n]S Jer 15:3;
S Eze 5:17;
33:27;
Am 4:6-10;
Rev 6:8
14:22 [o]S Jer 41:16
[p]S Eze 12:16
[q]Eze 20:43
[r]Eze 31:16;
32:31
14:23 [s]S Jer 22:8-9;
Eze 8:6-18; S 9:9
15:2 [t]Ps 80:8-16;
Isa 5:1-7; 27:2-6;
Jer 2:21;
Hos 10:1;
S Jn 15:2
15:3 [u]Jer 13:10
[v]S Isa 22:23
15:4 [w]Eze 17:3-10;
19:14; Jn 15:6
15:7 [x]S Lev 26:17;
Ps 34:16;
Eze 14:8
[y]S Eze 5:2
[z]S Eze 5:4
[a]Isa 24:18;
Am 9:1-4
15:8 [b]S Eze 14:13
[c]Eze 17:20;
18:24
16:2 [d]S Isa 57:12;
Eze 23:36
[e]Eze 8:17; 20:4;

22:2 16:3 [f]Ge 11:25-29; Eze 21:30 [g]S Ge 12:18 [h]S Ge 15:16
[i]ver 45; S Ge 10:15; S Dt 7:1; Jos 24:14-15 16:4 [j]Hos 2:3

14:20 *neither son nor daughter.* When God comes in judgment against a nation or people, no one can count on another's righteousness—not even that of his parents—to deliver him.

14:21 *my four dreadful judgments.* See note on 1:5. *sword and famine and wild beasts and plague.* Cf. the "four horsemen of the Apocalypse" (see Rev 6:1–8, and especially Rev 6:8).

14:23 *You.* Plural; i.e., the exiles in Babylon. *will be consoled.* When the exiles see the wickedness of those brought to Babylon from Jerusalem, they will know that God's judgment on the city was just.

15:2 *vine.* For Israel as a vine see Ps 80:8–13; cf. Lk 20:9–19; Jn 15:1–17.

15:3 *Do they make pegs from it to hang things on?* See Isa 22:23–25.

15:4 *is it then useful for anything?* Whereas Isaiah (5:1–7) and Jeremiah (2:21) express divine disappointment over Israel's failure to produce good fruit, Ezekiel typically laments her total uselessness.

15:7 *Although they have come out of the fire.* A reference to the siege of Jerusalem in 597 B.C., which resulted in the exile of which Ezekiel was a part (see 1:2; 2Ki 24:10–16). *fire will yet consume them.* Prophecy threatening another and more devastating siege—Ezekiel's main message before 586 (see 5:2,4; 10:2,7).

16:3 Cf. Dt 26:5. *Your ancestry and birth.* Jerusalem had a centuries-old, pre-Israelite history (Ge 14:18), and the city long resisted Israelite conquest (Jos 15:63). It became fully Israelite only after David's conquest (2Sa 5:6–9). *father . . . mother.* A reference to Jerusalem's non-Israelite origin generally, not to any specific individuals. *Amorite.* Cf. v. 45. Like the Canaanites, the Amorites were pre-Israelite, Semitic inhabitants of Palestine (Ge 48:22; Jos 5:1; 10:5; Jdg 1:34–36). *Hittite.* The Hittites were non-Semitic residents of Canaan, who earlier had flourished in Asia Minor during the second millennium B.C. (see Ge 23:10–20; 26:34; 1Sa 26:6; 2Sa 11:2–27; 1Ki 11:1).

16:4 *rubbed with salt.* This practice has been observed among Palestinian Arab peasants as late as A.D. 1918.

cord was not cut, nor were you washed with water to make you clean, nor were you rubbed with salt or wrapped in cloths. [5]No one looked on you with pity or had compassion enough to do any of these things for you. Rather, you were thrown out into the open field, for on the day you were born you were despised.

[6]" 'Then I passed by and saw you kicking about in your blood, and as you lay there in your blood I said to you, "Live!"[a][k] [7]I made you grow[l] like a plant of the field. You grew up and developed and became the most beautiful of jewels.[b] Your breasts were formed and your hair grew, you who were naked and bare.[m]

[8]" 'Later I passed by, and when I looked at you and saw that you were old enough for love, I spread the corner of my garment[n] over you and covered your nakedness. I gave you my solemn oath and entered into a covenant[o] with you, declares the Sovereign Lord,[p] and you became mine.[p]

[9]" 'I bathed[c] you with water and washed[q] the blood from you and put ointments on you. [10]I clothed you with an embroidered[r] dress and put leather sandals on you. I dressed you in fine linen[s] and covered you with costly garments.[t] [11]I adorned you with jewelry:[u] I put bracelets[v] on your arms and a necklace[w] around your neck, [12]and I put a ring on your nose,[x] earrings[y] on your ears and a beautiful crown[z] on your head.[a] [13]So you were adorned with gold and silver; your clothes[b] were of fine linen and costly fabric and embroidered cloth. Your food was fine flour, honey and olive oil.[c] You became very beautiful and rose to be a queen.[d] [14]And your fame[e] spread among the nations on account of your beauty,[f] because the splendor I had given you made your beauty perfect, declares the Sovereign Lord.[g]

[15]" 'But you trusted in your beauty and used your fame to become a prostitute. You lavished your favors on anyone who passed by[h] and your beauty became his.[d][i] [16]You took some of your garments to make gaudy high places,[j] where you carried on your prostitution.[k] Such things should not happen, nor should they ever occur. [17]You also took the fine jewelry I gave you, the jewelry made of my gold and silver, and you made for yourself male idols and engaged in prostitution with them.[l] [18]And you took your embroidered clothes to put on them, and you offered my oil and incense[m] before them. [19]Also the food I provided for you—the fine flour, olive oil and honey I gave you to eat—you offered as fragrant incense before them. That is what happened, declares the Sovereign Lord.[n]

[20]" 'And you took your sons and daughters[o] whom you bore to me[p] and sacrificed them as food to the idols. Was your

---

16:6 [k]ver 22; S Ex 19:4; Eze 18:23,32
16:7 [l]S Dt 1:10 [m]S Ex 1:7
16:8 [n]Ru 3:9 [over 59]; S Jer 11:10; Mal 2:14 [p]Jer 2:2; Hos 2:7, 19-20
16:9 [q]S Ru 3:3
16:10 [r]S Ex 26:36; S Isa 19:9 [s]Eze 27:16 [t]ver 18; S Isa 3:23
16:11 [u]S Jer 4:30; Eze 23:40 [v]Isa 3:19; Eze 23:42 [w]S Ge 41:42; S Ps 73:6
16:12 [x]Isa 3:21 [y]S Ge 35:4 [z]S Isa 28:5; S Jer 13:18 [a]Pr 1:9; S Isa 3:19
16:13 [b]Est 5:1

16:13 [c]1Sa 10:1 [d]Dt 32:13-14; S 1Ki 4:21; S Est 2:9,17
16:14 [e]1Ki 10:24 [f]S Est 1:11; S Ps 48:2; S La 2:15 [g]S Eze 5:5
16:15 [h]ver 25 [i]S Isa 57:8; S Jer 2:20; Eze 23:3; 27:3
16:16 [j]S Isa 57:7 [k]S 2Ki 23:7
16:17 [l]S Eze 7:20; Hos 2:13
16:18 [m]S Jer 44:5
16:19 [n]Hos 2:8
16:20 [o]S Jer 7:31 [p]Ex 13:2

[a]6 A few Hebrew manuscripts, Septuagint and Syriac; most Hebrew manuscripts *"Live!" And as you lay there in your blood I said to you, "Live!"* [b]7 Or *became mature* [c]9 Or *I had bathed* [d]15 Most Hebrew manuscripts; one Hebrew manuscript (see some Septuagint manuscripts) *by. Such a thing should not happen*

---

wrapped in cloths. Cf. Lk 2:7.
16:5 *thrown out into the open field.* Abandoned to die. Exposure of infants, common in ancient pagan societies, was abhorrent to Israel.
16:6 *blood. Of childbirth. Live!* God's basic desire for all people, summed up in one word (see 18:23,32; 1Ti 2:4; 2Pe 3:9).
16:7 *hair.* Pubic hair (see Isa 7:20).
16:8 *spread the corner of my garment.* Symbolic of entering a marriage relationship (see notes on Dt 22:30; Ru 3:9). *covenant.* Since the maiden symbolizes Jerusalem, this does not refer to the Sinai covenant but to marriage as a covenant (see Mal 2:14).
16:9 *blood.* Menstrual blood, indicating sexual maturity (see NIV text note on v. 7).
16:10 *embroidered dress ... leather sandals ... fine linen.* Representative of the very best garments. *embroidered dress.* See 27:16,24; colored, variegated material fit for a queen (see Ps 45:14). *leather sandals.* The same kind of leather was used to cover the tabernacle ("hides of sea cows," Ex 25:5; 26:14).
16:11 *bracelets on your arms.* See Ge 24:22.
16:12 *ring.* Not piercing the nose but worn on the outer part of the nose (see Ge 24:47). *earrings.* Circular ear ornaments, worn by men (Nu 31:50). The Hebrew for this word is not the same as that used in Ge 35:4; Ex 32:2–3. *crown.*

The wedding crown (see SS 3:11, where the groom wears it).
16:13 *gold and silver.* Cf. Hos 2:8. *fine flour.* Used in offerings, therefore of high quality (see v. 19; 46:14). *olive oil.* Cf. Hos 2:8. For the combination of honey and oil see Dt 32:13. *You became very beautiful.* Cf. Eph 5:27.
16:14 *your fame spread.* Especially in the time of David and Solomon.
16:15 *prostitute.* The accusation of prostitution referred both to spiritual turning away from the Lord and to physical involvement with the fertility rites of Canaanite paganism (cf. Jer 3:1–5; Hos 4:13–14; 9:1). *favors.* Sexual favors. Verb and noun forms of the Hebrew for this word occur 23 times in this chapter. *anyone who passed by.* Cf. Ge 38:14–16.
16:16 *garments.* All of the Lord's previous gifts were used by Jerusalem in prostituting herself. Cloths of some kind were needed in the Asherah cult practices (see 2Ki 23:7). They may have been used as curtains or as bedding (see Am 2:7–8).
16:17 *male idols.* Phallic symbols or pictures of naked men (see 23:14).
16:20 *sons and daughters ... sacrificed.* See 20:26,31; 23:37; 2Ki 21:6; 23:10; Jer 7:31; 19:5; 32:35. Laws against child sacrifice are recorded in Lev 18:21; 20:2; Dt 12:31; 18:10.

prostitution not enough? [q] 21You slaughtered my children and sacrificed them [e] to the idols. [r] 22In all your detestable practices and your prostitution you did not remember the days of your youth, [s] when you were naked and bare, [t] kicking about in your blood. [u]

23" 'Woe! [v] Woe to you, declares the Sovereign LORD. In addition to all your other wickedness, 24you built a mound for yourself and made a lofty shrine [w] in every public square. [x] 25At the head of every street [y] you built your lofty shrines and degraded your beauty, offering your body with increasing promiscuity to anyone who passed by. [z] 26You engaged in prostitution [a] with the Egyptians, [b] your lustful neighbors, and provoked [c] me to anger with your increasing promiscuity. [d] 27So I stretched out my hand [e] against you and reduced your territory; I gave you over [f] to the greed of your enemies, the daughters of the Philistines, [g] who were shocked by your lewd conduct. 28You engaged in prostitution with the Assyrians [h] too, because you were insatiable; and even after that, you still were not satisfied. [i] 29Then you increased your promiscuity to include Babylonia, [f][j] a land of merchants, but even with this you were not satisfied. [k]

30" 'How weak-willed you are, declares the Sovereign LORD, when you do all these things, acting like a brazen prostitute! [l] 31When you built your mounds at the head of every street and made your lofty shrines [m] in every public square, you were unlike a prostitute, because you scorned payment.

32" 'You adulterous wife! You prefer strangers to your own husband! 33Every prostitute receives a fee, [n] but you give gifts [o] to all your lovers, bribing them to come to you from everywhere for your illicit favors. [p] 34So in your prostitution you are the opposite of others; no one runs after you for your favors. You are the very opposite, for you give payment and none is given to you.

35" 'Therefore, you prostitute, hear the word of the LORD! 36This is what the Sovereign LORD says: Because you poured out your wealth [g] and exposed your nakedness in your promiscuity with your lovers, and because of all your detestable idols, and because you gave them your children's blood, [q] 37therefore I am going to gather all your lovers, with whom you found pleasure, those you loved as well as those you hated. I will gather them against you from all around and will strip [r] you in front of them, and they will see all your nakedness. [s] 38I will sentence you to the punishment of women who commit adultery and who shed blood; [t] I will bring upon you the blood vengeance of my wrath and jealous anger. [u] 39Then I will hand you over [v] to your lovers, and they will tear down your mounds and destroy your lofty shrines. They will strip you of your clothes and take your fine jewelry and leave you naked and bare. [w] 40They will bring a mob against you, who will stone [x] you and hack you to pieces with their swords. 41They will burn down [y] your houses and inflict punishment on you in the sight of many women. [z] I will put a stop [a] to your prostitution, and you will no longer pay your lovers. 42Then my wrath against you will subside and my jealous anger will turn away from you; I will be calm and no longer angry. [b]

43" 'Because you did not remember [c] the days of your youth but enraged me with all these things, I will surely bring down [d] on your head what you have done, declares the Sovereign LORD. Did you not add lewdness to all your other detestable practices? [e]

44" 'Everyone who quotes proverbs [f]

16:20
qPs 106:37-38;
S Isa 57:5;
Eze 23:37
16:21
rS 2Ki 17:17;
S Jer 19:5
16:22 sS Ps 25:7;
S 88:15; Jer 2:2;
Hos 2:15; 11:1
tHos 2:3 uver 6
16:23 vEze 24:6
16:24 wver 31;
Isa 57:7
xPs 78:58;
S Jer 2:20; 3:2;
S 44:21;
Eze 20:28
16:25 yS Jer 3:2
zver 15; S Pr 9:14
16:26
aS Isa 23:17
bS Jer 3:1;
cS 1Ki 14:9;
S Eze 8:17
dS Isa 57:8;
Jer 11:15;
Eze 20:8;
23:19-21
16:27
eEze 20:33;
25:13 /S Jer 34:20
gS 2Ch 28:18
16:28
hS 2Ki 16:7
iIsa 57:8
16:29 /S Jer 3:1;
Eze 23:14-17
kNa 3:16
16:30 /S Jer 3:3
16:31 mS ver 24
16:33
nS Ge 30:15
oIsa 30:6; 57:9
pHos 8:9-10

16:36
qS Jer 19:5;
Eze 23:10
16:37 rHos 2:3
sS Isa 47:3;
S Jer 13:22;
Eze 23:22;
Hos 2:10; 8:10;
Rev 17:16
16:38
tS Ge 38:24
uS Lev 20:10;
Ps 79:3,5;
Eze 23:25;
Zep 1:17
16:39
vS 2Ki 18:11
wEze 21:31;
Hos 2:3
16:40 xJn 8:5,7
16:41
yS Dt 13:16;
S Jer 19:13
zEze 23:10
aEze 22:15;
23:27,48
16:42
bS Isa 40:1-2; 54:9;

S Eze 5:13; 39:29 16:43 cS Ex 15:24; Ps 78:42 dEze 22:31
eEze 11:21 16:44 fS Ps 49:4

e21 Or and made them pass through the fire   f29 Or Chaldea   g36 Or lust

---

16:24 mound . . . lofty shrine. Cultic prostitution was moved from the high places (v. 15), which were outside the towns, into Jerusalem.

16:26 lustful. The Hebrew is more graphic: "having oversized organs." The language reflects both God's and Ezekiel's disgust with Jerusalem's apostasy. neighbors. Nowhere else in the OT are the Egyptians called "neighbors."

16:27 reduced your territory. After the 701 B.C. siege of Jerusalem, the Assyrian king Sennacherib gave some of Jerusalem's territory to the Philistines.

16:33 you give gifts to all your lovers. Jerusalem's perversity is here pictured as worse than adultery and ordinary prostitution (see also v. 34).

16:37 strip you. A reversal of the marriage covering (v. 8) and a return to the state described in v. 7.

16:38 sentence you. The punishment was death (see Lev 20:10; Dt 22:22) by stoning (see v. 40; Dt 22:21-24; Jn 8:5-7) or burning (Ge 38:24).

16:39 your mounds . . . your lofty shrines. The cultic centers within the city (see v. 24).

16:40 mob . . . will stone you. Cf. 23:47.

16:41 burn down your houses. A common form of punishment (see Jdg 12:1; 15:6). no longer pay your lovers. See v. 33.

16:44 Like mother, like daughter. Referring to Jerusalem's continual and seemingly hereditary tendency toward evil (cf. vv. 3,45).

will quote this proverb about you: "Like mother, like daughter." [45]You are a true daughter of your mother, who despised[g] her husband[h] and her children; and you are a true sister of your sisters, who despised their husbands and their children. Your mother was a Hittite and your father an Amorite.[i] [46]Your older sister[j] was Samaria, who lived to the north of you with her daughters; and your younger sister, who lived to the south of you with her daughters, was Sodom.[k] [47]You not only walked in their ways and copied their detestable practices, but in all your ways you soon became more depraved than they.[l] [48]As surely as I live, declares the Sovereign[m] LORD, your sister Sodom[n] and her daughters never did what you and your daughters have done.[o]

[49]" 'Now this was the sin of your sister Sodom:[p] She and her daughters were arrogant,[q] overfed and unconcerned;[r] they did not help the poor and needy.[s] [50]They were haughty[t] and did detestable things before me. Therefore I did away with them as you have seen.[u] [51]Samaria did not commit half the sins you did. You have done more detestable things than they, and have made your sisters seem righteous by all these things you have done.[v] [52]Bear your disgrace, for you have furnished some justification for your sisters. Because your sins were more vile than theirs, they appear more righteous[w] than you. So then, be ashamed and bear[x] your disgrace, for you have made your sisters appear righteous.

[53]" 'However, I will restore[y] the fortunes of Sodom and her daughters and of Samaria and her daughters, and your fortunes along with them,[z] [54]so that you may bear your disgrace[a] and be ashamed of all you have done in giving them comfort. [55]And your sisters, Sodom with her daughters and Samaria with her daughters, will return to what they were before; and you and your daughters will return to what you were before.[b] [56]You would not even men-

tion your sister Sodom in the day of your pride, [57]before your wickedness was uncovered. Even so, you are now scorned[c] by the daughters of Edom[h][d] and all her neighbors and the daughters of the Philistines—all those around you who despise you. [58]You will bear the consequences of your lewdness and your detestable practices, declares the LORD.[e]

[59]" 'This is what the Sovereign LORD says: I will deal with you as you deserve, because you have despised my oath by breaking the covenant.[f] [60]Yet I will remember the covenant[g] I made with you in the days of your youth,[h] and I will establish an everlasting covenant[i] with you. [61]Then you will remember your ways and be ashamed[j] when you receive your sisters, both those who are older than you and those who are younger. I will give them to you as daughters,[k] but not on the basis of my covenant with you. [62]So I will establish my covenant[l] with you, and you will know that I am the LORD.[m] [63]Then, when I make atonement[n] for you for all you have done, you will remember and be ashamed[o] and never again open your mouth[p] because of your humiliation, declares the Sovereign LORD.[q]' "

Two Eagles and a Vine

17 The word of the LORD came to me: [2]"Son of man, set forth an allegory and tell the house of Israel a parable.[r] [3]Say to them, 'This is what the Sovereign LORD says: A great eagle[s] with powerful wings, long feathers and full plumage of varied colors came to Lebanon.[t] Taking hold of the top of a cedar, [4]he broke off[u] its topmost shoot and carried it away to a land of merchants, where he planted it in a city of traders.

[5]" 'He took some of the seed of your

16:45
[g] S Eze 14:5
[h] Jer 44:19 /ver 3;
Eze 23:2
16:46 /S Jer 3:7
[k] Ge 13:10-13;
S 18:20;
Jer 3:8-11;
Eze 23:4;
Rev 11:8
16:47 /S Eze 5:7
16:48
[m] S Ge 15:2
[n] S Ge 19:25
[o] Mt 10:15;
11:23-24
16:49 [p] S Isa 1:10
[q] Ps 138:6;
Eze 28:2
[r] Isa 22:13
[s] S Ge 13:13;
Eze 18:7,12,16;
Am 6:4-6;
Lk 12:16-20;
16:19; Jas 5:5
16:50 [t] Ps 18:27
[u] Ge 18:20-21;
S 19:5
16:51
[v] Jer 3:8-11;
Eze 5:6-7; 23:11
16:52 [w] S Jer 3:11
[x] Eze 23:35
16:53 [y] S Dt 30:3;
Isa 19:24-25;
S Jer 48:47
[z] Eze 39:25
16:54 [a] S Jer 2:26
16:55
[b] Eze 36:11;
Mal 3:4
16:57
[c] S Ps 137:3
[d] 2Ki 16:6
16:58 [e] Eze 23:49
16:59 /S ver 8;
Eze 17:19
16:60
[g] S Ge 6:18;
S 9:15 /S Ps 25:7;
S Jer 2:2
[i] S Ge 9:9;
Eze 37:26
16:61 /ver 63;
Eze 20:43; 43:10;
44:13 [k] S Isa 43:6
16:62
[l] S Dt 29:14
[m] S Jer 24:7;
Eze 20:37,43-44;
34:25; 37:20;
Hos 2:19-20
16:63 [n] Ps 65:3;
78:38; 79:9
[o] Eze 36:31-32
[p] Ro 3:19
[q] Ps 39:9;
Da 9:7-8
17:2
[r] S Jdg 14:12;
S Eze 20:49
17:3 [s] S Dt 28:49;
Jer 49:22; Da 7:4;

Hos 8:1 [t] S Jer 22:23 **17:4** [u] S Isa 10:33

[h] **57** Many Hebrew manuscripts and Syriac; most Hebrew manuscripts, Septuagint and Vulgate *Aram*

16:46 *daughters.* Suburbs or satellite cities.
16:47 *more depraved than they.* The Bible frequently compares a city or people to Sodom (see v. 46) as the epitome of evil and degradation (see Dt 29:23; 32:32; Isa 1:9–10; 3:9; Jer 23:14; La 4:6; Mt 10:15; 11:23–24; Jude 7).
16:49 *sin of your sister Sodom.* Here social injustice rather than sexual perversion (Ge 19) is highlighted.
16:56 *day of your pride.* Referring to a time long before Ezekiel, when Jerusalem (as an Israelite city) was still relatively uncorrupted—as in the days of David and the early years of Solomon.
16:57 *scorned by the daughters of Edom.* The OT frequently condemns Edom for this (see 25:12–14; 35; Isa 63:1; Obadiah).

16:59 *covenant.* See v. 8 and note.
16:60 *everlasting covenant.* See 37:26; Isa 55:3; Jer 32:40.
17:2 *allegory . . . parable.* The allegory is in vv. 3–10, the explanation in vv. 11–21.
17:3 *great eagle.* Nebuchadnezzar (see v. 12). *Lebanon.* Jerusalem (see v. 12). *cedar.* David's dynasty; his royal family.
17:4 *topmost shoot.* Jehoiachin. *land of merchants.* The country of Babylonia (see v. 12; 16:29). *city of traders.* Babylon.
17:5 *seed.* Zedekiah son of Josiah; he was the brother of Jehoahaz and Jehoiakim and uncle of Jehoiachin (see 2Ki 23–24). *planted it.* Made him king (2Ki 24:17).

land and put it in fertile soil. He planted it like a willow by abundant water,[v] [6]and it sprouted and became a low, spreading vine. Its branches[w] turned toward him, but its roots remained under it. So it became a vine and produced branches and put out leafy boughs.[x]

[7]" 'But there was another great eagle with powerful wings and full plumage. The vine now sent out its roots toward him from the plot where it was planted and stretched out its branches to him for water.[y] [8]It had been planted in good soil by abundant water so that it would produce branches,[z] bear fruit and become a splendid vine.'

[9]"Say to them, 'This is what the Sovereign LORD says: Will it thrive? Will it not be uprooted and stripped of its fruit so that it withers? All its new growth will wither. It will not take a strong arm or many people to pull it up by the roots.[a] [10]Even if it[b] is transplanted, will it thrive? Will it not wither completely when the east wind strikes it—wither away in the plot where it grew?[c] '"

[11]Then the word of the LORD came to me: [12]"Say to this rebellious house, 'Do you not know what these things mean?[d]' Say to them: 'The king of Babylon went to Jerusalem and carried off her king and her nobles,[e] bringing them back with him to Babylon.[f] [13]Then he took a member of the royal family and made a treaty[g] with him, putting him under oath.[h] He also carried away the leading men[i] of the land, [14]so that the kingdom would be brought low,[j] unable to rise again, surviving only by keeping his treaty. [15]But the king rebelled[k] against him by sending his envoys to Egypt[l] to get horses and a large army.[m] Will he succeed? Will he who does such things escape? Will he break the treaty and yet escape?[n]

[16]" 'As surely as I live, declares the Sovereign LORD, he shall die[o] in Babylon, in

the land of the king who put him on the throne, whose oath he despised and whose treaty he broke.[p] [17]Pharaoh[q] with his mighty army and great horde will be of no help to him in war, when ramps[r] are built and siege works erected to destroy many lives.[s] [18]He despised the oath by breaking the covenant. Because he had given his hand in pledge[t] and yet did all these things, he shall not escape.

[19]" 'Therefore this is what the Sovereign LORD says: As surely as I live, I will bring down on his head my oath that he despised and my covenant that he broke.[u] [20]I will spread my net[v] for him, and he will be caught in my snare. I will bring him to Babylon and execute judgment[w] upon him there because he was unfaithful[x] to me. [21]All his fleeing troops will fall by the sword,[y] and the survivors[z] will be scattered to the winds.[a] Then you will know that I the LORD have spoken.[b]

[22]" 'This is what the Sovereign LORD says: I myself will take a shoot[c] from the very top of a cedar and plant it; I will break off a tender sprig from its topmost shoots and plant it on a high and lofty mountain.[d] [23]On the mountain heights[e] of Israel I will plant it; it will produce branches and bear fruit[f] and become a splendid cedar. Birds of every kind will nest in it; they will find shelter in the shade of its branches.[g] [24]All the trees of the field[h] will know that I the LORD bring down[i] the tall tree and make the low tree grow tall. I dry up the green tree and make the dry tree flourish.[j]

" 'I the LORD have spoken, and I will do it.[k] '"

The Soul Who Sins Will Die

18 The word of the LORD came to me: [2]"What do you people mean by

17:5 vDt 8:7-9; Ps 1:3; Isa 44:4; Eze 31:5
17:6 wS Isa 18:5 xS Job 5:3
17:7 yEze 31:4
17:8 zJob 18:19; Mal 4:1
17:9 aJer 42:10; Am 2:9
17:10 bS Job 1:19; Hos 12:1; 13:15 cS Eze 15:4
17:12 dS Eze 12:9 eS 2Ki 24:15 fS Dt 21:10; S 2Ch 36:10; Eze 24:19
17:13 gS Ex 23:32; S Jer 37:1 h2Ch 36:13 iIsa 3:2
17:14 jEze 29:14
17:15 kJer 52:3 lS Isa 30:2; S Jer 37:5 mS Dt 17:16 nS Ps 56:7; S Isa 30:5; Jer 34:3; 38:18; Eze 29:16
17:16 oS Jer 52:11; Eze 12:13
17:17 pS 2Ki 24:17 qJer 37:7 rS Eze 4:2 sS Isa 36:6; Jer 37:5; Eze 29:6-7
17:18 tS 2Ki 10:15; 1Ch 29:24
17:19 uJer 7:9; S Eze 16:59; 21:23; Hos 10:4
17:20 vS Eze 12:13; 32:3 wS Jer 2:35 xS Eze 15:8
17:21 yS Eze 12:14 z2Ki 25:11 aS Lev 26:33; S 2Ki 25:5; Zec 2:6 bS Jer 27:8
17:22 cS 2Ki 19:30; S Isa 4:2 dver 23; Isa 2:2; S Jer 23:5; Eze 20:40; 36:1, 36; 37:22; 40:2; 43:12
17:23 eS ver 22; S Jer 31:12 fS Isa 27:6 gPs 92:12;

18:2 S Isa 2:2; Eze 31:6; Da 4:12; Hos 14:5-7; S Mt 13:32 17:24 hS Ps 96:12; Isa 2:13 iS Ps 52:5 jS Nu 17:8; Da 5:21 kS 1Sa 2:7-8; Eze 19:12; 21:26; 22:14; 37:13; Am 9:11

17:6 *low, spreading vine.* No longer a tall cedar, because thousands of Judah's leading citizens had been deported (see 2Ki 24:15–16; see also Jer 52:28). But see note on 15:2.
17:7 *another great eagle.* An Egyptian pharaoh, either Psammetichus II (595–589 B.C.) or Hophra (589–570). Hophra, mentioned in Jer 44:30, is probably the pharaoh who offered help to Jerusalem in 586 (see Jer 37:5). If the fact that ch. 17 is located between ch. 8 (dated 592) and ch. 20 (dated 591) is chronologically meaningful, Psammetichus is meant. *sent out its roots toward him.* Zedekiah appealed to Egypt for military aid (v. 15), an act of rebellion against Nebuchadnezzar (see 2Ki 24:20).
17:10 *east wind.* The hot, dry wind known as the khamsin, which withers vegetation (see 19:12). Here it stands for Nebuchadnezzar and his Babylonian forces.

17:12 *this rebellious house.* See 2:3 and note.
17:15 *Will he break the treaty and yet escape?* The point of the chapter (see vv. 16,18).
17:16 *he shall die in Babylon.* See 2Ki 25:7.
17:19 *my oath . . . my covenant.* The king of Judah would have sworn faithfulness to the treaty in the name of the Lord. To swear such an oath and then violate it was to despise God.
17:22 *I myself.* A beautiful Messianic promise follows, using the previous imagery in a totally new and unexpected way. *shoot.* A member of David's family (cf. Isa 11:1; Zec 3:8; 6:12). *cedar.* See note on v. 3. *plant it.* Make him king (see v. 5). *high and lofty mountain.* Jerusalem.
17:23 *Birds . . . will nest in it.* See Mk 4:32.
18:2 *this proverb.* Cf. Jer 31:29, which indicates that the proverb arose first in Jerusalem. Jeremiah predicted the ces-

quoting this proverb about the land of Israel:

" 'The fathers eat sour grapes,
  and the children's teeth are set on
    edge'? [1]

[3]"As surely as I live, declares the Sovereign LORD, you will no longer quote this proverb [m] in Israel. [4]For every living soul belongs to me, the father as well as the son—both alike belong to me. The soul who sins [n] is the one who will die. [o]

[5]"Suppose there is a righteous man
  who does what is just and right.
[6]He does not eat at the mountain [p]
    shrines
  or look to the idols [q] of the house of
    Israel.
He does not defile his neighbor's wife
  or lie with a woman during her
    period. [r]
[7]He does not oppress [s] anyone,
  but returns what he took in pledge [t]
    for a loan.
He does not commit robbery [u]
  but gives his food to the hungry [v]
  and provides clothing for the naked. [w]
[8]He does not lend at usury
  or take excessive interest. [i] [x]
He withholds his hand from doing
    wrong
  and judges fairly [y] between man and
    man.
[9]He follows my decrees [z]
  and faithfully keeps my laws.

That man is righteous; [a]
  he will surely live, [b]
        declares the Sovereign LORD.

[10]"Suppose he has a violent son, who sheds blood [c] or does any of these other things [j] [11](though the father has done none of them):

"He eats at the mountain shrines. [d]
He defiles his neighbor's wife.
[12]He oppresses the poor [e] and needy.
He commits robbery.
He does not return what he took in
    pledge. [f]
He looks to the idols.
He does detestable things. [g]
[13]He lends at usury and takes excessive
    interest. [h]

Will such a man live? He will not! Because he has done all these detestable things, he will surely be put to death and his blood will be on his own head. [i]

[14]"But suppose this son has a son who sees all the sins his father commits, and though he sees them, he does not do such things: [j]

[15]"He does not eat at the mountain
    shrines [k]
  or look to the idols [l] of the house of
    Israel.

Cross-references (center column):

18:2 [i]S Job 21:19; Isa 3:15; Jer 31:29
18:3 [m]S Ps 49:4
18:4 [n]S 2Ki 14:6; S Pr 13:21 [o]ver 20; S Ge 18:23; S Ex 17:14; S Job 21:20; Isa 42:5; Eze 33:8; S Ro 6:23
18:6 [p]S Eze 6:2 [q]Dt 4:19; S Eze 6:13; 20:24; Am 5:26 [r]S Lev 12:2; S 15:24
18:7 [s]Ex 22:21; Mal 3:5; Jas 5:4 [t]S Ex 22:26 [u]S Ex 20:15 [v]S Job 22:7 [w]Dt 15:11; S Eze 16:49; S Mt 25:36; Lk 3:11
18:8 [x]S Ex 18:21; 22:25; S Lev 25:35-37; Dt 23:19-20 [y]S Jer 22:3; Zec 8:16
18:9 [z]S Lev 19:37

[a]Hab 2:4 [b]S Lev 18:5; S Eze 11:12; 20:11; Am 5:4
18:10 [c]S Ex 21:12; Eze 22:6
18:11 [d]Eze 22:9
18:12 [e]S Ex 22:22; S Job 24:9; Am 4:1 [f]S Ex 22:27 [g]2Ki 21:11; Isa 59:6-7; S Jer 22:17; S Eze 16:49; Hab 2:6

18:13 [h]Ex 22:25 [i]S Lev 20:9; Eze 33:4-5; Hos 12:14 18:14 [j]2Ch 34:21; S Pr 23:24 18:15 [k]Eze 22:9 [l]S Ps 24:4

[i]8 Or take interest; similarly in verses 13 and 17
[j]10 Or things to a brother

---

sation of the proverb, and Ezekiel said its end had come. *about the land of Israel.* And about the fate of those who have suffered loss. *The fathers . . . on edge.* The proverb, though it expresses self-pity, fatalism and despair, and though it mocks the justice of God, had its origin in Israelite belief in corporate solidarity (see Ex 20:5; 34:7 and Ezekiel's own words in chs. 16; 23). In La 5:7 the thought appears as a sincere confession. *set on edge.* The Hebrew for this phrase perhaps means "blunted" or "worn" (cf. Ecc 10:10), but it may refer to the sensation in the mouth when eating something bitter or sour.
18:3 *As surely as I live.* A divine oath, revealing God's unalterable intention. It is used often in Ezekiel (5:11; 14:16,18,20; 16:48; 17:16,19; 20:3,31,33; 33:11,27; 34:8; 35:6,11).
18:4 *The soul who sins is the one who will die.* Or "Only the soul . . ." Ezekiel spoke out against a false use the people were making of a doctrine of inherited guilt (perhaps based on a false understanding of Ex 20:5; 34:7). What follows is his description of three men, standing for three generations, who break the three/four-generation pattern. *soul.* "Life" or "person," not used here to distinguish spirit from body.
18:5 *righteous man.* The first generation that keeps the law. The following 15 commandments are partly ceremonial but are mostly moral injunctions. See the Ten Commandments in Ex 20 and Dt 5; cf. Ps 15:2-5; 24:3-6; Isa 33:15.
18:6 *eat at the mountain shrines.* Eating meat sacrificed to idols on the high places (see 6:3; Hos 4:13). *look to.* Seek

help from (see 23:27; 33:25; Ps 121:1). *idols.* See note on 6:4. *defile.* Adultery (condemned in Ex 20:14; Dt 22:22; Lev 18:20; 20:10) is here associated with a menstrual prohibition (see Lev 15:19-24; 18:19; 20:18), which is absent from the two listings that follow (cf. vv. 11,15).
18:7 *oppress.* The rich taking advantage of the poor. *returns what he took in pledge.* See Ex 22:26; Dt 24:12-13; Am 2:8. *robbery.* See the commandment against stealing in Ex 20:15; Dt 5:1. This is violent ("armed") robbery rather than secret theft or burglary (see Lev 19:13). *food to the hungry.* See Dt 15:7-11; Mt 25:31-46.
18:8 *lend at usury.* See 22:12; Ps 15:5; Pr 28:8. What is forbidden in Ex 22:25; Lev 25:35-37; Dt 23:19 is interest on loans to the needy. Dt 23:20 allows an Israelite to "charge a foreigner interest"; Ezekiel condemns usury. (Interest on modern commercial loans is a different matter.)
18:9 *That man is righteous; he will surely live.* After the checklist of commandments has been gone over, the verdict is rendered (cf. Ps 15:5; 24:5). *live.* See note on 16:6. This is life as more than mere existence; it includes communion with God (see Ps 63:3; 73:27-28).
18:10 *violent son.* Evil, second generation. About half (eight) of the previous commandments follow, but in a different order.
18:13 *his blood will be on his own head.* He is held responsible for his own sin (see Lev 20:9,11-12,16,27).
18:14 *a son.* Righteous, third generation. Twelve commandments follow.

He does not defile his neighbor's wife.
16He does not oppress anyone
 or require a pledge for a loan.
He does not commit robbery
 but gives his food to the hungry[m]
 and provides clothing for the naked.[n]
17He withholds his hand from sin[k]
 and takes no usury or excessive
  interest.
He keeps my laws[o] and follows my
  decrees.

He will not die for his father's sin; he will surely live. 18But his father will die for his own sin, because he practiced extortion, robbed his brother and did what was wrong among his people.

19"Yet you ask, 'Why does the son not share the guilt of his father?' Since the son has done what is just and right and has been careful to keep all my decrees, he will surely live.[p] 20The soul who sins is the one who will die.[q] The son will not share the guilt of the father, nor will the father share the guilt of the son. The righteousness of the righteous man will be credited to him, and the wickedness of the wicked will be charged against him.[r]

21"But if[s] a wicked man turns away from all the sins he has committed and keeps all my decrees[t] and does what is just and right, he will surely live; he will not die.[u] 22None of the offenses he has committed will be remembered against him. Because of the righteous things he has done, he will live.[v] 23Do I take any pleasure in the death of the wicked? declares the Sovereign LORD. Rather, am I not pleased[w] when they turn from their ways and live?[x]

24"But if a righteous man turns[y] from his righteousness and commits sin and does the same detestable things the wicked man does, will he live? None of the righteous things he has done will be remem-

bered. Because of the unfaithfulness[z] he is guilty of and because of the sins he has committed, he will die.[a]

25"Yet you say, 'The way of the Lord is not just.'[b] Hear, O house of Israel: Is my way unjust?[c] Is it not your ways that are unjust? 26If a righteous man turns from his righteousness and commits sin, he will die for it; because of the sin he has committed he will die. 27But if a wicked man turns away from the wickedness he has committed and does what is just and right, he will save his life.[d] 28Because he considers all the offenses he has committed and turns away from them, he will surely live; he will not die.[e] 29Yet the house of Israel says, 'The way of the Lord is not just.' Are my ways unjust, O house of Israel? Is it not your ways that are unjust?

30"Therefore, O house of Israel, I will judge you, each one according to his ways, declares the Sovereign LORD. Repent![f] Turn away from all your offenses; then sin will not be your downfall.[g] 31Rid[h] yourselves of all the offenses you have committed, and get a new heart[i] and a new spirit. Why[j] will you die, O house of Israel?[k] 32For I take no pleasure in the death of anyone, declares the Sovereign LORD. Repent[l] and live![m]

A Lament for Israel's Princes

19 "Take up a lament[n] concerning the princes[o] of Israel 2and say:

" 'What a lioness[p] was your mother
 among the lions!
She lay down among the young lions
 and reared her cubs.[q]
3She brought up one of her cubs,

Cross-reference column:

18:16 [m]Isa 58:7
[n]S Ex 22:27;
Ps 41:1;
Isa 58:10;
S Eze 16:49
18:17 [o]S Ps 1:2
18:19 [p]Ex 20:5;
Dt 5:9; Jer 15:4;
Zec 1:3-6
18:20
[q]S Nu 15:31
[r]Dt 24:16;
S 1Ki 8:32;
2Ki 14:6;
Isa 3:11;
S Eze 7:27;
S 14:14;
S Mt 16:27;
Jn 9:2
18:21 [s]Jer 18:8
[t]S Ge 26:5
[u]S Eze 13:22;
36:27
18:22
[v]Ps 18:20-24;
S Isa 43:25;
Da 4:27;
Mic 7:19
18:23
[w]Ps 147:11
[x]S Job 37:23;
S La 3:33;
S Eze 16:6;
Mic 7:18;
S 1Ti 2:4
18:24
[y]S Jer 34:16

[z]S Eze 15:8
[a]S 1Sa 15:11;
2Ch 24:17-20;
S Job 35:8;
Pr 21:16;
S Eze 3:20;
20:27;
2Pe 2:20-22
18:25 [b]Jer 2:29
[c]S Ge 18:25;
Jer 12:1;
Eze 33:17;
Zep 3:5;
Mal 2:17;
3:13-15
18:27
[d]S Isa 1:18;
S Eze 13:22
18:28 [e]S Isa 55:7
18:30 [f]S Isa 1:27;
S Jer 35:15;
Mt 3:2 [g]Eze 7:3;
24:14; 33:20;
Hos 12:6;
1Pe 1:17
18:31 [h]S Jdg 6:8
[i]Ps 51:10
[j]Jer 27:13
[k]S Isa 1:16-17;
S Eze 11:19;
36:26
18:32
[l]S Job 22:23;

Isa 55:7; Mal 3:7 [m]S 2Ch 7:14; S Job 37:23; S Eze 16:6;
33:11 19:1 [n]ver 14; Jer 7:29; 9:10,20; Eze 26:17; 27:2,32;
28:12; 32:2,16; Am 5:1 [o]S 2Ki 24:6 19:2 [p]S Nu 23:24
[q]S Ge 49:9

[k]17 Septuagint (see also verse 8); Hebrew *from the poor*

18:21 *But if a wicked man turns . . . and keeps . . . he will surely live.* Verses 1–20 indicate that the chain of inherited guilt can be broken, and vv. 21–29 teach that the power of guilt accumulated within a person's life can be overcome.
18:24 *But if a righteous man turns.* See Heb 2:3; 2Pe 2:20–22 for warnings against those who knowingly and willfully turn from righteousness.
18:26 *If a righteous man.* Verses 26–29 repeat the argument developed in vv. 21–25.
18:30 *Therefore.* Concluding, summary oracle. *each one.* While the house of Israel as a whole was guilty, God's judgment would be just and individual. *Repent!* Second call to repentance (see 14:6).
18:31 *get a new heart.* What had been promised unconditionally (11:19; 36:26) is here portrayed as attainable but not inevitable (cf. the same tension between Php 2:12 and 2:13).

18:32 *I take no pleasure.* Verse 23 is echoed in this final, grand summary, called by some the most important message in the whole book of Ezekiel (see note on 16:6).
19:1 *lament.* A metered (three beats plus two beats) chant usually composed for funerals of fallen leaders (as in 2Sa 1:17–27), but often used sarcastically by the OT prophets to lament or to ironically predict the death of a nation (see Isa 14:4–21; Am 5:1–3). See also 2:10. *princes.* Kings.
19:2 *lioness.* Although a lament, this chapter is an allegory like that in ch. 17 (to which it is related in content). Ch. 17 gives an interpretation, but this one does not. The lioness may be a personification of Israel (see v. 1), Judah (see 4:6; 8:1,17; 9:9) or Jerusalem (see 5:5), all of which may be considered to be mother to the kings (see vv. 10–14).
19:3 *one of her cubs.* Jehoahaz (see 2Ki 23:31–34; Jer 22:10–12), who reigned only three months. *devoured men.* A reference to his oppressive policies (see Jer 22:13).

and he became a strong lion.
He learned to tear the prey
and he devoured men.
4The nations heard about him,
and he was trapped in their pit.
They led him with hooks[r]
to the land of Egypt.[s]

5" 'When she saw her hope unfulfilled,
her expectation gone,
she took another of her cubs[t]
and made him a strong lion.[u]
6He prowled among the lions,
for he was now a strong lion.
He learned to tear the prey
and he devoured men.[v]
7He broke down[1] their strongholds
and devastated[w] their towns.
The land and all who were in it
were terrified by his roaring.
8Then the nations[x] came against him,
those from regions round about.
They spread their net[y] for him,
and he was trapped in their pit.[z]
9With hooks[a] they pulled him into a cage
and brought him to the king of Babylon.[b]
They put him in prison,
so his roar[c] was heard no longer
on the mountains of Israel.[d]

10" 'Your mother was like a vine in your vineyard[m][e]
planted by the water;[f]
it was fruitful and full of branches
because of abundant water.[g]
11Its branches were strong,
fit for a ruler's scepter.
It towered high
above the thick foliage,
conspicuous for its height
and for its many branches.[h]
12But it was uprooted[i] in fury
and thrown to the ground.
The east wind[j] made it shrivel,
it was stripped of its fruit;
its strong branches withered
and fire consumed them.[k]
13Now it is planted in the desert,[l]
in a dry and thirsty land.[m]
14Fire spread from one of its main[n] branches
and consumed[n] its fruit.
No strong branch is left on it
fit for a ruler's scepter.'[o]

This is a lament[p] and is to be used as a lament."

Rebellious Israel

20 In the seventh year, in the fifth
month on the tenth day, some of
the elders of Israel came to inquire[q] of the
LORD, and they sat down in front of me.[r]
2Then the word of the LORD came to
me: 3"Son of man, speak to the elders[s] of
Israel and say to them, 'This is what the
Sovereign LORD says: Have you come to
inquire[t] of me? As surely as I live, I will
not let you inquire of me, declares the Sovereign LORD.[u]'
4"Will you judge them? Will you judge
them, son of man? Then confront them
with the detestable practices of their fathers[v] 5and say to them: 'This is what the
Sovereign LORD says: On the day I chose[w]
Israel, I swore with uplifted hand[x] to the
descendants of the house of Jacob and revealed myself to them in Egypt. With
uplifted hand I said to them, "I am the
LORD your God.[y]" 6On that day I swore[z]
to them that I would bring them out of
Egypt into a land I had searched out for

19:4 [r]S Job 41:2 [s]2Ki 23:33-34; 2Ch 36:4; S La 4:20 **19:5** [t]S Ge 49:9 [u]2Ki 23:34 **19:6** [v]2Ki 24:9; 2Ch 36:9 **19:7** [w]Eze 29:10; 30:12 **19:8** [x]2Ki 24:2 [y]S Eze 12:13 [z]2Ki 24:11; S La 4:20 **19:9** [a]S 2Ki 19:28 [b]S 2Ki 25:7; S 2Ch 36:6 [c]Zec 11:3 [d]S 2Ki 24:15 **19:10** [e]S Ge 49:22 [f]S Jer 17:8 [g]Ps 80:8-11 **19:11** [h]Eze 31:3; Da 4:11 **19:12** [i]S Dt 29:28 [j]S Ge 41:6 [k]S Isa 27:11; S Eze 17:24; 28:17; Hos 13:15 **19:13** [l]Eze 20:35; Hos 2:14 [m]Hos 2:3 **19:14** [n]Eze 20:47 [o]S Eze 15:4 [p]S ver 1 **20:1** [q]S Ge 25:22 [r]Eze 1:1-2; S 8:1; 21:1 **20:3** [s]S Eze 7:26 [t]S Ge 25:22; Eze 14:3 [u]S 1Sa 28:6; Isa 1:15; Am 8:12; Mic 3:7 **20:4** [v]S Eze 16:2; 22:2; Mt 23:32 **20:5** [w]S Dt 7:6 [x]S Ge 14:22; S Nu 14:30 [y]S Lev 11:44 **20:6** [z]S Ex 6:8

[1] *7* Targum (see Septuagint); Hebrew *He knew*
[m] *10* Two Hebrew manuscripts; most Hebrew manuscripts *your blood*
[n] *14* Or *from under its*

19:5 *another of her cubs.* Perhaps Jehoiachin (who reigned only three months, 2Ki 24:8), but probably Zedekiah (of whom v. 7 appears a more likely description). Both were taken to Babylon (v. 9). If the reference is to Jehoiachin (2Ki 24:15), this was a true lament; if to Zedekiah, it was a prediction (2Ki 25:7).
19:10 *Your mother was like a vine.* The one previously pictured as a lioness (v. 2) is here a vine (see 15:2 and note; 17:7).
19:12 *east wind.* Nebuchadnezzar and his army (see note on 17:10).
19:13 *desert.* Babylonia—which to Israel seemed like a desert (see 20:35).
19:14 *Fire.* Rebellion (see 2Ki 24:20). *one of its main branches.* Zedekiah. *to be used as a lament.* Indicates repeated use (see Ps 137:1).
20:1 *seventh year . . . fifth month . . . tenth day.* Aug. 14, 591 B.C., the third date (see 1:2; 8:1). Since Ezekiel had received many revelations before this (see opening verses of chs. 12–18), the date must emphasize the importance of this chapter. Like chs. 16 and 23, it presents a negative view of Israel's history; unlike them, it does not employ allegory. *elders of Israel.* See notes on 8:1; 14:1. *inquire.* See v. 3 and note on 14:3.
20:3 *As surely as I live.* See note on 18:3. *inquire.* See note on 14:3.
20:5 *I chose.* The only occurrence of the word "choose" (election vocabulary) in Ezekiel. Verses 5–26 present Israel's history in three acts (vv. 5–9, Egypt; vv. 10–17, Desert, Part 1; vv. 18–26, Desert, Part 2); but see note on v. 28. Each act has four scenes: (1) revelation, (2) rebellion, (3) wrath, (4) reconsideration. *With uplifted hand.* A symbolic act accompanying the swearing of an oath (see vv. 15,23,42). *I am the LORD your God.* See Ex 3:6,14–15 and notes.
20:6 *land flowing with milk and honey.* See note on Ex 3:8. *most beautiful of all lands.* Cf. Dt 8:7–10; Jer 3:19 for the land's natural beauty. Its real beauty lay in being selected as God's dwelling place (Dt 12:5,11).

them, a land flowing with milk and honey,[a] the most beautiful of all lands.[b] [7]And I said to them, "Each of you, get rid of the vile images[c] you have set your eyes on, and do not defile yourselves with the idols[d] of Egypt. I am the LORD your God.[e]"

[8]"'But they rebelled against me and would not listen to me;[f] they did not get rid of the vile images they had set their eyes on, nor did they forsake the idols of Egypt.[g] So I said I would pour out my wrath on them and spend my anger against them in Egypt.[h] [9]But for the sake of my name I did what would keep it from being profaned[i] in the eyes of the nations they lived among and in whose sight I had revealed myself to the Israelites by bringing them out of Egypt.[j] [10]Therefore I led them out of Egypt and brought them into the desert.[k] [11]I gave them my decrees and made known to them my laws, for the man who obeys them will live by them.[l] [12]Also I gave them my Sabbaths[m] as a sign[n] between us,[o] so they would know that I the LORD made them holy.[p]

[13]"'Yet the people of Israel rebelled[q] against me in the desert. They did not follow my decrees but rejected my laws[r]—although the man who obeys them will live by them—and they utterly desecrated my Sabbaths.[s] So I said I would pour out my wrath[t] on them and destroy[u] them in the desert.[v] [14]But for the sake of my name I did what would keep it from being profaned[w] in the eyes of the nations in whose sight I had brought them out.[x] [15]Also with uplifted hand I swore[y] to them in the desert that I would not bring them into the land I had given them—a land flowing with milk and honey, most beautiful of all lands[z]— [16]because they rejected my laws[a] and did not follow my decrees and desecrated my Sab-

baths. For their hearts[b] were devoted to their idols.[c] [17]Yet I looked on them with pity and did not destroy[d] them or put an end to them in the desert. [18]I said to their children in the desert, "Do not follow the statutes of your fathers[e] or keep their laws or defile yourselves[f] with their idols. [19]I am the LORD your God;[g] follow my decrees and be careful to keep my laws.[h] [20]Keep my Sabbaths[i] holy, that they may be a sign[j] between us. Then you will know that I am the LORD your God.[k]"

[21]"'But the children rebelled against me: They did not follow my decrees, they were not careful to keep my laws[l]—although the man who obeys them will live by them—and they desecrated my Sabbaths. So I said I would pour out my wrath on them and spend my anger[m] against them in the desert.[n] [22]But I withheld[o] my hand, and for the sake of my name[p] I did what would keep it from being profaned in the eyes of the nations in whose sight I had brought them out. [23]Also with uplifted hand I swore to them in the desert that I would disperse them among the nations and scatter[q] them through the countries, [24]because they had not obeyed my laws but had rejected my decrees[r] and desecrated my Sabbaths,[s] and their eyes lusted after[t] their fathers' idols.[u] [25]I also gave them over[v] to statutes that were not good and laws they could not live by;[w] [26]I let them become defiled through their gifts—the sacrifice[x] of every firstborn[o]—that I might fill them with horror so they would know that I am the LORD.[y]'

[27]"Therefore, son of man, speak to the people of Israel and say to them, 'This is what the Sovereign LORD says: In this also

---

20:6 aS Ex 3:8
bS Dt 8:7;
Da 8:9; 11:41;
Mal 3:12
20:7 cEx 20:4
dS Eze 6:9
eS Ex 20:2;
Lev 18:3;
Dt 29:18
20:8 fS Jer 7:26
gS Jer 11:10;
S Eze 7:8; S 16:26
hS Ex 32:7;
Dt 9:7;
S Isa 63:10
20:9 iS Isa 48:11
jEze 36:22; 39:7
20:10
kS Ex 13:18; 19:1
20:11
lEx 20:1-23;
Lev 18:5;
Dt 4:7-8;
S Eze 18:9;
S Ro 10:5
20:12
mS Ex 20:10
nS Ex 31:13
oJer 17:22
pS Lev 20:8
20:13 qPs 78:40
rS Jer 6:19; 11:8
sver 24 tS Dt 9:8
uS Ex 32:10
vLev 26:15,43;
S Nu 14:29;
Ps 95:8-10;
Isa 56:6
20:14
wS Isa 48:11
xEze 36:23
20:15 yS Dt 1:34
zNu 14:22-23;
Ps 95:11; 106:26;
Heb 3:11
20:16 aJer 11:8;
Am 2:4
bS Nu 15:39 cver
24; S Eze 6:4;
Am 5:26
20:17 dS Jer 4:27
20:18
eS 2Ch 30:7;
Zec 1:4
fS Ps 106:39
20:19 gS Ex 20:2
hDt 5:32-33;
6:1-2; S 8:1;
11:1; S 12:1
20:20
iS Ex 20:10
jS Ex 31:13
kJer 17:22
20:21 lS Jer 7:26
mNu 25:3
nS Eze 7:8
20:22 oPs 78:38
pS Isa 48:11
20:23
qS Lev 26:33;

20:24 rAm 2:4 sver 13 tS Eze 6:9 uS ver 16;
S Eze 2:3; S 18:6 **20:25** vS Ps 81:12; Ro 1:28 wIsa 66:4;
2Th 2:11 **20:26** xS Lev 18:21 yLev 20:2-5; 2Ki 17:17

S Ps 9:11

o26 Or —making every firstborn pass through the fire

20:7 idols. See note on 6:4.
20:8 But they rebelled. See vv. 13,21; see also Jos 24:14. So I said I would pour out my wrath on them. An internal refrain (see vv. 13,21); see also note on 7:8. spend my anger against. See note on 5:13.
20:9 for the sake of my name. See vv. 14,22,44. Name and person are closely connected in the Bible. God's name is his identity and reputation—that by which he is known. The phrase used here is equivalent to "for my own sake" (cf. Isa 37:35; 43:25). God's acts of deliverance—past and future—identify him, revealing his true nature (see 36:22; Ps 23:3; Isa 48:9). profaned. By ridicule (see Nu 14:15-16).
20:10 desert. Act Two (see note on v. 5).
20:11 will live. See vv. 13,21; contrast v. 25. See notes on 16:6; 18:9; see also Lev 18:5 and note.
20:12 Sabbaths as a sign. Israel's observance of the Sabbath was to serve as a sign that she was the Lord's holy

people (see Ex 31:13-17). Ezekiel highlights the Sabbath (see 22:8,26; 23:38; 44:24; 45:17; 46:3), as did Jeremiah (Jer 17:19-27; cf. Ne 13:17-18). Jewish legalism later corrupted the Sabbath law (see Mt 12:1-14).
20:13 desecrated. By not observing the Sabbath-rest (see Jer 17:21-23) or by not observing it in the manner and spirit God intended (see Am 8:5).
20:18 I said to their children. Act Three (see note on v. 5). God began anew with the second generation in the desert (see Nu 14:26-35).
20:25-26 Cf. the principle of divine working in Ro 1:24-32.
20:26 sacrifice of every firstborn. See v. 31 and note on 16:20. so they would know that I am the LORD. God will go to any lengths to get his people to acknowledge him (see note on 5:13).

your fathers[z] blasphemed[a] me by forsaking me:[b] 28When I brought them into the land[c] I had sworn to give them and they saw any high hill or any leafy tree, there they offered their sacrifices, made offerings that provoked me to anger, presented their fragrant incense and poured out their drink offerings.[d] 29Then I said to them: What is this high place[e] you go to?' " (It is called Bamah[p] to this day.)

Judgment and Restoration

30"Therefore say to the house of Israel: 'This is what the Sovereign LORD says: Will you defile yourselves[f] the way your fathers did and lust after their vile images?[g] 31When you offer your gifts—the sacrifice of your sons[h] in[q] the fire—you continue to defile yourselves with all your idols to this day. Am I to let you inquire of me, O house of Israel? As surely as I live, declares the Sovereign LORD, I will not let you inquire of me.[i]

32" 'You say, "We want to be like the nations, like the peoples of the world, who serve wood and stone." But what you have in mind will never happen. 33As surely as I live, declares the Sovereign LORD, I will rule over you with a mighty hand and an outstretched arm[j] and with outpoured wrath.[k] 34I will bring you from the nations[l] and gather[m] you from the countries where you have been scattered—with a mighty hand[n] and an outstretched arm and with outpoured wrath.[o] 35I will bring you into the desert[p] of the nations and there, face to face, I will execute judgment[q] upon you. 36As I judged your fathers in the desert of the land of Egypt, so I will judge you, declares the Sovereign LORD.[r] 37I will take note of you as you

pass under my rod,[s] and I will bring you into the bond of the covenant.[t] 38I will purge[u] you of those who revolt and rebel against me. Although I will bring them out of the land where they are living, yet they will not enter the land of Israel. Then you will know that I am the LORD.[v]

39" 'As for you, O house of Israel, this is what the Sovereign LORD says: Go and serve your idols,[w] every one of you! But afterward you will surely listen to me and no longer profane my holy name[x] with your gifts and idols.[y] 40For on my holy mountain, the high mountain of Israel,[z] declares the Sovereign LORD, there in the land the entire house of Israel will serve me, and there I will accept them. There I will require your offerings[a] and your choice gifts,[r] along with all your holy sacrifices.[b] 41I will accept you as fragrant incense[c] when I bring you out from the nations and gather[d] you from the countries where you have been scattered, and I will show myself holy[e] among you in the sight of the nations.[f] 42Then you will know that I am the LORD,[g] when I bring you into the land of Israel,[h] the land I had sworn with uplifted hand to give to your fathers.[i] 43There you will remember your conduct[j] and all the actions by which you have defiled yourselves, and you will loathe yourselves[k] for all the evil you have done.[l] 44You will know that I am the LORD, when I deal with you for my name's

20:27
[z]S Ps 78:57
[a]S Nu 15:30;
Ro 2:24
[b]S Eze 18:24
20:28 [c]Ne 9:23;
Ps 78:55,58
[d]S Jer 2:7; S 3:6;
S 19:13;
S Eze 6:13
20:29
[e]Eze 16:16; 43:7
20:30 [f]ver 43
[g]S Jdg 2:16-19;
S Jer 16:12
20:31
[h]S Eze 16:20
[i]Ps 106:37-39;
S Jer 7:31;
S Eze 14:3;
Am 8:12;
Zec 7:13
20:33
[j]S Eze 16:27
[k]Jer 21:5;
Eze 25:16
20:34 [l]2Co 6:17
[m]S Dt 30:4;
S Ps 106:47
[n]S Isa 31:3
[o]Isa 27:12-13;
S Jer 44:6;
S La 2:4;
S Eze 6:14
20:35
[p]S Eze 19:13
[q]S 1Sa 12:7;
S Job 22:4;
S Jer 2:35
20:36
[r]Nu 11:1-35;
14:28-30;
1Co 10:5-10

20:37
[s]S Lev 27:32
[t]S Eze 16:62
20:38
[u]Eze 34:17-22;
Am 9:9-10
[v]Ps 95:11;
Jer 44:14;
S Eze 13:9;
23:49; Hos 2:14;
Zec 13:8-9;
Mal 3:3; 4:1-3;
Heb 4:3
20:39
[w]S Jer 44:25
[x]S Ex 20:7;
S Eze 13:19
[y]Eze 43:7;
Am 4:4
20:40
[z]S Eze 17:22;

34:14 [a]S Isa 60:7 [b]S Isa 56:7; Mal 3:4 20:41 [c]S 2Co 2:14
[d]S Dt 30:4 [e]Eze 28:25; 36:23 [f]S Isa 5:16; S Eze 11:17;
2Co 6:17 20:42 [g]Eze 38:23 [h]S Jer 23:8; Eze 34:13; 36:24
[i]Jer 30:3; Eze 34:27; 37:21 20:43 [j]Eze 14:22 [k]S Lev 26:41
[l]S Eze 6:9; S 16:61; Hos 5:15

[p]29 Bamah means high place.   [q]31 Or —making your
sons pass through   [r]40 Or and the gifts of your
firstfruits

20:28 *When I brought them into the land.* Apparently Act Four in Ezekiel's history (see note on v. 5), but it is not carried through with the same schematic consistency.
20:30 *Will you . . . ?* The point of the chapter: "How will you act?"
20:31 *inquire.* See note on 14:3.
20:32 *like the nations.* The temptation to lose its uniqueness was always present for Israel (see 1Sa 8:5). *will never happen.* As happened to those who were exiled to Egypt (see Jer 44:15–19).
20:33 *mighty hand . . . outstretched arm.* Terminology of the exodus (cf. Dt 4:34; 5:15; 7:19; 11:2; 26:8).
20:35 *desert of the nations.* Exile among the nations would be for Israel like a return to the desert through which she journeyed on the way to the promised land (see Hos 2:14).
20:37 *pass under my rod.* The way a shepherd counts or separates his flock (see Jer 33:13; Mt 25:32–33). *I will bring you into the bond of the covenant.* As he had in the Sinai Desert (see 16:60,62).
20:38 *purge.* As in the first desert experience, many were

not allowed to enter the land (see Nu 14:26–35).
20:39 *Go and serve your idols.* Irony; the opposite is meant (cf. 1Ki 22:15; Am 4:4).
20:40 *my holy mountain.* Mentioned only here in Ezekiel, it refers to Jerusalem or Zion (see Ps 2:6; 3:4; 15:1; see also Isa 11:9; 56:7; 57:13; 65:11; Ob 16; Zep 3:11). *entire house of Israel.* Includes the northern kingdom, which fell in 722–721 B.C. (see 11:15; 36:10). *I will require.* See Dt 23:21 ("demand"); Mic 6:8. *offerings.* Possibly refers to a prescribed contribution. The other 19 occurrences in Ezekiel of the Hebrew for this word are confined to chs. 44–48, where the reference is to the land set aside for the temple and priests (see 45:1; 48:8–10, "portion") or to the special gifts for the priests (see 44:30). *choice gifts.* Voluntary contributions (but see NIV text note).
20:41 *as fragrant incense.* Either in a metaphorical sense (as in Eph 5:2) or in a literal sense (as in 6:13). *bring you out.* Cf. v. 34.
20:43 *you will remember . . . and . . . loathe yourselves.* A thorough repentance (see 6:9; 16:63; 36:31; Lk 15: 17–19).

sake[m] and not according to your evil ways and your corrupt practices, O house of Israel, declares the Sovereign LORD.[n] ' "

Prophecy Against the South

[45]The word of the LORD came to me: [46]"Son of man, set your face toward[o] the south; preach against the south and prophesy against[p] the forest of the southland.[q] [47]Say to the southern forest:[r] 'Hear the word of the LORD. This is what the Sovereign LORD says: I am about to set fire to you, and it will consume[s] all your trees, both green and dry. The blazing flame will not be quenched, and every face from south to north[t] will be scorched by it.[u] [48]Everyone will see that I the LORD have kindled it; it will not be quenched.[v] ' "

[49]Then I said, "Ah, Sovereign LORD![w] They are saying of me, 'Isn't he just telling parables?[x] ' "

Babylon, God's Sword of Judgment

21 The word of the LORD came to me:[y] [2]"Son of man, set your face against[z] Jerusalem and preach against the sanctuary.[a] Prophesy against[b] the land of Israel [3]and say to her: 'This is what the LORD says: I am against you.[c] I will draw my sword[d] from its scabbard and cut off from you both the righteous and the wicked.[e] [4]Because I am going to cut off the righteous and the wicked, my sword[f] will be unsheathed against everyone from south to north.[g] [5]Then all people will know that I the LORD have drawn my sword[h] from its scabbard; it will not return[i] again.'[j]

[6]"Therefore groan, son of man! Groan before them with broken heart and bitter grief.[k] [7]And when they ask you, 'Why are you groaning?[l] you shall say, 'Because of the news that is coming. Every heart will melt[m] and every hand go limp;[n] every spirit will become faint[o] and every knee become as weak as water.'[p] It is coming! It will surely take place, declares the Sovereign LORD."

[8]The word of the LORD came to me: [9]"Son of man, prophesy and say, 'This is what the Lord says:

" 'A sword, a sword,
    sharpened and polished—
[10]sharpened for the slaughter,[q]
    polished to flash like lightning!

" 'Shall we rejoice in the scepter of my son Judah? The sword despises every such stick.[r]

[11]" 'The sword is appointed to be
    polished,[s]
  to be grasped with the hand;
it is sharpened and polished,
  made ready for the hand of the
    slayer.
[12]Cry out and wail, son of man,
  for it is against my people;
  it is against all the princes of Israel.
They are thrown to the sword
  along with my people.
Therefore beat your breast.[t]

[13]" 'Testing will surely come. And what if the scepter of Judah, which the sword

---

Cross references (center column):

20:44 [m]Ps 109:21; Isa 43:25; Eze 36:22
[n]S Eze 16:62; 36:32
20:46 [o]S Eze 4:3; S 13:17
[p]Eze 21:2; Am 7:16
[q]Isa 30:6; Jer 13:19
20:47 [r]S 2Ki 19:23
[s]Eze 19:14
[t]Eze 21:4
[u]Isa 9:18-19; S 13:8
20:48 [v]S Jer 7:20; Eze 21:5,32; 23:25
20:49 [w]S Eze 4:14
[x]S Jdg 14:12; S Ps 78:2; S Eze 12:9; Mt 13:13; S Jn 16:25
21:1 [y]S Eze 20:1
21:2 [z]S Eze 13:17
[a]Eze 9:6
[b]Jer 26:11-12; S Eze 20:46
21:3 [c]S Jer 21:13
[d]S Isa 27:1; S Eze 14:21
21:4 [e]ver 9-11; S Job 9:22; S Isa 57:1; Jer 47:6-7
[f]S Lev 26:25; S Jer 25:27
[g]S Eze 20:47
21:5 [h]S Isa 34:5
[i]ver 30
[j]S Eze 20:47-48; Na 1:9
21:6 [k]ver 12; S Isa 22:4; Jer 30:6; S Eze 9:4
21:7 [l]S Job 23:2
[m]S Jos 7:5
[n]S Jer 47:3; Eze 22:14
[o]S Ps 6:2
[p]S Lev 26:36;
[q]S Job 11:16 **21:10** [q]Ps 110:5-6; Isa 34:5-6 [r]Dt 32:41 **21:11** [s]Jer 46:4 **21:12** [t]Jer 31:19

20:44 *for my name's sake.* Summarizes and concludes the oracle (see note on v. 9).
20:46 *set your face.* A posture required eight times of Ezekiel (here; 13:17; 21:2; 25:2; 28:21; 29:2; 35:2; 38:2). *toward the south.* Toward Judah and Jerusalem, the object of all of Ezekiel's prophesying in these chapters. Any Babylonian invasion would traverse Palestine from north to south (see 26:7).
20:47 *set fire.* Common figurative language for invading forces (see Isa 10:16–19; Jer 15:14; 17:4,27; 21:14; see also note on 15:7). *both green and dry.* All trees (cf. 17:24; Lk 23:31). *from south to north.* Expresses totality, not direction; equivalent to saying, "from the border on the right to that on the left."
20:49 *parables.* See note on 17:2; for other ridiculing of the prophet see 12:21–28; 33:32.
21:2 *set your face.* See note on 20:46. *against the sanctuary.* See 9:6 and note.
21:3 *I am against you.* See note on 5:8. *my sword.* For the sword of the Lord's judgment see Isa 31:8; 34:6; 66:16. This is the first of five sword oracles (see vv. 8–17, 18–24, 25–27, 28–32). Here the sword refers to Babylon and Nebuchadnezzar (v. 19). *both the righteous and the wicked.* Indicates the completeness of the judgment that is about to come on Israel. No one will escape its devastating effects, not

even the righteous in the land. Contrast God's deliverance of Noah (Ge 6:7–8) and Lot (Ge 18:23; 19:12–13).
21:4 *from south to north.* See note on 20:47.
21:6 *groan . . . with broken heart and bitter grief.* Ezekiel's display of intense grief is to serve as another prophetic sign and as an occasion for a new message of impending judgment.
21:7 *when they ask you.* Cf. 12:9 for the people's response to Ezekiel's behavior. This is Ezekiel's seventh symbolic act (see Introduction: Literary Features).
21:9 *A sword, a sword.* A sword song (see note on v. 3), possibly accompanied by dancing or symbolic actions. Such songs may have been sung by warriors about to go into battle (see note on 2Sa 1:18).
21:10b To think that the Babylonians would conquer every other country except Judah was a false hope. *scepter.* Represents rule, government or kingdom. *my son Judah.* Corresponds to "my people" in v. 12 (see Ge 49:9). *sword.* Babylon and Nebuchadnezzar (v. 19).
21:11 *slayer.* Nebuchadnezzar (v. 19).
21:12 *Cry out and wail . . . beat your breast.* Eighth symbolic act (see Introduction: Literary Features).
21:13 *come.* On Judah. *what if the scepter . . . does not continue?* See note on v. 10b. The question anticipates the final interruption of Davidic kingship, which came in 586

despises, does not continue? declares the
Sovereign LORD.'

[14]"So then, son of man, prophesy
   and strike your hands[u] together.
Let the sword strike twice,
   even three times.
It is a sword for slaughter—
   a sword for great slaughter,
   closing in on them from every side.[v]
[15]So that hearts may melt[w]
   and the fallen be many,
I have stationed the sword for
   slaughter[s]
   at all their gates.
Oh! It is made to flash like lightning,
   it is grasped for slaughter.[x]
[16]O sword, slash to the right,
   then to the left,
   wherever your blade is turned.
[17]I too will strike my hands[y] together,
   and my wrath[z] will subside.
I the LORD have spoken.[a] "

[18]The word of the LORD came to me:
[19]"Son of man, mark out two roads for the
sword[b] of the king of Babylon to take,
both starting from the same country. Make
a signpost[c] where the road branches off to
the city. [20]Mark out one road for the sword
to come against Rabbah of the Ammonites[d] and another against Judah and fortified Jerusalem. [21]For the king of Babylon
will stop at the fork in the road, at the
junction of the two roads, to seek an
omen: He will cast lots[e] with arrows, he
will consult his idols,[f] he will examine the
liver.[g] [22]Into his right hand will come the
lot for Jerusalem, where he is to set up

battering rams, to give the command to
slaughter, to sound the battle cry,[h] to set
battering rams against the gates, to build a
ramp[i] and to erect siege works.[j] [23]It will
seem like a false omen to those who have
sworn allegiance to him, but he will
remind[k] them of their guilt[l] and take
them captive.

[24]"Therefore this is what the Sovereign
LORD says: 'Because you people have
brought to mind your guilt by your open
rebellion, revealing your sins in all that you
do—because you have done this, you will
be taken captive.

[25]" 'O profane and wicked prince of Israel, whose day has come,[m] whose time of
punishment has reached its climax,[n] [26]this
is what the Sovereign LORD says: Take off
the turban, remove the crown.[o] It will not
be as it was: The lowly will be exalted and
the exalted will be brought low.[p] [27]A ruin!
A ruin! I will make it a ruin! It will not be
restored until he comes to whom it rightfully belongs;[q] to him I will give it.'[r]

[28]"And you, son of man, prophesy and
say, 'This is what the Sovereign LORD says
about the Ammonites[s] and their insults:

" 'A sword,[t] a sword,
   drawn for the slaughter,
polished to consume
   and to flash like lightning!
[29]Despite false visions concerning you
   and lying divinations[u] about you,
it will be laid on the necks
   of the wicked who are to be slain,

Cross references (center column):

21:14 [u]ver 17; S Nu 24:10
[v]S Eze 6:11; 30:24
21:15 [w]S 2Sa 17:10
[x]Ps 22:14
21:17 [y]ver 14; Eze 22:13
[z]S Eze 5:13
[a]S Eze 6:11; S 16:42
21:19 [b]S Eze 14:21; 32:11 [c]Jer 31:21
21:20 [d]S Dt 3:11
21:21 [e]S Pr 16:33
[f]Zec 10:2
[g]Nu 22:7; S 23:23
21:22 [h]S Jer 4:16
[i]Jer 32:24
[j]S 2Ki 25:1; S Eze 4:2; 26:9
21:23 [k]S Nu 5:15
[l]S Eze 17:19
21:25 [m]Eze 22:4
[n]Eze 35:5
21:26 [o]S Isa 28:5; S Jer 13:18
[p]S Ps 75:7; Isa 40:4; S Eze 17:24; S Mt 23:12
21:27 [q]Ge 49:10
[r]Ps 2:6; Jer 23:5-6; Eze 37:24; Hag 2:21-22
21:28 [s]S Ge 19:38; Zep 2:8
[t]S Jer 12:12
21:29 [u]Jer 27:9

---

[s]15 Septuagint; the meaning of the Hebrew for this word
is uncertain.

Study notes (bottom):

B.C. (see vv. 25–27).

21:14 *strike your hands.* See 6:11 and note. *Let the sword
strike twice.* Cf. 2Ki 13:18–19.

21:17 *strike my hands.* In scorn and in harmony with
God's command to Ezekiel in v. 14.

21:19 *king of Babylon.* Nebuchadnezzar. *same country.*
Babylon, or possibly Aram (Syria)—Nebuchadnezzar headquartered at Riblah in northern Aram (see 2Ki 25:6).

21:20 *Rabbah.* Capital of Ammon (Jer 49:2); modern Amman (capital of Jordan).

21:21 *cast lots with arrows.* Divination with arrows, for
the purpose of seeking good omens for the coming campaign—a practice not elsewhere mentioned in the Bible.
Apparently arrows were labeled (e.g., "Rabbah," "Jerusalem"), placed into a quiver and drawn out, one with each
hand. Right-hand selection was seen as a good omen (see v.
22). *idols.* The Hebrew for this word is translated "household gods" in Ge 31:19. Consulting them is referred to in
Hos 3:4; Zec 10:2. The household gods of Ge 31:19–35
were small enough to hide in a saddle, but others were
life-size (1Sa 19:13–16). *examine the liver.* Looking at the
color and configurations of sheep livers to foretell the future
was common in ancient Babylonia and Rome, but the practice is not mentioned elsewhere in the Bible.

21:23 *false omen.* The leaders of Jerusalem, once submis-

sive to Nebuchadnezzar but now in rebellion (2Ki 24:20),
hoped that the result of the omen-seeking (vv. 21–22) was
misleading.

21:25 *prince of Israel.* Zedekiah (see note on 7:27).

21:26 *turban.* Only here is it mentioned as royal headwear.
Elsewhere it is worn by priests (Ex 28:4,37,39; 29:6;
39:28,31; Lev 8:9; 16:4), as a setting for the crown (Ex
28:36–37; 29:6; 39:31; Lev 8:9). It was made of fine linen
(Ex 28:39; 39:28). *lowly...exalted...exalted...brought
low.* A common Biblical expression for the reversal of human
conditions because of the intervention of the Lord (see
17:24; 1Sa 2:7–8; Lk 1:52–53).

21:27 *A ruin! A ruin!...a ruin!* Threefold repetition for
emphasis (see Isa 6:3; Jer 7:4). *until he comes to whom it
rightfully belongs.* The Messiah; apparently an allusion to Ge
49:10 (see note there). Or possibly the reference is to Nebuchadnezzar, translating "... whose is the judgment" or
". . . who pronounces sentence" (see 2Ki 25:6).

21:28 *Ammonites.* See v. 20. After judgment on Jerusalem, the foreigners would be dealt with (cf. Isa 10:5). *their
insults.* See 25:3,6; also cf. 36:15. *A sword, a sword.* Nebuchadnezzar's (see vv. 9,19 and notes).

21:29 *false visions...lying divinations.* Apparently Ammon also had false prophets of peace (see v. 10 and note;
13:10; Jer 6:14; 8:11–12). *it.* The sword.

whose day has come,
    whose time of punishment has
        reached its climax. *v*
30Return the sword to its scabbard. *w*
    In the place where you were created,
    in the land of your ancestry, *x*
    I will judge you.
31I will pour out my wrath upon you
    and breathe*y* out my fiery anger *z*
        against you;
    I will hand you over to brutal men,
    men skilled in destruction. *a*
32You will be fuel for the fire, *b*
    your blood will be shed in your land,
    you will be remembered*c* no more;
    for I the LORD have spoken.' "

Jerusalem's Sins

22 The word of the LORD came to me:
2"Son of man, will you judge her?
Will you judge this city of bloodshed? *d*
Then confront her with all her detestable
practices *e* 3and say: 'This is what the Sovereign LORD says: O city that brings on
herself doom by shedding blood*f* in her
midst and defiles herself by making idols,
4you have become guilty because of the
blood you have shed*g* and have become
defiled by the idols you have made. You
have brought your days to a close, and the
end of your years has come. *h* Therefore I
will make you an object of scorn*i* to the
nations and a laughingstock to all the
countries. *j* 5Those who are near and those
who are far away will mock you, O infamous city, full of turmoil. *k*

6" 'See how each of the princes of Israel
who are in you uses his power to shed
blood. *l* 7In you they have treated father
and mother with contempt; *m* in you they
have oppressed the alien *n* and mistreated
the fatherless and the widow. *o* 8You have
despised my holy things and desecrated my
Sabbaths. *p* 9In you are slanderous men*q*
bent on shedding blood; *r* in you are those
who eat at the mountain shrines*s* and
commit lewd acts. *t* 10In you are those
who dishonor their fathers' bed; *u* in you

are those who violate women during their
period, *v* when they are ceremonially unclean. *w* 11In you one man commits a detestable offense with his neighbor's wife, *x*
another shamefully defiles his daughter-in-
law, *y* and another violates his sister, *z* his
own father's daughter. *a* 12In you men accept bribes*b* to shed blood; you take
usury*c* and excessive interest*t* and make
unjust gain from your neighbors *d* by extortion. And you have forgotten*e* me, declares the Sovereign LORD. *f*

13" 'I will surely strike my hands*g* together at the unjust gain *h* you have made
and at the blood*i* you have shed in your
midst. *j* 14Will your courage endure*k* or
your hands*l* be strong in the day I deal
with you? I the LORD have spoken, *m* and I
will do it. *n* 15I will disperse you among the
nations and scatter*o* you through the
countries; and I will put an end to*p* your
uncleanness. *q* 16When you have been
defiled*u* in the eyes of the nations, you will
know that I am the LORD.' "

17Then the word of the LORD came to
me: 18"Son of man, the house of Israel has
become dross*r* to me; all of them are the
copper, tin, iron and lead left inside a furnace. *s* They are but the dross of silver. *t*
19Therefore this is what the Sovereign
LORD says: 'Because you have all become
dross, *u* I will gather you into Jerusalem.
20As men gather silver, copper, iron, lead
and tin into a furnace to melt it with a fiery
blast, so will I gather you in my anger and
my wrath and put you inside the city and
melt you. *v* 21I will gather you and I will
blow*w* on you with my fiery wrath, and
you will be melted inside her. *x* 22As silver
is melted*y* in a furnace, so you will be
melted inside her, and you will know that I

Cross references (center column)

21:29 *v*ver 25;
Eze 22:28; 35:5
21:30 *w*ver 5;
Jer 47:6
*x*S Eze 16:3
21:31 *y*Ps 18:15;
S Isa 11:4
*z*Ps 79:6;
Eze 22:20-21
*a*S Jer 4:7;
51:20-23;
S Eze 16:39
21:32
*b*S Eze 20:47-48;
Mal 4:1
*c*Eze 25:10
22:2 *d*Eze 24:6,
9; Hos 4:2;
Na 3:1; Hab 2:12
*e*S Eze 16:2;
23:36
22:3 *f*ver 6,13,
27; Eze 23:37,45;
24:6
22:4
*g*S 2Ki 21:16
*h*Eze 21:25
*i*S Ps 137:3
*j*Ps 44:13-14;
S Eze 5:14
22:5 *k*S Isa 22:2
22:6 *l*S Eze 11:6;
18:10; 33:25
22:7 *m*S Dt 5:16;
Mic 7:6
*n*S Ex 23:9
*o*S Ex 22:21-22
22:8 *p*S Eze 20:8;
Eze 23:38-39
22:9
*q*S Lev 19:16
*r*Isa 59:3;
S Eze 11:6;
Hos 4:2; 6:9
*s*Eze 18:11
*t*Eze 23:29;
Hos 4:10,14
22:10 *u*Lev 18:7

*v*S Lev 12:2
*w*S Lev 18:8,19
22:11 *x*S Jer 5:8
*y*S Ge 11:31;
Lev 18:15
*z*S Lev 18:9;
S 2Sa 13:14
*a*Eze 18:6
22:12
*b*S Ex 18:21;
Dt 27:25;
Ps 26:10;
Isa 5:23;
Am 5:12; Mic 7:3
*c*S Eze 18:8
*d*Lev 19:13
*e*Ps 106:21;
S Isa 17:10;
S 57:11
*f*S Eze 11:6
22:13
*g*S Nu 24:10;
S Eze 21:17
*h*S ver 27;
S Isa 33:15 *i*S ver
3 *i*S Eze 6:11

22:14 *k*Ps 76:7; Joel 2:11; Na 1:6; Mal 3:2 *l*S Eze 7:17
*m*Eze 24:14 *n*S Eze 17:24 22:15 *o*S Lev 26:33; Dt 4:27;
Zec 7:14 *p*S Eze 16:41 *q*Eze 24:11 22:18 *r*S Ps 119:119
*s*Isa 48:10 *t*Jer 6:28-30 22:19 *u*S Ps 119:119 22:20
*v*Hos 8:10; Mal 3:2 22:21 *w*Isa 40:7; Hag 1:9 *x*Ps 68:2;
Eze 21:31 22:22 *y*S Isa 1:25

*t*12 Or usury and interest   *u*16 Or When I have
allotted you your inheritance

21:30 *Return the sword.* Addressing Nebuchadnezzar.
21:31 *brutal men.* The people of the East, as in 25:4.
22:2 *will you judge her?* Cf. 20:4. *this city.* Jerusalem, the
usual focal point of Ezekiel's prophecy (see 5:5).
22:3 *shedding blood . . . making idols.* Two categories of
sins are developed: social injustices and idol worship. *idols.*
See note on 6:4.
22:6 *princes of Israel.* Leaders generally, not kings; contrast 21:12 with 19:1.
22:7 *mistreated the fatherless and the widow.* Cf. Isa
1:17.
22:8 *Sabbaths.* A major concern in Ezekiel (see note on
20:12).

22:9 *eat at the mountain shrines and commit lewd acts.*
See notes on 6:3; 16:15; 18:6.
22:10 *violate women.* Cf. 18:6.
22:11 *detestable offense.* All the sins mentioned in this
verse were specifically forbidden in the law (Lev 18:7–20;
20:10–21; Dt 22:22–23,30; 27:22).
22:12 *usury and excessive interest.* See note on 18:8.
22:13 *strike my hands.* In anger (see 21:14,17).
22:18 *dross.* For references to Jerusalem as a furnace see
Isa 1:21–26; Jer 6:27–30. Typically, imagery used by others
to represent purifying was used by Ezekiel to picture total
destruction (see note on 15:4).

the LORD have poured out my wrath[z] upon you.'"[a]

[23]Again the word of the LORD came to me: [24]"Son of man, say to the land, 'You are a land that has had no rain or showers[v] in the day of wrath.'[b] [25]There is a conspiracy[c] of her princes[w] within her like a roaring lion[d] tearing its prey; they devour people,[e] take treasures and precious things and make many widows[f] within her. [26]Her priests do violence to my law[g] and profane my holy things; they do not distinguish between the holy and the common;[h] they teach that there is no difference between the unclean and the clean;[i] and they shut their eyes to the keeping of my Sabbaths, so that I am profaned[j] among them.[k] [27]Her officials[l] within her are like wolves[m] tearing their prey; they shed blood and kill people[n] to make unjust gain.[o] [28]Her prophets whitewash[p] these deeds for them by false visions and lying divinations.[q] They say, 'This is what the Sovereign LORD says'—when the LORD has not spoken.[r] [29]The people of the land practice extortion and commit robbery;[s] they oppress the poor and needy and mistreat the alien,[t] denying them justice.[u]

[30]"I looked for a man among them who would build up the wall[v] and stand before me in the gap on behalf of the land so I would not have to destroy it, but I found none.[w] [31]So I will pour out my wrath on them and consume them with my fiery anger,[x] bringing down[y] on their own heads all they have done, declares the Sovereign LORD.[z]"

Two Adulterous Sisters

23 The word of the LORD came to me: [2]"Son of man, there were two women, daughters of the same mother.[a] [3]They became prostitutes in Egypt,[b] en-

gaging in prostitution[c] from their youth.[d] In that land their breasts were fondled and their virgin bosoms caressed.[e] [4]The older was named Oholah, and her sister was Oholibah. They were mine and gave birth to sons and daughters. Oholah is Samaria, and Oholibah is Jerusalem.[f]

[5]"Oholah engaged in prostitution while she was still mine; and she lusted after her lovers, the Assyrians[g]—warriors[h] [6]clothed in blue, governors and commanders, all of them handsome young men, and mounted horsemen. [7]She gave herself as a prostitute to all the elite of the Assyrians and defiled herself with all the idols of everyone she lusted after.[i] [8]She did not give up the prostitution she began in Egypt,[j] when during her youth men slept with her, caressed her virgin bosom and poured out their lust upon her.[k]

[9]"Therefore I handed her over[l] to her lovers,[m] the Assyrians, for whom she lusted.[n] [10]They stripped[o] her naked, took away her sons and daughters and killed her with the sword. She became a byword among women,[p] and punishment was inflicted[q] on her.[r]

[11]"Her sister Oholibah saw this,[s] yet in her lust and prostitution she was more depraved than her sister.[t] [12]She too lusted after the Assyrians—governors and commanders, warriors in full dress, mounted horsemen, all handsome young men.[u] [13]I saw that she too defiled herself; both of them went the same way.[v]

[14]"But she carried her prostitution still further. She saw men portrayed on a

---

22:22 [z]S Eze 7:8
[a]S Isa 64:7
22:24 [b]Eze 24:13
22:25 [c]Jer 11:9
[d]S Ps 22:13
[e]Hos 6:9
[f]Jer 15:8; 18:21
22:26
[g]Hos 9:7-8;
Zep 3:4;
Mal 2:7-8
[h]Eze 42:20;
44:23
[i]S Lev 20:25
/S Lev 18:21;
S Eze 13:19 [k]ver
8; S 1Sa 2:12-17;
Jer 2:8,26;
Hag 2:11-14
22:27
[l]S Jer 26:10;
[m]S ver 3;
S Eze 11:6;
33:25; 34:2-3;
Mic 3:2,10 [o]ver
13; S Ge 37:24;
S Isa 1:23;
S Jer 12:2;
S 51:13;
Eze 33:31
22:28
[p]S Eze 13:10
[q]S La 2:14;
S 4:13;
S Eze 21:29
[r]S Eze 13:2,6-7
22:29
[s]S Ps 62:10
[t]S Ex 22:21
[u]S Isa 5:7
22:30
[v]S Eze 13:5
[w]Ps 106:23;
S Isa 64:7; Jer 5:1
22:31
[x]Ex 32:10;
S Isa 30:27;
S La 4:11
[y]Eze 16:43
[z]Eze 7:8-9;
Ro 2:8
23:2 [a]S Jer 3:7;
S Eze 16:45
23:3 [b]Jos 24:14

[c]S Lev 17:7;
S Isa 1:21
[d]S Ps 25:7
[e]S Eze 16:15
23:4 /S Eze 16:46
23:5 [g]S 2Ki 16:7;
Hos 5:13
[h]Hos 8:9
23:7 [i]Isa 57:8;
Hos 5:3; 6:10
23:8 /Ex 32:4
[k]S Eze 16:15

23:9 [l]S 2Ki 18:11 [m]S Jer 4:30 [n]Hos 11:5 23:10 [o]Hos 2:10
[p]Eze 16:41 [q]Jer 42:10 [r]Eze 16:36 23:11 [s]S Jer 3:7
[t]Jer 3:8-11; S Eze 16:51 23:12 [u]2Ki 16:7-15; S 2Ch 28:16;
S Eze 16:15,28 23:13 [v]S 2Ki 17:19; Hos 12:2

[v]24 Septuagint; Hebrew *has not been cleansed or rained
on*   [w]25 Septuagint; Hebrew *prophets*

22:25 *princes.* Ezekiel begins to speak plainly concerning the "dross" of vv. 18–22. All of Jerusalem's leaders and people were included: princes (here), priests (v. 26), officials (v. 27), prophets (v. 28), people (v. 29). *like a roaring lion.* Cf. v. 27; 13:4; Zep 3:3.
22:26 *distinguish between the holy and the common.* The main duty of priests (see 44:23). *Sabbaths.* See note on v. 8.
22:28 *whitewash.* See 13:10 and note.
22:29 *people of the land.* See 7:27 and note.
22:30 *I looked for a man.* Cf. Isa 51:18; 59:16; 63:5. *stand before me in the gap.* See note on 13:5. To intercede with God in behalf of the people was part of a prophet's task (Ge 20:7; 1Sa 12:23; Jer 37:3; 42:2). Some interpret the task here as teaching, particularly calling the people to repentance. Cf. the task of the prophetic "watchman" (3:17–21; 33:1–6).
23:4 *Oholah.* Means "her tent." *Oholibah.* Means "My tent is in her." Cf. the two sisters of Jer 3:6–12. "Tent" could stand for Canaanite high places, for the Lord's taber-

nacle (except that Ezekiel never uses the word elsewhere for the legitimate shrine) or for Israel's tent-dwelling origin.
23:5 *prostitution.* Here represents political alliances with pagan powers—not idolatry as in ch. 16 (see note on 16:15). The graphic language of the chapter underscores God's and Ezekiel's disgust with Israel for playing the worldly game of international politics rather than relying on the Lord for her security—as clear a case of religious prostitution as idolatry. *Assyrians.* See 2Ki 15:19.
23:8 *in Egypt.* Cf. 20:5–8. Israel's entire history was marked by unfaithfulness. For her attachment to Egypt see Ex 17:3; Nu 11:5,18,20; 14:2–4; 21:5.
23:10 *stripped her naked.* A reference to the fall of Samaria to the Assyrians in 722–721 B.C.
23:14 *men portrayed on a wall.* Arousal through pictures was even more perverted (see 16:17 and note). *portrayed in red.* Jeremiah, too, noted red interior decorations with disfavor (Jer 22:14).

wall,[w] figures of Chaldeans[x] portrayed in
red,[x] 15with belts[y] around their waists
and flowing turbans on their heads; all of
them looked like Babylonian chariot officers, natives of Chaldea.[y] 16As soon as she
saw them, she lusted after them and sent
messengers[z] to them in Chaldea.[a] 17Then
the Babylonians[b] came to her, to the bed
of love, and in their lust they defiled her.
After she had been defiled by them, she
turned away from them in disgust.[c]
18When she carried on her prostitution
openly and exposed her nakedness,[d] I
turned away[e] from her in disgust, just as I
had turned away from her sister.[f] 19Yet
she became more and more promiscuous
as she recalled the days of her youth, when
she was a prostitute in Egypt. 20There she
lusted after her lovers, whose genitals were
like those of donkeys and whose emission
was like that of horses. 21So you longed for
the lewdness of your youth, when in Egypt
your bosom was caressed and your young
breasts fondled.[z] [g]

22"Therefore, Oholibah, this is what the
Sovereign LORD says: I will stir up your
lovers[h] against you, those you turned
away from in disgust, and I will bring them
against you from every side[i]— 23the Babylonians[j] and all the Chaldeans,[k] the men
of Pekod[l] and Shoa and Koa, and all the
Assyrians with them, handsome young
men, all of them governors and commanders, chariot officers and men of high rank,
all mounted on horses.[m] 24They will come
against you with weapons,[a] chariots and
wagons[n] and with a throng of people; they
will take up positions against you on every
side with large and small shields and with
helmets. I will turn you over to them for
punishment,[o] and they will punish you according to their standards. 25I will direct
my jealous anger[p] against you, and they
will deal with you in fury. They will cut off
your noses and your ears, and those of you
who are left will fall by the sword. They
will take away your sons and daughters,[q]
and those of you who are left will be consumed by fire.[r] 26They will also strip[s] you
of your clothes and take your fine jewelry.[t] 27So I will put a stop[u] to the lewdness
and prostitution you began in Egypt. You
will not look on these things with longing
or remember Egypt anymore.

28"For this is what the Sovereign LORD
says: I am about to hand you over[v] to
those you hate, to those you turned away
from in disgust. 29They will deal with you
in hatred and take away everything you
have worked for. They will leave you
naked[w] and bare, and the shame of your
prostitution will be exposed.[x] Your lewdness[y] and promiscuity[z] 30have brought
this upon you, because you lusted after the
nations and defiled yourself with their
idols.[a] 31You have gone the way of your
sister; so I will put her cup[b] into your
hand.[c]

32"This is what the Sovereign LORD
says:

"You will drink your sister's cup,
a cup large and deep;
it will bring scorn and derision,[d]
for it holds so much.[e]
33You will be filled with drunkenness and sorrow,
the cup of ruin and desolation,
the cup of your sister Samaria.[f]
34You will drink it[g] and drain it dry;
you will dash it to pieces
and tear your breasts.

I have spoken, declares the Sovereign
LORD.[h]

35"Therefore this is what the Sovereign
LORD says: Since you have forgotten[i] me
and thrust me behind your back,[j] you
must bear[k] the consequences of your
lewdness and prostitution."

36The LORD said to me: "Son of man,
will you judge Oholah and Oholibah? Then
confront[l] them with their detestable practices,[m] 37for they have committed adultery
and blood is on their hands. They committed adultery with their idols; they even
sacrificed their children, whom they bore
to me,[b] as food for them.[n] 38They have

23:14 [w]S Eze 8:10 [x]Jer 22:14; Na 2:3
23:15 [y]S Isa 5:27
23:16 [z]S Isa 57:9 [a]S Eze 6:9
23:17 [b]Jer 40:9 [c]S Eze 16:29
23:18 [d]S Isa 57:8 [e]Ps 78:59; 106:40; Jer 6:8 [f]Jer 12:8; Am 5:21
23:21 [g]S Eze 16:26
23:22 [h]S Jer 4:30 [i]S Eze 16:37
23:23 [j]2Ki 20:14-18; S Jer 40:9 [k]S Ge 11:28 [l]Jer 50:21 [m]S 2Ki 24:2
23:24 [n]Jer 47:3; Eze 26:7,10; Na 2:4 [o]Jer 39:5-6
23:25 [p]S Dt 29:20 [q]ver 47; Eze 24:21 [r]S Jer 12:9; S Eze 16:38; S 20:47-48
23:26 [s]S Jer 13:22 [t]S Isa 3:18-23; S Eze 16:39
23:27 [u]S Eze 16:41
23:28 [v]S Jer 34:20
23:29 [w]Mic 1:11 [x]S Jer 13:27 [y]S Eze 22:9 [z]Dt 28:48; S Eze 16:36
23:30 [a]Ps 106:37-38; Zep 3:1
23:31 [b]S Jer 25:15 [c]2Ki 21:13
23:32 [d]Ps 44:13; Hos 7:16 [e]Ps 60:3; Isa 51:17; Jer 25:15
23:33 [f]Jer 25:15-16; S Eze 12:19
23:34 [g]S Ps 16:5 [h]S Jer 25:27
23:35 [i]S Dt 32:18; S Isa 17:10 [j]S 1Ki 14:9; S 2Ch 29:6 [k]Eze 16:52
23:36 [l]S Eze 16:2 [m]Isa 58:1; S Eze 22:2; Mic 3:8
23:37 [n]S Eze 16:36

[x] *14* Or *Babylonians* [y] *15* Or *Babylonia*; also in verse 16 [z] *21* Syriac (see also verse 3); Hebrew *caressed because of your young breasts* [a] *24* The meaning of the Hebrew for this word is uncertain. [b] *37* Or *even made the children they bore to me pass through* ⌊*the fire*⌋

23:15 *belts.* Cf. Isa 5:27 for similar Assyrian military equipment.
23:20 *genitals.* See note on 16:26.
23:23 *Babylonians . . . Chaldeans.* Often identified with one another (see 1:3 and NIV text note there; 12:13), here distinguished (as in v. 15), probably because the Chaldeans were relative newcomers. *Pekod.* Aramaic people located east of Babylon. *Shoa and Koa.* Babylonian allies of uncertain origin and location.
23:24 *their standards.* Which were cruel and gruesome (see v. 25).
23:25 *fire.* See notes on 15:7; 20:47.
23:27 *in Egypt.* See note on v. 8.
23:31 *cup.* Filled with the anger of the Lord. To drink it was to die. For a development of the imagery cf. Ps 75:8; Isa 51:17,22; Jer 25:15–29; 49:12; La 4:21; Ob 16; Hab 2:16; Mt 20:22; 26:39; Rev 14:10.
23:37 *sacrificed their children.* See note on 16:20.

also done this to me: At that same time they defiled my sanctuary[o] and desecrated my Sabbaths.[p] 39On the very day they sacrificed their children to their idols, they entered my sanctuary and desecrated[q] it. That is what they did in my house.[r]

40"They even sent messengers for men who came from far away,[s] and when they arrived you bathed yourself for them, painted your eyes[t] and put on your jewelry.[u] 41You sat on an elegant couch,[v] with a table[w] spread before it on which you had placed the incense[x] and oil that belonged to me.[y]

42"The noise of a carefree[z] crowd was around her; Sabeans[c a] were brought from the desert along with men from the rabble, and they put bracelets[b] on the arms of the woman and her sister and beautiful crowns on their heads.[c] 43Then I said about the one worn out by adultery, 'Now let them use her as a prostitute,[d] for that is all she is.' 44And they slept with her. As men sleep with a prostitute, so they slept with those lewd women, Oholah and Oholibah. 45But righteous men will sentence them to the punishment of women who commit adultery and shed blood,[e] because they are adulterous and blood is on their hands.[f]

46"This is what the Sovereign LORD says: Bring a mob[g] against them and give them over to terror and plunder.[h] 47The mob will stone them and cut them down with their swords; they will kill their sons and daughters[i] and burn[j] down their houses.[k]

48"So I will put an end[l] to lewdness in the land, that all women may take warning and not imitate you.[m] 49You will suffer the penalty for your lewdness and bear the consequences of your sins of idolatry.[n]

Then you will know that I am the Sovereign LORD.[o]"

The Cooking Pot

24 In the ninth year, in the tenth month on the tenth day, the word of the LORD came to me:[p] 2"Son of man, record[q] this date, this very date, because the king of Babylon has laid siege to Jerusalem this very day.[r] 3Tell this rebellious house[s] a parable[t] and say to them: 'This is what the Sovereign LORD says:

  " 'Put on the cooking pot;[u] put it on
      and pour water into it.
4Put into it the pieces of meat,
    all the choice pieces—the leg and the
      shoulder.
Fill it with the best of these bones;[v]
5 take the pick of the flock.[w]
Pile wood beneath it for the bones;
    bring it to a boil
    and cook the bones in it.[x]

6"'For this is what the Sovereign LORD says:

  " 'Woe[y] to the city of bloodshed,[z]
    to the pot now encrusted,
    whose deposit will not go away!
Empty it piece by piece
    without casting lots[a] for them.[b]

7"'For the blood she shed is in her
    midst:
    She poured it on the bare rock;
  she did not pour it on the ground,
    where the dust would cover it.[c]
8To stir up wrath and take revenge
    I put her blood on the bare rock,
    so that it would not be covered.

Cross references

23:38
[o]S Lev 15:31
[p]S Ne 10:31
23:39
[q]S 2Ki 21:4
[r]S Jer 7:10;
Eze 22:8
23:40 [s]S Isa 57:9
[t]2Ki 9:30
[u]S Jer 4:30;
Eze 16:13-19;
Hos 2:13
23:41 [v]S Est 1:6;
S Pr 7:17
[w]Isa 65:11;
Eze 41:22; 44:16;
Mal 1:7,12
[x]Isa 57:9; S 65:3;
S Jer 44:5
[y]S Nu 18:12
23:42 [z]S Ps 73:5
[a]S 2Ch 9:1
[b]S Ge 24:30
[c]S Eze 16:11-12
23:43 [d]ver 3
23:45
[e]S Eze 22:3
[f]S Lev 20:10;
S Eze 16:38;
Hos 2:2; 6:5
23:46 [g]Eze 16:40
[h]S Dt 28:25;
S Jer 25:9
23:47 [i]S ver 25
[j]2Ch 36:19;
S Jer 34:22
[k]S 2Ch 36:17
23:48 [l]Eze 16:41
[m]2Pe 2:6
23:49 [n]Eze 24:13

[o]S Eze 7:4;
S 9:10; 16:58;
S 20:38
24:1 [p]S Eze 8:1;
26:1; 29:17
24:2 [q]Isa 30:8;
Hab 2:2
[r]2Ki 25:1;
S Jer 39:1
24:3 [s]S Isa 1:2;
S Eze 2:3,6
[t]S Eze 20:49
[u]S Eze 11:3
24:4 [v]S Eze 11:7
24:5
[w]S Isa 34:12;
Jer 52:10
[x]Jer 52:24-27;
Mic 3:2-3
24:6
[y]S Eze 16:23
[z]S Eze 22:2
[a]S Job 6:27;
Joel 3:3; Ob 1:11;
Na 3:10
24:7 [c]S Lev 17:13

[c]42 Or drunkards

23:38 *defiled my sanctuary.* See ch. 8. *Sabbaths.* See note on 22:8.
23:40 *They even sent messengers for men.* Possibly a reference to the Jerusalem summit meeting in Zedekiah's time (Jer 27). *you.* Jerusalem. *painted your eyes.* By daubing them with kohl, a soot-like compound, to draw attention to the eyes.
23:41 *couch, with a table spread before it.* Ready for a banquet (see Isa 21:5; also Pr 9:2).
23:42 *Sabeans.* Men from Sheba, located at the southwest corner of the Arabian peninsula (modern Yemen), known for trading (see Job 6:19; see also Eze 27:22; 38:13; 1Ki 10:1-10). But see NIV text note.
24:1 *ninth year . . . tenth month . . . tenth day.* Jan. 15, 588 B.C.; Ezekiel's fourth date (see 1:2; 8:1; 20:1).
24:2 *record this date . . . because.* God revealed to Ezekiel what was happening in Jerusalem.
24:3 *rebellious house.* The last occurrence of this condemning phrase in Ezekiel (see 2:5,6,8; 3:9,26-27;

12:2-3,9,25; 17:12). Jerusalem's rebellion would soon be crushed. *parable.* Cf. 17:2; 20:49. *cooking pot.* The image of 11:3-12, a discussion of the remnant, here pictures total destruction. The cooking pot is Jerusalem (cf. 11:3).
24:4 *choice pieces.* The people of Jerusalem who thought they were spared the exile in 597 B.C. because of their goodness (see 11:3 and note).
24:5 *wood.* Nebuchadnezzar's siege equipment.
24:6 *city of bloodshed.* Cf. 22:3. *encrusted.* Representing Jerusalem's irredeemable situation. *without casting lots for them.* After the siege of Jerusalem in 597, perhaps the Babylonians had cast lots to see whom they would take away into exile. Now everyone would go.
24:7 *blood . . . on the bare rock.* Jerusalem had brazenly left on display the blood she unjustly shed (cf. Isa 3:9). For uncovered blood see Ge 4:10; Job 16:18; Isa 26:21.
24:8 *wrath.* God's wrath. What Jerusalem had begun (v. 7), God would complete through judgment. Compare Ex 8:32 with Ex 9:12.

9 " 'Therefore this is what the Sovereign LORD says:

" 'Woe to the city of bloodshed!
I, too, will pile the wood high.
10So heap on the wood
and kindle the fire.
Cook the meat well,
mixing in the spices;
and let the bones be charred.
11Then set the empty pot on the coals
till it becomes hot and its copper glows
so its impurities may be melted
and its deposit burned away. *d*
12It has frustrated all efforts;
its heavy deposit has not been removed,
not even by fire.

13 " 'Now your impurity is lewdness. Because I tried to cleanse you but you would not be cleansed *e* from your impurity, you will not be clean again until my wrath against you has subsided. *f*

14 " 'I the LORD have spoken. *g* The time has come for me to act. *h* I will not hold back; I will not have pity, *i* nor will I relent. *j* You will be judged according to your conduct and your actions, *k* declares the Sovereign LORD. *l* ' "

Ezekiel's Wife Dies

15The word of the LORD came to me: 16"Son of man, with one blow *m* I am about to take away from you the delight of your eyes. *n* Yet do not lament or weep or shed any tears. *o* 17Groan quietly; *p* do not mourn for the dead. Keep your turban *q* fastened and your sandals *r* on your feet; do not cover the lower part of your face *s* or eat the customary food of mourners. *t* "

18So I spoke to the people in the morning, and in the evening my wife died. The next morning I did as I had been commanded. *u*

19Then the people asked me, "Won't you tell us what these things have to do with us? *v* "

20So I said to them, "The word of the LORD came to me: 21Say to the house of Israel, 'This is what the Sovereign LORD says: I am about to desecrate my sanctuary *w*—the stronghold in which you take pride, *x* the delight of your eyes, *y* the object of your affection. The sons and daughters *z* you left behind will fall by the sword. *a* 22And you will do as I have done. You will not cover the lower part of your face *b* or eat the customary food of mourners. *c* 23You will keep your turbans *d* on your heads and your sandals *e* on your feet. You will not mourn *f* or weep but will waste away *g* because of *d* your sins and groan among yourselves. *h* 24Ezekiel *i* will be a sign *j* to you; you will do just as he has done. When this happens, you will know that I am the Sovereign LORD.'

25"And you, son of man, on the day I take away their stronghold, their joy and glory, the delight of their eyes, *k* their heart's desire, *l* and their sons and daughters *m* as well— 26on that day a fugitive will come to tell you *n* the news. 27At that time your mouth will be opened; you will speak with him and will no longer be silent. *o* So you will be a sign to them, and they will know that I am the LORD. *p* "

A Prophecy Against Ammon

25 The word of the LORD came to me: 2"Son of man, set your face

Cross references (center column)

24:11 *d* Jer 21:10
24:13
e S Isa 22:14
f Jer 6:28-30;
La 1:9;
S Eze 16:42;
22:24; 23:36-49;
Hos 7:1; Zec 6:8
24:14 *g* S Eze 22:14
h S Nu 11:23
i S Eze 8:18
j S Job 27:22
k Eze 36:19;
Zec 8:14
l S Isa 3:11;
S Eze 18:30
24:16
m S Ps 39:10 *n* ver 21; Ps 84:1;
S La 2:4
o Jer 13:17; 16:5;
S 22:10
24:17 *p* Ps 39:9
q S Ex 28:39;
S Isa 3:20
r S Isa 20:2
s S Lev 13:45 *t* ver 22; S Jer 16:7
24:18
u S Eze 12:7
24:19 *v* Eze 12:9;
37:18
24:21
w S Lev 26:31;
S Eze 7:24
x S Lev 26:19
y S ver 16; Ps 27:4
z S Eze 23:25
a Jer 7:14,15;
Hos 9:12,16;
Mal 2:12
24:22
b S Lev 13:45
c Jer 16:7
24:23
d S Ex 28:39;
S Isa 3:20
e S Isa 20:2
f Ex 33:4
g S Lev 26:16
h Ps 78:64
24:24 *i* Eze 1:3
j S Isa 20:3;
Eze 12:11
24:25 *k* S La 2:4
l S Ps 20:4
m Dt 28:32;
Jer 11:22
24:26
n S 1Sa 4:12;
Job 1:15-19
24:27 *o* Da 10:15
p S Eze 3:26;
33:22

d 23 Or *away in*

Footnotes

24:11 *empty pot.* Jerusalem, emptied of inhabitants, would be set to the torch, in a vain final effort at purification.
24:13 *lewdness.* See 16:27; 22:9.
24:16 *blow.* Some swiftly fatal disease, one that often reached plague proportions (see Ex 9:14; Nu 14:37). *delight of your eyes.* The object of loving attention (see vv. 21,25)—apparently a conventional way of referring to a man's wife.
24:17 *Keep your turban fastened.* The mourner normally removed it and put dust on his head (see Jos 7:6; 1Sa 4:12). *sandals on your feet.* To remove them showed grief (see 2Sa 15:30). *cover . . . face.* A gesture of shame (Mic 3:7) or uncleanness (Lev 13:45). *food of mourners.* The funeral meal (see Jer 16:7).
24:19 *Then the people asked me.* The third time that the people responded to Ezekiel's behavior (see 12:9; 21:7).
24:21 *desecrate.* By letting Nebuchadnezzar burn it down.
24:24 *Ezekiel.* The prophet speaks of himself in the third person. Elsewhere his name occurs only in 1:3. *sign.* See note on 12:6.
24:26 *fugitive.* The first of the exiles of 586 B.C. *news.*

About the siege—its beginning (verifying the accuracy of vv. 1–2) and its ending (see note on 33:21).
24:27 *no longer be silent.* Ezekiel's wife died the same day the temple was burned (Aug. 14, 586 B.C.; see 2Ki 25:8–9). See notes on 3:26; 33:21. *sign.* See note on 12:6.
25:1–32:32 Oracles against the nations. Frequently in the prophets, God's word of judgment on Israel is accompanied by oracles of judgment on the nations. These make clear that, while judgment begins "with the family of God" (1Pe 4:17), the pagan nations would not escape God's wrath. Often these judgments are implicit messages of salvation for Israel (see 28:25–26) since the Lord's victories over hostile powers remove an enemy of his people or punish them for their cruel attacks on his people. In the case of Ezekiel there are seven oracles (the seventh of which has seven parts, each introduced by the phrase "The word of the LORD came to me"; see Introduction: Outline).
25:2 *set your face.* See note on 20:46. *Ammonites.* Ammon (part of modern Jordan) was immediately east of Israel (see 21:20; see also Jer 9:26; 49:1–6; Am 1:13–15; Zep 2:8–11). For hostile Ammonite action during this time and

against q the Ammonites r and prophesy against them. s ³Say to them, 'Hear the word of the Sovereign LORD. This is what the Sovereign LORD says: Because you said "Aha! t" over my sanctuary when it was desecrated u and over the land of Israel when it was laid waste and over the people of Judah when they went into exile, v ⁴therefore I am going to give you to the people of the East w as a possession. They will set up their camps x and pitch their tents among you; they will eat your fruit and drink your milk. y ⁵I will turn Rabbah z into a pasture for camels and Ammon into a resting place for sheep. a Then you will know that I am the LORD. ⁶For this is what the Sovereign LORD says: Because you have clapped your hands b and stamped your feet, rejoicing with all the malice of your heart against the land of Israel, c ⁷therefore I will stretch out my hand d against you and give you as plunder e to the nations. I will cut you off from the nations and exterminate you from the countries. I will destroy f you, and you will know that I am the LORD. g ' "

A Prophecy Against Moab

⁸"This is what the Sovereign LORD says: 'Because Moab h and Seir i said, "Look, the house of Judah has become like all the other nations," ⁹therefore I will expose the flank of Moab, beginning at its frontier towns—Beth Jeshimoth j, Baal Meon k and Kiriathaim l—the glory of that land. ¹⁰I will give Moab along with the Ammonites to the people of the East as a possession, so that the Ammonites will not be remembered m among the nations; ¹¹and I

will inflict punishment on Moab. Then they will know that I am the LORD.' " n

A Prophecy Against Edom

¹²"This is what the Sovereign LORD says: 'Because Edom o took revenge on the house of Judah and became very guilty by doing so, ¹³therefore this is what the Sovereign LORD says: I will stretch out my hand p against Edom and kill its men and their animals. q I will lay it waste, and from Teman r to Dedan s they will fall by the sword. t ¹⁴I will take vengeance on Edom by the hand of my people Israel, and they will deal with Edom in accordance with my anger u and my wrath; they will know my vengeance, declares the Sovereign LORD.' " v

A Prophecy Against Philistia

¹⁵"This is what the Sovereign LORD says: 'Because the Philistines w acted in vengeance and took revenge with malice x in their hearts, and with ancient hostility sought to destroy Judah, ¹⁶therefore this is what the Sovereign LORD says: I am about to stretch out my hand against the Philistines, y and I will cut off the Kerethites z and destroy those remaining along the coast. a ¹⁷I will carry out great vengeance b on them and punish c them in my wrath. Then they will know that I am the LORD, d when I take vengeance on them. e f ' "

A Prophecy Against Tyre

26 In the eleventh year, on the first day of the month, the word of the

25:2 qS Eze 13:17; 29:2 rS Eze 21:28 sJer 49:1-6
25:3 tS Ps 35:21; Eze 26:2; 36:2 uZep 2:8 vS Pr 17:5
25:4 wS Ge 25:6; S Jdg 6:3 xS Nu 31:10 yDt 28:33,51; S Jdg 6:33
25:5 zS Dt 3:11 aS Isa 17:2
25:6 bS Nu 24:10 cS Eze 6:11; Ob 1:12; Zep 2:8
25:7 dZep 1:4 eS Nu 14:3 fEze 21:31 gver 13-14,17; Am 1:14-15
25:8 hS Ge 19:37; S Dt 23:6; S Isa 16:6 iS Ge 14:6
25:9 jS Nu 33:49 kS Nu 32:3; S Jos 13:17 lS Nu 32:37; S Jos 13:19
25:10 mEze 21:32
25:11 nIsa 15:9; 16:1-14; Jer 48:1; Am 2:1-3
25:12 oS 2Sa 8:13-14; S 2Ch 28:17; S Isa 11:14
25:13 pS Ex 7:5; S Eze 16:27 qEze 29:8 rS Ge 36:11,15,34 sJer 25:23 tS Jer 49:10; S Eze 14:17
25:14 uEze 35:11 vS Ps 137:7; Eze 32:29; 35:2-3; 36:5; Am 1:11; Ob 1:1, 10-16; Mal 1:4
25:15 wS Jos 13:3; S 2Ch 28:18 xS Ps 73:8
25:16 yS 2Ch 26:6; Am 1:8

26 zS 1Sa 30:14 aS Eze 20:33 26:17 bS Nu 31:3 cJer 44:13 dS Ex 6:2; S 8:22 eS Isa 11:14 fS Isa 14:30; Jer 47:7; Joel 3:4

later see 2Ki 24:2; Ne 4:7.
25:3 *Aha!* A cry of malicious joy (cf. 26:2; 36:2; Ps 35:21–25).
25:4 *people of the East.* Probably nomadic tribes of the desert east of Ammon, though this could be a reference to Nebuchadnezzar and his army (see 21:31).
25:5 *Rabbah.* See note on 21:20. *pasture . . . resting place.* A common OT description for destroyed cities (see Isa 34:13–15; Zep 2:13–15). The sites were returned to the conditions they were in before the cities were built, representing the undoing of human efforts.
25:6 *clapped your hands.* See 6:11 and note.
25:7 *I will stretch out my hand against.* See note on 6:14. *plunder to the nations.* Cf. 26:5; 34:28. *cut you off.* Cf. v. 16.
25:8 *Moab.* Immediately to the south of Ammon, east of the Dead Sea (see Isa 15–16; Jer 48; Am 2:1–3; Zep 2:8–11). *Seir.* Edom, a country south of Moab and south of the Dead Sea (see ch. 35, especially v. 15; 36:5; Isa 34:5–17; 63:1–6; Jer 49:7–11; Am 1:11–12). *like all the other nations.* Israel wanted to be like the nations (see 20:32 and note), but when the nations saw Judah in her apparent vulnerability and lost their awe of her, they failed to take her

God seriously (cf. La 4:12).
25:9 *flank of Moab.* Lower hills rising from the Dead Sea, visible from Jerusalem. *Beth Jeshimoth.* A town in the plains of Moab. *Baal Meon.* A major Moabite town mentioned in an inscribed monument of Mesha, king of Moab (see chart on "Ancient Texts Relating to the OT," p. 5). *Kiriathaim.* A city also mentioned in the Mesha inscription (cf. 2Ki 3:4–5).
25:12 *Edom.* See note on v. 8. *took revenge.* By not harboring Judah's refugees after 586 B.C. (see Ob 11–14).
25:13 *Teman.* A district near Petra in central Edom (see Jer 49:7,20; Am 1:12; Ob 9; Hab 3:3). *Dedan.* A tribe and territory in southern Edom (see 27:20; 38:13; Isa 21:13; Jer 49:8).
25:15 *Philistines.* Inhabitants of the coastal plain along the Mediterranean west of Judah (1Sa 6:17), who strove for control of Canaan until subdued by David. Their hostility to Israel continued, however (see Isa 14:29–31; Jer 47; Am 1:6–8; Zep 2:4–7), until Nebuchadnezzar deported them.
25:16 *Kerethites.* Related to, if not identical with, the Philistines (see 1Sa 30:14 and note; 2Sa 8:18; 15:18; 20:7). *coast.* Of the Mediterranean.
26:1 *eleventh year . . . first day.* The number of the month is missing. The entire year dates from Apr. 23, 587, to Apr.

LORD came to me:[g] [2]"Son of man, because Tyre[h] has said of Jerusalem, 'Aha![i] The gate to the nations is broken, and its doors have swung open to me; now that she lies in ruins I will prosper,' [3]therefore this is what the Sovereign LORD says: I am against you, O Tyre, and I will bring many nations against you, like the sea[j] casting up its waves. [4]They will destroy[k] the walls of Tyre[l] and pull down her towers; I will scrape away her rubble and make her a bare rock. [5]Out in the sea[m] she will become a place to spread fishnets,[n] for I have spoken, declares the Sovereign LORD. She will become plunder[o] for the nations,[p] [6]and her settlements on the mainland will be ravaged by the sword. Then they will know that I am the LORD.

[7]"For this is what the Sovereign LORD says: From the north I am going to bring against Tyre Nebuchadnezzar[e][q] king of Babylon, king of kings,[r] with horses and chariots,[s] with horsemen and a great army. [8]He will ravage your settlements on the mainland with the sword; he will set up siege works[t] against you, build a ramp[u] up to your walls and raise his shields against you. [9]He will direct the blows of his battering rams against your walls and demolish your towers with his weapons.[v] [10]His horses will be so many that they will cover you with dust. Your walls will tremble at the noise of the war horses, wagons and chariots[w] when he enters your gates as men enter a city whose walls have been broken through. [11]The hoofs[x] of his horses will trample all your streets; he will kill your people with the sword, and your strong pillars[y] will fall to the ground.[z] [12]They will plunder your

wealth and loot your merchandise; they will break down your walls and demolish your fine houses and throw your stones, timber and rubble into the sea.[a] [13]I will put an end[b] to your noisy songs,[c] and the music of your harps[d] will be heard no more.[e] [14]I will make you a bare rock, and you will become a place to spread fishnets. You will never be rebuilt,[f] for I the LORD have spoken, declares the Sovereign LORD.

[15]"This is what the Sovereign LORD says to Tyre: Will not the coastlands[g] tremble[h] at the sound of your fall, when the wounded groan[i] and the slaughter takes place in you? [16]Then all the princes of the coast will step down from their thrones and lay aside their robes and take off their embroidered[j] garments. Clothed[k] with terror, they will sit on the ground,[l] trembling[m] every moment, appalled[n] at you. [17]Then they will take up a lament[o] concerning you and say to you:

" 'How you are destroyed, O city of renown,
peopled by men of the sea!
You were a power on the seas,
you and your citizens;
you put your terror
on all who lived there.[p]
[18]Now the coastlands tremble[q]
on the day of your fall;
the islands in the sea
are terrified at your collapse.'[r]

[19]"This is what the Sovereign LORD says: When I make you a desolate city, like cities no longer inhabited, and when I

26:1 [g]S Eze 24:1; 29:1; 30:20
26:2 [h]S Jos 19:29; 2Sa 5:11 [i]S Eze 25:3
26:3 [j]ver 19; Isa 5:30; Jer 50:42; 51:42 [k]S Isa 23:1, 11 [l]Am 1:10
26:5 [m]Eze 27:32 [n]Eze 47:10 [o]S Nu 14:3; Eze 29:19 [p]Zec 9:2-4
26:7 [q]Jer 27:6; 39:1 [r]S Ezr 7:12 [s]S Eze 23:24; Na 2:3-4
26:8 [t]S Jer 6:6 [u]S Jer 33:4
26:9 [v]S Eze 21:22
26:10 [w]S Jer 4:13; S 46:9; S Eze 23:24
26:11 [x]Isa 5:28 [y]S Jer 43:13 [z]S Isa 26:5

26:12 [a]Isa 23:8; S Jer 4:7; Eze 27:3-27; 28:8; Isa 1:8
26:13 [b]S Jer 7:34 [c]S Isa 23:7 [d]S Ps 137:2; S Isa 14:11 [e]S Job 30:31; S Jer 16:9; S 25:10; Rev 18:22
26:14 [f]S Job 12:14; Mal 1:4
26:15 [g]Isa 41:5; Eze 27:35 [h]S Jer 49:21 [i]S Job 24:12
26:16 [j]S Ex 26:36 [k]S Job 8:22 [l]S Job 2:8,13 [m]Hos 11:10 [n]S Lev 26:32; Eze 32:10
26:17 [o]S Eze 19:1 [p]Isa 14:12
26:18 [q]S Ps 46:6; S Jer 49:21

[r]Isa 23:5; S 41:5; Eze 27:35

[e]7 Hebrew *Nebuchadrezzar,* of which *Nebuchadnezzar* is a variant; here and often in Ezekiel and Jeremiah

13, 586 B.C. The oracle must date from the end of that year, in the 11th (Feb. 13, 586) or the 12th month (Mar. 15, 586). See note on 33:21. This is the fifth date in the book (see 1:2; 8:1; 20:1; 24:1).
26:2 *Tyre.* The island capital of Phoenicia, present-day Lebanon. It was involved in an anti-Assyrian coalition in 594 B.C. (see Jer 27:3). Ezekiel, more than any other prophet, prophesied against Tyre (see chs. 27-28; but see Isa 23; Jer 25:22; 47:4; Joel 3:4-5; Am 1:9-10; Zec 9:2-4). *Aha!* See note on 25:3. *gate to the nations.* Because of its geographical location, its political importance and the central role it played in international trade. The anti-Assyrian summit meeting was held there (see Jer 27).
26:3 *I am against you.* See note on 5:8. *like the sea casting up its waves.* For invading armies likened to waves of the sea cf. Isa 17:12-13. Since Tyre was an island, the metaphor is especially appropriate here.
26:5 *plunder for the nations.* Cf. 25:7; 34:28.
26:7 *north.* The direction from which Nebuchadnezzar would descend on Tyre after first marching his army up the Euphrates River valley rather than across the Arabian Desert (cf. Jer 1:13). *I am going to bring.* A clear indication of God's

sovereignty over the nations (cf. 28:7; 29:8). *Nebuchadnezzar.* The first of four references to him in Ezekiel (see 29:18-19; 30:10). He ruled from 605 to 562 B.C., and his name means "O (god) Nabu, protect my son" or "O (god) Nabu, protect my boundary." Jeremiah and Ezekiel both proclaimed that this pagan king would be used by God to do his work (see Jer 25:9; 27:6).
26:8 *siege.* Nebuchadnezzar's 15-year siege of Tyre began shortly after the fall of Jerusalem. There is no record that Tyre fell at this time (see note on 29:18).
26:14 *never be rebuilt.* Eventually fulfilled by Alexander's devastating siege in 332 B.C. (see note on Isa 23:1).
26:16 *princes of the coast.* Called kings in 27:35, they were probably trading partners with Tyre. *lay aside their robes.* Usually mourners tore their clothes (Job 2:12) and put on sackcloth, but cf. the king of Nineveh (Jnh 3:6). *Clothed with terror.* Because of political shock waves from the fall of such a powerful city (cf. 7:27; Ps 35:26; 109:29).
26:17 *lament.* See note on 19:1.
26:19 *ocean depths.* The primeval, chaotic mass—the "deep" of Ge 1:2. Tyre's collapse into the sea is described in almost cosmic terms.

bring the ocean depths[s] over you and its vast waters cover you,[t] [20]then I will bring you down with those who go down to the pit,[u] to the people of long ago. I will make you dwell in the earth below, as in ancient ruins, with those who go down to the pit, and you will not return or take your place[f] in the land of the living.[v] [21]I will bring you to a horrible end and you will be no more.[w] You will be sought, but you will never again be found, declares the Sovereign LORD."[x]

A Lament for Tyre

27 The word of the LORD came to me: [2]"Son of man, take up a lament[y] concerning Tyre. [3]Say to Tyre,[z] situated at the gateway to the sea,[a] merchant of peoples on many coasts, 'This is what the Sovereign LORD says:

" 'You say, O Tyre,
"I am perfect in beauty.[b]"
[4]Your domain was on the high seas;
    your builders brought your beauty to
        perfection.[c]
[5]They made all your timbers
    of pine trees from Senir[g]; [d]
they took a cedar from Lebanon[e]
    to make a mast for you.
[6]Of oaks[f] from Bashan
    they made your oars;
of cypress wood[h] from the coasts of
        Cyprus[i] [g]
    they made your deck, inlaid with
        ivory.
[7]Fine embroidered linen[h] from Egypt
    was your sail
    and served as your banner;
your awnings were of blue and purple[i]
    from the coasts of Elishah.[j]

[8]Men of Sidon and Arvad[k] were your
        oarsmen;
    your skilled men, O Tyre, were
        aboard as your seamen.[l]
[9]Veteran craftsmen of Gebal[j] [m] were on
        board
    as shipwrights to caulk your seams.
All the ships of the sea[n] and their
        sailors
    came alongside to trade for your
        wares.

[10]" 'Men of Persia,[o] Lydia[p] and Put[q]
    served as soldiers in your army.
They hung their shields[r] and helmets
        on your walls,
    bringing you splendor.
[11]Men of Arvad and Helech
    manned your walls on every side;
men of Gammad
    were in your towers.
They hung their shields around your
        walls;
    they brought your beauty to
        perfection.[s]

[12]" 'Tarshish[t] did business with you because of your great wealth of goods;[u] they exchanged silver, iron, tin and lead for your merchandise.

[13]" 'Greece,[v] Tubal and Meshech[w] traded with you; they exchanged slaves[x] and articles of bronze for your wares.

[14]" 'Men of Beth Togarmah[y] exchanged work horses, war horses and mules for your merchandise.

[15]" 'The men of Rhodes[k] [z] traded with

Cross references (center column):

26:19 [s]S Ge 7:11; [t]S ver 3; Isa 8:7-8
26:20 [u]Nu 16:30; Ps 28:1; 88:6; Eze 31:14; 32:18; Am 9:2; Jnh 2:2,6; [v]S Job 28:13; S Isa 14:9-10; Eze 32:24,30
26:21 [w]S Jer 51:64; Da 11:19; [x]Jer 20:4; Eze 27:36; 28:19; Rev 18:21
27:2 [y]S Eze 19:1
27:3 [z]S Ps 83:7; [a]ver 33; Hos 9:13
[b]S Isa 23:9; S Eze 16:15
27:4 [c]Eze 28:12
27:5 [d]S Dt 3:9; [e]S Isa 2:13
27:6 [f]Nu 21:33; S Ps 29:9; Jer 22:20; Zec 11:2; [g]S Ge 10:4; Isa 23:12
27:7 [h]S Ex 26:36; S Isa 19:9; [i]S Ex 25:4; Jer 10:9; [j]Ge 10:4

27:8 [k]Ge 10:18; [l]1Ki 9:27
27:9 [m]S Jos 13:5; [n]S Ps 104:26
27:10 [o]2Ch 36:20; Ezr 1:1; Eze 38:5; Da 8:20; [p]S Isa 66:19; [q]S Ge 10:6; Eze 30:5; Na 3:9; [r]SS 4:4
27:11 [s]ver 27
27:12 [t]S Ge 10:4; [u]ver 18,33
27:13 [v]Joel 3:6; [w]Ge 10:2; Isa 66:19; Eze 32:26; 38:2; 39:1; [x]Rev 18:13
27:14 [y]S Ge 10:3
27:15 [z]S Ge 10:7

Text notes:

[f]20 Septuagint; Hebrew return, and I will give glory
[g]5 That is, Hermon   [h]6 Targum; the Masoretic Text has a different division of the consonants.   [i]6 Hebrew Kittim   [j]9 That is, Byblos   [k]15 Septuagint; Hebrew Dedan

---

Study notes (bottom):

26:20 pit. The grave, "the earth below" (cf. Ps 69:15). people of long ago. Those long dead (Ps 143:3; La 3:6). not return or take your place in the land of the living. As Israel would (see 37:1–14).
26:21 See 27:36; 28:19.
27:2 lament. See note on 19:1.
27:3 I am perfect in beauty. See 28:12; cf. 28:2 for a similar prideful statement. Since Tyre is described as a stately ship in the following verses, some translate, "You are a ship, perfect in beauty."
27:4 brought your beauty to perfection. See v. 11.
27:5 Senir. Amorite name for Hermon, the Anti-Lebanon mountain (or range) famed for cedar.
27:6 Bashan. See note on 39:18. Cyprus. The Hebrew word Kittim (see NIV text note) was originally the name of a town in southern Cyprus colonized by Phoenicia.
27:7 Elishah. A city on the east side of Cyprus; also the oldest name for Cyprus (but see note on Ge 10:4).
27:8 Sidon. A harbor city 25 miles north of Tyre, which sometimes rivaled her in political and commercial importance (see note on 28:21). Arvad. Another Phoenician island-city, off the Mediterranean coast and north of Sidon.

27:9 Gebal. Byblos, an important ancient city on the coast between Sidon and Arvad (see NIV text note and 1Ki 5:18).
27:10 Lydia. In Asia Minor. Put. Libya, in North Africa, west of Egypt. soldiers. The ship image is abandoned, and Tyre is now described literally—as a city (see "walls" and "towers" in this and the next verse), complete with a mercenary army gathered from the whole world.
27:11 Arvad. See note on v. 8. Helech. Cilicia, the mountainous region in southeast Asia Minor. The name occurs only here in the Bible. Gammad. Either (1) northern Asia Minor, or (2) a coastal town near Arvad. It is not mentioned elsewhere in the Bible.
27:12 Tarshish. Traditionally located on the coast of southern Spain, but the island of Sardinia has also been suggested. Passages such as 1Ki 10:22; Jnh 1:3 imply that it was a long distance from the Canaanite coast. The list of places in vv. 12–23 generally follows a west-to-east direction.
27:13 Tubal and Meshech. Both in Asia Minor.
27:14 Beth Togarmah. In eastern Asia Minor, present-day Armenia (see 38:6). work horses. Asia Minor was known for its horses (see 1Ki 10:28 and NIV text notes there).
27:15 Rhodes. A large island off the southwest coast of

you, and many coastlands[a] were your customers; they paid you with ivory[b] tusks and ebony.

16"'Aram[c] did business with you because of your many products; they exchanged turquoise,[d] purple fabric, embroidered work, fine linen,[e] coral[f] and rubies for your merchandise.

17"'Judah and Israel traded with you; they exchanged wheat[g] from Minnith[h] and confections,[m] honey, oil and balm[i] for your wares.[j]

18"'Damascus,[k] because of your many products and great wealth of goods,[l] did business with you in wine from Helbon and wool from Zahar.

19"'Danites and Greeks[m] from Uzal[n] bought your merchandise; they exchanged wrought iron, cassia[o] and calamus for your wares.

20"'Dedan[p] traded in saddle blankets with you.

21"'Arabia[q] and all the princes of Kedar[r] were your customers; they did business with you in lambs, rams and goats.

22"'The merchants of Sheba[s] and Raamah traded with you; for your merchandise they exchanged the finest of all kinds of spices[t] and precious stones, and gold.[u]

23"'Haran,[v] Canneh and Eden[w] and merchants of Sheba, Asshur[x] and Kilmad traded with you. 24In your marketplace they traded with you beautiful garments, blue fabric, embroidered work and multicolored rugs with cords twisted and tightly knotted.

25"'The ships of Tarshish[y] serve
    as carriers for your wares.
You are filled with heavy cargo
    in the heart of the sea.[z]
26Your oarsmen take you
    out to the high seas.
But the east wind[a] will break you to
        pieces
    in the heart of the sea.
27Your wealth,[b] merchandise and wares,
    your mariners, seamen and
        shipwrights,
your merchants and all your soldiers,
    and everyone else on board
will sink into the heart of the sea[c]
    on the day of your shipwreck.
28The shorelands will quake[d]
    when your seamen cry out.
29All who handle the oars
    will abandon their ships;
the mariners and all the seamen
    will stand on the shore.
30They will raise their voice
    and cry bitterly over you;
they will sprinkle dust[e] on their heads
    and roll[f] in ashes.[g]
31They will shave their heads[h] because of
        you
    and will put on sackcloth.
They will weep[i] over you with anguish
        of soul
    and with bitter mourning.[j]
32As they wail and mourn over you,

27:15
aS Jer 25:22
bIKi 10:22;
Rev 18:12
27:16 cJdg 10:6;
Isa 7:1-8
dEx 28:18;
39:11; Eze 28:13
eS Eze 16:10
fJob 28:18
27:17 gS IKi 5:9
hJdg 11:33
iS Ge 43:11
jAc 12:20
27:18
kS Ge 14:15;
Eze 47:16-18
lS ver 12
27:19
mS Ge 10:2
nGe 10:27
oS Ex 30:24
27:20 pS Ge 10:7
27:21
qS 2Ch 9:14
rS Ge 25:13;
Isa 21:17
27:22
sS Ge 10:7,28
tS Ge 43:11
uRev 18:12
27:23
vS Ge 11:26
wS Isa 37:12
xS Ge 10:22;
S Nu 24:24

27:25
yS Ge 10:4;
Isa 2:16 fn
zRev 18:3
27:26
aS Ge 41:6;
Jer 18:17
27:27 bPr 11:4
cEze 28:8
27:28
dS Jer 49:21
27:30 eS Jos 7:6;
S 2Sa 1:2
fS Jer 6:26
gRev 18:18-19
27:31
hS Lev 13:40;
S Job 1:20;
S Isa 3:17;
S Jer 48:37
iS Isa 16:9;
Rev 18:15
jS Est 4:1;

Job 3:20; Isa 22:12; Jer 6:26; S La 2:10; S Eze 7:18

l 16 Most Hebrew manuscripts; some Hebrew manuscripts and Syriac *Edom*   m 17 The meaning of the Hebrew for this word is uncertain.

Asia Minor that served as gateway to the Aegean islands. It was an early major trading center (see Ac 21:1).

27:16 *Aram.* Syria. Since Damascus, the capital of Aram, is mentioned in v. 18, perhaps Edom is meant here (see NIV text note; see also 25:12 and note).

27:17 *Israel traded with you.* In the past. Since 722–721 B.C. Israel had ceased to exist as a political state. *Minnith.* An Ammonite town, apparently famous for its wheat; "wheat from Minnith" possibly denoted a superior quality of wheat. *balm.* Gum or oil from one of several plants; a product of Gilead (see Ge 37:25; Jer 8:22; 46:11).

27:18 *Damascus.* Capital of Aram (see note on v. 16; see also Isa 7:8). *Helbon.* A town north of Damascus, still in existence and still a wine-making center. The name occurs only here in the Bible. *Zahar.* Modern Ṣahra, an area northwest of Damascus, where grazing is still common today.

27:19 *Danites.* A term that Homer used for Greeks. Some read (as does the Septuagint) "and wine from" for "Danites and Greeks from." *Uzal.* See Ge 10:27; 1Ch 1:21; perhaps Yemen or the area between Haran and the Tigris. *cassia.* Similar to the cinnamon tree. The only other Biblical mention of it is in Ex 30:24, where it appears in a list of aromatic plants. *calamus.* An aromatic reed.

27:20 *Dedan.* See note on 25:13.

27:21 *Arabia and . . . Kedar.* A general expression for the

Bedouin tribes from Aram to the Arabian Desert. For Kedar see Isa 42:11; 60:7; Jer 49:28.

27:22 *Sheba.* See note on 23:42. *Raamah.* A city in southern Arabia.

27:23 *Haran.* A city east of Carchemish, in present-day eastern Turkey. It was well-known in ancient times as a center both for trade and for the worship of the moon-god Sin. From here Abraham moved to Canaan (see Ge 11:31; 12:4). *Canneh.* Of uncertain location, presumably in Mesopotamia. It is often identified with Calneh (Isa 10:9; Am 6:2). *Eden.* A district south of Haran, mentioned in connection with Haran in 2Ki 19:12. See Beth Eden in Am 1:5. *Sheba.* See note on 23:42. *Asshur.* Can mean the city, the country (Assyria) or the people (Assyrians). Here it is probably the city south of Nineveh that gave its name to the country. *Kilmad.* If a town, it is yet unidentified; presumably in Mesopotamia. Some read "all Media."

27:25 *Tarshish.* See note on v. 12. The ship image is resumed (see notes on vv. 3,10).

27:26 *east wind.* Disastrous at sea (Ps 48:7) as well as on land (Jer 18:17). It possibly symbolizes Nebuchadnezzar (as in 17:10; 19:12).

27:30 *dust on their heads.* See 26:16 for a similar scene. *roll in ashes.* Cf. Mic 1:10.

27:31 *shave their heads.* Cf. 7:18; Isa 15:2; 22:12.

they will take up a lament [k]
concerning you:
"Who was ever silenced like Tyre,
surrounded by the sea? [l] "
33When your merchandise went out on
the seas, [m]
you satisfied many nations;
with your great wealth [n] and your wares
you enriched the kings of the earth.
34Now you are shattered by the sea
in the depths of the waters;
your wares and all your company
have gone down with you. [o]
35All who live in the coastlands [p]
are appalled [q] at you;
their kings shudder with horror
and their faces are distorted with
fear. [r]
36The merchants among the nations hiss
at you; [s]
you have come to a horrible end
and will be no more. [t] ' "

A Prophecy Against the King of Tyre

28 The word of the LORD came to me:
2"Son of man [u], say to the ruler of
Tyre, 'This is what the Sovereign LORD
says:

" 'In the pride of your heart
you say, "I am a god;
I sit on the throne [v] of a god
in the heart of the seas." [w]
But you are a man and not a god,
though you think you are as wise as a
god. [x]
3Are you wiser than Daniel [n] ? [y]
Is no secret hidden from you?
4By your wisdom and understanding
you have gained wealth for yourself
and amassed gold and silver
in your treasuries. [z]
5By your great skill in trading [a]
you have increased your wealth, [b]
and because of your wealth
your heart has grown proud. [c]

6" 'Therefore this is what the Sovereign
LORD says:

27:32
[k]S Eze 19:1
[l]Isa 23:1-6;
Eze 26:5
27:33 [m]S ver 3
[n]S ver 12;
Eze 28:4-5
27:34 [o]Zec 9:4
27:35
[p]S Eze 26:15
[q]S Lev 26:32;
S Job 18:20
[r]S Eze 26:17-18;
32:10
27:36 [s]Jer 19:8;
S 49:17; S 50:13;
Zep 2:15
[t]S Ps 37:10,36;
S Eze 26:21
28:2 [u]S Isa 13:11
[v]S Isa 14:13
[w]Zep 2:15
[x]S Ge 3:5;
S Ps 9:20; 82:6-7;
S Eze 16:49;
2Th 2:4
28:3
[y]S Eze 14:14;
Da 1:20; 2:20-23,
28; 5:11-12
28:4 [z]Isa 10:13;
Zec 9:3
28:5 [a]S Isa 23:8
[b]S Jer 9:23;
S Eze 27:33
[c]S Job 31:25;
Ps 52:7; 62:10;
Hos 12:8; 13:6

28:7 [d]Eze 30:11;
31:12; 32:12;
Hab 1:6 [e]Jer 9:23
[f]S Eze 7:24
28:8 [g]S Ps 55:23;
Eze 32:30
[h]Rev 18:7
[i]S Eze 26:12;
27:27
28:9 [j]S Isa 31:3
[k]S Eze 16:49
28:10
[l]S 1Sa 14:6;
S Jer 9:26;
Eze 32:19,24
28:12
[m]S Eze 19:1
[n]Eze 27:2-4
28:13 [o]S Ge 2:8
[p]Eze 31:8-9
[q]Rev 17:4
[r]S Eze 27:16
[s]Isa 14:11;
Rev 21:20
28:14 [t]Ex 30:26;
40:9
[u]Ex 25:17-20

" 'Because you think you are wise,
as wise as a god,
7I am going to bring foreigners against
you,
the most ruthless of nations; [d]
they will draw their swords against your
beauty and wisdom [e]
and pierce your shining splendor. [f]
8They will bring you down to the pit, [g]
and you will die a violent death [h]
in the heart of the seas. [i]
9Will you then say, "I am a god,"
in the presence of those who kill
you?
You will be but a man, not a god, [j]
in the hands of those who slay you. [k]
10You will die the death of the
uncircumcised [l]
at the hands of foreigners.

I have spoken, declares the Sovereign
LORD.' "

11The word of the LORD came to me:
12"Son of man, take up a lament [m] concerning the king of Tyre and say to him:
'This is what the Sovereign LORD says:

" 'You were the model of perfection,
full of wisdom and perfect in
beauty. [n]
13You were in Eden, [o]
the garden of God; [p]
every precious stone [q] adorned you:
ruby, topaz and emerald,
chrysolite, onyx and jasper,
sapphire, [o] turquoise [r] and beryl. [p]
Your settings and mountings [q] were
made of gold;
on the day you were created they
were prepared. [s]
14You were anointed [t] as a guardian
cherub, [u]
for so I ordained you.
You were on the holy mount of God;

[n]3 Or Daniel; the Hebrew spelling may suggest a person
other than the prophet Daniel.   [o]13 Or lapis lazuli
[p]13 The precise identification of some of these precious
stones is uncertain.   [q]13 The meaning of the Hebrew
for this phrase is uncertain.

28:2 *ruler of Tyre.* May refer to the city of Tyre as ruler, or
to Ittobaal, the king then ruling Tyre (see v. 12). *pride.* Cf.
27:3; Pr 16:18; Ac 12:21–23.
28:3 *Daniel.* See note on 14:14.
28:7 *foreigners.* The Babylonians; see next phrase.
28:8 *pit.* Cf. Job 33:22,24; see note on 26:20.
28:10 *uncircumcised.* Used here in the sense of barbarian
or uncouth. The Phoenicians, like the Israelites and the
Egyptians, practiced circumcision (see 31:18; 32:19).
28:12 *lament.* See note on 19:1. king of Tyre. Cf. v. 2, but
see note on Isa 14:12–15. *model of perfection.* "Model" is
lit. "seal," as in Hag 2:23, where Zerubbabel is called God's
"signet ring." With cutting irony Ezekiel depicts the proud

king of Tyre as the first man created, radiant with wisdom
and beauty.
28:13 *You were in Eden.* Like Adam (Ge 2:15). Ezekiel
continues to use imagery of the creation and the fall to
picture the career of the king of Tyre (see 31:9,16,18). *every
precious stone.* Unlike Adam, who was naked (Ge 2:25), the
king is pictured as a fully clothed priest, ordained (v. 14) to
guard God's holy place. The 9 stones are among the 12 worn
by the priest (Ex 28:17–20). (The Septuagint lists all 12.)
settings and mountings. For the precious stones. *on the day
you were created.* Cf. v. 15; Ge 5:2.
28:14 *as a guardian cherub.* Cf. v. 16. The Genesis account has cherubim (plural) stationed at the border of the

you walked among the fiery stones.
¹⁵You were blameless in your ways
from the day you were created
till wickedness was found in you.
¹⁶Through your widespread trade
you were filled with violence,^v
and you sinned.
So I drove you in disgrace from the
mount of God,
and I expelled you, O guardian
cherub,^w
from among the fiery stones.
¹⁷Your heart became proud^x
on account of your beauty,
and you corrupted your wisdom
because of your splendor.
So I threw you to the earth;
I made a spectacle of you before
kings.^y
¹⁸By your many sins and dishonest trade
you have desecrated your sanctuaries.
So I made a fire^z come out from you,
and it consumed you,
and I reduced you to ashes^a on the
ground
in the sight of all who were
watching.^b
¹⁹All the nations who knew you
are appalled^c at you;
you have come to a horrible end
and will be no more.^d ' ''

A Prophecy Against Sidon

²⁰The word of the LORD came to me:
²¹"Son of man, set your face against^e Si-
don;^f prophesy against her ²²and say:
'This is what the Sovereign LORD says:

" 'I am against you, O Sidon,
and I will gain glory^g within you.

They will know that I am the LORD,
when I inflict punishment^h on her
and show myself holyⁱ within her.
²³I will send a plague upon her
and make blood flow in her streets.
The slain will fall within her,
with the sword against her on every
side.
Then they will know that I am the
LORD.^j

²⁴ "No longer will the people of Israel
have malicious neighbors who are painful
briers and sharp thorns.^k Then they will
know that I am the Sovereign LORD.

²⁵ 'This is what the Sovereign LORD
says: When I gather^l the people of Israel
from the nations where they have been
scattered,^m I will show myself holyⁿ
among them in the sight of the nations.
Then they will live in their own land,
which I gave to my servant Jacob.^o ²⁶They
will live there in safety^p and will build
houses and plant^q vineyards; they will live
in safety when I inflict punishment^r on all
their neighbors who maligned them. Then
they will know that I am the LORD their
God.^s ' ''

A Prophecy Against Egypt

29 In the tenth year, in the tenth
month on the twelfth day, the
word of the LORD came to me:^t ²"Son of
man, set your face against^u Pharaoh king
of Egypt^v and prophesy against him and
against all Egypt.^w ³Speak to him and say:
'This is what the Sovereign LORD says:

" 'I am against you, Pharaoh^x king of
Egypt,

Cross references (center column)

28:16
^vS Ge 6:11;
Hab 2:17
^wS Ge 3:24
28:17 ^xIsa 10:12;
Eze 16:49; 31:10
^yS Eze 19:12
28:18 ^zOb 1:18
^aMal 4:3
^bZec 9:2-4
28:19
^cS Lev 26:32
^dS Jer 51:64;
S Eze 26:21
28:21
^eS Eze 13:17
^fS Ge 10:15;
S Jer 25:22
28:22 ^gEze 39:13

^hEze 30:19
ⁱS Lev 10:3
28:23
^jS Eze 5:17;
38:22
28:24 ^kS Isa 5:6;
S Eze 2:6
28:25
^lPs 106:47;
Jer 32:37
^mS Isa 11:12
ⁿS Eze 20:41
^oJer 12:15; 23:8;
S Eze 11:17;
34:27; 37:25
28:26
^pS Eze 25:18;
S 1Ki 4:25;
S Jer 17:25
^qS Dt 20:6
^rS Ps 149:9
^sS Isa 65:21;
S Jer 32:15;
Eze 38:8;
39:26-27;
Hos 2:15; 11:11;
Am 9:14-15
29:1 ^tver 17;
S Eze 26:1
29:2 ^uS Eze 25:2
^vS Jer 25:19
^wIsa 19:1-17;
Jer 46:2;
Eze 30:1-26;
31:1-18; 32:1-32
29:3 ^xJer 44:30

---

garden after the expulsion of Adam and Eve (Ge 3:24). Some
read "with" instead of "as." *holy mount of God.* Cf. v. 16.
This does not reflect the Genesis story. See Isa 14:13 for the
figure of God dwelling on a mountain. *fiery stones.* The
precious stones (v. 13; cf. Rev 4:1–16; 21:15–21).
28:15 *You were blameless . . . till.* The parallel to Ge 2–3
is clear (see Ge 6:9; 17:1).
28:16 *widespread trade . . . filled with violence.* Tyre's
major crime.
28:17 *threw you to the earth.* Expulsion from the heavenly
garden.
28:21 *set your face.* See note on 20:46. *Sidon.* See 27:8
and note. This is the only time in the OT that Sidon is
mentioned apart from Tyre (cf. Isa 23:1–4; Jer 47:4; Joel
3:4; Zec 9:2).
28:22 *I am against you.* Possibly because of Sidon's involvement in the Jerusalem summit conference (Jer 27:3;
see note on 5:8). *I will gain glory within you.* The Lord's
glory would be recognized in Sidon's punishment.
28:24 *painful briers.* For references to Israel's enemies as
briers see Nu 33:55; Jos 23:13.
28:25 *When I gather . . . Israel.* A frequent promise in
Ezekiel and later (see 11:17; 20:34,41–42; 29:13; 34:13;

36:24; 37:21; 38:8; 39:27; Ne 1:9; Zec 10:8,10). *my
servant Jacob.* Cf. 37:25. For the promise see Ge 28:13;
35:12; Ps 105:10–11.
28:26 *live there in safety.* A perennial ideal that had
become an especially meaningful promise (cf. 34:28; 38:8,
11,14; 39:26; Lev 25:18–19; Jer 23:6; 32:37; 33:16).
houses . . . vineyards. Basic necessities of the good life (cf. Isa
65:21; Jer 29:5,28; Am 9:14).
29:1 *tenth year . . . tenth month . . . twelfth day.* Jan. 7,
587 B.C.; the sixth date in Ezekiel (see 1:2; 8:1; 20:1; 24:1;
26:1). This is the first of seven oracles against Egypt, all of
which are dated, except one (30:1). They represent divine
and prophetic anger at Egypt's actions (or nonactions) at this
time.
29:2 *set your face.* See note on 20:46. *Pharaoh.* Hophra,
589–570 B.C. (see Jer 44:30).
29:3 *I am against you.* See note on 5:8. *great monster.* Or
"crocodile"; pictured as being in the Nile. See note on Ex
4:3; see also Job 41:1 and NIV text note; Isa 27:1 ("monster"). *your streams.* Nile delta and canals (cf. Isa 7:18;
19:6; 37:25). *You say.* Boasts inscribed on Egyptian monuments (such as in Shelley's "Ozymandias") had become
proverbial.

you great monster[y] lying among your
streams.
You say, "The Nile[z] is mine;
I made it for myself."
[4]But I will put hooks[a] in your jaws
and make the fish of your streams
stick to your scales.
I will pull you out from among your
streams,
with all the fish sticking to your
scales.[b]
[5]I will leave you in the desert,
you and all the fish of your streams.
You will fall on the open field
and not be gathered[c] or picked up.
I will give you as food
to the beasts of the earth and the
birds of the air.[d]

[6]Then all who live in Egypt will know that
I am the LORD.

" 'You have been a staff of reed[e] for the
house of Israel. [7]When they grasped you
with their hands, you splintered[f] and you
tore open their shoulders; when they
leaned on you, you broke and their backs
were wrenched.[r] [g]

[8]" 'Therefore this is what the Sovereign
LORD says: I will bring a sword against you
and kill your men and their animals.[h]
[9]Egypt will become a desolate wasteland.
Then they will know that I am the LORD.

" 'Because you said, "The Nile[i] is
mine; I made it,["] [10]therefore I am against
you[k] and against your streams, and I will
make the land of Egypt[l] a ruin and a desolate waste[m] from Migdol[n] to Aswan,[o] as
far as the border of Cush.[s][p] [11]No foot of
man or animal will pass through it; no one
will live there for forty years.[q] [12]I will
make the land of Egypt desolate[r] among
devastated lands, and her cities will lie
desolate forty years among ruined cities.

And I will disperse the Egyptians among
the nations and scatter them through the
countries.[s]

[13]" 'Yet this is what the Sovereign LORD
says: At the end of forty years I will gather
the Egyptians from the nations where they
were scattered. [14]I will bring them back
from captivity and return them to Upper
Egypt,[t][t] the land of their ancestry. There
they will be a lowly[u] kingdom.[v] [15]It will
be the lowliest of kingdoms and will never
again exalt itself above the other nations.[w]
I will make it so weak that it will never
again rule over the nations. [16]Egypt will no
longer be a source of confidence[x] for the
people of Israel but will be a reminder[y] of
their sin in turning to her for help.[z] Then
they will know that I am the Sovereign
LORD.[a] ' "

[17]In the twenty-seventh year, in the first
month on the first day, the word of the
LORD came to me:[b] [18]"Son of man, Nebuchadnezzar[c] king of Babylon drove his
army in a hard campaign against Tyre;
every head was rubbed bare[d] and every
shoulder made raw.[e] Yet he and his army
got no reward from the campaign he led
against Tyre. [19]Therefore this is what the
Sovereign LORD says: I am going to give
Egypt to Nebuchadnezzar king[f] of Babylon, and he will carry off its wealth. He
will loot and plunder[g] the land as pay for
his army.[h] [20]I have given him Egypt[i] as a
reward for his efforts because he and his
army did it for me, declares the Sovereign
LORD.[j]

[21]"On that day I will make a horn[u][k]

Cross references (center column):

29:3 [y]S Ps 68:30; S 74:13; Eze 32:2 [z]S Jer 46:8
29:4 [a]S 2Ki 19:28; S Job 41:2 [b]Eze 38:4
29:5 [c]S Jer 8:2 [d]S Jer 7:33; 34:20; Eze 31:13; 32:4-6; 39:4
29:6 [e]S 2Ki 18:21
29:7 [f]2Ki 18:21; Isa 36:6 [g]Jer 17:5; Eze 17:15-17
29:8 [h]Eze 25:13; 32:11-13
29:9 [i]S Jer 46:8 [/]Eze 30:7-8,13-19
29:10 [k]S Jer 21:13 [l]S Eze 30:6 [m]S Jer 46:19 [n]S Ex 14:2 [o]Eze 30:6 [p]Isa 18:1; Eze 30:4
29:11 [q]Eze 32:13
29:12 [r]S Isa 34:10

[s]S Jer 46:19; Eze 30:7,23,26
29:14 [t]S Isa 11:11; Eze 30:14 [u]Eze 17:14 [v]S Isa 19:22; Jer 46:26
29:15 [w]Zec 10:11
29:16 [x]2Ch 32:10 [y]S Nu 5:15 [z]S La 4:17 [a]Isa 20:5; S 30:2; Hos 8:13
29:17 [b]S ver 1; S Eze 24:1; 30:20; 40:1
29:18 [c]Jer 27:6; 39:1 [d]S Lev 13:40; S Job 1:20; S Jer 48:37 [e]Ge 49:15
29:19 [/]S Isa 19:4 [g]S Eze 26:5 [h]Jer 43:10-13; Eze 30:4,10, 24-25; 32:11
29:20 [/]S Isa 43:3 [/]Isa 10:6-7; 45:1; S Jer 25:9

29:21 [k]S Ps 132:17; S Lk 1:69

Text notes (center column bottom):

[r]7 Syriac (see also Septuagint and Vulgate); Hebrew and
you caused their backs to stand   [s]10 That is, the
upper Nile region   [t]14 Hebrew to Pathros
[u]21 Horn here symbolizes strength.

29:4 *hooks.* Cf. 19:4. *fish of your streams.* Egypt's conquered territories or mercenaries.
29:5 *food to the beasts.* Particularly frustrating to the
pharaoh's great hopes for an afterlife, as symbolized by the
pyramids and expressed in the Egyptian "Book of the Dead."
29:6 *You have been a staff of reed.* A comparison made
earlier (see Isa 36:6). Hophra briefly but unsuccessfully diverted the Babylonians from laying siege to Jerusalem (see Jer
37:1–10).
29:8 *sword.* Nebuchadnezzar's (see note on 21:3). For the
entire expression, which is not found in other prophetic
books, see 6:3; 11:8; 14:17; 33:2; see also Lev 26:25.
29:10 *Migdol.* Location unknown; probably in northern
Egypt (see Jer 44:1; 46:14). *Aswan.* A town in southern
Egypt. "From Migdol to Aswan" (see 30:6) probably indicated all Egypt, just as "from Dan to Beersheba" meant all
Israel (see, e.g., Jdg 20:1; 1Sa 3:20).
29:11 *forty years.* Sometimes used to signify a long and
difficult period (cf. 4:6).

29:14 *Upper Egypt.* Southern Egypt (see 30:14; Jer 44:1,
15).
29:17 The second oracle against Egypt (see note on v. 1).
twenty-seventh year . . . first month . . . first day. Apr. 26,
571 B.C.; the seventh date in Ezekiel (see v. 1; 1:2; 8:1;
20:1; 24:1; 26:1) and the latest date given in the book.
Since the remaining dated oracles are in more or less chronological order, the date is mentioned here probably because of
the subject matter (Egypt).
29:18 *hard campaign.* Nebuchadnezzar besieged Tyre for
15 years, from 586 to 571 B.C. (see 26:7–14). *every head
was rubbed bare.* Probably from the leather helmets.
29:19 *I am going to give.* God's sovereignty over the
nations is again proclaimed.
29:21 *make a horn grow for.* Revive the strength of (see
NIV text note). The passage is not a Messianic prophecy.
open your mouth. Ezekiel's muteness (3:26; 24:27) would
be removed, and this word anticipates that of 33:22.

grow for the house of Israel, and I will open your mouth[l] among them. Then they will know that I am the LORD.[m]"

A Lament for Egypt

30 The word of the LORD came to me: 2"Son of man, prophesy and say: 'This is what the Sovereign LORD says:

" 'Wail[n] and say,
"Alas for that day!"
3For the day is near,[o]
the day of the LORD[p] is near—
a day of clouds,
a time of doom for the nations.
4A sword will come against Egypt,[q]
and anguish will come upon Cush.[v][r]
When the slain fall in Egypt,
her wealth will be carried away
and her foundations torn down.[s]

5Cush and Put,[t] Lydia and all Arabia,[u] Libya[w] and the people[v] of the covenant land will fall by the sword along with Egypt.[w]
6" 'This is what the LORD says:

" 'The allies of Egypt will fall
and her proud strength will fail.
From Migdol to Aswan[x]
they will fall by the sword within her,
declares the Sovereign LORD.
7" 'They will be desolate
among desolate lands,
and their cities will lie
among ruined cities.[y]
8Then they will know that I am the LORD,
when I set fire[z] to Egypt
and all her helpers are crushed.[a]

9" 'On that day messengers will go out from me in ships to frighten Cush[b] out of her complacency. Anguish[c] will take hold of them on the day of Egypt's doom, for it is sure to come.[d]

10" 'This is what the Sovereign LORD says:

" 'I will put an end to the hordes of Egypt
by the hand of Nebuchadnezzar[e] king of Babylon.[f]
11He and his army—the most ruthless of nations[g]—
will be brought in to destroy the land.
They will draw their swords against Egypt
and fill the land with the slain.[h]
12I will dry up[i] the streams of the Nile[j] and sell the land to evil men;
by the hand of foreigners
I will lay waste[k] the land and everything in it.

I the LORD have spoken.

13" 'This is what the Sovereign LORD says:

" 'I will destroy the idols[l]
and put an end to the images in Memphis.[x][m]
No longer will there be a prince in Egypt,[n]
and I will spread fear throughout the land.
14I will lay[o] waste Upper Egypt,[y]
set fire to Zoan[p]
and inflict punishment on Thebes.[z][q]
15I will pour out my wrath on Pelusium,[a]
the stronghold of Egypt,
and cut off the hordes of Thebes.
16I will set fire[r] to Egypt;
Pelusium will writhe in agony.
Thebes will be taken by storm;

Cross references

29:21 *l*Eze 33:22
*m*S Eze 3:27
30:2 *n*S Isa 13:6; Jas 5:1
30:3 *o*S Eze 7:7; Joel 1:15; 2:1,11; Ob 1:15 *p*ver 18; S Eze 7:12,19; 32:7; 34:12
30:4 *q*Jer 25:19; Da 11:43 *r*S Ge 10:6; S Eze 29:10 *s*S Eze 29:19
30:5 *t*S Eze 27:10 *u*S 2Ch 9:14 *v*Jer 25:20 *w*Na 3:9
30:6 *x*Eze 29:10
30:7 *y*S Eze 29:12
30:8 *z*S Jer 49:27; Eze 39:6; Am 1:4, 7,10; Na 1:6 *a*S Eze 29:9
30:9 *b*S Ge 10:6 *c*Isa 23:5 *d*Eze 32:9-10; Zep 2:12
30:10 *e*Jer 39:1 *f*S Eze 29:19
30:11 *g*S Eze 28:7 *h*ver 24-25
30:12 *i*S Isa 19:6 *j*S Jer 46:8; Eze 29:9 *k*S Eze 19:7
30:13 *l*S Jer 43:12; S Eze 6:6 *m*S Isa 19:13 *n*Zec 10:11
30:14 *o*S Eze 29:14 *p*S Nu 13:22 *q*S Jer 46:25
30:16 *r*S Jos 7:15

v4 That is, the upper Nile region; also in verses 5 and 9   *w5* Hebrew *Cub*   *x13* Hebrew *Noph*; also in verse 16   *y14* Hebrew *waste Pathros*   *z14* Hebrew *No*; also in verses 15 and 16   *a15* Hebrew *Sin*; also in verse 16

30:1 The third oracle against Egypt (see note on 29:1). No date is given, but it was probably between January and April of 587 B.C. Compare 29:1 with 30:20. Jerusalem was under siege at this time.

30:2–3 *that day . . . the day of the LORD.* The day of God's coming in judgment (see 7:7 and note). Egypt's judgment is announced.

30:3 *the day is near.* Cf. Isa 13:6. *day of clouds.* Cf. Joel 2:2; Zep 1:15.

30:4 *sword.* Nebuchadnezzar's (see v. 10; see also note on 21:3).

30:5 *Put.* Libya, in Africa (see note on 27:10). *Lydia.* Not in Asia Minor (see note on 27:10) but somewhere in northern Africa. *people of the covenant land.* Apparently Jews living in Egypt (see Jer 44).

30:6 *From Migdol to Aswan.* See note on 29:10.

30:8 *set fire to.* Make war on.

30:9 *messengers . . . in ships.* See Isa 18 for a similar oracle on Cush, involving ships on the Nile.

30:11 *most ruthless of nations.* A common phrase for the Babylonians, who were known for their cruelty (see 2Ki 25:7).

30:13 *idols.* See note on 6:4. *Memphis.* Located 15 miles south of Cairo, Memphis was a former capital of Egypt and one of her largest cities. The list of towns reveals no discernible pattern but is a literary device used to underscore the scope of the destruction (cf. Isa 10:9–11,27–32; Mic 1:10–15; Zep 2:4). *prince.* King.

30:14 *Upper Egypt.* See 29:14 and note. *Zoan.* A city in northeast Egypt in the delta region; also called Rameses (see Ex 1:11), Avaris and Tanis (see Isa 19:11,13; 30:4). *Thebes.* Capital of Upper Egypt; present-day Luxor and Karnak (see NIV text note).

30:15 *Pelusium.* A fortress in the eastern delta region of the Nile (see NIV text note).

Memphis[s] will be in constant
distress.
[17]The young men of Heliopolis[b][t] and
Bubastis[c]
will fall by the sword,
and the cities themselves will go into
captivity.
[18]Dark will be the day at Tahpanhes[u]
when I break the yoke of Egypt; [v]
there her proud strength will come to
an end.
She will be covered with clouds,
and her villages will go into
captivity. [w]
[19]So I will inflict punishment[x] on Egypt,
and they will know that I am the
LORD.' "

[20]In the eleventh year, in the first month
on the seventh day, the word of the LORD
came to me:[y] [21]"Son of man, I have broken the arm[z] of Pharaoh[a] king of Egypt. It
has not been bound up for healing[b] or put
in a splint so as to become strong enough
to hold a sword. [22]Therefore this is what
the Sovereign LORD says: I am against
Pharaoh king of Egypt.[c] I will break both
his arms, the good arm as well as the broken one, and make the sword fall from his
hand.[d] [23]I will disperse the Egyptians
among the nations and scatter them
through the countries.[e] [24]I will strength-
en[f] the arms of the king of Babylon and
put my sword[g] in his hand, but I will
break the arms of Pharaoh, and he will
groan[h] before him like a mortally wounded man. [25]I will strengthen the arms of the
king of Babylon, but the arms of Pharaoh
will fall limp. Then they will know that I
am the LORD, when I put my sword[i] into
the hand of the king of Babylon and he
brandishes it against Egypt.[j] [26]I will disperse the Egyptians among the nations and
scatter them through the countries. Then
they will know that I am the LORD. [k]"

Cross references (center column)

30:16
[s]S Isa 19:13
30:17 [t]Ge 41:45
30:18 [u]S Jer 43:7
[v]S Lev 26:13;
S Isa 9:4 [w]S ver 3
30:19 [x]Eze 28:22
30:20
[y]S Eze 26:1;
S 29:17; 31:1;
32:1
30:21
[z]S Jer 48:25
[a]S Jer 44:30
[b]Jer 30:13; 46:11
30:22
[c]S Ge 15:18;
S Jer 46:25
[d]Ps 37:17;
Zec 11:17
30:23
[e]S Eze 29:12
30:24 [f]Zec 10:6,
12; 12:5
[g]S Eze 21:14;
Zep 2:12
[h]Jer 51:52
30:25
[i]1 Ch 21:12
[j]S Isa 10:5; 45:1,
5; S Eze 29:19
30:26
[k]S Eze 29:12

31:1 [l]Jer 52:5
[m]S Eze 30:20;
32:17
31:3 [n]S Jer 50:18
[o]S 2Ki 19:23;
Hab 2:17;
Zec 11:1
[p]Isa 10:34;
S Eze 19:11
31:4 [q]Eze 17:7
[r]Da 4:10
31:5 [s]ver 10
[t]S Nu 24:6;
S Eze 17:5
31:6
[u]S Ge 31:7-9
[v]S Eze 17:23;
S Mt 13:32
31:7 [w]S Job 14:9
31:8 [x]Ps 80:10
[y]S Ge 30:37

A Cedar in Lebanon

31 In the eleventh year,[l] in the third
month on the first day, the word of
the LORD came to me: [m] 2"Son of man, say
to Pharaoh king of Egypt and to his hordes:

" 'Who can be compared with you in
majesty?
[3]Consider Assyria, [n] once a cedar in
Lebanon, [o]
with beautiful branches
overshadowing the forest;
it towered on high,
its top above the thick foliage. [p]
[4]The waters[q] nourished it,
deep springs made it grow tall;
their streams flowed
all around its base
and sent their channels
to all the trees of the field. [r]
[5]So it towered higher[s]
than all the trees of the field;
its boughs increased
and its branches grew long,
spreading because of abundant
waters. [t]
[6]All the birds of the air
nested in its boughs,
all the beasts of the field
gave birth[u] under its branches;
all the great nations
lived in its shade. [v]
[7]It was majestic in beauty,
with its spreading boughs,
for its roots went down
to abundant waters. [w]
[8]The cedars[x] in the garden of God
could not rival it,
nor could the pine trees
equal its boughs,
nor could the plane trees[y]
compare with its branches—
no tree in the garden of God

[b]17 Hebrew *Awen* (or *On*)   [c]17 Hebrew *Pi Beseth*

30:17 *Heliopolis.* Greek name (meaning "city of the sun")
for On (see NIV text note), located six miles northeast of
Cairo. *Bubastis.* At one time the capital of Lower (northern)
Egypt; located 40 miles northeast of Cairo.
30:18 *Dark.* A common Biblical metaphor describing ruin,
destruction or death. *Tahpanhes.* In extreme northeast
Egypt. Johanan son of Kareah and his men fled there after the
murder of Gedaliah (see Jer 43:4–7). *covered with clouds.*
See v. 3 and note; 32:7.
30:20 The fourth oracle against Egypt (see note on 29:1).
eleventh year . . . first month . . . seventh day. Apr. 29, 587
B.C.; the eighth date in Ezekiel (see 1:2; 8:1; 20:1; 24:1;
26:1; 29:1,17).
30:21 *broken the arm.* Refers to Pharaoh Hophra's defeat
by Nebuchadnezzar the previous year (see notes on 29:6; Jer
37:10).
30:24 *put my sword in his hand.* See note on 21:3.

31:1 The fifth oracle against Egypt (see note on 29:1).
eleventh year . . . third month . . . first day. June 21, 587
B.C.; the ninth date in Ezekiel (see 1:2; 8:1; 20:1; 24:1;
26:1; 29:1,17; 30:20).
31:3 *Consider Assyria.* A great nation that had fallen. In
609 B.C. Pharaoh Neco went to Carchemish to help the
Assyrian empire, which was reeling from Babylonian attacks.
The effort failed and Assyria passed from history. *once a
cedar.* The beginning of another allegory (see Ezekiel's allegorical use of the cedar in ch. 17). *Lebanon.* Known for its
cedars (see vv. 15–18; Jdg 9:15; 1Ki 4:33; 5:6; 2Ki 14:9;
Ezr 3:7; Ps 29:5; 92:12; 104:16).
31:4 *waters.* The Tigris and Euphrates. *deep springs.* Or
"the deep" (see note on 26:19).
31:6 *birds of the air.* See 17:23 and note; see also Da 4:12.
31:8 *garden of God.* The note of pride is introduced (see v.
10; cf. 28:13).

could match its beauty. *z*

⁹I made it beautiful
with abundant branches,
the envy of all the trees of Eden *a*
in the garden of God. *b*

¹⁰ 'Therefore this is what the Sovereign
LORD says: Because it towered on high,
lifting its top above the thick foliage, and
because it was proud *c* of its height, ¹¹I
handed it over to the ruler of the nations,
for him to deal with according to its
wickedness. I cast it aside, *d* ¹²and the
most ruthless of foreign nations *e* cut it
down and left it. Its boughs fell on the
mountains and in all the valleys; *f* its
branches lay broken in all the ravines of
the land. All the nations of the earth came
out from under its shade and left it. *g* ¹³All
the birds of the air settled on the fallen
tree, and all the beasts of the field were
among its branches. *h* ¹⁴Therefore no other
trees by the waters are ever to tower
proudly on high, lifting their tops above
the thick foliage. No other trees so well-
watered are ever to reach such a height;
they are all destined *i* for death, *j* for the
earth below, among mortal men, with
those who go down to the pit. *k*

¹⁵ 'This is what the Sovereign LORD
says: On the day it was brought down to
the grave *d* I covered the deep springs with
mourning for it; I held back its streams,
and its abundant waters were restrained.
Because of it I clothed Lebanon with
gloom, and all the trees of the field withered away. *l* ¹⁶I made the nations tremble *m* at the sound of its fall when I brought
it down to the grave with those who go
down to the pit. Then all the trees *n* of
Eden, *o* the choicest and best of Lebanon,
all the trees that were well-watered, were
consoled *p* in the earth below. *q* ¹⁷Those
who lived in its shade, its allies among the
nations, had also gone down to the grave
with it, joining those killed by the sword. *r*

¹⁸ 'Which of the trees of Eden can be

compared with you in splendor and majesty? Yet you, too, will be brought down
with the trees of Eden to the earth below;
you will lie among the uncircumcised, *s*
with those killed by the sword.

" 'This is Pharaoh and all his hordes, declares the Sovereign LORD.' "

A Lament for Pharaoh

32 In the twelfth year, in the twelfth
month on the first day, the word of
the LORD came to me: *t* ²"Son of man,
take up a lament *u* concerning Pharaoh
king of Egypt and say to him:

" 'You are like a lion *v* among the
nations;
you are like a monster *w* in the seas *x*
thrashing about in your streams,
churning the water with your feet
and muddying the streams. *y*

³" 'This is what the Sovereign LORD
says:

" 'With a great throng of people
I will cast my net over you,
and they will haul you up in my
net. *z*
⁴I will throw you on the land
and hurl you on the open field.
I will let all the birds of the air settle on
you
and all the beasts of the earth gorge
themselves on you. *a*
⁵I will spread your flesh on the
mountains
and fill the valleys *b* with your
remains.
⁶I will drench the land with your flowing
blood *c*
all the way to the mountains,
and the ravines will be filled with
your flesh. *d*
⁷When I snuff you out, I will cover the
heavens

Cross references (center column):

31:8 *z*Ge 2:8-9
31:9 *a*S Ge 2:8
*b*S Ge 13:10;
Eze 28:13
31:10
*c*S Isa 2:11;
S 14:13-14;
S Eze 28:17
31:11 *d*Da 5:20
31:12
*e*S Eze 28:7
*f*Eze 32:5; 35:8
*g*Eze 32:11-12;
Da 4:14
31:13
*h*S Isa 18:6;
S Eze 29:5; 32:4
31:14 *i*S Ps 49:14
*j*S Ps 82:7
*k*S Nu 14:11;
Ps 63:9;
S Eze 26:20;
32:24
31:15 *l*S 2Sa 1:21
31:16
*m*S Jer 49:21
*n*S Isa 14:8
*o*S Ge 2:8
*p*S Eze 14:22
*q*S Isa 14:15;
Eze 32:18
31:17 *r*Ps 9:17

31:18 *s*S Jer 9:26
32:1 *t*S Eze 31:1;
33:21
32:2 *u*2Sa 1:17;
3:33; 2Ch 35:25;
S Eze 19:1
*v*S Ki 24:1;
Na 2:11-13
*w*S Job 3:8;
S Ps 74:13
*x*S Ge 1:21 *y*ver
13; Job 41:31;
S Eze 29:3; 34:18
32:3
*z*S Eze 12:13;
Hab 1:15
32:4 *a*S Isa 18:6;
Eze 31:12-13;
39:4-5,17
32:5
*b*S Eze 31:12
32:6 *c*S Isa 34:3
*d*S Eze 29:5

31:11 *ruler of the nations.* Probably Nabopolassar; or possibly Nebuchadnezzar. *its wickedness.* Pride (see v. 10; Ge
11:1–8).
31:12 *most ruthless.* Babylon (see note on 30:11).
31:15 *grave.* See NIV text note. *deep springs.* See note on
v. 4.
31:16 *nations tremble.* As at Tyre's fall (see 27:35; 28:19).
were consoled. Because the mightiest of trees had joined
them in the "grave" (Sheol).
31:17 *those killed by the sword.* Those who met a premature death.
31:18 *you.* The Egyptian pharaoh. *you, too.* It would happen to Pharaoh as it had happened to Assyria. *uncircumcised.* See note on 28:10.
32:1 The sixth oracle against Egypt (see note on 29:1).

twelfth year . . . twelfth month . . . first day. Mar. 3, 585
B.C.; the tenth date in Ezekiel (see 1:2; 8:1; 20:1; 24:1;
26:1; 29:1,17; 30:20; 31:1). If the Septuagint and Syriac
are followed ("eleventh year"), then the chronological order
of the Egypt oracles is preserved (and the date would be Mar.
13, 586). Cf. 29:1; 30:20; 31:1; see v. 17 and note.
32:2 *lament.* See note on 19:1. *lion among the nations.* A
figure for royalty and grandeur (see 19:1–9). *monster.* See
29:3 and note. *seas . . . streams.* Canals of the Nile (see note
on 29:3).
32:3 *cast my net.* Earlier it was Zedekiah over whom God's
net was thrown (see 12:13; 17:20; 19:8).
32:4 *I will throw.* God's actions here are very similar to
those described in 29:3–5.
32:7 *I will cover the heavens.* The first of seven clauses

and darken their stars;
I will cover the sun with a cloud,
    and the moon will not give its light. *e*
[8]All the shining lights in the heavens
    I will darken*f* over you;
I will bring darkness over your land,*g*
    declares the Sovereign Lord.
[9]I will trouble the hearts of many peoples
    when I bring about your destruction
        among the nations,
    among*e* lands you have not known.
[10]I will cause many peoples to be appalled
        at you,
    and their kings will shudder with
        horror because of you
    when I brandish my sword*h* before
        them.
On the day*i* of your downfall
    each of them will tremble
    every moment for his life.*j*

[11]" 'For this is what the Sovereign Lord
says:

" 'The sword*k* of the king of Babylon*l*
    will come against you. *m*
[12]I will cause your hordes to fall
    by the swords of mighty men—
    the most ruthless of all nations. *n*
They will shatter the pride of Egypt,
    and all her hordes will be
        overthrown.*o*
[13]I will destroy all her cattle
    from beside abundant waters
no longer to be stirred by the foot of
        man
    or muddied by the hoofs of cattle. *p*
[14]Then I will let her waters settle
    and make her streams flow like oil,
        declares the Sovereign Lord.
[15]When I make Egypt desolate
    and strip the land of everything in it,
when I strike down all who live there,
    then they will know that I am the
        Lord. *q*

[16]"This is the lament*r* they will chant
for her. The daughters of the nations will

Cross references (center column)

32:7
*e*S Isa 13:10;
34:4; S Eze 30:3;
Joel 2:2,31; 3:15;
S Mt 24:29;
Rev 8:12
32:8 /S Ps 102:26
*g*S Job 9:7;
S Jer 4:23;
Joel 2:10
32:10
*h*S Isa 30:32
*i*S Jer 46:10
/S Eze 26:16;
S 27:35; 30:9;
Rev 18:9-10
32:11
*k*S Eze 21:19
/S Isa 19:4;
S Jer 46:13
*m*S Eze 29:19
32:12
*n*S Eze 28:7
*o*Eze 31:11-12
32:13 *p*S ver 2;
S Eze 29:8,11
32:15 *q*Ex 7:5;
S 14:4,18;
Ps 107:33-34
32:16
*r*S Ge 50:10;
S Eze 19:1
32:17 *s*S ver 1
32:18 *t*Jer 1:10
*u*Eze 26:20;
S 31:14,16;
Mic 1:8
32:19 *v*ver
29-30;
S Eze 28:10
32:20 *w*Ps 28:3
*x*Eze 31:17-18
32:21 *y*S Isa 14:9
*z*Eze 28:10
32:23
*a*S Isa 14:15
*b*Na 1:14
32:24
*c*S Ge 10:22
*d*S Jer 49:37
*e*S Job 28:13
/S Eze 26:20
32:25 *g*Eze 28:10
32:26 *h*S Eze 27:13

chant it; for Egypt and all her hordes they
will chant it, declares the Sovereign
Lord."

[17]In the twelfth year, on the fifteenth
day of the month, the word of the Lord
came to me:*s* [18]"Son of man, wail for the
hordes of Egypt and consign*t* to the earth
below both her and the daughters of
mighty nations, with those who go down
to the pit.*u* [19]Say to them, 'Are you more
favored than others? Go down and be laid
among the uncircumcised.'*v* [20]They will
fall among those killed by the sword. The
sword is drawn; let her be dragged*w* off
with all her hordes.*x* [21]From within the
grave*fy* the mighty leaders will say of
Egypt and her allies, 'They have come
down and they lie with the uncircumcised,*z* with those killed by the sword.'

[22]"Assyria is there with her whole army;
she is surrounded by the graves of all her
slain, all who have fallen by the sword.
[23]Their graves are in the depths of the pit*a*
and her army lies around her grave.*b* All
who had spread terror in the land of the
living are slain, fallen by the sword.

[24]"Elam*c* is there, with all her hordes
around her grave. All of them are slain,
fallen by the sword.*d* All who had spread
terror in the land of the living*e* went down
uncircumcised to the earth below. They
bear their shame with those who go down
to the pit.*f* [25]A bed is made for her among
the slain, with all her hordes around her
grave. All of them are uncircumcised,*g*
killed by the sword. Because their terror
had spread in the land of the living, they
bear their shame with those who go down
to the pit; they are laid among the slain.

[26]"Meshech and Tubal*h* are there, with
all their hordes around their graves. All of
them are uncircumcised, killed by the
sword because they spread their terror in
the land of the living. [27]Do they not lie

*e*9 Hebrew; Septuagint *bring you into captivity among
the nations,* / *to* †*21* Hebrew *Sheol*; also in verse 27

---

threatening the darkness associated with the day of the Lord
(see Joel 2:2,10,31; 3:15; Am 5:18-20; Zep 1:15).
32:9 *trouble the hearts.* This and the next verse reflect the
fear brought about whenever great world powers fall,
reminding lesser nations that they are even more vulnerable.
Cf. similar feelings aroused by Tyre's fall (26:16-18; 27:35;
28:19).
32:10 *my sword.* See note on 21:3.
32:11 *king of Babylon.* Nebuchadnezzar (cf. 21:19).
32:12 *most ruthless of all nations.* Babylon (see note on
30:11).
32:14 *streams flow like oil.* Their surface undisturbed by
any form of life. This is the only place in the Bible where this
eerie metaphor is used to describe desolation.

32:16 *daughters of the nations.* A world chorus of professional wailers (see Jer 9:17-18).
32:17 The seventh and last oracle against Egypt (see note
on 29:1). *twelfth year . . . fifteenth day.* No month is given
(as in 26:1; 40:1). The whole year dates from Apr. 13, 586,
to Apr. 1, 585 b.c. The Septuagint suggests the first month,
the 15th day of which would be Apr. 27, 586.
32:18 *earth below.* Same as "grave" (Sheol) in 31:15.
daughters of mighty nations. See note on v. 16.
32:19 *uncircumcised.* See note on 28:10.
32:24 *Elam.* A country east of Assyria; in present-day
Iran.
32:26 *Meshech and Tubal.* Peoples and territories in Asia
Minor.

with the other uncircumcised[i] warriors who have fallen, who went down to the grave with their weapons of war, whose swords were placed under their heads? The punishment for their sins rested on their bones, though the terror of these warriors had stalked through the land of the living.

[28]"You too, O Pharaoh, will be broken and will lie among the uncircumcised, with those killed by the sword.

[29]"Edom[j] is there, her kings and all her princes; despite their power, they are laid with those killed by the sword. They lie with the uncircumcised, with those who go down to the pit.[k]

[30]"All the princes of the north[l] and all the Sidonians[m] are there; they went down with the slain in disgrace despite the terror caused by their power. They lie uncircumcised[n] with those killed by the sword and bear their shame with those who go down to the pit.[o]

[31]"Pharaoh—he and all his army—will see them and he will be consoled[p] for all his hordes that were killed by the sword, declares the Sovereign LORD. [32]Although I had him spread terror in the land of the living, Pharaoh[q] and all his hordes will be laid among the uncircumcised, with those killed by the sword, declares the Sovereign LORD."[r]

Ezekiel a Watchman

33 The word of the LORD came to me: [2]"Son of man, speak to your countrymen and say to them: 'When I bring the sword[s] against a land, and the people of the land choose one of their men and make him their watchman,[t] [3]and he sees the sword coming against the land and blows the trumpet[u] to warn the people, [4]then if anyone hears the trumpet but does not take warning[v] and the sword comes

---

32:27 [Eze 28:10
32:29 [S Ps 137:7;
Isa 34:5-15;
Jer 49:7;
Eze 35:15; Ob 1:1
[k] Eze 25:12-14
32:30 [S Isa 14:31;
Jer 25:26;
Eze 38:6; 39:2
[m] S Ge 10:15;
S Jer 25:22
[n] Eze 28:10
[o] S Eze 26:20;
S 28:8
32:31 [p] S Eze 14:22
32:32 [q] S Jer 44:30
[r] S Job 3:14
33:2 [s] S Lev 26:25;
S Jer 12:12
[t] S 1Sa 14:16;
Isa 21:6-9;
S Jer 51:12
33:3 [u] S Ex 20:18;
S Nu 10:7;
Hos 5:8; 8:1
33:4 [v] 2Ch 25:16

[w] S Lev 20:9;
S Jer 6:17;
Zec 1:4; Ac 18:6
33:5 [x] S Lev 20:9
[y] S Ex 9:21
33:6 [z] Isa 56:10-11;
S Eze 3:18
33:7 [a] S Isa 52:8
[b] Jer 1:17; 26:2
33:8 [c] ver 14
[d] S Isa 3:11;
S Eze 18:4
33:9 [e] S Ps 7:12
[f] Eze 3:17-19
33:10 [g] S Lev 26:16
[h] S Lev 26:39;
S Eze 4:17
33:11 [i] S La 3:33
[j] S 2Ch 30:9;
S Isa 19:22;
S Jer 3:12
[k] Jer 44:7-8;
S Eze 18:23;
Hos 11:8;
Joel 2:12;
S 1Ti 2:4
33:12 [l] ver 2
[m] 2Ch 7:14;
S Eze 3:20;
S 18:21

---

and takes his life, his blood will be on his own head. [w] [5]Since he heard the sound of the trumpet but did not take warning, his blood will be on his own head. [x] If he had taken warning, he would have saved himself. [y] [6]But if the watchman sees the sword coming and does not blow the trumpet to warn the people and the sword comes and takes the life of one of them, that man will be taken away because of his sin, but I will hold the watchman accountable for his blood.' [z]

[7]"Son of man, I have made you a watchman[a] for the house of Israel; so hear the word I speak and give them warning from me. [b] [8]When I say to the wicked, 'O wicked man, you will surely die,' [c] and you do not speak out to dissuade him from his ways, that wicked man will die for[g] his sin, and I will hold you accountable for his blood. [d] [9]But if you do warn the wicked man to turn from his ways and he does not do so, [e] he will die for his sin, but you will have saved yourself. [f]

[10]"Son of man, say to the house of Israel, 'This is what you are saying: "Our offenses and sins weigh us down, and we are wasting away[g] because of[h] them. How then can we live?" [h] ' [11]Say to them, 'As surely as I live, declares the Sovereign LORD, I take no pleasure in the death of the wicked, but rather that they turn from their ways and live. [i] Turn! [j] Turn from your evil ways! Why will you die, O house of Israel?' [k]

[12]"Therefore, son of man, say to your countrymen, [l] 'The righteousness of the righteous man will not save him when he disobeys, and the wickedness of the wicked man will not cause him to fall when he turns from it. The righteous man, if he sins, will not be allowed to live because of his former righteousness.' [m] [13]If I

g 8 Or *in;* also in verse 9   **h** 10 Or *away in*

32:30 *Sidonians.* See note on 28:21.

33:1—48:35 A section depicting consolation for Israel (see Introduction: Outline).

33:1—37:28 Sermons and oracles of comfort following the fall of Jerusalem. Interspersed are words of warning and judgment (e.g., 33:23—29; 34:1—19; 35; 36:1—7), some of which may have been intended to comfort a downtrodden people.

33:2 *your countrymen.* Fellow Israelites in exile with Ezekiel. *sword.* The invading army. *people of the land.* Full citizens who owned land and served in the army (see 7:27; 12:19; 45:16,22; 46:3). *watchman.* A figure introduced in ch. 3 and expanded in ch. 18 (see note on 3:16).

33:3 *trumpet.* An instrument made from a ram's horn (Jos 6:4,6,13), used to warn of approaching danger (Ne 4:18—20; Jer 4:19; Am 3:6) and to announce the beginnings

of religious periods (e.g., Day of Atonement, Lev 25:9; New Moon festival, Ps 81:3).

33:4 *his blood will be on his own head.* See note on 18:13.

33:6 *his blood.* His life, blood being the life principle (see Ge 9:5; 42:22).

33:7 *house of Israel.* Both the nation and the individuals. Compare vv. 7—9 with 3:17—19.

33:10 *Our offenses and sins.* The first time the exiles expressed consciousness of sin. Previously they had blamed their fathers (18:2) and even God (18:19,25).

33:11 *As surely as I live.* See note on 18:3. *I take no pleasure.* The question of 18:23 is now a statement. God's basic intention for his creation is life, not death (see note on 16:6). *Turn!* The third call for repentance (see 14:6; 18:30).

33:12—20 Deals with the same subject as 18:21—24 —namely, that the individual, whether righteous or wicked, has a choice to live righteously each day.

tell the righteous man that he will surely live, but then he trusts in his righteousness and does evil, none of the righteous things he has done will be remembered; he will die for the evil he has done. [n] [14]And if I say to the wicked man, 'You will surely die,' but he then turns away from his sin and does what is just [o] and right— [15]if he gives back what he took in pledge [p] for a loan, returns what he has stolen, [q] follows the decrees that give life, and does no evil, he will surely live; he will not die. [r] [16]None of the sins [s] he has committed will be remembered against him. He has done what is just and right; he will surely live. [t]

[17]"Yet your countrymen say, 'The way of the Lord is not just.' But it is their way that is not just. [18]If a righteous man turns from his righteousness and does evil, [u] he will die for it. [v] [19]And if a wicked man turns away from his wickedness and does what is just and right, he will live by doing so. [w] [20]Yet, O house of Israel, you say, 'The way of the Lord is not just.' But I will judge each of you according to his own ways." [x]

Jerusalem's Fall Explained

[21]In the twelfth year of our exile, in the tenth month on the fifth day, a man who had escaped [y] from Jerusalem came to me and said, "The city has fallen! [z]" [22]Now the evening before the man arrived, the hand of the Lord was upon me, [a] and he opened my mouth [b] before the man came to me in the morning. So my mouth was opened and I was no longer silent. [c]

[23]Then the word of the Lord came to me: [24]"Son of man, the people living in those ruins [d] in the land of Israel are saying, 'Abraham was only one man, yet he possessed the land. But we are many; [e] surely the land has been given to us as our possession.' [f] [25]Therefore say to them,

'This is what the Sovereign Lord says: Since you eat [g] meat with the blood [h] still in it and look to your idols and shed blood, should you then possess the land? [i] [26]You rely on your sword, you do detestable things, [j] and each of you defiles his neighbor's wife. [k] Should you then possess the land?'

[27]Say this to them: 'This is what the Sovereign Lord says: As surely as I live, those who are left in the ruins will fall by the sword, those out in the country I will give to the wild animals to be devoured, and those in strongholds and caves will die of a plague. [l] [28]I will make the land a desolate waste, and her proud strength will come to an end, and the mountains [m] of Israel will become desolate so that no one will cross them. [n] [29]Then they will know that I am the Lord, when I have made the land a desolate [o] waste because of all the detestable things they have done.' [p]

[30]"As for you, son of man, your countrymen are talking together about you by the walls and at the doors of the houses, saying to each other, 'Come and hear the message that has come from the Lord.' [31]My people come to you, as they usually do, and sit before [q] you to listen to your words, but they do not put them into practice. With their mouths they express devotion, but their hearts are greedy [r] for unjust gain. [s] [32]Indeed, to them you are nothing more than one who sings love songs [t] with a beautiful voice and plays an instrument well, for they hear your words but do not put them into practice. [u]

[33]"When all this comes true—and it surely will—then they will know that a prophet has been among them. [v] "

33:13
[n]Heb 10:38;
2Pe 2:20-21
33:14 [o]S Jer 22:3
33:15
[p]S Ex 22:26
[q]Ex 22:1-4;
S Lev 6:2-5
[r]Isa 55:7;
Jer 18:7-8;
S Lk 19:8
33:16
[s]S Jer 50:20
[t]S Isa 43:25
33:18 [u]Jer 18:10
[v]S Eze 3:20
33:19 [w]S ver 14-15
33:20
[x]S Job 34:11
33:21 [y]Eze 24:26
[z]S 2Ki 25:4,10;
Jer 39:1-2;
52:4-7;
S Eze 32:1
33:22 [a]S Eze 1:3
[b]Eze 29:21;
Lk 1:64
[c]Eze 3:26-27;
S 24:27
33:24 [d]Eze 36:4
[e]S Dt 1:10
[f]Isa 51:2;
Jer 40:7;
Eze 11:15;
Lk 3:8; Ac 7:5

33:25 [g]Jer 7:21
[h]S Ge 9:4
[i]Jer 7:9-10;
S Eze 22:6,27
33:26 [j]Jer 41:7
[k]Eze 22:11
33:27 [l]1Sa 13:6;
Isa 2:19;
S Jer 42:22;
S Eze 7:15;
S 14:21; 39:4
33:28
[m]S Isa 41:15
[n]S Ge 6:7;
Jer 9:10
33:29
[o]S Lev 26:34
[p]S Jer 18:16;
S 44:22;
Eze 36:4;
Mic 7:13
33:31 [q]S Eze 8:1
[r]Ps 119:36
[s]Ps 78:36-37;
S Isa 29:13;
S 33:15;
S Jer 3:10; S 6:17;
S Eze 22:27;
Mt 13:22;
1Jn 3:18

33:32 [t]S 1Ki 4:32 [u]Mk 6:20 **33:33** [v]S 1Sa 3:20; S Jer 28:9;
S Eze 2:5

33:15 *gives back what he took in pledge . . . returns what he has stolen.* See note on 18:7. *decrees that give life.* The purpose of God's law was to foster and protect life (cf. 20:13,21). *he will surely live.* The entire section is Ezekiel's answer to the despairing question of v. 10.
33:17 *The way of the Lord is not just.* Cf. 18:25,29.
33:21 *twelfth year . . . tenth month . . . fifth day.* Jan. 8, 585 b.c., five months after the Jerusalem temple was burned. See date in 2Ki 25:8, which in modern reckoning is Aug. 14, 586. The journey between Jerusalem and Babylon could be made in four months (Ezr 7:9). *man who had escaped.* The first of the exiles of 586 (see 24:26, "fugitive"). A Jerusalem Jew would not "escape" to Babylonian captivity. *The city has fallen!* With this statement all of Ezekiel's previous prophecies were fulfilled and vindicated. He was then sent with a new mission: pastoral comfort.
33:22 *no longer silent.* The muteness that had come upon him at the beginning of his ministry was lifted (see 3:26 and note).

33:24 *people living in those ruins.* The residents of Jerusalem not exiled in 586 b.c. *Abraham was only one man . . . But we are many.* A boast by the unrepentant, similar to that of 11:15 (cf. Lk 3:8).
33:25 *eat meat with the blood.* Forbidden in Ge 9:4; Lev 7:26–27; 17:10; Dt 12:16,23. *look to your idols.* See note on 18:6.
33:27 *As surely as I live.* See note on 18:3. *sword . . . wild animals . . . plague.* Cf. the threefold threat in 5:12; 7:15; 12:16 and the fourfold threat in 14:12–21.
33:30–33 Words of assurance meant for Ezekiel alone.
33:31 *sit before you.* As the elders had (8:1; 14:1). *greedy.* The people were waiting for Ezekiel to tell them how they could personally profit from the situation rather than what God's larger designs were for them (cf. Mt 20:20–28).
33:32 *one who sings.* May indicate that Ezekiel chanted his oracles (see 2Ki 3:15; Isa 5:1), but more likely the prophet was using a metaphor. *they hear . . . but do not . . . practice.* See Isa 29:13; Mt 21:28–32; cf. Jas 1:22–25.

Shepherds and Sheep

34 The word of the LORD came to me: 2"Son of man, prophesy against the shepherds of Israel; prophesy and say to them: 'This is what the Sovereign LORD says: Woe to the shepherds of Israel who only take care of themselves! Should not shepherds take care of the flock? *w* 3You eat the curds, clothe yourselves with the wool and slaughter the choice animals, but you do not take care of the flock. *x* 4You have not strengthened the weak or healed *y* the sick or bound up *z* the injured. You have not brought back the strays or searched for the lost. You have ruled them harshly and brutally. *a* 5So they were scattered because there was no shepherd, *b* and when they were scattered they became food for all the wild animals. *c* 6My sheep wandered over all the mountains and on every high hill. *d* They were scattered *e* over the whole earth, and no one searched or looked for them. *f*

7" 'Therefore, you shepherds, hear the word of the LORD: 8As surely as I live, declares the Sovereign LORD, because my flock lacks a shepherd and so has been plundered *g* and has become food for all the wild animals, *h* and because my shepherds did not search for my flock but cared for themselves rather than for my flock, *i* 9therefore, O shepherds, hear the word of the LORD: 10This is what the Sovereign LORD says: I am against *j* the shepherds and will hold them accountable for my flock. I will remove them from tending the flock so that the shepherds can no longer feed themselves. I will rescue *k* my flock from their mouths, and it will no longer be food for them. *l*

11" 'For this is what the Sovereign LORD says: I myself will search for my sheep *m* and look after them. 12As a shepherd *n* looks after his scattered flock when he is with them, so will I look after my sheep. I will rescue them from all the places where they were scattered on a day of clouds and darkness. *o* 13I will bring them out from the nations and gather *p* them from the countries, and I will bring them into their own land. *q r s t* I will pasture them on the mountains of Israel, in the ravines and in all the settlements in the land. *u v w* 14I will tend them in a good pasture, and the mountain heights of Israel *x* will be their grazing land. There they will lie down in good grazing land, and there they will feed in a rich pasture *y* on the mountains of Israel. *z* 15I myself will tend my sheep and have them lie down, *a* declares the Sovereign LORD. *b* 16I will search for the lost and bring back the strays. I will bind up *c* the injured and strengthen the weak, *d* but the sleek and the strong I will destroy. *e* I will shepherd the flock with justice. *f*

17" 'As for you, my flock, this is what the Sovereign LORD says: I will judge between one sheep and another, and between rams and goats. *g* 18Is it not enough *h* for you to feed on the good pasture? Must you also trample the rest of your pasture with your feet? *i* Is it not enough for you to drink clear water? Must you also muddy the rest with your feet?

Cross references (center column)

34:2 wPs 78:70-72; Isa 40:11; Jer 3:15; S 23:1; Mic 3:11; Jn 10:11; 21:15-17; Jude 1:12
34:3 xIsa 56:11; S Eze 22:27; Am 6:4; Zec 11:5
34:4 yS Isa 3:7 zS Isa 1:6 aver 16; S Lev 25:43; Mic 3:3; Zec 11:15-17
34:5 bS Nu 27:17 cver 28; S Isa 56:9; Ac 20:29
34:6 dS Jer 50:6 eS Lev 26:33; S Ps 95:10; S Jer 10:21 /2Ch 18:16; Ps 142:4; Hos 7:13; S Mt 9:36; 18:12-13; Lk 15:5; 1Pe 2:25
34:8 gS Jdg 2:14 hS Isa 56:9 /Jude 1:12
34:10 /S Jer 21:13 kS Ps 72:14
/1Sa 2:29-30; S Jer 23:2; Zec 10:3
34:11 mS Ps 119:176
34:12 nIsa 40:11; S Jer 31:10; Zec 10:3; Lk 19:10 oS Eze 32:7
34:13 pS Ge 48:21; S Dt 30:4 qMic 4:6 rS Jer 11:17 sS Jer 23:8 tS Isa 60:21 uS Eze 28:25; 36:24 vS Jer 50:19 wJer 23:3
34:14 xS Eze 20:40 yPs 23:2; S 37:3 zS Isa 65:10; Eze 36:29-30;
37:22; Am 9:14; Mic 7:14 **34:15** aZep 3:13 bPs 23:1-2; · · S Jer 33:12; Mic 5:4 **34:16** cS Ps 147:3 dMic 4:6; Zep 3:19 eLk 19:10 /Isa 10:16; S Jer 31:8; Lk 5:32 **34:17** gMt 25:32-33 **34:18** hS Ge 30:15 /S Eze 32:2

Study notes

34:2 *shepherds of Israel.* Those responsible for providing leadership, especially the kings and their officials (see 2Sa 7:7; Jer 25:18–19), but also the prophets and priests (see Isa 56:11; Jer 23:9–11). Ezekiel had earlier singled out the princes, priests and prophets for special rebuke (ch. 22). To call a king a shepherd was common throughout the ancient Near East. For David's rise from shepherd to shepherd-king see Ps 78:70–71. For condemnation of the shepherds cf. Jer 23:1–4.

34:3 *eat . . . clothe . . . slaughter.* Legitimate rewards for shepherds. Their crime was that they did not care for the flock.

34:4 *searched for the lost.* Cf. Jer 50:6; Mt 18:12–14; Lk 15:4; 19:10.

34:5 *scattered.* Often used by Ezekiel to describe Israel's exile and dispersion (11:16–17; 12:15; 20:23,34,41; 22:15; 28:25). *no shepherd.* A picture used often in the Bible (e.g., Mk 6:34).

34:8 *wild animals.* Hostile foreign nations; but see v. 28, where they are contrasted.

34:10 *I am against the shepherds.* See note on 5:8.

34:11 *I myself will search for my sheep.* Having dealt with the faithless shepherds (vv. 1–10), the Lord committed himself to shepherd his flock (see Jer 23:3–4).

34:12 *from all the places.* Babylon was not the only place where the Israelites had gone (see Jer 43:1–7). *day of clouds and darkness.* The day of the Lord that had come upon Israel when Jerusalem fell in August of 586 B.C. (see 7:7 and note).

34:13 *I will bring them out.* The promises of restoration—begun in 11:17 and repeated in 20:34,41–42; 28:25—find special emphasis in this part (chs. 33–39) of Ezekiel (see 36:24; 37:21; 38:8; 39:27). *mountains of Israel.* Compare the tone of 6:3–7 with judgment now past (see v. 12). The mountains perhaps represented the scene of salvation.

34:14 *I will tend them.* See Isa 40:11; Jn 10:11.

34:16 *the sleek and the strong.* Those with power who had fattened themselves by oppressing the other "sheep" (see vv. 17–22).

34:17 *rams and goats.* People of power and influence who were oppressing poorer Israelites. This prophetic word shows the same concern for social justice found elsewhere in the prophets (see Isa 3:13–15; 5:8; Am 5:12; 6:1–7; Mic 2:1–5). Cf. the treatment of slaves Jeremiah observed (Jer 34:8–11).

[19]Must my flock feed on what you have trampled and drink what you have muddied with your feet?

[20]" 'Therefore this is what the Sovereign LORD says to them: See, I myself will judge between the fat sheep and the lean sheep.[j] [21]Because you shove with flank and shoulder, butting all the weak sheep with your horns[k] until you have driven them away, [22]I will save my flock, and they will no longer be plundered. I will judge between one sheep and another. [23]I will place over them one shepherd, my servant David, and he will tend[m] them; he will tend them and be their shepherd.[n] [24]I the LORD will be their God,[o] and my servant David[p] will be prince among them.[q] I the LORD have spoken.[r]

[25]" 'I will make a covenant[s] of peace[t] with them and rid the land of wild beasts[u] so that they may live in the desert and sleep in the forests in safety.[v] [26]I will bless[w] them and the places surrounding my hill.[i] I will send down showers in season;[x] there will be showers of blessing.[y] [27]The trees of the field will yield their fruit[z] and the ground will yield its crops;[a] the people will be secure[b] in their land. They will know that I am the LORD, when I break the bars of their yoke[c] and rescue them from the hands of those who enslaved them.[d] [28]They will no longer be plundered by the nations, nor will wild animals devour them. They will live in safety,[e] and no one will make them afraid.[f] [29]I will provide for them a land renowned[g] for its crops, and they will no longer be victims of famine[h] in the land or bear the scorn[i] of the nations.[j] [30]Then

they will know that I, the LORD their God, am with them and that they, the house of Israel, are my people, declares the Sovereign LORD.[k] [31]You my sheep,[l] the sheep of my pasture,[m] are people, and I am your God, declares the Sovereign LORD.' "

A Prophecy Against Edom

35 The word of the LORD came to me: [2]"Son of man, set your face against Mount Seir;[n] prophesy against it [3]and say: 'This is what the Sovereign LORD says: I am against you, Mount Seir, and I will stretch out my hand[o] against you and make you a desolate waste.[p] [4]I will turn your towns into ruins[q] and you will be desolate. Then you will know that I am the LORD.[r]

[5]" 'Because you harbored an ancient hostility and delivered the Israelites over to the sword[s] at the time of their calamity,[t] the time their punishment reached its climax,[u] [6]therefore as surely as I live, declares the Sovereign LORD, I will give you over to bloodshed[v] and it will pursue you.[w] Since you did not hate bloodshed, bloodshed will pursue you. [7]I will make Mount Seir a desolate waste[x] and cut off from it all who come and go.[y] [8]I will fill your mountains with the slain; those killed by the sword will fall on your hills and in your valleys and in all your ravines.[z] [9]I will make you desolate forever;[a] your

---

Cross references (center column):

34:20 /Mt 25:32
34:21 kS Dt 33:17
34:22 /Ps 72:12-14; Jer 23:2-3; Eze 20:37-38
34:23 mIsa 40:11; nS Isa 31:4; Mic 5:4
34:24 oEze 36:28; pPs 89:49; qS Isa 53:4; rJer 23:4-5; Zec 13:7
34:25 sS Eze 16:62; tS Ps 55:12; uLev 26:6; vS Lev 25:18; Isa 11:6-9; Hos 2:18
34:26 wS Ge 12:2; xPs 68:9; Joel 2:23; yDt 11:13-15; S 28:12; Isa 44:3
34:27 zS Ps 72:16; aS Job 14:9; bS Ps 67:6; cS Nu 24:21; dS Lev 26:13; dS Jer 30:8; S Eze 20:42; S 28:25
34:28 eS Jer 32:37; fS Jer 30:10; S Eze 28:26; 39:26; Hos 11:11; Am 9:15; Zep 3:13; Zec 14:11
34:29 gS Isa 4:2; hEze 36:29; iS Ps 137:3; Eze 36:6; Joel 2:19; jEze 36:15
34:30 kS Eze 14:11; 37:27
34:31 lS Ps 28:9; mS Jer 23:1
35:2 nS Ge 14:6

35:3 oS Jer 6:12; pS Isa 34:10; Eze 25:12-14 35:4 qJer 44:2; rver 9; S Jer 49:10 35:5 sS Ps 63:10; tOb 1:13; uPs 137:7; S Eze 21:29 35:6 vS Isa 34:3; wIsa 63:2-6 35:7 xS Jer 46:19; yS Jer 49:17 35:8 zS Eze 31:12 35:9 aOb 1:10

i26 Or I will make them and the places surrounding my hill a blessing

---

34:23 my servant David. A ruler like David and from his line (see Ps 89:4,20,29; Jer 23:5-6).
34:24 prince. The Lord announced a theocracy, a kingdom where he would be King and the earthly king a "prince" (cf. 37:25; 44:3; 45:7,16-17,22; 46:2-18; 48:21-22).
34:25 covenant of peace. Cf. 37:26. All of God's covenants aim at peace (see Ge 26:28-31; Nu 25:12; Isa 54:10; Mal 2:5). This covenant (the "new covenant" spoken of by Jeremiah, 31:31-34) looks to the final peace, initiated by Christ (Php 4:7) and still awaiting final fulfillment. "Peace" (Hebrew shalom) is more than absence of hostility; it is fullness of life enjoyed in complete security. sleep in the forests. Often dangerous (see Ps 104:20-21; Jer 5:6).
34:26 showers in season. Autumn rains, which signal the beginning of the rainy season, and spring rains, which come at the end (cf. Jer 5:24). showers of blessing. Blessing, the power of life promised to God's people through Abraham (Ge 12:1-3), is beautifully symbolized in the life-giving effects of rain.
34:27 bars of their yoke. The bars were wooden pegs inserted down through holes in the yoke and tied below the animal's neck with cords (Isa 58:6) to form a collar (cf.

30:18; Lev 26:13; Jer 27:2; 28:10-13). The entire picture represents foreign domination.
34:29 scorn of the nations. See 22:4.
34:30 I, the LORD their God, am with them . . . they . . . are my people. Covenant language (cf. 11:20; Ex 6:7; Hos 1:9), though the exact wording of this verse has no parallel elsewhere in Ezekiel.
35:2 set your face against. See note on 20:46. Mount Seir. Edom (v. 15), Israel's relative (Jacob and Esau being twins, Ge 25:21-30) and constant enemy, from whom brotherhood was sought but seldom found (cf. Am 1:11). Edom had to be dealt with before Israel could find peace (cf. Ge 32-33). See 25:12 and note; Isa 63:1-6.
35:3 I am against you. See note on 5:8.
35:5 ancient hostility. Beginning with Jacob's deception of Isaac for Esau's blessing (Ge 27; see especially v. 41) and continuing later (Nu 20:14-21; 2Sa 8:13-14; 1Ki 9:26-28). time of their calamity. Edom looted Jerusalem in 586 B.C. (see Ob 11-14).
35:6 as surely as I live. See note on 18:3. bloodshed will pursue you. Retributive justice based on Ge 9:6.
35:9 desolate forever. To experience no restoration like Egypt (see 29:13-16).

towns will not be inhabited. Then you will know that I am the LORD. *b*

10 " 'Because you have said, "These two nations and countries will be ours and we will take possession *c* of them," even though I the LORD was there, 11 therefore as surely as I live, declares the Sovereign LORD, I will treat you in accordance with the anger *d* and jealousy you showed in your hatred of them and I will make myself known among them when I judge you. *e* 12 Then you will know that I the LORD have heard all the contemptible things you have said against the mountains of Israel. You said, "They have been laid waste and have been given over to us to devour." ' 13 You boasted *g* against me and spoke against me without restraint, and I heard it. *h* 14 This is what the Sovereign LORD says: While the whole earth rejoices, I will make you desolate. *i* 15 Because you rejoiced *j* when the inheritance of the house of Israel became desolate, that is how I will treat you. You will be desolate, O Mount Seir, *k* you and all of Edom. *l* Then they will know that I am the LORD.' "

A Prophecy to the Mountains of Israel

36 "Son of man, prophesy to the mountains of Israel *m* and say, 'O mountains of Israel, hear the word of the LORD. 2 This is what the Sovereign LORD says: *n* The enemy said of you, "Aha! *o* The ancient heights *p* have become our possession." ' 3 Therefore prophesy and say, 'This is what the Sovereign LORD says: Because they ravaged *r* and hounded you from every side so that you became the possession of the rest of the nations and

the object of people's malicious talk and slander, *s* 4 therefore, O mountains of Israel, hear the word of the Sovereign LORD: This is what the Sovereign LORD says to the mountains and hills, to the ravines and valleys, *t* to the desolate ruins *u* and the deserted *v* towns that have been plundered and ridiculed *w* by the rest of the nations around you *x*— 5 this is what the Sovereign LORD says: In my burning *y* zeal I have spoken against the rest of the nations, and against all Edom, for with glee and with malice in their hearts they made my land their own possession so that they might plunder its pastureland.' *z* 6 Therefore prophesy concerning the land of Israel and say to the mountains and hills, to the ravines and valleys: 'This is what the Sovereign LORD says: I speak in my jealous wrath because you have suffered the scorn of the nations. *a* 7 Therefore this is what the Sovereign LORD says: I swear with uplifted hand *b* that the nations around you will also suffer scorn. *c*

8 " 'But you, O mountains of Israel, will produce branches and fruit *d* for my people Israel, for they will soon come home. 9 I am concerned for you and will look on you with favor; you will be plowed and sown, *e* 10 and I will multiply the number of people upon you, even the whole house of Israel. The towns will be inhabited and the ruins *f* rebuilt. *g* 11 I will increase the number of men and animals upon you, and they will be fruitful *h* and become numerous. I will settle people *i* on you as in the past *j* and will make you prosper more than before. *k* Then you will know that I am the LORD. 12 I will cause people, my people Israel, to walk upon you. They will

Cross references (center column)

35:9
b S Isa 34:5-6;
S Jer 49:13
35:10
c S Ps 83:12;
Eze 36:2,5
35:11 *d* Eze 25:14
e S Ps 9:16;
Ob 1:15; S Mt 7:2
35:12 *f* S Jer 50:7
35:13
g S Jer 49:16
h Da 11:36
35:14 *i* Jer 51:48
35:15 *j* Eze 36:5;
Ob 1:12 *k* ver 3
l S Isa 34:5-6,11;
Jer 50:11-13;
S La 4:21;
S Eze 32:29
36:1
m S Eze 17:22
36:2 *n* Eze 6:2-3
o S Eze 25:3
p S Dt 32:13
q S Eze 35:10
36:3 *r* Ob 1:13

s Ps 44:13-14;
S La 2:16; 3:62
36:4 *t* Eze 6:3
u Eze 33:24
v S Lev 26:43
w S Jer 2:26
x Dt 11:11;
S Ps 79:4;
S Eze 33:28-29
36:5 *y* S Dt 29:20
z Isa 66:16;
Jer 25:31; 50:11;
Eze 25:12-14;
S 35:10,15;
38:22; Joel 3:2,14
36:6 *a* Ps 123:3-4;
Eze 34:29
36:7 *b* S Nu 14:30
c S Jer 25:9
36:8 *d* S Isa 4:2;
S 27:6; Eze 47:12
36:9 *e* ver 34-36;
Jer 31:27
36:10 *f* S Isa 49:8
g Isa 49:17-23;
S Jer 30:18
36:11 *h* S Ge 1:22
i S Isa 49:19
j Mic 7:14
k Lev 26:9;
Job 42:13;
S Jer 31:28;
S Eze 16:55;
Zec 10:8

35:10 *These two nations.* Israel and Judah.
35:11 *as surely as I live.* See note on 18:3.
35:13 *You boasted against me.* Cf. Ob 12; Zep 2:8,10; also Ps 35:26; Jer 48:26,42.
36:1–15 The comforting counterpart to ch. 6. Verses 1–7 announce punishment for the nations, vv. 8–15 restoration for Israel.
36:2 *The enemy said of you.* See 25:3; 26:2. *Aha!* See note on 25:3. *ancient heights.* The promised land, of which the elevated region between the Jordan Valley and the Mediterranean coast was the central core.
36:3 *rest of the nations.* All nations that in the past had conquered parts of Israel—until finally they took full possession.
36:4 *mountains . . . hills . . . ravines . . . valleys.* See 6:3 and note on 1:5.
36:5 *my burning zeal.* The Lord was personally offended by the ridicule of the nations because it was his special land they were mocking and plundering (see "my land" later in the verse). *Edom.* Singled out because of their long-standing hostility to Israel (see ch. 35, especially vv. 2,5 and notes).
36:7 *with uplifted hand.* See 20:5 and note.

36:8 *branches and fruit.* Signs of productivity (see 17:8, 23) and the Lord's restored favor (see Lev 26:3–5); to be contrasted with Edom's desolation in 35:3,7,15. *soon.* As judgment neared (7:7; 12:23), a speedy return of the exiles was announced.
36:9 *I . . . will look on you with favor.* Cf. Lev 26:9 for the identical clause in a similar context.
36:10 *even the whole house of Israel.* In this chapter (as in 37:15–23) Ezekiel is speaking of the restoration of all Israel.
36:11 *be fruitful and become numerous.* Identical terminology to the divine blessing at creation (Ge 1:22,28; see Ge 8:17; 9:1,7) and the subsequent covenant blessing (see Ge 17:6; 35:11; 48:3–4; Ex 1:7). *Then you will know that I am the LORD.* These words of recognition, used throughout the book to express God's revelation through judgment, here point to God's self-disclosure in salvation (see note on 5:13; cf. 34:30).
36:12 *walk upon you.* The mountains of Israel are still being addressed. *deprive them of their children.* The mountains are poetically pictured as having contributed to the depopulation brought by the exile. This may refer to the fact that Palestine contained the Canaanites and their religious

possess you, and you will be their inheritance; *l* you will never again deprive them of their children.

[13] 'This is what the Sovereign LORD says: Because people say to you, "You devour men *m* and deprive your nation of its children," [14]therefore you will no longer devour men or make your nation childless, declares the Sovereign LORD. [15]No longer will I make you hear the taunts of the nations, and no longer will you suffer the scorn of the peoples or cause your nation to fall, declares the Sovereign LORD. *n* ' "

[16]Again the word of the LORD came to me: [17]"Son of man, when the people of Israel were living in their own land, they defiled it by their conduct and their actions. Their conduct was like a woman's monthly uncleanness *o* in my sight. *p* [18]So I poured out *q* my wrath on them because they had shed blood in the land and because they had defiled it with their idols. [19]I dispersed them among the nations, and they were scattered *r* through the countries; I judged them according to their conduct and their actions. *s* [20]And wherever they went among the nations they profaned *t* my holy name, for it was said of them, 'These are the LORD's people, and yet they had to leave his land.' *u* [21]I had concern for my holy name, which the house of Israel profaned among the nations where they had gone. *v*

[22]"Therefore say to the house of Israel, 'This is what the Sovereign LORD says: It is not for your sake, O house of Israel, that I am going to do these things, but for the

sake of my holy name, *w* which you have profaned *x* among the nations where you have gone. *y* [23]I will show the holiness of my great name, *z* which has been profaned *a* among the nations, the name you have profaned among them. Then the nations will know that I am the LORD, *b* declares the Sovereign LORD, when I show myself holy *c* through you before their eyes. *d*

[24]" 'For I will take you out of the nations; I will gather you from all the countries and bring you back into your own land. *e* [25]I will sprinkle *f* clean water on you, and you will be clean; I will cleanse *g* you from all your impurities *h* and from all your idols. *i* [26]I will give you a new heart *j* and put a new spirit in you; I will remove from you your heart of stone *k* and give you a heart of flesh. *l* [27]And I will put my Spirit *m* in you and move you to follow my decrees *n* and be careful to keep my laws. *o* [28]You will live in the land I gave your forefathers; you will be my people, *p* and I will be your God. *q* [29]I will save you from all your uncleanness. I will call for the grain and make it plentiful and will not bring famine *r* upon you. [30]I will increase the fruit of the trees and the crops of the field, so that you will no longer suffer disgrace among the nations because of famine. *s* [31]Then you will remember your evil ways and wicked deeds, and you will loathe

---

36:12
*l*Eze 47:14,22
36:13
*m*S Nu 13:32
36:15
*n*Ps 89:50-51;
Isa 54:4;
S Eze 34:29
36:17 *o*S Lev 5:2;
S 12:2
*p*Ps 106:37-38;
S Jer 2:7
36:18
*q*S 2Ch 34:21
36:19 *r*Dt 28:64
*s*Lev 18:24-28;
S Eze 7:8;
S 24:14; 39:24
36:20
*t*S Lev 18:21;
S Eze 13:19;
Ro 2:24
*u*Isa 52:5;
S Jer 33:24;
S Eze 12:16
36:21 *v*Ps 74:18;
Isa 48:9
36:22
*w*S Isa 37:35;
S Eze 20:44
*x*Ro 2:24*
*y*Dt 9:5-6;
Ps 106:8;
S Eze 20:9
36:23 *z*S Nu 6:27
*a*S Isa 37:23
*b*S Ps 46:10
*c*S Eze 20:41
*d*Ps 126:2;
S Isa 5:16;
Eze 20:14; 38:23;
39:7,27-28
36:24
*e*S Isa 43:5-6;
S Eze 34:13;
37:21
36:25
*f*S Lev 14:7;
S 16:14-15;
Heb 9:13
*g*S Ps 51:2,7
*h*S Ezr 6:21
*i*Isa 2:18;
Joel 3:21;
Zec 3:4; 13:2;
S Ac 22:16
36:26 *j*Jer 24:7
*k*S Jer 5:3

*l*S Ps 51:10; S Eze 18:31; S 2Co 3:3 **36:27** *m*S Isa 44:3;
Joel 2:29; Jn 3:5 *n*S Eze 18:21 *o*Jer 50:20; 1Th 4:8 **36:28**
*p*Jer 30:22; 31:33 *q*S Eze 11:17; S 14:11; 34:24; 37:14,27;
Zec 8:8 **36:29** *r*Eze 34:29 **36:30** *s*Lev 26:4-5;
S Eze 34:13-14; Hos 2:21-22

---

centers ("high places"), which had led Israel astray and so brought God's wrath down on his people (see 6:3 and note).
36:16–38 Summarizes all that Ezekiel prophesied concerning Israel.
36:18 *shed blood . . . defiled it with their idols.* A summary reference to Israel's social injustices and idolatrous religious practices (see 22:3 and note). *idols.* See note on 6:4.
36:20 *they profaned my holy name.* Because Israel had been removed from her land, it seemed to the nations that her God was unable to protect and preserve his people (cf. Nu 14:15–16; 2Ki 18:32–35; 19:10–12).
36:22 *It is not for your sake.* Not because God did not care for Israel, but because they did not deserve what he was about to do (cf. Dt 9:4–6). Statements like these make Ezekiel a preacher of pure grace. *for the sake of my holy name.* The reason given in ch. 20 for the withholding of divine punishment (see 20:9,14,22) is here given as a reason for divine restoration.
36:23 *Then the nations will know that I am the LORD.* The ultimate purpose of God's plans with Israel is that the whole world may know the true God.
36:24 *I will take . . . gather . . . bring you back.* The first of four stages of restoration in this central passage of Ezekiel: return of the exiles.
36:25 *I will sprinkle clean water.* For sprinkling with water

as a ritual act of cleansing see Ex 30:19–20; Lev 14:51; Nu 19:18; cf. Zec 13:1; Heb 10:22. *I will cleanse.* See v. 33; 37:23; Jer 33:8. *idols.* See note on 6:4.
36:26–27 Contains "new covenant" terminology (see Jer 31:33–34).
36:26 *new heart.* See notes on 11:19; 18:31. *put a new spirit in you.* Transform your mind and heart. Here and in 11:19 God declared that he would bring about the change. In 18:31 (see note there) he called on his people to effect the change. What he requires of his people he always provides. *heart of flesh.* "Flesh" in the OT is often a symbol for weakness and frailty (Isa 31:3); in the NT it often stands for the sinful nature as a God-opposing force (as in Ro 8:5–8). Here it stands (in opposition to stone) for a pliable, teachable heart.
36:27 *my Spirit.* God bestows his Spirit to enable the human spirit to do his will. Verses 25–27 are closely paralleled in Ps 51:7–11.
36:28 *my people . . . your God.* Covenant language (see 11:20 and note).
36:29 *from all your uncleanness.* From cultic and moral defilement (see v. 25; 37:23). *I will call.* As at the beginning when God called creation into being (cf. Ge 1:5,8,10).
36:30 *disgrace.* As in v. 15.
36:31 *Then you will remember.* God's undeserved grace leads to recollection and repentance (cf. 6:9; 16:63; 20:43;

yourselves for your sins and detestable practices.[t] [32]I want you to know that I am not doing this for your sake, declares the Sovereign LORD. Be ashamed[u] and disgraced for your conduct, O house of Israel![v]

[33]"This is what the Sovereign LORD says: On the day I cleanse[w] you from all your sins, I will resettle your towns, and the ruins[x] will be rebuilt.[y] [34]The desolate land will be cultivated instead of lying desolate in the sight of all who pass through it. [35]They will say, "This land that was laid waste has become like the garden of Eden;[z] the cities that were lying in ruins, desolate and destroyed, are now fortified and inhabited.[a]" [36]Then the nations around you that remain will know that I the LORD have rebuilt what was destroyed and have replanted what was desolate. I the LORD have spoken, and I will do it.[b]

[37]"This is what the Sovereign LORD says: Once again I will yield to the plea[c] of the house of Israel and do this for them: I will make their people as numerous as sheep,[d] [38]as numerous as the flocks for offerings[e] at Jerusalem during her appointed feasts. So will the ruined cities be filled with flocks of people. Then they will know that I am the LORD.[f]"

The Valley of Dry Bones

37 The hand of the LORD was upon me,[g] and he brought me out by the Spirit[h] of the LORD and set me in the middle of a valley;[i] it was full of bones.[j] [2]He led me back and forth among them, and I saw a great many bones on the floor of the valley, bones that were very dry. [3]He asked me, "Son of man, can these bones live?"

I said, "O Sovereign LORD, you alone know.[k]"

[4]Then he said to me, "Prophesy to these bones and say to them, 'Dry bones, hear the word of the LORD![l] [5]This is what the Sovereign LORD says to these bones: I will make breath[j] enter you, and you will come to life.[m] [6]I will attach tendons to you and make flesh come upon you and cover you with skin; I will put breath in you, and you will come to life. Then you will know that I am the LORD.[n]'"

[7]So I prophesied as I was commanded. And as I was prophesying, there was a noise, a rattling sound, and the bones came together, bone to bone. [8]I looked, and tendons and flesh appeared on them and skin covered them, but there was no breath in them.

[9]Then he said to me, "Prophesy to the breath;[o] prophesy, son of man, and say to it, 'This is what the Sovereign LORD says: Come from the four winds,[p] O breath, and breathe into these slain, that they may live.'" [10]So I prophesied as he commanded[q] me, and breath entered them; they came to life and stood up on their feet—a vast army.[r]

[11]Then he said to me: "Son of man, these bones are the whole house of Israel. They say, 'Our bones are dried up and our hope is gone; we are cut off.'[s] [12]Therefore prophesy and say to them: 'This is what

[j]5 The Hebrew for this word can also mean *wind* or *spirit* (see verses 6-14).

Cross references

36:31 [r]Isa 6:5; S Jer 31:19; S Eze 6:9
36:32 [u]Eze 16:63 [v]Dt 9:5
36:33 [w]S Lev 16:30 [x]S Lev 26:31 [y]S Isa 49:8
36:35 [z]S Ge 2:8 [a]Am 9:14
36:36 [b]S Jer 42:10; S Eze 17:22; 37:14; 39:27-28
36:37 [c]Zec 10:6; 13:9 [d]Ps 102:17; Jer 29:12-14
36:38 [e]1Ki 8:63; 2Ch 35:7-9 [f]S Ex 6:2
37:1 [g]S Eze 1:3 [h]S Eze 11:24; Lk 4:1; Ac 8:39 [i]Jer 7:32 [j]S Jer 8:2; Eze 40:1
37:3 [k]Dt 32:39; S 1Sa 2:6; Isa 26:19; 1Co 15:35
37:4 [l]Jer 22:29
37:5 [m]S Ge 2:7; Ps 104:29-30; Rev 11:11
37:6 [n]S Ex 6:2; Eze 38:23
37:9 [o]ver 14; Ps 104:30; Isa 32:15; Eze 39:29; Zec 12:10
[p]Jer 49:36; Da 7:2; 8:8; 11:4; Zec 2:6; 6:5; Rev 7:1
37:10 [q]S Eze 12:7
[r]Rev 11:11
37:11 [s]S Job 17:15; S La 3:54

Study notes

Ps 130:4).

36:32 *not . . . for your sake.* See note on v. 22.

36:33 *On the day.* Connects the promise of cleansing (vv. 24–32) and the promise of repopulation (vv. 33–36).

36:35 *garden of Eden.* Primeval fertility is suggested (cf. 28:13; 31:9). *fortified.* In contrast to 38:11.

36:36 *nations . . . will know.* See note on v. 23.

36:37 *yield to the plea.* Allowing petitions to come to him again, God reversed his earlier refusals to hear (cf. 14:3; 20:3,31).

36:38 *as numerous as the flocks for offerings.* See 1Ki 8:63; 1Ch 29:21; 2Ch 35:7 for the appropriateness of the comparison.

37:1–28 One of Ezekiel's major visions. Surprisingly no date is given (as in 1:2; 8:1; 40:1), but the event must have occurred sometime after 586 B.C.

37:1 *hand of the LORD.* See note on 1:3. *Spirit of the LORD.* Used elsewhere in Ezekiel only in 11:5; usually simply "the Spirit," as in 8:3; 11:1,24. *valley.* The Hebrew for this word is the same as that translated "plain" in 3:22–23; 8:4. Ezekiel now received a message of hope, where he had previously heard God's word of judgment. *bones.* Verse 11 interprets them as symbolizing Israel's apparently hopeless condition in exile.

37:2 *a great many bones.* Symbolizing the whole community of exiles. *very dry.* Long dead, far beyond the reach of resuscitation (1Ki 17:17–24; 2Ki 4:18–37; but see 2Ki 13:21).

37:4 *Prophesy to these bones.* Ezekiel had previously prophesied to inanimate objects (mountains, 6:2; 36:1; forests, 20:47) and now prophesied to lifeless bones and the "breath" (v. 9).

37:6 *tendons . . . flesh . . . skin . . . breath.* Lists of four items are common in Ezekiel (see note on 1:5).

37:7 *rattling sound.* Probably the sound of the bones coming together, but possibly recalling the sound accompanying God's presence, as in 3:12–13 ("rushing sound").

37:8 *but there was no breath.* This visionary re-creation of God's people recalls the two-step creation of man in Ge 2:7, where man was first formed from the dust and then received the breath of life.

37:9 *breath.* See NIV text note on v. 5. *four.* See note on 1:5. *slain.* What Ezekiel saw was a battlefield strewn with the bones of the fallen (see v. 10).

37:11 *Our bones . . . cut off.* A sense of utter despair, to which the vision offers hope.

37:12 *graves.* The imagery shifts from a scattering of bones on a battlefield (see note on v. 9) to a cemetery with sealed graves.

the Sovereign LORD says: O my people, I am going to open your graves and bring you up from them; I will bring you back to the land of Israel. [t] [13]Then you, my people, will know that I am the LORD, [u] when I open your graves and bring you up from them. [v] [14]I will put my Spirit [w] in you and you will live, and I will settle [x] you in your own land. Then you will know that I the LORD have spoken, and I have done it, declares the LORD. [y] ' "

One Nation Under One King

[15]The word of the LORD came to me: [16]"Son of man, take a stick of wood and write on it, 'Belonging to Judah and the Israelites [z] associated with him. [a] ' Then take another stick of wood, and write on it, 'Ephraim's stick, belonging to Joseph and all the house of Israel associated with him.' [17]Join them together into one stick so that they will become one in your hand. [b]

[18]"When your countrymen ask you, 'Won't you tell us what you mean by this?' [c] [19]say to them, 'This is what the Sovereign LORD says: I am going to take the stick of Joseph—which is in Ephraim's hand—and of the Israelite tribes associated with him, and join it to Judah's stick, making them a single stick of wood, and they will become one in my hand.' [d] [20]Hold before their eyes the sticks you have written on [21]and say to them, 'This is what the Sovereign LORD says: I will take the Israelites out of the nations where they have gone. I will gather them from all around and bring them back into their own land. [e] [22]I will make them one nation in the land, on the mountains of Israel. [f] There will be

one king over all of them and they will never again be two nations or be divided into two kingdoms. [g] [23]They will no longer defile [h] themselves with their idols and vile images or with any of their offenses, for I will save them from all their sinful backsliding, [k] [i] and I will cleanse them. They will be my people, and I will be their God. [j]

[24] " 'My servant David [k] will be king [l] over them, and they will all have one shepherd. [m] They will follow my laws and be careful to keep my decrees. [n] [25]They will live in the land I gave to my servant Jacob, the land where your fathers lived. [o] They and their children and their children's children will live there forever, [p] and David my servant will be their prince forever. [q] [26]I will make a covenant of peace [r] with them; it will be an everlasting covenant. [s] I will establish them and increase their numbers, [t] and I will put my sanctuary among them [u] forever. [v] [27]My dwelling place [w] will be with them; I will be their God, and they will be my people. [x] [28]Then the nations will know that I the LORD make Israel holy, [y] when my sanctuary is among them forever. [z] [a] ' "

A Prophecy Against Gog

38 The word of the LORD came to me: [2]"Son of man, set your face against Gog, [b] of the land of Magog, [c] the chief

Cross references (center column)

37:12 [t]ver 21; Dt 32:39; 1Sa 2:6; Isa 26:19; Jer 29:14; Hos 13:14; Am 9:14-15; Zep 3:20; Zec 8:8
37:13 [u]S Ex 6:2 [v]S Eze 17:24; Hos 13:14
37:14 [w]S ver 9; S Isa 11:2; Joel 2:28-29 [x]S Jer 43:2 [y]Eze 36:27-28, 36; Rev 11:11
37:16 [z]S 1Ki 12:20; 2Ch 10:17-19 [a]Nu 17:2-3; 2Ch 15:9
37:17 [b]ver 24; Isa 11:13; S Jer 50:4; Hos 1:11
37:18 [c]S Eze 24:19
37:19 [d]Zec 10:6
37:21 [e]S ver 12; S Isa 43:5-6; S Eze 20:42; 39:27; Mic 4:6
37:22 [f]S Eze 17:22; S 34:13-14
37:23 [g]Isa 11:13; Jer 33:24; S 50:4; Hos 1:11 [h]Eze 43:7 [i]S Jer 7:24 [j]Eze 11:18; S 36:28; Na 2:2
37:24 [k]Isa 55:4; Hos 3:5 [l]S 1Sa 13:14; S Isa 32:1 [m]Zec 13:7 [n]Ps 78:70-71; S Jer 30:21; S Eze 21:27
37:25 [o]S Eze 28:25 [p]S Ezr 9:12; Am 9:15 [q]S Ps 89:3-4; Isa 11:1; S Eze 34:23-24
37:26 [r]S Nu 25:12 [s]S Ge 9:16; S Dt 29:14;

S Heb 13:20 [t]S Jer 30:19 [u]Lev 26:11 [v]S Eze 16:62 **37:27** [w]S Lev 26:11 [x]S Eze 34:30; S 36:28; S 2Co 6:16* **37:28** [y]S Ex 31:13 [z]Hos 1:10-11 [a]Eze 43:9; Zep 3:15 **38:2** [b]ver 14; Eze 39:11 [c]S Ge 10:2

[k]23 Many Hebrew manuscripts (see also Septuagint); most Hebrew manuscripts *all their dwelling places where they sinned*

37:14 *I will settle you in your own land.* These words make it clear that the Lord is not speaking here of a resurrection from the dead but of the national restoration of Israel.
37:16 *take a stick.* Ezekiel's last symbolic act involving a material object (cf. 4:1,3,9; 5:1). *write on it.* Zec 11:7 seems to be based on this passage in Ezekiel.
37:17 *Join them together.* The sticks may have been miraculously joined, or Ezekiel may have joined the sticks together in his hand.
37:18 *Won't you tell us . . . ?* The symbolic act successfully aroused the people's curiosity (see 12:9; 21:7; 24:19).
37:19 *they will become one in my hand.* God would duplicate Ezekiel's symbolic act by uniting the two kingdoms separated since Solomon's death (see 1Ki 12). For similar prophecies of the reunion of Israel see 33:23,29; Jer 3:18; 23:5-6; Hos 1:11; Am 9:11.
37:22 *mountains of Israel.* See 6:2-3; 34:13; 36:1. *one king.* Only here and in v. 24 is the word "king" used of the future ruler. Usually "prince" is used (see note on 34:24), as in v. 25. See 7:27 and note; see also 44:3; 45:7-9 and frequently in chs. 45-48, where the ruler in the ideal age is always referred to as "prince."
37:23 *idols.* The old and basic offense (see note on 6:4).

backsliding. Cf. Jer 2:19; 3:22. *cleanse.* Cf. 36:25 for the same notion. *my people . . . their God.* See note on 11:20.
37:24 *My servant David.* As in 34:23 (see note there) the coming Messianic ruler is called David because he would be a descendant of David and would achieve for Israel what David had—except more fully. *king.* See note on v. 22. *shepherd.* As in 34:23 the coming ruler is likened to a shepherd who cares for his flock (cf. Jn 10, especially v. 16).
37:25 *my servant Jacob.* See 28:25 and note.
37:26 *covenant of peace.* See 34:25 and note. *everlasting covenant.* See 16:60 and note. The phrase occurs 16 times in the OT, referring at times to the Noahic covenant (Ge 9:16), the Abrahamic (Ge 17:7,13,19), the Davidic (2Sa 23:5) and the "new" (Jer 32:40). Cf. the covenant with Phinehas (Nu 25:12-13). *put my sanctuary among them.* As he had done before. This word is further developed in Ezekiel's vision of the future age, in which the rebuilt sanctuary would have central position (chs. 40-48). See vv. 27-28.
38:1 This statement, repeated often for receiving God's word, stands as an introduction to chs. 38-39, which are a unit. The future restoration of Israel under the reign of the house of David (ch. 37) will bring about a massive coalition of world powers to destroy God's kingdom. But the vast host

prince of¹ Meshech and Tubal; *d* prophesy against him ³and say: 'This is what the Sovereign LORD says: I am against you, O Gog, chief prince of *m* Meshech and Tubal. *e* ⁴I will turn you around, put hooks *f* in your jaws and bring you out with your whole army—your horses, your horsemen fully armed, and a great horde with large and small shields, all of them brandishing their swords. *g* ⁵Persia, Cush *n h* and Put *i* will be with them, all with shields and helmets, ⁶also Gomer *j* with all its troops, and Beth Togarmah *k* from the far north *l* with all its troops—the many nations with you.

⁷" 'Get ready; be prepared, *m* you and all the hordes gathered about you, and take command of them. ⁸After many days *n* you will be called to arms. In future years you will invade a land that has recovered from war, whose people were gathered from many nations *o* to the mountains of Israel, which had long been desolate. They had been brought out from the nations, and now all of them live in safety. *p* ⁹You and all your troops and the many nations with you will go up, advancing like a storm; *q* you will be like a cloud *r* covering the land. *s*

¹⁰" 'This is what the Sovereign LORD says: On that day thoughts will come into your mind *t* and you will devise an evil scheme. *u* ¹¹You will say, "I will invade a land of unwalled villages; I will attack a peaceful and unsuspecting people *v*—all of them living without walls and without gates and bars. *w* ¹²I will plunder and loot and turn my hand against the resettled ruins and the people gathered from the nations, rich in livestock and goods, living at the center of the land." ¹³Sheba *x* and Dedan *y* and the merchants of Tarshish *z* and all her villages *o* will say to you, "Have you come to plunder? Have you gathered your hordes to loot, to carry off silver and gold, to take away livestock and goods and to seize much plunder? *a* " '

¹⁴"Therefore, son of man, prophesy and say to Gog: 'This is what the Sovereign LORD says: In that day, when my people Israel are living in safety, *b* will you not take notice of it? ¹⁵You will come from your place in the far north, *c* you and many nations with you, all of them riding on horses, a great horde, a mighty army. *d* ¹⁶You will advance against my people Israel like a cloud *e* that covers the land. *f* In days to come, O Gog, I will bring you

Cross references

38:2
d S Eze 27:13
38:3 *e* Eze 39:1
38:4 *f* S 2Ki 19:28
g S Isa 43:17;
Eze 29:4; 39:2;
Da 11:40
38:5 *h* S Ge 10:6
i S Ge 10:6;
S Eze 27:10
38:6 *j* S Ge 10:2
k S Ge 10:3
l S Eze 32:30
38:7 *m* S Isa 8:9
38:8 *n* Isa 24:22
o S Isa 11:11 *p* ver
14; Jer 23:6;
S Eze 28:26;
Joel 3:1
38:9 *q* Isa 25:4;
28:2 *r* ver 16;
Jer 4:13; Joel 2:2
s Rev 20:8

38:10
t S Jer 17:10
u Ps 36:4; Mic 2:1
38:11
v S Ge 34:25
w Jer 49:31;
Zec 2:4
38:13 *x* S Ge 10:7
y S Ge 25:3
z S Ge 10:4
a Isa 10:6; 33:23;
S Jer 15:13
38:14 *b* S ver 8;
S Lev 25:18;
S Jer 16:15;
Zec 2:5
38:15 *c* Eze 32:30
d Eze 39:2;
Rev 20:8
38:16 *e* S ver 9
f Joel 3:11

¹2 Or *the prince of Rosh,*   *m*3 Or *Gog, prince of Rosh,*   *n*5 That is, the upper Nile region   *o*13 Or *her strong lions*

---

that comes against Jerusalem will end up as dead bodies strewn over the fields of the promised land. Palestine will become the cemetery of the enemy hordes (cf. ch. 37).

38:2 *Son of man.* See note on 2:1. *set your face.* See note on 20:46. *Gog.* Apparently a leader or king whose name appears only here and in Rev 20:8. Several identifications have been attempted, notably Gyges, king of Lydia (c. 660 B.C.). Possibly the name is purposely vague, standing for a mysterious, as yet undisclosed, enemy of God's people. *of the land of Magog.* In Ge 10:2; 1Ch 1:5 Magog is one of the sons of Japheth, thus the name of a people. In Eze 39:6 it appears to refer to a people. But since the Hebrew prefix *ma-* can mean "place of," Magog may here simply mean "land of Gog." Israel had long experienced the hostility of the Hamites and other Semitic peoples; the future coalition here envisioned will include—and in fact be led by—peoples descended from Japheth (cf. Ge 10). *chief prince.* Military commander-in-chief. The NIV text note gives the possible translation "prince of Rosh," and if it is correct, Rosh is probably the name of an unknown people or place. Identification with Russia is unlikely, and in any case cannot be proven. *Meshech and Tubal.* These sons of Japheth (see Ge 10:2; 1Ch 1:5) are probably located in eastern Asia Minor (cf. 27:13; 32:26). They are peoples and territories to the north of Israel (cf. vv. 6,15; 39:2). As in the days of the Assyrians and Babylonians, the major attack will come from the north.

38:3 *I am against you.* See note on 5:8.

38:4 *I will turn you around.* Emphasis is on the fact that God is completely in control of all that is to follow. *put hooks in your jaws.* As with Pharaoh in 29:4, Gog is likened to a beast led around by God.

38:5 *Cush.* See NIV text note. The invading forces from the north (see v. 2 and note) are joined by armies from the south. *Put.* Libya (Africa).

38:6 *Gomer.* Another of Gog's northern allies (see note on v. 2), mentioned in Ge 10:3 and 1Ch 1:6 as one of the sons of Japheth. According to non-Biblical sources, these peoples originated north of the Black Sea. *Beth Togarmah.* See note on 27:14. According to Ge 10:3; 1Ch 1:6 Togarmah is one of the children of Gomer.

38:8 *After many days . . . In future years.* After all the events of national restoration, the immigration and settlement in Israel as described in chs. 34–37 will be completed.

38:9 *like a cloud.* Jeremiah similarly describes the invasion from the north in Jer 4:13.

38:10 *On that day.* A phrase common to other prophetic writings but found only here in Ezekiel; it refers to the day of Gog's invasion of Israel. *thoughts will come into your mind.* The divine initiative (v. 4) is paralleled, as it often is in Scripture, by human action (cf. Dt 31:3; Isa 10:6–7). *evil scheme.* A raiding expedition (see v. 12).

38:11 *land of unwalled villages.* Speaks of a blissfully peaceful, ideal future time when walls no longer will be needed. See Zec 2:4–5, which assumes, as does this passage, that the Lord alone is sufficient protection (cf. 36:35–36).

38:12 *center of the land.* The Hebrew for "center" also means "navel," a graphic image for the belief that Israel was the vital link between God and the world (the idea occurs also in 5:5). The word occurs elsewhere in the Bible only in Jdg 9:37. Since the Hebrew for "land" can also mean "earth," theologically Jerusalem is both the center of the land of Israel and the center of the earth.

38:13 *Sheba.* Southwest corner of the Arabian peninsula (modern Yemen), known for trading (Job 6:19; see 23:42; 27:22; 1Ki 10:1–2). *Dedan.* See note on 25:13. *Tarshish.* See note on 27:12.

against my land, so that the nations may know me when I show myself holy[g] through you before their eyes.[h]

17" 'This is what the Sovereign LORD says: Are you not the one I spoke of in former days by my servants the prophets of Israel? At that time they prophesied for years that I would bring you against them. 18This is what will happen in that day: When Gog attacks the land of Israel, my hot anger will be aroused, declares the Sovereign LORD. 19In my zeal and fiery wrath I declare that at that time there shall be a great earthquake[i] in the land of Israel.[j] 20The fish of the sea, the birds of the air, the beasts of the field, every creature that moves along the ground, and all the people on the face of the earth will tremble[k] at my presence. The mountains will be overturned,[l] the cliffs will crumble[m] and every wall will fall to the ground.[n] 21I will summon a sword[o] against Gog on all my mountains, declares the Sovereign LORD. Every man's sword will be against his brother.[p] 22I will execute judgment[q] upon him with plague and bloodshed;[r] I will pour down torrents of rain, hailstones[s] and burning sulfur[t] on him and on his troops and on the many nations with him.[u] 23And so I will show my greatness and my holiness, and I will make myself known in the sight of many nations. Then they will know that I am the LORD.[v]'

39 "Son of man, prophesy against Gog[w] and say: 'This is what the Sovereign LORD says: I am against you, O Gog, chief prince of[p] Meshech[x] and Tubal.[y] 2I will turn you around and drag you along. I will bring you from the far north[z] and send you against the mountains of Israel.[a] 3Then I will strike your bow[b] from your left hand and make your arrows[c] drop from your right hand. 4On the moun-

tains of Israel you will fall, you and all your troops and the nations with you. I will give you as food to all kinds of carrion birds[d] and to the wild animals.[e] 5You will fall in the open field, for I have spoken, declares the Sovereign LORD.[f] 6I will send fire[g] on Magog[h] and on those who live in safety in the coastlands,[i] and they will know[j] that I am the LORD.

7" 'I will make known my holy name among my people Israel. I will no longer let my holy name be profaned,[k] and the nations will know[l] that I the LORD am the Holy One in Israel.[m] 8It is coming! It will surely take place, declares the Sovereign LORD. This is the day[n] I have spoken of.

9" 'Then those who live in the towns of Israel will go out and use the weapons for fuel and burn them up—the small and large shields, the bows and arrows,[o] the war clubs and the spears. For seven years they will use them for fuel.[p] 10They will not need to gather wood from the fields or cut it from the forests, because they will use the weapons for fuel. And they will plunder[q] those who plundered them and loot those who looted them, declares the Sovereign LORD.[r]

11" 'On that day I will give Gog a burial place in Israel, in the valley of those who travel east toward[q] the Sea.[r] It will block the way of travelers, because Gog and all his hordes will be buried[s] there. So it will be called the Valley of Hamon Gog.[s][t]

12" 'For seven months the house of Israel will be burying them in order to cleanse the land.[u] 13All the people of the land will bury them, and the day I am

---

Cross references (center column):

38:16
gS Lev 10:3
hIsa 29:23;
Eze 39:21
38:19 /Isa 24:18;
Joel 2:10; 3:16;
S Rev 6:12
/Ps 18:7;
S Eze 5:13;
Hag 2:6,21
38:20
kS Ex 15:14
/Isa 42:15
mJob 14:18
nS Ps 76:8;
Hos 4:3; Na 1:5
38:21 oIsa 66:16;
Jer 25:29
pS 1Sa 14:20;
S 2Ch 20:23;
Hag 2:22
38:22 qIsa 66:16;
Jer 25:31;
S Eze 36:5
rS Eze 14:19;
S 28:23
sS Ex 9:18;
Ps 18:12;
Rev 16:21
tS Ge 19:24;
S Rev 9:17
uS Eze 13:11
38:23
vEze 20:42;
S 36:23; S 37:6
39:1 wRev 20:8
xS Ge 10:2
yS Eze 27:13;
S 38:2,3
39:2
zS Eze 32:30
aS Eze 38:4,15
39:3 bHos 1:5;
Am 2:15 cPs 76:3

39:4 dS Ge 40:19
ever 17-20;
S Jer 25:33;
S Eze 29:5;
S 33:27
39:5 /S Eze 32:4
39:6 gS Eze 30:8;
Rev 20:9
hS Ge 10:2
iS Jer 25:22
/S Ex 6:7
39:7 kS Ex 20:7;
S Eze 13:19
/S Isa 49:26
mS Isa 12:6;
S 54:5;
S Eze 20:9;
S 36:23
39:8 nEze 7:6
39:9 oPs 76:3
pS Ps 46:9
39:10 qS Ex 3:22
rS Isa 14:2;

S 33:1; Hab 2:8 39:11 sS Isa 34:3 tS Eze 38:2 39:12
uDt 21:23

p1 Or *Gog, prince of Rosh,*   q11 Or *of*   r11 That is, the Dead Sea   s11 *Hamon Gog* means *hordes of Gog.*

Footnotes (bottom):

38:17 *Are you not the one I spoke of . . . ?* Probably a general reference to earlier prophecies of divine judgment on the nations arrayed against God and his people.
38:19 *earthquake.* Signaling the mighty presence of God, who comes to overwhelm the great army invading his land.
38:20 The fourfold listing of the animal world indicates the totality of nature (see note on 1:5; cf. Ge 9:2; 1Ki 4:33; Job 12:7–8 for similar listings).
38:21 *I will summon a sword.* God's sword of judgment (Isa 34:5–6; Jer 25:29). *Every man's sword will be against his brother.* The coalition of Israel's enemies will turn on itself, as did the armies that attacked Judah in the time of Jehoshaphat (2Ch 20:22–23).
38:22 The list of divine weapons suggests that God will intervene directly without the benefit of an earthly army.
39:1 *Gog, chief prince of Meshech.* See note on 38:2. While vv. 1–16 add new details, the same basic events as those in ch. 38 are described.
39:2 *from the far north.* As in 38:6,15.

39:3 *bow.* Cf. Jer 6:23. The Lord will disarm Israel's enemies before they can shoot an arrow.
39:4 *food to all kinds of carrion birds.* A theme expanded in vv. 17–20.
39:6 *I will send fire.* See 30:8 and note.
39:9 *burn them up.* Cf. Ps 46:9, where God does the burning. *seven.* A symbolic number signifying the finality of this great battle against God's people, as well as indicating the size of the invading armies.
39:11 *toward.* The NIV text note reading "of" seems preferable, since the other three times this preposition occurs "east of" is meant (see Ge 2:14; 4:16; 1Sa 13:5).
39:12 *seven.* As in v. 9, the number seven symbolizes totality, completeness and finality, and it also reveals the large number of invaders. *cleanse the land.* Ritual purity is a basic element in Ezekiel's theology (see 22:26; 24:13; 36:25,33; 37:23). Corpses were especially unclean (see Lev 5:2; 21:1,11; 22:4; Nu 5:2; 6:6–12; 19:16; 31:19).
39:13 *people of the land.* See 7:27 and note, though here

glorified ^{v} will be a memorable day for them, declares the Sovereign LORD.

14" 'Men will be regularly employed to cleanse the land. Some will go throughout the land and, in addition to them, others will bury those that remain on the ground. At the end of the seven months they will begin their search. 15As they go through the land and one of them sees a human bone, he will set up a marker beside it until the gravediggers have buried it in the Valley of Hamon Gog. 16(Also a town called Hamonah^t will be there.) And so they will cleanse the land.'

17"Son of man, this is what the Sovereign LORD says: Call out to every kind of bird ^{w} and all the wild animals: 'Assemble and come together from all around to the sacrifice I am preparing for you, the great sacrifice on the mountains of Israel. There you will eat flesh and drink blood. ^{x} 18You will eat the flesh of mighty men and drink the blood of the princes of the earth as if they were rams and lambs, goats and bulls—all of them fattened animals from Bashan. ^{y} 19At the sacrifice ^{z} I am preparing for you, you will eat fat till you are glutted and drink blood till you are drunk. 20At my table you will eat your fill of horses and riders, mighty men and soldiers of every kind,' declares the Sovereign LORD. ^{a}

21"I will display my glory among the nations, and all the nations will see the punishment I inflict and the hand I lay upon them. ^{b} 22From that day forward the house of Israel will know that I am the LORD their God. 23And the nations will know that the people of Israel went into exile for their sin, because they were unfaithful to me. So I hid my face from them and handed them over to their enemies, and they all fell by the sword. ^{c} 24I dealt with them according to their uncleanness and their offenses, and I hid my face from them. ^{d}

25"Therefore this is what the Sovereign LORD says: I will now bring Jacob back from captivity $^{u e}$ and will have compassion^f on all the people of Israel, and I will be zealous for my holy name. ^{g} 26They will forget their shame and all the unfaithfulness they showed toward me when they lived in safety^h in their land with no one to make them afraid. ^{i} 27When I have brought them back from the nations and have gathered them from the countries of their enemies, I will show myself holy through them in the sight of many nations. ^{j} 28Then they will know that I am the LORD their God, for though I sent them into exile among the nations, I will gather them ^{k} to their own land, not leaving any behind. ^{l} 29I will no longer hide my face ^{m} from them, for I will pour out my Spirit ^{n} on the house of Israel, declares the Sovereign LORD. ^{o}"

Cross references

39:13 ^{v}Eze 28:22
39:17 ^{w}S Job 15:23
^{x}S Eze 32:4
39:18 ^{y}S Ps 22:12; Jer 51:40
39:19 ^{z}S Lev 3:9
39:20 ^{a}S Isa 56:9; S Jer 12:9; Rev 19:17-18
39:21 ^{b}Ex 9:16; Isa 37:20; S Eze 38:16
39:23 ^{c}Isa 1:15; 59:2; S Jer 22:8-9; S 44:23
39:24 ^{d}2Ki 17:23; Jer 2:17,19; 4:18; S Eze 7:22; Da 9:7
39:25 ^{e}S Jer 33:7 /S Jer 30:18 ^{f}Isa 27:12-13; S Eze 16:53
39:26 ^{h}S 1Ki 4:25; S Jer 32:37; S Eze 38:8 ^{i}Isa 17:2; Eze 34:28; Mic 4:4
39:27 ^{j}S Eze 37:21
39:28 ^{k}Ps 147:2 ^{l}S Eze 36:23,36
39:29 ^{m}S Dt 31:17 ^{n}S Isa 11:2; S Eze 37:9; S Ac 2:17 ^{o}S Eze 16:42

Text notes

^{t}16 Hamonah means horde. ^{u}25 Or now restore the fortunes of Jacob

Study notes

a special class may not be implied.

39:14 Men will be regularly employed. After the seven-month burial period observed by all the people, special squads will be hired full time to ensure total cleansing of the land—by marking for burial any human bones that may have been missed. Total ritual purity is the aim.

39:15 marker. Probably of stone, either a large one or a heap of smaller ones.

39:17 Call out to every kind of bird . . . to the sacrifice. Various interpretations are: 1. Since the enemies are all dead and buried, this section (vv. 17–20) is perhaps to be understood as poetic imagery. 2. However, if the passage reverts back to v. 4, a more literal interpretation is possible—the dead bodies were not all buried at once. 3. Verses 17–20 involve a restating of vv. 9–16, employing a different figure (see Isa 34:6; Jer 46:10; Zep 1:7). The metaphor of sacrifice suggests a consecration to the Lord in judgment, as with Jericho (see Jos 6:17 and NIV text note).

39:18 You will eat the flesh of mighty men. A gory description of what birds of prey commonly do (see previous note and Rev 19:17–21). as if they were. The bodies of the victims are compared to animals commonly used for sacrifices. Bashan. Rich pastureland east of the Sea of Galilee, known for its sleek cattle (Dt 32:14; Ps 22:12; Am 4:1) and its oak trees (27:6; Isa 2:13).

39:19 eat fat . . . drink blood. Further indication that this is the Lord's sacrificial feast, in that fat and blood were normally reserved for God (see 44:15; Lev 3:17).

39:20 my table. Sacrificial altar. See 40:38–43 and 41:22 for description of the tables in the new temple.

39:21 my glory. God's visible presence in the world (see note on 1:28). Here that visibility is due to divine intervention in history.

39:22–23 the house of Israel will know . . . And the nations will know. As God had made himself known to Israel and the nations through his saving acts in Israel's behalf (see Ex 6:7; 7:5,17; 10:2; 14:18; 16:6–7,12; Jos 3:10; 4:24; cf. Jos 2:9–11; 5:1), so now Israel and the nations will see him again at work as he judges his people for their sin (see v. 27).

39:23 I hid my face. Expression of divine displeasure (see Ps 30:7; Isa 54:8; 57:17).

39:24 their uncleanness and their offenses. Spelled out especially in ch. 22, but also throughout chs. 6–24.

39:25 Jacob. The nation of Israel, as in 20:5. The parallelism within the verse supports this identity. my holy name. See note on 20:9.

39:26 They will forget their shame. The remembrance of shame previously called for (6:9; 20:43; 36:31) is here erased.

39:27 I will show myself holy through them. God will reveal himself anew in a restored, holy people (cf. 20:41; 28:25; 36:23).

39:28 Then they will know. See note on v. 22.

39:29 I will pour out my Spirit. The gift of God's enabling Spirit (see 11:19; 36:26–27; 37:14).

The New Temple Area

40 In the twenty-fifth year of our exile, at the beginning of the year, on the tenth of the month, in the fourteenth year after the fall of the city*ᵖ*—on that very day the hand of the LORD was upon me*q* and he took me there. ²In visions*ʳ* of God he took me to the land of Israel and set me on a very high mountain,*ˢ* on whose south side were some buildings that looked like a city. ³He took me there, and I saw a man whose appearance was like bronze;*ᵗ* he was standing in the gateway with a linen cord and a measuring rod*ᵘ* in his hand. ⁴The man said to me, "Son of man, look with your eyes and hear with your ears and pay attention to everything I am going to show you,*ᵛ* for that is why you have been brought here. Tell*ʷ* the house of Israel everything you see.*ˣ*"

The East Gate to the Outer Court

⁵I saw a wall completely surrounding the temple area. The length of the measuring rod in the man's hand was six long cubits, each of which was a cubit*ᵛ* and a handbreadth.*ʷ* He measured*ʸ* the wall; it was one measuring rod thick and one rod high.

⁶Then he went to the gate facing east.*ᶻ* He climbed its steps and measured the threshold of the gate; it was one rod deep.*ˣ* ⁷The alcoves*ᵃ* for the guards were one rod long and one rod wide, and the projecting walls between the alcoves were five cubits thick. And the threshold of the

gate next to the portico facing the temple was one rod deep.

⁸Then he measured the portico of the gateway; ⁹it*ᵛ* was eight cubits deep and its jambs were two cubits thick. The portico of the gateway faced the temple.

¹⁰Inside the east gate were three alcoves on each side; the three had the same measurements, and the faces of the projecting walls on each side had the same measurements. ¹¹Then he measured the width of the entrance to the gateway; it was ten cubits and its length was thirteen cubits. ¹²In front of each alcove was a wall one cubit high, and the alcoves were six cubits square. ¹³Then he measured the gateway from the top of the rear wall of one alcove to the top of the opposite one; the distance was twenty-five cubits from one parapet opening to the opposite one. ¹⁴He measured along the faces of the projecting walls all around the inside of the gateway—sixty cubits. The measurement was up to the portico*ᶻ* facing the courtyard.*ᵃ ᵇ* ¹⁵The distance from the entrance of the gateway to the far end of its portico was fifty cubits. ¹⁶The alcoves and the projecting walls inside the gateway were surmounted by narrow parapet openings all around, as was the portico; the openings

---

40:1 *p*S 2Ki 25:7; Jer 39:1-10; 52:4-11 *q*S Eze 1:3; S 29:17
40:2 *r*S Ex 24:10; Da 7:1,7 *s*S Jer 31:12; S Eze 17:22; Rev 21:10
40:3 *t*S Eze 1:7; Rev 1:15 *u*Eze 47:3; Zec 2:1-2; Rev 11:1; 21:15
40:4 *v*S Dt 6:6 *x*Eze 44:5
40:5 *y*Eze 42:20
40:6 *z*S Eze 8:16
40:7 *a*ver 36

40:14 *b*S Ex 27:9

v5 The common cubit was about 1 1/2 feet (about 0.5 meter). *w5* That is, about 3 inches (about 8 centimeters) *x6* Septuagint; Hebrew *deep, the first threshold, one rod deep* *y8,9* Many Hebrew manuscripts, Septuagint, Vulgate and Syriac; most Hebrew manuscripts *gateway facing the temple; it was one rod deep.* *9Then he measured the portico of the gateway; it* *z14* Septuagint; Hebrew *projecting wall* *a14* The meaning of the Hebrew for this verse is uncertain.

40:1 *twenty-fifth year . . . beginning . . . tenth.* Apr. 28, 573 B.C. *of our exile.* All the dates in the book of Ezekiel (see chart on "Dates in Ezekiel," p. 1227) are reckoned from the 597 exile, but only here and in 33:21 is the exile specifically mentioned (see 1:2). *the beginning of the year.* Hebrew *Rosh Hashanah,* the well-known New Year festival. It has long occurred in the fall (in either September or October), but since throughout the book Ezekiel uses a different and older religious calendar, the spring date as given above is correct (see note on Lev 23:24). *hand of the LORD was upon me.* See note on 1:3.
40:2 *visions of God.* Introduces all three of Ezekiel's major visions (see 1:1; 8:3). *very high mountain.* Mount Zion, also seen as extraordinarily high in other prophetic visions (17:22; Isa 2:2; Mic 4:1; Zec 14:10). Height here signifies importance, as the earthly seat of God's reign. *on whose south side.* With the city located on its southern slopes, the mountain is to the north (cf. Ps 48; see Ps 48:2 and note).
40:3 *like bronze.* Indicates the man was other than human. *in the gateway.* Presumably of the outer court (see vv. 17-19). *linen cord.* Used for longer measurements such as those in 47:3. *measuring rod.* Used for shorter measurements—about ten feet and four inches long.
40:5 *wall completely surrounding the temple area.* Separating the sacred from the secular. *six long cubits.* In using

the long cubit (seven handbreadths, or about 21 inches), which was older than the shorter cubit (six handbreadths, or about 18 inches), Ezekiel was returning to more ancient standards for the new community (see 2Ch 3:3).
40:6 *gate facing east.* The gate of the outer court. The three gates (east, north, south) of the outer court were similar to the three in the inner court (v. 32), having six alcoves for the guards (three on each side) and a portico (vv. 8-9). Comparable gate plans have been discovered at Megiddo, Gezer and Hazor, all dating from the time of Solomon (see 1Ki 9:15). The guards kept out anyone who might profane the temple area (see Ezr 2:62). *climbed its steps.* The first of three sets of stairs leading to the temple. This one had seven steps (v. 22); the next one (inner court), eight (v. 31); the last (temple), ten (v. 49; see NIV text note)— possibly indicating increasing degrees of "holiness" (sacredness).
40:9 *portico of the gateway faced the temple.* The reverse position of the porticoes of the inner court gates, which faced away from the temple (v. 34).
40:10 *three alcoves.* The alcoves for the guards, mentioned in v. 7.
40:16 *palm trees.* As in Solomon's temple (see 1Ki 6:29, 32,35).

Ezekiel's Temple

A. Wall (40:5,16-20)
B. East gate (40:6-14,16)
C. Portico (40:8)
D. Outer court (40:17)
E. Pavement (40:17)
F. Inner court (40:19)
G. North gate (40:20-22)
H. Inner court (40:23)
I. South gate (40:24-26)
J. South inner court (40:27)
K. Gateway (40:28-31)
L. Gateway (40:32-34)
M. Gateway (40:35-38)
N. Priests' rooms (40:44-45)

O. Court (40:47)
P. Temple portico (40:48-49)
Q. Outer sanctuary (41:1-2)
R. Most Holy Place (41:3-4)
S. Temple walls (41:5-7, 9, 11)
T. Base (41:8)
U. Open area (41:10)
V. West building (41:12)
W. Priests' rooms (42:1-10)
X. Altar (43:13-17)

AA. Rooms for preparing sacrifices (40:39-43)
BB. Ovens (46:19-20)
CC. Kitchens (46:21-24)

Ezekiel uses a long or "royal" cubit, 20.4 inches or 51.81 cm ("cubit and a handbreadth," Eze 40:5), as opposed to the standard Hebrew cubit of 17.6 inches or 44.7 cm.

Scripture describes a floor plan, but provides few height dimensions. This artwork shows an upward projection of the temple over the floor plan. This temple existed only in a vision of Ezekiel (Eze 40:2), and has never actually been built as were the temples of Solomon, Zerubbabel and Herod.

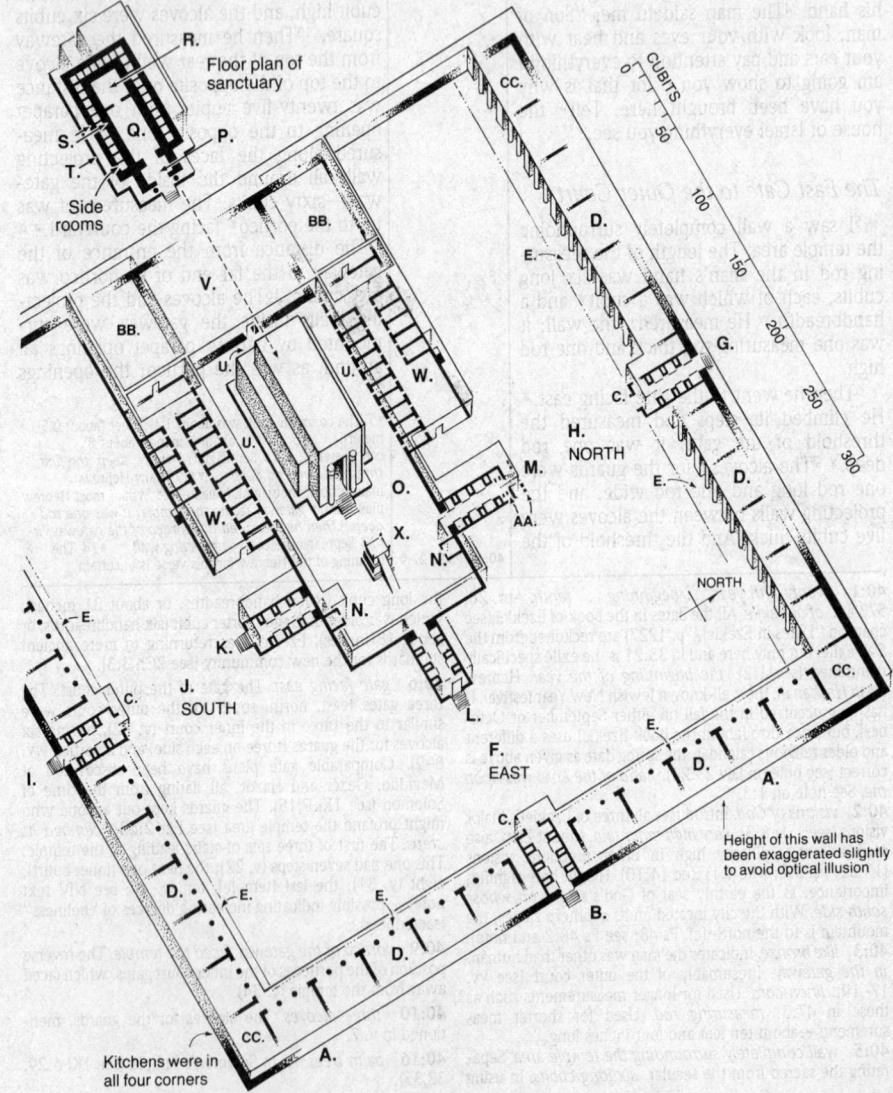

Floor plan of sanctuary

Side rooms

Height of this wall has been exaggerated slightly to avoid optical illusion

Kitchens were in all four corners

all around faced inward. The faces of the projecting walls were decorated with palm trees. c

The Outer Court

[17]Then he brought me into the outer court. d There I saw some rooms and a pavement that had been constructed all around the court; there were thirty rooms e along the pavement. f [18]It abutted the sides of the gateways and was as wide as they were long; this was the lower pavement. [19]Then he measured the distance from the inside of the lower gateway to the outside of the inner court; g it was a hundred cubits h on the east side as well as on the north.

The North Gate

[20]Then he measured the length and width of the gate facing north, leading into the outer court. [21]Its alcoves i—three on each side—its projecting walls and its portico j had the same measurements as those of the first gateway. It was fifty cubits long and twenty-five cubits wide. [22]Its openings, its portico k and its palm tree decorations had the same measurements as those of the gate facing east. Seven steps led up to it, with its portico opposite them. l [23]There was a gate to the inner court facing the north gate, just as there was on the east. He measured from one gate to the opposite one; it was a hundred cubits. m

The South Gate

[24]Then he led me to the south side and I saw a gate facing south. He measured its jambs and its portico, and they had the same measurements n as the others. [25]The gateway and its portico had narrow openings all around, like the openings of the others. It was fifty cubits long and twenty-five cubits wide. o [26]Seven steps led up to it, with its portico opposite them; it had palm tree decorations on the faces of the projecting walls on each side. p [27]The inner court q also had a gate facing south, and he measured from this gate to the outer gate

on the south side; it was a hundred cubits. r

Gates to the Inner Court

[28]Then he brought me into the inner court through the south gate, and he measured the south gate; it had the same measurements s as the others. [29]Its alcoves, t its projecting walls and its portico had the same measurements as the others. The gateway and its portico had openings all around. It was fifty cubits long and twenty-five cubits wide. u [30](The porticoes v of the gateways around the inner court were twenty-five cubits wide and five cubits deep.) [31]Its portico w faced the outer court; palm trees decorated its jambs, and eight steps led up to it. x

[32]Then he brought me to the inner court on the east side, and he measured the gateway; it had the same measurements y as the others. [33]Its alcoves, z its projecting walls and its portico had the same measurements as the others. The gateway and its portico had openings all around. It was fifty cubits long and twenty-five cubits wide. [34]Its portico a faced the outer court; palm trees decorated the jambs on either side, and eight steps led up to it.

[35]Then he brought me to the north gate b and measured it. It had the same measurements c as the others, [36]as did its alcoves, d its projecting walls and its portico, and it had openings all around. It was fifty cubits long and twenty-five cubits wide. [37]Its portico b e faced the outer court; palm trees decorated the jambs on either side, and eight steps led up to it. f

The Rooms for Preparing Sacrifices

[38]A room with a doorway was by the portico in each of the inner gateways, where the burnt offerings g were washed. [39]In the portico of the gateway were two tables on each side, on which the burnt offerings, h sin offerings i and guilt offer-

40:16 c ver 21-22; 2Ch 3:5; Eze 41:26	
40:17 d Rev 11:2	
e Eze 41:6	
f Eze 42:1	
40:19 g Eze 46:1	
h ver 23,27	
40:21 i ver 7 j ver 30	
40:22 k ver 49	
l S ver 16,26	
40:23 m S ver 19	
40:24 n ver 32,35	
40:25 o ver 33	
40:26 p S ver 22	
40:27 q ver 32	

r S ver 19	
40:28 s ver 35	
40:29 t ver 7 u ver 25	
40:30 v ver 21	
40:31 w ver 22	
x ver 34,37	
40:32 y S ver 24	
40:33 z ver 7	
40:34 a ver 22	
40:35 b Eze 44:4; 47:2 c S ver 24	
40:36 d ver 7	
40:37 e ver 22	
f ver 34	
40:38 g S 2Ch 4:6; Eze 42:13	
40:39 h Eze 46:2	
i Lev 4:3,28	

b 37 Septuagint (see also verses 31 and 34); Hebrew jambs

40:17 *thirty rooms.* The exact location of these rooms is not given. They were probably intended for the people's use (see Jer 35:2,4).

40:19 *hundred cubits.* Over 170 feet separated the outer wall from the inner wall and was the width of the outer court.

40:20 *gate facing north.* Both it and the south gate (v. 24) were identical to the east gate.

40:22 *Seven steps.* See note on v. 6.

40:28 *south gate.* Of the inner wall, which is not described but must be assumed. *it had the same measurements as the*

others. In both the outer walls (see note on v. 6).

40:34 *eight steps.* See note on v. 6.

40:38 *portico in each of the inner gateways.* The porticoes of the inner gateways were on the side of the outer court, facing away from the temple. *washed.* The inner parts and the legs were washed (Lev 1:9).

40:39 *burnt offerings.* Probably one of the oldest kinds of sacrifice. The entire animal was burned in consecration to God (see Lev 1). *sin offerings and guilt offerings.* Discussed in Lev 4–7. The fellowship offerings, which were more festive, are notable by their absence from this listing (see 43:27; 45:17; 46:2,12).

ings[j] were slaughtered.[k] [40]By the outside wall of the portico of the gateway, near the steps at the entrance to the north gateway were two tables, and on the other side of the steps were two tables. [41]So there were four tables on one side of the gateway and four on the other—eight tables in all—on which the sacrifices were slaughtered. [42]There were also four tables of dressed stone[l] for the burnt offerings, each a cubit and a half long, a cubit and a half wide and a cubit high. On them were placed the utensils for slaughtering the burnt offerings and the other sacrifices.[m] [43]And double-pronged hooks, each a handbreadth long, were attached to the wall all around. The tables were for the flesh of the offerings.

Rooms for the Priests

[44]Outside the inner gate, within the inner court, were two rooms, one[c] at the side of the north gate and facing south, and another at the side of the south[d] gate and facing north. [45]He said to me, "The room facing south is for the priests who have charge of the temple,[n] [46]and the room facing north[o] is for the priests who have charge of the altar.[p] These are the sons of Zadok,[q] who are the only Levites who may draw near to the LORD to minister before him.[r]"

[47]Then he measured the court: It was square—a hundred cubits long and a hundred cubits wide. And the altar was in front of the temple.[s]

The Temple

[48]He brought me to the portico of the temple[t] and measured the jambs of the portico; they were five cubits wide on either side. The width of the entrance was fourteen cubits and its projecting walls were[e] three cubits wide on either side. [49]The portico[u] was twenty cubits wide, and twelve[f] cubits from front to back. It was reached by a flight of stairs,[g] and there were pillars[v] on each side of the jambs.

40:39 /S Lev 7:1
kver 42
40:42 /Ex 20:25
mver 39
40:45 n1Ch 9:23
40:46 oEze 42:13
pNu 18:5
qS 2Sa 8:17;
S Ezr 7:2
rNu 16:5;
Eze 43:19; 44:15;
45:4; 48:11
40:47
sEze 41:13-14
40:48 t1Ki 6:2
40:49 uver 22;
1Ki 6:3
vS 1Ki 7:15

41:1 wver 23
41:2 x2Ch 3:3
41:4 y1Ki 6:20
zS Ex 26:33;
Heb 9:3-8
41:6 aEze 40:17
b5 1Ki 6:5
41:7 c1Ki 6:8

41 Then the man brought me to the outer sanctuary[w] and measured the jambs; the width of the jambs was six cubits[h] on each side.[i] [2]The entrance was ten cubits wide, and the projecting walls on each side of it were five cubits wide. He also measured the outer sanctuary; it was forty cubits long and twenty cubits wide.[x]

[3]Then he went into the inner sanctuary and measured the jambs of the entrance; each was two cubits wide. The entrance was six cubits wide, and the projecting walls on each side of it were seven cubits wide. [4]And he measured the length of the inner sanctuary; it was twenty cubits, and its width was twenty cubits across the end of the outer sanctuary.[y] He said to me, "This is the Most Holy Place.[z]"

[5]Then he measured the wall of the temple; it was six cubits thick, and each side room around the temple was four cubits wide. [6]The side rooms were on three levels, one above another, thirty[a] on each level. There were ledges all around the wall of the temple to serve as supports for the side rooms, so that the supports were not inserted into the wall of the temple.[b] [7]The side rooms all around the temple were wider at each successive level. The structure surrounding the temple was built in ascending stages, so that the rooms widened as one went upward. A stairway[c] went up from the lowest floor to the top floor through the middle floor.

[8]I saw that the temple had a raised base all around it, forming the foundation of the side rooms. It was the length of the rod, six long cubits. [9]The outer wall of the side rooms was five cubits thick. The open area between the side rooms of the temple [10]and the ⌊priests'⌋ rooms was twenty cubits wide all around the temple. [11]There were entrances to the side rooms from the

c44 Septuagint; Hebrew were rooms for singers, which were   d44 Septuagint; Hebrew east
e48 Septuagint; Hebrew entrance was
f49 Septuagint; Hebrew eleven   g49 Hebrew; Septuagint Ten steps led up to it   h1 The common cubit was about 1 1/2 feet (about 0.5 meter).   i1 One Hebrew manuscript and Septuagint; most Hebrew manuscripts side, the width of the tent

---

40:46 sons of Zadok. For the distinction between the sons of Zadok and the Levites see the fuller discussion in the notes on 44:15-31.

40:47 altar. Described in 43:13-17.

40:48 portico. Similar to the portico in Solomon's temple but slightly larger (see 1Ki 6:3).

40:49 pillars. Called Jakin and Boaz in Solomon's temple (see 1Ki 7:21).

41:1 outer sanctuary. Or nave, the largest of the three rooms comprising the temple (see 1Ki 6:3-5, where it is

called the main hall). This outer sanctuary was identical in size to Solomon's (see 1Ki 6:17).

41:3 he went into the inner sanctuary. Only the angel, not Ezekiel, entered the Most Holy Place. Lev 16 forbids any but the high priest to enter it, and then only once a year (see Heb 9:7). six cubits wide. Note the progressive narrowness of the door openings as one approaches the inner sanctuary (40:48, 14 cubits; 41:2, 10 cubits).

41:6 thirty on each level. These 90 side rooms were probably storerooms for the priests, possibly for the tithes (see Mal 3:10).

open area, one on the north and another on the south; and the base adjoining the open area was five cubits wide all around.

[12]The building facing the temple courtyard on the west side was seventy cubits wide. The wall of the building was five cubits thick all around, and its length was ninety cubits.

[13]Then he measured the temple; it was a hundred cubits long, and the temple courtyard and the building with its walls were also a hundred cubits long. [14]The width of the temple courtyard on the east, including the front of the temple, was a hundred cubits. [d]

[15]Then he measured the length of the building facing the courtyard at the rear of the temple, including its galleries [e] on each side; it was a hundred cubits.

The outer sanctuary, the inner sanctuary and the portico facing the court, [16]as well as the thresholds and the narrow windows [f] and galleries around the three of them—everything beyond and including the threshold was covered with wood. The floor, the wall up to the windows, and the windows were covered. [g] [17]In the space above the outside of the entrance to the inner sanctuary and on the walls at regular intervals all around the inner and outer sanctuary [18]were carved [h] cherubim [i] and palm trees. [j] Palm trees alternated with cherubim. Each cherub had two faces: [k] [19]the face of a man toward the palm tree on one side and the face of a lion toward the palm tree on the other. They were carved all around the whole temple. [l] [20]From the floor to the area above the entrance, cherubim and palm trees were carved on the wall of the outer sanctuary.

[21]The outer sanctuary [m] had a rectangular doorframe, and the one at the front of the Most Holy Place was similar. [22]There was a wooden altar [n] three cubits high and two cubits square [j]; its corners, its base [k] and its sides were of wood. The man said to me, "This is the table [o] that is before the Lord." [23]Both the outer sanctuary [p] and the Most Holy Place had double doors. [q]

[24]Each door had two leaves—two hinged leaves [r] for each door. [25]And on the doors of the outer sanctuary were carved cherubim and palm trees like those carved on the walls, and there was a wooden overhang on the front of the portico. [26]On the sidewalls of the portico were narrow windows with palm trees carved on each side. The side rooms of the temple also had overhangs. [s]

Rooms for the Priests

42 Then the man led me northward into the outer court and brought me to the rooms [t] opposite the temple courtyard [u] and opposite the outer wall on the north side. [v] [2]The building whose door faced north was a hundred cubits[1] long and fifty cubits wide. [3]Both in the section twenty cubits from the inner court and in the section opposite the pavement of the outer court, gallery [w] faced gallery at the three levels. [x] [4]In front of the rooms was an inner passageway ten cubits wide and a hundred cubits [m] long. Their doors were on the north. [y] [5]Now the upper rooms were narrower, for the galleries took more space from them than from the rooms on the lower and middle floors of the building. [6]The rooms on the third floor had no pillars, as the courts had; so they were smaller in floor space than those on the lower and middle floors. [7]There was an outer wall parallel to the rooms and the outer court; it extended in front of the rooms for fifty cubits. [8]While the row of rooms on the side next to the outer court was fifty cubits long, the row on the side nearest the sanctuary was a hundred cubits long. [9]The lower rooms had an entrance [z] on the east side as one enters them from the outer court.

[10]On the south side [n] along the length of the wall of the outer court, adjoining the temple courtyard [a] and opposite the outer

Cross references (center column)

41:14 [d]Eze 40:47
41:15 [e]Eze 42:3
41:16 [f]1Ki 6:4
[g]ver 25-26;
1Ki 6:15;
Eze 42:3
41:18 [h]S 1Ki 6:18
[i]Ex 37:7;
S 2Ch 3:7
[j]S 1Ki 6:29; 7:36
[k]Eze 10:21
41:19 [l]S Eze 10:14
41:21 [m]ver 1
41:22 [n]S Ex 30:1
[o]S Ex 25:23;
S Eze 23:41
41:23 [p]ver 1
[q]1Ki 6:32

41:24 [r]1Ki 6:34
41:26 [s]ver
15-16; Eze 40:16
42:1 [t]ver 13
[u]S Ex 27:9;
Eze 41:12-14
42:3 [w]Eze 41:15
[x]Eze 41:16
42:4 [y]Eze 46:19
42:9 [z]Eze 44:5;
46:19
42:10 [a]Eze 41:12-14

[1]2 Septuagint; Hebrew *long* [k]22 Septuagint; Hebrew *length* [l]2 The common cubit was about 1 1/2 feet (about 0.5 meter). [m]4 Septuagint and Syriac; Hebrew *and one cubit* [n]10 Septuagint; Hebrew *Eastward*

41:13 *hundred.* The 100-cubit symmetry stood for perfection.

41:16 *everything . . . was covered with wood.* As in Solomon's temple (1Ki 6:15).

41:18 *cherubim.* Who served as guards (cf. Ge 3:24). These, as opposed to those mentioned in ch. 10, have only two faces—a man's and a lion's (see 1Ki 6:29,32,35).

41:22 *wooden altar.* As the great altar stood outside the temple proper (43:13–17), so a smaller altar (3'5" square by 5' high) stood outside the Most Holy Place. It served as a

table, no doubt to hold the bread of the Presence (Ex 25:30; Lev 24:5–9; see 1Ki 6:20). Ezekiel makes no mention of an altar of incense or of lampstands, such as were found in Solomon's temple and in the tabernacle before it. Also not included are the "Sea" (1Ki 7:23) and the ark of the covenant.

41:23 *double doors.* Folding doors, so that the entry could be made still narrower.

42:1 *rooms opposite the temple courtyard.* Their function is described in vv. 13–14. They have no parallel in Solomon's temple as described in 1Ki 6.

wall, were rooms [b] [11]with a passageway in front of them. These were like the rooms on the north; they had the same length and width, with similar exits and dimensions. Similar to the doorways on the north [12]were the doorways of the rooms on the south. There was a doorway at the beginning of the passageway that was parallel to the corresponding wall extending eastward, by which one enters the rooms.

[13]Then he said to me, "The north [c] and south rooms [d] facing the temple courtyard [e] are the priests' rooms, where the priests who approach the LORD will eat the most holy offerings. There they will put the most holy offerings—the grain offerings, [f] the sin offerings [g] and the guilt offerings [h]—for the place is holy. [i] [14]Once the priests enter the holy precincts, they are not to go into the outer court until they leave behind the garments [j] in which they minister, for these are holy. They are to put on other clothes before they go near the places that are for the people. [k] "

[15]When he had finished measuring what was inside the temple area, he led me out by the east gate [l] and measured the area all around: [16]He measured the east side with the measuring rod; it was five hundred cubits. [o] [17]He measured the north side; it was five hundred cubits [p] by the measuring rod. [18]He measured the south side; it was five hundred cubits by the measuring rod. [19]Then he turned to the west side and measured; it was five hundred cubits by the measuring rod. [20]So he measured [m] the area [n] on all four sides. It had a wall around it, [o] five hundred cubits long and

five hundred cubits wide, [p] to separate the holy from the common. [q]

The Glory Returns to the Temple

43 Then the man brought me to the gate facing east, [r] [2]and I saw the glory of the God of Israel coming from the east. His voice was like the roar of rushing waters, [s] and the land was radiant with his glory. [t] [3]The vision I saw was like the vision I had seen when he [q] came to destroy the city and like the visions I had seen by the Kebar River, and I fell facedown. [4]The glory [u] of the LORD entered the temple through the gate facing east. [v] [5]Then the Spirit [w] lifted me up [x] and brought me into the inner court, and the glory [y] of the LORD filled the temple. [z]

[6]While the man was standing beside me, I heard someone speaking to me from inside the temple. [7]He said: "Son of man, this is the place of my throne [a] and the place for the soles of my feet. This is where I will live among the Israelites forever. The house of Israel will never again defile [b] my holy name—neither they nor their kings—by their prostitution [r] and the lifeless idols [s] of their kings at their high places. [c] [8]When they placed their threshold next to my threshold and their doorposts beside my doorposts, with only a wall between me and them, they defiled my holy name by their detestable practices.

[o] *16* See Septuagint of verse 17; Hebrew *rods*; also in verses 18 and 19.   [p] *17* Septuagint; Hebrew *rods*   [q] *3* Some Hebrew manuscripts and Vulgate; most Hebrew manuscripts *I*   [r] *7* Or *their spiritual adultery*; also in verse 9   [s] *7* Or *the corpses*; also in verse 9

Cross-references (center column)

42:10 [b]ver 1
42:13 [c]Eze 40:46
[d]ver 1
[e]Eze 41:12-14
[f]Jer 41:5
[g]S Lev 10:17
[h]Lev 14:13
[i]S Ex 29:31;
S Lev 6:29; 7:6;
10:12-13;
Nu 18:9-10
42:14
[j]Lev 16:23;
Eze 44:19
[k]Ex 29:9;
S Lev 8:7-9
42:15 [l]Eze 43:1
42:20 [m]Eze 40:5
[n]Eze 43:12
[o]Zec 2:5

[p]Eze 45:2;
Rev 21:16
[q]S Eze 22:26
43:1
[r]S 1Ch 9:18;
S Eze 8:16;
42:15; 44:1
43:2 [s]S Ps 18:4;
S Rev 1:15
[t]Isa 6:3;
Rev 18:1; 21:11
43:4 [u]Eze 1:28
[v]Eze 10:19; 44:2
43:5
[w]S Eze 11:24
[x]S Eze 3:12
[y]S Ex 16:7
[z]S Isa 6:4
43:7 [a]S Jer 3:17
[b]S Eze 37:23
[c]S Lev 26:30;
S Eze 20:29,39

42:13 *priests who approach the LORD.* The sons of Zadok (see 40:6 and note on 44:15). *eat the most holy offerings.* The priests normally received partial maintenance by being allowed to eat certain sacrifices (see Lev 2:3; 5:13; 6:16, 26,29; 7:6,10).
42:20 *five hundred cubits long and five hundred cubits wide.* Perfect symmetry in the ideal temple's total area.
43:2 *I saw the glory.* The high point of chs. 40–48. The temple had been prepared for this moment, and all that follows flows from this appearance. *coming from the east.* The direction Ezekiel had seen God leave (see 11:23). In the book of Ezekiel God's glory is always active (see vv. 4–5; 3:23; 9:3; 10:4,18; 44:4). *like the roar of rushing waters.* Ezekiel experienced an audition as well as a vision. For the comparison see 1:24; Rev 1:15; 14:2; 19:6. *the land was radiant with his glory.* God's visible glory is always described as being very bright (see 10:4; Lk 2:9; Rev 21:11,23).
43:3 *like the vision I had seen.* And yet it was different; for no creatures or wheels are mentioned here. *when he came to destroy the city.* See ch. 9. *by the Kebar River.* See ch. 1. *I fell facedown.* See 1:28; 3:23; 9:8; 11:13; 44:4.
43:4 *through the gate facing east.* See note on v. 2.
43:5 *Then the Spirit lifted me up.* With God being nearer, the function of the guiding angel was taken over by the Spirit of God. Ezekiel was transported into the inner court but not

into the temple (cf. 3:14; 8:3; 11:1,24). *filled the temple.* As at the consecration of Solomon's temple (1Ki 8:11; see Ex 40:34–35; Isa 6:4).
43:6 *someone.* God, but out of reverence not named here, preserving an air of awe and mystery.
43:7 *place of my throne.* See Isa 6:1; Jer 3:17. *place for the soles of my feet.* See 1Ch 28:2; Ps 99:5; 132:7; Isa 60:13; La 2:1. *I will live among the Israelites forever.* Renewing the promise of 37:26–28 (see v. 9; 1Ki 6:13; Zec 2:11). *prostitution.* As the NIV text note indicates, the word can stand either for the sacred prostitution in the Canaanite religion (Baalism) or for spiritual apostasy from true worship of the Lord (see note on 16:15). *lifeless idols.* As the NIV text note indicates, the reference is either to idols or to monuments or graves of past kings. Fourteen kings of Judah were buried in Jerusalem, possibly near (too near for Ezekiel) the temple area (see 2Ki 21:18,26; 23:30).
43:8 *their threshold next to my threshold.* Solomon's temple was surrounded by many of his own private structures (see 1Ki 7:1–12). The distinction between God's holy temple and the rest of the world is a central idea in the book of Ezekiel (see v. 12; 44:23). *So I destroyed them.* As elsewhere in Ezekiel, the unstable practices of the people and their kings brought about their destruction (see 5:11; 18:10–12; and especially 22:1–15).

So I destroyed them in my anger. [9]Now let them put away from me their prostitution and the lifeless idols of their kings, and I will live among them forever. [d]

[10]"Son of man, describe the temple to the people of Israel, that they may be ashamed [e] of their sins. Let them consider the plan, [11]and if they are ashamed of all they have done, make known to them the design of the temple—its arrangement, its exits and entrances—its whole design and all its regulations [t] and laws. Write these down before them so that they may be faithful to its design and follow all its regulations. [f]

[12]"This is the law of the temple: All the surrounding area [g] on top of the mountain will be most holy. [h] Such is the law of the temple.

The Altar

[13]"These are the measurements of the altar [i] in long cubits, that cubit being a cubit [u] and a handbreadth [v]: Its gutter is a cubit deep and a cubit wide, with a rim of one span [w] around the edge. And this is the height of the altar: [14]From the gutter on the ground up to the lower ledge it is two cubits high and a cubit wide, and from the smaller ledge up to the larger ledge it is four cubits high and a cubit wide. [15]The altar hearth [j] is four cubits high, and four horns [k] project upward from the hearth. [16]The altar hearth is square, twelve cubits long and twelve cubits wide. [l] [17]The upper ledge [m] also is square, fourteen cubits long and fourteen cubits wide, with a rim of half a cubit and a gutter of a cubit all around. The steps [n] of the altar face east. [o]"

[18]Then he said to me, "Son of man, this is what the Sovereign Lord says: These will be the regulations for sacrificing burnt offerings [p] and sprinkling blood [q] upon the altar when it is built: [19]You are to give a young bull [r] as a sin offering to the priests, who are Levites, of the family of Zadok, [s] who come near [t] to minister before me, declares the Sovereign Lord. [20]You are to take some of its blood and put it on the four horns of the altar [u] and on the four corners of the upper ledge [v] and all around the rim, and so purify the altar [w] and make atonement for it. [21]You are to take the bull for the sin offering and burn it in the designated part of the temple area outside the sanctuary. [x]

[22]"On the second day you are to offer a male goat without defect for a sin offering, and the altar is to be purified as it was purified with the bull. [23]When you have finished purifying it, you are to offer a young bull and a ram from the flock, both without defect. [y] [24]You are to offer them before the Lord, and the priests are to sprinkle salt [z] on them and sacrifice them as a burnt offering to the Lord.

[25]"For seven days [a] you are to provide a male goat daily for a sin offering; you are also to provide a young bull and a ram from the flock, both without defect. [b] [26]For seven days they are to make atonement for the altar and cleanse it; thus they will dedicate it. [27]At the end of these days, from the eighth day [c] on, the priests are to present your burnt offerings [d] and fellowship offerings [x] [e] on the altar. Then I will accept you, declares the Sovereign Lord."

The Prince, the Levites, the Priests

44 Then the man brought me back to the outer gate of the sanctuary, the one facing east, [f] and it was shut. [2]The

---

Cross references (center column):

43:9 [d]Eze 37:26-28
43:10 [e]S Eze 16:61
43:11 [f]Eze 44:5
43:12 [g]Eze 42:20 [h]S Eze 17:22
43:13 [i]S Ex 20:24; 2Ch 4:1
43:15 [j]Isa 29:2 [k]S Ex 27:2
43:16 [l]Rev 21:16
43:17 [m]ver 20; Eze 45:19 [n]Ex 20:26 [o]S Ex 27:1
43:18 [p]Ex 40:29 [q]Lev 1:5,11; Heb 9:21-22
43:19 [r]S Lev 4:3 [s]S 2Sa 8:17; S Ezr 7:2 [t]Nu 16:40; S Eze 40:46
43:20 [u]S Lev 4:7 [v]S ver 17 [w]Lev 16:19
43:21 [x]Ex 29:14; Heb 13:11
43:23 [y]Ex 29:1; S Lev 22:20
43:24 [z]S Lev 2:13; Mk 9:49-50
43:25 [a]S Lev 8:33 [b]S Ex 29:37 [c]Lev 9:1 [d]S Isa 60:7 [e]S Ex 32:6; S Lev 17:5
44:1 [f]S Eze 43:1

Footnotes (text notes):

[t]11 Some Hebrew manuscripts and Septuagint; most Hebrew manuscripts *regulations and its whole design*   [u]13 The common cubit was about 1 1/2 feet (about 0.5 meter).   [v]13 That is, about 3 inches (about 8 centimeters)   [w]13 That is, about 9 inches (about 22 centimeters)   [x]27 Traditionally *peace offerings*

43:12 *This is the law.* Refers to the contents of chs. 40–42.
43:13 *altar.* Alluded to in 40:47 and here described in detail. Although the material is not mentioned, dressed stones were probably to be used. Ex 20:24–26 allowed an altar to be made of earth, but use of dressed stones for those altars was strictly forbidden (see notes on Ex 20:24–25). Solomon's altar was bronze (1Ki 8:64). Ezekiel's altar, much larger than Solomon's, was over 20 feet tall, made up of three slabs of decreasing size, like a pyramid or Babylonian ziggurat: the "lower ledge" (v. 14), two cubits high; the "larger ledge" (v. 14), four cubits high; and the "altar hearth" (v. 15), four cubits high.
43:15 *altar hearth.* The Hebrew for this term appears only here in the OT and may also mean "mountain of God" or "lion of God"; it is a variant of a form that appears in Isa 29:1–2. *four horns.* Stone projections from each of the four corners of the altar hearth. On earlier altars they afforded a

refuge of last resort for an accused person (see Ex 21:12–14; 1Ki 1:50–51; 2:28–29).
43:17 *steps of the altar.* Forbidden in Ex 20:26 but here required because of the size (see note on v. 13).
43:18 *burnt offerings.* See note on 40:39. *sprinkling blood.* See Ex 29:16; Lev 4:6; 5:9.
43:19 *sin offering.* To cleanse the altar from the pollution of human sin (see note on 40:39). *of the family of Zadok.* See note on 44:15.
43:21 *outside the sanctuary.* As prescribed in Ex 29:14; Lev 4:12,21; 8:17; 9:11; 16:27. This action foreshadows one aspect of Christ's sacrifice (see Heb 13:11–13).
43:22 *purified.* By the sprinkling of the blood (see v. 20).
43:27 *fellowship offerings.* After the seven-day consecration by burnt offerings and sin offerings, the altar was ready for the celebration of the more festive fellowship offerings where the people partook of some of the meat (see Lev 3).

LORD said to me, "This gate is to remain shut. It must not be opened; no one may enter through it. ^{g} It is to remain shut because the LORD, the God of Israel, has entered through it. ^{3}The prince himself is the only one who may sit inside the gateway to eat in the presence ^{h} of the LORD. He is to enter by way of the portico of the gateway and go out the same way. ^{i} "

^{4}Then the man brought me by way of the north gate ^{j} to the front of the temple. I looked and saw the glory of the LORD filling the temple ^{k} of the LORD, and I fell facedown. ^{l}

^{5}The LORD said to me, "Son of man, look carefully, listen closely and give attention to everything I tell you concerning all the regulations regarding the temple of the LORD. Give attention to the entrance ^{m} of the temple and all the exits of the sanctuary. ^{n} ^{6}Say to the rebellious house ^{o} of Israel, 'This is what the Sovereign LORD says: Enough of your detestable practices, O house of Israel! ^{7}In addition to all your other detestable practices, you brought foreigners uncircumcised in heart ^{p} and flesh into my sanctuary, desecrating my temple while you offered me food, fat and blood, and you broke my covenant. ^{q} ^{8}Instead of carrying out your duty in regard to my holy things, you put others in charge of my sanctuary. ^{r} ^{9}This is what the Sovereign LORD says: No foreigner uncircumcised in heart and flesh is to enter my sanctuary, not even the foreigners who live among the Israelites. ^{s}

^{10} 'The Levites who went far from me when Israel went astray ^{t} and who wan-

dered from me after their idols must bear the consequences of their sin. ^{u} ^{11}They may serve in my sanctuary, having charge of the gates of the temple and serving in it; they may slaughter the burnt offerings ^{v} and sacrifices for the people and stand before the people and serve them. ^{w} ^{12}But because they served them in the presence of their idols and made the house of Israel fall ^{x} into sin, therefore I have sworn with uplifted hand ^{y} that they must bear the consequences of their sin, declares the Sovereign LORD. ^{z} ^{13}They are not to come near to serve me as priests or come near any of my holy things or my most holy offerings; they must bear the shame ^{a} of their detestable practices. ^{b} ^{14}Yet I will put them in charge of the duties of the temple and all the work that is to be done in it. ^{c}

^{15} 'But the priests, who are Levites and descendants of Zadok ^{d} and who faithfully carried out the duties of my sanctuary when the Israelites went astray from me, are to come near to minister before me; they are to stand before me to offer sacrifices of fat ^{e} and blood, declares the Sovereign LORD. ^{f} ^{16}They alone are to enter my sanctuary; they alone are to come near my table ^{g} to minister before me and perform my service. ^{h}

^{17} 'When they enter the gates of the inner court, they are to wear linen clothes; ^{i} they must not wear any woolen garment while ministering at the gates of the inner court or inside the temple. ^{18}They are to wear linen turbans ^{j} on their heads and linen undergarments ^{k} around their waists. They must not wear anything

---

44:2 ^{g}Eze 43:4-5
44:3
^{h}S Ex 24:9-11
^{i}Eze 46:2,8
44:4 /S Eze 40:35
^{k}S Isa 6:4;
S Eze 10:4;
Rev 15:8 /Da 8:17
44:5 ^{m}S Eze 42:9
^{n}Eze 40:4;
43:10-11
44:6 ^{o}S Eze 3:9
44:7
^{p}S Lev 26:41
^{q}Ge 17:14;
Ex 12:48;
Lev 22:25
44:8 ^{r}Lev 22:2;
Nu 18:7
44:9 ^{s}Joel 3:17;
Zec 14:21
44:10 ^{t}Ps 95:10

^{u}Nu 18:23
44:11
^{v}2Ch 29:34
^{w}Nu 3:5-37;
S 16:9;
S 1Ch 26:12-19
44:12
^{x}S Jer 18:15
^{y}Ps 106:26
^{z}2Ki 16:10-16;
Jer 14:10
44:13
^{a}S Eze 16:61
^{b}Nu 18:3;
Hos 5:1
44:14 ^{c}1Sa 2:36;
2Ki 23:9;
S 1Ch 23:28-32
44:15
^{d}S 2Sa 8:17;
S Ezr 7:2
^{e}S Ex 29:13
/S Jer 33:18;
S Eze 40:46;
Zec 3:7
44:16
^{g}S Eze 41:22
^{h}Lev 3:16-17;
17:5-6; Nu 18:5;
S 1Sa 2:35;
Zec 3:7
44:17 ^{i}Rev 19:8
44:18
/S Ex 28:39;
S Isa 3:20
^{k}S Ex 28:42

44:2 *It is to remain shut because.* The reason given here is that God entered through the east gate (43:1–2), thus making it holy. Related reasons may be that God would never again leave as before (10:19; 11:23) and that sun worship would be made impossible (see 8:16). Today the east gate (called the Golden Gate) of the sacred Moslem area (*Haram esh-Sharif*) in Jerusalem is likewise sealed shut as a result of a later but possibly related tradition.

44:3 *prince.* The first mention of the prince in chs. 40–48 (see 34:24 and note). *to eat.* Probably his part of the fellowship offering (see Lev 7:15; Dt 12:7; see also Eze 43:27 and note). While this honor is accorded the prince, it is significant that he is given no other part in the ceremonial functions, reserved now solely for the priests (see 2Ch 26:16–20). *by way of the portico.* From the inside of the outer court.

44:7 *uncircumcised in heart.* Spiritually unfit.

44:9 *No foreigner uncircumcised . . . is to enter my sanctuary.* Nehemiah enforced this restriction when he dismissed Tobiah (Ne 13:8), an Ammonite (Ne 2:10; see Dt 23:3). Foreigners could, however, be a part of Israel (see 47:22).

44:10 *Levites.* Members of the tribe of Levi served as priests from the earliest days (see Dt 33:8–11; Jdg 17:13). *when Israel went astray.* The reference is mainly to the period of the monarchy, especially to the last years, during which Ezekiel so often criticized the people's idolatry (see

6:3–6; 14:3–11; 16:18–21; 23:36–49; 36:17–18; 37:23).

44:11 *stand before the people.* Cf. standing before the Lord (see v. 15); the Levites still had an honorable position.

44:15 *Zadok.* Traced his Levitical lineage to Aaron through Aaron's son Eleazar (1Ch 6:50–53). He served as priest under David, along with Abiathar (see 2Sa 8:17 and note; 15:24–29; 20:25). He supported Solomon (as opposed to Abiathar, who pledged himself to Adonijah) and thus secured for himself and his descendants the privilege of serving in the Jerusalem temple (see 1Ki 1). Later the Zadokites were removed from office, but the Qumran (Dead Sea Scrolls) community remained loyal to them. *who faithfully carried out.* A distinction Ezekiel did not make in his oracles of judgment (see 7:26; 22:26 and the thrust of all of ch. 8). In chs. 40–48, however, the Zadokites received special consideration because of their faithfulness.

44:16 *They alone are to enter.* This elevation of the Zadokites and demotion of the Levites were part of the concern for ritual purity, a major theme of chs. 40–48. Only the fittest were to serve. *my table.* Either the table that held the bread (see 41:22 and note) or the large altar on which the Lord's food was presented (v. 7).

44:17 *linen.* Cooler than wool (see v. 18).

44:18 *turbans.* Ezekiel wore one (24:17).

that makes them perspire.[l] [19]When they go out into the outer court where the people are, they are to take off the clothes they have been ministering in and are to leave them in the sacred rooms, and put on other clothes, so that they do not consecrate[m] the people by means of their garments.[n]

[20]"'They must not shave[o] their heads or let their hair grow long, but they are to keep the hair of their heads trimmed.[p] [21]No priest is to drink wine when he enters the inner court.[q] [22]They must not marry widows or divorced women; they may marry only virgins of Israelite descent or widows of priests.[r] [23]They are to teach my people the difference between the holy and the common[s] and show them how to distinguish between the unclean and the clean.[t]

[24]"'In any dispute, the priests are to serve as judges[u] and decide it according to my ordinances. They are to keep my laws and my decrees for all my appointed feasts,[v] and they are to keep my Sabbaths holy.[w]

[25]"'A priest must not defile himself by going near a dead person; however, if the dead person was his father or mother, son or daughter, brother or unmarried sister, then he may defile himself.[x] [26]After he is cleansed, he must wait seven days.[y] [27]On the day he goes into the inner court of the sanctuary[z] to minister in the sanctuary, he is to offer a sin offering[a] for himself, declares the Sovereign LORD.

[28]"'I am to be the only inheritance[b] the priests have. You are to give them no possession in Israel; I will be their posses-

sion. [29]They will eat[c] the grain offerings, the sin offerings and the guilt offerings; and everything in Israel devoted[y] to the LORD[d] will belong to them.[e] [30]The best of all the firstfruits[f] and of all your special gifts will belong to the priests. You are to give them the first portion of your ground meal[g] so that a blessing[h] may rest on your household.[i] [31]The priests must not eat anything, bird or animal, found dead[j] or torn by wild animals.[k]

Division of the Land

45 "'When you allot the land as an inheritance,[l] you are to present to the LORD a portion of the land as a sacred district, 25,000 cubits long and 20,000[z] cubits wide; the entire area will be holy.[m] [2]Of this, a section 500 cubits square[n] is to be for the sanctuary, with 50 cubits around it for open land. [3]In the sacred district, measure off a section 25,000 cubits[a] long and 10,000 cubits[b] wide. In it will be the sanctuary, the Most Holy Place. [4]It will be the sacred portion of the land for the priests,[o] who minister in the sanctuary and who draw near to minister before the LORD. It will be a place for their houses as well as a holy place for the sanctuary.[p] [5]An area 25,000 cubits long and 10,000 cubits wide will belong to the Levites, who serve in the temple, as their possession for towns to live in.[c] [q]

[6]"'You are to give the city as its prop-

Cross references (center column)

44:18 [l]S Lev 16:4
44:19 [m]S Lev 6:27
[n]Ex 39:27-29;
Lev 6:10-11;
S Eze 42:14
44:20 [o]Eze 5:1
[p]S Lev 21:5;
Nu 6:5
44:21 [q]S Lev 10:9
44:22 [r]Lev 21:7
44:23 [s]S Eze 22:26
[t]S Ge 7:2;
Lev 13:50; 15:31;
Jer 15:19;
Hag 2:11-13
44:24 [u]Dt 17:8-9;
19:17; 21:5;
S 1Ch 23:4
[v]S Lev 23:2
[w]2Ch 19:8
44:25 [x]Lev 21:1-4
44:26 [y]Nu 19:14
44:27 [z]S Nu 3:28
[a]S Lev 4:28;
Nu 6:11
44:28 [b]S Nu 18:20;
Dt 18:1-2;
S Jos 13:33

44:29 [c]Lev 6:16
[d]S Lev 27:21
[e]Nu 18:9,14;
S Jos 13:14
44:30 [f]Nu 18:12-13;
S 2Ch 31:5
[g]S Nu 15:18-21
[h]S Lev 25:21
[i]S 2Ch 31:10;
Ne 10:35-37
44:31 [j]S Lev 11:39
[k]S Ex 22:31;
S Lev 11:40
45:1 [l]S Nu 34:13
[m]Eze 48:8-9,20
45:2 [n]Eze 42:20
45:4 [o]S Eze 40:46
[p]Eze 48:10-11
45:5 [q]Eze 48:13

[y]29 The Hebrew term refers to the irrevocable giving over of things or persons to the LORD. [z]1 Septuagint (see also verses 3 and 5 and 48:9); Hebrew 10,000 [a]3 That is, about 7 miles (about 12 kilometers) [b]3 That is, about 3 miles (about 5 kilometers) [c]5 Septuagint; Hebrew temple; they will have as their possession 20 rooms

Study notes

44:19 *take off the clothes.* In the interest of ritual purity.

44:20 *must not shave their heads.* Because it was a mourning ritual (7:18) that rendered the mourner unclean (see Lev 21:1–5). *or let their hair grow long.* Because it implied the taking of a vow that might prevent the priest from serving (see Nu 6:5; Ac 21:23–26).

44:23 *difference between the holy and the common.* One of Ezekiel's central concerns. The important task of declaring God's will on matters of clean and unclean food, the fitness of sacrificial animals and ritual purity either had been done for pay (see Mic 3:11) or had been neglected altogether (see Jer 2:8; Eze 22:26). See Hag 2:10–13 for a positive example.

44:24 *priests are to serve as judges.* One of their functions from earliest days (see NIV text note on 1Sa 4:18; see also 2Ch 19:8–11).

44:25 *dead person.* Contact with the dead made a person ceremonially unclean (Lev 21:1–3; Hag 2:13).

44:28 *no possession.* The statement that priests were not to own land agrees with Nu 18:20,23–24; Dt 10:9; Jos 13:14,33; 18:7.

44:31 *found dead.* This restriction applied to all Israel according to Lev 7:24.

45:1 *When you allot the land.* Envisioned a new acquisition and redistribution of the land. *present to the LORD.* The entire square area in the center of the land was to be set aside for the Lord. *20,000 cubits.* With the 5,000-cubit city area (v. 6) it was a perfect square. *entire area will be holy.* Set apart for the Lord and owned by no tribe.

45:2 *section 500 cubits square.* The temple area discussed in 42:16–20. *open land.* An unoccupied strip of land that served as a buffer between the more holy and the less holy, though the whole area was holy (see 42:20).

45:3 *measure off a section.* The middle strip of the holy square was specifically for the temple.

45:4 *land for the priests.* Not to own (see 44:28) but to live on.

45:5 *area . . . to the Levites.* A section of equal size just to the north was for the Levites to dwell on, even though it was in the holy area. The Levites, as opposed to the Zadokite priests, could hold land as a possession.

45:6 *city.* The former Jerusalem contained the temple area. The new holy city would not, but would be adjacent to the temple. *5,000 cubits wide.* The southernmost section of the city completed the perfectly square area. *it will belong to the whole house of Israel.* Not to any one tribe or person as in

erty an area 5,000 cubits wide and 25,000 cubits long, adjoining the sacred portion; it will belong to the whole house of Israel. *r*

7 " 'The prince will have the land bordering each side of the area formed by the sacred district and the property of the city. It will extend westward from the west side and eastward from the east side, running lengthwise from the western to the eastern border parallel to one of the tribal portions. *s* 8This land will be his possession in Israel. And my princes will no longer oppress my people but will allow the house of Israel to possess the land according to their tribes. *t*

9 " 'This is what the Sovereign LORD says: You have gone far enough, O princes of Israel! Give up your violence and oppression *u* and do what is just and right. *v* Stop dispossessing my people, declares the Sovereign LORD. 10You are to use accurate scales, *w* an accurate ephah *d x* and an accurate bath. *e* 11The ephah *y* and the bath are to be the same size, the bath containing a tenth of a homer *f* and the ephah a tenth of a homer; the homer is to be the standard measure for both. 12The shekel *g* is to consist of twenty gerahs. *z* Twenty shekels plus twenty-five shekels plus fifteen shekels equal one mina. *h*

Offerings and Holy Days

13 " 'This is the special gift you are to offer: a sixth of an ephah from each homer of wheat and a sixth of an ephah from each homer of barley. 14The prescribed portion of oil, measured by the bath, is a tenth of a bath from each cor (which consists of ten baths or one homer, for ten baths are equivalent to a homer). 15Also one sheep is to be taken from every flock of two hundred from the well-watered pastures of Israel. These will be used for the grain offerings, burnt offerings *a* and fellowship offerings *i* to make atonement *b* for the people, declares the Sovereign LORD. 16All the

people of the land will participate in this special gift for the use of the prince in Israel. 17It will be the duty of the prince to provide the burnt offerings, grain offerings and drink offerings at the festivals, the New Moons *c* and the Sabbaths *d*—at all the appointed feasts of the house of Israel. He will provide the sin offerings, grain offerings, burnt offerings and fellowship offerings to make atonement for the house of Israel. *e*

18 " 'This is what the Sovereign LORD says: In the first month *f* on the first day you are to take a young bull without defect *g* and purify the sanctuary. *h* 19The priest is to take some of the blood of the sin offering and put it on the doorposts of the temple, on the four corners of the upper ledge *i* of the altar *j* and on the gateposts of the inner court. 20You are to do the same on the seventh day of the month for anyone who sins unintentionally *k* or through ignorance; so you are to make atonement for the temple.

21 " 'In the first month on the fourteenth day you are to observe the Passover, *l* a feast lasting seven days, during which you shall eat bread made without yeast. 22On that day the prince is to provide a bull as a sin offering for himself and for all the people of the land. *m* 23Every day during the seven days of the Feast he is to provide seven bulls and seven rams *n* without defect as a burnt offering to the LORD, and a male goat for a sin offering. *o* 24He is to provide as a grain offering *p* an ephah for each bull and an ephah for each ram, along with a hin *j* of oil for each ephah. *q*

25 " 'During the seven days of the Feast, *r* which begins in the seventh month

Cross references (center column)

45:6
r Eze 48:15-18
45:7 *s* Eze 48:21
45:8
t S Nu 26:53;
Eze 46:18
45:9 *u* Ps 12:5
v S Jer 22:3;
Zec 7:9-10; 8:16
45:10
w Dt 25:15;
S Pr 11:1;
Am 8:4-6;
Mic 6:10-11
x S Lev 19:36
45:11 *y* Isa 5:10
45:12 *z* Ex 30:13;
Lev 27:25;
Nu 3:47
45:15 *a* S Lev 1:4
b Lev 6:30

45:17
c S Nu 10:10
d S Lev 23:38;
Isa 66:23
e S 1Ki 8:62;
S 2Ch 31:3;
Eze 46:4-12
45:18 *f* Ex 12:2
g S Lev 22:20;
Heb 9:14
h S Lev 16:33
45:19
i S Eze 43:17
j Lev 16:18-19
45:20 *k* Lev 4:27
45:21
l S Ex 12:11
45:22 *m* Lev 4:14
45:23
n S Nu 22:40;
S Job 42:8
o Nu 28:16-25
45:24
p Nu 28:12-13
q Eze 46:5-7
45:25 *r* Dt 16:13

Footnotes

d 10 An ephah was a dry measure.　　*e* 10 A bath was a liquid measure.　　*f* 11 A homer was a dry measure.　　*g* 12 A shekel weighed about 2/5 ounce (about 11.5 grams).　　*h* 12 That is, 60 shekels; the common mina was 50 shekels.　　*i* 15 Traditionally *peace offerings*; also in verse 17　　*j* 24 That is, probably about 4 quarts (about 4 liters)

---

former days.
45:7 *The prince will have the land.* A considerable portion of territory. In view of the next verse (cf. 46:18) the generous allotment should have kept the prince from greed like that of Ahab (see 1Ki 21). The prince was also responsible for sizable offerings (v. 17).
45:9 *O princes of Israel!* The language of this verse is reminiscent of the preaching Ezekiel did before 586 B.C. (see 22:6).
45:10 *You are to use accurate scales.* Israel was not to repeat the economic injustices of the past. The OT often warns against cheating in weights and measures (see Lev 19:35-36; Dt 25:13-16; Mic 6:10-12).
45:11 *same size.* A little more than half a bushel. *homer.* About six bushels.

45:13 *special gift.* Given to the prince as distinct from the gifts given to the priests (44:30). The prince is to use these gifts in part for the offerings to the Lord (see v. 16).
45:17 *drink offerings.* Usually wine is meant (see Nu 15:5; Hos 9:4); but wine is not mentioned here, though oil is (vv. 14,24).
45:18–46:24 This entire section involves so many variations from Pentateuchal law that the rabbis spent a great deal of effort trying to reconcile them. For example, the provision in 45:18 for an annual purification of the temple does not seem to take into consideration the Day of Atonement ritual of Lev 16.
45:19 *priest.* High priest.
45:22 *sin offering.* See note on 40:39.
45:25 *the Feast, which begins in the seventh month.* In

on the fifteenth day, he is to make the same provision for sin offerings, burnt offerings, grain offerings and oil. *s*

46 " 'This is what the Sovereign LORD says: The gate of the inner court *t* facing east *u* is to be shut on the six working days, but on the Sabbath day and on the day of the New Moon *v* it is to be opened. ²The prince is to enter from the outside through the portico *w* of the gateway and stand by the gatepost. The priests are to sacrifice his burnt offering *x* and his fellowship offerings. *k* He is to worship at the threshold of the gateway and then go out, but the gate will not be shut until evening. *y* ³On the Sabbaths *z* and New Moons the people of the land are to worship in the presence of the LORD at the entrance to that gateway. *a* ⁴The burnt offering the prince brings to the LORD on the Sabbath day is to be six male lambs and a ram, all without defect. ⁵The grain offering given with the ram is to be an ephah, *l* and the grain offering with the lambs is to be as much as he pleases, along with a hin *m* of oil for each ephah. *b* ⁶On the day of the New Moon *c* he is to offer a young bull, six lambs and a ram, all without defect. *d* ⁷He is to provide as a grain offering one ephah with the bull, one ephah with the ram, and with the lambs as much as he wants to give, along with a hin of oil with each ephah. *e* ⁸When the prince enters, he is to go in through the portico *f* of the gateway, and he is to come out the same way. *g*

⁹" 'When the people of the land come before the LORD at the appointed feasts, *h* whoever enters by the north gate to worship is to go out the south gate; and whoever enters by the south gate is to go out the north gate. No one is to return through the gate by which he entered, but each is

to go out the opposite gate. ¹⁰The prince is to be among them, going in when they go in and going out when they go out. *i*

¹¹" 'At the festivals and the appointed feasts, the grain offering is to be an ephah with a bull, an ephah with a ram, and with the lambs as much as one pleases, along with a hin of oil for each ephah. *j* ¹²When the prince provides *k* a freewill offering *l* to the LORD—whether a burnt offering or fellowship offerings—the gate facing east is to be opened for him. He shall offer his burnt offering or his fellowship offerings as he does on the Sabbath day. Then he shall go out, and after he has gone out, the gate will be shut. *m*

¹³" 'Every day you are to provide a year-old lamb without defect for a burnt offering to the LORD; morning by morning *n* you shall provide it. *o* ¹⁴You are also to provide with it morning by morning a grain offering, consisting of a sixth of an ephah with a third of a hin of oil *p* to moisten the flour. The presenting of this grain offering to the LORD is a lasting ordinance. *q* ¹⁵So the lamb and the grain offering and the oil shall be provided morning by morning for a regular *r* burnt offering. *s*

¹⁶" 'This is what the Sovereign LORD says: If the prince makes a gift from his inheritance to one of his sons, it will also belong to his descendants; it is to be their property by inheritance. *t* ¹⁷If, however, he makes a gift from his inheritance to one of his servants, the servant may keep it until the year of freedom; *u* then it will revert to the prince. His inheritance belongs to his sons only; it is theirs. ¹⁸The prince must not take *v* any of the inheritance *w* of the

---

k 2 Traditionally *peace offerings;* also in verse 12
l 5 That is, probably about 3/5 bushel (about 22 liters)
m 5 That is, probably about 4 quarts (about 4 liters)

Cross references (center column):

45:25
s Lev 23:34-43;
Nu 29:12-38
46:1 *t* S Eze 40:19
u S 1Ch 9:18 *v* ver
6; Isa 66:23
46:2 *w* ver 8
x Eze 40:39 *y* ver
12; S Eze 44:3
46:3 *z* S Isa 66:23
a Lk 1:10
46:5 *b* ver 11
46:6 *c* ver 1;
S Nu 10:10
d S Lev 22:20
46:7 *e* Eze 45:24
46:8 *f* ver 2
g Eze 44:3
46:9
h S Ex 23:14;
S 34:20

46:10
i 2Sa 6:14-15;
Ps 42:4
46:11 *j* ver 5
46:12
k S Eze 45:17
l S Lev 7:16 *m* ver
2
46:13 *n* S Ps 5:3
o Ex 29:38;
S Nu 28:3
46:14 *p* Nu 15:6
q Da 8:11
46:15
r S Ex 29:42
s S Ex 29:38;
Nu 28:5-6
46:16 *t* 2Ch 21:3
46:17
u S Lev 25:10
46:18 *v* 1Sa 8:14
w S Lev 25:23;
Eze 45:8;
Mic 2:1-2

---

some respects the most important of the festivals—called the Feast of Ingathering (Ex 23:16; 34:22) and the Feast of Tabernacles (Dt 16:16).

46:1 *gate of the inner court.* While the east gate of the outer court was permanently closed (44:2), the east gate of the inner court could be opened on festival days.

46:2 *through the portico of the gateway.* The portico of the gate of the inner court faced the outer court. *stand by the gatepost.* Which had been ritually cleansed (45:19). From there the prince could observe the sacrifices being performed on the great altar in the inner court, but he was not allowed into the inner court itself.

46:3 *at the entrance to that gateway.* But in the outer court.

46:4 *six male lambs and a ram.* Another example of a difference from Pentateuchal laws (see note on 45:18–46:24). Nu 28:9 calls for two lambs and no ram on the Sabbath.

46:5 *ephah.* Contrast Nu 28:9.

46:6 *day of the New Moon.* The first day of the month.

Contrast the requirement of Nu 28:11.

46:7 *as a grain offering one ephah.* Contrast Nu 28:12.

46:9 *whoever enters by the north gate.* These appear to be crowd control measures. If so, the new era would see masses of people thronging the sanctuary on the festival day.

46:12 *freewill offering.* Above and beyond what was required of the prince.

46:13 *morning by morning.* Contrast Nu 28:3–8, where the daily sacrifice consists of one lamb in the morning and one in the evening (see 1Ch 16:40; 2Ch 13:11; 31:3). A different custom appears in 2Ki 16:15, where a burnt offering was offered in the mornings, a grain offering in the evenings.

46:14 *sixth of an ephah . . . third of a hin.* Contrast Nu 28:5.

46:16 *his descendants.* Ezekiel pictured a hereditary rulership.

46:17 *until the year of freedom.* The Year of Jubilee—held, theoretically, every 50th year (see Lev 25:8–15, especially v. 13).

people, driving them off their property. He is to give his sons their inheritance out of his own property, so that none of my people will be separated from his property.' "

19Then the man brought me through the entrance[x] at the side of the gate to the sacred rooms facing north,[y] which belonged to the priests, and showed me a place at the western end. 20He said to me, "This is the place where the priests will cook the guilt offering and the sin offering and bake the grain offering, to avoid bringing them into the outer court and consecrating[z] the people."[a]

21He then brought me to the outer court and led me around to its four corners, and I saw in each corner another court. 22In the four corners of the outer court were enclosed[n] courts, forty cubits long and thirty cubits wide; each of the courts in the four corners was the same size. 23Around the inside of each of the four courts was a ledge of stone, with places for fire built all around under the ledge. 24He said to me, "These are the kitchens where those who minister at the temple will cook the sacrifices of the people."

The River From the Temple

47 The man brought me back to the entrance of the temple, and I saw water[b] coming out from under the threshold of the temple toward the east (for the temple faced east). The water was coming down from under the south side of the temple, south of the altar.[c] 2He then brought me out through the north gate[d] and led me around the outside to the outer

gate facing east, and the water was flowing from the south side.

3As the man went eastward with a measuring line[e] in his hand, he measured off a thousand cubits[o] and then led me through water that was ankle-deep. 4He measured off another thousand cubits and led me through water that was knee-deep. He measured off another thousand and led me through water that was up to the waist. 5He measured off another thousand, but now it was a river[f] that I could not cross, because the water had risen and was deep enough to swim in—a river that no one could cross.[g] 6He asked me, "Son of man, do you see this?"

Then he led me back to the bank of the river. 7When I arrived there, I saw a great number of trees on each side of the river.[h] 8He said to me, "This water flows toward the eastern region and goes down into the Arabah,[p][i] where it enters the Sea.[q] When it empties into the Sea,[q] the water there becomes fresh.[j] 9Swarms of living creatures will live wherever the river flows. There will be large numbers of fish, because this water flows there and makes the salt water fresh; so where the river flows everything will live.[k] 10Fishermen[l] will stand along the shore; from En Gedi[m] to En Eglaim there will be places for spreading nets.[n] The fish will be of many kinds[o]—like the fish of the Great Sea.[r][p] 11But the swamps and marshes will not become fresh; they will be left for salt.[q] 12Fruit trees of all kinds will grow on both

Cross references

46:19
x S Eze 42:9
y Eze 42:4
46:20
z S Lev 6:27 ; a ver 24; Zec 14:20
47:1 b S Isa 55:1
c Ps 46:4;
Joel 3:18;
Rev 22:1
47:2
d S Eze 40:35

47:3 e S Eze 40:3
47:5 f S Ge 2:10
g Isa 11:9;
Hab 2:14
47:7 h ver 12;
Rev 22:2
47:8 i S Dt 1:1;
S 3:17 j Isa 41:18
47:9 k Isa 12:3;
55:1; Jn 4:14;
7:37-38
47:10 l S Isa 19:8;
Mt 4:19
m S Jos 15:62
n Eze 26:5
o Ps 104:25;
Mt 13:47
p S Nu 34:6
47:11
q S Dt 29:23

n22 The meaning of the Hebrew for this word is uncertain. o3 That is, about 1,500 feet (about 450 meters) p8 Or *the Jordan Valley* q8 That is, the Dead Sea r10 That is, the Mediterranean; also in verses 15, 19 and 20

46:18 *The prince must not take.* See note on 45:7.

46:19–24 Fits well after 42:13–14, where other rooms for priests are described. The provisions here are a fitting conclusion to the sacrifice laws. The priests' area (vv. 19–20) was to be kept separate from the cooking areas of the Levites (vv. 21–24).

47:1 *man.* The angelic guide (40:3), who here appears for the last time, concluded Ezekiel's visionary tour of the new temple. *entrance of the temple.* Ezekiel was standing in the inner court. *water.* The rest of this section (vv. 1–12) makes it clear that healing, life-nurturing water is meant (see Ps 36:8; 46:4 and notes; see also Joel 3:18; Zec 13:1; 14:8; Rev 22:1–2). In the larger background was the river flowing from the Garden of Eden (Ge 2:10).

47:2 *brought me out through the north gate.* Because the east gate was closed (44:2).

47:5 *measured off another thousand.* For a total of four measurings (see note on 1:5). *river that no one could cross.* Amazing, in that a stream fed by no tributaries does not increase as it flows.

47:7 *great number of trees.* Reminiscent of Eden (Ge 2:9).

47:8 *toward the eastern region.* Contrast Zec 14:8. *Arabah.* Here the waterless region between Jerusalem and the Dead Sea (see NIV text note). *the Sea.* Usually means the Mediterranean Sea, but here obviously the Dead Sea is intended (see NIV text note). *becomes fresh.* The Hebrew says, figuratively, "becomes healed." That this lowest (1,300 feet below sea level) and saltiest (25 percent) body of water in the world should sustain such an abundance of life indicates the wonderful renewing power of this "river of the water of life" (Rev 22:1).

47:9 *Swarms of living creatures.* Overtones of Ge 1:20–21 point to a new creation.

47:10 *En Gedi.* Means "spring of the goat"; a strong spring midway along the western side of the Dead Sea. *En Eglaim.* Means "spring of the two calves." It is possibly Ain Feshkha, at the northwestern corner of the Dead Sea, though some suggest a location on the east bank. *the Great Sea.* See NIV text note.

47:11 *they will be left for salt.* Perhaps to provide the salt needed in the sacrifices (43:24).

47:12 *Every month they will bear.* A marvelous extension of the promises in 34:27; 36:30 (see Am 9:13).

banks of the river.[r] Their leaves will not wither, nor will their fruit[s] fail. Every month they will bear, because the water from the sanctuary[t] flows to them. Their fruit will serve for food and their leaves for healing.[u]"

The Boundaries of the Land

[13]This is what the Sovereign LORD says: "These are the boundaries[v] by which you are to divide the land for an inheritance among the twelve tribes of Israel, with two portions for Joseph.[w] [14]You are to divide it equally among them. Because I swore with uplifted hand to give it to your forefathers, this land will become your inheritance.[x]

[15]"This is to be the boundary of the land:[y]

"On the north side it will run from the Great Sea[z] by the Hethlon road[a] past Lebo[s] Hamath to Zedad, [16]Berothah[t][b] and Sibraim (which lies on the border between Damascus and Hamath),[c] as far as Hazer Hatticon, which is on the border of Hauran. [17]The boundary will extend from the sea to Hazar Enan,[u] along the northern border of Damascus, with the border of Hamath to the north. This will be the north boundary.[d]

[18]"On the east side the boundary will run between Hauran and Damascus, along the Jordan between Gilead and the land of Israel, to the eastern

sea and as far as Tamar.[v] This will be the east boundary.[e]

[19]"On the south side it will run from Tamar as far as the waters of Meribah Kadesh,[f] then along the Wadi of Egypt,[g] to the Great Sea.[h] This will be the south boundary.

[20]"On the west side, the Great Sea will be the boundary to a point opposite Lebo[w] Hamath.[i] This will be the west boundary.[j]

[21]"You are to distribute this land among yourselves according to the tribes of Israel. [22]You are to allot it as an inheritance[k] for yourselves and for the aliens[l] who have settled among you and who have children. You are to consider them as native-born Israelites; along with you they are to be allotted an inheritance among the tribes of Israel.[m] [23]In whatever tribe the alien settles, there you are to give him his inheritance," declares the Sovereign LORD.[n]

The Division of the Land

48 "These are the tribes, listed by name: At the northern frontier, Dan[o] will have one portion; it will follow the Hethlon road[p] to Lebo[x] Hamath;[q] Hazar Enan and the northern border of Damascus next to Hamath will be part of

Cross references

47:12 [r]ver 7; Rev 22:2 [s]S Ps 1:3 [t]S Isa 55:1 [u]S Ge 2:9; S Jer 17:8; Eze 36:8
47:13 [v]Nu 34:2-12 [w]S Ge 48:16; S 49:26
47:14 [x]S Ge 12:7; S Dt 1:8; S Eze 36:12
47:15 [y]Nu 34:2 [z]ver 19; S Nu 34:6 [a]Eze 48:1
47:16 [b]2Sa 8:8 [c]Nu 13:21; S Jer 49:23; Eze 48:1
47:17 [d]Eze 48:1
47:18 [e]S Eze 27:18
47:19 [f]Dt 32:51 [g]S Ge 15:18; Isa 27:12 [h]S ver 15; Eze 48:28
47:20 [i]S Nu 13:21; Eze 48:1 [j]Nu 34:6
47:22 [k]S Eze 36:12 [l]S Dt 24:19; S Isa 14:1; Mal 3:5 [m]S Lev 24:22; Nu 15:29; 26:55-56; Isa 56:6-7; Ro 10:12; Eph 2:12-16; 3:6; Col 3:11
47:23 [n]S Dt 10:19
48:1 [o]S Ge 30:6 [p]Eze 47:15-17 [q]S Eze 47:20

Translation notes

[s]15 Or past the entrance to [t]15,16 See Septuagint and Ezekiel 48:1; Hebrew road to go into Zedad, [16]Hamath, Berothah [u]Hebrew Enon, a variant of Enan [v]18 Septuagint and Syriac; Hebrew Israel. You will measure to the eastern sea [w]20 Or opposite the entrance to [x]1 Or to the entrance to

---

47:13 *two portions for Joseph.* Since the tribe of Levi received none (44:28), Ephraim and Manasseh, Joseph's two sons adopted by Jacob (Ge 48:17-20), each received an allotment (see 48:4-5).

47:14 *Because I swore.* A reference to the covenant made with Abram (Ge 15:9-21; see Eze 20:5; 36:28).

47:15 *This is to be the boundary.* Approximates Israel's borders at the time of David and Solomon, except that Transjordan is not included (see v. 18)—which, in any event, was never within the boundaries of the promised land proper. The following specified boundaries closely resemble those in Nu 34:1-12. *Hethlon road.* Probably situated on the Mediterranean coast, somewhere in present-day Lebanon. *Lebo Hamath.* See NIV text note. Lebo, however, probably does not mean "entrance," but should be identified with modern Lebweh, about 15 miles northeast of Baalbek and 20 miles southwest of Kadesh on the Orontes River, near Riblah. At one time Lebo must have served as a fortress guarding the southern route to Hamath. Perhaps the phrase should be translated "Lebo of Hamath." It is often referred to in Scripture as the northern limit of Israel (see v. 20; 48:1; Nu 13:21; 34:8; Jos 13:5; 1Ki 8:65; 2Ki 14:25; Am 6:14). *Zedad.* Mentioned in Nu 34:8 but otherwise unknown. **47:16** *Berothah.* Probably to be identified with the Berothai of 2Sa 8:8, but otherwise unknown. *Sibraim.* Location unknown; probably the Sepharvaim of 2Ki 17:24; 18:34. *Damascus.* Capital of Aram (Syria); according to v. 17 it was

included in Israel. *Hamath.* A city about 120 miles north of Damascus on the Orontes River. *Hazer Hatticon.* Means "the middle enclosure." Its location is unknown, but it is possibly the same as Hazar Enan in v. 17.

47:18 *eastern sea.* The Dead Sea (see Joel 2:20; Zec 14:8). *Tamar.* Means "(place of) palms" (see v. 19; 48:28); mentioned in Ge 14:7 (Hazazon Tamar) and 1 Ki 9:18 (see NIV text note) and identified with En Gedi (see note on v. 10) in 2Ch 20:2.

47:19 *Meribah Kadesh.* A district about 50 miles south of Beersheba, identified with Kadesh Barnea in Nu 34:4. *Wadi of Egypt.* The Wadi el-Arish, a deeply cut riverbed with seasonal flow that runs from the Sinai north-northwest until it enters the Mediterranean, 50 miles south of Gaza. It marked the southernmost extremity of Solomon's kingdom (1Ki 8:65).

47:22 *You are to consider them as native-born Israelites.* A gracious inclusiveness that went beyond the provision of 14:7. It reflects the same universalism that is found in such prophecies as Isa 56:3-8.

48:1 *Dan.* Occupies its historical location as the northernmost tribe (see the phrase "from Dan to Beersheba," giving northern and southern boundaries—e.g., in Jdg 20:1; 1Sa 3:20). Dan was born to Rachel's maidservant Bilhah (Ge 35:25). *Hethlon . . . Lebo Hamath.* See note on 47:15. *Hazar Enan.* See note on 47:16.

its border from the east side to the west side.

2"Asher[r] will have one portion; it will border the territory of Dan from east to west.

3"Naphtali[s] will have one portion; it will border the territory of Asher from east to west.

4"Manasseh[t] will have one portion; it will border the territory of Naphtali from east to west.

5"Ephraim[u] will have one portion; it will border the territory of Manasseh[v] from east to west.[w]

6"Reuben[x] will have one portion; it will border the territory of Ephraim from east to west.

7"Judah[y] will have one portion; it will border the territory of Reuben from east to west.

8"Bordering the territory of Judah from east to west will be the portion you are to present as a special gift. It will be 25,000 cubits[y] wide, and its length from east to west will equal one of the tribal portions; the sanctuary will be in the center of it.[z]

9"The special portion you are to offer to the LORD will be 25,000 cubits long and 10,000 cubits[z] wide.[a] 10This will be the sacred portion for the priests. It will be 25,000 cubits long on the north side, 10,-000 cubits wide on the west side, 10,000 cubits wide on the east side and 25,000 cubits long on the south side. In the center of it will be the sanctuary of the LORD.[b] 11This will be for the consecrated priests, the Zadokites,[c] who were faithful in serving me[d] and did not go astray as the Levites did when the Israelites went astray.[e] 12It will be a special gift to them from the sacred portion of the land, a most holy portion, bordering the territory of the Levites.

13"Alongside the territory of the priests, the Levites will have an allotment 25,000 cubits long and 10,000 cubits wide. Its total length will be 25,000 cubits and its width 10,000 cubits.[f] 14They must not sell or exchange any of it. This is the best

of the land and must not pass into other hands, because it is holy to the LORD.[g]

15"The remaining area, 5,000 cubits wide and 25,000 cubits long, will be for the common use of the city, for houses and for pastureland. The city will be in the center of it 16and will have these measurements: the north side 4,500 cubits, the south side 4,500 cubits, the east side 4,500 cubits, and the west side 4,500 cubits.[h] 17The pastureland for the city will be 250 cubits on the north, 250 cubits on the south, 250 cubits on the east, and 250 cubits on the west. 18What remains of the area, bordering on the sacred portion and running the length of it, will be 10,000 cubits on the east side and 10,000 cubits on the west side. Its produce will supply food for the workers of the city.[i] 19The workers from the city who farm it will come from all the tribes of Israel. 20The entire portion will be a square, 25,000 cubits on each side. As a special gift you will set aside the sacred portion, along with the property of the city.

21"What remains on both sides of the area formed by the sacred portion and the city property will belong to the prince. It will extend eastward from the 25,000 cubits of the sacred portion to the eastern border, and westward from the 25,000 cubits to the western border. Both these areas running the length of the tribal portions will belong to the prince, and the sacred portion with the temple sanctuary will be in the center of them.[j] 22So the property of the Levites and the property of the city will lie in the center of the area that belongs to the prince. The area belonging to the prince will lie between the border of Judah and the border of Benjamin.

23"As for the rest of the tribes: Benjamin[k] will have one portion; it will extend from the east side to the west side.

24"Simeon[l] will have one portion; it

48:2
[r]Jos 19:24-31
48:3
[s]Jos 19:32-39
48:4 [r]Jos 17:1-11
48:5 [u]Jos 16:5-9
[v]Jos 17:7-10
[w]Jos 17:17
48:6
[x]Jos 13:15-21
48:7 [y]Jos 15:1-63
48:8 [z]ver 21
48:9 [a]S Eze 45:1
48:10 [b]ver 21;
S Eze 45:3-4
48:11
[c]S 2Sa 8:17
[d]S Lev 8:35
[e]Eze 14:11;
S 44:15
48:13 [f]Eze 45:5

48:14
[g]S Lev 25:34;
27:10,28
48:16
[h]Rev 21:16
48:18 [i]Eze 45:6
48:21 [j]ver 8,10;
Eze 45:7
48:23
[k]Jos 18:11-28
48:24
[l]S Ge 29:33;
Jos 19:1-9

[y]8 That is, about 7 miles (about 12 kilometers)
[z]9 That is, about 3 miles (about 5 kilometers)

48:2 *Asher.* Born to Leah's maidservant Zilpah (Ge 35:26). The tribes descended from maidservants were placed farthest from the sanctuary (see Dan, v. 1; Naphtali, v. 3; Gad, v. 27).

48:3 *Naphtali.* Born to Rachel's maidservant Bilhah (see note on v. 2).

48:4 *Manasseh.* See note on 47:13.

48:5 *Ephraim.* See note on 47:13.

48:6 *Reuben.* Leah's firstborn (Ge 29:31).

48:7 *Judah.* Son of Leah (Ge 35:23). He had the most prestigious place, bordering the central holy portion (v. 8), because his tribe was given the Messianic promise (Ge 49:8–12).

48:8–22 An expansion of 45:1–8.

48:9 *10,000 cubits wide.* The width of the entire sacred district was 20,000 cubits (see 45:1). This must refer to the width of either the priests' or the Levites' area. The Septuagint reads "20,000."

48:11 *Zadokites, who were faithful.* See note on 44:15.

48:14 *not sell or exchange.* Since it was the Lord's, it was not to be an object of commerce.

48:19 *from all the tribes of Israel.* The sacred district was national property, not the prince's private domain.

48:23 *Benjamin.* Rachel's son (Ge 35:24).

48:24 *Simeon.* Leah's son (Ge 35:23).

will border the territory of Benjamin from east to west.

^{25}"Issachar ^{m} will have one portion; it will border the territory of Simeon from east to west.

^{26}"Zebulun ^{n} will have one portion; it will border the territory of Issachar from east to west.

^{27}"Gad ^{o} will have one portion; it will border the territory of Zebulun from east to west.

^{28}"The southern boundary of Gad will run south from Tamar ^{p} to the waters of Meribah Kadesh, then along the Wadi of Egypt, to the Great Sea. ^{a} ^{q}

^{29}"This is the land you are to allot as an inheritance to the tribes of Israel, and these will be their portions," declares the Sovereign LORD. ^{r}

The Gates of the City

^{30}"These will be the exits of the city: Beginning on the north side, which is 4,-500 cubits long, ^{31}the gates of the city will

be named after the tribes of Israel. The three gates on the north side will be the gate of Reuben, the gate of Judah and the gate of Levi.

^{32}"On the east side, which is 4,500 cubits long, will be three gates: the gate of Joseph, the gate of Benjamin and the gate of Dan.

^{33}"On the south side, which measures 4,500 cubits, will be three gates: the gate of Simeon, the gate of Issachar and the gate of Zebulun.

^{34}"On the west side, which is 4,500 cubits long, will be three gates: the gate of Gad, the gate of Asher and the gate of Naphtali. ^{s}

^{35}"The distance all around will be 18,-000 cubits.

"And the name of the city from that time on will be:

THE LORD IS THERE. ^{t} "

48:25 ^{m}Jos 19:17-23
48:26 ^{n}Jos 19:10-16
48:27 ^{o}Jos 13:24-28
48:28 ^{p}S Ge 14:7 ^{q}S Nu 34:6; Eze 47:19
48:29 ^{r}S Eze 45:1
48:34 ^{s}S 2Ch 4:4; Rev 21:12-13
48:35 ^{t}S Isa 12:6; S 24:23; S Jer 3:17; 14:9; Joel 3:21; Rev 3:12; S 21:3

^{a}28 That is, the Mediterranean

48:25 *Issachar.* Leah's son (Ge 35:23).
48:26 *Zebulun.* Leah's son (Ge 35:23).
48:27 *Gad.* Son of Zilpah, Leah's maid (see note on v. 2).
48:28 *Tamar.* See note on 47:18. *Meribah Kadesh.* See note on 47:19. *Wadi of Egypt.* See note on 47:19.
48:31 *Reuben . . . Judah . . . Levi.* The three most influential tribes—Reuben, the firstborn; Judah, the Messianic tribe; Levi, the tribe of the priesthood—had gates together

on the north side. Since Levi was included in this list, Joseph (v. 32) represented Ephraim and Manasseh (see note on 47:13) in order to keep the number at 12. For the gates cf. Rev 21:12-14.
48:35 *THE LORD IS THERE.* The great decisive word concerning the holy city; in Hebrew *Yahweh-Shammah,* a possible wordplay on *Yerushalayim,* the Hebrew pronunciation of Jerusalem. For other names of Jerusalem see 23:4; Isa 1:26; 60:14; 62:2-4,12; Jer 3:17; 33:16; Zec 8:3.

DANIEL

Author, Date and Authenticity

The book mentions Daniel as its author in several passages, such as 9:2 and 10:2. That Jesus concurred is clear from his reference to " 'the abomination that causes desolation,' spoken of through the prophet Daniel" (Mt 24:15), quoting 9:27; 11:31; 12:11. The book was probably completed c. 530 B.C., shortly after the capture of Babylon by Cyrus in 539.

The widely held view that the book of Daniel is largely fictional rests mainly on the modern philosophical assumption that long-range predictive prophecy is impossible. Therefore all fulfilled predictions in Daniel, it is claimed, had to have been composed no earlier than the Maccabean period (second century B.C.), after the fulfillments had taken place. But objective evidence excludes this hypothesis on several counts:

1. To avoid fulfillment of long-range predictive prophecy in the book, the adherents of the late-date view usually maintain that the four empires of chs. 2 and 7 are Babylon, Media, Persia and Greece. But in the mind of the author, "the Medes and Persians" (5:28) together constituted the second in the series of four kingdoms (2:36-43). Thus it becomes clear that the four empires are the Babylonian, Medo-Persian, Greek and Roman. See chart on "Identification of the Four Kingdoms," p. 1311.

2. The language itself argues for a date earlier than the second century. Linguistic evidence from the Dead Sea Scrolls (which furnish authentic samples of Hebrew and Aramaic writing from the second century B.C.; see "The Time between the Testaments," p. 1431) demonstrates that the Hebrew and Aramaic chapters of Daniel must have been composed centuries earlier. Furthermore, as recently demonstrated, the Persian and Greek words in Daniel do not require a late date. Some of the technical terms appearing in ch. 3 were already so obsolete by the second century B.C. that translators of the Septuagint (the Greek translation of the OT) translated them incorrectly.

3. Several of the fulfillments of prophecies in Daniel could not have taken place by the second century anyway, so the prophetic element cannot be dismissed. The symbolism connected with the fourth kingdom makes it unmistakably predictive of the Roman empire (see 2:33; 7:7,19), which did not take control of Syro-Palestine until 63 B.C. Also, the prophecy concerning the coming of "the Anointed One, the ruler," 483 years after "the issuing of the decree to restore and rebuild Jerusalem" (9:25), works out to the time of Jesus' ministry.

Objective evidence, therefore, appears to exclude the late-date hypothesis and indicates that there is insufficient reason to deny Daniel's authorship.

Theme

The theological theme of the book is God's sovereignty: "The Most High God is sovereign over the kingdoms of men" (5:21). Daniel's visions always show God as triumphant (7:11,26-27; 8:25; 9:27; 11:45; 12:13). The climax of his sovereignty is described in Revelation: "The kingdom of the world has become the kingdom of our Lord and of his Christ, and he will reign for ever and ever" (Rev 11:15; cf. Da 2:44; 7:27).

Literary Form

The book is made up primarily of historical narrative (found mainly in chs. 1-6) and apocalyptic (revelatory) material (found mainly in chs. 7-12). The latter may be defined as symbolic, visionary, prophetic literature, usually composed during oppressive conditions and being chiefly eschatological in theological content. Apocalyptic literature is primarily a literature of encouragement to the people of God (see Introduction to Zechariah: Literary Form; see also Introduction to Revelation: Literary Form). For the symbolic use of numbers in apocalyptic literature see Introduction to Revelation: Distinctive Feature.

Daniel's Training in Babylon

1 In the third year of the reign of Jehoia-kim[a] king of Judah, Nebuchadnez-zar[b] king of Babylon[c] came to Jerusalem and besieged it.[d] 2And the Lord delivered Jehoiakim king of Judah into his hand, along with some of the articles from the temple of God. These he carried[e] off to the temple of his god in Babylonia[a] and put in the treasure house of his god.[f]

3Then the king ordered Ashpenaz, chief of his court officials, to bring in some of the Israelites from the royal family and the no-bility[g]— 4young men without any physi-cal defect, handsome,[h] showing aptitude for every kind of learning,[i] well informed, quick to understand, and qualified to serve in the king's palace. He was to teach them the language[j] and literature of the Babylo-nians.[b] 5The king assigned them a daily amount of food and wine[k] from the king's table.[l] They were to be trained for three years,[m] and after that they were to enter the king's service.[n]

6Among these were some from Judah: Daniel,[o] Hananiah, Mishael and Azariah.[p] 7The chief official gave them new names: to Daniel, the name Belteshazzar;[q] to Hananiah, Shadrach; to Mishael, Me-shach; and to Azariah, Abednego.[r]

8But Daniel resolved not to defile[s] him-self with the royal food and wine, and he asked the chief official for permission not to defile himself this way. 9Now God had caused the official to show favor[t] and sympathy[u] to Daniel, 10but the official told Daniel, "I am afraid of my lord the king,

who has assigned your[c] food and drink.[v] Why should he see you looking worse than the other young men your age? The king would then have my head because of you."

11Daniel then said to the guard whom the chief official had appointed over Dan-iel, Hananiah, Mishael and Azariah, 12"Please test[w] your servants for ten days: Give us nothing but vegetables to eat and water to drink. 13Then compare our ap-pearance with that of the young men who eat the royal food, and treat your servants in accordance with what you see."[x] 14So he agreed to this and tested[y] them for ten days.

15At the end of the ten days they looked healthier and better nourished than any of the young men who ate the royal food.[z] 16So the guard took away their choice food and the wine they were to drink and gave them vegetables instead.[a]

17To these four young men God gave knowledge and understanding[b] of all kinds of literature and learning.[c] And Daniel could understand visions and dreams of all kinds.[d]

18At the end of the time[e] set by the king to bring them in, the chief official presented them to Nebuchadnezzar. 19The king talked with them, and he found none equal to Daniel, Hananiah, Mishael and Azariah; so they entered the king's ser-vice.[f] 20In every matter of wisdom and understanding about which the king ques-tioned them, he found them ten times bet-

1:1 aS Jer 46:2
bS 2Ki 24:1;
S Jer 28:14
cJer 50:1
d2Ki 24:1;
S 2Ch 36:6;
Jer 35:11
1:2 eS 2Ki 24:13
fS 2Ch 36:7;
Jer 27:19-20;
Zec 5:5-11
1:3 gS 2Ki 20:18;
S 24:15; Isa 39:7
1:4 hS Ge 39:6
iver 17 /S Ezr 4:7
1:5 kver 8,10
lS Est 2:9 mver 18
nver 19;
S Est 2:5-6
1:6 oS Ge 14:14
pDa 2:17,25
1:7 qDa 2:26;
4:8; 5:12; 10:1
rS Isa 39:7;
Da 2:49; 3:12
1:8 sS Eze 4:13-14
1:9 tS Ge 39:21;
S Pr 16:7
uS 1Ki 8:50

1:10 vver 5
1:12 wRev 2:10
1:13 xver 10
1:14 yRev 2:10
1:15 zEx 23:25
1:16 aver 12-13
1:17 bS Job 12:13
cDa 2:23;
Col 1:9; Jas 1:5
dDa 2:19,30;
5:11; 7:1; 8:1
1:18 ever 5
1:19 fS Ge 41:46

a2 Hebrew *Shinar*   b4 Or *Chaldeans*   c10 The
Hebrew for *your* and *you* in this verse is plural.

1:1 *third year.* According to the Babylonian system of computing the years of a king's reign, the third year of Jehoiakim would have been 605 B.C., since his first full year of kingship began on New Year's Day after his accession in 608. But according to the Judahite system, which counted the year of accession as the first year of reign, this was the fourth year of Jehoiakim (Jer 25:1; 46:2).
1:2 *carried off.* Judah was exiled to Babylonia because she disobeyed God's word regarding covenant-keeping, the sab-bath years and idolatry (see Lev 25:1–7; 26:27–35; 2Ch 36:14–21). The first deportation (605 B.C.) included Daniel, and the second (597) included Ezekiel. A third deportation took place in 586, when the Babylonians destroyed Jerusa-lem and the temple.
1:4 *language and literature of the Babylonians.* Including the classical literature in Sumerian and Akkadian cuneiform, a complicated syllabic writing system. But the language of normal communication in multiracial Babylon was Aramaic, written in an easily learned alphabetic script (see 2:4).
1:6 *Daniel.* Means "God is (my) Judge." *Hananiah.* Means "The LORD shows grace." *Mishael.* Means "Who is what God is?" *Azariah.* Means "The LORD helps."
1:7 *Belteshazzar.* Probably means, in Babylonian, "Bel (i.e., Marduk), protect his life!" *Shadrach.* Probably means "command of Aku (Sumerian moon-god)." *Meshach.* Prob-

ably means "Who is what Aku is?" *Abednego.* Means "ser-vant of Nego/Nebo (i.e., Nabu)."
1:8 *royal food and wine.* Israelites considered food from Nebuchadnezzar's table to be contaminated because the first portion of it was offered to idols. Likewise a portion of the wine was poured out on a pagan altar. Ceremonially unclean animals were used and were neither slaughtered nor pre-pared according to the regulations of the law. *he asked . . . not to defile himself.* He demonstrated the courage of his convictions.
1:9 *God had caused the official to show favor . . . to Daniel.* The careers of Joseph and Daniel were similar in many respects (see Ge 39–41).
1:12 *test your servants.* Daniel used good judgment by offering an alternative instead of rebelling. *ten.* Often had the symbolic significance of completeness.
1:17 With God's help, Daniel and his friends mastered the Babylonian literature on astrology and divination by dreams. But in the crucial tests of interpretation and prediction (see 2:3–11; 4:7), all the pagan literature proved worthless. Only by God's special revelation (2:17–28) was Daniel able to interpret correctly.
1:20 *ten.* See note on v. 12. *magicians.* See note on Ge 41:8.

ter than all the magicians[g] and enchanters in his whole kingdom.[h]

[21]And Daniel remained there until the first year of King Cyrus.[i]

Nebuchadnezzar's Dream

2 In the second year of his reign, Nebuchadnezzar had dreams;[j] his mind was troubled[k] and he could not sleep.[l] [2]So the king summoned the magicians,[m] enchanters, sorcerers[n] and astrologers[d][o] to tell him what he had dreamed.[p] When they came in and stood before the king, [3]he said to them, "I have had a dream that troubles[q] me and I want to know what it means.[e]"

[4]Then the astrologers answered the king in Aramaic,[f][r] "O king, live forever![s] Tell your servants the dream, and we will interpret it."

[5]The king replied to the astrologers, "This is what I have firmly decided:[t] If you do not tell me what my dream was and interpret it, I will have you cut into pieces[u] and your houses turned into piles of rubble.[v] [6]But if you tell me the dream and explain it, you will receive from me gifts and rewards and great honor.[w] So tell me the dream and interpret it for me."

[7]Once more they replied, "Let the king tell his servants the dream, and we will interpret it."

[8]Then the king answered, "I am certain that you are trying to gain time, because you realize that this is what I have firmly decided: [9]If you do not tell me the dream, there is just one penalty[x] for you. You have conspired to tell me misleading and wicked things, hoping the situation will change. So then, tell me the dream, and I will know that you can interpret it for me."[y]

[10]The astrologers[z] answered the king, "There is not a man on earth who can do what the king asks! No king, however great and mighty, has ever asked such a thing of any magician or enchanter or astrologer.[a] [11]What the king asks is too difficult. No one can reveal it to the king ex-

cept the gods,[b] and they do not live among men."

[12]This made the king so angry and furious[c] that he ordered the execution[d] of all the wise men of Babylon. [13]So the decree was issued to put the wise men to death, and men were sent to look for Daniel and his friends to put them to death.[e]

[14]When Arioch, the commander of the king's guard, had gone out to put to death the wise men of Babylon, Daniel spoke to him with wisdom and tact. [15]He asked the king's officer, "Why did the king issue such a harsh decree?" Arioch then explained the matter to Daniel. [16]At this, Daniel went in to the king and asked for time, so that he might interpret the dream for him.

[17]Then Daniel returned to his house and explained the matter to his friends Hananiah, Mishael and Azariah.[f] [18]He urged them to plead for mercy[g] from the God of heaven[h] concerning this mystery,[i] so that he and his friends might not be executed with the rest of the wise men of Babylon. [19]During the night the mystery[j] was revealed to Daniel in a vision.[k] Then Daniel praised the God of heaven[l] [20]and said:

> "Praise be to the name of God for ever
>   and ever;[m]
>   wisdom and power[n] are his.
> [21]He changes times and seasons;[o]
>   he sets up kings[p] and deposes[q]
>   them.
> He gives wisdom[r] to the wise
>   and knowledge to the discerning.[s]
> [22]He reveals deep and hidden things;[t]
>   he knows what lies in darkness,[u]
>   and light[v] dwells with him.
> [23]I thank and praise you, O God of my
>   fathers:[w]
>   You have given me wisdom[x] and
>   power,
> you have made known to me what we
>   asked of you,

Cross references

1:20 *g*S Ge 41:8; *h*S 1Ki 4:30; Est 2:15; S Eze 28:3; Da 2:13,28; 4:18; 6:3;
1:21 *i*S 2Ch 36:22; Da 6:28; 10:1
2:1 *j*ver 3; S Ge 20:3; S Job 33:15,18; Da 4:5 *k*Ge 41:8 *l*S Est 6:1
2:2 *m*S Ge 41:8 *n*Ex 7:11; Jer 27:9 *o*S ver 10; S Isa 19:3; S 44:25 *p*Da 4:6
2:3 *q*Da 4:5
2:4 *r*S Ezr 4:7 *s*S Ne 2:3
2:5 *t*Ge 41:32 *u*ver 12 *v*Ezr 6:11; Da 3:29
2:6 *w*ver 48; Da 5:7,16
2:9 *x*Est 4:11 *y*Isa 41:22-24
2:10 *z*ver 2; Da 3:8; 4:7 *a*ver 27; Da 5:8

2:11 *b*S Ge 41:38
2:12 *c*Da 3:13,19 *d*ver 5
2:13 *e*S Da 1:20; 5:19
2:17 *f*S Da 1:6
2:18 *g*S Isa 37:4 *h*Ezr 1:2; Ne 1:4; Jnh 1:9; Rev 11:13 *i*ver 23; Jer 33:3
2:19 *j*ver 28 *k*S Job 33:15; S Da 1:17
*l*S Jos 22:33
2:20 *m*S Ps 113:2; 145:1-2 *n*S Job 9:4; S Jer 32:19
2:21 *o*Da 7:25 *p*Da 4:17 *q*S Job 12:19; Ps 75:6-7; Ro 13:1 *r*S Ps 119:34; Jas 1:5 *s*S 2Sa 14:17
2:22 *t*S Ge 40:8; S Job 12:22; Da 5:11; 1Co 2:10 *u*Job 12:22; Ps 139:11-12; Jer 23:24; S Heb 4:13 *v*Isa 45:7; Jas 1:17
2:23 *w*S Ge 31:5; S Ex 3:15 *x*S Da 1:17

d2 Or *Chaldeans*; also in verses 4, 5 and 10   **e**3 Or *was*   **f**4 The text from here through chapter 7 is in Aramaic.

1:21 *first year of King Cyrus.* Over Babylon (539 B.C.). Daniel was still living in the year 537 (10:1), so he saw the exiles return to Judah from Babylonian captivity.

2:1 *second year of . . . Nebuchadnezzar.* 604 B.C.

2:4 *Aramaic.* Since the astrologers were of various racial backgrounds, they communicated in Aramaic, the language everyone understood. From here to the end of ch. 7 the entire narrative is in Aramaic. These six chapters deal with matters of importance to the Gentile nations of the Near East and were written in a language understandable to all. But the last five chapters (8–12) revert to Hebrew, since they deal with special concerns of the chosen people.

2:11 *do not live among men.* Are not readily accessible.

2:14 *Arioch.* Meaning uncertain. It is also the name of a Mesopotamian king who lived centuries earlier (Ge 14:1,9).

2:18 *God of heaven.* See note on Ezr 1:2. *mystery.* A key word in Daniel (2:19,27–30,47; 4:9). It also appears often in the writings (Dead Sea Scrolls) of the Qumran sect (see "The Time between the Testaments," p. 1431). The Greek equivalent is used in the NT to refer to the secret purposes of God that he reveals only to his chosen prophets and apostles (see note on Ro 11:25).

2:22 *light dwells with him.* See Ps 36:9.

you have made known to us the dream of the king. *y* "

Daniel Interprets the Dream

24Then Daniel went to Arioch, *z* whom the king had appointed to execute the wise men of Babylon, and said to him, "Do not execute the wise men of Babylon. Take me to the king, and I will interpret his dream for him."

25Arioch took Daniel to the king at once and said, "I have found a man among the exiles *a* from Judah *b* who can tell the king what his dream means."

26The king asked Daniel (also called Belteshazzar), *c* "Are you able to tell me what I saw in my dream and interpret it?"

27Daniel replied, "No wise man, enchanter, magician or diviner can explain to the king the mystery he has asked about, *d* 28but there is a God in heaven who reveals mysteries. *e* He has shown King Nebuchadnezzar what will happen in days to come. *f* Your dream and the visions that passed through your mind *g* as you lay on your bed *h* are these: *i*

29"As you were lying there, O king, your mind turned to things to come, and the revealer of mysteries showed you what is going to happen. *j* 30As for me, this mystery has been revealed *k* to me, not because I have greater wisdom than other living men, but so that you, O king, may know the interpretation and that you may understand what went through your mind.

31"You looked, O king, and there before you stood a large statue—an enormous, dazzling statue, *l* awesome *m* in appearance. 32The head of the statue was made of pure gold, its chest and arms of silver, its belly and thighs of bronze, 33its legs of iron, its feet partly of iron and partly of baked clay. 34While you were watching, a rock was cut out, but not by human hands. *n* It struck the statue on its feet of iron and clay and smashed *o* them. *p* 35Then the iron, the clay, the bronze, the silver and the gold were broken to pieces at the same time and became like chaff on

a threshing floor in the summer. The wind swept them away *q* without leaving a trace. But the rock that struck the statue became a huge mountain *r* and filled the whole earth. *s*

36"This was the dream, and now we will interpret it to the king. *t* 37You, O king, are the king of kings. *u* The God of heaven has given you dominion *v* and power and might and glory; 38in your hands he has placed mankind and the beasts of the field and the birds of the air. Wherever they live, he has made you ruler over them all. *w* You are that head of gold.

39"After you, another kingdom will rise, inferior to yours. Next, a third kingdom, one of bronze, will rule over the whole earth. *x* 40Finally, there will be a fourth kingdom, strong as iron—for iron breaks and smashes everything—and as iron breaks things to pieces, so it will crush and break all the others. *y* 41Just as you saw that the feet and toes were partly of baked clay and partly of iron, so this will be a divided kingdom; yet it will have some of the strength of iron in it, even as you saw iron mixed with clay. 42As the toes were partly iron and partly clay, so this kingdom will be partly strong and partly brittle. 43And just as you saw the iron mixed with baked clay, so the people will be a mixture and will not remain united, any more than iron mixes with clay.

44"In the time of those kings, the God of heaven will set up a kingdom that will never be destroyed, nor will it be left to another people. It will crush *z* all those kingdoms *a* and bring them to an end, but it will itself endure forever. *b* 45This is the meaning of the vision of the rock *c* cut out of a mountain, but not by human hands *d*—a rock that broke the iron, the bronze, the clay, the silver and the gold to pieces.

"The great God has shown the king what will take place in the future. *e* The dream is true *f* and the interpretation is trustworthy."

46Then King Nebuchadnezzar fell pros-

2:23 *y*S Eze 28:3
2:24 *z*ver 14
2:25 *a*S Dt 21:10
*b*S Da 1:6; 5:13; 6:13
2:26 *c*S Da 1:7
2:27 *d*S ver 10; S Ge 41:8
2:28 *e*S Ge 40:8; Jer 10:7; Am 4:13
*f*S Ge 49:1; Da 10:14;
Mt 24:6; Rev 1:1;
22:6 *g*Da 4:5
*h*S Ps 5:4
*i*S Eze 28:3; S Da 1:20
2:29 *j*S Ge 41:25
2:30 *k*Isa 45:3; S Da 1:17; Am 4:13
2:31 *l*Hab 1:7
*m*Isa 25:3-5
2:34 *n*S Job 12:19; Zec 4:6
*o*S Job 34:24 *p*ver 44-45; Ps 2:9; S Isa 60:12; Da 8:25

2:35 *q*Ps 1:4; 37:10; S Isa 17:13; 41:15-16 *r*Isa 2:3; Mic 4:1 *s*Zec 12:3
2:36 *t*S Ge 40:12
2:37 *u*S Ezr 7:12
*v*S Jer 27:7; Da 4:26
2:38 *w*S Jer 27:6; Da 4:21-22; 5:18
2:39 *x*Da 7:5
2:40 *y*Da 7:7,23
2:44 *z*S Ge 27:29; Ps 2:9; S 110:5; Mt 21:43-44; 1Co 15:24 *a*S 1Sa 9:20; Hag 2:22
*b*Ps 145:13; S Isa 9:7; Da 4:34; 6:26; 7:14,27; Ob 1:21; Mic 4:7,13; S Lk 1:33; Rev 11:15
2:45 *c*S Isa 28:16
*d*Da 8:25
*e*S Ge 41:25
*f*Rev 22:6

2:32–43 See map No. 7b and map No. 13 at the end of the Study Bible. The gold head represents the Neo-Babylonian empire (v. 38; see Jer 51:7); the silver chest and arms, the Medo-Persian empire established by Cyrus in 539 B.C. (the date of the fall of Babylon); the bronze belly and thighs, the Greek empire established by Alexander the Great c. 330; the iron legs and feet, the Roman empire. The toes (v. 41) are understood by some to represent a later confederation of states occupying the territory formerly controlled by the Roman empire. The diminishing value of the metals from gold to silver to bronze to iron represents the decreasing power and grandeur (v. 39) of the rulers of the successive

empires, from the absolute despotism of Nebuchadnezzar to the democratic system of checks and balances that characterized the Roman senates and assemblies. The metals also symbolize a growing degree of toughness and endurance, with each successive empire lasting longer than the preceding one.

2:35 broken to pieces. See Mt 21:44.

2:44 The fifth kingdom is the eternal kingdom of God, built on the ruins of the sinful empires of man. Its authority will extend over "the whole earth" (v. 35) and ultimately over "a new heaven and a new earth" (Rev 21:1).

trate[g] before Daniel and paid him honor and ordered that an offering[h] and incense be presented to him. [47]The king said to Daniel, "Surely your God is the God of gods[i] and the Lord of kings[j] and a revealer of mysteries,[k] for you were able to reveal this mystery.[l] "

[48]Then the king placed Daniel in a high[m] position and lavished many gifts on him. He made him ruler over the entire province of Babylon and placed him in charge of all its wise men.[n] [49]Moreover, at Daniel's request the king appointed Shadrach, Meshach and Abednego administrators over the province of Babylon,[o] while Daniel himself remained at the royal court.[p]

The Image of Gold and the Fiery Furnace

3 King Nebuchadnezzar made an image[q] of gold, ninety feet high and nine feet[g] wide, and set it up on the plain of Dura in the province of Babylon. [2]He then summoned the satraps,[r] prefects, governors, advisers, treasurers, judges, magistrates and all the other provincial officials[s] to come to the dedication of the image he had set up. [3]So the satraps, prefects, governors, advisers, treasurers, judges, magistrates and all the other provincial officials assembled for the dedication of the image that King Nebuchadnezzar had set up, and they stood before it.

[4]Then the herald loudly proclaimed, "This is what you are commanded to do, O peoples, nations and men of every language:[t] [5]As soon as you hear the sound of the horn, flute, zither, lyre, harp,[u] pipes and all kinds of music, you must fall down and worship the image[v] of gold that King Nebuchadnezzar has set up.[w] [6]Whoever does not fall down and worship will immediately be thrown into a blazing furnace."[x]

[7]Therefore, as soon as they heard the sound of the horn, flute, zither, lyre, harp and all kinds of music, all the peoples, na-

tions and men of every language fell down and worshiped the image of gold that King Nebuchadnezzar had set up.[y]

[8]At this time some astrologers[h][z] came forward and denounced the Jews. [9]They said to King Nebuchadnezzar, "O king, live forever![a] [10]You have issued a decree,[b] O king, that everyone who hears the sound of the horn, flute, zither, lyre, harp, pipes and all kinds of music must fall down and worship the image of gold,[c] [11]and that whoever does not fall down and worship will be thrown into a blazing furnace. [12]But there are some Jews whom you have set over the affairs of the province of Babylon—Shadrach, Meshach and Abednego[d]—who pay no attention[e] to you, O king. They neither serve your gods nor worship the image of gold you have set up."[f]

[13]Furious[g] with rage, Nebuchadnezzar summoned Shadrach, Meshach and Abednego. So these men were brought before the king, [14]and Nebuchadnezzar said to them, "Is it true, Shadrach, Meshach and Abednego, that you do not serve my gods[h] or worship the image[i] of gold I have set up? [15]Now when you hear the sound of the horn, flute, zither, lyre, harp, pipes and all kinds of music, if you are ready to fall down and worship the image I made, very good. But if you do not worship it, you will be thrown immediately into a blazing furnace. Then what god[j] will be able to rescue[k] you from my hand?"

[16]Shadrach, Meshach and Abednego[l] replied to the king, "O Nebuchadnezzar, we do not need to defend ourselves before you in this matter. [17]If we are thrown into the blazing furnace, the God we serve is able to save[m] us from it, and he will rescue[n] us from your hand, O king. [18]But even if he does not, we want you to know, O king, that we will not serve your gods or worship the image of gold you have set up.[o] "

Cross references (center column)

2:46 [g]Da 8:17; Ac 10:25
[h]Ac 14:13
2:47 [i]S Dt 10:17; Da 11:36 /Da 4:25; 1Ti 6:15 [k]S ver 22,28 /Da 4:9; 1Co 14:25
2:48 [m]S 2Ki 25:28 [n]S ver 6; S Est 8:2; S Da 1:20; 4:9; 5:11; 8:27
2:49 [o]S Da 1:7; 3:30 [p]Da 6:2
3:1 [q]ver 14; S Isa 46:6; Jer 16:20; Hab 2:19
3:2 [r]S Est 1:1 [s]ver 27; Da 6:7
3:4 [t]Da 4:1; 6:25; Rev 10:11
3:5 [u]S Ge 4:21 [v]Rev 13:12 [w]ver 10,15
3:6 [x]ver 11,15, 21; Jer 29:22; Da 5:19; 6:7; Mt 13:42,50; Rev 13:15

3:7 [y]S ver 5
3:8 [z]S Isa 19:3; S Da 2:10
3:9 [a]S Ne 2:3; Da 5:10; 6:6
3:10 [b]Da 6:12 [c]ver 4-6
3:12 [d]S Da 2:49 [e]Da 6:13 /S Est 3:3
3:13 [g]S Da 2:12
3:14 [h]Isa 46:1; Jer 50:2 [i]S ver 1
3:15 /S Isa 36:18-20 [k]S 2Ch 32:15
3:16 /S Da 1:7
3:17 [m]S Ge 48:16; S Ps 18:48; 27:1-2 [n]S Job 5:19; Da 6:20
3:18 [o]ver 28; S Ex 1:17; S Jos 24:15

[g]1 Aramaic *sixty cubits high and six cubits wide* (about 27 meters high and 2.7 meters wide)   [h]8 Or *Chaldeans*

2:48 Cf. the story of Joseph (Ge 41:41–43).
3:1 *image of gold.* Large statues of this kind were not made of solid gold but were plated with gold. *ninety feet high.* Including the lofty pedestal on which it no doubt stood. *Dura.* Either the name of a place now marked by a series of mounds (located a few miles south of Babylon) or a common noun meaning "walled enclosure."
3:2 The seven classifications of government officials were to pledge full allegiance to the newly established empire as they stood before the image. The image probably represented the god Nabu, whose name formed the first element in Nebuchadnezzar's name (in Akkadian *Nabu-kudurri-usur*,

meaning "Nabu, protect my son!" or "Nabu, protect my boundary!").
3:5 The words for "zither," "harp" and "pipes" are the only Greek loanwords in Daniel. Greek musicians and instruments are mentioned in Assyrian inscriptions written before the time of Nebuchadnezzar.
3:12 *They neither serve your gods nor worship the image.* They obeyed the word of God (Ex 20:3–5) above the word of the king.
3:17 See Heb 11:34.
3:18 *if he does not.* Whether God decides to rescue them (v. 17) or not, their faith is fully resigned to his will.

¹⁹Then Nebuchadnezzar was furious with Shadrach, Meshach and Abednego, and his attitude toward them changed. He ordered the furnace heated seven [p] times hotter than usual ²⁰and commanded some of the strongest soldiers in his army to tie up Shadrach, Meshach and Abednego [q] and throw them into the blazing furnace. ²¹So these men, wearing their robes, trousers, turbans and other clothes, were bound and thrown into the blazing furnace. ²²The king's command was so urgent and the furnace so hot that the flames of the fire killed the soldiers who took up Shadrach, Meshach and Abednego, [r] ²³and these three men, firmly tied, fell into the blazing furnace.

²⁴Then King Nebuchadnezzar leaped to his feet in amazement and asked his advisers, "Weren't there three men that we tied up and threw into the fire?"

They replied, "Certainly, O king."

²⁵He said, "Look! I see four men walking around in the fire, unbound and unharmed, and the fourth looks like a son of the gods."

²⁶Nebuchadnezzar then approached the opening of the blazing furnace and shouted, "Shadrach, Meshach and Abednego, servants of the Most High God, [s] come out! Come here!"

So Shadrach, Meshach and Abednego came out of the fire, ²⁷and the satraps, prefects, governors and royal advisers [t] crowded around them. [u] They saw that the fire [v] had not harmed their bodies, nor was a hair of their heads singed; their robes were not scorched, and there was no smell of fire on them.

²⁸Then Nebuchadnezzar said, "Praise be to the God of Shadrach, Meshach and Abednego, who has sent his angel [w] and rescued [x] his servants! They trusted [y] in him and defied the king's command and were willing to give up their lives rather than serve or worship any god except their own God. [z] ²⁹Therefore I decree [a] that the people of any nation or language who say anything against the God of Shadrach, Meshach and Abednego be cut into pieces and their houses be turned into piles of rub-

ble, [b] for no other god can save [c] in this way."

³⁰Then the king promoted Shadrach, Meshach and Abednego in the province of Babylon. [d]

Nebuchadnezzar's Dream of a Tree

4 King Nebuchadnezzar,

To the peoples, nations and men of every language, [e] who live in all the world:

May you prosper greatly! [f]

²It is my pleasure to tell you about the miraculous signs [g] and wonders that the Most High God [h] has performed for me.

³How great are his signs,
    how mighty his wonders! [i]
His kingdom is an eternal kingdom;
    his dominion endures [j] from
        generation to generation.

⁴I, Nebuchadnezzar, was at home in my palace, contented [k] and prosperous. ⁵I had a dream [l] that made me afraid. As I was lying in my bed, [m] the images and visions that passed through my mind [n] terrified me. [o] ⁶So I commanded that all the wise men of Babylon be brought before me to interpret [p] the dream for me. ⁷When the magicians, [q] enchanters, astrologers [i] and diviners [r] came, I told them the dream, but they could not interpret it for me. [s] ⁸Finally, Daniel came into my presence and I told him the dream. (He is called Belteshazzar, [t] after the name of my god, and the spirit of the holy gods [u] is in him.)

⁹I said, "Belteshazzar, chief [v] of the magicians, I know that the spirit of the holy gods [w] is in you, and no mystery is too difficult for you. Here is my dream; interpret it for me. ¹⁰These are the visions I saw while lying in my bed: [x] I looked, and there before me stood a tree in the middle of the land. Its height was enormous. [y] ¹¹The tree

3:19
[p]Lev 26:18-28
3:20 [q]S Da 1:7
3:22 [r]S Da 1:7
3:26 [s]Da 4:2,34
3:27 [t]ver 2;
Da 6:7
[u]Ps 91:3-11;
S Isa 43:2;
Heb 11:32-34
[v]Da 6:23
3:28 [w]S Ps 34:7;
Da 6:22; Ac 5:19
[x]S Ps 97:10;
Ac 12:11
[y]S Dt 31:20;
S Job 13:15;
S Ps 26:1; 84:12
[z]S ver 18
3:29 [a]Da 6:26

[b]S Ezr 6:11
[c]Da 6:27
3:30 [d]S Da 2:49
4:1 [e]S Da 3:4
[f]Da 6:25
4:2 [g]Ps 74:9
[h]S Da 3:26
4:3 [i]S Ps 105:27;
Da 6:27 [j]Da 2:44
4:4 [k]Ps 30:6;
S Isa 32:9
4:5 [l]S Da 2:1
[m]Ps 4:4 [n]Da 2:28
over 19;
S Ge 41:8;
S Job 3:26;
Da 2:3; 5:6
4:6 [p]Da 2:2
4:7 [q]S Ge 41:8
[r]S Isa 44:25;
S Da 2:2
[s]S Da 2:10
4:8 [t]S Da 1:7
[u]S Ge 41:38
4:9 [v]Da 2:48
[w]Da 5:11-12
4:10 [x]S ver 5;
Ps 4:4
[y]Eze 31:3-4

[i]7 Or *Chaldeans*

3:19 The temperature was controlled by the number of bellows forcing air into the fire chamber. Therefore sevenfold intensification was achieved by seven bellows pumping at the same time. But the expression "seven times hotter than usual" may have been figurative for "as hot as possible" (seven signifies completeness).
3:25 See Ps 91:9–12. *son of the gods.* Nebuchadnezzar was speaking as a pagan polytheist and was content to conceive of the fourth figure as a lesser heavenly being (v. 28)

sent by the all-powerful God of the Israelites.
3:29 See 2:5.
4:1–3 Nebuchadnezzar reached this conclusion after the experiences of vv. 4–37. The language of his confession may reflect Daniel's influence.
4:8 *after the name of my god.* See note on 1:7. Bel ("lord") was a title for the god Marduk.
4:10 *tree.* Interpreted in v. 22.
4:11 *grew large and strong.* In one of Nebuchadnezzar's

grew large and strong and its top touched the sky; it was visible to the ends of the earth.[z] [12]Its leaves were beautiful, its fruit abundant, and on it was food for all. Under it the beasts of the field found shelter, and the birds of the air lived in its branches;[a] from it every creature was fed.

[13]"In the visions I saw while lying in my bed,[b] I looked, and there before me was a messenger,[i] a holy one,[c] coming down from heaven. [14]He called in a loud voice: 'Cut down the tree[d] and trim off its branches; strip off its leaves and scatter its fruit. Let the animals flee from under it and the birds from its branches.[e] [15]But let the stump and its roots, bound with iron and bronze, remain in the ground, in the grass of the field.

4:11
[z]S Eze 19:11;
31:5
4:12
[a]S Eze 17:23;
S Mt 13:32
4:13 [b]ver 10;
Da 7:1 [c]S ver 23;
S Dt 33:2
4:14 [d]S Job 24:20
[e]S Eze 31:12;
S Mt 3:10

4:16 [f]ver 23,32
4:17 [g]ver 2,25;
Ps 83:18
[h]S Ps 103:19;
Jer 27:5-7;
Da 2:21; 5:18-21;
Ro 13:1
[i]Da 11:21;
Mt 23:12

" 'Let him be drenched with the dew of heaven, and let him live with the animals among the plants of the earth. [16]Let his mind be changed from that of a man and let him be given the mind of an animal, till seven times[k] pass by for him.[f]

[17]" 'The decision is announced by messengers, the holy ones declare the verdict, so that the living may know that the Most High[g] is sovereign[h] over the kingdoms of men and gives them to anyone he wishes and sets over them the lowliest[i] of men.'

[18]"This is the dream that I, King Nebuchadnezzar, had. Now, Belteshazzar, tell me what it means, for none of the wise men in my kingdom

[i]13 Or *watchman*; also in verses 17 and 23   [k]16 Or *years*; also in verses 23, 25 and 32

---

building inscriptions, Babylon is compared to a spreading tree (cf. v. 22). *its top touched the sky.* A phrase often used of Mesopotamian temple-towers (see also note on Ge 11:4).
4:13 *messenger.* Angel. See NIV text note.
4:15 *let the stump . . . remain.* Implies that the tree will be revived later (see v. 26).

4:16 *seven.* Signifies completeness. *times.* See NIV text note. The term referred to a given season of the year, and so to the year as a whole (see 7:25). For example, every recurrent spring meant that another full year had elapsed since the previous spring. Alternatively, "times" can refer to indefinite periods.

The Neo-Babylonian Empire
626-539 B.C.

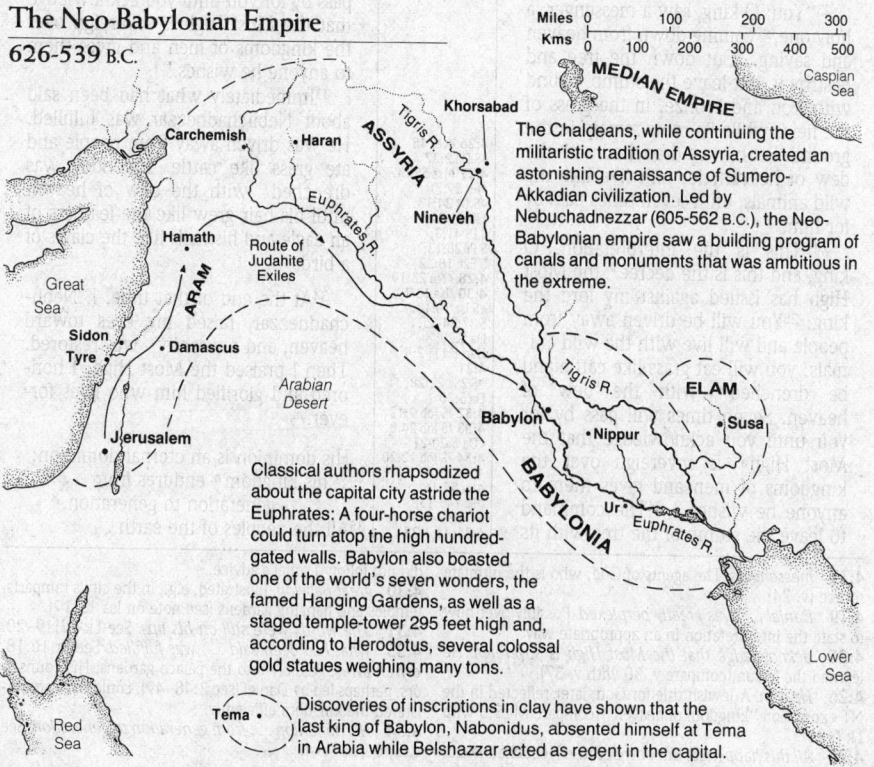

The Chaldeans, while continuing the militaristic tradition of Assyria, created an astonishing renaissance of Sumero-Akkadian civilization. Led by Nebuchadnezzar (605-562 B.C.), the Neo-Babylonian empire saw a building program of canals and monuments that was ambitious in the extreme.

Classical authors rhapsodized about the capital city astride the Euphrates: A four-horse chariot could turn atop the high hundred-gated walls. Babylon also boasted one of the world's seven wonders, the famed Hanging Gardens, as well as a staged temple-tower 295 feet high and, according to Herodotus, several colossal gold statues weighing many tons.

Discoveries of inscriptions in clay have shown that the last king of Babylon, Nabonidus, absented himself at Tema in Arabia while Belshazzar acted as regent in the capital.

can interpret it for me.[j] But you can,[k] because the spirit of the holy gods[l] is in you."[m]

Daniel Interprets the Dream

[19]Then Daniel (also called Belteshazzar) was greatly perplexed for a time, and his thoughts terrified[n] him. So the king said, "Belteshazzar, do not let the dream or its meaning alarm you."[o]

Belteshazzar answered, "My lord, if only the dream applied to your enemies and its meaning to your adversaries! [20]The tree you saw, which grew large and strong, with its top touching the sky, visible to the whole earth, [21]with beautiful leaves and abundant fruit, providing food for all, giving shelter to the beasts of the field, and having nesting places in its branches for the birds of the air[p]— [22]you, O king, are that tree![q] You have become great and strong; your greatness has grown until it reaches the sky, and your dominion extends to distant parts of the earth.[r]

[23]"You, O king, saw a messenger, a holy one,[s] coming down from heaven and saying, 'Cut down the tree and destroy it, but leave the stump, bound with iron and bronze, in the grass of the field, while its roots remain in the ground. Let him be drenched with the dew of heaven; let him live like the wild animals, until seven times pass by for him.'[t] [u]

[24]"This is the interpretation, O king, and this is the decree[v] the Most High has issued against my lord the king: [25]You will be driven away from people and will live with the wild animals; you will eat grass like cattle and be drenched[w] with the dew of heaven. Seven times will pass by for you until you acknowledge that the Most High[x] is sovereign over the kingdoms of men and gives them to anyone he wishes.[y] [26]The command to leave the stump of the tree with its roots[z] means that your kingdom will be restored to you when you acknowledge that Heaven rules.[a] [27]Therefore, O king, be pleased to accept my advice: Renounce your sins by doing what is right, and your wickedness by being kind to the oppressed.[b] It may be that then your prosperity[c] will continue.[d]"

The Dream Is Fulfilled

[28]All this happened[e] to King Nebuchadnezzar. [29]Twelve months later, as the king was walking on the roof of the royal palace of Babylon, [30]he said, "Is not this the great Babylon I have built as the royal residence, by my mighty power and for the glory[f] of my majesty?"[g]

[31]The words were still on his lips when a voice came from heaven, "This is what is decreed for you, King Nebuchadnezzar: Your royal authority has been taken from you.[h] [32]You will be driven away from people and will live with the wild animals; you will eat grass like cattle. Seven times will pass by for you until you acknowledge that the Most High is sovereign over the kingdoms of men and gives them to anyone he wishes."[i]

[33]Immediately what had been said about Nebuchadnezzar was fulfilled. He was driven away from people and ate grass like cattle. His body was drenched[j] with the dew of heaven until his hair grew like the feathers of an eagle and his nails like the claws of a bird.[k]

[34]At the end of that time, I, Nebuchadnezzar, raised my eyes toward heaven, and my sanity[l] was restored. Then I praised the Most High; I honored and glorified him who lives forever.[m]

His dominion is an eternal dominion;
    his kingdom[n] endures from
        generation to generation.[o]
[35]All the peoples of the earth

4:18 [i]S Ge 41:8; Da 5:8,15
[k]S Ge 41:15
[l]S Ge 41:38 [m]ver 7-9; S Da 1:20
4:19 [n]S ver 5; S Ge 41:8;
Da 7:15,28; 8:27; 10:16-17
[o]S Ge 40:12
4:21 [p]S Eze 31:6
4:22 [q]S 2Sa 12:7
[r]Jer 27:7;
Da 5:18-19
4:23 [s]ver 13;
Da 8:13 [t]Da 5:21
[u]S Eze 31:3-4
4:24 [v]Job 40:12;
Ps 107:40;
Jer 40:2
4:25 [w]S Job 24:8
[x]S ver 17
[y]Jer 27:5;
S Da 2:47; 5:21

4:26 [z]ver 15
[a]S Da 2:37
4:27 [b]Isa 55:6-7
[c]Jer 29:7
[d]S Dt 24:13;
1Ki 21:29;
S Ps 41:3;
S Pr 28:13;
S Eze 18:22
4:28 [e]Nu 23:19
4:30 [f]Isa 13:19
[g]S Isa 10:13;
S 37:24-25;
Da 5:20;
Hab 1:11; 2:4
4:31 [h]S 2Sa 22:28;
Da 5:20
4:32 [i]S Job 9:12
4:33 [j]S Job 24:8
[k]Da 5:20-21
4:34 [l]S Job 12:20
[m]Da 12:7
[n]Isa 37:16
[o]Ps 145:13;
S Da 2:44; 5:21;
6:26; Lk 1:33

4:17 *messengers.* The agents of God, who is the ultimate source (v. 24).

4:19 *Daniel . . . was greatly perplexed.* Possibly over how to state the interpretation in an appropriate way.

4:25 *acknowledge that the Most High is sovereign.* He learned the lesson (compare v. 30 with v. 37).

4:26 *Heaven.* A Jewish title for God, later reflected in the NT expression "kingdom of heaven" (compare Mt 5:3 with Lk 6:20).

4:28 *All this happened.* But only because Nebuchadnezzar

did not follow Daniel's advice.

4:30 *great Babylon.* Illustrated, e.g., in the city's ramparts, temples and hanging gardens (see note on Isa 13:19).

4:31 *The words were still on his lips.* See Lk 12:19–20.

4:33 *what had been said . . . was fulfilled.* See Pr 16:18. *driven away.* Possibly into the palace gardens. His counselors, perhaps led by Daniel (see 2:48–49), could have administered the kingdom efficiently.

4:34 *His dominion . . . from generation to generation.* See v. 3; 6:26; 7:14.

are regarded as nothing. *p*
He does as he pleases *q*
 with the powers of heaven
 and the peoples of the earth.
No one can hold back *r* his hand *s*
 or say to him: "What have you
 done?" *t*

³⁶At the same time that my sanity was restored, my honor and splendor were returned to me for the glory of my kingdom. *u* My advisers and nobles sought me out, and I was restored to my throne and became even greater than before. ³⁷Now I, Nebuchadnezzar, praise and exalt *v* and glorify *w* the King of heaven, because everything he does is right and all his ways are just. *x* And those who walk in pride *y* he is able to humble. *z*

The Writing on the Wall

5 King Belshazzar *a* gave a great banquet *b* for a thousand of his nobles *c* and drank wine with them. ²While Belshazzar was drinking *d* his wine, he gave orders to bring in the gold and silver goblets *e* that Nebuchadnezzar his father¹ had taken from the temple in Jerusalem, so that the king and his nobles, his wives and his concubines *f* might drink from them. *g* ³So they brought in the gold goblets that had been taken from the temple of God in Jerusalem, and the king and his nobles, his wives and his concubines drank from them. ⁴As they drank the wine, they praised the gods *h* of gold and silver, of bronze, iron, wood and stone. *i*

⁵Suddenly the fingers of a human hand appeared and wrote on the plaster of the wall, near the lampstand in the royal palace. The king watched the hand as it wrote. ⁶His face turned pale *j* and he was so frightened *k* that his knees knocked *l* together and his legs gave way. *m*

⁷The king called out for the enchanters, *n* astrologers *m o* and diviners *p* to be brought and said to these wise *q* men of Babylon, "Whoever reads this writing and tells me what it means will be clothed in

purple and have a gold chain placed around his neck, *r* and he will be made the third *s* highest ruler in the kingdom." *t*

⁸Then all the king's wise men *u* came in, but they could not read the writing or tell the king what it meant. *v* ⁹So King Belshazzar became even more terrified *w* and his face grew more pale. His nobles were baffled.

¹⁰The queen, *n* hearing the voices of the king and his nobles, came into the banquet hall. "O king, live forever!" *x* she said. "Don't be alarmed! Don't look so pale! ¹¹There is a man in your kingdom who has the spirit of the holy gods *y* in him. In the time of your father he was found to have insight and intelligence and wisdom *z* like that of the gods. *a* King Nebuchadnezzar your father—your father the king, I say—appointed him chief of the magicians, enchanters, astrologers and diviners. *b* ¹²This man Daniel, whom the king called Belteshazzar, *c* was found to have a keen mind and knowledge and understanding, and also the ability to interpret dreams, explain riddles *d* and solve difficult problems. *e* Call for Daniel, and he will tell you what the writing means. *f* "

¹³So Daniel was brought before the king, and the king said to him, "Are you Daniel, one of the exiles my father the king brought from Judah? *g* ¹⁴I have heard that the spirit of the gods *h* is in you and that you have insight, intelligence and outstanding wisdom. *i* ¹⁵The wise men and enchanters were brought before me to read this writing and tell me what it means, but they could not explain it. *j* ¹⁶Now I have heard that you are able to give interpretations and to solve difficult problems. *k* If you can read this writing and tell me what it means, you will be clothed in purple and have a gold chain placed around your neck, *l* and you will be made the third highest ruler in the kingdom." *m*

¹⁷Then Daniel answered the king, "You may keep your gifts for yourself and give

---

4:35 *p*S Isa 40:17
*q*Dt 21:8;
Ps 115:3;
S 135:6; Jnh 1:14
*r*S Isa 14:27
*s*S Dt 32:39
*t*S Job 9:4;
S Isa 14:24;
S 45:9; Da 5:21;
Ro 9:20
4:36 *u*S Pr 22:4;
Da 5:18
4:37 *v*S Ex 15:2
*w*S Ps 34:3
*x*Dt 32:4;
Ps 33:4-5
*y*Ps 18:27;
S 119:21
*z*S Job 31:4;
40:11-12;
S Isa 13:11;
Da 5:23;
Mt 23:12
5:1 *a*ver 30;
Da 7:1; 8:1
*b*S 1Ki 3:15
*c*Jer 50:35
5:2 *d*S Isa 21:5
*e*S 2Ki 24:13;
S 2Ch 36:10;
S Jer 52:19
*f*S Est 2:14
*g*S Est 1:7; Da 1:2
5:4 *h*Jdg 16:24
*i*S Est 1:10;
Ps 135:15-18;
Hab 2:19;
Rev 9:20
5:6 *j*S Job 4:15
*k*S Da 4:5
*l*S Isa 7:2
*m*S Ps 22:14;
Eze 7:17
5:7 *n*S Ge 41:8
*o*S Isa 19:3
*p*Isa 44:25
*q*Jer 50:35;
Da 4:6-7

*r*S Ge 41:42
*s*Est 10:3
*t*Da 2:5-6,48
5:8 *u*S Ex 8:18
*v*S Da 2:10;
S 4:18
5:9 *w*S Ps 48:5;
S Isa 21:4
5:10 *x*S Ne 2:3;
S Da 3:9
5:11 *y*S Ge 41:38
*z*ver 14;
S Da 1:17
*a*S Da 2:22
*b*Da 2:47-48
5:12 *c*S Da 1:7
*d*S Nu 12:8
*e*ver 14-16; Da 6:3
S Ge 28:3
5:13 *g*S Est 2:5-6;
Da 6:13
5:14 *h*S Ge 41:38
*i*S Da 2:22
5:15 *j*S Da 4:18
5:16 *k*S Ge 41:15
*l*S Ge 41:42
*m*S Est 5:3;
S Da 2:6

12 Or *ancestor*, or *predecessor*; also in verses 11, 13 and 18   *m* 7 Or *Chaldeans*; also in verse 11   *n* 10 Or *queen mother*

4:36 See Job 42:10,12.
4:37 *those who walk in pride he is able to humble.* See Pr 3:34; Jas 4:10; 1Pe 5:5–6.
5:1–4 The orgy of revelry and blasphemy on such occasions is confirmed by the ancient Greek historians Herodotus and Xenophon.
5:1 *King.* Belshazzar (meaning "Bel, protect the king!") was the son and viceroy of Nabonidus. He is called the "son" of Nebuchadnezzar (v. 22), but the Aramaic term could also mean "grandson" or "descendant" or even "successor" (see NIV text note on v. 22). See also note on v. 10 and NIV text

note on v. 2.
5:5 *Suddenly.* See notes on 4:31; 1Th 5:3.
5:7 *third highest ruler in the kingdom.* Nabonidus was first, Belshazzar second.
5:10 *queen.* See NIV text note. She could have been (1) the wife of Nebuchadnezzar, or (2) the daughter of Nebuchadnezzar and wife of Nabonidus, or (3) the wife of Nabonidus but not the daughter of Nebuchadnezzar.
5:11 *the time of your father.* Nebuchadnezzar died in 562 B.C.; the year is now 539.
5:17 *keep your gifts for yourself.* See Ge 14:23 and note.

your rewards to someone else. [n] Nevertheless, I will read the writing for the king and tell him what it means.

[18]"O king, the Most High God gave your father Nebuchadnezzar [o] sovereignty and greatness and glory and splendor. [p] [19]Because of the high position he gave him, all the peoples and nations and men of every language dreaded and feared him. Those the king wanted to put to death, he put to death; [q] those he wanted to spare, he spared; those he wanted to promote, he promoted; and those he wanted to humble, he humbled. [r] [20]But when his heart became arrogant and hardened with pride, [s] he was deposed from his royal throne [t] and stripped [u] of his glory. [v] [21]He was driven away from people and given the mind of an animal; he lived with the wild donkeys and ate grass like cattle; and his body was drenched with the dew of heaven, until he acknowledged that the Most High God is sovereign [w] over the kingdoms of men and sets over them anyone he wishes. [x]

[22]"But you his son, [o] O Belshazzar, have not humbled [y] yourself, though you knew all this. [23]Instead, you have set yourself up against [z] the Lord of heaven. You had the goblets from his temple brought to you, and you and your nobles, your wives [a] and your concubines drank wine from them. You praised the gods of silver and gold, of bronze, iron, wood and stone, which cannot see or hear or understand. [b] But you did not honor the God who holds in his hand your life [c] and all your ways. [d] [24]Therefore he sent the hand that wrote the inscription.

[25]"This is the inscription that was written:

MENE, MENE, TEKEL, PARSIN [p]

[26]"This is what these words mean:

Mene [q]: God has numbered the days [e] of your reign and brought it to an end. [f]

[27]Tekel [r]: You have been weighed on the scales [g] and found wanting. [h]

[28]Peres [s]: Your kingdom is divided and given to the Medes [i] and Persians." [j]

[29]Then at Belshazzar's command, Daniel was clothed in purple, a gold chain was placed around his neck, [k] and he was proclaimed the third highest ruler in the kingdom. [l]

[30]That very night Belshazzar, [m] king [n] of the Babylonians, [t] was slain, [o] [31]and Darius [p] the Mede [q] took over the kingdom, at the age of sixty-two.

Daniel in the Den of Lions

6 It pleased Darius [r] to appoint 120 satraps [s] to rule throughout the kingdom, [2]with three administrators over them, one of whom was Daniel. [t] The satraps were made accountable [u] to them so that the king might not suffer loss. [3]Now Daniel so distinguished himself among the administrators and the satraps by his exceptional qualities that the king planned to set him over the whole kingdom. [v] [4]At this, the administrators and the satraps tried to find grounds for charges [w] against Daniel in his conduct of government affairs, but they were unable to do so. They could find no corruption in him, because he was trustworthy and neither corrupt nor negligent. [5]Finally these men said, "We will never find any basis for charges against this man Daniel unless it has something to do with the law of his God." [x]

[6]So the administrators and the satraps went as a group to the king and said: "O King Darius, live forever! [y] [7]The royal administrators, prefects, satraps, advisers and

---

5:17 [n]S 2Ki 5:16
5:18 [o]S Jer 28:14
[p]S Jer 27:7;
S Da 2:37-38;
S 4:36
5:19 [q]Da 2:12-13;
S 3:6 [r]S Da 4:22
5:20 [s]Da 4:30
[t]Jer 43:10
[u]Jer 13:18;
S Da 4:31
[v]S Job 40:12;
Isa 14:13-15;
Eze 31:10-11;
Da 8:8
5:21 [w]S Eze 17:24
[x]Da 4:16-17,35
5:22 [y]S Ex 10:3
5:23 [z]S Isa 14:13;
S Jer 50:29
[a]Jer 44:9
[b]Ps 115:4-8;
Hab 2:19;
Rev 9:20
[c]Job 12:10;
Ac 17:28
[d]S Job 31:4;
S Isa 13:11;
Jer 10:23; S 48:26
5:26 [e]Jer 27:7
[f]Isa 13:6

5:27 [g]S Job 6:2
[h]Ps 62:9
5:28 [i]Isa 13:17
[j]S Jer 27:7;
50:41-43;
Da 6:28
5:29 [k]S Ge 41:42
[l]S Da 2:6
5:30 [m]S ver 1
[n]Jer 50:35
[o]S Isa 21:9;
S Jer 51:31
5:31 [p]Jer 50:41;
Da 6:1; 9:1; 11:1
[q]S Isa 13:3
6:1 [r]S Da 5:31
[s]S Est 1:1
6:2 [t]Da 2:48-49
[u]Ezr 4:22
6:3 [v]S Ge 41:41;
S Est 10:3;
S Da 1:20;
5:12-14
6:4 [w]Jer 20:10
6:5 [x]Ac 24:13-16
6:6 [y]S Ne 2:3

[o]22 Or *descendant;* or *successor*   [p]25 Aramaic *UPARSIN* (that is, *AND PARSIN*)   [q]26 *Mene* can mean *numbered* or *mina* (a unit of money).   [r]27 *Tekel* can mean *weighed* or *shekel.*   [s]28 *Peres* (the singular of *Parsin*) can mean *divided* or *Persia* or *a half mina* or *a half shekel.*   [t]30 Or *Chaldeans*

5:21 *until he acknowledged.* See note on 4:25.
5:22–23 Three charges were brought against Belshazzar: (1) He sinned not through ignorance but through disobedience and pride (v. 22); (2) he defied God by desecrating the sacred vessels (v. 23a); and (3) he praised idols and so did not honor God (v. 23b).
5:26–28 See NIV text notes. Three weights (mina, shekel, and half mina/shekel) may be intended, symbolizing three rulers (respectively): (1) Nebuchadnezzar, (2) either Evil-Merodach (2Ki 25:27; Jer 52:31) or Nabonidus, and (3) Belshazzar.
5:27 *weighed on the scales.* Measured in the light of God's standards (cf. Job 31:6; Ps 62:9; Pr 24:12).
5:28 *Medes and Persians.* The second kingdom of the

series of four predicted in ch. 2 (see Introduction: Author, Date and Authenticity).
5:30 *That very night.* See Pr 29:1; Lk 12:20.
5:31 *Darius the Mede.* Perhaps another name for Gubaru, referred to in Babylonian inscriptions as the governor that Cyrus put in charge of the newly conquered Babylonian territories. Or "Darius the Mede" may have been Cyrus's throne name in Babylon (see NIV text note on 6:28; see also 1Ch 5:26 for a similar phenomenon). *took over the kingdom.* The head of gold is now no more, as predicted in 2:39.
6:7 The conspirators lied in stating that "all" the royal administrators supported the proposed decree, since they knew that Daniel (totally unaware of the proposal) was the foremost of the three administrators.

governors[z] have all agreed that the king should issue an edict and enforce the decree that anyone who prays to any god or man during the next thirty days, except to you, O king, shall be thrown into the lions' den.[a] [8]Now, O king, issue the decree and put it in writing so that it cannot be altered—in accordance with the laws of the Medes and Persians, which cannot be repealed."[b] [9]So King Darius put the decree in writing.

[10]Now when Daniel learned that the decree had been published, he went home to his upstairs room where the windows opened toward[c] Jerusalem. Three times a day he got down on his knees[d] and prayed, giving thanks to his God, just as he had done before.[e] [11]Then these men went as a group and found Daniel praying and asking God for help.[f] [12]So they went to the king and spoke to him about his royal decree: "Did you not publish a decree that during the next thirty days anyone who prays to any god or man except to you, O king, would be thrown into the lions' den?"

The king answered, "The decree stands—in accordance with the laws of the Medes and Persians, which cannot be repealed."[g]

[13]Then they said to the king, "Daniel, who is one of the exiles from Judah,[h] pays no attention[i] to you, O king, or to the decree you put in writing. He still prays three times a day." [14]When the king heard this, he was greatly distressed;[j] he was determined to rescue Daniel and made every effort until sundown to save him.

[15]Then the men went as a group to the king and said to him, "Remember, O king, that according to the law of the Medes and Persians no decree or edict that the king issues can be changed."[k]

[16]So the king gave the order, and they brought Daniel and threw him into the lions' den.[l] The king said to Daniel, "May your God, whom you serve continually, rescue[m] you!"

[17]A stone was brought and placed over the mouth of the den, and the king sealed[n] it with his own signet ring and with the rings of his nobles, so that Daniel's situation might not be changed. [18]Then the king returned to his palace and

spent the night without eating[o] and without any entertainment being brought to him. And he could not sleep.[p]

[19]At the first light of dawn, the king got up and hurried to the lions' den. [20]When he came near the den, he called to Daniel in an anguished voice, "Daniel, servant of the living God, has your God, whom you serve continually, been able to rescue you from the lions?"[q]

[21]Daniel answered, "O king, live forever![r] [22]My God sent his angel,[s] and he shut the mouths of the lions.[t] They have not hurt me, because I was found innocent in his sight.[u] Nor have I ever done any wrong before you, O king."

[23]The king was overjoyed and gave orders to lift Daniel out of the den. And when Daniel was lifted from the den, no wound[v] was found on him, because he had trusted[w] in his God.

[24]At the king's command, the men who had falsely accused Daniel were brought in and thrown into the lions' den,[x] along with their wives and children.[y] And before they reached the floor of the den, the lions overpowered them and crushed all their bones.[z]

[25]Then King Darius wrote to all the peoples, nations and men of every language[a] throughout the land:

"May you prosper greatly![b]

[26]"I issue a decree that in every part of my kingdom people must fear and reverence[c] the God of Daniel.[d]

"For he is the living God[e]
    and he endures forever;[f]
his kingdom will not be destroyed,
    his dominion will never end.[g]
[27]He rescues and he saves;[h]
    he performs signs and wonders[i]
    in the heavens and on the earth.
He has rescued Daniel
    from the power of the lions."[j]

[28]So Daniel prospered during the reign of Darius and the reign of Cyrus[u][k] the Persian.[l]

Daniel's Dream of Four Beasts

7 In the first year of Belshazzar[m] king of Babylon, Daniel had a dream, and vi-

[u]28 Or *Darius, that is, the reign of Cyrus*

6:7 [z]S Da 3:2
[a]Ps 59:3; 64:2-6;
S Da 3:6
6:8 [b]S Est 1:19
6:10 [c]S 1Ki 8:29
[d]Ps 95:6 [e]Mt 6:6;
Ac 5:29
6:11 [f]1Ki 8:48-50;
Ps 55:17;
1Th 5:17-18
6:12 [g]S Est 1:19;
Da 3:8-12
6:13 [h]S Eze 14:14;
Da 2:25 [i]S Est 3:8
6:14 [j]Mk 6:26
6:15 [k]S Est 8:8
6:16 [l]S ver 7
[m]S Job 5:19;
Ps 37:39-40;
S 97:10
6:17 [n]Mt 27:66

6:18 [o]S 2Sa 12:17;
Da 10:3
[p]S Est 6:1
6:20 [q]S Da 3:17
6:21 [r]S Ne 2:3;
Da 3:9
6:22 [s]S Ge 32:1;
S Da 3:28 [t]ver 27; S Ps 91:11-13;
Heb 11:33
[u]Ac 12:11;
2Ti 4:17
6:23 [v]Da 3:27
[w]S 1Ch 5:20;
S Isa 12:2
6:24
[x]Dt 19:18-19;
Est 7:9-10;
Ps 54:5
[y]Dt 24:16;
2Ki 14:6
[z]S Isa 38:13
6:25 [a]S Da 3:4
[b]Da 4:1
6:26 [c]S Ps 5:7
[d]S Est 8:17;
Ps 99:1-3;
Da 3:29
[e]S Jos 2:11;
S 3:10
[f]S Jer 10:10;
Da 12:7; Rev 1:18
[g]S Da 2:44
6:27 [h]Da 3:29
[i]S Da 4:3
[j]S ver 22
6:28
[k]S 2Ch 36:22;
S Da 1:21
[l]S Da 5:28
7:1 [m]S Da 5:1

6:10 *toward Jerusalem.* See 2Ch 6:38–39. *Three times a day.* See Ps 55:17.
6:16 *serve continually.* See 1Co 15:58.
6:23 *he . . . trusted in his God.* That the lions were ravenously hungry (v. 24) was no obstacle to the Lord's rewarding

Daniel's faith by saving his life.
6:24 *along with their wives and children.* In accordance with Persian custom.
7:1 *first year of Belshazzar.* Probably 553 B.C. The events of ch. 7 preceded those of ch. 5.

sions[n] passed through his mind[o] as he was lying on his bed.[p] He wrote[q] down the substance of his dream.

[2]Daniel said: "In my vision at night I looked, and there before me were the four winds of heaven[r] churning up the great sea. [3]Four great beasts,[s] each different from the others, came up out of the sea.

[4]"The first was like a lion,[t] and it had the wings of an eagle.[u] I watched until its wings were torn off and it was lifted from the ground so that it stood on two feet like a man, and the heart of a man was given to it.

[5]"And there before me was a second beast, which looked like a bear. It was raised up on one of its sides, and it had three ribs in its mouth between its teeth. It was told, 'Get up and eat your fill of flesh!'[v]

[6]"After that, I looked, and there before me was another beast, one that looked like a leopard.[w] And on its back it had four wings like those of a bird. This beast had four heads, and it was given authority to rule.

[7]"After that, in my vision[x] at night I looked, and there before me was a fourth beast—terrifying and frightening and very powerful. It had large iron[y] teeth; it crushed and devoured its victims and trampled[z] underfoot whatever was left.[a] It was different from all the former beasts, and it had ten horns.[b]

[8]"While I was thinking about the horns, there before me was another horn, a little[c] one, which came up among them; and three of the first horns were uprooted before it. This horn had eyes like the eyes of a man[d] and a mouth that spoke boastfully.[e]

[9]"As I looked,

"thrones were set in place,

and the Ancient of Days[f] took his seat.[g]
His clothing was as white as snow;[h]
    the hair of his head was white like wool.[i]
His throne was flaming with fire,
    and its wheels[j] were all ablaze.
[10]A river of fire[k] was flowing,
    coming out from before him.[l]
Thousands upon thousands attended him;
    ten thousand times ten thousand stood before him.
The court was seated,
    and the books[m] were opened.

[11]"Then I continued to watch because of the boastful words the horn was speaking.[n] I kept looking until the beast was slain and its body destroyed and thrown into the blazing fire.[o] [12](The other beasts had been stripped of their authority, but were allowed to live for a period of time.)

[13]"In my vision at night I looked, and there before me was one like a son of man,[p] coming[q] with the clouds of heaven.[r] He approached the Ancient of Days and was led into his presence. [14]He was given authority,[s] glory and sovereign power; all peoples, nations and men of every language worshiped him.[t] His dominion is an everlasting dominion that will not pass away, and his kingdom[u] is one that will never be destroyed.[v]

The Interpretation of the Dream

[15]"I, Daniel, was troubled in spirit, and the visions that passed through my mind disturbed me.[w] [16]I approached one of those standing there and asked him the true meaning of all this.

"So he told me and gave me the interpretation[x] of these things: [17]'The four

Cross references (center column)

7:1 [n]S Eze 40:2
[o]S Da 1:17
[p]Ps 4:4;
S Da 4:13
[q]S Jer 36:4
7:2 [r]S Eze 37:9;
Da 8:8; 11:4;
Rev 7:1
7:3 [s]Rev 13:1
7:4 [t]S 2Ki 24:1;
Ps 7:2; Jer 4:7;
Rev 13:2
[u]S Eze 17:3
7:5 [v]Da 2:39
7:6 [w]Rev 13:2
7:7 [x]S Eze 40:2
[y]S Da 2:40
[z]Da 8:10 [a]Da 8:7
[b]S Rev 12:3
7:8 [c]Da 8:9
[d]Rev 9:7
[e]S Ps 12:3;
Rev 13:5-6

7:9 [f]ver 22
[g]S 1Ki 22:19;
2Ch 18:18;
Mt 19:28;
Rev 4:2; 20:4
[h]S Mt 28:3
[i]Rev 1:14
[j]S Eze 1:15; 10:6
7:10 [k]Ps 50:3;
97:3; Isa 30:27
[l]S Dt 33:2;
Ps 68:17;
Jude 1:14;
Rev 5:11
[m]S Ex 32:32;
S Ps 56:8;
Rev 20:11-15
7:11 [n]Rev 13:5-6
[o]Rev 19:20
7:13 [p]S Eze 1:5;
S 2:1; Mt 8:20*;
Rev 1:13*;
14:14* [q]Isa 13:6;
Zep 1:14;
Mal 3:2; 4:1
[r]S Dt 33:26;
S Rev 1:7
7:14 [s]S Mt 28:18
[t]Ps 72:11; 102:22
[u]S Isa 16:5
[v]S Da 2:44;
Heb 12:28;
Rev 11:15
7:15 [w]S Job 4:15;
S Da 4:19
7:16 [x]Da 8:16;
9:22; Zec 1:9

Footnotes (bottom)

7:2 *the great sea.* The world of nations and peoples (see also vv. 3,17).

7:3 *beasts.* The insignia or symbols of many Gentile nations were beasts (or birds) of prey (see v. 17).

7:4—7 The lion with an eagle's wings is a cherub (see note on Ge 3:24), symbolizing the Neo-Babylonian empire. The rest of v. 4 perhaps reflects the humbling experience of Nebuchadnezzar, as recorded in ch. 4. The bear (v. 5), raised up on one of its sides, refers to the superior status of the Persians in the Medo-Persian federation. The three ribs may represent the three principal conquests: Lydia (546 B.C.), Babylon (539) and Egypt (525). The leopard with four wings (v. 6) represents the speedy conquests of Alexander the Great (334–330), and the four heads correspond to the four main divisions into which his empire fell after his untimely death in 323 (see 8:22): Macedon and Greece (under Antipater and Cassander), Thrace and Asia Minor (under Lysimachus), Syria (under Seleucus I), Palestine and Egypt (under Ptolemy I). The fourth, unnamed, beast (v. 7), with its

irresistible power and surpassing all its predecessors, points to the Roman empire. Its ten horns correspond to the ten toes of 2:41–42.

7:7 *ten horns.* Indicative of the comprehensiveness of the beast's sphere of authority (see note on 1:12).

7:8 *another horn, a little one.* The antichrist, or a world power sharing in the characteristics of the antichrist. *mouth that spoke boastfully.* See 11:36; 2Th 2:4; Rev 13:5–6.

7:9 *Ancient of Days.* God. *throne . . . wheels.* See Eze 1:15–21,26–27.

7:10 *Thousands . . . ten thousand.* See 1Sa 18:7 and note.

7:13 *like a son of man.* See Rev 1:13. This is the first reference to the Messiah as the Son of Man, a title that Jesus applied to himself. He will be enthroned as ruler over the whole earth (previously misruled by the four kingdoms of men), and his kingdom "will never be destroyed" (v. 14), whether on earth or in heaven. *coming with the clouds of heaven.* See Mk 14:62; Rev 1:7.

7:16 *one of those standing there.* An angel.

great beasts are four kingdoms that will rise from the earth. [18]But the saints[y] of the Most High will receive the kingdom[z] and will possess it forever—yes, for ever and ever.' [a]

[19]"Then I wanted to know the true meaning of the fourth beast, which was different from all the others and most terrifying, with its iron teeth and bronze claws—the beast that crushed and devoured its victims and trampled underfoot whatever was left. [20]I also wanted to know about the ten horns[b] on its head and about the other horn that came up, before which three of them fell—the horn that looked more imposing than the others and that had eyes and a mouth that spoke boastfully.[c] [21]As I watched, this horn was waging war against the saints and defeating them,[d] [22]until the Ancient of Days came and pronounced judgment in favor of the saints of the Most High, and the time came when they possessed the kingdom. [e]

[23]"He gave me this explanation: 'The fourth beast is a fourth kingdom that will appear on earth. It will be different from all the other kingdoms and will devour the whole earth, trampling it down and crushing it.[f] [24]The ten horns[g] are ten kings who will come from this kingdom. After them another king will arise, different from the earlier ones; he will subdue three kings. [25]He will speak against the Most High[h] and oppress his saints[i] and try to change the set times[j] and the laws. The saints will be handed over to him for a time, times and half a time.[v] [k]

[26]" 'But the court will sit, and his power will be taken away and completely destroyed[l] forever. [27]Then the sovereignty, power and greatness of the kingdoms[m] un-

7:18 [y]S Ps 16:3; [z]S Ps 49:14; [a]Isa 60:12-14; Lk 12:32; Heb 12:28; Rev 2:26; 20:4
7:20 [b]Rev 17:12
[c]Rev 13:5-6
7:21 [d]Rev 13:7

7:22 [e]Mk 8:35
7:23 [f]S Da 2:40
7:24 [g]Rev 17:12
7:25 [h]S Isa 37:23; Da 11:36
[i]Rev 16:6
[j]Da 2:21; Mk 1:15; Lk 21:8; Ac 1:6-7
[k]Da 8:24; 12:7; S Rev 11:2
7:26 [l]Rev 19:20
7:27 [m]S Isa 14:2

[v]25 Or for a year, two years and half a year

7:18 saints. Exalted privileges will be enjoyed by Christ's followers during the Messianic kingdom age (Mt 19:28–29; Lk 22:29–30). See also Rev 1:6; 20:4–6.
7:24 ten kings. All the political powers (see note on 1:12) that will arise out of the fourth kingdom—not necessarily simultaneously (but see 2:44). three kings. Some of the ten. Three often signified a small, indefinite number.
7:25 He. See note on v. 8. a time, times and half a time. See NIV text note.
7:27 handed over to the saints. For their benefit. God and

Identification of the Four Kingdoms

Chronology of Major Empires in Daniel

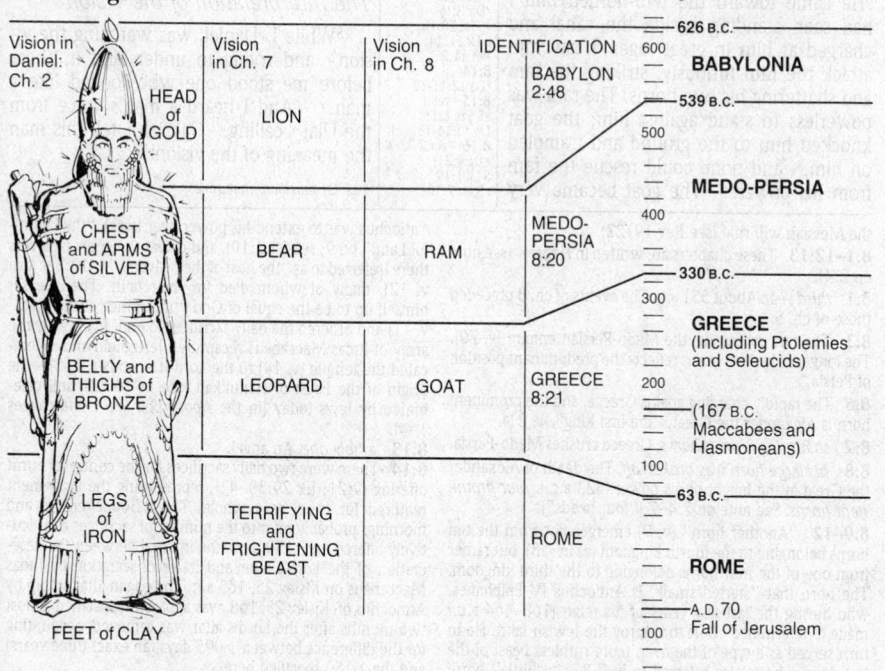

Vision in Daniel: Ch. 2	Vision in Ch. 7	Vision in Ch. 8	IDENTIFICATION		
HEAD of GOLD	LION		BABYLON 2:48	600	626 B.C. BABYLONIA
					539 B.C.
				500	
CHEST and ARMS of SILVER	BEAR	RAM	MEDO-PERSIA 8:20	400	MEDO-PERSIA
				300	330 B.C.
BELLY and THIGHS of BRONZE	LEOPARD	GOAT	GREECE 8:21	200	GREECE (Including Ptolemies and Seleucids)
					(167 B.C. Maccabees and Hasmoneans)
				100	63 B.C.
LEGS of IRON	TERRIFYING and FRIGHTENING BEAST		ROME		ROME
FEET of CLAY				100	A.D. 70 Fall of Jerusalem

der the whole heaven will be handed over to the saints,[n] the people of the Most High.[o] His kingdom will be an everlasting[p] kingdom, and all rulers will worship[q] and obey him.'

28"This is the end of the matter. I, Daniel, was deeply troubled[r] by my thoughts,[s] and my face turned pale,[t] but I kept the matter to myself."

Daniel's Vision of a Ram and a Goat

8 In the third year of King Belshazzar's[u] reign, I, Daniel, had a vision,[v] after the one that had already appeared to me. [2]In my vision I saw myself in the citadel of Susa[w] in the province of Elam;[x] in the vision I was beside the Ulai Canal. [3]I looked up,[y] and there before me was a ram[z] with two horns, standing beside the canal, and the horns were long. One of the horns was longer than the other but grew up later. [4]I watched the ram as he charged toward the west and the north and the south. No animal could stand against him, and none could rescue from his power.[a] He did as he pleased[b] and became great.

[5]As I was thinking about this, suddenly a goat with a prominent horn between his eyes came from the west, crossing the whole earth without touching the ground. [6]He came toward the two-horned ram I had seen standing beside the canal and charged at him in great rage. [7]I saw him attack the ram furiously, striking the ram and shattering his two horns. The ram was powerless to stand against him; the goat knocked him to the ground and trampled on him,[c] and none could rescue the ram from his power.[d] [8]The goat became very

great, but at the height of his power his large horn was broken off,[e] and in its place four prominent horns grew up toward the four winds of heaven.[f]

[9]Out of one of them came another horn, which started small[g] but grew in power to the south and to the east and toward the Beautiful Land.[h] [10]It grew until it reached[i] the host of the heavens, and it threw some of the starry host down to the earth[j] and trampled[k] on them. [11]It set itself up to be as great as the Prince[l] of the host;[m] it took away the daily sacrifice[n] from him, and the place of his sanctuary was brought low.[o] [12]Because of rebellion, the host of the saints,[w] and the daily sacrifice were given over to it. It prospered in everything it did, and truth was thrown to the ground.[p]

[13]Then I heard a holy one[q] speaking, and another holy one said to him, "How long will it take for the vision to be fulfilled[r]—the vision concerning the daily sacrifice, the rebellion that causes desolation, and the surrender of the sanctuary and of the host that will be trampled[s] underfoot?"

[14]He said to me, "It will take 2,300 evenings and mornings; then the sanctuary will be reconsecrated."[t]

The Interpretation of the Vision

[15]While I, Daniel, was watching the vision[u] and trying to understand it, there before me stood one who looked like a man.[v] [16]And I heard a man's voice from the Ulai[w] calling, "Gabriel,[x] tell this man the meaning of the vision."[y]

7:27 [n] 1Co 6:2
[o] Ge 14:18
[p] S 2Sa 7:13;
Ps 145:13;
S Da 2:44; S 4:34;
S Lk 1:33;
Rev 11:15; 22:5
[q] S Ps 22:27;
72:11; 86:9
7:28 [r] S Isa 21:3;
S Da 4:19
[s] S Ps 13:2
[t] S Job 4:15
8:1 [u] S Da 5:1
[v] S Da 1:17
8:2 [w] S Ezr 4:9;
S Est 2:8
[x] S Ge 10:22
8:3 [y] Da 10:5
[z] Rev 13:11
8:4 [a] Isa 41:3
[b] Da 11:3,16
8:7 [c] S Da 7:7
[d] Da 11:11,16

8:8
[e] 2Ch 26:16-21;
S Da 5:20
[f] S Da 7:2; Rev 7:1
8:9 [g] Da 7:8;
[h] S Eze 20:6;
Da 11:16
8:10 [i] S Isa 14:13
[j] Rev 8:10; 12:4
[k] S Da 7:7
8:11 [l] ver 25
[m] Da 11:36-37
[n] Eze 46:13-14
[o] Da 11:31; 12:11
8:12 [p] S Isa 48:1
8:13 [q] S Dt 33:2;
S Da 4:23
[r] Da 12:6
[s] S Isa 28:18;
S Lk 21:24;
Rev 11:2
8:14
[t] Da 12:11-12
8:15 [u] ver 1
[v] S Eze 2:1;
Da 10:16-18
8:16 [w] ver 2
[x] Da 9:21;
S Lk 1:19
[y] S Da 7:16

[w] 12 Or *rebellion, the armies*

---

the Messiah will rule (see Rev 19–22).

8:1–12:13 These chapters are written in Hebrew (see note on 2:4).

8:1 *third year.* About 551 B.C. The events of ch. 8 preceded those of ch. 5.

8:3 The ram represents the Medo-Persian empire (v. 20). The longer of his two horns reflects the predominant position of Persia.

8:5 The rapidly charging goat is Greece, and the prominent horn is Alexander the Great, "the first king" (v. 21).

8:7 *shattering his two horns.* Greece crushes Medo-Persia.

8:8 *his large horn was broken off.* The death of Alexander the Great at the height of his power (323 B.C.). *four prominent horns.* See note on 7:4–7 ("four heads").

8:9–12 "Another horn" (v. 9) emerges not from the ten horns belonging to the fourth kingdom (as in 7:8), but rather from one of the four horns belonging to the third kingdom. The horn that "started small" is Antiochus IV Epiphanes, who during the last few years of his reign (168–164 B.C.) made a determined effort to destroy the Jewish faith. He in turn served as a type of the even more ruthless beast of the last days, who is also referred to in 7:8 as a "little" horn.

Antiochus was to extend his power over Israel, "the Beautiful Land" (v. 9; see Jer 3:19), and defeat the godly believers there (referred to as "the host of the heavens," v. 10; see also v. 12), many of whom died for their faith. Then he set himself up to be the equal of God ("the Prince of the host," v. 11) and ordered the daily sacrifices to end. Eventually the army of Judas Maccabeus recaptured Jerusalem and rededicated the temple (v. 14) to the Lord (December, 165)—the origin of the Feast of Hanukkah (see Jn 10:22), still celebrated by Jews today (in the Apocrypha see 1 Maccabees 1–4).

8:13 *a holy one.* An angel.

8:14 There were two daily sacrifices for the continual burnt offering (9:21; Ex 29:38–42), representing the atonement required for Israel as a whole. The 2,300 evenings and mornings probably refer to the number of sacrifices consecutively offered on 1,150 days, the interval between the desecration of the Lord's altar and its reconsecration by Judas Maccabeus on Kislev 25, 165 B.C. The pagan altar set up by Antiochus on Kislev 25, 168, was apparently installed almost two months after the Lord's altar was removed, accounting for the difference between 1,095 days (an exact three years) and the 1,150 specified here.

17 As he came near the place where I was standing, I was terrified and fell prostrate.[z] "Son of man," he said to me, "understand that the vision concerns the time of the end."[a]

18 While he was speaking to me, I was in a deep sleep, with my face to the ground.[b] Then he touched me and raised me to my feet.[c]

19 He said: "I am going to tell you what will happen later in the time of wrath,[d] because the vision concerns the appointed time[e] of the end.[x][f] 20 The two-horned ram that you saw represents the kings of Media and Persia.[g] 21 The shaggy goat is the king of Greece,[h] and the large horn between his eyes is the first king.[i] 22 The four horns that replaced the one that was broken off represent four kingdoms that will emerge from his nation but will not have the same power.

23 "In the latter part of their reign, when rebels have become completely wicked, a stern-faced king, a master of intrigue, will arise. 24 He will become very strong, but not by his own power. He will cause astounding devastation and will succeed in whatever he does. He will destroy the mighty men and the holy people.[j] 25 He will cause deceit[k] to prosper, and he will consider himself superior. When they feel secure, he will destroy many and take his stand against the Prince of princes.[l] Yet he will be destroyed, but not by human power.[m]

26 "The vision of the evenings and mornings that has been given you is true,[n] but seal[o] up the vision, for it concerns the distant future."[p]

27 I, Daniel, was exhausted and lay ill[q] for several days. Then I got up and went about the king's business.[r] I was appalled[s] by the vision; it was beyond understanding.

Daniel's Prayer

9 In the first year of Darius[t] son of Xerxes[y][u] (a Mede by descent), who was made ruler over the Babylonian[z] kingdom— 2 in the first year of his reign, I, Daniel, understood from the Scriptures, according to the word of the LORD given to Jeremiah the prophet, that the desolation of Jerusalem would last seventy[v] years. 3 So I turned to the Lord God and pleaded with him in prayer and petition, in fasting,[w] and in sackcloth and ashes.[x]

4 I prayed to the LORD my God and confessed:[y]

"O Lord, the great and awesome God,[z] who keeps his covenant of love[a] with all who love him and obey his commands, 5 we have sinned[b] and done wrong.[c] We have been wicked and have rebelled; we have turned away[d] from your commands and laws.[e] 6 We have not listened[f] to your servants the prophets,[g] who spoke in your name to our kings, our princes and our fathers,[h] and to all the people of the land.

7 "Lord, you are righteous,[i] but this day we are covered with shame[j]—the men of Judah and people of Jerusalem and all Israel, both near and far, in all the countries where you have scattered[k] us because of our unfaithfulness[l] to you.[m] 8 O LORD, we and our kings, our princes and our fathers are covered with shame because we have sinned against you.[n] 9 The Lord our God is merciful and forgiving,[o] even though we have rebelled against him;[p] 10 we have not obeyed the LORD our God or kept the laws he gave us through his servants the prophets.[q] 11 All Israel has transgressed[r] your law[s] and turned away, refusing to obey you.

"Therefore the curses[t] and sworn judgments[u] written in the Law of Moses, the servant of God, have been poured out on us, because we have sinned[v] against you. 12 You have fulfilled[w] the words spoken against us and against our rulers by bringing upon us great disaster.[x] Under the whole heaven nothing has ever been done like[y] what has been done to

[x] *19* Or *because the end will be at the appointed time*
[y] *1* Hebrew *Ahasuerus* [z] *1* Or *Chaldean*

8:17 [z]Eze 1:28; 44:4; S Da 2:46; Rev 1:17 [a]ver 19; Hab 2:3 **8:18** [b]Da 10:9 [c]S Eze 2:2; Da 10:16-18; Zec 4:1 **8:19** [d]S Isa 10:25 [e]S Ps 102:13 [f]Hab 2:3 **8:20** [g]S Eze 27:10 **8:21** [h]Da 10:20 [i]Da 11:3 **8:24** [j]S Da 7:25; 11:36 **8:25** [k]Da 11:23 [l]Da 11:36 [m]S Da 2:34; 11:21 **8:26** [n]Da 10:1 [o]S Isa 8:16; S 29:11; Rev 10:4; 22:10 [p]Da 10:14 **8:27** [q]Da 10:8 [r]S Da 2:48 [s]S Isa 21:3; S Da 4:19 **9:1** [t]S Da 5:31 [u]S Ezr 4:6 **9:2** [v]S 2Ch 36:21; Jer 29:10; Zec 1:12; 7:5 **9:3** [w]S 2Ch 20:3 [x]S 2Sa 13:19; S Ne 1:4; Jer 29:12; Da 10:12; Jnh 3:6 **9:4** [y]S 1Ki 8:30 [z]S Dt 7:21 [a]Dt 7:9; S 1Ki 8:23 **9:5** [b]S Jer 8:14 [c]Ps 106:6 [d]Isa 53:6 [e]ver 11; La 1:20; S 3:42 **9:6** [f]S 2Ki 18:12 [g]S 2Ch 36:16; S Jer 44:5; Jas 5:10; Rev 10:7 [h]S 2Ch 29:6 **9:7** [i]S Ezr 9:15; S Isa 42:6 [j]Ezr 9:7; Ps 44:15 [k]Dt 4:27; Am 9:9 [l]S Dt 7:3 [m]S Jer 3:25; S 24:9; S Eze 39:23-24 **9:8** [n]S Ne 9:33; S Jer 14:20; S Eze 16:63 **9:9** [o]S Ex 34:7; S 2Sa 24:14; Jer 42:12 [p]S Ne 9:17; Jer 14:7 **9:10** [q]2Ki 17:13-15; S 18:12; Rev 10:7 **9:11** [r]S Jer 2:29 [s]2Ki 22:16 [t]S Dt 11:26; S 13:15; S 28:15 [u]2Ki 17:23 [v]Isa 1:4-6; Jer 8:5-10 **9:12** [w]S Isa 44:26; Zec 1:6 [x]S Jer 44:23 [y]Jer 30:7

8:17 *Son of man.* See note on Eze 2:1.
8:23–25 A description of Antiochus IV and his rise to power by intrigue and deceit (he was not the rightful successor to the Seleucid throne).
8:25 *Prince of princes.* God. *destroyed, but not by human power.* Antiochus died in 164 B.C. at Tabae in Persia through illness or accident; God "destroyed" him.
9:1 *first year.* 539–538 B.C. *Xerxes.* See NIV text note; not the later Xerxes of the book of Esther.
9:2 *Jeremiah . . . seventy years.* See note on Jer 25:11–12.
9:3–19 Daniel's prayer contains humility (v. 3), worship (v. 4), confession (vv. 5–15) and petition (vv. 16–19).
9:3 *sackcloth and ashes.* See note on Ge 37:34.
9:11 *curses . . . written in the Law.* See Lev 26:33; Dt 28:63–67.

Jerusalem.[z] [13]Just as it is written in the Law of Moses, all this disaster has come upon us, yet we have not sought the favor of the LORD[a] our God by turning from our sins and giving attention to your truth.[b] [14]The LORD did not hesitate to bring the disaster[c] upon us, for the LORD our God is righteous in everything he does;[d] yet we have not obeyed him.[e]

[15]"Now, O Lord our God, who brought your people out of Egypt with a mighty hand[f] and who made for yourself a name[g] that endures to this day, we have sinned, we have done wrong. [16]O Lord, in keeping with all your righteous acts,[h] turn away[i] your anger and your wrath[j] from Jerusalem,[k] your city, your holy hill.[l] Our sins and the iniquities of our fathers have made Jerusalem and your people an object of scorn[m] to all those around us.

[17]"Now, our God, hear the prayers and petitions of your servant. For your sake, O Lord, look with favor[n] on your desolate sanctuary. [18]Give ear,[o] O God, and hear;[p] open your eyes and see[q] the desolation of the city that bears your Name.[r] We do not make requests of you because we are righteous, but because of your great mercy.[s] [19]O Lord, listen! O Lord, forgive![t] O Lord, hear and act! For your sake,[u] O my God, do not delay, because your city and your people bear your Name."

The Seventy "Sevens"

[20]While I was speaking and praying, confessing[v] my sin and the sin of my people Israel and making my request to the LORD my God for his holy hill[w]— [21]while I was still in prayer, Gabriel,[x] the man I had seen in the earlier vision, came to me in swift flight about the time of the evening sacrifice.[y] [22]He instructed me and said to me, "Daniel, I have now come to give you insight and understanding.[z] [23]As soon as you began to pray,[a] an answer was given, which I have come to tell you, for you are highly esteemed.[b] Therefore, consider the message and understand the vision:[c]

[24]"Seventy 'sevens'[a] are decreed for your people and your holy city[d] to finish[b] transgression, to put an end to sin, to atone[e] for wickedness, to bring in everlasting righteousness,[f] to seal up vision and prophecy and to anoint the most holy.[c]

[25]"Know and understand this: From the issuing of the decree[d] to restore and rebuild[g] Jerusalem until the Anointed One,[e] [h] the ruler,[i] comes, there will be seven 'sevens,' and sixty-two 'sevens.' It will be rebuilt with streets and a trench, but in times of trouble.[j] [26]After the sixty-two 'sevens,' the Anointed One will be cut off[k] and will have nothing.[f] The people of the ruler who will come will destroy the city and the sanctuary. The end will come like a flood:[l] War will continue until the end, and desolations[m] have been decreed.[n] [27]He will confirm a covenant with many for one 'seven.'[g] In the middle of the 'seven'[g] he will put an end to sacrifice

---

Cross references (center column):

9:12 [z]Jer 44:2-6; Eze 5:9; Da 12:1; Joel 2:2; Zec 7:12
9:13 [a]S Dt 4:29; S Isa 31:1; Jer 2:30
[b]S Isa 9:13; S 44:27
9:14 [c]S Jer 18:8; [d]S Ge 18:25; S 2Ch 12:6; S Jer 12:1; [e]S Ne 9:33; S Jer 32:23; S 40:3
9:15 [f]S Ex 3:20; S Jer 32:21 [g]S Ne 9:10
9:16 [h]S Jdg 5:11; Ps 31:1; [i]S Isa 5:25; [j]S Ps 85:3 [k]Jer 32:32 [l]S Ex 15:17; S Ps 48:1 [m]S Ps 39:8; S Eze 5:14
9:17 [n]Nu 6:24-26; Ps 80:19
9:18 [o]S Ps 5:1 [p]Ps 116:1 [q]Ps 80:14 [r]S Dt 28:10; S Isa 37:17; Jer 7:10-12; 25:29 [s]Lk 18:13
9:19 [t]Ps 44:23 [u]S 1Sa 12:22
9:20 [v]S Ezr 10:1

[w]S ver 3; Ps 145:18; S Isa 58:9
9:21 [x]S Da 8:16; S Lk 1:19 [y]S Ex 29:39
9:22 [z]S Da 7:16; 10:14; Am 3:7
9:23 [a]S Isa 65:24 [b]Da 10:19; Lk 1:28 [c]Da 10:11-12; Mt 24:15
9:24 [d]S Isa 1:26 [e]S Isa 53:10 [f]S Isa 56:1; Heb 9:12
9:25 [g]S Ezr 4:24; S 6:15 [h]Mt 1:17; Jn 4:25 [i]S 1Sa 13:14 [j]S Ezr 3:3
9:26 [k]S Isa 53:8; Mt 16:21

[l]Isa 28:2; Da 11:10; Na 1:8 [m]Ps 46:8 [n]Isa 61:1; S Eze 4:5-6; Hag 2:23; Zec 4:14

[a]24 Or 'weeks'; also in verses 25 and 26   [b]24 Or restrain   [c]24 Or Most Holy Place; or most holy One   [d]25 Or word   [e]25 Or an anointed one; also in verse 26   [f]26 Or off and will have no one; or off, but not for himself   [g]27 Or 'week'

9:18 *because of your great mercy.* God answers prayer because of his grace, not because of our works.
9:20 *While I was speaking.* See Isa 65:24.
9:24 *sevens.* Probably seven-year periods of time, making a total of 490 years, but the numbers may be symbolic. Of the six purposes mentioned (all to be fulfilled through the Messiah), some believe that the last three were not achieved by the crucifixion and resurrection of Christ but await his further action: the establishment of everlasting righteousness (on earth), the complete fulfillment of vision and prophecy, and the anointing of the "most holy" (see NIV text note).
9:25-27 The time between the decree authorizing the rebuilding of Jerusalem (v. 25) and the coming of the Messiah ("the Anointed One") was to be 69 (7 plus 62) "sevens," or 483 years (see note on Ezr 7:11). The "seven 'sevens' " may refer to the period of the complete restoration of Jerusalem (partially narrated in Ezra and Nehemiah) and the "sixty-two 'sevens' " to the period between that restoration and the Messiah's coming to Israel. The final (70th) "seven" is not mentioned specifically until v. 27, following the prophecy of the destruction of Jerusalem by "the people

of the ruler who will come" (Titus in A.D. 70). Therefore, while many hold that the 70th "seven" was fulfilled during Christ's earthly ministry and the years immediately following, others conclude that there is an indeterminate interval between the 69th and the 70th "seven"—a period of "war" and "desolation" (v. 26). According to this latter opinion, in the 70th "seven" the little horn or beast of the last days (referred to here as the one who sets up an "abomination that causes desolation" and who is the antitype of the Roman Titus) will establish a covenant for seven years with the Jews (the "many") but will violate the covenant halfway through that period (but see also note on v. 27). The cutting off of the Anointed One (v. 26) refers to the crucifixion of Christ.
9:27 *He will confirm a covenant ... will put an end to sacrifice.* According to some, a reference to the Messiah's ("the Anointed One," v. 26) instituting the new covenant and putting "an end" to the OT sacrificial system; according to others, a reference to the antichrist's ("the [ultimate] ruler who will come," v. 26) making a treaty with the Jews in the future and then disrupting their system of worship. *abomination that causes desolation.* See note on 11:31.

and offering. And on a wing of the temple, he will set up an abomination that causes desolation, until the end that is decreed[o] is poured out on him."[h]"[i]

Daniel's Vision of a Man

10 In the third year of Cyrus[p] king of Persia, a revelation was given to Daniel (who was called Belteshazzar).[q] Its message was true[r] and it concerned a great war.[j] The understanding of the message came to him in a vision.

[2]At that time I, Daniel, mourned[s] for three weeks. [3]I ate no choice food; no meat or wine touched my lips;[t] and I used no lotions at all until the three weeks were over.

[4]On the twenty-fourth day of the first month, as I was standing on the bank[u] of the great river, the Tigris,[v] [5]I looked up[w] and there before me was a man dressed in linen,[x] with a belt of the finest gold[y] around his waist. [6]His body was like chrysolite,[z] his face like lightning,[a] his eyes like flaming torches,[b] his arms and legs like the gleam of burnished bronze,[c] and his voice[d] like the sound of a multitude.

[7]I, Daniel, was the only one who saw the vision; the men with me did not see it,[e] but such terror overwhelmed them that they fled and hid themselves. [8]So I was left alone,[f] gazing at this great vision; I had no strength left,[g] my face turned deathly pale[h] and I was helpless.[i] [9]Then I heard him speaking, and as I listened to him, I fell into a deep sleep, my face to the ground.[j]

[10]A hand touched me[k] and set me trembling on my hands and knees.[l] [11]He said, "Daniel, you who are highly esteemed,[m] consider carefully the words I am about to speak to you, and stand up,[n] for I have now been sent to you." And when he said this to me, I stood up trembling.

[12]Then he continued, "Do not be afraid,[o] Daniel. Since the first day that you set your mind to gain understanding and to humble[p] yourself before your God, your

words[q] were heard, and I have come in response to them.[r] [13]But the prince[s] of the Persian kingdom resisted me twenty-one days. Then Michael,[t] one of the chief princes, came to help me, because I was detained there with the king of Persia. [14]Now I have come to explain[u] to you what will happen to your people in the future,[v] for the vision concerns a time yet to come."[w]

[15]While he was saying this to me, I bowed with my face toward the ground and was speechless.[x] [16]Then one who looked like a man[k] touched my lips, and I opened my mouth and began to speak.[y] I said to the one standing before me, "I am overcome with anguish[z] because of the vision, my lord, and I am helpless. [17]How can I, your servant, talk with you, my lord? My strength is gone and I can hardly breathe."[a]

[18]Again the one who looked like a man touched[b] me and gave me strength.[c] [19]"Do not be afraid, O man highly esteemed,"[d] he said. "Peace![e] Be strong now; be strong."[f]

When he spoke to me, I was strengthened and said, "Speak, my lord, since you have given me strength."[g]

[20]So he said, "Do you know why I have come to you? Soon I will return to fight against the prince of Persia, and when I go, the prince of Greece[h] will come; [21]but first I will tell you what is written in the Book of Truth.[i] (No one supports me against them except Michael,[j] your

11 prince. [1]And in the first year of Darius[k] the Mede, I took my stand to support and protect him.)

The Kings of the South and the North

[2]"Now then, I tell you the truth:[l] Three more kings will appear in Persia, and

9:27 oS Isa 10:22
10:1 pS Da 1:21
qS Da 1:7
rDa 8:26
10:2 sS Ezr 9:4
10:3 tS Da 6:18
10:4 uDa 12:5
vS Ge 2:14
10:5 wDa 8:3;
xS Eze 9:2;
Rev 15:6
yJer 10:9
10:6 zS Ex 28:20
aMt 17:2; S 28:3
bJob 41:19;
Rev 19:12
cS Eze 1:7;
S Rev 1:15
dS Eze 1:24
10:7
e2Ki 6:17-20;
Ac 9:7
10:8 fGe 32:24
Da 8:27
gS Job 4:15
hHab 3:16
10:9 iDa 8:18;
Mt 17:6
10:10 kJer 1:9
lRev 1:17
10:11 mS Ge 6:9;
Da 9:23
nS Eze 2:1
10:12
oS Mt 14:27
pS Lev 16:31;
S Da 9:3

qS Isa 65:24
rDa 9:20
10:13 sIsa 24:21
tver 21; Da 12:1;
S Jude 1:9
10:14 uS Da 9:22
vS Eze 12:27
wS Da 2:28;
8:26; Hab 2:3
10:15
xEze 24:27;
Lk 1:20
10:16 yS Isa 6:7;
Jer 1:9;
Da 8:15-18
zS Isa 21:3
10:17 aS Da 4:19
10:18 bver 16
cS Da 8:18
10:19 dS Da 9:23
eJdg 6:23;
S Isa 35:4 fJos 1:9
gIsa 6:1-8
10:20 hDa 8:21;
11:2
10:21 iDa 11:2
jS ver 13;
S Jude 1:9
11:1 kS Da 5:31
11:2 lDa 10:21

h[27] Or it   i[27] Or And one who causes desolation will come upon the pinnacle of the abominable temple, until the end that is decreed is poured out on the desolated city,   j[1] Or true and burdensome   k[16] Most manuscripts of the Masoretic Text; one manuscript of the Masoretic Text, Dead Sea Scrolls and Septuagint Then something that looked like a man's hand

---

10:1 third year of Cyrus. The third year after his conquest of Babylonia in 539 B.C.
10:3 See 1:8–16.
10:5–6 See Rev 1:12–16.
10:7 Cf. Ac 9:7.
10:13 prince of the Persian kingdom. Apparently a demon exercising influence over the Persian realm in the interests of Satan (see also v. 20). His resistance was finally overcome by the archangel Michael, "the great prince who protects" the people of God (12:1).

10:20 prince of Greece. See note on v. 13. This spiritual power will also be opposed.
10:21 Book of Truth. See 12:1; perhaps a reference to the divine record of the destinies of all human beings (see note on Ex 32:32).
11:1 Darius the Mede. See note on 5:31.
11:2 Three more kings. Cambyses (530–522 B.C.), Pseudo-Smerdis or Gaumata (522) and Darius I (522–486). fourth. Xerxes I (486–465), who attempted to conquer Greece in 480 (see note on Est 1:1).

then a fourth, who will be far richer than all the others. When he has gained power by his wealth, he will stir up everyone against the kingdom of Greece. *m* ³Then a mighty king will appear, who will rule with great power and do as he pleases. *n* ⁴After he has appeared, his empire will be broken up and parceled out toward the four winds of heaven. *o* It will not go to his descendants, nor will it have the power he exercised, because his empire will be uprooted *p* and given to others.

⁵"The king of the South will become strong, but one of his commanders will become even stronger than he and will rule his own kingdom with great power. ⁶After some years, they will become allies. The daughter of the king of the South will go to the king of the North to make an alliance, but she will not retain her power, and he and his power¹ will not last. In those days she will be handed over, together with her royal escort and her father *m* and the one who supported her.

⁷"One from her family line will arise to take her place. He will attack the forces of the king of the North *q* and enter his fortress; he will fight against them and be victorious. ⁸He will also seize their gods, *r* their metal images and their valuable articles of silver and gold and carry them off to Egypt. *s* For some years he will leave the king of the North alone. ⁹Then the king of the North will invade the realm of the king of the South but will retreat to his own country. ¹⁰His sons will prepare for war and assemble a great army, which will sweep on like an irresistible flood *t* and carry the battle as far as his fortress.

¹¹"Then the king of the South will march out in a rage and fight against the king of the North, who will raise a large army, but it will be defeated. *u* ¹²When the army is carried off, the king of the South will be filled with pride and will slaughter many thousands, yet he will not remain triumphant. ¹³For the king of the North will muster another army, larger than the first; and after several years, he will advance with a huge army fully equipped.

¹⁴"In those times many will rise against the king of the South. The violent men among your own people will rebel in fulfillment of the vision, but without success. ¹⁵Then the king of the North will come and build up siege ramps *v* and will capture a fortified city. The forces of the South will be powerless to resist; even their best troops will not have the strength to stand. ¹⁶The invader will do as he pleases; *w* no one will be able to stand against him. *x* He will establish himself in the Beautiful Land and will have the power to destroy it. *y* ¹⁷He will determine to come with the might of his entire kingdom and will make an alliance with the king of the South. And he will give him a daughter in marriage in order to overthrow the kingdom, but his plans *n* will not succeed *z* or help him. ¹⁸Then he will turn his attention to the coastlands *a* and will take many of them, but a commander will put an end to his insolence and will turn his insolence back upon him. *b* ¹⁹After this, he will turn back toward the fortresses of his own country

Cross references (center column)

11:2
m S Da 10:20
11:3 *n* S Da 8:4, 21
11:4 *o* S Da 7:2; 8:22 *p* S Jer 42:10
11:7 *q* ver 6
11:8 *r* Isa 37:19; S 46:1-2 *s* Jer 43:12
11:10 *t* Isa 8:8; Jer 46:8; S Da 9:26

11:11 *u* Da 8:7-8
11:15 *v* S Eze 4:2
11:16 *w* S Da 8:4 *x* S Jos 1:5; S Da 8:7 *y* S Da 8:9
11:17 *z* S Ps 20:4
11:18 *a* S Isa 66:19; S Jer 25:22 *b* Hos 12:14

16 Or *offspring*   m 6 Or *child* (see Vulgate and Syriac)   n 17 Or *but she*

11:3 *mighty king.* Alexander the Great (336–323).
11:4 *four winds.* See note on 7:4–7 ("four heads").
11:5 *king of the South.* Ptolemy I Soter (323–285 B.C.) of Egypt. *one of his commanders.* Seleucus I Nicator (311–280). *his own kingdom.* Initially Babylonia, to which he then added extensive territories both east and west.
11:6 *daughter of the king of the South.* Berenice, daughter of Ptolemy II Philadelphus (285–246 B.C.) of Egypt. *king of the North.* Antiochus II Theos (261–246) of Syria. *alliance.* A treaty cemented by the marriage of Berenice to Antiochus. *she will not retain her power, and he . . . will not last.* Antiochus's former wife, Laodice, conspired to have Berenice and Antiochus put to death. *her father.* Berenice's father Ptolemy died at about the same time.
11:7 *One from her family line.* Berenice's brother, Ptolemy III Euergetes (246–221 B.C.) of Egypt, who did away with Laodice. *king of the North.* Seleucus II Callinicus (246–226 B.C.) of Syria. *his fortress.* Either (1) Seleucia (see Ac 13:4), which was the port of Antioch, or (2) Antioch itself.
11:8 *their gods.* Images of Syrian deities, and also of Egyptian gods that the Persian Cambyses had carried off after conquering Egypt in 525 B.C.
11:10 *His sons.* Seleucus III Ceraunus (226–223 B.C.) and

Antiochus III (the Great) (223–187), sons of Seleucus II. *his fortress.* Ptolemy's fortress at Raphia in southern Palestine.
11:11 *king of the South.* Ptolemy IV Philopator (221–203 B.C.) of Egypt. *king of the North.* Antiochus III. *defeated.* At Raphia in 217.
11:12 *slaughter many thousands.* The historian Polybius records that Antiochus lost nearly 10,000 infantrymen at Raphia.
11:14 *king of the South.* Ptolemy V Epiphanes (203–181 B.C.) of Egypt. *violent men among your own people.* Jews who joined the forces of Antiochus. *without success.* The Ptolemaic general Scopas crushed the rebellion in 200.
11:15 *fortified city.* The Mediterranean port of Sidon.
11:16 *The invader.* Antiochus, who was in control of Palestine by 197 B.C. *Beautiful Land.* See note on 8:9–12.
11:17 *he will give him a daughter in marriage.* Antiochus gave his daughter Cleopatra I in marriage to Ptolemy V in 194 B.C.
11:18 *he.* Antiochus. *coastlands.* Asia Minor and perhaps also mainland Greece. *commander.* The Roman consul Lucius Cornelius Scipio Asiaticus, who defeated Antiochus at Magnesia in Asia Minor in 190 B.C.
11:19 *stumble and fall.* Antiochus died in 187 B.C. while

but will stumble and fall,[c] to be seen no more.[d]

[20]"His successor will send out a tax collector to maintain the royal splendor.[e] In a few years, however, he will be destroyed, yet not in anger or in battle.

[21]"He will be succeeded by a contemptible[f] person who has not been given the honor of royalty.[g] He will invade the kingdom when its people feel secure, and he will seize it through intrigue. [22]Then an overwhelming army will be swept away[h] before him; both it and a prince of the covenant will be destroyed.[i] [23]After coming to an agreement with him, he will act deceitfully,[j] and with only a few people he will rise to power. [24]When the richest provinces feel secure, he will invade them and will achieve what neither his fathers nor his forefathers did. He will distribute plunder, loot and wealth among his followers.[k] He will plot the overthrow of fortresses—but only for a time.

[25]"With a large army he will stir up his strength and courage against the king of the South. The king of the South will wage war with a large and very powerful army, but he will not be able to stand because of the plots devised against him. [26]Those who eat from the king's provisions will try to destroy him; his army will be swept away, and many will fall in battle. [27]The two kings, with their hearts bent on evil,[l] will sit at the same table and lie[m] to each other, but to no avail, because an end will still come at the appointed time.[n] [28]The king of the North will return to his own country with great wealth, but his heart will be set

against the holy covenant. He will take action against it and then return to his own country.

[29]"At the appointed time he will invade the South again, but this time the outcome will be different from what it was before. [30]Ships of the western coastlands[o][o] will oppose him, and he will lose heart.[p] Then he will turn back and vent his fury[q] against the holy covenant. He will return and show favor to those who forsake the holy covenant.

[31]"His armed forces will rise up to desecrate the temple fortress and will abolish the daily sacrifice.[r] Then they will set up the abomination that causes desolation.[s] [32]With flattery he will corrupt those who have violated the covenant, but the people who know their God will firmly resist[t] him.

[33]"Those who are wise will instruct[u] many, though for a time they will fall by the sword or be burned or captured or plundered.[v] [34]When they fall, they will receive a little help, and many who are not sincere[w] will join them. [35]Some of the wise will stumble, so that they may be refined,[x] purified and made spotless until the time of the end, for it will still come at the appointed time.

The King Who Exalts Himself

[36]"The king will do as he pleases. He will exalt and magnify himself[y] above every god and will say unheard-of things[z] against the God of gods.[a] He will be suc-

Cross references (center column)

11:19 cS Ps 27:2; S 46:2
dPs 37:36; S Eze 26:21
11:20 eIsa 60:17
11:21 fDa 4:17
gS Da 8:25
11:22 hS Isa 28:15
iDa 8:10-11
11:23 jDa 8:25
11:24 kNe 9:25
11:27 lPs 64:6
mPs 12:2; Jer 9:5
nHab 2:3

11:30 oS Ge 10:4
pS 1Sa 17:32
qS Job 15:13
11:31 rHos 3:4
sS Jer 19:4;
Da 8:11-13;
S 9:27;
Mt 24:15*;
Mk 13:14*
11:32 tMic 5:7-9
11:33 uDa 12:3;
Mal 2:7
vMt 24:9;
Jn 16:2;
Heb 11:32-38
11:34 wMt 7:15;
Ro 16:18
11:35
xS Job 28:1;
S Ps 78:38;
S Isa 48:10;
Da 12:10;
Zec 13:9; Jn 15:2
11:36 yJude 1:16
zRev 13:5-6
aS Dt 10:17;
S Isa 14:13-14;
S Da 7:25;
8:11-12,25;
2Th 2:4

o30 Hebrew of Kittim

---

attempting to plunder a temple in the province of Elymais.
11:20 *His successor.* Seleucus IV Philopator (187–175 B.C.), son and successor of Antiochus the Great. *tax collector.* Seleucus's finance minister, Heliodorus. *he will be destroyed.* Seleucus was the victim of a conspiracy engineered by Heliodorus.
11:21 *contemptible person.* Seleucus's younger brother, Antiochus IV Epiphanes (175–164 B.C.). *not been given the honor of royalty.* Antiochus seized power while the rightful heir to the throne, the son of Seleucus (later to become Demetrius I), was still very young. *kingdom.* Syro-Palestine.
11:22 *prince of the covenant.* Either the high priest Onias III, who was murdered in 170 B.C., or, if the Hebrew for this phrase is translated "confederate prince," Ptolemy VI Philometor (181–146) of Egypt.
11:23 *he.* Antiochus.
11:24 *richest provinces.* Either of Palestine or of Egypt. *fortresses.* In Egypt.
11:25 *king of the South.* Ptolemy VI.
11:26 *his army.* That of Ptolemy.
11:27 *two kings.* Antiochus and Ptolemy, who was living in Antiochus's custody.
11:28 *against the holy covenant.* In 169 B.C. Antiochus plundered the temple in Jerusalem, set up a garrison there and massacred many Jews in the city.

11:30 *Ships of the western coastlands.* Roman vessels under the command of Popilius Laenas. *those who forsake the holy covenant.* Apostate Jews (see also v. 32).
11:31 *abomination that causes desolation.* See 9:27; 12:11; the altar to the pagan god Zeus Olympius, set up in 168 B.C. by Antiochus Epiphanes and prefiguring a similar abomination that Jesus predicted would be erected (see note on Mt 24:15; see also Lk 21:20).
11:33 *Those who are wise.* The godly leaders of the Jewish resistance movement, also called the Hasidim. *fall by the sword or be burned or captured or plundered.* See Heb 11:36–38.
11:34 *a little help.* The early successes of the guerrilla uprising (168 B.C.) that originated in Modein, 17 miles northwest of Jerusalem, under the leadership of Mattathias and his son Judas Maccabeus. In December, 165, the altar of the temple was rededicated.
11:35 *time of the end.* See v. 40; 12:4,9. Daniel concludes his predictions about Antiochus Epiphanes and begins to prophesy concerning the more distant future.
11:36 From here to the end of ch. 11 the antichrist (see notes on 7:8; 9:27) is in view. The details of this section do not fit what is known of Antiochus Epiphanes. See 2Th 2:4; cf. Rev 13:5–8.

cessful until the time of wrath[b] is completed, for what has been determined must take place.[c] 37He will show no regard for the gods of his fathers or for the one desired by women, nor will he regard any god, but will exalt himself above them all. 38Instead of them, he will honor a god of fortresses; a god unknown to his fathers he will honor with gold and silver, with precious stones and costly gifts. 39He will attack the mightiest fortresses with the help of a foreign god and will greatly honor those who acknowledge him. He will make them rulers over many people and will distribute the land at a price.[p]

40"At the time of the end the king of the South[d] will engage him in battle, and the king of the North will storm[e] out against him with chariots and cavalry and a great fleet of ships. He will invade many countries and sweep through them like a flood.[f] 41He will also invade the Beautiful Land.[g] Many countries will fall, but Edom,[h] Moab[i] and the leaders of Ammon will be delivered from his hand. 42He will extend his power over many countries; Egypt will not escape. 43He will gain control of the treasures of gold and silver and all the riches of Egypt,[j] with the Libyans[k] and Nubians in submission. 44But reports

from the east and the north will alarm him, and he will set out in a great rage to destroy and annihilate many. 45He will pitch his royal tents between the seas at[q] the beautiful holy mountain.[l] Yet he will come to his end, and no one will help him.

The End Times

12 "At that time Michael,[m] the great prince who protects your people, will arise. There will be a time of distress[n] such as has not happened from the beginning of nations until then. But at that time your people—everyone whose name is found written in the book[o]—will be delivered.[p] 2Multitudes who sleep in the dust of the earth will awake:[q] some to everlasting life, others to shame and everlasting contempt.[r] 3Those who are wise[r,s] will shine[t] like the brightness of the heavens, and those who lead many to righteousness,[u] like the stars for ever and ever.[v] 4But you, Daniel, close up and seal[w] the words of the scroll until the time of the end.[x] Many will go here and there[y] to increase knowledge."

5Then I, Daniel, looked, and there be-

Cross references (center column)

11:36
[b]S Isa 10:25; 26:20
[c]Eze 35:13; S Da 8:24
11:40 [d]S Isa 21:1
[e]Isa 5:28
[f]S Isa 8:7; S Eze 38:4
11:41
[g]S Eze 20:6; Mal 3:12
[h]S Isa 11:14
[i]S Jer 48:47
11:43 [j]S Eze 30:4
[k]2Ch 12:3; Na 3:9

11:45 [l]S Isa 2:2, 4; Da 8:9
12:1
[m]S Da 10:13; Jude 1:9
[n]S Da 9:12; S Mt 24:21; Mk 13:19; Rev 16:18
[o]S Ex 32:32; S Ps 56:8; S Jer 17:13; S Lk 10:20
[p]Jer 30:7
12:2 [q]Jn 11:24
[r]S Isa 26:19; Mt 25:46
12:3 [s]S Da 11:33
[t]Mt 13:43; Jn 5:35; Php 2:15
[u]S Isa 6:7
[v]S Pr 4:18; 1Co 15:42
12:4 [w]S Isa 8:16
[x]ver 9,13; Rev 22:10
[y]Jer 5:1

p39 Or *land for a reward*　　q45 Or *the sea and*
r3 Or *who impart wisdom*

11:37 *the one desired by women.* Usually interpreted as either Tammuz (see note on Eze 8:14) or the Messiah. **11:40–45** Conflicts to be waged between the antichrist and his political enemies. He will meet his end at the "beautiful holy mountain" (v. 45), Jerusalem's temple mount, doubtless in connection with the battle of Armageddon (Rev 16:13–16).

12:1 *Michael.* See note on 10:13. *time of distress.* See Jer 30:7; Mt 24:21 and note; cf. Rev 16:18. *book.* See 10:21; see also notes on Ps 9:5; 51:1; 69:28.
12:2 The first clear reference to a resurrection of both the righteous and the wicked. Cf. Jn 5:24–30. *everlasting life.* The phrase occurs only here in the OT.
12:5 *two others.* Two was the minimum number of wit-

Ptolemies and Seleucids

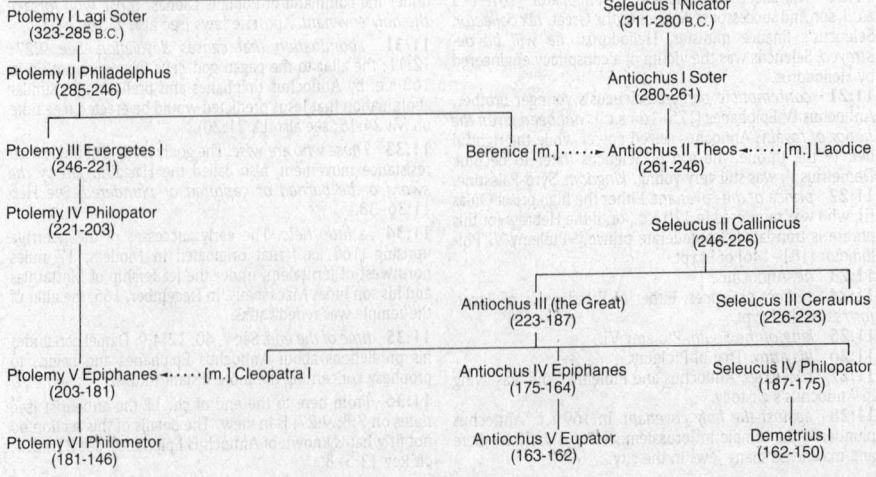

fore me stood two others, one on this bank of the river and one on the opposite bank.[z] [6]One of them said to the man clothed in linen,[a] who was above the waters of the river, "How long will it be before these astonishing things are fulfilled?"[b]

[7]The man clothed in linen, who was above the waters of the river, lifted his right hand[c] and his left hand toward heaven, and I heard him swear by him who lives forever,[d] saying, "It will be for a time, times and half a time.[s][e] When the power of the holy people[f] has been finally broken, all these things will be completed.[g]"

[8]I heard, but I did not understand. So I asked, "My lord, what will the outcome of all this be?"

[9]He replied, "Go your way, Daniel, because the words are closed up and sealed[h] until the time of the end.[i] [10]Many will be purified, made spotless and refined,[j] but the wicked will continue to be wicked.[k] None of the wicked will understand, but those who are wise will understand.[l]

[11]"From the time that the daily sacrifice[m] is abolished and the abomination that causes desolation[n] is set up, there will be 1,290 days.[o] [12]Blessed is the one who waits[p] for and reaches the end of the 1,335 days.[q]

[13]"As for you, go your way till the end.[r] You will rest,[s] and then at the end of the days you will rise to receive your allotted inheritance.[t] [u]"

Cross references (center column):

12:5 [z]Da 10:4
12:6 [a]S Eze 9:2
[b]Da 8:13
12:7 [c]S Ge 14:22
[d]S Da 6:26;
[e]S Da 7:25;
S Rev 11:2
[f]S Da 8:24
[g]Lk 21:24;
Rev 10:7

12:9 [h]S Isa 29:11
[i]S ver 4
12:10 [j]S Isa 1:25;
S Da 11:35
[k]S Isa 32:7;
Rev 22:11
[l]Hos 14:9
12:11
[m]S Ex 29:38
[n]S Da 8:11;
S 9:27;
Mt 24:15*;
Mk 13:14*
[o]Rev 11:2
12:12
[p]S Isa 30:18
[q]S Eze 4:5-6;
Da 8:14
12:13 [r]S ver 4
[s]Isa 57:2

[r]Ps 16:5; Rev 14:13 [u]Mt 10:22; Jas 1:12

[s]7 Or *a year, two years and half a year*

---

nesses to an oath (see v. 7; Dt 19:15).
12:7 *time, times and half a time.* See NIV text note; cf. 7:25.
12:11–12 Apparently representing either (1) further calculations relating to the persecutions of Antiochus Epiphanes (see 8:14; 11:28 and notes) or (2) further end-time calculations.
12:13 *rest.* Die (see Job 3:17).

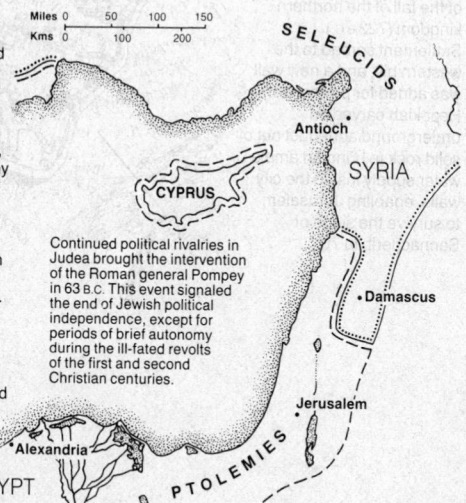

Soon after the death of Alexander the Great in 323 B.C., his generals divided his empire into four parts, two of which—Egypt and Syria—were under the rule of the Ptolemies and Seleucids respectively. Palestine was controlled from Egypt by the Ptolemaic dynasty from 323 to 198, and was subsequently governed by the Seleucids of Syria from 198 to 142.

The Diadochi, as the successors of Alexander were called, struggled bitterly for power over his domain. At first Ptolemy I seized his own satrapy, Egypt and North Africa, which had splendid resources and natural defense capabilities. Seleucus gained Syria and Mesopotamia, and by 301 Lysimachus held Thrace and Asia Minor and Cassander ruled Macedon. The situation changed again by 277, when only three major Hellenistic kingdoms stabilized in Egypt, in Syria, and in Macedonia under the Antigonids (277-168). Each continued until the eventual triumph of Rome.

Da 11 treats the "king of the South" and the "king of the North," describing their conflicts, wars and alliances. Their hostility toward the people of God culminated in the "abomination that causes desolation" (Da 11:31), identified historically with the reign of Antiochus IV Epiphanes (175-164). The Maccabean revolt followed, leading eventually to the founding of the Hasmonean dynasty.

Continued political rivalries in Judea brought the intervention of the Roman general Pompey in 63 B.C. This event signaled the end of Jewish political independence, except for periods of brief autonomy during the ill-fated revolts of the first and second Christian centuries.

Miles 0   50   100   150
Kms 0   100   200

SELEUCIDS
Antioch
SYRIA
CYPRUS
Damascus
Jerusalem
Alexandria
EGYPT
PTOLEMIES

Borders shown } PTOLEMIES – – – – –
c. 240 B.C.   } SELEUCIDS ················

The Book of the Twelve, or the Minor Prophets

In Ecclesiasticus (an Apocryphal book written c. 190 B.C.), Jesus ben Sira spoke of "the twelve prophets" (Ecclesiasticus 49:10) as a unit parallel to Isaiah, Jeremiah and Ezekiel. He thus indicated that these 12 prophecies were at that time thought of as a unit and were probably already written together on one scroll, as is the case in later times. Josephus (*Against Apion,* 1.8.3) also was aware of this grouping. Augustine (*The City of God,* 18.25) called them the "Minor Prophets," referring to the small size of these books by comparison with the major prophetic books and not at all suggesting that they are of minor importance.

In the traditional Jewish canon these works are arranged in what was thought to be their chronological order: (1) the books that came from the period of Assyrian power (Hosea, Joel, Amos, Obadiah, Jonah, Micah), (2) those written about the time of the decline of Assyria (Nahum, Habakkuk, Zephaniah) and (3) those dating from the postexilic era (Haggai, Zechariah, Malachi). On the other hand, their order in the Septuagint (the earliest Greek translation of the OT) is: Hosea, Amos, Micah, Joel, Obadiah, Jonah, Nahum, Habakkuk, Zephaniah, Haggai, Zechariah, Malachi (the order of the first six was probably determined by length, except for Jonah, which is placed last among them because of its different character).

In any event, it appears that within a century after the composition of Malachi the Jews had brought together the 12 shorter prophecies to form a book (scroll) of prophetic writings, which was received as canonical and paralleled the three major prophetic books of Isaiah, Jeremiah and Ezekiel. The great Greek manuscripts Alexandrinus and Vaticanus place the Twelve before the major prophets, but in the traditional Jewish canon and in all modern versions they appear after them.

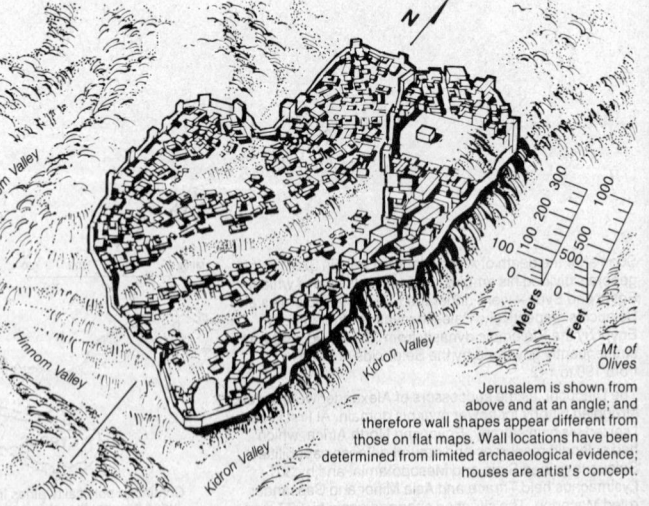

Jerusalem during the Time of the Prophets
c. 750—586 B.C.

Refugees arrived in Jerusalem about the time of the fall of the northern kingdom (722 B.C.). Settlement spread to the western hill, and a new wall was added for protection. Hezekiah carved an underground aqueduct out of solid rock to bring an ample water supply inside the city walls, enabling Jerusalem to survive the siege of Sennacherib in 701.

Jerusalem is shown from above and at an angle; and therefore wall shapes appear different from those on flat maps. Wall locations have been determined from limited archaeological evidence; houses are artist's concept.

HOSEA

Author and Date

Hosea son of Beeri prophesied about the middle of the eighth century B.C., his ministry beginning during or shortly after that of Amos. Amos threatened God's judgment on Israel at the hands of an unnamed enemy; Hosea identifies that enemy as Assyria (7:11; 8:9; 10:6; 11:11). Judging from the kings mentioned in 1:1, Hosea must have prophesied for at least 38 years, though almost nothing is known about him from sources outside his book. He was the only one of the writing prophets to come from the northern kingdom (Israel), and his prophecy is primarily directed to that kingdom. But since his prophetic activity is dated by reference to kings of Judah, the book was probably written in Judah after the fall of the northern capital, Samaria (722-721)—an idea suggested by references to Judah throughout the book (1:7,11; 4:15; 5:5,10,13; 6:4,11; 10:11; 11:12; 12:2). Whether Hosea himself authored the book that preserves his prophecies is not known. The book of Hosea stands first in the division of the Bible called the Book of the Twelve (in the Apocrypha; see Ecclesiasticus 49:10) or the Minor Prophets (a name referring to the brevity of these books as compared to Isaiah, Jeremiah and Ezekiel).

Background

Hosea lived in the tragic final days of the northern kingdom, during which six kings (following Jeroboam II) reigned within 25 years (2Ki 15:8-17:41). Four (Zechariah, Shallum, Pekahiah, Pekah) were murdered by their successors while in office, and one (Hoshea) was captured in battle; only one (Menahem) was succeeded on the throne by his son. These kings, given to Israel by God "in anger" and taken away "in wrath" (13:11), floated away "like a twig on the surface of the waters" (10:7). "Bloodshed" followed "bloodshed" (4:2). Assyria was expanding westward, and Menahem accepted that world power as overlord and paid tribute (2Ki 15:19-20). But shortly afterward, in 733 B.C., Israel was dismembered by Assyria because of the intrigue of Pekah (who had gained Israel's throne by killing Pekahiah, Menahem's son and successor). Only the territories of Ephraim and western Manasseh were left to the king of Israel. Then, because of the disloyalty of Hoshea (Pekah's successor), Samaria was captured and its people exiled in 722-721, bringing the northern kingdom to an end.

Theme and Message

The first part of the book (chs. 1-3) narrates the family life of Hosea as a symbol (similar to the symbolism in the lives of Isaiah, Jeremiah and Ezekiel) to convey the message the prophet had from the Lord for his people. God ordered Hosea to marry an adulterous wife, Gomer, and their three children were each given a symbolic name representing part of the ominous message. Ch. 2 alternates between Hosea's relation to Gomer and its symbolic representation of God's relation to Israel. The children are told to drive the unfaithful mother out of the house; but it was her reform, not her riddance, that was sought. The prophet was ordered to continue loving her, and he took her back and kept her in isolation for a while (ch. 3). The affair graphically represents the Lord's relation to the Israelites (cf. 2:4,9,18), who had been disloyal to him by worshiping Canaanite deities as the source of their abundance. Israel was to go through a period of exile (cf. 7:16; 8:14; 9:3,6,17; 11:5). But the Lord still loved his covenant people and longed to take them back, as Hosea took back Gomer. This return is described with imagery recalling the exodus from Egypt and settlement in Canaan (cf. 1:11; 2:14-23; 3:5; 11:10-11; 14:4-7). Hosea saw Israel's past experiences with the Lord as the fundamental pattern, or type, of God's future dealings with his people.

The second part of the book (chs. 4-14) gives the details of Israel's involvement in Canaanite religion, but a systematic outline of the material is difficult. Like other prophetic books, Hosea carried a call to repentance. Israel's alternative to destruction was to forsake her idols and return to the Lord (chs. 6;

14). Information gleaned from materials discovered at Ugarit (dating from the 15th century B.C.; see chart on "Ancient Texts Relating to the OT," p. 5) and from the writings of the early Christian historian Eusebius enables us to know more clearly the religious practices against which Hosea protested.

Hosea saw the failure to acknowledge God (4:6; 13:4) as Israel's basic problem. God's relation to Israel was that of love (2:19; 4:1; 6:6; 10:12; 12:6). The intimacy of the covenant relationship between God and Israel, illustrated in the first part of the book by the husband-wife relationship, is later amplified by the father-child relationship (11:1-4). Disloyalty to God was spiritual adultery (4:13-14; 5:4; 9:1; cf. Jer 3). Israel had turned to Baal worship and had sacrificed at the pagan high places, which included associating with the sacred prostitutes at the sanctuaries (4:14) and worshiping the calf image at Samaria (8:5; 10:5-6; 13:2). There was also international intrigue (5:13; 7:8-11) and materialism. Yet despite God's condemnation and the harshness of language with which the unavoidable judgment was announced, the major purpose of the book is to proclaim God's compassion and love that cannot—finally—let Israel go.

Special Problems

The book of Hosea has at least two perplexing problems. The first concerns the nature of the story told in chs. 1-3 and the character of Gomer. While some interpreters have thought the story to be merely an allegory of the relation between God and Israel, others claim, more plausibly, that the story is to be taken literally. Among the latter, some insist that Gomer was faithful at first and later became unfaithful, others that she was unfaithful even before the marriage.

The second problem of the book is the relation of ch. 3 to ch. 1. Despite the fact that no children are mentioned in ch. 3, some interpreters claim that the two chapters are different accounts of the same episode. The traditional interpretation, however, is more likely, namely, that ch. 3 is a sequel to ch. 1—i.e., after Gomer proved unfaithful, Hosea was instructed to take her back.

Outline

1 The word of the LORD that came[a] to Hosea son of Beeri during the reigns of Uzziah,[b] Jotham,[c] Ahaz[d] and Hezekiah,[e] kings of Judah,[f] and during the reign of Jeroboam[g] son of Jehoash[a] king of Israel:[h]

Hosea's Wife and Children

[2]When the LORD began to speak through Hosea, the LORD said to him, "Go, take to yourself an adulterous[i] wife and children of unfaithfulness, because the land is guilty of the vilest adultery[j] in departing from the LORD." [3]So he married Gomer[k] daughter of Diblaim, and she conceived and bore him a son.

[4]Then the LORD said to Hosea, "Call him Jezreel,[l] because I will soon punish the house of Jehu for the massacre at Jezreel, and I will put an end to the kingdom of Israel. [5]In that day I will break Israel's bow in the Valley of Jezreel.[m]"

[6]Gomer[n] conceived again and gave birth to a daughter. Then the LORD said to Hosea, "Call her Lo-Ruhamah,[b][o] for I will no longer show love to the house of Israel,[p] that I should at all forgive them. [7]Yet I will show love to the house of Judah; and I will save them—not by bow,[q] sword or battle, or by horses and horsemen, but by the LORD their God.[r]"

[8]After she had weaned Lo-Ruhamah,[s] Gomer had another son. [9]Then the LORD said, "Call him Lo-Ammi,[c] for you are not my people, and I am not your God.[t]

[10]"Yet the Israelites will be like the sand on the seashore, which cannot be measured or counted.[u] In the place where it was said to them, 'You are not my people,' they will be called 'sons of the living God.'[v][w] [11]The people of Judah and the people of Israel will be reunited,[x] and they will appoint one leader[y] and will come up out of the land,[z] for great will be the day of Jezreel.[a]

2 "Say of your brothers, 'My people,' and of your sisters, 'My loved one.'[b]

Israel Punished and Restored

[2]"Rebuke your mother,[c] rebuke her,
    for she is not my wife,
    and I am not her husband.
Let her remove the adulterous[d] look
        from her face
    and the unfaithfulness from between
        her breasts.
[3]Otherwise I will strip[e] her naked
    and make her as bare as on the day
        she was born;[f]
I will make her like a desert,[g]
    turn her into a parched land,

Cross references (center column)

1:1 [a]S Jer 1:2
[b]S 2Ki 14:21
[c]S 1Ch 3:12
[d]S 1Ch 3:13
[e]S 1Ch 3:13
[f]Isa 1:1; Mic 1:1
[g]S 2Ki 13:13
[h]Am 1:1
1:2 [i]S Jer 3:1;
Hos 2:2,5; 3:1
[j]Dt 31:16;
Jer 3:14;
Eze 23:3-21;
Hos 5:3
1:3 [k]ver 6
1:4 [l]ver 11;
S 1Sa 29:1;
1Ki 18:45;
2Ki 10:1-14;
Hos 2:22
1:5 [m]S Jos 15:56;
S 1Sa 29:1;
2Ki 15:29
1:6 [n]ver 3 [o]ver
6; Hos 2:23
[p]Hos 2:4
1:7 [q]S Ps 44:6
[r]Zec 4:6
1:8 [s]S ver 6

1:9 [t]ver 10;
S Eze 11:19-20;
1Pe 2:10
1:10
[u]S Ge 22:17;
S Jer 33:22 [v]S ver
9; Hos 2:23;
Ro 9:26*
[w]S Jos 3:10
1:11 [x]S Isa 11:12,
13 [y]Jer 23:5-8;
30:9
[z]S Eze 37:15-28
[a]S ver 4
2:1 [b]ver 23;
1Pe 2:10
2:2 [c]ver 5;
S Isa 50:1;
S Hos 1:2; 4:5
[d]S Isa 1:21;
S Eze 23:45

2:3 [e]S Eze 16:37 [f]Eze 16:4,22 [g]Isa 32:13-14

[a]I Hebrew *Joash*, a variant of *Jehoash*   [b]6 *Lo-Ruhamah* means *not loved*.   [c]9 *Lo-Ammi* means *not my people*.

1:1 *word of the LORD.* A claim of authority paralleling that of Joel (1:1), Micah (1:1) and Zechariah (1:1,7). *Hosea.* Means "salvation." *Uzziah.* Reigned 792–740 B.C. *Jotham.* 750–732. *Ahaz.* 735–715. *Hezekiah.* 729–686. Some of the reigns overlapped, with the co-regency of Ahaz and Hezekiah being the longest (see note on Isa 36:1). *Jeroboam.* Jeroboam II, 793–753. Hosea was a contemporary of Isaiah, Amos and Micah (see the similar first verse in their prophecies).
1:2 *take an adulterous wife.* See Introduction: Special Problems. *unfaithfulness.* The one great sin of which the Lord (through Hosea) accuses Israel.
1:3 *Gomer.* Not mentioned outside this book. *him.* The omission of this word in vv. 6, 9 may indicate that Hosea was not the father of Gomer's next two children.
1:4 *Jezreel.* Means "God scatters," here used to reinforce the announcement of judgment on the reigning house (see notes on v. 11; 2:22). Jeroboam II was of the dynasty of Jehu (841–814 B.C.), which was established at Jezreel by the overthrow of Ahab's son Joram (2Ki 9:14–37; cf. 1Ki 19:16–17). Jehu's dynasty ended with the murder of Zechariah in 753 (2Ki 15:8–10).
1:5 *Israel's bow.* Israel's military power, broken in 724 B.C., though Samaria held out under siege for some two years longer (2Ki 17:5–6).
1:6 *Lo-Ruhamah.* See NIV text note. The naming represents a reversal of the love (compassion) that God had earlier shown to Israel (Ex 33:19; Dt 7:6–8) but that later was promised again (2:23).
1:7 *Judah . . . I will save.* They were saved from Assyria by the Lord in 722–721 B.C. and again in 701 (see 2Ki 19:32–36).

1:9 *Lo-Ammi.* See NIV text note. The naming represents a break in the covenant relationship between the Lord and Israel (see Ex 6:7; Jer 7:23), which later, however, would be restored (v. 10; 2:1,23). The warnings became more severe in moving from the first to the third child.
1:10 Cited in Ro 9:26; 1Pe 2:10 and applied to the mission to the Gentiles. *Yet.* The threatened punishment (vv. 4–9) would be for only a limited time, and a period of blessing would follow. *sand on the seashore.* See the promise to Abraham and Jacob (Ge 22:17; 32:12; cf. Jer 33:22; Heb 11:12). *sons.* Contrasts with "children of unfaithfulness" (v. 2; 2:4). *living God.* Contrasts with idols—"which are not God" (Dt 32:17).
1:11 *reunited.* Israel and Judah would become one nation again. *out of the land.* Possibly the land of exile (cf. Ex 1:10). Another interpretation is that they would spring up from the ground as plants do. *Jezreel.* Here "God scatters" (see note on v. 4) refers to sowing or planting, indicating a reversal of the meaning of the first child's name (see 2:21–23).
2:1 *My people . . . My loved one.* The negatives associated with the names of Hosea's children (see NIV text notes on 1:6,9) are dropped.
2:2 *not my wife.* The marriage was broken by unfaithfulness, but reconciliation, not divorce, was sought (cf. vv. 7–15).
2:3 *strip her.* The husband supplied the wife's clothing (see Ex 21:10; Eze 16:10), and here her unfaithfulness was exposed (see Jer 13:26; Eze 16:39). *bare.* As Israel was when the Lord "found" her in Egypt—in slavery and with nothing (cf. Eze 16:4–8; Na 3:5).

and slay her with thirst.
⁴I will not show my love to her
    children, [h]
    because they are the children of
    adultery. [i]
⁵Their mother has been unfaithful
    and has conceived them in disgrace.
She said, 'I will go after my lovers, [j]
    who give me my food and my water,
    my wool and my linen, my oil and
    my drink.' [k]
⁶Therefore I will block her path with
    thornbushes;
I will wall her in so that she cannot
    find her way. [l]
⁷She will chase after her lovers but not
    catch them;
she will look for them but not find
    them. [m]
Then she will say,
    'I will go back to my husband [n] as at
    first, [o]
for then I was better off [p] than now.'
⁸She has not acknowledged [q] that I was
    the one
who gave her the grain, the new
    wine and oil, [r]
who lavished on her the silver and
    gold [s] —
which they used for Baal. [t]

⁹"Therefore I will take away my grain [u]
    when it ripens,
and my new wine [v] when it is ready.
I will take back my wool and my linen,
    intended to cover her nakedness.

¹⁰So now I will expose [w] her lewdness
    before the eyes of her lovers; [x]
    no one will take her out of my
    hands. [y]
¹¹I will stop [z] all her celebrations: [a]
    her yearly festivals, her New Moons,
    her Sabbath days—all her appointed
    feasts. [b]
¹²I will ruin her vines [c] and her fig trees, [d]
    which she said were her pay from her
    lovers; [e]
I will make them a thicket, [f]
    and wild animals will devour them. [g]
¹³I will punish her for the days
    she burned incense [h] to the Baals; [i]
she decked herself with rings and
    jewelry, [j]
and went after her lovers, [k]
    but me she forgot, [l] "
              declares the LORD. [m]

¹⁴"Therefore I am now going to allure
    her;
I will lead her into the desert [n]
    and speak tenderly to her.
¹⁵There I will give her back her vineyards,
    and will make the Valley of Achor [d] [o]
    a door of hope.
There she will sing [e] [p] as in the days of
    her youth, [q]
as in the day she came up out of
    Egypt. [r]

¹⁶"In that day," declares the LORD,
    "you will call me 'my husband'; [s]

2:4 [h]S Eze 8:18; Hos 1:6 [i]Hos 5:7	
2:5 [j]S Jer 3:6; [k]S Hos 1:2 [k]Jer 44:17-18	
2:6 [l]S Job 3:23; S 19:8; S La 3:9	
2:7 [m]Hos 5:13 [n]S Isa 54:5 [o]Jer 2:2; S 3:1 [p]S Eze 16:8	
2:8 [q]S Isa 1:3 [r]S Nu 18:12 [s]S Dt 8:18 [t]ver 13; Eze 16:15-19; Hos 8:4	
2:9 [u]Hos 8:7 [v]Hos 9:2	
2:10 [w]Eze 23:10 [x]Jer 13:26 [y]S Eze 16:37	
2:11 [z]Jer 7:34 [a]S Isa 24:8 [b]S Isa 1:14; Jer 16:9; Hos 3:4; 9:5; Am 5:21; 8:10	
2:12 [c]S Isa 7:23; S Jer 8:13 [d]S Jer 5:17 [e]S Jer 3:1 [f]S Isa 5:6 [g]Hos 5:7; 13:8	
2:13 [h]Isa 65:7 [i]ver 8; S Jer 7:9; Hos 11:2 [j]S Eze 16:17; S 23:40 [k]Hos 4:13 [l]Hos 4:6; 8:14; 13:6 [m]S Jer 44:17; Hos 13:1	
2:14 [n]S Eze 19:13	
2:15 [o]S Jos 7:24, 26 [p]Ex 15:1-18 [q]S Jer 2:2; S Eze 16:22 [r]S Eze 28:26; Hos 12:9	
2:16 [s]S Isa 54:5	

[d]15 *Achor* means *trouble.*   [e]15 Or *respond*

2:4 *children of adultery.* See 1:2. This contrasts with being "sons" of the Lord (1:10; 11:1).

2:5 *go after.* The wife was chasing other men (see Jer 3:2; Eze 16:33). *lovers.* See vv. 7,10. The reference is to Canaanite deities (such as Baal), whose worshipers hoped to gain agricultural fertility. *who give my food . . . my drink.* Ugaritic texts attribute crops to rain given by Baal. *wool . . . linen . . . oil . . . drink.* The agricultural staples of Palestine. Israel does not know the true source of her blessings.

2:6 *block her path.* Rather than punish Israel with death (cf. Dt 22:21; Eze 16:39–40; Na 3:5–7), the Lord would isolate her.

2:7 *chase.* A cultic term in Hosea; elsewhere the Hebrew for this word is translated "press on" or "pursue" (6:3; 8:3; 12:1). *look for.* See 5:6,15. *not find.* See 5:6. *go back.* The Hebrew for this expression often means "repent." *my husband.* The Lord.

2:8 *She has not acknowledged.* The Canaanites attributed grain, wine and oil to Baal. *silver and gold.* Used for making idols (see 8:4; 9:6; 13:2). *Baal.* The Canaanite god who was believed to control the weather and the fertility of crops, animals and man (see note on Jdg 2:13).

2:9 *take away.* By withholding the fruits of field and flock, the Lord made known the true source of those blessings.

2:10 *expose her lewdness.* The unfaithful wife was exposed to public shame (see La 1:8; Eze 16:37; 23:39). *no one will take her.* Baal had no power.

2:11 *stop . . . celebrations.* In exile these joyous seasons

would be only a memory. *yearly festivals.* See Ex 23:14–17; Dt 16:16. See also chart on "OT Feasts and Other Sacred Days," p. 176. *New Moons.* See 2Ki 4:23; Isa 1:13; Am 8:5. *Sabbath.* See Ex 20:8–11.

2:12 *pay from her lovers.* The harlot's pay (see 9:1; Dt 23:18; Eze 16:33; Mic 1:7). Israel attributed her agricultural products to the false gods she worshiped, rather than to the Lord (see Dt 11:13–14). *thicket.* See Isa 5:5–6; 7:23; 32:13; Mic 3:12.

2:13 *days.* Festival days. *Baals.* See v. 17; 11:2. Hosea used the plural here, suggesting the idols at the many local shrines (see Jer 2:23; 9:14). *went after.* See note on v. 5. *forgot.* The opposite of "know" in Hosea (cf. 13:4–6).

2:14 *into the desert.* For a second betrothal (see vv. 19–20). It refers back to the days of Israel's desert wandering, before she was tempted by the Baals in Canaan. *speak tenderly to.* Reassure, encourage, comfort (cf. Ge 34:3; Ru 2:13; Isa 40:2). God continually shows love in the midst of judgment.

2:15 *Valley of Achor.* Near Jericho (see Jos 7:1–26; 15:7; Isa 65:10). As the prophet reversed the meaning of the names of his children, so also the meaning of Achor (see NIV text note)—where God first judged his people in the promised land—became a symbol of new opportunity.

2:16–17 *husband . . . master . . . Baals.* A play on words. Of the two Hebrew words for husband, one (master) is identical with the name of the god Baal (see NIV text note on v. 16). There will be such a vigorous reaction against Baal

you will no longer call me 'my
　　master. f '
17I will remove the names of the Baals
　　from her lips; t
　　no longer will their names be
　　　invoked. u
18In that day I will make a covenant for
　　them
　　with the beasts of the field and the
　　　birds of the air
　　and the creatures that move along
　　　the ground. v
　　Bow and sword and battle
　　I will abolish w from the land,
　　so that all may lie down in safety. x
19I will betroth y you to me forever;
　　I will betroth you in g righteousness
　　　and justice, z
　　in h love and compassion. a
20I will betroth you in faithfulness,
　　and you will acknowledge b the
　　　LORD. c
21"In that day I will respond,"
　　declares the LORD—
　　"I will respond d to the skies,
　　and they will respond to the earth;
22and the earth will respond to the grain,
　　the new wine and oil, e
　　and they will respond to Jezreel. i f
23I will plant g her for myself in the land;

I will show my love to the one I
　　called 'Not my loved one.j h'
I will say to those called 'Not my
　　people,k' 'You are my
　　people'; i
and they will say, 'You are my
　　God.j '"

Hosea's Reconciliation With His Wife

3 The LORD said to me, "Go, show your
love to your wife again, though she is
loved by another and is an adulteress. k
Love her as the LORD loves the Israelites,
though they turn to other gods and love
the sacred raisin cakes. l "

2So I bought her for fifteen shekelsl of
silver and about a homer and a lethekm of
barley. 3Then I told her, "You are to live
withn me many days; you must not be a
prostitute or be intimate with any man,
and I will live withn you."

4For the Israelites will live many days
without king or prince, m without sacri-
ficen or sacred stones, o without ephod p
or idol. q 5Afterward the Israelites will re-

Cross references (center column)

2:17 rEx 23:13;
Ps 16:4
uS Jos 23:7;
Zec 13:2
2:18 vS Job 5:22
wS Ps 46:9;
S Isa 2:4;
Zec 9:10
xS Job 5:23;
S Jer 23:6;
Eze 34:25
2:19 yS Isa 62:4;
2Co 11:2
zS Isa 1:27
aS Isa 54:8
2:20 bJer 31:34;
Hos 4:1; 6:6;
13:4 cS Eze 16:8
2:21 dIsa 55:10;
Zec 8:12;
Mal 3:10-11
2:22
eS Jer 31:12;
Hos 14:7;
Joel 2:19
fS Eze 36:29-30;
S Hos 1:4
2:23 gS Jer 31:27

hS Hos 1:6 iS ver
1; S Isa 19:25;
S Hos 1:10
jS Jer 29:12;
Ro 9:25*
1Pe 2:10
3:1 kS Hos 1:2
lS 2Sa 6:19
3:4 mHos 13:11
nDa 11:31;
S Hos 2:11
oHos 10:1
pS Ex 25:7
qJdg 17:5-6;
18:14-17;
S La 2:9; Zec 10:2

Footnotes (center column)

l 16 Hebrew baal g 19 Or with; also in verse 20
h 19 Or with i 22 Jezreel means God plants.
j 23 Hebrew Lo-Ruhamah k 23 Hebrew Lo-Ammi
l 2 That is, about 6 ounces (about 170 grams)
m 2 That is, probably about 10 bushels (about 330 liters)
n 3 Or wait for

---

worship that this Hebrew word for "master" will no longer
be used of the Lord.
2:18 *make a covenant.* See 6:7; 8:1. Animals, the instruments of destruction in v. 12, as well as birds and insects,
would no longer threaten life. Nature and history combine in
a picture of peace (see Isa 11:6–9; 65:25). *Bow and sword.*
See 1:5. War is terminated. *land.* Israel (see 1:2; 4:1,3; 9:3;
10:1). *lie down in safety.* See Jer 33:16; Eze 34:24–28.
2:19–20 Rather than money, these five traits necessary to
the covenant relationship make up the bride-price (see Ex
22:16–17; Dt 22:23–29; 1Sa 18:25; 2Sa 3:14).
2:19 *righteousness.* See 10:12; Jer 23:6; Am 6:12; Mic
6:5. *justice.* See Am 5:24. *love.* See 4:1; 6:4; 10:12; 12:6.
compassion. A reversal of God's threatened withdrawal of
compassion (see 1:6 and NIV text note). "Lo-Ruhamah"
means lit. "not shown compassion" (cf. Ps 51:1; 103:3–14).
2:20 *faithfulness.* Dependability (see Dt 32:4; Ps 88:11).
acknowledge. The Hebrew for this word can refer to intimate marital relations (Ge 19:8; Nu 31:17–18,35), but it
also refers to active acknowledgment of a covenant partner
(see 4:1,6; 5:4; 6:3,6; 8:2; 11:3; 13:4).
2:21 *respond.* The woman (Israel) responded to the Lord's
overtures (see NIV text note on v. 15); now God responded
to her new behavior. The land also responded in becoming
productive (vv. 21–22).
2:22 *Jezreel.* Here used in the sense "God plants" (see NIV
text note and v. 23; see also note on 1:11). The threats
represented by the names of the children are turned into
blessings (see 1:10). The terms of the covenant were: "I will
take you as my own people, and I will be your God" (Ex 6:7;
see note on Zec 8:8).
2:23 *You are my God.* The people respond to God's gra-
ciousness. This verse is quoted in part in Ro 9:25; 1Pe 2:10
and applied to Gentiles coming into the church.

3:1 *said to me.* Ch. 3 is narrated in the first person, ch. 1 in
the third person. *Go . . . love . . . your wife.* Hosea's love for
unfaithful Gomer illustrated God's love for unfaithful Israel.
God's love for Israel (see 11:1; 14:4) is the basic theme of
the book. *other gods.* See Ex 20:3; Dt 31:20. *raisin cakes.*
Offered to Baal in thanksgiving for harvest.
3:2 Gomer had evidently become a slave, and Hosea
bought her back. *fifteen shekels.* Half the usual price of a
slave (Ex 21:7,32) or of the redemption value of a woman's
vow (Lev 27:4). *lethek.* See NIV text note. Comparison with
prices in 2Ki 7:1,16,18 suggests that half was paid in money
(silver) and half in produce (barley)—for a total value of 30
shekels.
3:3–5 A picture of exile and return.
3:3 *many days.* Not forever. There would be an "afterward" (v. 5), a future. *live with.* Suggests a period of isolation
(see NIV text note; see also 2:6), comparable to Israel's exile.
3:4 *king.* See 1:4; 5:1; 8:4,10; 10:15; 13:10–11. *prince.*
See 5:10; 7:3,5; 8:4; 13:10. *without sacrifice.* See 6:6;
8:11,13. *sacred stones.* See 10:1–2; Dt 16:22; 1Ki 14:23;
2Ki 17:10; Mic 5:13. *ephod.* Here an image associated with
idols (see Jdg 8:27; 17:5). *idol.* See Ge 31:30; 1Sa 19:13,16.
3:5 *return.* A basic word in Hosea's vocabulary (see 2:7;
5:4; 6:1; 7:10; 11:5; 12:6; 14:1–2). *seek.* Israel's repentance is envisioned (cf. 5:15)—the reverse of her present
stubborn rebellion (7:10). *LORD their God.* See 12:9; 13:4;
Jer 50:4. *David their king.* The Messianic king from the
dynasty of David (see Jer 30:9; Eze 34:24). After the death of
Solomon, Israel (the northern kingdom) had abandoned the
Davidic kings. *his blessings.* The vineyards and olive groves
that had been taken away (see 2:12–13,21) and all of God's
gifts (see Jer 31:12–14). *last days.* The Hebrew for this
phrase occurs 13 times in the OT, sometimes simply meaning the future ("days to come," Ge 49:1), but most of the

turn and seek[r] the LORD their God and David their king.[s] They will come trembling[t] to the LORD and to his blessings in the last days.[u]

The Charge Against Israel

4 Hear the word of the LORD, you Israelites,
  because the LORD has a charge[v] to bring
  against you who live in the land:[w]
"There is no faithfulness,[x] no love,
  no acknowledgment[y] of God in the land.[z]
[2]There is only cursing,[o] lying[a] and murder,[b]
  stealing[c] and adultery;[d]
they break all bounds,
  and bloodshed follows bloodshed.[e]
[3]Because of this the land mourns,[p][f]
  and all who live in it waste away;[g]
the beasts of the field and the birds of the air
  and the fish of the sea are dying.[h]

[4]"But let no man bring a charge,
  let no man accuse another,
for your people are like those
  who bring charges against a priest.[i]
[5]You stumble[j] day and night,
  and the prophets stumble with you.
So I will destroy your mother[k]—
[6] my people are destroyed from lack of knowledge.[l]

"Because you have rejected knowledge,

  I also reject you as my priests;
because you have ignored the law[m] of your God,
  I also will ignore your children.
[7]The more the priests increased,
  the more they sinned against me;
they exchanged[q] their[r] Glory[n] for something disgraceful.[o]
[8]They feed on the sins of my people
  and relish their wickedness.[p]
[9]And it will be: Like people, like priests.[r]
I will punish both of them for their ways
  and repay them for their deeds.[r]

[10]"They will eat but not have enough;[s]
  they will engage in prostitution[t] but not increase,
because they have deserted[u] the LORD
  to give themselves [11]to prostitution,[v]
to old wine[w] and new,
  which take away the understanding[x]
  [12]of my people.
They consult a wooden idol[y]
  and are answered by a stick of wood.[z]
A spirit of prostitution[a] leads them astray;[b]

3:5 [r]S Dt 4:29; S Isa 9:13; S 10:20; Hos 5:15; Mic 4:1-2 [s]S 1Sa 13:14 [t]S Ps 18:45 [u]S Dt 4:30; S Jer 50:4-5; Hos 11:10
4:1 [v]S Job 10:2; S Jer 2:9 [w]Joel 1:2,14 [x]S Pr 24:2 [y]S Pr 10:21; S Isa 1:3; Jer 7:28; S Hos 2:20 [z]S Jer 51:5
4:2 [a]Isa 59:3; Hos 7:3; 10:4; 11:12 [b]Hos 5:2; 6:9 [c]Hos 7:1 [d]S Jer 9:2 [e]S 2Ki 21:16; S Isa 1:15; S Eze 22:2,9; Hos 5:2; 10:13
4:3 [f]S Jer 4:28 [g]S Isa 15:6; S 33:9 [h]S Jer 4:25; S 9:10; S Eze 38:20; Zep 1:3
4:4 [i]Dt 17:12; S Eze 3:26
4:5 [j]S Eze 7:19; S 14:7 [k]S Hos 2:2
4:6 [l]S Pr 10:21; S Isa 1:3; S Hos 2:13; Mal 2:7-8

[m]Hos 8:1,12
4:7 [n]Hab 2:16 [o]Hos 9:11; 10:1, 6; 13:6
4:8 [p]S Isa 56:11; Hos 14:1;
Mic 3:11
4:9 [q]S Isa 24:2 [r]Jer 5:31; Hos 8:13; 9:9,15; 10:10; 12:2

4:10 [s]S Lev 26:26; S Isa 55:2; Mic 6:14 [t]S Eze 22:9 [u]Hos 7:14; 9:17 4:11 [v]ver 14; Hos 5:4 [w]S Lev 10:9; S 1Sa 25:36 [x]S Pr 20:1 4:12 [y]Jer 2:27 [z]Hab 2:19 [a]S Nu 15:39 [b]S Isa 44:20

[o]2 That is, to pronounce a curse upon   [p]3 Or dries up   [q]7 Syriac and an ancient Hebrew scribal tradition; Masoretic Text I will exchange   [r]7 Masoretic Text; an ancient Hebrew scribal tradition my

---

time, as no doubt here, referring to the Messianic age ("afterward," Joel 2:28; cf. Ac 2:17; Heb 1:2).
4:1–14:9 Deals with Israel's involvement in Canaanite religion, her moral sins and her international intrigues.
4:1 *Hear the word.* See, e.g., Isa 1:10; Jer 2:4; Eze 6:3. *charge.* As the Lord's spokesman, Hosea brought charges against unfaithful, covenant-breaking Israel (cf. v. 4; Isa 3:13; Jer 2:9; Mic 6:2). *faithfulness.* Loyalty to the covenant Lord (Jos 24:14) and right dealing with men (Pr 3:3). *love.* See 2:19; 10:12. *acknowledgment of God.* See 2:20 and note; 5:4; 6:6.
4:2 *cursing . . . adultery.* The sins detailed (paralleled in Jer 7:9) transgress the Ten Commandments (see Ex 20:13–16; Dt 5:17–20). *bloodshed.* Includes (1) murder (see 6:8–9), (2) the assassinations following the death of Jeroboam II when three kings reigned in one year (2Ki 15:10–14) and (3) human sacrifice (Ps 106:38; Eze 16:20–21; 23:37). Where God is not acknowledged (v. 1), moral uprightness disappears.
4:3 *land mourns.* God's judgment on man's sin affects all living things in man's world (see, e.g., Isa 24:3–6; Jer 4:23–28). *waste away.* See Isa 19:8; Jer 14:2; 15:9; Joel 1:10.
4:4–9 An indictment against the priests, whose duty it was to be guardians of God's law and to furnish religious instruction (see Dt 31:9–13; 33:10; 2Ch 17:8–9; Ezr 7:6,10; Jer 18:18). Hosea warned the priests not to lodge charges against the people for bringing God's judgment down on the

nation, for they themselves were guilty, and the people could also bring charges against them—as Hosea proceeded to do (see v. 9; Isa 28:7; Jer 2:26; 4:9; 23:11).
4:5 *stumble.* See 5:5. *prophets.* See Mic 2:6,11; 3:5–7. *your mother.* The nation (see 2:2,5; Isa 50:1).
4:6 *my people.* Israel (see vv. 8,12; 2:1,23; 6:11; 11:7; Mic 6:3). *destroyed from lack of knowledge.* Partly because the priests had failed to teach God's word to the people. *rejected knowledge . . . reject you.* Punishment in kind. *law of your God.* Israel's source of life (see Dt 32:47), which the priests should have been faithfully promoting.
4:7 *their Glory.* God (see Ps 106:20).
4:8 *feed on the sins.* Priests devoured the sacrifices (1Sa 2:13–17), profiting from the continuation of the sin rather than helping to cure it (see 8:13).
4:9 *Like people, like priests.* Without exception, all would be punished for their sins.
4:10 *eat but not have enough.* The punishment fit the sin. *prostitution.* See vv. 12,18; 2:4; 6:10; 9:1; Ps 106:39. Instead of giving themselves to the Lord, they gave themselves to prostitution.
4:11 *old wine.* See 7:5; 9:10; 14:7. *new.* See 2:8–9,22; 7:14; 9:2.
4:12 *wooden idol.* An image of a god (see Jer 2:27; 10:8; Hab 2:19). *stick of wood.* Either the wooden idol or a diviner's rod (see Eze 21:21). *spirit of prostitution.* See 5:4. Hebrew idioms often describe inner tendencies in terms of "spirit."

they are unfaithful[c] to their God.
13They sacrifice on the mountaintops
and burn offerings on the hills,
under oak,[d] poplar and terebinth,
where the shade is pleasant.[e]
Therefore your daughters turn to
prostitution[f]
and your daughters-in-law to
adultery.[g]

14"I will not punish your daughters
when they turn to prostitution,
nor your daughters-in-law
when they commit adultery,
because the men themselves consort
with harlots[h]
and sacrifice with shrine
prostitutes[i] —
a people without understanding[j] will
come to ruin![k]

15"Though you commit adultery, O Israel,
let not Judah become guilty.

"Do not go to Gilgal;[l]
do not go up to Beth Aven.[s] [m]
And do not swear, 'As surely as the
LORD lives!'[n]

16The Israelites are stubborn,[o]
like a stubborn heifer.[p]
How then can the LORD pasture them
like lambs[q] in a meadow?

17Ephraim is joined to idols;

leave him alone!
18Even when their drinks are gone,
they continue their prostitution;
their rulers dearly love shameful
ways.

19A whirlwind[r] will sweep them away,
and their sacrifices will bring them
shame.[s]

Judgment Against Israel

5 "Hear this, you priests!
Pay attention, you Israelites!
Listen, O royal house!
This judgment[t] is against you:
You have been a snare[u] at Mizpah,
a net[v] spread out on Tabor.
2The rebels are deep in slaughter.[w]
I will discipline all of them.[x]
3I know all about Ephraim;
Israel is not hidden[y] from me.
Ephraim, you have now turned to
prostitution;
Israel is corrupt.[z]

4"Their deeds do not permit them
to return[a] to their God.
A spirit of prostitution[b] is in their heart;
they do not acknowledge[c] the LORD.
5Israel's arrogance testifies[d] against
them;

4:12 cS Ps 73:27
4:13 dS Isa 1:29
eS Jer 3:6;
Hos 10:8; 11:2
fJer 2:20;
Am 7:17
gHos 2:13
4:14 hS ver 11
iS Ge 38:21;
Hos 9:10
jS Pr 10:21 kver 19
4:15 lHos 9:15;
12:11; Am 4:4;
5:5 mS Jos 7:2;
S Hos 5:8
nS Jer 4:2
4:16 oS Ex 32:9
pS Jer 31:18
qIsa 5:17; 7:25

4:19 rHos 12:1;
13:15 sver 13-14;
Isa 1:29
5:1 tS Job 10:2
uHos 6:9; 9:8
vS Jer 5:26
5:2 wS Hos 4:2
xHos 9:15
5:3 yAm 5:12
zS Eze 23:7;
S Hos 1:2; 6:10
5:4 aHos 7:10
bS Hos 4:11
cS Jer 4:22;
S Hos 4:6
5:5 dS Isa 3:9;
S Jer 2:19;
Hos 7:10

s15 Beth Aven means house of wickedness (a name for Bethel, which means house of God).

4:13 sacrifice. See 8:13. mountaintops. Places commonly chosen for pagan altars (see 10:8; Dt 12:2; 1Ki 14:23; 2Ki 17:10; Jer 2:20; 3:6). Clay tablets from Ugarit (see chart on "Ancient Texts Relating to the OT," p. 5) tell of fertility rites carried out by the Canaanites at the high places. oak ... terebinth. Trees noted for their shade. turn to prostitution. Canaanite fertility rites involved sexual activity (v. 14) that led to general erosion of morals.
4:14 not punish. The men would punish their women for immorality, but God would have no part in their hypocrisy. harlots. Common prostitutes (see Ge 34:31; Lev 21:14; Eze 16:31). shrine prostitutes. Women of the sanctuaries who served as partners for men in cultic sexual activity (cf. Ge 38:21–22; Dt 23:18). without understanding. Contrast 14:9.
4:15 Judah. An aside warning (see Introduction: Author and Date). guilty. See 10:2; 13:1; 14:1. Do not go. The nation as a whole was addressed. Gilgal. A site near Jericho (see 9:15; 12:11; Jos 4:19–20; 1Sa 11:13–15) where the Israelites had established a religious shrine. Beth Aven. A sarcastic substitute name for Bethel (see NIV text note; see also 5:8), site of one of the cult centers established by Jeroboam I (1Ki 12:29). As surely as the LORD lives. A form of solemn oath (see Jdg 8:19; Ru 3:13; 1Sa 14:39; 26:10,16; Jer 4:2; 38:16). Though proper in itself—since it invoked the true God (see Dt 6:13; 10:20; Jos 23:7)—it was here forbidden because it was being used deceitfully, as though the Israelites were truly honoring the Lord (see Jer 5:2).
4:16 stubborn. See Ne 9:29; Zec 7:11. stubborn heifer. See 10:11; Jer 2:20; an apt figure for unruly Israel (see 11:4; Jer 31:18).
4:17 Ephraim. Israel, the northern kingdom. idols. The

golden calf (8:5; 13:2; 1Ki 12:28) and the cult of Baal (2:8,13). leave him alone. Nothing could be done to help (see 2Sa 16:11; 2Ki 23:18).
4:19 A whirlwind will sweep them away. Lit. "The wind will catch them up with its wings," probably a metaphor from the threshing floor (see 13:3; Ps 1:4) for the sudden violence that would bring the exile. Since the Hebrew for the words "wind" and "spirit" is the same, there is a possible play on words with the "spirit of prostitution" (v. 12; 5:4). shame. By means of their sacrifices they hoped to flourish, but God's punishment for their idolatry would bring into disgrace among the nations (see 10:6).
5:1 priests ... Israelites ... royal house. The three groups addressed were all responsible for maintaining justice, but it miscarried at their hands. snare ... net. Devices for catching animals and birds, here used as metaphors for those who by economic and legal devices took cruel advantage of innocent people (see Job 18:8–10; Ps 140:5; Pr 29:5; La 1:13). Mizpah. Either (1) Mizpah in Gilead east of the Jordan (Ge 31:43–49) or (2) Mizpah in Benjamin (1Sa 7:5–6; 10:17). Tabor. A mountain at the southeastern edge of the Jezreel Valley. Reference must have been to well-known events that illustrated Israel's corruption.
5:2 discipline. A significant word in the prophets for God's corrective action against his people (see Isa 26:16; Jer 2:30; 5:3; 7:28).
5:3 Ephraim. Israel, the northern kingdom. prostitution. See 1:2; 4:10,18.
5:4 Their deeds. See 4:9; 7:2; 9:15; 12:2. Persistent sin can make repentance impossible (see Jer 13:23; Jn 8:34; Ro 6:6,16). spirit of prostitution. See 4:12. not acknowledge the LORD. See 4:6; Isa 1:2–4.

the Israelites, even Ephraim,
  stumble *e* in their sin;
Judah also stumbles with them. *f*
6When they go with their flocks and
    herds
  to seek the LORD, *g*
they will not find him;
  he has withdrawn *h* himself from
    them.
7They are unfaithful *i* to the LORD;
  they give birth to illegitimate *j*
    children.
Now their New Moon festivals *k*
  will devour *l* them and their fields.

8"Sound the trumpet *m* in Gibeah, *n*
  the horn in Ramah. *o*
Raise the battle cry in Beth Aven *t* ; *p*
  lead on, O Benjamin.
9Ephraim will be laid waste *q*
  on the day of reckoning. *r*
Among the tribes of Israel
  I proclaim what is certain. *s*
10Judah's leaders are like those
  who move boundary stones. *t*
I will pour out my wrath *u* on them
  like a flood of water.
11Ephraim is oppressed,
  trampled in judgment,
  intent on pursuing idols. *u* *v*
12I am like a moth *w* to Ephraim,
  like rot *x* to the people of Judah.

13"When Ephraim *y* saw his sickness,
  and Judah his sores,
then Ephraim turned to Assyria, *z*
  and sent to the great king for help. *a*

But he is not able to cure *b* you,
  not able to heal your sores. *c*
14For I will be like a lion *d* to Ephraim,
  like a great lion to Judah.
I will tear them to pieces *e* and go
    away;
  I will carry them off, with no one to
    rescue them. *f*
15Then I will go back to my place *g*
  until they admit their guilt. *h*
And they will seek my face; *i*
  in their misery *j* they will earnestly
    seek me. *k*"

Israel Unrepentant

6 "Come, let us return *l* to the LORD.
  He has torn us to pieces *m*
  but he will heal us; *n*
he has injured us
  but he will bind up our wounds. *o*
2After two days he will revive us; *p*
  on the third day *q* he will restore *r* us,
  that we may live in his presence.
3Let us acknowledge the LORD;
  let us press on to acknowledge him.
As surely as the sun rises,
  he will appear;
he will come to us like the winter
    rains, *s*

Cross references (center column)

5:5 *e*S Eze 14:7
  *f*Hos 14:1
5:6 *g*Mic 6:6-7
  *h*S Pr 1:28;
Isa 1:15; Eze 8:6;
Mal 1:10
5:7 *i*S Isa 24:16;
Hos 6:7 /Hos 2:4
  *k*Isa 1:14
  *l*S Hos 2:11-12
5:8 *m*S Nu 10:2;
S Jer 4:21;
S Eze 33:3
  *n*Jdg 19:12;
Hos 9:9; 10:9
  *o*S Isa 10:29
  *p*S Jos 7:2;
Hos 4:15; 10:5
5:9 *q*S Isa 7:16
  *r*Isa 37:3;
Hos 9:11-17
  *s*Isa 46:10;
Zec 1:6
5:10 *t*S Dt 19:14
  *u*S Eze 7:8
5:11 *v*Hos 9:16;
Mic 6:16
5:12
  *w*S Job 13:28;
S Isa 51:8
  *x*S Job 18:16
5:13 *y*S Isa 7:16
  *z*S Eze 23:5;
Hos 7:11; 8:9;
12:1 *a*S La 5:6;
Hos 7:8; 10:6

  *b*S Isa 3:7;
Hos 14:3
  *c*Hos 2:7
5:14
  *d*S Job 10:16;
S Jer 4:7; Am 3:4
  *e*Hos 6:1
  *f*S Dt 32:39;
Mic 5:8
5:15 *g*S Isa 18:4
  *h*S Lev 26:40
  *i*S Nu 21:7;
S Ps 24:6;
S Hos 3:5
  *j*Ps 50:15;
S Jer 2:27
  *k*Isa 64:9;
S Eze 20:43
6:1 *l*S Isa 10:20;
S 19:22

*m*S Job 16:9; La 3:11; Hos 5:14 *n*S Nu 12:13; S Jer 3:22
*o*S Dt 32:39; S Job 5:18; S Jer 30:17; Hos 14:4 6:2 *p*S 30:5;
S 80:18 *q*S Mt 16:21 *r*S Ps 71:20 6:3 *s*S Job 4:3; Joel 2:23

*t*8 *Beth Aven* means *house of wickedness* (a name for
Bethel, which means *house of God*). *u*11 The
meaning of the Hebrew for this word is uncertain.

Study notes (bottom)

5:5 *arrogance.* Stubborn rebellion against the Lord (see Dt
1:43; 1Sa 15:23; Ne 9:16; Job 35:12; Ps 10:2; Eze
16:56–57). *testifies.* In the case God presented against his
people (see 4:1 and note). *stumble.* Experience calamity (see
4:5). *Judah.* See Introduction: Author and Date.
5:6 *seek the LORD.* Go to him with prayer and sacrifices (see
3:5; Am 5:4–5). *not find him.* Offering sacrifices in their
situation was useless (see 2:7; cf. Isa 1:10–14; Am
5:21–25; Mic 6:6–8). The Lord would be "found" by Israel
only when she turned to him with integrity of heart (see 3:5;
5:15; Dt 4:29–31; Jer 29:13).
5:7 *unfaithful.* See Jer 5:11. *illegitimate children.* Children
they had prayed to the Baals for and had credited to their
fertility rites. *New Moon.* Usually a festive occasion (see,
e.g., 2:11; 1Sa 20:5,18; Am 8:5; Col 2:16), but now a time
of judgment. Or the meaning may be that one month would
be sufficient to accomplish their punishment.
5:8 Some interpreters suggest that the Aramean (Syrian)-Ephraimite (Israelite) war (2Ki 16:5–9; Isa 7:1–9) forms
the background of this oracle. *trumpet.* Made of a ram's
horn, which here sounds the alarm that an army is approaching (see 8:1). *Gibeah.* Two miles north of Jerusalem. *Ramah.*
North of Gibeah. *Beth Aven.* See note on 4:15. *lead on, O
Benjamin.* Thought to be the Benjamite war cry (see Jdg
5:14).
5:9 *waste.* See Jer 25:11,38.
5:10 *move boundary stones.* Judah had seized Israelite

territory (1Ki 15:16–22; see Dt 19:14; 27:17; Pr 22:28;
23:10; Isa 5:8; Mic 2:2). *my wrath.* See 13:11.
5:12 *moth . . . rot.* Both consume (see Job 13:28).
5:13 *sickness . . . sores.* Metaphors for the national
wounds the two nations had suffered at the hands of their
enemies (see Isa 1:5–6; 17:4,11; Jer 30:12–13). *turned to
Assyria.* Assyrian records tell of the tribute paid to Tiglath-
Pileser III by the Israelite kings Menaheem and Hoshea (cf.
2Ki 15:19–20; 17:3). *not able to cure.* The alliances were
worthless.
5:14 *lion.* See 13:7. The Lord might use human agents (Isa
10:5–6), but he would be responsible for Israel's punishment, from which there was no escape (see Isa 5:29; 42:22;
Am 9:1–4; Mic 5:8).
5:15 *go back to my place.* God threatened to withdraw
from Israel until, out of desperation, she truly repented. This
idea sets the stage for the prophet's next theme.
6:1 *let us return.* A shallow (see v. 4) proposal of repentance (using phrases from 5:13–15), in which Israel acknowledged that God, not Assyria (cf. 5:13), was the true physician
(cf. 7:1).
6:2 *two days . . . third day.* A brief time. Israel supposed
that God's wrath would only be temporary.
6:3 *acknowledge the LORD.* A key concept in Hosea (see v.
6; 2:8,20; 4:1,6; 5:4). *like the winter rains . . . spring rains.*
Israel believed that, as surely as seasonal rains fell, reviving
the earth, God's favor would return and restore her.

like the spring rains that water the
earth. ' ”

4"What can I do with you, Ephraim? u
What can I do with you, Judah?
Your love is like the morning mist,
like the early dew that disappears. v
5Therefore I cut you in pieces with my
prophets,
I killed you with the words of my
mouth; w
my judgments flashed like lightning
upon you. x
6For I desire mercy, not sacrifice, y
and acknowledgment z of God rather
than burnt offerings. a
7Like Adam, v they have broken the
covenant b —
they were unfaithful c to me there.
8Gilead is a city of wicked men, d
stained with footprints of blood.
9As marauders lie in ambush for a man, e
so do bands of priests;
they murder f on the road to Shechem,
committing shameful crimes. g
10I have seen a horrible h thing
in the house of Israel.
There Ephraim is given to prostitution
and Israel is defiled. i

11"Also for you, Judah,
a harvest j is appointed.

"Whenever I would restore the
fortunes k of my people,

7 1whenever I would heal Israel,
the sins of Ephraim are exposed
and the crimes of Samaria revealed. l
They practice deceit, m
thieves break into houses, n
bandits rob in the streets; o
2but they do not realize
that I remember p all their evil
deeds. q
Their sins engulf them; r
they are always before me.

3"They delight the king with their
wickedness,
the princes with their lies. s
4They are all adulterers, t
burning like an oven
whose fire the baker need not stir
from the kneading of the dough till it
rises.
5On the day of the festival of our king
the princes become inflamed with
wine, u
and he joins hands with the
mockers. v
6Their hearts are like an oven; w
they approach him with intrigue.
Their passion smolders all night;
in the morning it blazes like a flaming
fire.
7All of them are hot as an oven;

Cross references

6:3 rPs 72:6;
Hos 11:10; 12:6
6:4 uHos 11:8
vHos 7:1; 13:3
6:5 wJer 1:9-10;
5:14; 23:29
xHeb 4:12
6:6 yS 1Sa 15:22;
S Isa 1:11;
Mt 9:13*; 12:7*;
Mk 12:33
zS Jer 4:22;
S Hos 2:20
aS Ps 40:6;
Mic 6:8
6:7 bS Ge 9:11;
S Jer 11:10;
Hos 8:1
cS Hos 5:7
6:8 dHos 12:11
6:9 ePs 10:8
fS Hos 4:2
gJer 5:30-31;
7:9-10;
S Eze 22:9;
S Hos 5:1; 7:1
6:10 hS Jer 5:30
iS Jer 23:14;
S Eze 23:7;
S Hos 5:3
6:11 jJer 51:33;
Joel 3:13
7:1 kS Ps 126:1;
Zep 2:7

lS Eze 24:13;
S Hos 6:4 mver 13
nS Ex 22:2;
Hos 4:2
oS Hos 6:9; 12:1
7:2 pS Jer 14:10;
S 44:21;
S Hos 8:13
qS Job 35:15;
Hos 9:15
rJer 2:19; 4:18
7:3 sJer 28:1-4;
S Hos 4:2; 10:13;
Mic 7:3
7:4 tS Jer 9:2
7:5 uS Isa 28:1,7
vS Ps 1:1

7:6 wPs 21:9

v 7 Or As at Adam; or Like men

6:4 *What can I do . . . ?* See Isa 5:4. God saw through
Israel's superficial repentance. *Ephraim.* Israel, the northern
kingdom. *Judah.* See Introduction: Author and Date. *love.*
See 2:19; see also note on v. 6. *morning mist . . . dew.*
Figurative for that which is temporary.
6:5 *my prophets.* God's spokesmen (see Jer 1:9; 15:19)
had denounced the people's sin. *words of my mouth.* The
judgments spoken by the Lord's faithful prophets. *like lightning.* See Dt 32:41.
6:6 *mercy.* Hebrew *hesed,* a word that can refer to right
conduct toward one's fellowman or loyalty to the Lord or
both—the sum of what God requires of his servants. Here it
perhaps refers to both. The same Hebrew word is translated
"love" in v. 4. *not sacrifice.* Sacrifice apart from faithfulness
to the Lord's will is wholly unacceptable to him (see 1Sa
15:22–23; Isa 1:11–20; Jer 7:21–22; Am 5:21–24; Mic
6:6–8; Mt 9:13; 12:7).
6:7 *Like Adam.* The allusion is uncertain, since Scripture
records no covenant with Adam. The NIV text note suggests
a place named Adam (Tell ed-Damiyeh) at the Jordan (see
Jos 3:16), as suggested by the reference to "there" at the end
of the sentence. A third interpretation takes Adam as "mankind" (see NIV text note). *broken the covenant.* See 8:1; Jos
7:11.
6:8 *Gilead.* See 12:11; Jdg 10:17; 12:7. *footprints of
blood.* The allusion is unclear, but Hosea may have been
referring to a more recent event than the bloodbath of Jdg
12:1–6—such as Pekah's rebellion against Pekahiah (see
2Ki 15:25).
6:9 *they murder.* The specific event is unknown.

6:10 *prostitution.* See chs. 2; 4.
6:11 *harvest.* A figure for God's judgments (see 8:7;
10:12–13; Jer 51:33; Joel 3:13; Mt 13:39; Rev 14:15).
restore the fortunes. Paralleling "heal" (7:1), the phrase
refers to the restoration of the wounded national body (see
Joel 3:1; Zep 3:20).
7:1 *heal.* See 5:13; 6:1; 11:3; 14:4; Jer 51:8–9. *sins.* See
4:8; 5:5; 8:13. *Ephraim.* Israel, the northern kingdom. *exposed . . . revealed.* God sees them. *crimes.* See v. 3. *Samaria.* Another name for the northern kingdom, of which
Samaria was the royal city, selected by Omri to be capital of
Israel (1Ki 16:24). *deceit.* See Jer 6:13; 8:10; probably refers
to both feigned repentance and treacherous foreign alliances.
thieves. See 4:2. *bandits.* See 6:9; Ge 49:19; Jer 18:22.
7:2 *I remember.* All is open before the Lord (see Ps 90:8),
but the wicked believe God does not see (see Ps 10:6,11;
14:1; Eze 8:12).
7:3 *delight the king.* Probably in conjunction with one of
the palace revolts (see 2Ki 15:8–30). *king . . . princes.*
Paired also in 3:4; 8:4; 13:10. *lies.* See 11:12; Ps 59:12; Na
3:1.
7:4 *adulterers.* See 3:1; 4:2,13; Jer 9:2; Eze 23:37. *fire.* A
metaphor for political intrigue (see vv. 6–7). The fire was
banked until ready to use; then it broke out. *baker.* Perhaps
the leader of the conspiracy.
7:5 *festival of our king.* Probably a coronation or birthday
that became a drunken party. King Elah died in drunkenness
(1Ki 16:9–10). *mockers.* See Pr 21:24. Isaiah (28:1–8,14)
condemned Israel's drunkenness and her scoffers.
7:6 The intrigue was kept secret until a suitable time.

they devour their rulers.
All their kings fall, *x*
    and none of them calls *y* on me.

8"Ephraim mixes *z* with the nations;
    Ephraim is a flat cake not turned
        over.
9Foreigners sap his strength, *a*
    but he does not realize it.
His hair is sprinkled with gray,
    but he does not notice.
10Israel's arrogance testifies against him, *b*
    but despite all this
he does not return *c* to the LORD his
        God
    or search *d* for him.

11"Ephraim is like a dove, *e*
    easily deceived and senseless—
now calling to Egypt, *f*
    now turning to Assyria. *g*
12When they go, I will throw my net *h*
        over them;
    I will pull them down like birds of
        the air.
When I hear them flocking together,
    I will catch them.
13Woe *i* to them,
    because they have strayed *j* from me!
Destruction to them,
    because they have rebelled against
        me!
I long to redeem them
    but they speak lies *k* against me. *l*
14They do not cry out to me from their
        hearts *m*
    but wail upon their beds.

They gather together *w* for grain and
        new wine *n*
    but turn away from me. *o*
15I trained *p* them and strengthened them,
    but they plot evil *q* against me.
16They do not turn to the Most High; *r*
    they are like a faulty bow. *s*
Their leaders will fall by the sword
    because of their insolent *t* words.
For this they will be ridiculed *u*
    in the land of Egypt. *v*

Israel to Reap the Whirlwind

8 "Put the trumpet *w* to your lips!
    An eagle *x* is over the house of the
        LORD
because the people have broken my
        covenant *y*
    and rebelled against my law. *z*
2Israel cries out to me,
    'O our God, we acknowledge you!'
3But Israel has rejected what is good;
    an enemy will pursue him. *a*
4They set up kings without my consent;
    they choose princes without my
        approval. *b*
With their silver and gold
    they make idols *c* for themselves
        to their own destruction.
5Throw out your calf-idol, O Samaria! *d*
    My anger burns against them.
How long will they be incapable of
        purity? *e*
6   They are from Israel!

w 14 Most Hebrew manuscripts; some Hebrew
manuscripts and Septuagint *They slash themselves*

7:7 *x*Hos 13:10
*y*ver 16;
S Ps 14:4;
S Isa 9:13;
Zep 1:6
7:8 *z*ver 11;
Ps 106:35;
S Hos 5:13
7:9 *a*Isa 1:7;
Hos 8:7
7:10 *b*Hos 5:5
*c*Hos 5:4 *d*ver 14;
S Isa 9:13
7:11 *e*S Ge 8:8
*f*ver 16; Hos 9:6
*g*S ver 8;
S Jer 2:18;
S La 5:6; Hos 9:3;
12:1
7:12 *h*S Eze 12:13;
S 32:3
7:13 *i*Hos 9:12
*j*Jer 14:10;
S Eze 34:4-6;
Hos 9:17
*k*S Ps 116:11 *l*ver
1; Jer 51:9;
Mt 23:37
7:14 *m*Jer 3:10

*n*Am 2:8 *o*S ver
10; S Hos 4:10;
9:1; 13:16
7:15 *p*Hos 11:3
*q*Ps 2:1; S 140:2;
Na 1:9,11
7:16 *r*S ver 7
*s*S Ps 78:9,57
*t*Mal 3:14
*u*S Eze 23:32
*v*S ver 11;
Hos 9:3; 11:5
8:1 *w*S Nu 10:2;
S Eze 33:3
*x*S Dt 28:49;
Jer 4:13
*y*S Jer 11:10
*z*S Hos 4:6; S 6:7
8:3 *a*S Mt 7:23;
Tit 1:16
8:4 *b*Hos 13:10
*c*S Hos 2:8;
13:1-2
8:5 *d*ver 6;
Hos 10:5
*e*Jer 13:27

7:7 *rulers . . . kings.* Four kings were assassinated in 20 years, Zechariah and Shallum in a seven-month period (2Ki 15:10–15). *none of them calls on me.* The reason for the shameful situation.
7:8 *flat cake.* A metaphor describing unwise policies. Baked on hot stones (cf. 1Ki 19:6), the cake was burned on the bottom and raw on the top.
7:9 *hair . . . gray.* He was old before his time, but ignored the danger signals. Tribute to Tiglath-Pileser (2Ki 15:19–20,29) and to Egypt had sapped the country economically.
7:10 *return.* See 3:5; 5:4; Am 4:6–11. *search.* See 2:7; 5:6.
7:11 *dove.* See 11:11, where a different image is intended. *senseless.* See Jer 5:21. Menahem turned to Assyria (2Ki 15:19–20), and Pekah to Egypt. Hoshea alternated in allegiance to both (2Ki 17:4).
7:12 *my net.* The Lord himself was the hunter—not the nations—and Israel was certain to be caught.
7:13 *Woe.* Often used in conjunction with threats of judgment (see 9:12). *Destruction.* See 9:6; Isa 13:6. *redeem.* See 13:14; also used for deliverance from Egypt (see, e.g., Ex 6:6; Mic 6:4). *lies.* Possibly of ascribing prosperity and destiny to gods other than the Lord.
7:14 *wail.* See Joel 1:13. *They gather together.* See NIV text note; cf. Lev 19:28; 21:5. *grain and new wine.* See 2:8,22; 9:1–2.

7:15 *I trained them.* As children (or, perhaps, as troops). *strengthened them.* Lit. "strengthened their arms" (see Eze 30:24–25).
7:16 *Most High.* See 11:7. *faulty bow.* See Ps 78:57. The arrow missed the mark; Israel missed her purpose for being. *ridiculed.* Egypt would fail to assist Israel and then would belittle God's power (see Dt 9:28). *Egypt.* See 8:13; 9:6; 11:5. There is no record of a forced exile of large numbers to Egypt. Some captives were taken there (2Ki 23:34; Jer 22:11–14), and some fugitives voluntarily went there (2Ki 25:26; Jer 42–44). A return from Egypt is envisioned in 11:11; Isa 11:11; 27:13; Zec 10:10.
8:1 *trumpet.* Of alarm (see 5:8; Joel 2:1; Am 3:6). *your.* The prophet's. *eagle.* Or "vulture," referring to Assyria. *house of the Lord.* The land of Israel, not just the temple (see 9:15 and note; cf. Ex 15:17). *covenant.* The demands of the covenant.
8:2 *we acknowledge you.* But their worship of the Lord was thoroughly corrupted by pagan notions and practices, as vv. 3–6 indicate (see Am 2:4,7–8; 3:14; 5:26).
8:4 *set up kings.* After Jeroboam II, five kings ruled over Israel in 13 years (2Ki 15:8–30), three of whom seized the throne by violence (see 7:7).
8:5 *calf-idol.* Jeroboam I (930–909 B.C.) had set up golden calves in Bethel and Dan, saying "Here are your gods" (see 1Ki 12:28–33 and note on 1Ki 12:28).
8:6 *a craftsman has made it.* For prophetic satire on idola-

This calf—a craftsman has made it;
  it is not God.[f]
It will be broken in pieces,
  that calf[g] of Samaria.[h]

[7]"They sow the wind
  and reap the whirlwind.[i]
The stalk has no head;
  it will produce no flour.[j]
Were it to yield grain,
  foreigners would swallow it up.[k]
[8]Israel is swallowed up;[l]
  now she is among the nations
  like a worthless[m] thing.
[9]For they have gone up to Assyria[n]
  like a wild donkey[o] wandering alone.
Ephraim has sold herself to lovers.[p]
[10]Although they have sold themselves
    among the nations,
  I will now gather them together.[q]
They will begin to waste away[r]
  under the oppression of the mighty
    king.

[11]"Though Ephraim built many altars for
    sin offerings,
  these have become altars for
    sinning.[s]
[12]I wrote for them the many things of my
    law,
  but they regarded them as something
    alien.[t]
[13]They offer sacrifices given to me
  and they eat[u] the meat,

but the LORD is not pleased with
    them.[v]
Now he will remember[w] their
    wickedness
  and punish their sins:[x]
They will return to Egypt.[y]
[14]Israel has forgotten[z] his Maker[a]
  and built palaces;
Judah has fortified many towns.
But I will send fire upon their cities
  that will consume their fortresses."[b]

Punishment for Israel

9 Do not rejoice, O Israel;
  do not be jubilant[c] like the other
    nations.
For you have been unfaithful[d] to your
    God;
  you love the wages of a prostitute[e]
    at every threshing floor.
[2]Threshing floors and winepresses will
    not feed the people;
  the new wine[f] will fail them.
[3]They will not remain[g] in the LORD's
    land;
  Ephraim will return to Egypt[h]
    and eat unclean[x] food in Assyria.[i]
[4]They will not pour out wine offerings[j]
    to the LORD,
  nor will their sacrifices please[k] him.
Such sacrifices will be to them like the
    bread of mourners;[l]

[x]3 That is, ceremonially unclean

8:6 [f]S Jer 16:20; Hos 14:3 [g]S Ex 32:4 [h]S ver 5
8:7 [i]S Job 4:8; Pr 22:8; Isa 66:15; Hos 10:12-13; Na 1:3; Gal 6:8 [j]S Dt 28:38; [S] Isa 17:11; Hos 9:16 [k]Hos 2:9; S 7:9
8:8 [l]Jer 51:34 [m]Jer 22:28
8:9 [n]S Jer 2:18 [o]S Ge 16:12 [p]S Jer 22:20; Eze 23:5; S Hos 5:13
8:10 [q]S Eze 16:37; S 22:20 [r]Jer 42:2
8:11 [s]Hos 10:1; 12:11
8:12 [t]S ver 1
8:13 [u]S Jer 7:21
[v]S Jer 6:20; Hos 9:4 [w]Hos 7:2; 9:9; Am 8:7 [x]S Hos 4:9 [y]Hos 9:3,6
8:14 [z]S Dt 32:18; S Isa 17:10; S Hos 2:13 [a]S Ps 95:6 [b]Jer 5:17; S 17:27; Am 2:5
9:1 [c]Isa 22:12-13 [d]S Ps 73:27; S Isa 24:16; S Hos 7:14; 10:5 [e]S Ge 30:15
9:2 [f]Isa 24:7; Hos 2:9; Joel 1:10
9:3 [g]Lev 25:23 [h]S Hos 7:16; S 8:13 [i]Eze 4:13; S Hos 7:11; 10:5; Am 7:17
9:4 [j]Joel 1:9,13; 2:14 [k]S Hos 8:13 [l]S Jer 16:7

try see Isa 40:20; 41:22–24; 44:9–20; see also Ps 115:4–8. Aaron (Ex 32:8) and Jeroboam I had said, "These are your gods"; but Hosea said, "It is not God."
8:7 *sow . . . reap.* A familiar proverb about the results of doing evil (see 10:13; Job 4:8; Ps 126:5–6; Pr 11:18; 22:8; 2Co 9:6; Gal 6:7). Israel sowed the wind of idolatry and reaped the whirlwind of Assyria. *stalk . . . flour.* The prophet played on the similar sound of the Hebrew words. *foreigners.* Assyria.
8:8 Israel was chosen to be God's own people (Ex 19:5; Am 3:2), but since she had conformed to the other nations, she lost her special identity and so became worthless to God.
8:9 *Ephraim has sold herself to lovers.* For the "prostitute's fees" of Assyrian protection. Menahem (2Ki 15:19) and Hoshea (2Ki 17:3), kings of Israel, paid tribute to Assyria.
8:10 Even though Israel paid tribute to Assyria, that would not buy her security, for God would send judgment by the king of Assyria. Israel's real "enemy" was the Lord himself (see 2:8–9,13; 7:12).
8:11 *built many altars.* To Baal.
8:13 *offer sacrifices.* See v. 2 and note. *eat the meat.* Some of the sacrifices were partly eaten by the offerer and priests (see Lev 7:11–18; Dt 12:7; Jer 7:21). *not pleased with them.* See note on 6:6. *Egypt.* Israel, who had trusted in Egypt and Assyria, would have to go back to "Egypt," i.e., into bondage in a foreign land, primarily Assyria (see 9:3). But see note on 7:16.
8:14 *Israel has forgotten.* The cause of all their problems (cf. Jdg 2:10). *built palaces . . . fortified many towns.* Israel's

trust was not in her Maker but in what she herself had accomplished. *Judah.* See Introduction: Author and Date. *fire.* See Am 1:4,7,10,14; 2:5.
9:1 This verse begins a section that was probably spoken at a harvest festival, such as the Feast of Tabernacles (Lev 23:33–43; Dt 16:13–15). *unfaithful.* See 1:2; 2:2–5. *wages of a prostitute.* See 2:5,12; not to be taken literally, but in the sense of spiritual adultery. *at every threshing floor.* Since the threshing floor at threshing time was a man's world—the threshers stayed there all night to protect the grain and feasted at the end of the day's labors—prostitutes were not uncommon visitors (see Ru 3:2–3 and notes).
9:3 *LORD's land.* The promised land, which the Lord claimed as his own (cf. Lev 25:23; Jos 22:19; Jer 2:7; Eze 38:16; Joel 1:6). *Ephraim.* Israel, the northern kingdom. *Egypt . . . Assyria.* Israel was threatened with exile to the lands it depended on—where the temple sacrifice could not be offered (see 8:13 and note). *unclean.* A foreign country was unclean (see NIV text note; see also Am 7:17 and NIV text note). What grew there was likewise unclean, because it was the product of fertility credited to pagan gods (see Eze 4:13).
9:4 *bread of mourners.* Unclean, like bread in a house where there had been a death (see Nu 19:14; Dt 26:14; Jer 16:7). All who touched it became ceremonially unclean. *not come into the temple of the LORD.* In exile Israel would have no place (not even those places established by Jeroboam I; 1Ki 12:28–33) where she could bring sacrifices to the Lord or celebrate her religious festivals (v. 5).

all who eat them will be unclean. *m*
This food will be for themselves;
it will not come into the temple of
the LORD. *n*

5What will you do *o* on the day of your
appointed feasts, *p*
on the festival days of the LORD?
6Even if they escape from destruction,
Egypt will gather them, *q*
and Memphis *r* will bury them. *s*
Their treasures of silver *t* will be taken
over by briers,
and thorns *u* will overrun their tents.
7The days of punishment *v* are coming,
the days of reckoning *w* are at hand.
Let Israel know this.
Because your sins *x* are so many
and your hostility so great,
the prophet is considered a fool, *y*
the inspired man a maniac. *z*
8The prophet, along with my God,
is the watchman over Ephraim, *y*
yet snares *a* await him on all his paths,
and hostility in the house of his
God. *b*
9They have sunk deep into corruption, *c*
as in the days of Gibeah. *d*
God will remember *e* their wickedness
and punish them for their sins. *f*

10"When I found Israel,
it was like finding grapes in the
desert;
when I saw your fathers,
it was like seeing the early fruit *g* on
the fig *h* tree.
But when they came to Baal Peor, *i*
they consecrated themselves to that
shameful idol *j*
and became as vile as the thing they
loved.

11Ephraim's glory *k* will fly away like a
bird *l* —
no birth, no pregnancy, no
conception. *m*
12Even if they rear children,
I will bereave *n* them of every one.
Woe *o* to them
when I turn away from them! *p*
13I have seen Ephraim, *q* like Tyre,
planted in a pleasant place. *r*
But Ephraim will bring out
their children to the slayer." *s*

14Give them, O LORD—
what will you give them?
Give them wombs that miscarry
and breasts that are dry. *t*

15"Because of all their wickedness in
Gilgal, *u*
I hated them there.
Because of their sinful deeds, *v*
I will drive them out of my house.
I will no longer love them; *w*
all their leaders are rebellious. *x*
16Ephraim *y* is blighted,
their root is withered,
they yield no fruit. *z*
Even if they bear children,
I will slay *a* their cherished offspring."
17My God will reject *b* them
because they have not obeyed *c* him;
they will be wanderers among the
nations. *d*

10 Israel was a spreading vine; *e*
he brought forth fruit for himself.
As his fruit increased,
he built more altars; *f*

9:4 *m*S Dt 26:14;
Hag 2:13-14
*n*S Eze 4:13-14
9:5 *o*Isa 10:3;
Jer 5:31
*p*S Hos 2:11
9:6 *q*S Hos 7:11;
S 8:13
*r*S Isa 19:13
*s*S Jer 42:22
*t*Zep 1:11
*u*Isa 5:6;
Hos 10:8
9:7 *v*Isa 34:8;
Jer 10:15;
Mic 7:4; Lk 21:22
*w*S Job 31:14
*x*Jer 16:18
*y*S 1Sa 10:11;
Isa 44:25;
S La 2:14;
Eze 14:9-10
*z*S Jer 29:26;
Hos 14:1
9:8 *a*S Hos 5:1
*b*S Eze 22:26
9:9 *c*Zep 3:7
*d*Jdg 19:16-30;
S Hos 5:8
*e*S Hos 8:13
*f*S Hos 4:9
9:10 *g*S SS 2:13
*h*S Isa 28:4
*i*Nu 25:1-5;
Ps 106:28-29
*j*Jer 11:13;
S Hos 4:14

9:11 *k*S Isa 17:3
*l*S Hos 4:7; 10:5
*m*ver 14
9:12 *n*ver 16;
S Eze 24:21
*o*Hos 7:13
*p*S Dt 31:17
9:13 *q*S Ps 78:67
*r*S Eze 27:3
*s*S Job 15:22;
S La 2:22
9:14 *t*ver 11;
Lk 23:29
9:15 *u*S Hos 4:15
*v*S Hos 7:2
*w*S Jer 12:8
*x*S Isa 1:23;
S Hos 4:9; 5:2
9:16 *y*S Hos 5:11
*z*S Job 15:32;
S Hos 8:7 *a*S ver 12
9:17 *b*S Jer 6:30
*c*S Hos 4:10
*d*S Dt 28:65;
S Hos 7:13

10:1 *e*S Eze 15:2 *f*S 1Ki 14:23

*y*8 Or *The prophet is the watchman over Ephraim, / the people of my God*

9:6 *Egypt.* See 7:16 and note. *Memphis.* The capital of Lower (northern) Egypt. *briers, and thorns.* Cf. a similar threat against Edom (Isa 34:13).
9:7 *inspired man.* See Mic 2:11; 3:8. *maniac.* See 2Ki 9:11; Jer 29:26; cf. 1Sa 21:15.
9:8 *watchman.* See Isa 56:10; Jer 6:17; Eze 3:17; 33:2-8. *snares . . . hostility.* Israel showed only hostility toward the watchmen (the true prophets) whom God sent to warn his people of the great dangers that threatened (see Jer 1:19; 11:19; 15:10; Am 7:10-12).
9:9 *corruption.* The word used of the Israelites who worshiped the golden calf (Ex 32:7; Dt 9:12; 32:5). *days of Gibeah.* A reference to the corrupt events of Jdg 19–21. *God will remember.* Sins unrepented of are remembered, as well as the accumulated sins of generations (see 13:12).
9:10 The covenant relation is traced back to the desert (see 2:14–15; 13:5; Dt 32:10). *grapes . . . fig.* Refreshing delicacies (see Isa 28:4; Mic 7:1). The images used here (grapes in the desert, early fruit of the fig tree) beautifully convey God's delight in Israel when she, out of all the nations, committed herself to him in covenant at Sinai. *Baal Peor.* A shortened

form of Beth Baal Peor. Peor was a mountain (Dt 3:29). Baal Peor refers to the god of Peor (Nu 25:1–4) and was used interchangeably with Beth Peor, "the temple of Peor" (see Dt 3:29; 4:3,46; Jos 13:20). Hosea refers here to the incident in Nu 25. *became . . . vile.* See Isa 5:2,4,7.
9:11 *Ephraim's glory.* Her large population and prosperity. The punishment fit the sin. Prostitution produces no increase (see 4:10).
9:12 *to them.* To the children.
9:13 *Tyre.* Noted for its wealth, pleasant environment and security (see Eze 27:2–26).
9:14 Hosea did not pray out of hateful vengeance against Israel, but because he shared God's holy wrath against her sins.
9:15 *Gilgal.* See note on 4:15. *drive them out of my house.* As the unfaithful wife was driven from the husband's house, so Israel was driven from God's "house" —i.e., his land (see 8:1 and note). *leaders . . . rebellious.* A wordplay in Hebrew.
9:17 *My God.* Hosea's words alone, for God was no longer Israel's God. *reject.* See 4:6; 2Ki 17:20. *wanderers.* Like Cain (Ge 4:14–15).

as his land prospered, *g*
  he adorned his sacred stones. *h*
²Their heart is deceitful, *i*
  and now they must bear their guilt. *j*
The LORD will demolish their altars *k*
  and destroy their sacred stones. *l*

³Then they will say, "We have no king
  because we did not revere the LORD.
But even if we had a king,
  what could he do for us?"
⁴They make many promises,
  take false oaths *m*
and make agreements; *n*
therefore lawsuits spring up
  like poisonous weeds *o* in a plowed
    field.
⁵The people who live in Samaria fear
  for the calf-idol *p* of Beth Aven. *z q*
Its people will mourn over it,
  and so will its idolatrous priests, *r*
those who had rejoiced over its
    splendor,
  because it is taken from them into
    exile. *s*
⁶It will be carried to Assyria *t*
  as tribute *u* for the great king. *v*
Ephraim will be disgraced; *w*
Israel will be ashamed *x* of its wooden
    idols. *a*
⁷Samaria and its king will float away *y*
  like a twig on the surface of the
    waters.
⁸The high places *z* of wickedness *b a* will
    be destroyed—
  it is the sin of Israel.
Thorns *b* and thistles will grow up
  and cover their altars. *c*
Then they will say to the mountains,
    "Cover us!" *d*
  and to the hills, "Fall on us!" *e*

⁹"Since the days of Gibeah, *f* you have
    sinned, *g* O Israel,
  and there you have remained. *c*
Did not war overtake
  the evildoers in Gibeah?
¹⁰When I please, I will punish *h* them;
  nations will be gathered against them
to put them in bonds for their double
    sin.
¹¹Ephraim is a trained heifer
  that loves to thresh;
so I will put a yoke *i*
  on her fair neck.
I will drive Ephraim,
  Judah must plow,
  and Jacob must break up the ground.
¹²Sow *j* for yourselves righteousness, *k*
  reap the fruit of unfailing love,
  and break up your unplowed ground; *l*
for it is time to seek *m* the LORD,
  until he comes
  and showers righteousness *n* on you.
¹³But you have planted wickedness,
  you have reaped evil, *o*
  you have eaten the fruit of
    deception. *p*
Because you have depended on your
    own strength
  and on your many warriors, *q*
¹⁴the roar of battle will rise against your
    people,
  so that all your fortresses will be
    devastated *r* —
as Shalman *s* devastated Beth Arbel on
    the day of battle,

Cross references (center column):

10:1 *g*Hos 13:15
*h*Hos 3:4; S 4:7;
S 8:11; 12:11
10:2 *i*1Ki 18:21
/Hos 13:16 *k*ver 8
*l*Mic 5:13
10:4 *m*S Hos 4:2
*n*S Eze 17:19;
Am 5:7 *o*Am 6:12
10:5 *p*S Ex 32:4;
S Isa 44:17-20
*q*ver 8; S Hos 5:8
*r*S 2Ki 23:5;
Zep 1:4
*s*S Jdg 18:17-18;
S Hos 8:5; S 9:1,
3,11
10:6 *t*S 2Ki 16:7;
Hos 11:5
*u*S Jdg 3:15
*v*S Hos 5:13
*w*Isa 30:3;
S Hos 4:7
*x*Jer 48:13
10:7 *y*ver 15;
Hos 13:11
10:8 *z*S Eze 6:6
*a*S ver 5;
1Ki 12:28-30;
S Hos 4:13
*b*S Hos 9:6 *c*ver
2; S Isa 32:13
*d*S Job 30:6;
Am 3:14-15
*e*Am 7:9;
Lk 23:30*;
Rev 6:16

10:9 *f*S Hos 5:8
*g*S Jos 7:11
10:10
*h*S Eze 5:13;
S Hos 4:9
10:11
*i*S Jer 15:12;
S 31:18
10:12 *j*S Ecc 11:1
*k*S Pr 11:18;
Jas 3:18 *l*Jer 4:3
*m*S Isa 19:22;
Hos 12:6
*n*S Isa 45:8
10:13 *o*S Job 4:8;
S Hos 7:3; 11:12;
Gal 6:7-8
*p*S Pr 11:18;
S Hos 8:7
*q*Ps 33:16
10:14 *r*S Isa 17:3;
Mic 5:11
*s*S 2Ki 17:3

Footnotes (center column):

z 5 *Beth Aven* means *house of wickedness* (a name for
Bethel, which means *house of God*). *a 6* Or *its
counsel*   *b 8* Hebrew *aven,* a reference to Beth Aven (a
derogatory name for Bethel)   *c 9* Or *there a stand was
taken*

10:1 *Israel.* The nation personified and called by the name
of its ancestor. *vine.* A frequent metaphor for Israel (Dt
32:32; Ps 80:8–11; Isa 5:1; Jer 2:21; cf. Jn 15:1). *prospered.* The prosperity during the period of Jeroboam II
(793–753 B.C.) was probably in view.
10:2 *Their heart is deceitful.* Israel formally called to God
(8:2), but they dishonored him by pagan worship.
10:3 *We have no king.* Such would soon be their condition
when Assyria destroyed the nation.
10:4 *They make many promises.* The last kings of Israel
were notoriously corrupt and deceitful.
10:5 *Samaria.* The royal city of Israel (see note on 7:1).
calf-idol of Beth Aven. The idol that Jeroboam set up at
Bethel (see NIV text note; see also 1Ki 12:32–33).
10:6 *Ephraim.* Israel, the northern kingdom.
10:8 *high places.* See 4:13–14. *wickedness.* See NIV text
note. *Cover us!... Fall on us!* Cries of utter despair; quoted
by Jesus (Lk 23:30) and alluded to in Rev 6:16 (see Isa 2:19).
10:9 *Gibeah.* See 9:9 and note. As war came on Gibeah, so
war and captivity would come on Israel.
10:11 *trained heifer.* Up to now Ephraim (Israel) had been
as contented as a young cow that ate while threshing grain.

But now God would cause Israel (here called both Ephraim
and Jacob) and Judah to do the heavy work of plowing and
harrowing under a yoke—a picture of going into the Assyrian
and Babylonian captivities. *Judah.* See Introduction: Author
and Date.
10:12 *reap the fruit of unfailing love.* If Israel would only
do what was right ("unfailing love" translates the Hebrew
word *hesed;* see note on 6:6), she would be blessed by God.
break up your unplowed ground. Be no longer unproductive,
but repentant, making a radical new beginning and becoming productive and fruitful. *righteousness.* God's covenant
blessings that in righteousness he would shower on his
people if they in righteousness were loyal to him, their
covenant Lord.
10:13 *deception.* Israel had been living a lie—and by lies
(see 7:3; 10:4; 12:1).
10:14 *Shalman devastated Beth Arbel.* The event is otherwise unknown, as are the names mentioned. Atrocities
against civilians were common in ancient warfare (cf. 9:13;
13:16; 2Ki 8:12–13; Ps 137:8–9; Isa 13:16; Am 1:13; Na
3:10).

when mothers were dashed to the
  ground with their children. [t]
[15]Thus will it happen to you, O Bethel,
  because your wickedness is great.
When that day dawns,
  the king of Israel will be completely
  destroyed. [u]

God's Love for Israel

11 "When Israel was a child, [v] I
  loved [w] him,
and out of Egypt I called my son. [x]
[2]But the more I [d] called Israel,
  the further they went from me. [e] [y]
They sacrificed to the Baals [z]
  and they burned incense to images. [a]
[3]It was I who taught Ephraim to walk,
  taking them by the arms; [b]
but they did not realize
  it was I who healed [c] them.
[4]I led them with cords of human
  kindness,
  with ties of love; [d]
I lifted the yoke [e] from their neck
  and bent down to feed [f] them. [g]

[5]"Will they not return to Egypt [h]
  and will not Assyria [i] rule over them
  because they refuse to repent? [j]
[6]Swords [k] will flash in their cities,
  will destroy the bars [l] of their gates
  and put an end to their plans.
[7]My people are determined to turn [m]
  from me. [n]
Even if they call to the Most High,
  he will by no means exalt them.

[8]"How can I give you up, [o] Ephraim? [p]
How can I hand you over, Israel?
How can I treat you like Admah?
  How can I make you like Zeboiim? [q]
My heart is changed within me;
  all my compassion [r] is aroused. [s]
[9]I will not carry out my fierce anger, [t]
  nor will I turn and devastate [u]
  Ephraim.
For I am God, and not man [v] —
  the Holy One [w] among you.
I will not come in wrath. [f]
[10]They will follow the LORD;
  he will roar [x] like a lion. [y]
When he roars,
  his children will come trembling [z]
  from the west. [a]
[11]They will come trembling
  like birds from Egypt,
  like doves [b] from Assyria. [c]
I will settle them in their homes," [d]
  declares the LORD.

Israel's Sin

[12]Ephraim has surrounded me with lies, [e]
  the house of Israel with deceit.
And Judah is unruly against God,
  even against the faithful [f] Holy One. [g]

12 [1]Ephraim [h] feeds on the wind; [i]
  he pursues the east wind all day

10:14
[r]S Isa 13:16;
Hos 13:16
10:15 [u]S ver 7
11:1 [v]S Jer 2:2;
S Eze 16:22
[w]S Dt 4:37
[x]S Ex 4:22;
Hos 12:9,13;
13:4; Mt 2:15*
11:2 [y]ver 7
[z]S Hos 2:13
[a]S 2Ki 17:15;
Isa 65:7;
S Jer 18:15;
S Hos 4:13; 13:1
11:3 [b]S Dt 1:31;
S 32:11; Hos 7:15
[c]S Ex 15:26;
Jer 30:17
11:4 [d]Jer 31:2-3
[e]S Lev 26:13
[f]Ex 16:32;
Ps 78:25
[g]Jer 31:20
11:5 [h]S Hos 7:16
[i]S Hos 10:6
[j]S Ex 13:17
11:6 [k]Hos 13:16
[l]S La 2:9
11:7 [m]S Isa 26:10
[n]ver 2; Jer 3:6-7;
8:5

11:8 [o]S Jer 7:29
[p]Hos 6:4
[q]S Ge 14:8;
S La 3:32
[r]S 1Ki 3:26;
S Ps 25:6
[s]S Eze 33:11;
Am 7:3
11:9 [t]Dt 13:17;
S Jer 18:8;
S 30:11 [u]La 3:22;
Mal 3:6
[v]S Nu 23:19
[w]S 2Ki 19:22;
S Isa 31:1
11:10
[x]S Isa 42:13
[y]S Isa 31:4
[z]S Ps 18:45
[a]S Hos 3:5;
S 6:1-3
11:11 [b]S Ge 8:8
[c]S Isa 11:11

[d]S Eze 28:26; S 34:25-28 **11:12** [e]S Hos 4:2 [f]S Dt 7:9
[g]S Hos 10:13 **12:1** [h]S Ps 78:67 [i]S Ge 41:6; S Eze 17:10

[d]2 Some Septuagint manuscripts; Hebrew *they*
[e]2 Septuagint; Hebrew *them*   [f]9 Or *come against any
city*

11:1 A third appeal to history (see 9:10; 10:9) traces God's
choice of Israel back to Egypt, the exodus from that country
(cf. 12:9; 13:4) having given birth to the nation. Israel's
response to the Lord is now illustrated by the wayward son
rather than by the unfaithful wife (chs. 1–3). For Israel as a
son see Ex 4:22–23; Isa 1:2–4; and for God as Father see Dt
32:6; Jer 2:14. Hosea saw God's love as the basis (cf. 3:1) for
the election of Israel. Matthew found in the call of Israel from
Egypt a typological picture of Jesus' coming from Egypt (see
Mt 2:15 and note).
11:2 *images.* See Dt 7:25; 12:3.
11:3 *Ephraim.* Israel, the northern kingdom. *walk.* This
picture of a father teaching his child to walk is one of the
most tender in the OT. *did not realize.* See 2:5–8. *healed.*
See 5:13; 6:1; 7:1.
11:4 The imagery is unclear, but the figure seems to change
to a farmer tending his work animals. Another interpretation
sees a continuation of the son image, with the father lifting
the son to his cheek. *feed them.* God supplied miraculous
food in the desert (see Ex 16; Dt 8:16).
11:5 *Egypt... Assyria.* See 8:13 and note; 9:3. The tender
tone (vv. 1–4) changes to threat of exile to the two countries
between which Israel had vacillated. It is ironic that the
people rescued from Egypt should be returned there because
of their disloyalty to the one who had rescued them.
11:7 *call to the Most High.* See 7:16.
11:8 The stubborn son was subject to stoning (Dt

21:18–21), but the Lord's compassion overcame his wrath
and he refused to destroy Ephraim (Israel). *Admah ... Zeboiim.* Cities of the plain (Ge 10:19; 14:2,8), overthrown
when Sodom was destroyed (Ge 19:24–25; Dt 29:23; Jer
49:18) and symbolizing total destruction.
11:9 *God, and not man.* Although Israel has been as
unreliable as man, God will not be untrue to the love he has
shown toward Israel (see vv. 1–4; see also 1Sa 15:29; Mal
3:6). Israel was to be punished, but not destroyed. *the Holy
One among you.* See notes on Isa 1:4; 6:1; cf. Isa 12:6.
God's holiness is alluded to only here in Hosea.
11:10 The return from exile. *roar like a lion.* Rather than
threatening destruction (cf. 5:14; 13:7), God's roar was now
a clear signal to return from exile. *the west.* The islands of
the sea (as well as coastlands).
11:11 *from Egypt ... Assyria.* See 9:3. *like birds ... like
doves.* Suggests swiftness of return (cf. Isa 60:8) and is not
derogatory, as was the earlier comparison to a silly dove
(7:11). *declares the LORD.* See 2:13,16,21.
11:12 *lies... deceit.* See 7:3; 10:13 and note. *Judah.* See
Introduction: Author and Date. *unruly against God.* See Jer
2:31.
12:1 *wind.* See 8:7; Ecc 1:14. *east wind.* See 13:15; Job
15:2; 27:21; Isa 27:8; Jer 18:17. Pursuing the wind symbolized Israel's futile foreign policy, which vacillated between Egypt (2Ki 17:4; Isa 30:6–7) and Assyria (cf. 5:13;
7:11; 8:9; 2Ki 17:3).

and multiplies lies and violence.*j*
He makes a treaty with Assyria *k*
and sends olive oil to Egypt. *l*
[2]The LORD has a charge *m* to bring against
Judah; *n*
he will punish*o* Jacob*g* according to
his ways
and repay him according to his
deeds. *p*
[3]In the womb he grasped his brother's
heel;*q*
as a man he struggled*r* with God.
[4]He struggled with the angel and
overcame him;
he wept and begged for his favor.
He found him at Bethel *s*
and talked with him there—
[5]the LORD God Almighty,
the LORD is his name*t* of renown!
[6]But you must return*u* to your God;
maintain love and justice, *v*
and wait for your God always. *w*

[7]The merchant uses dishonest scales; *x*
he loves to defraud.
[8]Ephraim boasts, *y*
"I am very rich; I have become
wealthy. *z*
With all my wealth they will not find in
me
any iniquity or sin."

[9]"I am the LORD your God,

who brought you, out of*h* Egypt; *a*
I will make you live in tents*b* again,
as in the days of your appointed
feasts.
[10]I spoke to the prophets,
gave them many visions
and told parables*c* through them." *d*

[11]Is Gilead wicked?*e*
Its people are worthless!
Do they sacrifice bulls in Gilgal?*f*
Their altars will be like piles of stones
on a plowed field.*g*
[12]Jacob fled to the country of Aram*i* ; *h*
Israel served to get a wife,
and to pay for her he tended sheep. *i*
[13]The LORD used a prophet to bring Israel
up from Egypt,*j*
by a prophet he cared for him. *k*
[14]But Ephraim has bitterly provoked him
to anger;
his Lord will leave upon him the guilt
of his bloodshed*l*
and will repay him for his
contempt. *m*

The LORD's Anger Against Israel

13 When Ephraim spoke, men
trembled; *n*

g2 *Jacob* means *he grasps the heel* (figuratively, *he deceives*). **h**9 Or *God / ever since you were in* **i**12 That is, Northwest Mesopotamia

12:1 *j*S Hos 4:19; *k*Hos 5:13; *l*S 2Ki 17:4
12:2 *m*S Job 10:2; Mic 6:2 *n*Am 2:4
*o*S Ex 32:34
*p*S Hos 4:9; S 9:15
12:3 *q*Ge 25:26 *r*Ge 32:24-29
12:4 *s*S Ge 12:8; S 35:15
12:5 *t*S Ex 3:15
12:6 *u*S Isa 19:22; Jer 4:1; Joel 2:12 *v*S Ps 106:3; S Jer 22:3 *w*S Eze 18:30; Hos 6:1-3; 10:12; Mic 7:7
12:7 *x*S Lev 19:36; Am 8:5
12:8 *y*S Eze 28:5 *z*Ps 62:10; Rev 3:17
12:9 *a*Lev 23:43; S Hos 2:15; S 11:1 *b*S Ne 8:17
12:10 *c*S Jdg 14:12; S Eze 20:49 *d*2Ki 17:13; Jer 7:25
12:11 *e*S Hos 6:8 *f*S Hos 4:15 *g*S Hos 8:11
12:12 *h*Ge 28:5 *i*S Ge 29:18
12:13 *j*S Hos 11:1 *k*Ex 13:3; 14:19-22; Isa 63:11-14
12:14 *l*S Eze 18:13 *m*Da 11:18
13:1 *n*Jdg 12:1

12:2 *charge.* See 4:1. *Judah.* See Introduction: Author and Date. *Jacob.* Israel (see 10:11). The Lord indicted both kingdoms—all the descendants of Father Jacob. In their deceitfulness, Israel and Judah were living up to the name of their forefather (see NIV text note).
12:3 *In the womb.* See Ge 25:26; 27:36. *grasped his brother's heel.* See NIV text note on v. 2. God's covenant people here relived the experiences of Father Jacob and now had to return to God, just as Jacob was called back to Bethel (Ge 35:1–15).
12:4 *struggled with the angel.* See Ge 32:22–28 and NIV text note on Ge 32:28. *Bethel.* See Ge 28:12–19; 35:1–15. In Hosea's time, Bethel was the most important royal sanctuary in the northern kingdom (cf. Am 7:13).
12:5 *LORD God Almighty.* Paralleled in Am 3:13; 6:14; 9:5.
12:6 *love.* Hebrew *hesed*; See 6:6 ("mercy") and note. *justice.* See Am 5:15,24; Mic 6:8.
12:7 *merchant.* As Hosea had played on the meaning of Jacob in v. 2, he here uses a wordplay on Canaan (the Hebrew for "merchant" sounds like Canaan) to charge that Israel was no better than a Canaanite.
12:8 *I am very rich.* Riches brought a sense of self-sufficiency (cf. 10:13; Dt 32:15–18). *not find in me any iniquity.* Like a dishonest merchant, Ephraim (Israel) was confident that her deceitfulness (cf. 11:12) would not come to light.
12:9 *I am the LORD your God.* See 13:4; cf. Ex 20:2. *tents.* As during the desert journey long ago (cf. 2:14–15). *appointed feasts.* Probably the Feast of Tabernacles (Lev 23:42–44), which commemorated the desert journey.
12:10 *spoke to the prophets.* See 6:5; Am 2:11; Heb 1:1. There had been ample warning. *visions.* Revelations (see Nu

12:6–8; Am 1:1). *parables.* Containing messages of warning from God (see 2Sa 12:1–4; Ps 78:2; Isa 5:1–7; Eze 17:2; 24:3).
12:11 *Gilead wicked.* See 6:8–9 and notes. Gilead was overrun by Assyria in 734–732 B.C. (2Ki 15:29). *Gilgal.* See 4:15; 9:15. The Hebrew contains a wordplay between "Gilgal" and "piles" (Hebrew *gallim*). Rather than assuring safety, the altars themselves would be destroyed. *on a plowed field.* Israelite farmers gathered into piles the stones turned up by their plows.
12:12 Jacob fled from Esau to Paddan Aram (Ge 28:2,5), serving Laban seven years for each wife (Ge 29:20–28), and then continued as Laban's herdsman (Ge 30:31; 31:41).
12:13 *prophet.* Moses (cf. Nu 12:6–8; Dt 18:15; 34:10). *cared for him.* As Jacob had cared for Laban's flocks, so the Lord cared for Israel during her desert wandering. Earlier leadership by the prophet Moses stands in contrast with Israel's present disregard for prophets (cf. 4:5; 6:5; 9:7).
12:14 *Ephraim ... provoked him.* Despite warnings. *bloodshed.* Cf. 1:4; 4:2; 5:2; 6:8. This may refer either to violence against the prophets or to human sacrifice (cf. 2Ki 17:17). In legal passages (Lev 20:11–27), "their blood will be on their own heads" describes guilt. The prophet made a contrast between past divine preservation and present divine anger that would bring punishment. *repay.* See Isa 65:7.
13:1 *When Ephraim spoke.* In accordance with Jacob's blessing (Ge 48:10–20), Ephraim became a powerful tribe (Jdg 8:1–3; 12:1–7; 1Sa 1:1–4), from which came such prominent leaders as Joshua (Jos 24:30) and Jeroboam I (1Ki 11:26; 12:20). *Israel.* The 12 tribes. *died.* The wages of sin was death (cf. Ro 6:23), and the end of the nation was at hand.

he was exalted[o] in Israel.
But he became guilty of Baal
  worship[p] and died.
2Now they sin more and more;
  they make[q] idols for themselves from
    their silver,[r]
cleverly fashioned images,
  all of them the work of craftsmen.[s]
It is said of these people,
  "They offer human sacrifice
  and kiss[t] the calf-idols.[u]"
3Therefore they will be like the morning
    mist,
  like the early dew that disappears,[v]
  like chaff[w] swirling from a threshing
    floor,[x]
  like smoke[y] escaping through a
    window.

4"But I am the LORD your God,
  who brought you out of[k] Egypt.[z]
You shall acknowledge[a] no God but
    me,[b]
  no Savior[c] except me.
5I cared for you in the desert,[d]
  in the land of burning heat.
6When I fed them, they were satisfied;
  when they were satisfied, they
    became proud;[e]
  then they forgot[f] me.[g]
7So I will come upon them like a lion,[h]
  like a leopard I will lurk by the path.
8Like a bear robbed of her cubs,[i]
  I will attack them and rip them open.
Like a lion[j] I will devour them;
  a wild animal will tear them apart.[k]

9"You are destroyed, O Israel,

because you are against me,[l] against
  your helper.[m]
10Where is your king,[n] that he may save
    you?
Where are your rulers in all your
    towns,
of whom you said,
  'Give me a king and princes'?[o]
11So in my anger I gave you a king,[p]
  and in my wrath I took him away.[q]
12The guilt of Ephraim is stored up,
  his sins are kept on record.[r]
13Pains as of a woman in childbirth[s]
  come to him,
but he is a child without wisdom;
when the time[t] arrives,
  he does not come to the opening of
    the womb.[u]

14"I will ransom them from the power of
    the grave[1];[v]
  I will redeem them from death.[w]
Where, O death, are your plagues?
  Where, O grave,[1] is your
    destruction?[x]

"I will have no compassion,
15 even though he thrives[y] among his
    brothers.
An east wind[z] from the LORD will
    come,
  blowing in from the desert;
his spring will fail
  and his well dry up.[a]
His storehouse will be plundered[b]

13:1 oS Jdg 8:1
pS Hos 11:2
13:2 qJer 44:8
rS Isa 46:6;
S Jer 10:4
sHos 14:3
t1Ki 19:18
uS Isa 44:17-20;
S Hos 8:4
13:3 vS Hos 6:4
wS Job 13:25;
Ps 1:4;
S Isa 17:13
xDa 2:35 yPs 68:2
13:4 zS Jer 2:6;
S Hos 12:9
aS Hos 2:20
bS Ex 20:3
cS Dt 28:29;
Ps 18:46;
Isa 43:11;
45:21-22
13:5 dS Dt 1:19
13:6 eS Eze 28:5
/S Dt 32:18;
S Isa 17:10
gDt 32:12-15;
S Pr 30:7-9;
S Jer 5:7;
S Hos 2:13; S 4:7
13:7
hS Job 10:16;
S Jer 4:7
13:8 i2Sa 17:8
/S 1Sa 17:34;
Ps 17:12
kPs 50:22;
S La 3:10;
S Hos 2:12

13:9 iJer 2:17-19
mS Dt 33:29
13:10 n2Ki 17:4;
Hos 7:7 oS 1Sa 8:6;
Hos 8:4
13:11
pS Nu 11:20
qS Jos 24:20;
S 1Sa 13:14;
S 1Ki 14:10;
Hos 3:4; S 10:7
13:12
rS Dt 32:34
13:13 sIsa 13:8;
Mic 4:9-10
t2Ki 19:3
uIsa 66:9
13:14
vS Ps 16:10;
49:15;

S Eze 37:12-13 wS Isa 25:8 x1Co 15:55* 13:15 yS Hos 10:1
zS Job 1:19; S Eze 9:12; S Hos 4:19 aS Jer 51:36 bJer 20:5

12 Or "Men who sacrifice / kiss   k4 Or God / ever
since you were in   114 Hebrew Sheol

13:2 idols. See 4:12; 8:5–6; 11:2. human sacrifice. See
2Ki 17:17; 23:10; Eze 20:26; Mic 6:7. For the sense of the
NIV text note see 1Ki 12:26–33. kiss. Show homage to (cf.
1Ki 19:18).
13:3 "Mist" and "dew" (see 6:4), "chaff" (see Ps 1:4;
35:5; Isa 17:13; 29:5) and "smoke" (see Ps 37:20; 68:2;
Isa 51:6) are all figurative for Ephraim, who was soon to
vanish as a nation.
13:4 I am the LORD. See 12:9; Ex 20:2–3; Dt 5:6. The
contrast is with Jeroboam's declaration, "Here are your
gods" (1Ki 12:28). acknowledge . . . God. See 4:1; 6:3; 8:2.
13:5 desert. See 2:14; 9:10.
13:6 satisfied. See Dt 6:11–12; 8:10–14; 11:15–16. forgot me. Cf. Dt 8:14; 31:20; 32:15,18.
13:7–8 The Lord, previously pictured as a shepherd
(4:16), would attack like the wild beasts that often ravaged
the flocks.
13:7 lion. See 5:14. leopard. See Jer 5:6; Rev 13:2.
13:8 bear robbed of her cubs. See 2Sa 17:8; 2Ki 2:24; Pr
17:12.
13:9 helper. See Ps 10:14; 30:10; 54:4.
13:10 Where is your king . . . ? Help is only from the Lord,
not from kings. The prophet likely alludes to the royal assassinations of his day (see 3:4; 7:7; 8:4; 10:3). Give me a king.
Though all Israel asked for a king in the days of Samuel (1Sa

8:5,20), the reference here is only to the northern monarchy. They selected Jeroboam I (1Ki 12:26) in preference to
the Davidic kings.
13:11 The monarchy is here considered a rebellion (see
1Sa 8:7).
13:12 guilt . . . stored up. See 9:9 and note; Job 14:17.
Ephraim. Israel, the northern kingdom. sins . . . on record.
See 7:2; Dt 32:34–35.
13:13 Pains as of . . . childbirth. Their helpless situation
was comparable to that of a woman in childbirth (see Isa
13:8; 21:3; 26:17; Jer 4:31; 13:21; Mic 4:9–10; Mt 24:8)
who cannot deliver the child (see 2Ki 19:3; Isa 37:3) and
consequently dies.
13:14 I will ransom. A promise of redemption from death.
death. The personified reference is to the death of the nation
(see v. 1). Paul applies this passage to resurrection (1Co
15:55). grave. See NIV text note. For a description of Sheol
see Job 3:13–19; Ps 18:5; 116:3; Isa 14:9–10; see also
notes on Ge 37:35; Jnh 2:2.
13:15 thrives. In Hebrew a wordplay on Ephraim (meaning
"fruitful"). The drought-bringing east wind (cf. Job 1:19; Isa
27:8; Jer 4:11; 13:24; 18:17) is here a figure for Assyria, an
instrument of the Lord (Isa 10:5,15). Assyria invaded the
northern kingdom in 734 B.C., then crushed it and exiled its
people in 722–721. all its treasures. See Na 2:9.

of all its treasures.

[16] The people of Samaria[c] must bear their guilt,[d]

because they have rebelled[e] against their God.

They will fall by the sword;[f]

their little ones will be dashed[g] to the ground,

their pregnant women[h] ripped open."

Repentance to Bring Blessing

14 Return,[i] O Israel, to the LORD your God.

Your sins[j] have been your downfall![k]

[2] Take words with you

and return to the LORD.

Say to him:

"Forgive[l] all our sins

and receive us graciously,[m]

that we may offer the fruit of our lips.[m][n]

[3] Assyria cannot save us;[o]

we will not mount war-horses.[p]

We will never again say 'Our gods'[q]

to what our own hands have made,[r]

for in you the fatherless[s] find compassion."

[4] "I will heal[t] their waywardness[u]

and love them freely,[v]

for my anger has turned away[w] from them.

[5] I will be like the dew[x] to Israel;

he will blossom like a lily.[y]

Like a cedar of Lebanon[z]

he will send down his roots;[a]

[6] his young shoots will grow.

His splendor will be like an olive tree,[b]

his fragrance like a cedar of Lebanon.[c]

[7] Men will dwell again in his shade.[d]

He will flourish like the grain.

He will blossom[e] like a vine,

and his fame will be like the wine[f] from Lebanon.[g]

[8] O Ephraim, what more have I[n] to do with idols?[h]

I will answer him and care for him.

I am like a green pine[i] tree;

your fruitfulness comes from me."

[9] Who is wise?[j] He will realize these things.

Who is discerning? He will understand them.[k]

The ways of the LORD are right;[l]

the righteous walk[m] in them,

but the rebellious stumble in them.

Cross references (center column)

13:16 [c]2Ki 17:5
[d]Hos 10:2
[e]S Hos 7:14
[f]Hos 11:6
[g]S 2Ki 8:12;
S Hos 10:14
[h]2Ki 15:16;
Isa 13:16;
Am 1:13
14:1 [i]S Isa 19:22;
S Jer 3:12
[j]S Hos 4:8
[k]S Hos 5:5; S 9:7
14:2 [l]S Ex 34:9
[m]Ps 51:16-17;
Mic 7:18-19
[n]Heb 13:15
14:3 [o]S Hos 5:13
[p]Ps 33:17;
S Isa 31:1;
Mic 5:10
[q]S 10:14; 68:5;
Hos 13:2
[r]ver 8;
Jer 49:11
S Hos 6:1
[s]Jer 2:19
[t]S Isa 55:1;
Jer 31:20;
Zep 3:17

[u]S Job 13:16
14:5 [x]S Ge 27:28;
S Isa 18:4
[y]S SS 2:1
[z]Isa 35:2
[a]Job 29:19
14:6 [b]Ps 52:8;
S Jer 11:16
[c]S Ps 92:12;
S SS 4:11
14:7 [d]Ps 91:1-4
[e]S Ge 40:10
[f]S Hos 2:22
[g]S Eze 17:23
14:8 [h]S ver 3
[i]S Isa 37:24
14:9 [j]S Ps 107:43
[k]S Pr 10:29;

[l]S Isa 1:28; Da 12:10 [l]Ps 111:7-8; Zep 3:5; Ac 13:10
[m]Isa 26:7

[m]8 Or offer our lips as sacrifices of bulls   [n]8 Or What more has Ephraim

---

13:16 *Samaria.* See 7:1 and note; 8:5–6; 10:5,7; here, the northern kingdom. *rebelled against.* See Ps 5:10; Eze 20:8,13,21. *little ones ... women.* For atrocities against women and children see 10:14; 2Ki 8:12; 15:16; Ps 137:8–9; Isa 13:16; Am 1:13; Na 3:10.

14:1 *Return.* Another appeal for repentance (see 10:12; 12:6). Unlike that of ch. 6, this repentance would have to be sincere in order for the people to receive the gracious response from the Lord promised in vv. 4–8 (cf. Ps 130:7–8; Isa 55:6–9).

14:2 *Take words.* None could appear empty-handed (Ex 23:15; 34:20), but animal sacrifices would not be enough. Only words of true repentance would be sufficient. *fruit of our lips.* As thank offerings to the Lord.

14:3 *fatherless.* Penitent Israel (see Ps 10:14; 68:5; La 5:3). *find compassion.* Cf. the name of the child Lo-Ruhamah (see 1:6 and note; see also 2:1,23).

14:4 *heal.* See 11:3. *waywardness.* See 11:7. *love.* See

3:1; 11:1,8–9. *love ... freely.* See Isa 54:6–8. *anger ... turned away.* Contrasts with the burning anger that brought destruction (see 8:5).

14:5 *dew.* Here not a symbol of transitoriness (cf. 6:4; 13:3) but of God's blessing (cf. Dt 33:13). *cedar of Lebanon.* See notes on Jdg 9:15; 1Ki 5:6; Isa 9:10. *cedar.* See Ps 80:9–11. *Lebanon.* See Ps 104:16; Isa 35:2; 60:13.

14:7 *shade.* Protection (cf. Jdg 9:15; SS 2:3; La 4:20; Eze 31:6). *vine.* See 10:1; Isa 5:1–7.

14:8 *Ephraim.* Israel, the northern kingdom. *tree.* Only here in the OT is God compared to a tree. For the point of the imagery see Eze 31:3–7; Da 4:12. *fruitfulness.* Ephraim ("fruitful"; cf. Ge 41:52) received his fruitfulness from the Lord (cf. 2:8).

14:9 *ways of the LORD.* See Ps 18:21. The prophet concludes by offering each reader the alternatives of walking or stumbling (cf. 4:5; 5:5)—of obedience or rebellion.

JOEL

Author

The prophet Joel cannot be identified with any of the 12 other figures in the OT who have the same name. He is not mentioned outside the books of Joel and Acts (Ac 2:16). The non-Biblical legends about him are unconvincing. His father, Pethuel (1:1), is also unknown. Judging from his concern with Judah and Jerusalem (see 2:32; 3:1,6,8,16-20), it seems likely that Joel lived in that area.

Date

The book contains no references to datable historical events, but a good case can be made for its being written in the ninth century B.C. Many interpreters, however, date the book as late as the postexilic period (sixth century), after Haggai and Zechariah. In either case, its message is not significantly affected by its dating.

The book of Joel has striking linguistic parallels to those of Amos, Micah, Zephaniah, Jeremiah and Ezekiel. The literary relationships of these books are determined by one's view of the date of Joel. If it was written early, the other prophets borrowed his phrases; if it was later, the reverse may have taken place. Some scholars maintain that all the prophets drew more or less from the religious literary traditions that they and their readers shared in common—liturgical and otherwise.

Message

Joel sees the massive locust plague and severe drought devastating Judah as a harbinger of the "great and dreadful day of the LORD" (2:31). (The locusts he mentions in 1:4; 2:25 are best understood as real, not as allegorical representations of the Babylonians, Medo-Persians, Greeks and Romans, as held by some interpreters.) Confronted with this crisis, he calls on everyone to repent: old and young (1:2-3), drunkards (1:5), farmers (1:11) and priests (1:13). He describes the locusts as the Lord's army and sees in their coming a reminder that the day of the Lord is near. He does not voice the popular notion that the day will be one of judgment on the nations but deliverance and blessing for Israel. Instead—with Isaiah (2:10-21), Jeremiah (4:6), Amos (5:18-20) and Zephaniah (1:7-18)—he describes the day as one of punishment for unfaithful Israel as well. Restoration and blessing will come only after judgment and repentance.

Outline

I. Title (1:1)
II. Judah Experiences a Foretaste of the Day of the Lord (1:2-2:17)
   A. A Call to Mourning and Prayer (1:2-14)
   B. The Announcement of the Day of the Lord (1:15-2:11)
   C. A Call to Repentance and Prayer (2:12-17)
III. Judah Is Assured of Salvation in the Day of the Lord (2:18-3:21)
   A. The Lord's Restoration of Judah (2:18-27)
   B. The Lord's Renewal of His People (2:28-32)
   C. The Coming of the Day of the Lord (ch. 3)
      1. The nations judged (3:1-16)
      2. God's people blessed (3:17-21)

1

The word of the LORD that came[a] to Joel[b] son of Pethuel.

An Invasion of Locusts

[2]Hear this,[c] you elders;[d]
listen, all who live in the land.[e]
Has anything like this ever happened in your days
or in the days of your forefathers?[f]
[3]Tell it to your children,[g]
and let your children tell it to their children,
and their children to the next generation.[h]
[4]What the locust[i] swarm has left
the great locusts have eaten;
what the great locusts have left
the young locusts have eaten;
what the young locusts have left[j]
other locusts[a] have eaten.[k]

[5]Wake up, you drunkards, and weep!
Wail, all you drinkers of wine;[l]
wail because of the new wine,
for it has been snatched[m] from your lips.
[6]A nation has invaded my land,
powerful and without number;[n]
it has the teeth[o] of a lion,
the fangs of a lioness.
[7]It has laid waste[p] my vines
and ruined my fig trees.[q]
It has stripped off their bark
and thrown it away,
leaving their branches white.

[8]Mourn like a virgin[b] in sackcloth[r]

grieving for the husband[c] of her youth.
[9]Grain offerings and drink offerings[s]
are cut off from the house of the LORD.
The priests are in mourning,[t]
those who minister before the LORD.
[10]The fields are ruined,
the ground is dried up[d];[u]
the grain is destroyed,
the new wine[v] is dried up,
the oil fails.[w]
[11]Despair, you farmers,[x]
wail, you vine growers;
grieve for the wheat and the barley,[y]
because the harvest of the field is destroyed.[z]
[12]The vine is dried up
and the fig tree is withered;[a]
the pomegranate,[b] the palm and the apple tree—
all the trees of the field—are dried up.[c]
Surely the joy of mankind
is withered away.

A Call to Repentance

[13]Put on sackcloth,[d] O priests, and mourn;
wail, you who minister[e] before the altar.
Come, spend the night in sackcloth,
you who minister before my God;
for the grain offerings and drink offerings[f]

Cross references

1:1 [a]S Jer 1:2
[b]Ac 2:16
1:2 [c]Hos 5:1
[d]Joel 2:16
[e]S Hos 4:1
[f]Joel 2:2
1:3 [g]S Ex 10:2
[h]S Ps 71:18
1:4 [i]S Ex 10:14
[j]S Ex 10:5
[k]S Ex 10:15;
S Dt 28:39;
Am 7:1; Na 3:15
1:5 [l]Joel 3:3
[m]S Isa 24:7
1:6 [n]Ps 105:34;
Joel 2:2,11,25
[o]Rev 9:8
1:7 [p]Isa 5:6
[q]Am 4:9
1:8 [r]ver 13;
Isa 22:12;
Am 8:10

1:9 [s]S Hos 9:4
[t]S Isa 22:12
1:10 [u]S Isa 5:6;
S 24:4; S Jer 3:3
[v]S Hos 9:2
[w]S Nu 18:12
1:11 [x]S Job 6:20;
Am 5:16
[y]S Ex 9:31
[z]S Isa 17:11
1:12 [a]S Isa 15:6
[b]S Ex 28:33
[c]S Isa 16:8;
Hag 2:19
1:13
[d]S Ge 37:34;
S Jer 4:8
[e]Joel 2:17 [f]ver 9;
S Hos 9:4;
Joel 2:14

[a]4 The precise meaning of the four Hebrew words used here for locusts is uncertain.   [b]8 Or young woman
[c]8 Or betrothed   [d]10 Or ground mourns

1:1 *The word of the LORD . . . came to Joel.* Joel's claim of prophetic authority is similar to that of several other prophets (see Jer 1:2; Eze 1:3; Hos 1:1; Jnh 1:1,3; 3:1; Mic 1:1; Zep 1:1; Hag 1:1; Zec 1:1; Mal 1:1). *Joel.* Means "The LORD is God"; cf. Elijah's name, which means "(My) God is the LORD."

1:2 *elders.* Either the older men of the community or the recognized officials (see v. 14; 2:16,28; see also note on Ex 3:16).

1:4 See 2:25.

1:5 *drunkards.* Although Joel calls for repentance, drunkenness is the only specific sin mentioned in the book. It suggests a self-indulgent life-style (cf. Isa 28:7–8; Am 4:1) pursued by those who value material things more than spiritual. *weep.* Various segments of the community (drunkards, here; general population, v. 8; farmers, v. 11; priests, v. 13) are called to mourn. The destruction of the vines by the locusts leaves the drunkards without a source of wine.

1:6 The locusts are compared here to a nation; cf. the ants and coneys in Pr 30:25–26, where the Hebrew word for "creatures" means lit. "(a) people." Elsewhere they are called the Lord's "army" (2:11,25). The reverse comparison—that of armies to locusts in regard to numbers—is as old as Ugaritic literature (15th century B.C.) and is common in the OT (see Jdg 6:5; 7:12; Jer 46:23; 51:14,27; Na 3:15).

without number. A phrase used to describe the locusts in the plague in Egypt (see Ps 105:34; see also Ex 10:4–6,12–15). *teeth.* Joel's comparison of the locusts' teeth to lions' teeth is reflected in Rev 9:8.

1:7 *my.* The personal pronouns here and elsewhere in Joel (vv. 6,13–14; 2:13–14,17–18,23,26–27; 3:2–5,17) offer a hint of hope, since they indicate that the people belong to the Lord (cf. Jos 22:19).

1:8 *virgin.* The community is addressed. In Israel, when a woman was pledged to be married to a man, he was called her husband and she his wife, though she was still a virgin (see Dt 22:23–24). This verse refers to such a husband who died before the marriage was consummated. *sackcloth.* See v. 13; Ge 37:34 and note.

1:9 *offerings.* The locusts have left nothing that can be offered as sacrifice. The grain offering (Lev 2:1–2) and the drink offering, which was a libation of wine (Lev 23:13), were part of the daily offering (Ex 29:40; Nu 28:5–8).

1:10 *dried up.* The destruction caused by the locusts was intensified by drought. *grain . . . new wine . . . oil.* An important OT triad, related to the agriculture of that day (see 2:19).

1:13 *your God.* See note on v. 7. The phrase occurs eight times in Joel (here; v. 14; 2:13; 2:14; 2:23; 2:26; 2:27; 3:17).

are withheld from the house of your
　　God.
¹⁴Declare a holy fast;[g]
　　call a sacred assembly.
Summon the elders
　　and all who live in the land[h]
to the house of the LORD your God,
　　and cry out[i] to the LORD.[j]

¹⁵Alas for that[k] day!
For the day of the LORD[l] is near;
　　it will come like destruction from the
　　Almighty.[e] [m]

¹⁶Has not the food been cut off[n]
　　before our very eyes—
joy and gladness[o]
　　from the house of our God?[p]
¹⁷The seeds are shriveled
　　beneath the clods.[f] [q]
The storehouses are in ruins,
　　the granaries have been broken
　　down,
for the grain has dried up.
¹⁸How the cattle moan!
　　The herds mill about
because they have no pasture;[r]
　　even the flocks of sheep are
　　suffering.[s]

¹⁹To you, O LORD, I call,[t]
　　for fire[u] has devoured the open
　　pastures[v]

and flames have burned up all the
　　trees of the field.
²⁰Even the wild animals pant for you;[w]
　　the streams of water have dried up[x]
　　and fire has devoured the open
　　pastures.[y]

An Army of Locusts

2 Blow the trumpet[z] in Zion;[a]
　　sound the alarm on my holy hill.[b]
Let all who live in the land tremble,
　　for the day of the LORD[c] is coming.
It is close at hand[d]—
² 　a day of darkness[e] and gloom,[f] [g]
　　a day of clouds[h] and blackness.[i]
Like dawn spreading across the
　　mountains
　　a large and mighty army[j] comes,
such as never was of old[k]
　　nor ever will be in ages to come.

³Before them fire[l] devours,
　　behind them a flame blazes.
Before them the land is like the garden
　　of Eden,[m]
　　behind them, a desert waste[n]—
nothing escapes them.
⁴They have the appearance of horses;[o]
　　they gallop along like cavalry.

Cross references (center column):

1:14 gS 2Ch 20:3
hS Hos 4:1
iJnh 3:8
j2Ch 20:4
1:15 kS Isa 2:12;
Jer 30:7; S 46:10;
S Eze 30:3;
Mal 4:5 lJoel 2:1,
11,31; 3:14;
Am 5:18;
Zep 1:14;
Zec 14:1
mS Ge 17:1
1:16 nIsa 3:7
oS Ps 51:8
pDt 12:7
1:17
qS Isa 17:10-11
1:18 rS Ge 47:4
sS Jer 9:10
1:19 tPs 50:15
uS Ps 97:3;
Am 7:4
vS Jer 9:10
1:20 wS Ps 42:1;
S 104:21
x1Ki 17:7
yJoel 2:22
2:1 zS Nu 10:2,7
aver 15
bS Ex 15:17
cS Joel 1:15;
Zep 1:14-16
dS Eze 12:23;
S 30:3; Ob 1:15
2:2 ever 10,31;
S Job 9:7;
S Isa 8:22;
S 13:10; Am 5:18
fS Da 9:12;
S Mt 24:21
gS Eze 34:12
hS Eze 38:9
iZep 1:15;
Rev 9:2 jS Joel 1:6
kJoel 1:2
2:3 lS Ps 97:3;
S Isa 1:31
mS Ge 2:8
nEx 10:12-15;

Ps 105:34-35; S Isa 14:17 2:4 oRev 9:7

e15 Hebrew *Shaddai* 　f17 The meaning of the Hebrew
for this word is uncertain.

Commentary (bottom, two columns):

1:14 *fast . . . assembly.* See 2:15. Fasting, required on the Day of Atonement (see note and NIV text note on Lev 16:29) and also practiced in times of calamity (see Jdg 20:26; 2Sa 12:16; Jer 14:12; Jnh 3:4–5; Zec 7:3), was a sign of penitence and humility. The Bible speaks against outward signs that do not reflect a corresponding inward belief or attitude (see Mt 6:1–8; 23:1–36).
1:15 *day of the LORD.* This phrase occurs five times in Joel and is the dominant theme (here; 2:1; 2:11; 2:31; 3:14). Six other prophets also use it: Isaiah (13:6,9), Ezekiel (13:5; 30:3), Amos (5:18,20), Obadiah (15), Zephaniah (1:7,14) and Malachi (4:5); and an equivalent expression occurs in Zec 14:1. Sometimes abbreviated as "that day," the term often refers to the decisive intervention of God in history, such as through the invasion of locusts in Joel or at the battle of Carchemish, 605 B.C. (see Jer 46:2,10). It can also refer to Christ's coming to consummate history (see Mal 4:5; Mt 11:24; 1Co 5:5; 2Co 1:14; 1Th 5:2; 2Pe 3:10). When the term is not used for divine judgments in the midst of history, it refers to the final day of the Lord, which generally has two aspects: (1) God's triumph over and punishment of his enemies and (2) his granting of rest (security) and blessing to his people. *destruction . . . Almighty.* The Hebrew for each of these two words is a pun on the other (as in Isa 13:6).
1:18 Cf. the description of a drought in Jer 14:5–6. *moan.* The Hebrew for this word is used for the groaning of Israel in Egypt (Ex 2:23) and of others in distress (Pr 29:2; Isa 24:7; La 1:4,8,11,21; Eze 9:4; 21:12). *mill about.* The Hebrew for this verb is used to describe Israel's confused movements in the desert (Ex 14:3). *even . . . sheep.* Sheep are the last to suffer, because they can even grub the grass roots out of the soil.

1:19–20 *fire.* Although the destruction caused by the locusts is elsewhere compared to that of a fire (see 2:3), here the prophet likely is describing the effects of a drought. In both cases he evokes the fire of God's judgment (see, e.g., Jer 4:4; 15:14; 17:27; Eze 5:4; 15:6–7; 20:47; 21:32; Hos 8:14; Am 1:4,7,10,12,14; 2:2,5).
2:1 *trumpet.* See v. 15. Made of a ram's or bull's horn, it was used to signal approaching danger (Jer 4:5; 6:1; Eze 33:3). Its sound brought trembling (from fear) to the people (see Am 3:6). *Zion.* See v. 15; 3:17. Here, parallel to God's "holy hill" (see note on Ps 2:6), it refers to Jerusalem as the capital of the nation.
2:2 *day of darkness.* Darkness is a common prophetic figure used of the day of the Lord (see Am 5:18,20) and is generally a metaphor for distress and suffering (see Isa 5:30; 8:22; 50:3; 59:9; Jer 2:6,31; 13:16; La 3:6; Eze 34:12). *dawn.* Usually suggests relief from sorrow or gloom, the end of darkness (cf. Isa 8:20; 58:8). Here, however, it is used as bitter irony, describing the locust infestation that spreads across the land like the light of dawn, which first lights up the eastern horizon and then spreads across the whole countryside.
2:3–11 The staccato character of the poetry is appropriate for the imagery of war.
2:3 *Before them.* Joel creates a special impact by using this phrase three times (twice in v. 3 and once in v. 10), "behind them" twice (v. 3) and "At the sight of them" once (v. 6). See Ge 2:8,15 (the garden before the fall); Ge 13:10 (the Jordan Valley before the destruction of Sodom); and Isa 51:3; Eze 28:13; 31:8–9,16,18; 36:35 (all of which describe a desert that has become like Eden).
2:4 *horses.* Whereas Job compared the horse to a locust

5With a noise like that of chariots p
    they leap over the mountaintops,
like a crackling fire q consuming stubble,
    like a mighty army drawn up for
        battle.

6At the sight of them, nations are in
        anguish; r
    every face turns pale. s
7They charge like warriors; t
    they scale walls like soldiers.
They all march in line, u
    not swerving v from their course.
8They do not jostle each other;
    each marches straight ahead.
They plunge through defenses
    without breaking ranks.
9They rush upon the city;
    they run along the wall.
They climb into the houses; w
    like thieves they enter through the
        windows. x

10Before them the earth shakes, y
    the sky trembles, z
the sun and moon are darkened, a
    and the stars no longer shine. b
11The Lord c thunders d
    at the head of his army; e
his forces are beyond number,
    and mighty are those who obey his
        command.
The day of the Lord is great; f
    it is dreadful.
    Who can endure it? g

Rend Your Heart

12"Even now," declares the Lord,
    "return h to me with all your heart, i

with fasting and weeping and
    mourning."

13Rend your heart j
    and not your garments. k
Return l to the Lord your God,
    for he is gracious and
        compassionate, m
slow to anger and abounding in love, n
    and he relents from sending
        calamity. o
14Who knows? He may turn p and have
        pity q
    and leave behind a blessing r —
grain offerings and drink offerings s
    for the Lord your God.

15Blow the trumpet t in Zion, u
    declare a holy fast, v
    call a sacred assembly. w
16Gather the people,
    consecrate x the assembly;
bring together the elders, y
    gather the children,
    those nursing at the breast.
Let the bridegroom z leave his room
    and the bride her chamber.
17Let the priests, who minister a before
        the Lord,
    weep b between the temple porch
        and the altar. c
Let them say, "Spare your people,
        O Lord.
Do not make your inheritance an
        object of scorn, d
    a byword e among the nations.

(Job 39:20), Joel does the opposite.
2:5 Mountains, though barriers to ordinary horses and chariots, are no deterrent to locusts.
2:6 *At the sight of them.* Parallels "Before them" (vv. 3,10). *in anguish.* Because of the famine that the locusts will cause.
2:9 *climb into the houses.* As in the Egyptian plague of locusts (Ex 10:6). Latticed windows with no glass would not stop them.
2:10 *earth shakes.* See Ps 68:8; 77:18; Isa 24:18–20; Jer 4:23–24; Am 8:8; Na 1:5–6. *sky trembles.* See 2Sa 22:8; Isa 13:13; Hag 2:21; Heb 12:26–28. *darkened.* Joel links God's judgment through the locusts to the cosmic phenomena of the day of the Lord.
2:11 Just as Isaiah saw the Assyrians (Isa 10:5–7; 13:4) and Jeremiah the Babylonians (Jer 25:9; 43:10) as the Lord's instruments, so Joel sees the locusts as the Lord's army (cf. Jos 5:14; Ps 68:7,17; Hab 3:8–9)—the army of the Lord with which he will come against his enemies in the day of the Lord (see 3:9–11). This passage parallels Zep 1:14 (cf. v. 31; 3:14; Mal 4:1,5). *thunders.* See 3:16. *great . . . dreadful.* Two ideas often associated in the OT, though sometimes the Hebrew word underlying "dreadful" means "awesome" (see Dt 7:21; 10:21; Ps 106:21–22). The terms are fre-

quently used to describe the day of the Lord (see v. 31; Mal 4:5). *Who can endure it?* See Na 1:6; Mal 3:2; Rev 6:17. There is no escape except in turning to God.

2:13 *gracious . . . abounding in love.* Recalls the great self-characterization of God in Ex 34:6–7, which runs like a golden thread through the OT (see note on Ex 34:6–7; see also Dt 4:31; Mic 7:18).
2:15 *trumpet.* Not an alarm as in v. 1, but a call to religious assembly (see Lev 23:24; 25:9; Nu 10:10; Jos 6:4–5; 2Ch 15:14; Ps 47:5; 81:3; 98:6; 150:3). *fast . . . assembly.* See note on 1:14.
2:16 As with the call to mourning in ch. 1, no segment of the community was exempt. *assembly.* The Hebrew for this word refers to the religious community (see Nu 16:3; 2Ch 30:2,4,13,23–25; Mic 2:5). *elders.* See note on 1:2. *chamber.* The place where the marriage was consummated.

2:17 *your inheritance.* Israel is God's special possession (see Ex 19:5 and note; see also Ex 15:17; 34:9). Judah is to plead, not her innocence, but that God's honor is at stake before the world (see Ex 32:12; Nu 14:13; Dt 9:28; Jos 7:9). *byword.* See note on 1Ki 9:7. *Where is their God?* A rhetorical question with sarcastic intent (see Ps 42:3,10; 79:10; 115:2; Mic 7:10).

Why should they say among the
  peoples,
'Where is their God?[f]' "

The Lord's Answer

[18]Then the Lord will be jealous[g] for his
  land
  and take pity[h] on his people.

[19]The Lord will reply[g] to them:

"I am sending you grain, new wine[i]
  and oil,[j]
  enough to satisfy you fully;[k]
never again will I make you
  an object of scorn[l] to the nations.

[20]"I will drive the northern army[m] far
  from you,
  pushing it into a parched and barren
  land,
with its front columns going into the
  eastern[n] sea[h]
and those in the rear into the western
  sea.[i]
And its stench[o] will go up;
  its smell will rise."

Surely he has done great things.[j]
[21] Be not afraid,[p] O land;
  be glad and rejoice.[q]
Surely the Lord has done great things.[r]
[22] Be not afraid, O wild animals,
  for the open pastures are becoming
  green.[s]
The trees are bearing their fruit;
  the fig tree[t] and the vine[u] yield their
  riches.[v]
[23]Be glad, O people of Zion,
  rejoice[w] in the Lord your God,

for he has given you
  the autumn rains in righteousness.[k] [x]
He sends you abundant showers,[y]
  both autumn[z] and spring rains,[a] as
  before.
[24]The threshing floors will be filled with
  grain;
  the vats will overflow[b] with new
  wine[c] and oil.

[25]"I will repay you for the years the
  locusts[d] have eaten[e] —
  the great locust and the young locust,
  the other locusts and the locust
  swarm[l] —
  my great army[f] that I sent among you.
[26]You will have plenty to eat, until you
  are full,[g]
  and you will praise[h] the name of the
  Lord your God,
  who has worked wonders[i] for you;
never again will my people be shamed.[j]
[27]Then you will know[k] that I am in
  Israel,
  that I am the Lord[l] your God,
  and that there is no other;
never again will my people be shamed.[m]

The Day of the Lord

[28]"And afterward,
  I will pour out my Spirit[n] on all
  people.[o]

Cross references (center column):

2:17 *f* S Ps 42:3
2:18
g S Isa 26:11;
Zec 1:14; 8:2
h S Ps 72:13
2:19 *i* Ps 4:7
j S Jer 31:12
k S Lev 26:5
l S Eze 34:29
2:20
m Jer 1:14-15
n Zec 14:8
o S Isa 34:3
2:21
p S Isa 29:22;
S 54:4;
Zep 3:16-17
q S Ps 9:2
r S Ps 126:3;
S Isa 25:1
2:22 *s* S Ps 65:12
t S 1Ki 4:25
u S Nu 16:14
v Joel 1:18-20;
Zec 8:12
2:23 *w* Ps 33:21;
97:12; 149:2;
Isa 12:6; 41:16;
66:14; Hab 3:18;
Zec 10:7
x S Isa 45:8
y S Job 36:28;
S Eze 34:26
z Ps 84:6
a S Lev 26:4;
S Ps 135:7;
Jas 5:7
2:24 *b* Lev 26:10;
Mal 3:10
c S Pr 3:10;
Joel 3:18;
Am 9:13
2:25
d S Ex 10:14;
Am 4:9
e S Dt 28:39
f S Joel 1:6
2:26 *g* S Lev 26:5
h S Lev 23:40;
S Isa 62:9
i S Ps 126:3;
S Isa 25:1
j S Isa 29:22
2:27 *k* S Ex 6:7
l S Ex 6:2;
S Isa 44:8;
Joel 3:17
m Isa 45:17; 54:4;
Zep 3:11
2:28 *n* S Isa 11:2; S 44:3 *o* S Nu 11:17; S Mk 1:8; Gal 3:14

g 18,19 Or Lord was jealous . . . / and took pity . . . /
19The Lord replied   *h* 20 That is, the Dead Sea
i 20 That is, the Mediterranean   *j* 20 Or rise. / Surely it
has done great things."   *k* 23 Or / the teacher for
righteousness: *l* 25 The precise meaning of the four
Hebrew words used here for locusts is uncertain.

2:18 Joel begins a new section by turning from the destruction caused by the locusts to the blessings God will give to a repentant people. *jealous.* See note on Ex 20:5. The Lord will respond to the prayer of v. 17 and arouse himself to defend his honor and have pity on his people.
2:19 *grain, new wine and oil.* See note on 1:10.
2:20 *northern army.* Since enemies in ancient times did not invade from the sea or across the desert, Canaan's geographical location made her vulnerable only from the south (Egypt) and from the north (Assyria and Babylon). The hordes of locusts are pictured here as a vast army of Israel's most feared enemies. *stench.* Because the locusts are now dead.
2:21–23 As there was a threefold call to grief (1:5,8,13), so there is a threefold call to joy: The land (v. 21), the wild animals (v. 22) and the people (v. 23) are called on to rejoice in the Lord's bounty.
2:22 The wild animals now find green open pastures (cf. 1:19–20). The same land, with its trees (see 1:7,12,19) that the locusts and drought had devastated, is now productive.
2:23 *autumn rains in righteousness.* See NIV text note. The religious sect at Qumran (which produced most of the Dead Sea Scrolls; see "The Time between the Testaments," p. 1431) hailed their most revered teacher of the law, whom they called the "Teacher of Righteousness," as the fulfill-

ment of this prophecy. The immediate context, however, seems to support the translation in the NIV text.
2:24 *threshing floors.* See note on Ru 1:22.
2:25 See 1:4.
2:26 *wonders.* God worked wonders for the people when they were in Egypt (see Ex 7:3), and now will work wonders in restoring the devastated land.
2:27 *Israel.* Probably refers to all God's people, with no distinction between the northern and southern kingdoms, as also in 3:2,16. *I am the Lord your God.* This clause recalls the covenant at Sinai (see Ex 20:2). *there is no other.* See note on Dt 4:35.
2:28–32 Quoted by Peter at Pentecost (Ac 2:16–21), but with a few variations from both the Hebrew text and the Septuagint (the Greek translation of the OT).
2:28 *afterward.* In the Messianic period, beyond the restoration just spoken of. *pour out my Spirit.* See v. 29; Isa 32:15; 44:3; Jer 31:33–34; Eze 36:26–27; 39:29; Zec 12:10–13:1. *all people.* All will participate without regard to sex, age or rank; and then Moses' wish (Nu 11:29) will be realized (cf. Gal 3:28). Peter extends the "all" of this verse and the "everyone" of v. 32 to the Gentiles ("all who are far off," Ac 2:39), who will not be excluded from the Spirit's outpouring or deliverance (cf. Ro 11:11–24). *prophesy . . . dream dreams . . . see visions.* See Nu 12:6.

Your sons and daughters will
prophesy, *p*
your old men will dream dreams, *q*
your young men will see visions.
²⁹Even on my servants, *r* both men and
women,
I will pour out my Spirit in those
days. *s*
³⁰I will show wonders in the heavens *t*
and on the earth, *u*
blood and fire and billows of smoke.
³¹The sun will be turned to darkness *v*
and the moon to blood
before the coming of the great and
dreadful day of the LORD. *w*
³²And everyone who calls
on the name of the LORD *x* will be
saved; *y*
for on Mount Zion *z* and in Jerusalem
there will be deliverance, *a*
as the LORD has said,
among the survivors *b*
whom the LORD calls. *c*

The Nations Judged

3 "In those days and at that time,
when I restore the fortunes *d* of
Judah *e* and Jerusalem,
²I will gather *f* all nations
and bring them down to the Valley of
Jehoshaphat. *m,g*
There I will enter into judgment *h*
against them
concerning my inheritance, my
people Israel,

for they scattered *i* my people among
the nations
and divided up my land.
³They cast lots *j* for my people
and traded boys for prostitutes;
they sold girls for wine *k*
that they might drink.

⁴"Now what have you against me, O
Tyre and Sidon *l* and all you regions of
Philistia? *m* Are you repaying me for something I have done? If you are paying me
back, I will swiftly and speedily return on
your own heads what you have done. *n*
⁵For you took my silver and my gold and
carried off my finest treasures to your temples. *o* ⁶You sold the people of Judah and
Jerusalem to the Greeks, *p* that you might
send them far from their homeland.

⁷"See, I am going to rouse them out of
the places to which you sold them, *q* and I
will return *r* on your own heads what you
have done. ⁸I will sell your sons *s* and
daughters to the people of Judah, *t* and
they will sell them to the Sabeans, *u* a nation far away." The LORD has spoken. *v*

⁹Proclaim this among the nations:
Prepare for war! *w*
Rouse the warriors! *x*
Let all the fighting men draw near
and attack.
¹⁰Beat your plowshares into swords

Cross references (center column)

2:28
p S 1Sa 19:20
q Jer 23:25
2:29 *r* l Co 12:13;
Gal 3:28
s S Eze 36:27
2:30 *t* Lk 21:11
u Mk 13:24-25
2:31 *v* S ver 2;
S Isa 22:5;
S Jer 4:23;
S Mt 24:29
w S Joel 1:15;
Ob 1:15; Mal 3:2;
4:1,5
2:32 *x* S Ge 4:26;
S Ps 105:1
y S Ps 106:8;
Ac 2:17-21*;
Ro 10:13*
z S Isa 46:13
a Ob 1:17
b S Isa 1:9; 11:11;
Mic 4:7; 7:18;
S Ro 9:27
c Ac 2:39
3:1 *d* S Dt 30:3;
S Jer 16:15;
S Eze 38:8;
Zep 3:20
e Jer 40:5
3:2 *f* Zep 3:8 *g* ver
12; S Isa 22:1
h S Isa 13:9;
S Jer 2:35;
S Eze 36:5

i S Ge 11:4;
S Lev 26:33
3:3 *j* S Job 6:27;
S Eze 24:6
k Joel 1:5; Am 2:6
3:4 *l* S Ge 10:15;
S Mt 11:21
m S Ps 87:4;
Isa 14:29-31;
Jer 47:1-7
n S Lev 26:28;
S Isa 34:8;
S Eze 25:15-17;
Zec 9:5-7
3:5 *o* S 1Ki 15:18;
S 2Ch 21:16-17
3:6 *p* Eze 27:13;
Zec 9:13
3:7 *q* S Isa 43:5-6;
Jer 23:8

r S Isa 66:6 **3:8** *s* Isa 60:14 *t* Isa 14:2 *u* S Ge 10:7; S 2Ch 9:1
v S Isa 23:1; S Jer 30:16 **3:9** *w* S Isa 8:9 *x* Jer 46:4

m 2 *Jehoshaphat* means *the* LORD *judges*; also in verse 12.

Study notes (bottom)

2:30–31 These cosmic events are often associated with the
day of the Lord (see Isa 13:9–10; 34:4; Mt 24:29; Rev 6:12;
8:8–9; 9:1–19; 14:14–20; 16:4,8–9).
2:30 *blood.* From war. *fire . . . smoke.* Signs of God's
presence (see Ge 15:17 and note; Ex 19:18).
2:31 *blood.* The moon will become blood-red.
2:32 *calls on the name of the* LORD. Worships God (cf. Ge
4:26; 12:8) and prays to him (see Ps 116:4). *saved.* Delivered from the wrath of God's judgment (see Mt 24:13). *as
the* LORD *has said.* Perhaps Joel is recalling God's covenant with David (see 2Sa 7; Ps 132:13–18). *survivors.* See
Zec 13:8–9; 14:2.
3:1 *In those days.* At the time of Israel's final redemption.
restore the fortunes of. Or "bring back from captivity" (see
vv. 6–7; see also Jer 29:14 and NIV text note).
3:2 *Valley of Jehoshaphat.* See v. 12. Called the "valley of
decision" in v. 14, it seems to be a symbolic name for a valley
near Jerusalem that is here depicted as the place of God's
ultimate judgment on the nations gathered against Jerusalem
(see NIV text note). There King Jehoshaphat had witnessed
one of the Lord's historic victories over the nations (see
2Ch 20:1–30). *my inheritance.* See note on 2:17. Eight
times in four verses (vv. 2–5) God uses "my," emphasizing
his covenant relationship with Israel. *Israel.* See note on
2:27.
3:3 *cast lots for my people.* This happened to Judah at the
time of the captivity (586 B.C.) and is mentioned in Ob 11.

The Israelites were treated by their enemies as mere chattel,
to be traded off for the pleasures of prostitution and wine.
3:4–8 A parenthetical interlude. In vv. 1–3,9–11 God
announces judgment against the nations hostile to Israel, but
here he addresses the nations directly.
3:4 *me.* The Lord. *Tyre . . . Sidon . . . Philistia.* Tyre had
sold Israelites as slaves (see Am 1:9), and Philistia had often
plundered Israel (see Jdg 13:1; 1Sa 5:1; 2Ch 21:16–17; Eze
25:15–17). God punished them by allowing Sidon to be
enslaved by Antiochus III in 345 B.C. and by allowing Tyre to
be besieged by the Babylonians in 586 and to be captured by
the Greeks (under Alexander the Great) in 332.
3:6 The Greeks were trading with the Phoenicians as early
as 800 B.C.
3:8 *Sabeans.* From Sheba, whose queen visited Solomon
(see 1Ki 10:1–13). *far away.* It was located in the southern
part of the Arabian peninsula (present-day Yemen).
3:9–21 In vv. 9–11 Joel is the speaker; in vv. 12–13 God
speaks; in vv. 14–16, Joel; and in vv. 17–21, God. When
Joel speaks, he does so as the spokesman of the Lord, who
has commissioned him to be his prophet.
3:9–11 Joel commands that the nations be told to prepare
for battle, for the Lord would come against them with his
invincible heavenly army and bring them into judgment (cf.
Eze 38–39; Rev 19).
3:10 The first part of this verse is the reverse of Isa 2:4 and
Mic 4:3, where the peaceful effect of God's reign is por-

and your pruning hooks[y] into
spears.[z]
Let the weakling[a] say,
"I am strong!"[b]
[11]Come quickly, all you nations from
every side,
and assemble[c] there.

Bring down your warriors,[d] O LORD!

[12]"Let the nations be roused;
let them advance into the Valley of
Jehoshaphat,[e]
for there I will sit
to judge[f] all the nations on every
side.
[13]Swing the sickle,[g]
for the harvest[h] is ripe.
Come, trample the grapes,[i]
for the winepress[j] is full
and the vats overflow—
so great is their wickedness!"

[14]Multitudes,[k] multitudes
in the valley[l] of decision!
For the day of the LORD[m] is near
in the valley of decision.[n]
[15]The sun and moon will be darkened,
and the stars no longer shine.[o]
[16]The LORD will roar[p] from Zion
and thunder from Jerusalem;[q]
the earth and the sky will tremble.[r]
But the LORD will be a refuge[s] for his
people,
a stronghold[t] for the people of Israel.

Blessings for God's People

[17]"Then you will know[u] that I, the LORD
your God,[v]
dwell in Zion,[w] my holy hill.[x]
Jerusalem will be holy;[y]
never again will foreigners invade
her.[z]

[18]"In that day the mountains will drip
new wine,[a]
and the hills will flow with milk;[b]
all the ravines of Judah will run with
water.[c]
A fountain will flow out of the LORD's
house[d]
and will water the valley of
acacias.[n][e]
[19]But Egypt[f] will be desolate,
Edom[g] a desert waste,
because of violence[h] done to the people
of Judah,
in whose land they shed innocent
blood.
[20]Judah will be inhabited forever[i]
and Jerusalem through all
generations.
[21]Their bloodguilt,[j] which I have not
pardoned,
I will pardon.[k]"

The LORD dwells in Zion![l]

3:10 [y]Isa 2:4
[z]S Nu 25:7
[a]Zec 12:8
[b]S Jos 1:6
3:11
[c]Eze 38:15-16;
Zep 3:8
[d]S Isa 13:3
3:12 [e]S ver 2
[f]S Ps 82:1;
S Isa 2:4
3:13 [g]Mk 4:29
[h]S Isa 17:5;
S Hos 6:11;
Mt 13:39;
Rev 14:15-19
[i]S Jer 25:30
[j]S Jdg 6:11;
S Rev 14:20
3:14 [k]Isa 13:4
[l]S Isa 22:1
[m]Isa 34:2-8;
S Joel 1:15;
S Zep 1:7
[n]S Isa 2:4;
S Eze 36:5
3:15 [o]S Job 9:7;
S Eze 32:7
3:16 [p]S Isa 42:13
[q]Am 1:2
[r]S Jdg 5:4;
S Isa 14:16;
S Eze 38:19
[s]S Ps 46:1;
S Isa 25:4;
Zec 12:8
[t]S 2Sa 22:3;
Jer 16:19;
Zec 9:12

3:17 [u]S Ex 6:7
[v]S Joel 2:27
[w]S Ps 74:2;
S Isa 4:3 [x]Ps 2:6;
S Isa 2:2;
S Eze 17:22
[y]S Jer 31:40
[z]S Isa 52:1;
S Eze 44:9;
Zec 9:8
3:18 [a]S Joel 2:24
[b]Ex 3:8; S SS 5:1
[c]S Isa 30:25;
35:6; S 44:3
[d]Rev 22:1-2

[e]S Nu 25:1; S Isa 25:6; S Jer 31:12; S Eze 47:1; Am 9:13
3:19 [f]S Isa 19:1 [g]S Isa 11:14; S 34:11 [h]S Jer 51:35; Ob 1:10
3:20 [i]S Ezr 9:12; Am 9:15 **3:21** [j]S Isa 1:15 [k]S Eze 36:25
[l]S Ps 74:2; Isa 59:20; S Eze 48:35; Zec 8:3

[n]*18* Or *Valley of Shittim*

---

trayed. Here God's enemies are summoned to their last great confrontation with him.

3:11 *assemble there.* In the Valley of Jehoshaphat for judgment (vv. 2,12).

3:13 As a result of the Lord's great army that had marched against Judah (2:3–11), there had been no harvest (2:3). That harvest was to be restored (2:19,22,24,26). In the final great day of the Lord, there will also be a harvest—the harvest of God's judgment on the nations. Rev 14:14–20 draws heavily on this picture of judgment.

3:14 *valley of decision.* The Valley of Jehoshaphat (judgment) of vv. 2,12. "Jehoshaphat" speaks of God's role as Judge (see note on v. 2). Here "decision" (from a different Hebrew word) refers to the heavenly Judge's decision or judicial decree. The valley is now viewed as the place where that decree will be executed.

3:15 See 2:10 and note.

3:16 *roar.* Like a lion, God will destroy the nations. The first two lines occur also in Am 1:2 (see Jer 25:30). *thunder.* As God at the head of his army had thundered against Jerusalem (2:11), so he will then thunder against Jerusalem's enemies, and he will do so from his royal city, from which he rules his "inheritance" (see v. 17; Am 1:2).

3:17–21 God blesses his people in a dual way: negatively, by destroying their enemies; and positively, by giving them good things.

3:17 *I . . . dwell in Zion.* The Lord himself will dwell with them (see v. 21). The same picture is found in 2:27; Ps 46:4 (cf. Rev 21:3). The final blessed state of the now unholy and vulnerable city will be God's abiding presence in her (see v. 21 and note; Rev 21). Then she will be holy and impregnable.

3:18 *In that day.* The same as "In those days" of v. 1. The Edenic lushness pictured in this verse is in great contrast to the drought in 1:10 (see Am 9:13). *A fountain will flow out of the LORD's house.* Flowing from God's presence, streams of blessing will refresh his people and make their place endlessly fruitful (cf. Ps 36:8; 46:4; 87:7; Eze 47:1–12; Rev 22:1–2). *acacias.* Since acacias flourish in dry soil, the picture is that of a well-watered desert.

3:19 *Egypt . . . Edom.* As old enemies of Israel, they here represent all the nations hostile to God's people. *desolate . . . desert waste.* Figures for the removal of all life-sustaining blessings, thus setting in sharp focus the contrasting destinies of God's people and the enemies of God's kingdom. This picture of desolation also recalls the earlier description of Judah's condition (2:3).

3:20 *will be inhabited forever.* When God's judgment and redemption are consummated, his kingdom will endure and flourish eternally.

3:21 This book of judgment ends on a promising and encouraging note: "The LORD dwells in Zion," and therefore all is right with those who trust in God and live with him.

AMOS

Author

Amos was from Tekoa (1:1), a small town about 6 miles south of Bethlehem and 11 miles from Jerusalem. He was not a man of the court like Isaiah, or a priest like Jeremiah. He earned his living from the flock and the sycamore-fig grove (1:1; 7:14-15). Whether he owned the flocks and groves or only worked as a hired hand is not known. His skill with words and the strikingly broad range of his general knowledge of history and the world preclude his being an ignorant peasant. Though his home was in Judah, he was sent to announce God's judgment on the northern kingdom (Israel). He probably ministered for the most part at Bethel (7:10-13; see note on Ge 12:8), Israel's main religious sanctuary, where the upper echelons of the northern kingdom worshiped.

The book brings his prophecies together in a carefully organized form intended to be read as a unit. It offers few, if any, clues as to the chronological order of his spoken messages—he may have repeated them on many occasions to reach everyone who came to worship. The book is addressed also to the southern kingdom (hence the references to Judah and Jerusalem).

Date and Historical Situation

According to the first verse, Amos prophesied during the reigns of Uzziah over Judah (792-740 B.C.) and Jeroboam II over Israel (793-753). The main part of his ministry was probably carried out c. 760-750. Both kingdoms were enjoying great prosperity and had reached new political and military heights (cf. 2Ki 14:23-15:7; 2Ch 26). It was also a time of idolatry, extravagant indulgence in luxurious living, immorality, corruption of judicial procedures and oppression of the poor. As a consequence, God would soon bring about the Assyrian captivity of the northern kingdom (722-721).

Israel at the time was politically secure and spiritually smug. About 40 years earlier, at the end of his ministry, Elisha had prophesied the resurgence of Israel's power (2Ki 13:17-19), and more recently Jonah had prophesied her restoration to a glory not known since the days of Solomon (2Ki 14:25). The nation felt sure, therefore, that she was in God's good graces. But prosperity increased Israel's religious and moral corruption. God's past punishments for unfaithfulness were forgotten, and his patience was at an end—which he sent Amos to announce.

With Amos, the messages of the prophets began to be preserved in permanent form, being brought together in books that would accompany Israel through the coming debacle and beyond. (Since Amos was a contemporary of Hosea and Jonah, see Introductions to those books.)

Theme and Message

The dominant theme is clearly stated in 5:24, which calls for social justice as the indispensable expression of true piety. Amos was a vigorous spokesman for God's justice and righteousness, whereas Hosea emphasized God's love, grace, mercy and forgiveness. Amos declared that God was going to judge his unfaithful, disobedient, covenant-breaking people. Despite his special choice of Israel and his kindnesses to her during the exodus and conquest and in the days of David and Solomon, his people continually failed to honor and obey him. The shrines at Bethel and other places of worship were often paganized, and Israel had a worldly view of even the ritual that the Lord himself had prescribed. They thought performance of the rites was all God required, and, with that done, they could do whatever they pleased—an essentially pagan notion. Without commitment to God's law, they had no basis for standards of conduct. Amos condemns all who make themselves powerful or rich at the expense of others. Those who had acquired two splendid houses (3:15), expensive furniture and richly furnished tables by cheating, perverting justice and crushing the poor would lose everything they had.

God's imminent judgment on Israel would not be a mere punitive blow to warn (as often before, 4:6-11), but an almost total destruction. The unthinkable was about to happen: Because they had not

faithfully consecrated themselves to his lordship, God would uproot his chosen people by the hands of a pagan nation. Even so, if they would repent, there was hope that "the Lord God Almighty (would) have mercy on the remnant" (5:15; see 5:4-6,14). In fact, the Lord had a glorious future for his people, beyond the impending judgment. The house of David would again rule over Israel—even extend its rule over many nations—and Israel would once more be secure in the promised land, feasting on wine and fruit (9:11-15). The God of Israel, the Lord of history, would not abandon his chosen people or his chosen program of redemption.

The God for whom Amos speaks is God of more than merely Israel. He governs all nations, bringing them into being (9:7) and calling them to account (1:3-2:3). He also uses one against another to carry out his purposes (6:14). He is the Great King who rules the whole universe (4:13; 5:8; 9:5-6). Because he is all-sovereign, the God of Israel holds the history and destiny of all peoples and of the world in his hands. Israel must know not only that he is the Lord of her future, but also that he is Lord over all, and that he has purposes and concerns that reach far beyond her borders. Israel had a unique, but not an exclusive, claim on God. She needed to remember not only his covenant commitments to her but also her covenant obligations to him. (See further the prophecy of Jonah.)

Outline

1 The words of Amos, one of the shepherds of Tekoa [a]—what he saw concerning Israel two years before the earthquake, [b] when Uzziah [c] was king of Judah
and Jeroboam [d] son of Jehoash [a] was king
of Israel. [e]

²He said:

"The LORD roars [f] from Zion
    and thunders [g] from Jerusalem; [h]
the pastures of the shepherds dry up, [b]
    and the top of Carmel [i] withers." [j]

Judgment on Israel's Neighbors

³This is what the LORD says:

"For three sins of Damascus, [k]
    even for four, I will not turn back ˌmy
        wrath, [l]
Because she threshed Gilead
    with sledges having iron teeth,
⁴I will send fire [m] upon the house of
        Hazael [n]
    that will consume the fortresses [o] of
        Ben-Hadad. [p]
⁵I will break down the gate [q] of
        Damascus;

I will destroy the king who is in [c] the
        Valley of Aven [d]
and the one who holds the scepter in
        Beth Eden. [r]
The people of Aram will go into exile
        to Kir, [s] "
                                says the LORD. [t]

⁶This is what the LORD says:

"For three sins of Gaza, [u]
    even for four, I will not turn back ˌmy
        wrath, [v]
Because she took captive whole
        communities
    and sold them to Edom, [w]
⁷I will send fire upon the walls of Gaza
    that will consume her fortresses.
⁸I will destroy the king [e] of Ashdod [x]
    and the one who holds the scepter in
        Ashkelon.
I will turn my hand [y] against Ekron,
    till the last of the Philistines [z] is

Cross references (center column)

1:1 ªS 2Sa 14:2
bZec 14:5
cS 2Ki 14:21;
S 2Ch 26:23
dS 2Ki 14:23
eS Hos 1:1
1:2 fS Isa 42:13
gS Ps 29:3
hJoel 3:16
iAm 9:3
jS Jer 12:4
1:3 kIsa 7:8; 8:4;
17:1-3 lver 6,9,
11,13; Am 2:6
1:4 mS Jer 49:27;
S Eze 30:8
nS 1Ki 19:17;
2Ki 8:7-15
oJer 17:27
p1Ki 20:1;
2Ki 6:24;
Jer 49:23-27
1:5 qJer 51:30

rS Isa 37:12
sS 2Ki 16:9;
S Isa 22:6;
Zec 9:1
tS Isa 7:16;
Jer 49:27
1:6 uS Ge 10:19;
1Sa 6:17; Zep 2:4
vS ver 3
wS Ge 14:6;
Ob 1:11
1:8 xS 2Ch 26:6
yPs 81:14
zS Eze 25:16

Footnotes

ª1 Hebrew Joash, a variant of Jehoash   b2 Or
shepherds mourn   c5 Or the inhabitants of
d5 Aven means wickedness.   e8 Or inhabitants

1:1 Amos. Apparently a shortened form of a name like
Amasiah (2Ch 17:16), meaning "The LORD carries" or "The
LORD upholds." shepherds. The Hebrew for this word occurs elsewhere in the OT only in reference to the king of
Moab (2Ki 3:4, where it is translated "raised sheep"). Cf.
7:14, where a different Hebrew word is used. Amos was not
a professional prophet who earned his living from his ministry; he stood outside religious institutions. Tekoa. See
Introduction: Author. saw. Received by divine revelation.
earthquake. Evidently a major shock, long remembered, and
probably the one mentioned in Zec 14:5. Reference to the
earthquake suggests that the author viewed it as a kind of
divine reinforcement of the words of judgment. Uzziah. See
Introduction: Date and Historical Situation; see also note on
Isa 6:1. Jeroboam. See Introduction: Date and Historical
Situation.
1:2–2:16 A series of oracles against the nations. After
pronouncing judgments on Israel's neighbors for various
atrocities—judgments that Israel would naturally applaud—Amos announces God's condemnation of his own
two kingdoms for despising God's laws. His listing of Israel's
sins under the same form of indictment used against the
other nations shockingly pictures Israel's sins alongside those
of her pagan neighbors.
1:2 A thematic verse, ominously announcing the main
thrust of Amos's message. roars. Amos, a shepherd, was sent
to Israel to warn her that he had heard a lion roar and that the
lion is none other than the Lord himself, who has only
wanted to be Israel's shepherd. For the use of this imagery in
other contexts see Jer 25:30; Joel 3:16. from Zion. The Lord
established his earthly throne in Jerusalem, among his special
people, and from there he announces his judgments on
them, as well as on the other nations. pastures . . . top of
Carmel. See 9:3. From the driest portion of the land to the
greenest, the Lord's judgment will be felt like a severe
drought that devastates the whole land.
1:3 For three sins . . . four. For their many sins, especially
the one named; see also vv. 6,9,11,13; 2:1,4,6. For similar
numerical expressions see Pr 6:16; 30:15,18,21,29; Mic

5:5. Damascus. Capital of the Aramean state directly north
of Israel and a constant enemy in that day. Her crime was
brutality to the conquered people of Gilead, Israel's territory
east of Galilee. threshed . . . sledges. Heads of grain were
threshed by driving a wooden sledge fitted with sharp teeth
over the cut grain (cf. Job 41:30; Isa 28:27; 41:15; see 2Ki
13:7 and note on Ru 1:22).
1:4 send fire . . . that will consume. See vv. 7,10,12;
2:2,5; cf. v. 14; a common description of the threat of divine
judgment, usually carried out by a devastating war that
resulted in the burning of major cities and fortresses. See the
judgments mentioned in Jer 17:27; 49:27; 50:32; Hos 8:
14. Hazael. King of Damascus c. 842–796 B.C. and founder
of a new line of kings (see 2Ki 8:7–15). fortresses. See vv.
7,10,12,14; 2:2,5; perhaps referring to the fortress-like palatial dwellings of the rich and powerful. Ben-Hadad. Son of
Hazael (2Ki 13:24) and the second king with this name (cf.
2Ki 8:14–15), ruling c. 796–775.
1:5 king. See v. 8; lit. "one who sits [enthroned]." Valley of
Aven. Possibly the Beqaa Valley between the Lebanon and
Anti-Lebanon mountains, but may refer to the river valley in
which Damascus is located, calling it the "valley of wickedness" (see NIV text note). Beth Eden. Probably Damascus,
the garden spot of that region. Kir. An unidentified place,
possibly in the vicinity of Elam (2Ki 16:9; Isa 22:6), from
which the Arameans of Damascus are said to have come
(9:7).
1:6 Gaza. One of the five Philistine cities (see map on p.
330); it guarded the entry to Palestine from Egypt. whole
communities. See v. 9; not just warriors captured in battle.
The reference may be to villages in south Judah on the trade
route from Edom to Gaza. to Edom. See v. 9; trading the
people like cattle to another country.
1:8 Ashdod . . . Ashkelon . . . Ekron. Three more cities of
the Philistine group (see note on v. 6). Gath, the fifth (cf.
6:2), may already have been subdued by Uzziah (see 2Ch
26:6). the last. There would be no remnant. Philistia was
finally destroyed by Nebuchadnezzar.

dead," [a]

says the Sovereign LORD. [b]

[9]This is what the LORD says:

"For three sins of Tyre, [c]
    even for four, I will not turn back ˌmy
        wrathˎ. [d]
Because she sold whole communities of
        captives to Edom,
    disregarding a treaty of brotherhood, [e]
[10]I will send fire upon the walls of Tyre
    that will consume her fortresses. [f] "

[11]This is what the LORD says:

"For three sins of Edom, [g]
    even for four, I will not turn back ˌmy
        wrathˎ.
Because he pursued his brother with a
        sword, [h]
    stifling all compassion, [f]
because his anger raged continually
    and his fury flamed unchecked, [i]
[12]I will send fire upon Teman [j]
    that will consume the fortresses of
        Bozrah. [k] "

[13]This is what the LORD says:

"For three sins of Ammon, [l]
    even for four, I will not turn back ˌmy
        wrathˎ.
Because he ripped open the pregnant
        women [m] of Gilead
    in order to extend his borders,
[14]I will set fire to the walls of Rabbah [n]
    that will consume [o] her fortresses
amid war cries [p] on the day of battle,
    amid violent winds [q] on a stormy day.
[15]Her king [g] will go into exile,
    he and his officials together, [r] "

                    says the LORD. [s]

1:8 [a]S Isa 34:8
[b]Isa 14:28-32;
Zep 2:4-7
1:9 [c]1Ki 5:1;
9:11-14;
Jer 25:22;
Joel 3:4;
S Mt 11:21 [d]ver 3
[e]S 1Ki 5:12
1:10
[f]Isa 23:1-18;
S 34:8; S Jer 47:4;
Eze 26:2-4;
Zec 9:1-4
1:11
[g]Nu 20:14-21;
S 2Ch 28:17;
S Ps 83:6
[h]S Ps 63:10
[i]S Eze 25:12-14;
Zec 1:15
1:12 [j]S Ge 36:11,
15 [k]S Isa 34:5;
63:1-6; Jer 25:21;
Eze 25:12-14;
35:1-15; Ob 1:1;
Mal 1:2-5
1:13 [l]S Ge 19:38;
S Eze 21:28
[m]S Ge 34:29;
S 2Ki 8:12;
S Hos 13:16
1:14 [n]S Dt 3:11
[o]Isa 30:30
[p]S Job 39:25
[q]Jer 23:19
1:15 [r]S Jer 25:21
[s]1Ch 20:1;
S Jer 49:1;
Eze 21:28-32;
25:2-7
2:1 [t]S Isa 16:6
[u]Isa 33:12
2:2 [v]Jer 48:24
[w]S Job 39:25
[x]S Jos 6:20
2:3 [y]S Ps 2:10
[z]S Isa 40:23
[a]Isa 15:1-9;
16:1-14; S 25:10;
Jer 48:1;
S Eze 25:8-11;
Zep 2:8-9
2:4 [b]2Ki 17:19;
Hos 12:2
[c]S Jer 6:19
[d]S Eze 20:24
[e]Isa 9:16
[f]S Ex 34:15;
S Dt 31:20;
S Ps 4:2
[g]S 2Ki 22:13;
S Jer 9:14;

---

2 This is what the LORD says:

"For three sins of Moab, [t]
    even for four, I will not turn back ˌmy
        wrathˎ.
Because he burned, as if to lime, [u]
    the bones of Edom's king,
[2]I will send fire upon Moab
    that will consume the fortresses of
        Kerioth. [h] [v]
Moab will go down in great tumult
    amid war cries [w] and the blast of the
        trumpet. [x]
[3]I will destroy her ruler [y]
    and kill all her officials with him," [z]

                    says the LORD. [a]

[4]This is what the LORD says:

"For three sins of Judah, [b]
    even for four, I will not turn back ˌmy
        wrathˎ.
Because they have rejected the law [c] of
        the LORD
    and have not kept his decrees, [d]
because they have been led astray [e] by
        false gods, [i] [f]
    the gods [j] their ancestors followed, [g]
[5]I will send fire [h] upon Judah
    that will consume the fortresses [i] of
        Jerusalem. [j] "

Judgment on Israel

[6]This is what the LORD says:

"For three sins of Israel,

S 16:12 **2:5** [h]S 2Ki 25:9; S 2Ch 36:19 [i]Am 3:11 [j]S Jer 17:27;
S Hos 8:14

[f]*11 Or* sword / *and destroyed his allies*   [g]*15 Or /*
Molech; Hebrew malcam   [h]*2 Or of her cities*
[i]*4 Or by lies*   [j]*4 Or lies*

1:9 *Tyre.* The senior Phoenician merchant city, allied to
Israel by a "treaty of brotherhood" in the days of David (1Ki
5:1), later in the time of Solomon (1Ki 5:12) and later still
during the reign of Ahab, whose father-in-law ruled Tyre and
Sidon (1Ki 16:30-31). *she sold.* Her crime was like Philistia's (v. 6).
1:10 *walls.* Tyre was an almost impregnable island, boastful of her security (cf. Eze 26:1-28:19).
1:11 *Edom.* The nation descended from Esau (Ge 36; cf.
Ge 25:23-30; 27:39-40). *brother.* Israel (cf. Ob 8-10).
Reference may be to treaty "brother" (see note on v. 9).
Edom's crime was in violating this relationship by persistent
hostility.
1:12 *Teman . . . Bozrah.* Major cities of Edom, the former
thought to be near Petra, the latter now identified with
Buseirah, 37 miles to the north. With their destruction,
Edom would lose its capacity for continual warfare.
1:13 *Ammon.* Judgment centered on Rabbah (see note on
Dt 3:11), modern Amman. Greed for land bred a brutal
genocide that would be punished by a tumult of men and
nature, leaving the state without leaders to continue such
practices.

1:14 Fulfilled through the Assyrians.
1:15 See Jer 49:3 and NIV text note on Jer 49:1.
2:1 *burned . . . the bones of Edom's king.* Thus depriving
the king's spirit of the rest that was widely believed to result
from decent burial.
2:2 *Kerioth.* Perhaps a plural noun meaning "cities" (see
NIV text note) or the name of a major town (see Jer 48:24)
and shrine of Chemosh, the national god of Moab (see 1Ki
11:7,33).
2:4 *rejected the law of the LORD.* Judah's sins differed in
kind from those of the other nations. Those nations violated
the generally recognized laws of humanity, but Judah disobeyed the revealed law of God. These sins may be included
in the indictment against Israel that follows.
2:5 *fire . . . consume the fortresses.* Judah's punishment is
the same as Aram's (1:4), Gaza's (1:7), Tyre's (1:10),
Edom's (1:12), Ammon's (1:14) and Moab's (2:2)—loss of
the defenses and wealth in which they trusted.
2:6 Israel's sins revealed the general moral deterioration of
the nation. *the righteous.* Probably those who were not in
debt and whom there was no lawful reason to sell (cf. Lev
25:39-43). *the needy.* God had commanded that they be

even for four, I will not turn back ⌐my
wrath¬. *k*
They sell the righteous for silver,
and the needy for a pair of sandals. *l*
7They trample on the heads of the poor
as upon the dust of the ground
and deny justice to the oppressed.
Father and son use the same girl
and so profane my holy name. *m*
8They lie down beside every altar
on garments taken in pledge. *n*
In the house of their god
they drink wine *o* taken as fines. *p*

9"I destroyed the Amorite *q* before them,
though he was tall *r* as the cedars
and strong as the oaks. *s*
I destroyed his fruit above
and his roots *t* below.

10"I brought you up out of Egypt, *u*
and I led *v* you forty years in the
desert *w*
to give you the land of the
Amorites. *x*
11I also raised up prophets *y* from among
your sons
and Nazirites *z* from among your
young men.
Is this not true, people of Israel?"
declares the LORD.
12"But you made the Nazirites drink wine
and commanded the prophets not to
prophesy. *a*

13"Now then, I will crush you
as a cart crushes when loaded with
grain. *b*
14The swift will not escape, *c*
the strong *d* will not muster their
strength,
and the warrior will not save his
life. *e*
15The archer *f* will not stand his ground,
the fleet-footed soldier will not get
away,
and the horseman *g* will not save his
life. *h*
16Even the bravest warriors *i*
will flee naked on that day,"
declares the LORD.

Witnesses Summoned Against Israel

3 Hear this word the LORD has spoken
against you, *j* O people of Israel—against the whole family I brought
up out of Egypt: *k*

2"You only have I chosen *l*
of all the families of the earth;
therefore I will punish *m* you
for all your sins. *n* "

3Do two walk together
unless they have agreed to do so?
4Does a lion roar *o* in the thicket
when he has no prey? *p*

Cross references

2:6 *k* S Am 1:3
l S Joel 3:3;
Am 8:6
2:7
m S Lev 18:21;
Am 5:11-12; 8:4
2:8 *n* S Ex 22:26;
Dt 24:12-13
o Hos 7:14;
Am 4:1; 6:6
p Hab 2:6
2:9
q Nu 21:23-26;
Jos 10:12
r S Isa 10:33
s S Ps 29:9;
Nu 13:32
t S 2Ki 19:30;
S Job 18:16;
S Eze 17:9
2:10 *u* S Ex 6:6;
20:2; Am 3:1
v S Dt 8:2
w S Dt 2:7
x S Ex 3:8;
S Nu 21:25;
S Jos 13:4;
Am 9:7
2:11 *y* Dt 18:18;
Jer 7:25
z S Jdg 13:5
2:12 *a* Isa 30:10;
Jer 11:21;
Am 7:12-13;
Mic 2:6
2:13
b Am 7:16-17
2:14 *c* S Job 11:20
d S 1Ki 20:11
e Ps 33:16;
Isa 30:16-17
2:15 *f* S Eze 39:3
g S Ex 15:21;
Zec 10:5
h Ecc 9:11
2:16 *i* Jer 48:41
3:1 *j* Zep 2:5
k S Am 2:10
3:2 *l* S Ex 19:6;
Dt 7:6; Lk 12:47
m ver 14
n S Jer 14:10;
Mic 2:3; 1Pe 4:17 **3:4** *o* S Isa 42:13 *p* Ps 104:21; S Hos 5:14

---

helped (Dt 15:7–11), but they were instead sold for failure to
repay a (perhaps paltry) debt, for which a pair of sandals had
been given in pledge (see 8:6).
2:7 *trample.* See 8:4. *poor . . . oppressed.* To care for them
and to protect them from injustice were clearly commanded
by Israel's law (Ex 23:6–8); also, throughout the ancient
Near East, kings were supposed to defend such people.
Father and son use the same girl. Whether the girl in question was a household servant (in which case father and son
used her as a family prostitute) is not clear. In any case, the
law required that if there were sexual relations with a girl, a
marriage was obligatory (Ex 22:16; Dt 22:28–29). For a
father and son to have sexual relations with the same girl or
woman was strictly forbidden (Lev 18:7–8,15; 20:11–12).
profane my holy name. Cf. Lev 18:21; 19:12; 20:3; 21:6;
22:2,32; Jer 34:16; Eze 20:9,14,22,39; 36:20–23; 39:7.
2:8 *beside every altar . . . In the house of their god.* Israelites who broke the laws protecting the powerless brazenly
used their wrongly gotten gains even in places supposed to
be holy. *garments taken in pledge.* The law prohibited keeping a man's cloak overnight as a pledge (Ex 22:26–27; Dt
24:12–13), or taking a widow's cloak at all (Dt 24:17). *fines.*
Claimed as restitution for damages suffered. Exorbitant
claims or even false charges of damage seem to be suggested.
2:9 *I destroyed.* Israel not only had known God's law but
had been specially favored by his powerful help. *Amorite.*
Here used for all the inhabitants of Canaan (see notes on Ge
10:16; 15:16; Jdg 6:10; see also Dt 7:1 and note). *his fruit
above and his roots below.* That is, totally.
2:10 *I brought you up.* See 3:1. God's great blessings to
Israel in the past added to her guilt, and now they are

recalled as a part of the Lord's indictment against his people.
2:11 *I also raised up prophets . . . and Nazirites.* Prophets,
as God's faithful spokesmen (Dt 18:15–19), and Nazirites, as
those uniquely dedicated to him (Nu 6:1–21; Jdg 13:5), are
singled out as special gifts to his people. These persons who
were outside the priesthood were used by God through word
and example to call his people to faithfulness.
2:12 *But you.* They showed utter disdain for God's faithful
servants and thus betrayed their callous insensitivity to God's
working among them (cf. 7:16).
2:13 A loaded cart crushes anything that falls beneath its
wheels.
2:14–16 No one who might be expected to stand his
ground or escape would be able to save himself.
2:16 *that day.* The day God comes in judgment—as he did
through the Assyrian invasion that swept the northern kingdom away.
3:1–5:17 Oracles that underscore the certainty of God's
judgment on Israel.
3:1 *Hear this word.* See 4:1; 5:1. The Lord calls his people
to account because of their sins. *I.* He now speaks more
directly than in 1:2–2:16.
3:2 *You only.* Israel's present strength and prosperity gave
rise to complacency about her privileged status as the Lord's
chosen people. She is shockingly reminded of the long-for-
gotten responsibilities her privileges entailed.
3:3–6 With these rhetorical questions (involving comparisons) Amos builds up to the statements of vv. 7–8, to explain
why he is speaking such terrifying words. Each picture is of
cause and effect, using figures drawn from daily life—and
culminating in divine action (v. 6).

Does he growl in his den
  when he has caught nothing?
[5]Does a bird fall into a trap on the
    ground
  where no snare[q] has been set?
Does a trap spring up from the earth
  when there is nothing to catch?
[6]When a trumpet[r] sounds in a city,
  do not the people tremble?
When disaster[s] comes to a city,
  has not the LORD caused it?[t]

[7]Surely the Sovereign LORD does nothing
  without revealing his plan[u]
  to his servants the prophets.[v]

[8]The lion[w] has roared[x] —
  who will not fear?
The Sovereign LORD has spoken —
  who can but prophesy?[y]

[9]Proclaim to the fortresses of Ashdod[z]
  and to the fortresses of Egypt:
"Assemble yourselves on the mountains
    of Samaria;[a]
  see the great unrest within her
  and the oppression among her
    people."

[10]"They do not know how to do right,[b] "
    declares the LORD,
  "who hoard plunder[c] and loot in
    their fortresses."[d]

[11]Therefore this is what the Sovereign
LORD says:

"An enemy will overrun the land;
  he will pull down your strongholds
  and plunder your fortresses.[e] "

[12]This is what the LORD says:

"As a shepherd saves from the lion's[f]
    mouth
  only two leg bones or a piece of an
    ear,
so will the Israelites be saved,
those who sit in Samaria
  on the edge of their beds
  and in Damascus on their
    couches.[k] [g] "

[13]"Hear this and testify[h] against the
house of Jacob," declares the Lord, the
LORD God Almighty.

[14]"On the day I punish[i] Israel for her
    sins,
  I will destroy the altars of Bethel;[j]
  the horns[k] of the altar will be cut off
  and fall to the ground.
[15]I will tear down the winter house[l]
  along with the summer house;[m]
the houses adorned with ivory[n] will be
    destroyed
  and the mansions[o] will be
    demolished,[p] "
      declares the LORD.[q]

Israel Has Not Returned to God

4 Hear this word, you cows of Bashan[r]
  on Mount Samaria,[s]
you women who oppress the poor[t]
  and crush the needy[u]
and say to your husbands,[v] "Bring us
    some drinks![w] "
[2]The Sovereign LORD has sworn by his
    holiness:

[k] [12] The meaning of the Hebrew for this line is uncertain.

Cross references (center column)

3:5
[q] S Ps 119:110
3:6 [r] S Nu 10:2;
S Job 39:24;
S Jer 4:21
[s] S Isa 31:2
[t] Isa 14:24-27
3:7 [u] Ge 18:17;
S 1Sa 3:7;
S Da 9:22;
Jn 15:15;
Rev 10:7
[v] S Jer 23:22
3:8 [w] S Isa 31:4
[x] S Isa 42:13
[y] S Jer 20:9;
Jnh 1:1-3; 3:1-3;
Ac 4:20
3:9 [z] S Jos 13:3;
S 2Ch 26:6
[a] Am 4:1; 6:1
3:10 [b] Am 5:7;
6:12 [c] Hab 2:8
[d] S Ps 36:3;
Mic 6:10; Zep 1:9
3:11 [e] Am 2:5;
6:14

3:12 [f] S 1Sa 17:34
[g] S Est 1:6;
Am 6:4
3:13 [h] Eze 2:7
3:14 [i] S ver 2;
S Lev 26:18
[j] S Ge 12:8;
Am 5:5-6
[k] S Ex 27:2
3:15 [l] Jer 36:22
[m] Jdg 3:20
[n] S 1Ki 22:39
[o] Am 5:11; 6:11
[p] S Isa 34:5
[q] Hos 10:5-8,
14-15
4:1 [r] S Ps 22:12
[s] S Am 3:9
[t] S Isa 58:6;
S Eze 18:12
[u] S Dt 24:14
[v] Jer 44:19
[w] S Am 2:8; 5:11;
8:6

3:8 *The lion.* Echoes 1:2. *who can but prophesy?* Amos speaks because God has spoken.
3:9 The rich and powerful of Philistia and Egypt are summoned to witness the Lord's indictment against those who store up ill-gotten riches in the fortresses of Samaria (see v. 15). *fortresses.* See note on 1:4. *great unrest.* The result of a violent, selfish power structure that was heedless of the justice called for in God's law.
3:10 *who hoard.* Cf. 2:6–8. The prosperity of Israel's wealthy depended on oppression and robbery. The following verses announce God's judgment on such greed (cf. Hab 2:6–11).
3:11 *enemy.* Assyria. *plunder your fortresses.* Those that Samaria's wealthy had greedily filled with plunder.
3:12 *As a shepherd saves . . . only two leg bones.* To prove to the owner that the sheep had been eaten by a wild animal, not stolen by the shepherd. *be saved.* Only a mutilated remnant would survive. The nation as such would be more than wounded—it would be destroyed. *those who sit.* In idle luxury (cf. 6:4). *in Damascus on their couches.* See NIV text note. Since at this time Israel had extended its influence over Damascus, the rich merchants of Samaria may have maintained luxurious houses also in Damascus along with market privileges in that city (cf. 1Ki 20:34).
3:13 *Hear . . . testify.* Addressed to those summoned in v.

9. The rich and powerful of Philistia and Egypt are called upon to hear the Lord's indictment of the rich and powerful in Samaria and to testify that his indictment is true and that his judgment is warranted. Even these pagans will agree with God's judgment.
3:14 *altars of Bethel.* Israel's sins were rooted in the false shrine built by Jeroboam I at Bethel (1Ki 12:26–33). *horns of the altar.* Even the last refuge for a condemned man (cf. 1Ki 1:50–53) will afford Israel no protection.
3:15 *winter house . . . summer house.* Cf. 6:11; further signs of opulence that would not benefit their owners on the day of God's judgment—nor would expensive imported decorations, carvings and inlays of ivory (cf. 6:4; 1Ki 22:39). Many examples of such carvings have been found in ruined palaces in Samaria and other cities.
4:1 *Hear this word.* See note on 3:1. *cows of Bashan.* Upper-class women, directly addressed, are compared with the best breed of cattle in ancient Canaan, which were raised (and pampered) in the pastures of northern Transjordan (cf. Ps 22:12; Eze 39:18). Whether the metaphor was intended as an insult or an ironic flattery is uncertain.
4:2 *The Sovereign LORD has sworn.* Stresses the solemnity of the situation and the certainty of the events. *by his holiness.* Contrasts with Israel's sin, reminding them of what they could have been (Ex 19:6) if they had faithfully kept

"The time[x] will surely come
  when you will be taken away[y] with
    hooks,[z]
  the last of you with fishhooks.
[3]You will each go straight out
    through breaks in the wall,[a]
  and you will be cast out toward
    Harmon,[1]"
                    declares the LORD.

[4]"Go to Bethel[b] and sin;
  go to Gilgal[c] and sin yet more.
Bring your sacrifices every morning,[d]
  your tithes[e] every three years.[m/]
[5]Burn leavened bread[g] as a thank
    offering
  and brag about your freewill
    offerings[h] —
boast about them, you Israelites,
  for this is what you love to do,"
                    declares the Sovereign LORD.

[6]"I gave you empty stomachs[n] in every
    city
  and lack of bread in every town,
  yet you have not returned to me,"
                    declares the LORD.[i]

[7]"I also withheld[j] rain from you
    when the harvest was still three
      months away.
I sent rain on one town,
  but withheld it from another.[k]
One field had rain;
  another had none and dried up.
[8]People staggered from town to town for
    water[l]
  but did not get enough[m] to drink,
  yet you have not returned[n] to me,"
                    declares the LORD.[o]

[9]"Many times I struck your gardens and
    vineyards,
  I struck them with blight and
    mildew.[p]
Locusts[q] devoured your fig and olive
    trees,[r]
  yet you have not returned[s] to me,"
                    declares the LORD.

[10]"I sent plagues[t] among you
    as I did to Egypt.[u]
I killed your young men[v] with the
    sword,
  along with your captured horses.
I filled your nostrils with the stench[w] of
    your camps,
  yet you have not returned to me,"[x]
                    declares the LORD.[y]

[11]"I overthrew some of you
    as I[o] overthrew Sodom and
      Gomorrah.[z]
You were like a burning stick[a] snatched
    from the fire,
  yet you have not returned to me,"
                    declares the LORD.[b]

[12]"Therefore this is what I will do to you,
    Israel,
  and because I will do this to you,
    prepare to meet your God, O Israel."

[13]He who forms the mountains,[c]
    creates the wind,[d]
  and reveals his thoughts[e] to man,
he who turns dawn to darkness,

Cross-reference notes (center column):

4:2 [x]Jer 31:31
[y]Am 6:8
[z]S 2Ki 19:28;
S 2Ch 33:11;
S Isa 19:8
4:3 [a]S Eze 12:5
4:4 [b]S Jos 7:2
[c]S Hos 4:15
[d]S Nu 28:3
[e]Dt 14:28
[f]S Eze 20:39;
Am 5:21-22
4:5 [g]S Lev 7:13
[h]S Lev 22:18-21
4:6 [i]S Isa 3:1;
S 9:13; S Jer 5:3;
Hag 2:17
4:7 [j]S Jer 3:3;
Zec 14:17
[k]Ex 9:4,26;
Dt 11:17;
S 2Ch 7:13;
S Isa 5:6
4:8 [l]S Eze 4:16-17
[m]Hag 1:6
[n]S Jer 3:7
[o]S Job 36:31;
S Jer 14:4

4:9 [p]S Dt 28:22
[q]S Ex 10:13;
S Joel 2:25
[r]Joel 1:7
[s]S Isa 9:13;
S Jer 3:10
4:10 [t]S Ex 9:3
[u]Ex 11:5
[v]S Isa 9:17
[w]S Isa 34:3
[x]S Dt 28:21
[y]S Isa 9:13
4:11 [z]S Ge 19:24;
S Jer 23:14
[a]S Isa 7:4;
Jude 1:23
[b]S Job 36:13
4:13 [c]Ps 65:6
[d]Ps 135:7
[e]S Da 2:28

13 Masoretic Text; with a different word division of the
Hebrew (see Septuagint) out, O mountain of oppression
[m]4 Or tithes on the third day   [n]6 Hebrew you
cleanness of teeth   [o]11 Hebrew God

---

their side of the covenant—as God had his. *hooks.* According to Assyrian reliefs (pictures engraved on stone), prisoners
of war were led away with a rope fastened to a hook that
pierced the nose or lower lip (cf. 2Ki 19:28; 2Ch 33:11; Eze
19:4,9; Hab 1:15). The Hebrew word here may, in fact,
refer to ropes.
4:3 *breaks in the wall.* See 2Ki 17:5. *Harmon.* Appears to
be a place-name, though it is not otherwise known (see NIV
text note).
4:4–5 Spoken in irony.
4:4 *Bethel . . . Gilgal.* These towns had historical importance as places where God's help was commemorated (cf. Ge
35:1–15; Jos 4:20–24), and both were popular places of
worship in Amos' day (5:5; cf. Hos 4:15; 9:15; 12:11).
sacrifices every morning. See Ex 29:38–42. *tithes.* Apparently the special tithe that was to be brought every three
years (cf. Dt 14:28; 26:12). *years.* See NIV text note. The
Hebrew word for "days" sometimes stands for years.
4:5 *leavened bread.* The burning of leavened bread in the
sacrifices was strictly forbidden (see Lev 6:17; 7:12). Either
Amos rebukes the Israelites for willful transgression of the
law, or he speaks of burning in a general way for offering
inappropriate gifts to the Lord. Leavened bread could accompany a fellowship offering (see Lev 7:13). *what you love to*

do. They loved the forms and rituals of religion but did not
love what God loves—goodness, mercy, kindness, justice
(see 5:15; Isa 5:7; 61:8; Mic 6:8).
4:6–11 In the past, God had used natural disasters to
discipline and warn his people, but those lessons were soon
forgotten (cf. Dt 28:22,39–40,42,48,56–57).
4:6 *I.* These were not simply natural disasters; they were
direct acts of God (3:6). *yet . . . me.* See vv. 8–11.
4:7–8 Lack of rain three months before harvest would
prevent full development of the grain.
4:9 *Locusts.* Cf. 7:1; Joel 1:4.
4:10 *plagues . . . as . . . Egypt.* See Ex 7:14–12:30.
4:11 *Sodom and Gomorrah.* Exemplified total destruction,
God's judgment on those cities (see Ge 19:24–25) having
already become proverbial (cf. Dt 29:23; Isa 1:9; 13:19; Jer
49:18; 50:40; Zep 2:9). *burning stick snatched from the
fire.* Saved only by God's grace (cf. Zec 3:2).
4:12 *prepare to meet your God.* Devastated Israel, brought
to her knees by the Assyrians, would meet the God she had
covenanted with at Sinai and had now so grievously offended.
4:13 See note on 5:8–9. The God of such power and
majesty is easily able to execute the judgment announced in
v. 12.

and treads the high places of the
earth[f] —
    the LORD God Almighty is his name.[g]

A Lament and Call to Repentance

5 Hear this word, O house of Israel, this
  lament[h] I take up concerning you:

[2]"Fallen is Virgin[i] Israel,
    never to rise again,
  deserted in her own land,
    with no one to lift her up.[j] "

[3]This is what the Sovereign LORD says:

"The city that marches out a thousand
    strong for Israel
  will have only a hundred left;
  the town that marches out a hundred
    strong
  will have only ten left.[k] "

[4]This is what the LORD says to the house
of Israel:

  "Seek[l] me and live;[m]
[5] do not seek Bethel,
  do not go to Gilgal,[n]
  do not journey to Beersheba.[o]
For Gilgal will surely go into exile,
  and Bethel will be reduced to
    nothing.[p] [p]"
[6]Seek[q] the LORD and live,[r]
  or he will sweep through the house
    of Joseph like a fire;[s]
it will devour,
  and Bethel[t] will have no one to
    quench it.[u]

[7]You who turn justice into bitterness[v]
  and cast righteousness[w] to the
    ground[x]
[8](he who made the Pleiades and Orion,[y]
  who turns blackness into dawn[z]
  and darkens day into night,[a]
who calls for the waters of the sea
  and pours them out over the face of
    the land—
  the LORD is his name[b] —
[9]he flashes destruction on the stronghold
  and brings the fortified city to ruin),[c]
[10]you hate the one who reproves in
    court[d]
  and despise him who tells the truth.[e]

[11]You trample on the poor[f]
  and force him to give you grain.
Therefore, though you have built stone
    mansions,[g]
  you will not live in them;[h]
though you have planted lush vineyards,
  you will not drink their wine.[i]
[12]For I know how many are your offenses
  and how great your sins.[j]

You oppress the righteous and take
    bribes[k]
  and you deprive the poor[l] of justice
    in the courts.[m]
[13]Therefore the prudent man keeps
    quiet[n] in such times,

4:13 /Mic 1:3
gS Isa 47:4;
Am 5:8,27; 9:6
5:1 hS Jer 4:8;
S Eze 19:1
5:2 iS 2Ki 19:21;
Jer 14:17
/Jer 50:32;
Am 8:14
5:3 kIsa 6:13;
Am 6:9
5:4 lS Dt 4:29
mDt 32:46-47;
Isa 55:3;
Jer 29:13;
S Eze 18:9
5:5 nISa 11:14;
S Hos 4:15
oGe 21:31;
Am 8:14
pS 1Sa 7:16;
S 8:2
5:6 qPs 22:26;
105:4; S Isa 31:1;
55:6; Zep 2:3
rver 14;
S Lev 18:5
sDt 4:24
tS Am 3:14
uS Jer 4:4

5:7 vIsa 5:20;
Am 6:12
wS Am 3:10
xS Hos 10:4
5:8 yS Ge 1:16;
S Job 38:31
zS Job 38:12;
Isa 42:16
aS Ps 104:20;
Am 8:9
bPs 104:6-9;
Jer 16:21;
S Am 4:13
5:9 cMic 5:11
5:10 dS Isa 29:21
eIKi 22:8;
Gal 4:16
5:11 /Am 8:6
gS Am 3:15
hS Dt 28:30;
Mic 1:6
/S Jdg 9:27;
S Am 4:1; 9:14;
Mic 6:15;
Zep 1:13

5:12 /Hos 5:3 kS Job 36:18; S Isa 1:23; S Eze 22:12
lS Jer 5:28 mS Job 5:4; S Isa 5:23; S Am 2:6-7 5:13
nS Est 4:14

p5 Or grief, or wickedness; Hebrew aven, a reference to
Beth Aven (a derogatory name for Bethel)

5:1 *Hear this word.* See note on 3:1. *this lament.* Amos
sorrowfully fashioned a lament as if Israel were already dead.
5:2 *Virgin Israel.* See Jer 18:13; 31:4,21; see also notes on
2Ki 19:21; Isa 23:12. *deserted.* Left like a dead body on the
open field (cf. Jer 9:22).
5:3 *city . . . town.* The Hebrew expression denotes communities of varying size, all of which would suffer.
5:4 *Seek.* See vv. 6,14. *live.* If they would seek the Lord,
they (or at least a remnant, v. 15) could yet escape the violent
death anticipated in Amos's lament.
5:5 *Bethel . . . Gilgal.* See note on 4:4. *Beersheba.* Located
in the south of Judah, it also had evidently become a place of
pilgrimage and idolatry (cf. 8:14). All shrines where the
worship of God was abused would be destroyed.
5:6 The places of idolatry were doomed; yet if Israel turned
to God, there was hope for her as a nation. Otherwise the
people, too, would be destroyed. *house of Joseph.* The
northern kingdom of Israel, dominated by the tribe of
Ephraim, descendants of Joseph (also in v. 15; 6:6). *Bethel.*
The main religious center of the northern kingdom (see
7:13; see also 3:14; 4:4; 7:10). The god the Israelites
worshiped there would be powerless to save the place when
the true God brought his judgment.
5:7 *You who turn justice into bitterness.* They corrupted
the procedures and institutions of justice (the courts), making them instruments of injustice ("bitterness"). Turning
God's order upside down is inevitable in a society that ig-

nores his law and despises true religion (see 6:12).
5:8–9 As in 4:13, a brief hymn is inserted (see 9:5–6).
Here Amos highlights the contrast between "you who turn"
good into bad (v. 7) and the One "who turns" night into day
and governs the order of the universe—and whose power
can smash the walls his people hide behind.
5:8 *Pleiades.* A group of seven stars (part of the constellation Taurus); always mentioned in connection with Orion
(see note on Job 9:9). *blackness into dawn . . . day into
night.* The orderly sequence of day and night (cf. Jer 31:35).
waters of the sea. The waters above the expanse (see 9:6; Ge
1:7; see also notes on Ps 36:8; 42:7; 104:3,13); alternatively, waters evaporated from the sea and condensed as
rain.
5:10 Continues the sentence begun in v. 7. This poetic
paragraph is continued and completed in vv. 12b–13, which
(in the Hebrew) use the third person, while the preceding
passage (vv. 11–12a) uses the second person. The indictment of vv. 7,10,12b–13 is therefore more objective and
descriptive, while that of vv. 11–12a is more direct and
pointed. *reproves . . . tells the truth.* Those who are concerned that the courts uphold justice.
5:11 *though you have built.* God would take away their
prized possessions acquired through wrongful gain. Their
prosperity would be turned to grief (cf. Dt 28:30,38–40).
5:13 *prudent man.* He knows he cannot change the state of
affairs, and therefore only awaits judgment.

for the times are evil. °

14Seek good, not evil,
that you may live. ᵖ
Then the LORD God Almighty will be
with you,
just as you say he is.
15Hate evil, ۹ love good; ʳ
maintain justice in the courts. ˢ
Perhaps ᵗ the LORD God Almighty will
have mercy ᵘ
on the remnant ᵛ of Joseph.

16Therefore this is what the Lord, the
LORD God Almighty, says:

"There will be wailing ʷ in all the
streets ˣ
and cries of anguish in every public
square.
The farmers ʸ will be summoned to
weep
and the mourners to wail.
17There will be wailing ᶻ in all the
vineyards,
for I will pass through ᵃ your midst,"
says the LORD. ᵇ

The Day of the LORD

18Woe to you who long
for the day of the LORD! ᶜ
Why do you long for the day of the
LORD? ᵈ
That day will be darkness, ᵉ not
light. ᶠ

19It will be as though a man fled from a
lion
only to meet a bear, ᵍ
as though he entered his house
and rested his hand on the wall
only to have a snake bite him. ʰ
20Will not the day of the LORD be
darkness, ⁱ not light—
pitch-dark, without a ray of
brightness? ʲ

21"I hate, ᵏ I despise your religious
feasts; ˡ
I cannot stand your assemblies. ᵐ
22Even though you bring me burnt
offerings ⁿ and grain offerings,
I will not accept them. ° ᵖ
Though you bring choice fellowship
offerings, ۹
I will have no regard for them. ۹ ʳ
23Away with the noise of your songs!
I will not listen to the music of your
harps. ˢ
24But let justice ᵗ roll on like a river,
righteousness ᵘ like a never-failing
stream! ᵛ

25"Did you bring me sacrifices ʷ and
offerings
forty years ˣ in the desert, O house of
Israel?
26You have lifted up the shrine of your
king,

Cross references

5:13 °Mic 2:3
5:14 ᵖS ver 6
5:15 ۹S Ps 52:3;
S 97:10; Ro 12:9
ʳS Ge 18:25
ˢS Isa 1:17;
S 29:21; Zec 8:16
ᵗS Jer 36:3
ᵘS Joel 2:14
ᵛMic 5:7,8; 7:18
5:16 ʷJer 9:17;
Am 8:3; Zep 1:10
ˣJer 7:34
ʸS Joel 1:11
5:17 ᶻS Ex 11:6
ᵃEx 12:12
ᵇIsa 16:10;
S Jer 48:33
5:18 ᶜS Isa 2:12;
S Joel 1:15
ᵈS Jer 30:5
ᵉS 1Sa 2:9;
S Joel 2:2
ᶠS Job 20:28;
Isa 5:19,30;
Jer 30:7

5:19 ᵍS La 3:10
ʰS Dt 32:24;
Job 20:24;
S Ecc 10:8;
Isa 24:17-18;
Jer 15:2-3; 48:44
5:20 ⁱS 1Sa 2:9
ʲS Isa 13:10;
S Eze 7:7;
Ob 1:15;
Zep 1:15
5:21 ᵏJer 44:4
ˡS Lev 26:31;
S Hos 2:11
ᵐS Eze 23:18
5:22 ⁿS Lev 26:31
°S Jer 7:21
ᵖS Ps 40:6
۹Jer 14:12;
S Am 4:4;
Mic 6:6-7
ʳIsa 1:11-16;
S 66:3
5:23 ˢAm 5:23
5:24 ᵗS Jer 22:3
ᵘS Isa 45:8
ᵛMic 6:8

5:25 ʷS Isa 43:23 ˣS Ex 16:35

۹22 Traditionally *peace offerings*

5:14 *Seek good.* Cf. "Seek me" (v. 4); see Isa 1:16–17 and note on Isa 1:17. *that you may live.* The purpose is more definitely expressed than in vv. 4,6, and the way to change is explicit. *with you.* As your security and source of blessing. **5:15** *Perhaps.* Emphasizes the danger of presuming on God's grace. Even a widespread change of attitude would need the test of time to prove its genuineness. *remnant.* Implies that a change now would benefit the individual survivors of the disaster, though the nation as a whole would perish.
5:16–17 A return to the theme of lament with which this section began (vv. 1–2). *streets . . . square . . . farmers . . . vineyards.* All will be affected by God's punishment. Even farmers, usually too busy for such things, would join the professional mourners in lament, and mourning would overflow from the cities to the vineyards. When the holy God "will pass through" (as he did in Egypt, Ex 12:12), punishment for the unholy and unjust will be inescapable (cf. Isa 6:5).
5:18 *day of the LORD.* The time when God will show himself the victor over the world, vindicating his claims to be the Lord over all the earth (see notes on 8:9; Isa 2:11,17,20). Israel expected to be exalted as his people and longed for that day to come. Amos warned that the day would come, but not as Israel expected—it would be a day of "darkness, not light" (v. 20) for her, because she had not been faithful to God. (Cf. "the day of our Lord Jesus Christ" and variations in 1Co 1:8; 3:12–15; 5:5; 2Co 1:14; Php 1:6,10; 2:16.) Amos speaks primarily of an imminent and decisive judg-

ment on Israel, not exclusively of the last day.
5:19–20 The two pictures (v. 19) emphasize vividly the inescapability of God's coming judgment.
5:21–27 Again God directly addresses Israel with the charge of unfaithfulness.
5:21–23 These three verses summarize and reject the current practice of religion in Israel. The institutions were not wrong in themselves; it was the worshipers and the ways they worshiped that were wrong. The people had no basis on which to come to God, because their conduct reflected disobedience of his law (see Isa 1:11–15 and note).
5:21 *I cannot stand.* Lit. "I do not inhale with delight."
5:24 *justice . . . righteousness.* Prerequisites for acceptance by God; but these are what Israel had rejected and scorned (cf. vv. 7,10,12b). *river . . . never-failing stream.* In contrast to stream beds that are dry much of the year. The simile is especially apt: As plant and animal life flourishes where there is water, so human life flourishes where there is justice and righteousness.
5:25 Israel's right relationship with the Lord was never established primarily by sacrifices. It was above all based on obedience (see 1Sa 15:22–23; cf. Ro 1:5). *forty years in the desert.* See Nu 14:32–35.
5:26 The obscure language of this verse speaks of Israelite idolatry, but whether it was in the desert long ago or more recently in the promised land, or both, is not clear. The NIV text note takes two nouns as proper names derived from Akkadian. The Septuagint (the Greek translation of the OT) represents a somewhat different text, which is followed by

the pedestal of your idols, y
the star of your god r —
which you made for yourselves.
²⁷Therefore I will send you into exile z
beyond Damascus,"
says the LORD, whose name is God
Almighty. a

Woe to the Complacent

6 Woe to you b who are complacent c
in Zion,
and to you who feel secure d on
Mount Samaria, e
you notable men of the foremost nation,
to whom the people of Israel come! f
²Go to Calneh g and look at it;
go from there to great Hamath, h
and then go down to Gath i in
Philistia.
Are they better off than j your two
kingdoms?
Is their land larger than yours?
³You put off the evil day
and bring near a reign of terror. k
⁴You lie on beds inlaid with ivory
and lounge on your couches. l
You dine on choice lambs
and fattened calves. m
⁵You strum away on your harps n like
David
and improvise on musical
instruments. o
⁶You drink wine p by the bowlful
and use the finest lotions,
but you do not grieve q over the ruin
of Joseph. r
⁷Therefore you will be among the first to
go into exile; s
your feasting and lounging will end. t

The LORD Abhors the Pride of Israel

⁸The Sovereign LORD has sworn by himself u—the LORD God Almighty declares:

"I abhor v the pride of Jacob w
and detest his fortresses; x
I will deliver up y the city
and everything in it. z "

⁹If ten a men are left in one house, they
too will die. ¹⁰And if a relative who is to
burn the bodies b comes to carry them out
of the house and asks anyone still hiding
there, "Is anyone with you?" and he says,
"No," then he will say, "Hush! c We must
not mention the name of the LORD."

¹¹For the LORD has given the command,
and he will smash d the great house e
into pieces
and the small house into bits. f

¹²Do horses run on the rocky crags?
Does one plow there with oxen?
But you have turned justice into
poison g
and the fruit of righteousness h into
bitterness i —
¹³you who rejoice in the conquest of Lo
Debar s
and say, "Did we not take Karnaim t
by our own strength? i "

¹⁴For the LORD God Almighty declares,
"I will stir up a nation k against you,
O house of Israel,
that will oppress you all the way

5:26 y S Eze 18:6;
S 20:16
5:27 z Am 6:7;
7:11,17; Mic 1:16
a Dt 32:17-19;
Jer 38:17;
S Am 4:13;
Ac 7:42-43*
6:1 b Lk 6:24
c Zep 1:12
d S Job 24:23
e S Am 3:9
f Isa 32:9-11
6:2 g Ge 10:10
h S 2Ki 17:24;
S Jer 49:23
i S Jos 11:22;
2Ch 26:6 j Na 3:8
6:3 k S Isa 56:12;
S Eze 12:22;
Am 9:10
6:4 l S Est 1:6;
S Pr 7:17
m S Isa 1:11;
S Eze 34:2-3;
S Am 3:12
6:5 n S Ps 137:2;
S Isa 14:11;
Am 5:23
o S 1Ch 15:16
6:6 p S Isa 28:1;
S Am 2:8
q S Eze 9:4
r S Eze 16:49
6:7 s S Am 5:27
t S Jer 16:9;
S La 4:5

6:8 u S Ge 22:16;
Heb 6:13
v S Lev 26:30
w S Ps 47:4
x S Jer 12:8
y Am 4:2
z S Lev 26:19;
Dt 32:19
6:9 a S Am 5:3
6:10
b S 1Sa 31:12
c Am 8:3
6:11 d S Isa 34:5
e S Am 3:15
f Isa 55:11
6:12 g Hos 10:4
h S Am 3:10
i S Isa 1:21;
S Am 5:7
6:13 j S Job 8:15;
Isa 28:14-15
6:14 k Jer 5:15

r 26 Or lifted up Sakkuth your king / and Kaiwan your
idols, / your star-gods; Septuagint lifted up the shrine of
Molech / and the star of your god Rephan, / their idols
s 13 Lo Debar means nothing.   t 13 Karnaim means
horns; horn here symbolizes strength.

Ac 7:42-43.
5:27 This punishment is the final one—exile from the
God-given land to remote foreign places.
6:1 *in Zion . . . on Mount Samaria.* Although Amos spoke
primarily to Israel, Judah (Zion) also deserved his rebuke (cf.
2:4–5), for Israel properly comprised all 12 tribes. *foremost
nation.* In Israel's self-complacent eyes in this time of her
newly recovered power and prosperity.
6:2 Perhaps Calneh and Hamath had fallen in Jeroboam II's
campaign (2Ki 14:28), and the wall of Gath had been broken
down by Uzziah (2Ch 26:6). These words may have been
spoken by the "people of Israel" (v. 1) who, when they came
before their notables, flattered their vanity and thus reinforced their arrogant complacency.
6:4 *ivory.* See 3:15 and note.
6:5 *like David.* See 1Sa 16:15–23; 2Sa 23:1.
6:6 *Joseph.* See note on 5:6.
6:8 *sworn by himself.* See note on Ge 22:16; cf. Heb
6:13–14. By this oath God declares that the verdict is final.
6:10–11 A fearful scene: Apparently a survivor is cowering
inside the house, the relative forbidding him even to pray
because God's wrath had fallen on the city.

6:10 *burn the bodies.* Reference may be to burning a
memorial fire in honor of the dead (see Jer 34:5). Cremation
was not generally practiced, being reserved primarily for
serious offenders (see Lev 20:14; 21:9; Jos 7:15,25; cf. 1Sa
31:11–13).
6:11 *great house . . . small house.* Cf. perhaps the "summer house" and "winter house" of 3:15.
6:12 *plow there with oxen.* The Hebrew for this phrase is
sometimes translated (with a slight textual change) "plow
the sea with oxen." Israel's perversion of justice flies in the
face of even common human wisdom about the right order of
things.
6:13 *Lo Debar . . . Karnaim.* See NIV text notes for Amos's
ironic play on the meanings of these place names. They seem
to have been regained from Hazael by Jehoash (2Ki
10:32–33; 13:25), then taken by the Assyrians ("a nation,"
v. 14) soon after Amos's day (2Ki 15:29)—beginning the
sequence of events that would lead to the loss of all territory
conquered by Jeroboam II.
6:14 *from Lebo Hamath to the valley of the Arabah.* From
the Orontes River in north Lebanon to the Dead Sea—thus
the whole land (cf. 2Ki 14:25).

from Lebo^u Hamath^l to the valley of the Arabah.^m"

Locusts, Fire and a Plumb Line

7 This is what the Sovereign LORD showed me:ⁿ He was preparing swarms of locusts^o after the king's share had been harvested and just as the second crop was coming up. ²When they had stripped the land clean,^p I cried out, "Sovereign LORD, forgive! How can Jacob survive?^q He is so small!^r"

³So the LORD relented.^s

"This will not happen," the LORD said.^t

⁴This is what the Sovereign LORD showed me: The Sovereign LORD was calling for judgment by fire;^u it dried up the great deep and devoured^v the land. ⁵Then I cried out, "Sovereign LORD, I beg you, stop! How can Jacob survive? He is so small!^w"

⁶So the LORD relented.^x

"This will not happen either," the Sovereign LORD said.^y

⁷This is what he showed me: The Lord was standing by a wall that had been built true to plumb, with a plumb line in his hand. ⁸And the LORD asked me, "What do you see,^z Amos?^a"

"A plumb line,^b" I replied.

Then the Lord said, "Look, I am setting a plumb line among my people Israel; I will spare them no longer.^c

⁹"The high places^d of Isaac will be destroyed
and the sanctuaries^e of Israel will be ruined;
with my sword I will rise against the house of Jeroboam.^f"

Amos and Amaziah

¹⁰Then Amaziah the priest of Bethel^g sent a message to Jeroboam^h king of Israel: "Amos is raising a conspiracyⁱ against you in the very heart of Israel. The land cannot bear all his words.^j ¹¹For this is what Amos is saying:

" 'Jeroboam will die by the sword,
and Israel will surely go into exile,^k
away from their native land.' "^l

¹²Then Amaziah said to Amos, "Get out, you seer!^m Go back to the land of Judah. Earn your bread there and do your prophesying there.ⁿ ¹³Don't prophesy anymore at Bethel,^o because this is the king's sanctuary and the temple^p of the kingdom.^q"

¹⁴Amos answered Amaziah, "I was neither a prophet^r nor a prophet's son, but

---

6:14 *l*S Nu 13:21
*m*S Am 3:11
7:1 *n*ver 7;
Am 8:1
*o*Ps 78:46;
S Jer 51:14;
S Joel 1:4
7:2 *p*S Ex 10:15
*q*S Isa 37:4
*r*S Eze 11:13;
S Am 4:9
7:3 *s*S Ex 32:14;
Dt 32:36;
S Jer 18:8; 26:19
*t*S Hos 11:8
7:4 *u*S Isa 66:16;
S Joel 1:19
*v*Dt 32:22
7:5 *w*S ver 1-2;
Joel 2:17
7:6 *x*S Ex 32:14;
S Jer 18:8;
Jnh 3:10
*y*Jer 42:10;
S Eze 9:8
7:8 *z*Jer 1:11,13
*a*Am 8:2
*b*S 2Ki 21:13

*c*S Jer 15:6;
Eze 7:2-9
7:9 *d*S Lev 26:30
*e*S Lev 26:31
*f*S 1Ki 13:34;
2Ki 15:9;
Isa 63:18;
S Hos 10:8
7:10 *g*S Jos 7:2
*h*S 2Ki 14:23
*i*Jer 38:4
*j*2Ki 14:24;
Jer 26:8-11
7:11 *k*S Am 5:27
*l*Jer 36:16
7:12 *m*S 1Sa 9:9
*n*Mt 8:34
7:13 *o*S Jos 7:2;
S 1Ki 12:29
*p*Jer 36:5
*q*S Jer 20:2;
S Am 2:12;

Ac 4:18 7:14 *r*S 1Sa 10:5; 2Ki 2:5; 4:38; Zec 13:5

^u*14* Or *from the entrance to*

7:1 *showed me.* Introduces reports of visions that convey God's message through things seen as well as heard (see vv. 4,7; 8:1; cf. 9:1). *locusts.* Cf. 4:9; Joel 1:4. *king's share.* Apparently the earlier crop, from which the royal taxes were taken. *second crop.* The growth that came up in the fields after the grains and early hay were harvested. On these the flocks and herds pastured until the summer drought stopped all growth (cf. 1Ki 18:5).
7:2 See v. 5. *How . . . survive?* Mass starvation would afflict all the people. *Jacob.* Israel. *so small.* Powerless to withstand the calamity. Amos makes no appeal to the Lord's covenant with Israel—perhaps because Israel's unfaithfulness had removed all right to such an appeal.
7:3 See v. 6. *the LORD relented.* In response to the prophetic intercession (cf. Ge 20:7)—but forgiveness is not offered.
7:4 *great deep.* Probably the Mediterranean Sea. *land.* Lit. "portion," probably referring to the promised land or, more precisely, to everything growing on the land (cf. Joel 1:19).
7:5 See note on v. 2.
7:6 See note on v. 3.
7:7 Israel is compared to a wall built true to plumb—what she should have been, after all the Lord had done for her.
7:8-9 In vv. 1-6 God proposed wholesale punishments amounting to total destruction, but relented at Amos's prayer—though without promise of forgiveness. Now the Lord is no longer open to such intercession (cf. Jer 7:16; 11:14; 14:11; 15:1).
7:8 *plumb line.* God's people had been "built" (v. 7) according to God's standards. They were expected to be true to those standards, but were completely out of plumb when tested (cf. 2Ki 21:13). *my people.* Here, for the first time in the book of Amos, the Lord calls Israel "my people" (see v.

15; 8:2; 9:10,14). *spare them no longer.* See 8:2.
7:9 *high places . . . sanctuaries . . . house.* The centers of religious and political pretension and of self-righteous pride would be wiped out. *Isaac.* Israel's (Jacob's) father, a way of referring to Israel found only in Amos (see v. 16). *Jeroboam.* The oracles of chs. 1-6 were spoken to the leading people of Israel and Samaria as a whole; here Amos names one man, the king.
7:11 Amaziah's words summarize Amos's message (see note on v. 17). *Jeroboam.* That is, his "house" (v. 9), the king's name also representing his dynasty. *will die.* Jeroboam died naturally (2Ki 14:29), but his son and successor Zechariah (2Ki 15:8) was assassinated (2Ki 15:10).
7:12 *seer.* Amaziah dismissed Amos as a prophet for hire whom he need not take seriously.
7:13 *king's sanctuary.* Amaziah served the king in Samaria, not Israel's heavenly King; hence he would not allow a prophetic word to be spoken against Jeroboam or his realm at the royal chapel.
7:14 *neither a prophet nor a prophet's son.* Amos denied any previous connection with the prophets or their disciples (see note on 1Ki 20:35). No one had hired him to come and announce judgment on Jeroboam and Israel. *shepherd.* See note on 1:1, but the Hebrew uses a different word here—one not found elsewhere in the OT. The Hebrew for this word is, however, related to a word for "cattle," suggesting that Amos may also have tended cattle. *sycamore-fig trees.* A large tree, yielding fig-like fruit as well as useful timber. To ensure good fruit, the gardener had to slit the top of each fig—which may be the procedure referred to by the obscure Hebrew word here rendered "took care of."

I was a shepherd, and I also took care of
sycamore-fig trees.[s] 15But the LORD took
me from tending the flock[t] and said to
me, 'Go,[u] prophesy[v] to my people Israel.'[w] 16Now then, hear[x] the word of the
LORD. You say,

" 'Do not prophesy against[y] Israel,
and stop preaching against the house
of Isaac.'

17"Therefore this is what the LORD says:

" 'Your wife will become a prostitute[z]
in the city,
and your sons and daughters will fall
by the sword.
Your land will be measured and divided
up,
and you yourself will die in a pagan[v]
country.
And Israel will certainly go into exile,[a]
away from their native land.[b]' "

A Basket of Ripe Fruit

8 This is what the Sovereign LORD
showed me:[c] a basket of ripe fruit.
2"What do you see,[d] Amos?[e]" he asked.
"A basket[f] of ripe fruit," I answered.
Then the LORD said to me, "The time is
ripe for my people Israel; I will spare them
no longer.[g]
3"In that day," declares the Sovereign
LORD, "the songs in the temple will turn to
wailing.[w][h] Many, many bodies—flung
everywhere! Silence![i]"

4Hear this, you who trample the needy
and do away with the poor[j] of the
land,[k]

5saying,

"When will the New Moon[l] be over
that we may sell grain,
and the Sabbath be ended
that we may market[m] wheat?"[n]—
skimping the measure,
boosting the price
and cheating[o] with dishonest
scales,[p]
6buying the poor[q] with silver
and the needy for a pair of sandals,
selling even the sweepings with the
wheat.[r]

7The LORD has sworn by the Pride of
Jacob:[s] "I will never forget[t] anything
they have done.[u]

8"Will not the land tremble[v] for this,
and all who live in it mourn?
The whole land will rise like the Nile;
it will be stirred up and then sink
like the river of Egypt.[w]

9"In that day," declares the Sovereign
LORD,

"I will make the sun go down at noon
and darken the earth in broad
daylight.[x]
10I will turn your religious feasts[y] into
mourning
and all your singing into weeping.[z]
I will make all of you wear sackcloth[a]
and shave[b] your heads.
I will make that time like mourning for
an only son[c]
and the end of it like a bitter day.[d]

7:14 [s]S 1Ki 10:27; S Isa 9:10 **7:15** [t]S Ge 37:2; S 2Sa 7:8 [u]S Isa 6:9 [v]S Jer 26:12 [w]Jer 7:1-2; S Eze 2:3-4 **7:16** [x]Jer 22:2 [y]S Eze 20:46; Mic 2:6 **7:17** [z]S Hos 4:13 [a]S Am 5:27 [b]S 2Ki 17:6; S Eze 4:13; S Hos 9:3; Am 2:12-13 **8:1** [c]S Am 7:1 **8:2** [d]Jer 1:13; 24:3 [e]Am 7:8 [f]S Ge 40:16 [g]S La 4:18; Eze 7:2-9 **8:3** [h]S Am 5:16 [i]Am 6:10 **8:4** [j]S Pr 30:14 [k]S Job 20:19; S Ps 14:4; S Am 2:7

8:5 [l]S Nu 10:10 [m]Isa 58:13 [n]S Ne 10:31 [o]S Ge 31:7 [p]Dt 25:15; 2Ki 4:23; Ne 13:15-16; Eze 45:10-12; S Hos 12:7; Mic 6:10-11; Zec 5:6 **8:6** [q]Am 5:11 [r]S Am 2:6; S 4:1 **8:7** [s]S Ps 47:4 [t]S Hos 8:13 [u]S Job 35:15 **8:8** [v]S Job 9:6; Jer 51:29 [w]Ps 18:7; S Jer 46:8; Am 9:5 **8:9** [x]S Job 5:14; Isa 59:9-10; Jer 13:16; 15:9; S Eze 32:7; S Am 5:8; Mic 3:6; Mt 27:45; Mk 15:33; Lk 23:44-45 **8:10** [y]S Lev 26:31

[z]S La 5:15; S Hos 2:11 [a]S Joel 1:8 [b]S Lev 13:40; S Isa 3:17 [c]S Ge 21:16 [d]S Jer 2:19; S Eze 7:18

v17 Hebrew *an unclean* **w**3 Or *"the temple singers will wail*

7:15 *tending.* Or "following" (as in 2Sa 7:8), the Hebrew for which stresses the location of the shepherd rather than his activity. *Go.* Amos was in Bethel because God had sent him to prophesy there.
7:16 *Do not prophesy.* Cf. 2:12.
7:17 Amos turned to condemn the priest personally. *prostitute.* With the exile of Amaziah, the death of his children and the loss of the family estate, Amaziah's wife would be reduced to prostitution to survive. *Your land.* Amaziah's private estate would be divided up and given to others. *pagan country.* Where his ceremonial purity as a priest would be defiled (see NIV text note). *And Israel . . . native land.* Amos repeats—verbatim in the Hebrew—the last two lines of Amaziah's earlier summary of Amos's message (v. 11).
8:1 *showed me.* See note on 7:1.
8:2 *ripe fruit . . . time is ripe.* A wordplay in Hebrew; Israel was ready to be plucked.
8:3 *that day.* See note on 5:18. *wailing . . . Silence!* There would be no thanksgiving songs for this harvest (contrast Lev 23:39–41)—only the silence of despair.
8:5 *New Moon . . . Sabbath.* The official religious festivals, when commerce ceased (cf. Nu 28:9–15; 2Ki 4:23). *skimping the measure, boosting the price . . . dishonest scales.* See Lev 19:35–36; Dt 25:13–16; Pr 11:1; 16:11; 20:10, 23.
8:6 See note on 2:6.
8:7 *sworn by the Pride of Jacob.* Israel took pride in the fact that the Lord was her God.
8:8 *rise like the Nile.* Because of the heavy seasonal rains in Ethiopia, the Nile in Egypt annually rose by as much as 25 feet, flooding the whole valley except for the towns and villages standing above it. Its waters carried a large amount of rich soil, which was deposited on the land—perhaps referred to by the words "stirred up."
8:9 *that day.* See note on 5:18. *darken the earth.* As elsewhere, the "day of the LORD" is described as one in which the cosmic (world) order is disrupted and light is turned to darkness (see Isa 13:10; 24:23; 34:4; 50:3; Eze 32:7–8; Joel 2:10,31; Mic 3:6), as if creation is being undone (see Jer 4:23).
8:10 *mourning.* Illustrated by King David (2Sa 18:33). *wear sackcloth . . . shave your heads.* Signs of mourning (see Ge 37:34; Jer 47:5). *only son.* On whose life the future of the family depended (cf. 2Sa 18:18). *bitter day.* The opposite of the "day of celebration" (Est 9:22).

11"The days are coming," *e* declares the
Sovereign LORD,
"when I will send a famine through
the land—
not a famine of food or a thirst for
water,
but a famine*f* of hearing the words
of the LORD.*g*
12Men will stagger from sea to sea
and wander from north to east,
searching for the word of the LORD,
but they will not find it.*h*

13"In that day

"the lovely young women and strong
young men*i*
will faint because of thirst.*j*
14They who swear by the shame*x* of
Samaria,*k*
or say, 'As surely as your god lives,
O Dan,'*l*
or, 'As surely as the god*y* of
Beersheba*m* lives'—
they will fall,*n*
never to rise again.*o*"

Israel to Be Destroyed

9 I saw the Lord standing by the altar,
and he said:

"Strike the tops of the pillars
so that the thresholds shake.
Bring them down on the heads*p* of all
the people;
those who are left I will kill with the
sword.
Not one will get away,
none will escape.*q*

2Though they dig down to the depths of
the grave,*z r*
from there my hand will take them.
Though they climb up to the heavens,*s*
from there I will bring them down.*t*
3Though they hide themselves on the top
of Carmel,*u*
there I will hunt them down and
seize them.*v*
Though they hide from me at the
bottom of the sea,*w*
there I will command the serpent*x* to
bite them.*y z*
4Though they are driven into exile by
their enemies,
there I will command the sword*a* to
slay them.
I will fix my eyes upon them
for evil*b* and not for good.*c*"*d*

5The Lord, the LORD Almighty,
he who touches the earth and it
melts,*e*
and all who live in it mourn—
the whole land rises like the Nile,
then sinks like the river of Egypt*f*—
6he who builds his lofty palace*a g* in the
heavens
and sets its foundation*b* on the earth,
who calls for the waters of the sea
and pours them out over the face of
the land—
the LORD is his name.*h*

7"Are not you Israelites

x 14 Or *by Ashima;* or *by the idol*   *y 14* Or *power*
z 2 Hebrew *to Sheol*   *a 6* The meaning of the Hebrew
for this phrase is uncertain.   *b 6* The meaning of the
Hebrew for this word is uncertain.

8:11 *e* Jer 30:3;
31:27 *f* S Isa 30:20
g S 1Sa 3:1;
S 28:6;
S 2Ch 15:3
8:12 *h* S Eze 20:3,
31
8:13 *i* S Isa 9:17
j Isa 41:17;
Hos 2:3
8:14 *k* Mic 1:5
l S 1Ki 12:29
m S Am 5:5
n S Ps 46:2
o S Am 5:2
9:1 *p* Ps 68:21
q Jer 11:11

9:2 *r* S Job 7:9;
S Eze 26:20
s Jer 51:53
t Ob 1:4
9:3 *u* Am 1:2
v Ps 139:8-10
w Ps 68:22
x Isa 27:1
y Jer 16:16-17
z S Ge 49:17;
S Job 11:20
9:4 *a* S Lev 26:33;
S Eze 5:12
b S Jer 21:10
c Jer 39:16;
S Eze 15:7
d S Jer 44:11
9:5 *e* S Ps 46:2
f S Am 8:8
9:6 *g* Jer 43:9
h Ps 104:1-3,5-6,
13; S Am 5:8

8:11 *days.* When God's judgment begins to take effect. *famine of hearing the words of the LORD.* In times of great distress Israel turned to the Lord for a prophetic word of hope or guidance (see, e.g., 2Ki 19:1–4,14; 22:13–14; Jer 21:2; Eze 14:3,7), but in the coming judgment the Lord will answer all such appeals with silence—the awful silence of God (see 1Sa 28:6; Eze 7:26; 20:1–3; Mic 3:4,7).
8:12 *sea to sea ... north to east.* Throughout the land of Israel, even to the Transjordan.
8:13 *thirst.* Both physical and spiritual. Their strength sapped, even the lovely girls and strong boys of the nation would faint and fall useless.
8:14 *They who swear.* By the gods of their various religious centers (see NIV text notes)—the false gods in which they trusted rather than in the Lord.
9:1 *I saw the Lord.* See note on 7:1. God is now poised on earth. *by the altar.* God is about to initiate the destruction from the very place from which the people expect to hear a word of peace and blessing. *tops of the pillars.* God will shatter the temple completely, from the decorated capitals down to the heavy stone thresholds. The next lines depict the destruction. Whether the vision shows the Lord at Jerusalem or at Bethel is unclear, but we know of no temple structure at Bethel.
9:2–4 These verses emphasize the impossibility of escape

from God's impending judgment. The imaginary extremes to which a person might go may be compared with those in Ps 139:7–12. God's domain includes every place, even the realm of the grave (v. 2).
9:3 *top of Carmel.* See note on 1:2. *serpent.* In pagan mythology, the fierce monster of the sea. If someone should seek to escape by hiding in the depths, he could still not evade God, for even there all are subject to him.
9:4 *driven ... by their enemies ... I will command.* Even those dispersed among the nations will not escape God's judgment. *I will fix my eyes ... for evil.* Contrast Ps 33:18; 34:15.
9:5 *The Lord ... who.* Introduces a hymnic reminder that Israel's God is the Creator and Sustainer of the universe, thus underlining the pronouncements of the previous verses (cf. 4:13; 5:8–9). *earth ... melts.* See note on Ps 46:6. *like the Nile.* See 8:8 and note.
9:6 *his lofty palace.* Contrasts the scale of God with the scale of man, whose structures fall at the movement of the earth (v. 5). See Ps 104:3 and note. *sea.* See 5:8 and note.
9:7 *Cushites.* A dark-skinned people who lived south of Egypt (cf. Jer 13:23 and NIV text note). *Did I not bring Israel up ... ?* See note on Ex 20:2. Israel could not rely on God's past blessings as an assurance of his future benevolence. Her stubborn rebelliousness robbed the exodus of all special

the same to me as the Cushites[c]?"[i]
　　　　　declares the LORD.
"Did I not bring Israel up from Egypt,
　the Philistines[j] from Caphtor[d] [k]
　and the Arameans from Kir?[l]

[8]"Surely the eyes of the Sovereign LORD
　are on the sinful kingdom.
I will destroy[m] it
　from the face of the earth—
yet I will not totally destroy
　the house of Jacob,"
　　　　　declares the LORD.[n]
[9]"For I will give the command,
　and I will shake the house of Israel
　among all the nations
as grain[o] is shaken in a sieve,[p]
　and not a pebble will reach the
　　ground.[q]
[10]All the sinners among my people
　will die by the sword,[r]
all those who say,
　'Disaster will not overtake or meet
　　us.'[s]

Israel's Restoration

[11]"In that day I will restore
　David's[t] fallen tent.[u]
I will repair its broken places,
　restore its ruins,[v]
　and build it as it used to be,[w]
[12]so that they may possess the remnant of
　Edom[x]

and all the nations that bear my
　name,[e] [y]"
　　declares the LORD, who will
　　　　　do these things.[z]

[13]"The days are coming," [a] declares the
LORD,

"when the reaper[b] will be overtaken by
　the plowman[c]
and the planter by the one treading[d]
　grapes.
New wine[e] will drip from the
　mountains
　and flow from all the hills.[f]
[14]I will bring[g] back my exiled[f] [h] people
　Israel;
they will rebuild the ruined cities[i]
　and live in them.
They will plant vineyards[j] and drink
　their wine;
they will make gardens and eat their
　fruit.[k]
[15]I will plant[l] Israel in their own land,[m]
　never again to be uprooted[n]
　from the land I have given them," [o]

　　　　　says the LORD your God.[p]

9:7 [f]S 2Ch 12:3; Isa 20:4; 43:3 [g]S Ge 10:14 [h]S Dt 2:23 [f]S 2Ki 16:9; S Isa 22:6; S Am 2:10
9:8 [m]S Jer 4:27 [n]S Jer 44:27
9:9 [o]Lk 22:31 [p]Isa 30:28 [q]S Jer 31:36; S Da 9:7
9:10 [r]Jer 49:37 [s]Jer 5:12; S 23:17; S Eze 20:38; S Am 6:3
9:11 [t]S Isa 7:2 [u]S Ge 26:22 [v]Ps 53:6; S Isa 49:8 [w]Ps 80:12; S Eze 17:24; Mic 7:8,11; Zec 12:7; 14:10
9:12 [x]S Nu 24:18
[y]Isa 43:7; Jer 25:29 [z]Ac 15:16-17*
9:13 [a]Jer 31:38; 33:14 [b]S Ru 2:3 [c]Lev 26:5 [d]S Jdg 9:27 [e]S Joel 2:24 [f]S Joel 3:18
9:14 [g]S Jer 29:14 [h]S Jer 33:7 [i]S Isa 32:18; S 49:8; S 61:4 [j]S 2Ki 19:29 [k]S Isa 62:9; S Jer 30:18; S 31:28; Eze 28:25-26; S 34:13-14; S Am 5:11
9:15 [l]S Eze 15:17; S Isa 60:21 [m]S Jer 23:8 [n]S Joel 3:20

[o]S Isa 65:9; S Jer 3:18; Ob 1:17 [p]S Jer 18:9; S 24:6; S 32:15; S Eze 28:26; S 34:25-28; S 37:12,25

[c]7 That is, people from the upper Nile region   [d]7 That is, Crete   [e]12 Hebrew; Septuagint so that the remnant of men / and all the nations that bear my name may seek the Lord   [f]14 Or will restore the fortunes of my

meaning for her; her journey from Egypt is reduced to no more significance than the movements of other peoples. *Philistines from Caphtor.* See note on Jer 47:4. *Kir.* See note on 1:5.

9:8 *sinful kingdom.* Israel, the chosen, whose disobedience was far worse than the sins of other nations (cf. 1:3–2:16; 3:1–2).

9:9 *sieve.* Separates the wheat from small stones and other refuse gathered with it when scooped up from the ground. *not a pebble will reach.* Only the grain drops through, the refuse being screened out to be discarded.

9:10 *All the sinners . . . will die.* For their persistent rebellion.

9:11 The verse is also regarded as Messianic in the Jewish Talmud. *I will restore.* Raises a hope underlying Amos's words—one that runs through the whole OT from Ge 3:15 on: God will bring blessing after judgment and will not ultimately reject Israel. *tent.* Lit. "hut" (or rough booth)—either the dynasty ("house") of David or the united kingdom of the 12 tribes (David's kingdom). The word "hut" may have been chosen to recall David's humble beginnings. *as it used to be.* In the days of David and Solomon.

9:12 *remnant of Edom.* Whatever is left of Israel's bitter enemy (see note on 1:11) after her punishment. *all the*

nations that bear my name. Refers to the extent of the rule of the Lord's anointed future King, recalling that David had reigned over many nations surrounding Israel. It represents the fulfillment of the Abrahamic and Davidic covenants. The Messiah will reign even over former enemies, of whom Edom is symbolic (see note on Isa 34:5). *will do these things.* God does what he says.

9:13–15 After all the forecasts of destruction, dearth and death (cf. 5:9,11,27), Amos's final words picture a glorious Edenic prosperity, when the seasons will run together so that sowing and reaping are without interval, and there will be a continuous supply of fresh produce (a reversal of the conditions portrayed in 4:6–11).

9:13 Note the similarity to Joel 3:18.

9:14–15 *I will bring . . . they will rebuild . . . They will plant . . . I will plant.* In the promised land, God will make his people productive, fruitful and secure.

9:14 *my . . . people.* See note on 7:8; contrast Hos 1:9, but cf. Hos 2:23. *rebuild the ruined cities.* See Isa 58:12 and note.

9:15 *never again.* When Israel is finally restored, she will never again be destroyed. *your God.* Contrast Hos 1:9, but cf. Hos 2:23.

OBADIAH

Author

The author's name is Obadiah, which means "servant (or worshiper) of the LORD." His was a common name (see 1Ki 18:3-16; 1Ch 3:21; 7:3; 8:38; 9:16; 12:9; 27:19; 2Ch 17:7; 34:12; Ezr 8:9; Ne 10:5; 12:25). Neither his father's name nor the place of his birth is given.

Date and Place of Writing

The date and place of composition are disputed. Dating the prophecy is mainly a matter of relating vv. 11-14 to one of two specific events in Israel's history:

1. The invasion of Jerusalem by Philistines and Arabs during the reign of Jehoram (853-841 B.C.); see 2Ki 8:20-22; 2Ch 21:8-20. In this case, Obadiah would be a contemporary of Elisha.

2. The Babylonian attacks on Jerusalem (605-586). Obadiah would then be a contemporary of Jeremiah. This alternative seems more likely.

The parallels between Ob 1-9 and Jer 49:7-22 have caused many to suggest some kind of interdependence between Obadiah and Jeremiah, but it may be that both prophets were drawing on a common source not otherwise known to us.

Unity and Theme

There is no compelling reason to doubt the unity of this brief prophecy. Its theme is that Edom, proud over her own security, has gloated over Israel's devastation by foreign powers. However, Edom's participation in that disaster will bring on God's wrath. She herself will be destroyed, but Mount Zion and Israel will be delivered, and God's kingdom will triumph.

Edom's hostile activities have spanned the centuries of Israel's existence. The following Biblical references are helpful in understanding the relation of Israel and Edom: Ge 27:41-45; 32:1-21; 33; 36; Ex 15:15; Nu 20:14-21; Dt 2:1-6; 23:7; 1Sa 22 with Ps 52; 2Sa 8:13-14; 2Ki 8:20-22; 14:7; Ps 83; Eze 35; Joel 3:18-19; Am 1:11-12; 9:12.

Since the Edomites are related to the Israelites (v. 10), their hostility is all the more reprehensible. Edom is fully responsible for her failure to assist Israel and for her open aggression. The fact that God rejected Esau (Ge 25:23; Mal 1:3; Ro 9:13) in no way exonerates the Edomites. Edom, smug in its mountain strongholds, will be dislodged and sacked. Israel will prosper because God is with her.

Outline

¹The vision*a* of Obadiah.

1–4pp — Jer 49:14–16
5–6pp — Jer 49:9–10

This is what the Sovereign LORD says about Edom*b*—

We have heard a message from the
LORD:
An envoy*c* was sent to the nations to
say,
"Rise, and let us go against her for
battle"*d*—

²"See, I will make you small*e* among the
nations;
you will be utterly despised.
³The pride*f* of your heart has deceived
you,
you who live in the clefts of the
rocks*a g*
and make your home on the heights,
you who say to yourself,
'Who can bring me down to the
ground?'*h*
⁴Though you soar like the eagle
and make your nest*i* among the
stars,
from there I will bring you down,"*j*
declares the LORD.*k*
⁵"If thieves came to you,
if robbers in the night—
Oh, what a disaster awaits you—
would they not steal only as much as
they wanted?
If grape pickers came to you,

would they not leave a few grapes?*l*
⁶But how Esau will be ransacked,
his hidden treasures pillaged!
⁷All your allies*m* will force you to the
border;
your friends will deceive and
overpower you;
those who eat your bread*n* will set a
trap for you,*b*
but you will not detect it.

⁸"In that day," declares the LORD,
"will I not destroy*o* the wise men of
Edom,
men of understanding in the
mountains of Esau?
⁹Your warriors, O Teman,*p* will be
terrified,
and everyone in Esau's mountains
will be cut down in the slaughter.
¹⁰Because of the violence*q* against your
brother Jacob,*r*
you will be covered with shame;
you will be destroyed forever.*s*
¹¹On the day you stood aloof
while strangers carried off his wealth
and foreigners entered his gates
and cast lots*t* for Jerusalem,
you were like one of them.*u*
¹²You should not look down*v* on your
brother
in the day of his misfortune,*w*
nor rejoice*x* over the people of Judah

a 3 Or *of Sela*   **b** 7 The meaning of the Hebrew for this clause is uncertain.

1:1 *a*S Isa 1:1;
*b*S Ge 25:14;
S Isa 11:14;
S 34:11; 63:1-6;
Jer 49:7-22;
S Eze 25:12-14;
S 32:29;
S Am 1:11-12
*c*Isa 18:2
*d*Jer 6:4-5
1:2 *e*Nu 24:18
1:3 *f*S Isa 16:6
*g*fn Isa 16:1
*h*S 2Ch 25:11-12
1:4 *i*S Isa 10:14
*j*S Isa 14:13
*k*S Job 20:6

1:5 *l*S Dt 4:27;
24:21; S Isa 24:13
1:7 *m*Jer 30:14
*n*S Ps 41:9
1:8 *o*Job 5:12;
Isa 29:14
1:9 *p*S Ge 36:11,
34
1:10 *q*S Joel 3:19
*r*Ps 137:7;
Am 1:11-12
*s*S Ps 137:7;
S Eze 25:12-14;
35:9
1:11 *t*S Job 6:27;
S Eze 24:6
*u*S Am 1:6
1:12 *v*Pr 24:17
*w*S Job 31:29
*x*S Eze 35:15

---

1 *vision.* Commonly used in the OT to designate a revelation from God. *Obadiah.* See Introduction: Author. *We.* Either (1) the editorial "we," or (2) the prophet's association of Israel with himself, or (3) other prophets' pronouncements against Edom. In any case, the rest of the verse sets the stage for Obadiah's prophetic message, which begins with v. 2. *message.* Or "report." An envoy had been sent to the nations, calling them to battle against Edom. Perhaps a conspiracy was under way between some of Edom's allies (v. 7). Although Edom feels secure (trusting in her mountain fortresses and her wise men, vv. 2–4,8–9), Obadiah announces God's judgment on her for her hostility to Israel.
2 *I will make you small.* Cf. the colloquial expression, "cut one down to size."
3 *rocks.* See NIV text note. Sela was the capital of Edom. Perhaps the later Petra (both Sela and Petra mean "rock" or "cliff"), this rugged site is located some 50 miles south of the southern end of the Dead Sea. See note on 2Ki 14:7.
4 *eagle.* A proud and regal bird, noted for strength, keenness of vision and power of flight. *stars.* Hyperbole for high, inaccessible places in the mountains.
5 *If thieves . . . If grape pickers.* For a similar oracle against Edom see Jer 49:9.
6 *hidden treasures.* The ancient Greek historian Diodorus Siculus indicates that the Edomites put their wealth—accumulated from trade—in vaults in the rocks.
7 *set a trap for you.* However the Hebrew for this expression is understood (see NIV text note), it must indicate some act of treachery on the part of previously trusted close

friends. Those who "eat bread with" are one's *com-panions* (Latin *cum,* "with," and *panis,* "bread"). See note on Ps 41:9.
8 *In that day.* The day of Edom's destruction; but the words also have an eschatological ring. Since in OT prophecy Edom was often emblematic of all the world powers hostile to God and his kingdom, her judgment anticipates God's complete removal of all such opposition in that day. *wise men.* In whom Edom put so much confidence for her security (see Jer 49:7). Eliphaz, one of Job's three friends, was a Temanite (see next note). *Esau.* Another name for Edom (see Ge 36:1).
9 *Teman.* A reference to all Edom, as in Jer 49:7,20 (see also Am 1:12). Teman means "south," and the name probably refers to Edom as the southland. Some, however, identify Teman with Tawilan, a site about three miles east of Petra.
10 *your brother Jacob.* Edom's violent crimes are all the more reprehensible because they were committed against the brother nation. *covered with shame.* A striking expression since shame is usually associated with nakedness.
11 See Introduction: Date and Place of Writing. *strangers . . . foreigners.* These terms put in relief the sin of Edom: He did not act like a brother (v. 12) but was like one of the strangers.
12–14 A rebuke of Edom's hostile actions. The eight rebukes in this section proceed from the general to the particular. See Eze 35:13 and Ps 137 for examples of Edom's reactions to Judah's misfortunes.

in the day of their destruction,[y]
nor boast[z] so much
    in the day of their trouble.[a]
[13]You should not march through the gates
        of my people
    in the day of their disaster,
nor look down on them in their
        calamity[b]
    in the day of their disaster,
nor seize their wealth
    in the day of their disaster.
[14]You should not wait at the crossroads
        to cut down their fugitives,[c]
nor hand over their survivors
    in the day of their trouble.

[15]"The day of the LORD is near[d]
    for all nations.
As you have done, it will be done to
        you;
    your deeds[e] will return upon your
        own head.
[16]Just as you drank[f] on my holy hill,[g]
    so all the nations will drink[h]
        continually;
    they will drink and drink
    and be as if they had never been.[i]
[17]But on Mount Zion will be
        deliverance;[j]
    it will be holy,[k]
    and the house of Jacob

will possess its inheritance.[l]
[18]The house of Jacob will be a fire
        and the house of Joseph a flame;
    the house of Esau will be stubble,
    and they will set it on fire[m] and
        consume[n] it.
There will be no survivors[o]
    from the house of Esau."
                                The LORD has spoken.

[19]People from the Negev will occupy
        the mountains of Esau,
and people from the foothills will
        possess
    the land of the Philistines.[p]
They will occupy the fields of Ephraim
        and Samaria,[q]
and Benjamin[r] will possess Gilead.
[20]This company of Israelite exiles who are
        in Canaan
    will possess the land, as far as
        Zarephath;[s]
    the exiles from Jerusalem who are in
        Sepharad
    will possess the towns of the Negev.[t]
[21]Deliverers[u] will go up on[c] Mount Zion
    to govern the mountains of Esau.
And the kingdom will be the
        LORD's.[v]

1:12 [y]S Pr 17:5
[z]Ps 137:7
[a]S Eze 25:6;
Mic 4:11; 7:8
1:13 [b]S Eze 35:5
1:14 [c]S 1Ki 18:4
1:15
[d]S Jer 46:10;
S Eze 30:3;
S Joel 2:31;
S Am 5:18
[e]S Jer 50:29;
Hab 2:8
1:16 [f]Isa 51:17
[g]S Ex 15:17
[h]Jer 25:15;
49:12;
S La 4:21-22
[i]S La 4:21;
S Eze 25:12-14
1:17 [j]S Ps 69:35;
S Isa 14:1-2;
Joel 2:32;
S Am 9:11-15
[k]S Ps 74:2;
S Isa 4:3

1:18 [m]S Isa 1:31
[n]Zec 12:6
[o]S Jer 49:10
1:19 [p]Isa 11:14
[q]S Jer 31:5
[r]S Nu 1:36
1:20
[s]1Ki 17:9-10;
Lk 4:26
[t]S Jer 33:13
1:21
[u]S Dt 28:29;
S Jdg 3:9
[v]S Ps 22:28;
47:9; 66:4;
S Da 2:44;
Zec 14:9,16;
Mal 1:14;
Rev 11:15

[c]21 Or *from*

---

15 *The day of the LORD is near for all nations.* If there was an eschatological glimmering in "in that day" (v. 8), it here becomes a strong ray. The day of the Lord brings judgment for the nations (including, but not limited to, Edom) and salvation for the house of Jacob. *upon your own head.* The situation will be reversed in retribution for Edom's hostility against God's people detailed in vv. 11–14. Ezekiel's denunciation of Edom (ch. 35) reflects a similar punishment-fits-the-crime principle.

16 *Just as you drank.* As the Edomites profaned the holy mountain by carousing, so the nations will drink and drink. Their drinking, however, is that of the bitter potion of God's judgment—which they will be compelled to keep on drinking. For drinking as punishment see Jer 25:15–16; 49:12.

17 *But on Mount Zion will be deliverance.* Beginning with this verse the blessings on the house of Jacob are mentioned. Eschatological references are twofold: judgment on God's enemies, blessing on God's people.

18 *Jacob . . . Joseph.* Previously it was stated that the Lord would destroy Edom, using other nations (v. 7); now it is to be done by God's people. *no survivors.* The final word to Esau is that his house (or nation) will be totally destroyed;

there will be no Edomite survivors. Yet compare Am 9:12 with Ac 15:17 and see note on Am 9:12.

19 *People . . . will occupy.* With Edom annihilated, others will occupy Edomite territory. Although not expressly identified, these are most likely the remnant of Israel referred to in the lines immediately following. *Negev.* See note on Ge 12:9. *Philistines.* See note on Ge 10:14. *Gilead.* See notes on Ge 31:21; SS 4:1.

20 *Zarephath.* See note on 1Ki 17:9. *Sepharad.* Usually taken to refer to Sardis in Asia Minor (present-day Turkey), though some think that Sparta (the city in Greece) might be meant.

21 *Deliverers.* Having developed the theme of possessing lands around Zion, the prophet now turns to the center. The "deliverers" come from Mount Zion and rule over the mountains of Esau. Mount Zion is exalted over the mountains of Esau. The Messiah, the Deliverer par excellence, may ultimately be in view. *the kingdom will be the LORD's.* The conclusion of the prophecy—and the final outcome of history. The last book of the Bible echoes this theme (Rev 11:15).

JONAH

Title

The book is named after its principal character, whose name means "dove"; see the simile used of Ephraim in Hos 7:11 to portray the northern kingdom as "easily deceived and senseless." See also Ps 68:13; 74:19 and notes.

Author

Though the book does not identify its author, tradition has ascribed it to the prophet himself, Jonah son of Amittai (1:1), from Gath Hepher (2Ki 14:25) in Zebulun (Jos 19:10,13). In view of its many similarities with the narratives about Elijah and Elisha, however, it may come from the same prophetic circles that originally composed the accounts about those prophets, perhaps in the eighth century B.C. (see Introduction to 1Kings: Author, Sources and Date).

Background

In the half-century during which the prophet Jonah ministered (800-750 B.C.), a significant event affected the northern kingdom of Israel: King Jeroboam II (793-753) restored her traditional borders, ending almost a century of sporadic seesaw conflict between Israel and Damascus.

Jeroboam, in God's good providence (2Ki 14:26-27), capitalized on Assyria's defeat of Damascus (in the latter half of the ninth century), which temporarily crushed that center of Aramean power. Prior to that time, not only had Israel been considerably reduced in size, but the king of Damascus had even been able to control internal affairs in the northern kingdom (2Ki 13:7). However, after the Assyrian campaign against Damascus in 797, Jehoash, king of Israel, had been able to recover the territory lost to the king of Damascus (2Ki 13:25). Internal troubles in Assyria subsequently allowed Jeroboam II to complete the restoration of Israel's northern borders. Nevertheless, Assyria remained the real threat from the north at this time.

The prophets of the Lord were speaking to Israel regarding these events. About 797 B.C. Elisha spoke to the king of Israel concerning future victories over Damascus (2Ki 13:14-19). A few years later Jonah prophesied the restoration that Jeroboam II accomplished (2Ki 14:25). But soon after Israel had triumphed, she began to gloat over her new-found power. Because she was relieved of foreign pressures—relief that had come in accordance with encouraging words from Elisha and Jonah—she felt jealously complacent about her favored status with God (Am 6:1). She focused her religion on expectations of the "day of the LORD" (Am 5:18-20), when God's darkness would engulf the other nations, leaving Israel to bask in his light.

It was in such a time that the Lord sent Amos and Hosea to announce to his people Israel that he would "spare them no longer" (Am 7:8; 8:2) but would send them into exile "beyond Damascus" (Am 5:27), i.e., to Assyria (Hos 9:3; 10:6; 11:5). During this time the Lord also sent Jonah to Nineveh to warn it of the imminent danger of divine judgment.

Since Jonah was a contemporary of Amos, see Introduction to Amos: Date and Historical Situation for additional details.

Date of Writing

For a number of reasons, including the preaching to Gentiles, the book is often assigned a postexilic date. At least, it is said, the book must have been written after the destruction of Nineveh in 612 B.C. But these considerations are not decisive. The similarity of this narrative to the Elijah-Elisha accounts has already been noted. One may also question whether mention of the repentance of Nineveh and the consequent averted destruction of the city would have had so much significance to the author after Nineveh's overthrow. And to suppose that proclaiming God's word to Gentiles had no relevance in

the eighth century is to overlook the fact that already in the previous century Elijah and Elisha had extended their ministries to foreign lands (1Ki 17:7-24; 2Ki 8:7-17). Moreover, the prophet Amos (c. 760-750) set God's redemptive work in behalf of Israel in the context of his dealings with the nations (Am 1:3-2:16; 9:7,12). Perhaps the third quarter of the eighth century is the most likely date for the book, after the public ministries of Amos and Hosea and before the fall of Samaria to Assyria in 722-721.

Interpretation

Many have questioned whether the book of Jonah is historical. The supposed legendary character of some of the events (e.g., the episode involving the great fish) has caused them to suggest alternatives to the traditional view that the book is historical, biographical narrative. Although their specific suggestions range from fictional short story to allegory to parable, they share the common assumption that the account sprang essentially from the author's imagination, despite its serious and gracious message.

Such interpretations, often based in part on doubt about the miraculous as such, too quickly dismiss (1) the similarities between the narrative of Jonah and other parts of the OT and (2) the pervasive concern of the OT writers, especially the prophets, for history. They also fail to realize that OT narrators had a keen ear for recognizing how certain past events in Israel's pilgrimage with God illumine (by way of analogy) later events. (For example, the events surrounding the birth of Moses illumine the exodus, those surrounding Samuel's birth illumine the series of events narrated in the books of Samuel, and the ministries of Moses and Joshua illumine those of Elijah and Elisha.) Similarly, the prophets recognized that the future events they announced could be illumined by reference to analogous events of the past. Overlooking these features in OT narrative and prophecy, many have supposed that a story that too neatly fits the author's purpose must therefore be fictional.

On the other hand, it must be acknowledged that Biblical narrators were more than historians. They interpretatively recounted the past with the unswerving purpose of bringing it to bear on the present and the future. In the portrayal of past events, they used their materials to achieve this purpose effectively. Nonetheless, the integrity with which they treated the past ought not to be questioned. The book of Jonah recounts real events in the life and ministry of the prophet himself.

Literary Characteristics

Unlike most other prophetic parts of the OT, this book is a narrative account of a single prophetic mission. Its treatment of that mission is thus similar to the accounts of the ministries of Elijah and Elisha found in 1,2 Kings, and to certain narrative sections of Isaiah, Jeremiah and Ezekiel.

As is often the case in Biblical narratives, the author has compressed much into a small space; 40 verses tell the entire story (eight additional verses of poetry are devoted to Jonah's prayer of thanksgiving). In its scope (a single extended episode), compactness, vividness and character delineation, it is much like the book of Ruth.

Also as in Ruth, the author uses structural symmetry effectively. The story is developed in two parallel cycles that call attention to a series of comparisons and contrasts (see Outline). The story's climax is Jonah's grand prayer of confession, "Salvation comes from the LORD"—the middle confession of three from his lips (1:9; 2:9; 4:2). The last sentence emphasizes that the Lord's word is final and decisive, while Jonah is left sitting in the hot, open country outside Nineveh.

The author uses the art of representative roles in a straightforward manner. In this story of God's loving concern for all people, Nineveh, the great menace to Israel, is representative of the Gentiles. Correspondingly, stubbornly reluctant Jonah represents Israel's jealousy of her favored relationship with God and her unwillingness to share the Lord's compassion with the nations.

The book depicts the larger scope of God's purpose for Israel: that she might rediscover the truth of his concern for the whole creation and that she might better understand her own role in carrying out that concern.

Outline

I. Jonah Flees His Mission (chs. 1-2)
    A. Jonah's Commission and Flight (1:1-3)
    B. The Endangered Sailors' Cry to Their Gods (1:4-6)
    C. Jonah's Disobedience Exposed (1:7-10)
    D. Jonah's Punishment and Deliverance (1:11-2:1; 2:10)
    E. His Prayer of Thanksgiving (2:2-9)

Jonah Flees From the Lord

1 The word of the Lord came to Jonah[a] son of Amittai:[b] 2"Go to the great city of Nineveh[c] and preach against it, because its wickedness has come up before me."

3But Jonah ran[d] away from the Lord and headed for Tarshish.[e] He went down to Joppa,[f] where he found a ship bound for that port. After paying the fare, he went aboard and sailed for Tarshish to flee from the Lord.[g]

4Then the Lord sent a great wind on the sea, and such a violent storm arose that the ship threatened to break up.[h] 5All the sailors were afraid and each cried out to his own god. And they threw the cargo into the sea to lighten the ship.[i]

But Jonah had gone below deck, where he lay down and fell into a deep sleep. 6The captain went to him and said, "How can you sleep? Get up and call[j] on your god! Maybe he will take notice of us, and we will not perish."[k]

7Then the sailors said to each other, "Come, let us cast lots to find out who is responsible for this calamity."[l] They cast lots and the lot fell on Jonah.[m]

8So they asked him, "Tell us, who is responsible for making all this trouble for us? What do you do? Where do you come from? What is your country? From what people are you?"

9He answered, "I am a Hebrew and I worship the Lord,[n] the God of heaven,[o] who made the sea[p] and the land.[q]"

10This terrified them and they asked, "What have you done?" (They knew he was running away from the Lord, because he had already told them so.)

11The sea was getting rougher and rougher. So they asked him, "What should

1:1 *a*Mt 12:39-41; 16:4; Lk 11:29-32 *b*2Ki 14:25
1:2 *c*S Ge 10:11; S Na 1:1
1:3 *d*Ps 139:7 *e*S Ge 10:4 *f*S Jos 19:46; Ac 9:36,43 *g*Ex 4:13; S Jer 20:9; S Am 3:8
1:4 *h*Ps 107:23-26
1:5 *i*Ac 27:18-19
1:6 *j*Jnh 3:8 *k*S Ps 107:28
1:7 *l*Nu 32:23; Jos 7:10-18; S 1Sa 14:42 *m*S Pr 16:33
1:9 *n*S Ps 96:9 *o*S Da 2:18; Ac 17:24 *p*S Ne 9:6 *q*S Ge 1:9

1:1 *The word of the Lord came.* See 3:1; a common phrase used to indicate the divine source of the prophet's revelation (see, e.g., 1Ki 17:8; Jer 1:2,4; Hos 1:1; Joel 1:1; Hag 1:1,3; Zec 1:1,7). *Jonah.* See Introduction: Title; Author.
1:2 *great city.* See 3:2; 4:11; see also note on 3:3. According to Ge 10:11-12, it was first built by Nimrod (perhaps along with Rehoboth Ir, Calah and Resen) and was traditionally known as the "great city." About 700 B.C. Sennacherib made it the capital of Assyria, which it remained until its fall in 612 (see Introduction to Nahum: Background). Nineveh is over 500 miles from Gath Hepher, Jonah's hometown. *its wickedness has come up.* Cf. Sodom and Gomorrah (Ge 18:20-21). Except for the violence (3:8) of Nineveh, her "evil ways" (3:8,10) are not described in Jonah. Nahum later states that Nineveh's sins included plotting evil against the Lord (Na 1:11), cruelty and plundering in war (Na 2:12-13; 3:1,19), prostitution and witchcraft (Na 3:4) and commercial exploitation (Na 3:16).

1:3 *ran away.* The reason is found in 4:2. The futility of trying to run away from the Lord is acknowledged in Ps 139:7,9-10. *Tarshish.* Perhaps the city of Tartessus in southwest Spain, a Phoenician mining colony near Gibraltar. By heading in the opposite direction from Nineveh, to what seemed like the end of the world, Jonah intended to escape his divinely appointed task.
1:4-5 Although Jonah's mission was to bring God's warning of impending judgment to the pagan world, his refusal to go to Nineveh brings these pagan sailors into peril.
1:4 *the Lord sent a great wind.* God's sovereign working in Jonah's mission is evident at several other points also: the fish (v. 17), the release of Jonah (2:10), the vine (4:6), the worm (4:7) and the wind (4:8).
1:5 *his own god.* Apparently the sailors, who may have come from various ports, worshiped several pagan gods.
1:6 *The captain went to him.* The pagan captain's concern for everyone on board contrasts with the believing prophet's

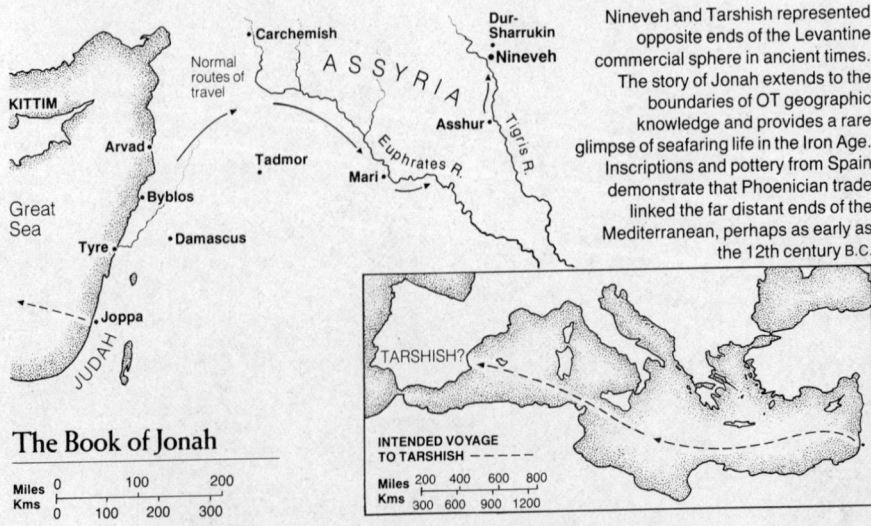

Nineveh and Tarshish represented opposite ends of the Levantine commercial sphere in ancient times. The story of Jonah extends to the boundaries of OT geographic knowledge and provides a rare glimpse of seafaring life in the Iron Age. Inscriptions and pottery from Spain demonstrate that Phoenician trade linked the far distant ends of the Mediterranean, perhaps as early as the 12th century B.C.

The Book of Jonah

Miles 0 100 200
Kms 0 100 200 300

INTENDED VOYAGE TO TARSHISH ----
Miles 200 400 600 800
Kms 300 600 900 1200

we do to you to make the sea calm down for us?"

¹²"Pick me up and throw me into the sea," he replied, "and it will become calm. I know that it is my fault that this great storm has come upon you." *r*

¹³Instead, the men did their best to row back to land. But they could not, for the sea grew even wilder than before. *s* ¹⁴Then they cried to the LORD, "O LORD, please do not let us die for taking this man's life. Do not hold us accountable for killing an innocent man, *t* for you, O LORD, have done as you pleased." *u* ¹⁵Then they took Jonah and threw him overboard, and the raging sea grew calm. *v* ¹⁶At this the men greatly feared *w* the LORD, and they offered a sacrifice to the LORD and made vows *x* to him.

¹⁷But the LORD provided *y* a great fish to swallow Jonah, *z* and Jonah was inside the fish three days and three nights.

Jonah's Prayer

2 From inside the fish Jonah prayed to the LORD his God. ²He said:

"In my distress I called *a* to the LORD, *b*
    and he answered me.
From the depths of the grave *a c* I called
    for help,

and you listened to my cry.
³You hurled me into the deep, *d*
    into the very heart of the seas,
    and the currents swirled about me;
all your waves *e* and breakers
    swept over me. *f*
⁴I said, 'I have been banished
    from your sight; *g*
yet I will look again
    toward your holy temple.' *h*
⁵The engulfing waters threatened me, *b*
    the deep surrounded me;
    seaweed was wrapped around my
        head. *i*
⁶To the roots of the mountains *j* I sank
        down;
    the earth beneath barred me in
        forever.
But you brought my life up from the
        pit, *k*
    O LORD my God.

⁷"When my life was ebbing away,
    I remembered *l* you, LORD,
and my prayer *m* rose to you,
    to your holy temple. *n*

⁸"Those who cling to worthless idols *o*
    forfeit the grace that could be theirs.

Cross references (center column):

1:12 *r*2Sa 24:17; 1Ch 21:17
1:13 *s*S Pr 21:30
1:14 *t*Dt 21:8; *u*S Da 4:35
1:15 *v*S Ps 107:29; Lk 8:24
1:16 *w*Mk 4:41; *x*S Nu 30:2; Ps 66:13-14
1:17 *y*Jnh 4:6,7; *z*Mt 12:40; 16:4; Lk 11:30
2:2 *a*La 3:55; *b*Ps 18:6; 120:1; *c*Ps 86:13

2:3 *d*S Ps 88:6; *e*S 2Sa 22:5; *f*S Ps 42:7
2:4 *g*Ps 31:22; Jer 7:15; *h*S 1Ki 8:48
2:5 *i*Ps 69:1-2
2:6 *j*Job 28:9; *k*S Job 17:16; S 33:18; S Ps 30:3
2:7 *l*Ps 77:11-13; *m*2Ch 30:27; *n*S Ps 11:4; 18:6
2:8 *o*S Dt 32:21; S 1Sa 12:21

*a*2 Hebrew *Sheol*   *b*5 Or *waters were at my throat*

---

refusal to carry God's warning to Nineveh.

1:7 *let us cast lots.* The casting of lots was a custom widely practiced in the ancient Near East. The precise method is unclear, though it appears that, for the most part, sticks or marked pebbles were drawn from a receptacle into which they had been "cast." *lot fell on Jonah.* By the lot of judgment the Lord exposed the guilty one (cf. Jos 7:14–26; 1Sa 14:38–44; Pr 16:33).

1:9 *Hebrew.* See note on Ge 14:13. *God of heaven, who made the sea and the land.* The sailors would have understood Jonah's words as being descriptive of the highest divinity. Their present experiences confirmed this truth, since, in the religions of the ancient Near East generally, the supreme god was master of the seas (see note on Jos 3:10). This is Jonah's first confessional statement, and, like those that follow (2:9d; 4:2), it is thoroughly orthodox. Though orthodox in his beliefs, Jonah refuses to fulfill his divine mission to Nineveh.

1:10 *What have you done?* This rhetorical question is really an accusation.

1:12 *throw me into the sea.* Jonah's readiness to die to save the terrified sailors contrasts with his later callous departure from Nineveh to watch from a safe distance while the city perishes—at least he still hoped it would perish (see 4:5).

1:13 *did their best to row.* The Hebrew uses the picturesque word meaning "to dig" (with oars) to indicate strenuous effort. The ship could be driven by sails, oars, or both. The reluctance of the sailors to throw Jonah into the sea stands in sharp contrast to Jonah's reluctance to warn Nineveh of impending judgment.

1:16 *greatly feared the LORD.* There is no evidence that the sailors renounced all other gods (contrast Naaman, 2Ki 5:15). Ancient pagans were ready to recognize the existence and power of many gods. At the least, however, the sailors acknowledged that the God of Israel was in control of the

present events, that he was the one who both stirred up and calmed the storm, and that at this moment he was the one to be recognized and worshiped.

1:17 *the LORD provided.* This characteristic phrase occurs also in 4:6–8. *great fish.* The Hebrew here and the Greek of Mt 12:40 are both general terms for a large fish, not necessarily a whale. This great fish is carefully distinguished from the sinister "serpent" of the sea (Am 9:3)—otherwise called "Leviathan" (Isa 27:1)—and the "monster of the deep" (Job 7:12; see Ps 74:13; Eze 32:2). *three days and three nights.* The phrase used here may, as in Mt 12:40, refer to a period of time including one full day and parts of two others (see notes on Mt 12:40; Lk 9:28; 1Co 15:4). In any case, the NT clearly uses Jonah's experience as a type (foreshadowing) of the burial and resurrection of Jesus, who was entombed for "three days and three nights" (Mt 12:40; see Mt 16:4; Lk 11:29–32).

2:2–9 A psalm of thanksgiving for deliverance from death in the sea. Jonah recalls his prayer for help as he was sinking into the depths. His gratitude is heightened by his knowledge that he deserved death but that God had shown him extraordinary mercy. The language of this song indicates that Jonah was familiar with the praise literature of the Psalms.

2:2 *grave.* Figurative for Jonah's near-death experience in the sea (see Ps 18:5; 30:3). See also note on Ge 37:35.

2:3 *You hurled me . . . your waves.* Jonah recognizes that the sailors (1:15) were agents of God's judgment.

2:4 *yet I will look again toward your holy temple.* The same note of hopeful expectation found in the prayers of the Psalms (e.g., Ps 5:7; 27:4). "Temple" here probably refers to the temple in Jerusalem, while "temple" in v. 7 refers to God's heavenly temple. The Israelites held these two residences of God in inseparable association (see 1Ki 8:38–39).

2:6 *pit.* The grave (see note on v. 2; see also Ps 30:3).

⁹But I, with a song of thanksgiving,ᵖ
will sacrifice ᵠ to you.
What I have vowed ʳ I will make good.
Salvation ˢ comes from the LORD."

¹⁰And the LORD commanded the fish,
and it vomited Jonah onto dry land.

Jonah Goes to Nineveh

3 Then the word of the LORD came to
Jonah ᵗ a second time: ²"Go to the
great city of Nineveh and proclaim to it the
message I give you."

³Jonah obeyed the word of the LORD
and went to Nineveh. Now Nineveh was a
very important city—a visit required three
days. ⁴On the first day, Jonah started into
the city. He proclaimed: ᵘ "Forty more
days and Nineveh will be overturned."
⁵The Ninevites believed God. They declared a fast, and all of them, from the
greatest to the least, put on sackcloth. ᵛ

⁶When the news reached the king of
Nineveh, he rose from his throne, took off
his royal robes, covered himself with sackcloth and sat down in the dust. ʷ ⁷Then he
issued a proclamation in Nineveh:

"By the decree of the king and his nobles:

　Do not let any man or beast, herd
or flock, taste anything; do not let
them eat or drink. ˣ ⁸But let man and
beast be covered with sackcloth. Let
everyone call ʸ urgently on God. Let
them give up ᶻ their evil ways ᵃ and

their violence. ᵇ ⁹Who knows? ᶜ God
may yet relent ᵈ and with compassion
turn ᵉ from his fierce anger ᶠ so that
we will not perish."

¹⁰When God saw what they did and
how they turned from their evil ways, he
had compassion ᵍ and did not bring upon
them the destruction ʰ he had threatened. ⁱ

Jonah's Anger at the LORD's Compassion

4 But Jonah was greatly displeased and
became angry.ʲ ²He prayed to the
LORD, "O LORD, is this not what I said
when I was still at home? That is why I
was so quick to flee to Tarshish. I knew ᵏ
that you are a gracious ˡ and compassionate God, slow to anger and abounding in
love, ᵐ a God who relents ⁿ from sending
calamity. ᵒ ³Now, O LORD, take away my
life,ᵖ for it is better for me to die ᵠ than to
live." ʳ

⁴But the LORD replied, "Have you any
right to be angry?" ˢ

⁵Jonah went out and sat down at a place
east of the city. There he made himself a
shelter, sat in its shade and waited to see
what would happen to the city. ⁶Then the
LORD God provided ᵗ a vine and made it
grow up over Jonah to give shade for his
head to ease his discomfort, and Jonah was
very happy about the vine. ⁷But at dawn
the next day God provided a worm, which
chewed the vine so that it withered. ᵘ

Cross references (center column)

2:9 ᵖS Ps 42:4; ᵠPs 50:14,23; Heb 13:15 ʳS Nu 30:2; Ps 116:14; S Ecc 5:4-5 ˢS Ex 15:2; S Ps 3:8
3:1 ᵗJnh 1:1
3:4 ᵘS Jer 18:7-10
3:5 ᵛDa 9:3; Mt 11:21; 12:41; Lk 11:32
3:6 ʷS Est 4:1-3; S Job 2:8,13;
3:7 ˣS 2Ch 20:3; S Ezr 10:6
3:8 ʸPs 130:1; Jnh 1:6 ᶻJer 25:5 ᵃJer 7:3
ᵇS Job 16:17
3:9 ᶜ2Sa 12:22 ᵈS Jer 18:8 ᵉS Joel 2:14 ᶠS Ps 85:3
3:10 ᵍS Am 7:6 ʰS Jer 18:8 ⁱS Ex 32:14
4:1 ʲver 4; Mt 20:11; Lk 15:28
4:2 ᵏJer 20:7-8 ˡS Dt 4:31; Ps 103:8 ᵐS Ex 22:27; Ps 86:5,15 ⁿS Nu 14:18 ᵒJoel 2:13
4:3 ᵖS Nu 11:15 ᵠS Job 7:15 ʳJer 8:3
4:4 ˢGe 4:6; Mt 20:11-15
4:6 ᵗS Jnh 1:17
4:7 ᵘJoel 1:12

2:9 *What I have vowed.* In the book of Psalms, prayers
were commonly accompanied by vows, usually involving
thank offerings (e.g., Ps 50:14; 56:12; 61:8; 65:1;
66:13–14; 116:12–19). *Salvation comes from the LORD.*
The climax of Jonah's thanksgiving prayer. It is Jonah's second confessional statement (see note on 1:9) and stands at
the literary midpoint of the book.
3:2 *proclaim to it the message I give you.* A prophet was
the bearer of a message from God, not primarily a foreteller of
coming events.
3:3 *obeyed.* But reluctantly, still wanting the Ninevites to
be destroyed (4:1–5). *very important city.* See 4:11, which
says the city had more than 120,000 inhabitants. Archaeological excavations indicate that the later imperial city of Nineveh was about eight miles around. The fact, however, that "a
visit required three days" may suggest a larger area, such as
the four-city complex of Nineveh, Rehoboth Ir, Calah and
Resen mentioned in Ge 10:11–12. Greater Nineveh covered
an area of some 60 miles in circumference. On the other
hand, "three days" may have been a conventional way of
describing a medium-length distance (see Ge 30:36; Ex
3:18; Jos 9:16–17).
3:5–6 *fast . . . sackcloth . . . dust.* Customary signs of
humbling oneself in repentance (see 1Ki 21:27; Ne 9:1).
3:5 *believed God.* This may mean that the Ninevites genuinely turned to the Lord (cf. Mt 12:41). On the other hand,
their belief in God may have gone no deeper than had the
sailors' fear of God (see note on 1:16). At least they took the

prophet's warning seriously and acted accordingly.
3:6 *king of Nineveh.* King of Assyria.
3:8 Inclusion of the domestic animals was unusual and
expressed the urgency with which the Ninevites sought
mercy.
3:9 God often responds in mercy to man's repentance by
canceling threatened punishment (v. 10). See note on Jer
18:7–10.
4:1 *angry.* Jonah was angry that God would have compassion on an enemy of Israel. He wanted God's goodness to be
shown only to Israelites, not to Gentiles.
4:2 *gracious . . . love.* See Ex 34:6–7 and note. Jonah again
uses a fixed, confessional formula (see note on 1:9). *slow to
anger.* In contrast, Jonah became angry quickly (vv. 1,9).
4:3 *take away my life.* Cf. 1Ki 19:4 (Elijah). To Jonah,
God's mercy to the Ninevites meant an end to Israel's favored standing with him. Jonah shortly before had rejoiced in
his deliverance from death, but now that Nineveh lives, he
prefers to die.
4:5 *shelter.* Apparently this shelter did not provide enough
shade since the next verse indicates that God provided a vine
to give more shade. *waited to see.* Jonah still hoped that
Nineveh would be destroyed.
4:6 *the LORD God provided.* This characteristic phrase occurs also in vv. 7–8; 1:17. *vine.* Probably a castor oil plant, a
shrub growing over 12 feet high with large, shady leaves.
God graciously increased the comfort of his stubbornly defiant prophet.

⁸When the sun rose, God provided a scorching east wind, and the sun blazed on Jonah's head so that he grew faint. He wanted to die,ᵛ and said, "It would be better for me to die than to live."

⁹But God said to Jonah, "Do you have a right to be angry about the vine?"ʷ

"I do," he said. "I am angry enough to die."

¹⁰But the LORD said, "You have been concerned about this vine, though you did not tend it or make it grow. It sprang up overnight and died overnight. ¹¹But Ninevehˣ has more than a hundred and twenty thousand people who cannot tell their right hand from their left, and many cattle as well. Should I not be concernedʸ about that great city?"

4:8 vS 1Ki 19:4
4:9 wver 4
4:11 xJnh 1:2; 3:2 yJnh 3:10

4:8 *better for me to die.* See note on v. 3.

4:10 *sprang up overnight and died overnight.* Indicative of fleeting value.

4:11 *cannot tell their right hand from their left.* Like small children (cf. Dt 1:39; Isa 7:15–16), the Ninevites needed God's fatherly compassion. *and many cattle as well.* God's concern extended even to domestic animals. *Should I not be concerned . . . ?* God had the first word (1:1), and he also has the last. The commission he gave Jonah displayed his mercy

and compassion to the Ninevites, and his last word to Jonah emphatically proclaimed that concern for every creature, both man and animal. Not only does the "LORD . . . preserve both man and beast" (Ps 36:6; see Ne 9:6; Ps 145:16), but he takes "no pleasure in the death of the wicked, but (desires) rather that they turn from their ways and live" (Eze 33:11; see Eze 18:21–23). Jonah and his countrymen traditionally rejoiced in God's special mercies to Israel but wished only his wrath on their enemies. God here rebukes such hardness and proclaims his own gracious benevolence.

MICAH

Author

Little is known about the prophet Micah beyond what can be learned from the book itself and Jer 26:18. Micah was from the town of Moresheth (1:1), probably Moresheth Gath (1:14) in southern Judah. The prophecy attests to Micah's deep sensitivity to the social ills of his day, especially as they affected the small towns and villages of his homeland.

Date

Micah prophesied sometime between 750 and 686 B.C. during the reigns of Jotham, Ahaz and Hezekiah, kings of Judah (1:1; Jer 26:18). He was therefore a contemporary of Isaiah (see Isa 1:1) and Hosea (see Hos 1:1). Micah predicted the fall of Samaria (1:6), which took place in 722-721. This would place his early ministry in the reigns of Jotham (750-732) and Ahaz (735-715). (The reigns of Jotham and Ahaz overlapped.) Micah's message reflects social conditions prior to the religious reforms under Hezekiah (715-686). (The reigns of Ahaz and Hezekiah seem to have overlapped from c. 729 to 715; see 2Ki 18:9 and note on Isa 36:1.)

Background

The background of the book is the same as that found in the earlier portions of Isaiah, though Micah does not exhibit the same knowledge of Jerusalem's political life as Isaiah does. Perhaps this is because he, like Amos, was from a Judahite village.

Israel was in an apostate condition. Micah predicted the fall of her capital, Samaria (1:5-7), and also foretold the inevitable desolation of Judah (1:9-16).

Three significant historical events occurred during this period:

1. In 734-732 B.C. Tiglath-Pileser III of Assyria led a military campaign against Aram (Syria), Philistia and parts of Israel and Judah. Ashkelon and Gaza were defeated. Judah, Ammon, Edom and Moab paid tribute to the Assyrian king, but Israel did not fare as well. According to 2Ki 15:29 the northern kingdom lost most of its territory, including all of Gilead and much of Galilee. Damascus fell in 732 and was annexed to the Assyrian empire.

2. In 722-721 Samaria fell, and the northern kingdom of Israel was conquered by Assyria.

3. In 701 Judah joined a revolt against Assyria and was overrun by King Sennacherib and his army, though Jerusalem was spared.

Literary Characteristics

Micah's style is similar to that of Isaiah. Both prophets use vigorous language and many figures of speech; both show great tenderness in threatening punishment and in promising justice. Micah makes frequent use of plays on words, 1:10-15 (see NIV text notes there) being the classic example.

Theme and Message

As the Outline shows, Micah's message alternates between oracles of doom and oracles of hope. The theme is judgment and deliverance by God. Micah also stresses that God hates idolatry, injustice, rebellion and empty ritualism, but he delights in pardoning the penitent. Finally, the prophet declares that Zion will have greater glory in the future than ever before. The Davidic kingdom, though it will seem to come to an end, will reach greater heights through the coming Messianic deliverer.

Outline

  I. Superscription (1:1)
  II. Judgment against Israel and Judah (1:2-3:12)

A. Introduction (1:2)
B. The Predicted Destruction (1:3-7)
C. Lamentation for the Destruction (1:8-16)
D. Corruption in Micah's Society (2:1-11)
E. Hope in the Midst of Gloom (2:12-13)
F. The Leaders Condemned (ch. 3)
III. Hope for Israel and Judah (chs. 4-5)
    A. The Coming Kingdom (ch. 4)
    B. The Coming King (5:1-5a)
    C. Victory for the People of God (5:5b-15)
IV. The Lord's Case against Israel (ch. 6)
    A. The Lord's Accusation (6:1-8)
    B. The Coming Judgment (6:9-16)
V. Gloom Turns to Triumph (ch. 7)
    A. Micah Laments the Corruption of His Society (7:1-6)
    B. Micah's Assurance of Hope (7:7)
    C. A Bright Future for God's People (7:8-13)
    D. Victory for God's Kingdom (7:14-20)

1 The word of the LORD that came to Micah of Moresheth[a] during the reigns of Jotham,[b] Ahaz[c] and Hezekiah,[d] kings of Judah[e]—the vision[f] he saw concerning Samaria and Jerusalem.

²Hear,[g] O peoples, all of you,[h]
　listen, O earth[i] and all who are in it,
that the Sovereign LORD may witness[j]
　against you,
　the Lord from his holy temple.[k]

Judgment Against Samaria and Jerusalem

³Look! The LORD is coming from his
　dwelling[l] place;
he comes down[m] and treads the high
　places of the earth.[n]
⁴The mountains melt[o] beneath him[p]
　and the valleys split apart,[q]
like wax before the fire,
　like water rushing down a slope.
⁵All this is because of Jacob's
　transgression,
　because of the sins of the house of
　　Israel.
What is Jacob's transgression?
　Is it not Samaria?[r]
What is Judah's high place?
　Is it not Jerusalem?

⁶"Therefore I will make Samaria a heap
　of rubble,

a place for planting vineyards.[s]
I will pour her stones[t] into the valley
　and lay bare her foundations.[u]
⁷All her idols[v] will be broken to
　pieces;[w]
all her temple gifts will be burned
　with fire;
I will destroy all her images.[x]
Since she gathered her gifts from the
　wages of prostitutes,[y]
as the wages of prostitutes they will
　again be used."

Weeping and Mourning

⁸Because of this I will weep[z] and wail;
　I will go about barefoot[a] and naked.
I will howl like a jackal
　and moan like an owl.
⁹For her wound[b] is incurable;[c]
　it has come to Judah.[d]
It[a] has reached the very gate[e] of my
　people,
　even to Jerusalem itself.
¹⁰Tell it not in Gath[b];
　weep not at all.[c]
In Beth Ophrah[d]
　roll in the dust.
¹¹Pass on in nakedness[f] and shame,

Cross-references (center column)

1:1 aver 14; Jer 26:18
bS 1Ch 3:12
cS 1Ch 3:13
dS 1Ch 3:13
eHos 1:1 /Isa 1:1
1:2 gS Dt 32:1
hPs 50:7
iS Jer 6:19
jS Ge 31:50; S Dt 4:26;
S Isa 1:2
kS Ps 11:4
1:3 /S Isa 18:4
mS Isa 64:1
nS Am 4:13
1:4 oS Ps 46:2,6
pS Job 9:5
qS Nu 16:31; Na 1:5
1:5 rAm 8:14

1:6 sS Dt 20:6
tS Am 5:11
uEze 13:14
1:7 vS Eze 6:6
wS Ex 32:20
xS Dt 9:21
yDt 23:17-18
1:8 zS Isa 15:3
aS Isa 20:2
1:9 bJer 46:11
cS Jer 10:19
dS 2Ki 18:13
eIsa 3:26
1:11 fEze 23:29

Footnotes

a9 Or He　b10 Gath sounds like the Hebrew for tell.
c10 Hebrew; Septuagint may suggest not in Acco. The Hebrew for in Acco sounds like the Hebrew for weep.
d10 Beth Ophrah means house of dust.

Commentary

1:1 Micah. Means "Who is like the LORD?" Moresheth. See Introduction: Author. Jotham, Ahaz and Hezekiah. See Introduction: Date. For background on these kings and the book of Micah see 2Ki 15:32–16:20; 18–20. Isaiah, Hosea and Micah prophesied at roughly the same time (see Isa 1:1; Hos 1:1). vision. See Isa 1:1 and note. Samaria and Jerusalem. The capitals of Israel and Judah respectively. The judgment predicted by Micah involved these nations and not just their capital cities.
1:2 Hear. The Hebrew for this word introduces prophetic addresses also in 3:1 and 6:1, where it is translated "Listen" (see also 3:9; 6:2). peoples . . . earth. All nations—an announcement that the day of the Lord is at hand, when God will call the nations to account. In view of that day Micah speaks in his prophecy of the impending judgments on Israel and Judah. holy temple. Heaven (see v. 3), as in Ps 11:4; Jnh 2:7; Hab 2:20.
1:3 The LORD is coming. An OT expression describing the Lord's intervention in history (see Ps 18:9; 96:13; 144:5; Isa 26:21; 31:4; 64:1–3). high places. May refer to mountains as well as to pagan shrines, since both are cited here (vv. 4–5). Cf. Am 4:13.
1:4 mountains melt. See Ps 97:5; Na 1:5.
1:5 Jacob's. Jacob was an alternate name for Israel (see Ge 32:28 and note; 35:10). Israel. Here (and in v. 13) specifically the northern kingdom, but Micah uses the name also for the southern kingdom (see 3:1,8–9; 5:1,3) or for the whole covenant people (see vv. 14–15; 2:12; 5:2; 6:2). high place. Pagan center of idolatry (see 2Ch 28:25).
1:6–7 God is the speaker. This prophecy was fulfilled during Micah's lifetime when Assyria destroyed Samaria in

722–721 B.C. (2Ki 17:6).
1:6 into the valley. Samaria was built on a hill (1Ki 16:24).
1:7 prostitutes. Prostitution is often an OT symbol for idolatry or spiritual unfaithfulness (Ex 34:15–16; Jdg 2:17; Eze 23:29–30). wages. The wealth that Samaria had gained from her idolatry will be taken by the Assyrians and placed in their own temples to be used again in the worship of idols.
1:8 this. The coming destruction of Samaria. barefoot. A sign of mourning (2Sa 15:30). It is possible that Micah actually walked stripped and barefoot through Jerusalem (cf. Isa 20:2). naked. Clothed only in a loincloth.
1:9 wound. The judgment about to overtake Samaria. incurable. See Isa 17:11 and note; Jer 30:12. gate. The Assyrian destruction of the northern kingdom will spread like a malignant disease to the gate of Jerusalem (v. 12). The gate was where the process of town government was carried on (see Ge 19:1 and note; Ru 4:1–4).
1:10–15 Several plays on words are explained in the NIV text notes. The towns mentioned lie in the Shephelah, i.e., the foothills (500–1,500 feet high) between the Mediterranean coastal plain and the mountains of Judah.
1:10 Tell it not in Gath. These words introduce a funeral lament over Judah. Micah did not want the pagan people in Gath to gloat over the downfall of God's people. Cf. 2Sa 1:20. roll in the dust. As a sign of grief over the coming catastrophe. See Isa 47:1 and note.
1:11 nakedness and shame. A reference to their future condition as prisoners (see Isa 20:4). will not come out. Because of the invasion, the people will not dare to go outside their houses.

you who live in Shaphir.[e]
Those who live in Zaanan[f]
    will not come out.
Beth Ezel is in mourning;
    its protection is taken from you.
[12]Those who live in Maroth[g] writhe in
        pain,
    waiting for relief,[g]
because disaster[h] has come from the
        LORD,
    even to the gate of Jerusalem.
[13]You who live in Lachish,[h] [i]
    harness the team to the chariot.
You were the beginning of sin
    to the Daughter of Zion,[j]
for the transgressions of Israel
    were found in you.
[14]Therefore you will give parting gifts[k]
    to Moresheth[l] Gath.
The town of Aczib[i][m] will prove
        deceptive[n]
    to the kings of Israel.
[15]I will bring a conqueror against you
    who live in Mareshah.[j] [o]
He who is the glory of Israel
    will come to Adullam.[p]
[16]Shave[q] your heads in mourning
    for the children in whom you delight;
make yourselves as bald as the vulture,
    for they will go from you into exile.[r]

Man's Plans and God's

2 Woe to those who plan iniquity,
    to those who plot evil[s] on their
        beds![t]
At morning's light they carry it out
    because it is in their power to do it.
[2]They covet fields[u] and seize them,[v]
    and houses, and take them.
They defraud[w] a man of his home,
    a fellowman of his inheritance.[x]

[3]Therefore, the LORD says:

"I am planning disaster[y] against this
        people,
    from which you cannot save
        yourselves.
You will no longer walk proudly,[z]
    for it will be a time of calamity.
[4]In that day men will ridicule you;
    they will taunt you with this
        mournful song:
'We are utterly ruined;[a]
    my people's possession is divided
        up.[b]
He takes it from me!
    He assigns our fields to traitors.'"

[5]Therefore you will have no one in the
        assembly of the LORD
    to divide the land[c] by lot.[d]

False Prophets

[6]"Do not prophesy," their prophets say.
    "Do not prophesy about these things;
    disgrace[e] will not overtake us.[f]"
[7]Should it be said, O house of Jacob:
    "Is the Spirit of the LORD angry?
    Does he do such things?"

"Do not my words do good[g]
    to him whose ways are upright?[h]
[8]Lately my people have risen up
    like an enemy.
You strip off the rich robe
    from those who pass by without a
        care,
    like men returning from battle.
[9]You drive the women of my people

Cross references (center column):

1:12 [g]Jer 14:19
[h]Jer 40:2
1:13 [i]S Jos 10:3
[j]S Ps 9:14
1:14 [k]2Ki 16:8
[l]S ver 1
[m]S Jos 15:44
[n]Jer 15:18
1:15 [o]Jos 15:44
[p]S Jos 12:15
1:16
[q]S Lev 13:40;
S Job 1:20
[r]S Dt 4:27;
S Am 5:27
2:1 [s]S Isa 29:20
[t]Ps 36:4
2:2 [u]Isa 5:8
[v]S Pr 30:14
[w]S Jer 22:17
[x]S 1Sa 8:14;
S Isa 1:23;
S Eze 46:18

2:3 [y]Jer 18:11;
S Am 3:1-2
[z]Isa 2:12
2:4 [a]S Lev 26:31;
S Jer 4:13
[b]S Jer 6:12
2:5 [c]Dt 32:13;
Jos 18:4
[d]S Nu 34:13
2:6 [e]Ps 44:13;
Jer 18:16; 19:8;
25:18; 29:18;
Mic 6:16
[f]S Am 2:12
2:7 [g]S Ps 119:65
[h]Ps 15:2; 84:11

Footnotes (center column):

[e]11 Shaphir means pleasant.   [f]11 Zaanan sounds like
the Hebrew for come out.   [g]12 Maroth sounds like the
Hebrew for bitter.   [h]13 Lachish sounds like the
Hebrew for team.   [i]14 Aczib means deception.
[j]15 Mareshah sounds like the Hebrew for conqueror.

Study notes (bottom):

1:12 has come. Micah foresees the future so clearly that to
him it seems as though it has already come.
1:13 Lachish. One of the largest towns in Judah (see Isa
36:2 and note). Later, Sennacherib was so proud of capturing
it that he decorated his palace at Nineveh with a relief
picturing his exploits. harness the team. In order to escape.
Daughter of Zion. A personification of Jerusalem and its
inhabitants.
1:14 parting gifts. The Hebrew for these words is translated "wedding gift" in 1Ki 9:16. Jerusalem must give up
Moresheth Gath, as a father gives a "wedding gift" to his
daughter when she marries. Aczib. See NIV text note. The
word "deceptive" is used in Jer 15:18 to describe a brook
that has dried up in summer. Like such a brook, the city of
Aczib will cease to exist. Israel. See note on 1:5.
1:15 Micah again represents God as speaking, as in vv.
6-7. glory of Israel. God himself (see 1Sa 15:29). will come
to Adullam. In judgment.
1:16 Israel was taken into exile by the Assyrians in
722-721 B.C., and Judah by the Babylonians in 586.
2:1-5 Directed primarily against wealthy landowners who

oppressed the poor.
2:1 power to do it. The rich, oppressing classes continued
to get rich at the expense of the poor because they controlled
the power structures of their society.
2:2 They covet. In violation of the tenth commandment
(see Ex 20:17 and note; Dt 5:21). inheritance. Land that
was to be the permanent possession of a particular family.
See Lev 25:10,13 (Year of Jubilee); Nu 27:1-11; 36:1-12
(Zelophehad's daughters); 1Ki 21:1-19 (Naboth's vineyard).
2:3 Therefore. Because of the sins of Israel's influential
classes, calamity will strike. disaster. The impending exile.
2:4 We . . . me. The rich landowners, on whom God's
judgment will fall. He. God. traitors. The treacherous Assyrians (see Isa 33:1 and note) who will capture the land.
2:5 you. The oppressing classes—the rich landowners. no
one . . . to divide the land. They will be cut off from all the
promises of the covenant people.
2:6 their prophets. The false prophets whose words were
addressed to Micah.
2:7 Verses 6-7a are spoken by Micah; vv. 7b-13 are
spoken by God.

from their pleasant homes. *i*
You take away my blessing
　from their children forever.
[10]Get up, go away!
　For this is not your resting place, *j*
because it is defiled, *k*
　it is ruined, beyond all remedy.
[11]If a liar and deceiver *l* comes and says,
　'I will prophesy for you plenty of
　　wine and beer,' *m*
he would be just the prophet for this
　people! *n*

Deliverance Promised

[12]"I will surely gather all of you, O Jacob;
　I will surely bring together the
　　remnant *o* of Israel.
I will bring them together like sheep in
　a pen,
　like a flock in its pasture;
　the place will throng with people. *p*
[13]One who breaks open the way will go
　up before *q* them;
they will break through the gate *r*
　and go out.
Their king will pass through before
　them,
　the LORD at their head."

Leaders and Prophets Rebuked

3 Then I said,
　"Listen, you leaders *s* of Jacob,
　you rulers of the house of Israel.
Should you not know justice,
[2]　you who hate good and love evil;
who tear the skin from my people
　and the flesh from their bones; *t*
[3]who eat my people's flesh, *u*
　strip off their skin
　and break their bones in pieces; *v*
who chop *w* them up like meat for the
　pan,
　like flesh for the pot? *x* "

Cross references (center column)

2:9 *i*Jer 10:20
2:10 *j*S Dt 12:9
*k*Lev 18:25-29;
Ps 106:38-39;
S La 4:15
2:11 *l*S 2Ch 36:16;
Jer 5:31
*m*S Lev 10:9
*n*Isa 30:10
2:12 *o*Mic 4:7;
5:7; 7:18
*p*S Ne 1:9
2:13 *q*S Isa 52:12
*r*S Isa 60:11
3:1 *s*S Jer 5:5
3:2 *t*Ps 53:4;
S Eze 22:27
3:3 *u*S Ps 14:4
*v*S Eze 34:4;
Zep 3:3
*w*S Job 24:14
*x*S Eze 11:7;
S 24:4-5

3:4 *y*S Dt 1:45;
S 1Sa 8:18;
S Isa 58:4;
S Jer 11:11
*z*S Dt 31:17
*a*S Job 15:31;
S Eze 8:18
3:5 *b*S Isa 3:12;
S 9:16; S 53:6
*c*S Jer 4:10
3:6 *d*Isa 8:19-22;
S Eze 12:24
*e*Isa 29:10
*f*S Eze 7:26;
S Am 8:11
3:7 *g*S Jer 6:15;
Mic 7:16
*h*S Isa 44:25
*i*S Est 6:12
*j*S Lev 13:45
*k*S Eze 20:3
3:8 *l*S Isa 57:12;
61:2
3:9 *m*Ps 58:1-2;
S Isa 1:23
3:10 *n*S Jer 22:13
*o*Isa 59:7;
Mic 7:2; Na 3:1;
Hab 2:12
*p*Jer 22:17;
S Eze 22:27
3:11 *q*S Ex 23:8;
S Lev 19:15;
Mal 2:9
*r*S Eze 13:19
*s*Isa 1:23;
S 56:11; Jer 6:13;
S La 4:13;
*t*S Hos 4:8,18
*t*S Isa 10:20
*u*Jer 7:4;
S Eze 34:2

[4]Then they will cry out to the LORD,
　but he will not answer them. *y*
At that time he will hide his face *z* from
　them
　because of the evil they have done. *a*

[5]This is what the LORD says:

"As for the prophets
　who lead my people astray, *b*
if one feeds them,
　they proclaim 'peace'; *c*
if he does not,
　they prepare to wage war against
　　him.
[6]Therefore night will come over you,
　　without visions,
　and darkness, without divination. *d*
The sun will set for the prophets, *e*
　and the day will go dark for them. *f*
[7]The seers will be ashamed *g*
　and the diviners disgraced. *h*
They will all cover *i* their faces
　because there is no answer from
　　God. *k* "

[8]But as for me, I am filled with power,
　with the Spirit of the LORD,
　and with justice and might,
to declare to Jacob his transgression,
　to Israel his sin. *l*
[9]Hear this, you leaders of the house of
　Jacob,
　you rulers of the house of Israel,
who despise justice
　and distort all that is right; *m*
[10]who build *n* Zion with bloodshed, *o*
　and Jerusalem with wickedness. *p*
[11]Her leaders judge for a bribe, *q*
　her priests teach for a price, *r*
　and her prophets tell fortunes for
　　money. *s*
Yet they lean *t* upon the LORD and say,
　"Is not the LORD among us?
　No disaster will come upon us." *u*
[12]Therefore because of you,

2:10 *resting place.* A place that could be regarded as one's own possession, where a people could settle in security (cf. Jos 1:13–15; 21:43–44; 22:4).
2:11 Anyone who promised greater affluence would gain a hearing.
2:12–13 Although Israel will be carried into captivity, a remnant will return (see note on Isa 1:9).
2:12 *Jacob . . . Israel.* Here perhaps the entire nation, north and south. Contrast 1:5; 3:1,9–10.
3:1–12 Verses 1–4 deal with the sins of the leaders of Israel, vv. 5–7 with the false prophets and vv. 9–12 with the leaders, priests and prophets.
3:1 *Jacob . . . Israel.* Both names refer to Judah here (see vv. 9–10).
3:2–3 *tear the skin . . . like flesh for the pot.* A series of figures of speech describing the cruel way the leaders treat the people.

3:2 *hate good and love evil.* Contrast Am 5:15; Ro 12:9.
3:4 *they.* The leaders. *he will not answer.* See v. 7. *hide his face.* See Dt 31:17; Isa 1:15 and note. Disobedience leads to separation from God.
3:5 *proclaim 'peace.'* The false prophets predicted peace for Judah while Micah predicted destruction and captivity (see v. 12; 4:10). See also Jer 6:13–14; 8:10–11.
3:7 *seers.* An older term for "prophets" (see note on 1Sa 9:9).
3:8 One of the chief purposes of Micah was to declare to Judah its sin. *filled . . . with the Spirit.* The prophets were Spirit-filled messengers (see Isa 48:16).
3:11 *for a bribe.* See Isa 1:23; 5:23.
3:12 The destruction of Jerusalem occurred in 586 B.C. This verse was quoted a century later in Jer 26:18. Jer 26:19 indicates that Micah's preaching may have been instrumental in the revival under King Hezekiah (see 2Ki 18:1–6; 2Ch

Zion will be plowed like a field,
Jerusalem will become a heap of
    rubble, *v*
the temple *w* hill a mound overgrown
    with thickets. *x*

The Mountain of the LORD

4:1–3pp — Isa 2:1–4

4 In the last days
the mountain *y* of the LORD's temple
    will be established
as chief among the mountains;
it will be raised above the hills, *z*
    and peoples will stream to it. *a*

²Many nations will come and say,

"Come, let us go up to the mountain of
    the LORD, *b*
to the house of the God of Jacob. *c*
He will teach us *d* his ways, *e*
    so that we may walk in his paths."
The law *f* will go out from Zion,
    the word of the LORD from Jerusalem.
³He will judge between many peoples
    and will settle disputes for strong
        nations far and wide. *g*
They will beat their swords into
    plowshares
and their spears into pruning hooks. *h*
Nation will not take up sword against
    nation,
    nor will they train for war *i*
        anymore. *j*
⁴Every man will sit under his own vine
    and under his own fig tree, *k*
and no one will make them afraid, *l*
    for the LORD Almighty has spoken. *m*
⁵All the nations may walk
    in the name of their gods; *n*
we will walk in the name of the LORD
    our God for ever and ever. *o*

The LORD's Plan

⁶"In that day," declares the LORD,

"I will gather the lame; *p*
I will assemble the exiles *q*
    and those I have brought to grief. *r*
⁷I will make the lame a remnant, *s*

those driven away a strong nation. *t*
The LORD will rule over them in Mount
    Zion *u*
from that day and forever. *v*

⁸As for you, O watchtower of the flock,
    O stronghold *k* of the Daughter of
    Zion,
the former dominion will be restored *w*
    to you;
kingship will come to the Daughter of
    Jerusalem. *x* "

⁹Why do you now cry aloud—
    have you no king? *y*
Has your counselor perished,
    that pain seizes you like that of a
        woman in labor? *z*
¹⁰Writhe in agony, O Daughter of Zion,
    like a woman in labor,
for now you must leave the city
    to camp in the open field.
You will go to Babylon; *a*
    there you will be rescued.
There the LORD will redeem *b* you
    out of the hand of your enemies.

¹¹But now many nations
    are gathered against you.
They say, "Let her be defiled,
    let our eyes gloat *c* over Zion!"
¹²But they do not know
    the thoughts of the LORD;
they do not understand his plan, *d*
    he who gathers them like sheaves to
        the threshing floor.

¹³"Rise and thresh, *e* O Daughter of Zion,
    for I will give you horns of iron;
I will give you hoofs of bronze
    and you will break to pieces many
        nations." *f*

You will devote their ill-gotten gains to
    the LORD, *g*
their wealth to the Lord of all the
    earth.

A Promised Ruler From Bethlehem

5 Marshal your troops, O city of
    troops, *1*

3:12 *v*S 2Ki 25:9;
S Isa 6:11
*w*S Jer 52:13
*x*S Lev 26:31;
S Jer 17:3; S 22:6;
S La 5:18;
S Eze 5:14
4:1 *y*S Ps 48:1;
Zec 8:3
*z*S Eze 17:22
*a*S Ps 22:27;
86:9; S Jer 3:17;
S 31:12;
S Da 2:35
4:2 *b*S Jer 31:6;
S Eze 20:40
*c*Zec 2:11; 14:16
*d*S Ps 119:171
*e*Ps 25:8-9;
S Isa 54:13
*f*S Dt 18:18
4:3 *g*S Isa 11:4
*h*Joel 3:10;
Zec 9:10
*i*S Ps 46:9
*j*Zec 8:20-22
4:4 *k*S 1Ki 4:25
*l*S Lev 26:6;
S Eze 39:26
*m*S Isa 1:20
4:5 *n*2Ki 17:29;
Ac 14:16
*o*Jos 24:14-15;
Isa 26:8;
Zec 10:12
4:6 *p*S Jer 31:8
*q*S Ps 106:47
*r*S Eze 34:13,16;
S 37:21; Zep 3:19
4:7 *s*S Joel 2:32;
S Mic 2:12

*t*S Ge 12:2
*u*S Isa 2:2
*v*S Da 2:44;
S 7:14; S Lk 1:33;
Rev 11:15
4:8 *w*S Isa 1:26
*x*Zec 9:9
4:9 *y*Jer 8:19
*z*S Ge 3:16;
Jer 30:6; 48:41
4:10 *a*S Dt 21:10;
2Ki 20:18;
Isa 43:14
*b*S Isa 48:20
4:11 *c*S La 2:16;
S Ob 1:12;
Mic 7:8
4:12
*d*S Ge 50:20;
S Isa 55:8;
Ro 11:33-34
4:13 *e*S Isa 21:10
*f*S Isa 45:1;
S Da 2:44
*g*S Isa 23:18

*k*8 Or *hill*   *1*1 Or *Strengthen your walls, O walled city*

29–31).
4:1–3 See notes on Isa 2:2–4, a passage that is almost the
same as these verses.
4:4 *vine and . . . fig tree.* A reference to the peaceful
security of the kingdom of God. See 1Ki 4:25; Zec 3:10. *no
one will make them afraid.* See Zep 3:13. Fear will be a thing
of the past.
4:5 *walk in the name of the LORD.* Confess, love, obey and
rely on the Lord. Cf. Zec 10:12.
4:6 *In that day.* The Messianic period (see v. 1; see also
note on Isa 2:11,17,20).

4:7 *remnant.* The people of God (see 2:12; see also note on
Isa 1:9).
4:8 *watchtower of the flock.* The capital city of David, the
shepherd-king. *former dominion.* The kingdom of David will
be restored under the Messiah.
4:9–13 In vv. 9–10 Micah foresees the collapse of the
monarchy and the impending exile in 586 B.C. as well as the
restoration beginning in 538. Verses 11–13 are a prophecy of
judgment against the gloating enemies of Jerusalem.
5:1 Jerusalem will be besieged, and her kings will be seized
and taken to Babylon (the last king, Zedekiah, was blinded;

for a siege is laid against us.
They will strike Israel's ruler
  on the cheek[h] with a rod.

2"But you, Bethlehem[i] Ephrathah,[j]
  though you are small among the
    clans[m] of Judah,
out of you will come for me
  one who will be ruler[k] over Israel,
whose origins[n] are from of old,[l]
  from ancient times.[o]" [m]

3Therefore Israel will be abandoned[n]
  until the time when she who is in
    labor gives birth
and the rest of his brothers return
  to join the Israelites.

4He will stand and shepherd his flock[o]
  in the strength of the LORD,
in the majesty of the name of the
    LORD his God.
And they will live securely, for then his
    greatness[p]
will reach to the ends of the earth.
5   And he will be their peace. [q]

Deliverance and Destruction

When the Assyrian invades[r] our land
  and marches through our fortresses,
we will raise against him seven
    shepherds,
  even eight leaders of men. [s]
6They will rule[p] the land of Assyria with
    the sword,
  the land of Nimrod[t] with drawn
    sword.[q] [u]
He will deliver us from the Assyrian
  when he invades our land
  and marches into our borders. [v]

7The remnant[w] of Jacob will be
  in the midst of many peoples
like dew[x] from the LORD,
  like showers on the grass,[y]
which do not wait for man

or linger for mankind.
8The remnant of Jacob will be among the
    nations,
  in the midst of many peoples,
like a lion among the beasts of the
    forest,[z]
  like a young lion among flocks of
    sheep,
which mauls and mangles[a] as it goes,
  and no one can rescue. [b]
9Your hand will be lifted up[c] in triumph
    over your enemies,
  and all your foes will be destroyed.

10"In that day," declares the LORD,

"I will destroy your horses from among
    you
  and demolish your chariots. [d]
11I will destroy the cities[e] of your land
  and tear down all your strongholds.[f]
12I will destroy your witchcraft
  and you will no longer cast spells. [g]
13I will destroy your carved images[h]
  and your sacred stones from among
    you; [i]
you will no longer bow down
  to the work of your hands.[j]
14I will uproot from among you your
    Asherah poles[r] [k]
  and demolish your cities.
15I will take vengeance[l] in anger and
    wrath
  upon the nations that have not
    obeyed me."

The LORD's Case Against Israel

6 Listen to what the LORD says:

"Stand up, plead your case before the
    mountains;[m]

m2 Or *rulers*   n2 Hebrew *goings out*   o2 Or *from days of eternity*   p6 Or *crush*   q6 Or *Nimrod in its gates*   r14 That is, symbols of the goddess Asherah

Cross references (center column)

5:1 hLa 3:30
5:2 iS Jn 7:42
/S Ge 35:16;
S 48:7
kS Nu 24:19;
S 1Sa 13:14;
S 2Sa 6:21;
S 2Ch 7:18
lPs 102:25
mMt 2:6*
5:3 nS Jer 7:29
5:4 oIsa 40:11;
49:9;
S Eze 34:11-15,
23; Mic 7:14
pIsa 52:13;
Lk 1:32
5:5 qS Isa 9:6;
S Lk 2:14;
Col 1:19-20
rIsa 8:7
sIsa 10:24-27
5:6 tGe 10:8
uZep 2:13
vNa 2:11-13
5:7 wS Am 5:15;
S Mic 2:12
xS Ps 133:3
yIsa 44:4

5:8 zS Ge 49:9
aMic 4:13;
Zec 10:5
bS Ps 50:22;
S Isa 5:29;
S Hos 5:14
5:9 cS Ps 10:12
5:10 dEx 15:4,
19; S Hos 14:3;
Hag 2:22;
Zec 9:10
5:11 eS Dt 29:23;
Isa 6:11 /S La 2:2;
S Hos 10:14;
Am 5:9
5:12
gDt 18:10-12;
Isa 2:6; 8:19
5:13 hNa 1:14
iHos 10:2
/S Isa 2:18;
S Eze 6:9;
Zec 13:2
5:14
kS Ex 34:13;
S Jdg 3:7;
S 2Ki 17:10
5:15 lS Isa 65:12
6:1 mS Ps 50:1;
S Eze 6:2

Notes (bottom)

see 2Ki 25:7).

5:2 In contrast to the dire prediction of v. 1, Micah shifts to a positive note. *Ephrathah.* The region in which Bethlehem was located (see Ru 1:2; 4:11; 1Sa 17:12). *ruler.* Ultimately Christ, who will rule (see note on 4:8) for God the Father. *origins . . . from of old.* His beginnings were much earlier than his human birth (see Jn 8:58). *from ancient times.* Within history (cf. 2Sa 7:12–16; Isa 9:6–7; Am 9:11), and even from eternity (see NIV text note).
5:3 *Israel will be abandoned.* Until the Messiah is born and begins his rule. *Israel.* See note on 1:5.
5:4 *strength . . . majesty.* The Messiah will shepherd and rule in the strength and majesty of God the Father.
5:5 *their peace.* Jesus is "our peace" (Eph 2:14). In addition to freedom from war, the Hebrew word for "peace" also connotes prosperity in the OT. See notes on Isa 9:6 ("Prince of Peace"); Lk 2:14. *Assyrian.* Symbolic of all the enemies of God's people in every age. See Isa 11:11; Zec 10:10–11. *we.*

The people of God. *seven . . . eight.* A figurative way of saying "many" (see note on Job 5:19).
5:6 *land of Nimrod.* Assyria. See Ge 10:8–11. *he.* The ruler of v. 2.
5:8 *lion.* Like the previous simile (v. 7) this pictures the inevitable progress of the people of God toward triumph over their enemies (v. 9).
5:10–14 In the Messianic era the people of God will not depend on weapons of war or pagan idols. The successes of his people are always achieved by dependence on him.
6:1–16 This chapter depicts a courtroom scene in which the Lord lodges a legal complaint against Israel. In vv. 1–2 the Lord summons the people to listen to his accusation and to prepare their defense against the charges that follow in vv. 9–16. The Lord speaks in vv. 3–5, poignantly reminding the people of his gracious acts in their behalf. In vv. 6–7 Israel is speaking, and in v. 8 Micah responds directly to the nation, answering the questions of vv. 6–7. God charges the people

let the hills hear what you have to say.

[2]Hear,[n] O mountains, the LORD's accusation;[o]
listen, you everlasting foundations of the earth.
For the LORD has a case[p] against his people;
he is lodging a charge[q] against Israel.

[3]"My people, what have I done to you? How have I burdened[r] you?[s] Answer me.
[4]I brought you up out of Egypt[t] and redeemed you from the land of slavery.[u]
I sent Moses[v] to lead you, also Aaron[w] and Miriam.[x]
[5]My people, remember what Balak[y] king of Moab counseled and what Balaam son of Beor answered.
Remember your journey, from Shittim[z] to Gilgal,[a]
that you may know the righteous acts[b] of the LORD."

[6]With what shall I come before[c] the LORD
and bow down before the exalted God?
Shall I come before him with burnt offerings,
with calves a year old?[d]
[7]Will the LORD be pleased with thousands of rams,[e]
with ten thousand rivers of oil?[f]
Shall I offer my firstborn[g] for my transgression,
the fruit of my body for the sin of my soul?[h]
[8]He has showed you, O man, what is good.
And what does the LORD require of you?
To act justly[i] and to love mercy
and to walk humbly[j] with your God.[k]

Israel's Guilt and Punishment

[9]Listen! The LORD is calling to the city—
and to fear your name is wisdom—
"Heed the rod[l] and the One who appointed it.[s]
[10]Am I still to forget, O wicked house,
your ill-gotten treasures
and the short ephah,[t] which is accursed?[m]
[11]Shall I acquit a man with dishonest scales,[n]
with a bag of false weights?[o]
[12]Her rich men are violent;[p]
her people are liars[q]
and their tongues speak deceitfully.[r]
[13]Therefore, I have begun to destroy[s] you,
to ruin you because of your sins.
[14]You will eat but not be satisfied;[t]
your stomach will still be empty.[u]
You will store up but save nothing,[u]
because what you save I will give to the sword.
[15]You will plant but not harvest;[v]
you will press olives but not use the oil on yourselves,
you will crush grapes but not drink the wine.[w]
[16]You have observed the statutes of Omri[x]
and all the practices of Ahab's[y] house,
and you have followed their traditions.[z]
Therefore I will give you over to ruin[a]
and your people to derision;
you will bear the scorn[b] of the nations.[v]"

Israel's Misery

7 What misery is mine!
I am like one who gathers summer fruit

6:2 [n]Dt 32:1
[o]S Hos 12:2
[p]S Isa 3:13
6:3 [q]Ps 50:7;
S Jer 2:9
6:3 [r]Jer 2:5
[s]Jer 2:5
6:4 [t]S Ex 3:10;
S 6:6 [u]Dt 7:8
[v]S Ex 4:16
[w]S Nu 33:1;
Ps 77:20
[x]S Ex 15:20
6:5 [y]S Nu 22:2
[z]S Nu 25:1
[a]S Dt 11:30;
Jos 5:9-10
[b]Jdg 5:11;
1Sa 12:7
6:6 [c]S Ps 95:2
[d]Ps 40:6-8;
51:16-17
6:7 [e]S Isa 1:11;
S 40:16
[f]Ps 50:8-10
[g]S Lev 18:21;
S 2Ki 3:27
[h]Hos 5:6;
S Am 5:22
6:8 [i]S Isa 1:17;
S Jer 22:3
[j]S 2Ki 22:19;
S Isa 57:15
[k]S Ge 5:22;
Dt 10:12-13;
1Sa 15:22;
Hos 6:6;
Zec 7:9-10;
Mt 9:13; 23:23;
Mk 12:33;
Lk 11:42

6:9 [l]S Ge 17:1;
Isa 11:4
6:10
[m]Eze 45:9-10;
S Am 3:10; 8:4-6
6:11
[n]S Lev 19:36
[o]S Dt 25:13
6:12 [p]S Isa 1:23
[q]S Ps 116:11;
Isa 3:8
[r]S Ps 35:20;
S Jer 9:3
6:13 [s]Isa 1:7;
6:11
6:14 [t]S Isa 9:20;
S Hos 4:10
[u]Isa 30:6
6:15 [v]S Dt 28:38;
Jer 12:13
[w]Job 24:11;
S Am 5:11;
Zep 1:13
6:16 [x]S 1Ki 16:25
[y]1Ki 16:29-33
[z]Jer 7:24
[a]S Jer 25:9
[b]S Dt 28:37;
S Jer 51:51;
S Mic 2:6

[s]9 The meaning of the Hebrew for this line is uncertain.   [t]10 An ephah was a dry measure.   [u]14 The meaning of the Hebrew for this word is uncertain.   [v]16 Septuagint; Hebrew scorn due my people

---

with specific wrongs in vv. 9–16.
6:1–2 *mountains . . . foundations of the earth.* Inanimate objects were called on as third-party witnesses because of their enduring nature and because they were witnesses to his covenant (see Dt 32:1; Jos 24:27; Isa 1:2 and note).
6:2 *Israel.* Primarily Judah here.
6:3 *My people.* Indicative of a tender rebuke (see also v. 5).
6:5 *Balak . . . Balaam.* See Nu 22–24. *Shittim to Gilgal.* See Jos 3:1; 4:19.
6:6 The same thought is expressed in 1Sa 15:22; Ps 51:16; Hos 6:6; Isa 1:11–15 (see note there). Micah does not deny the desirability of sacrifices but shows that it does no good to offer them without obedience.
6:8 *man.* The use of the singular makes the accusation

personal, though Micah is speaking to all Israel (see also Dt 10:12–13). *act justly . . . love mercy.* The kind of obedience God expects from his covenant people.
6:9 *city.* Jerusalem.
6:10 *ephah.* About half a bushel.
6:11 See Pr 11:1; 20:23; Hos 12:7; Am 8:5.
6:12 *Her.* Jerusalem's.
6:13 *Therefore.* See note on 2:3.
6:16 *Omri . . . Ahab's.* 1Ki 16:25,30 says that they did more evil than all the kings who preceded them.
7:1–20 The speakers in this chapter are Micah (vv. 1–7), Zion (vv. 8–10), Micah (vv. 11–13), perhaps Zion (v. 14), God (v. 15), Micah (vv. 16–20). The chapter begins on a note of gloom but ends with a statement of hope.

at the gleaning of the vineyard;
there is no cluster of grapes to eat,
none of the early figs[c] that I crave.
[2]The godly have been swept from the
land;[d]
not one[e] upright man remains.
All men lie in wait[f] to shed blood;[g]
each hunts his brother[h] with a net.[i]
[3]Both hands are skilled in doing evil;[j]
the ruler demands gifts,
the judge accepts bribes,[k]
the powerful dictate what they
desire—
they all conspire together.
[4]The best of them is like a brier,[l]
the most upright worse than a thorn[m]
hedge.
The day of your watchmen has come,
the day God visits you.
Now is the time of their confusion.[n]
[5]Do not trust a neighbor;
put no confidence in a friend.[o]
Even with her who lies in your embrace
be careful of your words.
[6]For a son dishonors his father,
a daughter rises up against her
mother,[p]
a daughter-in-law against her
mother-in-law—
a man's enemies are the members of
his own household.[q]

[7]But as for me, I watch[r] in hope[s] for
the LORD,
I wait for God my Savior;
my God will hear[t] me.

Israel Will Rise

[8]Do not gloat over me,[u] my enemy!
Though I have fallen, I will rise.[v]
Though I sit in darkness,
the LORD will be my light.[w]
[9]Because I have sinned against him,
I will bear the LORD's wrath,[x]
until he pleads my case[y]
and establishes my right.
He will bring me out into the light;[z]
I will see his righteousness.[a]
[10]Then my enemy will see it
and will be covered with shame,[b]
she who said to me,

"Where is the LORD your God?"[c]
My eyes will see her downfall;[d]
even now she will be trampled[e]
underfoot
like mire in the streets.

[11]The day for building your walls[f] will
come,
the day for extending your
boundaries.
[12]In that day people will come to you
from Assyria[g] and the cities of Egypt,
even from Egypt to the Euphrates
and from sea to sea
and from mountain to mountain.[h]
[13]The earth will become desolate because
of its inhabitants,
as the result of their deeds.[i]

Prayer and Praise

[14]Shepherd[j] your people with your
staff,[k]
the flock of your inheritance,
which lives by itself in a forest,
in fertile pasturelands.[w][l]
Let them feed in Bashan[m] and Gilead[n]
as in days long ago.[o]

[15]"As in the days when you came out of
Egypt,
I will show them my wonders.[p]"

[16]Nations will see and be ashamed,[q]
deprived of all their power.
They will lay their hands on their
mouths[r]
and their ears will become deaf.
[17]They will lick dust[s] like a snake,
like creatures that crawl on the
ground.
They will come trembling[t] out of their
dens;
they will turn in fear[u] to the LORD
our God
and will be afraid of you.
[18]Who is a God[v] like you,
who pardons sin[w] and forgives[x] the
transgression
of the remnant[y] of his inheritance?[z]
You do not stay angry[a] forever

7:1 cS SS 2:13
7:2 dS Ps 12:1
eS Jer 2:29; 8:6
fPs 10:8
gS Pr 6:17;
S Mic 3:10
hS Isa 3:5
iS Jer 5:26
7:3 jS Pr 4:16
kS Ex 23:8;
S Eze 22:12
7:4 lS Nu 33:55;
S Eze 2:6
mS 2Sa 23:6
nS Job 31:14;
Isa 22:5;
S Hos 9:7
7:5 oJer 9:4
7:6 pS Eze 22:7
qMt 10:35-36*;
S Mk 13:12
7:7 rS Isa 21:8
sPs 130:5;
Isa 25:9 /S Ps 4:3
7:8 uS Ps 22:17;
S Pr 24:17;
S Mic 4:11
vPs 20:8; 37:24;
S Am 9:11
wS 2Sa 22:29;
Isa 9:2
7:9 xLa 3:39-40
yS Ps 119:154
zS Ps 107:10
aIsa 46:13
7:10 bS Ps 35:26

cS Ps 42:3
dS Isa 51:23
eS 2Sa 22:43;
S Job 40:12;
S Isa 5:5;
Zec 10:5
7:11 fIsa 54:11;
S Am 9:11
7:12 gS Isa 11:11
hIsa 19:23-25;
60:4
7:13
iIsa 3:10-11;
S Eze 12:19;
S 33:28-29
7:14 jS Ps 28:9;
S Mic 5:4
kPs 23:4 lPs 95:7
mS Isa 33:9
nS SS 4:1;
S Jer 50:19
oEze 36:11
7:15 pS Ex 3:20;
Ps 78:12
7:16 qIsa 26:11
rS Jdg 18:19
7:17 sS Ge 3:14
t2Sa 22:46
uIsa 25:3; Mic 7:10
7:18 vS Ex 8:10;
S 1Sa 2:2
wS Isa 43:25;
S Jer 50:20;
Zec 3:4
xS 2Ch 6:21;
Ps 103:8-13
yS Joel 2:32;
S Am 5:15;
S Mic 2:12
zS Ex 34:9
aS Ps 103:9;
S Isa 54:9

w 14 Or *in the middle of Carmel*

7:1–2 Looking for the godly is like looking for summer fruit when the harvest has ended (see also Jer 8:20).
7:4 *day of your watchmen.* The day of judgment that the prophets warned about (see Jer 6:17; Eze 3:17–21). *visits you.* For punishment.
7:6 The family unit was disintegrating.
7:8 *me.* Zion. *my enemy.* Other nations. *Though I have fallen.* Micah foresees the destruction of Zion in 586 B.C.
7:14 *inheritance.* Israel (see also v. 18; Ps 94:14).
7:15–17 It is possible that these verses constitute a prayer

that God will show his wonders again as in the exodus, that the nations will see and be ashamed, and that they will turn to the Lord in fear.
7:16 When the nations see God's power at the Messiah's coming, they will be amazed.
7:17 *lick dust like a snake.* A picture of defeat.
7:18–20 The conclusion to the whole book, not just to ch. 7.
7:18 *Who is a God like you . . . ?* Perhaps a pun on Micah's name (see note on 1:1). Cf. Ex 15:11; Ps 89:6.

but delight to show mercy. [b]

[19]You will again have compassion on us;
you will tread our sins underfoot
and hurl all our iniquities [c] into the
depths of the sea. [d]

[20]You will be true to Jacob,
and show mercy to Abraham, [e]
as you pledged on oath to our fathers [f]
in days long ago. [g]

7:18
[b]S 2Ch 30:9;
S Jer 31:20;
32:41;
S Eze 18:23
7:19 [c]S Isa 43:25
[d]S Jer 31:34

7:20 [e]Gal 3:16 [f]Dt 7:8; Lk 1:72 [g]Ps 108:4

7:19 *iniquities into the depths of the sea.* See note on Isa 38:17.

7:20 *Jacob . . . Abraham.* God had sworn to Abraham (Ge 22:17) and Jacob (Ge 28:14) that their descendants would be as numerous as the dust of the earth and the sand on the seashore, and he had promised Abraham that he would be the father of many nations (Ge 17:5; cf. Lk 1:54–55). All believers are ultimately included in this promise (Ro 4; Gal 3:6–29; Heb 11:12).

NAHUM

Author

The book contains the "vision of Nahum" (1:1), whose name means "comfort" and is related to the name Nehemiah, meaning "The LORD comforts" or "comfort of the LORD." (Nineveh's fall, which is Nahum's theme, would bring comfort to Judah.) Nothing is known about him except his hometown (Elkosh), and even its general location is uncertain.

Date

In 3:8-10 the author speaks of the fall of Thebes, which happened in 663 B.C., as already past. In all three chapters Nahum prophesied Nineveh's fall, which was fulfilled in 612. Nahum therefore uttered this oracle between 663 and 612, perhaps near the end of this period since he represents the fall of Nineveh as imminent (2:1; 3:14,19). This would place him during the reign of Josiah and make him a contemporary of Zephaniah and the young Jeremiah.

Background

Assyria (represented by Nineveh, 1:1) had already destroyed Samaria (722-721 B.C.), resulting in the captivity of the northern kingdom of Israel, and posed a present threat to Judah. The Assyrians were brutally cruel, their kings often being depicted as gloating over the gruesome punishments inflicted on conquered peoples. They conducted their wars with shocking ferocity, uprooted whole populations as state policy and deported them to other parts of their empire. The leaders of conquered cities were tortured and horribly mutilated before being executed (see note on 3:3). No wonder the dread of Assyria fell on all her neighbors!

About 700 B.C. King Sennacherib made Nineveh the capital of the Assyrian empire, and it remained the capital until it was destroyed in 612. Jonah had announced its destruction earlier (Jnh 3:4), but the people repented and the destruction was temporarily averted. Not long after that, however, Nineveh reverted to its extreme wickedness, brutality and pride. The brutality reached its peak under Ashurbanipal (669-627), the last great ruler of the Assyrian empire. After his death, Assyria's influence and power waned rapidly until 612, when Nineveh was overthrown (see notes on 1:14; 2:1). (Further historical information is given in notes throughout the book.)

Recipients

Some words are addressed to Judah (see 1:12-13,15), but most are addressed to Nineveh (see 1:11,14; 2:1,13; 3:5-17,19) or its king (3:18). The book, however, was meant for Judahite readers.

Literary Style

The contents are primarily judicial (judgment oracles), with appropriate descriptions and vocabulary, as well as intense moods, sights and sounds. The language is poetic, with frequent use of metaphors and similes, vivid word pictures, repetition and many short—often staccato—phrases (see, e.g., 3:2-3). Rhetorical questions punctuate the flow of thought, which has a marked stress on moral indignation toward injustice.

Theological Themes

The focal point of the entire book is the Lord's judgment on Nineveh for her oppression, cruelty, idolatry and wickedness. The book ends with the destruction of the city.

According to Ro 11:22, God is not only kind but also stern. In Nahum, God is not only "slow to anger" (1:3) and "a refuge . . . for those who trust in him" (1:7), but also one who "will not leave the guilty unpunished" (1:3). God's righteous and just kingdom will ultimately triumph, for kingdoms built on wickedness and tyranny must eventually fall, as Assyria did.

In addition, Nahum declares the universal sovereignty of God. God is Lord of history and of all nations; as such he controls their destinies.

Outline

I. Title (1:1)
II. Nineveh's Judge (1:2-15)
  A. The Lord's Kindness and Sternness (1:2-8)
  B. Nineveh's Overthrow and Judah's Joy (1:9-15)
III. Nineveh's Judgment (ch. 2)
  A. Nineveh Besieged (2:1-10)
  B. Nineveh's Desolation Contrasted with Her Former Glory (2:11-13)
IV. Nineveh's Total Destruction (ch. 3)
  A. Nineveh's Sins (3:1-4)
  B. Nineveh's Doom (3:5-19)

1 An oracle[a] concerning Nineveh. [b] The book of the vision[c] of Nahum the Elkoshite.

The Lord's Anger Against Nineveh

[2] The Lord is a jealous[d] and avenging God;
   the Lord takes vengeance[e] and is filled with wrath.
The Lord takes vengeance on his foes
   and maintains his wrath against his enemies.[f]
[3] The Lord is slow to anger[g] and great in power;
   the Lord will not leave the guilty unpunished. [h]
His way is in the whirlwind[i] and the storm,[j]
   and clouds[k] are the dust of his feet.
[4] He rebukes[l] the sea and dries it up;[m]
   he makes all the rivers run dry.
Bashan and Carmel[n] wither
   and the blossoms of Lebanon fade.
[5] The mountains quake[o] before him
   and the hills melt away.[p]
The earth trembles[q] at his presence,
   the world and all who live in it.[r]
[6] Who can withstand[s] his indignation?
   Who can endure[t] his fierce anger?[u]
His wrath is poured out like fire;[v]
   the rocks are shattered[w] before him.

[7] The Lord is good,[x]
   a refuge in times of trouble.[y]
He cares for[z] those who trust in him,[a]

[8] but with an overwhelming flood[b]
he will make an end of ˌNinevehˌ;
   he will pursue his foes into darkness.

[9] Whatever they plot[c] against the Lord
   he[a] will bring to an end;
   trouble will not come a second time.
[10] They will be entangled among thorns[d]
   and drunk[e] from their wine;
   they will be consumed like dry stubble.[b][f]
[11] From you, ˌO Nineveh,ˌ has one come forth
   who plots evil against the Lord
   and counsels wickedness.

[12] This is what the Lord says:

"Although they have allies and are numerous,
   they will be cut off[g] and pass away.
Although I have afflicted you, ˌO Judah,ˌ
   I will afflict you no more. [h]
[13] Now I will break their yoke[i] from your neck
   and tear your shackles away."[j]

[14] The Lord has given a command concerning you, ˌNinevehˌ:
   "You will have no descendants to bear your name.[k]
I will destroy the carved images[l] and cast idols
   that are in the temple of your gods.

[a] 9 Or What do you foes plot against the Lord? / He
[b] 10 The meaning of the Hebrew for this verse is uncertain.

Cross references (center column):

1:1 [a]S Isa 13:1; 19:1; Jer 23:33-34 [b]S Ge 10:11; S Jer 50:18; Na 2:8; 3:7 [c]S Isa 1:1
1:2 [d]S Ex 20:5 [e]S Ge 4:24; S Dt 32:41; Ps 94:1 /S Dt 7:10
1:3 [g]S Ne 9:17 [h]S Ex 34:7 [i]S Ex 14:21; S 2Ki 2:1 [j]S Ps 50:3 [k]S 2Sa 22:10; S Ps 104:3
1:4 [l]S 2Sa 22:16 [m]S Ex 14:22 [n]S Isa 33:9
1:5 [o]S Ex 19:18; S Job 9:6 [p]S Mic 1:4 [q]S Joel 2:10 [r]S Eze 38:20
1:6 [s]S Ps 130:3 [t]S Eze 22:14 [u]S Ps 76:7 [v]S Isa 5:24-25; S 42:25; S Jer 10:10 [w]1Ki 19:11
1:7 [x]S Jer 33:11 [y]S Jer 17:17 [z]S Ps 1:6 [a]S Ps 22:9
1:8 [b]S Isa 8:7; S Da 9:26
1:9 [c]S Hos 7:15
1:10 [d]S 2Sa 23:6 [e]S Isa 49:26 [f]S Isa 5:24; Mal 4:1
1:12 [g]S Isa 10:34 [h]Isa 54:6-8; S La 3:31-32
1:13 [i]S Isa 9:4 [j]S Job 12:18; S Ps 107:14
1:14 [k]S Isa 14:22 [l]Mic 5:13

Study notes (bottom):

1:1 The title of the book. *oracle*. See note on Isa 13:1. *Nineveh*. See Introduction: Background; see also notes on Jnh 1:2; 3:3. Here the capital city stands for the entire Assyrian empire. *vision*. See note on Isa 1:1. *Nahum the Elkoshite*. See Introduction: Author.
1:2–3 The covenant name Yahweh ("the Lord") is emphasized.
1:2 *jealous*. See note on Ex 20:5. *avenging ... vengeance ... vengeance*. God acts justly in judgment toward all who oppose him and his kingdom. The repetition is for emphasis.
1:3 *the guilty*. Such as Nineveh. *whirlwind ... storm ... clouds*. See notes on Ps 18:7–15; 68:4; 77:16–19; 104:3–4.
1:4 *rebukes the sea and dries it up*. As at the crossing of the Red Sea (Ex 14). *makes all the rivers run dry*. As at the crossing of the Jordan (Jos 3). *Bashan ... Carmel ... Lebanon*. See notes on SS 7:5; Isa 2:13; 33:9; 35:2; Am 4:1. These three places were noted for their fertility, vineyards and trees, but at the Lord's word they wither.
1:5 *mountains ... hills ... earth ... world*. Emblems of stability and permanence.
1:6 *Who can withstand ... ? Who can endure ... ?* Rhetorical questions. If mountains quake before the Lord (v. 5), what human being can think that he is not vulnerable? Cf. Ro 2:3–5.
1:7 *those who trust in him*. Such as Judah.
1:8 *overwhelming flood*. Symbolic of an invading army (see Isa 8:7–8). *end ... darkness*. In 612 b.c. that end came for

Nineveh, and the darkness enveloped her. Through the ministry of Jonah, Nineveh had formerly experienced the light of God. But she later rejected it, and the result was the darkness of judgment.
1:9 *they plot*. See note on v. 11. *trouble will not come a second time*. God never permitted the Assyrians a second victory over the Judahites; the first was the fall of Samaria (722–721 b.c.) and of the northern kingdom (Sennacherib's invasion in 701 was not a complete victory; see 2Ki 18:13–19:37; Isa 36–37).
1:10 *drunk from their wine*. See 3:11 and note; but perhaps the line here should read: "and drenched as with their wine,/yet they ..." (see NIV text note).
1:11 *one ... who plots evil*. Possibly the Assyrian king Ashurbanipal (669–627 b.c.), the last great Assyrian emperor, whose western expeditions succeeded in subduing Egypt and to whom King Manasseh had to submit as a vassal (see 2Ch 33:11–13).
1:12 *they*. The Assyrians. *I have afflicted you*. God had used Assyria as the rod of his anger against his covenant-breaking people in the days of Ahaz (Isa 10:5) and again in the time of Manasseh.
1:13 *I will break their yoke*. Judah was Assyria's vassal; that yoke would be broken.
1:14 *I will prepare your grave*. God used the Babylonians, the Medes and the Scythians to dig Nineveh's grave in 612 b.c. For the fulfillment of this prophecy see Eze 32:22–23.

I will prepare your grave,[m]
  for you are vile."

[15]Look, there on the mountains,
    the feet of one who brings good
      news,[n]
    who proclaims peace![o]
  Celebrate your festivals,[p] O Judah,
    and fulfill your vows.
  No more will the wicked invade you;[q]
    they will be completely destroyed.

Nineveh to Fall

2 An attacker[r] advances against you,
    Nineveh.
  Guard the fortress,
    watch the road,
    brace yourselves,
    marshal all your strength!

[2]The LORD will restore[s] the splendor[t] of
    Jacob
  like the splendor of Israel,
    though destroyers have laid them waste
    and have ruined their vines.

[3]The shields of his soldiers are red;
    the warriors are clad in scarlet.[u]
  The metal on the chariots flashes
    on the day they are made ready;
    the spears of pine are brandished.[c]
[4]The chariots[v] storm through the streets,

rushing back and forth through the
      squares.
  They look like flaming torches;
    they dart about like lightning.

[5]He summons his picked troops,
    yet they stumble[w] on their way.
  They dash to the city wall;
    the protective shield is put in place.
[6]The river gates[x] are thrown open
    and the palace collapses.
[7]It is decreed[d] that the city
    be exiled and carried away.
  Its slave girls moan[y] like doves
    and beat upon their breasts.[z]
[8]Nineveh is like a pool,
    and its water is draining away.
  "Stop! Stop!" they cry,
    but no one turns back.
[9]Plunder the silver!
    Plunder the gold!
  The supply is endless,
    the wealth from all its treasures!
[10]She is pillaged, plundered, stripped!
    Hearts melt,[a] knees give way,
    bodies tremble, every face grows
      pale.[b]

[11]Where now is the lions' den,[c]

Cross references

1:14 mS Jer 28:8;
Eze 32:22-23
1:15 nIsa 40:9;
Ro 10:15
oS Isa 52:7;
Ac 10:36
pLev 23:2-4
qS Isa 52:1
2:1 rJer 51:20
2:2 sS Eze 37:23
tIsa 60:15
2:3
uS Eze 23:14-15
2:4 vS Jer 4:13;
S Eze 23:24

2:5 wJer 46:12
2:6 xIsa 45:1;
Na 3:13
2:7 yS Ge 8:8;
S Isa 59:11
zIsa 32:12
2:10 aS Jos 2:11;
S 7:5 bS Isa 29:22
2:11 cIsa 5:29

[c]3 Hebrew; Septuagint and Syriac / *the horsemen rush to and fro*   [d]7 The meaning of the Hebrew for this word is uncertain.

1:15 *mountains.* Of Jerusalem and Judah. *feet of one who brings good news.* This verse sets forth a principle that is applicable in several contexts of deliverance. Here the reference is to the good news of deliverance from the Assyrian threat; in Isa 52:7, deliverance from Babylonian exile; in Ro 10:15, deliverance from sin through the gospel ("good news") of Christ. *Celebrate your festivals.* In the joy of your deliverance. *fulfill your vows.* Those you uttered in the time of distress (see note on Ps 7:17). *No more will the wicked invade you.* The Assyrian invasion in the days of Manasseh was the last. *wicked.* See note on Dt 13:13. *completely destroyed.* Fulfilled in 612 when Nineveh fell (see note on v. 14).
2:1 *attacker.* Refers to the alliance of the Babylonians, the Medes and the Scythians—particularly the Medes under Cyaxares and the Babylonians under Nabopolassar. *Guard the fortress . . . marshal all your strength!* Probably irony, touched with sarcasm. *road.* By which the enemies will come.
2:2 *restore the splendor of Jacob . . . Israel.* The whole nation will be restored and united again.
2:3 *his soldiers.* Those of the attacker (v. 1), or perhaps those of Nineveh itself. *red.* Either (1) the color of the shields, or (2) a reference to blood on them, or (3) the result of the reflection of the sun shining on them. *brandished.* Ready to use.
2:4 *chariots . . . rushing.* Refers to either (1) the Assyrian war chariots and their unprecedented speed as the Assyrians take frantic but vain steps to defend themselves, or (2) the chariots of Nineveh's invaders.
2:5 *He.* Probably the king of Assyria. *city wall.* A moat 150 feet wide had to be filled in before reaching Nineveh's wall, which was almost 8 miles long with 15 gates. Then battering

rams were moved up. *protective shield.* Of the defenders—a framework covered with hides to deflect stones and arrows directed by the invaders at the defenders on the wall.
2:6 *river gates.* Perhaps the dams on the Khoser River, which ran through the city to the Tigris River. They were either already in place, or quickly built, to back up the river water, then suddenly released so the flood would damage the walls. *palace collapses.* One ancient historian (the author of the *Babylonian Chronicles*) speaks of a flood that washed away some of the wall, making it easier for the invaders to enter the city.
2:7 *slave girls.* Possibly temple prostitutes, whose places of business and idols were being destroyed.
2:8 *like a pool . . . water is draining away.* Some think that this refers to the Tigris and the smaller rivers encircling and running through parts of the city, and to a system of dams to make the city more impenetrable. Others take the language less literally as a reference to Nineveh's people fleeing, like water draining from a pool.
2:9 The cry of the invaders.
2:10 *pillaged, plundered, stripped.* The Hebrew for all three words is similar. The *Babylonian Chronicles* confirms the fact that a great quantity of plunder was carried off by the invaders. *Hearts melt.* The powerful, insolent Ninevites become helpless with fear.
2:11-13 Nahum ironically contrasts the devastated and desolate city of Nineveh with its former glory and power, expressed in figurative terms.
2:11 *lion and lioness.* Cf. Isa 5:29; Jer 4:7; Hos 5:14; Mic 5:8. The lion is an appropriate image to apply to Assyria because of the rapacious ways of the Assyrian monarchs and because Nineveh contained numerous lion sculptures.

the place where they fed their young,
　where the lion and lioness went,
　and the cubs, with nothing to fear?
[12]The lion killed [d] enough for his cubs
　and strangled the prey for his mate,
filling his lairs [e] with the kill
　and his dens with the prey. [f]

[13]"I am against [g] you,"
　declares the LORD Almighty.
"I will burn up your chariots in
　smoke, [h]
and the sword [i] will devour your
　young lions.
I will leave you no prey on the earth.
The voices of your messengers
　will no longer be heard." [j]

Woe to Nineveh

3 Woe to the city of blood, [k]
　full of lies, [l]
full of plunder,
　never without victims!
[2]The crack of whips,
　the clatter of wheels,
galloping horses
　and jolting chariots!
[3]Charging cavalry,
　flashing swords
　and glittering spears!
Many casualties,
　piles of dead,
bodies without number,
　people stumbling over the
　　corpses [m]—
[4]all because of the wanton lust of a
　harlot,
　alluring, the mistress of sorceries, [n]
who enslaved nations by her
　prostitution [o]
and peoples by her witchcraft.

[5]"I am against [p] you," declares the LORD
　Almighty.
"I will lift your skirts [q] over your
　face.
I will show the nations your
　nakedness [r]
　and the kingdoms your shame.
[6]I will pelt you with filth, [s]
I will treat you with contempt [t]
　and make you a spectacle. [u]
[7]All who see you will flee [v] from you and
　say,
'Nineveh [w] is in ruins [x]—who will
　mourn for her?' [y]
Where can I find anyone to comfort [z]
　you?"

[8]Are you better than [a] Thebes, [e] [b]
　situated on the Nile, [c]
with water around her?
The river was her defense,
　the waters her wall.
[9]Cush [f] [d] and Egypt were her boundless
　strength;
Put [e] and Libya [f] were among her
　allies.
[10]Yet she was taken captive [g]
　and went into exile.
Her infants were dashed [h] to pieces
　at the head of every street.
Lots [i] were cast for her nobles,
　and all her great men were put in
　chains. [j]
[11]You too will become drunk; [k]
you will go into hiding [l]
and seek refuge from the enemy.

[12]All your fortresses are like fig trees
　with their first ripe fruit; [m]
　when they are shaken,

Cross references

2:12 [d]S Jer 51:34
[e]S Jer 4:7
[f]S Isa 37:18
2:13
[g]Isa 10:5-13;
S Jer 21:13;
Na 3:5 [h]Ps 46:9
[i]S 2Sa 2:26
[j]S Mic 5:6
3:1 [k]S Eze 22:2;
S Mic 3:10
[l]Ps 12:2
3:3 [m]2Ki 19:35;
Isa 34:3; Jer 47:3
3:4 [n]S Isa 47:9
[o]S Isa 23:17;
Eze 16:25-29

3:5 [p]S Na 2:13
[q]S Isa 20:4;
Jer 13:22
[r]S Isa 47:3
3:6 [s]S Ex 29:14;
S Job 9:31
[t]S 1Sa 2:30;
S Jer 51:37
[u]Isa 14:16
3:7 [v]S Isa 13:14;
S 31:9 [w]S Na 1:1
[x]S Job 3:14
[y]S Jer 15:5
[z]S Isa 51:19
3:8 [a]Am 6:2
[b]S Jer 46:25
[c]Isa 19:6-9
3:9 [d]S Ge 10:6;
S 2Ch 12:3
[e]S Eze 27:10
[f]Eze 30:5
3:10 [g]S Isa 20:4
[h]S 2Ki 8:12;
S Isa 13:16;
Hos 13:16
[i]S Job 6:27;
S Eze 24:6
[j]S Jer 40:1
3:11 [k]S Isa 49:26
[l]S Isa 2:10
3:12 [m]S SS 2:13

[e]8 Hebrew *No Amon*　[f]9 That is, the upper Nile
region

2:12 *filling his lairs . . . with the prey.* Nineveh was filled with the spoils of war from many conquered nations.

2:13 *I will burn up.* Nineveh's fall will not be caused by merely natural forces or the superior power of her attackers; it will be an act of God. Nineveh had been put on trial, found guilty and sentenced to destruction. *voices . . . no longer be heard.* History has confirmed this prediction.

3:1 *city of blood.* Nineveh's bloody massacres of her conquered rivals were well known. *never without victims.* The Assyrians were noted for their ruthlessness, brutality and terrible atrocities. Many of their victims were beheaded, impaled or burned.

3:3 *piles of dead.* The Assyrian king Shalmaneser III boasted of erecting a pyramid of chopped-off heads in front of an enemy's city. Other Assyrian kings stacked corpses like cordwood by the gates of defeated cities. Nahum's description of the cruel Assyrians is apropos.

3:4 *harlot.* Probably a reference to the chief love goddess of Nineveh and, by extension, to the city as a whole. The lure of luxury and wealth brought multitudes to Nineveh. *sorceries . . . witchcraft.* See Dt 18:10.

3:5 *lift your skirts over your face.* The punishment of prostitutes and adulteresses.

3:6 Nineveh will be humiliated.

3:7 *who . . . ? Where . . . ?* Rhetorical questions. Nineveh will receive no sympathy.

3:8 *Thebes.* See NIV text note. *No Amon* means "city of (the god) Amon." Thebes was the great capital of Upper Egypt. Its site is occupied today by the towns of Luxor and Karnak. It was destroyed by the Assyrians in 663 B.C.

3:9 *Put.* A neighbor of Egypt, but its location is uncertain.

3:10 *her great men were put in chains.* Assyrian kings often did this; e.g., King Ashurbanipal gave this description of his treatment of a captured leader: "I . . . put a dog chain on him and made him occupy a kennel at the eastern gate of Nineveh."

3:11 *will become drunk.* Probably from the cup of God's wrath.

3:12 *like fig trees with their first ripe fruit.* A simile for the eagerness with which the victors gather the rich loot of Nineveh. *figs fall into the mouth of the eater.* Nineveh's fortresses will finally fall just as easily.

the figs[n] fall into the mouth of the
    eater.
[13]Look at your troops—
    they are all women![o]
The gates[p] of your land
    are wide open to your enemies;
    fire has consumed their bars. [q]

[14]Draw water for the siege,[r]
    strengthen your defenses![s]
Work the clay,
    tread the mortar,
    repair the brickwork!
[15]There the fire[t] will devour you;
    the sword[u] will cut you down
    and, like grasshoppers, consume you.
Multiply like grasshoppers,
    multiply like locusts![v]
[16]You have increased the number of your
    merchants
    till they are more than the stars of the
    sky,
but like locusts[w] they strip the land
    and then fly away.

[17]Your guards are like locusts,[x]
    your officials like swarms of locusts
    that settle in the walls on a cold
    day—
but when the sun appears they fly
    away,
    and no one knows where.

[18]O king of Assyria, your shepherds[g]
    slumber;[y]
    your nobles lie down to rest. [z]
Your people are scattered[a] on the
    mountains
    with no one to gather them.
[19]Nothing can heal your wound;[b]
    your injury is fatal.
Everyone who hears the news about
    you
    claps his hands[c] at your fall,
for who has not felt
    your endless cruelty? [d]

3:12 [n]S Isa 28:4
3:13 [o]S Isa 19:16
[p]S Na 2:6
[q]S Isa 45:2
3:14 [r]S 2Ch 32:4
[s]Na 2:1
3:15 [t]S Isa 27:1
[u]S 2Sa 2:26
[v]S Jer 51:14;
S Joel 1:4
3:16 [w]S Ex 10:13

3:17 [x]Jer 51:27
3:18 [y]Ps 76:5-6;
S Jer 25:27
[z]Isa 56:10
[a]S 1Ki 22:17
3:19
[b]S Jer 30:13;
S Mic 1:9
[c]S Job 27:23;
S La 2:15;
Zep 2:15
[d]Isa 37:18

[g]18 Or rulers

3:13 *your troops . . . are all women!* They are weak and
unable to stand against the invading armies. *their bars.* The
bars of the gates.
3:14 *Draw water.* A normal preparation for siege. *strength-
en your defenses!* Irony, the point being that it will do no
good (see note on 2:1).
3:15 *There.* Inside your strong fortifications. *fire will devour you.* Confirmed by history and archaeology. Assyria's
king died in the flames of his palace.
3:16 *your merchants . . . are more than the stars.* Speaks of
Assyria's vast trading and commercial enterprises. *they strip
the land.* In the time of Nineveh's adversity the merchants
stripped the land of its treasures, and the trade network was
destroyed.
3:17 *locusts.* Feared by the farmers of the ancient Near
East, because they came in huge swarms and devoured

everything in their path. Their activity provided an apt simile
for the exploitative actions of Nineveh's officials during her
destruction. *no one knows where.* Thus will Nineveh's officials disappear, without a trace. Interestingly, for centuries
no one knew where Nineveh itself lay buried; in 1845 it was
finally uncovered by archaeologists.
3:18 *O king.* The reigning king at the time of Nineveh's fall
was Sin-Shar-Ishkun; so these words are prophetically addressed to him. *shepherds.* Leaders. *lie down to rest.* Die.
people are scattered. The age-old scene of refugees fleeing a
place of destruction is repeated at Nineveh.
3:19 *your injury is fatal.* Nineveh was so totally destroyed
that it was never rebuilt, and within a few centuries it was
covered with windblown sand. So that "great city" (Jnh 1:2;
cf. 3:2) fell in 612 b.c., never to rise again—all in fulfillment
of God's word through his prophet Nahum.

HABAKKUK

Author

Little is known about Habakkuk except that he was a contemporary of Jeremiah and a man of vigorous faith rooted deeply in the religious traditions of Israel. The account of his ministering to the needs of Daniel in the lions' den in the Apocryphal book *Bel and the Dragon* is legendary rather than historical.

Date

The prediction of the coming Babylonian invasion (1:6) indicates that Habakkuk lived in Judah toward the end of Josiah's reign (640-609 b.c.) or at the beginning of Jehoiakim's (609-598). The prophecy is generally dated a little before or after the battle of Carchemish (605), when Egyptian forces, who had earlier gone to the aid of the last Assyrian king, were routed by the Babylonians under Nabopolassar and Nebuchadnezzar and were pursued as far as the Egyptian border (Jer 46). Habakkuk, like Jeremiah, probably lived to see the initial fulfillment of his prophecy when Jerusalem was attacked by the Babylonians in 597.

Message

Among the prophetic writings, Habakkuk is somewhat unique in that it includes no oracle addressed to Israel. It contains, rather, a dialogue between the prophet and God (see Outline). (The book of Jonah, while narrative, presents an account of conflict between the Lord and one of his prophets.) In the first two chapters, Habakkuk argues with God over his ways that appear to him unfathomable, if not unjust. Having received replies, he responds with a beautiful confession of faith (ch. 3).

This account of wrestling with God is, however, not just a fragment from a private journal that has somehow entered the public domain. It was composed for Israel. No doubt it represented the voice of the godly in Judah, struggling to comprehend the ways of God. God's answers therefore spoke to all who shared Habakkuk's troubled doubts. And Habakkuk's confession became a public expression—as indicated by its liturgical notations (see note on 3:1).

Habakkuk was perplexed that wickedness, strife and oppression were rampant in Judah but God seemingly did nothing. When told that the Lord was preparing to do something about it through the "ruthless" Babylonians (1:6), his perplexity only intensified: How could God, who is "too pure to look on evil" (1:13), appoint such a nation "to execute judgment" (1:12) on a people "more righteous than themselves" (1:13)?

God makes it clear, however, that eventually the corrupt destroyer will itself be destroyed. In the end, Habakkuk learns to rest in God's appointments and await his working in a spirit of worship.

Literary Features

The author wrote clearly and with great feeling, and penned many memorable phrases (2:2,4,14,20; 3:2,17-19). The book was popular during the intertestamental period; a complete commentary on its first two chapters has been found among the Dead Sea Scrolls (see "The Time between the Testaments," p. 1431).

Outline

I. Title (1:1)
II. Habakkuk's First Complaint: Why does the evil in Judah go unpunished? (1:2-4)
III. God's Answer: The Babylonians will punish Judah (1:5-11)
IV. Habakkuk's Second Complaint: How can a just God use wicked Babylon to punish a people more righteous than themselves? (1:12-2:1)

1 The oracle[a] that Habakkuk the prophet received.

Habakkuk's Complaint

2How long,[b] O LORD, must I call for help,
but you do not listen?[c]
Or cry out to you, "Violence!"
but you do not save?[d]
3Why do you make me look at injustice?
Why do you tolerate[e] wrong?[f]
Destruction and violence[g] are before me;
there is strife,[h] and conflict abounds.
4Therefore the law[i] is paralyzed,
and justice never prevails.
The wicked hem in the righteous,
so that justice[j] is perverted.[k]

The LORD's Answer

5"Look at the nations and watch—
and be utterly amazed.[l]
For I am going to do something in your days
that you would not believe,
even if you were told.[m]
6I am raising up the Babylonians,[a] [n]
that ruthless and impetuous people,
who sweep across the whole earth[o]
to seize dwelling places not their own.[p]
7They are a feared and dreaded people;[q]
they are a law to themselves
and promote their own honor.
8Their horses are swifter[r] than leopards,
fiercer than wolves[s] at dusk.

Their cavalry gallops headlong;
their horsemen come from afar.
They fly like a vulture swooping to devour;
9 they all come bent on violence.
Their hordes[b] advance like a desert wind
and gather prisoners[t] like sand.
10They deride kings
and scoff at rulers.[u]
They laugh at all fortified cities;
they build earthen ramps[v] and capture them.
11Then they sweep past like the wind[w]
and go on—
guilty men, whose own strength is their god."[x]

Habakkuk's Second Complaint

12O LORD, are you not from everlasting?[y]
My God, my Holy One,[z] we will not die.[a]
O LORD, you have appointed[b] them to execute judgment;
O Rock,[c] you have ordained them to punish.
13Your eyes are too pure[d] to look on evil;
you cannot tolerate wrong.[e]
Why then do you tolerate[f] the treacherous?[g]
Why are you silent while the wicked swallow up those more righteous than themselves?[h]
14You have made men like fish in the sea,
like sea creatures that have no ruler.

Cross references

1:1 [a]S Na 1:1
1:2 [b]S Ps 6:3
[c]Ps 13:1-2; 22:1-2 [d]Jer 14:9; Zec 1:12
1:3 [e]ver 13 [f]S Job 9:23 [g]Jer 20:8 [h]S Ps 55:9
1:4 [i]Ps 119:126 [j]S Isa 29:21 [k]S Job 19:7; S Isa 1:23; 5:20; S Eze 9:9
1:5 [l]S Isa 29:9 [m]Ac 13:41*
1:6 [n]S Dt 28:49; S 2Ki 24:2 [o]Rev 20:9 [p]S Jer 13:20; S 21:7
1:7 [q]Isa 18:7; Jer 39:5-9
1:8 [r]S Jer 4:13 [s]S Ge 49:27
1:9 [t]Hab 2:5
1:10 [u]S 2Ch 36:6 [v]S Jer 33:4
1:11 [w]Jer 4:11-12 [x]S Da 4:30
1:12 [y]S Ge 21:33 [z]Isa 31:1; 37:23 [a]Ps 118:17 [b]Isa 10:6 [c]S Ge 49:24; S Ex 33:22
1:13 [d]Ps 18:26 [e]S La 3:34-36 [f]ver 3 [g]S Ps 25:3 [h]S Job 21:7

[a]6 Or Chaldeans   [b]9 The meaning of the Hebrew for this word is uncertain.

1:1 *oracle.* Such as the two found here (vv. 5–11; 2:2–20). Oracles were frequently received in visions. The Hebrew word for "oracle" (possibly meaning "burden," but perhaps only "pronouncement") often refers to revelations containing warnings of impending doom (cf. Isa 15:1; 19:1; 22:1), but in Zec 9:1; 12:1; Mal 1:1 it refers to messages that also contain hope. *Habakkuk.* The name is probably Babylonian and refers to a kind of garden plant. *prophet.* Habakkuk is called a prophet also in 3:1, tying ch. 3 closely to chs. 1–2.
1:2–2:20 A dialogue between the prophet and God. The basic theme is age-old: Why does evil seem to go unpunished? Why does God not respond to prayer?
1:2 *Violence!* At this time Judah was probably under King Jehoiakim, who was ambitious, cruel and corrupt. Habakkuk describes the social corruption and spiritual apostasy of Judah in the late seventh century B.C.
1:3 *you tolerate.* See v. 13. The prophet was amazed that God seemed to condone cruelty and violence.
1:4 *law is paralyzed ... justice is perverted.* Because wealthy landowners controlled the courts through bribery.
1:5 *would not believe.* To the people of Judah it was incredible that God would give them over to the arrogant Babylonians.
1:6 The apostate nation of Judah is to be punished by an invasion of the Babylonians, a powerful people who regained

their independence from Assyria in 626 B.C., destroyed Assyrian power completely in 612–605, and flourished until 539. In this context, the Chaldeans (see NIV text note) are synonymous with the newly resurgent Babylonians. *seize dwelling places.* See 2:6–8.
1:7 *promote their own honor.* A mark of arrogance.
1:8 The speed with which Babylon conquered her enemies had become proverbial.
1:9 *gather prisoners like sand.* Like their Assyrian predecessors, the Babylonians deported conquered peoples as a matter of deliberate national policy (see 2:5).
1:10 *build earthen ramps.* A siege method.
1:11 *whose own strength is their god.* The Babylonians were so proud and confident of their military might that it had virtually become their god (see v. 16).
1:12 Habakkuk cannot see the justice in Judah's being punished by an even more wicked nation, and thinks that the Babylonians surely would not be allowed to conquer Judah completely. *from everlasting.* See Ps 90:2. LORD, *you have appointed them.* The prophet recognizes Babylon as God's agent of judgment (cf. Isa 7:18–20; 44:28–45:1).
1:13 A classic statement of the problem of evil within the context of Israel's faith: Why does evil appear to flourish unchecked by a just and holy God? *treacherous ... wicked.* The Babylonians. *those more righteous.* Judah.

15 The wicked[i] foe pulls all of them up with hooks,[j]
he catches them in his net,[k]
he gathers them up in his dragnet;
and so he rejoices and is glad.
16 Therefore he sacrifices to his net
and burns incense[l] to his dragnet,
for by his net he lives in luxury
and enjoys the choicest food.
17 Is he to keep on emptying his net,
destroying nations without mercy?[m]

2 I will stand at my watch[n]
and station myself on the ramparts;[o]
I will look to see what he will say[p] to me,
and what answer I am to give to this complaint.[c] [q]

The LORD's Answer

2 Then the LORD replied:

"Write[r] down the revelation
and make it plain on tablets
so that a herald[d] may run with it.
3 For the revelation awaits an appointed time;[s]
it speaks of the end[t]
and will not prove false.
Though it linger, wait[u] for it;
it[e] will certainly come and will not delay.[v]

4 "See, he is puffed up;
his desires are not upright—
but the righteous[w] will live by his faith[f] [x]—
5 indeed, wine[y] betrays him;
he is arrogant[z] and never at rest.
Because he is as greedy as the grave[g]
and like death is never satisfied,[a]
he gathers to himself all the nations
and takes captive[b] all the peoples.

6 "Will not all of them taunt[c] him with ridicule and scorn, saying,

" 'Woe to him who piles up stolen goods
and makes himself wealthy by extortion![d]
How long must this go on?'
7 Will not your debtors[h] suddenly arise?
Will they not wake up and make you tremble?
Then you will become their victim.[e]
8 Because you have plundered many nations,
the peoples who are left will plunder you.[f]
For you have shed man's blood;[g]
you have destroyed lands and cities
and everyone in them.[h]

9 "Woe to him who builds[i] his realm by unjust gain[j]
to set his nest[k] on high,
to escape the clutches of ruin!
10 You have plotted the ruin[l] of many peoples,

1:15 [i]Jer 5:26 [j]S Isa 19:8 [k]S Job 18:8; Jer 16:16 **1:16** [l]Jer 44:8 **1:17** [m]S Isa 14:6; 19:8 **2:1** [n]S Isa 21:8 [o]S Ps 48:13 [p]Ps 85:8 [q]S Ps 5:3; S Eze 3:17 **2:2** [r]S Isa 30:8; S Jer 36:2; S Eze 24:2; S Ro 4:24; Rev 1:19 **2:3** [s]Da 11:27 [t]Da 8:17 [u]S Ps 27:14 [v]S Eze 12:25 **2:4** [w]S Eze 18:9 [x]Ro 1:17*; Gal 3:11*; Heb 10:37-38* **2:5** [y]S Pr 20:1 [z]S Isa 2:11 [a]S Pr 27:20; S 30:15-16 [b]Hab 1:9 **2:6** [c]S Isa 14:4 [d]Am 2:8 **2:7** [e]S Pr 29:1 **2:8** [f]Isa 33:1; Jer 50:17-18; S Ob 1:15; Zec 2:8-9 [g]ver 17 [h]S Eze 39:10 **2:9** [i]S Jer 22:13 [j]S Jer 51:13 [k]S Job 39:27; S Isa 10:14 **2:10** [l]Jer 26:19

[c]1 Or *and what to answer when I am rebuked* [d]2 Or *so that whoever reads it* [e]3 Or *Though he linger, wait for him; / he* [f]4 Or *faithfulness* [g]5 Hebrew *Sheol* [h]7 Or *creditors*

1:15 *hooks.* See note on Am 4:2. *catches them in his net.* Babylon's victims are as powerless as fish swimming into a net. Mesopotamian reliefs portray, in symbolic fashion, conquering rulers capturing the enemy in fishnets.
1:16 See note on v. 11.
2:1 *I will stand at my watch.* The figure of a guard looking out from a tower and expecting a response to his challenge. Any rebuke (see NIV text note) would be for questioning God's justice. *ramparts.* The walls of Jerusalem.
2:2–3 *revelation.* See 1Ch 17:15; Pr 29:18. The Hebrew for this word refers specifically to a prophet's vision (see, e.g., Isa 1:1).
2:2 *so that a herald may run with it.* Lit. "so that he who reads it may run," i.e., so that a messenger may run to deliver the message and read it to those to whom he has been sent.
2:3 *wait for it.* The following message deals with the fall of Babylon in 539 B.C., about 66 years after Habakkuk's prophecy. The Lord tells Habakkuk (and Judah) that fulfillment of the prophecy may "linger," but that he and the people are to expect it (see 3:16).
2:4 *he.* Collective for the Babylonians, but with special reference to their king. *but.* In contrast to the Babylonians, whose desires are not upright. *the righteous will live by his faith.* See NIV text note; see also Isa 26, especially vv. 1–6. In light of God's revelation about how (and when) he is working, his people are to wait patiently and live by faith—trusting in their sovereign God. The clause is quoted frequently in the NT to support the teaching that people are saved by grace through faith (Ro 1:17; Gal 3:11; cf. Eph 2:8) and should live by faith (Heb 10:38–39). It became the rallying cry of the Protestant Reformation in the 16th century. The same principle that was applicable in the realm of national deliverance is applicable in the area of spiritual deliverance (salvation).
2:5 *greedy as the grave.* The grave never says, "Enough" (Pr 30:15–16).
2:6–20 This taunt falls into two halves of ten (Hebrew) lines each (vv. 6–14 and vv. 15–20), each half concluding with a significant theological statement (vv. 14,20). Together these two statements set the five "woes" pronounced against Babylon (vv. 6,9,12,15,19; cf. Isa 5:8–23; Mt 23:13–32; Lk 6:24–26; Rev 9:12; 11:14) in a larger frame of reference.
2:6 *all of them taunt him.* The threatened victims of the Babylonian onslaught, especially Judah, will taunt ruthless Babylon. *Woe.* The Babylonians' greed for conquest is condemned.
2:8 *you have shed man's blood.* See v. 17. Therefore Babylon's blood would be shed (see note on Ge 9:6).
2:9 *Woe.* The Babylonians' pride in building is condemned. *nest on high.* Like the eagle building an inaccessible nest, the Babylonians thought their empire to be unconquerable (see Ob 3–4; cf. Isa 14:4,13–15).

shaming[m] your own house and
forfeiting your life.
[11]The stones[n] of the wall will cry out,
and the beams of the woodwork will
echo it.

[12]"Woe to him who builds a city with
bloodshed[o]
and establishes a town by crime!
[13]Has not the LORD Almighty determined
that the people's labor is only fuel for
the fire,[p]
that the nations exhaust themselves
for nothing?[q]
[14]For the earth will be filled with the
knowledge of the glory[r] of the
LORD,
as the waters cover the sea.[s]

[15]"Woe to him who gives drink[t] to his
neighbors,
pouring it from the wineskin till they
are drunk,
so that he can gaze on their naked
bodies.
[16]You will be filled with shame[u] instead
of glory.[v]
Now it is your turn! Drink[w] and be
exposed[i] ![x]
The cup[y] from the LORD's right hand is
coming around to you,
and disgrace will cover your glory.
[17]The violence[z] you have done to
Lebanon will overwhelm you,
and your destruction of animals will
terrify you.[a]

For you have shed man's blood;[b]
you have destroyed lands and cities
and everyone in them.

[18]"Of what value[c] is an idol,[d] since a
man has carved it?
Or an image[e] that teaches lies?
For he who makes it trusts in his own
creation;
he makes idols that cannot speak.[f]
[19]Woe to him who says to wood, 'Come
to life!'
Or to lifeless stone, 'Wake up!'[g]
Can it give guidance?
It is covered with gold and silver;[h]
there is no breath in it.[i]
[20]But the LORD is in his holy temple;[j]
let all the earth be silent[k] before
him."

Habakkuk's Prayer

3 A prayer of Habakkuk the prophet. On
shigionoth.[i] [l]

[2]LORD, I have heard[m] of your fame;
I stand in awe[n] of your deeds,
O LORD.[o]
Renew[p] them in our day,
in our time make them known;
in wrath remember mercy.[q]

[3]God came from Teman,[r]

Cross references
2:10 [m]ver 16;
[S] Na 3:6
2:11
[n]S Jos 24:27;
Zec 5:4; Lk 19:40
2:12 [o]S Eze 22:2;
S Mic 3:10
2:13 [p]Isa 50:11
[q]S Isa 47:13
2:14 [r]S Ex 16:7;
S Nu 14:21
[s]S Isa 11:9
2:15 [t]S Pr 23:20
2:16 [u]S ver 10
[v]S Eze 23:32-34;
Hos 4:7
[w]S Lev 10:9
[x]S La 4:21
[y]S Ps 16:5;
S Isa 51:22
2:17 [z]S Jer 51:35
[a]S Jer 50:15

[b]ver 8
2:18
[c]1Sa 12:21
[d]S Jdg 10:14;
S Isa 40:19;
S Jer 5:21;
S 14:22
[e]S Lev 26:1
[f]Ps 115:4-5;
Jer 10:14;
1Co 12:2
2:19 [g]1Ki 18:27
[h]S Jer 10:4
[i]S Da 5:4,23;
S Hos 4:12
2:20 [j]S Ps 11:4
[k]S Isa 41:1
3:1 [l]Ps 7 Title
3:2 [m]S Job 26:14;
Ps 44:1
[n]S Ps 119:120
[o]S Ps 90:16
[p]Ps 85:6
[q]Isa 54:8
3:3 [r]S Ge 36:11,
15

[i]16 Masoretic Text; Dead Sea Scrolls, Aquila, Vulgate and
Syriac (see also Septuagint) and stagger   [i]1 Probably a
literary or musical term

2:11 *The stones ... will cry out, and the beams.* The
stones and beams in Babylonian houses were purchased with
plunder, and thus testified against the occupants.
2:12 *Woe.* Babylonian injustice is condemned.
2:13 *fuel for the fire.* The cities built by the labor of the
Babylonians (v. 12) will be burned.
2:14 The Lord's future destruction of proud Babylon and all
her worldly glory will cause his greater glory to be known
throughout the world (see Ex 14:4,17-18; Isa 11:9; Rev
17:1-19:4).
2:15 Cf. Ge 9:20-22. *Woe.* Babylonian violence is condemned. Her rapacious treatment of her neighbors, which
stripped them of all their wealth (cf. what she later did to
Jerusalem, 2Ki 25:8-21), is compared to one who makes his
neighbor drunk so he can take lewd pleasure from the man's
nakedness.
2:16 *be filled with shame ... be exposed.* The Lord will do
to Babylon what she has done to others. *cup from the LORD's
right hand.* A symbol of divine retribution (see Isa 51:17,22;
Jer 25:15-17; La 4:21; Rev 14:10; 16:19).
2:17 *violence you have done to Lebanon.* The Babylonians
apparently had ravaged the cedar forests of Lebanon to adorn
their temples and palaces (cf. Isa 14:8). *destruction of animals.* Assyrian inscriptions record hunting expeditions in the
Lebanon range, and such sport may have been indulged in by
the invading Babylonians as well. Babylonian violence was
destructive of all forms of life, not only of lands and cities.
2:18 *idols.* The Hebrew for this word means "godlets" or

"nonentities" (cf. Isa 41:29; 44:9; Jer 10:15 and the condemnation of idolatry in Ex 20:4-5; Ps 115:4-8).
2:19 *Woe.* Babylonian idolatry is condemned.
2:20 *But.* The stone and wood idols of the nations (v. 19)
are silent before people, but the people of the world are to be
silent before the true God, who is about to judge (cf. Isa
41:1; Zep 1:7; Zec 2:13). *holy temple.* Heaven.
3:1 In the strict sense, petition is found in this prayer only
in v. 2 but, as with many of the psalms, it is set in a larger
context of recollection (vv. 3-15) and expression of confidence and trust (vv. 16-19). In fact, Habakkuk's prayer
appears to have been used as a psalm; note the psalm-like
heading (v. 1) and the musical and/or literary notations (vv.
1,3,9,13,19).
3:2 *heard of your fame.* In vv. 3-15 Habakkuk recalls a
poetic celebration of God's mighty saving acts of
old—perhaps one he had heard at the temple (see v. 16).
3:3 *God came.* When celebrating the exodus, the OT poets
(and poet-prophets) combined recollections of the mighty
acts of God with conventional images of a fearsome manifestation of the Lord. He came down with his heavenly host and
rode on the mighty thunderstorm as his chariot, with his
arrows flying in all directions, a cloudburst of rain descending
on the earth and the mountains quaking before him (see Dt
33:2; Jdg 5:4-5; Ps 18:7-15; 68:4-10,32-35; 77:16-19;
Mic 1:3-4). Such figures characterize many of the references
in the following verses. *Teman.* Means "southland." God is
pictured as coming from the area south of Judah during the

the Holy One[s] from Mount Paran.[t]
        Selah[k]
His glory covered the heavens[u]
  and his praise filled the earth.[v]
[4]His splendor was like the sunrise;[w]
  rays flashed from his hand,
  where his power[x] was hidden.
[5]Plague[y] went before him;
  pestilence followed his steps.
[6]He stood, and shook the earth;
  he looked, and made the nations
    tremble.
  The ancient mountains crumbled[z]
  and the age-old hills[a] collapsed.[b]
  His ways are eternal.[c]
[7]I saw the tents of Cushan in distress,
  the dwellings of Midian[d] in
    anguish.[e]

[8]Were you angry with the rivers,[f]
  O LORD?
  Was your wrath against the streams?
  Did you rage against the sea[g]
  when you rode with your horses
  and your victorious chariots?[h]
[9]You uncovered your bow,
  you called for many arrows.[i]   Selah
  You split the earth with rivers;
[10] the mountains saw you and
    writhed.[j]
  Torrents of water swept by;
  the deep roared[k]
  and lifted its waves[l] on high.

[11]Sun and moon stood still[m] in the
  heavens
  at the glint of your flying arrows,[n]

at the lightning[o] of your flashing
  spear.
[12]In wrath you strode through the earth
  and in anger you threshed[p] the
    nations.
[13]You came out[q] to deliver[r] your people,
  to save your anointed[s] one.
  You crushed[t] the leader of the land of
    wickedness,
  you stripped him from head to foot.
                     Selah
[14]With his own spear you pierced his
  head
  when his warriors stormed out to
    scatter us,[u]
  gloating as though about to devour
  the wretched[v] who were in hiding.
[15]You trampled the sea[w] with your
  horses,
  churning the great waters.[x]

[16]I heard and my heart pounded,
  my lips quivered at the sound;
  decay crept into my bones,
  and my legs trembled.[y]
  Yet I will wait patiently[z] for the day of
    calamity
  to come on the nation invading us.
[17]Though the fig tree does not bud
  and there are no grapes on the vines,
  though the olive crop fails
  and the fields produce no food,[a]
  though there are no sheep in the pen
  and no cattle in the stalls,[b]
[18]yet I will rejoice in the LORD,[c]
  I will be joyful in God my Savior.[d]

3:3 [s]Isa 31:1
[t]S Nu 10:12
[u]S Ps 8:1
[v]Ps 48:10
3:4 [w]S Isa 18:4
[x]S Job 9:6
3:5 [y]S Lev 26:25
3:6 [z]S Ps 46:2
[a]Ge 49:26
[b]S Ex 19:18;
Ps 18:7; 114:1-6
[c]S Ge 21:33
3:7 [d]S Ge 25:2;
S Nu 25:15;
Jdg 7:24-25
[e]Ex 15:14
3:8 [f]S Ex 7:20
[g]S Ps 77:16
[h]S 2Ki 2:11;
S Ps 68:17
3:9 [i]S Dt 32:23;
Ps 7:12-13
3:10 /S Ps 77:16
[k]Ps 98:7
[l]S Ps 93:3
3:11 [m]Jos 10:13
[n]Ps 18:14

[o]S Ps 144:6;
Zec 9:14
3:12 [p]S Isa 41:15
3:13 [q]S Ex 13:21
[r]S Ps 20:6; S 28:8
[s]S 2Sa 23:1
[t]Ps 68:21; 110:6
3:14 [u]Jdg 7:22
[v]Ps 64:2-5
3:15 [w]S Job 9:8
[x]S Ps 15:8
3:16 [y]S Job 4:14
[z]S Ps 37:7
3:17
[a]Joel 1:10-12,18
[b]Jer 5:17
3:18 [c]Ps 97:12;
S Isa 61:10;
Php 4:4
[d]S Ex 15:2;
S Lk 1:47

[k]3 A word of uncertain meaning; possibly a musical term;
also in verses 9 and 13

---

exodus. *Mount Paran.* See Dt 33:2; probably northwest of the Gulf of Aqaba and south of Kadesh Barnea, between Edom and Sinai. *filled the earth.* See note on 2:14.

3:5 *Plague . . . pestilence.* Means of divine punishment (cf. Ex 7:14–12:30; Lev 26:25; Ps 91:3,6).

3:6 God's presence was frequently marked by earthquakes (see Ex 19:18; Ps 18:7; Jer 4:24–26; 10:10). Landslides may also be alluded to here.

3:7 *Cushan . . . Midian.* Arab tribes living near Edom. *distress . . . anguish.* When Israel was delivered from Egypt under Moses, neighboring peoples were filled with fear (see Ex 15:14–16; Jos 2:9–10).

3:8 Poetic allusions to the plague on the Nile (Ex 7:20–24) and/or the stopping of the Jordan (Jos 3:15–17), and to the parting of the Red Sea (Ex 14:15–31). But see note on v. 3.

3:9 *arrows.* Probably thunderbolts unleashed by the heavenly archer. *split the earth with rivers.* Caused by the accompanying thunderstorms.

3:11 *Sun and moon stood still.* Probably an allusion to the victory at Gibeon (Jos 10:12–13), indicating that God's triumph over his enemies would be just as complete as on that occasion.

3:12 *threshed.* See note on Am 1:3.

3:13 *deliver your people.* God fought against the nations of

Canaan (v. 12) but delivered his people. *save.* By giving victory to. *anointed one.* The covenant nation, the "kingdom of priests" (Ex 19:6), which God came to deliver. He destroyed the enemy, and in this great act of wrath (v. 12) remembered mercy (v. 2). *leader of the land of wickedness.* Pharaoh (see Ex 14:5–9).

3:14–15 Another reference to the destruction of the Egyptians in the Red Sea. God will likewise vanquish present foes.

3:15 *horses.* See v. 8 and note.

3:16 Hearing the hymnic recollection of God's mighty deeds of old in Israel's behalf (vv. 3–15) fills the prophet with an awe so profound that he feels physically weak. Alternatively, it is possible that the message from the Lord that Babylon would be sent against Judah (1:5–11) had so devastated him that he felt ill—until he heard the Lord's further word. *wait patiently.* See note on 2:3. *nation invading us.* Babylonia.

3:17 Probably anticipates the awful results of the imminent Babylonian invasion and devastation.

3:18–19 Habakkuk has learned the lesson of faith (2:4)—to trust in God's providence regardless of circumstances. He declares that even if God should send suffering and loss, he would still rejoice in his Savior-God—one of the strongest affirmations of faith in all Scripture.

¹⁹The Sovereign LORD is my strength; *e*
he makes my feet like the feet of a
deer,

3:19 *e*S Dt 33:29;
Ps 46:1-5

/S Dt 32:13;
Ps 18:33

he enables me to go on the heights. *f*

For the director of music. On my
stringed instruments.

3:19 *makes my feet like the feet of a deer.* Gives me
sure-footed confidence. *director.* Probably the conductor of
the temple musicians. This chapter may have formed part of
the temple prayers that were chanted with the accompaniment of instruments (see 1Ch 16:4–7). *stringed instruments.* Including harp and lyre (Ps 33:2; 92:3; 144:9).

ZEPHANIAH

Author

The prophet Zephaniah was evidently a person of considerable social standing in Judah and was probably related to the royal line. The prophecy opens with a statement of the author's ancestry (1:1), which in itself is an unusual feature of the Hebrew prophetic tradition. Zephaniah was the fourth-generation descendant of Hezekiah, a notable king of Judah from 715 to 686 B.C. Apart from this statement, nothing more is said about his background. Whereas the prophet Micah dealt carefully and sympathetically with the problems of the common people of Judah, Zephaniah's utterances show a much greater familiarity with court circles and current political issues. Zephaniah was probably familiar with the writings of such prominent eighth-century prophets as Isaiah and Amos, whose utterances he reflects, and he may also have been aware of the ministry of the young Jeremiah.

Date

According to 1:1, Zephaniah prophesied during the reign of King Josiah (640-609 B.C.), making him a contemporary of Jeremiah, Nahum and perhaps Habakkuk. His prophecy is probably to be dated relatively early in Josiah's reign, before that king's attempt at reform (and while conditions brought about by the reigns of Manasseh and Amon still prevailed) and before the Assyrian king Ashurbanipal's death in 627 (while Assyria was still powerful, though threatened).

Background

See Introductions to Jeremiah and Nahum: Background; see also 2Ki 22:1-23:30; 2Ch 34-35 and notes.

Purpose and Theme

The intent of the author was to announce to Judah God's approaching judgment. A Scythian incursion into Canaan may have provided the immediate occasion. This fierce, horse-mounted people originated in what is now southern Russia, but by the seventh century B.C. had migrated across the Caucasus and settled in and along the northern territories of the Assyrian empire. Alternately the enemies and allies of Assyria, they seem to have thrust south along the Mediterranean sometime in the 620s, destroying Ashkelon and Ashdod and halting at the Egyptian border only because of a payoff by Pharaoh Psamtik (Psammetichus). Ultimately, however, the destruction prophesied by Zephaniah came at the hands of the Babylonians after they had overpowered Assyria and brought that ancient power to its end.

Zephaniah's main theme is the coming of the day of the Lord (see notes on Isa 2:11,17,20; Joel 1:15; 2:2; Am 5:18; 8:9), when God will severely punish the nations, including apostate Judah. He portrays the stark horror of that ordeal with the same graphic imagery found elsewhere in the prophets. But he also makes it clear that God will yet be merciful toward his people; like many other prophets, he ends his pronouncements of doom on the positive note of Judah's restoration.

Outline

I. Introduction (1:1-3)
   A. Title: The Prophet Identified (1:1)
   B. Prologue: Double Announcement of Total Judgment (1:2-3)
II. The Day of the Lord Coming on Judah and the Nations (1:4-18)
   A. Judgment on the Idolaters in Judah (1:4-9)
   B. Wailing throughout Jerusalem (1:10-13)
   C. The Inescapable Day of the Lord's Wrath (1:14-18)

1 The word of the LORD that came to Zephaniah son of Cushi, the son of Gedaliah, the son of Amariah, the son of Hezekiah, during the reign of Josiah[a] son of Amon[b] king of Judah:

Warning of Coming Destruction

2 "I will sweep away everything
   from the face of the earth,"[c]
            declares the LORD.
3 "I will sweep away both men and
      animals;[d]
   I will sweep away the birds of the
      air[e]
   and the fish of the sea.
The wicked will have only heaps of
   rubble[a]
   when I cut off man from the face of
      the earth,"[f]
            declares the LORD.[g]

Against Judah

4 "I will stretch out my hand[h] against
      Judah
   and against all who live in Jerusalem.
I will cut off from this place every
   remnant of Baal,[i]
   the names of the pagan and the
      idolatrous priests[j] —
5 those who bow down on the roofs
   to worship the starry host,[k]
those who bow down and swear by the
      LORD
   and who also swear by Molech,[b][l]

6 those who turn back from following[m]
      the LORD
   and neither seek[n] the LORD nor
      inquire[o] of him.
7 Be silent[p] before the Sovereign LORD,
   for the day of the LORD[q] is near.
The LORD has prepared a sacrifice;[r]
   he has consecrated those he has
      invited.
8 On the day of the LORD's sacrifice
   I will punish[s] the princes
   and the king's sons[t]
and all those clad
   in foreign clothes.
9 On that day I will punish
   all who avoid stepping on the
      threshold,[c][u]
who fill the temple of their gods
   with violence and deceit.[v]

10 "On that day,[w]" declares the LORD,
   "a cry will go up from the Fish
      Gate,[x]
   wailing[y] from the New Quarter,
   and a loud crash from the hills.
11 Wail,[z] you who live in the market
      district[d];
   all your merchants will be wiped out,
   all who trade with[e] silver will be
      ruined.[a]
12 At that time I will search Jerusalem
   with lamps

Cross references

1:1 a2Ki 22:1; 2Ch 34:1-35:25 bS 1Ch 3:14
1:2 cS Ge 6:7
1:3 dJer 50:3 eS Jer 4:25 fver 18; S Hos 4:3 gS Eze 14:17
1:4 hS Jer 6:12 iMic 5:13; Zep 2:11 jS Jer 15:6; S Hos 10:5
1:5 kS Jer 8:2 lS Lev 18:21; Jer 5:7
1:6 mIsa 1:4; Jer 2:13 nS Isa 9:13 oS Hos 7:7
1:7 pS Isa 41:1 qver 14; Isa 13:6; S Eze 7:19; S Joel 3:14; S Am 5:18-20 rS Lev 3:9; S Jer 46:10
1:8 sIsa 24:21 tJer 39:6
1:9 uS 1Sa 5:5 vS Am 3:10
1:10 wIsa 22:5 xS 2Ch 33:14 yS Am 5:16
1:11 zJas 5:1 aHos 9:6

Notes

a3 The meaning of the Hebrew for this line is uncertain. b5 Hebrew Malcam, that is, Milcom c9 See 1 Samuel 5:5. d11 Or the Mortar e11 Or in

---

1:1 *The word of the LORD.* A common introductory phrase in the prophets (see, e.g., Jer 1:4; Hos 1:1; Mic 1:1). *Zephaniah.* Means "The LORD hides" or "The LORD protects," perhaps referring to God's protection of Zephaniah during the infamous reigns of Manasseh and Amon, the predecessors of good King Josiah. *son of . . . Hezekiah.* From the author's pedigree, scholars suggest that he was in his early 20s when he began to prophesy. He is more closely identified with the ruling class than was Isaiah, although Isaiah also moved regularly in court circles and was perhaps of noble birth.
1:2–3 *sweep away.* Zephaniah speaks of the coming catastrophe in language reminiscent of God's utterances prior to the flood (Ge 6:7). But this time it will be by God's fire (v. 18; 3:8).
1:3 *heaps of rubble.* See NIV text note. Alternatively, the sense may be that God will place formidable obstacles in the paths of the wicked and destroy them completely.
1:4–6 Seems to indicate that Zephaniah's main ministry took place before 621 B.C., since the practices condemned here were abolished in Josiah's reforms (2Ki 23:4–16). Perhaps Zephaniah's message was partly instrumental in motivating King Josiah and the people to undertake the reforms (cf. 2Ch 34:1–7).
1:4 Judah is censured for its unrepentant participation in the gross idolatry of Baal. *this place.* Jerusalem, where Zephaniah probably lived. *Baal.* See note on Jdg 2:13.
1:5 *on the roofs.* See 2Ki 23:12; Jer 19:13. *worship the starry host.* See Dt 4:15–19; 2Ki 17:16; 21:3; Isa 47:13.

swear by the LORD . . . by Molech. Syncretism (worship of one's own god along with other gods). *Molech.* Worshiped by the Ammonites, his rituals sometimes involved child sacrifice. Molech worship was forbidden to the Israelites (Lev 18:21; 20:1–5). Despite this, Solomon set up an altar to Molech on the Mount of Olives (1Ki 11:7). Manasseh established the rituals in the Valley of Ben Hinnom (2Ch 33:6; Jer 7:31; 32:35).
1:7 *Be silent before the Sovereign LORD.* See Hab 2:20. *day of the LORD.* Zephaniah's main theme (see Introduction: Purpose and Theme); not of deliverance for Judah, but of divine vengeance on the idolatrous covenant nation. *sacrifice.* The victim is Judah. *consecrated.* Since the coming slaughter of judgment is called a sacrifice, God's preparation of his guests is called his consecration of them—in preparation for their feasting on the plunder. *those . . . invited.* The pagan conquerors (mainly Babylon).
1:9 *avoid stepping on the threshold.* Perhaps referring to a pagan custom that began in the time of Samuel (see NIV text note).
1:10–13 Wailing throughout the city (contrast 3:14–17).
1:10 Merchants who had grown rich through corrupt business practices would be destroyed. *Fish Gate.* See note on Ne 3:3. *New Quarter.* See note on Ne 11:9.
1:11 *market district.* May have been an area in the Tyropoeon Valley, just south of Mount Moriah, where some foreign merchants lived (see 1Ki 20:34 and note).
1:12 *search Jerusalem with lamps.* The Babylonians later dragged people from houses, streets, sewers and tombs,

and punish those who are
    complacent, [b]
who are like wine left on its dregs, [c]
who think, 'The Lord will do nothing, [d]
    either good or bad.' [e]
[13]Their wealth will be plundered, [f]
    their houses demolished.
They will build houses
    but not live in them;
they will plant vineyards
    but not drink the wine. [g]

The Great Day of the Lord

[14]"The great day of the Lord [h] is near [i] —
    near and coming quickly.
Listen! The cry on the day of the Lord
    will be bitter,
    the shouting of the warrior there.
[15]That day will be a day of wrath,
    a day of distress and anguish,
    a day of trouble and ruin,
    a day of darkness [j] and gloom,
    a day of clouds and blackness, [k]
[16]a day of trumpet and battle cry [l]
    against the fortified cities
    and against the corner towers. [m]
[17]I will bring distress [n] on the people
    and they will walk like blind [o] men,
because they have sinned against the
    Lord.
Their blood will be poured out [p] like
    dust
    and their entrails like filth. [q]
[18]Neither their silver nor their gold
    will be able to save them
    on the day of the Lord's wrath. [r]
In the fire of his jealousy [s]
    the whole world will be consumed, [t]
for he will make a sudden end
    of all who live in the earth. [u]"

2 Gather together, [v] gather together,
  O shameful [w] nation,

[2]before the appointed time arrives
    and that day sweeps on like chaff, [x]
before the fierce anger [y] of the Lord
    comes upon you,
before the day of the Lord's wrath [z]
    comes upon you.
[3]Seek [a] the Lord, all you humble of the
    land,
you who do what he commands.
Seek righteousness, [b] seek humility; [c]
    perhaps you will be sheltered [d]
    on the day of the Lord's anger.

Against Philistia

[4]Gaza [e] will be abandoned
    and Ashkelon [f] left in ruins.
At midday Ashdod will be emptied
    and Ekron uprooted.
[5]Woe to you who live by the sea,
    O Kerethite [g] people;
the word of the Lord is against you, [h]
    O Canaan, land of the Philistines.

"I will destroy you,
    and none will be left." [i]

[6]The land by the sea, where the
    Kerethites [f] dwell,
will be a place for shepherds and
    sheep pens. [j]
[7]It will belong to the remnant [k] of the
    house of Judah;
    there they will find pasture.
In the evening they will lie down
    in the houses of Ashkelon.
The Lord their God will care for them;
    he will restore their fortunes. [g] [l]

Against Moab and Ammon

[8]"I have heard the insults [m] of Moab [n]
    and the taunts of the Ammonites, [o]

1:12 [b]Am 6:1
[c]Jer 48:11
[d]S 2Ki 21:16;
S Eze 8:12
[e]S Job 22:13
1:13
[f]S 2Ki 24:13;
Jer 15:13
[g]Dt 28:30,39;
La 5:2; S Am 5:11
1:14 [h]S ver 7;
S Joel 1:15
[i]S Eze 7:7;
S Da 7:13
1:15 [j]S 1Sa 2:9
[k]S Isa 22:5;
Joel 2:2;
Mk 13:24-25
1:16 [l]S Jer 4:19
[m]S Dt 28:52;
S Isa 2:15;
S Joel 2:1
1:17 [n]S Dt 28:52
[o]S Isa 59:10
[p]Ps 79:3
[q]S Ps 83:10
1:18
[r]S Job 20:20;
S 40:11; S Jer 4:4;
S Eze 7:19
[s]S Dt 29:20 [t]S ver
2-3; Zep 3:8
[u]S Ge 6:7;
S Eze 7:11
2:1 [v]2Ch 20:4;
Joel 1:14
[w]S Jer 3:3; 6:15

2:2 [x]Isa 17:13;
Hos 13:3
[y]S Jer 10:25;
S La 4:11
[z]S Jer 4:4;
S Eze 7:19
2:3 [a]S Am 5:6
[b]S Isa 1:17
[c]Ps 45:4 [d]Ps 57:1
2:4 [e]S Ge 10:19;
S Am 1:6,7-8;
Zec 9:5-7
[f]Jer 47:5
2:5 [g]S 1Sa 30:14
[h]S Lev 26:31;
Am 3:1
[i]S Isa 14:30
2:6 [j]S Isa 5:17
2:7 [k]S Ge 45:7
[l]S Dt 30:3;
Ps 126:4;
Jer 32:44;
S Hos 6:11;
S Joel 3:1;
Am 1:6-8
2:8 [m]S Jer 48:27
[n]S Ge 19:37;
S Isa 16:6
[o]S Eze 21:28

[f]6 The meaning of the Hebrew for this word is uncertain.
[g]7 Or will bring back their captives

where they had hidden. *The Lord will do nothing.* A typical
depiction of the arrogance of the wicked (see note on Ps
10:11).
1:13 The assets of those who have become wealthy
through dishonesty will be exposed and plundered (see Dt
28:30).
1:14–18 In a dramatic passage of great lyrical power, the
Lord describes the destruction that will sweep the earth in
the day of God's wrath.
1:15 *darkness . . . blackness.* See Am 5:18–20.
1:17 *like blind men.* See Dt 28:28–29.
1:18 *Neither . . . silver nor . . . gold will . . . save them.* In
the day of God's judgment, material wealth cannot buy
deliverance from punishment.
2:1–3 The prophet's exhortation to repent. This call to
repentance and the later indictment of Jerusalem for refusal
to repent (see 3:6–8 and note) frame the series of judgments
that illustratively detail God's acts in the coming day of the
Lord (2:4–3:5).

2:2 *like chaff.* See note on Ps 1:4.
2:3 *Seek the Lord.* Even though destruction is imminent,
there is still time to be sheltered from the calamity if only the
nation will repent. *humble.* Those who abandon the arrogance of their idolatry and wickedness and humble themselves in repentance before God.
2:4–3:8 God's coming judgment on the nations—including Jerusalem (cf. Am 1–2).
2:4 *Gaza . . . Ashkelon . . . Ashdod . . . Ekron.* See notes on
Jos 13:3; Jdg 3:3; Am 1:6,8.
2:5 *Kerethite.* See note on 1Sa 30:14. *Canaan.* See note on
Ge 10:6. *I . . . left.* The Lord's announced purpose.
2:6 The once-populous Philistine cities will revert to pastureland. *Kerethites.* See NIV text note.
2:7 The faithful remnant of Judah will occupy this land and
graze their flocks on it. *restore their fortunes.* See NIV text
note. Here and in vv. 9,11 the prophet anticipates the ultimate outcome of the day of the Lord, which he spells out
more fully in 3:9–20.

who insulted[p] my people
  and made threats against their land.[q]
[9]Therefore, as surely as I live,"
  declares the LORD Almighty, the God
    of Israel,
"surely Moab[r] will become like
    Sodom,[s]
  the Ammonites[t] like Gomorrah—
a place of weeds and salt pits,
  a wasteland forever.
The remnant of my people will
    plunder[u] them;
  the survivors[v] of my nation will
    inherit their land.[w]"

[10]This is what they will get in return for
    their pride,[x]
  for insulting[y] and mocking the
    people of the LORD Almighty.[z]
[11]The LORD will be awesome[a] to them
  when he destroys all the gods[b] of the
    land.[c]
The nations on every shore will worship
    him,[d]
  every one in its own land.

Against Cush

[12]"You too, O Cushites,[h][e]
  will be slain by my sword.[f]"

Against Assyria

[13]He will stretch out his hand against the
    north
  and destroy Assyria,[g]
leaving Nineveh[h] utterly desolate
  and dry as the desert.[i]
[14]Flocks and herds[j] will lie down there,
    creatures of every kind.
  The desert owl[k] and the screech owl[l][m]
    will roost on her columns.

Their calls will echo through the
    windows,
  rubble will be in the doorways,
    the beams of cedar will be exposed.
[15]This is the carefree[n] city
    that lived in safety.[o]
She said to herself,
  "I am, and there is none besides
    me."[p]
What a ruin she has become,
  a lair for wild beasts![q]
All who pass by her scoff[r]
  and shake their fists.[s]

The Future of Jerusalem

3 Woe to the city of oppressors,[t]
    rebellious[u] and defiled![v]
[2]She obeys[w] no one,
  she accepts no correction.[x]
She does not trust[y] in the LORD,
  she does not draw near[z] to her God.
[3]Her officials are roaring lions,[a]
  her rulers are evening wolves,[b]
  who leave nothing for the morning.[c]
[4]Her prophets are arrogant;
  they are treacherous[d] men.
Her priests profane the sanctuary
  and do violence to the law.[e]
[5]The LORD within her is righteous;[f]
  he does no wrong.[g]
Morning by morning[h] he dispenses his
    justice,
  and every new day he does not fail,[i]
  yet the unrighteous know no
    shame.[j]

[6]"I have cut off nations;

2:8 [p]Eze 25:3
  [q]S La 3:61
2:9 [r]S Dt 23:6;
  Isa 15:1-16:14;
  Jer 48:1-47;
  Eze 25:8-11
  [s]Dt 29:23;
  Isa 13:19;
  Jer 49:18
  [t]Jer 49:1-6;
  Eze 25:1-7
  [u]S Isa 11:14
  [v]S 2Ki 19:31
  [w]S Am 2:1-3
2:10 [x]S Job 40:12;
  S Isa 16:6
  [y]S Jer 48:27
  [z]S Ps 9:6
2:11 [a]S Joel 2:11
  [b]S Zep 1:4
  [c]S 1Ch 19:1;
  Eze 25:6-7
  [d]Ps 86:9;
  S Isa 12:4;
  Zep 3:9
2:12 [e]S Ge 10:6;
  S Isa 20:4
  [f]S Jer 46:10
2:13 [g]S Isa 10:5
  [h]S Ge 10:11;
  S Na 1:1
  [i]S Mic 5:6;
  Zec 10:11
2:14 [j]S Isa 5:17
  [k]S Isa 14:23
  [l]Rev 18:2
  [m]S Ps 102:6
2:15 [n]S Isa 32:9
  [o]Isa 47:8
  [p]Eze 28:2
  [q]Jer 49:33
  [r]S Isa 28:22;
  S Na 3:19
  [s]S Eze 27:36
3:1 [t]S Jer 6:6
  [u]S Dt 21:18
  [v]S Eze 23:30
3:2 [w]S Jer 22:21
  [x]S Lev 26:23;
  S Jer 7:28
  [y]S Dt 1:32
  [z]S Ps 73:28
3:3 [a]S Ps 22:13
  [b]S Ge 49:27
  [c]S Mic 3:3
3:4 [d]S Ps 25:3;
  S Isa 48:8;
  Jer 3:20; 9:4;
  Mal 2:10
  [e]S Jer 23:11;
  S Eze 22:26
3:5 [f]S Ezr 9:15 [g]Dt 32:4 [h]S Ps 5:3 [i]S La 3:23 [j]S Jer 3:3;
  S Eze 18:25

[h]12 That is, people from the upper Nile region

2:8 *Moab... Ammonites.* See notes on Ge 19:36–38; Am 1:13. For the hostility of Ammon and Moab toward Israel see Am 1:13–15; 2:1–3. They had often threatened to occupy Israelite territory (see Jdg 11:12–13; Eze 25:3–6).
2:9 *Sodom... Gomorrah.* See Ge 19. They were used in the OT to typify complete destruction at the hands of God (see Dt 29:23; Isa 13:19; Jer 49:18), and their mention added ominous overtones to the prophet's description of the day of the Lord. *weeds.* A symbol of depopulation (see Isa 7:23–25). *remnant... will inherit their land.* See note on v. 7.
2:10 *in return for their pride, for insulting and mocking.* In reprisal, the faithful remnant will occupy Ammonite and Moabite territory.
2:11 *nations... will worship him.* See 3:9 and note.
2:12 *You too.* Without elaboration, the prophet simply announces God's purpose against Egypt (see v. 5 and note). *Cushites.* See NIV text note. Egypt was ruled from 715 to 663 B.C. by a Cushite dynasty. *my sword.* Probably Babylon.
2:13 *north.* Although Nineveh was east of Judah, Assyrian armies normally invaded Canaan from the north, having first marched west along the Euphrates. *Nineveh.* See the books

of Jonah and Nahum. Since Nineveh was destroyed in 612 B.C., Zephaniah's ministry had to be before that date. *utterly desolate.* Even the site of Nineveh was later forgotten—until discovered through modern excavations.
2:15 *I am... none besides me.* See Isa 47:10. Assyria's boast belongs properly to God alone (see Isa 45:5–6,18,21). *has become.* Anticipating Nineveh's impending destruction.
3:1 *city.* Apostate Jerusalem is condemned for its sins. *oppressors.* See Jer 22:3.
3:3–4 *officials... rulers... prophets... priests.* All classes of Judah's leaders are castigated for indulging in conduct completely opposed to their vocations and responsibilities (see Jer 1:18 and note).
3:3 *roaring lions... evening wolves.* Those in power are rapacious.
3:4 *arrogant... treacherous men.* Claiming to be prophets of the Lord, they proclaimed only lies (see Jer 5:31; 14:14; 23:16,32). *priests... do violence to the law.* They should have been teachers of the law (see Dt 31:9–13; 2Ch 17:8–9; 19:8; Ezr 7:6; Jer 2:8; 18:18; Mal 2:7).
3:6–8 Jerusalem's refusal to repent (see 2:1–3 and note).
3:6 *I have cut off nations.* The destruction of other nations

their strongholds are demolished.
I have left their streets deserted,
with no one passing through.
Their cities are destroyed; *k*
no one will be left—no one at all.
7 I said to the city,
'Surely you will fear me
and accept correction!' *l*
Then her dwelling would not be cut off,
nor all my punishments come upon
her.
But they were still eager
to act corruptly *m* in all they did.
8 Therefore wait *n* for me," declares the
LORD,
"for the day I will stand up to
testify. *i*
I have decided to assemble *o* the
nations, *p*
to gather the kingdoms
and to pour out my wrath *q* on them—
all my fierce anger. *r*
The whole world will be consumed *s*
by the fire of my jealous anger.

9 "Then will I purify the lips of the
peoples,
that all of them may call *t* on the
name of the LORD *u*
and serve *v* him shoulder to shoulder.
10 From beyond the rivers of Cush *j* *w*
my worshipers, my scattered people,
will bring me offerings. *x*
11 On that day you will not be put to
shame *y*
for all the wrongs you have done to
me, *z*
because I will remove from this city
those who rejoice in their pride. *a*
Never again will you be haughty
on my holy hill. *b*

12 But I will leave within you
the meek *c* and humble,
who trust *d* in the name of the LORD.
13 The remnant *e* of Israel will do no
wrong; *f*
they will speak no lies, *g*
nor will deceit be found in their
mouths. *h*
They will eat and lie down *i*
and no one will make them afraid. *j* "

14 Sing, O Daughter of Zion; *k*
shout aloud, *l* O Israel!
Be glad and rejoice *m* with all your heart,
O Daughter of Jerusalem!
15 The LORD has taken away your
punishment,
he has turned back your enemy.
The LORD, the King of Israel, is with
you; *n*
never again will you fear *o* any
harm. *p*
16 On that day they will say to Jerusalem,
"Do not fear, O Zion;
do not let your hands hang limp. *q*
17 The LORD your God is with you,
he is mighty to save. *r*
He will take great delight *s* in you,
he will quiet you with his love, *t*
he will rejoice over you with
singing." *u*

18 "The sorrows for the appointed feasts
I will remove from you;
they are a burden and a reproach to
you. *k*
19 At that time I will deal
with all who oppressed *v* you;

3:6 *k* S Lev 26:31
3:7 *l* S Jer 7:28
m S Hos 9:9
3:8 *n* S Ps 27:14
o S Joel 3:11
p S Isa 2:3
q Ps 79:6;
Rev 16:1
r S Jer 10:25;
S La 4:11
s S Zep 1:18
3:9 *t* S Zep 2:11
u S Ge 4:26
v S Isa 19:18
3:10 *w* S Ge 10:6;
S Ps 68:31
x S 2Ch 32:23;
S Isa 60:7
3:11
y S Isa 29:22;
S Joel 2:26-27
z S Ge 50:15
a S Ps 59:12
b S Ex 15:17;
S Lev 26:19

3:12 *c* Isa 14:32
d S Jer 29:12;
Na 1:7
3:13 *e* S Isa 10:21
f Ps 119:3;
S Isa 4:3
g S Jer 33:16;
Rev 14:5
h S Job 16:17
i Eze 34:15;
Zep 2:7
j S Lev 26:6;
S Eze 34:25-28
3:14 *k* S Ps 9:14;
Zec 2:10
l S Ps 95:1;
Isa 12:6; Zec 2:10
m S Ps 9:2;
S Isa 51:11
3:15
n Eze 37:26-28
o S Isa 54:14
p Zec 9:9
3:16
q S 2Ki 19:26;
S Job 4:3;
Isa 35:3-4;
Heb 12:12
3:17 *r* S Isa 63:1;
S Joel 2:21
s S Dt 28:63;
S Isa 62:4
t S Hos 14:4
u S Isa 40:1
3:19 *v* S Isa 14:2

g 8 Septuagint and Syriac; Hebrew *will rise up to plunder*   *j* 10 That is, the upper Nile region   *k* 18 Or "I will gather you who mourn for the appointed feasts; / your reproach is a burden to you

---

was meant to serve as a warning to wanton Judah, but to no avail (see v. 7). *will be.* Or "is."
3:7 *eager to act corruptly.* See, e.g., Jer 7:13,25–26.
3:8 *wait.* A sarcastic statement to Judah to wait for the threatened catastrophe. *to testify.* To lodge accusations (see Ps 50:7)—and then proceed to execute judgments. *I have decided.* Or "For I have decided." The Lord concludes his announcement of judgment with a general declaration of his intent.
3:9–20 A three-stanza oracle (vv. 9–13, 14–17, 18–20) announcing redemption that will follow God's judgment.
3:9–13 The Lord gives assurance that the nations will be purified, the scattered remnant restored and Jerusalem purged.
3:9 God's fearful judgment of the nations will effect (or be followed by) their purification so that they will call on his name and serve him. Israel's God will be acknowledged by the nations, and God's people will be held in honor by them (cf. vv. 19–20).
3:10 *Cush.* See NIV text note; the most distant area imaginable. The most widely dispersed will be restored. *bring me offerings.* Rather than to Baal and Molech (cf. 1:4–5).

3:11 *me,/because.* In the Hebrew, this new line begins the same as the first line of v. 9. Hence it may be better to read: "me./Then." Thus vv. 9–11a constitute a three-line unit (in Hebrew) and vv. 11b,c–12 a three-line unit. The latter speaks of a purified Jerusalem. Verse 13 is a summary conclusion. *my holy hill.* Mount Zion (see Ps 2:6).
3:13 *no one will make them afraid.* Quoted verbatim from Mic 4:4.
3:14–17 Joy in the restored city (in two parts: vv. 14–15 and vv. 16–17)—the prophet's reassurance (contrast 1:10–13).
3:14 *Daughter of Zion . . . of Jerusalem.* Personification of Jerusalem and its inhabitants.
3:15 *your enemy.* All those arrayed against Israel. *The LORD, the King of Israel.* See Isa 44:6; see also Introduction to Psalms: Theology.
3:16 *do not let your hands hang limp.* Do not be discouraged.
3:18–20 Summary announcement of restoration—the Lord's final assurance.
3:18 *appointed feasts.* See Lev 23.

I will rescue the lame
  and gather those who have been
    scattered. ᵂ
I will give them praise ˣ and honor
  in every land where they were put to
    shame.
²⁰At that time I will gather you;
  at that time I will bring ʸ you home.

I will give you honor ᶻ and praise ᵃ
  among all the peoples of the earth
when I restore your fortunes¹ ᵇ
  before your very eyes,"
                                    says the LORD.

3:19
ᵂS Eze 34:16;
S Mic 4:6
ˣIsa 60:18
3:20
ʸS Jer 29:14;
S Eze 37:12

ᶻIsa 56:5; 66:22
ᵃS Dt 26:19;
S Isa 60:18
ᵇS Joel 3:1

¹20 Or *I bring back your captives*

3:20 *give you honor and praise.* See Ge 12:2–3.

HAGGAI

Author

Haggai was a prophet who, along with Zechariah, encouraged the returned exiles to rebuild the temple (see Ezr 5:1-2; 6:14). "Haggai" means "festal," which may indicate that the prophet was born during one of the three pilgrimage feasts (Unleavened Bread, Pentecost or Weeks, and Tabernacles; cf. Dt 16:16). Based on 2:3 (see note there) Haggai may have witnessed the destruction of Solomon's temple. If so, he must have been in his early 70s during his ministry.

Background

In 538 B.C. the conqueror of Babylon, Cyrus king of Persia, issued a decree allowing the Jews to return to Jerusalem and rebuild the temple (see Ezr 1:2-4; 6:3-5). Led by Zerubbabel (but see note on Ezr 1:8, "Sheshbazzar"), about 50,000 Jews journeyed home and began work on the temple. About two years later (536) they completed the foundation amid great rejoicing (Ezr 3:8-10). Their success aroused the Samaritans and other neighbors who feared the political and religious implications of a rebuilt temple in a thriving Jewish state. They therefore opposed the project vigorously and managed to halt work until Darius the Great became king of Persia in 522 B.C. (Ezr 4:1-5,24).

Darius was interested in the religions of his empire, and Haggai and Zechariah began to preach in his second year, 520 B.C. (see 1:1; Zec 1:1). The Jews were more to blame for their inactivity than their opponents, and Haggai tried to arouse them from their lethargy. When the governor of Trans-Euphrates and other officials tried to interfere with the rebuilding efforts, Darius fully supported the Jews (Ezr 5:3-6; 6:6-12). In 516 B.C. the temple was finished and dedicated (Ezr 6:15-18).

Date

The messages of Haggai were given during a four-month period in 520 B.C., the second year of King Darius. The first message was delivered on the first day of the sixth month (Aug. 29), the last on the 24th day of the ninth month (Dec. 18). See notes on 1:1; 2:1,10; see also Introduction to Zechariah: Dates.

Themes and Teaching

Next to Obadiah, Haggai is the shortest book in the OT, but its teachings are none the less significant. Haggai clearly shows the consequences of disobedience (1:6,11; 2:16-17) and obedience (2:7-9,19). When the people give priority to God and his house, they are blessed rather than cursed. Obedience brings the encouragement and strength of the Spirit of God (2:4-5).

Ch. 2 speaks of the coming of the Messiah, called the "desired of all nations" in v. 7 (but see note there). His coming would fill the rebuilt temple with glory (see 2:9 and note). The Lord made Zerubbabel his "signet ring" as a guarantee that the Messiah would come (see 2:23 and note). These passages are linked with the judgment of the nations at Christ's second coming, when the nations will be shaken and kingdoms overthrown (see 2:6-7,21-22 and notes; cf. Heb 12:25-29).

Literary Features

Like Malachi, Haggai uses a number of questions to highlight key issues (see 1:4,9; 2:3,19). He also makes effective use of repetition: "Give careful thought" occurs in 1:5,7; 2:15,18, and "I am with you" in 1:13; 2:4. "I will shake the heavens and the earth" is found in 2:6,21. The major sections of the book are marked off by the date on which the word of the Lord came "to" (or "through") Haggai (1:1; 2:1,10,20).

Several times the prophet appears to echo other Scriptures (compare 1:6 with Dt 28:38-39 and 2:17 with Dt 28:22). The threefold use of "Be strong" in 2:4 (see note there) reflects the encouragement given in Jos 1:6-7,9,18.

Outline

A Call to Build the House of the LORD

1 In the second year of King Darius,^{a} on the first day of the sixth month, the word of the LORD came through the prophet Haggai^b to Zerubbabel^c son of Shealtiel, governor^d of Judah, and to Joshua^{ae} son of Jehozadak,^{f} the high priest:^{g}

^{2}This is what the LORD Almighty^h says: "These people^i say, 'The time has not yet come for the LORD's house to be built.'^{j}'"

^{3}Then the word of the LORD came through the prophet Haggai:^{k} ^{4}"Is it a time for you yourselves to be living in your paneled houses,^{l} while this house remains a ruin?^{m}"

^{5}Now this is what the LORD Almighty says: "Give careful thought^n to your ways. ^{6}You have planted much, but have harvested little.^{o} You eat, but never have enough.^{p} You drink, but never have your fill.^{q} You put on clothes, but are not warm. You earn wages,^{r} only to put them in a purse with holes in it."

^{7}This is what the LORD Almighty says: "Give careful thought^s to your ways. ^{8}Go up into the mountains and bring down timber^t and build the house, so that I may take pleasure^u in it and be honored,^{v}" says the LORD. ^{9}"You expected much, but see, it turned out to be little.^{w} What you brought home, I blew^x away. Why?" declares the LORD Almighty. "Because of my

house, which remains a ruin,^{y} while each of you is busy with his own house. ^{10}Therefore, because of you the heavens have withheld^z their dew^a and the earth its crops.^{b} ^{11}I called for a drought^c on the fields and the mountains,^{d} on the grain, the new wine,^{e} the oil^f and whatever the ground produces, on men and cattle, and on the labor of your hands.^{g}"

^{12}Then Zerubbabel^h son of Shealtiel, Joshua son of Jehozadak, the high priest, and the whole remnant^i of the people obeyed^j the voice of the LORD their God and the message of the prophet Haggai, because the LORD their God had sent him. And the people feared^k the LORD.

^{13}Then Haggai,^{l} the LORD's messenger,^{m} gave this message of the LORD to the people: "I am with^n you," declares the LORD. ^{14}So the LORD stirred up^o the spirit of Zerubbabel^p son of Shealtiel, governor of Judah, and the spirit of Joshua son of Jehozadak,^{q} the high priest, and the spirit of the whole remnant^r of the people. They came and began to work on the house of the LORD Almighty, their God, ^{15}on the twenty-fourth day of the sixth month^s in the second year of King Darius.^{t}

1:1 ^{a}S Ezr 4:24
^{b}S Ezr 5:1
^{c}S 1Ch 3:19;
Mt 1:12-13
^{d}Ezr 5:3;
S Ne 5:14
^{e}S Ezr 2:2
^{f}S 1Ch 6:15;
S Ezr 3:2 ^{g}Zec 3:8
1:2 ^{h}Isa 13:4
^{i}S Isa 29:13
^{j}Ezr 1:2
1:3 ^{k}S Ezr 5:1
1:4 ^{l}S 2Sa 7:2
^{m}ver 9; Jer 33:12
1:5 ^{n}ver 7;
La 3:40;
Hag 2:15,18
1:6 ^{o}S Lev 26:20;
S Isa 5:10
^{p}S Isa 9:20;
S 55:2 ^{q}Am 4:8
^{r}Hag 2:16;
Zec 8:10
1:7 ^{s}S ver 5
1:8 ^{t}S 1Ch 14:1
^{u}S Job 22:3;
Ps 132:13-14
^{v}S Ex 29:43;
Jer 13:11
1:9 ^{w}S Dt 28:38;
S Isa 5:10
^{x}S Ps 103:16;
S Eze 22:21

^{y}S ver 4;
S Ne 13:11
1:10 ^{z}S Dt 28:24
^{a}S Ge 27:28;
1Ki 17:1
^{b}Lev 26:19;
Dt 28:23
1:11 ^{c}S Dt 11:26;
S 28:22; S Ru 1:1;
S 1Ki 17:1;
S Isa 5:6 ^{d}Isa 7:25
^{e}S Dt 28:51;
Ps 4:7
^{f}S Nu 18:12
^{g}Hag 2:17
1:12 ^{h}ver 1 ^{i}ver
14; S Isa 1:9;
Hag 2:2

/S Job 36:11; S Isa 50:10; Mt 28:20 ^{k}S Dt 31:12; S Isa 1:2
1:13 ^{l}ver 1 ^{m}S Nu 27:21; S 2Ch 36:15 ^{n}S Ge 26:3;
S Nu 14:9; S Mt 28:20; Ro 8:31 **1:14** ^{o}S Ezr 1:5 ^{p}S Ezr 5:2
^{q}S 1Ch 6:15 ^{r}S ver 12 **1:15** ^{s}ver 1; Hag 2:10,20 ^{t}S Ezr 4:24

^{a} 1 A variant of *Jeshua*; here and elsewhere in Haggai

1:1 *second year . . . first day . . . sixth month.* Aug. 29, 520 B.C. *King Darius.* Darius Hystaspis (or Hystaspes) ruled Persia from 522 to 486 B.C. It was he who prepared the trilingual inscription on the Behistun (Bisitun) cliff wall (located in modern Iran), through which cuneiform languages were deciphered. *first day.* The New Moon was the day on which prophets were sometimes consulted (see 2Ki 4:22–23 and note on Isa 1:14). *Zerubbabel.* See note on Ezr 1:8, "Sheshbazzar." *Shealtiel.* According to 1Ch 3:17–19 he was Zerubbabel's grandfather (in Hebrew "son" sometimes means "grandson"). *Joshua.* Mentioned with Zerubbabel also in vv. 12,14; 2:2,4. *Jehozadak.* Had been taken captive by Nebuchadnezzar (1Ch 6:15).

1:2 LORD *Almighty.* Used more than 90 times in Haggai, Zechariah and Malachi. See note on Isa 13:4. *These people.* See 2:14. Because of their sin, the nation is not called "my people" (see Isa 6:9; 8:6,11–12; Jer 14:10–11; see also note on Hos 1:9). *time has not yet come.* After the foundation of the temple had been laid in 536 B.C. (see Ezr 3:8–10), opposition hindered and then halted the work until 520 (see Ezr 4:1–5,24).

1:4 *paneled houses.* Usually connected with royal dwellings, which had cedar paneling (1Ki 7:3,7; Jer 22:14).

1:6 *planted much . . . harvested little.* A curse for disobedience (see Dt 28:38–39). Lev 26:20 also describes the unfruitfulness of a land judged by God. *drink . . . fill.* Cf. Isa 55:1–2. The people experience futility in all their activities, legitimate or illegitimate (cf. Hos 4:10–11). *purse with holes.* Famine causes prices to rise sharply.

1:8 *mountains . . . timber.* Perhaps wood from the hills around Jerusalem was to supplement the cedar wood already purchased from Lebanon (see Ezr 3:7). *take pleasure in it.* And in the sacrifices offered there (contrast Isa 1:11). *be honored.* An obedient nation would bring praise and honor to God (see Jer 13:11).

1:9 *busy with.* Lit. "running to."

1:10 *dew.* Normally abundant, and often as valuable as rain (see 2Sa 1:21; 1Ki 17:1).

1:11 *mountains.* The hills were cultivated, especially through terracing (see Ps 104:13–15; Isa 7:25; Joel 3:18). *the grain, the new wine, the oil.* The three basic crops of the land, often mentioned in a context of blessing or cursing (see Dt 7:13; 11:14; 28:51; Hos 2:8,22). Olive oil was used as food, ointment or medicine. *men and cattle.* The drought affected men and cattle and so could be said to be "on" them too.

1:12 *remnant.* See note on Isa 1:9. *feared the LORD.* Showing reverence, respect and obedience (see Dt 31:12–13; Mal 1:6; 3:5,16).

1:13 *messenger.* A title for prophets (see 2Ch 36:15; Isa 42:19 and note) or priests (see Mal 2:7). *I am with you.* A sure indication of success (see 2:4; Nu 14:9; Ge 26:3 and note).

1:14 *stirred up the spirit.* The Hebrew for this expression is translated "moved (the) heart" in Ezr 1:5, where God stirred up many of these same people to return home and rebuild the temple.

1:15 *twenty-fourth day of the sixth month.* Sept. 21, 520 B.C.

The Promised Glory of the New House

2 On the twenty-first day of the seventh month, [u] the word of the LORD came through the prophet Haggai: [v] 2"Speak to Zerubbabel [w] son of Shealtiel, governor of Judah, to Joshua son of Jehozadak, [x] the high priest, and to the remnant [y] of the people. Ask them, 3'Who of you is left who saw this house [z] in its former glory? How does it look to you now? Does it not seem to you like nothing? [a] 4But now be strong, O Zerubbabel,' declares the LORD. 'Be strong, [b] O Joshua son of Jehozadak, [c] the high priest. Be strong, all you people of the land,' declares the LORD, 'and work. For I am with [d] you,' declares the LORD Almighty. 5'This is what I covenanted [e] with you when you came out of Egypt. [f] And my Spirit [g] remains among you. Do not fear.' [h]

6"This is what the LORD Almighty says: 'In a little while [i] I will once more shake the heavens and the earth, [j] the sea and the dry land. 7I will shake all nations, and the desired [k] of all nations will come, and I will fill this house [l] with glory, [m]' says the LORD Almighty. 8'The silver is mine and

the gold [n] is mine,' declares the LORD Almighty. 9'The glory [o] of this present house [p] will be greater than the glory of the former house,' says the LORD Almighty. 'And in this place I will grant peace, [q]' declares the LORD Almighty."

Blessings for a Defiled People

10On the twenty-fourth day of the ninth month, [r] in the second year of Darius, the word of the LORD came to the prophet Haggai: 11"This is what the LORD Almighty says: 'Ask the priests [s] what the law says: 12If a person carries consecrated meat [t] in the fold of his garment, and that fold touches some bread or stew, some wine, oil or other food, does it become consecrated? [u]' "

The priests answered, "No."

13Then Haggai said, "If a person defiled by contact with a dead body touches one of these things, does it become defiled?"

"Yes," the priests replied, "it becomes defiled. [v]"

14Then Haggai said, " 'So it is with this people [w] and this nation in my sight,' de-

Cross references

2:1 [u]ver 10,20; S Lev 23:34; Jn 7:37 [v]S Ezr 5:1
2:2 [w]Hag 1:1 [x]S 1Ch 6:15 [y]S Hag 1:12
2:3 [z]S Ezr 3:12; S Isa 60:7 [a]Zec 4:10
2:4 [b]S 1Ch 28:20; Zec 8:9; S Eph 6:10 [c]S 1Ch 6:15 [d]S Ex 33:14; S Nu 14:9; S 2Sa 5:10; Ac 7:9
2:5 [e]S Ge 6:18 [f]S Ex 29:46 [g]S Ne 9:20 [h]S Ge 15:1; 1Ch 28:20; S Ezr 5:2; Zec 8:13
2:6 [i]S Isa 10:25 [j]S Ex 19:18; S Job 9:6; S Isa 14:16; S Eze 38:19; Heb 12:26*
2:7 [k]S 1Sa 9:20 [l]S Isa 60:7 [m]S Ex 16:7; S 29:43; Lk 2:32
2:8 [n]S 1Ch 29:2
2:9 [o]S Ps 85:9; S Isa 11:10 [p]S Ezr 3:12; S Isa 60:7 [q]S Lev 26:6; S Isa 60:17
2:10 [r]S ver 1; S Hag 1:15

2:11 [s]S Lev 10:10-11; Dt 17:8-11; 33:8; S Jer 18:18 2:12 [t]Jer 11:15 [u]S Ge 7:2; S Lev 6:27; Mt 23:19 2:13 [v]Lev 22:4-6; Nu 19:13 2:14 [w]S Isa 29:13

2:1 *twenty-first day of the seventh month.* Oct. 17, 520 B.C., the last day of the Feast of Tabernacles. It was a time to celebrate the summer harvest (see Lev 23:34–43), though the crops were meager (see 1:11; cf. Jn 7:37). Solomon had dedicated the temple during this feast (1Ki 8:2).

2:3 *is left.* Some of the older exiles (perhaps including Haggai himself) had seen Solomon's magnificent temple, destroyed by the Babylonians 66 years earlier. *this house in its former glory.* See vv. 7,9. Zerubbabel's temple was considered a continuation of Solomon's. *seem ... like nothing.* Cf. the reaction when the foundation of the temple was finished (Ezr 3:12).

2:4 *be strong ... work.* David used these words in 1Ch 28:20 when he encouraged Solomon to build the temple. Joshua son of Nun had been exhorted with similar words (Jos 1:6–7,9,18). *I am with you.* See 1:13 and note; 1Ch 28:20. The same God who helped Solomon will empower Zerubbabel and the people.

2:5 *my Spirit.* The Holy Spirit had rested on Moses and the 70 elders as they had led the people out of Egypt and through the desert (see Nu 11:16–17,25; Isa 63:11). See also Zec 4:6 and note. *Do not fear.* See notes on v. 4; Jos 1:18; Isa 41:10.

2:6 An announcement of the coming day of God's judgment on the nations—which the fall of Persia to Alexander the Great (333–330 B.C.) would foreshadow. Heb 12:26–27 relates this verse to the judgment of the nations at the second coming of Christ. The background for the shaking of the nations here and in vv. 21–22 is the judgment on Egypt at the Red Sea. Cf. also Isa 14:16–17.

2:7 *desired ... will come.* "Desired" can refer to individuals, as in 1Sa 9:20; Da 9:23 (where the same Hebrew verb is translated "highly esteemed"); 11:37. Thus it may have Messianic significance (cf. Mal 3:1). The same Hebrew word can also refer to articles of value, however (see 2Ch 20:25;

32:27)—such as the contribution of King Darius to the temple (Ezr 6:8). If that is the intent here, the bringing of the "riches of the nations" to Zion in Isa 60:5 is a close parallel (see note there). *fill ... with glory.* "Glory" can refer to material splendor (see Isa 60:7,13 and notes) or to the presence of God (Ex 40:34–35; 1Ki 8:10–11). The latter references connect the glory of the Lord with the cloud that filled the sanctuary. When Christ came to the earthly temple, God's presence was evident as never before (see Lk 2:27, 32).

2:8 *silver ... gold.* God provided for Solomon's temple (1Ch 29:2,7) and for Zerubbabel's (Ezr 6:5).

2:9 *glory ... greater.* Ultimately because the Messiah would be present there (see v. 7 and note). *this place.* Probably Jerusalem (see Isa 60:17 and note). *I will grant peace.* Probably an allusion to the priestly benediction (see Nu 6:26).

2:10 *twenty-fourth day ... ninth month.* Dec. 18, 520 B.C.—when winter crops were planted.

2:11 *priests.* They were consulted about the precise meaning of the law (see Jer 18:18; Mal 2:7–9).

2:12 *consecrated meat.* Meat from an animal set apart for a sacrifice. *does it become consecrated?* A question about transmitting holiness. Consecrated meat made the garment "holy" because it was in direct contact with that garment (see Lev 6:27), but the garment could not pass on that holiness to a third object. Cf. Eze 46:20.

2:13 *does it become defiled?* Ceremonial uncleanness is transmitted much more easily than holiness. Anything touched by an unclean person becomes unclean (see Nu 19:11–13,22).

2:14 *this people.* See 1:2 and note. *Whatever they do ... is defiled.* Even though the people were back in the holy land, that holiness did not make them pure. They needed to obey the Lord, particularly with regard to rebuilding the temple. See notes on vv. 12–13.

clares the LORD. 'Whatever they do and whatever they offer[x] there is defiled.

15 " 'Now give careful thought[y] to this from this day on[b]—consider how things were before one stone was laid[z] on another in the LORD's temple.[a] 16When anyone came to a heap[b] of twenty measures, there were only ten. When anyone went to a wine vat[c] to draw fifty measures, there were only twenty.[d] 17I struck all the work of your hands[e] with blight,[f] mildew and hail,[g] yet you did not turn[h] to me," declares the LORD.[i] 18'From this day on, from this twenty-fourth day of the ninth month, give careful thought[j] to the day when the foundation[k] of the LORD's temple was laid. Give careful thought: 19Is there yet any seed left in the barn? Until now, the vine and the fig tree, the pomegranate[l] and the olive tree have not borne fruit.[m]

" 'From this day on I will bless[n] you.' "

Zerubbabel the LORD's Signet Ring

20The word of the LORD came to Haggai[o] a second time on the twenty-fourth day of the month:[p] 21"Tell Zerubbabel[q] governor of Judah that I will shake[r] the heavens and the earth. 22I will overturn[s] royal thrones and shatter the power of the foreign kingdoms.[t] I will overthrow chariots[u] and their drivers; horses and their riders[v] will fall, each by the sword of his brother.[w]

23 " 'On that day,[x] declares the LORD Almighty, 'I will take you, my servant[y] Zerubbabel[z] son of Shealtiel,' declares the LORD, 'and I will make you like my signet ring,[a] for I have chosen you,' declares the LORD Almighty.' "

2:14 xS Ps 51:17;
S Isa 1:13
2:15 yS Hag 1:5
zS Ezr 3:10
aEzr 4:24
2:16 bS Ru 3:7
cS Job 24:11;
S Isa 5:2
dS Dt 28:38;
S Isa 5:10;
S Hag 1:6
2:17 eHag 1:11
fS Dt 28:22
gS Ex 9:18;
Ps 78:48
hS Isa 9:13;
S Jer 3:10
iS Am 4:6
2:18 jS Hag 1:5
kS Ezr 3:11
2:19 lS Ex 28:33
mS Joel 1:12
nS Ge 12:2;
S Lev 25:21;
Ps 128:1-6;
S Joel 2:14

2:20 oS Ezr 5:1
pS ver 1;
S Hag 1:15
2:21 qS Ezr 5:2
rS Isa 14:16;
Eze 38:19-20
2:22
sS Ge 19:25;

S Job 2:13 tS Da 2:44 uS Mic 5:10 vS Ex 15:21 wS Jdg 7:22;
S Eze 38:21 2:23 xIsa 2:11; 10:20; Zec 4:10 yS Isa 20:3;
S Da 9:24-26 zMt 1:12 aS Ge 38:18; S Ex 28:9; 2Co 1:22

b15 Or to the days past

2:15 *before one stone was laid.* Before the 24th day of the sixth month (1:15).

2:16 *heap.* Probably of grain (see Jer 50:26). *only ten ... only twenty.* The poor harvests were related to the sin of the people. See 1:11; Isa 5:10 and note. *wine vat.* A trough into which grape juice flowed. See note on Isa 16:10.

2:17 *blight, mildew.* Mentioned as a curse for disobedience in Dt 28:22. See also 1Ki 8:37; Am 4:9. The blight was probably caused by a scorching east wind (see Ge 41:6 and note). *hail.* Sent to destroy the fields and livestock of Egypt (see Ex 9:25; Ps 78:47–48). *you did not turn.* See Am 4:9.

2:18 *when the foundation ... was laid.* The same potential for blessing existed at the time when the foundation of the temple was laid in 536 B.C. (Ezr 3:11). This is a warning not to fail again.

2:19 *vine ... fig tree ... pomegranate ... olive tree.* Grapes, figs and pomegranates ripened in August and September, and olives from September to November. These harvests, like the earlier grain crops, had produced little. See 1:11 and note. *I will bless you.* Because of their response to Haggai's message, future abundance is assured. Cf. Mal 3:10.

2:20 See note on v. 10.

2:21 *shake ... the earth.* See v. 6 and note.

2:22 *overturn ... overthrow.* The Hebrew for these words is used with reference to Sodom and Gomorrah (see Ge 19:25; Am 4:11). *chariots ... horses ... riders.* Cf. the destruction of Pharaoh's army at the Red Sea (Ex 15:1,4,19, 21). *each by ... his brother.* The plight of the armies of Midian (Jdg 7:22), Gog (Eze 38:21) and the nations fighting against Jerusalem in the last days (Zec 14:13).

2:23 *On that day.* The day of the Lord. See Isa 2:11,17,20; 10:20,27; Zec 2:11 and notes. *my servant.* Applied to prophets (see Isa 20:3 and note), political leaders (Isa 22:20) and the Messiah (see Isa 41:8–9; 42:1 and notes). *signet ring.* A kind of seal that functioned as a signature (see Est 8:8) and was worn on one's finger (Est 3:10). Like other seals (cf. Ge 38:18) it could be used as a pledge or guarantee of full payment. Its mention here probably reverses the curse placed on King Jehoiachin in Jer 22:24 (cf. Jdg 17:2). Zerubbabel would then be a guarantee that someday the Messiah descended from David will come (cf. Mt 1:1,12). In 2Co 1:22 the Holy Spirit is the seal guaranteeing the believer's future inheritance (cf. Eph 1:13–14). *chosen you.* See Isa 41:8–9; 42:1 and notes.

ZECHARIAH

Background

Zechariah's prophetic ministry took place in the postexilic period, the time of the Jewish restoration from Babylonian captivity. For historical details see Introduction to Haggai: Background.

Author and Unity

Like Jeremiah (1:1) and Ezekiel (1:3), Zechariah was not only a prophet (1:1) but also a priest. He was born in Babylonia and was among those who returned to Judah in 538 B.C. under the leadership of Zerubbabel and Joshua (his grandfather Iddo is named among the returnees in Ne 12:4). At a later time, when Joiakim was high priest, Zechariah apparently succeeded Iddo (1:1,7) as head of that priestly family (Ne 12:10-16). Since the grandson succeeded the grandfather, it has been suggested that the father (Berekiah, 1:1,7) died at an early age.

Zechariah was a contemporary of Haggai (Ezr 5:1; 6:14) but continued his ministry long after him (compare 1:1 and 7:1 with Hag 1:1; see also Ne 12:1-16). His young age (see 2:4) in the early period of his ministry makes it possible that he ministered even into the reign of Artaxerxes I (465-424 B.C.).

Most likely Zechariah wrote the entire book that bears his name. Some have questioned his authorship of chs. 9-14—citing differences in style and other compositional features, and giving historical and chronological references that allegedly require a different date and author from those of chs. 1-8. All these objections, however, can be explained in other satisfactory ways, so there is no compelling reason to question the unity of the book.

Dates

The dates of Zechariah's recorded messages are best correlated with those of Haggai and with other historical events as follows:

1. Haggai's first message (Hag 1:1-11; Ezr 5:1) — Aug. 29, 520 B.C.
2. Resumption of the building of the temple (Hag 1:12-15; Ezr 5:2) — Sept. 21, 520
   (The rebuilding seems to have been hindered from 536 to c. 530 [Ezr 4:1-5], and the work ceased altogether from c. 530 to 520 [Ezr 4:24].)
3. Haggai's second message (Hag 2:1-9) — Oct. 17, 520
4. Beginning of Zechariah's preaching (1:1-6) — Oct./Nov., 520
5. Haggai's third message (Hag 2:10-19) — Dec. 18, 520
6. Haggai's fourth message (Hag 2:20-23) — Dec. 18, 520
7. Tattenai's letter to Darius concerning the rebuilding of the temple (Ezr 5:3-6:14) — 519-518
   (There must have been a lapse of time between the resumption of the building and Tattenai's appearance.)
8. Zechariah's eight night visions (1:7-6:8) — Feb. 15, 519
9. Joshua crowned (6:9-15) — Feb. 16 (?), 519
10. Repentance urged, blessings promised (chs. 7-8) — Dec. 7, 518
11. Dedication of the temple (Ezr 6:15-18) — Mar. 12, 516
12. Zechariah's final prophecy (chs. 9-14) — After 480 (?)

Occasion and Purpose

The occasion is the same as that of the book of Haggai (see Background; Dates). The chief purpose of Zechariah (and Haggai) was to rebuke the people of Judah and to encourage and motivate them to complete the rebuilding of the temple (4:8-10; Hag 1-2), though both prophets were clearly

interested in spiritual renewal as well. In addition, the purpose of the eight night visions (1:7-6:8) is explained in 1:3,5-6: The Lord said that if Judah would return to him, he would return to them. Furthermore, his word would continue to be fulfilled.

Theological Teaching

The theological teaching of the book is related to its Messianic as well as its apocalyptic and eschatological motifs. Regarding the Messianic emphasis, Zechariah foretold Christ's coming in lowliness (6:12), his humanity (6:12; 13:7), his rejection and betrayal for 30 pieces of silver (11:12-13), his crucifixion (struck by the "sword" of the Lord; 13:7), his priesthood (6:13), his kingship (6:13; 9:9; 14:9,16), his coming in glory (14:4), his building of the Lord's temple (6:12-13), his reign (9:10; 14) and his establishment of enduring peace and prosperity (3:10; 9:9-10). These Messianic passages give added significance to Jesus' words in Lk 24:25-27,44.

Concerning the apocalyptic and eschatological emphasis, Zechariah foretold the siege of Jerusalem (12:1-3; 14:1-2), the initial victory of Judah's enemies (14:2), the Lord's defense of Jerusalem (14:3-4), the judgment on the nations (12:9; 14:3), the topographical changes in Judah (14:4-5), the celebration of the Feast of Tabernacles in the Messianic kingdom age (14:16-19) and the ultimate holiness of Jerusalem and her people (14:20-21).

There is also theological significance in the prophet's name, which means "The Lord (Yahweh) remembers." "The Lord" is the personal, covenant name of God and is a perpetual testimony to his faithfulness to his promises (see note on Ex 3:14). He "remembers" his covenant promises and takes action to fulfill them. In the book of Zechariah God's promised deliverance from Babylonian exile, including a restored kingdom community and a functioning temple (the earthly throne of the divine King), leads into even grander pictures of the salvation and restoration to come through the Messiah.

Finally, the book as a whole teaches the sovereignty of God in history, over people and nations—past, present and future.

Literary Form and Themes

The book is primarily a mixture of exhortation (call to repentance, 1:2-6), prophetic visions (1:7-6:8) and judgment and salvation oracles (chs. 9-14). The prophetic visions of 1:7-6:8 are called apocalyptic (revelatory) literature, which is essentially a literature of encouragement to God's people. When the apocalyptic section is read along with the salvation (or deliverance) oracles in chs. 9-14, it becomes obvious that the dominant emphasis of the book is encouragement because of the glorious future that awaits the people of God.

In fact, encouragement is the book's central theme—primarily encouragement to complete the rebuilding of the temple. Various means are used to accomplish this end, and these function as subthemes. For example, great stress is laid on the coming of the Messiah and the overthrow of all anti-kingdom forces by him so that God's rule can be finally and fully established on earth. The then-current local scene thus becomes the basis for contemplating the universal, eschatological picture.

Outline

Part I (chs. 1-8)

B. The Rebuke by the Lord (7:4-7)
C. The Command to Repent (7:8-14)
D. The Restoration of Israel to God's Favor (8:1-17)
E. Kingdom Joy and Jewish Favor (8:18-23)

Part II (chs. 9-14)

V. Two Prophetic Oracles: The Great Messianic Future and the Full Realization of God's Kingdom (chs. 9-14)
  A. The First Oracle: The Advent and Rejection of the Messiah (chs. 9-11)
      1. The advent of the Messianic King (chs. 9-10)
      2. The rejection of the Messianic Shepherd-King (ch. 11)
  B. The Second Oracle: The Advent and Reception of the Messiah (chs. 12-14)
      1. The deliverance and conversion of Israel (chs. 12-13)
      2. The Messiah's coming and his kingdom (ch. 14)

A Call to Return to the LORD

1 In the eighth month of the second year of Darius,[a] the word of the LORD came to the prophet Zechariah[b] son of Berekiah,[c] the son of Iddo:[d]

2"The LORD was very angry[e] with your forefathers. 3Therefore tell the people: This is what the LORD Almighty says: 'Return[f] to me,' declares the LORD Almighty, 'and I will return to you,'[g] says the LORD Almighty. 4Do not be like your forefathers,[h] to whom the earlier prophets[i] proclaimed: This is what the LORD Almighty says: 'Turn from your evil ways[j] and your evil practices.' But they would not listen or pay attention to me,[k] declares the LORD.[l] 5Where are your forefathers now? And the prophets, do they live forever? 6But did not my words[m] and my decrees, which I commanded my servants the prophets, overtake your forefathers?[n]

"Then they repented and said, 'The LORD Almighty has done to us what our ways and practices deserve,[o] just as he determined to do.'"[p]

The Man Among the Myrtle Trees

7On the twenty-fourth day of the eleventh month, the month of Shebat, in the second year of Darius, the word of the LORD came to the prophet Zechariah son of Berekiah, the son of Iddo.[q]

8During the night I had a vision—and there before me was a man riding a red[r] horse! He was standing among the myrtle trees in a ravine. Behind him were red, brown and white horses.[s] 9I asked, "What are these, my lord?"

The angel[t] who was talking with me answered, "I will show you what they are."[u]

10Then the man standing among the myrtle trees explained, "They are the ones the LORD has sent to go throughout the earth."[v]

11And they reported to the angel of the LORD,[w] who was standing among the myrtle trees, "We have gone throughout the earth and found the whole world at rest and in peace."[x]

12Then the angel of the LORD said, "LORD Almighty, how long[y] will you withhold mercy[z] from Jerusalem and from the towns of Judah,[a] which you have been angry with these seventy[b] years?" 13So the LORD spoke[c] kind and comforting words[d] to the angel who talked with me.[e]

14Then the angel who was speaking to me said, "Proclaim this word: This is what the LORD Almighty says: 'I am very jealous[f] for Jerusalem and Zion, 15but I am

Cross references

1:1 ᵃS Ezr 4:24; S 6:15 ᵇS Ezr 5:1 ᶜMt 23:35; Lk 11:51 ᵈver 7; S Ne 12:4
1:2 ᵉS 2Ch 36:16
1:3 ᶠS Job 22:23 ᵍMal 3:7; Jas 4:8
1:4 ʰS 2Ch 36:15 ⁱZec 7:7 ʲS Isa 41:17:13; Ps 106:6; S 2Ch 7:14; S Jer 23:22 ᵏS 2Ch 24:19; Ps 78:8; S Jer 6:17; 17:23 ˡS Eze 20:18; S 33:4
1:6 ᵐS Isa 44:26 ⁿS Dt 28:2; S Da 9:12; S Hos 5:9 ᵒJer 12:14-17; La 2:17 ᵖJer 23:20; 39:16; S 44:17
1:7 ᵠS ver 1
1:8 ʳRev 6:4 ˢZec 6:2-7
1:9 ᵗZec 4:1,4-5; 5:5 ᵘS Da 7:16
1:10 ᵛZec 6:5-8
1:11 ʷGe 16:7 ˣS Isa 14:7
1:12 ʸS Ps 6:3 ᶻPs 40:11 ᵃS Jer 40:5 ᵇS 2Ch 36:21; S Da 9:2
1:13 ᶜS Isa 35:4 ᵈS Job 15:11 ᵉZec 4:1
1:14 ᶠS Isa 26:11; S Joel 2:18

1:1 eighth month of the second year. October-November, 520 B.C. Haggai also began his prophetic ministry in Darius's second year, on the first day of the sixth month, i.e., on Aug. 29, 520 (Hag 1:1). the word of the LORD. A technical phrase for the prophetic word of revelation (see 9:1; 12:1; Jer 1:2; Eze 1:3; Hos 1:1; Joel 1:1; Jnh 1:1; 3:1; Mic 1:1; Zep 1:1; Hag 1:1; Mal 1:1). See also note on 6:9. prophet. One called by God to be his spokesman (see note on Ex 7:1–2). Iddo. See v. 7; Ezr 5:1; 6:14; Ne 12:4,16; see also Introduction: Author.

1:2 very angry with your forefathers. The Lord was angry because of the covenant-breaking sins of the Jews' preexilic forefathers, resulting in the destruction of Jerusalem and the temple in 586 B.C., followed by exile to Babylonia. God's anger should not be explained away, for to deny that God has genuine emotions is to deprive him of one of the clear marks of personality.

1:3 Return to me . . . and I will return to you. Cf. 7:13. If the people of Zechariah's day would change their course and go in the opposite direction from that of their forefathers (v. 4), the Lord would return to them with blessing instead of with a curse (see v. 16; see also Jer 18:7–10).

1:4 earlier prophets. Such as Isaiah (see Isa 45:22), Jeremiah (see Jer 18:11) and Ezekiel (see Eze 33:11). See also 7:7,12; Jer 25:4–5; 35:15.

1:5 do they live forever? No, but God's words through them live on to be fulfilled (see v. 6).

1:6 did not my words . . . overtake your forefathers? Cf. Isa 40:6–8; 55:10–11. For the imagery of "overtake" see Dt 28:2 ("accompany" is lit. "overtake"),15,45. my servants the prophets. See 2Ki 9:7; 17:13,23; 21:10; 24:2; Ezr 9:11; Jer 7:25 and note; 25:4; Eze 38:17; Da 9:6,10; Am 3:7. they repented. Apparently a reference to what hap-

pened to some of the preexilic forefathers and/or their offspring during the exile and immediately afterward (cf. Ezr 9; 10:1–17; Da 9:1–19).

1:7–17 The first vision. Although God's covenant people are troubled while the oppressing nations are at ease, God is jealous (see note on Ex 20:5) for his people and will restore them and their towns and the temple. The imagery of the first vision is reflected in that of the eighth and final vision (6:1–8).

1:7 twenty-fourth day of . . . Shebat. Feb. 15, 519 B.C., about three months after the date of v. 1.

1:8 During the night. Zechariah had all eight visions (1:7–6:8) in one night. vision. Not a dream (see 4:1). The visions were given to Zechariah while he was fully awake. man riding. The angel of the Lord (v. 11). He must not be confused with the interpreting angel, who is mentioned in vv. 9,13–14,19; 2:3; 4:1,4–5; 5:5,10; 6:4–5. horses. Perhaps angelic messengers (v. 10).

1:11 angel of the LORD. See note on Ge 16:7. at rest. Cf. 6:8. While the Persian empire as a whole was secure and at ease by this time (v. 15), the Jews in Judah were oppressed and still under foreign domination (v. 12).

1:12 seventy years. See 7:5 and note; Jer 25:11–12 and note; 29:10; cf. 2Ch 36:21; Ezr 1:1; Da 9:2.

1:13 comforting words. Those of vv. 14–17.

1:14 jealous. See 8:2. Through the use of such language the Lord's love for Judah is shown (see note on Ex 20:5; cf. Jas 4:4). The key idea is that of God vindicating Judah for the violations against her (v. 15).

1:15 added to the calamity. God was angry with Israel and used the Assyrians (Isa 10:5) and Babylonians (Isa 47:6; Jer 25:9) to punish her, but they went too far by trying to destroy the Jews as a people.

very angry with the nations that feel secure.*g* I was only a little angry,*h* but they added to the calamity.'*i*

16"Therefore, this is what the LORD says: 'I will return*j* to Jerusalem with mercy, and there my house will be rebuilt. And the measuring line*k* will be stretched out over Jerusalem,' declares the LORD Almighty.*l*

17"Proclaim further: This is what the LORD Almighty says: 'My towns will again overflow with prosperity, and the LORD will again comfort*m* Zion and choose*n* Jerusalem.' "*o*

Four Horns and Four Craftsmen

18Then I looked up—and there before me were four horns! 19I asked the angel who was speaking to me, "What are these?"

He answered me, "These are the horns*p* that scattered Judah, Israel and Jerusalem."

20Then the LORD showed me four craftsmen. 21I asked, "What are these coming to do?"

He answered, "These are the horns that scattered Judah so that no one could raise his head, but the craftsmen have come to terrify them and throw down these horns of the nations who lifted up their horns*q* against the land of Judah to scatter its people."*r*

A Man With a Measuring Line

2 Then I looked up—and there before me was a man with a measuring line in his hand! 2I asked, "Where are you going?"

He answered me, "To measure Jerusalem, to find out how wide and how long it is."*s*

3Then the angel who was speaking to me left, and another angel came to meet him 4and said to him: "Run, tell that young man, 'Jerusalem will be a city without walls*t* because of the great number*u* of men and livestock in it.*v* 5And I myself will be a wall*w* of fire*x* around it,' declares the LORD, 'and I will be its glory*y* within.'*z a*

6"Come! Come! Flee from the land of the north," declares the LORD, "for I have scattered*b* you to the four winds of heaven,"*c* declares the LORD.*d*

7"Come, O Zion! Escape,*e* you who live in the Daughter of Babylon!"*f* 8For this is what the LORD Almighty says: "After he has honored me and has sent me against the nations that have plundered you—for whoever touches you touches the apple of his eye*g*— 9I will surely raise my hand against them so that their slaves will plunder them.*a h* Then you will know that the LORD Almighty has sent me.*i*

10"Shout*j* and be glad, O Daughter of Zion.*k* For I am coming,*l* and I will live among you,"*m* declares the LORD.*n* 11Many nations will be joined with the LORD in that day and will become my people.*o* I will live among you and you will know that the LORD Almighty has sent me to you.*p* 12The LORD will inherit*q* Judah*r* as his portion in the holy land and

---

1:15 *g*Jer 48:11
*h*S 2Ch 28:9
*i*S Ps 69:26;
123:3-4;
S Am 1:11
1:16 *j*S Job 38:5;
*k*S Isa 40:1
Zec 2:1-2
*l*S Ezr 1:1
1:17 *m*S Isa 40:1
*n*S Isa 14:1
*o*S Ezr 9:9;
S Ps 51:18;
Isa 54:8-10;
S 61:4
1:19 *p*Am 6:13
1:21
*q*S 1Ki 22:11;
Ps 75:4
*r*S Ps 75:10;
S Isa 54:16-17;
Zec 12:9

2:2 *s*S Eze 40:3;
S Zec 1:16;
Rev 21:15
2:4 *t*S Eze 38:11
*u*S Isa 49:20;
S Jer 30:19;
S 33:22
*v*Zec 14:11
2:5 *w*S Isa 26:1;
Eze 42:20
*x*S Isa 10:17
*y*S Ps 85:9;
S Isa 11:10;
S 24:23;
Rev 21:23
*z*S Ps 125:2
*a*S Ps 46:5;
S Eze 38:14
2:6 *b*S Ps 44:11
*c*S Eze 17:21;
S 37:9
*d*Mt 24:31;
Mk 13:27
2:7 *e*S Isa 42:7
*f*S Isa 48:20;
Jer 3:18
2:8 *g*S Dt 32:10
2:9 *h*S Isa 14:2;
S Jer 12:14;
S Hab 2:8
*i*S Isa 48:16;
Zec 4:9; 6:15
2:10 *j*S Zep 3:14
*k*S Isa 23:12;
S Zep 3:14
*l*Zec 9:9
*m*S Ex 25:8;
Lev 26:12;
S Nu 23:21;
Zec 8:3

*n*S Rev 21:3 **2:11** *o*S Jer 24:7; S Mic 4:2; Zec 8:8,20-22
*p*Zec 4:9; 6:15 **2:12** *q*S Ex 34:9; Ps 33:12; Jer 10:16
*r*Jer 40:5

a*8,9* Or *says after . . . eye:* *9"I . . . plunder them."*

1:16 *I will return.* See note on v. 3. *mercy.* Or "motherly compassion" (also in v. 12). *my house will be rebuilt.* See Ezr 6:14–16. *measuring line.* A symbol of restoration (cf. Jer 31:38–40).

1:17 *choose Jerusalem.* See 2:12; 3:2.

1:18–21 The second vision. The nations that devastated Israel (v. 19) will in turn be destroyed by other nations.

1:18 *four.* If the number is to be taken literally, the reference is probably to Assyria, Egypt, Babylonia and Medo-Persia. *horns.* Symbolic of strength in general (Ps 18:2), or the strength of a country, i.e., its king (Ps 89:17; Da 7:7–8; 8:20–21; Rev 17:12), or, as here (see v. 21), the power of a nation in general.

1:20 *four craftsmen.* If the number is to be understood literally, probably the reference is to Egypt, Babylonia, Persia and Greece. What is clear is that all Judah's enemies will ultimately be defeated (v. 21).

2:1–13 The third vision. There will be full restoration and blessing for the covenant people, temple and city.

2:1 *measuring line.* See note on 1:16.

2:4 *young man.* Evidently Zechariah. *without walls.* The city's population will overflow to the point that it will be as

though it had no walls (see 10:8,10; see also note on Isa 49:19–20).

2:5 *wall of fire.* Here symbolic of divine protection (see Ex 13:21 and note; Isa 4:5–6 and note). *glory.* See Ex 40:34.

2:6 *land of the north.* Babylon (v. 7) invaded Judah from the north (Jer 1:14; 4:6; 6:1,22; 10:22). *to the four winds.* In all directions. The exiles would return from north, south, east and west (Isa 43:5–6; 49:12).

2:7 *Zion.* Jerusalem's exiles in Babylon. *Escape . . . Babylon.* Cf. Rev 18:4–8.

2:8 *apple of his eye.* See note on Dt 32:10.

2:9 *hand.* Power.

2:10 See 9:9. *I will live among you.* See v. 11; 8:3; Lev 26:11–12; Eze 37:27; Jn 1:14; 2 Co 6:16; Rev 21:3.

2:11 *Many nations.* In fulfillment of the promise to Abraham (Ge 12:3; cf. Zec. 8:20–23; Ge 18:18; 22:18; Isa 2:2–4; 60:3). *that day.* The day of the Lord (see 3:10; see also note on Isa 2:11,17,20).

2:12 *holy land.* This designation occurs only here in Scripture. The land was rendered holy chiefly because it was the site of the earthly throne and sanctuary of the holy King, who dwelt there among his covenant people. See note on Ex 3:5. *choose Jerusalem.* See 1:17; 3:2.

will again choose[s] Jerusalem. [13]Be still[t] before the LORD, all mankind, because he has roused himself from his holy dwelling. [u]'"

Clean Garments for the High Priest

3 Then he showed me Joshua[b][v] the high priest standing before the angel of the LORD, and Satan[c][w] standing at his right side to accuse him. [2]The LORD said to Satan, "The LORD rebuke you,[x] Satan! The LORD, who has chosen[y] Jerusalem, rebuke you! Is not this man a burning stick[z] snatched from the fire?"[a]

[3]Now Joshua was dressed in filthy clothes as he stood before the angel. [4]The angel said to those who were standing before him, "Take off his filthy clothes."

Then he said to Joshua, "See, I have taken away your sin,[b] and I will put rich garments[c] on you."

[5]Then I said, "Put a clean turban[d] on his head." So they put a clean turban on his head and clothed him, while the angel of the LORD stood by.

[6]The angel of the LORD gave this charge to Joshua: [7]"This is what the LORD Almighty says: 'If you will walk in my ways

and keep my requirements,[e] then you will govern my house[f] and have charge[g] of my courts, and I will give you a place among these standing here. [h]

[8]" 'Listen, O high priest[i] Joshua and your associates seated before you, who are men symbolic[j] of things to come: I am going to bring my servant, the Branch.[k] [9]See, the stone I have set in front of Joshua![l] There are seven eyes[d][m] on that one stone,[n] and I will engrave an inscription on it,' says the LORD Almighty, 'and I will remove the sin[o] of this land in a single day.

[10]" 'In that day each of you will invite his neighbor to sit[p] under his vine and fig tree,[q]' declares the LORD Almighty."

The Gold Lampstand and the Two Olive Trees

4 Then the angel who talked with me returned and wakened[r] me, as a man is wakened from his sleep.[s] [2]He asked me, "What do you see?"[t]

2:12 [s]S Dt 12:5; S Isa 14:1
2:13 [t]S Ex 14:14; S Isa 41:1; [u]S Dt 26:15
3:1 [v]S Ezr 2:2; Zec 6:11; [w]S 2Sa 24:1; S 2Ch 18:21; S Ps 109:6; S Mt 4:10
3:2 [x]Jude 1:9; [y]S Isa 14:1; [z]S Isa 7:4; [a]Jude 1:23
3:4 [b]S Zec 12:13; S Eze 36:25; S Mic 7:18; [c]S Ge 41:42; S Ps 132:9; S Isa 52:1; Rev 19:8
3:5 [d]S Eze 29:6
3:7 [e]S Lev 8:35 /Dt 17:8-11; S Eze 44:15-16 [g]2Ch 23:6 [h]Jer 15:19; Zec 6:15
3:8 [i]Hag 1:1 /S Dt 28:46; S Eze 12:11 [k]S Isa 4:2; S 49:3; S Eze 17:22
3:9 [l]S Ezr 2:2 [m]S 2Ch 16:9 [n]Isa 28:16 [o]S 2Sa 12:13; S Jer 50:20
3:10 [p]S Job 11:18 [q]S Nu 16:14; S 1Ki 4:25; Mic 4:4
4:1 [r]S Da 8:18 [s]Jer 31:26 **4:2** [t]S Jer 1:13

b [1] A variant of *Jeshua*; here and elsewhere in Zechariah
c [1] *Satan* means *accuser*.   **d** [9] Or *facets*

2:13 *Be still before the LORD.* See Hab 2:20; Zep 1:7. *roused himself.* To judge (cf. v. 9).

3:1–10 The fourth vision. Israel will be cleansed and restored as a priestly nation (see Ex 19:6 and note).

3:1 *Joshua.* The same person's name is spelled "Jeshua" in Ezra and Nehemiah (see NIV text note; Ezr 2:2; Ne 7:7; see also NIV text note on Hag 1:1). Here he represents the sinful nation of Israel (see vv. 8–9). The names "Joshua" and "Jeshua" were common in ancient times. The Greek equivalent is spelled "Jesus" in English, and all three forms of the name mean "The LORD saves" (see NIV text note on Mt 1:21). *standing before.* Ministering before—as priest (see Dt 10:8; 2Ch 29:11; Eze 44:15). *angel of the LORD.* See 1:11; see also note on Ge 16:7. *Satan.* See NIV text note; cf. Job 1:6–12; 2:1–7; Rev 12:10. *right side.* See Ps 109:6. *accuse.* The Hebrew for this word has the same root as the Hebrew for "Satan."

3:2 *rebuke . . . rebuke.* Repeated for emphasis (see 4:7; see also note on Isa 40:1). *chosen Jerusalem.* See 1:17; 2:12. *burning stick snatched from the fire.* The Jews were retrieved from the fire of Babylonian exile to carry out God's future purpose for them (see Am 4:11; see also Zec 13:8–9; Dt 4:20 and note; 7:7–8; 1Ki 8:51; Isa 48:10; Jer 11:4; 30:7; Rev 12:13–16).

3:4 *those who were standing before him.* Probably angels (see also v. 7). *Take off his filthy clothes.* Thus depriving him of his priestly office. The act is here symbolic also of the removal of sin (see note on v. 9).

3:5 *Put a clean turban on his head.* Thus reinstating him into his high-priestly function so that Israel once again has a divinely authorized priestly mediator. On the front of the turban were the words: "HOLY TO THE LORD" (Ex 28:36; 39:30; cf. 14:20).

3:7 If Joshua and his priestly associates are faithful, they will be co-workers with the angels in the carrying out of God's purposes for Zion and Israel. *these standing here.* See note on v. 4.

3:8 *associates.* Fellow priests. *my servant.* See notes on Ex 14:31; Ps 18 title; Isa 41:8–9; 42:1–4; 42:1; Ro 1:1. *Branch.* A Messianic title (see 6:12; Isa 4:2 and note; 11:1; Jer 23:5; 33:15).

3:9 *stone.* Probably another figure of the Messiah (cf. Ps 118:22–23; Isa 8:13–15; 28:16 and note; Da 2:35,45; Mt 21:42; Eph 2:19–22; 1Pe 2:6–8). *seven eyes.* Perhaps symbolic of infinite intelligence (omniscience). See note on 4:10. *I will remove the sin of this land.* The symbolic act of v. 4 is now explained. "Land" stands for the people of Israel. For the cleansing spoken of here see also 12:10–13:1. *in a single day.* Ultimately Good Friday, though some believe the reference also includes Christ's second coming.

3:10 *that day.* The day of the Lord (see 2:11; see also note on Isa 2:11,17,20). *sit under his vine and fig tree.* A proverbial picture of peace, security and contentment (see 2Ki 18:31; Mic 4:4 and note).

4:1–14 The fifth vision. The Jews are encouraged to rebuild the temple by being reminded of their divine resources. The light from the lampstand in the tabernacle/temple represents the reflection of God's glory in the consecration and the holy service of God's people (see note on Ex 25:31)—made possible only by the power of God's Spirit (see v. 6; the oil, v. 12). This enabling power will equip and sustain Zerubbabel in the rebuilding of the temple (vv. 6–10). And in the performance of their offices, Zerubbabel and Joshua (as representatives of the royal and priestly mediatorial offices) will channel the Spirit's enablement to God's people (vv. 11–14).

4:1 *wakened me.* On the same night (see note on 1:8).

4:2 *What do you see?* See 5:2; see also Jer 1:11 and note. The vision here was probably of seven lamps arranged around a large bowl that served as a bountiful reservoir of oil. The "seven channels to the lights" conveyed the oil from the bowl to the lamps. But the text is also open to a different interpretation, namely, that the "channels" are "lips" or "spouts" that hold the wicks of these oil lamps, and that each

I answered, "I see a solid gold lamp-stand[u] with a bowl at the top and seven lights[v] on it, with seven channels to the lights. [3]Also there are two olive trees[w] by it, one on the right of the bowl and the other on its left."

[4]I asked the angel who talked with me, "What are these, my lord?"

[5]He answered, "Do you not know what these are?"

"No, my lord," I replied.[x]

[6]So he said to me, "This is the word of the Lord to Zerubbabel:[y] 'Not[z] by might nor by power,[a] but by my Spirit,'[b] says the Lord Almighty.

[7]"What[e] are you, O mighty mountain? Before Zerubbabel you will become level ground.[c] Then he will bring out the cap-stone[d] to shouts[e] of 'God bless it! God bless it!' "

[8]Then the word of the Lord came to me: [9]"The hands of Zerubbabel have laid the foundation[f] of this temple; his hands will also complete it.[g] Then you will know that the Lord Almighty has sent me[h] to you.

[10]"Who despises the day[i] of small things?[j] Men will rejoice when they see

4:2 uS Ex 25:31;
Rev 1:12 vRev 4:5
4:3 wver 11;
S Ps 1:3;
S Rev 11:4
4:5 xS Zec 1:9
4:6 yS 1Ch 3:19;
S Ezr 5:2
zS 1Sa 13:22;
S 1Ki 19:12
aS 1Sa 2:9
bS Ne 9:20;
Isa 11:2-4;
S Da 2:34;
Hos 1:7
4:7 cS Ps 26:12;
Jer 51:25
dS Ps 118:22
eS 1Ch 15:28
4:9 fS Ezr 3:11
gEzr 3:8; S 6:15;
Zec 6:12
4:10 iS Hag 2:23
jHag 2:3

kS Ezr 5:1;
S Ne 12:1;
S Job 38:5
lS 2Ch 16:9;
Rev 5:6
4:11 mS ver 3;
S Rev 11:4
4:14 nEx 29:7;
40:15; S Ps 45:7;
S Isa 20:3;
S Da 9:24-26
5:1 oS Ps 40:7;
S Jer 36:2;
Rev 5:1
5:2 pS Jer 1:13
5:3 qIsa 24:6;
34:2; 43:28;
Mal 3:9; 4:6

the plumb line in the hand of Zerubbabel.[k]

"(These seven are the eyes[l] of the Lord, which range throughout the earth.)"

[11]Then I asked the angel, "What are these two olive trees[m] on the right and the left of the lampstand?"

[12]Again I asked him, "What are these two olive branches beside the two gold pipes that pour out golden oil?"

[13]He replied, "Do you not know what these are?"

"No, my lord," I said.

[14]So he said, "These are the two who are anointed[n] to[f] serve the Lord of all the earth."

The Flying Scroll

5 I looked again—and there before me was a flying scroll![o]

[2]He asked me, "What do you see?"[p] I answered, "I see a flying scroll, thirty feet long and fifteen feet wide.[g]"

[3]And he said to me, "This is the curse[q] that is going out over the whole land; for

e7 Or Who   f14 Or two who bring oil and
g2 Hebrew twenty cubits long and ten cubits wide (about 9 meters long and 4.5 meters wide)

---

of these lamps had seven of them (thus a total of 49 flames). In any event, the bowl represents an abundant supply of oil, symbolizing the fullness of God's power through his Spirit, and the "seven . . . seven" represents the abundant light shining from the lamps (seven being the number of fullness or completeness).

4:3 two olive trees. Cf. Rev 11:4. The two olive trees stand for the priestly and royal offices and symbolize a continuing supply of oil. The two olive branches (v. 12) stand for Joshua the priest (ch. 3) and Zerubbabel from the royal house of David (ch. 4; cf. v. 14). These two leaders were to do God's work (e.g., on the temple and in the lives of the people) in the power of his Spirit (v. 6). The combination of the priestly and royal lines and their functions points ultimately to the Messianic King-Priest and his offices and functions (cf. 6:13).

4:4 these. The two olive trees of v. 3, as v. 11 makes clear. The answer to the question is postponed until v. 14.

4:6 Not by might nor by power. Even though Zerubbabel does not possess the royal might and power that David and Solomon had enjoyed. by my Spirit. Interprets the symbolism of the oil (v. 12). The angel encouraged Zerubbabel to complete the rebuilding of the temple (vv. 7–10) and assured him of the Spirit's enablement.

4:7 mountain . . . level ground. Faith in the power of God's Spirit can overcome mountainous obstacles. The figurative mountain probably included opposition (Ezr 4:1–5,24) and the people's unwillingness to persevere (Hag 1:14; 2:1–5). Cf. the same or similar imagery in Isa 40:4; 41:15; 49:11; Mt 17:20; 21:21; Mk 11:23; 1Co 13:2; 2Co 10:4. cap-stone. The final stone to be put in place (see Ps 118:22), marking the completion of the restoration temple by Zerubbabel (see v. 9). God bless it! God bless it! Repeated for emphasis (see 3:2; see also note on Isa 40:1).

4:8 See note on 6:9.

4:9 laid the foundation. In 537–536 b.c. (Ezr 3:8–11; 5:16). complete it. In 516 (Ezr 6:14–16).

4:10 day of small things. Some thought the work on the

temple was insignificant (Ezr 3:12; Hag 2:3), but God was in the rebuilding program and, by his Spirit (v. 6), would enable Zerubbabel to finish it. plumb line. The meaning of the Hebrew for this phrase is uncertain. If "plumb line" is correct, the text states that the people would rejoice when they saw this implement in Zerubbabel's hand to complete the task. But the Hebrew for these words may also be rendered "separated (i.e., chosen) stone," referring to the capstone of v. 7. seven . . . eyes. See note on 3:9. God oversees the whole earth and is therefore in control of the situation in Judah.

4:14 The meaning of the vision is now explained. two . . . anointed. Zerubbabel from the royal line of David and Joshua the priest. The oil (v. 12) used in anointing symbolizes the Holy Spirit (v. 6). The combination of ruler and priest points ultimately to the Messianic King-Priest (cf. 6:13; Ps 110; Heb 7). Lord of all the earth. The master of the circumstances in which Zerubbabel and the people found themselves.

5:1–4 The sixth vision. Lawbreakers are condemned by the law they have broken; sinners will be purged from the land.

5:1 flying. Unrolled and waving like a banner, for all to read. scroll. See note on Ex 17:14.

5:2 What do you see? See 4:2; see also Jer 1:11 and note. thirty . . . fifteen. Unusually large (especially in its width), for all to see. Such a bold, clear message of judgment against sin should spur the people on to repentance and righteousness.

5:3 curse. See Dt 27:26 and note. on one side . . . on the other. Like the two tablets of the law (Ex 32:15), the scroll is inscribed on both sides (cf. Eze 2:9–10; Rev 5:1). thief. He breaks the eighth commandment (Ex 20:15). everyone who swears falsely. See 8:17. Such a person violates the third commandment (compare v. 4 with Ex 20:7). Although theft and perjury may have been the most common forms of lawbreaking at the time, they are probably intended as representative sins. The people of Judah had been guilty of infrac-

according to what it says on one side, every thief^r will be banished, and according to what it says on the other, everyone who swears falsely^s will be banished. ⁴The LORD Almighty declares, 'I will send it out, and it will enter the house of the thief and the house of him who swears falsely^t by my name. It will remain in his house and destroy it, both its timbers and its stones.^u'"

The Woman in a Basket

⁵Then the angel who was speaking to me came forward and said to me, "Look up and see what this is that is appearing."

⁶I asked, "What is it?"

He replied, "It is a measuring basket.^{hv}" And he added, "This is the iniquityⁱ of the people throughout the land."

⁷Then the cover of lead was raised, and there in the basket sat a woman! ⁸He said, "This is wickedness," and he pushed her back into the basket and pushed the lead cover down over its mouth.^w

⁹Then I looked up—and there before me were two women, with the wind in their wings! They had wings like those of a stork,^x and they lifted up the basket between heaven and earth.

¹⁰"Where are they taking the basket?" I asked the angel who was speaking to me.

¹¹He replied, "To the country of Babylonia^{jy} to build a house^z for it. When it is ready, the basket will be set there in its place."^a

Four Chariots

6 I looked up again—and there before me were four chariots^b coming out from between two mountains—mountains of bronze! ²The first chariot had red horses, the second black,^c ³the third white,^d and the fourth dappled—all of them powerful. ⁴I asked the angel who was speaking to me, "What are these, my lord?"

⁵The angel answered me, "These are the four spirits^{ke} of heaven, going out from standing in the presence of the Lord of the whole world.^f ⁶The one with the black horses is going toward the north country, the one with the white horses toward the west,^l and the one with the dappled horses toward the south."

⁷When the powerful horses went out, they were straining to go throughout the earth.^g And he said, "Go throughout the earth!" So they went throughout the earth.

⁸Then he called to me, "Look, those going toward the north country have given my Spirit^m rest^h in the land of the north."ⁱ

A Crown for Joshua

⁹The word of the LORD came to me: ¹⁰"Take silver and gold from the exiles Heldai, Tobijah and Jedaiah, who have arrived from Babylon.^j Go the same day to

Cross references

5:3 ^rEx 20:15;
Mal 3:8 ^sEx 20:7;
Isa 48:1
5:4 ^tZec 8:17
^uLev 14:34-45;
S Pr 3:33;
S Hab 2:9-11;
Mal 3:5
5:6 ^vMic 6:10
5:8 ^wMic 6:11
5:9 ^xLev 11:19
5:11 ^yS Ge 10:10
^zJer 29:5,28
^aS Da 1:2

6:1 ^bver 5;
S 2Ki 2:11
6:2 ^cRev 6:5
6:3 ^dRev 6:2
6:5 ^eS Eze 37:9;
Mt 24:31;
Rev 7:1
^fS Jos 3:11
6:7 ^gIsa 43:6;
Zec 1:8
6:8 ^hS Eze 5:13;
S 24:13
ⁱS Zec 1:10
6:10
^jEzr 7:14-16;
Jer 28:6

Footnotes

^h6 Hebrew *an ephah*; also in verses 7-11   ^l6 Or *appearance*   ⁱ11 Hebrew *Shinar*   ^k5 Or *winds*   ^l6 Or *horses after them*   ^m8 Or *spirit*

Study notes

tions against the whole law (cf. Jas 2:10).

5:4 *it will enter . . . and destroy.* "It" refers to the curse (v. 3). God's word, whether promise (ch. 4) or warning (as here), always accomplishes its purpose (cf. Ps 147:15; Isa 55:10–11; Heb 4:12–13).

5:5–11 The seventh vision. Not only must flagrant, persistent sinners be removed from the land (vv. 1–4), but the whole sinful system will be removed—apparently to a more fitting place (Babylonia).

5:6 *measuring basket.* See NIV text note. A normal ephah-sized container would not be large enough to hold a person. This one was undoubtedly enlarged (like the flying scroll of vv. 1–2) for the purpose of the vision. *iniquity.* See v. 8 ("wickedness").

5:7 *woman.* Perhaps the reason the people's wickedness was personified as a woman (cf. also Rev 17:3–6) is that the Hebrew word for "wickedness" (v. 8) is feminine in gender.

5:8 *wickedness.* A general term denoting moral, religious and civil evil—frequently used as an antonym of righteousness (e.g., Pr 13:6; Eze 33:12). The whole evil system was to be destroyed (cf. 2Th 2:6–8).

5:9 *two women.* Divinely chosen agents. *wind.* Also an instrument of God (Ps 104:3–4). The removal of wickedness would be the work of God alone.

5:11 *Babylonia.* See Ge 10:10 and NIV text note; 11:2 and NIV text note; Rev 17–18. Babylonia, a land of idolatry, was an appropriate locale for wickedness—but not Israel, where God chose to dwell with his people. Only after purging it of

its evil would the promised land truly be the "holy land" (2:12).

6:1–8 The eighth and last vision. It corresponds to the first (1:7–17), though there are differences in details, such as in the order and colors of the horses. As in the first vision, the Lord is depicted as the one who controls the events of history. He will conquer the nations that oppress Israel.

6:1 *four chariots.* Angelic spirits as agents of divine judgment (v. 5). *two mountains.* Possibly Mount Zion and the Mount of Olives, with the Kidron Valley between them. *bronze.* Perhaps symbolic of judgment (cf. Nu 21:9).

6:2–3 *red . . . black . . . white . . . dappled.* The horses may signify various divine judgments on the earth (see note on v. 8). See also Rev 6:1–8 and note on Rev 6:2.

6:4 *these.* The chariots, with the horses harnessed to them.

6:5 *four spirits.* See note on v. 1. *Lord of the whole world.* See note on 4:14.

6:8 *north country.* Primarily Babylonia, but also the direction from which most of Israel's foes invaded Palestine (see note on 2:6). *my Spirit.* If the alternative translation in the NIV text note ("spirit") is taken, the meaning is that the angelic beings dispatched to the north have triumphed and thus have pacified or appeased God's spirit (i.e., his anger; cf. Ecc 10:4, where the same Hebrew word is translated "anger"). See 1:15, where God's displeasure was aroused against oppressive nations. In either case, since conquest was announced in the north, victory was assured over all enemies.

the house of Josiah son of Zephaniah. ¹¹Take the silver and gold and make a crown,ᵏ and set it on the head of the high priest, Joshuaˡ son of Jehozadak. ᵐ ¹²Tell him this is what the LORD Almighty says: 'Here is the man whose name is the Branch,ⁿ and he will branch out from his place and build the temple of the LORD. ᵒ ¹³It is he who will build the temple of the LORD, and he will be clothed with majesty and will sit and rule on his throne. And he will be a priestᵖ on his throne. And there will be harmony between the two.' ¹⁴The crown will be given to Heldai,ⁿ Tobijah, Jedaiah and Henᵒ son of Zephaniah as a memorialᑫ in the temple of the LORD. ¹⁵Those who are far away will come and help to build the temple of the LORD,ʳ and you will know that the LORD Almighty has sent me to you.ˢ This will happen if you diligently obeyᵗ the LORD your God."

Justice and Mercy, Not Fasting

7 In the fourth year of King Darius, the word of the LORD came to Zechariahᵘ on the fourth day of the ninth month, the month of Kislev.ᵛ ²The people of Bethel had sent Sharezer and Regem-Melech, together with their men, to entreatʷ the

LORDˣ ³by asking the priests of the house of the LORD Almighty and the prophets, "Should I mournʸ and fast in the fifthᶻ month, as I have done for so many years?"

⁴Then the word of the LORD Almighty came to me: ⁵"Ask all the people of the land and the priests, 'When you fastedᵃ and mourned in the fifth and seventhᵇ months for the past seventy years,ᶜ was it really for me that you fasted? ⁶And when you were eating and drinking, were you not just feasting for yourselves?ᵈ ⁷Are these not the words the LORD proclaimed through the earlier prophetsᵉ when Jerusalem and its surrounding towns were at restᶠ and prosperous, and the Negev and the western foothillsᵍ were settled?' "ʰ

⁸And the word of the LORD came again to Zechariah: ⁹"This is what the LORD Almighty says: 'Administer true justice;ᶦ show mercy and compassion to one another.ʲ ¹⁰Do not oppress the widowᵏ or the fatherless, the alienˡ or the poor. ᵐ In your hearts do not think evil of each other.'ⁿ

¹¹"But they refused to pay attention;

Cross references (center column)

6:11 ᵏPs 21:3
ˡS Ezr 2:2;
S Zec 3:1
ᵐS 1Ch 6:15;
S Ezr 3:2
6:12 ⁿS Isa 4:2;
S Eze 17:22
ᵒEzr 3:8-10;
Zec 4:6-9
6:13 ᵖS Ps 110:4
6:14 ᑫS Ex 28:12
6:15 ʳIsa 60:10
ˢZec 2:9-11
ᵗIsa 58:12;
Jer 7:23;
S Zec 3:7
7:1 ᵘS Ezr 5:1
ᵛNe 1:1
7:2 ʷJer 26:19;
Zec 8:21

ˣHag 2:10-14
7:3 ʸZec 12:12-14
ᶻ2Ki 25:9;
Jer 52:12-14
7:5 ᵃIsa 58:5
ᵇ2Ki 25:25
ᶜS Da 9:2
7:6 ᵈS Isa 43:23
7:7 ᵉIsa 1:11-20;
Zec 1:4;ᶠJer 22:21
ᵍS Jer 17:26
ʰJer 44:4-5
7:9 ᶦS Jer 22:3;
42:5; Zec 8:16
ʲS Dt 22:1
7:10 ᵏJer 49:11
ˡS Ex 22:21
ᵐS Lev 25:17;
Isa 1:23
ⁿS Ex 22:22;
S Job 35:8;
S Isa 1:17;
S Eze 45:9;
S Mic 6:8

ⁿ14 Syriac; Hebrew *Helem* ᵒ14 Or *and the gracious one, the*

6:9–15 The fourth and fifth visions were concerned with the high priest and the civil governor (in the Davidic line). Zechariah now relates the message of those two visions to the Messianic King-Priest.
6:9 Introduces a prophetic oracle (see 4:8; 7:4,8; 8:1,18; see also note on 1:1).
6:10 *silver and gold.* Gifts for the temple (cf. Ezr 6:5; Hag 2:8).
6:11 *crown.* The Hebrew for this word is not the same as that used for the high priest's turban, and is not referring to an ornate crown with many diadems (cf. Rev 19:12). The royal crowning of the high priest foreshadows the goal and consummation of prophecy—the crowning and reign of the Messianic King-Priest (see vv. 12–13; cf. Ps 110:4; Heb 7:1–3).
6:12 *Here is the man.* Cf. Pilate's introduction of Jesus in Jn 19:5. *Branch.* See note on 3:8. According to the Aramaic Targum (a paraphrase), the Jerusalem Talmud (a collection of religious instruction) and the Midrash (practical exposition), Jews regarded this verse as Messianic. *branch out.* The NIV here reflects the wordplay in the Hebrew text. *temple.* Cf. Isa 2:2–3; Eze 40–43; Hag 2:6–9.
6:13 *his throne.* See 2Sa 7:16; Isa 9:7 and note; Lk 1:32. *priest on his throne.* The coming Davidic King will also be a priest. *two.* Probably the royal and priestly offices. Such a combination was not normally possible in Israel. For this reason, the sect of Qumran (see "The Time between the Testaments," p. 1431) expected two Messianic figures—a high-priest Messiah and a Davidic one. But the two offices and functions would in fact be united in the one person of the Messiah (cf. Ps 110; Heb 7).
6:14 *Hen.* Means "gracious one" (see NIV text note), perhaps another name for Josiah—to honor him for his hospitality (v. 10).
6:15 *Those who are far away will . . . help.* Cf. Isa 60:4–7.

7:1 *fourth year . . . fourth day . . . ninth month.* Dec. 7, 518 B.C.—not quite two years after the eight night visions (see note on 1:7).
7:3 *prophets.* Including Zechariah. *I.* The people of Bethel collectively. *fast in the fifth month.* See note on 8:19. *so many years.* "The past seventy years" (v. 5).
7:4–7 A rebuke for selfish and insincere fasting on the part of the people and the priests.
7:4,8 See note on 6:9.
7:5 *fasted . . . fifth and seventh.* See note on 8:19. *seventy years.* See 1:12 and note. Since these fasts commemorated events related to the destruction of Jerusalem and the temple (see note on 8:19), the 70 years here are to be reckoned from 586 B.C. Strictly speaking, 68 years had transpired; 70 is thus a round number.
7:6 *for yourselves.* Cf. Isa 1:11–17; 58:1–7,13–14.
7:7,12 *earlier prophets.* See note on 1:4.
7:7 *Negev.* See note on Ge 12:9. *western foothills.* Sloping toward the Mediterranean.
7:9–10 Four tests of faithful covenant living, consisting of a series of social, moral and ethical commands.
7:9 *justice.* The proper ordering of all society (cf. 8:16; see Isa 42:1,4; Mic 6:8). *mercy.* Or "faithful love" (cf. Hos 10:12; 12:6). *compassion.* See note on 1:16.
7:10 *oppress.* Oppression is denounced frequently in the OT (e.g., Am 2:6–8; 4:1; 5:11–12,21–24; 8:4–6). *widow . . . fatherless . . . alien . . . poor.* For the Biblical concern for such people see, e.g., Dt 10:18; Isa 1:17 and note; Jer 5:28; Jas 1:27; 1Jn 3:16–18. In the ancient Near East, the ideal king was expected to protect the oppressed and needy members of society. *think evil of each other.* In 8:17 the almost identical Hebrew is translated "plot evil against your neighbor," which is probably the sense here as well.
7:11 *they.* The preexilic forefathers, as the reference to the "earlier prophets" in v. 12 shows. *stubbornly they turned*

stubbornly° they turned their backs° and stopped up their ears.° ¹²They made their hearts as hard as flint° and would not listen to the law or to the words that the LORD Almighty had sent by his Spirit through the earlier prophets.° So the LORD Almighty was very angry.°

¹³" 'When I called, they did not listen;° so when they called, I would not listen,'° says the LORD Almighty.° ¹⁴"I scattered° them with a whirlwind° among all the nations, where they were strangers. The land was left so desolate behind them that no one could come or go.° This is how they made the pleasant land desolate.°' "

The LORD Promises to Bless Jerusalem

8 Again the word of the LORD Almighty came to me. ²This is what the LORD Almighty says: "I am very jealous° for Zion; I am burning with jealousy for her."

³This is what the LORD says: "I will return° to Zion° and dwell in Jerusalem.° Then Jerusalem will be called the City of Truth,° and the mountain° of the LORD Almighty will be called the Holy Mountain.°"

⁴This is what the LORD Almighty says: "Once again men and women of ripe old age will sit in the streets of Jerusalem,° each with cane in hand because of his age. ⁵The city streets will be filled with boys and girls playing there.°' "

⁶This is what the LORD Almighty says:

"It may seem marvelous to the remnant of this people at that time,° but will it seem marvelous to me?°' declares the LORD Almighty.

⁷This is what the LORD Almighty says: "I will save my people from the countries of the east and the west.° ⁸I will bring them back° to live° in Jerusalem; they will be my people,° and I will be faithful and righteous to them as their God.°"

⁹This is what the LORD Almighty says: "You who now hear these words spoken by the prophets° who were there when the foundation° was laid for the house of the LORD Almighty, let your hands be strong° so that the temple may be built. ¹⁰Before that time there were no wages° for man or beast. No one could go about his business safely° because of his enemy, for I had turned every man against his neighbor. ¹¹But now I will not deal with the remnant of this people as I did in the past," ° declares the LORD Almighty.

¹²"The seed will grow well, the vine will yield its fruit,° the ground will produce its crops,° and the heavens will drop their dew.° I will give all these things as an inheritance° to the remnant of this people.° ¹³As you have been an object of cursing° among the nations, O Judah and

7:11 °S Isa 9:9; ⁿS Jer 32:33; ⁿS Jer 5:3; 8:5; 11:10; S 17:23; S Eze 5:6
7:12 ʳS Jer 5:3; 17:1; S Eze 11:19 ˢS Ne 9:29 ᵗS Jer 42:21; S Da 9:12
7:13 ᵘS Jer 7:27 ᵛIsa 1:15; S Jer 11:11; 14:12; S Mic 3:4 ʷS Pr 1:28; S La 3:44; S Eze 20:31
7:14 ˣS Lev 26:33; Dt 4:27; 28:64-67; S Ps 44:11 ʸJer 23:19 ᶻS Isa 33:8 S 44:6; ᵃS Eze 12:19
8:2 ᵇS Joel 2:18 8:3 ᶜZec 1:16 ᵈS Isa 52:8; ᵉS Zec 2:10 ᶠS Ps 15:2; S Isa 1:26; S 48:1; S Jer 33:16 ᵍS Jer 26:18 ʰS Isa 1:26; S Mic 4:1
8:4 ⁱS Isa 65:20 8:5 ʲS Jer 30:20; 31:13
8:6 ᵏPs 118:23; 126:1-3 ˡJer 32:17,27 8:7 ᵐPs 107:3; S Isa 11:11; S 43:5 8:8 ⁿS Eze 37:12; Zec 10:10 °S Jer 31:24 ᵖS Isa 51:16; S Eze 11:19-20; S 36:28; S Zec 2:11;

Heb 8:10 ᵠJer 11:4; Zec 10:6 8:9 ʳS Ezr 5:1 ˢS Ezr 3:11 ᵗS Hag 2:4 8:10 ᵘS Isa 5:10; S Hag 1:6 ᵛS 2Ch 15:5 8:11 ʷIsa 12:1 8:12 ˣS Ps 85:12; S Joel 2:22 ʸS Ps 67:6 ᶻS Ge 27:28 ᵃS Ps 65:13; S Isa 60:21; Ob 1:17 ᵇS Hos 2:21 8:13 ᶜS Nu 5:27; S Dt 13:15; S Ps 102:8; Jer 42:18

their backs. See Dt 9:6,13,27. *stopped up their ears.* See Ps 58:4; Isa 6:10 and note; cf. Isa 33:15.
7:12 *hard as flint.* See Eze 3:8-9. *words . . . sent by his Spirit.* The words of the prophets were inspired by God's Spirit (cf. Ne 9:30; 2Pe 1:21). *very angry.* See 1:2,15.
7:13 See note on 1:3.
7:14 *scattered them.* One of the curses for covenant disobedience (Dt 28:36-37,64-68; see note on Dt 28:64). *whirlwind.* See Pr 1:27; Isa 40:24; Hos 4:19. *land . . . desolate.* See Dt 28:41-42,45-52. *This is how.* By their sins. *pleasant land.* Cf. Ps 106:24; Jer 3:19.
8:1-23 Ten promises of blessing, each beginning with "This is what the LORD (Almighty) says" (vv. 2,3,4,6,7,9, 14,18,20,23).
8:1,18 See note on 6:9.
8:2 *jealous.* See 1:14; see also note on Ex 20:5.
8:3 *I will return.* See 1:3 and note; 1:16. *dwell.* See note on 2:10. *the City of Truth.* Cf. v. 16; see Isa 1:26 and note. *the Holy Mountain.* Cf. 14:20-21.
8:4-5 See Isa 11:6-9 and note; 65:20-25.
8:6,11-12 *remnant.* See notes on Isa 1:9; 10:20-22.
8:6 *will it seem marvelous to me?* See Ge 18:14 and note; Jer 32:17,27.
8:7 *save my people.* Deliver them from exile, bondage and dispersion (cf. Isa 11:11-12; 43:5-7; Jer 30:7-11; 31:7-8). *from the countries of the east and west.* Lit. "from the land of the sunrise and from the land of the going in of the sun," i.e., from everywhere—wherever the people are (cf. Ps 50:1; 113:3; Mal 1:11).

8:8 *they will be my people, and I will be . . . their God.* Covenant terminology, pertaining to intimate fellowship in a covenant relationship (see 13:9; Ge 17:7 and note; Ex 6:7; 29:45-46; Lev 11:45; 22:33; 25:38; 26:12 and note; 26:45; Nu 15:41; Dt 29:13; Jer 24:7; 31:33; 32:38; Eze 34:30-31; 36:28; 37:27; Hos 1:9-10; 2:23; 2Co 6:16; Heb 8:10; Rev 21:3). *faithful and righteous.* Judah's restoration to covenant favor and blessing rests on the faithfulness (dependability) and righteousness of God.
8:9 *prophets.* Including Haggai (1:1) and Zechariah (1:1; cf. Ezr 5:1-2). *hands be strong.* See v. 13. The Hebrew for this expression is translated "be encouraged" in Jdg 7:11.
8:10 *Before that time.* Before the temple foundation was laid (see v. 9). *no wages.* See Hag 1:6-11; 2:15-19. *enemy.* For example, the Samaritans (Ezr 4:1-5).
8:11 *But now.* The reasons for discouragement have passed; God will now provide the grounds for encouragement.
8:12 Contrast with Hag 1:10-11. In Hag 2:19 God had predicted just such a reversal as is depicted here. Fertility and bounty are part of the covenant blessings for obedience promised in Lev 26:3-10; Dt 28:11-12; cf. Eze 34:25-27.
8:13 *object of cursing among the nations.* Part of the covenant curses for disobedience threatened in Dt 28:15-68 (see Dt 28:37); cf. Jer 24:9; 25:18. *Judah and Israel.* The whole nation will experience this deliverance and blessing (cf. Jer 31:1-31; Eze 37:15-28). *blessing.* See vv. 20-23; cf. Ge 12:2. *hands be strong.* See note on v. 9.

Israel, so will I save[d] you, and you will be a blessing.[e] Do not be afraid,[f] but let your hands be strong.[g]"

[14]This is what the LORD Almighty says: "Just as I had determined to bring disaster[h] upon you and showed no pity when your fathers angered me," says the LORD Almighty, [15]"so now I have determined to do good[i] again to Jerusalem and Judah.[j] Do not be afraid. [16]These are the things you are to do: Speak the truth[k] to each other, and render true and sound judgment[l] in your courts; [m] [17]do not plot evil[n] against your neighbor, and do not love to swear falsely.[o] I hate all this," declares the LORD.

[18]Again the word of the LORD Almighty came to me. [19]This is what the LORD Almighty says: "The fasts of the fourth,[p] fifth,[q] seventh[r] and tenth[s] months will become joyful[t] and glad occasions and happy festivals for Judah. Therefore love truth[u] and peace."

[20]This is what the LORD Almighty says: "Many peoples and the inhabitants of many cities will yet come, [21]and the inhabitants of one city will go to another and say, 'Let us go at once to entreat[v] the LORD and seek[w] the LORD Almighty. I myself am going.' [22]And many peoples and powerful nations will come to Jerusalem to seek the LORD Almighty and to entreat him." [x]

[23]This is what the LORD Almighty says: "In those days ten men from all languages and nations will take firm hold of one Jew by the hem of his robe and say, 'Let us go with you, because we have heard that God is with you.' " [y]

Judgment on Israel's Enemies

An Oracle[z]

9 The word of the LORD is against the
land of Hadrach
and will rest upon Damascus[a] —
for the eyes of men and all the tribes of
Israel
are on the LORD— [p]
[2]and upon Hamath[b] too, which borders
on it,
and upon Tyre[c] and Sidon,[d] though
they are very skillful.
[3]Tyre has built herself a stronghold;
she has heaped up silver like dust,
and gold like the dirt of the streets.[e]
[4]But the Lord will take away her
possessions
and destroy[f] her power on the sea,
and she will be consumed by fire.[g]

27:32-36; 28:18

p / Or Damascus. / For the eye of the LORD is on all mankind, / as well as on the tribes of Israel,

---

Cross references column:

8:13 [d]S Ps 48:8
[e]S Ge 12:2;
S Joel 2:14
[f]S Hag 2:5 [g]ver 9
8:14
[h]S Eze 24:14
8:15 [i]ver 13;
S Jer 29:11;
Mic 7:18-20
[j]Jer 31:28; 32:42
8:16 [k]S Ps 15:2;
S Jer 33:16;
S Eph 4:25
[l]S Eze 18:8
[m]S Eze 45:9;
S Am 5:15;
S Zec 7:9
8:17 [n]Pr 3:29
[o]S Pr 6:16-19;
S Jer 7:9; Zec 5:4
8:19 [p]S 2Ki 25:7;
Jer 39:2
[q]S Jer 52:12
[r]2Ki 25:25
[s]Jer 52:4
[t]Ps 30:11 [u]ver 16
8:21 [v]S Zec 7:2
[w]Jer 26:19

8:22 [x]S Ps 86:9;
117:1; Isa 2:2-3;
S 44:5; S 45:14;
49:6; S Zec 2:11
8:23
[y]S Ps 102:22;
S Isa 14:1;
S 45:14; S 56:3;
1Co 14:25
[z]S Isa 13:1;
Jer 23:33
9:1 [a]Isa 17:1;
S Am 1:5
9:2 [b]S Jer 49:23
[c]Eze 28:1-19
[d]S Ge 10:15
9:3 [e]Job 27:16;
S Eze 28:4
9:4 [f]S Isa 23:11
[g]S Isa 23:1;
Jer 25:22;
Eze 26:3-5;

8:14–17 Verses 14–15 specify God's part in the people's restoration to favor and blessing; vv. 16–17 delineate their part.
8:14 *your fathers angered me.* See note on 1:2.
8:15 *do good.* See vv. 12–13.
8:16–17 See 7:9–10. Such moral and ethical behavior sums up the character of those who are in covenant relationship with the Lord.
8:16 *courts.* Lit. "gates" (see Ge 19:1 and note; 2Sa 18:24).
8:17 *swear falsely.* Perjure oneself (see note on 5:3). *I hate all this.* Pr 6:16–19 lists seven things the Lord hates, three of which relate directly to vv. 16–17 here: "a lying tongue," "a heart that devises wicked schemes" and "a false witness who pours out lies."
8:19 See 7:2–6. *fourth.* The fast that lamented the breaching of the walls of Jerusalem by Nebuchadnezzar (2 Ki 25:3–4; Jer 39:2; 52:6–7). *fifth.* Commemorated the burning of the temple and the other important buildings (2Ki 25:8–10; Jer 52:12–14). *seventh.* Marked the anniversary of Gedaliah's assassination (2Ki 25:22–25; Jer 41:1–3). *tenth.* Mourned the beginning of Nebuchadnezzar's siege of Jerusalem (2Ki 25:1; Jer 39:1; 52:4; Eze 24:1–2). *happy festivals.* Cf. Isa 65:18–19; Jer 31:10–14.
8:20–23 For similar predictions about Gentiles seeking the Lord see 2:11 and note; Isa 2:2–4; Mic 4:1–5.
8:22 *powerful.* Or "numerous" (as in Ex 1:9; NIV text note on Isa 53:12); anticipates a fulfillment of the promise of Gentile blessing in the Abrahamic covenant (Ge 12:3; Gal 3:8,26–29; see also Isa 55:5; 56:6–7; cf. Mk 11:17).
8:23 *ten.* One way of indicating a large or complete number in Hebrew (see Ge 31:7 and note; Lev 26:26; Nu 14:22;

1Sa 1:8; Ne 4:12). *Jew.* The word, used of the people of the kingdom of Judah after the exile, occurs first in Jer 32:12. *we have heard that God is with you.* True godliness attracts others to the Lord (see Ge 26:28; 30:27; see also notes on Ge 39:2–6; 1Co 14:24).

9:1–8 Probably a prophetic description of the Lord's march south to Jerusalem, destroying the traditional enemies of Israel. As history shows, the agent of his judgment was Alexander the Great (333 B.C.).
9:1 *An Oracle/The word of the LORD.* The Hebrew for this phrase occurs only two other times in the OT (12:1; Mal 1:1), making it likely that Zec 9–14 and Malachi were written during the same general period (see Introduction: Date). *Hadrach.* Hatarikka, north of Hamath on the Orontes River (see v. 2). *Damascus.* The leading city-state of the Arameans. *eyes . . . on the LORD.* The thought may be that the eyes of men, especially all the tribes of Israel, are turned toward the Lord (for deliverance).
9:2 *upon Hamath too.* Judgment will rest upon Hamath, just as upon Hadrach and Damascus. Hamath is modern Hama. See Am 6:2. *it.* Damascus. *Tyre and Sidon.* Phoenician (modern Lebanese) coastal cities. Their judgment (vv. 3–4) is also foretold in Isa 23; Eze 26:3–14; 28:20–24; Am 1:9–10.
9:3 *stronghold.* The Hebrew for this word is a pun on the Hebrew for "Tyre" (meaning "rock"). The stronghold was Tyre's island fortress (Isa 23:4; Eze 26:5). It fell (v. 4) to Alexander in 332 B.C. *silver like dust . . . gold like the dirt.* Cf. 1Ki 10:21,27. Tyre was a center of trade and commerce, and her wealth was proverbial (see Isa 23:2–3,8,18; Eze 26:12; 27:3–27,33; 28:4–5,7,12–14,16–18).

⁵Ashkelon ʰ will see it and fear;
  Gaza will writhe in agony,
  and Ekron too, for her hope will
    wither.
  Gaza will lose her king
  and Ashkelon will be deserted.
⁶Foreigners will occupy Ashdod,
  and I will cut off ⁱ the pride of the
    Philistines.
⁷I will take the blood from their mouths,
  the forbidden food from between
    their teeth.
  Those who are left will belong to our
    God ʲ
  and become leaders in Judah,
  and Ekron will be like the Jebusites. ᵏ
⁸But I will defend ˡ my house
  against marauding forces. ᵐ
  Never again will an oppressor overrun
    my people,
  for now I am keeping watch. ⁿ

The Coming of Zion's King

⁹Rejoice greatly, O Daughter of Zion! ᵒ
  Shout, ᵖ Daughter of Jerusalem!
  See, your king ᑫ comes to you, ᑫ
  righteous and having salvation, ʳ
  gentle and riding on a donkey, ˢ
  on a colt, the foal of a donkey. ᵗ
¹⁰I will take away the chariots from
    Ephraim
  and the war-horses from Jerusalem,

and the battle bow will be broken. ᵘ
  He will proclaim peace ᵛ to the nations.
  His rule will extend from sea to sea
  and from the River ʳ to the ends of
    the earth. ˢ ʷ
¹¹As for you, because of the blood of my
    covenant ˣ with you,
  I will free your prisoners ʸ from the
    waterless pit. ᶻ
¹²Return to your fortress, ᵃ O prisoners of
    hope;
  even now I announce that I will
    restore twice ᵇ as much to you.
¹³I will bend Judah as I bend my bow ᶜ
  and fill it with Ephraim. ᵈ
  I will rouse your sons, O Zion,
  against your sons, O Greece, ᵉ
  and make you like a warrior's
    sword. ᶠ

The LORD Will Appear

¹⁴Then the LORD will appear over them; ᵍ
  his arrow will flash like lightning. ʰ
  The Sovereign LORD will sound the
    trumpet; ⁱ
  he will march in the storms ʲ of the
    south,
¹⁵ and the LORD Almighty will shield ᵏ
    them.

9:5 ʰJer 47:5
9:6 ⁱS Isa 14:30
9:7 ʲS Job 25:2
  ᵏS Jer 47:1;
  S Joel 3:4;
  S Zep 2:4
9:8 ˡS Isa 26:1
  ᵐZec 14:21
  ⁿS Isa 52:1;
  S 54:14;
  S Joel 3:17
9:9 ᵒS Isa 62:11
  ᵖS 1Ki 1:39
  ᑫS Ps 24:7;
  S 149:2; Mic 4:8
  ʳIsa 9:6-7;
  43:3-11;
  Jer 23:5-6;
  Zep 3:14-15;
  Zec 2:10
  ˢS Ge 49:11;
  S 1Ki 1:33
  ᵗMt 21:5⁵;
  Jn 12:15⁵
9:10 ᵘHos 1:7;
  2:18; Mic 4:3;
  5:10; Zec 10:4
  ᵛS Isa 2:4
  ʷPs 72:8
9:11 ˣS Ex 24:8;
  S Mt 26:28;
  S Lk 22:20
  ʸS Isa 10:4;
  S 42:7 ᶻJer 38:6
9:12 ᵃS Joel 3:16
  ᵇS Dt 21:17;
  S Isa 40:2
9:13
  ᶜS 2Sa 22:35
  ᵈS Isa 49:2
  ᵉS Joel 3:6
  ᶠS Jer 51:20
9:14 ᵍIsa 31:5
  ʰPs 18:14;
  S Hab 3:11
  ⁱS Lev 25:9;
  S Mt 24:31
  ʲIsa 21:1; 66:15
9:15 ᵏIsa 31:5;
  37:35; Zec 12:8

ᑫ9 Or *King* ʳ10 That is, the Euphrates ˢ10 Or *the end of the land*

9:5-7 The Philistine cities were greatly alarmed at Alexander's steady advance.
9:5 *her hope will wither.* As the northernmost city of Philistia, Ekron would be the first to suffer. Her hope that Tyre would stem the tide would meet with disappointment.
9:6 *Foreigners.* People of mixed nationality; they characterized the postexilic period (Ne 13:23-24). *l.* God. *Philistines.* See note on Ge 10:14. At one time their control of Canaan was so extensive that the land was eventually named after them ("Palestine").
9:7 *blood.* Of idolatrous sacrifices. *forbidden food.* Ceremonially unclean food. *Jebusites.* These ancient inhabitants of Jerusalem (see note on Ge 10:16) were absorbed into Judah (e.g., Araunah in 2Sa 24:16-24; 1Ch 21:18-26). So would it be with a remnant of the Philistines.
9:8 *defend my house against marauding forces.* See 2:5. Alexander spared the temple and the city of Jerusalem. *oppressor.* The Hebrew for this word is translated "slave driver" in Ex 3:7; 5:6,10 and elsewhere; thus it echoes the Egyptian bondage motif. *keeping watch.* See Ex 3:7; Ps 32:8.
9:9 Quoted in the NT as Messianic and as referring ultimately to the Triumphal Entry of Jesus into Jerusalem (Mt 21:5; Jn 12:15). *Daughter of Zion.* A personification of Jerusalem and its inhabitants. *your king.* The Davidic ("your") Messianic King. *righteous.* Conforming to the divine standard of morality and ethics, particularly as revealed in the Mosaic legislation; a characteristic of the ideal king (see 2Sa 23:3-4; Ps 72:1-3; Isa 9:7; 11:4-5; 53:11; Jer 23:5-6; 33:15-16). *gentle.* Or "humble" (cf. Isa 53:2-3,7; Mt 11:29). *riding on a donkey.* A suitable choice, since the donkey was a lowly animal of peace (contrast the war-horse

of v. 10) as well as a princely mount (Jdg 10:4; 12:14; 2Sa 16:2) before the horse came into common use. The royal mount used by David and his sons was the mule (2Sa 18:9; 1Ki 1:33).
9:10 *take away the chariots . . . war-horses . . . battle bow.* A similar era of disarmament is foreseen in Isa 2:4; 9:5-7; 11:1-10; Mic 5:10-11. *Ephraim.* See note on v. 13. *peace to the nations.* In sharp contrast to Alexander's empire, which was founded on bloodshed, the Messianic King will establish a universal kingdom of peace as the ultimate fulfillment of the Abrahamic covenant (cf. 14:16; see Ge 12:3; 18:18; 22:18). *His rule will extend from . . . to.* It will be universal (see Ps 22:27-28; 72:8-11; Isa 45:22; 52:10).
9:11 *blood of my covenant with you.* Probably the Mosaic covenant (Ex 24:3-8). *prisoners.* Perhaps those still in Babylonia, the land of exile. *waterless pit.* Cf. Ge 37:24; Jer 38:6.
9:12 *fortress.* Either (1) Jerusalem (Zion) and environs or (2) God himself (cf. 2:5). *hope.* In the future delivering King (vv. 9-10). *twice as much.* Full or complete restoration (cf. Isa 61:7).
9:13 See note on 10:4. The Lord compares himself to a warrior who uses Judah as his bow and Ephraim (the northern kingdom) as his arrow. *your sons, O Zion.* The Maccabees (see note on Da 11:34). *your sons, O Greece.* The Seleucids of Syria (after the breakup of Alexander's empire).
9:14 See Ps 18:7-15; Hab 3:3-15. *trumpet.* Probably a reference to thunder (cf. Ex 19:16-19). *south.* In the region of Mount Sinai, where the Mosaic covenant was given (see v. 11) and where the Lord's dwelling was (see Jdg 5:4-5; Ps 68:8; Hab 3:3).

They will destroy
and overcome with slingstones. *l*
They will drink and roar as with wine; *m*
they will be full like a bowl *n*
used for sprinkling[t] the corners *o* of
the altar.
[16] The LORD their God will save them on
that day *p*
as the flock of his people.
They will sparkle in his land
like jewels in a crown. *q*
[17] How attractive and beautiful they will
be!
Grain will make the young men
thrive,
and new wine the young women.

The LORD Will Care for Judah

10 Ask the LORD for rain in the
springtime;
it is the LORD who makes the storm
clouds.
He gives showers of rain *r* to men,
and plants of the field *s* to everyone.
[2] The idols *t* speak deceit,
diviners *u* see visions that lie;
they tell dreams *v* that are false,
they give comfort in vain. *w*
Therefore the people wander like sheep
oppressed for lack of a shepherd. *x*

[3] "My anger burns against the shepherds,
and I will punish the leaders; *y*
for the LORD Almighty will care
for his flock, the house of Judah,
and make them like a proud horse in
battle. *z*

[4] From Judah will come the
cornerstone, *a*
from him the tent peg, *b*
from him the battle bow, *c*
from him every ruler.
[5] Together they[u] will be like mighty men
trampling the muddy streets in
battle. *d*
Because the LORD is with them,
they will fight and overthrow the
horsemen. *e*

[6] "I will strengthen *f* the house of Judah
and save the house of Joseph.
I will restore them
because I have compassion *g* on
them. *h*
They will be as though
I had not rejected them,
for I am the LORD their God
and I will answer *i* them.
[7] The Ephraimites will become like
mighty men,
and their hearts will be glad as with
wine. *j*
Their children will see it and be joyful;
their hearts will rejoice *k* in the LORD.
[8] I will signal *l* for them
and gather them in.
Surely I will redeem them;
they will be as numerous *m* as before.
[9] Though I scatter them among the
peoples,
yet in distant lands they will
remember me. *n*

Cross references (center column):

9:15 *l* Zec 14:3
m Zec 10:7
n Zec 14:20
o S Ex 27:2
9:16 *p* S Isa 10:20
q S Jer 31:11
10:1 *r* S Lev 26:4;
S 1Ki 8:36;
S Ps 104:13;
S 135:7
s S Job 14:9
10:2 *t* Eze 21:21
u S Isa 44:25
v Jer 23:16
w S Isa 40:19
x S Nu 27:17;
S Jer 23:1;
S Hos 3:4;
S Mt 9:36
10:3 *y* Isa 14:9;
S Jer 25:34
z S Eze 34:8-10

10:4 *a* S Ps 118:22;
S Ac 4:11
b S Isa 22:23
c S Zec 9:10
10:5 *d* S 2Sa 22:43;
S Mic 7:10
e S Am 2:15;
S Mic 5:8;
Hag 2:22;
Zec 12:4
10:6 *f* S Eze 30:24
g S Ps 102:13;
S Isa 14:1
h S Eze 36:37;
37:19;
S Zec 8:7-8
i Ps 34:17;
Isa 58:9; 65:24;
Zec 13:9
10:7 *j* Zec 9:15
k S Isa 2:1;
S Isa 60:5;
S Joel 2:23
10:8 *l* Isa 5:26
m S Jer 33:22;
S Eze 36:11
10:9 *n* S Isa 44:21;
S Eze 6:9

---

t 15 Or bowl, / like together. / s They u 4,5 Or ruler, all of them

---

9:15 The Apocryphal book 1 Maccabees (3:16–24; 4:6–16; 7:40–50) records a partial fulfillment of this verse. *slingstones.* Hurled at defenders on the city wall and onto the inhabitants inside. *bowl used for sprinkling.* See Ex 27:1–3; Lev 4:6–7.

9:16 *that day.* See note on 2:11.

10:1 *it is the LORD who ... gives showers ... plants.* The Lord, not the Canaanite god Baal, is the one who controls the weather and the rain, giving life and fertility to the land (see Jer 14:22; Am 5:8). Therefore God's people are to pray to and trust in him. See further Isa 55:10–12; Hos 2:8; 6:3; Joel 2:21–27; Mt 5:45.

10:2 *idols.* Household gods (see Ge 31:19 and note). They were used for divination during the period of the judges (Jdg 17:5; 18:14–20). *diviners.* Included among false prophets, they were the occult counterpart to true prophets. Cf. Jer 23:30–32; 27:9–10. Resorting to such sources for information and guidance is expressly forbidden in Dt 18:9–14 because God provided true prophets (and ultimately the Messianic Prophet) for that purpose (Dt 18:15–22; see Jn 4:25; 6:14; Ac 3:22–23,26; see also note on Ge 30:27). *people wander like sheep. lack of a shepherd.* Spiritual leadership is missing (cf. Mk 6:34). "Shepherd" is primarily a royal motif, whether referring to human kings (2Sa 5:2; Isa 44:28; Jer 23:2–4) or to God as King (Ps 23:1; 100:3; Eze 34:11–16) or to the Messianic,

Davidic King (Eze 34:23–24; Jn 10:11–16; Heb 13:20; 1Pe 5:4).

10:3 *I will punish the leaders.* Cf. Eze 34:1–10. *like a proud horse.* Triumphant.

10:4 Probably Messianic (indicated by the Aramaic Targum). *From Judah.* See Ge 49:10; Jer 30:21; Mic 5:2. *cornerstone.* See note on 3:9; see especially Isa 28:16; Eph 2:20. *tent peg.* The ruler as the support of the state (see note on Isa 22:23; see also Isa 22:24). *battle bow.* Part of the Divine Warrior terminology (cf. 9:13; Ps 7:12; 45:5; La 2:4; 3:12; Hab 3:9).

10:5 *they.* Judah (v. 4), i.e., its people. *the LORD is with them.* See Jos 1:5; Jer 1:8,19; 15:20. *overthrow.* Partly fulfilled in the Maccabean victories (during the period between the OT and the NT).

10:6 *Judah ... Joseph.* The people of the southern and northern kingdoms will be reunited (see note on 8:13).

10:7 *Ephraimites.* See note on 9:13. *glad as with wine.* Cf. Ps 104:15.

10:8 *signal.* Lit. "whistle," a continuation of the shepherd metaphor (see Jdg 5:16). *redeem.* The Hebrew for this word is often used of ransoming from slavery or captivity (see Isa 35:10; Mic 6:4; cf. 1Pe 1:18–19). *as numerous as before.* See Ex 1:6–20.

10:9 *they will remember me.* According to the meaning of Zechariah's name, "the LORD remembers" (his covenant

They and their children will survive,
 and they will return.
10I will bring them back from Egypt
 and gather them from Assyria.^o
I will bring them to Gilead^p and
 Lebanon,
 and there will not be room^q enough
 for them.
11They will pass through the sea of
 trouble;
the surging sea will be subdued
and all the depths of the Nile will dry
 up.^r
Assyria's pride^s will be brought down
 and Egypt's scepter^t will pass away.^u
12I will strengthen^v them in the LORD
 and in his name they will walk,^w"
 declares the LORD.

11 Open your doors, O Lebanon,^x
 so that fire^y may devour your
 cedars!
2Wail, O pine tree, for the cedar has
 fallen;
the stately trees are ruined!
Wail, oaks^z of Bashan;
 the dense forest^a has been cut
 down!^b
3Listen to the wail of the shepherds;
 their rich pastures are destroyed!

10:10
oS Isa 11:11;
S Zec 8:8
pS Jer 50:19
qS Isa 49:19
10:11
rIsa 19:5-7;
S 51:10 sZep 2:13
tEze 30:13
uEze 29:15
10:12
vS Eze 30:24
wS Mic 4:5
11:1 xS Eze 31:3
yS 2Ch 36:19;
Zec 12:6
11:2 zS Isa 2:13
aIsa 32:19
bS Isa 10:34

11:3 cS Isa 5:29
dJer 2:15; 50:44;
Eze 19:9
11:4 eS Jer 25:34
11:5 fJer 50:7;
S Eze 34:2-3
11:6 gZec 14:13
hIsa 9:19-21;
S Jer 13:14;
S La 2:21; 5:8;
S Mic 5:8; 7:2-6
11:7 iS Jer 25:34
11:8 jS Eze 14:5
11:9 kS Jer 43:11
lS Isa 9:20
11:10 mver 7
nS Ps 89:39;
Jer 14:21

Listen to the roar of the lions;^c
 the lush thicket of the Jordan is
 ruined!^d

Two Shepherds

4This is what the LORD my God says:
"Pasture the flock marked for slaughter.^e
5Their buyers slaughter them and go unpunished. Those who sell them say, 'Praise
the LORD, I am rich!' Their own shepherds
do not spare them.^f 6For I will no longer
have pity on the people of the land," declares the LORD. "I will hand everyone
over to his neighbor^g and his king. They
will oppress the land, and I will not rescue
them from their hands."^h

7So I pastured the flock marked for
slaughter,ⁱ particularly the oppressed of
the flock. Then I took two staffs and called
one Favor and the other Union, and I pastured the flock. 8In one month I got rid of
the three shepherds.

The flock detested^j me, and I grew
weary of them 9and said, "I will not be
your shepherd. Let the dying die, and the
perishing perish.^k Let those who are left
eat^l one another's flesh."

10Then I took my staff called Favor^m and
broke it, revokingⁿ the covenant I had

---

people and promises). Now they will remember him.
10:10 *Egypt . . . Assyria.* See v. 11. Probably representing
all the countries where the Israelites are dispersed, these two
evoke memories of slavery and exile. *gather them.* See Isa
11:11–16; Eze 39:27–29. *Gilead.* See note on Ge 31:21;
see also SS 6:5; Jer 50:19; Mic 7:14. *Lebanon.* See 2Ki
19:23; Isa 33:9 and note; 35:2 and note; Jer 22:6. *not be
room enough.* See v. 8; 2:4; see also note on Isa 49:19–20.
10:11 *pass through the sea of trouble.* As at the Red Sea
(see Ex 14:22 and note).
11:1–3 Some interpret this brief poem as a taunt song
anticipating the lament that will be sung over the destruction
of the nations' power and arrogance (ch. 10), represented by
the cedar, the pine and the oak (vv. 1–2). Their kings are
represented by the shepherds and the lions (v. 3). Understood in this way, vv. 1–3 would provide the conclusion to
the preceding section. Other interpreters, however, without
denying the presence of figurative language, see the piece
more literally as a description of the devastation of Syro-
Palestine due to the rejection of the Messianic Good Shepherd (vv. 4–14). Verses 1–3 would then furnish the introduction to the next section. The geography of the
text—Lebanon, Bashan and Jordan—would seem to favor
this interpretation. Part of the fulfillment would be the destruction and further subjugation of the area by the Romans,
including the fall of Jerusalem in A.D. 70 and of Masada in 73.
Understood in this way, the passage is in sharp contrast with
ch. 10 and its prediction of Israel's full deliverance and
restoration to the covenant land. Now the scene is one of
desolation for the land (vv. 1–3), followed by the threat of
judgment and disaster for both land and people (vv. 4–6).
11:1 *Lebanon.* See 10:10 and note.
11:2 *Bashan.* See note on Isa 2:13. The Israelites took this
region from the Amorite king, Og, at the time of the conquest
of Canaan (Nu 21:33–35). It was allotted to the half-tribe of

Manasseh (Jos 13:29–30; 17:5). *dense forest.* Of Lebanon.
11:3 If the language is figurative, the shepherds and lions
represent the rulers or leaders of the Jews (see v. 5; 10:3; cf.
Jer 25:34–36). *lush thicket of the Jordan.* Where the lions
had their lairs.
11:4–14 The reason for the judgment on Israel in vv. 1–3
is now given, namely, the people's rejection of the Messianic
Shepherd-King. Just as the Servant in the "servant songs"
(see note on Isa 42:1–4) is rejected, so here the Good
Shepherd (a royal figure) is rejected. The same Messianic
King is in view in both instances.
11:4 *says.* To Zechariah. *flock.* Israel.
11:5 *buyers.* The sheep (the Jews) are bought as slaves by
outsiders. Part of the fulfillment came in A.D. 70 and the
following years. *Those who sell them.* "Their own shepherds
(rulers or leaders)."
11:6 *land.* Palestine. *king.* Perhaps the Roman emperor (cf.
Jn 19:15). *They.* Includes the Romans prophetically.
11:7 *I.* Zechariah, as a type (foreshadowing) of the Messianic Shepherd-King. *called one Favor.* To ensure divine
favor on the flock. *Union.* See Eze 37:15–28. Such unity
would be the result of the gracious leadership of the Good
Shepherd. (For the significance of the subsequent breaking of
the two staffs see vv. 10,14.)
11:8 *got rid of the three shepherds.* Although the three
cannot be specifically identified, the Good Shepherd will
dispose of all such unfit leaders. *I grew weary of them.* Cf. Isa
1:13–14.
11:9 *Let the dying die.* The Good Shepherd terminates his
providential care of the sheep. *eat one another's flesh.* According to Josephus, this actually happened during the Roman siege of Jerusalem in A.D. 70 (cf. also La 4:10).
11:10 *covenant.* Apparently a covenant of security and
restraint, by which the Shepherd had been holding back the
nations from his people (cf. Eze 34:25; Hos 2:18). Now,

made with all the nations. 11 It was revoked
on that day, and so the afflicted of the flock
who were watching me knew it was the
word of the LORD.

12 I told them, "If you think it best, give
me my pay; but if not, keep it." So they
paid me thirty pieces of silver.[o]

13 And the LORD said to me, "Throw it to
the potter"—the handsome price at which
they priced me! So I took the thirty pieces
of silver[p] and threw them into the house
of the LORD to the potter.[q]

14 Then I broke my second staff called
Union, breaking the brotherhood between
Judah and Israel.

15 Then the LORD said to me, "Take
again the equipment of a foolish shepherd.
16 For I am going to raise up a shepherd
over the land who will not care for the
lost, or seek the young, or heal the injured,
or feed the healthy, but will eat the meat
of the choice sheep, tearing off their hoofs.

17 "Woe to the worthless shepherd,[r]
who deserts the flock!
May the sword strike his arm[s] and his
right eye!
May his arm be completely withered,
his right eye totally blinded!"[t]

11:12 [o]S Ge 23:16; Mt 26:15
11:13 [p]S Ex 21:32 [q]Mt 27:9-10*; Ac 1:18-19
11:17 [r]Jer 23:1 [s]S Eze 30:21-22 [t]S Jer 23:1

[u]S Isa 13:1
12:1 [v]S Ge 1:8; S Ps 104:2; S Jer 51:15 [w]Ps 102:25; Heb 1:10 [x]S Isa 57:16
12:2 [y]S Ps 75:8 [z]S Ps 60:3; S Isa 51:23 [a]Zec 14:14
12:3 [b]Isa 66:18; Zec 14:2 [c]S Isa 28:16; Da 2:34-35 [d]S Isa 29:8
12:4 [e]Ps 76:6; S Zec 10:5
12:5 [f]S Eze 30:24
12:6 [g]Isa 10:17-18; S Zec 11:1 [h]Ob 1:18

Jerusalem's Enemies to Be Destroyed

An Oracle[u]

12 This is the word of the LORD concerning Israel. The LORD, who
stretches out the heavens,[v] who lays the
foundation of the earth,[w] and who forms
the spirit of man[x] within him, declares:
2 "I am going to make Jerusalem a cup[y]
that sends all the surrounding peoples reeling.[z] Judah[a] will be besieged as well as
Jerusalem. 3 On that day, when all the nations[b] of the earth are gathered against
her, I will make Jerusalem an immovable
rock[c] for all the nations. All who try to
move it will injure[d] themselves. 4 On that
day I will strike every horse with panic and
its rider with madness," declares the LORD.
"I will keep a watchful eye over the house
of Judah, but I will blind all the horses of
the nations.[e] 5 Then the leaders of Judah
will say in their hearts, 'The people of
Jerusalem are strong,[f] because the LORD
Almighty is their God.'

6 "On that day I will make the leaders of
Judah like a firepot[g] in a woodpile, like a
flaming torch among sheaves. They will
consume[h] right and left all the surround-

however, the nations (e.g., the Romans) will be permitted to overrun them.

11:11 *the afflicted of the flock.* Probably the faithful few, who recognize the authoritative word of the Lord (see also v. 7, where the same Hebrew phrase is rendered "the oppressed of the flock"). *it.* Probably Israel's affliction by the nations. *word of the LORD.* The faithful discern that what happens (e.g., the judgment on Jerusalem and the temple in A.D. 70) is a fulfillment of God's prophetic word—as a result of such actions as those denounced in Mt 23, which led to the rejection of the Good Shepherd.

11:12 *give me my pay.* Refers to the severance of the relationship. *keep it.* A more emphatic way of ending the relationship. *thirty pieces of silver.* The price of a slave among the Israelites in ancient times (see note on Ex 21:32); also, a way of indicating a trifling amount.

11:13 *handsome price.* Irony and sarcasm. *threw them into the house of the LORD to the potter.* For the NT use of vv. 12–13 see Mt 26:14–15; 27:3–10; see also note on Mt 27:9.

11:14 *broke my second staff called Union.* Signifying the dissolution of the covenant nation, particularly of the unity between the south and the north. The breaking up of the nation into parties hostile to each other was characteristic of later Jewish history; it greatly hindered the popular cause in the war against Rome (cf. Jn 11:48).

11:15 *again.* See v. 7. *foolish shepherd.* With the Shepherd of the Lord's choice removed from the scene, a foolish and worthless (v. 17) shepherd replaces him. A selfish, greedy, corrupt leader will arise and afflict the flock (the people of Israel).

11:16 *seek the young.* Cf. Ge 33:13; Isa 40:11. *tearing off their hoofs.* Apparently in a greedy search for the last edible piece.

11:17 *worthless shepherd.* See note on v. 15. This counterfeit shepherd may have found a partial historical fulfillment in such leaders as Simeon bar Kosiba or Kokhba (who led the Jewish revolt against the Romans in A.D. 132–135 and who was hailed as the Messiah by Rabbi Akiba). But it would seem that the final stage of the progressive fulfillment of the complete prophecy awaits the rise of the final antichrist (cf. Eze 34:2–4; Da 11:36–39; Jn 5:43; 2Th 2:3–10; Rev 13:1–8). *deserts the flock.* Contrast the Good Shepherd of Jn 10:11–16. *May his arm be completely withered.* May his power be paralyzed. *his right eye totally blinded.* May his intelligence be nullified. Thus this leader will be powerless to fight.

12:1–14:21 This second oracle in Part II of the book revolves around two scenes: the final siege of Jerusalem, and the Messiah's return to defeat Israel's enemies and establish his kingdom.

12:1 *An Oracle.* See note on 9:1. *Israel.* The whole nation, not just the northern kingdom. Judah and Jerusalem, however, are the main focus of attention. *The LORD, who stretches . . . lays . . . forms.* This description of the Lord's creative power shows that he is able to perform what he predicts; it also strengthens the royal and sovereign authority of the message.

12:2 *cup that sends all . . . reeling.* See note on Isa 51:17.

12:3 *that day.* See note on 2:11. The phrase is used often in chs. 12–14 (12:4,6,8–9,11; 13:1–2,4; 14:4,6,8–9,13, 20–21). *all the nations . . . gathered against her.* See 14:2, 12; Joel 3:9–16; cf. Rev 16:16–21.

12:4 *panic . . . madness . . . blind.* Listed in Dt 28:28 among Israel's curses for disobeying the stipulations of the covenant. Now these curses are turned against Israel's enemies. *watchful eye.* See Ps 32:8; 33:18.

12:6 Like a fire destroying wood and sheaves of grain, Judah's discerning leaders (see v. 5) will consume their enemies (cf. Jdg 15:3–5; see note on Isa 1:31).

ing peoples, but Jerusalem will remain intact[i] in her place.

7"The LORD will save the dwellings of Judah first, so that the honor of the house of David and of Jerusalem's inhabitants may not be greater than that of Judah.[j] 8On that day the LORD will shield[k] those who live in Jerusalem, so that the feeblest[l] among them will be like David, and the house of David will be like God,[m] like the Angel of the LORD going before[n] them. 9On that day I will set out to destroy all the nations[o] that attack Jerusalem.[p]

Mourning for the One They Pierced

10"And I will pour out on the house of David and the inhabitants of Jerusalem a spirit[v][q] of grace and supplication.[r] They will look on[w] me, the one they have pierced,[s] and they will mourn for him as one mourns for an only child,[t] and grieve bitterly for him as one grieves for a firstborn son.[u] 11On that day the weeping[v] in Jerusalem will be great, like the weeping of Hadad Rimmon in the plain of Megiddo.[w] 12The land will mourn,[x] each clan by itself, with their wives by themselves: the clan of the house of David and their wives, the clan of the house of Nathan and their wives, 13the clan of the house of Levi and their wives, the clan of Shimei and their wives, 14and all the rest of the clans and their wives.[y]

Cross references (center column)

12:6 iZec 14:10
12:7 jJer 30:18;
S Am 9:11
12:8 kS Ps 91:4;
S Joel 3:16;
S Zec 9:15
lJoel 3:10
mPs 82:6
nMic 7:8
12:9 oS Isa 29:7
pS Zec 1:21;
14:2-3
12:10 qS Eze 37:9
rIsa 44:3;
S Eze 39:29;
Joel 2:28-29
sS Ps 22:16;
Jn 19:34,37*
tJdg 11:34
uS Ge 21:16;
Jer 31:19
12:11 vJer 50:4
w2Ki 23:29
12:12 xMt 24:30;
Rev 1:7
12:14 yZec 7:3
13:1 zJer 17:13
aS Lev 16:30;
S Ps 51:2;
Heb 9:14
13:2 bS Jer 43:12;
S Eze 6:6;
S 36:25;
S Hos 2:17
cS Mic 5:13
d1Ki 22:22;
Jer 23:14-15
13:3 eS Jer 28:16
fDt 13:6-11;
18:20; S Ne 6:14;
Jer 23:34;
S Eze 14:9
13:4 gS Jer 6:15
hMt 3:4
iS 1Ki 18:7;
S Isa 20:2
jS Eze 12:24
13:5 kS Am 7:14
13:7 lS Isa 34:5;
Jer 47:6
mIsa 40:11;
S 53:4; Eze 37:24

Cleansing From Sin

13 "On that day a fountain[z] will be opened to the house of David and the inhabitants of Jerusalem, to cleanse[a] them from sin and impurity.

2"On that day, I will banish the names of the idols[b] from the land, and they will be remembered no more,"[c] declares the LORD Almighty. "I will remove both the prophets[d] and the spirit of impurity from the land. 3And if anyone still prophesies, his father and mother, to whom he was born, will say to him, 'You must die, because you have told lies[e] in the LORD's name.' When he prophesies, his own parents will stab him.[f]

4"On that day every prophet will be ashamed[g] of his prophetic vision. He will not put on a prophet's garment[h] of hair[i] in order to deceive.[j] 5He will say, 'I am not a prophet. I am a farmer; the land has been my livelihood since my youth.[x][k] 6If someone asks him, 'What are these wounds on your body[y]?' he will answer, 'The wounds I was given at the house of my friends.'

The Shepherd Struck, the Sheep Scattered

7"Awake, O sword,[l] against my shepherd,[m]

v10 Or the Spirit   w10 Or to   x5 Or farmer; a man sold me in my youth   y6 Or wounds between your hands

---

12:8 like David. Like a great warrior. like God. Cf. Ex 4:16; 7:1. like the Angel of the LORD. See Ge 48:16 and note; Ex 14:19; 23:20; 32:34; 33:2,14–15,22; Hos 12:3–4; see also Ge 16:7 and note.
12:10 a spirit. See NIV text note; see also Isa 32:15 and note; 44:3; 59:20–21; Jer 31:31,33; Eze 36:26–27; 39:29; Joel 2:28–29. look on. See NIV text note. The emphasis seems to be on looking "to" the Messiah in faith (cf. Nu 21:9; Isa 45:22; Jn 3:14–15). pierced. Cf. Ps 22:16; Isa 53:5; Jn 19:34; partly fulfilled in Jn 19:37. mourns for an only child. Cf. Jer 6:26. grieves for a firstborn son. Cf. Ex 11:5–6.
12:11 Hadad Rimmon. The name of either (1) a place near Megiddo, where the people mourned the death of King Josiah (2Ch 35:20–27; see v. 22 there for the plain of Megiddo and vv. 24–25 for the mourning), or (2) a Semitic storm god (see 2Ki 5:18), whose name means "Hadad the thunderer" in Babylonian (as in the Epic of Gilgamesh, 11:98; see also Eze 8:14 for an example of the practice of weeping for a Babylonian deity).
12:12 Nathan. David's son (2Sa 5:14; cf. Lk 3:31).
12:13 Shimei. Son of Gershon, the son of Levi (Nu 3:17–18,21). The repentance and mourning are led, then, by the civil (royal) and religious leaders.
13:1 cleanse them from sin. See 3:4–9; one of the provisions of the new covenant (Jer 31:34; Eze 36:25).
13:2 names of the idols. The influence and fame, and even the very existence, of the idols. prophets. False prophecy was still a problem in the postexilic period (see Ne 6:12–14)

and would again be a problem in the future (see Mt 24:4–5, 11,23–24; 2Th 2:2–4).
13:3 lies. False prophecies. parents will stab him. In obedience to Dt 13:6–9. The Hebrew for "stab" is the same as the verb for "pierced" in 12:10, perhaps indicating that the feelings and actions exhibited in piercing the Messiah will now be directed toward the false prophets.
13:4–6 Because of the stern measures just mentioned, a false prophet will be reluctant to identify himself as such and will be evasive in his responses to interrogation. To help conceal his true identity, he will not wear a "prophet's garment of hair" (v. 4), such as Elijah wore (2Ki 1:8; see also Mt 3:4). Instead, to avoid the death penalty (v. 3), he will deny being a prophet and will claim to have been a farmer since his youth (v. 5). And if a suspicious person notices marks on his body and inquires about them (v. 6), he will claim he received them in a scuffle with friends (or perhaps as discipline from his parents during childhood). Apparently the accuser suspects that the false prophet's wounds were self-inflicted to arouse his prophetic ecstasy in idolatrous rites (as in 1Ki 18:28; cf. also Lev 19:28; 21:5 and note; Dt 14:1; Jer 16:6; 41:5; 48:37).
13:5 the land . . . my youth. If the alternative translation in the NIV text note is taken, the meaning is that someone sold him as a slave while still young.
13:6 Some take this verse as Messianic, but the interpretation given above seems preferable from the context (e.g., v. 5).
13:7 my shepherd. The royal (Messianic) Good Shepherd

against the man who is close to me!"
declares the LORD Almighty.

"Strike the shepherd,
    and the sheep will be scattered, ^{n}
    and I will turn my hand against the
        little ones.
^{8}In the whole land," declares the LORD,
    "two-thirds will be struck down and
        perish;
    yet one-third will be left in it. ^{o}
^{9}This third I will bring into the fire; ^{p}
    I will refine them like silver ^{q}
    and test them like gold. ^{r}
They will call^s on my name^t
    and I will answer^u them;
I will say, 'They are my people,' ^{v}
    and they will say, 'The LORD is our
        God. ^{w} ' "

The LORD Comes and Reigns

14 A day of the LORD^x is coming
        when your plunder^y will be di-
vided among you.

^{2}I will gather all the nations^z to Jerusalem to fight against it; ^{a} the city will be
captured, the houses ransacked, and the
women raped. ^{b} Half of the city will go into
exile, but the rest of the people will not be
taken from the city. ^{c}

^{3}Then the LORD will go out and fight^d
against those nations, as he fights in the
day of battle. ^{e} ^{4}On that day his feet will
stand on the Mount of Olives,^{f} east of
Jerusalem, and the Mount of Olives will be
split^g in two from east to west, forming a

great valley, with half of the mountain
moving north and half moving south. ^{5}You
will flee by my mountain valley, for it will
extend to Azel. You will flee as you fled
from the earthquake$^{z\,h}$ in the days of Uzziah king of Judah. Then the LORD my God
will come, ^{i} and all the holy ones with
him. ^{j}

^{6}On that day there will be no light, ^{k} no
cold or frost. ^{7}It will be a unique^l day,
without daytime or nighttime^m—a day
known to the LORD. When evening comes,
there will be light. ^{n}

^{8}On that day living water^o will flow^p
out from Jerusalem, half to the eastern^q
sea^a and half to the western sea, ^{b} in summer and in winter. ^{r}

^{9}The LORD will be king^s over the whole
earth. ^{t} On that day there will be one
LORD, and his name the only name. ^{u}

^{10}The whole land, from Geba^v to Rimmon, ^{w} south of Jerusalem, will become
like the Arabah. But Jerusalem will be
raised up^x and remain in its place, ^{y} from
the Benjamin Gate^z to the site of the First
Gate, to the Corner Gate, ^{a} and from the
Tower of Hananel^b to the royal wine-

Cross references

13:7 ^{n}S 2Sa 17:2;
Mt 26:31*;
Mk 14:27*
13:8
^{o}S Eze 5:2-4,12;
Zec 14:2
13:9 ^{p}S Isa 4:4;
33:14; Mal 3:2
^{q}S Ps 12:6;
S Da 11:35;
1Pe 1:6-7
^{r}S Job 6:29;
S Jer 6:27
^{s}S Ps 50:15
^{t}Ps 105:1
^{u}S Ps 86:7;
S Isa 30:19;
S Zec 10:6
^{v}S Lev 26:12;
S Jer 30:22
^{w}S Isa 44:5;
S Jer 29:12;
S Eze 20:38
14:1 ^{x}Isa 13:6;
S Joel 1:15;
Mal 4:1
^{y}S Isa 23:18
14:2 ^{z}S Isa 2:3;
S Zec 12:3
^{a}S Eze 5:8
^{b}S Ge 34:29;
S La 5:11
^{c}Isa 13:6;
S Zec 13:8
14:3
^{d}Zec 9:14-15
^{e}S Isa 8:9;
S Zec 12:9
14:4 ^{f}Eze 11:23
^{g}S Nu 16:31

14:5 ^{h}Am 1:1
^{i}Isa 29:6;
66:15-16
^{j}S Dt 33:2;
Mt 16:27; 25:31;
Jude 14
14:6
^{k}S Isa 13:10;
S Jer 4:23
14:7 ^{l}Jer 30:7
^{m}Rev 21:23-25;
22:5
^{n}S Isa 13:10;
S 30:26

14:8 ^{o}Eze 47:1-12; Jn 7:38; Rev 22:1-2 ^{p}S Isa 30:25
^{q}Joel 2:20 ^{r}S Ge 8:22 **14:9** ^{s}S Ps 22:28; S Ob 1:21 ^{t}S Dt 6:4;
Ps 47:7; Isa 45:24; Rev 11:15 ^{u}Hab 2:14; Eph 4:5-6 **14:10**
^{v}1Ki 15:22 ^{w}S Jos 15:32 ^{x}Isa 2:2-4; Jer 30:18; S Am 9:11
^{y}Zec 12:6 ^{z}S Jer 20:2 ^{a}S 2Ki 14:13 ^{b}S Ne 3:1

^{z}5 Or ^{5}*My mountain valley will be blocked and will
extend to Azel. It will be blocked as it was blocked
because of the earthquake* ^{a}8 That is, the Dead Sea
^{b}8 That is, the Mediterranean

(cf. the true Shepherd of 11:4–14; contrast the foolish and
worthless shepherd of 11:15–17). *Strike the shepherd.* In
11:17 it was the worthless shepherd who was to be struck;
now it is the Good Shepherd (cf. also 12:10). *sheep will be
scattered.* In fulfillment of the curses for covenant disobedience (Dt 28:64; 29:24–25). This part of the verse is quoted
by Jesus not long before his arrest (Mt 26:31; Mk 14:27) and
applied to the scattering of the apostles (Mt 26:56; Mk
14:49–50), who in turn are probably typological of the
dispersion of the Jews in A.D. 70 and the subsequent years.
13:8–9 These verses depict a refining process for Israel (see
note on Isa 48:10).
13:8 *one-third.* A remnant, thus revealing God's mercy in
the midst of judgment.
13:9 *They are my people . . . The LORD is our God.* See note
on 8:8. They will be restored to proper covenant relationship
with the Lord (see also Eze 20:30–44).
14:1 *your . . . you.* Jerusalem (v. 2) is the object of the
plunder.
14:2 *all the nations . . . fight against it.* See v. 12; see also
note on 12:3.
14:3 *day of battle.* Any occasion when the Lord supernaturally intervenes to deliver his people, such as at the Red Sea
(see note on Ex 14:14).
14:4 *Mount of Olives.* Called by this name elsewhere in
the OT only in 2Sa 15:30. This prophecy is probably referred
to in Ac 1:11–12. *east.* Thus it faced the temple mount and,
being about 2,700 feet high, rose about 200 feet above it. Cf.

Eze 11:23; 43:1–2.
14:5 *Azel.* The name of a place east of Jerusalem, marking
the eastern end of the newly formed valley. The location is
unknown. *holy ones.* May include both believers and angels.
They will accompany our Lord when he comes (cf. Mt
25:31; 1Th 3:13; Jude 14; Rev 19:14).
14:7 *unique day.* Due to the topographical, cosmic and
cataclysmic changes. See also Isa 60:19–20 and notes; cf.
Rev 21:23–25; 22:5.
14:8 *living water will flow.* Perhaps both literal and symbolic (cf. Ps 46:4; 65:9; Isa 8:6; Jer 2:13; Eze 47:1–12; Joel
3:18; Jn 4:10–14; 7:38; Rev 22:1–2).
14:9 *The LORD will be king over the whole earth.* A pervasive theological theme in Scripture. *one LORD.* See Dt 6:4; Isa
43:11 and notes.
14:10 *Geba.* About six miles north-northeast of Jerusalem
at the northern boundary of Judah (2Ki 23:8). *Rimmon.* Also
called En Rimmon (Ne 11:29; cf. Jos 15:32), it was about 35
miles south-southwest of Jerusalem, where the hill country
of Judah slopes away into the Negev. *Arabah.* See note on Dt
1:1. All the land around Jerusalem is to be leveled. *Jerusalem
will be raised up.* See note on Isa 2:2–4. The elevation may
be both physical and in prominence. *Benjamin Gate . . . First
Gate . . . Tower of Hananel.* All were probably at the northeastern part of the city wall (cf. Jer 31:38; 37:12–13; 38:7).
Corner Gate. At the northwest corner (cf. Jer 31:38). *royal
winepresses.* Just south of the city. Thus the whole city is
included.

presses. 11It will be inhabited;[c] never
again will it be destroyed. Jerusalem will
be secure.[d]
12This is the plague with which the
LORD will strike[e] all the nations that
fought against Jerusalem: Their flesh will
rot while they are still standing on their
feet, their eyes will rot in their sockets, and
their tongues will rot in their mouths.[f]
13On that day men will be stricken by the
LORD with great panic.[g] Each man will
seize the hand of another, and they will
attack each other.[h] 14Judah[i] too will fight
at Jerusalem. The wealth of all the surrounding nations will be collected[j]—great
quantities of gold and silver and clothing.
15A similar plague[k] will strike the horses
and mules, the camels and donkeys, and
all the animals in those camps.
16Then the survivors[l] from all the nations that have attacked Jerusalem will go
up year after year to worship[m] the King,[n]
the LORD Almighty, and to celebrate the
Feast of Tabernacles.[o] 17If any of the peoples of the earth do not go up to Jerusalem
to worship[p] the King, the LORD Almighty,
they will have no rain.[q] 18If the Egyptian
people do not go up and take part, they
will have no rain. The LORD[c] will bring on
them the plague[r] he inflicts on the nations
that do not go up to celebrate the Feast of
Tabernacles.[s] 19This will be the punishment of Egypt and the punishment of all
the nations that do not go up to celebrate
the Feast of Tabernacles.[t]
20On that day HOLY TO THE LORD[u] will
be inscribed on the bells of the horses, and
the cooking pots[v] in the LORD's house will
be like the sacred bowls[w] in front of the
altar. 21Every pot in Jerusalem and Judah
will be holy[x] to the LORD Almighty, and
all who come to sacrifice will take some of
the pots and cook in them. And on that
day[y] there will no longer be a Canaanite[d][z] in the house[a] of the LORD Almighty.[b]

14:11 [c]Zec 2:4 [d]S Ps 48:8; S Eze 34:25-28 **14:12** [e]S Isa 11:4 [f]ver 18; S Lev 26:16; S Dt 28:22; Job 18:13 **14:13** [g]S Ge 35:5 [h]S Jdg 7:22; S Zec 11:6 **14:14** [i]Zec 12:2 [j]S Isa 23:18 **14:15** [k]ver 12 **14:16** [l]S 2Ki 19:31 [m]S Ps 22:29; S 86:9; S Isa 19:21 [n]S Ob 1:21 [o]S Ex 23:16; Isa 60:6-9; S Mic 4:2 **14:17** [p]S 2Ch 32:23 [q]S Jer 14:4; S Am 4:7 **14:18** [r]S Ge 27:29 [s]S ver 12 **14:19** [t]S Ezr 3:4 **14:20** [u]S Ex 39:30 [v]S Eze 46:20 [w]Zec 9:15 **14:21** [x]S Jer 31:40; Ro 14:6-7; 1Co 10:31 [y]Ne 8:10 [z]Zec 9:8 [a]S Ne 11:1 [b]S Eze 44:9

c *18* Or *part, then the LORD* d *21* Or *merchant*

14:11 *inhabited.* See 2:4. *never again . . . destroyed.* As at the time of the exile to Babylonia (see Isa 43:28 and note). *Jerusalem will be secure.* See Jer 31:40.

14:12 *plague.* See Isa 37:36 and note. *nations that fought against Jerusalem.* See v. 2; see also note on 12:3.

14:13 *great panic . . . attack each other.* See note on Jdg 7:22.

14:14 *gold and silver and clothing.* The plunder of battle, thus reversing the situation in v. 1.

14:15 A similar plague will strike the beasts of burden, preventing the people from using them to escape.

14:16 See Isa 2:2–4 and note. *Feast of Tabernacles.* See notes on Ex 23:16; Ps 81:3. Of the three great pilgrimage festivals (see Ex 23:14–17), perhaps Tabernacles was selected as the one for representatives of the various Gentile nations because it was the last and greatest festival of the Hebrew calendar, gathering up into itself the year's worship. (See note on Eze 45:25.) It was to be a time of grateful rejoicing (Lev 23:40; Dt 16:13–15; Ne 8:17). Beginning with the period of Ezra and Nehemiah, the reading and teaching of "the Book of the Law of God" became an integral part of the festivities (Ne 8:18; cf. Isa 2:3). The festival seems to speak of the final, joyful regathering and restoration of Israel, as well as of the ingathering of the nations. See chart on "OT Feasts and Other Sacred Days," p. 176.

14:17 *no rain.* One of the curses for covenant disobedience (Dt 28:22–24; cf. Zec 9:11–10:1).

14:18 *Egyptian people . . . will have no rain.* See NIV text note. With either reading, the withholding of rain may still be included, for drought would cause even the Nile inundation to fail.

14:20 *HOLY TO THE LORD.* Engraved on the gold plate worn on the high priest's turban (Ex 28:36–38) as a reminder of his consecration to the Lord's service. See note on 3:5. God's original purpose for Israel (see Ex 19:6 and note) will be realized.

14:21 *Every pot in Jerusalem . . . holy.* See Joel 3:17. Even common things become holy when they are used for God's service. *Canaanite.* Represents anyone who is morally or spiritually unclean—anyone who is not included among the chosen people of God (cf. Isa 35:8; Eze 43:7; 44:9; Rev 21:27).

MALACHI

Author

The book is ascribed to Malachi, whose name means "my messenger." Since the term occurs in 3:1, and since both prophets and priests were called messengers of the Lord (see 2:7; Hag 1:13), some have thought "Malachi" to be only a title that tradition has given the author. The view has been supported by appeal to the early Greek translation (the Septuagint), which translates the term in 1:1 "his messenger" rather than as a proper noun. The matter, however, remains uncertain, and it is still very likely that Malachi was in fact the author's name.

Background

Spurred on by the prophetic activity of Haggai and Zechariah, the returned exiles under the leadership of their governor Zerubbabel finished the temple in 516 B.C. In 458 the community was strengthened by the coming of Ezra the priest and several thousand more Jews. King Artaxerxes of Persia encouraged Ezra to develop the temple worship (Ezr 7:17) and to make sure the law of Moses was being obeyed (Ezr 7:25-26).

Thirteen years later (445) the same Persian king permitted his cupbearer Nehemiah to return to Jerusalem and rebuild the walls (Ne 6:15). As newly appointed governor, Nehemiah also spearheaded reforms to help the poor (Ne 5:2-13), and he convinced the people to shun mixed marriages, to keep the Sabbath (Ne 10:30-31) and to bring their tithes and offerings faithfully (Ne 10:37-39).

In 433 B.C. Nehemiah returned to the service of the Persian king, and during his absence the Jews fell into sin once more. Later, however, Nehemiah came back to Jerusalem to discover that the tithes were ignored, the Sabbath was broken, the people had intermarried with foreigners, and the priests had become corrupt (Ne 13:7-31). Several of these sins are condemned by Malachi (see 1:6-14; 2:14-16; 3:8-11).

Date

The similarity between the sins denounced in Nehemiah and those denounced in Malachi suggest that the two leaders were contemporaries. Malachi may have been written after Nehemiah returned to Persia in 433 B.C. or during his second period as governor. Since the governor mentioned in 1:8 (see note there) probably was not Nehemiah, the first alternative may be more likely. Malachi was most likely the last prophet of the OT era (though some place Joel later).

Themes and Theology

Although the Jews had been allowed to return from exile and rebuild the temple, several discouraging factors brought about a general religious malaise: (1) Their land remained but a small province in the backwaters of the Persian empire, (2) the glorious future announced by the prophets (including the other postexilic prophets, Haggai and Zechariah) had not (yet) been realized, and (3) their God had not (yet) come to his temple (3:1) with majesty and power (as celebrated in Ps 68) to exalt his kingdom in the sight of the nations. Doubting God's covenant love (1:2) and no longer trusting his justice (2:17; 3:14-15), the Jews of the restored community began to lose hope. So their worship degenerated into a listless perpetuation of mere forms, and they no longer took the law seriously.

Malachi rebukes their doubt of God's love (1:2-5) and the faithlessness of both priests (1:6-2:9) and people (2:10-16). To their charge that God is unjust ("Where is the God of justice?" 2:17) because he has failed to come in judgment to exalt his people, Malachi answers with an announcement and a warning. The Lord they seek will come—but he will come "like a refiner's fire" (3:1-4). He will come to judge—but he will judge his people first (3:5).

Because the Lord does not change in his commitments and purpose, Israel has not been completely destroyed for her persistent unfaithfulness (3:6). But only through repentance and reformation will she

again experience God's blessing (3:6-12). Those who honor the Lord will be spared when he comes to judge (3:16-18).

In conclusion, Malachi once more reassures and warns his readers that "the day ['that great and dreadful day of the LORD,' 4:5] is coming" and that "it will burn like a furnace" (4:1). In that day the righteous will rejoice, and "you will trample down the wicked" (4:1-3). So "remember the law of my servant Moses" (4:4). To prepare his people for that day the Lord will send "the prophet Elijah" to call them back to the godly ways of their forefathers (4:5-6).

Literary Features

Malachi is called an "oracle" (see 1:1 and note) and is written in what might be called lofty prose. The text features a series of questions asked by both God and the people. Frequently the Lord's statements are followed by sarcastic questions introduced by "But you ask" (1:2,6-7; 2:14,17; 3:7-8,13; cf. 1:13). In each case the Lord's response is given.

Repetition is a key element in the book. The name "LORD Almighty" occurs 20 times. The book begins with a description of the wasteland of Edom (1:3-4) and ends with a warning of Israel's destruction (4:6).

Several vivid figures are employed within the book of Malachi. The priests sniff contemptuously at the altar of the Lord (1:13), and the Lord spreads on their faces the offal from their sacrifices (2:3). As Judge, "he will be like a refiner's fire or a launderer's soap" (3:2), but for the righteous "the sun of righteousness will rise with healing in its wings. And you will go out and leap like calves released from the stall" (4:2).

Outline

1 An oracle:[a] The word[b] of the LORD to Israel through Malachi.[a]

Jacob Loved, Esau Hated

[2]"I have loved[c] you," says the LORD. "But you ask,[d] 'How have you loved us?'

"Was not Esau Jacob's brother?" the LORD says. "Yet I have loved Jacob,[e] [3]but Esau I have hated,[f] and I have turned his mountains into a wasteland[g] and left his inheritance to the desert jackals.[h]"

[4]Edom[i] may say, "Though we have been crushed, we will rebuild[j] the ruins."

But this is what the LORD Almighty says: "They may build, but I will demolish.[k] They will be called the Wicked Land, a people always under the wrath of the LORD.[l] [5]You will see it with your own eyes and say, 'Great[m] is the LORD—even beyond the borders of Israel!'[n]

Blemished Sacrifices

[6]"A son honors his father,[o] and a servant his master.[p] If I am a father, where is the honor due me? If I am a master, where is the respect[q] due me?" says the LORD Almighty.[r] "It is you, O priests, who show contempt for my name.

"But you ask,[s] 'How have we shown contempt for your name?'

[7]"You place defiled food[t] on my altar.

"But you ask,[u] 'How have we defiled you?'

"By saying that the LORD's table[v] is contemptible. [8]When you bring blind animals for sacrifice, is that not wrong? When you sacrifice crippled or diseased animals,[w] is that not wrong? Try offering them to your governor! Would he be pleased[x] with you? Would he accept you?" says the LORD Almighty.[y]

[9]"Now implore God to be gracious to us. With such offerings[z] from your hands, will he accept[a] you?"—says the LORD Almighty.

[10]"Oh, that one of you would shut the temple doors,[b] so that you would not light useless fires on my altar! I am not pleased[c] with you," says the LORD Almighty, "and I will accept[d] no offering[e] from your hands. [11]My name will be great[f] among the nations,[g] from the rising to the setting of the sun.[h] In every place incense[i] and pure offerings[j] will be brought to my name, because my name will be great among the nations," says the LORD Almighty.

[12]"But you profane it by saying of the Lord's table,[k] 'It is defiled,' and of its food,[l] 'It is contemptible.' [13]And you say, 'What a burden!'[m] and you sniff at it contemptuously,[n]" says the LORD Almighty.

"When you bring injured, crippled or diseased animals and offer them as sacrifices,[o] should I accept them from your hands?"[p] says the LORD. [14]"Cursed is the

Cross references

1:1 [a]S Na 1:1 [b]Ac 7:38; Ro 3:1-2; 1Pe 4:11
1:2 [c]S Dt 4:37 [d]ver 6,7; Mal 2:14,17; 3:7, 13 [e]S Jer 46:27; Ro 9:13*
1:3 [f]Lk 14:26 [g]S Isa 34:10 [h]S Isa 13:22
1:4 [i]S Isa 11:14; S 34:11 /[j]Isa 9:10 [k]S Isa 34:5 [l]S La 4:22; S Eze 25:12-14; S 26:14
1:5 [m]Ps 35:27; 48:1; Mic 5:4 [n]Isa 45:22; 52:10; S Am 1:11-12
1:6 [o]S Lev 20:9; Mt 15:4; 23:9 [p]Lk 6:46 [q]S Dt 31:12; S Isa 1:2 [r]Job 5:17 [s]S ver 2
1:7 [t]ver 12; Lev 21:6 [u]S ver 2 [v]S Eze 23:41

1:8 [w]S Lev 1:3; S Dt 15:21 [x]S Ge 32:20 [y]S Isa 43:23
1:9 [z]Lev 23:33-44; Ps 51:17; Mic 6:6-8; Ro 12:1; Heb 13:16 [a]S Jer 6:20
1:10 [b]2Ch 28:24 [c]S Hos 5:6 [d]Lev 22:20 [e]ver 13; Isa 1:11-14; Jer 14:12; Mal 2:12
1:11 [f]S Isa 24:15; 56:6 [g]S Isa 6:3; S 12:4 [h]S Ps 113:3; S Mt 8:11 [i]Isa 60:6-7;

Rev 5:8; 8:3 /[j]S Isa 19:21; Heb 13:15 1:12 [k]S Eze 41:22 /[l]S ver 7 1:13 [m]Isa 43:22-24 [n]S Nu 14:11 [o]S ver 10 [p]S Dt 15:21

[a]1 Malachi means my messenger.

1:1 *oracle.* See Zec 9:1 and note; 12:1; see also Hab 1:1 and note.

1:2 *loved you.* The Lord's reassuring word to his disheartened people.

1:3 *Esau I have hated.* If Israel doubts God's covenant love, she should consider the contrast between God's ways with her and his ways with Jacob's brother Esau (Edom). Paul explains God's love for Jacob and hatred for Esau on the basis of election (Ro 9:10–13). God chose Jacob but not Esau. For the use of "love" and "hate" here, cf. how Leah was "hated" in that Jacob loved Rachel more (Ge 29:31,33; cf. Dt 21:16–17). Likewise, believers are to "hate" their parents (Lk 14:26) in the sense that they love Christ even more (Mt 10:37). *wasteland.* Malachi's words about Edom echo those of the earlier prophets (see Isa 34:5–15; Jer 49:7–22; Eze 25:12–14; 35:1–15; Obadiah). Between c. 550 and 400 B.C. the Nabatean Arabs gradually forced the Edomites from their homeland.

1:4 *Edom may say.* Her proud self-reliance has not assured her security and will not secure her future (cf. Jer 49:16).

1:5 *Great . . . Israel.* When she sees the ultimate fate of Edom, doubting Israel will acknowledge that the Lord is the great Ruler over all the nations.

1:6–2:9 The Lord rebukes the priests.

1:6 *son honors his father.* Cf. Isa 1:2–3. *priests, who show contempt for my name.* Contrast 2:5; cf. Isa 1:4.

1:7 *food.* The offerings (see v. 12; Lev 21:8,21). *defiled you.* By offering defiled sacrifices they defile the Lord himself.

the Lord's table. The altar (see v. 12; Eze 44:16). Since the priests ate from the sacrifices, the altar was also the table from which they got their food. *contemptible.* As the priests considered the Lord's altar and its sacrifices (v. 12) contemptible, so the Lord would cause the priests to be considered contemptible by the people (see 2:9 and note).

1:8 *blind . . . crippled.* Animals with defects or serious flaws were unacceptable as sacrifices (see Dt 15:21). *governor.* Probably the Persian governor.

1:10 *shut the temple doors.* Better no sacrifices than sacrifices offered with contempt (cf. Isa 1:11–15).

1:11 *great among the nations.* Cf. v. 14. God's judgment on Edom (v. 5) and other nations demonstrates his superiority over their gods, and it ultimately will evoke their recognition of him (see Zep 2:11). *incense and pure offerings.* Cf. the acceptable offerings presented by foreigners in Isa 56:6–7; 60:7. Some interpreters understand "incense" to mean "prayer" (cf. Rev 5:8) and "offerings" to mean "praise" (cf. Heb 13:15).

1:12 *defiled . . . contemptible.* See v. 7.

1:13 *sniff at it contemptuously.* Cf. the behavior of Eli's sons in 1Sa 2:15–17. *injured . . . diseased.* See v. 8 and note.

1:14 *vows . . . a blemished animal.* An animal sacrificed in fulfillment of a vow had to be a male without defect or blemish (see Lev 22:18–23). *great king.* See Zec 14:9. *my name . . . feared.* More than the governor of v. 8 (see v. 11 and note).

cheat who has an acceptable male in his flock and vows to give it, but then sacrifices a blemished animal[q] to the Lord. For I am a great king,[r] says the LORD Almighty,[s] "and my name is to be feared[t] among the nations.[u]

Admonition for the Priests

2 "And now this admonition is for you, O priests.[v] 2If you do not listen,[w] and if you do not set your heart to honor[x] my name," says the LORD Almighty, "I will send a curse[y] upon you, and I will curse your blessings.[z] Yes, I have already cursed them, because you have not set your heart to honor me.

3"Because of you I will rebuke[b] your descendants[c]; I will spread on your faces the offal[a] from your festival sacrifices, and you will be carried off with it.[b] 4And you will know that I have sent you this admonition so that my covenant with Levi[c] may continue," says the LORD Almighty. 5"My covenant was with him, a covenant[d] of life and peace,[e] and I gave them to him; this called for reverence[f] and he revered me and stood in awe of my name. 6True instruction[g] was in his mouth and nothing false was found on his lips. He walked[h] with me in peace[i] and uprightness,[j] and turned many from sin.[k]

7"For the lips of a priest[l] ought to preserve knowledge, and from his mouth men should seek instruction[m]—because he is the messenger[n] of the LORD Almighty.

8But you have turned from the way[o] and by your teaching have caused many to stumble;[p] you have violated the covenant[q] with Levi," [r] says the LORD Almighty. 9"So I have caused you to be despised[s] and humiliated[t] before all the people, because you have not followed my ways but have shown partiality[u] in matters of the law." [v]

Judah Unfaithful

10Have we not all all one Father[d]?[w] Did not one God create us?[x] Why do we profane the covenant[y] of our fathers by breaking faith[z] with one another?

11Judah has broken faith. A detestable[a] thing has been committed in Israel and in Jerusalem: Judah has desecrated the sanctuary the LORD loves,[b] by marrying[c] the daughter of a foreign god.[d] 12As for the man who does this, whoever he may be, may the LORD cut him off[e] from the tents of Jacob[e]—even though he brings offerings[g] to the LORD Almighty.

13Another thing you do: You flood the LORD's altar with tears.[h] You weep and

1:14 qEx 12:5; S Lev 22:18-21
rPs 95:3; S Ob 1:21; 1Ti 6:15
sJer 46:18
tS Dt 28:58
uPs 72:8-11
2:1 vver 7
2:2 wJer 13:17
xMt 15:7-9; Jn 5:23; 1Ti 6:16; Rev 5:12-13
yS Dt 11:26; S 28:20
zNu 6:23-27
2:3 aS Eze 29:14; S Lev 4:11; S Job 9:31
bJ Ki 14:10
2:4 cS Nu 3:12
2:5 dDt 33:9; Ps 25:10; 103:18; S Mt 26:28; S Lk 22:20; Heb 7:22
eS Nu 25:12
fS Dt 14:23; S 28:58; Ps 119:161; Heb 12:28
2:6 gS Dt 33:10
hS Ge 5:22
iLk 2:14; S Jn 14:27; Gal 5:22
jS Ps 25:21
kS Ro 11:14; Jas 5:19-20
2:7 lS Jer 18:18
mS Lev 10:11; S 2Ch 17:7
nS Nu 27:21; S 2Ch 36:15; Mt 11:10; Mk 1:2
2:8 oS Ex 32:8; Jer 2:8
pS Jer 18:15
qJer 33:21; S Eze 22:26
rS Hos 4:6
2:9 sS Lev 2:30; S Ps 22:6; S Jer 51:37
tS Ps 35:4;

Jer 3:25; Ac 8:32-33 uS Ex 18:16; S Lev 19:15; Ac 10:34; Ro 2:11 vS 1Sa 2:17 **2:10** wS Ex 4:22; Mt 5:16; 6:4,18; Lk 11:2; 1Co 8:6 xS Job 4:17; Isa 43:1 yEx 19:5; S 2Ki 17:15; Jer 31:32 zS Zep 3:3-4 **2:11** aS Isa 1:13; S 48:8 bS Dt 4:37 cS Ne 13:23 dS Ex 34:16; Jer 3:7-9 **2:12** eS 1Sa 2:30-33; S Eze 24:21 fS Nu 24:5; 2Sa 20:1 gS Mal 1:10 **2:13** hS Jer 11:11

b3 Or cut off (see Septuagint)   c3 Or will blight your grain   d10 Or father   e12 Or 12May the LORD cut off from the tents of Jacob anyone who gives testimony in behalf of the man who does this

---

2:2 curse your blessings. It was the function of the priests to pronounce God's blessing on the people (see Nu 6:23–27), but their blessings will become curses so that their uniquely priestly function will be worse than useless.
2:3 spread on your faces. To disgrace you (see Na 3:6). offal. The entrails of an animal that were taken "outside the camp" and burned along with its hide and flesh (see Ex 29:14; Lev 8:17; 16:27).
2:4 Levi. The priests were chosen from the tribe of Levi (see Nu 3:12–13; Ne 13:29).
2:5 covenant of life and peace. An allusion to the covenant with Phinehas, Aaron's grandson, in Nu 25:10–13. Phinehas defended God's honor by killing two offenders involved in the idolatry and immorality connected with the Baal of Peor (Nu 25:1–3). he revered me. Phinehas showed this by his zeal for God (see Nu 25:13).
2:6–7 instruction. Priests were responsible to teach the law of Moses (see Lev 10:11; see also notes on Zep 3:4; Hag 2:11).
2:6 peace and uprightness. Linked together also in Ps 37:37, but here "walked with me in peace and uprightness" probably refers to covenant loyalty.
2:7 messenger. As teacher of the law and as one through whom people could inquire of God (see notes on 3:1; Hag 1:13).
2:8 violated the covenant. By unfaithful teaching, but also, it seems, by intermarriage with foreigners (see Ezr 9:1; 10:18–22; Ne 13:27–29). with Levi. See v. 4 and note on

v. 5.
2:9 despised. In Hebrew the same word that is translated "contemptible" in 1:7,12 (see note on 1:7). shown partiality. Forbidden in Lev 19:15. The priests were to be like God in this respect (see Dt 10:17).
2:10–16 Malachi rebukes the people—in a passage framed by references to "breaking faith." Two examples of their sin are specifically mentioned: marrying pagan women and divorce.
2:10 one Father. See Isa 63:16. create us. As his special people (see Isa 43:1 and note). covenant of our fathers. The covenant God made with their forefathers at Mount Sinai. breaking faith. One could not even trust his own fellow Israelites or national leaders—like the priests.
2:11 daughter of a foreign god. A pagan woman. Such marriages were strictly forbidden in the covenant law because they would lead to apostasy (see Ex 34:15–16; Dt 7:3–4; 1Ki 11:1–6; cf. Jos 23:12–13). Ezra and Nehemiah both wrestled with this problem (Ezr 9:1–2; Ne 13:23–29).
2:12 The alternative given in the NIV text note (particularly "gives testimony") is supported, e.g., by the use of the same Hebrew verb in Ge 30:33; Dt 5:20; Ru 1:21; 1Sa 12:3; 2Sa 1:16; Isa 3:9; Jer 14:7. On this reading, the one to be cut off is the one who speaks in defense of the wrongdoer. tents of Jacob. A figurative expression for the community (see Jer 30:18).
2:13 weep and wail. Because the Lord does not respond to their sacrifices with blessing, they add wailing to their

wail[i] because he no longer pays attention[j] to your offerings or accepts them with pleasure from your hands.[k] [14]You ask,[l] "Why?" It is because the LORD is acting as the witness[m] between you and the wife of your youth,[n] because you have broken faith with her, though she is your partner, the wife of your marriage covenant.[o]

[15]Has not ˌthe LORDˌ made them one?[p] In flesh and spirit they are his. And why one? Because he was seeking godly offspring.[f][q] So guard yourself[r] in your spirit, and do not break faith[s] with the wife of your youth.

[16]"I hate divorce,[t]" says the LORD God of Israel, "and I hate a man's covering himself[g] with violence[u] as well as with his garment," says the LORD Almighty.

So guard yourself in your spirit,[v] and do not break faith.

The Day of Judgment

[17]You have wearied[w] the LORD with your words.

"How have we wearied him?" you ask.[x]

By saying, "All who do evil are good in the eyes of the LORD, and he is pleased[y] with them" or "Where is the God of justice?[z]"

3 "See, I will send my messenger,[a] who will prepare the way before me.[b]

Then suddenly the Lord[c] you are seeking will come to his temple; the messenger of the covenant,[d] whom you desire,[e] will come," says the LORD Almighty.

[2]But who can endure[f] the day of his coming?[g] Who can stand[h] when he appears? For he will be like a refiner's fire[i] or a launderer's soap.[j] [3]He will sit as a refiner and purifier of silver;[k] he will purify[l] the Levites and refine them like gold and silver.[m] Then the LORD will have men who will bring offerings in righteousness,[n] [4]and the offerings[o] of Judah and Jerusalem will be acceptable to the LORD, as in days gone by, as in former years.[p]

[5]"So I will come near to you for judgment. I will be quick to testify against sorcerers,[q] adulterers[r] and perjurers,[s] against those who defraud laborers of their wages,[t] who oppress the widows[u] and the fatherless, and deprive aliens[v] of justice, but do not fear[w] me," says the LORD Almighty.

Robbing God

[6]"I the LORD do not change.[x] So you, O

2:13 *i*Ps 39:12
/Ps 66:18;
Jer 14:12
*k*Isa 58:2
2:14 /S Mal 1:2
*m*S Ge 21:30;
S Jos 24:22
*n*S Pr 5:18
*o*S Eze 16:8;
Heb 13:4
2:15 *p*S Ge 2:24;
Mt 19:4-6
*q*S Dt 14:2;
1Co 7:14
*r*S Dt 4:15
*s*S Isa 54:6;
1Co 7:10;
Heb 13:4
2:16 *t*S Dt 24:1;
Mt 5:31-32;
19:4-9;
Mk 10:4-5
*u*S Ge 6:11;
34:25; S Pr 4:17;
S Isa 58:4
*v*Ps 51:10
2:17 *w*S Isa 1:14
*x*S Mal 1:2
*y*Ps 5:4
*z*S Ge 18:25;
S Eze 18:25
3:1 *a*S Nu 27:21;
S 2Ch 36:15
*b*S Isa 40:3;
S Mt 3:3; 11:10*;
Mk 1:2*;
Lk 7:27*

*c*Mic 5:2
*d*S Isa 42:6
*e*S 1Sa 9:20
3:2 /S Eze 22:14;
Rev 6:17
*g*S Eze 7:7;
S Da 7:13;
S Joel 2:31;
S Mt 16:27;
Jas 5:8; 2Pe 3:4;
S Rev 1:7
*h*S 1Sa 6:20
/S Isa 1:31;
S 30:30;
S Zec 13:9;
Mt 3:10-12

/S Job 9:30 **3:3** *k*S Da 12:10; S 1Co 3:13 /S 1Ch 23:28;
S Isa 1:25 *m*S Job 28:1; S Ps 12:6; 1Pe 1:7; Rev 3:18
*n*S Ps 132:9 **3:4** *o*2Ch 7:12; Ps 51:19; Mal 1:11 *p*S 2Ch 7:3;
S Eze 20:40 **3:5** *q*S Ex 7:11; S Isa 47:9 *r*Ex 20:14; Jas 2:11;
2Pe 2:12-14 *s*Lev 19:11-12; S Jer 7:9 *t*S Lev 19:13; Jas 5:4
*u*S Ex 22:22 *v*S Ex 22:21; S Dt 24:19; S Eze 22:7
*w*S Dt 31:12; S Isa 1:2 **3:6** *x*S Nu 23:19; S Heb 7:21; Jas 1:17

*f*15 Or *15But the one ˌwho is our fatherˌ did not do this, not as long as life remained in him. And what was he seeking? An offspring from God *g*16 Or his wife

prayers.

2:14 *witness . . . marriage covenant.* Marriage was a covenant (see Pr 2:17; Eze 16:8), and covenants were affirmed before witnesses (see notes on Dt 30:19; 1Sa 20:23; Isa 8:1–2).

2:15 *one.* See Ge 2:24 and note. *godly offspring.* Marriage "sanctifies" the children (see 1Co 7:14 and note). If the alternative translation in the NIV text note is taken, this verse refers to Abraham, who "married" the foreigner Hagar in order to have a son (Ge 16:1–4). But Abraham did not divorce Sarah, who had suggested the union with Hagar in the first place.

2:16 *I hate divorce.* See Isa 50:1 and note. *violence.* See 3:5.

2:17–4:6 The second half of Malachi's prophecy speaks of God's coming to his people. They had given up on God (see 2:17, which introduces this section) and had grown religiously cynical and morally corrupt. So God's coming will mean judgment and purification as well as redemption.

2:17 *wearied the LORD with your words.* In Isa 43:24 Israel's sins had wearied God. *All who do evil are good.* Such was the depth of their cynicism. *Where is . . . justice?* Cf. the sarcastic taunts of Isa 5:19.

3:1 *my messenger.* The Hebrew for these words is *mal'aki*; it is normally used of a priest or prophet (see Hag 1:13 and note). This is fulfilled in John the Baptist (see Mt 11:10; Mk 1:2; Lk 1:76). *who will prepare the way.* When the Lord comes, it will be to purify (v. 3) and judge (v. 5), but he will mercifully send one before him to prepare his people (see

4:5–6 and notes; see also Isa 40:3 and note). *the Lord you are seeking . . . whom you desire, will come.* See Hag 2:7 and note. *messenger of the covenant.* The Messiah, who as the Lord's representative will confirm and establish the covenant (see note on Isa 42:6).

3:2 *day of his coming.* The day of the Lord (see 4:1; see also note on Isa 2:11,17,20). Malachi announces the Lord's coming to complete God's work in history, especially the work he outlines in the rest of his book. His word is fulfilled in the accomplishments of the Messiah. *Who can stand . . . ?* Those who desire the Lord's coming must know that clean hands and a pure heart are required (cf. Ps 24:3–4; Isa 33:14–15). *refiner's fire.* See Isa 1:25; Zec 13:8–9 and notes. *launderer's soap.* See Isa 7:3 and note. White clothes signified purity (cf. Mk 9:3; Rev 3:5).

3:3 *purify the Levites.* Those who are supposed to be "messengers" of the Lord and who serve at the altar will be purged of their sins and unfaithfulness—such as the Lord has rebuked in 1:6–2:9.

3:4 *be acceptable.* See 1:8 and note. *days gone by.* Probably the time of Moses and Phinehas (see note on 2:5).

3:5 When he comes, the Lord will both purify the Levites (vv. 3–4) and judge the people. *sorcerers.* Common in the ancient Near East (see Ex 7:11; Dt 18:10).

3:6 *do not change.* See Jas 1:17. Contrary to what many in Malachi's day were thinking, God remains faithful to his covenant. *not destroyed.* In contrast to Edom (1:3–5) and in spite of Israel's history of unfaithfulness.

descendants of Jacob, are not destroyed.[y] [7]Ever since the time of your forefathers you have turned away[z] from my decrees and have not kept them. Return[a] to me, and I will return to you," [b] says the LORD Almighty.

"But you ask,[c] 'How are we to return?'

[8]"Will a man rob[d] God? Yet you rob me.

"But you ask, 'How do we rob you?'

"In tithes[e] and offerings. [9]You are under a curse[f]—the whole nation of you—because you are robbing me. [10]Bring the whole tithe[g] into the storehouse,[h] that there may be food in my house. Test me in this," says the LORD Almighty, "and see if I will not throw open the floodgates[i] of heaven and pour out[j] so much blessing[k] that you will not have room enough for it.[l] [11]I will prevent pests from devouring[m] your crops, and the vines in your fields will not cast their fruit,[n]" says the LORD Almighty. [12]"Then all the nations will call you blessed,[o] for yours will be a delightful land," [p] says the LORD Almighty.[q]

[13]"You have said harsh things[r] against me," says the LORD.

"Yet you ask,[s] 'What have we said against you?'

[14]"You have said, 'It is futile[t] to serve[u] God. What did we gain by carrying out his requirements[v] and going about like mourners[w] before the LORD Almighty? [15]But now we call the arrogant[x] blessed. Certainly the evildoers[y] prosper,[z] and even those who challenge God escape.' "

[16]Then those who feared the LORD talked with each other, and the LORD listened and heard.[a] A scroll[b] of remembrance was written in his presence concerning those who feared[c] the LORD and honored his name.

[17]"They will be mine,[d]" says the LORD Almighty, "in the day when I make up my treasured possession.[h][e] I will spare[f] them, just as in compassion a man spares his son[g] who serves him. [18]And you will again see the distinction between the righteous[h] and the wicked, between those who serve God and those who do not.[i]

The Day of the LORD

4 "Surely the day is coming;[j] it will burn like a furnace.[k] All the arrogant[l] and every evildoer will be stubble,[m] and that day that is coming will set them on fire,[n]" says the LORD Almighty. "Not a root or a branch[o] will be left to them. [2]But for you who revere my name,[p] the sun of righteousness[q] will rise with healing[r] in its wings. And you will go out and leap[s] like calves released from the stall. [3]Then you will trample[t] down the wicked; they will be ashes[u] under the soles of your feet

3:6 [y]S Job 34:15;
S Hos 11:9
3:7 [z]S Ex 32:8;
S Jer 7:26;
Ac 7:51
[a]S Isa 44:22;
S Eze 18:32
[b]S Zec 1:3;
Jas 4:8 [c]S Mal 1:2
3:8 [d]S Zec 5:3
[e]S Lev 27:30;
Nu 18:21;
S Ne 13:10-12;
Lk 18:12
3:9 [f]S Dt 11:26;
28:15-68;
S Zec 5:3
3:10 [g]S Ex 22:29
[h]S Ne 13:12
[i]S Mal 1:7:2
/Isa 44:3
[k]S Lev 25:21;
S Joel 2:14;
2Co 9:8-11
[l]S Joel 2:24
3:11
[m]S Ex 10:15;
S Dt 28:39
[n]S Ex 23:26
3:12
[o]S Dt 28:3-12;
Isa 61:9
[p]S Isa 62:4;
S Eze 20:6
[q]S 2Ch 31:10
3:13 [r]Mal 2:17
[s]S Mal 1:2
3:14 [t]Ps 73:13;
S Isa 57:10
[u]Ps 100:2;
Jn 13:16;
Ro 12:11
[v]S Jos 22:5;
S Isa 1:14
[w]Isa 58:3
3:15
[x]S Ps 119:21
[y]Ps 14:1; 36:1-2;
Jer 7:10
[z]S Job 21:7

3:16 [a]S Ps 34:15
[b]S Ex 32:32;
S Ps 56:8; S 87:6;
S Lk 10:20
[c]S Dt 28:58;
S 31:12;
Ps 33:18;
S Pr 1:7;

3:16 [d]Isa 43:21 [e]S Ex 8:22; S Dt 7:6; S Ro 8:14;
S Tit 2:14 /Ne 13:22; Ps 103:13; Isa 26:20; Lk 15:1-32
[g]Ro 8:32 **3:18** [h]S Ge 18:25 [i]Dt 32:4; Mt 25:32-33,41 **4:1**
[j]S Da 7:13; S Joel 2:31; Mt 11:14; Ac 2:20 [k]S Isa 31:9
[l]S Isa 2:12 [m]S Isa 5:24; S Na 1:10 [n]S Isa 1:31 [o]S 2Ki 10:11;
S Eze 17:8; S Mt 3:10 **4:2** [p]S Dt 28:58; Ps 61:5; 111:9;
Rev 14:1 [q]S Ps 118:27; S Isa 9:2; S 45:8; Lk 1:78; Eph 5:14
[r]S 2Ch 7:14; S Isa 30:26; S Mt 4:23; Rev 22:2 [s]S Isa 35:6 **4:3**
[t]S Job 40:12; Ps 18:40-42 [u]Eze 28:18

[h] 17 Or Almighty, "my treasured possession, in the day when I act

3:7 *Return . . . and I will return.* If the Lord is to come for Israel's redemption, she must repent.
3:9 *curse.* See 2:2 and note.
3:10 *storehouse.* The treasury rooms of the sanctuary (see 1Ki 7:51; 2Ch 31:11-12; Ne 13:12). *floodgates of heaven.* Elsewhere the idiom refers to abundant provision of food (see 2Ki 7:2,19; Ps 78:23-24). *pour out . . . blessing.* The promised covenant blessing (see Dt 28:12; cf. Isa 44:3).
3:11 *pests . . . cast their fruit.* Examples of the threatened covenant curses (see Dt 28:39-40).
3:12 *call you blessed.* In fulfillment of the promise to Abraham (see Ge 12:2-3; see also Isa 61:9 and note).
3:14 *It is futile to serve God.* Because the redemption they longed for had not yet been realized. *like mourners.* In sackcloth and ashes.
3:15 *arrogant.* Evildoers—those who challenge God (see note on Ps 10:11). *blessed.* In their unbelief, the Jews call blessed those whom the godly know to be cursed (see Ps 119:21)—but it is they who will be called blessed if they repent (v. 12). *evildoers prosper . . . escape.* Note the psalmist's struggle with the prosperity of the wicked in Ps 73:3, 9-12.
3:16 *those who feared the LORD.* Those who had not given way to doubts and cynicism. *talked with each other.* In the face of the widespread complaining against God (vv. 14-15), they sought mutual encouragement in fellowship. *scroll of*

remembrance. Analogous to the records of notable deeds kept by earthly rulers (see Est 6:1-3; Isa 4:3; Da 7:10; 12:1). *honored his name.* Contrast the priests (1:12) and many among the people (vv. 14-15; 2:17).
3:17 *my treasured possession.* See note on Ex 19:5. *spare them.* In the day of judgment (see 4:1-2). *who serves him.* Cf. 1:6.
3:18 *you will again see.* As they apparently do not now see; hence their cynicism. *the righteous and the wicked.* See 2:17 and note.
4:1 *the day.* The day of the Lord (see v. 5; 3:2 and note). *burn like a furnace.* See 3:2-3; Isa 1:31; 66:15-16 and notes. *arrogant.* See 3:15 and note. *stubble . . . fire.* See Isa 47:14 and John the Baptist's prophecy about the work of Christ in Mt 3:12. *Not a root or a branch.* Nothing of them will be left (see Eze 17:8-9).
4:2 *sun of righteousness.* God and his glory are compared with the sun in Isa 60:1,19 (see notes there). Christ is the "rising sun" from heaven (see Lk 1:78-79; see also Isa 9:2 and note). *righteousness . . . healing.* Salvation and renewal are intended (see Isa 45:8; 46:13; 53:5; Jer 30:17 and notes). *its wings.* The sun's rays (cf. Ps 139:9). *like calves released from the stall.* Frisky young calves often frolic about when released from confinement.
4:3 *trample . . . the wicked.* As one treads the winepress (see Isa 63:2-3 and notes).

on the day when I do these things," says the LORD Almighty.

4"Remember the law[v] of my servant Moses, the decrees and laws I gave him at Horeb[w] for all Israel.[x]

5"See, I will send you the prophet Elijah[y] before that great and dreadful day of the LORD comes.[z] 6He will turn the hearts of the fathers to their children,[a] and the hearts of the children to their fathers; or else I will come and strike[b] the land with a curse."[c]

4:4 [v]S Dt 28:61;
S Ps 147:19;
Mt 5:17; 7:12;
Ro 2:13; 4:15;
Gal 3:24
[w]S Ex 3:1
[x]S Ex 20:1
4:5 [y]S 1Ki 17:1;
S Mt 11:14;
16:14

[z]S Joel 2:31 4:6 [a]Lk 1:17 [b]S Isa 11:4; Rev 19:15
[c]S Dt 11:26; S 13:15; S Jos 6:17; S 23:15; S Zec 5:3

4:4 *Remember the law.* A final exhortation to those who impatiently wait for the Lord's coming. *my servant.* See Ex 14:31; Dt 34:5; Jdg 2:8; Ps 18 title; Isa 20:3; 41:8–9; 42:1 and notes. *Horeb.* Mount Sinai (cf. Ex 3:1).
4:5 See 3:1 and note. *Elijah.* As Elijah came before Elisha (whose ministry was one of judgment and redemption), so "Elijah" will be sent to prepare God's people for the Lord's coming. John the Baptist ministered "in the spirit and power of Elijah" (Lk 1:17; see Mt 11:13–14; 17:12–13; Mk

9:11–13). And some feel that Elijah may also be one of the two witnesses in Rev 11:3. *great and dreadful day.* See v. 1; 3:2 and note; Joel 2:11,31.
4:6 *turn the hearts.* Cf. Ge 18:19; Dt 7:9–11. According to Lk 1:17 John the Baptist sought to accomplish this. *curse.* Total destruction. If Israel does not repent, she will be dealt with as God had dealt with Edom (see Isa 34:5; cf. Mal 1:3–4).

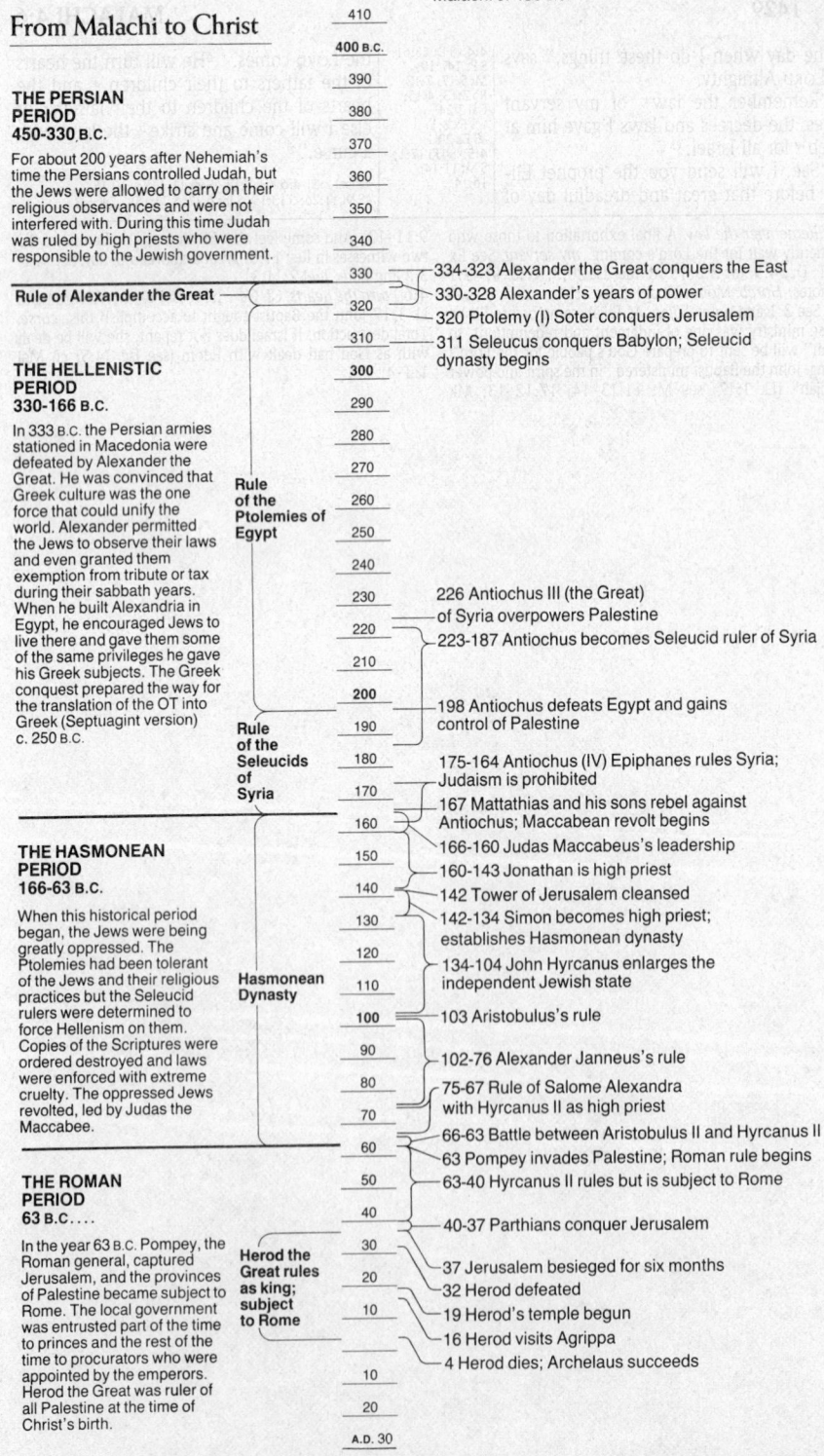

Malachi c. 430 B.C.

From Malachi to Christ

THE PERSIAN PERIOD
450-330 B.C.

For about 200 years after Nehemiah's time the Persians controlled Judah, but the Jews were allowed to carry on their religious observances and were not interfered with. During this time Judah was ruled by high priests who were responsible to the Jewish government.

Rule of Alexander the Great

THE HELLENISTIC PERIOD
330-166 B.C.

In 333 B.C. the Persian armies stationed in Macedonia were defeated by Alexander the Great. He was convinced that Greek culture was the one force that could unify the world. Alexander permitted the Jews to observe their laws and even granted them exemption from tribute or tax during their sabbath years. When he built Alexandria in Egypt, he encouraged Jews to live there and gave them some of the same privileges he gave his Greek subjects. The Greek conquest prepared the way for the translation of the OT into Greek (Septuagint version) c. 250 B.C.

Rule of the Ptolemies of Egypt

Rule of the Seleucids of Syria

THE HASMONEAN PERIOD
166-63 B.C.

When this historical period began, the Jews were being greatly oppressed. The Ptolemies had been tolerant of the Jews and their religious practices but the Seleucid rulers were determined to force Hellenism on them. Copies of the Scriptures were ordered destroyed and laws were enforced with extreme cruelty. The oppressed Jews revolted, led by Judas the Maccabee.

Hasmonean Dynasty

THE ROMAN PERIOD
63 B.C....

In the year 63 B.C. Pompey, the Roman general, captured Jerusalem, and the provinces of Palestine became subject to Rome. The local government was entrusted part of the time to princes and the rest of the time to procurators who were appointed by the emperors. Herod the Great was ruler of all Palestine at the time of Christ's birth.

Herod the Great rules as king; subject to Rome

410
400 B.C.
390
380
370
360
350
340
330
320
310
300
290
280
270
260
250
240
230
220
210
200
190
180
170
160
150
140
130
120
110
100
90
80
70
60
50
40
30
20
10
10
20
A.D. 30

334-323 Alexander the Great conquers the East
330-328 Alexander's years of power
320 Ptolemy (I) Soter conquers Jerusalem
311 Seleucus conquers Babylon; Seleucid dynasty begins

226 Antiochus III (the Great) of Syria overpowers Palestine
223-187 Antiochus becomes Seleucid ruler of Syria

198 Antiochus defeats Egypt and gains control of Palestine

175-164 Antiochus (IV) Epiphanes rules Syria; Judaism is prohibited
167 Mattathias and his sons rebel against Antiochus; Maccabean revolt begins
166-160 Judas Maccabeus's leadership
160-143 Jonathan is high priest
142 Tower of Jerusalem cleansed
142-134 Simon becomes high priest; establishes Hasmonean dynasty
134-104 John Hyrcanus enlarges the independent Jewish state
103 Aristobulus's rule
102-76 Alexander Janneus's rule
75-67 Rule of Salome Alexandra with Hyrcanus II as high priest
66-63 Battle between Aristobulus II and Hyrcanus II
63 Pompey invades Palestine; Roman rule begins
63-40 Hyrcanus II rules but is subject to Rome
40-37 Parthians conquer Jerusalem
37 Jerusalem besieged for six months
32 Herod defeated
19 Herod's temple begun
16 Herod visits Agrippa
4 Herod dies; Archelaus succeeds

The Time between the Testaments

The time between the Testaments was one of ferment and change—a time of the realignment of traditional power blocs and the passing of a Near Eastern cultural tradition that had been dominant for almost 3,000 years.

In Biblical history, the approximately 400 years that separate the time of Nehemiah from the birth of Christ are known as the intertestamental period (c. 432-5 B.C.). Sometimes called the "silent" years, they were anything but silent. The events, literature and social forces of these years would shape the world of the NT.

History

With the Babylonian captivity, Israel ceased to be an independent nation and became a minor territory in a succession of larger empires. Very little is known about the latter years of Persian domination because the Jewish historian Josephus, our primary source for the intertestamental period, all but ignores them.

With Alexander the Great's acquisition of Palestine (332 B.C.), a new and more insidious threat to Israel emerged. Alexander was committed to the creation of a world united by Greek language and culture, a policy followed by his successors. This policy, called Hellenization, had a dramatic impact on the Jews.

At Alexander's death (323 B.C.) the empire he won was divided among his generals. Two of them founded dynasties—the Ptolemies in Egypt and the Seleucids in Syria and Mesopotamia—that would contend for control of Palestine for over a century.

The rule of the Ptolemies was considerate of Jewish religious sensitivities, but in 198 B.C. the Seleucids took control and paved the way for one of the most heroic periods in Jewish history.

The early Seleucid years were largely a continuation of the tolerant rule of the Ptolemies, but Antiochus IV Epiphanes (whose title means "God made manifest" and who ruled 175-164 B.C.) changed that when he attempted to consolidate his fading empire through a policy of radical Hellenization. While a segment of the Jewish aristocracy had already adopted Greek ways, the majority of Jews were outraged.

Antiochus's atrocities were aimed at the eradication of Jewish religion. He prohibited some of the central elements of Jewish practice, attempted to destroy all copies of the Torah (the Pentateuch) and required offerings to the Greek god Zeus. His crowning outrage was the erection of a statue of Zeus and the sacrificing of a pig in the Jerusalem temple itself.

Opposition to Antiochus was led by Mattathias, an elderly villager from a priestly family, and his five sons: Judas (Maccabeus), Jonathan, Simon, John and Eleazar. Mattathias destroyed a Greek altar established in his village, Modein, and killed Antiochus's emissary. This triggered the Maccabean revolt, a 24-year war (166-142 B.C.) that resulted in the independence of Judah until the Romans took control in 63 B.C.

The victory of Mattathias's family was a hollow one, however. With the death of his last son, Simon, the Hasmonean dynasty that they founded soon evolved into an aristocratic, Hellenistic regime sometimes hard to distinguish from that of the Seleucids. During the reign of Simon's son, John Hyrcanus, the orthodox Jews who had supported the Maccabees fell out of favor. With only a few exceptions, the rest of the Hasmoneans supported the Jewish Hellenizers. The Pharisees were actually persecuted by Alexander Janneus (102-76 B.C.).

The Hasmonean dynasty ended when, in 63 B.C., an expanding Roman empire intervened in a dynastic clash between the two sons of Janneus, Aristobulus II and Hyrcanus II. Pompey, the general who subdued the East for Rome, took Jerusalem after a three-month siege of the temple area, massacring priests in the performance of their duties and entering the Most Holy Place. This sacrilege began Roman rule in a way that Jews could neither forgive nor forget.

Literature

During these unhappy years of oppression and internal strife, the Jewish people produced a sizable body of literature that both recorded and addressed their era. Three of the more significant works are the Septuagint, the Apocrypha and the Dead Sea Scrolls.

Septuagint. Jewish legend says that 72 scholars, under the sponsorship of Ptolemy Philadelphus (c. 250 B.C.), were brought together on the island of Pharos, near Alexandria, where they produced a Greek translation of the OT in 72 days. From this tradition the Latin word for 70, "Septuagint," became the

name attached to the translation. The Roman numeral for 70, LXX, is used as an abbreviation for it.

Behind the legend lies the probability that at least the Torah (the five books of Moses) was translated into Greek c. 250 B.C. for the use of the Greek-speaking Jews of Alexandria. The rest of the OT and some noncanonical books were also included in the LXX before the dawning of the Christian era, though it is difficult to be certain when.

The Septuagint quickly became the Bible of the Jews outside Palestine who, like the Alexandrians, no longer spoke Hebrew. It would be difficult to overestimate its influence. It made the Scriptures available both to the Jews who no longer spoke their ancestral language and to the entire Greek-speaking world. It later became the Bible of the early church. Also, its widespread popularity and use contributed to the retention of the Apocrypha by some branches of Christendom.

Apocrypha. Derived from a Greek word that means "hidden," Apocrypha has acquired the meaning "false," but in a technical sense it describes a specific body of writings. This collection consists of a variety of books and additions to canonical books that, with the exception of 2 Esdras (c. A.D. 90), were written during the intertestamental period. Their recognition as authoritative in Roman and Eastern Christianity is the result of a complex historical process.

The canon of the OT accepted by Protestants today was very likely established by the dawn of the second century A.D., though after the fall of Jerusalem and the destruction of the temple in 70. The precise scope of the OT was discussed among the Jews until the Council of Jamnia (c. 90). This Hebrew canon was not accepted by the early church, which used the Septuagint. In spite of disagreements among some of the church fathers as to which books were canonical and which were not, the Apocryphal books continued in common use by most Christians until the Reformation. During this period most Protestants decided to follow the original Hebrew canon while Rome, at the Council of Trent (1546) and more recently at the First Vatican Council (1869-70), affirmed the larger "Alexandrian" canon that includes the Apocrypha.

The Apocryphal books have retained their place primarily through the weight of ecclesiastical authority, without which they would not commend themselves as canonical literature. There is no clear evidence that Jesus or the apostles ever quoted any Apocryphal works as Scripture (but see note on Jude 14). The Jewish community that produced them repudiated them, and the historical surveys in the apostolic sermons recorded in Acts completely ignore the period they cover. Even the sober, historical account of 1 Maccabees is tarnished by numerous errors and anachronisms.

There is nothing of theological value in the Apocryphal books that cannot be duplicated in canonical Scripture, and they contain much that runs counter to its teachings. Nonetheless, this body of literature does provide a valuable source of information for the study of the intertestamental period.

Dead Sea Scrolls. In the spring of 1947 an Arab shepherd chanced upon a cave in the hills overlooking the northwestern shore of the Dead Sea that contained what has been called "the greatest manuscript discovery of modern times." The documents and fragments of documents found in those caves, dubbed the "Dead Sea Scrolls," included OT books, a few books of the Apocrypha, apocalyptic works, pseudepigrapha (books that purport to be the work of ancient heroes of the faith), and a number of books peculiar to the sect that produced them.

Approximately a third of the documents are Biblical, with Psalms, Deuteronomy and Isaiah—the books quoted most often in the NT—occurring most frequently. One of the most remarkable finds was a complete 24-foot-long scroll of Isaiah.

The Scrolls have made a significant contribution to the quest for a form of the OT texts most accurately reflecting the original manuscripts; they provide copies 1,000 years closer to the originals than were previously known. The understanding of Biblical Hebrew and Aramaic and knowledge of the development of Judaism between the Testaments have been increased significantly. Of great importance to readers of the Bible is the demonstration of the care with which OT texts were copied, thus providing objective evidence for the general reliability of those texts.

Social Developments

The Judaism of Jesus' day is, to a large extent, the result of changes that came about in response to the pressures of the intertestamental period.

Diaspora. The Diaspora (dispersion) of Israel begun in the exile accelerated during these years until a writer of the day could say that Jews filled "every land and sea."

Jews outside Palestine, cut off from the temple, concentrated their religious life in the study of the Torah and the life of the synagogue (see below). The missionaries of the early church began their Gentile ministries among the Diaspora, using their Greek translation of the OT.

Sadducees. In Palestine, the Greek world made its greatest impact through the party of the Sadducees. Made up of aristocrats, it became the temple party. Because of their position, the Sadducees had a vested interest in the status quo.

Relatively few in number, they wielded disproportionate political power and controlled the high priesthood. They rejected all religious writings except the Torah, as well as any doctrine (such as the resurrection) not found in those five books.

Synagogue. During the exile, Israel was cut off from the temple, divested of nationhood and surrounded by pagan religious practices. Her faith was threatened with extinction. Under these circumstances, the exiles turned their religious focus from what they had lost to what they retained— the Torah and the belief that they were God's people. They concentrated on the law rather than nationhood, on personal piety rather than sacramental rectitude, and on prayer as an acceptable replacement for the sacrifices denied to them.

When they returned from the exile, they brought with them this new form of religious expression, as well as the synagogue (its center), and Judaism became a faith that could be practiced wherever the Torah could be carried. The emphases on personal piety and a relationship with God, which characterized synagogue worship, not only helped preserve Judaism but also prepared the way for the Christian gospel.

Pharisees. As the party of the synagogue, the Pharisees strove to reinterpret the law. They built a "hedge" around it to enable Jews to live righteously before God in a world that had changed drastically since the days of Moses. Although they were comparatively few in number, the Pharisees enjoyed the support of the people and influenced popular opinion if not national policy. They were the only party to survive the destruction of the temple in A.D. 70 and were the spiritual progenitors of modern Judaism.

Essenes. An almost forgotten Jewish sect until the discovery of the Dead Sea Scrolls, the Essenes were a small, separatist group that grew out of the conflicts of the Maccabean age. Like the Pharisees, they stressed strict legal observance, but they considered the temple priesthood corrupt and rejected much of the temple ritual and sacrificial system. Mentioned by several ancient writers, the precise nature of the Essenes is still not certain, though it is generally agreed that the Qumran community that produced the Dead Sea Scrolls was an Essene group.

Because they were convinced that they were the true remnant, these Qumran Essenes had separated themselves from Judaism at large and devoted themselves to personal purity and preparation for the final war between the "Sons of Light and the Sons of Darkness." They practiced an apocalyptic faith, looking back to the contributions of their "Teacher of Righteousness" and forward to the coming of two, and possibly three, Messiahs. The destruction of the temple in A.D. 70, however, seems to have delivered a death blow to their apocalyptic expectations.

Attempts have been made to equate aspects of the beliefs of the Qumran community with the origins of Christianity. Some have seen a prototype of Jesus in their "Teacher of Righteousness," and both John the Baptist and Jesus have been assigned membership in the sect. There is, however, only a superficial, speculative base for these conjectures.

THE NEW
TESTAMENT

The Synoptic Gospels

A careful comparison of the four Gospels reveals that Matthew, Mark and Luke are noticeably similar, while John is quite different. The first three Gospels agree extensively in language, in the material they include, and in the order in which events and sayings from the life of Christ are recorded. (Chronological order does not appear to have been rigidly followed in any of the Gospels, however.) Because of this agreement, these three books are called the Synoptic Gospels (*syn,* "together with"; *optic,* "seeing"; thus "seeing together"). For an example of agreement in content see Mt 9:2-8; Mk 2:3-12; Lk 5:18-26. An instance of verbatim agreement is found in Mt 10:22a; Mk 13:13a; Lk 21:17. A mathematical comparison shows that 91 percent of Mark's Gospel is contained in Matthew, while 53 percent of Mark is found in Luke. Such agreement raises questions as to the origin of the Synoptic Gospels. Did the authors rely on a common source? Were they interdependent? Questions such as these constitute what is known as the Synoptic Problem. Several suggested solutions have been advanced:

1. *The use of oral tradition.* Some have thought that tradition had become so stereotyped that it provided a common source from which all the Gospel writers drew.

2. *The use of an early Gospel.* Some have postulated that the Synoptic authors all had access to an earlier Gospel, now lost.

3. *The use of written fragments.* Some have assumed that written fragments had been composed concerning various events from the life of Christ and that these were used by the Synoptic authors.

4. *Mutual dependence.* Some have suggested that the Synoptic writers drew from each other with the result that what they wrote was often very similar.

5. *The use of two major sources.* The most common view currently is that the Gospel of Mark and a hypothetical document, called *Quelle* (German for "source") or *Q,* were used by Matthew and Luke as sources for most of the materials included in their Gospels.

6. *The priority and use of Matthew.* Another view suggests that the other two Synoptics drew from Matthew as their main source.

7. *A combination of most of the above.* This theory assumes that the authors of the Synoptic Gospels made use of oral tradition, written fragments, mutual dependence on other Synoptic writers or on their Gospels, and the testimony of eyewitnesses.

Dating the Synoptic Gospels

MARK ═══╗
         MATTHEW   LUKE

ASSUMPTION A
Matthew and Luke used
Mark as a major source

> **View No. 1**
> Mark written in the 50s
> or early 60s
>
>> (1) Matthew written in
>>   late 50s or the 60s
>>
>> (2) Luke written 59-63
>
> **View No. 2**
> Mark written 65-70
>
>> (1) Matthew written in the 70s
>>
>> (2) Luke written in the 70s

MARK | MATTHEW | LUKE

ASSUMPTION B
Matthew and Luke did not
use Mark as a source

> **View No. 1**
> Mark could have been written
> anytime between 50 and 70
>
> **View No. 2**
> Mark written 65-70
>
>> (1) Matthew written early 50s
>>   (see Introduction to Matthew:
>>   Date and Place of Writing)
>>
>> (2) Luke written 59-63 (see Introduction
>>   to Luke: Date and Place of Writing)

MATTHEW

See "The Synoptic Gospels," p. 1437.

Author

The early church fathers were unanimous in holding that Matthew, one of the 12 apostles, was the author of this Gospel. However, the results of modern critical studies—in particular those that stress Matthew's alleged dependence on Mark for a substantial part of his Gospel—have caused some Biblical scholars to abandon Matthean authorship. Why, they ask, would Matthew, an eyewitness to the events of our Lord's life, depend so heavily on Mark's account? The best answer seems to be that he agreed with it and wanted to show that the apostolic testimony to Christ was not divided.

Matthew, whose name means "gift of the LORD," was a tax collector who left his work to follow Jesus (9:9-13). In Mark and Luke he is called by his other name, Levi.

Date and Place of Writing

The Jewish nature of Matthew's Gospel may suggest that it was written in Palestine, though many think it may have originated in Syrian Antioch. Some have argued on the basis of its Jewish characteristics that it was written in the early church period, possibly the early part of A.D. 50, when the church was largely Jewish and the gospel was preached to Jews only (Ac 11:19). However, those who have concluded that both Matthew and Luke drew extensively from Mark's Gospel date it later—after the Gospel of Mark had been in circulation for a period of time. See chart on "Dating the Synoptic Gospels," p. 1437. Accordingly, some feel that Matthew would have been written in the late 50s or in the 60s. Others, who assume that Mark was written between 65 and 70, place Matthew in the 70s or even later.

Recipients

Since his Gospel was written in Greek, Matthew's readers were obviously Greek-speaking. They also seem to have been Jews. Many elements point to Jewish readership: Matthew's concern with fulfillment of the OT (he has more quotations from and allusions to the OT than any other NT author); his tracing of Jesus' descent from Abraham (1:1-17); his lack of explanation of Jewish customs (especially in contrast to Mark); his use of Jewish terminology (e.g., "kingdom of heaven" and "Father in heaven," where "heaven" reveals the Jewish reverential reluctance to use the name of God); his emphasis on Jesus' role as "Son of David" (1:1; 9:27; 12:23; 15:22; 20:30-31; 21:9,15; 22:41-45). This does not mean, however, that Matthew restricts his Gospel to Jews. He records the coming of the Magi (non-Jews) to worship the infant Jesus (2:1-12), as well as Jesus' statement that the "field is the world" (13:38). He also gives a full statement of the Great Commission (28:18-20). These passages show that, although Matthew's Gospel is Jewish, it has a universal outlook.

Purpose

Matthew's main purpose is to prove to his Jewish readers that Jesus is their Messiah. He does this primarily by showing how Jesus in his life and ministry fulfilled the OT Scriptures. Although all the Gospel writers quote the OT, Matthew includes nine additional proof texts (1:22-23; 2:15; 2:17-18; 2:23; 4:14-16; 8:17; 12:17-21; 13:35; 27:9-10) to drive home his basic theme: Jesus is the fulfillment of the OT predictions of the Messiah. Matthew even finds the history of God's people in the OT recapitulated in some aspects of Jesus' life (see, e.g., his quotation of Hos 11:1 in 2:15). To accomplish his purpose Matthew also emphasizes Jesus' Davidic lineage (see Recipients above).

Structure

The way the material is arranged reveals an artistic touch. The whole Gospel is woven around five great discourses: (1) chs. 5-7; (2) ch. 10; (3) ch. 13; (4) ch. 18; (5) chs. 24-25. That this is deliberate

is clear from the refrain that concludes each discourse: "When Jesus had finished saying these things," or similar words (7:28; 11:1; 13:53; 19:1; 26:1). The narrative sections, in each case, appropriately lead up to the discourses. The Gospel has a fitting prologue (chs. 1-2) and a challenging epilogue (28:16-20).

The fivefold division may suggest that Matthew has modeled his book on the structure of the Pentateuch (the first five books of the OT). He may also be presenting the gospel as a new Torah and Jesus as a new and greater Moses.

Outline

The Genealogy of Jesus

1:1–17pp — Lk 3:23–38
1:3–6pp — Ru 4:18–22
1:7–11pp — 1Ch 3:10–17

1 A record of the genealogy of Jesus Christ the son of David,ᵃ the son of Abraham:ᵇ

2Abraham was the father of Isaac, ᶜ
 Isaac the father of Jacob, ᵈ
 Jacob the father of Judah and his brothers, ᵉ
3Judah the father of Perez and Zerah, whose mother was Tamar, ᶠ
 Perez the father of Hezron,
 Hezron the father of Ram,
4Ram the father of Amminadab,
 Amminadab the father of Nahshon,
 Nahshon the father of Salmon,
5Salmon the father of Boaz, whose mother was Rahab, ᵍ
 Boaz the father of Obed, whose mother was Ruth,
 Obed the father of Jesse,
6and Jesse the father of King David. ʰ

David was the father of Solomon, whose mother had been Uriah's wife, ⁱ
7Solomon the father of Rehoboam,
 Rehoboam the father of Abijah,
 Abijah the father of Asa,
8Asa the father of Jehoshaphat,
 Jehoshaphat the father of Jehoram,
 Jehoram the father of Uzziah,
9Uzziah the father of Jotham,
 Jotham the father of Ahaz,

 Ahaz the father of Hezekiah,
10Hezekiah the father of Manasseh, ʲ
 Manasseh the father of Amon,
 Amon the father of Josiah,
11and Josiah the father of Jeconiahᵃ and his brothers at the time of the exile to Babylon. ᵏ

12After the exile to Babylon:
 Jeconiah was the father of Shealtiel, ˡ
 Shealtiel the father of Zerubbabel, ᵐ
13Zerubbabel the father of Abiud,
 Abiud the father of Eliakim,
 Eliakim the father of Azor,
14Azor the father of Zadok,
 Zadok the father of Akim,
 Akim the father of Eliud,
15Eliud the father of Eleazar,
 Eleazar the father of Matthan,
 Matthan the father of Jacob,
16and Jacob the father of Joseph, the husband of Mary, ⁿ of whom was born Jesus, who is called Christ. ᵒ

17Thus there were fourteen generations in all from Abraham to David, fourteen from David to the exile to Babylon, and fourteen from the exile to the Christ. ᵇ

The Birth of Jesus Christ

18This is how the birth of Jesus Christ came about: His mother Mary was pledged to be married to Joseph, but before they came together, she was found to be with child through the Holy Spirit. ᵖ 19Because

Cross references

1:1 *a*2Sa 7:12-16;
Isa 9:6,7; 11:1;
Jer 23:5,6;
S Mt 9:27;
Lk 1:32,69;
Rev 22:16
*b*Ge 22:18;
S Gal 3:16
1:2 *c*Ge 21:3,12
*d*Ge 25:26
*e*Ge 29:35; 49:10
1:3 *f*Ge 38:27-30
1:5 *g*S Heb 11:31
1:6 *h*1Sa 16:1;
17:12 *i*2Sa 12:24

1:10 *j*2Ki 20:21
1:11
*k*2Ki 24:14-16;
Jer 27:20; 40:1;
Da 1:1,2
1:12 *l*1Ch 3:17
*m*1Ch 3:19;
Ezr 3:2
1:16 *n*Lk 1:27
*o*Mt 27:17
1:18 *p*Lk 1:35

ᵃ*11* That is, Jehoiachin; also in verse 12   ᵇ*17* Or *Messiah*. "The Christ" (Greek) and "the Messiah" (Hebrew) both mean "the Anointed One."

1:1–16 For a comparison of Matthew's genealogy with Luke's see note on Lk 3:23–38. The types of people mentioned in this genealogy reveal the broad scope of those who make up the people of God as well as the genealogy of Jesus.
1:1 *the son of David.* A Messianic title (see note on 9:27) found several times in this Gospel (in 1:20 it is not a Messianic title). *the son of Abraham.* Because Matthew was writing to Jews, it was important to identify Jesus in this way.
1:4 *Amminadab.* Father-in-law of Aaron (Ex 6:23).
1:5 *Rahab.* See Jos 2. Since quite a long time had elapsed between Rahab and David and because of Matthew's desire for systematic organization (see note on v. 17), many of the generations between these two ancestors were assumed, but not listed, by Matthew.
1:8 *Jehoram the father.* Matthew calls Jehoram the father of Uzziah, but from 2Ch 21:4–26:23 it is clear that, again, several generations were assumed (Ahaziah, Joash and Amaziah) and that "father" is used in the sense of "forefather."
1:11 *Josiah the father.* Similarly (see note on v. 8), Josiah is called the father of Jeconiah (i.e., Jehoiachin; see NIV text note), whereas he was actually the father of Jehoiakim and the grandfather of Jehoiachin (2Ch 36:1–9).
1:12 *Shealtiel the father.* See note on 1 Ch. 3:19.
1:16 Matthew does not say that Joseph was the father of Jesus but only that he was the husband of Mary and that

Jesus was born of her. In this genealogy Matthew shows that, although Jesus is not the physical son of Joseph, he is the legal son and therefore a descendant of David.
1:17 *fourteen generations ... fourteen ... fourteen.* These divisions reflect two characteristics of Matthew's Gospel: (1) an apparent fondness for numbers and (2) concern for systematic arrangement. The number 14 may have been chosen because it is twice seven (the number of completeness) and/or because it is the numerical value of the name David (see note on Rev 13:18). For the practice of telescoping genealogies to achieve the desired number of names see Introduction to 1 Chronicles: Genealogies.
1:18 *pledged to be married.* There were no sexual relations during a Jewish betrothal period, but it was a much more binding relationship than a modern engagement and could be broken only by divorce (see v. 19). In Dt 22:24 a betrothed woman is called a "wife," though the preceding verse speaks of her as being "pledged to be married." Matthew uses the terms "husband" (v. 19) and "wife" (v. 24) of Joseph and Mary before they were married.
1:19 *righteous.* To Jews this meant being zealous in keeping the law. *divorce her quietly.* He would sign the necessary legal papers but not have her judged publicly and stoned (see Dt 22:23–24).

Joseph her husband was a righteous man and did not want to expose her to public disgrace, he had in mind to divorce[q] her quietly.

20But after he had considered this, an angel[r] of the Lord appeared to him in a dream[s] and said, "Joseph son of David, do not be afraid to take Mary home as your wife, because what is conceived in her is from the Holy Spirit. 21She will give birth to a son, and you are to give him the name Jesus,[c][t] because he will save his people from their sins."[u]

22All this took place to fulfill[v] what the Lord had said through the prophet: 23"The virgin will be with child and will give birth to a son, and they will call him Immanuel"[d][w]—which means, "God with us."

24When Joseph woke up, he did what the angel[x] of the Lord had commanded him and took Mary home as his wife. 25But he had no union with her until she gave birth to a son. And he gave him the name Jesus.[y]

The Visit of the Magi

2 After Jesus was born in Bethlehem in Judea,[z] during the time of King Herod,[a] Magi[e] from the east came to Jerusalem 2and asked, "Where is the one who has been born king of the Jews?[b] We saw his star[c] in the east[f] and have come to worship him."

3When King Herod heard this he was disturbed, and all Jerusalem with him. 4When he had called together all the people's chief priests and teachers of the law, he asked them where the Christ[g] was to be born. 5"In Bethlehem[d] in Judea," they replied, "for this is what the prophet has written:

6" 'But you, Bethlehem, in the land of Judah,
are by no means least among the rulers of Judah;
for out of you will come a ruler
who will be the shepherd of my people Israel.'[h]" [e]

7Then Herod called the Magi secretly and found out from them the exact time the star had appeared. 8He sent them to Bethlehem and said, "Go and make a careful search for the child. As soon as you find him, report to me, so that I too may go and worship him."

9After they had heard the king, they went on their way, and the star they had seen in the east[i] went ahead of them until it stopped over the place where the child was. 10When they saw the star, they were overjoyed. 11On coming to the house, they

Cross references

1:19 qDt 24:1
1:20 rS Ac 5:19
sS Mt 27:19
1:21 tS Lk 1:31
uPs 130:8;
S Lk 2:11;
S Jn 3:17;
Ac 5:31;
S Ro 11:14;
Tit 2:14
1:22 vMt 2:15,
17,23; 4:14;
8:17; 12:17;
21:4; 26:54,56;
27:9; Lk 4:21;
21:22; 24:44;
Jn 13:18; 19:24,
28,36
1:23 wIsa 7:14;
8:8,10
1:24 xS Ac 5:19
1:25 yver 21;
S Lk 1:31
2:1 zLk 2:4-7
aLk 1:5
2:2 bJer 23:5;
Mt 27:11;
Mk 15:2;
Lk 23:38;
Jn 1:49; 18:33-37
cNu 24:17

2:5 dJn 7:42
2:6 eMic 5:2;
2Sa 5:2

Text notes

c21 Jesus is the Greek form of Joshua, which means the LORD saves.   d23 Isaiah 7:14   e1 Traditionally Wise Men   f2 Or star when it rose   g4 Or Messiah   h6 Micah 5:2   i9 Or seen when it rose

Study notes

1:20 in a dream. The phrase occurs five times in the first two chapters of Matthew (here; 2:12–13,19,22) and indicates the means the Lord used for speaking to Joseph. son of David. Perhaps a hint that the message of the angel related to the expected Messiah. take Mary home as your wife. They were legally bound to each other, but not yet living together as husband and wife. what is conceived in her is from the Holy Spirit. This agrees perfectly with the announcement to Mary (Lk 1:35), except that the latter is more specific (see note on Lk 1:26–35).
1:22 fulfill. Twelve times (here; 2:15,23; 3:15; 4:14; 5:17; 8:17; 12:17; 13:14,35; 21:4; 27:9) Matthew speaks of the OT being fulfilled, i.e., of events in NT times that were prophesied in the OT—a powerful testimony to the divine origin of Scripture and its accuracy even in small details. In the fulfillments we also see the writer's concern for linking the gospel with the OT.
1:23 See note on Isa 7:14. This is the first of at least 47 quotations, most of them Messianic, that Matthew takes from the OT (see NIV text notes throughout Matthew).
2:1 Bethlehem in Judea. A village about five miles south of Jerusalem. Matthew says nothing of the events in Nazareth (cf. Lk 1:26–56). Possibly wanting to emphasize Jesus' Davidic background, he begins with the events that happened in David's city. It is called "Bethlehem in Judea," not to distinguish it from the town of the same name about seven miles northwest of Nazareth, but to emphasize that Jesus came from the tribe and territory that produced the line of Davidic kings. That Jews expected the Messiah to be born in Bethlehem and to be from David's family is clear from Jn 7:42. King Herod. Herod the Great (37–4 B.C.), to be distin-

guished from the other Herods in the Bible (see chart on "House of Herod," p. 1443). Herod was a non-Jew, an Idumean, who was appointed king of Judea by the Roman Senate in 40 B.C. and gained control in 37. Like most rulers of the day, he was ruthless, murdering his wife, his three sons, mother-in-law, brother-in-law, uncle and many others—not to mention the babies in Bethlehem (v. 16). His reign was also noted for splendor, as seen in the many theaters, amphitheaters, monuments, pagan altars, fortresses and other buildings he erected or refurbished—including the greatest work of all, the rebuilding of the temple in Jerusalem, begun in 19 B.C. and finished 68 years after his death. Magi. Probably astrologers, perhaps from Persia or southern Arabia, both of which are east of Palestine. Jerusalem. Since they were looking for the "king of the Jews" (v. 2), they naturally came to the Jewish capital city (see map No. 8 at the end of the Study Bible).
2:2 king of the Jews. Indicates the Magi were Gentiles. Matthew shows that people of all nations acknowledged Jesus as "king of the Jews" and came to worship him as Lord. star. Probably not an ordinary star, planet or comet, though some scholars have identified it with the conjunction of Jupiter and Saturn.
2:4 chief priests. Sadducees (see note on 3:7) who were in charge of worship at the temple in Jerusalem. teachers of the law. The Jewish scholars of the day, professionally trained in the development, teaching and application of OT law. Their authority was strictly human and traditional.
2:6 This prophecy from Micah had been given seven centuries earlier.
2:11 house. Contrary to tradition, the Magi did not visit

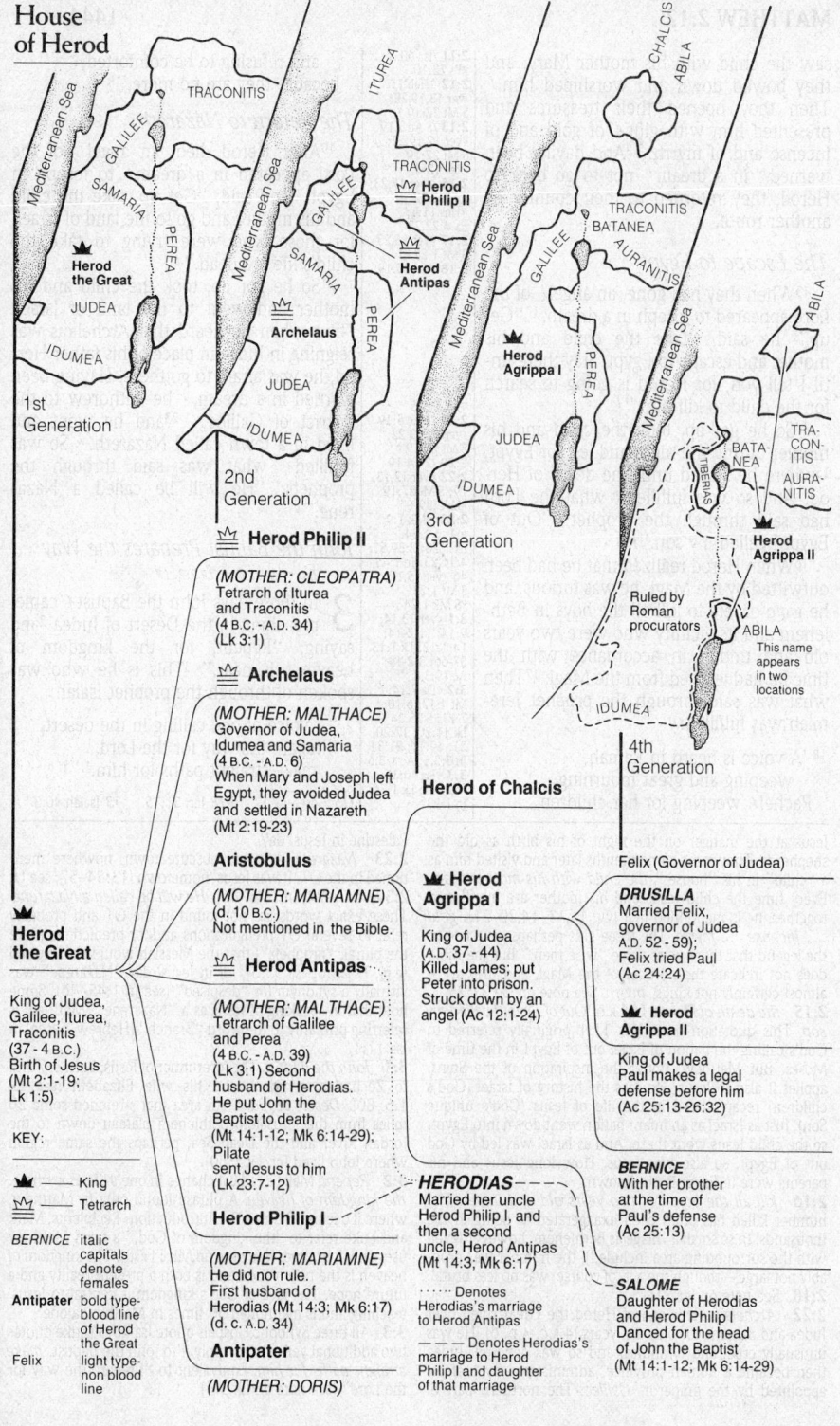

House of Herod

Mediterranean Sea

TRACONITIS

GALILEE
SAMARIA
PEREA

👑 **Herod the Great**

JUDEA

IDUMEA

1st Generation

ITUREA
TRACONITIS

TRACONITIS

♔ **Herod Philip II**

Mediterranean Sea

GALILEE
SAMARIA
PEREA

♔ **Herod Antipas**

Archelaus

JUDEA

IDUMEA

2nd Generation

CHALCIS
ABILA

TRACONITIS
BATANEA

GALILEE
AURANITIS

Mediterranean Sea

👑 **Herod Agrippa I**

PEREA

JUDEA

IDUMEA

ABILA

3rd Generation

BATA-
NEA
TIBERIAS

TRA-
CONI-
TIS
AURA-
NITIS

ABILA
This name appears in two locations

Ruled by Roman procurators

IDUMEA

Mediterranean Sea

👑 **Herod Agrippa II**

4th Generation

👑 **Herod the Great**

King of Judea, Galilee, Iturea, Traconitis (37 - 4 B.C.)
Birth of Jesus (Mt 2:1-19; Lk 1:5)

KEY:

👑 —— King

♔ —— Tetrarch

BERNICE italic capitals denote females

Antipater bold type- blood line of Herod the Great

Felix light type- non blood line

♔ **Herod Philip II**

(MOTHER: CLEOPATRA)
Tetrarch of Iturea and Traconitis
(4 B.C. - A.D. 34)
(Lk 3:1)

♔ **Archelaus**

(MOTHER: MALTHACE)
Governor of Judea, Idumea and Samaria
(4 B.C. - A.D. 6)
When Mary and Joseph left Egypt, they avoided Judea and settled in Nazareth
(Mt 2:19-23)

Aristobulus

(MOTHER: MARIAMNE)
(d. 10 B.C.)
Not mentioned in the Bible.

♔ **Herod Antipas**

(MOTHER: MALTHACE)
Tetrarch of Galilee and Perea
(4 B.C. - A.D. 39)
(Lk 3:1) Second husband of Herodias.
He put John the Baptist to death
(Mt 14:1-12; Mk 6:14-29);
Pilate sent Jesus to him
(Lk 23:7-12)

Herod Philip I

(MOTHER: MARIAMNE)
He did not rule.
First husband of Herodias (Mt 14:3; Mk 6:17)
(d. c. A.D. 34)

Antipater

(MOTHER: DORIS)

Herod of Chalcis

👑 **Herod Agrippa I**

King of Judea
(A.D. 37 - 44)
Killed James; put Peter into prison.
Struck down by an angel (Ac 12:1-24)

HERODIAS
Married her uncle Herod Philip I, and then a second uncle, Herod Antipas (Mt 14:3; Mk 6:17)

········· Denotes Herodias's marriage to Herod Antipas

——— Denotes Herodias's marriage to Herod Philip I and daughter of that marriage

---

Felix (Governor of Judea)

DRUSILLA
Married Felix, governor of Judea
A.D. 52 - 59);
Felix tried Paul
(Ac 24:24)

👑 **Herod Agrippa II**

King of Judea
Paul makes a legal defense before him
(Ac 25:13-26:32)

BERNICE
With her brother at the time of Paul's defense
(Ac 25:13)

SALOME
Daughter of Herodias and Herod Philip I
Danced for the head of John the Baptist
(Mt 14:1-12; Mk 6:14-29)

saw the child with his mother Mary, and they bowed down and worshiped him.*f* Then they opened their treasures and presented him with gifts*g* of gold and of incense and of myrrh. ¹²And having been warned*h* in a dream*i* not to go back to Herod, they returned to their country by another route.

The Escape to Egypt

¹³When they had gone, an angel*j* of the Lord appeared to Joseph in a dream.*k* "Get up," he said, "take the child and his mother and escape to Egypt. Stay there until I tell you, for Herod is going to search for the child to kill him."*l*

¹⁴So he got up, took the child and his mother during the night and left for Egypt, ¹⁵where he stayed until the death of Herod. And so was fulfilled*m* what the Lord had said through the prophet: "Out of Egypt I called my son."*j n*

¹⁶When Herod realized that he had been outwitted by the Magi, he was furious, and he gave orders to kill all the boys in Bethlehem and its vicinity who were two years old and under, in accordance with the time he had learned from the Magi. ¹⁷Then what was said through the prophet Jeremiah was fulfilled:*o*

¹⁸"A voice is heard in Ramah,
    weeping and great mourning,
  Rachel*p* weeping for her children

and refusing to be comforted,
  because they are no more."*k q*

The Return to Nazareth

¹⁹After Herod died, an angel*r* of the Lord appeared in a dream*s* to Joseph in Egypt ²⁰and said, "Get up, take the child and his mother and go to the land of Israel, for those who were trying to take the child's life are dead."*t*

²¹So he got up, took the child and his mother and went to the land of Israel. ²²But when he heard that Archelaus was reigning in Judea in place of his father Herod, he was afraid to go there. Having been warned in a dream,*u* he withdrew to the district of Galilee,*v* ²³and he went and lived in a town called Nazareth.*w* So was fulfilled*x* what was said through the prophets: "He will be called a Nazarene."*y*

John the Baptist Prepares the Way

3:1–12pp — Mk 1:3–8; Lk 3:2–17

3 In those days John the Baptist*z* came, preaching in the Desert of Judea ²and saying, "Repent, for the kingdom of heaven*a* is near." ³This is he who was spoken of through the prophet Isaiah:

"A voice of one calling in the desert,
  'Prepare the way for the Lord,
    make straight paths for him.' "*l b*

Cross references

2:11 *f* Isa 60:3
  g Ps 72:10
2:12 *h* Heb 11:7
  i ver 13,19,22;
  S Mt 27:19
2:13 *j* S Ac 5:19
  k ver 12,19,22;
  S Mt 27:19
  l Rev 12:4
2:15 *m* ver 17,23;
  S Mt 1:22
  n Hos 11:1;
  Ex 4:22,23
2:17 *o* ver 15,23;
  S Mt 1:22
2:18 *p* Ge 35:19

q Jer 31:15
2:19 *r* S Ac 5:19
  s ver 12,13,22;
  S Mt 27:19
2:20 *t* Ex 4:19
2:22 *u* ver 12,13,
  19; S Mt 27:19
  v Lk 2:39
2:23 *w* Mk 1:9;
  6:1; S 1:24;
  Lk 1:26; 2:39,51;
  4:16,23; Jn 1:45,
  46 *x* ver 15,17;
  S Mt 1:22
  y S Mk 1:24
3:1 *z* ver 13,14;
  9:14; 11:2-14;
  14:1-12; Lk 1:13,
  57-66; 3:2-19;
  Ac 19:3,4
3:2 *a* Da 7:14;
  Mt 4:17; 6:10;
  7:21; S 25:34;
  Lk 11:20; 17:20,
  21; 19:11; 21:31;
  Jn 3:3,5; Ac 1:3,6
3:3 *b* Isa 40:3;
  Mal 3:1; Lk 1:76;
  Jn 1:23

i 15 Hosea 11:1   *k* 18 Jer. 31:15   *l* 3 Isaiah 40:3

Jesus at the manger on the night of his birth as did the shepherds. They came some months later and visited him as a "child" in his "house." *the child with his mother Mary.* Every time the child Jesus and his mother are mentioned together, he is mentioned first (vv. 11,13–14,20–21). *gold . . . incense . . . myrrh.* The three gifts perhaps gave rise to the legend that there were three "wise men." But the Bible does not indicate the number of the Magi, and they were almost certainly not kings. *myrrh.* See note on Ge 37:25.

2:15 *the death of Herod.* In 4 B.C. *Out of Egypt I called my son.* This quotation from Hos 11:1 originally referred to God's calling the nation of Israel out of Egypt in the time of Moses. But Matthew, under the inspiration of the Spirit, applies it also to Jesus. He sees the history of Israel (God's children) recapitulated in the life of Jesus (God's unique Son). Just as Israel as an infant nation went down into Egypt, so the child Jesus went there. And as Israel was led by God out of Egypt, so also was Jesus. How long Jesus and his parents were in Egypt is not known.

2:16 *kill all the boys . . . two years old and under.* The number killed has often been exaggerated as being in the thousands. In so small a village as Bethlehem, however (even with the surrounding area included), the number was probably not large—though the act, of course, was no less brutal.

2:18 See note on Jer 31:15.

2:22 *Archelaus.* This son of Herod the Great ruled over Judea and Samaria for only ten years (4 B.C.-A.D. 6). He was unusually cruel and tyrannical and so was deposed. Judea then became a Roman province, administered by prefects appointed by the emperor. *Galilee.* The northern part of

Palestine in Jesus' day.

2:23 *Nazareth.* A rather obscure town, nowhere mentioned in the OT. It was Jesus' hometown (13:54–57; see Lk 2:39; 4:16–24; Jn 1:45–46). *He will be called a Nazarene.* These exact words are not found in the OT and probably refer to several OT prefigurations and/or predictions (note the plural, "prophets") that the Messiah would be despised (e.g., Ps 22:6; Isa 53:3), for in Jesus' day "Nazarene" was virtually a synonym for "despised" (see Jn 1:45–46). Some hold that in speaking of Jesus as a "Nazarene," Matthew is referring primarily to the word "Branch" (Hebrew *neṣer*) in Isa 11:1.

3:1 *John the Baptist.* The forerunner of Jesus, born c. 7 B.C. to Zechariah, a priest, and his wife Elizabeth (see Lk 1:5–80). *Desert of Judea.* An area that stretched some 20 miles from the Jerusalem-Bethlehem plateau down to the Jordan River and the Dead Sea, perhaps the same region where John lived (cf. Lk 1:80).

3:2 *Repent.* Make a radical change in one's life as a whole. *the kingdom of heaven.* A phrase found only in Matthew, where it occurs 33 times. See Introduction: Recipients. Mark and Luke refer to "the kingdom of God," a term Matthew uses only four times (see note on Mk 11:30). The kingdom of heaven is the rule of God and is both a present reality and a future hope. The idea of God's kingdom is central to Jesus' teaching and is mentioned 50 times in Matthew alone.

3:3 All three Synoptic Gospels quote Isa 40:3 (Luke quotes two additional verses) and apply it to John the Baptist. *make straight paths for him.* Equivalent to "Prepare the way for the Lord" (see note on Lk 3:4).

4John's[c] clothes were made of camel's hair, and he had a leather belt around his waist.[d] His food was locusts[e] and wild honey. 5People went out to him from Jerusalem and all Judea and the whole region of the Jordan. 6Confessing their sins, they were baptized[f] by him in the Jordan River.

7But when he saw many of the Pharisees and Sadducees coming to where he was baptizing, he said to them: "You brood of vipers![g] Who warned you to flee from the coming wrath?[h] 8Produce fruit in keeping with repentance.[i] 9And do not think you can say to yourselves, 'We have Abraham as our father.'[j] I tell you that out of these stones God can raise up children for Abraham. 10The ax is already at the root of the trees, and every tree that does not produce good fruit will be cut down and thrown into the fire.[k]

11"I baptize you with[m] water for repentance.[l] But after me will come one who is more powerful than I, whose sandals I am not fit to carry. He will baptize you with the Holy Spirit[m] and with fire.[n] 12His winnowing fork is in his hand, and he will clear his threshing floor, gathering his wheat into the barn and burning up the chaff with unquenchable fire."[o]

The Baptism of Jesus

3:13–17pp — Mk 1:9–11; Lk 3:21,22; Jn 1:31–34

13Then Jesus came from Galilee to the Jordan to be baptized by John.[p] 14But John tried to deter him, saying, "I need to be baptized by you, and do you come to me?" 15Jesus replied, "Let it be so now; it is

m11 Or in

Cross-references (center column):

3:4 cS Mt 3:1
d2Ki 1:8
eLev 11:22
3:6 fver 11; S Mk 1:4
3:7 gMt 12:34; 23:33 hS Ro 1:18
3:8 iAc 26:20
3:9 jS Lk 3:8

3:10 kMt 7:19; Lk 3:9; 13:6–9; Jn 15:2,6
3:11 lver 6; S Mk 1:4 mS Mk 1:8 nIsa 4:4; Ac 2:3,4
3:12 oMt 13:30; S 25:41
3:13 pS Mt 3:1; S Mk 1:4

3:4 *locusts and wild honey.* A man living in the desert did not hesitate to eat insects, and locusts were among the clean foods (Lev 11:21–22). John's simple food, clothing and lifestyle were a visual protest against self-indulgence.
3:6 *Jordan River.* See note on Mk 1:5.
3:7 *Pharisees and Sadducees.* The Pharisees (see notes on Mk 2:16; Lk 5:17) were a legalistic and separatistic group who strictly, but often hypocritically, kept the law of Moses and the unwritten "tradition of the elders" (15:2). The Sadducees (see notes on Mk 12:18; Lk 20:27; Ac 4:1) were more worldly and politically minded, and were theologically unorthodox—among other things denying the resurrection,

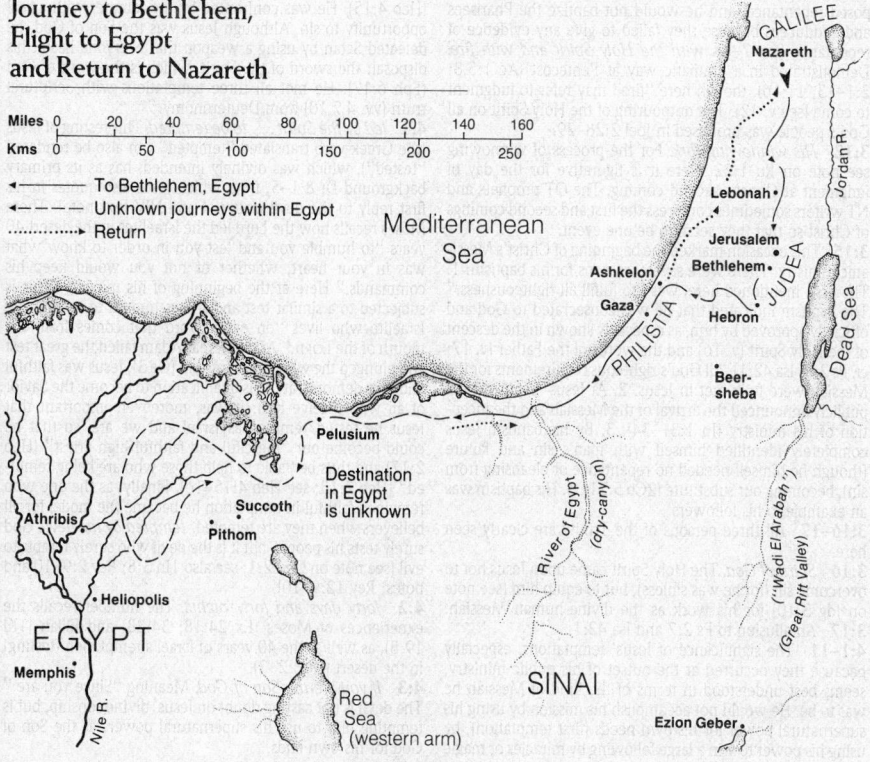

Journey to Bethlehem, Flight to Egypt and Return to Nazareth

Miles 0   20   40   60   80   100   120   140   160
Kms   0   50   100   150   200   250

◄—— To Bethlehem, Egypt
◄— — — Unknown journeys within Egypt
············► Return

Mediterranean Sea

GALILEE
Nazareth
Lebonah
Jerusalem
Bethlehem
Ashkelon
Gaza
Hebron
JUDEA
PHILISTIA
Beer-sheba
Jordan R.
Dead Sea

Pelusium
Destination in Egypt is unknown
Succoth
Pithom
Athribis
Heliopolis
EGYPT
Memphis
Nile R.
Red Sea (western arm)
River of Egypt (dry-canyon)
SINAI
Ezion Geber
("Wadi El Arabah")
(Great Rift Valley)

proper for us to do this to fulfill all righteousness." Then John consented.

¹⁶As soon as Jesus was baptized, he went up out of the water. At that moment heaven was opened,^q and he saw the Spirit of God^r descending like a dove and lighting on him. ¹⁷And a voice from heaven^s said, "This is my Son,^t whom I love; with him I am well pleased."^u

The Temptation of Jesus

4:1–11pp — Mk 1:12,13; Lk 4:1–13

4 Then Jesus was led by the Spirit into the desert to be tempted^v by the devil.^w ²After fasting forty days and forty nights,^x he was hungry. ³The tempter^y came to him and said, "If you are the Son of God,^z tell these stones to become bread."

⁴Jesus answered, "It is written: 'Man does not live on bread alone, but on every

word that comes from the mouth of God.'ⁿ"^a

⁵Then the devil took him to the holy city^b and had him stand on the highest point of the temple. ⁶"If you are the Son of God,"^c he said, "throw yourself down. For it is written:

" 'He will command his angels
concerning you,
and they will lift you up in their
hands,
so that you will not strike your foot
against a stone.'^o"^d

⁷Jesus answered him, "It is also written: 'Do not put the Lord your God to the test.'^p"^e

Cross references:
3:16 ^qEze 1:1; Jn 1:51; Ac 7:56; 10:11; Rev 4:1; 19:11 ^rIsa 11:2; 42:1
3:17 ^sDt 4:12; Mt 17:5; Jn 12:28 ^tPs 2:7; Ac 13:33; Heb 1:1-5; 5:5; 2Pe 1:17,18 ^uIsa 42:1; Mt 12:18; 17:5; Mk 1:11; 9:7; Lk 3:22; 9:35; 2Pe 1:17
4:1 ^vHeb 4:15 ^wGe 3:1-7
4:2 ^xEx 34:28; 1Ki 19:8
4:3 ^y1Th 3:5 ^zS Mt 3:17; 14:33; 16:16; 27:54; Mk 3:11; Lk 1:35; 22:70; Jn 1:34,49; 5:25; 11:27; 20:31; Ac 9:20; Ro 1:4; 1Jn 5:10-13,20; Rev 2:18
4:4 ^aDt 8:3; Jn 4:34
4:5 ^bNe 11:1; Da 9:24; Mt 27:53 **4:6** ^cS ver 3 ^dPs 91:11,12
4:7 ^eDt 6:16

n4 Deut. 8:3   o6 Psalm 91:11,12   p7 Deut. 6:16

---

angels and spirits (Ac 23:8).
3:9 *We have Abraham as our father.* See Jn 8:39. Salvation does not come as a birthright (even for the Jews) but through faith in Christ (Ro 2:28–29; Gal 3:7,9,29).
3:10 *The ax is already at the root of the trees.* Judgment is near.
3:11 *with water for repentance.* John's baptism presupposed repentance, and he would not baptize the Pharisees and Sadducees because they failed to give any evidence of repentance (vv. 7–8). *with the Holy Spirit and with fire.* Demonstrated in a dramatic way at Pentecost (Ac 1:5,8; 2:1–13; 11:16), though here "fire" may refer to judgment to come (see v. 12). The outpouring of the Holy Spirit on all God's people was promised in Joel 2:28–29.
3:12 *His winnowing fork.* For the process of winnowing see note on Ru 1:22. Here it is figurative for the day of judgment at Christ's second coming. The OT prophets and NT writers sometimes compress the first and second comings of Christ so that they seem to be one event.
3:15 This occasion marked the beginning of Christ's Messianic ministry. There were several reasons for his baptism: 1. The first, mentioned here, was "to fulfill all righteousness." The baptism indicated that he was consecrated to God and officially approved by him, as especially shown in the descent of the Holy Spirit (v. 16) and the words of the Father (v. 17; cf. Ps 2:7; Isa 42:1). All God's righteous requirements for the Messiah were fully met in Jesus. 2. At Jesus' baptism John publicly announced the arrival of the Messiah and the inception of his ministry (Jn 1:31–34). 3. By his baptism Jesus completely identified himself with man's sin and failure (though he himself needed no repentance or cleansing from sin), becoming our substitute (2Co 5:21). 4. His baptism was an example to his followers.
3:16–17 All three persons of the Trinity are clearly seen here.
3:16 *Spirit of God.* The Holy Spirit came upon Jesus not to overcome sin (for he was sinless), but to equip him (see note on Jdg 3:10) for his work as the divine-human Messiah.
3:17 An allusion to Ps 2:7 and Isa 42:1.
4:1–11 The significance of Jesus' temptations, especially because they occurred at the outset of his public ministry, seems best understood in terms of the kind of Messiah he was to be. He would not accomplish his mission by using his supernatural power for his own needs (first temptation), by using his power to win a large following by miracles or magic

(second temptation) or by compromising with Satan (third temptation). Jesus had no inward desire or inclination to sin, for these in themselves are sin (Mt 5:22,28). Because he was God he did not sin in any way, whether by actions or word or inner desire (2Co 5:21; Heb 7:26; 1Pe 2:22; 1Jn 3:5). Yet Jesus' temptation was real, not merely symbolic. He was "tempted in every way, just as we are—yet was without sin" (Heb 4:15). He was confronted by the tempter with a real opportunity to sin. Although Jesus was the Son of God, he defeated Satan by using a weapon that everyone has at his disposal: the sword of the Spirit, which is the word of God (Eph 6:17). He met all three temptations with Scriptural truth (vv. 4,7,10) from Deuteronomy.
4:1 *led by the Spirit . . . to be tempted.* This testing of Jesus (the Greek verb translated "tempted" can also be rendered "tested"), which was divinely intended, has as its primary background Dt 8:1–5, from which Jesus also quotes in his first reply to the devil (see v. 4 and NIV text note). There Moses recalls how the Lord led the Israelites in the desert 40 years "to humble you and test you in order to know what was in your heart, whether or not you would keep his commands." Here at the beginning of his ministry Jesus is subjected to a similar test and shows himself to be the true Israelite who lives "on every word that comes from the mouth of the LORD." And whereas Adam failed the great test and plunged the whole race into sin (Ge 3), Jesus was faithful and thus demonstrated his qualification to become the Savior of all who receive him. It was, moreover, important that Jesus be tested/tempted as Israel and we are, so that he could become our "merciful and faithful high priest" (Heb 2:17) and thus be "able to help those who are being tempted" (Heb 2:15; see Heb 4:15–16). Finally, as the one who remained faithful in temptation he became the model for all believers when they are tempted. *tempted by the devil.* God surely tests his people, but it is the devil who surely tempts to evil (see note on Ge 22:1; see also 1Jn 3:8; Rev 2:9–10 and notes; Rev 12:9–10).
4:2 *forty days and forty nights.* The number recalls the experiences of Moses (Ex 24:18; 34:28) and Elijah (1Ki 19:8), as well as the 40 years of Israel's temptation (testing) in the desert (Dt 8:2–3).
4:3 *If you are the Son of God.* Meaning "Since you are." The devil is not casting doubt on Jesus' divine sonship, but is tempting him to use his supernatural powers as the Son of God for his own ends.

8Again, the devil took him to a very high
mountain and showed him all the kingdoms of the world and their splendor.
9"All this I will give you," he said, "if you
will bow down and worship me."
10Jesus said to him, "Away from me, Satan![f] For it is written: 'Worship the Lord
your God, and serve him only.'[q]"[g]
11Then the devil left him,[h] and angels
came and attended him.[i]

Jesus Begins to Preach

12When Jesus heard that John had been
put in prison,[j] he returned to Galilee.[k]
13Leaving Nazareth, he went and lived in
Capernaum,[l] which was by the lake in the
area of Zebulun and Naphtali— 14to fulfill[m] what was said through the prophet
Isaiah:

15"Land of Zebulun and land of Naphtali,
the way to the sea, along the Jordan,
Galilee of the Gentiles—
16the people living in darkness
have seen a great light;
on those living in the land of the
shadow of death
a light has dawned."[r][n]

17From that time on Jesus began to
preach, "Repent, for the kingdom of
heaven[o] is near."

The Calling of the First Disciples

4:18–22pp — Mk 1:16–20; Lk 5:2–11; Jn 1:35–42

18As Jesus was walking beside the Sea of
Galilee,[p] he saw two brothers, Simon
called Peter[q] and his brother Andrew.
They were casting a net into the lake, for
they were fishermen. 19"Come, follow
me,"[r] Jesus said, "and I will make you
fishers of men." 20At once they left their
nets and followed him.[s]

4:10 [f]1Ch 21:1; Job 1:6-9; Mt 16:23; Mk 4:15; Lk 10:18; 13:16; 22:3,31; Ro 16:20; 2Co 2:11; 11:14; 2Th 2:9; Rev 12:9 [g]Dt 6:13
4:11 [h]Jas 4:7 [i]Mt 26:53; Lk 22:43; Heb 1:14
4:12 [j]Mt 14:3 [k]Mk 1:14
4:13 [l]Mk 1:21; 9:33; Lk 4:23,31; Jn 2:12; 4:46,47
4:14 [m]S Mt 1:22
4:16 [n]Isa 9:1,2; Lk 2:32; Jn 1:4,5, 9
4:17 [o]S Mt 3:2
4:18 [p]Mt 15:29; Mk 7:31; Jn 6:1 [q]Mt 16:17,18
4:19 [r]ver 20,22; Mt 8:22; Mk 10:21,28,52; Lk 5:28; Jn 1:43; 21:19,22
4:20 [s]S ver 19

[q] *10* Deut. 6:13 [r] *16* Isaiah 9:1,2

4:4 Just as God gave the Israelites manna in a supernatural way (Dt 8:3), so also man must rely on God for spiritual feeding. Jesus relied on his Father, not his own miracle power, for provision of food.
4:5 See note on Lk 4:2. *highest point of the temple.* See note on Lk 4:9. *temple.* The temple, including the entire temple area, had been rebuilt by Herod the Great (see note on 2:1; see also Jn 2:20). The courtyard had been greatly enlarged, to about 330 by 500 yards. To accomplish this a huge platform had been erected to compensate for the sharp falling off of the land to the southeast. An enormous retaining wall made of massive stones was built to support the platform. On the platform stood the temple building, porches and courtyards flanked by beautiful colonnades.
4:12 See map No. 9 at the end of the Study Bible. *John had been put in prison.* See Mk 1:14 and note on Lk 3:20. The reason for John's imprisonment is given in 14:3–4.
4:13 *Capernaum.* Although not mentioned in the OT, it was evidently a sizable town in Jesus' day. Peter's house there became Jesus' base of operations during his extended ministry in Galilee (see Mk 2:1; 9:33). A fifth-century basilica now stands over the supposed site of Peter's house, and a fourth-century synagogue is located a short distance from it.
4:15–16 Another Messianic prophecy from Isaiah. Jesus spent most of his public ministry "in the area of Zebulun and Naphtali" (v. 13), which is north and west of the Sea of Galilee.
4:17 *Repent.* Jesus began his public ministry with the same message as that of John the Baptist (3:2). The people must repent because God's reign was drawing near in the person and ministry of Jesus Christ.
4:18 *Sea of Galilee.* See note on Mk 1:16. *net.* A circular casting net used either from a boat or while standing in shallow water.

Jesus' Baptism and Temptation

Events surrounding Jesus' baptism reveal the intense religious excitement and social ferment of the early days of John the Baptist's ministry. Herod had been rapacious and extravagant; Roman military occupation was harsh. Some agitation centered around the change of procurators from Gratus to Pilate in A.D. 26. Most of the people hoped for a religious solution to their low political fortunes, and when they heard of a new prophet, they flocked out into the desert to hear him. The religious sect (Essenes) from Qumran professed similar doctrines of repentance and baptism. Jesus was baptized at Bethany on the other side of the Jordan (see Jn 1:28). John also baptized at "Aenon near Salim" (Jn 3:23).

The temptation took place in (1) the desert region of the lower Jordan Valley, (2) a high mountain (possibly one of the abrupt cliffs near Jericho that present an unsurpassed panorama) and (3) the pinnacle of the temple, from which the priests sounded the trumpet to call the city's attention to important events.

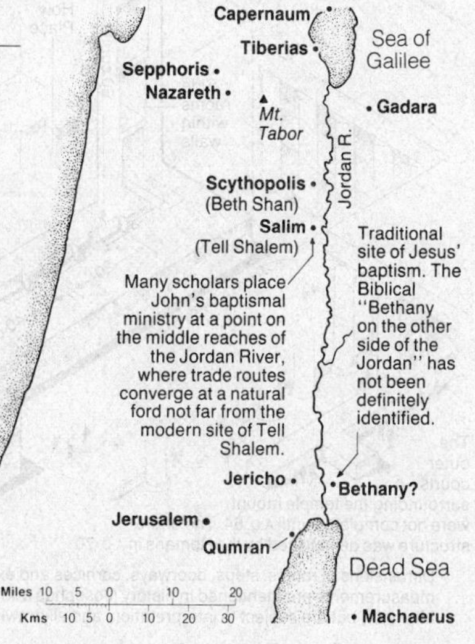
Capernaum
Tiberias
Sea of Galilee
Sepphoris
Nazareth
Mt. Tabor
Gadara
Jordan R.
Scythopolis (Beth Shan)
Salim (Tell Shalem)
Traditional site of Jesus' baptism. The Biblical "Bethany on the other side of the Jordan" has not been definitely identified.
Many scholars place John's baptismal ministry at a point on the middle reaches of the Jordan River, where trade routes converge at a natural ford not far from the modern site of Tell Shalem.
Jericho
Bethany?
Jerusalem
Qumran
Dead Sea
Machaerus
Miles 10 5 0 10 20
Kms 10 5 0 10 20 30

²¹Going on from there, he saw two other brothers, James son of Zebedee and his brother John.[t] They were in a boat with their father Zebedee, preparing their nets. Jesus called them, ²²and immediately they left the boat and their father and followed him.[u]

Jesus Heals the Sick

²³Jesus went throughout Galilee,[v] teaching in their synagogues,[w] preaching the good news[x] of the kingdom,[y] and healing every disease and sickness among the people.[z] ²⁴News about him spread all over Syria,[a] and people brought to him all who were ill with various diseases, those suffering severe pain, the demon-possessed,[b] those having seizures,[c] and the paralyzed,[d] and he healed them. ²⁵Large crowds from Galilee, the Decapolis,[s]

Jerusalem, Judea and the region across the Jordan followed him.[e]

The Beatitudes

5:3–12pp — Lk 6:20–23

5 Now when he saw the crowds, he went up on a mountainside and sat down. His disciples came to him, ²and he began to teach them, saying:

³"Blessed are the poor in spirit,
    for theirs is the kingdom of heaven.[f]
⁴Blessed are those who mourn,
    for they will be comforted.[g]
⁵Blessed are the meek,
    for they will inherit the earth.[h]
⁶Blessed are those who hunger and thirst
    for righteousness,

4:21 [t]Mt 17:1; 20:20; 26:37; Mk 3:17; 13:3; Lk 8:51; Jn 21:2
4:22 [u]S ver 19
4:23 [v]Mk 1:39; Lk 4:15,44
[w]Mt 9:35; 13:54; Mk 1:21;
Lk 4:15; Jn 6:59; 18:20 [x]Mk 1:14
[y]S Mt 3:2;
Ac 20:25; 28:23, 31 [z]Mt 8:16; 14:14; 15:30; Mk 3:10;
Lk 7:22; Ac 10:38
4:24 [a]S Lk 2:2
[b]Mt 8:16,28; 9:32; 12:22; 15:22; Mk 1:32; 5:15,16,18
[c]Mt 17:15
[d]Mt 8:6; 9:2; Mk 2:3

4:25 [e]Mk 3:7,8; Lk 6:17
5:3 [f]ver 10,19; S Mt 25:34
5:4 [g]Isa 61:2,3; Rev 7:17

5:5 [h]Ps 37:11; Ro 4:13

[s]25 That is, the Ten Cities

4:20 See note on Mk 1:17.
4:21 *preparing their nets.* Washing, mending and hanging the nets up to dry in preparation for the next day's work.
4:23 *teaching . . . preaching . . . healing.* Jesus' threefold ministry. The synagogues (see note on Mk 1:21) provided a place for him to teach on the Sabbath. During the week he

preached to larger crowds in the open air.
4:24 *Syria.* The area north of Galilee and between Damascus and the Mediterranean Sea. *those having seizures.* The Greek word for this expression originally meant "moonstruck" and reflects the ancient superstition that seizures were caused by changes of the moon. *the paralyzed.* A

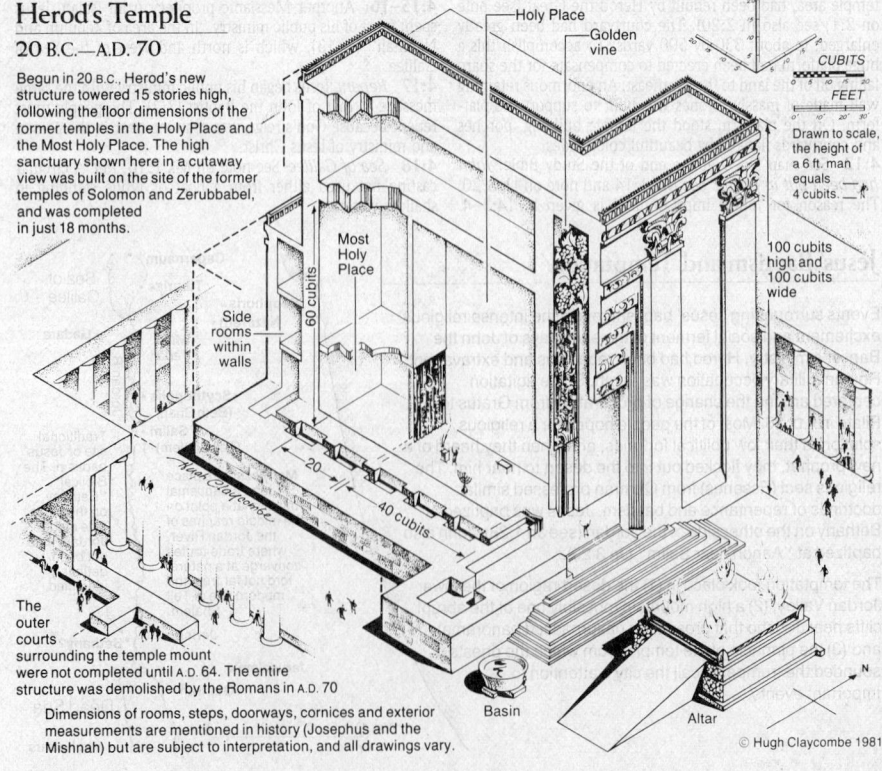

Herod's Temple

20 B.C.—A.D. 70

Begun in 20 B.C., Herod's new structure towered 15 stories high, following the floor dimensions of the former temples in the Holy Place and the Most Holy Place. The high sanctuary shown here in a cutaway view was built on the site of the former temples of Solomon and Zerubbabel, and was completed in just 18 months.

Holy Place

Golden vine

CUBITS

FEET

Drawn to scale, the height of a 6 ft. man equals 4 cubits.

100 cubits high and 100 cubits wide

Most Holy Place

60 cubits

Side rooms within walls

20

40 cubits

The outer courts surrounding the temple mount were not completed until A.D. 64. The entire structure was demolished by the Romans in A.D. 70

Basin

Altar

N

Dimensions of rooms, steps, doorways, cornices and exterior measurements are mentioned in history (Josephus and the Mishnah) but are subject to interpretation, and all drawings vary.

© Hugh Claycombe 1981

for they will be filled. *i*

7Blessed are the merciful,

for they will be shown mercy. *j*

8Blessed are the pure in heart, *k*

for they will see God. *l*

9Blessed are the peacemakers, *m*

for they will be called sons of God. *n*

10Blessed are those who are persecuted

because of righteousness, *o*

for theirs is the kingdom of heaven. *p*

11"Blessed are you when people insult you, *q* persecute you and falsely say all kinds of evil against you because of me. *r* 12Rejoice and be glad, *s* because great is your reward in heaven, for in the same way they persecuted the prophets who were before you. *t*

Salt and Light

13"You are the salt of the earth. But if the salt loses its saltiness, how can it be made salty again? It is no longer good for anything, except to be thrown out and trampled by men. *u*

14"You are the light of the world. *v* A city on a hill cannot be hidden. 15Neither do people light a lamp and put it under a bowl. Instead they put it on its stand, and it gives light to everyone in the house. *w* 16In the same way, let your light shine before men, *x* that they may see your good deeds *y* and praise *z* your Father in heaven.

The Fulfillment of the Law

17"Do not think that I have come to abolish the Law or the Prophets; I have not come to abolish them but to fulfill them. *a* 18I tell you the truth, until heaven and earth disappear, not the smallest letter, not

---

Cross references (center column):

5:6 *i*Isa 55:1,2
5:7 *j*S Jas 2:13
5:8 *k*Ps 24:3,4; 73:1 *l*Ps 17:15; 42:2; Heb 12:14; Rev 22:4
5:9 *m*Jas 3:18; S Ro 14:19 *n*ver 44,45; S Ro 8:14
5:10 *o*S 1Pe 3:14 *p*ver 3,19; S Mt 25:34
5:11 *q*Isa 51:7 *r*S Jn 15:21
5:12 *s*Ps 9:2; Ac 5:41; S 2Co 6:10; 12:10; Col 1:24; Jas 1:2; 1Pe 1:6; 4:13,16 *t*2Ch 36:16; Mt 23:31,37; Ac 7:52; 1Th 2:15; Heb 11:32-38

5:13 *u*Mk 9:50; Lk 14:34,35
5:14 *v*Jn 8:12
5:15 *w*Mk 4:21; Lk 8:16; 11:33
5:16 *x*1Co 10:31; Php 1:11

*y*S Tit 2:14 *z*S Mt 9:8 5:17 *a*Jn 10:34,35; Ro 3:31

---

transliteration of the Greek that has come directly into English. Greek physicians were among the best in ancient times, and many of our medical terms come from their language.

4:25 *the Decapolis.* A league of free cities (see NIV text note) characterized by high Greek culture. All but one, Scythopolis (Beth Shan), were east of the Sea of Galilee and the Jordan River. The league stretched from a point northeast of the Sea of Galilee southward to Philadelphia (modern Amman).

5:1–7:29 The Sermon on the Mount is the first of five great discourses in Matthew (chs. 5–7; 10; 13; 18; 24–25). It contains three types of material: (1) beatitudes, i.e., declarations of blessedness (5:1–12), (2) ethical admonitions (5:13–20; 6:1–7:23) and (3) contrasts between Jesus' ethical teaching and Jewish legalistic traditions (5:21–48). The Sermon ends with a short parable stressing the importance of practicing what has just been taught (7:24–27) and an expression of amazement by the crowds at the authority with which Jesus spoke (7:28–29).

Opinion differs as to whether the Sermon is a summary of what Jesus taught on one occasion or a compilation of teachings presented on numerous occasions. Matthew possibly took a single sermon and expanded it with other relevant teachings of Jesus. Thirty-four of the verses in Matthew's Sermon occur in different contexts in Luke than the apparently parallel Sermon on the Plain (Lk 6:17–49).

The Sermon on the Mount's call to moral and ethical living is so high that some have dismissed it as being completely unrealistic or have projected its fulfillment to the future kingdom. There is no doubt, however, that Jesus (and Matthew) gave the sermon as a standard for all Christians, realizing that its demands cannot be met in our own power. It is also true that Jesus occasionally used hyperbole to make his point (see, e.g., note on 5:29–30).

5:1 *mountainside.* The exact location is uncertain. It may have been the gently sloping hillside at the northwest corner of the Sea of Galilee, not far from Capernaum (see note on Lk 6:20–49). The new law, like the old (Ex 19:3), was given from a mountain. *sat down.* It was the custom for Jewish rabbis to be seated while teaching (see Mk 4:1; 9:35; Lk 4:20; 5:3; Jn 8:2). *disciples.* Lit. "learners."

5:3 *Blessed.* The word means more than "happy," because happiness is an emotion often dependent on outward circumstances. "Blessed" here refers to the ultimate well-being

and distinctive spiritual joy of those who share in the salvation of the kingdom of God. See notes on Ps 1:1; Rev 1:3. *poor in spirit.* In contrast to the spiritually proud and self-sufficient. *theirs is the kingdom of heaven.* The kingdom is not something earned. It is more a gift than a recompense.

5:5 *meek.* This beatitude is taken from Ps 37:11 and refers not so much to an attitude toward man as to a disposition before God, namely, humility.

5:8 *heart.* The center of one's being, including mind, will and emotions (see note on Ps 4:7).

5:13 *salt.* Used for flavoring and preserving.

5:15 *lamp.* In Jesus' day people used small clay lamps that burned olive oil drawn up by a wick (see note on Ex 25:37). *bowl.* A peck-sized bowl that held ground meal or flour.

5:16 *Father in heaven.* Matthew uses the term "Father in heaven" or "heavenly Father" 17 times, whereas Mark and Luke use the term only once each, and John does not use it at all.

5:17 *the Law.* The first five books of the Jewish Scriptures (our OT). *the Prophets.* Not only the Latter Prophets—Isaiah, Jeremiah and Ezekiel, which we call Major Prophets, and the 12 Minor Prophets (lumped together by the Jews as "the Book of the Twelve")—but also the so-called Former Prophets (Joshua, Judges, Samuel and Kings). Taken together, "the Law" and "the Prophets" designated the entire OT, including the Writings, the third section of the Hebrew Bible. See 13:35, where Matthew introduces a quotation from the Writings (Ps 78:2) with "what was spoken through the prophet." *fulfill.* Jesus fulfilled the Law in the sense that he gave it its full meaning. He emphasized its deep, underlying principles and total commitment to it rather than mere external acknowledgment and obedience.

5:18–20 Jesus is not speaking against observing all the requirements of the Law, but against hypocritical, Pharisaical legalism. Such legalism was not the keeping of all details of the Law but the hollow sham of keeping laws externally, to gain merit before God, while breaking them inwardly. It was following the letter of the Law while ignoring its spirit. Jesus repudiates the Pharisees' interpretation of the Law and their view of righteousness by works. He preaches a righteousness that comes only through faith in him and his work. In the verses that follow, he gives six examples of Pharisaical externalism.

5:18 *smallest letter.* One word in Greek (*iota*), which we use when we say, "It doesn't make one iota of difference." It

the least stroke of a pen, will by any means disappear from the Law until everything is accomplished.[b] [19]Anyone who breaks one of the least of these commandments[c] and teaches others to do the same will be called least in the kingdom of heaven, but whoever practices and teaches these commands will be called great in the kingdom of heaven. [20]For I tell you that unless your righteousness surpasses that of the Pharisees and the teachers of the law, you will certainly not enter the kingdom of heaven.[d]

Murder

5:25,26pp — Lk 12:58,59

[21]"You have heard that it was said to the people long ago, 'Do not murder,[t] [e] and anyone who murders will be subject to judgment.' [22]But I tell you that anyone who is angry[f] with his brother[u] will be subject to judgment.[g] Again, anyone who says to his brother, 'Raca,'[v] is answerable to the Sanhedrin.[h] But anyone who says, 'You fool!' will be in danger of the fire of hell.[i]

[23]"Therefore, if you are offering your gift at the altar and there remember that your brother has something against you, [24]leave your gift there in front of the altar. First go and be reconciled to your brother; then come and offer your gift.

[25]"Settle matters quickly with your adversary who is taking you to court. Do it while you are still with him on the way, or he may hand you over to the judge, and the judge may hand you over to the officer, and you may be thrown into prison. [26]I tell you the truth, you will not get out until you have paid the last penny.[w]

Adultery

[27]"You have heard that it was said, 'Do not commit adultery.'[x] [j] [28]But I tell you

that anyone who looks at a woman lustfully has already committed adultery with her in his heart.[k] [29]If your right eye causes you to sin,[l] gouge it out and throw it away. It is better for you to lose one part of your body than for your whole body to be thrown into hell. [30]And if your right hand causes you to sin,[m] cut it off and throw it away. It is better for you to lose one part of your body than for your whole body to go into hell.

Divorce

[31]"It has been said, 'Anyone who divorces his wife must give her a certificate of divorce.'[y] [n] [32]But I tell you that anyone who divorces his wife, except for marital unfaithfulness, causes her to become an adulteress, and anyone who marries the divorced woman commits adultery.[o]

Oaths

[33]"Again, you have heard that it was said to the people long ago, 'Do not break your oath,[p] but keep the oaths you have made to the Lord.'[q] [34]But I tell you, Do not swear at all:[r] either by heaven, for it is God's throne;[s] [35]or by the earth, for it is his footstool; or by Jerusalem, for it is the city of the Great King.[t] [36]And do not swear by your head, for you cannot make even one hair white or black. [37]Simply let your 'Yes' be 'Yes,' and your 'No,' 'No';[u] anything beyond this comes from the evil one.[v]

An Eye for an Eye

[38]"You have heard that it was said, 'Eye for eye, and tooth for tooth.'[z] [w] [39]But I tell you, Do not resist an evil person. If some-

---

Cross references:

5:18 [b]Ps 119:89; Isa 40:8; 55:11; Mt 24:35; Mk 13:31; Lk 16:17; 21:33
5:19 [c]Jas 2:10
5:20 [d]Isa 26:2; Mt 18:3; Jn 3:5
5:21 [e]Ex 20:13; 21:12; Dt 5:17
5:22 [f]Ecc 7:9; 1Co 13:5; Eph 4:26; Jas 1:19,20 [g]1Jn 3:15 [h]Mt 26:59; Jn 11:47; Ac 5:21,27,34,41; 6:12 [i]Mt 18:9; Mk 9:43,48; Lk 16:24; Jas 3:6
5:27 [j]Ex 20:14; Dt 5:18
5:28 [k]Pr 6:25; 2Pe 2:14
5:29 [l]ver 30; Mt 18:6,8,9; Mk 9:42-47; Lk 17:2; Ro 14:21; 1Co 8:13; 2Co 6:3; 11:29
5:30 [m]S ver 29
5:31 [n]Dt 24:1-4
5:32 [o]S Lk 16:18
5:33 [p]Lev 19:12 [q]Nu 30:2; Dt 23:21; Mt 23:16-22
5:34 [r]Jas 5:12 [s]Isa 66:1; Mt 23:22
5:35 [t]Ps 48:2
5:37 [u]Jas 5:12 [v]Mt 6:13; 13:19, 38; Jn 17:15; Eph 6:16; 2Th 3:3; 1Jn 2:13,14; 3:12; 5:18,19
5:38 [w]Ex 21:24; Lev 24:20; Dt 19:21

Footnotes:

[t]*21* Exodus 20:13   [u]*22* Some manuscripts *brother without cause*   [v]*22* An Aramaic term of contempt   [w]*26* Greek *kodrantes*   [x]*27* Exodus 20:14   [y]*31* Deut. 24:1   [z]*38* Exodus 21:24; Lev. 24:20; Deut. 19:21

---

is the nearest Greek equivalent to the Hebrew *yodh*, the smallest letter of the Hebrew alphabet (see Ps 119:73 title). *least stroke of a pen.* The Greek word for this phrase means "horn" and was used to designate the slight embellishment or extension of certain letters of the Hebrew alphabet (somewhat like the bottom of a "j").

5:21 *it was said.* The contrast that Jesus sets up (vv. 21,27,31,33,38,43) is not between the OT and his teaching (he has just established the validity of the OT Law). Rather, it is between externalistic interpretation of the rabbinic tradition on the one hand, and Jesus' correct interpretation of the Law on the other. *murder.* Several Hebrew and Greek verbs mean "kill." The ones used here and in Ex 20:13 specifically mean "murder."

5:22 *Raca.* May be related to the Aramaic word for "empty" and mean "Empty-head!" *Sanhedrin.* See note on Mk 14:55. *hell.* The Greek word is *ge(h)enna*, which derives its

name from a deep ravine south of Jerusalem, the "Valley of (the Sons of) Hinnom" (Hebrew *ge hinnom*). During the reigns of the wicked Ahaz and Manasseh, human sacrifices to the Ammonite god Molech were offered there. Josiah desecrated the valley because of the pagan worship there (2Ki 23:10; see Jer 7:31–32; 19:6). It became a sort of perpetually burning city dump and later a figure for the place of final punishment.

5:26 *penny.* The smallest Roman copper coin.

5:29–30 Jesus is not teaching self-mutilation, for even a blind man can lust. The point is that we should deal with sin as necessary.

5:32 *except for marital unfaithfulness.* See note on 19:3. Neither Mk 10:11–12 nor Lk 16:18 mentions this exception.

5:38 See notes on Ex 21:23–25; Lev 24:20.

one strikes you on the right cheek, turn to him the other also.[x] [40]And if someone wants to sue you and take your tunic, let him have your cloak as well. [41]If someone forces you to go one mile, go with him two miles. [42]Give to the one who asks you, and do not turn away from the one who wants to borrow from you.[y]

Love for Enemies

[43]"You have heard that it was said, 'Love your neighbor[a][z] and hate your enemy.'[a] [44]But I tell you: Love your enemies,[b] and pray for those who persecute you,[b] [45]that you may be sons[c] of your Father in heaven. He causes his sun to rise on the evil and the good, and sends rain on the righteous and the unrighteous.[d] [46]If you love those who love you, what reward will you get?[e] Are not even the tax collectors doing that? [47]And if you greet only your brothers, what are you doing more than others? Do not even pagans do that? [48]Be perfect, therefore, as your heavenly Father is perfect.[f]

Giving to the Needy

6 "Be careful not to do your 'acts of righteousness' before men, to be seen by them.[g] If you do, you will have no reward from your Father in heaven.

[2]"So when you give to the needy, do not announce it with trumpets, as the hypocrites do in the synagogues and on the streets, to be honored by men. I tell you the truth, they have received their reward in full. [3]But when you give to the needy, do not let your left hand know what your right hand is doing, [4]so that your giving may be in secret. Then your Father, who sees what is done in secret, will reward you.[h]

Prayer

6:9–13pp — Lk 11:2–4

[5]"And when you pray, do not be like the hypocrites, for they love to pray standing[i] in the synagogues and on the street

corners to be seen by men. I tell you the truth, they have received their reward in full. [6]But when you pray, go into your room, close the door and pray to your Father,[j] who is unseen. Then your Father, who sees what is done in secret, will reward you. [7]And when you pray, do not keep on babbling[k] like pagans, for they think they will be heard because of their many words.[l] [8]Do not be like them, for your Father knows what you need[m] before you ask him.

[9]"This, then, is how you should pray:

" 'Our Father[n] in heaven,
hallowed be your name,
[10]your kingdom[o] come,
your will be done[p]
on earth as it is in heaven.
[11]Give us today our daily bread.[q]
[12]Forgive us our debts,
as we also have forgiven our
debtors.[r]
[13]And lead us not into temptation,[s]
but deliver us from the evil one.[c][t]

[14]For if you forgive men when they sin against you, your heavenly Father will also forgive you.[u] [15]But if you do not forgive men their sins, your Father will not forgive your sins.[v]

Fasting

[16]"When you fast,[w] do not look somber[x] as the hypocrites do, for they disfigure their faces to show men they are fasting. I tell you the truth, they have received their reward in full. [17]But when you fast, put oil on your head and wash your face, [18]so that it will not be obvious to men that you are fasting, but only to your Father, who is unseen; and your Father, who sees what is done in secret, will reward you.[y]

5:39 xLk 6:29;
Ro 12:17,19;
1Pe 3:9
5:42 yDt 15:8;
Lk 6:30
5:43 zLev 19:18;
Mt 19:19; 22:39;
Mk 12:31;
Lk 10:27;
Ro 13:9;
Gal 5:14; Jas 2:8
aDt 23:6;
Ps 139:21,22
5:44 bLk 6:27,
28; 23:34;
Jn 15:20;
Ac 7:60; Ro 8:35;
12:14; 1Co 4:12;
1Pe 2:23
5:45 cver 9;
Lk 6:35;
S Ro 8:14 dJob
25:3
5:46 eLk 6:32
5:48 fLev 19:2;
1Pe 1:16
6:1 gMt 5:16;
23:5
6:4 hver 6,18;
Col 3:23,24
6:5 iMk 11:25;
Lk 18:10-14

6:6 jLk 4:33
6:7 kEcc 5:2
lLki 18:26-29
6:8 mver 32
6:9 nJer 3:19;
Mal 2:10;
1Pe 1:17
6:10 oS Mt 3:2
pS Mt 26:39
6:11 qPr 30:8
6:12
rMt 18:21-35
6:13 sJas 1:13
tS Mt 5:37
6:14
uMt 18:21-35;
Mk 11:25,26;
Eph 4:32;
Col 3:13
6:15 vMt 18:35
6:16 wLev 16:29,
31; 23:27-32;
Nu 29:7
xIsa 58:5;
Zec 7:5; 8:19
6:18 yver 4,6

a43 Lev. 19:18   b44 Some late manuscripts *enemies,
bless those who curse you, do good to those who hate
you*   c13 Or *from evil*; some late manuscripts *one, /
for yours is the kingdom and the power and the glory
forever. Amen.*

5:40 *tunic . . . cloak.* The first was an undergarment, the second a loose outer one.
5:41 *forces.* The Greek verb comes from a Persian word meaning "press into service" and is used in 27:32, where the Roman soldiers pressed Simon into service to carry Jesus' cross.
5:46 *tax collectors.* Traditionally known as "publicans," these were local men employed by Roman tax contractors to collect taxes for them. Because they worked for Rome and often demanded unreasonable payments, the tax collectors gained a bad reputation and were generally hated and considered traitors.
5:48 *Be perfect.* Christ sets up the high ideal of perfect love

(see vv. 43–47)—not that we can fully attain it in this life. That, however, is God's high standard for us.
6:1 *acts of righteousness.* This verse introduces the discussion of three acts of righteousness: (1) giving (vv. 2–4), (2) praying (vv. 5–15) and (3) fasting (vv. 16–18).
6:10 *your kingdom come.* A reference to the future consummation of the kingdom.
6:11 *bread.* Represents the necessities, but not the luxuries, of life.
6:12 *debts.* Moral debts, i.e., sins (see note on Lk 11:4).
6:17 *put oil on your head and wash your face.* Jews put ashes on their heads when fasting. Putting oil on the head and washing the face were reserved for joyous occasions.

Treasures in Heaven

6:22,23pp — Lk 11:34–36

19"Do not store up for yourselves treasures on earth,[z] where moth and rust destroy,[a] and where thieves break in and steal. 20But store up for yourselves treasures in heaven,[b] where moth and rust do not destroy, and where thieves do not break in and steal.[c] 21For where your treasure is, there your heart will be also.[d]

22"The eye is the lamp of the body. If your eyes are good, your whole body will be full of light. 23But if your eyes are bad, your whole body will be full of darkness. If then the light within you is darkness, how great is that darkness!

24"No one can serve two masters. Either he will hate the one and love the other, or he will be devoted to the one and despise the other. You cannot serve both God and Money.[e]

Do Not Worry

6:25–33pp — Lk 12:22–31

25"Therefore I tell you, do not worry[f] about your life, what you will eat or drink; or about your body, what you will wear. Is not life more important than food, and the body more important than clothes? 26Look at the birds of the air; they do not sow or reap or store away in barns, and yet your heavenly Father feeds them.[g] Are you not much more valuable than they?[h] 27Who of you by worrying can add a single hour to his life[d]?[i]

28"And why do you worry about clothes? See how the lilies of the field grow. They do not labor or spin. 29Yet I tell you that not even Solomon in all his splendor[j] was dressed like one of these. 30If that is how God clothes the grass of the field, which is here today and tomorrow is thrown into the fire, will he not much more clothe you, O you of little faith?[k] 31So do not worry, saying, 'What shall we eat?' or 'What shall we drink?' or 'What shall we wear?' 32For the pagans run after all these things, and your heavenly Father

knows that you need them.[l] 33But seek first his kingdom[m] and his righteousness, and all these things will be given to you as well.[n] 34Therefore do not worry about tomorrow, for tomorrow will worry about itself. Each day has enough trouble of its own.

Judging Others

7:3–5pp — Lk 6:41,42

7 "Do not judge, or you too will be judged.[o] 2For in the same way you judge others, you will be judged, and with the measure you use, it will be measured to you.[p]

3"Why do you look at the speck of sawdust in your brother's eye and pay no attention to the plank in your own eye? 4How can you say to your brother, 'Let me take the speck out of your eye,' when all the time there is a plank in your own eye? 5You hypocrite, first take the plank out of your own eye, and then you will see clearly to remove the speck from your brother's eye.

6"Do not give dogs what is sacred; do not throw your pearls to pigs. If you do, they may trample them under their feet, and then turn and tear you to pieces.

Ask, Seek, Knock

7:7–11pp — Lk 11:9–13

7"Ask and it will be given to you;[q] seek and you will find; knock and the door will be opened to you. 8For everyone who asks receives; he who seeks finds;[r] and to him who knocks, the door will be opened.

9"Which of you, if his son asks for bread, will give him a stone? 10Or if he asks for a fish, will give him a snake? 11If you, then, though you are evil, know how to give good gifts to your children, how much more will your Father in heaven give good gifts[s] to those who ask him! 12So in everything, do to others what you would have them do to you,[t] for this sums up the Law and the Prophets.[u]

[d]27 Or *single cubit to his height*

6:19 [z]Pr 23:4;
Lk 12:16-21;
Heb 13:5
[a]S Jas 5:2,3
6:20 [b]Mt 19:21;
Lk 12:33; 16:9;
18:22; 1Ti 6:19
[c]Lk 12:33
6:21 [d]Lk 12:34
6:24 [e]Lk 16:13
6:25 [f]ver 27,28,
31,34; Lk 10:41;
12:11,22
6:26 [g]Job 38:41;
Ps 104:21;
136:25; 145:15;
147:9
[h]Mt 10:29-31
6:27 [i]Ps 39:5
6:29 [j]1Ki 10:4-7
6:30 [k]Mt 8:26;
14:31; 16:8;
Lk 12:28

6:32 [l]ver 8
6:33 [m]S Mt 3:2
[n]Ps 37:4;
Mt 19:29
7:1 [o]Lk 6:37;
Ro 14:4,10,13;
1Co 4:5; 5:12;
Jas 4:11,12
7:2 [p]Eze 35:11;
Mk 4:24;
Lk 6:38; Ro 2:1
7:7 [q]1Ki 3:5;
Mt 18:19; 21:22;
Jn 14:13,14;
15:7,16; 16:23,
24; Jas 1:5-8; 4:2,
3; 5:16; 1Jn 3:22;
5:14,15
7:8 [r]Pr 8:17;
Jer 29:12,13
7:11 [s]Jas 1:17
7:12 [t]Lk 6:31
[u]Ro 13:8-10;
Gal 5:14

6:19 *moth and rust.* Representative of all agents and processes that destroy worldly possessions.
6:28 *lilies.* Here represents flowers generally.
6:30 *thrown into the fire.* Grass was commonly used to heat the clay ovens of Palestine.
7:1 The Christian is not to judge hypocritically or self-righteously, as can be seen from the context (v. 5). The same thought is expressed in 23:13–39 (cf. Ro 2:1). To obey Christ's commands in this chapter, we must first evaluate a person's character—whether he is a "dog" (v. 6) or a false prophet (v. 15), or whether his life shows fruit (v. 16). Scripture repeatedly exhorts believers to evaluate carefully

and choose between good and bad people and things (sexually immoral, 1Co 5:9; those who masquerade as angels of light, 2Co 11:14; dogs, Php 3:2; false prophets, 1Jn 4:1). The Christian is to "test everything" (1Th 5:21).
7:6 Teaching should be given in accordance with the spiritual capacity of the learners. *dogs.* The unclean dogs of the street were held in low esteem.
7:12 The so-called Golden Rule is found in negative form in rabbinic Judaism and also in Hinduism, Buddhism and Confucianism. It occurred in various forms in Greek and Roman ethical teaching. Jesus stated it in positive form. *the Law and the Prophets.* See note on 5:17.

The Narrow and Wide Gates

13"Enter through the narrow gate. v For wide is the gate and broad is the road that leads to destruction, and many enter through it. 14But small is the gate and narrow the road that leads to life, and only a few find it.

A Tree and Its Fruit

15"Watch out for false prophets. w They come to you in sheep's clothing, but inwardly they are ferocious wolves. x 16By their fruit you will recognize them. y Do people pick grapes from thornbushes, or figs from thistles? z 17Likewise every good tree bears good fruit, but a bad tree bears bad fruit. 18A good tree cannot bear bad fruit, and a bad tree cannot bear good fruit. a 19Every tree that does not bear good fruit is cut down and thrown into the fire. b 20Thus, by their fruit you will recognize them.

21"Not everyone who says to me, 'Lord, Lord,' c will enter the kingdom of heaven, d but only he who does the will of my Father who is in heaven. e 22Many will say to me on that day, f 'Lord, Lord, did we not prophesy in your name, and in your name drive out demons and perform many miracles?' g 23Then I will tell them plainly, 'I never knew you. Away from me, you evildoers!' h

The Wise and Foolish Builders

7:24-27pp — Lk 6:47-49

24"Therefore everyone who hears these words of mine and puts them into practice i is like a wise man who built his house on the rock. 25The rain came down, the streams rose, and the winds blew and beat against that house; yet it did not fall, because it had its foundation on the rock. 26But everyone who hears these words of mine and does not put them into practice is like a foolish man who built his house on sand. 27The rain came down, the streams

rose, and the winds blew and beat against that house, and it fell with a great crash."

28When Jesus had finished saying these things, j the crowds were amazed at his teaching, k 29because he taught as one who had authority, and not as their teachers of the law.

The Man With Leprosy

8:2-4pp — Mk 1:40-44; Lk 5:12-14

8 When he came down from the mountainside, large crowds followed him. 2A man with leprosy e l came and knelt before him m and said, "Lord, if you are willing, you can make me clean."

3Jesus reached out his hand and touched the man. "I am willing," he said. "Be clean!" Immediately he was cured f of his leprosy. 4Then Jesus said to him, "See that you don't tell anyone. n But go, show yourself to the priest o and offer the gift Moses commanded, p as a testimony to them."

The Faith of the Centurion

8:5-13pp — Lk 7:1-10

5When Jesus had entered Capernaum, a centurion came to him, asking for help. 6"Lord," he said, "my servant lies at home paralyzed q and in terrible suffering."

7Jesus said to him, "I will go and heal him."

8The centurion replied, "Lord, I do not deserve to have you come under my roof. But just say the word, and my servant will be healed. r 9For I myself am a man under authority, with soldiers under me. I tell this one, 'Go,' and he goes; and that one, 'Come,' and he comes. I say to my servant, 'Do this,' and he does it."

10When Jesus heard this, he was astonished and said to those following him, "I tell you the truth, I have not found anyone in Israel with such great faith. s 11I say to

---

e2 The Greek word was used for various diseases affecting the skin—not necessarily leprosy.   f3 Greek made clean

---

Cross references (center column):

7:13 vLk 13:24; Jn 10:7,9
7:15 wJer 23:16; Mt 24:24; Lk 6:26; 2Pe 2:1; 1Jn 4:1; Rev 16:13
xEze 22:27; Ac 20:29
7:16 yMt 12:33; Lk 6:44 zJas 3:12
7:18 aLk 6:43
7:19 bS Mt 3:10
7:21 cHos 8:2; Mt 25:11; S Jn 13:13; 1Co 12:3
dS Mt 3:2
eMt 12:50; Ro 2:13; Jas 1:22; 1Jn 3:18
7:22 fS Mt 10:15
gLk 10:20; 1Co 13:1-3
7:23 hPs 6:8; Mt 25:12,41; Lk 13:25-27
7:24 iver 21; Jas 1:22-25

7:28 jMt 11:1; 13:53; 19:1; 26:1
kMt 13:54; 22:33; Mk 1:22; 6:2; 11:18; Lk 4:32; Jn 7:46
8:2 lLev 13:45; 26:6; Lk 5:12; 17:12 mMt 9:18; 15:25; 18:26; 20:20
8:4 nMt 9:30; 12:16; Mk 5:43; 7:36; S 8:30; Lk 4:41
oLk 17:14
pLev 14:2-32
8:6 qS Mt 4:24
8:8 rPs 107:20
8:10 sMt 15:28

Study notes (bottom):

7:22 *prophesy.* In the NT this verb primarily means to give a message from God, not necessarily to predict. *demons.* See note on Mk 1:23.

7:29 *authority.* The teachers of the law quoted other rabbis to support their own teaching (see note on 2:4), but Jesus spoke with divine authority.

8:2 *leprosy.* See NIV text note and Lev 13-14. *make me clean.* Leprosy made a person ceremonially unclean as well as physically afflicted (see note on Lk 5:12-16).

8:4 *don't tell anyone.* Perhaps for several reasons: (1) Jesus did not want to be considered just a miracle worker, (2) he did not want his teaching ministry hindered by too much publicity being given to his healing miracles, and (3) he did not want his death to come prematurely, i.e., before he had finished his ministry. See 9:30; 12:16; Mk 1:44; 5:43;

7:36; Lk 8:56. *show yourself to the priest.* See note on Lk 5:14. *them.* The priests.

8:5 *centurion.* A Roman military officer in charge of 100 soldiers. In Luke's account (Lk 7:1-5) Jewish elders and friends of the centurion came to Jesus on his behalf, but Matthew does not mention these intermediaries. A parallel situation was the flogging of Jesus by Pilate, in which the act was obviously not carried out by Pilate himself but by the Roman soldiers at Pilate's command (27:26, lit. "he flogged Jesus").

8:8 *I do not deserve to have you come under my roof.* According to rabbinical law, a Jew ceremonially defiled himself by entering a Gentile's house. But the centurion's statement may also reveal his own sense of moral guilt in the presence of Jesus.

you that many will come from the east and the west,[t] and will take their places at the feast with Abraham, Isaac and Jacob in the kingdom of heaven.[u] 12But the subjects of the kingdom[v] will be thrown outside, into the darkness, where there will be weeping and gnashing of teeth."[w]

13Then Jesus said to the centurion, "Go! It will be done just as you believed it would."[x] And his servant was healed at that very hour.

Jesus Heals Many

8:14–16pp — Mk 1:29–34; Lk 4:38–41

14When Jesus came into Peter's house, he saw Peter's mother-in-law lying in bed with a fever. 15He touched her hand and the fever left her, and she got up and began to wait on him.

16When evening came, many who were demon-possessed were brought to him, and he drove out the spirits with a word and healed all the sick.[y] 17This was to fulfill[z] what was spoken through the prophet Isaiah:

"He took up our infirmities
and carried our diseases."[g] [a]

The Cost of Following Jesus

8:19–22pp — Lk 9:57–60

18When Jesus saw the crowd around him, he gave orders to cross to the other side of the lake.[b] 19Then a teacher of the law came to him and said, "Teacher, I will follow you wherever you go."

20Jesus replied, "Foxes have holes and birds of the air have nests, but the Son of Man[c] has no place to lay his head."

21Another disciple said to him, "Lord, first let me go and bury my father."

22But Jesus told him, "Follow me,[d] and let the dead bury their own dead."

Jesus Calms the Storm

8:23–27pp — Mk 4:36–41; Lk 8:22–25
8:23–27Ref — Mt 14:22–33

23Then he got into the boat and his dis-

ciples followed him. 24Without warning, a furious storm came up on the lake, so that the waves swept over the boat. But Jesus was sleeping. 25The disciples went and woke him, saying, "Lord, save us! We're going to drown!"

26He replied, "You of little faith,[e] why are you so afraid?" Then he got up and rebuked the winds and the waves, and it was completely calm.[f]

27The men were amazed and asked, "What kind of man is this? Even the winds and the waves obey him!"

The Healing of Two Demon-possessed Men

8:28–34pp — Mk 5:1–17; Lk 8:26–37

28When he arrived at the other side in the region of the Gadarenes,[h] two demon-possessed[g] men coming from the tombs met him. They were so violent that no one could pass that way. 29"What do you want with us,[h] Son of God?" they shouted. "Have you come here to torture us before the appointed time?"[i]

30Some distance from them a large herd of pigs was feeding. 31The demons begged Jesus, "If you drive us out, send us into the herd of pigs."

32He said to them, "Go!" So they came out and went into the pigs, and the whole herd rushed down the steep bank into the lake and died in the water. 33Those tending the pigs ran off, went into the town and reported all this, including what had happened to the demon-possessed men. 34Then the whole town went out to meet Jesus. And when they saw him, they pleaded with him to leave their region.[j]

Jesus Heals a Paralytic

9:2–8pp — Mk 2:3–12; Lk 5:18–26

9 Jesus stepped into a boat, crossed over and came to his own town.[k] 2Some men brought to him a paralytic,[l] lying on

Cross references (center column)

8:11 [t]Ps 107:3; Isa 49:12; 59:19; Mal 1:11
[u]Lk 13:29
8:12 [v]Mt 13:38 [w]Mt 13:42,50; 22:13; 24:51; 25:30; Lk 13:28
8:13 [x]S Mt 9:22
8:16 [y]S Mt 4:23, 24
8:17 [z]S Mt 1:22 [a]Isa 53:4
8:18 [b]Mk 4:35
8:20 [c]Da 7:13; Mt 12:8,32,40; 16:13,27,28; 17:9; 19:28; Mk 2:10; 8:31
8:22 [d]S Mt 4:19

8:26 [e]S Mt 6:30 [f]Ps 65:7; 89:9; 107:29
8:28 [g]S Mt 4:24
8:29 [h]Jdg 11:12; 2Sa 16:10; 1Ki 17:18; Mk 1:24; Lk 4:34; Jn 2:4 [i]2Pe 2:4
8:34 [j]Lk 5:8; Ac 16:39
9:1 [k]Mt 4:13
9:2 [l]S Mt 4:24

[g]17 Isaiah 53:4   [h]28 Some manuscripts *Gergesenes*; others *Gerasenes*

8:11 The universality of the gospel is one of Matthew's themes (see especially 28:19–20).
8:18 *the other side.* The east side.
8:20 *Son of Man.* See note on Mk 8:31.
8:22 *let the dead bury their own dead.* Let the spiritually dead bury the physically dead. The time of Jesus' ministry was short and demanded full attention and commitment. This statement stresses the radical demands of Jesus' discipleship, since Jews placed great importance on the duty of children to bury their parents.
8:24 *furious storm.* See note on Mk 4:37. *But Jesus was sleeping.* See note on Lk 8:23.
8:28 *region of the Gadarenes.* The region around the city of Gadara, six miles southeast of the Sea of Galilee. Mark and

Luke identify the region by the capital city Gerasa, located about 35 miles southeast of the Sea. *two.* Mark (5:2) and Luke (8:27) mention only one Gadarene demoniac.
8:29 *appointed time.* The time of their judgment (see notes on Mk 5:10 and Lk 8:31).
8:30 *herd of pigs.* Large numbers of Gentiles lived in Galilee. Normally Jews did not raise pigs, since they were considered the most "unclean" of all animals.
8:32 Though Jesus seemingly consented to the demons' request, the pigs carried the demons into the depths of the sea—perhaps symbolic of the Abyss (see Lk 8:31 and note).
8:34 *pleaded with him to leave.* They were probably more concerned about their financial loss than about the deliverance of the miserable demon-possessed man.

a mat. When Jesus saw their faith,[m] he said to the paralytic, "Take heart,[n] son; your sins are forgiven."[o]

3At this, some of the teachers of the law said to themselves, "This fellow is blaspheming!"[p]

4Knowing their thoughts,[q] Jesus said, "Why do you entertain evil thoughts in your hearts? 5Which is easier: to say, 'Your sins are forgiven,' or to say, 'Get up and walk'? 6But so that you may know that the Son of Man[r] has authority on earth to forgive sins. . . ." Then he said to the paralytic, "Get up, take your mat and go home." 7And the man got up and went home. 8When the crowd saw this, they were filled with awe; and they praised God,[s] who had given such authority to men.

The Calling of Matthew

9:9–13pp — Mk 2:14–17; Lk 5:27–32

9As Jesus went on from there, he saw a man named Matthew sitting at the tax collector's booth. "Follow me,"[t] he told him, and Matthew got up and followed him.

10While Jesus was having dinner at Matthew's house, many tax collectors and "sinners" came and ate with him and his disciples. 11When the Pharisees saw this, they asked his disciples, "Why does your teacher eat with tax collectors and 'sinners'?"[u]

12On hearing this, Jesus said, "It is not the healthy who need a doctor, but the sick. 13But go and learn what this means: 'I desire mercy, not sacrifice.'[i][v] For I have not come to call the righteous, but sinners."[w]

Jesus Questioned About Fasting

9:14–17pp — Mk 2:18–22; Lk 5:33–39

14Then John's[x] disciples came and asked him, "How is it that we and the Pharisees fast,[y] but your disciples do not fast?"

15Jesus answered, "How can the guests of the bridegroom mourn while he is with them?[z] The time will come when the bridegroom will be taken from them; then they will fast.[a]

16"No one sews a patch of unshrunk cloth on an old garment, for the patch will pull away from the garment, making the tear worse. 17Neither do men pour new wine into old wineskins. If they do, the skins will burst, the wine will run out and the wineskins will be ruined. No, they pour new wine into new wineskins, and both are preserved."

A Dead Girl and a Sick Woman

9:18–26pp — Mk 5:22–43; Lk 8:41–56

18While he was saying this, a ruler came and knelt before him[b] and said, "My daughter has just died. But come and put your hand on her,[c] and she will live." 19Jesus got up and went with him, and so did his disciples.

20Just then a woman who had been subject to bleeding for twelve years came up behind him and touched the edge of his cloak.[d] 21She said to herself, "If I only touch his cloak, I will be healed."

22Jesus turned and saw her. "Take heart,[e] daughter," he said, "your faith has healed you."[f] And the woman was healed from that moment.[g]

23When Jesus entered the ruler's house and saw the flute players and the noisy crowd,[h] 24he said, "Go away. The girl is not dead[i] but asleep."[j] But they laughed at him. 25After the crowd had been put outside, he went in and took the girl by the hand, and she got up.[k] 26News of this spread through all that region.[l]

Jesus Heals the Blind and Mute

27As Jesus went on from there, two blind men followed him, calling out, "Have mercy on us, Son of David!"[m] 28When he had gone indoors, the blind men came to him, and he asked them, "Do you believe that I am able to do this?"

"Yes, Lord," they replied.[n]

29Then he touched their eyes and said, "According to your faith will it be done to

Cross references (center column)

9:2 m S ver 22
n Jn 16:33
o Lk 7:48
9:3 p Mt 26:65; Jn 10:33
9:4 q Ps 94:11; Mt 12:25; Lk 6:8; 9:47; 11:17; Jn 2:25
9:6 r S Mt 8:20
9:8 s Mt 5:16; 15:31; Lk 7:16; 13:13; 17:15; 23:47; Jn 15:8; Ac 4:21; 11:18; 21:20
9:9 t S Mt 4:19
9:11 u Mt 11:19; Lk 5:30; 15:2; 19:7; Gal 2:15
9:13 v Hos 6:6; Mic 6:6–8; Mt 12:7
w Lk 19:10; 1Ti 1:15
9:14 x S Mt 3:1
y Mt 11:18,19; Lk 18:12
9:15 z Jn 3:29

a Ac 13:2,3; 14:23
9:18 b S Mt 8:2
c S Mk 5:23
9:20 d Mt 14:36; Mk 3:10; 6:56; Lk 6:19
9:22 e ver 2; Jn 16:33 /ver 29; Mt 8:13; Mk 10:52; Lk 7:50; 17:19; 18:42 g Mt 15:28
9:23 h 2Ch 35:25; Jer 9:17,18
9:24 i Ac 20:10 /Da 12:2; Ps 76:5; Jn 11:11–14; Ac 7:60; 13:36; 1Co 11:30; 15:6, 18,20; 1Th 4:13–16
9:25 k S Lk 7:14
9:26 l ver 31; Mt 4:24; 14:1; Mk 1:28,45; Lk 4:14,37; 5:15; 7:17
9:27 m S Mt 1:1; 12:23; 15:22; 20:30,31; 21:9, 15; 22:42; Mk 10:47
9:28 n Ac 14:9

i13 Hosea 6:6

Study notes (bottom)

9:1 *his own town.* Capernaum (see note on 4:13).
9:3 *blaspheming.* Here the term includes usurping God's prerogative to forgive sins (see note on Mk 2:7).
9:10 *tax collectors.* See note on 5:46.
9:17 *new wineskins.* In ancient times goatskins were used to hold wine. As the fresh grape juice fermented, the wine would expand, and the new wineskin would stretch. But a used skin, already stretched, would break. Jesus brings a newness that cannot be confined within the old forms.
9:18 *ruler.* From Mark and Luke we know that he was a synagogue ruler named Jairus (see note on Mk 5:22).

9:20 *subject to bleeding for twelve years.* See note on Mk 5:25.
9:22 *healed.* See note on Mk 5:34.
9:23 *flute players.* Musicians hired to play in mourning ceremonies. *noisy crowd.* Mourners hired to wail and lament.
9:24 *not dead but asleep.* See note on Lk 8:52.
9:27 *Son of David.* A popular Jewish title for the coming Messiah (e.g., 12:23; 20:30; 21:9; 22:41–45; see note on 1:1).

you"; *o* ³⁰and their sight was restored. Jesus warned them sternly, "See that no one knows about this." *p* ³¹But they went out and spread the news about him all over that region. *q*

³²While they were going out, a man who was demon-possessed *r* and could not talk *s* was brought to Jesus. ³³And when the demon was driven out, the man who had been mute spoke. The crowd was amazed and said, "Nothing like this has ever been seen in Israel." *t*

³⁴But the Pharisees said, "It is by the prince of demons that he drives out demons." *u*

The Workers Are Few

³⁵Jesus went through all the towns and villages, teaching in their synagogues, preaching the good news of the kingdom and healing every disease and sickness. *v* ³⁶When he saw the crowds, he had compassion on them, *w* because they were harassed and helpless, like sheep without a shepherd. *x* ³⁷Then he said to his disciples, "The harvest *y* is plentiful but the workers are few. *z* ³⁸Ask the Lord of the harvest, therefore, to send out workers into his harvest field."

Jesus Sends Out the Twelve

10:2–4pp — Mk 3:16–19; Lk 6:14–16; Ac 1:13
10:9–15pp — Mk 6:8–11; Lk 9:3–5; 10:4–12
10:19–22pp — Mk 13:11–13; Lk 21:12–17
10:26–33pp — Lk 12:2–9
10:34,35pp — Lk 12:51–53

10 He called his twelve disciples to him and gave them authority to drive out evil *j* spirits *a* and to heal every disease and sickness. *b*

²These are the names of the twelve apostles: first, Simon (who is called Peter) and his brother Andrew; James son of Zebedee, and his brother John; ³Philip and Bartholomew; Thomas and Matthew the tax collector; James son of Alphaeus, and Thaddaeus; ⁴Simon the Zealot and Judas Iscariot, who betrayed him. *c*

⁵These twelve Jesus sent out with the

following instructions: "Do not go among the Gentiles or enter any town of the Samaritans. *d* ⁶Go rather to the lost sheep of Israel. *e* ⁷As you go, preach this message: 'The kingdom of heaven *f* is near.' ⁸Heal the sick, raise the dead, cleanse those who have leprosy, *k* drive out demons. Freely you have received, freely give. ⁹Do not take along any gold or silver or copper in your belts; *g* ¹⁰take no bag for the journey, or extra tunic, or sandals or a staff; for the worker is worth his keep. *h*

¹¹"Whatever town or village you enter, search for some worthy person there and stay at his house until you leave. ¹²As you enter the home, give it your greeting. *i* ¹³If the home is deserving, let your peace rest on it; if it is not, let your peace return to you. ¹⁴If anyone will not welcome you or listen to your words, shake the dust off your feet *j* when you leave that home or town. ¹⁵I tell you the truth, it will be more bearable for Sodom and Gomorrah *k* on the day of judgment *l* than for that town. *m* ¹⁶I am sending you out like sheep among wolves. *n* Therefore be as shrewd as snakes and as innocent as doves. *o*

¹⁷"Be on your guard against men; they will hand you over to the local councils *p* and flog you in their synagogues. *q* ¹⁸On my account you will be brought before governors and kings *r* as witnesses to them and to the Gentiles. ¹⁹But when they arrest you, do not worry about what to say or how to say it. *s* At that time you will be given what to say, ²⁰for it will not be you speaking, but the Spirit of your Father *t* speaking through you.

²¹"Brother will betray brother to death, and a father his child; children will rebel against their parents *u* and have them put to death. *v* ²²All men will hate you because of me, *w* but he who stands firm to the end will be saved. *x* ²³When you are persecuted in one place, flee to another. I tell you the

Cross references

9:29 *o*S ver 22
9:30 *p*S Mt 8:4
9:31 *q*S ver 26; Mk 7:36
9:32 *r*S Mt 4:24
*s*Mt 12:22-24
9:33 *t*Mk 2:12
9:34 *u*Mt 12:24
9:35 *v*S Mt 4:23
9:36 *w*Mt 14:14; 15:32; Mk 8:2
*x*Nu 27:17; 1Ki 22:17; Eze 34:5,6; Zec 10:2
9:37 *y*Jn 4:35
*z*Lk 10:2
10:1
*a*Mk 3:13-15; 6:7; Lk 4:36; 9:1
*b*S Mt 4:23
10:4
*c*Mt 26:14-16,25, 47; 27:3; Mk 14:10; Jn 6:71; 12:4; 13:2,26,27; Ac 1:16
10:5 *d*1Ki 16:24; 2Ki 17:24; Lk 9:52; 10:33; 17:16; Jn 4:4-26, 39,40; 8:48; Ac 8:5,25
10:6 *e*Jer 50:6; Mt 15:24
10:7 *f*S Mt 3:2
10:9 *g*Lk 22:35
10:10
*h*S 1Ti 5:18
10:12 *i*1Sa 25:6
10:14 *j*Ne 5:13; Mk 6:11; Lk 9:5; 10:11; Ac 13:51; 18:6
10:15 *k*Ge 18:20; 19:24; 2Pe 2:6; Jude 7 *l*Mt 12:36; Ac 17:31; 2Pe 2:9; 3:7; 1Jn 4:17; Jude 6
*m*Mt 11:22,24
10:16 *n*Lk 10:3; Ac 20:29
*o*S 1Co 14:20
10:17 *p*S Mt 5:22 *q*Mt 23:34; Mk 13:9; Ac 5:40; 22:19; 26:11
10:18
*r*Ac 25:24-26
10:19 *s*Ex 4:12; Ac 4:8
10:20 *t*Lk 12:11, 12; Ac 4:8
10:21 *u*ver 35, 36; Mic 7:6
*v*Mk 13:12
10:22
*w*S Jn 15:21
*x*Mt 24:13; Mk 13:13; Lk 21:19; Rev 2:10

i / Greek *unclean* *k 8* The Greek word was used for various diseases affecting the skin—not necessarily leprosy.

Study notes

10:2–4 See notes on Lk 6:14–16.
10:2 *apostles.* See note on Mk 6:30.
10:4 *the Zealot.* Either a description of Simon's religious zeal or a reference to his membership in the party of the Zealots, a Jewish revolutionary group violently opposed to Roman rule over Palestine.
10:5 *Do not go.* The good news about the kingdom was to be proclaimed first to Jews only. After his death and resurrection, Jesus commanded the message to be taken to all nations (28:19; cf. 21:43). *Samaritans.* A mixed-blood race resulting from the intermarriage of Israelites left behind when the people of the northern kingdom were exiled and Gentiles brought into the land by the Assyrians (2Ki 17:24). Bitter

hostility existed between Jews and Samaritans in Jesus' day (see Jn 4:9).
10:14 *shake the dust off your feet.* A symbolic act practiced by the Pharisees when they left an "unclean" Gentile area. Here it represented an act of solemn warning to those who rejected God's message (see notes on Lk 9:5; Ac 13:51; cf. Ac 18:6).
10:15 *Sodom and Gomorrah.* See Ge 19:23–29.
10:17 *local councils.* The lower courts, connected with local synagogues, that tried less serious cases and flogged those found guilty.
10:23 The saying seems to teach that the gospel will continue to be preached to the Jews until Christ's second

truth, you will not finish going through the cities of Israel before the Son of Man comes. *y*

24"A student is not above his teacher, nor a servant above his master. *z* 25It is enough for the student to be like his teacher, and the servant like his master. If the head of the house has been called Beelzebub, *1a* how much more the members of his household!

26"So do not be afraid of them. There is nothing concealed that will not be disclosed, or hidden that will not be made known. *b* 27What I tell you in the dark, speak in the daylight; what is whispered in your ear, proclaim from the roofs. 28Do not be afraid of those who kill the body but cannot kill the soul. Rather, be afraid of the One *c* who can destroy both soul and body in hell. 29Are not two sparrows sold for a penny *m*? Yet not one of them will fall to the ground apart from the will of your Father. 30And even the very hairs of your head are all numbered. *d* 31So don't be afraid; you are worth more than many sparrows. *e*

32"Whoever acknowledges me before men, *f* I will also acknowledge him before my Father in heaven. 33But whoever disowns me before men, I will disown him before my Father in heaven. *g*

34"Do not suppose that I have come to bring peace to the earth. I did not come to bring peace, but a sword. 35For I have come to turn

" 'a man against his father,
   a daughter against her mother,
a daughter-in-law against her
      mother-in-law *h*—
36 a man's enemies will be the members
      of his own household.' *n i*

37"Anyone who loves his father or mother more than me is not worthy of me; anyone who loves his son or daughter

---

Cross references (center column):

10:23 *y* S Lk 17:30
10:24 *z* S Jn 13:16
10:25
10:26 *a* S Mk 3:22
10:26 *b* Mk 4:22;
Lk 8:17
10:28 *c* Isa 8:12,
13; Heb 10:31
10:30
10:31 *d* 1Sa 14:45;
2Sa 14:11;
1Ki 1:52;
Lk 21:18;
Ac 27:34
10:31 *e* Mt 6:26;
12:12
10:32 *f* Ro 10:9
10:33 *g* Mk 8:38;
2Ti 2:12
10:35 *h* ver 21
10:36 *i* Mic 7:6

10:37 *j* Lk 14:26
10:38 *k* Mt 16:24;
Lk 14:27
10:39 *l* S Jn 12:25
10:40 *m* Ex 16:8;
Mt 18:5; Gal 4:14
n Lk 9:48; 10:16;
12:44; 13:20
10:42 *o* Pr 14:31;
19:17; Mt 25:40;
Mk 9:41;
Ac 10:4;
Heb 6:10
11:1 *p* S Mt 7:28
11:2 *q* S Mt 3:1
r Mt 14:3
11:3 *s* Ps 118:26;
Jn 11:27;
Heb 10:37
11:5 *t* Isa 35:4-6;
61:1; Mt 15:31;
Lk 4:18,19
11:6 *u* Mt 13:21;
26:31
11:7 *v* S Mt 3:1
w Mt 3:1

---

more than me is not worthy of me; *j* 38and anyone who does not take his cross and follow me is not worthy of me. *k* 39Whoever finds his life will lose it, and whoever loses his life for my sake will find it. *l*

40"He who receives you receives me, *m* and he who receives me receives the one who sent me. *n* 41Anyone who receives a prophet because he is a prophet will receive a prophet's reward, and anyone who receives a righteous man because he is a righteous man will receive a righteous man's reward. 42And if anyone gives even a cup of cold water to one of these little ones because he is my disciple, I tell you the truth, he will certainly not lose his reward." *o*

Jesus and John the Baptist
11:2–19pp — Lk 7:18–35

11 After Jesus had finished instructing his twelve disciples, *p* he went on from there to teach and preach in the towns of Galilee. *o*

2When John *q* heard in prison *r* what Christ was doing, he sent his disciples 3to ask him, "Are you the one who was to come, *s* or should we expect someone else?"

4Jesus replied, "Go back and report to John what you hear and see: 5The blind receive sight, the lame walk, those who have leprosy *p* are cured, the deaf hear, the dead are raised, and the good news is preached to the poor. *t* 6Blessed is the man who does not fall away on account of me." *u*

7As John's *v* disciples were leaving, Jesus began to speak to the crowd about John: "What did you go out into the desert *w* to see? A reed swayed by the wind? 8If not, what did you go out to see? A man dressed

---

1 25 Greek *Beezeboul* or *Beelzeboul*   *m 29* Greek *an assarion*   *n 36* Micah 7:6   *o 1* Greek *in their towns*   *p 5* The Greek word was used for various diseases affecting the skin—not necessarily leprosy.

---

coming.
10:25 *Beelzebub.* The prince of demons (12:24); the Greek form of the Hebrew name Baal-Zebub ("lord of flies"; see 2Ki 1:2), a parody on and mockery of the actual epithet, Baal-Zebul ("Exalted Baal" or "Prince Baal"; see NIV text note). The name came to be used of Satan.
10:28 *hell.* See note on 5:22.
10:34 At first glance this saying sounds like a contradiction of Isa 9:6 ("Prince of Peace"), Lk 2:14 ("on earth peace to men") and Jn 14:27 ("Peace I leave with you"). It is true that Christ came to bring peace—peace between the believer and God, and peace among men. Yet the inevitable result of Christ's coming is conflict—between Christ and the antichrist, between light and darkness, between Christ's children and the devil's children. This conflict can occur even between members of the same family (vv. 35–36).

10:38 *take his cross.* The first mention of the cross in Matthew's Gospel. The cross was an instrument of death and here symbolizes the necessity of total commitment—even unto death—on the part of Jesus' disciples (see note on Mk 8:34).
10:41 *prophet.* John was the last prophet of the old covenant.
11:1 While the 12 apostles were carrying out their first mission, Jesus continued his ministry in Galilee.
11:3 *the one who was to come.* The Messiah. *expect someone else.* See note on Lk 7:19.
11:4 *report to John what you hear and see.* See note on Lk 7:22.
11:5 *the good news is preached to the poor.* See note on Lk 7:22.
11:6 *the man who does not fall away.* See note on Lk 7:23.

in fine clothes? No, those who wear fine clothes are in kings' palaces. 9Then what did you go out to see? A prophet?ˣ Yes, I tell you, and more than a prophet. 10This is the one about whom it is written:

" 'I will send my messenger ahead of you,ʸ
who will prepare your way before you.'q z

11I tell you the truth: Among those born of women there has not risen anyone greater than John the Baptist; yet he who is least in the kingdom of heaven is greater than he. 12From the days of John the Baptist until now, the kingdom of heaven has been forcefully advancing, and forceful men lay hold of it. 13For all the Prophets and the Law prophesied until John.ᵃ 14And if you are willing to accept it, he is the Elijah who was to come.ᵇ 15He who has ears, let him hear.ᶜ

16"To what can I compare this generation? They are like children sitting in the marketplaces and calling out to others:

17" 'We played the flute for you,
and you did not dance;
we sang a dirge,
and you did not mourn.'

18For John came neither eatingᵈ nor drinking,ᵉ and they say, 'He has a demon.' 19The Son of Man came eating and drinking, and they say, 'Here is a glutton and a drunkard, a friend of tax collectors and "sinners." 'ᶠ But wisdom is proved right by her actions."

Woe on Unrepentant Cities

11:21–23pp — Lk 10:13-15

20Then Jesus began to denounce the cities in which most of his miracles had been performed, because they did not repent. 21"Woe to you, Korazin! Woe to you, Bethsaida!ᵍ If the miracles that were per-

formed in you had been performed in Tyre and Sidon,ʰ they would have repented long ago in sackcloth and ashes.ⁱ 22But I tell you, it will be more bearable for Tyre and Sidon on the day of judgment than for you.ʲ 23And you, Capernaum,ᵏ will you be lifted up to the skies? No, you will go down to the depths.ʳⁱ If the miracles that were performed in you had been performed in Sodom, it would have remained to this day. 24But I tell you that it will be more bearable for Sodom on the day of judgment than for you."ᵐ

Rest for the Weary

11:25–27pp — Lk 10:21,22

25At that time Jesus said, "I praise you, Father,ⁿ Lord of heaven and earth, because you have hidden these things from the wise and learned, and revealed them to little children.ᵒ 26Yes, Father, for this was your good pleasure.

27"All things have been committed to meᵖ by my Father.q No one knows the Son except the Father, and no one knows the Father except the Son and those to whom the Son chooses to reveal him.ʳ

28"Come to me,ˢ all you who are weary and burdened, and I will give you rest.ᵗ 29Take my yoke upon you and learn from me,ᵘ for I am gentle and humble in heart, and you will find rest for your souls.ᵛ 30For my yoke is easy and my burden is light."ʷ

Lord of the Sabbath

12:1–8pp — Mk 2:23–28; Lk 6:1–5
12:9–14pp — Mk 3:1–6; Lk 6:6–11

12 At that time Jesus went through the grainfields on the Sabbath. His disciples were hungry and began to pick some heads of grainˣ and eat them. 2When the Pharisees saw this, they said to him, "Look! Your disciples are doing what is unlawful on the Sabbath."ʸ

Cross references (center column):

11:9 ˣMt 14:5; 21:26; Lk 1:76; 7:26
11:10 ʸJn 3:28 ᶻMal 3:1; Mk 1:2; Lk 7:27
11:13 ᵃLk 16:16
11:14 ᵇMal 4:5; Mt 17:10-13; Mk 9:11-13; Lk 1:17; Jn 1:21
11:15 ᶜMt 13:9, 43; Mk 4:23; Lk 14:35; S Rev 2:7
11:18 ᵈMt 3:4 ᵉS Lk 1:15
11:19 ᶠS Mt 9:11
11:21 ᵍMk 6:45; 8:22; Lk 9:10; Jn 1:44; 12:21
ʰJoel 3:4; Am 1:9; Mt 15:21; Mk 3:8; Lk 6:17; Ac 12:20 ⁱJnh 3:5-9
11:22 ʲver 24; Mt 10:15
11:23 ᵏS Mt 4:13 ˡIsa 14:13-15
11:24 ᵐS Mt 10:15
11:25 ⁿMt 16:17; Lk 22:42; 23:34; Jn 11:41; 12:27, 28 ᵒS Mt 13:11; 1Co 1:26-29
11:27 ᵖS Mt 28:18 qS Jn 3:35 ʳJn 10:15; 17:25, 26
11:28 ˢJn 7:37 ᵗEx 33:14
11:29 ᵘJn 13:15; Php 2:5; 1Pe 2:21; 1Jn 2:6 ᵛPs 116:7; Jer 6:16
11:30 ʷ1Jn 5:3
12:1 ˣDt 23:25
12:2 ʸver 10; Ex 20:10; 23:12; Dt 5:14; Lk 13:14; 14:3; Jn 5:10; 7:23; 9:16

q10 Mal. 3:1   r23 Greek *Hades*

11:11 *greater than he.* John belonged to the age of the old covenant, which was preparatory to Christ. The least NT saint has a higher privilege in Christ as a part of his bride (the church, Eph 5:25–27,32) than John the Baptist, who was only a friend of the bridegroom (Jn 3:29). Another view, however, stresses the expression "he who is least," holding that the key to its meaning is found in 18:4—"whoever humbles himself like this child." Such a person, though "least," is regarded by God as even greater than John the Baptist.
11:12 *forceful men lay hold of it.* They enter the kingdom and become Christ's disciples. To do this takes spiritual courage, vigor, power and determination because of ever-present persecution.
11:17 *played the flute.* As at a wedding. *sang a dirge.* As at a funeral. The latter symbolized the ministry of John, the

former that of Jesus. The Jews were like children who refused to respond on either occasion.
11:19 *wisdom is proved right by her actions.* Apparently means that God (wisdom) had sent both John and Jesus in specific roles, and that this would be vindicated by the miraculous works of Jesus (see v. 20). See note on Lk 7:35.
11:21 *Korazin.* Mentioned in the Bible only twice (here and in Lk 10:13), it was near the Sea of Galilee, probably about two miles north of Capernaum. *Bethsaida.* On the northeast shore of the Sea of Galilee. Philip the tetrarch rebuilt Bethsaida and named it "Julias," after Julia, daughter of Caesar Augustus. *Tyre and Sidon.* Cities on the Phoenician coast north of Palestine.
11:23 *Capernaum.* See note on Lk 10:15.
12:1 *grainfields.* Of wheat or barley, the latter eaten by poorer people.

3 He answered, "Haven't you read what
David did when he and his companions
were hungry?[z] 4 He entered the house of
God, and he and his companions ate the
consecrated bread—which was not lawful
for them to do, but only for the priests.[a]
5 Or haven't you read in the Law that on
the Sabbath the priests in the temple desecrate the day[b] and yet are innocent? 6 I tell
you that one[s] greater than the temple is
here.[c] 7 If you had known what these
words mean, 'I desire mercy, not sacrifice,'[t][d] you would not have condemned
the innocent. 8 For the Son of Man[e] is Lord
of the Sabbath."

9 Going on from that place, he went into
their synagogue, 10 and a man with a shriveled hand was there. Looking for a reason
to accuse Jesus,[f] they asked him, "Is it
lawful to heal on the Sabbath?"[g]

11 He said to them, "If any of you has a
sheep and it falls into a pit on the Sabbath,
will you not take hold of it and lift it out?[h]
12 How much more valuable is a man than
a sheep![i] Therefore it is lawful to do good
on the Sabbath."

13 Then he said to the man, "Stretch out
your hand." So he stretched it out and it
was completely restored, just as sound as
the other. 14 But the Pharisees went out
and plotted how they might kill Jesus.[j]

God's Chosen Servant

15 Aware of this, Jesus withdrew from
that place. Many followed him, and he
healed all their sick,[k] 16 warning them not
to tell who he was.[l] 17 This was to fulfill[m]
what was spoken through the prophet
Isaiah:

18 "Here is my servant whom I have
chosen,
the one I love, in whom I delight;[n]
I will put my Spirit on him,[o]
and he will proclaim justice to the
nations.
19 He will not quarrel or cry out;
no one will hear his voice in the
streets.
20 A bruised reed he will not break,
and a smoldering wick he will not
snuff out,
till he leads justice to victory.
21 In his name the nations will put their
hope."[u][p]

Jesus and Beelzebub

12:25–29pp — Mk 3:23–27; Lk 11:17–22

22 Then they brought him a demon-possessed man who was blind and mute, and
Jesus healed him, so that he could both
talk and see.[q] 23 All the people were astonished and said, "Could this be the Son of
David?"[r]

24 But when the Pharisees heard this,
they said, "It is only by Beelzebub,[v][s] the
prince of demons, that this fellow drives
out demons."[t]

25 Jesus knew their thoughts[u] and said
to them, "Every kingdom divided against
itself will be ruined, and every city or
household divided against itself will not
stand. 26 If Satan[v] drives out Satan, he is
divided against himself. How then can his
kingdom stand? 27 And if I drive out demons by Beelzebub,[w] by whom do your
people[x] drive them out? So then, they will
be your judges. 28 But if I drive out demons
by the Spirit of God, then the kingdom of
God[y] has come upon you.

29 "Or again, how can anyone enter a
strong man's house and carry off his
possessions unless he first ties up the
strong man? Then he can rob his house.

30 "He who is not with me is against me,
and he who does not gather with me scatters.[z] 31 And so I tell you, every sin and
blasphemy will be forgiven men, but the
blasphemy against the Spirit will not be
forgiven.[a] 32 Anyone who speaks a word
against the Son of Man will be forgiven,
but anyone who speaks against the Holy
Spirit will not be forgiven, either in this
age[b] or in the age to come.[c]

33 "Make a tree good and its fruit will be
good, or make a tree bad and its fruit will
be bad, for a tree is recognized by its

12:3 [z] 1Sa 21:6
12:4 [a] Lev 24:5,9
12:5 [b] Nu 28:9,10; Jn 7:22,23
12:6 [c] ver 41,42
12:7 [d] Hos 6:6; Mic 6:6-8; Mt 9:13
12:8 [e] S Mt 8:20
12:10 [f] Mk 3:2; 12:13; Lk 11:54; 14:1; 20:20 [g] S ver 2
12:11 [h] Lk 14:5
12:12 [i] Mt 6:26; 10:31
12:14 [j] Ge 37:18; Ps 71:10; Mt 26:4; 27:1; Mk 3:6; Lk 6:11; Jn 5:18; 7:1,19; 11:53
12:15 [k] S Mt 4:23
12:16 [l] S Mt 8:4
12:17 [m] S Mt 1:22
12:18 [n] S Mt 3:17 [o] S Jn 3:34
12:21 [p] Isa 42:1-4
12:22 [q] S Mt 4:24
12:23 [r] S Mt 9:27
12:24 [s] S Mk 3:22 [t] Mt 9:34
12:25 [u] S Mt 9:4
12:26 [v] S Mt 4:10
12:27 [w] ver 24 [x] Ac 19:13
12:28 [y] S Mt 3:2
12:30 [z] Mk 9:40; Lk 11:23
12:31 [a] Mk 3:28,29; Lk 12:10
12:32 [b] Tit 2:12 [c] Mk 10:30; Lk 20:34,35; Eph 1:21; Heb 6:5

[s] *6* Or *something;* also in verses 41 and 42 [t] *7* Hosea 6:6 [u] *21* Isaiah 42:1-4 [v] *24* Greek *Beezeboul* or *Beelzeboul;* also in verse 27

12:3 *what David did.* See note on Mk 2:25.
12:4 *consecrated bread.* Each Sabbath, 12 fresh loaves of bread were to be set on a table in the Holy Place (Ex 25:30; Lev 24:5–9). The old loaves were eaten by the priests.
12:5 *desecrate the day.* By doing work associated with the sacrifices.
12:8 *the Son of Man is Lord of the Sabbath.* See note on Lk 6:5.
12:10 *heal on the Sabbath.* The rabbis prohibited healing on the Sabbath, unless it was feared the victim would die before the next day.
12:16 *not to tell who he was.* See note on 8:4.
12:20 Jesus mends broken lives (see v. 15; Jn 4:4–42; 8:3–11).
12:23 *the Son of David.* See note on 9:27.
12:24 *Beelzebub.* See note on 10:25.
12:31 *blasphemy against the Spirit will not be forgiven.* The context (vv. 24,28,32) suggests that the "unpardonable sin" was attributing to Satan Christ's authenticating miracles done in the power of the Holy Spirit (see note on Mk 3:29).

fruit.d 34You brood of vipers,e how can you who are evil say anything good? For out of the overflow of the heart the mouth speaks.f 35The good man brings good things out of the good stored up in him, and the evil man brings evil things out of the evil stored up in him. 36But I tell you that men will have to give account on the day of judgment for every careless word they have spoken. 37For by your words you will be acquitted, and by your words you will be condemned."g

The Sign of Jonah

12:39–42pp — Lk 11:29–32
12:43–45pp — Lk 11:24–26

38Then some of the Pharisees and teachers of the law said to him, "Teacher, we want to see a miraculous signh from you."i

39He answered, "A wicked and adulterous generation asks for a miraculous sign! But none will be given it except the sign of the prophet Jonah.j 40For as Jonah was three days and three nights in the belly of a huge fish,k so the Son of Manl will be three days and three nights in the heart of the earth.m 41The men of Ninevehn will stand up at the judgment with this generation and condemn it; for they repented at the preaching of Jonah,o and now onew greater than Jonah is here. 42The Queen of the South will rise at the judgment with this generation and condemn it; for she camep from the ends of the earth to listen to Solomon's wisdom, and now one greater than Solomon is here.

43"When an evilx spirit comes out of a man, it goes through arid places seeking rest and does not find it. 44Then it says, 'I will return to the house I left.' When it arrives, it finds the house unoccupied, swept clean and put in order. 45Then it goes and takes with it seven other spirits more wicked than itself, and they go in

and live there. And the final condition of that man is worse than the first.q That is how it will be with this wicked generation."

Jesus' Mother and Brothers

12:46–50pp — Mk 3:31–35; Lk 8:19–21

46While Jesus was still talking to the crowd, his motherr and brotherss stood outside, wanting to speak to him. 47Someone told him, "Your mother and brothers are standing outside, wanting to speak to you."y

48He replied to him, "Who is my mother, and who are my brothers?" 49Pointing to his disciples, he said, "Here are my mother and my brothers. 50For whoever does the will of my Father in heavent is my brother and sister and mother."

The Parable of the Sower

13:1–15pp — Mk 4:1–12; Lk 8:4–10
13:16,17pp — Lk 10:23,24
13:18–23pp — Mk 4:13–20; Lk 8:11–15

13 That same day Jesus went out of the houseu and sat by the lake. 2Such large crowds gathered around him that he got into a boatv and sat in it, while all the people stood on the shore. 3Then he told them many things in parables, saying: "A farmer went out to sow his seed. 4As he was scattering the seed, some fell along the path, and the birds came and ate it up. 5Some fell on rocky places, where it did not have much soil. It sprang up quickly, because the soil was shallow. 6But when the sun came up, the plants were scorched, and they withered because they had no root. 7Other seed fell among thorns, which grew up and choked the plants. 8Still other seed fell on good soil, where it produced a crop—a hundred,w

Cross references (center column)

12:33 dMt 7:16, 17; Lk 6:43,44
12:34 eMt 3:7; 23:33 /Mt 15:18; Lk 6:45
12:37 gJob 15:6; Pr 10:14; 18:21; Jas 3:2
12:38 hS Jn 2:11; S 4:48 iMt 16:1; Mk 8:11,12; Lk 11:16; Jn 2:18; 6:30; 1Co 1:22
12:39 jMt 16:4; Lk 11:29
12:40 kJnh 1:17 /S Mt 8:20 mS Mt 16:21
12:41 nJnh 1:2 oJnh 3:5
12:42 p1Ki 10:1; 2Ch 9:1

12:45 q2Pe 2:20
12:46 rMt 1:18; 2:11,13,14,20; Lk 1:43; 2:33,34, 48,51; Jn 2:1,5; 19:25,26 sMt 13:55; Jn 2:12; 7:3,5; Ac 1:14; 1Co 9:5; Gal 1:19
12:50 tMt 6:10; Jn 15:14
13:1 uver 36; Mt 9:28
13:2 vLk 5:3
13:8 wGe 26:12

w41 Or *something*; also in verse 42   x43 Greek *unclean*   y47 Some manuscripts do not have verse 47.

12:38 *miraculous sign.* The Pharisees wanted to see a spectacular miracle, preferably in the sky (see Lk 11:16), as the sign that Jesus was the Messiah. Instead, he cites them a "sign" from history.

12:39 *adulterous.* Referring to spiritual, not physical, adultery, in the sense that their generation had become unfaithful to its spiritual husband (God).

12:40 *three days and three nights.* Including at least part of the first day and part of the third day, a common Jewish reckoning of time. See note on Lk 24:46. *huge fish.* The Greek word does not mean "whale" but rather "sea creature," i.e., a huge fish (see note on Jnh 1:17).

12:41–42 *one greater than Jonah . . . one greater than Solomon.* See note on Lk 11:31–32.

12:42 *Queen of the South.* In 1Ki 10:1 she is called the queen of Sheba, a country in southwest Arabia, now called

Yemen.

12:43–45 See note on Lk 11:24.

12:46 *mother and brothers.* See note on Lk 8:19.

12:50 *whoever does the will of my Father.* See note on Mk 3:34.

13:3–9 See vv. 18–23 for the interpretation of this first parable.

13:3 *parables.* Our word "parable" comes from the Greek *parabole,* which means "a placing beside"—and thus a comparison or an illustration. Its most common use in the NT is for the illustrative stories that Jesus drew from nature and human life. The Synoptic Gospels contain about 30 of these stories. John's Gospel contains no parables but uses other figures of speech (see notes on Mk 4:2; Lk 8:4).

13:5 *rocky places.* Not ground covered with small stones, but shallow soil on top of solid rock.

sixty or thirty times what was sown. [9]He who has ears, let him hear." [x]

[10]The disciples came to him and asked, "Why do you speak to the people in parables?"

[11]He replied, "The knowledge of the secrets of the kingdom of heaven [y] has been given to you, [z] but not to them. [12]Whoever has will be given more, and he will have an abundance. Whoever does not have, even what he has will be taken from him. [a] [13]This is why I speak to them in parables:

"Though seeing, they do not see;
　　though hearing, they do not hear or
　　　　understand. [b]

[14]In them is fulfilled [c] the prophecy of Isaiah:

" 'You will be ever hearing but never
　　　　understanding;
　　you will be ever seeing but never
　　　　perceiving.
[15]For this people's heart has become
　　　　calloused;
　　they hardly hear with their ears,
　　and they have closed their eyes.
Otherwise they might see with their
　　　　eyes,
　　hear with their ears,
　　understand with their hearts
　　and turn, and I would heal them.' [z] [d]

[16]But blessed are your eyes because they see, and your ears because they hear. [e] [17]For I tell you the truth, many prophets and righteous men longed to see what you see [f] but did not see it, and to hear what you hear but did not hear it.

[18]"Listen then to what the parable of the sower means: [19]When anyone hears the message about the kingdom [g] and does not understand it, the evil one [h] comes and snatches away what was sown in his heart. This is the seed sown along the path. [20]The one who received the seed that fell on rocky places is the man who hears the word and at once receives it with joy. [21]But since he has no root, he lasts only a short time. When trouble or persecution

comes because of the word, he quickly falls away. [i] [22]The one who received the seed that fell among the thorns is the man who hears the word, but the worries of this life and the deceitfulness of wealth [j] choke it, making it unfruitful. [23]But the one who received the seed that fell on good soil is the man who hears the word and understands it. He produces a crop, yielding a hundred, sixty or thirty times what was sown." [k]

The Parable of the Weeds

[24]Jesus told them another parable: "The kingdom of heaven is like [l] a man who sowed good seed in his field. [25]But while everyone was sleeping, his enemy came and sowed weeds among the wheat, and went away. [26]When the wheat sprouted and formed heads, then the weeds also appeared.

[27]"The owner's servants came to him and said, 'Sir, didn't you sow good seed in your field? Where then did the weeds come from?'

[28]" 'An enemy did this,' he replied.

"The servants asked him, 'Do you want us to go and pull them up?'

[29]" 'No,' he answered, 'because while you are pulling the weeds, you may root up the wheat with them. [30]Let both grow together until the harvest. At that time I will tell the harvesters: First collect the weeds and tie them in bundles to be burned; then gather the wheat and bring it into my barn.' " [m]

The Parables of the Mustard Seed and the Yeast

13:31,32pp — Mk 4:30–32
13:31–33pp — Lk 13:18–21

[31]He told them another parable: "The kingdom of heaven is like [n] a mustard seed, [o] which a man took and planted in his field. [32]Though it is the smallest of all your seeds, yet when it grows, it is the largest of garden plants and becomes a

---

13:9 [x]S Mt 11:15
13:11 [y]S Mt 3:2
　[z]Mt 11:25;
　16:17; 19:11;
　Jn 6:65;
　1Co 2:10,14;
　Col 1:27;
　1Jn 2:20,27
13:12
　[a]S Mt 25:29
13:13 [b]Dt 29:4;
　Jer 5:21; Eze 12:2
13:14 [c]ver 35;
　S Mt 1:22
13:15 [d]Isa 6:9,
　10; Jn 12:40;
　Ac 28:26,27;
　Ro 11:8
13:16 [e]Mt 16:17
13:17 [f]Jn 8:56;
　Heb 11:13;
　1Pe 1:10-12
13:19 [g]Mt 4:23
　[h]S Mt 5:37

13:21 [i]Mt 11:6;
　26:31
13:22 [j]Mt 19:23;
　1Ti 6:9,10,17
13:23 [k]ver 8
13:24 [l]ver 31,33,
　45,47; Mt 18:23;
　20:1; 22:2; 25:1;
　Mk 4:26,30
13:30 [m]Mt 3:12
13:31 [n]S ver 24
　[o]Mt 17:20;
　Lk 17:6

[z]15 Isaiah 6:9,10

13:13–14 Jesus speaks in parables because of the spiritual dullness of the people (see note on Lk 8:4).
13:24–30 See vv. 36–43 for the interpretation.
13:24 *The kingdom of heaven is like.* This phrase introduces six of the seven parables in this chapter (all but the parable of the sower).
13:25 *weeds.* Probably darnel, which looks very much like wheat while it is young, but can later be distinguished. This parable does not refer to unbelievers in the professing church. The field is the world (v. 38). Thus the people of the kingdom live side by side with the people of the evil one.

13:31–32 Although the kingdom will seem to have an insignificant beginning, it will eventually spread throughout the world.
13:32 *the smallest . . . the largest.* The mustard seed is not the smallest seed known today, but it was the smallest seed used by Palestinian farmers and gardeners, and under favorable conditions the plant could reach some ten feet in height. *a tree . . . its branches.* Likely an allusion to Da 4:21, suggesting that the kingdom of heaven will expand to world dominion and people from all nations will find rest in it (cf. Da 2:35,44–45; 7:27; Rev 11:15).

tree, so that the birds of the air come and perch in its branches." *p*

33He told them still another parable: "The kingdom of heaven is like *q* yeast that a woman took and mixed into a large amount *a* of flour *r* until it worked all through the dough." *s*

34Jesus spoke all these things to the crowd in parables; he did not say anything to them without using a parable. *t* 35So was fulfilled *u* what was spoken through the prophet:

"I will open my mouth in parables,
I will utter things hidden since the
    creation of the world." *b v*

The Parable of the Weeds Explained

36Then he left the crowd and went into the house. His disciples came to him and said, "Explain to us the parable *w* of the weeds in the field."

37He answered, "The one who sowed the good seed is the Son of Man. *x* 38The field is the world, and the good seed stands for the sons of the kingdom. The weeds are the sons of the evil one, *y* 39and the enemy who sows them is the devil. The harvest *z* is the end of the age, *a* and the harvesters are angels. *b*

40"As the weeds are pulled up and burned in the fire, so it will be at the end of the age. 41The Son of Man *c* will send out his angels, *d* and they will weed out of his kingdom everything that causes sin and all who do evil. 42They will throw them into the fiery furnace, where there will be weeping and gnashing of teeth. *e* 43Then the righteous will shine like the sun *f* in the kingdom of their Father. He who has ears, let him hear. *g*

The Parables of the Hidden Treasure and the Pearl

44"The kingdom of heaven is like *h* treasure hidden in a field. When a man found it, he hid it again, and then in his joy went and sold all he had and bought that field. *i* 45"Again, the kingdom of heaven is

13:32
*p*Ps 104:12;
Eze 17:23; 31:6;
Da 4:12
13:33 *q*S ver 24
*r*Ge 18:6 *s*Gal 5:9
13:34 *t*S Jn 16:25
13:35 *u*ver 14;
S Mt 1:22
*v*Ps 78:2;
Ro 16:25,26;
1Co 2:7; Eph 3:9;
Col 1:26
13:36 *w*Mt 15:15
13:37 *x*S Mt 8:20
13:38 *y*Jn 8:44,
45; 1Jn 3:10
13:39 *z*Joel 3:13
*a*Mt 24:3; 28:20
*b*Rev 14:15
13:41 *c*S Mt 8:20
*d*Mt 24:31
13:42 *e*S Mt 8:12
13:43 *f*Da 12:3
*g*S Mt 11:15
13:44 *h*S ver 24
*i*Isa 55:1;
Mt 19:21;
Php 3:7,8

13:45 *j*S ver 24
13:47 *k*S ver 24
*l*Mt 22:10
13:49 *m*Mt 25:32
13:50 *n*S Mt 8:12
13:53 *o*S Mt 7:28
13:54 *p*S Mt 4:23
*q*S Mt 7:28
13:55 *r*Lk 3:23;
Jn 6:42
*s*S Mt 12:46
*t*S Mt 12:46
13:57 *u*Jn 6:61
*v*Lk 4:24; Jn 4:44

like *j* a merchant looking for fine pearls. 46When he found one of great value, he went away and sold everything he had and bought it.

The Parable of the Net

47"Once again, the kingdom of heaven is like *k* a net that was let down into the lake and caught all kinds *l* of fish. 48When it was full, the fishermen pulled it up on the shore. Then they sat down and collected the good fish in baskets, but threw the bad away. 49This is how it will be at the end of the age. The angels will come and separate the wicked from the righteous *m* 50and throw them into the fiery furnace, where there will be weeping and gnashing of teeth. *n*

51"Have you understood all these things?" Jesus asked.

"Yes," they replied.

52He said to them, "Therefore every teacher of the law who has been instructed about the kingdom of heaven is like the owner of a house who brings out of his storeroom new treasures as well as old."

A Prophet Without Honor

13:54-58pp — Mk 6:1-6

53When Jesus had finished these parables, *o* he moved on from there. 54Coming to his hometown, he began teaching the people in their synagogue, *p* and they were amazed. *q* "Where did this man get this wisdom and these miraculous powers?" they asked. 55"Isn't this the carpenter's son? *r* Isn't his mother's *s* name Mary, and aren't his brothers *t* James, Joseph, Simon and Judas? 56Aren't all his sisters with us? Where then did this man get all these things?" 57And they took offense *u* at him.

But Jesus said to them, "Only in his hometown and in his own house is a prophet without honor." *v*

58And he did not do many miracles there because of their lack of faith.

a 33 Greek *three satas* (probably about 1/2 bushel or 22 liters)   *b 35* Psalm 78:2

13:33 In the Bible, yeast usually symbolizes that which is evil or unclean (see note on Mk 8:15). Here, however, it is a symbol of growth. As yeast permeates a batch of dough, so the kingdom of heaven spreads through a person's life. Or it may signify the growth of the kingdom by the inner working of the Holy Spirit (using God's word).
13:44-45 These two parables teach the same truth: The kingdom is of such great value that one should be willing to give up all he has in order to gain it. Jesus did not imply that one can purchase the kingdom with money or good deeds.
13:44 *treasure hidden in a field.* In ancient times it was common to hide treasure in the ground since there were no

banks—though there were "bankers" (Mt 25:27).
13:47-51 The parable of the net teaches the same general lesson as the parable of the weeds: There will be a final separation of the righteous and the wicked. The parable of the weeds also emphasizes that we are not to try to make such a separation now and that this is entirely the Lord's business (vv. 28-30,41-42).
13:54 *his hometown.* Nazareth.
13:55 *carpenter's son.* The word translated "carpenter" could mean "stonemason." (Apparently Joseph was not living at the time of this incident.) *brothers.* Sons born to Joseph and Mary after Jesus.

John the Baptist Beheaded

14:1–12pp — Mk 6:14–29

14 At that time Herod[w] the tetrarch heard the reports about Jesus,[x] [2]and he said to his attendants, "This is John the Baptist;[y] he has risen from the dead! That is why miraculous powers are at work in him."

[3]Now Herod had arrested John and bound him and put him in prison[z] because of Herodias, his brother Philip's wife,[a] [4]for John had been saying to him: "It is not lawful for you to have her."[b] [5]Herod wanted to kill John, but he was afraid of the people, because they considered him a prophet.[c]

[6]On Herod's birthday the daughter of Herodias danced for them and pleased Herod so much [7]that he promised with an oath to give her whatever she asked. [8]Prompted by her mother, she said, "Give me here on a platter the head of John the Baptist." [9]The king was distressed, but because of his oaths and his dinner guests, he ordered that her request be granted [10]and had John beheaded[d] in the prison. [11]His head was brought in on a platter and given to the girl, who carried it to her mother. [12]John's disciples came and took his body and buried it.[e] Then they went and told Jesus.

Jesus Feeds the Five Thousand

14:13–21pp — Mk 6:32–44; Lk 9:10–17; Jn 6:1–13
14:13–21Ref — Mt 15:32–38

[13]When Jesus heard what had happened, he withdrew by boat privately to a solitary place. Hearing of this, the crowds followed him on foot from the towns. [14]When Jesus landed and saw a large

14:1 wMk 8:15;
Lk 3:1,19; 13:31;
23:7,8; Ac 4:27;
12:1 xLk 9:7-9
14:2 yS Mt 3:1
14:3 zMt 4:12;
11:2 aLk 3:19,20
14:4 bLev 18:16;
20:21
14:5 cS Mt 11:9
14:10 dMt 17:12
14:12 eAc 8:2

crowd, he had compassion on them[f] and healed their sick.[g]

[15]As evening approached, the disciples came to him and said, "This is a remote place, and it's already getting late. Send the crowds away, so they can go to the villages and buy themselves some food."

[16]Jesus replied, "They do not need to go away. You give them something to eat."

[17]"We have here only five loaves[h] of bread and two fish," they answered.

[18]"Bring them here to me," he said. [19]And he directed the people to sit down on the grass. Taking the five loaves and the two fish and looking up to heaven, he gave thanks and broke the loaves.[i] Then he gave them to the disciples, and the disciples gave them to the people. [20]They all ate and were satisfied, and the disciples picked up twelve basketfuls of broken pieces that were left over. [21]The number of those who ate was about five thousand men, besides women and children.

Jesus Walks on the Water

14:22–33pp — Mk 6:45–51; Jn 6:15–21
14:34–36pp — Mk 6:53–56

[22]Immediately Jesus made the disciples get into the boat and go on ahead of him to the other side, while he dismissed the crowd. [23]After he had dismissed them, he went up on a mountainside by himself to pray.[j] When evening came, he was there alone, [24]but the boat was already a considerable distance[c] from land, buffeted by the waves because the wind was against it. [25]During the fourth watch of the night Jesus went out to them, walking on the lake. [26]When the disciples saw him walking on the lake, they were terrified. "It's a

14:14 fS Mt 9:36
gS Mt 4:23
14:17 hMt 16:9
14:19 iISa 9:13;
Mt 26:26;
Mk 8:6; Lk 9:16;
24:30; Ac 2:42;
1Co 10:16;
1Ti 4:4
14:23 jS Lk 3:21

c24 Greek *many stadia*

14:1 *tetrarch*. The ruler of a fourth part of a region. Herod the tetrarch (Herod Antipas) was one of several sons of Herod the Great. When Herod the Great died, his kingdom (see map on p. 1542) was divided among four of his sons. Herod Antipas ruled over Galilee and Perea (4 B.C.-A.D. 39). Matthew correctly refers to him as tetrarch here, as Luke regularly does (Lk 3:19; 9:7; Ac 13:1). But in v. 9 Matthew calls him "king"—as Mark also does (Mk 6:14)—because that was his popular title among the Galileans, as well as in Rome.

14:3 *Herodias*. A granddaughter of Herod the Great. First she married her uncle, Herod Philip (Herod the Great also had another son named Philip), who lived in Rome. While a guest in their home, Herod Antipas persuaded Herodias to leave her husband for him. Marriage to one's brother's wife, while the brother was still living, was forbidden by the Mosaic law (Lev 18:16). *Philip*. The son of Herod the Great and Mariamne, the daughter of Simon the high priest, and thus a half-brother of Herod Antipas, born to Malthace (see chart on "House of Herod," p. 1443).

14:6 *the daughter of Herodias*. Salome, according to Jose-

phus. She later married her granduncle, the other Philip (son of Herod the Great), who ruled the northern territories (Lk 3:1). At this time Salome was a young woman of marriageable age. Her dance was unquestionably lascivious, and the performance pleased both Herod and his guests.

14:8 *platter*. A flat wooden dish on which meat was served.

14:13–21 See Mk 6:32–44; Lk 9:10–17; Jn 6:1–13 and notes.

14:21 *besides women and children*. Matthew alone notes this. He was writing to the Jews, who did not permit women and children to eat with men in public. So they were in a place by themselves.

14:25 *fourth watch*. 3:00–6:00 A.M. According to Roman reckoning the night was divided into four watches: (1) 6:00–9:00 P.M., (2) 9:00-midnight, (3) midnight–3:00 A.M. and (4) 3:00–6:00 A.M. (see note on Mk 13:35). The Jews had only three watches during the night: (1) sunset–10:00 P.M., (2) 10:00 P.M.–2:00 A.M. and (3) 2:00 A.M.-sunrise (see Jdg 7:19; 1Sa 11:11).

ghost,"[k] they said, and cried out in fear.
27But Jesus immediately said to them:
"Take courage![l] It is I. Don't be afraid."[m]

28"Lord, if it's you," Peter replied, "tell me to come to you on the water."

29"Come," he said.

Then Peter got down out of the boat, walked on the water and came toward Jesus. 30But when he saw the wind, he was afraid and, beginning to sink, cried out, "Lord, save me!"

31Immediately Jesus reached out his hand and caught him. "You of little faith,"[n] he said, "why did you doubt?"

32And when they climbed into the boat, the wind died down. 33Then those who were in the boat worshiped him, saying, "Truly you are the Son of God."[o]

34When they had crossed over, they landed at Gennesaret. 35And when the men of that place recognized Jesus, they sent word to all the surrounding country. People brought all their sick to him 36and begged him to let the sick just touch the edge of his cloak,[p] and all who touched him were healed.

Clean and Unclean

15:1–20pp — Mk 7:1–23

15 Then some Pharisees and teachers of the law came to Jesus from Jerusalem and asked, 2"Why do your disciples break the tradition of the elders? They don't wash their hands before they eat!"[q]

3Jesus replied, "And why do you break the command of God for the sake of your tradition? 4For God said, 'Honor your father and mother'[d][r] and 'Anyone who curses his father or mother must be put to death.'[e][s] 5But you say that if a man says to his father or mother, 'Whatever help you might otherwise have received from me is a gift devoted to God,' 6he is not to 'honor his father[f]' with it. Thus you nullify the word of God for the sake of your tradition. 7You hypocrites! Isaiah was right when he prophesied about you:

8" 'These people honor me with their lips,
    but their hearts are far from me.
9They worship me in vain;

their teachings are but rules taught by men.'[g][u]"

10Jesus called the crowd to him and said, "Listen and understand. 11What goes into a man's mouth does not make him 'unclean,'[v] but what comes out of his mouth, that is what makes him 'unclean.'"[w]

12Then the disciples came to him and asked, "Do you know that the Pharisees were offended when they heard this?"

13He replied, "Every plant that my heavenly Father has not planted[x] will be pulled up by the roots. 14Leave them; they are blind guides.[h][y] If a blind man leads a blind man, both will fall into a pit."[z]

15Peter said, "Explain the parable to us."[a]

16"Are you still so dull?"[b] Jesus asked them. 17"Don't you see that whatever enters the mouth goes into the stomach and then out of the body? 18But the things that come out of the mouth come from the heart,[c] and these make a man 'unclean.' 19For out of the heart come evil thoughts, murder, adultery, sexual immorality, theft, false testimony, slander.[d] 20These are what make a man 'unclean'; but eating with unwashed hands does not make him 'unclean.' "

The Faith of the Canaanite Woman

15:21–28pp — Mk 7:24–30

21Leaving that place, Jesus withdrew to the region of Tyre and Sidon.[f] 22A Canaanite woman from that vicinity came to him, crying out, "Lord, Son of David,[g] have mercy on me! My daughter is suffering terribly from demon-possession."[h]

23Jesus did not answer a word. So his disciples came to him and urged him, "Send her away, for she keeps crying out after us."

24He answered, "I was sent only to the lost sheep of Israel."[i]

25The woman came and knelt before him.[j] "Lord, help me!" she said.

26He replied, "It is not right to take the

Cross references (center column)

14:26 *k* Lk 24:37
14:27 *l* Mt 9:2; Ac 23:11;
m Da 10:12;
Mt 17:7; 28:10;
Lk 1:13,30; 2:10;
Ac 18:9; 23:11;
Rev 1:17
14:31 *n* S Mt 6:30
14:33 *o* Ps 2:7; S Mt 4:3
14:36 *p* S Mt 9:20
15:2 *q* Lk 11:38
15:4 *r* Ex 20:12; Dt 5:16; Eph 6:2
s Ex 21:17; Lev 20:9

15:9 *t* Col 2:20-22
u Isa 29:13; Mal 2:2
15:11 *v* S Ac 10:14,15
w ver 18
15:13 *x* Isa 60:21; 61:3
15:14 *y* Mt 23:16, 24; Ro 2:19
z Lk 6:39
15:15 *a* Mt 13:36
15:16 *b* Mt 16:9
15:18 *c* Mt 12:34; Lk 6:45; Jas 3:6
15:19 *d* Gal 5:19-21
15:20 *e* Ro 14:14
15:21 *f* S Mt 11:21
15:22 *g* S Mt 9:27
h S Mt 4:24
15:24 *i* Mt 10:6, 23; Ro 15:8
15:25 *j* S Mt 8:2

Text notes (center column, bottom)

d 4 Exodus 20:12; Deut. 5:16   **e** 4 Exodus 21:17; Lev. 20:9   **f** 6 Some manuscripts *father or his mother*   **g** 9 Isaiah 29:13   **h** 14 Some manuscripts *guides of the blind*

14:34 *Gennesaret.* Either the narrow plain, about four miles long and less than two miles wide, on the west side of the Sea of Galilee near the north end (north of Magdala), or a town in the plain. The plain was considered a garden spot of Palestine, fertile and well watered.
15:2 *the tradition of the elders.* After the Babylonian captivity, the Jewish rabbis began to make meticulous rules and regulations governing the daily life of the people. These were

interpretations and applications of the law of Moses, handed down from generation to generation. In Jesus' day this "tradition of the elders" was in oral form. It was not until c. A.D. 200 that it was put into writing in the Mishnah. *wash.* See Mk 7:1–4.
15:5–6 See notes on Mk 7:11,13.
15:7–20 See Mk 7:6–23 and notes.
15:26 *children's.* "The lost sheep of Israel" (v. 24). *their*

children's bread and toss it to their dogs."

27"Yes, Lord," she said, "but even the dogs eat the crumbs that fall from their masters' table."

28Then Jesus answered, "Woman, you have great faith!*k* Your request is granted." And her daughter was healed from that very hour.

Jesus Feeds the Four Thousand

15:29–31pp — Mk 7:31–37
15:32–39pp — Mk 8:1–10
15:32–39Ref — Mt 14:13–21

29Jesus left there and went along the Sea of Galilee. Then he went up on a mountainside and sat down. 30Great crowds came to him, bringing the lame, the blind, the crippled, the mute and many others, and laid them at his feet; and he healed them.*l* 31The people were amazed when they saw the mute speaking, the crippled made well, the lame walking and the blind seeing. And they praised the God of Israel.*m*

32Jesus called his disciples to him and said, "I have compassion for these people;*n* they have already been with me three days and have nothing to eat. I do not want to send them away hungry, or they may collapse on the way."

33His disciples answered, "Where could we get enough bread in this remote place to feed such a crowd?"

34"How many loaves do you have?" Jesus asked.

"Seven," they replied, "and a few small fish."

35He told the crowd to sit down on the ground. 36Then he took the seven loaves and the fish, and when he had given thanks, he broke them*o* and gave them to the disciples, and they in turn to the people. 37They all ate and were satisfied. Afterward the disciples picked up seven basketfuls of broken pieces that were left over.*p* 38The number of those who ate was four thousand, besides women and children. 39After Jesus had sent the crowd away, he got into the boat and went to the vicinity of Magadan.

15:28 *k*S Mt 9:22
15:30 *l*S Mt 4:23
15:31 *m*S Mt 9:8
15:32 *n*S Mt 9:36
15:36
*o*S Mt 14:19
15:37 *p*Mt 16:10

16:1 *q*S Ac 4:1
*r*S Mt 12:38
16:3
*s*Lk 12:54-56
16:4 *t*Mt 12:39
16:6 *u*Lk 12:1
16:8 *v*S Mt 6:30
16:9
*w*Mt 14:17-21
16:10
*x*Mt 15:34-38
16:12 *y*S Ac 4:1

The Demand for a Sign

16:1–12pp — Mk 8:11–21

16 The Pharisees and Sadducees*q* came to Jesus and tested him by asking him to show them a sign from heaven.*r*

2He replied,*i* "When evening comes, you say, 'It will be fair weather, for the sky is red,' 3and in the morning, 'Today it will be stormy, for the sky is red and overcast.' You know how to interpret the appearance of the sky, but you cannot interpret the signs of the times.*s* 4A wicked and adulterous generation looks for a miraculous sign, but none will be given it except the sign of Jonah."*t* Jesus then left them and went away.

The Yeast of the Pharisees and Sadducees

5When they went across the lake, the disciples forgot to take bread. 6"Be careful," Jesus said to them. "Be on your guard against the yeast of the Pharisees and Sadducees."*u*

7They discussed this among themselves and said, "It is because we didn't bring any bread."

8Aware of their discussion, Jesus asked, "You of little faith,*v* why are you talking among yourselves about having no bread? 9Do you still not understand? Don't you remember the five loaves for the five thousand, and how many basketfuls you gathered?*w* 10Or the seven loaves for the four thousand, and how many basketfuls you gathered?*x* 11How is it you don't understand that I was not talking to you about bread? But be on your guard against the yeast of the Pharisees and Sadducees." 12Then they understood that he was not telling them to guard against the yeast used in bread, but against the teaching of the Pharisees and Sadducees.*y*

Peter's Confession of Christ

16:13–16pp — Mk 8:27–29; Lk 9:18–20

13When Jesus came to the region of

i 2 Some early manuscripts do not have the rest of verse 2 and all of verse 3.

---

dogs. The Greek says "little dogs," meaning a pet dog in the home, and Jesus' point was that the gospel was to be given first to Jews. The woman understood Jesus' implication and was willing to settle for "crumbs." Jesus rewarded her faith (v. 28).

15:29–39 See Mk 7:31–8:10 and notes.

15:37 The feeding of the 5,000 is recorded in all four Gospels, but the feeding of the 4,000 is only in Matthew and Mark. The 12 baskets mentioned in the accounts of the feeding of the 5,000 were possibly the lunch baskets of the

12 apostles. The seven baskets mentioned here were possibly larger.

15:39 *Magadan.* Also called Magdala, the home of Mary Magdalene. Mark (8:10) has "Dalmanutha."

16:4 *the sign of Jonah.* See 12:39–40 and note on Lk 11:30.

16:6 *yeast of the Pharisees and Sadducees.* See v. 12.

16:12 Matthew often explains the meaning of Jesus' words (cf. 17:13).

16:13 *Caesarea Philippi.* To be distinguished from the

Caesarea Philippi, he asked his disciples, "Who do people say the Son of Man is?"

14They replied, "Some say John the Baptist;z others say Elijah; and still others, Jeremiah or one of the prophets."a

15"But what about you?" he asked. "Who do you say I am?"

16Simon Peter answered, "You are the Christ,i the Son of the living God."b

17Jesus replied, "Blessed are you, Simon son of Jonah, for this was not revealed to you by man,c but by my Father in heaven.d 18And I tell you that you are Peter,k e and on this rock I will build my church,f and the gates of Hadesl will not overcome it.m 19I will give you the keysg of the kingdom of heaven; whatever you bind on earth will ben bound in heaven, and whatever you loose on earth will ben loosed in heaven."h 20Then he warned his disciples not to tell anyonei that he was the Christ.

Jesus Predicts His Death

16:21–28pp — Mk 8:31 — 9:1; Lk 9:22–27

21From that time on Jesus began to explain to his disciples that he must go to Jerusalemj and suffer many thingsk at the hands of the elders, chief priests and teachers of the law,l and that he must be killedm and on the third dayn be raised to life.o

22Peter took him aside and began to

rebuke him. "Never, Lord!" he said. "This shall never happen to you!"

23Jesus turned and said to Peter, "Get behind me, Satan!p You are a stumbling block to me; you do not have in mind the things of God, but the things of men."

24Then Jesus said to his disciples, "If anyone would come after me, he must deny himself and take up his cross and follow me.q 25For whoever wants to save his lifeo will lose it, but whoever loses his life for me will find it.r 26What good will it be for a man if he gains the whole world, yet forfeits his soul? Or what can a man give in exchange for his soul? 27For the Son of Mans is going to comet in his Father's glory with his angels, and then he will reward each person according to what he has done.u 28I tell you the truth, some who are standing here will not taste death before they see the Son of Man coming in his kingdom."

The Transfiguration

17:1–8pp — Lk 9:28–36
17:1–13pp — Mk 9:2–13

17 After six days Jesus took with him Peter, James and Johnv the brother

Cross references:
16:14 *z* S Mt 3:1; *a* Mk 6:15; Jn 1:21
16:16 *b* S Mt 4:3; Ps 42:2; Jer 10:10; Ac 14:15; 2Co 6:16; 1Th 1:9; 1Ti 3:15; Heb 10:31; 12:22
16:17 *c* 1Co 15:50; Eph 6:12; Heb 2:14; *d* S Mt 13:11
16:18 *e* Jn 1:42; *f* S Eph 2:20; Rev 3:7
16:19 *g* Isa 22:22; *h* Mt 18:18; Jn 20:23
16:20 *i* S Mk 8:30
16:21 *j* S Lk 9:51; *k* Ps 22:6; Isa 53:3; Mt 26:67,68; Mk 10:34; Lk 17:25; Jn 18:22,23; 19:3; *l* Mt 27:1,2; *m* Ac 2:23; 3:13; *n* Hos 6:2; Mt 12:40; Jn 2:19; 1Co 15:3,4; *o* Mt 17:22,23; Mk 9:31; Lk 9:22; 18:31-33; 24:6,7
16:23 *p* S Mt 4:10
16:24 *q* Mt 10:38; Lk 14:27
16:25 *r* S Jn 12:25
16:27 *s* S Mt 8:20; *t* S Lk 17:30; Jn 14:3; Ac 1:11; *u* S 1Co 1:7; S 1Th 2:19; 4:16; S Rev 1:7; 22:7,

12,20 *u* 2Ch 6:23; Job 34:11; Ps 62:12; Jer 17:10; Eze 18:20; 1Co 3:12-15; 2Co 5:10; Rev 22:12 17:1 *v* S Mt 4:21

i 16 Or Messiah; also in verse 20 **k** *18 Peter means rock.* **l** *18 Or hell* **m** *18 Or not prove stronger than it* **n** *19 Or have been* **o** *25 The Greek word means either life or soul; also in verse 26.*

---

magnificent city of Caesarea, which Herod the Great had built on the coast of the Mediterranean. Caesarea Philippi, rebuilt by Herod's son Philip (who named it after Tiberius Caesar and himself), was north of the Sea of Galilee, near the slopes of Mount Hermon. Originally it was called Paneas (the ancient name survives today as Banias) in honor of the Greek god Pan, whose shrine was located there. The region was especially pagan.

16:18 *Peter . . . rock . . . church.* In the Greek "Peter" is *petros* and "rock" is *petra.* The rock on which the church is built may be Peter's inspired (v. 17) confession of faith in Jesus as the Messiah, "the Son of the living God," or it may be Peter himself, since Eph 2:20 indicates that the church is "built on the foundation of the apostles and prophets." *church.* In the Gospels this word is used only by Matthew (here and twice in 18:17). In the Septuagint it is used for the congregation of Israel. In Greek circles of Jesus' day it indicated the assembly of free, voting citizens in a city (cf. Ac 19:32,38,41). *Hades.* The Greek name for the place of departed spirits, generally equivalent to the Hebrew *Sheol* (see note on Ge 37:35). The "gates of Hades" may mean the "powers of death," i.e., all forces opposed to Christ and his kingdom (but see note on Job 17:16).

16:19 *keys.* Perhaps Peter used these keys on the day of Pentecost (Ac 2) when he announced that the door of the kingdom was unlocked to Jews and proselytes and later when he acknowledged that it was also opened to Gentiles (Ac 10). *bind . . . loose.* Not authority to determine, but to announce, guilt or innocence (see 18:18 and the context there; cf. Ac 5:3,9).

16:20 *not to tell.* Because of the false concepts of the Jews, who looked for an exclusively national and political Messiah, Jesus told his disciples not to publicize Peter's confession, lest it precipitate a revolution against Rome (see note on 8:4).

16:21 *began.* The beginning of a new emphasis in Jesus' ministry. Instead of teaching the crowds in parables, he concentrated on preparing the disciples for his coming suffering and death.

16:23 *Satan.* A loanword from Hebrew, meaning "adversary" or "accuser" (see NIV text note on Job 1:6; see also note on Rev 2:9).

16:24 *take up his cross.* See note on 10:38.

16:28 There are two main interpretations of this verse: 1. It is a prediction of the transfiguration, which happened a week later (17:1) and which demonstrated that Jesus will return in his Father's glory (16:27). 2. It refers to the day of Pentecost and the rapid spread of the gospel described in the book of Acts. The context seems to favor the first view. See note on 2Pe 1:16.

17:1–9 The transfiguration was: (1) a revelation of the glory of the Son of God, a glory hidden now but to be fully revealed when he returns; (2) a confirmation of the difficult teaching given to the disciples at Caesarea Philippi (16:13–20); and (3) a beneficial experience for the disciples, who were discouraged after having been reminded so recently of Jesus' impending suffering and death (16:21). See notes on Mk 9:2–7; Lk 9:28–35.

17:1 *six days.* Mark also says "six days"(Mk 9:2), counting just the days between Peter's confession and the transfiguration, whereas Luke, counting all the days involved, says,

of James, and led them up a high mountain by themselves. [2]There he was transfigured before them. His face shone like the sun, and his clothes became as white as the light. [3]Just then there appeared before them Moses and Elijah, talking with Jesus.

[4]Peter said to Jesus, "Lord, it is good for us to be here. If you wish, I will put up three shelters—one for you, one for Moses and one for Elijah."

[5]While he was still speaking, a bright cloud enveloped them, and a voice from the cloud said, "This is my Son, whom I love; with him I am well pleased. [w] Listen to him!"[x]

[6]When the disciples heard this, they fell facedown to the ground, terrified. [7]But Jesus came and touched them. "Get up," he said. "Don't be afraid."[y] [8]When they looked up, they saw no one except Jesus.

[9]As they were coming down the mountain, Jesus instructed them, "Don't tell anyone[z] what you have seen, until the Son of Man[a] has been raised from the dead."[b] [10]The disciples asked him, "Why then do the teachers of the law say that Elijah must come first?"

[11]Jesus replied, "To be sure, Elijah comes and will restore all things.[c] [12]But I tell you, Elijah has already come,[d] and they did not recognize him, but have done to him everything they wished.[e] In the same way the Son of Man is going to suffer[f] at their hands." [13]Then the disciples understood that he was talking to them about John the Baptist.[g]

The Healing of a Boy With a Demon

17:14–19pp — Mk 9:14–28; Lk 9:37–42

[14]When they came to the crowd, a man approached Jesus and knelt before him. [15]"Lord, have mercy on my son," he said. "He has seizures[h] and is suffering greatly. He often falls into the fire or into the water. [16]I brought him to your disciples, but they could not heal him."

[17]"O unbelieving and perverse generation," Jesus replied, "how long shall I stay with you? How long shall I put up with you? Bring the boy here to me." [18]Jesus rebuked the demon, and it came out of the boy, and he was healed from that moment.

[19]Then the disciples came to Jesus in private and asked, "Why couldn't we drive it out?"

[20]He replied, "Because you have so little faith. I tell you the truth, if you have faith[i] as small as a mustard seed,[j] you can say to this mountain, 'Move from here to there' and it will move.[k] Nothing will be impossible for you.[p]"

[22]When they came together in Galilee, he said to them, "The Son of Man[l] is going to be betrayed into the hands of men. [23]They will kill him,[m] and on the third day[n] he will be raised to life."[o] And the disciples were filled with grief.

The Temple Tax

[24]After Jesus and his disciples arrived in Capernaum, the collectors of the two-drachma tax[p] came to Peter and asked, "Doesn't your teacher pay the temple tax[q]?"

[25]"Yes, he does," he replied.

When Peter came into the house, Jesus was the first to speak. "What do you think, Simon?" he asked. "From whom do the

---

Cross references (center column):

17:5 [w]S Mt 3:17
[x]Ac 3:22,23
17:7 [y]S Mt 14:27
17:9 [z]S Mk 8:30
[a]S Mt 8:20
[b]S Mt 16:21
17:11 [c]Mal 4:6;
Lk 1:16,17
17:12 [d]S Mt 11:14
[e]Mt 14:3,10
[f]S Mt 16:21
17:13 [g]S Mt 3:1

17:15 [h]Mt 4:24
17:20 [i]S Mt 21:21
[j]Mt 13:31;
Lk 17:6
[k]1Co 13:2
17:22 [l]S Mt 8:20
17:23 [m]Ac 2:23;
3:13 [n]S Mt 16:21
[o]S Mt 16:21
17:24 [p]Ex 30:13

[p]20 Some manuscripts you. [21]But this kind does not go out except by prayer and fasting. [q]24 Greek the two drachmas

---

"About eight days" (Lk 9:28). *Peter, James and John.* These three disciples had an especially close relationship to Jesus (see 26:37; Mk 5:37). *high mountain.* Its identity is unknown. However, the reference to Caesarea Philippi (16:13) may suggest that it was Mount Hermon, which was just northeast of Caesarea Philippi (see note on Lk 9:28). *by themselves.* Luke adds "to pray" (Lk 9:28).
17:2 *he was transfigured.* His appearance changed. The three disciples saw Jesus in his glorified state (see Jn 17:5; 2Pe 1:17).
17:3 *Moses and Elijah.* Moses appears as the representative of the old covenant and the promise of salvation, which was soon to be fulfilled in the death of Jesus. Elijah appears as the appointed restorer of all things (Mal 4:5–6; Mk 9:11–13). Lk 9:31 says that they talked about Christ's death. See note on Lk 9:30.
17:4 *three shelters.* See notes on Mk 9:5; Lk 9:33.
17:5 *them.* Jesus, Moses and Elijah. *This is my Son, whom I love; with him I am well pleased.* The same words spoken from heaven at Jesus' baptism (3:17). No mere man, but the very Son of God, was transfigured.

17:6 *terrified.* Primarily with a sense of awe at the presence and majesty of God.
17:10 The traditional eschatology of the teachers of the law, based on Mal 4:5–6, held that Elijah must appear before the coming of the Messiah. The disciples reasoned that if Jesus really was the Messiah, as the transfiguration proved him to be, why had not Elijah appeared?
17:12 *In the same way.* As John the Baptist was not recognized and was killed, so Jesus would be rejected and killed.
17:13 See note on 16:12.
17:15 *seizures.* See note on 4:24.
17:18 Not all seizures were the result of demon possession, but these were.
17:20 *mustard seed.* See 13:31–32 and notes.
17:22 The second prediction of Christ's death, the first being in 16:21.
17:24 *two-drachma tax.* The annual temple tax required of every male 20 years of age and older (Ex 30:13; 2Ch 24:9; Ne 10:32). It was worth half a shekel (approximately two days' wages) and was used for the upkeep of the temple.

kings of the earth collect duty and
taxes[q]—from their own sons or from others?"
26"From others," Peter answered.
"Then the sons are exempt," Jesus said
to him. 27"But so that we may not offend[r]
them, go to the lake and throw out your
line. Take the first fish you catch; open its
mouth and you will find a four-drachma
coin. Take it and give it to them for my tax
and yours."

The Greatest in the Kingdom of Heaven

18:1–5pp — Mk 9:33–37; Lk 9:46–48

18 At that time the disciples came to
Jesus and asked, "Who is the greatest in the kingdom of heaven?"
2He called a little child and had him
stand among them. 3And he said: "I tell
you the truth, unless you change and
become like little children,[s] you will never
enter the kingdom of heaven.[t] 4Therefore,
whoever humbles himself like this child is
the greatest in the kingdom of heaven.[u]
5"And whoever welcomes a little child
like this in my name welcomes me.[v] 6But
if anyone causes one of these little ones
who believe in me to sin,[w] it would be
better for him to have a large millstone
hung around his neck and to be drowned
in the depths of the sea.[x]
7"Woe to the world because of the
things that cause people to sin! Such things
must come, but woe to the man through
whom they come![y] 8If your hand or your
foot causes you to sin,[z] cut it off and
throw it away. It is better for you to enter
life maimed or crippled than to have two
hands or two feet and be thrown into eternal fire. 9And if your eye causes you to
sin,[a] gouge it out and throw it away. It is
better for you to enter life with one eye
than to have two eyes and be thrown into
the fire of hell.[b]

The Parable of the Lost Sheep

18:12–14pp — Lk 15:4–7

10"See that you do not look down on
one of these little ones. For I tell you that
their angels[c] in heaven always see the face
of my Father in heaven.[r]
12"What do you think? If a man owns a
hundred sheep, and one of them wanders
away, will he not leave the ninety-nine on
the hills and go to look for the one that
wandered off? 13And if he finds it, I tell
you the truth, he is happier about that one
sheep than about the ninety-nine that did
not wander off. 14In the same way your
Father in heaven is not willing that any of
these little ones should be lost.

A Brother Who Sins Against You

15"If your brother sins against you,[s] go
and show him his fault,[d] just between the
two of you. If he listens to you, you have
won your brother over. 16But if he will not
listen, take one or two others along, so that
'every matter may be established by the
testimony of two or three witnesses.'[t] [e]
17If he refuses to listen to them, tell it to
the church;[f] and if he refuses to listen
even to the church, treat him as you would
a pagan or a tax collector.[g]
18"I tell you the truth, whatever you
bind on earth will be[u] bound in heaven,
and whatever you loose on earth will be[u]
loosed in heaven.[h]
19"Again, I tell you that if two of you on
earth agree about anything you ask for, it
will be done for you[i] by my Father in
heaven. 20For where two or three come
together in my name, there am I with
them."[j]

The Parable of the Unmerciful Servant

21Then Peter came to Jesus and asked,
"Lord, how many times shall I forgive my
brother when he sins against me?[k] Up to
seven times?"[l]
22Jesus answered, "I tell you, not seven
times, but seventy-seven times.[v] [m]
23"Therefore, the kingdom of heaven is
like[n] a king who wanted to settle accounts[o] with his servants. 24As he began

[r] *10* Some manuscripts *heaven.* [11] *The Son of Man came to save what was lost.* [s] *15* Some manuscripts do not have *against you.* [t] *16* Deut. 19:15 [u] *18* Or *have been* [v] *22* Or *seventy times seven*

17:25 [q]Mt 22:17-21; Ro 13:7 **17:27** [r]Jn 6:61 **18:3** [s]Mt 19:14; 1Pe 2:2 [t]S Mt 3:2 **18:4** [u]S Mk 9:35 **18:5** [v]Mt 10:40 **18:6** [w]S Mt 5:29 [x]Mk 9:42; Lk 17:2 **18:7** [y]Lk 17:1 **18:8** [z]S Mt 5:29 **18:9** [a]S Mt 5:29 [b]S Mt 5:22

18:10 [c]Ge 48:16; Ps 34:7; Ac 12:11,15; Heb 1:14 **18:15** [d]Lev 19:17; Lk 17:3; Gal 6:1; Jas 5:19,20 **18:16** [e]Nu 35:30; Dt 17:6; 19:15; Jn 8:17; 2Co 13:1; 1Ti 5:19; Heb 10:28 **18:17** [f]1Co 6:1-6 [g]S Ro 16:17 **18:18** [h]Mt 16:19; Jn 20:23 **18:19** [i]S Mt 7:7 **18:20** [j]S Mt 28:20 **18:21** [k]S Mt 6:14 [l]Lk 17:4 **18:22** [m]Ge 4:24 **18:23** [n]S Mt 13:24 [o]Mt 25:19

17:26 *the sons are exempt.* The implication is that Peter and the rest of the disciples belonged to God's royal household, but unbelieving Jews did not (see 21:43).
18:3 *like little children.* Trusting and unpretentious.
18:6 *large millstone.* Lit. "a millstone of a donkey," i.e., a millstone turned by a donkey—far larger and heavier than the small millstones (24:41) used by women each morning in their homes.
18:10 *their angels.* Guardian angels not exclusively for children, but for God's people in general (Ps 34:7; 91:11; Heb 1:14).
18:15 *brother.* A fellow believer.
18:17 *church.* The local congregation. Here and 16:18 are the only two places where the Gospels speak of the "church." *pagan.* For the Jews this meant any Gentile. *tax collector.* See note on 5:46. This verse establishes one basis for excommunication.
18:18 See note on 16:19.
18:22 *seventy-seven times.* Times without number (see NIV text note).

the settlement, a man who owed him ten thousand talents[w] was brought to him. [25]Since he was not able to pay,[p] the master ordered that he and his wife and his children and all that he had be sold[q] to repay the debt.

[26]"The servant fell on his knees before him.[r] 'Be patient with me,' he begged, 'and I will pay back everything.' [27]The servant's master took pity on him, canceled the debt and let him go.

[28]"But when that servant went out, he found one of his fellow servants who owed him a hundred denarii.[x] He grabbed him and began to choke him. 'Pay back what you owe me!' he demanded.

[29]"His fellow servant fell to his knees and begged him, 'Be patient with me, and I will pay you back.'

[30]"But he refused. Instead, he went off and had the man thrown into prison until he could pay the debt. [31]When the other servants saw what had happened, they were greatly distressed and went and told their master everything that had happened.

[32]"Then the master called the servant in. 'You wicked servant,' he said, 'I canceled all that debt of yours because you begged me to. [33]Shouldn't you have had mercy on your fellow servant just as I had on you?' [34]In anger his master turned him over to the jailers to be tortured, until he should pay back all he owed.

[35]"This is how my heavenly Father will treat each of you unless you forgive your brother from your heart."[s]

Divorce

19:1–9pp — Mk 10:1–12

19 When Jesus had finished saying these things,[t] he left Galilee and went into the region of Judea to the other side of the Jordan. [2]Large crowds followed him, and he healed them[u] there.

[3]Some Pharisees came to him to test him. They asked, "Is it lawful for a man to divorce his wife[v] for any and every reason?"

[4]"Haven't you read," he replied, "that

at the beginning the Creator 'made them male and female,'[y][w] [5]and said, 'For this reason a man will leave his father and mother and be united to his wife, and the two will become one flesh'[z]?[x] [6]So they are no longer two, but one. Therefore what God has joined together, let man not separate."

[7]"Why then," they asked, "did Moses command that a man give his wife a certificate of divorce and send her away?"[y]

[8]Jesus replied, "Moses permitted you to divorce your wives because your hearts were hard. But it was not this way from the beginning. [9]I tell you that anyone who divorces his wife, except for marital unfaithfulness, and marries another woman commits adultery."[z]

[10]The disciples said to him, "If this is the situation between a husband and wife, it is better not to marry."

[11]Jesus replied, "Not everyone can accept this word, but only those to whom it has been given.[a] [12]For some are eunuchs because they were born that way; others were made that way by men; and others have renounced marriage[a] because of the kingdom of heaven. The one who can accept this should accept it."

The Little Children and Jesus

19:13–15pp — Mk 10:13–16; Lk 18:15–17

[13]Then little children were brought to Jesus for him to place his hands on them[b] and pray for them. But the disciples rebuked those who brought them.

[14]Jesus said, "Let the little children come to me, and do not hinder them, for the kingdom of heaven belongs[c] to such as these."[d] [15]When he had placed his hands on them, he went on from there.

The Rich Young Man

19:16–29pp — Mk 10:17–30; Lk 18:18–30

[16]Now a man came up to Jesus and

Cross references (center column):

18:25 [p]Lk 7:42
[q]Lev 25:39;
2Ki 4:1; Ne 5:5,8
18:26 [r]S Mt 8:2
18:35
[s]S Mt 6:14;
S Jas 2:13
19:1 [t]S Mt 7:28
19:2 [u]S Mt 4:23
19:3 [v]Mt 5:31

19:4 [w]Ge 1:27;
5:2
19:5 [x]Ge 2:24;
1Co 6:16;
Eph 5:31
19:7 [y]Dt 24:1-4;
Mt 5:31
19:9 [z]S Lk 16:18
19:11
[a]S Mt 13:11;
1Co 7:7-9,17
19:13
[b]S Mk 5:23
19:14
[c]S Mt 25:34
[d]Mt 18:3;
1Pe 2:2

Footnotes:

[w]24 That is, millions of dollars   [x]28 That is, a few dollars   [y]4 Gen. 1:27   [z]5 Gen. 2:24   [a]12 Or have made themselves eunuchs

---

18:25 For this practice of selling into slavery see Ex 21:2; Lev 25:39; 2Ki 4:1; Ne 5:5; Isa 50:1.
18:35 *forgive.* The one main teaching of the parable.
19:1 *the other side of the Jordan.* The east side, known later as Transjordan or Perea and today simply as Jordan. Jesus now began ministering there (see note on Lk 13:22).
19:3 *for any and every reason.* This last part of the question is not in the parallel passage in Mark (10:2). Matthew possibly included it because he was writing to the Jews, who were aware of the dispute between the schools of Shammai and Hillel over the interpretation of Dt 24:1–4. Shammai held that "something indecent" meant "marital unfaithful-

ness"—the only allowable cause for divorce. Hillel (c. 60 B.C.-A.D. 20) emphasized the preceding clause, "who becomes displeasing to him." He would allow a man to divorce his wife if she did anything he disliked—even if she burned his food while cooking it. Jesus clearly took the side of Shammai (see v. 9), but only after first pointing back to God's original ideal for marriage in Ge 1:27; 2:24.
19:10–12 See 1Co 7:7–8,26,32–35.
19:16 *what good thing must I do . . . ?* The rich man was thinking in terms of righteousness by works. Jesus had to correct this misunderstanding first before answering the question more fully. *eternal life.* The first use of this term in

asked, "Teacher, what good thing must I do to get eternal life *e*?"*f*

17"Why do you ask me about what is good?" Jesus replied. "There is only One who is good. If you want to enter life, obey the commandments."*g*

18"Which ones?" the man inquired.

Jesus replied, " 'Do not murder, do not commit adultery,*h* do not steal, do not give false testimony, 19honor your father and mother,'*b i* and 'love your neighbor as yourself.'*c*'*j*

20"All these I have kept," the young man said. "What do I still lack?"

21Jesus answered, "If you want to be perfect,*k* go, sell your possessions and give to the poor,*l* and you will have treasure in heaven.*m* Then come, follow me."

22When the young man heard this, he went away sad, because he had great wealth.

23Then Jesus said to his disciples, "I tell you the truth, it is hard for a rich man*n* to enter the kingdom of heaven. 24Again I tell you, it is easier for a camel to go through the eye of a needle than for a rich man to enter the kingdom of God."

25When the disciples heard this, they were greatly astonished and asked, "Who then can be saved?"

26Jesus looked at them and said, "With man this is impossible, but with God all things are possible."*o*

27Peter answered him, "We have left everything to follow you!*p* What then will there be for us?"

28Jesus said to them, "I tell you the truth, at the renewal of all things, when the Son of Man sits on his glorious throne,*q* you who have followed me will also sit on twelve thrones, judging the twelve tribes of Israel.*r* 29And everyone who has left houses or brothers or sisters or father or mother*d* or children or fields for my sake will receive a hundred times as

much and will inherit eternal life.*s* 30But many who are first will be last, and many who are last will be first.*t*

The Parable of the Workers in the Vineyard

20 "For the kingdom of heaven is like*u* a landowner who went out early in the morning to hire men to work in his vineyard.*v* 2He agreed to pay them a denarius for the day and sent them into his vineyard.

3About the third hour he went out and saw others standing in the marketplace doing nothing. 4He told them, 'You also go and work in my vineyard, and I will pay you whatever is right.' 5So they went.

"He went out again about the sixth hour and the ninth hour and did the same thing. 6About the eleventh hour he went out and found still others standing around. He asked them, 'Why have you been standing here all day long doing nothing?'

7" 'Because no one has hired us,' they answered.

"He said to them, 'You also go and work in my vineyard.'

8"When evening came,*w* the owner of the vineyard said to his foreman, 'Call the workers and pay them their wages, beginning with the last ones hired and going on to the first.'

9"The workers who were hired about the eleventh hour came and each received a denarius. 10So when those came who were hired first, they expected to receive more. But each one of them also received a denarius. 11When they received it, they began to grumble*x* against the landowner. 12'These men who were hired last worked only one hour,' they said, 'and you have made them equal to us who have borne

Cross references

19:16
e S Mt 25:46
f Lk 10:25
19:17 *g* Lev 18:5
19:18 *h* Jas 2:11
19:19
i Ex 20:12-16;
Dt 5:16-20
j Lev 19:18;
S Mt 5:43
19:21 *k* Mt 5:48
l S Ac 2:45
m S Mt 6:20
19:23
n Mt 13:22;
1Ti 6:9,10
19:26
o Ge 18:14; Job
42:2; Jer 32:17;
Lk 1:37; 18:27;
Ro 4:21
19:27 *p* S Mt 4:19
19:28
q Mt 20:21; 25:31
r Lk 22:28-30;
Rev 3:21; 4:4;
20:4

19:29 *s* Mt 6:33;
S 25:46
19:30 *t* Mt 20:16;
Mk 10:31;
Lk 13:30
20:1 *u* S Mt 13:24
v Mt 21:28,33
20:8 *w* Lev 19:13;
Dt 24:15
20:11 *x* Jnh 4:1

b 19 Exodus 20:12-16; Deut. 5:16-20   *c 19* Lev. 19:18
d 29 Some manuscripts *mother or wife*

Matthew's Gospel (see v. 29; 25:46). In John it occurs much more frequently, often taking the place of the term "kingdom of God (or heaven)" used in the Synoptics, which treat the following three expressions as synonymous: (1) eternal life (v. 16; Mk 10:17; Lk 18:18), (2) entering the kingdom of heaven (v. 23; Mk 10:24; Lk 18:24) and (3) being saved (vv. 25–26; Mk 10:26–27; Lk 18:26–27).

19:17 *There is only One who is good.* The good is not something to be done as meritorious in itself. God alone is good, and all other goodness derives from him—even the keeping of the commandments, which Jesus proceeded to enumerate (vv. 18–20). *If you want to enter life, obey the commandments.* "To enter life" is the same as "to get eternal life" (v. 16). The requirement to "obey the commandments" is not to establish one's merit before God but is to be an expression of true faith. The Bible always teaches

that salvation is a gift of God's grace received through faith (see Eph 2:8).

19:21 *go, sell your possessions.* In his listing of the commandments, Jesus omitted "Do not covet." This was the rich man's main problem and was preventing him from entering life.

19:24 *camel to go through the eye of a needle.* See note on Mk 10:25.

19:28 *judging.* Governing or ruling (cf. the OT "judge"; see Introduction to Judges: Title).

20:2 *a denarius.* The usual daily wage. A Roman soldier also received one denarius a day.

20:3 *third hour.* 9:00 A.M.

20:5 *sixth hour . . . ninth hour.* Noon and 3:00 P.M. respectively.

20:6 *eleventh hour.* 5:00 P.M.

the burden of the work and the heat^y of the day.'

13"But he answered one of them, 'Friend,^z I am not being unfair to you. Didn't you agree to work for a denarius? 14Take your pay and go. I want to give the man who was hired last the same as I gave you. 15Don't I have the right to do what I want with my own money? Or are you envious because I am generous?'^a

16"So the last will be first, and the first will be last."^b

Jesus Again Predicts His Death

20:17–19pp — Mk 10:32–34; Lk 18:31–33

17Now as Jesus was going up to Jerusalem, he took the twelve disciples aside and said to them, 18"We are going up to Jerusalem,^c and the Son of Man^d will be betrayed to the chief priests and the teachers of the law.^e They will condemn him to death 19and will turn him over to the Gentiles to be mocked and flogged^f and crucified.^g On the third day^h he will be raised to life!"^i

A Mother's Request

20:20–28pp — Mk 10:35–45

20Then the mother of Zebedee's sons^j came to Jesus with her sons and, kneeling down,^k asked a favor of him.

21"What is it you want?" he asked.

She said, "Grant that one of these two sons of mine may sit at your right and the other at your left in your kingdom."^l

22"You don't know what you are asking," Jesus said to them. "Can you drink the cup^m I am going to drink?"

"We can," they answered.

23Jesus said to them, "You will indeed drink from my cup,^n but to sit at my right or left is not for me to grant. These places

belong to those for whom they have been prepared by my Father."

24When the ten heard about this, they were indignant^o with the two brothers. 25Jesus called them together and said, "You know that the rulers of the Gentiles lord it over them, and their high officials exercise authority over them. 26Not so with you. Instead, whoever wants to become great among you must be your servant,^p 27and whoever wants to be first must be your slave— 28just as the Son of Man^q did not come to be served, but to serve,^r and to give his life as a ransom^s for many."

Two Blind Men Receive Sight

20:29–34pp — Mk 10:46–52; Lk 18:35–43

29As Jesus and his disciples were leaving Jericho, a large crowd followed him. 30Two blind men were sitting by the roadside, and when they heard that Jesus was going by, they shouted, "Lord, Son of David,^t have mercy on us!"

31The crowd rebuked them and told them to be quiet, but they shouted all the louder, "Lord, Son of David, have mercy on us!"

32Jesus stopped and called them. "What do you want me to do for you?" he asked.

33"Lord," they answered, "we want our sight."

34Jesus had compassion on them and touched their eyes. Immediately they received their sight and followed him.

The Triumphal Entry

21:1–9pp — Mk 11:1–10; Lk 19:29–38
21:4–9pp — Jn 12:12–15

21 As they approached Jerusalem and came to Bethphage on the Mount of Olives,^u Jesus sent two disciples, 2saying to them, "Go to the village ahead of you, and at once you will find a donkey

Cross references (center column)

20:12 ^yJnh 4:8; Lk 12:55; Jas 1:11
20:13 ^zMt 22:12; 26:50
20:15 ^aDt 15:9; Mk 7:22
20:16 ^bS Mt 19:30
20:18 ^cS Lk 9:51 ^dS Mt 8:20 ^eMt 27:1,2
20:19 ^fS Mt 16:21 ^gS Ac 2:23 ^hS Mt 16:21 ^iS Mt 16:21
20:20 ^jS Mt 4:21 ^kS Mt 8:2
20:21 ^lMt 19:28
20:22 ^mIsa 51:17,22; Jer 49:12; Mt 26:39,42; Mk 14:36; Lk 22:42; Jn 18:11
20:23 ^nAc 12:2; Rev 1:9

20:24 ^oLk 22:24,25
20:26 ^pS Mk 9:35
20:28 ^qS Mt 8:20 ^rIsa 42:1; Lk 12:37; 22:27; Jn 13:13–16; 2Co 8:9; Php 2:7 ^sEx 30:12; Isa 44:22; 53:10; Mt 26:28; 1Ti 2:6; Tit 2:14; Heb 9:28; 1Pe 1:18,19
20:30 ^tS Mt 9:27
21:1 ^uMt 24:3; 26:30; Mk 14:26; Lk 19:37; 21:37; 22:39; Jn 8:1; Ac 1:12

20:17–19 See Mk 10:32–34; Lk 18:31–33 and notes.
20:19 *and will turn him over to the Gentiles to be mocked and flogged and crucified.* An additional statement in this third prediction of the passion. Jesus would not be killed by the Jews, which would have been by stoning, but would be crucified by the Romans. All three predictions include his resurrection on the third day (16:21; 17:23).
20:20 *mother of Zebedee's sons.* Mark has "James and John, the sons of Zebedee," asking the question (Mk 10:35–37), yet there is no contradiction. The three joined in making the petition.
20:22 *drink the cup.* A figure of speech meaning to "undergo" or "experience." Here the reference is to suffering (cf. 26:39). The same figure of speech is used in Jer 25:15; Eze 23:32; Hab 2:16; Rev 14:10; 16:19; 18:6 for divine wrath or judgment.
20:28 *ransom.* The Greek word was used most commonly for the price paid to redeem a slave. Similarly, Christ paid the

ransom price of his own life to free us from the slavery of sin. *for.* Here the Greek for this preposition emphasizes the substitutionary nature of Christ's death. *many.* Christ "gave himself as a ransom for all men" (1Ti 2:6). Salvation is offered to "all," but only the "many" (i.e., the elect) receive it.
20:29 *Jericho.* See note on Mk 10:46.
20:30 *Two blind men.* The other Synoptics mention only one (see note on 8:28). *Son of David.* A Messianic title (see note on 9:27).
21:1 *Jerusalem.* See map No. 9 at the end of the Study Bible. *Bethphage.* The name means "house of figs." It is not mentioned in the OT, and in the NT only in connection with the Triumphal Entry. In the Talmud it is spoken of as being near Jerusalem.
21:2 *donkey.* An animal symbolic of humility, peace and Davidic royalty (see notes on Zec 9:9; Lk 19:30). See also note on Mk 11:2.

tied there, with her colt by her. Untie them and bring them to me. ³If anyone says anything to you, tell him that the Lord needs them, and he will send them right away."

⁴This took place to fulfill ᵛ what was spoken through the prophet:

⁵"Say to the Daughter of Zion,
    'See, your king comes to you,
gentle and riding on a donkey,
    on a colt, the foal of a donkey.' " ᵉ ʷ

⁶The disciples went and did as Jesus had instructed them. ⁷They brought the donkey and the colt, placed their cloaks on them, and Jesus sat on them. ⁸A very large crowd spread their cloaks ˣ on the road, while others cut branches from the trees and spread them on the road. ⁹The crowds that went ahead of him and those that followed shouted,

"Hosanna ᶠ to the Son of David!" ʸ

"Blessed is he who comes in the name of the Lord!" ᵍ ᶻ

"Hosanna ᶠ in the highest!" ᵃ

¹⁰When Jesus entered Jerusalem, the whole city was stirred and asked, "Who is this?"

¹¹The crowds answered, "This is Jesus, the prophet ᵇ from Nazareth in Galilee."

Jesus at the Temple
21:12–16pp — Mk 11:15–18; Lk 19:45–47

¹²Jesus entered the temple area and drove out all who were buying ᶜ and selling there. He overturned the tables of the money changers ᵈ and the benches of those selling doves. ᵉ ¹³"It is written," he said to them, " 'My house will be called a house of prayer,' ʰ ᶠ but you are making it a 'den of robbers.' ⁱ " ᵍ

¹⁴The blind and the lame came to him at the temple, and he healed them. ʰ ¹⁵But when the chief priests and the teachers of the law saw the wonderful things he did and the children shouting in the temple area, "Hosanna to the Son of David," ⁱ they were indignant. ʲ

¹⁶"Do you hear what these children are saying?" they asked him.

"Yes," replied Jesus, "have you never read,

" 'From the lips of children and infants you have ordained praise'ʲ ?" ᵏ

¹⁷And he left them and went out of the city to Bethany, ˡ where he spent the night.

The Fig Tree Withers
21:18–22pp — Mk 11:12–14,20–24

¹⁸Early in the morning, as he was on his way back to the city, he was hungry. ¹⁹Seeing a fig tree by the road, he went up to it but found nothing on it except leaves. Then he said to it, "May you never bear fruit again!" Immediately the tree withered. ᵐ

²⁰When the disciples saw this, they were amazed. "How did the fig tree wither so quickly?" they asked.

²¹Jesus replied, "I tell you the truth, if you have faith and do not doubt, ⁿ not only can you do what was done to the fig tree, but also you can say to this mountain, 'Go,

---

Cross references (center column):

21:4 ᵛS Mt 1:22
21:5 ʷZec 9:9; Isa 62:11
21:8 ˣ2Ki 9:13
21:9 ʸver 15; S Mt 9:27; ᶻPs 118:26; Mt 23:39
ᵃLk 2:14
21:11 ᵇDt 18:15; Lk 7:16,39; 24:19; Jn 1:21, 25; 6:14; 7:40
21:12 ᶜDt 14:26
ᵈEx 30:13
ᵉLev 1:14

21:13 ᶠIsa 56:7
ᵍJer 7:11
21:14 ʰS Mt 4:23
21:15 ⁱver 9; S Mt 9:27
ʲLk 19:39
21:16 ᵏPs 8:2
21:17 ˡMt 26:6; Mk 11:1; Lk 24:50; Jn 11:1, 18; 12:1
21:19 ᵐIsa 34:4; Jer 8:13
21:21 ⁿMt 17:20; Lk 17:6; 1Co 13:2; Jas 1:6

e5 Zech. 9:9   19 A Hebrew expression meaning "Save!" which became an exclamation of praise; also in verse 15   g9 Psalm 118:26   h13 Isaiah 56:7   i13 Jer. 7:11   j16 Psalm 8:2

21:7 *Jesus sat on them.* He sat on the cloaks. We know from Mark (11:2) and Luke (19:30) that he rode the colt. Typically, a mother donkey followed her offspring closely. Matthew mentions two animals, while the other Gospels have only one (see note on 8:28).

21:8 *spread their cloaks on the road.* An act of royal homage (see 2Ki 9:13).

21:9 These are three separate quotations, not necessarily spoken at the same time. *Hosanna.* See note on Ps 118:25–26; both prayer and praise (see NIV text note). *Son of David.* See note on 9:27. *in the highest.* That is, may those in heaven sing "Hosanna" (see Ps 148:1–2; Lk 2:14).

21:12–17 In the Synoptics the cleansing of the temple occurs during the last week of Jesus' ministry; in John it takes place during the first few months (Jn 2:12–16). Two explanations are possible: 1. There were two cleansings, one at the beginning and the other at the end of Jesus' public ministry. 2. There was only one cleansing, which took place during Passion Week but which John placed at the beginning of his account for theological reasons—to show that God's judgment was operative through the Messiah from the outset of his ministry. However, different details are present in the

two accounts (the selling of cattle and sheep in Jn 2:14, the whip in Jn 2:15, and the statements of Jesus in Mt 21:13; Jn 2:16). From Matthew's and Luke's accounts we might assume that the cleansing of the temple took place on Sunday, following the so-called Triumphal Entry (21:1–11). But Mark (11:15–19) clearly indicates that it was on Monday. Matthew often compressed narratives.

21:12 *temple area.* The "buying and selling" took place in the large outer court of the Gentiles, which covered several acres (see note on Mk 11:15).

21:13 *house of prayer.* See note on Mk 11:17.

21:17 *Bethany.* A village on the eastern slope of the Mount of Olives, about two miles from Jerusalem and the final station on the road from Jericho to Jerusalem.

21:18–22 See note on vv. 12–17; another example of compressing narratives. Mark (11:12–14,20–25) places the cursing of the fig tree on Monday morning and the disciples' finding it withered on Tuesday morning. In Matthew's account the tree withered as soon as Jesus cursed it, emphasizing the immediacy of judgment. For the theological meaning of this event see note on Mk 11:14.

throw yourself into the sea,' and it will be
done. 22If you believe, you will receive
whatever you ask for[o] in prayer."

The Authority of Jesus Questioned

21:23–27pp — Mk 11:27–33; Lk 20:1–8

23Jesus entered the temple courts, and,
while he was teaching, the chief priests
and the elders of the people came to him.
"By what authority[p] are you doing these
things?" they asked. "And who gave you
this authority?"

24Jesus replied, "I will also ask you one
question. If you answer me, I will tell you
by what authority I am doing these things.
25John's baptism—where did it come
from? Was it from heaven, or from men?"

They discussed it among themselves and
said, "If we say, 'From heaven,' he will
ask, 'Then why didn't you believe him?'
26But if we say, 'From men'—we are afraid
of the people, for they all hold that John
was a prophet."[q]

27So they answered Jesus, "We don't
know."

Then he said "Neither will I tell you by
what authority I am doing these things.

The Parable of the Two Sons

28"What do you think? There was a
man who had two sons. He went to the
first and said, 'Son, go and work today in
the vineyard.'[r]

29" 'I will not,' he answered, but later
he changed his mind and went.

30"Then the father went to the other
son and said the same thing. He answered,
'I will, sir,' but he did not go.

31"Which of the two did what his father
wanted?"

"The first," they answered.

Jesus said to them "I tell you the truth,
the tax collectors[s] and the prostitutes[t] are
entering the kingdom of God ahead of you.
32For John came to you to show you the
way of righteousness,[u] and you did not
believe him, but the tax collectors[v] and
the prostitutes[w] did. And even after you
saw this, you did not repent[x] and believe
him.

21:22 [o]S Mt 7:7 **21:23** [p]Ac 4:7; 7:27 **21:26** [q]S Mt 11:9 **21:28** [r]ver 33; Mt 20:1 **21:31** [s]Lk 7:29 [t]Lk 7:50 **21:32** [u]Mt 3:1-12 [v]Lk 3:12,13; 7:29 [w]Lk 7:36-50 [x]Lk 7:30

The Parable of the Tenants

21:33–46pp — Mk 12:1–12; Lk 20:9–19

33"Listen to another parable: There was
a landowner who planted[y] a vineyard. He
put a wall around it, dug a winepress in it
and built a watchtower.[z] Then he rented
the vineyard to some farmers and went
away on a journey.[a] 34When the harvest
time approached, he sent his servants[b] to
the tenants to collect his fruit.

35"The tenants seized his servants; they
beat one, killed another, and stoned a
third.[c] 36Then he sent other servants[d] to
them, more than the first time, and the
tenants treated them the same way. 37Last
of all, he sent his son to them. 'They will
respect my son,' he said.

38"But when the tenants saw the son,
they said to each other, 'This is the heir.[e]
Come, let's kill him[f] and take his inheritance.'[g] 39So they took him and threw him
out of the vineyard and killed him.

40"Therefore, when the owner of the
vineyard comes, what will he do to those
tenants?"

41"He will bring those wretches to a
wretched end,"[h] they replied, "and he
will rent the vineyard to other tenants,[i]
who will give him his share of the crop at
harvest time."

42Jesus said to them, "Have you never
read in the Scriptures:

" 'The stone the builders rejected
has become the capstone[k];
the Lord has done this,
and it is marvelous in our eyes'[l] ?[j]

43"Therefore I tell you that the kingdom
of God will be taken away from you[k] and
given to a people who will produce its
fruit. 44He who falls on this stone will be
broken to pieces, but he on whom it falls
will be crushed."[m][l]

45When the chief priests and the Pharisees heard Jesus' parables, they knew he
was talking about them. 46They looked for
a way to arrest him, but they were afraid of
the crowd because the people held that he
was a prophet.[m]

21:33 [y]Ps 80:8 [z]Isa 5:1-7 [a]Mt 25:14,15 **21:34** [b]Mt 22:3 **21:35** [c]2Ch 24:21; Mt 23:34,37; Heb 11:36,37 **21:36** [d]Mt 22:4 **21:38** [e]Heb 1:2 [f]S Mt 12:14 [g]Ps 2:8 **21:41** [h]Mt 8:11, 12 [i]S Ac 13:46 **21:42** [j]Ps 118:22, 23; S Ac 4:11 **21:43** [k]Mt 8:12 **21:44** [l]S Lk 2:34 **21:46** [m]S ver 11, 26

[k]*42* Or *cornerstone* [l]*42* Psalm 118:22,23
[m]*44* Some manuscripts do not have verse 44.

21:23 *By what authority . . . ?* See note on Lk 20:2.
21:25 *from heaven, or from men?* See notes on Mk 11:30; Lk 20:3.
21:33 *watchtower.* For guarding the vineyard, especially when the grapes ripened, and for shelter. The rabbis specified that it was to be a raised wooden platform, 15 feet high and 6 feet square.
21:35–37 The tenants are the Jews, or their leaders. The servants represent the OT prophets, many of whom were killed. The son represents Christ, who was condemned to death by the religious leaders.
21:41 *other tenants.* Gentiles, to whom Paul turned when the Jews, for the most part, rejected the gospel (Ac 13:46; 18:6). By the second century the church was composed almost entirely of Gentiles.
21:44 *will be broken to pieces.* See note on Lk 20:18.

The Parable of the Wedding Banquet

22:2–14Ref — Lk 14:16–24

22 Jesus spoke to them again in parables, saying: 2"The kingdom of heaven is like[n] a king who prepared a wedding banquet for his son. 3He sent his servants[o] to those who had been invited to the banquet to tell them to come, but they refused to come.

4"Then he sent some more servants[p] and said, 'Tell those who have been invited that I have prepared my dinner: My oxen and fattened cattle have been butchered, and everything is ready. Come to the wedding banquet.'

5"But they paid no attention and went off—one to his field, another to his business. 6The rest seized his servants, mistreated them and killed them. 7The king was enraged. He sent his army and destroyed those murderers[q] and burned their city.

8"Then he said to his servants, 'The wedding banquet is ready, but those I invited did not deserve to come. 9Go to the street corners[r] and invite to the banquet anyone you find.' 10So the servants went out into the streets and gathered all the people they could find, both good and bad,[s] and the wedding hall was filled with guests.

11"But when the king came in to see the guests, he noticed a man there who was not wearing wedding clothes. 12'Friend,'[t] he asked, 'how did you get in here without wedding clothes?' The man was speechless.

13"Then the king told the attendants, 'Tie him hand and foot, and throw him outside, into the darkness, where there will be weeping and gnashing of teeth.'[u]

14"For many are invited, but few are chosen."[v]

Paying Taxes to Caesar

22:15–22pp — Mk 12:13–17; Lk 20:20–26

15Then the Pharisees went out and laid plans to trap him in his words. 16They sent their disciples to him along with the Herodians.[w] "Teacher," they said, "we know you are a man of integrity and that you teach the way of God in accordance with the truth. You aren't swayed by men, because you pay no attention to who they are. 17Tell us then, what is your opinion? Is it right to pay taxes[x] to Caesar or not?"

18But Jesus, knowing their evil intent, said, "You hypocrites, why are you trying to trap me? 19Show me the coin used for paying the tax." They brought him a denarius, 20and he asked them, "Whose portrait is this? And whose inscription?"

21"Caesar's," they replied.

Then he said to them, "Give to Caesar what is Caesar's,[y] and to God what is God's."

22When they heard this, they were amazed. So they left him and went away.[z]

Marriage at the Resurrection

22:23–33pp — Mk 12:18–27; Lk 20:27–40

23That same day the Sadducees,[a] who say there is no resurrection,[b] came to him with a question. 24"Teacher," they said, "Moses told us that if a man dies without having children, his brother must marry the widow and have children for him.[c] 25Now there were seven brothers among

---

22:7 *burned their city.* A common military practice; here possibly an allusion to the destruction of Jerusalem in A.D. 70.

22:11 *not wearing wedding clothes.* It has been conjectured that it may have been the custom for the host to provide the guests with wedding garments. This would have been necessary for the guests at this banquet in particular, for they were brought in directly from the streets (vv. 9–10). The failure of the man in question to avail himself of a wedding garment was therefore an insult to the host, who had made the garments available.

22:13 *throw him outside, into the darkness . . . weeping . . . gnashing of teeth.* Expressions depicting severe punishment. Whereas the first part of the parable (vv. 2–10) spoke of God's rejection of national Israel (cf. 21:43–45), the latter part (vv. 11–13) deals with the responsibility of the individual. The wedding garment no doubt speaks of the righteousness that God, the gracious host, provides for all who accept his invitation. God issues an undeserved invitation to undeserving people, and in addition provides the righteousness the invitation demands.

22:15–17 The Pharisees were ardent nationalists, opposed to Roman rule, while the hated Herodians, as their name indicates, supported the Roman rule of the Herods. Now, however, the Pharisees enlisted the help of the Herodians to trap Jesus in his words. After trying to put him off guard with flattery, they sprang their question: "Is it right to pay taxes to Caesar or not?" (v. 17). If he said "No," the Herodians would report him to the Roman governor and he would be executed for treason. If he said "Yes," the Pharisees would denounce him to the people as disloyal to his nation.

22:19 *denarius.* The common Roman coin of that day (see note on 20:2). On one side was the portrait of Emperor Tiberius and on the other the inscription in Latin: "Tiberius Caesar Augustus, son of the divine Augustus." The coin was issued by Caesar and was used for paying tax to him.

22:21 *to God what is God's.* In distinguishing clearly between Caesar and God, Jesus also protested against the false and idolatrous claims made on the coins (see previous note).

22:24 *Moses told us.* Jesus quoted from the Pentateuch when arguing with the Sadducees, since those books had special authority for them (see note on Mk 12:18). The reference (Dt 25:5–6) is to the levirate law (from Latin *levir,* "brother-in-law"), which was given to protect the widow and guarantee continuance of the family line.

us. The first one married and died, and since he had no children, he left his wife to his brother. 26The same thing happened to the second and third brother, right on down to the seventh. 27Finally, the woman died. 28Now then, at the resurrection, whose wife will she be of the seven, since all of them were married to her?"

29Jesus replied, "You are in error because you do not know the Scriptures d or the power of God. 30At the resurrection people will neither marry nor be given in marriage; e they will be like the angels in heaven. 31But about the resurrection of the dead—have you not read what God said to you, 32'I am the God of Abraham, the God of Isaac, and the God of Jacob'n?f He is not the God of the dead but of the living."

33When the crowds heard this, they were astonished at his teaching. g

The Greatest Commandment

22:34-40pp — Mk 12:28-31

34Hearing that Jesus had silenced the Sadducees, h the Pharisees got together. 35One of them, an expert in the law, i tested him with this question: 36"Teacher, which is the greatest commandment in the Law?"

37Jesus replied: " 'Love the Lord your God with all your heart and with all your soul and with all your mind.'o/ 38This is the first and greatest commandment. 39And the second is like it: 'Love your neighbor as yourself.'pk 40All the Law and the Prophets hang on these two commandments." l

Whose Son Is the Christ?

22:41-46pp — Mk 12:35-37; Lk 20:41-44

41While the Pharisees were gathered together, Jesus asked them, 42"What do you think about the Christq? Whose son is he?"

"The son of David," m they replied.

43He said to them, "How is it then that David, speaking by the Spirit, calls him 'Lord'? For he says,

44" 'The Lord said to my Lord:

"Sit at my right hand
until I put your enemies
under your feet." ' r n

45If then David calls him 'Lord,' how can he be his son?" 46No one could say a word in reply, and from that day on no one dared to ask him any more questions. o

Seven Woes

23:1-7pp — Mk 12:38,39; Lk 20:45,46
23:37-39pp — Lk 13:34,35

23 Then Jesus said to the crowds and to his disciples: 2"The teachers of the law p and the Pharisees sit in Moses' seat. 3So you must obey them and do everything they tell you. But do not do what they do, for they do not practice what they preach. 4They tie up heavy loads and put them on men's shoulders, but they themselves are not willing to lift a finger to move them. q

5"Everything they do is done for men to see: r They make their phylacteries s s wide and the tassels on their garments t long; 6they love the place of honor at banquets and the most important seats in the synagogues; u 7they love to be greeted in the marketplaces and to have men call them 'Rabbi.' v

8"But you are not to be called 'Rabbi,' for you have only one Master and you are all brothers. 9And do not call anyone on earth 'father,' for you have one Father, w and he is in heaven. 10Nor are you to be called 'teacher,' for you have one Teacher, the Christ. q 11The greatest among you will be your servant. x 12For whoever exalts himself will be humbled, and whoever humbles himself will be exalted. y

13"Woe to you, teachers of the law and Pharisees, you hypocrites! z You shut the kingdom of heaven in men's faces. You

---

Cross references (center column):

22:29 dJn 20:9
22:30 eMt 24:38
22:32 fEx 3:6; Ac 7:32
22:33 gS Mt 7:28
22:34 hS Ac 4:1
22:35 iLk 7:30; 10:25; 11:45; 14:3
22:37 jDt 6:5
22:39 kLev 19:18; S Mt 5:43
22:40 lMt 7:12; Lk 10:25-28
22:42 mS Mt 9:27

22:44 nPs 110:1; 1Ki 5:3; Ac 2:34,35; 1Co 15:25; Heb 1:13; 10:13
22:46 oMk 12:34; Lk 20:40
23:2 pEzr 7:6,25
23:4 qLk 11:46; Ac 15:10; Gal 6:13
23:5 rMt 6:1,2,5,16 sEx 13:9; Dt 6:8 tNu 15:38; Dt 22:12
23:6 uLk 11:43; 14:7; 20:46
23:7 vver 8; Mt 26:25,49; Mk 9:5; 10:51; Jn 1:38,49; 3:2, 26; 20:16
23:9 wMal 1:6; Mt 6:9; 7:11
23:11 xS Mk 9:35
23:12 yISa 2:8; Ps 18:27; Pr 3:34; Isa 57:15; Eze 21:26; Lk 1:52; 14:11
23:13 zver 15,23, 25,27,29

---

n32 Exodus 3:6   o37 Deut. 6:5   p39 Lev. 19:18
q42,10 Or *Messiah*   r44 Psalm 110:1   s5 That is, boxes containing Scripture verses, worn on forehead and arm

---

22:25-40 See Mk 12:18-31; Lk 20:27-40 and notes.

22:37,39 *Love.* The Greek verb is not *phileo*, which expresses friendly affection, but *agapao*, the commitment of devotion that is directed by the will and can be commanded as a duty.

22:37 *with all your heart . . . soul . . . mind.* With your whole being. The Hebrew of Dt 6:5 has "heart . . . soul . . . strength," but some manuscripts of the Septuagint (the Greek translation of the OT) add "mind." Jesus combined all four terms in Mk 12:30.

22:40 *the Law and the Prophets.* The entire OT (see note

on 5:17).

22:41-46 See notes on Mk 12:35-40; Lk 20:44-47.

23:2 *sit in Moses' seat.* The authorized successors of Moses as teachers of the law.

23:5 *phylacteries.* These boxes (see NIV text note) contained four passages (Ex 13:1-10; 13:11-16; Dt 6:4-9; 11:13-21).

23:8-10 The warning is against seeking titles of honor to foster pride. Obviously, we should avoid unreasonable literalism in applying such commands.

yourselves do not enter, nor will you let those enter who are trying to.[t] [a]

15"Woe to you, teachers of the law and Pharisees, you hypocrites! You travel over land and sea to win a single convert,[b] and when he becomes one, you make him twice as much a son of hell[c] as you are.

16"Woe to you, blind guides![d] You say, 'If anyone swears by the temple, it means nothing; but if anyone swears by the gold of the temple, he is bound by his oath.'[e] 17You blind fools! Which is greater: the gold, or the temple that makes the gold sacred?[f] 18You also say, 'If anyone swears by the altar, it means nothing; but if anyone swears by the gift on it, he is bound by his oath.' 19You blind men! Which is greater: the gift, or the altar that makes the gift sacred?[g] 20Therefore, he who swears by the altar swears by it and by everything

on it. 21And he who swears by the temple swears by it and by the one who dwells[h] in it. 22And he who swears by heaven swears by God's throne and by the one who sits on it.[i]

23"Woe to you, teachers of the law and Pharisees, you hypocrites! You give a tenth[j] of your spices—mint, dill and cummin. But you have neglected the more important matters of the law—justice, mercy and faithfulness.[k] You should have practiced the latter, without neglecting the former. 24You blind guides![l] You strain out a gnat but swallow a camel.

25"Woe to you, teachers of the law and Pharisees, you hypocrites! You clean the outside of the cup and dish,[m] but inside

---

23:13 [a]Lk 11:52
23:15 [b]Ac 2:11;
6:5; 13:43
[c]S Mt 5:22
23:16 [d]ver 24;
Isa 9:16;
Mt 15:14
[e]Mt 5:33-35
23:17 [f]Ex 30:29
23:19 [g]Ex 29:37

23:21 [h]1Ki 8:13;
Ps 26:8
23:22 [i]Ps 11:4;
Mt 5:34
23:23 [j]Lev 27:30
[k]Mic 6:8;
Lk 11:42
23:24 [l]ver 16
23:25 [m]Mk 7:4

[t] 13 Some manuscripts to. 14Woe to you, teachers of the law and Pharisees, you hypocrites! You devour widows' houses and for a show make lengthy prayers. Therefore you will be punished more severely.

23:15 *twice as much a son of hell as you are.* Doubly zealous for ritual purification, which fostered pride and false security and brought no salvation.
23:23 Jesus does not criticize the observance of the minutiae of the law (he says, "without neglecting" them), but he does criticize the hypocrisy often involved (see note on

5:18–20).
23:24 *strain out.* The strict Pharisee would carefully strain his drinking water through a cloth to be sure he did not swallow a gnat, the smallest of unclean animals. But, figuratively, he would swallow a camel—one of the largest.

Jewish Sects

PHARISEES

Their roots can be traced to the second century B.C.—to the Hasidim.

1. Along with the Torah, they accepted as equally inspired and authoritative, all material contained within the oral tradition.
2. On free will and determination, they held to a mediating view that made it impossible for either free will or the sovereignty of God to cancel out the other.
3. They accepted a rather developed hierarchy of angels and demons.
4. They taught that there was a future for the dead.
5. They believed in the immortality of the soul and in reward and retribution after death.
6. They were champions of human equality.
7. The emphasis of their teaching was ethical rather than theological.

SADDUCEES

They probably had their beginning during the Hasmonean period (166-63 B.C.). Their demise occurred c. A.D. 70 with the fall of Jerusalem.

1. They denied that the oral law was authoritative and binding.
2. They interpreted Mosaic law more literally than did the Pharisees.
3. They were very exacting in Levitical purity.
4. They attributed all to free will.
5. They argued there is neither resurrection of the dead nor a future life.
6. They rejected a belief in angels and demons.
7. They rejected the idea of a spiritual world.
8. Only the books of Moses were canonical Scripture.

ESSENES

They probably originated among the Hasidim, along with the Pharisees, from whom they later separated (I Maccabees 2:42; 7:13). They were a group of very strict and zealous Jews who took part with the Maccabeans in a revolt against the Syrians, c. 165-155 B.C.

1. They followed a strict observance of the purity laws of the Torah.
2. They were notable for their communal ownership of property.
3. They had a strong sense of mutual responsibility.
4. Daily worship was an important feature along with a daily study of their sacred scriptures.
5. Solemn oaths of piety and obedience had to be taken.
6. Sacrifices were offered on holy days and during sacred seasons.
7. Marriage was not condemned in principle but was avoided.
8. They attributed all that happened to fate.

ZEALOTS

They originated during the reign of Herod the Great c. 6 B.C. and ceased to exist in A.D. 73 at Masada.

1. They opposed payment of tribute for taxes to a pagan emperor, saying that allegiance was due only to God.
2. They held a fierce loyalty to the Jewish traditions.
3. They were opposed to the use of the Greek language in Palestine.
4. They prophesied the coming of the time of salvation.

they are full of greed and self-indulgence. [n] [26]Blind Pharisee! First clean the inside of the cup and dish, and then the outside also will be clean.

[27]"Woe to you, teachers of the law and Pharisees, you hypocrites! You are like whitewashed tombs, [o] which look beautiful on the outside but on the inside are full of dead men's bones and everything unclean. [28]In the same way, on the outside you appear to people as righteous but on the inside you are full of hypocrisy and wickedness.

[29]"Woe to you, teachers of the law and Pharisees, you hypocrites! You build tombs for the prophets [p] and decorate the graves of the righteous. [30]And you say, 'If we had lived in the days of our forefathers, we would not have taken part with them in shedding the blood of the prophets.' [31]So you testify against yourselves that you are the descendants of those who murdered the prophets. [q] [32]Fill up, then, the measure [r] of the sin of your forefathers! [s]

[33]"You snakes! You brood of vipers! [t] How will you escape being condemned to hell? [u] [34]Therefore I am sending you prophets and wise men and teachers. Some of them you will kill and crucify; [v] others you will flog in your synagogues [w] and pursue from town to town. [x] [35]And so upon you will come all the righteous blood that has been shed on earth, from the blood of righteous Abel [y] to the blood of Zechariah son of Berekiah, [z] whom you murdered between the temple and the altar. [a] [36]I tell you the truth, all this will come upon this generation. [b]

[37]"O Jerusalem, Jerusalem, you who kill the prophets and stone those sent to you, [c] how often I have longed to gather your children together, as a hen gathers her chicks under her wings, [d] but you were not willing. [38]Look, your house is left to you desolate. [e] [39]For I tell you, you will not

see me again until you say, 'Blessed is he who comes in the name of the Lord.' [u]'/

Signs of the End of the Age
24:1–51pp — Mk 13:1–37; Lk 21:5–36

24 Jesus left the temple and was walking away when his disciples came up to him to call his attention to its buildings. [2]"Do you see all these things?" he asked. "I tell you the truth, not one stone here will be left on another; [g] every one will be thrown down."

[3]As Jesus was sitting on the Mount of Olives, [h] the disciples came to him privately. "Tell us," they said, "when will this happen, and what will be the sign of your coming [i] and of the end of the age?" [j]

[4]Jesus answered: "Watch out that no one deceives you. [k] [5]For many will come in my name, claiming, 'I am the Christ, [v]' and will deceive many. [l] [6]You will hear of wars and rumors of wars, but see to it that you are not alarmed. Such things must happen, but the end is still to come. [7]Nation will rise against nation, and kingdom against kingdom. [m] There will be famines [n] and earthquakes in various places. [8]All these are the beginning of birth pains.

[9]"Then you will be handed over to be persecuted [o] and put to death, [p] and you will be hated by all nations because of me. [q] [10]At that time many will turn away from the faith and will betray and hate each other, [11]and many false prophets [r] will appear and deceive many people. [s] [12]Because of the increase of wickedness, the love of most will grow cold, [13]but he who stands firm to the end will be saved. [t] [14]And this gospel of the kingdom [u] will be preached in the whole world [v] as a testimony to all nations, and then the end will come.

[15]"So when you see standing in the holy place [w] 'the abomination that causes deso-

Cross references (center column)
23:25 [n]Lk 11:39
23:27 [o]Lk 11:44; Ac 23:3
23:29 [p]Lk 11:47, 48
23:31 [q]S Mt 5:12
23:32 [r]1Th 2:16 [s]Eze 20:4
23:33 [t]Mt 3:7; 12:34 [u]S Mt 5:22
23:34 [v]2Ch 36:15,16; Lk 11:49 [w]S Mt 10:17 [x]Mt 10:23
23:35 [y]Ge 4:8; Heb 11:4 [z]Zec 1:1 [a]2Ch 24:21
23:36 [b]Mt 10:23; 24:34; Lk 11:50, 51
23:37 [c]2Ch 24:21; S Mt 5:12 [d]Ps 57:1; 61:4; Isa 31:5
23:38 [e]1Ki 9:7,8; Jer 22:5

23:39 [f]Ps 118:26; Mt 21:9
24:2 [g]Lk 19:44
24:3 [h]S Mt 21:1 [i]S Lk 17:30 [j]Mt 13:39; 28:20
24:4 [k]S Mk 13:5
24:5 [l]ver 11,23, 24; 1Jn 2:18
24:7 [m]Isa 19:2 [n]Ac 11:28
24:9 [o]Mt 10:17 [p]Jn 16:2 [q]S Jn 15:21
24:11 [r]S Mt 7:15 [s]S Mk 13:5
24:13 [t]S Mt 10:22
24:14 [u]S Mt 4:23 [v]S Ro 10:18; Lk 2:1; 4:5; Ac 11:28; 17:6; Rev 3:10; 16:14
24:15 [w]S Ac 6:13

[u]39 Psalm 118:26   [v]5 Or *Messiah*; also in verse 23

23:27 *whitewashed tombs.* A person who stepped on a grave became ceremonially unclean (see Nu 19:16), so graves were whitewashed to make them easily visible, especially at night.
23:35 *Abel to ... Zechariah.* The murder of Abel is recorded in Ge 4:8 and that of Zechariah son of Jehoiada in 2Ch 24:20–22 (Chronicles comes at the close of the OT according to the Hebrew arrangement). The expression was somewhat like our "from Genesis to Revelation." Jesus was summing up the history of martyrdom in the OT.
24:1–25:46 The Olivet discourse, the fifth and last of the great discourses in Matthew's Gospel (see notes on 5:1–7:29; Mk 13:1–37).
24:2 *not one stone ... left.* Fulfilled literally in A.D. 70, when the Romans under Titus completely destroyed Jerusalem and the temple buildings. Stones were even pried apart

to collect the gold leaf that melted from the roof when the temple was set on fire. See note on Mk 13:1. *thrown down.* Excavations in 1968 uncovered large numbers of these stones, toppled from the walls by the invaders.
24:3 *Mount of Olives.* A ridge a little more than a mile long, beyond the Kidron Valley east of Jerusalem and rising about 200 feet above the city (see note on Mk 11:1). *when will this happen, and what will be the sign of your coming and of the end of the age?* Jesus deals with these questions but does not distinguish them sharply. However, it appears that the description of the end of the age is discussed in vv. 4–14, the destruction of Jerusalem in vv. 15–22 (see Lk 21:20) and Christ's coming in vv. 23–31.
24:8 *birth pains.* The rabbis spoke of "birth pains," i.e., sufferings, that would precede the coming of the Messiah.
24:15 *the abomination that causes desolation.* The detest-

lation,'[w][x] spoken of through the prophet
Daniel—let the reader understand—
16then let those who are in Judea flee to
the mountains. 17Let no one on the roof of
his house[y] go down to take anything out
of the house. 18Let no one in the field go
back to get his cloak. 19How dreadful it
will be in those days for pregnant women
and nursing mothers![z] 20Pray that your
flight will not take place in winter or on
the Sabbath. 21For then there will be great
distress, unequaled from the beginning of
the world until now—and never to be
equaled again.[a] 22If those days had not
been cut short, no one would survive, but
for the sake of the elect[b] those days will be
shortened. 23At that time if anyone says to
you, 'Look, here is the Christ!' or, 'There
he is!' do not believe it.[c] 24For false
Christs and false prophets will appear and
perform great signs and miracles[d] to deceive even the elect—if that were possible.
25See, I have told you ahead of time.

26"So if anyone tells you, 'There he is,
out in the desert,' do not go out; or, 'Here
he is, in the inner rooms,' do not believe it.
27For as lightning[e] that comes from the
east is visible even in the west, so will be
the coming[f] of the Son of Man.[g]
28Wherever there is a carcass, there the
vultures will gather.[h]

29"Immediately after the distress of
those days

" 'the sun will be darkened,
and the moon will not give its light;
the stars will fall from the sky,
and the heavenly bodies will be
shaken.'[x][i]

30"At that time the sign of the Son of
Man will appear in the sky, and all the
nations of the earth will mourn.[j] They
will see the Son of Man coming on the
clouds of the sky,[k] with power and great
glory. 31And he will send his angels[l] with
a loud trumpet call,[m] and they will gather
his elect from the four winds, from one
end of the heavens to the other.

32"Now learn this lesson from the fig
tree: As soon as its twigs get tender and its
leaves come out, you know that summer is
near. 33Even so, when you see all these
things, you know that it[y] is near, right at
the door.[n] 34I tell you the truth, this generation[z] will certainly not pass away until
all these things have happened.[o] 35Heaven
and earth will pass away, but my words
will never pass away.[p]

The Day and Hour Unknown

24:37–39pp — Lk 17:26,27
24:45–51pp — Lk 12:42–46

36"No one knows about that day or
hour, not even the angels in heaven, nor
the Son,[a] but only the Father.[q] 37As it was
in the days of Noah,[r] so it will be at the
coming of the Son of Man. 38For in the
days before the flood, people were eating
and drinking, marrying and giving in marriage,[s] up to the day Noah entered the
ark; 39and they knew nothing about what
would happen until the flood came and
took them all away. That is how it will be
at the coming of the Son of Man.[t] 40Two
men will be in the field; one will be taken
and the other left.[u] 41Two women will be
grinding with a hand mill; one will be tak-
en and the other left.[v]

42"Therefore keep watch, because you
do not know on what day your Lord will
come.[w] 43But understand this: If the
owner of the house had known at what
time of night the thief was coming,[x] he

24:15 [x]Da 9:27; 11:31; 12:11
24:17 [y]1Sa 9:25; Mt 10:27; Lk 12:3; Ac 10:9
24:19 [z]Lk 23:29
24:21 [a]Eze 5:9; Da 12:1; Joel 2:2
24:22 [b]ver 24,31
24:23 [c]Lk 17:23; 21:8
24:24 [d]Ex 7:11, 22; 2Th 2:9-11; Rev 13:13; 16:14; 19:20
24:27 [e]Lk 17:24 [f]S Lk 17:30 [g]S Mt 8:20
24:28 [h]Lk 17:37
24:29 [i]Isa 13:10; 34:4; Eze 32:7; Joel 2:10,31; Zep 1:15; Rev 6:12,13; 8:12
24:30 [j]Rev 1:7 [k]S Rev 1:7
24:31 [l]Mt 13:41 [m]Isa 27:13; Zec 9:14; 1Co 15:52; 1Th 4:16; Rev 8:2; 10:7; 11:15
24:33 [n]Jas 5:9
24:34 [o]Mt 16:28; S 23:36
24:35 [p]S Mt 5:18
24:36 [q]Ac 1:7
24:37 [r]Ge 6:5; 7:6-23
24:38 [s]Mt 22:30
24:39 [t]S Lk 17:30
24:40 [u]Lk 17:34
24:41 [v]Lk 17:35
24:42 [w]Mt 25:13; Lk 12:40
24:43 [x]S Lk 12:39

[w] *15* Daniel 9:27; 11:31; 12:11 [x] *29* Isaiah 13:10; 34:4 [y] *33* Or *he* [z] *34* Or *race* [a] *36* Some manuscripts do not have *nor the Son.*

able thing causing the desolation of the holy place. The primary reference in Daniel (see NIV text note for references) was to 168 B.C., when Antiochus Epiphanes erected a pagan altar to Zeus on the sacred altar in the temple of Jerusalem. According to some, there were still two more stages in the progressive fulfillment of the predictions in Daniel and Matthew: (1) the Roman destruction of the temple in A.D. 70 and (2) the setting up of an image of the antichrist in Jerusalem (see 2Th 2:4; Rev 13:14–15; see also notes on Da 9:25–27; 11:31).
24:16 *the mountains.* The Transjordan mountains, where Pella was located. Christians in Jerusalem fled to that area during the Roman siege shortly before A.D. 70. Some believe a similar fleeing will occur in a future tribulation period (identified with Daniel's 70th "seven," Da 9:27).
24:20 *or on the Sabbath.* Matthew alone includes this because he was writing to Jews, who were forbidden to travel more than about half a mile on the Sabbath.
24:21 *great distress, unequaled.* Josephus, the Jewish historian who was there, describes the destruction of Jerusalem in almost identical language. Some believe the reference is also to a future period of great distress (see Da 12:1).
24:22 *the elect.* The people of God. *days . . . cut short.* Some hold that this statement means that the distress will be of such intensity that, if allowed to continue, it will destroy everyone. Others believe that Christ is referring to the cutting short of a previously determined time period (such as the 70th "seven" of Da 9:27 or the 42 months of Rev 11:2; 13:5).
24:28 *there the vultures will gather.* The coming of Christ will be as obvious as the gathering of vultures around a carcass (see note on Lk 17:37, where the saying is used in a slightly different sense).
24:29 See note on Mk 13:25.
24:30 *Son of Man.* See note on Mk 8:31.
24:34 *this generation.* See NIV text note; see also note on Mk 13:30.
24:36 *nor the Son.* See note on Mk 13:32.

would have kept watch and would not have let his house be broken into. ⁴⁴So you also must be ready,*y* because the Son of Man will come at an hour when you do not expect him.

⁴⁵"Who then is the faithful and wise servant,*z* whom the master has put in charge of the servants in his household to give them their food at the proper time? ⁴⁶It will be good for that servant whose master finds him doing so when he returns.*a* ⁴⁷I tell you the truth, he will put him in charge of all his possessions.*b* ⁴⁸But suppose that servant is wicked and says to himself, 'My master is staying away a long time,' ⁴⁹and he then begins to beat his fellow servants and to eat and drink with drunkards.*c* ⁵⁰The master of that servant will come on a day when he does not expect him and at an hour he is not aware of. ⁵¹He will cut him to pieces and assign him a place with the hypocrites, where there will be weeping and gnashing of teeth.*d*

The Parable of the Ten Virgins

25 "At that time the kingdom of heaven will be like*e* ten virgins who took their lamps*f* and went out to meet the bridegroom.*g* ²Five of them were foolish and five were wise.*h* ³The foolish ones took their lamps but did not take any oil with them. ⁴The wise, however, took oil in jars along with their lamps. ⁵The bridegroom was a long time in coming, and they all became drowsy and fell asleep.*i*

⁶"At midnight the cry rang out: 'Here's the bridegroom! Come out to meet him!'

⁷"Then all the virgins woke up and trimmed their lamps. ⁸The foolish ones said to the wise, 'Give us some of your oil; our lamps are going out.'*j*

⁹" 'No,' they replied, 'there may not be enough for both us and you. Instead, go to those who sell oil and buy some for yourselves.'

¹⁰"But while they were on their way to buy the oil, the bridegroom arrived. The virgins who were ready went in with him to the wedding banquet.*k* And the door was shut.

¹¹"Later the others also came. 'Sir! Sir!' they said. 'Open the door for us!'

¹²"But he replied, 'I tell you the truth, I don't know you.'*l*

¹³"Therefore keep watch, because you do not know the day or the hour.*m*

The Parable of the Talents
25:14–30Ref — Lk 19:12–27

¹⁴"Again, it will be like a man going on a journey,*n* who called his servants and entrusted his property to them. ¹⁵To one he gave five talents*b* of money, to another two talents, and to another one talent, each according to his ability.*o* Then he went on his journey. ¹⁶The man who had received the five talents went at once and put his money to work and gained five more. ¹⁷So also, the one with the two talents gained two more. ¹⁸But the man who had received the one talent went off, dug a hole in the ground and hid his master's money.

¹⁹"After a long time the master of those servants returned and settled accounts with them.*p* ²⁰The man who had received the five talents brought the other five. 'Master,' he said, 'you entrusted me with five talents. See, I have gained five more.'

²¹"His master replied, 'Well done, good and faithful servant! You have been faithful with a few things; I will put you in charge of many things.*q* Come and share your master's happiness!'

²²"The man with the two talents also came. 'Master,' he said, 'you entrusted me with two talents; see, I have gained two more.'

²³"His master replied, 'Well done, good and faithful servant! You have been faithful with a few things; I will put you in charge of many things.*r* Come and share your master's happiness!'

²⁴"Then the man who had received the one talent came. 'Master,' he said, 'I knew that you are a hard man, harvesting where you have not sown and gathering where you have not scattered seed. ²⁵So I was afraid and went out and hid your talent in the ground. See, here is what belongs to you.'

24:44 *y*1Th 5:6
24:45 *z*Mt 25:21, 23
24:46 *a*Rev 16:15
24:47 *b*Mt 25:21, 23
24:49 *c*Lk 21:34
24:51 *d*S Mt 8:12
25:1 *e*S Mt 13:24
/Lk 12:35-38;
Ac 20:8; Rev 4:5
*g*Rev 19:7; 21:2
25:2 *h*Mt 24:45
25:5 *i*1Th 5:6
25:8 *j*Lk 12:35
25:10 *k*Rev 19:9

25:12 *l*ver 41;
S Mt 7:23
25:13 *m*Mt 24:42,44;
Mk 13:35;
Lk 12:40
25:14 *n*Mt 21:33;
Lk 19:12
25:15 *o*Mt 18:24, 25
25:19 *p*Mt 18:23
25:21 *q*ver 23;
Mt 24:45,47;
Lk 16:10
25:23 *r*ver 21

*b*15 A talent was worth more than a thousand dollars.

25:1 *ten virgins.* The bridesmaids, who were responsible for preparing the bride to meet the bridegroom. *lamps.* Torches that consisted of a long pole with oil-drenched rags at the top. (Small clay lamps would have been of little use in an outdoor procession.)
25:3 *oil.* Olive oil.
25:7 *trimmed.* The charred ends of the rags were cut off and oil was added.

25:9 *there may not be enough.* Torches required large amounts of oil in order to keep burning, and the oil had to be replenished about every 15 minutes.
25:15 *talent.* The term was first used for a unit of weight (about 75 pounds), then for a unit of coinage. The present-day use of "talent" to indicate an ability or gift is derived from this parable (see note on Lk 19:13).

CHILDHOOD

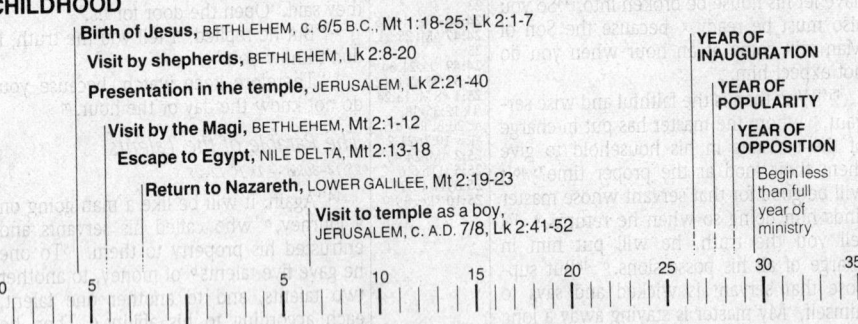

Birth of Jesus, BETHLEHEM, C. 6/5 B.C., Mt 1:18-25; Lk 2:1-7

Visit by shepherds, BETHLEHEM, Lk 2:8-20

Presentation in the temple, JERUSALEM, Lk 2:21-40

Visit by the Magi, BETHLEHEM, Mt 2:1-12

Escape to Egypt, NILE DELTA, Mt 2:13-18

Return to Nazareth, LOWER GALILEE, Mt 2:19-23

Visit to temple as a boy, JERUSALEM, C. A.D. 7/8, Lk 2:41-52

YEAR OF INAUGURATION

YEAR OF POPULARITY

YEAR OF OPPOSITION

Begin less than full year of ministry

10 — 5 — B.C. | A.D. — 5 — 10 — 15 — 20 — 25 — 30 — 35

Dotted lines leading to the timeline are meant to define sequence of events only. Exact dates, even year dates, are generally unknown.

Jesus baptized
JORDAN RIVER
C. A.D. 26
Mt 3:13-17; Mk 1:9-11;
Lk 3:21-23; Jn 1:29-39

Jesus tempted by Satan
DESERT
Mt 4:1-11; Mk 1:12-13;
Lk 4:1-13

Jesus' first miracle
CANA
Jn 2:1-11

4 fishermen become Jesus' followers
SEA OF GALILEE
AT CAPERNAUM
A.D. 27
Mt 4:18-22; Mk 1:16-20;
Lk 5:1-11

Jesus heals Peter's mother-in-law
CAPERNAUM
Mt 8:14-17; Mk 1:29-34;
Lk 4:38-41

YEAR OF INAUGURATION — YEAR OF POPULARITY

A.D. 27

FALL	WINTER	SPRING	SUMMER	FALL	WINTER

28

Jesus' cleansing of the temple
A.D. 27
Jn 2:14-22

Jesus and Nicodemus
JERUSALEM
A.D. 27
Jn 3:1-21

Jesus talks to the Samaritan woman
SAMARIA
Jn 4:5-42

Jesus heals a nobleman's son
CANA
Jn 4:46-54

The people of Jesus' hometown try to kill him
NAZARETH
Lk 4:16-31

Jesus begins his first preaching trip through Galilee
Mt 4:23-25; Mk 1:35-39;
Lk 4:42-44

Matthew decides to follow Jesus
CAPERNAUM
Mt 9:9-13; Mk 2:13-17;
Lk 5:27-32

Jesus chooses the 12 disciples
A.D. 28
Mk 3:13-19; Lk 6:12-15

Jesus preaches the "Sermon on the Mount"
Mt 5:1-7:29; Lk 6:20-49

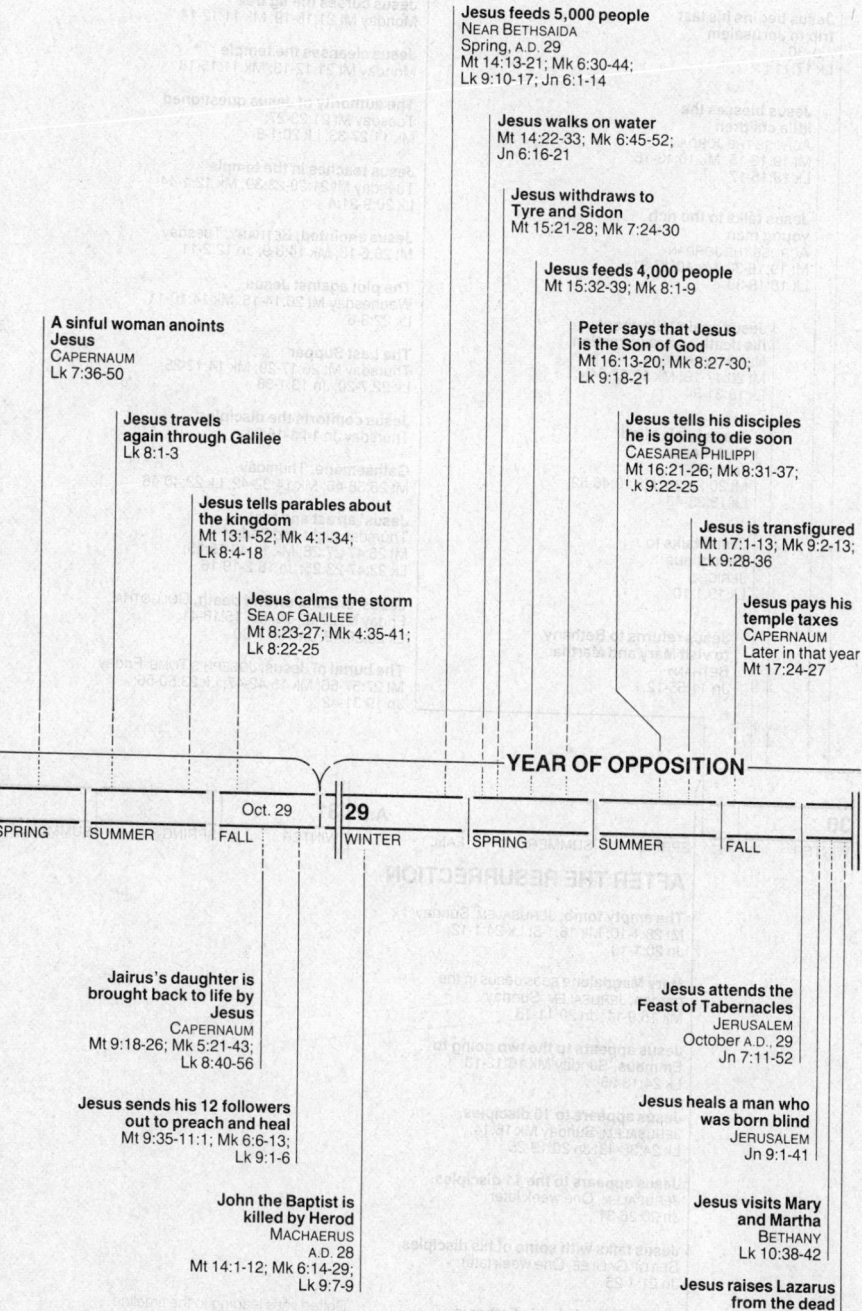

Jesus feeds 5,000 people
NEAR BETHSAIDA
Spring, A.D. 29
Mt 14:13-21; Mk 6:30-44;
Lk 9:10-17; Jn 6:1-14

Jesus walks on water
Mt 14:22-33; Mk 6:45-52;
Jn 6:16-21

**Jesus withdraws to
Tyre and Sidon**
Mt 15:21-28; Mk 7:24-30

Jesus feeds 4,000 people
Mt 15:32-39; Mk 8:1-9

**Peter says that Jesus
is the Son of God**
Mt 16:13-20; Mk 8:27-30;
Lk 9:18-21

**Jesus tells his disciples
he is going to die soon**
CAESAREA PHILIPPI
Mt 16:21-26; Mk 8:31-37;
Lk 9:22-25

Jesus is transfigured
Mt 17:1-13; Mk 9:2-13;
Lk 9:28-36

**Jesus pays his
temple taxes**
CAPERNAUM
Later in that year
Mt 17:24-27

**A sinful woman anoints
Jesus**
CAPERNAUM
Lk 7:36-50

**Jesus travels
again through Galilee**
Lk 8:1-3

**Jesus tells parables about
the kingdom**
Mt 13:1-52; Mk 4:1-34;
Lk 8:4-18

Jesus calms the storm
SEA OF GALILEE
Mt 8:23-27; Mk 4:35-41;
Lk 8:22-25

— YEAR OF OPPOSITION —

| SPRING | SUMMER | FALL | Oct. 29 | **29** WINTER | SPRING | SUMMER | FALL |

**Jairus's daughter is
brought back to life by
Jesus**
CAPERNAUM
Mt 9:18-26; Mk 5:21-43;
Lk 8:40-56

**Jesus sends his 12 followers
out to preach and heal**
Mt 9:35-11:1; Mk 6:6-13;
Lk 9:1-6

**John the Baptist is
killed by Herod**
MACHAERUS
A.D. 28
Mt 14:1-12; Mk 6:14-29;
Lk 9:7-9

**Jesus attends the
Feast of Tabernacles**
JERUSALEM
October A.D. 29
Jn 7:11-52

**Jesus heals a man who
was born blind**
JERUSALEM
Jn 9:1-41

**Jesus visits Mary
and Martha**
BETHANY
Lk 10:38-42

**Jesus raises Lazarus
from the dead**
BETHANY
Winter, A.D. 29
Jn 11:1-44

Jesus begins his last trip to Jerusalem
A.D. 30
Lk 17:11

Jesus blesses the little children
ACROSS THE JORDAN
Mt 19:13-15; Mk 10:13-16;
Lk 18:15-17

Jesus talks to the rich young man
ACROSS THE JORDAN
Mt 19:16-30; Mk 10:17-31;
Lk 18:18-30

Jesus again tells about his death and resurrection
NEAR THE JORDAN
Mt 20:17-19; Mk 10:32-34;
Lk 18:31-34

Jesus heals blind Bartimaeus
JERICHO
Mt 20:29-34; Mk 10:46-52;
Lk 18:35-43

Jesus talks to Zacchaeus
JERICHO
Lk 19:1-10

Jesus returns to Bethany to visit Mary and Martha
BETHANY
Jn 11:55-12:1

The Triumphal Entry, JERUSALEM, Sunday
Mt 21:1-11; Mk 11:1-10; Lk 19:29-44;
Jn 12:12-19

Jesus curses the fig tree
Monday Mt 21:18-19; Mk 11:12-14

Jesus cleanses the temple
Monday Mt 21:12-13; Mk 11:15-18

The authority of Jesus questioned
Tuesday Mt 21:23-27;
Mk 11:27-33; Lk 20:1-8

Jesus teaches in the temple
Tuesday Mt 21:28-23:39; Mk 12:1-44;
Lk 20:9-21:4

Jesus anointed, BETHANY, Tuesday
Mt 26:6-13; Mk 14:3-9; Jn 12:2-11

The plot against Jesus
Wednesday Mt 26:14-16; Mk 14:10-11;
Lk 22:3-6

The Last Supper
Thursday Mt 26:17-29; Mk 14:12-25;
Lk 22:7-20; Jn 13:1-38

Jesus comforts the disciples
Thursday Jn 14:1-16:33

Gethsemane, Thursday
Mt 26:36-46; Mk 14:32-42; Lk 22:40-46

Jesus' arrest and trial
Thursday night and Friday
Mt 26:47-27:26; Mk 14:43-15:15;
Lk 22:47-23:25; Jn 18:2-19:16

Jesus' crucifixion and death, GOLGOTHA,
Friday Mt 27:27-56; Mk 15:16-41;
Lk 23:26-49; Jn 19:17-30

The burial of Jesus, JOSEPH'S TOMB, Friday
Mt 27:57-66; Mk 15:42-47; Lk 23:50-56;
Jn 19:31-42

| 30 | | | | A.D. | 31 | | |
| WINTER | SPRING | SUMMER | FALL | | WINTER | SPRING | SUMMER |

AFTER THE RESURRECTION

The empty tomb, JERUSALEM, Sunday
Mt 28:1-10; Mk 16:1-8; Lk 24:1-12;
Jn 20:1-10

Mary Magdalene sees Jesus in the garden, JERUSALEM, Sunday
Mk 16:9-11; Jn 20:11-18

Jesus appears to the two going to Emmaus, Sunday Mk 16:12-13;
Lk 24:13-35

Jesus appears to 10 disciples,
JERUSALEM, Sunday Mk 16:14;
Lk 24:36-43; Jn 20:19-25

Jesus appears to the 11 disciples,
JERUSALEM, One week later
Jn 20:26-31

Jesus talks with some of his disciples,
SEA OF GALILEE, One week later
Jn 21:1-25

Jesus ascends to his Father in heaven, MT OF OLIVES, 40 days later
Mt 28:16-20; Mk 16:19-20; Lk 24:44-53

Dotted lines leading to the timeline
are meant to define sequence of events only.
Exact dates, even year dates, are generally unknown.

26"His master replied, 'You wicked, lazy servant! So you knew that I harvest where I have not sown and gather where I have not scattered seed? 27Well then, you should have put my money on deposit with the bankers, so that when I returned I would have received it back with interest.

28" 'Take the talent from him and give it to the one who has the ten talents. 29For everyone who has will be given more, and he will have an abundance. Whoever does not have, even what he has will be taken from him.s 30And throw that worthless servant outside, into the darkness, where there will be weeping and gnashing of teeth.'t

The Sheep and the Goats

31"When the Son of Man comesu in his glory, and all the angels with him, he will sit on his thronev in heavenly glory. 32All the nations will be gathered before him, and he will separatew the people one from another as a shepherd separates the sheep from the goats.x 33He will put the sheep on his right and the goats on his left.

34"Then the King will say to those on his right, 'Come, you who are blessed by my Father; take your inheritance, the kingdomy prepared for you since the creation of the world.z 35For I was hungry and you gave me something to eat, I was thirsty and you gave me something to drink, I was a stranger and you invited me in,a 36I needed clothes and you clothed me,b I was sick and you looked after me,c I was in prison and you came to visit me.'d

37"Then the righteous will answer him, 'Lord, when did we see you hungry and feed you, or thirsty and give you something to drink? 38When did we see you a stranger and invite you in, or needing clothes and clothe you? 39When did we see you sick or in prison and go to visit you?'

40"The King will reply, 'I tell you the truth, whatever you did for one of the least of these brothers of mine, you did for me.'e

41"Then he will say to those on his left, 'Depart from me,f you who are cursed, into the eternal fireg prepared for the devil and his angels.h 42For I was hungry and you gave me nothing to eat, I was thirsty and you gave me nothing to drink, 43I was a stranger and you did not invite me in, I needed clothes and you did not clothe me, I was sick and in prison and you did not look after me.'

44"They also will answer, 'Lord, when did we see you hungry or thirsty or a stranger or needing clothes or sick or in prison, and did not help you?'

45"He will reply, 'I tell you the truth, whatever you did not do for one of the least of these, you did not do for me.'i

46"Then they will go away to eternal punishment, but the righteous to eternal life.j " k

The Plot Against Jesus

26:2–5pp — Mk 14:1,2; Lk 22:1,2

26 When Jesus had finished saying all these things,l he said to his disciples, 2"As you know, the Passoverm is two days away—and the Son of Man will be handed over to be crucified.

3Then the chief priests and the elders of the people assembledn in the palace of the high priest, whose name was Caiaphas,o 4and they plotted to arrest Jesus in some sly way and kill him.p 5"But not during the Feast," they said, "or there may be a riotq among the people."

Jesus Anointed at Bethany

26:6–13pp — Mk 14:3–9
26:6–13Ref — Lk 7:37,38; Jn 12:1–8

6While Jesus was in Bethanyr in the home of a man known as Simon the Leper,

---

Cross references (center column):

25:29 sMt 13:12; Mk 4:25; Lk 8:18; 19:26
25:30 tS Mt 8:12
25:31 uS Lk 17:30 vMt 19:28
25:32 wMal 3:18 xEze 34:17,20
25:34 yS Mt 3:2; 5:3,10,19; 19:14; S Ac 20:32; 1Co 15:50; Gal 5:21; Jas 2:5 zHeb 4:3; 9:26; Rev 13:8; 17:8
25:35 aJob 31:32; Heb 13:2
25:36 bIsa 58:7; Eze 18:7; Jas 2:15,16 cJas 1:27 d2Ti 1:16

25:40 eS Mt 10:40,42; Heb 13:2 fS Mt 7:23 gIsa 66:24; Mt 3:12; S 5:22; Mk 9:43,48; Lk 3:17; Jude 7 h2Pe 2:4
25:45 iPr 14:31; 17:5
25:46 jMt 19:29; Jn 3:15,16,36; 17:2,3; Ro 2:7; Gal 6:8; 1Jn 1:2; 5:11,13,20 kDa 12:2; Jn 5:29; Ac 24:15; Ro 2:7, 8; Gal 6:8
26:1 lS Mt 7:28
26:2 mS Jn 11:55
26:3 nPs 2:2 over 57; Lk 3:2; Jn 11:47-53; 18:13,14,24,28; Ac 4:6
26:4 pS Mt 12:14
26:5 qMt 27:24
26:6 rS Mt 21:17

Study notes (bottom):

25:27 bankers. The Greek for this word comes from trapeza ("table"), a word seen on the front of banks in Greece today. Bankers sat at small tables and changed money (cf. 21:12). interest. The Greek for this word was first used in the sense of offspring, interest being the "offspring" of invested money.

25:31–46 The two most widely accepted interpretations of this judgment are: 1. It will occur at the beginning of an earthly millennial kingdom (vv. 31,34). Its purpose will be to determine who will be allowed to enter the kingdom (v. 34) The criterion for judgment will be the kind of treatment shown to the Jewish people ("these brothers of mine," v. 40) during the preceding great tribulation period (vv. 35–40, 42–45). Ultimately, how a person treats the Jewish people will reveal whether or not he is saved (vv. 41,46). 2. The judgment referred to occurs at the great white throne at the end of the age (Rev 20:11–15). Its purpose will be to determine who will be allowed to enter the eternal kingdom of the saved and who will be consigned to eternal punishment in hell (vv. 34,46). The basis for judgment will be whether love is shown to God's people (see 1Jn 3:14–15).

25:34–40 Rewards in the kingdom of heaven are given to those who serve without thought of reward. There is no hint of merit here, for God gives out of grace, not debt.

26:2 Passover. See note on Mk 14:1.

26:3 Caiaphas. High priest A.D. 18–36 and the son-in-law of Annas (Jn 18:13), a former high priest, who served 6–15.

26:5 there may be a riot. Hundreds of thousands of Jewish pilgrims came to Jerusalem for Passover, and riots were not unknown. The religious leaders (v. 3) knew that many people admired Jesus.

26:6 Simon the Leper. Not mentioned elsewhere, though

7a woman came to him with an alabaster jar of very expensive perfume, which she poured on his head as he was reclining at the table.

8When the disciples saw this, they were indignant. "Why this waste?" they asked. 9"This perfume could have been sold at a high price and the money given to the poor."

10Aware of this, Jesus said to them, "Why are you bothering this woman? She has done a beautiful thing to me. 11The poor you will always have with you,ˢ but you will not always have me. 12When she poured this perfume on my body, she did it to prepare me for burial.ᵗ 13I tell you the truth, wherever this gospel is preached throughout the world, what she has done will also be told, in memory of her."

Judas Agrees to Betray Jesus

26:14–16pp — Mk 14:10,11; Lk 22:3–6

14Then one of the Twelve—the one called Judas Iscariotᵘ—went to the chief priests 15and asked, "What are you willing to give me if I hand him over to you?" So they counted out for him thirty silver coins.ᵛ 16From then on Judas watched for an opportunity to hand him over.

The Lord's Supper

26:17–19pp — Mk 14:12–16; Lk 22:7–13
26:20–24pp — Mk 14:17–21
26:26–29pp — Mk 14:22–25; Lk 22:17–20; 1Co 11:23–25

17On the first day of the Feast of Unleavened Bread,ʷ the disciples came to Jesus and asked, "Where do you want us to make preparations for you to eat the Passover?"ˣ

18He replied, "Go into the city to a certain man and tell him, 'The Teacher says: My appointed timeʸ is near. I am going to celebrate the Passover with my disciples at your house.' " 19So the disciples did as Jesus had directed them and prepared the Passover.

20When evening came, Jesus was reclining at the table with the Twelve. 21And while they were eating, he said, "I tell you the truth, one of you will betray me."ᶻ

22They were very sad and began to say to him one after the other, "Surely not I, Lord?"

23Jesus replied, "The one who has dipped his hand into the bowl with me will betray me.ᵃ 24The Son of Man will go just as it is written about him.ᵇ But woe to that man who betrays the Son of Man! It would be better for him if he had not been born."

25Then Judas, the one who would betray him,ᶜ said, "Surely not I, Rabbi?"ᵈ

Jesus answered, "Yes, it is you."ᶜ

26While they were eating, Jesus took bread, gave thanks and broke it,ᵉ and gave it to his disciples, saying, "Take and eat; this is my body."

27Then he took the cup,ᶠ gave thanks and offered it to them, saying, "Drink from it, all of you. 28This is my blood of theᵈ covenant,ᵍ which is poured out for many for the forgiveness of sins.ʰ 29I tell you, I will not drink of this fruit of the vine from now on until that day when I drink it anew with youⁱ in my Father's kingdom."

30When they had sung a hymn, they went out to the Mount of Olives.ʲ

Jesus Predicts Peter's Denial

26:31–35pp — Mk 14:27–31; Lk 22:31–34

31Then Jesus told them, "This very night

Cross references (center column)

26:11 ˢDt 15:11
26:12 ᵗJn 19:40
26:14 ᵘver 25, 47; S Mt 10:4
26:15 ᵛEx 21:32; Zec 11:12
26:17 ʷEx 12:18-20 ˣDt 16:5-8
26:18 ʸMk 14:35,41; Jn 7:6,8,30; 8:20; 12:23; 13:1; 17:1
26:21 ᶻLk 22:21-23; Jn 13:21
26:23 ᵃPs 41:9; Jn 13:18
26:24 ᵇver 31, 54,56; Isa 53; Da 9:26; Mk 9:12; Lk 24:25-27,46; Ac 17:2,3; 26:22,23; 1Pe 1:10,11
26:25 ᶜS Mt 10:4 ᵈS Mt 23:7
26:26 ᵉS Mt 14:19
26:27 ᶠ1Co 10:16
26:28 ᵍEx 24:6-8; Zec 9:11; Mal 2:5; Heb 9:20; 10:29; S 13:20 ʰS Mt 20:28; Mk 1:4
26:29 ⁱAc 10:41
26:30 ʲS Mt 21:1

ᶜ25 Or *"You yourself have said it"* ᵈ28 Some manuscripts *the new*

Simon was a common Jewish name in the first century. He was probably a well-known victim of leprosy who had been healed by Jesus.
26:7 *alabaster jar.* Most "alabaster" of ancient times was actually marble (see note on Mk 14:3).
26:10 *beautiful.* The Greek word has an aesthetic as well as an ethical meaning.
26:14 *Iscariot.* See note on Mk 3:19.
26:15 *thirty silver coins.* Equivalent to 120 denarii. Laborers customarily received one denarius for a day's work (see 20:1–16).
26:17 *the first day of the Feast of Unleavened Bread.* The 14th of Nisan (March-April), it was also called the preparation of the Passover. The Passover meal was eaten the evening of the 14th after sunset—and therefore technically on the 15th, since the Jewish day ended at sunset. The Feast of Unleavened Bread lasted seven days, from the 15th to the 21st of Nisan (see Lev 23:5–6), but in the time of Christ the entire period, Nisan 14–21, was referred to under that name (see note on Mk 14:12).

26:18–30 These verses clearly indicate that Jesus ate the Passover meal with his disciples the night before his crucifixion. For more information on the Lord's Supper see notes on Mk 14:22,24.
26:20 *reclining at the table.* See note on Mk 14:18.
26:23 *dipped his hand into the bowl with me.* It was the custom—still practiced by some in the Middle East—to take a piece of bread, or a piece of meat wrapped in bread, and dip it into a bowl of sauce (made of stewed fruit) on the table. *will betray me.* In that culture, as among Arabs today, to eat with a person was tantamount to saying, "I am your friend and will not hurt you." This fact made Judas's deed all the more despicable (cf. Ps 41:9).
26:24 *as it is written about him.* See note on Mk 14:21.
26:26–28 See note on Mk 14:22.
26:30 *hymn.* The Passover fellowship was concluded with the second half of the Hallel Psalms (Ps 115–118).
26:31 *all fall away.* Not Peter only, but all the eleven (Judas had previously withdrawn, Jn 13:30). The meaning of the words "fall away" is seen in Peter's denial (vv. 69–75) and in

you will all fall away on account of me,[k] for it is written:

" 'I will strike the shepherd,
    and the sheep of the flock will be scattered.'[e] [l]

32But after I have risen, I will go ahead of you into Galilee."[m]

33Peter replied, "Even if all fall away on account of you, I never will."

34"I tell you the truth," Jesus answered, "this very night, before the rooster crows, you will disown me three times."[n]

35But Peter declared, "Even if I have to die with you,[o] I will never disown you." And all the other disciples said the same.

Gethsemane

26:36–46pp — Mk 14:32–42; Lk 22:40–46

36Then Jesus went with his disciples to a place called Gethsemane, and he said to them, "Sit here while I go over there and pray." 37He took Peter and the two sons of Zebedee[p] along with him, and he began to be sorrowful and troubled. 38Then he said to them, "My soul is overwhelmed with sorrow[q] to the point of death. Stay here and keep watch with me."[r]

39Going a little farther, he fell with his face to the ground and prayed, "My Father, if it is possible, may this cup[s] be taken from me. Yet not as I will, but as you will."[t]

40Then he returned to his disciples and found them sleeping. "Could you men not keep watch with me[u] for one hour?" he asked Peter. 41"Watch and pray so that you will not fall into temptation.[v] The spirit is willing, but the body is weak."

42He went away a second time and prayed, "My Father, if it is not possible for this cup to be taken away unless I drink it, may your will be done."[w]

43When he came back, he again found them sleeping, because their eyes were heavy. 44So he left them and went away once more and prayed the third time, saying the same thing.

45Then he returned to the disciples and

said to them, "Are you still sleeping and resting? Look, the hour[x] is near, and the Son of Man is betrayed into the hands of sinners. 46Rise, let us go! Here comes my betrayer!"

Jesus Arrested

26:47–56pp — Mk 14:43–50; Lk 22:47–53

47While he was still speaking, Judas,[y] one of the Twelve, arrived. With him was a large crowd armed with swords and clubs, sent from the chief priests and the elders of the people. 48Now the betrayer had arranged a signal with them: "The one I kiss is the man; arrest him." 49Going at once to Jesus, Judas said, "Greetings, Rabbi!"[z] and kissed him.

50Jesus replied, "Friend,[a] do what you came for."[f]

Then the men stepped forward, seized Jesus and arrested him. 51With that, one of Jesus' companions reached for his sword,[b] drew it out and struck the servant of the high priest, cutting off his ear.[c]

52"Put your sword back in its place," Jesus said to him, "for all who draw the sword will die by the sword.[d] 53Do you think I cannot call on my Father, and he will at once put at my disposal more than twelve legions of angels?[e] 54But how then would the Scriptures be fulfilled[f] that say it must happen in this way?"

55At that time Jesus said to the crowd, "Am I leading a rebellion, that you have come out with swords and clubs to capture me? Every day I sat in the temple courts teaching,[g] and you did not arrest me. 56But this has all taken place that the writings of the prophets might be fulfilled."[h] Then all the disciples deserted him and fled.

Before the Sanhedrin

26:57–68pp — Mk 14:53–65; Jn 18:12,13,19–24

57Those who had arrested Jesus took him to Caiaphas,[i] the high priest, where the teachers of the law and the elders had

Cross references (center column)

26:31 [k]Mt 11:6; 13:21 [l]Zec 13:7; Jn 16:32
26:32 [m]Mt 28:7, 10,16
26:34 [n]ver 75; Jn 13:38
26:35 [o]Jn 13:37
26:37 [p]S Mt 4:21
26:38 [q]S Jn 12:27 [r]ver 40,41
26:39 [s]S Mt 20:22 [t]ver 42; Ps 40:6-8; Isa 50:5; Mt 6:10; Jn 4:34; 5:30; 6:38
26:40 [u]ver 38
26:41 [v]Mt 6:13
26:42 [w]S ver 39

26:45 [x]S ver 18
26:47 [y]S Mt 10:4
26:49 [z]ver 25; S Mt 23:7
26:50 [a]Mt 20:13; 22:12
26:51 [b]Lk 22:36, 38 [c]Jn 18:10
26:52 [d]Ge 9:6; Ex 21:12; Rev 13:10
26:53 [e]2Ki 6:17; Da 7:10; Mt 4:11
26:54 [f]S ver 24; S Mt 1:22
26:55 [g]Mk 12:35; Lk 21:37; Jn 7:14, 28; 18:20
26:56 [h]S ver 24; S Mt 1:22
26:57 [i]S ver 3

[e]31 Zech. 13:7   [f]50 Or "Friend, why have you come?"

---

the terrified flight of the other disciples (v. 56). *I will strike the shepherd.* See note on Zec 13:7.

26:32 *into Galilee.* Cf. 10:16–20; Mk 16:7; Jn 21:1–23.

26:34 *before the rooster crows.* The reference may be to the third of the Roman watches into which the night was divided (see note on 14:25; see also Mk 13:35). Or it may simply refer to early morning when the rooster crows.

26:36 *Gethsemane.* The name means "oil press," a place for squeezing the oil from olives.

26:39 *cup.* A symbol of deep sorrow and suffering. Here it

refers to his Father's face being turned away from him when he who had no sin was made sin (i.e., a sin offering) for us (see 27:46; 2Co 5:21).

26:41 See note on Mk 14:38.

26:48 *the one I kiss.* See note on Lk 22:47.

26:49 *Rabbi.* Hebrew word for "(my) teacher."

26:53 *legions.* A Roman legion had 6,000 soldiers.

26:54 *Scriptures be fulfilled.* In view of v. 56 probably a reference to Zec 13:7.

26:57—27:26 For a summary of the two stages (religious and civil) of the trial of Jesus see note on Mk 14:53–15:15.

assembled. 58But Peter followed him at a distance, right up to the courtyard of the high priest.' He entered and sat down with the guards*k* to see the outcome.

59The chief priests and the whole Sanhedrin*l* were looking for false evidence against Jesus so that they could put him to death. 60But they did not find any, though many false witnesses*m* came forward.

Finally two*n* came forward 61and declared, "This fellow said, 'I am able to destroy the temple of God and rebuild it in three days.'"*o*

62Then the high priest stood up and said to Jesus, "Are you not going to answer? What is this testimony that these men are bringing against you?" 63But Jesus remained silent.*p*

The high priest said to him, "I charge you under oath*q* by the living God:*r* Tell us if you are the Christ,*s* *s* the Son of God."*t*

64"Yes, it is as you say,"*u* Jesus replied. "But I say to all of you: In the future you will see the Son of Man sitting at the right hand of the Mighty One*v* and coming on the clouds of heaven."*w*

65Then the high priest tore his clothes*x* and said, "He has spoken blasphemy! Why do we need any more witnesses? Look, now you have heard the blasphemy. 66What do you think?"

"He is worthy of death,"*y* they answered.

67Then they spit in his face and struck him with their fists.*z* Others slapped him 68and said, "Prophesy to us, Christ. Who hit you?"*a*

Peter Disowns Jesus

26:69-75pp — Mk 14:66-72; Lk 22:55-62; Jn 18:16-18,25-27

69Now Peter was sitting out in the courtyard, and a servant girl came to him. "You also were with Jesus of Galilee," she said.

70But he denied it before them all. "I

don't know what you're talking about," he said.

71Then he went out to the gateway, where another girl saw him and said to the people there, "This fellow was with Jesus of Nazareth."

72He denied it again, with an oath: "I don't know the man!"

73After a little while, those standing there went up to Peter and said, "Surely you are one of them, for your accent gives you away."

74Then he began to call down curses on himself and he swore to them, "I don't know the man!"

Immediately a rooster crowed. 75Then Peter remembered the word Jesus had spoken: "Before the rooster crows, you will disown me three times."*b* And he went outside and wept bitterly.

Judas Hangs Himself

27 Early in the morning, all the chief priests and the elders of the people came to the decision to put Jesus to death.*c* 2They bound him, led him away and handed him over*d* to Pilate, the governor.*e*

3When Judas, who had betrayed him,*f* saw that Jesus was condemned, he was seized with remorse and returned the thirty silver coins*g* to the chief priests and the elders. 4"I have sinned," he said, "for I have betrayed innocent blood."

"What is that to us?" they replied. "That's your responsibility."*h*

5So Judas threw the money into the temple*i* and left. Then he went away and hanged himself.*j*

6The chief priests picked up the coins and said, "It is against the law to put this into the treasury, since it is blood money." 7So they decided to use the money to buy the potter's field as a burial place for foreigners. 8That is why it has been called the Field of Blood*k* to this day. 9Then what

Cross references (center column)

26:58 *l* ver 69; Mk 14:66; Lk 22:55;
Jn 18:15
k Mk 15:16; Lk 11:21; Jn 7:32, 45,46
26:59 *l* S Mt 5:22
26:60 *m* Ps 27:12; 35:11; Ac 6:13
n Dt 19:15
26:61 *o* S Jn 2:19
26:63 *p* S Mk 14:61
q Lev 5:1
r S Mt 16:16
s Lk 22:67
t S Mt 4:3
26:64 *u* Mt 27:11; Lk 22:70
v S Mk 16:19
w S Rev 1:7
26:65 *x* S Mk 14:63
26:66 *y* Lev 24:16; Jn 19:7
26:67 *z* S Mt 16:21
26:68 *a* Lk 22:63-65

26:75 *b* ver 34; Jn 13:38
27:1 *c* S Mt 12:14; Mk 15:1; Lk 22:66
27:2 *d* Mt 20:19 *e* Mk 15:1; Lk 13:1; Ac 3:13; 1Ti 6:13
27:3 *f* S Mt 10:4 *g* Mt 26:14,15
27:4 *h* ver 24
27:5 *i* Lk 1:9,21 *j* Ac 1:18
27:8 *k* Ac 1:19

g 63 Or *Messiah*; also in verse 68

26:59 *Sanhedrin.* See note on Mk 14:55.
26:61 *I am able to destroy the temple of God.* Evidently an intentional distortion of Jesus' words (Jn 2:19).
26:63 *I charge you under oath.* Jesus refused to answer the question of v. 62 (see v. 63a). But when the high priest used this form, he was legally obliged to reply.
26:65 *tore his clothes.* Ordinarily the high priest was forbidden by law to do this (Lev 10:6; 21:10), but this was considered a highly unusual circumstance. The high priest interpreted Jesus' answer in v. 64 as blasphemy (see note on Mk 14:64).
26:67-68 Mark reports that they blindfolded Jesus (Mk 14:65), which explains the mocking command: "Prophesy ... Who hit you?"

26:73 *your accent gives you away.* Peter had a decidedly Galilean accent that was conspicuous in Jerusalem.
27:1 *Early in the morning.* The Sanhedrin could not have a legal session at night, so at daybreak a special meeting was held to make the death sentence (see 26:66) official.
27:2 *handed him over to Pilate.* The Sanhedrin had been deprived by the Roman government of the right to carry out capital punishment, except in the case of a foreigner who invaded the sacred precincts of the temple. So Jesus had to be handed over to Pilate for execution. For additional information about Pilate see note on Mk 15:1.
27:3-10 See Ac 1:16-19.
27:5 *hanged himself.* See note on Ac 1:18.
27:8 *called the Field of Blood.* Cf. "the Valley of Slaugh-

was spoken by Jeremiah the prophet was fulfilled:[l] "They took the thirty silver coins, the price set on him by the people of Israel, [10]and they used them to buy the potter's field, as the Lord commanded me."[h][m]

Jesus Before Pilate

27:11-26pp — Mk 15:2-15; Lk 23:2,3; 18-25; Jn 18:29-19:16

[11]Meanwhile Jesus stood before the governor, and the governor asked him, "Are you the king of the Jews?"[n]

"Yes, it is as you say," Jesus replied.

[12]When he was accused by the chief priests and the elders, he gave no answer.[o] [13]Then Pilate asked him, "Don't you hear the testimony they are bringing against you?"[p] [14]But Jesus made no reply,[q] not even to a single charge—to the great amazement of the governor.

[15]Now it was the governor's custom at the Feast to release a prisoner[r] chosen by the crowd. [16]At that time they had a notorious prisoner, called Barabbas. [17]So when the crowd had gathered, Pilate asked them, "Which one do you want me to release to you: Barabbas, or Jesus who is called Christ?"[s] [18]For he knew it was out of envy that they had handed Jesus over to him.

[19]While Pilate was sitting on the judge's seat,[t] his wife sent him this message: "Don't have anything to do with that innocent[u] man, for I have suffered a great deal today in a dream[v] because of him."

[20]But the chief priests and the elders persuaded the crowd to ask for Barabbas and to have Jesus executed.[w]

[21]"Which of the two do you want me to release to you?" asked the governor.

"Barabbas," they answered.

[22]"What shall I do, then, with Jesus who is called Christ?"[x] Pilate asked.

They all answered, "Crucify him!"

[23]"Why? What crime has he committed?" asked Pilate.

But they shouted all the louder, "Crucify him!"

[24]When Pilate saw that he was getting nowhere, but that instead an uproar[y] was starting, he took water and washed his hands[z] in front of the crowd. "I am innocent of this man's blood,"[a] he said. "It is your responsibility!"[b]

[25]All the people answered, "Let his blood be on us and on our children!"[c]

[26]Then he released Barabbas to them. But he had Jesus flogged,[d] and handed him over to be crucified.

The Soldiers Mock Jesus

27:27-31pp — Mk 15:16-20

[27]Then the governor's soldiers took Jesus into the Praetorium[e] and gathered the whole company of soldiers around him. [28]They stripped him and put a scarlet robe on him,[f] [29]and then twisted together a crown of thorns and set it on his head. They put a staff in his right hand and knelt in front of him and mocked him. "Hail, king of the Jews!" they said.[g] [30]They spit on him, and took the staff and struck him on the head again and again.[h] [31]After they had mocked him, they took off the robe and put his own clothes on him. Then they led him away to crucify him.[i]

The Crucifixion

27:33-44pp — Mk 15:22-32; Lk 23:33-43; Jn 19:17-24

[32]As they were going out,[j] they met a man from Cyrene,[k] named Simon, and they forced him to carry the cross.[l] [33]They came to a place called Golgotha (which means The Place of the Skull).[m] [34]There they offered Jesus wine to drink, mixed with gall;[n] but after tasting it, he refused to drink it. [35]When they had crucified him, they divided up his clothes by casting lots.[i][o] [36]And sitting down, they kept

27:9 [l]S Mt 1:22
27:10 [m]Zec 11:12,13; Jer 32:6-9
27:11 [n]S Mt 2:2
27:12
[o]S Mk 14:61
27:13 [p]Mt 26:62
27:14
[q]S Mk 14:61
27:15 [r]Jn 18:39
27:17 [s]ver 22; Mt 1:16
27:19 [t]Jn 19:13 [u]ver 24 [v]Ge 20:6; Nu 12:6; 1Ki 3:5; Job 33:14-16; Mt 1:20; 2:12,13, 19,22
27:20 [w]Ac 3:14
27:22 [x]Mt 1:16

27:24 [y]Mt 26:5 [z]Ps 26:6 [a]Dt 21:6-8 [b]ver 4
27:25 [c]Jos 2:19; S Ac 5:28
27:26 [d]Isa 53:5; Jn 19:1
27:27 [e]Jn 18:28, 33; 19:9
27:28 [f]Jn 19:2
27:29 [g]Isa 53:3; Jn 19:2,3
27:30 [h]S Mt 16:21
27:31 [i]Isa 53:7
27:32 [j]Heb 13:12 [k]Ac 2:10; 6:9; 11:20; 13:1 [l]Mk 15:21; Lk 23:26
27:33 [m]Jn 19:17
27:34 [n]ver 48; Ps 69:21
27:35 [o]Ps 22:18

[h]10 See Zech. 11:12,13; Jer. 19:1-13; 32:6-9.   [i]35 A few late manuscripts *lots that the word spoken by the prophet might be fulfilled: "They divided my garments among themselves and cast lots for my clothing"* (Psalm 22:18)

---

ter" in Jer 19:6.

27:9 *Jeremiah.* The quotation that follows seems to be a combining of Zec 11:12-13 and Jer 19:1-13 (or perhaps Jer 18:2-12 or Jer 32:6-9). But Matthew attributes it to the major prophet Jeremiah, just as Mark (1:2-3) quotes Mal 3:1 and Isa 40:3 but attributes them to the major prophet Isaiah.

27:15 *the governor's custom.* Of which nothing is known outside the Gospels.

27:19 This incident is found only in Matthew's Gospel.

27:26 *flogged.* Roman floggings were so brutal that sometimes the victim died before crucifixion.

27:27 *Praetorium.* The governor's official residence in Jerusalem (see note on Mk 15:16).

27:28 *scarlet robe.* The outer cloak of a Roman soldier.

27:29 *staff.* A mock scepter.

27:32 *Cyrene.* A city in North Africa. *Simon . . . to carry the cross.* See note on Mk 15:21.

27:33 *Golgotha.* See note on Mk 15:22.

27:34 *mixed with gall.* Tradition says that the women of Jerusalem customarily furnished this pain-killing narcotic to prisoners who were crucified. Jesus refused to drink it because he wanted to be fully conscious until his death (v. 50).

27:35 *crucified.* See note on Mk 15:24. *casting lots.* Explained more precisely in Jn 19:23-24.

watch[p] over him there. [37]Above his head they placed the written charge against him: THIS IS JESUS, THE KING OF THE JEWS. [38]Two robbers were crucified with him,[q] one on his right and one on his left. [39]Those who passed by hurled insults at him, shaking their heads[r] [40]and saying, "You who are going to destroy the temple and build it in three days,[s] save yourself![t] Come down from the cross, if you are the Son of God!"[u]

[41]In the same way the chief priests, the teachers of the law and the elders mocked him. [42]"He saved others," they said, "but he can't save himself! He's the King of Israel![v] Let him come down now from the cross, and we will believe[w] in him. [43]He trusts in God. Let God rescue him[x] now if he wants him, for he said, 'I am the Son of God.'" [44]In the same way the robbers who were crucified with him also heaped insults on him.

The Death of Jesus

27:45–56pp — Mk 15:33–41; Lk 23:44–49

[45]From the sixth hour until the ninth hour darkness[y] came over all the land. [46]About the ninth hour Jesus cried out in a loud voice, *"Eloi, Eloi,*[i] *lama sabachthani?"*—which means, "My God, my God, why have you forsaken me?"[k] [z]

[47]When some of those standing there heard this, they said, "He's calling Elijah." [48]Immediately one of them ran and got a sponge. He filled it with wine vinegar,[a] put it on a stick, and offered it to Jesus to drink. [49]The rest said, "Now leave him alone. Let's see if Elijah comes to save him."

[50]And when Jesus had cried out again in a loud voice, he gave up his spirit.[b]

[51]At that moment the curtain of the temple[c] was torn in two from top to bottom. The earth shook and the rocks split.[d]

[52]The tombs broke open and the bodies of many holy people who had died were raised to life. [53]They came out of the tombs, and after Jesus' resurrection they went into the holy city[e] and appeared to many people.

[54]When the centurion and those with him who were guarding[f] Jesus saw the earthquake and all that had happened, they were terrified, and exclaimed, "Surely he was the Son[l] of God!"[g]

[55]Many women were there, watching from a distance. They had followed Jesus from Galilee to care for his needs.[h] [56]Among them were Mary Magdalene, Mary the mother of James and Joses, and the mother of Zebedee's sons.[i]

The Burial of Jesus

27:57–61pp — Mk 15:42–47; Lk 23:50–56; Jn 19:38–42

[57]As evening approached, there came a rich man from Arimathea, named Joseph, who had himself become a disciple of Jesus. [58]Going to Pilate, he asked for Jesus' body, and Pilate ordered that it be given to him. [59]Joseph took the body, wrapped it in a clean linen cloth, [60]and placed it in his own new tomb[j] that he had cut out of the rock. He rolled a big stone in front of the entrance to the tomb and went away. [61]Mary Magdalene and the other Mary were sitting there opposite the tomb.

The Guard at the Tomb

[62]The next day, the one after Preparation Day, the chief priests and the Pharisees went to Pilate. [63]"Sir," they said, "we remember that while he was still alive that deceiver said, 'After three days I will rise again.'[k] [64]So give the order for the tomb to be made secure until the third day. Otherwise, his disciples may come and steal the

Cross references (center column):

27:36 *p*ver 54
27:38 *q*Isa 53:12
27:39 *r*Ps 22:7; 109:25; La 2:15
27:40 *s*S Jn 2:19
*t*ver 42 *u*Mt 4:3,6
27:42 *v*Jn 1:49; 12:13 *w*S Jn 3:15
27:43 *x*Ps 22:8
27:45 *y*Am 8:9
27:46 *z*Ps 22:1
27:48 *a*ver 34; Ps 69:21
27:50 *b*Jn 19:30
27:51 *c*Ex 26:31-33; Heb 9:3,8; 10:19, 20 *d*ver 54

27:53 *e*S Mt 4:5
27:54 *f*ver 36 *g*S Mt4:3; 17:5
27:55 *h*Lk 8:2,3
27:56 *i*Mk 15:47; Lk 24:10; Jn 19:25
27:60 *j*Mt 27:66; 28:2; Mk 16:4; Ac 13:29
27:63 *k*S Mt 16:21

146 Some manuscripts *Eli, Eli*   k46 Psalm 22:1
154 Or *a son*

27:37 See note on Mk 15:26.
27:45 *From the sixth hour until the ninth hour.* From noon until 3:00 P.M.
27:46 *Eloi, Eloi, lama sabachthani?* A mixture of Aramaic and Hebrew, translated by Matthew for his readers (see note on Mk 15:34).
27:49 See note on Mk 15:35.
27:51 *curtain.* The inner curtain that separated the Holy Place from the Most Holy Place. The tearing of the curtain signified Christ's making it possible for believers to go directly into God's presence (see Heb 9:1–14; 10:14–22).
27:52–53 An incident found only in Matthew's Gospel, perhaps symbolic of Christ's conquering death through his redemptive work on the cross.
27:54 *centurion.* See note on 8:5. *Son of God.* It cannot be determined whether the centurion made a fully Christian confession, or whether he was only acknowledging that,

since the gods had so obviously acted to vindicate this judicial victim, Jesus must be one especially favored by them (see NIV text note). But in view of the ridicule voiced by the Jews (v. 40), it seems probable that Matthew intended the former. See note on Lk 23:47.
27:56 See note on Mk 15:40.
27:57 *Arimathea.* A village in the hill country of Ephraim, about 20 miles northwest of Jerusalem.
27:58 *asked for Jesus' body.* See note on Lk 23:52.
27:59–60 See note on Mk 15:46.
27:62 *The next day, the one after Preparation Day.* Saturday, the Sabbath. Friday was the preparation day for the Sabbath (sunset Friday to sunset Saturday).
27:64 *This last deception will be worse than the first.* The first would be that Jesus was the Messiah, the second that he had risen as the Son of God.

body[l] and tell the people that he has been raised from the dead. This last deception will be worse than the first."

65"Take a guard,"[m] Pilate answered. "Go, make the tomb as secure as you know how." 66So they went and made the tomb secure by putting a seal[n] on the stone[o] and posting the guard.[p]

The Resurrection

28:1–8pp — Mk 16:1–8; Lk 24:1–10

28 After the Sabbath, at dawn on the first day of the week, Mary Magdalene[q] and the other Mary[r] went to look at the tomb.

2There was a violent earthquake,[s] for an angel[t] of the Lord came down from heaven and, going to the tomb, rolled back the stone[u] and sat on it. 3His appearance was like lightning, and his clothes were white as snow.[v] 4The guards were so afraid of him that they shook and became like dead men.

5The angel said to the women, "Do not be afraid,[w] for I know that you are looking for Jesus, who was crucified. 6He is not here; he has risen, just as he said.[x] Come and see the place where he lay. 7Then go quickly and tell his disciples: 'He has risen from the dead and is going ahead of you into Galilee.[y] There you will see him.' Now I have told you."

8So the women hurried away from the tomb, afraid yet filled with joy, and ran to tell his disciples. 9Suddenly Jesus met them.[z] "Greetings," he said. They came to him, clasped his feet and worshiped him. 10Then Jesus said to them, "Do not

be afraid. Go and tell my brothers[a] to go to Galilee; there they will see me."

The Guards' Report

11While the women were on their way, some of the guards[b] went into the city and reported to the chief priests everything that had happened. 12When the chief priests had met with the elders and devised a plan, they gave the soldiers a large sum of money, 13telling them, "You are to say, 'His disciples came during the night and stole him away[c] while we were asleep.' 14If this report gets to the governor,[d] we will satisfy him and keep you out of trouble." 15So the soldiers took the money and did as they were instructed. And this story has been widely circulated among the Jews to this very day.

The Great Commission

16Then the eleven disciples went to Galilee, to the mountain where Jesus had told them to go.[e] 17When they saw him, they worshiped him; but some doubted. 18Then Jesus came to them and said, "All authority in heaven and on earth has been given to me.[f] 19Therefore go and make disciples of all nations,[g] baptizing them in[m] the name of the Father and of the Son and of the Holy Spirit,[h] 20and teaching[i] them to obey everything I have commanded you. And surely I am with you[j] always, to the very end of the age."[k]

m19 Or into; see Acts 8:16; 19:5; Romans 6:3; 1 Cor. 1:13; 10:2 and Gal. 3:27.

Cross references

27:64 lMt 28:13
27:65 mver 66; Mt 28:11
27:66 nDa 6:17
over 60; Mt 28:2
pMt 28:11
28:1 qLk 8:2
rMt 27:56
28:2 sMt 27:51
tJn 20:12;
S Ac 5:19
uMt 27:60
28:3 vDa 7:9;
10:6; Mk 9:3;
S Jn 20:12
28:5 wver 10;
S Mt 14:27
28:6 xS Mt 16:21
28:7 yver 10,16;
Mt 26:32
28:9 zJn 20:14-18
28:10 aMt 12:50;
25:40; Mk 3:34;
Jn 20:17;
Ro 8:29;
Heb 2:11-13,17
28:11 bMt 27:65, 66
28:13 cMt 27:64
28:14 dS Mt 27:2
28:16 ever 7,10;
Mt 26:32
28:18 fDa 7:13, 14; Lk 10:22;
Jn 3:35; S 13:13;
17:2; 1Co 15:27;
Eph 1:20-22;
Php 2:9,10
28:19 gIsa 49:6;
Mk 16:15,16;
Lk 24:47; Ac 1:8;
14:21 hAc 1:8;
2:38; 8:16;
Ro 6:3,4;
Gal 3:27;
Col 2:12
28:20 iJn 14:26;
Ac 2:42 jDt 31:6;
1Ki 8:57;
Hag 1:13;
Mt 18:20;
Ac 18:10
kMt 13:39; 24:3

Study notes

27:65 Take a guard. Pilate granted them a guard of Roman soldiers (28:4,11–12).

28:1 first day of the week. See note on Lk 24:1. the other Mary. The wife of Clopas and sister of the mother of Jesus (see 27:56; Jn 19:25).

28:2 There was. The sense is "Now there had been." It is clear from the parallel accounts (Mk 16:2–6; Lk 24:1–7; Jn 20:1) that the events of vv. 2–4 occurred before the women actually arrived at the tomb. a violent earthquake. Only Matthew mentions this earthquake and the one at Jesus' death (27:51,54).

28:11–15 Only Matthew tells of the posting of the guard (27:62–66), and he follows up by telling of their report.

28:16 eleven. Judas had committed suicide (27:5). had told them. See v. 10.

28:19 all nations. Contrast 10:5–6. baptizing them. As a sign of their union with and commitment to Christ (see notes on Ac 2:38; Ro 6:3–4).

28:20 with you. Matthew ends with the reassuring and empowering words of him who came to earth to be "God with us" (1:23).

MARK

See "The Synoptic Gospels," p. 1437.

Author

Although there is no direct internal evidence of authorship, it was the unanimous testimony of the early church that this Gospel was written by John Mark. The most important evidence comes from Papias (c. A.D. 140), who quotes an even earlier source as saying: (1) Mark was a close associate of Peter, from whom he received the tradition of the things said and done by the Lord; (2) this tradition did not come to Mark as a finished, sequential account of the life of our Lord, but as the preaching of Peter—preaching directed to the needs of the early Christian communities; (3) Mark accurately preserved this material. The conclusion drawn from this tradition is that the Gospel of Mark largely consists of the preaching of Peter arranged and shaped by John Mark (see note on Ac 10:37).

John Mark in the NT

It is generally agreed that the Mark who is associated with Peter in the early non-Biblical tradition is also the John Mark of the NT. The first mention of him is in connection with his mother, who had a house in Jerusalem that served as a meeting place for believers (Ac 12:12). When Paul and Barnabas returned to Antioch from Jerusalem after the famine visit, Mark accompanied them (Ac 12:25). Mark next appears as a "helper" to Paul and Barnabas on their first missionary journey (Ac 13:5), but he deserted them at Perga, in Pamphylia, to return to Jerusalem (Ac 13:13). Paul must have been deeply disappointed with Mark's actions on this occasion, because when Barnabas proposed taking Mark on the second journey, Paul flatly refused, a refusal that broke up their working relationship (Ac 15:36-39). Barnabas took Mark, who was his cousin, and departed for Cyprus. No further mention is made of either of them in the book of Acts. Mark reappears in Paul's letter to the Colossians written from Rome. Paul sends a greeting from Mark and adds: "You have received instructions about him; if he comes to you, welcome him" (Col 4:10; see Phm 24, written about the same time). At this point Mark was apparently beginning to win his way back into Paul's confidence. By the end of Paul's life, Mark had fully regained Paul's favor (see 2Ti 4:11).

Date of Composition

Some, who hold that Matthew and Luke used Mark as a major source, have suggested that Mark may have been composed in the 50s or early 60s. Others have felt that the content of the Gospel and statements made about Mark by the early church fathers indicate that the book was written shortly before the destruction of Jerusalem in A.D. 70. See chart on "Dating the Synoptic Gospels," p. 1437.

Place of Origin

According to early church tradition, Mark was written "in the regions of Italy" (Anti-Marcionite Prologue) or, more specifically, in Rome (Irenaeus and Clement of Alexandria). These same authors closely associate Mark's writing of the Gospel with the apostle Peter. The above evidence is consistent with (1) the historical probability that Peter was in Rome during the last days of his life and was martyred there, and (2) the Biblical evidence that Mark also was in Rome about the same time and was closely associated with Peter (see 2Ti 4:11; 1Pe 5:13, where the word "Babylon" is probably a cryptogram for Rome).

Recipients

The evidence points to the church at Rome or at least to Gentile readers. Mark explains Jewish customs (7:2-4; 15:42), translates Aramaic words (3:17; 5:41; 7:11,34; 15:22) and seems to have

a special interest in persecution and martyrdom (8:34-38; 13:9-13)—subjects of special concern to Roman believers. A Roman destination would explain the almost immediate acceptance of this Gospel and its rapid dissemination.

Occasion and Purpose

Since Mark's Gospel is traditionally associated with Rome, it may have been occasioned by the persecutions of the Roman church in the period c. A.D. 64-67. The famous fire of Rome in 64—probably set by Nero himself but blamed on Christians—resulted in widespread persecution. Even martyrdom was not unknown among Roman believers. Mark may be writing to prepare his readers for this suffering by placing before them the life of our Lord. There are many references, both explicit and veiled, to suffering and discipleship throughout his Gospel (see 1:12-13; 3:22,30; 8:34-38; 10:30,33-34,45; 13:8,11-13).

Emphases

1. *The cross.* Both the human cause (12:12; 14:1-2; 15:10) and the divine necessity (8:31; 9:31; 10:33) of the cross are emphasized by Mark.

2. *Discipleship.* Special attention should be paid to the passages on discipleship that arise from Jesus' predictions of his passion (8:34-9:1; 9:35-10:31; 10:42-45).

3. *The teachings of Jesus.* Although Mark records far fewer actual teachings of Jesus than the other Gospel writers, there is a remarkable emphasis on Jesus as teacher. The words "teacher," "teach" or "teaching," and "Rabbi" are applied to Jesus in Mark 39 times.

4. *The Messianic secret.* On several occasions Jesus warns his disciples or the person for whom he has worked a miracle to keep silent about who he is or what he has done (1:34,44; 3:12; 5:43; 7:36-37; 8:26,30; 9:9).

5. *Son of God.* Although Mark emphasizes the humanity of Jesus (see 3:5; 6:6,31,34; 7:34; 8:12,33; 10:14; 11:12), he does not neglect his deity (see 1:1,11; 3:11; 5:7; 9:7; 12:1-11; 13:32; 15:39).

Special Characteristics

Mark's Gospel is a simple, succinct, unadorned, yet vivid account of Jesus' ministry, emphasizing more what Jesus did than what he said. Mark moves quickly from one episode in Jesus' life and ministry to another, often using the adverb "immediately" (see note on 1:12). The book as a whole is characterized as "The beginning of the gospel" (1:1). The life, death and resurrection of Christ comprise the "beginning," of which the apostolic preaching in Acts is the continuation.

Outline

I. The Beginnings of Jesus' Ministry (1:1-13)
    A. His Forerunner (1:1-8)
    B. His Baptism (1:9-11)
    C. His Temptation (1:12-13)
II. Jesus' Ministry in Galilee (1:14-6:29)
    A. Early Galilean Ministry (1:14-3:12)
        1. Call of the first disciples (1:14-20)
        2. Miracles in Capernaum (1:21-34)
        3. A tour of Galilee (1:35-45)
        4. Ministry in Capernaum (2:1-22)
        5. Sabbath controversy (2:23-3:12)
    B. Later Galilean Ministry (3:13-6:29)
        1. Selection of the 12 apostles (3:13-19)
        2. Teachings in Capernaum (3:20-35)
        3. Parables of the kingdom (4:1-34)
        4. Trip across the Sea of Galilee (4:35-5:20)
        5. More Galilean miracles (5:21-43)
        6. Unbelief in Jesus' hometown (6:1-6)
        7. Six apostolic teams tour Galilee (6:7-13)
        8. King Herod's reaction to Jesus' ministry (6:14-29)
III. Withdrawals from Galilee (6:30-9:32)
    A. To the Eastern Shore of the Sea of Galilee (6:30-52)
    B. To the Western Shore of the Sea of Galilee (6:53-7:23)

John the Baptist Prepares the Way

1:2–8pp — Mt 3:1–11; Lk 3:2–16

1 The beginning of the gospel about Jesus Christ, the Son of God.ᵃ ᵃ

²It is written in Isaiah the prophet:

"I will send my messenger ahead of
    you,
    who will prepare your way"ᵇ ᵇ —
³"a voice of one calling in the desert,
'Prepare the way for the Lord,
    make straight paths for him.' "ᶜ ᶜ

⁴And so Johnᵈ came, baptizing in the desert region and preaching a baptism of repentanceᵉ for the forgiveness of sins.ᶠ ⁵The whole Judean countryside and all the people of Jerusalem went out to him. Confessing their sins, they were baptized by him in the Jordan River. ⁶John wore clothing made of camel's hair, with a leather belt around his waist,ᵍ and he ate locustsʰ and wild honey. ⁷And this was his message: "After me will come one more powerful than I, the thongs of whose sandals I am not worthy to stoop down and untie.ⁱ

⁸I baptize you withᵈ water, but he will baptize you with the Holy Spirit."ʲ

The Baptism and Temptation of Jesus

1:9–11pp — Mt 3:13–17; Lk 3:21,22
1:12,13pp — Mt 4:1–11; Lk 4:1–13

⁹At that time Jesus came from Nazarethᵏ in Galilee and was baptized by Johnˡ in the Jordan. ¹⁰As Jesus was coming up out of the water, he saw heaven being torn open and the Spirit descending on him like a dove.ᵐ ¹¹And a voice came from heaven: "You are my Son,ⁿ whom I love; with you I am well pleased."ᵒ

¹²At once the Spirit sent him out into the desert, ¹³and he was in the desert forty days,ᵖ being tempted by Satan. q He was with the wild animals, and angels attended him.

The Calling of the First Disciples

1:16–20pp — Mt 4:18–22; Lk 5:2–11; Jn 1:35–42

¹⁴After Johnʳ was put in prison, Jesus went into Galilee,ˢ proclaiming the good news of God.ᵗ ¹⁵"The time has come,"ᵘ

Cross references:
1:1 ᵃS Mt 4:3
1:2 ᵇMal 3:1; Mt 11:10; Lk 7:27
1:3 ᶜIsa 40:3; Jn 1:23
1:4 ᵈS Mt 3:1 ᵉver 8; Jn 1:26, 33; Ac 1:5,22; 11:16; 13:24; 18:25; 19:3,4 ᶠLk 1:77
1:6 ᵍ2Ki 1:8 ʰLev 11:22
1:7 ⁱAc 13:25
1:8 ʲIsa 44:3; Joel 2:28; Jn 1:33; Ac 1:5; 2:4; 11:16; 19:4-6
1:9 ᵏS Mt 2:23 ˡS Mt 3:1
1:10 ᵐJn 1:32 ⁿS Mt 3:17 ᵒS Mt 3:17
1:13 ᵖEx 24:18; 1Ki 19:8 qS Mt 4:10; Heb 4:15
1:14 ʳS Mt 3:1 ˢMt 4:12 ᵗMt 4:23
1:15 ᵘRo 5:6; Gal 4:4; Eph 1:10

ᵃ*1* Some manuscripts do not have *the Son of God.*
ᵇ*2* Mal. 3:1   ᶜ*3* Isaiah 40:3   ᵈ*8* Or *in*

1:1 *The beginning.* See Introduction: Special Characteristics; suggests the opening verse of Genesis (see Jn 1:1). *gospel.* From the Old English *godspel,* "good story" or "good news," which accurately translates the Greek. The good news is that God has provided salvation through the life, death and resurrection of Jesus Christ. *Jesus.* See NIV text note on Mt 1:21. *Christ.* See NIV text note on Mt 1:17.
1:2–3 *in Isaiah the prophet.* The quotation that immediately follows (see first two poetry lines) comes from Mal 3:1 but is followed by one from Isa 40:3 (see note on Mt 27:9). Understanding the ministry of Jesus must begin with the OT. What Isaiah says about God applies to Jesus, his Son (v. 1). The passages cited speak of the messenger, the desert and the Lord, each of which is stressed in vv. 4–8.
1:4 *John came.* Mark, like John, has no nativity narrative, but begins with the ministry of John the Baptist. The name John means "The Lord is gracious." *baptizing.* John's practice of baptizing those who came to him in repentance was so characteristic of his ministry that he became known as "the Baptist" or "the Baptizer." *the desert region.* The arid region west of the Dead Sea, whose inhabitants included those who wrote and preserved the Dead Sea Scrolls. *repentance.* Involves deliberate turning from sin to righteousness, and John's emphasis on repentance recalls the preaching of the prophets (e.g., Hos 3:4–5). God always grants forgiveness when there is repentance. *baptism.* John was preaching repentance-baptism, i.e., baptism that was preceded or accompanied by repentance. Baptism was not new to John's audience. They knew of baptism for Gentile converts, but had not heard that the descendants of Abraham (Jews) needed to repent and be baptized.
1:5 *whole ... all.* Obvious hyperbole, indicating the high interest created by John's preaching. For centuries Israel had had no prophet. *Jordan River.* The principal river in Palestine, beginning in the snows of Mount Hermon and ending in the Dead Sea. Its closest point to Jerusalem is about 20 miles.
1:6 *camel's hair ... leather belt.* Worn by Elijah and other prophets (2Ki 1:8; cf. Zec 13:4). *locusts and wild honey.* See

note on Mt 3:4.
1:7–8 *message.* Mark's account of John's message is brief (cf. Mt 3:7–12; Lk 3:7–17) and focuses on the coming of the powerful One.
1:8 *baptize you with the Holy Spirit.* See note on Mt 3:11.
1:9 *At that time.* Jesus probably began his public ministry c. A.D. 27, when he was approximately 30 years old (Lk 3:23). As far as we know, he had spent most of his previous life in Nazareth. *Nazareth.* See note on Mt 2:23. *baptized by John.* For the significance of Jesus' baptism see Mt 3:15 and note.
1:10–11 All three persons of the Trinity are involved: (1) the Father speaks, (2) the Son is baptized, and (3) the Holy Spirit descends on the Son.
1:10 *the Spirit descending on him.* Jesus' anointing for ministry—an anointing he claimed in the synagogue at Nazareth (Lk 4:18). *like a dove.* Symbolizing the gentleness, purity and guilelessness of the Holy Spirit (see Mt 10:16).
1:11 An allusion to Ps 2:7 and Isa 42:1. *a voice.* God sometimes spoke directly from heaven (see 9:7; Jn 12:28–29). *You are my Son.* In v. 1 Mark proclaims Jesus as the Son of God; here God the Father himself proclaims Jesus as his Son.
1:12 *At once.* A distinctive characteristic of Mark's style is his use (some 47 times) of a Greek word that has been variously translated "at once," "immediately," "quickly," "just then" (see, e.g., vv. 18,20,23,28–29,42–43).
1:13 *forty.* See note on Mt 4:2. *tempted.* See notes on Mt 4:1–11. *Satan.* See notes on Ge 3:1; Zec 3:1; Rev 2:9–10; 12:9–10. *wild animals.* In Jesus' day there were many more wild animals—including lions—in Palestine than today. Only Mark reports their presence in this connection; he emphasizes that God kept Jesus safe in the desert. *angels attended him.* As they had attended Israel in the desert (see Ex 23:20,23; 32:34).
1:14 *After John was put in prison.* See Mt 4:12 and note on Lk 3:20. *the good news of God.* The good news from, as well as about, God.
1:15 *The kingdom of God.* See note on Mt 3:2. *is near.*

he said. "The kingdom of God is near. Repent and believe[v] the good news!"[w]

16As Jesus walked beside the Sea of Galilee, he saw Simon and his brother Andrew casting a net into the lake, for they were fishermen. 17"Come, follow me," Jesus said, "and I will make you fishers of men." 18At once they left their nets and followed him.[x]

19When he had gone a little farther, he saw James son of Zebedee and his brother John in a boat, preparing their nets. 20Without delay he called them, and they left their father Zebedee in the boat with the hired men and followed him.

Jesus Drives Out an Evil Spirit

1:21–28pp — Lk 4:31–37

21They went to Capernaum, and when the Sabbath came, Jesus went into the synagogue and began to teach.[y] 22The people were amazed at his teaching, because he taught them as one who had authority, not as the teachers of the law.[z] 23Just then a man in their synagogue who was possessed with an evil[e] spirit cried out, 24"What do you want with us,[a] Jesus of Nazareth?[b] Have you come to destroy us? I know who you are—the Holy One of God!"[c]

25"Be quiet!" said Jesus sternly. "Come out of him!"[d] 26The evil spirit shook the man violently and came out of him with a shriek.[e]

27The people were all so amazed[f] that they asked each other, "What is this? A new teaching—and with authority! He even gives orders to evil spirits and they obey him." 28News about him spread quickly over the whole region[g] of Galilee.

Jesus Heals Many

1:29–31pp — Mt 8:14,15; Lk 4:38,39
1:32–34pp — Mt 8:16,17; Lk 4:40,41

29As soon as they left the synagogue,[h] they went with James and John to the home of Simon and Andrew. 30Simon's mother-in-law was in bed with a fever, and they told Jesus about her. 31So he went to her, took her hand and helped her up.[i] The fever left her and she began to wait on them.

32That evening after sunset the people brought to Jesus all the sick and demon-possessed.[j] 33The whole town gathered at the door, 34and Jesus healed many who had various diseases.[k] He also drove out many demons, but he would not let the demons speak because they knew who he was.[l]

Cross references (center column):
1:15 vS Jn 3:15; wAc 20:21
1:18 xS Mt 4:19
1:21 yver 39; S Mt 4:23; S Mk 10:1
1:22 zS Mt 7:28,29
1:24 aS Mt 8:29; bMt 2:23; Lk 24:19; Jn 1:45,46; Ac 4:10; 24:5; cPs 16:10; Isa 41:14,16,20; Lk 1:35; Jn 6:69; Ac 3:14; 1Jn 2:20
1:25 dver 34
1:26 eMk 9:20
1:27 fMk 10:24,32
1:28 gS Mt 9:26
1:29 hver 21,23
1:31 iS Lk 7:14
1:32 jS Mt 4:24
1:34 kS Mt 4:23; lMk 3:12; Ac 16:17,18

e23 Greek *unclean*; also in verses 26 and 27

The coming of Christ (the King) brings the kingdom near to the people.

1:16 *Sea of Galilee.* A beautiful lake, almost 700 feet below sea level, 14 miles long and 6 miles wide, fed by the waters of the upper Jordan River. It was also called the Lake of Gennesaret (Lk 5:1) and the Sea of Tiberias (Jn 6:1; 21:1). In OT times it was known as the Sea of Kinnereth (e.g., Nu 34:11). *Simon.* Probably a contraction of the OT name Simeon (see NIV text note on Ac 15:14). Jesus gave Simon the name Peter (3:16; Mt 16:18; Jn 1:42). *net.* See note on Mt 4:18.

1:17 *Come, follow me.* The call to discipleship is definite and demands a response of total commitment. This was not Jesus' first encounter with Simon and Andrew (see Jn 1:35–42). *fishers of men.* Evangelists (see Lk 5:10).

1:21 *Capernaum.* See note on Mt 4:13. *synagogue.* A very important religious institution among the Jews of that day. Originating during the exile, it provided a place where Jews could study the Scriptures and worship God. A synagogue could be established in any town where there were at least ten married Jewish men. *began to teach.* Jesus, like Paul (see Ac 13:15; 14:1; 17:2; 18:4), took advantage of the custom that allowed visiting teachers to participate in the worship service by invitation of the synagogue leaders.

1:22 *amazed.* Mark frequently reported the amazement that Jesus' teaching and actions produced (see 2:12; 5:20, 42; 6:2,51; 7:37; 10:26; 11:18; see also 15:5). In these instances it was Christ's inherent authority that amazed. He did not quote human authorities, as did the teachers of the law, because his authority was directly from God. *teachers of the law.* See note on Mt 2:4.

1:23 *a man in their synagogue . . . cried out.* It was actually the demon who cried out. *possessed by an evil spirit.* Demonic possession intended to torment and destroy those who are created in God's image, but the demon recognized that Jesus was a powerful adversary, capable of destroying the forces of Satan.

1:24 *the Holy One of God.* Apart from the parallel in Lk 4:34, the title is used elsewhere only in Jn 6:69 and points to Christ's divine origin rather than his Messiahship (see Lk 1:35). The name was perhaps used by the demons in accordance with the occult belief that the precise use of a person's name gave certain control over him. The man was possessed by more than one demon (see 5:9), but only one spoke.

1:25 *Be quiet!* Lit. "Be muzzled!" Jesus' superior power silences the shrieks of the demon-possessed man.

1:27 *with authority.* Jesus' authority in how he taught (v. 22) and in what he did (here) impressed the people.

1:29 *to the home of Simon and Andrew.* Jesus and the disciples probably went there for a meal, since the main Sabbath meal was served immediately following the synagogue service.

1:30 *Simon's mother-in-law.* 1Co 9:5 speaks of Peter's being married.

1:32 *the people brought.* They waited until the Sabbath was over (after sunset) before carrying anything (see Jer 17:21–22).

1:34 *because they knew who he was.* Luke says, "because they knew he was the Christ" (Lk 4:41). Jesus probably wanted first to show by word and deed the kind of Messiah he was (in contrast to popular notions) before he clearly declared himself, and he would not let the demons frustrate this intent.

Jesus Prays in a Solitary Place

1:35–38pp — Lk 4:42,43

35Very early in the morning, while it was still dark, Jesus got up, left the house and went off to a solitary place, where he prayed. *m* 36Simon and his companions went to look for him, 37and when they found him, they exclaimed: "Everyone is looking for you!"

38Jesus replied, "Let us go somewhere else—to the nearby villages—so I can preach there also. That is why I have come." *n* 39So he traveled throughout Galilee, preaching in their synagogues *o* and driving out demons. *p*

A Man With Leprosy

1:40–44pp — Mt 8:2–4; Lk 5:12–14

40A man with leprosy*f* came to him and begged him on his knees, *q* "If you are willing, you can make me clean."

41Filled with compassion, Jesus reached out his hand and touched the man. "I am willing," he said. "Be clean!" 42Immediately the leprosy left him and he was cured.

43Jesus sent him away at once with a strong warning: 44"See that you don't tell this to anyone. *r* But go, show yourself to the priest *s* and offer the sacrifices that Moses commanded for your cleansing, *t* as a testimony to them." 45Instead he went out and began to talk freely, spreading the news. As a result, Jesus could no longer

enter a town openly but stayed outside in lonely places. *u* Yet the people still came to him from everywhere. *v*

Jesus Heals a Paralytic

2:3–12pp — Mt 9:2–8; Lk 5:18–26

2 A few days later, when Jesus again entered Capernaum, the people heard that he had come home. 2So many *w* gathered that there was no room left, not even outside the door, and he preached the word to them. 3Some men came, bringing to him a paralytic, *x* carried by four of them. 4Since they could not get him to Jesus because of the crowd, they made an opening in the roof above Jesus and, after digging through it, lowered the mat the paralyzed man was lying on. 5When Jesus saw their faith, he said to the paralytic, "Son, your sins are forgiven." *y*

6Now some teachers of the law were sitting there, thinking to themselves, 7"Why does this fellow talk like that? He's blaspheming! Who can forgive sins but God alone?" *z*

8Immediately Jesus knew in his spirit that this was what they were thinking in their hearts, and he said to them, "Why are you thinking these things? 9Which is easier: to say to the paralytic, 'Your sins are forgiven,' or to say, 'Get up, take your mat and walk'? 10But that you may know that the Son of Man *a* has authority on

---

Cross references (center column):

1:35 *m*S Lk 3:21
1:38 *n*Isa 61:1
1:39 *o*S Mt 4:23
*p*S Mt 4:24
1:40 *q*Mk 10:17
1:44 *r*S Mt 8:4
*s*Lev 13:49
*t*Lev 14:1-32

1:45 *u*Lk 5:15,16
*v*Mk 2:13;
Lk 5:17; Jn 6:2
2:2 *w*ver 13;
Mk 1:45
2:3 *x*S Mt 4:24
2:5 *y*Lk 7:48
2:7 *z*Isa 43:25
2:10 *a*S Mt 8:20

---

*f*40 The Greek word was used for various diseases affecting the skin—not necessarily leprosy.

1:36 *companions.* Andrew, James, John and perhaps Philip and Nathanael (cf. Jn 1:43–45).

1:39 *throughout Galilee.* The first of what seem to be three tours of Galilee (second tour, Lk 8:1; third tour, Mk 6:6 and Mt 11:1).

1:40 *leprosy.* See NIV text note and Lev 13–14.

1:41 *touched the man.* An act that, according to Mosaic law, brought defilement (see Lev 13, especially vv. 45–46; cf. Lev 5:2). Jesus' compassion for the man superseded ceremonial considerations.

1:44 *don't tell this to anyone.* See notes on Mt 8:4; 16:20. *go, show yourself to the priest.* See note on Lk 5:14. *a testimony to them.* The sacrifices were to be evidence to the priests and the people that the cure was real and that Jesus respected the law. The healing was also a testimony to Jesus' divine power, since Jews believed that only God could cure leprosy (see 2Ki 5:1–14).

1:45 *no longer enter a town openly.* Jesus' growing popularity with the people (see 1:28; 3:7–8; Lk 7:17) and the increasing opposition from Jewish leaders (see 2:6–7,16, 23–24; 3:2,6,22) finally made it necessary for him to withdraw from Galilee into surrounding territories.

2:1 *home.* When in Capernaum, Jesus probably made his home at Peter's house (see 1:21,29).

2:2 *So many gathered.* The same enthusiasm that greeted Jesus earlier (1:32–33,37) was evident at his return.

2:3 *a paralytic.* Nothing definite can be said about the

nature of the man's affliction beyond the fact that he could not walk. The determination of the four men to reach Jesus suggests that his condition was desperate.

2:4 *they made an opening in the roof.* A typical Palestinian house had a flat roof accessible by means of an outside staircase. The roof was often made of a thick layer of clay (packed with a stone roller), supported by mats of branches across wood beams.

2:5 *When Jesus saw their faith.* Jesus recognized that the bold action of the paralyzed man and his friends gave evidence of faith. *Son, your sins are forgiven.* Jesus first met the man's deepest need: forgiveness.

2:7 *He's blaspheming! Who can forgive sins but God alone?* In Jewish theology even the Messiah could not forgive sins, and Jesus' forgiveness of sin was a claim to deity—which they considered to be blasphemous (see note on 14:64).

2:9 *Which is easier . . . ?* Jesus' point probably was that neither forgiving sins nor healing was easier. Both are equally impossible to men and equally easy to God.

2:10 *But that you may know.* Probably spoken to the teachers of the law. The words "He said to the paralytic" are parenthetical to explain a change in the persons addressed. For a discussion of the title "Son of Man" see note on 8:31. It is clear that one purpose of miracles was to give evidence of Jesus' deity. See the use of miraculous signs in John's Gospel (2:11; 20:30–31).

earth to forgive sins . . . ." He said to the paralytic, [11]"I tell you, get up, take your mat and go home." [12]He got up, took his mat and walked out in full view of them all. This amazed everyone and they praised God, [b] saying, "We have never seen anything like this!" [c]

The Calling of Levi

2:14–17pp — Mt 9:9–13; Lk 5:27–32

[13]Once again Jesus went out beside the lake. A large crowd came to him, [d] and he began to teach them. [14]As he walked along, he saw Levi son of Alphaeus sitting at the tax collector's booth. "Follow me," [e] Jesus told him, and Levi got up and followed him.

[15]While Jesus was having dinner at Levi's house, many tax collectors and "sinners" were eating with him and his disciples, for there were many who followed him. [16]When the teachers of the law who were Pharisees[f] saw him eating with the "sinners" and tax collectors, they asked his disciples: "Why does he eat with tax collectors and 'sinners'?" [g]

[17]On hearing this, Jesus said to them, "It is not the healthy who need a doctor, but the sick. I have not come to call the righteous, but sinners." [h]

Cross references (center column)

2:12 [b]S Mt 9:8
[c]Mt 9:33
2:13 [d]Mk 1:45; Lk 5:15; Jn 6:2
2:14 [e]S Mt 4:19
[g]S Mt 9:11
2:16 [f]Ac 23:9
2:17 [h]Lk 19:10; 1Ti 1:15

2:18 [i]S Mt 6:16–18; Ac 13:2
2:20 [j]Lk 17:22
2:23 [k]Dt 23:25
2:24 [l]S Mt 12:2

Jesus Questioned About Fasting

2:18–22pp — Mt 9:14–17; Lk 5:33–38

[18]Now John's disciples and the Pharisees were fasting. [i] Some people came and asked Jesus, "How is it that John's disciples and the disciples of the Pharisees are fasting, but yours are not?"

[19]Jesus answered, "How can the guests of the bridegroom fast while he is with them? They cannot, so long as they have him with them. [20]But the time will come when the bridegroom will be taken from them, [j] and on that day they will fast.

[21]"No one sews a patch of unshrunk cloth on an old garment. If he does, the new piece will pull away from the old, making the tear worse. [22]And no one pours new wine into old wineskins. If he does, the wine will burst the skins, and both the wine and the wineskins will be ruined. No, he pours new wine into new wineskins."

Lord of the Sabbath

2:23–28pp — Mt 12:1–8; Lk 6:1–5
3:1–6pp — Mt 12:9–14; Lk 6:6–11

[23]One Sabbath Jesus was going through the grainfields, and as his disciples walked along, they began to pick some heads of grain. [k] [24]The Pharisees said to him, "Look, why are they doing what is unlawful on the Sabbath?" [l]

2:12 *This amazed everyone.* See note on 1:22.
2:14 *Levi son of Alphaeus.* Matthew (see Mt 9:9; 10:3). His given name was probably Levi, and Matthew ("gift of the LORD") his apostolic name. *tax collector's booth.* Levi was a tax collector (see note on Lk 3:12) under Herod Antipas, tetrarch of Galilee. The tax collector's booth where Jesus found Levi was probably a toll booth on the major international road that went from Damascus through Capernaum to the Mediterranean coast and to Egypt (see the "way of the sea," Isa 9:1). *Levi got up and followed.* See note on Lk 5:28.
2:15 *sinners.* Notoriously evil people as well as those who refused to follow the Mosaic law as interpreted by the teachers of the law. The term was commonly used of tax collectors, adulterers, robbers and the like. *were eating.* To eat with a person was a sign of friendship.
2:16 *teachers of the law who were Pharisees.* Not all teachers of the law were Pharisees—successors of the Hasidim, pious Jews who joined forces with the Maccabees during the struggle for freedom from Syrian oppression (166–142 B.C.). They first appear under the name Pharisees during the reign of John Hyrcanus (135–105). Although some, no doubt, were godly, most of those who came into conflict with Jesus were hypocritical, envious, rigid and formalistic. According to Pharisaism, God's grace extended only to those who kept his law. See notes on Mt 3:7; Lk 5:17. *tax collectors.* Jewish tax collectors were regarded as outcasts. They could not serve as witnesses or as judges and were expelled from the synagogue. In the eyes of the Jewish community their disgrace extended to their families. See note on Mt 5:46.
2:17 *I have not come to call the righteous, but sinners.* A self-righteous man does not realize his need for salvation, but

an admitted sinner does.
2:18 *John's disciples.* John the Baptist's disciples may have been fasting because he was in prison (see 1:14), or this may have been a practice among them as an expression of repentance, intended to hasten the coming of redemption announced by John. *disciples of the Pharisees.* Pharisees as such were not teachers, but some were also "scribes" (teachers of the law), who often had disciples. Or perhaps the phrase is used in a nontechnical way to refer to people influenced by the Pharisees. *fasting.* In the Mosaic law only the fast of the Day of Atonement was required (Lev 16:29, 31; 23:27–32; Nu 29:7). After the Babylonian exile four other yearly fasts were observed by the Jews (Zec 7:5; 8:19). In Jesus' time the Pharisees fasted twice a week (see Lk 18:12).
2:19 *How can the guests of the bridegroom fast while he is with them?* Jesus compared his disciples with the guests of a bridegroom. A Jewish wedding was a particularly joyous occasion, and the celebration associated with it often lasted a week. It was unthinkable to fast during such festivities, because fasting was associated with sorrow.
2:20 *when the bridegroom will be taken from them.* Jesus is the bridegroom, who would be taken from them by death, and then fasting would be in order.
2:22 *new wineskins.* See note on Mt 9:17.
2:23 *pick some heads of grain.* There was nothing wrong in the action itself, which comes under the provision of Dt 23:25.
2:24 *what is unlawful on the Sabbath.* According to Jewish tradition (in the Mishnah), harvesting (which is what Jesus' disciples technically were doing) was forbidden on the Sabbath. See Ex 34:21.

²⁵He answered, "Have you never read what David did when he and his companions were hungry and in need? ²⁶In the days of Abiathar the high priest, *m* he entered the house of God and ate the consecrated bread, which is lawful only for priests to eat. *n* And he also gave some to his companions." *o*

²⁷Then he said to them, "The Sabbath was made for man, *p* not man for the Sabbath. *q* ²⁸So the Son of Man *r* is Lord even of the Sabbath."

3 Another time he went into the synagogue, *s* and a man with a shriveled hand was there. ²Some of them were looking for a reason to accuse Jesus, so they watched him closely *t* to see if he would heal him on the Sabbath. *u* ³Jesus said to the man with the shriveled hand, "Stand up in front of everyone."

⁴Then Jesus asked them, "Which is lawful on the Sabbath: to do good or to do evil, to save life or to kill?" But they remained silent.

⁵He looked around at them in anger and, deeply distressed at their stubborn hearts, said to the man, "Stretch out your hand." He stretched it out, and his hand was completely restored. ⁶Then the Phari-

sees went out and began to plot with the Herodians *v* how they might kill Jesus. *w*

Crowds Follow Jesus

3:7–12pp — Mt 12:15,16; Lk 6:17–19

⁷Jesus withdrew with his disciples to the lake, and a large crowd from Galilee followed. *x* ⁸When they heard all he was doing, many people came to him from Judea, Jerusalem, Idumea, and the regions across the Jordan and around Tyre and Sidon. *y* ⁹Because of the crowd he told his disciples to have a small boat ready for him, to keep the people from crowding him. ¹⁰For he had healed many, *z* so that those with diseases were pushing forward to touch him. *a* ¹¹Whenever the evil⁸ spirits saw him, they fell down before him and cried out, "You are the Son of God." *b* ¹²But he gave them strict orders not to tell who he was. *c*

The Appointing of the Twelve Apostles

3:16–19pp — Mt 10:2–4; Lk 6:14–16; Ac 1:13

¹³Jesus went up on a mountainside and called to him those he wanted, and they came to him. *d* ¹⁴He appointed

Cross references (center column):

2:26 *m* 1Ch 24:6; 2Sa 8:17
n Lev 24:5-9
o 1Sa 21:1-6
2:27 *p* Ex 23:12; Dt 5:14 *q* Col 2:16
2:28 *r* S Mt 8:20
3:1 *s* S Mt 4:23; Mk 1:21
3:2 *t* S Mt 12:10
u Lk 14:1

3:6 *v* Mt 22:16; Mk 12:13
w S Mt 12:14
3:7 *x* Mt 4:25
3:8 *y* S Mt 11:21
3:10 *z* S Mt 4:23
a S Mt 9:20
3:11 *b* S Mt 4:3; Mk 1:23,24
3:12 *c* S Mt 8:4; Mk 1:24,25,34; Ac 16:17,18
3:13 *d* Mt 5:1

⁸*11* Greek *unclean;* also in verse 30

2:25 *what David did.* See 1Sa 21:1–6. The relationship between the OT incident and the apparent infringement of the Sabbath by the disciples lies in the fact that on both occasions godly men did something forbidden. Since, however, it is always "lawful" to do good and to save life (even on the Sabbath), both David and the disciples were within the spirit of the law (see Isa 58:6–7; Lk 6:6–11; 13:10–17; 14:1–6).

2:26 *In the days of Abiathar the high priest.* According to 1Sa 21:1, Ahimelech, Abiathar's father, was then high priest (see note on 2Sa 8:17). *consecrated bread.* See note on Mt 12:4.

2:27 *The Sabbath was made for man, not man for the Sabbath.* Jewish tradition had so multiplied the requirements and restrictions for keeping the Sabbath that the burden had become intolerable. Jesus cut across these traditions and emphasized the God-given purpose of the Sabbath—a day intended for man (for spiritual, mental and physical restoration; see Ex 20:8–11).

2:28 See note on Lk 6:5.

3:1–6 A demonstration that Jesus is Lord of the Sabbath (see 2:28).

3:2 *Some of them.* The Pharisees (v. 6; cf. Lk 6:7). *to accuse Jesus.* Jesus' presence demanded a decision about his preaching, his acts and his person. The hostility, first seen in 2:6–7, continues to spread. See note on v. 6. *to see if he would heal him on the Sabbath.* An indication that the Pharisees believed in Jesus' power to perform miracles. The question was not "Could he?" but "Would he?" Jewish tradition prescribed that aid could be given the sick on the Sabbath only when the person's life was threatened, which obviously was not the case here. See notes on 2:25; Lk 13:14.

3:4 *to do good or to do evil, to save life or to kill?* Jesus asks: Which is better, to preserve life by healing or to destroy

life by refusing to heal? The question is ironic since, whereas Jesus was ready to heal, the Pharisees were plotting to put him to death. It is obvious who was guilty of breaking the Sabbath. *they remained silent.* See 12:34.

3:6 *the Pharisees . . . began to plot.* The decision to seek Jesus' death was not the result of this incident alone, but was the response to a series of incidents (see 2:6–7,16–17,24). The plotting of the Pharisees and the Herodians is seen again on Tuesday of Passion Week (12:13). *Herodians.* Influential Jews who favored the Herodian dynasty, meaning they were supporters of Rome, from which the Herods received their authority. They joined the Pharisees in opposing Jesus because they feared he might have an unsettling political influence on the people. See note on Mt 22:15–17.

3:8 Here we see impressive evidence of Jesus' rapidly growing popularity among the people. This geographical list indicates that the crowds came not only from the areas in the vicinity of Capernaum but also from considerable distances. The regions mentioned included virtually all of Israel and its surrounding neighbors. Mark tells of Jesus' work in all these regions except Idumea (see 1:14, Galilee; 5:1 and 10:1, the region across the Jordan; 7:24,31, Tyre and Sidon; 10:1, Judea; 11:11, Jerusalem). *Idumea.* The Greek form of the Hebrew "Edom," but here referring to an area in western Palestine south of Judea, not to earlier Edomite territory. (See map on p. 1542).

3:11 *the evil spirits.* See note on 1:23. *You are the Son of God.* The evil spirits recognized who Jesus was, but they did not believe in him (see note on 1:24).

3:12 *not to tell who he was.* The time for revealing Jesus' identity had not yet come (see 1:34 and note; see also notes on Mt 8:4; 16:20), and demons were hardly the proper channel for such disclosure.

3:14 *designating them apostles.* See note on 6:30. *that they might be with him.* The training of the Twelve included

twelve—designating them apostles[h][e] —that they might be with him and that he might send them out to preach [15]and to have authority to drive out demons.[f] [16]These are the twelve he appointed: Simon (to whom he gave the name Peter);[g] [17]James son of Zebedee and his brother John (to them he gave the name Boanerges, which means Sons of Thunder); [18]Andrew, Philip, Bartholomew, Matthew, Thomas, James son of Alphaeus, Thaddaeus, Simon the Zealot [19]and Judas Iscariot, who betrayed him.

Jesus and Beelzebub

3:23–27pp — Mt 12:25–29; Lk 11:17–22

[20]Then Jesus entered a house, and again a crowd gathered,[h] so that he and his disciples were not even able to eat.[i] [21]When his family heard about this, they went to take charge of him, for they said, "He is out of his mind."[j]

[22]And the teachers of the law who came down from Jerusalem[k] said, "He is possessed by Beelzebub[i]![l] By the prince of demons he is driving out demons."[m]

[23]So Jesus called them and spoke to them in parables:[n] "How can Satan[o] drive out Satan? [24]If a kingdom is divided against itself, that kingdom cannot stand. [25]If a house is divided against itself, that house cannot stand. [26]And if Satan opposes himself and is divided, he cannot stand; his end has come. [27]In fact, no one can enter a strong man's house and carry off his possessions unless he first ties up the strong man. Then he can rob his house.[p] [28]I tell you the truth, all the sins and blas-

phemies of men will be forgiven them. [29]But whoever blasphemes against the Holy Spirit will never be forgiven; he is guilty of an eternal sin."[q]

[30]He said this because they were saying, "He has an evil spirit."

Jesus' Mother and Brothers

3:31–35pp — Mt 12:46–50; Lk 8:19–21

[31]Then Jesus' mother and brothers arrived.[r] Standing outside, they sent someone in to call him. [32]A crowd was sitting around him, and they told him, "Your mother and brothers are outside looking for you."

[33]"Who are my mother and my brothers?" he asked.

[34]Then he looked at those seated in a circle around him and said, "Here are my mother and my brothers! [35]Whoever does God's will is my brother and sister and mother."

The Parable of the Sower

4:1–12pp — Mt 13:1–15; Lk 8:4–10
4:13–20pp — Mt 13:18–23; Lk 8:11–15

4 Again Jesus began to teach by the lake.[s] The crowd that gathered around him was so large that he got into a boat and sat in it out on the lake, while all the people were along the shore at the water's edge. [2]He taught them many things by parables,[t] and in his teaching said: [3]"Listen! A farmer went out to sow his seed.[u] [4]As he was scattering the seed, some fell along the path, and the birds came and ate it up. [5]Some fell on rocky

Cross references (center column)

3:14 *e*S Mk 6:30
3:15 *f*S Mt 10:1
3:16 *g*Jn 1:42
3:20 *h*ver 7
*i*Mk 6:31
3:21 *j*Jn 10:20;
Ac 26:24
3:22 *k*Mt 15:1
*l*Mt 10:25;
11:18; 12:24;
Jn 7:20; 8:48,
52;10:20
*m*Mt 9:34
3:23 *n*Mk 4:2
*o*S Mt 4:10
3:27 *p*Isa 49:24,
25

3:29 *q*Mt 12:31,
32; Lk 12:10
3:31 *r*ver 21
4:1 *s*Mk 2:13;
3:7
4:2 *t*ver 11;
Mk 3:23
4:3 *u*ver 26

h 14 Some manuscripts do not have *designating them apostles*. *i 22* Greek *Beezeboul* or *Beelzeboul*

---

not only instruction and practice in various forms of ministry but also continuous association and intimate fellowship with Jesus himself.

3:16–19 See notes on Lk 6:14–16.

3:17 *Sons of Thunder.* Probably descriptive of their dispositions (see notes on 10:37; Lk 9:54–55).

3:18 *Thaddaeus.* Apparently the same as "Judas son of James" (see Lk 6:16; Ac 1:13). *the Zealot.* See note on Mt 10:4.

3:19 *Iscariot.* Probably means "the man from Kerioth," the town Kerioth Hezron (Jos 15:25), 12 miles south of Hebron (Jer 48:24). For Judas' betrayal of Jesus see 14:10–11, 43–46.

3:20 *a house.* Probably the home of Peter and Andrew (see 1:29; 2:1).

3:21 *his family . . . went to take charge of him.* No doubt they had come to Capernaum from Nazareth, some 30 miles away (see v. 31).

3:22 *Beelzebub.* See note on Mt 10:25.

3:23 *parables.* In this context the word is used in the general sense of comparisons (see note on 4:2).

3:27 *enter a strong man's house and carry off his possessions.* Jesus was doing this very thing when he freed people from Satan's control.

3:28 *I tell you the truth.* A solemn affirmation used by Jesus to strengthen his assertions (see 8:12; 9:1,41; 10:15,29; 11:23; 12:43; 13:30; 14:9,18,25,30).

3:29 *whoever blasphemes against the Holy Spirit will never be forgiven.* Jesus identifies this sin in v. 30 (cf. v. 22)—the teachers of the law attributed Jesus' healing to Satan's power rather than the Holy Spirit (see note on Mt 12:31).

3:31 *Jesus' mother and brothers.* See note on Lk 8:19.

3:34 *Whoever does God's will.* Membership in God's spiritual family, evidenced by obedience to him, is more important than membership in our human families (see note on 10:30).

4:1 *sat in it.* Sitting was the usual position for Jewish teachers (see Mt 5:1; Lk 5:3; Jn 8:2).

4:2 *parables.* Usually stories out of ordinary life used to illustrate spiritual or moral truth, sometimes in the form of brief similes, comparisons (see note on 3:23), analogies or proverbial sayings. Ordinarily they had a single main point, and not every detail was meant to have significance. See notes on Mt 13:3; Lk 8:4.

4:3–8 In that day seed was broadcast by hand—which, by its nature, scattered some seed on unproductive ground (see note on Lk 8:5).

Jerusalem

During the Ministry of Jesus

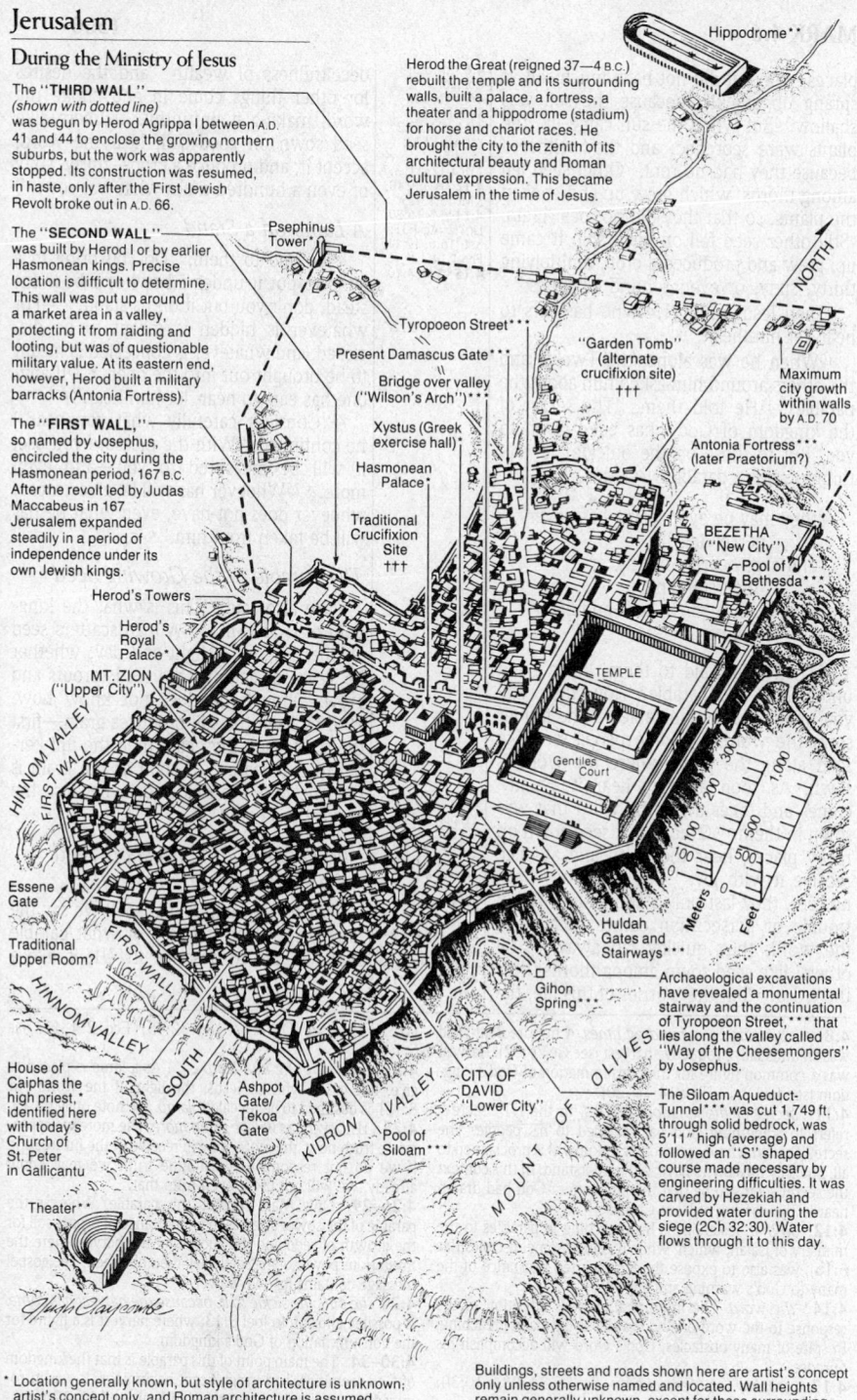

The **"THIRD WALL"**
(shown with dotted line)
was begun by Herod Agrippa I between A.D. 41 and 44 to enclose the growing northern suburbs, but the work was apparently stopped. Its construction was resumed, in haste, only after the First Jewish Revolt broke out in A.D. 66.

The **"SECOND WALL"**
was built by Herod I or by earlier Hasmonean kings. Precise location is difficult to determine. This wall was put up around a market area in a valley, protecting it from raiding and looting, but was of questionable military value. At its eastern end, however, Herod built a military barracks (Antonia Fortress).

The **"FIRST WALL,"**
so named by Josephus, encircled the city during the Hasmonean period, 167 B.C. After the revolt led by Judas Maccabeus in 167 Jerusalem expanded steadily in a period of independence under its own Jewish kings.

Herod the Great (reigned 37—4 B.C.) rebuilt the temple and its surrounding walls, built a palace, a fortress, a theater and a hippodrome (stadium) for horse and chariot races. He brought the city to the zenith of its architectural beauty and Roman cultural expression. This became Jerusalem in the time of Jesus.

Hippodrome **

Psephinus Tower *

NORTH

Tyropoeon Street ***

Present Damascus Gate ***

"Garden Tomb" (alternate crucifixion site) †††

Maximum city growth within walls by A.D. 70

Bridge over valley ("Wilson's Arch") ***

Xystus (Greek exercise hall)

Hasmonean Palace *

Traditional Crucifixion Site †††

Herod's Towers

Herod's Royal Palace *

MT. ZION ("Upper City")

Antonia Fortress *** (later Praetorium?)

BEZETHA ("New City")

Pool of Bethesda ***

TEMPLE

Gentiles Court

HINNOM VALLEY

FIRST WALL

Essene Gate

Traditional Upper Room?

FIRST WALL

HINNOM VALLEY

SOUTH

House of Caiphas the high priest,* identified here with today's Church of St. Peter in Gallicantu

Theater **

Ashpot Gate/ Tekoa Gate

Pool of Siloam ***

KIDRON VALLEY

CITY OF DAVID ("Lower City")

Gihon Spring ***

Huldah Gates and Stairways ***

MOUNT OF OLIVES

Meters — Feet

100 200 300
100 500 1,000
500

Archaeological excavations have revealed a monumental stairway and the continuation of Tyropoeon Street, *** that lies along the valley called "Way of the Cheesemongers" by Josephus.

The Siloam Aqueduct-Tunnel *** was cut 1,749 ft. through solid bedrock, was 5'11" high (average) and followed an "S" shaped course made necessary by engineering difficulties. It was carved by Hezekiah and provided water during the siege (2Ch 32:30). Water flows through it to this day.

* Location generally known, but style of architecture is unknown; artist's concept only, and Roman architecture is assumed.

** Location and architecture unknown, but referred to in written history; shown here for illustrative purposes.

*** Ancient feature has remained, or appearance has been determined from evidence.

Buildings, streets and roads shown here are artist's concept only unless otherwise named and located. Wall heights remain generally unknown, except for those surrounding the Temple Mount.

DEEP VALLEYS on the east, south and west permitted urban expansion only to the north.

places, where it did not have much soil. It sprang up quickly, because the soil was shallow. 6But when the sun came up, the plants were scorched, and they withered because they had no root. 7Other seed fell among thorns, which grew up and choked the plants, so that they did not bear grain. 8Still other seed fell on good soil. It came up, grew and produced a crop, multiplying thirty, sixty, or even a hundred times."*v*

9Then Jesus said, "He who has ears to hear, let him hear."*w*

10When he was alone, the Twelve and the others around him asked him about the parables. 11He told them, "The secret of the kingdom of God*x* has been given to you. But to those on the outside*y* everything is said in parables 12so that,

" 'they may be ever seeing but never
    perceiving,
and ever hearing but never
    understanding;
otherwise they might turn and be
    forgiven!'*i* "*z*

13Then Jesus said to them, "Don't you understand this parable? How then will you understand any parable? 14The farmer sows the word.*a* 15Some people are like seed along the path, where the word is sown. As soon as they hear it, Satan*b* comes and takes away the word that was sown in them. 16Others, like seed sown on rocky places, hear the word and at once receive it with joy. 17But since they have no root, they last only a short time. When trouble or persecution comes because of the word, they quickly fall away. 18Still others, like seed sown among thorns, hear the word; 19but the worries of this life, the

deceitfulness of wealth*c* and the desires for other things come in and choke the word, making it unfruitful. 20Others, like seed sown on good soil, hear the word, accept it, and produce a crop—thirty, sixty or even a hundred times what was sown."

A Lamp on a Stand

21He said to them, "Do you bring in a lamp to put it under a bowl or a bed? Instead, don't you put it on its stand?*d* 22For whatever is hidden is meant to be disclosed, and whatever is concealed is meant to be brought out into the open.*e* 23If anyone has ears to hear, let him hear."*f*

24"Consider carefully what you hear," he continued. "With the measure you use, it will be measured to you—and even more.*g* 25Whoever has will be given more; whoever does not have, even what he has will be taken from him."*h*

The Parable of the Growing Seed

26He also said, "This is what the kingdom of God is like.*i* A man scatters seed on the ground. 27Night and day, whether he sleeps or gets up, the seed sprouts and grows, though he does not know how. 28All by itself the soil produces grain—first the stalk, then the head, then the full kernel in the head. 29As soon as the grain is ripe, he puts the sickle to it, because the harvest has come."*j*

The Parable of the Mustard Seed

4:30–32pp — Mt 13:31,32; Lk 13:18,19

30Again he said, "What shall we say the kingdom of God is like,*k* or what parable shall we use to describe it? 31It is like a

Cross-reference column

4:8 *v*Jn 15:5; Col 1:6
4:9 *w*ver 23; S Mt 11:15
4:11 *x*S Mt 3:2 *y*1Co 5:12,13; Col 4:5; 1Th 4:12; 1Ti 3:7
4:12 *z*Isa 6:9,10; S Mt 13:13-15
4:14 *a*Mk 16:20; Lk 1:2; Ac 4:31; 8:4; 16:6; 17:11; Php 1:14
4:15 *b*S Mt 4:10

4:19 *c*Mt 19:23; 1Ti 6:9,10,17; 1Jn 2:15-17
4:21 *d*S Mt 5:15
4:22 *e*Jer 16:17; Mt 10:26; Lk 8:17; 12:2
4:23 *f*ver 9; S Mt 11:15
4:24 *g*S Mt 7:2
4:25 *h*S Mt 25:29
4:26 *i*S Mt 13:24
4:29 *j*Rev 14:15
4:30 *k*S Mt 13:24

*i*12 Isaiah 6:9,10

4:8 *multiplying . . . a hundred times.* A hundredfold yield was an unusually productive harvest (see Ge 26:12). Harvest was a common figure for the consummation of God's kingdom (see Joel 3:13; Rev 14:14–20).

4:11 *secret of the kingdom of God.* In the NT "secret" refers to something God has revealed to his people. The secret (that which was previously unknown) is proclaimed to all, but only those who have faith understand. In this context the secret seems to be that the kingdom of God had drawn near in the coming of Jesus Christ.

4:12 *so that.* Jesus likens his preaching in parables to the ministry of Isaiah, which, while it gained some disciples (Isa 8:16), was also to expose the hardhearted resistance of the many to God's warning and appeal.

4:14 *the word.* The interpretation calls attention to the response to the word of God that Jesus has been preaching. In spite of many obstacles, God's word will accomplish his purpose.

4:17 *trouble or persecution.* See 8:34–38; 10:30; 13:9–13.

4:19 *deceitfulness of wealth.* Prosperity tends to give a false sense of self-sufficiency, security and well-being

(10:17–25; see Dt 8:17–18; 32:15; Ecc 2:4–11; Jas 5:1–6).

4:21 *Do you bring in a lamp . . . ?* As a lamp is placed to give, not hide, light, so Jesus, the light of the world (Jn 8:12), is destined to be revealed. *lamp.* See note on Mt 5:15.

4:25 *Whoever has will be given more.* The more we appropriate truth now, the more we will receive in the future; and if we do not respond to what little truth we may know already, we will not profit even from that.

4:26–29 Only Mark records this parable. Whereas the parable of the sower stresses the importance of proper soil for the growth of seed and the success of the harvest, here the mysterious power of the seed itself is emphasized. The gospel message contains its own power.

4:29 *he puts the sickle to it, because the harvest has come.* A possible allusion to Joel 3:13, where harvest is a figure for the consummation of God's kingdom.

4:30–34 The main point of this parable is that the kingdom of God seemingly had insignificant beginnings. It was introduced by the despised and rejected Jesus and his 12 unimpressive disciples. But a day will come when its true greatness and power will be seen by all the world.

mustard seed, which is the smallest seed you plant in the ground. [32]Yet when planted, it grows and becomes the largest of all garden plants, with such big branches that the birds of the air can perch in its shade."

[33]With many similar parables Jesus spoke the word to them, as much as they could understand. [l] [34]He did not say anything to them without using a parable. [m] But when he was alone with his own disciples, he explained everything.

Jesus Calms the Storm
4:35–41pp — Mt 8:18,23–27; Lk 8:22–25

[35]That day when evening came, he said to his disciples, "Let us go over to the other side." [36]Leaving the crowd behind, they took him along, just as he was, in the boat. [n] There were also other boats with him. [37]A furious squall came up, and the waves broke over the boat, so that it was nearly swamped. [38]Jesus was in the stern, sleeping on a cushion. The disciples woke him and said to him, "Teacher, don't you care if we drown?"

[39]He got up, rebuked the wind and said to the waves, "Quiet! Be still!" Then the wind died down and it was completely calm.

[40]He said to his disciples, "Why are you so afraid? Do you still have no faith?" [o] [41]They were terrified and asked each

Cross references (center column):
- 4:33 [l]Jn 16:12
- 4:34 [m]S Jn 16:25
- 4:36 [n]ver 1; Mk 3:9; 5:2,21; 6:32,45
- 4:40 [o]Mt 14:31; Mk 16:14
- 5:2 [p]Mk 4:1 [q]Mk 1:23
- 5:7 [r]S Mt 8:29 [s]S Mt 4:3; Lk 1:32; 6:35; Ac 16:17; Heb 7:1
- 5:9 [t]ver 15

other, "Who is this? Even the wind and the waves obey him!"

The Healing of a Demon-possessed Man
5:1–17pp — Mt 8:28–34; Lk 8:26–37
5:18–20pp — Lk 8:38,39

[5] They went across the lake to the region of the Gerasenes. [k] [2]When Jesus got out of the boat, [p] a man with an evil[1] spirit [q] came from the tombs to meet him. [3]This man lived in the tombs, and no one could bind him any more, not even with a chain. [4]For he had often been chained hand and foot, but he tore the chains apart and broke the irons on his feet. No one was strong enough to subdue him. [5]Night and day among the tombs and in the hills he would cry out and cut himself with stones.

[6]When he saw Jesus from a distance, he ran and fell on his knees in front of him. [7]He shouted at the top of his voice, "What do you want with me, [r] Jesus, Son of the Most High God? [s] Swear to God that you won't torture me!" [8]For Jesus had said to him, "Come out of this man, you evil spirit!"

[9]Then Jesus asked him, "What is your name?"

"My name is Legion," [t] he replied, "for

[k]1 Some manuscripts Gadarenes; other manuscripts Gergesenes   [l]2 Greek unclean; also in verses 8 and 13

4:31 See notes on Mt 13:31–32.

4:34 He did not say anything to them without using a parable. Jesus used parables to illustrate truths, stimulate thinking and awaken spiritual perception. The people in general were not ready for the full truth of the gospel. When alone with his disciples Jesus taught more specifically, but even they usually needed to have things explained.

4:35–41 Although miracles are hard for modern man to accept, the NT makes it clear that Jesus is Lord not only over his church but also over all creation.

4:35 to the other side. Jesus left the territory of Galilee to go to the region of the Gerasenes (5:1).

4:37 A furious squall came up. Situated in a basin surrounded by mountains, the Sea of Galilee is particularly susceptible to sudden, violent storms. Cool air from the Mediterranean is drawn down through the narrow mountain passes and clashes with the hot, humid air lying over the lake.

4:38 sleeping on a cushion. The picture of Jesus, exhausted and asleep on the cushion customarily kept under the coxswain's seat, is characteristic of Mark's human touch.

4:41 Who is this? In view of what Jesus had just done, the only answer to this rhetorical question was: He is the very Son of God! God's presence, as well as his power, was demonstrated (see Ps 65:7; 107:25–30; Pr 30:4). Mark indicates his answer to this question in the opening line of his Gospel (1:1). By such miracles Jesus sought to establish and increase the disciples' faith in his deity.

5:1 across the lake. The east side of the lake, a territory largely inhabited by Gentiles, as indicated by the presence of the large herd of pigs—animals Jews considered "unclean"

and therefore unfit to eat. region of the Gerasenes. Gerasa, located about 35 miles southeast of the Sea of Galilee, may have had holdings on the eastern shore of the Sea, giving its name to a small village there now known as Khersa. About one mile south is a fairly steep slope within 40 yards of the shore, and about two miles from there are cavern tombs that appear to have been used as dwellings.

5:3 lived in the tombs. It was not unusual for the same cave to provide burial for the dead and shelter for the living. Very poor people often lived in such caves.

5:4 he had often been chained. Though the villagers no doubt chained him partly for their own protection, this harsh treatment added to his humiliation.

5:5 he would cry out and cut himself with stones. Every word in the story emphasizes the man's pathetic condition as well as the purpose of demonic possession—to torment and destroy the divine likeness with which man was created.

5:7 What do you want with me . . . ? A way of saying, "What do we have in common?" Similar expressions are found in the OT (e.g., 2Sa 16:10; 19:22), where they mean, "Mind your own business!" The demon was speaking, using the voice of the possessed man. Son of the Most High God. See note on 1:24. Swear to God that you won't torture me! The demon sensed that he was to be punished and used the strongest basis for an oath that he knew, though his appeal to God was strangely ironic.

5:9 My name is Legion . . . for we are many. A Roman legion was made up of 6,000 men. Here the term suggests that the man was possessed by numerous demons and perhaps also represents the many powers opposed to Jesus, who embodies the power of God.

we are many." [10]And he begged Jesus again and again not to send them out of the area.

[11]A large herd of pigs was feeding on the nearby hillside. [12]The demons begged Jesus, "Send us among the pigs; allow us to go into them." [13]He gave them permission, and the evil spirits came out and went into the pigs. The herd, about two thousand in number, rushed down the steep bank into the lake and were drowned.

[14]Those tending the pigs ran off and reported this in the town and countryside, and the people went out to see what had happened. [15]When they came to Jesus, they saw the man who had been possessed by the legion[u] of demons,[v] sitting there, dressed and in his right mind; and they were afraid. [16]Those who had seen it told

the people what had happened to the demon-possessed man—and told about the pigs as well. [17]Then the people began to plead with Jesus to leave their region.

[18]As Jesus was getting into the boat, the man who had been demon-possessed begged to go with him. [19]Jesus did not let him, but said, "Go home to your family and tell them[w] how much the Lord has done for you, and how he has had mercy on you." [20]So the man went away and began to tell in the Decapolis[m][x] how much Jesus had done for him. And all the people were amazed.

A Dead Girl and a Sick Woman

5:22–43pp — Mt 9:18–26; Lk 8:41–56

[21]When Jesus had again crossed over by boat to the other side of the lake,[y] a large

5:15 *u*ver 9 *v*ver 16,18; S Mt 4:24

5:19 *w*S Mt 8:4
5:20 *x*Mt 4:25; Mk 7:31
5:21 *y*Mt 9:1

*m*20 That is, the Ten Cities

5:10 *not to send them out of the area.* The demons were fearful of being sent into eternal punishment, i.e., "into the Abyss" (Lk 8:31).
5:13 *He gave them permission.* See note on Mt 8:32.
5:16 *and told about the pigs as well.* In addition to the remarkable change in the demon-possessed man, the drown-

ing of the pigs seemed to be a major concern, no doubt because it was so dramatic and brought considerable financial loss to the owners.
5:17 *plead with Jesus to leave their region.* Fear of further loss may have motivated this response, but also the fact that a powerful force was at work in their midst that they could

---

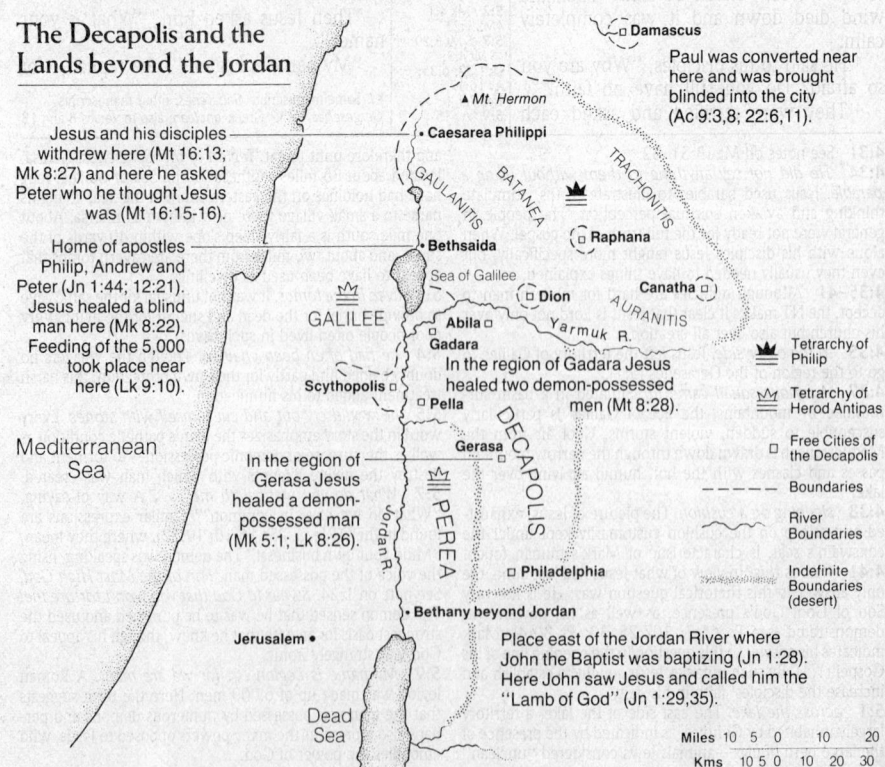

The Decapolis and the Lands beyond the Jordan

Paul was converted near here and was brought blinded into the city (Ac 9:3,8; 22:6,11).

Jesus and his disciples withdrew here (Mt 16:13; Mk 8:27) and here he asked Peter who he thought Jesus was (Mt 16:15-16).

Home of apostles Philip, Andrew and Peter (Jn 1:44; 12:21). Jesus healed a blind man here (Mk 8:22). Feeding of the 5,000 took place near here (Lk 9:10).

In the region of Gadara Jesus healed two demon-possessed men (Mt 8:28).

In the region of Gerasa Jesus healed a demon-possessed man (Mk 5:1; Lk 8:26).

Place east of the Jordan River where John the Baptist was baptizing (Jn 1:28). Here John saw Jesus and called him the "Lamb of God" (Jn 1:29,35).

Damascus
Mt. Hermon
Caesarea Philippi
GAULANITIS
BATANEA
TRACHONITIS
Bethsaida
Raphana
Sea of Galilee
Canatha
Dion
AURANITIS
GALILEE
Abila
Yarmuk R.
Gadara
Scythopolis
Pella
DECAPOLIS
Gerasa
Jordan R.
PEREA
Philadelphia
Bethany beyond Jordan
Jerusalem
Mediterranean Sea
Dead Sea

Tetrarchy of Philip
Tetrarchy of Herod Antipas
Free Cities of the Decapolis
Boundaries
River Boundaries
Indefinite Boundaries (desert)

Miles 10 5 0   10   20
Kms   10 5 0   10 20 30

crowd gathered around him while he was by the lake.[z] 22Then one of the synagogue rulers,[a] named Jairus, came there. Seeing Jesus, he fell at his feet 23and pleaded earnestly with him, "My little daughter is dying. Please come and put your hands on[b] her so that she will be healed and live." 24So Jesus went with him.

A large crowd followed and pressed around him. 25And a woman was there who had been subject to bleeding[c] for twelve years. 26She had suffered a great deal under the care of many doctors and had spent all she had, yet instead of getting better she grew worse. 27When she heard about Jesus, she came up behind him in the crowd and touched his cloak, 28because she thought, "If I just touch his clothes,[d] I will be healed." 29Immediately her bleeding stopped and she felt in her body that she was freed from her suffering.[e]

30At once Jesus realized that power[f] had gone out from him. He turned around in the crowd and asked, "Who touched my clothes?"

31"You see the people crowding against you," his disciples answered, "and yet you can ask, 'Who touched me?'"

32But Jesus kept looking around to see who had done it. 33Then the woman, knowing what had happened to her, came and fell at his feet and, trembling with fear,

told him the whole truth. 34He said to her, "Daughter, your faith has healed you.[g] Go in peace[h] and be freed from your suffering."

35While Jesus was still speaking, some men came from the house of Jairus, the synagogue ruler.[i] "Your daughter is dead," they said. "Why bother the teacher any more?"

36Ignoring what they said, Jesus told the synagogue ruler, "Don't be afraid; just believe."

37He did not let anyone follow him except Peter, James and John the brother of James.[j] 38When they came to the home of the synagogue ruler,[k] Jesus saw a commotion, with people crying and wailing loudly. 39He went in and said to them, "Why all this commotion and wailing? The child is not dead but asleep."[l] 40But they laughed at him.

After he put them all out, he took the child's father and mother and the disciples who were with him, and went in where the child was. 41He took her by the hand[m] and said to her, "Talitha koum!" (which means, "Little girl, I say to you, get up!").[n] 42Immediately the girl stood up and walked around (she was twelve years old). At this they were completely astonished. 43He gave strict orders not to let anyone know about this,[o] and told them to give her something to eat.

Cross references

5:21 [z]Mk 4:1
5:22 [a]ver 35,36, 38; Lk 13:14; Ac 13:15; 18:8,17
5:23 [b]Mt 19:13; Mk 6:5; 7:32; 8:23; 16:18; Lk 4:40; 13:13; S Ac 6:6
5:25 [c]Lev 15:25-30
5:28 [d]S Mt 9:20
5:29 [e]ver 34
5:30 [f]Lk 5:17; 6:19
5:34 [g]S Mt 9:22 [h]S Ac 15:33
5:35 [i]S ver 22
5:37 [j]S Mt 4:21
5:38 [k]S ver 22
5:39 [l]S Mt 9:24
5:41 [m]Mk 1:31 [n]S Lk 7:14
5:43 [o]S Mt 8:4

---

not comprehend.

5:19 *tell them how much the Lord has done for you.* This is in marked contrast to Jesus' exhortation to silence in the case of the man cleansed of leprosy (1:44; see 1:34; 3:12; see also note on Mt 8:4), perhaps because the healing of the demoniac was in Gentile territory, where there was little danger that Messianic ideas about Jesus might be circulated.

5:20 *Decapolis.* See note on Mt 4:25.

5:21 *the other side of the lake.* Jesus returned to the west side of the lake, perhaps to Capernaum.

5:22 *synagogue rulers.* A ruler of the synagogue was a layman whose responsibilities were administrative and included such things as looking after the building and supervising the worship. Though there were exceptions (see Ac 13:15), most synagogues had only one ruler. Sometimes the title was honorary, with no administrative responsibilities assigned.

5:25 *subject to bleeding for twelve years.* The precise nature of the woman's problem is not known. Her existence was wretched because she was shunned by people generally, since anyone having contact with her was made ceremonially unclean (Lev 15:25-33).

5:26 *She had suffered a great deal under the care of many doctors.* The Jewish Talmud preserves a record of medicines and treatments prescribed for illnesses of this sort.

5:28 *If I just touch his clothes.* Although it needed to be bolstered by physical contact, her faith was rewarded (v. 34; cf. Ac 19:12).

5:30 *power had gone out from him.* The woman was healed because God graciously determined to heal her

through the power then active in Jesus.

5:32 *kept looking around to see who had done it.* Jesus would not allow the woman to recede into the crowd without publicly commending her faith and assuring her that she was permanently healed.

5:34 *healed.* The Greek for "healed" actually means "saved." Here both physical healing ("be freed from your suffering") and spiritual salvation ("go in peace") are meant. The two are often seen together in Mark's Gospel (see 2:1–12; 3:1–6).

5:37 *Peter, James and John.* These three disciples had an especially close relationship to Jesus (see note on Ac 3:1).

5:38 *people crying and wailing loudly.* It was customary for professional mourners to be brought in at the time of death. In this case, however, it is not certain that enough time had elapsed for professional mourners to have been secured.

5:39 *not dead but asleep.* See note on Lk 8:52.

5:41 *Talitha koum!* Mark is the only Gospel writer who here preserves the original Aramaic—one of the languages of Palestine in the first century A.D. and probably the language Jesus and his disciples ordinarily spoke (they may also have spoken Hebrew and Greek).

5:43 *not to let anyone know.* In the vicinity of Galilee Jesus often cautioned people whom he healed not to spread the story of the miracle. His great popularity with the people, coupled with the growing opposition from the religious leaders, could have precipitated a crisis before Jesus' ministry was completed (see 1:44; 5:19; 7:36; 8:26).

A Prophet Without Honor

6:1–6pp — Mt 13:54–58

6 Jesus left there and went to his hometown,[p] accompanied by his disciples. [2]When the Sabbath came,[q] he began to teach in the synagogue,[r] and many who heard him were amazed.[s]

"Where did this man get these things?" they asked. "What's this wisdom that has been given him, that he even does miracles! [3]Isn't this the carpenter? Isn't this Mary's son and the brother of James, Joseph,[n] Judas and Simon?[t] Aren't his sisters here with us?" And they took offense at him.[u]

[4]Jesus said to them, "Only in his hometown, among his relatives and in his own house is a prophet without honor."[v] [5]He could not do any miracles there, except lay his hands on[w] a few sick people and heal them. [6]And he was amazed at their lack of faith.

Jesus Sends Out the Twelve

6:7–11pp — Mt 10:1,9–14; Lk 9:1,3–5

Then Jesus went around teaching from village to village.[x] [7]Calling the Twelve to him,[y] he sent them out two by two[z] and gave them authority over evil[o] spirits.[a]

[8]These were his instructions: "Take nothing for the journey except a staff—no bread, no bag, no money in your belts. [9]Wear sandals but not an extra tunic. [10]Whenever you enter a house, stay there until you leave that town. [11]And if any place will not welcome you or listen to

you, shake the dust off your feet[b] when you leave, as a testimony against them."

[12]They went out and preached that people should repent.[c] [13]They drove out many demons and anointed many sick people with oil[d] and healed them.

John the Baptist Beheaded

6:14–29pp — Mt 14:1–12
6:14–16pp — Lk 9:7–9

[14]King Herod heard about this, for Jesus' name had become well known. Some were saying,[p] "John the Baptist[e] has been raised from the dead, and that is why miraculous powers are at work in him."

[15]Others said, "He is Elijah."[f]

And still others claimed, "He is a prophet,[g] like one of the prophets of long ago."[h]

[16]But when Herod heard this, he said, "John, the man I beheaded, has been raised from the dead!"

[17]For Herod himself had given orders to have John arrested, and he had him bound and put in prison.[i] He did this because of Herodias, his brother Philip's wife, whom he had married. [18]For John had been saying to Herod, "It is not lawful for you to have your brother's wife."[j] [19]So Herodias nursed a grudge against John and wanted to kill him. But she was not able to, [20]because Herod feared John and protected him, knowing him to be a righteous and holy man.[k] When Herod heard John, he

Cross-references (center column)

6:1 [p]S Mt 2:23
6:2 [q]Mk 1:21
  [r]S Mt 4:23
  [s]S Mt 7:28
6:3 [t]S Mt 12:46
  [u]Mt 11:6; Jn 6:61
6:4 [v]Lk 4:24;
  Jn 4:44
6:5 [w]S Mk 5:23
6:6 [x]Mt 9:35;
  Mk 1:39;
  Lk 13:22
6:7 [y]Mk 3:13
  [z]Dt 17:6; Lk 10:1
  [a]S Mt 10:1

6:11 [b]S Mt 10:14
6:12 [c]Lk 9:6
6:13 [d]S Jas 5:14
6:14 [e]S Mt 3:1
6:15 [f]Mal 4:5
  [g]S Mt 21:11
  [h]Mt 16:14;
  Mk 8:28
6:17 [i]Mt 4:12;
  11:2; Lk 3:19,20
6:18 [j]Lev 18:16;
  20:21
6:20 [k]S Mt 11:9

[n]3 Greek *Joses*, a variant of *Joseph*   [o]7 Greek *unclean*
[p]14 Some early manuscripts *He was saying*

6:1 *his hometown.* Though Mark does not specifically mention Nazareth, it is obviously meant (see note on 1:9).

6:2 *teach in the synagogue.* See note on 1:21. *were amazed.* See note on 1:22.

6:3 *carpenter.* Matthew reports that Jesus was called "the carpenter's son" (Mt 13:55); only in Mark is Jesus himself referred to as a carpenter. The Greek word can also apply to a mason or smith, but it seems to have its usual meaning ("carpenter") here. The question is derogatory, meaning, "Is he not a common worker with his hands like the rest of us?" *brother of James, Joseph, Judas and Simon.* See note on Lk 8:19. *they took offense at him.* They saw no reason to believe that he was different from them, much less that he was specially anointed by God.

6:5 *He could not do any miracles there.* It was not that Jesus did not have power to perform miracles at Nazareth, but that he chose not to in such a climate of unbelief (v. 6).

6:6 *he was amazed.* See note on Lk 7:9.

6:7 *two by two.* The purpose of going in pairs may have been to bolster credibility by having the testimony of more than one witness (cf. Dt 17:6), as well as to provide mutual support during their training period.

6:8 *no bread, no bag, no money in your belts.* They were to depend entirely on the hospitality of those to whom they testified (see v. 10).

6:9 *not an extra tunic.* At night an extra tunic was helpful as a covering to protect from the cold night air, and the implication here is that the disciples were to trust in God to provide lodging each night.

6:11 *shake the dust off your feet.* See note on Mt 10:14.

6:12–13 *preached . . . . drove out many demons.* This mission marks the beginning of the disciples' own ministry in Jesus' name (see 3:14–15), and their message was precisely the same as his (1:15).

6:12 *repent.* See note on 1:4.

6:13 *anointed many sick people with oil.* In the ancient world olive oil was widely used as a medicine (see Isa 1:6; Lk 10:34; Jas 5:14).

6:14 *King Herod.* See note on Mt 14:1. Mark may here have used the title "king" sarcastically (since Herod was actually a tetrarch), or perhaps he simply used Herod's popular title.

6:15 *He is Elijah.* See Mal 4:5.

6:16 *John . . . has been raised from the dead!* Herod, disturbed by an uneasy conscience and disposed to superstition, feared that John had come back to haunt him.

6:17 *John arrested . . . and put in prison.* See 1:14; Lk 3:19–20. Josephus says that John was imprisoned at Machaerus, the fortress in Perea on the eastern side of the Dead Sea. *Herodias.* See note on Mt 14:3. *Philip.* See note on Mt 14:3.

was greatly puzzled q; yet he liked to listen to him.

21Finally the opportune time came. On his birthday Herod gave a banquet l for his high officials and military commanders and the leading men of Galilee. m 22When the daughter of Herodias came in and danced, she pleased Herod and his dinner guests.

The king said to the girl, "Ask me for anything you want, and I'll give it to you." 23And he promised her with an oath, "Whatever you ask I will give you, up to half my kingdom." n

24She went out and said to her mother, "What shall I ask for?"

"The head of John the Baptist," she answered.

25At once the girl hurried in to the king with the request: "I want you to give me right now the head of John the Baptist on a platter."

26The king was greatly distressed, but because of his oaths and his dinner guests, he did not want to refuse her. 27So he immediately sent an executioner with orders to bring John's head. The man went, beheaded John in the prison, 28and brought back his head on a platter. He presented it to the girl, and she gave it to her mother. 29On hearing of this, John's disciples came and took his body and laid it in a tomb.

Jesus Feeds the Five Thousand

6:32–44pp — Mt 14:13–21; Lk 9:10–17; Jn 6:5–13
6:32–44Ref — Mk 8:2–9

30The apostles o gathered around Jesus and reported to him all they had done and taught. p 31Then, because so many people were coming and going that they did not

Cross-reference column:
6:21 lEst 1:3; 2:18 mLk 3:1
6:23 nEst 5:3,6; 7:2
6:30 oMt 10:2; Lk 9:10; 17:5; 22:14; 24:10; Ac 1:2,26
pLk 9:10

6:31 qMk 3:20
6:32 rver 45; S Mk 4:36
6:34 sS Mt 9:36
6:37 t2Ki 4:42-44
6:38 uMt 15:34; Mk 8:5
6:41 vS Mt 14:19

even have a chance to eat, q he said to them, "Come with me by yourselves to a quiet place and get some rest."

32So they went away by themselves in a boat r to a solitary place. 33But many who saw them leaving recognized them and ran on foot from all the towns and got there ahead of them. 34When Jesus landed and saw a large crowd, he had compassion on them, because they were like sheep without a shepherd. s So he began teaching them many things.

35By this time it was late in the day, so his disciples came to him. "This is a remote place," they said, "and it's already very late. 36Send the people away so they can go to the surrounding countryside and villages and buy themselves something to eat."

37But he answered, "You give them something to eat." t

They said to him, "That would take eight months of a man's wages r! Are we to go and spend that much on bread and give it to them to eat?"

38"How many loaves do you have?" he asked. "Go and see."

When they found out, they said, "Five—and two fish." u

39Then Jesus directed them to have all the people sit down in groups on the green grass. 40So they sat down in groups of hundreds and fifties. 41Taking the five loaves and the two fish and looking up to heaven, he gave thanks and broke the loaves. v Then he gave them to his disciples to set before the people. He also divided the two fish among them all. 42They all ate and

q20 Some early manuscripts he did many things
r37 Greek take two hundred denarii

6:22 *the daughter of Herodias.* See note on Mt 14:6.
6:23 *up to half my kingdom.* A proverbial reference to generosity, not to be taken literally (see Est 5:3,6). Generosity suited the occasion and would win the approval of the guests.
6:30 *apostles.* In Mark's Gospel the word occurs only here and in 3:14 (in some manuscripts). The apostles were Jesus' authorized agents or representatives (see note on Heb 3:1). In the NT the word is sometimes used quite generally (see Jn 13:16, where the Greek *apostolos* is translated "messenger"). In the technical sense it is used (1) of the Twelve (3:14)—in which sense it is also applied to Paul (Rom 1:1)—and (2) of a larger group including Barnabas (Ac 14:14), James the Lord's brother (Gal 1:19), and possibly Andronicus and Junias (Ro 16:7). *reported to him all they had done and taught.* Because he had commissioned them as his representatives. They were returning from a third preaching tour in Galilee (see note on 1:39).
6:32 *they went away by themselves in a boat.* John reports that they went to the other side of the Sea of Galilee (Jn 6:1). Luke, more specifically, says they went to Bethsaida (Lk 9:10), which locates the feeding of the 5,000 on the

northeast shore (see note on 7:24).
6:33 *ran on foot . . . and got there ahead of them.* Perhaps a strong headwind slowed down the boat so that the people had time to go on foot around the lake and arrive before the boat.
6:37 *eight months of a man's wages.* See NIV text note. The usual pay for a day's work was one denarius (see Mt 20:2), meaning that about 200 denarii would be earned in eight months.
6:39 *green grass.* Grass is green around the Sea of Galilee after the late winter or early spring rains.
6:40 *groups of hundreds and fifties.* Recalls the order of the Mosaic camp in the desert (e.g., Ex 18:21). The word translated "groups" means "garden plots," a picturesque figure (v. 39).
6:42 *all ate and were satisfied.* Attempts to explain away this miracle (e.g., by suggesting that Jesus and his disciples shared their lunch and the crowd followed their good example) are inadequate. If Jesus was, as he claimed to be, God incarnate, the miracle presents no difficulties. God had promised that when the true Shepherd came the desert would become rich pasture where the sheep would be gath-

were satisfied, ⁴³and the disciples picked up twelve basketfuls of broken pieces of bread and fish. ⁴⁴The number of the men who had eaten was five thousand.

Jesus Walks on the Water

6:45–51pp — Mt 14:22–32; Jn 6:15–21
6:53–56pp — Mt 14:34–36

⁴⁵Immediately Jesus made his disciples get into the boat *w* and go on ahead of him to Bethsaida, *x* while he dismissed the crowd. ⁴⁶After leaving them, he went up on a mountainside to pray. *y*

⁴⁷When evening came, the boat was in the middle of the lake, and he was alone on land. ⁴⁸He saw the disciples straining at the oars, because the wind was against them. About the fourth watch of the night he went out to them, walking on the lake. He was about to pass by them, ⁴⁹but when they saw him walking on the lake, they thought he was a ghost. *z* They cried out, ⁵⁰because they all saw him and were terrified.

Immediately he spoke to them and said, "Take courage! It is I. Don't be afraid." *a* ⁵¹Then he climbed into the boat *b* with them, and the wind died down. *c* They were completely amazed, ⁵²for they had not understood about the loaves; their hearts were hardened. *d*

⁵³When they had crossed over, they landed at Gennesaret and anchored there. *e* ⁵⁴As soon as they got out of the boat, people recognized Jesus. ⁵⁵They ran throughout that whole region and carried

the sick on mats to wherever they heard he was. ⁵⁶And wherever he went—into villages, towns or countryside—they placed the sick in the marketplaces. They begged him to let them touch even the edge of his cloak, *f* and all who touched him were healed.

Clean and Unclean

7:1–23pp — Mt 15:1–20

7 The Pharisees and some of the teach-
ers of the law who had come from Jerusalem gathered around Jesus and ²saw some of his disciples eating food with hands that were "unclean," *g* that is, un-washed. ³(The Pharisees and all the Jews do not eat unless they give their hands a ceremonial washing, holding to the tradi-tion of the elders. *h* ⁴When they come from the marketplace they do not eat unless they wash. And they observe many other traditions, such as the washing of cups, pitchers and kettles.⁵) *i*

⁵So the Pharisees and teachers of the law asked Jesus, "Why don't your disciples live according to the tradition of the el-ders *j* instead of eating their food with 'un-clean' hands?"

⁶He replied, "Isaiah was right when he prophesied about you hypocrites; as it is written:

" 'These people honor me with their lips,

Cross-references (center column)

6:45 *w* ver 32; *x* S Mt 11:21
6:46 *y* S Lk 3:21
6:49 *z* Lk 24:37
6:50 *a* S Mt 14:27
6:51 *b* ver 32; *c* Mk 4:39
6:52 *d* Mk 8:17-21
6:53 *e* Jn 6:24,25

6:56 *f* S Mt 9:20
7:2 *g* Ac 10:14, 28; 11:8; Ro 14:14
7:3 *h* ver 5,8,9, 13; Lk 11:38
7:4 *i* Mt 23:25; Lk 11:39
7:5 *j* S ver 3; Gal 1:14; Col 2:8

⁵4 Some early manuscripts *pitchers, kettles and dining couches*

---

ered and fed (Eze 34:23–31), and here the Messiah feasts with followers in the desert (cf. Isa 25:6–9). Jesus is the Shepherd who provides for all our needs so that we lack nothing (cf. Ps 23:1).

6:43 *twelve basketfuls of broken pieces of bread and fish.* Bread was regarded by Jews as a gift of God, and it was required that scraps that fell on the ground during a meal be picked up. The fragments were collected in small wicker baskets that were carried as a part of daily attire. Each of the disciples returned with his basket full (see 8:8; see also note on Mt 15:37).

6:44 *men.* Lit. "males," as in all four Gospels. Matthew further emphasizes the point by adding "besides women and children" (Mt 14:21). *five thousand.* The size of the crowd is amazing in light of the fact that the neighboring towns of Capernaum and Bethsaida probably had a population of only 2,000–3,000 each.

6:45 *go on ahead of him.* John indicates that the people were ready to take Jesus by force and make him king (Jn 6:14–15), and Jesus therefore sent his disciples across the lake while he slipped away into the hills to pray.

6:48 *fourth watch.* 3:00–6:00 A.M. See 13:35; see also note on Mt 14:25. *walking on the lake.* A special display of the majestic presence and power of the transcendent Lord, who rules over the sea (see Ps 89:9; Isa 51:10,15; Jer 31:35).

6:49 *a ghost.* Popular Jewish superstition held that the appearance of spirits during the night brought disaster. The disciples' terror was prompted by what they may have thought was a water spirit.

6:52 *they had not understood about the loaves.* Had they understood the feeding of the 5,000, they would not have been amazed at Jesus' walking on the water or his calming the waves. *their hearts were hardened.* They were showing themselves to be similar to Jesus' opponents, who also exhib-ited hardness of heart (3:5). See 8:17–21; see also note on Ex 4:21.

6:53 *Gennesaret.* See note on Mt 14:34.

6:56 *touch even the edge of his cloak.* See note on 5:28.

7:1 *The Pharisees . . . had come down from Jerusalem.* Another delegation of fact-finding religious leaders from Jerusalem (see 3:22) sent to investigate the Galilean activi-ties of Jesus. See notes on 2:16; Mt 2:4.

7:3 *ceremonial washing.* See note on Jn 2:6. *the tradition of the elders.* Considered to be binding (see v. 5 and note on Mt 15:2).

7:4 *marketplace.* Where Jews would come into contact with Gentiles, or with Jews who did not observe the ceremonial law, and thus become ceremonially unclean.

7:6 *Isaiah . . . prophesied.* Isaiah roundly denounced the religious leaders of his day (Isa 29:13), and Jesus uses a quotation from this prophet to describe the tradition of the elders as "rules taught by men" (v. 7).

but their hearts are far from me.
[7]They worship me in vain;
their teachings are but rules taught by men.’[t][k]

[8]You have let go of the commands of God and are holding on to the traditions of men.”[l]

[9]And he said to them: “You have a fine way of setting aside the commands of God in order to observe[u] your own traditions![m] [10]For Moses said, ‘Honor your father and your mother,’[v][n] and, ‘Anyone who curses his father or mother must be put to death.’[w][o] [11]But you say[p] that if a man says to his father or mother: ‘Whatever help you might otherwise have received from me is Corban’ (that is, a gift devoted to God), [12]then you no longer let him do anything for his father or mother. [13]Thus you nullify the word of God[q] by your tradition[r] that you have handed down. And you do many things like that.”

[14]Again Jesus called the crowd to him and said, “Listen to me, everyone, and understand this. [15]Nothing outside a man can make him ‘unclean’ by going into him. Rather, it is what comes out of a man that makes him ‘unclean.’[x]”

[17]After he had left the crowd and entered the house, his disciples asked him[s] about this parable. [18]“Are you so dull?” he asked. “Don’t you see that nothing that enters a man from the outside can make him ‘unclean’? [19]For it doesn’t go into his heart but into his stomach, and then out of his body.” (In saying this, Jesus declared all foods[t] “clean.”)[u]

[20]He went on: “What comes out of a man is what makes him ‘unclean.’ [21]For from within, out of men’s hearts, come evil thoughts, sexual immorality, theft, murder, adultery, [22]greed,[v] malice, deceit, lewdness, envy, slander, arrogance and folly. [23]All these evils come from inside and make a man ‘unclean.’ ”

The Faith of a Syrophoenician Woman

7:24–30pp — Mt 15:21–28

[24]Jesus left that place and went to the vicinity of Tyre.[y][w] He entered a house and did not want anyone to know it; yet he could not keep his presence secret. [25]In fact, as soon as she heard about him, a woman whose little daughter was possessed by an evil[z] spirit[x] came and fell at his feet. [26]The woman was a Greek, born in Syrian Phoenicia. She begged Jesus to drive the demon out of her daughter.

[27]“First let the children eat all they want,” he told her, “for it is not right to take the children’s bread and toss it to their dogs.”

[28]“Yes, Lord,” she replied, “but even

7:7 [k]Isa 29:13
7:8 [l]S ver 3
7:9 [m]S ver 3
7:10 [n]Ex 20:12; Dt 5:16 [o]Ex 21:17; Lev 20:9
7:11 [p]Mt 23:16, 18
7:13 [q]S Heb 4:12 [r]S ver 3
7:17 [s]Mk 9:28
7:19 [t]Ro 14:1-12; Col 2:16; 1Ti 4:3-5 [u]S Ac 10:15
7:22 [v]Mt 20:15
7:24 [w]S Mt 11:21
7:25 [x]S Mt 4:24

[t]*6,7* Isaiah 29:13 [u]*9* Some manuscripts *set up* [v]*10* Exodus 20:12; Deut. 5:16 [w]*10* Exodus 21:17; Lev. 20:9 [x]*15* Some early manuscripts *‘unclean.’ [16]If anyone has ears to hear, let him hear.* [y]*24* Many early manuscripts *Tyre and Sidon* [z]*25* Greek *unclean*

7:8 *the commands of God . . . the traditions of men.* Jesus clearly contrasts the two. God’s commands are found in Scripture and are binding; the traditions of the elders (v. 3) are not Biblical and therefore not authoritative or binding.
7:10 The fifth commandment is cited in both its positive and negative forms.
7:11 *Corban.* The transliteration of a Hebrew word meaning “offering.” By using this word in a religious vow an irresponsible Jewish son could formally dedicate to God (i.e., to the temple) his earnings that otherwise would have gone for the support of his parents. The money, however, did not necessarily have to go for religious purposes. The Corban formula was simply a means of circumventing the clear responsibility of children toward their parents as prescribed in the law. The teachers of the law held that the Corban oath was binding, even when uttered rashly. The practice was one of many traditions that adhered to the letter of the law while ignoring its spirit. *(that is, a gift devoted to God).* By explaining this Hebrew word, Mark reveals that he is addressing Gentile readers, probably Romans primarily.
7:13 *Thus you nullify the word of God by your tradition.* The teachers of the law appealed to Nu 30:1–2 in support of the Corban vow, but Jesus categorically rejects the practice of using one Biblical teaching to nullify another. The scribal interpretation of Nu 30:1–2 satisfied the letter of the passage but missed the meaning of the law as a whole. God never intended obedience to one command to nullify another.
7:16 See NIV text note on v. 15. Although this verse is present in the majority of the Greek manuscripts, it does not occur in the most ancient ones. It appears to be a scribal addition derived from either 4:9 or 4:23.
7:19 *(In saying this, Jesus declared all foods “clean.”)* Mark adds this parenthetical comment to help his readers see the significance of Jesus’ pronouncement for them (see Ac 10:9–16).
7:20 *‘unclean.’* Jesus replaced the normal Jewish understandings of defilement with the truth that defilement comes from an impure heart, not the violation of external rules. Fellowship with God is not interrupted by unclean hands or food, but by sin (see vv. 21–23).
7:24 *Tyre.* A Gentile city located in Phoenicia (modern Lebanon), which bordered Galilee to the northwest. A journey of about 30 miles from Capernaum would have brought Jesus to the vicinity of Tyre. *did not want anyone to know.* Ever since the feeding of the 5,000 (6:30–44) Jesus and his disciples had been, for the most part, skirting the region of Galilee. His purpose was to avoid the opposition in Galilee and to secure opportunity to teach his disciples privately (9:30–31). The regions to which he withdrew were: (1) the northeastern shore of the Sea of Galilee (6:30–53), (2) Phoenicia (7:24–30), (3) the Decapolis (7:31–8:10) and (4) Caesarea Philippi (8:27–9:32).
7:26 *Greek.* Here probably equivalent to “Gentile.” *Syrian Phoenicia.* At that time Phoenicia belonged administratively to Syria. Mark possibly used the term to distinguish this woman from the Libyan-Phoenicians of North Africa.
7:27 *the children’s bread and toss it to their dogs.* See note on Mt 15:26.

the dogs under the table eat the children's crumbs."

²⁹Then he told her, "For such a reply, you may go; the demon has left your daughter."

³⁰She went home and found her child lying on the bed, and the demon gone.

The Healing of a Deaf and Mute Man

7:31-37pp — Mt 15:29-31

³¹Then Jesus left the vicinity of Tyre[y] and went through Sidon, down to the Sea of Galilee[z] and into the region of the Decapolis.[a][a] ³²There some people brought to him a man who was deaf and could hardly talk,[b] and they begged him to place his hand on[c] the man.

³³After he took him aside, away from the crowd, Jesus put his fingers into the man's ears. Then he spit[d] and touched the man's tongue. ³⁴He looked up to heaven[e] and with a deep sigh[f] said to him, "Eph-phatha!" (which means, "Be opened!").

³⁵At this, the man's ears were opened, his tongue was loosened and he began to speak plainly.[g]

³⁶Jesus commanded them not to tell anyone.[h] But the more he did so, the more they kept talking about it. ³⁷People were overwhelmed with amazement. "He has done everything well," they said. "He even makes the deaf hear and the mute speak."

Jesus Feeds the Four Thousand

8:1-9pp — Mt 15:32-39
8:1-9Ref — Mk 6:34-44
8:11-21pp — Mt 16:1-12

8 During those days another large crowd gathered. Since they had nothing to eat, Jesus called his disciples to him and said, ²"I have compassion for these people;[i] they have already been with me three days and have nothing to eat. ³If I

Cross references (center column):

7:31 [y]ver 24; S Mt 11:21; [z]S Mt 4:18; [a]Mt 4:25; Mk 5:20
7:32 [b]Mt 9:32; Lk 11:14; [c]S Mk 5:23
7:33 [d]Mk 8:23
7:34 [e]Mk 6:41; Jn 11:41; [f]Mk 8:12
7:35 [g]Isa 35:5,6
7:36 [h]S Mt 8:4
8:2 [i]S Mt 9:36

[a]31 That is, the Ten Cities

7:28 *Yes, Lord.* The only time in this Gospel that Jesus is addressed as "Lord."

7:31 *left the vicinity of Tyre and went through Sidon, down to the Sea of Galilee.* Apparently Jesus went north from Tyre to Sidon (about 25 miles) and then southeast through the territory of Herod Philip to the east side of the Sea of Galilee. The route was circuitous possibly to avoid entering Galilee, where Herod Antipas was in power (see 6:17-29) and where many people wanted to take Jesus by force and make him king (Jn 6:14-15). Herod had intimated a hostile interest in Jesus (6:14-16). *Decapolis.* See notes on v. 24; Mt 4:25.

7:34 *Ephphatha!* An Aramaic word that Mark translates for his Gentile readers.

7:35 *the man's ears were opened . . . he began to speak plainly.* Jesus was doing what God had promised to do when

he came to redeem his people (see Isa 35:5-6).

7:36 *not to tell anyone.* See 1:44; see also notes on 5:19, 43; Mt 8:4; 16:20.

8:1-10 Although there are striking similarities between this account and 6:34-44, they are two distinct incidents, as indicated by the fact that Jesus himself refers to two feedings (see vv. 18-20). The differences in details are as definite as the similarities.

8:1 *another large crowd gathered.* Since this incident took place in the region of the Decapolis (see 7:31), the crowd probably was made up of both Jews and Gentiles.

8:2 *I have compassion for these people.* As Jesus had compassion because the people were like sheep without a shepherd (6:34), he now has compassion because they had been so long without food.

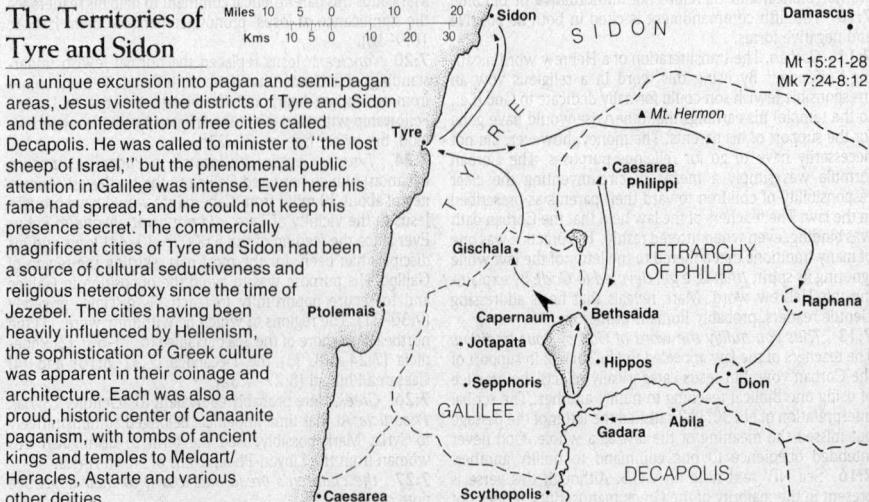

The Territories of Tyre and Sidon

Miles 10 5 0   10   20
Kms 10 5 0   10   20 30

Mt 15:21-28
Mk 7:24-8:12

In a unique excursion into pagan and semi-pagan areas, Jesus visited the districts of Tyre and Sidon and the confederation of free cities called Decapolis. He was called to minister to "the lost sheep of Israel," but the phenomenal public attention in Galilee was intense. Even here his fame had spread, and he could not keep his presence secret. The commercially magnificent cities of Tyre and Sidon had been a source of cultural seductiveness and religious heterodoxy since the time of Jezebel. The cities having been heavily influenced by Hellenism, the sophistication of Greek culture was apparent in their coinage and architecture. Each was also a proud, historic center of Canaanite paganism, with tombs of ancient kings and temples to Melqart/Heracles, Astarte and various other deities.

Map labels: Sidon, SIDON, Damascus, Mt. Hermon, Tyre, TYRE, Caesarea Philippi, Gischala, TETRARCHY OF PHILIP, Raphana, Ptolemais, Capernaum, Bethsaida, Jotapata, Hippos, Sepphoris, Dion, GALILEE, Gadara, Abila, DECAPOLIS, Caesarea, Scythopolis

send them home hungry, they will collapse
on the way, because some of them have
come a long distance."
4His disciples answered, "But where in
this remote place can anyone get enough
bread to feed them?"
5"How many loaves do you have?"
Jesus asked.
"Seven," they replied.
6He told the crowd to sit down on the
ground. When he had taken the seven
loaves and given thanks, he broke them
and gave them to his disciples to set before
the people, and they did so. 7They had a
few small fish as well; he gave thanks for
them also and told the disciples to distribute them.[j] 8The people ate and were satisfied. Afterward the disciples picked up
seven basketfuls of broken pieces that were
left over.[k] 9About four thousand men
were present. And having sent them away,
10he got into the boat with his disciples
and went to the region of Dalmanutha.
11The Pharisees came and began to
question Jesus. To test him, they asked
him for a sign from heaven.[l] 12He sighed
deeply[m] and said, "Why does this generation ask for a miraculous sign? I tell you
the truth, no sign will be given to it."
13Then he left them, got back into the boat
and crossed to the other side.

The Yeast of the Pharisees and Herod

14The disciples had forgotten to bring
bread, except for one loaf they had with
them in the boat. 15"Be careful," Jesus
warned them. "Watch out for the yeast[n]
of the Pharisees[o] and that of Herod."[p]
16They discussed this with one another
and said, "It is because we have no
bread."
17Aware of their discussion, Jesus asked
them: "Why are you talking about having
no bread? Do you still not see or understand? Are your hearts hardened?[q] 18Do
you have eyes but fail to see, and ears but
fail to hear? And don't you remember?
19When I broke the five loaves for the five
thousand, how many basketfuls of pieces
did you pick up?"
"Twelve,"[r] they replied.
20"And when I broke the seven loaves
for the four thousand, how many basketfuls of pieces did you pick up?"
They answered, "Seven."[s]
21He said to them, "Do you still not understand?"[t]

The Healing of a Blind Man at Bethsaida

22They came to Bethsaida,[u] and some
people brought a blind man[v] and begged
Jesus to touch him. 23He took the blind
man by the hand and led him outside the
village. When he had spit[w] on the man's
eyes and put his hands on[x] him, Jesus
asked, "Do you see anything?"
24He looked up and said, "I see people;
they look like trees walking around."
25Once more Jesus put his hands on the
man's eyes. Then his eyes were opened,
his sight was restored, and he saw everything clearly. 26Jesus sent him home, saying, "Don't go into the village.[b]"

8:7 [j]Mt 14:19 **8:8** [k]ver 20 **8:11** [l]S Mt 12:38 **8:12** [m]Mk 7:34 **8:15** [n]1Co 5:6-8 [o]Lk 12:1 [p]S Mt 14:1; Mk 12:13 **8:17** [q]Isa 6:9,10; Mk 6:52 **8:19** [r]Mt 14:20; Mk 6:41-44; Lk 9:17; Jn 6:13 **8:20** [s]ver 6-9; Mt 15:37 **8:21** [t]Mk 6:52 **8:22** [u]S Mt 11:21 [v]Mk 10:46; Jn 9:1 **8:23** [w]Mk 7:33 [x]S Mk 5:23

[b]*26* Some manuscripts *Don't go and tell anyone in the village*

8:4 *where . . . can anyone get enough bread to feed them?* The disciples' question reflects their inadequacy and acknowledges that Jesus alone could feed the people. They had not forgotten his feeding of the 5,000 (6:34–44) and were probably simply giving back to him the task of procuring bread. Alternatively, their question may reveal their spiritual dullness—they were slow learners.
8:8 *seven basketfuls.* See note on Mt 15:37.
8:9 *four thousand men.* See note on 6:44.
8:10 *Dalmanutha.* South of the Plain of Gennesaret a cave has been found bearing the name "Talmanutha," perhaps the spot where Jesus landed. Matthew says Jesus went to the vicinity of Magadan (Mt 15:39; see note there). Dalmanutha and Magadan (or Magdala), located on the western shore of the Sea of Galilee, may be names for the same place or for two places located close to each other.
8:11 *Pharisees.* See note on 2:16. *sign from heaven.* The Pharisees wanted more compelling proof of Jesus' divine authority than his miracles, but he refused to perform such a sign because the request came from unbelief.
8:13 *the other side.* The eastern shore of the Sea of Galilee.
8:15 *yeast of the Pharisees and that of Herod.* Here, as generally in the NT (Mt 16:6,11; Lk 12:1; 1Co 5:6–8; Gal 5:9; but Mt 13:33 seems to be an exception—see note there), yeast is a symbol of evil or corruption. The metaphor includes the idea of a tiny amount of yeast being able to ferment a large amount of dough. In this context it refers to the evil disposition of both the Pharisees and Herod Antipas (see Lk 23:8), who called for Jesus to produce a sign, i.e., a proof of his divine authority (see note on v. 11).
8:18–20 These verses imply two feeding narratives (see note on vv. 1–10).
8:22 *Bethsaida.* See note on Mt 11:21.
8:24 *like trees walking around.* The man had no doubt bumped into trees in his blindness; now he dimly sees something like tree trunks moving about.
8:25 *Once more Jesus put his hands on the man's eyes.* This second laying on of hands is unique in Jesus' healing ministry. *he saw everything clearly.* Giving sight to the blind was another indication that Jesus was doing what God had promised to do when he came to bring salvation (Isa 35:5).
8:26 *Don't go into the village.* So as not to broadcast what Jesus had done for him and precipitate a crisis before Jesus had completed his ministry. See 1:44; see also notes on 5:19,43; Mt 8:4; 16:20.

Peter's Confession of Christ

8:27–29pp — Mt 16:13–16; Lk 9:18–20

27Jesus and his disciples went on to the villages around Caesarea Philippi. On the way he asked them, "Who do people say I am?"

28They replied, "Some say John the Baptist;[y] others say Elijah;[z] and still others, one of the prophets."

29"But what about you?" he asked. "Who do you say I am?"

Peter answered, "You are the Christ.[c]"[a]

30Jesus warned them not to tell anyone about him.[b]

Jesus Predicts His Death

8:31 — 9:1pp — Mt 16:21–28; Lk 9:22–27

31He then began to teach them that the Son of Man[c] must suffer many things[d] and be rejected by the elders, chief priests and teachers of the law,[e] and that he must be killed[f] and after three days[g] rise again.[h] 32He spoke plainly[i] about this, and Peter took him aside and began to rebuke him.

33But when Jesus turned and looked at his disciples, he rebuked Peter. "Get behind me, Satan!"[j] he said. "You do not have in mind the things of God, but the things of men."

34Then he called the crowd to him along with his disciples and said: "If anyone would come after me, he must deny himself and take up his cross and follow me.[k] 35For whoever wants to save his life[d] will lose it, but whoever loses his life for me and for the gospel will save it.[l] 36What good is it for a man to gain the whole world, yet forfeit his soul? 37Or what can a man give in exchange for his soul? 38If anyone is ashamed of me and my words in this adulterous and sinful generation, the Son of Man[m] will be ashamed of him[n] when he comes[o] in his Father's glory with the holy angels."

9 And he said to them, "I tell you the truth, some who are standing here will not taste death before they see the kingdom of God come[p] with power."[q]

The Transfiguration

9:2–8pp — Lk 9:28–36
9:2–13pp — Mt 17:1–13

2After six days Jesus took Peter, James and John[r] with him and led them up a

Cross references

8:28 [y]S Mt 3:1
[z]Mal 4:5
8:29 [a]Jn 6:69; 11:27
8:30 [b]S Mt 8:4; 16:20; 17:9; Mk 9:9; Lk 9:21
8:31 [c]S Mt 8:20
[d]S Mt 16:21
[e]Mt 27:1,2
[f]Ac 2:23; 3:13
[g]S Mt 16:21
[h]S Mt 16:21
8:32 [i]Jn 18:20
8:33 [j]S Mt 4:10
8:34 [k]Mt 10:38; Lk 14:27
8:35 [l]S Jn 12:25
8:38 [m]S Mt 8:20
[n]Mt 10:33; Lk 12:9
[o]S 1Th 2:19
9:1 [p]Mk 13:30; Lk 22:18
[q]Mt 24:30; 25:31
9:2 [r]S Mt 4:21

[c]29 Or *Messiah.* "The Christ" (Greek) and "the Messiah" (Hebrew) both mean "the Anointed One." [d]35 The Greek word means either *life* or *soul;* also in verse 36.

8:27 *Caesarea Philippi.* See notes on 7:24; Mt 16:13.
8:29 *Christ.* See NIV text note. Because popular Jewish ideas associated with the term "Christ" were largely political and national, Jesus seldom used it. Of its seven occurrences in Mark, only three appear in the sayings of Jesus (9:41; 12:35; 13:21), and in none of these does he use the title of himself (with the possible exception of 9:41). Mark identifies Jesus as the Christ in 1:1.
8:30 *not to tell anyone about him.* See 1:44; see also notes on 5:19,43; Mt 8:4; 16:20.
8:31–10:52 A new section begins in 8:31 and centers on three predictions of Jesus' death (8:31; 9:31; 10:33–34). It indicates a geographical shift from Galilee, where most of Jesus' public ministry reported by Mark took place, to Jerusalem and the closing days of Jesus' life on earth. In this section Jesus defines the true meaning of "Christ" as the title applies to him.
8:31 *Son of Man.* Jesus' most common title for himself, used 81 times in the Gospels and never used by anyone but Jesus. In Da 7:13–14 the Son of Man is pictured as a heavenly figure who in the end times is entrusted by God with authority, glory and sovereign power. That Jesus used "Son of Man" as a Messianic title by his use of it (v. 31) in juxtaposition to Peter's use of "Christ" (v. 29). See note on Da 7:13. *must suffer.* As predicted in the Suffering Servant passage in Isa 52:13–53:12 (see Mk 9:9,12,31; 10:33–34; 14:21,41). *elders.* The lay members of the Sanhedrin, the high court of the Jews. *chief priests.* See note on Mt 2:4. These included the ruling high priest, Caiaphas; the former high priest, Annas; and the high priestly families. *teachers of the law.* See note on Mt 2:4. Representatives of the three groups mentioned here constituted the Sanhedrin.
8:32 *Peter . . . began to rebuke him.* Suffering and rejection had no place in Peter's conception of the Messiah, and

he rebuked Jesus for teaching what to him seemed not only inconceivable but terribly wrong.
8:33 *Satan.* Peter's attempt to dissuade Jesus from going to the cross held the same temptation Satan gave at the outset of Jesus' ministry (see Mt 4:8–10), so Jesus severely rebuked him.
8:34 *deny himself.* Cease to make self the object of his life and actions. *take up his cross.* The picture is of a man, already condemned, required to carry the beam of his own cross to the place of execution (see Jn 19:17). Cross-bearing is a willingness to suffer and die for the Lord's sake. *and follow me.* Implying that his own death would be by crucifixion.
8:35 *save his life.* Physical life may be saved by denying Jesus, but eternal life will be lost. Conversely, discipleship may result in the loss of physical life, but that loss is insignificant when compared with gaining eternal life.
8:36 *the whole world.* All the things that could possibly be achieved or acquired in this life. *soul.* That is, eternal life (also in v. 37).
8:38 *ashamed of me and my words.* Contrast Ro 1:16. A person who is more concerned about fitting into and pleasing his own "adulterous and sinful generation" than about following and pleasing Christ will have no part in God's kingdom. *Son of Man.* See note on 8:31. *when he comes in his Father's glory.* See 2Th 1:6–10. The situation in which Jesus is rejected, humiliated and put to death will be reversed when he returns in glory as the Judge of all men.
9:1 *I tell you the truth.* See note on 3:28. *not taste death before they see the kingdom of God come with power.* See note on Mt 16:28. *kingdom of God.* See note on Mt 3:2.
9:2 *After six days.* See note on Mt 17:1. *Peter, James and John.* See note on 5:37. *a high mountain.* See note on Lk 9:28. *transfigured.* See note on Mt 17:2.

high mountain, where they were all alone. There he was transfigured before them. [3]His clothes became dazzling white,[s] whiter than anyone in the world could bleach them. [4]And there appeared before them Elijah and Moses, who were talking with Jesus.

[5]Peter said to Jesus, "Rabbi,[t] it is good for us to be here. Let us put up three shelters—one for you, one for Moses and one for Elijah." [6](He did not know what to say, they were so frightened.)

[7]Then a cloud appeared and enveloped them, and a voice came from the cloud:[u] "This is my Son, whom I love. Listen to him!"[v]

[8]Suddenly, when they looked around, they no longer saw anyone with them except Jesus.

[9]As they were coming down the mountain, Jesus gave them orders not to tell anyone[w] what they had seen until the Son of Man[x] had risen from the dead. [10]They kept the matter to themselves, discussing what "rising from the dead" meant.

[11]And they asked him, "Why do the teachers of the law say that Elijah must come first?"

[12]Jesus replied, "To be sure, Elijah does come first, and restores all things. Why then is it written that the Son of Man[y] must suffer much[z] and be rejected?[a] [13]But I tell you, Elijah has come,[b] and they have done to him everything they wished, just as it is written about him."

The Healing of a Boy With an Evil Spirit

9:14–28; 30–32pp — Mt 17:14–19; 22,23; Lk 9:37–45

[14]When they came to the other disciples, they saw a large crowd around them and the teachers of the law arguing with them. [15]As soon as all the people saw Jesus, they were overwhelmed with wonder and ran to greet him.

[16]"What are you arguing with them about?" he asked.

[17]A man in the crowd answered, "Teacher, I brought you my son, who is possessed by a spirit that has robbed him of speech. [18]Whenever it seizes him, it throws him to the ground. He foams at the mouth, gnashes his teeth and becomes rigid. I asked your disciples to drive out the spirit, but they could not."

[19]"O unbelieving generation," Jesus replied, "how long shall I stay with you? How long shall I put up with you? Bring the boy to me."

[20]So they brought him. When the spirit saw Jesus, it immediately threw the boy into a convulsion. He fell to the ground and rolled around, foaming at the mouth.[c] [21]Jesus asked the boy's father, "How long has he been like this?"

"From childhood," he answered. [22]"It has often thrown him into fire or water to kill him. But if you can do anything, take pity on us and help us."

[23]"'If you can'?" said Jesus. "Everything is possible for him who believes."[d]

[24]Immediately the boy's father ex-

Cross references (center column):

9:3 [s]S Mt 28:3
9:5 [t]S Mt 23:7
9:7 [u]Ex 24:16
[v]S Mt 3:17
9:9 [w]S Mk 8:30
[x]S Mt 8:20
9:12 [y]S Mt 8:20
[z]S Mt 16:21
[a]Lk 23:11
9:13 [b]S Mt 11:14

9:20 [c]Mk 1:26
9:23
[d]S Mt 21:21; Mk 11:23; Jn 11:40

9:4 *Elijah and Moses.* See notes on Mt 17:3; Lk 9:30.
9:5 *Rabbi.* Hebrew word for "(my) teacher." *three shelters.* Peter may have desired to erect new tents of meeting where God could again communicate with his people (see Ex 29:42). Or he may have been thinking of the booths used at the Feast of Tabernacles (Lev 23:42). In any case, he seemed eager to find fulfillment of the promised glory then, prior to the sufferings that Jesus had announced as necessary.
9:7 *a voice came from the cloud.* The cloud is frequently a symbol of God's presence to protect and guide (e.g., Ex 16:10; 19:9; 24:15–18; 33:9–10). *Listen to him!* The full sense includes obeying him. When God is involved, the only true hearing is obedient hearing (see Jas 1:22–25).
9:9 *not to tell anyone.* After Jesus' resurrection the disciples were to tell everyone what they had experienced, for Jesus' finished work would have demonstrated his true and full character as the Messiah. *Son of Man.* See note on 8:31.
9:10 *what "rising from the dead" meant.* As Jews they were familiar with the doctrine of the resurrection; it was the resurrection of the Son of Man that baffled them, because their theology had no place for a suffering and dying Messiah.
9:11 *Elijah must come first.* See note on Mt 17:10.
9:12 *Elijah does come first, and restores all things.* A reference to the coming of Elijah, or one like him, in preparation for the coming of the Messiah (see note on Mt 17:10). *Son of Man.* See note on 8:31. *must suffer much and be*

rejected. Just as "Elijah" (John the Baptist; see note on v. 13) has been rejected (see note on Mt 17:12).
9:13 *Elijah has come.* A reference to John the Baptist (see Mt 17:13). *they.* Herod and Herodias (see 6:17–29). John, like Elijah, was opposed by a weak ruler and his wicked consort. *as it is written about him.* What Scripture says about Elijah in his relationship to Ahab and Jezebel (1Ki 19:1–10). There is no prediction of suffering associated with Elijah's ministry in the end times. However, what happened to Elijah under the threats of Jezebel foreshadowed what would happen to John the Baptist. The order of events suggested in vv. 11–13 is as follows: (1) Elijah ministered in the days of wicked Jezebel; (2) Elijah was a type of John the Baptist, who in turn suffered at the hands of Herodias; (3) the Son of Man suffered and was rejected a short time after John was beheaded.
9:14 *the other disciples.* The nine besides Peter, James and John (see v. 2).
9:18 Demonic possession was responsible for the boy's condition (see vv. 20,25–26).
9:22 *to kill him.* See notes on 5:5,13.
9:23 *If you can? . . . Everything is possible for him who believes.* The question was not whether Jesus had the power to heal the boy but whether the father had faith to believe it. A person who truly believes will set no limits on what God can do.

claimed, "I do believe; help me overcome my unbelief!"

25When Jesus saw that a crowd was running to the scene,*e* he rebuked the evil*e* spirit. "You deaf and mute spirit," he said, "I command you, come out of him and never enter him again."

26The spirit shrieked, convulsed him violently and came out. The boy looked so much like a corpse that many said, "He's dead." 27But Jesus took him by the hand and lifted him to his feet, and he stood up.

28After Jesus had gone indoors, his disciples asked him privately,*f* "Why couldn't we drive it out?"

29He replied, "This kind can come out only by prayer.*f* "

30They left that place and passed through Galilee. Jesus did not want anyone to know where they were, 31because he was teaching his disciples. He said to them, "The Son of Man*g* is going to be betrayed into the hands of men. They will kill him,*h* and after three days*i* he will rise."*/* 32But they did not understand what he meant*k* and were afraid to ask him about it.

Who Is the Greatest?

9:33–37pp — Mt 18:1–5; Lk 9:46–48

33They came to Capernaum.*/* When he was in the house,*m* he asked them, "What were you arguing about on the road?" 34But they kept quiet because on the way they had argued about who was the greatest.*n*

35Sitting down, Jesus called the Twelve and said, "If anyone wants to be first, he

must be the very last, and the servant of all."*o*

36He took a little child and had him stand among them. Taking him in his arms,*p* he said to them, 37"Whoever welcomes one of these little children in my name welcomes me; and whoever welcomes me does not welcome me but the one who sent me."*q*

Whoever Is Not Against Us Is for Us

9:38–40pp — Lk 9:49,50

38"Teacher," said John, "we saw a man driving out demons in your name and we told him to stop, because he was not one of us."*r*

39"Do not stop him," Jesus said. "No one who does a miracle in my name can in the next moment say anything bad about me, 40for whoever is not against us is for us.*s* 41I tell you the truth, anyone who gives you a cup of water in my name because you belong to Christ will certainly not lose his reward.*t*

Causing to Sin

42"And if anyone causes one of these little ones who believe in me to sin,*u* it would be better for him to be thrown into the sea with a large millstone tied around his neck.*v* 43If your hand causes you to sin,*w* cut it off. It is better for you to enter life maimed than with two hands to go into hell,*x* where the fire never goes out.*gy* 45And if your foot causes you to

Cross references (center column)

9:25 *ever* 15
9:28 /Mk 7:17
9:31 *g*S Mt 8:20
*h*ver 12; Ac 2:23;
3:13 /S Mt 16:21
/S Mt 16:21
9:32 *k*Lk 2:50;
9:45; 18:34;
Jn 12:16
9:33 /S Mt 4:13
*m*Mk 1:29
9:34 *n*Lk 22:24

9:35 *o*Mt 18:4;
Mk 10:43;
Lk 22:26
9:36 *p*Mk 10:16
9:37 *q*S Mt 10:40
9:38
*r*Nu 11:27-29
9:40 *s*Mt 12:30;
Lk 11:23
9:41 *t*S Mt 10:42
9:42 *u*S Mt 5:29
*v*Mt 18:6;
Lk 17:2
9:43 *w*S Mt 5:29
*x*Mt 5:30; 18:8
*y*S Mt 25:41

*e*25 Greek *unclean*   *f*29 Some manuscripts *prayer and fasting*   *g*43 Some manuscripts *out,* 44*where* / *" 'their worm does not die, / and the fire is not quenched.'*

9:24 *I do believe; help me overcome my unbelief!* Since faith is never perfect, belief and unbelief are often mixed.
9:25 *When Jesus saw that a crowd was running to the scene, he rebuked the evil spirit.* As much as possible, Jesus wanted to avoid further publicity.
9:29 *This kind.* Seems to suggest that there are different kinds of demons. *only by prayer.* The disciples apparently had taken for granted the power given to them or had come to believe that it was inherent in them. Lack of prayer indicated they had forgotten that their power over the demonic spirits was from Jesus (see 3:15; 6:7,13).
9:30 *passed through Galilee.* Jesus' public ministry in and around Galilee was completed (see note on 7:24), and he was now on his way to Jerusalem to suffer and die (see 10:32–34). As he had been doing for several months, Jesus continued to focus his teaching ministry on the Twelve (v. 31).
9:31 *Son of Man.* See note on 8:31.
9:32 *they did not understand.* See v. 10; 8:32–33.
9:33 *Capernaum.* See notes on 1:21; Mt 4:13. *the house.* Probably the one belonging to Peter and Andrew (see 1:29).
9:34 *they kept quiet.* No doubt due to embarrassment. *who was the greatest.* Questions of rank and status are normal and played an important role in the life of Jewish groups at this time, but they had no place in Jesus' value

system (see v. 35; 10:42–45).
9:35 *Sitting down.* See note on 4:1.
9:38 *not one of us.* The man apparently was a believer, but he was not one of the exclusive company of the Twelve. Nevertheless he acted in Jesus' name and had done what the disciples, on at least one occasion, had not been able to do (see vv. 14–18,28).
9:39 *Do not stop him.* Jesus' view of discipleship was far more inclusive than the narrow view held by the Twelve.
9:41 *I tell you the truth.* See note on 3:28. *gives you a cup of water.* God remembers even small acts of kindness extended to believers because they are believers. *his reward.* Including God's approval.
9:42 *one of these little ones who believe in me.* Perhaps the little children mentioned in vv. 36–37, or the man mentioned in v. 38. Jesus' point is clear: To cause even those whom we might consider to be the least of believers to sin will bring serious judgment. *millstone.* A heavy stone slab turned by a donkey in grinding grain.
9:43 *cut it off.* Hyperbole, a figure of speech that exaggerates to make its point, is used here to emphasize the need for drastic action. Often sin can be conquered only by radical "spiritual surgery." *life.* Eternal life in the presence of God. *hell.* See note on Mt 5:22.
9:44,46 See NIV text notes on vv. 43,45. Verses 44,46 are

sin,[z] cut it off. It is better for you to enter life crippled than to have two feet and be thrown into hell.[h][a] 47And if your eye causes you to sin,[b] pluck it out. It is better for you to enter the kingdom of God with one eye than to have two eyes and be thrown into hell,[c] 48where

" 'their worm does not die,
   and the fire is not quenched.'[i] [d]

49Everyone will be salted[e] with fire.

50"Salt is good, but if it loses its saltiness, how can you make it salty again?[f] Have salt in yourselves,[g] and be at peace with each other."[h]

Divorce

10:1–12pp — Mt 19:1–9

10 Jesus then left that place and went into the region of Judea and across the Jordan.[i] Again crowds of people came to him, and as was his custom, he taught them.[j]

2Some Pharisees[k] came and tested him by asking, "Is it lawful for a man to divorce his wife?"

3"What did Moses command you?" he replied.

4They said, "Moses permitted a man to

write a certificate of divorce and send her away."[l]

5"It was because your hearts were hard[m] that Moses wrote you this law," Jesus replied. 6"But at the beginning of creation God 'made them male and female.'[i][n] 7"For this reason a man will leave his father and mother and be united to his wife,[k] 8and the two will become one flesh.'[l][o] So they are no longer two, but one. 9Therefore what God has joined together, let man not separate."

10When they were in the house again, the disciples asked Jesus about this. 11He answered, "Anyone who divorces his wife and marries another woman commits adultery against her.[p] 12And if she divorces her husband and marries another man, she commits adultery."[q]

The Little Children and Jesus

10:13–16pp — Mt 19:13–15; Lk 18:15–17

13People were bringing little children to Jesus to have him touch them, but the disciples rebuked them. 14When Jesus saw

---

Cross references (center column)

9:45 [z]S Mt 5:29
[a]Mt 18:8
9:47 [b]S Mt 5:29
[c]Mt 5:29; 18:9
9:48 [d]Isa 66:24;
S Mt 25:41
9:49 [e]Lev 2:13
9:50 [f]Mk 5:13;
Lk 14:34,35
[g]Col 4:6
[h]Ro 12:18;
2Co 13:11;
1Th 5:13
10:1 [i]Mk 1:5;
Jn 10:40; 11:7
[j]S Mt 4:23;
Mk 2:13; 4:2;
6:6,34
10:2 [k]Mk 2:16

10:4 [l]Dt 24:1–4;
Mt 5:31
10:5 [m]Ps 95:8;
Heb 3:15
10:6 [n]Ge 1:27;
5:2
10:8 [o]Ge 2:24;
1Co 6:16
10:11 [p]S Lk 16:18
10:12 [q]Ro 7:3;
1Co 7:10,11

[h]45 Some manuscripts *hell,* [40]*where / " 'their worm does not die, / and the fire is not quenched.'*
[i]48 Isaiah 66:24   [j]6 Gen. 1:27   [k]7 Some early manuscripts do not have *and be united to his wife.*
[l]8 Gen. 2:24

Notes (bottom)

not found in important early manuscripts of the NT. Verses 44,46 are identical with v. 48.
9:47 *kingdom of God.* See note on Mt 3:2.
9:48 Isa 66:24 speaks of the punishment for rebellion against God. As the final word of Isaiah's message, the passage became familiar as a picture of endless destruction. *worm does not die.* Worms were always present in the rubbish dump (see note on Mt 5:22).
9:49 The saying may mean that everyone who enters hell will suffer its fire, or (if only loosely connected with the preceding) it may mean that every Christian in this life can expect to undergo the fire of suffering and purification.
9:50 *Salt is good.* The distinctive mark of discipleship typified by salt is allegiance to Jesus and the gospel (see 8:35,38; see also note on Mt 5:13). *be at peace with each other.* Strife is resolved and peace restored when we recognize in one another a common commitment to Jesus and the gospel.
10:1 *region of Judea.* The Greek and Roman equivalent to the OT land of Judah, essentially the southern part of Palestine (now exclusive of Idumea), which formerly had been the southern kingdom. For Jesus' ministry in Judea see note on Lk 9:51. *Jordan.* See note on 1:5. Jesus' journey took him south from Capernaum, over the mountains of Samaria into Judea and then east across the Jordan into Perea, where he was in the territory of Herod Antipas (see note on Mt 14:1). For Jesus' ministry in Perea see note on Lk 13:22.
10:2 *Pharisees.* See note on 2:16. *came and tested him.* The question of the Pharisees was hostile. It was for unlawful divorce and remarriage that John the Baptist denounced Herod Antipas and Herodias (see 6:17–18), and this rebuke cost him first imprisonment and then his life. Jesus was now within Herod's jurisdiction, and the Pharisees may have hoped that Jesus' reply would cause the tetrarch to seize him as he had John. *Is it lawful . . . to divorce his wife?* Jews of

that day generally agreed that divorce was lawful, the only debated issue being the proper grounds for it (see note on Mt 19:3).
10:5 *because your hearts were hard.* Divorce was an accommodation to human weakness and was used to bring order in a society that had disregarded God's will, but it was not the standard God had originally intended, as vv. 6–9 clearly indicate. The purpose of Dt 24:1 was not to make divorce acceptable, but to reduce the hardship of its consequences.
10:6 *at the beginning of creation.* Jesus goes back to the time before human sin to show God's original intention. God instituted marriage as a great unifying blessing, bonding the male and female in his creation.
10:8 *no longer two, but one.* The deduction drawn by Jesus affirms the ideal of the permanence of marriage.
10:9 *Therefore what God has joined together.* Jesus grounds the sanctity of marriage in the authority of God himself, and his "No" to divorce safeguards against human selfishness, which always threatens to destroy marriage.
10:11 *Anyone who divorces his wife.* In Jewish practice divorce was effected by the husband himself, not by a judicial authority or court. *commits adultery against her.* A simple declaration of divorce on the part of a husband could not release him from the divine law of marriage and its moral obligations—this enduring force of the marriage bond was unrecognized in rabbinic courts. But see note on Mt 19:3; see also Mt 19:9, where an exception is mentioned. 1Co 7:15 may contain another exception (see notes on 1Co 7:12,15).
10:12 *she commits adultery.* In this historical and geographical context, Jesus' pronouncements confirm the bold denunciation by John the Baptist and equally condemn Herod Antipas and Herodias.
10:14 *kingdom of God.* See note on Mt 3:2. *belongs to*

this, he was indignant. He said to them, "Let the little children come to me, and do not hinder them, for the kingdom of God belongs to such as these.[r] [15]I tell you the truth, anyone who will not receive the kingdom of God like a little child will never enter it."[s] [16]And he took the children in his arms,[t] put his hands on them and blessed them.

The Rich Young Man

10:17–31pp — Mt 19:16–30; Lk 18:18–30

[17]As Jesus started on his way, a man ran up to him and fell on his knees[u] before him. "Good teacher," he asked, "what must I do to inherit eternal life?"[v]

[18]"Why do you call me good?" Jesus answered. "No one is good—except God alone. [19]You know the commandments: 'Do not murder, do not commit adultery, do not steal, do not give false testimony, do not defraud, honor your father and mother.'[m]"[w]

[20]"Teacher," he declared, "all these I have kept since I was a boy."

[21]Jesus looked at him and loved him. "One thing you lack," he said. "Go, sell everything you have and give to the poor,[x] and you will have treasure in heaven.[y] Then come, follow me."[z]

[22]At this the man's face fell. He went away sad, because he had great wealth.

[23]Jesus looked around and said to his disciples, "How hard it is for the rich[a] to enter the kingdom of God!"

[24]The disciples were amazed at his words. But Jesus said again, "Children, how hard it is[n] to enter the kingdom of God![b] [25]It is easier for a camel to go through the eye of a needle than for a rich man to enter the kingdom of God."[c]

[26]The disciples were even more amazed, and said to each other, "Who then can be saved?"

[27]Jesus looked at them and said, "With man this is impossible, but not with God; all things are possible with God."[d]

[28]Peter said to him, "We have left everything to follow you!"[e]

[29]"I tell you the truth," Jesus replied, "no one who has left home or brothers or sisters or mother or father or children or fields for me and the gospel [30]will fail to receive a hundred times as much[f] in this

Cross references (center column)

10:14 [r]S Mt 25:34
10:15 [s]Mt 18:3
10:16 [f]Mk 9:36
10:17 [u]Mk 1:40
[v]Lk 10:25; S Ac 20:32
10:19 [w]Ex 20:12-16; Dt 5:16-20
10:21 [x]S Ac 2:45
[y]Mt 6:20; Lk 12:33
[z]S Mt 4:19
10:23 [a]Ps 52:7; 62:10; Mk 4:19; 1Ti 6:9,10,17
10:24 [b]Mt 7:13, 14; Jn 3:5
10:25 [c]Lk 12:16-20; 16:19-31
10:27 [d]S Mt 19:26
10:28 [e]S Mt 4:19
10:30 [f]Mt 6:33

[m]19 Exodus 20:12-16; Deut. 5:16-20   [n]24 Some manuscripts *is for those who trust in riches*

---

such as these. The kingdom of God belongs to those who, like children, are prepared to receive the kingdom as a gift of God (see note on v. 15).

10:15 *I tell you the truth.* See note on 3:28. *like a little child.* The point of comparison is the usual openness and receptivity of children. The kingdom of God must be received as a gift; it cannot be achieved by human effort. It may be entered only by those who know they are helpless, without claim or merit.

10:16 *and blessed them.* Jesus visually demonstrated that the blessings of the kingdom are freely given.

10:17 *a man.* Mark does not identify the man, but Luke (18:18) calls him a "ruler," meaning he was probably a member of an official council or court, and Matthew (19:20) says he was "young." *what must I do . . . ?* The rich man was thinking in terms of earning righteousness to merit eternal life, but Jesus taught that it was a gift to be received (see v. 15). *eternal life.* See note on Mt 19:16.

10:18 *Why do you call me good?* Jesus was not denying his own goodness but was forcing the man to recognize that his only hope was in total reliance on God, who alone can give eternal life. He may also have been encouraging the young man to consider the full identity and nature of the One he was addressing.

10:19 *do not defraud.* The prohibition of fraud may have represented the tenth commandment (against covetousness). If so, Jesus here mentions all six commandments that prohibit wrong actions and attitudes against one's fellowman (see Ex 20:12–16; Dt 5:16–21). *since I was a boy.* Probably a reference to the age of 13, when a Jewish boy assumed personal

responsibility for obeying the commandments.

10:21 *Jesus . . . loved him.* Jesus recognized the man's earnestness. His response was not intended to shame him by exposing failure to understand the spiritual depth of the commandments but was an expression of genuine love. *One thing you lack . . . Go, sell everything.* The young man's primary problem was his wealth (see v. 22), and therefore Jesus' prescription was to rid him of it. There is no indication that Jesus' command to him was meant for all Christians. It applies only to those who have the same spiritual problem. *treasure in heaven.* The gift of eternal life, or salvation. This treasure is not to be earned by self-denial or giving of one's material goods but is to be received by following Jesus. In giving away his wealth, the young man would have removed the obstacle that kept him from trusting in Jesus.

10:22 *He went away sad, because he had great wealth.* The tragic decision to turn away reflected a greater love for his possessions than for eternal life (cf. 4:19).

10:25 *eye of a needle.* The camel was the largest animal found in Palestine. The vivid contrast between the largest animal and the smallest opening represents what, humanly speaking, is impossible.

10:27 *With man this is impossible, but not with God.* Salvation is totally the work of God. Every attempt to enter the kingdom on the basis of achievement or merit is futile. Apart from the grace of God, no one can be saved.

10:29 *I tell you the truth.* See note on 3:28. *gospel.* See note on 1:1.

10:30 *this present age . . . the age to come.* These two terms take in all of time from the fall of man to the eternal state. The present age is evil (Gal 1:4), but the coming righteous age will begin with the second advent of Christ and continue forever. *a hundred times as much . . . and with them persecutions.* The life of discipleship is a combination of promise and persecution, blessing and suffering. God takes nothing from a Christian without making multiplied restora-

10:20 *all these I have kept.* The man spoke sincerely, because for him keeping the law was a matter of external conformity. That the law also required inner obedience, which no one can fully satisfy, apparently escaped him completely. Paul speaks of having had a similar outlook before his conversion (Php 3:6).

present age (homes, brothers, sisters, mothers, children and fields—and with them, persecutions) and in the age to come,^{g} eternal life.^{h} ^{31}But many who are first will be last, and the last first."^{i}

Jesus Again Predicts His Death

10:32–34pp — Mt 20:17–19; Lk 18:31–33

^{32}They were on their way up to Jerusalem, with Jesus leading the way, and the disciples were astonished, while those who followed were afraid. Again he took the Twelve^j aside and told them what was going to happen to him. ^{33}"We are going up to Jerusalem,"^{k} he said, "and the Son of Man^l will be betrayed to the chief priests and teachers of the law.^{m} They will condemn him to death and will hand him over to the Gentiles, ^{34}who will mock him and spit on him, flog him^n and kill him.^{o} Three days later^p he will rise."^{q}

The Request of James and John

10:35–45pp — Mt 20:20–28

^{35}Then James and John, the sons of Zebedee, came to him. "Teacher," they said, "we want you to do for us whatever we ask."

^{36}"What do you want me to do for you?" he asked.

^{37}They replied, "Let one of us sit at your right and the other at your left in your glory."^{r}

^{38}"You don't know what you are asking,"^{s} Jesus said. "Can you drink the cup^t I drink or be baptized with the baptism I am baptized with?"^{u}

^{39}"We can," they answered.

Jesus said to them, "You will drink the cup I drink and be baptized with the baptism I am baptized with,^{v} ^{40}but to sit at my right or left is not for me to grant. These places belong to those for whom they have been prepared."

^{41}When the ten heard about this, they became indignant with James and John. ^{42}Jesus called them together and said, "You know that those who are regarded as rulers of the Gentiles lord it over them, and their high officials exercise authority over them. ^{43}Not so with you. Instead, whoever wants to become great among you must be your servant,^{w} ^{44}and whoever wants to be first must be slave of all. ^{45}For even the Son of Man did not come to be served, but to serve,^{x} and to give his life as a ransom for many."^{y}

Blind Bartimaeus Receives His Sight

10:46–52pp — Mt 20:29–34; Lk 18:35–43

^{46}Then they came to Jericho. As Jesus and his disciples, together with a large

Cross references

10:30 ^{g}S Mt 12:32; ^{h}S Mt 25:46
10:31 ^{i}S Mt 19:30
10:32 ^{j}Mk 3:16-19
10:33 ^{k}S Lk 9:51; ^{l}S Mt 8:20; ^{m}Mt 27:1,2
10:34 ^{n}S Mt 16:21; ^{o}Ac 2:23; 3:13; ^{p}S Mt 16:21; ^{q}S Mt 16:21
10:37 ^{r}Mt 19:28
10:38 ^{s}Job 38:2; ^{t}S Mt 20:22; ^{u}Lk 12:50
10:39 ^{v}Ac 12:2; Rev 1:9
10:43 ^{w}S Mk 9:35
10:45 ^{x}S Mt 20:28; ^{y}S Mt 20:28

Study notes

tion in a new and glorious form. Paradoxically, fellowship with other believers develops most deeply in persecution. *eternal life.* Beyond the conflicts of history is the triumph assured to those who belong to God.
10:31 *first will be last.* A warning against pride in sacrificial accomplishments such as Peter had manifested (v. 28).
10:32 *on their way up to Jerusalem.* This last journey to Jerusalem began in a city called Ephraim (cf. Jn 11:54) and took Jesus into Galilee (Lk 17:11), south through Perea to Jericho (Lk 18:35), then to Bethany (Lk 19:29) and finally to Jerusalem (Lk 19:41). *those who followed.* Probably pilgrims on their way to the Passover in Jerusalem. *the Twelve.* See 3:16–19 and notes on Lk 6:14–16.
10:33–34 *Gentiles, who will . . . kill him.* The word "crucify" does not occur in any of the passion predictions in Mark's Gospel, but the statement that Jesus would be handed over to Gentiles to be killed by them suggests crucifixion, since this was the usual means of Roman execution of non-Romans.
10:33 *Son of Man . . . chief priests . . . teachers of the law.* See notes on 8:31; Mt 2:4.
10:35–45 Parallel to 9:33–37. Both passages deal with true greatness and both follow a prediction of Jesus' suffering and death. Both also show how spiritually undiscerning the disciples were.
10:35–36 *want . . . want.* James's and John's desire for position and power would be realized only if they willingly submitted to servanthood (see "wants . . . wants" in vv. 43–44).
10:35 *James and John, the sons of Zebedee.* See 1:19; 3:17.
10:37 *sit at your right and the other at your left.* Positions of prestige and power.

10:38 *drink the cup I drink.* A Jewish expression that meant to share someone's fate. In the OT the cup of wine was a common metaphor for God's wrath against human sin and rebellion (Ps 75:8; Isa 51:17–23; Jer 25:15–28; 49:12; 51:7). Accordingly, the cup Jesus had to drink refers to divine punishment of sins that he bore in place of sinful mankind (see 10:45; 14:36). *be baptized with the baptism I am baptized with.* The image of baptism is parallel to that of the cup, referring to his suffering and death as a baptism (see Lk 12:50; cf. Ro 6:3–4 for the figure).
10:40 *is not for me to grant.* Jesus would not usurp his Father's authority.
10:41 *the ten.* The other disciples. *indignant.* Possibly because they desired the positions of prestige and power for themselves.
10:43 *Not so with you.* Jesus overturns the value structure of the world. The life of discipleship is to be characterized by humble and loving service.
10:45 A key verse in Mark's Gospel. Jesus came to this world as a servant—indeed, the Servant—who would suffer and die for our redemption, as Isaiah clearly predicted (Isa 52:13–53:12). *Son of Man.* See note on 8:31. *ransom.* Means "the price paid for release (from bondage)." Jesus gave his life to release us from bondage to sin and death. *for.* That is, "in place of," pointing to Christ's substitutionary death. See note on Mt 20:28. *many.* In contrast to the one life given for our ransom.
10:46 *Jericho.* A very ancient city located five miles west of the Jordan and about 15 miles northeast of Jerusalem. In Jesus' time OT Jericho was largely abandoned, but a new city, south of the old one, had been built by Herod the Great. *leaving the city.* Luke says Jesus "approached the city" (Lk 18:35). He may have been referring to the new Jericho,

crowd, were leaving the city, a blind man, Bartimaeus (that is, the Son of Timaeus), was sitting by the roadside begging. [47]When he heard that it was Jesus of Nazareth,[z] he began to shout, "Jesus, Son of David,[a] have mercy on me!"

[48]Many rebuked him and told him to be quiet, but he shouted all the more, "Son of David, have mercy on me!"

[49]Jesus stopped and said, "Call him."

So they called to the blind man, "Cheer up! On your feet! He's calling you." [50]Throwing his cloak aside, he jumped to his feet and came to Jesus.

[51]"What do you want me to do for you?" Jesus asked him.

The blind man said, "Rabbi,[b] I want to see."

[52]"Go," said Jesus, "your faith has healed you."[c] Immediately he received his sight and followed[d] Jesus along the road.

The Triumphal Entry

11:1–10pp — Mt 21:1–9; Lk 19:29–38
11:7–10pp — Jn 12:12–15

11 As they approached Jerusalem and came to Bethphage and Bethany[e] at the Mount of Olives,[f] Jesus sent two of his disciples, [2]saying to them, "Go to the village ahead of you, and just as you enter it, you will find a colt tied there, which no one has ever ridden.[g] Untie it and bring it here. [3]If anyone asks you, 'Why are you doing this?' tell him, 'The Lord needs it and will send it back here shortly.'"

10:47
zS Mk 1:24
aS Mt 9:27
10:51 bS Mt 23:7
10:52 cS Mt 9:22
dS Mt 4:19
11:1 eS Mt 21:17
fS Mt 21:1
11:2 gNu 19:2;
Dt 21:3; 1Sa 6:7

11:4 hMk 14:16
11:9 iPs 118:25,
26; Mt 23:39
11:10 jLk 2:14
11:11 kMt 21:12,
17

[4]They went and found a colt outside in the street, tied at a doorway.[h] As they untied it, [5]some people standing there asked, "What are you doing, untying that colt?" [6]They answered as Jesus had told them to, and the people let them go. [7]When they brought the colt to Jesus and threw their cloaks over it, he sat on it. [8]Many people spread their cloaks on the road, while others spread branches they had cut in the fields. [9]Those who went ahead and those who followed shouted,

"Hosanna![o]"

"Blessed is he who comes in the name of the Lord!"[p][i]

[10]"Blessed is the coming kingdom of our father David!"

"Hosanna in the highest!"[j]

[11]Jesus entered Jerusalem and went to the temple. He looked around at everything, but since it was already late, he went out to Bethany with the Twelve.[k]

Jesus Clears the Temple

11:12–14pp — Mt 21:18–22
11:15–18pp — Mt 21:12–16; Lk 19:45–47; Jn 2:13–16

[12]The next day as they were leaving Bethany, Jesus was hungry. [13]Seeing in the distance a fig tree in leaf, he went to find out if it had any fruit. When he reached it,

o9 A Hebrew expression meaning "Save!" which became an exclamation of praise; also in verse 10 p9 Psalm 118:25,26

---

while Matthew (20:29) and Mark may have meant the old city. *a blind man . . . begging.* The presence of a blind beggar just outside the city gates, on a road pilgrims followed on the way to Jerusalem, was a common sight in that day.
10:47 *Nazareth.* See note on Mt 2:23. *Son of David.* A Messianic title (see Isa 11:1–3; Jer 23:5–6; Eze 34:23–24; and notes on Mt 1:1; 9:27). This is the only place in Mark where it is used to address Jesus.
10:51 *Rabbi.* Hebrew word for "(my) teacher."
11:1–11 At this point a new section in the Gospel of Mark begins. Jesus arrives in Jerusalem, and the rest of his ministry takes place within the confines of the Holy City. The Triumphal Entry, which inaugurates Passion Week, is a deliberate Messianic action, and the clue to its understanding is found in Zec 9:9 (quoted in Mt 21:5; Jn 12:15). Jesus purposefully offers himself as the Messiah, knowing that this will provoke Jewish leaders to take action against him.
11:1 *Bethphage.* See note on Mt 21:1. *Bethany.* See note on Mt 21:17. *Mount of Olives.* Directly east of Jerusalem, it rises to a height of about 2,700 feet, some 200 feet higher than Mount Zion. Its summit commands a magnificent view of the city and especially of the temple.
11:2 *the village ahead.* Probably Bethphage. *colt.* The Greek word can mean the young of any animal, but here it means the colt of a donkey (see Mt 21:2; Jn 12:15). *which no one has ever ridden.* Unused animals were regarded as especially suitable for religious purposes (see Nu 19:2; Dt 21:3; 1Sa 6:7).

11:3 *If anyone asks you.* The message concerning the colt is not directed specifically to the owner but to anyone who might question the disciples' action. *Lord.* See note on Lk 19:31.
11:8 *branches.* The word means "leaves" or "leafy branches," which were readily available in nearby fields. Only John mentions palm branches (Jn 12:13), which apparently came from Jericho, since they are not native to Jerusalem.
11:9 *Hosanna.* See note on Ps 118:25. *Blessed is he who comes.* A quotation of Ps 118:26, one of the Hallel ("Praise") Psalms sung at Passover and especially fitting for this occasion.
11:10 *the coming kingdom of our father David.* The Messianic kingdom promised to David's son (2Sa 7:11–14).
11:11 *temple.* See note on Mt 4:5. *went out to Bethany.* Apparently Jesus spent each night through Thursday of Passion Week in Bethany at the home of his friends Mary, Martha and Lazarus (see 11:19; 14:13; Mt 21:17; Jn 12:1–3). *the Twelve.* See 3:16–19 and notes on Lk 6:14–16.
11:12 *The next day.* Monday of Passion Week. *Bethany.* See note on Mt 21:17.
11:13 *not the season for figs.* Fig trees around Jerusalem normally begin to get leaves in March or April but do not produce figs until their leaves are all out in June. This tree was an exception in that it was already, at Passover time, full of leaves.

he found nothing but leaves, because it was not the season for figs.[l] [14]Then he said to the tree, "May no one ever eat fruit from you again." And his disciples heard him say it.

[15]On reaching Jerusalem, Jesus entered the temple area and began driving out those who were buying and selling there. He overturned the tables of the money changers and the benches of those selling doves, [16]and would not allow anyone to carry merchandise through the temple courts. [17]And as he taught them, he said, "Is it not written:

" 'My house will be called
    a house of prayer for all nations'[q]?[m]

But you have made it 'a den of robbers.'[r] "[n]

[18]The chief priests and the teachers of the law heard this and began looking for a way to kill him, for they feared him,[o] because the whole crowd was amazed at his teaching.[p]

[19]When evening came, they[s] went out of the city.[q]

The Withered Fig Tree

11:20–24pp — Mt 21:19–22

[20]In the morning, as they went along,

they saw the fig tree withered from the roots. [21]Peter remembered and said to Jesus, "Rabbi,[r] look! The fig tree you cursed has withered!"

[22]"Have[t] faith in God," Jesus answered. [23]"I tell you the truth, if anyone says to this mountain, 'Go, throw yourself into the sea,' and does not doubt in his heart but believes that what he says will happen, it will be done for him.[s] [24]Therefore I tell you, whatever you ask for in prayer, believe that you have received it, and it will be yours.[t] [25]And when you stand praying, if you hold anything against anyone, forgive him, so that your Father in heaven may forgive you your sins.[u]"[u]

The Authority of Jesus Questioned

11:27–33pp — Mt 21:23–27; Lk 20:1–8

[27]They arrived again in Jerusalem, and while Jesus was walking in the temple courts, the chief priests, the teachers of the law and the elders came to him. [28]"By what authority are you doing these things?" they asked. "And who gave you authority to do this?"

11:13 *l*Lk 13:6-9
11:17 *m*Isa 56:7
*n*Jer 7:11
11:18 *o*Mt 21:46;
Mk 12:12;
Lk 20:19
*p*S Mt 7:28
11:19 *q*Lk 21:37

11:21 *r*S Mt 23:7
11:23
*s*S Mt 21:21
11:24 *t*S Mt 7:7
11:25 *u*S Mt 6:14

q17 Isaiah 56:7   *r17* Jer. 7:11   *s19* Some early manuscripts *he*   *t22* Some early manuscripts *If you have*   *u25* Some manuscripts *sins. 26But if you do not forgive, neither will your Father who is in heaven forgive your sins.*

11:14 *May no one ever eat fruit from you again.* Perhaps the incident was a parable of judgment, with the fig tree representing Israel (see Hos 9:10; Na 3:12). A tree full of leaves normally should have fruit, but this one was cursed because it had none. The fact that the cleansing of the temple (vv. 15–19) is sandwiched between the two parts of the account of the fig tree (vv. 12–14 and vv. 20–25) may underscore the theme of judgment (see note on v. 21). The only application Jesus makes, however, is as an illustration of believing prayer (vv. 21–25).
11:15–19 All three Synoptic writers mention a cleansing of the temple at the end of Jesus' ministry. Only John has one at the beginning. See notes on Mt 21:12–17; Jn 2:14–17.
11:15 *the temple area.* The court of the Gentiles, the only part of the temple in which Gentiles could worship God and gather for prayer (see v. 17). *buying and selling.* Pilgrims coming to the Passover Feast needed animals that met the ritual requirements for sacrifice, and the vendors set up their animal pens and money tables in the court of the Gentiles. *the tables of the money changers.* Pilgrims needed their money changed into the local currency because the annual temple tax had to be paid in that currency. Also, the Mishnah (see note on Mt 15:2) required Tyrian currency for some offerings. *those selling doves.* Doves were required for the purification of women (Lev 12:6; Lk 2:22–24), the cleansing of those with certain skin diseases (Lev 14:22), and other purposes (Lev 15:14,29). They were also the usual offering of the poor (Lev 5:7).
11:16 *to carry merchandise through the temple courts.* A detail found only in Mark. Apparently the temple area was being used as a shortcut between the city and the Mount of Olives. See note on v. 27.
11:17 *a house of prayer for all nations.* Isa 56:7 assured godly non-Jews that they would be allowed to worship God

in the temple. By allowing the court of the Gentiles to become a noisy, smelly marketplace, the Jewish religious leaders were interfering with God's provision. *a den of robbers.* Not only because they took financial advantage of the people but because they robbed the temple of its sanctity.
11:18 *chief priests and the teachers of the law.* See note on Mt 2:4. *began looking for a way to kill him.* See note on 3:6. They regarded Jesus as a dangerous threat to their whole way of life.
11:19 *went out of the city.* To Bethany (see note on v. 11).
11:20 *In the morning.* Tuesday morning of Passion Week. *withered from the roots.* This detail indicates that the destruction was total (see Job 18:16) and that no one in the future would eat fruit from the tree. It served as a vivid warning of the judgment to come in A.D. 70 (see 13:2 and note on Mt 24:2).
11:21 *Rabbi.* Hebrew word for "(my) teacher." *fig tree you cursed.* See note on v. 14. *has withered.* Perhaps prophetic of the fate of the Jewish authorities who were now about to reject their Messiah.
11:23 *I tell you the truth.* See note on 3:28. *this mountain . . . into the sea.* The Mount of Olives, from which the Dead Sea is visible.
11:26 This verse is not found in the earliest and best manuscripts of the NT (see NIV text note on v. 25), probably having been inserted from Mt 6:15.
11:27 *temple courts.* Several courts surrounded the main temple buildings, including the court of the women, the court of the men (Israelite), and the court of the Gentiles (see v. 16). *the chief priests, the teachers of the law and the elders.* See note on 8:31.
11:28 *authority.* The Sanhedrin was asking why Jesus performed what appeared to be an official act if he possessed no official status (see note on Lk 20:2).

²⁹Jesus replied, "I will ask you one question. Answer me, and I will tell you by what authority I am doing these things. ³⁰John's baptism—was it from heaven, or from men? Tell me!"

³¹They discussed it among themselves and said, "If we say, 'From heaven,' he will ask, 'Then why didn't you believe him?' ³²But if we say, 'From men' . . . .'" (They feared the people, for everyone held that John really was a prophet.) ᵛ

³³So they answered Jesus, "We don't know."

Jesus said, "Neither will I tell you by what authority I am doing these things."

The Parable of the Tenants

12:1–12pp — Mt 21:33–46; Lk 20:9–19

12 He then began to speak to them in parables: "A man planted a vineyard. ʷ He put a wall around it, dug a pit for the winepress and built a watchtower. Then he rented the vineyard to some farmers and went away on a journey. ²At harvest time he sent a servant to the tenants to collect from them some of the fruit of the vineyard. ³But they seized him, beat him and sent him away empty-handed. ⁴Then he sent another servant to them; they struck this man on the head and treated him shamefully. ⁵He sent still another, and that one they killed. He sent many others; some of them they beat, others they killed.

⁶"He had one left to send, a son, whom he loved. He sent him last of all, ˣ saying, 'They will respect my son.'

⁷"But the tenants said to one another, 'This is the heir. Come, let's kill him, and the inheritance will be ours.' ⁸So they took

him and killed him, and threw him out of the vineyard.

⁹"What then will the owner of the vineyard do? He will come and kill those tenants and give the vineyard to others. ¹⁰Haven't you read this scripture:

" 'The stone the builders rejected
  has become the capstoneᵛ ; ʸ
¹¹the Lord has done this,
  and it is marvelous in our eyes' ʷ?" ᶻ

¹²Then they looked for a way to arrest him because they knew he had spoken the parable against them. But they were afraid of the crowd; ᵃ so they left him and went away. ᵇ

Paying Taxes to Caesar

12:13–17pp — Mt 22:15–22; Lk 20:20–26

¹³Later they sent some of the Pharisees and Herodiansᶜ to Jesus to catch himᵈ in his words. ¹⁴They came to him and said, "Teacher, we know you are a man of integrity. You aren't swayed by men, because you pay no attention to who they are; but you teach the way of God in accordance with the truth. Is it right to pay taxes to Caesar or not? ¹⁵Should we pay or shouldn't we?"

But Jesus knew their hypocrisy. "Why are you trying to trap me?" he asked. "Bring me a denarius and let me look at it." ¹⁶They brought the coin, and he asked them, "Whose portrait is this? And whose inscription?"

"Caesar's," they replied.

¹⁷Then Jesus said to them, "Give to Caesar what is Caesar's and to God what is God's." ᵉ

11:32 ᵛS Mt 11:9
12:1 ʷIsa 5:1-7
12:6 ˣHeb 1:1-3
12:10 ʸS Ac 4:11
12:11 ᶻPs 118:22,23
12:12 ᵃS Mk 11:18 ᵇMt 22:22
12:13 ᶜMt 22:16; Mk 3:6 ᵈS Mt 12:10
12:17 ᵉRo 13:7

ᵛ10 Or cornerstone   ʷ11 Psalm 118:22,23

11:30 *from heaven, or from men?* "Heaven" was a common Jewish term for God, often substituted for the divine name to avoid a possible misuse of it (see Ex 20:7). Jesus' question implied that his authority, like that of John's baptism, came from God.

12:1–12 Most of Jesus' parables make one main point. This one is rather complex, and the details fit the social situation in Jewish Galilee in the first century. Large estates, owned by absentee landlords, were put in the hands of local peasants who cultivated the land as tenant farmers. The parable exposed the planned attempt on Jesus' life, and God's judgment on the planners. See notes on Mt 21:35–37,41.

12:1 *parables.* See note on 4:2. *A man planted a vineyard.* The description reflects the language of Isa 5:1–2 where the vineyard clearly symbolizes Israel. *watchtower.* See note on Mt 21:33.

12:7 *the inheritance will be ours.* Jewish law provided that a piece of property unclaimed by an heir would be declared "ownerless," and could be claimed by anyone. The tenants assumed that the son came as heir to claim his property, and

that if he were slain, they could claim the land.

12:9 *others.* See note on Mt 21:41.

12:10 *capstone.* See note on Ps 118:22.

12:12 *against them.* The representatives of the Sanhedrin mentioned in 11:27.

12:13–17 This incident probably took place on Tuesday of Passion Week in one of the temple courts (see chart on "Passion Week," p. 1524).

12:13 *Pharisees.* See note on 2:16. *Herodians.* See note on 3:6. The plan to destroy Jesus, which had originated early in his Galilean ministry, had now matured and was gaining momentum in Jerusalem.

12:14 *pay taxes to Caesar.* Jews in Judea were required to pay tribute money to the emperor. The tax was highly unpopular, and some Jews flatly refused to pay it, believing that payment was an admission of Roman right to rule. See note on Mt 22:15–17.

12:15 *denarius.* See notes on 6:37; Mt 22:19.

12:17 *Give to Caesar what is Caesar's.* See note on Mt 22:21. There are obligations to the state that do not infringe on our obligations to God (see Ro 13:1–7; 1Ti 2:1–6; Tit 3:1–2; 1Pe 2:13–17).

And they were amazed at him.

Marriage at the Resurrection

12:18–27pp — Mt 22:23–33; Lk 20:27–38

18Then the Sadducees,f who say there is no resurrection,g came to him with a question. 19"Teacher," they said, "Moses wrote for us that if a man's brother dies and leaves a wife but no children, the man must marry the widow and have children for his brother.h 20Now there were seven brothers. The first one married and died without leaving any children. 21The second one married the widow, but he also died, leaving no child. It was the same with the third. 22In fact, none of the seven left any children. Last of all, the woman died too. 23At the resurrectionx whose wife will she be, since the seven were married to her?"

24Jesus replied, "Are you not in error because you do not know the Scripturesi or the power of God? 25When the dead rise, they will neither marry nor be given in marriage; they will be like the angels in heaven.j 26Now about the dead rising—have you not read in the book of Moses, in the account of the bush, how God said to him, 'I am the God of Abraham, the God of Isaac, and the God of Jacob'y?k 27He is not the God of the dead, but of the living. You are badly mistaken!"

The Greatest Commandment

12:28–34pp — Mt 22:34–40

28One of the teachers of the lawl came and heard them debating. Noticing that Jesus had given them a good answer, he asked him, "Of all the commandments, which is the most important?"

29"The most important one," answered Jesus, "is this: 'Hear, O Israel, the Lord our God, the Lord is one.z 30Love the Lord your God with all your heart and with all your soul and with all your mind and with all your strength.'a m 31The second is this: 'Love your neighbor as yourself.'b n There is no commandment greater than these."

32"Well said, teacher," the man replied. "You are right in saying that God is one and there is no other but him.o 33To love him with all your heart, with all your understanding and with all your strength, and to love your neighbor as yourself is more important than all burnt offerings and sacrifices."p

34When Jesus saw that he had answered wisely, he said to him, "You are not far from the kingdom of God."q And from then on no one dared ask him any more questions.r

Whose Son Is the Christ?

12:35–37pp — Mt 22:41–46; Lk 20:41–44
12:38–40pp — Mt 23:1–7; Lk 20:45–47

35While Jesus was teaching in the temple courts,s he asked, "How is it that the teachers of the law say that the Christc is the son of David?t 36David himself, speaking by the Holy Spirit,u declared:

" 'The Lord said to my Lord:
　"Sit at my right hand
　until I put your enemies
　　under your feet." 'd v

37David himself calls him 'Lord.' How then can he be his son?"

The large crowdw listened to him with delight.

38As he taught, Jesus said, "Watch out

Cross references (center column)

12:18 /S Ac 4:1
gAc 23:8;
1Co 15:12
12:19 hDt 25:5
12:24
i2Ti 3:15–17
12:25
j1Co 15:42,49,52
12:26 kEx 3:6
12:28
lLk 10:25–28;
20:39

12:30 mDt 6:4,5
12:31
nLev 19:18;
S Mt 5:43
12:32 oDt 4:35,
39; Isa 45:6,14;
46:9
12:33
pISa 15:22;
Hos 6:6;
Mic 6:6–8;
Heb 10:8
12:34 qS Mt 3:2
rMt 22:46;
Lk 20:40
12:35
sS Mt 26:55
tS Mt 9:27
12:36 u2Sa 23:2
vPs 110:1;
S Mt 22:44
12:37 wJn 12:9

Text notes

x23 Some manuscripts *resurrection, when men rise from the dead.* y26 Exodus 3:6 z29 Or *the Lord our God is one Lord* a30 Deut. 6:4,5 b31 Lev. 19:18 c35 Or *Messiah* d36 Psalm 110:1

12:18 *Sadducees.* A Jewish party that represented the wealthy and sophisticated classes. They were located largely in Jerusalem and made the temple and its administration their primary interest. Though they were small in number, in Jesus' time they exerted powerful political and religious influence. See notes on Mt 3:7; Lk 20:27; Ac 4:1. *who say there is no resurrection.* They denied the resurrection, accepted only the five books of Moses as authoritative and flatly rejected the oral tradition (see note on Mt 15:2). These beliefs set them against the Pharisees and common Jewish piety.

12:19 See note on Mt 22:24.

12:26 *book of Moses.* The Pentateuch, the first five books of the OT. *in the account of the bush.* A common way of referring to Ex 3:1–6 (see Ro 11:2, where "about Elijah" refers to 1Ki 19:1–10).

12:28 *which is the most important?* Jewish rabbis counted 613 individual statutes in the law, and attempted to differentiate between "heavy" (or "great") and "light" (or "little") commands.

12:29 The first quotation came to be known as the Shema,

named after the first word of Dt 6:4 in Hebrew, which means "hear." The Shema became the Jewish confession of faith, which was recited by pious Jews every morning and evening. To this day it begins every synagogue service.

12:31 To the Shema Jesus joined the commandment from Lev 19:18 to show that love for neighbor is a natural and logical outgrowth of love for God. *neighbor.* See Lk 10:25–37.

12:33 *all burnt offerings and sacrifices.* The comparison was undoubtedly suggested by the fact that the discussion took place in the temple courtyard (see 11:27).

12:34 *kingdom of God.* See note on Mt 3:2.

12:35 *temple courts.* See note on 11:27. *Christ.* See NIV text note on Mt 1:17. *son of David.* See note on 10:47. Most of the people knew that the Messiah was to be from the family of David.

12:36 *The Lord said to my Lord.* God said to David's Lord, i.e., David's superior—ultimately the Messiah (see note on Ps 110:1). The purpose of the quotation was to show that the Messiah was more than a descendant of David—he was David's Lord.

for the teachers of the law. They like to walk around in flowing robes and be greeted in the marketplaces, 39and have the most important seats in the synagogues and the places of honor at banquets.ˣ 40They devour widows' houses and for a show make lengthy prayers. Such men will be punished most severely."

The Widow's Offering

12:41–44pp — Lk 21:1–4

41Jesus sat down opposite the place where the offerings were putʸ and watched the crowd putting their money into the temple treasury. Many rich people threw in large amounts. 42But a poor widow came and put in two very small copper coins,ᵉ worth only a fraction of a penny.ᶠ

43Calling his disciples to him, Jesus said, "I tell you the truth, this poor widow has put more into the treasury than all the others. 44They all gave out of their wealth; but she, out of her poverty, put in everything—all she had to live on."ᶻ

Signs of the End of the Age

13:1–37pp — Mt 24:1–51; Lk 21:5–36

13 As he was leaving the temple, one of his disciples said to him, "Look, Teacher! What massive stones! What magnificent buildings!"

2"Do you see all these great buildings?" replied Jesus. "Not one stone here will be left on another; every one will be thrown down."ᵃ

3As Jesus was sitting on the Mount of Olivesᵇ opposite the temple, Peter, James, Johnᶜ and Andrew asked him privately, 4"Tell us, when will these things happen? And what will be the sign that they are all about to be fulfilled?"

5Jesus said to them: "Watch out that no one deceives you.ᵈ 6Many will come in my name, claiming, 'I am he,' and will deceive many. 7When you hear of wars and rumors of wars, do not be alarmed. Such things must happen, but the end is still to come. 8Nation will rise against nation, and kingdom against kingdom. There will be earthquakes in various places, and famines. These are the beginning of birth pains.

9"You must be on your guard. You will be handed over to the local councils and flogged in the synagogues.ᵉ On account of me you will stand before governors and kings as witnesses to them. 10And the gospel must first be preached to all nations. 11Whenever you are arrested and brought to trial, do not worry beforehand about what to say. Just say whatever is given you at the time, for it is not you speaking, but the Holy Spirit.ᶠ

12"Brother will betray brother to death, and a father his child. Children will rebel against their parents and have them put to death.ᵍ 13All men will hate you because of

---

Cross references (center column):

12:39 ˣLk 11:43
12:41 ʸ2Ki 12:9; Jn 8:20
12:44 ᶻ2Co 8:12

13:2 ᵃLk 19:44
13:3 ᵇS Mt 21:1
ᶜS Mt 4:21
13:5 ᵈver22; Jer 29:8; Eph 5:6; 2Th 2:3,10-12; 1Ti 4:1; 2Ti 3:13; 1Jn 4:6
13:9 ᵉS Mt 10:17
13:11 ᶠMt 10:19, 20; Lk 12:11,12
13:12 ᵍMic 7:6; Mt 10:21; Lk 12:51-53

ᵉ42 Greek *two lepta*   ᶠ42 Greek *kodrantes*

Study notes (bottom):

12:38 *flowing robes.* The teachers of the law wore long, white linen robes that were fringed and almost reached to the ground.

12:39 *most important seats in the synagogues.* A reference to the bench in front of the "ark" that contained the sacred scrolls. Those who sat there could be seen by all the worshipers in the synagogue.

12:40 *devour widows' houses.* Since the teachers of the law were not paid a regular salary, they were dependent on the generosity of patrons for their livelihood. Such a system was open to abuses, and widows were especially vulnerable to exploitation.

12:41 *the temple treasury.* Located in the court of the women. Both men and women were allowed in this court, but women could go no farther into the temple buildings. It contained 13 trumpet-shaped receptacles for contributions brought by worshipers.

12:42 *very small copper coins.* The smallest coins then in circulation in Palestine. Though her offering was meager, the widow brought "all she had" (v. 44; see note on 2Co 8:12).

12:43 *I tell you the truth.* See note on 3:28.

13:1–37 The Olivet discourse, as this chapter of Mark is commonly called, falls into five sections: (1) Jesus' prophecy of the destruction of the temple and the questions of the disciples (vv. 1–4); (2) warnings against deceivers and false signs of the end (vv. 5–23); (3) the coming of the Son of Man (vv. 24–27); (4) the lesson of the fig tree (vv. 28–31); (5) exhortation to watchfulness (vv. 32–37).

13:1 *massive stones.* According to Josephus (*Antiquities,* 15.11.3), they were white, and some of them were 37 feet long, 12 feet high and 18 feet wide.

13:2 See note on Mt 24:2.

13:3 *Mount of Olives.* See note on 11:1. *Peter, James, John and Andrew.* See 1:16–20.

13:4 The disciples thought that the destruction of the temple would be one of the events that ushered in the end times (see Mt 24:3). *the sign.* The way by which the disciples might know that the destruction of the temple was about to take place and that the end of the age was approaching.

13:5 *Watch out.* It is clear from such words as "Watch out," "You must be on your guard" (v. 9), "So be on your guard" (v. 23), "Be on guard! Be alert!" (v. 33), "Therefore keep watch" (v. 35) and "Watch!" (v. 37) that one of the main purposes of the Olivet discourse was to alert the disciples to the danger of deception.

13:6 *I am he.* That is, the Messiah.

13:7 *the end.* Not the destruction of Jerusalem but the end of the age (see Mt 24:3).

13:8 *birth pains.* See note on Mt 24:8.

13:9 *local councils.* The religious courts made up of the synagogue elders. *flogged.* Infraction of Jewish regulations was punishable by flogging, the maximum penalty being 39 strokes with the whip (see 2Co 11:23–24).

13:10 *first.* Before the end of the age (see Mt 24:14).

13:13 *firm to the end.* Such perseverance is a sure indication of salvation (cf. Heb 3:14; 6:11–12; 10:36).

me,[h] but he who stands firm to the end will be saved.[i]

14"When you see 'the abomination that causes desolation'[g][j] standing where it[h] does not belong—let the reader understand—then let those who are in Judea flee to the mountains. 15Let no one on the roof of his house go down or enter the house to take anything out. 16Let no one in the field go back to get his cloak. 17How dreadful it will be in those days for pregnant women and nursing mothers![k] 18Pray that this will not take place in winter, 19because those will be days of distress unequaled from the beginning, when God created the world,[l] until now—and never to be equaled again.[m] 20If the Lord had not cut short those days, no one would survive. But for the sake of the elect, whom he has chosen, he has shortened them. 21At that time if anyone says to you, 'Look, here is the Christ[i]!' or, 'Look, there he is!' do not believe it.[n] 22For false Christs and false prophets[o] will appear and perform signs and miracles[p] to deceive the elect—if that were possible. 23So be on your guard;[q] I have told you everything ahead of time.

24"But in those days, following that distress,

" 'the sun will be darkened,
    and the moon will not give its light;
25the stars will fall from the sky,
    and the heavenly bodies will be
        shaken.'[j][r]

26"At that time men will see the Son of Man coming in clouds[s] with great power and glory. 27And he will send his angels and gather his elect from the four winds, from the ends of the earth to the ends of the heavens.[t]

28"Now learn this lesson from the fig tree: As soon as its twigs get tender and its leaves come out, you know that summer is near. 29Even so, when you see these things happening, you know that it is near, right at the door. 30I tell you the truth, this generation[k][u] will certainly not pass away until all these things have happened.[v] 31Heaven and earth will pass away, but my words will never pass away.[w]

The Day and Hour Unknown

32"No one knows about that day or hour, not even the angels in heaven, nor the Son, but only the Father.[x] 33Be on guard! Be alert[l]![y] You do not know when that time will come. 34It's like a man going away: He leaves his house and puts his servants[z] in charge, each with his assigned task, and tells the one at the door to keep watch.

35"Therefore keep watch because you do not know when the owner of the house will come back—whether in the evening, or at midnight, or when the rooster crows, or at dawn. 36If he comes suddenly, do not

Cross references (center column)

13:13
  [h]S Jn 15:21
  [i]S Mt 10:22
13:14 [j]Da 9:27;
  11:31; 12:11
13:17 [k]Lk 23:29
13:19 [l]Mk 10:6
  [m]Da 9:26; 12:1;
  Joel 2:2
13:21 [n]Lk 17:23;
  21:8
13:22 [o]S Mt 7:15
  [p]S Jn 4:48;
  2Th 2:9,10
13:23 [q]2Pe 3:17
13:25 [r]Isa 13:10;
  34:4; S Mt 24:29

13:26 [s]S Rev 1:7
13:27 [t]Zec 2:6
13:30 [u]Lk 17:25
  [v]Mk 9:1
13:31
  [w]S Mt 5:18
13:32 [x]Ac 1:7;
  1Th 5:1,2
13:33 [y]1Th 5:6
13:34 [z]Mt 25:14

Text notes (bottom of center column)

[g]14 Daniel 9:27; 11:31; 12:11 [h]14 Or he; also in verse 29 [i]21 Or Messiah [j]25 Isaiah 13:10; 34:4 [k]30 Or race [l]33 Some manuscripts alert and pray

Study notes (bottom)

13:14 the abomination that causes desolation. See notes on Da 9:25–27; Mt 24:15. standing where it does not belong. See 2Th 2:4. let those who are in Judea flee to the mountains. See note on Mt 24:16.
13:15 roof of his house. See notes on 2:4; Lk 17:31.
13:16 cloak. See note on Mt 5:40.
13:17 pregnant women and nursing mothers. Representative of anyone forced to flee under especially difficult circumstances.
13:18 in winter. The time when heavy rains caused streams to become swollen and impossible to cross, preventing many from reaching a place of refuge.
13:19 days of distress unequaled. See note on Mt 24:21.
13:20 the elect. The people of God.
13:21 Christ. See NIV text note on Mt 1:17.
13:24 in those days. A common OT expression having to do with the end time (see Jer 3:16,18; 31:29; 33:15–16; Joel 3:1; Zec 8:23). distress. See v. 19 and note on Mt 24:21.
13:25 The description in vv. 24–25 does not necessarily refer to a complete breakup of the universe. It was language commonly used to describe God's awful judgment on a fallen world (see Isa 13:10; 24:21–23; 34:4; Eze 32:7–8; Joel 2:10,31; 3:15; Am 8:9).
13:26 Son of Man. See note on 8:31. coming in clouds with great power and glory. A reference to Christ's second coming (see 8:38; 2Th 1:6–10; Rev 19:11–16).

13:27 angels. See note on Ge 16:7; cf. Rev 14:14–16. gather his elect. In the OT God is spoken of as gathering his scattered people (Dt 30:3–4; Isa 43:6; Jer 32:37; Eze 34:13; 36:24).
13:28 the fig tree. See note on 11:13.
13:29 these things. The signs listed in vv. 5–23 precede the destruction of Jerusalem and/or the end of the age. it. Probably a reference to the second coming of Christ (see Lk 21:31 and NIV text note on Mt 24:33).
13:30 I tell you the truth. See note on 3:28. generation. See NIV text note. If the term is understood as a normal life span, it may refer either to the generation in which Jesus lived while on earth or to the generation living when these signs begin to occur (see note on Lk 21:32).
13:32 No one knows. A map of the future would be a hindrance, not a help, to faith. Certain signs have been given, but not for the purpose of making detailed, sequential predictions. that day. An OT expression for the day of the Lord's appearance (Am 8:3,9,13; 9:11; Mic 4:6; 5:10; 7:11), referring to the coming of the Son of Man (v. 26). angels. See note on Ge 16:7. nor the Son. While on earth, even Jesus lived by faith, and obedience was the hallmark of his ministry.
13:35 in the evening, or at midnight, or when the rooster crows, or at dawn. The four watches of the night used by the Romans (see note on Mt 14:25).

let him find you sleeping. [37]What I say to you, I say to everyone: 'Watch!' " [a]

Jesus Anointed at Bethany

14:1–11pp — Mt 26:2–16
14:1,2,10,11pp — Lk 22:1–6
14:3–8Ref — Jn 12:1–8

14 Now the Passover [b] and the Feast of Unleavened Bread were only two days away, and the chief priests and the teachers of the law were looking for some sly way to arrest Jesus and kill him. [c] 2"But not during the Feast," they said, "or the people may riot."

3While he was in Bethany, [d] reclining at the table in the home of a man known as Simon the Leper, a woman came with an alabaster jar of very expensive perfume, made of pure nard. She broke the jar and poured the perfume on his head. [e]

4Some of those present were saying indignantly to one another, "Why this waste of perfume? 5It could have been sold for more than a year's wages [m] and the money given to the poor." And they rebuked her harshly.

6"Leave her alone," said Jesus. "Why are you bothering her? She has done a beautiful thing to me. 7The poor you will always have with you, and you can help

13:37
[a]Lk 12:35-40
14:1 [b]S Jn 11:55
[c]S Mt 12:14
14:3 [d]S Mt 21:17
[e]Lk 7:37-39

14:7 [f]Dt 15:11
14:8 [g]Jn 19:40
14:9
[h]S Mt 24:14;
Mk 16:15
14:10
[i]Mk 3:16-19
[j]S Mt 10:4
14:12
[k]Ex 12:1-11;
Dt 16:1-4;
1Co 5:7

them any time you want. [f] But you will not always have me. 8She did what she could. She poured perfume on my body beforehand to prepare for my burial. [g] 9I tell you the truth, wherever the gospel is preached throughout the world, [h] what she has done will also be told, in memory of her."

10Then Judas Iscariot, one of the Twelve, [i] went to the chief priests to betray Jesus to them. [j] 11They were delighted to hear this and promised to give him money. So he watched for an opportunity to hand him over.

The Lord's Supper

14:12–26pp — Mt 26:17–30; Lk 22:7–23
14:22–25pp — 1Co 11:23–25

12On the first day of the Feast of Unleavened Bread, when it was customary to sacrifice the Passover lamb, [k] Jesus' disciples asked him, "Where do you want us to go and make preparations for you to eat the Passover?"

13So he sent two of his disciples, telling them, "Go into the city, and a man carrying a jar of water will meet you. Follow him. 14Say to the owner of the house he

m5 Greek than three hundred denarii

14:1 *Passover.* The Jewish festival commemorating the time when the angel of the Lord passed over the homes of the Hebrews rather than killing their firstborn sons as he did in the Egyptian homes (see Ex 12:13,23,27). The lambs or kids used in the feast were killed on the 14th of Nisan (March–April), and the meal was eaten the same evening between sundown and midnight. Since the Jewish day began at sundown, the Passover Feast took place on the 15th of Nisan. *Feast of Unleavened Bread.* This feast followed Passover and lasted seven days (see Ex 12:15–20; 23:15; 34:18; Dt 16:1–8). *chief priests.* See note on 8:31. *teachers of the law.* See note on Mt 2:4.

14:2 *not during the Feast.* During Passover and the week-long Feast of Unleavened Bread the population of Jerusalem increased from about 50,000 to several hundred thousand. It would have been too risky to apprehend Jesus with so large and excitable a crowd present.

14:3–9 In John's Gospel this incident occurred before Passion Week began (see Jn 12:1). Matthew and Mark may place it here to contrast the hatred of the religious leaders and the betrayal by Judas with the love and devotion of the woman who anointed Jesus.

14:3 *Bethany.* See note on Mt 21:17. *reclining at the table.* The usual posture for eating a banquet meal. *Simon the Leper.* See note on Mt 26:6. *a woman.* We know from John's Gospel (12:3) that she was Mary, the sister of Martha and Lazarus. *alabaster jar.* A sealed flask with a long neck that was broken off when the contents were used and that contained enough ointment for one application. *nard.* A perfume made from the aromatic oil extracted from the root of a plant grown chiefly in India. *poured the perfume on his head.* Anointing was a common custom at feasts (see Ps 23:5; Lk 7:46). The woman's action expressed her deep devotion to Jesus.

14:4 *Some of those present.* Matthew (26:8) identifies

them as the disciples, while John (12:4–5) singles out Judas Iscariot.

14:5 *given to the poor.* It was a Jewish custom to give gifts to the poor on the evening of Passover (see Jn 13:29).

14:7 *The poor you will always have with you.* This did not express lack of concern for the poor, for their needs lay close to Jesus' heart (see Mt 6:2–4; Lk 4:18; 6:20; 14:13,21; 18:22; Jn 13:29).

14:8 *to prepare for my burial.* It was a normal Jewish custom to anoint a body with aromatic oils in preparing it for burial (see 16:1). Jesus seems to anticipate suffering a criminal's death, for only in that circumstance was there no anointing of the body.

14:9 *I tell you the truth.* See note on 3:28. *gospel.* See note on 1:1.

14:10 *Judas Iscariot.* See note on 3:19. *chief priests.* See note on 8:31. This was an unexpected opportunity that they seized, even though they had intended not to apprehend Jesus during the Feast (see v. 2).

14:11 *money.* Thirty silver coins (Mt 26:15).

14:12 *the first day of the Feast of Unleavened Bread.* Ordinarily this would mean the 15th of Nisan, the day after Passover (see note on v. 1). However, the added phrase, "when it was customary to sacrifice the Passover lamb," makes it clear that the 14th of Nisan is meant because Passover lambs were killed on that day (Ex 12:6). The entire eight-day celebration was sometimes referred to as the Feast of Unleavened Bread, and there is evidence that the 14th of Nisan may have been loosely referred to as the "first day of Unleavened Bread."

14:13 *two of his disciples.* Peter and John (Lk 22:8). *man carrying a jar.* He would easily have been identified because customarily only women carried water jars.

14:14 *Where is my guest room . . . ?* It was a Jewish custom that anyone in Jerusalem who had a room available

enters, 'The Teacher asks: Where is my guest room, where I may eat the Passover with my disciples?' [15]He will show you a large upper room, *l* furnished and ready. Make preparations for us there."

[16]The disciples left, went into the city and found things just as Jesus had told them. So they prepared the Passover.

[17]When evening came, Jesus arrived with the Twelve. [18]While they were reclining at the table eating, he said, "I tell you the truth, one of you will betray me—one who is eating with me."

[19]They were saddened, and one by one they said to him, "Surely not I?"

[20]"It is one of the Twelve," he replied, "one who dips bread into the bowl with me. *m* [21]The Son of Man *n* will go just as it is written about him. But woe to that man who betrays the Son of Man! It would be better for him if he had not been born."

[22]While they were eating, Jesus took bread, gave thanks and broke it, *o* and gave it to his disciples, saying, "Take it; this is my body."

[23]Then he took the cup, gave thanks and offered it to them, and they all drank from it. *p*

[24]"This is my blood of the *n* covenant, *q* which is poured out for many," he said to them. [25]"I tell you the truth, I will not drink again of the fruit of the vine until that day when I drink it anew in the kingdom of God." *r*

[26]When they had sung a hymn, they went out to the Mount of Olives. *s*

Cross references (center column):
14:15 *l* Ac 1:13
14:20 *m* Jn 13:18-27
14:21 *n* S Mt 8:20
14:22 *o* S Mt 14:19
14:23 *p* 1Co 10:16
14:24 *q* S Mt 26:28
14:25 *r* S Mt 3:2
14:26 *s* S Mt 21:1

14:27 *t* Zec 13:7
14:28 *u* Mk 16:7
14:30 *v* ver 66-72; Lk 22:34;
14:31 *w* Lk 22:33; Jn 13:37
14:33 *x* S Mt 4:21
14:34 *y* Jn 12:27
14:35 *z* ver 41; S Mt 26:18

Jesus Predicts Peter's Denial

14:27–31pp — Mt 26:31–35

[27]"You will all fall away," Jesus told them, "for it is written:

" 'I will strike the shepherd,
    and the sheep will be scattered.' *o t*

[28]But after I have risen, I will go ahead of you into Galilee." *u*

[29]Peter declared, "Even if all fall away, I will not."

[30]"I tell you the truth," Jesus answered, "today—yes, tonight—before the rooster crows twice *p* you yourself will disown me three times." *v*

[31]But Peter insisted emphatically, "Even if I have to die with you, *w* I will never disown you." And all the others said the same.

Gethsemane

14:32–42pp — Mt 26:36–46; Lk 22:40–46

[32]They went to a place called Gethsemane, and Jesus said to his disciples, "Sit here while I pray." [33]He took Peter, James and John *x* along with him, and he began to be deeply distressed and troubled. [34]"My soul is overwhelmed with sorrow to the point of death," *y* he said to them. "Stay here and keep watch."

[35]Going a little farther, he fell to the ground and prayed that if possible the hour *z* might pass from him. [36]*Abba,* *q* Fa-

n24 Some manuscripts *the new*   *o27* Zech. 13:7
p30 Some early manuscripts do not have *twice.*
q36 Aramaic for *Father*

---

would give it upon request to a pilgrim to celebrate the Passover. It appears that Jesus had made previous arrangements with the owner of the house.
14:15 *Make preparations.* These would include food for the meal: unleavened bread, wine, bitter herbs, sauce and the lamb.
14:17 *When evening came.* Thursday of Passion Week.
14:18 *reclining at the table eating.* Originally the Passover meal was eaten standing (Ex 12:11), but in Jesus' time it was customary to eat it while reclining. *I tell you the truth.* See note on 3:28.
14:20 *dips bread into the bowl with me.* See note on Mt 26:23.
14:21 *Son of Man.* See note on 8:31. *as it is written about him.* Jesus no doubt had the "suffering servant" passage of Isa 53 in mind.
14:22 The NT gives four accounts of the Lord's Supper (Mt 26:26–28; Mk 14:22–24; Lk 22:19–20; 1Co 11:23–25). Matthew's account is very much like Mark's, and Luke's and Paul's have similarities. All the accounts include the taking of the bread; the thanksgiving or blessing; the breaking of the bread; the saying, "This is my body"; the taking of the cup; and the explanation of the relation of blood to the covenant. Only Paul and Luke record Jesus' command to continue to celebrate the Supper. *this is my body.* The bread represented his body, given for them (see Lk 22:19; 1Co 11:24).

14:23 *gave thanks.* The word "Eucharist" is derived from the Greek term used here.
14:24 *my blood of the covenant.* The cup represents the blood of Jesus, which, in turn, represents his poured-out life (i.e., his death). God's commitments to his people in the new covenant are possible only through Christ's atoning death (see Jer 31:31–34; Heb 8:8–12; see also note on Lk 22:20). See note on Ex 24:7. *for many.* See note on Ro 5:15.
14:25 *I tell you the truth.* See note on 3:28. *kingdom of God.* See note on Mt 3:2.
14:26 *a hymn.* See note on Mt 26:30. *Mount of Olives.* See note on 11:1.
14:30 *I tell you the truth.* See note on 3:28. *crows twice.* See NIV text notes here and on v. 72.
14:32 *Gethsemane.* A garden or orchard on the lower slopes of the Mount of Olives, one of Jesus' favorite places (see Lk 22:39; Jn 18:2). The name is Hebrew and means "oil press," i.e., a place for squeezing the oil from olives.
14:33 *Peter, James and John.* See note on 5:37.
14:36 *Abba, Father.* Expressive of an especially close relationship to God (see also NIV text note). *this cup.* The chalice of death and of God's wrath that Jesus took from the Father's hand in fulfillment of his mission. What Jesus dreaded was not death as such, but the manner of his death as the one who was taking the sin of mankind upon himself. See note on 10:38.

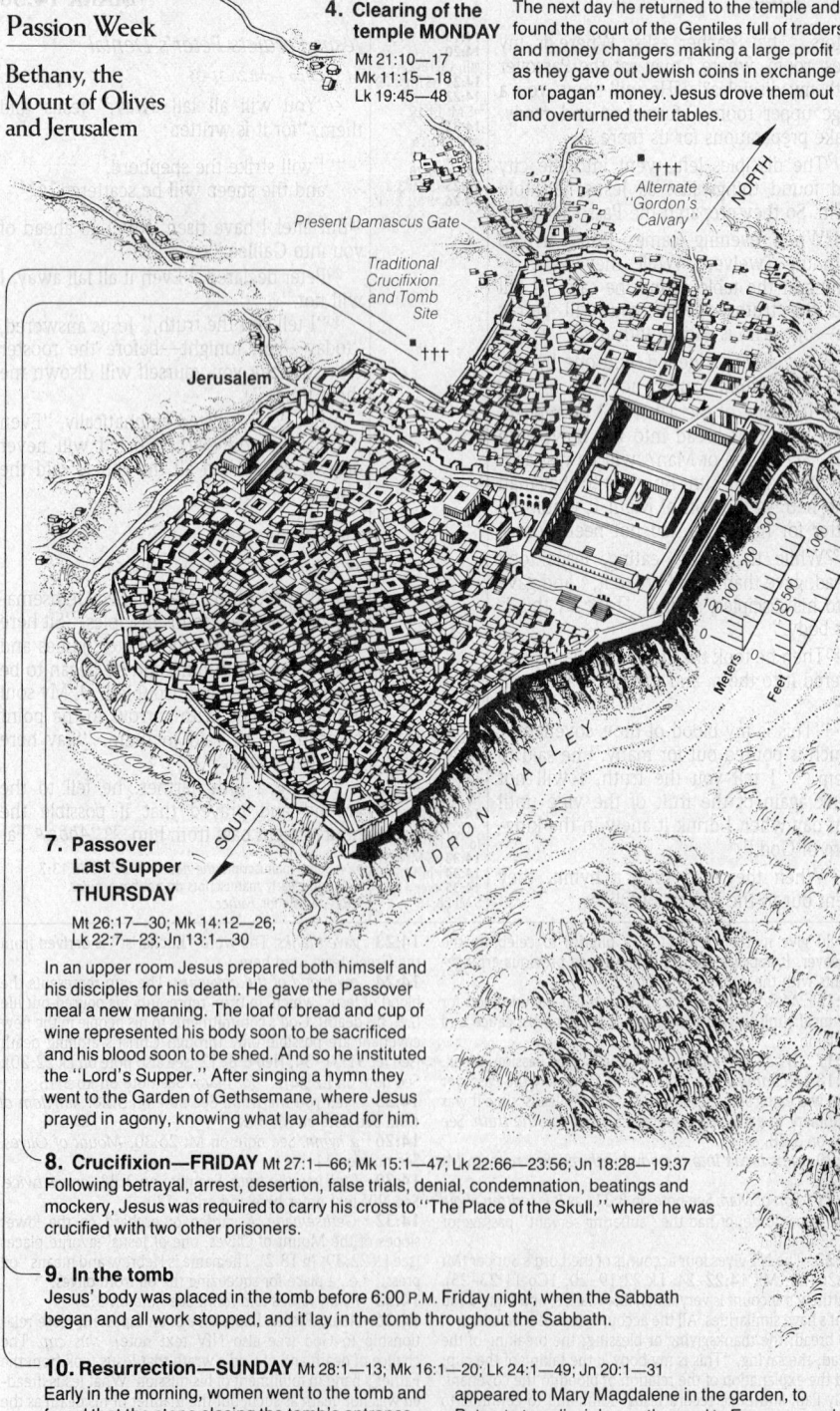

Passion Week

Bethany, the
Mount of Olives
and Jerusalem

4. Clearing of the temple MONDAY
Mt 21:10—17
Mk 11:15—18
Lk 19:45—48

The next day he returned to the temple and found the court of the Gentiles full of traders and money changers making a large profit as they gave out Jewish coins in exchange for "pagan" money. Jesus drove them out and overturned their tables.

†††
Alternate
'Gordon's
Calvary'

NORTH

Present Damascus Gate

Traditional
Crucifixion
and Tomb
Site

†††

Jerusalem

Meters
Feet
0 100 200 300
0 500 1,000

KIDRON VALLEY

SOUTH

**7. Passover
Last Supper
THURSDAY**

Mt 26:17—30; Mk 14:12—26;
Lk 22:7—23; Jn 13:1—30

In an upper room Jesus prepared both himself and his disciples for his death. He gave the Passover meal a new meaning. The loaf of bread and cup of wine represented his body soon to be sacrificed and his blood soon to be shed. And so he instituted the "Lord's Supper." After singing a hymn they went to the Garden of Gethsemane, where Jesus prayed in agony, knowing what lay ahead for him.

8. Crucifixion—FRIDAY Mt 27:1—66; Mk 15:1—47; Lk 22:66—23:56; Jn 18:28—19:37
Following betrayal, arrest, desertion, false trials, denial, condemnation, beatings and mockery, Jesus was required to carry his cross to "The Place of the Skull," where he was crucified with two other prisoners.

9. In the tomb
Jesus' body was placed in the tomb before 6:00 P.M. Friday night, when the Sabbath began and all work stopped, and it lay in the tomb throughout the Sabbath.

10. Resurrection—SUNDAY Mt 28:1—13; Mk 16:1—20; Lk 24:1—49; Jn 20:1—31
Early in the morning, women went to the tomb and found that the stone closing the tomb's entrance had been rolled back. An angel told them Jesus was alive and gave them a message. Jesus appeared to Mary Magdalene in the garden, to Peter, to two disciples on the road to Emmaus, and later that day to all the disciples but Thomas. His resurrection was established as a fact.

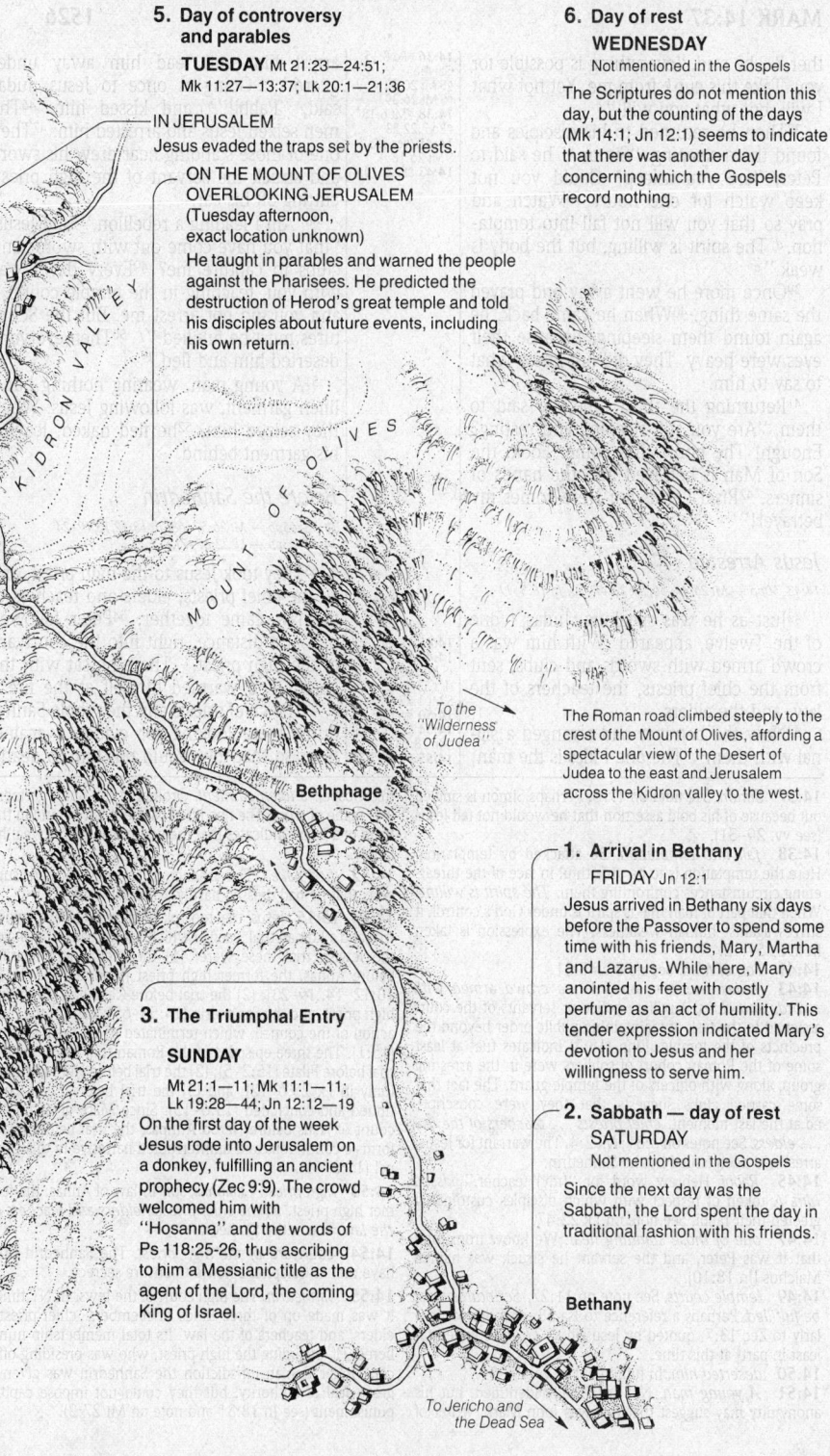

5. Day of controversy and parables

TUESDAY Mt 21:23—24:51;
Mk 11:27—13:37; Lk 20:1—21:36

IN JERUSALEM
Jesus evaded the traps set by the priests.

ON THE MOUNT OF OLIVES
OVERLOOKING JERUSALEM
(Tuesday afternoon,
exact location unknown)

He taught in parables and warned the people
against the Pharisees. He predicted the
destruction of Herod's great temple and told
his disciples about future events, including
his own return.

6. Day of rest
WEDNESDAY
Not mentioned in the Gospels

The Scriptures do not mention this
day, but the counting of the days
(Mk 14:1; Jn 12:1) seems to indicate
that there was another day
concerning which the Gospels
record nothing.

KIDRON VALLEY

MOUNT OF OLIVES

To the
"Wilderness
of Judea"

Bethphage

The Roman road climbed steeply to the
crest of the Mount of Olives, affording a
spectacular view of the Desert of
Judea to the east and Jerusalem
across the Kidron valley to the west.

1. Arrival in Bethany
FRIDAY Jn 12:1

Jesus arrived in Bethany six days
before the Passover to spend some
time with his friends, Mary, Martha
and Lazarus. While here, Mary
anointed his feet with costly
perfume as an act of humility. This
tender expression indicated Mary's
devotion to Jesus and her
willingness to serve him.

2. Sabbath — day of rest
SATURDAY
Not mentioned in the Gospels

Since the next day was the
Sabbath, the Lord spent the day in
traditional fashion with his friends.

3. The Triumphal Entry

SUNDAY

Mt 21:1—11; Mk 11:1—11;
Lk 19:28—44; Jn 12:12—19

On the first day of the week
Jesus rode into Jerusalem on
a donkey, fulfilling an ancient
prophecy (Zec 9:9). The crowd
welcomed him with
"Hosanna" and the words of
Ps 118:25-26, thus ascribing
to him a Messianic title as the
agent of the Lord, the coming
King of Israel.

Bethany

To Jericho and
the Dead Sea

ther,"*a* he said, "everything is possible for you. Take this cup*b* from me. Yet not what I will, but what you will."*c*

³⁷Then he returned to his disciples and found them sleeping. "Simon," he said to Peter, "are you asleep? Could you not keep watch for one hour? ³⁸Watch and pray so that you will not fall into temptation.*d* The spirit is willing, but the body is weak."*e*

³⁹Once more he went away and prayed the same thing. ⁴⁰When he came back, he again found them sleeping, because their eyes were heavy. They did not know what to say to him.

⁴¹Returning the third time, he said to them, "Are you still sleeping and resting? Enough! The hour*f* has come. Look, the Son of Man is betrayed into the hands of sinners. ⁴²Rise! Let us go! Here comes my betrayer!"

Jesus Arrested

14:43–50pp — Mt 26:47–56; Lk 22:47–50; Jn 18:3–11

⁴³Just as he was speaking, Judas,*g* one of the Twelve, appeared. With him was a crowd armed with swords and clubs, sent from the chief priests, the teachers of the law, and the elders.

⁴⁴Now the betrayer had arranged a signal with them: "The one I kiss is the man;

Cross references (center column)
14:36 *a*Ro 8:15; Gal 4:6
*b*S Mt 20:22
*c*S Mt 26:39
14:38 *d*Mt 6:13
*e*Ro 7:22,23
14:41 *f*ver 35; S Mt 26:18
14:43 *g*S Mt 10:4

14:45 *h*S Mt 23:7
14:49
*i*S Mt 26:55
*j*Isa 53:7–12; S Mt 1:22
14:50 *k*ver 27
14:54 *l*S Mt 26:3
*m*Jn 18:18
14:55 *n*S Mt 5:22

arrest him and lead him away under guard." ⁴⁵Going at once to Jesus, Judas said, "Rabbi!"*h* and kissed him. ⁴⁶The men seized Jesus and arrested him. ⁴⁷Then one of those standing near drew his sword and struck the servant of the high priest, cutting off his ear.

⁴⁸"Am I leading a rebellion," said Jesus, "that you have come out with swords and clubs to capture me? ⁴⁹Every day I was with you, teaching in the temple courts,*i* and you did not arrest me. But the Scriptures must be fulfilled."*j* ⁵⁰Then everyone deserted him and fled.*k*

⁵¹A young man, wearing nothing but a linen garment, was following Jesus. When they seized him, ⁵²he fled naked, leaving his garment behind.

Before the Sanhedrin

14:53–65pp — Mt 26:57–68; Jn 18:12,13,19–24
14:61–63pp — Lk 22:67–71

⁵³They took Jesus to the high priest, and all the chief priests, elders and teachers of the law came together. ⁵⁴Peter followed him at a distance, right into the courtyard of the high priest.*l* There he sat with the guards and warmed himself at the fire.*m* ⁵⁵The chief priests and the whole Sanhedrin*n* were looking for evidence against Jesus so that they could put him to death,

---

14:37 *Simon.* See note on 1:16. Perhaps Simon is singled out because of his bold assertion that he would not fail Jesus (see vv. 29–31).

14:38 *fall into temptation.* Be attacked by temptation. Here the temptation is to be unfaithful in face of the threatening circumstances confronting them. *The spirit is willing.* When that part of man that is spirit is under God's control, it strives against human weakness. The expression is taken from Ps 51:12.

14:41 *Son of Man.* See note on 8:31.

14:43 *Judas.* See note on 3:19. *a crowd armed with swords and clubs.* Auxiliary police or servants of the court assigned to the task of maintaining public order beyond the precincts of the temple. John (18:3) indicates that at least some of the Roman cohort of soldiers were in the arresting group, along with officers of the temple guard. The fact that some carried clubs suggests that they were conscripted at the last moment. *chief priests . . . teachers of the law . . . elders.* See notes on 8:31; Mt 2:4. The warrant for Jesus' arrest had been issued by the Sanhedrin.

14:45 *Rabbi.* Hebrew word for "(my) teacher." *kissed him.* A token of respect with which disciples customarily greeted their rabbi. See note on Lk 22:47.

14:47 *one of those standing near.* We know from John that it was Peter, and the servant he struck was named Malchus (Jn 18:10).

14:49 *temple courts.* See note on 11:27. *Scriptures must be fulfilled.* Perhaps a reference to Isa 53, or more particularly to Zec 13:7, quoted by Jesus in v. 27 and fulfilled (at least in part) at this time.

14:50 *deserted him.* In fulfillment of vv. 27–31.

14:51 *A young man.* Not specifically identified, but his anonymity may suggest that this was John Mark, writer of

this Gospel. *a linen garment.* Ordinarily the outer garment was made of wool. The fine linen garment left behind in the hand of a guard indicates that the youth was from a wealthy family.

14:52 *fled naked.* The absence of an undergarment suggests that he had dressed hastily to follow Jesus.

14:53–15:15 Jesus' trial took place in two stages: a Jewish trial and a Roman trial, each of which had three episodes. For the Jewish trial these were: (1) the preliminary hearing before Annas, the former high priest (reported only in Jn 18:12–14, 19–23); (2) the trial before Caiaphas, the ruling high priest, and the Sanhedrin (14:53–65); and (3) the final action of the council, which terminated its all-night session (15:1). The three episodes of the Roman trial were: (1) the trial before Pilate (15:2–5); (2) the trial before Herod Antipas (only in Lk 23:6–12); and (3) the trial before Pilate continued and concluded (15:6–15). Since Mark gives no account of Jesus before Herod Antipas, the trial before Pilate forms a continuous and uninterrupted narrative in this Gospel (15:2–15).

14:53 *high priest.* Caiaphas, son-in-law of Annas, the former high priest. *all the chief priests, elders and teachers of the law.* The entire Sanhedrin.

14:54 *courtyard of the high priest.* The Sanhedrin may have met at Caiaphas's house to ensure secrecy.

14:55 *Sanhedrin.* The high court of the Jews. In NT times it was made up of three kinds of members: chief priests, elders, and teachers of the law. Its total membership numbered 71, including the high priest, who was presiding officer. Under Roman jurisdiction the Sanhedrin was given a great deal of authority, but they could not impose capital punishment (see Jn 18:31 and note on Mt 27:2).

but they did not find any. [56]Many testified falsely against him, but their statements did not agree.

[57]Then some stood up and gave this false testimony against him: [58]"We heard him say, 'I will destroy this man-made temple and in three days will build another,[o] not made by man.'" [59]Yet even then their testimony did not agree.

[60]Then the high priest stood up before them and asked Jesus, "Are you not going to answer? What is this testimony that these men are bringing against you?" [61]But Jesus remained silent and gave no answer.[p]

Again the high priest asked him, "Are you the Christ,[r] the Son of the Blessed One?"[q]

[62]"I am," said Jesus. "And you will see the Son of Man sitting at the right hand of the Mighty One and coming on the clouds of heaven."[r]

[63]The high priest tore his clothes.[s] "Why do we need any more witnesses?" he asked. [64]"You have heard the blasphemy. What do you think?"

They all condemned him as worthy of death.[t] [65]Then some began to spit at him; they blindfolded him, struck him with their fists, and said, "Prophesy!" And the guards took him and beat him.[u]

Peter Disowns Jesus

14:66–72pp — Mt 26:69–75; Lk 22:56–62; Jn 18:16–18,25–27

[66]While Peter was below in the court-yard,[v] one of the servant girls of the high priest came by. [67]When she saw Peter warming himself,[w] she looked closely at him.

"You also were with that Nazarene, Jesus,"[x] she said.

[68]But he denied it. "I don't know or understand what you're talking about,"[y] he said, and went out into the entryway.[s]

[69]When the servant girl saw him there, she said again to those standing around, "This fellow is one of them." [70]Again he denied it.[z]

After a little while, those standing near said to Peter, "Surely you are one of them, for you are a Galilean."[a]

[71]He began to call down curses on himself, and he swore to them, "I don't know this man you're talking about."[b]

[72]Immediately the rooster crowed the second time.[t] Then Peter remembered the word Jesus had spoken to him: "Before the rooster crows twice[u] you will disown me three times."[c] And he broke down and wept.

Jesus Before Pilate

15:2–15pp — Mt 27:11–26; Lk 23:2,3,18–25; Jn 18:29–19:16

15 Very early in the morning, the chief priests, with the elders, the teachers of the law[d] and the whole Sanhedrin,[e] reached a decision. They bound Jesus, led

Cross references (center column)

14:58 *o*S Jn 2:19
14:61 *p*Isa 53:7;
Mt 27:12,14;
Mk 15:5;
Lk 23:9; Jn 19:9
*q*Mt 16:16;
Jn 4:25,26
14:62 *r*S Rev 1:7
14:63 *s*Lev 10:6;
21:10; Nu 14:6;
Ac 14:14
14:64 *t*Lev 24:16
14:65
*u*S Mt 16:21

14:66 *v*ver 54
14:67 *w*ver 54
*x*S Mk 1:24
14:68 *y*ver 30,72
14:70 *z*ver 30,68,
72 *a*Ac 2:7
14:71 *b*ver 30,72
14:72 *c*ver 30,68
15:1 *d*Mt 27:1;
Lk 22:66
*e*S Mt 5:22

*t*61 Or *Messiah*   *s*68 Some early manuscripts *entryway and the rooster crowed*   *t*72 Some early manuscripts do not have *the second time.*   *u*72 Some early manuscripts do not have *twice.*

14:56 *Many testified falsely against him.* In Jewish judicial procedure, witnesses functioned as the prosecution. *did not agree.* According to Dt 19:15 a person could not be convicted unless two or more witnesses gave testimony, which assumes that their testimonies had to agree.
14:58 There is no statement by Jesus precisely like this in the Gospels. It is probably an allusion to what is reported in Jn 2:19.
14:61 *Christ.* See NIV text note. *Son of the Blessed One.* "The Blessed One" was a way of referring to God without pronouncing his name (see note on 11:30). The title was therefore equivalent to "Son of God," though in this context it would seem not to refer to deity but to royal Messiahship, since in popular Jewish belief the Messiah was to be a man, not God.
14:62 *Son of Man.* See note on 8:31. This Son of Man saying brings together Da 7:13 and Ps 110:1.
14:63 *tore his clothes.* A sign of great grief or shock (see Ge 37:29; 2Ki 18:37; 19:1). In the case of the high priest it was a form of judicial act expressing the fact that he regarded Jesus' answer as blasphemous (see note on Mt 26:65).
14:64 *blasphemy.* The sin of blasphemy not only involved reviling the name of God (see Lev 24:10–16) but also included any affront to his majesty or authority (see Mk 2:7; 3:28–29; Jn 5:18; 10:33). Jesus' claim to be the Messiah and, in fact, to have majesty and authority belonging only to God was therefore regarded by Caiaphas as blasphemy, for

which the Mosaic law prescribed death by stoning (Lev 24:16).
14:65 *began to spit at him . . . struck him with their fists.* Conventional gestures of rejection and condemnation (Nu 12:14; Dt 25:9; Job 30:10; Isa 50:6). *they blindfolded him.* An old interpretation of Isa 11:2–4 held that the Messiah could judge by smell without the aid of sight. *Prophesy!* Say who it was that struck you!
14:66 *below.* While Jesus was being beaten in an upstairs room of Caiaphas's house, Peter was below in the courtyard. *one of the servant girls.* The doorkeeper (Jn 18:16).
14:67 *Nazarene.* See note on Mt 2:23.
14:68 *I don't know or understand what you're talking about.* Common in Jewish law for a formal, legal denial.
14:70 *Galilean.* Galileans were easily identified by their dialect. Peter's speech showed him to be a Galilean, and his presence among the Judeans in the courtyard suggested he was a follower of Jesus.
15:1 *Very early in the morning.* The working day of a Roman official began at daylight. *morning.* Friday of Passion Week. *Sanhedrin.* See note on 14:55. *reached a decision.* Apparently to accuse Jesus before the civil authority for treason rather than blasphemy (see Lk 23:1–14 and note on Lk 23:2). *Pilate.* The Roman governor of Judea from A.D. 26 to 36, whose official residence was in Caesarea, on the Mediterranean coast. (In 1961 archaeologists working at Caesarea unearthed a stone contemporary with Pilate and

him away and handed him over to Pilate.*f*

2"Are you the king of the Jews?"*g* asked Pilate.

"Yes, it is as you say," Jesus replied.

3The chief priests accused him of many things. 4So again Pilate asked him, "Aren't you going to answer? See how many things they are accusing you of."

5But Jesus still made no reply,*h* and Pilate was amazed.

6Now it was the custom at the Feast to release a prisoner whom the people requested. 7A man called Barabbas was in prison with the insurrectionists who had committed murder in the uprising. 8The crowd came up and asked Pilate to do for them what he usually did.

9"Do you want me to release to you the king of the Jews?"*i* asked Pilate, 10knowing it was out of envy that the chief priests had handed Jesus over to him. 11But the chief priests stirred up the crowd to have Pilate release Barabbas*j* instead.

12"What shall I do, then, with the one you call the king of the Jews?" Pilate asked them.

13"Crucify him!" they shouted.

14"Why? What crime has he committed?" asked Pilate.

But they shouted all the louder, "Crucify him!"

15Wanting to satisfy the crowd, Pilate

15:1 /S Mt 27:2
15:2 gver 9,12, 18,26; S Mt 2:2
15:5 hS Mk 14:61
15:9 /S ver 2
15:11 /Ac 3:14

released Barabbas to them. He had Jesus flogged,*k* and handed him over to be crucified.

The Soldiers Mock Jesus
15:16–20pp — Mt 27:27–31

16The soldiers led Jesus away into the palace*l* (that is, the Praetorium) and called together the whole company of soldiers. 17They put a purple robe on him, then twisted together a crown of thorns and set it on him. 18And they began to call out to him, "Hail, king of the Jews!"*m* 19Again and again they struck him on the head with a staff and spit on him. Falling on their knees, they paid homage to him. 20And when they had mocked him, they took off the purple robe and put his own clothes on him. Then they led him out*n* to crucify him.

The Crucifixion
15:22–32pp — Mt 27:33–44; Lk 23:33–43; Jn 19:17–24

21A certain man from Cyrene,*o* Simon, the father of Alexander and Rufus,*p* was passing by on his way in from the country, and they forced him to carry the cross.*q* 22They brought Jesus to the place called Golgotha (which means The Place of the Skull). 23Then they offered him wine mixed with myrrh,*r* but he did not take it. 24And they crucified him. Dividing up his

15:15 kIsa 53:6
15:16 /Jn 18:28, 33; 19:9
15:18 mS ver 2
15:20 nHeb 13:12
15:21 oS Mt 27:32 pRo 16:13 qMt 27:32; Lk 23:26
15:23 rver 36; Ps 69:21; Pr 31:6

---

inscribed with his name.) When he came to Jerusalem, he stayed in the magnificent palace built by Herod the Great, located west and a little south of the temple area. Mark uses the word "Praetorium" to indicate this palace in v. 16, and it was here that the Roman trial of Jesus took place.

15:2 *asked Pilate.* Judgment in a Roman court was the sole responsibility of the imperial magistrate.

15:3 *many things.* See note on Lk 23:2. Multiple charges were common in criminal cases.

15:4 *Aren't you going to answer?* If Jesus made no defense, according to Roman law Pilate would have to pronounce against him.

15:6 *custom.* See note on Jn 18:39.

15:7 *Barabbas.* Probably a member of the Zealots, a revolutionary Jewish group. *in the uprising.* Nothing from other sources is known about this insurrection, though Mark speaks of it as if it was well known. Under the Roman prefects such revolts were common (see Lk 13:1).

15:13 *Crucify.* See note on v. 24.

15:15 *flogged.* The Romans used a whip made of several strips of leather into which were embedded (near the ends) pieces of bone and lead. The Jews limited the number of stripes to a maximum of 40 (in practice to 39 in case of a miscount), but no such limitation was recognized by the Romans, and victims of Roman floggings often did not survive.

15:16 *Praetorium.* The word was used originally of a general's tent, or of the headquarters in a military camp (see note on v. 1). *the whole company.* The soldiers quartered in the Praetorium were recruited from non-Jewish inhabitants of Palestine and assigned to the military governor.

15:17 *purple robe.* Probably an old military cloak, whose

color suggested royalty (see Mt 27:28). *crown of thorns.* Made of a prickly plant (the Greek word means simply "briers"), of which there are many in Palestine. Both robe and crown were parts of the mock royal attire placed on Jesus.

15:18 *Hail, king of the Jews!* A mocking salutation that corresponded to "Hail, Caesar!"

15:19 *spit on him.* Probably a parody on the kiss of homage that was customary in the Near East when in the presence of royalty.

15:21 *Cyrene.* An important city of Libya in North Africa that had a large Jewish population. *Simon.* Probably a Jew who was in Jerusalem to celebrate the Passover (cf. "Jews of Cyrene" in Ac 6:9). *Alexander and Rufus.* Only mentioned by Mark, but referred to in such a way as to suggest that they were known by those to whom he wrote. Rufus may be the same person spoken of in Ro 16:13. *carry the cross.* Men condemned to death were usually forced to carry a beam of the cross, often weighing 30 or 40 pounds, to the place of crucifixion. Jesus started out by carrying his (see Jn 19:17), but he had been so weakened by flogging that Simon was pressed into service.

15:22 *The Place of the Skull.* It may have been a small hill (though the Gospels say nothing of a hill) that looked like a skull, or it may have been so named because of the many executions that took place there.

15:23 *wine mixed with myrrh.* The Talmud gives evidence that incense was mixed with wine to deaden pain (see Pr 31:6). Myrrh is a spice derived from plants native to the Arabian deserts and parts of Africa (see note on Ge 37:25).

15:24 *crucified.* A Roman means of execution in which the victim was nailed to a cross. Heavy, wrought-iron nails were

clothes, they cast lots ^{s} to see what each would get.

^{25}It was the third hour when they crucified him. ^{26}The written notice of the charge against him read: THE KING OF THE JEWS. ^{t} ^{27}They crucified two robbers with him, one on his right and one on his left. ^{v} ^{29}Those who passed by hurled insults at him, shaking their heads ^{u} and saying, "So! You who are going to destroy the temple and build it in three days, ^{v} ^{30}come down from the cross and save yourself!"

^{31}In the same way the chief priests and the teachers of the law mocked him ^{w} among themselves. "He saved others," they said, "but he can't save himself! ^{32}Let this Christ, $^{w\,x}$ this King of Israel, ^{y} come down now from the cross, that we may see and believe." Those crucified with him also heaped insults on him.

The Death of Jesus

15:33–41pp — Mt 27:45–56; Lk 23:44–49

^{33}At the sixth hour darkness came over the whole land until the ninth hour. ^{z} ^{34}And at the ninth hour Jesus cried out in a loud voice, *"Eloi, Eloi, lama sabachthani?"* —which means, "My God, my God, why have you forsaken me?" $^{x\,a}$

^{35}When some of those standing near heard this, they said, "Listen, he's calling Elijah."

^{36}One man ran, filled a sponge with wine vinegar, ^{b} put it on a stick, and offered it to Jesus to drink. "Now leave him alone. Let's see if Elijah comes to take him down," he said.

^{37}With a loud cry, Jesus breathed his last. ^{c}

^{38}The curtain of the temple was torn in two from top to bottom. ^{d} ^{39}And when the centurion, ^{e} who stood there in front of Jesus, heard his cry and ^{y} saw how he died, he said, "Surely this man was the Son ^{z} of God!" ^{f}

^{40}Some women were watching from a distance. ^{g} Among them were Mary Magdalene, Mary the mother of James the younger and of Joses, and Salome. ^{h} ^{41}In Galilee these women had followed him and cared for his needs. Many other women who had come up with him to Jerusalem were also there. ^{i}

The Burial of Jesus

15:42–47pp — Mt 27:57–61; Lk 23:50–56; Jn 19:38–42

^{42}It was Preparation Day (that is, the day before the Sabbath). ^{j} So as evening approached, ^{43}Joseph of Arimathea, a promi-

---

Cross references (center column):

15:24 ^{s}Ps 22:18
15:26 ^{t}S ver 2
15:29 ^{u}Ps 22:7; 109:25 ^{v}S Jn 2:19
15:31 ^{w}Ps 22:7
15:32 ^{x}S Mk 14:61 ^{y}S ver 2
15:33 ^{z}Am 8:9
15:34 ^{a}Ps 22:1

15:36 ^{b}ver 23; Ps 69:21
15:37 ^{c}Jn 19:30
15:38 ^{d}Heb 10:19,20 ^{e}ver 45 /Mk 1:1,11; 9:7; S Mt 4:3
15:40 ^{g}Ps 38:11 ^{h}Mk 16:1; Lk 24:10; Jn 19:25
15:41 ^{i}Mt 27:55, 56; Lk 8:2,3
15:42 ^{j}Mt 27:62; Jn 19:31

^{v}27 Some manuscripts *left,* 28and the scripture was fulfilled which says, "He was counted with the lawless ones" (Isaiah 53:12) ^{w}32 Or *Messiah* ^{x}34 Psalm 22:1 ^{y}39 Some manuscripts do not have *heard his cry and.* ^{z}39 Or *a son*

---

driven through the wrists and the heel bones. If the life of the victim lingered too long, death was hastened by breaking his legs (see Jn 19:33). Archaeologists have discovered the bones of a crucified man, near Jerusalem, dating between A.D. 7 and 66, which shed light on the position of the victim when nailed to the cross. Only slaves, the basest of criminals, and offenders who were not Roman citizens were executed in this manner. First-century authors vividly describe the agony and disgrace of being crucified. *Dividing up his clothes.* It was the accepted right of the executioner's squad to claim the minor possessions of the victim. Jesus' clothing probably consisted of an under and an outer garment, a belt, sandals and possibly a head covering.

15:26 *charge against him.* It was customary to write the charge on a wooden board that was carried before the victim as he walked to the place of execution, and then the board was affixed to the cross above his head. THE KING OF THE JEWS. The wording of the charge differs slightly in the Gospels, but all agree that Jesus was crucified for claiming to be the king of the Jews.

15:27 *two robbers.* According to Roman law, robbery was not a capital offense. Mark's term must signify men guilty of insurrection, crucified for high treason.

15:28 The earlier and more reliable Greek manuscripts do not have this verse (see NIV text note on v. 27). It was probably added from Lk 22:37 (quoting Isa 53:12). Mark does not include many OT quotations.

15:29 See note on 14:58.

15:32 *Christ.* See NIV text note on Mt 1:17. *Those crucified with him.* One of the criminals later repented and asked to be included in Jesus' kingdom (Lk 23:39–43).

15:33 *sixth hour.* 12:00 noon. *ninth hour.* 3:00 P.M.

15:34 The words were spoken in Aramaic (but with some Hebrew characteristics), one of the languages commonly spoken in Palestine in Jesus' day. They reveal how deeply Jesus felt his abandonment by God as he bore the sins of mankind (but see introduction to Ps 22 and note on Ps 22:1).

15:35 *Elijah.* The bystanders mistook the first words of Jesus' cry ("Eloi, Eloi") to be a cry for Elijah. It was commonly believed that Elijah would come in times of critical need to protect the innocent and rescue the righteous (v. 36).

15:36 *wine vinegar.* A sour wine used by laborers and soldiers.

15:37 *With a loud cry.* The strength of the cry indicates that Jesus did not die the ordinary death of those crucified, who normally suffered long periods of complete agony, exhaustion and then unconsciousness before dying.

15:38 *curtain of the temple.* The curtain that separated the Holy Place from the Most Holy Place (Ex 26:31–33). The tearing of the curtain indicated that Christ had entered heaven itself for us so that we too may now enter God's very presence (Heb 9:8–10,12; 10:19–20).

15:39 *centurion.* A commander of 100 men in the Roman army. *saw how he died.* See note on v. 37. *the Son of God.* See notes on Mt 27:54; Lk 23:47.

15:40 *Mary Magdalene.* From 16:9 and Lk 8:2 we learn that Jesus had driven seven demons from her. *Mary the mother of James the younger and of Joses.* See v. 47; 16:1. *Salome.* Probably the wife of Zebedee and the mother of James and John (see Mt 27:56).

15:42 *Preparation Day.* Friday. Since it was now late in the afternoon, there was an urgency to get Jesus' body down from the cross before sundown, when the Sabbath began.

15:43 *Arimathea.* See note on Mt 27:57. *Council.* The

nent member of the Council,[k] who was himself waiting for the kingdom of God,[l] went boldly to Pilate and asked for Jesus' body. [44]Pilate was surprised to hear that he was already dead. Summoning the centurion, he asked him if Jesus had already died. [45]When he learned from the centurion[m] that it was so, he gave the body to Joseph. [46]So Joseph bought some linen cloth, took down the body, wrapped it in the linen, and placed it in a tomb cut out of rock. Then he rolled a stone against the entrance of the tomb.[n] [47]Mary Magdalene and Mary the mother of Joses[o] saw where he was laid.

The Resurrection

16:1–8pp. — Mt 28:1–8; Lk 24:1–10

16 When the Sabbath was over, Mary Magdalene, Mary the mother of James, and Salome bought spices[p] so that they might go to anoint Jesus' body. [2]Very early on the first day of the week, just after sunrise, they were on their way to the tomb [3]and they asked each other, "Who will roll the stone away from the entrance of the tomb?"[q]

[4]But when they looked up, they saw that the stone, which was very large, had been rolled away. [5]As they entered the tomb, they saw a young man dressed in a white robe[r] sitting on the right side, and they were alarmed.

[6]"Don't be alarmed," he said. "You are looking for Jesus the Nazarene,[s] who was crucified. He has risen! He is not here. See

the place where they laid him. [7]But go, tell his disciples and Peter, 'He is going ahead of you into Galilee. There you will see him,[t] just as he told you.' "[u]

[8]Trembling and bewildered, the women went out and fled from the tomb. They said nothing to anyone, because they were afraid.

[The most reliable early manuscripts and other ancient witnesses do not have Mark 16:9–20.]

[9]When Jesus rose early on the first day of the week, he appeared first to Mary Magdalene,[v] out of whom he had driven seven demons. [10]She went and told those who had been with him and who were mourning and weeping. [11]When they heard that Jesus was alive and that she had seen him, they did not believe it.[w]

[12]Afterward Jesus appeared in a different form to two of them while they were walking in the country.[x] [13]These returned and reported it to the rest; but they did not believe them either.

[14]Later Jesus appeared to the Eleven as they were eating; he rebuked them for their lack of faith and their stubborn refusal to believe those who had seen him after he had risen.[y]

[15]He said to them, "Go into all the world and preach the good news to all creation.[z] [16]Whoever believes and is baptized will be saved, but whoever does not

Cross references (center column)

15:43 [k]S Mt 5:22 /S Mt 3:2; Lk 2:25,38
15:45 [m]ver 39
15:46 [n]Mk 16:3
15:47 [o]ver 40
16:1 [p]Lk 23:56; Jn 19:39,40
16:3 [q]Mk 15:46
16:5 [r]S Jn 20:12
16:6 [s]S Mk 1:24

16:7 [t]Jn 21:1-23 [u]Mk 14:28
16:9 [v]Mk 15:47; Jn 20:11-18
16:11 [w]ver 13, 14; Lk 24:11
16:12 [x]Lk 24:13-32
16:14 [y]Lk 24:36-43
16:15 [z]Mt 28:18-20; Lk 24:47,48; Ac 1:8

Sanhedrin (see note on 14:55). *kingdom of God.* See note on Mt 3:2. *Pilate.* See note on v. 1. *asked for Jesus' body.* See note on Lk 23:52.

15:44 *surprised.* Crucified men often lived two or three days before dying, and the early death of Jesus was therefore extraordinary.

15:45 *he gave the body to Joseph.* The release of the body of one condemned for high treason, and especially to one who was not an immediate relative, was quite unusual.

15:46 *tomb cut out of rock.* Matthew tells us that the tomb belonged to Joseph and that it was new, i.e., it had not been used before (Mt 27:60). The location of the tomb was in a garden very near the site of the crucifixion (see Jn 19:41). There is archaeological evidence that the traditional site of the burial of Jesus (the Church of the Holy Sepulchre in Jerusalem) was a cemetery during the first century A.D. *stone.* A disc-shaped stone that rolled in a sloped channel.

16:1 *Sabbath was over.* About 6:00 P.M. Saturday evening. No purchases were possible on the Sabbath. *Mary Magdalene, Mary the mother of James, and Salome.* See note on 15:40. *spices.* Embalming was not practiced by the Jews. These spices were brought as an act of devotion and love. *to anoint Jesus' body.* The women had no expectation of Jesus' resurrection.

16:3 *Who will roll the stone away . . . ?* Setting the large stone in place was a relatively easy task, but once it had

slipped into the groove cut in bedrock in front of the entrance it was very difficult to remove.

16:5 *As they entered the tomb.* Inside the large opening of the facade of the tomb was a forechamber, at the back of which a low rectangular opening led to the burial chamber. *young man dressed in a white robe.* Identified by Matthew (28:2) as an angel. See note on Lk 24:4.

16:6 *crucified.* See note on 15:24. *He has risen!* The climax of Mark's Gospel is the resurrection, without which Jesus' death, though noble, would be indescribably tragic. But in the resurrection he is declared to be the Son of God with power (Ro 1:4).

16:7 *and Peter.* Jesus showed special concern for Peter, in view of his confident boasting and subsequent denials (14:29–31,66–72). *just as he told you.* See 14:28.

16:9–20 Serious doubt exists as to whether these verses belong to the Gospel of Mark. They are absent from important early manuscripts and display certain peculiarities of vocabulary, style and theological content that are unlike the rest of Mark. His Gospel probably ended at 16:8, or its original ending has been lost.

16:9 *Mary Magdalene.* See note on 15:40.

16:12–13 A shortened account of the two men going to Emmaus (see Lk 24:13–35).

16:14 *the Eleven.* Judas Iscariot had committed suicide (see Mt 27:5).

16:16 *baptized.* See notes on 1:4; Ro 6:3–4.

believe will be condemned. [a] [17]And these signs [b] will accompany those who believe: In my name they will drive out demons; [c] they will speak in new tongues; [d] [18]they will pick up snakes [e] with their hands; and when they drink deadly poison, it will not hurt them at all; they will place their hands on [f] sick people, and they will get well."

[19]After the Lord Jesus had spoken to

them, he was taken up into heaven [g] and he sat at the right hand of God. [h] [20]Then the disciples went out and preached everywhere, and the Lord worked with them and confirmed his word by the signs [i] that accompanied it.

16:16 [a]Jn 3:16, 18,36; Ac 16:31
16:17 [b]S Jn 4:48 [c]Mk 9:38; Lk 10:17; Ac 5:16; 8:7; 16:18; 19:13-16 [d]Ac 2:4; 10:46; 19:6; 1Co 12:10, 28,30; 13:1; 14:2-39
16:18 [e]Lk 10:19; Ac 28:3-5 [f]S Ac 6:6

16:19 [g]Lk 24:50,51; Jn 6:62; Ac 1:9-11; 1Ti 3:16 [h]Ps 110:1; Mt 26:64; Ac 2:33; 5:31; Ro 8:34; Col 3:1; Heb 1:3; 12:2
16:20 [i]S Jn 4:48

16:18 *drink deadly poison.* No occurrence of drinking deadly poison without harm is found in the NT.

16:19 *right hand of God.* A position of authority second only to God's (see 14:62; Ps 110:1).

LUKE

See "The Synoptic Gospels," p. 1437.

Author

The author's name does not appear in the book, but much unmistakable evidence points to Luke. This Gospel is a companion volume to the book of Acts, and the language and structure of these two books indicate that both were written by the same person. They are addressed to the same individual, Theophilus, and the second volume refers to the first (Ac 1:1). Certain sections in Acts use the pronoun "we" (Ac 16:10-17; 20:5-15; 21:1-18; 27:1-28:16), indicating that the author was with Paul when the events described in these passages took place. By process of elimination, Paul's "dear friend Luke, the doctor" (Col 4:14), and "fellow worker" (Phm 24) becomes the most likely candidate. His authorship is supported by the uniform testimony of early Christian writings (e.g., the Muratorian Canon, A.D. 170, and the works of Irenaeus, c. 180).

Luke was probably a Gentile by birth, well educated in Greek culture, a physician by profession, a companion of Paul at various times from his second missionary journey to his first imprisonment in Rome, and a loyal friend who remained with the apostle after others had deserted (2Ti 4:11).

Antioch (of Syria) and Philippi are among the places suggested as his hometown.

Recipient and Purpose

The Gospel is specifically directed to Theophilus (1:3), whose name means "one who loves God" and almost certainly refers to a particular person rather than to lovers of God in general. The use of "most excellent" with the name further indicates an individual, and supports the idea that he was a Roman official or at least of high position and wealth. He was possibly Luke's patron, responsible for seeing that the writings were copied and distributed. Such a dedication to the publisher was common at that time.

Theophilus, however, was more than a publisher. The message of this Gospel was intended for his own instruction (1:4) as well as the instruction of those among whom the book would be circulated. The fact that the Gospel was initially directed to Theophilus does not narrow or limit its purpose. It was written to strengthen the faith of all believers and to answer the attacks of unbelievers. It was presented to displace disconnected and ill-founded reports about Jesus. Luke wanted to show that the place of the Gentile Christian in God's kingdom is based on the teaching of Jesus. He wanted to commend the preaching of the gospel to the whole world.

Date and Place of Writing

The two most commonly suggested periods for dating the Gospel of Luke are: (1) A.D. 59-63, and (2) the 70s or the 80s (see chart on "Dating the Synoptic Gospels," p. 1437).

The place of writing was probably Rome, though Achaia, Ephesus and Caesarea also have been suggested. The place to which it was sent would, of course, depend on the residence of Theophilus. By its detailed designations of places in Palestine, the Gospel seems to be intended for readers who were unfamiliar with that land. Antioch, Achaia and Ephesus are possible destinations.

Style

Luke had outstanding command of the Greek language. His vocabulary is extensive and rich, and his style at times approaches that of classical Greek (as in the preface, 1:1-4), while at other times it is quite Semitic (1:5-2:52)—often like the Greek translation of the OT. His vocabulary seems to reveal geographical and cultural sensitivity, in that it varies with the particular land or people being described. When Luke refers to Peter in a Jewish setting, he uses more Semitic language than when he refers to Paul in a Hellenistic setting.

Characteristics

The third Gospel presents the works and teachings of Jesus that are especially important for understanding the way of salvation. Its scope is complete from the birth of Christ to his ascension, its arrangement is orderly, and it appeals to both Jews and Gentiles. The writing is characterized by literary excellence, historical detail and warm, sensitive understanding of Jesus and of those around him.

Since the Synoptic Gospels (Matthew, Mark and Luke) report many of the same episodes in Jesus' life, one would expect much similarity in their accounts. The dissimilarities reveal the distinctive emphases of the separate writers. Luke's characteristic themes include: (1) universality, recognition of Gentiles as well as Jews in God's plan; (2) emphasis on prayer, especially Jesus' praying before important occasions (see note on 3:21); (3) joy at the announcement of the gospel or "good news" (see note on 1:14); (4) special concern for the role of women; (5) special interest in the poor (some of the rich were included among Jesus' followers, but he seemed closest to the poor); (6) concern for sinners (Jesus was a friend to those deep in sin); (7) stress on the family circle (Jesus' activity included men, women and children, with the setting frequently in the home); (8) repeated use of the title "Son of Man" (e.g., 19:10); (9) emphasis on the Holy Spirit (see note on 4:1).

Sources

Although Luke acknowledges that many others had written of Jesus' life (1:1), he does not indicate that he relied on these reports for his own writing. He used personal investigation and arrangement, based on testimony from "eyewitnesses and servants of the word" (1:2)—including the preaching and oral accounts of the apostles. His language differences from the other Synoptics and his blocks of distinctive material (e.g., 10:1-18:14; 19:1-28) indicate independent work, though he obviously used some of the same sources.

Plan

Luke's account of Jesus' ministry can be divided into three major parts: (1) the events that occurred in and around Galilee (4:14-9:50), (2) those that took place in Judea and Perea (9:51-19:27), and (3) those of the final week in Jerusalem (19:28-24:53). Luke's uniqueness is especially seen in the amount of material devoted to Jesus' closing ministry in Judea and Perea. This material is predominantly made up of accounts of Jesus' discourses. Sixteen of the 23 parables that occur in Luke are found here (9:51-18:14; 19:1-28). Of the 20 miracles recorded in Luke, only 4 appear in these sections. Already in the ninth chapter (see note on 9:51), Jesus is seen anticipating his final appearance in Jerusalem and his crucifixion (see note on 13:22).

The main theme of the Gospel is the nature of Jesus' Messiahship and mission, and a key verse is 19:10.

Outline

Introduction

1:1–4Ref — Ac 1:1

1 Many have undertaken to draw up an account of the things that have been fulfilled[a] among us, [2]just as they were handed down to us by those who from the first[a] were eyewitnesses[b] and servants of the word.[c] [3]Therefore, since I myself have carefully investigated everything from the beginning, it seemed good also to me to write an orderly account[d] for you, most excellent[e] Theophilus,[f] [4]so that you may know the certainty of the things you have been taught.[g]

The Birth of John the Baptist Foretold

[5]In the time of Herod king of Judea[h] there was a priest named Zechariah, who belonged to the priestly division of Abijah;[i] his wife Elizabeth was also a descendant of Aaron. [6]Both of them were upright in the sight of God, observing all the Lord's commandments and regulations blamelessly.[j] [7]But they had no children, because Elizabeth was barren; and they were both well along in years.

[8]Once when Zechariah's division was on duty and he was serving as priest before God,[k] [9]he was chosen by lot,[l] according

to the custom of the priesthood, to go into the temple of the Lord and burn incense.[m] [10]And when the time for the burning of incense came, all the assembled worshipers were praying outside.[n]

[11]Then an angel[o] of the Lord appeared to him, standing at the right side of the altar of incense.[p] [12]When Zechariah saw him, he was startled and was gripped with fear.[q] [13]But the angel said to him: "Do not be afraid,[r] Zechariah; your prayer has been heard. Your wife Elizabeth will bear you a son, and you are to give him the name John.[s] [14]He will be a joy and delight to you, and many will rejoice because of his birth,[t] [15]for he will be great in the sight of the Lord. He is never to take wine or other fermented drink,[u] and he will be filled with the Holy Spirit[v] even from birth.[b][w] [16]Many of the people of Israel will he bring back to the Lord their God. [17]And he will go on before the Lord,[x] in the spirit and power of Elijah,[y] to turn the hearts of the fathers to their children[z] and the disobedient to the wisdom of the righteous—to make ready a people prepared for the Lord."[a]

[18]Zechariah asked the angel, "How can I

Cross references (center column)

1:2 aMk 1:1; Jn 15:27; Ac 1:21,22 bHeb2:3; 1Pe 5:1; 2Pe 1:16; 1Jn 1:1 cS Mk 4:14
1:3 dAc 11:4 eAc 24:3; 26:25 fAc 1:1
1:4 gJn 20:31; Ac 2:42
1:5 hMt 2:1 iCh 24:10
1:6 jGe 6:9; Dt 5:33; 1Ki 9:4; Lk 2:25
1:8 k1Ch 24:19; 2Ch 8:14
1:9 lAc 1:26

mEx 30:7,8; 1Ch 23:13; 2Ch 29:11; Ps 141:2
1:10 nLev 16:17
1:11 oS Ac 5:19 pEx 30:1-10
1:12 qJdg 6:22, 23; 13:22
1:13 rver 30; S Mt 14:27 sver 60,63; S Mt 3:1
1:14 tver 58
1:15 uNu 6:3; Lev 10:9; Jdg 13:4; Lk 7:33 vver 41,67; Ac 2:4; 4:8,31; 6:3,5; 9:17; 11:24; Eph 5:18; S Ac 10:44 wJer 1:5; Gal 1:15
1:17 xver 76 yS Mt 11:14 zMal 4:5,6 aS Mt 3:3

a *1 Or been surely believed*   b *15 Or from his mother's womb*

1:1–4 Using language similar to classical Greek, Luke begins with a formal preface, common to historical works of that time, in which he states his purpose for writing and identifies the recipient. He acknowledges other reports on the subject, shows the need for this new work and states his method of approach and sources of information.
1:1 *things . . . fulfilled among us.* Things prophesied in the OT and now fully accomplished.
1:2 *handed down.* A technical term for passing on information as authoritative tradition. *eyewitnesses and servants of the word.* Luke, though not an eyewitness himself, received testimony from those who were eyewitnesses and were dedicated to spreading the gospel. Apostolic preaching and interviews with other individuals associated with Jesus' ministry were available to him.
1:3 *carefully investigated.* Luke's account was exact in historical detail, having been checked in every way. Inspiration by the Holy Spirit did not rule out human effort. The account is complete, extending back to the very beginning of Jesus' earthly life. It has an orderly, meaningful arrangement that is generally chronological. *most excellent.* Paul used this respectful term for governors Felix (Ac 24:3) and Festus (Ac 26:25). *Theophilus.* See Introduction: Recipient and Purpose.
1:4 *so that you may know.* Cf. John's purpose for writing (Jn 20:31).
1:5 *Herod king of Judea.* Herod the Great reigned 37–4 B.C., and his kingdom included Samaria, Galilee, much of Perea and Coele-Syria (see note on Mt 2:1). The time referred to here is probably c. 7–6. *Zechariah . . . Elizabeth.* Both were of priestly descent from the line of Aaron. *priestly division of Abijah.* From the time of David the priests were organized into 24 divisions, and Abijah was one of the "heads of the priestly families" (Ne 12:12; see 1Ch 24:10).

1:6 *upright . . . blamelessly.* They were not sinless, but were faithful and sincere in keeping God's ordinances. Simeon (2:25) and Joseph (Mt 1:19) are given similar praise.
1:7 *no children.* See note on v. 25.
1:9 It was one of the priest's duties to keep the incense burning on the altar in front of the Most Holy Place. He supplied it with fresh incense before the morning sacrifice and again after the evening sacrifice (Ex 30:6–8). Ordinarily a priest would have this privilege very infrequently, and sometimes never, since duty assignments were determined by lot. *chosen by lot.* See notes on Ne 11:1; Pr 16:33; Jnh 1:7; Ac 1:26.
1:11 *angel of the Lord.* See v. 19. *right side of the altar.* The south side, since the altar faced east.
1:12 *fear.* A common reaction, as with Gideon (Jdg 6:22–23) and Manoah (Jdg 13:22).
1:13 *Do not be afraid.* This word of reassurance is given many times in both OT and NT (see, e.g., v. 30; 2:10 and note; 5:10; 8:50; 12:7,32; Ge 15:1; 21:17; 26:24; Dt 1:21; Jos 8:1). *John.* The name (derived from Hebrew) means "The Lord is gracious."
1:14 *joy.* A keynote of these opening chapters (vv. 14,44, 47,58; 2:10).
1:15 *wine or other fermented drink.* It appears likely that John was to be subject to the Nazirite vow of abstinence from alcoholic drinks (Nu 6:1–4). If so, he was a lifelong Nazirite, as were Samson (Jdg 13:4–7) and Samuel (1Sa 1:11).
1:17 *Elijah.* John was not Elijah returning in the flesh (Jn 1:21), but he functioned like that OT preacher of repentance and was therefore a fulfillment of Mal 4:5–6 (see Mt 11:14; 17:10–13). *to turn the hearts of the fathers to their children.* See note on Mal 4:6. *people prepared for the Lord.* John helped fulfill Isaiah's prophecy (Isa 40:3–5), as Luke shows in 3:4–6.

be sure of this?[b] I am an old man and my wife is well along in years." [c]

19The angel answered, "I am Gabriel.[d] I stand in the presence of God, and I have been sent to speak to you and to tell you this good news. 20And now you will be silent and not able to speak[e] until the day this happens, because you did not believe my words, which will come true at their proper time."

21Meanwhile, the people were waiting for Zechariah and wondering why he stayed so long in the temple. 22When he came out, he could not speak to them. They realized he had seen a vision in the temple, for he kept making signs[f] to them but remained unable to speak.

23When his time of service was completed, he returned home. 24After this his wife Elizabeth became pregnant and for five months remained in seclusion. 25"The Lord has done this for me," she said. "In these days he has shown his favor and taken away my disgrace[g] among the people."

The Birth of Jesus Foretold

26In the sixth month, God sent the angel Gabriel[h] to Nazareth,[i] a town in Galilee, 27to a virgin pledged to be married to a man named Joseph,[j] a descendant of David. The virgin's name was Mary. 28The angel went to her and said, "Greetings, you who are highly favored! The Lord is with you."

29Mary was greatly troubled at his words and wondered what kind of greeting this might be. 30But the angel said to her, "Do not be afraid,[k] Mary, you have found favor with God.[l] 31You will be with child and give birth to a son, and you are to give him the name Jesus.[m] 32He will be great and will be called the Son of the Most High.[n] The Lord God will give him the throne of his father David,[o] 33and he will reign over the house of Jacob forever; his kingdom[p] will never end." [q]

34"How will this be," Mary asked the angel, "since I am a virgin?"

35The angel answered, "The Holy Spirit will come upon you,[r] and the power of the Most High[s] will overshadow you. So the holy one[t] to be born will be called[c] the Son of God.[u] 36Even Elizabeth your relative is going to have a child[v] in her old age, and she who was said to be barren is in her sixth month. 37For nothing is impossible with God." [w]

38"I am the Lord's servant," Mary answered. "May it be to me as you have said." Then the angel left her.

Mary Visits Elizabeth

39At that time Mary got ready and hurried to a town in the hill country of Judea,[x] 40where she entered Zechariah's home and greeted Elizabeth. 41When Elizabeth heard Mary's greeting, the baby leaped in her womb, and Elizabeth was filled with the Holy Spirit.[y] 42In a loud

---

1:18 bGe 15:8
cver 34; Ge 17:17
1:19 dver 26;
Da 8:16; 9:21
1:20 eEx 4:11;
Eze 3:26
1:22 fver 62
1:25 gGe 30:23;
Isa 4:1
1:26 hS ver 19
iS Mt 2:23
1:27 jMt 1:16,18,
20; Lk 2:4
1:30 kver 13;
S Mt 14:27
lGe 6:8
1:31 mIsa 7:14;
Mt 1:21,25;
Lk 2:21
1:32 nver 35,76;
S Mk 5:7
oS Mt 1:1
1:33 pMt 28:18
q2Sa 7:16;
Ps 89:3,4; Isa 9:7;
Jer 33:17;
Da 2:44; 7:14,27;
Mic 4:7; Heb 1:8
1:35 rMt 1:18
sver 32,76;
S Mk 5:7
tS Mk 1:24
uS Mt 4:3
1:36 vver 24
1:37
wS Mt 19:26
xver 65
1:41 yS ver 15

---

c35 Or So the child to be born will be called holy,

1:18 *How can I be sure . . . ?* Like Abraham (Ge 15:8), Gideon (Jdg 6:17) and Hezekiah (2Ki 20:8), Zechariah asked for a sign (cf. 1Co 1:22).

1:19 *Gabriel.* The name can mean "God is my hero" or "mighty man of God." Only two angels are identified by name in Scripture: Gabriel (Da 8:16; 9:21) and Michael (Da 10:13,21; Jude 9; Rev 12:7).

1:21 *the people were waiting for Zechariah.* They were waiting for him to come out of the Holy Place and pronounce the Aaronic blessing (Nu 6:24–26).

1:23 *his time of service.* Each priest was responsible for a week's service at the temple once every six months. *home.* See v. 39.

1:24 *remained in seclusion.* In joy, devotion and gratitude that the Lord had taken away her childlessness.

1:25 *The Lord . . . has shown his favor and taken away my disgrace.* Not only did lack of children deprive the parents of personal happiness, but it was generally considered to indicate divine disfavor and often brought social reproach (see Ge 16:2, Sarai; 25:21, Rebekah; 30:23, Rachel; 1Sa 1:1–18, Hannah; see also Lev 20:20–21; Ps 128:3; Jer 22:30).

1:26–35 This section speaks clearly of the virginal conception of Jesus (vv. 27,34–35; see Mt 1:18–25). The conception was the work of the Holy Spirit; the eternal Second Person of the Trinity, while remaining God, also "became flesh" (Jn 1:14). From conception he was fully God and fully man.

1:26 *In the sixth month.* That is, from the time of John's conception. *Nazareth.* See note on Mt 2:23.

1:27 *pledged to be married.* See note on Mt 1:18.

1:28 *Greetings.* Ave in the Latin Vulgate (from which comes "Ave Maria").

1:31 *Jesus.* See NIV text note on Mt 1:21 for the meaning of this name.

1:32 *the Son of the Most High.* This title has two senses: (1) the divine Son of God and (2) the Messiah born in time. His Messiahship is clearly referred to in the following context (vv. 32b–33). *Most High.* A title frequently used of God in both the OT and NT (see vv. 35,76; 6:35; 8:28; Ge 14:19 and note; 2Sa 22:14; Ps 7:10). *throne.* Promised in the OT to the Messiah descended from David (2Sa 7:13,16; Ps 2:6–7; 89:26–27; Isa 9:6–7). *his father David.* Mary was a descendant of David, as was Joseph (see Mt 1:16); so Jesus could rightly be called a "son" of David.

1:33 *forever.* See Ps 45:6; Rev 11:15. *his kingdom will never end.* Although Christ's role as mediator will one day be finished (see 1Co 15:24–28), the kingdom of the Father and Son, as one, will never end.

1:34 *How will this be . . . ?* Mary did not ask in disbelief, as Zechariah did (v. 20). See v. 45.

1:35 *holy one.* Jesus never sinned (2Co 5:21; Heb 4:15; 7:26; 1Pe 2:22; 1Jn 3:5).

1:36 *Elizabeth your relative.* It is not known whether she was a cousin, aunt or other relation.

voice she exclaimed: "Blessed are you among women, *z* and blessed is the child you will bear! [43]But why am I so favored, that the mother of my Lord *a* should come to me? [44]As soon as the sound of your greeting reached my ears, the baby in my womb leaped for joy. [45]Blessed is she who has believed that what the Lord has said to her will be accomplished!"

Mary's Song

1:46–53pp — 1Sa 2:1–10

[46]And Mary said:

"My soul glorifies the Lord *b*
[47] and my spirit rejoices in God my
　　Savior, *c*
[48]for he has been mindful
　　of the humble state of his servant. *d*
From now on all generations will call
　　me blessed, *e*
[49] for the Mighty One has done great
　　things *f* for me—
　　holy is his name. *g*
[50]His mercy extends to those who fear
　　him,
　　from generation to generation. *h*
[51]He has performed mighty deeds with
　　his arm; *i*
　　he has scattered those who are proud
　　in their inmost thoughts. *j*
[52]He has brought down rulers from their
　　thrones
　　but has lifted up the humble. *k*
[53]He has filled the hungry with good
　　things *l*
　　but has sent the rich away empty.
[54]He has helped his servant Israel,
　　remembering to be merciful *m*
[55]to Abraham and his descendants *n*
　　forever,
　　even as he said to our fathers."

[56]Mary stayed with Elizabeth for about three months and then returned home.

The Birth of John the Baptist

[57]When it was time for Elizabeth to have her baby, she gave birth to a son. [58]Her neighbors and relatives heard that the Lord had shown her great mercy, and they shared her joy.

[59]On the eighth day they came to circumcise *o* the child, and they were going to name him after his father Zechariah, [60]but his mother spoke up and said, "No! He is to be called John." *p*

[61]They said to her, "There is no one among your relatives who has that name."

[62]Then they made signs *q* to his father, to find out what he would like to name the child. [63]He asked for a writing tablet, and to everyone's astonishment he wrote, "His name is John." *r* [64]Immediately his mouth was opened and his tongue was loosed, and he began to speak, *s* praising God. [65]The neighbors were all filled with awe, and throughout the hill country of Judea *t* people were talking about all these things. [66]Everyone who heard this wondered about it, asking, "What then is this child going to be?" For the Lord's hand was with him. *u*

Zechariah's Song

[67]His father Zechariah was filled with the Holy Spirit *v* and prophesied: *w*

[68]"Praise be to the Lord, the God of
　　Israel, *x*
　　because he has come and has
　　redeemed his people. *y*
[69]He has raised up a horn *d z* of salvation
　　for us

*d*69 *Horn* here symbolizes strength.

Cross references (center column)

1:42 *z*Jdg 5:24
1:43 *a*S Jn 13:13
1:46 *b*Ps 34:2,3
1:47 *c*Ps 18:46;
Isa 17:10; 61:10;
Hab 3:18;
1Ti 1:1; 2:3; 4:10
1:48 *d*ver 38;
Ps 138:6
*e*Lk 11:27
1:49 *f*Ps 71:19
*g*Ps 111:9
1:50 *h*Ex 20:6;
Ps 103:17
1:51 *i*Ps 98:1;
Isa 40:10
*j*Ge 11:8;
Ex 18:11;
2Sa 22:28;
Jer 13:9; 49:16
1:52 *k*S Mt 23:12
1:53 *l*Ps 107:9
1:54 *m*Ps 98:3
1:55 *n*S Gal 3:16

1:59 *o*Ge 17:12;
Lev 12:3;
Lk 2:21; Php 3:5
1:60 *p*ver 13,63;
S Mt 3:1
1:62 *q*ver 22
1:63 *r*ver 13,60;
S Mt 3:1
1:64 *s*ver 20;
Eze 24:27
1:65 *t*ver 39
1:66 *u*Ge 39:2;
Ac 11:21
1:67 *v*S ver 15
*w*Joel 2:28
1:68 *x*Ge 24:27;
1Ki 8:15;
Ps 72:18
*y*Ps 111:9;
Lk 7:16
1:69 *z*1Sa 2:1,10;
2Sa 22:3; Ps 18:2;
89:17; 132:17;
Eze 29:21

1:44 *for joy.* In some mysterious way the Holy Spirit produced this remarkable response in the unborn baby.
1:46–55 One of four hymns preserved in Lk 1–2 (see vv. 68–79; 2:14; 2:29–32 and notes). This hymn of praise is known as the Magnificat because in the Latin Vulgate translation the opening word is *Magnificat,* which means "glorifies." This song is like a psalm, and should also be compared with the song of Hannah (1Sa 2:1–10; see note on 1Sa 2:1).
1:50 *those who fear him.* Those who revere God and live in harmony with his will.
1:51 *his arm.* A figurative description of God's powerful acts. God does not have a body; he is spirit (Jn 4:24).
1:53 *hungry.* Both physically and spiritually (Mt 5:6; Jn 6:35). The coming of God's kingdom will bring changes affecting every area of life.
1:54 *remembering to be merciful.* The song ends with an assurance that God will be true to his promises to his people (see Ge 22:16–18).
1:56 *three months.* Mary evidently remained with Elizabeth until John's birth and then returned to her home in Nazareth.

Nazareth.
1:59 *name him after his father.* An accepted practice in that day, as seen in Josephus (*Life*, 1).
1:62 *they made signs to his father.* Apparently assuming that since he was mute he was also deaf.
1:63 *a writing tablet.* Probably a small wooden board covered with wax.
1:67 *filled with the Holy Spirit . . . prophesied.* Prophecy not only predicts but also proclaims God's word. Both Zechariah and Elizabeth (vv. 41–45) were enabled by the Holy Spirit to express what otherwise they could not have formulated.
1:68–79 This hymn is called Benedictus ("Praise be") because the opening word in the Latin Vulgate translation is *Benedictus.* Whereas the Magnificat (see note on 1:46–55) is similar to a psalm, the Benedictus is more like a prophecy.
1:68 *redeemed his people.* Not limited to national security (v. 71), but including moral and spiritual salvation (vv. 75, 77).
1:69 *horn.* Indicates strength (see NIV text note), as in the

in the house of his servant David[a]

70(as he said through his holy prophets of long ago),[b]

71salvation from our enemies
and from the hand of all who hate us—

72to show mercy to our fathers[c]
and to remember his holy covenant,[d]

73 the oath he swore to our father Abraham:[e]

74to rescue us from the hand of our enemies,
and to enable us to serve him[f] without fear[g]

75 in holiness and righteousness[h] before him all our days.

76And you, my child, will be called a prophet[i] of the Most High;[j]
for you will go on before the Lord to prepare the way for him,[k]

77to give his people the knowledge of salvation
through the forgiveness of their sins,[l]

78because of the tender mercy of our God,
by which the rising sun[m] will come to us from heaven

79to shine on those living in darkness and in the shadow of death,[n]
to guide our feet into the path of peace."[o]

80And the child grew and became strong in spirit;[p] and he lived in the desert until he appeared publicly to Israel.

The Birth of Jesus

2 In those days Caesar Augustus[q] issued a decree that a census should be taken of the entire Roman world.[r] 2(This was the first census that took place while Quirinius was governor of Syria.)[s] 3And everyone went to his own town to register.

4So Joseph also went up from the town of Nazareth in Galilee to Judea, to Bethlehem[t] the town of David, because he belonged to the house and line of David. 5He went there to register with Mary, who was pledged to be married to him[u] and was expecting a child. 6While they were there, the time came for the baby to be born, 7and she gave birth to her firstborn, a son. She wrapped him in cloths and placed him in a manger, because there was no room for them in the inn.

The Shepherds and the Angels

8And there were shepherds living out in the fields nearby, keeping watch over their flocks at night. 9An angel[v] of the Lord appeared to them, and the glory of the Lord shone around them, and they were terrified. 10But the angel said to them, "Do not be afraid.[w] I bring you good news of great

Cross references

1:69 [a]S Mt 1:1
1:70 [b]Jer 23:5; Ac 3:21; Ro 1:2
1:72 [c]Mic 7:20 [d]Ps 105:8,9; 106:45; Eze 16:60
1:73 [e]Ge 22:16-18
1:74 [f]Heb 9:14 [g]Jn 4:18
1:75 [h]Eph 4:24
1:76 [i]S Mt 11:9 [j]ver 32,35; S Mk 5:7 [k]ver 17; S Mt 3:3
1:77 [l]Jer 31:34; Mt 1:21; Mk 1:4
1:78 [m]Mal 4:2
1:79 [n]Ps 107:14; Isa 9:2; 59:9; Mt 4:16; S Ac 26:18 [o]S Lk 2:14
1:80 [p]Lk 2:40,52
2:1 [q]Lk 3:1; Mt 22:17 [r]S Mt 24:14
2:2 [s]Mt 4:24; Ac 15:23,41; 21:3; Gal 1:21
2:4 [t]S Jn 7:42
2:5 [u]Lk 1:27
2:9 [v]S Ac 5:19
2:10 [w]S Mt 14:27

---

horn of an animal (Dt 33:17; Ps 22:21; Mic 4:13). Jesus, the Messiah from the house of David, has the power to save. **1:74** *to rescue us.* No doubt including liberation from all oppression and bondage as well as deliverance from sin. **1:76** *called a prophet of the Most High.* Whereas Jesus will be called "the Son of the Most High" (see v. 32 and note). *prepare the way.* See note on 3:4. **1:78** *the rising sun.* A reference to the coming of the Messiah (see also similar figures in Nu 24:17; Isa 9:2; 60:1; Mal 4:2). Zechariah not only praised his own son, the "prophet of the Most High" (vv. 76–77), but also gave honor to the coming Messiah (vv. 78–79). **1:79** *those living in darkness.* The lost, separated from God (Isa 9:1–2; Mt 4:16). *peace.* See note on 2:14. **1:80** *lived in the desert.* John's parents, old at his birth, probably died while he was young, and he apparently grew up in the Desert of Judea, which lies between Jerusalem and the Dead Sea. *until he appeared publicly.* John's preaching and announcing the coming of the Messiah marked his public appearance. He was about 30 years old when he began his ministry (see note on 3:23). **2:1** Luke is the only Gospel writer who relates his narrative to dates of world history. *Caesar Augustus.* The first and (according to many) greatest Roman emperor (31 B.C.-A.D. 14). Having replaced the republic with an imperial form of government, he expanded the empire to include the entire Mediterranean world, established the famed *Pax Romana* ("Roman Peace") and ushered in the golden age of Roman literature and architecture. Augustus (which means "exalted") was a title voted to him by the Roman senate in 27 B.C. *census.* Used for military service and taxation. Jews, however, were exempt from Roman military service. God used

the decree of a pagan emperor to fulfill the prophecy of Mic 5:2. *Roman world.* See map No. 13 at the end of the Study Bible. **2:2** *Quirinius.* This official was possibly in office for two terms, first 6–4 B.C. and then A.D. 6–9. A census is associated with each term. This is the first; Ac 5:37 refers to the second. **2:3** *own town.* Probably the town of their ancestral origin. **2:4** *Nazareth . . . Bethlehem.* Bethlehem, the town where David was born (1Sa 17:12; 20:6), was at least a three-day trip from Nazareth. *Judea.* The Greco-Roman designation for the southern part of Palestine, earlier included in the kingdom of Judah. **2:5** *with Mary.* Mary too was of the house of David and probably was required to enroll. In Syria, the Roman province in which Palestine was located, women 12 years of age and older were required to pay a poll tax and therefore to register. *pledged to be married.* See note on Mt 1:18. **2:7** *cloths.* Strips of cloth were regularly used to wrap a newborn infant. *manger.* The feeding trough of the animals. This is the only indication that Christ was born in a stable. Very early tradition suggests that it was a cave, perhaps used as a stable. **2:8** *living out in the fields.* Does not necessarily mean it was summer, the dry season. The flocks reserved for temple sacrifice were kept in the fields near Bethlehem throughout the year. *keeping watch.* Against thieves and predatory animals. **2:9** *An angel of the Lord.* A designation used throughout the birth narratives (see 1:11; Mt 1:20,24; 2:13,19). The angel in 1:11 is identified as Gabriel (1:19; see 1:26). **2:10** *Do not be afraid.* Fear was the common reaction to angelic appearances (see note on 1:13), and encouragement

joy that will be for all the people. [11]Today in the town of David a Savior[x] has been born to you; he is Christ[e][y] the Lord.[z] [12]This will be a sign[a] to you: You will find a baby wrapped in cloths and lying in a manger."

[13]Suddenly a great company of the heavenly host appeared with the angel, praising God and saying,

[14]"Glory to God in the highest,
  and on earth peace[b] to men on
    whom his favor rests."

[15]When the angels had left them and gone into heaven, the shepherds said to one another, "Let's go to Bethlehem and see this thing that has happened, which the Lord has told us about."

[16]So they hurried off and found Mary and Joseph, and the baby, who was lying in the manger.[c] [17]When they had seen him, they spread the word concerning what had been told them about this child, [18]and all who heard it were amazed at what the shepherds said to them. [19]But Mary treasured up all these things and pondered them in her heart.[d] [20]The shepherds returned, glorifying and praising God[e] for all the things they had heard and seen, which were just as they had been told.

Jesus Presented in the Temple

[21]On the eighth day, when it was time to circumcise him,[f] he was named Jesus,

the name the angel had given him before he had been conceived.[g]

[22]When the time of their purification according to the Law of Moses[h] had been completed, Joseph and Mary took him to Jerusalem to present him to the Lord [23](as it is written in the Law of the Lord, "Every firstborn male is to be consecrated to the Lord"[f]),[i] [24]and to offer a sacrifice in keeping with what is said in the Law of the Lord: "a pair of doves or two young pigeons."[g][j]

[25]Now there was a man in Jerusalem called Simeon, who was righteous and devout.[k] He was waiting for the consolation of Israel,[l] and the Holy Spirit was upon him. [26]It had been revealed to him by the Holy Spirit that he would not die before he had seen the Lord's Christ. [27]Moved by the Spirit, he went into the temple courts. When the parents brought in the child Jesus to do for him what the custom of the Law required,[m] [28]Simeon took him in his arms and praised God, saying:

[29]"Sovereign Lord, as you have
    promised,[n]
  you now dismiss[h] your servant in
    peace.[o]
[30]For my eyes have seen your salvation,[p]
[31] which you have prepared in the sight
    of all people,

2:11 ×S Mt 1:21;
Ac 5:31; 13:23;
S Ro 11:14;
1Ti 4:10;
1Jn 4:14
yMt 1:16; 16:16,
20; Jn 11:27;
Ac 2:36; 3:20;
S 9:22
zS Jn 13:13
2:12 a1Sa 2:34;
10:7; 2Ki 19:29;
Ps 86:17; Isa 7:14
2:14 bIsa 9:6;
52:7; 53:5;
Mic 5:5; Lk 1:79;
S Jn 14:27;
Ro 5:1; Eph 2:14,
17
2:16 cver 7
2:19 dver 51
2:20 eS Mt 9:8
2:21 fS Lk 1:59

gS Lk 1:31
2:22 hLev 12:2-8
2:23 iEx 13:2,12,
15; Nu 3:13
2:24 jLev 12:8
2:25 kLk 1:6 iver
38; Isa 52:9;
Lk 23:51
2:27 mver 22
2:29 nver 26
oAc 2:24
2:30 pIsa 40:5;
52:10; Lk 3:6

e11 Or Messiah. "The Christ" (Greek) and "the Messiah" (Hebrew) both mean "the Anointed One"; also in verse 26. f23 Exodus 13:2,12 g24 Lev. 12:8 h29 Or promised, / now dismiss

was needed.

2:11 town of David. Bethlehem. Savior. Many Jews were looking for a political leader to deliver them from Roman rule, while others were hoping for a savior to deliver them from sickness and physical hardship. But this announcement concerns the Savior who would deliver from sin and death (see Mt 1:21; Jn 4:42). Christ. See NIV text note. the Lord. A designation originally reserved for God but later applied to the Messiah as well (see Ac 2:36; Php 2:11).
2:14 See note on 1:46–55. This brief hymn is called the Gloria in Excelsis Deo, from the first words of the Latin Vulgate translation (meaning "Glory to God in the Highest"). The angels recognized the glory and majesty of God by giving praise to him. in the highest. A reference to heaven, where God dwells (cf. Mt 6:9). peace to men on whom his favor rests. Peace is not assured to all, but only to those pleasing to God—the objects of his good pleasure (see Luke's use of the words "pleased" and "pleasure" elsewhere: 3:22; 10:21; 12:32). The Roman world was experiencing the Pax Romana ("Roman Peace"), marked by external tranquillity. But the angels proclaimed a deeper, more lasting peace than that—a peace of mind and soul made possible by the Savior (v. 11). Peace with God is received by faith in Christ (Ro 5:1), and it is on believers that "his favor rests." The Davidic Messiah was called "Prince of Peace" (Isa 9:6), and Christ promised peace to his disciples (Jn 14:27). But Christ also brought conflict (the "sword"; see Mt 10:34–36; cf. Lk 12:49), for peace with God involves opposition to Satan and his work

(Jas 4:4).
2:20 praising God. A term often used by Luke (1:64; 2:13,28; 5:25–26; 7:16; 13:13; 17:15,18; 18:43; 19:37; 23:47; 24:53).
2:22 their purification. Following the birth of a son, the mother had to wait 40 days before going to the temple to offer sacrifice for her purification. If she could not afford a lamb and a pigeon (or dove), then two pigeons (or doves) would be acceptable (Lev 12:2–8; cf. Lev 5:11). to Jerusalem. The distance from Bethlehem to Jerusalem was only about five miles. present him to the Lord. The firstborn of both man and animal were to be dedicated to the Lord (see v. 23; Ex 13:12–13). The animals were sacrificed, but the human beings were to serve God throughout their lives. The Levites actually served in the place of all the firstborn males in Israel (see Nu 3:11–13; 8:17–18).
2:25 the consolation of Israel. The comfort the Messiah would bring to his people at his coming (see vv. 26,38; 23:51; 24:21; Isa 40:1–2; Mt 5:4). the Holy Spirit was upon him. Not in the way common to all believers after Pentecost. Simeon was given a special insight by the Spirit so that he would recognize the "Christ."
2:29–32 See note on 1:46–55. This hymn of Simeon has been called the Nunc Dimittis, from the first words of the Latin Vulgate translation, meaning "[You] now dismiss."
2:31 all people. As a Gentile himself, Luke was careful to emphasize the truth that salvation was offered for the Gentiles (v. 32) as well as for Jews.

³²a light for revelation to the Gentiles
and for glory to your people Israel." *q*

³³The child's father and mother marveled at what was said about him. ³⁴Then Simeon blessed them and said to Mary, his mother: *r* "This child is destined to cause the falling *s* and rising of many in Israel, and to be a sign that will be spoken against, ³⁵so that the thoughts of many hearts will be revealed. And a sword will pierce your own soul too."

³⁶There was also a prophetess, *t* Anna, the daughter of Phanuel, of the tribe of Asher. She was very old; she had lived with her husband seven years after her marriage, ³⁷and then was a widow until she was eighty-four. *i u* She never left the temple but worshiped night and day, fasting and praying. *v* ³⁸Coming up to them at that very moment, she gave thanks to God and spoke about the child to all who were looking forward to the redemption of Jerusalem. *w*

³⁹When Joseph and Mary had done everything required by the Law of the Lord, they returned to Galilee to their own town of Nazareth. *x* ⁴⁰And the child grew and became strong; he was filled with wisdom, and the grace of God was upon him. *y*

The Boy Jesus at the Temple

⁴¹Every year his parents went to Jerusalem for the Feast of the Passover. *z* ⁴²When he was twelve years old, they went up to the Feast, according to the custom. ⁴³After the Feast was over, while his parents were returning home, the boy Jesus stayed behind in Jerusalem, but they were unaware of it. ⁴⁴Thinking he was in their company, they traveled on for a day. Then they began looking for him among their relatives and friends. ⁴⁵When they did not find him, they went back to Jerusalem to look for him. ⁴⁶After three days they found him in the temple courts, sitting among the teachers, listening to them and asking them questions. ⁴⁷Everyone who heard him was amazed *a* at his understanding and his answers. ⁴⁸When his parents saw him, they were astonished. His mother *b* said to him, "Son, why have you treated us like this? Your father *c* and I have been anxiously searching for you."

⁴⁹"Why were you searching for me?" he asked. "Didn't you know I had to be in my Father's house?" *d* ⁵⁰But they did not understand what he was saying to them. *e*

⁵¹Then he went down to Nazareth with them *f* and was obedient to them. But his mother treasured all these things in her heart. *g* ⁵²And Jesus grew in wisdom and stature, and in favor with God and men. *h*

John the Baptist Prepares the Way

3:2–10pp — Mt 3:1–10; Mk 1:3–5
3:16,17pp — Mt 3:11,12; Mk 1:7,8

3 In the fifteenth year of the reign of Tiberius Caesar—when Pontius Pi-

i 37 Or widow for eighty-four years

Cross references (center column):

2:32 *q* Isa 42:6; 49:6; Ac 13:47; 26:23
2:34 *r* S Mt 12:46 *s* Isa 8:14; Mt 21:44; 1Co 1:23; 2Co 2:16; Gal 5:11; 1Pe 2:7, 8
2:36 *t* S Ac 21:9
2:37 *u* 1Ti 5:9 *v* Ac 13:3; 14:23; 1Ti 5:5
2:38 *w* ver 25; Isa 40:2; 52:9; Lk 1:68; 24:21
2:39 *x* ver 51; S Mt 2:23
2:40 *y* ver 52; Lk 1:80
2:41 *z* Ex 23:15; Dt 16:1–8; Lk 22:8
2:47 *a* S Mt 7:28
2:48 *b* S Mt 12:46 *c* Lk 3:23; 4:22
2:49 *d* Jn 2:16
2:50 *e* S Mk 9:32
2:51 *f* ver 39; S Mt 2:23 *g* ver 19
2:52 *h* ver 40; 1Sa 2:26; Pr 3:4; Lk 1:80

2:33 *child's father.* Luke, aware of the virgin birth of Jesus (1:26–35), is referring to Joseph as Jesus' legal father.

2:34 *falling and rising of many in Israel.* Christ raises up those who believe in him, but is a stumbling block for those who disbelieve (see 20:17–18; 1Co 1:23; 1Pe 2:6–8). *sign . . . spoken against.* Christ points to the Father and his love for sinners, and those who oppose him also oppose the Father.

2:35 *sword will pierce your own soul too.* The word "too" indicates that Mary, as well as Jesus, would suffer deep anguish—the first reference in this Gospel to Christ's suffering and death.

2:36 *prophetess.* Other prophetesses were Miriam (Ex 15:20), Deborah (Jdg 4:4), Huldah (2Ki 22:14) and the daughters of Philip (Ac 21:9). *Anna.* Same name as OT Hannah (1Sa 1:2), which means "gracious." Anna praised God for the child Jesus as Hannah had praised God for the child Samuel (1Sa 2:1–10).

2:37 *never left the temple.* Herod's temple was quite large and included rooms for various uses, and Anna may have been allowed to live in one of them. This statement, however, probably means that she spent her waking hours attending and worshiping in the temple.

2:38 *Jerusalem.* The holy city of God's chosen people (Isa 40:2; 52:9); here it stands for Israel as a whole.

2:39 *they returned to Galilee.* Luke does not mention the coming of the Magi, the danger from Herod, or the flight to and return from Egypt (cf. Mt 2:1–23).

2:41 *Feast of the Passover.* Annual attendance at three feasts by all adult males (normally accompanied by their families) was commanded in the law: Passover, Pentecost and Tabernacles (see notes on Ex 23:14–17; Dt 16:16). Distance prevented many from attending all three, but most Jews tried to be at Passover.

2:42 *twelve years old.* At age 12 boys began preparing to take their places in the religious community the following year.

2:46 *three days.* One day traveling away from Jerusalem, a second traveling back and a third looking for him. *the teachers.* The rabbis, experts in Judaism.

2:49 *in my Father's house.* Jesus pointed to his personal duty to his Father in heaven. He contrasted his "my Father" with Mary's "Your father" (v. 48). At 12 years of age he was aware of his unique relationship to God. But he was also obedient to his earthly parents (v. 51).

2:52 Luke appears to have borrowed the words of 1Sa 2:26. *And Jesus grew.* Although Jesus was God, there is no indication that he had all knowledge and wisdom from birth. He seems to have matured like any other boy.

3:1–2 Historians frequently dated an event by giving the year of the ruler's reign in which the event happened.

3:1 *fifteenth year.* Several possible dates could be indicated by this description, but the date A.D. 25–26 (Tiberius had authority in the provinces beginning in 11) best fits the chronology of the life of Christ. The other rulers named do not help pinpoint the beginning of John's ministry, but only

late[i] was governor of Judea, Herod[j] tetrarch of Galilee, his brother Philip tetrarch of Iturea and Traconitis, and Lysanias tetrarch of Abilene— [2]during the high priesthood of Annas and Caiaphas,[k] the word of God came to John[l] son of Zechariah[m] in the desert. [3]He went into all the country around the Jordan, preaching a baptism of repentance for the forgiveness of sins.[n] [4]As is written in the book of the words of Isaiah the prophet:

"A voice of one calling in the desert,
'Prepare the way for the Lord,
    make straight paths for him.
[5]Every valley shall be filled in,
    every mountain and hill made low.
The crooked roads shall become
    straight,
    the rough ways smooth.
[6]And all mankind will see God's
    salvation.' "[j] [o]

[7]John said to the crowds coming out to be baptized by him, "You brood of vipers![p] Who warned you to flee from the coming wrath?[q] [8]Produce fruit in keeping with repentance. And do not begin to say to yourselves, 'We have Abraham as our father.'[r] For I tell you that out of these stones God can raise up children for Abraham. [9]The ax is already at the root of the trees, and every tree that does not produce good fruit will be cut down and thrown into the fire."[s]

[10]"What should we do then?"[t] the crowd asked.

[11]John answered, "The man with two tunics should share with him who has none, and the one who has food should do the same."[u]

[12]Tax collectors also came to be baptized.[v] "Teacher," they asked, "what should we do?"

[13]"Don't collect any more than you are required to,"[w] he told them.

[14]Then some soldiers asked him, "And what should we do?"

He replied, "Don't extort money and don't accuse people falsely[x]—be content with your pay."

[15]The people were waiting expectantly and were all wondering in their hearts if John[y] might possibly be the Christ.[k] [z] [16]John answered them all, "I baptize you with[l] water.[a] But one more powerful than I will come, the thongs of whose sandals I am not worthy to untie. He will baptize you with the Holy Spirit and with fire.[b] [17]His winnowing fork[c] is in his hand to clear his threshing floor and to gather the wheat into his barn, but he will burn up the chaff with unquenchable fire."[d]

Cross references (center column):

3:1 [i]S Mt 27:2
[j]S Mt 14:1
3:2 [k]S Mt 26:3
[l]S Mt 3:1
[m]Lk 1:13
3:3 [n]ver 16;
S Mk 1:4
3:6 [o]Isa 40:3-5;
Ps 98:2;
Isa 42:16; 52:10;
Lk 2:30
3:7 [p]Mt 12:34;
23:33 [q]S Ro 1:18
3:8 [r]Isa 51:2;
Lk 19:9; Jn 8:33,
39; Ac 13:26;
Ro 4:1,11,12,16,
17; 9:7,8; Gal 3:7
3:9 [s]S Mt 3:10
3:10 [t]ver 12,14;
Ac 2:37; 16:30
3:11 [u]Isa 58:7;
Eze 18:7
3:12 [v]Lk 7:29
3:13 [w]Lk 19:8
3:14 [x]Ex 23:1;
Lev 19:11
3:15 [y]S Mt 3:1
[z]Jn 1:19,20;
Ac 13:25
3:16 [a]ver 3;
S Mk 1:4
[b]Jn 1:26,33;
Ac 1:5; 2:3;
11:16; 19:4
3:17 [c]Isa 30:24
[d]Mt 13:30;
S 25:41

[i]6 Isaiah 40:3-5　　[k]15 Or Messiah　　[l]16 Or in

---

serve to indicate the general historical period. *Pontius Pilate.* The Roman prefect who then ruled in Judea, Samaria and Idumea. *Herod tetrarch of Galilee.* At the death of Herod the Great (4 B.C.), his sons—Archelaus, Herod Antipas and Herod Philip—were given jurisdiction over his divided kingdom. Herod Antipas became the tetrarch of Galilee and Perea (see note on Mt 14:1). *Lysanias tetrarch of Abilene.* Nothing more is known of this Lysanias than that his name has been found in certain inscriptions.

3:2 *the high priesthood of Annas and Caiaphas.* Annas was high priest from A.D. 6 until he was deposed by the Roman official Gratus in 15. He was followed by his son Eleazar, his son-in-law Caiaphas and then four more sons. Even though Rome had replaced Annas, the Jews continued to recognize his authority (see Jn 18:13; Ac 4:6); so Luke included his name as well as that of the Roman appointee, Caiaphas. *word of God.* The source of John's preaching and authority for his baptizing. God's message came to John as it came to the OT prophets (cf. Jer 1:2; Eze 1:3; Hos 1:1; Joel 1:1). *desert.* Refers to a desolate, uninhabited area, not necessarily a sandy, waterless place.

3:3 *baptism of repentance.* See note on Mt 3:11. John's baptism represented a change of heart, which includes sorrow for sin and a determination to lead a holy life. *forgiveness of sins.* Christ would deliver the repentant person from sin's penalty by dying on the cross.

3:4 *Prepare the way.* Before a king made a journey to a distant country, the roads he would travel were improved. Similarly, preparation for the Messiah was made in a moral and spiritual way by the ministry of John, which focused on repentance and forgiveness of sin and the need for a Savior.

3:6 *all mankind.* God's salvation was to be made known to both Jews and Gentiles—a major theme of Luke's Gospel (see note on 2:31).

3:7 *the coming wrath.* A reference to both the destruction of Jerusalem (21:20–23), which occurred in A.D. 70, and the final judgment (Jn 3:36). But see notes on 1Th 1:10; 5:9.

3:9 *ax . . . at the root.* A symbolic way of saying that judgment is near for those who give no evidence of repentance. *fire.* A symbol of judgment (Mt 7:19; 13:40–42).

3:11 *two tunics.* A tunic was something like a long undershirt. Since two such garments were not needed, the second should be given to a person in need of one (see 9:3).

3:12 *Tax collectors.* Taxes were collected for the Roman government by Jewish agents, who were especially detested for helping the pagan conqueror and for frequently defrauding their own people.

3:14 *soldiers.* Limited military forces were allowed for certain Jewish leaders and institutions (such as those of Herod Antipas, the police guard of the temple, and escorts for tax collectors). The professions of tax collector and soldier as such were not condemned, but the common unethical practices associated with them were.

3:16 *baptize you with the Holy Spirit.* Fulfilled at Pentecost (Ac 1:5; 2:4,38). *and with fire.* Here fire is associated with judgment (v. 17). See also the fire of Pentecost (Ac 2:3) and the fire of testing (1Co 3:13).

3:17 *His winnowing fork.* See note on Ru 1:22. The chaff represents the unrepentant and the wheat the righteous. Many Jews thought that only pagans would be judged and punished when the Messiah came, but John declared that judgment would come to all who did not repent—including Jews.

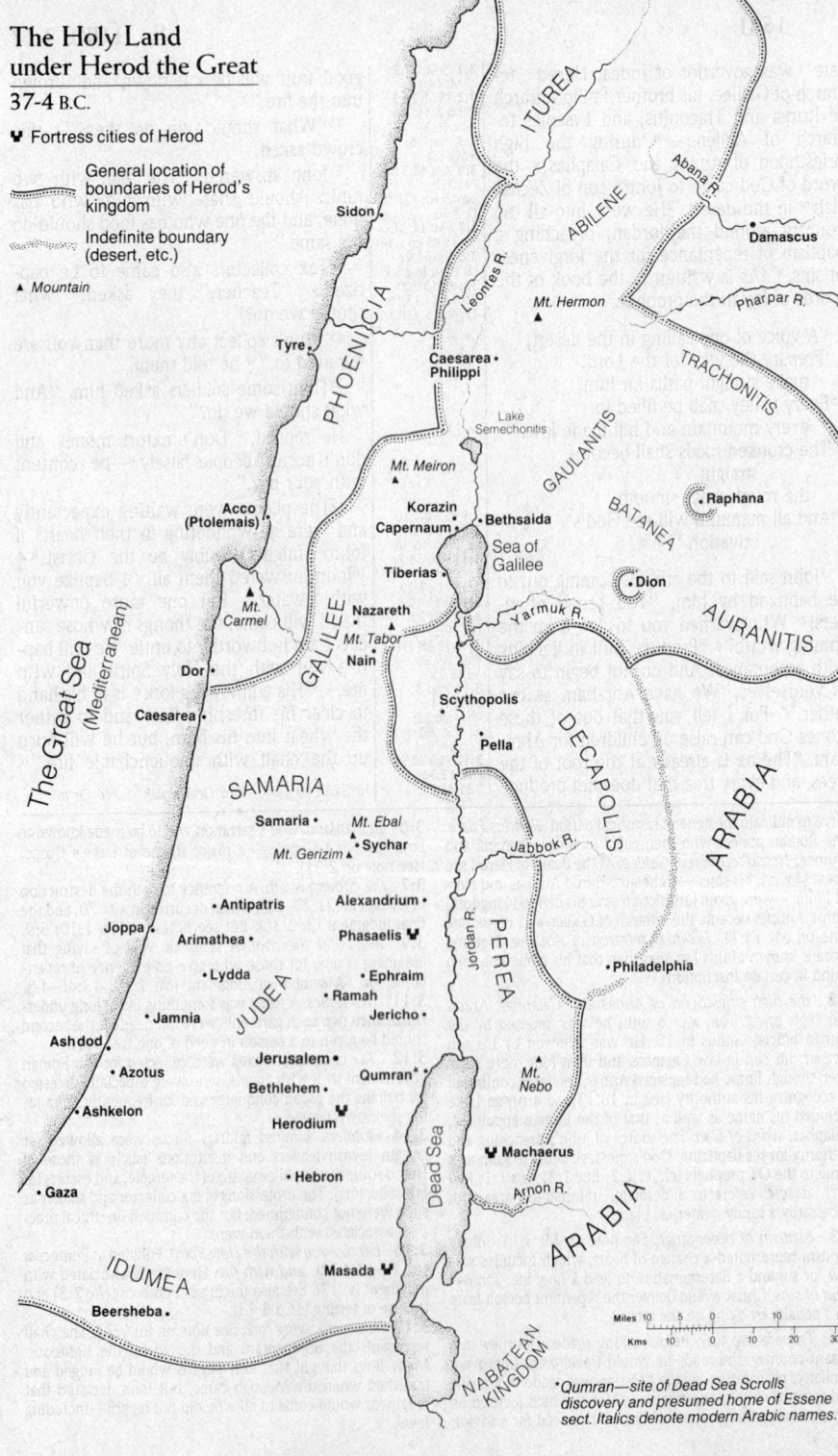

The Holy Land under Herod the Great

37-4 B.C.

♆ Fortress cities of Herod

General location of boundaries of Herod's kingdom

Indefinite boundary (desert, etc.)

▲ Mountain

The Great Sea (Mediterranean)

ITUREA

ABILENE

Abana R.

Damascus

Pharpar R.

Sidon

Leontes R.

TRACHONITIS

Mt. Hermon

Tyre

PHOENICIA

Caesarea Philippi

Lake Semechonitis

GAULANITIS

BATANEA

Raphana

Acco (Ptolemais)

Mt. Meiron ▲

Korazin

Capernaum • Bethsaida

Sea of Galilee

Tiberias

Dion

AURANITIS

Mt. Carmel ▲

GALILEE

Nazareth

Mt. Tabor ▲

Nain •

Yarmuk R.

Dor •

Scythopolis •

DECAPOLIS

ARABIA

Caesarea •

Pella •

SAMARIA

Samaria • Mt. Ebal ▲

Mt. Gerizim ▲ • Sychar

Jabbok R.

• Antipatris

Alexandrium ♆

Joppa •

Arimathea •

Phasaelis ♆

PEREA

• Philadelphia

• Lydda

• Ephraim

JUDEA

• Ramah

Jericho •

Jamnia •

Ashdod •

Jerusalem •

Qumran* •

Mt. Nebo ▲

Azotus •

Bethlehem •

Ashkelon •

Herodium ♆

Dead Sea

♆ Machaerus

Arnon R.

• Gaza

Hebron •

ARABIA

IDUMEA

Masada ♆

Beersheba •

Miles 10 5 0   10   20

Kms 10   0   10   20   30

NABATEAN KINGDOM

*Qumran—site of Dead Sea Scrolls discovery and presumed home of Essene sect. Italics denote modern Arabic names.

¹⁸And with many other words John exhorted the people and preached the good news to them.

¹⁹But when John rebuked Herod[e] the tetrarch because of Herodias, his brother's wife, and all the other evil things he had done, ²⁰Herod added this to them all: He locked John up in prison.[f]

The Baptism and Genealogy of Jesus

3:21,22pp — Mt 3:13–17; Mk 1:9–11
3:23–38pp — Mt 1:1–17

²¹When all the people were being baptized, Jesus was baptized too. And as he was praying,[g] heaven was opened ²²and the Holy Spirit descended on him[h] in bodily form like a dove. And a voice came from heaven: "You are my Son,[i] whom I love; with you I am well pleased."[j]

²³Now Jesus himself was about thirty years old when he began his ministry.[k] He was the son, so it was thought, of Joseph,[l]

the son of Heli, ²⁴the son of Matthat,
the son of Levi, the son of Melki,
the son of Jannai, the son of Joseph,
²⁵the son of Mattathias, the son of Amos,
the son of Nahum, the son of Esli,
the son of Naggai, ²⁶the son of Maath,
the son of Mattathias, the son of Semein,
the son of Josech, the son of Joda,
²⁷the son of Joanan, the son of Rhesa,
the son of Zerubbabel,[m] the son of Shealtiel,

the son of Neri, ²⁸the son of Melki,
the son of Addi, the son of Cosam,
the son of Elmadam, the son of Er,
²⁹the son of Joshua, the son of Eliezer,
the son of Jorim, the son of Matthat,
the son of Levi, ³⁰the son of Simeon,
the son of Judah, the son of Joseph,
the son of Jonam, the son of Eliakim,
³¹the son of Melea, the son of Menna,
the son of Mattatha, the son of Nathan,[n]
the son of David, ³²the son of Jesse,
the son of Obed, the son of Boaz,
the son of Salmon,[m] the son of Nahshon,
³³the son of Amminadab, the son of Ram,[n]
the son of Hezron, the son of Perez,[o]
the son of Judah, ³⁴the son of Jacob,
the son of Isaac, the son of Abraham,
the son of Terah, the son of Nahor,[p]
³⁵the son of Serug, the son of Reu,
the son of Peleg, the son of Eber,
the son of Shelah, ³⁶the son of Cainan,
the son of Arphaxad,[q] the son of Shem,
the son of Noah, the son of Lamech,[r]
³⁷the son of Methuselah, the son of Enoch,
the son of Jared, the son of Mahalalel,
the son of Kenan,[s] ³⁸the son of Enosh,

Cross references (margin)

3:19 [e]ver 1; S Mt 14:1
3:20 [f]S Mt 14:3,4
3:21 [g]Mt 14:23; Mk 1:35; 6:46; Lk 5:16; 6:12; 9:18,28; 11:1
3:22 [h]Isa 42:1; Jn 1:32,33; Ac 10:38
[i]S Mt 3:17
[j]S Mt 3:17
3:23 [k]Mt 4:17; Ac 1:1 [l]Lk 1:27
3:27 [m]Mt 1:12
3:31 [n]2Sa 5:14; 1Ch 3:5
3:33 [o]Ru 4:18-22; 1Ch 2:10-12
3:34 [p]Ge 11:24,26
3:36 [q]Ge 11:12 [r]Ge 5:28-32
3:37 [s]Ge 5:12-25

[m]32 Some early manuscripts *Sala*   [n]33 Some manuscripts *Amminadab, the son of Admin, the son of Arni*; other manuscripts vary widely.

3:19 *rebuked Herod . . . because of Herodias.* Herod Antipas had married the daughter of Aretas IV of Arabia, but divorced her to marry his own niece, Herodias, who was already his brother's (Herod Philip's) wife (see Mt 14:3; Mk 6:17).

3:20 *locked John up in prison.* According to Josephus, John was imprisoned in Machaerus, east of the Dead Sea (*Antiquities*, 18.5.2). This did not occur until sometime after the beginning of Jesus' ministry (see Jn 3:22–24), but Luke mentions it here in order to conclude his section on John's ministry before beginning his account of the beginning of Jesus' ministry (see also Mt 4:12; Mk 1:14). He later briefly alludes to John's death (9:7–9).

3:21 *baptized.* See note on Mt 3:15. *as he was praying.* Only Luke notes Jesus' praying at the time of his baptism. Jesus in prayer is one of the special themes of Luke (see 5:16; 6:12; 9:18,28–29; 11:1; 22:32,41; 23:34,46).

3:22 *Holy Spirit descended.* Luke specifies "in bodily form." To John, it was a sign (see Jn 1:32–34; see also note on Mk 1:10). *You are my son, whom I love.* See Ps 2:7; Isa 42:1; Heb 1:5. Two other times the Gospel writers record the declarations of a voice from heaven addressing Jesus: (1) on the Mount of Transfiguration (9:35), and (2) in the temple area during Jesus' final week (Jn 12:28).

3:23–38 There are several differences between Luke's genealogy and Matthew's (1:2–16). Matthew begins with Abraham (the father of the Jewish people), while Luke traces the line in the reverse order and goes back to Adam, showing Jesus' relationship to the whole human race (see note on 2:31). From Abraham to David, the genealogies of Matthew and Luke are almost the same, but from David on they are different. Some scholars suggest that this is because Matthew traces the legal descent of the house of David using only heirs to the throne, while Luke traces the complete line of Joseph to David. A more likely explanation, however, is that Matthew follows the line of Joseph (Jesus' legal father), while Luke emphasizes that of Mary (Jesus' blood relative). Although tracing a genealogy through the mother's side was unusual, so was the virgin birth. Luke's explanation here that Jesus was the son of Joseph, "so it was thought" (v. 23), brings to mind his explicit virgin birth statement (1:34–35) and suggests the importance of the role of Mary in Jesus' genealogy.

3:23 *about thirty years old.* Luke, a historian, relates the beginning of Jesus' public ministry both to world history (see vv. 1–2) and to the rest of Jesus' life. Thirty was the age when a Levite undertook his service (Nu 4:47) and when a man was considered mature. *so it was thought.* Luke had already affirmed the virgin birth (1:34–35), and here makes clear again that Joseph was not Jesus' physical father.

the son of Seth, the son of Adam, the son of God. *t*

The Temptation of Jesus

4:1–13pp — Mt 4:1–11; Mk 1:12,13

4 Jesus, full of the Holy Spirit, *u* returned from the Jordan *v* and was led by the Spirit *w* in the desert, ²where for forty days *x* he was tempted by the devil. *y* He ate nothing during those days, and at the end of them he was hungry.

³The devil said to him, "If you are the Son of God, *z* tell this stone to become bread."

⁴Jesus answered, "It is written: 'Man does not live on bread alone.' *o* "*a*

⁵The devil led him up to a high place and showed him in an instant all the kingdoms of the world. *b* ⁶And he said to him, "I will give you all their authority and splendor, for it has been given to me, *c* and I can give it to anyone I want to. ⁷So if you worship me, it will all be yours."

⁸Jesus answered, "It is written: 'Worship the Lord your God and serve him only.' *p* "*d*

⁹The devil led him to Jerusalem and had him stand on the highest point of the temple. "If you are the Son of God," he said, "throw yourself down from here. ¹⁰For it is written:

" 'He will command his angels concerning you

to guard you carefully;
¹¹they will lift you up in their hands,
so that you will not strike your foot
against a stone.' *q* "*e*

¹²Jesus answered, "It says: 'Do not put the Lord your God to the test.' *r* "*f*

¹³When the devil had finished all this tempting, *g* he left him *h* until an opportune time.

Jesus Rejected at Nazareth

¹⁴Jesus returned to Galilee *i* in the power of the Spirit, and news about him spread through the whole countryside. *j* ¹⁵He taught in their synagogues, *k* and everyone praised him.

¹⁶He went to Nazareth, *l* where he had been brought up, and on the Sabbath day he went into the synagogue, *m* as was his custom. And he stood up to read. *n* ¹⁷The scroll of the prophet Isaiah was handed to him. Unrolling it, he found the place where it is written:

¹⁸"The Spirit of the Lord is on me, *o*
because he has anointed me
to preach good news *p* to the poor.
He has sent me to proclaim freedom for
the prisoners
and recovery of sight for the blind,

Cross references

3:38 *t*Ge 5:1,2, 6-9
4:1 *u*ver 14,18; S Lk 1:15,35; 3:16,22; 10:21
*v*Lk 3:3,21
*w*Eze 37:1; Lk 2:27
4:2 *x*Ex 34:28; 1Ki 19:8
*y*Heb 4:15
4:3 *z*S Mt 4:3
4:4 *a*Dt 8:3
4:5 *b*S Mt 24:14
4:6 *c*Jn 12:31; 14:30; 1Jn 5:19
4:8 *d*Dt 6:13
4:11 *e*Ps 91:11, 12
4:12 *f*Dt 6:16
4:13 *g*Heb 4:15
*h*Jn 14:30
4:14 *i*Mt 4:12
*j*S Mt 9:26
4:15 *k*S Mt 4:23
*l*S Mt 2:23
*m*Mt 13:54
*n*S 1Ti 4:13
4:18 *o*S Jn 3:34
*p*Mk 16:15

*o*4 Deut. 8:3   *p*8 Deut. 6:13   *q*11 Psalm 91:11,12   *r*12 Deut. 6:16

Study notes

4:1 *full of the Holy Spirit.* Luke emphasizes the Holy Spirit not only in his Gospel (1:35,41,67; 2:25–27; 3:16,22; 4:14,18; 10:21; 11:13; 12:10,12) but also in Acts, where the Spirit is mentioned 57 times. *in the desert.* The Desert of Judea (see Mt 3:1; see also note on 1:80).

4:2 *he was tempted.* See notes on Mt 4:1–11; Heb 2:18; 4:15. Luke states that Jesus was tempted for the 40 days he was fasting, and the three specific temptations recounted in Matthew and Luke seem to have occurred at the close of this period—when Jesus' hunger was greatest and his resistance lowest. The sequence of the second and third temptations differs in Matthew and Luke. Matthew probably followed the chronological order, since at the end of the mountain temptation (Matthew's third) Jesus told Satan to leave (Mt 4:10). To emphasize a certain point the Gospel writers often bring various events together, not intending to give chronological sequence. Perhaps Luke's focus here is geographical, as he concludes with Jesus in Jerusalem.

4:3 *If you are.* See note on Mt 4:3. *tell this stone to become bread.* The devil always makes his temptations seem attractive.

4:7 *worship me.* The devil was tempting Jesus to avoid the sufferings of the cross, which he came specifically to endure (Mk 10:45). The temptation offered an easy shortcut to world dominion.

4:9 *the highest point of the temple.* Either the southeast corner of the temple colonnade, from which there was a drop of some 100 feet to the Kidron Valley below, or the pinnacle of the temple proper. *If you are.* See note on Mt 4:3. *throw*

yourself down. Satan was tempting Jesus to test God's faithfulness and to attract public attention dramatically.

4:10 *For it is written.* This time Satan also quoted Scripture, though he misused Ps 91:11–12.

4:12 Jesus answered with Scripture, as he had on each of the other two occasions, quoting from Deuteronomy (see NIV text notes here).

4:13 *he left him until an opportune time.* Satan continued his testing throughout Jesus' ministry (see Mk 8:33), culminating in the supreme test at Gethsemane.

4:14 *in the power of the Spirit.* See note on v. 1.

4:15 *taught in their synagogues.* See note on Mk 1:21.

4:16 *He went to Nazareth.* Not at the start of his ministry but perhaps almost a year later (v. 23 presupposes that Jesus had already been ministering). Probably all the events of Jn 1:19–4:42 occurred between Lk 4:13 and 4:14. *as was his custom.* Jesus' custom of regular worship sets an example for all his followers. *to read.* Jesus probably read from Isaiah in Hebrew, and then he or someone else paraphrased it in Aramaic, one of the other common languages of the day.

4:17 *The scroll of the prophet Isaiah.* The books of the OT were written on scrolls, kept in a special place in the synagogue and handed to the reader by a special attendant. The passage Jesus read about the Messiah (Isa 61:1–2) may have been one he chose to read, or it may have been the assigned passage for the day.

4:18 This verse tells of the Messiah's ministry of preaching and healing—to meet every human need. *he has anointed me.* Not with literal oil (see Ex 30:22–31), but with the Holy Spirit.

to release the oppressed,
19 to proclaim the year of the Lord's favor." [s] [q]

20Then he rolled up the scroll, gave it back to the attendant and sat down. [r] The eyes of everyone in the synagogue were fastened on him, 21and he began by saying to them, "Today this scripture is fulfilled [s] in your hearing."

22All spoke well of him and were amazed at the gracious words that came from his lips. "Isn't this Joseph's son?" they asked. [t]

23Jesus said to them, "Surely you will quote this proverb to me: 'Physician, heal yourself! Do here in your hometown [u] what we have heard that you did in Capernaum.' " [v]

24"I tell you the truth," he continued, "no prophet is accepted in his hometown. [w] 25I assure you that there were many widows in Israel in Elijah's time, when the sky was shut for three and a half years and there was a severe famine throughout the land. [x] 26Yet Elijah was not sent to any of them, but to a widow in Zarephath in the region of Sidon. [y] 27And there were many in Israel with leprosy [t] in the time of Elisha the prophet, yet not one of them was cleansed—only Naaman the Syrian." [z]

28All the people in the synagogue were furious when they heard this. 29They got up, drove him out of the town, [a] and took him to the brow of the hill on which the town was built, in order to throw him down the cliff. 30But he walked right through the crowd and went on his way. [b]

Cross references

4:19 [q]Isa 61:1,2; Lev 25:10; Ps 102:20; 103:6; Isa 42:7; 49:8,9; 58:6
4:20 [r]ver 17; S Mt 26:55
4:21 [s]S Mt 1:22
4:22 [t]Mt 13:54, 55; Jn 6:42; 7:15
4:23 [u]ver 16; S Mt 2:23
[v]Mk 1:21-28; 2:1-12
4:24 [w]Mt 13:57; Jn 4:44
4:25 [x]1Ki 17:1; 18:1; Jas 5:17,18; Rev 11:6
[y]1Ki 17:8-16; S Mt 11:21
4:27 [z]2Ki 5:1-14; Ac 7:58; Heb 13:12
4:30 [b]Jn 8:59; 10:39
4:31 [c]ver 23; S Mt 4:13
4:32 [d]S Mt 7:28
[e]ver 36; Mt 7:29
4:34 [f]S Mt 8:29
[g]S Mk 1:24
[h]Jas 2:19
4:35 [i]ver 41; S Mk 1:24
[j]ver 39,41; Mt 8:26; Lk 8:24
4:36 [k]S Mt 7:28
[l]ver 32; Mt 7:29; S Mt 10:1
4:37 [m]ver 14; S Mt 9:26
4:39 [n]ver 35,41

Jesus Drives Out an Evil Spirit

4:31–37pp — Mk 1:21–28

31Then he went down to Capernaum, [c] a town in Galilee, and on the Sabbath began to teach the people. 32They were amazed at his teaching, [d] because his message had authority. [e]

33In the synagogue there was a man possessed by a demon, an evil [u] spirit. He cried out at the top of his voice, 34"Ha! What do you want with us, [f] Jesus of Nazareth? [g] Have you come to destroy us? I know who you are [h]—the Holy One of God!" [i]

35"Be quiet!" Jesus said sternly. [j] "Come out of him!" Then the demon threw the man down before them all and came out without injuring him.

36All the people were amazed [k] and said to each other, "What is this teaching? With authority [l] and power he gives orders to evil spirits and they come out!" 37And the news about him spread throughout the surrounding area. [m]

Jesus Heals Many

4:38–41pp — Mt 8:14–17
4:38–43pp — Mk 1:29–38

38Jesus left the synagogue and went to the home of Simon. Now Simon's mother-in-law was suffering from a high fever, and they asked Jesus to help her. 39So he bent over her and rebuked [n] the fever, and it left her. She got up at once and began to wait on them.

40When the sun was setting, the people

---

[s]*19* Isaiah 61:1,2   [t]*27* The Greek word was used for various diseases affecting the skin—not necessarily leprosy.   [u]*33* Greek *unclean*; also in verse 36

4:19 *the year of the Lord's favor.* Not a calendar year, but the period when salvation would be proclaimed—the Messianic age. This quotation from Isa 61:1–2 alludes to the Year of Jubilee (Lev 25:8–55), when once every 50 years slaves were freed, debts were canceled and ancestral property was returned to the original family. Isaiah predicted primarily the liberation of Israel from the future Babylonian captivity, but Jesus proclaimed liberation from sin and all its consequences.
4:20 *sat down.* It was customary to stand while reading Scripture (v. 16) but to sit while teaching (see Mt 5:1; 26:55; Jn 8:2; Ac 16:13).
4:23 *hometown.* Nazareth. Although Jesus was born in Bethlehem, he was brought up in Nazareth, in Galilee (1:26; 2:39,51; Mt 2:23). *Capernaum.* See note on Mt 4:13.
4:26–27 Mention of Jesus' reference to God's helping two non-Israelites (1Ki 17:1–15; 2Ki 5:1–14) reflects Luke's special concern for the Gentiles. Jesus' point was that when Israel rejected God's messenger of redemption, God sent him to the Gentiles—and so it will be again if they refuse to accept Jesus (see 10:13–15; Ro 9–11).
4:26 *Sidon.* One of the oldest Phoenician cities, 20 miles north of Tyre. Jesus later healed a Gentile woman's daughter in this region (Mt 15:21–28).

4:28 *furious.* Because of Jesus' condemnation of Israel and favorable attitude toward Gentiles.
4:30 *walked right through the crowd.* Luke does not explain whether the escape was miraculous or simply the result of Jesus' commanding presence. In any case, his time (to die) had not yet come (Jn 7:30).
4:32 See note on Mk 1:22.
4:33 *possessed by a demon.* To pagans, "demon" meant a supernatural being, whether good or bad, but Luke makes it clear that this was an evil spirit. Such a demon could cause mental disorder (Jn 10:20), violent action (Lk 8:26–29), bodily disease (13:11,16) and rebellion against God (Rev 16:14).
4:34 *Holy One of God.* See note on Mk 1:24.
4:38 *Simon's mother-in-law.* Peter was married (1Co 9:5). *a high fever.* All three Synoptics tell of this miracle (Mt 8:14–15; Mk 1:29–31), but only Luke, the doctor, uses the more specific phrase "high fever."
4:40 *When the sun was setting.* The Sabbath (v. 31) was over at sundown (about 6:00 P.M.). Until then, according to the tradition of the elders, Jews could not travel more than about two-thirds of a mile or carry a burden. Only after sundown could they carry the sick to Jesus, and their eager-

brought to Jesus all who had various kinds of sickness, and laying his hands on each one,[o] he healed them.[p] [41]Moreover, demons came out of many people, shouting, "You are the Son of God!"[q] But he rebuked[r] them and would not allow them to speak,[s] because they knew he was the Christ.[v]

[42]At daybreak Jesus went out to a solitary place. The people were looking for him and when they came to where he was, they tried to keep him from leaving them. [43]But he said, "I must preach the good news of the kingdom of God[t] to the other towns also, because that is why I was sent." [44]And he kept on preaching in the synagogues of Judea.[w][u]

4:40 [o]S Mk 5:23
[p]S Mt 4:23
4:41 [q]S Mt 4:3
[r]S ver 35
[s]S Mt 8:4
4:43 [t]S Mt 3:2
4:44 [u]S Mt 4:23

5:1 [v]S Mk 4:14; S Heb 4:12
5:3 [w]Mt 13:2
5:4 [x]Jn 21:6
5:5 [y]Lk 8:24,45; 9:33,49; 17:13

The Calling of the First Disciples

5:1–11pp — Mt 4:18–22; Mk 1:16–20; Jn 1:40–42

5 One day as Jesus was standing by the Lake of Gennesaret,[x] with the people crowding around him and listening to the word of God,[v] [2]he saw at the water's edge two boats, left there by the fishermen, who were washing their nets. [3]He got into one of the boats, the one belonging to Simon, and asked him to put out a little from shore. Then he sat down and taught the people from the boat.[w]

[4]When he had finished speaking, he said to Simon, "Put out into deep water, and let down[v] the nets for a catch."[x]

[5]Simon answered, "Master,[y] we've worked hard all night and haven't caught

[v]41 Or Messiah   [w]44 Or the land of the Jews; some manuscripts Galilee   [x]1 That is, Sea of Galilee
[y]4 The Greek verb is plural.

---

ness is seen in the fact that they set out while the sun was still setting.
4:41 because they knew he was the Christ. See note on Mk 1:34.
4:42 solitary place. Mark includes the words "where he prayed" (Mk 1:35).

4:43 kingdom of God. Luke's first use of this phrase; it occurs over 30 times in his Gospel. Some of its different meanings in the Bible are: the eternal kingship of God; the presence of the kingdom in the person of Jesus, the King; the approaching spiritual form of the kingdom; the future kingdom. See note on Mt 3:2.

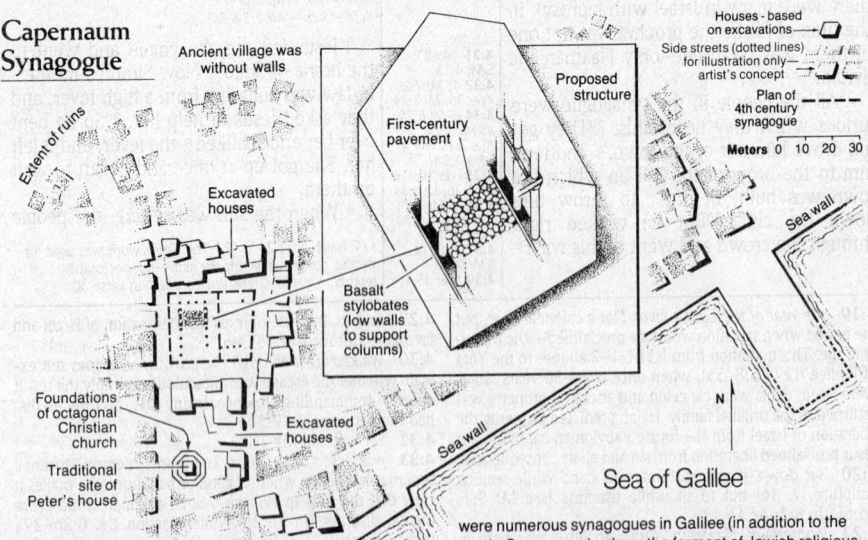

Capernaum Synagogue

Ancient village was without walls

Proposed structure

First-century pavement

Houses - based on excavations

Side streets (dotted lines) for illustration only—artist's concept

Plan of 4th century synagogue

Meters 0 10 20 30

Extent of ruins

Excavated houses

Basalt stylobates (low walls to support columns)

Sea wall

Foundations of octagonal Christian church

Excavated houses

Sea wall

Traditional site of Peter's house

N

Sea of Galilee

Capernaum was more than a seaside fishing village in the days of Jesus. It was the place that Christ chose to be the center of his ministry to the entire region of Galilee, and it possessed ideal characteristics as a point of dissemination for the gospel.

There were good reasons for this. The town itself was named Kephar Nahum, "village of (perhaps the prophet), Nahum" and was the centerpiece of a densely populated region having a bicultural flavor. On the one hand, there

were numerous synagogues in Galilee (in addition to the one in Capernaum), where the ferment of Jewish religious life was profound. On the other hand, there was Hellenism, a pervasive culture already centuries old and potent in its paganism—a lifestyle that influenced manners, dress, architecture and political institutions as well.

Recent archaeological work at Capernaum has revealed a section of the pavement of a first-century synagogue below the still-existing ruins of the fourth-century one on the site. A private house later made into a church and a place of pilgrimage has yielded some evidence that may link it to the site of Simon Peter's house (Lk 4:38).

anything.^{z} But because you say so, I will let down the nets."

^{6}When they had done so, they caught such a large number of fish that their nets began to break.^{a} ^{7}So they signaled their partners in the other boat to come and help them, and they came and filled both boats so full that they began to sink.

^{8}When Simon Peter saw this, he fell at Jesus' knees and said, "Go away from me, Lord; I am a sinful man!"^{b} ^{9}For he and all his companions were astonished at the catch of fish they had taken, ^{10}and so were James and John, the sons of Zebedee, Simon's partners.

Then Jesus said to Simon, "Don't be afraid;^{c} from now on you will catch men." ^{11}So they pulled their boats up on shore, left everything and followed him.^{d}

The Man With Leprosy

5:12-14pp — Mt 8:2-4; Mk 1:40-44

^{12}While Jesus was in one of the towns, a man came along who was covered with leprosy.$^{z\,e}$ When he saw Jesus, he fell with his face to the ground and begged him, "Lord, if you are willing, you can make me clean."

^{13}Jesus reached out his hand and touched the man. "I am willing," he said. "Be clean!" And immediately the leprosy left him.

^{14}Then Jesus ordered him, "Don't tell anyone,^{f} but go, show yourself to the priest and offer the sacrifices that Moses commanded^g for your cleansing, as a testimony to them."

^{15}Yet the news about him spread all the more,^{h} so that crowds of people came to hear him and to be healed of their sicknesses. ^{16}But Jesus often withdrew to lonely places and prayed.^{i}

Jesus Heals a Paralytic

5:18-26pp — Mt 9:2-8; Mk 2:3-12

^{17}One day as he was teaching, Pharisees and teachers of the law,^{j} who had come from every village of Galilee and from Judea and Jerusalem, were sitting there. And the power of the Lord was present for him to heal the sick.^{k} ^{18}Some men came carrying a paralytic on a mat and tried to take him into the house to lay him before Jesus. ^{19}When they could not find a way to do this because of the crowd, they went up on the roof and lowered him on his mat through the tiles into the middle of the crowd, right in front of Jesus.

^{20}When Jesus saw their faith, he said, "Friend, your sins are forgiven."^{l}

^{21}The Pharisees and the teachers of the

5:5 ^{z}Jn 21:3
5:6 ^{a}Jn 21:11
5:8 ^{b}Ge 18:27; Job 42:6; Isa 6:5
5:10 ^{c}S Mt 14:27
5:11 ^{d}ver 28; S Mt 4:19
5:12 ^{e}S Mt 8:2

5:14 ^{f}S Mt 8:4
^{g}Lev 14:2-32
5:15 ^{h}S Mt 9:26
5:16 ^{i}S Lk 3:21
5:17 ^{j}Mt 15:1; Lk 2:46
^{k}Mk 5:30; Lk 6:19
5:20 ^{l}Lk 7:48,49

^{z}12 The Greek word was used for various diseases affecting the skin—not necessarily leprosy.

4:44 This summary statement includes not only what has just been described (from v. 14 on) but also what lay ahead in Jesus' ministry. No express mention is made in the Synoptics of the early Judean ministry recorded in John (2:13–4:3), though it may be reflected in Mt 23:37 and Lk 13:34. *Judea.* Some manuscripts, as well as the parallel accounts (Mt 4:23; Mk 1:39), mention Galilee instead of Judea (see NIV text note). In writing to a Gentile (see Introduction: Recipient and Purpose), Luke possibly used "Judea" to refer to the whole of Palestine, the land of the Jews (23:5; Ac 10:37; 11:1,29; 26:20).
5:1 *Lake of Gennesaret.* Luke is the only one who calls it a lake. The other Gospel writers call it the Sea of Galilee, and John twice calls it the Sea of Tiberias (Jn 6:1; 21:1).
5:2 *washing their nets.* After each period of fishing, the nets were washed, stretched and prepared for use again.
5:3 *sat down.* The usual position for teaching (see note on 4:20). The boat provided an ideal arrangement, removed from the press of the crowd but near enough to be seen and heard.
5:7 *their partners.* See v. 10.
5:8 *Go away from me, Lord.* The nearer one comes to God, the more he feels his own sinfulness and unworthiness—as did Abraham (Ge 18:27), Job (42:6) and Isaiah (6:5).
5:11 *left everything and followed him.* This was not the first time these men had been with Jesus (see Jn 1:40–42; 2:1–2). Their periodic and loose association now became a closely knit fellowship as they followed the Master. The scene is the same as Mt 4:18–22 and Mk 1:16–20, but the accounts relate events from different hours of the morning.
5:12–16 The healing of the man with leprosy is described in all three of the Synoptic Gospels, but the setting is different

in each. In Matthew (8:1–4) it is part of a collection of miracles; in Mark (1:40–45) and Luke it is probably one incident that occurred on the first tour of Galilee.
5:12 *covered with leprosy.* See NIV text note; see also NIV text note on Lev 13:2. Luke alone notes the extent of his disease. The Greek term was used in medical literature, though not concerning leprosy.
5:14 *Don't tell anyone.* See notes on Mt 8:4; 16:20. *but go, show yourself to the priest.* By this command Jesus urged the man to keep the law, to provide further proof for the actual healing, to testify to the authorities concerning his ministry and to supply ritual certification of cleansing so the man could be reinstated into society. *a testimony to them.* See note on Mk 1:44.
5:17 *Pharisees and teachers of the law.* See notes on Mt 2:4; 3:7; Mk 2:16. Opposition was rising in Galilee from these religious leaders. *Pharisees.* Mentioned here for the first time in Luke. Their name meaning "separated ones," they numbered about 6,000 and were spread over the whole of Palestine. They were teachers in the synagogues, religious examples in the eyes of the people and self-appointed guardians of the law and its proper observance. They considered the interpretations and regulations handed down by tradition to be virtually as authoritative as Scripture (Mk 7:8–13). Already Jesus had run counter to the Jewish leaders in Jerusalem (Jn 5:16–18). Now they came to a home in Capernaum (Mk 2:1–6) to hear and watch him. *teachers of the law.* "Scribes," who studied, interpreted and taught the law (both written and oral). The majority of these teachers belonged to the party of the Pharisees.
5:19 *roof.* See note on Mk 2:4. *tiles.* Probably ceiling tiles.
5:21 *this fellow . . . speaks blasphemy.* See note on Mk

law began thinking to themselves, "Who is this fellow who speaks blasphemy? Who can forgive sins but God alone?" [m]

[22]Jesus knew what they were thinking and asked, "Why are you thinking these things in your hearts? [23]Which is easier: to say, 'Your sins are forgiven,' or to say, 'Get up and walk'? [24]But that you may know that the Son of Man [n] has authority on earth to forgive sins. . . ." He said to the paralyzed man, "I tell you, get up, take your mat and go home." [25]Immediately he stood up in front of them, took what he had been lying on and went home praising God. [26]Everyone was amazed and gave praise to God. [o] They were filled with awe and said, "We have seen remarkable things today."

The Calling of Levi

5:27–32pp — Mt 9:9–13; Mk 2:14–17

[27]After this, Jesus went out and saw a tax collector by the name of Levi sitting at his tax booth. "Follow me," [p] Jesus said to him, [28]and Levi got up, left everything and followed him. [q]

[29]Then Levi held a great banquet for Jesus at his house, and a large crowd of tax collectors [r] and others were eating with them. [30]But the Pharisees and the teachers of the law who belonged to their sect [s] complained to his disciples, "Why do you eat and drink with tax collectors and 'sinners'?" [t]

[31]Jesus answered them, "It is not the healthy who need a doctor, but the sick. [32]I have not come to call the righteous, but sinners to repentance." [u]

5:21 mIsa 43:25
5:24 nS Mt 8:20
5:26 oS Mt 9:8
5:27 pS Mt 4:19
5:28 qver 11;
S Mt 4:19
5:29 rLk 15:1
5:30 sAc 23:9
rS Mt 9:11
5:32 uS Jn 3:17

5:33 vLk 7:18;
Jn 1:35; 3:25,26
5:34 wJn 3:29
5:35 xLk 9:22;
17:22; Jn 16:5-7
6:1 yDt 23:25
6:2 zS Mt 12:2
6:3 aIsa 21:6
6:4 bLev 24:5,9

Jesus Questioned About Fasting

5:33–39pp — Mt 9:14–17; Mk 2:18–22

[33]They said to him, "John's disciples [v] often fast and pray, and so do the disciples of the Pharisees, but yours go on eating and drinking."

[34]Jesus answered, "Can you make the guests of the bridegroom [w] fast while he is with them? [35]But the time will come when the bridegroom will be taken from them; [x] in those days they will fast."

[36]He told them this parable: "No one tears a patch from a new garment and sews it on an old one. If he does, he will have torn the new garment, and the patch from the new will not match the old. [37]And no one pours new wine into old wineskins. If he does, the new wine will burst the skins, the wine will run out and the wineskins will be ruined. [38]No, new wine must be poured into new wineskins. [39]And no one after drinking old wine wants the new, for he says, 'The old is better.' "

Lord of the Sabbath

6:1–11pp — Mt 12:1–14; Mk 2:23–3:6

6 One Sabbath Jesus was going through the grainfields, and his disciples began to pick some heads of grain, rub them in their hands and eat the kernels. [y] [2]Some of the Pharisees asked, "Why are you doing what is unlawful on the Sabbath?" [z]

[3]Jesus answered them, "Have you never read what David did when he and his companions were hungry? [a] [4]He entered the house of God, and taking the consecrated bread, he ate what is lawful only for priests to eat. [b] And he also gave some to his companions." [5]Then Jesus said to

---

2:7. The Pharisees considered blasphemy to be the most serious sin a man could commit (see note on Mk 14:64).
5:23 *Which is easier: to say . . . ?* See notes on Mk 2:9–10.
5:24 *that you may know.* Jesus' power to heal was a visible affirmation of his power to forgive sins.
5:27 *a tax collector.* See note on 3:12. *tax booth.* The place where customs were collected (see note on Mk 2:14).
5:28 *left everything and followed him.* Since Jesus had been ministering in Capernaum for some time, Levi probably had known him previously (see note on v. 11).
5:29 *a great banquet.* When Levi began to follow Jesus, he did not do it secretly.
5:30 *Pharisees . . . complained.* They probably stood outside and registered their complaints from a distance. *eat . . . with tax collectors and 'sinners.'* See note on Mk 2:15.
5:31 *not the healthy who need a doctor, but the sick.* Not to imply that the Pharisees were "the healthy," but that a person must recognize himself as a sinner before he can be spiritually healed (see note on Mk 2:17).
5:33 *John's disciples . . . fast and pray.* John the Baptist had grown up in the desert and learned to subsist on a meager, austere diet of locusts and wild honey. His ministry

was characterized by a sober message and a strenuous schedule. For a contrast between Jesus' ministry and John the Baptist's see 7:24–28; Mt 11:1–19. The Pharisees also had rigorous lifestyles (see notes on 18:12). But Jesus went to banquets, and his disciples enjoyed a freedom not known by the Pharisees. *fast.* See note on Mk 2:18. While Jesus rejected fasting legalistically for display (cf. Isa 58:3–11), he himself fasted privately and permitted its voluntary use for spiritual benefit (Mt 4:2; 6:16–18).
5:35 See notes on Mk 2:19–20.
5:36 *parable.* See notes on Mt 13:3; Mk 4:2.
5:37 *old wineskins.* See note on Mt 9:17.
5:39 *The old is better.* Jesus was indicating the reluctance of some people to change from their traditional religious ways and try the gospel.
6:1 *going through the grainfields.* See note on Mk 2:23.
6:3 *what David did.* See note on Mk 2:25.
6:4 *consecrated bread.* See note on Mt 12:4.
6:5 *Son of Man.* See note on Mk 8:31. *Lord of the Sabbath.* Jesus has the authority to overrule laws concerning the Sabbath, particularly as interpreted by the Pharisees (see Mt 12:8; Mk 2:27).

them, "The Son of Man c is Lord of the Sabbath."

6On another Sabbath d he went into the synagogue and was teaching, and a man was there whose right hand was shriveled. 7The Pharisees and the teachers of the law were looking for a reason to accuse Jesus, so they watched him closely e to see if he would heal on the Sabbath. f 8But Jesus knew what they were thinking g and said to the man with the shriveled hand, "Get up and stand in front of everyone." So he got up and stood there.

9Then Jesus said to them, "I ask you, which is lawful on the Sabbath: to do good or to do evil, to save life or to destroy it?"

10He looked around at them all, and then said to the man, "Stretch out your hand." He did so, and his hand was completely restored. 11But they were furious h and began to discuss with one another what they might do to Jesus.

The Twelve Apostles

6:13–16pp — Mt 10:2–4; Mk 3:16–19; Ac 1:13

12One of those days Jesus went out to a mountainside to pray, and spent the night praying to God. i 13When morning came, he called his disciples to him and chose twelve of them, whom he also designated apostles: j 14Simon (whom he named Peter), his brother Andrew, James, John, Philip, Bartholomew, 15Matthew, k Thomas, James son of Alphaeus, Simon who was called the Zealot, 16Judas son of James, and Judas Iscariot, who became a traitor.

Cross-references (center column):
6:5 cS Mt 8:20
6:6 dver 1
6:7 eS Mt 12:10
/S Mt 12:2
6:8 gS Mt 9:4
6:11 hJn 5:18
6:12 iS Lk 3:21
6:13 jS Mk 6:30
6:15 kMt 9:9

6:17 lMt 4:25;
S Mt 11:21;
Mk 3:7,8
6:19 mS Mt 9:20
nMk 5:30;
Lk 5:17
6:20 oS Mt 25:34
6:21 pIsa 55:1,2;
Mt 5:6 qIsa 61:2,
3; Mt 5:4;
Rev 7:17
6:22 rJn 9:22;
16:2 sIsa 51:7
tS Jn 15:21
6:23 uS Mt 5:12
vS Mt 5:12
6:24 wJas 5:1
xLk 16:25
6:25 yIsa 65:13

Blessings and Woes

6:20–23pp — Mt 5:3–12

17He went down with them and stood on a level place. A large crowd of his disciples was there and a great number of people from all over Judea, from Jerusalem, and from the coast of Tyre and Sidon, l 18who had come to hear him and to be healed of their diseases. Those troubled by evil a spirits were cured, 19and the people all tried to touch him, m because power was coming from him and healing them all. n

20Looking at his disciples, he said:

"Blessed are you who are poor,
    for yours is the kingdom of God. o
21Blessed are you who hunger now,
    for you will be satisfied. p
Blessed are you who weep now,
    for you will laugh. q
22Blessed are you when men hate you,
    when they exclude you r and insult you s
    and reject your name as evil,
        because of the Son of Man. t

23"Rejoice in that day and leap for joy, u because great is your reward in heaven. For that is how their fathers treated the prophets. v

24"But woe to you who are rich, w
    for you have already received your
        comfort. x
25Woe to you who are well fed now,
    for you will go hungry. y
Woe to you who laugh now,

a 18 Greek unclean

6:8 stand in front of everyone. So there would be no question about the healing.
6:9 which is lawful on the Sabbath . . . ? Jesus had been enduring questions and attacks from the Pharisees and now took the initiative by putting the questions to everyone in the synagogue (see note on Mk 3:4).
6:10 He looked around at them. Jesus wanted to see whether anyone objected to his question or the implied answer, but no one was bold enough to do so.
6:11 they were furious. Because they could not withstand Jesus' reasoning. Already they were plotting to take his life (Jn 5:18). See note on Mk 3:6.
6:12 Characteristically, Jesus spent the night in prayer before the important work of selecting his 12 apostles.
6:13 he called his disciples. Among those who came to hear Jesus as a group who regularly followed him and were committed to his teachings. At least 72 men were included, since this many disciples were sent out on an evangelistic campaign (10:1,17). Later, 120 believers waited and worshiped in Jerusalem following the ascension (Ac 1:15). From such disciples Jesus at this time chose 12 to be his apostles, meaning "ones sent with a special commission" (see notes on Mk 6:30; 1Co 1:1; Heb 3:1).
6:14–16 Lists of the apostles appear also in Mt 10:2–4; Mk 3:16–19; Ac 1:13. Although the order of the names varies, Peter is always first and Judas Iscariot last.

6:14 Bartholomew. Seems to be (in the Synoptics) the same as Nathanael (in John). Nathanael is associated with Philip in Jn 1:45.
6:15 Matthew. Another name for Levi. James son of Alphaeus. Probably the same as James the younger (Mk 15:40). the Zealot. See note on Mt 10:4.
6:16 Judas son of James. Another name for Thaddaeus (Mt 10:3; Mk 3:18). Judas Iscariot. Probably the only one from Judea, the rest coming from Galilee (see note on Mk 3:19).
6:17 stood on a level place. Perhaps a plateau, which would satisfy both this context and that in Mt 5:1.
6:20–49 Luke's Sermon on the Plain, apparently parallel to Matthew's Sermon on the Mount (Mt 5–7). Although this sermon is much shorter than the one in Matthew, they both begin with the Beatitudes and end with the lesson of the builders. Some of Matthew's Sermon is found in other portions of Luke (e.g., 11:2–4; 12:22–31,33–34), suggesting that the material may have been given on various occasions in Jesus' preaching.
6:20–23 See Mt 5:3–12. The Beatitudes go deeper than material poverty (v. 20) and physical hunger (v. 21). Matthew's account indicates that Jesus spoke of poverty "in spirit" (Mt 5:3) and hunger "for righteousness" (Mt 5:6).
6:24–26 This section is a point-by-point negative counterpart of vv. 20–22.

for you will mourn and weep. [z]

26Woe to you when all men speak well of
you,

for that is how their fathers treated
the false prophets. [a]

Love for Enemies

6:29,30pp — Mt 5:39–42

27"But I tell you who hear me: Love
your enemies, do good to those who hate
you, [b] 28bless those who curse you, pray
for those who mistreat you. [c] 29If someone
strikes you on one cheek, turn to him the
other also. If someone takes your cloak, do
not stop him from taking your tunic.
30Give to everyone who asks you, and if
anyone takes what belongs to you, do not
demand it back. [d] 31Do to others as you
would have them do to you. [e]

32"If you love those who love you, what
credit is that to you? [f] Even 'sinners' love
those who love them. 33And if you do good
to those who are good to you, what credit
is that to you? Even 'sinners' do that.
34And if you lend to those from whom you
expect repayment, what credit is that to
you? [g] Even 'sinners' lend to 'sinners,' expecting to be repaid in full. 35But love your
enemies, do good to them, [h] and lend to
them without expecting to get anything
back. Then your reward will be great, and
you will be sons [i] of the Most High, [j] because he is kind to the ungrateful and
wicked. 36Be merciful, [k] just as your Father [l] is merciful.

Judging Others

6:37–42pp — Mt 7:1–5

37"Do not judge, and you will not be
judged. [m] Do not condemn, and you will
not be condemned. Forgive, and you will
be forgiven. [n] 38Give, and it will be given
to you. A good measure, pressed down,
shaken together and running over, will be
poured into your lap. [o] For with the measure you use, it will be measured to
you." [p]

39He also told them this parable: "Can a
blind man lead a blind man? Will they not

both fall into a pit? [q] 40A student is not
above his teacher, but everyone who is fully trained will be like his teacher. [r]

41"Why do you look at the speck of sawdust in your brother's eye and pay no attention to the plank in your own eye?
42How can you say to your brother, 'Brother, let me take the speck out of your eye,'
when you yourself fail to see the plank in
your own eye? You hypocrite, first take the
plank out of your eye, and then you will
see clearly to remove the speck from your
brother's eye.

A Tree and Its Fruit

6:43,44pp — Mt 7:16,18,20

43"No good tree bears bad fruit, nor
does a bad tree bear good fruit. 44Each tree
is recognized by its own fruit. [s] People do
not pick figs from thornbushes, or grapes
from briers. 45The good man brings good
things out of the good stored up in his
heart, and the evil man brings evil things
out of the evil stored up in his heart. For
out of the overflow of his heart his mouth
speaks. [t]

The Wise and Foolish Builders

6:47–49pp — Mt 7:24–27

46"Why do you call me, 'Lord, Lord,' [u]
and do not do what I say? [v] 47I will show
you what he is like who comes to me and
hears my words and puts them into practice. [w] 48He is like a man building a house,
who dug down deep and laid the foundation on rock. When a flood came, the torrent struck that house but could not shake
it, because it was well built. 49But the one
who hears my words and does not put
them into practice is like a man who built
a house on the ground without a foundation. The moment the torrent struck that
house, it collapsed and its destruction was
complete."

The Faith of the Centurion

7:1–10pp — Mt 8:5–13

7 When Jesus had finished saying all
this [x] in the hearing of the people, he

6:25 [z]Pr 14:13
6:26 [a]S Mt 7:15
6:27 [b]ver 35;
Mt 5:44;
Ro 12:20
6:28 [c]S Mt 5:44
6:30 [d]Dt 15:7,8,
10; Pr 21:26
6:31 [e]Mt 7:12
6:32 [f]Mt 5:46
6:34 [g]Mt 5:42
6:35 [h]ver 27
[i]S Ro 8:14
[j]S Mk 5:7
6:36 [k]Jas 2:13
[l]Mt 5:48; 6:1;
Lk 11:2; 12:32;
Ro 8:15; Eph 4:6;
1Pe 1:17;
1Jn 1:3; 3:1
6:37 [m]S Mt 7:1
[n]Mt 6:14
6:38 [o]Ps 79:12;
Isa 65:6,7
[p]S Mt 7:2

6:39 [q]Mt 15:14
6:40 [r]S Jn 13:16
6:44 [s]Mt 12:33
6:45 [t]Pr 4:23;
Mt 12:34,35;
Mk 7:20
6:46 [u]S Jn 13:13
[v]Mal 1:6;
Mt 7:21
6:47 [w]Lk 8:21;
11:28;
Jas 1:22-25
7:1 [x]Mt 7:28

6:27 *Love your enemies.* The heart of Jesus' teaching is
love. While the Golden Rule (v. 31) is sometimes expressed
in negative form outside the Bible, Jesus not only forbids
treating others spitefully but also commands that we love
everyone—even our enemies.
6:29 *turn to him the other.* We are not to have a retaliatory
attitude. *cloak . . . tunic.* The cloak was the outer coat, under
which the tunic was worn.
6:36 *just as your Father is merciful.* God's perfection
should be our example and goal (see Mt 5:48).
6:37 *Do not judge.* Jesus did not relieve his followers of the

need for discerning right and wrong (cf. vv. 43–45), but he
condemned unjust and hypocritical judging of others.
6:38 *poured into your lap.* Probably refers to the way the
outer garment was worn, leaving a fold over the belt that
could be used as a large pocket to hold a measure of
wheat.
6:41 *speck . . . plank.* Jesus used hyperbole (a figure of
speech that overstates for emphasis) to sharpen the contrast
and to emphasize how foolish and hypocritical it is for us to
criticize someone for a fault while remaining blind to our
own considerable faults.

entered Capernaum. [2]There a centurion's servant, whom his master valued highly, was sick and about to die. [3]The centurion heard of Jesus and sent some elders of the Jews to him, asking him to come and heal his servant. [4]When they came to Jesus, they pleaded earnestly with him, "This man deserves to have you do this, [5]because he loves our nation and has built our synagogue." [6]So Jesus went with them.

He was not far from the house when the centurion sent friends to say to him: "Lord, don't trouble yourself, for I do not deserve to have you come under my roof. [7]That is why I did not even consider myself worthy to come to you. But say the word, and my servant will be healed.[y] [8]For I myself am a man under authority, with soldiers under me. I tell this one, 'Go,' and he goes; and that one, 'Come,' and he comes. I say to my servant, 'Do this,' and he does it."

[9]When Jesus heard this, he was amazed at him, and turning to the crowd following him, he said, "I tell you, I have not found such great faith even in Israel." [10]Then the men who had been sent returned to the house and found the servant well.

Jesus Raises a Widow's Son

7:11–16Ref — 1Ki 17:17–24; 2Ki 4:32–37; Mk 5:21–24,35–43; Jn 11:1–44

[11]Soon afterward, Jesus went to a town called Nain, and his disciples and a large crowd went along with him. [12]As he approached the town gate, a dead person was being carried out—the only son of his mother, and she was a widow. And a large crowd from the town was with her.

[13]When the Lord[z] saw her, his heart went out to her and he said, "Don't cry."

[14]Then he went up and touched the coffin, and those carrying it stood still. He said, "Young man, I say to you, get up!"[a] [15]The dead man sat up and began to talk, and Jesus gave him back to his mother.

[16]They were all filled with awe[b] and praised God.[c] "A great prophet[d] has appeared among us," they said. "God has come to help his people."[e] [17]This news about Jesus spread throughout Judea[b] and the surrounding country.[f]

Jesus and John the Baptist

7:18–35pp — Mt 11:2–19

[18]John's[g] disciples[h] told him about all these things. Calling two of them, [19]he sent them to the Lord to ask, "Are you the one who was to come, or should we expect someone else?"

[20]When the men came to Jesus, they said, "John the Baptist sent us to you to ask, 'Are you the one who was to come, or should we expect someone else?' "

[21]At that very time Jesus cured many who had diseases, sicknesses[i] and evil spirits, and gave sight to many who were blind. [22]So he replied to the messengers, "Go back and report to John what you have seen and heard: The blind receive sight, the lame walk, those who have leprosy[c] are cured, the deaf hear, the dead are raised, and the good news is preached to the poor.[j] [23]Blessed is the man who does not fall away on account of me."

[b]17 Or the land of the Jews   [c]22 The Greek word was used for various diseases affecting the skin—not necessarily leprosy.

7:7 yPs 107:20

7:13 zver 19; Lk 10:1; 13:15; 17:5; 22:61; 24:34; Jn 11:2
7:14 aMt 9:25; Mk 1:31; Lk 8:54; Jn 11:43; Ac 9:40
7:16 bLk 1:65 cS Mt 9:8 dver 39; S Mt 21:11 eLk 1:68
7:17 fS Mt 9:26
7:18 gS Mt 3:1 hS Lk 5:33
7:21 iS Mt 4:23
7:22 jIsa 29:18, 19; 35:5,6; 61:1, 2; Lk 4:18

7:2 centurion's servant. The centurion was probably a member of Herod Antipas's forces, which were organized in Roman fashion, ordinarily in companies of 100 men. Roman centurions referred to in the NT showed characteristics to be admired (e.g., Ac 10:2; 23:17–18; 27:43). This centurion showed genuine concern for his slave, and he was admired by the Jews, who spoke favorably of him even though he was a Gentile (see vv. 5,9).
7:3 elders of the Jews. Highly respected Jews of the community, though not necessarily rulers of the synagogue. They were willing to come and plead for the centurion. In Matthew's account (Mt 8:5–13) the centurion speaks with Jesus himself, while in Luke's account he speaks with Jesus through his friends (see note on Mt 8:5).
7:6 I do not deserve to have you come under my roof. See note on Mt 8:8.
7:9 he was amazed. The amazement of Jesus is only mentioned twice, here because of belief and at Nazareth because of unbelief (Mk 6:6).
7:14 coffin. The man was probably carried in an open coffin, suggested by Jewish custom and the fact that he sat up in response to Jesus' command. This is the first of three instances of Jesus' raising someone from the dead, the others

being Jairus's daughter (8:40–56) and Lazarus (Jn 11:38–44).
7:18 John's disciples. Despite John the Baptist's imprisonment, his disciples kept in contact with him and continued his ministry.
7:19 should we expect someone else? John had announced the coming of the Christ, but now he himself had been languishing in prison for months, and the work of Jesus had not brought the results John apparently expected. His disappointment was natural. He wanted reassurance—and perhaps also wanted to urge Jesus to further action.
7:22 report to John what you have seen and heard. In answer, Jesus pointed to his healing and life-restoring miracles. He did not give promises but clearly observable evidence—evidence that reflected the predicted ministry of the Messiah. the good news is preached to the poor. In Jesus' review of his works, he used an ascending scale of impressive deeds, ending with the dead raised and the good news preached to the poor. In this way, Jesus reminded John that these were the things predicted of the Messiah in the Scriptures (see Isa 29:18–21; 35:5–6; 61:1; see also Lk 4:18).
7:23 the man who does not fall away. Jesus did not want discouragement and doubt to ensnare John.

24After John's messengers left, Jesus began to speak to the crowd about John: "What did you go out into the desert to see? A reed swayed by the wind? 25If not, what did you go out to see? A man dressed in fine clothes? No, those who wear expensive clothes and indulge in luxury are in palaces. 26But what did you go out to see? A prophet?k Yes, I tell you, and more than a prophet. 27This is the one about whom it is written:

" 'I will send my messenger ahead of
    you,
who will prepare your way before
    you.'d l

28I tell you, among those born of women there is no one greater than John; yet the one who is least in the kingdom of Godm is greater than he."

29(All the people, even the tax collectors, when they heard Jesus' words, acknowledged that God's way was right, because they had been baptized by John.n 30But the Pharisees and experts in the lawo rejected God's purpose for themselves, because they had not been baptized by John.)

31"To what, then, can I compare the people of this generation? What are they like? 32They are like children sitting in the marketplace and calling out to each other:

" 'We played the flute for you,
    and you did not dance;
we sang a dirge,
    and you did not cry.'

33For John the Baptist came neither eating bread nor drinking wine,p and you say,

'He has a demon.' 34The Son of Man came eating and drinking, and you say, 'Here is a glutton and a drunkard, a friend of tax collectors and "sinners." 'q 35But wisdom is proved right by all her children."

Jesus Anointed by a Sinful Woman

7:37–39Ref — Mt 26:6–13; Mk 14:3–9; Jn 12:1–8
7:41,42Ref — Mt 18:23–34

36Now one of the Pharisees invited Jesus to have dinner with him, so he went to the Pharisee's house and reclined at the table. 37When a woman who had lived a sinful life in that town learned that Jesus was eating at the Pharisee's house, she brought an alabaster jar of perfume, 38and as she stood behind him at his feet weeping, she began to wet his feet with her tears. Then she wiped them with her hair, kissed them and poured perfume on them.

39When the Pharisee who had invited him saw this, he said to himself, "If this man were a prophet,r he would know who is touching him and what kind of woman she is—that she is a sinner."

40Jesus answered him, "Simon, I have something to tell you."

"Tell me, teacher," he said.

41"Two men owed money to a certain moneylender. One owed him five hundred denarii,e and the other fifty. 42Neither of them had the money to pay him back, so he canceled the debts of both. Now which of them will love him more?"

43Simon replied, "I suppose the one who had the bigger debt canceled."

"You have judged correctly," Jesus said. 44Then he turned toward the woman

---

7:26 kS Mt 11:9
7:27 lMal 3:1;
Mt 11:10; Mk 1:2
7:28 mS Mt 3:2
7:29 nMt 21:32;
Mk 1:5; Lk 3:12
7:30 oS Mt 22:35
7:33 pLk 1:15

7:34 qLk 5:29,
30; 15:1,2
7:39 rver 16;
S Mt 21:11

d27 Mal. 3:1   e41 A denarius was a coin worth about a day's wages.

7:24 *What did you go . . . to see?* John was not a weak messenger, swayed by the pressures of human opinion. On the contrary, he was a true prophet.
7:26 *more than a prophet.* John was the unique prophet sent to prepare the way for the Messiah.
7:28 *one who is least in the kingdom of God.* See note on Mt 11:11.
7:30 *experts in the law.* A designation used by Luke (see 10:25,37; 11:45–46,52; 14:3; see also Mt 22:35) for the "scribes" (the teachers of the law), most of whom were Pharisees (see note on 5:17). *rejected God's purpose.* Tax collectors had shown their willingness to repent by accepting John's baptism, whereas the Pharisees showed their rejection of God's message by refusing to be baptized.
7:32 *like children sitting in the marketplace.* People had rejected both John and Jesus, but for different reasons—like children who refuse to play either a joyful game or a mournful one. They would not associate with John when he followed the strictest of rules or with Jesus when he freely associated with all kinds of people.
7:34 *a friend of tax collectors and "sinners."* Jesus ate and talked with people who were religious and social outcasts.

He even called a tax collector to be an apostle (5:27–32).
7:35 *wisdom is proved right by all her children.* In contrast to the rejection by foolish critics, spiritually wise persons could see that the ministries of both John and Jesus were godly, despite their differences. See note on Mt 11:19.
7:36 *one of the Pharisees.* See note on 5:17. His motive may have been to entrap Jesus rather than to learn from him.
7:37 *a woman who had lived a sinful life.* A prostitute. She must have heard Jesus preach, and in repentance she determined to lead a new life. She came out of love and gratitude, in the understanding that she could be forgiven. *alabaster jar.* A long-necked, globular bottle. *perfume.* A perfumed ointment.
7:38 *stood behind him at his feet.* Jesus reclined on a couch with his feet extended away from the table, which made it possible for the woman to wipe his feet with her hair and still not disturb him. *poured perfume on them.* The anointing, perhaps originally intended for Jesus' head, was instead applied to his feet. A similar act was performed by Mary of Bethany just over a week before the crucifixion (Jn 12:3).
7:41 *five hundred denarii.* See NIV text note.

and said to Simon, "Do you see this woman? I came into your house. You did not give me any water for my feet,^{s} but she wet my feet with her tears and wiped them with her hair. ^{45}You did not give me a kiss,^{t} but this woman, from the time I entered, has not stopped kissing my feet. ^{46}You did not put oil on my head,^{u} but she has poured perfume on my feet. ^{47}Therefore, I tell you, her many sins have been forgiven—for she loved much. But he who has been forgiven little loves little."

^{48}Then Jesus said to her, "Your sins are forgiven."^{v}

^{49}The other guests began to say among themselves, "Who is this who even forgives sins?"

^{50}Jesus said to the woman, "Your faith has saved you;^{w} go in peace."^{x}

The Parable of the Sower
8:4-15pp — Mt 13:2-23; Mk 4:1-20

8 After this, Jesus traveled about from one town and village to another, proclaiming the good news of the kingdom of God.^{y} The Twelve were with him, ^{2}and also some women who had been cured of evil spirits and diseases: Mary (called Magdalene)^z from whom seven demons had come out; ^{3}Joanna the wife of Cuza, the manager of Herod's^a household; Susanna; and many others. These women were

helping to support them out of their own means.

^{4}While a large crowd was gathering and people were coming to Jesus from town after town, he told this parable: ^{5}"A farmer went out to sow his seed. As he was scattering the seed, some fell along the path; it was trampled on, and the birds of the air ate it up. ^{6}Some fell on rock, and when it came up, the plants withered because they had no moisture. ^{7}Other seed fell among thorns, which grew up with it and choked the plants. ^{8}Still other seed fell on good soil. It came up and yielded a crop, a hundred times more than was sown."

When he said this, he called out, "He who has ears to hear, let him hear."^{b}

^{9}His disciples asked him what this parable meant. ^{10}He said, "The knowledge of the secrets of the kingdom of God has been given to you,^{c} but to others I speak in parables, so that,

" 'though seeing, they may not see;
though hearing, they may not understand.'^{f} ^{d}

^{11}"This is the meaning of the parable: The seed is the word of God.^{e} ^{12}Those along the path are the ones who hear, and then the devil comes and takes away the word from their hearts, so that they may

7:44 ^{s}Ge 18:4; 19:2; 43:24; Jdg 19:21; Jn 13:4-14; 1Ti 5:10
7:45 ^{t}Lk 22:47, 48; S Ro 16:16
7:46 ^{u}Ps 23:5; Ecc 9:8
7:48 ^{v}Mt 9:2
7:50 ^{w}S Mt 9:22 ^{x}S Ac 15:33
8:1 ^{y}S Mt 4:23
8:2 ^{z}Mt 27:55,56
8:3 ^{a}S Mt 14:1
8:8 ^{b}S Mt 11:15
8:10 ^{c}S Mt 13:11 ^{d}Isa 6:9;
8:11 ^{e}S Heb 4:12
^{f}*10* Isaiah 6:9

7:44 *water for my feet.* The minimal gesture of hospitality.
7:47 *for she loved much.* Her love was evidence of her forgiveness, but not the basis for it. Verse 50 clearly states that she was saved by faith. See Eph 1:7.
7:50 *Your faith has saved you.* Her sins were forgiven and she could experience God's peace (see 1:79 and note on 2:14).
8:1 *Jesus traveled about.* Jesus' ministry had been centered in Capernaum, and much of his preaching was in synagogues, but now he traveled again from town to town on a second tour of the Galilean countryside. For the first tour see 4:43-44; Mt 4:23-25; Mk 1:38-39. For the third tour see note on 9:1-6. *kingdom of God.* See note on 4:43.
8:2 *Mary (called Magdalene).* Her hometown was Magdala. She is not to be confused with the sinful woman of ch. 7 or Mary of Bethany (Jn 11:1).
8:3 *Susanna.* Nothing more is known of her. *helping to support them.* Jesus and his disciples did not provide for themselves by miracles, but were supported by the service and means of such grateful people as these women.
8:4 *parable.* From this point on Jesus used parables (see notes on Mt 13:3; Mk 4:2) more extensively as a means of teaching. They were particularly effective and easy to remember because he used familiar scenes. Although parables clarified Jesus' teaching, they also included hidden meanings needing further explanation. These hidden meanings challenged the sincerely interested to further inquiry, and taught truths that Jesus wanted to conceal from unbelievers (see v. 10). From parables Jesus' enemies could find no direct statements to use against him. The parable of the sower is one of three parables recorded in each of the Synop-

tic Gospels (Mt 13:1-23; Mk 4:1-20). The others are those of the mustard seed (13:19; Mt 13:31-32; Mk 4:30-32) and of the vineyard (20:9-19; Mt 21:33-46; Mk 12:1-12).
8:5 *to sow his seed.* In Eastern practice the seed was sometimes sown first and the field plowed afterward. Roads and pathways went directly through many fields, and the traffic made much of the surface too hard for seed to take root in.
8:6 *on rock.* On a thin layer of soil that covered solid rock. Any moisture that fell there soon evaporated, and the germinating seed withered and died (see Mt 13:5-6).
8:8 *a hundred times more.* Luke's version is more abbreviated than Matthew's (13:8) and Mark's (4:8), but the point is the same: The quantity of increase depends on the quality of soil. *let him hear.* A challenge for listeners to understand the message and appropriate it for themselves.
8:9 *His disciples.* They included "the Twelve and the others" (Mk 4:10).
8:10 *secrets of the kingdom of God.* Truths that can be known only by revelation from God (cf. Eph 3:2-5; 1Pe 1:10-12). See note on Mk 4:11. *though seeing, they may not see.* This quotation from Isaiah (6:9) does not express a desire that some would not understand, but simply states the sad truth that those who are not willing to receive Jesus' message will find the truth hidden from them. Their ultimate fate is implied in the fuller quotation in Mt 13:14-15 (see note on Mk 4:12).
8:11 *the word of God.* The message that comes from God.
8:12 *may not believe.* The devil's purpose is that people will not hear with understanding and therefore will not appropriate the message and be saved.

not believe and be saved. [13]Those on the rock are the ones who receive the word with joy when they hear it, but they have no root. They believe for a while, but in the time of testing they fall away.[f] [14]The seed that fell among thorns stands for those who hear, but as they go on their way they are choked by life's worries, riches[g] and pleasures, and they do not mature. [15]But the seed on good soil stands for those with a noble and good heart, who hear the word, retain it, and by persevering produce a crop.

A Lamp on a Stand

[16]"No one lights a lamp and hides it in a jar or puts it under a bed. Instead, he puts it on a stand, so that those who come in can see the light.[h] [17]For there is nothing hidden that will not be disclosed, and nothing concealed that will not be known or brought out into the open.[i] [18]Therefore consider carefully how you listen. Whoever has will be given more; whoever does not have, even what he thinks he has will be taken from him."[j]

Jesus' Mother and Brothers

8:19–21pp — Mt 12:46–50; Mk 3:31–35

[19]Now Jesus' mother and brothers came to see him, but they were not able to get near him because of the crowd. [20]Someone told him, "Your mother and brothers[k] are standing outside, wanting to see you."

[21]He replied, "My mother and brothers are those who hear God's word and put it into practice."[l]

Cross references:
8:13 [f]Mt 11:6
8:14 [g]Mt 19:23; 1Ti 6:9,10,17
8:16 [h]S Mt 5:15
8:17 [i]Mt 10:26; Mk 4:22; Lk 12:2
8:18 [j]S Mt 25:29
8:20 [k]Jn 7:5
8:21 [l]Lk 6:47; 11:28; Jn 14:21
8:24 [m]S Lk 5:5 [n]Lk 4:35,39,41 [o]Ps 107:29; Jnh 1:15
8:28 [p]S Mt 8:29

Jesus Calms the Storm

8:22–25pp — Mt 8:23–27; Mk 4:36–41
8:22–25Ref — Mk 6:47–52; Jn 6:16–21

[22]One day Jesus said to his disciples, "Let's go over to the other side of the lake." So they got into a boat and set out. [23]As they sailed, he fell asleep. A squall came down on the lake, so that the boat was being swamped, and they were in great danger.

[24]The disciples went and woke him, saying, "Master, Master,[m] we're going to drown!"

He got up and rebuked[n] the wind and the raging waters; the storm subsided, and all was calm.[o] [25]"Where is your faith?" he asked his disciples.

In fear and amazement they asked one another, "Who is this? He commands even the winds and the water, and they obey him."

The Healing of a Demon-possessed Man

8:26–37pp — Mt 8:28–34
8:26–39pp — Mk 5:1–20

[26]They sailed to the region of the Gerasenes,[g] which is across the lake from Galilee. [27]When Jesus stepped ashore, he was met by a demon-possessed man from the town. For a long time this man had not worn clothes or lived in a house, but had lived in the tombs. [28]When he saw Jesus, he cried out and fell at his feet, shouting at the top of his voice, "What do you want with me,[p] Jesus, Son of the Most High

[g]26 Some manuscripts *Gadarenes*; other manuscripts *Gergesenes*; also in verse 37

8:13 *They believe for a while.* This kind of belief is superficial and does not save. It is similar to what James calls "dead" (Jas 2:17,26) or "useless" faith (Jas 2:20).

8:16 *lights a lamp.* Although Jesus couched much of his message in parables, he intended that the disciples make the truths known as widely as possible (see note on 11:33). *puts it on a stand.* See note on Mt 5:15.

8:17 This verse explains v. 16. It is the destiny of the truth to be made known (cf. 12:2). The disciples were to begin a proclamation that would become universal.

8:18 *consider carefully how you listen.* The disciples heard not only for themselves but also for those to whom they would minister (see Mk 4:24; cf. Jas 1:19–22). Truth that is not understood and appropriated will be lost (19:26), but truth that is used will be multiplied.

8:19 *Jesus' mother and brothers came.* See note on Mk 3:21. More is known about their motive from Mk 3:21, 31–32. The family, thinking he was "out of his mind," probably wanted to get him away from his heavy schedule. *brothers.* Did not believe in Jesus at this time (Jn 7:5). Various interpretations concerning their relationship to Jesus arose in the early church: They were sons of Joseph by a previous marriage (according to Epiphanius) or were cousins (said Jerome). The most natural conclusion (suggested by

Helvidius) is that they were the sons of Joseph and Mary, younger half brothers of Jesus. Four of these brothers are named in Mk 6:3, where sisters are also mentioned. Since Joseph is not mentioned here, it is likely that he had died.

8:21 Jesus' reply was not meant to reject his natural family but to emphasize the higher priority of his spiritual relationship to those who believed in him.

8:23 *squall.* See note on Mk 4:37.

8:26 *region of the Gerasenes.* The Gospels describe the location of this event in two ways: (1) the region of the Gerasenes (see note on Mk 5:1); (2) the region of the Gadarenes (see note on Mt 8:28). Some manuscripts of Matthew, Mark and Luke read "Gergesenes" (see NIV text note here), but this spelling may have been introduced in an attempt to resolve the differences.

8:27 *demon-possessed man.* See note on 4:33. Matthew (8:28) refers to two demon-possessed men, but Mark (5:2) and Luke probably mention only the one who was prominent and did the talking. *tombs.* An isolated burial ground avoided by most people (but see note on Mk 5:3).

8:28 *Son of the Most High God.* Cf. 1:32; 4:34. The title "Most High God" was commonly used by Gentiles (see Ge 14:19 and note; Ac 16:17); its use here perhaps indicates that this man was not a Jew (but see note on Mk 1:24).

God? q I beg you, don't torture me!" 29For Jesus had commanded the evil h spirit to come out of the man. Many times it had seized him, and though he was chained hand and foot and kept under guard, he had broken his chains and had been driven by the demon into solitary places.

30Jesus asked him, "What is your name?"

"Legion," he replied, because many demons had gone into him. 31And they begged him repeatedly not to order them to go into the Abyss. r

32A large herd of pigs was feeding there on the hillside. The demons begged Jesus to let them go into them, and he gave them permission. 33When the demons came out of the man, they went into the pigs, and the herd rushed down the steep bank into the lake s and was drowned.

34When those tending the pigs saw what had happened, they ran off and reported this in the town and countryside, 35and the people went out to see what had happened. When they came to Jesus, they found the man from whom the demons had gone out, sitting at Jesus' feet, t dressed and in his right mind; and they were afraid. 36Those who had seen it told the people how the demon-possessed u man had been cured. 37Then all the people of the region of the Gerasenes asked Jesus to leave them, v because they were overcome with fear. So he got into the boat and left.

38The man from whom the demons had gone out begged to go with him, but Jesus sent him away, saying, 39"Return home and tell how much God has done for you." So the man went away and told all over town how much Jesus had done for him.

A Dead Girl and a Sick Woman

8:40–56pp — Mt 9:18–26; Mk 5:22–43

40Now when Jesus returned, a crowd welcomed him, for they were all expecting him. 41Then a man named Jairus, a ruler of the synagogue, w came and fell at Jesus' feet, pleading with him to come to his house 42because his only daughter, a girl of about twelve, was dying.

As Jesus was on his way, the crowds almost crushed him. 43And a woman was there who had been subject to bleeding x for twelve years, i but no one could heal her. 44She came up behind him and touched the edge of his cloak, y and immediately her bleeding stopped.

45"Who touched me?" Jesus asked.

When they all denied it, Peter said, "Master, z the people are crowding and pressing against you."

46But Jesus said, "Someone touched me; a I know that power has gone out from me." b

47Then the woman, seeing that she could not go unnoticed, came trembling and fell at his feet. In the presence of all the people, she told why she had touched him and how she had been instantly healed. 48Then he said to her, "Daughter, your faith has healed you. c Go in peace." d

49While Jesus was still speaking, someone came from the house of Jairus, the synagogue ruler. e "Your daughter is dead," he said. "Don't bother the teacher any more."

50Hearing this, Jesus said to Jairus, "Don't be afraid; just believe, and she will be healed."

51When he arrived at the house of Jairus, he did not let anyone go in with him except Peter, John and James, f and the child's father and mother. 52Meanwhile, all the people were wailing and mourning g for her. "Stop wailing," Jesus said "She is not dead but asleep." h

Cross references

8:28 qS Mk 5:7
8:31 rRev 9:1,2, 11; 11:7; 17:8; 20:1,3
8:33 sver 22,23
8:35 tLk 10:39
8:36 uS Mt 4:24
8:37 vAc 16:39

8:41 wver 49; S Mk 5:22
8:43 xLev 15:25-30
8:44 yS Mt 9:20
8:45 zS Lk 5:5
8:46 aMt 14:36; Mk 3:10 bLk 5:17; 6:19
8:48 cS Mt 9:22 dS Ac 15:33
8:49 ever 41
8:51 fS Mt 4:21
8:52 gLk 23:27 hS Mt 9:24

h29 Greek unclean   i43 Many manuscripts years, and she had spent all she had on doctors

8:30 What is your name? Jesus asked the man his name, but it was the demons who replied, thus showing they were in control. Legion. See note on Mk 5:9.
8:31 Abyss. A place of confinement for evil spirits and for Satan (see note on Rev 9:1).
8:32 pigs. Pigs were unclean to Jews, and eating them was forbidden (Lev 11:7–8), but this was the Decapolis, a predominantly Gentile territory. he gave them permission. See note on Mt 8:32.
8:39 Return home and tell how much God has done for you. Although the man wanted to follow Jesus, he was directed to make the miracle known in his own native territory. There was no danger here of interference with Jesus' ministry (see note on Mk 5:19).
8:41 ruler of the synagogue. The ruler was responsible for conducting services, selecting participants and maintaining

order (see note on Mk 5:22).
8:43 bleeding. The hemorrhage had made her ceremonially unclean for 12 years (see Lev 15:19–30). no one could heal her. Comparison with Mk 5:26 shows the restraint of Luke the physician in describing the failure of doctors to help her.
8:45 Who touched me? For the woman's good and for a testimony to the crowd, Jesus insisted that the miracle be made known.
8:46 power has gone out. See note on Mk 5:30.
8:48 Daughter. A tender address used nowhere else in Jesus' recorded words (cf. 23:28). Go in peace. Cf. 7:50.
8:50 will be healed. See note on Mk 5:34.
8:52 wailing and mourning. See note on Mk 5:38. not dead but asleep. Jesus meant that she was not permanently dead (see Jn 11:11–14 for a similar statement about

53They laughed at him, knowing that she was dead. 54But he took her by the hand and said, "My child, get up!" [i] 55Her spirit returned, and at once she stood up. Then Jesus told them to give her something to eat. 56Her parents were astonished, but he ordered them not to tell anyone what had happened. [j]

Jesus Sends Out the Twelve

9:3–5pp — Mt 10:9–15; Mk 6:8–11
9:7–9pp — Mt 14:1,2; Mk 6:14–16

9 When Jesus had called the Twelve together, he gave them power and authority to drive out all demons [k] and to cure diseases, [l] 2and he sent them out to preach the kingdom of God [m] and to heal the sick. 3He told them: "Take nothing for the journey—no staff, no bag, no bread, no money, no extra tunic. [n] 4Whatever house you enter, stay there until you leave that town. 5If people do not welcome you, shake the dust off your feet when you leave their town, as a testimony against them." [o] 6So they set out and went from village to village, preaching the gospel and healing people everywhere.

7Now Herod [p] the tetrarch heard about all that was going on. And he was perplexed, because some were saying that John [q] had been raised from the dead, [r] 8others that Elijah had appeared, [s] and still others that one of the prophets of long ago had come back to life. [t] 9But Herod said, "I beheaded John. Who, then, is this I hear such things about?" And he tried to see him. [u]

8:54 [i] S Lk 7:14
8:56 [j] S Mt 8:4
9:1 [k] S Mt 10:1
  [l] S Mt 4:23;
    Lk 5:17
9:2 [m] S Mt 3:2
9:3 [n] Lk 10:4;
    22:35
9:5 [o] S Mt 10:14
9:7 [p] S Mt 14:1
  [q] S Mt 3:1 [r] ver 19
9:8 [s] S Mt 11:14
  [t] ver 19; Jn 1:21
9:9 [u] Lk 23:8

Jesus Feeds the Five Thousand

9:10–17pp — Mt 14:13–21; Mk 6:32–44; Jn 6:5–13
9:13–17Ref — 2Ki 4:42–44

10When the apostles [v] returned, they reported to Jesus what they had done. Then he took them with him and they withdrew by themselves to a town called Bethsaida, [w] 11but the crowds learned about it and followed him. He welcomed them and spoke to them about the kingdom of God, [x] and healed those who needed healing.

12Late in the afternoon the Twelve came to him and said, "Send the crowd away so they can go to the surrounding villages and countryside and find food and lodging, because we are in a remote place here."

13He replied, "You give them something to eat."

They answered, "We have only five loaves of bread and two fish—unless we go and buy food for all this crowd." 14(About five thousand men were there.)

But he said to his disciples, "Have them sit down in groups of about fifty each." 15The disciples did so, and everybody sat down. 16Taking the five loaves and the two fish and looking up to heaven, he gave thanks and broke them. [y] Then he gave them to the disciples to set before the people. 17They all ate and were satisfied, and the disciples picked up twelve basketfuls of broken pieces that were left over.

9:10 [v] S Mk 6:30
   [w] S Mt 11:21
9:11 [x] ver 2;
    S Mt 3:2
9:16 [y] S Mt 14:19
9:18 [z] S Lk 3:21

Peter's Confession of Christ

9:18–20pp — Mt 16:13–16; Mk 8:27–29
9:22–27pp — Mt 16:21–28; Mk 8:31 — 9:1

18Once when Jesus was praying [z] in pri-

Lazarus).

8:56 *ordered them not to tell.* See notes on Mt 8:4; Mk 5:43. Further publicity at this time concerning a raising from the dead would have been counterproductive to Jesus' ministry.

9:1–6 A new phase of Jesus' ministry began when he sent out the apostles to do the type of preaching, teaching and healing that they had observed him doing (Mt 9:35). This was the third tour of Galilee by Jesus and his disciples (see note on 8:1). On the first tour Jesus traveled with the four fishermen; on the second all 12 were with him; on the third Jesus traveled alone after sending out the Twelve two by two.

9:1 *the Twelve.* The apostles (see 6:13). *power and authority.* Special power to heal (see 5:17; 8:46) and authority in teaching and control over evil spirits. *demons.* Evil spirits (see note on 4:33).

9:3 *Take nothing.* No excess baggage that would encumber travel, not even the usual provisions. They were to be entirely dependent on the people with whom they were staying (see note on Mk 6:8).

9:4 *stay there.* They were not to move from house to house, seeking better lodging, but use only one home as headquarters while preaching in a community.

9:5 *shake the dust off your feet.* A sign of repudiation for their rejection of God's message and a gesture showing

separation from everything associated with the place (see 10:11; see also notes on Mt 10:14; Ac 13:51).

9:7 *Herod the tetrarch.* See note on Mt 14:1. *John had been raised from the dead.* See note on Mk 6:16. Luke does not give details about John's death (see Mt 14:1–12; Mk 6:17–29), which occurred about this time, but simply notes that it had taken place (v. 9).

9:8 *Elijah had appeared.* See notes on 1:17; Mk 9:12.

9:9 *he tried to see him.* Herod's desire to see Jesus was not fulfilled until Jesus' trial (23:8–12).

9:10–17 The feeding of the 5,000 is the only miracle besides Jesus' resurrection that is reported in all four Gospels (see notes on Mk 6:30–44; Jn 6:1–14).

9:10 *Bethsaida.* See note on Mt 11:21. Jesus must have retired to a remote area near the town (v. 12).

9:12 *Late in the afternoon.* After the preaching and healing, the question was raised about food and lodging because they were in an isolated place. Jesus may have introduced the question (see Jn 6:5), but the Synoptics indicate that the disciples were also concerned.

9:14 *sit down in groups of about fifty.* See note on Mk 6:40.

9:17 *picked up twelve basketfuls of broken pieces.* This act served as an example of avoiding wastefulness and as a demonstration that everyone had been adequately fed (see note on Mk 6:43).

vate and his disciples were with him, he asked them, "Who do the crowds say I am?"

[19]They replied, "Some say John the Baptist;[a] others say Elijah; and still others, that one of the prophets of long ago has come back to life."[b]

[20]"But what about you?" he asked. "Who do you say I am?"

Peter answered, "The Christ[i] of God."[c]

[21]Jesus strictly warned them not to tell this to anyone.[d] [22]And he said, "The Son of Man[e] must suffer many things[f] and be rejected by the elders, chief priests and teachers of the law,[g] and he must be killed[h] and on the third day[i] be raised to life."[j]

[23]Then he said to them all: "If anyone would come after me, he must deny himself and take up his cross daily and follow me.[k] [24]For whoever wants to save his life will lose it, but whoever loses his life for me will save it.[l] [25]What good is it for a man to gain the whole world, and yet lose or forfeit his very self? [26]If anyone is ashamed of me and my words, the Son of Man will be ashamed of him[m] when he comes in his glory and in the glory of the

Father and of the holy angels.[n] [27]I tell you the truth, some who are standing here will not taste death before they see the kingdom of God."

The Transfiguration

9:28–36pp — Mt 17:1–8; Mk 9:2–8

[28]About eight days after Jesus said this, he took Peter, John and James[o] with him and went up onto a mountain to pray.[p] [29]As he was praying, the appearance of his face changed, and his clothes became as bright as a flash of lightning. [30]Two men, Moses and Elijah, [31]appeared in glorious splendor, talking with Jesus. They spoke about his departure,[q] which he was about to bring to fulfillment at Jerusalem. [32]Peter and his companions were very sleepy,[r] but when they became fully awake, they saw his glory and the two men standing with him. [33]As the men were leaving Jesus, Peter said to him, "Master,[s] it is good for us to be here. Let us put up three shelters—one for you, one for Moses and one for Elijah." (He did not know what he was saying.)

[34]While he was speaking, a cloud appeared and enveloped them, and they

Cross-references (center column)

9:19 [a]S Mt 3:1
[b]ver 7,8
9:20 [c]Jn 1:49;
6:66-69; 11:27
9:21 [d]S Mk 8:30
9:22 [e]S Mt 8:20
/S Mt 16:21
[g]Mt 27:1,2
[h]Ac 2:23; 3:13
/S Mt 16:21
/S Mt 16:21
9:23 [k]Mt 10:38;
Lk 14:27
9:24 [l]S Jn 12:25
9:26 [m]Mt 10:33;
Lk 12:9; 2Ti 2:12

[n]S Mt 16:27
9:28 [o]S Mt 4:21
[p]S Lk 3:21
9:31 [q]2Pe 1:15
9:32 [r]Mt 26:43
9:33 [s]S Lk 5:5

[i]20 Or Messiah

9:18 *Who do the crowds say I am?* The report brought by the disciples was the same as the one that reached Herod (see vv. 7–8). This event occurred to the north, outside Herod's territory, in the vicinity of Caesarea Philippi (see Mt 16:13 and note; see also note on Mk 7:24).

9:20 *Peter answered.* He was the spokesman for the disciples. *The Christ of God.* See NIV text note on 2:11. This predicted Deliverer (the Messiah) had been awaited for centuries (see Jn 4:25; see also notes on Mt 16:18; Mk 8:29).

9:21 *warned them not to tell.* The people had false notions about the Messiah and needed to be taught further before Jesus identified himself explicitly to the public. He had a crucial schedule to keep and could not be interrupted by premature reactions (see notes on Mt 8:4; 16:20; Mk 1:34).

9:22 *Son of Man.* See note on Mk 8:31. *must suffer.* Jesus' first explicit prediction of his death (for later references see v. 44; 12:50; 17:25; 18:31–33; cf. 24:7,25–27).

9:23 *take up his cross daily.* To follow Jesus requires self-denial, complete dedication and willing obedience. Luke emphasizes continued action, and "daily" is not mentioned explicitly in the parallel accounts (Mt 16:24–26; Mk 8:34). Disciples from Galilee knew what the cross meant, for hundreds of men had been executed by this means in their region.

9:24 *whoever loses his life for me.* A saying of Jesus found in all four Gospels and in two Gospels more than once (Mt 10:38–39; 16:24–25; Mk 8:34–35; Lk 14:26–27; 17:33; and, in slightly different form, Jn 12:25). No other saying of Jesus is given such emphasis.

9:26 *If anyone is ashamed.* See 12:9; see also note on Mk 8:38.

9:27 See note on Mt 16:28. *kingdom of God.* See note on Mt 3:2.

9:28 *About eight days.* Frequently used to indicate a week (e.g., Jn 20:26 in the Greek; see note on Mt 17:1). *Peter, John and James.* These three were also with Jesus at the healing of Jairus's daughter (8:51) and in his last visit to Gethsemane (Mk 14:33). *onto a mountain.* Although Mount Tabor is the traditional site of the Mount of Transfiguration, its distance from Caesarea Philippi (the vicinity of the last scene), its height (about 1,800 feet) and its occupation by a fortress make it unlikely. Mount Hermon fits the context much better by being both closer and higher (over 9,000 feet; see Mk 9:2). *pray.* Again Luke points out the place of prayer in an important event.

9:30 *Moses and Elijah.* Moses, the great OT deliverer and lawgiver, and Elijah, the representative of the prophets. Moses' work had been finished by Joshua, Elijah's by Elisha (another form of the name Joshua). They now spoke with Jesus (whose Hebrew name was Joshua) about the "exodus" he was about to accomplish, by which he would deliver his people from the bondage of sin and bring to fulfillment the work of both Moses and Elijah (see note on 1Ki 19:16).

9:31 *departure.* Greek *exodos,* a euphemism for Jesus' approaching death. It may also link Jesus' saving death and resurrection with God's saving of his people out of Egypt.

9:32 *sleepy.* Perhaps the event was at night. *saw his glory.* See note on Ex 33:18.

9:33 *three shelters.* Temporary structures to prolong the visit of the three important persons: lawgiver, prophet and Messiah. The idea was not appropriate, however, because Jesus had a task to finish in his few remaining days on earth (see note on Mk 9:5).

were afraid as they entered the cloud. 35A voice came from the cloud, saying, "This is my Son, whom I have chosen;[t] listen to him."[u] 36When the voice had spoken, they found that Jesus was alone. The disciples kept this to themselves, and told no one at that time what they had seen.[v]

The Healing of a Boy With an Evil Spirit

9:37–42,43–45pp — Mt 17:14–18; 22,23; Mk 9:14–27; 30–32

37The next day, when they came down from the mountain, a large crowd met him. 38A man in the crowd called out, "Teacher, I beg you to look at my son, for he is my only child. 39A spirit seizes him and he suddenly screams; it throws him into convulsions so that he foams at the mouth. It scarcely ever leaves him and is destroying him. 40I begged your disciples to drive it out, but they could not."

41"O unbelieving and perverse generation,"[w] Jesus replied, "how long shall I stay with you and put up with you? Bring your son here."

42Even while the boy was coming, the demon threw him to the ground in a convulsion. But Jesus rebuked the evil[k] spirit, healed the boy and gave him back to his father. 43And they were all amazed at the greatness of God.

While everyone was marveling at all that Jesus did, he said to his disciples, 44"Listen carefully to what I am about to tell you: The Son of Man is going to be betrayed into the hands of men."[x] 45But they did not understand what this meant. It was hidden from them, so that they did not grasp it,[y] and they were afraid to ask him about it.

Who Will Be the Greatest?

9:46–48pp — Mt 18:1–5
9:46–50pp — Mk 9:33–40

46An argument started among the disciples as to which of them would be the greatest.[z] 47Jesus, knowing their thoughts,[a] took a little child and had him stand beside him. 48Then he said to them, "Whoever welcomes this little child in my name welcomes me; and whoever welcomes me welcomes the one who sent me.[b] For he who is least among you all—he is the greatest."[c]

49"Master,"[d] said John, "we saw a man driving out demons in your name and we tried to stop him, because he is not one of us."

50"Do not stop him," Jesus said, "for whoever is not against you is for you."[e]

Samaritan Opposition

51As the time approached for him to be taken up to heaven,[f] Jesus resolutely set out for Jerusalem.[g] 52And he sent messengers on ahead, who went into a Samaritan[h] village to get things ready for him; 53but the people there did not welcome him, because he was heading for Jerusalem. 54When the disciples James and John[i] saw this, they asked, "Lord, do you want us to call fire down from heaven to destroy them!?"[j] 55But Jesus turned and rebuked them, 56and[m] they went to another village.

Cross references (center column):

9:35 [t]Isa 42:1 [u]S Mt 3:17
9:36 [v]Mt 17:9
9:41 [w]Dt 32:5
9:44 [x]S ver 22
9:45 [y]S Mk 9:32

9:46 [z]Lk 22:24
9:47 [a]S Mt 9:4
9:48 [b]S Mt 10:40 [c]S Mk 9:35
9:49 [d]S Lk 5:5
9:50 [e]Mt 12:30; Lk 11:23
9:51 [f]S Mk 16:19 [g]Lk 13:22; 17:11; 18:31; 19:28
9:52 [h]S Mt 10:5
9:54 [i]S Mt 4:21 [j]2Ki 1:10,12

---

[k]42 Greek unclean [l]54 Some manuscripts them, even as Elijah did [m]55,56 Some manuscripts them. And he said, "You do not know what kind of spirit you are of, for the Son of Man did not come to destroy men's lives, but to save them." 56And

---

9:35 whom I have chosen. Or "the Chosen One," related to a Palestinian Jewish title found in Dead Sea Scrolls literature, and possibly echoing Isa 42:1. See 23:35. have chosen. Parallel to "love" (Mt 17:5; see 2Pe 1:17).

9:39 A spirit seizes him. This evil spirit was causing seizures (Mt 17:15) and a speechless condition (Mk 9:17). Evil spirits were responsible for many kinds of affliction (see note on 4:33).

9:44 Another prediction of Jesus' coming death (see note on v. 22), an indication of how it will be brought about (see 22:21).

9:46 which . . . would be the greatest. A subject that arose on a number of occasions (see 22:24; see also Mk 10:35–45).

9:48 he who is least . . . is the greatest. A person will become great as he sincerely and unpretentiously looks away from self to revere God.

9:49 not one of us. Jesus shifts the pronoun to "you" in v. 50, which may mean that the man had a relationship to Jesus of which the disciples were unaware (see note on Mk 9:38).

9:50 whoever is not against you is for you. Spoken in the context of opposition to the disciples' work (cf. 11:23, set in

a different context).

9:51 set out for Jerusalem. Lit. "set his face to go to Jerusalem" (cf. Isa 50:7). Luke emphasizes Jesus' determination to complete his mission (see note on 13:22). This journey to Jerusalem, however, is not the one that led to his crucifixion but marks the beginning of a period of ministry in Judea, of which Jerusalem was the central city. Mk 10:1 notes this departure for Judea, which John more specifically describes as a journey to Jerusalem during the time of the Feast of Tabernacles (Jn 7:1–10). The Judean ministry (see Introduction: Outline) is recounted in 9:51–13:21 and Jn 7:10–10:39.

9:52 a Samaritan village. Samaritans were particularly hostile to Jews who were on their way to observe religious festivals in Jerusalem. It was at least a three-day journey from Galilee to Jerusalem through Samaria, and Samaritans refused overnight shelter for the pilgrims. Because of this antipathy, Jews traveling between Galilee and Jerusalem frequently went on the east side of the Jordan River.

9:54 call fire down. As Elijah had (2Ki 1:9–16). James and John were known as "Sons of Thunder" (Mk 3:17).

9:55 rebuked them. See note on 2Ki 1:10.

The Cost of Following Jesus

9:57–60pp — Mt 8:19–22

57As they were walking along the road,[k] a man said to him, "I will follow you wherever you go."

58Jesus replied. "Foxes have holes and birds of the air have nests, but the Son of Man[l] has no place to lay his head."

59He said to another man, "Follow me."[m]

But the man replied, "Lord, first let me go and bury my father."

60Jesus said to him, "Let the dead bury their own dead, but you go and proclaim the kingdom of God."[n]

61Still another said, "I will follow you, Lord; but first let me go back and say good-by to my family."[o]

62Jesus replied, "No one who puts his hand to the plow and looks back is fit for service in the kingdom of God."

Jesus Sends Out the Seventy-two

10:4–12pp — Lk 9:3–5
10:13–15,21,22pp — Mt 11:21–23,25–27
10:23,24pp — Mt 13:16,17

10 After this the Lord[p] appointed seventy-two[q] others and sent them two by two[r] ahead of him to every town and place where he was about to go.[s] 2He told them, "The harvest is plentiful, but the workers are few. Ask the Lord of the harvest, therefore, to send out workers into his harvest field.[t] 3Go! I am sending you out like lambs among wolves.[u] 4Do not take a purse or bag or sandals; and do not greet anyone on the road.

5"When you enter a house, first say, 'Peace to this house.' 6If a man of peace is there, your peace will rest on him; if not, it will return to you. 7Stay in that house, eating and drinking whatever they give you, for the worker deserves his wages.[v] Do not move around from house to house.

8"When you enter a town and are welcomed, eat what is set before you.[w] 9Heal the sick who are there and tell them, 'The kingdom of God[x] is near you.' 10But when you enter a town and are not welcomed, go into its streets and say, 11'Even the dust of your town that sticks to our feet we wipe off against you.[y] Yet be sure of this: The kingdom of God is near.'[z] 12I tell you, it will be more bearable on that day for Sodom[a] than for that town.[b]

13"Woe to you,[c] Korazin! Woe to you, Bethsaida! For if the miracles that were performed in you had been performed in Tyre and Sidon, they would have repented long ago, sitting in sackcloth[d] and ashes. 14But it will be more bearable for Tyre and Sidon at the judgment than for you. 15And you, Capernaum,[e] will you be lifted up to the skies? No, you will go down to the depths.[o]

16"He who listens to you listens to me; he who rejects you rejects me; but he who rejects me rejects him who sent me."[f]

17The seventy-two[g] returned with joy and said, "Lord, even the demons submit to us in your name."[h]

18He replied, "I saw Satan[i] fall like lightning from heaven.[j] 19I have given you authority to trample on snakes[k] and scorpions and to overcome all the power of the

---

9:57 [k]ver 51
9:58 [l]S Mt 8:20
9:59 [m]S Mt 4:19
9:60 [n]S Mt 3:2
9:61 [o]1Ki 19:20
10:1 [p]S Lk 7:13
[q]Lk 9:1,2,51,52
[r]Mk 6:7 [s]Mt 10:1
10:2 [t]Mt 9:37, 38; Jn 4:35
10:3 [u]Mt 10:16

10:7 [v]S 1Ti 5:18
10:8 [w]1Co 10:27
10:9 [x]S Mt 3:2
10:11 [y]S Mt 10:14 [z]ver 9
10:12 [a]S Mt 10:15 [b]Mt 11:24
10:13 [c]Lk 6:24-26 [d]S Rev 11:3
10:15 [e]S Mt 4:13
10:16 [f]S Mt 10:40
10:17 [g]ver 1 [h]S Mk 16:17
10:18 [i]S Mt 4:10 [j]Isa 14:12; Rev 9:1; 12:8,9
10:19 [k]Mk 16:18; Ac 28:3-5

---

[n]*1 Some manuscripts seventy; also in verse 17
[o]*15 Greek Hades*

9:57 *As they were walking.* Continuing their journey through Samaria to Jerusalem.

9:59 *bury my father.* If his father had already died, the man would have been occupied with the burial then. But evidently he wanted to wait until after his father's death, which might have been years away. Jesus told him that the spiritually dead could bury the physically dead, and that the spiritually alive should be busy proclaiming the kingdom of God.

10:1 *appointed seventy-two.* Recorded only in Luke, though similar instructions were given to the Twelve (Mt 9:37–38; 10:7–16; Mk 6:7–11; cf. Lk 9:3–5). Certain differences in early manuscripts make it unclear as to whether the number was 72 or 70 (see NIV text note). Jesus covered Judea with his message (see note on 9:51) as thoroughly as he had Galilee. *two by two.* During his ministry in Galilee, Jesus had also sent out the Twelve two by two (see 9:1–6; Mk 6:7 and notes), a practice continued in the early church (Ac 13:2; 15:27,39–40; 17:14; 19:22).

10:4 *Do not take a purse or bag or sandals.* They were to travel light, without moneybag, luggage or extra sandals. *do not greet.* They were not to stop along the way to visit and exchange customary lengthy greetings. The mission was urgent.

10:7 *Do not move around.* See note on 9:4.

10:9 *The kingdom of God is near.* The heart of Jesus' message (see notes on 4:43; Mt 3:2).

10:11 *dust . . . we wipe off.* See note on 9:5.

10:12 *more bearable . . . for Sodom.* Although Sodom was so sinful that God destroyed it (Ge 19:24–28; Jude 7), the people who heard the message of Jesus and his disciples were even more accountable, because they had the gospel of the kingdom preached to them. *that day.* Judgment day.

10:13 *Korazin . . . Bethsaida.* See note on Mt 11:21.

10:14 *Tyre and Sidon.* Gentile cities in Phoenicia, north of Galilee, which had not had opportunity to witness Jesus' miracles and hear his preaching as the people had in most of Galilee (see note on v. 12).

10:15 *Capernaum.* Jesus' headquarters on the north shore of Galilee (see Mt 4:13 and note), whose inhabitants had many opportunities to see and hear Jesus. Therefore the condemnation for their rejection was the greater.

10:18 *Satan fall.* Even the demons were driven out by the disciples (v. 17), which meant that Satan was suffering defeat.

10:19 *snakes and scorpions . . . power of the enemy.* The snakes and scorpions may represent evil spirits; the enemy is Satan himself.

enemy; nothing will harm you. 20However, do not rejoice that the spirits submit to you, but rejoice that your names are written in heaven." [l]

21At that time Jesus, full of joy through the Holy Spirit, said, "I praise you, Father, Lord of heaven and earth, because you have hidden these things from the wise and learned, and revealed them to little children. [m] Yes, Father, for this was your good pleasure.

22"All things have been committed to me by my Father. [n] No one knows who the Son is except the Father, and no one knows who the Father is except the Son and those to whom the Son chooses to reveal him." [o]

23Then he turned to his disciples and said privately, "Blessed are the eyes that see what you see. 24For I tell you that many prophets and kings wanted to see what you see but did not see it, and to hear what you hear but did not hear it." [p]

The Parable of the Good Samaritan

10:25–28pp — Mt 22:34–40; Mk 12:28–31

25On one occasion an expert in the law stood up to test Jesus. "Teacher," he asked, "what must I do to inherit eternal life?" [q]

26"What is written in the Law?" he replied. "How do you read it?"

27He answered: " 'Love the Lord your God with all your heart and with all your soul and with all your strength and with all your mind' [p] ; [r] and, 'Love your neighbor as yourself.' [q] " [s]

28"You have answered correctly," Jesus replied. "Do this and you will live." [t]

29But he wanted to justify himself, [u] so he asked Jesus, "And who is my neighbor?"

Cross-references (center column):

10:20
/S Rev 20:12
10:21
m 1Co 1:26-29
10:22
n S Mt 28:18
o Jn 1:18
10:24
p 1Pe 1:10-12
10:25
q Mt 19:16;
Lk 18:18
10:27 r Dt 6:5
s Lev 19:18;
S Mt 5:43
10:28 t S Ro 7:10
10:29 u Lk 16:15

10:31
v Lev 21:1-3
10:33
w S Mt 10:5
10:38 x Jn 11:1;
12:2
10:39 y Jn 11:1;
12:3 z Lk 8:35
10:40 a Mk 4:38

30In reply Jesus said: "A man was going down from Jerusalem to Jericho, when he fell into the hands of robbers. They stripped him of his clothes, beat him and went away, leaving him half dead. 31A priest happened to be going down the same road, and when he saw the man, he passed by on the other side. [v] 32So too, a Levite, when he came to the place and saw him, passed by on the other side. 33But a Samaritan, [w] as he traveled, came where the man was; and when he saw him, he took pity on him. 34He went to him and bandaged his wounds, pouring on oil and wine. Then he put the man on his own donkey, took him to an inn and took care of him. 35The next day he took out two silver coins [r] and gave them to the innkeeper. 'Look after him,' he said, 'and when I return, I will reimburse you for any extra expense you may have.'

36"Which of these three do you think was a neighbor to the man who fell into the hands of robbers?"

37The expert in the law replied, "The one who had mercy on him."

Jesus told him, "Go and do likewise."

At the Home of Martha and Mary

38As Jesus and his disciples were on their way, he came to a village where a woman named Martha [x] opened her home to him. 39She had a sister called Mary, [y] who sat at the Lord's feet [z] listening to what he said. 40But Martha was distracted by all the preparations that had to be made. She came to him and asked, "Lord, don't you care [a] that my sister has left me to do the work by myself! Tell her to help me!"

p 27 Deut. 6:5   q 27 Lev. 19:18   r 35 Greek *two denarii*

10:20 Man's salvation is more important than power to overcome the evil one or escape his harm. *your names are written.* Salvation is recorded in heaven (see Ps 69:28; Da 12:1; Php 4:3; Heb 12:23; Rev 3:5).

10:25 *expert in the law.* A scholar well versed in Scripture asked a common question (18:18; cf. Mt 22:35), either to take issue with Jesus or simply to see what kind of teacher he was. See note on 7:30.

10:27 *Love . . . God . . . Love your neighbor.* Elsewhere Jesus uses these words in reply to another question (Mt 22:35–40; Mk 12:28–32), putting the same two Scriptures together (Dt 6:5; Lev 19:18). Whether a fourfold love (heart, soul, strength and mind, as here and in Mk 12:30) or threefold (Dt 6:5; Mt 22:37; Mk 12:33), the significance is that total devotion is demanded.

10:29 *to justify himself.* The answer to his first question was obviously one he knew, so to gain credibility he asked for an interpretation. In effect he said, "But the real question is: Who is my neighbor?"

10:30 *Jerusalem to Jericho.* A distance of 17 miles and a descent from about 2,500 feet above sea level to about 800 feet below sea level. The road ran through rocky, desert country, which provided places for robbers to waylay defenseless travelers.

10:31–33 *priest . . . Levite . . . Samaritan.* It is significant that the person Jesus commended was neither the religious leader nor the lay associate, but a hated foreigner. Jews viewed Samaritans as half-breeds, both physically (see note on Mt 10:5) and spiritually (see notes on Jn 4:20,22). Samaritans and Jews practiced open hostility (see note on 9:52), but Jesus asserted that love knows no national boundaries.

10:35 *two silver coins.* Two days' wages, which would keep a man up to two months in an inn.

10:36 *Which . . . was a neighbor to the man . . . ?* The question now became: Who proves he is the good neighbor by his actions?

10:38 *a village.* Bethany, about two miles from Jerusalem, was the home of Mary and Martha (Jn 12:1–3).

⁴¹"Martha, Martha," the Lord answered, "you are worried[b] and upset about many things, ⁴²but only one thing is needed.[s c] Mary has chosen what is better, and it will not be taken away from her."

Jesus' Teaching on Prayer

11:2–4pp — Mt 6:9–13
11:9–13pp — Mt 7:7–11

11 One day Jesus was praying[d] in a certain place. When he finished, one of his disciples said to him, "Lord,[e] teach us to pray, just as John taught his disciples."

²He said to them, "When you pray, say:

" 'Father,[t]
hallowed be your name,
your kingdom[f] come.[u]
³Give us each day our daily bread.
⁴Forgive us our sins,
    for we also forgive everyone who sins
        against us.[v g]
And lead us not into temptation.[w' ' h]

⁵Then he said to them, "Suppose one of you has a friend, and he goes to him at midnight and says, 'Friend, lend me three loaves of bread, ⁶because a friend of mine on a journey has come to me, and I have nothing to set before him.'

⁷"Then the one inside answers, 'Don't bother me. The door is already locked, and my children are with me in bed. I can't get up and give you anything.' ⁸I tell you, though he will not get up and give him the bread because he is his friend, yet because of the man's boldness[x] he will get up and give him as much as he needs.[i]

⁹"So I say to you: Ask and it will be given to you;[j] seek and you will find;

knock and the door will be opened to you. ¹⁰For everyone who asks receives; he who seeks finds; and to him who knocks, the door will be opened.

¹¹"Which of you fathers, if your son asks for[y] a fish, will give him a snake instead? ¹²Or if he asks for an egg, will give him a scorpion? ¹³If you then, though you are evil, know how to give good gifts to your children, how much more will your Father in heaven give the Holy Spirit to those who ask him!"

Jesus and Beelzebub

11:14,15; 17–22; 24–26pp — Mt 12:22,24–29; 43–45
11:17–22pp — Mk 3:23–27

¹⁴Jesus was driving out a demon that was mute. When the demon left, the man who had been mute spoke, and the crowd was amazed.[k] ¹⁵But some of them said, "By Beelzebub,[z l] the prince of demons, he is driving out demons."[m] ¹⁶Others tested him by asking for a sign from heaven.[n]

¹⁷Jesus knew their thoughts[o] and said to them: "Any kingdom divided against itself will be ruined, and a house divided against itself will fall. ¹⁸If Satan[p] is divided against himself, how can his kingdom stand? I say this because you claim that I drive out demons by Beelzebub. ¹⁹Now if I drive out demons by Beelzebub, by whom do your followers drive them out? So then, they will be your judges. ²⁰But if I drive out demons by the finger of God,[q] then

Cross-references (center column)

10:41
[b]Mt 6:25-34;
Lk 12:11,22
10:42 [c]Ps 27:4
11:1 [d]S Lk 3:21
[e]S Jn 13:13
11:2 [f]S Mt 3:2
11:4 [g]Mt 18:35;
Mk 11:25
[h]Mt 26:41;
Jas 1:13
11:8 [i]Lk 18:1-6
11:9 [j]S Mt 7:7

11:14 [k]Mt 9:32,
33
11:15 [l]S Mk 3:22
[m]Mt 9:34
11:16
[n]S Mt 12:38
11:17 [o]S Mt 9:4
11:18 [p]S Mt 4:10
11:20 [q]Ex 8:19

Text notes

[s]42 Some manuscripts *but few things are needed—or only one*   [t]2 Some manuscripts *Our Father in heaven*   [u]2 Some manuscripts *come. May your will be done on earth as it is in heaven.*   [v]4 Greek *everyone who is indebted to us*   [w]4 Some manuscripts *temptation but deliver us from the evil one*   [x]8 Or *persistence*   [y]11 Some manuscripts *for bread, will give him a stone; or if he asks for*   [z]15 Greek *Beezeboul* or *Beelzeboul;* also in verses 18 and 19

11:1 *Jesus was praying.* Not only on special occasions (e.g., baptism, 3:21; choosing the Twelve, 6:12; Gethsemane, 22:41) but also as a regular practice (5:16; Mt 14:23; Mk 1:35). *teach us to pray.* The Lord's model prayer was given here in answer to a request, and is similar to Mt 6:9–13, where it is a part of the Sermon on the Mount. Six petitions are included in the prayer as given in the Sermon on the Mount by Matthew (combining the last two petitions into one), whereas five appear in the prayer in Luke.
11:4 *Forgive us our sins.* Mt 6:12 has "debts," but the meaning is the same as "sins." Jesus taught this truth on other occasions as well (Mt 18:35; Mk 11:25). The prayer is a pattern for believers, who have already been forgiven for their sins. Jesus speaks here of daily forgiveness, which is necessary to restore broken communion with God.
11:5–13 Jesus now urged boldness (or persistence; see NIV text note on v. 8) in prayer (vv. 5–8) and gave assurance that God answers prayer (vv. 9–13). The argument is from the lesser to the greater (see v. 13).
11:13 *give the Holy Spirit.* Mt 7:11 has "give good gifts," meaning spiritual gifts. Luke emphasizes the work of the

Spirit, the greatest of God's gifts.
11:14 *demon that was mute.* See note on 4:33. This evil spirit caused muteness. The probable parallel passage in Matthew (12:22–30; see also Mk 3:20–27) indicates that the man was also blind.
11:15 *Beelzebub, the prince of demons.* Satan (v. 18). See note on Mt 10:25.
11:16 *a sign from heaven.* Jesus had just healed a mute. Here was their sign, and they would not recognize it.
11:17 *kingdom divided against itself.* If Satan gave power to Jesus, who opposed him in every way, Satan would be supporting an attack upon himself.
11:19 *by whom do your followers . . . ?* Jesus did not say whether the followers of the Pharisees (see Mt 12:24) actually drove out demons (see note on v. 24); but they claimed to drive them out by the power of God, and Jesus claimed the same. So to accuse Jesus of using Satanic power was implicitly to condemn their own followers as well. *your judges.* They will condemn you for your accusation against them.
11:20 *the kingdom of God has come.* In the sense that the King was present in the person of Jesus (see note on 4:43)

the kingdom of God[r] has come to you.
21"When a strong man, fully armed, guards his own house, his possessions are safe. 22But when someone stronger attacks and overpowers him, he takes away the armor in which the man trusted and divides up the spoils.

23"He who is not with me is against me, and he who does not gather with me, scatters.[s]

24"When an evil[a] spirit comes out of a man, it goes through arid places seeking rest and does not find it. Then it says, 'I will return to the house I left.' 25When it arrives, it finds the house swept clean and put in order. 26Then it goes and takes seven other spirits more wicked than itself, and they go in and live there. And the final condition of that man is worse than the first."[t]

27As Jesus was saying these things, a woman in the crowd called out, "Blessed is the mother who gave you birth and nursed you."[u]

28He replied, "Blessed rather are those who hear the word of God[v] and obey it."[w]

The Sign of Jonah
11:29–32pp — Mt 12:39–42

29As the crowds increased, Jesus said, "This is a wicked generation. It asks for a miraculous sign,[x] but none will be given it except the sign of Jonah.[y] 30For as Jonah was a sign to the Ninevites, so also will the Son of Man be to this generation. 31The Queen of the South will rise at the judg-

ment with the men of this generation and condemn them; for she came from the ends of the earth to listen to Solomon's wisdom,[z] and now one[b] greater than Solomon is here. 32The men of Nineveh will stand up at the judgment with this generation and condemn it; for they repented at the preaching of Jonah,[a] and now one greater than Jonah is here.

The Lamp of the Body
11:34,35pp — Mt 6:22,23

33"No one lights a lamp and puts it in a place where it will be hidden, or under a bowl. Instead he puts it on its stand, so that those who come in may see the light.[b] 34Your eye is the lamp of your body. When your eyes are good, your whole body also is full of light. But when they are bad, your body also is full of darkness. 35See to it, then, that the light within you is not darkness. 36Therefore, if your whole body is full of light, and no part of it dark, it will be completely lighted, as when the light of a lamp shines on you."

Six Woes

37When Jesus had finished speaking, a Pharisee invited him to eat with him; so he went in and reclined at the table.[c] 38But the Pharisee, noticing that Jesus did not first wash before the meal,[d] was surprised.

39Then the Lord[e] said to him, "Now then, you Pharisees clean the outside of the cup and dish, but inside you are full of

11:20 [r]S Mt 3:2
11:23 [s]Mt 12:30; Mk 9:40; Lk 9:50
11:26 [t]2Pe 2:20
11:27 [u]Lk 23:29
11:28 [v]S Heb 4:12; [w]Pr 8:32; Lk 6:47; 8:21; Jn 14:21
11:29 [x]ver 16; S Mt 12:38 [y]Jnh 1:17; Mt 16:4

11:31 [z]1Ki 10:1; 2Ch 9:1
11:32 [a]Jnh 3:5
11:33 [b]S Mt 5:15
11:37 [c]Lk 7:36; 14:1
11:38 [d]Mk 7:3,4
11:39 [e]S Lk 7:13

[a]24 Greek *unclean*　[b]31 Or *something*; also in verse 32

and that the powers of evil were being overthrown.

11:22 *someone stronger attacks.* Jesus was stronger than Beelzebub, and by his exorcism of demons he demonstrated that he had overpowered Satan and disarmed him. It was therefore foolish to suggest that Jesus had cast out demons by Satan's power.

11:23 The one who does not intentionally support Jesus opposes him, making neutrality impossible. Even the worker in 9:50, whom the disciples described as "not one of us," was apparently a believer, acting in Jesus' name (see note on Mk 9:38), and Jesus did not condemn him.

11:24 *evil spirit comes out.* Jesus is perhaps referring to the work of Jewish exorcists, who claimed to cast out demons (cf. v. 19) but who rejected the kingdom of God and whose exorcisms were therefore ineffective. See Mt 12:43–45, where Jesus makes a similar comment about the Jewish nation of that day.

11:25 *finds the house swept clean.* The place had been cleaned up but left unoccupied. A life reformed but lacking God's presence is open to reoccupancy by evil.

11:29 *asks for a miraculous sign.* On several occasions Jews asked for miraculous signs (v. 16; Mt 12:38; Mk 8:11), but Jesus rejected their requests because they had wrong motives.

11:30 *as Jonah was a sign.* Jonah spent three days (see note on Mt 12:40) "buried" in the huge fish, just as Jesus would

be buried for three days before his resurrection.

11:31–32 *one greater than Solomon . . . one greater than Jonah.* Jesus argued from the lesser to the greater. If the queen of Sheba responded positively to the wisdom of Solomon, and the men of Nineveh to the preaching of Jonah, how much more should the people of Jesus' day have responded to the ministry of Jesus, who is infinitely greater than Solomon or Jonah!

11:31 *The Queen of the South.* The queen of Sheba (see 1Ki 10:1–10 and notes).

11:33 *a bowl.* A container holding about one peck. *may see the light.* A lamp is meant to give light to those who are near it (see v. 36). Jesus had publicly exhibited the light of the gospel for all to see, but the Jews requested more spectacular signs. The problem was not with any failure on Jesus' part in giving light; it was with the faulty vision of the Jews.

11:34 *your eyes are good.* Those asking for a sign do not need more light; they need good eyes to allow the light to enter.

11:38 *did not first wash.* Especially for ceremonial cleansing, not commanded in the law but added in the tradition of the Pharisees (Mk 7:3; cf. Mt 15:9).

11:39 *clean the outside.* Engage in ceremonial washings of the body. *greed and wickedness.* These Pharisees were more concerned about keeping ceremonies than about being moral (cf. Mk 7:20–23).

greed and wickedness.*f* 40You foolish people!*g* Did not the one who made the outside make the inside also? 41But give what is inside the dish,*c* to the poor,*h* and everything will be clean for you.*i*

42"Woe to you Pharisees, because you give God a tenth*j* of your mint, rue and all other kinds of garden herbs, but you neglect justice and the love of God.*k* You should have practiced the latter without leaving the former undone.*l*

43"Woe to you Pharisees, because you love the most important seats in the synagogues and greetings in the marketplaces.*m*

44"Woe to you, because you are like unmarked graves,*n* which men walk over without knowing it."

45One of the experts in the law*o* answered him, "Teacher, when you say these things, you insult us also."

46Jesus replied, "And you experts in the law, woe to you, because you load people down with burdens they can hardly carry, and you yourselves will not lift one finger to help them.*p*

47"Woe to you, because you build tombs for the prophets, and it was your forefathers who killed them. 48So you testify that you approve of what your forefathers did; they killed the prophets, and you build their tombs.*q* 49Because of this, God in his wisdom*r* said, 'I will send them prophets and apostles, some of whom they will kill and others they will persecute.'*s* 50Therefore this generation will be held responsible for the blood of all the prophets that

has been shed since the beginning of the world, 51from the blood of Abel*t* to the blood of Zechariah,*u* who was killed between the altar and the sanctuary. Yes, I tell you, this generation will be held responsible for it all.*v*

52"Woe to you experts in the law, because you have taken away the key to knowledge. You yourselves have not entered, and you have hindered those who were entering."*w*

53When Jesus left there, the Pharisees and the teachers of the law began to oppose him fiercely and to besiege him with questions, 54waiting to catch him in something he might say.*x*

Warnings and Encouragements
12:2–9pp — Mt 10:26–33

12 Meanwhile, when a crowd of many thousands had gathered, so that they were trampling on one another, Jesus began to speak first to his disciples, saying: "Be on your guard against the yeast of the Pharisees, which is hypocrisy.*y* 2There is nothing concealed that will not be disclosed, or hidden that will not be made known.*z* 3What you have said in the dark will be heard in the daylight, and what you have whispered in the ear in the inner rooms will be proclaimed from the roofs.

4"I tell you, my friends,*a* do not be afraid of those who kill the body and after that can do no more. 5But I will show you

*c*41 Or *what you have*

Cross references (center column)
11:39 *f*Mt 23:25, 26; Mk 7:20-23
11:40 *g*Lk 12:20; 1Co 15:36
11:41 *h*Lk 12:33
11:42 *j*Lk 18:12
*k*Dt 6:5; Mic 6:8
*l*Mt 23:23
11:43 *m*Mt 23:6, 7; Lk 14:7; 20:46
11:44 *n*Mt 23:27
11:45 *o*S Mt 22:35
11:46 *p*S Mt 23:4
11:48
*q*Mt 23:29-32; Ac 7:51-53
11:49 *r*1Co 1:24, 30; Col 2:3
*s*Mt 23:34

11:51 *t*Ge 4:8
*u*2Ch 24:20,21
*v*Mt 23:35,36
11:52 *w*Mt 23:13
11:54
*x*S Mt 12:10
12:1 *y*Mt 16:6, 11,12
12:2 *z*S Mk 4:22
12:4 *a*Jn 15:14, 15

Notes (bottom)

11:40 *make the inside also.* The inside of man (the "heart" and inner righteousness) is more important than the outside (ceremonial cleansing).

11:41 *the dish.* Supplied from the figures of speech used in v. 39. *everything will be clean.* Giving from the heart makes everything else right. If one gives to the poor, his heart is no longer in the grip of "greed and wickedness" (v. 39).

11:44 *unmarked graves.* The Jews whitewashed their tombs so that no one would accidentally touch them and be defiled (cf. Nu 19:16; Mt 23:27). Just as touching a grave resulted in ceremonial uncleanness, associating with the Pharisees could result in moral uncleanness.

11:45 *experts in the law.* See note on 7:30.

11:46 *load people down.* By adding rules and regulations to the authenic law of Moses (see note on Mt 15:2) and doing nothing to help others keep them (Mt 23:4), while inventing ways for themselves to circumvent them.

11:47 *tombs for the prophets.* Outwardly the Jews appeared to honor the prophets in building or rebuilding memorials, but inwardly they rejected the Christ the prophets announced. They lived in opposition to the teachings of the prophets, just as their forefathers had done.

11:49 *God in his wisdom said.* Not a quotation from the OT or any other known book. It may refer to God speaking through Jesus, or it may be referring in quotation form to God's decision to send prophets and apostles even though he knew they would be rejected.

11:51 *blood of Abel . . . Zechariah.* See note on Mt 23:35.

11:52 *the key to knowledge.* The very persons who should have opened the people's minds concerning the law obscured their understanding by faulty interpretation and an erroneous system of theology. They kept themselves and the people in ignorance of the way of salvation, or, as Matthew's account puts it, they "shut the kingdom of heaven in men's faces" (Mt 23:13).

11:54 *waiting to catch him.* The determination of the religious leaders to trap Jesus is evident throughout Luke (6:11; 19:47-48; 20:19-20; 22:2).

12:1 *yeast of the Pharisees.* See note on Mk 8:15.

12:2 *nothing concealed that will not be disclosed.* In this context the meaning is that nothing hidden through hypocrisy will fail to be made known.

12:3 *inner rooms.* Storerooms were surrounded by other rooms so that no one could dig in from outside.

12:4 *after that can do no more.* Encouragement in the face of persecution (see Mt 10:28).

12:5 *power to throw you into hell.* God alone has this power. The Greek word for "hell" is *ge(h)enna* (see note on Mt 5:22), not to be confused with Hades, the general name for the place of the dead. In the NT *ge(h)enna* is used only in Matthew, Mark, Jas 3:6 and here. *fear him.* Respect his authority, stand in awe of his majesty and trust in him. Verses 6–7 give the basis for trust.

whom you should fear: Fear him who, after the killing of the body, has power to throw you into hell. Yes, I tell you, fear him.[b] [6]Are not five sparrows sold for two pennies[d]? Yet not one of them is forgotten by God. [7]Indeed, the very hairs of your head are all numbered.[c] Don't be afraid; you are worth more than many sparrows.[d]

[8]"I tell you, whoever acknowledges me before men, the Son of Man will also acknowledge him before the angels of God.[e] [9]But he who disowns me before men will be disowned[f] before the angels of God. [10]And everyone who speaks a word against the Son of Man[g] will be forgiven, but anyone who blasphemes against the Holy Spirit will not be forgiven.[h]

[11]"When you are brought before synagogues, rulers and authorities, do not worry about how you will defend yourselves or what you will say,[i] [12]for the Holy Spirit will teach you at that time what you should say."[j]

The Parable of the Rich Fool

[13]Someone in the crowd said to him, "Teacher, tell my brother to divide the inheritance with me."

[14]Jesus replied, "Man, who appointed me a judge or an arbiter between you?" [15]Then he said to them, "Watch out! Be on your guard against all kinds of greed; a man's life does not consist in the abundance of his possessions."[k]

[16]And he told them this parable: "The ground of a certain rich man produced a good crop. [17]He thought to himself, 'What shall I do? I have no place to store my crops.'

[18]"Then he said, 'This is what I'll do. I will tear down my barns and build bigger ones, and there I will store all my grain and my goods. [19]And I'll say to myself, "You have plenty of good things laid up for

many years. Take life easy; eat, drink and be merry."'

[20]"But God said to him, 'You fool![l] This very night your life will be demanded from you.[m] Then who will get what you have prepared for yourself?'[n]

[21]"This is how it will be with anyone who stores up things for himself but is not rich toward God."[o]

Do Not Worry

12:22-31pp — Mt 6:25-33

[22]Then Jesus said to his disciples: "Therefore I tell you, do not worry about your life, what you will eat; or about your body, what you will wear. [23]Life is more than food, and the body more than clothes. [24]Consider the ravens: They do not sow or reap, they have no storeroom or barn; yet God feeds them.[p] And how much more valuable you are than birds! [25]Who of you by worrying can add a single hour to his life[e]? [26]Since you cannot do this very little thing, why do you worry about the rest?

[27]"Consider how the lilies grow. They do not labor or spin. Yet I tell you, not even Solomon in all his splendor[q] was dressed like one of these. [28]If that is how God clothes the grass of the field, which is here today, and tomorrow is thrown into the fire, how much more will he clothe you, O you of little faith![r] [29]And do not set your heart on what you will eat or drink; do not worry about it. [30]For the pagan world runs after all such things, and your Father[s] knows that you need them.[t] [31]But seek his kingdom,[u] and these things will be given to you as well.[v]

[32]"Do not be afraid,[w] little flock, for your Father has been pleased to give you the kingdom.[x] [33]Sell your possessions and give to the poor.[y] Provide purses for your-

Cross references (center column)

12:5 *b* Heb 10:31
12:7 *c* S Mt 10:30
d Mt 12:12
12:8 *e* Lk 15:10
12:9 *f* Mk 8:38;
2Ti 2:12
12:10 *g* S Mt 8:20
h Mt 12:31,32;
S 1Jn 5:16
12:11 *i* Mt 10:17,
19; Lk 21:12,14
12:12 *j* Ex 4:12;
Mt 10:20;
Mk 13:11;
Lk 21:15
12:15 *k* Job
20:20; 31:24;
Ps 62:10

12:20 *l* Jer 17:11;
Lk 11:40 *m* Job
27:8 *n* Ps 39:6;
49:10
12:21 *o* ver 33
12:24 *p* Job
38:41; Ps 147:9
12:27
q 1Ki 10:4-7
12:28 *r* S Mt 6:30
12:30 *s* S Lk 6:36
t Mt 6:8
12:31 *u* S Mt 3:2
v Mt 19:29
12:32
w S Mt 14:27
x S Mt 25:34
12:33 *y* S Ac 2:45

[d]6 Greek *two assaria*　　[e]25 Or *single cubit to his height*

12:6 *five sparrows sold for two pennies.* God even cares for little birds, sold cheaply for food. Three words used for Roman coins are *denarius* (Mt 18:28), *assarion* (Mt 10:29) and *kodrantes* (Mt 5:26), very loosely related to each other as are a 50-cent piece, nickel and penny. The coins here are *assaria*, so the transaction would be something like five birds for two nickels.

12:8 *acknowledges me.* When a person acknowledges that Jesus is the Messiah, the Son of God (Mt 16:16; 1Jn 2:22), Jesus acknowledges that the individual is his loyal follower (cf. Mt 7:21).

12:9 *will be disowned.* See 9:26; 2Ti 2:12; cf. Mt 7:21; 25:41-46. The same word is used in Peter's denial (22:34, "deny"; 22:61, "disown").

12:10 *blasphemes against the Holy Spirit.* See note on Mt 12:31; cf. Mk 3:28-29.

12:13 *divide the inheritance.* Dt 21:17 gave the general rule that an elder son received double a younger one's portion. Disputes over such matters were normally settled by rabbis. This man's request of Jesus was selfish and materialistic. There is no indication that the man had been listening seriously to what Jesus had been saying (cf. vv. 1-11). Jesus replied with a parable about the consequences of greed.

12:16 *parable.* See note on 8:4.

12:20 *fool!* A strong word (11:40; Eph 5:17).

12:31 *seek his kingdom.* Since v. 32 suggests that Jesus is speaking to believers, who already possess the kingdom, this command probably means that Christians should seek the spiritual benefits of the kingdom rather than the material goods of the world (cf. Mt 6:33).

12:33 *give to the poor.* The danger of riches and the need for giving are characteristic themes in Luke (3:11; 6:30; 11:41; 14:13-14; 16:9; 18:22; 19:8).

selves that will not wear out, a treasure in heaven [z] that will not be exhausted, where no thief comes near and no moth destroys. [a] 34For where your treasure is, there your heart will be also. [b]

Watchfulness

12:35,36pp — Mt 25:1-13; Mk 13:33-37
12:39,40; 42-46pp — Mt 24:43-51

35"Be dressed ready for service and keep your lamps burning, 36like men waiting for their master to return from a wedding banquet, so that when he comes and knocks they can immediately open the door for him. 37It will be good for those servants whose master finds them watching when he comes. [c] I tell you the truth, he will dress himself to serve, will have them recline at the table and will come and wait on them. [d] 38It will be good for those servants whose master finds them ready, even if he comes in the second or third watch of the night. 39But understand this: If the owner of the house had known at what hour the thief [e] was coming, he would not have let his house be broken into. 40You also must be ready, [f] because the Son of Man will come at an hour when you do not expect him."

41Peter asked, "Lord, are you telling this parable to us, or to everyone?"

42The Lord [g] answered, "Who then is the faithful and wise manager, whom the master puts in charge of his servants to give them their food allowance at the proper time? 43It will be good for that servant whom the master finds doing so when he returns. 44I tell you the truth, he will put him in charge of all his possessions. 45But suppose the servant says to himself, 'My master is taking a long time in coming,' and he then begins to beat the

menservants and maidservants and to eat and drink and get drunk. 46The master of that servant will come on a day when he does not expect him and at an hour he is not aware of. [h] He will cut him to pieces and assign him a place with the unbelievers.

47"That servant who knows his master's will and does not get ready or does not do what his master wants will be beaten with many blows. [i] 48But the one who does not know and does things deserving punishment will be beaten with few blows. [j] From everyone who has been given much, much will be demanded; and from the one who has been entrusted with much, much more will be asked.

Not Peace but Division

12:51-53pp — Mt 10:34-36

49"I have come to bring fire on the earth, and how I wish it were already kindled! 50But I have a baptism [k] to undergo, and how distressed I am until it is completed! [l] 51Do you think I came to bring peace on earth? No, I tell you, but division. 52From now on there will be five in one family divided against each other, three against two and two against three. 53They will be divided, father against son and son against father, mother against daughter and daughter against mother, mother-in-law against daughter-in-law and daughter-in-law against mother-in-law." [m]

Interpreting the Times

54He said to the crowd: "When you see a cloud rising in the west, immediately you say, 'It's going to rain,' and it does. [n] 55And when the south wind blows, you say, 'It's going to be hot,' and it is. 56Hypocrites! You know how to interpret the appearance

Cross references (center column)

12:33 [z]S Mt 6:20
[a]S Jas 5:2
12:34 [b]Mt 6:21
12:37 [c]Mt 24:42, 46; 25:13
[d]S Mt 20:28
12:39 [e]Mt 6:19; 1Th 5:2; 2Pe 3:10; Rev 3:3; 16:15
12:40 [/]Mk 13:33; Lk 21:36
12:42 [g]S Lk 7:13
12:46 [h]ver 40
12:47 [i]Dt 25:2
12:48 [j]Lev 5:17; Nu 15:27-30
12:50 [k]Mk 10:38
[l]S Jn 19:30
12:53 [m]Mic 7:6; Mt 10:21
12:54 [n]Mt 16:2

Study notes (bottom)

12:37 *dress himself to serve.* The master reverses the normal roles and serves the servants (cf. 22:27; Mk 10:45; Jn 13:4-5,12-16).

12:38 *second or third watch.* Night was divided into four watches (Mk 13:35) and three by the Jews (Jdg 7:19); see note on Mt 14:25. These were probably the last two of the Jewish watches. The banquet would have begun in the first watch.

12:40 Christ's return is certain, but the time is not known (cf. Mt 24:36).

12:41 Jesus taught the people in parables but used a more direct approach with the disciples. However, he did not intend these warnings of watchfulness just for the disciples (see Mk 13:37). In the following verses he emphasizes the duty to fulfill responsibilities.

12:42 *wise manager.* An outstanding slave (v. 43) was sometimes left in charge of an estate (see 16:1).

12:46-48 *cut him to pieces . . . beaten with many blows . . . beaten with few blows.* Three grades of punishment that the judge will mete out in proportion to both the privileges

each person has enjoyed and his response to those privileges (see Ro 2:12-16).

12:49 *fire.* Applied figuratively in different ways in the NT (see note on 3:16). Here it is associated with judgment (v. 49) and division (v. 51). Judgment falls on the wicked, who are separated from the righteous.

12:50 *baptism.* The suffering that Jesus was to endure on the cross (see note on Mk 10:38). *until it is completed.* The words from the cross would pronounce the completion (Jn 19:28,30). Jesus wished that the hour of suffering were already past.

12:51 *division.* See note on Mt 10:34.

12:54-56 Wind from the west was from the Mediterranean Sea; from the south it was from the desert. Although people could use such indicators to forecast the weather, they could not recognize the signs of spiritual crisis, the coming of the Messiah, the threat of his death, the coming confrontation with Rome, and the eternal consequences these events would have for their own lives.

of the earth and the sky. How is it that you don't know how to interpret this present time?[o]

[57]"Why don't you judge for yourselves what is right? [58]As you are going with your adversary to the magistrate, try hard to be reconciled to him on the way, or he may drag you off to the judge, and the judge turn you over to the officer, and the officer throw you into prison.[p] [59]I tell you, you will not get out until you have paid the last penny.[f] "[q]

Repent or Perish

13 Now there were some present at that time who told Jesus about the Galileans whose blood Pilate[r] had mixed with their sacrifices. [2]Jesus answered, "Do you think that these Galileans were worse sinners than all the other Galileans because they suffered this way?[s] [3]I tell you, no! But unless you repent, you too will all perish. [4]Or those eighteen who died when the tower in Siloam[t] fell on them—do you think they were more guilty than all the others living in Jerusalem? [5]I tell you, no! But unless you repent,[u] you too will all perish."

[6]Then he told this parable: "A man had a fig tree, planted in his vineyard, and he went to look for fruit on it, but did not find any.[v] [7]So he said to the man who took care of the vineyard, 'For three years now I've been coming to look for fruit on this fig tree and haven't found any. Cut it down![w] Why should it use up the soil?'

[8]"'Sir,' the man replied, 'leave it alone for one more year, and I'll dig around it and fertilize it. [9]If it bears fruit next year, fine! If not, then cut it down.' "

Cross-references (center column)

12:56 [o]Mt 16:3
12:58 [p]Mt 5:25
12:59 [q]Mt 5:26; Mk 12:42
13:1 [r]S Mt 27:2
13:2 [s]Jn 9:2,3
13:4 [t]Jn 9:7,11
13:5 [u]Mt 3:2; Ac 2:38
13:6 [v]Isa 5:2; Jer 8:13; Mt 21:19
13:7 [w]S Mt 3:10

13:10 [x]S Mt 4:23
13:11 [y]ver 16
13:13 [z]S Mk 5:23
13:14 [a]S Mt 12:2 [b]S Mk 5:22 [c]Ex 20:9
13:15 [d]Lk 14:5
13:16 [e]S Lk 3:8 [f]S Mt 4:10
13:17 [g]Isa 66:5
13:18 [h]S Mt 3:2 [i]S Mt 13:24

A Crippled Woman Healed on the Sabbath

[10]On a Sabbath Jesus was teaching in one of the synagogues,[x] [11]and a woman was there who had been crippled by a spirit for eighteen years.[y] She was bent over and could not straighten up at all. [12]When Jesus saw her, he called her forward and said to her, "Woman, you are set free from your infirmity." [13]Then he put his hands on her,[z] and immediately she straightened up and praised God.

[14]Indignant because Jesus had healed on the Sabbath,[a] the synagogue ruler[b] said to the people, "There are six days for work.[c] So come and be healed on those days, not on the Sabbath."

[15]The Lord answered him, "You hypocrites! Doesn't each of you on the Sabbath untie his ox or donkey from the stall and lead it out to give it water?[d] [16]Then should not this woman, a daughter of Abraham,[e] whom Satan[f] has kept bound for eighteen long years, be set free on the Sabbath day from what bound her?"

[17]When he said this, all his opponents were humiliated,[g] but the people were delighted with all the wonderful things he was doing.

The Parables of the Mustard Seed and the Yeast

13:18,19pp — Mk 4:30–32
13:18–21pp — Mt 13:31–33

[18]Then Jesus asked, "What is the kingdom of God[h] like?[i] What shall I compare it to? [19]It is like a mustard seed, which a man took and planted in his garden. It

[f]59 Greek lepton

12:57 *judge for yourselves.* Despite the insistence of the Pharisees, despite the Roman system, and even despite the pressure of family, a person must accept God on his terms. The signs of the times called for immediate decision—before judgment came on the Jewish nation.
12:58 *be reconciled . . . or.* Settle accounts before it is too late.
12:59 *last penny.* Greek *lepton.* If a *kodrantes* is compared to a penny (see note on v. 6), this coin corresponds to half a penny.
13:1 *the Galileans.* The incident is otherwise unknown, but having people killed while offering sacrifices in the temple fits the reputation of Pilate. These Galileans may have broken an important Roman regulation, which led to their bloody punishment.
13:2,4 *worse sinners . . . more guilty.* In ancient times it was often assumed that a calamity would befall only those who were extremely sinful (see Jn 9:1–2; see also Job 4:7; 22:5, where Eliphaz falsely accused Job). But Jesus pointed out that all are sinners who must repent or face a fearful end.
13:4 *those eighteen.* Another unknown incident. *the tower in Siloam.* Built inside the southeast section of Jerusalem's

wall.
13:6 *fig tree.* Probably refers to the Jewish nation (see note on Mk 11:14), but it may also apply to the individual soul.
13:7 *For three years.* A period of ample opportunity.
13:11 *crippled by a spirit.* Various disorders were caused by evil spirits (see note on 4:33). The description of this woman's infirmity suggests that the bones of her spine were rigidly fused together.
13:12 *set free.* The spirit had been cast out, and the woman was freed from the bond of Satan and from her physical handicap.
13:14 *healed on the Sabbath.* A focal point of attack against Jesus was his conduct on the Sabbath (see 6:6–11; 14:1–6; Mt 12:1–8,11–12; Jn 5:1–18; see also Ex 20:9–10). *synagogue ruler.* See note on 8:41.
13:15 *untie his ox.* They had more regard for the needs of an animal than for the far greater need of a person. Jesus called his critics "hypocrites" because they pretended zeal for the law, but their motive was to attack him and his healing.
13:19 *mustard seed.* See notes on Mt 13:31–32; Mk 4:31. Trees in Scripture are sometimes symbols of nations

grew and became a tree,[j] and the birds of the air perched in its branches." [k]

20Again he asked, "What shall I compare the kingdom of God to? 21It is like yeast that a woman took and mixed into a large amount[g] of flour until it worked all through the dough." [l]

The Narrow Door

22Then Jesus went through the towns and villages, teaching as he made his way to Jerusalem. [m] 23Someone asked him, "Lord, are only a few people going to be saved?"

He said to them, 24"Make every effort to enter through the narrow door, [n] because many, I tell you, will try to enter and will not be able to. 25Once the owner of the house gets up and closes the door, you will stand outside knocking and pleading, 'Sir, open the door for us.'

"But he will answer, 'I don't know you or where you come from.' [o]

26"Then you will say, 'We ate and drank with you, and you taught in our streets.'

27"But he will reply, 'I don't know you or where you come from. Away from me, all you evildoers!' [p]

28"There will be weeping there, and gnashing of teeth, [q] when you see Abraham, Isaac and Jacob and all the prophets in the kingdom of God, but you yourselves thrown out. 29People will come from east and west[r] and north and south, and will take their places at the feast in the king-

dom of God. 30Indeed there are those who are last who will be first, and first who will be last." [s]

Jesus' Sorrow for Jerusalem

13:34,35pp — Mt 23:37-39
13:34,35Ref — Lk 19:41

31At that time some Pharisees came to Jesus and said to him, "Leave this place and go somewhere else. Herod[t] wants to kill you."

32He replied, "Go tell that fox, 'I will drive out demons and heal people today and tomorrow, and on the third day I will reach my goal.'[u] 33In any case, I must keep going today and tomorrow and the next day—for surely no prophet[v] can die outside Jerusalem!

34"O Jerusalem, Jerusalem, you who kill the prophets and stone those sent to you, how often I have longed to gather your children together, as a hen gathers her chicks under her wings, [w] but you were not willing! 35Look, your house is left to you desolate.[x] I tell you, you will not see me again until you say, 'Blessed is he who comes in the name of the Lord.'[h]"[y]

Jesus at a Pharisee's House

14:8-10Ref — Pr 25:6,7

14 One Sabbath, when Jesus went to eat in the house of a prominent Pharisee, [z] he was being carefully

---

Cross references (center column):

13:19 /Lk 17:6
kS Mt 13:32
13:21 /1Co 5:6
13:22 mS Lk 9:51
13:24 nMt 7:13
13:25 oMt 7:23; 25:10-12
13:27 pS Mt 7:23
13:28 qS Mt 8:12
13:29 rS Mt 8:11

13:30 sS Mt 19:30
13:31 tS Mt 14:1
13:32 uS Heb 2:10
13:33 vS Mt 21:11
13:34 wS Mt 23:37
13:35 xJer 12:17; 22:5 yPs 118:26; Lk 19:38
14:1 zLk 7:36; 11:37

g21 Greek three satas (probably about 1/2 bushel or 22 liters)   h35 Psalm 118:26

(see Eze 17:23; 31:6; Da 4:12,21).
13:21 *yeast.* See note on Mt 13:33. Its permeating quality is emphasized here as it works from the inside to affect all the dough. This parable speaks of the powerful influence of God's kingdom. *large amount.* See NIV text note; same amount as used by Sarah in Ge 18:6 (see NIV text note there).
13:22 *through the towns and villages.* See chart on "The Life of Christ," p. 1480. Somewhere between the events of 11:1 and 13:21 Jesus left Judea and began his work in and around Perea, which is recorded in 13:22–19:27; Mt 19:1–20:28; Mk 10; Jn 10:40–42. During the last part of the Perean ministry, it appears that he went north to Galilee and then traveled south again through Perea to Jericho and to Jerusalem. Some of Jesus' sayings that Luke attributes to the period of ministry in Perea are found in different settings in Matthew (7:13–14,22–23). Perhaps he repeated various sayings on different occasions. *as he made his way to Jerusalem.* Where he would die. Although Jesus was ministering throughout Perea, his eyes were constantly set on the Holy City and his ultimate destiny.
13:23 *only a few . . . saved?* Perhaps the questioner had observed that in spite of the very large crowds that came to hear Jesus' preaching and be healed, there were only a few followers who were loyal. Jesus did not answer directly, but warned that many would try to enter after it was too late.
13:27 *I don't know you.* See Mt 7:23; 25:12.
13:29 *People . . . from east and west and north and south.*

From the four corners of the world (Ps 107:3) and from among all people, including Gentiles.
13:31 *Herod wants to kill you.* See note on Mt 14:1. Jesus was probably in Perea, which was under Herod's jurisdiction (see note on 3:1). The Pharisees wanted to frighten Jesus into leaving this area and going to Judea.
13:32 *fox.* A crafty animal. *today and tomorrow.* In Semitic usage this phrase could refer to an indefinite but limited period of time. *reach my goal.* Jesus' life had a predetermined plan that would be carried out, and no harm could come to him until his purpose was accomplished (cf. 4:43; 9:22).
13:33 *outside Jerusalem.* Jesus' hour had not yet come (see 2:38; Jn 7:30; 8:20; cf. Jn 8:59; 10:39; 11:54). He would die in Jerusalem as had numerous prophets before him.
13:34 *how often . . . !* This lament over Jerusalem may suggest that Jesus was in Jerusalem more often than the Synoptics indicate (cf. 4:44; 5:1; 7:10; 10:22). However, the statement in vv. 34–35 may have been uttered some distance from Jerusalem, i.e., in Perea. According to Mt 23:37–38, the same utterance was spoken on Tuesday of Passion Week. Jesus repeated many of his teachings and sayings.
13:35 *house is left . . . desolate.* God will abandon his temple and his city (see 21:20,24; Jer 12:7; 22:5). *not see me again until.* See Zec 12:10; Rev 1:7; cf. Isa 45:23; Ro 14:11; Php 2:10–11.
14:1 *One Sabbath.* Of seven recorded miracles on the Sabbath, Luke includes five (4:31,38; 6:6; 13:14; 14:1); the

watched.[a] ²There in front of him was a man suffering from dropsy. ³Jesus asked the Pharisees and experts in the law,[b] "Is it lawful to heal on the Sabbath or not?"[c] ⁴But they remained silent. So taking hold of the man, he healed him and sent him away.

⁵Then he asked them, "If one of you has a son[i] or an ox that falls into a well on the Sabbath day, will you not immediately pull him out?"[d] ⁶And they had nothing to say.

⁷When he noticed how the guests picked the places of honor at the table,[e] he told them this parable: ⁸"When someone invites you to a wedding feast, do not take the place of honor, for a person more distinguished than you may have been invited. ⁹If so, the host who invited both of you will come and say to you, 'Give this man your seat.' Then, humiliated, you will have to take the least important place. ¹⁰But when you are invited, take the lowest place, so that when your host comes, he will say to you, 'Friend, move up to a better place.' Then you will be honored in the presence of all your fellow guests. ¹¹For everyone who exalts himself will be humbled, and he who humbles himself will be exalted."[f]

¹²Then Jesus said to his host, "When you give a luncheon or dinner, do not invite your friends, your brothers or relatives, or your rich neighbors; if you do, they may invite you back and so you will be repaid. ¹³But when you give a banquet, invite the poor, the crippled, the lame, the blind,[g] ¹⁴and you will be blessed. Although they cannot repay you, you will be

repaid at the resurrection of the righteous."[h]

The Parable of the Great Banquet

14:16–24Ref — Mt 22:2–14

¹⁵When one of those at the table with him heard this, he said to Jesus, "Blessed is the man who will eat at the feast[i] in the kingdom of God."[j]

¹⁶Jesus replied: "A certain man was preparing a great banquet and invited many guests. ¹⁷At the time of the banquet he sent his servant to tell those who had been invited, 'Come, for everything is now ready.'

¹⁸"But they all alike began to make excuses. The first said, 'I have just bought a field, and I must go and see it. Please excuse me.'

¹⁹"Another said, 'I have just bought five yoke of oxen, and I'm on my way to try them out. Please excuse me.'

²⁰"Still another said, 'I just got married, so I can't come.'

²¹"The servant came back and reported this to his master. Then the owner of the house became angry and ordered his servant, 'Go out quickly into the streets and alleys of the town and bring in the poor, the crippled, the blind and the lame.'[k]

²²"'Sir,' the servant said, 'what you ordered has been done, but there is still room.'

²³"Then the master told his servant, 'Go out to the roads and country lanes and make them come in, so that my house will be full. ²⁴I tell you, not one of those men

---

Cross references (center column):

14:1 [a]S Mt 12:10
14:3 [b]S Mt 22:35
[c]S Mt 12:2
14:5 [d]Lk 13:15
14:7 [e]S Lk 11:43
14:11 [f]S Mt 23:12
14:13 [g]ver 21

14:14 [h]Ac 24:15
14:15 [i]Isa 25:6; Mt 26:29; Lk 13:29; Rev 19:9 [j]S Mt 3:2
14:21 [k]ver 13

i 5 Some manuscripts donkey

---

other two are Jn 5:10; 9:14. Concerning the vigil of the Pharisees see note on 13:14. Sabbath meals were prepared the day before.

14:2 *dropsy.* An accumulation of fluid that would indicate illness affecting other parts of the body. The Greek for this word is a medical term found only here in the NT (see Introduction: Author).

14:3 *experts in the law.* See notes on 5:17; 7:30. By questioning them before the miracle, Jesus made it difficult for them to protest afterward.

14:5 *has a son.* See NIV text note. The reading "donkey" matches well with the "ox that falls into a well." But in Dt 5:14 the law is specified for both humans and animals; one category opens with "son" and another with "ox." Jesus' action was "unlawful" only according to rabbinic interpretations, not according to the Mosaic law itself.

14:7 *places of honor.* Maneuvering for better seats may also have caused trouble at the Last Supper (22:24).

14:11 *humbles himself will be exalted.* A basic principle repeated often in the Bible (see 11:43; 18:14; 20:46; 2Ch 7:14–15; Pr 3:34; 25:6- 7; Mt 18:4; 23:12; Jas 4:10; 1Pe 5:6).

14:14 *resurrection of the righteous.* All will be resurrected (Da 12:2; Jn 5:28–29; Ac 24:15). Some hold that the

resurrection of the righteous (1Co 15:23; 1Th 4:16; Rev 20:4–6) is distinct from the "general" resurrection (1Co 15:12,21; Heb 6:2; Rev 20:11–15). *the righteous.* Those who have been pronounced so by God on the basis of Christ's atonement and who have evidenced their faith by their actions (cf. Mt 25:34–40).

14:15 *feast in the kingdom.* The great Messianic banquet to come. Association of the future kingdom with a feast was common (13:29; Isa 25:6; Mt 8:11; 25:1–10; 26:29; Rev 19:9).

14:16 *Jesus replied.* Jesus used the man's remark as the occasion for a parable warning that not everyone would enter the kingdom.

14:18 *bought a field.* The initial invitation must have been accepted, but when the final invitation came (by Jewish custom the announcement that came when the feast was ready), other interests took priority. None of the "reasons" given was genuine. For example, one did not buy a field without first seeing it, nor oxen without first trying them out (v. 19).

14:24 *those men who were invited.* Without explicitly mentioning them, Jesus warned the Jews that refusal to accept God's invitation would result in their rejection and the inclusion of Gentiles instead (see 20:9–19).

who were invited will get a taste of my banquet.' " *l*

The Cost of Being a Disciple

25Large crowds were traveling with Jesus, and turning to them he said: 26"If anyone comes to me and does not hate his father and mother, his wife and children, his brothers and sisters—yes, even his own life—he cannot be my disciple. *m* 27And anyone who does not carry his cross and follow me cannot be my disciple. *n*

28"Suppose one of you wants to build a tower. Will he not first sit down and estimate the cost to see if he has enough money to complete it? 29For if he lays the foundation and is not able to finish it, everyone who sees it will ridicule him, 30saying, 'This fellow began to build and was not able to finish.'

31"Or suppose a king is about to go to war against another king. Will he not first sit down and consider whether he is able with ten thousand men to oppose the one coming against him with twenty thousand? 32If he is not able, he will send a delegation while the other is still a long way off and will ask for terms of peace. 33In the same way, any of you who does not give up everything he has cannot be my disciple. *o*

34"Salt is good, but if it loses its saltiness, how can it be made salty again? *p* 35It is fit neither for the soil nor for the manure pile; it is thrown out. *q*

"He who has ears to hear, let him hear." *r*

The Parable of the Lost Sheep

15:4–7pp — Mt 18:12–14

15 Now the tax collectors *s* and "sinners" were all gathering around to

hear him. 2But the Pharisees and the teachers of the law muttered, "This man welcomes sinners and eats with them." *t*

3Then Jesus told them this parable: *u* 4"Suppose one of you has a hundred sheep and loses one of them. Does he not leave the ninety-nine in the open country and go after the lost sheep until he finds it? *v* 5And when he finds it, he joyfully puts it on his shoulders 6and goes home. Then he calls his friends and neighbors together and says, 'Rejoice with me; I have found my lost sheep.' *w* 7I tell you that in the same way there will be more rejoicing in heaven over one sinner who repents than over ninety-nine righteous persons who do not need to repent. *x*

The Parable of the Lost Coin

8"Or suppose a woman has ten silver coins *j* and loses one. Does she not light a lamp, sweep the house and search carefully until she finds it? 9And when she finds it, she calls her friends and neighbors together and says, 'Rejoice with me; I have found my lost coin.' *y* 10In the same way, I tell you, there is rejoicing in the presence of the angels of God over one sinner who repents." *z*

The Parable of the Lost Son

11Jesus continued: "There was a man who had two sons. *a* 12The younger one said to his father, 'Father, give me my share of the estate.' *b* So he divided his property *c* between them.

13"Not long after that, the younger son got together all he had, set off for a distant country and there squandered his wealth *d* in wild living. 14After he had spent every-

Cross references (center column)

14:24 *l* Mt 21:43; Ac 13:46
14:26 *m* Mt 10:37; S Jn 12:25
14:27 *n* Mt 10:38; Lk 9:23
14:33 *o* Php 3:7,8
14:34 *p* Mk 9:50
14:35 *q* Mt 5:13
r S Mt 11:15
15:1 *s* Lk 5:29

15:2 *t* S Mt 9:11
15:3 *u* Mt 13:3
15:4 *v* Ps 23; 119:176; Jer 31:10; Eze 34:11–16; Lk 5:32; 19:10
15:6 *w* ver 9
15:7 *x* ver 10
15:9 *y* ver 6
15:10 *z* ver 7
15:11 *a* Mt 21:28
15:12 *b* Dt 21:17 *c* ver 30
15:13 *d* ver 30; Lk 16:1

j 8 Greek ten drachmas, each worth about a day's wages

14:26 *hate his father.* A vivid hyperbole, meaning that one must love Jesus even more than his immediate family (see Mal 1:2–3 for another use of the figure). See Mt 10:37.
14:27 *carry his cross.* See 9:23; Mt 10:38 and notes.
14:28 *estimate the cost.* Jesus did not want a blind, naive commitment that expected only blessings. As a builder estimates costs or a king evaluates military strength (v. 31), so a person must consider what Jesus expects of his followers.
14:33 *give up everything he has.* The cost, Jesus warned, is complete surrender to him.
14:34 *Salt is good.* See note on Mk 9:50.
15:1 *tax collectors and "sinners."* See notes on 3:12; Mk 2:15.
15:2 *muttered.* Complained among themselves, but not openly. *eats with them.* More than simple association, eating with a person indicated acceptance and recognition (cf. Ac 11:3; 1 Co 5:11; Gal 2:12).
15:3 *this parable.* Jesus responded with a story that contrasted the love of God with the exclusiveness of the Pharisees.
15:4 *the lost sheep.* The shepherd theme was familiar from

Ps 23; Isa 40:11; Eze 34:11–16.
15:7 *rejoicing in heaven.* God's concern and joy at the sinner's repentance are set in stark contrast to the attitude of the Pharisees and the teachers of the law (v. 2). *righteous . . . do not need to repent.* Probably irony: those who think they are righteous (such as the Pharisees and the teachers of the law) and feel no need to repent.
15:8 *ten silver coins.* See NIV text note. A *drachma* was a Greek coin approximately equivalent to the Roman denarius, worth about an average day's wages (Mt 20:2). *search carefully.* Near Eastern houses frequently had no windows and only earthen floors, making the search for a single coin difficult.
15:12 *share of the estate.* The father might divide the inheritance (double to the older son; see Dt 21:17 and note on Lk 12:13) but retain the income from it until his death. But to give a younger son his portion of the inheritance upon request was highly unusual.
15:13 *got together all he had.* The son's motive becomes apparent when he departs, taking with him all his possessions and leaving nothing behind to come back to. He wants

thing, there was a severe famine in that whole country, and he began to be in need. [15]So he went and hired himself out to a citizen of that country, who sent him to his fields to feed pigs. [e] [16]He longed to fill his stomach with the pods that the pigs were eating, but no one gave him anything.

[17]"When he came to his senses, he said, 'How many of my father's hired men have food to spare, and here I am starving to death! [18]I will set out and go back to my father and say to him: Father, I have sinned[f] against heaven and against you. [19]I am no longer worthy to be called your son; make me like one of your hired men.' [20]So he got up and went to his father.

"But while he was still a long way off, his father saw him and was filled with compassion for him; he ran to his son, threw his arms around him and kissed him.[g]

[21]"The son said to him, 'Father, I have sinned against heaven and against you.[h] I am no longer worthy to be called your son.[k]'

[22]"But the father said to his servants,

'Quick! Bring the best robe[i] and put it on him. Put a ring on his finger[j] and sandals on his feet. [23]Bring the fattened calf and kill it. Let's have a feast and celebrate. [24]For this son of mine was dead and is alive again;[k] he was lost and is found.' So they began to celebrate.[l]

[25]"Meanwhile, the older son was in the field. When he came near the house, he heard music and dancing. [26]So he called one of the servants and asked him what was going on. [27]'Your brother has come,' he replied, 'and your father has killed the fattened calf because he has him back safe and sound.'

[28]"The older brother became angry[m] and refused to go in. So his father went out and pleaded with him. [29]But he answered his father, 'Look! All these years I've been slaving for you and never disobeyed your orders. Yet you never gave me even a young goat so I could celebrate with my friends. [30]But when this son of yours who has squandered your property[n] with pros-

Cross references (center column)

15:15 [e]Lev 11:7
15:18 [f]Lev 26:40; Mt 3:2
15:20 [g]Ge 45:14, 15; 46:29; Ac 20:37
15:21 [h]Ps 51:4
15:22 [i]Zec 3:4; Rev 6:11 [j]Ge 41:42
15:24 [k]Eph 2:1, 5; 5:14; 1Ti 5:6 [l]ver 32
15:28 [m]Jnh 4:1
15:30 [n]ver 12,13

[k]21 Some early manuscripts *son. Make me like one of your hired men.*

---

to be free of parental restraint and to spend his share of the family wealth as he pleases. *wild living.* More specific in v. 30, though the older brother may have exaggerated because of his bitter attitude.

15:15 *to feed pigs.* The ultimate indignity for a Jew; not only was the work distasteful but pigs were "unclean" animals (Lev 11:7).

15:16 *pods.* Seeds of the carob tree.

15:22-23 *best robe . . . ring . . . sandals . . . feast.* Each was a sign of position and acceptance (cf. Ge 41:42; Zec 3:4): a long robe of distinction, a signet ring of authority,

sandals like a son (slaves went barefoot), and the fattened calf for a special occasion.

15:28 *The older brother.* The forgiving love of the father symbolizes the divine mercy of God, and the older brother's resentment is like the attitude of the Pharisees and teachers of the law who opposed Jesus.

15:29 *even a young goat.* Cheaper food than a fattened calf.

15:30 *this son of yours.* The older brother would not even recognize him as his brother, so bitter was his hatred.

Parables of Jesus

	MATTHEW	MARK	LUKE
Lamp under a bowl	5:14-15	4:21-22	8:16; 11:33
Wise and foolish builders	7:24-27		6:47-49
New cloth on an old coat	9:16	2:21	5:36
New wine in old wineskins	9:17	2:22	5:37-38
Sower and the soils	13:3-8,18-23	4:3-8,14-20	8:5-8,11-15
Weeds	13:24-30, 36-43		
Mustard seed	13:31-32	4:30-32	13:18-19
Yeast	13:33		13:20-21
Hidden treasure	13:44		
Valuable pearl	13:45-46		
Net	13:47-50		
Owner of a house	13:52		
Lost sheep	18:12-14		15:4-7
Unmerciful servant	18:23-34		
Workers in the vineyard	20:1-16		
Two sons	21:28-32		
Tenants	21:33-44	12:1-11	20:9-18
Wedding banquet	22:2-14		
Fig tree	24:32-35	13:28-29	21:29-31

titutes[o] comes home, you kill the fattened calf for him!'

³¹" 'My son,' the father said, 'you are always with me, and everything I have is yours. ³²But we had to celebrate and be glad, because this brother of yours was dead and is alive again; he was lost and is found.' "[p]

The Parable of the Shrewd Manager

16 Jesus told his disciples: "There was a rich man whose manager was accused of wasting his possessions.[q] ²So he called him in and asked him, 'What is this I hear about you? Give an account of your management, because you cannot be manager any longer.'

³"The manager said to himself, 'What shall I do now? My master is taking away my job. I'm not strong enough to dig, and I'm ashamed to beg— ⁴I know what I'll do

15:30 [o]Pr 29:3
15:32 [p]ver 24; Mal 3:17
16:1 [q]Lk 15:13, 30

so that, when I lose my job here, people will welcome me into their houses.'

⁵"So he called in each one of his master's debtors. He asked the first, 'How much do you owe my master?'

⁶" 'Eight hundred gallons[l] of olive oil,' he replied.

"The manager told him, 'Take your bill, sit down quickly, and make it four hundred.'

⁷"Then he asked the second, 'And how much do you owe?'

" 'A thousand bushels[m] of wheat,' he replied.

"He told him, 'Take your bill and make it eight hundred.'

⁸"The master commended the dishonest manager because he had acted shrewdly.

[l]6 Greek *one hundred batous* (probably about 3 kiloliters)
[m]7 Greek *one hundred korous* (probably about 35 kiloliters)

15:31 *everything I have is yours.* The father's love included both brothers. The parable might better be called the parable of "The Father's Love" rather than "The Prodigal Son." It shows a contrast between the self-centered exclusiveness of the Pharisees, who failed to understand God's love, and the concern and joy of God at the repentance of sinners.
15:32 *dead and is alive.* A beautiful picture of the return of the younger son, which also pictures Christian conversion (see Ro 6:13; Eph 2:1,5). The words "lost and is found" are often used to mean "perished and saved" (19:10; Mt 10:6; 18:10–14).
16:1 *disciples.* Perhaps more than just the Twelve (see 6:13; 10:1). *manager.* A steward who handled all the business affairs of the owner. *wasting.* He had squandered his master's possessions, just as the prodigal ("wasteful") son (15:13).
16:3 *What shall I do now?* The dishonest manager (v. 8) had no scruples against using his position for his own benefit,

even if it meant cheating his master. Knowing he would lose his job, the manager planned for his future by discounting the debts owed to his master in order to obligate the debtors to himself. Interpreters disagree as to whether his procedure of discounting was in itself dishonest. Was he giving away what really belonged to his master, or was he forgoing interest payments his master did not have a right to charge? Originally the manager may have overcharged the debtors, a common way of circumventing the Mosaic law that prohibited taking interest from fellow Jews (Dt 23:19). So, to reduce the debts, he may have returned the figures to their initial amounts, which would both satisfy his master and gain the good favor of the debtors. In any event, the point remains the same: He was shrewd enough to use the means at his disposal to plan for his future well-being.
16:6 *Eight hundred gallons of olive oil.* The yield of about 450 olive trees.
16:7 *thousand bushels of wheat.* The approximate yield of

	MATTHEW	MARK	LUKE
Faithful and wise servant	24:45-51		12:42-48
Ten virgins	25:1-13		
Talents (minas)	25:14-30		19:12-27
Sheep and goats	25:31-46		
Growing seed		4:26-29	
Watchful servants		13:35-37	12:35-40
Moneylender			7:41-43
Good Samaritan			10:30-37
Friend in need			11:5-8
Rich fool			12:16-21
Unfruitful fig tree			13:6-9
Lowest seat at the feast			14:7-14
Great banquet			14:16-24
Cost of discipleship			14:28-33
Lost coin			15:8-10
Lost (prodigal) son			15:11-32
Shrewd manager			16:1-8
Rich man and Lazarus			16:19-31
Master and his servant			17:7-10
Persistent widow			18:2-8
Pharisee and tax collector			18:10-14

For the people of this world[r] are more shrewd[s] in dealing with their own kind than are the people of the light.[t] [9]I tell you, use worldly wealth[u] to gain friends for yourselves, so that when it is gone, you will be welcomed into eternal dwellings.[v]

[10]"Whoever can be trusted with very little can also be trusted with much,[w] and whoever is dishonest with very little will also be dishonest with much. [11]So if you have not been trustworthy in handling worldly wealth,[x] who will trust you with true riches? [12]And if you have not been trustworthy with someone else's property, who will give you property of your own?

[13]"No servant can serve two masters. Either he will hate the one and love the other, or he will be devoted to the one and despise the other. You cannot serve both God and Money."[y]

[14]The Pharisees, who loved money,[z] heard all this and were sneering at Jesus.[a] [15]He said to them, "You are the ones who justify yourselves[b] in the eyes of men, but God knows your hearts.[c] What is highly valued among men is detestable in God's sight.

Additional Teachings

[16]"The Law and the Prophets were proclaimed until John.[d] Since that time, the good news of the kingdom of God is being preached,[e] and everyone is forcing his way into it. [17]It is easier for heaven and

earth to disappear than for the least stroke of a pen to drop out of the Law.[f]

[18]"Anyone who divorces his wife and marries another woman commits adultery, and the man who marries a divorced woman commits adultery.[g]

The Rich Man and Lazarus

[19]"There was a rich man who was dressed in purple and fine linen and lived in luxury every day.[h] [20]At his gate was laid a beggar[i] named Lazarus, covered with sores [21]and longing to eat what fell from the rich man's table.[j] Even the dogs came and licked his sores.

[22]"The time came when the beggar died and the angels carried him to Abraham's side. The rich man also died and was buried. [23]In hell,[n] where he was in torment, he looked up and saw Abraham far away, with Lazarus by his side. [24]So he called to him, 'Father Abraham,[k] have pity on me and send Lazarus to dip the tip of his finger in water and cool my tongue, because I am in agony in this fire.'[l]

[25]"But Abraham replied, 'Son, remember that in your lifetime you received your good things, while Lazarus received bad things,[m] but now he is comforted here and you are in agony.[n] [26]And besides all this, between us and you a great chasm has been fixed, so that those who want to go

Cross references (center column)

16:8 [r]Ps 17:14
[s]Ps 18:26
[t]Jn 12:36;
Eph 5:8; 1Th 5:5
16:9 [u]ver 11,13
[v]Mt 19:21;
Lk 12:33
16:10 [w]Mt 25:21,23;
Lk 19:17
16:11 [x]ver 9,13
16:13 [y]ver 9,11;
Mt 6:24
16:14 [z]S 1Ti 3:3
[a]Lk 23:35
16:15 [b]Lk 10:29
[c]S Rev 2:23
16:16 [d]Mt 5:17;
11:12,13
[e]S Mt 4:23

16:17 [f]S Mt 5:18
16:18 [g]Mt 5:31,
32; 19:9;
Mk 10:11;
Ro 7:2,3;
1Co 7:10,11
16:19 [h]Eze 16:49
16:20 [i]Ac 3:2
16:21 [j]Mt 15:27;
Lk 15:16
16:24 [k]ver 30;
S Lk 3:8
[l]S Mt 5:22
16:25 [m]Ps 17:14
[n]Lk 6:21,24,25

[n]23 Greek *Hades*

---

about 100 acres.

16:8 *people of the light.* God's people (Jn 12:36; Eph 5:8; 1Th 5:5).

16:9 *use worldly wealth.* God's people should be alert to make use of what God has given them. *to gain friends.* By helping those in need, who in the future will show their gratitude when they welcome their benefactors into heaven ("eternal dwellings"). In this way worldly wealth may be wisely used to gain eternal benefit.

16:10 *trusted with much.* Cf. 19:17; Mt 25:21. Faithfulness is not determined by the amount entrusted but by the character of the person who uses it.

16:11 *true riches.* The things of highest value, ultimately those of the spirit, the eternal.

16:13 *two masters.* See Mt 6:24; cf. Jas 4:4.

16:16 *until John.* The ministry of John the Baptist, which prepared the way for Jesus the Messiah, was the dividing line between the old covenant and the new (see notes on Jer 31:31–34; Heb 8:6–12). *forcing his way.* The meaning is disputed, but it probably speaks of the fierce earnestness with which people were responding to the gospel of the kingdom. Multitudes were coming to hear Jesus and to receive his message (see Mt 11:12).

16:17 The ministry of Jesus (introducing the new covenant era) was a fulfillment of the law (defining the old covenant era) in the most minute detail (cf. 21:33). *least stroke of a pen.* See notes on Mt 5:17–18.

16:18 *divorces his wife.* See Mt 5:31–32; 19:9; Mk 10:11–12; 1Co 7:10–11. Jesus affirms the continuing au-

thority of the law: For example, adultery was still adultery, still unlawful and still sinful. Matthew's treatment is fuller in that (1) it shows that the law was given because of man's hardened heart in regard to divorce, and (2) it includes one exception as permissible grounds for divorce—marital unfaithfulness (Mt 19:9).

16:19 *a rich man.* Sometimes given the name Dives (from the Latin for "rich man"). *purple and fine linen.* Characteristic of costly garments.

16:20 *Lazarus.* Not the Lazarus Jesus raised from the dead (Jn 11:43–44). If this is a parable, it is the only one in which Jesus gave a name to one of the characters. *covered with sores.* The Greek for this phrase is a common medical term found only here in the NT (see Introduction: Author).

16:22 *Abraham's side.* The Talmud mentions both paradise (see 23:43) and Abraham's side (traditionally "bosom") as the home of the righteous. Abraham's side refers to the place of blessedness to which the righteous dead go to await future vindication. Its bliss is the quality of blessedness reserved for people like Abraham.

16:23 *hell.* See NIV text note. Hades is the place to which the wicked dead go to await the final judgment. That torment begins in Hades is evident from the plight of the rich man. The location of Abraham's side is not specified, but it is separated from Hades by an impassable chasm. Hades includes the torment that characterizes hell (fire, Rev 20:10; agony, Rev 14:11; separation, Mt 8:12). Some understand Jesus' description of Abraham's side and Hades in a less literal way.

from here to you cannot, nor can anyone cross over from there to us.'

27"He answered, 'Then I beg you, father, send Lazarus to my father's house, 28for I have five brothers. Let him warn them,*o* so that they will not also come to this place of torment.'

29"Abraham replied, 'They have Moses*p* and the Prophets;*q* let them listen to them.'

30" 'No, father Abraham,'*r* he said, 'but if someone from the dead goes to them, they will repent.'

31"He said to him, 'If they do not listen to Moses and the Prophets, they will not be convinced even if someone rises from the dead.' "

Sin, Faith, Duty

17 Jesus said to his disciples: "Things that cause people to sin*s* are bound to come, but woe to that person through whom they come.*t* 2It would be better for him to be thrown into the sea with a millstone tied around his neck than for him to cause one of these little ones*u* to sin.*v* 3So watch yourselves.

"If your brother sins, rebuke him,*w* and if he repents, forgive him.*x* 4If he sins against you seven times in a day, and seven times comes back to you and says, 'I repent,' forgive him."*y*

5The apostles*z* said to the Lord,*a* "Increase our faith!"

6He replied, "If you have faith as small as a mustard seed,*b* you can say to this mulberry tree, 'Be uprooted and planted in the sea,' and it will obey you.*c*

7"Suppose one of you had a servant plowing or looking after the sheep. Would he say to the servant when he comes in from the field, 'Come along now and sit down to eat'? 8Would he not rather say, 'Prepare my supper, get yourself ready and wait on me*d* while I eat and drink; after that you may eat and drink'? 9Would he thank the servant because he did what he was told to do? 10So you also, when you have done everything you were told to do, should say, 'We are unworthy servants; we have only done our duty.' "*e*

Ten Healed of Leprosy

11Now on his way to Jerusalem,*f* Jesus traveled along the border between Samaria and Galilee.*g* 12As he was going into a village, ten men who had leprosy*o h* met him. They stood at a distance*i* 13and called out in a loud voice, "Jesus, Master,*j* have pity on us!"

14When he saw them, he said, "Go, show yourselves to the priests."*k* And as they went, they were cleansed.

15One of them, when he saw he was healed, came back, praising God*l* in a loud voice. 16He threw himself at Jesus' feet and thanked him—and he was a Samaritan.*m*

17Jesus asked, "Were not all ten cleansed? Where are the other nine? 18Was no one found to return and give praise to God except this foreigner?" 19Then he said to him, "Rise and go; your faith has made you well."*n*

The Coming of the Kingdom of God

17:26,27pp — Mt 24:37-39

20Once, having been asked by the Pharisees when the kingdom of God would come,*o* Jesus replied, "The kingdom of God does not come with your careful observation, 21nor will people say, 'Here it is,'

Cross references (center column)

16:28 *o*Ac 2:40; 20:23; 1Th 4:6
16:29 *p*S Lk 24:27,44; Jn 1:45; 5:45-47; Ac 15:21
*q*Lk 4:17; 24:27,44; Jn 1:45
16:30 *r*ver 24; S Lk 3:8
17:1 *s*S Mt 5:29
*t*Mt 18:7
17:2 *u*Mk 10:24; Lk 10:21
*v*S Mt 5:29
17:3 *w*S Mt 18:15
*x*Eph 4:32; Col 3:13
17:4 *y*Mt 18:21,22
17:5 *z*S Mk 6:30
*a*S Lk 7:13
17:6 *b*Mt 13:31; 17:20; Lk 13:19
*c*S Mt 21:21; Mk 9:23

17:8 *d*Lk 12:37
17:10 *e*1Co 9:16
17:11 *f*S Lk 9:51
*g*Lk 9:51,52; Jn 4:3,4
17:12 *h*S Mt 8:2
*i*Lev 13:45,46
17:13 *j*S Lk 5:5
17:14 *k*Lev 14:2; Mt 8:4
17:15 *l*S Mt 9:8
17:16 *m*S Mt 10:5
17:19 *n*S Mt 9:22
17:20 *o*S Mt 3:2

o 12 The Greek word was used for various diseases affecting the skin—not necessarily leprosy.

16:28 *I have five brothers.* For the first time the rich man showed concern for others.

16:29 *Moses and the Prophets.* A way of designating the whole OT. The rich man had failed to pay attention to Scripture and its teaching, and feared his brothers would do the same.

16:30 *someone from the dead.* The story may suggest that Lazarus was intended, but Luke's account seems to imply that Jesus was speaking also of his own resurrection (cf. v. 31; 9:22). If a person's mind is closed and Scripture is rejected, no evidence—not even a resurrection—will change him.

17:2 *millstone.* A heavy stone for grinding grain. *one of these little ones.* Either young in the faith or young in age (cf. 10:21; Mt 18:6; Mk 10:24).

17:3 *your brother.* See Mt 18:15-17; cf. Mt 12:50.

17:4 *seven times.* That is, forgiveness is to be unlimited (cf. Ps 119:164; Mt 18:21-22).

17:5 *Increase our faith!* They felt incapable of measuring up to the standards set forth in vv. 1-4. They wanted greater

faith to lay hold of the power to live up to Jesus' standards.

17:6 See Mt 17:20; Mk 11:23; see also notes on Mt 13:31-32; Mk 4:31.

17:7 *a servant.* A slave, used to illustrate performance of duty (cf. 12:37).

17:11 *border between Samaria and Galilee.* From this point Jesus seems to have journeyed to Perea, where he ministered on his way south to Jerusalem (see notes on 9:51; 13:22).

17:14 *show yourselves to the priests.* Normal procedure after a cure (see Lev 13:2-3; 14:2-32).

17:16 *Samaritan.* See note on 10:31-33. Normally Jews did not associate with Samaritans (Jn 4:9), but leprosy broke down social barriers while erecting others (see notes on Lev 13:2,4,45-46).

17:19 *your faith has made you well.* See Mt 9:22. The phrase may also be rendered "your faith has saved you" (7:50). The fact that the Samaritan returned to thank Jesus may indicate that he had received salvation in addition to the physical healing all ten had received (cf. 7:50; 8:48,50).

or 'There it is,'[p] because the kingdom of
God is within[p] you."
[22]Then he said to his disciples, "The
time is coming when you will long to see
one of the days of the Son of Man,[q] but
you will not see it.[r] [23]Men will tell you,
'There he is!' or 'Here he is!' Do not go
running off after them.[s] [24]For the Son of
Man in his day[q] will be like the lightning,[t] which flashes and lights up the sky
from one end to the other. [25]But first he
must suffer many things[u] and be rejected[v]
by this generation.[w]
[26]"Just as it was in the days of Noah,[x]
so also will it be in the days of the Son of
Man. [27]People were eating, drinking, marrying and being given in marriage up to the
day Noah entered the ark. Then the flood
came and destroyed them all.
[28]"It was the same in the days of Lot.[y]
People were eating and drinking, buying
and selling, planting and building. [29]But
the day Lot left Sodom, fire and sulfur
rained down from heaven and destroyed
them all.
[30]"It will be just like this on the day the
Son of Man is revealed.[z] [31]On that day no
one who is on the roof of his house, with
his goods inside, should go down to get
them. Likewise, no one in the field should
go back for anything.[a] [32]Remember Lot's
wife![b] [33]Whoever tries to keep his life will
lose it, and whoever loses his life will preserve it.[c] [34]I tell you, on that night two
people will be in one bed; one will be tak-
en and the other left. [35]Two women will
be grinding grain together; one will be tak-
en and the other left.[r]"[d]
[37]"Where, Lord?" they asked.
He replied, "Where there is a dead
body, there the vultures will gather."[e]

The Parable of the Persistent Widow

18 Then Jesus told his disciples a parable to show them that they should
always pray and not give up.[f] [2]He said:
"In a certain town there was a judge who
neither feared God nor cared about men.
[3]And there was a widow in that town who
kept coming to him with the plea, 'Grant
me justice[g] against my adversary.'
[4]"For some time he refused. But finally
he said to himself, 'Even though I don't
fear God or care about men, [5]yet because
this widow keeps bothering me, I will see
that she gets justice, so that she won't
eventually wear me out with her coming!'"[h]
[6]And the Lord[i] said, "Listen to what
the unjust judge says. [7]And will not God
bring about justice for his chosen ones,
who cry out[j] to him day and night? Will
he keep putting them off? [8]I tell you, he

17:21 [p]ver 23 **17:22** [q]S Mt 8:20 [r]S Lk 5:35 **17:23** [s]Mt 24:23; Lk 21:8 **17:24** [t]Mt 24:27 **17:25** [u]S Mt 16:21 [v]Lk 9:22; 18:32 [w]Mk 13:30; Lk 21:32 **17:26** [x]Ge 6:5-8; 7:6-24 **17:28** [y]Ge 19:1-28 **17:30** [z]Mt 10:23; S 16:27; 24:3,27, 37,39; 25:31; S 1Co 1:7; S 1Th 2:19; 2Th 1:7; 2:8; 2Pe 3:4; S Rev 1:7 **17:31** [a]Mt 24:17, 18 **17:32** [b]Ge 19:26 **17:33** [c]S Jn 12:25 **17:35** [d]Mt 24:41 **17:37** [e]Mt 24:28 **18:1** [f]Isa 40:31; Lk 11:5-8; S Ac 1:14; S Ro 1:10; 12:12; Eph 6:18; Col 4:2; 1Th 5:17 **18:3** [g]Isa 1:17 **18:5** [h]Lk 11:8 **18:6** [i]S Lk 7:13 **18:7** [j]Ex 22:23; Ps 88:1; Rev 6:10

[p]*21* Or *among* [q]*24* Some manuscripts do not have *in his day.* [r]*35* Some manuscripts *left.* [36]*Two men will be in the field; one will be taken and the other left.*

17:21 *the kingdom of God is within you.* Probably indicating that the kingdom is spiritual and internal (Mt 23:26), rather than physical and external (cf. Jn 18:36). But see NIV text note (cf. 19:11; 21:7; Ac 1:6), meaning that the kingdom is present in the person of its king, Jesus (see also note on 4:43). However, the immediate context (v. 20) may favor the former interpretation, namely, that the kingdom is spiritual and so not visible. If this is the correct view, the pronoun "you" in the phrase "within you" is to be taken in a general sense rather than as referring to the unbelieving Pharisees personally. The kingdom certainly was not within them.
17:22 *long to see.* In time of trouble, believers will desire to experience the day when Jesus returns in his glory and delivers his people from their distress.
17:23 *Do not go running off after them.* Do not leave your work in order to pursue predictions of Christ's second advent.
17:24 *like the lightning.* His coming will be sudden, unexpected and public (cf. 12:40).
17:25 *he must suffer.* Jesus repeatedly foretold his coming death (5:35; 9:22,43–45; 12:50; 13:32–33; 18:32; 24:7; see Mt 16:21), which had to occur before his glorious return.
17:28 *in the days of Lot.* See Ge 18:16–19:28.
17:30 *Son of Man is revealed.* At Jesus' second coming he will be plainly visible to all (1Co 1:7; 2Th 1:7; 1Pe 1:7,13; 4:13).
17:31 *on the roof of his house.* It was customary to relax on the flat rooftop. When the final hour comes, however, the individual there should not be thinking of going into the house to retrieve some material objects. Matthew and Mark refer similarly to flight at the fall of Jerusalem, and indirectly to the end time (Mt 24:17–18; Mk 13:15), but here the reference is explicitly to Jesus' return (see v. 30; cf. 21:21).
17:33 *whoever loses his life will preserve it.* See note on 9:24 (cf. Mt 10:39).
17:35 *taken.* Could refer to being "taken to/from destruction" or "taken into the kingdom." What is clear is that no matter how close two people may be in life, they have no guarantee of the same eternal destiny. One may go to judgment and condemnation, the other to salvation, reward and blessing.
17:37 *Where . . . there the vultures will gather.* A proverb. See note on Mt 24:28. In response to the disciples' question, Jesus explains that these things will take place wherever there are people to whom the event pertains.
18:2 *nor cared about men.* Unconcerned about the needs of others or about their opinion of him.
18:3 *a widow.* Particularly helpless and vulnerable because she had no family to uphold her cause. Only justice and her own persistence were in her favor.
18:7 *will not God bring about justice . . . ?* If an unworthy judge who feels no constraint of right or wrong is compelled by persistence to deal justly with a helpless individual, how much more will God answer prayer! *keep putting them off.* God will not delay his support of the chosen ones when they are right. He is not like the unjust judge, who had to be badgered until he wearied and gave in.
18:8 *will he find faith . . . ?* Particularly faith that perseveres in prayer and loyalty (see Mt 24:12–13). Christ makes a second application that looks forward to the time of his second coming. A period of spiritual decline and persecution is assumed—a time that will require perseverance such

will see that they get justice, and quickly. However, when the Son of Man[k] comes,[l] will he find faith on the earth?"

The Parable of the Pharisee and the Tax Collector

[9]To some who were confident of their own righteousness[m] and looked down on everybody else,[n] Jesus told this parable: [10]"Two men went up to the temple to pray,[o] one a Pharisee and the other a tax collector. [11]The Pharisee stood up[p] and prayed about[s] himself: 'God, I thank you that I am not like other men—robbers, evildoers, adulterers—or even like this tax collector. [12]I fast[q] twice a week and give a tenth[r] of all I get.'

[13]"But the tax collector stood at a distance. He would not even look up to heaven, but beat his breast[s] and said, 'God, have mercy on me, a sinner.'[t]

[14]"I tell you that this man, rather than the other, went home justified before God. For everyone who exalts himself will be humbled, and he who humbles himself will be exalted."[u]

The Little Children and Jesus

18:15–17pp — Mt 19:13–15; Mk 10:13–16

[15]People were also bringing babies to Jesus to have him touch them. When the disciples saw this, they rebuked them. [16]But Jesus called the children to him and said, "Let the little children come to me, and do not hinder them, for the kingdom of God belongs to such as these. [17]I tell you the truth, anyone who will not receive the kingdom of God like a little child[v] will never enter it."

The Rich Ruler

18:18–30pp — Mt 19:16–29; Mk 10:17–30

[18]A certain ruler asked him, "Good teacher, what must I do to inherit eternal life?"[w]

[19]"Why do you call me good?" Jesus answered. "No one is good—except God alone. [20]You know the commandments: 'Do not commit adultery, do not murder, do not steal, do not give false testimony, honor your father and mother.'[t] "[x]

[21]"All these I have kept since I was a boy," he said.

[22]When Jesus heard this, he said to him, "You still lack one thing. Sell everything you have and give to the poor,[y] and you will have treasure in heaven.[z] Then come, follow me."

[23]When he heard this, he became very sad, because he was a man of great wealth. [24]Jesus looked at him and said, "How hard it is for the rich to enter the kingdom of God![a] [25]Indeed, it is easier for a camel to go through the eye of a needle than for a rich man to enter the kingdom of God."

[26]Those who heard this asked, "Who then can be saved?"

[27]Jesus replied, "What is impossible with men is possible with God."[b]

[28]Peter said to him, "We have left all we had to follow you!"[c]

[29]"I tell you the truth," Jesus said to them, "no one who has left home or wife or brothers or parents or children for the sake of the kingdom of God [30]will fail to receive many times as much in this age and, in the age to come,[d] eternal life."[e]

Jesus Again Predicts His Death

18:31–33pp — Mt 20:17–19; Mk 10:32–34

[31]Jesus took the Twelve aside and told them, "We are going up to Jerusalem,[f] and everything that is written by the prophets[g] about the Son of Man[h] will be fulfilled. [32]He will be handed over to the Gentiles.[i] They will mock him, insult him,

---

18:8 [k]S Mt 8:20 [l]S Mt 16:27
18:9 [m]Lk 16:15 [n]Isa 65:5
18:10 [o]Ac 3:1
18:11 [p]Mt 6:5; Mk 11:25
18:12 [q]Isa 58:3; Mt 9:14 [r]Mal 3:8; Lk 11:42
18:13 [s]Isa 66:2; Jer 31:19; Lk 23:48 [t]Lk 5:32; 1Ti 1:15
18:14 [u]S Mt 23:12
18:17 [v]Mt 11:25; 18:3
18:18 [w]Lk 10:25
18:20 [x]Ex 20:12-16; Dt 5:16-20; Ro 13:9
18:22 [y]S Ac 2:45 [z]S Mt 6:20
18:24 [a]Pr 11:28
18:27 [b]S Mt 19:26
18:28 [c]S Mt 4:19
18:30 [d]S Mt 12:32 [e]S Mt 25:46
18:31 [f]S Lk 9:51 [g]Ps 22; Isa 53 [h]S Mt 8:20
18:32 [i]Lk 23:1

[s]*11* Or *to*   [t]*20* Exodus 20:12-16; Deut. 5:16-20

18:10 *to pray.* Periods for prayer were scheduled daily in connection with the morning and evening sacrifices. People could also go to the temple at any time for private prayer.
18:12 *fast twice a week.* Fasting was not commanded in the Mosaic law except for the fast on the Day of Atonement. However, the Pharisees also fasted on Mondays and Thursdays (see 5:33; Mt 6:16; 9:14; Mk 2:18; Ac 27:9). *a tenth of all I get.* As a typical first-century Pharisee, he tithed all that he acquired, not merely what he earned.
18:13 *have mercy on me.* The verb used here means "to be propitiated" (see note on 1Jn 2:2). The tax collector does not plead his good works but the mercy of God in forgiving his sin.
18:14 *justified before God.* God reckoned him to be righteous, i.e., his sins were forgiven and he was credited with righteousness—not his own (v. 9) but that which comes

from God.
18:17 *like a little child.* With total dependence, full trust, frank openness and complete sincerity (see Mt 18:3; 19:14; Mk 10:15; cf. 1Pe 2:2). See note on Mk 10:15.
18:18–27 For this event see notes on Mk 10:17–27.
18:18 *eternal life.* See note on Mt 19:16.
18:30 *this age . . . the age to come.* The present age of sin and misery and the future age to be inaugurated by the return of the Messiah.
18:31 *everything that is written by the prophets.* Sometimes referred to as the third prediction of Jesus' death, though the total number is more than three (see note on 17:25). The first distinct prediction is in 9:22 and the second in 9:43–45. The Messiah's death had been predicted and/or prefigured centuries before (e.g., Ps 22; Isa 53; Zec 13:7; see Lk 24:27; Mt 26:24,31,54). *Son of Man.* See note on Mk 8:31.

spit on him, flog him[j] and kill him.[k] 33On
the third day[l] he will rise again."[m]
34The disciples did not understand any
of this. Its meaning was hidden from them,
and they did not know what he was talking about.[n]

A Blind Beggar Receives His Sight

18:35–43pp — Mt 20:29–34; Mk 10:46–52

35As Jesus approached Jericho,[o] a blind
man was sitting by the roadside begging.
36When he heard the crowd going by, he
asked what was happening. 37They told
him, "Jesus of Nazareth is passing by."[p]
38He called out, "Jesus, Son of David,[q]
have mercy[r] on me!"
39Those who led the way rebuked him
and told him to be quiet, but he shouted all
the more, "Son of David, have mercy on
me!"[s]
40Jesus stopped and ordered the man to
be brought to him. When he came near,
Jesus asked him, 41"What do you want me
to do for you?"
"Lord, I want to see," he replied.
42Jesus said to him, "Receive your sight;
your faith has healed you."[t] 43Immedi-
ately he received his sight and followed
Jesus, praising God. When all the people
saw it, they also praised God.[u]

Zacchaeus the Tax Collector

19 Jesus entered Jericho[v] and was
passing through. 2A man was there
by the name of Zacchaeus; he was a chief
tax collector and was wealthy. 3He wanted
to see who Jesus was, but being a short
man he could not, because of the crowd.
4So he ran ahead and climbed a sycamore-
fig[w] tree to see him, since Jesus was coming that way.[x]
5When Jesus reached the spot, he
looked up and said to him, "Zacchaeus,
come down immediately. I must stay at
your house today." 6So he came down at
once and welcomed him gladly.
7All the people saw this and began to
mutter, "He has gone to be the guest of a
'sinner.' "[y]
8But Zacchaeus stood up and said to the
Lord,[z] "Look, Lord! Here and now I give
half of my possessions to the poor, and if I
have cheated anybody out of anything,[a] I
will pay back four times the amount."[b]
9Jesus said to him, "Today salvation has
come to this house, because this man, too,
is a son of Abraham.[c] 10For the Son of
Man came to seek and to save what was
lost."[d]

The Parable of the Ten Minas

19:12–27Ref — Mt 25:14–30

11While they were listening to this, he
went on to tell them a parable, because he
was near Jerusalem and the people thought
that the kingdom of God[e] was going to
appear at once.[f] 12He said: "A man of noble birth went to a distant country to have
himself appointed king and then to return.
13So he called ten of his servants[g] and
gave them ten minas.[u] 'Put this money to
work,' he said, 'until I come back.'

[u] *13* A mina was about three months' wages.

18:32 [j]S Mt 16:21 [k]S Ac 2:23
18:33 [l]S Mt 16:21 [m]S Mt 16:21
18:34 [n]S Mk 9:32
18:35 [o]Lk 19:1
18:37 [p]Lk 19:4
18:38 [q]ver 39; S Mt 9:27 [r]Mt 17:15; Lk 18:13
18:39 [s]ver 38
18:42 [t]S Mt 9:22
18:43 [u]S Mt 9:8; Lk 13:17
19:1 [v]Lk 18:35
19:4 [w]1Ki 10:27; 1Ch 27:28; Isa 9:10 [x]Lk 18:37
19:7 [y]S Mt 9:11
19:8 [z]S Lk 7:13 [a]Lk 3:12,13 [b]Ex 22:1; Lev 6:4,5; Nu 5:7; 2Sa 12:6; Eze 33:14,15
19:9 [c]S Lk 3:8
19:10 [d]Eze 34:12,16; S Jn 3:17
19:11 [e]S Mt 3:2 [f]Lk 17:20; Ac 1:6
19:13 [g]Mk 13:34

18:35 *approached Jericho.* See note on Mk 10:46. *a blind man.* Bartimaeus (Mk 10:46). Matthew reports that two blind men were healed (see note on Mt 8:28). Probably since one was the spokesman and more outstanding, Mark and Luke did not record the presence of the other.

18:38–39 *Son of David.* A Messianic title (see Mt 22:41–45; Mk 12:35; Jn 7:42; see also 2Sa 7:12–13; Ps 89:3–4; Am 9:11; Mt 12:23; 21:15–16).

18:42 *your faith.* See note on 17:19.

19:1 *entered Jericho.* See note on Mk 10:46.

19:2 *chief tax collector.* A position referred to only here in the Bible, probably designating one in charge of a district, with other tax collectors under him. The region was prosperous at this time, so it is no wonder that Zacchaeus had grown rich. See notes on 3:12; Mk 2:14–15.

19:4 *a sycamore-fig tree.* A sturdy tree from 30 to 40 feet high, with a short trunk and spreading branches, capable of holding a grown man. (See note on Am 7:14.)

19:5 *I must stay at your house.* Implies a divine necessity.

19:8 *four times.* Almost the extreme repayment required under the law in case of theft (Ex 22:1; 2Sa 12:6; cf. Pr 6:31).

19:9 *son of Abraham.* A true Jew—not only of the lineage of Abraham but one who also walks "in the footsteps" of Abraham's faith (Ro 4:12). Jesus recognized the tax collector as such, though Jewish society excluded him.

19:10 A key verse in Luke's Gospel. *Son of Man.* A Messianic title (Da 7:13) used only by Jesus in the four Gospels, by Stephen (Ac 7:56) and in John's vision (Rev 1:13). See Introduction: Plan; see also note on Mk 8:31. *to seek and to save.* An important summary of Jesus' purpose—to bring salvation, meaning eternal life (18:18), and the kingdom of God (18:25). See note on 15:32.

19:11 *kingdom . . . was going to appear.* They expected the Messiah to appear in power and glory and to set up his earthly kingdom, defeating all their political and military enemies.

19:12 *to have himself appointed king.* A rather unusual procedure, but the Herods did just that when they went to Rome to be appointed rulers over the Jews. Similarly, Jesus was soon to depart and in the future is to return as King. During his absence, his servants are entrusted with their master's affairs (for a similar parable see Mt 25:14–30).

19:13 *ten minas.* See NIV text note. One talent equaled 60 minas (see Mt 25:15) and a mina equaled 100 drachmas, each drachma being worth about a day's wages (see note on 15:8). Thus the total amount was valued at between two and three years' average wages, and a tenth would be about three months' wages. This was small, however, compared with the amounts mentioned in the parable recorded in Matthew. Here all ten are given the same amount.

14"But his subjects hated him and sent a delegation after him to say, 'We don't want this man to be our king.'

15"He was made king, however, and returned home. Then he sent for the servants to whom he had given the money, in order to find out what they had gained with it.

16"The first one came and said, 'Sir, your mina has earned ten more.'

17"'Well done, my good servant!'ʰ his master replied. 'Because you have been trustworthy in a very small matter, take charge of ten cities.'ⁱ

18"The second came and said, 'Sir, your mina has earned five more.'

19"His master answered, 'You take charge of five cities.'

20"Then another servant came and said, 'Sir, here is your mina; I have kept it laid away in a piece of cloth. 21I was afraid of you, because you are a hard man. You take out what you did not put in and reap what you did not sow.'ʲ

22"His master replied, 'I will judge you by your own words,ᵏ you wicked servant! You knew, did you, that I am a hard man, taking out what I did not put in, and reaping what I did not sow?ˡ 23Why then didn't you put my money on deposit, so that when I came back, I could have collected it with interest?'

24"Then he said to those standing by, 'Take his mina away from him and give it to the one who has ten minas.'

25"'Sir,' they said, 'he already has ten!'

26"He replied, 'I tell you that to everyone who has, more will be given, but as for

19:17 ʰPr 27:18 /Lk 16:10
19:21 /Mt 25:24
19:22 ᵏ2Sa 1:16; Job 15:6 /Mt 25:26
19:26 ᵐS Mt 25:29
19:28 ⁿMk 10:32; S Lk 9:51
19:29 ᵒS Mt 21:17 ᵖS Mt 21:1
19:32 ᵍLk 22:13
19:36 ʳ2Ki 9:13
19:37 ˢS Mt 21:1
19:38 ᵗPs 118:26; Lk 13:35

the one who has nothing, even what he has will be taken away.ᵐ 27But those enemies of mine who did not want me to be king over them—bring them here and kill them in front of me.'"

The Triumphal Entry

19:29–38pp — Mt 21:1–9; Mk 11:1–10
19:35–38pp — Jn 12:12–15

28After Jesus had said this, he went on ahead, going up to Jerusalem.ⁿ 29As he approached Bethphage and Bethanyᵒ at the hill called the Mount of Olives,ᵖ he sent two of his disciples, saying to them, 30"Go to the village ahead of you, and as you enter it, you will find a colt tied there, which no one has ever ridden. Untie it and bring it here. 31If anyone asks you, 'Why are you untying it?' tell him, 'The Lord needs it.'"

32Those who were sent ahead went and found it just as he had told them.ᵍ 33As they were untying the colt, its owners asked them, "Why are you untying the colt?"

34They replied, "The Lord needs it."

35They brought it to Jesus, threw their cloaks on the colt and put Jesus on it. 36As he went along, people spread their cloaksʳ on the road.

37When he came near the place where the road goes down the Mount of Olives,ˢ the whole crowd of disciples began joyfully to praise God in loud voices for all the miracles they had seen:

38"Blessed is the king who comes in the name of the Lord!"ᵛ ᵗ

ᵛ38 Psalm 118:26

19:14 *sent a delegation.* Such an incident had occurred over 30 years earlier in the case of Archelaus (Josephus, *Wars,* 2.6.1; *Antiquities,* 17.9.3), as well as in a number of other instances. This aspect of the story may have been included to warn the Jews against rejecting Jesus as King.
19:22 *You knew ... that I am a hard man ... ?* The master did not admit to the statement of the servant, but repeated it in a question. If this was the opinion of the servant, he should have acted accordingly.
19:26 *more will be given ... what he has will be taken away.* See 8:18; 17:33; Mt 13:12. Those who seek spiritual gain in the gospel, for themselves and others, will become richer, and those who neglect or squander what is given them will become impoverished, losing even what they have.
19:27 *those enemies of mine ... kill them.* Perhaps a reference to Jerusalem's destruction in A.D. 70. The punishment of those who rebelled and actively opposed the king (v. 14) was much more severe than that of the negligent servant.
19:28–44 The Triumphal Entry occurred on Sunday of Passion Week. See charts on "The Life of Christ," p. 1480, and "Passion Week," p. 1524.
19:29 *Bethphage.* A village near the road going from Jericho to Jerusalem. *Bethany.* Another village about two miles

southeast of Jerusalem (Jn 11:18), and the home of Mary, Martha and Lazarus. *Mount of Olives.* A ridge a little more than a mile long, separated from Jerusalem by the Kidron Valley—to the east of the city (see notes on Zec 14:4; Mk 11:1). *two of his disciples.* Not named here or in the parallel passages (Mt 21:1; Mk 11:1; cf. Jn 12:14).

19:30 *village.* Probably Bethphage. *colt.* In other accounts a donkey colt (Jn 12:15) is specified and the mother of the colt (Mt 21:7) with him. Luke uses a Greek word that the Septuagint frequently employed to translate the Hebrew word for "donkey." Jesus chooses to enter Jerusalem this time mounted on a donkey to claim publicly that he was the chosen Son of David to sit on David's throne (1Ki 1:33,44), the one of whom the prophets had spoken (Zec 9:9). *which no one has ever ridden.* One that had not been put to secular use (Nu 19:2; 1Sa 6:7).

19:31 *The Lord.* Either God or, more likely, Jesus himself, here claiming his own unique status as Israel's Lord.

19:37 *all the miracles.* The raising of Lazarus and the healing of blind Bartimaeus were recent examples, but included also would be the works recorded in John on various occasions in Jerusalem, as well as the whole of his ministry in Galilee (cf. Mt 21:14; Jn 12:17).

"Peace in heaven and glory in the highest!" *u*

³⁹Some of the Pharisees in the crowd said to Jesus, "Teacher, rebuke your disciples!" *v*

⁴⁰"I tell you," he replied, "if they keep quiet, the stones will cry out." *w*

⁴¹As he approached Jerusalem and saw the city, he wept over it *x* ⁴²and said, "If you, even you, had only known on this day what would bring you peace—but now it is hidden from your eyes. ⁴³The days will come upon you when your enemies will build an embankment against you and encircle you and hem you in on every side. *y* ⁴⁴They will dash you to the ground, you and the children within your walls. *z* They will not leave one stone on another, *a* because you did not recognize the time of God's coming *b* to you."

Jesus at the Temple

19:45,46pp — Mt 21:12–16; Mk 11:15–18; Jn 2:13–16

⁴⁵Then he entered the temple area and began driving out those who were selling. ⁴⁶"It is written," he said to them, " 'My house will be a house of prayer' *w; c* but you have made it 'a den of robbers.' *x* " *d*

⁴⁷Every day he was teaching at the temple. *e* But the chief priests, the teachers of the law and the leaders among the people were trying to kill him. *f* ⁴⁸Yet they could not find any way to do it, because all the people hung on his words.

Cross references (center column)

19:38 *u* S Lk 2:14
19:39 *v* Mt 21:15, 16
19:40 *w* Hab 2:11
19:41 *x* Isa 22:4; Lk 13:34,35
19:43 *y* Isa 29:3; Jer 6:6; Eze 4:2; 26:8; Lk 21:20
19:44 *z* Ps 137:9
a Lk 21:6
b 1Pe 2:12
19:46 *c* Isa 56:7
d Jer 7:11
19:47 *e* S Mt 26:55
f S Mt 12:14; Mk 11:18

20:1 *g* S Mt 26:55
h Lk 8:1
20:2 *i* Jn 2:18; Ac 4:7; 7:27
20:4 *j* S Mk 1:4
20:6 *k* Lk 7:29
l S Mk 11:9
20:9 *m* Isa 5:1-7
n Mt 25:14

The Authority of Jesus Questioned

20:1–8pp — Mt 21:23–27; Mk 11:27–33

20 One day as he was teaching the people in the temple courts *g* and preaching the gospel, *h* the chief priests and the teachers of the law, together with the elders, came up to him. ²"Tell us by what authority you are doing these things," they said. "Who gave you this authority?" *i*

³He replied, "I will also ask you a question. Tell me, ⁴John's baptism *j*—was it from heaven, or from men?"

⁵They discussed it among themselves and said, "If we say, 'From heaven,' he will ask, 'Why didn't you believe him?' ⁶But if we say, 'From men,' all the people *k* will stone us, because they are persuaded that John was a prophet." *l*

⁷So they answered, "We don't know where it was from."

⁸Jesus said, "Neither will I tell you by what authority I am doing these things."

The Parable of the Tenants

20:9–19pp — Mt 21:33–46; Mk 12:1–12

⁹He went on to tell the people this parable: "A man planted a vineyard, *m* rented it to some farmers and went away for a long time. *n* ¹⁰At harvest time he sent a servant to the tenants so they would give him some of the fruit of the vineyard. But the tenants beat him and sent him away empty-handed. ¹¹He sent another servant, but

w 46 Isaiah 56:7   *x* 46 Jer. 7:11

19:43 *your enemies will build an embankment.* See 21:20; fulfilled when the Romans took Jerusalem in A.D. 70, using an embankment to besiege the city. The description is reminiscent of OT predictions (Isa 29:3; 37:33; Eze 4:1–3).
19:44 *the time of God's coming to you.* God came to the Jews in the person of Jesus the Messiah, but they failed to recognize him and rejected him (see Jn 1:10–11; cf. Lk 20:13–16).
19:45 Mark (11:11–17) makes clear that this cleansing occurred the day after the Triumphal Entry, i.e., on Monday of Passion Week. *the temple area.* The outer court (of the Gentiles), where animals for sacrifice were sold at unfair prices. John records a cleansing of the temple at the beginning of Jesus' ministry (Jn 2:13–25), but the Synoptics (see Mt 21:12–13; Mk 11:15–17) speak only of a cleansing at the close of Jesus' ministry (see notes on Mt 21:12–17; Jn 2:14–17).
19:47 *chief priests.* See 3:2; 22:52; 23:4; 24:20. They were part of the Sanhedrin, the ruling Jewish council (see note on Mk 14:55). *were trying to kill him.* See 20:19–20 (cf. Jn 7:1; 11:53–57).
20:1 The events of 20:1–21:36 all occurred on Tuesday of Passion Week—a long day of controversy. *One day.* Not specified, but Mark's parallel accounts (Mk 11:19–20, 27–33) indicate that this day (Tuesday) followed the cleansing of the temple (Monday), which followed the Triumphal Entry (Sunday). *chief priests.* See 19:47 and note on Mt 2:4.

teachers of the law. See 5:30 and notes on 5:17; Mt 2:4. *elders.* See note on Mt 15:2. Each of these groups was represented in the Jewish council, the Sanhedrin (see 22:66).
20:2 *Who gave you this authority?* They had asked this of John the Baptist (Jn 1:19–25) and of Jesus early in his ministry (Jn 2:18–22). Here the reference is to the cleansing of the temple, which not only defied the authority of the Jewish leaders but also hurt their monetary profits. The leaders may also have been looking for a way to discredit Jesus in the eyes of the people or raise suspicion of him as a threat to the authority of Rome.
20:3 *John's baptism . . . from heaven, or from men?* By replying with a question, Jesus put the burden on his opponents—indicating only two alternatives: The work of John was either God-inspired or man-devised. By refusing to answer, they placed themselves in an awkward position. *from heaven.* See note on Mk 11:30.
20:10 *he sent a servant.* This parable (v. 9) is reminiscent of Isa 5:1–7. The servants who were sent to the tenants represent the prophets God sent in former times who were rejected (see Ne 9:26; Jer 7:25–26; 25:4–7; Mt 23:34; Ac 7:52; Heb 11:36–38). *give him some of the fruit.* In accordance with a kind of sharecropping agreement, a fixed amount was due the landowner. At the proper time he would expect to receive his share.

that one also they beat and treated shamefully and sent away empty-handed. 12He
sent still a third, and they wounded him
and threw him out.
13"Then the owner of the vineyard said,
'What shall I do? I will send my son,
whom I love;[o] perhaps they will respect
him.'
14"But when the tenants saw him, they
talked the matter over. 'This is the heir,'
they said. 'Let's kill him, and the inheritance will be ours.' 15So they threw him
out of the vineyard and killed him.
"What then will the owner of the vineyard do to them? 16He will come and kill
those tenants[p] and give the vineyard to
others."
When the people heard this, they said,
"May this never be!"
17Jesus looked directly at them and
asked, "Then what is the meaning of that
which is written:

> " 'The stone the builders rejected
> has become the capstone[y]'[z]?[q]

18Everyone who falls on that stone will be
broken to pieces, but he on whom it falls
will be crushed."[r]
19The teachers of the law and the chief
priests looked for a way to arrest him[s]
immediately, because they knew he had
spoken this parable against them. But they
were afraid of the people.[t]

Paying Taxes to Caesar

20:20–26pp — Mt 22:15–22; Mk 12:13–17

20Keeping a close watch on him, they
sent spies, who pretended to be honest.
They hoped to catch Jesus in something he
said[u] so that they might hand him over to
the power and authority of the governor.[v]
21So the spies questioned him: "Teacher,
we know that you speak and teach what is
right, and that you do not show partiality
but teach the way of God in accordance
with the truth.[w] 22Is it right for us to pay
taxes to Caesar or not?"
23He saw through their duplicity and
said to them, 24"Show me a denarius.
Whose portrait and inscription are on it?"
25"Caesar's," they replied.
He said to them, "Then give to Caesar
what is Caesar's,[x] and to God what is
God's."
26They were unable to trap him in what
he had said there in public. And astonished
by his answer, they became silent.

The Resurrection and Marriage

20:27–40pp — Mt 22:23–33; Mk 12:18–27

27Some of the Sadducees,[y] who say
there is no resurrection,[z] came to Jesus
with a question. 28"Teacher," they said,
"Moses wrote for us that if a man's brother
dies and leaves a wife but no children, the
man must marry the widow and have children for his brother.[a] 29Now there were
seven brothers. The first one married a
woman and died childless. 30The second
31and then the third married her, and in
the same way the seven died, leaving no
children. 32Finally, the woman died too.
33Now then, at the resurrection whose
wife will she be, since the seven were married to her?"
34Jesus replied, "The people of this age
marry and are given in marriage. 35But
those who are considered worthy of taking
part in that age[b] and in the resurrection
from the dead will neither marry nor be
given in marriage, 36and they can no

20:13 [o]S Mt 3:17 **20:16** [p]Lk 19:27 **20:17** [q]Ps 118:22; S Ac 4:11 **20:18** [r]Isa 8:14, 15 **20:19** [s]Lk 19:47 [t]S Mk 11:18 **20:20** [u]S Mt 12:10 [v]Mt 27:2

20:21 [w]Jn 3:2 **20:25** [x]Lk 23:2; Ro 13:7 **20:27** [y]S Ac 4:1 [z]Ac 23:8; 1 Co 15:12 **20:28** [a]Dt 25:5 **20:35** [b]S Mt 12:32

[y] *17* Or *cornerstone* [z] *17* Psalm 118:22

20:13 *my son, whom I love.* The specific reference to the beloved son makes clearer the intended application of the son in the parable to the Son, Jesus Christ (see 3:22; Mt 17:5).
20:14 *inheritance will be ours.* See note on Mk 12:7.
20:16 *give the vineyard to others.* See note on Mt 21:41.
20:17 *the capstone.* See note on Ps 118:22.
20:18 *will be broken to pieces.* As a pot dashed against a stone is broken, and as one lying beneath a falling stone is crushed, so those who reject Jesus the Messiah will be doomed (see Isa 8:14; cf. Da 2:34–35,44; Lk 2:34).
20:19 *teachers of the law.* The "scribes." For their opposition to Jesus see 5:30; 9:22; 19:47; 22:2; 23:10.
20:20 *authority of the governor.* Fearing to take action themselves, the Jewish religious leaders hoped to draw from Jesus some statement that would bring action from the Roman officials and remove him from his contact with the people.
20:22 *taxes to Caesar.* To agree to the taxes demanded by Caesar would disappoint the people, but to advise no payment would disturb the Roman officials. The questioners hoped to trap Jesus with this dilemma.
20:24 *a denarius.* A Roman coin worth about a day's wages (see note on Mt 22:19).
20:25 *to God what is God's.* See note on Mt 22:21.
20:27 *Sadducees.* An aristocratic, politically minded group, willing to compromise with secular and pagan leaders. They controlled the high priesthood at this time and held the majority of the seats in the Sanhedrin. They did not believe in the resurrection or an afterlife, and they rejected the oral tradition taught by the Pharisees (Josephus, *Antiquities,* 13.10.6.). See notes on Mt 2:4; 3:7; Mk 12:18; Ac 4:1.
20:28 *the man must marry the widow.* The levirate law (see note on Mt 22:24; cf. Ge 38:8).
20:34–35 *this age . . . that age.* See note on 18:30.
20:36 *like the angels.* The resurrection order cannot be assumed to follow present earthly lines. In the new age there will be no marriage, no procreation and no death. *children of the resurrection.* Those who are to take part in the resurrection of the righteous (cf. Mt 22:23–33; Mk 12:18–27; Ac 4:1–2; 23:6–10).

longer die; for they are like the angels. They are God's children,[c] since they are children of the resurrection. 37But in the account of the bush, even Moses showed that the dead rise, for he calls the Lord 'the God of Abraham, and the God of Isaac, and the God of Jacob.'[a][d] 38He is not the God of the dead, but of the living, for to him all are alive."

39Some of the teachers of the law responded, "Well said, teacher!" 40And no one dared to ask him any more questions.[e]

Whose Son Is the Christ?

20:41–47pp — Mt 22:41–23:7; Mk 12:35–40

41Then Jesus said to them, "How is it that they say the Christ[b] is the Son of David?[f] 42David himself declares in the Book of Psalms:

" 'The Lord said to my Lord:
    "Sit at my right hand
43until I make your enemies
    a footstool for your feet." '[c][g]

44David calls him 'Lord.' How then can he be his son?"

45While all the people were listening, Jesus said to his disciples, 46"Beware of the teachers of the law. They like to walk around in flowing robes and love to be greeted in the marketplaces and have the most important seats in the synagogues and the places of honor at banquets.[h] 47They devour widows' houses and for a show make lengthy prayers. Such men will be punished most severely."

Cross-references (center column)
20:36 cS Jn 1:12
20:37 dEx 3:6
20:40 eMt 22:46; Mk 12:34
20:41 fS Mt 1:1
20:43 gPs 110:1; S Mt 22:44
20:46 hS Lk 11:43
21:1 iMt 27:6; Jn 8:20
21:4 j2Co 8:12
21:6 kLk 19:44
21:8 lLk 17:23

The Widow's Offering

21:1–4pp — Mk 12:41–44

21 As he looked up, Jesus saw the rich putting their gifts into the temple treasury.[i] 2He also saw a poor widow put in two very small copper coins.[d] 3"I tell you the truth," he said, "this poor widow has put in more than all the others. 4All these people gave their gifts out of their wealth; but she out of her poverty put in all she had to live on."[j]

Signs of the End of the Age

21:5–36pp — Mt 24; Mk 13
21:12–17pp — Mt 10:17–22

5Some of his disciples were remarking about how the temple was adorned with beautiful stones and with gifts dedicated to God. But Jesus said, 6"As for what you see here, the time will come when not one stone will be left on another;[k] every one of them will be thrown down."

7"Teacher," they asked, "when will these things happen? And what will be the sign that they are about to take place?"

8He replied: "Watch out that you are not deceived. For many will come in my name, claiming, 'I am he,' and, 'The time is near.' Do not follow them.[l] 9When you hear of wars and revolutions, do not be frightened. These things must happen first, but the end will not come right away."

10Then he said to them: "Nation will rise against nation, and kingdom against

a37 Exodus 3:6   b41 Or Messiah   c43 Psalm 110:1   d2 Greek two lepta

---

20:37 account of the bush. Since Scripture chapters and verses were not used at the time of Christ, the passage was identified in this way, referring to Moses' experience with the burning bush (Ex 3:2).
20:39 Well said, teacher! Even though there was great animosity against Jesus, the teachers of the law (who were Pharisees) sided with Jesus against the Sadducees on the matter of resurrection.
20:44 David calls him 'Lord.' If the Messiah was a descendant of David, how could this honored king refer to his offspring as Lord? Unless Jesus' opponents were ready to admit that the Messiah was also the divine Son of God, they could not answer his question. See also note on Ps 110:1.
20:46 flowing robes . . . important seats. See notes on Mk 12:38–39.
20:47 devour widows' houses. They take advantage of this defenseless group by fraud and schemes for selfish gain. punished most severely. Cf. 12:47–48. The higher the esteem of men, the more severe the demands of true justice; and the more hypocrisy (Mt 23:1–36), the greater the condemnation.
21:1 the temple treasury. In the court of women 13 boxes, shaped like inverted megaphones, were positioned to receive the donations of the worshipers.
21:2 very small copper coins. Jewish coins worth very little.

21:3–4 See note on 2Co 8:12.
21:5–36 See note on Mk 13:1–37.
21:5 how the temple was adorned. One stone at the southwest corner was some 36 feet long. "Whatever was not overlaid with gold was purest white" (Josephus, Jewish War, 5.5.6.). Herod gave a golden vine for one of its decorations. Its grape clusters were as tall as a man. The full magnificence of the temple as elaborated and adorned by Herod has only recently come to light through archaeological investigations on the temple hill.
21:6 not one stone . . . left. Fulfilled in A.D. 70 when the Romans took Jerusalem and burned the temple (see note on Mt 24:2).
21:7 when . . . ? Mark reports that this question was asked by four disciples: Peter, James, John and Andrew (Mk 13:3). Matthew gives the question in a fuller form, including an inquiry for the sign of Jesus' coming and the end of the age (Mt 24:3). what will be the sign . . . ? What would be the indication that these things are about to happen?
21:8 I am he. I am Jesus the Messiah (having come a second time). The time. The end time.
21:9 the end will not come right away. Refers to the end of the age (see Mt 24:3,6). All the events listed in vv. 8–18 are characteristic of the entire present age, not just signs of the end of the age.

kingdom. *m* 11There will be great earthquakes, famines and pestilences in various
places, and fearful events and great signs
from heaven. *n*

12"But before all this, they will lay hands
on you and persecute you. They will deliver you to synagogues and prisons, and
you will be brought before kings and governors, and all on account of my name.
13This will result in your being witnesses to
them. *o* 14But make up your mind not to
worry beforehand how you will defend
yourselves. *p* 15For I will give you *q* words
and wisdom that none of your adversaries
will be able to resist or contradict. 16You
will be betrayed even by parents, brothers,
relatives and friends, *r* and they will put
some of you to death. 17All men will hate
you because of me. *s* 18But not a hair of
your head will perish. *t* 19By standing firm
you will gain life. *u*

20"When you see Jerusalem being surrounded by armies, *v* you will know that
its desolation is near. 21Then let those who
are in Judea flee to the mountains, let
those in the city get out, and let those in
the country not enter the city. *w* 22For this
is the time of punishment *x* in fulfillment *y*
of all that has been written. 23How dreadful it will be in those days for pregnant
women and nursing mothers! There will
be great distress in the land and wrath
against this people. 24They will fall by the

sword and will be taken as prisoners to all
the nations. Jerusalem will be trampled *z*
on by the Gentiles until the times of the
Gentiles are fulfilled.

25"There will be signs in the sun, moon
and stars. On the earth, nations will be in
anguish and perplexity at the roaring and
tossing of the sea. *a* 26Men will faint from
terror, apprehensive of what is coming on
the world, for the heavenly bodies will be
shaken. *b* 27At that time they will see the
Son of Man *c* coming in a cloud *d* with
power and great glory. 28When these
things begin to take place, stand up and lift
up your heads, because your redemption is
drawing near." *e*

29He told them this parable: "Look at
the fig tree and all the trees. 30When they
sprout leaves, you can see for yourselves
and know that summer is near. 31Even so,
when you see these things happening, you
know that the kingdom of God *f* is near.

32"I tell you the truth, this generation *e g*
will certainly not pass away until all these
things have happened. 33Heaven and earth
will pass away, but my words will never
pass away. *h*

34"Be careful, or your hearts will be
weighed down with dissipation, drunkenness and the anxieties of life, *i* and that
day will close on you unexpectedly *j* like a

Cross-references (center column)

21:10 *m*2Ch 15:6;
Isa 19:2
21:11 *n*Isa 29:6;
Joel 2:30
21:13 *o*Php 1:12
21:14 *p*Lk 12:11
21:15
*q*S Lk 12:12
21:16 *r*Lk 12:52,
53
21:17 *s*S Jn 15:21
21:18
*t*S Mt 10:30
21:19
*u*S Mt 10:22
21:20
*v*S Lk 19:43
21:21 *w*Lk 17:31
21:22 *x*Isa 63:4;
Da 9:24-27;
Hos 9:7
*y*S Mt 1:22

21:24 *z*Isa 5:5;
63:18; Da 8:13;
Rev 11:2
21:25 *a*2Pe 3:10,
12
21:26
*b*S Mt 24:29
21:27 *c*S Mt 8:20
*d*S Rev 1:7
21:28 *e*Lk 18:7
21:31 *f*S Mt 3:2
21:32 *g*Lk 11:50;
17:25
21:33 *h*S Mt 5:18
21:34 *i*Mk 4:19
*j*Lk 12:40,46;
1Th 5:2-7

*e*32 Or *race*

21:11 *signs from heaven.* See v. 25. For prophetic descriptions of celestial signs accompanying the day of the Lord see
note on Mk 13:25.
21:12 *deliver you to synagogues.* Synagogues were used
not only for worship and school, but also for community
administration and confinement while awaiting trial.
21:15 *none . . . will be able to resist.* See Ac 6:9–10.
21:18 Although persecution and death may come, God is
in control, and the ultimate outcome will be eternal victory.
not a hair of your head will perish. In view of v. 16 this
cannot refer to physical safety. The figure indicates that there
will be no real, i.e., spiritual, loss.
21:19 See note on Mk 13:13.
21:20 *surrounded by armies.* See 19:43. The sign that the
end was near (cf. v. 7) would be the surrounding of Jerusalem with armies. Associated with this event would be the
"abomination that causes desolation" (Mt 24:15).
21:21 *flee to the mountains.* When an army surrounds a
city, it is natural to seek protection inside the walls, but Jesus
directs his followers to seek the safety of the mountains
because the city was doomed to destruction (see note on Mt
24:16).
21:22 *time of punishment.* God's retributive justice as the
consequence of faithlessness (cf. Isa 63:4; Jer 5:29; Hos
9:7).
21:24 *times of the Gentiles.* The Gentiles would have both
spiritual opportunities (Mk 13:10; cf. Lk 20:16; Ro 11:25)
and domination of Jerusalem, but these times will end when
God's purpose for the Gentiles has been fulfilled.
21:27 *At that time . . . Son of Man coming.* The time of

Christ's second coming (see Da 7:13). Often the predictions
in this discourse refer ultimately to the end times, while at
the same time describing the more imminent destruction of
Jerusalem in A.D. 70.
21:28 *lift up your heads.* Do not be downcast at the
appearance of these signs, but look up in joy, hope and trust.
redemption. Final, completed redemption.
21:29 *Look at the fig tree.* The coming of spring is announced by the greening of the trees (cf. Mt 24:32–35; Mk
13:28–31). In a similar way, one can anticipate the coming
of the kingdom when its signs are seen. But "kingdom" is
used in different ways (see note on 4:43). The reference in v.
31 is to the future kingdom.
21:32 *this generation.* If the reference is to the destruction
of Jerusalem, which occurred about 40 years after Jesus
spoke these words, "generation" is used in its ordinary sense
of a normal life span. All these things were fulfilled in a
preliminary sense in the A.D. 70 destruction of Jerusalem. If
the reference is to the second coming of Christ, "generation"
might indicate the Jewish people as a race (see NIV text
note), who were promised existence to the very end. Or it
might refer to the future generation alive at the beginning of
these things. It does not mean that Jesus had a mistaken
notion he was going to return immediately.
21:34 *that day.* When Christ returns and the future aspect
of God's kingdom is inaugurated (cf. v. 31). *close on you
unexpectedly.* Does not mean that Christ's second coming
will be completely unannounced, since there will be introductory signs (vv. 28,31).
21:35 *the whole earth.* The second coming of Christ will

trap. 35For it will come upon all those who
live on the face of the whole earth. 36Be
always on the watch, and pray[k] that you
may be able to escape all that is about to
happen, and that you may be able to stand
before the Son of Man."

37Each day Jesus was teaching at the
temple,[l] and each evening he went out[m]
to spend the night on the hill called the
Mount of Olives,[n] 38and all the people
came early in the morning to hear him at
the temple.[o]

Judas Agrees to Betray Jesus

22:1,2pp — Mt 26:2–5; Mk 14:1,2,10,11

22 Now the Feast of Unleavened
Bread, called the Passover, was approaching,[p] 2and the chief priests and the
teachers of the law were looking for some
way to get rid of Jesus,[q] for they were
afraid of the people. 3Then Satan[r] entered
Judas, called Iscariot,[s] one of the Twelve.
4And Judas went to the chief priests and
the officers of the temple guard[t] and discussed with them how he might betray
Jesus. 5They were delighted and agreed to
give him money.[u] 6He consented, and
watched for an opportunity to hand Jesus
over to them when no crowd was present.

21:36 [k]Mt 26:41
21:37 [l]S Mt 26:55 [m]Mk 11:19 [n]S Mt 21:1
21:38 [o]Jn 8:2
22:1 [p]S Jn 11:55
22:2 [q]S Mt 12:14
22:3 [r]S Mt 4:10 [s]S Mt 10:4
22:4 [t]ver 52; Ac 4:1; 5:24
22:5 [u]Zec 11:12
22:7 [v]Ex 12:18-20; Dt 16:5-8; S Mk 14:12
22:8 [w]Ac 3:1,11; 4:13,19; 8:14
22:13 [x]Lk 19:32
22:14 [y]S Mk 6:30 [z]Mt 26:20; Mk 14:17,18
22:15 [a]S Mt 16:21
22:16 [b]S Lk 14:15

The Last Supper

22:7–13pp — Mt 26:17–19; Mk 14:12–16
22:17–20pp — Mt 26:26–29; Mk 14:22–25; 1Co 11:23–25
22:21–23pp — Mt 26:21–24; Mk 14:18–21; Jn 13:21–30
22:25–27pp — Mt 20:25–28; Mk 10:42–45
22:33,34pp — Mt 26:33–35; Mk 14:29–31; Jn 13:37,38

7Then came the day of Unleavened
Bread on which the Passover lamb had to
be sacrificed.[v] 8Jesus sent Peter and
John,[w] saying, "Go and make preparations
for us to eat the Passover."

9"Where do you want us to prepare for
it?" they asked.

10He replied, "As you enter the city, a
man carrying a jar of water will meet you.
Follow him to the house that he enters,
11and say to the owner of the house, 'The
Teacher asks: Where is the guest room,
where I may eat the Passover with my disciples?' 12He will show you a large upper
room, all furnished. Make preparations
there."

13They left and found things just as Jesus
had told them.[x] So they prepared the Passover.

14When the hour came, Jesus and his
apostles[y] reclined at the table.[z] 15And he
said to them, "I have eagerly desired to eat
this Passover with you before I suffer.[a]
16For I tell you, I will not eat it again until
it finds fulfillment in the kingdom of
God."[b]

17After taking the cup, he gave thanks

---

involve the whole of mankind, whereas the fall of Jerusalem did not.

21:37 *Each day.* Each day during the final week of his life, from his Triumphal Entry to the time of the Passover (Sunday-Thursday). *Mount of Olives.* See notes on 19:29; Mt 21:17.

22:1 *Feast of Unleavened Bread . . . Passover.* "Passover" was used in two different ways: (1) a specific meal begun at twilight on the 14th of Nisan (Lev 23:4–5), and (2) the week following the Passover meal (Eze 45:21), otherwise known as the Feast of Unleavened Bread, a week in which no leaven was allowed (Ex 12:15–20; 13:3–7). By NT times the two names for the week-long festival were virtually interchangeable.

22:2 *the chief priests and the teachers of the law.* See 20:1.

22:3 *Satan entered Judas.* In the Gospels this expression is used on two separate occasions: (1) before Judas went to the chief priests and offered to betray Jesus (here), and (2) during the Last Supper (Jn 13:27). Thus the Gospel writers depict Satan's control over Judas, who had never displayed a high motive of service or commitment to Jesus.

22:4 *officers of the temple guard.* All of these were Jews selected mostly from the Levites.

22:7 *Passover lamb had to be sacrificed.* On the 14th of Nisan between 2:30 and 5:30 P.M. in the court of the priests—Thursday of Passion Week.

22:10 *a man carrying a jar.* It was extraordinary to see a man carrying a jar of water, since this was normally women's work.

22:11 *The Teacher asks.* This form of address may have been chosen because the owner was a follower already known to Jesus.

22:13 *as Jesus had told them.* It may be that Jesus had made previous arrangements with the man in order to make sure that the Passover meal would not be interrupted. Since Jesus did not identify ahead of time just where he would observe Passover, Judas was unable to inform the enemy, who might have interrupted this important occasion.

22:14–30 It appears that Luke does not attempt to be strictly chronological in his account of the Last Supper. He records the most important part of the occasion first—the sharing of the bread and the cup. Then he tells of Jesus' comments about his betrayer and about the argument over who would be greatest, though both of these subjects seem to have been introduced earlier. John's Gospel (13:26–30), e.g., indicates that Judas had already left the room before the bread and cup of the Lord's Supper were shared, but Luke does not tell when he left.

22:14 *reclined at the table.* See note on Mk 14:3.

22:16 *until it finds fulfillment.* Jesus yearned to keep this Passover with his disciples because it was the last occasion before he himself was to be slain as the perfect "Passover lamb" (1Co 5:7) and thus fulfill this sacrifice for all time. Jesus would eat no more Passover meals until the coming of the future kingdom. After this he will renew fellowship with those who through the ages have commemorated the Lord's Supper. Finally the fellowship will be consummated in the great Messianic "wedding supper" to come (Rev 19:9).

22:17 *After taking the cup.* Either the first of the four cups shared during regular observance of the Passover meal, or the third cup.

and said, "Take this and divide it among you. 18For I tell you I will not drink again of the fruit of the vine until the kingdom of God comes."

19And he took bread, gave thanks and broke it, c and gave it to them, saying, "This is my body given for you; do this in remembrance of me."

20In the same way, after the supper he took the cup, saying, "This cup is the new covenant d in my blood, which is poured out for you. 21But the hand of him who is going to betray me is with mine on the table. e 22The Son of Man f will go as it has been decreed, g but woe to that man who betrays him." 23They began to question among themselves which of them it might be who would do this.

24Also a dispute arose among them as to which of them was considered to be greatest. h 25Jesus said to them, "The kings of the Gentiles lord it over them; and those who exercise authority over them call themselves Benefactors. 26But you are not to be like that. Instead, the greatest among you should be like the youngest, i and the one who rules like the one who serves. j 27For who is greater, the one who is at the table or the one who serves? Is it not the one who is at the table? But I am among you as one who serves. k 28You are those who have stood by me in my trials. 29And I confer on you a kingdom, l just as my Father conferred one on me, 30so that you may eat and drink at my table in my king-

dom m and sit on thrones, judging the twelve tribes of Israel. n

31"Simon, Simon, Satan has asked o to sift you f as wheat. p 32But I have prayed for you, q Simon, that your faith may not fail. And when you have turned back, strengthen your brothers." r

33But he replied, "Lord, I am ready to go with you to prison and to death." s

34Jesus answered, "I tell you, Peter, before the rooster crows today, you will deny three times that you know me."

35Then Jesus asked them, "When I sent you without purse, bag or sandals, t did you lack anything?"

"Nothing," they answered.

36He said to them, "But now if you have a purse, take it, and also a bag; and if you don't have a sword, sell your cloak and buy one. 37It is written: 'And he was numbered with the transgressors' g; u and I tell you that this must be fulfilled in me. Yes, what is written about me is reaching its fulfillment."

38The disciples said, "See, Lord, here are two swords."

"That is enough," he replied.

Jesus Prays on the Mount of Olives

22:40–46pp — Mt 26:36–46; Mk 14:32–42

39Jesus went out as usual v to the Mount of Olives, w and his disciples followed him. 40On reaching the place, he said to them,

---

Cross references (center column):

22:19 cS Mt 14:19
22:20 dEx 24:8; Isa 42:6; Jer 31:31-34; Zec 9:11; 2Co 3:6; Heb 8:6; 9:15
22:21 ePs 41:9
22:22 fS Mt 8:20 gAc 2:23; 4:28
22:24 hMk 9:34; Lk 9:46
22:26 iIPe 5:5 jS Mk 9:35
22:27 kS Mt 20:28
22:29 lS Mt 25:34; 2Ti 2:12
22:30 mS Lk 14:15 nS Mt 19:28
22:31 oJob 1:6-12 pAm 9:9
22:32 qJn 17:9, 15; S Ro 8:34 rJn 21:15-17
22:33 sJn 11:16
22:35 tMt 10:9, 10; Lk 9:3; 10:4
22:37 uIsa 53:12
22:39 vLk 21:37 wS Mt 21:1

t31 The Greek is plural. g37 Isaiah 53:12

22:18 *until the kingdom of God comes.* See notes on v. 16; 4:43.
22:19 *is.* Represents or signifies. *given for you.* Anticipating his substitutionary sacrifice on the cross. *in remembrance of me.* Just as the Passover was a constant reminder and proclamation of God's redemption of Israel from bondage in Egypt, so the keeping of Christ's command would be a remembering and proclaiming of the deliverance of believers from the bondage of sin through Christ's atoning work on the cross.
22:20 *after the supper.* Mentioned only here and in 1Co 11:25; see note on 1Co 11:23–26. *took the cup.* See note on Mk 14:24. *new covenant.* Promised through the prophet Jeremiah (31:31–34)—the fuller administration of God's saving grace, founded on and sealed by the death of Jesus ("in my blood"). See note on 1Co 11:25.
22:25 *Benefactors.* A title assumed by or voted for rulers in Egypt, Syria and Rome as a display of honor, but frequently not representing actual service rendered.
22:26 *like the one who serves.* Jesus urges and exemplifies servant leadership—a trait that was as uncommon then as it is now.
22:28 *in my trials.* Including temptations (cf. 4:13), hardships (9:58) and rejection (Jn 1:11).
22:29 *confer on you a kingdom.* The following context (v. 30) indicates that this kingdom is the future form of the kingdom (see notes on 4:43; Mt 3:2).
22:30 *sit on thrones.* As they shared in Jesus' trials, so they will share in his rule (2Ti 2:12). *judging.* Leading or ruling.

See NIV text note on Jdg 2:16. *the twelve tribes of Israel.* See Mt 19:28.
22:31 *sift you.* See NIV text note. Satan wanted to test the disciples, hoping to bring them to spiritual ruin.
22:36 *a purse . . . a bag.* Cf. previous instructions (9:3; 10:4). Until now they had been dependent on generous hospitality, but future opposition would require them to be prepared to pay their own way. *buy one.* An extreme figure of speech used to warn them of the perilous times about to come. They would need defense and protection, as Paul did when he appealed to Caesar (Ac 25:11) as the one who "bears the sword" (Ro 13:4).
22:37 *numbered with the transgressors.* Jesus was soon to be arrested as a criminal, in fulfillment of prophetic Scripture, and his disciples would also be in danger for being his followers.
22:38 *". . . two swords." "That is enough."* Sensing that the disciples had taken him too literally, Jesus ironically closes the discussion with a curt "That's plenty!" Not long after this, Peter was rebuked for using a sword (v. 50).
22:39 *Mount of Olives.* See 21:37; Jn 18:2. Matthew specifies Gethsemane (Mt 26:36), and John, an olive grove (Jn 18:1). The place apparently was located on the lower slopes of the Mount of Olives.
22:40 *temptation.* Here refers to severe trial of the kind referred to in vv. 28–38, which might lead to a faltering of their faith.

"Pray that you will not fall into temptation." [x] [41] He withdrew about a stone's throw beyond them, knelt down [y] and prayed, [42] "Father, if you are willing, take this cup [z] from me; yet not my will, but yours be done." [a] [43] An angel from heaven appeared to him and strengthened him. [b] [44] And being in anguish, he prayed more earnestly, and his sweat was like drops of blood falling to the ground. [h]

[45] When he rose from prayer and went back to the disciples, he found them asleep, exhausted from sorrow. [46] "Why are you sleeping?" he asked them. "Get up and pray so that you will not fall into temptation." [c]

Jesus Arrested

22:47–53pp — Mt 26:47–56; Mk 14:43–50; Jn 18:3–11

[47] While he was still speaking a crowd came up, and the man who was called Judas, one of the Twelve, was leading them. He approached Jesus to kiss him, [48] but Jesus asked him, "Judas, are you betraying the Son of Man with a kiss?"

[49] When Jesus' followers saw what was going to happen, they said, "Lord, should we strike with our swords?" [d] [50] And one of them struck the servant of the high priest, cutting off his right ear.

[51] But Jesus answered, "No more of this!" And he touched the man's ear and healed him.

[52] Then Jesus said to the chief priests, the officers of the temple guard, [e] and the elders, who had come for him, "Am I leading a rebellion, that you have come with swords and clubs? [53] Every day I was with you in the temple courts, [f] and you did not lay a hand on me. But this is your hour [g]—when darkness reigns." [h]

Peter Disowns Jesus

22:55–62pp — Mt 26:69–75; Mk 14:66–72; Jn 18:16–18,25–27

[54] Then seizing him, they led him away and took him into the house of the high priest. [i] Peter followed at a distance. [j] [55] But when they had kindled a fire in the middle of the courtyard and had sat down together, Peter sat down with them. [56] A servant girl saw him seated there in the firelight. She looked closely at him and said, "This man was with him."

[57] But he denied it. "Woman, I don't know him," he said.

[58] A little later someone else saw him and said, "You also are one of them."

"Man, I am not!" Peter replied.

[59] About an hour later another asserted, "Certainly this fellow was with him, for he is a Galilean." [k]

[60] Peter replied, "Man, I don't know what you're talking about!" Just as he was speaking, the rooster crowed. [61] The Lord [l] turned and looked straight at Peter. Then Peter remembered the word the Lord had spoken to him: "Before the rooster crows today, you will disown me three times." [m] [62] And he went outside and wept bitterly.

The Guards Mock Jesus

22:63–65pp — Mt 26:67,68; Mk 14:65; Jn 18:22,23

[63] The men who were guarding Jesus began mocking and beating him. [64] They blindfolded him and demanded, "Prophesy! Who hit you?" [65] And they said many other insulting things to him. [n]

Cross references

22:40 [x] Mt 6:13
22:41 [y] Lk 18:11
22:42 [z] S Mt 20:22 [a] S Mt 26:39
22:43 [b] Mt 4:11; Mk 1:13
22:46 [c] ver 40
22:49 [d] ver 38
22:52 [e] ver 4
22:53 [f] S Mt 26:55 [g] Jn 12:27 [h] Mt 8:12; Jn 1:5; 3:20
22:54 [i] Mt 26:57; Mk 14:53 [j] Mt 26:58; Mk 14:54; Jn 18:15
22:59 [k] Lk 23:6
22:61 [l] S Lk 7:13 [m] ver 34
22:65 [n] S Mt 16:21

---

[h] 44 Some early manuscripts do not have verses 43 and 44.

22:42 *this cup.* The cup of suffering (Mt 20:22–23; cf. Isa 51:17; Eze 23:33). See note on Mk 14:36.

22:43 *An angel.* Matthew and Mark tell of angels ministering to Jesus at the close of his fasting and temptations (Mt 4:11; Mk 1:13), but Luke does not. Here Luke tells of the strengthening presence of an angel, but the other Gospels do not.

22:44 *drops of blood.* Probably perspiration in large drops like blood, or possibly hematidrosis, the actual mingling of blood and sweat as in cases of extreme anguish, strain or sensitivity.

22:47 *a crowd came up.* They were sent by the chief priests, elders (Mt 26:47) and teachers of the law (Mk 14:43), and they carried swords and clubs. Included was a detachment of soldiers with officials of the Jews (v. 52; Jn 18:3). *to kiss him.* This signal had been prearranged to identify Jesus to the authorities (Mt 26:48). It was unnecessary because Jesus identified himself (Jn 18:5), but Judas acted out his plan anyway.

22:50 *the servant of the high priest.* Malchus by name; Simon Peter struck the blow (Jn 18:10).

22:51 *healed him.* Jesus rectified the wrong done by his follower. No faith on the part of Malchus was involved, but to allow such action would have been contrary to the teaching of Jesus.

22:53 *this is your hour.* It was the time appointed for Jesus' enemies to apprehend him, the time when the forces of darkness (the powers of evil) would do their worst to defeat God's plan.

22:54 *house of the high priest.* See notes on 3:2; Mk 14:53; 15:15.

22:59 *he is a Galilean.* Recognized by his speech (Mt 26:73) and identified by a relative of Malchus, the high priest's slave (Jn 18:26).

22:61 *The Lord ... looked straight at Peter.* Peter was outside in the enclosed courtyard, and perhaps Jesus was being taken from the trial by Caiaphas to the Sanhedrin when Jesus caught Peter's eye. *Peter remembered.* The words spoken by Jesus (v. 34).

Jesus Before Pilate and Herod

22:67–71pp — Mt 26:63–66; Mk 14:61–63; Jn 18:19–21
23:2,3pp — Mt 27:11–14; Mk 15:2–5; Jn 18:29–37
23:18–25pp — Mt 27:15–26; Mk 15:6–15; Jn 18:39 – 19:16

66At daybreak the council o of the elders of the people, both the chief priests and teachers of the law, met together, p and Jesus was led before them. 67"If you are the Christ, i" they said, "tell us."

Jesus answered, "If I tell you, you will not believe me, 68and if I asked you, you would not answer. q 69But from now on, the Son of Man will be seated at the right hand of the mighty God." r

70They all asked, "Are you then the Son of God?" s

He replied, "You are right in saying I am." t

71Then they said, "Why do we need any more testimony? We have heard it from his own lips."

23 Then the whole assembly rose and led him off to Pilate. u 2And they began to accuse him, saying, "We have found this man subverting our nation. v He opposes payment of taxes to Caesar w and claims to be Christ, j a king." x

3So Pilate asked Jesus, "Are you the king of the Jews?"

"Yes, it is as you say," Jesus replied.

4Then Pilate announced to the chief priests and the crowd, "I find no basis for a charge against this man." y

5But they insisted, "He stirs up the people all over Judea k by his teaching. He started in Galilee z and has come all the way here."

6On hearing this, Pilate asked if the man was a Galilean. a 7When he learned that Jesus was under Herod's jurisdiction, he sent him to Herod, b who was also in Jerusalem at that time.

8When Herod saw Jesus, he was greatly pleased, because for a long time he had been wanting to see him. c From what he had heard about him, he hoped to see him perform some miracle. 9He plied him with many questions, but Jesus gave him no answer. d 10The chief priests and the teachers of the law were standing there, vehemently accusing him. 11Then Herod and his soldiers ridiculed and mocked him. Dressing him in an elegant robe, e they sent him back to Pilate. 12That day Herod and Pilate became friends f—before this they had been enemies.

13Pilate called together the chief priests, the rulers and the people, 14and said to them, "You brought me this man as one who was inciting the people to rebellion. I have examined him in your presence and have found no basis for your charges against him. g 15Neither has Herod, for he sent him back to us; as you can see, he has done nothing to deserve death. 16Therefore, I will punish him h and then release him. l "

18With one voice they cried out, "Away with this man! Release Barabbas to us!" i 19(Barabbas had been thrown into prison

---

22:66 oS Mt 5:22
pMt 27:1;
Mk 15:1
22:68 qLk 20:3-8
22:69
rS Mk 16:19
22:70 sS Mt 4:3
tMt 27:11;
Lk 23:3
23:1 uS Mt 27:2
23:2 vver 14
wLk 20:22
xJn 19:12
23:4 yver 14,22,41; Mt 27:23;
Jn 18:38;
1Ti 6:13;
S 2Co 5-21
23:5 zMk 1:14

23:6 aLk 22:59
23:7 bS Mt 14:1
23:8 cLk 9:9
23:9
dS Mk 14:61
23:11
eMk 15:17-19;
Jn 19:2,3
23:12 fAc 4:27
23:14 gS ver 4
23:16 hver 22;
Mt 27:26;
Jn 19:1;
Ac 16:37;
2Co 11:23,24
23:18 iAc 3:13,14

i67 Or *Messiah*   j2 Or *Messiah*; also in verses 35 and 39   k5 Or *over the land of the Jews*   l16 Some manuscripts *him.* 17Now *he was obliged to release one man to them at the Feast.*

22:66 *At daybreak.* Only after daylight could a legal trial take place for the whole council (Sanhedrin) to pass the death sentence.
22:67 *If you are the Christ.* This demand is related to a question asked later: "Are you then the Son of God?" (v. 70).
22:71 *We have heard it.* The reaction to Jesus' reply makes clear that his answer was a strong affirmative. Mark has simply, "I am" (Mk 14:62). It was blasphemy to claim to be the Messiah and the Son of God—unless, of course, the claim was true (see note on Mk 14:64).
23:1 *the whole assembly.* The body of the Sanhedrin (Mt 26:59; 27:1) who had met at the earliest hint of dawn (22:66). *led him off to Pilate.* See note on Mt 27:2. *Pilate.* See note on Mk 15:1. The Roman governor had his main headquarters in Caesarea, but he was in Jerusalem during Passover to prevent trouble from the large number of Jews assembled for the occasion.
23:2 *subverting our nation.* Large crowds followed Jesus, but he was not misleading them or turning them against Rome. *opposes payment of taxes.* Another untrue charge (see 20:25). *claims to be Christ, a king.* Jesus claimed to be the Messiah, but not a political or military king, the kind Rome would be anxious to eliminate.
23:3 *Yes.* Jesus affirms that he is a king, but then explains that his kingdom is not the kind that characterizes this world

(Jn 18:33–38).
23:5 *Judea.* See NIV text note; may here refer to the whole of the land of the Jews (including Galilee) or to the southern section only, where the region of Judea proper was governed by Pilate (see note on 4:44).
23:7 *Herod's jurisdiction.* See note on 3:1. Although Pilate and Herod were rivals, Pilate did not want to handle this case; so he sent Jesus to Herod (cf. v. 12). *in Jerusalem.* Herod's main headquarters was in Tiberias on the Sea of Galilee; but, like Pilate, he had come to Jerusalem because of the crowds at Passover.
23:8 *wanting to see him.* Herod was worried about Jesus' identity (9:7–9) and had desired to kill him (13:31), though the two had never met. There is no record that Jesus ever preached in Tiberias, where Herod's residence was located.
23:11 *elegant robe.* See note on Mk 15:17.
23:16 *I will punish him.* Although Pilate found Jesus "not guilty" as charged, he was willing to have him illegally beaten in order to satisfy the chief priests and the people and to warn against any possible trouble in the future. Scourging, though not intended to kill, was sometimes fatal (see note on Mk 15:15).
23:18 *Barabbas.* Means "son of Abba." Pilate offered a choice between Jesus and an obviously evil, dangerous criminal (see Mt 27:15–20; Mk 15:6–11; Jn 18:39–40).

for an insurrection in the city, and for murder.)

20Wanting to release Jesus, Pilate appealed to them again. 21But they kept shouting, "Crucify him! Crucify him!"

22For the third time he spoke to them: "Why? What crime has this man committed? I have found in him no grounds for the death penalty. Therefore I will have him punished and then release him."*j*

23But with loud shouts they insistently demanded that he be crucified, and their shouts prevailed. 24So Pilate decided to grant their demand. 25He released the man who had been thrown into prison for insurrection and murder, the one they asked for, and surrendered Jesus to their will.

The Crucifixion

23:33–43pp — Mt 27:33–44; Mk 15:22–32; Jn 19:17–24

26As they led him away, they seized Simon from Cyrene,*k* who was on his way in from the country, and put the cross on him and made him carry it behind Jesus.*l* 27A large number of people followed him, including women who mourned and wailed*m* for him. 28Jesus turned and said to them, "Daughters of Jerusalem, do not weep for me; weep for yourselves and for your children.*n* 29For the time will come when you will say, 'Blessed are the barren women, the wombs that never bore and the breasts that never nursed!'*o* 30Then

" 'they will say to the mountains, "Fall on us!"

and to the hills, "Cover us!" '*m**p*

31For if men do these things when the tree

is green, what will happen when it is dry?"*q*

32Two other men, both criminals, were also led out with him to be executed.*r* 33When they came to the place called the Skull, there they crucified him, along with the criminals—one on his right, the other on his left. 34Jesus said, "Father,*s* forgive them, for they do not know what they are doing."*n**t* And they divided up his clothes by casting lots.*u*

35The people stood watching, and the rulers even sneered at him.*v* They said, "He saved others; let him save himself if he is the Christ of God, the Chosen One."*w*

36The soldiers also came up and mocked him.*x* They offered him wine vinegar*y* 37and said, "If you are the king of the Jews,*z* save yourself."

38There was a written notice above him, which read: THIS IS THE KING OF THE JEWS.*a*

39One of the criminals who hung there hurled insults at him: "Aren't you the Christ? Save yourself and us!"*b*

40But the other criminal rebuked him. "Don't you fear God," he said, "since you are under the same sentence? 41We are punished justly, for we are getting what our deeds deserve. But this man has done nothing wrong."*c*

42Then he said, "Jesus, remember me when you come into your kingdom.*o*"*d*

43Jesus answered him, "I tell you the

Cross references

23:22 *j*ver 16
23:26 *k*S Mt 27:32
/Mk 15:21;
Jn 19:17
23:27 *m*Lk 8:52
23:28
*n*Lk 19:41-44;
21:23,24
23:29 *o*Mt 24:19
23:30 *p*Hos 10:8;
Isa 2:19; Rev 6:16

23:31 *q*Eze 20:47
23:32 *r*Isa 53:12;
Mt 27:38;
Mk 15:27;
Jn 19:18
23:34
*s*S Mt 11:25
*t*S Mt 5:44
*u*Ps 22:18
23:35 *v*Ps 22:17
*w*Isa 42:1
23:36 *x*Ps 22:7
*y*Ps 69:21;
Mt 27:48
23:37 *z*Lk 4:3,9
23:38 *a*S Mt 2:2
23:39 *b*ver 35,37
23:41 *c*S ver 4
23:42
*d*S Mt 16:27

m30 Hosea 10:8   *n34* Some early manuscripts do not have this sentence.   *o42* Some manuscripts *come with your kingly power*

23:19 *insurrection . . . murder.* This particular uprising is otherwise unknown but, coupled with murder, it shows the gravity of his deeds (see Jn 18:40).

23:22 *third time.* See vv. 4,14.

23:25 *surrendered Jesus.* Luke's account is abbreviated. Pilate had already handed Jesus over to the soldiers for scourging before he was convicted (Jn 19:1–5). He now handed him over for crucifixion.

23:26 *Simon.* His sons, Rufus and Alexander (Mk 15:21), must have been known in Christian circles at a later time, and perhaps were associated with the church at Rome (Ro 16:13). *Cyrene.* A leading city of Libya, west of Egypt. *put the cross on him.* See note on Mk 15:21.

23:28 *weep for yourselves and for your children.* Because of the terrible suffering to befall Jerusalem some 40 years later when the Romans would besiege the city and utterly destroy the temple.

23:29 *Blessed are the barren.* It would be better not to have children than to have them experience such suffering. Cf. Jer 16:1–4; 1Co 7:25–35.

23:30 *Fall on us!* People would seek escape through destruction in death rather than continuing suffering and judgment (cf. Hos 10:8; Rev 6:16).

23:31 *tree is green . . . dry.* If they treat the Messiah this way when the "tree" is well-watered and green, what will

their plight be when he is withdrawn from them and they suffer for their rejection in the dry period?

23:32 *both criminals.* See note on v. 18.

23:33 *the Skull.* Latin *Calvaria,* hence the name "Calvary" (see note on Mk 15:22). *crucified.* See note on Mk 15:24.

23:34 *divided up his clothes.* Any possessions an executed person had with him were taken by the executioners. Unwittingly the soldiers (cf. Jn 19:23–24) were fulfilling the words of Ps 22:18 (but see introduction to Ps 22 and notes on Ps 22:17,20–21).

23:35 *the Chosen One.* See note on 9:35.

23:36 *wine vinegar.* A sour drink carried by the soldiers for the day. Jesus refused a sedative drink (Mt 27:34; Mk 15:23) but later was given the vinegar drink when he cried out in thirst (Jn 19:28–30). Luke shows that it was offered in mockery.

23:38 *written notice.* Indicated the crime for which a person was dying. This was Pilate's way of mocking the Jewish leaders as well as announcing what Jesus had been accused of. *KING OF THE JEWS.* See note on Mk 15:26.

23:39 *One of the criminals.* See note on Mk 15:32.

23:43 *paradise.* In the Septuagint (the Greek translation of the OT) the word designated a garden (Ge 2:8–10) or forest (Ne 2:8), but in the NT (used only here and in 2Co 12:4; Rev 2:7) it refers to the place of bliss and rest between death and

truth, today you will be with me in paradise." *e*

Jesus' Death

23:44–49pp — Mt 27:45–56; Mk 15:33–41

⁴⁴It was now about the sixth hour, and darkness came over the whole land until the ninth hour, *f* ⁴⁵for the sun stopped shining. And the curtain of the temple *g* was torn in two. *h* ⁴⁶Jesus called out with a loud voice, *i* "Father, into your hands I commit my spirit." *j* When he had said this, he breathed his last. *k*

⁴⁷The centurion, seeing what had happened, praised God *l* and said, "Surely this was a righteous man." ⁴⁸When all the people who had gathered to witness this sight saw what took place, they beat their breasts *m* and went away. ⁴⁹But all those who knew him, including the women who had followed him from Galilee, *n* stood at a distance, *o* watching these things.

Jesus' Burial

23:50–56pp — Mt 27:57–61; Mk 15:42–47; Jn 19:38–42

⁵⁰Now there was a man named Joseph, a member of the Council, a good and up-

---

Cross references (center column):

23:43 *e*2Co 12:3, 4; Rev 2:7
23:44 *f*Am 8:9
23:45 *g*Ex 26:31-33; Heb 9:3,8
23:46 *h*Heb 10:19,20
23:46 *i*Mt 27:50 /Ps 31:5; 1Pe 2:23
23:47 *k*Jn 19:30 *l*S Mt 9:8
23:48 *m*Lk 18:13
23:49 *n*Lk 8:2 *o*Ps 38:11

23:51 *p*Lk 2:25, 38
23:54 *q*Mt 27:62
23:55 *r*ver 49
23:56 *s*Mk 16:1; Lk 24:1
*t*Ex 12:16; 20:10
24:1 *u*Lk 23:56
24:3 *v*ver 23,24

---

right man, ⁵¹who had not consented to their decision and action. He came from the Judean town of Arimathea and he was waiting for the kingdom of God. *p* ⁵²Going to Pilate, he asked for Jesus' body. ⁵³Then he took it down, wrapped it in linen cloth and placed it in a tomb cut in the rock, one in which no one had yet been laid. ⁵⁴It was Preparation Day, *q* and the Sabbath was about to begin.

⁵⁵The women who had come with Jesus from Galilee *r* followed Joseph and saw the tomb and how his body was laid in it. ⁵⁶Then they went home and prepared spices and perfumes. *s* But they rested on the Sabbath in obedience to the commandment. *t*

The Resurrection

24:1–10pp — Mt 28:1–8; Mk 16:1–8; Jn 20:1–8

24 On the first day of the week, very early in the morning, the women took the spices they had prepared *u* and went to the tomb. ²They found the stone rolled away from the tomb, ³but when they entered, they did not find the body of the Lord Jesus. *v* ⁴While they were won-

---

Study notes:

resurrection (cf. Lk 16:22; 2Co 12:2).
23:44 *about the sixth hour . . . the ninth hour.* From noon to three in the afternoon, by the Jewish method of designating time. Jesus had been put on the cross at the third hour (9:00 A.M., Mk 15:25). The "sixth hour" of John (Jn 19:14) may be Roman time (6:00 A.M.), when Pilate gave his decision (but see note on Jn 19:14).
23:45 *curtain of the temple.* The curtain between the Holy Place and the Most Holy Place. Its tearing symbolized Christ's opening the way directly to God (Heb 9:3,8; 10:19–22).
23:47 *praised God.* Either for having publicly vindicated Jesus by mighty signs from heaven, or out of fear (see Mt 27:54) to appease the heavenly Judge and thus ward off a divine penalty for having carried out an unjust judgment. *this was a righteous man.* Or "this man was the Righteous One." Matthew and Mark report the centurion's words as "this man was the Son (or son) of God." "The Righteous One" and "the Son of God" would have been essentially equivalent terms. Similarly, "the son of God" and "a righteous man" would have been virtual equivalents. Which one the centurion intended is difficult to determine (see note on Mt 27:54). It seems clear, however, that the Gospel writers saw in his declaration a vindication of Jesus, and since the centurion was the Roman official in charge of the crucifixion, his testimony was viewed as significant (see also the declarations of Pilate: vv. 4,14–15,22; Mt 27:23–24).
23:48 *beat their breasts.* A sign of anguish, grief or contrition (cf. 18:13).
23:49 *the women . . . from Galilee.* See Mt 27:55–56; Mk 15:40–41; Jn 19:25; cf. Lk 24:10.
23:50 *Joseph, a member of the Council.* Either Joseph was not present at the meeting of the Sanhedrin (22:66), or he did not support the vote to have Jesus killed (see v. 51). Mk 14:64 suggests he was not present, for the decision was supported by "all."
23:51 *Arimathea.* See note on Mt 27:57. *waiting for the kingdom of God.* See 2:25.

23:52 The remains of an executed criminal often were left unburied or at best put in a dishonored place in a pauper's field. A near relative, such as a mother, might ask for the body, but it was a courageous gesture for Joseph, a member of the Sanhedrin, to ask for Jesus' body.
23:53 *in which no one had yet been laid.* Rock-hewn tombs were usually made to accommodate several bodies. This one, though finished, had not yet been used. See notes on 19:30; Mk 15:46.
23:54 *Preparation Day.* Friday, the day before the Sabbath, when preparation was made for keeping the Sabbath. It could be used for Passover preparation, but since in this instance it is followed by the Sabbath, it indicates Friday.
23:55 *The women.* See v. 49; 24:10; cf. 8:2–3. They saw where Jesus was buried and would not mistake the location when they returned.
23:56 *spices and perfumes.* Yards of cloth and large quantities of spices were used in preparing a body for burial. Seventy-five pounds of myrrh and aloes were already used on that first evening (Jn 19:39). More was purchased for the return of the women after the Sabbath.
24:1 *first day of the week.* Sunday began by Jewish time at sundown on Saturday. Spices could then be bought (Mk 16:1), and they were ready to set out early the next day. When the women started out, it was dark (Jn 20:1), and by the time they arrived at the tomb, it was still early dawn (see Mt 28:1; Mk 16:2).
24:2 *the stone rolled away.* A tomb's entrance was ordinarily closed to keep vandals and animals from disturbing the bodies. This stone, however, had been sealed by Roman authority for a different reason (see Mt 27:62–66).
24:4 *two men.* They looked like men, but their clothes were remarkable (see 9:29; Ac 1:10; 10:30). Other reports referring to them call them angels (v. 23; see also Jn 20:12). Although Matthew speaks of one angel (not two, Mt 28:2) and Mark of a young man in white (Mk 16:5), this is not strange because frequently only the spokesman is noted and an accompanying figure is not mentioned. Words and pos-

dering about this, suddenly two men in clothes that gleamed like lightning*w* stood beside them. [5]In their fright the women bowed down with their faces to the ground, but the men said to them, "Why do you look for the living among the dead? [6]He is not here; he has risen! Remember how he told you, while he was still with you in Galilee:*x* [7]'The Son of Man*y* must be delivered into the hands of sinful men, be crucified and on the third day be raised again.'"*z* [8]Then they remembered his words.*a*

[9]When they came back from the tomb, they told all these things to the Eleven and to all the others. [10]It was Mary Magdalene, Joanna, Mary the mother of James, and the others with them*b* who told this to the apostles.*c* [11]But they did not believe*d* the women, because their words seemed to them like nonsense. [12]Peter, however, got up and ran to the tomb. Bending over, he saw the strips of linen lying by themselves,*e* and he went away,*f* wondering to himself what had happened.

On the Road to Emmaus

[13]Now that same day two of them were going to a village called Emmaus, about seven miles*p* from Jerusalem.*g* [14]They were talking with each other about everything that had happened. [15]As they talked and discussed these things with each other, Jesus himself came up and walked along with them;*h* [16]but they were kept from recognizing him.*i*

[17]He asked them, "What are you discussing together as you walk along?"

They stood still, their faces downcast.

24:4 *w*S Jn 20:12
24:6 *x*Mt 17:22, 23; Lk 9:22; 24:44
24:7 *y*S Mt 8:20 *z*S Mt 16:21
24:8 *a*Jn 2:22
24:10 *b*Lk 8:1-3 *c*S Mk 6:30
24:11 *d*Mk 16:11

24:12 *e*Jn 20:3-7 *f*Jn 20:10
24:13 *g*Mk 16:12
24:15 *h*ver 36
24:16 *i*Jn 20:14; 21:4

p13 Greek *sixty stadia* (about 11 kilometers)

ture (seated, Jn 20:12; standing, Lk 24:4) often change in the course of events, so these variations are not necessarily contradictory. They are merely evidence of independent accounts.
24:6 *while . . . in Galilee.* Jesus had predicted his death and resurrection on a number of occasions (9:22), but the disci-

ples failed to comprehend or accept what he was saying.
24:9 *to the Eleven and to all the others.* "Eleven" is sometimes used to refer to the group of apostles (Ac 1:26; 2:14) after the betrayal by Judas. Judas was dead at the time the apostles first met the risen Christ, but the group was still called the Twelve (Jn 20:24). The "others" included disci-

Resurrection Appearances

EVENT	DATE	Matthew	Mark	Luke	John	Acts	I Corinthians
At the empty tomb outside Jerusalem	Early Sunday morning	28:1-10	16:1-8	24:1-12	20:1-9		
To Mary Magdalene at the tomb	Early Sunday morning		16:9-11		20:11-18		
To two travelers on the road to Emmaus	Sunday at midday			24:13-32			
To Peter in Jerusalem	During the day on Sunday			24:34		15:5	
To the ten disciples in the upper room	Sunday evening		16:14	24:36-43	20:19-25		
To the eleven disciples in the upper room	One week later				20:26-31	15:5	
To seven disciples fishing on the Sea of Galilee	One day at daybreak				21:1-23		
To the eleven disciples on the mountain in Galilee	Some time later	28:16-20	16:15-18				
To more than 500	Some time later					15:6	
To James	Some time later					15:7	
At the Ascension on the Mt. of Olives	Forty days after the resurrection			24:44-49		1:3-8	

[18]One of them, named Cleopas,[j] asked him, "Are you only a visitor to Jerusalem and do not know the things that have happened there in these days?"

[19]"What things?" he asked.

"About Jesus of Nazareth,"[k] they replied. "He was a prophet,[l] powerful in word and deed before God and all the people. [20]The chief priests and our rulers[m] handed him over to be sentenced to death, and they crucified him; [21]but we had hoped that he was the one who was going to redeem Israel.[n] And what is more, it is the third day[o] since all this took place. [22]In addition, some of our women amazed us.[p] They went to the tomb early this morning [23]but didn't find his body. They came and told us that they had seen a vision of angels, who said he was alive. [24]Then some of our companions went to the tomb and found it just as the women had said, but him they did not see."[q]

[25]He said to them, "How foolish you are, and how slow of heart to believe all that the prophets have spoken! [26]Did not the Christ[q] have to suffer these things and then enter his glory?"[r] [27]And beginning with Moses[s] and all the Prophets,[t] he explained to them what was said in all the Scriptures concerning himself.[u]

[28]As they approached the village to which they were going, Jesus acted as if he were going farther. [29]But they urged him strongly, "Stay with us, for it is nearly evening; the day is almost over." So he went in to stay with them.

[30]When he was at the table with them, he took bread, gave thanks, broke it[v] and began to give it to them. [31]Then their eyes were opened and they recognized him,[w] and he disappeared from their sight. [32]They asked each other, "Were not our hearts burning within us[x] while he talked with us on the road and opened the Scriptures[y] to us?"

[33]They got up and returned at once to Jerusalem. There they found the Eleven and those with them, assembled together [34]and saying, "It is true! The Lord[z] has risen and has appeared to Simon."[a] [35]Then the two told what had happened on the way, and how Jesus was recognized by them when he broke the bread.[b]

Jesus Appears to the Disciples

[36]While they were still talking about this, Jesus himself stood among them and said to them, "Peace be with you."[c]

[37]They were startled and frightened, thinking they saw a ghost.[d] [38]He said to them, "Why are you troubled, and why do doubts rise in your minds? [39]Look at my hands and my feet. It is I myself! Touch me and see;[e] a ghost does not have flesh and bones, as you see I have."

[40]When he had said this, he showed them his hands and feet. [41]And while they still did not believe it because of joy and amazement, he asked them, "Do you have anything here to eat?" [42]They gave him a piece of broiled fish, [43]and he took it and ate it in their presence.[f]

[44]He said to them, "This is what I told you while I was still with you:[g] Everything must be fulfilled[h] that is written

---

Cross references (center column):

24:18 /Jn 19:25
24:19 kS Mk 1:24; lS Mt 21:11
24:20 mLk 23:13
24:21 nLk 1:68; 2:38; 21:28; oS Mt 16:21
24:22 pver 1-10
24:24 qver 12
24:26 rHeb 2:10; 1Pe 1:11
24:27 sGe 3:15; Nu 21:9; Dt 18:15; tIsa 7:14; 9:6; 40:10,11; 53; Eze 34:23; Da 9:24; Mic 7:20; Mal 3:1; uJn 1:45
24:30 vS Mt 14:19
24:31 wver 16
24:32 xPs 39:3; yver 27,45
24:34 zS Lk 7:13; a1Co 15:5
24:35 bver 30,31
24:36 cJn 20:19, 21,26; S 14:27
24:37 dMk 6:49
24:39 eJn 20:27; 1Jn 1:1
24:43 fAc 10:41
24:44 gLk 9:45; 18:34; hS Mt 1:22; 16:21; Lk 9:22, 44; 18:31-33; 22:37

[q]26 Or Messiah; also in verse 46

---

ples who, for the most part, came from Galilee.

24:10 *Mary Magdalene.* See note on 8:2. She is named first in most of the lists of women (Mt 27:56; Mk 15:40); but cf. Jn 19:25) and was the first to see the risen Christ (Jn 20:13-18). *Joanna.* See 8:3. She is named by only Luke at this point (Mark is the only one who adds Salome at this time, Mk 16:1). *Mary the mother of James.* See Mk 16:1. She is the "other Mary" of Mt 28:1. The absence of the mother of Jesus is significant. She was probably with John (cf. Jn 19:27).

24:12 *Peter . . . ran.* John's Gospel (20:3-9) includes another disciple, John himself.

24:13 *two of them.* One was named Cleopas (v. 18).

24:16 *kept from recognizing him.* By special divine intervention.

24:19 *a prophet.* They had respect for Jesus as a man of God, but after his death they apparently were reluctant to call him the Messiah.

24:21 *to redeem Israel.* To set the Jewish nation free from bondage to Rome and usher in the kingdom of God (1:68; 2:38; 21:28,31; cf. Tit 2:14; 1Pe 1:18). *the third day.* A reference either to the Jewish belief that after the third day the soul left the body or to Jesus' remark that he would be resurrected on the third day (9:22).

24:23 *vision of angels.* See note on v. 4.

24:24 *some of our companions.* See v. 12 and note.

24:27 *Moses and all the Prophets.* A way of designating the whole of the OT Scriptures.

24:28 *as if he were going farther.* If they had not invited him in, he apparently would have continued on by himself.

24:31 *their eyes were opened.* Cf. v. 16; more than a matter of simple recognition.

24:33 *the Eleven and those with them.* See note on v. 9.

24:36 *Jesus himself stood among them.* Behind locked doors (Jn 20:19), indicating that his body was of a different order. It was the glorified body of the resurrection (cf. Mk 16:12). *Peace be with you.* The traditional greeting, now given new significance by the resurrection.

24:39 *my hands and my feet.* Indicating that Jesus' feet as well as his hands were nailed to the cross (see note on Mk 15:24; cf. Jn 20:20,27).

24:42 *a piece of broiled fish.* Demonstrating that he had a physical body that could consume food.

24:44 *Law of Moses, the Prophets and the Psalms.* The three parts of the Hebrew OT (Psalms was the first book of the third section, called the Writings), indicating that Christ (the Messiah) was foretold in the whole OT.

about me in the Law of Moses,[i] the Prophets[j] and the Psalms."[k]

[45]Then he opened their minds so they could understand the Scriptures. [46]He told them, "This is what is written: The Christ will suffer[l] and rise from the dead on the third day, [m] [47]and repentance and forgiveness of sins will be preached in his name[n] to all nations, [o] beginning at Jerusalem. [p] [48]You are witnesses[q] of these things. [49]I am going to send you what my Father has promised;[r] but stay in the city until you have been clothed with power from on high."

The Ascension

[50]When he had led them out to the vicinity of Bethany, [s] he lifted up his hands and blessed them. [51]While he was blessing them, he left them and was taken up into heaven.[t] [52]Then they worshiped him and returned to Jerusalem with great joy. [53]And they stayed continually at the temple, [u] praising God.

24:44	[i]S ver 27
	[j]S ver 27 [k]Ps 2; 16; 22; 69; 72; 110; 118
24:46	
	[l]S Mt 16:21 [m]S Mt 16:21
24:47	[n]Ac 5:31; 10:43; 13:38 [o]Mt 28:19; Mk 13:10 [p]Isa 2:3
24:48	[q]S Jn 15:27; Ac 1:8; 2:32; 4:20; 5:32; 13:31; 1Pe 5:1
24:49	[r]S Jn 14:16; Ac 1:4
24:50	[s]S Mt 21:17
24:51	[t]2Ki 2:11 **24:53** [u]S Ac 2:46

24:45 *opened their minds.* By explaining the OT Scriptures (cf. v. 27).

24:46 *suffer . . . rise from the dead . . . third day.* The OT depicts the Messiah as one who would suffer (Ps 22; Isa 53) and rise from the dead on the third day (Ps 16:9–11; Isa 53:10–11; compare Jnh 1:17 with Mt 12:40).

24:47 *repentance and forgiveness of sins.* See Ac 5:31; 10:43; 13:38; 26:18. The prediction of Christ's death and resurrection (v. 46) is joined with the essence of man's response (repentance) and the resulting benefit (forgiveness; cf. Isa 49:6; Ac 13:47; 26:22–23). *beginning at Jerusalem.* Cf. Ac 1:8.

24:49 *what my Father has promised.* Cf. Joel 2:28–29. The reference is to the coming power of the Spirit, fulfilled in Ac 2:4.

24:50 *Bethany.* A village on the Mount of Olives (see notes on 19:29; Mt 21:17).

24:51 *taken up into heaven.* Different from his previous disappearances (4:30; 24:3; Jn 8:59). They saw him ascend into a cloud (Ac 1:9).

24:53 *at the temple.* During the period of time immediately following Christ's ascension the believers met continually at the temple (Ac 2:46; 3:1; 5:21,42), where many rooms were available for meetings (see note on 2:37).

JOHN

See "The Synoptic Gospels," p. 1437.

Author

The author is the apostle John, "the disciple whom Jesus loved" (13:23; 19:26; 20:2; 21:7,20,24). He was prominent in the early church but is not mentioned by name in this Gospel—which would be natural if he wrote it, but hard to explain otherwise. The author knew Jewish life well, as seen from references to popular Messianic speculations (e.g., 1:20-21; 7:40-42), to the hostility between Jews and Samaritans (4:9), and to Jewish customs, such as the duty of circumcision on the eighth day taking precedence over the prohibition of working on the Sabbath (see note on 7:22). He knew the geography of Palestine, locating Bethany about 15 stadia (about two miles) from Jerusalem (11:18) and mentioning Cana, a village not referred to in any earlier writing known to us (2:1; 21:2). The Gospel of John has many touches that were obviously based on the recollections of an eyewitness—such as the house at Bethany being filled with the fragrance of the broken perfume jar (12:3). Early writers such as Irenaeus and Tertullian say that John wrote this Gospel, and all other evidence agrees (see Introduction to 1 John: Author).

Date

In general, two views of the dating of this Gospel have been advocated:

1. The traditional view places it toward the end of the first century, c. A.D. 85 or later (see Introduction to 1 John: Date).

2. More recently, some scholars have suggested an earlier date, perhaps as early as the 50s and no later than 70.

The first view may be supported by reference to the statement of Clement of Alexandria that John wrote to supplement the accounts found in the other Gospels (Eusebius, *Ecclesiastical History,* 6.14.7), and thus his Gospel is later than the first three. It has also been argued that the seemingly more developed theology of the fourth Gospel indicates that it originated later.

The second view has found favor because it has been felt more recently that John wrote independently of the other Gospels. This does not contradict the statement of Clement referred to above. Also, those who hold this view point out that developed theology does not necessarily argue for a late origin. The theology of Romans (written c. 57) is every bit as developed as that in John. Further, the statement in 5:2 that there "is" (rather than "was") a pool "near the Sheep Gate" may suggest a time before 70, when Jerusalem was destroyed. Others, however, observe that John elsewhere sometimes used the present tense when speaking of the past.

Purpose and Emphases

Some interpreters have felt that John's aim was to set forth a version of the Christian message that would appeal to Greek thinkers. Others have seen a desire to supplement (or correct) the Synoptic Gospels, to combat some form of heresy, to oppose the continuing followers of John the Baptist or to achieve a similar goal. But the writer himself states his main purpose clearly: "These are written that you may believe that Jesus is the Christ, the Son of God, and that by believing you may have life in his name" (20:31). He may have had Greek readers mainly in mind, some of whom were being exposed to heretical influence, but his primary intention was evangelistic. It is possible to understand "may believe" in the sense of "may continue to believe"—in which case the purpose would be to build up believers as well as to win new converts.

For the main emphases of the book see notes on 1:4,7,9,14,19,49; 2:4,11; 3:27; 4:34; 6:35; 13:1-17:26; 13:31; 17:12,5; 20:31.

Outline

The Word Became Flesh

1 In the beginning was the Word,[a] and the Word was with God,[b] and the Word was God.[c] [2]He was with God in the beginning.[d]

[3]Through him all things were made; without him nothing was made that has been made.[e] [4]In him was life,[f] and that life was the light[g] of men. [5]The light shines in the darkness,[h] but the darkness has not understood[a] it.[i]

[6]There came a man who was sent from God; his name was John.[j] [7]He came as a witness to testify[k] concerning that light, so that through him all men might believe.[l] [8]He himself was not the light; he came only as a witness to the light. [9]The true light[m] that gives light to every man[n] was coming into the world.[b]

[10]He was in the world, and though the world was made through him,[o] the world did not recognize him. [11]He came to that which was his own, but his own did not receive him.[p] [12]Yet to all who received him, to those who believed[q] in his name,[r]

he gave the right to become children of God[s]— [13]children born not of natural descent,[c] nor of human decision or a husband's will, but born of God.[t]

[14]The Word became flesh[u] and made his dwelling among us. We have seen his glory,[v] the glory of the One and Only,[d] who came from the Father, full of grace[w] and truth.[x]

[15]John testifies[y] concerning him. He cries out, saying, "This was he of whom I said, 'He who comes after me has surpassed me because he was before me.'"[z] [16]From the fullness[a] of his grace[b] we have all received one blessing after another. [17]For the law was given through Moses;[c] grace and truth came through Jesus Christ.[d] [18]No one has ever seen God,[e] but

1:1 aIsa 55:11; Rev 19:13
bJn 17:5; 1Jn 1:2
cPhp 2:6
1:2 dGe 1:1; Jn 8:58; 17:5,24; 1Jn 1:1; Rev 1:8
1:3 ever 10; 1Co 8:6; Col 1:16; Heb 1:2
1:4 fS Jn 5:26; 6:57; 11:25; 14:6; Ac 3:15; Heb 7:16; 1Jn 1:1,2; 5:20; Rev 1:18
gPs 36:9; Jn 3:19; 8:12; 9:5; 12:46
1:5 hPs 18:28 iJn 3:19
1:6 jS Mt 3:1
1:7 kver 15,19, 32; Jn 3:26; 5:33 lver 12; S Jn 3:15
1:9 m1Jn 2:8 nIsa 49:6
1:10 oS ver 3
1:11 pIsa 53:3
1:12 qver 7; S Jn 3:15 rS 1Jn 3:23
sDt 14:1; S Ro 8:14; 8:16, 21; Eph 5:1; 1Jn 3:1,2
1:13 tJn 3:6; Tit 3:5; Jas 1:18; 1Pe 1:23; 1Jn 3:9; 4:7; 5:1, 4

1:14 uGal 4:4; Php 2:7,8; 1Ti 3:16; Heb 2:14; 1Jn 1:1,2; 4:2 vEx 33:18; 40:34 wS Ro 3:24 xJn 14:6 1:15 yver 7 zver 30; Mt 3:11 1:16 aEph 1:23; Col 1:19; 2:9 bS Ro 3:24 1:17 cDt 32:46; Jn 7:19 dver 14 1:18 eEx 33:20; Jn 6:46; Col 1:15; 1Ti 6:16; 1Jn 4:12

a5 Or darkness, and the darkness has not overcome b9 Or This was the true light that gives light to every man who comes into the world   c13 Greek of bloods d14 Or the Only Begotten

1:1 *In the beginning.* See Ge 1:1. *Word.* Greeks used this term not only of the spoken word but also of the unspoken word, the word still in the mind—the reason. When they applied it to the universe, they meant the rational principle that governs all things. Jews, on the other hand, used it as a way of referring to God. Thus John used a term that was meaningful to both Jews and Gentiles. *with God.* The Word was distinct from the Father. *was God.* In the fullest sense (see note on Ro 9:5). The prologue (vv. 1–18) begins and ends with a ringing affirmation of his deity (see note on v. 18).
1:4 *life.* One of the great concepts of this Gospel. The term is found 36 times in John, while no other NT book uses it more than 17 times. Life is Christ's gift (10:28), and he, in fact, is "the life" (14:6). *light of men.* This Gospel also links light with Christ, from whom comes all spiritual illumination. He is the "light of the world," who holds out wonderful hope for man (8:12). For an OT link between life and light see Ps 36:9.
1:5 *darkness.* The stark contrast between light and darkness is a striking theme in this Gospel (see, e.g., 12:35).
1:6 *John.* In this Gospel the name John always refers to John the Baptist.
1:7 *as a witness to testify.* John the Baptist's singular ministry was to testify to Jesus (10:41). "Witness" is another important concept in this Gospel. The noun ("witness" or "testimony") is used 14 times (in Matthew not at all, in Mark three times, in Luke once) and the verb ("testify") 33 times (found once each in Matthew and Luke, not at all in Mark)—in both cases more often than anywhere else in the NT. John (the author) thereby emphasizes that the facts about Jesus are amply attested. *that through him all men might believe.* People were not to believe "in" John the Baptist but "through" him. Similarly, the writer's purpose was to draw them to belief in Christ (20:31); he uses the verb "believe" 98 times.
1:9 John is referring to the incarnation of Christ. *world.* Another common word in John's writings, found 78 times in this Gospel and 24 times in his letters (only 47 times in all of Paul's writings). It can mean the universe, the earth, the

people on earth, most people, people opposed to God, or the human system opposed to God's purposes. John emphasizes the word by repetition, and moves without explanation from one meaning to another (see, e.g., 17:5,14–15 and notes).
1:12 *he gave the right.* Membership in God's family is by grace alone—the gift of God (see Eph 2:8–9). It is never a human achievement, as v. 13 emphasizes; yet the imparting of the gift is dependent on man's reception of it, as the words "received" and "believed" make clear.
1:14 *became.* Indicates transition; the Word existed before he became man. *flesh.* A strong, almost crude, word that stresses the reality of Christ's manhood. *made his dwelling among us. We have seen his glory.* The Greek for "made his dwelling" is connected with the word for "tent/tabernacle"; the verse would have reminded John's Jewish readers of the Tent of Meeting, which was filled by the glory of God (Ex 40:34–35). Christ revealed his glory to his disciples by the miracles he performed (see 2:11) and by his death and resurrection. *grace and truth.* The corresponding Hebrew terms are often translated "(unfailing) love and faithfulness" (see notes on Ps 26:3; Pr 16:6). *grace.* A significant Christian concept (see notes on Jnh 4:2; Gal 1:3; Eph 1:2), though John never uses the word after the prologue (vv. 1–18). *truth.* A word John uses 25 times and links closely with Jesus, who is the truth (14:6).
1:15 *cries out.* The present tense indicates that John the Baptist's preaching still sounded in people's ears, though he was killed long before this Gospel was written. *he was before me.* In ancient times the older person was given respect and regarded as greater than the younger. People would normally have ranked Jesus lower in respect than John, who was older. John the Baptist explains that this is only apparent, since Jesus, as the Word, existed before he was born on earth.
1:18 *God the One and Only.* An explicit declaration of Christ's deity (see vv. 1,14 and notes; 3:16). *has made him known.* Sometimes in the OT people are said to have seen God (e.g., Ex 24:9–11). But we are also told that no one can see God and live (Ex 33:20). Therefore, since no human

God the One and Only,[e,f]f who is at the Father's side, has made him known.

John the Baptist Denies Being the Christ

[19]Now this was John's[g] testimony when the Jews[h] of Jerusalem sent priests and Levites to ask him who he was. [20]He did not fail to confess, but confessed freely, "I am not the Christ.[g]"[i]

[21]They asked him, "Then who are you? Are you Elijah?"[j]

He said, "I am not."

"Are you the Prophet?"[k]

He answered, "No."

[22]Finally they said, "Who are you? Give us an answer to take back to those who sent us. What do you say about yourself?"

[23]John replied in the words of Isaiah the prophet, "I am the voice of one calling in the desert,[l] 'Make straight the way for the Lord.'"[h][m]

[24]Now some Pharisees who had been sent [25]questioned him, "Why then do you baptize if you are not the Christ, nor Elijah, nor the Prophet?"

[26]"I baptize with[i] water," [n] John replied, "but among you stands one you do not know. [27]He is the one who comes after me,[o] the thongs of whose sandals I am not worthy to untie."[p]

[28]This all happened at Bethany on the other side of the Jordan,[q] where John was baptizing.

Jesus the Lamb of God

[29]The next day John saw Jesus coming toward him and said, "Look, the Lamb of God,[r] who takes away the sin of the world![s] [30]This is the one I meant when I said, 'A man who comes after me has surpassed me because he was before me.'[t] [31]I myself did not know him, but the reason I came baptizing with water was that he might be revealed to Israel."

[32]Then John gave this testimony: "I saw the Spirit come down from heaven as a dove and remain on him.[u] [33]I would not have known him, except that the one who

Cross references
1:18 /Jn 3:16,18; 1Jn 4:9
1:19 gS Mt 3:1 hJn 2:18; 5:10, 16; 6:41,52; 7:1; 10:24
1:20 /Jn 3:28; Lk 3:15,16
1:21 /S Mt 11:14 kDt 18:15
1:23 /Mt 3:1 mIsa 40:3
1:26 nS Mk 1:4
1:27 over 15,30 pMk 1:7
1:28 qJn 3:26; 10:40
1:29 rver 36; Ge 22:8; Isa 53:7; 1Pe 1:19; Rev 5:6; 13:8 sS Jn 3:17
1:30 tver 15,27
1:32 uMt 3:16

Footnotes
e 18 Or the Only Begotten   f 18 Some manuscripts but the only (or only begotten) Son   g 20 Or Messiah. "The Christ" (Greek) and "the Messiah" (Hebrew) both mean "the Anointed One"; also in verse 25.
h 23 Isaiah 40:3   i 26 Or in; also in verses 31 and 33

---

being can see God as he really is, those who saw God saw him in a form he took on himself temporarily for the occasion. Now, however, Christ has made him known.

1:19 *the Jews.* The phrase occurs about 70 times in this Gospel. It is used in a favorable sense (e.g., 4:22) and in a neutral sense (e.g., 2:6). But generally John used it of the Jewish leaders who were hostile to Jesus (e.g., 8:48). Here it refers to the delegation sent by the Sanhedrin to look into the activities of an unauthorized teacher. *Levites.* Descendants of the tribe of Levi, who were assigned to specific duties in connection with the tabernacle and temple (Nu 3:17–37). They also had teaching responsibilities (2Ch 35:3; Ne 8:7–9), and it was probably in this role that they were sent with the priests to John the Baptist.

1:20 *I.* Emphatic, contrasting John the Baptist (or Baptizer) with someone else. Throughout the following verses this emphatic "I" occurs frequently, and almost invariably there is an implied contrast with Jesus, who is always given the higher place.

1:21 *Are you Elijah? . . . I am not.* The Jews remembered that Elijah had not died (2Ki 2:11) and believed that the same prophet would come back to earth to announce the end time. In this sense, John properly denied that he was Elijah. When Jesus later said the Baptist was Elijah (Mt 11:14; 17:10–13), he meant it in the sense that John was a fulfillment of the prophecy of Mal 4:5 (cf. Lk 1:17). *the Prophet.* The prophet of Dt 18:15,18. The Jewish people expected a variety of persons to be associated with the coming of the Messiah. John the Baptist emphatically denies being the Prophet. He had come to testify about Jesus, yet they kept asking him about himself. His answers became progressively more terse.

1:23 The Baptist applied the prophecy of Isa 40:3 to his own ministry of calling people to repent in preparation for the coming of the Messiah. The men of Qumran (the community that produced the Dead Sea Scrolls; see "The Time between the Testaments," p. 1431) applied the same words to themselves, but they prepared for the Lord's coming by

isolating themselves from the world to secure their own salvation. John concentrated on helping people come to the Messiah (the Christ).

1:24 *Pharisees.* The conservative religious party, who probed deeper than the rest of the delegation (v. 19). See notes on Mt 3:7; Mk 2:16; Lk 5:17.

1:25 *the Christ.* Means "the Anointed One" (see NIV text note on v. 20). In OT times anointing signified being set apart for service, particularly as king (cf. 1Sa 16:1,13; 26:11) or priest (Ex 40:13–15; Lev 4:3). But people were looking for not just *an* anointed one but *the* Anointed One, the Messiah.

1:27 *whose sandals I am not worthy to untie.* A menial task, fit for a slave. Disciples would perform all sorts of service for their rabbis (teachers), but loosing sandal thongs was expressly excluded.

1:28 *Bethany.* The Bethany mentioned elsewhere in the Gospels was only about two miles from Jerusalem. The site of this other Bethany is not known, except that it was located on the east side of the Jordan.

1:29 *Lamb of God.* An expression found in the Bible only here and in v. 36. Many suggestions have been made as to its precise meaning (e.g., the lamb offered at Passover, or the lamb of Isa 53:7, of Jer 11:19 or of Ge 22:8). But the expression seems to be a general reference to sacrifice, not the name for a particular offering. John was saying that Jesus would be the sacrifice that would atone for the sin of the world.

1:31 *I . . . did not know him.* John the Baptist, who "lived in the desert until he appeared publicly to Israel" (Lk 1:80), may not have known Jesus at all. But the words probably mean only that he did not know that Jesus was the Messiah until he saw the sign mentioned in vv. 32–33.

1:32 See note on Mt 3:15 for Jesus' baptism.

1:33 *he . . . will baptize with the Holy Spirit.* John baptized with water, but Jesus would baptize with the Spirit. If a specific event is intended by these words, the fulfillment was the sending of the Holy Spirit on the day of Pentecost (Ac 2).

sent me to baptize with water[v] told me, 'The man on whom you see the Spirit come down and remain is he who will baptize with the Holy Spirit.'[w] 34I have seen and I testify that this is the Son of God."[x]

Jesus' First Disciples

1:40–42pp — Mt 4:18–22; Mk 1:16–20; Lk 5:2–11

35The next day John[y] was there again with two of his disciples. 36When he saw Jesus passing by, he said, "Look, the Lamb of God!"[z]

37When the two disciples heard him say this, they followed Jesus. 38Turning around, Jesus saw them following and asked, "What do you want?"

They said, "Rabbi"[a] (which means Teacher), "where are you staying?"

39"Come," he replied, "and you will see."

So they went and saw where he was staying, and spent that day with him. It was about the tenth hour.

40Andrew, Simon Peter's brother, was one of the two who heard what John had said and who had followed Jesus. 41The first thing Andrew did was to find his brother Simon and tell him, "We have found the Messiah" (that is, the Christ).[b] 42And he brought him to Jesus.

Jesus looked at him and said, "You are Simon son of John. You will be called[c] Cephas" (which, when translated, is Peter[j]).[d]

Jesus Calls Philip and Nathanael

43The next day Jesus decided to leave

for Galilee. Finding Philip,[e] he said to him, "Follow me."[f]

44Philip, like Andrew and Peter, was from the town of Bethsaida.[g] 45Philip found Nathanael[h] and told him, "We have found the one Moses wrote about in the Law,[i] and about whom the prophets also wrote[j]—Jesus of Nazareth,[k] the son of Joseph."[l]

46"Nazareth! Can anything good come from there?"[m] Nathanael asked.

"Come and see," said Philip.

47When Jesus saw Nathanael approaching, he said of him, "Here is a true Israelite,[n] in whom there is nothing false."[o]

48"How do you know me?" Nathanael asked.

Jesus answered, "I saw you while you were still under the fig tree before Philip called you."

49Then Nathanael declared, "Rabbi,[p] you are the Son of God;[q] you are the King of Israel."[r]

50Jesus said, "You believe[k] because I told you I saw you under the fig tree. You shall see greater things than that." 51He then added, "I tell you[l] the truth, you[l] shall see heaven open,[s] and the angels of God ascending and descending[t] on the Son of Man."[u]

Jesus Changes Water to Wine

2 On the third day a wedding took place at Cana in Galilee.[v] Jesus' mother[w] was there, 2and Jesus and his disciples had also been invited to the wedding. 3When

Cross references (center column)

1:33 [v]S Mk 1:4; [w]S Mk 1:8
1:34 [x]ver 49; S Mt 4:3
1:35 [y]S Mt 3:1
1:36 [z]S ver 29
1:38 [a]ver 49; S Mt 23:7
1:41 [b]Jn 4:25
1:42 [c]Ge 17:5, 15; 32:28; 35:10; [d]Mt 16:18
1:43 [e]Mt 10:3; Jn 6:5-7; 12:21, 22; 14:8,9; [f]S Mt 4:19
1:44 [g]S Mt 11:21
1:45 [h]Jn 21:2; [i]S Lk 24:27; [j]S Lk 24:27; [k]S Mk 1:24; [l]Lk 3:23
1:46 [m]Jn 7:41, 42,52
1:47 [n]Ro 9:4,6; [o]Ps 32:2
1:49 [p]ver 38; S Mt 23:7; [q]ver 34; S Mt 4:3; [r]S Mt 2:2; 27:42; Jn 12:13
1:51 [s]S Mt 3:16; [t]Ge 28:12; [u]S Mt 8:20
2:1 [v]Jn 4:46; 21:2; [w]S Mt 12:46

Text notes (center column, bottom)

[j]42 Both *Cephas* (Aramaic) and *Peter* (Greek) mean *rock.* [k]50 Or *Do you believe . . . ?* [l]51 The Greek is plural.

1:34 *Son of God.* See vv. 14,18; 3:16; 20:31.
1:35 *two.* One was Andrew (v. 40). The other is not named, but from early times it has been thought that he was the author of this Gospel. *his disciples.* In the sense that they had been baptized by John and looked to him as their religious teacher.
1:36 *Lamb of God.* See note on v. 29.
1:39 *tenth hour.* 4:00 P.M.
1:41 *the Messiah.* See note on v. 25.
1:42 *Peter.* See NIV text note. In the Gospels, Peter was anything but a rock; he was impulsive and unstable. In Acts, he was a pillar of the early church. Jesus named him not for what he was but for what, by God's grace, he would become.
1:44 *Bethsaida.* See note on Mt 11:21.
1:45 *son of Joseph.* Not a denial of the virgin birth of Christ (Mt 1:18,20,23,25; Lk 1:35). Joseph was Jesus' legal, though not his natural, father.
1:46 *Nazareth.* See 7:52; see also note on Mt 2:23.
1:47 *a true Israelite.* See 2:24–25.
1:48 *fig tree.* Its shade was a favorite place for study and prayer in hot weather.
1:49 *Son of God.* See vv. 14,18,34; 3:16; 20:31. At the beginning of Jesus' ministry Nathanael acknowledged Jesus

with this meaningful title; later it was used in mockery (Mt 27:40; cf. Jn 19:7). *King of Israel.* See 12:13. In Mk 15:32 "Christ" and "King of Israel" are equated.
1:51 *heaven open.* In Jesus' ministry the disciples will see heaven's (God's) testimony to Jesus as plainly as if they heard an announcement from heaven concerning him. *the angels of God ascending and descending.* As in Jacob's dream (see Ge 28:12 and note), thus marking Jesus as God's elect one through whom redemption comes to the world—perhaps identifying Jesus as *the* true Israelite (see v. 47). *Son of Man.* Jesus' favorite self-designation (see notes on Mk 8:31; Lk 6:5; 19:10).
2:1 *a wedding.* Little is known of how a wedding was performed in first-century Palestine, but clearly the feast was very important and might go on for a week. To fail in proper hospitality was a serious offense. *Cana.* Mentioned only in John's Gospel (2:11; 4:46,50; 21:2). It was west of the Sea of Galilee, but the exact location is unknown.
2:3 *When the wine was gone.* More than a minor social embarrassment, since the family had an obligation to provide a feast of the socially required standard. There was no great variety in beverages, and people normally drank water or wine.

Miracles of Jesus

Healing	MATTHEW	MARK	LUKE	JOHN
Man with leprosy	8:2-4	1:40-42	5:12-13	
Roman centurion's servant	8:5-13		7:1-10	
Peter's mother-in-law	8:14-15	1:30-31	4:38-39	
Two men from Gadara	8:28-34	5:1-15	8:27-35	
Paralyzed man	9:2-7	2:3-12	5:18-25	
Woman with bleeding	9:20-22	5:25-29	8:43-48	
Two blind men	9:27-31			
Man mute and possessed	9:32-33			
Man with a shriveled hand	12:10-13	3:1-5	6:6-10	
Man blind, mute and possessed	12:22		11:14	
Canaanite woman's daughter	15:21-28	7:24-30		
Boy with a demon	17:14-18	9:17-29	9:38-43	
Two blind men (one named)	20:29-34	10:46-52	18:35-43	
Deaf mute		7:31-37		
Man possessed, synagogue		1:23-26	4:33-35	
Blind man at Bethsaida		8:22-26		
Crippled woman			13:11-13	
Man with dropsy			14:1-4	
Ten men with leprosy			17:11-19	
The high priest's servant			22:50-51	
Official's son at Capernaum				4:46-54
Sick man, pool of Bethesda				5:1-9
Man born blind				9:1-7

Command over the forces of nature	MATTHEW	MARK	LUKE	JOHN
Calming the storm	8:23-27	4:37-41	8:22-25	
Walking on the water	14:25	6:48-51		6:19-21
5,000 people fed	14:15-21	6:35-44	9:12-17	6:5-13
4,000 people fed	15:32-38	8:1-9		
Coin in the fish's mouth	17:24-27			
Fig tree withered	21:18-22	11:12-14, 20-25		
Catch of fish			5:4-11	
Water turned into wine				2:1-11
Another catch of fish				21:1-11

Bringing the dead back to life	MATTHEW	MARK	LUKE	JOHN
Jairus's daughter	9:18-19, 23-25	5:22-24, 38-42	8:41-42, 49-56	
Widow's son at Nain			7:11-15	
Lazarus				11:1-44

the wine was gone, Jesus' mother said to him, "They have no more wine."

[4]"Dear woman,[x] why do you involve me?"[y] Jesus replied. "My time[z] has not yet come."

[5]His mother said to the servants, "Do whatever he tells you."[a]

[6]Nearby stood six stone water jars, the kind used by the Jews for ceremonial washing,[b] each holding from twenty to thirty gallons.[m]

[7]Jesus said to the servants, "Fill the jars with water"; so they filled them to the brim.

[8]Then he told them, "Now draw some out and take it to the master of the banquet."

They did so, [9]and the master of the banquet tasted the water that had been turned into wine.[c] He did not realize where it had come from, though the servants who had drawn the water knew. Then he called the bridegroom aside [10]and said, "Everyone brings out the choice wine first and then the cheaper wine after the guests have had too much to drink; but you have saved the best till now."

[11]This, the first of his miraculous signs,[d] Jesus performed at Cana in Galilee. He thus revealed his glory,[e] and his disciples put their faith in him.[f]

Jesus Clears the Temple

2:14–16pp — Mt 21:12,13; Mk 11:15–17; Lk 19:45,46

[12]After this he went down to Capernaum[g] with his mother[h] and brothers[i]

and his disciples. There they stayed for a few days.

[13]When it was almost time for the Jewish Passover,[j] Jesus went up to Jerusalem.[k] [14]In the temple courts he found men selling cattle, sheep and doves,[l] and others sitting at tables exchanging money.[m] [15]So he made a whip out of cords, and drove all from the temple area, both sheep and cattle; he scattered the coins of the money changers and overturned their tables. [16]To those who sold doves he said, "Get these out of here! How dare you turn my Father's house[n] into a market!"

[17]His disciples remembered that it is written: "Zeal for your house will consume me."[n][o]

[18]Then the Jews[p] demanded of him, "What miraculous sign[q] can you show us to prove your authority to do all this?"[r]

[19]Jesus answered them, "Destroy this temple, and I will raise it again in three days."[s]

[20]The Jews replied, "It has taken forty-six years to build this temple, and you are going to raise it in three days?" [21]But the temple he had spoken of was his body.[t] [22]After he was raised from the dead, his disciples recalled what he had said.[u] Then they believed the Scripture[v] and the words that Jesus had spoken.

[23]Now while he was in Jerusalem at the Passover Feast,[w] many people saw the miraculous signs[x] he was doing and be-

Cross references (center column)

2:4 [x]Jn 19:26
[y]S Mt 8:29
[z]S Mt 26:18
2:5 [a]Ge 41:55
2:6 [b]Mk 7:3,4;
Jn 3:25
2:9 [c]Jn 4:46
2:11 [d]ver 23;
Mt 12:38; Jn 3:2;
S 4:48; 6:2,14,26,
30; 12:37; 20:30
[e]Jn 1:14
[f]Ex 14:31
2:12 [g]S Mt 4:13
[h]S Mt 12:46
[i]S Mt 12:46
2:13 [j]S Jn 11:55
[k]Dt 16:1-6;
Lk 2:41
2:14 [l]Lev 1:14;
Dt 14:26
[m]Dt 14:25
2:16 [n]Lk 2:49
2:17 [o]Ps 69:9
2:18 [p]S Jn 1:19
[q]S ver 11
[r]S Mt 12:38
2:19
[s]S Mt 16:21;
26:61; 27:40;
Mk 14:58; 15:29;
Ac 6:14
2:21 [t]1Co 6:19
2:22 [u]Lk 24:5-8;
Jn 12:16; 14:26
[v]Ps 16:10;
S Lk 24:27
2:23 [w]ver 13
[x]S ver 11

[m]6 Greek *two to three metretes* (probably about 75 to 115 liters)   [n]17 Psalm 69:9

2:4 *My time has not yet come.* Several similar expressions scattered through this Gospel (7:6,8,30; 8:20) picture Jesus moving inevitably toward the destiny for which he had come: the time of his sacrificial death on the cross. At the crucifixion and resurrection Jesus' time had truly come (12:23,27; 13:1; 16:32; 17:1).

2:6 *ceremonial washing.* Jews became ceremonially defiled during the normal circumstances of daily life, and were cleansed by pouring water over the hands. For a lengthy feast with many guests a large amount of water was required for this purpose. *holding.* Refers to capacity, not actual content.

2:11 *signs.* John always refers to Jesus' miracles as "signs," a word emphasizing the significance of the action rather than the marvel (see, e.g., 4:54; 6:14; 9:16; 11:47). They revealed Jesus' glory (see 1:14; cf. Isa 35:1–2; Joel 3:18; Am 9:13).

2:12 *went down.* Situated on the shore of the lake, Capernaum was at a lower level than Cana. *brothers.* See note on Lk 8:19.

2:13 *Passover.* See Ex 12 and notes on Ex 12:11–23; see also notes on Mt 26:17,18–30; Mk 14:1,12; Lk 22:1; and chart on "OT Feasts and Other Sacred Days," p. 176. Passover was one of the annual feasts that all Jewish men were required to celebrate in Jerusalem (Dt 16:16). See note on 5:1.

2:14–17 Matthew, Mark and Luke record a cleansing of the temple toward the end of Jesus' ministry (see note on Mt 21:12–17).

2:14 *cattle, sheep and doves.* Required for sacrifices. Jews who came great distances had to be able to buy sacrificial animals near the temple. The merchants, however, were selling them in the outer court of the temple itself, the one place where Gentiles could come to pray. *exchanging money.* Many coins had to be changed into currency acceptable to the temple authorities, which made money changers necessary (see note on Mk 11:15). They should not, however, have been working in the temple itself.

2:19 The Jews thought Jesus was referring to the literal temple, but John tells us that he was not (v. 21). Years later Jesus was accused of saying that he would destroy the temple and raise it again (Mt 26:60–61; Mk 14:57–59), and mockers repeated the charge as he hung on the cross (Mt 27:40; Mk 15:29). The same misunderstanding may have been behind the charge against Stephen (Ac 6:14).

2:20 *forty-six years.* The temple was not finally completed until A.D. 64. The meaning is that work had been going on for 46 years. Since it had begun in 20 B.C., the year of the event recorded here is A.D. 26.

2:22 *recalled.* See 14:26.

2:23 *the Passover Feast.* See note on v. 13. *name.* In ancient times an individual's "name" summed up his whole person (see NIV text note).

lieved[y] in his name.[o] 24But Jesus would not entrust himself to them, for he knew all men. 25He did not need man's testimony about man,[z] for he knew what was in a man.[a]

Jesus Teaches Nicodemus

3 Now there was a man of the Pharisees named Nicodemus,[b] a member of the Jewish ruling council.[c] 2He came to Jesus at night and said, "Rabbi,[d] we know[e] you are a teacher who has come from God. For no one could perform the miraculous signs[f] you are doing if God were not with him."[g]

3In reply Jesus declared, "I tell you the truth, no one can see the kingdom of God unless he is born again.[p][h][i]

4"How can a man be born when he is old?" Nicodemus asked. "Surely he cannot enter a second time into his mother's womb to be born!"

5Jesus answered, "I tell you the truth, no one can enter the kingdom of God unless he is born of water and the Spirit.[j][k] 6Flesh gives birth to flesh, but the Spirit gives birth to spirit.[l] 7You should not be surprised at my saying, 'You[r] must be born again.' 8The wind blows wherever it pleases. You hear its sound, but you cannot tell where it comes from or where it is going. So it is with everyone born of the Spirit."[m]

9"How can this be?"[n] Nicodemus asked.

10"You are Israel's teacher,"[o] said Jesus, "and do you not understand these things? 11I tell you the truth, we speak of what we know,[p] and we testify to what we have seen, but still you people do not accept our testimony.[q] 12I have spoken to you of

earthly things and you do not believe; how then will you believe if I speak of heavenly things? 13No one has ever gone into heaven[r] except the one who came from heaven[s]—the Son of Man.[s][t] 14Just as Moses lifted up the snake in the desert,[u] so the Son of Man must be lifted up,[v] 15that everyone who believes[w] in him may have eternal life.[t][x]

16"For God so loved[y] the world that he gave[z] his one and only Son,[u][a] that whoever believes[b] in him shall not perish but have eternal life.[c] 17For God did not send his Son into the world[d] to condemn the world, but to save the world through him.[e] 18Whoever believes in him is not condemned,[f] but whoever does not believe stands condemned already because he has not believed in the name of God's one and only Son.[v][g] 19This is the verdict: Light[h] has come into the world, but men loved darkness instead of light because their deeds were evil.[i] 20Everyone who does evil hates the light, and will not come into the light for fear that his deeds will be exposed.[j] 21But whoever lives by the truth comes into the light, so that it may be seen plainly that what he has done has been done through God."[w]

John the Baptist's Testimony About Jesus

22After this, Jesus and his disciples went

Cross references (center column)

2:23 y S Jn 3:15
2:25 z Isa 11:3
a Dt 31:21;
1Ki 8:39;
S Mt 9:4; Jn 6:61,
64; 13:11
3:1 b Jn 7:50;
19:39 c Lk 23:13
3:2 d S Mt 23:7
ever 11 f S Jn 2:11
g Jn 10:38; 14:10,
11; Ac 2:22;
10:38
3:3 h S Jn 1:13
i S Mt 3:2
3:5 j S Ac 22:16
k Tit 3:5
3:6 l S Jn 1:13;
1Co 15:50
3:8
m 1Co 2:14-16
3:9 n Jn 6:52,60
3:10 o Lk 2:46
3:11 p Jn 1:18;
7:16,17 q ver 32
3:13 r Pr 30:4;
Ac 2:34;
Eph 4:8-10 s ver
31; Jn 6:38,42;
Heb 4:14; 9:24
t S Mt 8:20
3:14 u Nu 21:8,9
v S Jn 12:32
3:15 w ver 16,36;
Ge 15:6;
Nu 14:11;
Mt 27:42;
Mk 1:15; Jn 1:7,
12; 2:23; 5:24;
7:38; 20:29;
Ac 13:39; 16:31;
Ro 3:22; 10:9,10;
1Jn 5:1,5,10 x ver
16,36;
S Mt 25:46;
Jn 20:31
3:16 y Ro 5:8;
Eph 2:4; 1Jn 4:9,
10 z Isa 9:6;
Ro 8:32
a Ge 22:12;
Jn 1:18 b S ver 15
c ver 36; Jn 6:29,
40; 11:25,26
3:17 d Jn 6:29,57;
10:36; 11:42;
17:8,21; 20:21
e Isa 53:11;
S Mt 1:21;
S Lk 2:11; 19:10;
Jn 1:29; 12:47;
S Ro 11:14;
1Ti 1:15; 2:5,6;
1Jn 2:2; 3:5
3:18 f Jn 5:24 g Jn 1:18; 1Jn 4:9 3:19 h S Jn 1:4 i Ps 52:3;
Jn 7:7 3:20 j Eph 5:11,13

Text notes (center column)

o 23 Or and believed in him   p 3 Or born from above; also in verse 7   q 6 Or but spirit   r 7 The Greek is plural.   s 13 Some manuscripts Man, who is in heaven   t 15 Or believes may have eternal life in him   u 16 Or his only begotten Son   v 18 Or God's only begotten Son   w 21 Some interpreters end the quotation after verse 15.

Study notes (bottom)

3:1 a man of the Pharisees. See notes on Mt 3:7; Mk 2:16; Lk 5:17.

3:2 at night. Perhaps Nicodemus was afraid to come by day. Or he may have wanted a long talk, which would have been difficult in the daytime with the crowds around Jesus.

3:3 born again. The Greek also may mean "born from above" (see NIV text note). Both meanings are consistent with Jesus' redeeming work.

3:5 kingdom of God. See note on Mt 3:2. born of water and the Spirit. A phrase understood in various ways: 1. It means much the same as "born of the Spirit" (v. 8; cf. Tit 3:5). 2. Water here refers to purification. 3. Water refers to baptism—that of John (1:31) or that of Jesus and his disciples (v. 22; 4:1–2).

3:7 You. See NIV text note. This assertion applies to everyone, not just Nicodemus. must. There are no exceptions. born again. See note on v. 3.

3:8 The Holy Spirit is sovereign. He works as he pleases in his renewal of the human heart.

3:11 we. The plural associates others, perhaps the disci-

ples, with Jesus. The words are true of Christians as well as of Christ. testimony. See note on 1:7.

3:13 the Son of Man. Jesus' favorite self-designation (see notes on Mk 8:31; Lk 6:5; 19:10).

3:14 the Son of Man must be lifted up. See notes on 12:31–32.

3:15 believes. See note on 1:7. eternal life. An infinitely high quality of life in living fellowship with God—both now and forever.

3:16 God so loved the world. The great truth that motivated God's plan of salvation (cf. 1Jn 4:9–10). All people on earth—or perhaps all creation (see note on 1:9). that he gave. See Isa 9:6. one and only Son. See 1:14,18; cf. Ge 22:2,16; Ro 8:32. Although believers are also called "sons of God" (2Co 6:18; Rev 21:7), Jesus is uniquely God's Son.

3:18 believes . . . does not believe. John is not speaking of momentary beliefs and doubts but of continuing, settled attitudes.

3:22 baptized. According to 4:2 only the disciples actually baptized.

out into the Judean countryside, where he spent some time with them, and baptized. [k] [23]Now John [l] also was baptizing at Aenon near Salim, because there was plenty of water, and people were constantly coming to be baptized. [24](This was before John was put in prison.) [m] [25]An argument developed between some of John's disciples and a certain Jew[x] over the matter of ceremonial washing. [n] [26]They came to John and said to him, "Rabbi, [o] that man who was with you on the other side of the Jordan—the one you testified[p] about —well, he is baptizing, and everyone is going to him."

[27]To this John replied, "A man can receive only what is given him from heaven. [28]You yourselves can testify that I said, 'I am not the Christ[y] but am sent ahead of him.' [q] [29]The bride belongs to the bridegroom. [r] The friend who attends the bridegroom waits and listens for him, and is full of joy when he hears the bridegroom's voice. That joy is mine, and it is now complete. [s] [30]He must become greater; I must become less.

[31]"The one who comes from above[t] is above all; the one who is from the earth belongs to the earth, and speaks as one from the earth. [u] The one who comes from heaven is above all. [32]He testifies to what he has seen and heard, [v] but no one accepts his testimony. [w] [33]The man who has accepted it has certified that God is truthful. [34]For the one whom God has sent[x] speaks the words of God, for God[z] gives the Spirit[y] without limit. [35]The Father loves the Son and has placed everything in his hands. [z] [36]Whoever believes in the Son has eternal life, [a] but whoever rejects the Son will not see life, for God's wrath remains on him." [a]

Jesus Talks With a Samaritan Woman

4 The Pharisees heard that Jesus was gaining and baptizing more disciples than John, [b] [2]although in fact it was not Jesus who baptized, but his disciples. [3]When the Lord[c] learned of this, he left Judea[d] and went back once more to Galilee.

[4]Now he had to go through Samaria. [e] [5]So he came to a town in Samaria called Sychar, near the plot of ground Jacob had given to his son Joseph. [f] [6]Jacob's well was there, and Jesus, tired as he was from the journey, sat down by the well. It was about the sixth hour.

[7]When a Samaritan woman came to

[x]25 Some manuscripts *and certain Jews* [y]28 Or *Messiah* [z]34 Greek *he* [a]36 Some interpreters end the quotation after verse 30.

Cross references:
3:22 [k]Jn 4:2
3:23 [l]S Mt 3:1
3:24 [m]Mt 4:12; 14:3
3:25 [n]Jn 2:6
3:26 [o]S Mt 23:7 [p]Jn 1:7
3:28 [q]Jn 1:20,23
3:29 [r]Mt 9:15
3:31 [s]Jn 16:24; 17:13; [t]Php 2:2; 1Jn 1:4; 2Jn 12
3:31 [t]ver 13
[u]Jn 8:23; 1Jn 4:5
3:32 [v]Jn 8:26; 15:15 [w]ver 11
3:34 [x]S ver 17 [y]Isa 42:1; Mt 12:18; Lk 4:18; Ac 10:38
3:35 [z]S Mt 28:18
3:36 [a]S ver 15; Jn 5:24; 6:47
4:1 [b]Jn 3:22,26
4:3 [c]S Lk 7:13 [d]Jn 3:22
4:4 [e]S Mt 10:5
4:5 [f]Ge 33:19; Jos 24:32

3:23 *Aenon.* Possibly about eight miles south of Scythopolis (Beth Shan), west of the Jordan.
3:25 *argument . . . over . . . ceremonial washing.* The Dead Sea (Qumran) Scrolls (see "The Time between the Testaments," p. 1431) show that some Jews were deeply interested in the right way to achieve ceremonial purification.
3:26 *testified.* See note on 1:7. John's disciples knew that he had testified about Jesus, but they loved their master and were envious of Jesus' success.
3:27 The words are true of both Jesus and John (and of everyone). Both had what God had given them, so there was no place for envy. *given.* The verb "to give" is used frequently in this Gospel (76 times), especially of the things the Father gives the Son.
3:29 *the bridegroom.* The most important man at a wedding, referring here to Jesus. The friend (best man) is there only to help the bridegroom, which describes the role of John the Baptist. *full of joy.* Not because he was on center stage, but because the bridegroom was there. John's joy was to hear of Jesus' success.
3:30 John the Baptist had been sent to prepare the way for the Messiah and here reaffirms his subordinate position.
3:31 *The one who comes from above.* Jesus, whose heavenly origin (cf. 1Co 15:47) meant much to John. *the one who is from the earth.* A general expression that could apply to anyone, but here it particularly refers to John the Baptist.
3:32 *what he has seen and heard.* Jesus taught from divine experience. *no one.* Does not mean that no person accepted what he said (see v. 33) but that people in general refused his teaching.
3:33 *certified.* When anyone accepts Christ's testimony, he accepts the truth that Jesus came from heaven and that God

was acting in him for the world's salvation. He thereby certifies that God is truthful.
3:34 *the one whom God has sent.* Jesus. *without limit.* Some hold that it is only to Jesus that the Spirit is given without limit. Others take the "he" (see NIV text note) as a reference to Christ's giving the Spirit without limit to believers.
3:36 *has.* Eternal life is a present possession, not something the believer will only obtain later (see note on v. 15). *God's wrath.* A strong expression, meaning that God is actively opposed to everything evil. The word "wrath" occurs only here in John's Gospel (see note on Ro 1:18). *remains.* A sinner cannot expect God's wrath eventually to fade away. God's opposition to evil is both total and permanent.
4:1 *Pharisees.* The religious leaders took a close interest in John the Baptist (see note on 1:24) and then also in Jesus.
4:2 The disciples did not baptize without Jesus' approval (3:22).
4:3 *left Judea.* Success (which aroused opposition; see 7:1), not failure, led Jesus to leave Judea.
4:4 *had to go.* The necessity lay in Jesus' mission, not in geography. *Samaria.* Here the whole region, not simply the city. Jews often avoided Samaria by crossing the Jordan and traveling on the east side (see notes on Mt 10:5; Lk 9:52).
4:5 *Sychar.* A small village near Shechem. Jacob bought some land in the vicinity of Shechem (Ge 33:18–19), and it was apparently this land that he gave to Joseph (Ge 48:21–22).
4:6 *Jacob's well.* Mentioned nowhere else in Scripture. *about the sixth hour.* About 12:00 noon.
4:7 *to draw water.* People normally drew water at the end of the day rather than in the heat of midday (see Ge 24:11 and note). But the practice is attested by Josephus, who says

draw water, Jesus said to her, "Will you give me a drink?"*g* 8(His disciples had gone into the town *h* to buy food.)

9The Samaritan woman said to him, "You are a Jew and I am a Samaritan *i* woman. How can you ask me for a drink?" (For Jews do not associate with Samaritans.*b*)

10Jesus answered her, "If you knew the gift of God and who it is that asks you for a drink, you would have asked him and he would have given you living water." *j*

11"Sir," the woman said, "you have nothing to draw with and the well is deep. Where can you get this living water? 12Are you greater than our father Jacob, who gave us the well *k* and drank from it himself, as did also his sons and his flocks and herds?"

13Jesus answered, "Everyone who drinks this water will be thirsty again, 14but whoever drinks the water I give him will never thirst. *l* Indeed, the water I give him will become in him a spring of water *m* welling up to eternal life." *n*

15The woman said to him, "Sir, give me this water so that I won't get thirsty *o* and have to keep coming here to draw water."

16He told her, "Go, call your husband and come back."

17"I have no husband," she replied.

Cross references:
4:7 *g*Ge 24:17; 1Ki 17:10
4:8 *h*ver 5,39
4:9 *i*S Mt 10:5
4:10 *j*Isa 44:3; 55:1; Jer 2:13; 17:13; Zec 14:8; Jn 7:37,38; Rev 7:17; 21:6; 22:1,17
4:12 *k*ver 6
4:14 *l*Jn 6:35 *m*Isa 12:3; 58:11; Jn 7:38 *n*S Mt 25:46
4:15 *o*Jn 6:34

4:19 *p*S Mt 21:11
4:20 *q*Dt 11:29; Jos 8:33 *r*Lk 9:53
4:21 *s*Jn 5:28; 16:2 *t*Mal 1:11; 1Ti 2:8
4:22 *u*2Ki 17:28-41 *v*Isa 2:3; Ro 3:1, 2; 9:4,5; 15:8,9
4:23 *w*Jn 5:25; 16:32 *x*Php 3:3
4:24 *y*Php 3:3
4:25 *z*Mt 1:16; Jn 1:41
4:26 *a*Jn 8:24; 9:35-37

Jesus said to her, "You are right when you say you have no husband. 18The fact is, you have had five husbands, and the man you now have is not your husband. What you have just said is quite true."

19"Sir," the woman said, "I can see that you are a prophet. *p* 20Our fathers worshiped on this mountain, *q* but you Jews claim that the place where we must worship is in Jerusalem." *r*

21Jesus declared, "Believe me, woman, a time is coming *s* when you will worship the Father neither on this mountain nor in Jerusalem. *t* 22You Samaritans worship what you do not know; *u* we worship what we do know, for salvation is from the Jews. *v* 23Yet a time is coming and has now come *w* when the true worshipers will worship the Father in spirit *x* and truth, for they are the kind of worshipers the Father seeks. 24God is spirit, *y* and his worshipers must worship in spirit and in truth."

25The woman said, "I know that Messiah" (called Christ) *z* "is coming. When he comes, he will explain everything to us."

26Then Jesus declared, "I who speak to you am he." *a*

b 9 Or do not use dishes Samaritans have used

---

that the young ladies whom Moses helped (Ex 2:15–17) came to draw water at noon.

4:9 The point of the NIV text note (and probably of the text) is that a Jew would become ceremonially unclean if he used a drinking vessel handled by a Samaritan, since the Jews held that all Samaritans were "unclean."

4:10 *gift.* The Greek for this word is used only here in this Gospel and emphasizes God's grace through Christ. Jesus gave life and gave it freely. *living water.* In 7:38–39 the term is explained as meaning the Holy Spirit, but here it refers to eternal life (see v. 14).

4:11 *deep.* Christian pilgrim sources as early as the fourth century mention a well in this area that was about 100 feet deep. When the present well was cleaned out in 1935, it was found to be 138 feet deep.

4:12 *our father Jacob.* Respect for the past prevented her from seeing the great opportunity of the present.

4:14 *welling up.* The expression is a vigorous one, with a meaning like "leaping up." Jesus was speaking of vigorous, abundant life (cf. 10:10).

4:15 Cf. the misunderstanding of Nicodemus (3:4). In both cases the way was opened for further instruction.

4:18 *five husbands.* The Jews held that a woman might be divorced twice or at the most three times. If the Samaritans had the same standard, the woman's life had been exceedingly immoral. Apparently she had not married her present partner.

4:19 *a prophet.* Because of his special insight.

4:20 *this mountain.* Perhaps the woman did not like the way the conversation was going and so began to argue. The proper place of worship had long been a source of debate between Jews and Samaritans. Samaritans held that "this mountain" (Mount Gerizim) was especially sacred. Abraham

and Jacob had built altars in the general vicinity (Ge 12:7; 33:20), and the people had been blessed from this mountain (Dt 11:29; 27:12). In the Samaritan Scriptures, Mount Gerizim (rather than Mount Ebal) was the mountain on which Moses had commanded an altar to be built (Dt 27:4–6). The Samaritans had built a temple on Mount Gerizim c. 400 B.C., which the Jews destroyed c. 128. Both actions, of course, increased hostility between the two groups.

4:22 *worship what you do not know.* The Samaritan Bible contained only the Pentateuch. They worshiped the true God, but their failure to accept much of his revelation meant that they knew little of him. *salvation is from the Jews.* The Messiah would be a Jew.

4:24 *God is spirit . . . worship in spirit and in truth.* The place of worship is irrelevant, because true worship must be in keeping with God's nature, which is spirit. In John's Gospel truth is associated with Christ (14:6; see note on 1:14), a fact that has great importance for the proper understanding of Christian worship.

4:25 *Messiah . . . will explain everything.* The woman's last attempt to evade the issue. The matter was too important, she reasoned, for people like Jesus and herself to work out. Understanding would have to await the coming of the Messiah (see note on 1:25). The Samaritans expected a Messiah, but their rejection of all the inspired writings after the Pentateuch meant that they knew little about him. They thought of him mainly as a teacher.

4:26 *I . . . am he.* The only occasion before his trial on which Jesus specifically said that he was the Messiah (but see Mk 9:41). The term did not have the political overtones in Samaria that it had in Judea, which may be part of the reason Jesus used the designation here.

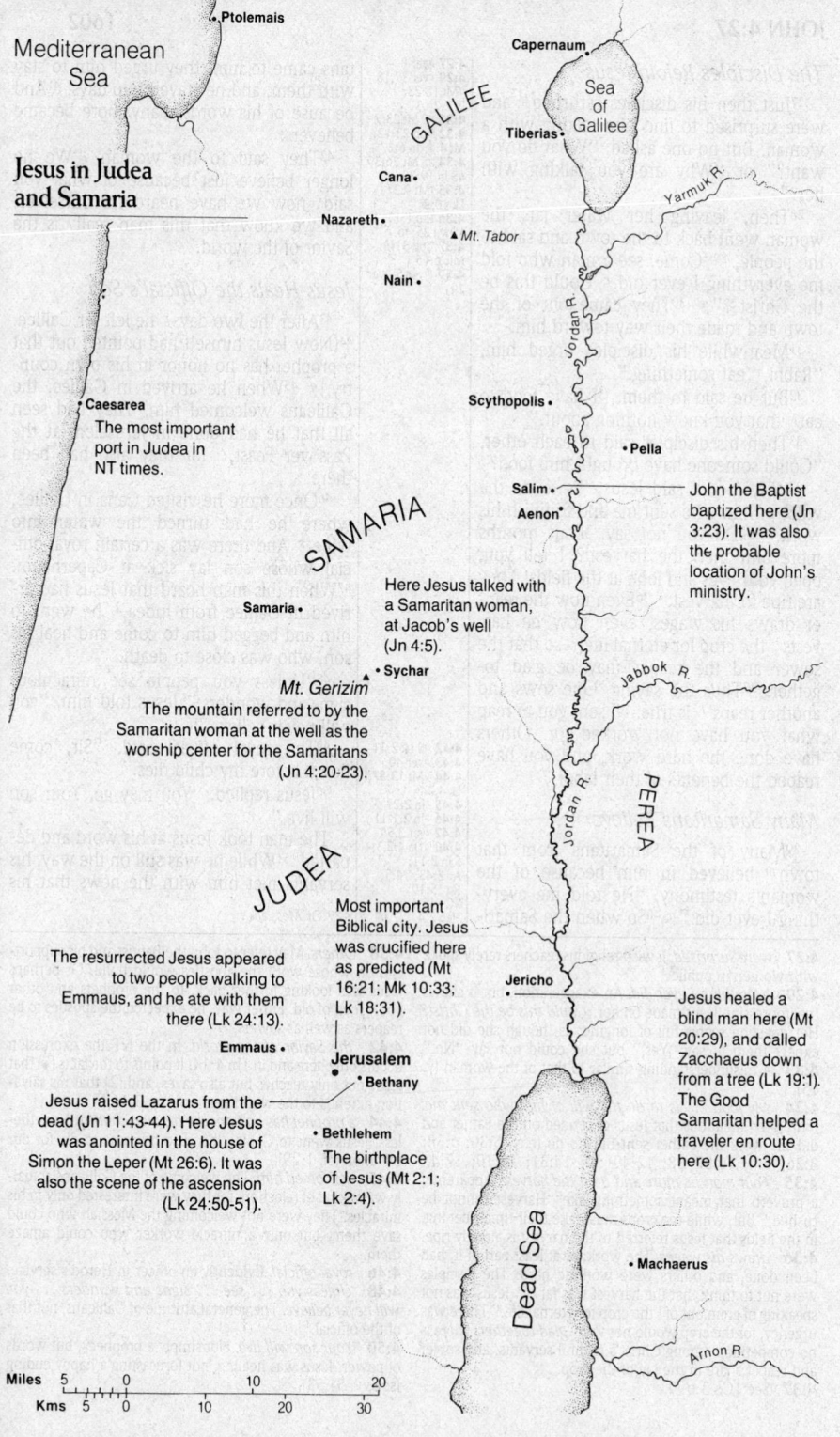

Jesus in Judea and Samaria

Mediterranean Sea

Ptolemais

GALILEE

Capernaum

Sea of Galilee

Tiberias

Cana

Nazareth

Nain

▲ Mt. Tabor

Jordan R.

Yarmuk R.

Caesarea
The most important port in Judea in NT times.

Scythopolis

Pella

SAMARIA

Salim

Aenon

John the Baptist baptized here (Jn 3:23). It was also the probable location of John's ministry.

Here Jesus talked with a Samaritan woman, at Jacob's well (Jn 4:5).

Samaria

Jabbok R.

Mt. Gerizim
The mountain referred to by the Samaritan woman at the well as the worship center for the Samaritans (Jn 4:20-23).

Sychar

PEREA

Jordan R.

JUDEA

Most important Biblical city. Jesus was crucified here as predicted (Mt 16:21; Mk 10:33; Lk 18:31).

The resurrected Jesus appeared to two people walking to Emmaus, and he ate with them there (Lk 24:13).

Emmaus

Jerusalem
Bethany

Jericho

Jesus healed a blind man here (Mt 20:29), and called Zacchaeus down from a tree (Lk 19:1). The Good Samaritan helped a traveler en route here (Lk 10:30).

Jesus raised Lazarus from the dead (Jn 11:43-44). Here Jesus was anointed in the house of Simon the Leper (Mt 26:6). It was also the scene of the ascension (Lk 24:50-51).

Bethlehem
The birthplace of Jesus (Mt 2:1; Lk 2:4).

Dead Sea

Machaerus

Arnon R.

Miles 5   0   10   20
Kms 5 0   10   20   30

The Disciples Rejoin Jesus

27Just then his disciples returned[b] and were surprised to find him talking with a woman. But no one asked, "What do you want?" or "Why are you talking with her?"

28Then, leaving her water jar, the woman went back to the town and said to the people, 29"Come, see a man who told me everything I ever did.[c] Could this be the Christ[c]?"[d] 30They came out of the town and made their way toward him.

31Meanwhile his disciples urged him, "Rabbi,[e] eat something."

32But he said to them, "I have food to eat[f] that you know nothing about."

33Then his disciples said to each other, "Could someone have brought him food?"

34"My food," said Jesus, "is to do the will[g] of him who sent me and to finish his work.[h] 35Do you not say, 'Four months more and then the harvest'? I tell you, open your eyes and look at the fields! They are ripe for harvest.[i] 36Even now the reaper draws his wages, even now he harvests[j] the crop for eternal life,[k] so that the sower and the reaper may be glad together. 37Thus the saying 'One sows and another reaps'[l] is true. 38I sent you to reap what you have not worked for. Others have done the hard work, and you have reaped the benefits of their labor."

Many Samaritans Believe

39Many of the Samaritans from that town[m] believed in him because of the woman's testimony, "He told me everything I ever did."[n] 40So when the Samari-

tans came to him, they urged him to stay with them, and he stayed two days. 41And because of his words many more became believers.

42They said to the woman, "We no longer believe just because of what you said; now we have heard for ourselves, and we know that this man really is the Savior of the world."[o]

Jesus Heals the Official's Son

43After the two days[p] he left for Galilee. 44(Now Jesus himself had pointed out that a prophet has no honor in his own country.)[q] 45When he arrived in Galilee, the Galileans welcomed him. They had seen all that he had done in Jerusalem at the Passover Feast,[r] for they also had been there.

46Once more he visited Cana in Galilee, where he had turned the water into wine.[s] And there was a certain royal official whose son lay sick at Capernaum. 47When this man heard that Jesus had arrived in Galilee from Judea,[t] he went to him and begged him to come and heal his son, who was close to death.

48"Unless you people see miraculous signs and wonders," Jesus told him, "you will never believe."[u]

49The royal official said, "Sir, come down before my child dies."

50Jesus replied, "You may go. Your son will live."

The man took Jesus at his word and departed. 51While he was still on the way, his servants met him with the news that his

Cross references (center column)

4:27 bver 8
4:29 cver 17,18
 dMt 12:23;
 Jn 7:26,31
4:31 eS Mt 23:7
4:32 fJob 23:12;
 Mt 4:4; Jn 6:27
4:34 gS Mt 26:39
 hS Jn 19:30
4:35 iMt 9:37;
 Lk 10:2
4:36 jRo 1:13
 kS Mt 25:46
4:37 lJob 31:8;
 Mic 6:15
4:39 mver 5 nver
 29

4:42 oS Lk 2:11
4:43 pver 40
4:44 qMt 13:57;
 Lk 4:24
4:45 rJn 2:23
4:46 sJn 2:1-11
4:47 tver 3,54
4:48 uDa 4:2,3;
 S Jn 2:11;
 Ac 2:43; 14:3;
 Ro 15:19;
 2Co 12:12;
 Heb 2:4

c29 Or Messiah

4:27 were surprised. Jewish religious teachers rarely spoke with women in public.
4:29 everything I ever did. An exaggeration, but it shows the impression Jesus made on her. Could this be the Christ? Her question seems full of longing, as though she did not expect them to say "Yes," but she could not say "No."
4:33 A misunderstanding similar to that of the woman (v. 15).
4:34 My food . . . is to do the will of him who sent me. John often mentions that Jesus depended on the Father and did the work the Father sent him to do (e.g., 5:30; 6:38; 8:26; 9:4; 10:37-38; 12:49-50; 14:31; 15:10; 17:4).
4:35 Four months more and then the harvest. Apparently a proverb that meant something like "Harvest cannot be rushed." But, while the crops must take their time ripening, in the fields that Jesus referred to the harvest is already ripe.
4:36 draws his wages. The work, or at least part of it, had been done, and others were working hard. The disciples were not to think that the harvest was far off. Jesus was not speaking of grain but of "the crop for eternal life." There was urgency, for the crop would not wait. glad together. There is no competition among Christ's faithful servants, and sower and reaper share in the joy of the crop.
4:37 See 1Co 3:6-9.

4:38 Others. May refer to John the Baptist and his supporters, on whose work the apostles would build. Or perhaps Jesus was looking further back, to the prophets and other godly men of old. Either way, he expected the apostles to be reapers as well as sowers.
4:42 the Savior of the world. In the NT the expression occurs only here and in 1Jn 4:14. It points to the facts (1) that Jesus not only teaches but also saves, and (2) that his salvation extends to the world (see note on 3:16).
4:44 a prophet has no honor in his own country. Nonetheless, Jesus went to Galilee, because he came to die for our salvation (cf. 1:29).
4:45 welcomed him. The welcome of the Galileans actually was a kind of rejection, for they were interested only in his miracles. They were not welcoming the Messiah who could save them, but only a miracle worker who could amaze them.
4:46 royal official. Evidently an officer in Herod's service.
4:48 Unless you . . . see . . . signs and wonders . . . you will never believe. The general attitude of Galileans, not that of the official.
4:50 Your son will live. Not simply a prophecy, but words of power. Jesus was healing, not forecasting a happy ending (see vv. 51,53).

boy was living. [52]When he inquired as to the time when his son got better, they said to him, "The fever left him yesterday at the seventh hour."

[53]Then the father realized that this was the exact time at which Jesus had said to him, "Your son will live." So he and all his household[v] believed.

[54]This was the second miraculous sign[w] that Jesus performed, having come from Judea to Galilee.

The Healing at the Pool

5 Some time later, Jesus went up to Jerusalem for a feast of the Jews. [2]Now there is in Jerusalem near the Sheep Gate[x] a pool, which in Aramaic[y] is called Bethesda[d] and which is surrounded by five covered colonnades. [3]Here a great number of disabled people used to lie—the blind, the lame, the paralyzed.[e] [5]One who was there had been an invalid for thirty-eight years. [6]When Jesus saw him lying there and learned that he had been in this condition for a long time, he asked him, "Do you want to get well?"

[7]"Sir," the invalid replied, "I have no one to help me into the pool when the water is stirred. While I am trying to get in, someone else goes down ahead of me."

[8]Then Jesus said to him, "Get up! Pick up your mat and walk."[z] [9]At once the man was cured; he picked up his mat and walked.

The day on which this took place was a Sabbath,[a] [10]and so the Jews[b] said to the man who had been healed, "It is the Sabbath; the law forbids you to carry your mat."[c]

[11]But he replied, "The man who made me well said to me, 'Pick up your mat and walk.'"

[12]So they asked him, "Who is this fellow who told you to pick it up and walk?"

[13]The man who was healed had no idea who it was, for Jesus had slipped away into the crowd that was there.

[14]Later Jesus found him at the temple and said to him, "See, you are well again. Stop sinning[d] or something worse may happen to you." [15]The man went away and told the Jews[e] that it was Jesus who had made him well.

Life Through the Son

[16]So, because Jesus was doing these things on the Sabbath, the Jews persecuted him. [17]Jesus said to them, "My Father[f] is

---

4:53 [v]S Ac 11:14
4:54 [w]S ver 48;
S Jn 2:11
5:2 [x]Ne 3:1;
12:39 [y]Jn 19:13,
17,20; 20:16;
Ac 21:40; 22:2;
26:14
5:8 [z]Mt 9:5,6

5:9 [a]Mt 12:1-14;
Jn 9:14
5:10 [b]ver 16
[c]Ne 13:15-22;
Jer 17:21;
S Mt 12:2
5:14 [d]Mk 2:5;
Jn 8:11
5:15 [e]S Jn 1:19
5:17 [f]Lk 2:49

---

[d]2 Some manuscripts *Bethzatha*; other manuscripts *Bethsaida*   [e]3 Some less important manuscripts *paralyzed—and they waited for the moving of the waters.* [4]From time to time an angel of the Lord would come down and stir up the waters. The first one into the pool after each such disturbance would be cured of whatever disease he had.

4:53 *believed.* Cf. the aim of this Gospel (20:31).
4:54 *the second miraculous sign.* There had, of course, already been many such signs (2:23; 3:2), but this was the second time Jesus performed a sign after coming from Judea to Galilee.
5:1 *Some time later.* An indefinite expression (cf. 6:1; 7:1). *a feast of the Jews.* Probably one of the three pilgrimage feasts to which all Jewish males were expected to go—Passover, Pentecost or Tabernacles. The identity of this feast is significant for the attempt to ascertain the number of Passovers included in Jesus' ministry, and thus the number of years his ministry lasted. John explicitly mentions at least three different Passovers: the first in 2:13,23 (see note on 2:13), the second in 6:4 and the third several times (e.g., in 11:55; 12:1). If three Passovers are accepted, the length of Jesus' ministry was between two and three years. However, if the feast of 5:1 was a fourth Passover or assumes that a fourth Passover had come and gone, Jesus' ministry would have lasted between three and four years.
5:2 *there is.* Not "was." This may mean that the pool was still in existence at the time this was being written, i.e., that John wrote before the destruction of Jerusalem. However, this falls short of proving the time of writing (see Introduction: Date). *Bethesda.* The manuscripts have a variety of names (see NIV text note), but one of the Dead Sea Scrolls seems to show that Bethesda is the right name. The site is generally identified with the twin pools near the present-day Saint Anne's Church. There would have been a colonnade on each of the four sides and another between the two pools.
5:3–4 See NIV text note. Verse 4 was doubtless inserted by a later copyist to explain why people waited by the pool in large numbers.

5:5 *invalid.* John does not say what the trouble was, but it was a form of paralysis or at least lameness.
5:6 *Do you want to get well?* The question was important. The man had not asked Jesus for help, and a beggar of that day could lose a sometimes profitable (and easy) income if he were cured. Or perhaps he had simply lost the will to be cured.
5:7 *when the water is stirred.* The man did not see Jesus as a potential healer, and his mind was set on the supposed curative powers of the water.
5:9 *the man was cured.* Ordinarily, faith in Jesus was essential to the cure (e.g., Mk 5:34), but here the man did not even know who Jesus was (v. 13). Jesus usually healed in response to faith, but he was not limited by a person's lack of it.
5:10 *the law forbids you to carry your mat.* It was not the law of Moses but their traditional interpretation of it that prohibited carrying loads of any kind on the Sabbath. The Jews had very strict regulations on keeping the Sabbath, but also had many curious loopholes that their lawyers made full use of (cf. Mt 23:4).
5:12 *this fellow.* The Jews were contrasting the authority of the law of God, which in their view prohibited the action, and that of a mere man (as they considered Jesus to be) who permitted it.
5:14 *something worse.* The eternal consequences of sin are more serious than any physical ailment.
5:16 *was doing.* The continuous action points to more than one incident, and the Jews apparently discerned a pattern. *persecuted.* John does not tell us what form the persecution took.
5:17 *My Father is always at his work.* Jesus' justification for

always at his work *g* to this very day, and I, too, am working." ¹⁸For this reason the Jews tried all the harder to kill him; *h* not only was he breaking the Sabbath, but he was even calling God his own Father, making himself equal with God. *i*

¹⁹Jesus gave them this answer: "I tell you the truth, the Son can do nothing by himself; *j* he can do only what he sees his Father doing, because whatever the Father does the Son also does. ²⁰For the Father loves the Son *k* and shows him all he does. Yes, to your amazement he will show him even greater things than these. *l* ²¹For just as the Father raises the dead and gives them life, *m* even so the Son gives life *n* to whom he is pleased to give it. ²²Moreover, the Father judges no one, but has entrusted all judgment to the Son, *o* ²³that all may honor the Son just as they honor the Father. He who does not honor the Son does not honor the Father, who sent him. *p*

²⁴"I tell you the truth, whoever hears my word and believes him who sent me *q* has eternal life *r* and will not be condemned; *s* he has crossed over from death to life. *t* ²⁵I tell you the truth, a time is coming and has now come *u* when the dead will hear *v* the voice of the Son of God and those who hear will live. ²⁶For as the Father has life in himself, so he has granted the Son to have life *w* in himself. ²⁷And he has given him authority to judge *x* because he is the Son of Man.

²⁸"Do not be amazed at this, for a time is coming *y* when all who are in their graves will hear his voice ²⁹and come out—those who have done good will rise to live, and those who have done evil will rise to be condemned. *z* ³⁰By myself I can do nothing; *a* I judge only as I hear, and my judgment is just, *b* for I seek not to please myself but him who sent me. *c*

Testimonies About Jesus

³¹"If I testify about myself, my testimony is not valid. *d* ³²There is another who testifies in my favor, *e* and I know that his testimony about me is valid.

³³"You have sent to John and he has testified *f* to the truth. ³⁴Not that I accept human testimony; *g* but I mention it that you may be saved. *h* ³⁵John was a lamp

5:17 *g* Jn 9:4; 14:10
5:18 *h* S Mt 12:14 *i* Jn 10:30,33; 19:7
5:19 *j* ver 30; S Jn 14:24
5:20 *k* Jn 3:35 *l* Jn 14:12
5:21 *m* Ro 4:17; 8:11; 2Co 1:9; Heb 11:19 *n* Jn 11:25
5:22 *o* ver 27; Ge 18:25; Jdg 11:27; Jn 9:39; S Ac 10:42
5:23 *p* Lk 10:16; S 1Jn 2:23
5:24 *q* S Mt 10:40; S Jn 3:15; S 3:17 *r* S Mt 25:46 *s* Jn 3:18 *t* 1Jn 3:14
5:25 *u* Jn 4:23; 16:32
5:26 *v* Jn 8:43,47 *w* Dt 30:20; Job 10:12; 33:4; Ps 36:9; S Jn 1:4
5:27 *x* S ver 22
5:28 *y* Jn 4:21; 16:2
5:29 *z* S Mt 25:46
5:30 *a* ver 19 *b* Isa 28:6; Jn 8:16 *c* S Mt 26:39
5:31 *d* Jn 8:14
5:32 *e* ver 37; Jn 8:18
5:33 *f* S Jn 1:7 **5:34** *g* 1Jn 5:9 *h* Ac 16:30,31; Eph 2:8; Tit 3:5

his action was his close relation to his Father. The Jews did not refer to God as "My Father," regarding the term as too intimate—though they might have used "Our Father" or, in prayer, "My Father in heaven." Jesus also exemplified the way the Sabbath should be observed. God does not stop his deeds of compassion on that day and neither did Jesus.
5:18 *his own Father.* Referring to a special relationship. The Jews did not object to the idea that God is the Father of all, but they strongly objected to Jesus' claim that he stood in a special relationship to the Father—a relationship so close as to make himself equal with God.
5:19 *can.* Because of who and what he was, it was not possible for Jesus to act except in dependence on the Father.
5:20 *the Father loves the Son.* Therefore the Father revealed to the Son his plans and purposes, and the Son obediently carried them out. *greater things.* The Son's activities in raising the dead and judging (see following verses).
5:21 *the Father raises the dead.* A firm belief among the Jews. They also held that he did not give this privilege to anyone else. Jesus claimed a prerogative that, according to his opponents, belonged only to God. *the Son gives life.* Probably refers to Christ's gift of abundant life here and now, though possibly also to the future resurrection (see 11:25–26).
5:22 *entrusted all judgment to the Son.* The Jews believed that the Father is Judge of the world, so this teaching seemed heretical to them.
5:24 *believes him . . . has eternal life.* Faith and life are connected (cf. 20:31). *has eternal life.* A present possession (see note on 3:15). *has crossed.* The decisive action has taken place, and the believer no longer belongs to death.
5:25 *is coming and has now come.* A reference not only to the future resurrection but also to the fact that Christ gives life now. The spiritually dead who hear him receive life from him.
5:26 *has life in himself.* Must be understood against the background of the OT, where life is spoken of as belonging to

God and as being his gift (Dt 30:20; Job 10:12; 33:4; Ps 16:11; 27:1; 36:9; etc.). The Son has been given the same kind of life that the Father possesses (cf. also 1Jn 5:11 for the benefit to man).
5:27 *authority to judge.* Granted to the Son by the Father. *Son of Man.* See note on 1:51.
5:28–29 A reference to the future raising of the dead.
5:29 *done good . . . live . . . done evil . . . condemned.* As always in Scripture, judgment is on the basis of works, though salvation, of course, is a gift from God in response to faith (cf. v. 24).
5:30 *By myself I can do nothing.* Jesus stresses his dependence on the Father (see note on v. 19). He judges only as he hears from the Father, which makes his judgment fair.
5:31–47 This section stresses the testimonies (see note on 1:7) of John the Baptist (v. 33), of the works of Jesus (v. 36), of God the Father (v. 37), of the Scriptures (v. 39) and of Moses (v. 46).
5:31 Jesus' testimony about himself required the support of all God's revelation. Otherwise, it would have been unacceptable.
5:32 *another.* The Father testifies concerning the Son. The Jews might not accept this testimony, but it was the testimony that mattered.
5:33 *You have sent to John.* A reference to the delegation from the Jewish leaders to John the Baptist (see 1:19). *he has testified.* The testimony of John was important, though not, of course, equal to the testimony of the Father. But had the Jews believed John, they would have believed Christ and would have been saved.
5:35 *John was.* The past tense may indicate that John was dead or at least imprisoned. In any case, his work was done. *burned and gave light.* John's giving light was costly to him. *for a time.* The Jewish leaders never came to grips with John's message, and their responses to him were always at best tentative and superficial.

that burned and gave light,[i] and you chose for a time to enjoy his light.

36"I have testimony weightier than that of John.[j] For the very work that the Father has given me to finish, and which I am doing,[k] testifies that the Father has sent me.[l] 37And the Father who sent me has himself testified concerning me.[m] You have never heard his voice nor seen his form,[n] 38nor does his word dwell in you,[o] for you do not believe[p] the one he sent.[q] 39You diligently study[f] the Scriptures[r] because you think that by them you possess eternal life.[s] These are the Scriptures that testify about me,[t] 40yet you refuse to come to me[u] to have life.

41"I do not accept praise from men,[v] 42but I know you. I know that you do not have the love of God in your hearts. 43I have come in my Father's name, and you do not accept me; but if someone else comes in his own name, you will accept him. 44How can you believe if you accept praise from one another, yet make no effort to obtain the praise that comes from the only God[g]?[w]

45"But do not think I will accuse you before the Father. Your accuser is Moses,[x] on whom your hopes are set.[y] 46If you believed Moses, you would believe me, for he wrote about me.[z] 47But since you do not believe what he wrote, how are you going to believe what I say?"[a]

Jesus Feeds the Five Thousand

6:1–13pp — Mt 14:13–21; Mk 6:32–44; Lk 9:10–17

6 Some time after this, Jesus crossed to the far shore of the Sea of Galilee (that is, the Sea of Tiberias), 2and a great crowd of people followed him because they saw the miraculous signs[b] he had performed on the sick. 3Then Jesus went up on a mountainside[c] and sat down with his disciples. 4The Jewish Passover Feast[d] was near.

5When Jesus looked up and saw a great crowd coming toward him, he said to Philip,[e] "Where shall we buy bread for these people to eat?" 6He asked this only to test him, for he already had in mind what he was going to do.

7Philip answered him, "Eight months' wages[h] would not buy enough bread for each one to have a bite!"

8Another of his disciples, Andrew, Simon Peter's brother,[f] spoke up, 9"Here is a boy with five small barley loaves and two small fish, but how far will they go among so many?"[g]

10Jesus said, "Have the people sit down." There was plenty of grass in that place, and the men sat down, about five thousand of them. 11Jesus then took the loaves, gave thanks,[h] and distributed to those who were seated as much as they wanted. He did the same with the fish.

12When they had all had enough to eat, he said to his disciples, "Gather the pieces that are left over. Let nothing be wasted." 13So they gathered them and filled twelve baskets with the pieces of the five barley loaves left over by those who had eaten. 14After the people saw the miraculous

5:35 [i]Da 12:3; 2Pe 1:19
5:36 [j]1Jn 5:9
  [k]Jn 14:11; 15:24
  [l]S Jn 3:17
5:37 [m]Jn 8:18
  [n]Dt 4:12;
  1Ti 1:17;
  S Jn 1:18
5:38 [o]1Jn 1:10;
  2:14 [p]Isa 26:10
  [q]S Jn 3:17
5:39 [r]Ro 2:17,18
  [s]S Mt 25:46
  [t]S Lk 24:27,44;
  Ac 13:27
5:40 [u]Jn 6:44
5:41 [v]ver 44
5:44 [w]S Ro 2:29
5:45 [x]Jn 9:28
  [y]Ro 2:17
5:46 [z]Ge 3:15;
  S Lk 24:27,44;
  Ac 26:22
5:47 [a]Lk 16:29,
  31

6:2 [b]S Jn 2:11
6:3 [c]ver 15
6:4 [d]S Jn 11:55
6:5 [e]S Jn 1:43
6:8 [f]Jn 1:40
6:9 [g]2Ki 4:43
6:11 [h]ver 23;
  S Mt 14:19

[f]39 Or *Study diligently* (the imperative)   [g]44 Some early manuscripts *the Only One*   [h]7 Greek *two hundred denarii*

5:36 *work.* The miracles of Jesus, which testified to what he is and to his divine mission (see 10:25).

5:37 *the Father . . . has himself testified . . . his voice.* Probably a reference to God's voice in the Scriptures (see vv. 38–39). God had also given his voice of approval at Jesus' baptism (see Mt 3:17). *not seen his form.* Probably refers to their lack of spiritual perception of who Jesus really is.

5:38 *you do not believe.* The Jews did not recognize what God was saying, as their failure to believe Jesus shows.

5:39 *You diligently study.* The Jewish leaders studied Scripture in minute detail. Despite their reverence for the very letter of Scripture (see notes on Mt 5:18–21), they did not recognize the one to whom Scripture bears supreme testimony.

5:41 *praise from men.* Jesus did not accept human praise any more than human testimony (v. 34).

5:42 *love of God.* May mean God's love for them or theirs for God. Probably it is the latter, but people's love for God is in response to his prior love for them (1Jn 4:19).

5:43–44 The Jews had their attention firmly fixed on people. Their emphasis on self-seeking and on human praise showed that they did not accept the one who came from God, and therefore they missed the praise that comes from God.

5:45 *Your accuser is Moses.* The Jews prided themselves

on their attachment to Moses, their great lawgiver. So it was an unexpected thrust for Jesus to say that Moses himself would accuse them before God.

5:46 *he wrote about me.* All the NT writers stressed, or assumed, that the OT, rightly read, points to Christ (cf. Lk 24:25–27,44). Jesus applied this truth specifically to the writings of Moses (see, e.g., notes on Ge 49:10; Ex 12:21; Lev 16:5; Nu 24:17; Dt 18:15).

6:1–15 The feeding of the 5,000 is the one miracle, apart from the resurrection, found in all four Gospels. It shows Jesus as the supplier of human need, and sets the stage for his testimony that he is the bread of life (v. 35).

6:1 *Some time after this.* See 5:1 and note. *Sea of Tiberias.* Probably the official Roman name, while Sea of Galilee was the popular name. The name came from the town of Tiberias (named after the emperor), founded c. A.D. 20, and probably was not much in use during Jesus' ministry.

6:2 *miraculous signs.* See note on 2:11.

6:4 *Passover.* See note on 2:13.

6:5 *Philip.* Since he came from nearby Bethsaida (1:44), it was appropriate to ask him.

6:9 *barley loaves.* Cheap bread, the food of the poor.

6:10 *about five thousand.* The number of men; women and children were not included (Mt 14:21).

6:12 *Gather the pieces.* See note on Mk 6:43.

sign[i] that Jesus did, they began to say, "Surely this is the Prophet who is to come into the world."[j] 15Jesus, knowing that they intended to come and make him king[k] by force, withdrew again to a mountain by himself.[l]

Jesus Walks on the Water

6:16–21pp — Mt 14:22–33; Mk 6:47–51

16When evening came, his disciples went down to the lake, 17where they got into a boat and set off across the lake for Capernaum. By now it was dark, and Jesus had not yet joined them. 18A strong wind was blowing and the waters grew rough. 19When they had rowed three or three and a half miles,[i] they saw Jesus approaching the boat, walking on the water;[m] and they were terrified. 20But he said to them, "It is I; don't be afraid."[n] 21Then they were

willing to take him into the boat, and immediately the boat reached the shore where they were heading.

22The next day the crowd that had stayed on the opposite shore of the lake[o] realized that only one boat had been there, and that Jesus had not entered it with his disciples, but that they had gone away alone.[p] 23Then some boats from Tiberias[q] landed near the place where the people had eaten the bread after the Lord had given thanks.[r] 24Once the crowd realized that neither Jesus nor his disciples were there, they got into the boats and went to Capernaum in search of Jesus.

Jesus the Bread of Life

25When they found him on the other

6:14 [i]S Jn 2:11 /Dt 18:15,18; Mt 11:3; S 21:11	
6:15 [k]Jn 18:36 /Mt 14:23; Mk 6:46	
6:19 [m]Job 9:8	
6:20 [n]S Mt 14:27	
6:22 [o]ver 2 [p]ver 15-21	
6:23 [q]ver 1 [r]ver 11	

[i]*19 Greek rowed twenty-five or thirty stadia (about 5 or 6 kilometers)*

6:13 *twelve baskets ... left over.* There was abundant supply.
6:14 *sign.* It pointed people to the Son of Man and the food for eternal life that he gives (v. 27), but they thought only of the Prophet, i.e., the prophet of Dt 18:15 who would be like Moses (see 1:21 and note). Through Moses, God had pro-

vided food and water for the people in the desert, and they expected the Prophet to do no more than this.
6:15 *make him king by force.* Jesus rejected the world's version of kingship as a temptation of the devil (Mt 4:8–10; see note on Jn 18:36).
6:19 *three or three and a half miles.* Mark says they were

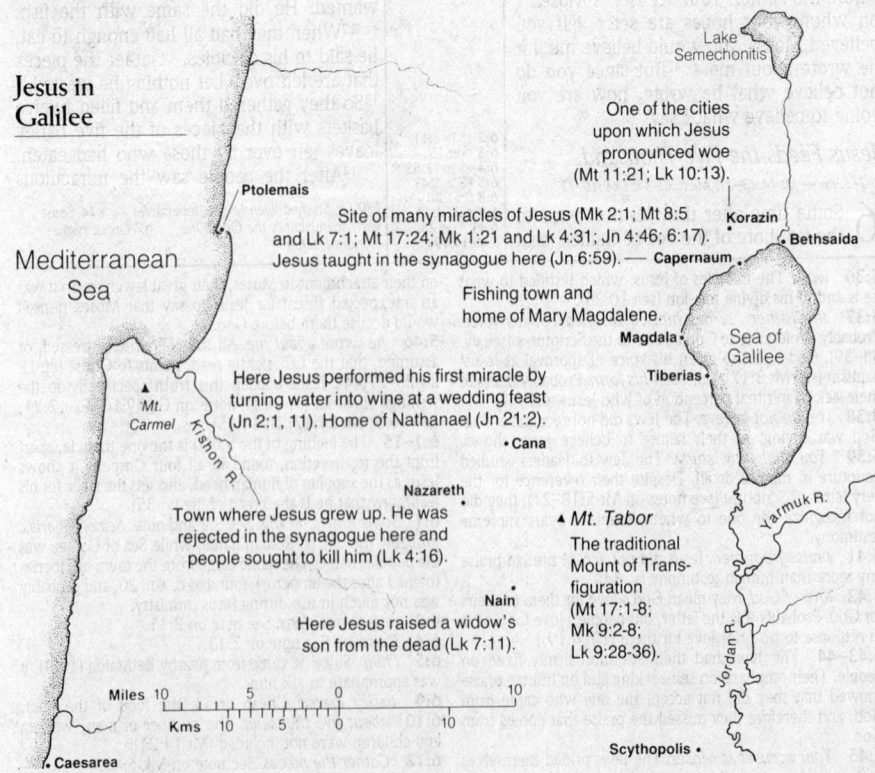

Jesus in Galilee

Mediterranean Sea

Lake Semechonitis

One of the cities upon which Jesus pronounced woe (Mt 11:21; Lk 10:13).

Korazin

Bethsaida

Ptolemais

Site of many miracles of Jesus (Mk 2:1; Mt 8:5 and Lk 7:1; Mt 17:24; Mk 1:21 and Lk 4:31; Jn 4:46; 6:17). Jesus taught in the synagogue here (Jn 6:59). — Capernaum

Fishing town and home of Mary Magdalene.

Magdala

Sea of Galilee

Mt. Carmel

Kishon R.

Here Jesus performed his first miracle by turning water into wine at a wedding feast (Jn 2:1, 11). Home of Nathanael (Jn 21:2).

Tiberias

Cana

Nazareth

Town where Jesus grew up. He was rejected in the synagogue here and people sought to kill him (Lk 4:16).

Mt. Tabor
The traditional Mount of Transfiguration (Mt 17:1-8; Mk 9:2-8; Lk 9:28-36).

Yarmuk R.

Nain
Here Jesus raised a widow's son from the dead (Lk 7:11).

Jordan R.

Miles 10 5 0 10
Kms 10 5 0 10

Caesarea

Scythopolis

side of the lake, they asked him, "Rabbi,*s* when did you get here?"

²⁶Jesus answered, "I tell you the truth, you are looking for me,*t* not because you saw miraculous signs*u* but because you ate the loaves and had your fill. ²⁷Do not work for food that spoils, but for food that endures*v* to eternal life,*w* which the Son of Man*x* will give you. On him God the Father has placed his seal*y* of approval."

²⁸Then they asked him, "What must we do to do the works God requires?"

²⁹Jesus answered, "The work of God is this: to believe*z* in the one he has sent."*a*

³⁰So they asked him, "What miraculous sign*b* then will you give that we may see it and believe you?*c* What will you do? ³¹Our forefathers ate the manna*d* in the desert; as it is written: 'He gave them bread from heaven to eat.'*i* "*e*

³²Jesus said to them, "I tell you the truth, it is not Moses who has given you the bread from heaven, but it is my Father who gives you the true bread from heaven. ³³For the bread of God is he who comes down from heaven*f* and gives life to the world."

³⁴"Sir," they said, "from now on give us this bread."*g*

³⁵Then Jesus declared, "I am*h* the bread of life.*i* He who comes to me will never go hungry, and he who believes*j* in me will never be thirsty.*k* ³⁶But as I told you, you have seen me and still you do not believe. ³⁷All that the Father gives me*l* will come to me, and whoever comes to me I will never drive away. ³⁸For I have come down from heaven*m* not to do my will but to do the will*n* of him who sent me.*o* ³⁹And this is the will of him who sent me, that I shall lose none of all that he has given me,*p* but raise them up at the last day.*q* ⁴⁰For my Father's will is that everyone who looks to the Son*r* and believes in him shall have eternal life,*s* and I will raise him up at the last day."

⁴¹At this the Jews began to grumble about him because he said, "I am the bread that came down from heaven." ⁴²They said, "Is this not Jesus, the son of Joseph,*t* whose father and mother we know?*u* How can he now say, 'I came down from heaven'?"*v*

⁴³"Stop grumbling among yourselves," Jesus answered. ⁴⁴"No one can come to me unless the Father who sent me draws him,*w* and I will raise him up at the last day. ⁴⁵It is written in the Prophets: 'They

6:25 *s* Mt 23:7
6:26 *t* ver 24 *u* ver 30; S Jn 2:11
6:27 *v* Isa 55:2 *w* ver 54; S Mt 25:46 *x* S Mt 8:20 *y* Ro 4:11; 1Co 9:2; 2Co 1:22; Eph 1:13; 4:30; 2Ti 2:19; Rev 7:3
6:29 *z* 1Jn 3:23 *a* S Jn 3:17
6:30 *b* S Jn 2:11 *c* S Mt 12:38
6:31 *d* Nu 11:7-9 *e* Ex 16:4,15; Ne 9:15; Ps 78:24; 105:40 *f* ver 50; Jn 3:13,31
6:34 *g* Jn 4:15

6:35 *h* Ex 3:14; Jn 8:12; 10:7,11; 11:25; 14:6; 15:1 *i* ver 48,51 *j* S Jn 3:15 *k* Jn 4:14
6:37 *l* ver 39; Jn 17:2,6,9,24
6:38 *m* Jn 3:13,31 *n* S Mt 26:39 *o* S Jn 3:17
6:39 *p* Isa 27:3; Jer 23:4; Jn 10:28; 17:12; 18:9 *q* ver 40,44, 54
6:40 *r* Jn 12:45 *s* S Mt 25:46
6:42 *t* Lk 4:22 *u* Jn 7:27,28 *v* ver 38,62
6:44 *w* ver 65; Jer 31:3; Jn 12:32 *i* 31 Exodus 16:4; Neh. 9:15; Psalm 78:24,25

"in the middle of the lake" (Mk 6:47). *terrified.* They thought they were seeing a ghost (Mt 14:26).
6:21 *immediately the boat reached the shore.* Some think that this was another miracle. In any event, the boat's safe arrival is implicitly credited to Jesus.
6:22–24 The crowd could not figure out what had happened to Jesus. But they wanted to see him again, so they looked for him in the most likely place, Capernaum.
6:27 *eternal life.* Not something to be achieved but to be received by faith in Christ (see vv. 28–29; see also note on 3:15). *Son of Man.* See note on Mk 8:31. Submission of the Son to the Father is one of John's major themes (see note on 4:34).
6:28 *What must we do . . . ?* They missed the point that eternal life is Christ's gift and were thinking in terms of achieving it by pious works.
6:29 *work of God.* Believing in Jesus Christ is the indispensable "work" God calls for—the one that leads to eternal life.
6:30 *What will you do?* They seek from Jesus a sign greater than the gift of manna that had accompanied Moses' ministry.
6:31 *manna.* A popular Jewish expectation was that when the Messiah came he would renew the sending of manna. The crowd probably reasoned that Jesus had done little compared to Moses. He had fed 5,000; Moses had fed a nation. He did it once; Moses did it for 40 years. He gave ordinary bread; Moses gave "bread from heaven."
6:32 Jesus corrected them, pointing out that the manna in the desert did not come from Moses but from God, and that the Father still "gives" (the present tense is important) the true bread from heaven (life through the Son).
6:33 *the bread of God.* Jesus moved the discussion to

something (and Someone) much more important than manna.
6:34 *this bread.* Probably another misunderstanding, like that by the woman at the well (4:15; cf. also Nicodemus, 3:4). Their minds ran along materialistic lines.
6:35 *I am.* The first of seven self-descriptions of Jesus introduced by "I am" (see 8:12; 9:5; 10:7,9; 10:11,14; 11:25; 14:6; 15:1,5). In the Greek the words are solemnly emphatic and echo Ex 3:14. *the bread of life.* May mean "the bread that is living" and/or "the bread that gives life." What is implied in v. 33 is now made explicit and repeated with minor variations in vv. 41,48,51.
6:36 Contrast 20:29.
6:37 God's action (see v. 44; 10:29; 17:6; 18:9), not man's (v. 28), is primary in salvation, and Christ's mercy is unfailing (see vv. 31–40; 10:28; 17:9,12,15,19; 18:9).
6:38 *I have come down from heaven.* Repeated six times in this context (vv. 33,38,41,50–51,58), emphasizing Jesus' divine origin. *to do the will of him who sent me.* See note on 4:34.
6:39 *I shall lose none.* The true believer will persevere because of Christ's firm hold on him (see Php 1:6). *the last day.* An expression found only in John in the NT (see vv. 40,44,54).
6:40 *eternal life.* See note on 3:15. *raise him up at the last day.* Death cannot destroy the life that Christ gives.
6:41 *the Jews.* See note on 1:19.
6:44 *draws.* People do not come to Christ strictly on their own initiative; the Father draws them.
6:45 *the Prophets.* The section of the OT from which the quotation is taken. *Everyone who . . . learns from him comes.* Only those who learn from God come to salvation, and all who learn from him are saved.

will all be taught by God.'[k][x] Everyone
who listens to the Father and learns from
him comes to me. 46No one has seen the
Father except the one who is from God;[y]
only he has seen the Father. 47I tell you the
truth, he who believes has everlasting
life.[z] 48I am the bread of life.[a] 49Your forefathers ate the manna in the desert, yet
they died.[b] 50But here is the bread that
comes down from heaven,[c] which a man
may eat and not die. 51I am the living
bread[d] that came down from heaven.[e] If
anyone eats of this bread, he will live forever. This bread is my flesh, which I will
give for the life of the world."[f]
52Then the Jews[g] began to argue sharply among themselves,[h] "How can this
man give us his flesh to eat?"
53Jesus said to them, "I tell you the
truth, unless you eat the flesh[i] of the Son
of Man[j] and drink his blood,[k] you have
no life in you. 54Whoever eats my flesh and
drinks my blood has eternal life, and I will
raise him up at the last day.[l] 55For my
flesh is real food and my blood is real
drink. 56Whoever eats my flesh and drinks
my blood remains in me, and I in him.[m]
57Just as the living Father sent me[n] and I
live because of the Father, so the one who
feeds on me will live because of me. 58This
is the bread that came down from heaven.
Your forefathers ate manna and died, but
he who feeds on this bread will live forever."[o] 59He said this while teaching in
the synagogue in Capernaum.

Many Disciples Desert Jesus

60On hearing it, many of his disciples[p]
said, "This is a hard teaching. Who can
accept it?"[q]
61Aware that his disciples were grumbling about this, Jesus said to them, "Does
this offend you?[r] 62What if you see the
Son of Man[s] ascend to where he was before![t] 63The Spirit gives life;[u] the flesh
counts for nothing. The words I have
spoken to you are spirit[l] and they are life.
64Yet there are some of you who do not
believe." For Jesus had known[v] from the
beginning which of them did not believe
and who would betray him.[w] 65He went
on to say, "This is why I told you that no
one can come to me unless the Father has
enabled him."[x]
66From this time many of his disciples[y]
turned back and no longer followed him.
67"You do not want to leave too, do
you?" Jesus asked the Twelve.[z]
68Simon Peter answered him,[a] "Lord,
to whom shall we go? You have the words
of eternal life.[b] 69We believe and know
that you are the Holy One of God."[c]
70Then Jesus replied, "Have I not chosen you,[d] the Twelve? Yet one of you is a
devil!"[e] 71(He meant Judas, the son of Si-

[k]45 Isaiah 54:13 [l]63 Or *Spirit*

6:45 [x]Isa 54:13; Jer 31:33,34; 1Co 2:13; 1Th 4:9; Heb 8:10,11; 10:16; 1Jn 2:27
6:46 [y]S Jn 1:18; 5:37; 7:29
6:47 [z]S Mt 25:46
6:48 [a]ver 35,51
6:49 [b]ver 31,58
6:50 [c]ver 33
6:51 [d]ver 35,48 [e]ver 41,58 [f]Heb 10:10
6:52 [g]S Jn 1:19 [h]Jn 7:43; 9:16; 10:19
6:53 [i]Mt 26:26 [j]S Mt 8:20 [k]Mt 26:28
6:54 [l]ver 39
6:56 [m]Jn 15:4-7; 1Jn 2:24; 3:24; 4:15
6:57 [n]S Jn 3:17
6:58 [o]ver 49-51; Jn 3:36; 5:24
6:60 [p]ver 66 [q]ver 52
6:61 [r]Mt 13:57
6:62 [s]S Mt 8:20 [t]S Mk 16:19; S Jn 3:13; 17:5
6:63 [u]2Co 3:6
6:64 [v]S Jn 2:25 [w]S Mt 10:4
6:65 [x]ver 37,44; S Mt 13:11
6:66 [y]ver 60
6:67 [z]Mt 10:2
6:68 [a]Mt 16:16 [b]ver 63; S Mt 25:46
6:69 [c]S Mk 1:24; 8:29; Lk 9:20
6:70 [d]Jn 15:16, 19 [e]Jn 13:27; 17:12

6:49 *they died.* Jesus' opponents had set their hearts (cf. v. 31) on that which could neither give nor sustain spiritual life.
6:50 *eat and not die.* Jesus' gift is in contrast; the life he gives is eternal.
6:51 *eats of this bread.* Appropriates Jesus as the sustenance of one's life. *my flesh, which I will give.* Looking forward to Calvary. Providing eternal life would be costly to the Giver. *world.* See note on 4:42.
6:53–58 Jesus' absolute statement that "unless you eat the flesh of the Son of Man and drink his blood, you have no life in you" (v. 53) precludes a direct reference to the Lord's Supper. He clearly does not teach that receiving that sacrament is the one requirement for eternal life or that it is the only ordinance through which Christ and his saving benefits are received. In this very discourse he emphasizes faith in response to testimony (see vv. 35,40,47,51). Flesh and blood here point to Christ as the crucified one and the source of life. Jesus speaks of faith's appropriation of himself as God's appointed sacrifice, not—at least not directly—of any ritual requirement.
6:54 *the last day.* See note on v. 39.
6:58 *the bread that came down from heaven.* As in v. 49, the value of the manna is limited and is contrasted with the heavenly food Christ gives. For the tenth time in this chapter reference is made to Jesus' coming down from heaven or to the bread from heaven.
6:60 *hard.* Hard to accept, not hard to understand. The thought of eating the flesh of the Son of Man and drinking his blood was doubtless shocking to most of Jesus' Jewish hearers (see note on vv. 53–58).
6:62 *Son of Man.* See notes on Mk 8:31; Lk 6:5; 19:10. *ascend.* Probably refers to the series of events that began with the cross, where Jesus was glorified (see note on 7:39). *where he was before.* Referring to Jesus' heavenly preexistence.
6:63 Cf. 3:5–6,8. *are spirit and . . . life.* Are the Spirit at work producing life.
6:65 Coming to Christ for salvation is never a merely human achievement (see vv. 37,39,44–45).
6:66 *From this time.* May also mean "For this reason" or both. *many . . . turned back.* Jesus had already made clear what discipleship meant, and many were not ready to receive life in the way he taught.
6:68 As in the Synoptic Gospels, Peter acts as spokesman. *words of eternal life.* The expression is general. Peter was not speaking of a formula but of the thrust of Jesus' teaching. He perceived the truth of v. 63.
6:69 *We believe and know.* Since the Greek verbs are in the perfect tense, they mean, "We have entered a state of belief and knowledge that has continued until the present time." *the Holy One of God.* Applied to Jesus in Mk 1:24; Lk 4:34 (see Ac 2:27).
6:70 *a devil.* Judas (v. 71) would oppose Christ in the spirit of Satan.
6:71 *Iscariot.* Means "a man from Kerioth" (in Judea; see Jos 15:25) and would apply equally to the father and the son (cf. 12:4). Judas seems to have been the only non-Galilean among the Twelve. *one of the Twelve.* And therefore one of the last persons likely to betray Jesus.

mon Iscariot,^f who, though one of the Twelve, was later to betray him.)^g

Jesus Goes to the Feast of Tabernacles

7 After this, Jesus went around in Galilee, purposely staying away from Judea because the Jews^h there were waiting to take his life.ⁱ ²But when the Jewish Feast of Tabernacles^j was near, ³Jesus' brothers^k said to him, "You ought to leave here and go to Judea, so that your disciples may see the miracles you do. ⁴No one who wants to become a public figure acts in secret. Since you are doing these things, show yourself to the world." ⁵For even his own brothers did not believe in him.^l

⁶Therefore Jesus told them, "The right time^m for me has not yet come; for you any time is right. ⁷The world cannot hate you, but it hates meⁿ because I testify that what it does is evil.^o ⁸You go to the Feast. I am not yet^m going up to this Feast, because for me the right time^p has not yet come." ⁹Having said this, he stayed in Galilee.

¹⁰However, after his brothers had left for the Feast, he went also, not publicly, but in secret. ¹¹Now at the Feast the Jews were

watching for him^q and asking, "Where is that man?"

¹²Among the crowds there was widespread whispering about him. Some said, "He is a good man."

Others replied, "No, he deceives the people."^r ¹³But no one would say anything publicly about him for fear of the Jews.^s

Jesus Teaches at the Feast

¹⁴Not until halfway through the Feast did Jesus go up to the temple courts and begin to teach.^t ¹⁵The Jews^u were amazed and asked, "How did this man get such learning^v without having studied?"^w

¹⁶Jesus answered, "My teaching is not my own. It comes from him who sent me.^x ¹⁷If anyone chooses to do God's will, he will find out^y whether my teaching comes from God or whether I speak on my own. ¹⁸He who speaks on his own does so to gain honor for himself,^z but he who works for the honor of the one who sent him is a man of truth; there is nothing false about him. ¹⁹Has not Moses given you the law?^a Yet not one of you keeps the law. Why are you trying to kill me?"^b

²⁰"You are demon-possessed,"^c the

Cross references (center column)

6:71 ^fS Mt 26:14
^gS Mt 10:4
7:1 ^hS Jn 1:19
ⁱver 19,25;
S Mt 12:14
7:2 ^jLev 23:34;
Dt 16:16
7:3 ^kS Mt 12:46
7:5 ^lPs 69:8;
Mk 3:21
7:6 ^mS Mt 26:18
7:7 ⁿJn 15:18,19
^oJn 3:19,20
7:8 ^pver 6;
S Mt 26:18

7:11 ^qJn 11:56
7:12 ^rver 40:43
7:13 ^sJn 9:22;
12:42; 19:38;
20:19
7:14 ^tver 28;
S Mt 26:55
7:15 ^uS Jn 1:19
^vAc 26:24
^wMt 13:54
7:16 ^xS Jn 14:24
7:17 ^yPs 25:14
7:18 ^zJn 5:41;
8:50,54
7:19 ^aDt 32:46;
Jn 1:17 ^bver 1;
S Mt 12:14
7:20 ^cS Mk 3:22

^m8 Some early manuscripts do not have *yet*.

7:1–8:59 In chs. 7–8 John records strong opposition to Jesus, including repeated references to threats on his life (7:1,13,19,25,30,32,44; 8:37,40,59). The apostle seems to have gathered the major arguments against the Messiahship of Jesus and here answers them.

7:1 *After this.* As in 5:1 and 6:1 the time is indefinite. However, 6:4 refers to the Passover Feast and 7:2 to the Feast of Tabernacles, making the interval about six months.

7:2 *Feast of Tabernacles.* The great feast in the Jewish year, celebrating the completion of harvest and commemorating God's goodness to the people during the desert wanderings (see Lev 23:43–43; Dt 16:13–15; cf. Zec 14:16–19). The name came from the leafy shelters in which people lived throughout the seven days of the Feast.

7:3 *brothers.* See note on Lk 8:19.

7:4 It is not clear whether the brothers claimed some knowledge of Jesus' miracles that other people did not have or whether they were suggesting that any claim to Messiahship must be decided in Jerusalem. Their advice was not given sincerely, for they did not believe in Jesus (v. 5).

7:6 *right time.* Jesus moved in accordance with the will of God (see note on 2:4).

7:7 *The world.* Either (1) people opposed to God or (2) the human system opposed to God's purposes (see note on 1:10). The brothers belonged to the world and therefore could not be the objects of its hatred. Jesus, however, rebuked the world and was hated accordingly.

7:8 *not yet.* See NIV text note. Jesus was not refusing to go to the Feast, but refusing to go in the way the brothers suggested—as a pilgrim. When he went, it would be to deliver a prophetic message from God, for which he awaited the "right time" (v. 6).

7:10 *not publicly.* Rejecting the brothers' suggestion to show himself (v. 4).

7:12 *whispering.* Because it was not safe to speak openly (cf. v. 13).

7:14 *halfway through the Feast.* When the crowds would be at their maximum. Teaching in the temple courts at such a time would reach many.

7:15 *The Jews.* Distinct from "the crowds" (v. 12), who were also Jews (see note on 1:19). *without having studied.* Under a rabbi. Jesus had never been the disciple of a recognized Jewish teacher.

7:16 *not my own.* The Father, from whom he came, had been his "rabbi" (see note on 4:34).

7:17 *chooses to do God's will.* Reflecting a whole attitude of life. A person sincerely set on doing God's will welcomes Jesus' teaching and believes in him (cf. 6:29). *he will find out.* Augustine commented, "Understanding is the reward of faith . . . What is 'If any man be willing to do his will'? It is the same thing as to believe."

7:18 *is a man of truth.* Or "is true." They should recognize that Jesus was not self-seeking. In this Gospel, no one is spoken of as being "true" except God the Father (3:33; 8:26) and Jesus (here). Once more John ranks Jesus with God.

7:19 *the law.* The Jews congratulated themselves on being the chosen recipients of the law (cf. Ro 2:17), but Jesus told them that they all broke the law of which they were so proud.

7:20 *You are demon-possessed.* The accusation of demon possession is made elsewhere in John (e.g., 8:48–52; 10:20–21; cf. Mt 12:24–32; Mk 3:22–30). *the crowd.* Probably the pilgrims who had come up to Jerusalem for the Feast—different from "the Jews" who were trying to kill Jesus (v. 1) and the Jerusalem mob that knew of the plot (v. 25).

crowd answered. "Who is trying to kill you?"

[21]Jesus said to them, "I did one miracle,[d] and you are all astonished. [22]Yet, because Moses gave you circumcision[e] (though actually it did not come from Moses, but from the patriarchs),[f] you circumcise a child on the Sabbath. [23]Now if a child can be circumcised on the Sabbath so that the law of Moses may not be broken, why are you angry with me for healing the whole man on the Sabbath? [24]Stop judging by mere appearances, and make a right judgment."[g]

Is Jesus the Christ?

[25]At that point some of the people of Jerusalem began to ask, "Isn't this the man they are trying to kill?[h] [26]Here he is, speaking publicly, and they are not saying a word to him. Have the authorities[i] really concluded that he is the Christ[n]?[j] [27]But we know where this man is from; [k] when the Christ comes, no one will know where he is from."

[28]Then Jesus, still teaching in the temple courts,[l] cried out, "Yes, you know me, and you know where I am from.[m] I am not here on my own, but he who sent me is true.[n] You do not know him, [29]but I know him[o] because I am from him and he sent me."[p]

[30]At this they tried to seize him, but no one laid a hand on him,[q] because his time

had not yet come.[r] [31]Still, many in the crowd put their faith in him.[s] They said, "When the Christ comes, will he do more miraculous signs[t] than this man?"

[32]The Pharisees heard the crowd whispering such things about him. Then the chief priests and the Pharisees sent temple guards to arrest him.

[33]Jesus said, "I am with you for only a short time,[u] and then I go to the one who sent me.[v] [34]You will look for me, but you will not find me; and where I am, you cannot come."[w]

[35]The Jews said to one another, "Where does this man intend to go that we cannot find him? Will he go where our people live scattered[x] among the Greeks,[y] and teach the Greeks? [36]What did he mean when he said, 'You will look for me, but you will not find me,' and 'Where I am, you cannot come'?"[z]

[37]On the last and greatest day of the Feast,[a] Jesus stood and said in a loud voice, "If anyone is thirsty, let him come to me and drink.[b] [38]Whoever believes[c] in me, as[o] the Scripture has said,[d] streams of living water[e] will flow from within him."[f] [39]By this he meant the Spirit,[g] whom those who believed in him were later to receive.[h] Up to that time the Spirit

---

Cross references (center column):

7:21 [d]ver 23; Jn 5:2-9
7:22 [e]Lev 12:3 / [f]Ge 17:10-14
7:24 [g]1Sa 16:7; Isa 11:3,4; Jn 8:15; 2Co 10:7
7:25 [h]ver 1; S Mt 12:14
7:26 [i]ver 48 / [j]Jn 4:29
7:27 [k]Mt 13:55; Lk 4:22; Jn 6:42
7:28 [l]ver 14 [m]Jn 8:14 [n]Jn 8:26,42
7:29 [o]S Mt 11:27 [p]S Jn 3:17
7:30 [q]ver 32,44; Jn 10:39
[r]S Mt 26:18
7:31 [s]Jn 8:30; 10:42; 11:45; 12:11,42 [t]S Jn 2:11
7:33 [u]Jn 12:35; 13:33; 16:16 [v]Jn 16:5,10,17,28
7:34 [w]ver 36; Jn 8:21; 13:33
7:35 [x]S Jas 1:1 [y]Jn 12:20; Ac 17:4; 18:4
7:36 [z]ver 34
7:37 [a]Lev 23:36 [b]Isa 55:1; Rev 22:17
7:38 [c]S Jn 3:15 [d]Isa 58:11 [e]S Jn 4:10 / [f]S Jn 4:14
7:39 [g]Joel 2:28; Jn 1:33; Ac 2:17, 33 [h]S Jn 20:22

---

[n]26 Or *Messiah*; also in verses 27, 31, 41 and 42
[o]37,38 Or / *If anyone is thirsty, let him come to me.* / *And let him drink,* [38]*who believes in me.* / *As*

7:21 *one miracle.* Evidently that of healing the lame man (5:1–9), as the discussion about the Sabbath shows.

7:22 *circumcision.* The requirement of circumcision was included in the law Moses gave (Ex 12:44,48; Lev 12:3), yet it did not originate with Moses but went back to Abraham (Ge 17:9–14). The Jews took such regulations as that in Lev 12:3 to mean that circumcision must be performed on the eighth day even if it was the Sabbath, a day on which no work should be done. This exception is of critical importance in understanding the controversy (v. 23). Jesus was not saying that the Sabbath should not be observed or that the Jewish regulations were too harsh. He was saying that his opponents did not understand what the Sabbath meant. The command to circumcise showed that sometimes work not only might be done on the Sabbath but must be done then. Deeds of mercy were in this category.

7:25 *people of Jerusalem.* An expression found only here and in Mk 1:5 in the NT, probably referring to the Jerusalem mob (see note on v. 20). They did not originate the plot against Jesus, but they knew of it.

7:26 *Have the authorities really concluded . . . ?* In Greek, the question is in a form that expects a negative answer. *the Christ.* See note on 1:25.

7:27 *no one will know where he is from.* Some Jews held that the OT gave the origin of the Messiah (cf. v. 42; Mt 2:4–6), but others believed that it did not.

7:28 *you know me.* Irony, because in a sense they knew Jesus and that he came from Nazareth, but in a deeper sense they did not know Jesus or the Father (8:19). Jesus men-

tioned again his dependence on the Father (cf. 4:34) and went on to declare that he had real knowledge of God and that they did not. Both his origin and mission were from God.

7:30 *they tried to seize him.* Jesus' enemies were powerless against him until his time came (see note on 2:4).

7:31 *crowd.* Of pilgrims (see note on v. 20). Many of them believed on the basis of the miraculous signs (cf. 6:26).

7:32 *the Pharisees.* See notes on Mt 3:7; Mk 2:16; Lk 5:17. *the chief priests.* There was only one ruling chief priest, but the Romans had deposed a number of chief priests, and these retained the title by courtesy.

7:33 *then I go.* Jesus changed the topic from his miracles to his death, to which he referred enigmatically (v. 34).

7:35 *scattered among the Greeks.* From the time of the exile, many Jews lived outside Palestine and were found in most cities throughout the Roman empire.

7:37 *the last . . . day of the Feast.* Either the seventh or the eighth day: This feast lasted seven days (Lev 23:34; Dt 16:13,15) but had a "closing assembly" on the eighth day (Lev 23:36). See note on Mk 14:12. *stood and said in a loud voice.* Teachers usually sat, so Jesus drew special attention to his message.

7:38 *living water.* See note on 4:10.

7:39 *the Spirit.* Explaining the "living water" (v. 38). *had not been given.* In the manner in which he would be given at Pentecost (see Ac 2). *glorified.* Here probably refers to Jesus' crucifixion, resurrection and exaltation (see note on 13:31). The fullness of the Spirit's work depends on Jesus' prior work of salvation.

had not been given, since Jesus had not yet been glorified. [i]

40On hearing his words, some of the people said, "Surely this man is the Prophet." [j]

41Others said, "He is the Christ."

Still others asked, "How can the Christ come from Galilee? [k] 42Does not the Scripture say that the Christ will come from David's family [p] [l] and from Bethlehem, [m] the town where David lived?" 43Thus the people were divided [n] because of Jesus. 44Some wanted to seize him, but no one laid a hand on him. [o]

Unbelief of the Jewish Leaders

45Finally the temple guards went back to the chief priests and Pharisees, who asked them, "Why didn't you bring him in?"

46"No one ever spoke the way this man does," [p] the guards declared.

47"You mean he has deceived you also?" [q] the Pharisees retorted. 48"Has any of the rulers or of the Pharisees believed in him? [r] 49No! But this mob that knows nothing of the law—there is a curse on them."

50Nicodemus, [s] who had gone to Jesus earlier and who was one of their own number, asked, 51"Does our law condemn anyone without first hearing him to find out what he is doing?"

52They replied, "Are you from Galilee, too? Look into it, and you will find that a prophet [q] does not come out of Galilee." [t]

[The earliest and most reliable manuscripts and other ancient witnesses do not have John 7:53–8:11.]

53Then each went to his own home.

8 But Jesus went to the Mount of Olives. [u] 2At dawn he appeared again in the temple courts, where all the people gathered around him, and he sat down to teach them. [v] 3The teachers of the law and the Pharisees brought in a woman caught in adultery. They made her stand before the group 4and said to Jesus, "Teacher, this woman was caught in the act of adultery. 5In the Law Moses commanded us to stone such women. [w] Now what do you say?" 6They were using this question as a trap, [x] in order to have a basis for accusing him. [y]

But Jesus bent down and started to write on the ground with his finger. 7When they kept on questioning him, he

Cross references

7:39 [i] Jn 12:23; 13:31,32
7:40 [j] S Mt 21:11
7:41 [k] ver 52; Jn 1:46
7:42 [l] S Mt 1:1 [m] Mic 5:2; Mt 2:5,6; Lk 2:4
7:43 [n] Jn 6:52; 9:16; 10:19
7:44 [o] ver 30
7:46 [p] S Mt 7:28
7:47 [q] ver 12
7:48 [r] Jn 12:42
7:50 [s] Jn 3:1; 19:39

7:52 [t] ver 41
8:1 [u] S Mt 21:1
8:2 [v] ver 20; S Mt 26:55
8:5 [w] Lev 20:10; Job 31:11
8:6 [x] Mt 22:15,18 [y] S Mt 12:10

[p] 42 Greek seed   [q] 52 Two early manuscripts the Prophet

7:40 people. The "crowd" of v. 20 (see note there).

7:42 Bethlehem. There were different ideas about the Messiah's place of origin (cf. v. 27).

7:46 the guards. They knew they would be in trouble for failing to make the arrest, but did not mention the hostility of part of the crowd, which would have given them something of an excuse before the Pharisees. They were favorably impressed by the teaching of Jesus and were not inclined to cause him trouble.

7:47 the Pharisees retorted. They must have been greatly irritated. Ordinarily the chief priests would have rebuked the temple guards.

7:49 this mob. The pilgrim crowd again (see note on v. 20). knows nothing. The Pharisees exaggerated the people's ignorance of Scripture (cf. v. 42). But the average Jew paid little attention to the minutiae that mattered so much to the Pharisees. The "traditions of the elders" were too great a burden for people who earned their living by hard physical work, and consequently these regulations were widely disregarded.

7:50–51 There is irony here. The Pharisees implied that no leader believed in Jesus, yet Nicodemus, "a member of the Jewish ruling council" (3:1), spoke up. They called for people to observe the law, but Nicodemus pointed to their own failure to keep the law.

7:52 a prophet does not come out of Galilee. See 1:46. They were angry—and wrong. Jonah came from Galilee, and perhaps other prophets as well. Moreover, the Pharisees overlooked the right of God to raise up prophets from wherever he chooses.

7:53–8:11 This story may not have belonged originally to the Gospel of John. It is absent from almost all the important early manuscripts, and those that have it sometimes place it

elsewhere (e.g., after Lk 21:38). But the story may well be authentic.

7:53 This verse (along with 8:1) shows that the story was originally attached to another narrative, since Jesus was not present at the meeting of the Sanhedrin described in vv. 45–52.

8:1 Mount of Olives. See note on Mk 11:1.

8:3 teachers of the law. See notes on Mt 2:4; Lk 5:17. a woman caught in adultery. This sin cannot be committed alone, so the question arises as to why only one offender was brought. The incident was staged to trap Jesus (v. 6), and provision had been made for the man to escape. The woman's accusers must have been especially eager to humiliate her, since they could have kept her in private custody while they spoke to Jesus.

8:4 caught in the act. Compromising circumstances were not sufficient evidence, as Jewish law required witnesses who had seen the act.

8:5 to stone such women. They altered the law a little. The manner of execution was not prescribed unless the woman was a betrothed virgin (Dt 22:23–24). And the law required the execution of both parties (Lev 20:10; Dt 22:22), not just the woman.

8:6 using this question as a trap. The Romans did not allow the Jews to carry out death sentences (18:31), so if Jesus had said to stone her, he could have been in conflict with the Romans. If he had said not to stone her, he could have been accused of being unsupportive of the law. started to write. We can only guess what Jesus wrote on the ground.

8:7 let him be the first. Jesus' answer disarmed them. Since he spoke of throwing a stone, he could not be accused of failure to uphold the law. But the qualification for throwing it prevented anyone from acting. without sin. The phrase is

straightened up and said to them, "If any one of you is without sin, let him be the first to throw a stone [z] at her." [a] ⁸Again he stooped down and wrote on the ground.

⁹At this, those who heard began to go away one at a time, the older ones first, until only Jesus was left, with the woman still standing there. ¹⁰Jesus straightened up and asked her, "Woman, where are they? Has no one condemned you?"

¹¹"No one, sir," she said.

"Then neither do I condemn you," [b] Jesus declared. "Go now and leave your life of sin." [c]

The Validity of Jesus' Testimony

¹²When Jesus spoke again to the people, he said, "I am [d] the light of the world. [e] Whoever follows me will never walk in darkness, but will have the light of life." [f]

¹³The Pharisees challenged him, "Here you are, appearing as your own witness; your testimony is not valid." [g]

¹⁴Jesus answered, "Even if I testify on my own behalf, my testimony is valid, for I know where I came from and where I am going. [h] But you have no idea where I come from [i] or where I am going. ¹⁵You judge by human standards; [j] I pass judgment on no one. [k] ¹⁶But if I do judge, my decisions are right, because I am not alone. I stand with the Father, who sent me. [l] ¹⁷In your own Law it is written that the testimony of two men is valid. [m] ¹⁸I am one who testifies for myself; my other witness is the Father, who sent me." [n]

¹⁹Then they asked him, "Where is your father?"

"You do not know me or my Father," [o] Jesus replied. "If you knew me, you would know my Father also." [p] ²⁰He spoke these words while teaching [q] in the temple area near the place where the offerings were put. [r] Yet no one seized him, because his time had not yet come. [s]

²¹Once more Jesus said to them, "I am going away, and you will look for me, and you will die [t] in your sin. Where I go, you cannot come." [u]

²²This made the Jews ask, "Will he kill himself? Is that why he says, 'Where I go, you cannot come'?"

²³But he continued, "You are from below; I am from above. You are of this world; I am not of this world. [v] ²⁴I told you that you would die in your sins; if you do not believe that I am ¸the one I claim to be, [r] [w] you will indeed die in your sins."

²⁵"Who are you?" they asked.

"Just what I have been claiming all along," Jesus replied. ²⁶"I have much to say in judgment of you. But he who sent me is reliable, [x] and what I have heard from him I tell the world." [y]

²⁷They did not understand that he was telling them about his Father. ²⁸So Jesus said, "When you have lifted up the Son of Man, [z] then you will know that I am ¸the one I claim to be¸ and that I do nothing on my own but speak just what the Father has taught me. [a] ²⁹The one who sent me is with me; he has not left me alone, [b] for I

Cross references

8:7 z Dt 17:7; Eze 16:40
a Ro 2:1,22
8:11 b Jn 3:17
c Jn 5:14
8:12 d S Jn 6:35
e S Jn 1:4
f Pr 4:18; Mt 5:14
8:13 g Jn 5:31
8:14 h Jn 13:3; 16:28 /Jn 7:28; 9:29
8:15 /S Jn 7:24
k Jn 3:17
8:16 l Jn 5:30
8:17 m S Mt 18:16
8:18 n Jn 5:37
8:19 o Jn 16:3
p S 1Jn 2:23
8:20 q S Mt 26:55
r Mk 12:41
s S Mt 26:18
8:21 t Eze 3:18
u Jn 7:34; 13:33
8:23 v Jn 3:31; 17:14
8:24 w Jn 4:26; 13:19
8:26 x Jn 7:28
y Jn 3:32; 15:15
8:28 z S Jn 12:32
a S Jn 14:24
8:29 b ver 16; Jn 16:32

r 24 Or I am he; also in verse 28

---

quite general and means "without any sin," not "without this sin."

8:9 *began to go away.* Because they were not "without sin" (v. 7). *the older ones.* They were the first to realize what was involved. But all the men were either conscience-stricken or afraid, and in the end only Jesus and the woman remained.

8:10 *Woman.* Not a harsh form of address (cf. its use in 19:26).

8:11 *Go now and leave your life of sin.* Jesus did not condone what the woman had done.

8:12 *I am.* See note on 6:35. *the light.* See 1:4 and note; 9:5; 12:46. It is also true that "God is light" (1Jn 1:5). And as Jesus' followers reflect the light that comes from him, they too are "the light of the world" (Mt 5:14; cf. Php 2:15). *darkness.* Both the darkness of this world and that of Satan. *the light of life.* "God is light" (1Jn 1:5); but Jesus is also the light from God that lights the way for life—as the pillar of fire lighted the way for the Israelites (see Ex 13:21; Ne 9:12).

8:13 *Pharisees.* See notes on Mt 3:7; Mk 2:16; Lk 5:17.

8:14 Jesus made two points in reply. First, he was qualified to bear testimony, whereas the Pharisees were not; and he knew both his origin and his destination, whereas they knew neither. (See note on vv. 16–18 for the second point.)

8:15 The judgment of the Pharisees was limited and world-

ly. In the sense they meant, Jesus made it clear that he did not judge at all. In the proper sense, of course, he did judge (v. 26).

8:16–18 Jesus' second point was that his testimony was not unsupported. The Father was with him, so he and the Father were the two witnesses required by the law (Dt 17:6; 19:15).

8:16 *the Father who sent me.* Jesus was always aware of his mission (see note on 4:34).

8:19 *If you knew me.* John makes it clear that the Word (Jesus) was with God and was God (1:1) and reveals God (1:18). Jesus here stresses that the Father is known through the Son and that to know the one is to know the other.

8:20 *his time.* See note on 2:4.

8:23 Things other than death divide people (cf., e.g., v. 47; 3:31; 15:19; 1Jn 3:10). *of.* Here denotes origin. Jesus was certainly in the world, but he was not of the world. They belonged to "this world"—Satan's domain (1Jn 5:19).

8:24 *believe.* See note on 1:7. *I am.* Jesus echoes God's great affirmation about himself (see v. 58; see also notes on 6:35; Ex 3:14).

8:28 *lifted up.* Normally used in the NT in the sense of "exalt," but John uses it of the crucifixion (see 3:14). *Son of Man.* See note on Mk 8:31. *I am.* See notes on vv. 24,58.

always do what pleases him." c 30Even as he spoke, many put their faith in him. d

The Children of Abraham

31To the Jews who had believed him, Jesus said, "If you hold to my teaching, e you are really my disciples. 32Then you will know the truth, and the truth will set you free." f

33They answered him, "We are Abraham's descendants s g and have never been slaves of anyone. How can you say that we shall be set free?"

34Jesus replied, "I tell you the truth, everyone who sins is a slave to sin. h 35Now a slave has no permanent place in the family, but a son belongs to it forever. i 36So if the Son sets you free, j you will be free indeed. 37I know you are Abraham's descendants. Yet you are ready to kill me, k because you have no room for my word. 38I am telling you what I have seen in the Father's presence, l and you do what you have heard from your father. t " m

39"Abraham is our father," they answered.

"If you were Abraham's children," n said Jesus, "then you would u do the things Abraham did. 40As it is, you are determined to kill me, o a man who has told you the truth that I heard from God. p Abraham did not do such things. 41You are doing the things your own father does." q

"We are not illegitimate children," they protested. "The only Father we have is God himself." r

The Children of the Devil

42Jesus said to them, "If God were your

Father, you would love me, s for I came from God t and now am here. I have not come on my own; u but he sent me. v 43Why is my language not clear to you? Because you are unable to hear what I say. 44You belong to your father, the devil, w and you want to carry out your father's desire. x He was a murderer from the beginning, not holding to the truth, for there is no truth in him. When he lies, he speaks his native language, for he is a liar and the father of lies. y 45Yet because I tell the truth, z you do not believe me! 46Can any of you prove me guilty of sin? If I am telling the truth, why don't you believe me? 47He who belongs to God hears what God says. a The reason you do not hear is that you do not belong to God."

The Claims of Jesus About Himself

48The Jews answered him, "Aren't we right in saying that you are a Samaritan b and demon-possessed?" c

49"I am not possessed by a demon," said Jesus, "but I honor my Father and you dishonor me. 50I am not seeking glory for myself; d but there is one who seeks it, and he is the judge. 51I tell you the truth, if anyone keeps my word, he will never see death." e

52At this the Jews exclaimed, "Now we know that you are demon-possessed! f Abraham died and so did the prophets, yet you say that if anyone keeps your word, he will never taste death. 53Are you greater than our father Abraham? g He died, and

Cross references

8:29 cIsa 50:5; Jn 4:34; 5:30; 6:38
8:30 dS Jn 7:31
8:31 eJn 15:7; 2Jn 9
8:32 fver 36; Ro 8:2; 2Co 3:17; Gal 5:1,13
8:33 gver 37,39; S Lk 3:8
8:34 hS Ro 6:16
8:35 iGal 4:30
8:36 jver 32
8:37 kver 39,40
8:38 lJn 5:19,30; 14:10,24 mver 41,44
8:39 nver 37; S Lk 3:8
8:40 oS Mt 12:14 pver 26
8:41 qver 38,44 rIsa 63:16; 64:8

8:42 sIJn 5:1 tS Jn 13:3 uJn 7:28 vS Jn 3:17
8:44 wIJn 3:8 xver 38,41 yGe 3:4; 4:9; 2Ch 18:21; Ps 5:6; 12:2
8:45 zJn 18:37
8:47 aJn 18:37; 1Jn 4:6
8:48 bS Mt 10:5 cver 52; S Mk 3:22
8:50 dver 54; Jn 5:41
8:51 eJn 11:26
8:52 fver 48; S Mk 3:22
8:53 gver 39; Jn 4:12

s33 Greek seed; also in verse 37   t38 Or presence. Therefore do what you have heard from the Father.   u39 Some early manuscripts "If you are Abraham's children," said Jesus, "then

Study notes

8:30 faith. Cf. 20:31.
8:31 believed. Here seems to mean "made a formal profession of faith." Their words show that these people were not true believers (see vv. 33,37).
8:32 the truth. Closely connected with Jesus (v. 36; 14:6), it is not philosophical truth but the truth that leads to salvation. free. Freedom from sin, not from ignorance (see v. 36).
8:33 have never been slaves. An amazing disregard of their Roman overlords.
8:34 a slave to sin. Because the sinner cannot break free by his own strength.
8:37 you are ready to kill me. See note on 7:1–8:59.
8:38 Note the contrast: "I . . . you"; "seen . . . heard"; "the Father . . . your father." Not until later (v. 44) did Jesus say who their father was, but it is clear even at this point that it was neither God nor Abraham as they claimed.
8:39–41 Their deeds revealed their parentage.
8:41 illegitimate. May have been a slander aimed at Jesus' virgin birth.
8:43 my language. The form of expression—the actual words. what I say. The content. The Jews were so convinced of their own preconceptions that they did not really hear what Jesus was saying (cf. v. 47).

8:44 your father, the devil. The Jews' relationship to Satan was now stated explicitly. Jesus clearly excluded the idea of the universal fatherhood of God. you want. Points to determination of will. Their problem was basically spiritual, not intellectual. Being oriented toward Satan, they were bent on murder (v. 37) and eventually would succeed (v. 28). truth. Foreign to Satan and those who are his (see 14:6).
8:46 Can . . . you prove me guilty of sin? The asking of the question was more significant than the Jews' failure to answer, in that it showed Jesus had a perfectly clear conscience.
8:47 hears what God says. See 10:3–4; 1Jn 4:6.
8:48 The Jews. See note on 1:19. a Samaritan. Probably to suggest that he was lax in Jewish observances—"No better than a Samaritan." Or it may be a reflection on the birth of Jesus—perhaps claiming that his father was a Samaritan. demon-possessed. See 10:20 and note on 7:20.
8:51 my word. The whole of Jesus' message, which when accepted brings deliverance from death.
8:53 Are you greater . . . ? The question was framed to expect the answer "No." This is ironic, since Jesus was indeed far greater than Abraham, even as he was greater than Moses (see 6:30–35 and notes).

so did the prophets. Who do you think you are?"

54Jesus replied, "If I glorify myself,[h] my glory means nothing. My Father, whom you claim as your God, is the one who glorifies me.[i] 55Though you do not know him,[j] I know him.[k] If I said I did not, I would be a liar like you, but I do know him and keep his word.[l] 56Your father Abraham[m] rejoiced at the thought of seeing my day; he saw it[n] and was glad."

57"You are not yet fifty years old," the Jews said to him, "and you have seen Abraham!"

58"I tell you the truth," Jesus answered, "before Abraham was born,[o] I am!"[p] 59At this, they picked up stones to stone him,[q] but Jesus hid himself,[r] slipping away from the temple grounds.

Jesus Heals a Man Born Blind

9 As he went along, he saw a man blind from birth. 2His disciples asked him, "Rabbi,[s] who sinned,[t] this man[u] or his parents,[v] that he was born blind?"

3"Neither this man nor his parents sinned," said Jesus, "but this happened so that the work of God might be displayed in his life.[w] 4As long as it is day,[x] we must do the work of him who sent me. Night is coming, when no one can work. 5While I am in the world, I am the light of the world."[y]

6Having said this, he spit[z] on the ground, made some mud with the saliva, and put it on the man's eyes. 7"Go," he

8:54 *h*ver 50
/Jn 16:14; 17:1,5
8:55 /ver 19
*k*Jn 7:28,29
/Jn 15:10
8:56 *m*ver 37,39;
Ge 18:18
*n*S Mt 13:17
8:58 *o*S Jn 1:2
*p*Ex 3:14; 6:3
8:59 *q*Ex 17:4;
Lev 24:16;
1Sa 30:6;
Jn 10:31; 11:8
*r*Jn 12:36
9:2 *s*S Mt 23:7
*t*ver 34; Lk 13:2;
Ac 28:4
*u*Eze 18:20
*v*Ex 20:5; Job
21:19
9:3 *w*Jn 11:4
9:4 *x*Jn 11:9;
12:35
9:5 *y*S Jn 1:4
9:6 *z*Mk 7:33;
8:23

told him, "wash in the Pool of Siloam"[a] (this word means Sent). So the man went and washed, and came home seeing.[b]

8His neighbors and those who had formerly seen him begging asked, "Isn't this the same man who used to sit and beg?"[c] 9Some claimed that he was.

Others said, "No, he only looks like him."

But he himself insisted, "I am the man."

10"How then were your eyes opened?" they demanded.

11He replied, "The man they call Jesus made some mud and put it on my eyes. He told me to go to Siloam and wash. So I went and washed, and then I could see."[d]

12"Where is this man?" they asked him. "I don't know," he said.

The Pharisees Investigate the Healing

13They brought to the Pharisees the man who had been blind. 14Now the day on which Jesus had made the mud and opened the man's eyes was a Sabbath.[e] 15Therefore the Pharisees also asked him how he had received his sight.[f] "He put mud on my eyes," the man replied, "and I washed, and now I see."

16Some of the Pharisees said, "This man is not from God, for he does not keep the Sabbath."[g]

But others asked, "How can a sinner do such miraculous signs?"[h] So they were divided.[i]

17Finally they turned again to the blind

9:7 *a*ver 11;
2Ki 5:10; Lk 13:4
*b*Isa 35:5;
Jn 11:37
9:8 *c*Ac 3:2,10
9:11 *d*ver 7
9:14
*e*Mt 12:1-14;
Jn 5:9
9:15 *f*ver 10
9:16 *g*S Mt 12:2
*h*S Jn 2:11
*i*S Jn 6:52

8:56 *my day.* All that was involved in the incarnation. Jesus probably was not referring to any one occasion but to Abraham's general joy in the fulfilling of the purposes of God in Christ, by which all nations on earth would receive blessing (Ge 18:18). *he saw it.* In faith, from afar.

8:57 *not yet fifty years old.* A generous allowance for Jesus' maximum possible age. Jesus was about 30 when he began his ministry (Lk 3:23).

8:58 *I am!* A solemnly emphatic declaration echoing God's great affirmation in Ex 3:14 (see vv. 24,28; see also note on 6:35). Jesus did not say "I was" but "I am," expressing the eternity of his being and his oneness with the Father (see 1:1). With this climactic statement Jesus concludes his speech that began with the related claim, "I am the light of the world" (v. 12).

8:59 *to stone him.* The Jews could not interpret Jesus' claim as other than blasphemy, for which stoning was the proper penalty (Lev 24:16).

9:1−12 Jesus performed more miracles of this kind than of any other. Giving sight to the blind was predicted as a Messianic activity (Isa 29:18; 35:5; 42:7). Thus these miracles were additional evidence that Jesus was the Messiah (20:31).

9:2 *who sinned . . . ?* The rabbis had developed the principle that "There is no death without sin, and there is no suffering without iniquity." They were even capable of thinking that a child could sin in the womb or that its soul

might have sinned in a preexistent state. They also held that terrible punishments came on certain people because of the sin of their parents. As the next verse shows, Jesus plainly contradicted these beliefs.

9:4 *we.* Not Jesus only.

9:5 *the light of the world.* See note on 8:12.

9:6 Jesus used variety in his cures.

9:7 *Siloam.* Already an ancient name (see NIV text note on Ne 3:15; see also Isa 8:6). A rock-cut pool on the southern end of the main ridge on which Jerusalem was built, it served as part of the major water system developed by King Hezekiah. *Sent.* Or "one who has been sent."

9:8 *begging.* Not mentioned previously, but it was about the only way a blind person of that day could support himself.

9:13 *Pharisees.* See notes on Mt 3:7; Mk 2:16; Lk 5:17.

9:14 *Sabbath.* Cf. 5:16 and the discussion that follows.

9:16 *Some . . . others.* The first group started from their entrenched position and ruled out the possibility of Jesus' being from God. The second started from the fact of the "miraculous signs" and ruled out the possibility of his being a sinner (cf. vv. 31–33).

9:17 *What have you to say about him?* It is curious that they put such a question to such a person; their doing so reflected their perplexity. *a prophet.* Probably the highest designation of which the man could think. He progressed in his thinking about Jesus: from a man (v. 11), to a prophet (v. 17) who might be followed by disciples (v. 27), to one "from

man, "What have you to say about him? It was your eyes he opened."

The man replied, "He is a prophet."[j]

[18]The Jews[k] still did not believe that he had been blind and had received his sight until they sent for the man's parents. [19]"Is this your son?" they asked. "Is this the one you say was born blind? How is it that now he can see?"

[20]"We know he is our son," the parents answered, "and we know he was born blind. [21]But how he can see now, or who opened his eyes, we don't know. Ask him. He is of age; he will speak for himself." [22]His parents said this because they were afraid of the Jews,[l] for already the Jews had decided that anyone who acknowledged that Jesus was the Christ[v] would be put out[m] of the synagogue.[n] [23]That was why his parents said, "He is of age; ask him."[o]

[24]A second time they summoned the man who had been blind. "Give glory to God,[w][p] they said. "We know this man is a sinner."[q]

[25]He replied, "Whether he is a sinner or not, I don't know. One thing I do know. I was blind but now I see!"

[26]Then they asked him, "What did he do to you? How did he open your eyes?"

[27]He answered, "I have told you already[r] and you did not listen. Why do you want to hear it again? Do you want to become his disciples, too?"

[28]Then they hurled insults at him and said, "You are this fellow's disciple! We are disciples of Moses![s] [29]We know that God spoke to Moses, but as for this fellow, we don't even know where he comes from."[t]

[30]The man answered, "Now that is remarkable! You don't know where he comes from, yet he opened my eyes. [31]We know that God does not listen to sinners. He listens to the godly man who does his will. [u] [32]Nobody has ever heard of opening the eyes of a man born blind. [33]If this man were not from God,[v] he could do nothing."

[34]To this they replied, "You were steeped in sin at birth;[w] how dare you lecture us!" And they threw him out.[x]

Spiritual Blindness

[35]Jesus heard that they had thrown him out, and when he found him, he said, "Do you believe[y] in the Son of Man?"[z]

[36]"Who is he, sir?" the man asked. "Tell me so that I may believe in him."[a]

[37]Jesus said, "You have now seen him; in fact, he is the one speaking with you."[b]

[38]Then the man said, "Lord, I believe," and he worshiped him.[c]

[39]Jesus said, "For judgment[d] I have come into this world,[e] so that the blind will see[f] and those who see will become blind."[g]

[40]Some Pharisees who were with him heard him say this and asked, "What? Are we blind too?"[h]

[41]Jesus said, "If you were blind, you would not be guilty of sin; but now that you claim you can see, your guilt remains.[i]

The Shepherd and His Flock

10 "I tell you the truth, the man who does not enter the sheep pen by

9:17 /S Mt 21:11
9:18 kS Jn 1:19
9:22 lS Jn 7:13
mver 34; Lk 6:22
nJn 12:42; 16:2
9:23 over 21
9:24 pJos 7:19
qver 16
9:27 rver 15
9:28 sJn 5:45
9:29 tJn 8:14

9:31
uGe 18:23-32;
Ps 34:15,16;
66:18; 145:19,20;
Pr 15:29; Isa
1:15; 59:1,2;
Jn 15:7;
Jas 5:16-18;
1Jn 5:14,15
9:33 vver 16;
Jn 3:2
9:34 wver 2 xver
22,35; Isa 66:5
9:35 yS Jn 3:15
zS Mt 8:20
9:36 aRo 10:14
9:37 bJn 4:26
9:38 cMt 28:9
9:39 dS Jn 5:22
eJn 3:19; 12:47
fLk 4:18
gMt 13:13
9:40 hRo 2:19
9:41 iJn 15:22,24

v22 Or Messiah   w24 A solemn charge to tell the truth (see Joshua 7:19)

God" (v. 33), to one who was properly to be worshiped (v. 38).

9:18 *The Jews.* See note on 1:19. In their prejudice they did not learn from the sign but tried to discredit the miracle.
9:21 *He is of age.* There was much to which the parents could not testify, but their emphasis on the son's responsibility showed their fear of getting involved.
9:22 *put out of the synagogue.* Excommunication is reported as early as the time of Ezra (10:8), but there is practically no information about the way it was practiced in NT times. The synagogue was the center of Jewish community life, so excommunication cut a person off from many social relationships (though, in some of its forms, at least in later times, not from worship).
9:24 *We.* Emphatic in the Greek.
9:27 *his disciples, too.* The man already counted himself a disciple.
9:30–33 Good reasoning from an unschooled man.
9:31 *God does not listen to sinners.* Cf. the remark of some of the Pharisees in v. 16.
9:34 *threw him out.* May mean "expelled him from their assembly" or, more probably, "excommunicated him" (see

note on v. 22).
9:35 *when he found him.* Jesus obviously had been looking for the man. *Son of Man.* See note on Mk 8:31.
9:36 The man was ready to follow any suggestion from his benefactor.
9:38 *I believe.* See 20:31 and note on 1:7. *Lord . . . he worshiped him.* The man was giving Jesus the reverence due to God.
9:39 It is unlikely that the conversation of vv. 35–38 took place in the presence of the Pharisees. The incident of vv. 39–41, therefore, probably occurred a little later. *For judgment.* In a sense Jesus did not come for judgment (3:17; 12:47), but his coming divides people, and this always brings a type of judgment. Those who reject his gift end up "blind."
9:40 *Pharisees.* They found it incredible that anyone would consider them spiritually blind.
9:41 The Pharisees' claim to sight showed their complete unawareness of their spiritual blindness and need. And, though they claimed to have sight, their actions were evidence of their blindness.
10:1–30 Should be understood in light of the OT (and ancient Near Eastern) concept of "shepherd," symbolizing a

the gate, but climbs in by some other way,
is a thief and a robber.[j] 2The man who
enters by the gate is the shepherd of his
sheep.[k] 3The watchman opens the gate for
him, and the sheep listen to his voice.[l] He
calls his own sheep by name and leads
them out.[m] 4When he has brought out all
his own, he goes on ahead of them, and his
sheep follow him because they know his
voice.[n] 5But they will never follow a
stranger; in fact, they will run away from
him because they do not recognize a
stranger's voice." 6Jesus used this figure of
speech,[o] but they did not understand
what he was telling them.[p]
7Therefore Jesus said again, "I tell you
the truth, I am[q] the gate[r] for the sheep.
8All who ever came before me[s] were
thieves and robbers,[t] but the sheep did
not listen to them. 9I am the gate; whoever
enters through me will be saved.[x] He will
come in and go out, and find pasture.
10The thief comes only to steal and kill and
destroy; I have come that they may have
life,[u] and have it to the full.[v]
11"I am[w] the good shepherd.[x] The good
shepherd lays down his life for the sheep.[y]
12The hired hand is not the shepherd who
owns the sheep. So when he sees the wolf
coming, he abandons the sheep and runs
away.[z] Then the wolf attacks the flock
and scatters it. 13The man runs away because he is a hired hand and cares nothing
for the sheep.
14"I am the good shepherd;[a] I know my
sheep[b] and my sheep know me— 15just as
the Father knows me and I know the Father[c]—and I lay down my life for the
sheep.[d] 16I have other sheep[e] that are not
of this sheep pen. I must bring them also.
They too will listen to my voice, and there
shall be one flock[f] and one shepherd.[g]
17The reason my Father loves me is that I
lay down my life[h]—only to take it up
again. 18No one takes it from me, but I lay
it down of my own accord.[i] I have authority to lay it down and authority to take
it up again. This command I received from
my Father."[j]
19At these words the Jews were again
divided.[k] 20Many of them said, "He is demon-possessed[l] and raving mad.[m] Why
listen to him?"
21But others said, "These are not the
sayings of a man possessed by a demon.[n]
Can a demon open the eyes of the
blind?"[o]

The Unbelief of the Jews

22Then came the Feast of Dedication[y] at
Jerusalem. It was winter, 23and Jesus was

10:1 [j]ver 8,10 **10:2** [k]ver 11,14; Mk 6:34 **10:3** [l]ver 4,5,14, 16,27 [m]ver 4,5, 14,16,27 **10:4** [n]S ver 3 **10:6** [o]S Jn 16:25, [p]S Mk 9:32 **10:7** [q]S Jn 6:35 [r]ver 9 **10:8** [s]Jer 23:1,2; Eze 34:2 [t]ver 1 **10:10** [u]S Jn 1:4; 3:15,16; 5:40; 20:31 [v]Ps 65:11; Ro 5:17 **10:11** [w]S Jn 6:35 [x]ver 14; Ps 23:1; Isa 40:11; Eze 34:11-16,23; Mt 2:6; Lk 12:32; Heb 13:20; 1Pe 2:25; 5:4; Rev 7:17 [y]ver 15, 17,18; Jn 15:13; 1Jn 3:16 **10:12** [z]Zec 11:16,17 **10:14** [a]S ver 11 [b]ver 27; Ex 33:12 **10:15** [c]Mt 11:27 [d]ver 11,17,18 **10:16** [e]Isa 56:8; Ac 10:34,35 [f]Jn 11:52; 17:20, 21; Eph 2:11-19 [g]Eze 34:23; 37:24 **10:17** [h]ver 11, 15,18 **10:18** [i]Mt 26:53 [j]Jn 15:10; Php 2:8; Heb 5:8 **10:19** [k]S Jn 6:52 **10:20** [l]S Mk 3:22 [m]2Ki 9:11; Jer 29:26; Mk 3:21 **10:21** [n]S Mt 4:24 [o]Ex 4:11; Jn 9:32,33

[x]*9* Or *kept safe* [y]*22* That is, Hanukkah

royal caretaker of God's people. God himself was called the "Shepherd of Israel" (Ps 80:1; cf. Ps 23:1; Isa 40:10–11; Eze 34:11–16), and he had given great responsibility to the leaders ("shepherds") of Israel, which they failed to respect. God denounced these false shepherds (see Isa 56:9–12; Eze 34) and promised to provide the true Shepherd, the Messiah, to care for the sheep (Eze 34:23).

10:1 *sheep pen.* A court surrounded by walls but open to the sky, and with only one entrance. The walls kept the sheep from wandering and protected them from wild animals.

10:3 *The watchman.* Apparently in charge of a large fold, where several flocks were kept. *his voice.* The sheep recognized the voice of their own shepherd and responded only to him. *his own sheep.* The shepherd did not call sheep randomly, but only those that belonged to him.

10:4 *he goes on ahead.* The Palestinian shepherd led his sheep (he did not drive them), and the sheep followed because they knew his voice.

10:7 *I am.* See note on 6:35.

10:8 *All . . . before me.* "False shepherds" like the Pharisees and the chief priests, not the true OT prophets (see note on vv. 1–30).

10:9 *the gate.* The one way into salvation. Inside there is safety, and one is able to go out and find pasture, i.e., the supply of all needs.

10:10 *thief.* His interest is in himself. Christ's interest is in his sheep, whom he enables to have life to the full (see note on 1:4).

10:11 *I am.* See note on 6:35. *lays down his life.* A Palestinian shepherd might risk danger for his sheep (see Ge 31:39; 1Sa 17:34–37), but he expected to come through alive. Jesus said that the good shepherd will die for his sheep.

10:12 *hired hand.* He is interested in wages, not sheep. In time of danger he runs away because of what he is (v. 13) and abandons the flock to predators.

10:14 *I know . . . my sheep know.* A deep mutual knowledge, like that of the Father and the Son.

10:15 *I lay down my life.* See v. 11; the fact of central importance.

10:16 *other sheep.* These already belonged to Christ, though they had not yet been brought to him. *not of this sheep pen.* Those outside Judaism. Here is a glimpse of the future worldwide scope of the church. *one flock.* All God's people have the same Shepherd (see 17:20–23).

10:17–18 That Christ would die for his people runs through this section of John's Gospel. Both the love and the plan of the Father are involved, as well as the authority he gave to the Son. Christ obediently chose to die; otherwise, no one would have had the power to kill him.

10:19 *divided.* See 7:43; 9:16.

10:20 *demon-possessed.* See note on 7:20.

10:21 Cf. 9:16.

10:22 *Feast of Dedication.* The commemoration of the dedication (see NIV text note) of the temple by Judas Maccabeus in December, 165 B.C., after it had been profaned by Antiochus Epiphanes. This was the last great deliverance the Jews had experienced. *It was winter.* A description for those unfamiliar with the Jewish calendar.

10:23 *Solomon's Colonnade.* See Ac 3:11; 5:12. It was a roofed structure—somewhat similar to a Greek stoa—commonly but erroneously thought to date back to Solomon's time.

in the temple area walking in Solomon's Colonnade.[p] [24]The Jews[q] gathered around him, saying, "How long will you keep us in suspense? If you are the Christ,[z] tell us plainly."[r]

[25]Jesus answered, "I did tell you,[s] but you do not believe. The miracles I do in my Father's name speak for me,[t] [26]but you do not believe because you are not my sheep.[u] [27]My sheep listen to my voice; I know them,[v] and they follow me.[w] [28]I give them eternal life,[x] and they shall never perish;[y] no one can snatch them out of my hand.[z] [29]My Father, who has given them to me,[a] is greater than all[a];[b] no one can snatch them out of my Father's hand. [30]I and the Father are one."[c]

[31]Again the Jews picked up stones to stone him,[d] [32]but Jesus said to them, "I have shown you many great miracles from the Father. For which of these do you stone me?"

[33]"We are not stoning you for any of these," replied the Jews, "but for blasphemy, because you, a mere man, claim to be God."[e]

[34]Jesus answered them, "Is it not written in your Law,[f] 'I have said you are gods'[b]?[g] [35]If he called them 'gods,' to whom the word of God[h] came—and the

Scripture cannot be broken[i]— [36]what about the one whom the Father set apart[j] as his very own[k] and sent into the world?[l] Why then do you accuse me of blasphemy because I said, 'I am God's Son'?[m] [37]Do not believe me unless I do what my Father does.[n] [38]But if I do it, even though you do not believe me, believe the miracles, that you may know and understand that the Father is in me, and I in the Father."[o] [39]Again they tried to seize him,[p] but he escaped their grasp.[q]

[40]Then Jesus went back across the Jordan[r] to the place where John had been baptizing in the early days. Here he stayed [41]and many people came to him. They said, "Though John never performed a miraculous sign,[s] all that John said about this man was true."[t] [42]And in that place many believed in Jesus.[u]

The Death of Lazarus

11 Now a man named Lazarus was sick. He was from Bethany,[v] the village of Mary and her sister Martha.[w] [2]This Mary, whose brother Lazarus now lay sick, was the same one who poured

---

Cross references (center column):

10:23 *p*Ac 3:11; 5:12
10:24 *q*S Jn 1:19 *r*Lk 22:67; Jn 16:25,29
10:25 *s*Jn 4:26; 8:58 *t*Jn 5:36; 14:11
10:26 *u*Jn 8:47
10:27 *v*ver 14 *w*ver 4
10:28 *x*S Mt 25:46 *y*Isa 66:22 *z*S Jn 6:39
10:29 *a*Jn 17:2,6, 24 *b*Jn 14:28
10:30 *c*Dt 6:4; Jn 17:21-23
10:31 *d*S Jn 8:59
10:33 *e*Lev 24:16; Mt 26:63-66; S 5:18
10:34 *f*Jn 8:17; 12:34; 15:25; Ro 3:19; 1Co 14:21 *g*Ps 82:6
10:35 *h*S Heb 4:12
10:36 *i*S Mt 5:18 *j*Jer 1:5 *k*Jn 6:69 *l*S Jn 3:17
10:37 *m*Jn 5:17,18 *n*ver 25
10:38 *o*Jn 14:10, 11,20; 17:21
10:39 *p*Jn 7:30 *q*Lk 4:30; Jn 8:59
10:40 *r*Jn 1:28
10:41 *s*S Jn 2:11
10:42 *u*S Jn 7:31
11:1 *v*S Mt 21:17 *w*Lk 10:38

---

[z]24 Or *Messiah*   [a]29 Many early manuscripts *What my Father has given me is greater than all*   [b]34 Psalm 82:6

10:24 *the Christ.* See note on 1:25 and cf. 20:31. This was the critical question, but it was not easy to answer because of the different ideas of Messiahship then in vogue.

10:25 *I did tell you.* Jesus had not specifically affirmed his Messiahship except to the Samaritan woman (4:26). He may have meant here that the general thrust of his teaching made his claim clear or that such statements as in 8:58 were sufficient. Or he may have been referring to the evidence of his whole manner of life (including the miracles)—all he had done in the Father's name (for the name see note on 2:23).

10:26 *not my sheep.* Their failure to believe arose from what they were.

10:27 *voice.* Cf. vv. 3–5. *I know them.* Cf. v. 14. *they follow.* Cf. vv. 4–5.

10:28 *eternal life.* Christ's gift (see note on 3:15). *never perish.* The Greek construction here is a strong denial that the sheep will ever perish. The sheep's security is in the power of the shepherd, who will let no one take them from him.

10:29 *My Father.* See note on 5:17. *can.* The Father's power ("hand") is greater than that of any enemy, making the sheep completely secure.

10:30 *one.* The Greek is neuter—"one thing," not "one person." The two are one in essence or nature, but they are not identical persons. This great truth is what warrants Jesus' "I am" declarations (see 8:24,28,58 and note on 6:35; see also 17:21–22).

10:31 *the Jews.* See note on 1:19. *to stone him.* They took Jesus' words as blasphemy, and therefore prepared to carry out the law (Lev 24:16), though without due process.

10:32 *great miracles.* Or "good deeds" (as, e.g., in Mt 5:16; 1Ti 5:10,25; 6:18). Although the reference here includes Jesus' miracles, the underlying Greek words refer to works in general that are fine and noble in character first of

all (see note on v. 38).

10:33 *blasphemy.* The Jewish leaders correctly understood the thrust of Jesus' words, but their preconceptions and unbelief prevented them from accepting his claim as true.

10:34 *your Law.* In its strictest sense the term meant the Pentateuch, but was often used, as here, of the whole OT. *you are gods.* The words Jesus quotes from Ps 82:6 refer to the judges (or other leaders or rulers), whose tasks were divinely appointed (see Ex 22:28 and NIV text note; Dt 1:17; 16:18; 2Ch 19:6).

10:35 *Scripture cannot be broken.* Jesus testified to the complete authority and reliability of the OT.

10:36 If there is any sense in which men can be spoken of as "gods" (as Ps 82:6 speaks of human rulers or judges), how much more may the term be used of him whom the Father set apart and sent!

10:37 *what my Father does.* The kind of works of compassion that the Father himself does.

10:38 *miracles.* Lit. "works." The miracles were a part of Jesus' works. It was Jesus' quality of life, not people's inability to explain his marvels, that he primarily spoke of here (see note on v. 32).

10:39 *they tried to seize him.* It is not clear if this was to arrest him for trial or to take him out for stoning. *he escaped.* John does not say why they failed, but he often makes it clear that Jesus could not be killed before the appointed time (see note on 2:4; see also Lk 4:30).

10:41 *all that John said.* For John the Baptist as a witness see 1:7 and note.

11:1 *Lazarus.* Mentioned only in chs. 11–12 of John's Gospel (the name is found also in the parable of Lk 16:19–31). The sisters are mentioned in Lk 10:38–42.

11:2 *poured perfume.* See 12:3.

perfume on the Lord and wiped his feet with her hair. x 3So the sisters sent word to Jesus, "Lord, the one you love y is sick."

4When he heard this, Jesus said, "This sickness will not end in death. No, it is for God's glory z so that God's Son may be glorified through it." 5Jesus loved Martha and her sister and Lazarus. 6Yet when he heard that Lazarus was sick, he stayed where he was two more days.

7Then he said to his disciples, "Let us go back to Judea." a

8"But Rabbi," b they said, "a short while ago the Jews tried to stone you, c and yet you are going back there?"

9Jesus answered, "Are there not twelve hours of daylight? A man who walks by day will not stumble, for he sees by this world's light. d 10It is when he walks by night that he stumbles, for he has no light."

11After he had said this, he went on to tell them, "Our friend e Lazarus has fallen asleep; f but I am going there to wake him up."

12His disciples replied, "Lord, if he sleeps, he will get better." 13Jesus had been speaking of his death, but his disciples thought he meant natural sleep. g

14So then he told them plainly, "Lazarus is dead, 15and for your sake I am glad I was not there, so that you may believe. But let us go to him."

16Then Thomas h (called Didymus) said to the rest of the disciples, "Let us also go, that we may die with him."

Jesus Comforts the Sisters

17On his arrival, Jesus found that Lazarus had already been in the tomb for four days. i 18Bethany j was less than two miles c from Jerusalem, 19and many Jews had come to Martha and Mary to comfort them in the loss of their brother. k 20When Martha heard that Jesus was coming, she went out to meet him, but Mary stayed at home. l

21"Lord," Martha said to Jesus, "if you had been here, my brother would not have died. m 22But I know that even now God will give you whatever you ask." n

23Jesus said to her, "Your brother will rise again."

24Martha answered, "I know he will rise again in the resurrection o at the last day." p

25Jesus said to her, "I am q the resurrection and the life. r He who believes s in me will live, even though he dies; 26and whoever lives and believes t in me will never die. u Do you believe this?"

27"Yes, Lord," she told him, "I believe that you are the Christ, d v the Son of God, w who was to come into the world." x 28And after she had said this, she went back and called her sister Mary aside. "The

---

11:2 xMk 14:3; Lk 7:38; Jn 12:3
11:3 yver 5,36
11:4 zver 40
11:7 aJn 10:40
11:8 bS Mt 23:7
cJn 8:59; 10:31
11:9 dJn 9:4; 12:35
11:11 ever 3
/S Mt 9:24
11:13 gMt 9:24
11:16 hMt 10:3; Jn 14:5; 20:24-28; 21:2; Ac 1:13

11:17 iver 6,39
11:18 jver 1; S Mt 21:17
11:19 kver 31; Job 2:11
11:20 lLk 10:38-42
11:21 mver 32,37
11:22 nver 41,42
11:24 oDa 12:2; Jn 5:28,29; Ac 24:15
pJn 6:39,40
11:25 qS Jn 6:35
rS Jn 1:4
sS Jn 1:4
11:26 tS Jn 3:15
uS Mt 25:46
11:27 vS Lk 2:11
wS Mt 4:3
xJn 6:14

c18 Greek *fifteen stadia* (about 3 kilometers)   d27 Or *Messiah*

11:3 *the one you love.* The relationship must have been exceptionally close.
11:4 Cf. 9:3. *This sickness will not end in death.* Thus predicting the raising of Lazarus (v. 44), since Jesus already knew of his death (v. 14). In fact, Lazarus must have died shortly after the messengers left Bethany, accounting for the "four days" of vv. 17,39: one day for the journey of the messengers, the two days when Jesus remained where he was (v. 6; see 10:40), and a day for Jesus' journey to Bethany. But see note on v. 17. *glory.* See notes on 7:39; 12:41; 13:31. Here God's Son would be glorified through what happened to Lazarus, partly because the miracle displays the glory of God (who alone can raise the dead; see 5:21) in Jesus (v. 40) and partly because it would help initiate events leading to the cross (vv. 46–53).
11:6 *he stayed where he was.* Jesus moved as the Father directed, not as people (here Mary and Martha) wished (cf. 2:3–4).
11:8 *the Jews.* See note on 1:19. *tried to stone you.* See note on 10:31. There was clear danger in going into Judea.
11:9 *twelve hours.* Enough time for what must be done, but no time for waste.
11:11 *fallen asleep.* A euphemism for death, used by the unbelieving world as well as by Christians.
11:15 *believe.* Cf. 20:31.
11:16 *Thomas ... Didymus.* The Hebrew word from which we get "Thomas" and the Greek word *Didymus* both mean "twin." We usually remember Thomas for his doubting, but he was also capable of devotion and courage.

11:17 *four days.* See note on v. 4. Many Jews believed that the soul remained near the body for three days after death in the hope of returning to it. If this idea was in the minds of these people, they obviously thought all hope was gone—Lazarus was irrevocably dead.
11:18 *less than two miles.* Reflects John's concern for accuracy.
11:19 *to comfort them.* Jewish custom provided for three days of very heavy mourning, then four of heavy mourning, followed by lighter mourning for the remainder of 30 days. It was usual for friends to visit the family to comfort them.
11:20 *she went out to meet him.* Perhaps because as the elder she was hostess.
11:21 Repeated by Mary in v. 32. Perhaps the sisters had said this to one another often as they awaited Jesus' arrival.
11:22 *whatever you ask.* This comment seems to mean that Martha hoped for an immediate resurrection in spite of the fact that Lazarus's body had already begun to decay. Nothing is too difficult for God to do.
11:25 *I am.* See note on 6:35. *life.* See note on 1:4. Jesus was saying more than that he gives resurrection and life. In some way these are identified with him, and his nature is such that final death is impossible for him. He is life (cf. 14:6; Ac 3:15; Heb 7:16). *He who believes ... will live.* See note on 1:7. Jesus not only is life but conveys life to the believer so that death will never triumph over him (cf. 1Co 15:54–57).
11:27 *I believe.* Martha is often remembered for her shortcoming recorded in Lk 10:40–41. But she was a woman of faith, as this magnificent declaration shows.

Teacher[y] is here," she said, "and is asking for you." [29]When Mary heard this, she got up quickly and went to him. [30]Now Jesus had not yet entered the village, but was still at the place where Martha had met him.[z] [31]When the Jews who had been with Mary in the house, comforting her,[a] noticed how quickly she got up and went out, they followed her, supposing she was going to the tomb to mourn there.

[32]When Mary reached the place where Jesus was and saw him, she fell at his feet and said, "Lord, if you had been here, my brother would not have died."[b]

[33]When Jesus saw her weeping, and the Jews who had come along with her also weeping, he was deeply moved[c] in spirit and troubled.[d] [34]"Where have you laid him?" he asked.

"Come and see, Lord," they replied.

[35]Jesus wept.[e]

[36]Then the Jews said, "See how he loved him!"[f]

[37]But some of them said, "Could not he who opened the eyes of the blind man[g] have kept this man from dying?"[h]

Jesus Raises Lazarus From the Dead

[38]Jesus, once more deeply moved,[i] came to the tomb. It was a cave with a stone laid across the entrance.[j] [39]"Take away the stone," he said.

"But, Lord," said Martha, the sister of the dead man, "by this time there is a bad odor, for he has been there four days."[k] [40]Then Jesus said, "Did I not tell you

that if you believed,[l] you would see the glory of God?"[m]

[41]So they took away the stone. Then Jesus looked up[n] and said, "Father,[o] I thank you that you have heard me. [42]I knew that you always hear me, but I said this for the benefit of the people standing here,[p] that they may believe that you sent me."[q]

[43]When he had said this, Jesus called in a loud voice, "Lazarus, come out!"[r] [44]The dead man came out, his hands and feet wrapped with strips of linen,[s] and a cloth around his face.[t]

Jesus said to them, "Take off the grave clothes and let him go."

The Plot to Kill Jesus

[45]Therefore many of the Jews who had come to visit Mary,[u] and had seen what Jesus did,[v] put their faith in him.[w] [46]But some of them went to the Pharisees and told them what Jesus had done. [47]Then the chief priests and the Pharisees[x] called a meeting[y] of the Sanhedrin.[z]

"What are we accomplishing?" they asked. "Here is this man performing many miraculous signs.[a] [48]If we let him go on like this, everyone will believe in him, and then the Romans will come and take away both our place[e] and our nation."

[49]Then one of them, named Caiaphas,[b] who was high priest that year,[c] spoke up, "You know nothing at all! [50]You do not realize that it is better for you that one

Cross references (center column):

11:28 [y]Mt 26:18; Jn 13:13
11:30 [z]ver 20
11:31 [a]ver 19
11:32 [b]ver 21
11:33 [c]ver 38 [d]S Jn 12:27
11:35 [e]Lk 19:41
11:36 [f]ver 3
11:37 [g]Jn 9:6,7 [h]ver 21,32
11:38 [i]ver 33 [j]Mt 27:60; Lk 24:2; Jn 20:1
11:39 [k]ver 17

11:40 [l]ver 23-25 [m]ver 4
11:41 [n]Jn 17:1 [o]S Mt 11:25
11:42 [p]Jn 12:30 [q]S Jn 3:17
11:43 [r]S Lk 7:14
11:44 [s]Jn 19:40 [t]Jn 20:7
11:45 [u]ver 19 [v]Jn 2:23 [w]Ex 14:31; S Jn 7:31
11:47 [x]ver 57 [y]Mt 26:3 [z]S Mt 5:22 [a]S Jn 2:11
11:49 [b]S Mt 26:3 [c]ver 51; Jn 18:13, 14

[e]48 Or temple

11:28 *The Teacher.* A significant description to be given by a woman. The rabbis would not teach women (cf. 4:27), but Jesus taught them frequently.
11:31 *to mourn there.* Wailing at a tomb was common, and the Jews immediately thought this was in Mary's mind. Because they followed her, Jesus got maximum publicity.
11:32 Cf. v. 21.
11:33 *weeping.* Both times the word denotes a loud expression of grief, i.e., "wailing." *troubled.* See note on 12:27; cf. 13:21.
11:35 *wept.* The Greek for this word is not the one for loud grief, as in v. 33, but one that denotes quiet weeping, i.e., "shed tears."
11:36 Cf. v. 5.
11:37 Their position was like that of Martha (v. 21) and Mary (v. 32), but they based it on Jesus' ability to give sight to the blind (cf. ch. 9).
11:39 *four days.* See notes on vv. 4,17.
11:40 *glory.* See note on v. 4.
11:44 *strips of linen.* Narrow strips, like bandages. Sometimes a shroud was used (see note on 19:40). *a cloth.* A separate item.
11:45 *many of the Jews . . . put their faith in him.* Perhaps some who had been opposed to Jesus now came to believe (see note on 1:19; cf. 20:31).
11:46 *Pharisees.* See notes on Mt 3:7; Mk 2:16; Lk 5:17.
11:47 *the chief priests and the Pharisees.* In all four

Gospels the Pharisees appear as Jesus' principal opponents throughout his public ministry. But they lacked political power, and it is the chief priests who were prominent in the events that led to Jesus' crucifixion. Here both groups are associated in a meeting of the Sanhedrin (see note on Mk 14:55). They did not deny the reality of the miraculous signs (see note on 2:11), but they did not understand their meaning, for they failed to believe.
11:48 *place.* Probably the temple (see NIV text note and Ac 6:13–14; 21:28), though sometimes the Jews used the expression to denote Jerusalem.
11:49 *Caiaphas.* High priest c. A.D. 18–36. He was the son-in-law of Annas (18:13), who had been deposed from the high priesthood by the Romans in A.D. 15. *high priest that year.* Means "high priest at that time." The high priesthood was not an annual office but one supposed to be held for life. *You know nothing at all!* A remark typical of Sadducean rudeness (Caiaphas, as high priest, was a Sadducee). Josephus says that Sadducees "in their intercourse with their peers are as rude as to aliens." For Sadducees see notes on Mt 2:4; 3:7; Mk 12:18; Lk 20:27; Ac 4:1.
11:50 *better.* Caiaphas was concerned with political expediency, not with guilt and innocence. He believed that one man, no matter how innocent, should perish rather than that the nation be put in jeopardy. Ironically, the Jews went ahead with their execution of Jesus, and in A.D. 70 the nation still perished.

man die for the people than that the whole nation perish." [d]

[51]He did not say this on his own, but as high priest that year he prophesied that Jesus would die for the Jewish nation, [52]and not only for that nation but also for the scattered children of God, to bring them together and make them one. [e] [53]So from that day on they plotted to take his life. [f]

[54]Therefore Jesus no longer moved about publicly among the Jews. [g] Instead he withdrew to a region near the desert, to a village called Ephraim, where he stayed with his disciples.

[55]When it was almost time for the Jewish Passover, [h] many went up from the country to Jerusalem for their ceremonial cleansing [i] before the Passover. [56]They kept looking for Jesus, [j] and as they stood in the temple area they asked one another, "What do you think? Isn't he coming to the Feast at all?" [57]But the chief priests and Pharisees had given orders that if anyone found out where Jesus was, he should report it so that they might arrest him.

Jesus Anointed at Bethany

12:1–8Ref — Mt 26:6–13; Mk 14:3–9; Lk 7:37–39

12 Six days before the Passover, [k] Jesus arrived at Bethany, [l] where Lazarus lived, whom Jesus had raised from the dead. [2]Here a dinner was given in Jesus' honor. Martha served, [m] while Lazarus was among those reclining at the table

with him. [3]Then Mary took about a pint [f] of pure nard, an expensive perfume; [n] she poured it on Jesus' feet and wiped his feet with her hair. [o] And the house was filled with the fragrance of the perfume.

[4]But one of his disciples, Judas Iscariot, who was later to betray him, [p] objected, [5]"Why wasn't this perfume sold and the money given to the poor? It was worth a year's wages. [g]" [6]He did not say this because he cared about the poor but because he was a thief; as keeper of the money bag, [q] he used to help himself to what was put into it.

[7]"Leave her alone," Jesus replied. "It was intended that she should save this perfume for the day of my burial. [r] [8]You will always have the poor among you, [s] but you will not always have me."

[9]Meanwhile a large crowd of Jews found out that Jesus was there and came, not only because of him but also to see Lazarus, whom he had raised from the dead. [t] [10]So the chief priests made plans to kill Lazarus as well, [11]for on account of him [u] many of the Jews were going over to Jesus and putting their faith in him. [v]

The Triumphal Entry

12:12–15pp — Mt 21:4–9; Mk 11:7–10; Lk 19:35–38

[12]The next day the great crowd that had come for the Feast heard that Jesus was on his way to Jerusalem. [13]They took palm

Cross references (center column):

11:50 [d]Jn 18:14
11:52 [e]Isa 49:6; Jn 10:16
11:53 [f]S Mt 12:14
11:54 [g]Jn 7:1
11:55 [h]Ex 12:13, 23,27; Mt 26:1,2; Mk 14:1; Jn 13:1
[i]2Ch 30:17,18
11:56 [j]Jn 7:11
12:1 [k]S Jn 11:55
[l]S Mt 21:17
12:2 [m]Lk 10:38-42
12:3 [n]Mk 14:3
[o]Jn 11:2
12:4 [p]S Mt 10:4
12:6 [q]Jn 13:29
12:7 [r]Jn 19:40
12:8 [s]Dt 15:11
12:9 [t]Jn 11:43,44
12:11 [u]ver 17, 18; Jn 11:45
[v]S Jn 7:31

[f]3 Greek a *litra* (probably about 0.5 liter)   [g]5 Greek three hundred *denarii*

11:51 *as high priest.* Caiaphas was not a private citizen but was God's high priest, and God overruled in what he said. *prophesied.* His words were true in a way he could not imagine. Prophecy in Scripture is the impartation of divinely revealed truth. In reality Caiaphas's words meant that Jesus' death would be for the nation, not by way of removing political trouble, but by taking away the sins of those who believed in him.

11:52 *for the scattered children of God.* Jesus' death would have effects far beyond the nation (cf. 1:29; 3:16; 4:42; 10:16; etc.).

11:54 *he withdrew.* Jesus was not to die before his "time" (see note on 2:4), but he would not act imprudently. Knowing the attitude of his opponents, he withdrew. He would die for others, but in his own time, not that of his enemies. *Ephraim.* If it was the city known as Ophrah, it was about 15 miles north of Jerusalem.

11:55 *Passover.* See notes on 2:13; 5:1. *ceremonial cleansing.* Especially important at a time like Passover, because without it, it would not be possible to keep the Feast (cf. 18:28; see note on 2:6).

11:56 *Isn't he coming . . . ?* The question expected the answer "No."

12:1–11 All four Gospels have an account of a woman anointing Jesus. John's account seems to tell of the same incident recorded in Mt 26:6–13 and Mk 14:3–9, while that in Lk 7:36–50 is different.

12:1 *Bethany.* See note on Mt 21:17.

12:3 *nard.* The name of both a plant and the fragrant oil it yielded. Since it was very expensive, Mary's act of devotion was costly. It was also an unusual act, both because she poured the oil on Jesus' feet (normally it was poured on the head) and because she used her hair to wipe them (a respectable woman did not unbind her hair in public). Further, it showed her humility, for it was a servant's work to attend to the feet (see notes on 1:27; 13:5).

12:4 *Judas Iscariot.* See note on 6:71.

12:6 *a thief.* The one passage from which we learn that Judas was dishonest. Yet he must have been thought to be a man of some reliability, for he was keeper of the money bag.

12:7 *save.* Probably the meaning is "save for this purpose." Perfume was normally associated with festivity, but it was also used in burials (see 19:39–40), and Jesus links it with his burial, which Mary's act unwittingly anticipates.

12:9 *Jews.* See note on 1:19.

12:10 The Jewish leaders previously had spoken of the death of one man (11:50), but now they wanted another death. Sin grows.

12:12 *great crowd.* Pilgrims who had come up from the country for the Passover Feast. Many of the pilgrims had doubtless seen and heard Jesus in Galilee, and they welcomed the opportunity to proclaim him as Messiah.

12:13 *palm branches.* Used in celebration of victory. John saw a multitude with palm branches in heaven (Rev 7:9). *Hosanna!* See NIV text note; see also note on Mt 21:9. *the name.* See note on 2:23. *Blessed is the King of Israel!* The

branches[w] and went out to meet him, shouting,

"Hosanna![h]"

"Blessed is he who comes in the name of the Lord!"[i] [x]

"Blessed is the King of Israel!"[y]

[14]Jesus found a young donkey and sat upon it, as it is written,

[15]"Do not be afraid, O Daughter of Zion; see, your king is coming, seated on a donkey's colt."[j] [z]

[16]At first his disciples did not understand all this.[a] Only after Jesus was glorified[b] did they realize that these things had been written about him and that they had done these things to him.

[17]Now the crowd that was with him[c] when he called Lazarus from the tomb and raised him from the dead continued to spread the word. [18]Many people, because they had heard that he had given this miraculous sign,[d] went out to meet him. [19]So the Pharisees said to one another, "See, this is getting us nowhere. Look how the whole world has gone after him!"[e]

Jesus Predicts His Death

[20]Now there were some Greeks[f] among those who went up to worship at the Feast. [21]They came to Philip, who was from Bethsaida[g] in Galilee, with a request. "Sir," they said, "we would like to see

Jesus." [22]Philip went to tell Andrew; Andrew and Philip in turn told Jesus.

[23]Jesus replied, "The hour[h] has come for the Son of Man to be glorified.[i] [24]I tell you the truth, unless a kernel of wheat falls to the ground and dies,[j] it remains only a single seed. But if it dies, it produces many seeds. [25]The man who loves his life will lose it, while the man who hates his life in this world will keep it[k] for eternal life.[l] [26]Whoever serves me must follow me; and where I am, my servant also will be.[m] My Father will honor the one who serves me.

[27]"Now my heart is troubled,[n] and what shall I say? 'Father,[o] save me from this hour'?[p] No, it was for this very reason I came to this hour. [28]Father, glorify your name!"

Then a voice came from heaven,[q] "I have glorified it, and will glorify it again." [29]The crowd that was there and heard it said it had thundered; others said an angel had spoken to him.

[30]Jesus said, "This voice was for your benefit,[r] not mine. [31]Now is the time for judgment on this world;[s] now the prince of this world[t] will be driven out. [32]But I, when I am lifted up from the earth,[u] will draw all men to myself."[v] [33]He said this to show the kind of death he was going to die.[w]

[34]The crowd spoke up, "We have heard

Cross-references

12:13 [w]Lev 23:40; [x]Ps 118:25,26; [y]S Jn 1:49
12:15 [z]Zec 9:9
12:16 [a]S Mk 9:32 [b]ver 23; Jn 2:22; 7:39
12:17 [c]Jn 11:42
12:18 [d]ver 11; Lk 19:37
12:19 [e]Jn 11:47,48
12:20 [f]Jn 7:35; Ac 11:20
12:21 [g]S Mt 11:21
12:23 [h]S Mt 26:18; Jn 13:32; 17:1
12:24 [i]1Co 15:36; Mk 8:35; Lk 14:26; 17:33
12:25 [k]Mt 10:39; [l]S Mt 25:46
12:26 [m]Jn 14:3; 17:24; 2Co 5:8; Php 1:23; 1Th 4:17
12:27 [n]Mt 26:38,39; Jn 11:33,38; 13:21 [o]S Mt 11:25 [p]ver 23
12:28 [q]S Mt 3:17
12:30 [r]Ex 19:9; Jn 11:42
12:31 [s]Jn 16:11 [t]Jn 14:30; 16:11; 2Co 4:4; Eph 2:2; 1Jn 4:4; 5:19
12:32 [u]ver34; Jn 3:14; 8:28 [v]Jn 6:44
12:33 [w]Jn 18:32; 21:19

[h]13 A Hebrew expression meaning "Save!" which became an exclamation of praise   [i]13 Psalm 118:25, 26   [j]15 Zech. 9:9

people's addition to the words of the psalm, which John alone records. It reflects his special interest in Jesus' royalty, which he brings out throughout the passion narrative.
12:14 *donkey.* See notes on Zec 9:9; Mt 21:2,7; Mk 11:2; Lk 19:30.
12:16 An example of the meaning of 16:13. *glorified.* See notes on v. 41; 11:4; 13:31. Only after the crucifixion and the coming of the Holy Spirit did the disciples appreciate the meaning of the prophecy and its fulfillment.
12:19 *Pharisees.* See notes on Mt 3:7; Mk 2:16; Lk 5:17.
12:20 *Greeks.* Probably "God-fearers," people attracted to Judaism by its monotheism and morality, but repelled by its nationalism and requirements such as circumcision. They worshiped in the synagogues but did not become proselytes.
12:21 *Philip.* A Greek name, which may be why they came to this disciple (though he was not the only one of the Twelve to have a Greek name). *to see.* Means "to have an interview with." After v. 22 John records no more about these Greeks (yet see note on v. 32). He regarded their coming as important but not their conversation with Jesus. Jesus came to die for the world, and the coming of these Gentiles indicates the scope of the effectiveness of his approaching crucifixion.
12:23 *The hour has come.* The hour to which everything else led (see note on 2:4). *glorified.* Jesus was speaking about his death on the cross and his subsequent resurrection and exaltation (see notes on v. 41; 11:4; 13:31).
12:24 *if it dies, it produces.* The principle of life through death is seen in the plant world. The kernel must perish as a

kernel if there is to be a plant.
12:25 *the man who hates his life . . . will keep it.* To love one's life here and now—to concentrate on one's own success—is to lose what matters (cf. Mt 16:24–25; Mk 8:34–35; Lk 9:23–24). Supremely, of course, the principle is seen in the cross of Jesus. *hates.* Love for God must be such that all other loves are, by comparison, hatred. *eternal life.* See note on 3:15.
12:27 *troubled.* John's equivalent to the agony in Gethsemane described in the other Gospels. *this hour.* Jesus faced the prospect of becoming sin (or a sin offering) for sinful people (2Co 5:21). He considered praying for God to save him from this death, but refused to pray it, because the very reason he had come was to die.
12:28 *Father, glorify your name!* His prayer was not for deliverance but for the Father to be glorified. The voice from heaven gave the answer. *name.* See note on 2:23.
12:31 *on this world.* The cross was God's judgment on the world. *the prince of this world.* Satan (cf. 16:11). The cross would seem to be his triumph; in fact, it was his defeat. Out of it would flow the greatest good ever to come to the world.
12:32 *lifted up.* See note on 3:14. The cross was the supreme exaltation of Jesus (see notes on v. 41; 13:31). *all men.* Christ will draw people to himself without regard for nationality, ethnic affiliation or status. It is significant that Greek Gentiles were present on this occasion (v. 20).
12:34 *the Law.* Here seems to mean OT Scripture in general (see note on 10:34), the reference being to passages

from the Law[x] that the Christ[k] will remain forever,[y] so how can you say, 'The
Son of Man[z] must be lifted up'?[a] Who is
this 'Son of Man'?"
35Then Jesus told them, "You are going
to have the light[b] just a little while longer.
Walk while you have the light,[c] before
darkness overtakes you.[d] The man who
walks in the dark does not know where he
is going. 36Put your trust in the light while
you have it, so that you may become sons
of light."[e] When he had finished speaking,
Jesus left and hid himself from them.[f]

The Jews Continue in Their Unbelief

37Even after Jesus had done all these miraculous signs[g] in their presence, they still
would not believe in him. 38This was to
fulfill the word of Isaiah the prophet:

"Lord, who has believed our message
and to whom has the arm of the Lord
been revealed?"[l] [h]

39For this reason they could not believe,
because, as Isaiah says elsewhere:

40"He has blinded their eyes
and deadened their hearts,
so they can neither see with their eyes,
nor understand with their hearts,
nor turn—and I would heal
them."[m] [i]

41Isaiah said this because he saw Jesus'
glory[j] and spoke about him.[k]

42Yet at the same time many even
among the leaders believed in him.[l] But
because of the Pharisees[m] they would not
confess their faith for fear they would be
put out of the synagogue;[n] 43for they
loved praise from men[o] more than praise
from God.[p]
44Then Jesus cried out, "When a man
believes in me, he does not believe in me
only, but in the one who sent me.[q]
45When he looks at me, he sees the one
who sent me.[r] 46I have come into the
world as a light,[s] so that no one who believes in me should stay in darkness.
47"As for the person who hears my
words but does not keep them, I do not
judge him. For I did not come to judge the
world, but to save it.[t] 48There is a judge
for the one who rejects me and does not
accept my words; that very word which I
spoke will condemn him[u] at the last day.
49For I did not speak of my own accord,
but the Father who sent me commanded
me[v] what to say and how to say it. 50I
know that his command leads to eternal
life.[w] So whatever I say is just what the
Father has told me to say."[x]

Jesus Washes His Disciples' Feet

13 It was just before the Passover
Feast.[y] Jesus knew that the time
had come[z] for him to leave this world and
go to the Father.[a] Having loved his own

12:34 [x]S Jn 10:34 [y]Ps 110:4; Isa 9:7; Eze 37:25; Da 7:14 [z]S Mt 8:20 [a]Jn 3:14
12:35 [b]ver 46 [c]Eph 5:8 [d]1Jn 1:6; 2:11
12:36 [e]ver 46; S Lk 16:8 [f]Jn 8:59
12:37 [g]S Jn 2:11
12:38 [h]Isa 53:1; Ro 10:16
12:40 [i]Isa 6:10; S Mt 13:13,15
12:41 [j]Isa 6:1-4 [k]Lk 24:27
12:42 [l]ver 11; Jn 7:48 [m]S Jn 7:13 [n]Jn 9:22
12:43 [o]1Sa 15:30 [p]S Ro 2:29
12:44 [q]S Mt 10:40; Jn 5:24
12:45 [r]S Jn 14:9
12:46 [s]S Jn 1:4
12:47 [t]S Jn 3:17
12:48 [u]Jn 5:45
12:49 [v]Jn 14:31
12:50 [w]S Mt 25:46 [x]S Jn 14:24
13:1 [y]S Jn 11:55 [z]S Mt 26:18 [a]Jn 16:28

[k]*34* Or *Messiah* [l]*38* Isaiah 53:1 [m]*40* Isaiah 6:10

such as Ps 89:36; 110:4; Isa 9:7; Da 7:14. *the Christ.* See note on 1:25. *Son of Man.* The only place in the Gospels where anyone other than Jesus used the expression, and even here Jesus is being quoted (see note on Mk 8:31).

12:35–36 *the light.* Light is closely identified with Jesus, as seen from the call to believe in the light (see notes on 1:4; 8:12).

12:37 *they still would not believe.* God's ancient people should have responded when God sent his Messiah. They should have seen the significance of the signs he did.

12:39 *could not believe.* Does not mean that the people in question had no choice. They purposely rejected God and chose evil, and v. 40 explains that God in turn brought on them a judicial blinding of eyes and hardening of hearts. Yet many Jewish leaders did believe in Jesus as the Messiah (v. 42).

12:40 These words from Isa 6:10 are quoted by Jesus (Mt 13:14–15; Mk 4:12; Lk 8:10) and by Paul (Ac 28:26–27).

12:41 *saw Jesus' glory.* Isaiah spoke primarily of the glory of God (Isa 6:3). John spoke of the glory of Jesus and made no basic distinction between the two, attesting Jesus' oneness with God. The thought of glory here is complex. There is the idea of majesty, and there is also the idea (which meant so much to John) that Jesus' death on the cross and his subsequent resurrection and exaltation show his real glory. Isaiah foresaw the rejection of Christ, as the passages quoted (Isa 53:1; 6:10) show. He spoke of the Messiah both in the words about blind eyes and hard hearts, on the one hand, and about healing, on the other. This is the cross and this is glory, for the cross and resurrection and exaltation portray both suffering and healing, rejection and triumph, humiliation and glory.

12:42 *many . . . leaders believed.* John does not give a picture of unrelieved gloom. Many Jewish leaders believed (see note on 1:7), though they remained secret believers for fear of excommunication (see note on 9:22).

12:44 *cried out.* The words are given special emphasis by being spoken in a loud voice. *believe in me.* John ends his story of the public ministry of Jesus with an appeal for belief. He does not say when Jesus spoke these words (they may have been uttered earlier), but they are a fitting close to this part of his account. *the one who sent me.* Jesus' mission, as well as the inseparability of the Father and the Son, is stressed throughout this Gospel.

12:46 *I have come into the world.* Points to both Jesus' preexistence and his mission. *light.* See notes on 1:4; 8:12.

12:47 *to judge.* Not the purpose of Jesus' coming, but judgment is the other side of salvation. It is not the purpose of the sun's shining to cast shadows, but when the sun shines, shadows are inevitable.

12:49 *the Father . . . commanded me what to say.* Jesus' hearers have a great responsibility. His "word" (v. 48) is that which the Father commanded him to say. To reject it, therefore, is to reject God.

12:50 *eternal life.* See note on 3:15. *So.* Jesus said what he did in order to fulfill the will of the Father—a wonderful note on which to end the account of Jesus' public ministry.

13:1–17:26 John has by far the longest account of the

who were in the world, he now showed them the full extent of his love. [n]

[2] The evening meal was being served, and the devil had already prompted Judas Iscariot, son of Simon, to betray Jesus. [b] [3] Jesus knew that the Father had put all things under his power, [c] and that he had come from God [d] and was returning to God; [4] so he got up from the meal, took off his outer clothing, and wrapped a towel around his waist. [e] [5] After that, he poured water into a basin and began to wash his disciples' feet, [f] drying them with the towel that was wrapped around him.

[6] He came to Simon Peter, who said to him, "Lord, are you going to wash my feet?"

[7] Jesus replied, "You do not realize now what I am doing, but later you will understand." [g]

[8] "No," said Peter, "you shall never wash my feet."

Jesus answered, "Unless I wash you, you have no part with me."

[9] "Then, Lord," Simon Peter replied, "not just my feet but my hands and my head as well!"

[10] Jesus answered, "A person who has had a bath needs only to wash his feet; his whole body is clean. And you are clean, [h]

though not every one of you." [i] [11] For he knew who was going to betray him, [j] and that was why he said not every one was clean.

[12] When he had finished washing their feet, he put on his clothes and returned to his place. "Do you understand what I have done for you?" he asked them. [13] "You call me 'Teacher' [k] and 'Lord,' [l] and rightly so, for that is what I am. [14] Now that I, your Lord and Teacher, have washed your feet, you also should wash one another's feet. [m] [15] I have set you an example that you should do as I have done for you. [n] [16] I tell you the truth, no servant is greater than his master, [o] nor is a messenger greater than the one who sent him. [17] Now that you know these things, you will be blessed if you do them. [p]

Jesus Predicts His Betrayal

[18] "I am not referring to all of you; [q] I know those I have chosen. [r] But this is to fulfill the scripture: [s] 'He who shares my bread [t] has lifted up his heel [u] against me.' [o] [v]

[19] "I am telling you now before it happens, so that when it does happen you will believe [w] that I am He. [x] [20] I tell you the

Cross references (center column):

13:2 [b] S Mt 10:4
13:3 [c] S Mt 28:18
[d] Jn 8:42; 16:27, 28,30; 17:8
13:4 [e] S Mt 20:28
13:5 [f] S Lk 7:44
13:7 [g] ver 12
13:10 [h] Jn 15:3

[i] ver 18
13:11 [j] S Mt 10:4
13:13 [k] Mt 26:18; Jn 11:28
[l] S Mt 28:18; Lk 1:43; 2:11; 6:46; 11:1; Ac 10:36; Ro 10:9,12; 14:9; 1Co 12:3; Php 2:11; Col 2:6
13:14 [m] 1Pe 5:5
13:15
[n] S Mt 11:29; S 1Ti 4:12
13:16
[o] Mt 10:24; Lk 6:40; Jn 15:20
13:17 [p] Mt 7:24, 25; Lk 11:28; Jas 1:25
13:18 [q] ver 10
[r] Jn 15:16,19
[s] S Mt 1:22
[t] Mt 26:23
[u] Jn 6:70 [v] Ps 41:9
13:19 [w] Jn 14:29; 16:4 [x] Jn 4:26; 8:24

[n] 1 Or *he loved them to the last*   [o] 18 Psalm 41:9

---

upper room, though curiously he says nothing about the institution of the Lord's Supper. Still we owe to him most of our information about what our Lord said to his disciples on that night. One feature of the discourse is Jesus' emphasis on love. The word occurs only six times in chs. 1–12 but 31 times in chs. 13–17.

13:1 *Passover Feast.* See notes on 2:13; 5:1. *the time.* See note on 2:4.

13:2 *evening meal.* Some believe that this feast was a fellowship meal eaten sometime before the Passover Feast. This would mean that the Last Supper could not have been the Passover meal as the Synoptic Gospels clearly indicate. However, this meal may have been the Passover Feast itself, in which case the accounts of the Synoptics and John would agree. *the devil.* See v. 27. *Judas Iscariot.* See note on 6:71.

13:3 *the Father had put all things under his power.* John again emphasizes the fulfillment of God's plan and Jesus' control of the situation.

13:5 *began to wash his disciples' feet.* A menial task (see note on 1:27), normally performed by a servant. On this occasion there was no servant and no one else volunteered. Jesus' action was during the meal, not upon arrival, done deliberately to emphasize a point. It was a lesson in humility, but it also set forth the principle of selfless service that was so soon to be exemplified in the cross. John alone tells of this incident, but Luke says that in rebuking the disciples over a quarrel concerning who would be the greatest, Jesus said, "I am among you as one who serves" (Lk 22:27). Jesus' life of service would culminate on the cross.

13:8 *No.* Characteristically, Peter objected, though apparently no one else did. He was a mixture of humility (he did not want Jesus to perform this lowly service for him) and pride (he tried to dictate to Jesus). *Unless I wash you.* Jesus' reply looks beyond the incident to what it symbolizes: Peter

needed a spiritual cleansing. The external washing was a picture of cleansing from sin, which Christians also sometimes need (see note on 1Jn 1:9).

13:9 *my hands and my head.* Peter's response was wholehearted, but he was still dictating to Jesus.

13:10 *only to wash his feet.* A man would bathe himself before going to a feast. When he arrived, he only needed to wash his feet to be entirely clean again.

13:11 *he knew.* Again John emphasizes Jesus' command of the situation.

13:13 *Teacher . . . Lord.* An instructor would normally be called "Teacher," but "Lord" referred to one occupying the supreme place. Jesus accepted both titles.

13:14–15 Some Christians believe that Christ intended to institute a foot-washing ordinance to be practiced regularly. Most Christians, however, interpret Christ's action here as providing an example of humble service.

13:14 *wash one another's feet.* Christians should be willing to perform the most menial services for one another.

13:16 With minor variations this saying, which Jesus used often, is found in 15:20; Mt 10:24; Lk 6:40 (cf. Lk 22:27).

13:18 *not referring to all of you.* Jesus was leading up to his prediction of the betrayal (v. 21). *shares my bread.* To eat bread together was a mark of close fellowship (see note on Ps 41:9). *lifted up his heel.* May be derived from a horse's preparing to kick, or perhaps something like shaking off the dust from one's feet (Lk 9:5; 10:11).

13:19 *so that . . . you will believe.* See 20:31. Jesus' concern was for the disciples, not himself. *I am He.* An emphatic form of speech, such as that in 8:58 (see note there).

13:20 *anyone I send . . . the one who sent me.* Jesus' mission is a common theme in this Gospel, and now the mission of his followers is linked with it (cf. 20:21).

truth, whoever accepts anyone I send accepts me; and whoever accepts me accepts the one who sent me." [y]

[21]After he had said this, Jesus was troubled in spirit [z] and testified, "I tell you the truth, one of you is going to betray me." [a]

[22]His disciples stared at one another, at a loss to know which of them he meant. [23]One of them, the disciple whom Jesus loved, [b] was reclining next to him. [24]Simon Peter motioned to this disciple and said, "Ask him which one he means."

[25]Leaning back against Jesus, he asked him, "Lord, who is it?" [c]

[26]Jesus answered, "It is the one to whom I will give this piece of bread when I have dipped it in the dish." Then, dipping the piece of bread, he gave it to Judas Iscariot, [d] son of Simon. [27]As soon as Judas took the bread, Satan entered into him. [e]

"What you are about to do, do quickly," Jesus told him, [28]but no one at the meal understood why Jesus said this to him. [29]Since Judas had charge of the money, [f] some thought Jesus was telling him to buy what was needed for the Feast, [g] or to give something to the poor. [h] [30]As soon as Judas had taken the bread, he went out. And it was night. [i]

Jesus Predicts Peter's Denial

13:37,38pp — Mt 26:33–35; Mk 14:29–31; Lk 22:33,34

[31]When he was gone, Jesus said, "Now is the Son of Man [j] glorified [k] and God is glorified in him. [l] [32]If God is glorified in him, [p] God will glorify the Son in himself, [m] and will glorify him at once.

[33]"My children, I will be with you only a little longer. You will look for me, and just as I told the Jews, so I tell you now: Where I am going, you cannot come. [n]

[34]"A new command [o] I give you: Love one another. [p] As I have loved you, so you must love one another. [q] [35]By this all men will know that you are my disciples, if you love one another." [r]

[36]Simon Peter asked him, "Lord, where are you going?" [s]

Jesus replied, "Where I am going, you cannot follow now, [t] but you will follow later." [u]

[37]Peter asked, "Lord, why can't I follow you now? I will lay down my life for you."

[38]Then Jesus answered, "Will you really lay down your life for me? I tell you the truth, before the rooster crows, you will disown me three times! [v]

Jesus Comforts His Disciples

14 "Do not let your hearts be troubled. [w] Trust [x] in God [q]; [y] trust also in me. [2]In my Father's house are many rooms; if it were not so, I would have told you. I am going there [z] to prepare a place for you. [3]And if I go and prepare a place for you, I will come back [a] and take you to be

---

Cross references (center column)

13:20 [y]S Mt 10:40
13:21 [z]S Jn 12:27 [a]Mt 26:21
13:23 [b]Jn 19:26; 20:2; 21:7,20
13:25 [c]Mt 26:22; Jn 21:20
13:26 [d]S Mt 10:4
13:27 [e]Lk 22:3
13:29 [f]Jn 12:6 [g]ver 1 [h]Jn 12:5
13:30 [i]Lk 22:53
13:31 [j]S Mt 8:20 [k]Jn 7:39; 12:23

[l]Jn 14:13; 17:4; 1Pe 4:11
13:32 [m]Jn 17:1
13:33 [n]S Jn 7:33, 34
13:34 [o]Jn 15:12; 1Jn 2:7-11; 3:11 [p]Lev 19:18; 1Th 4:9; 1Pe 1:22 [q]Jn 15:12; Eph 5:2; 1Jn 4:10, 11
13:35 [r]1Jn 3:14; 4:20
13:36 [s]Jn 16:5 [t]ver 33; Jn 14:2 [u]Jn 21:18,19; 2Pe 1:14
13:38 [v]Jn 18:27
14:1 [w]ver 27 [x]S Jn 3:15 [y]Ps 4:5; 36; 16:5
14:2 [z]Jn 13:33,
14:3 [a]ver 18,28; S Mt 16:27

[p]32 Many early manuscripts do not have If God is glorified in him.   [q]1 Or You trust in God

---

13:21 *troubled.* See 11:33. Though he knew of it long before it happened, Jesus was grieved by the betrayal of a friend.

13:22 *at a loss.* The disciples' astonishment shows that Judas had concealed his contacts with the high priests. No one suspected him (see v. 28), but all seem to have thought that the betrayal would be involuntary (see Mk 14:19).

13:23 *the disciple whom Jesus loved.* Usually thought to be John, the author of this Gospel (see 19:26; 20:2; 21:7, 20). The expression does not, of course, mean that Jesus did not love the others, but that there was a special bond with this man. *reclining.* At a dinner, guests reclined on couches, leaning on the left elbow with the head toward the table.

13:26 *the one to whom I . . . give . . . bread . . . dipped . . . in the dish.* Evidently Judas was near Jesus, possibly in the seat of honor. John used Judas's full name (see note on 6:71) in recording this solemn moment.

13:27 *As soon as Judas took the bread.* Evidently the critical moment. If the giving of the bread to Judas was a mark of honor, it also seems to have been a final appeal—which Judas did not accept. *Satan.* The name is used only here in John (cf. v. 2). *do quickly.* Jesus' words once more indicate his control. He would die as he directed, not as his opponents determined.

13:29 *the Feast.* See v. 1 and note on v. 2. *the poor.* See 12:5.

13:30 *night.* In light of John's emphasis on the conflict between light and darkness, this may have been more than a time note—picturing also the darkness of Judas's soul.

13:31 *Son of Man.* See note on Mk 8:31. *glorified.* See v. 32 and note on 7:39. Here the idea of glory includes a reference to Jesus' sacrificial death on the cross and the glorious salvation that would result. *God is glorified in him.* The glory of the Father is closely bound to that of the Son.

13:34 *A new command.* In a sense it was an old one (see Lev 19:18), but for Christ's disciples it was new, because it was the mark of their brotherhood, created by Christ's great love for them (cf. Mt 22:37–39; Mk 12:30–31; Lk 10:27). *As I have loved you.* Our standard is Christ's love for us.

13:35 *love.* The distinguishing mark of Christ's followers (cf. 1Jn 3:23; 4:7–8,11–12,19–21).

13:36 *where are you going?* Peter seems to have ignored Jesus' words about love and was more concerned about his Master's departure. In Jesus' reply "you" in v. 33 is singular and thus personal to Peter, whereas in v. 33 the word is plural.

13:37 *I will lay down my life.* Words similar to those of the *good* shepherd in 10:11. Peter was characteristically sure of himself, when in fact he would not at this time lay down his life for Jesus. Exactly the opposite would be true.

13:38 *you will disown me three times.* Peter's denial is prophesied in all four Gospels (Mt 26:33–35; Mk 14:29–31; Lk 22:31–34).

14:1 *Do not . . . be troubled.* The apostles had just received disturbing news (13:33,36). *Trust.* The antidote for a troubled heart.

14:2 *my Father's house.* Heaven. *rooms.* Lit. "dwelling places," implying permanence.

14:3 *I will come back.* Jesus comes in many ways, but the

with me that you also may be where I am.[b] [4]You know the way to the place where I am going."

Jesus the Way to the Father

[5]Thomas[c] said to him, "Lord, we don't know where you are going, so how can we know the way?"

[6]Jesus answered, "I am[d] the way[e] and the truth[f] and the life.[g] No one comes to the Father except through me.[h] [7]If you really knew me, you would know[r] my Father as well.[i] From now on, you do know him and have seen him."

[8]Philip[j] said, "Lord, show us the Father and that will be enough for us."

[9]Jesus answered: "Don't you know me, Philip, even after I have been among you such a long time? Anyone who has seen me has seen the Father.[k] How can you say, 'Show us the Father'? [10]Don't you believe that I am in the Father, and that the Father is in me?[l] The words I say to you are not just my own.[m] Rather, it is the Father, living in me, who is doing his work. [11]Believe me when I say that I am in the Father and the Father is in me; or at least believe on the evidence of the miracles themselves.[n] [12]I tell you the truth, anyone who has faith[o] in me will do what I have been doing.[p] He will do even greater things than these, because I am go-

ing to the Father. [13]And I will do whatever you ask[q] in my name, so that the Son may bring glory to the Father. [14]You may ask me for anything in my name, and I will do it.

Jesus Promises the Holy Spirit

[15]"If you love me, you will obey what I command.[r] [16]And I will ask the Father, and he will give you another Counselor[s] to be with you forever— [17]the Spirit of truth.[t] The world cannot accept him,[u] because it neither sees him nor knows him. But you know him, for he lives with you and will be[s] in you. [18]I will not leave you as orphans;[v] I will come to you.[w] [19]Before long, the world will not see me anymore, but you will see me.[x] Because I live, you also will live.[y] [20]On that day[z] you will realize that I am in my Father,[a] and you are in me, and I am in you.[b] [21]Whoever has my commands and obeys them, he is the one who loves me.[c] He who loves me will be loved by my Father,[d] and I too will love him and show myself to him."

[22]Then Judas[e] (not Judas Iscariot) said, "But, Lord, why do you intend to show yourself to us and not to the world?"[f]

[23]Jesus replied, "If anyone loves me, he

Cross references:

14:3 [b]S Jn 12:26
14:5 [c]S Jn 11:16
14:6 [d]S Jn 6:35
[e]Jn 10:9;
Eph 2:18;
Heb 10:20
[f]Jn 1:14 [g]S Jn 1:4
[h]Ac 4:12
14:7 [i]Jn 1:18;
S 1Jn 2:23
14:8 [j]S Jn 1:43
14:9 [k]Isa 9:6;
Jn 1:14; 12:45;
2Co 4:4; Php 2:6;
Col 1:15; Heb 1:3
14:10 [l]ver 11,20;
Jn 10:38; 17:21
[m]S ver 24
14:11 [n]Jn 5:36;
10:38
14:12 [o]Mt 21:21
[p]Lk 10:17
14:13 [q]S Mt 7:7
14:15 [r]ver 21,23;
Ps 103:18;
Jn 15:10;
1Jn 2:3-5; 3:22,
24; 5:3; 2Jn 6;
Rev 12:17; 14:12
14:16 [s]ver 26;
Jn 15:26; 16:7
14:17 [t]Jn 15:26;
16:13; 1Jn 4:6;
5:6 [u]1Co 2:14
14:18 [v]1Ki 6:13
[w]ver 3,28;
S Mt 16:27
14:19 [x]Jn 7:33,
34; 16:16
[y]Jn 6:57
14:20 [z]Jn 16:23,
26 [a]ver 10,11;
Jn 10:38; 17:21
14:21 [b]S Ro 8:10
[c]S ver 15
[d]Dt 7:13;
Jn 16:27; 1Jn 2:5
14:22 [e]Lk 6:16;
Ac 1:13 [f]Ac 10:41

[r]7 Some early manuscripts *If you really have known me, you will know* [s]17 Some early manuscripts *and is*

---

primary reference here is to his second advent.
14:4 *way.* See v. 6.
14:5 *Thomas.* He was honest, and plainly told the Lord he did not understand (see note on 11:16).
14:6 *I am.* See note on 6:35. *the way.* To God. Jesus is not one way among many, but the way (cf. Ac 4:12; Heb 10:19–20). In the early church, Christianity was sometimes called "the Way" (e.g., Ac 9:2; 19:9,23). *the truth.* A key emphasis in this Gospel (see note on 1:14). *the life.* See note on 1:4. Very likely the statement means "I am the way (to the Father) in that I am the truth and the life."
14:7 *me . . . my Father.* Once more Jesus stresses the intimate connection between the Father and himself. Jesus brought a full revelation of the Father (cf. 1:18), so that the apostles had real knowledge of him.
14:10 *not just my own.* Jesus' teaching was not of human origin, and there was an inseparable connection between his words and his work.
14:11 *Believe . . . that I am in the Father and the Father is in me.* Saving faith is trust in a person, but it must also have factual content. Faith includes believing that Jesus is one with the Father.
14:12 *greater things.* Miracles (see v. 11). These depended on Jesus' going to the Father, because they are works done in the strength of the Holy Spirit, whom Jesus would send from the Father (15:26; cf. 14:16–17).
14:13 *in my name.* Not simply prayer that mentions Jesus' name but prayer in accordance with all that the person who bears the name is (see note on 2:23). It is prayer aimed at carrying forward the work Jesus did—prayer that he himself will answer (see also v. 14).
14:15 *love . . . obey.* Love, like faith (Jas 2:14–26), cannot

be separated from obedience.
14:16 *the Father . . . will give you.* The first of a series of important passages about the Holy Spirit (v. 26; 15:26; 16:7–15), the gift of the Father. *another.* Besides Jesus. *Counselor.* Or "Helper." It is a legal term, but with a broader meaning than "counsel for the defense" (see 1Jn 2:1). It referred to any person who helped someone in trouble with the law. The Spirit will always stand by Christ's people.
14:17 *the Spirit of truth.* In essence and in action the Spirit is characterized by truth. He brings people to the truth of God. All three persons of the Trinity are linked with truth. See also the Father (4:23–24; cf. Ps 31:5; Isa 65:16) and the Son (14:6). *The world.* Which takes no notice of the Spirit of God (cf. 1Co 2:14). But the Spirit was "with" Jesus' disciples and would be "in" them. Some believe the latter relationship (indwelling) specifically anticipates the coming of the Holy Spirit on the day of Pentecost (Ac 2; cf. Ro 8:9).
14:18 *I will come to you.* The words relate to the coming of the Spirit, but Jesus also speaks of his own appearances after the resurrection and at his second coming (see vv. 3, 19, 28; 16:22).
14:19 *the world . . . but you.* The cross separated the world (who would not see Jesus thereafter) from the disciples (who would). *Because I live, you also will live.* The life of the Christian always depends on the life of Christ (cf. 1:4; 3:15).
14:20 *On that day you will realize.* The resurrection would radically change their thinking.
14:21 *obeys . . . loves.* Love for Christ and keeping his commands cannot be separated (see note on v. 15). *loved by my Father . . . I too will love him.* The love of the Father cannot be separated from that of the Son.
14:22 *why . . . ?* He (and, for that matter, the others)

will obey my teaching.*g* My Father will love him, and we will come to him and make our home with him.*h* 24He who does not love me will not obey my teaching. These words you hear are not my own; they belong to the Father who sent me.*i*

25"All this I have spoken while still with you. 26But the Counselor,*j* the Holy Spirit, whom the Father will send in my name,*k* will teach you all things*l* and will remind you of everything I have said to you.*m* 27Peace I leave with you; my peace I give you.*n* I do not give to you as the world gives. Do not let your hearts be troubled*o* and do not be afraid.

28"You heard me say, 'I am going away and I am coming back to you.'*p* If you loved me, you would be glad that I am going to the Father,*q* for the Father is greater than I.*r* 29I have told you now before it happens, so that when it does happen you will believe.*s* 30I will not speak with you much longer, for the prince of this world*t* is coming. He has no hold on me, 31but the world must learn that I love the Father and that I do exactly what my Father has commanded me.*u*

"Come now; let us leave."

14:23 *g*S ver 15
*h*S Ro 8:10
14:24 *i*ver 10;
Dt 18:18;
Jn 5:19; 7:16;
8:28; 12:49,50
14:26 *j*ver 16;
Jn 15:26; 16:7
*k*Ac 2:33
*l*Jn 16:13;
1Jn 2:20,27
*m*Jn 2:22
14:27 *n*Nu 6:26;
Ps 85:8; Mal 2:6;
S Lk 2:14; 24:36;
Jn 16:33;
Php 4:7; Col 3:15
*o*ver 1
14:28 *p*ver 2-4,
18; S Mt 16:27
*q*Jn 5:18
*r*Jn 10:29
14:29 *s*Jn 13:19;
16:4
14:30 *t*S Jn 12:31
14:31 *u*Jn 10:18;
12:49

15:1 *v*S Jn 6:35
*w*Ps 80:8-11;
Isa 5:1-7
15:2 *x*ver 6;
S Mt 3:10
*y*Ps 92:14;
Mt 3:8; 7:20;
Gal 5:22;
Eph 5:9; Php 1:11
15:3 *z*Jn 13:10;
17:17; Eph 5:26
15:4 *a*S Jn 6:56
15:5 *b*ver 16
15:6 *c*ver 2;
Eze 15:4;
S Mt 3:10
15:7 *d*ver 4;
S Jn 6:56
*e*S Mt 7:7

The Vine and the Branches

15 "I am*v* the true vine,*w* and my Father is the gardener. 2He cuts off every branch in me that bears no fruit,*x* while every branch that does bear fruit*y* he prunes† so that it will be even more fruitful. 3You are already clean because of the word I have spoken to you.*z* 4Remain in me, and I will remain in you.*a* No branch can bear fruit by itself; it must remain in the vine. Neither can you bear fruit unless you remain in me.

5"I am the vine; you are the branches. If a man remains in me and I in him, he will bear much fruit;*b* apart from me you can do nothing. 6If anyone does not remain in me, he is like a branch that is thrown away and withers; such branches are picked up, thrown into the fire and burned.*c* 7If you remain in me*d* and my words remain in you, ask whatever you wish, and it will be given you.*e* 8This is to my Father's glory,*f* that you bear much fruit, showing yourselves to be my disciples.*g*

9"As the Father has loved me,*h* so have I loved you. Now remain in my love. 10If

15:8 *f*S Mt 9:8 *g*Jn 8:31 **15:9** *h*Jn 17:23,24,26

† *2 The Greek for* prunes *also means* cleans.

---

probably looked for Jesus to fulfill popular Messianic expectations. It was not easy, therefore, to understand how that would mean showing himself to the disciples but not to the world.

14:23 *loves . . . obey . . . love.* Again love and obedience are linked (cf. vv. 15,21).

14:24 Once more the close relationship between Jesus' words and the Father's is stressed (see v. 10; 7:16).

14:26 *Counselor.* See note on v. 16. *Holy Spirit.* His normal title in the NT (though only here and at 1:33 in this Gospel)—emphasizing his holiness, rather than his power or greatness. *whom the Father will send.* Both the Father and the Son are involved in the sending (see 15:26). *name.* See notes on v. 13; 2:23. *remind you of everything I have said to you.* Crucial for the life of the church—and for the writing of the NT.

14:27 *Peace . . . my peace.* A common Hebrew greeting (20:19,21,26), which Jesus uses here in an unusual way. The term speaks, in effect, of the salvation that Christ's redemptive work will achieve for his disciples—total well-being and inner rest of spirit, in fellowship with God. All true peace is his gift, which the repetition emphasizes. *I do not give . . . as the world gives.* In its greetings of peace the world can only express a longing or wish. But Jesus' peace is real and present. *troubled.* See note on v. 1.

14:28 *heard me say.* Cf. v. 3. *the Father is greater than I.* Revealing the subordinate role Jesus accepted as a necessary part of the incarnation. The statement must be understood in the light of the unity between the Father and the Son (10:30).

14:30 *prince of this world.* See note on 12:31. *has no hold on me.* Satan has a hold on people because of their fallen state. Since Christ was sinless, Satan could have no hold on him.

14:31 *I do exactly what my Father has commanded me.*

Jesus had stressed the importance of his followers being obedient (vv. 15,21,23), and he set the example. With these words he goes to fulfill his mission (chs. 18–19).

15:1 *I am.* See note on 6:35. *the true vine.* The vine is frequently used in the OT as a symbol of Israel (e.g., Ps 80:8–16; Isa 5:1–7; Jer 2:21). When this imagery is used, Israel is often shown as lacking in some way. Jesus, however, is "the true vine."

15:2 *cuts off.* A reference to judgment (see note on v. 6). *prunes.* Pruning produces fruitfulness. In the NT the figure of good fruit represents the product of a godly life (see Mt 3:8; 7:16–20) or virtues of character (see Gal 5:22–23; Eph 5:9; Php 1:11).

15:3 *clean.* See NIV text note on v. 2. *the word.* Sums up the message of Jesus.

15:4 *Remain in me.* The believer has no fruitfulness apart from his union and fellowship with Christ. A branch out of contact with the vine is lifeless.

15:5 *I am the vine.* See note on v. 1. The repetition gives emphasis. *remains in me and I in him.* A living union with Christ is absolutely necessary; without it there is nothing.

15:6 *thrown into the fire and burned.* Judged (see note on v. 2). In light of such passages as 6:39; 10:27–28, these branches probably do not represent true believers. Genuine salvation is evidenced by a life of fruitfulness (see v. 10 and notes on vv. 2,4; see also Heb 6:9, "things that accompany salvation").

15:7 *my words remain in you.* It is impossible to pray correctly apart from knowing and believing the teachings of Christ. *ask whatever you wish.* See 14:13 and note.

15:8 *to my Father's glory.* The Father is glorified in the work of the Son (13:31–32), and he is also glorified in the fruit-bearing of disciples (see Mt 7:20; Lk 6:43–45).

15:10 *obey . . . as I have obeyed.* Again the importance of obedience (cf. 14:15,21,23), and again the example of Christ

you obey my commands, *i* you will remain in my love, just as I have obeyed my Father's commands and remain in his love. ¹¹I have told you this so that my joy may be in you and that your joy may be complete. *j* ¹²My command is this: Love each other as I have loved you. *k* ¹³Greater love has no one than this, that he lay down his life for his friends. *l* ¹⁴You are my friends *m* if you do what I command. *n* ¹⁵I no longer call you servants, because a servant does not know his master's business. Instead, I have called you friends, for everything that I learned from my Father I have made known to you. *o* ¹⁶You did not choose me, but I chose you and appointed you *p* to go and bear fruit *q*—fruit that will last. Then the Father will give you whatever you ask in my name. *r* ¹⁷This is my command: Love each other. *s*

The World Hates the Disciples

¹⁸"If the world hates you, *t* keep in mind that it hated me first. ¹⁹If you belonged to the world, it would love you as its own. As it is, you do not belong to the world, but I have chosen you *u* out of the world. That is why the world hates you. *v* ²⁰Remember the words I spoke to you: 'No servant is greater than his master.' *u w* If they persecuted me, they will persecute you also. *x* If they obeyed my teaching, they will obey yours also. ²¹They will treat

you this way because of my name, *y* for they do not know the One who sent me. *z* ²²If I had not come and spoken to them, *a* they would not be guilty of sin. Now, however, they have no excuse for their sin. *b* ²³He who hates me hates my Father as well. ²⁴If I had not done among them what no one else did, *c* they would not be guilty of sin. *d* But now they have seen these miracles, and yet they have hated both me and my Father. ²⁵But this is to fulfill what is written in their Law: *e* 'They hated me without reason.' *v f*

²⁶"When the Counselor *g* comes, whom I will send to you from the Father, *h* the Spirit of truth *i* who goes out from the Father, he will testify about me. *j* ²⁷And you also must testify, *k* for you have been with me from the beginning. *l*

16 "All this *m* I have told you so that you will not go astray. *n* ²They will put you out of the synagogue; *o* in fact, a time is coming when anyone who kills you will think he is offering a service to God. *p* ³They will do such things because they have not known the Father or me. *q* ⁴I have told you this, so that when the time comes you will remember *r* that I warned

---

Cross references (center column):

15:10 *i* S Jn 14:15
15:11 *j* S Jn 3:29
15:12 *k* ver 17; S Jn 13:34
15:13 *l* Ge 44:33; Jn 10:11; Ro 5:7, 8
15:14 *m* Job 16:20; Pr 18:24; Lk 12:4
n Mt 12:50
15:15 *o* Jn 8:26
15:16 *p* ver 19; Jn 13:18 *q* ver 5 *r* S Mt 7:7
15:17 *s* ver 12
15:18 *t* Isa 66:5; Jn 7:7; 1Jn 3:13
15:19 *u* ver 16 *v* Jn 17:14
15:20
w S Jn 13:16
x 2Ti 3:12

15:21 *y* Isa 66:5; Mt 5:10,11; 10:22; Lk 6:22; Ac 5:41; 1Pe 4:14; Rev 2:3
z Jn 16:3
15:22 *a* Eze 2:5; 3:7 *b* Jn 9:41; Ro 1:20; 2:1
15:24 *c* Jn 5:36 *d* Jn 9:41
15:25
e S Jn 10:34
f Ps 35:19; 69:4; 109:3
15:26 *g* Jn 14:16 *h* Jn 14:26; 16:7 *i* S Jn 14:17 *j* 1Jn 5:7
15:27
k S Lk 24:48; Jn 21:24; 1Jn 1:2; 4:14 *l* S Lk 1:2
16:1
m Jn 15:18-27
n Mt 11:6
16:2 *o* Jn 9:22; 12:42 *p* Isa 66:5;

Ac 26:9,10; Rev 6:9 **16:3** *q* Jn 15:21; 17:25; 1Jn 3:1 **16:4** *r* Jn 13:19; 14:29

u 20 John 13:16   *v 25* Psalms 35:19; 69:4

(cf. 14:31). *my love . . . his love.* See vv. 12,14. Obedience and love go together (see 1Jn 2:5; 5:2–3).

15:11 *joy.* Mentioned previously in this Gospel only in 3:29, but one of the characteristic notes of the upper room discourse (16:20–22,24; 17:13). The Christian way is never dreary, for Jesus desires his disciples' joy to be complete.

15:13 Christ's love was not only in words but also in his sacrificial death.

15:15 *servants . . . friends.* A servant is simply an agent, doing what his master commands and often not understanding his master's purpose. But Jesus takes his friends into his confidence. *everything . . . I have made known to you.* From 16:12 we learn that though Jesus had let his disciples know as much as they were able to absorb of the Father's plan, the revelation was not yet complete. The Spirit would make other things known in due course.

15:16 *I chose you . . . bear fruit . . . ask.* Disciples normally chose the particular rabbi to whom they wanted to be attached, but it was not so with Jesus' disciples. He chose them, and for a purpose—the bearing of fruit. We usually desire a strong prayer life in order that we may be fruitful, but here it is the other way around. Jesus enables us to bear fruit, and then the Father will hear our prayers. *name.* See notes on 2:23; 14:13.

15:18–19 *world.* Here refers to the human system that opposes God's purpose (see note on 1:9).

15:19 *you do not belong.* The believer's essential being, his new life, comes specially from God, and therefore he is not the same as those who oppose God.

15:21 *They will treat you this way.* Because Christians do not belong to the world, persecution from the world is

inevitable. The basic reason is the world's ignorance and rejection of the Father (cf. 16:3). *name.* See note on 2:23.

15:22 *no excuse.* Privilege and responsibility go together. The Jews had had the great privilege of having the Son of God among them—in addition to having received God's special revelation in the OT. Their rejection of Jesus left them totally guilty and without excuse. Had he not come to them they would still have been sinners, but they would not have been guilty of rejecting him directly (see v. 24).

15:25 *to fulfill what is written.* In the end God's purpose is always accomplished, despite the belief of sinful men that they have successfully opposed it. *Law.* See notes on 10:34; 12:34.

15:26 *Counselor.* See note on 14:16. *I will send.* See notes on 14:16,26. *Spirit of truth.* See note on 14:17. *goes out from the Father.* Probably refers to the Spirit's being sent to do the Father's work on earth rather than to his eternal relationship with the Father. *testify.* See note on 1:7.

15:27 *you also.* Emphatic. Believers bear their testimony to Christ in the power of the Spirit. But it is their testimony, and they are responsible for bearing it. *from the beginning.* The apostles bore the definitive testimony, for they were uniquely chosen and taught by Christ and were eyewitnesses of his glory (see Lk 24:48; Ac 10:39,41).

16:2 *put you out of the synagogue.* See note on 9:22. *a service to God.* Religious people have often persecuted others in the strong conviction that this was right (see Ac 26:9–11; Gal 1:13–14).

16:3 *the Father.* See note on 5:17. *or me.* Again the Father and the Son are linked. Not to know Christ is to be ignorant of the Father.

you. I did not tell you this at first because I was with you. [s]

The Work of the Holy Spirit

[5]"Now I am going to him who sent me, [t] yet none of you asks me, 'Where are you going?' [u] [6]Because I have said these things, you are filled with grief. [v] [7]But I tell you the truth: It is for your good that I am going away. Unless I go away, the Counselor [w] will not come to you; but if I go, I will send him to you. [x] [8]When he comes, he will convict the world of guilt [w] in regard to sin and righteousness and judgment: [9]in regard to sin, [y] because men do not believe in me; [10]in regard to righteousness, [z] because I am going to the Father, [a] where you can see me no longer; [11]and in regard to judgment, because the prince of this world [b] now stands condemned.

[12]"I have much more to say to you, more than you can now bear. [c] [13]But when he, the Spirit of truth, [d] comes, he will guide you into all truth. [e] He will not speak on his own; he will speak only what he hears, and he will tell you what is yet to come. [14]He will bring glory to me by taking from what is mine and making it known to you. [15]All that belongs to the Father is mine. [f] That is why I said the

Spirit will take from what is mine and make it known to you.

[16]"In a little while [g] you will see me no more, and then after a little while you will see me." [h]

The Disciples' Grief Will Turn to Joy

[17]Some of his disciples said to one another, "What does he mean by saying, 'In a little while you will see me no more, and then after a little while you will see me,' [i] and 'Because I am going to the Father'?" [j] [18]They kept asking, "What does he mean by 'a little while'? We don't understand what he is saying."

[19]Jesus saw that they wanted to ask him about this, so he said to them, "Are you asking one another what I meant when I said, 'In a little while you will see me no more, and then after a little while you will see me'? [20]I tell you the truth, you will weep and mourn [k] while the world rejoices. You will grieve, but your grief will turn to joy. [l] [21]A woman giving birth to a child has pain [m] because her time has come; but when her baby is born she forgets the anguish because of her joy that a child is born into the world. [22]So with you: Now is your time of grief, [n] but I will see you again [o] and you will rejoice, and no

[w] 8 Or will expose the guilt of the world

Cross references (center column)

16:4 [s]Jn 15:27
16:5 [t]ver 10,17, 28; Jn 7:33
[u]Jn 13:36; 14:5
16:6 [v]ver 22
16:7 [w]Jn 14:16, 26; 15:26
[x]Jn 7:39; 14:26
16:9 [y]Jn 15:22
16:10 [z]Ac 3:14; 7:52; Ro 1:17; 3:21,22; 1Pe 3:18
[a]S ver 5
16:11
[b]S Jn 12:31
16:12 [c]Mk 4:33; 1Co 3:2
16:13
[d]S Jn 14:17
[e]Ps 25:5; Jn 14:26
16:15 [f]Jn 17:10

16:16 [g]S Jn 7:33
[h]ver 22; Jn 14:18-24
16:17 [i]ver 16
[j]ver 5
16:20
[k]Mk 16:10; Lk 23:27
[l]Jn 20:20
16:21 [m]Isa 13:8; 21:3; 26:17; Mic 4:9; 1Th 5:3
16:22 [n]ver 6
[o]ver 16

Study notes

16:5 *none of you asks me, 'Where are you going?'* Peter had asked such a question (13:36), but quickly turned his attention to another subject. His concern had been with what would happen to himself and the others and not for where Jesus was going.

16:6 *you are filled with grief.* Because of his announced departure.

16:7 *Unless I go away.* Jesus did not say why the Spirit would not come until he went away, but clearly taught that his saving work on the cross was necessary before the sending of the Spirit. *Counselor.* See note on 14:16. *I will send him.* See note on 14:26.

16:8 *he will convict the world.* The work the Spirit does in the world (see NIV text note). The NT normally speaks of his work in believers.

16:9 *in regard to sin.* Apart from the Spirit's convicting work, people can never see themselves as sinners. *because men do not believe.* May mean that their sin is their failure to believe, or that their unbelief is a classic example of sin. Typically, John may have had both of these in mind.

16:10 *in regard to righteousness.* The righteousness brought about by Christ's sacrificial death (cf. Ro 1:17; 3:21–22). No one but the Holy Spirit can reveal to a person that a righteous status before God does not depend on good works but on Christ's death on the cross. *because I am going to the Father.* The ascension, which as part of Christ's exaltation placed God's seal of approval on Christ's redemptive act.

16:11 *in regard to judgment.* Jesus was speaking of the defeat of Satan, which was a form of judgment, not simply a victory. More than power is in question. God acts with justice. *prince of this world.* See note on 12:31.

16:12 *more than you can now bear.* This may mean "more than you can understand now," or "more than you can

perform without the Spirit's help" (to live out Christ's teaching requires the enabling presence of the Spirit).

16:13 *Spirit of truth.* See note on 14:17. *only what he hears.* We are not told whether he hears from the Father or the Son, but it obviously does not matter, for the verse stresses the close relationship among the three. *what is yet to come.* Probably means the whole Christian way or revelation (presented and preserved in the apostolic writings), still future at the time Jesus spoke.

16:14 *glory to me.* See note on 1:14. The Spirit draws no attention to himself but promotes the glory of Christ.

16:15 *All that belongs to the Father is mine.* Cf. 17:10. The three Persons are closely related.

16:16 *a little while . . . a little while.* Few doubt that the first phrase refers to the interval before the crucifixion. But interpretations differ as to whether the second refers to the interval preceding the resurrection or the coming of the Spirit or the second coming of Christ. It seems that the language here best fits the resurrection.

16:17 *going to the Father.* See v. 10. Jesus had not linked this with "a little while," but the apostles saw them as connected.

16:20 *weep.* The same verb for loud wailing as in 11:33, which carries the idea of deep sorrow and its outward expression.

16:21 *A woman giving birth.* Giving birth usually causes both pain and joy (cf. Isa 26:17–19; 66:7–14; Hos 13:13–14).

16:22 *I will see you again.* As in v. 16, probably a reference to Jesus' appearances after his resurrection. *no one will take away your joy.* The resurrection would change things permanently, bringing a joy that cannot be removed by the world's assaults.

one will take away your joy. *p* 23In that day *q* you will no longer ask me anything. I tell you the truth, my Father will give you whatever you ask in my name. *r* 24Until now you have not asked for anything in my name. Ask and you will receive, *s* and your joy will be complete. *t*

25"Though I have been speaking figuratively, *u* a time is coming *v* when I will no longer use this kind of language but will tell you plainly about my Father. 26In that day you will ask in my name. *w* I am not saying that I will ask the Father on your behalf. 27No, the Father himself loves you because you have loved me *x* and have believed that I came from God. *y* 28I came from the Father and entered the world; now I am leaving the world and going back to the Father." *z*

29Then Jesus' disciples said, "Now you are speaking clearly and without figures of speech. *a* 30Now we can see that you know all things and that you do not even need to have anyone ask you questions. This makes us believe *b* that you came from God." *c*

31"You believe at last!" *x* Jesus answered. 32"But a time is coming, *d* and has come, when you will be scattered, *e* each to his own home. You will leave me all alone. *f* Yet I am not alone, for my Father is with me. *g*

33"I have told you these things, so that in me you may have peace. *h* In this world you will have trouble. *i* But take heart! I have overcome *j* the world."

Jesus Prays for Himself

17 After Jesus said this, he looked toward heaven *k* and prayed:

"Father, the time has come. *l* Glorify your Son, that your Son may glorify you. *m* 2For you granted him authority over all people *n* that he might give eternal life *o* to all those you have given him. *p* 3Now this is eternal life: that they may know you, *q* the only true God, and Jesus Christ, whom you have sent. *r* 4I have brought you glory *s* on earth by completing the work you gave me to do. *t* 5And now, Father, glorify me *u* in your presence with the glory I had with you *v* before the world began. *w*

Jesus Prays for His Disciples

6"I have revealed you *v x* to those whom you gave me *y* out of the world. They were yours; you gave them to me and they have obeyed your word.

Cross references (center column):

16:22 *p* ver 20; Jer 31:12
16:23 *q* ver 26; Jn 14:20 *r* S Mt 7:7
16:24 *s* S Mt 7:7 *t* S Jn 3:29
16:25 *u* ver 29; Ps 78:2; Eze 20:49; Mt 13:34; Mk 4:33,34; Jn 10:6 *v* ver 2
16:26 *w* ver 23,24
16:27 *x* Jn 14:21, 23 *y* ver 30; S Jn 13:3
16:28 *z* ver 5,10, 17; Jn 13:3
16:29 *a* S ver 25
16:30 *b* 1Ki 17:24 *c* ver 27; S Jn 13:3
16:32 *d* ver 2,25 *e* Mt 26:31 *f* Mt 26:56 *g* Jn 8:16,29

16:33 *h* S Jn 14:27 *i* Jn 15:18-21 *j* Ro 8:37; 1Jn 4:4; 5:4; Rev 2:7,11, 17,26; 3:5,12,21; 21:7
17:1 *k* Jn 11:41 *l* S Mt 26:18 *m* Jn 12:23; 13:31,32
17:2 *n* S Mt 28:18 *o* S Mt 25:46 *p* ver 6,9,24; Da 7:14; Jn 6:37,39
17:3 *q* S Php 3:8 *r* ver 8,18,21,23, 25; S Jn 3:17
17:4 *s* Jn 13:31 *t* S Jn 19:30
17:5 *u* ver 1 *v* Php 2:6 *w* S Jn 1:2

17:6 *x* ver 26; Jn 1:18 *y* S ver 2

x 31 Or *"Do you now believe?"*   *y 6* Greek *your name;* also in verse 26

16:23 *you will no longer ask me anything.* Seems to mean asking for information (rather than asking in prayer), which would not be necessary after the resurrection. Jesus then moved on to the subject of prayer. However, Jesus may have been saying that his disciples previously had been praying to Christ, but after his death and resurrection they were to go directly to the Father and pray in Christ's name (see vv. 24,26–27 and notes). *name.* See notes on 2:23; 14:13.

16:24 *Until now.* Previously they had asked the Father or Christ, but they had not asked the Father in Christ's name. *your joy.* See note on 15:11.

16:25 *I have been speaking figuratively.* Throughout the discourse, not just in the immediately preceding words. *a time is coming.* After the resurrection.

16:26 *in my name.* See notes on 2:23; 14:13. *I am not saying that I will ask.* Not a contradiction of Ro 8:34; Heb 7:25; 1Jn 2:1. Those passages mean that Christ's presence in heaven as the crucified and risen Lord is itself an intercession. Here the teaching is that there will be no need for him to make petitions in our behalf.

16:27 *the Father himself loves you.* Christ is explaining why the disciples can come directly to the Father in prayer. It is because the disciples have loved and trusted in Jesus, and in love God will hear their requests in Jesus' name.

16:29 *without figures of speech.* See v. 25 and note.

16:30 *believe that you came from God.* Two recurring themes of this Gospel: believing (see note on 1:7) and Jesus' coming from God (see notes on 4:34; 17:3,8).

16:32 *you will be scattered.* The disciples had faith, but not enough to stand firm in face of disaster. Jesus knew they would fail; however, his church is not built on people's

strength but on God's ability to use people even after they have failed.

16:33 Notice the contrasts: between "in me" and "in this world" (see note on 1:10) and between "peace" and "trouble." *I have overcome.* Just before his death Jesus affirms his final victory.

17:1–26 Jesus' longest recorded prayer.

17:1 *he looked toward heaven.* The customary attitude in prayer (11:41; Ps 123:1; Mk 7:34), though sometimes the person prostrated himself (see Mt 26:39). *Father.* Used of God in John's Gospel 122 times. *the time.* See note on 2:4. *Glorify . . . glorify.* See notes on 1:14; 7:39; 13:31. The glory of the Father and that of the Son are closely connected, and the death by which Jesus would glorify God would lead to eternal life for believers (v. 2).

17:2 *granted.* The thought of giving is stressed in this chapter (vv. 4,6–9,11–12,14,22,24); see note on 3:27. *that he might give eternal life.* See note on 3:15. *those you have given him.* Again God's initiative in salvation is stressed.

17:3 *sent.* Again the mission of Jesus is mentioned.

17:4 *I have brought you glory.* Christ's mission was not self-centered. *the work you gave me.* Jesus emphasized the supreme place of the Father.

17:5 *glorify me . . . with the glory I had with you.* Jesus asks the Father to return him to his previous position of glory, to exchange humiliation for glorification. This occurred at Christ's resurrection and exaltation to God's right hand. *world.* The universe (see notes on v. 14; 1:9). "World" occurs 18 times in this prayer.

17:6 *I have revealed you.* See NIV text note and notes on 2:23; 14:13; cf. 1:18. *those whom you gave me.* Again the divine initiative (cf. 6:44).

7Now they know that everything you have given me comes from you. 8For I gave them the words you gave me[z] and they accepted them. They knew with certainty that I came from you,[a] and they believed that you sent me.[b] 9I pray for them.[c] I am not praying for the world, but for those you have given me,[d] for they are yours. 10All I have is yours, and all you have is mine.[e] And glory has come to me through them. 11I will remain in the world no longer, but they are still in the world,[f] and I am coming to you.[g] Holy Father, protect them by the power of your name—the name you gave me—so that they may be one[h] as we are one.[i] 12While I was with them, I protected them and kept them safe by that name you gave me. None has been lost[j] except the one doomed to destruction[k] so that Scripture would be fulfilled.[l]

13"I am coming to you now,[m] but I say these things while I am still in the world, so that they may have the full measure of my joy[n] within them. 14I

have given them your word and the world has hated them,[o] for they are not of the world any more than I am of the world.[p] 15My prayer is not that you take them out of the world but that you protect them from the evil one.[q] 16They are not of the world, even as I am not of it.[r] 17Sanctify[z] them by the truth; your word is truth.[s] 18As you sent me into the world,[t] I have sent them into the world.[u] 19For them I sanctify myself, that they too may be truly sanctified.[v]

Jesus Prays for All Believers

20"My prayer is not for them alone. I pray also for those who will believe in me through their message, 21that all of them may be one,[w] Father, just as you are in me and I am in you.[x] May they also be in us so that the world may believe that you have sent me.[y] 22I have given them the glory that you gave me,[z] that they may be one as we are one:[a] 23I in them and you in me.

17:8 [z]ver 14,26; S Jn 14:24
[a]S Jn 13:3 [b]ver 3, 18,21,23,25; S Jn 3:17
17:9 [c]Lk 22:32 [d]S ver 2
17:10 [e]Jn 16:15
17:11 [f]Jn 13:1 [g]ver 13; Jn 7:33 [h]ver 21-23; Ps 133:1 [i]Jn 10:30
17:12 [j]S Jn 6:39 [k]Jn 6:70 [l]S Mt 1:22
17:13 [m]ver 11 [n]S Jn 3:29
17:14 [o]Jn 15:19 [p]ver 16; Jn 8:23
17:15 [q]S Mt 5:37
17:16 [r]ver 14
17:17 [s]S Jn 15:3; 2Sa 7:28; 1Ki 17:24
17:18 [t]ver 3,8, 21,23,25; S Jn 3:17 [u]Jn 20:21
17:19 [v]ver 17
17:21 [w]Jer 32:39 [x]ver 11; Jn 10:38 [y]ver 3,8,18,23, 25; S Jn 3:17
17:22 [z]Jn 1:14 [a]S Jn 14:20

[z] 17 Greek hagiazo (set apart for sacred use or make holy); also in verse 19

17:7 everything . . . comes from you. Only as people see the Father at work in Jesus do they have a proper concept of God. The disciples had at last reached this understanding. **17:8** Three things about the disciples are mentioned: 1. They accepted the teaching (unlike the Pharisees and others who heard it but did not receive it). 2. They knew with certainty Jesus' divine origin. Acceptance of the revelation led them further into truth. 3. They believed (see note on 1:7; cf. 1:12; 20:31).
17:9 not . . . for the world. The only prayer Jesus could pray for the world was that it cease to be worldly (i.e., opposed to God), and this he did pray (vv. 21,23).
17:11 Holy Father. A form of address found only here in the NT (but cf. 1Pe 1:15–16; Rev 4:8; 6:10). The name suggests both remoteness and nearness; God is both awe-inspiring and loving. that they may be one. The latter part of the prayer strongly emphasizes unity. Here the unity is already given, not something to be achieved. The meaning is "that they continually be one" rather than "that they become one." The unity is to be like that between the Father and the Son. It is much more than unity of organization, but the church's present divisions are the result of the failures of Christians.
17:12 I protected them. Christ's power is adequate for every need. the one doomed to destruction. Lit. "the son of destruction" (see 2Th 2:3), i.e., one belonging to the sphere of damnation and destined for destruction (but predestination is not here in view).
17:13 my joy. See note on 15:11.
17:14 the world. The world is hostile to God and God's people (see notes on v. 5; 1:9). not of the world. They do not have the mind-set of the world, i.e., hostility to God, for they have been "born of the Spirit" (3:8) and are "children of God" (1:12).
17:15 not that you take them out of the world. The world is where Jesus' disciples are to do their work; Jesus does not wish them to be taken from it until that work is done (see v. 18). the evil one. Especially active in the world (1Jn 5:19),

making God's protection indispensable.
17:17 Sanctify. See NIV text note. the truth; your word. Sanctification and revelation (as recorded in God's word) go together. For the connection of Christ's teaching with truth cf. 8:31–32.
17:18 As you sent me . . . I have sent them. Jesus' mission is one of the dominant themes of this Gospel and is given as the pattern for his followers. into the world. We may long for heaven, but it is on earth that our work is done.
17:19 I sanctify myself. This statement appears to be unparalleled. In the Septuagint (the Greek translation of the OT) the verb is used of consecrating priests (Ex 28:41) and sacrifices (Ex 28:38; Nu 18:9). Jesus solemnly "sets himself apart to do God's will," which at this point meant his death. that they too may be . . . sanctified. Jesus died on the cross not only to save us but also to consecrate us to God's service (see NIV text note on v. 17).
17:20 those who will believe in me. Jesus had just spoken of the mission and the sanctification of his followers (vv. 18–19). He was confident that they would spread the gospel, and he prayed for those who would believe as a result. All future believers are included in this prayer.
17:21 that all of them may be one. See note on v. 11. Father. See note on v. 1. that the world may believe. The unity of believers should have an effect on outsiders, to convince them of the mission of Christ. Jesus' prayer is a rebuke of the groundless and often bitter divisions among believers.
17:22 the glory. See note on v. 1. Believers are to be characterized by humility and service, just as Christ was, and it is on them that God's glory rests. that they may be one as we are one. Again the Lord emphasized the importance of unity among his followers, and again the standard is the unity of the Father and the Son.
17:23 I in them and you in me. There are two indwellings: that of the Son in believers, and that of the Father in the Son. It is because the latter is a reality that the former can take place. complete unity. Again the emphasis on unity has an

May they be brought to complete unity to let the world know that you sent me[b] and have loved them[c] even as you have loved me.

24"Father, I want those you have given me[d] to be with me where I am,[e] and to see my glory,[f] the glory you have given me because you loved me before the creation of the world.[g]

25"Righteous Father, though the world does not know you,[h] I know you, and they know that you have sent me.[i] 26I have made you known to them,[j] and will continue to make you known in order that the love you have for me may be in them[k] and that I myself may be in them."

Jesus Arrested

18:3–11pp — Mt 26:47–56; Mk 14:43–50; Lk 22:47–53

18 When he had finished praying, Jesus left with his disciples and crossed the Kidron Valley.[l] On the other side there was an olive grove,[m] and he and his disciples went into it.[n]

2Now Judas, who betrayed him, knew the place, because Jesus had often met there with his disciples.[o] 3So Judas came to the grove, guiding[p] a detachment of soldiers and some officials from the chief priests and Pharisees.[q] They were carrying torches, lanterns and weapons.

4Jesus, knowing all that was going to happen to him,[r] went out and asked them, "Who is it you want?"[s]

5"Jesus of Nazareth,"[t] they replied.

"I am he," Jesus said. (And Judas the traitor was standing there with them.) 6When Jesus said, "I am he," they drew back and fell to the ground.

7Again he asked them, "Who is it you want?"[u]

And they said, "Jesus of Nazareth."

8"I told you that I am he," Jesus answered. "If you are looking for me, then let these men go." 9This happened so that the words he had spoken would be fulfilled: "I have not lost one of those you gave me."[a] [v]

10Then Simon Peter, who had a sword, drew it and struck the high priest's servant, cutting off his right ear. (The servant's name was Malchus.)

11Jesus commanded Peter, "Put your sword away! Shall I not drink the cup[w] the Father has given me?"

Jesus Taken to Annas

18:12,13pp — Mt 26:57

12Then the detachment of soldiers with its commander and the Jewish officials[x] arrested Jesus. They bound him 13and brought him first to Annas, who was the father-in-law of Caiaphas,[y] the high priest that year. 14Caiaphas was the one who had

---

17:23 bver 3,8, 18,21,25;
S Jn 3:17
cJn 16:27
17:24 dS ver 2
eS Jn 12:26
fJn 1:14 gver 5;
S Mt 25:34;
S Jn 1:2
17:25 hJn 15:21;
16:3 iver 3,8,18, 21,23; S Jn 3:17;
16:27
17:26 jver 6
kJn 15:9
18:1 l2Sa 15:23
mver 26;
S Mt 21:1
nMt 26:36
18:2 oLk 21:37; 22:39
18:3 pAc 1:16
qver 12

18:4 rJn 6:64; 13:1,11 sver 7
18:5 tS Mk 1:24
18:7 uver 4
18:9 vS Jn 6:39
18:11 wS Mt 20:22
18:12 xver 3
18:13 yver 24;
S Mt 26:3

a9 John 6:39

---

evangelistic aim. This time it is connected not only with the mission of Jesus but also with God's love for people and for Christ.

17:24 *Father.* See note on v. 1. *I want.* Means "I will that." Jesus said, "I will"—his last will and testament for his followers. Where he himself was concerned, he prayed, "not what I will, but what you will" (Mk 14:36). *to be with me.* The Christian's greatest blessing. *my glory.* Perhaps used here to refer to Jesus' eternal splendor (see 1Jn 3:2). Or Jesus' prayer may have been that in the life to come they might fully appreciate the glory of his lowly service (cf. Eph 2:7).

17:25 *Righteous Father.* A form of address found only here in the NT (cf. "Holy Father," v. 11). *they know.* They did not know God directly and personally, but they knew God had sent Christ. To recognize God in Christ's mission is a great advance over anything the world can know.

18:1 *crossed the Kidron Valley.* East of Jerusalem and dry except during the rainy season.

18:2 *Judas.* See note on 6:71. *officials from the chief priests and Pharisees.* Equivalent to the temple guard sent by the Sanhedrin. *torches.* Resinous pieces of wood fastened together. *lanterns.* Terra-cotta holders into which household lamps could be inserted.

18:4 *knowing all that was going to happen to him.* Jesus was not taken by surprise.

18:5 *I am.* See 6:35; 8:58 and notes. *with them.* John does not let us forget where Judas belonged.

18:6 *fell to the ground.* They came to arrest a meek peasant and instead were met in the dim light by a majestic person.

18:8 *I am.* The threefold repetition (vv. 5,6,8) emphasizes the solemn words. *let these men go.* Jesus cared for the disciples even as he was going to his death. Twice he had made the arresting party say plainly that he was the one they wanted (vv. 4–5,7).

18:9 *would be fulfilled.* Words normally used in quoting Scripture, and Jesus' words are on the same level. See 6:39; 17:12.

18:10 *Simon Peter.* It is to John that we owe the information that the man with the sword (the Greek for this word refers to a short sword) was Peter, and that the man he wounded was named Malchus.

18:11 *the cup.* Often points to suffering (Ps 75:8; Eze 23:31–34) and the wrath of God (Isa 51:17,22; Jer 25:15; Rev 14:10; 16:19). *the Father has given me.* The Synoptic Gospels also speak of the cup at the time of Jesus' prayer at Gethsemane (Mt 26:39; Mk 14:36; Lk 22:42), and John says it came from the Father. God was in control.

18:12 *bound him.* The reason for the bonds is not much clear. Perhaps their use was standard procedure, much like the modern use of handcuffs.

18:13 *Annas.* Had been deposed from the high priesthood by the Romans in A.D. 15 but was probably still regarded by many as the true high priest. In Jewish law a man could not be sentenced on the day his trial was held. The two examinations—this one (mentioned only by John) and that before Caiaphas—may have been conducted to give some form of legitimacy to what was done. *high priest that year.* See note on 11:49.

18:14 *Caiaphas . . . had advised the Jews.* A reference to

advised the Jews that it would be good if one man died for the people. *z*

Peter's First Denial

18:16–18pp — Mt 26:69,70; Mk 14:66–68; Lk 22:55–57

15Simon Peter and another disciple were following Jesus. Because this disciple was known to the high priest, *a* he went with Jesus into the high priest's courtyard, *b* 16but Peter had to wait outside at the door. The other disciple, who was known to the high priest, came back, spoke to the girl on duty there and brought Peter in.

17"You are not one of his disciples, are you?" the girl at the door asked Peter.

He replied, "I am not." *c*

18It was cold, and the servants and officials stood around a fire *d* they had made to keep warm. Peter also was standing with them, warming himself. *e*

The High Priest Questions Jesus

18:19–24pp — Mt 26:59–68; Mk 14:55–65; Lk 22:63–71

19Meanwhile, the high priest questioned Jesus about his disciples and his teaching. 20"I have spoken openly to the world," Jesus replied. "I always taught in synagogues *f* or at the temple, *g* where all the Jews come together. I said nothing in secret. *h* 21Why question me? Ask those who heard me. Surely they know what I said."

22When Jesus said this, one of the officials *i* nearby struck him in the face. *j* "Is this the way you answer the high priest?" he demanded.

23"If I said something wrong," Jesus replied, "testify as to what is wrong. But if I spoke the truth, why did you strike me?" *k* 24Then Annas sent him, still bound, to Caiaphas *l* the high priest. *b*

Peter's Second and Third Denials

18:25–27pp — Mt 26:71–75; Mk 14:69–72; Lk 22:58–62

25As Simon Peter stood warming himself, *m* he was asked, "You are not one of his disciples, are you?"

He denied it, saying, "I am not." *n*

26One of the high priest's servants, a relative of the man whose ear Peter had cut off, *o* challenged him, "Didn't I see you with him in the olive grove?" *p* 27Again Peter denied it, and at that moment a rooster began to crow. *q*

Jesus Before Pilate

18:29–40pp — Mt 27:11–18,20–23; Mk 15:2–15; Lk 23:2,3,18–25

28Then the Jews led Jesus from Caiaphas to the palace of the Roman governor. *r* By now it was early morning, and to avoid

Center column references:

18:14 *z*Jn 11:49-51
18:15 *a*S Mt 26:3
*b*Mt 26:58; Mk 14:54; Lk 22:54
18:17 *c*ver 25
18:18 *d*Jn 21:9 *e*Mk 14:54,67
18:20 *f*S Mt 4:23 *g*Mt 26:55 *h*Jn 7:26

18:22 *i*ver 3 /Mt 16:21; Jn 19:3
18:23 *k*Mt 5:39; Ac 23:2-5
18:24 *l*ver 13; S Mt 26:3
18:25 *m*ver 18 *n*ver 17
18:26 *o*ver 10 *p*ver 1
18:27 *q*Jn 13:38
18:28 *r*S Mt 27:2

b24 Or *(Now Annas had sent him, still bound, to Caiaphas the high priest.)*

11:49–50. For John it was this unconscious prophecy that mattered most about Caiaphas. John may also have been hinting that a fair trial could not be expected from a man who had already said that putting Jesus to death was expedient. **18:15** *another disciple.* Perhaps John himself. *known to the high priest.* Refers to more than casual acquaintance; he had entrée into the high priest's house and could bring Peter in.
18:17 *the girl at the door.* All four Gospels tell us that Peter's first challenge came from a slave girl, the most unimportant person imaginable. Her question expected the answer "No." Peter took the easy way out. The other Gospels seem to indicate that the other denials followed immediately, but it is likely that there were intervals during which other things happened (see Lk 22:58–59).
18:18 *Peter also was standing with them.* On a cold night he would have been conspicuous if he had stayed away from the fire.
18:19 *questioned.* Not legal, since witnesses were supposed to be brought in first to establish guilt. The accused was not required to prove his innocence. Perhaps Annas regarded this as a preliminary inquiry, not a trial.
18:20 *I have spoken openly.* It should not have been difficult to find witnesses (v. 21). *nothing in secret.* Not a denial that he taught the disciples privately, but a denial that he had secretly taught them subversive teaching different from his public message.
18:22 *struck.* Another illegality. The word apparently means a blow with the open hand—a slap.
18:23 *testify.* A legal term, indicating an invitation to act in proper legal form. John stresses the importance of testimony throughout his Gospel (see note on 1:7).
18:25 *he was asked.* Lit. "they asked him." Some find a

difficulty in that Mt 26:71 says another girl asked this question, whereas Mk 14:69 says it was the same girl, and Lk 22:58 that it was a man. But with a group of servants talking around a fire, several would doubtless take up and repeat such a question, which could be the meaning of John's "they." As on the first occasion (v. 17) the question anticipated the answer "No." The servants probably did not really expect to find a follower of Jesus in the high priest's courtyard, but the question seemed worth asking.
18:26 *a relative.* Another piece of information we owe to John. A relative would have a deeper interest in the swordsman than other people had. But the light in the garden would have been dim, as in the courtyard (a charcoal fire glows, but does not have flames). *Didn't I see you . . . ?* Expected the answer "Yes."
18:27 *a rooster began to crow.* The fulfillment of the prophecy in 13:38.
18:28 *the Roman governor.* John says little about the Jewish phase of Jesus' trial but much about the Roman trial (see note on Mk 14:53–15:15). It is possible that John was in the Praetorium, the governor's official residence, for this trial. *early morning.* The chief priests evidently held a second session of the Sanhedrin after daybreak to give some appearance of legality to what they did (Mk 15:1). This occasion would have been immediately after that, perhaps between 6:00 A.M. and 7:00 A.M. *ceremonial uncleanness.* A result of entering a Gentile residence. *to eat the Passover.* Does not mean that the time of the Passover meal had not yet come, for this would contradict the Synoptic Gospels, which have Jesus eating the Passover meal the night before. The term "Passover" was used to refer to the whole festival of Passover and Unleavened Bread, which lasted seven days and included a number of meals.

ceremonial uncleanness the Jews did not enter the palace;[s] they wanted to be able to eat the Passover.[t] 29So Pilate came out to them and asked, "What charges are you bringing against this man?"

30"If he were not a criminal," they replied, "we would not have handed him over to you."

31Pilate said, "Take him yourselves and judge him by your own law."

"But we have no right to execute anyone," the Jews objected. 32This happened so that the words Jesus had spoken indicating the kind of death he was going to die[u] would be fulfilled.

33Pilate then went back inside the palace,[v] summoned Jesus and asked him, "Are you the king of the Jews?"[w]

34"Is that your own idea," Jesus asked, "or did others talk to you about me?"

35"Am I a Jew?" Pilate replied. "It was your people and your chief priests who handed you over to me. What is it you have done?"

36Jesus said, "My kingdom[x] is not of this world. If it were, my servants would fight to prevent my arrest by the Jews.[y] But now my kingdom is from another place."[z]

37"You are a king, then!" said Pilate.

Jesus answered, "You are right in saying I am a king. In fact, for this reason I was born, and for this I came into the world, to testify to the truth.[a] Everyone on the side of truth listens to me."[b]

38"What is truth?" Pilate asked. With this he went out again to the Jews and said, "I find no basis for a charge against him.[c] 39But it is your custom for me to release to you one prisoner at the time of the Passover. Do you want me to release 'the king of the Jews'?"

40They shouted back, "No, not him! Give us Barabbas!" Now Barabbas had taken part in a rebellion.[d]

Jesus Sentenced to be Crucified

19:1–16pp — Mt 27:27–31; Mk 15:16–20

19 Then Pilate took Jesus and had him flogged.[e] 2The soldiers twisted together a crown of thorns and put it on his head. They clothed him in a purple robe 3and went up to him again and again, saying, "Hail, king of the Jews!"[f] And they struck him in the face.[g]

4Once more Pilate came out and said to the Jews, "Look, I am bringing him out[h] to you to let you know that I find no basis for a charge against him."[i] 5When Jesus came out wearing the crown of thorns and the purple robe,[j] Pilate said to them, "Here is the man!"

6As soon as the chief priests and their officials saw him, they shouted, "Crucify! Crucify!"

But Pilate answered, "You take him and crucify him.[k] As for me, I find no basis for a charge against him."[l]

7The Jews insisted, "We have a law, and according to that law he must die,[m] be-

Cross-references (center column)

18:28 [s]ver 33; Jn 19:9 [t]Jn 11:55
18:32 [u]Mt 20:19; 26:2; Jn 3:14; 8:28; 12:32,33
18:33 [v]ver 28, 29; Jn 19:9 [w]Lk 23:3; S Mt 2:2
18:36 [x]S Mt 3:2 [y]Mt 26:53 [z]Lk 17:21; Jn 6:15
18:37 [a]Jn 3:32 [b]Jn 8:47; 1Jn 4:6

18:38 [c]S Lk 23:4
18:40 [d]Ac 3:14
19:1 [e]Dt 25:3; Isa 50:6; 53:5; Mt 27:26
19:3 [f]Mt 27:29 [g]Jn 18:22
19:4 [h]Jn 18:38 [i]ver 6; S Lk 23:4
19:5 [j]ver 2
19:6 [k]Ac 3:13 [l]ver 4; S Lk 23:4
19:7 [m]Lev 24:16

18:29 *Pilate.* The Roman governor (see note on Mk 15:1). He showed himself tolerant of Jewish ways. *What charges . . . ?* A normal question at the beginning of a trial, but it was difficult to answer, because the Jews had no charge that would stand up in a Roman court of law.

18:31 *Take him yourselves.* In other words, no Roman charge, no Roman trial. *no right to execute anyone.* They were looking for an execution, not a fair trial. The restriction was important, for otherwise Rome's supporters could be quietly removed by local legal executions. Sometimes the Romans seem to have condoned local executions (e.g., of Stephen, Ac 7), but normally they retained the right to inflict the death penalty.

18:32 *the kind of death he was going to die.* Cf. 12:32–33 and "must" in 12:34. Jewish execution was by stoning, but Jesus' death was to be by crucifixion, whereby he would bear the curse (Dt 21:22–23). The Romans, not the Jews, had to put Jesus to death. God was overruling in the whole process.

18:33 *Are you the king of the Jews?* Pilate's first words to Jesus, identical in all four Gospels. One glance was enough to show him that a dangerous rebel existed only in the imaginations of Jesus' enemies.

18:34 *Is that your own idea . . . ?* If so, Pilate's question (v. 33) had meant, "Are you a rebel?" If the question had originated with the Jews, it meant, "Are you the Messianic King?"

18:36 *My kingdom.* Jesus agrees that he has a kingdom, but asserts that it is not the kind of kingdom that has soldiers

to fight for it. It was not built, nor is it maintained, by military might.

18:37 *to testify to the truth.* Two of this Gospel's important ideas (see 1:7 and note; 1:14 and note; 14:6).

18:38 *What is truth?* Pilate may have been jesting, and meant, "What does truth matter?" Or he may have been serious, and meant, "It is not easy to find truth. What is it?" Either way, it was clear to him that Jesus was no rebel. *no basis for a charge against him.* Teaching the truth was not a criminal offense.

18:39 *it is your custom.* Prisoners are known to have been released on special occasions in other places. *the king of the Jews.* John keeps his emphasis on the note of royalty. Pilate may have hoped that the use of the title would influence people toward the way he wanted them to decide.

18:40 *Barabbas.* A rebel and a murderer (Lk 23:19). The name is Aramaic and means "son of Abba," i.e., "son of the father"; in place of this man, the "Son of the Father" died.

19:1 Pilate hoped a flogging would satisfy the Jews and enable him to release Jesus (see note on Mk 15:15).

19:2 *thorns.* A general term relating to any thorny plant. *purple.* A color used by royalty.

19:6 *You . . . crucify him.* The petulant utterance of an exasperated man, for the Jews could not carry out this form of execution. *I find no basis.* For the third time Pilate proclaimed Jesus' innocence (see 18:38; 19:4). Luke also records this threefold proclamation (Lk 23:4,14,22).

19:7 *he must die.* Apparently referring to the penalty for

cause he claimed to be the Son of God." [n]

[8]When Pilate heard this, he was even more afraid, [9]and he went back inside the palace. [o] "Where do you come from?" he asked Jesus, but Jesus gave him no answer. [p] [10]"Do you refuse to speak to me?" Pilate said. "Don't you realize I have power either to free you or to crucify you?"

[11]Jesus answered, "You would have no power over me if it were not given to you from above. [q] Therefore the one who handed me over to you [r] is guilty of a greater sin."

[12]From then on, Pilate tried to set Jesus free, but the Jews kept shouting, "If you let this man go, you are no friend of Caesar. Anyone who claims to be a king [s] opposes Caesar."

[13]When Pilate heard this, he brought Jesus out and sat down on the judge's seat [t] at a place known as the Stone Pavement (which in Aramaic [u] is Gabbatha). [14]It was the day of Preparation [v] of Passover Week, about the sixth hour. [w]

"Here is your king," [x] Pilate said to the Jews.

[15]But they shouted, "Take him away! Take him away! Crucify him!"

"Shall I crucify your king?" Pilate asked.

"We have no king but Caesar," the chief priests answered.

[16]Finally Pilate handed him over to them to be crucified. [y]

The Crucifixion

19:17–24pp — Mt 27:33–44; Mk 15:22–32; Lk 23:33–43

So the soldiers took charge of Jesus. [17]Carrying his own cross, [z] he went out to the place of the Skull [a] (which in Aramaic [b] is called Golgotha). [18]Here they crucified him, and with him two others [c]—one on each side and Jesus in the middle.

[19]Pilate had a notice prepared and fastened to the cross. It read: JESUS OF NAZARETH, [d] THE KING OF THE JEWS. [e] [20]Many of the Jews read this sign, for the place where Jesus was crucified was near the city, [f] and the sign was written in Aramaic, Latin and Greek. [21]The chief priests of the Jews protested to Pilate, "Do not write 'The King of the Jews,' but that this man claimed to be king of the Jews." [g]

[22]Pilate answered, "What I have written, I have written."

[23]When the soldiers crucified Jesus, they took his clothes, dividing them into four shares, one for each of them, with the un-

Cross references (center column)

19:7 [n]Mt 26:63-66; Jn 5:18; 10:33
19:9 [o]Jn 18:33 [p]S Mk 14:61
19:11 [q]S Ro 13:1 [r]Jn 18:28-30; Ac 3:13
19:12 [s]Lk 23:2
19:13 [t]Mt 27:19 [u]S Jn 5:2
19:14 [v]Mt 27:62 [w]Mk 15:25 [x]ver 19,21
19:16 [y]Mt 27:26; Mk 15:15; Lk 23:25
19:17 [z]Ge 22:6; Lk 14:27; 23:26 [a]Lk 23:33 [b]S Jn 5:2
19:18 [c]Lk 23:32
19:19 [d]S Mk 1:24 [e]ver 14,21
19:20 [f]Heb 13:12
19:21 [g]ver 14

---

blasphemy (Lev 24:16).

19:8 *even more afraid.* Pilate was evidently superstitious, and this charge frightened him.

19:9 *Jesus gave him no answer.* The reason is not clear, but Jesus had answered other questions readily. Perhaps Pilate would not have understood the answer or would not have believed it.

19:10 *I have power.* Pilate was incredulous and very conscious of his authority. His second question indicates his personal responsibility for crucifying Jesus.

19:11 Jesus' last words to Pilate. *from above.* All earthly authority comes ultimately from God. *a greater sin.* That of Caiaphas (not Judas, who was only a means). But "greater" implies that there was a lesser sin, so Pilate's sin was also real.

19:12 *no friend of Caesar.* Some people had official status as "Friends of Caesar," but the term seems to be used here in the general sense. There was an implied threat that if he released Jesus, Pilate would be accused before Caesar. His record was such that he could not face such a prospect without concern.

19:13 *the Stone Pavement.* Not a translation of *Gabbatha,* which seems to mean "the hill of the house," but a different name for the same place.

19:14 *day of Preparation.* Normally Friday was the day people prepared for the Sabbath. Here the meaning is Friday of Passover week. *about the sixth hour.* About noon. Mk 15:25 says that Jesus was crucified at "the third hour." It is possible that Mark's Gospel contains a copyist's error, for the Greek numerals for three and six could be confused. Or it may be that John was using Roman time, in which case the appearance before Pilate would have been at 6:00 A.M. and the crucifixion at 9:00 A.M. (the third hour according to Jewish reckoning; see Mk 15:33). For other time references see Mt 27:45–46; Mk 15: 33–34; Lk 23:44. *Here is your*

king. John does not let us forget the sovereignty of Jesus. Pilate did not mean the expression seriously, but John did. *the Jews.* See note on 1:19.

19:15 *We have no king but Caesar.* More irony. They rejected any suggestion that they were rebels against Rome, but expressed the truth of their spiritual condition.

19:17 *Carrying his own cross.* A cross might be shaped like a *T,* an *X,* a *Y,* or an *I,* as well as like the traditional form. A condemned man would normally carry a beam of it to the place of execution. Somewhere along the way Simon of Cyrene took Jesus' cross (Mk 15:21), probably because Jesus was weakened by the flogging. *Golgotha.* Aramaic for "the skull." The name of the site is given in both Greek and Aramaic ("Calvary") is from the Latin with the same meaning). See note on Mk 15:22.

19:18 *they crucified him.* See note on Mk 15:24. As with the scourging, John describes this horror with one Greek word. None of the Gospel writers dwells on the physical sufferings of Jesus. *one on each side.* Perhaps meant as a final insult, but it brings out the important truth that in his death Jesus was identified with sinners.

19:19 *a notice.* A placard stating the crime for which a man was executed was often fastened to his cross. THE KING OF THE JEWS. Again the royalty theme.

19:20 *Aramaic.* One of the languages of the Jewish people at that time (along with Hebrew). *Latin.* The official language of Rome. *Greek.* The common language of communication throughout the empire. The threefold inscription may account for the slight differences in wording in the four Gospels.

19:22 Pilate must have a sufficient reason for the execution, and he was not above mocking the Jews, but for John his insistence may also have served to underscore that Jesus' kingship is final and unalterable.

19:23 *undergarment.* A type of shirt, reaching from the

dergarment remaining. This garment was seamless, woven in one piece from top to bottom.

24"Let's not tear it," they said to one another. "Let's decide by lot who will get it."

This happened that the scripture might be fulfilled[h] which said,

"They divided my garments among them
and cast lots for my clothing."[c] [i]

So this is what the soldiers did.

25Near the cross[j] of Jesus stood his mother,[k] his mother's sister, Mary the wife of Clopas, and Mary Magdalene.[l] 26When Jesus saw his mother[m] there, and the disciple whom he loved[n] standing nearby, he said to his mother, "Dear woman, here is your son," 27and to the disciple, "Here is your mother." From that time on, this disciple took her into his home.

The Death of Jesus

19:29,30pp — Mt 27:48,50; Mk 15:36,37; Lk 23:36

28Later, knowing that all was now completed,[o] and so that the Scripture would be fulfilled,[p] Jesus said, "I am thirsty."[A] A jar of wine vinegar[q] was there, so they soaked a sponge in it, put the sponge on a stalk of the hyssop plant, and lifted it to Jesus' lips. 30When he had received the drink, Jesus said, "It is finished."[r] With

that, he bowed his head and gave up his spirit.

31Now it was the day of Preparation,[s] and the next day was to be a special Sabbath. Because the Jews did not want the bodies left on the crosses[t] during the Sabbath, they asked Pilate to have the legs broken and the bodies taken down. 32The soldiers therefore came and broke the legs of the first man who had been crucified with Jesus, and then those of the other.[u] 33But when they came to Jesus and found that he was already dead, they did not break his legs. 34Instead, one of the soldiers pierced[v] Jesus' side with a spear, bringing a sudden flow of blood and water.[w] 35The man who saw it[x] has given testimony, and his testimony is true.[y] He knows that he tells the truth, and he testifies so that you also may believe. 36These things happened so that the scripture would be fulfilled:[z] "Not one of his bones will be broken,"[d] [a] 37and, as another scripture says, "They will look on the one they have pierced."[e] [b]

The Burial of Jesus

19:38–42pp — Mt 27:57–61; Mk 15:42–47; Lk 23:50–56

38Later, Joseph of Arimathea asked Pilate for the body of Jesus. Now Joseph was a disciple of Jesus, but secretly because he feared the Jews.[c] With Pilate's permission, he came and took the body away. 39He was accompanied by Nicodemus,[d] the

---

Cross references (center column):

19:24 [h]ver 28, 36,37; S Mt 1:22
[i]Ps 22:18
19:25 [j]Mt 27:55, 56 [k]S Mt 12:46
[l]Lk 8:2; Jn 20:1, 18
19:26 [m]S Mt 12:46 [n]S Jn 13:23
19:28 [o]S ver 30; Jn 13:1 [p]ver 24, 36,37; S Mt 1:22
19:29 [q]Ps 69:21
19:30 [r]Lk 12:50; Jn 4:34; 17:4

19:31 [s]ver 14,42 [t]Dt 21:23; Jos 8:29; 10:26, 27
19:32 [u]ver 18
19:34 [v]Zec 12:10; Rev 1:7 [w]1Jn 5:6, 8
19:35 [x]S Lk 24:48 [y]Jn 15:27; 21:24
19:36 [z]ver 24,28, 37; S Mt 1:22 [a]Ex 12:46; Nu 9:12; Ps 34:20
19:37 [b]Zec 12:10; Rev 1:7
19:38 [c]S Jn 7:13
19:39 [d]Jn 3:1; 7:50

[c]24 Psalm 22:18   [d]36 Exodus 12:46; Num. 9:12; Psalm 34:20   [e]37 Zech. 12:10

Footnotes:

neck to the knees or ankles. *seamless.* Therefore too valuable to be cut up.
19:24 See introduction to Ps 22 and notes on Ps 22:17, 20–21.
19:25 *Clopas.* Mentioned only here in the NT. *Mary Magdalene.* Appears in the crucifixion and resurrection story in all four Gospels, but apart from that we read of her only in Lk 8:2–3.
19:26 *disciple whom he loved.* John (see note on 13:23).
19:27 *took her into his home.* And so took responsibility for her. It may be that Jesus' brothers still did not believe in him (see 7:5).
19:28 *I am thirsty.* May refer to Ps 69:21 (cf. Ps 22:15).
19:29 *wine vinegar.* Equivalent to cheap wine, the drink of ordinary people. *a sponge.* A useful way of giving drink to one on a cross, and may indicate forethought and compassion on someone's part. *hyssop.* The name given to a number of plants. See also note on Ex 12:22.
19:30 *It is finished.* Apparently the loud cry of Mt 27:50; Mk 15:37. Jesus died as a victor and had completed what he came to do. *gave up his spirit.* An unusual way of describing death, perhaps suggesting an act of will.
19:31 *Preparation.* See note on v. 14. *a special Sabbath.* The Sabbath that fell at Passover time. The Passover meal had been eaten on Thursday evening, the day of Preparation was Friday, and the Sabbath came on Saturday. *the Jews.* See note on 1:19. *to have the legs broken.* To hasten death, because the victim then could not put any weight on his legs

and breathing would be difficult.
19:34 *pierced Jesus' side.* Probably to make doubly sure that Jesus was dead, but perhaps simply an act of brutality (see v. 37; Isa 53:5; Zec 12:10; cf. Ps 22:16). *blood and water.* The result of the spear piercing the pericardium (the sac that surrounds the heart) and the heart itself.
19:35 *The man who saw it.* Either John himself or someone he regarded as reliable. Obviously he considered the incident important, and comments that it was well attested. *testifies . . . believe.* See note on 1:7.
19:36–37 *scripture.* Again John observes God's overruling in the fulfillment of Scripture. It was extraordinary that Jesus was the only one of the three whose legs were not broken and that he suffered an unusual spear thrust that did not break a bone.
19:38 *Joseph.* A rich disciple (Mt 27:57), and a member of the Sanhedrin who had not agreed to Jesus' condemnation (Lk 23:51). *Arimathea.* See note on Mt 27:57. *secretly.* It would have been hard for a member of the Sanhedrin to support Jesus' cause openly. Jesus' closest followers all ran away (Mk 14:50), and it was left to Joseph and Nicodemus to provide for his burial. *With Pilate's permission.* Otherwise people could take away their crucified friends before they died and revive them.
19:39 *Nicodemus.* John alone tells us that he joined Joseph in the burial. *seventy-five pounds.* A very large amount, such as was used in royal burials (cf. 2Ch 16:14).

man who earlier had visited Jesus at night. Nicodemus brought a mixture of myrrh and aloes, about seventy-five pounds.[f] [40]Taking Jesus' body, the two of them wrapped it, with the spices, in strips of linen.[e] This was in accordance with Jewish burial customs.[f] [41]At the place where Jesus was crucified, there was a garden, and in the garden a new tomb, in which no one had ever been laid. [42]Because it was the Jewish day of Preparation[g] and since the tomb was nearby,[h] they laid Jesus there.

The Empty Tomb

20:1–8pp — Mt 28:1–8; Mk 16:1–8; Lk 24:1–10

20 Early on the first day of the week, while it was still dark, Mary Magdalene[i] went to the tomb and saw that the stone had been removed from the entrance.[j] [2]So she came running to Simon Peter and the other disciple, the one Jesus loved,[k] and said, "They have taken the Lord out of the tomb, and we don't know where they have put him!"[l]

[3]So Peter and the other disciple started for the tomb.[m] [4]Both were running, but the other disciple outran Peter and reached the tomb first. [5]He bent over and looked in[n] at the strips of linen[o] lying there but did not go in. [6]Then Simon Peter, who was behind him, arrived and went into the tomb. He saw the strips of linen lying there, [7]as well as the burial cloth that had been around Jesus' head.[p] The cloth was

19:40 [e]Lk 24:12; Jn 11:44; 20:5,7 /Mt 26:12
19:42 [g]ver 14,31 [h]ver 20,41
20:1 [i]ver 18; Lk 8:2; Jn 19:25 /Mt 27:60,66
20:2 [k]S Jn 13:23 [l]ver 13
20:3 [m]Lk 24:12
20:5 [n]ver 11 [o]S Jn 19:40
20:7 [p]Jn 11:44
20:8 [q]ver 4
20:9 [r]Mt 22:29; Jn 2:22 [s]Lk 24:26,46; Ac 2:24
20:11 [t]ver 5
20:12 [u]Mt 28:2,3; Mk 16:5; Lk 24:4; Ac 1:10; S 5:19; 10:30
20:13 [v]ver 15 [w]ver 2
20:14 [x]Mk 16:9 [y]Lk 24:16; Jn 21:4
20:15 [z]ver 13
20:16 [a]S Jn 5:2 [b]S Mt 23:7

folded up by itself, separate from the linen. [8]Finally the other disciple, who had reached the tomb first,[q] also went inside. He saw and believed. [9](They still did not understand from Scripture[r] that Jesus had to rise from the dead.)[s]

Jesus Appears to Mary Magdalene

[10]Then the disciples went back to their homes, [11]but Mary stood outside the tomb crying. As she wept, she bent over to look into the tomb[t] [12]and saw two angels in white,[u] seated where Jesus' body had been, one at the head and the other at the foot.

[13]They asked her, "Woman, why are you crying?"[v]

"They have taken my Lord away," she said, "and I don't know where they have put him."[w] [14]At this, she turned around and saw Jesus standing there,[x] but she did not realize that it was Jesus.[y]

[15]"Woman," he said, "why are you crying?[z] Who is it you are looking for?"

Thinking he was the gardener, she said, "Sir, if you have carried him away, tell me where you have put him, and I will get him."

[16]Jesus said to her, "Mary."

She turned toward him and cried out in Aramaic,[a] "Rabboni!"[b] (which means Teacher).

[17]Jesus said, "Do not hold on to me, for I have not yet returned to the Father. Go

[f]39 Greek a hundred litrai (about 34 kilograms)

19:40 *strips of linen.* Thin strips like bandages. There was also a shroud, a large sheet (Mt 27:59; Mk 15:46; Lk 23:53).

19:41 *a new tomb.* Joseph's own tomb (Mt 27:60).

19:42 *Preparation.* See note on v. 14. *nearby.* Haste was necessary, since it was near sunset, when the Sabbath would start and no work could be done.

20:1 *while it was still dark.* Mark says it was "just after sunrise" (Mk 16:2). Perhaps the women came in groups, with Mary Magdalene coming very early. Or John may refer to the time of leaving home, Mark to that of arrival at the tomb. *Mary Magdalene.* See note on 19:25; cf. Mk 16:9.

20:2 *to Simon Peter.* Despite his denials, Peter was still the leading figure among the disciples. *the one Jesus loved.* John (see note on 13:23). *we.* Indicates that there were others with Mary (see Mt 28:1; Mk 16:1; Lk 24:10), though John does not identify them. *have put him.* Mary had no thought of resurrection.

20:7 *folded up.* An orderly arrangement, not in disarray, as would have resulted from a grave robbery.

20:8 *He saw and believed.* Cf. v. 29. John did not say what he believed, but it must have been that Jesus was resurrected.

20:9 *Scripture.* First they came to know of the resurrection through what they saw in the tomb; only later did they see it in Scripture. It is obvious they did not make up a story of resurrection to fit a preconceived understanding of Scriptural prophecy. *had to rise.* It was in Scripture and thus the will of

God.

20:11 *Mary.* Perhaps Jesus appeared first to Mary because she needed him most at that time. *crying.* As in 11:33, it means "wailing," a loud expression of grief.

20:12 *two angels.* Matthew has one angel (Mt 28:2), Mark a young man (Mk 16:5) and Luke two men who were angels (Lk 24:4,23). See note on Lk 24:4.

20:14 *did not realize that it was Jesus.* A number of times the risen Jesus was not recognized (21:4; Mt 28:17; Lk 24:16,37). He may have looked different, or he may intentionally have prevented recognition.

20:16 *Mary.* Cf. 10:3–4. *Rabboni.* A strengthened form of *Rabbi,* and in the NT found elsewhere only in Mk 10:51 (in the Greek). Although the word means "(my) teacher," there are few if any examples of its use in ancient Judaism as a form of address other than in calling on God in prayer. However, John's explanation casts doubt on any thought that Mary intended to address Jesus as God here.

20:17 *for I have not yet returned.* The meaning appears to be that the ascension was still some time off. Mary would have opportunity to see Jesus again, so she need not cling to him. Alternatively, Jesus may be reminding Mary that after his crucifixion she cannot have him with her except through the Holy Spirit (see 16:5–16). *my brothers.* Probably the disciples (cf. v. 18; Mt 12:50). The members of his family did not believe in him (7:5), though they became disciples not long after this (Ac 1:14). *my Father and your Father.* God is Father both of Christ and of believers, but in different senses

instead to my brothers[c] and tell them, 'I am returning to my Father[d] and your Father, to my God and your God.' "

[18]Mary Magdalene[e] went to the disciples[f] with the news: "I have seen the Lord!" And she told them that he had said these things to her.

Jesus Appears to His Disciples

[19]On the evening of that first day of the week, when the disciples were together, with the doors locked for fear of the Jews,[g] Jesus came and stood among them and said, "Peace[h] be with you!"[i] [20]After he said this, he showed them his hands and side.[j] The disciples were overjoyed[k] when they saw the Lord.

[21]Again Jesus said, "Peace be with you![l] As the Father has sent me,[m] I am sending you."[n] [22]And with that he breathed on them and said, "Receive the Holy Spirit.[o] [23]If you forgive anyone his sins, they are forgiven; if you do not forgive them, they are not forgiven."[p]

Jesus Appears to Thomas

[24]Now Thomas[q] (called Didymus), one of the Twelve, was not with the disciples when Jesus came. [25]So the other disciples told them, "We have seen the Lord!"

But he said to them, "Unless I see the nail marks in his hands and put my finger where the nails were, and put my hand into his side,[r] I will not believe it."[s]

[26]A week later his disciples were in the house again, and Thomas was with them.

Though the doors were locked, Jesus came and stood among them and said, "Peace[t] be with you!"[u] [27]Then he said to Thomas, "Put your finger here; see my hands. Reach out your hand and put it into my side. Stop doubting and believe."[v]

[28]Thomas said to him, "My Lord and my God!"

[29]Then Jesus told him, "Because you have seen me, you have believed;[w] blessed are those who have not seen and yet have believed."[x]

[30]Jesus did many other miraculous signs[y] in the presence of his disciples, which are not recorded in this book.[z] [31]But these are written that you may[g] believe[a] that Jesus is the Christ, the Son of God,[b] and that by believing you may have life in his name.[c]

Jesus and the Miraculous Catch of Fish

21 Afterward Jesus appeared again to his disciples,[d] by the Sea of Tiberias.[h][e] It happened this way: [2]Simon Peter, Thomas[f] (called Didymus), Nathanael[g] from Cana in Galilee,[h] the sons of Zebedee,[i] and two other disciples were together. [3]"I'm going out to fish," Simon Peter told them, and they said, "We'll go with you." So they went out and got into the boat, but that night they caught nothing.[j]

[4]Early in the morning, Jesus stood on

Cross references (center column):

20:17
c S Mt 28:10
d Jn 7:33
20:18 e S ver 1
f Lk 24:10,22,23
20:19 g S Jn 7:13
h S Jn 14:27 i ver 21,26;
Lk 24:36-39
20:20 j Lk 24:39, 40; Jn 19:34
k Jn 16:20,22
20:21 l ver 19
m S Jn 3:17
n Mt 28:19;
Jn 17:18
20:22 o Jn 7:39;
Ac 2:38; 8:15-17;
19:2; Gal 3:2
20:23
p Mt 16:19; 18:18
20:24
q S Jn 11:16
20:25 r ver 20
s Mk 16:11

20:26 t S Jn 14:27
u ver 21
20:27 v ver 25;
Lk 24:40
20:29 w S Jn 3:15
x 1Pe 1:8
20:30 y S Jn 2:11
z Jn 21:25
20:31 a S Jn 3:15;
19:35 b S Mt 4:3
c S Mt 25:46
21:1 d ver 14;
Jn 20:19,26
e Jn 6:1
21:2 f S Jn 11:16
g Jn 1:45 h Jn 2:1
i S Mt 4:21
21:3 j Lk 5:5

g31 Some manuscripts may continue to   h1 That is, Sea of Galilee

---

(see 1:12,14,18,34).
20:19 *disciples.* Probably includes others besides the apostles, "the Twelve" (v. 24). *the Jews.* See note on 1:19. *Peace be with you!* The normal Hebrew greeting (cf. Da 10:19). Because of their behavior the previous Friday, they may have expected rebuke and censure; but Jesus calmed their fears (see note on 14:27).
20:20 *his hands and side.* Where the wounds were (John does not refer to the wounds in the feet). According to Lk 24:37 they thought they were seeing a ghost. Jesus was clearly identifying himself.
20:21 *Peace be with you!* See note on v. 19. *I am sending you.* See note on 17:18.
20:22 *Receive the Holy Spirit.* Thus anticipating what happened 50 days later on the day of Pentecost (Ac 2). The disciples needed God's help to carry out the commission they had just been given.
20:23 Lit. "Those whose sins you forgive have already been forgiven; those whose sins you do not forgive have not been forgiven." God does not forgive people's sins because we do so, nor does he withhold forgiveness because we do. Rather, those who proclaim the gospel are in effect forgiving or not forgiving sins, depending on whether the hearers accept or reject Jesus Christ.
20:24 *Thomas.* See note on 11:16.
20:25 *Unless I see . . . and put . . . I will not believe.* Hardheaded skepticism can scarcely go further than this.

20:26 *Peace.* See vv. 19,21 and note on 14:27.
20:28 *My Lord and my God!* The high point of faith (see note on 1:1).
20:29 *those who have not seen and yet have believed.* Would have been very few at this time. All whom John mentions had seen in some sense. The words, of course, apply to future believers as well.
20:30 *miraculous signs.* See note on 2:11. John had selected from among many. *in the presence of his disciples.* Those who could testify to what he had done. John again stresses testimony (see note on 1:7).
20:31 *that you may believe.* Expresses John's evangelistic purpose. *believe.* See note on 1:7. *Jesus is the Christ, the Son of God.* Faith has content. *the Christ.* See note on 1:25. This whole Gospel is written to show the truth of Jesus' Messiahship and to present him as the Son of God, so that the readers may believe in him. *that by believing you may have life.* Another expression of purpose—to bring about faith that leads to life (see notes on 1:4; 3:15). *name.* Represents all that he is and stands for (see note on 2:23).
21:1 *Sea of Tiberias.* See note on 6:1.
21:2 *Simon Peter.* See note on Mk 1:16. *Thomas.* See note on 11:16. *sons of Zebedee.* Not named in this Gospel (see Mt 4:21).
21:3 *that night.* Nighttime was favored by fishermen in ancient times (as Aristotle, e.g., informs us).
21:4 *did not realize that it was Jesus.* Cf. Mary Magdalene

the shore, but the disciples did not realize that it was Jesus. *k*

⁵He called out to them, "Friends, haven't you any fish?"

"No," they answered.

⁶He said, "Throw your net on the right side of the boat and you will find some." When they did, they were unable to haul the net in because of the large number of fish. *l*

⁷Then the disciple whom Jesus loved *m* said to Peter, "It is the Lord!" As soon as Simon Peter heard him say, "It is the Lord," he wrapped his outer garment around him (for he had taken it off) and jumped into the water. ⁸The other disciples followed in the boat, towing the net full of fish, for they were not far from shore, about a hundred yards. *i* ⁹When they landed, they saw a fire *n* of burning coals there with fish on it, *o* and some bread.

¹⁰Jesus said to them, "Bring some of the fish you have just caught."

¹¹Simon Peter climbed aboard and dragged the net ashore. It was full of large fish, 153, but even with so many the net was not torn. ¹²Jesus said to them, "Come and have breakfast." None of the disciples dared ask him, "Who are you?" They knew it was the Lord. ¹³Jesus came, took the bread and gave it to them, and did the same with the fish. *p* ¹⁴This was now the third time Jesus appeared to his disciples *q* after he was raised from the dead.

Jesus Reinstates Peter

¹⁵When they had finished eating, Jesus

21:4 *k*Lk 24:16;
Jn 20:14
21:6 *l*Lk 5:4-7
21:7 *m*S Jn 13:23
21:9 *n*Jn 18:18
*o*ver 10,13
21:13 *p*ver 9
21:14 *q*Jn 20:19,
26

21:15 *r*Mt 26:33,
35; Jn 13:37
*s*Lk 12:32
21:16 *r*2Sa 5:2;
Eze 34:2; Mt 2:6;
S Jn 10:11;
Ac 20:28;
1Pe 5:2,3
21:17 *u*Jn 13:38
*v*Jn 16:30 *w*S ver
16
21:19 *x*Jn 12:33;
18:32 *y*Jn 13:36;
2Pe 1:14
*z*S Mt 4:19
21:20 *a*ver 7;
S Jn 13:23
*b*Jn 13:25
21:22
*c*S Mt 16:27 *d*ver
19; S Mt 4:19

---

said to Simon Peter, "Simon son of John, do you truly love me more than these?"

"Yes, Lord," he said, "you know that I love you." *r*

Jesus said, "Feed my lambs." *s*

¹⁶Again Jesus said, "Simon son of John, do you truly love me?"

He answered, "Yes, Lord, you know that I love you."

Jesus said, "Take care of my sheep." *t*

¹⁷The third time he said to him, "Simon son of John, do you love me?"

Peter was hurt because Jesus asked him the third time, "Do you love me?" *u* He said, "Lord, you know all things; *v* you know that I love you."

Jesus said, "Feed my sheep. *w* ¹⁸I tell you the truth, when you were younger you dressed yourself and went where you wanted; but when you are old you will stretch out your hands, and someone else will dress you and lead you where you do not want to go." ¹⁹Jesus said this to indicate the kind of death *x* by which Peter would glorify God. *y* Then he said to him, "Follow me!" *z*

²⁰Peter turned and saw that the disciple whom Jesus loved *a* was following them. (This was the one who had leaned back against Jesus at the supper and had said, "Lord, who is going to betray you?") *b* ²¹When Peter saw him, he asked, "Lord, what about him?"

²²Jesus answered, "If I want him to remain alive until I return, *c* what is that to you? You must follow me." *d* ²³Because of

i 8 Greek *about two hundred cubits* (about 90 meters)

(see note on 20:14).

21:7 *disciple whom Jesus loved.* See note on 13:23. *his outer garment.* It is curious that he put on this garment (the word appears only here in the NT) preparatory to jumping into the water. But Jews regarded a greeting as a religious act that could be done only when one was clothed. Peter may have been preparing himself to greet the Lord.

21:9 *burning coals.* Lit. "charcoal," as in 18:18 ("fire"; see note on 18:26).

21:11 *Peter . . . dragged the net ashore.* Appears to mean that Peter headed up the effort, for the whole group had not been able previously to haul the net into the boat (v. 6). *the net was not torn.* In contrast to the nets mentioned in Lk 5:6.

21:14 *the third time.* The third appearance to a group of disciples (20:19–23,24–29), though there had been other appearances to individuals.

21:15–17 *love.* The Greek word for "love" in Jesus' first two questions is different from that in his third question and in all Peter's answers. It is uncertain whether a distinction in meaning is intended since John often made slight word variations, apparently for stylistic reasons. Also, no distinction is made between these two words elsewhere in this Gospel. In this passage, however, they occur together, and the variations seem too deliberate to be explained on stylistic

grounds. "Truly love" refers to a love in which the entire personality, including the will, is involved. "Love" refers to spontaneous natural affection or fondness in which emotion plays a more prominent role than will. Whatever interpretation is adopted, the important thing is that in so serious a matter as the reinstatement of Peter, the great question was whether he loved Jesus.

21:15 *more than these.* May mean "more than you love these men" or "more than these men love me" or "more than you love these things" (i.e., the fishing gear). Perhaps the second is best, for Peter had claimed a devotion above that of the others (cf. 13:37; Mt 26:33; Mk 14:29). Peter did not take up the comparison, and Jesus did not explain it. *Feed my lambs.* Probably means much the same as "Take care of my sheep" (v. 16) and "Feed my sheep" (v. 17).

21:17 *you know all things.* Peter's replies stress Christ's knowledge, not his own grasp of the situation.

21:18 *stretch out your hands.* The early church understood this as a prophecy of crucifixion.

21:19 *the kind of death.* Peter would be a martyr. Tradition indicates that he was crucified upside down.

21:20 *disciple whom Jesus loved.* See note on 13:23. *was following.* He was doing what Peter was twice told to do (vv. 19,22). *at the supper.* See 13:23–25.

21:22 *until I return.* A clear declaration of the second

this, the rumor spread among the brothers *e* that this disciple would not die. But Jesus did not say that he would not die; he only said, "If I want him to remain alive until I return, what is that to you?"

24This is the disciple who testifies to

coming.

these things *f* and who wrote them down. We know that his testimony is true. *g*

25Jesus did many other things as well. *h* If every one of them were written down, I suppose that even the whole world would not have room for the books that would be written.

21:23 *e*S Ac 1:16

21:24 *f*S Jn 15:27
*g*Jn 19:35
21:25 *h*Jn 20:30

21:24 *disciple who testifies.* Testimony is important throughout this Gospel (see note on 1:7). We now learn that it was the beloved disciple who was the witness behind the account. *these things.* Must refer to the whole book. *who wrote them down.* The beloved disciple was not only the witness but also the actual author. *We know.* Evidently written by contemporaries in a position to know the truth. **21:25** *many other things.* As in 20:30 we are assured that the author has been selective. *even the whole world would not have room.* Our historical knowledge of Jesus is at best partial, but we have been given all we need to know.

Major Archaeological Finds
Relating to the NT

SITE OR ARTIFACT	LOCATION	RELATING SCRIPTURE
ISRAEL		
Herod's temple	Jerusalem	Lk 1:9
Herod's winter palace	Jericho	Mt 2:4
The Herodium (possible site of Herod's tomb)	Near Bethlehem	Mt 2:19
Masada	Southwest of Dead Sea	cf. Lk 21:20
Early synagogue	Capernaum	Mk 1:21
Pool of Siloam	Jerusalem	Jn 9:7
Pool of Bethesda	Jerusalem	Jn 5:2
Pilate inscription	Caesarea	Lk 3:1
Inscription: Gentile entrance of temple sanctuary	Jerusalem	Ac 21:27-29
Skeletal remains of crucified man	Jerusalem	Lk 23:33
Peter's house	Capernaum	Mt 8:14
Jacob's well	Nablus	Jn 4:5-6
ASIA MINOR		
Derbe inscription	Kerti Hüyük	Ac 14:20
Sergius Paulus inscription	Antioch in Pisidia	Ac 13:6-7
Zeus altar (Satan's throne?)	Pergamum	Rev 2:13
Fourth-century B.C. walls	Assos	Ac 20:13-14
Artemis temple and altar	Ephesus	Ac 19:27-28
Ephesian theater	Ephesus	Ac 19:29
Silversmith shops	Ephesus	Ac 19:24
Artemis statues	Ephesus	Ac 19:35
GREECE		
Erastus inscription	Corinth	Ro 16:23
Synagogue inscription	Corinth	Ac 18:4
Meat market inscription	Corinth	1Co 10:25
Cult dining rooms (in Asklepius and Demeter temples)	Corinth	1Co 8:10
Court (*bema*)	Corinth	Ac 18:12
Marketplace (*bema*)	Philippi	Ac 16:19
Starting gate for races	Isthmia	1Co 9:24,26
Gallio inscription	Delphi	Ac 18:12
Egnatian Way	Kavalla (Neapolis), Philippi, Apollonia, Thessalonica	Cf. Ac 16:11-12; 17:1
Politarch inscription	Thessalonica	Ac 17:6
ITALY		
Tomb of Augustus	Rome	Lk 2:1
Mamertime Prison	Rome	2Ti 1:16-17; 2:9; 4:6-8
Appian Way	Puteoli to Rome	Ac 28:13-16
Golden House of Nero	Rome	Cf. Ac 25:10; 1Pe 2:13
Arch of Titus	Rome	Cf. Lk 19:43-44; 21:6,20

ACTS

Author

Although the author does not name himself, evidence outside the Scriptures and inferences from the book itself lead to the conclusion that the author was Luke.

The earliest of the external testimonies appears in the Muratorian Canon (c. A.D. 170), where the explicit statement is made that Luke was the author of both the third Gospel and the "Acts of All the Apostles." Eusebius (c. 325) lists information from numerous sources to identify the author of these books as Luke (*Ecclesiastical History,* 3.4).

Within the writing itself are some clues as to who the author was:

1. *Luke, the companion of Paul.* In the description of the happenings in Acts, certain passages make use of the pronoun "we." At these points the author includes himself as a companion of Paul in his travels (16:10-17; 20:5-15; 21:1-18; 27:1-28:16). A historian as careful with details as this author proves to be would have good reason for choosing to use "we" in some places and "they" elsewhere. The author was therefore probably present with Paul at the particular events described in the "we" sections.

These "we" passages include the period of Paul's two-year imprisonment at Rome (ch. 28). During this time Paul wrote, among other letters, Philemon and Colossians. In them he sends greetings from his companions, and Luke is included among them (Phm 23-24; Col 4:10-17). In fact, after eliminating those who, for one reason or another, would not fit the requirements for the author of Acts, Luke is left as the most likely candidate.

2. *Luke, the physician.* Although it cannot be proved that the author of Acts was a physician simply from his vocabulary, the words he uses and the traits and education reflected in his writings fit well his role as a physician (see, e.g., note on 28:6). It is true that the doctor of the first century did not have as specialized a vocabulary as that of doctors today, but there are some usages in Luke-Acts that seem to suggest that a medical man was the author of these books. And it should be remembered that Paul uses the term "doctor" in describing Luke (Col 4:14).

Date

Two dates are possible for the writing of this book: (1) c. A.D. 63, soon after the last event recorded in the book, and (2) c. 70 or even later.

The earlier date is supported by:

1. *Silence about later events.* While arguments from silence are not conclusive, it is perhaps significant that the book contains no allusion to events that happened after the close of Paul's two-year imprisonment in Rome: e.g., the burning of Rome and the persecution of the Christians there (A.D. 64), the martyrdom of Peter and Paul (possibly 67) and the destruction of Jerusalem (70).

2. *No outcome of Paul's trial.* If Luke knew the outcome of the trial Paul was waiting for (28:30), why did he not record it at the close of Acts? Perhaps it was because he had brought the history up to date.

Those who prefer the later date hold that 1:8 reveals one of the purposes Luke had in writing his history, and that this purpose influenced the way the book ended. Luke wanted to show how the church penetrated the world of his day in ever-widening circles (Jerusalem, Judea, Samaria, the ends of the earth) until it reached Rome, the world's political and cultural center. On this understanding, mention of the martyrdom of Paul (c. A.D. 67) and of the destruction of Jerusalem (70) was not pertinent. This would allow for the writing of Acts c. 70 or even later.

Recipient

The recipient of the book, Theophilus, is the same person addressed in the first volume, the Gospel of Luke (see Introduction to Luke: Recipient and Purpose).

Importance

The book of Acts provides a bridge for the writings of the NT. As a second volume to Luke's Gospel, it joins what Jesus "began to do and to teach" (1:1) as told in the Gospels with what he continued to do and teach through the apostles' preaching and the establishment of the church. Besides linking the Gospel narratives on the one hand and the apostolic letters on the other, it supplies an account of the life of Paul from which we can learn the setting for his letters. Geographically its story spans the lands between Jerusalem, where the church began, and Rome, the political center of the empire. Historically it recounts the first 30 years of the church. It is also a bridge that ties the church in its beginning with each succeeding age. This book may be studied to gain an understanding of the principles that ought to govern the church of any age.

Theme and Purpose

The theme of the work is best summarized in 1:8. It was ordinary procedure for a historian at this time to begin a second volume by summarizing the first volume and indicating the contents anticipated in his second volume. Luke summarized his first volume in 1:1-3; the theme of his second volume is presented in the words of Jesus: "You will be my witnesses in Jerusalem, and in all Judea and Samaria, and to the ends of the earth." This is, in effect, an outline of the book of Acts (see Plan and Outline).

The main purposes of the book appear to be:

1. *To present a history.* The significance of Acts as a historical account of Christian origins cannot be overestimated. It tells of the founding of the church, the spread of the gospel, the beginnings of congregations, and evangelistic efforts in the apostolic pattern. One of the unique aspects of Christianity is its firm historical foundation. The life and teachings of Jesus Christ are established in the four Gospel narratives, and the book of Acts provides a coordinated account of the beginnings of the church.

2. *To give a defense.* One finds embedded in Acts a record of Christian defenses made to both Jews (e.g., 4:8-12) and Gentiles (e.g., 25:8-11), with the underlying purpose of conversion. It shows how the early church coped with pagan and Jewish thought, the Roman government and Hellenistic society.

Luke probably wrote this work as Paul awaited trial in Rome. If his case came to court, what better court brief could Paul have had than a life of Jesus, a history of the beginnings of the church (including the activity of Paul) and an early collection of Paul's letters?

3. *To provide a guide.* Luke had no way of knowing how long the church would continue on this earth, but as long as it pursues its course, the book of Acts will be one of its major guides. In Acts we see basic principles being applied to specific situations in the context of problems and persecutions. These same principles continue to be applicable until Christ returns.

4. *To depict the triumph of Christianity in the face of bitter persecution.* The success of the church in carrying the gospel from Jerusalem to Rome and in planting local churches across the Roman empire demonstrated that Christianity was not a mere work of man. God was in it (see 5:35-39).

Characteristics

1. *Accurate historical detail.* Every page of Acts abounds with sharp, precise details, to the delight of the historian. The account covers a period of about 30 years and reaches across the lands from Jerusalem to Rome. Luke's description of these times and places is filled with all kinds of people and cultures, a variety of governmental administrations, court scenes in Caesarea, and dramatic events involving such centers as Antioch, Ephesus, Athens, Corinth and Rome. Barbarian country districts and Jewish centers are included as well. Yet in each instance archaeological findings reveal that Luke uses the proper terms for the time and place being described. Hostile criticism has not succeeded in disproving the detailed accuracy of Luke's political and geographical designations.

2. *Literary excellence.* Not only does Luke have a large vocabulary compared with other NT writers, but he also uses these words in literary styles that fit the cultural settings of the events he is recording. At times he employs good, classical Greek; at other times the Aramaic of first-century Palestine shows through his expressions. This is an indication of Luke's careful practice of using language appropriate to the time and place being described. Aramaisms are used when Luke is describing happenings that took place in Palestine (chs. 1-12). When, however, Paul departs for Hellenistic lands beyond the territories where Aramaic-speaking people live, Aramaisms cease.

3. *Dramatic description.* Luke's skillful use of speeches contributes to the drama of his narrative. Not only are they carefully spaced and well balanced between Peter and Paul, but the speeches of a number of other individuals add variety and vividness to the account. Luke's use of details brings the

action to life. Nowhere in ancient literature is there an account of a shipwreck superior to Luke's with its nautical details (ch. 27). The book is vivid and fast-moving throughout.

4. *Objective account.* Luke's careful arrangement of material need not detract from the accuracy of his record. He demonstrates the objectivity of his account by recording the failures as well as the successes, the bad as well as the good, in the early church. Not only is the discontent between the Grecian Jews and the Hebraic Jews recorded (6:1) but also the discord between Paul and Barnabas (15:39). Divisions and differences are recognized (15:2; 21:20-21).

Plan and Outline

Luke weaves together different interests and emphases as he relates the beginnings and expansion of the church. The design of his book revolves around (1) key persons: Peter and Paul; (2) important topics and events: the role of the Holy Spirit, pioneer missionary outreach to new fields, conversions, the growth of the church, and life in the Christian community; (3) significant problems: conflict between Jews and Gentiles, persecution of the church by some Jewish elements, trials before Jews and Romans, confrontations with Gentiles, and other hardships in the ministry; (4) geographical advances: five significant stages (see the quotations in the outline; see also map of "The Spread of the Gospel," p. 1668).

I. Peter and the Beginnings of the Church in Palestine (chs. 1-12)
   A. "Throughout Judea, Galilee and Samaria" (1:1-9:31; see 9:31)
      1. Introduction (1:1-2)
      2. Christ's postresurrection ministry (1:3-11)
      3. The period of waiting for the Holy Spirit (1:12-26)
      4. The filling with the Spirit (ch. 2)
      5. The healing of the lame man and the resultant arrest of Peter and John (3:1-4:31)
      6. The community of goods (4:32-5:11)
      7. The arrest of the 12 apostles (5:12-42)
      8. The choice of the Seven (6:1-7)
      9. Stephen's arrest and martyrdom (6:8-7:60)
      10. The scattering of the Jerusalem believers (8:1-4)
      11. Philip's ministry (8:5-40)
        a. In Samaria (8:5-25)
        b. To the Ethiopian eunuch (8:26-40)
      12. Saul's conversion (9:1-31)
   B. "As far as Phoenicia, Cyprus and Antioch"(9:32-12:25; see 11:19)
      1. Peter's ministry on the Mediterranean coast (9:32-11:18)
        a. To Aeneas and Dorcas (9:32-43)
        b. To Cornelius (10:1-11:18)
      2. The new Gentile church in Antioch (11:19-30)
      3. Herod's persecution of the church and his subsequent death (ch. 12)
II. Paul and the Expansion of the Church from Antioch to Rome (chs. 13-28)
   A. "Throughout the region of Phrygia and Galatia" (13:1-15:35; see 16:6)
      1. Paul's first missionary journey (chs. 13-14)
      2. The Jerusalem conference (15:1-35)
   B. "Over to Macedonia" (15:36-21:16; see 16:9)
      1. Paul's second missionary journey (15:36-18:22)
      2. Paul's third missionary journey (18:23-21:16)
   C. "To Rome" (21:17-28:31; see 28:14)
      1. Paul's imprisonment in Jerusalem (21:17-23:35)
        a. Arrest (21:17-22:29)
        b. Trial before the Sanhedrin (22:30-23:11)
        c. Transfer to Caesarea (23:12-35)
      2. Paul's imprisonment in Caesarea (chs. 24-26)
        a. Trial before Felix (ch. 24)
        b. Trial before Festus (25:1-12)
        c. Hearing before Festus and Agrippa (25:13-26:32)
      3. Voyage to Rome (27:1-28:15)
      4. Two years under house arrest in Rome (28:16-31)

Jesus Taken Up Into Heaven

1 In my former book,[a] Theophilus, I wrote about all that Jesus began to do and to teach[b] [2]until the day he was taken up to heaven,[c] after giving instructions[d] through the Holy Spirit to the apostles[e] he had chosen.[f] [3]After his suffering, he showed himself to these men and gave many convincing proofs that he was alive. He appeared to them[g] over a period of forty days and spoke about the kingdom of God.[h] [4]On one occasion, while he was eating with them, he gave them this command: "Do not leave Jerusalem, but wait[i] for the gift my Father promised, which you have heard me speak about.[j] [5]For John baptized with[a] water,[k] but in a few days you will be baptized with the Holy Spirit."[l]

[6]So when they met together, they asked him, "Lord, are you at this time going to restore[m] the kingdom to Israel?"

[7]He said to them: "It is not for you to know the times or dates the Father has set by his own authority.[n] [8]But you will receive power when the Holy Spirit comes on you;[o] and you will be my witnesses[p]

in Jerusalem, and in all Judea and Samaria,[q] and to the ends of the earth."[r]

[9]After he said this, he was taken up[s] before their very eyes, and a cloud hid him from their sight.

[10]They were looking intently up into the sky as he was going, when suddenly two men dressed in white[t] stood beside them. [11]"Men of Galilee,"[u] they said, "why do you stand here looking into the sky? This same Jesus, who has been taken from you into heaven, will come back[v] in the same way you have seen him go into heaven."

Matthias Chosen to Replace Judas

[12]Then they returned to Jerusalem[w] from the hill called the Mount of Olives,[x] a Sabbath day's walk[b] from the city. [13]When they arrived, they went upstairs to the room[y] where they were staying. Those present were Peter, John, James and Andrew; Philip and Thomas, Bartholomew and Matthew; James son of Alphaeus and Simon the Zealot, and Judas son of James.[z] [14]They all joined together constantly in

Cross references (center column)

1:1 aLk 1:1-4
bLk 3:23
1:2 cver 9,11;
S Mk 16:19
dMt 28:19,20
eS Mk 6:30
fJn 13:18; 15:16,
19
1:3 gMt 28:17;
Lk 24:34,36;
Jn 20:19,26;
21:1,14; 1 Co
15:5-7 hS Mt 3:2
1:4 iPs 27:14
/Lk 24:49;
Jn 14:16; Ac 2:33
1:5 kS Mk 1:4
/S Mk 1:8
1:6 mMt 17:11;
Ac 3:21
1:7 nDt 29:29;
Ps 102:13;
Mt 24:36
1:8 oAc 2:1-4
pS Lk 24:48

qAc 8:1-25
rS Mt 28:19
1:9 sver 2;
S Mk 16:19
1:10 tS Jn 20:12
1:11 uAc 2:7
vS Mt 16:27
1:12 wLk 24:52
xS Mt 21:1
1:13 yAc 9:37;
20:8 zMt 10:2-4;
Mk 3:16-19;
Lk 6:14-16

a5 Or in   b12 That is, about 3/4 mile (about 1,100 meters)

1:1 *my former book.* The Gospel of Luke. Acts was addressed to the same patron, Theophilus (see Introduction to Luke: Recipient and Purpose). *began to do and to teach.* An apt summation of Luke's Gospel, implying that Jesus' work continues in Acts through his own personal interventions and the ministry of the Holy Spirit.

1:2 *taken up to heaven.* The last scene of Luke's Gospel (24:50–52) and the opening scene of this second volume (vv. 6–11). The ascension occurred 40 days after the resurrection (v. 3). *through the Holy Spirit.* Jesus' postresurrection instruction of his apostles was carried on through the Holy Spirit, and succeeding statements make it clear that what the apostles were to accomplish was likewise to be done through the Spirit (vv. 4–5,8; see Lk 24:49; Jn 20:22; see also Introduction to Judges: Theme and Theology). Luke characteristically stresses the Holy Spirit's work and enabling power (e.g., v. 8; 2:4,17; 4:8,31; 5:3; 6:3,5; 7:55; 8:16; 9:17,31; 10:44; 13:2,4; 15:28; 16:6; 19:2,6; see note on Lk 4:1).

1:3 *many convincing proofs.* See the resurrection appearances (Mt 28:1–20; Lk 24:1–53; Jn 20:1–29; 1Co 15:3–8). *kingdom of God.* The heart of Jesus' preaching (see notes on Mt 3:2; Lk 4:43).

1:4 *the gift my Father promised.* The Holy Spirit (see Jn 14:26; 15:26–27; 16:12–13).

1:5 *John baptized with water.* See Lk 3:16. *in a few days.* The day of Pentecost came ten days later, when the baptism with the Holy Spirit occurred (2:1–4).

1:6 *restore the kingdom to Israel?* Like their fellow countrymen, they were looking for the deliverance of the people of Israel from foreign domination and for the establishment of an earthly kingdom. The reference to the coming of the Spirit had caused them to wonder if the new age was about to dawn.

1:7 *the times or dates.* The elapsing time or the character of coming events (see 1Th 5:1).

1:8 A virtual outline of Acts: The apostles were to be witnesses in Jerusalem (chs. 1–7), Judea and Samaria (chs. 8–9) and the ends of the earth—including Caesarea, Antioch, Asia Minor, Greece and Rome (chs. 10–28). However, they were not to begin this staggering task until they had been equipped with the power of the Spirit (vv. 4–5). *my witnesses.* An important theme throughout Acts (2:32; 3:15; 5:32; 10:39; 13:31; 22:15). *Judea.* The region in which Jerusalem was located. *Samaria.* The adjoining region to the north.

1:10 *two men dressed in white.* A common description of angels.

1:11 *Men of Galilee.* All the Twelve were from Galilee except Judas, and he was no longer present. *in the same way.* In the same resurrection body and in clouds and "great glory" (Mt 24:30).

1:12 *Mount of Olives.* The ascension occurred on the eastern slope of the mount between Jerusalem and Bethany (Lk 19:28–29,37; see notes on Zec 14:4; Mk 11:1; Lk 19:29). *Sabbath day's walk.* See NIV text note. This distance was drawn from rabbinical reasoning based on several OT passages (Ex 16:29; Nu 35:5; Jos 3:4). A faithful Jew was to travel no farther on the Sabbath.

1:13 *room.* Probably an upper room of a large house, such as the one where the Last Supper was held (Mk 14:15) or that of Mary, mother of Mark (see note on 12:12). *Bartholomew.* Apparently John calls him Nathanael (see Jn 1:45–49; 21:2). *James son of Alphaeus.* The same as James the younger (Mk 15:40). *Zealot.* See note on Mt 10:4. *Judas son of James.* Not Judas Iscariot, but the same as Thaddaeus (Mt 10:3; Mk 3:18).

1:14 *with the women.* Possibly wives of the apostles (cf. 1Co 9:5) and those listed as ministering to Jesus (Mt 27:55; Lk 8:2–3; 24:22). *Mary the mother of Jesus.* Last mentioned here in Scripture. *brothers.* See note on Lk 8:19. These brothers would include James, who later became important in the church (12:17; 15:13; Gal 2:9).

prayer, [a] along with the women [b] and Mary the mother of Jesus, and with his brothers. [c]

[15] In those days Peter stood up among the believers [c] (a group numbering about a hundred and twenty) [16] and said, "Brothers, [d] the Scripture had to be fulfilled [e] which the Holy Spirit spoke long ago through the mouth of David concerning Judas, [f] who served as guide for those who arrested Jesus— [17] he was one of our number [g] and shared in this ministry." [h]

[18] (With the reward [i] he got for his wickedness, Judas bought a field; [j] there he fell headlong, his body burst open and all his intestines spilled out. [19] Everyone in Jerusalem heard about this, so they called that field in their language [k] Akeldama, that is, Field of Blood.)

[20] "For," said Peter, "it is written in the book of Psalms,

" 'May his place be deserted;
    let there be no one to dwell in it,' [d] [l]

and,

" 'May another take his place of
    leadership.' [e] [m]

[21] Therefore it is necessary to choose one of the men who have been with us the whole time the Lord Jesus went in and out among us, [22] beginning from John's baptism [n] to the time when Jesus was taken up from us. For one of these must become a witness [o] with us of his resurrection."

[23] So they proposed two men: Joseph called Barsabbas (also known as Justus) and Matthias. [24] Then they prayed, [p] "Lord, you know everyone's heart. [q] Show us [r] which of these two you have chosen [25] to take over this apostolic ministry, which Judas left to go where he belongs." [26] Then they cast lots, and the lot fell to Matthias; so he was added to the eleven apostles. [s]

The Holy Spirit Comes at Pentecost

2 When the day of Pentecost [t] came, they were all together [u] in one place. [2] Suddenly a sound like the blowing of a violent wind came from heaven and filled the whole house where they were sitting. [v] [3] They saw what seemed to be tongues of fire that separated and came to rest on each of them. [4] All of them were filled with

Cross references (center column):

1:14 aAc 2:42; 4:24; 6:4; S Lk 18:1; S Ro 1:10
bLk 23:49,55
cS Mt 12:46
1:16 dAc 6:3; 11:1,12,29; 14:2; 18:18,27; 21:7; S 22:5; S Ro 7:1
ever 20;
S Mt 1:22
/S Mt 10:4
1:17 gJn 6:70,71
hver 25
1:18 iMt 26:14,15 /Mt 27:3-10
1:19 kS Jn 5:2
1:20 /Ps 69:25
mPs 109:8

1:22 nS Mk 1:4
over 8;
S Lk 24:48
1:24 pAc 6:6; 13:3; 14:23
qS Rev 2:23
rlSa 14:41
1:26 sAc 2:14
2:1 tLev 23:15,16; Ac 20:16;
1Co 16:8
uAc 1:14
2:2 vAc 4:31

c15 Greek brothers   d20 Psalm 69:25   e20 Psalm 109:8

1:16 *the Scripture had to be fulfilled.* For the Scripture referred to see NIV text notes on v. 20. Both before and after Christ came, numerous psalms were viewed as Messianic. What happened in the psalmist's experience was typical of the experiences of the Messiah. No doubt Jesus' instruction in Lk 24:27,45–47 included these Scriptures.

1:18 *Judas bought a field.* Judas bought the field indirectly: The money he returned to the priests (Mt 27:3) was used to purchase the potter's field (Mt 27:7). *fell headlong.* Mt 27:5 reports that Judas hanged himself. It appears that when the body finally fell, either because of decay or because someone cut it down, it was in a decomposed condition and so broke open in the middle. Another possibility is that "hanged" in Mt 27:5 means "impaled" (see NIV text note on Est 2:23) and that the gruesome results of Judas's suicide are described here.

1:19 *Akeldama.* An Aramaic term, no doubt adopted by people who knew the circumstances, for the field was purchased with Judas's blood money (Mt 27:3–8).

1:20 *it is written.* Two passages of Scripture (see NIV text notes) were put together to suggest that Judas had left a vacancy that had to be filled.

1:21 *went in and out among us.* Ministered publicly.

1:22 *a witness with us of his resurrection.* Apparently several met this requirement. On this occasion, however, the believers were selecting someone to become an official witness to the resurrection—thus, a 12th apostle (v. 25).

1:23 *Barsabbas.* Means "son of (the) Sabbath." This patronymic was used for two early Jewish Christians, possibly brothers. One was Joseph (here); the other was Judas, a prophet in Jerusalem who was sent to Antioch with Silas (15:22,32). *Justus.* Joseph's Hellenistic name. Nothing more is known of him.

1:26 *cast lots.* See Pr 16:33. By casting lots they were able to allow God the right of choice. The use of rocks or sticks to designate the choice was common (see 1Ch 26:13–16; see

also notes on Ne 11:1; Jnh 1:7). This is the Bible's last mention of casting lots.

2:1 *day of Pentecost.* The 50th day after the Sabbath of Passover week (Lev 23:15–16), thus the first day of the week. Pentecost is also called the Feast of Weeks (Dt 16:10), the Feast of Harvest (Ex 23:16) and the day of firstfruits (Nu 28:26). *they were all together.* The nearest antecedent of "they" is the 11 apostles (plus Matthias), but the reference is probably to all those mentioned in 1:13–15. *in one place.* Evidently not the upstairs room where they were staying (1:13) but perhaps some place in the temple precincts, for the apostles were "continually at the temple" when it was open (Lk 24:53; see note there).

2:2 *violent wind.* Breath or wind is a symbol of the Spirit of God (see Eze 37:9,14; Jn 3:8). The coming of the Spirit is marked by audible (wind) and visible (fire) signs. *whole house.* May refer to the temple (cf. 7:47).

2:3 *tongues.* A descriptive metaphor appropriate to the context, in which several languages are about to be spoken. *fire.* A symbol of the divine presence (see Ex 3:2 and note), it was also associated with judgment (see Mt 3:12).

2:4 *All of them.* Could refer either to the apostles or to the 120. Those holding that the 120 are meant point to the fulfillment of Joel's prophecy (vv. 17–18) as involving more than the 12 apostles. The nearest reference, however, is to the apostles (see note on v. 1), and the narrative continues with Peter and the 11 standing to address the crowd (v. 14). *filled with the Holy Spirit.* A fulfillment of 1:5,8; see also Jesus' promise in Lk 24:49. Their spirits were completely under the control of the Spirit; their words were his words. *in other tongues.* The Spirit enabled them to speak in languages they had not previously learned (see NIV text note). Two other examples of speaking in tongues are found in Acts (10:46; 19:6). One extended NT passage deals with this spiritual gift (1Co 12–14). Not all agree, however, that these other passages refer to speaking in known languages. The gift

the Holy Spirit[w] and began to speak in other tongues[f][x] as the Spirit enabled them.

[5]Now there were staying in Jerusalem God-fearing[y] Jews from every nation under heaven. [6]When they heard this sound, a crowd came together in bewilderment, because each one heard them speaking in his own language. [7]Utterly amazed,[z] they asked: "Are not all these men who are speaking Galileans?[a] [8]Then how is it that each of us hears them in his own native language? [9]Parthians, Medes and Elamites; residents of Mesopotamia, Judea and Cappadocia,[b] Pontus[c] and Asia,[d] [10]Phrygia[e] and Pamphylia,[f] Egypt and the parts of Libya near Cyrene;[g] visitors from Rome [11](both Jews and converts to Judaism); Cretans and Arabs—we hear them declaring the wonders of God in our own

tongues!" [12]Amazed and perplexed, they asked one another, "What does this mean?"

[13]Some, however, made fun of them and said, "They have had too much wine.[g]"[h]

Peter Addresses the Crowd

[14]Then Peter stood up with the Eleven, raised his voice and addressed the crowd: "Fellow Jews and all of you who live in Jerusalem, let me explain this to you; listen carefully to what I say. [15]These men are not drunk, as you suppose. It's only nine in the morning![i] [16]No, this is what was spoken by the prophet Joel:

[17]" 'In the last days, God says,

Cross references
2:4 [w]S Lk 1:15; [x]S Mk 16:17
2:5 [y]Lk 2:25; Ac 8:2
2:7 [z]ver 12
[a]Ac 1:11
2:9 [b]1Pe 1:1
[c]Ac 18:2; 1Pe 1:1
[d]Ac 16:6; 19:10; Ro 16:5; 1Co 16:19; 2Co 1:8; Rev 1:4
2:10 [e]Ac 16:6; 18:23 [f]Ac 13:13; 14:24; 15:38
[g]S Mt 27:32

2:13 [h]1Co 14:23; Eph 5:18
2:15 [i]1Th 5:7

[f]4 Or *languages*; also in verse 11　　[g]13 Or *sweet wine*

had particular relevance here, where people of different nationalities and languages were gathered.
2:5 *God-fearing Jews.* Devout Jews from different parts of the world but assembled now in Jerusalem either as visitors or as current residents (cf. Lk 2:25).
2:6 *speaking in his own language.* Jews from different parts

of the world would understand the Aramaic of their homeland. Also the Greek language was common to all parts of the world. But more than this was occurring; they heard the apostles speak in languages native to the different places represented.
2:9 *Parthians.* Inhabitants of the territory from the Tigris to

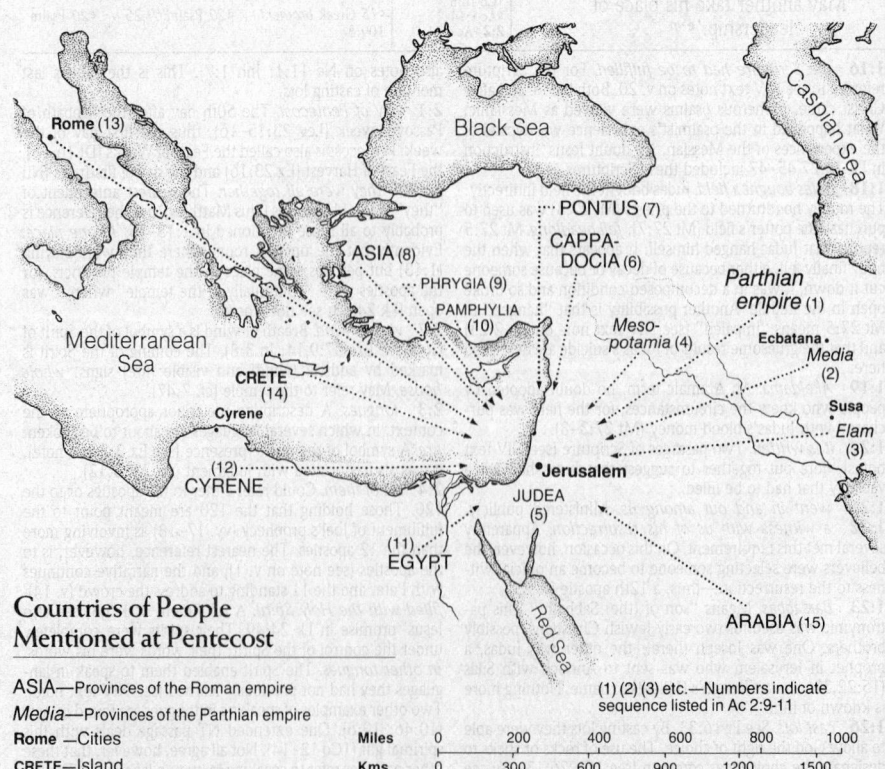

Countries of People Mentioned at Pentecost

ASIA—Provinces of the Roman empire
Media—Provinces of the Parthian empire
Rome —Cities
CRETE—Island

(1) (2) (3) etc.—Numbers indicate sequence listed in Ac 2:9-11

| | Miles | 0 | 200 | 400 | 600 | 800 | 1000 |
| | Kms | 0 | 300 | 600 | 900 | 1200 | 1500 |

I will pour out my Spirit on all
people. /
Your sons and daughters will
prophesy, *k*
your young men will see visions,
your old men will dream dreams.
18Even on my servants, both men and
women,
I will pour out my Spirit in those
days,
and they will prophesy. /
19I will show wonders in the heaven
above
and signs on the earth below, *m*
blood and fire and billows of smoke.
20The sun will be turned to darkness
and the moon to blood *n*
before the coming of the great and
glorious day of the Lord.
21And everyone who calls
on the name of the Lord *o* will be
saved.' *h p*

22"Men of Israel, listen to this: Jesus of
Nazareth *q* was a man accredited by God
to you by miracles, wonders and signs, *r*
which God did among you through him, *s*
as you yourselves know. 23This man was
handed over to you by God's set purpose
and foreknowledge; *t* and you, with the
help of wicked men, *i* put him to death by
nailing him to the cross. *u* 24But God raised
him from the dead, *v* freeing him from the
agony of death, because it was impossible

for death to keep its hold on him. *w* 25David
said about him:

" 'I saw the Lord always before me.
Because he is at my right hand,
I will not be shaken.
26Therefore my heart is glad and my
tongue rejoices;
my body also will live in hope,
27because you will not abandon me to the
grave,
nor will you let your Holy One see
decay. *x*
28You have made known to me the paths
of life;
you will fill me with joy in your
presence.'*j y*

29"Brothers, *z* I can tell you confidently
that the patriarch *a* David died and was
buried, *b* and his tomb is here *c* to this day.
30But he was a prophet and knew that God
had promised him on oath that he would
place one of his descendants on his
throne. *d* 31Seeing what was ahead, he
spoke of the resurrection of the Christ, *k*
that he was not abandoned to the grave,
nor did his body see decay. *e* 32God has
raised this Jesus to life, *f* and we are all
witnesses *g* of the fact. 33Exalted *h* to the

Cross references (center column):

2:17 /Nu 11:25;
Isa 44:3;
Eze 39:29;
Jn 7:37-39;
Ac 10:45
*k*S Ac 21:9
2:18 /Ac 21:9-12
2:19 *m*Lk 21:11
2:20 *n*S Mt 24:29
2:21 *o*Ge 4:26;
26:25; Ps 105:1;
Ac 9:14; 1Co 1:2;
2Ti 2:22 *p*Joel
2:28-32;
Ro 10:13
2:22 *q*S Mk 1:24
*r*S Jn 4:48
*s*S Jn 3:2
2:23 *t*Isa 53:10;
Ac 3:18; 4:28
*u*Mt 16:21;
Lk 24:20; Ac 3:13
2:24 *v*ver 32;
Ac 13:30,33,34,
37; 17:31;
Ro 6:4; 8:11;
10:9; 1Co 6:14;
15:15; Eph 1:20;
Col 2:12;
Heb 13:20;
1Pe 1:21

*w*Jn 20:9
2:27 *x*ver 31;
Ac 13:35
2:28 *y*Ps 16:8-11
2:29 *z*S Ac 22:5
*a*Ac 7:8,9
*b*Ac 13:36;
1Ki 2:10
*c*Ne 3:16
2:30 *d*S Mt 1:1
2:31 *e*Ps 16:10
2:32 *f*S ver 24
*g*S Lk 24:48
2:33 *h*S Php 2:9

Text notes:

h21 Joel 2:28-32   *i23* Or of those not having the law
(that is, Gentiles)   *j28* Psalm 16:8-11   *k31* Or
Messiah. "The Christ" (Greek) and "the Messiah"
(Hebrew) both mean "the Anointed One"; also in verse
36.

India. *Medes. Elamites.* Media lay east of Mesopotamia, northwest of
Persia and south-southwest of the Caspian Sea. *Elamites.*
Elam was north of the Persian Gulf, bounded on the west by
the Tigris. *Mesopotamia.* Between the Euphrates and Tigris
rivers. *Judea.* The homeland of the Jews, perhaps used here
in the OT sense "from the river of Egypt to . . . the Euphrates" (Ge 15:18), including Galilee. *Cappadocia, Pontus and
Asia.* Districts in Asia Minor.
2:10 *Phrygia and Pamphylia.* Districts in Asia Minor.
Egypt. Contained a great number of Jews. Two out of the five
districts of Alexandria were Jewish. *Libya.* A region west of
Egypt. *Cyrene.* The capital of a district of Libya called
Cyrenaica. *Rome.* Thousands of Jews lived in Rome.
2:11 *converts to Judaism.* Gentiles who undertook the full
observance of the Mosaic law were received into full fellowship with the Jews. *Cretans.* Represented an island lying
south-southeast of Greece. *Arabs.* From a region to the east.
The kingdom of the Nabatean Arabs lay between the Red Sea
and the Euphrates, with Petra as its capital. *we hear them
declaring.* Not a miracle of hearing but of speaking. The
believers were declaring God's wonders in the native languages of the various visiting Jews.
2:14-40 The pattern and themes of the message that
follows became common in the early church: (1) an explanation of events (vv. 14–21); (2) the gospel of Jesus Christ—his
death, resurrection and exaltation (vv. 22–36); (3) an exhortation to repentance and baptism (vv. 37–40). The outline of
this sermon is similar to those in chs. 3; 10; 13.
2:14 *with the Eleven.* The apostles had been baptized with
the Holy Spirit and had spoken in other languages to various

groups. Now they stood with Peter, who served as their
spokesman.
2:15 *only nine in the morning!* On a festival day such as
Pentecost, the Jew would not break his fast until at least
10:00 A.M. So it was extremely unlikely that a group of men
would be drunk at such an early hour.
2:17–18 *all people . . . sons . . . daughters . . . young men
. . . old men . . . men . . . women.* The Spirit is bestowed on
all, irrespective of sex, age and rank.
2:17 *last days.* See Isa 2:2; Hos 3:5; Mic 4:1; see also
notes on 1Ti 4:1; 2Ti 3:1; Heb 1:1; 1Pe 1:20; 1Jn 2:18. In
the passage quoted from Joel the Hebrew has "afterward"
and the Septuagint "after these things." Peter interprets the
passage as referring specifically to the latter days of the new
covenant (see Jer 31:33–34; Eze 36:26–27; 39:29) in contrast to the former days of the old covenant. The age of
Messianic fulfillment has arrived. *my Spirit.* See note on 1:2.
2:21 *everyone who calls.* Cf. v. 39; includes faith and
response rather than merely using words (Mt 7:21).
2:22 *accredited . . . by miracles, wonders and signs.* The
mighty works done by Jesus were signs that the Messiah had
come.
2:23 *wicked men.* See NIV text note; here, however, the
Gentiles were acting in an evil way.
2:27 *not abandon me to the grave.* David referred ultimately to the Messiah (v. 31). God would not allow his
physical body to decompose.
2:29 *his tomb is here.* The tomb of David could be seen in
Jerusalem. It still contained the remains of David's body. The
words of Ps 16:8–11 did not fully apply to him.

right hand of God,[f] he has received from the Father[j] the promised Holy Spirit[k] and has poured out[l] what you now see and hear. [34]For David did not ascend to heaven, and yet he said,

" 'The Lord said to my Lord:
"Sit at my right hand
[35]until I make your enemies
a footstool for your feet." ' [1] [m]

[36]"Therefore let all Israel be assured of this: God has made this Jesus, whom you crucified, both Lord[n] and Christ."[o]

[37]When the people heard this, they were cut to the heart and said to Peter and the other apostles, "Brothers, what shall we do?"[p]

[38]Peter replied, "Repent and be baptized,[q] every one of you, in the name of Jesus Christ for the forgiveness of your sins.[r] And you will receive the gift of the Holy Spirit.[s] [39]The promise is for you and your children[t] and for all who are far off[u]—for all whom the Lord our God will call."

[40]With many other words he warned them; and he pleaded with them, "Save yourselves from this corrupt generation."[v] [41]Those who accepted his message were

baptized, and about three thousand were added to their number[w] that day.

The Fellowship of the Believers

[42]They devoted themselves to the apostles' teaching[x] and to the fellowship, to the breaking of bread[y] and to prayer.[z] [43]Everyone was filled with awe, and many wonders and miraculous signs were done by the apostles.[a] [44]All the believers were together and had everything in common.[b] [45]Selling their possessions and goods, they gave to anyone as he had need.[c] [46]Every day they continued to meet together in the temple courts.[d] They broke bread[e] in their homes and ate together with glad and sincere hearts, [47]praising God and enjoying the favor of all the people.[f] And the Lord added to their number[g] daily those who were being saved.

Peter Heals the Crippled Beggar

3 One day Peter and John[h] were going up to the temple[i] at the time of prayer—at three in the afternoon.[j] [2]Now a man crippled from birth[k] was being car-

2:33 [s]S Mk 16:19 /Ac 1:4 [k]Jn 7:39; 14:26; 15:26 /Ac 10:45
2:35 [m]Ps 110:1; S Mt 22:44
2:36 [n]S Mt 28:18 [o]S Lk 2:11
2:37 [p]Lk 3:10, 12,14; Ac 16:30
2:38 [q]ver 41; Ac 8:12,16,36,38; 9:18; 10:48; 16:15,33; 19:5; 22:16; Col 2:12 [r]Jer 36:3; Mk 1:4; S Lk 24:47; Ac 3:19 [s]S Jn 20:22
2:39 [t]Isa 44:3; 65:23 [u]Isa 57:19; Ac 10:45; Eph 2:13
2:40 [v]Dt 32:5; Php 2:15
2:41 [w]ver 47; Ac 4:4; 5:14; 6:1, 7; 9:31,35,42; 11:21,24; 14:1; 21; 16:5; 17:12
2:42 [x]Mt 28:20 [y]S Mt 14:19 [z]S Ac 1:14
2:43 [a]Ac 5:12
2:44 [b]Ac 4:32
2:45 [c]Mt 19:21; Lk 12:33; 18:22; Ac 4:34,35; 6:1
2:46 [d]Lk 24:53; Ac 3:1; 5:21,42 [e]ver 42; S Mt 14:19
2:47 [f]S Ro 14:18 [g]S ver 41

3:1 [h]S Lk 22:8 [i]Ac 2:46 /Ps 55:17; Ac 10:30 **3:2** [k]Ac 14:8

[1]35 Psalm 110:1

2:33 *promised Holy Spirit.* See note on 1:4. *has poured out.* See v. 17; Joel 2:28.
2:34 *The Lord said to my Lord.* The Lord (God) said to my Lord (the Son of David, the Messiah). According to Peter, David addressed his descendant with uncommon respect because he, through the inspiration of the Spirit, recognized how great and divine he would be (Mt 22:41–45). Not only was he to be resurrected (vv. 31–32) but he was to be exalted to God's right hand (vv. 33–35). And his presence there was now being demonstrated by the sending of the Holy Spirit (v. 33; Jn 16:7). See also note on Ps 110:1.
2:37 *cut to the heart.* Reflects both belief in Jesus and regret over former rejection.
2:38 *Repent and be baptized.* Repentance was important in the message of the forerunner, John the Baptist (Mk 1:4; Lk 3:3), in the preaching of Jesus (Mk 1:15; Lk 13:3) and in the directions Jesus left just before his ascension (Lk 24:47). So also baptism was important to John the Baptizer (Mk 1:4), in the instructions of Jesus (Mt 28:18–19) and in the preaching recorded in Acts—where it was associated with belief (8:12; 18:8), acceptance of the word (v. 41) and repentance (here). *in the name of Jesus Christ.* Not a contradiction to the fuller formula given in Mt 28:19. In Acts the abbreviated form emphasizes the distinctive quality of this baptism, for Jesus is now included in a way that he was not in John's baptism (19:4–5). *for the forgiveness of your sins.* Not that baptism effects forgiveness. Rather, forgiveness comes through that which is symbolized by baptism (see Ro 6:3–4 and note). *Holy Spirit.* Two gifts are now given: the forgiveness of sins (see also 22:16) and the Holy Spirit. The promise of the indwelling gift of the Holy Spirit is given to all Christians (cf. Ro 8:9–11; 1Co 12:13).
2:41 *their number.* The number of believers.
2:42 *apostles' teaching.* Included all that Jesus himself taught (Mt 28:20), especially the gospel, which was cen-

tered in his death, burial and resurrection (see vv. 23–24; 3:15; 4:10; 1Co 15:1–4). It was a unique teaching in that it came from God and was clothed with the authority conferred on the apostles (2Co 13:10; 1Th 4:2). Today it is available in the books of the NT. *the fellowship.* The corporate fellowship of believers in worship. *breaking of bread.* Although this phrase is used of an ordinary meal in v. 46 (see Lk 24:30,35), the Lord's Supper seems to be indicated here (see note on 20:7; cf. 1Co 10:16; 11:20). *prayer.* Acts emphasizes the importance of prayer in the Christian life—private as well as public (1:14; 3:1; 6:4; 10:4,31; 12:5; 16:13,16).
2:44 *believers were together.* The unity of the early church. *everything in common.* See 4:34–35. This was a voluntary sharing to provide for those who did not have enough for the essentials of living (see good and bad examples of sharing, 4:36–5:9).
2:46 *broke bread in their homes.* Here the daily life of Christians is described, distinguishing their activity in the temple from that in their homes, where they ate their meals—not the Lord's Supper—with gladness and generosity. *glad and sincere hearts.* The fellowship, oneness and sharing enjoyed in the early church are fruits of the Spirit. Joy is to be the mood of the believer (see note on 16:34).
3:1 *Peter and John.* Among the foremost apostles (Gal 2:9). Along with John's brother, James, they had been especially close to Jesus (Mk 9:2; 13:3; 14:33; Lk 22:8). Arrested together (4:3), they were also together in Samaria (8:14). *time of prayer.* The three stated times of prayer for later Judaism were midmorning (the third hour, 9:00 A.M.), the time of the evening sacrifice (the ninth hour, 3:00 P.M.) and sunset.
3:2 *gate called Beautiful.* The favorite entrance to the temple court, it was probably the bronze-sheathed gate that is elsewhere called the Nicanor Gate. Apparently it led from

ried to the temple gate[l] called Beautiful, where he was put every day to beg[m] from those going into the temple courts. [3]When he saw Peter and John about to enter, he asked them for money. [4]Peter looked straight at him, as did John. Then Peter said, "Look at us!" [5]So the man gave them his attention, expecting to get something from them.

[6]Then Peter said, "Silver or gold I do not have, but what I have I give you. In the name of Jesus Christ of Nazareth,[n] walk." [7]Taking him by the right hand, he helped him up, and instantly the man's feet and ankles became strong. [8]He jumped to his feet and began to walk. Then he went with them into the temple courts, walking and jumping,[o] and praising God. [9]When all the people[p] saw him walking and praising God, [10]they recognized him as the same man who used to sit begging at the temple gate called Beautiful,[q] and they were filled with wonder and amazement at what had happened to him.

Peter Speaks to the Onlookers

[11]While the beggar held on to Peter and John,[r] all the people were astonished and came running to them in the place called Solomon's Colonnade.[s] [12]When Peter saw this, he said to them: "Men of Israel, why does this surprise you? Why do you stare at us as if by our own power or godliness we had made this man walk? [13]The God of Abraham, Isaac and Jacob,[t] the God of our fathers,[u] has glorified his servant Jesus. You handed him over[v] to be killed, and

you disowned him before Pilate,[w] though he had decided to let him go.[x] [14]You disowned the Holy[y] and Righteous One[z] and asked that a murderer be released to you.[a] [15]You killed the author of life, but God raised him from the dead.[b] We are witnesses[c] of this. [16]By faith in the name of Jesus,[d] this man whom you see and know was made strong. It is Jesus' name and the faith that comes through him that has given this complete healing to him, as you can all see.

[17]"Now, brothers,[e] I know that you acted in ignorance,[f] as did your leaders.[g] [18]But this is how God fulfilled[h] what he had foretold[i] through all the prophets,[j] saying that his Christ[m] would suffer.[k] [19]Repent, then, and turn to God, so that your sins may be wiped out,[l] that times of refreshing may come from the Lord, [20]and that he may send the Christ,[m] who has been appointed for you—even Jesus. [21]He must remain in heaven[n] until the time comes for God to restore everything,[o] as he promised long ago through his holy prophets.[p] [22]For Moses said, 'The Lord your God will raise up for you a prophet like me from among your own people; you must listen to everything he tells you.[q] [23]Anyone who does not listen to him will be completely cut off from among his people.'[n][r]

[24]"Indeed, all the prophets[s] from Samuel on, as many as have spoken, have foretold these days. [25]And you are heirs[t] of

Cross references (center column)

3:2 [l]Lk 16:20
[m]Jn 9:8
3:6 [n]ver16; S Mk 1:24;
3:8 [o]Isa 35:6; Ac 14:10
3:9 [p]Ac 4:16,21
3:10 [q]ver 2
3:11 [r]S Lk 22:8
[s]Jn 10:23; Ac 5:12
3:13 [t]Ex 3:6
[u]Ac 5:30; 7:32; 22:14 [v]Ac 2:23

[w]S Mt 27:2
[x]S Lk 23:4
[y]S Mk 1:24; Ac 4:27 [z]Ac 7:52
[a]Mk 15:11; Lk 23:18-25
3:15 [b]S Ac 2:24
[c]S Lk 24:48
3:16 [d]ver 6
3:17 [e]S Ac 22:5
[f]Lk 23:34
[g]Ac 13:27
3:18 [h]S Mt 1:22
[i]Ac 2:23
[j]S Lk 24:27
[k]Ac 17:2,3; 26:22,23
[l]Ps 51:1; Isa 43:25; 44:22; S Ac 2:38
3:20 [m]S Lk 2:11
3:21 [n]Ac 1:11
[o]Mt 17:11;
Ac 1:6 [p]Lk 1:70
3:22 [q]Dt 18:15, 18; Ac 7:37
3:23 [r]Dt 18:19
3:24 [s]S Lk 24:27
3:25 [t]Ac 2:39

[m]18 Or Messiah; also in verse 20   [n]23 Deut. 18:15,18,19

---

the court of the Gentiles to the court of women, on the east wall of the temple proper.
3:6 *In the name of Jesus Christ.* Not by power of their own, but by the authority of the Messiah.
3:7 *he helped him up.* But he had faith to be healed (v. 16).
3:8 *into the temple courts.* From the outer court (for Gentiles also) into the court of women, containing the treasury (Mk 12:41–44), and then into the court of Israel (see map No. 8 at the end of the Study Bible). From the outer court, nine gates led into the inner courts.
3:11 *Solomon's Colonnade.* A porch along the inside of the wall enclosing the outer court, with rows of 27-foot-high stone columns and a roof of cedar (see note on Jn 10:23).
3:12–26 See note on 2:14–40.
3:13 *his servant Jesus.* A reminder of the suffering servant prophesied in Isa 52:13–53:12 (see Mt 12:18; Ac 4:27,30). *disowned him.* Voted against Jesus, spurned him, denied him and refused to acknowledge him as the true Messiah. *Pilate . . . had decided to let him go.* See Jn 19:12.
3:14 *Holy and Righteous One.* Blameless in relation to God and man.
3:15 *You killed . . . God raised . . . We are witnesses.* A recurring theme in the speeches of Acts (see 2:23–24; 4:10; 5:30–32; 10:39–41; 13:28–29; cf. 1Co 15:1–4).
3:18 *foretold through all the prophets.* Echoes what Jesus

had said (Lk 24:26–27). The suffering was prophesied (compare Isa 53:7–8 with Ac 8:32–33; Ps 2:1–2 with Ac 4:25–26; Ps 22:1 with Mt 27:46; see also 1Pe 1:11).
3:19 *Repent.* Repentance is a change of mind and will arising from sorrow for sin and leading to transformation of life (see note on 2:38). *turn to God.* Subsequent to repentance and not completely identical with it. See 11:21 ("believe and turn") and 26:20 ("repent and turn"; see also 9:35; 14:15; 15:19; 26:18; 28:27). In the strictest sense, repentance is turning from sin, and faith is turning to God. However, the word "turn" is not always used with such precision. *your sins . . . wiped out.* Your sins will be forgiven as a result of repentance.
3:22–26 *raise up . . . raised up.* Christ is the fulfillment of prophecies made relative to Moses, David and Abraham. He was to be a prophet like Moses (vv. 22–23), he was foretold in Samuel's declarations concerning David (v. 24; see note there), and he was to bring blessing to all people as promised to Abraham (vv. 25–26).
3:24 *prophets from Samuel on.* Samuel anointed David to be king and spoke of the establishment of his kingdom (1Sa 16:13; cf. 13:14; 15:28; 28:17). Nathan's prophecy (2Sa 7:12–16) was ultimately Messianic (see Ac 13:22–23,34; Heb 1:5).
3:25 *offspring.* The word is singular, ultimately signifying Christ (see Gal 3:16).

the prophets and of the covenant[u] God made with your fathers. He said to Abraham, 'Through your offspring all peoples on earth will be blessed.'[o][v] 26When God raised up[w] his servant, he sent him first[x] to you to bless you by turning each of you from your wicked ways."

Peter and John Before the Sanhedrin

4 The priests and the captain of the temple guard[y] and the Sadducees[z] came up to Peter and John while they were speaking to the people. 2They were greatly disturbed because the apostles were teaching the people and proclaiming in Jesus the resurrection of the dead.[a] 3They seized Peter and John, and because it was evening, they put them in jail[b] until the next day. 4But many who heard the message believed, and the number of men grew[c] to about five thousand.

5The next day the rulers,[d] elders and teachers of the law met in Jerusalem. 6Annas the high priest was there, and so were Caiaphas,[e] John, Alexander and the other men of the high priest's family. 7They had Peter and John brought before them and began to question them: "By what power or what name did you do this?"

8Then Peter, filled with the Holy Spirit,[f] said to them: "Rulers and elders of the people![g] 9If we are being called to account today for an act of kindness shown to a cripple[h] and are asked how he was healed, 10then know this, you and all the people of Israel: It is by the name of Jesus Christ of Nazareth,[i] whom you crucified but whom God raised from the dead,[j] that this man stands before you healed. 11He is

" 'the stone you builders rejected,

which has become the capstone.[p]'[q][k]

12Salvation is found in no one else, for there is no other name under heaven given to men by which we must be saved."[l]

13When they saw the courage of Peter and John[m] and realized that they were unschooled, ordinary men,[n] they were astonished and they took note that these men had been with Jesus.[o] 14But since they could see the man who had been healed standing there with them, there was nothing they could say. 15So they ordered them to withdraw from the Sanhedrin[p] and then conferred together. 16"What are we going to do with these men?"[q] they asked. "Everybody living in Jerusalem knows they have done an outstanding miracle,[r] and we cannot deny it. 17But to stop this thing from spreading any further among the people, we must warn these men to speak no longer to anyone in this name."

18Then they called them in again and commanded them not to speak or teach at all in the name of Jesus.[s] 19But Peter and John replied, "Judge for yourselves whether it is right in God's sight to obey you rather than God.[t] 20For we cannot help speaking[u] about what we have seen and heard."[v]

21After further threats they let them go. They could not decide how to punish them, because all the people[w] were praising God[x] for what had happened. 22For the man who was miraculously healed was over forty years old.

The Believers' Prayer

23On their release, Peter and John went

Cross references (center column):

3:25 uRo 9:4,5; vGe 12:3; 22:18; 26:4; 28:14
3:26 wver 22; S Ac 2:24; xAc 13:46; Ro 1:16
4:1 yLk 22:4; zMt 3:7; 16:1,6; 22:23,34; Ac 5:17; 23:6-8
4:2 aAc 17:18
4:3 bAc 5:18
4:4 cS Ac 2:41
4:5 dLk 23:13
4:6 eS Mt 26:3
4:8 fS Lk 1:15; gver 5; Lk 23:13
4:9 hAc 3:6
4:10 iS Mk 1:24; jS Ac 2:24
4:11 kPs 118:22; Isa 28:16; Zec 10:4; Mt 21:42; Eph 2:20; 1Pe 2:7
4:12 lS Mt 1:21; Jn 14:6; Ac 10:43; S Ro 11:14; 1Ti 2:5
4:13 mS Lk 22:8; nMt 11:25; oMk 3:14
4:15 pS Mt 5:22
4:16 qJn 11:47; rAc 3:6-10
4:18 sAm 7:13; Ac 5:40
4:19 tAc 5:29
4:20 uJob 32:18; Jer 20:9; Am 3:8; vS Lk 24:48
4:21 wAc 5:26; xS Mt 9:8

o25 Gen. 22:18; 26:4   p11 Or cornerstone
q11 Psalm 118:22

4:1 *priests.* Those who were serving that week in the temple precincts (see note on Lk 1:23). *captain of the temple guard.* A member of one of the leading priestly families; next in rank to the high priest (see 5:24,26; Lk 22:4,52). *Sadducees.* A Jewish sect whose members came from the priestly line and controlled the temple. They did not believe in the resurrection or a personal Messiah, but held that the Messianic age—an ideal time—was then present and must be preserved. The high priest, one of their number, presided over the Sanhedrin (see 5:17; 23:6-8; Mt 22:23-33). See also notes on Mt 3:7; Mk 12:18; Lk 20:27.
4:3 *evening.* The evening sacrifices ended about 4:00 P.M., and the temple gates would be closed at that time. Any judgments involving life and death must be begun and concluded in daylight hours.
4:4 *men.* Lit. "males." *five thousand.* A growth from the 3,000 at Pentecost (2:41); see later growth (5:14; 6:7).
4:5 *rulers, elders and teachers of the law.* The three groups making up the Sanhedrin, Israel's supreme court (see Lk 22:66; see also notes on Mt 2:4; 15:2; Mk 14:55; Lk 5:17).
4:6 *Annas.* High priest A.D. 6–15, but deposed by the Romans and succeeded by his son, Eleazar, then by his

son-in-law, Caiaphas (18–36), who was also called Joseph. However, Annas was still recognized by the Jews as high priest (Lk 3:2; cf. Jn 18:13, 24). *John.* May be Jonathan son of Annas, who was appointed high priest in A.D. 36. Others suggest it was Johanan ben Zaccai, who became the president of the Great Synagogue after the fall of Jerusalem. *Alexander.* Not further identified.
4:8 *filled with the Holy Spirit.* See note on 2:4.
4:11 *the stone . . . rejected.* Fulfillment of prophecy was an important element in early Christian sermons and defenses. Jesus had also used Ps 118:22 (Mt 21:42; see 1Pe 2:7 and cf. Ro 9:33; Isa 28:16).
4:12 *no other name.* See 10:43; Jn 14:6; 1Ti 2:5; see also NIV text note on Mt 1:21.
4:13 *courage.* A certain boldness characterized the assurance, authority and forthrightness of the apostles (2:29; 4:29; 28:31), and shared by the believers (4:31). *unschooled, ordinary men.* Peter and John had not been trained in the rabbinic schools, nor did they hold official positions in recognized religious circles.
4:20 *cannot help speaking.* See 5:29.
4:23 *went back.* Probably to the same upper room where

back to their own people and reported all that the chief priests and elders had said to them. [24]When they heard this, they raised their voices together in prayer to God.[y] "Sovereign Lord," they said, "you made the heaven and the earth and the sea, and everything in them.[z] [25]You spoke by the Holy Spirit through the mouth of your servant, our father David:[a]

" 'Why do the nations rage
    and the peoples plot in vain?
[26]The kings of the earth take their stand
    and the rulers gather together
against the Lord
    and against his Anointed One.[r] [s] [b]

[27]Indeed Herod[c] and Pontius Pilate[d] met together with the Gentiles and the people[t] of Israel in this city to conspire against your holy servant Jesus,[e] whom you anointed. [28]They did what your power and will had decided beforehand should happen.[f] [29]Now, Lord, consider their threats and enable your servants to speak your word with great boldness.[g] [30]Stretch out your hand to heal and perform miraculous signs and wonders[h] through the name of your holy servant Jesus."[i]

[31]After they prayed, the place where they were meeting was shaken.[j] And they were all filled with the Holy Spirit[k] and spoke the word of God[l] boldly. [m]

The Believers Share Their Possessions

[32]All the believers were one in heart and mind. No one claimed that any of his possessions was his own, but they shared everything they had. [n] [33]With great power the apostles continued to testify[o] to the resurrection[p] of the Lord Jesus, and much grace[q] was upon them all. [34]There were no needy persons among them. For from time to time those who owned lands or houses sold them,[r] brought the money from the sales [35]and put it at the apostles' feet,[s] and it was distributed to anyone as he had need.[t]

[36]Joseph, a Levite from Cyprus, whom the apostles called Barnabas[u] (which means Son of Encouragement), [37]sold a field he owned and brought the money and put it at the apostles' feet. [v]

Ananias and Sapphira

5 Now a man named Ananias, together with his wife Sapphira, also sold a piece of property. [2]With his wife's full knowledge he kept back part of the money for himself,[w] but brought the rest and put it at the apostles' feet.[x]

[3]Then Peter said, "Ananias, how is it that Satan[y] has so filled your heart[z] that you have lied to the Holy Spirit[a] and have kept for yourself some of the money you received for the land?[b] [4]Didn't it belong to you before it was sold? And after it was sold, wasn't the money at your disposal?[c] What made you think of doing such a

Cross references (center column)

4:24 [y]S Ac 1:14
[z]Ne 9:6; Job 41:11; Isa 37:16
4:25 [a]Ac 1:16
4:26 [b]Ps 2:1,2; Da 9:25; Lk 4:18; Ac 10:38; Heb 1:9
4:27 [c]S Mt 14:1
[d]S Mt 27:2; Lk 23:12 [e]ver 30; Ac 3:13,14
4:28 [f]Ac 2:23
4:29 [g]ver 13,31; Ps 138:3; Ac 9:27; 13:46; 14:3; 28:31; Eph 6:19; Php 1:14
4:30 [h]S Jn 4:48 [i]ver 27
4:31 [j]Ac 2:2 [k]S Lk 1:15 [l]S Heb 4:12 [m]S ver 29

4:32 [n]Ac 2:44
4:33 [o]S Lk 24:48 [p]Ac 1:22 [q]S Ro 3:24
4:34 [r]Mt 19:21; Ac 2:45
4:35 [s]ver 37; Ac 5:2 [t]Ac 2:45; 6:1
4:36 [u]Ac 9:27; 11:22,30; 13:2; 1Co 9:6; Gal 2:1, 9,13
4:37 [v]ver 35; Ac 5:2
5:2 [w]Jos 7:11 [x]Ac 4:35,37
5:3 [y]S Mt 4:10 [z]Jn 13:2,27 [a]ver 9 [b]Dt 23:21
5:4 [c]Dt 23:22

[r]26 That is, Christ or Messiah   [s]26 Psalm 2:1,2
[t]27 The Greek is plural.

---

the apostles had met before (1:13) and where the congregation may have continued to meet (12:12).
4:24 *Sovereign Lord.* See Lk 2:29.
4:27 *Herod.* Herod Antipas, tetrarch of Galilee and Perea (Lk 23:7–15). *Pontius Pilate.* Roman procurator of Judea (Lk 23:1–24).
4:28 *decided beforehand.* Not that God had compelled them to act as they did, but he willed to use them and their freely chosen acts to accomplish his saving purpose.
4:30 *holy servant.* See note on 3:13.
4:31 *was shaken.* An immediate sign that the prayers had been heard (see 16:26). *filled with the Holy Spirit.* See note on 2:4. *spoke the word of God.* They continued preaching the gospel despite the warnings of the council (see note on v. 13).
4:32 *one in heart and mind.* In complete accord, extending to their attitude toward personal possessions (see 2:44).
4:33 *testify to the resurrection.* As significant as the death of Christ was, the most compelling event was the resurrection—an event about which the disciples could not keep silent.
4:34 *those who owned lands or houses sold them.* See note on 2:44.
4:36 *Levite.* Although Levites owned no inherited land in Palestine, these regulations may not have applied to the Levites in other countries (Cyprus). So perhaps Barnabas sold

land he owned in Cyprus and brought the proceeds to the apostles (v. 37). Or he may have been married, and the land sold may have been from his wife's property. It is also possible that the prohibition against Levite ownership of land in Palestine was no longer observed. *Cyprus.* An island in the eastern part of the Mediterranean Sea. Jews had settled there from Maccabean times. *Barnabas.* Used here as a good example of giving. In this way Luke introduces the one who will become an important companion of Paul (see 13:1–4). For other significant contributions of this greathearted leader to the life and ministry of the early church see 9:27; 11:22, 25; 15:37–39.
5:1 *Ananias . . . Sapphira.* Given as bad examples of sharing (Barnabas was the good example; see on 4:36). Love of praise for (pretended) generosity and love for money led to the first recorded sin in the life of the church. It is a warning to the readers that "God cannot be mocked" (Gal 6:7). Compare this divine judgment at the beginning of the church era with God's judgments on Nadab and Abihu (Lev 10:2), on Achan (Jos 7:25) and on Uzzah (2Sa 6:7).
5:2 *kept back part.* They had a right to keep back whatever they chose, but to make it appear that they had given all when they had not was sinful.
5:3 *Satan has so filled your heart.* The continuing activity of Satan is noted (see Lk 22:3; Jn 13:2,27; 1Pe 5:8). *lied to the Holy Spirit.* A comparison with v. 4 shows that the Holy Spirit is regarded as God himself present with his people.

thing? You have not lied to men but to God." d

⁵When Ananias heard this, he fell down and died. e And great fear f seized all who heard what had happened. ⁶Then the young men came forward, wrapped up his body, g and carried him out and buried him.

⁷About three hours later his wife came in, not knowing what had happened. ⁸Peter asked her, "Tell me, is this the price you and Ananias got for the land?"

"Yes," she said, "that is the price." h

⁹Peter said to her, "How could you agree to test the Spirit of the Lord? i Look! The feet of the men who buried your husband are at the door, and they will carry you out also."

¹⁰At that moment she fell down at his feet and died. j Then the young men came in and, finding her dead, carried her out and buried her beside her husband. k ¹¹Great fear l seized the whole church and all who heard about these events.

The Apostles Heal Many

¹²The apostles performed many miraculous signs and wonders m among the people. And all the believers used to meet together n in Solomon's Colonnade. o ¹³No one else dared join them, even though they were highly regarded by the people. p ¹⁴Nevertheless, more and more men and women believed in the Lord and were added to their number. q ¹⁵As a result, people brought the sick into the streets and laid them on beds and mats so that at least Peter's shadow might fall on some of them

Cross references (center column)

5:4 dLev 6:2
5:5 ever 10;
Ps 5:6 fver 11
5:6 gJn 19:40
5:8 hver 2
5:9 iver 3
5:10 jver 5 kver 6
5:11 lver 5; Ac 19:17
5:12 mS Jn 4:48; Ac 2:43 nAc 4:32 oJn 10:23; Ac 3:11
5:13 pAc 2:47; 4:21
5:14 qS Ac 2:41

5:15 rAc 19:12
5:16 sMt 8:16; S Mk 16:17
5:17 tAc 15:5 uS Ac 4:1
5:18 vAc 4:3
5:19 wGe 16:7; Ex 3:2; Mt 1:20; 2:13,19; 28:2; Lk 1:11; 2:9; S Jn 20:12; Ac 8:26; 10:3; 12:7,23; 27:23 xAc 16:26 yPs 34:7
5:20 zJn 6:63,68
5:21 aAc 4:5,6 bver 27,34,41; S Mt 5:22
5:22 cAc 12:18, 19
5:24 dAc 4:1

as he passed by. r ¹⁶Crowds gathered also from the towns around Jerusalem, bringing their sick and those tormented by evil u spirits, and all of them were healed. s

The Apostles Persecuted

¹⁷Then the high priest and all his associates, who were members of the party t of the Sadducees, u were filled with jealousy. ¹⁸They arrested the apostles and put them in the public jail. v ¹⁹But during the night an angel w of the Lord opened the doors of the jail x and brought them out. y ²⁰"Go, stand in the temple courts," he said, "and tell the people the full message of this new life." z

²¹At daybreak they entered the temple courts, as they had been told, and began to teach the people.

When the high priest and his associates a arrived, they called together the Sanhedrin b—the full assembly of the elders of Israel—and sent to the jail for the apostles. ²²But on arriving at the jail, the officers did not find them there. c So they went back and reported, ²³"We found the jail securely locked, with the guards standing at the doors; but when we opened them, we found no one inside." ²⁴On hearing this report, the captain of the temple guard and the chief priests d were puzzled, wondering what would come of this.

²⁵Then someone came and said, "Look! The men you put in jail are standing in the temple courts teaching the people." ²⁶At that, the captain went with his officers and brought the apostles. They did not use

u 16 Greek unclean

5:9 to test the Spirit of the Lord. If no dire consequences had followed this act of sin, the results among the believers would have been serious when the deceit became known. Not only would dishonesty appear profitable, but the conclusion that the Spirit could be deceived would follow. It was important to set the course properly at the outset in order to leave no doubt that God will not tolerate such hypocrisy and deceit.

5:11 church. The first use of the term in Acts. It can denote either the local congregation (8:1; 11:22; 13:1) or the universal church (see 20:28). The Greek word for "church" (ekklesia) was already being used for political and other assemblies (see 19:32,40) and, in the Septuagint (the Greek translation of the OT), for Israel when gathered in religious assembly.

5:12 Solomon's Colonnade. See note on 3:11.

5:13 No one else dared join them. Because of the fate of Ananias and his wife, no pretenders or halfhearted followers risked identification with the believers. Luke cannot mean that no one joined the Christian community, since v. 14 indicates that many were coming to Christ.

5:14 more men and women believed. See 4:4. This is the first specific mention of women believing (cf. 8:3,12; 9:2;

13:50; 16:1,13–14; 17:4,12,34; 18:2; 21:5; but cf. also 1:14).

5:15 Peter's shadow. Parallels such items as Paul's handkerchiefs (19:12) and the edge of Jesus' cloak (Mt 9:20)—not that any of these material objects had magical qualities, but the least article or shadow represented a direct means of contact with Jesus or his apostles.

5:17 high priest. The official high priest recognized by Rome was Caiaphas, but the Jews considered Annas, Caiaphas's father-in-law, to be the actual high priest since the high priesthood was to be held for life (see note on 4:6). his associates. His family members. party of the Sadducees. See note on 4:1.

5:18 in the public jail. To await trial the next day.

5:19 angel of the Lord. This phrase is used four other times in Acts: (1) Stephen speaks of him (7:30–38); (2) he guides Philip (8:26); (3) he liberates Peter (12:7–10); (4) he strikes down Herod (12:23). See also Mt 1:20–24; 2:13,19; 28:2; Lk 1:11–38; 2:9.

5:21 Sanhedrin. The supreme Jewish court, consisting of 70 to 100 men (71 being the proper number). They sat in a semicircle, backed by three rows of disciples of the "learned men," with the clerks of the court standing in front.

5:24 captain of the temple guard. See note on 4:1.

force, because they feared that the people *e* would stone them.

27Having brought the apostles, they made them appear before the Sanhedrin*f* to be questioned by the high priest. 28"We gave you strict orders not to teach in this name,"*g* he said. "Yet you have filled Jerusalem with your teaching and are determined to make us guilty of this man's blood."*h*

29Peter and the other apostles replied: "We must obey God rather than men!*i* 30The God of our fathers*j* raised Jesus from the dead*k*—whom you had killed by hanging him on a tree.*l* 31God exalted him to his own right hand*m* as Prince and Savior*n* that he might give repentance and forgiveness of sins to Israel.*o* 32We are witnesses of these things,*p* and so is the Holy Spirit,*q* whom God has given to those who obey him."

33When they heard this, they were furious*r* and wanted to put them to death. 34But a Pharisee named Gamaliel,*s* a teacher of the law,*t* who was honored by all the people, stood up in the Sanhedrin and ordered that the men be put outside for a little while. 35Then he addressed them: "Men of Israel, consider carefully what you intend to do to these men. 36Some time ago Theudas appeared, claiming to be somebody, and about four hundred men rallied to him. He was killed, all his followers were dispersed, and it all came to nothing. 37After him, Judas the

Galilean appeared in the days of the census*u* and led a band of people in revolt. He too was killed, and all his followers were scattered. 38Therefore, in the present case I advise you: Leave these men alone! Let them go! For if their purpose or activity is of human origin, it will fail.*v* 39But if it is from God, you will not be able to stop these men; you will only find yourselves fighting against God."*w*

40His speech persuaded them. They called the apostles in and had them flogged.*x* Then they ordered them not to speak in the name of Jesus, and let them go.

41The apostles left the Sanhedrin, rejoicing*y* because they had been counted worthy of suffering disgrace for the Name.*z* 42Day after day, in the temple courts*a* and from house to house, they never stopped teaching and proclaiming the good news*b* that Jesus is the Christ.*v* *c*

The Choosing of the Seven

6 In those days when the number of disciples was increasing,*d* the Grecian Jews*e* among them complained against the Hebraic Jews because their widows*f* were being overlooked in the daily distribution of food.*g* 2So the Twelve gathered all the disciples*h* together and said, "It would not be right for us to neglect the ministry of the word of God*i* in order to wait on tables. 3Brothers,*j* choose seven men from

Cross references (center column):

5:26 *e*Ac 4:21
5:27 *f*S Mt 5:22
5:28 *g*Ac 4:18
    *h*Mt 23:35;
    27:25; Ac 2:23,
    36; 3:14,15; 7:52
5:29 *i*Ex 1:17;
    Ac 4:19
5:30 *j*S Ac 3:13
    *k*S Ac 2:24
    *l*Ac 10:39; 13:29;
    Gal 3:13
5:31 *m*S Mk 16:19
    *n*S Lk 2:11
    *o*S Mt 1:21;
    Mk 1:4;
    Lk 24:47;
    Ac 2:38; 3:19;
    10:43
5:32 *p*S Lk 24:48
    *q*Jn 15:26
5:33 *r*Ac 2:37;
    7:54
5:34 *s*Ac 22:3
    *t*Lk 2:46; 5:17

5:37 *u*Lk 2:1,2
5:38 *v*Mt 15:13
5:39
    *w*2Ch 13:12;
    Pr 21:30;
    Isa 46:10;
    Ac 7:51; 11:17
5:40 *x*S Mt 10:17
5:41 *y*S Mt 5:12
    *z*S Jn 15:21
5:42 *a*S Ac 2:46
    *b*S Ac 13:32
    *c*S Ac 9:22
6:1 *d*S Ac 2:41
    *e*Ac 9:29
    *f*Ac 9:39,41;
    1Ti 5:3 *g*Ac 4:35
6:2 *h*S Ac 11:26
    *i*S Heb 4:12
6:3 *j*S Ac 1:16

*v*42 Or *Messiah*

Footnotes (bottom):

5:28 *make us guilty of this man's blood.* Probably a reference to the apostles' repeated declaration that some of the Jews and some of their leaders had killed Jesus (2:23; 3:13–15; 4:10–11; cf. Mt 27:25).
5:30 *tree.* Used to describe the cross (1Pe 2:24; see Dt 21:22–23). Like its Hebrew counterpart, the Greek for this word could refer to a tree, a pole, a wooden beam or some similar object.
5:32 *so is the Holy Spirit . . . given to those who obey him.* See Jn 15:26–27. The disciples' testimony was directed and confirmed by the Holy Spirit, who convicts the world through the word (Jn 16:8–11) and is given to those who respond to God with "the obedience that comes from faith" (Ro 1:5; see note on 6:7).
5:34 *a Pharisee named Gamaliel.* The most famous Jewish teacher of his time and traditionally listed among the "heads of the schools." Possibly he was the grandson of Hillel. Like Hillel (see note on Mt 19:3), he was moderate in his views, a characteristic that is apparent in his cautious recommendation on this occasion. Saul (Paul) was one of his students (22:3).
5:36 *Theudas.* We know of him from no other historical source.
5:37 *Judas the Galilean.* The Jewish historian Josephus refers to him as a man from Gamala in Gaulanitis who refused to give tribute to Caesar. His revolt was crushed, but a movement, started in his time, may have lived on in the party of the Zealots (see 1:13 and note on Mt 10:4). *days of*

the census. Not the first census of Quirinius, noted by Luke in his Gospel (2:2), but the one in A.D. 6.
5:40 *flogged.* Beaten with the Jewish penalty of "forty lashes minus one" (2Co 11:24).
6:1 *the number of disciples was increasing.* A considerable length of time may have transpired since the end of ch. 5. The church continued to grow (see 5:14), but this gave rise to inevitable problems, both from within (6:1–7) and from without (6:8–7:60). At this stage of its development, the church was entirely Jewish in its composition. However, there were two groups of Jews within the fellowship: 1. *Grecian Jews.* Hellenists—those born in lands other than Palestine who spoke the Greek language and were more Grecian than Hebraic in their attitudes and outlook. 2. *Hebraic Jews.* Those who spoke the Aramaic and/or Hebrew language(s) of Palestine and preserved Jewish culture and customs. *daily distribution of food.* Help was needed by widows who had no one to care for them and so became the church's responsibility (cf. 4:35; 11:28–29; see also 1Ti 5:3–16).
6:2 *the Twelve.* At this early stage, the apostles were responsible for church life in general, including the ministry of the word of God and the care of the needy. *tables.* The early church was concerned about a spiritual ministry ("word of God" and "prayer"; see v. 4) and a material ministry ("wait on tables").
6:3 *choose seven men.* The church elected them (v. 5), and the apostles "ordained" them (v. 6). In this way they

among you who are known to be full of the Spirit[k] and wisdom. We will turn this responsibility over to them[l] [4]and will give our attention to prayer[m] and the ministry of the word."

[5]This proposal pleased the whole group. They chose Stephen,[n] a man full of faith and of the Holy Spirit;[o] also Philip,[p] Procorus, Nicanor, Timon, Parmenas, and Nicolas from Antioch, a convert to Judaism. [6]They presented these men to the apostles, who prayed[q] and laid their hands on them.[r]

[7]So the word of God spread.[s] The number of disciples in Jerusalem increased rapidly,[t] and a large number of priests became obedient to the faith.

Stephen Seized

[8]Now Stephen, a man full of God's grace and power, did great wonders and miraculous signs[u] among the people. [9]Opposition arose, however, from members of the Synagogue of the Freedmen (as it was called)—Jews of Cyrene[v] and Alexandria as well as the provinces of Cilicia[w] and

Asia.[x] These men began to argue with Stephen, [10]but they could not stand up against his wisdom or the Spirit by whom he spoke.[y]

[11]Then they secretly[z] persuaded some men to say, "We have heard Stephen speak words of blasphemy against Moses and against God."[a]

[12]So they stirred up the people and the elders and the teachers of the law. They seized Stephen and brought him before the Sanhedrin.[b] [13]They produced false witnesses,[c] who testified, "This fellow never stops speaking against this holy place[d] and against the law. [14]For we have heard him say that this Jesus of Nazareth will destroy this place[e] and change the customs Moses handed down to us."[f]

[15]All who were sitting in the Sanhedrin[g] looked intently at Stephen, and they saw that his face was like the face of an angel.

Stephen's Speech to the Sanhedrin

7 Then the high priest asked him, "Are these charges true?"

Cross references

6:3 [k]S Lk 1:15 /Ex 18:21; Ne 13:13
6:4 [m]S Ac 1:14
6:5 [n]ver 8; Ac 7:55-60; 11:19; 22:20 [o]S Lk 1:15 [p]Ac 8:5-40; 21:8
6:6 [q]S Ac 1:24 [r]Nu 8:10; 27:18; Ac 9:17; 19:6; 28:8; 1Ti 4:14; S Mk 5:23
6:7 [s]Ac 12:24; 19:20 [t]S Ac 2:41
6:8 [u]S Jn 4:48
6:9 [v]S Mt 27:32 [w]Ac 15:23,41; 22:3; 23:34

[x]S Ac 2:9
6:10 [y]Lk 21:15
6:11 [z]1Ki 21:10 [a]Mt 26:59-61
6:12 [b]S Mt 5:22
6:13 [c]Ex 23:1; Ps 27:12 [d]Mt 24:15; Ac 7:48; 21:28
6:14 [e]S Jn 2:19 [f]Ac 15:1; 21:21; 26:3; 28:17
6:15 [g]S Mt 5:22

were appointed to their work. *full of the Spirit.* See note on 2:4.

6:5 *They chose Stephen . . . Nicolas.* It is significant that all seven of the men chosen had Greek names. The murmuring had come from the Greek-speaking segment of the church; so those elected to care for the work came from their number so as to represent their interests fairly. Only Stephen and Philip of the Seven receive further notice (Stephen, 6:8–7:60; Philip, 8:5–40; 21:8–9). *from Antioch, a convert to Judaism.* It is significant that a proselyte was included in the number and that Luke points out his place of origin as Antioch, the city to which the gospel was soon to be taken and which was to become the "headquarters" for the forthcoming Gentile missionary effort.

6:6 *prayed and laid their hands on them.* Laying on of hands was used in the OT period to confer blessing (Ge 48:13–20), to transfer guilt from sinner to sacrifice (Lev 1:4) and to commission a person for a new responsibility (Nu 27:23). In the NT period, laying on of hands was observed in healing (28:8; Mk 1:41), blessing (Mk 10:16), ordaining or commissioning (Ac 6:6; 13:3; 1Ti 5:22) and imparting of spiritual gifts (Ac 8:17; 19:6; 1Ti 4:14; 2Ti 1:6). These seven men were appointed to responsibilities turned over to them by the Twelve. The Greek word used to describe their responsibility ("wait on") is the verb from which the noun "deacon" comes. Later one reads of deacons in Php 1:1; 1Ti 3:8–13. The Greek noun for "deacon" can also be translated "minister" or "servant." The men appointed on this occasion were simply called the Seven (21:8), just as the apostles were called the Twelve. It is disputed whether the Seven were the first deacons or were later replaced by deacons (see note on 1Ti 3:8).

6:7 One of a series of progress reports given periodically throughout the book of Acts (1:15; 2:41; 4:4; 5:14; 6:7; 9:31; 12:24; 16:5; 19:20; 28:31). *a large number of priests.* Though involved by lineage and life service in the priestly observances of the old covenant, they accepted the preaching of the apostles, which proclaimed a sacrifice that made the old sacrifices unnecessary (Heb 8:13; 10:1–4,

11–14). *became obedient to the faith.* Responded to the commands of the gospel. To believe is to obey God. Faith itself is obedience, but faith also produces obedience (Eph 2:8–10; Jas 2:14–26).

6:8 *great wonders and miraculous signs.* Until now, Acts told of only the apostles working miracles (2:43; 3:4–8; 5:12). But now, after the laying on of the apostles' hands, Stephen too is reported as working miraculous signs. Philip also will soon do the same (8:6).

6:9 *Freedmen.* Persons who had been freed from slavery. They came from different Hellenistic areas. *Cyrene.* The chief city in Libya and north Africa (see note on 2:10), halfway between Alexandria and Carthage. One of its population groups was Jewish (see 11:19–21). *Alexandria.* Capital of Egypt and second only to Rome in the empire. Two out of five districts in Alexandria were Jewish. *Cilicia.* A Roman province in the southeast corner of Asia Minor adjoining Syria. Tarsus, the birthplace of Paul, was one of its principal towns. *Asia.* A Roman province in the western part of Asia Minor. Ephesus, where Paul later ministered for a few years, was its capital. *These men began to argue.* Since Saul was from Tarsus, this may have been the synagogue he attended, and he may have been among those who argued with Stephen. He was present when Stephen was stoned (7:58).

6:11 *blasphemy against Moses and against God.* Since Stephen declared that the worship of God was no longer to be restricted to the temple (7:48–49), his opponents twisted these words to trump up an accusation that Stephen was attacking the temple, the law, Moses and, ultimately, God.

6:12 *the elders and the teachers of the law.* See notes on Mt 2:4; 15:2; Lk 5:17. *Sanhedrin.* See note on Mk 14:55.

6:13 *speaking against this holy place and against the law.* Similar to the charges brought against Christ (see Mt 26:61). Stephen may have referred to Jesus' words as recorded in Jn 2:19, and the words may have been misunderstood or purposely misinterpreted (v. 14), as at the trial of Jesus.

7:1 *high priest.* Probably Caiaphas (see Mt 26:57–66), but see note on 4:6; cf. Jn 18:19, 24. *Are these charges true?* See notes on 6:11,13.

²To this he replied: "Brothers and fathers,[h] listen to me! The God of glory[i] appeared to our father Abraham while he was still in Mesopotamia, before he lived in Haran.[j] ³'Leave your country and your people,' God said, 'and go to the land I will show you.'[w][k]

⁴"So he left the land of the Chaldeans and settled in Haran. After the death of his father, God sent him to this land where you are now living.[l] ⁵He gave him no inheritance here,[m] not even a foot of ground. But God promised him that he and his descendants after him would possess the land,[n] even though at that time Abraham had no child. ⁶God spoke to him in this way: 'Your descendants will be strangers in a country not their own, and they will be enslaved and mistreated four hundred years.[o] ⁷But I will punish the nation they serve as slaves,' God said, 'and afterward they will come out of that country and worship me in this place.'[x][p] ⁸Then he gave Abraham the covenant of circumcision.[q] And Abraham became the father of Isaac and circumcised him eight days after his birth.[r] Later Isaac became the father of Jacob,[s] and Jacob became the father of the twelve patriarchs.[t]

⁹"Because the patriarchs were jealous of Joseph,[u] they sold him as a slave into Egypt.[v] But God was with him[w] ¹⁰and rescued him from all his troubles. He gave Joseph wisdom and enabled him to gain the goodwill of Pharaoh king of Egypt; so

he made him ruler over Egypt and all his palace.[x]

¹¹"Then a famine struck all Egypt and Canaan, bringing great suffering, and our fathers could not find food.[y] ¹²When Jacob heard that there was grain in Egypt, he sent our fathers on their first visit.[z] ¹³On their second visit, Joseph told his brothers who he was,[a] and Pharaoh learned about Joseph's family.[b] ¹⁴After this, Joseph sent for his father Jacob and his whole family,[c] seventy-five in all.[d] ¹⁵Then Jacob went down to Egypt, where he and our fathers died.[e] ¹⁶Their bodies were brought back to Shechem and placed in the tomb that Abraham had bought from the sons of Hamor at Shechem for a certain sum of money.[f]

¹⁷"As the time drew near for God to fulfill his promise to Abraham, the number of our people in Egypt greatly increased.[g] ¹⁸Then another king, who knew nothing about Joseph, became ruler of Egypt.[h] ¹⁹He dealt treacherously with our people and oppressed our forefathers by forcing them to throw out their newborn babies so that they would die.[i]

²⁰"At that time Moses was born, and he was no ordinary child.[y] For three months he was cared for in his father's house.[j] ²¹When he was placed outside, Pharaoh's daughter took him and brought him up as her own son.[k] ²²Moses was educated in all

Cross-references (center column):

7:2 [h]Ac 22:1 /Ps 29:3 [i]Ge 11:31; 15:7
7:3 [k]Ge 12:1
7:4 [l]Ge 12:5
7:5 [m]Heb 11:13 [n]Ge 12:7; 17:8; 26:3
7:6 [o]Ex 1:8-11; 12:40
7:7 [p]Ge 15:13, 14; Ex 3:12
7:8 [q]Ge 17:9-14 [r]Ge 21:2-4 [s]Ge 25:26 [t]Ge 29:31-35; 30:5-13,17-24; 35:16-18,22-26
7:9 [u]Ge 37:4,11 [v]Ge 37:28; Ps 105:17 [w]Ge 39:2,21,23; Hag 2:4

7:10 [x]Ge 41:37-43; Ps 105:20-22
7:11 [y]Ge 41:54
7:12 [z]Ge 42:1,2
7:13 [a]Ge 45:1-4 [b]Ge 45:16
7:14 [c]Ge 45:9,10 [d]Ge 46:26,27; Ex 1:5; Dt 10:22
7:15 [e]Ge 46:5-7; 49:33; Ex 1:6
7:16 [f]Ge 23:16-20; 33:18,19; 50:13; Jos 24:32
7:17 [g]Ex 1:7; Ps 105:24
7:18 [h]Ex 1:8
7:19 [i]Ex 1:10-22
7:20 [j]Ex 2:2; Heb 11:23
7:21 [k]Ex 2:3-10

[w]3 Gen. 12:1   [x]7 Gen. 15:13,14   [y]20 Or *was fair in the sight of God*

7:2 *Abraham . . . in Mesopotamia, before he lived in Haran.* Abraham's call came in Ur, not Haran (cf. Ge 15:7; Ne 9:7). Or perhaps he was called first in Ur, and then later his call was renewed in Haran (see note on Jer 15:19–21).

7:4 *land of the Chaldeans.* A district in southern Babylonia, the name was later applied to a region that included all Babylonia. *After the death of his father.* Ge 11:26 does not mean that all three sons—Abraham, Nahor and Haran—were born to Terah in the same year when he was 70 years old. See Ge 11:26–12:1. It may be that Haran was Terah's firstborn and that Abraham was born 60 years later. Thus the death of Terah at 205 years of age could have occurred just before Abraham, at 75, left Haran.

7:6 *four hundred years.* A round number for the length of Israel's stay in Egypt (Ex 12:40–41 has 430 years). That four generations would represent considerably less than 400 years is not a necessary conclusion (see note on Ge 15:16). Ex 6:16–20 makes Moses the great-grandson of Levi, son of Jacob and brother of Joseph. This would make four generations from Levi to Moses. But in 1Ch 7:22–27 a list of ten names represents the generations between Ephraim, the son of Joseph, and Joshua. The ten generations at 40 years each would equal 400 years, the same period of time noted as four generations. But one list is abbreviated and the other gives a full genealogy.

7:8 *covenant of circumcision.* See notes on Ge 17:10–11. The essential conditions for the religion of Israel were already

fulfilled long before the temple was built and their present religious customs began. *twelve patriarchs.* See Ge 35:23–26.

7:9 *they sold him.* Israel consistently rejected God's favored individuals. Stephen builds his case about Jesus' rejection by noting Joseph's rejection by his brothers (Ge 37:12–36).

7:13 *second visit.* See Ge 43.

7:14 *Jacob and his whole family, seventy-five in all.* Although the Hebrew Bible uses the number 70 (Ge 46:27; Ex 1:5; Dt 10:22), the Greek translation of the OT (the Septuagint) adds at Ge 46:20 the names of two sons of Manasseh, two of Ephraim, and one grandson of each. This makes the number 75 and is the number that Stephen uses.

7:16 Stephen greatly compresses OT accounts of two land purchases (by Abraham and Jacob) and two burial places (at Hebron and Shechem). According to the OT, Abraham purchased land at Hebron (Ge 23:17–18), where he (Ge 25:9–11), Isaac (Ge 35:29) and Jacob (Ge 50:13) were buried. Jacob bought land at Shechem (Ge 33:19), where Joseph was later buried (Jos 24:32). Josephus preserves a tradition that Joseph's brothers were buried at Hebron. Stephen's rhetorical device (by which he recalls that Jacob and the 12 patriarchs were not buried in Egypt but in Canaan) is strange to modern ears but would have been well understood by his hearers.

7:18 *another king, who knew nothing about Joseph.* See note on Ex 1:8.

the wisdom of the Egyptians[l] and was powerful in speech and action.

23"When Moses was forty years old, he decided to visit his fellow Israelites. 24He saw one of them being mistreated by an Egyptian, so he went to his defense and avenged him by killing the Egyptian. 25Moses thought that his own people would realize that God was using him to rescue them, but they did not. 26The next day Moses came upon two Israelites who were fighting. He tried to reconcile them by saying, 'Men, you are brothers; why do you want to hurt each other?'

27"But the man who was mistreating the other pushed Moses aside and said, 'Who made you ruler and judge over us?[m] 28Do you want to kill me as you killed the Egyptian yesterday?'[z] 29When Moses heard this, he fled to Midian, where he settled as a foreigner and had two sons.[n]

30"After forty years had passed, an angel appeared to Moses in the flames of a burning bush in the desert near Mount Sinai. 31When he saw this, he was amazed at the sight. As he went over to look more closely, he heard the Lord's voice:[o] 32'I am the God of your fathers,[p] the God of Abraham, Isaac and Jacob.'[a] Moses trembled with fear and did not dare to look.[q]

33"Then the Lord said to him, 'Take off your sandals; the place where you are standing is holy ground.[r] 34I have indeed seen the oppression of my people in Egypt. I have heard their groaning and have come down to set them free. Now come, I will send you back to Egypt.'[b][s]

35"This is the same Moses whom they had rejected with the words, 'Who made you ruler and judge?'[t] He was sent to be their ruler and deliverer by God himself,

through the angel who appeared to him in the bush. 36He led them out of Egypt[u] and did wonders and miraculous signs[v] in Egypt, at the Red Sea[c][w] and for forty years in the desert.[x]

37"This is that Moses who told the Israelites, 'God will send you a prophet like me from your own people.'[d][y] 38He was in the assembly in the desert, with the angel[z] who spoke to him on Mount Sinai, and with our fathers;[a] and he received living words[b] to pass on to us.[c]

39"But our fathers refused to obey him. Instead, they rejected him and in their hearts turned back to Egypt.[d] 40They told Aaron, 'Make us gods who will go before us. As for this fellow Moses who led us out of Egypt—we don't know what has happened to him!'[e][e] 41That was the time they made an idol in the form of a calf. They brought sacrifices to it and held a celebration in honor of what their hands had made.[f] 42But God turned away[g] and gave them over to the worship of the heavenly bodies.[h] This agrees with what is written in the book of the prophets:

" 'Did you bring me sacrifices and
        offerings
    forty years in the desert, O house of
        Israel?
43You have lifted up the shrine of Molech
    and the star of your god Rephan,
    the idols you made to worship.
Therefore I will send you into exile'[f][i]
    beyond Babylon.

44"Our forefathers had the tabernacle of

Cross references (center column):

7:22 [l]1Ki 4:30; Isa 19:11
7:27 [m]Ge 19:9; Nu 16:13
7:29 [n]Ex 2:11-15
7:31 [o]Ex 3:1-4
7:32 [p]S Ac 3:13
[q]Ex 3:6
7:33 [r]Ex 3:5; Jos 5:15
7:34 [s]Ex 3:7-10
7:35 [t]ver 27

7:36 [u]Ex 12:41; 33:1 [v]Ex 11:10; S Jn 4:48
[w]Ex 14:21
[x]Ex 15:25; 17:5,6
7:37 [y]Dt 18:15, 18; Ac 3:22
7:38 [z]ver 53
[a]Ex 19:17; Lev 27:34
[b]Dt 32:45-47; Heb 4:12 [c]Ro 3:2
7:39 [d]Nu 14:3,4
7:40 [e]Ex 32:1,23
7:41 [f]Ex 32:4-6; Ps 106:19,20; Rev 9:20
7:42 [g]Jos 24:20; Isa 63:10
[h]Jer 19:13
7:43
[i]Am 5:25-27

[z]28 Exodus 2:14 [a]32 Exodus 3:6 [b]34 Exodus 3:5,7,8,10 [c]36 That is, Sea of Reeds [d]37 Deut. 18:15 [e]40 Exodus 32:1 [f]43 Amos 5:25-27

Study notes (bottom):

7:22 *Moses was educated in all the wisdom of the Egyptians.* Not explicitly stated in the OT but to be expected if he grew up in the household of Pharaoh's daughter. Both Philo and Josephus speak of Moses' great learning.

7:23 *Moses was forty.* Moses was 80 years old when sent to speak before Pharaoh (Ex 7:7) and 120 years old when he died (Dt 34:7). Stephen's words agree with a tradition that at his first departure from Egypt he was 40 years of age.

7:29 *fled to Midian.* Rejected by his own people, Moses feared that they would inform the Egyptians, and this led to his flight to Midian (Ex 2:15), the land flanking the Gulf of Aqaba on both sides. *had two sons.* Gershom and Eliezer (Ex 2:22; 18:3–4; 1Ch 23:15).

7:30 *After forty years.* Plus the 40 years of v. 23, making the 80 years of Ex 7:7. *Mount Sinai.* Called Horeb in Ex 3:1 (see note there).

7:35 *the same Moses . . . sent to be their ruler and deliverer.* Israel rejected Moses, their deliverer, just as the Jews of Stephen's day were rejecting Jesus, their deliverer. Yet both were sent by God. *angel who appeared to him in the bush.* See Ex 3:2.

7:37 *prophet like me.* See 3:22–23; see also note on Dt 18:15.

7:38 *angel who spoke to him.* According to Jewish interpretation at that time, the law was given to Moses by angel mediation—after the manner of the original call of Moses (see Ex 3:2; see also v. 53; Gal 3:19; Heb 2:2). *he received living words to pass on to us.* Moses was the mediator between God and man on Mount Sinai.

7:39 *refused to obey him.* Another rejection of God's representative and his commands.

7:40 *Make us gods.* While Moses was on Sinai receiving the law, the people made the golden calf, rejecting God and his representative (Ex 32:1). The people had not traveled far from the idolatry of Egypt.

7:42 *God . . . gave them over.* See note on Ro 1:24.

7:43 Stephen quotes Am 5:25–27 as translated in the Septuagint, except that he replaces Damascus with Babylon in view of the fact that the final exile of Israel from the promised land was carried out by the Babylonians (Amos was speaking first of the Assyrian exile of the northern kingdom).

7:44–50 Because he had been accused of "speaking

the Testimony[j] with them in the desert. It had been made as God directed Moses, according to the pattern he had seen.[k] [45]Having received the tabernacle, our fathers under Joshua brought it with them when they took the land from the nations God drove out before them.[l] It remained in the land until the time of David,[m] [46]who enjoyed God's favor and asked that he might provide a dwelling place for the God of Jacob.[g][n] [47]But it was Solomon who built the house for him.[o]

[48]"However, the Most High[p] does not live in houses made by men.[q] As the prophet says:

[49]" 'Heaven is my throne,
    and the earth is my footstool.[r]
What kind of house will you build for
    me?
                          says the Lord.
Or where will my resting place be?
[50]Has not my hand made all these
    things?'[h][s]

[51]"You stiff-necked people,[t] with uncircumcised hearts[u] and ears! You are just like your fathers: You always resist the Holy Spirit! [52]Was there ever a prophet your fathers did not persecute?[v] They even killed those who predicted the coming of the Righteous One. And now you have betrayed and murdered him[w]— [53]you who have received the law that was put into effect through angels[x] but have not obeyed it."

The Stoning of Stephen

[54]When they heard this, they were furi-

Cross-references (center column):

7:44 /Ex 38:21; Nu 1:50; 17:7
kEx 25:8,9,40
7:45 /Jos 3:14-17; 18:1; 23:9; 24:18; Ps 44:2
m2Sa 7:2,6
7:46 n2Sa 7:8-16; 1Ki 8:17; Ps 132:1-5
7:47 o1Ki 6:1-38
7:48 pS Mk 5:7
q1Ki 8:27; 2Ch 2:6
7:49 rMt 5:34,35
7:50 sIsa 66:1,2
7:51 tEx 32:9; 33:3,5
uLev 26:41; Dt 10:16; Jer 4:4; 9:26
wAc 3:14; 1Th 2:15
7:53 xver 38; Gal 3:19; Heb 2:2

7:54 yAc 5:33
7:55 zS Lk 1:15
aS Mk 16:19
7:56 bS Mt 3:16
cS Mt 8:20
7:58 dLk 4:29
eLev 24:14,16
/Dt 17:7
gAc 22:20
hAc 8:1
7:59 iPs 31:5; Lk 23:46
7:60 /Lk 22:41; Ac 9:40
kS Mk 5:44
/S Mt 9:24
8:1 mAc 7:58
nver 4; Ac 11:19
oAc 9:31
8:3 pAc 7:58
qAc 9:1,13,21; 22:4,19; 26:10, 11; 1Co 15:9; Gal 1:13,23; Php 3:6; 1Ti 1:13
8:4 rver 1

---

ous[y] and gnashed their teeth at him. [55]But Stephen, full of the Holy Spirit,[z] looked up to heaven and saw the glory of God, and Jesus standing at the right hand of God.[a] [56]"Look," he said, "I see heaven open[b] and the Son of Man[c] standing at the right hand of God."

[57]At this they covered their ears, yelling at the top of their voices, they all rushed at him, [58]dragged him out of the city[d] and began to stone him.[e] Meanwhile, the witnesses[f] laid their clothes[g] at the feet of a young man named Saul.[h]

[59]While they were stoning him, Stephen prayed, "Lord Jesus, receive my spirit."[i] [60]Then he fell on his knees[j] and cried out, "Lord, do not hold this sin against them."[k] When he had said this, he fell asleep.[l]

8 And Saul[m] was there, giving approval to his death.

The Church Persecuted and Scattered

On that day a great persecution broke out against the church at Jerusalem, and all except the apostles were scattered[n] throughout Judea and Samaria.[o] [2]Godly men buried Stephen and mourned deeply for him. [3]But Saul[p] began to destroy the church.[q] Going from house to house, he dragged off men and women and put them in prison.

Philip in Samaria

[4]Those who had been scattered[r]

g46 Some early manuscripts *the house of Jacob*
h50 Isaiah 66:1,2

---

against the holy place" (6:13), Stephen concludes his recital with a word about the sanctuary. Presumably, he had been preaching that the risen Christ had now replaced the temple as the mediation of God's saving presence among his people and as the one (the "place") through whom they (and "all nations," Mk 11:17) could come to God in prayer (see note on 6:13).

7:44 *tabernacle of the Testimony.* So called by Stephen because the primary contents of the desert tabernacle were the ark of the covenant and the two covenant tablets it contained, which were called "the Testimony" (see Ex 25:16,21 and notes).

7:49 Isaiah reminded Israel that all creation is the temple that God himself had made. Stephen recalls that word to remind his hearers that ultimately God builds his own temple.

7:51 *uncircumcised hearts and ears.* Though physically circumcised, they were acting like the uncircumcised pagan nations around them. They were not truly consecrated to the Lord.

7:53 *law that was put into effect through angels.* See note on v. 38.

7:55 *full of the Holy Spirit.* See note on 2:4; see also 6:5.

7:56 *Son of Man.* See note on Mk 8:31. Jesus used this title

of himself (see Mk 2:10) to emphasize his relationship to Messianic prediction (Mt 25:31; Da 7:13–14). It is unusual for someone other than Jesus to apply this term to Christ (see also Rev 1:13).

7:58 *laid their clothes at the feet of . . . Saul.* Some have thought that this marked Saul as being in charge of the execution. In any case, it is Luke's way of introducing the main character of the second section of the book.

7:60 *do not hold this sin against them.* Compare with Jesus' words (Lk 23:34).

8:1 *giving approval.* See 22:20. *all except the apostles.* For the apostles to stay in Jerusalem would be an encouragement to those in prison and a center of appeal to those scattered. The church now went underground. *scattered throughout Judea and Samaria.* The beginning of the fulfillment of the commission in 1:8—not by the church's plan, but by events beyond the believers' control. See map of "The Spread of the Gospel," p. 1668.

8:3 *began to destroy.* See 22:4. The Greek underlying this phrase sometimes describes the ravages of wild animals.

8:4 *preached the word.* Many witnesses to the gospel went everywhere proclaiming the good news. The number of witnesses multiplied, and the territory covered was expanded greatly (cf. 11:19–20).

preached the word wherever they went.*s* ⁵Philip*t* went down to a city in Samaria and proclaimed the Christ*i* there. ⁶When the crowds heard Philip and saw the miraculous signs he did, they all paid close attention to what he said. ⁷With shrieks, evil*j* spirits came out of many,*u* and many paralytics and cripples were healed.*v* ⁸So there was great joy in that city.

Simon the Sorcerer

⁹Now for some time a man named Simon had practiced sorcery*w* in the city and amazed all the people of Samaria. He boasted that he was someone great,*x* ¹⁰and all the people, both high and low, gave him their attention and exclaimed, "This man is the divine power known as the Great Power."*y* ¹¹They followed him because he had amazed them for a long time with his magic. ¹²But when they believed Philip as he preached the good news of the kingdom of God*z* and the name of Jesus Christ, they were baptized,*a* both men and women. ¹³Simon himself believed and was baptized. And he followed Philip everywhere, astonished by the great signs and miracles*b* he saw.

¹⁴When the apostles in Jerusalem heard that Samaria*c* had accepted the word of God,*d* they sent Peter and John*e* to them. ¹⁵When they arrived, they prayed for them that they might receive the Holy Spirit,*f* ¹⁶because the Holy Spirit had not yet come upon any of them;*g* they had simply been baptized into*k* the name of the Lord Jesus.*h* ¹⁷Then Peter and John placed their hands on them,*i* and they received the Holy Spirit.*j*

i5 Or Messiah   *17 Greek unclean*   *k16 Or in*

Cross references (center column):

8:4 *s*Ac 15:35
8:5 *t*Ac 6:5; 21:8
8:7 *u*S Mk 16:17
*v*S Mt 4:24
8:9 *w*Ac 13:6
*x*Ac 5:36
8:10 *y*Ac 14:11; 28:6

8:12 *z*S Mt 3:2
*a*S Ac 2:38
8:13 *b*ver 6; Ac 19:11
8:14 *c*ver 1
*d*S Heb 4:12
*e*S Lk 22:8
8:15 *f*S Jn 20:22
8:16 *g*S Ac 10:44; 19:2
*h*Mt 28:19;
S Ac 2:38
8:17 *i*S Ac 6:6
*j*S Jn 20:22

8:5 *Philip.* One of the Seven in the Jerusalem church (6:5), who now becomes an evangelist, proclaiming the Christ (Messiah); see also 21:8. Philip is an example of one of those who were scattered. *a city in Samaria.* Some manuscripts have "the city of Samaria," a reference to the old capital Samaria, renamed Sebaste or Neapolis (modern Nablus).

8:9 *Simon.* In early Christian literature the "sorcerer" (Simon Magus) is described as the arch-heretic of the church and the "father" of Gnostic teaching.
8:10 *the Great Power.* Simon claimed to be either God himself or, more likely, his chief representative.
8:13 *Simon himself believed and was baptized.* It is dif-

Philip's and Peter's Missionary Journeys

▷———▶ Philip's First Journey
Ac 8:5-13

▷—·—·—▶ Philip's Second Journey
Ac 8:26-40

■———▶ Peter's Journey
Ac 9:32-10:48

▷··········▶ Ethiopian's Journey
Ac 8:26-39

Miles 10 5 0 10 20
Kms 10 5 0 10 20 30

Caesarea

Samaria (Sebaste)

Mt. Gerizim

Jordan R.

Antipatris

Joppa

Mediterranean Sea

Lydda

Jamnia

Jerusalem

Azotus

Traditional place of baptism

Betogabris

Bethsura

Dead Sea

Neapolis

Gaza

18When Simon saw that the Spirit was given at the laying on of the apostles' hands, he offered them money 19and said, "Give me also this ability so that everyone on whom I lay my hands may receive the Holy Spirit."

20Peter answered: "May your money perish with you, because you thought you could buy the gift of God with money! k 21You have no part or share l in this ministry, because your heart is not right m before God. 22Repent n of this wickedness and pray to the Lord. Perhaps he will forgive you for having such a thought in your heart. 23For I see that you are full of bitterness and captive to sin."

24Then Simon answered, "Pray to the Lord for me o so that nothing you have said may happen to me."

25When they had testified and proclaimed the word of the Lord, p Peter and John returned to Jerusalem, preaching the gospel in many Samaritan villages. q

Philip and the Ethiopian

26Now an angel r of the Lord said to Philip, s "Go south to the road—the desert road—that goes down from Jerusalem to Gaza." 27So he started out, and on his way he met an Ethiopian1 t eunuch, u an important official in charge of all the treasury of Candace, queen of the Ethiopians. This man had gone to Jerusalem to worship, v 28and on his way home was sitting in his chariot reading the book of Isaiah the prophet. 29The Spirit told w Philip, "Go to that chariot and stay near it."

30Then Philip ran up to the chariot and heard the man reading Isaiah the prophet.

8:20 kDa 5:17; Mt 10:8; Ac 2:38
8:21 lNe 2:20
mPs 78:37
8:22 nAc 2:38
8:24 oEx 8:8; Nu 21:7; 1Ki 13:6; Jer 42:2
8:25 pS Ac 13:48 qver 40
8:26 rS Ac 5:19 sAc 6:5
8:27 tPs 68:31; 87:4; Zep 3:10 uIsa 56:3-5 v1Ki 8:41-43; Jn 12:20
8:29 wAc 10:19; 11:12; 13:2; 20:23; 21:11

8:33 xIsa 53:7,8
8:35 yMt 5:2 zLk 24:27; Ac 17:2; 18:28; 28:23 aS Ac 13:32
8:36 bS Ac 2:38; 10:47
8:39 c1Pe 18:12; 2Ki 2:16; Eze 3:12,14; 8:3; 11:1,24; 43:5; 2Co 12:2; 1Th 4:17; Rev 12:5

"Do you understand what you are reading?" Philip asked.

31"How can I," he said, "unless someone explains it to me?" So he invited Philip to come up and sit with him.

32The eunuch was reading this passage of Scripture:

"He was led like a sheep to the
    slaughter,
    and as a lamb before the shearer is
    silent,
    so he did not open his mouth.
33In his humiliation he was deprived of
    justice.
Who can speak of his descendants?
For his life was taken from the
    earth." m x

34The eunuch asked Philip, "Tell me, please, who is the prophet talking about, himself or someone else?" 35Then Philip began y with that very passage of Scripture z and told him the good news a about Jesus.

36As they traveled along the road, they came to some water and the eunuch said, "Look, here is water. Why shouldn't I be baptized?" n b 38And he gave orders to stop the chariot. Then both Philip and the eunuch went down into the water and Philip baptized him. 39When they came up out of the water, the Spirit of the Lord suddenly took Philip away, c and the eunuch did not see him again, but went on his way rejoicing. 40Philip, however, appeared at Azotus

l27 That is, from the upper Nile region   m33 Isaiah 53:7,8   n36 Some late manuscripts baptized?" 37Philip said, "If you believe with all your heart, you may." The eunuch answered, "I believe that Jesus Christ is the Son of God."

---

ficult to know whether Simon's faith was genuine. Even though Luke says Simon believed, Peter's statement that Simon had no part in the apostles' ministry because his heart was not "right before God" (v. 21) casts some doubt.
8:14 had accepted the word of God. Were obedient to the gospel proclaimed by Philip. sent Peter and John. The Jerusalem church assumed the responsibility of inspecting new evangelistic efforts and the communities of believers they produced (see 11:22).
8:16 not yet come upon any of them. Since the day of Pentecost, those who "belong to Christ" (Ro 8:9) also have the Holy Spirit. But the Spirit had not yet been manifest to the Christians in Samaria by the usual signs. This deficiency was now graciously supplied (v. 17).
8:17 placed their hands on them. See v. 18; 19:1–7; cf. 2Ti 1:6; see also note on 6:6.
8:18 he offered them money. Simon had boasted of having great powers before (see v. 10 and note), and now he tried to buy this magical power he believed the apostles possessed.
8:23 full of bitterness. See Dt 29:18.
8:26 an angel of the Lord. Cf. v. 29; see note on 5:19. from Jerusalem to Gaza. A distance of about 50 miles.
8:27 an Ethiopian. Ethiopia corresponded in this period to

Nubia, from the upper Nile region at the first cataract (Aswan) to Khartoum. Candace. The traditional title of the queen mother, responsible for performing the secular duties of the reigning king—who was thought to be too sacred for such activities. gone to Jerusalem to worship. If not a full-fledged proselyte (Dt 23:1), the Ethiopian was a Gentile God-fearer.
8:30 heard the man reading. It was customary practice to read aloud.
8:34 who is the prophet talking about . . . ? Beginning with Isa 53 (see v. 35), Philip may have identified the suffering servant with the Davidic Messiah of Isa 11 or with the Son of Man (Da 7:13).
8:35 good news. The way of salvation through Jesus Christ.
8:36 they came to some water. There were several possibilities: a brook in the Valley of Elah (which David crossed to meet Goliath, 1Sa 17:40); the Wadi el-Hasi just north of Gaza; water from a spring or one of the many pools in the area.
8:37 See NIV text note on v. 36.
8:39 rejoicing. Joy is associated with salvation in Acts (see note on 16:34).

and traveled about, preaching the gospel in all the towns *d* until he reached Caesarea. *e*

Saul's Conversion

9:1–19pp — Ac 22:3–16; 26:9–18

9 Meanwhile, Saul was still breathing out murderous threats against the Lord's disciples. *f* He went to the high priest ²and asked him for letters to the synagogues in Damascus, *g* so that if he found any there who belonged to the Way, *h* whether men or women, he might take them as prisoners to Jerusalem. ³As he neared Damascus on his journey, suddenly a light from heaven flashed around him. *i* ⁴He fell to the ground and heard a voice *j* say to him, "Saul, Saul, why do you persecute me?"

⁵"Who are you, Lord?" Saul asked.

"I am Jesus, whom you are persecuting," he replied. ⁶"Now get up and go into the city, and you will be told what you must do." *k*

⁷The men traveling with Saul stood there speechless; they heard the sound *l* but did not see anyone. *m* ⁸Saul got up from the ground, but when he opened his eyes he could see nothing. *n* So they led him by the hand into Damascus. ⁹For three days he was blind, and did not eat or drink anything.

¹⁰In Damascus there was a disciple named Ananias. The Lord called to him in a vision, *o* "Ananias!"

"Yes, Lord," he answered.

¹¹The Lord told him, "Go to the house of Judas on Straight Street and ask for a man from Tarsus *p* named Saul, for he is praying. ¹²In a vision he has seen a man named Ananias come and place his hands on *q* him to restore his sight."

¹³"Lord," Ananias answered, "I have heard many reports about this man and all the harm he has done to your saints *r* in Jerusalem. *s* ¹⁴And he has come here with authority from the chief priests *t* to arrest all who call on your name." *u*

¹⁵But the Lord said to Ananias, "Go! This man is my chosen instrument *v* to carry my name before the Gentiles *w* and their kings *x* and before the people of Israel. ¹⁶I will show him how much he must suffer for my name." *y*

¹⁷Then Ananias went to the house and entered it. Placing his hands on *z* Saul, he said, "Brother Saul, the Lord—Jesus, who appeared to you on the road as you were coming here—has sent me so that you may see again and be filled with the Holy Spirit." *a* ¹⁸Immediately, something like scales fell from Saul's eyes, and he could see again. He got up and was baptized, *b* ¹⁹and after taking some food, he regained his strength.

Saul in Damascus and Jerusalem

Saul spent several days with the disciples *c* in Damascus. *d* ²⁰At once he began

---

8:40 *d* ver 25
e Ac 10:1,24; 12:19; 21:8,16; 23:23,33; 25:1,4,6,13
9:1 *f* S Ac 8:3
9:2 *g* Isa 17:1; Jer 49:23
h Ac 19:9,23; 22:4; 24:14,22
9:3 *i* 1Co 15:8
9:4 *j* Isa 6:8
9:6 *k* ver 16; Eze 3:22
9:7 *l* Jn 12:29
m Da 10:7
9:8 *n* ver 18
9:10 *o* Ac 10:3, 17,19; 12:9; 16:9,10; 18:9

9:11 *p* ver 30; Ac 11:25; 21:39; 22:3
9:12 *q* S Mk 5:23
9:13 *r* ver 32; Ac 26:10; Ro 1:7; 15:25,26,31; 16:2,15; Eph 1:1; Php 1:1
s S Ac 8:3
9:14 *t* ver 2,21
u S Ac 2:21
9:15 *v* Ac 13:2; Ro 1:1; Gal 1:15; 1Ti 1:12
w Ro 11:13; 15:15,16; Gal 1:16; 2:7,8
x Ac 25:22,23; 26:1
9:16 *y* Ac 20:23; 21:11; 2Co 6:4-10; 11:23-27; 2Ti 1:8; 2:3,9
9:17 *z* S Ac 6:6
a S Lk 1:15
9:18 *b* S Ac 2:38
9:19 *c* S Ac 11:26
d Ac 26:20

8:40 *Azotus.* OT Ashdod (see 1Sa 5:1), one of the five Philistine cities. It was about 19 miles from Gaza and 60 miles from Caesarea. *Caesarea.* Rebuilt by Herod and with an excellent harbor, it served as the headquarters of the Roman procurators. The account leaves Philip in Caesarea at this time; his next appearance is 20 years later, and he is still located in the same place (21:8).

9:1 *Saul.* Introduced at the stoning of Stephen (7:58), he was born in Tarsus and trained under Gamaliel (22:3). See note on Php 3:4–14. *murderous threats.* We do not know that Saul was directly involved in the death of anyone other than Stephen (8:1), but there appear to have been similar cases (22:4; 26:10). *high priest.* Probably Caiaphas (see note on 4:6) and the members of the Sanhedrin, who had authority over Jews both in Judea and elsewhere.

9:2 *Damascus.* Located in the Roman province of Syria, it was the nearest important city outside Palestine. It also had a large Jewish population. The distance from Jerusalem to Damascus was about 150 miles, four to six days' travel. *the Way.* A name for Christianity occurring a number of times in Acts (16:17; 18:25–26; 19:9,23; 22:4; 24:14,22; see 2Pe 2:2). Jesus called himself "the way" (Jn 14:6). *prisoners to Jerusalem.* Where the full authority of the Sanhedrin could be exercised in trial for either acquittal or death.

9:3 *a light from heaven.* "About noon" (26:13).

9:4 *why do you persecute me?* To persecute the church is to persecute Christ, for the church is his body (see 1Co 12:27; Eph 1:22–23).

9:5 *Who are you, Lord?* In rabbinic tradition such a voice

from heaven would have been understood as the voice of God himself. The solemn repetition of Saul's name and the bright light suggested to him that he was in the presence of deity.

9:7 *heard the sound.* Those with Saul heard the sound but "did not understand" what the voice was saying (22:9); cf. Da 10:7).

9:10 *Ananias.* Mentioned elsewhere only in 22:12. His was a common name (5:1; 23:2). The Greek form is derived from the Hebrew name Hananiah, meaning "The Lord is gracious/shows grace" (see Da 1:6).

9:11 *Straight Street.* Probably followed the same route of the long, straight street that today runs through the city from east to west. It is a decided contrast to the numerous crooked streets of the city (see map of "Roman Damascus," p. 1661). *Tarsus.* See note on 22:3. *praying.* Prayer is often associated with visions in Luke and Acts (see 10:9–11; Lk 1:10; 3:21; 9:28).

9:13,32 *saints.* See notes on Ro 1:7; Php 1:1.

9:15 *before the Gentiles.* See Ro 1:13–14. *their kings.* Agrippa (26:1) and Caesar at Rome (25:11–12; 28:19).

9:17 *Jesus, who appeared to you.* The Damascus road experience was not merely a vision. The resurrected Christ actually appeared to Saul, and on this fact Saul based his qualification to be an apostle (1Co 9:1; 15:8).

9:20 *At once.* Following his baptism. *synagogues.* It became Saul's regular practice to preach at every opportunity in the synagogues (13:5; 14:1; 17:1–2,10; 18:4,19; 19:8). *Jesus is the Son of God.* Saul's message was a declaration of

to preach in the synagogues *e* that Jesus is the Son of God. *f* 21All those who heard him were astonished and asked, "Isn't he the man who raised havoc in Jerusalem among those who call on this name? *g* And hasn't he come here to take them as prisoners to the chief priests?" *h* 22Yet Saul grew more and more powerful and baffled the Jews living in Damascus by proving that Jesus is the Christ. *o i*

23After many days had gone by, the Jews conspired to kill him, *j* 24but Saul learned of their plan. *k* Day and night they kept close watch on the city gates in order to kill him. 25But his followers took him by night and lowered him in a basket through an opening in the wall. *l*

26When he came to Jerusalem, *m* he tried to join the disciples, but they were all afraid of him, not believing that he really

was a disciple. 27But Barnabas *n* took him and brought him to the apostles. He told them how Saul on his journey had seen the Lord and that the Lord had spoken to him, *o* and how in Damascus he had preached fearlessly in the name of Jesus. *p* 28So Saul stayed with them and moved about freely in Jerusalem, speaking boldly in the name of the Lord. 29He talked and debated with the Grecian Jews, *q* but they tried to kill him. *r* 30When the brothers *s* learned of this, they took him down to Caesarea *t* and sent him off to Tarsus. *u*

31Then the church throughout Judea, Galilee and Samaria *v* enjoyed a time of peace. It was strengthened; and encouraged by the Holy Spirit, it grew in numbers, *w* living in the fear of the Lord.

9:20 *e*Ac 13:5, 14; 14:1; 17:2, 10,17; 18:4,19; 19:8 *f*S Mt 4:3 9:21 *g*S Ac 8:3 *h*ver 14 9:22 *i*S Lk 2:11; Ac 5:42; 17:3; 18:5,28 9:23 *j*S Ac 20:3 9:24 *k*Ac 20:3, 19; 23:16,30 9:25 *l*1Sa 19:12; 2Co 11:32,33 9:26 *m*Ac 22:17; 26:20; Gal 1:17, 18	9:27 *n*S Ac 4:36 *o*ver 3-6 *p*ver 20, 22 9:29 *q*Ac 6:1 *r*2Co 11:26 9:30 *s*S Ac 1:16 *t*S Ac 8:40 *u*S ver 11 9:31 *v*Ac 8:1 *w*S Ac 2:41

*o*22 Or *Messiah*

what he himself had become convinced of on the Damascus road: Christ's deity and Messiahship (see NIV text note on v. 22).
9:23 *After many days.* Three years (Gal 1:17–18). It is probable that the major part of this period was spent in Arabia, away from Damascus, though the borders of Arabia

extended to the environs of Damascus. *the Jews conspired to kill him.* Upon his return to Damascus, the governor under Aretas gave orders for his arrest (2Co 11:32). The absence of Roman coins struck in Damascus between A.D. 34 and 62 may indicate that Aretas was in control during that period.
9:25 *lowered him in a basket.* See 2Co 11:33 (cf. Jos 2:15;

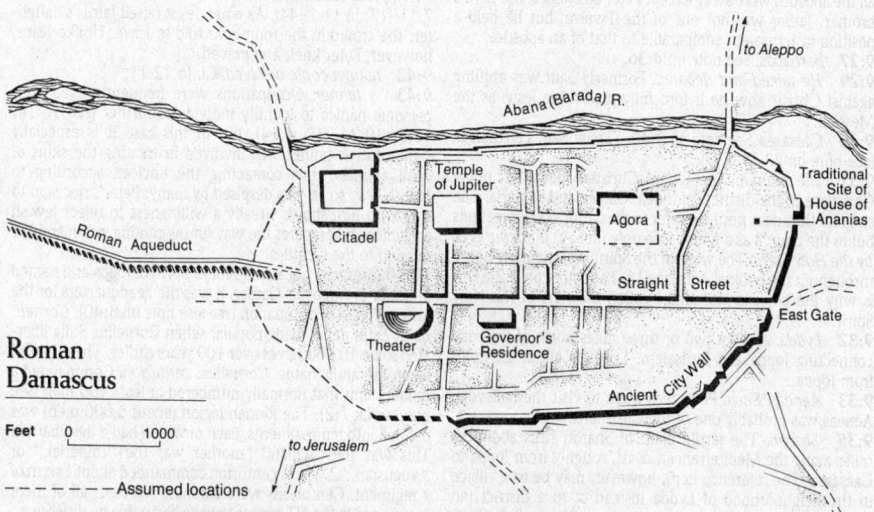

Roman Damascus

Feet 0 1000

– – – – – Assumed locations

Damascus represented much more to Saul, the strict Pharisee, than another stop on his campaign of repression. It was the hub of a vast commercial network with far-flung lines of caravan trade reaching into north Syria, Mesopotamia, Anatolia, Persia and Arabia. If the new "Way" of Christianity flourished in Damascus, it would quickly reach all these places. From the viewpoint of the Sanhedrin and of Saul, the arch-persecutor, it had to be stopped in Damascus.

The city itself was a veritable oasis, situated in a plain watered by the Biblical rivers Abana and Pharpar.

Roman architecture overlaid the Hellenistic town plan with a great temple to Jupiter and a mile-long colonnaded street, the "Straight Street" of Ac 9:11. The city gates and a section of the town wall may still be seen today, as well as the lengthy bazaar that runs along the line of the ancient street.

The dominant political figure at the time of Paul's escape from Damascus (2 Co 11:32-33) was Aretas IV, king of the Nabateans (9 B.C.-A.D. 40), though normally the Decapolis cities were attached to the province of Syria and were thus under the influence of Rome.

Aeneas and Dorcas

[32] As Peter traveled about the country, he went to visit the saints[x] in Lydda. [33] There he found a man named Aeneas, a paralytic who had been bedridden for eight years. [34] "Aeneas," Peter said to him, "Jesus Christ heals you.[y] Get up and take care of your mat." Immediately Aeneas got up. [35] All those who lived in Lydda and Sharon[z] saw him and turned to the Lord.[a]

[36] In Joppa[b] there was a disciple named Tabitha (which, when translated, is Dorcas[p]), who was always doing good[c] and helping the poor. [37] About that time she became sick and died, and her body was washed and placed in an upstairs room.[d] [38] Lydda was near Joppa; so when the disciples[e] heard that Peter was in Lydda, they sent two men to him and urged him, "Please come at once!"

[39] Peter went with them, and when he arrived he was taken upstairs to the room. All the widows[f] stood around him, crying and showing him the robes and other clothing that Dorcas had made while she was still with them.

[40] Peter sent them all out of the room;[g] then he got down on his knees[h] and prayed. Turning toward the dead woman, he said, "Tabitha, get up."[i] She opened her eyes, and seeing Peter she sat up. [41] He took her by the hand and helped her to her feet. Then he called the believers and the widows and presented her to them alive. [42] This became known all over Joppa, and many people believed in the Lord.[j] [43] Peter stayed in Joppa for some time with a tanner named Simon.[k]

Cornelius Calls for Peter

10 At Caesarea[l] there was a man named Cornelius, a centurion in what was known as the Italian Regiment. [2] He and all his family were devout and God-fearing;[m] he gave generously to those in need and prayed to God regularly. [3] One

9:32 xS ver 13
9:34 yAc 3:6,16; 4:10
9:35 z1Ch 5:16; 27:29; SS 2:1; Isa 33:9; 35:2; 65:10 aS Ac 2:41
9:36 bJos 19:46; 2Ch 2:16; Ezr 3:7; Jnh 1:3; Ac 10:5
c1Ti 2:10; Tit 3:8
9:37 dAc 1:13; 20:8
9:38 eS Ac 11:26
9:39 fAc 6:1; 1Ti 5:3

9:40 gMt 9:25
hLk 22:41; Ac 7:60
iS Lk 7:14
9:42 jS Ac 2:41
9:43 kAc 10:6
10:1 lS Ac 8:40
10:2 mver 22,35; Ac 13:16,26

p.36 Both *Tabitha* (Aramaic) and *Dorcas* (Greek) mean *gazelle.*

1Sa 19:12).

9:26 *he came to Jerusalem.* From Gal 1:19 we learn that all the apostles were away except Peter and James, the Lord's brother. James was not one of the Twelve, but he held a position in Jerusalem comparable to that of an apostle.

9:27 *Barnabas.* See note on 4:36.

9:29 *He talked and debated.* Formerly Saul was arguing against Christ; now he is forcefully presenting Jesus as the Messiah.

9:30 *Caesarea.* See note on 8:40. *Tarsus.* Saul's birthplace (see note on 22:3).

9:31 *the church.* The whole Christian body, including Christians in the districts of Judea, Galilee and Samaria. The singular thus does not refer to the various congregations but to the church as a whole (see note on 5:11). *encouraged by the Holy Spirit.* The work of the Spirit is particularly noted throughout the book of Acts (see 13:2 and note on 1:2). This is why the book is sometimes called the Acts of the Holy Spirit.

9:32 *Lydda.* A town two or three miles north of the road connecting Joppa and Jerusalem. Lydda is about 12 miles from Joppa.

9:33 *Aeneas.* Since Peter was there to visit the believers, Aeneas was probably one of the Christians.

9:35 *Sharon.* The fertile plain of Sharon runs about 50 miles along the Mediterranean coast, roughly from Joppa to Caesarea. The reference here, however, may be to a village in the neighborhood of Lydda instead of to a district (an Egyptian papyrus refers to a town by that name in Palestine).

9:36 *Joppa.* About 38 miles from Jerusalem, the main seaport of Judea. Today it is known as Jaffa and is a suburb of Tel Aviv.

9:37 *body was washed.* In preparation for burial, a custom common to both Jews (Purification of the Dead) and Greeks. *upstairs room.* If burial was delayed, it was customary to lay the body in an upper room. In Jerusalem the body had to be buried the day the person died, but outside Jerusalem up to three days might be allowed for burial.

9:38 *near Joppa.* See note on v. 32. *come at once!* Whether for consolation or for a miracle, Peter was urged to hurry in order to arrive before the burial.

9:40 *sent them all out.* Cf. 1Ki 17:23; 2Ki 4:33. Peter had been present on all three occasions recorded in Scripture when Jesus raised individuals from the dead (Mt 9:25; Lk 7:11–17; Jn 11:1–44). As when Jesus raised Jairus's daughter, the crowd in the room was told to leave. Unlike Jesus, however, Peter knelt and prayed.

9:42 *many people believed.* Cf. Jn 12:11.

9:43 *a tanner.* Occupations were frequently used with personal names to identify individuals further (see 16:14; 18:3; 19:24; 2Ti 4:14), but in this case it is especially significant. A tanner was involved in treating the skins of dead animals, thus contacting the unclean according to Jewish law; so he was despised by many. Peter's decision to stay with him shows already a willingness to reject Jewish prejudice and prepares the way for his coming vision and the mission to the Gentiles.

10:1 *Caesarea.* Located 30 miles north of Joppa and named in honor of Augustus Caesar, it was the headquarters for the Roman forces of occupation (see also note on 8:40). *Cornelius.* A Latin name made popular when Cornelius Sulla liberated some 10,000 slaves over 100 years earlier. These had all taken his family name, Cornelius. *centurion.* Commanded a military unit that normally numbered at least 100 men (see note on Lk 7:2). The Roman legion (about 6,000 men) was divided into ten regiments, each of which had a designation. This was the "Italian" (another was the "Imperial," or "Augustan," 27:1). A centurion commanded about a sixth of a regiment. Centurions were carefully selected; all of them mentioned in the NT appear to have had noble qualities (e.g., Lk 7:5). The Roman centurions provided necessary stability to the entire Roman system.

10:2 *devout.* In spite of all his good deeds, Cornelius needed to hear the way of salvation from a human messenger. The role of the angel (v. 3) was to bring Cornelius and Peter together (cf. 8:26; 9:10). *God-fearing.* The term used of one who was not a full Jewish proselyte but who believed in one God and respected the moral and ethical teachings of the Jews.

10:3 *about three in the afternoon.* Another indication that Cornelius followed Jewish religious practices. Three in the afternoon was a Jewish hour of prayer (see 3:1)—the hour of

day at about three in the afternoon[n] he had a vision.[o] He distinctly saw an angel[p] of God, who came to him and said, "Cornelius!"

[4]Cornelius stared at him in fear. "What is it, Lord?" he asked.

The angel answered, "Your prayers and gifts to the poor have come up as a memorial offering[q] before God.[r] [5]Now send men to Joppa[s] to bring back a man named Simon who is called Peter. [6]He is staying with Simon the tanner,[t] whose house is by the sea."

[7]When the angel who spoke to him had gone, Cornelius called two of his servants and a devout soldier who was one of his attendants. [8]He told them everything that had happened and sent them to Joppa.[u]

Peter's Vision

10:9–32Ref — Ac 11:5–14

[9]About noon the following day as they were on their journey and approaching the city, Peter went up on the roof[v] to pray. [10]He became hungry and wanted something to eat, and while the meal was being prepared, he fell into a trance.[w] [11]He saw heaven opened[x] and something like a large sheet being let down to earth by its four corners. [12]It contained all kinds of four-footed animals, as well as reptiles of the earth and birds of the air. [13]Then a voice told him, "Get up, Peter. Kill and eat."

[14]"Surely not, Lord!"[y] Peter replied. "I have never eaten anything impure or unclean."[z]

[15]The voice spoke to him a second time, "Do not call anything impure that God has made clean."[a]

[16]This happened three times, and immediately the sheet was taken back to heaven.

[17]While Peter was wondering about the meaning of the vision,[b] the men sent by Cornelius[c] found out where Simon's house was and stopped at the gate. [18]They called out, asking if Simon who was known as Peter was staying there.

[19]While Peter was still thinking about the vision,[d] the Spirit said[e] to him, "Simon, three[q] men are looking for you. [20]So get up and go downstairs. Do not hesitate to go with them, for I have sent them."[f]

[21]Peter went down and said to the men, "I'm the one you're looking for. Why have you come?"

[22]The men replied, "We have come from Cornelius the centurion. He is a righteous and God-fearing man,[g] who is respected by all the Jewish people. A holy angel told him to have you come to his house so that he could hear what you have to say."[h] [23]Then Peter invited the men into the house to be his guests.

Peter at Cornelius' House

The next day Peter started out with them, and some of the brothers[i] from Joppa went along.[j] [24]The following day he arrived in Caesarea.[k] Cornelius was expecting them and had called together his relatives and close friends. [25]As Peter entered the house, Cornelius met him and fell at his feet in reverence. [26]But Peter made him get up. "Stand up," he said, "I am only a man myself."[l]

[27]Talking with him, Peter went inside and found a large gathering of people.[m] [28]He said to them: "You are well aware that it is against our law for a Jew to asso-

Cross references (center column)

10:3 [n]Ps 55:17; Ac 3:1 [o]S Ac 9:10 [p]S Ac 5:19
10:4 [q]Ps 20:3; S Mt 10:42; 26:13 [r]Rev 8:4
10:5 [s]S Ac 9:36
10:6 [t]Ac 9:43
10:8 [u]S Ac 9:36
10:9 [v]S Mt 24:17
10:10 [w]Ac 22:17
10:11 [x]S Mt 3:16
10:14 [y]Ac 9:5
[z]Lev 11:4-8, 13-20; 20:25; Dt 14:3-20; Eze 4:14
10:15 [a]ver 28; Ge 9:3; Mt 15:11; Lk 11:41; Ac 11:9; Ro 14:14,17,20; 1Co 10:25; 1Ti 4:3,4; Tit 1:15
10:17 [b]S Ac 9:10 [c]ver 7,8
10:19 [d]S Ac 9:10 [e]S Ac 8:29
10:20 [f]Ac 15:7-9
10:22 [g]ver 2 [h]Ac 11:14
10:23 [i]S Ac 1:16 [j]ver 45; Ac 11:12
10:24 [k]S Ac 8:40
10:26 [l]Ac 14:15; Rev 19:10; 22:8,9
10:27 [m]ver 24

[q]*19* One early manuscript *two*; other manuscripts do not have the number.

Footnotes (bottom)

the evening incense. *a vision.* Not a dream or trance but a revelation through an angel to Cornelius while at prayer (see v. 30; see also note on 9:11).
10:4 *memorial offering.* A portion of the grain offering burned on the altar was called a "memorial" (Lev 2:2).
10:5–6 *Joppa . . . Simon the tanner.* See notes on 9:36,43.
10:9 *roof to pray.* It was customary for eastern houses to have flat roofs with outside stairways. The roof was used as a convenient place for relaxation and privacy.
10:10 *fell into a trance.* A state of mind God produced and used to communicate with Peter. It was not merely imagination or a dream. Peter's consciousness was heightened to receive the vision from God.
10:12 *all kinds of four-footed animals.* Including animals both clean and unclean according to Lev 11.
10:14 *Surely not, Lord!* So deeply ingrained was the observance of the laws of clean and unclean that Peter refused to obey immediately. *impure or unclean.* Anything common (impure) was forbidden by the law to be eaten.
10:15 *God has made clean.* Jesus had already laid the

groundwork for setting aside the laws of clean and unclean food (Mt 15:11; see 1Ti 4:3–5).
10:16 *three times.* To make a due impression on Peter.
10:23 *invited the men into the house.* By providing lodging for them, Peter was already taking the first step toward accepting Gentiles. Such intimate relationship with Gentiles was contrary to prescribed Jewish practice. *The next day.* It was too late in the day to start out on the long journey to Caesarea (see note on v. 1). *some of the brothers.* Six in number (11:12), they were Jewish in background (10:45).
10:26 *I am only a man.* Possibly Cornelius was only intending to honor Peter as one having a rank superior to his own, since he was God's messenger. But Peter allowed no chance for misunderstanding—he was not to be worshiped as more than a created being.
10:28 *God has shown me.* Peter recognized that his vision had deeper significance than declaring invalid the distinction between clean and unclean meat; he saw that the barrier between Jew and Gentile had been removed (see Eph 2:11–22).

ciate with a Gentile or visit him. *n* But God has shown me that I should not call any man impure or unclean. *o* 29So when I was sent for, I came without raising any objection. May I ask why you sent for me?"

30Cornelius answered: "Four days ago I was in my house praying at this hour, at three in the afternoon. Suddenly a man in shining clothes *p* stood before me 31and said, 'Cornelius, God has heard your prayer and remembered your gifts to the poor. 32Send to Joppa for Simon who is called Peter. He is a guest in the home of Simon the tanner, who lives by the sea.' 33So I sent for you immediately, and it was good of you to come. Now we are all here in the presence of God to listen to everything the Lord has commanded you to tell us."

34Then Peter began to speak: "I now

realize how true it is that God does not show favoritism *q* 35but accepts men from every nation who fear him and do what is right. *r* 36You know the message *s* God sent to the people of Israel, telling the good news *t* of peace *u* through Jesus Christ, who is Lord of all. *v* 37You know what has happened throughout Judea, beginning in Galilee after the baptism that John preached— 38how God anointed *w* Jesus of Nazareth with the Holy Spirit and power, and how he went around doing good and healing *x* all who were under the power of the devil, because God was with him. *y* 39"We are witnesses *z* of everything he did in the country of the Jews and in Jerusalem. They killed him by hanging him on a tree, *a* 40but God raised him from the dead *b* on the third day and caused him to be seen. 41He was not seen by all the

10:28 *n*Jn 4:9; 18:28; Ac 11:3
*o*S ver 14,15; Ac 15:8,9
10:30
*p*S Jn 20:12

10:34 *q*Dt 10:17; 2Ch 19:7; Job 34:19; Mk 12:14; Ro 2:11; Gal 2:6; Eph 6:9; Col 3:25; Jas 2:1; 1Pe 1:17
10:35 *r*Ac 15:9
10:36 *s*1Jn 1:5
*t*S Ac 13:32
*u*S Lk 2:14
*v*S Mt 28:18
10:38 *w*S Ac 4:26
*x*S Mt 4:23
*y*S Jn 3:2
10:39 *z*ver 41; S Lk 24:48
*a*S Ac 5:30
10:40 *b*S Ac 2:24

10:30 *Four days ago.* The Jews counted a part of a day as a day: (1) the day the angel appeared to Cornelius, (2) the day the messengers came to Joppa and Peter received a vision, (3) the day the group set out from Joppa and (4) the day they arrived at Cornelius's house. *a man in shining clothes.* Common language to describe an angel when appearing in the

form of a man.
10:34 *God does not show favoritism.* God does not favor an individual because of his station in life, his nationality or his material possessions (see note on Jas 2:1). He does, however, respect his character and judge his work. This is evident because God "accepts men from every nation who

---

Timeline of Paul's Life

Lines, brackets and dotted lines help show sequence of events, but are not meant to point to precise months or days within a given year, since exact dating is difficult.

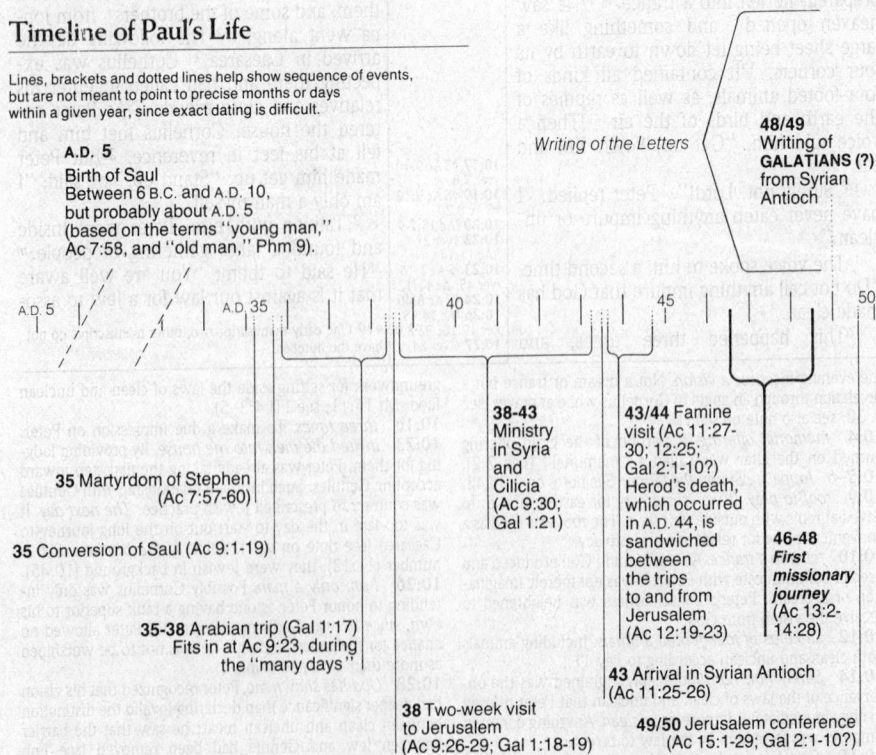

A.D. 5
Birth of Saul
Between 6 B.C. and A.D. 10, but probably about A.D. 5 (based on the terms "young man," Ac 7:58, and "old man," Phm 9).

Writing of the Letters

48/49
Writing of
GALATIANS (?)
from Syrian
Antioch

35 Martyrdom of Stephen (Ac 7:57-60)

35 Conversion of Saul (Ac 9:1-19)

35-38 Arabian trip (Gal 1:17)
Fits in at Ac 9:23, during the "many days"

38-43
Ministry
in Syria
and
Cilicia
(Ac 9:30;
Gal 1:21)

38 Two-week visit
to Jerusalem
(Ac 9:26-29; Gal 1:18-19)

43/44 Famine
visit (Ac 11:27-30; 12:25)
Gal 2:1-10?)
Herod's death,
which occurred
in A.D. 44, is
sandwiched
between
the trips
to and from
Jerusalem
(Ac 12:19-23)

43 Arrival in Syrian Antioch
(Ac 11:25-26)

49/50 Jerusalem conference
(Ac 15:1-29; Gal 2:1-10?)

46-48
*First
missionary
journey*
(Ac 13:2-14:28)

people,[c] but by witnesses whom God had already chosen—by us who ate[d] and drank with him after he rose from the dead. [42]He commanded us to preach to the people[e] and to testify that he is the one whom God appointed as judge of the living and the dead.[f] [43]All the prophets testify about him[g] that everyone[h] who believes[i] in him receives forgiveness of sins through his name."[j]

[44]While Peter was still speaking these words, the Holy Spirit came on[k] all who heard the message. [45]The circumcised believers who had come with Peter[l] were astonished that the gift of the Holy Spirit had been poured out[m] even on the Gentiles. [n] [46]For they heard them speaking in tongues[r][o] and praising God.

Then Peter said, [47]"Can anyone keep these people from being baptized with water?[p] They have received the Holy Spirit just as we have."[q] [48]So he ordered that they be baptized in the name of Jesus Christ.[r] Then they asked Peter to stay with them for a few days.

Peter Explains His Actions

11 The apostles and the brothers[s] throughout Judea heard that the Gentiles also had received the word of God.[t] [2]So when Peter went up to Jerusalem, the circumcised believers[u] criticized him [3]and said, "You went into the house of uncircumcised men and ate with them."[v]

[4]Peter began and explained everything to them precisely as it had happened: [5]"I was in the city of Joppa praying, and in a

10:41 [c]Jn 14:17, 22 [d]Lk 24:43; Jn 21:13; Ac 1:4
10:42 [e]Mt 28:19, 20 [f]S Jn 5:22; Ac 17:31; Ro 14:9; 2Co 5:10; 2Ti 4:1; 1Pe 4:5
10:43 [g]Isa 53:11; Ac 26:22 [h]Ac 15:9 [i]S Jn 3:15 [j]S Lk 24:27
10:44 [k]Ac 8:15, 16; 11:15; 15:8; 19:6; S Lk 1:15
10:45 [l]ver 23 [m]Ac 2:33,38 [n]Ac 11:18; 15:8
10:46 [o]S Mk 16:17

10:47 [p]Ac 8:36 [q]S Jn 20:22; Ac 11:17
10:48 [r]S Ac 2:38
11:1 [s]S Ac 1:16 [t]S Heb 4:12
11:2 [u]Ac 10:45
11:3 [v]Ac 10:25, 28; Gal 2:12

[r]46 Or *other languages*

---

fear him and do what is right" (v. 35). Cornelius already worshiped the true God, but this was not enough: He lacked faith in Christ (v. 36).
10:36 *peace.* Between God and man (reconciliation). *Lord of all.* Lord of both Jew and Gentile (see vv. 34–35).
10:37 *after the baptism that John preached.* Similar to the

outline of Mark's Gospel, Peter's sermon begins with John's baptism and continues to the resurrection of Jesus. This is significant since the early church fathers viewed Mark as the "interpreter" of Peter (see Introduction to Mark: Author). See previous summaries of Peter's preaching (2:14–41; 3:12–26; 4:8–12; 5:29–32); see also note on 2:14–40.

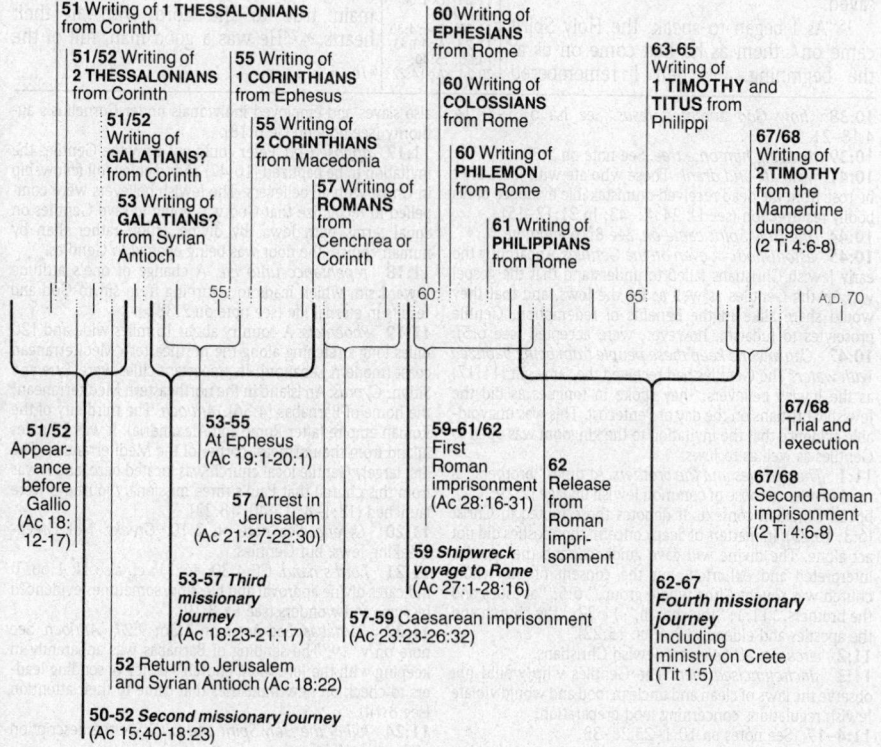

51 Writing of **1 THESSALONIANS** from Corinth

51/52 Writing of **2 THESSALONIANS** from Corinth

51/52 Writing of **GALATIANS?** from Corinth

53 Writing of **GALATIANS?** from Syrian Antioch

55 Writing of **1 CORINTHIANS** from Ephesus

55 Writing of **2 CORINTHIANS** from Macedonia

57 Writing of **ROMANS** from Cenchrea or Corinth

60 Writing of **EPHESIANS** from Rome

60 Writing of **COLOSSIANS** from Rome

60 Writing of **PHILEMON** from Rome

61 Writing of **PHILIPPIANS** from Rome

63-65 Writing of **1 TIMOTHY** and **TITUS** from Philippi

67/68 Writing of **2 TIMOTHY** from the Mamertime dungeon (2 Ti 4:6-8)

55   60   65   A.D. 70

51/52 Appearance before Gallio (Ac 18:12-17)

53-55 At Ephesus (Ac 19:1-20:1)

57 Arrest in Jerusalem (Ac 21:27-22:30)

59-61/62 First Roman imprisonment (Ac 28:16-31)

62 Release from Roman imprisonment

67/68 Trial and execution

67/68 Second Roman imprisonment (2 Ti 4:6-8)

59 *Shipwreck voyage to Rome* (Ac 27:1-28:16)

53-57 *Third missionary journey* (Ac 18:23-21:17)

57-59 Caesarean imprisonment (Ac 23:23-26:32)

62-67 *Fourth missionary journey* Including ministry on Crete (Tit 1:5)

52 Return to Jerusalem and Syrian Antioch (Ac 18:22)

50-52 *Second missionary journey* (Ac 15:40-18:23)

trance I saw a vision. *w* I saw something like a large sheet being let down from heaven by its four corners, and it came down to where I was. [6]I looked into it and saw four-footed animals of the earth, wild beasts, reptiles, and birds of the air. [7]Then I heard a voice telling me, 'Get up, Peter. Kill and eat.'

[8]"I replied, 'Surely not, Lord! Nothing impure or unclean has ever entered my mouth.'

[9]"The voice spoke from heaven a second time, 'Do not call anything impure that God has made clean.' *x* [10]This happened three times, and then it was all pulled up to heaven again.

[11]"Right then three men who had been sent to me from Caesarea *y* stopped at the house where I was staying. [12]The Spirit told *z* me to have no hesitation about going with them. *a* These six brothers *b* also went with me, and we entered the man's house. [13]He told us how he had seen an angel *c* appear in his house and say, 'Send to Joppa for Simon who is called Peter. [14]He will bring you a message *d* through which you and all your household *e* will be saved.'

[15]"As I began to speak, the Holy Spirit came on *f* them as he had come on us at the beginning. *g* [16]Then I remembered

what the Lord had said: 'John baptized with *s* water, *h* but you will be baptized with the Holy Spirit.' *i* [17]So if God gave them the same gift *j* as he gave us, *k* who believed in the Lord Jesus Christ, who was I to think that I could oppose God?"

[18]When they heard this, they had no further objections and praised God, saying, "So then, God has granted even the Gentiles repentance unto life." *l*

The Church in Antioch

[19]Now those who had been scattered by the persecution in connection with Stephen *m* traveled as far as Phoenicia, Cyprus and Antioch, *n* telling the message only to Jews. [20]Some of them, however, men from Cyprus *o* and Cyrene, *p* went to Antioch *q* and began to speak to Greeks also, telling them the good news *r* about the Lord Jesus. [21]The Lord's hand was with them, *s* and a great number of people believed and turned to the Lord. *t*

[22]News of this reached the ears of the church at Jerusalem, and they sent Barnabas *u* to Antioch. [23]When he arrived and saw the evidence of the grace of God, *v* he was glad and encouraged them all to remain true to the Lord with all their hearts. *w* [24]He was a good man, full of the

Cross references (center column):

11:5 *w*Ac 10:9-32; S 9:10
11:9 *x*S Ac 10:15
11:11 *y*S Ac 8:40
11:12 *z*S Ac 8:29 *a*Ac 15:9; Ro 3:22 *b*ver 1,29; S Ac 1:16
11:13 *c*S Ac 5:19
11:14 *d*Ac 10:36 *e*Jn 4:53; Ac 16:15,31-34; 18:8; 1Co 1:11, 16
11:15 *f*S Ac 10:44 *g*Ac 2:4
11:16 *h*S Mk 1:4 *i*S Mk 1:8
11:17 *j*Ac 2:38 *k*Ac 10:45,47
11:18 *l*Ro 10:12, 13; 2Co 7:10
11:19 *m*Ac 8:1,4 *n*ver 26,27; Ac 13:1; 14:26; 18:22; Gal 2:11
11:20 *o*Ac 4:36 *p*S Mt 27:32 *q*S ver 19 *r*S Ac 13:32
11:21 *s*Lk 1:66 *t*S Ac 2:41
11:22 *u*S Ac 4:36
11:23 *v*Ac 13:43; 14:26; 15:40; 20:24 *w*Ac 14:22

s 16 Or *in*

10:38 *how God anointed Jesus.* See Isa 61:1–3; Lk 4:18–21.

10:39 *hanging him on a tree.* See note on 5:30.

10:41 *who ate and drank.* Those who ate with Jesus after he rose from the dead received unmistakable evidence of his bodily resurrection (see Lk 24:42–43; Jn 21:12–15).

10:44 *the Holy Spirit came on.* See 8:16 and note.

10:45 *astonished . . . even on the Gentiles.* Apparently the early Jewish Christians failed to understand that the gospel was for the Gentiles as well as for the Jews, and that they would share alike in the benefits of redemption. Gentile proselytes to Judaism, however, were accepted (see 6:5).

10:47 *Can anyone keep these people from being baptized with water?* The Gentiles had received the same gift (11:17) as the Jewish believers; they spoke in tongues as did the Jewish Christians on the day of Pentecost. This was unavoidable evidence that the invitation to the kingdom was open to Gentiles as well as to Jews.

11:1 *The apostles and the brothers.* At times "brothers" is used to refer to those of common Jewish lineage (2:29; 7:2), but in Christian contexts it denotes those united in Christ (6:3; 10:23). In matters of deep concern, the apostles did not act alone. The divine will gave guidance, and the apostles interpreted and exhorted, but the consent of the whole church was sought ("the whole group," 6:5; "apostles and the brothers," 11:1; "the church," 11:22; "the church and the apostles and elders," 15:4; cf. 15:22).

11:2 *circumcised believers.* Jewish Christians.

11:3 *uncircumcised men.* The Gentiles who would not observe the laws of clean and unclean food and would violate Jewish regulations concerning food preparation.

11:4–17 See notes on 10:1–23,28–33.

11:14 *you and all your household.* Not only the family but

also slaves and employed individuals under Cornelius's authority (see note on Ge 6:18).

11:17 *oppose God.* Peter could not deny the Gentiles the invitation to be baptized (10:47) and to enjoy full fellowship in Christ with all believers. The Jewish believers were compelled to recognize that God was going to save Gentiles on equal terms with Jews. By divine action rather than by human choice, the door was being opened to Gentiles.

11:18 *repentance unto life.* A change of one's attitude toward sin, which leads to a turning from sin to God and results in eternal life (see note on 2:38).

11:19 *Phoenicia.* A country about 15 miles wide and 120 miles long stretching along the northeastern Mediterranean coast (modern Lebanon). Its important cities were Tyre and Sidon. *Cyprus.* An island in the northeastern Mediterranean; the home of Barnabas (4:36). *Antioch.* The third city of the Roman empire (after Rome and Alexandria). It was 15 miles inland from the northeast corner of the Mediterranean. The first largely Gentile local church was located here, and it was from this church that Paul's three missionary journeys were launched (13:1–4; 15:40; 18:23).

11:20 *Cyrene.* See note on 2:10. *Greeks.* Not Greek-speaking Jews, but Gentiles.

11:21 *Lord's hand.* Cf. 4:30; 13:11; cf. also Lk 1:66. It indicates divine approval and blessing, sometimes evidenced by signs and wonders (see Ex 8:19).

11:22 *Barnabas.* See notes on 4:36; 9:27. *Antioch.* See note on v. 19. The sending of Barnabas was apparently in keeping with the Jerusalem church's policy of sending leaders to check on new ministries that came to their attention (see 8:14).

11:24 *full of the Holy Spirit and faith.* See the description of Stephen (6:5).

Holy Spirit[x] and faith, and a great number of people were brought to the Lord.[y]

[25]Then Barnabas went to Tarsus[z] to look for Saul, [26]and when he found him, he brought him to Antioch. So for a whole year Barnabas and Saul met with the church and taught great numbers of people. The disciples[a] were called Christians first[b] at Antioch.

[27]During this time some prophets[c] came down from Jerusalem to Antioch. [28]One of them, named Agabus,[d] stood up and through the Spirit predicted that a severe famine would spread over the entire Roman world.[e] (This happened during the reign of Claudius.)[f] [29]The disciples,[g] each according to his ability, decided to provide help[h] for the brothers[i] living in Judea. [30]This they did, sending their gift to the elders[j] by Barnabas[k] and Saul.[l]

Peter's Miraculous Escape From Prison

12 It was about this time that King Herod[m] arrested some who belonged to the church, intending to persecute them. [2]He had James, the brother of John,[n] put to death with the sword.[o] [3]When he saw that this pleased the Jews,[p] he proceeded to seize Peter also. This happened during the Feast of Unleavened Bread.[q] [4]After arresting him, he put him in prison, handing him over to be guarded by four squads of four soldiers each. Herod

intended to bring him out for public trial after the Passover.[r]

[5]So Peter was kept in prison, but the church was earnestly praying to God for him.[s]

[6]The night before Herod was to bring him to trial, Peter was sleeping between two soldiers, bound with two chains,[t] and sentries stood guard at the entrance. [7]Suddenly an angel[u] of the Lord appeared and a light shone in the cell. He struck Peter on the side and woke him up. "Quick, get up!" he said, and the chains fell off Peter's wrists.[v]

[8]Then the angel said to him, "Put on your clothes and sandals." And Peter did so. "Wrap your cloak around you and follow me," the angel told him. [9]Peter followed him out of the prison, but he had no idea that what the angel was doing was really happening; he thought he was seeing a vision.[w] [10]They passed the first and second guards and came to the iron gate leading to the city. It opened for them by itself,[x] and they went through it. When they had walked the length of one street, suddenly the angel left him.

[11]Then Peter came to himself[y] and said, "Now I know without a doubt that the Lord sent his angel and rescued me[z] from Herod's clutches and from everything the Jewish people were anticipating."

[12]When this had dawned on him, he went to the house of Mary the mother of

Cross references (center column)

11:24 xS Lk 1:15
yS Ac 2:41
11:25 zS Ac 9:11
11:26 aver 29;
Ac 6:1,2; 9:19,26,
38; 13:52
bAc 26:28;
1Pe 4:16
11:27 cAc 13:1;
15:32; 1Co 11:4;
12:28,29; 14:29,
32,37; S Eph 4:11
11:28 dAc 21:10
eS Mt 24:14
fAc 18:2
11:29 gS ver 26
hRo 15:26;
2Co 8:1-4; 9:2
iver 1,12;
S Ac 1:16
11:30 jAc 14:23;
15:2,22; 20:17;
1Ti 5:17; Tit 1:5;
Jas 5:14; 1Pe 5:1;
2Jn 1 kS Ac 4:36
lAc 12:25
12:1 mS Mt 14:1
12:2 nS Mt 4:21
oMk 10:39
12:3 pAc 24:27;
25:9 qEx 12:15;
23:15; Ac 20:6

12:4 rS Jn 11:55
12:5 sS Ac 1:14;
Ro 15:30,31;
Eph 6:18;
12:6 tAc 21:33
12:7 uS Ac 5:19
vPs 107:14;
Ac 16:26
12:9 wS Ac 9:10
12:10 xAc 5:19;
16:26
12:11 yLk 15:17
zPs 34:7;
Da 3:28; 6:22;
2Co 1:10; 2Pe 2:9

Study notes (bottom)

11:25 *Tarsus.* See 9:11,30 and note on 22:3.

11:26 *whole year.* Luke notes definite periods of time (18:11; 19:8,10; 24:27; 28:30). *Christians.* Whether adopted by believers or invented by enemies as a term of reproach, it is an apt title for those "belonging to Christ" (the meaning of the term).

11:27 *prophets.* The first mention of the gift of prophecy in Acts. Prophets preach, exhort, explain or, as in this case, foretell (see 13:1; 15:32; 19:6; 21:9–10; Ro 12:6; 1Co 12:10; 13:2,8; 14:3,6,29–37; see also notes on Jnh 3:2; Zec 1:1; Eph 4:11).

11:28 *Agabus.* Later foretells Paul's imprisonment (21:10). In Acts, prophets are engaged in foretelling (v. 27; 21:9–10) at least as often as in "forthtelling" (15:32).

11:30 *elders.* First reference to them in Acts (see notes on 1Ti 3:1; 5:17). Since the apostles are not mentioned, they may have been absent from Jerusalem at this time.

12:1 *about this time.* Some hold that the events recorded in ch. 12 group together matters concerning Herod and may not be in strict chronological order. For example, the arrival of Barnabas and Saul in Jerusalem (11:30) may have followed Herod's persecution and Peter's release from prison. Since the date of Herod's death was A.D. 44, these events would probably have occurred in 43. According to this view, the famine of 11:28 occurred c. 46, following Herod's death (v. 23). Others hold that such juggling of events is not necessary. Thus the relief gift of 11:30 came before Herod's death in 44, and the return of Barnabas and Saul (v. 25) followed Herod's death. According to the former view, the

Jerusalem visit of Gal 2:1–10 was the famine visit of v. 25; 11:30. According to the latter view, the Gal 2:1 visit was the Jerusalem council visit of 15:1–29. *King Herod.* Agrippa I, grandson of Herod the Great (see notes on Mt 2:1; 14:1) and son of Aristobulus. He was a nephew of Herod Antipas, who had beheaded John the Baptist (Mt 14:3–12) and had tried Jesus (Lk 23:8–12). When Antipas was exiled, Agrippa received his tetrarchy as well as those of Philip and Lysanias (see Lk 3:1). In A.D. 41 Judea and Samaria were added to his realm.

12:2 *James.* Brother of John the apostle and son of Zebedee (Mt 4:21). This event took place about ten years after Jesus' death and resurrection. Jesus had warned of their coming suffering (Mt 20:23). *death with the sword.* Beheaded, like John the Baptist.

12:3 *Feast of Unleavened Bread.* See note on Lk 22:1.

12:4 *four squads.* One company of four soldiers for each of the four watches of the night. *Passover.* Another way of referring to the whole week of the festival (see note on Lk 22:1).

12:7 *a light shone.* The glory of the Lord (see Lk 2:9).

12:9 *prison.* Probably the tower of Antonia, located at the northwest corner of the temple—the "barracks" where Paul was later held (see 21:34).

12:12 *Mary.* The aunt of Barnabas (see Col 4:10). Apparently her home was a gathering place for Christians. It may have been the location of the upper room where the Last Supper was held (see Mk 14:13–15; see also Ac 1:13) and the place of prayer in 4:31. *John . . . Mark.* See note on v. 25.

The Spread of the Gospel

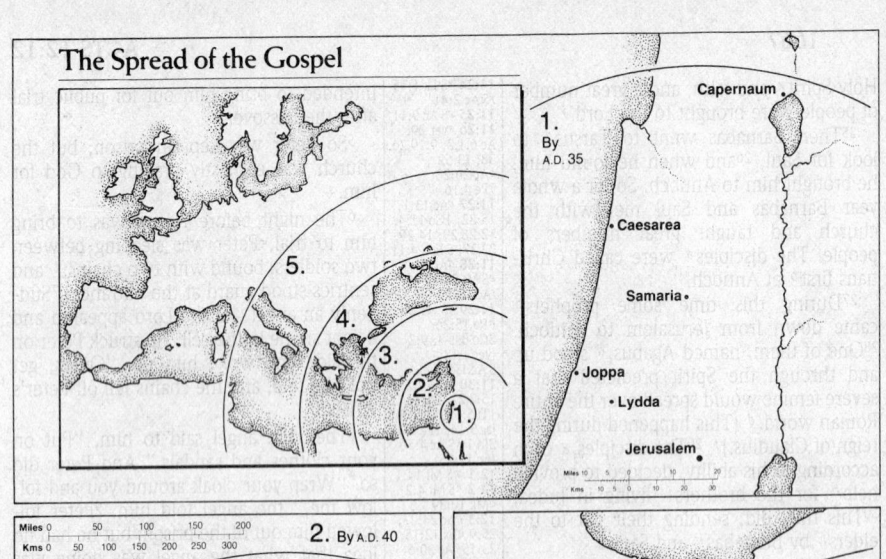

1.
By
A.D. 35

Capernaum

Caesarea

Samaria

Joppa

Lydda

Jerusalem

Miles 10   5   0   10   20
Kms 10 5 0   10   20   30

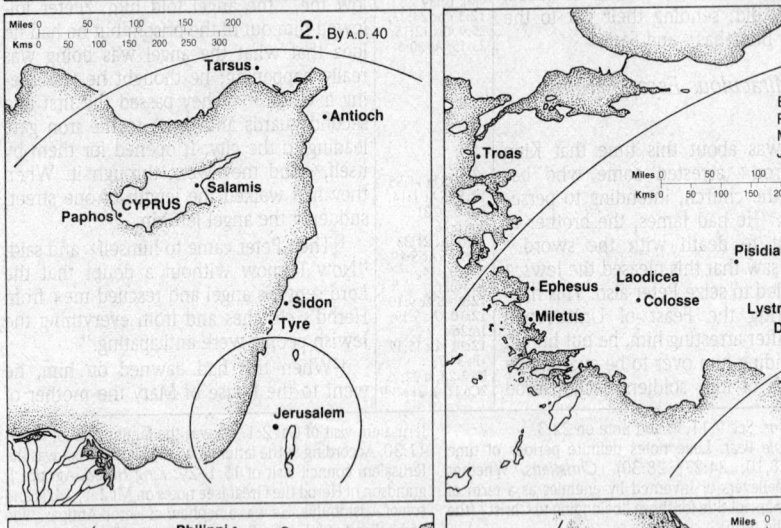

2. By A.D. 40

Miles 0   50   100   150   200
Kms 0 50 100 150 200 250 300

Tarsus

Antioch

CYPRUS   Salamis

Paphos

Sidon
Tyre

Jerusalem

3.

By A.D. 48
Paul's First
Missionary
Journey

Miles 0   50   100   150   200
Kms 0 50 100 150 200 250 300

Troas

Ephesus   Laodicea   Pisidian Antioch
         Colosse   Iconium
Miletus   Lystra
                               Derbe

CYPRUS

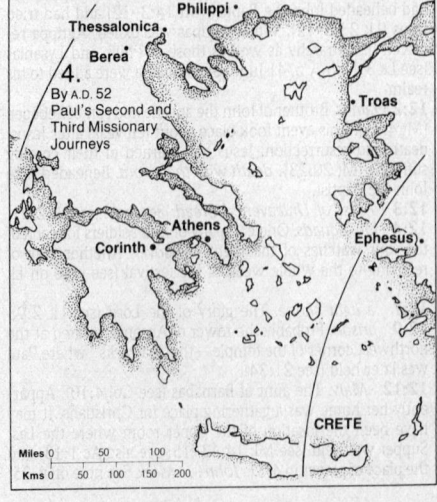

Philippi
Thessalonica
Berea

4.

By A.D. 52
Paul's Second and
Third Missionary
Journeys

Troas

Athens
Corinth   Ephesus

Miles 0   50   100
Kms 0 50 100 150 200

CRETE

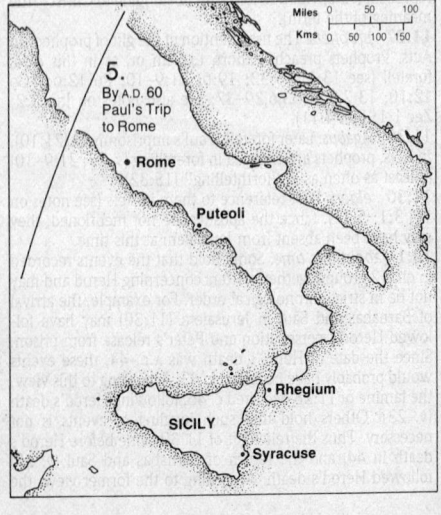

Miles 0   50   100
Kms 0 50 100 150

5.
By A.D. 60
Paul's Trip
to Rome

Rome

Puteoli

Rhegium

SICILY

Syracuse

John, also called Mark,[a] where many people had gathered and were praying.[b] [13]Peter knocked at the outer entrance, and a servant girl named Rhoda came to answer the door.[c] [14]When she recognized Peter's voice, she was so overjoyed[d] she ran back without opening it and exclaimed, "Peter is at the door!"

[15]"You're out of your mind," they told her. When she kept insisting that it was so, they said, "It must be his angel."[e]

[16]But Peter kept on knocking, and when they opened the door and saw him, they were astonished. [17]Peter motioned with his hand[f] for them to be quiet and described how the Lord had brought him out of prison. "Tell James[g] and the brothers[h] about this," he said, and then he left for another place.

[18]In the morning, there was no small commotion among the soldiers as to what had become of Peter. [19]After Herod had a thorough search made for him and did not find him, he cross-examined the guards and ordered that they be executed.[i]

Herod's Death

Then Herod went from Judea to Caesarea[j] and stayed there a while. [20]He had been quarreling with the people of Tyre and Sidon;[k] they now joined together and

sought an audience with him. Having secured the support of Blastus, a trusted personal servant of the king, they asked for peace, because they depended on the king's country for their food supply.[l]

[21]On the appointed day Herod, wearing his royal robes, sat on his throne and delivered a public address to the people. [22]They shouted, "This is the voice of a god, not of a man." [23]Immediately, because Herod did not give praise to God, an angel[m] of the Lord struck him down,[n] and he was eaten by worms and died.

[24]But the word of God[o] continued to increase and spread.[p]

[25]When Barnabas[q] and Saul had finished their mission,[r] they returned from[t] Jerusalem, taking with them John, also called Mark.[s]

Barnabas and Saul Sent Off

13 In the church at Antioch[t] there were prophets[u] and teachers:[v] Barnabas,[w] Simeon called Niger, Lucius of Cyrene,[x] Manaen (who had been brought up with Herod[y] the tetrarch) and Saul. [2]While they were worshiping the Lord and fasting, the Holy Spirit said,[z] "Set apart for me Barnabas and Saul for the work[a] to which I have called them."[b] [3]So after they

[t]25 Some manuscripts to

Cross references (center column)

12:12 [a]ver 25; Ac 13:5,13; 15:37,39; Col 4:10; 2Ti 4:11; Phm 24; 1Pe 5:13 [b]ver 5
12:13 [c]Jn 18:16, 17
12:14 [d]Lk 24:41
12:15 [e]S Mt 18:10
12:17 [f]Ac 13:16; 19:33; 21:40 [g]S Ac 15:13 [h]S Ac 1:16
12:19 [i]Ac 16:27 [j]S Ac 8:40
12:20 [k]S Mt 11:21
[l]1Ki 5:9,11; Eze 27:17
12:23 [m]S Ac 5:19 [n]1Sa 25:38; 2Sa 24:16,17; 2Ki 19:35
12:24 [o]S Heb 4:12 [p]Ac 6:7; 19:20
12:25 [q]S Ac 4:36 [r]Ac 11:30 [s]S ver 12
13:1 [t]S Ac 11:19 [u]S Ac 11:27 [v]S Eph 4:11 [w]S Ac 4:36 [x]S Mt 27:32 [y]S Mt 14:1
13:2 [z]S Ac 8:29 [a]Ac 14:26 [b]Ac 9:15; 22:21

Study notes (bottom)

12:13 *Rhoda.* A hired servant, but in sympathy with the family and the church.

12:15 *his angel.* Reflects the belief that everyone has a personal angel who ministers to him (cf. Mt 18:10; Heb 1:14), adding the idea that such an angel occasionally showed himself and that his appearance resembled the person under his care.

12:16 *they were astonished.* Though they had been "earnestly praying to God for him" (v. 5).

12:17 *James.* The Lord's brother, a leader in the Jerusalem church (Gal 1:19). James, the brother of John, had been killed (see v. 2).

12:19 *Caesarea.* Not only a headquarters for Roman procurators, but Agrippa used it as his capital when no procurators were assigned to Judea (see notes on 8:40; 10:1).

12:20 *Tyre and Sidon.* The leading cities of Phoenicia (Lebanon today). They were dependent on the grainfields of Galilee for their food. *Blastus.* The treasurer; not otherwise known.

12:21 *On the appointed day.* A festival Herod was celebrating in honor of Claudius Caesar (Josephus, *Antiquities*, 19.8.2). *wearing his royal robes.* The historian Josephus describes a silver robe, dazzling bright, that Herod wore that day. When people acclaimed him a god, he did not deny it. He was seized with violent pains, was carried out and died five days later (Josephus, *Antiquities*, 19.8.2).

12:23 *angel of the Lord.* See note on v. 7. *eaten by worms.* A miserable death associated with Herod's acceptance of acclaim to be divine, but may also be seen as divine retribution for his persecution of the church.

12:24 *the word of God . . . spread.* Third summary report of progress (see 6:7; 9:31). Three more follow (16:5; 19:20;

28:31).

12:25 *John . . . Mark.* See v. 12. He was perhaps the young man who fled on the night of Jesus' arrest (Mk 14:51–52). He wrote the second Gospel (see Introduction to Mark: Author; John Mark in the NT) and accompanied Barnabas and Saul on the first part of their first missionary journey (see notes on 15:38–39).

13:1 *prophets.* See note on 11:27. The special gift of inspiration experienced by OT prophets (Dt 18:18–20; 2Pe 1:21) was known in the NT as well (2:17–18; 1Co 14:29–32; Eph 3:5). The prophets are second to the apostles in Paul's lists (1Co 12:28–29; Eph 2:20; 4:11; but cf. Lk 11:49; Ro 12:6; 1Co 12:10). *teachers.* See 11:26; 15:35; 18:11; 20:20; 28:31; 1Co 12:28–29; Eph 4:11. *Barnabas . . . Saul.* The church leaders at Antioch, perhaps listed in the order of their importance. *Barnabas.* See note on 4:36. He was sent originally to Antioch by the church in Jerusalem (11:22), had recently returned from taking alms to Jerusalem (12:25) and was a recognized leader in the church at Antioch. *Simeon called Niger.* "Simeon" suggests Jewish background; in that case, Niger (Latin for "black") may indicate his dark complexion. *Lucius of Cyrene.* Lucius is a Latin name. In the second group of preachers coming to Antioch, some were from Cyrene (11:20), capital of Libya (see 6:9 and note). *Manaen.* In Hebrew, Menahem. Since he was the foster brother of Herod Antipas, he would be able to tell of the thoughts and actions of Herod (see Lk 9:7–9).

13:2 *worshiping the Lord and fasting.* Paul's first missionary journey did not result from a planning session but from the Spirit's initiative as the leaders worshiped (see v. 4). The communication from the Holy Spirit may have come through the prophets.

13:3 *placed their hands on them.* For the purpose of

had fasted and prayed, they placed their hands on them[c] and sent them off. [d]

On Cyprus

[4]The two of them, sent on their way by the Holy Spirit,[e] went down to Seleucia and sailed from there to Cyprus.[f] [5]When they arrived at Salamis, they proclaimed the word of God[g] in the Jewish synagogues.[h] John[i] was with them as their helper.

[6]They traveled through the whole island until they came to Paphos. There they met a Jewish sorcerer[j] and false prophet[k] named Bar-Jesus, [7]who was an attendant of the proconsul,[l] Sergius Paulus. The proconsul, an intelligent man, sent for Barnabas and Saul because he wanted to hear the word of God. [8]But Elymas the sorcerer[m] (for that is what his name means) opposed them and tried to turn the proconsul[n] from the faith. [o] [9]Then Saul, who was also called Paul, filled with the Holy Spirit,[p] looked straight at Elymas and said, [10]"You are a child of the devil[q] and an enemy of everything that is right! You are full of all kinds of deceit and trickery. Will you never stop perverting the right ways of the Lord?[r] [11]Now the hand of the Lord is against you.[s] You are going to be blind, and for a time you will be unable to see the light of the sun." [t]

Immediately mist and darkness came over him, and he groped about, seeking someone to lead him by the hand. [12]When the proconsul[u] saw what had happened, he believed, for he was amazed at the teaching about the Lord.

In Pisidian Antioch

[13]From Paphos,[v] Paul and his companions sailed to Perga in Pamphylia,[w] where John[x] left them to return to Jerusalem. [14]From Perga they went on to Pisidian Antioch.[y] On the Sabbath[z] they entered the synagogue[a] and sat down. [15]After the reading from the Law[b] and the Prophets, the synagogue rulers sent word to them, saying, "Brothers, if you have a message of encouragement for the people, please speak."

[16]Standing up, Paul motioned with his hand[c] and said: "Men of Israel and you Gentiles who worship God, listen to me! [17]The God of the people of Israel chose our fathers; he made the people prosper during their stay in Egypt, with mighty power he led them out of that country,[d] [18]he endured their conduct[u][e] for about forty

[u]18 Some manuscripts and cared for them

13:3 [c]S Ac 6:6
[d]Ac 14:26
13:4 [e]ver 2,3
[f]Ac 4:36
13:5 [g]S Heb 4:12
[h]S Ac 9:20
[i]S Ac 12:12
13:6 [j]Ac 8:9
[k]S Mt 7:15
13:7 [l]ver 8,12;
Ac 18:12; 19:38
13:8 [m]Ac 8:9
[n]S ver 7
[o]Isa 30:11;
Ac 6:7
13:9 [p]S Lk 1:15
13:10
[q]Mt 13:38;
Jn 8:44 [r]Hos 14:9
13:11 [s]Ex 9:3;
1Sa 5:6,7; Ps 32:4

[t]Ge 19:10,11;
2Ki 6:18
13:12 [u]S ver 7
13:13 [v]ver 6
[w]S Ac 2:10
[x]S Ac 12:12
13:14 [y]Ac 14:19,
21 [z]ver 27,42,44;
Ac 16:13; 18:4
[a]S Ac 9:20
13:15 [b]Ac 15:21
13:16
[c]S Ac 12:17
13:17 [d]Ex 6:6,7;
Dt 7:6-8
13:18 [e]Dt 1:31

---

separating the two for the designated work (see 14:26 for the completion of the mission). Fasting and prayer accompany this appointment (see 14:23; cf. Lk 2:37).

13:4 See map No. 11 at the end of the Study Bible. *Seleucia.* The seaport of Antioch (16 miles to the west, and 5 miles upstream from the mouth of the Orontes River). *Cyprus.* Many Jews lived there, and the gospel had already been preached there (11:19–20; see note on 11:19).

13:5 *Salamis.* A town on the east coast of the central plain of Cyprus, near modern Famagusta. *John.* John Mark, a cousin of Barnabas (see Col 4:10); see also note on 12:25.

13:6 *Paphos.* At the western end of Cyprus, nearly 100 miles from Salamis. It was the headquarters for Roman rule. *Bar-Jesus.* "Bar" is Aramaic for "son of "; "Jesus" is derived from the Greek for "Joshua" (see NIV text note on Mt 1:21).

13:7 *proconsul.* Since Cyprus was a Roman senatorial province, a proconsul was assigned to it.

13:8 *Elymas.* A Semitic name meaning "sorcerer" or "magician" or "wise man" (probably a self-assumed designation).

13:9 *Saul . . . called Paul.* The names mean "asked [of God]" and "little" respectively. It was customary to have a given name, in this case Saul (Hebrew, Jewish background), and a later name, in this case Paul (Roman, Hellenistic background). From now on Saul is called Paul in Acts. This may be due to Saul's success in preaching to Paulus or to the fact that he is now entering the Gentile phase of his ministry. The order in which they are mentioned now changes from "Barnabas and Saul" to "Paul and Barnabas." Upon their return to the Jerusalem church, however, the order reverts to "Barnabas and Paul" (15:12).

13:12 *he believed.* He was convinced by the miracle and the message.

13:13 *Perga in Pamphylia.* Perga was the capital of Pamphylia, a coastal province of Asia Minor between the provinces of Lycia and Cilicia, and was 5 miles inland and 12 miles east of the important seaport Attalia. *John left them.* Homesickness to get back to Jerusalem, an illness of Paul necessitating a change in plans and a trip to Galatia, and a change in leadership from Barnabas to Paul have all been suggested as reasons for John Mark's return. Paul's dissatisfaction with his departure is noted later (15:37–39).

13:14 *Pisidian.* See note on 14:24. *Antioch.* Named after Antiochus, king of Syria after the death of Alexander the Great. It was 110 miles from Perga and was at the hub of good roads and trade. The city had a large Jewish population. It was a Roman colony, which meant that a contingent of retired military men was settled there. They were given free land and were made citizens of the city of Rome, with all the accompanying privileges. *synagogue.* Paul's regular practice was to begin his preaching in the synagogue as long as the Jews would allow it (see v. 5; 14:1; 17:1,10,17; 18:4,19; 19:8). His reason for doing so was grounded in his understanding of God's redemptive plan (see v. 46; Ro 1:16; 2:9–10; see also Ro 9–11). He was not neglecting his Gentile mission, for the God-fearers (Gentiles committed to worshiping the one true God) were part of the audience. Moreover, the synagogue provided a ready-made preaching situation with a building, regularly scheduled meetings and a people who knew the OT Scriptures. It was customary to invite visitors, and especially visiting rabbis (such as Paul), to address the gathering.

13:15 *the Law and the Prophets.* Sections from the OT were read, followed by exposition and exhortation. *rulers.* Those who were responsible for calling readers and preachers, arranging the service and maintaining order.

13:16 *Gentiles who worship God.* See note on 10:2.

years in the desert,^{f} ^{19}he overthrew seven nations in Canaan^g and gave their land to his people^h as their inheritance.^{i} ^{20}All this took about 450 years.

"After this, God gave them judges^j until the time of Samuel the prophet.^{k} ^{21}Then the people asked for a king,^{l} and he gave them Saul^m son of Kish, of the tribe of Benjamin,^{n} who ruled forty years. ^{22}After removing Saul,^{o} he made David their king.^{p} He testified concerning him: 'I have found David son of Jesse a man after my own heart;^{q} he will do everything I want him to do.'^{r}

^{23}"From this man's descendants^s God has brought to Israel the Savior^t Jesus,^{u} as he promised.^{v} ^{24}Before the coming of Jesus, John preached repentance and baptism to all the people of Israel.^{w} ^{25}As John was completing his work,^{x} he said: 'Who do you think I am? I am not that one.^{y} No, but he is coming after me, whose sandals I am not worthy to untie.'^{z}

^{26}"Brothers,^{a} children of Abraham,^{b} and you God-fearing Gentiles, it is to us that this message of salvation^c has been sent. ^{27}The people of Jerusalem and their rulers did not recognize Jesus,^{d} yet in condemning him they fulfilled the words of the prophets^e that are read every Sabbath. ^{28}Though they found no proper ground for a death sentence, they asked Pilate to have him executed.^{f} ^{29}When they had carried out all that was written about him,^{g} they took him down from the tree^h and laid him in a tomb.^{i} ^{30}But God raised him from the dead,^{j} ^{31}and for many days he was seen by those who had traveled with him from Galilee to Jerusalem.^{k} They are now his witnesses^l to our people.

^{32}"We tell you the good news:^{m} What God promised our fathers^n ^{33}he has fulfilled for us, their children, by raising up Jesus.^{o} As it is written in the second Psalm:

" 'You are my Son;
today I have become your
Father.^{v}'^{w}^{p}

^{34}The fact that God raised him from the

dead, never to decay, is stated in these words:

" 'I will give you the holy and sure
blessings promised to
David.'^{x} ^{q}

^{35}So it is stated elsewhere:

" 'You will not let your Holy One see
decay.'^{y} ^{r}

^{36}"For when David had served God's purpose in his own generation, he fell asleep;^{s} he was buried with his fathers^t and his body decayed. ^{37}But the one whom God raised from the dead^u did not see decay.

^{38}"Therefore, my brothers, I want you to know that through Jesus the forgiveness of sins is proclaimed to you.^{v} ^{39}Through him everyone who believes^w is justified from everything you could not be justified from by the law of Moses.^{x} ^{40}Take care that what the prophets have said does not happen to you:

^{41}" 'Look, you scoffers,
wonder and perish,
for I am going to do something in your
days
that you would never believe,
even if someone told you.'^{z} "^{y}

^{42}As Paul and Barnabas were leaving the synagogue,^{z} the people invited them to speak further about these things on the next Sabbath. ^{43}When the congregation was dismissed, many of the Jews and devout converts to Judaism followed Paul and Barnabas, who talked with them and urged them to continue in the grace of God.^{a}

^{44}On the next Sabbath almost the whole city gathered to hear the word of the Lord. ^{45}When the Jews saw the crowds, they were filled with jealousy and talked abusively^b against what Paul was saying.^{c}

^{46}Then Paul and Barnabas answered them boldly: "We had to speak the word

---

Cross references (center column):

13:18 ^{f}Nu 14:33; Ps 95:10; Ac 7:36
13:19 ^{g}Dt 7:1
^{h}Jos 19:51;
Ac 7:45 ^{i}Ps 78:55
13:20 ^{j}Jdg 2:16
^{k}1Sa 3:19,20;
Ac 3:24
13:21 ^{l}1Sa 8:5,19
^{m}1Sa 10:1
^{n}1Sa 9:1,2
13:22 ^{o}1Sa 15:23,26
^{p}1Sa 16:13;
Ps 89:20
^{q}1Sa 13:14;
Jer 3:15
^{r}Isa 44:28
13:23 ^{s}Mt 1:1
^{t}S Lk 2:11
^{u}Mt 1:21 ^{v}ver 32; 2Sa 7:11; 22:51; Jer 30:9
13:24 ^{w}S Mk 1:4
13:25 ^{x}Ac 20:24
^{y}Jn 1:20
^{z}Mt 3:11; Jn 1:27
13:26 ^{a}S Ac 22:5
^{b}S Lk 3:8
^{c}Ac 4:12; 28:28
13:27 ^{d}Ac 3:17
^{e}S Lk 24:27;
S Mt 1:22
13:28 ^{f}Mt 27:20-25;
Ac 3:14
13:29 ^{g}S Mt 1:22;
Lk 18:31
^{h}S Ac 5:30
^{i}Lk 23:53
13:30 ^{j}S Mt 16:21;
28:6; S Ac 2:24
13:31 ^{k}Mt 28:16
^{l}S Lk 24:48
13:32 ^{m}Isa 40:9;
52:7; Ac 5:42;
8:35; 10:36;
14:7,15,21;
17:18 ^{n}Ac 26:6;
Ro 1:2; 4:13; 9:4
13:33 ^{o}S Ac 2:24
^{p}Ps 2:7;
S Mt 3:17
13:34 ^{q}Isa 55:3
13:35 ^{r}Ps 16:10;
Ac 2:27
13:36 ^{s}S Mt 9:24
^{t}2Sa 7:12;
1Ki 2:10;
2Ch 29:28;
Ac 2:29
13:37 ^{u}S Ac 2:24
13:38 ^{v}S Lk 24:47;
Ac 2:38
13:39 ^{w}S Jn 3:15
^{x}Ro 3:28
13:41 ^{y}Hab 1:5
13:42 ^{z}ver 14
13:43
^{a}S Ac 11:23;
14:22; S Ro 3:24
13:45 ^{b}Ac 18:6;
1Pe 4:4; Jude 10
^{c}S 1Th 2:16

^{v}33 Or have begotten you ^{w}33 Psalm 2:7
^{x}34 Isaiah 55:3 ^{y}35 Psalm 16:10 ^{z}41 Hab. 1:5

13:20 *about 450 years.* The 400 years of the "stay in Egypt" (v. 17; see note on 7:6) plus the 40 years in the desert and the time between the crossing of the Jordan and the distribution of the land (see Jos 14–19).
13:23 *as he promised.* See, e.g., Isa 11:1–16.
13:29–31 *tree . . . tomb . . . God raised . . . witnesses.* See note on 3:14.
13:31 *many days.* Forty days (see 1:3).
13:33 *today I have become your Father.* Here refers to the resurrection of Jesus (see NIV text note here and note on Ps

2:7–9; cf. Ro 1:4).
13:35 *not let your Holy One see decay.* Quoted also in Peter's sermon at Pentecost (see note on 2:27).
13:39 *justified from.* Justification combines two aspects: (1) the forgiveness of sins (here); (2) the gift of righteousness (Ro 3:21–22).
13:46 *had to speak . . . to you first.* Since the gospel came from and was for the Jews first and since Paul was himself a Jew with great compassion for his people (Ro 9:1–5; 10:1–3). See note on v. 14.

of God to you first. *d* Since you reject it and do not consider yourselves worthy of eternal life, we now turn to the Gentiles. *e* 47For this is what the Lord has commanded us:

" 'I have made you*a* a light for the
        Gentiles,*f*
    that you*a* may bring salvation to the
        ends of the earth.'*b*"*g*

48When the Gentiles heard this, they were glad and honored the word of the Lord; *h* and all who were appointed for eternal life believed.

49The word of the Lord *i* spread through the whole region. 50But the Jews incited the God-fearing women of high standing and the leading men of the city. They stirred up persecution against Paul and Barnabas, and expelled them from their region. *j* 51So they shook the dust from their feet *k* in protest against them and went to

Iconium. *l* 52And the disciples *m* were filled with joy and with the Holy Spirit. *n*

In Iconium

14 At Iconium *o* Paul and Barnabas went as usual into the Jewish synagogue. *p* There they spoke so effectively that a great number *q* of Jews and Gentiles believed. 2But the Jews who refused to believe stirred up the Gentiles and poisoned their minds against the brothers. *r* 3So Paul and Barnabas spent considerable time there, speaking boldly *s* for the Lord, who confirmed the message of his grace by enabling them to do miraculous signs and wonders. *t* 4The people of the city were divided; some sided with the Jews, others with the apostles. *u* 5There was a plot afoot among the Gentiles and Jews, *v* together with their leaders, to mistreat them and stone them. *w* 6But they found out about it

13:46 *d*ver 26; Ac 3:26
*e*Mt 21:41; Ac 18:6; 23:21; 26:20; 28:28; Ro 11:11
13:47 *f*S Lk 2:32
*g*Isa 49:6
13:48 *h*ver 49; Ac 8:25; 15:35, 36; 19:10,20
13:49 *i*S ver 48
13:50 *j*S 1Th 2:16
13:51 *k*S Mt 10:14

*l*Ac 14:1,19,21; 16:2; 2Ti 3:11
13:52 *m*S Ac 11:26
*n*S Lk 1:15
14:1 *o*S Ac 13:51
*p*S Ac 9:20
*q*S Ac 2:41
14:2 *r*S Ac 1:16
14:3 *s*S Ac 4:29
*t*S Jn 4:48
14:4 *u*Ac 17:4,5; 28:24
14:5 *v*S Ac 20:3
*w*ver 19

*a*47 The Greek is singular.   *b*47 Isaiah 49:6

13:48 *all who were appointed for eternal life believed.* Possession of eternal life involves both human faith and divine appointment.
13:51 *shook the dust.* To show the severance of responsibility and the repudiation of those who had rejected their message and had brought suffering to the servants of the Lord (see note on Lk 9:5). *Iconium.* Modern Konya; it was an important crossroads and agricultural center in the central plain of the province of Galatia.
13:52 *filled . . . with the Holy Spirit.* See note on 2:4.
14:1 *great number.* At first there was good success, then bitter opposition from the Jews (v. 2). But these evidently failed in their initial attempt, for Paul and Barnabas remained there a considerable time (v. 3). A second wave of persecution was planned, involving violence (v. 5).
14:3 *confirmed . . . by . . . miraculous signs.* A major

purpose of miracles was to confirm the truth of the words and the approval of God.
14:4 *apostles.* Both Paul and Barnabas are called apostles (see v. 14; see also note on Mk 6:30). The term is used here not of the Twelve but in the broader sense to refer to persons sent on a mission, i.e., missionaries (see 13:2–3).
14:5 *stone them.* A Jewish mode of execution for blasphemy. Probably mob action was planned here.
14:6 *Lycaonian cities.* Lycaonia was a district east of Pisidia, north of the Taurus Mountains. It was part of the Roman province of Galatia. *Lystra.* A Roman colony (see note on 13:14) and probable home of Timothy (though he was known in Iconium as well), it was about 20 miles from Iconium and 130 miles from Antioch. *Derbe.* About 60 miles from Lystra; home of Gaius (see 20:4 and note on 14:20).

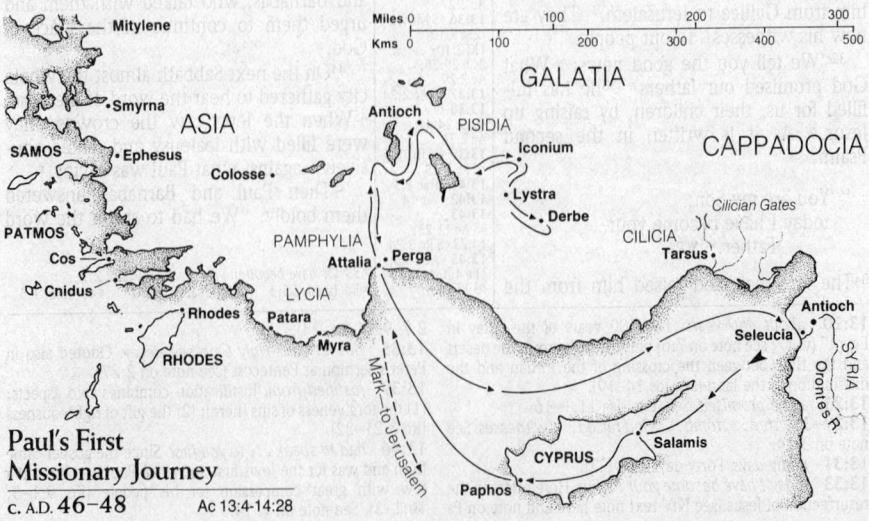

Paul's First Missionary Journey
c. A.D. 46–48   Ac 13:4–14:28

and fled[x] to the Lycaonian cities of Lystra and Derbe and to the surrounding country, [7]where they continued to preach[y] the good news.[z]

In Lystra and Derbe

[8]In Lystra there sat a man crippled in his feet, who was lame from birth[a] and had never walked. [9]He listened to Paul as he was speaking. Paul looked directly at him, saw that he had faith to be healed[b] [10]and called out, "Stand up on your feet!"[c] At that, the man jumped up and began to walk.[d]

[11]When the crowd saw what Paul had done, they shouted in the Lycaonian language, "The gods have come down to us in human form!"[e] [12]Barnabas they called Zeus, and Paul they called Hermes because he was the chief speaker.[f] [13]The priest of Zeus, whose temple was just outside the city, brought bulls and wreaths to the city gates because he and the crowd wanted to offer sacrifices to them.

[14]But when the apostles Barnabas and Paul heard of this, they tore their clothes[g] and rushed out into the crowd, shouting: [15]"Men, why are you doing this? We too are only men,[h] human like you. We are bringing you good news,[i] telling you to turn from these worthless things[j] to the living God,[k] who made heaven and earth[l] and sea and everything in them.[m] [16]In the past, he let[n] all nations go their own way.[o] [17]Yet he has not left himself without testimony:[p] He has shown kindness by giving you rain from heaven and crops in their seasons;[q] he provides you

with plenty of food and fills your hearts with joy."[r] [18]Even with these words, they had difficulty keeping the crowd from sacrificing to them.

[19]Then some Jews[s] came from Antioch and Iconium[t] and won the crowd over. They stoned Paul[u] and dragged him outside the city, thinking he was dead. [20]But after the disciples[v] had gathered around him, he got up and went back into the city. The next day he and Barnabas left for Derbe.

The Return to Antioch in Syria

[21]They preached the good news[w] in that city and won a large number[x] of disciples. Then they returned to Lystra, Iconium[y] and Antioch, [22]strengthening the disciples and encouraging them to remain true to the faith.[z] "We must go through many hardships[a] to enter the kingdom of God," they said. [23]Paul and Barnabas appointed elders[c][b] for them in each church and, with prayer and fasting,[c] committed them to the Lord,[d] in whom they had put their trust. [24]After going through Pisidia, they came into Pamphylia,[e] [25]and when they had preached the word in Perga, they went down to Attalia.

[26]From Attalia they sailed back to Antioch,[f] where they had been committed to the grace of God[g] for the work they had now completed.[h] [27]On arriving there, they gathered the church together and reported all that God had done through them[i] and how he had opened the door[j] of faith to

14:6	xMt 10:23
14:7	yAc 16:10
	zver 15,21; S Ac 13:32
14:8	aAc 3:2
14:9	bMt 9:28, 29; 13:58
14:10	cEze 2:1
	dAc 3:8
14:11	eAc 8:10; 28:6
14:12	fEx 7:1
14:14	gS Mk 14:63
14:15	hS Ac 10:26 iver 7,21; S Ac 13:32 jISa 12:21; 1Th 1:9 kSt 16:16 lGe 1:1 mPs 146:6; Rev 14:7
14:16	nAc 17:30 oPs 81:12; Mic 4:5
14:17	pRo 1:20 qDt 11:14; Job 5:10; Ps 65:10
	rPs 4:7
14:19	sAc 13:45 tS Ac 13:51 u2Co 11:25; 2Ti 3:11
14:20	vver 22, 28; S Ac 11:26
14:21	wS Ac 13:32 xS Ac 2:41 yS Ac 13:51
14:22	zAc 11:23; 13:43 aJn 16:33; 1Th 3:3; 2Ti 3:12
14:23	bS Ac 11:30 cAc 13:3 dAc 20:32
14:24	eS Ac 2:10
14:26	fS Ac 11:19 gS Ac 11:23 hAc 13:1,3
14:27	iAc 15:4, 12; 21:19 jICo 16:9; 2Co 2:12; Col 4:3; Rev 3:8

c23 Or Barnabas ordained elders; or Barnabas had elders elected

---

14:12 Zeus ... Hermes. Zeus was the patron god of the city, and his temple was there. People who came to bring sacrifices to Zeus apparently decided to make an offering to Paul and Barnabas instead. The identification of Zeus with Barnabas may indicate that his appearance was more imposing, and Paul was identified as the god Hermes (the Roman Mercury) because he was the spokesman (see 28:6). This incident may have been occasioned by an ancient legend that told of a supposed visit to the same general area by Zeus and Hermes. They were, however, not recognized by anyone except an old couple. So the people of Lystra were determined not to allow such an oversight to happen again.
14:13 city gates. The Greek for this expression can refer to the temple gates, the city gates or house gates.
14:14 tore their clothes. A Jewish way of expressing great anguish (see Ge 37:29,34).
14:15 worthless things. Used in the OT to denote false gods (see 1Sa 12:21).
14:19 They stoned Paul. Within the city rather than at the usual place of execution outside the walls (cf. 2Co 12:2).
14:20 disciples had gathered around him. Young Timothy may have been present (see 2Ti 3:10–11). Derbe. A border town in the southeastern part of the Lycaonian region of Galatia (see note on v. 6). An inscription naming the city has

been discovered about 30 miles east of what was previously thought to be the city site.
14:23 appointed. The Greek for this word (used also in 2Co 8:19) can mean (1) to stretch out the hand, (2) to appoint by show of hands or (3) to appoint or elect without regard to the method. In 6:6 the appointment of the Seven included selection by the church and presentation to the apostles, who prayed and laid their hands on them. Because these were new churches, at least partly pagan in background, Paul and Barnabas may have both selected and appointed the elders.
14:24 Pisidia. A district about 120 miles long and 50 miles wide, north of Pamphylia (13:13–14). Bandits frequented the region (see perhaps 2Co 11:26). Pamphylia. A district 80 miles long and 20 miles at the widest part, on the southern coast of Asia Minor. After A.D. 74 Pisidia was included in the Roman province of Pamphylia (see 13:13).
14:25 Perga. See note on 13:13. Attalia. The best harbor on the coast of Pamphylia (see 13:13).
14:26 Antioch. See 11:20; see also note on 11:19.
14:27 opened the door of faith. God had brought Gentiles to faith—had, as it were, opened the door for them to believe (cf. 11:18).

the Gentiles. 28And they stayed there a long time with the disciples. *k*

The Council at Jerusalem

15 Some men *l* came down from Judea to Antioch and were teaching the brothers: *m* "Unless you are circumcised, *n* according to the custom taught by Moses, *o* you cannot be saved." 2This brought Paul and Barnabas into sharp dispute and debate with them. So Paul and Barnabas were appointed, along with some other believers, to go up to Jerusalem *p* to see the apostles and elders *q* about this question. 3The church sent them on their way, and as they traveled through Phoenicia *r* and Samaria, they told how the Gentiles had been converted. *s* This news made all the brothers very glad. 4When they came to Jerusalem, they were welcomed by the church and the apostles and elders, to whom they reported everything God had done through them. *t*

5Then some of the believers who belonged to the party *u* of the Pharisees *v* stood up and said, "The Gentiles must be circumcised and required to obey the law of Moses." *w*

6The apostles and elders met to consider this question. 7After much discussion, Pe-

ter got up and addressed them: "Brothers, you know that some time ago God made a choice among you that the Gentiles might hear from my lips the message of the gospel and believe. *x* 8God, who knows the heart, *y* showed that he accepted them by giving the Holy Spirit to them, *z* just as he did to us. 9He made no distinction between us and them, *a* for he purified their hearts by faith. *b* 10Now then, why do you try to test God *c* by putting on the necks of the disciples a yoke *d* that neither we nor our fathers have been able to bear? 11No! We believe it is through the grace *e* of our Lord Jesus that we are saved, just as they are."

12The whole assembly became silent as they listened to Barnabas and Paul telling about the miraculous signs and wonders *f* God had done among the Gentiles through them. *g* 13When they finished, James *h* spoke up: "Brothers, listen to me. 14Simon *d* has described to us how God at first showed his concern by taking from the Gentiles a people for himself. *i* 15The words of the prophets are in agreement with this, as it is written:

16"'After this I will return

Cross references

14:28
k S Ac 11:26
15:1 *l* ver 24; Gal 2:12
m S Ac 1:16 *n* ver 5; Gal 5:2,3
o S Ac 6:14
15:2 *p* Gal 2:2
q S Ac 11:30
15:3 *r* Ac 11:19
s Ac 14:27
15:4 *t* ver 12; Ac 14:27; 21:19
15:5 *u* Ac 5:17
v Mt 3:7 *w* ver 1

15:7 *x* Ac 10:1-48
15:8 *y* S Rev 2:23
z S Ac 10:44,47
15:9 *a* Ac 10:28, 34; 11:12
b Ac 10:43
15:10 *c* Ac 5:9
d S Mt 23:4; Gal 5:1
15:11
e S Ro 3:24; Gal 2:16; Eph 2:5-8
15:12 *f* S Jn 4:48
g ver 4; Ac 14:27; 21:19
15:13 *h* Ac 12:17; 21:18; 1Co 15:7; Gal 1:19; 2:9,12
15:14 *i* 2Pe 1:1

d 14 Greek *Simeon*, a variant of *Simon*; that is, Peter

14:28 *long time.* Probably more than a year.

15:1 *Some men.* Probably from "the party of the Pharisees" (v. 5). These were believers who insisted that before a person could become a true Christian he must keep the law of Moses, and the test of such compliance was circumcision. *from Judea.* Meant that these Judaizers (or legalists) were given a hearing, not that they correctly represented the apostles and elders of Jerusalem (cf. v. 24).

15:2 *go up to Jerusalem.* See notes on 12:1; Gal 2:1. Those who hold that Gal 2:1–10 refers to the famine visit of 11:27–30; 12:25 argue that since Gal 2:2 says that the visit mentioned there was occasioned by a revelation, it must refer to Agabus's prediction of the coming famine (11:27–28). Those who believe that Gal 2:1–10 refers to the Jerusalem council visit of 15:1–22 assert that the famine visit occurred at the time of Herod Agrippa's death in A.D. 44 (11:27–30; 12:25). Thus Saul's conversion, which was 14 years earlier (Gal 2:1), would have occurred in 30, the probable year of Christ's crucifixion—which obviously seems too early.

15:4–22 The sequence of meetings described in vv. 4–22 is: (1) a general meeting of welcome and report (vv. 4–5); (2) a meeting of the leaders (perhaps to one side) while the church was still assembled (vv. 6–11); (3) a meeting of the apostles, the elders and the whole assembly (vv. 12–22).

15:4 The first meeting was a report, cordially received, about the work done among the Gentiles.

15:5 *believers who belonged to the party of the Pharisees.* Some Pharisees became Christians and brought their Judaic beliefs with them. They believed that Gentiles must first become converts to Judaism and be circumcised (see v. 1), and then they would be eligible to be saved by faith. Perhaps some of them had gone to Antioch and now returned to present their case.

15:7 *Peter got up.* After a period of considerable discussion by the apostles and elders, Peter addressed them. *Gentiles might hear.* Peter's argument was his own experience: God had sent him to preach to the Gentiles (10:28–29).

15:8 *giving the Holy Spirit to them.* The irrefutable proof of God's acceptance (see 10:44,47; 11:17–18).

15:9 *purified their hearts by faith.* Peter's way of saying what Paul affirmed (Ro 5:1; cf. Gal 2:15–16).

15:10 *a yoke.* The law (see Gal 5:1; cf. Mt 11:28–29).

15:11 *through the grace of our Lord.* No circumcision was required. *we are saved, just as they are.* See Ro 3:9.

15:12 *assembly became silent.* See note on vv. 4–22. Apparently the people had remained in place while the apostles and elders met. The assembly had not remained quiet during that time, but now they became silent to listen to the leaders. *Barnabas and Paul.* The order here puts Barnabas first (perhaps reflecting his importance in Jerusalem), whereas in the account of the missionary journey the order was "Paul and Barnabas" after the events on the island of Cyprus (13:7,9,13,42). *miraculous signs and wonders.* See 8:19–20; 14:3.

15:13 *James.* The brother of the Lord. His argument added proof from Scripture.

15:14 *Simon.* Peter (see v. 7). James uses Peter's Hebrew name in its Hebrew form (Simeon; see NIV text note). *a people for himself.* A new community largely made up of Gentiles but including Jews as well (Jn 10:16; cf. 1Pe 2:9–10).

15:15 *prophets.* Specifically Am 9:11–12 (see NIV text note on Am 9:12).

15:16 *After this I will return.* Some have taken this quotation from Amos as setting forth a sequence of the end times, including (1) the church age (taking out "a people for himself," v. 14), (2) the restoration of Israel as a nation (v. 16)

and rebuild David's fallen tent.
Its ruins I will rebuild,
    and I will restore it,
[17]that the remnant of men may seek the
        Lord,
    and all the Gentiles who bear my
        name,
    says the Lord, who does these things'[e] [i]
[18]   that have been known for ages.[f] [k]

[19]"It is my judgment, therefore, that we
should not make it difficult for the Gentiles
who are turning to God. [20]Instead we
should write to them, telling them to abstain from food polluted by idols,[l] from
sexual immorality,[m] from the meat of
strangled animals and from blood.[n] [21]For
Moses has been preached in every city
from the earliest times and is read in the
synagogues on every Sabbath."[o]

The Council's Letter to Gentile Believers

[22]Then the apostles and elders,[p] with
the whole church, decided to choose some
of their own men and send them to Antioch[q] with Paul and Barnabas. They chose
Judas (called Barsabbas) and Silas,[r] two
men who were leaders among the brothers. [23]With them they sent the following
letter:

    The apostles and elders, your brothers,

    To the Gentile believers in Antioch,[s]
    Syria[t] and Cilicia:[u]

    Greetings.[v]

    [24]We have heard that some went
out from us without our authorization
and disturbed you, troubling your
minds by what they said.[w] [25]So we all

agreed to choose some men and send
them to you with our dear friends Barnabas and Paul— [26]men who have
risked their lives[x] for the name of our
Lord Jesus Christ. [27]Therefore we are
sending Judas and Silas[y] to confirm by
word of mouth what we are writing.
[28]It seemed good to the Holy Spirit[z]
and to us not to burden you with anything beyond the following requirements: [29]You are to abstain from
food sacrificed to idols, from blood,
from the meat of strangled animals
and from sexual immorality.[a] You will
do well to avoid these things.

    Farewell.

[30]The men were sent off and went
down to Antioch, where they gathered the
church together and delivered the letter.
[31]The people read it and were glad for its
encouraging message. [32]Judas and Silas,[b]
who themselves were prophets,[c] said
much to encourage and strengthen the
brothers. [33]After spending some time
there, they were sent off by the brothers
with the blessing of peace[d] to return to
those who had sent them.[g] [35]But Paul and
Barnabas remained in Antioch, where they
and many others taught and preached[e] the
word of the Lord.[f]

Disagreement Between Paul and Barnabas

[36]Some time later Paul said to Barnabas,
"Let us go back and visit the brothers in all
the towns[g] where we preached the word

Cross references (center column):

15:17 [i]Am 9:11,12
15:18 [k]Isa 45:21
15:20
[l]1Co 8:7-13;
10:14-28;
Rev 2:14,20
[m]1Co 10:7,8;
Rev 2:14,20 [n]ver
29; Ge 9:4;
Lev 3:17; 7:26;
17:10-13; 19:26;
Dt 12:16,23
15:21 [o]Ac 13:15;
2Co 3:14,15
15:22
[p]S Ac 11:30
[q]S Ac 11:19 [r]ver
27,32,40;
Ac 16:19,25,29;
2Co 1:19;
1Th 1:1; 2Th 1:1;
1Pe 5:12
15:23 [s]ver 1;
S Ac 11:19
[t]S Lk 2:2 [u]ver 41;
S Ac 6:9
[v]Ac 23:25,26;
Jas 1:1
15:24 [w]ver 1;
Gal 1:7; 5:10

15:26
[x]Ac 9:23-25;
14:19; 1Co 15:30
15:27 [y]S ver 22
15:28 [z]Ac 5:32
15:29 [a]ver 20;
Ac 21:25
15:32 [b]S ver 22
[c]S Ac 11:27
15:33 [d]1Sa 1:17;
Mk 5:34;
Lk 7:50;
Ac 16:36;
1Co 16:11
15:35 [e]Ac 8:4
[f]S Ac 13:48
15:36 [g]Ac 13:4,
13,14,51; 14:1,6,
24,25

Footnotes:

[e]17 Amos 9:11,12   [f]17,18 Some manuscripts
things'— / [18]known to the Lord for ages is his work
[g]33 Some manuscripts them, [34]but Silas decided to
remain there

Bottom notes (two columns):

and (3) the final salvation of the Gentiles (vv. 17–18). Others
declare that the quotation merely confirms God's intent to
save Gentiles.

15:19 *not make it difficult.* Circumcision was not required,
but four stipulations were laid down (see note on v. 20).
These were in areas where the Gentiles had particular weaknesses and where the Jews were particularly repulsed by
Gentile violations. It would help both the individual and the
relationship between Gentile and Jew if these requirements
were observed. They involved divine directives that the Jews
believed were given before the Mosaic laws.

15:20 *food polluted by idols.* See v. 29; 1Co 8:7–13; Rev
2:14,20. *sexual immorality.* A sin taken too lightly by the
Greeks and also associated with certain pagan religious festivals. *meat of strangled animals.* Thus retaining the blood
that was forbidden to be eaten (see Ge 9:4). *blood.* Expressly
forbidden in Jewish law (see Lev 17:10–12). Reference here
may be to consuming blood apart from meat.

15:22 *apostles and elders, with the whole church.* Apparently there was unanimous agreement with the choice of

messengers and with the contents of the letter (vv. 23–29).
Judas (called Barsabbas). The same surname as that of Joseph
Barsabbas (see 1:23 and note). The two may have been
brothers. *Silas.* A leader in the Jerusalem church, a prophet
(v. 32) and a Roman citizen (16:37).

15:23 *in Antioch, Syria and Cilicia.* Antioch was the leading city of the combined provinces of Syria and Cilicia.

15:28 *seemed good to the Holy Spirit and to us.* Prior
authority is given to the Spirit (whose working in the assembly is thus claimed), but there was also agreement among the
apostles, elders and brothers (vv. 22–23).

15:29 *abstain from food . . . sexual immorality.* See note
on v. 20.

15:32 *prophets.* One of the primary functions of prophets
in the early church was, as here indicated, to encourage and
strengthen the brothers.

15:33 *those who had sent them.* The Jerusalem church
(see v. 22).

15:34 See NIV text note on v. 33.

15:36 *towns where we preached the word.* Towns of the
first missionary journey (see 13:4–14:26).

of the Lord[h] and see how they are doing."
[37]Barnabas wanted to take John, also called
Mark,[i] with them, [38]but Paul did not
think it wise to take him, because he had
deserted them[j] in Pamphylia and had not
continued with them in the work. [39]They
had such a sharp disagreement that they
parted company. Barnabas took Mark and
sailed for Cyprus, [40]but Paul chose Silas[k]
and left, commended by the brothers to
the grace of the Lord.[l] [41]He went through
Syria[m] and Cilicia,[n] strengthening the
churches.[o]

Timothy Joins Paul and Silas

16 He came to Derbe and then to Lystra,[p] where a disciple named Timothy[q] lived, whose mother was a Jewess
and a believer,[r] but whose father was a
Greek. [2]The brothers[s] at Lystra and Iconium[t] spoke well of him. [3]Paul wanted to
take him along on the journey, so he circumcised him because of the Jews who
lived in that area, for they all knew that his
father was a Greek.[u] [4]As they traveled
from town to town, they delivered the
decisions reached by the apostles and elders[v] in Jerusalem[w] for the people to

Reference column:
15:36
hS Ac 13:48
15:37
iS Ac 12:12
15:38 jAc 13:13
15:40 kS ver 22
lS Ac 11:23
15:41 mver 23;
S Lk 2:2
nS Ac 6:9
oAc 16:5
16:1 pAc 14:6
q1Co 4:17;
16:10; 2Co 1:1,
19; Php 1:1;
2:19; 1Th 3:2,6;
1Ti 1:2,18;
2Ti 1:2,5,6
r2Ti 1:5
16:2 sver 40;
S Ac 1:16
tS Ac 13:51
16:3 uGal 2:3
16:4 vS Ac 11:30
wAc 15:2

xAc 15:28,29
16:5 yAc 9:31;
15:41 zS Ac 2:41
16:6 aAc 2:10;
18:23 bAc 18:23;
Gal 1:2; 3:1
cS Ac 2:9
16:7 dRo 8:9;
Gal 4:6;
Php 1:19;
1Pe 1:11
16:8 ever 11;
Ac 20:5;
2Co 2:12;
2Ti 4:13
16:9 fS Ac 9:10
gAc 19:21,29;
20:1,3; Ro 15:26;

obey.[x] [5]So the churches were strengthened[y] in the faith and grew daily in numbers.[z]

Paul's Vision of the Man of Macedonia

[6]Paul and his companions traveled
throughout the region of Phrygia[a] and
Galatia,[b] having been kept by the Holy
Spirit from preaching the word in the province of Asia.[c] [7]When they came to the
border of Mysia, they tried to enter Bithynia, but the Spirit of Jesus[d] would not
allow them to. [8]So they passed by Mysia
and went down to Troas.[e] [9]During the
night Paul had a vision[f] of a man of Macedonia[g] standing and begging him, "Come
over to Macedonia and help us." [10]After
Paul had seen the vision, we[h] got ready at
once to leave for Macedonia, concluding
that God had called us to preach the gospel[i] to them.

Lydia's Conversion in Philippi

[11]From Troas[j] we put out to sea and

1Co 16:5; 1Th 1:7,8 16:10 hver 10-17; 20:5-15; 21:1-18;
27:1-28:16 iAc 14:7 16:11 jS ver 8

15:38 *he had deserted them.* Mark had turned back at
Perga and did not go to Antioch, Iconium, Lystra and Derbe
(see note on 13:13).
15:39 *they parted company.* Barnabas and Mark do not
appear again in Acts. However, in 1Co 9:6 Paul names
Barnabas as setting a noble example in working to support
himself. Also in Gal 2:11–13 another scene is described in
Antioch that includes Barnabas. Mark evidently returned
from his work with Barnabas and became associated with
Peter (see 1Pe 5:13). During Paul's first imprisonment, Mark
was included in Paul's group (see Col 4:10; Phm 24). By the
end of Paul's life he came to admire Mark so much that he
requested him to come to be with him during his final days
(2Ti 4:11; see Introduction to Mark: John Mark in the NT).
Cyprus. The island of Barnabas's birthplace (cf. 4:36).
15:40 *Silas.* Had returned to Jerusalem with Judas after
delivering the Jerusalem letter (vv. 32–33). His presence in
Antioch now indicates that, after reporting to those who had
sent him, he came back to Antioch to participate in the
church's work there.
16:1 See map No. 11 at the end of the Study Bible. *Derbe.*
See notes on 14:6,20. Paul had approached Derbe on the
first trip from the opposite direction, so the order of towns is
reversed here. *Lystra.* See note on 14:6. *Timothy.* Since Paul
addressed him as a young man some 15 years later (see 1Ti
4:12), he must have been in his teens at this time. *father was
a Greek.* Statements concerning his mother's faith (here and
in 2Ti 1:5) and silence concerning any faith on his father's
part suggest that the father was neither a convert to Judaism
nor a believer in Christ.
16:3 *he circumcised him.* As a matter of expediency so that
his work among the Jews might be more effective. This was
different from Titus's case (see Gal 2:3), where circumcision
was refused because some were demanding it as necessary
for salvation.
16:6 *his companions.* Silas and Timothy. *Phrygia.* The
district was formerly the Hellenistic territory of Phrygia, but

it had more recently been divided between the Roman provinces of Asia and Galatia. Iconium and Antioch were in
Galatian Phrygia. *Galatia.* The name had been used to denote
the Hellenistic kingdom, but in 25 B.C. it had been expanded
considerably to become the Roman province of that name.
Asia. This, too, had been a smaller area formerly but now
was a Roman province including the Hellenistic districts of
Mysia, Lydia, Caria and parts of Phrygia.
16:7 *Mysia.* In the northeast part of the province of Asia
Luke uses these old Hellenistic names, but Paul preferred the
provincial (Roman) names. *Bithynia.* A senatorial province
formed after 74 B.C., it was east of Mysia. *Spirit of Jesus.* As
the "Holy Spirit" was used at times interchangeably with
"God" (see 5:3–4), so here "Holy Spirit" is used interchangeably with "Spirit of Jesus." *not allow.* The Spirit may
have led in any of a number of ways: vision, circumstances,
good sense or use of the prophetic gift.
16:8 *Troas.* Located ten miles from ancient Troy. Alexandria Troas (its full name) was a Roman colony and an
important seaport for connections between Macedonia and
Greece on the one hand and Asia Minor on the other. Paul
returned to Troas following his work in Ephesus on his third
journey (see 2Co 2:12). At some time—on Paul's second
journey or on his third—a church was started there, for Paul
ministered to believers in Troas when he returned from his
third journey on his way to Jerusalem (20:5–12).
16:9 *vision.* One of the ways God gave direction (cf. 10:3).
man of Macedonia. Macedonia had become a Roman province in 148 B.C. There is no indication that the man of the
vision is Luke, as some have suggested, but he does join the
group at this point.
16:10 *we got ready.* This is where the "we" passages of
Acts begin (see Introduction: Author). The conclusion is that
Luke is informing the reader that he had joined the party at
Troas.
16:11 *Samothrace.* An island in the northeastern Aegean
Sea. It was a convenient place for boats to anchor rather than

sailed straight for Samothrace, and the next day on to Neapolis. [12]From there we traveled to Philippi,[k] a Roman colony and the leading city of that district of Macedonia.[l] And we stayed there several days.

[13]On the Sabbath[m] we went outside the city gate to the river, where we expected to find a place of prayer. We sat down and began to speak to the women who had gathered there. [14]One of those listening was a woman named Lydia, a dealer in purple cloth from the city of Thyatira,[n] who was a worshiper of God. The Lord opened her heart[o] to respond to Paul's message. [15]When she and the members of her household[p] were baptized,[q] she invited us to her home. "If you consider me a believer in the Lord," she said, "come and stay at my house." And she persuaded us.

16:12	[k]Ac 20:6; Php 1:1; 1Th 2:2
	[l]S ver 9
16:13	
	[m]S Ac 13:14
16:14	[n]Rev 1:11; 2:18,24
	[o]Lk 24:45
16:15	
	[p]S Ac 11:14
	[q]S Ac 2:38
16:16	[r]ver 13
	[s]Dt 18:11; 1Sa 28:3,7
16:17	[t]S Mk 5:7
16:18	
	[u]S Mk 16:17
16:19	[v]ver 16; Ac 19:25,26
	[w]S Ac 15:22
	[x]Ac 8:3; 17:6; 21:30; Jas 2:6

Paul and Silas in Prison

[16]Once when we were going to the place of prayer,[r] we were met by a slave girl who had a spirit[s] by which she predicted the future. She earned a great deal of money for her owners by fortune-telling. [17]This girl followed Paul and the rest of us, shouting, "These men are servants of the Most High God,[t] who are telling you the way to be saved." [18]She kept this up for many days. Finally Paul became so troubled that he turned around and said to the spirit, "In the name of Jesus Christ I command you to come out of her!" At that moment the spirit left her.[u]

[19]When the owners of the slave girl realized that their hope of making money[v] was gone, they seized Paul and Silas[w] and dragged[x] them into the marketplace to face the authorities. [20]They brought them

---

risk sailing at night. *Neapolis.* The seaport for Philippi, ten miles away; modern Kavalla.
16:12 *Philippi.* A city in eastern Macedonia named after Philip II, father of Alexander the Great (see map of "Philippi," p. 1801). Since it was a Roman colony, it was independent of provincial administration and had a governmental

organization modeled after that of Rome (see note on 13:14). Many retired legionnaires from the Roman army settled there, but few Jews. See Introduction to Philippians: Recipients. *leading city.* Thessalonica was the capital of Macedonia. But Macedonia had four districts, and Philippi was in the first of these. Amphipolis, however, was the first city of

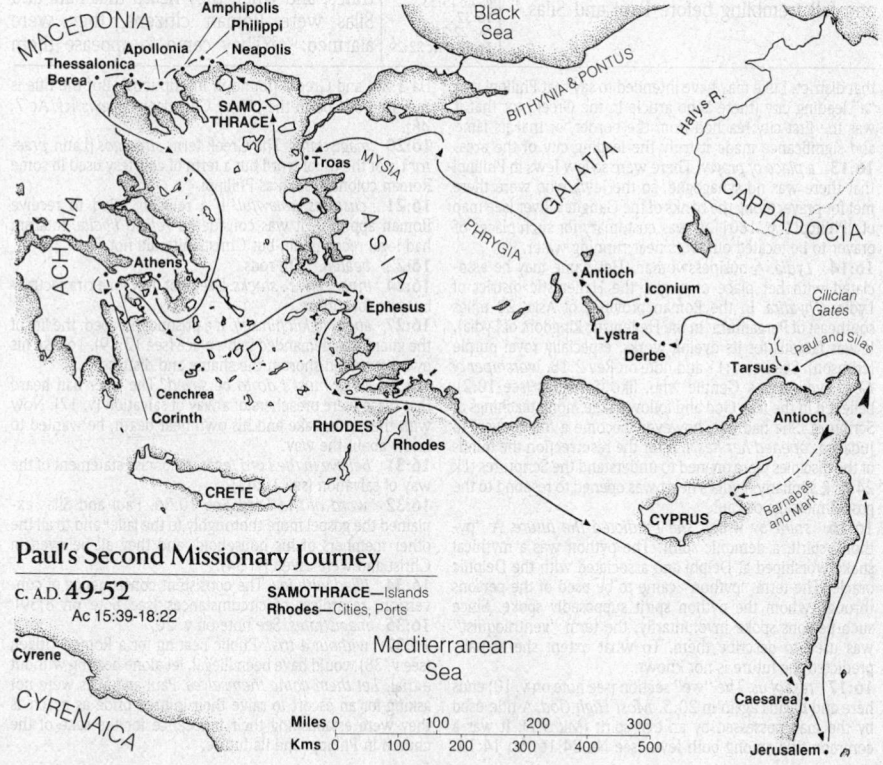

Paul's Second Missionary Journey

C. A.D. **49-52**
Ac 15:39-18:22

SAMOTHRACE—Islands
Rhodes—Cities, Ports

Mediterranean
Sea

Miles 0   100   200   300
Kms 0   100   200   300   400   500

before the magistrates and said, "These men are Jews, and are throwing our city into an uproar[y] [21]by advocating customs unlawful for us Romans[z] to accept or practice."[a]

[22]The crowd joined in the attack against Paul and Silas, and the magistrates ordered them to be stripped and beaten.[b] [23]After they had been severely flogged, they were thrown into prison, and the jailer[c] was commanded to guard them carefully. [24]Upon receiving such orders, he put them in the inner cell and fastened their feet in the stocks.[d]

[25]About midnight[e] Paul and Silas[f] were praying and singing hymns[g] to God, and the other prisoners were listening to them. [26]Suddenly there was such a violent earthquake that the foundations of the prison were shaken.[h] At once all the prison doors flew open,[i] and everybody's chains came loose.[j] [27]The jailer woke up, and when he saw the prison doors open, he drew his sword and was about to kill himself because he thought the prisoners had escaped.[k] [28]But Paul shouted, "Don't harm yourself! We are all here!"

[29]The jailer called for lights, rushed in and fell trembling before Paul and Silas.[l]

[30]He then brought them out and asked, "Sirs, what must I do to be saved?"[m]

[31]They replied, "Believe[n] in the Lord Jesus, and you will be saved[o]—you and your household."[p] [32]Then they spoke the word of the Lord to him and to all the others in his house. [33]At that hour of the night[q] the jailer took them and washed their wounds; then immediately he and all his family were baptized.[r] [34]The jailer brought them into his house and set a meal before them; he[s] was filled with joy because he had come to believe in God—he and his whole family.

[35]When it was daylight, the magistrates sent their officers to the jailer with the order: "Release those men." [36]The jailer[t] told Paul, "The magistrates have ordered that you and Silas be released. Now you can leave. Go in peace."[u]

[37]But Paul said to the officers: "They beat us publicly without a trial, even though we are Roman citizens,[v] and threw us into prison. And now do they want to get rid of us quietly? No! Let them come themselves and escort us out."

[38]The officers reported this to the magistrates, and when they heard that Paul and Silas were Roman citizens, they were alarmed.[w] [39]They came to appease them

---

Cross references (center column):

16:20 [y]Ac 17:6
16:21 [z]ver 12
[a]Est 3:8
16:22
[b]2Co 11:25;
1Th 2:2
16:23 [c]ver 27,36
16:24 [d]Job 13:27; 33:11;
Jer 20:2,3; 29:26
16:25 [e]Ps 119:
55,62 [f]S Ac 15:22
[g]S Eph 5:19
16:26 [h]Ac 4:31
[i]Ac 5:19; 12:10
[j]Ac 12:7
16:27 [k]Ac 12:19
16:29
[l]S Ac 15:22

16:30 [m]Ac 2:37
16:31 [n]S Jn 3:15
[o]S Ro 11:14
[p]S Ac 11:14
16:33 [q]ver 25
[r]S Ac 2:38
16:34
[s]S Ac 11:14
16:36 [t]ver 23,27
[u]S Ac 15:33
16:37
[v]Ac 22:25-29
16:38 [w]Ac 22:29

---

that district. Luke may have intended to say that Philippi was "a" leading city (there is no article in the Greek), or that it was the first city reached from the border, or that its fame and significance made it truly the leading city of the area.
16:13 *a place of prayer.* There were so few Jews in Philippi that there was no synagogue, so the Jews who were there met for prayer along the banks of the Gangites River (see map of "Philippi," p. 1801). It was customary for such places of prayer to be located outdoors near running water.
16:14 *Lydia.* A businesswoman. Her name may be associated with her place of origin, the Hellenistic district of Lydia. *Thyatira.* In the Roman province of Asia, 20 miles southeast of Pergamum (in the Hellenistic kingdom of Lydia). It was famous for its dyeing works, especially royal purple (crimson). See Rev 1:11 and note on Rev 2:18. *worshiper of God.* Lydia was a Gentile who, like Cornelius (see 10:2), believed in the true God and followed the moral teachings of Scripture. She had not, however, become a full convert to Judaism. *opened her heart.* After the resurrection the minds of the disciples were opened to understand the Scriptures (Lk 24:45); similarly, Lydia's heart was opened to respond to the gospel message of Paul.
16:16 *spirit by which she predicted the future.* A "python" spirit, a demonic spirit. The python was a mythical snake worshiped at Delphi and associated with the Delphic oracle. The term "python" came to be used of the persons through whom the python spirit supposedly spoke. Since such persons spoke involuntarily, the term "ventriloquist" was used to describe them. To what extent she actually predicted the future is not known.
16:17 *rest of us.* The "we" section (see note on v. 10) ends here and begins again in 20:5. *Most High God.* A title used by the man possessed by an evil spirit (Mk 5:7). It was a common title among both Jews (see Nu 24:16; Isa 14:14;

Da 3:26) and Greeks (found in inscriptions). But the title is not used of God in the NT by Christians or Jews (cf. Ac 7:48).
16:20 *magistrates.* The Greek term *strategos* (Latin *praetor*), not the usual word but a term of courtesy used in some Roman colonies, such as Philippi.
16:21 *customs unlawful.* If a religion failed to receive Roman approval, it was considered *religio illicita.* Judaism had legal recognition, but Christianity did not.
16:22 *beaten.* With rods.
16:24 *inner cell . . . stocks.* Used not only for extra security but also for torture.
16:27 *about to kill himself.* If a prisoner escaped, the life of the guard was demanded in his place (see 12:19). To take his own life would shorten the shame and distress.
16:30 *what must I do to be saved?* The jailer had heard that these were preachers of a way of salvation (v. 17). Now with the earthquake and his own near death, he wanted to know about the way.
16:31 *Believe in the Lord Jesus.* A concise statement of the way of salvation (see 10:43).
16:32 *word of the Lord.* See 10:36. Paul and Silas explained the gospel more thoroughly to the jailer and to all the other members of his household, and they all believed in Christ and were saved (v. 34).
16:34 *filled with joy.* The consistent consequence of conversion, regardless of circumstances (see note on 8:39).
16:35 *magistrates.* See note on v. 20.
16:37 *without a trial.* Public beating for a Roman citizen (see v. 38) would have been illegal, let alone beating without a trial. *Let them come themselves.* Paul and Silas were not asking for an escort to salve their injured pride as much as they were establishing their innocence for the sake of the church in Philippi and its future.

and escorted them from the prison, requesting them to leave the city. *x* 40After Paul and Silas came out of the prison, they went to Lydia's house,*y* where they met with the brothers*z* and encouraged them. Then they left.

In Thessalonica

17 When they had passed through Amphipolis and Apollonia, they came to Thessalonica,*a* where there was a Jewish synagogue. 2As his custom was, Paul went into the synagogue,*b* and on three Sabbath*c* days he reasoned with them from the Scriptures,*d* 3explaining and proving that the Christ*h* had to suffer*e* and rise from the dead.*f* "This Jesus I am proclaiming to you is the Christ,*h*"*g* he said. 4Some of the Jews were persuaded and joined Paul and Silas,*h* as did a large number of God-fearing Greeks and not a few prominent women.

5But the Jews were jealous; so they rounded up some bad characters from the marketplace, formed a mob and started a riot in the city.*i* They rushed to Jason's*j* house in search of Paul and Silas in order to bring them out to the crowd.*i* 6But when they did not find them, they dragged*k* Jason and some other brothers*l* before the city officials, shouting: "These men who have caused trouble all over the world*m* have now come here,*n* 7and Jason has welcomed them into his house. They are all defying Caesar's decrees, saying that

there is another king, one called Jesus."*o* 8When they heard this, the crowd and the city officials were thrown into turmoil. 9Then they made Jason*p* and the others post bond and let them go.

In Berea

10As soon as it was night, the brothers sent Paul and Silas*q* away to Berea.*r* On arriving there, they went to the Jewish synagogue.*s* 11Now the Bereans were of more noble character than the Thessalonians,*t* for they received the message with great eagerness and examined the Scriptures*u* every day to see if what Paul said was true.*v* 12Many of the Jews believed, as did also a number of prominent Greek women and many Greek men.*w*

13When the Jews in Thessalonica learned that Paul was preaching the word of God at Berea,*x* they went there too, agitating the crowds and stirring them up. 14The brothers*y* immediately sent Paul to the coast, but Silas*z* and Timothy*a* stayed at Berea. 15The men who escorted Paul brought him to Athens*b* and then left with instructions for Silas and Timothy to join him as soon as possible.*c*

In Athens

16While Paul was waiting for them in Athens, he was greatly distressed to see that the city was full of idols. 17So he reasoned in the synagogue*d* with the Jews

Cross references (center column)

16:39 *x*Mt 8:34; Lk 8:37
16:40 *y*ver 14
17:1 *z*ver 2; S Ac 1:16
*a*ver 11,13; Php 4:16;
1Th 1:1; 2Th 1:1; 2Ti 4:10
17:2 *b*S Ac 9:20
*c*S Ac 13:14
*d*Ac 8:35; 18:28
17:3 *e*Lk 24:26; Ac 3:18
*f*Lk 24:46; S Ac 2:24
*g*S Ac 9:22
17:4 *h*S Ac 15:22
17:5 *i*ver 13;
S 1Th 2:16
*j*Ro 16:21
17:6 *k*S Ac 16:19
*l*S Ac 1:16
*m*S Mt 24:14
*n*Ac 16:20

17:7 *o*Lk 23:2; Jn 19:12
17:9 *p*ver 5
17:10 *q*S Ac 15:22 *r*ver 13; Ac 20:4
*s*S Ac 9:20
17:11 *t*S ver 1
*u*Lk 16:29; Jn 5:39 *v*Dt 29:29
17:12 *w*S Ac 2:41
17:13 *x*S Heb 4:12
17:14 *y*S Ac 9:30
*z*S Ac 15:22
*a*S Ac 16:1
17:15 *b*ver 16, 21,22; Ac 18:1; 1Th 3:1 *c*Ac 18:5
17:17 *d*S Ac 9:20

*h*3 Or *Messiah*   *i*5 Or *the assembly of the people*

17:1 *Amphipolis . . . Thessalonica.* The Egnatian Way crossed the whole of present-day northern Greece east-west and included Philippi, Amphipolis, Apollonia and Thessalonica on its route. At several locations, such as Kavalla (Neapolis), Philippi and Apollonia, the road is still visible today. If a person traveled about 30 miles a day, each city could be reached after one day's journey. *Thessalonica.* About 100 miles from Philippi. It was the capital of the province of Macedonia and had a population of more than 200,000, including a colony of Jews (and a synagogue). All these contributed to Paul's decision to preach there. See Introduction to 1 Thessalonians: The City and the Church. **17:2** *synagogue.* See note on 13:14. *three Sabbath days.* These two weeks represent the time spent in the synagogue reasoning with the Jews, not Paul's total time in Thessalonica. An analysis of the Thessalonian letters reveals that Paul had taught them much more doctrine than would have been possible in two or three weeks. **17:4** *God-fearing Greeks.* See notes on 10:2; 16:14. *prominent women.* Perhaps the wives of the leading men of the city, but women who deserve notice and position in their own right (see also v. 12). **17:5** *were jealous.* Because of the large number of people (including some Jews, many God-fearing Gentiles and many prominent women) who responded to Paul's ministry (cf. 13:45). *Jason's house.* Paul had probably been staying there. **17:6** *city officials.* The Greek term *politarch* (lit. "city ruler"), used here and in v. 8, is found nowhere else in Greek

literature, but it was discovered in 1835 in a Greek inscription on an arch that had spanned the Egnatian Way on the west side of Thessalonica. (The arch was destroyed in 1867, but the block with the inscription was rescued and is now in the British Museum in London.) The term has since been found in 16 other inscriptions in surrounding towns of Macedonia, and elsewhere. **17:7** *defying Caesar's decrees.* Blasphemy was the gravest accusation for a Jew, but treason—to support a rival king above Caesar—was the worst accusation for a Roman. **17:9** *post bond.* Jason was forced to guarantee a peaceful, quiet community, or he would face the confiscation of his properties and perhaps even death. **17:10** *Paul and Silas.* It has been suggested that Timothy was left at Philippi and rejoined Paul and Silas at Berea (compare v. 10 with v. 14). *Berea.* Modern Verria, located 50 miles from Thessalonica in another district of Macedonia. *synagogue.* See note on 13:14. **17:14** *the coast.* One might conclude that Paul went by boat to Athens. But the road to Athens is also a coast road, and Paul may have walked the distance after having been escorted to the coast (some 20 miles). In any event, Christian companions stayed with him until reaching Athens. **17:15** *Athens.* Five centuries before Paul, Athens had been at the height of its glory in art, philosophy and literature. She had retained her reputation in philosophy through the years and still maintained a leading university in Paul's day. **17:17** *synagogue.* See note on 13:14. *God-fearing Greeks.*

and the God-fearing Greeks, as well as in the marketplace day by day with those who happened to be there. ¹⁸A group of Epicurean and Stoic philosophers began to dispute with him. Some of them asked, "What is this babbler trying to say?" Others remarked, "He seems to be advocating foreign gods." They said this because Paul was preaching the good news *e* about Jesus and the resurrection.*f* ¹⁹Then they took him and brought him to a meeting of the Areopagus,*g* where they said to him, "May we know what this new teaching*h* is that you are presenting? ²⁰You are bringing some strange ideas to our ears, and we want to know what they mean." ²¹(All the Athenians*i* and the foreigners who lived there spent their time doing nothing but talking about and listening to the latest ideas.)

²²Paul then stood up in the meeting of the Areopagus*j* and said: "Men of Athens! I see that in every way you are very religious.*k* ²³For as I walked around and looked carefully at your objects of worship, I even found an altar with this inscription: TO AN UNKNOWN GOD. Now what you worship as something unknown*l* I am going to proclaim to you.

²⁴"The God who made the world and everything in it*m* is the Lord of heaven and earth*n* and does not live in temples built by hands.*o* ²⁵And he is not served by human hands, as if he needed anything, because he himself gives all men life and breath and everything else.*p* ²⁶From one man he made every nation of men, that they should inhabit the whole earth; and he determined the times set for them and the exact places where they should live.*q* ²⁷God did this so that men would seek him and perhaps reach out for him and find him, though he is not far from each one of us.*r* ²⁸'For in him we live and move and have our being.'*s* As some of your own poets have said, 'We are his offspring.'*t*

²⁹"Therefore since we are God's offspring, we should not think that the divine being is like gold or silver or stone—an image made by man's design and skill.*u* ³⁰In the past God overlooked*v* such ignorance,*w* but now he commands all people everywhere to repent.*x* ³¹For he has set a day when he will judge*y* the world with justice*z* by the man he has appointed.*a* He has given proof of this to all men by raising him from the dead."*b*

³²When they heard about the resurrection of the dead,*c* some of them sneered, but others said, "We want to hear you again on this subject." ³³At that, Paul left the Council. ³⁴A few men became follow-

Cross references (center column):

17:18 *e*S Ac 13:32 /ver 31,32; Ac 4:2
17:19 *g*ver 22 *h*Mk 1:27
17:21 *i*S ver 15
17:22 *j*ver 19 *k*ver 16
17:23 *l*Jn 4:22
17:24 *m*Isa 42:5; Ac 14:15
*n*Dt 10:14; Isa 66:1,2; Mt 11:25
17:25 *o*1Ki 8:27; Ac 7:48
*p*Ps 50:10-12; Isa 42:5
17:26 *q*Dt 32:8; Job 12:23
17:27 *r*Dt 4:7; Isa 55:6; Jer 23:23,24
17:28 *s*Dt 30:20; Job 12:10; Da 5:23 *t*Epimenides; Aratus, Phaenomena, 5
17:29 *u*Isa 40:18-20; Ro 1:23
17:30 *v*Ac 14:16; Ro 3:25 *w*ver 23; 1Pe 1:14
*x*Lk 24:47; Tit 2:11,12
17:31 *y*S Mt 10:15 *z*Ps 9:8; 96:13; 98:9 *a*S Ac 10:42 *b*S Ac 2:24
17:32 *c*ver 18,31

See note on 10:2.

17:18 *Epicurean . . . philosophers.* Originally they taught that the supreme good is happiness—but not mere momentary pleasure or temporary gratification. By Paul's time, however, this philosophy had degenerated into a more sensual system of thought. *Stoic philosophers.* They taught that people should live in accord with nature, recognize their own self-sufficiency and independence, and suppress their desires. At its best, Stoicism had some admirable qualities, but, like Epicureanism, by Paul's time it had degenerated into a system of pride. *babbler.* The Greek word meant "seed picker," a bird picking up seeds here and there. Then it came to refer to the loafer in the marketplace who picked up whatever scraps of learning he could find and paraded them without digesting them himself.

17:19 *Areopagus.* Means "hill of Ares." Ares was the Greek god of thunder and war (the Roman equivalent was Mars). The Areopagus was located just west of the acropolis and south of the Agora and had once been the site of the meeting of the Court or Council of the Areopagus. Earlier the Council governed a Greek city-state, but by NT times the Areopagus retained authority only in the areas of religion and morals and met in the Royal Portico at the northwest corner of the Agora. They considered themselves the custodians of teachings that introduced new religions and foreign gods.

17:22 *religious.* Or "superstitious." The Greek for this word could be used to congratulate a person or to criticize him, depending on whether the person using it included himself in the circle of individuals he was describing. The Athenians would not know which meaning to take until Paul continued. In this context it is clear that Paul wanted to be complimentary in order to gain a hearing.

17:23 TO AN UNKNOWN GOD. The Greeks were fearful of offending any god by failing to give him attention; so they felt they could cover any omissions by the label "unknown god." Other Greek writers confirm that such altars could be seen in Athens—a striking point of contact for Paul.

17:24 *The God who made the world.* Thus a personal Creator, in contrast with the views of pantheistic Stoicism.

17:26 *From one man he made every nation.* All people are of one family (whether Athenians or Romans, Greeks or barbarians, Jews or Gentiles). *determined the times.* He planned the exact times when nations should emerge and decline. *places where they should live.* He also planned the specific area to be occupied by each nation. He is God, the Designer (things were not left to Chance, as the Epicureans thought).

17:28 *some of your own poets.* There are two quotations here: (1) "In him we live and move and have our being," from the Cretan poet Epimenides (c. 600 B.C.) in his *Cretica,* and (2) "We are his offspring," from the Cilician poet Aratus (c. 315–240) in his *Phaenomena,* as well as from Cleanthes (331–233) in his *Hymn to Zeus.* Paul quotes Greek poets elsewhere as well (see 1Co 15:33; Tit 1:12 and notes).

17:30 *overlooked such ignorance.* God had not judged them for worshiping false gods in their ignorance (see v. 31).

17:31 *the man he has appointed.* Jesus, the Son of Man (see Da 7:13; cf. Mt 25:31–46; Ac 10:42).

17:32 *resurrection of the dead.* Immortality of the soul was accepted by the Greeks, but not resurrection of a dead body.

17:33 *the Council.* The meeting of the Areopagites.

17:34 *Dionysius.* Later tradition states, though it cannot be proved, that he became bishop of Athens. *Damaris.* Some have suggested that she must have been a foreign, educated woman to have been present at a public meeting such as the

ers of Paul and believed. Among them was Dionysius, a member of the Areopagus, ^{d} also a woman named Damaris, and a number of others.

In Corinth

18 After this, Paul left Athens ^{e} and went to Corinth. ^{f} ^{2}There he met a Jew named Aquila, a native of Pontus, who had recently come from Italy with his wife Priscilla, ^{g} because Claudius ^{h} had ordered all the Jews to leave Rome. Paul went to see them, ^{3}and because he was a tentmaker as they were, he stayed and worked with them. ^{i} ^{4}Every Sabbath ^{j} he reasoned in the synagogue, ^{k} trying to persuade Jews and Greeks.

^{5}When Silas ^{l} and Timothy ^{m} came from Macedonia, ^{n} Paul devoted himself exclusively to preaching, testifying to the Jews that Jesus was the Christ. ^{j} ^{o} ^{6}But when the Jews opposed Paul and became abusive, ^{p} he shook out his clothes in protest ^{q} and said to them, "Your blood be on your own heads! ^{r} I am clear of my responsibility. ^{s} From now on I will go to the Gentiles." ^{t}

^{7}Then Paul left the synagogue and went next door to the house of Titius Justus, a worshiper of God. ^{u} ^{8}Crispus, ^{v} the syna-

gogue ruler, ^{w} and his entire household ^{x} believed in the Lord; and many of the Corinthians who heard him believed and were baptized.

^{9}One night the Lord spoke to Paul in a vision: ^{y} "Do not be afraid; ^{z} keep on speaking, do not be silent. ^{10}For I am with you, ^{a} and no one is going to attack and harm you, because I have many people in this city." ^{11}So Paul stayed for a year and a half, teaching them the word of God. ^{b}

^{12}While Gallio was proconsul ^{c} of Achaia, ^{d} the Jews made a united attack on Paul and brought him into court. ^{13}"This man," they charged, "is persuading the people to worship God in ways contrary to the law."

^{14}Just as Paul was about to speak, Gallio said to the Jews, "If you Jews were making a complaint about some misdemeanor or serious crime, it would be reasonable for me to listen to you. ^{15}But since it involves questions about words and names and your own law ^{e}—settle the matter yourselves. I will not be a judge of such things." ^{16}So he had them ejected from the court. ^{17}Then they all turned on Sosthenes ^{f} the synagogue ruler ^{g} and beat

Cross references (center column)

17:34 ^{d}ver 19,22
18:1 ^{e}S Ac 17:15
^{f}Ac 19:1;
1Co 1:2; 2Co 1:1,
23; 2Ti 4:20
18:2 ^{g}ver 19,26;
Ro 16:3;
1Co 16:19;
2Ti 4:19
^{h}Ac 11:28
18:3 ^{i}Ac 20:34;
1Co 4:12;
1Th 2:9; 2Th 3:8
18:4 ^{j}S Ac 13:14
^{k}S Ac 9:20
18:5 ^{l}S Ac 15:22
^{m}S Ac 16:1
^{n}S Ac 16:9;
17:14,15
^{o}S Ac 9:22
18:6 ^{p}S Ac 13:45
^{q}S Mt 10:14
^{r}2Sa 1:16;
^{s}Eze 33:4
^{s}Eze 3:17-19;
Ac 20:26
^{t}S Ac 13:46
18:7 ^{u}Ac 16:14
18:8 ^{v}1Co 1:14

^{w}S Mk 5:22
^{x}S Ac 11:14
18:9 ^{y}S Ac 9:10
^{z}S Mt 14:27
18:10
^{a}S Mt 28:20
18:11
^{b}S Heb 4:12
18:12 ^{c}Ac 13:7,
8,12; 19:38 ^{d}ver
27; Ro 15:26;
1Co 16:15;
2Co 9:2; 1Th 1:7,
8
18:15 ^{e}Ac 23:29;
25:11,19
18:17 ^{f}1Co 1:1
^{g}ver 8

15 Or *Messiah;* also in verse 28

Study notes (bottom)

Areopagus. It is also possible that she was a God-fearing Gentile who had heard Paul at the synagogue (v. 17).

18:1 *went to Corinth.* Either by land along the isthmus (a distance of about 50 miles) or by sea from Piraeus, the port of Athens, to Cenchrea, on the eastern shore of the isthmus of Corinth. See Introduction to 1 Corinthians: The City of Corinth; see also map of "Corinth," p. 1733.

18:2 *Pontus.* In the northeastern region of Asia Minor, a province lying along the Black Sea between Bithynia and Armenia (see 2:9). *Priscilla.* The diminutive form of Prisca. Since no mention is made of a conversion and since a partnership is established in work (see v. 3), it is likely that they were already Christians. They may have been converted in Rome by those returning from Pentecost or by others at a later time. *Claudius.* Emperor of Rome (A.D. 41–54). *ordered all the Jews to leave Rome.* Recorded in Suetonius (*Claudius,* 25). The expulsion order was given, Suetonius writes, because of "their [the Jews'] continual tumults instigated by Chrestus" (a common misspelling of "Christ"). "Chrestus" refers to Christ, the riots obviously were "about" him rather than led "by" him.

18:3 *tentmaker.* Paul would have been taught this trade as a youth. It was the Jewish custom to provide manual training for sons, whether rich or poor.

18:4 *synagogue.* See note on 13:14.

18:5 *Silas and Timothy came from Macedonia.* Paul instructed these two to come to him at Athens (17:15). Evidently they did (1Th 3:1), but they may have been sent back to Macedonia almost immediately to check on the churches—perhaps Silas to Philippi and Timothy to Thessalonica.

18:7 *Titius Justus.* Titius was a common Roman name. Justus is used to distinguish him from the Titus of 2Co 2:13; 7:13–14; 8:16,23. *worshiper of God.* Like Titus, an uncir-

cumcised Gentile, but attending the synagogue.

18:8 *Crispus.* Paul baptized him (1Co 1:14). *synagogue ruler.* See note on 13:15. *believed and were baptized.* The response to the gospel, a process going on daily, as the tense of the Greek verbs indicates.

18:9 *in a vision.* Paul had seen the Lord in a resurrection body at his conversion (9:4–6; 1Co 15:8) and in the temple at Jerusalem in a trance (22:17–18). Now he sees him in a vision (see 23:11).

18:11 *a year and a half.* During this time he may also have taken the gospel to the neighboring districts of Achaia (2Co 1:1).

18:12 *Gallio.* The brother of Seneca, the philosopher, who was the tutor of Nero. Gallio was admired as a man of exceptional fairness and calmness. From an inscription found at Delphi, it is known that Gallio was proconsul of Achaia in A.D. 51–52. This information enables us to date Paul's visit to Corinth on his second journey as well as his writing of the Thessalonian letters.

18:13 *contrary to the law.* The Jews were claiming that Paul was advocating a religion not recognized by Roman law as Judaism was. If he had been given the opportunity to speak, he could have argued that the gospel he was preaching was the faith of his fathers (see 24:14–15; 26:6–7) and thus authorized by Roman law.

18:17 *they all turned on Sosthenes.* It is not clear whether the Greeks beat Sosthenes, seeing the occasion as an opportunity to vent their feelings against the Jews, or the Jews beat their own synagogue ruler because he was unsuccessful in presenting their case—probably the former. A Sosthenes is included with Paul in the writing of 1 Corinthians (1:1). Perhaps he was the second ruler of the synagogue at Corinth to become a Christian in response to Paul's preaching (see v. 8).

him in front of the court. But Gallio showed no concern whatever.

Priscilla, Aquila and Apollos

[18]Paul stayed on in Corinth for some time. Then he left the brothers[h] and sailed for Syria,[i] accompanied by Priscilla and Aquila.[j] Before he sailed, he had his hair cut off at Cenchrea[k] because of a vow he had taken.[l] [19]They arrived at Ephesus,[m] where Paul left Priscilla and Aquila. He himself went into the synagogue and reasoned with the Jews. [20]When they asked him to spend more time with them, he declined. [21]But as he left, he promised, "I will come back if it is God's will."[n] Then he set sail from Ephesus. [22]When he landed at Caesarea,[o] he went up and greeted the church and then went down to Antioch.[p]

[23]After spending some time in Antioch, Paul set out from there and traveled from place to place throughout the region of Galatia[q] and Phrygia,[r] strengthening all the disciples.[s]

[24]Meanwhile a Jew named Apollos,[t] a native of Alexandria, came to Ephesus.[u] He was a learned man, with a thorough knowledge of the Scriptures. [25]He had been instructed in the way of the Lord, and he spoke with great fervor[k][v] and taught about Jesus accurately, though he knew only the baptism of John.[w] [26]He began to speak boldly in the synagogue. When Priscilla and Aquila[x] heard him, they invited him to their home and explained to him the way of God more adequately.

[27]When Apollos wanted to go to Achaia,[y] the brothers[z] encouraged him

Cross references

18:18 [h]ver 27; S Ac 1:16
[i]S Lk 2:2 /S ver 2
[k]Ro 16:1 [l]Nu 6:2, 5,18; Ac 21:24
18:19 [m]ver 21, 24; Ac 19:1,17, 26; 1Co 15:32; 16:8; Eph 1:1; 1Ti 1:3; Rev 1:11; 2:1
18:21 [n]Ro 1:10; 15:32; 1Co 4:19; Jas 4:15
18:22 [o]S Ac 8:40 [p]S Ac 11:19
18:23 [q]S Ac 16:6 [r]Ac 2:10; 16:6 [s]Ac 14:22; 15:32, 41
18:24 [t]Ac 19:1; 1Co 1:12; 3:5,6, 22; 4:6; 16:12; Tit 3:13 [u]S ver 19
18:25 [v]Ro 12:11 [w]S Mk 1:4
18:26 [x]S ver 2
18:27 [y]S ver 12 [z]ver 18; S Ac 1:16

[k]25 Or *with fervor in the Spirit*

18:18 *Priscilla and Aquila.* The order of the names used here (but cf. v. 2) may indicate the prominent role of Priscilla or her higher social position (see Ro 16:3; 2Ti 4:19). *a vow he had taken.* Grammatically this could refer to Aquila, but the emphasis on Paul and his activity makes Paul more probable. It was probably a temporary Nazirite vow (see Nu 6:1–21). Different vows were frequently taken to express thanks for deliverance from grave dangers. Shaving the head marked the end of a vow.

18:19 *Ephesus.* Leading commercial city of Asia Minor, the capital of provincial Asia and the warden of the temple of Artemis (Diana). See Introduction to Ephesians: The City of

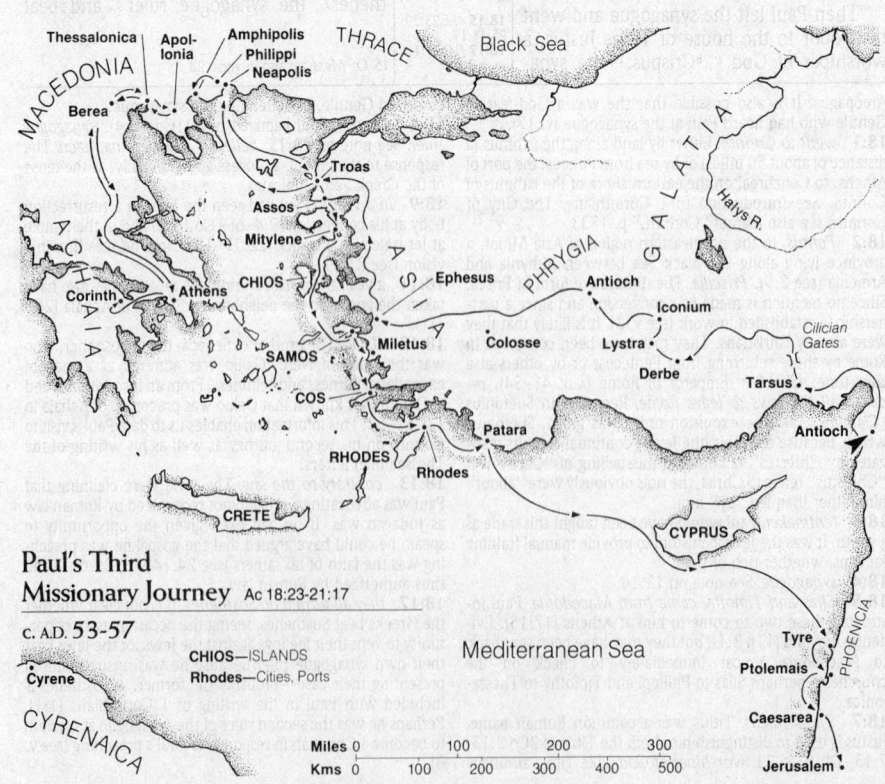

Paul's Third Missionary Journey Ac 18:23–21:17

c. A.D. 53-57

CHIOS—ISLANDS
Rhodes—Cities, Ports

Thessalonica, Apollonia, Amphipolis, Philippi, Neapolis, THRACE, Black Sea, MACEDONIA, Berea, Troas, Assos, Mitylene, ACHAIA, Corinth, Athens, CHIOS, Ephesus, PHRYGIA, Antioch, Iconium, GALATIA, Halys R., ASIA, Miletus, Colosse, Lystra, Derbe, Cilician Gates, Tarsus, SAMOS, COS, Patara, Antioch, RHODES, Rhodes, CYPRUS, PHOENICIA, CRETE, Mediterranean Sea, Tyre, Ptolemais, Cyrene, CYRENAICA, Caesarea, Jerusalem

Miles 0   100   200   300
Kms 0   100   200   300   400   500

and wrote to the disciples there to welcome him. On arriving, he was a great help to those who by grace had believed. [28]For he vigorously refuted the Jews in public debate, proving from the Scriptures[a] that Jesus was the Christ.[b]

Paul in Ephesus

19 While Apollos[c] was at Corinth,[d] Paul took the road through the interior and arrived at Ephesus.[e] There he found some disciples [2]and asked them, "Did you receive the Holy Spirit[f] when[1] you believed?"

They answered, "No, we have not even heard that there is a Holy Spirit."

[3]So Paul asked, "Then what baptism did you receive?"

"John's baptism," they replied.

[4]Paul said, "John's baptism[g] was a baptism of repentance. He told the people to believe in the one coming after him, that is, in Jesus."[h] [5]On hearing this, they were baptized into[m] the name of the Lord Jesus.[i] [6]When Paul placed his hands on them,[j] the Holy Spirit came on them,[k]

and they spoke in tongues[n][l] and prophesied. [7]There were about twelve men in all.

[8]Paul entered the synagogue[m] and spoke boldly there for three months, arguing persuasively about the kingdom of God.[n] [9]But some of them[o] became obstinate; they refused to believe and publicly maligned the Way.[p] So Paul left them. He took the disciples[q] with him and had discussions daily in the lecture hall of Tyrannus. [10]This went on for two years,[r] so that all the Jews and Greeks who lived in the province of Asia[s] heard the word of the Lord.[t]

[11]God did extraordinary miracles[u] through Paul, [12]so that even handkerchiefs and aprons that had touched him were taken to the sick, and their illnesses were cured[v] and the evil spirits left them.

[13]Some Jews who went around driving out evil spirits[w] tried to invoke the name of the Lord Jesus over those who were demon-possessed. They would say, "In the name of Jesus,[x] whom Paul preaches, I command you to come out." [14]Seven sons

Cross references (center column)

18:28 [a]Ac 8:35;
17:2 [b]ver 5;
S Ac 9:22
19:1 [c]S Ac 18:24
[d]S Ac 18:1
[e]S Ac 18:19
19:2 [f]S Jn 20:22
19:4 [g]S Mk 1:4
[h]Jn 1:7
19:5 [i]S Ac 2:38
19:6 [j]S Ac 6:6
[k]S Ac 10:44

[l]S Mk 16:17
19:8 [m]S Ac 9:20
[n]S Mt 3:2;
Ac 28:23
19:9 [o]Ac 14:4
[p]ver 23; S Ac 9:2
[q]ver 30;
S Ac 11:26
19:10 [r]Ac 20:31
[s]ver 22,26,27;
S Ac 2:9
[t]S Ac 13:48
19:11 [u]Ac 8:13
19:12 [v]Ac 5:15
19:13 [w]Mt 12:27
[x]Mk 9:38

[1] Or *after*   [m] 5 Or *in*   [n] 6 Or *other languages*

Ephesus; see also map of "Ephesus" there. *Paul left Priscilla and Aquila.* They would give valuable aid upon Paul's return, providing advice as to where and how the work there could be started. *synagogue.* See note on 13:14.

18:22 *greeted the church.* Could refer to a congregation in Caesarea, but the explanation that "he went up" makes it more likely that it was the church in Jerusalem, some 2,500 feet above sea level.

18:23 See map No. 11 at the end of the Study Bible. *region of Galatia and Phrygia.* The same route he had taken when starting on his second missionary journey, but in the reverse order (16:6). The use of the phrase may indicate the southern part of Galatia in the Phrygian area (see note on 16:6).

18:24 *Alexandria.* In Egypt. It was the second most important city in the Roman empire and had a large Jewish population.

18:25 *baptism of John.* It was not in the name of Jesus (see also 19:2–4). Apollos knew something about Jesus, but basically he, like John, was still looking forward to the coming of the Messiah. His baptism was based on repentance rather than on faith in the finished work of Christ.

18:27 *Achaia.* The Roman province with Corinth as its capital.

19:1 *Apollos was at Corinth.* Apollos was introduced at Ephesus (18:24) in the absence of Paul; he moved to Corinth before Paul returned to Ephesus. But later Apollos came back to Ephesus during Paul's ministry there (see 1Co 16:12). *through the interior.* Not the lower direct route down the Lycus and Meander valleys but the upper Phrygian route approaching Ephesus from a more northerly direction. If Paul got to northern Galatia, which is unlikely, it must have been on one of these trips through the interior (see 16:6; 18:23). *Ephesus.* See note on 18:19. *some disciples.* These 12 (v. 7) seem to have been followers of Jesus, but indirectly through John the Baptist or some of his followers. Or perhaps they had received their teaching from Apollos himself in his earlier state of partial understanding (see 18:26). Like Apollos, they had a limited understanding of the gospel (see note on 18:25).

19:2 *receive the Holy Spirit.* Paul finds that they were not informed about the Holy Spirit at all (vv. 3–6).

19:4 *John's baptism.* See notes on Mt 3:11,15. *baptism of repentance.* A summation of John's teaching. It was preparatory and provisional, stressing man's sinfulness and thus creating a sense of need for the gospel. John's baptism looked forward to Jesus, who by his death would make possible the forgiveness of sins (see note on Mk 1:4).

19:6 *placed his hands on them.* See note on 6:6. *Holy Spirit came on them . . . spoke in tongues and prophesied.* The same experience the disciples had at Pentecost (2:4,11) and the Gentiles had in Caesarea (10:46).

19:8 *three months.* Much longer than the three Sabbaths in Thessalonica (17:2), but the same approach: Jews first, then Greeks (see note on 13:14).

19:9 *the Way.* See note on 9:2. *lecture hall of Tyrannus.* See map of "Ephesus," p. 1789; probably a school used regularly by Tyrannus, a philosopher or rhetorician. Instruction was probably given in the cooler, morning hours. One Greek manuscript adds that Paul did his instructing from 11:00 A.M. to 4:00 P.M. This would have been the hot time of the day, but the hall was available and the people were not at their regular work.

19:10 *two years.* Two years and three months (see v. 8) was the longest stay in one missionary location that Luke records. By Jewish reckoning, any part of a year is considered a year; so this period can be spoken of as three years (20:31). *all . . . in the province of Asia heard.* One of the elements of Paul's missionary strategy is seen here. Many of the cities where Paul planted churches were strategic centers that, when evangelized, served as focal points from which the gospel radiated out to the surrounding areas. Other examples are Antioch in Pisidia (see 13:14), Thessalonica (see 17:1), Athens (see 17:15) and Corinth (see 18:1).

19:12 *handkerchiefs.* Probably used by Paul in his trade of leatherworking: one for tying around his head, the other around his waist. Cf. 5:15.

19:14 *Sceva, a Jewish chief priest.* May have been related to the high priestly family of Jerusalem. But more likely he

of Sceva, a Jewish chief priest, were doing this. 15One day, the evil spirit answered them, "Jesus I know, and I know about Paul, but who are you?" 16Then the man who had the evil spirit jumped on them and overpowered them all. He gave them such a beating that they ran out of the house naked and bleeding.

17When this became known to the Jews and Greeks living in Ephesus, they were all seized with fear, and the name of the Lord Jesus was held in high honor. 18Many of those who believed now came and openly confessed their evil deeds. 19A number who had practiced sorcery brought their scrolls together and burned them publicly. When they calculated the value of the scrolls, the total came to fifty thousand drachmas. 20In this way the word of the Lord a spread widely and grew in power. b

21After all this had happened, Paul decided to go to Jerusalem, c passing through Macedonia d and Achaia. e "After I have been there," he said, "I must visit Rome also." f 22He sent two of his helpers, g Timothy h and Erastus, i to Macedonia, while he stayed in the province of Asia j a little longer.

The Riot in Ephesus

23About that time there arose a great disturbance about the Way. k 24A silversmith named Demetrius, who made silver shrines of Artemis, brought in no little business for the craftsmen. 25He called them together, along with the workmen in related trades, and said: "Men, you know

we receive a good income from this business. l 26And you see and hear how this fellow Paul has convinced and led astray large numbers of people here in Ephesus m and in practically the whole province of Asia. n He says that man-made gods are no gods at all. o 27There is danger not only that our trade will lose its good name, but also that the temple of the great goddess Artemis will be discredited, and the goddess herself, who is worshiped throughout the province of Asia and the world, will be robbed of her divine majesty."

28When they heard this, they were furious and began shouting: "Great is Artemis of the Ephesians!" p 29Soon the whole city was in an uproar. The people seized Gaius q and Aristarchus, r Paul's traveling companions from Macedonia, s and rushed as one man into the theater. 30Paul wanted to appear before the crowd, but the disciples t would not let him. 31Even some of the officials of the province, friends of Paul, sent him a message begging him not to venture into the theater.

32The assembly was in confusion: Some were shouting one thing, some another. u Most of the people did not even know why they were there. 33The Jews pushed Alexander to the front, and some of the crowd shouted instructions to him. He motioned v for silence in order to make a defense before the people. 34But when they realized he was a Jew, they all shouted in

Cross references

19:17 yS Ac 18:19
zAc 5:5,11
19:20 aS Ac 13:48
bAc 6:7; 12:24
19:21 cAc 20:16, 22; 21:4,12,15; Ro 15:25
dS Ac 16:9
eS Ac 18:12
fRo 15:24,28
19:22 gAc 13:5
hS Ac 16:1
iRo 16:23;
2Ti 4:20 jver 10, 26,27; S Ac 2:9
19:23 kS Ac 9:2

19:25 lAc 16:16, 19,20
19:26 mS Ac 18:19
nS Ac 2:9
oDt 4:28;
Ps 115:4;
Isa 44:10-20;
Jer 10:3-5;
Ac 17:29;
1Co 8:4; Rev 9:20
19:28 pS Ac 18:19
19:29 qAc 20:4;
Ro 16:23;
1Co 1:14
rAc 20:4; 27:2;
Col 4:10; Phm 24
sS Ac 16:9
19:30 tS Ac 11:26
19:32 uAc 21:34
19:33 vS Ac 12:17

o19 A drachma was a silver coin worth about a day's wages.

took this title himself to make further impression with his magical wiles. Drawn by Paul's ability to drive out evil spirits, Jewish exorcists wanted to copy his work (cf. 13:6).

19:19 scrolls. Such documents bearing alleged magical formulas and secret information have been unearthed. Ephesus was a center for magical incantations. fifty thousand drachmas. The high price (see NIV text note) was not due to the quality of the books but to the supposed power gained by their secret rigmarole of words and names.

19:22 Erastus. An important figure at Corinth, "the city's director of public works" at one time (see note on Ro 16:23). He is located later at Corinth also (2Ti 4:20). Just now he returns to Corinth by way of Macedonia with Timothy.

19:24 silversmith named Demetrius. Each trade had its guild, and Demetrius was probably a responsible leader of the guild for the manufacture of silver shrines and images. Artemis. The Greek name for the Roman goddess Diana. The Ephesian Artemis, however, was very different from the Greco-Roman goddess. She had taken on the characteristics of Cybele, the mother goddess of fertility worshiped in Asia Minor and served by many prostitute priestesses. A meteorite may be the basis of the many-breasted image of heavenly workmanship claimed for Artemis (v. 35). (Some have identified the objects that cover the torso of the image as ostrich

eggs.) Reproductions of the original image from the time of the emperor Domitian (A.D. 81–96) have been found in Ephesus.

19:25 a good income. Since the temple of Artemis was one of the seven wonders of the ancient world, people came from far and wide to view it. Their purchase of silver shrines and images produced a lucrative business for the craftsmen.

19:27 temple of the great goddess. See map of "Ephesus," p. 1789; the glory of Ephesus: 425 feet long and 220 feet wide, having 127 white marble columns 62 feet high and less than 4 feet apart. In the inner sanctuary was the many-breasted image supposedly dropped from heaven.

19:29 Aristarchus. Traveled later with Paul from Corinth to Jerusalem (20:3–4), and also accompanied Paul on the voyage from Jerusalem to Rome (27:1–2; Col 4:10).

19:31 officials of the province. Greek Asiarchon, members of a council of men of wealth and influence elected to promote the worship of the emperor. Paul had friends in this highest circle.

19:33 Alexander. Pushed forward by the Jews either to make clear the disassociation of the Jews from the Christians and/or to accuse the Christians further of an offense against the Greeks. The crowd recognized that the Jews were not worshipers of Artemis any more than the Christians.

unison for about two hours: "Great is Artemis of the Ephesians!" *w*

35The city clerk quieted the crowd and said: "Men of Ephesus, *x* doesn't all the world know that the city of Ephesus is the guardian of the temple of the great Artemis and of her image, which fell from heaven? 36Therefore, since these facts are undeniable, you ought to be quiet and not do anything rash. 37You have brought these men here, though they have neither robbed temples *y* nor blasphemed our goddess. 38If, then, Demetrius and his fellow craftsmen *z* have a grievance against anybody, the courts are open and there are proconsuls. *a* They can press charges. 39If there is anything further you want to bring up, it must be settled in a legal assembly. 40As it is, we are in danger of being charged with rioting because of today's events. In that case we would not be able to account for this commotion, since there is no reason for it." 41After he had said this, he dismissed the assembly.

19:34 *w*ver 28
19:35
*x*S Ac 18:19
19:37 *y*Ro 2:22
19:38 *z*ver 24
*a*Ac 13:7,8,12;
18:12

20:1 *b*S Ac 11:26
*c*S Ac 16:9
*d*ver 19;
Ac 9:23,24; 14:5;
23:12,15,30;
25:3; 2Co 11:26;
S 1Th 2:16
*e*S Lk 2:2
*f*S Ac 16:9
20:4 *g*S Ac 19:29
*h*S Ac 17:1
*i*S Ac 19:29
*j*S Ac 16:1
*k*Eph 6:21;
Col 4:7; Tit 3:12
*l*Ac 21:29;
2Ti 4:20
*m*S Ac 2:9
20:5 *n*S Ac 16:10
*o*S Ac 16:8
20:6 *p*S Ac 16:12
*q*S Ac 16:8
20:7 *r*1Co 16:2;
Rev 1:10

Through Macedonia and Greece

20 When the uproar had ended, Paul sent for the disciples *b* and, after encouraging them, said good-by and set out for Macedonia. *c* 2He traveled through that area, speaking many words of encouragement to the people, and finally arrived in Greece, 3where he stayed three months. Because the Jews made a plot against him *d* just as he was about to sail for Syria, *e* he decided to go back through Macedonia. *f* 4He was accompanied by Sopater son of Pyrrhus from Berea, Aristarchus *g* and Secundus from Thessalonica, *h* Gaius *i* from Derbe, Timothy *j* also, and Tychicus *k* and Trophimus *l* from the province of Asia. *m* 5These men went on ahead and waited for us *n* at Troas. *o* 6But we sailed from Philippi *p* after the Feast of Unleavened Bread, and five days later joined the others at Troas, *q* where we stayed seven days.

Eutychus Raised From the Dead at Troas

7On the first day of the week *r* we came

19:35 *city clerk.* The secretary of the city who published the decisions of the civic assembly. He was the most important local official and the chief executive officer of the assembly, acting as go-between for Ephesus and the Roman authorities.
19:38 *courts . . . proconsuls.* Probably general terms, not intended to refer to more than one court or one proconsul. As capital city of the province of Asia, Ephesus was the headquarters for the proconsul.
19:39 *legal assembly.* The regular civil meeting ordinarily held three times a month.
20:1 *said good-by and set out.* Paul wanted to: (1) leave Ephesus, (2) preach in Troas on his way to Macedonia, (3) meet Titus at Troas with a report from Corinth (see 2Co 2:12–13) and (4) continue collecting the offering for Judea (see 1Co 16:1–4; 2 Co 8:1–9:15; Ro 15:25–28).
20:2 *He traveled through that area.* May cover a considerable period. He may have gone to Illyricum (see Ro 15:19) at this time.
20:3 *three months.* Probably a reference to the stay in Corinth, the capital of Achaia. These would be the winter months when ships did not sail regularly. Paul probably wrote Romans at this time (see Introduction to Romans: Occasion). *a plot against him.* The Jews were determined to take Paul's life; also, at this time he was carrying the offering for the Christians in Judea, so there would have been a temptation for theft as well. The port at Cenchrea would have provided a convenient place for Paul's enemies to detect him as he entered a ship to embark for Syria.
20:4 These men seem to be the delegates appointed to accompany Paul and the money given for the needy in Judea (see note on 2Co 8:23). Three were from Macedonia, two from Galatia and two from Asia. Luke may have joined them at Philippi ("we sailed," v. 6; see note on 16:10). *Sopater.* May be the same as Sosipater (Ro 16:21). *Aristarchus.* See note on 19:29. *Secundus.* Not mentioned elsewhere. His name means "second," as Tertius (see Ro 16:22) means "third" and Quartus (see Ro 16:23) means "fourth." *Gaius*

from Derbe. A Gaius from Macedonia was associated with Aristarchus (see 19:29), but the grouping of the names in pairs (after the reference to Sopater) indicates that this Gaius was associated with Roman Galatia and is different from the Macedonia Gaius. *Timothy.* May have represented more than one particular church. He was from Lystra but had been responsible for working in other churches (1Co 16:10–11; Php 2:19–23). *Tychicus.* A constant help to Paul, especially in association with the churches of Asia (Eph 6:21–22; Col 4:7–9; 2Ti 4:12; Tit 3:12). *Trophimus.* Appears again in 21:29 (see 2Ti 4:20). He was an Ephesian, and it is implied that he was a Gentile.
20:5 *Troas.* Was to be the rendezvous for Paul and those who went on ahead by sea from Neapolis, the seaport of Philippi (16:11). Paul and his immediate companions stayed in Philippi before sailing a week later.
20:6 *from Philippi.* From the seaport, Neapolis, about ten miles away. *Feast of Unleavened Bread.* Began with Passover and lasted a week. Paul spent the period in Philippi. Formerly he had hoped to reach Jerusalem sooner (see 19:21), but now he hoped to arrive there for Pentecost (see 20:16). *five days later.* The voyage from Neapolis to Troas took five days. It had taken about two days the other direction (16:11). *seven days.* Although Paul was in a hurry to arrive at Jerusalem by Pentecost, he remained seven days at Troas. This might have been because of a ship schedule, but more likely the delay was in order to meet with the believers on the first day of the week to break bread.
20:7 *first day of the week.* Sunday. Although some maintain that they met on Saturday evening since the Jewish day began at six o'clock the previous evening, there is no indication that Luke is using the Jewish method of reporting time to tell of happenings in this Hellenistic city. *to break bread.* Here indicates the Lord's Supper, since breaking bread was the expressed purpose for this formal gathering. The Lord's Supper had been commanded (Lk 22:19), and it was observed regularly (see 2:42).

together to break bread.[s] Paul spoke to the people and, because he intended to leave the next day, kept on talking until midnight. [8]There were many lamps in the upstairs room[t] where we were meeting. [9]Seated in a window was a young man named Eutychus, who was sinking into a deep sleep as Paul talked on and on. When he was sound asleep, he fell to the ground from the third story and was picked up dead. [10]Paul went down, threw himself on the young man[u] and put his arms around him. "Don't be alarmed," he said. "He's alive!"[v] [11]Then he went upstairs again and broke bread[w] and ate. After talking until daylight, he left. [12]The people took the young man home alive and were greatly comforted.

Paul's Farewell to the Ephesian Elders

[13]We went on ahead to the ship and sailed for Assos, where we were going to take Paul aboard. He had made this arrangement because he was going there on foot. [14]When he met us at Assos, we took him aboard and went on to Mitylene. [15]The next day we set sail from there and arrived off Kios. The day after that we crossed over to Samos, and on the following day arrived at Miletus.[x] [16]Paul had decided to sail past Ephesus[y] to avoid spending time in the province of Asia,[z] for he

was in a hurry to reach Jerusalem,[a] if possible, by the day of Pentecost.[b]

[17]From Miletus,[c] Paul sent to Ephesus for the elders[d] of the church. [18]When they arrived, he said to them: "You know how I lived the whole time I was with you,[e] from the first day I came into the province of Asia.[f] [19]I served the Lord with great humility and with tears,[g] although I was severely tested by the plots of the Jews.[h] [20]You know that I have not hesitated to preach anything[i] that would be helpful to you but have taught you publicly and from house to house. [21]I have declared to both Jews[j] and Greeks that they must turn to God in repentance[k] and have faith in our Lord Jesus.[l]

[22]"And now, compelled by the Spirit, I am going to Jerusalem,[m] not knowing what will happen to me there. [23]I only know that in every city the Holy Spirit warns me[n] that prison and hardships are facing me.[o] [24]However, I consider my life worth nothing to me,[p] if only I may finish the race[q] and complete the task[r] the Lord Jesus has given me[s]—the task of testifying to the gospel of God's grace.[t]

[25]"Now I know that none of you among whom I have gone about preaching the kingdom[u] will ever see me again.[v] [26]Therefore, I declare to you today that I am innocent of the blood of all men.[w] [27]For I have not hesitated to proclaim to you the whole will of God.[x] [28]Keep watch

Cross references

20:7 [s]S Mt 14:19
20:8 [t]Ac 1:13; 9:37
20:10 [u]1Ki 17:21; 2Ki 4:34 [v]Mt 9:23,24
20:11 [w]ver 7; S Mt 14:19
20:15 [x]ver 17; 2Ti 4:20
20:16 [y]S Ac 18:19 [z]S Ac 2:9
[a]S Ac 19:21 [b]S Ac 2:1
20:17 [c]ver 15 [d]S Ac 11:30
20:18 [e]Ac 18:19-21; 19:1-41 [f]S Ac 2:9
20:19 [g]Ps 6:6 [h]S ver 3
20:20 [i]ver 27; Ps 40:10; Jer 26:2; 42:4
20:21 [j]Ac 18:5 [k]S Ac 2:38 [l]Ac 24:24; 26:18; Eph 1:15; Col 2:5; Phm 5
20:22 [m]ver 16
20:23 [n]S Ac 8:29; 21:4 [o]S Ac 9:16
20:24 [p]Ac 21:13 [q]2Ti 4:7 [r]2Co 4:1 [s]Gal 1:1; Tit 1:3 [t]S Ac 11:23
20:25 [u]S Mt 4:23 [v]ver 38
20:26 [w]Eze 3:17-19; Ac 18:6
20:27 [x]S ver 20

20:9 *Eutychus.* A name common among the freedman class (see note on 6:9).

20:10 *He's alive!* As Peter had raised Tabitha (9:40), so Paul raised Eutychus.

20:13 *Assos.* On the opposite side of the peninsula from Troas—about 20 miles away by land. The coastline, however, was about 40 miles. Thus Paul was not far behind the ship that sailed around the peninsula.

20:14 *Mitylene.* After the first day of sailing, they put into this harbor on the southeast shore of the island of Lesbos.

20:15 *Kios.* The second night they spent off the shore of this larger island, which lay along the west coast of Asia Minor. *Samos.* Crossing the mouth of the bay that leads to Ephesus, they came on the third day to Samos, one of the most important islands in the Aegean. *Miletus.* Thirty miles south of Ephesus, the destination of the ship Paul was on. He would have had to change ships to put into Ephesus, which would have lost time (see v. 16). If he had come to Ephesus, he would have had to visit a number of families, which would have taken more time. If trouble should arise, as the riot of a year ago (19:23–41), even more time would be lost. It could not be risked.

20:16 *by the day of Pentecost.* Fifty days from Passover. Five days plus seven days (v. 6) plus four days (vv. 13–15) had already gone by, leaving only about two-thirds of the time for the remainder of the trip.

20:17 *elders of the church.* The importance of the leadership of elders has been evident throughout Paul's ministry. He had delivered the famine gift from the church at Antioch

to the elders of the Jerusalem church (11:30). He had appointed elders on his first missionary journey (see 14:23) and had addressed the holders of this office later in Philippi (Php 1:1, "overseers"). He requested the Ephesian elders to meet with him on this solemn occasion (see v. 28). Some years later he wrote down instruction about the elders' qualifications (1Ti 3; Tit 1).

20:19 *with tears.* See v. 31. Paul's ministry at Ephesus was conducted with emotional fervency and a sense of urgency.

20:22 *compelled by the Spirit.* Paul did not go to Jerusalem against the direction of the Spirit, as some have suggested, but because of the guidance of the Spirit. People pleaded with him not to go (21:4,12), not because the Spirit prohibited his going but because the Spirit revealed the capture that awaited him there (21:11–12).

20:25 *none of you ... will ever see me again.* Not a message from God but what Paul anticipated. He had been mistaken before in his plans: He had intended to stay in Ephesus until Pentecost, but he had to leave earlier (see v. 1; 1Co 16:8–9). His prophetic power was not used to foresee his own future, just as his healing power was not used to heal his own disease (see 2Co 12:7–9). As it turned out, it seems that Paul did revisit Ephesus (see 1Ti 1:3).

20:28 *overseers. Be shepherds.* The "elders" (v. 17) were called "overseers" and told to pastor ("shepherd") the flock—demonstrating that the same men could be called "elders," "overseers" or "pastors." *his own blood.* Lit. "the blood of his own one," a term of endearment (such as "his own dear one," referring to his own Son).

over yourselves and all the flock[y] of which the Holy Spirit has made you overseers.[p] [z] Be shepherds of the church of God,[q] [a] which he bought[b] with his own blood.[c] [29]I know that after I leave, savage wolves[d] will come in among you and will not spare the flock.[e] [30]Even from your own number men will arise and distort the truth in order to draw away disciples[f] after them. [31]So be on your guard! Remember that for three years[g] I never stopped warning each of you night and day with tears.[h]

[32]"Now I commit you to God[i] and to the word of his grace, which can build you up and give you an inheritance[j] among all those who are sanctified.[k] [33]I have not coveted anyone's silver or gold or clothing.[l] [34]You yourselves know that these hands of mine have supplied my own needs and the needs of my companions.[m] [35]In everything I did, I showed you that by this kind of hard work we must help the weak, remembering the words the Lord Jesus himself said: 'It is more blessed to give than to receive.'"

[36]When he had said this, he knelt down with all of them and prayed.[n] [37]They all wept as they embraced him and kissed him.[o] [38]What grieved them most was his statement that they would never see his face again.[p] Then they accompanied him to the ship.[q]

On to Jerusalem

21 After we[r] had torn ourselves away from them, we put out to sea and sailed straight to Cos. The next day we went to Rhodes and from there to Patara.

[2]We found a ship crossing over to Phoenicia,[s] went on board and set sail. [3]After sighting Cyprus and passing to the south of it, we sailed on to Syria.[t] We landed at Tyre, where our ship was to unload its cargo. [4]Finding the disciples[u] there, we stayed with them seven days. Through the Spirit[v] they urged Paul not to go on to Jerusalem. [5]But when our time was up, we left and continued on our way. All the disciples and their wives and children accompanied us out of the city, and there on the beach we knelt to pray.[w] [6]After saying good-by to each other, we went aboard the ship, and they returned home.

[7]We continued our voyage from Tyre[x] and landed at Ptolemais, where we greeted the brothers[y] and stayed with them for a day. [8]Leaving the next day, we reached Caesarea[z] and stayed at the house of Philip[a] the evangelist,[b] one of the Seven. [9]He had four unmarried daughters who prophesied.[c]

[10]After we had been there a number of days, a prophet named Agabus[d] came down from Judea. [11]Coming over to us, he took Paul's belt, tied his own hands and feet with it and said, "The Holy Spirit says,[e] 'In this way the Jews of Jerusalem will bind[f] the owner of this belt and will hand him over to the Gentiles.'"[g]

[12]When we heard this, we and the people there pleaded with Paul not to go up to Jerusalem. [13]Then Paul answered, "Why are you weeping and breaking my heart? I am ready not only to be bound,

---

p.28 Traditionally *bishops*   **q.28** Many manuscripts *of the Lord*

Cross references (center column)

20:28 [y]ver 29; S Jn 21:16
[z]S 1Ti 3:1
[a]S 1Co 10:32
[b]S 1Co 6:20
[c]S Ro 3:25
20:29 [d]Eze 34:5; Mt 7:15 [e]ver 28
20:30 [f]S Ac 11:26
20:31 [g]Ac 19:10 [h]ver 19
20:32 [i]Ac 14:23 [j]S Eph 1:14; S Mt 25:34; Col 1:12; 3:24; Heb 9:15; 1Pe 1:4 [k]Ac 26:18
20:33 [l]1Sa 12:3; 1Co 9:12; 2Co 2:17; 7:2; 11:9; 12:14-17; 1Th 2:5
20:34 [m]S Ac 18:3
20:36 [n]Lk 22:41; Ac 9:40; 21:5
20:37 [o]S Lk 15:20
20:38 [p]ver 25 [q]Ac 21:5
21:1 [r]S Ac 16:10

21:2 [s]Ac 11:19
21:3 [t]S Lk 2:2
21:4 [u]S Ac 11:26 [v]ver 11; Ac 20:23
21:5 [w]Lk 22:41; Ac 9:40; 20:36
21:7 [x]Ac 12:20 [y]S Ac 1:16
21:8 [z]S Ac 8:40 [a]Ac 6:5; 8:5-40 [b]Eph 4:11; 2Ti 4:5
21:9 [c]Ex 15:20; Jdg 4:4; Ne 6:14; Lk 2:36; Ac 2:17; 1Co 11:5
21:10 [d]Ac 11:28
21:11 [e]S Ac 8:29 [f]ver 33 [g]1Ki 22:11; Isa 20:2-4; Jer 13:1-11; Mt 20:19

20:31 *three years.* See note on 19:10.

20:32 *are sanctified.* Positional sanctification (see 26:18; see also note on 1Co 1:2).

20:34 *supplied my own needs.* Paul had worked in Thessalonica (1Th 2:9) and Corinth (Ac 18:3).

20:35 *remembering the words the Lord Jesus himself said.* A formula regularly used in the early church to introduce a quotation from Jesus (1 Clement 46:7). This is a rare instance of a saying of Jesus not found in the canonical Gospels.

21:1 *sailed straight to Cos.* Favorable winds took them to a stopping place for the night at this island. *Rhodes.* The leading city on the island of Rhodes, once noted for its harbor colossus, one of the seven wonders of the ancient world (but demolished over two centuries before Paul arrived there). It took them a day to get to Rhodes. *Patara.* On the southern coast of Lycia. Paul changed ships from a vessel that hugged the shore of Asia Minor to one going directly to Tyre and Phoenicia.

21:3 *Cyprus.* See 13:4. *Tyre.* Paul had passed through this Phoenician area at least once before (15:3; cf. Mk 7:24).

21:4 *seven days.* These, added to the 29 days since the Passover in Philippi, would leave only two weeks until Pentecost. *urged Paul not to go.* The Spirit warned of the coming trials in store for Paul at Jerusalem. Because of these warn-

ings, Paul's brothers urged him not to go on, knowing that trials lay ahead. But Paul felt "compelled by the Spirit" to go (20:22).

21:7 *Ptolemais.* The modern city of Acco, north of and across the bay from Mount Carmel. It was one day's journey from Tyre on the north and another 35 miles to Caesarea on the south.

21:8 *Caesarea.* A Gentile city, the capital of Roman Judea (see note on 10:1). *Philip the evangelist.* Philip's evangelistic work may have focused on Caesarea for almost 25 years (see note on 8:40). "Evangelist" is a title used only here and in Eph 4:11; 2Ti 4:5.

21:9 *unmarried daughters.* They may have been dedicated in a special way to serving the Lord. *prophesied.* See 1Co 11:5; 12:8-10; cf. Lk 2:36. For OT prophetesses see Ex 15:20; Jdg 4:4; 2Ki 22:14; Ne 6:14.

21:10 *prophet named Agabus.* Evidently he held the office of prophet, as Philip held the office of evangelist (v. 8). This is the same prophet who had been in Antioch prophesying the coming famine in Jerusalem some 15 years earlier (11:27–29).

21:12 *we and the people there.* Now Luke, in the company of travelers with Paul, joins in urging Paul not to go to Jerusalem.

but also to die[h] in Jerusalem for the name of the Lord Jesus."[i] [14]When he would not be dissuaded, we gave up[j] and said, "The Lord's will be done."[k]

[15]After this, we got ready and went up to Jerusalem.[l] [16]Some of the disciples from Caesarea[m] accompanied us and brought us to the home of Mnason, where we were to stay. He was a man from Cyprus[n] and one of the early disciples.

Paul's Arrival at Jerusalem

[17]When we arrived at Jerusalem, the brothers[o] received us warmly.[p] [18]The next day Paul and the rest of us went to see James,[q] and all the elders[r] were present. [19]Paul greeted them and reported in detail what God had done among the Gentiles[s] through his ministry.[t]

[20]When they heard this, they praised God. Then they said to Paul: "You see, brother, how many thousands of Jews have believed, and all of them are zealous[u] for the law.[v] [21]They have been informed that you teach all the Jews who live among the Gentiles to turn away from Moses,[w] telling them not to circumcise their children[x] or live according to our customs.[y] [22]What shall we do? They will certainly hear that you have come, [23]so do what we tell you. There are four men with us who have made a vow.[z] [24]Take these men, join in their purification rites[a] and pay their expenses, so that they can have their heads shaved.[b] Then everybody will know there is no truth in these reports about you, but

that you yourself are living in obedience to the law. [25]As for the Gentile believers, we have written to them our decision that they should abstain from food sacrificed to idols, from blood, from the meat of strangled animals and from sexual immorality."[c]

[26]The next day Paul took the men and purified himself along with them. Then he went to the temple to give notice of the date when the days of purification would end and the offering would be made for each of them.[d]

Paul Arrested

[27]When the seven days were nearly over, some Jews from the province of Asia saw Paul at the temple. They stirred up the whole crowd and seized him,[e] [28]shouting, "Men of Israel, help us! This is the man who teaches all men everywhere against our people and our law and this place. And besides, he has brought Greeks into the temple area and defiled this holy place."[f] [29](They had previously seen Trophimus[g] the Ephesian[h] in the city with Paul and assumed that Paul had brought him into the temple area.)

[30]The whole city was aroused, and the people came running from all directions. Seizing Paul,[i] they dragged him[j] from the temple, and immediately the gates were shut. [31]While they were trying to kill him, news reached the commander of the Roman troops that the whole city of Jerusalem was in an uproar. [32]He at once took

Cross references (center column)

21:13 [h]Ac 20:24 [i]S Jn 15:21; S Ac 9:16
21:14 [j]Ru 1:18 [k]S Mt 26:39
21:15 [l]S Ac 19:21
21:16 [m]S Ac 8:40 [n]ver 3,4
21:17 [o]S Ac 9:30 [p]Ac 15:4
21:18 [q]S Ac 15:13 [r]S Ac 11:30
21:19 [s]Ac 14:27; 15:4,12 [t]Ac 1:17
21:20 [u]Ac 22:3; Ro 10:2 Gal 1:14; Php 3:6 [v]Ac 15:1, 5
21:21 [w]ver 28 [x]Ac 15:19-21; 1Co 7:18,19 [y]S Ac 6:14
21:23 [z]Nu 6:2,5, 18; Ac 18:18
21:24 [a]ver 26; Ac 24:18 [b]Ac 18:18

21:25 [c]Ac 15:20, 29
21:26 [d]Nu 6:13-20; Ac 24:18
21:27 [e]Jer 26:8; Ac 24:18; 26:21; S 1Th 2:16
21:28 [f]Mt 24:15; Ac 6:13; 24:5,6
21:29 [g]Ac 20:4; 2Ti 4:20 [h]S Ac 18:19
21:30 [i]Ac 26:21 [j]S Ac 16:19

Footnotes

21:14 *Lord's will be done.* May mean that they finally recognized that it was the Lord's will for Paul to go to Jerusalem.
21:16 *Mnason.* Must have been a disciple of some means to be able to accommodate Paul and a group of about nine men traveling with him.
21:17 *arrived at Jerusalem.* No more than a day or two before Pentecost. *the brothers received us warmly.* May indicate the grateful reception of the offering as well.
21:18 *James.* The brother of the Lord, author of the letter of James and leader of the church in Jerusalem (see Gal 1:19; 2:9). He is called an apostle but was not one of the Twelve.
21:23 *made a vow.* They were evidently under the temporary Nazirite vow and became unclean before the completion time of the vow (perhaps from contact with a dead body); cf. Nu 6:2–12.
21:24 *purification rites.* In some instances the rites included the offering of sacrifices. Such rites were observed by choice by some Jewish Christians but were not required of Christians, whether Jew or Gentile. *pay their expenses.* Paul's part in sponsoring these men would include (1) paying part or all of the expenses of the sacrificial victims (in this case eight pigeons and four lambs, Nu 6:9–12) and (2) going to the temple to notify the priest when their days of purification would be fulfilled so the priests would be prepared to sacrifice their offerings (v. 26). *living in obedience to the law.* Paul had earlier taken a vow himself (18:18); he had

been a Jew to the Jews (see 1Co 9:20–21), and Timothy had been circumcised (16:3). However, Paul was very careful not to sacrifice Christian principle in any act of obedience to the law (he would not have Titus circumcised, Gal 2:3).
21:27 *seven days.* Cf. Nu 6:9. These were the days required for purification, shaving their heads at the altar, the sacrifice of a sin offering and burnt offering for each, and announcing the completion to the priests. *Jews from the province of Asia.* Paul had suffered already from the hands of Asian Jews (20:19).
21:28 *brought Greeks into the temple area.* Explicitly forbidden according to inscribed stone markers (still in existence). Any Gentiles found within the bounds of the court of Israel would be killed. But there is no evidence that Paul had brought anyone other than Jews into the area.
21:29 *Trophimus.* Paul probably did not take him into the forbidden area. If he had, they should have attacked Trophimus rather than Paul.
21:30 *gates were shut.* By order of the temple officer to prevent further trouble inside the sacred precincts.
21:31 *commander.* Greek *chiliarch,* a commander of 1,000 (a regiment), Claudius Lysias by name (23:26), who was stationed at the Fortress of Antonia (see note on v. 37).
21:32 *some officers.* Centurions. Since the plural is used, it is likely that at least two centurions and 200 soldiers were involved.

some officers and soldiers and ran down to the crowd. When the rioters saw the commander and his soldiers, they stopped beating Paul. *k*

³³The commander came up and arrested him and ordered him to be bound *l* with two *m* chains. *n* Then he asked who he was and what he had done. ³⁴Some in the crowd shouted one thing and some another, *o* and since the commander could not get at the truth because of the uproar, he ordered that Paul be taken into the barracks. *p* ³⁵When Paul reached the steps, *q* the violence of the mob was so great he had to be carried by the soldiers. ³⁶The crowd that followed kept shouting, "Away with him!" *r*

Paul Speaks to the Crowd

22:3–16pp — Ac 9:1–22; 26:9–18

³⁷As the soldiers were about to take Paul into the barracks, *s* he asked the commander, "May I say something to you?" "Do you speak Greek?" he replied. ³⁸"Aren't you the Egyptian who started a revolt and led four thousand terrorists out into the desert *t* some time ago?" *u*

³⁹Paul answered, "I am a Jew, from Tarsus *v* in Cilicia, *w* a citizen of no ordinary city. Please let me speak to the people."

⁴⁰Having received the commander's permission, Paul stood on the steps and motioned *x* to the crowd. When they were all silent, he said to them in Aramaic *r*: *y*

22 ¹"Brothers and fathers, *z* listen now to my defense."

²When they heard him speak to them in Aramaic, *a* they became very quiet.

Then Paul said: ³"I am a Jew, *b* born in Tarsus *c* of Cilicia, *d* but brought up in this city. Under *e* Gamaliel *f* I was thoroughly trained in the law of our fathers *g* and was just as zealous *h* for God as any of you are today. ⁴I persecuted *i* the followers of this Way *j* to their death, arresting both men and women and throwing them into prison, *k* ⁵as also the high priest and all the Council *l* can testify. I even obtained letters from them to their brothers *m* in Damascus, *n* and went there to bring these people as prisoners to Jerusalem to be punished.

⁶"About noon as I came near Damascus, suddenly a bright light from heaven flashed around me. *o* ⁷I fell to the ground and heard a voice say to me, 'Saul! Saul! Why do you persecute me?'

⁸'Who are you, Lord?' I asked.

"'I am Jesus of Nazareth, *p* whom you are persecuting,' he replied. ⁹My companions saw the light, *q* but they did not understand the voice *r* of him who was speaking to me.

¹⁰"'What shall I do, Lord?' I asked.

"'Get up,' the Lord said, 'and go into Damascus. There you will be told all that you have been assigned to do.' *s* ¹¹My companions led me by the hand into Damascus, because the brilliance of the light had blinded me. *t*

¹²"A man named Ananias came to see me. *u* He was a devout observer of the law and highly respected by all the Jews living there. *v* ¹³He stood beside me and said, 'Brother Saul, receive your sight!' And at

21:32 *k*Ac 23:27
21:33 *l*ver 11
*m*Ac 12:6
*n*Ac 20:23;
22:29; Eph 6:20;
2Ti 2:9
21:34 *o*Ac 19:32
*p*ver 37;
Ac 22:24; 23:10, 16,32
21:35 *q*ver 40
21:36 *r*Lk 23:18; Jn 19:15;
Ac 22:22
21:37 *s*S ver 34
21:38 *t*Mt 24:26
*u*Ac 5:36
21:39 *v*S Ac 9:11
*w*S Ac 6:9
21:40
*x*S Ac 12:17
*y*S Jn 5:2
22:1 *z*Ac 7:2
22:2 *a*Ac 21:40;
S Jn 5:2

22:3 *b*Ac 21:39
*c*S Ac 9:11
*d*S Ac 6:9
*e*Lk 10:39
*f*Ac 5:34 *g*Ac 26:5
*h*1Ki 19:10;
S Ac 21:20
22:4 *i*S Ac 8:3
*j*S Ac 9:2 *k*ver 19, 20
22:5 *l*Lk 22:66
*m*Ac 1:16; 2:29;
13:26; 23:1;
28:17,21;
S Ro 7:1; 9:3
*n*Ac 9:2
22:6 *o*Ac 9:3
22:8 *p*S Mk 1:24
22:9 *q*Ac 26:13
*r*Ac 9:7
22:10 *s*Ac 16:30
22:11 *t*Ac 9:8
22:12 *u*Ac 9:17
*v*Ac 10:22

r40 Or possibly Hebrew; also in 22:2

21:33 *two chains.* Probably his hands were chained to a soldier on either side.
21:37 *barracks.* The Fortress of Antonia was connected to the northern end of the temple area by two flights of steps. The tower overlooked the temple area.
21:38 *the Egyptian who started a revolt.* Josephus tells of an Egyptian false prophet who some years earlier had led 4,000 (Josephus, through a misreading of a Greek capital letter, says 30,000) out to the Mount of Olives. Roman soldiers killed hundreds, but the leader escaped. *terrorists.* The Greek here is a loanword from Latin *sicarii,* meaning "dagger-men," who were violent assassins.
21:39 *Tarsus.* See note on 11:1.
21:40 *Aramaic.* More likely Aramaic than Hebrew (see NIV text note), since Aramaic was the most commonly used language among Palestinian Jews.
22:1 *Brothers.* See note on 11:1.
22:2 *Aramaic.* See note on 21:40. Actually, if he had spoken in Hebrew, they would have become quieter in order not to miss a single word, because it would have been more difficult for them to understand.
22:3 *born in Tarsus.* Paul had citizenship in Tarsus (21:39) as well as being a Roman citizen. "No ordinary city" (21:39) was used by Euripides to describe Athens. Tarsus was 10

miles inland on the Cydnus River and 30 miles from the mountains, which were cut by a deep, narrow gorge called the Cilician Gates. It was an important commercial center, university city and crossroads of travel. *brought up in this city.* Paul must have come to Jerusalem at an early age. Another translation ("brought up in this city at the feet of Gamaliel, being thoroughly trained according to the law of our fathers") would suggest that Paul came to Jerusalem when he was old enough to begin training under Gamaliel. *Gamaliel.* The most honored rabbi of the first century. Possibly he was the grandson of Hillel (see also 5:34–40).
22:4 *I persecuted the followers.* See 9:1–4.
22:5 *high priest.* Caiaphas, the high priest over 20 years earlier, was now dead, and Ananias was high priest (see 23:2); but the records of the high priest would show Paul's testimony to be true.
22:6 *About noon.* A detail not included in the earlier account (9:1–22).
22:8 *Who are you, Lord?* See note on 9:5. *persecuting.* See note on 9:4.
22:9 *did not understand the voice.* They heard the sound (9:7) but did not understand what was said.
22:12 *Ananias . . . devout observer of the law.* Important to this audience (see note on Lk 1:6).

that very moment I was able to see him.
14"Then he said: 'The God of our fathers[w] has chosen you to know his will
and to see[x] the Righteous One[y] and to
hear words from his mouth. 15You will be
his witness[z] to all men of what you have
seen[a] and heard. 16And now what are you
waiting for? Get up, be baptized[b] and
wash your sins away,[c] calling on his
name.'[d]
17"When I returned to Jerusalem[e] and
was praying at the temple, I fell into a
trance[f] 18and saw the Lord speaking.
'Quick!' he said to me. 'Leave Jerusalem
immediately, because they will not accept
your testimony about me.'
19" 'Lord,' I replied, 'these men know
that I went from one synagogue to another
to imprison[g] and beat[h] those who believe
in you. 20And when the blood of your martyr[s] Stephen was shed, I stood there giving my approval and guarding the clothes
of those who were killing him.'[i]
21"Then the Lord said to me, 'Go; I will
send you far away to the Gentiles.' "[j]

Paul the Roman Citizen

22The crowd listened to Paul until he
said this. Then they raised their voices and
shouted, "Rid the earth of him![k] He's not
fit to live!"[l]
23As they were shouting and throwing
off their cloaks[m] and flinging dust into the
air,[n] 24the commander ordered Paul to be
taken into the barracks.[o] He directed[p]
that he be flogged and questioned in order
to find out why the people were shouting
at him like this. 25As they stretched him
out to flog him, Paul said to the centurion
standing there, "Is it legal for you to flog a
Roman citizen who hasn't even been
found guilty?"[q]
26When the centurion heard this, he
went to the commander and reported it.
"What are you going to do?" he asked.
"This man is a Roman citizen."
27The commander went to Paul and
asked, "Tell me, are you a Roman citizen?"
"Yes, I am," he answered.
28Then the commander said, "I had to
pay a big price for my citizenship."
"But I was born a citizen," Paul replied.
29Those who were about to question
him[r] withdrew immediately. The commander himself was alarmed when he
realized that he had put Paul, a Roman
citizen,[s] in chains.[t]

Before the Sanhedrin

30The next day, since the commander
wanted to find out exactly why Paul was
being accused by the Jews,[u] he released
him[v] and ordered the chief priests and all
the Sanhedrin[w] to assemble. Then he
brought Paul and had him stand before
them.
23 Paul looked straight at the Sanhedrin[x] and said, "My brothers,[y] I
have fulfilled my duty to God in all good
conscience[z] to this day." 2At this the high

22:14 [w]S Ac 3:13 [x]S 1Co 15:8 [y]Ac 7:52 **22:15** [z]Ac 23:11; 26:16 [a]ver 14 **22:16** [b]S Ac 2:38 [c]Lev 8:6; Ps 51:2; Eze 36:25; Jn 3:5; 1Co 6:11; Eph 5:26; Tit 3:5; Heb 10:22; 1Pe 3:21 [d]Ro 10:13 **22:17** [e]Ac 9:26 [f]Ac 10:10 **22:19** [g]ver 4; S Ac 8:3 [h]S Mt 10:17 **22:20** [i]Ac 7:57-60; 8:1 **22:21** [j]S Ac 9:15; S 13:46 **22:22** [k]Ac 21:36 [l]Ac 25:24 **22:23** [m]Ac 7:58 [n]2Sa 16:13 **22:24** [o]S Ac 21:34 [p]ver 29 **22:25** [q]Ac 16:37 **22:29** [r]ver 24 [s]ver 24,25; Ac 16:38 [t]S Ac 21:33 **22:30** [u]Ac 23:28 [v]Ac 21:33 [w]S Mt 5:22 **23:1** [x]Ac 22:30 [y]S Ac 22:5 [z]Ac 24:16; 1Co 4:4; 2Co 1:12; 1Ti 1:5,19; 3:9; 2Ti 1:3; Heb 9:14; 10:22; 13:18; 1Pe 3:16, 21

[s]20 Or *witness*

22:14 *to see the Righteous One.* Cf. 3:14. To see the resurrected Jesus was all-important to Paul (see 26:16; 1Co 9:1; 15:8). It was that experience that had convinced him of the truth of the gospel and that became the foundation of his theology.
22:16 *wash your sins away.* Baptism is the outward sign of an inward work of grace. The reality and the symbol are closely associated in the NT (see 2:38; Tit 3:5; 1Pe 3:21). The outward rite, however, does not produce the inward grace (cf. Ro 2:28–29; Eph 2:8–9; Php 3:4–9). See note on Ro 6:3–4.
22:17 *When I returned to Jerusalem.* Refers to the visit described in 9:26; Gal 1:17–18. *at the temple, I fell into a trance.* See Peter's trance (10:10; 11:5; cf. 2Co 12:3). Paul was not a blasphemer of the temple but continued to hold it in high honor.
22:20 *giving my approval.* Does not necessarily mean that Paul had to be a member of the Sanhedrin, though some have thought so (see note on 26:10). He could show his approval by allowing them to put their cloaks at his feet.
22:24 *commander.* See note on 21:31. *barracks.* See note on 21:37. *that he be flogged.* Not with the rod, as at Philippi (16:22–24), but with the scourge, a merciless instrument of torture. It was legal to use it to force a confession from a slave or alien but never from a Roman citizen. The scourge consisted of a whip of leather thongs with pieces of bone or metal attached to the ends.
22:25 *they stretched him out.* The Greek word used for tying a person to a post for whipping. *centurion.* See note on 10:1. *Roman citizen.* According to Roman law, all Roman citizens were assured exclusion from all degrading forms of punishment: beating with rods, scourging, crucifixion.
22:28 *pay a big price.* There were three ways to obtain Roman citizenship: (1) receive it as a reward for some outstanding service to Rome; (2) buy it at a considerable price; (3) be born into a family of Roman citizens. How Paul's father or an earlier ancestor had gained citizenship, no one knows. By 171 B.C. a large number of Jews were citizens of Tarsus, and in the time of Pompey (106–48) some of these could have received Roman citizenship as well. Cf. 16:37.
22:30 *he released him.* Paul was no longer bound, and presumably he would have been free completely if the Sanhedrin had not wished to detain him. *chief priests.* Those of the high priestly line of descent (mainly Sadducees), but the Sanhedrin now included a considerable number of Pharisees. These men constituted the ruling body of the Jews. The Jewish court was respected by the Roman governor, whose approval had to be obtained before sentencing to capital punishment.
23:1 *Sanhedrin.* See note on 5:21. *brothers.* Fellow Jews (see note on 11:1). *good conscience.* A consistent claim of Paul.
23:2 *Ananias.* High priest A.D. 47–59, son of Nebedaeus. He is not to be confused with the high priest Annas (A.D.

priest Ananias[a] ordered those standing near Paul to strike him on the mouth.[b] [3]Then Paul said to him, "God will strike you, you whitewashed wall![c] You sit there to judge me according to the law, yet you yourself violate the law by commanding that I be struck!"[d]

[4]Those who were standing near Paul said, "You dare to insult God's high priest?"

[5]Paul replied, "Brothers, I did not realize that he was the high priest; for it is written: 'Do not speak evil about the ruler of your people.'[t] "[e]

[6]Then Paul, knowing that some of them were Sadducees[f] and the others Pharisees, called out in the Sanhedrin, "My brothers,[g] I am a Pharisee,[h] the son of a Pharisee. I stand on trial because of my hope in the resurrection of the dead."[i] [7]When he said this, a dispute broke out between the Pharisees and the Sadducees, and the assembly was divided. [8](The Sadducees say that there is no resurrection,[j] and that there are neither angels nor spirits, but the Pharisees acknowledge them all.)

[9]There was a great uproar, and some of the teachers of the law who were Pharisees[k] stood up and argued vigorously. "We find nothing wrong with this man,"[l] they said. "What if a spirit or an angel has spoken to him?"[m] [10]The dispute became so violent that the commander was afraid Paul would be torn to pieces by them. He ordered the troops to go down and take him away from them by force and bring him into the barracks.[n]

[11]The following night the Lord stood near Paul and said, "Take courage![o] As you have testified about me in Jerusalem, so you must also testify in Rome."[p]

The Plot to Kill Paul

[12]The next morning the Jews formed a conspiracy[q] and bound themselves with an oath not to eat or drink until they had killed Paul.[r] [13]More than forty men were involved in this plot. [14]They went to the chief priests and elders and said, "We have taken a solemn oath not to eat anything until we have killed Paul.[s] [15]Now then, you and the Sanhedrin[t] petition the commander to bring him before you on the pretext of wanting more accurate information about his case. We are ready to kill him before he gets here."

[16]But when the son of Paul's sister heard of this plot, he went into the barracks[u] and told Paul.

[17]Then Paul called one of the centurions and said, "Take this young man to the commander; he has something to tell him." [18]So he took him to the commander.

The centurion said, "Paul, the prisoner,[v] sent for me and asked me to bring this young man to you because he has something to tell you."

[19]The commander took the young man by the hand, drew him aside and asked, "What is it you want to tell me?"

[20]He said: "The Jews have agreed to ask you to bring Paul before the Sanhedrin[w] tomorrow on the pretext of wanting more accurate information about him.[x] [21]Don't give in to them, because more than forty[y] of them are waiting in ambush for him. They have taken an oath not to eat or drink until they have killed him.[z] They are ready now, waiting for your consent to their request."

[22]The commander dismissed the young man and cautioned him, "Don't tell anyone that you have reported this to me."

Paul Transferred to Caesarea

[23]Then he called two of his centurions

Cross references

23:2 [a]Ac 24:1
[b]Jn 18:22
23:3 [c]Mt 23:27
[d]Lev 19:15;
Dt 25:1,2; Jn 7:51
23:5 [e]Ex 22:28
23:6 [f]ver 7,8;
S Ac 4:1
[g]S Ac 22:5
[h]Ac 26:5; Php 3:5
[i]Ac 24:15,21;
26:8
23:8 [j]Mt 22:23;
1Co 15:12
23:9 [k]Mk 2:16
[l]ver 29;
Jer 26:16;
S Lk 23:4;
Ac 25:25; 26:31;
28:18 [m]Ac 22:7,
17,18
23:10
[n]S Ac 21:34
23:11
[o]S Mt 14:27
[p]Ac 19:21; 28:23

23:12 [q]S Ac 20:3
[r]ver 14,21,30;
Ac 25:3
23:14 [s]ver 12
23:15 [t]ver 1;
Ac 22:30
23:16 [u]ver 10;
S Ac 21:34
23:18 [v]S Eph 3:1
23:20 [w]ver 1
[x]ver 14,15
23:21 [y]ver 13
[z]ver 12,14

[t]5 Exodus 22:28

Study notes

6–15; see note on Lk 3:2). Ananias was noted for cruelty and violence. When the revolt against Rome broke out, he was assassinated by his own people.

23:3 *whitewashed wall!* Having an attractive exterior but filled with unclean contents, such as tombs holding dead bodies (see Mt 23:27); or walls that look substantial but fall before the winds (see Eze 13:10–12). It is a metaphor for a hypocrite.

23:5 *I did not realize that he was the high priest.* Explained in different ways: 1. Paul had poor eyesight (suggested by such passages as Gal 4:15; 6:11) and failed to see that the one who presided was the high priest. 2. He failed to discern that the one who presided was the high priest because on some occasions others had sat in his place. 3. He was using pure irony: A true high priest would not give such an order. 4. He refused to acknowledge that Ananias was the high priest under these circumstances.

23:6 *Sadducees.* See notes on 4:1; Mt 3:7; Mk 12:18; Lk

20:27. They denied the resurrection and angels and spirits (v. 8). *Pharisees.* See notes on Mt 3:7; Mk 2:16; Lk 5:17.
23:10 *commander.* See note on 21:31. *barracks.* See note on 21:37.
23:11 *the Lord stood near.* In times of crisis and need for strength, Paul was given help (see 18:9; 22:18; 27:23).
23:12 *bound themselves with an oath.* Probably these were from the Zealots or the "terrorists" (see note on 21:38) later responsible for revolt against Rome.
23:17 *centurions.* See note on 10:1. *commander.* See note on 21:31.
23:22 *Don't tell anyone.* For the boy's own safety and because of the commander's plans to transfer Paul under cover of night (see v. 23).
23:23 *soldiers . . . horsemen . . . spearmen.* Heavily armed infantry, cavalry and lightly armed soldiers. The commander assigned 470 men to protect Paul, the Roman citizen (cf. 22:25–29)—but the Greek for "spearmen" is an ob-

and ordered them, "Get ready a detachment of two hundred soldiers, seventy horsemen and two hundred spearmen[u] to go to Caesarea[a] at nine tonight.[b] 24Provide mounts for Paul so that he may be taken safely to Governor Felix."[c]

25He wrote a letter as follows:

26Claudius Lysias,

To His Excellency,[d] Governor Felix:

Greetings.[e]

27This man was seized by the Jews and they were about to kill him,[f] but I came with my troops and rescued him,[g] for I had learned that he is a Roman citizen.[h] 28I wanted to know why they were accusing him, so I brought him to their Sanhedrin.[i] 29I found that the accusation had to do with questions about their law,[j] but there was no charge against him[k] that deserved death or imprisonment. 30When I was informed[l] of a plot[m] to be carried out against the man, I sent him to you at once. I also ordered his accusers[n] to present to you their case against him.

31So the soldiers, carrying out their orders, took Paul with them during the night and brought him as far as Antipatris. 32The next day they let the cavalry[o] go on with

him, while they returned to the barracks.[p] 33When the cavalry[q] arrived in Caesarea,[r] they delivered the letter to the governor[s] and handed Paul over to him. 34The governor read the letter and asked what province he was from. Learning that he was from Cilicia,[t] 35he said, "I will hear your case when your accusers[u] get here." Then he ordered that Paul be kept under guard[v] in Herod's palace.

The Trial Before Felix

24 Five days later the high priest Ananias[w] went down to Caesarea with some of the elders and a lawyer named Tertullus, and they brought their charges[x] against Paul before the governor.[y] 2When Paul was called in, Tertullus presented his case before Felix: "We have enjoyed a long period of peace under you, and your foresight has brought about reforms in this nation. 3Everywhere and in every way, most excellent[z] Felix, we acknowledge this with profound gratitude. 4But in order not to weary you further, I would request that you be kind enough to hear us briefly.

5"We have found this man to be a troublemaker, stirring up riots[a] among the Jews[b] all over the world. He is a ringleader of the Nazarene[c] sect[d] 6and even tried to desecrate the temple;[e] so we seized him.

Cross references

23:23 aS Ac 8:40
bver 33
23:24 cver 26, 33; Ac 24:1-3,10; 25:14
23:26 dLk 1:3; Ac 24:3; 26:25
eAc 15:23
23:27 fAc 21:32
gAc 21:33
hAc 22:25-29
23:28 iAc 22:30
23:29 jAc 18:15; 25:19 kS ver 9
23:30 lver 20,21
mS Ac 20:3 nver 35; Ac 24:19; 25:16
23:32 over 23
pS Ac 21:34
23:33 qver 23,24
rS Ac 8:40 sver 26
23:34 tS Ac 6:9; 21:39
23:35 uver 30; Ac 24:19; 25:16
vAc 24:27
24:1 wAc 23:2
xAc 23:30,35
yS Ac 23:24
24:3 zLk 1:3; Ac 23:26; 26:25
24:5 aAc 16:20; 17:6 bAc 21:28
cS Mk 1:24 dver 14; Ac 26:5; 28:22
24:6 eAc 21:28

u23 The meaning of the Greek for this word is uncertain.

---

scure word and could perhaps be translated "additional mounts and pack animals" (see NIV text note).
23:27 for I had learned that he is a Roman citizen. Inserted to gain the commander's favor with Rome, but not a true statement, because the commander did not learn of Paul's citizenship until he was about to scourge him to gain information.
23:30 ordered his accusers to present to you their case. He anticipated that the order would be given by the time the letter was delivered.
23:31 Antipatris. Rebuilt by Herod the Great and named for his father. It was a military post between Samaria and Judea—30 miles from Jerusalem.
23:33 Caesarea. The headquarters of Roman rule for Samaria and Judea—28 miles from Antipatris.
23:34 The governor. Antonius Felix. The emperor Claudius had appointed him governor of Judea c. A.D. 52, a time when Felix's brother was the emperor's favorite minister. The brothers had formerly been slaves, then freedmen, then high officials in government. The historian Tacitus said of Felix, "He held the power of a tyrant with the disposition of a slave." He married three queens in succession, one of whom was Drusilla (see note on 24:24). from Cilicia. If Paul had come from a province nearby, Felix might have turned him over for trial under another's jurisdiction.
23:35 Herod's palace. Erected as a royal residence by Herod the Great but now used as a Roman praetorium—the place for the official business of the emperor and/or to house personnel directly responsible to the emperor. Praetoria were located in Rome (Php 1:13), Ephesus, Jerusalem (Jn 18:28),

Caesarea and other parts of the empire.
24:1 Five days later. After the departure from Jerusalem. This would allow just enough time for a messenger to go from Caesarea to Jerusalem, the Sanhedrin to appoint their representatives, and the appointees to make the return journey to Caesarea. Ananias. See note on 23:2. The high priest himself made the 60-mile journey to supervise the case personally. elders. The Sanhedrin was made up of both the religious and the political councils. See notes on Ex 3:16; 2Sa 3:17; Joel 1:12; Mt 15:2. lawyer. Lit. "orator." In a court trial one trained in forensic rhetoric would serve as an attorney at law. Tertullus. A common variant of the name Tertius. Possibly he was a Roman but more likely a Hellenistic Jew familiar with the procedures of the Roman court.
24:2-3 long period of peace . . . with profound gratitude. The expected eulogy with which to introduce a speech before a judge. In his six years in office Felix had eliminated bands of robbers, thwarted organized assassins and crushed a movement led by an Egyptian (see note on 21:38). But in general his record was not good. He was recalled by Rome two years later because of misrule. His reforms and improvements are hard to identify historically.
24:5 troublemaker . . . ringleader of the Nazarene sect. To excite dissension in the empire was treason against Caesar. To be a leader of a religious sect without Roman approval was contrary to law. the Nazarene sect. Christianity.
24:6 tried to desecrate the temple. The charge is now qualified by "an attempt," rather than the former claim (see note on 21:28).

8By examining him yourself you will be able to learn the truth about all these charges we are bringing against him."

9The Jews joined in the accusation, asserting that these things were true.

10When the governor motioned for him to speak, Paul replied: "I know that for a number of years you have been a judge over this nation; so I gladly make my defense. 11You can easily verify that no more than twelve days ago I went up to Jerusalem to worship. 12My accusers did not find me arguing with anyone at the temple, or stirring up a crowd in the synagogues or anywhere else in the city. 13And they cannot prove to you the charges they are now making against me. 14However, I admit that I worship the God of our fathers as a follower of the Way, which they call a sect. I believe everything that agrees with the Law and that is written in the Prophets, 15and I have the same hope in God as these men, that there will be a resurrection of both the righteous and the wicked. 16So I strive always to keep my conscience clear before God and man.

17"After an absence of several years, I came to Jerusalem to bring my people gifts for the poor and to present offerings. 18I was ceremonially clean when they found me in the temple courts doing this. There was no crowd with me, nor was I involved in any disturbance. 19But there are some

Jews from the province of Asia, who ought to be here before you and bring charges if they have anything against me. 20Or these who are here should state what crime they found in me when I stood before the Sanhedrin— 21unless it was this one thing I shouted as I stood in their presence: 'It is concerning the resurrection of the dead that I am on trial before you today.' "

22Then Felix, who was well acquainted with the Way, adjourned the proceedings. "When Lysias the commander comes," he said, "I will decide your case." 23He ordered the centurion to keep Paul under guard but to give him some freedom and permit his friends to take care of his needs.

24Several days later Felix came with his wife Drusilla, who was a Jewess. He sent for Paul and listened to him as he spoke about faith in Christ Jesus. 25As Paul discoursed on righteousness, self-control and the judgment to come, Felix was afraid and said, "That's enough for now! You may leave. When I find it convenient, I will send for you." 26At the same time he was hoping that Paul would offer him a bribe, so he sent for him frequently and talked with him.

27When two years had passed, Felix was

Cross-references (center column)

24:9 /S 1Th 2:16
24:10
g S Ac 23:24
24:11 h Ac 21:27; ver 1
24:12 i Ac 25:8; 28:17 /ver 18
24:13 k Ac 25:7
24:14 l S Ac 3:13 m S Ac 9:2 n S ver 5 o Ac 26:6,22; 28:23
24:15 p Ac 23:6; 28:20 q S Mt 25:46
24:16 r S Ac 23:1
24:17 s Ac 11:29, 30; Ro 15:25-28, 31; 1 Co 16:1-4, 15; 2Co 8:1-4; Gal 2:10
24:18 t Ac 21:26 u ver 12

24:19 v S Ac 2:9 w Ac 23:30
24:21 x Ac 23:6
24:22 y S Ac 9:2
24:23 z Ac 23:35 a Ac 28:16 b Ac 23:16; 27:3
24:24 c S Ac 20:21
24:25 d Gal 5:23; 1Th 5:6; 1Pe 4:7; 5:8; 2Pe 1:6 e Ac 10:42 f Jer 36:16

v6-8 Some manuscripts him and wanted to judge him according to our law. 7But the commander, Lysias, came and with the use of much force snatched him from our hands 8and ordered his accusers to come before you. By

---

24:7 See NIV text note on vv. 6–8.
24:10 Paul's reserved introduction lacks the flattery employed by Tertullus (vv. 2–4).
24:11 *twelve days ago.* Paul answers each accusation. He was not a troublemaker, and he had not been involved in disturbances. He had but recently arrived in Jerusalem. He had spent five days in Caesarea and nearly seven in Jerusalem.
24:14 *worship . . . God . . . as a follower of the Way.* Paul admits to his part in the Way, but he still believes the Law and the Prophets. He shares the same hope as the Jews—resurrection and judgment (v. 15).
24:16 *conscience clear.* See note on 23:1.
24:17 *to bring my people gifts for the poor.* The only explicit reference in Acts to the collection that was so important to Paul (see note on 20:4). *to present offerings.* May refer to Paul's help in sponsoring those who were fulfilling their vows (see 21:24). He also may have intended to present offerings for himself.
24:19 *Jews from the province of Asia.* See 21:27–29. The absence of these Asian Jews would seem to suggest that they could not substantiate their accusations.
24:21 *concerning the resurrection.* Paul again introduces the point of contention between the Pharisees and Sadducees.
24:22 *well acquainted with the Way.* Felix could not have governed Judea and Samaria for six years without becoming familiar with the place and activities of the Christians.
24:23 *to give him some freedom.* Perhaps Paul was under

house arrest similar to what he experienced while waiting trial in Rome (28:30–31), since he was a Roman citizen who had not been found guilty of any crime.
24:24 *Drusilla.* Felix's third wife, daughter of Herod Agrippa I. At age 15 she married Azizus, king of Emesa, but deserted him for Felix a year later. Her son, also named Agrippa, died in the eruption of Vesuvius (A.D. 79).
24:25 *Felix was afraid.* Hearing of righteousness, self-control and the judgment, Felix looked at his past life and was filled with fear. He had a spark of sincerity and concern. *When I find it convenient.* Lust, pride, greed and selfish ambition made it continually inconvenient to change.
24:26 *offer him a bribe.* Felix supposed that Paul had access to considerable funds. He had heard of his bringing an offering to the Jewish Christians in Palestine (see v. 17). So he wanted Paul to give him money in order to secure his release. Paul no longer had the money, nor would he offer a bribe if he had it.
24:27 *Felix was succeeded by . . . Festus.* Felix was recalled to Rome in A.D. 59/60 to answer for disturbances and irregularities in his rule, such as his handling of riots between Jewish and Syrian inhabitants. Festus is not mentioned in existing historical records before his arrival in Palestine. He died in office after two years, but his record for that time shows wisdom and honesty superior to both his predecessor, Felix, and his successor, Albinus. *to grant a favor to the Jews.* Felix did not want to incite more anger among the Jews, whom he would be facing in Roman court shortly. To release Paul from prison would do just that.

succeeded by Porcius Festus,[g] but because Felix wanted to grant a favor to the Jews,[h] he left Paul in prison.[i]

The Trial Before Festus

25 Three days after arriving in the province, Festus[j] went up from Caesarea[k] to Jerusalem, [2]where the chief priests and Jewish leaders appeared before him and presented the charges against Paul.[l] [3]They urgently requested Festus, as a favor to them, to have Paul transferred to Jerusalem, for they were preparing an ambush to kill him along the way.[m] [4]Festus answered, "Paul is being held[n] at Caesarea,[o] and I myself am going there soon. [5]Let some of your leaders come with me and press charges against the man there, if he has done anything wrong."

[6]After spending eight or ten days with them, he went down to Caesarea, and the next day he convened the court[p] and ordered that Paul be brought before him.[q] [7]When Paul appeared, the Jews who had come down from Jerusalem stood around him, bringing many serious charges against him,[r] which they could not prove.[s]

[8]Then Paul made his defense: "I have done nothing wrong against the law of the Jews or against the temple[t] or against Caesar."

[9]Festus, wishing to do the Jews a favor,[u] said to Paul, "Are you willing to go up to Jerusalem and stand trial before me there on these charges?"[v]

[10]Paul answered: "I am now standing before Caesar's court, where I ought to be tried. I have not done any wrong to the Jews,[w] as you yourself know very well. [11]If, however, I am guilty of doing anything deserving death, I do not refuse to die. But if the charges brought against me by these Jews are not true, no one has the right to hand me over to them. I appeal to Caesar!"[x]

[12]After Festus had conferred with his council, he declared: "You have appealed to Caesar. To Caesar you will go!"

Festus Consults King Agrippa

[13]A few days later King Agrippa and Bernice arrived at Caesarea[y] to pay their respects to Festus. [14]Since they were spending many days there, Festus discussed Paul's case with the king. He said: "There is a man here whom Felix left as a prisoner.[z] [15]When I went to Jerusalem, the chief priests and elders of the Jews brought charges against him[a] and asked that he be condemned.

[16]"I told them that it is not the Roman custom to hand over any man before he has faced his accusers and has had an opportunity to defend himself against their charges.[b] [17]When they came here with me, I did not delay the case, but convened the court the next day and ordered the

Cross references (center column)
24:27 [g]Ac 25:1, 4,9,14 [h]Ac 12:3; 25:9 [i]Ac 23:35; 25:14
25:1 [j]S Ac 24:27 [k]S Ac 8:40
25:2 [l]ver 15; Ac 24:1
25:3 [m]S Ac 20:3
25:4 [n]Ac 24:23 [o]S Ac 8:40
25:6 [p]ver 17 [q]ver 10
25:7 [r]Mk 15:3; Lk 23:2,10; Ac 24:5,6 [s]Ac 24:13
25:8 [t]Ac 6:13; 24:12; 28:17
25:9 [u]Ac 24:27; 12:3
25:10 [v]ver 20 [w]ver 8
25:11 [x]ver 21, 25; Ac 26:32; 28:19
25:13 [y]S Ac 8:40
25:14 [z]Ac 24:27
25:15 [a]ver 2; Ac 24:1
25:16 [b]ver 4,5; Ac 23:30

25:1 *from Caesarea to Jerusalem.* Sixty miles, a two-day trip. Festus was anxious to go immediately to the center of Jewish rule and worship.

25:2 *chief priests and Jewish leaders.* The Sanhedrin (see note on Mk 14:55).

25:3 *an ambush.* Probably the same group that had earlier made a vow to take Paul's life (see note on 23:12).

25:6 *convened the court.* To make his decision binding as a formal ruling.

25:7 *which they could not prove.* Again, as in the first hearing, Paul's adversaries produced no witnesses or evidence of any kind.

25:8 *nothing . . . against the law.* Paul had respect for the law (see Ro 7:12; 8:3–4; 1Co 9:20). *against the temple.* See notes on 21:28–29. Paul had not defied its customs by taking Trophimus into forbidden areas (21:29). Jesus had prophesied its destruction, but he was not responsible for its plight (Lk 21:5–6). *against Caesar.* Paul proclaimed the kingdom of God but not as a political rival of Rome (cf. 17:6–7). He advocated respect for law and order (see Ro 13:1–7) and prayer for civil rulers (see 1Ti 2:2).

25:9 *Are you willing to go up to Jerusalem . . . ?* Obviously not. Festus had said that the trial would be before him; so Paul insisted that he was then standing in the Roman civil court (v. 10). He wanted to keep his trial there rather than suffer at the hands of a Jewish religious court. As a Roman citizen, he could refuse to go to a local provincial court; instead he looked to a higher Roman court.

25:11 *I appeal to Caesar!* Nero had become the emperor by this time. It was the right of every Roman citizen to have his case heard before Caesar himself (or his representative) in Rome. This was the highest court of appeal, and winning such a case could have led to more than just Paul's acquittal. It could have resulted in official recognition of Christianity as distinct from Judaism.

25:12 *his council.* The officials and legal experts who made up the advisory council for the Roman governor.

25:13 *King Agrippa.* Herod Agrippa II. He was 17 years old at the death of his father in A.D. 44 (12:23). Being too young to succeed his father, he was replaced by several Galilean procurators. Eight years later, however, a gradual extension of territorial authority began. Ultimately he ruled over territory north and northeast of the Sea of Galilee, over several Galilean cities and over some cities in Perea. At the Jewish revolt, when Jerusalem fell, he was on the side of the Romans. He died c. A.D. 100—the last of the Herods. *Bernice.* The oldest daughter of Agrippa I, she was 16 years old at his death. When only 13, she married her uncle, Herod of Chalcis, and had two sons. When Herod died, she lived with her brother, Agrippa II. To silence rumors that she was living in incest with her brother, she married Polemon, king of Cilicia, but left him soon to return to Agrippa. She became the mistress of the emperor Vespasian's son Titus but was later ignored by him. *to pay their respects.* It was customary for rulers to pay a complimentary visit to a new ruler at the time of his assignment. It was advantageous to each that they get along (cf. Herod Antipas and Pilate, Lk 23:6–12).

man to be brought in. *c* 18When his accusers got up to speak, they did not charge him with any of the crimes I had expected. 19Instead, they had some points of dispute *d* with him about their own religion *e* and about a dead man named Jesus who Paul claimed was alive. 20I was at a loss how to investigate such matters; so I asked if he would be willing to go to Jerusalem and stand trial there on these charges. *f* 21When Paul made his appeal to be held over for the Emperor's decision, I ordered him held until I could send him to Caesar." *g*

22Then Agrippa said to Festus, "I would like to hear this man myself."

He replied, "Tomorrow you will hear him." *h*

Paul Before Agrippa

26:12–18pp — Ac 9:3–8; 22:6–11

23The next day Agrippa and Bernice *i* came with great pomp and entered the audience room with the high ranking officers and the leading men of the city. At the command of Festus, Paul was brought in. 24Festus said: "King Agrippa, and all who are present with us, you see this man! The whole Jewish community *j* has petitioned me about him in Jerusalem and here in Caesarea, shouting that he ought not to live any longer. *k* 25I found he had done nothing deserving of death, *l* but because he made his appeal to the Emperor *m* I decided to send him to Rome. 26But I have nothing definite to write to His Majesty about him. Therefore I have brought him before all of you, and especially before you, King Agrippa, so that as a result of this investigation I may have something to write. 27For I think it is unreasonable to send on a prisoner without specifying the charges against him."

26 Then Agrippa said to Paul, "You have permission to speak for yourself." *n*

So Paul motioned with his hand *o* and began his defense: 2"King Agrippa, I consider myself fortunate to stand before you *p* today as I make my defense against all the accusations of the Jews, *q* 3and especially so because you are well acquainted with all the Jewish customs *r* and controversies. *s* Therefore, I beg you to listen to me patiently.

4"The Jews all know the way I have lived ever since I was a child, *t* from the beginning of my life in my own country, and also in Jerusalem. 5They have known me for a long time *u* and can testify, if they are willing, that according to the strictest sect *v* of our religion, I lived as a Pharisee. *w* 6And now it is because of my hope *x* in what God has promised our fathers *y* that I am on trial today. 7This is the promise our twelve tribes *z* are hoping to see fulfilled as they earnestly serve God day and night. *a* O king, it is because of this hope that the Jews are accusing me. *b* 8Why should any of you consider it incredible that God raises the dead? *c*

9"I too was convinced *d* that I ought to do all that was possible to oppose *e* the name of Jesus of Nazareth. *f* 10And that is just what I did in Jerusalem. On the authority of the chief priests I put many of the saints *g* in prison, *h* and when they were put to death, I cast my vote against them. *i* 11Many a time I went from one synagogue to another to have them pun-

---

25:17 *c*ver 6,10
25:19 *d*Ac 18:15;
23:29 *e*Ac 17:22
25:20 *f*ver 9
25:21 *g*ver 11,12
25:22 *h*Ac 9:15;
Ac 26:30
25:24 *i*ver 2,3,7
*k*Ac 22:22
25:25 *l*S Ac 23:9
*m*S ver 11

26:1 *n*Ac 9:15;
25:22
*o*S Ac 12:17
26:2 *p*Ps 119:46
*q*Ac 24:1,5; 25:2,
7,11
26:3 *r*ver 7;
S Ac 6:14
*s*Ac 25:19
26:4 *t*Gal 1:13,
14; Php 3:5
26:5 *u*Ac 22:3
*v*S Ac 24:5
*w*Ac 23:6;
Php 3:5
26:6 *x*Ac 23:6;
24:15; 28:20
*y*S Ac 13:32;
Ro 15:8
26:7 *z*Jas 1:1
*a*1Th 3:10;
1Ti 5:5 *b*ver 2
26:8 *c*Ac 23:6
26:9 *d*1Ti 1:13
*e*Jn 16:2
*f*S Jn 15:21
26:10 *g*S Ac 9:13
*h*S Ac 8:3; 9:2,14,
21 *i*Ac 22:20

25:19 *religion.* Or "superstition," the same word used by Paul in 17:22 (see note there).

25:22 *I would like to hear.* Agrippa had been wishing to hear Paul (cf. Antipas wanting to see Jesus, Lk 9:9; 23:8).

25:23 *audience room.* Not the judgment hall, for this was not a court trial. It was in an auditorium appropriate for the pomp of the occasion, with a king, his sister, the Roman governor and the outstanding leaders of both the Jews and the Roman government present. *high ranking officers.* Five regiments were stationed at Caesarea, so their five commanders would be in attendance (see note on 21:31).

25:26 *I have nothing definite.* Festus was required to send Caesar an explicit report on the case when an appeal was made. He hoped for some help from Agrippa in this matter. This was not an official trial but a special hearing to satisfy the curiosity of Agrippa and provide an assessment for Festus. *especially before you, King Agrippa.* He would be sensitive to differences between Pharisees and Sadducees, expectations of the Messiah, differences between Jews and Christians, and Jewish customs pertinent to these problems.

26:1 *permission to speak.* Agrippa gave the permission because Festus allowed him to have charge of the hearing.

26:3 *well acquainted with all the Jewish customs.* Agrippa as king controlled the temple treasury and the investments of the high priest, and could appoint the high priest. He was consulted by the Romans on religious matters. This is one of the reasons Festus wanted him to assess Paul.

26:5 *I lived as a Pharisee.* Cf. Gal 1:14.

26:6 *my hope in what God has promised.* Including God's kingdom, the Messiah and the resurrection (see v. 8).

26:8 Paul had been speaking to Agrippa but at this point must have addressed others as well, such as Festus and the commanders (see note on 21:31), who did not believe in the resurrection. Agrippa was also allied with the Sadducees, whom he appointed high priests, and was likely to reject both the resurrection of Christ and resurrection in general.

26:10 *I cast my vote against them.* Does not necessarily mean that Paul was a member of the Sanhedrin (see note on 22:20). He may have been appointed to a commission to carry out the prosecution (see v. 12), where his vote was given.

26:11 *force them to blaspheme.* He tried to force them either to curse Jesus or to confess publicly that Jesus is the Son of God, in which case they could be condemned for

ished,[j] and I tried to force them to blaspheme. In my obsession against them, I even went to foreign cities to persecute them.

[12]"On one of these journeys I was going to Damascus with the authority and commission of the chief priests. [13]About noon, O king, as I was on the road, I saw a light from heaven, brighter than the sun, blazing around me and my companions. [14]We all fell to the ground, and I heard a voice[k] saying to me in Aramaic,[w][l] 'Saul, Saul, why do you persecute me? It is hard for you to kick against the goads.'

[15]"Then I asked, 'Who are you, Lord?'

"'I am Jesus, whom you are persecuting,' the Lord replied. [16]'Now get up and stand on your feet.[m] I have appeared to you to appoint you as a servant and as a witness of what you have seen of me and what I will show you.[n] [17]I will rescue you[o] from your own people and from the Gentiles.[p] I am sending you to them [18]to open their eyes[q] and turn them from darkness to light,[r] and from the power of Satan to God, so that they may receive forgiveness of sins[s] and a place among those who are sanctified by faith in me.'[t]

[19]"So then, King Agrippa, I was not disobedient[u] to the vision from heaven. [20]First to those in Damascus,[v] then to those in Jerusalem[w] and in all Judea, and to the Gentiles[x] also, I preached that they should repent[y] and turn to God and prove their repentance by their deeds.[z] [21]That is why the Jews seized me[a] in the temple courts and tried to kill me.[b] [22]But I have had God's help to this very day, and so I stand here and testify to small and great

alike. I am saying nothing beyond what the prophets and Moses said would happen[c]— [23]that the Christ[x] would suffer[d] and, as the first to rise from the dead,[e] would proclaim light to his own people and to the Gentiles."[f]

[24]At this point Festus interrupted Paul's defense. "You are out of your mind,[g] Paul!" he shouted. "Your great learning[h] is driving you insane."

[25]"I am not insane, most excellent[i] Festus," Paul replied. "What I am saying is true and reasonable. [26]The king is familiar with these things,[j] and I can speak freely to him. I am convinced that none of this has escaped his notice, because it was not done in a corner. [27]King Agrippa, do you believe the prophets? I know you do."

[28]Then Agrippa said to Paul, "Do you think that in such a short time you can persuade me to be a Christian?"[k]

[29]Paul replied, "Short time or long—I pray God that not only you but all who are listening to me today may become what I am, except for these chains."[l]

[30]The king rose, and with him the governor and Bernice[m] and those sitting with them. [31]They left the room, and while talking with one another, they said, "This man is not doing anything that deserves death or imprisonment."[n]

[32]Agrippa said to Festus, "This man could have been set free[o] if he had not appealed to Caesar."[p]

Paul Sails for Rome

27 When it was decided that we[q] would sail for Italy,[r] Paul and

[w]14 Or Hebrew   [x]23 Or Messiah

Cross references (center column)

26:11
/S Mt 10:17
26:14 kAc 9:7
/S Jn 5:2
26:16 mEze 2:1;
Da 10:11
nAc 22:14,15
26:17 oJer 1:8,19
pS Ac 9:15;
S 13:46
26:18 qIsa 35:5
rPs 18:28;
Isa 42:7,16;
Eph 5:8;
Col 1:13; 1Pe 2:9
sLk 24:47;
Ac 2:38
tS Ac 20:21
26:19 uIsa 50:5
26:20
vAc 9:19-25
wAc 9:26-29;
22:17-20
xS Ac 9:15;
S 13:46 yAc 3:19
zJer 18:11;
35:15; Mt 3:8;
Lk 3:8
26:21 aAc 21:27,
30 bAc 21:31

26:22
cS Lk 24:27,44;
Ac 10:43; 24:14
26:23
dS Mt 16:21
e1Co 15:20,23;
Col 1:18; Rev 1:5
fS Lk 2:32
26:24
gS Jn 10:20;
S 1Co 4:10
hJn 7:15
26:25
iS Ac 23:26
26:26 jver 3
26:28 kAc 11:26
26:29
lS Ac 21:33
26:30 mAc 25:23
26:31 nS Ac 23:9
26:32 oAc 28:18
pS Ac 25:11
27:1 qS Ac 16:10
rAc 18:2; 25:12,
25

Study notes (bottom)

blasphemy, a sufficient cause for death (see Mt 26:63–66).
26:12 *I was going to Damascus.* Again Paul gives an account of his conversion (see 9:1–19; 22:4–21 and notes).
26:14 *I heard a voice.* See notes on 9:7; 22:9. *to kick against the goads.* A Greek proverb for useless resistance—the ox succeeds only in hurting itself.
26:17 *to them.* Not only to the Jews but also to the Gentiles (see 22:21; Gal 1:15–16). His mission was from God (Gal 1:1).
26:18 *from darkness to light.* A figure especially characteristic of Paul (see Ro 13:12; 2Co 4:6; Eph 5:8–14; Col 1:13; 1Th 5:5). *are sanctified.* Positional sanctification (see notes on 20:32; 1Co 1:2).
26:22 *the prophets and Moses.* The OT Scriptures (Lk 24:27,44).
26:23 *the first to rise from the dead.* The firstfruits of the dead—to die no more (see 1Co 15:20; Col 1:18). *to the Gentiles.* Cf. Isa 49:6.
26:24 *You are out of your mind.* See Jn 10:20; 1Co 14:23. The governor felt that Paul's education and reading of the sacred Scriptures had led him to a mania about prophecy and resurrection.
26:26 *not done in a corner.* This gospel is based on actual

events, lived out in historical times and places. The king must himself attest to the truth of what Paul has affirmed.
26:27 *do you believe the prophets?* King Agrippa was faced with a dilemma. If he said "Yes," Paul would press him to recognize their fulfillment in Jesus; if he said "No," he would be in trouble with the devout Jews, who accepted the message of the prophets as the very word of God.
26:28 *in such a short time you can persuade me to be a Christian?* His question is an evasion of Paul's question and an answer to what he anticipates Paul's next question to be. His point is that he will not be persuaded by such a brief statement.
26:29 *these chains.* Paul was still bound as a prisoner.
27:1 See map No. 11 at the end of the Study Bible. *we would sail.* The "we" narrative (see note on 16:10) begins again (the last such reference appeared in 21:18). Probably Luke has spent the two years of Paul's Caesarean imprisonment nearby, and now he joins those ready to sail. *centurion named Julius.* Otherwise unknown. Perhaps he was given the specific duties of an imperial courier, which included delivering prisoners for trial. *Imperial Regiment.* The Roman legions were designated by number, and each of the regiments also had designations. The identification "Augustan,"

some other prisoners were handed over to a centurion named Julius, who belonged to the Imperial Regiment.ˢ ²We boarded a ship from Adramyttium about to sail for ports along the coast of the province of Asia,ᵗ and we put out to sea. Aristarchus,ᵘ a Macedonianᵛ from Thessalonica,ʷ was with us.

³The next day we landed at Sidon;ˣ and Julius, in kindness to Paul,ʸ allowed him to go to his friends so they might provide for his needs.ᶻ ⁴From there we put out to sea again and passed to the lee of Cyprus because the winds were against us.ᵃ ⁵When we had sailed across the open sea off the coast of Ciliciaᵇ and Pamphylia,ᶜ we landed at Myra in Lycia. ⁶There the centurion found an Alexandrian shipᵈ sailing for Italyᵉ and put us on board. ⁷We made slow headway for many days and had difficulty arriving off Cnidus. When the wind did not allow us to hold our course,ᶠ we sailed to the lee of Crete,ᵍ opposite Salmone. ⁸We moved along the coast with difficulty and came to a place called Fair Havens, near the town of Lasea.

⁹Much time had been lost, and sailing had already become dangerous because by now it was after the Fast.ʸʰ So Paul warned them, ¹⁰"Men, I can see that our voyage is going to be disastrous and bring great loss to ship and cargo, and to our own lives also."ⁱ ¹¹But the centurion, instead of listening to what Paul said, followed the advice of the pilot and of the owner of the ship. ¹²Since the harbor was unsuitable to winter in, the majority decided that we should sail on, hoping to reach Phoenix and winter there. This was

27:1 ˢAc 10:1
27:2 ᵗS Ac 2:9
      ᵘS Ac 19:29
      ᵛS Ac 16:9
      ʷS Ac 17:1
27:3 ˣMt 11:21
      ʸver 43
      ᶻAc 24:23; 28:16
27:4 ᵃver 7
27:5 ᵇS Ac 6:9
      ᶜS Ac 2:10
27:6 ᵈAc 28:11
      ᵉver 1; Ac 18:2;
25:12,25

27:7 ᶠver 4 ᵍver
12,13,21; Tit 1:5
27:9
ʰLev 16:29-31;
23:27-29;
Nu 29:7
27:10 ⁱver 21

ʸ9 That is, the Day of Atonement (Yom Kippur)

or "Imperial" (belonging to the empire), was common (see note on 10:1).
27:2 *Adramyttium.* A harbor on the west coast of the province of Asia, southeast of Troas, east of Assos. *ports along the coast.* At one of these stops, Julius would plan to transfer to a ship going to Rome. *Aristarchus.* See 19:29; 20:4; see also Phm 24 and Col 4:10, indicating he was in Rome with Paul later.
27:3 *Sidon.* About 70 miles north of Caesarea.
27:4 *the lee of Cyprus.* They sought the protecting shelter of the island by sailing north on the eastern side of the island, then west along the northern side. *winds were against us.* Prevailing winds in summer were westerly.
27:5 *Cilicia and Pamphylia.* Adjoining provinces on the southern shore of Asia Minor. From Sidon to Myra along this coast would normally be a voyage of 10 to 15 days. *Myra in Lycia.* The growing importance of the city of Myra was associated with the development of navigation. Instead of

hugging the coast from point to point, more ships were daring to run directly from Alexandria in Egypt to harbors like Myra on the southern coast of Asia Minor. It was considerably out of the way on the trip to Rome from Egypt, but the prevailing westerly wind would not allow a direct voyage toward the west. Myra became an important grain-storage city as well.
27:6 *Alexandrian ship.* A ship from Egypt (with grain cargo, v. 38) bound for Rome. Paul and the others could have remained on the first ship and continued up the coast to Macedonia, then taken the land route over the Egnatian Way across Greece and on to Rome, entering Italy at the port of Brundisium. But Julius chose to change ships here, accepting the opportunity of a voyage direct to Rome. Some suggest that Aristarchus from Macedonia stayed with the first ship and went to his home area to tell of Paul's coming imprisonment in Rome. If so, he later joined Paul in Rome (see note on v. 2).

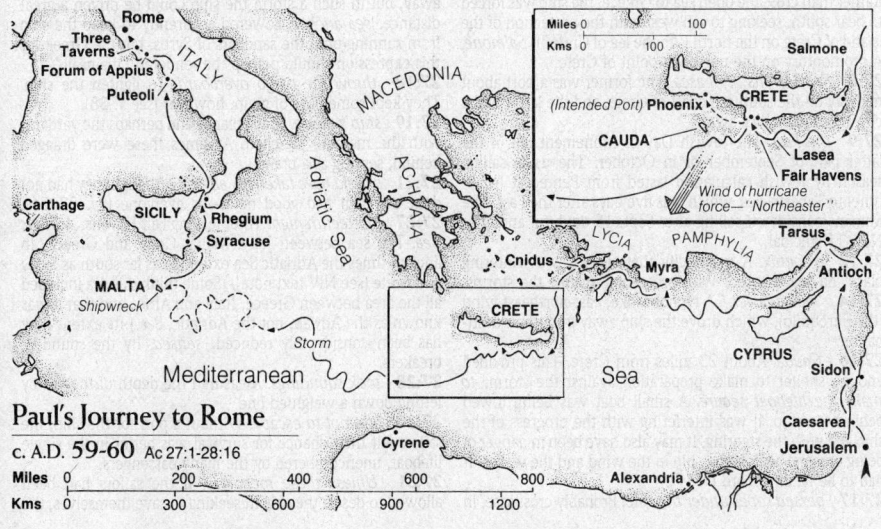

Paul's Journey to Rome
c. A.D. **59-60** Ac 27:1-28:16

a harbor in Crete,^{j} facing both southwest and northwest.

The Storm

^{13}When a gentle south wind began to blow, they thought they had obtained what they wanted; so they weighed anchor and sailed along the shore of Crete. ^{14}Before very long, a wind of hurricane force,^{k} called the "northeaster," swept down from the island. ^{15}The ship was caught by the storm and could not head into the wind; so we gave way to it and were driven along. ^{16}As we passed to the lee of a small island called Cauda, we were hardly able to make the lifeboat^l secure. ^{17}When the men had hoisted it aboard, they passed ropes under the ship itself to hold it together. Fearing that they would run aground^m on the sandbars of Syrtis, they lowered the sea anchor and let the ship be driven along. ^{18}We took such a violent battering from the storm that the next day they began to throw the cargo overboard.^{n} ^{19}On the third day, they threw the ship's tackle overboard with their own hands. ^{20}When neither sun nor stars appeared for many days and the storm continued raging, we finally gave up all hope of being saved.

^{21}After the men had gone a long time without food, Paul stood up before them and said: "Men, you should have taken my advice^o not to sail from Crete; ^{p} then you would have spared yourselves this damage and loss. ^{22}But now I urge you to keep up your courage,^{q} because not one of you will be lost; only the ship will be destroyed. ^{23}Last night an angel^r of the God whose I am and whom I serve^s stood beside me^t ^{24}and said, 'Do not be afraid, Paul. You must stand trial before Caesar; ^{u} and God has graciously given you the lives of all who sail with you.' ^{v} ^{25}So keep up your courage,^{w} men, for I have faith in God that it will happen just as he told me. ^{x} ^{26}Nevertheless, we must run aground^y on some island." ^{z}

The Shipwreck

^{27}On the fourteenth night we were still being driven across the Adriatic^z Sea, when about midnight the sailors sensed they were approaching land. ^{28}They took soundings and found that the water was a hundred and twenty feet^a deep. A short time later they took soundings again and found it was ninety feet^b deep. ^{29}Fearing that we would be dashed against the rocks, they dropped four anchors from the stern and prayed for daylight. ^{30}In an attempt to escape from the ship, the sailors let the lifeboat^a down into the sea, pretending they were going to lower some anchors from the bow. ^{31}Then Paul said to the cen-

---

27:12 /S ver 7
27:14 kMk 4:37
27:16 /ver 30
27:17 mver 26,39
27:18 nver 19, 38; Jnh 1:5
27:21 over 10
pS ver 7

27:22 qver 25,36
27:23 rS Ac 5:19
sRo 1:9 tAc 18:9; 23:11; 2Ti 4:17
27:24 uAc 23:11
vver 44
27:25 wver 22,36
xRo 4:20,21
27:26 yver 17,39
zAc 28:1
27:30 aver 16

z27 In ancient times the name referred to an area extending well south of Italy. a28 Greek *twenty orguias* (about 37 meters) b28 Greek *fifteen orguias* (about 27 meters)

27:7 *Cnidus.* From Myra to Cnidus at the southeast point of Asia Minor was about 170 miles. The trip probably took another 10 to 15 days. *Crete.* An island 160 miles long. Rather than cross the open sea to Greece, the ship was forced to bear south, seeking to sail west with the protection of the island of Crete on the north ("to the lee of Crete"). *Salmone.* A promontory on the northeast point of Crete.

27:8 *Fair Havens . . . Lasea.* The former was a port about midway on the southern coast of Crete, and the latter was a city about five miles away.

27:9 *the Fast.* The Jewish Day of Atonement fell in the latter part of September or in October. The usual sailing season by Jewish calculation lasted from Pentecost (May-June) to Tabernacles, which was five days after the Fast. The Romans considered sailing after Sept. 15 doubtful and after Nov. 11 suicidal.

27:12 *Phoenix.* A major city that served as a wintering place, having a harbor with protection against the storms.

27:14 *"northeaster."* A typhoon-like, east-northeast wind (the Euroquilo), which drove the ship away from their destination.

27:16 *Cauda.* About 23 miles from Crete. This provided enough shelter to make preparation against the storm. *to make the lifeboat secure.* A small boat was being towed behind the ship. It was interfering with the progress of the ship and with the steering. It may also have been in danger of being crushed against the ship in the wind and the waves. It had to be taken aboard (v. 17).

27:17 *passed ropes under the ship.* Probably crosswise, in order to keep the ship from being broken apart by the storm. *Syrtis.* A long stretch of desolate banks of quicksand along northern Africa off the coast of Tunis and Tripoli—still far away, but in such a storm the ship could be driven a great distance. *sea anchor.* Lowered apparently to keep the ship from running onto the sandbars of Syrtis, but the Greek for this expression should perhaps be rendered "mainsail."

27:18 *throw the cargo overboard.* To lighten the ship. They kept some bags of grain, however (see v. 38).

27:19 *ship's tackle.* Spars, planks and perhaps the yardarm with the mainsail attached. At times these were dragged behind, serving as a brake.

27:21 *should have taken my advice.* Although they had not done so, Paul had good news for everyone (vv. 22–26).

27:27 *fourteenth night.* After leaving Fair Havens. *Adriatic Sea.* The sea between Italy, Malta, Crete and Greece. In ancient times the Adriatic Sea extended as far south as Sicily and Crete (see NIV text note). (Some think this sea included all the area between Greece, Italy and Africa and that it was known as the Adrian, not the Adriatic, Sea.) Its extent now has been considerably reduced. *sensed.* By the sound of breakers.

27:28 *took soundings.* Measured the depth of the sea by letting down a weighted line.

27:30 *attempt to escape.* Without a port for the ship, the sailors felt their chance for survival was better in the single lifeboat, unencumbered by the many passengers.

27:31 *Unless these men stay.* If the sailors had been allowed to desert the ship in seeking to save themselves, the

turion and the soldiers, "Unless these men stay with the ship, you cannot be saved." [b] ³²So the soldiers cut the ropes that held the lifeboat and let it fall away.

³³Just before dawn Paul urged them all to eat. "For the last fourteen days," he said, "you have been in constant suspense and have gone without food—you haven't eaten anything. ³⁴Now I urge you to take some food. You need it to survive. Not one of you will lose a single hair from his head." [c] ³⁵After he said this, he took some bread and gave thanks to God in front of them all. Then he broke it [d] and began to eat. ³⁶They were all encouraged [e] and ate some food themselves. ³⁷Altogether there were 276 of us on board. ³⁸When they had eaten as much as they wanted, they lightened the ship by throwing the grain into the sea. [f]

³⁹When daylight came, they did not recognize the land, but they saw a bay with a sandy beach, [g] where they decided to run the ship aground if they could. ⁴⁰Cutting loose the anchors, [h] they left them in the sea and at the same time untied the ropes that held the rudders. Then they hoisted the foresail to the wind and made for the beach. ⁴¹But the ship struck a sandbar and ran aground. The bow stuck fast and would not move, and the stern was broken to pieces by the pounding of the surf. [i]

⁴²The soldiers planned to kill the prisoners to prevent any of them from swimming away and escaping. ⁴³But the centurion wanted to spare Paul's life [j] and kept them

from carrying out their plan. He ordered those who could swim to jump overboard first and get to land. ⁴⁴The rest were to get there on planks or on pieces of the ship. In this way everyone reached land in safety. [k]

Ashore on Malta

28 Once safely on shore, we [l] found out that the island [m] was called Malta. ²The islanders showed us unusual kindness. They built a fire and welcomed us all because it was raining and cold. ³Paul gathered a pile of brushwood and, as he put it on the fire, a viper, driven out by the heat, fastened itself on his hand. ⁴When the islanders saw the snake hanging from his hand, [n] they said to each other, "This man must be a murderer; for though he escaped from the sea, Justice has not allowed him to live." [o] ⁵But Paul shook the snake off into the fire and suffered no ill effects. [p] ⁶The people expected him to swell up or suddenly fall dead, but after waiting a long time and seeing nothing unusual happen to him, they changed their minds and said he was a god. [q]

⁷There was an estate nearby that belonged to Publius, the chief official of the island. He welcomed us to his home and for three days entertained us hospitably. ⁸His father was sick in bed, suffering from fever and dysentery. Paul went in to see him and, after prayer, [r] placed his hands on him [s] and healed him. [t] ⁹When this had happened, the rest of the sick on the island came and were cured. ¹⁰They honored us [u] in many ways and when we were ready to

Cross references

27:31 [b] ver 24
27:34
[c] S Mt 10:30
27:35
[d] S Mt 14:19
27:36 [e] ver 22,25
27:38 [f] ver 18;
Jnh 1:5
27:39 [g] Ac 28:1
27:40 [h] ver 29
27:41 [i] 2Co 11:25
27:43 [j] ver 3

27:44 [k] ver 22,31
28:1 [l] S Ac 16:10
[m] Ac 27:26,39
28:4 [n] Mk 16:18
[o] Lk 13:2,4
28:5 [p] Lk 10:19
28:6 [q] Ac 14:11
28:8 [r] Jas 5:14,15
[s] S Ac 6:6
[t] Ac 9:40
28:10 [u] Ps 15:4

---

passengers would have been unable to beach the ship the following day.

27:33 *haven't eaten anything.* No provisions had been distributed nor regular meals eaten since the storm began.

27:35 *took some bread and gave thanks.* Paul gave two good examples: He ate food for physical nourishment and gave thanks to God. To give thanks before a meal was common practice among God's people (see Lk 9:16; 24:30; 1Ti 4:4–5).

27:37 *276 of us on board.* To note the number on board may have been necessary in preparation for the distribution of food or perhaps for the coming attempt to get ashore. The number is not extraordinary for the time. Josephus refers to a ship that had 600 aboard (*Life*, 15).

27:38 *lightened the ship.* They threw overboard the remaining bags of wheat (see v. 18), which had probably been kept for food supply. The lighter the ship, the farther it could sail in to shore.

27:40 *untied the ropes that held the rudders.* In order to lower the stern rudders into place so the ship could be steered toward the sandy shore. Ancient ships had a steering oar on either side of the stern.

27:42 *soldiers planned to kill the prisoners.* If a prisoner escaped, the life of his guard was taken in his place. The soldiers did not want to risk having a prisoner escape.

27:43 Once more the centurion is to be admired for stopping this plan and trusting the prisoners.

28:1 *Malta.* Known as Melita by the Greeks and Romans. It was included in the province of Sicily and is located 58 miles south of that large island.

28:2 *islanders.* Lit. "barbarians"; all non-Greek-speaking people were called this by Greeks. Far from being uncivilized tribesmen, they were Phoenician in ancestry and used a Phoenician dialect but were thoroughly Romanized. *raining and cold.* It was the end of October or the beginning of November.

28:3 *a viper.* Must have been known to the islanders to be poisonous.

28:6 *to swell up.* The usual medical term for inflammation; it is used only by Luke in the NT (see Introduction to Luke: Author). *said he was a god.* Parallel to the Lystrans' attempt to worship Paul and Barnabas (14:11–18).

28:7 *Publius.* A Roman name, but the first name and not the family name. It must have been what the islanders called him. *chief official.* The "first man" of Malta, a technical term for the top authority. Luke's designation is accurate here, as elsewhere, even though the Greek term used is not a common one. Cf. also "proconsul" (Greek *anthypatos*, 13:7), "magistrates" (Greek *strategoi*, 16:20), "city officials" (Greek *politarchs*, 17:6), "officials of the province" (Greek *Asiarchon*, 19:31).

sail, they furnished us with the supplies we needed.

Arrival at Rome

[11]After three months we put out to sea in a ship that had wintered in the island. It was an Alexandrian ship[v] with the figurehead of the twin gods Castor and Pollux. [12]We put in at Syracuse and stayed there three days. [13]From there we set sail and arrived at Rhegium. The next day the south wind came up, and on the following day we reached Puteoli. [14]There we found some brothers[w] who invited us to spend a week with them. And so we came to Rome. [15]The brothers[x] there had heard that we were coming, and they traveled as far as the Forum of Appius and the Three Taverns to meet us. At the sight of these men Paul thanked God and was encouraged. [16]When we got to Rome, Paul was allowed to live by himself, with a soldier to guard him.[y]

Paul Preaches at Rome Under Guard

[17]Three days later he called together the leaders of the Jews.[z] When they had assembled, Paul said to them: "My brothers,[a] although I have done nothing against our people[b] or against the customs of our ancestors,[c] I was arrested in Jerusalem and handed over to the Romans. [18]They examined me[d] and wanted to release me,[e] because I was not guilty of any crime deserving death.[f] [19]But when the Jews objected, I was compelled to appeal to Caesar[g]—not that I had any charge to

bring against my own people. [20]For this reason I have asked to see you and talk with you. It is because of the hope of Israel[h] that I am bound with this chain."[i]

[21]They replied, "We have not received any letters from Judea concerning you, and none of the brothers[j] who have come from there has reported or said anything bad about you. [22]But we want to hear what your views are, for we know that people everywhere are talking against this sect."[k]

[23]They arranged to meet Paul on a certain day, and came in even larger numbers to the place where he was staying. From morning till evening he explained and declared to them the kingdom of God[l] and tried to convince them about Jesus[m] from the Law of Moses and from the Prophets.[n] [24]Some were convinced by what he said, but others would not believe.[o] [25]They disagreed among themselves and began to leave after Paul had made this final statement: "The Holy Spirit spoke the truth to your forefathers when he said[p] through Isaiah the prophet:

[26]" 'Go to this people and say,
    "You will be ever hearing but never
        understanding;
    you will be ever seeing but never
        perceiving."
[27]For this people's heart has become
        calloused;[q]
    they hardly hear with their ears,
    and they have closed their eyes.
Otherwise they might see with their
        eyes,
    hear with their ears,

Cross references (center column)

28:11 [v]Ac 27:6
28:14 [w]S Ac 1:16
28:15 [x]S Ac 1:16
28:16 [y]Ac 24:23; 27:3
28:17 [z]Ac 25:2
[a]S Ac 22:5
[b]S Ac 25:8
[c]S Ac 6:14
28:18 [d]Ac 22:24
[e]Ac 26:31,32
[f]S Ac 23:9
28:19
[g]S Ac 25:11

28:20 [h]Ac 26:6,7
[i]S Ac 21:33
28:21 [j]S Ac 22:5
28:22 [k]S Ac 24:5
28:23 [l]S Mt 3:2;
Ac 19:8 [m]Ac 17:3
[n]S Ac 8:35
28:24 [o]Ac 14:4; 17:4,5
28:25 [p]S Heb 3:7
28:27 [q]Ps 119:70

28:11 *After three months.* They had to remain here until the sailing season opened in late February or early March. *Castor and Pollux.* The two "sons of Zeus" (Greek *Dioscuroi*), the guardian deities of sailors.
28:12 *Syracuse.* The leading city on the island of Sicily, situated on the east coast.
28:13 *Rhegium.* A town on the coast of Italy, near the southwestern tip and close to the narrowest point of the strait separating that country from Sicily, opposite Messina. Around the promontory north of the town was the whirlpool of Charybdis and the rock of Scylla. Coming from his triumph in Judea, the general Titus landed here on his way to Rome. *Puteoli.* Modern Pozzuoli, almost 200 miles from Rhegium. It was situated in the northern part of the Bay of Naples and was the chief port of Rome, though 75 miles away. The population included Jews as well as Christians.
28:14 *spend a week.* As at Troas (20:6) and Tyre (21:4), Paul was with them for one or perhaps two Sundays to observe the keeping of the Lord's Supper and to teach and preach. Either the centurion had business to care for or he was free to delay the journey at Paul's request (see 27:42–43; see also 27:3). *Rome.* See map of "Rome," p. 1702.
28:15 *Forum of Appius.* A small town 43 miles from Rome,

noted for its wickedness. Some Roman Christians came this far to meet Paul. Beyond this they would not be certain of the way he would come. *Three Taverns.* A town 33 miles from Rome. Other Roman believers met Paul here. The term "tavern" was used to designate any kind of shop.
28:16 *live by himself.* "In his own rented house" (v. 30). He had committed no flagrant crime and was not a politically dangerous rival. So he was allowed to have his own living quarters, but a guard was with him at all times, perhaps chained to him (Eph 6:20; Php 1:13–14,17; Col 4:3,18; Phm 10,13).
28:17 *leaders of the Jews.* The decree of the emperor Claudius (see 18:2) had been allowed to lapse, and Jews had returned to Rome with their leaders. *My brothers.* An epithet that recognized the common Jewish blood he shared with them. Cf. the usage in v. 15, referring to brothers in Christ.
28:20 *the hope of Israel.* See note on 26:6.
28:22 *we want to hear . . . your views.* The Jews in Rome were well aware of the dispute over whether Jesus was the Messiah. They wanted to hear Paul's presentation, and he was eager to present it before the arrival of adverse opinions from the Jewish leaders of Jerusalem.
28:23 *Law of Moses . . . Prophets.* The OT Scriptures (see Lk 24:27,44).

understand with their hearts
and turn, and I would heal them.' c r

28"Therefore I want you to know that
God's salvation s has been sent to the Gentiles, t and they will listen!" d

30For two whole years Paul stayed there
in his own rented house and welcomed all

who came to see him. 31Boldly u and without hindrance he preached the kingdom of
God v and taught about the Lord Jesus
Christ.

28:27 r Isa 6:9, 10; S Mt 13:15	
28:28 s Lk 2:30 t S Ac 13:46	
28:31 u S Ac 4:29 v ver 23; S Mt 4:23	

c27 Isaiah 6:9,10   d28 Some manuscripts listen!"
29After he said this, the Jews left, arguing vigorously
among themselves.

28:28 *God's salvation has been sent to the Gentiles.* The main thought of the book of Acts. The gospel is meant for all. And Paul was a chosen vessel to carry the message to Gentiles as well as to Jews.

28:29 See NIV text note on v. 28.

28:30 *two whole years.* Paul served the Lord (v. 31) during the full period of waiting for his accusers to press the trial in Rome. There are a number of indications that he was released from this imprisonment: 1. Acts stops abruptly at

this time. 2. Paul wrote to churches expecting to visit them soon; so he must have anticipated a release (see Php 2:24; Phm 22). 3. A number of the details in the Pastoral Letters do not fit into the historical setting given in the book of Acts. Following the close of the book, these details indicate a return to Asia Minor, Crete and Greece. 4. Tradition indicates that Paul went to Spain. Even if he did not go, the very fact that a tradition arose suggests a time when he could have taken that journey. See map of "Paul's Fourth Missionary Journey," p. 1836.

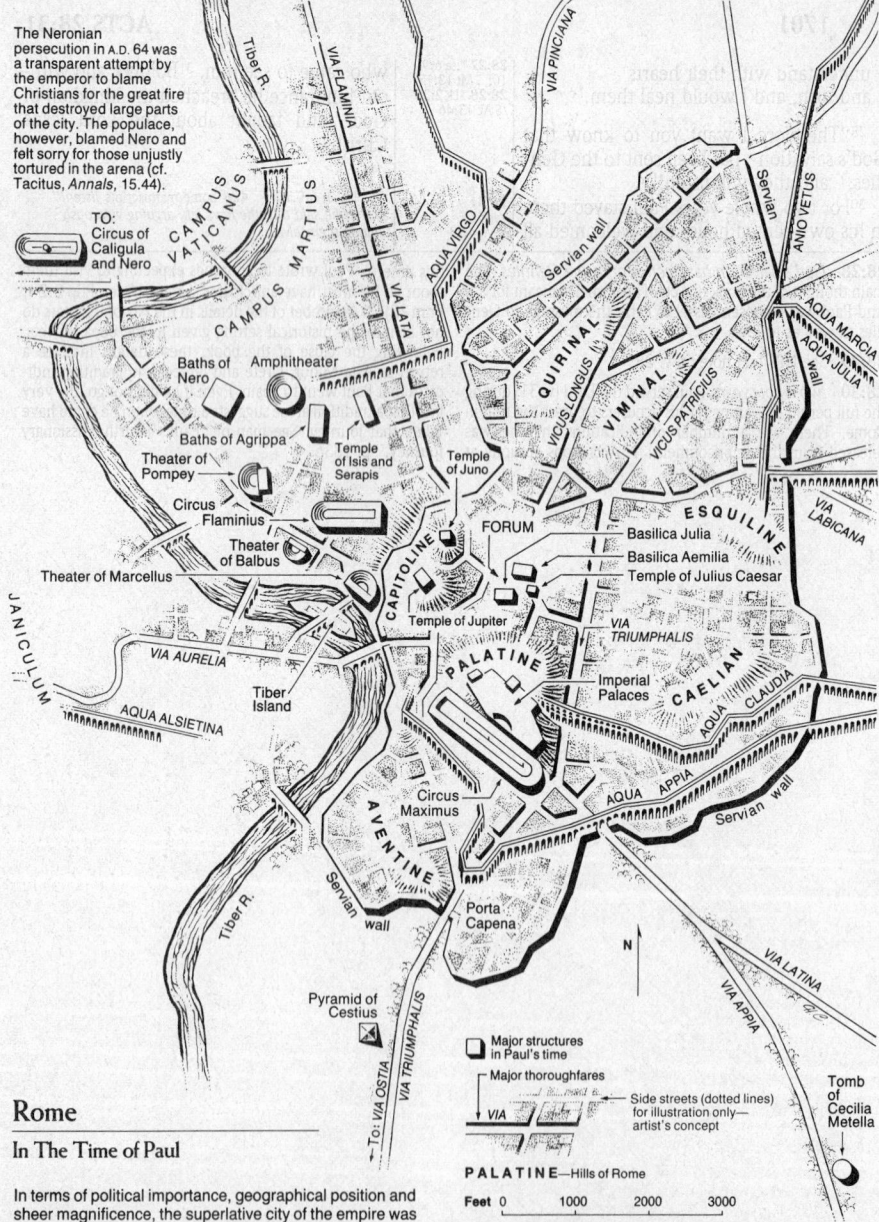

Rome

In The Time of Paul

In terms of political importance, geographical position and sheer magnificence, the superlative city of the empire was Rome, the capital.

Located on a series of jutting foothills and low-lying eminences (the "seven hills") east of a bend in the Tiber River some 18 miles from the Mediterranean, Rome was celebrated for its impressive public buildings, aqueducts, baths, theaters and thoroughfares, many of which led from distant provinces. The city of the first Christian century had spread far beyond its fourth-century B.C. "Servian" walls and lay unwalled, secure in its greatness.

The most prominent features were the Capitoline hill, with temples to Jupiter and Juno, and the nearby Palatine, adorned with imperial palaces, including Nero's "Golden House." Both hills overlooked the Roman Forum, the hub of the entire empire.

Alternatively described as the glorious crowning achievement of mankind and as the sewer of the universe where all the scum from every corner of the empire gathered, Rome had reasons for both civic pride in its architecture and shame for staggering urban social problems not unlike those of cities today.

The apostle Paul entered the city from the south on the Via Appia. He first lived under house arrest and then, after a period of freedom, as a condemned prisoner in the Mamertime dungeon near the Forum. Remarkably, Paul was able to proclaim the gospel among all classes of people, from the palace to the prison. According to tradition, he was executed at a spot on the Ostian Way outside Rome in A.D. 68.

ROMANS

Author

The writer of this letter was the apostle Paul (see 1:1). No voice from the early church was ever raised against his authorship. The letter contains a number of historical references that agree with known facts of Paul's life. The doctrinal content of the book is typical of Paul, which is evident from a comparison with other letters he wrote.

Date and Place of Writing

The book was probably written in the early spring of A.D. 57. Very likely Paul was on his third missionary journey, ready to return to Jerusalem with the offering from the mission churches for poverty-stricken believers in Jerusalem (see 15:25-27). In 15:26 it is suggested that Paul had already received contributions from the churches of Macedonia and Achaia, so he either was at Corinth or had already been there. Since he had not yet been at Corinth (on his third missionary journey) when he wrote 1 Corinthians (cf. 1Co 16:1-4), and the collection issue had still not been resolved when he wrote 2 Corinthians (2Co 8-9), the writing of Romans must follow that of 1,2 Corinthians (dated c. 55).

The most likely place of writing is either Corinth or Cenchrea (about six miles away) because of references to Phoebe of Cenchrea (16:1) and to Gaius, Paul's host (16:23), who was probably a Corinthian (see 1Co 1:14). Erastus (16:23) may also have been a Corinthian (see 2Ti 4:20).

Recipients

The original recipients of the letter were the people of the church at Rome (1:7), who were predominantly Gentile. Jews, however, must have constituted a substantial minority of the congregation (see 4:1; chs. 9-11; see also note on 1:13). Perhaps Paul originally sent the entire letter to the Roman church, after which he or someone else used a shorter form (chs. 1-14 or 1-15) for more general distribution. See note on 2Pe 3:15.

Major Theme

Paul's primary theme in Romans is the basic gospel, God's plan of salvation and righteousness for all mankind, Jew and Gentile alike (1:16-17). Although justification by faith has been suggested by some as the theme, it would seem that a broader theme states the message of the book more adequately. "Righteousness from God" (1:17) includes justification by faith, but it also embraces such related ideas as guilt, sanctification and security.

Purpose

Paul's purposes for writing this letter were varied:

1. He wrote to prepare the way for his coming visit to Rome and his proposed mission to Spain (1:10-15; 15:22-29).

2. He wrote to present the basic system of salvation to a church that had not received the teaching of an apostle before.

3. He sought to explain the relationship between Jew and Gentile in God's overall plan of redemption. The Jewish Christians were being rejected by the larger Gentile group in the church (14:1) because the Jewish believers still felt constrained to observe dietary laws and sacred days (14:2-6).

Occasion

When Paul wrote this letter, he was probably at Corinth (Ac 20:2-3) on his third missionary journey. His work in the eastern Mediterranean was almost finished (see 15:18-23), and he greatly desired to visit the Roman church (see 1:11-12; 15:23-24). At this time, however, he could not go to Rome because he felt he must personally deliver the collection taken among the Gentile churches for the

poverty-stricken Christians of Jerusalem (see 15:25-28). So instead of going to Rome, he sent a letter to prepare the Christians there for his intended visit in connection with a mission to Spain (see 15:23-24). For many years Paul had wanted to visit Rome to minister there (see 1:13-15), and this letter served as a careful and systematic theological introduction to that hoped-for personal ministry. Since he was not acquainted directly with the Roman church, he says little about its problems (but see 14:1-15:13; cf. also 13:1-7; 16:17-18).

Content

Paul begins by surveying the spiritual condition of all mankind. He finds Jews and Gentiles alike to be sinners and in need of salvation. That salvation has been provided by God through Jesus Christ and his redemptive work on the cross. It is a provision, however, that must be received by faith—a principle by which God has always dealt with mankind, as the example of Abraham shows. Since salvation is only the beginning of Christian experience, Paul moves on to show how the believer is freed from sin, law and death—a provision made possible by his union with Christ in both death and resurrection and by the indwelling presence and power of the Holy Spirit. Paul then shows that Israel too, though presently in a state of unbelief, has a place in God's sovereign redemptive plan. Now she consists of only a remnant, allowing for the conversion of the Gentiles, but the time will come when "all Israel will be saved" (11:26). The letter concludes with an appeal to the readers to work out their Christian faith in practical ways, both in the church and in the world. None of Paul's other letters states so profoundly the content of the gospel and its implications for both the present and the future.

Special Characteristics

1. *The most systematic of Paul's letters.* It reads more like an elaborate theological essay than a letter.
2. *Emphasis on Christian doctrine.* The number and importance of the theological themes touched upon are impressive: sin, salvation, grace, faith, righteousness, justification, sanctification, redemption, death and resurrection.
3. *Widespread use of OT quotations.* Although Paul regularly quotes from the OT in his letters, in Romans the argument is sometimes carried along by such quotations (see especially chs. 9-11).
4. *Deep concern for Israel.* Paul writes about her present status, her relationship to the Gentiles and her final salvation.

Outline

I. Introduction (1:1-15)
II. Theme: Righteousness from God (1:16-17)
III. The Unrighteousness of All Mankind (1:18-3:20)
  A. Gentiles (1:18-32)
  B. Jews (2:1-3:8)
  C. Summary: All People (3:9-20)
IV. Righteousness Imputed: Justification (3:21-5:21)
  A. Through Christ (3:21-26)
  B. Received by Faith (3:27-4:25)
    1. The principle established (3:27-31)
    2. The principle illustrated (ch. 4)
  C. The Fruits of Righteousness (5:1-11)
  D. Summary: Man's Unrighteousness Contrasted with God's Gift of Righteousness (5:12-21)
V. Righteousness Imparted: Sanctification (chs. 6-8)
  A. Freedom from Sin's Tyranny (ch. 6)
  B. Freedom from the Law's Condemnation (ch. 7)
  C. Life in the Power of the Holy Spirit (ch. 8)
VI. God's Righteousness Vindicated: The Problem of the Rejection of Israel (chs. 9-11)
  A. The Justice of the Rejection (9:1-29)
  B. The Cause of the Rejection (9:30-10:21)
  C. Facts That Lessen the Difficulty (ch. 11)
    1. The rejection is not total (11:1-10)
    2. The rejection is not final (11:11-24)
    3. God's ultimate purpose is mercy (11:25-36)

1 Paul, a servant of Christ Jesus, called to be an apostle[a] and set apart[b] for the gospel of God[c]— 2the gospel he promised beforehand[d] through his prophets[e] in the Holy Scriptures[f] 3regarding his Son, who as to his human nature[g] was a descendant of David,[h] 4and who through the Spirit[a] of holiness was declared with power to be the Son of God[b][i] by his resurrection from the dead:[j] Jesus Christ our Lord.[k] 5Through him and for his name's sake, we received grace[l] and apostleship to call people from among all the Gentiles[m] to the obedience that comes from faith.[n] 6And you also are among those who are called to belong to Jesus Christ.[o]

7To all in Rome who are loved by God[p] and called to be saints:[q]

Grace and peace to you from God our Father and from the Lord Jesus Christ.[r]

Paul's Longing to Visit Rome

8First, I thank my God through Jesus Christ for all of you,[s] because your faith is being reported all over the world.[t] 9God, whom I serve[u] with my whole heart in preaching the gospel of his Son, is my witness[v] how constantly I remember you 10in my prayers at all times;[w] and I pray that now at last by God's will[x] the way may be opened for me to come to you.[y]

11I long to see you[z] so that I may impart to you some spiritual gift[a] to make you strong— 12that is, that you and I may be mutually encouraged by each other's faith. 13I do not want you to be unaware,[b] brothers,[c] that I planned many times to come to you (but have been prevented from doing so until now)[d] in order that I might have a harvest among you, just as I have had among the other Gentiles.

14I am obligated[e] both to Greeks and non-Greeks, both to the wise and the foolish. 15That is why I am so eager to preach the gospel also to you who are at Rome.[f]

16I am not ashamed of the gospel,[g] because it is the power of God[h] for the salvation of everyone who believes:[i] first for the Jew,[j] then for the Gentile.[k] 17For in the gospel a righteousness from God is revealed,[l] a righteousness that is by faith[m] from first to last,[c] just as it is written: "The righteous will live by faith."[d][n]

God's Wrath Against Mankind

18The wrath of God[o] is being revealed from heaven against all the godlessness

Cross references

1:1 [a]S 1Co 1:1
[b]S Ac 9:15
[c]Ro 15:16;
S 2Co 2:12; 11:7;
1Th 2:8,9;
1Pe 4:17
1:2 [d]S Ac 13:32;
Tit 1:2 [e]Lk 1:70;
Ro 3:21 /Gal 3:8
1:3 [g]S Jn 1:14;
Ro 9:5 [h]S Mt 1:1
1:4 [i]S Mt 4:3
/S Ac 2:24
[k]1Co 1:2
1:5 [l]1Ti 1:14
[m]S Ac 9:15
[n]Ac 6:7;
Ro 16:26
1:6 [o]Jude 1;
Rev 17:14
1:7 [p]Ro 8:39;
1Th 1:4
[q]S Ac 9:13
[r]1Co 1:3;
Eph 1:2; 1Ti 1:2;
Tit 1:4; 1Pe 1:2
1:8 [s]1Co 1:4;
Eph 1:16;
1Th 2:13;
2Th 1:3; 2Ti 1:3
[t]S Ro 10:18;
16:19
1:9 [u]2Ti 1:3
[v]Job 16:19;
Jer 42:5;
2Co 1:23;
Gal 1:20;
Php 1:8; 1Th 2:5,
10
1:10 [w]1Sa 12:23;
S Lk 18:1;
S Ac 1:14;
Eph 1:16;
Php 1:4; Col 1:9;
2Th 1:11;
2Ti 1:3; Phm 4
[x]S Ac 18:21 [y]ver
13; Ro 15:32

1:11 [z]Ro 15:23
[a]1Co 1:7;
12:1-31

1:13 [b]S Ro 11:25 [c]S Ro 7:1 [d]Ro 15:22,23 1:14 [e]1Co 9:16
1:15 [f]Ro 15:20 1:16 [g]2Ti 1:8 [h]1Co 1:18 [i]S Jn 3:15
/Ac 3:26; 13:46 [k]S Ac 13:46; Ro 2:9,10 1:17 [l]Ro 3:21;
Php 3:9 [m]S Ro 9:30 [n]Hab 2:4; Gal 3:11; Heb 10:38 1:18
[o]Jn 3:36; Ro 5:9; Eph 5:6; Col 3:6; 1Th 1:10; Rev 19:15

[a]4 Or who as to his spirit   [b]4 Or was appointed to be
the Son of God with power   [c]17 Or is from faith to
faith   [d]17 Hab. 2:4

1:1 *Paul.* In ancient times writers put their names at the beginning of letters. For more information on Paul see notes on Ac 9:1; Php 3:4–14. *servant.* The Greek for this word means (1) a "slave," who completely belongs to his owner and has no freedom to leave, and (2) a "servant," who willingly chooses to serve his master. See notes on Ex 14:31; Ps 18 title; Isa 41:8–9; 42:1. *apostle.* One specially commissioned by Christ (see notes on Mk 6:30; 1Co 1:1; Heb 3:1). *gospel.* See note on Mk 1:1.
1:2 *prophets.* Not just the writers of the prophetic books, for the whole OT prophesied about Jesus (see Lk 24:27,44). *Holy Scriptures.* The OT.
1:7 *saints.* The basic idea of the Greek for this word is "holiness." All Christians are saints in that they are positionally "set apart" to God and are experientially being made increasingly "holy" by the Holy Spirit (see note on 1Co 1:2). *Grace.* See notes on Jnh 4:2; Gal 1:3; Eph 1:2. *peace.* See notes on Jn 14:27; 20:19; Gal 1:3; Eph 1:2.
1:8 *thank.* Paul often began his letters with thanks (see 1Co 1:4; Eph 1:16; Php 1:3; Col 1:3; 1Th 1:2; 2Th 1:3; 2Ti 1:3; Phm 4). *through Jesus Christ.* The Christian must go through Christ not only for requests to God (see Jn 15:16) but also to give thanks. *all over the world.* Every place where the gospel has been preached.
1:9 *gospel of his Son.* The same as the "gospel of God" (v. 1).
1:12 *mutually.* Paul's genuine humility is seen in his desire to be ministered to by the believers at Rome as well as to minister to them.
1:13 *harvest.* New converts as well as spiritual growth by those already converted. *among you . . . among the other*

Gentiles. Suggests that the church at Rome was predominantly Gentile.
1:14 *Greeks.* Those Gentiles who spoke Greek or followed the Greek way of life, even though they may have been Latin-speaking citizens of the Roman empire. *non-Greeks.* Lit. "barbarians," a word that probably imitated the unintelligible sound of their languages to Greek ears. They were the other Gentiles to whom Paul ministered.
1:16–17 The theme of the entire book.
1:16 *not ashamed.* Not even in the capital city of the Roman empire (see v. 15). *gospel.* See note on Mk 1:1. *first.* Not only in time but also in privilege. "Salvation is from the Jews" (Jn 4:22), and the Messiah was a Jew. The "very words of God" (3:2), the covenants, law, temple worship, revelation of the divine glory, and Messianic prophecies came to them (9:3–5). These privileges, however, were not extended to the Jews because of their superior merit or because of God's partiality toward them. It was necessary that the invasion of this world by the gospel begin at a particular point with a particular people, who in turn were responsible to carry that gospel to the other nations.
1:17 *righteousness.* The state of being "in the right" in relation to God (see notes on 2:13; 3:21,24).
1:18–3:20 In developing the theme of righteousness from God (1:17; 3:21–5:21), Paul sets the stage by showing that all have sinned and therefore need the righteousness that only God can provide. He shows the sin of the Gentiles (1:18–32) and the sin of the Jews (2:1–3:8) and then summarizes the sin of all—Gentile and Jew alike (3:9–20).
1:18–20 No one—not even one who has not heard of the Bible or of Christ—has an excuse for not honoring God,

and wickedness of men who suppress the truth by their wickedness, [19]since what may be known about God is plain to them, because God has made it plain to them. [p] [20]For since the creation of the world God's invisible qualities—his eternal power and divine nature—have been clearly seen, being understood from what has been made, [q] so that men are without excuse. [r]

[21]For although they knew God, they neither glorified him as God nor gave thanks to him, but their thinking became futile and their foolish hearts were darkened. [s] [22]Although they claimed to be wise, they became fools [t] [23]and exchanged the glory of the immortal God for images [u] made to look like mortal man and birds and animals and reptiles.

[24]Therefore God gave them over [v] in the sinful desires of their hearts to sexual impurity for the degrading of their bodies with one another. [w] [25]They exchanged the truth of God for a lie, [x] and worshiped and served created things [y] rather than the Creator—who   is   forever   praised. [z] Amen. [a]

[26]Because of this, God gave them over [b] to shameful lusts. [c] Even their women exchanged natural relations for unnatural ones. [d] [27]In the same way the men also abandoned natural relations with women and were inflamed with lust for one another. Men committed indecent acts with other men, and received in themselves the due penalty for their perversion. [e]

[28]Furthermore, since they did not think it worthwhile to retain the knowledge of God, he gave them over [f] to a depraved mind, to do what ought not to be done. [29]They have become filled with every kind of wickedness, evil, greed and depravity. They are full of envy, murder, strife, deceit and malice. They are gossips, [g] [30]slanderers, God-haters, insolent, arrogant and boastful; they invent ways of doing evil; they disobey their parents; [h] [31]they are senseless, faithless, heartless, [i] ruthless. [32]Although they know God's righteous decree that those who do such things deserve death, [j] they not only continue to do these very things but also approve [k] of those who practice them.

God's Righteous Judgment

2 You, therefore, have no excuse, [l] you who pass judgment on someone else, for at whatever point you judge the other, you are condemning yourself, because you who pass judgment do the same things. [m] [2]Now we know that God's judgment against those who do such things is based on truth. [3]So when you, a mere man, pass judgment on them and yet do the same things, do you think you will escape God's judgment? [4]Or do you show contempt for the riches [n] of his kindness, [o] tolerance [p] and patience, [q] not realizing that God's kindness leads you toward repentance? [r]

[5]But because of your stubbornness and your unrepentant heart, you are storing up

1:19 [p]Ac 14:17
1:20 [q]Ps 19:1-6
[r]Ro 2:1
1:21 [s]Ge 8:21; Jer 2:5; 17:9; Eph 4:17,18
1:22 [t]1Co 1:20, 27; 3:18,19
1:23 [u]Dt 4:16, 17; Ps 106:20; Jer 2:11; Ac 17:29
1:24 [v]ver 26,28; Ps 81:12; Eph 4:19
[w]1Pe 4:3
1:25 [x]Isa 44:20
[y]Jer 10:14; 13:25; 16:19,20
[z]Ro 9:5; 2Co 11:31
[a]S Ro 11:36
1:26 [b]ver 24,28
[c]Eph 4:19; 1Th 4:5
[d]Lev 18:22,23
1:27 [e]Lev 18:22; 20:13; 1Co 6:18

1:28 [f]ver 24,26
1:29 [g]2Co 12:20; 1Ti 5:13; Jas 3:2; 3Jn 10
1:30 [h]2Ti 3:2
1:31 [i]2Ti 3:3
1:32 [j]S Ro 6:23
[k]Ps 50:18; Lk 11:48; Ac 8:1; 22:20
2:1 [l]Ro 1:20
[m]2Sa 12:5-7; S Mt 7:1,2
2:4 [n]Ro 9:23; 11:33; Eph 1:7, 18; 2:7; 3:8,16; Col 2:2
[o]Ro 11:22
[p]Ro 3:25
[q]Ex 34:6; Ro 9:22; 1Ti 1:16; 1Pe 3:20; 2Pe 3:15
[r]2Pe 3:9

because the whole created world reveals him.
1:18 *wrath of God.* Not a petulant, irrational burst of anger, such as humans often exhibit, but a holy, just revulsion against what is contrary to and opposes his holy nature and will. *is being revealed.* God's wrath is not limited to the end-time judgment of the wicked (1Th 1:10; Rev 19:15; 20:11–15). Here the wrath of God is his abandonment of the wicked to their sins (vv. 24–32). *the truth.* The truth about God revealed in the creation order.
1:21 *knew God.* From seeing his revelation in creation (vv. 19–20). The fact that these people were idolaters (v. 23) and knew God only through the creation order indicates that they were Gentiles. *gave thanks.* For earthly blessings, such as sun, rain and crops (see Mt 5:45; Ac 14:17).
1:23 *glory.* God's unique majesty (see Isa 48:11), which fallen mankind has lost sight of and for which they have substituted deities of their own devising, patterned after various creatures.
1:24,26,28 *God gave them over.* God allowed sin to run its course as an act of judgment.
1:25 *Amen.* Can mean either "Yes indeed, it is so" or "So be it" (see 9:5; 11:36; 15:33; 16:27; see also note on Dt 27:15; cf. 1Ki 1:36).
1:26 *their women.* Not necessarily their wives.
1:27 *Homosexual practice is sinful in God's eyes. The OT also condemns the practice (see Lev 18:22).
1:28 *knowledge of God.* See vv. 19,21. *a depraved mind.* The intent precedes the act (see v. 21; Mk 7:20–23).

1:32 *they know.* Their outrageous conduct was not due to total ignorance of what God required but to self-will and rebellion. *approve.* The extreme of sin is applauding, rather than regretting, the sins of others.
2:1–16 In this section Paul sets forth principles that govern God's judgment. God judges (1) according to truth (v. 2), (2) according to deeds (vv. 6–11) and (3) according to the light a person has (vv. 12–15). These principles lay the groundwork for Paul's discussion of the guilt of the Jews (vv. 17–29).
2:1 *no excuse.* Paul's teaching about judging agrees with that of Jesus (see note on Mt 7:1), who did not condemn judging as such, but hypocritical judging. *you who pass judgment.* A warning that had special relevance for Jews, who were inclined to look down on Gentiles because of their ignorance of God's revelation in the OT and because of their immoral lives.
2:2 *we know.* An expression Paul frequently used that assumed the persons addressed agreed with the statement that followed (see 3:19; 7:14; 8:22,28; 1Co 8:1,4; 2Co 5:1; 1Ti 1:8).
2:3 Jesus also condemned this attitude (Mt 7:3; cf. Lk 18:9).
2:4 The purpose of God's kindness is to give opportunity for repentance (2Pe 3:9). The Jews had misconstrued his patience to be a lack of intent to judge.
2:5 *day of God's wrath.* Judgment at the end of time in contrast to the judgment discussed in 1:18–32.

wrath against yourself for the day of God's wrath[s], when his righteous judgment[t] will be revealed. [6]God "will give to each person according to what he has done."[e][u] [7]To those who by persistence in doing good seek glory, honor[v] and immortality,[w] he will give eternal life.[x] [8]But for those who are self-seeking and who reject the truth and follow evil,[y] there will be wrath and anger.[z] [9]There will be trouble and distress for every human being who does evil:[a] first for the Jew, then for the Gentile;[b] [10]but glory, honor and peace for everyone who does good: first for the Jew, then for the Gentile.[c] [11]For God does not show favoritism.[d]

[12]All who sin apart from the law will also perish apart from the law, and all who sin under the law[e] will be judged by the law. [13]For it is not those who hear the law who are righteous in God's sight, but it is those who obey[f] the law who will be declared righteous. [14](Indeed, when Gentiles, who do not have the law, do by nature things required by the law,[g] they are a law for themselves, even though they do not have the law, [15]since they show that the requirements of the law are written on their hearts, their consciences also bearing witness, and their thoughts now accusing, now even defending them.) [16]This will take place on the day when God will judge men's secrets[h] through Jesus Christ,[i] as my gospel[j] declares.

The Jews and the Law

[17]Now you, if you call yourself a Jew; if

you rely on the law and brag about your relationship to God;[k] [18]if you know his will and approve of what is superior because you are instructed by the law; [19]if you are convinced that you are a guide for the blind, a light for those who are in the dark, [20]an instructor of the foolish, a teacher of infants, because you have in the law the embodiment of knowledge and truth— [21]you, then, who teach others, do you not teach yourself? You who preach against stealing, do you steal?[l] [22]You who say that people should not commit adultery, do you commit adultery? You who abhor idols, do you rob temples?[m] [23]You who brag about the law,[n] do you dishonor God by breaking the law? [24]As it is written: "God's name is blasphemed among the Gentiles because of you."[f][o]

[25]Circumcision has value if you observe the law,[p] but if you break the law, you have become as though you had not been circumcised.[q] [26]If those who are not circumcised keep the law's requirements,[r] will they not be regarded as though they were circumcised?[s] [27]The one who is not circumcised physically and yet obeys the law will condemn you[t] who, even though you have the[g] written code and circumcision, are a lawbreaker.

[28]A man is not a Jew if he is only one outwardly,[u] nor is circumcision merely outward and physical.[v] [29]No, a man is a Jew if he is one inwardly; and circumcision is circumcision of the heart,[w] by the

2:5 sPs 110:5; Rev 6:17 tJude 6
2:6 uPs 62:12; S Mt 16:27
2:7 vver 10
w1Co 15:53,54; 2Ti 1:10
xS Mt 25:46
2:8 y2Th 2:12
zEze 22:31
2:9 aPs 32:10
bver 10; Ro 1:16
2:10 cver 9; Ro 1:16
2:11 dS Ac 10:34
2:12 eRo 3:19; 6:14; 1Co 9:20, 21; Gal 4:21; 5:18; S Ro 7:4
2:13 flas 1:22,23, 25
2:14 gAc 10:35
2:16 hEcc 12:14; 1Co 4:5
iAc 10:42
jRo 16:25; 2Ti 2:8
2:17 kver 23; Jer 8:8; Mic 3:11; Jn 5:45; Ro 9:4
2:21 lMt 23:3,4
2:22 mAc 19:37
2:23 nS ver 17
2:24 olsa 52:5; Eze 36:22; 2Pe 2:2
2:25 pver 13,27; Gal 5:3 qJer 4:4; 9:25,26
2:26 rRo 8:4 sS 1Co 7:19
2:27 tMt 12:41, 42
2:28 uMt 3:9; Jn 8:39; Ro 9:6,7 vGal 6:15
2:29 wDt 30:6

e6 Psalm 62:12; Prov. 24:12   f24 Isaiah 52:5; Ezek. 36:22   g27 Or who, by means of a

---

2:6–7 Paul is not contradicting his continual emphasis in all his writings, including Romans, that a person is saved not by what he does but by faith in what Christ does for him. Rather, he is discussing the principle of judgment according to deeds (see note on vv. 1–16). If anyone persists in doing good deeds (i.e., lives a perfect life), he will receive eternal life. No one can do this, but if anyone could, God would give him life, since God judges according to what a person does.
2:9 *first for the Jew.* With spiritual privilege comes spiritual responsibility (see Am 3:2; Lk 12:48).
2:11 A basic teaching of both the OT and the NT.
2:12 *law.* The Mosaic law. "All who sin apart from the law" refers to Gentiles. God judges according to the light available to people. Gentiles will not be condemned for not obeying a law they did not possess. Their judgment will be on other grounds (see 1:18–20; 2:15; cf. Am 1:3–2:3).
2:13 *will be declared righteous.* At God's pronouncement of acquittal on judgment day (see note on 3:24).
2:14 *by nature.* By natural impulse without the external constraint of the Mosaic law. *things required by the law.* Does not mean that pagans fulfilled the requirements of the Mosaic law but refers to practices in pagan society that agreed with the law, such as caring for the sick and elderly, honoring parents and condemning adultery. *law for themselves.* The moral nature of pagans, enlightened by conscience (v. 15), functioned for them as the Mosaic law did for

the Jews.
2:16 This verse should be read with v. 13, as the parentheses around vv. 14–15 indicate.
2:17–24 The presentation takes the form of a dialogue. Paul knew how a self-righteous Jew thought, for he had been one himself. He cites one advantage after another that Jews considered to be unqualified assets. But those assets became liabilities when there was no correspondence between profession and practice. Paul applied to the Jew the principles of judgment set forth in vv. 1–16 (see note on those verses).
2:19–20 *the blind . . . infants.* Gentiles, to whom Jews regarded themselves as vastly superior because they (the Jews) possessed the Mosaic law.
2:22 *do you rob temples?* See Ac 19:37. Large amounts of wealth were often stored in pagan temples.
2:25 *Circumcision.* A sign of the covenant that God made with Israel (see Lev 12:3) and a pledge of the covenant blessing (see Ge 17 and notes on Ge 17:10–11). The Jews had come to regard circumcision as a guarantee of God's favor.
2:27 If a Gentile's deeds excelled those of a Jew in righteousness, that very fact condemned the Jew, who had an immeasurably better set of standards in the law of Moses.
2:29 *by the Spirit.* The true sign of belonging to God is not an outward mark on the physical body, but the regenerating power of the Holy Spirit within—what Paul meant by

Spirit,[x] not by the written code.[y] Such a
man's praise is not from men, but from
God.[z]

God's Faithfulness

3 What advantage, then, is there in being a Jew, or what value is there in
circumcision? 2Much in every way![a] First
of all, they have been entrusted with the
very words of God.[b]
3What if some did not have faith?[c] Will
their lack of faith nullify God's faithfulness?[d] 4Not at all! Let God be true,[e] and
every man a liar.[f] As it is written:

"So that you may be proved right when
you speak
and prevail when you judge."[h] [g]

5But if our unrighteousness brings out
God's righteousness more clearly,[h] what
shall we say? That God is unjust in bringing his wrath on us? (I am using a human
argument.)[i] 6Certainly not! If that were
so, how could God judge the world?[j]
7Someone might argue, "If my falsehood
enhances God's truthfulness and so increases his glory,[k] why am I still condemned as a sinner?"[l] 8Why not say—as
we are being slanderously reported as saying and as some claim that we say—"Let
us do evil that good may result"?[m] Their
condemnation is deserved.

No One Is Righteous

9What shall we conclude then? Are we
any better[i]?[n] Not at all! We have already
made the charge that Jews and Gentiles
alike are all under sin.[o] 10As it is written:

"There is no one righteous, not even
one;
11 there is no one who understands,
no one who seeks God.
12All have turned away,
they have together become
worthless;
there is no one who does good,
not even one."[j] [p]
13"Their throats are open graves;
their tongues practice deceit."[k] [q]
"The poison of vipers is on their
lips."[l] [r]
14 "Their mouths are full of cursing and
bitterness."[m] [s]
15"Their feet are swift to shed blood;
16 ruin and misery mark their ways,
17and the way of peace they do not
know."[n] [t]
18 "There is no fear of God before their
eyes."[o] [u]

19Now we know that whatever the law
says,[v] it says to those who are under the
law,[w] so that every mouth may be silenced[x] and the whole world held accountable to God.[y] 20Therefore no one
will be declared righteous in his sight by
observing the law;[z] rather, through the
law we become conscious of sin.[a]

Righteousness Through Faith

21But now a righteousness from God,[b]
apart from law, has been made known, to
which the Law and the Prophets testify.[c]

2:29 [x]Php 3:3; Col 2:11 [y]Ro 7:6; 2Co 3:6 [z]Jn 5:44; 12:43; 1Co 4:5; 2Co 10:18; Gal 1:10; 1Th 2:4; 1Pe 3:4 **3:2** [a]Ro 9:4,5 [b]Dt 4:8; Ps 147:19; Ac 7:38 **3:3** [c]Ro 10:16; Heb 4:2 [d]2Ti 2:13 **3:4** [e]Jn 3:33 [f]Ps 116:11 [g]Ps 51:4 **3:5** [h]Ro 5:8 [i]Ro 6:19; Gal 3:15 **3:6** [j]Ge 18:25; Ro 2:16 **3:7** [k]ver 4 [l]Ro 9:19 **3:8** [m]Ro 6:1 **3:9** [n]ver 1 [o]ver 19,23; 1Ki 8:46; 2Ch 6:36; Ps 106:6; Ro 5:12; 11:32; Gal 3:22 **3:12** [p]Ps 14:1-3; 53:1-3; Ecc 7:20 **3:13** [q]Ps 5:9 [r]Ps 140:3 **3:14** [s]Ps 10:7 **3:17** [t]Isa 59:7,8 **3:18** [u]Ps 36:1 **3:19** [v]S Jn 10:34 [w]S Ro 2:12 [x]Ps 63:11; 107:42; Eze 16:63 [y]ver 9 **3:20** [z]Ac 13:39; Gal 2:16 [a]S Ro 4:15 **3:21** [b]Isa 46:13; Jer 23:6; Ro 1:17; 9:30 [c]Ac 10:43; Ro 1:2

h *4* Psalm 51:4 **i** *9* Or *worse* **j** *12* Psalms 14:1-3; 53:1-3; Eccles. 7:20 **k** *13* Psalm 5:9 **l** *13* Psalm 140:3 **m** *14* Psalm 10:7 **n** *17* Isaiah 59:7,8 **o** *18* Psalm 36:1

"circumcision of the heart" (see Dt 30:6).
3:2 *First of all.* Paul does not discuss the other advantages of being a Jew until 9:4–5. *entrusted.* The advantage of having the very words of God involves a duty.
3:3 *God's faithfulness.* God is faithful to his promises and would punish Israel for its unbelief (v. 5; see 2Ti 2:13).
3:4 God's punishment of sin exhibits his faithfulness to his righteous character.
3:5 *brings out God's righteousness.* By contrast, in showing it up against the dark background of man's sin. *a human argument.* "Human" in the sense of its weakness and absurdity.
3:6 *judge.* On judgment day. *the world.* All moral creatures (also in v. 19)—a more limited reference than in 1:20.
3:9 *Are we any better?* Are Jews better than Gentiles in the sight of God? *all.* Nine times in four verses (vv. 9–12) Paul mentions the universality of sin ("all," two times; "no one," four times; "not even one," two times; "together," once). *under sin.* Under its power and condemnation.
3:10–18 A collection of OT quotations that underscores Paul's charge that both Jews and Gentiles are under the power of sin. Several factors explain why the citations are not always verbatim: 1. NT quotations sometimes gave the general sense and were not meant to be word-for-word. 2. Quotation marks were not used in Greek. 3. The quotations were often taken from the Greek translation (the Septuagint) of the Hebrew OT, because Greek readers were not familiar with the Hebrew Bible. 4. Sometimes the NT writer, in order to drive home his point, would purposely (under the inspiration of the Holy Spirit) enlarge, abbreviate or adapt an OT passage or combine two or more passages.
3:11 *understands.* About God and what is right.
3:13 *open graves.* Expressing the corruption of the heart.
3:18 *fear of God.* Awesome reverence for God; the source of all godliness (see note on Ge 20:11).
3:19 *we know.* See note on 2:2. *law.* The OT (as in Jn 10:34; 15:25; 1Co 14:21). *those who are under the law.* Jews. *every mouth . . . whole world.* Jews as well as Gentiles are guilty.
3:20 *declared righteous.* See notes on v. 24; 2:13.
3:21–5:21 Having shown that all (both Gentiles and Jews) are unrighteous (1:18–3:20), Paul now shows that God has provided a righteousness for mankind.
3:21 *But now.* There are two possible meanings: (1) temporal—all of time is divided into two periods, and in the "now" period the righteousness from God has been made known; (2) logical—the contrast is between the righteousness gained by observing the law (which is impossible, v. 20) and the righteousness provided by God. *the Law and the Prophets testify.* See Ge 15:6; Ps 32:1–2; Hab 2:4.

²²This righteousness from God _d_ comes through faith _e_ in Jesus Christ _f_ to all who believe. _g_ There is no difference, _h_ ²³for all have sinned _i_ and fall short of the glory of God, ²⁴and are justified _j_ freely by his grace _k_ through the redemption _l_ that came by Christ Jesus. ²⁵God presented him as a sacrifice of atonement, _p_ _m_ through faith in his blood. _n_ He did this to demonstrate his justice, because in his forbearance he had left the sins committed beforehand unpunished _o_— ²⁶he did it to demonstrate his justice at the present time, so as to be just and the one who justifies those who have faith in Jesus.

²⁷Where, then, is boasting? _p_ It is excluded. On what principle? On that of observing the law? No, but on that of faith. ²⁸For we maintain that a man is justified by faith apart from observing the law. _q_ ²⁹Is God the God of Jews only? Is he not the God of Gentiles too, _r_ Yes, of Gentiles too, ³⁰since there is only one God, who will justify the circumcised by faith and the uncircumcised through that same faith. _s_

³¹Do we, then, nullify the law by this faith? Not at all! Rather, we uphold the law.

Abraham Justified by Faith

4 What then shall we say _t_ that Abraham, our forefather, _u_ discovered in this matter? ²If, in fact, Abraham was justified by works, he had something to boast about—but not before God. _v_ ³What does the Scripture say? "Abraham believed God, and it was credited to him as righteousness." _q_ _w_

⁴Now when a man works, his wages are not credited to him as a gift, _x_ but as an obligation. ⁵However, to the man who does not work but trusts God who justifies the wicked, his faith is credited as righteousness. _y_ ⁶David says the same thing when he speaks of the blessedness of the

---

3:22 _d_ Ro 1:17
_e_ S Ro 9:30
_f_ Gal 2:16; 3:22
_g_ S Jn 3:15;
Ro 4:11; 10:4
_h_ Ro 10:12;
Gal 3:28;
Col 3:11
3:23 _i_ S ver 9
3:24 _j_ S Ro 4:25
_k_ Jn 1:14,16,17;
Ro 4:16; 5:21;
6:14; 11:5;
2Co 12:9;
Eph 2:8; 4:7;
Tit 2:11;
Heb 4:16
_l_ Ps 130:7;
1Co 1:30;
Gal 4:5; Eph 1:7,
14; Col 1:14;
Heb 9:12
3:25 _m_ Ex 25:17;
Lev 16:10;
Ps 65:3;
Heb 2:17; 9:28;
1Jn 4:10
_n_ Ac 20:28;
Ro 5:9; Eph 1:7;
Heb 9:12,14;
13:12; 1Pe 1:19;
Rev 1:5
_o_ Ac 14:16; 17:30
3:27 _p_ Ro 2:17,
23; 4:2;
1Co 1:29-31;
Eph 2:9
3:28 _q_ Ac 13:39;
Ro 3:20,21;
Gal 2:16; 3:11;
Eph 2:9; Jas 2:20,

24,26 **3:29** _r_ Ac 10:34,35; Ro 9:24; 10:12; 15:9; Gal 3:28
3:30 _s_ Ro 4:11,12; Gal 3:8 **4:1** _t_ S Ro 8:31 _u_ S Lk 3:8 **4:2** _v_ 1Co 1:31 **4:3** _w_ ver 5,9,22; Ge 15:6; Gal 3:6; Jas 2:23 **4:4** _x_ Ro 11:6 **4:5** _y_ ver 3,9,22; S Ro 9:30

p _25_ Or _as the one who would turn aside his wrath, taking away sin_   **q** _3_ Gen. 15:6; also in verse 22

3:22–23 _There is no difference . . . glory of God._ A parenthetical thought: All who believe are "justified freely" (v. 24), not "all have sinned . . . and are justified freely" (vv. 23–24).

3:22 _no difference._ Between Jews and Gentiles (see 10:12).

3:23 _glory of God._ What God intended man to be. The glory that man had before the fall (see Ge 1:26–28; Ps 8:5–6; cf. Eph 4:24; Col 3:10) the believer will again have through Christ (see Heb 2:5–9).

3:24 _justified._ Paul uses this verb 22 times, mostly in 2:13–5:1; Gal 2–3. It is translated "justify" in all cases except two (2:13; 3:20, where it is translated "declared righteous"). The term describes what happens when someone believes in Christ as his Savior: From the negative viewpoint, God declares the person to be not guilty; from the positive viewpoint, he declares him to be righteous. He cancels the guilt of the person's sin and credits righteousness to him. Paul emphasizes two points in this regard: 1. No one lives a perfectly good, holy, righteous life. On the contrary, "there is no one righteous" (v. 10), and "all have sinned and fall short of the glory of God" (v. 23). "Therefore no one will be declared righteous in his [God's] sight by observing the law" (v. 20). 2. But even though all are sinners and not sons, God will declare everyone who puts his trust in Jesus not guilty but righteous. This legal declaration is valid because Christ died to pay the penalty for our sin and lived a life of perfect righteousness that can in turn be imputed to us. This is the central theme of Romans and is stated in the theme verse, 1:17 ("a righteousness from God"). Christ's righteousness (his obedience to God's law and his sacrificial death) will be credited to believers as their own. Paul uses the word "credited" nine times in ch. 4 alone. _freely by his grace._ The central thought in justification is that, although man clearly and totally deserves to be declared guilty (vv. 9–19), because of his trust in Christ God declares him righteous. This is stated in several ways here: (1) "freely" (as a gift, for nothing), (2) "by his grace," (3) "through the redemption that came by Christ Jesus" and (4) "through faith"

(v. 25). _redemption._ A word taken from the slave market—the basic idea is that of obtaining release by payment of a ransom. Paul uses this word to refer to release from guilt, with its liability for judgment, and to deliverance from slavery to sin, because Christ in his death paid the ransom for us.

3:25 _sacrifice of atonement._ The Greek for this phrase speaks of a sacrifice that satisfies the righteous wrath of God. Without this appeasement ("propitiation") all people are justly destined for eternal punishment. See NIV text note here; see also note on 1Jn 2:2. _faith in his blood._ Saving faith looks to Jesus Christ in his sacrificial death for us.

3:25b–26 The sins of God's people, punished symbolically in the animal sacrifices of the OT period, would be totally punished in the once-for-all sacrifice of Christ on the cross.

3:28 _by faith._ When Luther translated this passage, he added the word "alone," which, though not in the Greek, accurately reflects the meaning (see note on Jas 2:14–26).

3:30 _only one God._ By appealing to the first article of Jewish faith ("the Lᴏʀᴅ is one," Dt 6:4), Paul argues that there is only one way of salvation for both Jew and Gentile, namely, faith in Christ.

3:31 Paul anticipated being charged with antinomianism (against law): If justification comes by faith alone, then is not the law rejected? He gives a more complete answer in chs. 6–7 and reasserts the validity of the law in 13:8–10.

4:1 _Abraham, our forefather._ The great patriarch of the Jewish nation, the true example of a justified person (see Jas 2:21–23). The Jews of Jesus' time used Abraham as an example of justification by works, but Paul holds him up as a shining example of righteousness by faith (see Gal 3:6–9).

4:3 The reference is to Ge 15:6, where nothing is mentioned about works. _credited._ Abraham had kept no law, rendered no service and performed no ritual that earned credit to his account before God. His belief in God, who had made promises to him, was credited to him as righteousness.

4:6–8 God does not continue to credit unrighteousness to the sinner who repents, but forgives him when he confesses (see Ps 32:3–5; Eze 18:23,27–28,32; 33:14–16).

man to whom God credits righteousness apart from works:

⁷"Blessed are they
   whose transgressions are forgiven,
   whose sins are covered.
⁸Blessed is the man
   whose sin the Lord will never count
     against him."[r][z]

⁹Is this blessedness only for the circumcised, or also for the uncircumcised?[a] We have been saying that Abraham's faith was credited to him as righteousness.[b] ¹⁰Under what circumstances was it credited? Was it after he was circumcised, or before? It was not after, but before! ¹¹And he received the sign of circumcision, a seal of the righteousness that he had by faith while he was still uncircumcised.[c] So then, he is the father[d] of all who believe[e] but have not been circumcised, in order that righteousness might be credited to them. ¹²And he is also the father of the circumcised who not only are circumcised but who also walk in the footsteps of the faith that our father Abraham had before he was circumcised.

¹³It was not through law that Abraham and his offspring received the promise[f] that he would be heir of the world,[g] but through the righteousness that comes by faith.[h] ¹⁴For if those who live by law are heirs, faith has no value and the promise is worthless,[i] ¹⁵because law brings wrath.[j] And where there is no law there is no transgression.[k]

¹⁶Therefore, the promise comes by faith, so that it may be by grace[l] and may be guaranteed[m] to all Abraham's offspring—not only to those who are of the law but also to those who are of the faith of Abraham. He is the father of us all.[n] ¹⁷As it is written: "I have made you a father of many nations."[s][o] He is our father in the sight of God, in whom he believed—the God who gives life[p] to the dead and calls[q] things that are not[r] as though they were.

¹⁸Against all hope, Abraham in hope believed and so became the father of many nations,[s] just as it had been said to him, "So shall your offspring be."[t][t] ¹⁹Without weakening in his faith, he faced the fact that his body was as good as dead[u]—since he was about a hundred years old[v]—and that Sarah's womb was also dead.[w] ²⁰Yet he did not waver through unbelief regarding the promise of God, but was strengthened[x] in his faith and gave glory to God,[y] ²¹being fully persuaded that God had power to do what he had promised.[z]

Cross references (center column):

4:8 [z]Ps 32:1,2; 103:12; 2Co 5:19
4:9 [a]Ro 3:30
    [b]S ver 3
4:11 [c]Ge 17:10, 11 [d]ver 16,17; S Lk 3:8 [e]S Ro 3:22
4:13 [f]S Ac 13:32; Gal 3:16,29 [g]Ge 17:4-6
[h]S Ro 9:30
4:14 [i]Gal 3:18
4:15 [j]Ro 7:7-25; 1Co 15:56; 2Co 3:7; Gal 3:10; S Ro 7:12 [k]Ro 3:20; 5:13; 7:7
4:16 [l]S Ro 3:24 [m]Ro 15:8 [n]ver 11; S Lk 3:8; S Gal 3:16
4:17 [o]Ge 17:5 [p]S Jn 5:21 [q]Isa 48:13 [r]1Co 1:28
4:18 [s]ver 17 [t]Ge 15:5
4:19 [u]Heb 11:11, 12 [v]Ge 17:17 [w]Ge 18:11
4:20 [x]1Sa 30:6 [y]S Mt 9:8
4:21 [z]Ge 18:14; S Mt 19:26

[r]8 Psalm 32:1,2   [s]17 Gen. 17:5   [t]18 Gen. 15:5

4:9 *circumcised.* Jews. *uncircumcised.* Gentiles.

4:10 *not after, but before!* Abraham was declared righteous (Ge 15) some 14 years before he was circumcised (Ge 17). See Gal 3:17 for a similar statement.

4:11 *sign.* Circumcision was, among other things, the outward sign of the righteousness that God had credited to Abraham for his faith. *So then.* Abraham is the "father" of believing Gentiles (the uncircumcised), because he believed and was justified before the rite of circumcision (the mark of Jews) was instituted.

4:12 *father of the circumcised.* Abraham is also the father of believing Jews. Thus his story shows that for Jew and Gentile alike there is only one way of justification—the way of faith.

4:13 *not through law.* Not on the condition that the promise be merited by works of the law. *his offspring.* All those of whom Abraham is said to be father (vv. 11–12). *heir of the world.* "World" here refers to the creation, as in 1:20. No express mention of this heirship is made in the Genesis account of Abraham. He is promised "offspring like the dust of the earth" (Ge 13:16) and possession of the land of Canaan (Ge 12:7; 13:14–15; 15:7,18–21; 17:8), and that all the peoples on earth will be blessed through him (Ge 12:3; 18:18) or his offspring (Ge 22:18). But since, as Genesis already makes clear, God purposed through Abraham and his offspring to work out the destiny of the whole world, it was implicit in the promises to Abraham that he and his offspring would "inherit the earth" (see Ps 37:9,11,22, 29,34; Mt 5:5). The full realization of this awaits the consummation of the Messianic kingdom at Christ's return.

4:14 *those who live by law.* Those whose claim to the inheritance is based on the fulfillment of the law. *promise.* See note on v. 13.

4:15 *law brings wrath.* The law, because it reveals sin and even stimulates it (see 7:7–11), produces wrath, not promise. *transgression.* Overstepping a clearly defined line. Where there is no law there is still sin, but it does not have the character of transgression.

4:16 A summary of the thought of vv. 11–12. For the close correlation between faith and grace see 3:24–25; Eph 2:8. *those who are of the law.* Jewish Christians. *those who are of the faith of Abraham.* Gentile Christians who share Abraham's faith but who, like Abraham, do not possess the law.

4:17 *in the sight of God.* God considers Abraham the father of Jews and believing Gentiles alike, no matter how others (especially the Jews) may see him. *the God who gives life to the dead.* The main reference is to the birth of Isaac through Abraham and Sarah, both of whom were far past the age of childbearing (see Ge 18:11). Secondarily Paul alludes also to the resurrection of Christ (see vv. 24–25). *calls things that are not.* God has the ability to create out of nothing, as he demonstrated in the birth of Isaac.

4:18 *Against all hope . . . in hope believed.* When all hope, as a human possibility, failed, Abraham placed his hope in God.

4:19 *Without weakening in his faith.* Abraham had some anxious moments (see Ge 17:17–18), but God did not count these against him. *faced the fact.* Faith does not refuse to face reality but looks beyond all difficulties to God and his promises. *Sarah's womb was also dead.* Sarah was ten years younger than Abraham (see Ge 17:17) but well past the age of bearing children.

4:20 *gave glory to God.* Because Abraham had faith to believe that God would do what he promised. Whereas works are man's attempt to establish a claim on God, faith brings glory to him.

²²This is why "it was credited to him as righteousness." *a* ²³The words "it was credited to him" were written not for him alone, ²⁴but also for us, *b* to whom God will credit righteousness—for us who believe in him *c* who raised Jesus our Lord from the dead. *d* ²⁵He was delivered over to death for our sins *e* and was raised to life for our justification. *f*

Peace and Joy

5 Therefore, since we have been justified *g* through faith, *h* we *u* have peace *i* with God through our Lord Jesus Christ, *j* ²through whom we have gained access *k* by faith into this grace in which we now stand. *l* And we *u* rejoice in the hope *m* of the glory of God. ³Not only so, but we *u* also rejoice in our sufferings, *n* because we know that suffering produces perseverance; *o* ⁴perseverance, character; and character, hope. ⁵And hope *p* does not disappoint us, because God has poured out his love *q* into our hearts by the Holy Spirit, *r* whom he has given us.

⁶You see, at just the right time, *s* when

we were still powerless, *t* Christ died for the ungodly. *u* ⁷Very rarely will anyone die for a righteous man, though for a good man someone might possibly dare to die. ⁸But God demonstrates his own love for us in this: While we were still sinners, Christ died for us. *v*

⁹Since we have now been justified *w* by his blood, *x* how much more shall we be saved from God's wrath *y* through him! ¹⁰For if, when we were God's enemies, *z* we were reconciled *a* to him through the death of his Son, how much more, having been reconciled, shall we be saved through his life! *b* ¹¹Not only is this so, but we also rejoice in God through our Lord Jesus Christ, through whom we have now received reconciliation. *c*

Death Through Adam, Life Through Christ

¹²Therefore, just as sin entered the

Cross references

4:22 *a*S ver 3
4:24 *b*Ps 102:18; Hab 2:2; Ro 15:4; 1Co 9:10; 10:11; 2Ti 3:16,17 *c*Ro 10:9; 1Pe 1:21 *d*S Ac 2:24
4:25 *e*Isa 53:5,6; Ro 5:6,8; 8:32; 2Co 5:21 *f*Isa 53:11; Ro 3:24; 5:1,9,16, 18; 8:30; 1Co 6:11; 2Co 5:15
5:1 *g*S Ro 4:25 *h*S Ro 3:28
5:2 *i*S Lk 2:14 *j*ver 10 *k*Eph 2:18; 3:12 *l*1Co 15:1
5:3 *m*S Heb 3:6 *n*S Mt 5:12
5:5 *o*S Heb 10:36 *p*Php 1:20; S Heb 3:6; 1Jn 3:2,3 *q*ver 8; Jn 3:16; Ro 8:39
5:6 *r*Ac 2:33; 10:45; Tit 3:5,6 *s*Mk 1:15; Gal 4:4; Eph 1:10
*t*ver 8,10
5:8 *u*Ro 4:25 *v*Jn 3:16; 15:13; 1Pe 3:18; 1Jn 3:16; 4:10
5:9 *w*S Ro 4:25 *x*S Ro 3:25 *y*S Ro 1:18
5:10 *z*Ro 11:28; Col 1:21 *a*ver 11; Ro 11:15; 2Co 5:18,19; Col 1:20,22 *b*Ro 8:34; Heb 7:25 **5:11** *c*S ver 10

u *1,2,3* Or *let us*

4:22 *This is why.* Abraham's faith was "credited to him as righteousness" because it was true faith, i.e., complete confidence in God's promise.

4:23 *not for him alone.* Abraham's experience was not private or individual but had broad implications. If justification by faith was true for him, it is universally true.

4:24 *but also for us.* As Abraham was justified because he believed in a God who brought life from the dead, so we will be justified by believing "in him who raised Jesus our Lord from the dead."

4:25 These words, which reflect the Septuagint (Greek) translation of Isa 53:12, are probably quoted from a Christian confessional formula.

5:1 *peace with God.* Not merely a subjective feeling (peace of mind) but primarily an objective status, a new relationship with God: Once we were his enemies, but now we are his friends (see v. 10; Eph 2:16; Col 1:21–22).

5:2 *access.* Jesus ushers us into the presence of God. The heavy curtain (of the temple) that separated man from God and God from man has been removed (see note on Mt 27:51). *hope of the glory of God.* The Christian's confidence that the purpose for which God created him will be ultimately realized (see note on 3:23).

5:3 *rejoice in our sufferings.* Not "because of" but "in." Paul does not advocate a morbid view of life but a joyous and triumphant one.

5:4 A Christian can rejoice in suffering because he knows that it is not meaningless. Part of God's purpose is to produce character in his children.

5:5 *hope does not disappoint us.* The believer's hope is not to be equated with unfounded optimism. On the contrary, it is the blessed assurance of our future destiny and is based on God's love, which is revealed to us by the Holy Spirit and objectively demonstrated to us in the death of Christ. Paul has moved from faith (v. 1) to hope (vv. 2,4–5) to love (v. 5; see 1Co 13:13; see also note on 1Th 1:3). *has poured out.* The verb indicates a present status resulting from a past action. When we first believed in Christ, the Holy Spirit poured out his love in our hearts, and his love for us contin-

ues to dwell in us.

5:6 *the right time.* The appointed moment in God's redemptive plan (Mk 1:15; Gal 4:4). *Christ died for the ungodly.* Christ's love is grounded in God's free grace and is not the result of any inherent worthiness found in its objects (mankind). In fact, it is lavished on us in spite of our undesirable character.

5:7 *righteous man . . . good man.* We were neither righteous nor good, but sinners, when Christ died for us (see v. 8; 3:10–12).

5:9 *by his blood.* By laying down his life as a sacrifice—a reference to Christ's death for our sins (see 3:25). *God's wrath.* The final judgment, as the verb "shall be saved" makes clear (cf. 1Th 1:9–10).

5:10 *God's enemies.* Man is the enemy of God, not the reverse. Thus the hostility must be removed from man if reconciliation is to be accomplished. God took the initiative in bringing this about through the death of his Son (see v. 11; Col 1:21–22). *reconciled.* To reconcile is "to put an end to hostility," and is closely related to the term "justify," as the parallelism in vv. 9–10 indicates:

v. 9	v. 10
justified	reconciled
by his blood	through the death of his Son
shall we be saved	shall we be saved

saved through his life. A reference to the unending life and ministry of the resurrected Christ for his people (see Heb 7:25). Since we were reconciled when we were God's enemies, we will be saved because Christ lives to keep us.

5:11 *we have now received reconciliation.* Reconciliation, like justification (v. 1), is a present reality for Christians and is something to rejoice about.

5:12–21 A contrast between Adam and Christ. Adam introduced sin and death into the world; Christ brought righteousness and life. The comparison begun in v. 12 is completed in v. 18; these two verses summarize the whole passage. These two men also sum up the message of the book up to this point. Adam stands for man's condemnation (1:18–3:20); Christ stands for the believer's justification

world through one man, *d* and death through sin, *e* and in this way death came to all men, because all sinned— *f* ¹³for before the law was given, sin was in the world. But sin is not taken into account when there is no law. *g* ¹⁴Nevertheless, death reigned from the time of Adam to the time of Moses, even over those who did not sin by breaking a command, as did Adam, *h* who was a pattern of the one to come. *i*

¹⁵But the gift is not like the trespass. For if the many died by the trespass of the one man, *j* how much more did God's grace and the gift that came by the grace of the one man, Jesus Christ, *k* overflow to the many! ¹⁶Again, the gift of God is not like the result of the one man's sin: The judgment followed one sin and brought condemnation, but the gift followed many trespasses and brought justification. ¹⁷For if, by the trespass of the one man, death *l* reigned through that one man, how much more will those who receive God's abundant provision of grace and of the gift of righteousness reign in life *m* through the one man, Jesus Christ.

¹⁸Consequently, just as the result of one

trespass was condemnation for all men, *n* so also the result of one act of righteousness was justification *o* that brings life *p* for all men. ¹⁹For just as through the disobedience of the one man *q* the many were made sinners, *r* so also through the obedience *s* of the one man the many will be made righteous.

²⁰The law was added so that the trespass might increase. *t* But where sin increased, grace increased all the more, *u* ²¹so that, just as sin reigned in death, *v* so also grace *w* might reign through righteousness to bring eternal life *x* through Jesus Christ our Lord.

Dead to Sin, Alive in Christ

6 What shall we say, then? *y* Shall we go on sinning so that grace may increase? *z* ²By no means! We died to sin; *a* how can we live in it any longer? ³Or don't you know that all of us who were baptized *b* into Christ Jesus were baptized into his death? ⁴We were therefore buried with him through baptism into death *c* in order that, just as Christ was raised from the dead *d* through the glory of the Father, we too may live a new life. *e*

Cross references (center column)

5:12 *d*ver 15,16, 17; Ge 3:1-7; 1Co 15:21,22
*e*ver 14,18; Ge 2:17; 3:19; S Ro 6:23 /S Ro 3:9
5:13 *g*S Ro 4:15
5:14 *h*Ge 3:11,12 *i*1Co 15:22,45
5:15 *j*ver 12,18, 19. *k*Ac 15:11
5:17 *l*S ver 12 *m*Jn 10:10

5:18 *n*S ver 12 *o*S Ro 4:25 *p*Isa 53:11
5:19 *q*ver 12 *r*S Ro 3:9 *s*S Php 2:8
5:20 *t*Ro 3:20; 7:7,8; Gal 3:19 *u*Ro 6:1; 1Ti 1:13,14
5:21 *v*ver 12,14; S Ro 6:16 *w*S Ro 3:24 *x*S Mt 25:46
6:1 *y*S Ro 8:31 *z*ver 15; Ro 3:5,8
6:2 *a*S ver 6; ver 10,11; S ver 18; Ro 8:13; Col 3:5; 1Pe 2:24
6:3 *b*S Mt 28:19
6:4 *c*S ver 6 *d*S Ac 2:24 *e*Ro 7:6; S 2Co 5:17; Eph 4:22-24; Col 3:10

Study notes (bottom)

(3:21–5:11).

5:12 *death.* Physical death is the penalty for sin. It is also the symbol of spiritual death, man's ultimate separation from God. *because all sinned.* Not a repetition of 3:23. The context shows that Adam's sin involved the rest of mankind in condemnation (vv. 18–19) and death (v. 15). We do not start life with even the possibility of living it sinlessly; we begin with a sinful nature (see Ge 8:21; Ps 51:5; 58:3; Eph 2:3).

5:13 *sin is not taken into account.* In the period when there was no (Mosaic) law, sin ("breaking a command," v. 14) was not charged against man (see 4:15). Death, however, continued to occur (v. 14). Since death is the penalty for sin, people between Adam and Moses were involved in the sin of someone else, namely, Adam (see note on v. 12).

5:14 *pattern.* Adam by his sin brought universal ruin on the human race. In this act he is the prototype of Christ, who through one righteous act (v. 18) brought universal blessing. The analogy is one of contrast.

5:15 *the many.* The same as "all men" in v. 12 (see Isa 53:11; Mk 10:45). *how much more.* A theme that runs through this section. God's grace is infinitely greater for good than is Adam's sin for evil.

5:16 *gift of God.* Salvation. *many trespasses.* The sins of the succeeding generations.

5:17 *will . . . reign in life.* The future reign of believers with Jesus Christ (2Ti 2:12; Rev 22:5).

5:18 *life for all men.* Does not mean that everyone eventually will be saved, but that salvation is available to all. To be effective, God's gracious gift must be received (see v. 17).

5:19 *made righteous.* A reference to a standing (status) before God (see 2Co 5:21), not to a change in character. The latter (the doctrine of sanctification) is developed in chs. 6–8.

5:20 *law was added.* Not to bring about redemption and to point up the need for it. The law made sin even more sinful by revealing what sin is in stark contrast to God's holiness.

6:1–8:39 In 3:21–5:21 Paul explains how God has provided for our redemption and justification. He next explains the doctrine of sanctification—the process by which believers grow to maturity in Christ. He treats this subject in three parts: (1) freedom from sin's tyranny (ch. 6), (2) freedom from the law's condemnation (ch. 7) and (3) life in the power of the Holy Spirit (ch. 8).

6:1 *Shall we go on sinning so that grace may increase?* This question arose out of what Paul had just said in 5:20: "Where sin increased, grace increased all the more." Such a question expresses an antinomian (against law) viewpoint. Apparently some objected to Paul's teaching of justification by faith alone because they thought it would lead to moral irresponsibility.

6:2 *died to sin.* The reference is to an event in the past and is explained in v. 3.

6:3–4 The when and how of the Christian's death to sin. In NT times baptism so closely followed conversion that the two were considered part of one event (see Ac 2:38 and note). So although baptism is not a means by which we enter into a vital faith relationship with Jesus Christ, it is closely associated with faith. Baptism depicts graphically what happens as a result of the Christian's union with Christ, which comes with faith—through faith we are united with Christ, just as through our natural birth we are united with Adam. As we fell into sin and became subject to death in father Adam, so we now have died and been raised again with Christ—which baptism symbolizes.

6:4 *buried with him through baptism into death.* Amplified in vv. 5–7. *through the glory of the Father.* By the power of God. God's glory is his divine excellence, his perfection. Any one of his attributes is a manifestation of his excellence. Thus his power is a manifestation of his glory, as is his righteousness (see 3:23). Glory and power are often closely related in the Bible (see Ps 145:11; Col 1:11; 1Pe 4:11; Rev 1:6; 4:11; 5:12–13; 7:12; 19:1). *live a new life.* Amplified in vv. 8–10.

5If we have been united with him like this in his death, we will certainly also be united with him in his resurrection.[f] 6For we know that our old self[g] was crucified with him[h] so that the body of sin[i] might be done away with,[v] that we should no longer be slaves to sin[j]— 7because anyone who has died has been freed from sin.[k]

8Now if we died with Christ, we believe that we will also live with him.[l] 9For we know that since Christ was raised from the dead,[m] he cannot die again; death no longer has mastery over him.[n] 10The death he died, he died to sin[o] once for all;[p] but the life he lives, he lives to God.

11In the same way, count yourselves dead to sin[q] but alive to God in Christ Jesus. 12Therefore do not let sin reign[r] in your mortal body so that you obey its evil desires. 13Do not offer the parts of your body to sin, as instruments of wickedness,[s] but rather offer yourselves to God, as those who have been brought from death to life; and offer the parts of your body to him as instruments of righteousness.[t] 14For sin shall not be your master,[u] because you are not under law,[v] but under grace.[w]

6:5 [f]ver 4,8; Ro 8:11; 2Co 4:10; Eph 2:6; Php 3:10,11; Col 2:12; 3:1; 2Ti 2:11 **6:6** [g]S Gal 5:24; Eph 4:22; Col 3:9 [h]S ver 2; ver 3-8; 2Co 4:10; Gal 2:20; 5:24; 6:14; Php 3:10; Col 2:12,20; 3:3 [i]Ro 7:24 [j]S ver 16 **6:7** [k]S ver 18 **6:8** [l]S ver 5 **6:9** [m]ver 4; S Ac 2:24 [n]Rev 1:18 **6:10** [o]S ver 2 [p]S Heb 7:27 **6:11** [q]S ver 2 **6:12** [r]ver 16 **6:13** [s]ver 16,19; Ro 7:5 [t]Ro 12:1; 2Co 5:14,15; 1Pe 2:24 **6:14** [u]S ver 16 [v]S Ro 2:12 [w]S Ro 3:24

Slaves to Righteousness

15What then? Shall we sin because we are not under law but under grace?[x] By no means! 16Don't you know that when you offer yourselves to someone to obey him as slaves, you are slaves to the one whom you obey[y]—whether you are slaves to sin,[z] which leads to death,[a] or to obedience, which leads to righteousness? 17But thanks be to God[b] that, though you used to be slaves to sin,[c] you wholeheartedly obeyed the form of teaching[d] to which you were entrusted. 18You have been set free from sin[e] and have become slaves to righteousness.[f]

19I put this in human terms[g] because you are weak in your natural selves. Just as you used to offer the parts of your body in slavery to impurity and to ever-increasing wickedness, so now offer them in slavery to righteousness[h] leading to holiness. 20When you were slaves to sin,[i] you were free from the control of righteousness.[j] 21What benefit did you reap at that time from the things you are now ashamed of? Those things result in death![k] 22But now

6:15 [x]ver 1,14 **6:16** [y]2Pe 2:19 [z]ver 6,12,14,17,20; Ge 4:7; Ps 51:5; 119:133; Jn 8:34; Ro 5:21; 7:14,23,25; 8:2; 2Pe 2:19 [a]S ver 23 **6:17** [b]Ro 1:8; S 2Co 2:14 [c]S ver 16 [d]2Ti 1:13 **6:18** [e]S ver 2; ver 7,22; Ro 8:2; 1Pe 4:1; S ver 16 [f]S ver 22 **6:19** [g]Ro 3:5; Gal 3:15 [h]S ver 13; S ver 22 **6:20** [i]S ver 16 [j]ver 16 **6:21** [k]S ver 23

[v]6 Or *be rendered powerless*

6:6 *our old self.* Our unregenerate self; what we once were. *body of sin.* The self in its pre-Christian state, dominated by sin. This is a figurative expression in which the old self is personified. It is a "body" that can be put to death. For the believer, this old self has been "rendered powerless" (see NIV text note) so that it can no longer enslave us to sin—whatever lingering vitality it may yet exert in its death throes.

6:7 *has died.* The believer's death with Christ to sin's ruling power. *freed from sin.* Set free from its shackles and power.

6:8 As resurrection followed death in the experience of Christ, so the believer who dies with Christ is raised to a new quality of moral life here and now. Resurrection in the sense of a new birth is already a fact, and it increasingly exerts itself in the believer's life.

6:10 *he died to sin once for all.* In his death Christ (for the sake of sinners) submitted to the "reign" of sin (5:21); but his death broke the judicial link between sin and death, and he passed forever from the sphere of sin's "reign." Having been raised from the dead, he now lives forever to glorify God. *to God.* For the glory of God.

6:11 *count yourselves.* The first step toward victory over sin in the believer's life (for the succeeding steps see note on vv. 12–13). He is dead to sin and alive to God, and by faith he is to live in the light of this truth. *in Christ.* The first occurrence in Romans of this phrase, which is found often in Paul's writings. True believers are "in Christ" because they have died with Christ and have been raised to new life with him.

6:12–13 A call for the Christian to become in experience what he already is in position—dead to sin (see vv. 5–7) and alive to God (see vv. 8–10). The second step toward the Christian's victory over sin is refusal to let sin reign in his life (v. 12). The third step is to offer himself to God (v. 13).

6:13 *offer.* Put yourselves in the service of, perhaps also echoing the language of sacrifice. *parts of your body.* All the separate capacities of your being (also in v. 19).

6:14 *sin shall not be your master.* Paul conceived of sin as a power that enslaves, and so personified it. *not under law.* The meaning is not that the Christian has been freed from all moral authority. He has, however, been freed from the law in the manner in which God's people were under law in the OT era. Law provides no enablement to resist the power of sin; it only condemns the sinner. But grace enables. *under grace.* For the disciplinary aspect of grace see Tit 2:11–12.

6:15–23 The question raised here seems to come from those who are afraid that the doctrine of justification by faith alone will remove all moral restraint. Paul rejects such a suggestion and shows that a Christian does not throw morality to the winds. To the contrary, he exchanges sin for righteousness as his master.

6:16 The contrast between sin and obedience suggests that sin is by nature disobedience to God.

6:17 *wholeheartedly obeyed.* Christian obedience is not forced or legalistic, but willing. *form of teaching.* May refer to a summary of the moral and ethical teachings of Christ that was given to new converts in the early church.

6:18 *slaves to righteousness.* A Christian has changed masters. Whereas he was formerly a slave to sin, he becomes a slave (a willing servant) to righteousness.

6:19 *I put this in human terms.* An apology for using an imperfect analogy. The word "slave" when applied to Christians, who are free in Christ, naturally presents problems.

6:22 *set free from sin.* See note on v. 6. *holiness.* Slavery to God produces holiness, and the end of the process is eternal life (viewed not in its present sense but in its final, future sense). There is no eternal life without holiness (see Heb

that you have been set free from sin[l] and have become slaves to God,[m] the benefit you reap leads to holiness, and the result is eternal life.[n] 23For the wages of sin is death,[o] but the gift of God is eternal life[p] in[w] Christ Jesus our Lord.

An Illustration From Marriage

7 Do you not know, brothers[q]—for I am speaking to men who know the law—that the law has authority over a man only as long as he lives? 2For example, by law a married woman is bound to her husband as long as he is alive, but if her husband dies, she is released from the law of marriage.[r] 3So then, if she marries another man while her husband is still alive, she is called an adulteress.[s] But if her husband dies, she is released from that law and is not an adulteress, even though she marries another man.

4So, my brothers, you also died to the law[t] through the body of Christ,[u] that you might belong to another,[v] to him who was raised from the dead, in order that we might bear fruit to God. 5For when we were controlled by the sinful nature,[x w] the sinful passions aroused by the law[x] were at work in our bodies,[y] so that we bore fruit for death.[z] 6But now, by dying to what once bound us, we have been

released from the law[a] so that we serve in the new way of the Spirit, and not in the old way of the written code.[b]

Struggling With Sin

7What shall we say, then?[c] Is the law sin? Certainly not![d] Indeed I would not have known what sin was except through the law.[e] For I would not have known what coveting really was if the law had not said, "Do not covet."[y f] 8But sin, seizing the opportunity afforded by the commandment,[g] produced in me every kind of covetous desire. For apart from law, sin is dead.[h] 9Once I was alive apart from law; but when the commandment came, sin sprang to life and I died. 10I found that the very commandment that was intended to bring life[i] actually brought death. 11For sin, seizing the opportunity afforded by the commandment,[j] deceived me,[k] and through the commandment put me to death. 12So then, the law is holy, and the commandment is holy, righteous and good.[l]

13Did that which is good, then, become death to me? By no means! But in order

Cross references

6:22 /S ver 18; [m]ver 18,19; Ro 7:25; 1Co 7:22; Eph 6:6; 1Pe 2:16
6:23 [o]ver 16,21; Ge 2:17; Pr 10:16; Eze 18:4; Ro 1:32; S 5:12; 7:5,13; 8:6,13; Gal 6:7,8; Jas 1:15
[p]S Mt 25:46
7:1 [q]S Ac 1:16; S 22:5; Ro 1:13; 1Co 1:10; 5:11; 6:6; 14:20,26; Gal 3:15; 6:18
7:2 [r]1Co 7:39
7:3 [s]S Lk 16:18
7:4 [t]ver 6; Gal 2:19; 3:23-25; 4:31; 5:1 [u]Col 1:22; [v]Gal 2:19,20
7:5 [w]S Gal 5:24; [x]Ro 7:7-11; [y]Ro 6:13; [z]S Ro 6:23
7:6 [a]S ver 4; [b]Ro 2:29; 2Co 3:6
7:7 [c]S Ro 8:31; [d]S ver 12; [e]S Ro 4:15; [f]Ex 20:17; Dt 5:21
7:8 [g]ver 11; [h]S Ro 4:15
7:10 [i]Lev 18:5; Lk 10:26-28; S Ro 10:5; Gal 3:12
7:11 [j]ver 8; [k]Ge 3:13
7:12 [l]ver 7,13,14,16; Ro 8:4; Gal 3:21; 1Ti 1:8; S Ro 4:15

[w]23 Or through   [x]5 Or the flesh; also in verse 25
[y]7 Exodus 20:17; Deut. 5:21

12:14). Anyone who has been justified will surely give evidence of that fact by the presence of holiness in his life. For other occurrences of the word "holiness" see v. 19; 1Co 1:30; 1Th 4:3–4,7; 2Th 2:13; 1Ti 2:15; Heb 12:14; 1Pe 1:2.
6:23 Two kinds of servitude are contrasted here. One brings death as its wages; the other results in eternal life, not as wages earned or merited, but as a gift of God. For the contrast between wages and gift see 4:4.
7:1 law. Perhaps Paul has in mind the Mosaic law, but his concern here is with the fundamental character of law as such.
7:2–3 These verses illustrate the principle set down in v. 1. Death decisively changes a person's relationship to the law.
7:4 So. Paul now draws the conclusion from the principle stated in v. 1 and illustrated in vv. 2–3. died to the law. The law's power to condemn no longer threatens the Christian, whose death here is to be understood in terms of 6:2–7. There, however, he dies to sin; here he dies to the law. The result is that the law has no more hold on him. through the body of Christ. His physical body (self) crucified. belong to another. The resurrected Christ (see 6:5). The purpose of this union is to produce the fruit of holiness.
7:5 controlled by the sinful nature. A condition, so far as Christians are concerned, that belongs to the past—the unregenerate state. aroused by the law. The law not only reveals sin; it also stimulates it. The natural tendency in man is to desire the forbidden thing. death. Physical death and, beyond that, spiritual death—final separation from God—were the fruit of our "union" with the law.
7:6 what once bound us. The law; see vv. 4,6. released from the law. In the sense of its condemnation (see note on v. 4). new way of the Spirit. See note on 8:4. old way of the

written code. Life under the OT law.
7:7 Is the law sin? This question was occasioned by the remarks about the law in vv. 4–6. I. Paul seems to be using the first person pronoun of himself, but also as representative of mankind in general (vv. 7–12) and of Christians in particular (vv. 13–25). I would not have known what sin was. The law fulfilled the important function of revealing the presence and fact of sin.
7:8 opportunity afforded by the commandment. See note on v. 5. sin is dead. Not nonexistent but not fully perceived.
7:9 Once I was alive. Paul reviews his own experience from the vantage point of his present understanding. Before he realized that the law condemned him to death, he was alive. Reference is to the time either before his bar mitzvah (see below) or before his conversion, when the true rigor of the law became clear to him (see Lk 18:20–21; Php 3:6). when the commandment came. When Paul came to the realization that he stood guilty before the law—a reference either to his bar mitzvah, when he, at age 13, assumed full responsibility for the law, or to the time when he became aware of the full force of the law (at his conversion). I died. Paul came to realize he was condemned to death, because law reveals sin, and sin's wages is death (6:23).
7:10 was intended to bring life. See Lev 18:5. As it worked out, law became the avenue through which sin entered—both in Paul's experience and in that of mankind. Instead of giving life, the law brought condemnation; instead of producing holiness, it stimulated sin.
7:12 the law is holy. Despite the despicable use that sin made of the law, the law was not to blame. The law is God's and as such is holy, righteous and good.
7:13–25 Whether Paul is describing a Christian or non-Christian experience has been hotly debated through the

that sin might be recognized as sin, it produced death in me[m] through what was good,[n] so that through the commandment sin might become utterly sinful.

[14]We know that the law is spiritual; but I am unspiritual,[o] sold[p] as a slave to sin.[q] [15]I do not understand what I do. For what I want to do I do not do, but what I hate I do.[r] [16]And if I do what I do not want to do, I agree that the law is good.[s] [17]As it is, it is no longer I myself who do it, but it is sin living in me.[t] [18]I know that nothing good lives in me, that is, in my sinful nature.[z][u] For I have the desire to do what is good, but I cannot carry it out. [19]For what I do is not the good I want to do; no, the evil I do not want to do—this I keep on doing.[v] [20]Now if I do what I do not want to do, it is no longer I who do it, but it is sin living in me that does it.[w]

[21]So I find this law at work:[x] When I want to do good, evil is right there with me. [22]For in my inner being[y] I delight in God's law;[z] [23]but I see another law at work in the members of my body, waging war[a] against the law of my mind and mak-

ing me a prisoner of the law of sin[b] at work within my members. [24]What a wretched man I am! Who will rescue me from this body of death?[c] [25]Thanks be to God—through Jesus Christ our Lord![d]

So then, I myself in my mind am a slave to God's law,[e] but in the sinful nature a slave to the law of sin.[f]

Life Through the Spirit

8 Therefore, there is now no condemnation[g] for those who are in Christ Jesus,[a][h] [2]because through Christ Jesus[i] the law of the Spirit of life[j] set me free[k] from the law of sin[l] and death. [3]For what the law was powerless[m] to do in that it was weakened by the sinful nature,[b][n] God did by sending his own Son in the likeness of sinful man[o] to be a sin offering.[c][p] And so he condemned sin in sinful man,[d] [4]in order that the righteous requirements[q] of the law might be fully met

Cross references (center column):
7:13 [m]S Ro 6:23; [n]S ver 12
7:14 [o]1Co 3:1; [p]1Ki 21:20,25; 2Ki 17:17; [q]S Ro 6:16
7:15 [r]ver 19; Gal 5:17
7:16 [s]S ver 12
7:17 [t]ver 20
7:18 [u]ver 25; S Gal 5:24
7:19 [v]ver 15
7:20 [w]ver 17
7:21 [x]ver 23,25
7:22 [y]Eph 3:16; [z]Ps 1:2; 40:8
7:23 [a]Gal 5:17; Jas 4:1; 1Pe 2:11
[b]S Ro 6:16
7:24 [c]Ro 6:6; 8:2
7:25 [d]S 2Co 2:14; [e]S Ro 6:22; [f]S Ro 6:16
8:1 [g]ver 34; [h]ver 39; S Ro 16:3
8:2 [i]Ro 7:25; [j]1Co 15:45; [k]Jn 8:32,36; S Ro 6:18; [l]S Ro 6:16; S 7:4
8:3 [m]Heb 7:18; 10:1-4; [n]Ro 7:18,19; S Gal 5:24; [o]S Php 2:7; [p]Heb 2:14,17
8:4 [q]Ro 2:26

Text notes:
[z]18 Or my flesh   [a]1 Some later manuscripts Jesus, who do not live according to the sinful nature but according to the Spirit,   [b]3 Or the flesh; also in verses 4, 5, 8, 9, 12 and 13   [c]3 Or man, for sin   [d]3 Or in the flesh

---

Commentary:

centuries. That he is speaking of the non-Christian life is suggested by: (1) the use of phrases such as "sold as a slave to sin" (v. 14), "I know that nothing good lives in me" (v. 18) and "What a wretched man I am!" (v. 24)—which do not seem to describe Christian experience; (2) the contrast between ch. 7 and ch. 8, making it difficult for the other view to be credible; (3) the problem of the value of conversion if one ends up in spiritual misery. In favor of the view that Paul is describing Christian experience are: (1) the use of the present tense throughout the passage; (2) Paul's humble opinion of himself (v. 18); (3) his high regard for God's law (vv. 14,16); (4) the location of this passage in the section of Romans where Paul is dealing with sanctification—the growth of the Christian in holiness.
7:13 Sin used a holy thing (law) for an unholy end (death). By this fact the contemptible nature of sin is revealed.
7:14 *spiritual.* The law had its origin in God. *I am.* The personal pronoun and the verb, taken together, suggest that Paul is describing his present (Christian) experience. *unspiritual.* Even a believer has the seeds of rebellion in his heart. *sold as a slave to sin.* A phrase so strong that many refuse to accept it as descriptive of a Christian. However, it may graphically point out the failure even of Christians to meet the radical ethical and moral demands of the gospel. It also points up the persistent nature of sin.
7:15 *I do not understand.* The struggle within creates tension, ambivalence and confusion.
7:16 *I agree that the law is good.* Even when Paul is rebellious and disobedient, the Holy Spirit reveals to him the essential goodness of the law.
7:17 *no longer I myself who do it.* Not an attempt to escape moral responsibility but a statement of the great control sin can have over a Christian's life.
7:18 *nothing good lives in me.* A reference to man's fallen nature, as the last phrase of the sentence indicates. Paul is not saying that no goodness at all exists in Christians.
7:20 *sin . . . does it.* See note on v. 17.
7:21 *law.* Here means "principle."
7:22 *I delight in God's law.* The Mosaic law or God's law

generally. It is difficult to see how a non-Christian could say this.
7:23 *another law.* A principle or force at work in Paul preventing him from giving obedience to God's law. *law of my mind.* His desire to obey God's law. *law of sin.* Essentially the same as "another law," mentioned above.
7:24 *body of death.* Figurative for the body of sin (6:6) that hung on him like a corpse and from which he could not gain freedom.
7:25 The first half of this verse is the answer to the question stated in v. 24—deliverance comes, not through legalistic effort, but through Christ. The last half is a summary of vv. 13–24. *I myself.* The real self—the inner being that delights in God's law (v. 22).
8:1 *condemnation.* The law brings condemnation because it points out, stimulates and condemns sin. But the Christian is no longer "under law" (6:14). *in Christ Jesus.* United with him, as explained in 6:1–10 (see note on 6:11).
8:2 *the law of the Spirit of life.* The controlling power of the Holy Spirit, who is life-giving. Paul uses the word "law" in several different ways in Romans—to mean, e.g., a controlling power (here); God's law (2:17–20; 9:31; 10:3–5); the Pentateuch (3:21b); the OT as a whole (3:19); a principle (3:27). *law of sin and death.* The controlling power of sin, which ultimately produces death.
8:3 *powerless to do.* The law was not able to overcome sin. It could point out, condemn and even stimulate sin, but it could not remove it. *in the likeness of sinful man.* Christ in his incarnation became truly a man, but, unlike all other men, was sinless. *in sinful man.* See NIV text note; "flesh" may refer either to man's flesh or to Christ's. If the latter, it states where God condemned sin, namely, in Christ's human (but not sinful) nature—the interpretation that seems more consistent with Paul's teaching.
8:4 *righteous requirements of the law.* The law still plays a role in the life of a believer—not, however, as a means of salvation but as a moral and ethical guide, obeyed out of love for God and by the power that the Spirit provides. This is the fulfillment of Jer 31:33–34 (a prophecy of the new cov-

in us, who do not live according to the sinful nature but according to the Spirit. [r]

[5]Those who live according to the sinful nature have their minds set on what that nature desires; [s] but those who live in accordance with the Spirit have their minds set on what the Spirit desires. [t] [6]The mind of sinful man [e] is death, [u] but the mind controlled by the Spirit is life [v] and peace; [7]the sinful mind [f] is hostile to God. [w] It does not submit to God's law, nor can it do so. [8]Those controlled by the sinful nature [x] cannot please God.

[9]You, however, are controlled not by the sinful nature [y] but by the Spirit, if the Spirit of God lives in you. [z] And if anyone does not have the Spirit of Christ, [a] he does not belong to Christ. [10]But if Christ is in you, [b] your body is dead because of sin, yet your spirit is alive because of righteousness. [11]And if the Spirit of him who raised Jesus from the dead [c] is living in you, he who raised Christ from the dead will also give life to your mortal bodies [d] through his Spirit, who lives in you.

[12]Therefore, brothers, we have an obligation—but it is not to the sinful nature, to live according to it. [e] [13]For if you live according to the sinful nature, you will die; [f]

but if by the Spirit you put to death the misdeeds of the body, [g] you will live, [h] [14]because those who are led by the Spirit of God [i] are sons of God. [j] [15]For you did not receive a spirit [k] that makes you a slave again to fear, [l] but you received the Spirit of sonship. [g] And by him we cry, "Abba, [h] Father." [m] [16]The Spirit himself testifies with our spirit [n] that we are God's children. [o] [17]Now if we are children, then we are heirs [p]—heirs of God and co-heirs with Christ, if indeed we share in his sufferings [q] in order that we may also share in his glory. [r]

Future Glory

[18]I consider that our present sufferings are not worth comparing with the glory that will be revealed in us. [s] [19]The creation waits in eager expectation for the sons of God [t] to be revealed. [20]For the creation was subjected to frustration, not by its own choice, but by the will of the one who subjected it, [u] in hope [21]that [i] the creation

8:4 [r]S Gal 5:16
8:5 [s]Gal 5:19-21
  [t]Gal 5:22-25
8:6 [u]S Ro 6:23
  [v]ver 13; Gal 6:8
8:7 [w]Jas 4:4
8:8 [x]S Gal 5:24
8:9 [y]S Gal 5:24
  [z]ver 11;
  1Co 6:19;
  2Ti 1:14
  [a]Jn 14:17;
  S Ac 16:7;
  1Jn 4:13
8:10 [b]ver 9;
  Ex 29:45;
  Jn 14:20,23;
  2Co 13:5;
  Gal 2:20;
  Eph 3:17;
  Col 1:27;
  Rev 3:20
8:11 [c]S Ac 2:24
  [d]Jn 5:21; S Ro 6:5
8:12 [e]ver 4;
  S Gal 5:24
8:13 [f]S Ro 6:23

8:14 [g]S Ro 6:2 [h]ver 6;
  Gal 6:8
  [i]S Gal 5:18
  [j]ver 19;
  Hos 1:10;
  Mal 3:17; Mt 5:9;
  S Jn 1:12;
  Gal 3:26; 4:5;
  Eph 1:5; Rev 21:7
8:15 [k]S Jn 20:22
  [l]S 2Ti 1:7
  [m]Mk 14:36;
  Gal 4:5,6
8:16 [n]2Co 1:22;
  Eph 1:13 [o]S ver
  14; S Jn 1:12
8:17
  [p]S Ac 20:32;
  Gal 3:29; 4:7;

Eph 3:6; Tit 3:7 [q]S 2Co 1:5 [r]2Ti 2:12; 1Pe 4:13 8:18
[s]2Co 4:17; 1Pe 4:13; 5:1 8:19 [t]S ver 14 8:20 [u]Ge 3:17-19;
5:29

[e]6 Or mind set on the flesh   [f]7 Or the mind set on
the flesh   [g]15 Or adoption   [h]15 Aramaic for Father
[i]20,21 Or subjected it in hope. [21]For

---

enant). *fully met.* Lit. "fulfilled." God's aim in sending his Son was that believers might be enabled to embody the true and full intentions of the law. *according to the Spirit.* How the law's righteous requirements can be fully met—by no longer letting the sinful nature hold sway but by yielding to the directing and empowering ministry of the Holy Spirit.
8:5–8 Two mind-sets are described here: that of the sinful nature and that of the Spirit. The former leads to death, the latter to life and peace. The sinful nature is bound up with death (v. 6), hostility to God (v. 7), insubordination (v. 7) and unacceptability to God (v. 8).
8:10 *your body is dead because of sin.* Even a Christian's body is subject to physical death, the consequence of sin. *your spirit is alive.* Or "the Spirit is life" (see v. 2). On this reading, "body" is understood as in 7:24. *because of righteousness.* Because the spirit of the Christian has been justified, it is not subject to death as is his body. The Christian is indwelt by the life-giving Spirit as a result of his justification.
8:11 For the close connection between the resurrection of Christ and that of believers see 1Co 6:14; 15:20,23; 2Co 4:14; Php 3:21; 1Th 4:14. *give life to your mortal bodies.* The resurrection of our bodies, guaranteed to believers by the indwelling presence of the Holy Spirit—whose presence is evidenced by a Spirit-controlled life (vv. 4–9), which in turn provides assurance that our resurrection is certain even now.
8:14 *sons of God.* God is the Father of all in the sense that he created all and his love and providential care are extended to all (see Mt 5:45). But not all are his children. Jesus said to the unbelieving Jews of his day, "You belong to your father, the devil" (Jn 8:44). People become children of God through faith in God's unique Son (see Jn 1:12–13), and being led by God's Spirit is the hallmark of this relationship.
8:15 *sonship.* The underlying word here is "adoption" (see

NIV text note). It occurs four other times in the NT (v. 23; 9:4; Gal 4:5 [see note there]; Eph 1:5). Adoption was common among the Greeks and Romans, who granted the adopted son all the privileges of a natural son, including inheritance rights. Christians are adopted sons by grace; Christ, however, is God's Son by nature. *Abba, Father.* Expressive of an especially close relationship to God (see also NIV text note).
8:16 *testifies with our spirit.* The inner testimony of the Holy Spirit to our relationship to Christ. *God's children.* The same as "sons of God," terms that in the NT are synonymous.
8:17 *heirs.* Those who have already entered, at least partially, into the possession of their inheritance. *co-heirs with Christ.* Everything really belongs to Christ, but by grace we share in what is his. *if indeed we share in his sufferings.* The Greek construction used here does not set forth a condition but states a fact. The meaning, then, is not that there is some doubt about sharing Christ's glory. Rather, despite the fact that Christians presently suffer, they are assured a future entrance into their inheritance.
8:19 *The creation.* Both animate and inanimate, but exclusive of human beings (see vv. 22–23, where "whole creation" and "we ourselves" are contrasted). *sons of God to be revealed.* Christians are already sons of God, but the full manifestation of all that this means will not come until the end (see 1Jn 3:1–2).
8:20 *was subjected to frustration.* A reference to Ge 3:17–19. *in hope.* A possible allusion to the promise of Ge 3:15.
8:21 *will be liberated from its bondage to decay.* The physical universe is not destined for destruction (annihilation) but for renewal (see 2Pe 3:13; Rev 21:1). And living things will no longer be subject to death and decay, as they are today.

itself will be liberated from its bondage to decay[v] and brought into the glorious freedom of the children of God. [w]

[22]We know that the whole creation has been groaning[x] as in the pains of childbirth right up to the present time. [23]Not only so, but we ourselves, who have the firstfruits of the Spirit,[y] groan[z] inwardly as we wait eagerly[a] for our adoption as sons, the redemption of our bodies. [b] [24]For in this hope we were saved. [c] But hope that is seen is no hope at all. [d] Who hopes for what he already has? [25]But if we hope for what we do not yet have, we wait for it patiently. [e]

[26]In the same way, the Spirit helps us in our weakness. We do not know what we ought to pray for, but the Spirit[f] himself intercedes for us[g] with groans that words cannot express. [27]And he who searches our hearts[h] knows the mind of the Spirit, because the Spirit intercedes[i] for the saints in accordance with God's will.

More Than Conquerors

[28]And we know that in all things God works for the good[j] of those who love him,[i] who[k] have been called[k] according to his purpose. [l] [29]For those God foreknew[m] he also predestined[n] to be conformed to the likeness of his Son, [o] that he might be the firstborn[p] among many

brothers. [30]And those he predestined,[q] he also called;[r] those he called, he also justified;[s] those he justified, he also glorified. [t]

[31]What, then, shall we say in response to this? [u] If God is for us,[v] who can be against us?[w] [32]He who did not spare his own Son,[x] but gave him up for us all—how will he not also, along with him, graciously give us all things? [33]Who will bring any charge[y] against those whom God has chosen? It is God who justifies. [34]Who is he that condemns?[z] Christ Jesus, who died[a]—more than that, who was raised to life[b]—is at the right hand of God[c] and is also interceding for us. [d] [35]Who shall separate us from the love of Christ?[e] Shall trouble or hardship or persecution or famine or nakedness or danger or sword?[f] [36]As it is written:

"For your sake we face death all day
    long;
we are considered as sheep to be
    slaughtered."[l] [g]

8:21 vAc 3:21;
2Pe 3:13;
Rev 21:1
wS Jn 1:12
8:22 xJer 12:4
8:23 yS 2Co 5:5
z2Co 5:2,4 aver
19; Gal 5:5 bver
11; Php 3:21
8:24 cJ Th 5:8;
Tit 3:7
dS 2Co 4:18
8:25 ePs 37:7
8:26 fver 15,16
gEph 6:18
8:27 hS Rev 2:23
iS ver 34
8:28 jGe 50:20;
Isa 38:17;
Jer 29:11 kver 30;
Ro 11:29;
1Co 1:9; Gal 1:6,
15; Eph 4:1,4;
1Th 2:12;
2Ti 1:9;
Heb 9:15;
1Pe 2:9; 2Pe 1:10
lEph 1:11; 3:11;
Heb 6:17
8:29 mRo 11:2;
1Pe 1:2 nEph 1:5,
11 o1Co 15:49;
2Co 3:18;
Php 3:21; 1Jn 3:2
pS Col 1:18

8:30 qEph 1:5,11
rS ver 28
sS Ro 4:25
tRo 9:23
8:31 uRo 4:1;
6:1; 7:7; 9:14,30
vEx 3:12;
Isa 41:10;
Hag 1:13
wPs 56:9; 118:6;
Isa 8:10;
Jer 20:11;
Heb 13:6
8:32 xGe 22:13;
Mal 3:17;

Jn 3:16; Ro 5:8 **8:33** yIsa 50:8,9 **8:34** zver 1 aRo 5:6-8
bS Ac 2:24 cS Mk 16:19 dver 27; Job 16:20; Isa 53:12;
Heb 7:25; 9:24; 1Jn 2:1 **8:35** ever 37-39 f1Co 4:11;
2Co 11:26,27 **8:36** gPs 44:22; 1Co 4:9; 15:30,31; 2Co 4:11;
6:9; 11:23

l28 Some manuscripts And we know that all things work
together for good to those who love God   k28 Or
works together with those who love him to bring about
what is good—with those who   l36 Psalm 44:22

8:22 *has been groaning.* Creation is personified as a woman in labor waiting for the birth of her child.
8:23 *firstfruits of the Spirit.* The Christian's possession of the Holy Spirit is not only evidence of his present salvation (vv. 14,16) but is also a pledge of his future inheritance—and not only a pledge but also the down payment on that inheritance (see 2Co 1:22; 5:5; Eph 1:14). *adoption as sons.* See note on v. 15. Christians are already God's children, but this is a reference to the full realization of our inheritance in Christ. *redemption of our bodies.* The resurrection, as the final stage of our adoption. The first stage was God's predestination of our adoption (see Eph 1:5); the second is our present inclusion as children of God (see v. 14; Gal 3:26).
8:24 *in this hope.* We are saved by faith (see Eph 2:8), not hope; but hope accompanies salvation.
8:26 *In the same way.* As hope sustains the believer in suffering, so the Holy Spirit helps him in prayer. *with groans that words cannot express.* In v. 23 it is the believer who groans; here it is the Holy Spirit. Whether Paul means words that are unspoken or words that cannot be expressed in human language is not clear—probably the former, though v. 27 seems to suggest the latter.
8:27 The relationship between the Holy Spirit and God the Father is so close that the Holy Spirit's prayers need not be audible. God knows his every thought.
8:28 *the good.* That which conforms us "to the likeness of his Son" (v. 29). *called.* Effectual calling: the call of God to which there is invariably a positive response.
8:29 *foreknew.* Some insist that the knowledge here is not abstract but is couched in love and mixed with purpose. They hold that God not only knew us before we had any knowledge of him but that he also knew us, in the sense of

choosing us by his grace, before the foundation of the world (see Eph 1:4; 2Ti 1:9 and notes). Others believe that Paul here refers to the fact that in eternity past God knew those who by faith would become his people. *predestined.* Predestination here is to moral conformity to the likeness of his Son. *that he might be the firstborn among many brothers.* The reason God foreknew, predestined and conformed believers to Christ's likeness is that the Son might hold the position of highest honor in the great family of God.
8:30 *predestined . . . glorified.* The sequence by which God carries out his predestination. *glorified.* Since this final stage is firmly grounded in God's set purpose, it is as certain as if it had already happened.
8:31 *If God is for us.* The form of the condition makes it clear that there is no doubt about it.
8:32 The argument (from the greater to the lesser) here is similar to that in 5:9–10. If God gave the supreme gift of his Son to save us, he will certainly also give whatever is necessary to bring to fulfillment the work begun at the cross. See note on Ge 22:16.
8:33–34 A court of law is in mind. No charge can be brought against the Christian because God has already pronounced a verdict of not guilty.
8:34 Three reasons are given as to why no one can condemn God's elect: (1) Christ died for us; (2) he is alive and seated at the right hand of God, the position of power; (3) he is interceding for us.
8:35–39 Paul wanted to show his readers that suffering does not separate believers from Christ but actually carries them along toward their ultimate goal.
8:36 Ps 44:22 is quoted to show that suffering has always been part of the experience of God's people.

37No, in all these things we are more than
conquerors[h] through him who loved us.[i]
38For I am convinced that neither death
nor life, neither angels nor demons,[m]
neither the present nor the future,[j] nor
any powers,[k] 39neither height nor depth,
nor anything else in all creation, will be
able to separate us from the love of God[l]
that is in Christ Jesus our Lord.[m]

God's Sovereign Choice

9 I speak the truth in Christ—I am not
lying,[n] my conscience confirms[o] it in
the Holy Spirit— 2I have great sorrow and
unceasing anguish in my heart. 3For I
could wish that I myself[p] were cursed[q]
and cut off from Christ for the sake of my
brothers,[r] those of my own race,[s] 4the
people of Israel.[t] Theirs is the adoption as
sons;[u] theirs the divine glory,[v] the covenants,[w] the receiving of the law,[x] the
temple worship[y] and the promises.[z]
5Theirs are the patriarchs,[a] and from them
is traced the human ancestry of Christ,[b]
who is God over all,[c] forever praised![n] [d]
Amen.
6It is not as though God's word[e] had
failed. For not all who are descended from
Israel are Israel.[f] 7Nor because they are
his descendants are they all Abraham's
children. On the contrary, "It is through
Isaac that your offspring will be reckoned."[o] [g] 8In other words, it is not the
natural children who are God's children,[h]
but it is the children of the promise who
are regarded as Abraham's offspring.[i] 9For
this was how the promise was stated: "At
the appointed time I will return, and Sarah
will have a son."[p] [j]
10Not only that, but Rebekah's children
had one and the same father, our father
Isaac.[k] 11Yet, before the twins were born
or had done anything good or bad[l]—in
order that God's purpose[m] in election
might stand: 12not by works but by him
who calls—she was told, "The older will
serve the younger."[q] [n] 13Just as it is written: "Jacob I loved, but Esau I hated."[r] [o]
14What then shall we say?[p] Is God unjust? Not at all![q] 15For he says to Moses,

8:37 [h]1Co 15:57 [i]Ro 5:8; Gal 2:20; Eph 5:2; Rev 1:5; 3:9 **8:38** [j]1Co 3:22 [k]Eph 1:21; Col 1:16; 1Pe 3:22 **8:39** [l]S Ro 5:8 [m]ver 1; S Ro 16:3 **9:1** [n]Ps 15:2; 2Co 11:10; Gal 1:20; 1Ti 2:7 [o]S Ro 1:9 **9:3** [p]Ex 32:32 [q]1Co 12:3; 16:22 [r]S Ac 22:5 [s]Ro 11:14 **9:4** [t]ver 6 [u]Ex 4:22; 6:7; Dt 7:6 [v]Heb 9:5 [w]Ge 17:2; Dt 4:13; Ac 3:25; Eph 2:12 [x]Ps 147:19 [y]Heb 9:1 [z]S Ac 13:32; S Gal 3:16 **9:5** [a]Ro 11:28 [b]Mt 1:1-16; Ro 1:3 [c]Jn 1:1; Col 2:9 [d]Ro 1:25; 2Co 11:31 **9:6** [e]S Heb 4:12 [f]Ro 2:28,29; Gal 6:16 **9:7** [g]Ge 21:12; Heb 11:18 **9:8** [h]S Ro 8:14 [i]S Gal 3:16 **9:9** [j]Ge 18:10,14 **9:10** [k]Ge 25:21 **9:11** [l]ver 16 [m]Ro 8:28 **9:12** [n]Ge 25:23 **9:13** [o]Mal 1:2,3 **9:14** [p]S Ro 8:31 [q]2Ch 19:7

[m] 38 Or *nor heavenly rulers* [n] 5 Or *Christ, who is over all. God be forever praised!* Or *Christ. God who is over all be forever praised!* [o] 7 Gen. 21:12 [p] 9 Gen. 18:10,14 [q] 12 Gen. 25:23 [r] 13 Mal. 1:2,3

8:37 *who loved us.* Referring especially to Christ's death on the cross.

8:39 *neither height nor depth.* It is impossible to get beyond God's loving reach. *nor anything else in all creation.* Includes all created things. Only God is not included, and he is the one who has justified us (v. 33).

9:1 *in the Holy Spirit.* Conscience is a reliable guide only when enlightened by the Holy Spirit.

9:3 *cursed.* The Greek for this word is *anathema,* and it means delivered over to the wrath of God for eternal destruction (see 1Co 12:3; 16:22; Gal 1:8–9). Such was Paul's great love for his fellow Jews. For a similar expression of love see Ex 32:32.

9:4 *people of Israel.* The descendants of Jacob (who was renamed Israel by God; see Ge 32:28). The name was used of the entire nation (see Jdg 5:7), then of the northern kingdom after the nation was divided (see 1Ki 12), the southern kingdom being called Judah. During the intertestamental period and later in NT times, Palestinian Jews used the title to indicate that they were the chosen people of God. Its use here is especially relevant because Paul is about to show that, despite Israel's unbelief and disobedience, God's promises to her are still valid. *adoption.* Israel had been accepted as God's son (see Ex 4:22–23; Jer 31:9; Hos 11:1). *glory.* The evidence of the presence of God among his people (see Ex 16:7,10; Lev 9:6,23; Nu 16:19). *covenants.* For example, the Abrahamic (Ge 15:17–21; 17:1–8); the Mosaic (Ex 19:5; 24:1–4), renewed on the plains of Moab (Dt 29:1–15), at Mounts Ebal and Gerizim (Jos 8:30–35) and at Shechem (Jos 24); the Levitical (Nu 25:12–13; Jer 33:21; Mal 2:4–5); the Davidic (2Sa 7; 23:5; Ps 89:3–4,28–29; 132:11–12); and the new (prophesied in Jer 31:31–40). *promises.* Especially those made to Abraham (Ge 12:7; 13:14–17; 17:4–8; 22:16–18) but also including the many OT Messianic promises (e.g., 2Sa 7:12,16; Isa 9:6–7; Jer 23:5; 31:31–34; Eze 34:23–24; 37:24–28).

9:5 *patriarchs.* Abraham, Isaac, Jacob and his sons. *Christ, who is God.* One of the clearest statements of the deity of Jesus Christ found in the entire NT, assuming the accuracy of the translation (see NIV text note). See also 1:4; Mt 1:23; 28:19; Lk 1:35; 5:20–21; Jn 1:1,3,10,14,18; 5:18; 2Co 13:14; Php 2:6; Col 1:15–20; 2:9; Tit 2:13; Heb 1:3,8; 2Pe 1:1; Rev 1:13–18; 22:13.

9:6 *God's word.* His clearly stated purpose, which has not failed, because "not all who are descended from Israel are Israel." Paul is not denying the election of all Israel (as a nation) but stating that within Israel there is a separation, that of unbelieving Israel and believing Israel. Physical descent is no guarantee of a place in God's family.

9:7 *descendants.* Physical descendants (e.g., Ishmael and his offspring).

9:8 *natural children.* Those merely biologically descended from Abraham. *God's children.* See v. 4. Not all Israelites were God's children. The reference is to the Israel of faith.

9:11 *done anything good or bad.* God's choice of Jacob was based on sovereign freedom, not on the fulfillment of any prior conditions. *God's purpose in election.* God's purpose embodied in his election (see note on Eph 1:4).

9:12 *not by works but by him who calls.* Before Rebekah's children were even born, God made a choice—a choice obviously not based on works. *calls.* See 8:28 and note.

9:13 *Jacob I loved, but Esau I hated.* Equivalent to "Jacob I chose, but Esau I rejected." In vv. 6–13 Paul is clearly dealing with personal and not national election—he is not portraying the nation Israel (Jacob) over the nation Edom (Esau)—though Mal 1:2–3 (see NIV text note) does speak of the nations. Paul's intention is evident in light of the problem he is addressing: How can God's promise stand when so many who comprise Israel (in the OT collective sense) are unbelieving and therefore cut off?

9:14 *Is God unjust?* Unjust to elect on the basis of his sovereign freedom, as with Jacob and Esau.

"I will have mercy on whom I have mercy,
and I will have compassion on whom I have compassion."[s] [r]

16It does not, therefore, depend on man's desire or effort, but on God's mercy.[s] 17For the Scripture says to Pharaoh: "I raised you up for this very purpose, that I might display my power in you and that my name might be proclaimed in all the earth."[t] [t] 18Therefore God has mercy on whom he wants to have mercy, and he hardens whom he wants to harden.[u]

19One of you will say to me:[v] "Then why does God still blame us?[w] For who resists his will?"[x] 20But who are you, O man, to talk back to God?[y] "Shall what is formed say to him who formed it,[z] 'Why did you make me like this?'"[u][a] 21Does not the potter have the right to make out of the same lump of clay some pottery for noble purposes and some for common use?[b]

22What if God, choosing to show his wrath and make his power known, bore with great patience[c] the objects of his wrath—prepared for destruction?[d] 23What if he did this to make the riches of his glory[e] known to the objects of his mercy, whom he prepared in advance for glory[f]— 24even us, whom he also called,[g] not only from the Jews but also from the Gentiles?[h] 25As he says in Hosea:

"I will call them 'my people' who are not my people;
and I will call her 'my loved one' who is not my loved one,"[v] [i]

26and,

"It will happen that in the very place where it was said to them,
'You are not my people,'
they will be called 'sons of the living God.'"[w][j]

27Isaiah cries out concerning Israel:

"Though the number of the Israelites be like the sand by the sea,[k]
only the remnant will be saved.[l]
28For the Lord will carry out his sentence on earth with speed and finality."[x] [m]

29It is just as Isaiah said previously:

"Unless the Lord Almighty[n]
had left us descendants,
we would have become like Sodom,
we would have been like Gomorrah."[y] [o]

Israel's Unbelief

30What then shall we say?[p] That the Gentiles, who did not pursue righteousness, have obtained it, a righteousness that is by faith;[q] 31but Israel, who pursued a

---

Cross references (center column):

9:15 [r]Ex 33:19
9:16 [s]Eph 2:8; Tit 3:5
9:17 [t]Ex 9:16; 14:4; Ps 76:10
9:18 [u]Ex 4:21; 7:3; 14:4,17; Dt 2:30; Jos 11:20; Ro 11:25
9:19 [v]Ro 11:19; 1Co 15:35; Jas 2:18 [w]Ro 3:7
9:20 [x]2Sa 16:10; 2Ch 20:6; Da 4:35 [y]Job 1:22; 9:12; 40:2 [z]Isa 64:8; Jer 18:6 [a]Isa 29:16; 45:9; 10:15
9:21 [b]2Ti 2:20
9:22 [c]S Ro 2:4 [d]Pr 16:4
9:23 [e]S Ro 2:4 /Ro 8:30
9:24 [g]S Ro 8:28 [h]S Ro 3:29
9:25 [i]Hos 2:23; 1Pe 2:10
9:26 [j]Hos 1:10; S Mt 16:16; S Ro 8:14
9:27 [k]Ge 22:17; Hos 1:10 [l]2Ki 19:4; Jer 44:14; 50:20; Joel 2:32; Ro 11:5
9:28 [m]Isa 10:22, 23
9:29 [n]Jas 5:4 [o]Isa 1:9; Ge 19:24-29; Dt 29:23; Isa 13:19; Jer 50:40
9:30 [p]S Ro 8:31 [q]Ro 1:17; 3:22; 4:5,13; 10:6; Gal 2:16; Php 3:9; Heb 11:7

[s]15 Exodus 33:19   [t]17 Exodus 9:16
[u]20 Isaiah 29:16; 45:9   [v]25 Hosea 2:23
[w]26 Hosea 1:10   [x]28 Isaiah 10:22,23
[y]29 Isaiah 1:9

9:15 Paul denies injustice in God's dealing with Isaac and Ishmael, and Jacob and Esau, by appealing to God's sovereign right to dispense mercy as he chooses.
9:16 *It.* God's choice, which is not controlled in any way by man. However, Paul makes it clear that the basis for Israel's rejection was her unbelief (see vv. 30–32).
9:17 *Pharaoh.* Pharaoh of the exodus. *raised you up.* Made him ruler of Egypt. *my name.* The character of God, particularly as revealed in the exodus (see Ex 15:13–18; Jos 2:10–11; 9:9; 1Sa 4:8).
9:18 The first part of this verse again echoes Ex 33:19 (see v. 15) and the last part such texts as Ex 7:3; 9:12; 14:4,17, in which God is said to harden the hearts of Pharaoh and the Egyptians. *on whom he wants to have mercy.* Cannot mean that God is arbitrary in his mercy, because Paul ultimately bases God's rejection of Israel on her unbelief (see vv. 30–32).
9:19 Someone may object: "If God determines whose heart is hardened and whose is not, how can God blame anyone for hardening his heart?"
9:20 *who are you, O man, to talk back to God?* Paul is not silencing all questioning of God by man, but he is speaking to those with an impenitent, God-defying attitude who want to make God answerable to man for what he does and who, by their questions, defame the character of God.
9:21 The analogy between God and the potter and between man and the pot should not be pressed to the extreme. The main point is the sovereign freedom of God in dealing with man.
9:22–23 An illustration of the principle stated in v. 21. The emphasis is on God's mercy, not his wrath.
9:22 No one can call God to account for what he does. But he does not exercise his freedom of choice arbitrarily, and he shows great patience even toward the objects of his wrath. In light of 2:4, the purpose of such patience is to bring about repentance.
9:23 *glory.* See note on 3:23.
9:25–26 In the original context these passages from Hosea refer to the spiritual restoration of Israel. But Paul finds in them the principle that God is a saving, forgiving, restoring God, who delights to take those who are "not my people" and make them "my people." Paul then applies this principle to Gentiles, whom God makes his people by sovereignly grafting them into covenant relationship (see ch. 11).
9:27–29 The two passages from Isaiah indicate that only a small remnant will survive from the great multitude of Israelites. God's calling includes both Jews and Gentiles (see v. 24), but the vast majority are Gentiles, as v. 30 suggests.
9:30–32 A new step in Paul's argument: The reason for Israel's rejection lay in the nature of her disobedience—she failed to obey her own God-given law, which in reality was pointing to Christ. She pursued the law—yet not by faith but by works. Thus the real cause of Israel's rejection was that she failed to believe.
9:31 *law of righteousness.* The law that prescribed the way to righteousness. Paul does not reject obedience to the law

law of righteousness,ʳ has not attained it.ˢ ³²Why not? Because they pursued it not by faith but as if it were by works. They stumbled over the "stumbling stone."ᵗ ³³As it is written:

"See, I lay in Zion a stone that causes men to stumble
and a rock that makes them fall,
and the one who trusts in him will never be put to shame."ᶻ ᵘ

10 Brothers, my heart's desireᵛ and prayer to God for the Israelites is that they may be saved. ²For I can testify about them that they are zealousʷ for God, but their zeal is not based on knowledge. ³Since they did not know the righteousness that comes from God and sought to establish their own, they did not submit to God's righteousness.ˣ ⁴Christ is the end of the lawʸ so that there may be righteousness for everyone who believes.ᶻ

⁵Moses describes in this way the righteousness that is by the law: "The man who does these things will live by

them."ᵃ ᵃ ⁶But the righteousness that is by faithᵇ says: "Do not say in your heart, 'Who will ascend into heaven?'ᵇ ᶜ (that is, to bring Christ down) ⁷or 'Who will descend into the deep?'ᵇ ᵈ (that is, to bring Christ up from the dead).ᵉ ⁸But what does it say? "The word is near you; it is in your mouth and in your heart,"ᶜ ᶠ that is, the word of faith we are proclaiming: ⁹That if you confessᵍ with your mouth, "Jesus is Lord,"ʰ and believeⁱ in your heart that God raised him from the dead,ʲ you will be saved. ᵏ ¹⁰For it is with your heart that you believe and are justified, and it is with your mouth that you confess and are saved. ¹¹As the Scripture says, "Anyone who trusts in him will never be put to shame."ᵈ ˡ ¹²For there is no difference between Jew and Gentileᵐ—the same Lord is Lord of allⁿ and richly blesses all who call on him, ¹³for,

---

Cross-references (center column):

9:31 ʳDt 6:25; Isa 51:1; Ro 10:2, 3; 11:7 ˢGal 5:4
9:32 ᵗ1Pe 2:8
9:33 ᵘIsa 8:14; 28:16; Ro 10:11; 1Pe 2:6,8
10:1 ᵛPs 20:4
10:2 ʷS Ac 21:20
10:3 ˣRo 1:17; S 9:31
10:4 ʸGal 3:24; Ro 7:1-4 ᶻS Ro 3:22
10:5 ᵃLev 18:5; Dt 4:1; 6:24; Ne 9:29; Pr 19:16; Isa 55:3; Eze 20:11,13,21; S Ro 7:10
10:6 ᵇS Ro 9:30 ᶜDt 30:12
10:7 ᵈDt 30:13 ᵉS Ac 2:24
10:8 ᶠDt 30:14
10:9 ᵍMt 10:32 ʰS Jn 13:13 ⁱS Jn 3:15 ʲS Ac 2:24 ᵏS Ro 11:14
10:11 ˡIsa 28:16; Ro 9:33
10:12 ᵐS Ro 3:22,29 ⁿS Mt 28:18

ᶻ33 Isaiah 8:14; 28:16   ᵃ5 Lev. 18:5
ᵇ6,7 Deut. 30:12-13   ᶜ8 Deut. 30:14
ᵈ11 Isaiah 28:16

---

but righteousness by works, the attempt to use the law to put God in one's debt.

9:32 *not by faith.* The failure of Israel was not that she pursued the wrong thing (i.e., righteous standing before God), but that she pursued it by works in a futile effort to merit God's favor rather than pursuing it by faith. *the "stumbling stone."* Jesus, the Messiah. God's rejection of Israel was not arbitrary but was based on Israel's rejection of God's way of gaining righteousness (faith).

9:33 The two passages from Isaiah, which are here combined, apparently were commonly used by early Christians in defense of Jesus' Messiahship (see 1Pe 2:4,6–8; see also Ps 118:22; Lk 20:17–18).

10:1 *prayer to God for the Israelites.* Paul often prayed for the churches (see Eph 1:15–23; Col 1:3; 1Th 1:2–3; 2Th 1:3). Here he prays for the salvation of his fellow countrymen.

10:2 *zealous for God.* The Jews' zeal for God (see Ac 21:20; 22:3; Gal 1:14) was commendable in that God was its object, but it was flawed because it was not based on right knowledge about God's way of salvation. Paul, before his conversion, was an example of such zeal (see Gal 1:14).

10:3 *righteousness that comes from God.* Righteous standing based on faith (see 1:17), which comes from God as a gift and cannot be earned by man's works. *their own.* Righteous standing based on mere human effort.

10:4 *Christ is the end of the law.* Although the Greek word for "end" (*telos*) can mean either (1) "termination," "cessation," or (2) "goal," "culmination," "fulfillment," it seems best here to understand it in the latter sense. Christ is the fulfillment of the law (see Mt 5:17) in the sense that he brought it to completion by obeying perfectly its demands and by fulfilling its types and prophecies. The Christian is no longer "under the law" (6:15), since Christ has freed him from its condemnation, but the law still plays a role in his life. He is liberated by the Holy Spirit to fulfill its moral demands (see 8:4). *righteousness.* The righteous standing before God that Christ makes available to everyone who believes (see notes on 1:17; 3:24).

10:5 *The man who does these things will live by them.* Lev

18:5 (see note there; see also Dt 6:25) speaks of the righteousness to which Israel was called under the Sinai covenant. Some understand Paul's purpose in quoting it here as describing the way of obtaining righteousness ("will live") by keeping the law (see 2:6–10). Others think that the reference is to Christ, who perfectly fulfilled the law's demands and thus makes salvation available to all who believe (see Heb 5:9).

10:6–7 The purpose of the OT quotation is to explain the nature of the righteousness that is by faith. It does not require heroic feats such as bringing Christ down from heaven or up from the grave. Dt 30:12–13 in its original context refers to the law, and Paul here applies the basic principle to Christ.

10:8 *The word is near you.* In the OT passage the "word" is God's word as found in the law. Paul takes the passage and applies it to the gospel, "the word of faith"—the main point being the accessibility of the gospel. Righteousness is gained by faith, not by deeds, and is readily available to anyone who will receive it freely from God through Christ.

10:9 *Jesus is Lord.* The earliest Christian confession of faith (cf. 1Co 12:3), probably used at baptisms. In view of the fact that "Lord" (Greek *kyrios*) is used over 6,000 times in the Septuagint (the Greek translation of the OT) to translate the name of Israel's God (Yahweh), it is clear that Paul, when using this word of Jesus, is ascribing deity to him. *in your heart.* In Biblical terms the heart is not merely the seat of the emotions and affections, but also of the intellect and will. *God raised him from the dead.* A bedrock truth of Christian doctrine (see 1Co 15:4,14,17) and the central thrust of apostolic preaching (see, e.g., Ac 2:31–32; 3:15; 4:10; 10:40). Christians believe not only that Jesus lived but also that he still lives. *will be saved.* In the future tense. Paul is thinking of final salvation—salvation at the last day.

10:10 Salvation involves inward belief ("with your heart") as well as outward confession ("with your mouth").

10:12 *no difference between Jew and Gentile.* In the sense that both are on the same footing as far as salvation is concerned (see v. 13).

10:13 Peter cited this same passage (Joel 2:32) on the day of Pentecost (Ac 2:21).

"Everyone who calls on the name of the Lord[o] will be saved."[e] [p]

[14]How, then, can they call on the one they have not believed in? And how can they believe in the one of whom they have not heard? And how can they hear without someone preaching to them? [15]And how can they preach unless they are sent? As it is written, "How beautiful are the feet of those who bring good news!"[f] [q]

[16]But not all the Israelites accepted the good news.[r] For Isaiah says, "Lord, who has believed our message?"[g][s] [17]Consequently, faith comes from hearing the message,[t] and the message is heard through the word of Christ.[u] [18]But I ask: Did they not hear? Of course they did:

"Their voice has gone out into all the
    earth,
their words to the ends of the
    world."[h] [v]

[19]Again I ask: Did Israel not understand? First, Moses says,

"I will make you envious[w] by those
    who are not a nation;
I will make you angry by a nation
    that has no understanding."[i] [x]

[20]And Isaiah boldly says,

"I was found by those who did not seek
    me;
I revealed myself to those who did
    not ask for me."[j] [y]

[21]But concerning Israel he says,

"All day long I have held out my hands

to a disobedient and obstinate people."[k] [z]

The Remnant of Israel

11 I ask then: Did God reject his people? By no means![a] I am an Israelite myself, a descendant of Abraham,[b] from the tribe of Benjamin.[c] [2]God did not reject his people,[d] whom he foreknew.[e] Don't you know what the Scripture says in the passage about Elijah—how he appealed to God against Israel: [3]"Lord, they have killed your prophets and torn down your altars; I am the only one left, and they are trying to kill me"[l]?[f] [4]And what was God's answer to him? "I have reserved for myself seven thousand who have not bowed the knee to Baal."[m] [g] [5]So too, at the present time there is a remnant[h] chosen by grace.[i] [6]And if by grace, then it is no longer by works;[j] if it were, grace would no longer be grace.[n]

[7]What then? What Israel sought so earnestly it did not obtain,[k] but the elect did. The others were hardened,[l] [8]as it is written:

"God gave them a spirit of stupor,
    eyes so that they could not see
    and ears so that they could not
      hear,[m]
to this very day."[o] [n]

Cross references (center column)

10:13 oS Ac 2:21
pJoel 2:32
10:15 qIsa 52:7;
Na 1:15
10:16 rHeb 4:2
sIsa 53:1;
Jn 12:38
10:17 tGal 3:2,5
uCol 3:16
10:18 vPs 19:4;
S Mt 24:14;
Ro 1:8; Col 1:6,
23; 1Th 1:8
10:19
wRo 11:11,14
xDt 32:21
10:20 yIsa 65:1;
Ro 9:30

10:21 zIsa 65:2;
Jer 35:17
11:1 aLev 26:44;
1Sa 12:22;
Ps 94:14;
Jer 31:37;
33:24-26
b2Co 11:22
cPhp 3:5
11:2 dS ver 1
eS Ro 8:29
11:3 f1Ki 19:10,
14
11:4 g1Ki 19:18
11:5 hS Ro 9:27
iS Ro 3:24
11:6 jRo 4:4
11:7 kRo 9:31
lver 25; S Ro 9:18
11:8
mS Mt 13:13-15
nDt 29:4;
Isa 29:10

e 13 Joel 2:32   f 15 Isaiah 52:7   g 16 Isaiah 53:1
h 18 Psalm 19:4   i 19 Deut. 32:21   j 20 Isaiah 65:1
k 21 Isaiah 65:2   l 3 1 Kings 19:10,14
m 4 1 Kings 19:18   n 6 Some manuscripts by grace. But
if by works, then it is no longer grace; if it were, work
would no longer be work.   o 8 Deut. 29:4;
Isaiah 29:10

10:14–15 Since it might be argued that Jews had never had a fair opportunity to hear and respond to the gospel, Paul, by means of a series of rhetorical questions, states (in reverse order) the conditions necessary to call on Christ and be saved: (1) a preacher sent from God, (2) proclamation of the message, (3) hearing the message, (4) believing the message.

10:15 *How beautiful are the feet of those who bring good news!* The quotation is from Isa 52:7, which refers to those who bring the exiles the good news of their imminent release from captivity in Babylon. Here it is applied to gospel preachers, who bring the good news of release from captivity to sin.

10:17 *word of Christ.* Either (1) the gospel concerning Christ, or (2) Christ speaking his message through his messengers.

10:18 *Their voice.* The quotation is from Ps 19:4, which refers to the testimony of the heavens to the glory of God. Here "their voice" is applied to gospel preachers and is used to show that Israel cannot offer the excuse that she did not have opportunity to hear, since preachers went everywhere. These words (originally used to describe God's revelation in nature) aptly describe the widespread preaching of the gospel, and Paul uses them to show that Jews had ample opportunity to hear the message of redemption.

10:19 *Did Israel not understand?* The quotation that follows (from Dt 32:21) answers this question by suggesting that the Gentiles, whom the Jews considered to be spiritually unenlightened, understood. Surely if they understood the message, the Jews could have. *those who are not a nation.* The Gentiles, those who are not a nation of God's forming in the sense that Israel was.

10:21 The responsibility for Israel's rejection as a nation rested with Israel herself. She had failed to meet God's requirement, namely, faith.

11:1 *reject.* Totally reject. There has always been a faithful remnant among the Jewish people.

11:2 *whom he foreknew.* See note on 8:29.

11:5 *remnant.* As it was in Elijah's day, so it was in Paul's day. Despite widespread apostasy, a faithful remnant of Jews remained. *chosen by grace.* The grounds for the existence of the remnant was not their good works but God's grace.

11:7 *What Israel sought so earnestly.* A righteous standing before God, which eluded the greater part of Israel. *the elect.* The faithful remnant among the Jews. *were hardened.* Because they refused the way of faith (see 9:31–32), God made them impervious to spiritual truth (see note on Isa 6:10)—a judicial hardening of Israel.

11:8 *to this very day.* The spiritual dullness of the Jews had continued from Isaiah's day to Paul's day.

9And David says:

"May their table become a snare and a
trap,
a stumbling block and a retribution
for them.
10May their eyes be darkened so they
cannot see,[o]
and their backs be bent forever."[p] [p]

Ingrafted Branches

11Again I ask: Did they stumble so as to
fall beyond recovery? Not at all![q] Rather,
because of their transgression, salvation
has come to the Gentiles[r] to make Israel
envious.[s] 12But if their transgression
means riches for the world, and their loss
means riches for the Gentiles,[t] how much
greater riches will their fullness bring!

13I am talking to you Gentiles. Inasmuch
as I am the apostle to the Gentiles,[u] I
make much of my ministry 14in the hope
that I may somehow arouse my own
people to envy[v] and save[w] some of them.
15For if their rejection is the reconciliation[x] of the world, what will their acceptance be but life from the dead?[y] 16If the
part of the dough offered as firstfruits[z] is
holy, then the whole batch is holy; if the
root is holy, so are the branches.

17If some of the branches have been broken off,[a] and you, though a wild olive
shoot, have been grafted in among the others[b] and now share in the nourishing sap
from the olive root, 18do not boast over
those branches. If you do, consider this:
You do not support the root, but the root
supports you.[c] 19You will say then,
"Branches were broken off so that I could
be grafted in." 20Granted. But they were
broken off because of unbelief, and you
stand by faith.[d] Do not be arrogant,[e] but
be afraid.[f] 21For if God did not spare the
natural branches, he will not spare you
either.

22Consider therefore the kindness[g] and
sternness of God: sternness to those who
fell, but kindness to you, provided that you
continue[h] in his kindness. Otherwise, you
also will be cut off.[i] 23And if they do not
persist in unbelief, they will be grafted in,
for God is able to graft them in again.[j]
24After all, if you were cut out of an olive
tree that is wild by nature, and contrary to

11:10 [o]ver 8 [p]Ps 69:22,23 **11:11** [q]ver 1 [r]S Ac 13:46 [s]ver 14; Ro 10:19 **11:12** [t]ver 25 **11:13** [u]S Ac 9:15 **11:14** [v]ver 11; Ro 10:19; 1Co 10:33; 1Th 2:16 [w]S Mt 1:21; S Lk 2:11; S Jn 3:17; Ac 4:12; 16:31; 1Co 1:21; 1Ti 2:4; Tit 3:5 **11:15** [x]S Ro 5:10 [y]Lk 15:24,32 **11:16** [z]Lev 23:10,17; Nu 15:18-21

11:17 [a]Jer 11:16; Jn 15:2 [b]Ac 2:39; Eph 2:11-13 **11:18** [c]Jn 4:22 **11:20** [d]1Co 10:12; 2Co 1:24 [e]1Ti 6:17 [f]1Pe 1:17 **11:22** [g]Ro 2:4 [h]1Co 15:2; Col 1:23; Heb 3:6 [i]Jn 15:2 **11:23** [j]2Co 3:16

[p]*10* Psalm 69:22,23

11:9–10 The passage from Ps 69:22–23 was probably originally spoken by David concerning his enemies; Paul uses it to describe the results of the divine hardening.
11:11 *their transgression.* The Jews' rejection of the gospel. *make Israel envious.* See v. 14; 10:19.
11:12 *riches for the world.* Equivalent to "riches for the Gentiles," a reference to the abundant benefits of salvation already enjoyed by believing Gentiles, which had come about because of the rejection of the gospel by the Jews. That rejection caused the apostles to turn to the Gentiles (see Ac 13:46–48; 18:6). *their loss.* Equivalent to "their transgression" (see note on v. 11), but focusing on the loss that this transgression entailed. *greater riches.* See note on v. 15. *their fullness.* The salvation of Israel (see vv. 26–27; see also the "fullness [NIV 'full number'] of the Gentiles," v. 25).
11:13 *apostle to the Gentiles.* See 1:5; Ac 9:15; Gal 1:16; 2:7,9.
11:15 *their rejection.* God's temporary and partial exclusion of the Jews. *reconciliation of the world.* Somewhat equivalent to "riches for the world" (see note on v. 12). *life from the dead.* Equivalent to "greater riches" in v. 12. The sequence of redemptive events is: The "transgression" and "loss" (v. 12) of Israel leads to the salvation of the Gentiles, which leads to the jealousy or envy of Israel, which leads to the "fullness" (v. 12) of Israel when the hardening is removed, which leads to even more riches for the Gentiles. But what are the "greater riches" (v. 12) for the Gentiles, which Paul describes here as "life from the dead"? Three views may be suggested: (1) an unprecedented spiritual awakening in the world; (2) the consummation of redemption at the resurrection of the dead; (3) a figurative expression describing the conversion of the Jews as a joyful and glorious event (like resurrection)—which will result in even greater blessing for the world. Of these three views the first seems least likely, since, before Israel's spiritual rebirth, the fullness of the Gentiles will already have come in (see v. 25). Since the Gentile mission will then be complete, there seems to be no place for a period of unprecedented spiritual awakening. The second view also seems unlikely, since the context suggests nothing of bodily resurrection.
11:16 The first half of this verse is a reference to Nu 15:17–21. Part of the dough made from the first of the harvested grain (firstfruits) was offered to the Lord. This consecrated the whole batch. *firstfruits.* The patriarchs. *whole batch.* The Jewish people. *holy.* Not that all Jews are righteous (i.e., saved) but that God will be true to his promises concerning them (see 3:3–4). Paul foresaw a future for Israel, even though she was for a time set aside. *root.* The patriarchs. *branches.* The Jewish people.
11:17 *branches.* Individual Jews. *wild olive shoot.* Gentile Christians. *grafted in.* The usual procedure was to insert a shoot or slip of a cultivated tree into a common or wild one. In vv. 17–24, however, the metaphor is used, "contrary to nature" (v. 24), of grafting a wild olive branch (the Gentiles) into the cultivated olive tree. Such a procedure is unnatural, which is precisely the point. Normally, such a graft would be unfruitful. *olive root.* The patriarchs. The whole olive tree represents the people of God.
11:18 *the root supports you.* The salvation of Gentile Christians is dependent on the Jews, especially the patriarchs (e.g., the Abrahamic covenant). See Jn 4:22.
11:19 *Branches.* Unbelieving Jews.
11:20 *be afraid.* On the fear of God see note on Ge 20:11; see also Pr 3:7; Php 2:12–13; Heb 4:1, "be careful"; 1Pe 1:17.
11:22 *kindness and sternness of God.* Any adequate doctrine of God must include these two elements. When we ignore his kindness, God seems a ruthless tyrant; when we ignore his sternness, he seems a doting Father.
11:23 *God is able to graft them in again.* Paul holds out hope for the Jews—God is able (see Mt 19:26; Mk 10:27; Lk 18:27).
11:24 *contrary to nature.* Paul recognized that such grafting was not commonly practiced (see note on v. 17). The

nature were grafted into a cultivated olive tree,[k] how much more readily will these, the natural branches, be grafted into their own olive tree!

All Israel Will Be Saved

[25] I do not want you to be ignorant[l] of this mystery,[m] brothers, so that you may not be conceited:[n] Israel has experienced a hardening[o] in part until the full number of the Gentiles has come in.[p] [26]And so all Israel will be saved,[q] as it is written:

"The deliverer will come from Zion;
　he will turn godlessness away from
　　Jacob.
[27]And this is[q] my covenant with them
　when I take away their sins."[r] [r]

[28]As far as the gospel is concerned, they are enemies[s] on your account; but as far as election is concerned, they are loved on account of the patriarchs,[t] [29]for God's gifts and his call[u] are irrevocable.[v] [30]Just as you who were at one time disobedient[w] to God have now received mercy as a result of their disobedience, [31]so they too have now become disobedient in order that they

too may now[s] receive mercy as a result of God's mercy to you. [32]For God has bound all men over to disobedience[x] so that he may have mercy on them all.

Doxology

[33]Oh, the depth of the riches[y] of the
　　wisdom and[t] knowledge of
　　God![z]
How unsearchable his judgments,
　and his paths beyond tracing out![a]
[34]"Who has known the mind of the Lord?
　Or who has been his counselor?"[u] [b]
[35]"Who has ever given to God,
　that God should repay him?"[v] [c]
[36]For from him and through him and to
　　him are all things.[d]
To him be the glory forever! Amen.[e]

Living Sacrifices

12 Therefore, I urge you,[f] brothers, in view of God's mercy, to offer your

Center cross-references

11:24 [k]Jer 11:16
11:25 [l]Ro 1:13; 1Co 10:1; 12:1; 2Co 1:8; 1Th 4:13 [m]S Ro 16:25 [n]Ro 12:16 [o]ver 7; S Ro 9:18 [p]Lk 21:24
11:26 [q]Isa 45:17; Jer 31:34
11:27 [r]Isa 59:20, 21; 27:9; Heb 8:10,12
11:28 [s]Ro 5:10 [t]Dt 7:8; 10:15; Ro 9:5
11:29 [u]S Ro 8:28 [v]S Heb 7:21
11:30 [w]S Eph 2:2
11:32 [x]S Ro 3:9
11:33 [y]S Ro 2:4 [z]Ps 92:5; Eph 3:10; Col 2:3 [a]Job 5:9; 11:7; Ps 139:6; Ecc 8:17; Isa 40:28
11:34 [b]Isa 40:13, 14; Job 15:8; 36:22; Jer 23:18; 1Co 2:16
11:35 [c]Job 41:11; 35:7
11:36 [d]1Co 8:6; 11:12; Col 1:16; Heb 2:10 [e]Ro 16:27; Eph 3:21; 1Ti 1:17; 1Pe 5:11; Jude 25; Rev 5:13;
7:12 12:1 [f]Eph 4:1; 1Pe 2:11

[q]27 Or will be　[r]27 Isaiah 59:20,21; 27:9; Jer. 31:33,34　[s]31 Some manuscripts do not have now.　[t]33 Or riches and the wisdom and the　[u]34 Isaiah 40:13　[v]35 Job 41:11

---

inclusion of Gentiles in the family of God is "contrary to nature" (cf. Eph 2:12). Obviously, the reasoning in this verse is more theological than horticultural. It would be difficult horticulturally to graft broken branches back into the parent tree, but the Jews really "belong" (historically and theologically) to the parent tree. Thus they will "much more readily . . . be grafted into their own olive tree."
11:25 *mystery.* The so-called mystery religions of Paul's day used the Greek word (*mysterion*) in the sense of something that was to be revealed only to the initiated. Paul himself, however, used it to refer to something formerly hidden or obscure but now revealed by God for all to know and understand (see 16:25; 1Co 2:7; 4:1; 13:2; 14:2; 15:51; Eph 1:9; 3:3–4,9; 5:32; 6:19; Col 1:26–27; 2:2; 4:3; 2Th 2:7; 1Ti 3:9,16). The word is used of (1) the incarnation (1Ti 3:16; see note there), (2) the death of Christ (1Co 2:1, NIV text note; 2:7, "secret wisdom"), (3) God's purpose to sum up all things in Christ (Eph 1:9) and especially to include both Jews and Gentiles in the NT church (Eph 3:3–6), (4) the change that will take place at the resurrection (1Co 15:51), and (5) the plan of God by which both Jew and Gentile, after a period of disobedience by both, will by his mercy be included in his kingdom (v. 25). *so that you may not be conceited.* God's merciful plan to include the Gentiles in his great salvation plan should humble them, not fill them with arrogance. *in part.* Israel's hardening is partial, not total. *until.* Israel's hardening is temporary, not permanent. *full number of the Gentiles.* The total number of the elect Gentiles.
11:26 *And so.* An emphatic statement that this is the way all Israel will be saved. *all Israel.* Three main interpretations of this phrase are: (1) the total number of elect Jews of every generation (equivalent to the "fullness" of Israel [v. 12], which is analogous to the "fullness ['full number'] of the Gentiles" [v. 25]); (2) the total number of the elect, both Jews and Gentiles, of every generation; (3) the great majority of Jews of the final generation. *will be saved.* The salvation of the Jews will, of course, be on the same basis as anyone's

salvation: personal faith in Jesus Christ, crucified and risen from the dead. *The deliverer will come from Zion.* The quotation is from Isa 59:20, where the deliverer ("Redeemer") seems to refer to God. The Talmud understood the text to be a reference to the Messiah, and Paul appears to use it in this way. *Zion.* See note on Gal 4:26.
11:27 *covenant.* The new covenant of Jer 31:31–34. *when I take away their sins.* See Jer 31:34; Zec 13:1. Just as salvation for Gentiles involves forgiveness of sins, so the Jews, when they are saved, are forgiven by the mercy of God—his forgiveness based only on their repentance and faith (see v. 23; Zec 12:10–13:1).
11:28 *they are enemies.* Only temporarily. *on your account.* Explained in v. 11. *loved on account of the patriarchs.* Not because any merit was passed on from the patriarchs to the Jewish people as a whole, but because God in love chose Israel and that choice was irrevocable.
11:29 *God's gifts and his call are irrevocable.* God does not change his mind with reference to his call. Even though Israel is presently in a state of unbelief, God's purpose will be fulfilled in her.
11:32 *all men.* Both groups under discussion (Jews and Gentiles). There has been a period of disobedience for each in order that God may have mercy on them all. Paul is in no way teaching universal salvation.
11:33–36 The doxology that ends this section of Romans is the natural outpouring of Paul's praise to God, whose wisdom and knowledge brought about his great plan for the salvation of both Jews and Gentiles.
12:1–16:27 Paul now turns to the practical application of all he has said previously in the letter. This does not mean that he has not said anything about Christian living up to this point. Chs. 6–8 have touched on this already, but now Paul goes into detail to show that Jesus Christ is to be Lord of every area of life. These chapters are not a postscript to the great theological discussions in chs. 1–11. In a real sense the entire letter has been directed toward the goal of showing that God demands our action as well as our believing and

bodies as living sacrifices,[g] holy and pleasing to God—this is your spiritual[w] act of worship. [2]Do not conform[h] any longer to the pattern of this world,[i] but be transformed by the renewing of your mind.[j] Then you will be able to test and approve what God's will is[k]—his good, pleasing[l] and perfect will.

[3]For by the grace given me[m] I say to every one of you: Do not think of yourself more highly than you ought, but rather think of yourself with sober judgment, in accordance with the measure of faith God has given you. [4]Just as each of us has one body with many members, and these members do not all have the same function,[n] [5]so in Christ we who are many form one body,[o] and each member belongs to all the others. [6]We have different gifts,[p] according to the grace given us. If a man's gift is prophesying,[q] let him use it in proportion to his[x] faith.[r] [7]If it is serving, let him serve; if it is teaching, let him teach;[s] [8]if it is encouraging, let him encourage;[t] if it is contributing to the needs of others, let him give generously;[u] if it is leadership, let

him govern diligently; if it is showing mercy, let him do it cheerfully.

Love

[9]Love must be sincere.[v] Hate what is evil; cling to what is good.[w] [10]Be devoted to one another in brotherly love.[x] Honor one another above yourselves.[y] [11]Never be lacking in zeal, but keep your spiritual fervor,[z] serving the Lord. [12]Be joyful in hope,[a] patient in affliction,[b] faithful in prayer.[c] [13]Share with God's people who are in need.[d] Practice hospitality.[e]

[14]Bless those who persecute you;[f] bless and do not curse. [15]Rejoice with those who rejoice; mourn with those who mourn.[g] [16]Live in harmony with one another.[h] Do not be proud, but be willing to associate with people of low position.[y] Do not be conceited.[i]

12:1 [g]Ro 6:13, 16,19; 1Co 6:20; 1Pe 2:5
12:2 [h]1Pe 1:14 [i]Co 1:20; 2Co 10:2; 1Jn 2:15 [j]Eph 4:23 [k]S Eph 5:17 [l]S 1Ti 5:4
12:3 [m]Ro 15:15; 1Co 15:10; Gal 2:9; Eph 3:7; 4:7; 1Pe 4:10,11
12:4 [n]1Co 12:12-14; Eph 4:16
12:5 [o]1Co 6:15; 10:17; 12:12,20, 27; Eph 2:16; 4:4,25; 5:30; Col 3:15
12:6 [p]1Co 7:7; 12:4,8-10 [q]S Eph 4:11 [r]1Pe 4:10,11
12:7 [s]S Eph 4:11
12:8 [t]Ac 11:23; 13:15; 15:32 [u]2Co 8:2; 9:5-13

12:9 [v]2Co 6:6; 1Ti 1:5 [w]Ps 97:10; Am 5:15; 1Th 5:21,22
12:10 [x]Ps 133:1; 1Th 4:9; Heb 13:1; 1Pe 1:22 [y]Php 2:3

12:11 [z]Ac 18:25 12:12 [a]Ro 5:2 [b]Heb 10:32,36 [c]S Lk 18:1
12:13 [d]S Ac 24:17 [e]2Ki 4:10; Job 31:32; 1Ti 3:2; 5:10; Heb 13:2; 1Pe 4:9 12:14 [f]S Mt 5:44 12:15 [g]Job 30:25
12:16 [h]S Ro 15:5 [i]ver 3; Ps 131:1; Isa 5:21; Jer 45:5; Ro 11:25

[w]1 Or reasonable   [x]6 Or in agreement with the
[y]16 Or willing to do menial work

---

thinking. Faith expresses itself in obedience.
12:1 *Therefore, I urge you.* Paul draws an important inference from the truth set forth in chs. 1–11. *God's mercy.* Much of the letter has been concerned with demonstrating this. *your bodies.* See 6:13 and note. *living sacrifices.* In contrast to dead animal sacrifices, or perhaps "living" in the sense of having the new life of the Holy Spirit (see 6:4). *spiritual act.* Not merely ritual activity but the involvement of heart, mind and will. *worship.* Obedient service.
12:2 *this world.* With all its evil and corruption (see Gal 1:4). *be transformed.* Here a process, not a single event. The same word is used in the transfiguration narratives (Mt 17:2–8; Mk 9:2–8) and in 2Co 3:18. *mind.* Thought and will as they relate to morality (see 1:28). *Then.* After the spiritual transformation just described has taken place. *God's will.* What God wants from the believer here and now. *good.* That which leads to the spiritual and moral growth of the Christian. *pleasing.* To God, not necessarily to us. *perfect.* No improvement can be made on the will of God.
12:3 *measure of faith.* The power given by God to each believer to fulfill various ministries in the church (see vv. 4–8). *God has given.* Since the power comes from God, there can be no basis for a superior attitude or self-righteousness.
12:4–8 Paul likens Christians to members of a human body. There are many members and each has a different function, but all are needed for the health of the body. The emphasis is on unity within diversity (see 1Co 12:12–31).
12:5 *in Christ.* The key to Paul's concept of Christian unity. It is only in Jesus Christ that any unity in the church is possible. True unity is spiritually based. See note on 6:11.
12:6 *gifts.* Greek *charismata*, referring to special gifts of grace—freely given by God to his people to meet the needs of the body (see notes on 1Co 1:7; 12:4). *prophesying.* See note on 1Co 12:10. *let him use it.* There is to be no false modesty that denies the existence of gifts or refuses to use them. *in proportion to his faith.* Probably means about the same thing as "measure of faith" in v. 3 (see note there).

12:7 *serving.* Any kind of service needed by the body of Christ or by any of its members. *teaching.* See notes on 1Co 12:28; Eph 4:11.
12:8 *encouraging.* Exhorting others with an uplifting, cheerful call to worthwhile accomplishment. The teacher often carried out this function. In teaching, the believer is shown what he must do; in encouraging, he is helped to do it. *contributing.* Giving what is one's own, or possibly distributing what has been given by others. *let him govern.* Possibly a reference to an elder. The Ephesian church had elders by about this time (see Ac 20:17; 1Th 5:12; 1Ti 5:17). *showing mercy.* Caring for the sick, the poor and the aged. *cheerfully.* Serving the needy should be a delight, not a chore.
12:9 *Love.* The Christian's love for fellow Christians and perhaps also for his fellowman. *sincere.* True love, not pretense. In view of the preceding paragraph, with its emphasis on social concern, the love Paul speaks of here is not mere emotion but is active love.
12:10 *brotherly love.* Love within the family of God. *Honor one another above yourselves.* Only a mind renewed by the Holy Spirit (see v. 2) could possibly do this (see Php 2:3).
12:11 *spiritual fervor.* Lit. "fervent in spirit." If "spirit" means "Holy Spirit" here, the reference would be to the fervor the Holy Spirit provides.
12:12 *Be joyful in hope.* The certainty of the Christian's hope is a cause for joy (see 5:5; see also 8:16–25; 1Pe 1:3–9). *patient.* Enduring triumphantly—necessary for a Christian, because affliction is his inevitable experience (see Jn 16:33). *faithful in prayer.* One must not only pray in hard times, but also maintain communion with God through prayer at all times (see Lk 18:1; 1Th 5:17).
12:13 *Share with God's people.* The Christian has social responsibility to all people, but especially to other believers (see Gal 6:10).
12:14 *Bless those who persecute you.* Paul is echoing Jesus' teaching in Mt 5:44; Lk 6:28.
12:15 Identification with others in their joys and in their sorrows is a Christian's privilege and responsibility.

17 Do not repay anyone evil for evil.[j] Be
careful to do what is right in the eyes of
everybody.[k] 18 If it is possible, as far as it
depends on you, live at peace with everyone.[l] 19 Do not take revenge,[m] my friends,
but leave room for God's wrath, for it is
written: "It is mine to avenge; I will
repay,"[z][n] says the Lord. 20 On the contrary:

"If your enemy is hungry, feed him;
if he is thirsty, give him something to
drink.
In doing this, you will heap burning
coals on his head."[a][o]

21 Do not be overcome by evil, but overcome evil with good.

Submission to the Authorities

13 Everyone must submit himself to
the governing authorities,[p] for
there is no authority except that which
God has established.[q] The authorities that
exist have been established by God.
2 Consequently, he who rebels against the
authority is rebelling against what God has
instituted,[r] and those who do so will bring
judgment on themselves. 3 For rulers hold
no terror for those who do right, but for
those who do wrong. Do you want to be
free from fear of the one in authority?
Then do what is right and he will commend you.[s] 4 For he is God's servant to do
you good. But if you do wrong, be afraid,
for he does not bear the sword for nothing.
He is God's servant, an agent of wrath to
bring punishment on the wrongdoer.[t]
5 Therefore, it is necessary to submit to the
authorities, not only because of possible
punishment but also because of conscience.[u]

6 This is also why you pay taxes,[v] for the
authorities are God's servants, who give
their full time to governing. 7 Give everyone what you owe him: If you owe taxes,
pay taxes;[w] if revenue, then revenue; if
respect, then respect; if honor, then honor.

Love, for the Day Is Near

8 Let no debt remain outstanding, except
the continuing debt to love one another,
for he who loves his fellowman has fulfilled the law.[x] 9 The commandments, "Do
not commit adultery," "Do not murder,"
"Do not steal," "Do not covet,"[b][y] and
whatever other commandment there may
be, are summed up[z] in this one rule:
"Love your neighbor as yourself."[c][a]
10 Love does no harm to its neighbor.
Therefore love is the fulfillment of the
law.[b]

11 And do this, understanding the

12:17 [j]ver 19; Pr 20:22; 24:29 [k]2Co 8:21
12:18 [l]S Mk 9:50; S Ro 14:19
12:19 [m]ver 17; Lev 19:18; Pr 20:22; 24:29 [n]Dt 32:35; Ge 50:19; 1Sa 26:10; Ps 94:1; Jer 51:36
12:20 [o]Pr 25:21, 22; Ex 23:4; Mt 5:44; Lk 6:27
13:1 [p]Tit 3:1; 1Pe 2:13,14 [q]Da 2:21; 4:17; Jn 19:11
13:2 [r]Ex 16:8
13:3 [s]1Pe 2:14
13:4 [t]1Th 4:6
13:5 [u]Pr 24:21, 22
13:6 [v]Mt 22:17
13:7 [w]Mt 17:25; Mt 22:17,21; Lk 23:2
13:8 [x]ver 10; S Mt 5:43; Jn 13:34; Col 3:14
13:9 [y]Ex 20:13-15,17; Dt 5:17-19,21 [z]Mt 7:12 [a]Lev 19:18; S Mt 5:43
13:10 [b]S ver 8; ver 9

[z]*19* Deut. 32:35 [a]*20* Prov. 25:21,22 [b]*9* Exodus 20:13-15,17; Deut. 5:17-19,21 [c]*9* Lev. 19:18

12:17 *Do not repay anyone evil for evil.* See Mt 5:39–42, 44–45; 1Th 5:15; 1Pe 3:9. *Be careful to do what is right in the eyes of everybody.* A possible reflection of Pr 3:4 in the Septuagint (the Greek translation of the OT). Christian conduct should never betray the high moral standards of the gospel, or it will provoke the disdain of unbelievers and bring the gospel into disrepute (see 2Co 8:21; 1Ti 3:7).
12:18 *If it is possible . . . live at peace.* Jesus pronounced a blessing on peacemakers (Mt 5:9), and believers are to cultivate peace with everyone to the extent that it depends on them.
12:20 *heap burning coals on his head.* Doing good to one's enemy (v. 21), instead of trying to take revenge, may bring about his repentance (see note on Pr 25:22).
13:1 *submit.* A significant word in vv. 1–7. *governing authorities.* The civil rulers, all of whom were probably pagans at the time Paul was writing. Christians may have been tempted not to submit to them and to claim allegiance only to Christ. *established by God.* Even the possibility of a persecuting state did not shake Paul's conviction that civil government is ordained by God.
13:2 *judgment.* Either divine judgment or, more likely, punishment by the governing authorities, since v. 3 ("For") explains this verse; see also v. 4.
13:3 *do what is right and he will commend you.* Paul is not stating that this will always be true but is describing the proper, ideal function of rulers. When civil rulers overstep their proper function, the Christian is to obey God rather than man (see Ac 4:19; 5:29).
13:4 *he is God's servant.* In the order of divine providence the ruler is God's servant (see Isa 45:1). *good.* Rulers exist for the benefit of society—to protect the general public by maintaining good order. *the sword.* The symbol of Roman authority on both the national and the international levels. Here we find the Biblical principle of using force for the maintenance of good order.
13:5 *because of conscience.* Civil authorities are ordained by God, and in order to maintain a good conscience Christians must duly honor them.
13:6 *you pay taxes.* Because rulers are God's agents, who function for the benefit of society in general.
13:8 *continuing debt.* To love is the one debt that is never paid off. No matter how much one has loved, he is under obligation to keep on loving. *one another.* Includes not only fellow Christians but all people, as the second half of the verse makes clear ("fellowman"). *the law.* The Mosaic law, which lays down both moral and social responsibilities.
13:9 Further explains the last statement of v. 8, namely, that love of neighbor encompasses all our social responsibilities. *your neighbor.* Jesus taught that our neighbor is anyone in need (see Lk 10:25–37), which is probably the idea Paul has in mind here. *as yourself.* Not a command to love ourselves but a recognition of the fact that we naturally do so.
13:11–14 In this section, as in other NT passages, the certain coming of the end of the present age is used to provide motivation for godly living (see, e.g., Mt 25:31–46; Mk 13:33–37; Jas 5:7–11; 2Pe 3:11–14).
13:11 *present time.* The time of salvation, the closing period of the present age, before the consummation of the kingdom. *The hour.* The time for action. *our salvation.* The full realization of salvation at the second coming of Jesus Christ (see 8:23; Heb 9:28; 1Pe 1:5). *is nearer now.* Every day brings us closer to the second advent of Christ.

present time. The hour has come[c] for you to wake up from your slumber,[d] because our salvation is nearer now than when we first believed. [12]The night is nearly over; the day is almost here.[e] So let us put aside the deeds of darkness[f] and put on the armor[g] of light. [13]Let us behave decently, as in the daytime, not in orgies and drunkenness,[h] not in sexual immorality and debauchery, not in dissension and jealousy.[i] [14]Rather, clothe yourselves with the Lord Jesus Christ,[j] and do not think about how to gratify the desires of the sinful nature.[d][k]

The Weak and the Strong

14 Accept him whose faith is weak,[l] without passing judgment on disputable matters. [2]One man's faith allows him to eat everything, but another man, whose faith is weak, eats only vegetables.[m] [3]The man who eats everything must not look down on[n] him who does not, and the man who does not eat everything must not condemn[o] the man who does, for God has accepted him. [4]Who are you to judge someone else's servant?[p] To his own master he stands or falls. And he will stand, for the Lord is able to make him stand.

[5]One man considers one day more sa-

cred than another;[q] another man considers every day alike. Each one should be fully convinced in his own mind. [6]He who regards one day as special, does so to the Lord. He who eats meat, eats to the Lord, for he gives thanks to God;[r] and he who abstains, does so to the Lord and gives thanks to God. [7]For none of us lives to himself alone[s] and none of us dies to himself alone. [8]If we live, we live to the Lord; and if we die, we die to the Lord. So, whether we live or die, we belong to the Lord.[t]

[9]For this very reason, Christ died and returned to life[u] so that he might be the Lord of both the dead and the living.[v] [10]You, then, why do you judge your brother? Or why do you look down on[w] your brother? For we will all stand before God's judgment seat.[x] [11]It is written:

" 'As surely as I live,'[y] says the Lord,
'every knee will bow before me;
    every tongue will confess to
        God.' "[e][z]

[12]So then, each of us will give an account of himself to God.[a]

Cross references

13:11 [c]1Co 7:29-31; 10:11; Jas 5:8; 1Pe 4:7; 1Jn 2:18; Rev 22:10 [d]Eph 5:14; 1Th 5:5,6
13:12 [e]Heb 10:25; 1Jn 2:8 /Eph 5:11 [g]Eph 6:11,13; 1Th 5:8
13:13 [h]S Eph 5:18 [i]Lk 21:34; Gal 5:20,21; Eph 5:18; 1Pe 4:3
13:14 [j]Gal 3:27; Eph 4:24; Col 3:10,12 [k]S Gal 5:24
14:1 [l]Ro 15:1; 1Co 8:9-12; 9:22
14:2 [m]ver 14
14:3 [n]ver 10; Lk 18:9 [o]ver 10, 13; Col 2:16
14:4 [p]S Mt 7:1
14:5 [q]Gal 4:10; Col 2:16
14:6 [r]S Mt 14:19; 1Co 10:30,31; 1Ti 4:3,4
14:7 [s]2Co 5:15; Gal 2:20
14:8 [t]Php 1:20
14:9 [u]Rev 1:18; 2:8 [v]S Ac 10:42; 2Co 5:15
14:10 [w]ver 3; S Mt 7:1 [x]S 2Co 5:10
14:11 [y]Isa 49:18 [z]Isa 45:23; Php 2:10,11
14:12 [a]Mt 12:36; 1Pe 4:5

[d]14 Or the flesh   [e]11 Isaiah 45:23

13:12 *The night.* The present evil age. *is nearly over; the day is almost here.* A clear example of the NT teaching of the "nearness" of the end times (see Mt 24:33; 1Co 7:29; Php 4:5; Jas 5:8–9; 1Pe 4:7; 1Jn 2:18). These texts do not mean that the early Christians believed that Jesus would return within a few years (and thus were mistaken). Rather, they regarded the death and resurrection of Christ as the crucial events of history that began the last days. Since the next great event in God's redemptive plan is the second coming of Jesus Christ, "the night," no matter how long chronologically it may last, is "nearly over." *the day.* The appearing of Jesus Christ, which ushers in the consummation of the kingdom.
13:14 *clothe yourselves with the Lord Jesus Christ.* See Gal 3:27. Paul exhorts believers to display outwardly what has already taken place inwardly—including practicing all the virtues associated with Christ.
14:1 *whose faith is weak.* Probably Jewish Christians at Rome who were unwilling to give up the observance of certain requirements of the law, such as dietary restrictions and the keeping of the Sabbath and other special days. Their concern was not quite the same as that of the Judaizers of Galatia. The Judaizers thought they could put God in their debt by works of righteousness and were trying to force this heretical teaching on the Galatian churches, but the "weak" Roman Christians did neither. They were not yet clear as to the status of OT regulations under the new covenant inaugurated by the coming of Christ. *without passing judgment on disputable matters.* Fellowship among Christians is not to be based on everyone's agreement on disputable questions. Christians do not agree on all matters pertaining to the Christian life, nor do they need to.
14:2 *One man's faith.* In contrast, Paul now describes the "strong" Christian. Here faith is used in the sense of assur-

ance or confidence. The strong Christian's understanding of the gospel allows him to recognize that one's diet has no spiritual significance.
14:4 *someone else's.* God's. A Christian must not reject a fellow Christian, who is also a servant of God. *To his own master he stands or falls.* The "weak" Christian is not the master of his "strong" brother, nor is the "strong" the master of the "weak." God is Master, and to him alone all believers are responsible.
14:5 *one day more sacred than another.* Some feel that this refers primarily to the Sabbath, but it is probably a reference to all the special days of the OT ceremonial law. *considers every day alike.* All days are to be dedicated to God through holy living and godly service. *fully convinced in his own mind.* The importance of personal conviction in disputable matters of conduct runs through this passage (see vv. 14,16,22–23).
14:6 The motivation behind the actions of both the strong and the weak is to be the same: Both should want to serve the Lord and give thanks for his provision.
14:7 *none of us lives to himself alone.* The reference is to "us" Christians. We do not live to please ourselves but the Lord. *none of us dies to himself alone.* Even in death the important thing is one's relationship to the Lord. Paul repeats the truths of this verse in v. 8.
14:9 *Lord.* See note on 10:9. Christ's Lordship over both the dead and the living arises out of his death and resurrection.
14:10 *why do you judge your brother?* Addressed to weak Christians. *why do you look down on your brother?* Addressed to strong Christians. *we will all.* Refers to every Christian. *God's judgment seat.* All Christians will be judged, and the judgment will be based on works (see 2Co 5:10; cf. 1Co 3:10–15).

¹³Therefore let us stop passing judgment[b] on one another. Instead, make up your mind not to put any stumbling block or obstacle in your brother's way.[c] ¹⁴As one who is in the Lord Jesus, I am fully convinced that no food[f] is unclean in itself.[d] But if anyone regards something as unclean, then for him it is unclean.[e] ¹⁵If your brother is distressed because of what you eat, you are no longer acting in love.[f] Do not by your eating destroy your brother for whom Christ died.[g] ¹⁶Do not allow what you consider good to be spoken of as evil.[h] ¹⁷For the kingdom of God is not a matter of eating and drinking,[i] but of righteousness, peace[j] and joy in the Holy Spirit,[k] ¹⁸because anyone who serves Christ in this way is pleasing to God and approved by men.[l]

¹⁹Let us therefore make every effort to do what leads to peace[m] and to mutual edification.[n] ²⁰Do not destroy the work of God for the sake of food.[o] All food is clean,[p] but it is wrong for a man to eat anything that causes someone else to stumble.[q] ²¹It is better not to eat meat or drink wine or to do anything else that will cause your brother to fall.[r]

²²So whatever you believe about these things keep between yourself and God. Blessed is the man who does not condemn[s] himself by what he approves. ²³But the man who has doubts[t] is condemned if he eats, because his eating is not from faith; and everything that does not come from faith is sin.

15 We who are strong ought to bear with the failings of the weak[u] and not to please ourselves. ²Each of us should please his neighbor for his good,[v] to build him up.[w] ³For even Christ did not please himself[x] but, as it is written: "The insults of those who insult you have fallen on me."[g][y] ⁴For everything that was written in the past was written to teach us,[z] so that through endurance and the encouragement of the Scriptures we might have hope.

⁵May the God who gives endurance and encouragement give you a spirit of unity[a] among yourselves as you follow Christ Jesus, ⁶so that with one heart and mouth

Cross references (center column):

14:13 *b*ver 1; S Mt 7:1 *c*S 2Co 6:3
14:14 *d*ver 20; S Ac 10:15 *e*1Co 8:7
14:15 *f*Eph 5:2 *g*ver 20; 1Co 8:11
14:16 *h*1Co 10:30
14:17 *i*1Co 8:8 /Isa 32:17 *k*Ro 15:13; Gal 5:22
14:18 *l*Lk 2:52; Ac 24:16; 2Co 8:21
14:19 *m*Ps 34:14; Ro 12:18; 1Co 7:15; 2Ti 2:22; Heb 12:14 *n*Ro 15:2; 1Co 14:3-5,12,17,26; 2Co 12:19; Eph 4:12,29
14:20 *o*ver 15 *p*ver 14; S Ac 10:15 *q*ver 13; 1Co 8:9-12
14:21 *r*S Mt 5:29

14:22 *s*1Jn 3:21
14:23 *t*ver 5
15:1 *u*Ro 14:1; 1Th 5:14
15:2 *v*S 1Co 10:24 *w*S Ro 14:19
15:3 *x*2Co 8:9 *y*Ps 69:9
15:4 *z*S Ro 4:23, 24

15:5 *a*Ro 12:16; 1Co 1:10; 2Co 13:11; Eph 4:3; Php 2:2; Col 3:14; 1Pe 3:8

*f*14 Or *that nothing*   *g*3 Psalm 69:9

14:13 *Instead.* The words that immediately follow are addressed to strong Christians. *obstacle.* Something that causes one to fall into sin.

14:14 *As one who is in the Lord Jesus, I am fully convinced.* Now that Paul was a Christian, the old food taboos no longer applied (see Mt 15:10–11,16–20; Mk 7:14–23). *no food is unclean in itself.* For Paul's teaching elsewhere on this subject see 1Ti 4:4; Tit 1:15. *if anyone regards something as unclean, then for him it is unclean.* Not to be generalized to mean that sin is only a matter of subjective opinion or conscience. Paul is not discussing conduct that in the light of Scripture is clearly sinful, but conduct concerning which Christians may legitimately differ (in this case, food regulations). With regard to such matters, decisions should be guided by conscience.

14:15 *love.* The key to proper settlement of disputes. *your brother for whom Christ died.* Christ so valued the weak brother as to die for him. Surely the strong Christian ought to be willing to make adjustments in his own behavior for the sake of such brothers.

14:16 *what you consider good.* From your own understanding of Christian liberty. *to be spoken of as evil.* To exercise freedom without responsibility can lead to evil results.

14:17 *kingdom of God.* See notes on Mt 3:2; Lk 4:43. *is not a matter of eating and drinking.* To be concerned with such trivial matters is to miss completely the essence of Christian living. *righteousness.* Righteous living. Paul's concern for the moral and ethical dimension of the Christian life stands out in all his letters. *peace.* See 5:1 and note. *joy in the Holy Spirit.* Joy given by the Holy Spirit.

14:19 *mutual edification.* The spiritual building up of individual Christians and of the church (see 1:11–12).

14:20 *work of God.* The weak Christian brother who as a redeemed person is God's work and in whom God continues to work (cf. Eph 2:10). *causes someone else to stumble.* Paul recognizes a strong Christian's right to certain freedoms, but qualifies it with the principle of regard for a weak brother's scruples.

14:22 *keep between yourself and God.* The strong Christian is not required to go against his convictions or change his standards. Yet he is not to flaunt his Christian freedom but keep it a private matter. *what he approves.* Probably a reference to the eating of certain foods.

14:23 *everything.* The matters discussed above, namely, conduct about which there can be legitimate differences of opinion between Christians.

15:1 *We who are strong.* Paul identifies himself with the strong Christians, those whose personal convictions allow them more freedom than the weak. *to bear.* Not merely to tolerate or put up with but to uphold lovingly. *failings.* Not sins, since in the matters under discussion there is no clear guidance in Scripture. *not to please ourselves.* Not that a Christian should never please himself, but that he should not insist on doing what he wants without regard to the scruples of other Christians.

15:3 *Christ did not please himself.* He came to do the will of the Father, not his own will. This involved suffering and even death (see Mt 20:28; Mk 10:45; 1Co 10:33–11:1; 2Co 8:9; Php 2:5–8). *The insults of those who insult you have fallen on me.* In the psalm quoted (69:9) "you" refers to God and "me" refers to the righteous sufferer, whom Paul identifies with Christ. The quotation serves to show how Christ did not please himself, but voluntarily bore man's hostility toward God.

15:4 Here Paul defends his application of Ps 69:9 to Christ. In so doing, he states a great truth concerning the purpose of Scripture: It was written for our instruction, so that as we patiently endure we might be encouraged to hold fast our hope in Christ (see 1Co 10:6,11).

15:5 *a spirit of unity among yourselves.* Not that believers should all come to the same conclusions on the matters of conscience discussed above, but that they might agree to disagree in love.

you may glorify[b] the God and Father[c] of our Lord Jesus Christ.

[7]Accept one another,[d] then, just as Christ accepted you, in order to bring praise to God. [8]For I tell you that Christ has become a servant of the Jews[he] on behalf of God's truth, to confirm the promises[f] made to the patriarchs [9]so that the Gentiles[g] may glorify God[h] for his mercy, as it is written:

"Therefore I will praise you among the
    Gentiles;
I will sing hymns to your name."[i] [i]

[10]Again, it says,

"Rejoice, O Gentiles, with his
    people."[j] [j]

[11]And again,

"Praise the Lord, all you Gentiles,
  and sing praises to him, all you
    peoples."[k] [k]

[12]And again, Isaiah says,

"The Root of Jesse[l] will spring up,
  one who will arise to rule over the
    nations;
the Gentiles will hope in him."[l] [m]

[13]May the God of hope fill you with all joy and peace[n] as you trust in him, so that you may overflow with hope by the power of the Holy Spirit.[o]

Paul the Minister to the Gentiles

[14]I myself am convinced, my brothers,

that you yourselves are full of goodness,[p] complete in knowledge[q] and competent to instruct one another. [15]I have written you quite boldly on some points, as if to remind you of them again, because of the grace God gave me[r] [16]to be a minister of Christ Jesus to the Gentiles[s] with the priestly duty of proclaiming the gospel of God,[t] so that the Gentiles might become an offering[u] acceptable to God, sanctified by the Holy Spirit.

[17]Therefore I glory in Christ Jesus[v] in my service to God.[w] [18]I will not venture to speak of anything except what Christ has accomplished through me in leading the Gentiles[x] to obey God[y] by what I have said and done— [19]by the power of signs and miracles,[z] through the power of the Spirit.[a] So from Jerusalem[b] all the way around to Illyricum, I have fully proclaimed the gospel of Christ.[c] [20]It has always been my ambition to preach the gospel[d] where Christ was not known, so that I would not be building on someone else's foundation.[e] [21]Rather, as it is written:

"Those who were not told about him
    will see,
and those who have not heard will
    understand."[m][f]

[22]This is why I have often been hindered from coming to you.[g]

15:6 [b]Ps 34:3 [c]Rev 1:6
15:7 [d]Ro 14:1
15:8 [e]Mt 15:24; Ac 3:25,26 [f]2Co 1:20
15:9 [g]S Ro 3:29 [h]S Mt 9:8 [i]2Sa 22:50; Ps 18:49
15:10 [j]Dt 32:43; Isa 66:10
15:11 [k]Ps 117:1
15:12 [l]S Rev 5:5 [m]Isa 11:10; Mt 12:21
15:13 [n]Ro 14:17 [o]ver 19; 1Co 2:4; 4:20; 1Th 1:5

15:14 [p]Eph 5:9 [q]S 2Co 8:7; 2Pe 1:12
15:15 [r]S Ro 12:3
15:16 [s]S Ac 9:15 [t]ver 19; S Ro 1:1 [u]Isa 66:20
15:17 [v]Php 3:3 [w]Heb 2:17
15:18 [x]Ac 15:12; 21:19; Ro 1:5 [y]Ro 16:26
15:19 [z]S Jn 4:48; Ac 19:11 [a]S ver 13 [b]Ac 22:17-21 [c]S 2Co 2:12
15:20 [d]Ro 1:15 [e]2Co 10:15,16
15:21 [f]Isa 52:15
15:22 [g]Ro 1:13

[h]8 Greek *circumcision*   [i]9 2 Samuel 22:50; Psalm 18:49   [j]10 Deut. 32:43   [k]11 Psalm 117:1   [l]12 Isaiah 11:10   [m]21 Isaiah 52:15

15:7 *just as Christ accepted you.* See 14:3,4,15.
15:8 *Christ has become a servant of the Jews.* Clearly revealed in his earthly ministry. He was sent to the Jewish people and largely limited his ministry to them (see Mt 15:24). God gave a special priority, so far as the gospel is concerned, to the Jews (see 3:1–8). *promises made to the patriarchs.* The covenant promises made to Abraham (Ge 12:1–3; 17:7; 18:19; 22:18), Isaac (Ge 26:3–4) and Jacob (Ge 28:13–15; 46:2–4).
15:9 *so that the Gentiles may glorify God.* From the beginning, God's redemptive work in and for Israel had in view the redemption of the Gentiles (see Ge 12:3). They would both see God's mighty and gracious acts for his people and hear the praises of God's people as they celebrated what God had done for them (a common theme in the Psalms; see Paul's quotations in vv. 9b–12 and note on Ps 9:1). Thus they would come to know the true God and glorify him for his mercy (see notes on Ps 46:10; 47:9). God's greatest and climactic act for Israel's salvation was the sending of the Messiah to fulfill the promises made to the patriarchs and so to gather in the great harvest of the Gentiles.
15:12 *Root of Jesse.* Jesse was the father of David (see 1Sa 16:5–13; Mt 1:6), and the Messiah was the "Son of David" (Mt 21:9). See Isa 11:1; Rev 5:5. *Gentiles will hope in him.* The Gentile mission of the early church was a fulfillment of this prophecy, as is the continuing evangelization of the nations.

15:13 *God of hope.* Any hope the Christian has comes from God. See note on 5:5. *by the power of the Holy Spirit.* Hope cannot be conjured up by man's effort; it is God's gift by his Spirit (see 8:24–25).
15:15 *as if to remind you of them again.* Since Paul had never preached or taught in Rome, he may be referring to Christian doctrine generally known in the church.
15:16 *minister of Christ Jesus to the Gentiles.* See note on 11:13. *priestly duty of proclaiming the gospel.* Paul's priestly function was different from that of the Levitical priests. They were involved with the rituals of the temple, whereas he preached the gospel. *an offering acceptable to God, sanctified by the Holy Spirit.* The offering Paul brought to God was the Gentile church.
15:17 *I glory.* Paul was not boasting of his own achievements but of what Christ had accomplished through him.
15:19 *signs and miracles.* See Ac 14:8–10; 16:16–18, 25–26; 20:9–12; 28:8–9; 2Co 12:12; Heb 2:3–4. *from Jerusalem.* The home of the mother church, where the gospel originated and its dissemination began (see Ac 1:8). *Illyricum.* A Roman province north of Macedonia (present-day Albania and Yugoslavia). Acts mentions nothing of his ministry there, and perhaps all he means is that he reached the border. *I have fully proclaimed the gospel.* Not everyone had heard the gospel in the eastern Mediterranean, but Paul believed that his work there had been completed and it was time to move on to other places.

Paul's Plan to Visit Rome

23But now that there is no more place for me to work in these regions, and since I have been longing for many years to see you,[h] 24I plan to do so when I go to Spain.[i] I hope to visit you while passing through and to have you assist[j] me on my journey there, after I have enjoyed your company for a while. 25Now, however, I am on my way to Jerusalem[k] in the service[l] of the saints[m] there. 26For Macedonia[n] and Achaia[o] were pleased to make a contribution for the poor among the saints in Jerusalem.[p] 27They were pleased to do it, and indeed they owe it to them. For if the Gentiles have shared in the Jews' spiritual blessings, they owe it to the Jews to share with them their material blessings.[q] 28So after I have completed this task and have made sure that they have received this fruit, I will go to Spain[r] and visit you on the way. 29I know that when I come to you,[s] I will come in the full measure of the blessing of Christ.

30I urge you, brothers, by our Lord Jesus Christ and by the love of the Spirit,[t] to join me in my struggle by praying to God for me.[u] 31Pray that I may be rescued[v] from the unbelievers in Judea and that my service[w] in Jerusalem may be acceptable to the saints[x] there, 32so that by God's will[y] I may come to you[z] with joy and together with you be refreshed.[a] 33The God of peace[b] be with you all. Amen.

Personal Greetings

16 I commend[c] to you our sister Phoebe, a servant[n] of the church in Cenchrea.[d] 2I ask you to receive her in the Lord[e] in a way worthy of the saints[f] and to give her any help she may need from you, for she has been a great help to many people, including me.

3Greet Priscilla[o] and Aquila,[g] my fellow workers[h] in Christ Jesus.[i] 4They risked their lives for me. Not only I but all the churches of the Gentiles are grateful to them.

5Greet also the church that meets at their house.[j]

Greet my dear friend Epenetus, who was the first convert[k] to Christ in the province of Asia.[l]

6Greet Mary, who worked very hard for you.

7Greet Andronicus and Junias, my relatives[m] who have been in prison with me.[n] They are outstanding among the apostles, and they were in Christ[o] before I was.

8Greet Ampliatus, whom I love in the Lord.

9Greet Urbanus, our fellow worker in Christ,[p] and my dear friend Stachys.

10Greet Apelles, tested and approved in Christ.[q]

Cross references

15:23 hAc 19:21; Ro 1:10,11
15:24 iver 28 /1Co 16:6; Tit 3:13
15:25 kS Ac 19:21
/S Ac 24:17
mS Ac 9:13
15:26 nS Ac 16:9
oS Ac 18:12
pS Ac 24:17
15:27 q1Co 9:11
15:28 rver 24
15:29 sRo 1:10, 11
15:30 tGal 5:22; Col 1:8
u2Co 1:11; Col 4:12
15:31 v2Co 1:10; 2Th 3:2;
2Ti 3:11; 2Pe 2:9
wver 25;
S Ac 24:17
xS Ac 9:13
15:32 yS Ac 18:21
zRo 1:10,13
a1Co 16:18; Phm 7
15:33 bRo 16:20; 2Co 13:11; Php 4:9; 1Th 5:23; 2Th 3:16; Heb 13:20

16:1 cS 2Co 3:1 dAc 18:18
16:2 ePhp 2:29
fS Ac 9:13
16:3 gS Ac 18:2 hS Php 2:25 iver 7,9,10; Ro 8:1,39; 1Co 1:30; 2Co 5:17; Gal 1:22; 5:6; Eph 1:13
16:5 /1Co 16:19; Col 4:15; Phm 2 k1Co 16:15 /S Ac 2:9
16:7 mver 11,21 nCol 4:10; Phm 23 oS ver 3

16:9 pS ver 3 16:10 qS ver 3

n / Or deaconess   o 3 Greek Prisca, a variant of Priscilla

15:22 *hindered from coming to you.* Paul's great desire to complete the missionary task in the eastern Mediterranean had prevented him from making a trip to Rome.

15:23 *no more place for me to work.* Because of the principle stated in v. 20. *longing for many years to see you.* See 1:11–15.

15:24 *to have you assist me on my journey there.* Paul wanted to use the Roman church as a base of operations for a mission to Spain. *enjoyed your company for a while.* More than a quick stop at Rome was contemplated (see 1:11–12).

15:25 *in the service of the saints there.* Paul wanted to present the gift (see v. 26) personally to the Jerusalem church. The gift included interpretation. It was not merely money; it represented the love and concern of the Gentile churches for their Jewish brothers and sisters. *saints.* Refers generally to believers in Jesus Christ (see note on 1:7).

15:26 *contribution.* See 1Co 16:1–4; 2Co 8–9.

15:27 *Jews' spiritual blessings.* Especially Christ and the gospel.

15:28 *this fruit.* The collection from the Gentile churches.

15:31 *Pray that I may be rescued from the unbelievers in Judea.* Paul wanted to go to Jerusalem. The delivery of the collection was important to him, but he had received warnings about what might happen to him there (see Ac 20:22–23). *may be acceptable.* Perhaps a reference to the way in which the money was to be distributed—often a delicate and difficult task.

15:32 *with you be refreshed.* See 1:11–12.

15:33 *God of peace.* See notes on 5:1; 1Th 5:23.

16:1 *our sister.* In the sense of being a fellow believer. *Phoebe.* Probably the carrier of the letter to Rome. *servant.* See NIV text note; one who serves or ministers in any way. When church related, as it is here, it probably refers to a specific office—woman deacon or deaconess. *Cenchrea.* A port located about six miles east of Corinth on the Saronic Gulf.

16:3 *Priscilla and Aquila.* Close friends of Paul who worked in the same trade of tentmaking (see Ac 18:2–3).

16:4 *risked their lives for me.* There is no other record of this in the NT or elsewhere, but it must have been widely known, as the last part of the verse indicates.

16:6 *Mary.* Six persons are known by this name in the NT. This one is unknown apart from this reference.

16:7 *Junias.* A feminine name. *among the apostles.* Two interpretations are given: 1. "Apostles" is used in a wider sense than the Twelve—to include preachers of the gospel recognized by the churches (see Ac 14:4,14; 1Th 2:7). 2. "Apostles" is preceded by the definite article, which may indicate that the Twelve are in view. In this case, the meaning would be that these two persons were outstanding "in the opinion of" the apostles.

16:8–10 *Ampliatus... Urbanus... Stachys... Apelles.* All common slave names found in the imperial household.

16:10 *Aristobulus.* Perhaps refers to the grandson of Herod the Great and brother of Herod Agrippa I.

Greet those who belong to the household[r] of Aristobulus.

[11]Greet Herodion, my relative.[s]

Greet those in the household[t] of Narcissus who are in the Lord.

[12]Greet Tryphena and Tryphosa, those women who work hard in the Lord.

Greet my dear friend Persis, another woman who has worked very hard in the Lord.

[13]Greet Rufus,[u] chosen[v] in the Lord, and his mother, who has been a mother to me, too.

[14]Greet Asyncritus, Phlegon, Hermes, Patrobas, Hermas and the brothers with them.

[15]Greet Philologus, Julia, Nereus and his sister, and Olympas and all the saints[w] with them.[x]

[16]Greet one another with a holy kiss.[y]

All the churches of Christ send greetings.

[17]I urge you, brothers, to watch out for those who cause divisions and put obstacles in your way that are contrary to the teaching you have learned.[z] Keep away from them.[a] [18]For such people are not serving our Lord Christ,[b] but their own appetites.[c] By smooth talk and flattery they deceive[d] the minds of naive people. [19]Everyone has heard[e] about your obedience, so I am full of joy over you; but I

want you to be wise about what is good, and innocent about what is evil.[f]

[20]The God of peace[g] will soon crush[h] Satan[i] under your feet.

The grace of our Lord Jesus be with you.[j]

[21]Timothy,[k] my fellow worker, sends his greetings to you, as do Lucius,[l] Jason[m] and Sosipater, my relatives.[n]

[22]I, Tertius, who wrote down this letter, greet you in the Lord.

[23]Gaius,[o] whose hospitality I and the whole church here enjoy, sends you his greetings.

Erastus,[p] who is the city's director of public works, and our brother Quartus send you their greetings.[p]

[25]Now to him who is able[q] to establish you by my gospel[r] and the proclamation of Jesus Christ, according to the revelation of the mystery[s] hidden for long ages past, [26]but now revealed and made known through the prophetic writings[t] by the command of the eternal God, so that all nations might believe and obey[u] him— [27]to the only wise God be glory forever through Jesus Christ! Amen.[v]

16:10 [r]S Ac 11:14
16:11 [s]ver 7,21
[t]S Ac 11:14
16:13 [u]Mk 15:21
[v]S 2Jn 1
16:15 [w]ver 2;
S Ac 9:13 [x]ver 14
16:16 [y]1Co 16:20;
2Co 13:12;
1Th 5:26;
1Pe 5:14
16:17 [z]Gal 1:8,9;
1Ti 1:3; 6:3
[a]Mt 18:15-17;
1Co 5:11;
2Th 3:6,14;
2Ti 3:5; Tit 3:10;
2Jn 10
16:18 [b]Ro 14:18
[c]Php 3:19
[d]2Sa 15:6;
Ps 12:2;
Isa 30:10; Col 2:4
16:19 [e]Ro 1:8

[f]S 1Co 14:20
16:20 [g]S Ro 15:33
[h]Ge 3:15
[i]S Mt 4:10
[j]2Co 13:14;
S Gal 6:18;
1Th 5:28;
Rev 22:21
16:21 [k]S Ac 16:1
[l]Ac 13:1
[m]Ac 17:5 [n]ver 7,
11
16:23 [o]S Ac 19:29
[p]Ac 19:22;
2Ti 4:20
16:25 [q]2Co 9:8;
Eph 3:20; Jude 24
[r]Ro 2:16; 2Ti 2:8
[s]Isa 48:6;
Eph 1:9; 3:3-6,9;
Col 1:26,27; 2:2;
1Ti 3:16

16:26 [t]Ro 1:2 [u]Ro 1:5 16:27 [v]S Ro 11:36

P.23 Some manuscripts their greetings. 24May the grace of our Lord Jesus Christ be with all of you. Amen.

16:11 *my relative.* Perhaps a reference to his being a Jew. *Narcissus.* Sometimes identified with Tiberius Claudius Narcissus, a wealthy freedman of the Roman emperor Tiberius.
16:12 *Tryphena and Tryphosa.* Perhaps sisters, even twins, because it was common for such persons to be given names from the same root. *Persis.* Means "Persian woman."
16:14–15 None of these persons can be further identified, except that they were slaves or freedmen in the Roman church.
16:16 *holy kiss.* See 1Co 16:20; 2Co 13:12; 1Th 5:26; 1Pe 5:14. Justin Martyr (A.D. 150) tells us that the holy kiss was a regular part of the worship service in his day. It is still a practice in some churches.
16:17–20 A theological application of the story of man's fall (Ge 3).
16:17 *those who cause divisions and put obstacles in your way.* Who these people were we cannot tell, but some of their characteristics are mentioned in v. 18.
16:19 *wise about what is good.* Christians are to be experts in doing good.
16:20 *God of peace.* See 15:33. *will soon crush Satan.* A reference to Satan's final doom (cf. Ge 3:15). For "soon" see note on 13:12.
16:21 *Jason.* Possibly the Jason mentioned in Ac 17:5–9. *Sosipater.* Probably Sopater son of Pyrrhus from Berea (see Ac 20:4).

16:22 *I, Tertius, who wrote down this letter.* Not mentioned elsewhere in the NT. He had functioned as Paul's secretary.
16:23 *Gaius.* Usually identified with Titius Justus, a God-fearer, in whose house Paul stayed while in Corinth (see Ac 18:7; 1Co 1:14). His full name would be Gaius Titius Justus. *here.* In Corinth. *Erastus.* At Corinth archaeologists have discovered a reused block of stone in a paved square, with the Latin inscription: "Erastus, commissioner of public works, bore the expense of this pavement." This may refer to the Erastus mentioned here. He may also be the same person referred to in Ac 19:22 and 2Ti 4:20, though it is difficult to be certain because the name was fairly common. *Quartus.* Means "fourth (son)."
16:25 *my gospel.* Not a gospel different from that preached by others, but a gospel Paul received by direct revelation (see Gal 1:12). *proclamation of Jesus Christ.* A description of the gospel; it is about Jesus Christ, who is its content. *mystery.* See note on 11:25. *for long ages.* From eternity past (see 1Co 2:6–10).
16:26 *revealed and made known through the prophetic writings.* See 1:2. *all nations.* The universality of the gospel (see Mt 28:19).
16:27 *to . . . God be glory.* The ultimate purpose of all things.

1 CORINTHIANS

Author and Date

Paul is acknowledged as the author both by the letter itself (1:1-2; 16:21) and by the early church fathers. His authorship was attested by Clement of Rome as early as A.D. 96, and today practically all NT scholars concur. The letter was written c. 55 toward the close of Paul's three-year residency in Ephesus (see 16:5-9; Ac 20:31). It is clear from his reference to staying at Ephesus until Pentecost (16:8) that he intended to remain there somewhat less than a year when he wrote 1 Corinthians.

The City of Corinth

It has been estimated that in Paul's day Corinth had a population of about 250,000 free persons, plus as many as 400,000 slaves. In a number of ways it was the chief city of Greece.

1. *Its commerce.* Located just off the Corinthian isthmus, it was a crossroads for travelers and traders. It had two harbors: (1) Cenchrea, six miles to the east on the Saronic Gulf, and (2) Lechaion, a mile and a half to the west on the Corinthian Gulf. Goods flowed across the isthmus on the Diolkos, a road by which smaller ships could be hauled fully loaded across the isthmus, and by which cargoes of larger ships could be transported by wagons from one side to the other. Goods flowed through the city from Italy and Spain to the west and from Asia Minor, Phoenicia and Egypt to the east.

2. *Its culture.* Although Corinth was not a university town like Athens, it was characterized nevertheless by typical Greek culture. Its people were interested in Greek philosophy and placed a high premium on wisdom.

3. *Its religion.* Corinth contained at least 12 temples. Whether they were all in use during Paul's time is not known for certain. One of the most infamous was the temple dedicated to Aphrodite, the goddess of love, whose worshipers practiced religious prostitution. About a fourth of a mile north of the theater stood the temple of Asclepius, the god of healing, and in the middle of the city the sixth-century B.C. temple of Apollo was located. In addition, the Jews had established a synagogue; the inscribed lintel of it has been found and placed in the museum at old Corinth.

4. *Its immorality.* Like any large commercial city, Corinth was a center for open and unbridled immorality. The worship of Aphrodite fostered prostitution in the name of religion. At one time 1,000 sacred prostitutes served her temple. So widely known did the immorality of Corinth become that the Greek verb "to Corinthianize" came to mean "to practice sexual immorality." In a setting like this it is no wonder that the Corinthian church was plagued with numerous problems.

Occasion and Purpose

Paul had received information from several sources concerning the conditions existing in the church at Corinth. Some members of the household of Chloe had informed him of the factions that had developed in the church (1:11). There were three individuals—Stephanas, Fortunatus and Achaicus—who had come to Paul in Ephesus to make some contribution to his ministry (16:17), but whether these were the ones from Chloe's household we do not know.

Some of those who had come had brought disturbing information concerning moral irregularities in the church (chs. 5-6). Immorality had plagued the Corinthian assembly almost from the beginning. From 5:9-10 it is apparent that Paul had written previously concerning moral laxness. He had urged believers "not to associate with sexually immoral people" (5:9). Because of misunderstanding he now finds it necessary to clarify his instruction (5:10-11) and to urge immediate and drastic action (5:3-5,13).

Other Corinthian visitors had brought a letter from the church that requested counsel on several subjects (see 7:1; cf. 8:1; 12:1; 16:1).

It is clear that, although the church was gifted (see 1:4-7), it was immature and unspiritual (3:1-4). Paul's purposes for writing were: (1) to instruct and restore the church in its areas of weakness,

correcting erroneous practices such as divisions (1:10-4:21), immorality (ch. 5; 6:12-20), litigation in pagan courts (6:1-8) and abuse of the Lord's Supper (11:17-34); (2) to correct false teaching concerning the resurrection (ch. 15); and (3) to give instruction concerning the offering for poverty-stricken believers in Jerusalem (16:1-4).

Theme

The letter revolves around the theme of problems in Christian conduct in the church. It thus has to do with progressive sanctification, the continuing development of holiness of character. Obviously Paul was personally concerned with the Corinthians' problems, revealing a true pastor's (shepherd's) heart.

Relevance

This letter is timely for the church today, both to instruct and to inspire. Most of the questions and problems that confronted the church at Corinth are still very much with us—problems like immaturity, instability, divisions, jealousy and envy, lawsuits, marital difficulties, sexual immorality and misuse of spiritual gifts. Yet in spite of this concentration on problems, the book contains some of the most familiar and beloved chapters in the entire Bible—e.g., ch. 13 (on love) and ch. 15 (on resurrection).

Corinth

In The Time of Paul

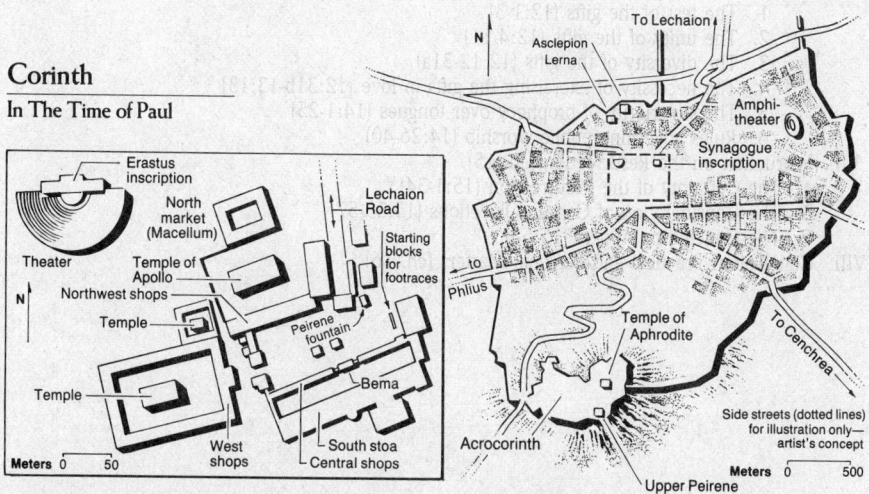

The city of Corinth, perched like a one-eyed Titan astride the narrow isthmus connecting the Greek mainland with the Peloponnese, was one of the dominant commercial centers of the Hellenic world as early as the eighth century B.C.

No city in Greece was more favorably situated for land and sea trade. With a high, strong citadel at its back, it lay between the Saronic Gulf and the Ionian Sea and ports at Lechaion and Cenchrea. A *diolkos*, or stone tramway for the overland transport of ships, linked the two seas. Crowning the Acrocorinth was the temple of Aphrodite, served, according to Strabo, by more than 1,000 pagan priestess-prostitutes.

By the time the gospel reached Corinth in the spring of A.D. 52, the city had a proud history of leadership in the Achaian League, and a spirit of revived Hellenism under Roman domination following the destruction of the city by Mummius in 146 B.C.

Paul's lengthy stay in Corinth brought him directly in contact with the major monuments of the *agora*, many of which still survive. The fountain-house of the spring *Peirene*, the temple of Apollo, the *macellum* or meat market (I Co 10:25) and the theater, the *bema* (Ac 18:12), and the unimpressive synagogue all played a part in the experience of the apostle. An inscription from the theater names the city official Erastus, probably the friend of Paul mentioned in Ro 16:23.

Outline

I. Introduction (1:1-9)
II. Divisions in the Church (1:10-4:21)
   A. The Fact of the Divisions (1:10-17)
   B. The Causes of the Divisions (1:18-4:13)
      1. A wrong conception of the Christian message (1:18-3:4)
      2. A wrong conception of Christian ministry and ministers (3:5-4:5)
      3. A wrong conception of the Christian (4:6-13)
   C. The Exhortation to End the Divisions (4:14-21)
III. Moral and Ethical Disorders in the Life of the Church (chs. 5-6)
   A. Laxity in Church Discipline (ch. 5)
   B. Lawsuits before Non-Christian Judges (6:1-11)
   C. Sexual Immorality (6:12-20)
IV. Instruction on Marriage (ch. 7)
   A. The Prologue: General Principles (7:1-7)
   B. The Problems of the Married (7:8-24)
   C. The Problems of the Unmarried (7:25-40)
V. Instruction on Questionable Practices (8:1-11:1)
   A. The Principles Involved (ch. 8)
   B. The Principles Illustrated (ch. 9)
   C. A Warning from the History of Israel (10:1-22)
   D. The Principles Applied (10:23-11:1)
VI. Instruction on Public Worship (11:2-14:40)
   A. Propriety in Worship (11:2-16)
   B. The Lord's Supper (11:17-34)
   C. Spiritual Gifts (chs. 12-14)
      1. The test of the gifts (12:1-3)
      2. The unity of the gifts (12:4-11)
      3. The diversity of the gifts (12:12-31a)
      4. The necessity of exercising the gifts in love (12:31b-13:13)
      5. The superiority of prophecy over tongues (14:1-25)
      6. Rules governing public worship (14:26-40)
VII. Instruction on the Resurrection (ch. 15)
   A. The Certainty of the Resurrection (15:1-34)
   B. The Consideration of Certain Objections (15:35-57)
   C. The Concluding Appeal (15:58)
VIII. Conclusion: Practical and Personal Matters (ch. 16)

1 Paul, called to be an apostle[a] of Christ Jesus by the will of God,[b] and our brother Sosthenes,[c]

²To the church of God[d] in Corinth,[e] to those sanctified in Christ Jesus and called[f] to be holy, together with all those everywhere who call on the name[g] of our Lord Jesus Christ—their Lord and ours:

³Grace and peace to you from God our Father and the Lord Jesus Christ.[h]

Thanksgiving

⁴I always thank God for you[i] because of his grace given you in Christ Jesus. ⁵For in him you have been enriched[j] in every way—in all your speaking and in all your knowledge[k]— ⁶because our testimony[l] about Christ was confirmed in you. ⁷Therefore you do not lack any spiritual gift[m] as you eagerly wait for our Lord Jesus Christ to be revealed.[n] ⁸He will keep you strong to the end, so that you will be blameless[o] on the day of our Lord Jesus Christ.[p] ⁹God, who has called you[q] into fellowship with his Son Jesus Christ our Lord,[r] is faithful.[s]

Divisions in the Church

¹⁰I appeal to you, brothers,[t] in the name of our Lord Jesus Christ, that all of you agree with one another so that there may be no divisions among you[u] and that you may be perfectly united[v] in mind and thought. ¹¹My brothers, some from Chloe's household[w] have informed me that there are quarrels among you. ¹²What I mean is this: One of you says, "I follow Paul";[x] another, "I follow Apollos";[y] another, "I follow Cephas[a]";[z] still another, "I follow Christ."

¹³Is Christ divided? Was Paul crucified for you? Were you baptized into[b] the name of Paul?[a] ¹⁴I am thankful that I did not baptize any of you except Crispus[b] and Gaius,[c] ¹⁵so no one can say that you were baptized into my name. ¹⁶(Yes, I also baptized the household[d] of Stephanas;[e] beyond that, I don't remember if I baptized anyone else.) ¹⁷For Christ did not send me to baptize,[f] but to preach the gospel—not with words of human wisdom,[g] lest the cross of Christ be emptied of its power.

Christ the Wisdom and Power of God

¹⁸For the message of the cross is foolish-

Cross references (center column)

1:1 [a]Ro 1:1; Eph 1:1; 2Ti 1:1
[b]S 2Co 1:1
[c]Ac 18:17
1:2 [d]S 1Co 10:32
[e]S Ac 18:1
[f]Ro 1:7
[g]S Ac 2:21
1:3 [h]S Ro 1:7
1:4 [i]S Ro 1:8
1:5 [j]2Co 9:11
[k]S 2Co 8:7
1:6 [l]2Th 1:10; 1Ti 2:6; Rev 1:2
1:7 [m]Ro 1:11; 1Co 12:1-31
[n]S Mt 16:27; S Lk 17:30; 1Th 1:10; S 2:19; Tit 2:13; Jas 5:7, 8; 1Pe 1:13; 2Pe 3:12; S Rev 1:7
1:8 [o]S 1Th 3:13
[p]Am 5:18; 1Co 5:5; Php 1:6, 10; 2:16; 1Th 5:2
1:9 [q]S Ro 8:28
[r]1Jn 1:3 sDt 7:9; Isa 49:7; 1Co 10:13; 1Th 5:24; 2Th 3:3; 2Ti 2:13;
1:10 [t]S Ro 7:1

[u]1Co 11:18
[v]S Ro 15:5
1:11 [w]S Ac 11:14
1:12 [x]1Co 3:4,22
[y]S Ac 18:24
[z]Jn 1:42;
1Co 3:22; 9:5
1:13 [a]S Mt 28:19
1:14 [b]Ac 18:8
[c]S Ac 19:29

1:16 [d]S Ac 11:14 [e]1Co 16:15 1:17 [f]Jn 4:2; S Ac 2:38
[g]1Co 2:1,4,13

[a]12 That is, Peter   [b]13 Or in; also in verse 15

1:1 *Paul.* The Greek custom was to begin a letter with the writer's name. For more information on Paul see notes on Ac 9:1; Php 3:4–14. *apostle of Christ Jesus.* See notes on Mk 6:30; Heb 3:1. Paul uses this title in all his letters (except Philippians, 1,2 Thessalonians and Philemon) to establish his authority as Christ's messenger—an authority that had been challenged (see ch. 9; 2Co 11). He reinforces his authority by adding "by the will of God," i.e., by divine initiative. *Sosthenes.* Perhaps the synagogue ruler at Corinth who was assaulted by the Greeks (Ac 18:17). If so, he obviously became a Christian—possibly while Paul was preaching at Corinth (Ac 18:18) or during Apollos's ministry there (Ac 19:1).
1:2 *church of God.* Used only by Paul and only in Ac 20:28, here and 2Co 1:1. Its OT counterpart is the expression "assembly (or community) of the LORD" (see Dt 23:1; see also Nu 16:3; 20:4; 1Ch 28:8). *sanctified.* Set apart for the Lord. It can also mean "made holy," which is done by (1) being declared holy through faith in Christ's atoning death on the cross (sometimes called positional sanctification), and (2) being made holy by the work of the Holy Spirit in the lives of Christians (sometimes called progressive sanctification). In spite of the fact that Paul found much in the Corinthian Christians to criticize, he still called them "sanctified"—not because of their conduct, but because of their relationship to Christ (positional sanctification).
1:3 *Grace and peace.* See notes on Jnh 4:2; Jn 14:27; 20:19; Gal 1:3; Eph 1:2.
1:4 *thank.* See Ro 1:8.
1:5 *speaking and . . . knowledge.* Gifts of the Spirit (see 12:8; see also 2Co 8:7).
1:6 *confirmed.* Paul's preaching about Christ had been accepted by the Corinthians, and they had proved it to be true.

1:7 *any spiritual gift.* Probably refers to the spiritual gifts of chs. 12–14. According to those chapters, a spiritual gift is a manifestation of the Holy Spirit enabling one to minister to the needs of Christ's body, the church (see 12:7–11; 14:3, 12,17). The Greek word used here stresses that it is a gift of grace.
1:8 *He.* God the Father. *the end.* Of the age, when Christ comes again. *on the day of our Lord Jesus Christ.* When he returns (v. 7; Php 1:6).
1:9 *God . . . is faithful.* He may be trusted to do what he has promised (1Th 5:24), namely, to keep believers "strong to the end" (v. 8).
1:10 *brothers.* In Christ believers have a unity similar to that of blood brothers and sisters. Paul is referring to both men and women (see 16:20; Ro 16:3,6–7,12–13,15).
1:11 *quarrels.* See Gal 5:19; Jas 4:12.
1:12 *Apollos.* He had carried on a fruitful ministry in Corinth (Ac 18:24–28; 19:1). *Cephas.* See NIV text notes here and on Jn 1:42. It has been suggested that those who followed Peter in Corinth were Jewish Christians.
1:13 *Is Christ divided?* See 12:12–13. *into the name of Paul.* Implies becoming a follower or intimate associate.
1:16 *household.* Other examples of households being baptized are those of Cornelius (Ac 10:24, 48), Lydia (Ac 16:15) and the Philippian jailer (Ac 16:33–34). The term may include family members, servants or anyone who lived in the house. *Stephanas.* See 16:15,17.
1:17 *not . . . to baptize.* Paul is not minimizing baptism; rather, he is asserting that his God-given task was primarily to preach. Jesus (Jn 4:2) and Peter (Ac 10:48) also had others baptize for them. *words of human wisdom.* Lit. "wisdom of speech." Paul's mission was not to couch the gospel in the language of the trained orator, who had studied the techniques of influencing people by persuasive arguments.

ness[h] to those who are perishing,[i] but to us who are being saved[j] it is the power of God.[k] 19For it is written:

"I will destroy the wisdom of the wise;
    the intelligence of the intelligent I
    will frustrate."[c][l]

20Where is the wise man?[m] Where is the scholar? Where is the philosopher of this age?[n] Has not God made foolish[o] the wisdom of the world? 21For since in the wisdom of God the world[p] through its wisdom did not know him, God was pleased through the foolishness of what was preached to save[q] those who believe.[r] 22Jews demand miraculous signs[s] and Greeks look for wisdom, 23but we preach Christ crucified:[t] a stumbling block[u] to Jews and foolishness[v] to Gentiles, 24but to those whom God has called,[w] both Jews and Greeks, Christ the power of God[x] and the wisdom of God.[y] 25For the foolishness[z] of God is wiser than man's wisdom, and the weakness[a] of God is stronger than man's strength.

26Brothers, think of what you were when you were called.[b] Not many of you were wise[c] by human standards; not many were influential; not many were of noble birth. 27But God chose[d] the foolish[e] things of the world to shame the wise; God chose the weak things of the world to shame the strong. 28He chose the lowly things of this world and the despised things—and the things that are not[f]—to nullify the things that are, 29so that no one may boast before him.[g] 30It is because of him that you are in Christ Jesus,[h] who has become for us wisdom from God—that is, our righteousness,[i] holiness[j] and redemption.[k] 31Therefore, as it is written: "Let him who boasts boast in the Lord."[d][l]

2 When I came to you, brothers, I did not come with eloquence or superior wisdom[m] as I proclaimed to you the testimony about God.[e] 2For I resolved to know nothing while I was with you except Jesus Christ and him crucified.[n] 3I came to you[o] in weakness[p] and fear, and with much trembling.[q] 4My message and my preaching were not with wise and persuasive words,[r] but with a demonstration of the Spirit's power,[s] 5so that your faith might not rest on men's wisdom, but on God's power.[t]

Wisdom From the Spirit

6We do, however, speak a message of

Cross references

1:18 [h]ver 21,23, 25; 1Co 2:14 [i]2Co 2:15; 4:3; 2Th 2:10 [j]Ac 2:47 [k]ver 24; Ro 1:16
1:19 [l]Isa 29:14
1:20 [m]Isa 19:11, 12 [n]1Co 2:6,8; 3:18; 2Co 4:4; Gal 1:4 [o]ver 27; Job 12:17; Isa 44:25; Jer 8:9; Ro 1:22; 1Co 3:18,19
1:21 [p]ver 27,28; 1Co 6:2; 11:32 [q]S Ro 11:14 [r]S Ro 3:22
1:22 [s]S Mt 12:38; S Jn 2:11; S 4:48
1:23 [t]1Co 2:2; Gal 3:1 [u]S Lk 2:34 [v]S ver 18
1:24 [w]S Ro 8:28 [x]ver 18; Ro 1:16 [y]ver 30; S Col 2:3
1:25 [z]S ver 18 [a]2Co 13:4
1:26 [b]S Ro 8:28 [c]ver 20
1:27 [d]Jas 2:5 [e]ver 20; Ro 1:22; 1Co 3:18,19
1:28 [f]Ro 4:17
1:29 [g]Eph 2:9
1:30 [h]S Ro 16:3 [i]Jer 23:5,6; 33:16; 2Co 5:21; Php 3:9 / 1Co 1:2 [j]S Ro 3:24
1:31 [l]Jer 9:23,24; Ps 34:2; 44:8; 2Co 10:17
2:1 [m]ver 4,13; 1Co 1:17
2:2 [n]Gal 6:14; 1Co 1:23
2:3 [o]Ac 18:1-18 [p]1Co 4:10; 9:22; 2Co 11:29,30; 12:5,9,10; 13:9 [q]S 2Co 7:15 2:4 [r]ver 1 [s]S Ro 15:13 2:5 [t]2Co 4:7; 6:7

[c]19 Isaiah 29:14   [d]31 Jer. 9:24   [e]1 Some manuscripts as I proclaimed to you God's mystery

---

1:19 The quotation is from Isa 29:14, where God denounced the policy of the "wise" in Judah in seeking an alliance with Egypt when threatened by King Sennacherib of Assyria. *the wise.* Aristides said that on every street in Corinth one met a so-called wise man, who had his own solutions to the world's problems.
1:20 *wise man.* Probably a reference to Gentile philosophers in general. *scholar.* Probably the Jewish teacher of the law (see note on Mt 2:4). *philosopher of this age.* Probably refers to the Greek sophists, who engaged in long and subtle disputes. *God made foolish the wisdom of the world.* All humanly devised philosophical systems end in meaninglessness because they have a wrong concept of God and his revelation.
1:21 *wisdom . . . foolishness.* Jesus expresses a similar thought in Lk 10:21. It is God's intention that worldly wisdom should not be the means of knowing him. *foolishness of what was preached.* Not that preaching is foolish, but that the message being preached (Christ crucified) is viewed by the world as foolish.
1:22 *Greeks look for wisdom.* True of Greeks in general, but especially of the Greek philosophers.
1:23 *Christ crucified.* See 2:2. *stumbling block to Jews.* They expected a triumphant, political Messiah (Ac 1:6), not a crucified one. *foolishness to Gentiles.* Greeks and Romans were sure that no reputable person would be crucified, so it was unthinkable that a crucified criminal could be the Savior.
1:24 *power.* See Ro 1:4,16; Mk 12:24. *wisdom.* See v. 30. The crucified Christ is the power that saves and the wisdom that transforms seeming folly into ultimate and highest discernment.
1:26–31 The Corinthian Christians themselves were living

proof that salvation does not depend on anything in man, so that when someone is saved, he must boast in the Lord (v. 31).
1:30 *because of him . . . you are in Christ.* It is God who has called you to union and communion with Christ. *righteousness.* It is by faith in Christ that we are justified (declared righteous); see Ro 5:19. *holiness.* See note on v. 2. *redemption.* See note on Ro 3:24.
2:1 *When I came to you.* On his initial trip to Corinth c. A.D. 51 (Ac 18). *with eloquence or superior wisdom.* See note on 1:17. Perhaps Apollos (Ac 18:24–28) had influenced the Corinthians in such a way that they were placing undue emphasis on eloquence and intellectual ability.
2:2 *know nothing . . . except Jesus Christ.* Paul resolved to make Christ the sole subject of his teaching and preaching while he was with them. *Jesus Christ.* See 1:30. *him crucified.* See 1:17–18,23.
2:4 *not with wise and persuasive words.* This does not give preachers a license to neglect study and preparation. Paul's letters reveal a great deal of knowledge in many areas of learning, and his eloquence is apparent in his address before the Areopagus (see Ac 17:22–31 and notes). Paul's point is that unless the Holy Spirit works in a listener's heart, the wisdom and eloquence of a preacher are ineffective. Paul's confidence as a preacher did not rest on intellectual and oratorical ability, as did that of the Greek orators (see note on 1:17). *demonstration.* The Greek word is used of producing proofs in an argument in court. Paul's preaching was marked by the convincing demonstration of the power of the Holy Spirit.
2:6 *mature.* Wise, developed Christians; contrast the "in-

wisdom among the mature,[u] but not the wisdom of this age[v] or of the rulers of this age, who are coming to nothing.[w] [7]No, we speak of God's secret wisdom, a wisdom[x] that has been hidden[y] and that God destined for our glory before time began. [8]None of the rulers of this age[z] understood it, for if they had, they would not have crucified the Lord of glory.[a] [9]However, as it is written:

"No eye has seen,
  no ear has heard,
no mind has conceived
  what God has prepared for those who
    love him"[f] [b] —

[10]but God has revealed[c] it to us by his Spirit.[d]

The Spirit searches all things, even the deep things of God. [11]For who among men knows the thoughts of a man[e] except the man's spirit[f] within him? In the same way no one knows the thoughts of God except the Spirit of God. [12]We have not received the spirit[g] of the world[h] but the Spirit who is from God, that we may understand what God has freely given us. [13]This is what we speak, not in words taught us by human wisdom[i] but in words taught by the Spirit, expressing spiritual truths in spiritual words.[g] [14]The man without the Spirit does not accept the things that come from the Spirit of God,[j] for they are foolishness[k] to him, and he cannot understand them, because they are spiritually dis-

cerned. [15]The spiritual[l] man makes judgments about all things, but he himself is not subject to any man's judgment:

[16]"For who has known the mind of the
    Lord
  that he may instruct him?"[h] [m]

But we have the mind of Christ.[n]

On Divisions in the Church

3 Brothers, I could not address you as spiritual[o] but as worldly[p]—mere infants[q] in Christ. [2]I gave you milk, not solid food,[r] for you were not yet ready for it.[s] Indeed, you are still not ready. [3]You are still worldly. For since there is jealousy and quarreling[t] among you, are you not worldly? Are you not acting like mere men? [4]For when one says, "I follow Paul," and another, "I follow Apollos,"[u] are you not mere men?

[5]What, after all, is Apollos?[v] And what is Paul? Only servants,[w] through whom you came to believe—as the Lord has assigned to each his task. [6]I planted the seed,[x] Apollos watered it, but God made it grow. [7]So neither he who plants nor he who waters is anything, but only God, who makes things grow. [8]The man who plants and the man who waters have one purpose, and each will be rewarded according to his own labor.[y] [9]For we are

(center column cross-references)

2:6 [u]Eph 4:13; Php 3:15; Col 4:12; Heb 5:14; 6:1; Jas 1:4 [v]ver 8; S 1Co 1:20 [w]Ps 146:4
2:7 [x]ver 1 [y]Ro 16:25
2:8 [z]ver 6; S 1Co 1:20 [a]Ps 24:7; Ac 7:2; Jas 2:1
2:9 [b]Isa 64:4; 65:17
2:10 [c]S Mt 13:11; 2Co 12:1,7; Gal 1:12; 2:2; Eph 3:3,5 [d]Jn 14:26
2:11 [e]Jer 17:9 [f]Pr 20:27
2:12 [g]Ro 8:15 [h]1Co 1:20,27; Jas 2:5
2:13 [i]ver 1,4; 1Co 1:17
2:14 [j]Jn 14:17 [k]S 1Co 1:18
2:15 [l]1Co 3:1; Gal 6:1
2:16 [m]Isa 40:13; S Ro 11:34 [n]Jn 15:15
3:1 [o]1Co 2:15 [p]Ro 7:14; 1Co 2:14 [q]1Co 14:20
3:2 [r]Heb 5:12-14; 1Pe 2:2 [s]Jn 16:12
3:3 [t]Ro 13:13; 1Co 1:11; Gal 5:20
3:4 [u]1Co 1:12
3:5 [v]S Ac 18:24 [w]1Co 4:1; 2Co 6:4; Eph 3:7; Col 1:23,25
3:6 [x]Ac 18:4-11; 1Co 4:15; 9:1; 15:1
3:8 [y]ver 14; Ps 18:20; 62:12;

Mt 25:21; 1Co 9:17

[f]9 Isaiah 64:4   [g]13 Or Spirit, interpreting spiritual truths to spiritual men   [h]16 Isaiah 40:13

---

fants" mentioned in 3:1 (see Heb 5:13–6:3).
2:7 *secret.* Cf. Ro 16:25–26; Eph 3:4–5; 1Ti 3:16. The secret, or mystery, was once hidden but is now known because God has revealed it to his people (v. 10). To unbelievers it is still hidden. *for our glory.* God's wisdom will cause every believer to share eventually in Christ's glory (Ro 8:17).
2:8 *rulers of this age.* Such as the chief priests (Lk 24:20), Pilate and Herod Antipas (cf. Ac 4:27). *crucified the Lord of glory.* The cross is here contrasted with the majesty of the victim.
2:9 *what God has prepared.* Probably not to be limited to either present or future blessing; both are involved (cf. vv. 7,12).
2:10 *Spirit searches all things.* Not in order to know them, for he knows all things. Instead he comprehends the depth of God's nature and his plans of grace; so he is fully competent to make the revelation claimed here.
2:12 *spirit of the world.* Cf. v. 6 ("wisdom of this age"); the spirit of human wisdom as alienated from God—the attitude of the sinful nature (Ro 8:6–7).
2:13 *words taught by the Spirit.* The message Paul proclaimed was expressed in words given by the Holy Spirit. Thus spiritual truth was aptly combined with fitting spiritual words. But see NIV text note.
2:14–3:4 This passage explains why many fail to apprehend true wisdom (2:9). It is because such wisdom is perceived by the spiritual (mature) Christian (2:14–16; cf. v.

6). The Corinthians, however, were worldly (infant) believers (3:1–4), and the proof of their immaturity was their division over human leaders (3:3–4).
2:14 *man without the Spirit.* Described in Jude 19 as one who follows "mere natural instincts" (cf. Ro 8:9). The non-Christian is basically dominated by the merely physical, worldly or natural life. Because he does not possess the Holy Spirit, he is not equipped to receive appreciatively truth that comes from the Spirit. Such a person needs the new birth (Jn 3:1–8; Tit 3:5–6). *foolishness.* See 1:18.
2:15 *spiritual.* Mature (v. 6). *not subject to any man's judgment.* One who does not have the Spirit is not qualified to judge the spiritual person. Thus believers are not rightfully subject to the opinions of unbelievers.
3:1 *Brothers.* See note on 1:10. *spiritual.* See note on 2:15. *worldly.* See note on 2:14–3:4.
3:2 *milk, not solid food.* See notes on Heb 5:12–14.
3:3 *like mere men.* Like men of the world instead of men of God. They were following merely human standards.
3:4 *I follow Paul . . . Apollos.* See 1:12.
3:6 *I planted.* See Ac 18:4–11. Paul's work was of a pioneer nature, preaching where no one had ever preached before. *Apollos watered.* See Ac 18:24–28. Apollos worked in the established church, edifying the converts Paul had won.
3:9 *God's field.* The people are God's farm. *God's building.* They are also depicted as God's temple (vv. 16–17). He owns the farm and the building where both Paul and Apollos

God's fellow workers;[z] you are God's field,[a] God's building.[b]

[10]By the grace God has given me,[c] I laid a foundation[d] as an expert builder, and someone else is building on it. But each one should be careful how he builds. [11]For no one can lay any foundation other than the one already laid, which is Jesus Christ.[e] [12]If any man builds on this foundation using gold, silver, costly stones, wood, hay or straw, [13]his work will be shown for what it is,[f] because the Day[g] will bring it to light. It will be revealed with fire, and the fire will test the quality of each man's work.[h] [14]If what he has built survives, he will receive his reward.[i] [15]If it is burned up, he will suffer loss; he himself will be saved, but only as one escaping through the flames.[j]

[16]Don't you know that you yourselves are God's temple[k] and that God's Spirit lives in you?[l] [17]If anyone destroys God's temple, God will destroy him; for God's temple is sacred, and you are that temple.

[18]Do not deceive yourselves. If any one of you thinks he is wise[m] by the standards of this age,[n] he should become a "fool" so that he may become wise. [19]For the wisdom of this world is foolishness[o] in God's sight. As it is written: "He catches the wise in their craftiness";[p] [20]and again, "The Lord knows that the thoughts of the wise are futile."[q] [21]So then, no more

boasting about men![r] All things are yours,[s] [22]whether Paul or Apollos[t] or Cephas[k][u] or the world or life or death or the present or the future[v]—all are yours, [23]and you are of Christ,[w] and Christ is of God.

Apostles of Christ

4 So then, men ought to regard us as servants[x] of Christ and as those entrusted[y] with the secret things[z] of God. [2]Now it is required that those who have been given a trust must prove faithful. [3]I care very little if I am judged by you or by any human court; indeed, I do not even judge myself. [4]My conscience[a] is clear, but that does not make me innocent.[b] It is the Lord who judges me.[c] [5]Therefore judge nothing[d] before the appointed time; wait till the Lord comes.[e] He will bring to light[f] what is hidden in darkness and will expose the motives of men's hearts. At that time each will receive his praise from God.[g]

[6]Now, brothers, I have applied these things to myself and Apollos for your benefit, so that you may learn from us the meaning of the saying, "Do not go beyond what is written."[h] Then you will not take pride in one man over against another.[i]

3:9 z Mk 16:20; 2Co 6:1; 1Th 3:2
a Isa 61:3
b Eph 2:20-22; 1Pe 2:5
3:10 c S Ro 12:3
d Ro 15:20; S Eph 2:20
3:11 e Isa 28:16; Eph 2:20
3:13 f 1Co 4:5
g S 1Co 1:8; 2Th 1:7-10; 2Ti 1:12,18; 4:8
h Nu 31:22,23; Jer 23:28,29; Mal 3:3; S 2Th 1:7
3:14 i S ver 8
3:15 j Jude 23
3:16 k 1Co 6:19; 2Co 6:16; Eph 2:21,22; Heb 3:6 /S Ro 8:9
3:18 m Isa 5:21; 1Co 8:2; Gal 6:3
n S 1Co 1:20
3:19 o ver 18; Ro 1:22; 1Co 1:20,27
p Job 5:13
3:20 q Ps 94:11

3:21 r 1Co 4:6
s Ro 8:32
3:22 t ver 5,6
u S 1Co 1:12
v Ro 8:38
3:23 w 1Co 15:23; 2Co 10:7; Gal 3:29
4:1 x S 1Co 3:5
y 1Co 9:17; Tit 1:7
z S Ro 16:25
4:4 a S Ac 23:1
b Ro 2:13
c 2Co 10:18
4:5 d S Mt 7:1,2
e S 1Th 2:19 /Job 12:22; Ps 90:8; 1Co 3:13

g S Ro 2:29 **4:6** h 1Co 1:19,31; 3:19,20 i 1Co 1:12; 3:4

i 19 Job 5:13   j 20 Psalm 94:11   k 22 That is, Peter

---

worked.

3:10 *I laid a foundation.* By preaching Christ and him crucified (2:2). *someone else.* Apollos.

3:12 *gold, silver, costly stones.* Precious, durable work that stands the test of divine judgment; symbolic of pure Christian doctrine and living. *wood, hay or straw.* Worthless work that will not stand the test; symbolic of weak, insipid teaching and life.

3:13 Cf. 4:5; 2Co 5:10. *the Day.* See note on 1:8. *fire.* God's judgment. The work of some believers will stand the test while that of others will disappear—emphasizing the importance of teaching the pure word of God.

3:15 *loss.* Of reward (v. 14). *as one escaping through the flames.* Perhaps a Greek proverbial phrase, meaning "by a narrow escape," with one's work burned up by the fire of God's pure justice and judgment.

3:16 *God's temple.* Paul does not mean here that each of his readers is a temple of the Holy Spirit. He says, "You yourselves (plural) are God's temple (singular)." In 6:19 he speaks of each Christian as a temple of the Holy Spirit.

3:17 *God will destroy him.* Strong language, indicating that such a foolish laborer is not one of the Lord's true servants. This is in contrast to the thought of v. 15, where the faulty Christian worker is saved, but his work is destroyed (he suffers loss of reward). In the context of chs. 1–4 Paul here refers to people who tear the local church apart by factions and quarrels (1:11–12). *sacred.* Holy, set apart for God's use and glory; so do not desecrate the church by breaking it up into various factions.

3:18 *become a "fool."* Turn away from human wisdom (from being "wise by the standards of this age"). Cf. 1:18. *become wise.* Cf. 1:21, 24.

3:21 *about men.* About being some man's disciple (see 1:12; 3:4; cf. 1:31; 4:6). *All things are yours.* All these Christian leaders belong to the whole church. No group can call one leader its very own (see vv. 22–23).

3:23 *you are of Christ.* You are united with and belong to Christ. *Christ is of God.* Christ is in union with God the Father (Jn 10:30) and with God the Holy Spirit (2Co 13:14). Similarly, Christians are in union with the church's true leaders (v. 22) and with Christ (v. 23), who in turn is in union with the other members of the Trinity.

4:1 *those entrusted.* The Greek underlying this phrase means "house manager" or "steward." *secret things.* Things that human wisdom cannot discover but that are now revealed by God to his people (see note on Ro 11:25).

4:3 *not even judge myself.* His judgment was merely human, and his conscience may be mistaken (v. 4). Only God is fully qualified to judge.

4:5 *appointed time.* When God will judge believers (see 3:13). *expose the motives.* Cf. Ps 19:12; 139:23–24; Heb 4:12–13.

4:6 *these things.* See 3:5–4:5. *the saying.* Perhaps a proverb common among the rabbis. *what is written.* In Scripture. Our view of man should be Biblical (cf. v. 7; 1:9, 31; 3:19–20; Ro 12:3). We should recognize man's weakness and ever-present limitations. *pride.* One of the root causes of divisions.

7For who makes you different from anyone else? What do you have that you did not receive?/ And if you did receive it, why do you boast as though you did not?

8Already you have all you want! Already you have become rich!k You have become kings—and that without us! How I wish that you really had become kings so that we might be kings with you! 9For it seems to me that God has put us apostles on display at the end of the procession, like men condemned to die l in the arena. We have been made a spectacle m to the whole universe, to angels as well as to men. 10We are fools for Christ,n but you are so wise in Christ!o We are weak, but you are strong!p You are honored, we are dishonored! 11To this very hour we go hungry and thirsty, we are in rags, we are brutally treated, we are homeless.q 12We work hard with our own hands.r When we are cursed, we bless;s when we are persecuted,t we endure it; 13when we are slandered, we answer kindly. Up to this moment we have become the scum of the earth, the refuse u of the world.

14I am not writing this to shame you,v but to warn you, as my dear children.w 15Even though you have ten thousand guardians in Christ, you do not have many fathers, for in Christ Jesus I became your fatherx through the gospel.y 16Therefore I urge you to imitate me.z 17For this reason I am sending to youa Timothy,b my sonc whom I love, who is faithful in the Lord.

He will remind you of my way of life in Christ Jesus, which agrees with what I teach everywhere in every church. d

18Some of you have become arrogant,e as if I were not coming to you.f 19But I will come to you very soon,g if the Lord is willing,h and then I will find out not only how these arrogant people are talking, but what power they have. 20For the kingdom of God is not a matter ofi talk but of power.j 21What do you prefer? Shall I come to you with a whip,k or in love and with a gentle spirit?

Expel the Immoral Brother!

5 It is actually reported that there is sexual immorality among you, and of a kind that does not occur even among pagans: A man has his father's wife.l 2And you are proud! Shouldn't you rather have been filled with grief m and have put out of your fellowship n the man who did this? 3Even though I am not physically present, I am with you in spirit. o And I have already passed judgment on the one who did this, just as if I were present. 4When you are assembled in the name of our Lord Jesusp and I am with you in spirit, and the power of our Lord Jesus is present, 5hand this man over q to Satan,r so that the sinful nature1 may be destroyed and his spirit saved on the day of the Lord.s

15 Or that his body; or that the flesh

Cross references

4:7 /Jn 3:27; Ro 12:3,6
4:8 kRev 3:17,18
4:9 lS Ro 8:36
mPs 71:7;
Heb 10:33
4:10
nS 1Co 1:18;
o1Co 3:18;
2Co 11:19
pS 1Co 2:3
4:11 qRo 8:35;
2Co 11:23-27
4:12 rS Ac 18:3
sRo 12:14;
1Pe 3:9
tS Mt 5:44
4:13 uJer 20:18;
La 3:45
4:14 v1Co 6:5;
15:34; 2Th 3:14
wS 1Th 2:11
4:15 xS ver 14
y1Co 9:12,14,18,
23; 15:1
4:16 z1Co 11:1;
Php 3:17; 4:9;
1Th 1:6; 2Th 3:7,
9
4:17 a1Co 16:10
bS Ac 16:1
cS 1Ti 1:2

dS 1Co 7:17
4:18 eJer 43:2
/ver 21
4:19 g1Co 16:5,
6; 2Co 1:15,16
hS Ac 18:21
4:20 iRo 14:17
/S Ro 15:13
4:21 k2Co 1:23;
2:1; 13:2,10
5:1 /Lev 18:8;
Dt 22:30; 27:20
5:2 m2Co 7:7-11
nver 13
5:3 oCol 2:5;
1Th 2:17
5:4 p2Th 3:6
5:5 q1Ti 1:20
rS Mt 4:10
sS 1Co 1:8

4:8 Paul uses irony and sarcasm here to get the Corinthians to see how poor they really are because of their haughtiness and spiritual immaturity in comparison with apostles.

4:9 *apostles.* See note on 1:1. *spectacle.* "Theater" is derived from the Greek word used here. Paul refers to the gladiatorial contests in the arena (or perhaps to the triumphal procession of a victorious Roman general). He pictures all the world and even angels looking on while the apostles are brought in last to fight to the death.

4:10 More irony.

4:11–13 A graphic description of Paul's condition in Ephesus right up to the writing of this letter.

4:12 *We work hard with our own hands.* Paul was a tentmaker by trade (Ac 18:3; cf. 20:34–35; 1Co 9:6,18). *we bless.* See Mt 5:44. *endure it.* Instead of retaliating.

4:14 *my dear children.* See v. 15.

4:15 *your father.* See 3:6,10.

4:18 *Some of you.* Some of the Corinthians who were trying to undercut Paul's authority (see 9:1–3) were teaching that he was unstable (2Co 1:17) and that his ministry was not important (2Co 10:10).

4:19 *arrogant.* See 5:2.

4:20 *kingdom of God.* God's present reign in the lives of his people—that dynamic new life in Christ (2Co 5:17), the power of the new birth (Jn 3:3–8), showing itself in a humble life, dedicated to Christ and his church. *not . . . of talk but of power.* Idle, empty talk is contrasted with the genuine power of the Holy Spirit.

5:1 *not . . . even among pagans.* The Roman orator Cicero states that incest was practically unheard of in Roman society. *his father's wife.* That this expression was used rather than "his mother" suggests that the woman was his stepmother. The OT prohibited such a marriage (Lev 18:8; Dt 22:30; 27:20).

5:2 *proud.* Evidently proud of their liberty—a distortion of grace. *put out of your fellowship.* Excommunicated from the church (cf. Jn 9:22).

5:4 *assembled in the name of our Lord Jesus.* The Corinthians are to pass judgment on the man by the authority of the Lord Jesus. *the power of our Lord Jesus is present.* Jesus' power is present through his word and his Holy Spirit.

5:5 *hand this man over to Satan.* Abandon this sinful man to the devil that he may afflict the man as he pleases. This abandonment to Satan was to be accomplished, not by some magical incantation, but by expelling the man from the church (see v. 13; also vv. 2,7,11). To expel him was to put him out in the devil's territory, severed from any connection with God's people. *so that the sinful nature may be destroyed.* So that being officially ostracized from the church will cause the man such anguish that he will repent and forsake his wicked way. For an alternative interpretation see NIV text note. In the latter view, Satan is allowed to bring physical affliction on the man, which would bring him to repentance. *his spirit saved.* Cf. 3:15. The person put out of the church may well be a Christian. *day of the Lord.* When Christ returns (see 1:7).

⁶Your boasting is not good.ᵗ Don't you know that a little yeastᵘ works through the whole batch of dough?ᵛ ⁷Get rid of the old yeast that you may be a new batch without yeast—as you really are. For Christ, our Passover lamb, has been sacrificed.ʷ ⁸Therefore let us keep the Festival, not with the old yeast, the yeast of malice and wickedness, but with bread without yeast,ˣ the bread of sincerity and truth.

⁹I have written you in my letter not to associateʸ with sexually immoral people— ¹⁰not at all meaning the people of this worldᶻ who are immoral, or the greedy and swindlers, or idolaters. In that case you would have to leave this world. ¹¹But now I am writing you that you must not associate with anyone who calls himself a brotherᵃ but is sexually immoral or greedy, an idolaterᵇ or a slanderer, a drunkard or a swindler. With such a man do not even eat.ᶜ

¹²What business is it of mine to judge those outsideᵈ the church? Are you not to judge those inside?ᵉ ¹³God will judge those outside. "Expel the wicked man from among you."ᵐᶠ

Lawsuits Among Believers

6 If any of you has a dispute with another, dare he take it before the ungodly for judgment instead of before the saints?ᵍ ²Do you not know that the saints will judge the world?ʰ And if you are to judge the world, are you not competent to judge trivial cases? ³Do you not know that we will judge angels? How much more the things of this life! ⁴Therefore, if you have disputes about such matters, appoint as judges even men of little account in the church!ⁿ ⁵I say this to shame you.ⁱ Is it possible that there is nobody among you wise enough to judge a dispute between believers?ʲ ⁶But instead, one brotherᵏ goes to law against another—and this in front of unbelievers!ˡ

⁷The very fact that you have lawsuits among you means you have been completely defeated already. Why not rather be wronged? Why not rather be cheated?ᵐ ⁸Instead, you yourselves cheat and do wrong, and you do this to your brothers.ⁿ

Cross references

5:6 ᵗJas 4:16
ᵘMt 16:6,12
ᵛGal 5:9
5:7 ʷEx 12:3-6, 21; Mk 14:12; 1Pe 1:19
5:8 ˣEx 12:14, 15; Dt 16:3
5:9 ʸEph 5:11; 2Th 3:6,14
5:10 ᶻ1Co 10:27
5:11 ᵃS Ro 7:1
ᵇ1Co 10:7,14
ᶜS Ro 16:17
5:12 ᵈS Mk 4:11
ᵉver 3-5; 1Co 6:1-4
5:13 ᶠDt 13:5; 17:7; 19:19; 22:21,24; 24:7; Jdg 20:13

6:1 ᵍMt 18:17
6:2 ʰMt 19:28; Lk 22:30; 1Co 5:12
6:5 ⁱS 1Co 4:14
ʲAc 1:15
6:6 ᵏS Ro 7:1
ˡ2Co 6:14,15; 1Ti 5:8
6:7 ᵐMt 5:39,40
6:8 ⁿ1Th 4:6

ᵐ13 Deut. 17:7; 19:19; 21:21; 22:21,24; 24:7
ⁿ4 Or matters, do you appoint as judges men of little account in the church?

5:6 *a little yeast . . . the whole batch of dough.* To illustrate Christian holiness and discipline, Paul alludes to the prohibition against the use of leaven (or yeast) in the bread eaten in the Passover Feast (see Ex 12:15). Leaven in Scripture usually symbolizes evil or sin (see note on Mk 8:15), and the church here is called on to get rid of the yeast of sin (v. 8) because they are an unleavened batch of dough—new creations in Christ (2Co 5:17).

5:7 *Get rid of the old yeast.* Perhaps refers to the Passover custom of sweeping all the (leavened) bread crumbs out of one's house before preparing the Passover meal. *without yeast—as you really are.* Positionally they were a new batch, already sanctified in God's sight (see 1:2; 6:11), but Paul calls on them to become holy also in conduct (see note on 1:2). *Christ, our Passover lamb.* In his death on the cross, Christ fulfilled the true meaning of the Jewish sacrifice of the Passover lamb (Isa 53:7; Jn 1:29). Christ, the Lamb of God, was crucified on Passover day, a celebration that began the evening before when the Passover meal was eaten (cf. Ex 12:8).

5:8 *let us keep the Festival.* Keeping the Feast of Unleavened Bread (which followed Passover) symbolizes living the Christian life in holy dedication to God (cf. Ro 12:1–2; 1Pe 2:5) and not getting involved in such sins as malice and wickedness and incestuous marriages.

5:9 *I have written you in my letter.* Paul here clarifies a previous letter (one not preserved). The Corinthians mistook that letter to mean that, on separating from sin, they should disassociate themselves from all immoral persons, including non-Christian people. Instead, Paul meant that they should separate from immoral persons in the church who claimed to be Christian brothers (vv. 10–11).

5:11 *With such a man do not even eat.* Calling oneself a Christian while continuing to live an immoral life is reprehensible and degrading, and gives a false testimony to Christ. If the true Christian has intimate association with someone who does this, the non-Christian world may assume that the

church approves such immoral, ungodly living and thus the name of Christ would be dishonored. Questions could arise concerning the true character of the Christian's own testimony (cf. Ro 16:17–18; 2Th 3:6, 14–15).

5:12 *judge those inside.* The church is to exercise spiritual discipline over the professing believers in the church (cf. Mt 18:15–18), but it is not to attempt to judge the unsaved world. There are governing authorities to do that (Ro 13:1–5), and the ultimate judgment of the world is to be left to God (v. 13; cf. Rev 20:11–15).

6:1 *a dispute with another.* Paul seems to be talking about various kinds of property court cases here (cf. the phrase "rather be cheated," v. 7), not criminal cases that should be handled by the state (Ro 13:3–4). *before the saints.* The Corinthians should take their property cases before qualified Christians for settlement. In Paul's day the Romans allowed the Jews to apply their own law in property matters, and since the Romans did not yet consider Christians as a separate class from the Jews, Christians no doubt had the same rights.

6:2 *saints will judge the world.* With Christ. Cf. Mt 19:28; 2Ti 2:12; Rev 20:4. *competent to judge trivial cases.* Paul views believers as fully competent to judge cases where Christians have claims against each other, because they view matters from a godly vantage point. In comparison with their future role in the judgment of the world and of angels, judgments concerning things of this life are insignificant.

6:3 *we will judge angels.* Cf. 2Pe 2:4,9; Jude 6.

6:4 *even men of little account.* See NIV text note. Either the verse suggests that the least in the church are capable of judging such small matters, or it asks ironically if believers should submit their cases to pagan judges, who really are not qualified to decide on cases between Christians.

6:7 *completely defeated.* Most likely by greed, retaliation and hatred, instead of practicing unselfishness, forgiveness and love—even willingness to suffer loss.

[9]Do you not know that the wicked will
not inherit the kingdom of God?[o] Do not
be deceived:[p] Neither the sexually immoral nor idolaters nor adulterers[q] nor male
prostitutes nor homosexual offenders[r]
[10]nor thieves nor the greedy nor drunkards
nor slanderers nor swindlers[s] will inherit
the kingdom of God. [11]And that is what
some of you were.[t] But you were
washed,[u] you were sanctified,[v] you were
justified[w] in the name of the Lord Jesus
Christ and by the Spirit of our God.

Sexual Immorality

[12]"Everything is permissible for
me"—but not everything is beneficial.[x]
"Everything is permissible for me"—but I
will not be mastered by anything. [13]"Food
for the stomach and the stomach for
food"—but God will destroy them both.[y]
The body is not meant for sexual immorality, but for the Lord,[z] and the Lord for the
body. [14]By his power God raised the Lord
from the dead,[a] and he will raise us also.[b]
[15]Do you not know that your bodies are
members of Christ himself?[c] Shall I then
take the members of Christ and unite them
with a prostitute? Never! [16]Do you not
know that he who unites himself with a
prostitute is one with her in body? For it is
said, "The two will become one flesh."[o][d]
[17]But he who unites himself with the Lord
is one with him in spirit.[e]

[18]Flee from sexual immorality.[f] All
other sins a man commits are outside his
body, but he who sins sexually sins against
his own body.[g] [19]Do you not know that
your body is a temple[h] of the Holy Spirit,
who is in you, whom you have received
from God? You are not your own;[i] [20]you
were bought at a price.[j] Therefore honor
God with your body.[k]

Marriage

7 Now for the matters you wrote about:
It is good for a man not to marry.[p][l]
[2]But since there is so much immorality,
each man should have his own wife, and

6:9 [o]S Mt 25:34 [p]Job 13:9; 1Co 15:33; Gal 6:7; Jas 1:16 [q]Lev 18:20; Dt 22:22 [r]Lev 18:22 **6:10** [s]1Ti 1:10; Rev 21:8; 22:15 **6:11** [t]S Eph 2:2 [u]S Ac 22:16 [v]1Co 1:2 [w]S Ro 4:25 **6:12** [x]1Co 10:23 **6:13** [y]Col 2:22 [z]ver 15,19; Ro 12:1 **6:14** [a]S Ac 2:24 [b]S Ro 6:5; Eph 1:19,20; 1Th 4:16 **6:15** [c]S Ro 12:5 **6:16** [d]Ge 2:24; Mt 19:5; Eph 5:31 **6:17** [e]Jn 17:21-23; Ro 8:9-11; Gal 2:20 **6:18** [f]ver 9; 1Co 5:1; 2Co 12:21; Gal 5:19; Eph 5:3; 1Th 4:3, 4; Heb 13:4 [g]Ro 6:12 **6:19** [h]Jn 2:21 [i]Ro 14:7,8 **6:20** [j]Ps 74:2; S Mt 20:28; Ac 20:28; 1Co 7:23; Rev 5:9; 14:4 [k]Php 1:20 **7:1** [l]ver 8,26

[o]*16* Gen. 2:24 [p]*1* Or "*It is good for a man not to have sexual relations with a woman.*"

6:9 *not inherit the kingdom of God.* Cf. Jn 3:3–5. *sexually immoral.* Paul here identifies three kinds of sexually immoral persons: adulterers, male prostitutes and males who practice homosexuality. In Ro 1:26 he adds the category of females who practice homosexuality. People who engage in such practices, as well as the other offenders listed in vv. 9–10, are explicitly excluded from God's kingdom (but see next note).

6:11 *some of you were. But.* God, however, does save and sanctify people like those described in vv. 9–10.

6:12 *Everything is permissible for me.* Paul is probably quoting some in the Corinthian congregation who boasted that they had a right to do anything they pleased. The apostle counters by observing that such "freedom" of action may not benefit the Christian. *not be mastered by anything.* One may become enslaved by those actions in which he "freely" indulges (see note on 10:23).

6:13 *Food for the stomach and the stomach for food.* Paul quotes some Corinthians again who were claiming that as the physical acts of eating and digesting food have no bearing on one's inner spiritual life, so the physical act of promiscuous sexual activity does not affect one's spiritual life. *The body is not meant for sexual immorality, but for the Lord.* Paul here declares the dignity of the human body: It is intended for the Lord. Although granting that food and the stomach are transitory, Paul denies that what one does with his body is unimportant. This is particularly true of the use of sex, which the Lord has ordained in wedlock for the good of mankind (cf. Heb 13:4).

6:14 *God raised the Lord . . . us also.* As an illustration of God's high regard for the body, Paul cites the resurrection of Christ's body and, eventually, the believer's body (15:51–53; 1Th 4:16–17). A body destined for resurrection should not be used for immorality.

6:15 *members of Christ.* See 12:27. It is not merely the spirit that is a member of Christ's body; it is the whole person, consisting of spirit and body. This fact gives dignity to the human body.

6:16 *one with her in body.* In a sexual relationship the two bodies become one (cf. Ge 2:24; Mt 19:5), and a new human being may emerge from the sexual union. Sexual relations outside the marriage bond are a gross perversion of the divinely established marriage union.

6:17 *one with him in spirit.* There is a higher union than the marriage bond: the believer's spiritual union with Christ, which is the perfect model for the kind of unity that should mark the marriage relationship (cf. Eph 5:21–33).

6:18 *other sins . . . are outside his body.* Perhaps means that in a unique way, sexual immorality gratifies one's physical body. Or, since the word "other" does not occur in the Greek text, Paul may be quoting a Corinthian slogan (see note on v. 12), which he refutes in the second half of the verse. *he who sins sexually sins against his own body.* The body is a temple of the Holy Spirit (v. 19); thus to use it in prostitution disgraces God's temple. Furthermore, the prostitutes of Corinth were dedicated to the service of Aphrodite, the goddess of love and sex.

6:19 *your body is a temple of the Holy Spirit.* The Christian should value his body as a sacred place where God dwells and should realize that by the Spirit's presence and power he can be helped against such sins as sexual immorality (Ro 8:9). *not your own.* Cf. 1Pe 2:9.

6:20 *honor God with your body.* Cf. 10:31; Ro 6:12–13; Col 3:17.

7:1 *matters you wrote about.* The Corinthians had written Paul, asking him a number of vexing questions (see 8:1; 12:1). *good for a man not to marry.* Because of the crisis at Corinth (v. 26). Elsewhere (Eph 5:22–33; Col 3:18–19; 1Ti 3:2,12; 5:14) Paul spoke strongly in favor of the married state, and in 1Ti 4:1–3 he taught that forbidding to marry would be a sign of the end-time apostasy. Another possible interpretation is that Paul is again (see notes on 6:12–13,18) quoting a slogan of the Corinthians (see NIV text note). He refutes this idea in v. 2 by stating that sexual relations have their proper expression in marriage.

7:2 *so much immorality.* Example: The temple to Aphrodite on the Acrocorinth, the rocky eminence above Corinth, at one time had in service 1,000 prostitute priestesses.

each woman her own husband. 3The husband should fulfill his marital duty to his
wife,[m] and likewise the wife to her husband. 4The wife's body does not belong to
her alone but also to her husband. In the
same way, the husband's body does not
belong to him alone but also to his wife.
5Do not deprive each other except by
mutual consent and for a time,[n] so that
you may devote yourselves to prayer. Then
come together again so that Satan[o] will
not tempt you[p] because of your lack of
self-control. 6I say this as a concession, not
as a command.[q] 7I wish that all men were
as I am.[r] But each man has his own gift
from God; one has this gift, another has
that.[s]

8Now to the unmarried and the widows
I say: It is good for them to stay unmarried,
as I am.[t] 9But if they cannot control themselves, they should marry,[u] for it is better
to marry than to burn with passion.

10To the married I give this command
(not I, but the Lord): A wife must not separate from her husband.[v] 11But if she does,
she must remain unmarried or else be reconciled to her husband.[w] And a husband
must not divorce his wife.

12To the rest I say this (I, not the
Lord):[x] If any brother has a wife who is
not a believer and she is willing to live
with him, he must not divorce her. 13And
if a woman has a husband who is not a
believer and he is willing to live with her,
she must not divorce him. 14For the unbelieving husband has been sanctified
through his wife, and the unbelieving wife
has been sanctified through her believing
husband. Otherwise your children would
be unclean, but as it is, they are holy.[y]

15But if the unbeliever leaves, let him do
so. A believing man or woman is not
bound in such circumstances; God has
called us to live in peace.[z] 16How do you
know, wife, whether you will save[a] your
husband?[b] Or, how do you know, husband, whether you will save your wife?

17Nevertheless, each one should retain
the place in life that the Lord assigned to
him and to which God has called him.[c]
This is the rule I lay down in all the
churches.[d] 18Was a man already circumcised when he was called? He should not
become uncircumcised. Was a man uncircumcised when he was called? He should
not be circumcised.[e] 19Circumcision is
nothing and uncircumcision is nothing.[f]
Keeping God's commands is what counts.
20Each one should remain in the situation
which he was in when God called him.[g]
21Were you a slave when you were called?
Don't let it trouble you—although if you

7:3 [m]Ex 21:10; 1Pe 3:7
7:5 [n]Ex 19:15; 1Sa 21:4,5 [o]S Mt 4:10 [p]1Th 3:5
7:6 [q]2Co 8:8
7:7 [r]ver 8; 1Co 9:5 [s]Mt 19:11,12; Ro 12:6; 1Co 12:4,11
7:8 [t]ver 1,26
7:9 [u]1Ti 5:14
7:10 [v]Mal 2:14-16; S Lk 16:18
7:11 [w]ver 39; Ro 7:2,3
7:12 [x]ver 6,10; 2Co 11:17
7:14 [y]Mal 2:15
7:15 [z]S Ro 14:19; 1Co 14:33
7:16 [a]S Ro 11:14 [b]1Pe 3:1
7:17 [c]Ro 12:3 [d]1Co 4:17; 14:33; 2Co 8:18; 11:28
7:18 [e]Ac 15:1,2
7:19 [f]Ro 2:25-27; Gal 5:6; 6:15; Col 3:11
7:20 [g]ver 24

7:3 *fulfill . . . marital duty.* Married couples should have normal sexual relations. Permanent abstention deprives the other partner of his or her natural right and may be conducive to temptation.
7:4 *In the same way.* Both husband and wife have conjugal rights and exclusive possession of the other in this area.
7:5 *Do not deprive each other.* Of sexual fulfillment. *Satan . . . not tempt you because of your lack of self-control.* The Christian deprived of normal sexual activity with his or her marriage partner may be tempted by Satan to sexual immorality. The normal God-given sexual drive in the human being is strong.
7:6 *concession, not as a command.* Although marriage is desirable and according to God's plan, it was not mandatory under the difficult circumstances at Corinth (see v. 26). In another situation (1Ti 5:14) Paul urges "the younger widows to marry."
7:10 *I give this command (not I, but the Lord).* Paul is citing a command from the Lord Jesus during his earthly ministry that married couples must stay together (Mt 5:32; 19:3–9; Mk 10:2–12; Lk 16:18). Paul probably heard such commands from other disciples (cf. Gal 1:18–19) or from Jesus himself by a special revelation.
7:11 *But if she does, she must remain unmarried or else be reconciled.* Paul argues that in the light of Christ's command she (or he) is not to marry again. Rather, the separated or divorced couple are to be reconciled. Clearly the ideal is that marriage should not be permanently disrupted.
7:12 *I say this (I, not the Lord).* Paul is not quoting a direct command from Jesus here. *any brother has a wife . . . not a believer.* The apostle is talking here (and in v. 13) about couples already married, when one of them becomes a Christian. If at all possible, they should remain together, unless the unbeliever, whether man or woman, refuses to remain (v. 15).
7:14 *the unbelieving husband . . . wife has been sanctified.* The unbelieving partner is influenced by the godly life of the Christian partner; so that family is under the holy influence of the believer and in that sense is sanctified. *your children . . . are holy.* They at least have the advantage of being under the sanctifying influence of one Christian parent (see v. 16) and so may be called holy. Some believe that such children are called holy because they are included with their parents in the new covenant in Christ, just as the children of Abraham were included in the covenant with their father (and so were circumcised).
7:15 *A believing man or woman is not bound in such circumstances.* The believer is not under obligation to try to continue living with the unbeliever. *live in peace.* If the unbeliever were forced to live with the believer, there would be no peace in the home.
7:17 *retain the place in life that the Lord assigned to him.* Each Christian is to live contentedly for the Lord in whatever economic, social and religious station in life God has placed him. See v. 18 for an example.
7:18 *circumcised . . . uncircumcised.* Jew . . . Gentile. In the religious sphere, Christian Jews should not try to obliterate physically the fact that they are Jews, and Christian Gentiles should not yield to Jewish pressure for circumcision (cf. Ac 15:1–5; Gal 5:1–3).
7:21 *Were you a slave . . . ?* In the social and economic sphere, the Christian slave should live contentedly in his situation, realizing that he has become free in Christ (v. 22; Jn 8:32, 36). *if you can gain your freedom, do so.* If a Christian slave has an opportunity to get his freedom, he should take advantage of it. In the Roman empire slaves were

can gain your freedom, do so. 22For he who was a slave when he was called by the Lord is the Lord's freedman; *h* similarly, he who was a free man when he was called is Christ's slave. *i* 23You were bought at a price; *j* do not become slaves of men. 24Brothers, each man, as responsible to God, should remain in the situation God called him to. *k*

25Now about virgins: I have no command from the Lord, *l* but I give a judgment as one who by the Lord's mercy *m* is trustworthy. 26Because of the present crisis, I think that it is good for you to remain as you are. *n* 27Are you married? Do not seek a divorce. Are you unmarried? Do not look for a wife. *o* 28But if you do marry, you have not sinned; *p* and if a virgin marries, she has not sinned. But those who marry will face many troubles in this life, and I want to spare you this.

29What I mean, brothers, is that the time is short. *q* From now on those who have wives should live as if they had none; 30those who mourn, as if they did not; those who are happy, as if they were not; those who buy something, as if it were not theirs to keep; 31those who use the things of the world, as if not engrossed in them. For this world in its present form is passing away. *r*

32I would like you to be free from concern. An unmarried man is concerned about the Lord's affairs *s*—how he can please the Lord. 33But a married man is concerned about the affairs of this world—how he can please his wife— 34and his interests are divided. An unmarried woman or virgin is concerned about the Lord's affairs: Her aim is to be devoted to the Lord in both body and spirit. *t* But a married woman is concerned about the affairs of this world—how she can please her husband. 35I am saying this for your own good, not to restrict you, but that you may live in a right way in undivided *u* devotion to the Lord.

36If anyone thinks he is acting improperly toward the virgin he is engaged to, and if she is getting along in years and he feels he ought to marry, he should do as he wants. He is not sinning. *v* They should get married. 37But the man who has settled the matter in his own mind, who is under no compulsion but has control over his own will, and who has made up his mind not to marry the virgin—this man also does the right thing. 38So then, he who marries the virgin does right, *w* but he who does not marry her does even better. *q*

39A woman is bound to her husband as

Reference column:

7:22 *h*Jn 8:32,36
    *i*S Ro 6:22
7:23 *j*S 1Co 6:20
7:24 *k*ver 20
7:25 *l*ver 6;
    2Co 8:8
    *m*2Co 4:1;
    1Ti 1:13,16
7:26 *n*ver 1,8
7:27 *o*ver 20,21
7:28 *p*ver 36
7:29 *q*ver 31;
    S Ro 13:11,12
7:31 *r*ver 29;
    S Heb 12:27
7:32 *s*1Ti 5:5

7:34 *t*Lk 2:37
7:35 *u*Ps 86:11
7:36 *v*ver 28
7:38 *w*Heb 13:4

---

*q*36-38 Or 36*If anyone thinks he is not treating his daughter properly, and if she is getting along in years, and he feels she ought to marry, he should do as he wants. He is not sinning. He should let her get married.* 37*But the man who has settled the matter in his own mind, who is under no compulsion but has control over his own will, and who has made up his mind to keep the virgin unmarried—this man also does the right thing.* 38*So then, he who gives his virgin in marriage does right, but he who does not give her in marriage does even better.*

---

sometimes freed by Roman patricians. There is nothing wrong with seeking to improve your condition, but be content at every stage.

7:22 *a free man . . . is Christ's slave.* A man who was not a Roman slave should realize that in a spiritual sense he belonged to Christ, and, because of his allegiance to Christ, he must not oppress the underprivileged slave. Cf. Eph 6:5, 9; Col 3:22; 4:1.

7:23 *bought at a price . . . not . . . slaves of men.* Christians in all stations of life should realize that their ultimate allegiance is not to men but to Christ, who bought them with his blood (6:20; 1Pe 1:18–19).

7:25 *Now about virgins.* Paul answers another major question the Corinthians had asked (v. 1). *I give a judgment as one who . . . is trustworthy.* Paul is not giving a direct command from Jesus here (as in v. 10; cf. Ac 20:35). In this matter, which is not a question of right and wrong, Paul expresses his own judgment. Even though he put it this way, he is certainly not denying that he wrote under the influence of divine inspiration (see v. 40). And since he writes under inspiration, what he recommends is clearly the better course of action.

7:26 *present crisis.* Probably a reference to the pressures of the Christian life in an immoral and particularly hostile environment (cf. vv. 2,28; 5:1; 2Ti 3:12). Paul's recommendation here does not apply to all times and all situations.

7:28 *many troubles.* Times of suffering and persecution for Christ, when being married would mean even greater hard-

ship in taking care of one's mate.

7:29 *time is short.* The time for doing the Lord's work has become increasingly short. Life is fleeting, as times of persecution remind us. Do not be unduly concerned with the affairs of this world (vv. 29–31) because material things are changing and disappearing (v. 31). Some think the reference is to the Lord's second coming.

7:34 *his interests are divided.* He cannot give undistracted service to Christ (v. 35). This is particularly true in times of persecution.

7:36–38 See NIV text note.

7:36 *he is acting improperly toward the virgin he is engaged to . . . getting along in years . . . They should get married.* In the light of hostility toward believers in Corinth, a man might refrain from marrying his fiancée. But if he then realizes that his fiancée is getting beyond her prime marriageable age and the situation thus seems unfair to her, it is perfectly proper for them to get married.

7:37 *has control over his own will . . . does the right thing.* The man who determines that there is no need for him to marry his fiancée under the circumstances has made a good decision too (v. 38). Paul may be referring to a man who has control of his passions, as in v. 7 (cf. v. 9).

7:39 *bound to her husband as long as he lives.* Marriage is a lifelong union (yet see the exception clause in Mt 19:9). *if her husband dies.* Death breaks the marriage bond, and a Christian is then free to marry another Christian ("he must belong to the Lord").

long as he lives.[x] But if her husband dies, she is free to marry anyone she wishes, but he must belong to the Lord.[y] [40]In my judgment,[z] she is happier if she stays as she is—and I think that I too have the Spirit of God.

Food Sacrificed to Idols

8 Now about food sacrificed to idols:[a] We know that we all possess knowledge.[r][b] Knowledge puffs up, but love builds up. [2]The man who thinks he knows something[c] does not yet know as he ought to know.[d] [3]But the man who loves God is known by God.[e]

[4]So then, about eating food sacrificed to idols:[f] We know that an idol is nothing at all in the world[g] and that there is no God but one.[h] [5]For even if there are so-called gods,[i] whether in heaven or on earth (as indeed there are many "gods" and many "lords"), [6]yet for us there is but one God,[j] the Father,[k] from whom all things came[l] and for whom we live; and there is but one Lord,[m] Jesus Christ, through whom all things came[n] and through whom we live. [7]But not everyone knows this.[o] Some people are still so accustomed to idols that

when they eat such food they think of it as having been sacrificed to an idol, and since their conscience is weak,[p] it is defiled. [8]But food does not bring us near to God;[q] we are no worse if we do not eat, and no better if we do.

[9]Be careful, however, that the exercise of your freedom does not become a stumbling block[r] to the weak.[s] [10]For if anyone with a weak conscience sees you who have this knowledge eating in an idol's temple, won't he be emboldened to eat what has been sacrificed to idols?[t] [11]So this weak brother, for whom Christ died, is destroyed[u] by your knowledge. [12]When you sin against your brothers[v] in this way and wound their weak conscience, you sin against Christ.[w] [13]Therefore, if what I eat causes my brother to fall into sin, I will never eat meat again, so that I will not cause him to fall.[x]

The Rights of an Apostle

9 Am I not free?[y] Am I not an apostle?[z] Have I not seen Jesus our Lord?[a] Are you not the result of my work in the

7:39 [x]Ro 7:2,3	
[y]2Co 6:14	
7:40 [z]ver 25	
8:1 [a]ver 4,7,10; Ac 15:20	
[b]Ro 15:14	
8:2 [c]1Co 3:18	
[d]1Co 13:8,9,12; 1Ti 6:4	
8:3 [e]Jer 1:5; Ro 8:29; Gal 4:9	
8:4 [f]ver 1,7,10; Ex 34:15	
[g]Ac 14:15; 1Co 10:19;	
Gal 4:8 [h]ver 6; Dt 6:4; Ps 86:10; Eph 4:6; 1Ti 2:5	
8:5 [i]2Th 2:4	
8:6 [j]S ver 4 [k]Mal 2:10	
[l]S Ro 11:36 [m]Eph 4:5 [n]S Jn 1:3	
8:7 [o]ver 1	
[p]Ro 14:14; 1Co 10:28	
8:8 [q]Ro 14:17	
8:9 [r]S 2Co 6:3; Gal 5:13 [s]Ro 14:1	
8:10 [t]ver 1,4,7	
8:11 [u]Ro 14:15, 20	
8:12 [v]Mt 18:6 [w]Mt 25:40,45	
8:13 [x]S Mt 5:29	
9:1 [y]ver 19 [z]S 1Co 1:1; 2Co 12:12 [a]S 1Co 15:8	

[r] 1 Or "We all possess knowledge," as you say

7:40 *as she is.* A widow. *I think that I too have the Spirit of God.* Paul writes as one convinced that he is guided by the Holy Spirit.

8:1 *Now about food.* Another matter the Corinthians had written about (see note on 7:1). *sacrificed to idols.* Offered on pagan altars. Meat left over from a sacrifice might be eaten by the priests, eaten by the offerer and his friends at a feast in the temple (see note on v. 10) or sold in the public meat market. Some Christians felt that if they ate such meat, they participated in pagan worship and thus compromised their testimony for Christ. Other Christians did not feel this way. *knowledge.* Explained in vv. 2–6. *Knowledge puffs up.* It fills one with false pride. *love builds up.* Explained in vv. 7–13. The Christian should love his brother who doubts.

8:2 *does not yet know.* The wisest and most knowledgeable Christian realizes that his knowledge is limited. God is the only one who knows all (cf. Ro 11:33–36).

8:3 *the man who loves God is known by God.* A person who tempers his knowledge with love toward God shows that he is really known and thus accepted by God as one of God's own redeemed (Gal 4:8–9; 1Jn 4:7–8).

8:4 *an idol is nothing.* It represents no real god and possesses no power (see Ps 115:4–7; 135:15–17; Isa 44:12–20). But there are demons behind them (10:20).

8:5 *so-called gods.* The alleged gods of Greek and Roman mythology. *many "gods" and many "lords."* Not that there actually are many gods and lords. This would contradict the consistent and emphatic teaching of Scripture that there is but one God (Dt 6:4). Paul is recognizing the obvious fact that there are many who are worshiped as gods—though they do not actually exist, to say nothing of being deities.

8:6 *from whom all things came . . . through whom all things came.* See Heb 2:10. God the Father is the ultimate source of all creation (Ac 4:24). God the Son is the dynamic one through whom, with the Father, all things came into existence (Jn 1:3; Col 1:16).

8:7 *knows this.* Knows that an idol has no personal reality.

since their conscience is weak, it is defiled. Christians who conceive of an idol as being real cannot rid themselves of this idea. Consequently, they think that in eating meat sacrificed on pagan altars they have involved themselves in pagan worship and thus have sinned against Christ.

8:9 *your freedom.* To eat meat sacrificed to idols because you know that an idol is nothing (v. 4). *the weak.* Those Christians whose consciences are weak, who think it is wrong to eat meat sacrificed to idols.

8:10 *eating in an idol's temple.* At the site of ancient Corinth, archaeologists have discovered two temples containing rooms apparently used for pagan feasts where meat offered to idols was eaten. To such feasts Christians may have been invited by pagan friends.

8:11 *this weak brother . . . is destroyed by your knowledge.* The weak Christian is influenced by the example of the stronger Christian and, though he feels it to be wrong, eats the meat that has been offered to an idol. The spiritual destruction that follows is explained in v. 12.

8:12 *wound their weak conscience.* Eating meat offered to idols when they feel it is wrong tends to blunt their consciences, so that doing what is wrong becomes much easier. The result may be moral tragedy. *you sin against Christ.* Because Christ died for your brother (v. 11), even as he died for you. It is also a sin against Christ because it breaks the unity of the members of his body (the church).

8:13 *I will never eat meat again.* Paul will forever refrain from engaging in the harmless practice of eating meat sacrificed to idols if it will cause his weak Christian brother, who feels it is wrong, also to eat that meat.

9:1 *Am I not free?* Do I not have the rights that any Christian has? *Am I not an apostle?* Some at Corinth (2Co 12:11–12) and elsewhere (Gal 1:1; 1:15–2:10) questioned Paul's genuine apostleship. To certify his apostleship Paul gives this proof: that he has seen the Lord Jesus (Ac 9:1–9; 22:6–16; 26:12–18), as was true of the other apostles (Ac 1:21–22). Furthermore, he adds that his ministry has pro-

Lord?[b] [2]Even though I may not be an apostle to others, surely I am to you! For you are the seal[c] of my apostleship in the Lord.

[3]This is my defense to those who sit in judgment on me. [4]Don't we have the right to food and drink?[d] [5]Don't we have the right to take a believing wife[e] along with us, as do the other apostles and the Lord's brothers[f] and Cephas[s]?[g] [6]Or is it only I and Barnabas[h] who must work for a living?

[7]Who serves as a soldier[i] at his own expense? Who plants a vineyard[j] and does not eat of its grapes? Who tends a flock and does not drink of the milk? [8]Do I say this merely from a human point of view? Doesn't the Law say the same thing? [9]For it is written in the Law of Moses: "Do not muzzle an ox while it is treading out the grain."[t][k] Is it about oxen that God is concerned?[l] [10]Surely he says this for us, doesn't he? Yes, this was written for us,[m] because when the plowman plows and the thresher threshes, they ought to do so in the hope of sharing in the harvest.[n] [11]If we have sown spiritual seed among you, is it too much if we reap a material harvest from you?[o] [12]If others have this right of support from you, shouldn't we have it all the more?

But we did not use this right.[p] On the contrary, we put up with anything rather than hinder[q] the gospel of Christ. [13]Don't you know that those who work in the temple get their food from the temple, and those who serve at the altar share in what is offered on the altar?[r] [14]In the same way, the Lord has commanded that those who preach the gospel should receive their living from the gospel.[s]

[15]But I have not used any of these rights.[t] And I am not writing this in the hope that you will do such things for me. I would rather die than have anyone deprive me of this boast.[u] [16]Yet when I preach the gospel, I cannot boast, for I am compelled to preach.[v] Woe to me if I do not preach the gospel! [17]If I preach voluntarily, I have a reward;[w] if not voluntarily, I am simply discharging the trust committed to me.[x] [18]What then is my reward? Just this: that in preaching the gospel I may offer it free of charge,[y] and so not make use of my rights[z] in preaching it.

[19]Though I am free[a] and belong to no man, I make myself a slave to everyone,[b] to win as many as possible.[c] [20]To the Jews I became like a Jew, to win the Jews.[d] To those under the law I became like one under the law (though I myself am not under the law),[e] so as to win those under the law. [21]To those not having the law I became like one not having the law[f] (though I am not free from God's law but am under Christ's law),[g] so as to win those not having the law. [22]To the weak I became weak, to win the weak.[h] I have become all things to all men[i] so that by all possible means I might save some.[j] [23]I do

Cross references (center column):

9:1 [b]1Co 3:6; 4:15
9:2 [c]2Co 3:2,3
9:4 [d]ver 14; S Ac 18:3
9:5 [e]1Co 7:7,8 /S Mt 12:46
[g]S 1Co 1:12
9:6 [h]S Ac 4:36
9:7 [i]2Ti 2:3,4 /Dt 20:6; Pr 27:18; 1Co 3:6,8
9:9 [k]Dt 25:4; 1Ti 5:18 /Dt 22:1-4; Pr 12:10
9:10 [m]S Ro 4:23,24 [n]Pr 11:25; 2Ti 2:6
9:11 [o]ver 14; Ro 15:27; Gal 6:6
9:12 [p]ver 15,18; S Ac 18:3 [q]2Co 6:3; 11:7-12
9:13 [r]Lev 6:16,26; Dt 18:1
9:14 [s]S 1Ti 5:18
9:15 [t]ver 12,18; S Ac 18:3 [u]2Co 11:9,10
9:16 [v]Ro 1:14; Ac 9:15; 26:16-18
9:17 [w]1Co 3:8,14 [x]1Co 4:1; Gal 2:7; Col 1:25
9:18 [y]2Co 11:7; 12:13 [z]ver 12,15
9:19 [a]ver 1 [b]2Co 4:5; Gal 5:13 [c]Mt 18:15; 1Pe 3:1
9:20 [d]Ac 16:3; 21:20-26; Ro 11:14 [e]S Ro 2:12
9:21 [f]Ro 2:12,14 [g]Gal 6:2
9:22 [h]S Ro 14:1; S 1Co 2:3 [i]1Co 10:33 /S Ro 11:14

[s]5 That is, Peter   [t]9 Deut. 25:4

---

duced true spiritual fruit (the Corinthians) for the Lord, which would confirm to them that he is indeed an apostle.
9:4 *right to food and drink.* Paul and Barnabas, as God's workers, have a right to have their food and other physical needs supplied at the church's expense (cf. vv. 6,13–14).
9:5 *take a believing wife along with us.* Paul asserts his right to be married, if he wishes. This does not mean that he was married, as some have imagined (see 7:7). Other apostles, including Peter (see Mk 1:30), had wives.
9:11 *material harvest.* Food, lodging and pay supplied by the Corinthians (cf. Gal 6:6). Paul here sets forth the principle that Christian workers should be paid for their labors.
9:12 *did not use this right.* The point of Paul's discussion in ch. 9. He had numerous rights that he did not claim because of his love for the Corinthians. Thus ch. 9 is an extended personal illustration of the practice advocated in ch. 8. Because of love for others, believers should be ready to surrender their rights.
9:13 *those who work in the temple.* The Corinthian believers would understand this illustration not only from their knowledge of the OT (cf. Lev 7:28–36; Nu 18:8–20) but also from the practice in pagan temples in Greece and Rome.
9:15 *this boast.* That he had preached the gospel without charge, so that they could not say that they had paid him for it.
9:16 *I am compelled to preach.* The Lord had laid on Paul the necessity of preaching the gospel (Ac 9:1–16;

26:16–18; see also Jer 20:9 and note).
9:18 *my reward... in preaching the gospel.* Paul's reward in preaching is not material things but the boasting that he has preached to the Corinthians without charge and has not taken advantage of the rights he deserves: food and drink, shelter and pay (vv. 3–12).
9:19 *I make myself a slave to everyone.* Not only did Paul not use his right to material support in preaching the gospel but he also deprived himself—curtailed his personal privileges and social and religious rights—in dealing with different kinds of people. *to win.* To bring to Christ.
9:20 *those under the law.* Those under the OT law and religious practices (the Jews). *I became like one under the law.* For the Jews' sake Paul conformed to the Jewish law (Ac 16:3; 18:18; 21:20–26).
9:21 *those not having the law.* Those who have not been raised under the OT law (the Gentiles). *I became like one not having the law.* Paul accommodated himself to Gentile culture when it did not violate his allegiance to Christ, though he still reckoned that he was under God's law and Christ's law. (By "Christ's law" Paul is probably referring to Christ's teachings, though the term is not necessarily restricted to them.)
9:22 *the weak.* Those whose consciences are weak (8:9–12). *I became weak.* Paul did not exercise his Christian freedom in such things as eating meat sacrificed to idols (8:9,13).

all this for the sake of the gospel, that I may share in its blessings.

24Do you not know that in a race all the runners run, but only one gets the prize?k Run l in such a way as to get the prize. 25Everyone who competes in the games goes into strict training. They do it to get a crown m that will not last; but we do it to get a crown that will last forever. n 26Therefore I do not run like a man running aimlessly; o I do not fight like a man beating the air. p 27No, I beat my body q and make it my slave so that after I have preached to others, I myself will not be disqualified for the prize. r

Warnings From Israel's History

10 For I do not want you to be ignorant s of the fact, brothers, that our forefathers were all under the cloud t and that they all passed through the sea. u 2They were all baptized into v Moses in the cloud and in the sea. 3They all ate the same spiritual food w 4and drank the same spiritual drink; for they drank from the spiritual rock x that accompanied them, and that rock was Christ. 5Nevertheless, God was not pleased with most of them;

their bodies were scattered over the desert. y

6Now these things occurred as examples u z to keep us from setting our hearts on evil things as they did. 7Do not be idolaters, a as some of them were; as it is written: "The people sat down to eat and drink and got up to indulge in pagan revelry." v b 8We should not commit sexual immorality, as some of them did—and in one day twenty-three thousand of them died. c 9We should not test the Lord, d as some of them did—and were killed by snakes. e 10And do not grumble, as some of them did f—and were killed g by the destroying angel. h

11These things happened to them as examples i and were written down as warnings for us, j on whom the fulfillment of the ages has come. k 12So, if you think you are standing firm, l be careful that you don't fall! 13No temptation has seized you except what is common to man. And God is faithful; m he will not let you be tempted beyond what you can bear. n But when you are tempted, he will also provide a

---

9:24 kPhp 3:14;
Col 2:18 lver 25,
26; Gal 2:2; 5:7;
Php 2:16;
2Ti 4:7; Heb 12:1
9:25 m2Ti 2:5
n2Ti 4:8;
Jas 1:12; 1Pe 5:4;
Rev 2:10; 3:11
9:26 oS ver 24
p1Ti 6:12
9:27 qRo 8:13
rver 24
10:1 sS Ro 11:25
tEx 13:21;
Ps 105:39
uEx 14:22,29;
Ps 66:6
10:2 vRo 6:3
10:3 wS Jn 6:31
10:4 xEx 17:6;
Nu 20:11;
Ps 78:15; 105:41

10:5 yNu 14:29;
Heb 3:17; Jude 5
10:6 zver 11
10:7 aver 14
bEx 32:4,6,19
10:8 cNu 25:1-9
10:9 dEx 17:2;
Ps 78:18; 95:9;
106:14 eNu 21:5,
6
10:10 fNu 16:41;
17:5,10
gNu 16:49
hEx 12:23;
1Ch 21:15;
Heb 11:28
10:11 iver 6
jS Ro 4:24
kS Ro 13:11
10:12 lRo 11:20;
2Co 1:24

10:13 mS 1Co 1:9 n2Pe 2:9

u6 Or types; also in verse 11   v7 Exodus 32:6

9:23 *blessings.* The blessings of realizing that he has been faithful to Christ in preaching, of hearing the Lord's "Well done" (Mt 25:21; Lk 19:17) and of seeing others come to Christ.

9:24 *race... runners.* The Corinthians were familiar with the foot races in their own Isthmian games, which occurred every other year and were second only to the Olympic games in importance. *prize.* In ancient times the prize was a perishable wreath (v. 25).

9:25 *crown that will last forever.* See 2Ti 4:8; Jas 1:12; 1Pe 5:4; Rev 2:10; 3:11; 4:10 and notes.

9:26 *not... running aimlessly.* See Php 3:14.

9:27 *I beat my body and make it my slave.* Here Paul uses the figure of boxing to represent the Christian life. He does not aimlessly beat the air, but he severely disciplines his own body in serving Christ. *not be disqualified for the prize.* Paul realizes that he must with rigor serve the Lord and battle against sin. If he fails in this, he may be excluded from the reward (see 3:10–15).

10:1 *under the cloud.* Under God's leadership and guidance (Ex 13:21–22; Nu 9:15–23; 14:14; Dt 1:33; Ps 78:14). His guidance did not fail them—he successfully led them through the sea (Ex 14:22,29).

10:2 As a people, they were united under God's redemptive program, and they submitted to Moses, God's appointed leader (Ex 14:31). *baptized.* A figure used to depict their submission to Moses as their deliverer and leader, just as Christian baptism depicts the believer's submission to Christ as Savior and Lord.

10:3–4 *spiritual food... spiritual drink.* The manna and the water from the rock are used as figures representing the spiritual sustenance that God continually provides for his people (Ex 16:2–36; 17:1–7; Nu 20:2–11; 21:16).

10:4 *that rock was Christ.* The rock, from which the water came, and the manna were symbolic of supernatural sustenance through Christ, the bread of life and the water of life

(Jn 4:14; 6:30–35).

10:5 *God was not pleased with most of them.* In spite of the remarkable privileges given to Israel (vv. 1–4), they failed to obey God, thus incurring his displeasure. Of the adults who came out of Egypt, only Caleb and Joshua were allowed to enter Canaan (Nu 14:22–24, 28–35; Jos 1:1–2).

10:6 *as they did.* What Paul has in mind is described in vv. 7–10.

10:7 *idolaters.* Referring to the incident of the golden calf (Ex 32:1–6). The people ate a ritual meal sacrificed to an idol (cf. ch. 8).

10:8 Refers to Israel's joining herself to Baal of Peor (Nu 25:1–9), participating in the worship of this god of the Moabites and engaging in sexual immorality with the prostitute virgins who worshiped this god. *twenty-three thousand.* The Hebrew and Greek (Septuagint) texts of Nu 25:9 have 24,000. It is clear that Paul is not striving for exactness. He is only speaking approximately. First-century writers were not as concerned about being precise as 20th-century authors often are.

10:10 *do not grumble.* As in Nu 16:41. *destroying angel.* Paul links the angel who brought the plague of Nu 16:46–50—because of the grumbling of the Israelites against Moses and Aaron (Nu 16:41)—with the destroying angel of Ex 12:23.

10:11 *written down as warnings.* See note on Ro 15:4. *fulfillment of the ages.* The period of time inaugurated by Christ's death and resurrection and continuing into the future until Christ's second coming and beyond. It is the period of fulfillment when all that God has been doing for his people throughout all previous ages comes to its fruition in the Messiah.

10:13 *temptation.* Temptation in itself is not sin. Jesus was tempted (Mt 4:1–11). Yielding to the temptation is sin. *stand up under it.* Through God's enablement to resist the temptation to sin.

way out so that you can stand up under it.

Idol Feasts and the Lord's Supper

[14]Therefore, my dear friends,[o] flee from idolatry.[p] [15]I speak to sensible people; judge for yourselves what I say. [16]Is not the cup of thanksgiving for which we give thanks a participation in the blood of Christ? And is not the bread that we break[q] a participation in the body of Christ?[r] [17]Because there is one loaf, we, who are many, are one body,[s] for we all partake of the one loaf.

[18]Consider the people of Israel: Do not those who eat the sacrifices[t] participate in the altar? [19]Do I mean then that a sacrifice offered to an idol is anything, or that an idol is anything?[u] [20]No, but the sacrifices of pagans are offered to demons,[v] not to God, and I do not want you to be participants with demons. [21]You cannot drink the cup of the Lord and the cup of demons too; you cannot have a part in both the Lord's table and the table of demons.[w] [22]Are we trying to arouse the Lord's jealousy?[x] Are we stronger than he?[y]

The Believer's Freedom

[23]"Everything is permissible"—but not

everything is beneficial.[z] "Everything is permissible"—but not everything is constructive. [24]Nobody should seek his own good, but the good of others.[a]

[25]Eat anything sold in the meat market without raising questions of conscience,[b] [26]for, "The earth is the Lord's, and everything in it."[w][c]

[27]If some unbeliever invites you to a meal and you want to go, eat whatever is put before you[d] without raising questions of conscience. [28]But if anyone says to you, "This has been offered in sacrifice," then do not eat it, both for the sake of the man who told you and for conscience' sake[x][e]— [29]the other man's conscience, I mean, not yours. For why should my freedom[f] be judged by another's conscience? [30]If I take part in the meal with thankfulness, why am I denounced because of something I thank God for?[g]

[31]So whether you eat or drink or whatever you do, do it all for the glory of God.[h] [32]Do not cause anyone to stumble,[i] whether Jews, Greeks or the church of

---

10:14 *o*Heb 6:9;
1Pe 2:11;
1Jn 2:7; Jude 3
*p*ver 7; 1Jn 5:21
10:16
*q*S Mt 14:19
*r*Mt 26:26-28;
1Co 11:23-25
10:17 *s*S Ro 12:5
10:18 *t*Lev 7:6,
14,15
10:19 *u*S 1Co 8:4
10:20 *v*Lev 17:7;
Dt 32:17;
Ps 106:37;
Rev 9:20
10:21
*w*2Co 6:15,16
10:22 *x*Dt 32:16,
21; 1Ki 14:22;
Ps 78:58; Jer 44:8
*y*Ecc 6:10;
Isa 45:9

10:23 *z*1Co 6:12
10:24 *a*ver 33;
S Ro 15:1,2;
1Co 13:5;
Php 2:4,21
10:25
*b*S Ac 10:15;
1Co 8:7
10:26 *c*Ps 24:1;
Ex 9:29; 19:5;
Job 41:11;
Ps 50:12; 1Ti 4:4
10:27 *d*Lk 10:7
10:28 *e*1Co 8:7,
10-12
10:29 *f*1Co 9:1,
19
10:30 *g*S Ro 14:6
10:31
*h*Zec 14:21;
Col 3:17;
1Pe 4:11

10:32 *i*S Mt 5:29; Ac 24:16; S 2Co 6:3

*w*26 Psalm 24:1   *x*28 Some manuscripts *conscience' sake, for "the earth is the Lord's and everything in it"*

10:14 *flee from idolatry.* Like that described in Ex 32:1–6. Corinthian Christians had come out of a background of paganism. Temples for the worship of Apollo, Asclepius, Demeter, Aphrodite and other pagan gods and goddesses were seen daily by the Corinthians as they engaged in the activities of everyday life. The worship of Aphrodite, with its many sacred prostitutes, was a particularly strong temptation.

10:16 *cup of thanksgiving.* One of the cups drunk at the Jewish Passover, at which time the Lord's Supper was instituted (Mt 26:17–30; Mk 14:12–26; Lk 22:7–23). *participation in the blood of Christ.* A memorial symbol of fellowship with the crucified Christ, not a literal drinking of his blood. When the Lord's Supper was instituted, Christ had not yet poured out his blood. The Lord's Supper is to remind us of him (11:25).

10:17 *one loaf.* The act of many believers partaking of one loaf of bread symbolizes the unity of the body of Christ, the church, which is nourished by the one bread of life (see Jn 6:33–58).

10:18 *those who eat the sacrifices participate in the altar.* When the people of Israel ate part of the sacrifice made at the altar (Lev 7:15; 8:31; Dt 12:17–18), they participated in the worship of God, who established the sacrifices and whose altar it was. Likewise when the pagans sacrificed, they did so to demons (vv. 20–21). Paul denies that the idol is anything, i.e., that it is a real deity (v. 19). Nor is a sacrifice offered to a so-called god anything, because the idol is nothing and the god being worshiped is no god at all. In reality, demons (not gods) were the objects of idol worship. God's people are warned that if they do eat meat sacrificed to idols, they should not eat it with pagans in their temple feasts, for to do so is to become "participants with demons" (v. 20).

10:22 *arouse the Lord's jealousy.* By sharing in pagan idolatry and worship (cf. Ex 20:5; Dt 32:21; Ps 78:58).

10:23 *not everything is constructive.* See note on 6:12. Personal freedom and desire for one's rights are not the only considerations. One must also consider "the good of others" (v. 24; cf. 8:1; Gal 6:2).

10:25 *Eat anything sold in the meat market.* Even if it has been sacrificed to an idol, because out in the public market it has lost its pagan religious significance.

10:26 A quotation from Ps 24:1 used at Jewish mealtimes as a blessing (cf. Ps 50:12; 89:11).

10:27 *eat whatever is put before you.* Whether or not it might be meat sacrificed to idols, ask no questions. As long as the subject has not been brought up, you are free to eat the meat, even if it had been offered to an idol.

10:28 *for the sake of the man who told you.* If the meat has been identified as meat sacrificed to idols and you eat it, the man—whether a believer or an unbeliever—might think you condone, or even are willing to participate in, the worship of the idols the meat has been offered to. *for conscience' sake.* In eating meat that has publicly been declared to have been sacrificed to idols, you may offend "the other man's conscience" (v. 29) by causing him to think it is all right to eat meat sacrificed to idols even though he has doubts about it. Or if he is an unbeliever, he may think that the Christian worships both God and a pagan idol.

10:29 *my freedom.* Cf. Ro 14:16. The exercise of one's personal freedom is to be governed by whether it will bring glory to God, whether it will build up the church of God and whether it will encourage the unsaved to receive Christ as Savior and Lord (vv. 31–33).

10:30 *something I thank God for.* Paul could thank God for meat sacrificed to idols, for the idol is nothing and the meat is a part of God's created world.

10:31 *all for the glory of God.* The all-inclusive principle that governs the discussion in chs. 8–10 is that God should be glorified in everything that is done.

God[j]— 33even as I try to please everybody in every way.[k] For I am not seeking
my own good but the good of many,[l] so
11 that they may be saved.[m] 1Follow
my example,[n] as I follow the example of Christ.[o]

Propriety in Worship

2I praise you[p] for remembering me in
everything[q] and for holding to the teachings,[y] just as I passed them on to you.[r]
3Now I want you to realize that the
head of every man is Christ,[s] and the head
of the woman is man,[t] and the head of
Christ is God.[u] 4Every man who prays or
prophesies[v] with his head covered dishonors his head. 5And every woman who
prays or prophesies[w] with her head uncovered dishonors her head—it is just as
though her head were shaved.[x] 6If a
woman does not cover her head, she
should have her hair cut off; and if it is a
disgrace for a woman to have her hair cut
or shaved off, she should cover her head.
7A man ought not to cover his head,[z]
since he is the image[y] and glory of God;
but the woman is the glory of man. 8For
man did not come from woman, but
woman from man;[z] 9neither was man
created for woman, but woman for man.[a]
10For this reason, and because of the angels, the woman ought to have a sign of
authority on her head.
11In the Lord, however, woman is not
independent of man, nor is man independent of woman. 12For as woman came
from man, so also man is born of woman.
But everything comes from God.[b] 13Judge
for yourselves: Is it proper for a woman to
pray to God with her head uncovered?
14Does not the very nature of things teach
you that if a man has long hair, it is a
disgrace to him, 15but that if a woman has

10:32 [j]Ac 20:28; 1Co 1:2; 11:16, 22; 15:9; 1Ti 3:5, 15
10:33 [k]Ro 15:2; 1Co 9:22 [l]S ver 24 [m]S Ro 11:14
11:1 [n]S 1Co 4:16 [o]Ro 15:3; 1Pe 2:21
11:2 [p]ver 17,22 [q]1Co 4:17 [r]ver 23; 1Co 15:2,3; 2Th 2:15; 3:6
11:3 [s]S Eph 1:22 [t]Ge 3:16; Eph 5:23 [u]1Co 3:23
11:4 [v]S Ac 11:27
11:5 [w]S Ac 21:9 [x]Dt 21:12
11:7 [y]Ge 1:26; 5:1; 9:6; Jas 3:9
11:8 [z]Ge 2:21-23; 1Ti 2:13
11:9 [a]Ge 2:18
11:12 [b]S Ro 11:36

[y]2 Or *traditions* [z]4-7 Or *4Every man who prays or prophesies with long hair dishonors his head. 5And every woman who prays or prophesies with no covering of hair on her head dishonors her head—she is just like one of the "shorn women." 6If a woman has no covering, let her be for now with short hair, but since it is a disgrace for a woman to have her hair shorn or shaved, she should grow it again. 7A man ought not to have long hair*

10:32 *Do not cause anyone to stumble.* The particular cause of stumbling Paul had in mind was that of eating meat offered to idols (see 8:13). Living to glorify God will result in doing what is beneficial for others, whether Christians ("the church of God") or non-Christians ("Jews, Greeks").

10:33 *please everybody in every way.* Paul does not mean that he will compromise the truths of the gospel in order to please everybody, but that he will consider his fellowman and not cause anyone's conscience to be offended by his daily life, thus keeping that person from receiving the gospel. *that they may be saved.* See 9:22.

11:1 Notice the order: (1) Christ is the supreme example (cf. 1Pe 2:21); (2) Christ's apostle follows his example ("as I follow"); (3) we are to follow the apostle's example.

11:3–16 The subject of this section is propriety in public worship, not male-female relations in general. Paul is concerned, however, that the proper relationship between husbands and wives be reflected in public worship. As in the previous section, he desires that all be done to the glory of God (10:31).

11:3 Some understand the term "head" to refer primarily to the concept of honor, in that one's physical head is the seat of his honor (cf. vv. 4–5). Thus as Christ honored God, man is to honor Christ, and woman is to honor her husband. Others see in the word "head" the idea of authority (which would also include the concept of honor). They point out that Paul clearly uses the term in the sense of authority in Eph 1:21–22 ("under his feet"; "head over everything"), in Eph 5:22–23 (where headship is seen in a context of submission) and in Col 1:18; 2:10. Thus as Christ is in authority over man and is therefore to be honored by man, so the husband is in a position of authority and is therefore to be honored by his wife.

11:4 The first use of "head" in this verse refers to man's physical head; the second refers to his spiritual Head (Christ)—or perhaps is intended in a double sense. In the culture of Paul's day, men uncovered their heads in worship to signify their respect for and submission to deity. When a man prayed or prophesied with his head covered, he failed to show the proper attitude toward Christ.

11:5–6 For a woman, taking off her head covering in public and exposing her hair was a sign of loose morals and sexual promiscuity. Paul says she might as well have her hair cut or shaved off. The shaved head indicated that the woman either had been publicly disgraced because of some shameful act or was openly flaunting her independence and her refusal to be in submission to her husband. Paul's message to her was: Show your respect for and submission to your husband by covering your head during public worship.

Some do not see in these verses a temporary cultural significance to the covering/uncovering of the head. They insist that, since Paul referred to the order of creation (vv. 7–9), his directive is not to be restricted to his time. Thus women of all times should wear a head covering.

Others find a lasting principle in the passage requiring wives, in all ways, to show respect for their husbands by submitting to their authority—not merely by a particular style of attire, but by godly lives. Man, who was created first, is to have authority over his wife (see 1Ti 2:11–14). The wife was made out of his body (Ge 2:21–24) to be his helper and companion (Ge 2:20). She is to honor her husband by submitting to him as her head (see v. 3).

Still others see these verses, not as a mandate for all marriages, but as reflecting marriage relationships at that time in Corinth and therefore giving a reason why the women there should have covered their heads (v. 10). They point to vv. 11–12 as a contrast, emphasizing equality and mutual dependence between men and women who are "in the Lord" (v. 11; see Gal 3:28; 1Pe 3:7).

11:10 *angels.* Perhaps mentioned here because they are interested in all aspects of the Christian's salvation and are sensitive to decorum in worship (cf. Eph 3:10; 1Ti 5:21). *sign of authority.* Understood by some to refer to the woman's authority as co-ruler with man in the creation (Ge 1:26–27). Others take the phrase to refer to the man's authority as properly recognized by the woman in her head covering.

11:13–14 *proper . . . the very nature of things.* Believers must be conscious of how their actions appear in their culture, in light of what is considered to be honorable behavior.

long hair, it is her glory? For long hair is given to her as a covering. [16]If anyone wants to be contentious about this, we have no other practice—nor do the churches of God. *c*

The Lord's Supper

11:23–25pp — Mt 26:26–28; Mk 14:22–24; Lk 22:17–20

[17]In the following directives I have no praise for you, *d* for your meetings do more harm than good. [18]In the first place, I hear that when you come together as a church, there are divisions *e* among you, and to some extent I believe it. [19]No doubt there have to be differences among you to show which of you have God's approval. *f* [20]When you come together, it is not the Lord's Supper you eat, [21]for as you eat, each of you goes ahead without waiting for anybody else. *g* One remains hungry, another gets drunk. [22]Don't you have homes to eat and drink in? Or do you despise the church of God *h* and humiliate those who have nothing? *i* What shall I say to you? Shall I praise you *j* for this? Certainly not!

[23]For I received from the Lord *k* what I also passed on to you: *l* The Lord Jesus, on

the night he was betrayed, took bread, [24]and when he had given thanks, he broke it and said, "This is my body, *m* which is for you; do this in remembrance of me." [25]In the same way, after supper he took the cup, saying, "This cup is the new covenant *n* in my blood; *o* do this, whenever you drink it, in remembrance of me." [26]For whenever you eat this bread and drink this cup, you proclaim the Lord's death until he comes. *p*

[27]Therefore, whoever eats the bread or drinks the cup of the Lord in an unworthy manner will be guilty of sinning against the body and blood of the Lord. *q* [28]A man ought to examine himself *r* before he eats of the bread and drinks of the cup. [29]For anyone who eats and drinks without recognizing the body of the Lord eats and drinks judgment on himself. [30]That is why many among you are weak and sick, and a number of you have fallen asleep. *s* [31]But if we judged ourselves, we would not come under judgment. *t* [32]When we are judged by the Lord, we are being disciplined *u* so that we will not be condemned with the world. *v*

[33]So then, my brothers, when you come

Cross references (center column)

11:16
c S 1Co 7:17;
S 10:32
11:17 *d* ver 2,22
11:18
e 1Co 1:10-12;
3:3
11:19 *f* 1Jn 2:19
11:21 *g* 2Pe 2:13;
Jude 12
11:22
h S 1Co 10:32
i Jas 2:6 /ver 2,17
11:23 *k* Gal 1:12
l S ver 2

11:24
m 1Co 10:16
11:25
n S Lk 22:20
o 1Co 10:16
11:26 *p* S 1Co 1:7
11:27
q Heb 10:29
11:28 *r* 2Co 13:5
11:30 *s* S Mt 9:24
11:31 *t* Ps 32:5;
1Jn 1:9
11:32 *u* Ps 94:12;
118:18; Pr 3:11,
12; Heb 12:7-10;
Rev 3:19
v Jn 15:18,19

Study notes (bottom section)

11:16 In worship services, Paul and the churches in general followed the common custom of the men wearing short hair and the women long hair. Paul was basing his remarks, particularly in vv. 13–16, on common custom in the churches.

11:17 *no praise.* Contrast v. 2.

11:18 *divisions.* Paul had already dealt with one aspect of these divisions (1:10–17).

11:19 *God's approval.* As deplorable as factions may be, they serve one good purpose: They distinguish those who are faithful and true in God's sight.

11:20 *not the Lord's Supper you eat.* Their intention was to eat the Lord's Supper, but it was profaned by their gluttony and discrimination.

11:21 *remains hungry . . . gets drunk.* The early church held the *agape* ("love") feast in connection with the Lord's Supper (cf. 2Pe 2:13; Jude 12). Perhaps the meal was something like a present-day potluck dinner. In good Greek style they brought food for all to share, the rich bringing more and the poor less, but because of their cliques the rich ate much and the poor were left hungry.

11:22 *Shall I praise you for this?* See v. 17.

11:23–26 Observe the similarity of Paul's words here with Mt 26:26–29; Mk 14:22–25; and especially Lk 22:17–20.

11:23 *I received from the Lord.* Paul does not necessarily mean that he received the message about the Lord's Supper directly from Christ. The information probably was passed on to him by others who had heard it from Jesus.

11:24 *had given thanks.* The Jewish practice at meals. This makes it a true Eucharist ("thanksgiving"). *my body.* The broken bread is a symbol of Christ's body given for sinners (Lk 22:19). *in remembrance of me.* As the Feast of Passover was a commemorative meal (see Ex 12:14), so also the Lord's Supper is a memorial supper, recalling and portraying Christ's death for sinners.

11:25 *after supper.* After the Passover supper. The Lord's Supper was first celebrated by Jesus in connection with the

Passover meal (cf. Mt 26:18–30 and parallels in Mark and Luke). *the cup.* A symbol of the new covenant in Jesus' blood (Lk 22:20; cf. Jer 31:31–34). (The old covenant was the Mosaic or Sinaitic covenant; see Ex 24:3–8.) By the use of this covenant sign God signifies his bestowal of salvation upon his people, sealed and paid for by the shedding of Jesus' blood.

11:26 *whenever you eat . . . and drink.* The Lord's Supper should be held periodically, but there is no explicit instruction as to how often. *until he comes.* Cf. Mt 26:29.

11:27 *in an unworthy manner.* In the irreverent and self-centered manner that characterized some of the Corinthians at their unruly *agape* supper (vv. 19–22).

11:28 *examine himself.* A person should test the attitude of his own heart and actions and his awareness of the significance of the Supper, thus making the Supper, under God, a spiritual means of grace.

11:29 *without recognizing the body of the Lord.* The word "body" may refer to either the Lord's physical body or the church as the body of Christ (see 12:13,27). The first view means that the person partakes of the Lord's Supper without recognizing that it symbolizes Christ's crucified body. But in that case, why is the blood not mentioned? The second view means that the participant is not aware of the nature of the church as the body of Christ, resulting in the self-centered actions of vv. 20–21. *judgment.* Not God's eternal judgment, which is to come on the unbeliever, but such disciplinary judgment as physical sickness and death (v. 30).

11:30 *have fallen asleep.* A common first-century figure of speech for death.

11:32 *disciplined.* As God's redeemed children we are disciplined—just as a human father disciplines his child—so that we might repent of our sins (cf. 2Co 7:10) and grow in grace (2Pe 3:18; Heb 12:7–11).

11:33 *come together to eat.* Another reference to the *agape* fellowship meal (see note on v. 21). Each person was to exercise restraint and wait to eat with the others. If a

together to eat, wait for each other. 34If anyone is hungry,[w] he should eat at home,[x] so that when you meet together it may not result in judgment.

And when I come[y] I will give further directions.

Spiritual Gifts

12 Now about spiritual gifts,[z] brothers, I do not want you to be ignorant.[a] 2You know that when you were pagans,[b] somehow or other you were influenced and led astray to mute idols.[c] 3Therefore I tell you that no one who is speaking by the Spirit of God says, "Jesus be cursed,"[d] and no one can say, "Jesus is Lord,"[e] except by the Holy Spirit.[f]

4There are different kinds of gifts, but the same Spirit.[g] 5There are different kinds of service, but the same Lord. 6There are different kinds of working, but the same God[h] works all of them in all men.[i]

7Now to each one the manifestation of the Spirit is given for the common good.[j] 8To one there is given through the Spirit the message of wisdom,[k] to another the message of knowledge[l] by means of the same Spirit, 9to another faith[m] by the same Spirit, to another gifts of healing[n] by that one Spirit, 10to another miraculous powers,[o] to another prophecy,[p] to another distinguishing between spirits,[q] to another speaking in different kinds of tongues,[a][r] and to still another the interpretation of tongues.[a] 11All these are the work of one and the same Spirit,[s] and he gives them to each one, just as he determines.

One Body, Many Parts

12The body is a unit, though it is made up of many parts; and though all its parts are many, they form one body.[t] So it is with Christ.[u] 13For we were all baptized[v]

11:34 [w]ver 21 [x]ver 22 [y]S 1Co 4:19 **12:1** [z]Ro 1:11; 1Co 1:7; 14:1,37 [a]S Ro 11:25 **12:2** [b]S Eph 2:2 [c]Ps 115:5; Jer 10:5; Hab 2:18,19 **12:3** [d]Ro 9:3; 1Co 16:22 [e]S Jn 13:13 [f]1Jn 4:2,3 **12:4** [g]ver 8-11; Ro 12:4-8; Eph 4:11; Heb 2:4 **12:6** [h]Eph 4:6 [i]S Php 2:13 **12:7** [j]1Co 14:12; Eph 4:12 **12:8** [k]1Co 2:6 [l]S 2Co 8:7 **12:9** [m]Mt 17:19, 20; 1Co 13:2 [n]ver 28,30; Mt 10:1 **12:10** [o]ver 28-30; Gal 3:5 [p]S Eph 4:11 [q]1Jn 4:1 [r]S Mk 16:17 **12:11** [s]S ver 4 **12:12** [t]S Ro 12:5 [u]ver 27 **12:13** [v]S Mk 1:8

[a] *10* Or *languages*; also in verse 28

person was too hungry, he should satisfy his hunger at home and not bring selfish and discriminatory practices into the church.

11:34 *when I come . . . further directions.* Paul suggests that they had other problems concerning the Lord's Supper that needed his attention, but he would take care of these later.

12:1 *Now about.* Suggests Paul is answering another question raised by the Corinthians in their letter (cf. 7:1; 8:1; 16:1). *spiritual gifts.* For a definition see note on 1:7, though a different Greek word is used there.

12:2 *led astray to mute idols.* At one time the Corinthians had been led by various influences to worship mute idols (cf. 10:19–20), but now they are to be led by the Holy Spirit.

12:3 *"Jesus be cursed" . . . "Jesus is Lord."* One who is regenerated by the Holy Spirit cannot pronounce a curse on Jesus; rather, he is the only one who from the heart can confess, "Jesus is Lord" (cf. Jn 20:28; also 1Jn 4:2–3). The Greek word for "Lord" here is used in the Greek translation of the OT (the Septuagint) to translate the Hebrew name *Yahweh* ("the LORD").

12:4–6 *same Spirit . . . same Lord . . . same God.* These verses, reflecting the Trinity, show the diversity and unity of spiritual gifts.

12:4 *gifts.* Gifts of grace produced by the indwelling Holy Spirit.

12:5 *service.* The Greek word in its various forms is used to indicate service to the Christian community, such as serving tables (Ac 6:2–3); it is also the word used a little later in the first-century Christian church for the office of deacon (Php 1:1).

12:6 *working.* The Greek word indicates power that is in operation. Spiritual gifts produce results that are obvious.

12:7 *to each one the manifestation . . . given for the common good.* Every member of the body of Christ has been given some spiritual gift that is an evidence of the Spirit's working in his life. All the gifts are intended to build up the members of the Christian community (see 1Pe 4:10–11). They are not to be used for selfish advantage, as some in the Corinthian community apparently were doing.

12:8 *To one . . . to another.* Not everyone has the same gift or all the gifts. *message of wisdom . . . knowledge.* Gifts that meet the need of the Christian community when knowledge or wisdom is required to make decisions or to choose proper courses of action.

12:9 *faith.* Not saving faith, which all Christians have, but faith to meet a specific need within the body of Christ. *gifts of healing.* Lit. "gifts of healings." The double plural may suggest different kinds of illnesses and the various ways God heals them.

12:10 *miraculous powers.* Lit. "deeds of power." In Scripture a miracle is an action that cannot be explained by natural means. It is an act of God intended as evidence of his power and purpose. *prophecy.* A communication of the mind of God imparted to a believer by the Holy Spirit. It may be a prediction (cf. Agabus, Ac 11:28; 21:10–11) or an indication of the will of God in a given situation (cf. 14:29–30; Ac 13:1–2). *distinguishing between spirits.* Since there can also be false prophecies that come from evil spirits, this gift is necessary in order to distinguish the true from the false (cf. 1Jn 4:1–6). *different kinds of tongues.* Since the Greek word for "tongues" means "languages" or "dialects," some understand it to refer to the ability to speak in unlearned human languages, as the apostles did on the day of Pentecost (Ac 2:4,6,11; cf. also 1Co 14:9–10). Others believe that in chs. 12–14 the term "tongues" refers to both earthly and heavenly languages, including ecstatic languages of praise and prayer (13:1; 14:2,10). *interpretation of tongues.* The communication of the message spoken in a tongue so that hearers can understand and be edified (cf. 14:5, 13,27–28).

12:11 *as he determines.* The Holy Spirit sovereignly determines which gift or gifts each believer should have.

12:12 *a unit . . . many parts.* This example illustrates the unity and diversity of the different spiritual gifts exercised by God's people, who are all members of the one body of Christ. *with Christ.* With Christ's body, the church, of which he is the head (Eph 1:22–23).

12:13 *all baptized by one Spirit into one body.* Spiritually baptized, regenerated by the Holy Spirit (Jn 3:3,5) and united with Christ as part of his body. *Jews or Greeks.* In Christ there is no racial or cultural distinction. *slave or free.* No social distinction. *all given the one Spirit to drink.* God has given all his people the Holy Spirit to indwell them (6:19)

by^b one Spirit^w into one body—whether Jews or Greeks, slave or free^x—and we were all given the one Spirit to drink.^y

¹⁴Now the body is not made up of one part but of many. ^z ¹⁵If the foot should say, "Because I am not a hand, I do not belong to the body," it would not for that reason cease to be part of the body. ¹⁶And if the ear should say, "Because I am not an eye, I do not belong to the body," it would not for that reason cease to be part of the body. ¹⁷If the whole body were an eye, where would the sense of hearing be? If the whole body were an ear, where would the sense of smell be? ¹⁸But in fact God has arranged^a the parts in the body, every one of them, just as he wanted them to be. ^b ¹⁹If they were all one part, where would the body be? ²⁰As it is, there are many parts, but one body. ^c

²¹The eye cannot say to the hand, "I don't need you!" And the head cannot say to the feet, "I don't need you!" ²²On the contrary, those parts of the body that seem to be weaker are indispensable, ²³and the parts that we think are less honorable we treat with special honor. And the parts that

are unpresentable are treated with special modesty, ²⁴while our presentable parts need no special treatment. But God has combined the members of the body and has given greater honor to the parts that lacked it, ²⁵so that there should be no division in the body, but that its parts should have equal concern for each other. ²⁶If one part suffers, every part suffers with it; if one part is honored, every part rejoices with it.

²⁷Now you are the body of Christ, ^d and each one of you is a part of it. ^e ²⁸And in the church^f God has appointed first of all apostles, ^g second prophets, ^h third teachers, then workers of miracles, also those having gifts of healing, ⁱ those able to help others, those with gifts of administration, ^j and those speaking in different kinds of tongues. ^k ²⁹Are all apostles? Are all prophets? Are all teachers? Do all work miracles? ³⁰Do all have gifts of healing? Do all speak in tongues^c? ^l Do all interpret? ³¹But eagerly desire^d ^m the greater gifts.

Cross references (center column):

12:13 ^wEph 2:18; ^xGal 3:28; Col 3:11; ^yJn 7:37-39
12:14 ^zver 12,20
12:18 ^aver 28
^bver 11
12:20 ^cver 12, 14; S Ro 12:5
12:27 ^dEph 1:23; 4:12; Col 1:18,24 ^eS Ro 12:5
12:28 ^fS 1Co 10:32 ^gS Eph 4:11 ^hS Eph 4:11 ⁱver 9 /Ro 12:6-8 ^kver 10; S Mk 16:17
12:30 ^lver 10
12:31 ^m1Co 14:1,39

^b13 Or with; or in   ^c30 Or other languages   ^d31 Or But you are eagerly desiring

---

so that their lives may overflow with the fruit of the Spirit (Gal 5:22–23; cf. Jn 7:37–39).

12:14–20 Addressed mainly to those who feel that their gifts are inferior and unimportant. Apparently the more spectacular gifts (such as tongues) had been glorified in the Corinthian church, making those who did not have them feel inferior.

12:14 As the human body must have diversity to work effectively as a whole, so the members of Christ's body have diverse gifts, the use of which can help bring about the accomplishment of Christ's united purpose. Each must properly exercise his gifts or effectively use his position for the good of the whole: e.g., the gift of the message of wisdom, the message of knowledge, the position of apostle, elder (1Pe 5:1), deacon (Ac 6:1–6).

12:18 Paul stresses the sovereign purpose of God in diversifying the parts of the body; by implication he is saying that God has arranged that different Christians in the body of Christ exercise different spiritual gifts, not the same gift. And this diversity is intended to accomplish God's unified purpose. God's method employs diversity to create unity.

12:21–26 Addressed mainly to those who feel that their gifts are superior and most important. These verses provide another indication that some gifts, like tongues, had been magnified as being preeminent.

12:21 The principle here is the interdependence of the parts of the body in the one whole. Christians in the body of Christ are mutually dependent as they exercise their distinctive functions.

12:22 *weaker are indispensable.* Christians who seem to have less important functions in the body of Christ are actually indispensable.

12:23 *the parts that we think are less honorable we treat with special honor.* Just as we give food to the stomach, though it is a less attractive part of the body, so we should give honor and support to the Christians in the church who have ordinary gifts (in their functions). *the parts that are unpresentable are treated with special modesty.* Christians

whose functions may be very obscure in the church are to be given special respect.

12:24 Persons with more spectacular gifts do not need to be given special honor.

12:25 *no division.* See 1:10–12.

12:26 *every part suffers.* In the body of Christ if one Christian suffers, all the Christians are affected (cf. Ac 12:1–5—the martyrdom of James and the imprisonment of Peter).

12:27 *you are the body of Christ.* Addressed to the local church at Corinth. Each local church is the body of Christ just as the universal church is Christ's body.

12:28 The list here differs somewhat from that in vv. 8–10 (see notes there). Paul notes three of the gifted individuals of Eph 4:11, then five of the spiritual gifts listed in vv. 8–10. The apostles and prophets were part of the foundation of the church (Eph 2:20), and teaching was associated with the pastoral office (Eph 4:11; 1Ti 3:2). These three gifted individuals are listed as "first," "second" and "third," indicating their importance in the church. The rest of the list is introduced with "then," indicating the variety that follows. Paul's lists of spiritual gifts seem to be largely random samples. Apart from v. 28a he does not rank them in importance since he has already insisted that all gifts are important (vv. 21–26). *apostles.* Those chosen by Christ during his earthly ministry to be with him and to go out and preach (Mk 3:14). They were also to be witnesses of the resurrection (Ac 1:21–22). The term may occasionally have been used in a broader sense (Ro 16:7; Gal 1:19). *miracles . . . healing . . . tongues.* See notes on vv. 9–10. *to help others.* Any act of helping others may be the product of a spiritual gift (cf. Ro 12:6–8), though the primary reference here is probably to a ministry to the poor, needy, sick and distressed (cf. Ac 6:1–6). *administration.* Those with gifts of administration were enabled by the Holy Spirit to organize and project plans and spiritual programs in the church.

12:29–30 *Are all apostles . . . ?* Christians have different gifts, and no one gift should be expected by everyone.

Love

And now I will show you the most excellent way.

13 If I speak in the tongues[e] [n] of men and of angels, but have not love, I am only a resounding gong or a clanging cymbal. [2]If I have the gift of prophecy[o] and can fathom all mysteries[p] and all knowledge,[q] and if I have a faith[r] that can move mountains,[s] but have not love, I am nothing. [3]If I give all I possess to the poor[t] and surrender my body to the flames,[f] [u] but have not love, I gain nothing.

[4]Love is patient,[v] love is kind. It does not envy, it does not boast, it is not proud.[w] [5]It is not rude, it is not self-seeking,[x] it is not easily angered,[y] it keeps no record of wrongs.[z] [6]Love does not delight in evil[a] but rejoices with the truth.[b] [7]It always protects, always trusts, always hopes, always perseveres.[c]

[8]Love never fails. But where there are prophecies,[d] they will cease; where there are tongues,[e] they will be stilled; where there is knowledge, it will pass away. [9]For we know in part[f] and we prophesy in part, [10]but when perfection comes,[g] the imperfect disappears. [11]When I was a child, I talked like a child, I thought like a child, I reasoned like a child. When I became a man, I put childish ways[h] behind me. [12]Now we see but a poor reflection as in a mirror;[i] then we shall see face to face.[j] Now I know in part; then I shall know fully, even as I am fully known.[k]

[13]And now these three remain: faith, hope and love.[l] But the greatest of these is love.[m]

Gifts of Prophecy and Tongues

14 Follow the way of love[n] and eagerly desire[o] spiritual gifts,[p] especially the gift of prophecy.[q] [2]For anyone who

Cross references

13:1 [n]ver 8; S Mk 16:17
13:2 [o]ver 8; S Eph 4:11; S Ac 11:27
[p]1Co 14:2
[q]S 2Co 8:7
[r]1Co 12:9
[s]Mt 17:20; 21:21
13:3 [t]Lk 19:8; S Ac 2:45
[u]Da 3:28
13:4 [v]1Th 5:14
[w]1Co 5:2
13:5 [x]S 1Co 10:24
[y]S Mt 5:22 [z]Job 14:16,17; Pr 10:12; 17:9; 1Pe 4:8
13:6 [a]2Th 2:12
[b]2Jn 4; 3Jn 3,4
13:7 [c]ver 8,13
13:8 [d]ver 2 [e]ver 1

13:9 [f]ver 12; S 1Co 8:2
13:10 [g]Php 3:12
13:11 [h]Ps 131:2
13:12 [i]Job 26:14; 36:26 [j]Ge 32:30; Job 19:26; 1Jn 3:2 [k]1Co 8:3; Gal 4:9
13:13 [l]Ro 5:2-5; Gal 5:5,6; Eph 4:2-5; Col 1:4,5;

1Th 1:3; 5:8; Heb 6:10-12 [m]Mt 22:37-40; 1Co 16:14; Gal 5:6; 1Jn 4:7-12,16 **14:1** [n]1Co 16:14 [o]ver 39; 1Co 12:31 [p]S 1Co 12:1 [q]ver 39; S Eph 4:11

[e]1 Or *languages* [f]3 Some early manuscripts *body that I may boast*

12:31 *eagerly desire the greater gifts.* See v. 28; 14:1,5, 12,39. If the alternative translation (see NIV text note) is correct, the Corinthians were apparently seeking status through the exercise of the gifts that seemed to them to be more important. *the most excellent way.* Paul now shows the right way to exercise all spiritual gifts—the way of love. He does not identify love as a gift; rather, it is a fruit of the Spirit (Gal 5:22).

13:1–3 *tongues ... prophecy ... faith ... give.* Paul selects four gifts as examples. He declares that even their most spectacular manifestations mean nothing unless motivated by love.

13:1 *tongues of men and of angels.* Paul uses hyperbole. Even if he could speak not only the various languages that human beings speak but even the languages used by angels—if he did not speak in love, it would be nothing but noise. *love.* The Greek for this word indicates a selfless concern for the welfare of others that is not called forth by any quality of lovableness in the person loved, but is the product of a will to love in obedience to God's command. It is like Christ's love manifested on the cross (cf. Jn 13:34–35; 1Jn 3:16).

13:2 *all mysteries and all knowledge.* Again Paul uses hyperbole to express the amount of understanding possessed. Even if one's gift is unlimited knowledge, if one does not possess and exercise that knowledge in love, he is nothing. *faith that can move mountains.* A special capacity to trust God to meet outstanding needs. Again Paul uses hyperbole.

13:3 *surrender my body to the flames.* A reference to suffering martyrdom through burning at the stake, as many early Christians experienced. Even the supreme sacrifice, if not motivated by love, accomplishes nothing.

13:4–7 Love is now described both positively and negatively.

13:4 *not proud.* See 8:1.

13:5 *not rude.* Perhaps an indirect reference to their unruly conduct in worship (11:18–22).

13:6 *does not delight in evil.* As they were doing in ch. 5.

13:8 *prophecies ... will cease; ... tongues ... will be stilled; ... knowledge ... will pass away.* These three will

cease because they are partial in nature (v. 9) and will be unnecessary when what is complete has come (v. 10).

13:10 *perfection.* The Greek for this word can mean "end," "fulfillment," "completeness" or "maturity." In this context the contrast is between the partial and the complete. Some refer the verse to the return of Christ, others to the death of the Christian, others to the maturity (or establishment) of the church (see the illustration in v. 11), still others to the completion of the canon of NT Scripture. Verse 12, however, seems to indicate that Paul is here speaking of Christ's second coming.

13:12 *we see but a poor reflection as in a mirror.* The imagery is of a polished metal (probably bronze) mirror in which one could receive only an imperfect reflection (cf. Jas 1:23)—in contrast to seeing the Lord directly and clearly in heaven. *know fully ... fully known.* The Christian will know the Lord to the fullest extent possible for a finite being, similar to the way the Lord knows the Christian fully and infinitely. This will not be true until the Lord returns.

13:13 *remain.* Now and forever. *faith, hope and love.* See note on 1Th 1:3. *the greatest of these is love.* Because God is love (1Jn 4:8) and has communicated his love to us (1Jn 4:10) and commands us to love one another (Jn 13:34–35). Love supersedes the gifts because it outlasts them all. Long after these sought-after gifts are no longer necessary, love will still be the governing principle that controls all that God and his redeemed people are and do.

14:1–5 The basic principle Paul insists on is that whatever is done in the church must contribute to the edification (building up) of the body. This is in keeping with the declaration in 12:7 that gifts are "given for the common good." It also is in agreement with the principle of love (ch. 13). What is spoken in the church, then, must be intelligible—it must be spoken in the vernacular language or at least be interpreted in the vernacular. Prophecy is therefore more desirable than tongues (unless an interpreter is present) because prophecy is spoken in the native language of the listeners.

14:1 *the way of love ... spiritual gifts.* Love is the means by which spiritual gifts are made effective. *especially the gift of prophecy.* See note on 12:10.

14:2 *tongue.* See NIV text note. The hearers cannot under-

speaks in a tongue[g] [r] does not speak to men but to God. Indeed, no one understands him;[s] he utters mysteries[t] with his spirit.[h] [3]But everyone who prophesies speaks to men for their strengthening,[u] encouragement[v] and comfort. [4]He who speaks in a tongue[w] edifies[x] himself, but he who prophesies[y] edifies the church. [5]I would like every one of you to speak in tongues,[i] but I would rather have you prophesy.[z] He who prophesies is greater than one who speaks in tongues,[i] unless he interprets, so that the church may be edified.[a]

[6]Now, brothers, if I come to you and speak in tongues, what good will I be to you, unless I bring you some revelation[b] or knowledge[c] or prophecy or word of instruction?[d] [7]Even in the case of lifeless things that make sounds, such as the flute or harp, how will anyone know what tune is being played unless there is a distinction in the notes? [8]Again, if the trumpet does not sound a clear call, who will get ready for battle?[e] [9]So it is with you. Unless you speak intelligible words with your tongue, how will anyone know what you are saying? You will just be speaking into the air. [10]Undoubtedly there are all sorts of languages in the world, yet none of them is without meaning. [11]If then I do not grasp

the meaning of what someone is saying, I am a foreigner to the speaker, and he is a foreigner to me.[f] [12]So it is with you. Since you are eager to have spiritual gifts,[g] try to excel in gifts that build up[h] the church.

[13]For this reason anyone who speaks in a tongue should pray that he may interpret what he says.[i] [14]For if I pray in a tongue, my spirit prays,[j] but my mind is unfruitful. [15]So what shall I do? I will pray with my spirit,[k] but I will also pray with my mind; I will sing[l] with my spirit, but I will also sing with my mind. [16]If you are praising God with your spirit, how can one who finds himself among those who do not understand[j] say "Amen"[m] to your thanksgiving,[n] since he does not know what you are saying? [17]You may be giving thanks well enough, but the other man is not edified.[o]

[18]I thank God that I speak in tongues more than all of you. [19]But in the church I would rather speak five intelligible words to instruct others than ten thousand words in a tongue.[p]

[20]Brothers, stop thinking like children.[q] In regard to evil be infants,[r] but in your

---

14:2 [r]S Mk 16:17 [s]ver 6-11,16 [t]1Co 13:2
14:3 [u]ver 4,5,12, 17,26; S Ro 14:19 [v]ver 31
14:4 [w]S Mk 16:17 [x]S ver 3 [y]S 1Co 13:2
14:5 [z]Nu 11:29 [a]S ver 3
14:6 [b]ver 26; Eph 1:17 [c]S 2Co 8:7 [d]Ro 6:17
14:8 [e]Nu 10:9; Jer 4:19
14:11 [f]Ge 11:7
14:12 [g]S 1Co 12:1 [h]S ver 3
14:13 [i]ver 5
14:14 [j]ver 2
14:15 [k]ver 2,14 [l]S Eph 5:19
14:16 [m]Dt 27:15-26; 1Ch 16:36; Ne 8:6; Ps 106:48; Rev 5:14; 7:12 [n]S Mt 14:19; 1Co 11:24
14:17 [o]S ver 3
14:19 [p]ver 6
14:20 [q]1Co 3:11; Eph 4:14; Heb 5:12,13; 1Pe 2:2 [r]Jer 4:22; Mt 10:16; Ro 16:19

[g]2 Or *another language*; also in verses 4, 13, 14, 19, 26 and 27   [h]2 Or *by the Spirit*   [i]5 Or *other languages*; also in verses 6, 18, 22, 23 and 39   [j]16 Or *among the inquirers*

---

stand what the person who speaks in a tongue is saying. Therefore what he says is a mystery unless it is interpreted. Only God understands it. *with his spirit.* It is not spoken from his mind (see vv. 14–17).

14:3 In prophesying the speaker can edify and encourage others (12:7).

14:4 *edifies himself.* This edification does not involve the mind since the speaker does not understand what he has said. It is a personal edification in the area of the emotions, of deepening conviction, of fuller commitment and greater love.

14:5 *like . . . you to speak in tongues.* Paul was not opposed to tongues-speaking if it was practiced properly. *He who prophesies is greater.* Because he serves the common good more effectively since what he says can be understood and thus edifies the church. *unless he interprets.* If the tongues-speaker also has the gift of interpretation, his speaking is as beneficial as prophecy, for then it can be understood (see v. 13).

14:6 *what good will I be . . . ?* It would be useless for a person to speak in tongues unless, by interpretation, he brings the church something understandable and edifying.

14:7 *flute or harp.* Instruments that were well known in Greece. *distinction in the notes.* For a person to recognize the tune and to understand and appreciate it, there must be a variety of notes so arranged as to create a meaningful tune. One note repeated monotonously cannot accomplish this.

14:8 *the trumpet . . . ready for battle.* All Greeks would be acquainted with the use of the trumpet for battle signals (cf. Homer's *Iliad*, 18.219), and the Jews would be familiar with the use of the ram's horn (Nu 10:9; Jos 6:4,9). Again, the notes sounded must convey a message.

14:9 *speak intelligible words.* Speak in the vernacular language of the listeners rather than in a tongue (or else provide an interpretation).

14:10 *all sorts of languages.* Some see vv. 10–11 as an indication that the tongues of chs. 12–14 were unlearned foreign languages.

14:12 *excel in gifts that build up the church.* The basic principle of ch. 14.

14:14 *mind is unfruitful.* When a person speaks in tongues or prays in tongues, the human mind does not produce the language.

14:15–17 *pray . . . sing . . . praising God . . . say "Amen" . . . thanksgiving.* Elements employed in OT (1Ch 16:36; Ne 5:13; 8:6; Ps 104:33; 136:1; 148:1) and NT worship (Ro 11:36; Eph 5:18–20). "Amen," meaning "It is true" or "So be it," is the believer's confession of agreement with the words spoken (cf. Gal 1:5). Thus it is important that a message in tongues be interpreted.

14:15 *pray with my spirit . . . with my mind . . . sing with my spirit . . . with my mind.* May mean that Paul will sometimes pray or sing with his spirit in a tongue; at other times he will pray or sing with his mind in his own language. Others believe that Paul was declaring his intention to pray or sing with both mind and spirit at the same time.

14:19 *But in the church.* Some believe that an interpretation is unnecessary when the gift of tongues is being used as a private prayer language. They base such a distinction on v. 18 (see v. 14) when compared with the phrase quoted here.

14:20 *In regard to evil be infants.* Just as in the case of infants, have no evil desires or wrong motives in wanting to excel in spiritual gifts (such as speaking in tongues) as an end in itself.

thinking be adults. 21In the Law s it is written:

"Through men of strange tongues
and through the lips of foreigners
I will speak to this people,
but even then they will not listen to
me,"k t
says the Lord.

22Tongues, then, are a sign, not for believers but for unbelievers; prophecy,u however, is for believers, not for unbelievers. 23So if the whole church comes together and everyone speaks in tongues, and some who do not understand l or some unbelievers come in, will they not say that you are out of your mind?v 24But if an unbeliever or someone who does not understand m comes in while everybody is prophesying, he will be convinced by all that he is a sinner and will be judged by all, 25and the secrets w of his heart will be laid bare. So he will fall down and worship God, exclaiming, "God is really among you!"x

Orderly Worship

26What then shall we say, brothers?y

When you come together, everyone z has a hymn,a or a word of instruction,b a revelation, a tongue c or an interpretation.d All of these must be done for the strengthening e of the church. 27If anyone speaks in a tongue, two—or at the most three—should speak, one at a time, and someone must interpret. 28If there is no interpreter, the speaker should keep quiet in the church and speak to himself and God.

29Two or three prophets f should speak, and the others should weigh carefully what is said.g 30And if a revelation comes to someone while he is sitting down, the first speaker should stop. 31For you can all prophesy in turn so that everyone may be instructed and encouraged. 32The spirits of prophets are subject to the control of prophets.h 33For God is not a God of disorder i but of peace.j

As in all the congregations k of the saints,l 34women should remain silent in the churches. They are not allowed to speak,m but must be in submission,n as the

Cross references (center column):
14:21 *s* ver 34; S Jn 10:34 *t* Dt 28:49; Isa 28:11,12
14:22 *u* ver 1
14:23 *v* Ac 2:13
14:25 *w* Ro 2:16 *x* Isa 45:14; Zec 8:23
14:26 *y* S Ro 7:1

z 1Co 12:7-10 *a* S Eph 5:19 *b* ver 6 *c* ver 2 *d* 1Co 12:10 *e* S Ro 14:19
14:29 *f* ver 32,37; S 1Co 13:2 *g* 1Co 12:10
14:32 *h* 1Jn 4:1
14:33 *i* ver 40 *j* S Ro 15:33 *k* S 1Co 7:17; S 10:32 *l* S Ac 9:13
14:34 *m* 1Co 11:5,13 *n* S Eph 5:22; 1Ti 2:11,12

k21 Isaiah 28:11,12   l23 Or some inquirers
m24 Or some inquirer

14:21–22 The passage from Isa 28 indicates that the foreign language of the Assyrians was a sign to unbelieving Israel that judgment was coming on them. Paul deduced from this fact that tongues were intended to be a sign for unbelievers (v. 22), as, e.g., in Ac 2:4–12. Similarly, prophecy was for believers (v. 22) since it communicated revealed truth to those disposed to receive it (cf. Mt 13:11–16).
14:21 *In the Law.* Cf. Ro 3:10–19, where Paul quotes from a number of passages from the OT, including Isaiah, and then in v. 19 collectively calls them "the law."
14:23 *some who do not understand.* Perhaps those who had become "inquirers" (see NIV text note) concerning the gospel but as yet did not really understand. *some unbelievers.* Those who have made no movement toward saving faith. The context is a meeting of the church in which everyone is speaking in tongues with the result that general confusion reigns. *out of your mind.* The visitors will be repulsed by the confusion, and the phenomenon meant to be an impressive sign will have a negative effect on the unsaved.
14:24 *everybody is prophesying.* Prophecy, spoken in the vernacular language and intended for believers, turns out to have a positive effect on unbelievers because they hear and understand and are convicted of their sins. (Yet see restrictions on prophesying in vv. 29–32 and notes there.)
14:26–27 *everyone . . . anyone . . . someone.* The stress here is again on the diversity and yet complementary nature of spiritual gifts. It is also apparent that every member could participate, not just certain leaders or officers.
14:26 *a hymn, or a word of instruction, a revelation, a tongue or an interpretation.* Elements that made up the worship service at Corinth. Some of these elements (the hymn and the word of instruction) came from OT and synagogue worship (cf. Mt 26:30; Lk 4:16–22). All parts of Christian worship should be edifying ("strengthening") to the church.
14:27–28 Three restrictions are placed on speaking in a tongue "in the church" (v. 28): 1. Only two or three should

do so in a meeting. 2. They should do so one at a time. 3. There must be interpretation.
14:28 *the speaker should keep quiet.* The implication seems to be that it was up to the one speaking in a tongue in the Corinthian church to make certain that there was in the audience someone to interpret his message.
14:29 *Two or three prophets should speak.* Apparently in turn (v. 31), as with the tongues-speakers (v. 27). *weigh carefully.* Judge. The prophets themselves were to decide whether the messages of their fellow prophets were valid (see note on v. 32).
14:30 *a revelation.* Not an inspired revelation intended to become a part of written Scripture. In OT times, Scriptural revelation came through prophets, and in NT times through apostles or close associates of apostles. Prophecy referred to in chs. 12–14 could come through any member of the church (vv. 26,29–31). It could be a prediction (Agabus, Ac 11:28; 21:10–11), a divine directive (Ac 13:1–2) or a message designed to strengthen, encourage or comfort (v. 3).
14:32 *control of prophets.* Prophecy (and tongues as well) was not an uncontrollable emotional ecstasy. Paul insists that these gifts should be controlled by the recipients themselves (vv. 15, 26–32). See notes on vv. 27–29.
14:33 *God . . . of peace.* See note on 1Th 5:23. *disorder.* Paul was concerned that disorderly and unregulated worship at Corinth would bring discredit on the name of the God who had called them in Christ to peace and unity. *in all the congregations of the saints.* A unique expression in the NT that stresses the universality and commonality of the whole visible church of God on earth. All congregations are to obey the directives that follow.
14:34–35 See note on 11:3–16. Some believe that in light of 11:3 there is a God-ordained order that is to be the basis for administration and authority. Women are to be in submission to their husbands both at home (see Eph 5:22) and in the church (see v. 34; 1Ti 2:11–12) regardless of their particular culture. According to this view, a timeless order

Law[o] says. [35]If they want to inquire about something, they should ask their own husbands at home; for it is disgraceful for a woman to speak in the church.

[36]Did the word of God[p] originate with you? Or are you the only people it has reached? [37]If anybody thinks he is a prophet[q] or spiritually gifted,[r] let him acknowledge that what I am writing to you is the Lord's command.[s] [38]If he ignores this, he himself will be ignored.[n]

[39]Therefore, my brothers, be eager[t] to prophesy,[u] and do not forbid speaking in tongues. [40]But everything should be done in a fitting and orderly[v] way.

The Resurrection of Christ

15 Now, brothers, I want to remind you of the gospel[w] I preached to you,[x] which you received and on which you have taken your stand. [2]By this gospel

you are saved,[y] if you hold firmly[z] to the word I preached to you. Otherwise, you have believed in vain.

[3]For what I received[a] I passed on to you[b] as of first importance[o]: that Christ died for our sins[c] according to the Scriptures,[d] [4]that he was buried,[e] that he was raised[f] on the third day[g] according to the Scriptures,[h] [5]and that he appeared to Peter,[p][i] and then to the Twelve.[j] [6]After that, he appeared to more than five hundred of the brothers at the same time, most of whom are still living, though some have fallen asleep.[k] [7]Then he appeared to James,[l] then to all the apostles,[m] [8]and last

Cross references
14:34 [o]ver 21; Ge 3:16
14:36 [p]S Heb 4:12
14:37 [q]S Ac 11:27; 1Co 13:2; 2Co 10:7
[r]1Co 2:15; S 12:1
[s]1Jn 4:6
14:39 [t]ver 1; 1Co 12:31 [u]ver 1; S Eph 4:11
14:40 [v]ver 33; Col 2:5
15:1 [w]Isa 40:9; Ro 2:16
[x]S 1Co 3:6; S Gal 1:8

15:2 [y]Ro 1:16 [z]S Ro 11:22
15:3 [a]Gal 1:12 [b]S 1Co 11:2
[c]Isa 53:5; Jn 1:29; S Gal 1:4; 1Pe 2:24
[d]S Mt 26:24; S Lk 24:27; S 24:44; Ac 17:2; 26:22,23

15:4 [e]Mt 27:59,60 [f]S Ac 2:24 [g]S Mt 16:21 [h]Jn 2:21,22; Ac 2:25,30,31 15:5 [i]Lk 24:34 [j]Mk 16:14; Lk 24:36-43 15:6 [k]ver 18,20; S Mt 9:24 15:7 [l]S Ac 15:13 [m]Lk 24:33,36,37; Ac 1:3,4

[n]38 Some manuscripts *If he is ignorant of this, let him be ignorant* [o]3 Or *you at the first* [p]5 Greek *Cephas*

---

was established at creation (see note on 11:5–6).

Others maintain that Paul's concern is that the church be strengthened (v. 26) by believers showing respect for others (see vv. 30–31) and for God (see v. 33) as they exercise their spiritual gifts. Such respect must necessarily take account of accepted social practices. If within a particular social order, it is disgraceful for a woman to speak in church—and it was in this case (v. 35)—then she shows disrespect by doing so and should remain silent. There were occasions, though—even in this culture—for women to speak in church. For example, in 11:5 Paul assumes that women pray and prophesy in public worship. Thus his purpose, according to this view, was not to define the role of women but to establish a fitting (vv. 34–35) and orderly (vv. 27–31) way of worship (v. 40).

Still others say that in this context Paul is discussing primarily the disruption of worship by women who become involved in noisy discussions surrounding tongues-speaking and prophecy. Instead of publicly clamoring for explanations, the wives were to discuss matters with their husbands at home (cf. v. 35). Paul does not altogether forbid women to speak in church (see 11:5). What he is forbidding is the disorderly speaking indicated in these verses.

14:36 Paul asks these rhetorical questions sarcastically, suggesting that the Corinthians were following their own practice in these matters rather than conforming to God's word.

14:37 *the Lord's command.* Paul's commands are the Lord's commands and are to be followed. In a situation where so much stress was being placed on gifts, Paul insists that any genuinely gifted person will recognize the apostle's God-given authority.

14:38 *he himself will be ignored.* Paul and the churches will ignore such a disobedient person, and so he will be regarded as an unbeliever.

14:39 *do not forbid speaking in tongues.* Paul's solution to the tongues problem in the Corinthian church was not to forbid tongues, but to correct the improper use of the gift.

14:40 *a fitting and orderly way.* As spelled out in vv. 26–35.

15:2 *if you hold firmly.* See note on Heb 3:14. *believed in vain.* If you are not persevering in the Christian faith, this is an evidence that you did not have saving faith in the first place (cf. Judas Iscariot, who eventually showed that he was not a true believer).

15:3–5 Two lines of evidence for the death and resurrec-

tion of Christ are given here: (1) the testimony of the OT (e.g., Ps 16:8–11; Isa 53:5–6,11) and (2) the testimony of eyewitnesses (Ac 1:21–22). Six resurrection appearances are listed here. The Gospels give more.

15:3 *what I received I passed on to you as of first importance.* Here Paul links himself with early Christian tradition. He was not its originator, nor did he receive it directly from the Lord. His source was other Christians. The verbs he uses are technical terms for receiving and transmitting tradition (see note on 11:23). What follows is the heart of the gospel: that Christ died for our sins (not for his own sins; cf. Heb 7:27), that he was buried (confirmation that he had really died) and that he was raised from the dead.

15:4 *on the third day.* Cf. Mt 12:40. The Jews counted parts of days as whole days. Thus the three days would include part of Friday afternoon, all of Saturday, and Sunday morning. A similar way of reckoning time is seen in Jn 20:26 (lit. "after eight days," NIV "a week later"); two Sundays are implied, one at each end of the expression.

15:5 *Peter . . . the Twelve.* The appearance to Peter is the one mentioned in Lk 24:34, which occurred on Easter Sunday. The appearance to the Twelve seems to have taken place on Sunday evening (see Lk 24:36–43; Jn 20:19–23). "The Twelve" seems to have been used to refer to the group of original apostles, even though Judas was no longer with them (notice, however, that the 11 disciples, the 11 apostles or "the Eleven" are referred to in Mt 28:16; Mk 16:14; Lk 24:9,33; Ac 1:26).

15:6 *more than five hundred . . . at the same time.* The appearance to this large group may be mentioned to help bolster the faith of those Corinthians who evidently had some doubts about the resurrection of Christ (cf. v. 12). This appearance may be the one in Galilee recorded in Mt 28:10, 16–20, where the Eleven and possibly more met the risen Lord. *some have fallen asleep.* A common expression at that time for physical death (cf. Ac 7:60).

15:7 *James.* Since this James is listed in addition to the apostles, he is not James son of Zebedee or James son of Alphaeus (Mt 10:2–3). This is James, the half-brother of Jesus (Mt 13:55), who did not believe in Christ before the resurrection (Jn 7:5) but afterward joined the apostolic band (Ac 1:14) and later became prominent in the Jerusalem church (Ac 15:13). It is not clear in Scripture when and where this appearance to James occurred. *to all the apostles.* For example, Ac 1:6–11.

of all he appeared to me also,[n] as to one abnormally born.

[9]For I am the least of the apostles[o] and do not even deserve to be called an apostle, because I persecuted[p] the church of God.[q] [10]But by the grace[r] of God I am what I am, and his grace to me[s] was not without effect. No, I worked harder than all of them[t]—yet not I, but the grace of God that was with me.[u] [11]Whether, then, it was I or they,[v] this is what we preach, and this is what you believed.

The Resurrection of the Dead

[12]But if it is preached that Christ has been raised from the dead,[w] how can some of you say that there is no resurrection[x] of the dead?[y] [13]If there is no resurrection of the dead, then not even Christ has been raised. [14]And if Christ has not been raised,[z] our preaching is useless and so is your faith. [15]More than that, we are then found to be false witnesses about God, for we have testified about God that he raised Christ from the dead.[a] But he did not raise him if in fact the dead are not raised. [16]For if the dead are not raised, then Christ has not been raised either. [17]And if Christ has

not been raised, your faith is futile; you are still in your sins.[b] [18]Then those also who have fallen asleep[c] in Christ are lost. [19]If only for this life we have hope in Christ, we are to be pitied more than all men.[d]

[20]But Christ has indeed been raised from the dead,[e] the firstfruits[f] of those who have fallen asleep.[g] [21]For since death came through a man,[h] the resurrection of the dead[i] comes also through a man. [22]For as in Adam all die, so in Christ all will be made alive.[j] [23]But each in his own turn: Christ, the firstfruits;[k] then, when he comes,[l] those who belong to him.[m] [24]Then the end will come, when he hands over the kingdom[n] to God the Father after he has destroyed all dominion, authority and power.[o] [25]For he must reign[p] until he has put all his enemies under his feet.[q] [26]The last enemy to be destroyed is death.[r] [27]For he "has put everything under his feet."[q][s] Now when it says that "everything" has been put under him, it is clear that this does not include God himself, who put everything under Christ.[t] [28]When he has done this, then the Son

Cross references column

15:8 [n]Ac 9:3-6, 17; 1Co 9:1; Gal 1:16
15:9 [o]2Co 12:11; Eph 3:8; 1Ti 1:15
[p]S Ac 8:3
[q]S 1Co 10:32
15:10 [r]S Ro 3:24
[s]S Ro 12:3
[t]2Co 11:23; Col 1:29
[u]S Php 2:13
15:11 [v]Gal 2:6
15:12 [w]ver 4
[x]S Jn 11:24
[y]Ac 17:32; 23:8; 2Ti 2:18
15:14 [z]1Th 4:14
15:15 [a]S Ac 2:24

15:17 [b]S Ro 4:25
15:18 [c]ver 6,20; S Mt 9:24
15:19 [d]S 1Co 4:9
15:20 [e]1Pe 1:3
[f]ver 23; S Ac 26:23 [g]ver 6,18; S Mt 9:24
15:21 [h]S Ro 5:12
[i]ver 12
15:22 [j]Ro 5:14-18; S 1Co 6:14
15:23 [k]ver 20
[l]ver 52; S 1Th 2:19
[m]S 1Co 3:23
15:24 [n]Da 2:44; 7:14,27; 2Pe 1:11
[o]Ro 8:38
15:25 [p]Isa 9:7; 52:7 [q]ver 27; S Mt 22:44
15:26 [r]2Ti 1:10; Rev 20:14; 21:4

15:27 [s]ver 25; Ps 8:6; S Mt 22:44 [t]S Mt 28:18
[q]27 Psalm 8:6

15:8 *last of all.* See Ac 9:1–8. This appearance to Paul came several years after the resurrection (perhaps c. A.D. 33). *one abnormally born.* Paul was not part of the original group of apostles. He had not lived with Christ as the others had. His entry into the apostolic office was not "normal." Furthermore, at his conversion he was abruptly snatched from his former way of life (Ac 9:3–6).

15:9 *church of God.* In persecuting the church, he was actually persecuting Christ (see Ac 9:4–5).

15:12–19 Some at Corinth were saying that there was no resurrection of the body, and Paul draws a number of conclusions from this false contention. If the dead do not rise from the grave, then (1) "not even Christ has been raised" (v. 13); (2) "our preaching is useless" (v. 14); (3) "so is your faith" (v. 14); (4) we are "false witnesses" that God raised Christ from the dead (v. 15); (5) "your faith is futile" (v. 17); (6) "you are still in your sins" (v. 17) and still carry the guilt and condemnation of sin; (7) "those also who have fallen asleep [have died] in Christ are lost" (v. 18); and (8) "we are to be pitied" who "only for this life . . . hope in Christ" (v. 19) and put up with persecution and hardship.

15:12 *Christ has been raised.* Christ was raised historically on the third day. Paul uses this same verb form (that expresses the certainty of Christ's bodily resurrection) a total of seven times in this passage (vv. 4,12–14,16–17,20).

15:20 *But Christ has indeed been raised.* Paul's categorical conclusion based on his evidence set forth in vv. 3–8. *firstfruits.* The first sheaf of the harvest given to the Lord (Lev 23:10–11,17,20) as a token that all the harvest belonged to the Lord and would be dedicated to him through dedicated lives. So Christ, who has been raised, is the guarantee of the resurrection of all of God's redeemed people (cf. 1Th 4:13–18).

15:21 *death came through a man.* Through Adam (Ge 3:17–19). *the resurrection of the dead comes also through a man.* Through Christ, the second Adam, "the last Adam"

(v. 45; cf. Ro 5:12–21).

15:22 *in Adam all die.* All who are "in Adam"—i.e., his descendants—suffer death. *in Christ all will be made alive.* All who are "in Christ"—i.e., who are related to him by faith—will be made alive at the resurrection (cf. Jn 5:25; 1Th 4:16–17; Rev 20:6).

15:23 *each in his own turn.* Christ, the firstfruits, was raised in his own time in history (c. A.D. 30), and those who are identified with Christ by faith will be raised at his second coming. His resurrection is the pledge that ours will follow.

15:24 *the end.* The second coming of Christ and all the events accompanying it. This includes his handing over the kingdom to the Father, following his destroying all dominion, authority and power of the persons and forces who oppose him.

15:25 *For he must reign.* During this process of Christ's destroying all dominion and handing over the kingdom to the Father, Christ must reign (Rev 20:1–6). Some take this to mean that Christ will literally reign with his saints for 1,000 years on the earth (cf. Isa 2:2–4; Mic 4:1–5). Others believe that this refers to Christ's reign over the course of history and in the lives of his people, who are spiritually raised, or born again. This reign is viewed as continuing throughout the present age. *under his feet.* An OT figure for complete conquest. Verse 25 is an allusion to Ps 110:1 (cf. Mt 22:44).

15:26 This destruction of death will occur at the end of the second-coming events after Christ conquers his enemies (Rev 19:11–21; 20:5–14), at the great white throne judgment (when death and Hades will be thrown into the lake of fire).

15:28 *the Son himself will be made subject to him.* The Son will be made subject to the Father in the sense that administratively, after he subjects all things to his power, he will then turn it all over to God the Father, the administrative head. This is not to suggest that the Son is in any way inferior to the Father. All three persons of the Trinity are equal in

himself will be made subject to him who put everything under him,[u] so that God may be all in all.[v]

[29]Now if there is no resurrection, what will those do who are baptized for the dead? If the dead are not raised at all, why are people baptized for them? [30]And as for us, why do we endanger ourselves every hour?[w] [31]I die every day[x]—I mean that, brothers—just as surely as I glory over you in Christ Jesus our Lord. [32]If I fought wild beasts[y] in Ephesus[z] for merely human reasons, what have I gained? If the dead are not raised,

"Let us eat and drink,
    for tomorrow we die."[r] [a]

[33]Do not be misled:[b] "Bad company corrupts good character."[c] [34]Come back to your senses as you ought, and stop sinning; for there are some who are ignorant of God[d]—I say this to your shame.[e]

The Resurrection Body

[35]But someone may ask,[f] "How are the dead raised? With what kind of body will

they come?"[g] [36]How foolish![h] What you sow does not come to life unless it dies.[i] [37]When you sow, you do not plant the body that will be, but just a seed, perhaps of wheat or of something else. [38]But God gives it a body as he has determined, and to each kind of seed he gives its own body.[j] [39]All flesh is not the same: Men have one kind of flesh, animals have another, birds another and fish another. [40]There are also heavenly bodies and there are earthly bodies; but the splendor of the heavenly bodies is one kind, and the splendor of the earthly bodies is another. [41]The sun has one kind of splendor, [k] the moon another and the stars another;[l] and star differs from star in splendor.

[42]So will it be[m] with the resurrection of the dead.[n] The body that is sown is perishable, it is raised imperishable;[o] [43]it is sown in dishonor, it is raised in glory;[p] it is sown in weakness, it is raised in power; [44]it is sown a natural body, it is raised a spiritual body.[q]

Cross references

15:28 [u]Php 3:21
[v]1Co 3:23
15:30
[w]2Co 11:26
15:31 [x]S Ro 8:36
15:32 [y]2Co 1:8
[z]S Ac 18:19
Lk 12:19
15:33 [b]S 1Co 6:9
[c]Pr 22:24,25
15:34 [d]S Gal 4:8
[e]S 1Co 4:14
15:35 [f]Ro 9:19

[g]Eze 37:3
15:36 [h]Lk 11:40;
12:20 [i]Jn 12:24
15:38 [j]Ge 1:11
15:41 [k]Ps 19:4-6
[l]Ps 8:1,3
15:42 [m]Da 12:3;
Mt 13:43 [n]ver 12
[o]ver 50,53,54
15:43 [p]Php 3:21;
Col 3:4
15:44 [q]ver 50

[r]32 Isaiah 22:13

---

deity and in dignity. The subordination referred to is one of function (see note on 11:3). The Father is supreme in the Trinity; the Son carries out the Father's will (e.g., in creation, redemption); the Spirit is sent by the Father and the Son to vitalize life, communicate God's truth, apply his salvation to people and enable them to obey God's will (or word). *so that God may be all in all.* The triune God will be shown to be supreme and sovereign in all things.
15:29 *those ... who are baptized for the dead.* The present tense suggests that at Corinth people were currently being baptized for the dead. But because Paul does not give any more information about the practice, many attempts have been made to interpret the concept. Three of these are: 1. Living believers were being baptized for believers who died before they were baptized, so that they too, in a sense, would not miss out on baptism. 2. Christians were being baptized in anticipation of the resurrection of the dead. 3. New converts were being baptized to fill the ranks of Christians who had died. At any rate, Paul mentions this custom almost in passing, using it in his arguments substantiating the resurrection of the dead, but without necessarily approving the practice. Probably the passage will always remain obscure.
15:30 *why do we endanger ourselves every hour?* If there is no resurrection, why should we suffer persecution and privation for Christ every day (cf. 2Co 11:23–29)?
15:32 *I fought wild beasts in Ephesus.* This statement can be taken literally or figuratively. But since from Ac 19 we have no evidence of Paul suffering imprisonment and having to face the lions, it is more likely that the expression means that the enemies in Ephesus were as ferocious as wild beasts. *Let us eat and drink, for tomorrow we die.* See Isa 22:13; a fitting philosophy of life if there is no resurrection.
15:33 A quotation from the Greek comedy *Thais* written by the Greek poet Menander, whose writings the Corinthians would know. The application of the quotation is that those who are teaching that there is no resurrection (v. 12) are the "bad company," and they are corrupting the "good character" of those who hold to the correct doctrine. Cf. Pr

13:20.
15:34 *stop sinning.* The sin of denying that there is a resurrection and thus doubting even the resurrection of Christ, all of which had a negative effect on the lives they were living. *some who are ignorant of God.* Even in the Corinthian church. This, Paul says, is a shameful situation.
15:35–49 In discussing the nature of the resurrection body, Paul compares it to plant life (vv. 36–38), to fleshly beings (v. 39) and to celestial and earthly physical bodies (vv. 40–41).
15:36–38 Plant organisms, though organized similarly in their own order, are different; the seed sown is related to the new plant that sprouts, but the new sprout has a different and genuinely new body that God has given it.
15:39 *All flesh is not the same.* Although there is much that is similar in the organizational character of fleshly beings, each species is different: man, animals, birds, fish.
15:40–41 Here the analogy involves inanimate objects of creation: the sun, moon and stars with their differing splendor, and the earthly bodies (possibly the great mountains, canyons and seas) with their splendor. In it all, God can take similar physical material and organize it differently to accomplish his purpose.
15:42–44 In applying these analogies, the apostle says that in the case of the resurrection of the dead, God will take a perishable, dishonorable, weak (and sinful) body—"a natural body" characterized by sin—and in the resurrection make it an imperishable, glorious, powerful body. "Spiritual body" does not mean a nonmaterial body but, from the analogies, a physical one similar to the present natural body organizationally, but radically different in that it will be imperishable, glorious and powerful, fit to live eternally with God. There is continuity, but there is also change.
15:44–49 The contrast here between the natural body and the spiritual body again follows from their two representatives (see notes on vv. 21–22). One is the first Adam, who had a natural body of the dust of the ground (Ge 2:7) and through whom a natural body is given to his descendants. The other is the last Adam, Christ, the life-giving spirit (cf. Jn

If there is a natural body, there is also a spiritual body. 45So it is written: "The first man Adam became a living being"s; r the last Adam,s a life-giving spirit. t 46The spiritual did not come first, but the natural, and after that the spiritual. u 47The first man was of the dust of the earth, v the second man from heaven. w 48As was the earthly man, so are those who are of the earth; and as is the man from heaven, so also are those who are of heaven. x 49And just as we have borne the likeness of the earthly man, y so shall we t bear the likeness of the man from heaven. z

50I declare to you, brothers, that flesh and blood a cannot inherit the kingdom of God, b nor does the perishable inherit the imperishable. c 51Listen, I tell you a mystery: d We will not all sleep, e but we will all be changed f— 52in a flash, in the twinkling of an eye, at the last trumpet. For the trumpet will sound, g the dead h will be raised imperishable, and we will be changed. 53For the perishable i must clothe itself with the imperishable, j and the mortal with immortality. 54When the perishable has been clothed with the imperishable, and the mortal with immortality, then the saying that is written will

come true: "Death has been swallowed up in victory." u k

55"Where, O death, is your victory?
Where, O death, is your sting?" v l

56The sting of death is sin, m and the power of sin is the law. n 57But thanks be to God! o He gives us the victory through our Lord Jesus Christ. p

58Therefore, my dear brothers, stand firm. Let nothing move you. Always give yourselves fully to the work of the Lord, q because you know that your labor in the Lord is not in vain. r

The Collection for God's People

16 Now about the collection s for God's people: t Do what I told the Galatian u churches to do. 2On the first day of every week, v each one of you should set aside a sum of money in keeping with his income, saving it up, so that when I come no collections will have to be made. w 3Then, when I arrive, I will give letters of introduction to the men you approve x and send them with your gift to Jerusalem. 4If it seems advisable for me to go also, they will accompany me.

s45 Gen. 2:7 t49 Some early manuscripts so let us u54 Isaiah 25:8 v55 Hosea 13:14

Cross references (center column)

15:45 rGe 2:7; sRo 5:14; tJn 5:21; 6:57,58; Ro 8:2
15:46 uver 44
15:47 vGe 2:7; 3:19; Ps 90:3; wJn 3:13,31
15:48 xPhp 3:20,21
15:49 yGe 5:3; zS Ro 8:29
15:50 aEph 6:12; Heb 2:14; bS Mt 25:34 cver 42,53,54
15:51 dI Co 13:2; 14:2 eS Mt 9:24 f2Co 5:4; Php 3:21
15:52 gS Mt 24:31 hJn 5:25
15:53 iver 42,50, 54 j2Co 5:2,4
15:54 kIsa 25:8; Heb 2:14; Rev 20:14
15:55 lHos 13:14
15:56 mS Ro 5:12 nS Ro 4:15
15:57 oS 2Co 2:14 pRo 8:37; Heb 2:14,15
15:58 q1Co 16:10 rIsa 65:23
16:1 sS Ac 24:17 tS Ac 9:13 uS Ac 16:6
16:2 vAc 20:7 w2Co 9:4,5
16:3 x2Co 3:1; 8:18,19

5:26) who through his death and resurrection will at the second coming give his redeemed people a spiritual body—physical, yet imperishable, without corruption, and adaptable to live with God forever (cf. Php 3:21). It will be a body similar to Christ's resurrected, glorified physical body (cf. Lk 24:36–43).
15:46 Adam, the earthly man, and his descendants received natural, earthly bodies. Christ, the last Adam, the man from heaven who became incarnate in a human body, received a glorified, spiritual body following his resurrection. Similarly, his redeemed people will receive a spiritual body.
15:50 Paul's final argument about the resurrection of the body: God's redeemed people must have newly organized, imperishable bodies to live with him. "Flesh and blood" stands for perishable, corrupt, weak, sinful human beings.
15:51 mystery. Things about the resurrection body that were not understood but are now revealed (see note on Ro 11:25). We will not all sleep. Some believers will not experience death and the grave. we will all be changed. All believers, whether alive when Jesus comes again or in the grave, will receive changed, imperishable bodies.
15:52 in a flash. The change to an imperishable body will occur instantly at the last trumpet call. Some refer this to the "loud trumpet call" of Mt 24:31 or the seventh trumpet of Rev 11:15, others to the rapture (the snatching away) of God's people (cf. 1Th 4:16), which they hold will take place before Christ's (and their) return to reign on earth (cf. Rev 19:11–16; 20:1–6). we will be changed. Paul lived in anticipation of Christ's return, as all believers should.
15:56 The sting of death is sin. It was sin that brought us under death's power—it was Adam's sin that brought his death and ultimately ours (see Ro 5:12). the power of sin is the law. The law of God gives sin its power, for it reveals our sin and condemns us because of our sin.

15:57 victory through our Lord Jesus Christ. Victory over the condemnation for sin that the law brought (v. 56) and over death and the grave (vv. 54–55), through the death and resurrection of Christ (cf. Ro 4:25).
15:58 Therefore. Because of Christ's resurrection and ours, we know that serving him is not empty, useless activity. your labor in the Lord is not in vain. Our effort is invested in the Lord's winning cause. He will also reward us at his second coming (Mt 25:21; cf. Lk 19:17).
16:1 Now about. Again an answer to one of the questions of the Corinthians (cf. 7:1; 8:1; 12:1). God's people. His people at Jerusalem (cf. v. 3; Ro 15:26). Galatian churches. The fact that the Galatian and Macedonian churches (2Co 8:1; 9:1–4) are involved, along with the Corinthians, indicates that the collection of this offering was quite widespread. The Jerusalem saints may have become poverty-stricken because of the famine recorded in Ac 11:28 (c. A.D. 44 or 46), or because of the persecution of Jerusalem Christians (cf. Ac 8:1).
16:2 On the first day of every week, each one of you should set aside. Every Sunday each person was to bring what he had set aside for the Lord's work—an amount proportionate to his income. Since it was to be brought on Sunday, the new day for worship (cf. Ac 20:7; Rev 1:10), probably it was collected at the worship service, not at home. Justin Martyr indicates (in his Apology, 1. 67–68) that in his time (c. A.D. 150) offerings were brought to the church on Sundays.
16:3 For proper financial accountability and responsibility these approved men would act as auditors and guardians of the funds the Corinthians gave (2Co 8:16–21).
16:4 If it seems advisable for me to go also. Possibly to take care of important missionary business, or to be there to explain about the gift when it arrives.

Personal Requests

5After I go through Macedonia, I will come to you*y*—for I will be going through Macedonia. *z* 6Perhaps I will stay with you awhile, or even spend the winter, so that you can help me on my journey, *a* wherever I go. 7I do not want to see you now and make only a passing visit; I hope to spend some time with you, if the Lord permits. *b* 8But I will stay on at Ephesus *c* until Pentecost, *d* 9because a great door for effective work has opened to me, *e* and there are many who oppose me.

10If Timothy*f* comes, see to it that he has nothing to fear while he is with you, for he is carrying on the work of the Lord, *g* just as I am. 11No one, then, should refuse to accept him. *h* Send him on his way*i* in peace*j* so that he may return to me. I am expecting him along with the brothers.

12Now about our brother Apollos: *k* I strongly urged him to go to you with the brothers. He was quite unwilling to go now, but he will go when he has the opportunity.

13Be on your guard; stand firm*l* in the faith; be men of courage; be strong. *m* 14Do everything in love. *n*

15You know that the household of Stephanas*o* were the first converts*p* in Achaia, *q* and they have devoted themselves to the service*r* of the saints. *s* I urge you, brothers, 16to submit*t* to such as these and to everyone who joins in the work, and labors at it. 17I was glad when Stephanas, Fortunatus and Achaicus arrived, because they have supplied what was lacking from you. *u* 18For they refreshed*v* my spirit and yours also. Such men deserve recognition. *w*

Final Greetings

19The churches in the province of Asia*x* send you greetings. Aquila and Priscilla*wy* greet you warmly in the Lord, and so does the church that meets at their house. *z* 20All the brothers here send you greetings. Greet one another with a holy kiss. *a*

21I, Paul, write this greeting in my own hand. *b*

16:5 *y*S 1Co 4:19
*z*S Ac 16:9
16:6 *a*Ro 15:24;
Tit 3:13
16:7 *b*S Ac 18:21
16:8 *c*S Ac 18:19
*d*S Ac 2:1
16:9 *e*S Ac 14:27
16:10 *f*S Ac 16:1
*g*1Co 15:58
16:11 *h*1Ti 4:12
*i*2Co 1:16; 3Jn 6
*j*S Ac 15:33
16:12
*k*S Ac 18:24

16:13 *l*1Co 1:8;
2Co 1:21;
Gal 5:1;
Php 1:27;
1Th 3:8; S Tit 1:9
*m*S Eph 6:10
16:14 *n*1Co 14:1
16:15 *o*1Co 1:16
*p*Ro 16:5
*q*S Ac 18:12
*r*S Ac 24:17
*s*S Ac 9:13
16:16 *t*1Th 5:12;
Heb 13:17
16:17
*u*2Co 11:9;
Php 2:30
16:18 *v*Ro 15:32;
Phm 7 *w*Php 2:29
16:19 *x*S Ac 2:9
*y*S Ac 18:2
*z*S Ro 16:5
16:20
*a*S Ro 16:16
16:21 *b*Gal 6:11;
Col 4:18;
2Th 3:17; Phm 19

w*19* Greek *Prisca*, a variant of *Priscilla*

16:5 *After I go through Macedonia.* After leaving Ephesus (v. 8), where he was when he wrote 1 Corinthians, Paul planned to go up to Macedonia, no doubt to visit the Philippians and others in northern Greece, and then to Corinth. He had originally planned to go to Corinth first and then to Macedonia but thought it best to change his plans (see 2Co 1:12–2:4).

16:6 *even spend the winter.* Probably the three-month stay in Greece mentioned in Ac 20:3. *help me on my journey.* With supplies and equipment, and certainly with prayers and goodwill. However, Paul had indicated earlier in the letter (9:7–12) that he did not want to be a financial burden to them.

16:8 *until Pentecost.* The 50th day (Pentecost means "50") after Passover, when the Jews celebrated the Feast of Firstfruits (Lev 23:10–16)—late spring.

16:9 *many who oppose me.* Probably a reference to the pagan craftsmen who made the silver shrines of Artemis and to the general populace whom they had stirred up (Ac 19:23–34).

16:10 *If Timothy comes.* In Ac 19:22 Paul sends Timothy (and Erastus) into Macedonia, after which Timothy was to go on to Corinth (1Co 4:17). *see to it that he has nothing to fear.* Timothy seems to have been somewhat timid (1Ti 4:12; 2Ti 1:7), and Paul wants the Corinthians to treat him kindly.

16:11 *brothers.* Possibly including Erastus (cf. Ac 19:22), who was a believer from Corinth and "the city's director of public works" (Ro 16:23; see note there).

16:12 *Now about . . . Apollos.* The Corinthians had asked Paul about Apollos (cf. the similar words, "now about," in 7:1; 8:1; 12:1; 16:1) and his coming to see them.

16:15 *household of Stephanas.* Evidently the Corinthians had little respect for this household that Paul had baptized (1:16). They were among the first converts in Achaia (Greece), along with the few individuals in Athens who had believed a short time earlier (Ac 17:34). *service.* The whole household of Stephanas was serving.

16:17 Probably the ones who had brought to the apostle the letter from the Corinthians referred to in 7:1. Their coming "supplied what was lacking" from the Corinthians, i.e., the affection of these three brothers supplied the affection Paul desired from the whole Corinthian church.

16:18 *refreshed my spirit and yours.* Perhaps through their willingness to come to get Paul's advice and to bring it back to them. At least a new relationship between Paul and the Corinthians was in the making.

16:19 *province of Asia.* The Roman province (presently in western Turkey) in which Ephesus and the surrounding cities were located (cf. Ac 19:10). During Paul's long ministry in Ephesus all in the province of Asia heard the word. The churches of Colosse, Laodicea and Hierapolis (cf. Col 4:13–16; Rev 1:11), which were located on the border of the province of Asia, may be included in the greetings, along with the other churches of Rev 2–3. *Aquila and Priscilla.* They had helped Paul found the church at Corinth (Ac 18:1–4). *warmly in the Lord.* Enthusiastically as fellow believers. *the church that meets at their house.* Aquila and Priscilla had left Corinth with Paul and had gone to Ephesus (Ac 18:18–19). Evidently they were still there, and a church was meeting at their house; it now sends greetings. House churches were common in this early period (cf. Ro 16:3–5; Phm 2).

16:20 *holy kiss.* The kiss of mutual respect and love in the Lord was evidently the public practice of early Christians—from a practice that was customary in the ancient East. Such a practice may have been used in the first-century A.D. synagogue—men kissing men, and women kissing women—and it would have been natural for the practice to have been continued in the early Jewish-Gentile churches.

16:21 *greeting in my own hand.* Paul now signs this letter, as was his habit (see Col 4:18; Phm 19), a mark of the authenticity of the letter (2Th 3:17). Someone else had been penning the letter for him up to this point (cf. Ro 16:22).

²²If anyone does not love the Lord ᶜ —a curse ᵈ be on him. Come, O Lord ˣ! ᵉ

²³The grace of the Lord Jesus be with you. ᶠ

²⁴My love to all of you in Christ Jesus. Amen. ʸ

| 16:22 ᶜEph 6:24 |
| ᵈRo 9:3 |
| ᵉRev 22:20 |
| 16:23 |
| ᶠS Ro 16:20 |

ˣ22 In Aramaic the expression *Come, O Lord* is *Marana tha.* ʸ24 Some manuscripts do not have *Amen.*

16:22 *a curse be on him.* May this person experience God's displeasure and wrath, since he has declared himself an unbeliever (Jn 3:36). This is not a curse based on things God has created (e.g., heaven and earth), an oath that Jesus forbids. Rather, it is a curse based on God as witness to the unbeliever's essential lack of love and obedience to God (see also Gal 1:8–9). *Come, O Lord!* See NIV text note; an expression used by the early church as a cry that the second coming of Christ may soon take place.

16:23 The apostle's usual benediction (see Gal 6:18; Eph 6:24; Php 4:23); a longer Trinitarian benediction is found in 2Co 13:14.

16:24 Although he has been severe with the Corinthians, Paul wants them to know that he loves them as believers in Christ Jesus.

2 CORINTHIANS

Author

Paul is the author of this letter (see 1:1; 10:1). It is stamped with his style and it contains more autobiographical material than any of his other writings.

Date

The available evidence indicates that the year A.D. 55 is a reasonable estimate for the writing of this letter. From 1Co 16:5-8 we conclude that 1 Corinthians was written from Ephesus before Pentecost (in the spring) and that 2 Corinthians was written later that same year before the onset of winter. 2Co 2:13; 7:5 indicate that it was written from Macedonia.

Recipients

The opening salutation of the letter states that it was addressed to the church in Corinth and to the Christians throughout Achaia (the Roman province comprising all the territory of Greece south of Macedonia).

Purpose

The Corinthian church had been infiltrated by false teachers who were challenging both Paul's personal integrity and his authority as an apostle. Because he had announced a change in his itinerary, with the result that he would now pay the Corinthians one (long) visit instead of two (short) visits, these adversaries were asserting that his word was not to be trusted. They were also saying that he was not a genuine apostle and that he was putting into his own pocket the money they had collected for the poverty-stricken believers in Jerusalem. Paul asks the Corinthians to consider that his personal life in their midst was always honorable and that his life-transforming message of salvation was true. He urges them to prepare for his impending visit by completing the collection they had started a year previously and by dealing with the troublemakers in their midst. He warns them that he means what he writes.

Structure

The structure of the letter relates primarily to Paul's impending third visit to Corinth. The letter falls naturally into three sections:
1. Paul explains the reason for the change of itinerary (chs. 1-7).
2. Paul encourages the Corinthians to complete the collection in preparation for his arrival (chs. 8-9).
3. Paul stresses the certainty of his coming, his authenticity as an apostle and his readiness as an apostle to exercise discipline if necessary (chs. 10-13).

Unity

Some have questioned the unity of this letter (see note on 2:3-4), but it forms a coherent whole, as the structure (above) shows. Tradition has been unanimous in affirming its unity (the early church fathers, e.g., knew the letter only in its present form). Furthermore, none of the early Greek manuscripts breaks up the book.

Outline

I. Primarily Apologetic: Paul's Explanation of His Conduct and Apostolic Ministry (chs. 1-7)
   A. Salutation (1:1-2)
   B. Thanksgiving for Divine Comfort in Affliction (1:3-11)
   C. The Integrity of Paul's Motives and Conduct (1:12-2:4)
   D. Forgiving the Offender at Corinth (2:5-11)

1 Paul, an apostle[a] of Christ Jesus by the will of God,[b] and Timothy[c] our brother,

To the church of God[d] in Corinth,[e] together with all the saints throughout Achaia:[f]

[2]Grace and peace to you from God our Father and the Lord Jesus Christ.[g]

The God of All Comfort

[3]Praise be to the God and Father of our Lord Jesus Christ,[h] the Father of compassion and the God of all comfort, [4]who comforts us[i] in all our troubles, so that we can comfort those in any trouble with the comfort we ourselves have received from God. [5]For just as the sufferings of Christ flow over into our lives,[j] so also through Christ our comfort overflows. [6]If we are distressed, it is for your comfort and salvation;[k] if we are comforted, it is for your comfort, which produces in you patient endurance of the same sufferings we suffer. [7]And our hope for you is firm, because we know that just as you share in our sufferings,[l] so also you share in our comfort.

[8]We do not want you to be uninformed,[m] brothers, about the hardships we suffered[n] in the province of Asia.[o] We were under great pressure, far beyond our ability to endure, so that we despaired even of life. [9]Indeed, in our hearts we felt the sentence of death. But this happened that we might not rely on ourselves but on God,[p] who raises the dead. [q] [10]He has delivered us from such a deadly peril,[r] and he will deliver us. On him we have set our hope[s] that he will continue to deliver us, [11]as you help us by your prayers.[t] Then many will give thanks[u] on our[a] behalf for the gracious favor granted us in answer to the prayers of many.

Paul's Change of Plans

[12]Now this is our boast: Our conscience[v] testifies that we have conducted ourselves in the world, and especially in our relations with you, in the holiness[w] and sincerity[x] that are from God. We have done so not according to worldly wisdom[y] but according to God's grace. [13]For we do not write you anything you cannot read or understand. And I hope that, [14]as you have understood us in part, you will come to understand fully that you can boast of us just as we will boast of you in the day of the Lord Jesus.[z]

[15]Because I was confident of this, I planned to visit you[a] first so that you might benefit twice.[b] [16]I planned to visit you on my way[c] to Macedonia[d] and to come back to you from Macedonia, and then to have you send me on my way[e] to Judea.[f] [17]When I planned this, did I do it lightly? Or do I make my plans in a worldly

1:1 aS 1Co 1:1
biCo 1:1;
Eph 1:1; Col 1:1;
2Ti 1:1
cS Ac 16:1
dS 1Co 10:32
eS Ac 18:1
fS Ac 18:12
1:2 gS Ro 1:7
1:3 hEph 1:3;
1Pe 1:3
1:4 iIsa 49:13;
51:12; 66:13;
2Co 7:6,7,13
1:5 jRo 8:17;
2Co 4:10;
Gal 6:17;
Php 3:10;
Col 1:24;
1Pe 4:13
1:6 k2Co 4:15
1:7 lS ver 5
1:8 mS Ro 11:25
n1Co 15:32
oS Ac 2:9

1:9 pJer 17:5,7
qS Jn 5:21
1:10 rS Ro 15:31
s1Ti 4:10
1:11 tRo 15:30;
Php 1:19
u2Co 4:15; 9:11
1:12 vS Ac 23:1
w1Th 2:10
x2Co 2:17
y1Co 1:17; 2:1,4,
13
1:14 zS 1Co 1:8
1:15 aS 1Co 4:19
bRo 1:11,13;
15:29
1:16 c1Co 16:5-7
dS Ac 16:9
e1Co 16:11;
3Jn 6 fAc 19:21

a / / Many manuscripts *your*

1:1 *apostle.* One specially commissioned by Christ (see notes on Mk 6:30; 1Co 1:1; Heb 3:1). *Timothy.* Evidently with Paul when this letter was written, but not necessarily a co-author. *our brother.* Our fellow believer, our brother in Christ (cf. Ac 9:17; Heb 2:11). *church of God.* The community of believers, the local representatives of the universal church (see note on 1Co 1:2). *saints.* Another term for God's people; it means "those who have been set apart as holy to the Lord" (see note on Ro 1:7). *Achaia.* Greece, as distinct from Macedonia in the north. Though the letter deals particularly with the situation in Corinth, it was also intended for Christians elsewhere in Greece. Presumably copies of the letter would be made in Corinth and circulated to them. **1:2** *Grace and peace.* See notes on Jnh 4:2; Jn 14:27; 20:19; Gal 1:3; Eph 1:2. **1:3** *God.* The source of our comfort. *comfort.* Consolation and encouragement. This comfort flows to believers when they suffer for Jesus' sake, and it equips them to comfort others who are in trouble (vv. 4–7). **1:8** *we suffered.* Throughout this letter Paul uses the editorial plural (we, us, our, ourselves). Except where the context plainly indicates otherwise, these plurals should be understood as referring to Paul alone. *Asia.* The Roman province of that name in western Asia Minor, now Turkish territory. The precise location where Paul's hardships occurred is not given, nor is the nature of affliction. **1:9** Paul's hardships were so life-threatening that he regarded his survival and recovery as tantamount to being raised from the dead. *rely . . . on God.* A key principle of this letter. God's grace is all-sufficient, and our weakness is pre-

cisely the opportunity for his power to be displayed (cf. 12:9–10). **1:12** In defending his trustworthiness against the slanders being spread about him, Paul appeals to the witness of his own conscience and to the Corinthians' firsthand knowledge of his character. He had spent 18 months with them when he first came to Corinth (Ac 18:11), so they could not plead ignorance of his integrity. **1:13** In keeping with their knowledge of Paul's character, they can trust what he writes from a distance: He means what he says. **1:14** *in part.* Some in Corinth had allowed their confidence in Paul and his apostolic authority to be shaken by the false apostles who had penetrated their ranks. *day of the Lord Jesus.* His return (cf. 1Th 2:19–20). **1:15** *that you might benefit twice.* Here and in v. 16 Paul refers to his change of itinerary. Originally he had planned to cross over by sea from Ephesus to Corinth, visiting the Corinthians before traveling north to Macedonia, and then, returning from Macedonia, to visit them a second time. This was when he was on good terms with them. What probably occurred was that he paid them a quick visit directly from Ephesus, a visit he had not contemplated and one that proved to be "painful" (2:1). That visit then gave rise to his letter that caused them sorrow (see 7:8–9). **1:17** *did I do it lightly?* Paul's opponents in Corinth had been attempting to persuade the Christians there that this change of plan was evidence that his word was not to be trusted, that he was fickle and unreliable. The two rhetorical

manner[g] so that in the same breath I say, "Yes, yes" and "No, no"?

[18]But as surely as God is faithful,[h] our message to you is not "Yes" and "No." [19]For the Son of God,[i] Jesus Christ, who was preached among you by me and Silas[b][j] and Timothy,[k] was not "Yes" and "No," but in him it has always[l] been "Yes." [20]For no matter how many promises[m] God has made, they are "Yes" in Christ. And so through him the "Amen"[n] is spoken by us to the glory of God.[o] [21]Now it is God who makes both us and you stand firm[p] in Christ. He anointed[q] us, [22]set his seal[r] of ownership on us, and put his Spirit in our hearts as a deposit, guaranteeing what is to come.[s]

[23]I call God as my witness[t] that it was in order to spare you[u] that I did not return to Corinth. [24]Not that we lord it over[v] your faith, but we work with you for your joy, because it is by faith you stand firm.[w]

2 [1]So I made up my mind that I would not make another painful visit to you.[x] [2]For if I grieve you,[y] who is left to make me glad but you whom I have grieved? [3]I wrote as I did[z] so that when I came I should not be distressed[a] by those who ought to make me rejoice. I had con-

fidence[b] in all of you, that you would all share my joy. [4]For I wrote you[c] out of great distress and anguish of heart and with many tears, not to grieve you but to let you know the depth of my love for you.

Forgiveness for the Sinner

[5]If anyone has caused grief,[d] he has not so much grieved me as he has grieved all of you, to some extent—not to put it too severely. [6]The punishment[e] inflicted on him by the majority is sufficient for him. [7]Now instead, you ought to forgive and comfort him,[f] so that he will not be overwhelmed by excessive sorrow. [8]I urge you, therefore, to reaffirm your love for him. [9]The reason I wrote you[g] was to see if you would stand the test and be obedient in everything.[h] [10]If you forgive anyone, I also forgive him. And what I have forgiven—if there was anything to forgive—I have forgiven in the sight of Christ for your sake, [11]in order that Satan[i] might not outwit us. For we are not unaware of his schemes.[j]

Ministers of the New Covenant

[12]Now when I went to Troas[k] to preach

1:17 g2Co 10:2, 3; 11:18
1:18 hS 1Co 1:9
1:19 iS Mt 4:3 /S Ac 15:22 kS Ac 16:1 /Heb 13:8
1:20 mRo 15:8 nS 1Co 14:16 oRo 15:9
1:21 pS 1Co 16:13 q1Jn 2:20,27
1:22 rGe 38:18; Eze 9:4; Hag 2:23 sS 2Co 5:5
1:23 tS Ro 1:9 u1Co 4:21; 2Co 2:1,3; 13:2, 10
1:24 v1Pe 5:3 wRo 11:20; 1Co 15:1
2:1 xS 2Co 1:23
2:2 y2Co 7:8
2:3 zver 4,9; 2Co 7:8,12 a2Co 12:21

b2Co 7:16; 8:22; Gal 5:10; 2Th 3:4; Phm 21
2:4 cver 3,9; 2Co 7:8,12
2:5 d1Co 5:1,2
2:6 e1Co 5:4,5; 2Co 7:11
2:7 fGal 6:1; Eph 4:32; Col 3:13
2:9 gver 3,4; 2Co 7:8,12
h2Co 7:15; 10:6
2:11 iS Mt 4:10 /Lk 22:31; 2Co 4:4; 1Pe 5:8, 9

2:12 kS Ac 16:8

b19 Greek Silvanus, a variant of Silas

---

questions are in effect his denial that he acts lightly and that he says "Yes" and "No" at the same time so that it is impossible to know what he means. In any case, his plan to visit the Corinthians had not been abandoned; it had simply been modified.

1:18 *not "Yes" and "No."* Paul now (vv. 18–20) appeals to the gospel message he had preached to them: Believing it, they had found it to be altogether true and entirely free from ambiguity, and by their experience of its dynamic power they had proved it to be one great affirmative in Christ, in whom all God's promises are "Yes."

1:20 *"Amen."* The "Amen" uttered by the congregation at the end of an offering of prayer or praise (cf. 1Co 14:16).

1:22 *seal.* See note on Hag 2:23. *deposit.* A part given as a guarantee that the whole will be forthcoming. The part is of the same kind as the whole. The first installment of a sum of money that has been inherited, e.g., assures the recipient that the whole will be received. This justifies the expansion of a single Greek word into several English words: "a deposit, guaranteeing what is to come."

1:23 *to spare you.* Paul's change of plans for visiting the Corinthian Christians had been motivated, not by a fickle and insensitive attitude, but by love and concern for them.

2:1 *another painful visit.* Paul had already made one painful visit to Corinth, and he wanted to avoid another such visit, though he was ready to exert his authority should it prove necessary (cf. 13:2). The occasion of this former painful visit is not known to us. It could not have been his original visit to Corinth at the time when the church there was founded in response to the preaching of the gospel. Therefore he must have paid a second visit, which is confirmed by 12:14; 13:1, where he states that the visit he is now about to make will be his third. The second visit probably took place between the writing of 1 and 2 Corinthians, though some hold that it occurred before 1 Corinthians was written.

2:3–4 *I wrote as I did . . . out of great distress and anguish.* This passage refers to a previous letter that had been sent to the Corinthians. The consensus of the church from the earliest times has been that this previous letter is 1 Corinthians. In more recent times, however, the hypothesis that the reference is to an intermediate letter, written after 1 Corinthians and before 2 Corinthians, has been widely accepted. Some advocates of this theory hold that the letter in question is now lost; others have identified it, in whole or in part, with the last four chapters of 2 Corinthians, contending that these chapters are out of harmony with the earlier ones and that they fit the description of a letter written "out of great distress and anguish." There is, however, no historical evidence that the unity of 2 Corinthians was questioned or that its integrity was doubted prior to modern times.

2:5–11 Speaks of a particular person who has been the cause of serious offense in Corinth and upon whom church discipline has been imposed. Paul admonishes the Corinthians that because the offender has shown genuine sorrow and repentance for his sin the punishment should be discontinued and he should be lovingly restored to their fellowship. Church discipline, important as it is, should not be allowed to develop into a form of graceless rigor in which there is no room for pardon and restoration. The offense in question probably took place during Paul's intermediate visit to Corinth (see note on v. 1) and was the occasion for his writing the severe letter demanding the punishment of the offender (see note on vv. 3–4). Another view is that the reference is to the incident recorded in 1Co 5.

2:12 *when I went to Troas.* Paul had traveled up from Ephesus to Troas, a city on the Aegean coast opposite the island of Tenedos, hoping to find Titus there and to receive news from him about the Corinthian church. But Titus, who, presumably, Paul knew would be following the same route in reverse, did not arrive in Troas; so Paul, anxious for news

the gospel of Christ[l] and found that the Lord had opened a door[m] for me, [13]I still had no peace of mind,[n] because I did not find my brother Titus[o] there. So I said good-by to them and went on to Macedonia.[p]

[14]But thanks be to God,[q] who always leads us in triumphal procession in Christ and through us spreads everywhere the fragrance[r] of the knowledge[s] of him. [15]For we are to God the aroma[t] of Christ among those who are being saved and those who are perishing.[u] [16]To the one we are the smell of death;[v] to the other, the fragrance of life. And who is equal to such a task?[w] [17]Unlike so many, we do not peddle the word of God for profit.[x] On the contrary, in Christ we speak before God with sincerity,[y] like men sent from God.[z]

3 Are we beginning to commend ourselves[a] again? Or do we need, like

some people, letters of recommendation[b] to you or from you? [2]You yourselves are our letter, written on our hearts, known and read by everybody.[c] [3]You show that you are a letter from Christ, the result of our ministry, written not with ink but with the Spirit of the living God,[d] not on tablets of stone[e] but on tablets of human hearts.[f]

[4]Such confidence[g] as this is ours through Christ before God. [5]Not that we are competent in ourselves[h] to claim anything for ourselves, but our competence comes from God.[i] [6]He has made us competent as ministers of a new covenant[j]—not of the letter[k] but of the Spirit; for the letter kills, but the Spirit gives life.[l]

2:12 /S Ro 1:1; 2Co 4:3,4; 8:18; 9:13; 1Th 3:2
mS Ac 14:27
2:13 n2Co 7:5
o2Co 7:6,13; 8:6, 16,23; 12:18; Gal 2:1,3; Tit 1:4
pS Ac 16:9
2:14 qRo 6:17; 7:25; 1Co 15:57; 2Co 9:15
rEze 20:41; Eph 5:2; Php 4:18
sS 2Co 8:7
2:15 tS ver 14; Ge 8:21; Ex 29:18; Nu 15:3
uS 1Co 1:18
2:16 vS Lk 2:34; 6
Jn 3:36 w2Co 3:5, 6
2:17 xS Ac 20:33; 2Co 4:2; 1Th 2:5
y1Co 5:8
z2Co 1:12; 12:19
3:1 aRo 16:1;
2Co 5:12; 10:12, 18; 12:11

bAc 18:27;

Ro 16:1; 1Co 16:3 3:2 c1Co 9:2 3:3 dS Mt 16:16 ever 7; Ex 24:12; 31:18; 32:15,16 fPr 3:3; 7:3; Jer 31:33; Eze 36:26
3:4 gS Eph 3:12 3:5 h2Co 2:16 i1Co 15:10 3:6 jS Lk 22:20
kRo 2:29; 7:6 lJn 6:63

from Corinth, "went on to Macedonia" (v. 13), perhaps to the city of Philippi.

2:13 *my brother.* Cf. 8:23. Paul held Titus in high esteem; he entrusted Titus with the organization of the collection of funds in Corinth for the relief of the poverty-stricken Christians of Jerusalem (8:6), and he chose him to bear this letter to the Corinthian Christians (8:16–17).

2:14 At this point Paul breaks off the narrative of his itinerary and in a characteristic manner allows his spontaneous spirit to carry him into a lengthy digression (the narrative is not resumed until 7:5). The digression, however, is quite relevant to the main tenor of this letter, for it is an immensely rich outpouring of triumphant faith in praise of the unfailing adequacy of the grace of God for every conceivable situation, no matter how threatening and destructive it may seem to be. *leads us in triumphal procession.* The imagery is that of a Roman triumph in which the victorious general would lead his soldiers and the captives they had taken in festive procession, while the people watched and applauded and the air was filled with the sweet smell released by the burning of spices in the streets. So the Christian, called to spiritual warfare, is triumphantly led by God in Christ, and it is through him that God spreads everywhere the "fragrance" of the knowledge of Christ.

2:16 *the smell of death . . . the fragrance of life.* As the gospel aroma is released in the world through Christian testimony, it is always sweet-smelling, even though it may be differently received. The two ultimate categories of mankind are "those who are being saved and those who are perishing" (v. 15). To the latter, testifying Christians are the smell of death, not because the gospel message has become evil-smelling or death-dealing, but because in rejecting the life-giving grace of God unbelievers choose death for themselves. To those who welcome the gospel of God's grace, Christians with their testimony are the fragrance of life. *who is equal to such a task?* For the answer see 3:5.

2:17 *we do not peddle the word of God for profit.* Paul is referring to false teachers who had infiltrated the Corinthian church. Such persons—themselves insincere, self-sufficient and boastful—artfully presented themselves in a persuasive manner, and their chief interest was to take money from gullible church members. Paul, by contrast, had preached the gospel sincerely and free of charge, taking care not to be a financial burden to the Corinthian believers (see 11:7–12; 1Co 9:7–15).

3:1 *Are we beginning to commend ourselves again?* Paul is sensitive to the fact that virtually everything he wrote or said was liable to be twisted and used in a hostile manner by the false teachers in Corinth. *letters of recommendation.* The appearance of vagrant impostors, who claimed to be teachers of apostolic truth, led to the need for letters of recommendation. Paul needed no such confirmation; but others, including the Corinthian intruders, did need authentication and, being themselves false, often resorted to unscrupulous methods for obtaining or forging letters of recommendation.

3:2 *known and read by everybody.* Because of the power of the gospel demonstrated by their transformed lives.

3:3 *letter from Christ.* Paul is no more than the instrument in the hands of the Master. *written not with ink.* As a parchment or papyrus document would be. *with the Spirit of the living God.* As though the Spirit were a substitute for ink! Ink fades and may easily be deleted or blocked out since it is no more than an inanimate fluid. But the Spirit of the living God is himself life and therefore life-giving (v. 6), and the life he gives is eternal and without defect. *not on tablets of stone.* As at Sinai (see note on v. 6). *on tablets of human hearts.* See Jer 31:33; Eze 11:19; 36:26. Paul explains the significance of this contrast between the old and the new covenants in vv. 7–18.

3:5 *our competence comes from God.* Answers the question in 2:16: "And who is equal to such a task?"

3:6 *ministers of.* Those who serve the cause of (see Ro 15:16; Col 1:7; 4:7; 1Ti 4:6). Paul will return to the theme of "this ministry" in 4:1. *new covenant.* Here Paul takes up the theme suggested by the mention of "tablets of human hearts" (v. 3). See Heb 8–10 and note on Heb 7:22. Paul's reference to ministers of a new covenant in contrast to the "ministry that brought death" (v. 7) may have been occasioned by his opponents in Corinth who were Judaizers, perhaps those who claimed to be associated with Peter (1Co 1:12) and who are referred to as Hebrews in 11:22 (see note there). *the letter.* The "tablets of stone" on which the letter of the law was originally written (see Ex 24:12; 31:18; 32:15–16). *the Spirit.* The writing of the law "with the Spirit of the living God . . . on tablets of human hearts," which was the promise of the new covenant as foretold by the prophets (see Jer 31:31–34; 32:39–40; Eze 11:19; 36:26). *the letter kills, but the Spirit gives life.* Does not mean that the external, literal sense of Scripture is deadly or unprofitable while

The Glory of the New Covenant

[7]Now if the ministry that brought death, [m] which was engraved in letters on stone, came with glory, so that the Israelites could not look steadily at the face of Moses because of its glory, [n] fading though it was, [8]will not the ministry of the Spirit be even more glorious? [9]If the ministry that condemns men[o] is glorious, how much more glorious is the ministry that brings righteousness! [p] [10]For what was glorious has no glory now in comparison with the surpassing glory. [11]And if what was fading away came with glory, how much greater is the glory of that which lasts!

[12]Therefore, since we have such a hope, [q] we are very bold. [r] [13]We are not like Moses, who would put a veil over his face[s] to keep the Israelites from gazing at it while the radiance was fading away. [14]But their minds were made dull, [t] for to

this day the same veil remains when the old covenant[u] is read. [v] It has not been removed, because only in Christ is it taken away. [15]Even to this day when Moses is read, a veil covers their hearts. [16]But whenever anyone turns to the Lord, [w] the veil is taken away. [x] [17]Now the Lord is the Spirit, [y] and where the Spirit of the Lord is, there is freedom. [z] [18]And we, who with unveiled faces all reflect[c a] the Lord's glory, [b] are being transformed into his likeness[c] with ever-increasing glory, which comes from the Lord, who is the Spirit.

Treasures in Jars of Clay

4 Therefore, since through God's mercy[d] we have this ministry, we do not lose heart. [e] [2]Rather, we have renounced secret and shameful ways;[f] we do not use deception, nor do we distort the word of God. [g] On the contrary, by setting

3:7 [m]ver 9; S Ro 4:15 [n]ver 13; Ex 34:29-35; Isa 42:21
3:9 [o]ver 7; Dt 27:26 [p]Ro 1:17; 3:21, 22
3:12 [q]Ro 5:4,5; 8:24,25 [r]S Ac 4:29
3:13 [s]ver 7; Ex 34:33
3:14 [t]Ro 11:7,8; 2Co 4:4
[u]Ac 13:15; 15:21 [v]ver 6
3:16 [w]Ro 11:23 [x]Ex 34:34; Isa 25:7
3:17 [y]Isa 61:1,2; Gal 4:6,7 [z]S Jn 8:32
3:18 [a]1Co 13:12 [b]Jn 17:22,24; 2Co 4:4,6 [c]S Ro 8:29
4:1 [d]1Co 7:25; 1Ti 1:13,16 [e]ver 16; Ps 18:45; Isa 40:31
4:2 [f]Ro 6:21; S 1Co 4:5 [g]2Co 2:17; S Heb 4:12

[c]*18* Or *contemplate*

---

the inner, spiritual (mystical or mythical) sense is vital. "The letter" is synonymous with the law as an external standard before which all people, because they are lawbreakers, stand guilty and condemned to death. Therefore it is described as the "ministry that brought death" and the "ministry that condemns" (vv. 7–8). On the other hand, the Spirit who gives life is the "Spirit of the living God" who, in fulfillment of the promise of the new covenant, writes that same law inwardly "on tablets of human hearts" (v. 3). He thus provides the believer with love for God's law, which previously he had hated, and with power to keep it, which previously he had not possessed.

3:7–18 Paul is defending his "ministry" of the new covenant in Christ (cf. v. 6; 4:1) and here compares the experiences of Moses, who mediated the old covenant of Sinai, and his own as a minister of the new covenant. But he now applies the word "ministry" to the law that was "engraved in letters on stone" and to the Spirit, who writes "on tablets of human hearts" (v. 3). The point of comparison is the fading glory that shone on Moses' face and the "ever-increasing glory" reflected in the faces of those who minister the new covenant. This contrast in regard to glory serves to highlight the temporary and inadequate character of the old covenant and the permanent and effective character of the new covenant.

3:7 *came with glory.* The law of the old covenant given at Sinai was in no way bad or evil; on the contrary, Paul describes it elsewhere as holy, righteous, good and spiritual (Ro 7:12,14). The evil is in the hearts and deeds of people who, as lawbreakers, bring upon themselves the condemnation of the law and the penalty of death—and the law engraved on stone could not purge away that evil. *its glory.* The glory of God surrounded the giving of the law and was reflected on the face of Moses when he descended from the mountain (see Ex 34:29–30).

3:8–9 *ministry of the Spirit . . . brings righteousness.* Giving life instead of death. "Righteousness" is here both objective (justification) and personal (sanctification).

3:11 *what was fading away.* Paul here applies the fading to the old covenant of Sinai, which was not to endure forever. In due course it was superseded by the unfading and much more glorious radiance belonging to the new covenant.

3:13 *Moses, who would put a veil over his face.* See Ex 34:33–35. The purpose of the veil was to prevent the Israelites from seeing the fading of the glory.

3:14 *to this day the same veil remains.* The veil that prevented them from seeing the fading of the glory on Moses' face is still with them, preventing them from recognizing the temporary and inadequate character of the old covenant—a "veil" that is removed only in Christ. Only those who have received the new covenant in Christ have the power to see how the new covenant has transcended and replaced the old covenant—because of its greater glory.

3:17 *the Lord is the Spirit.* This statement should be linked with what was said at the end of v. 6: "the Spirit gives life." It is only by turning to the Lord (v. 16) that the condemnation and the sentence of death pronounced by the law on the lawbreaker are annulled and replaced by the free life-giving grace of the new covenant. There is a close relationship between the Spirit of Christ and the Holy Spirit. Both are said to dwell in the believer (Ro 8:9; Gal 2:20). In Ro 8:9–10 the Spirit, the Spirit of God, the Spirit of Christ, and Christ all seem to be used interchangeably. In Ac 16:6–7 the Holy Spirit and the Spirit of Jesus appear to be one and the same. Perhaps this is because the Holy Spirit proceeds from the Father and the Son, and the first two persons of the Trinity accomplish their purposes through the Spirit.

3:18 *with unveiled faces.* In contrast to Moses. *being transformed into his likeness with ever-increasing glory.* Christ himself is the glory of God in the fullness of its radiance (Heb 1:3); his is the eternal and unfading glory, which he had with the Father before the world began (Jn 17:5). We who believe are made partakers of this glory by being gradually transformed into the likeness of Christ. The reference here is to the process of Christian sanctification.

4:1 *this ministry.* See 3:6 and note. *we do not lose heart.* When God through his mercy calls and commissions his servants, he also supplies the strength necessary for them to persevere in the face of hardships and persecutions.

4:2 *we have renounced secret and shameful ways.* Paul is referring to the false teachers in Corinth. By contrast, he is able to appeal to the conscience of every one of them and also to his integrity in the sight of God, because his practice was always that of setting forth the truth plainly, i.e., without veiling it or resorting to deception (cf. 1:12,18–24).

forth the truth plainly we commend our-selves to every man's conscience[h] in the sight of God. [3]And even if our gospel[i] is veiled,[j] it is veiled to those who are per-ishing.[k] [4]The god[l] of this age[m] has blind-ed[n] the minds of unbelievers, so that they cannot see the light of the gospel of the glory of Christ,[o] who is the image of God.[p] [5]For we do not preach ourselves,[q] but Jesus Christ as Lord,[r] and ourselves as your servants[s] for Jesus' sake. [6]For God, who said, "Let light shine out of dark-ness,"[d t] made his light shine in our hearts[u] to give us the light of the knowl-edge of the glory of God in the face of Christ.[v]

[7]But we have this treasure in jars of clay[w] to show that this all-surpassing power is from God[x] and not from us. [8]We are hard pressed on every side,[y] but not crushed; perplexed,[z] but not in despair; [9]persecuted,[a] but not abandoned;[b] struck down, but not destroyed.[c] [10]We always carry around in our body the death of Jesus,[d] so that the life of Jesus may also be revealed in our body.[e] [11]For we who are

alive are always being given over to death for Jesus' sake,[f] so that his life may be revealed in our mortal body. [12]So then, death is at work in us, but life is at work in you.[g]

[13]It is written: "I believed; therefore I have spoken."[e h] With that same spirit of faith[i] we also believe and therefore speak, [14]because we know that the one who raised the Lord Jesus from the dead[j] will also raise us with Jesus[k] and present us with you in his presence.[l] [15]All this is for your benefit, so that the grace that is reaching more and more people may cause thanksgiving[m] to overflow to the glory of God.

[16]Therefore we do not lose heart.[n] Though outwardly we are wasting away, yet inwardly[o] we are being renewed[p] day by day. [17]For our light and momentary troubles are achieving for us an eternal glory that far outweighs them all.[q] [18]So we

---

Cross-reference column:

4:2 [h]2Co 5:11
4:3 [i]S 2Co 2:12
/2Co 3:14
[k]S 1Co 1:18
4:4 [l]S Jn 12:31
[m]S 1Co 1:20
[n]2Co 3:14 over 6
[o]S Jn 14:9
4:5 [q]1Co 1:13
[r]1Co 1:23
[s]1Co 9:19
4:6 [t]Ge 1:3;
Ps 18:28
[u]2Pe 1:19 [v]ver 4
4:7 [w]Job 4:19;
Isa 64:8; 2Ti 2:20
[x]Jdg 7:2;
1Co 2:5; 2Co 6:7
4:8 [y]2Co 7:5
[z]Gal 4:20
4:9 [a]Jn 15:20;
Ro 8:35
[b]Heb 13:5
[c]Ps 37:24;
Pr 24:16
4:10 [d]S Ro 6:6;
S 2Co 1:5
[e]S Ro 6:5

4:11 [f]Ro 8:36
4:12 [g]2Co 13:9
4:13 [h]Ps 116:10
[i]1Co 12:9
4:14 [j]S Ac 2:24
[k]1Th 4:14
[l]Eph 5:27;
Col 1:22; Jude 24
4:15 [m]2Co 1:11;
9:11
4:16 [n]ver 1;
Ps 18:45

[o]Ro 7:22 [p]Ps 103:5; Isa 40:31; Col 3:10 4:17 [q]Ps 30:5;
Ro 8:18; 1Pe 1:6,7

[d]6 Gen. 1:3   [e]13 Psalm 116:10

4:3 *if our gospel is veiled.* See 3:13–18.
4:4 *god of this age.* The devil, who is the archenemy of God and the unseen power behind all unbelief and ungodli-ness. Those who follow him have in effect made him their god. *this age.* Used in contrast to the future eternal age when God's creation will be forever purged of all that now mars and defiles it. In Gal 1:4 it is called the "present evil age." *blinded the minds of unbelievers.* Paul continues to use the imagery of the veil that covers the divine glory so that those who reject the gospel fail to see that glory (3:12–18). *image of God.* Christ, who is both the incarnate Son and the Second Person of the Trinity, authentically displays God to us, for he is the very radiance of divine glory (Heb 1:3). He is the image of God in which man was originally created and into which redeemed mankind is being gloriously transformed (3:18), until at last, when Christ comes again at the end of this age, we who believe will be like him (1Jn 3:2).
4:5 *we do not preach ourselves.* As did the false teachers, puffed up with self-importance. Paul does not lord it over their faith (1:24), for there is only one Lord, Jesus Christ, and he is the theme of Paul's preaching.
4:6 *Let light shine out of darkness.* God said this at the creation (Ge 1:2–4), and God says it again in the new creation or new birth (see 5:17; Jn 3:3,7; 1Pe 1:3) as the darkness of sin is dispelled by the light of the gospel. *the light of the knowledge of the glory of God.* The light that now shines in Paul's heart (qualifying him to be a proclaimer of Christ) is the knowledge of the glory of God as it was displayed in the face of Christ—who has come, not just from an earthly tabernacle, but from the glorious presence of God in heaven itself (see Jn 1:14).
4:7 *this treasure.* The gospel. *jars of clay.* It was customary to conceal treasure in clay jars, which had little value or beauty and did not attract attention to themselves and their precious contents. Here they represent Paul's human frailty and unworthiness. *all-surpassing power is from God and not from us.* The idea that the absolute insufficiency of man reveals the total sufficiency of God pervades this letter.
4:10 *We always carry around in our body the death of*

Jesus. The frailty of the "clay jar" of Paul's humanity (v. 7) is plainly seen in the constant hardships and persecutions with which he is buffeted for the sake of the gospel and through which he shares in Christ's suffering (see 1:5; Ro 8:17; Php 3:10; Col 1:24).
4:11 *that his life may be revealed in our mortal body.* The reference is to Christ's resurrection life and power. Once again (see note on v. 7), human weakness provides the occasion for the triumph of divine power, and daily "dying" magnifies the wonder of daily resurrection life (see 1:9).
4:13 *I believed; therefore I have spoken.* See NIV text note. Faith leads to testimony. Paul therefore tirelessly la-bored and journeyed to bring the gospel message to others.
4:16 *Therefore we do not lose heart.* Repeating the statement in v. 1. The intervening paragraphs explain why the apostle continues to have a cheerful heart, and the remaining verses of the chapter summarize the argument he has developed. *wasting away.* Because of the hardships to which he is subjected. *being renewed.* Because of the inex-tinguishable flame of the resurrection life of Jesus burning within. Moreover, the inward renewal overcomes the out-ward destruction, and ultimately overcomes even death it-self.
4:17 *light and momentary troubles.* Seen in the perspec-tive of eternity, the Christian's difficulties, whatever they may be, diminish in importance. *eternal glory that far out-weighs them all.* By comparison, the eternal glory is far greater than all the suffering one may face in this life (cf. Ro 8:18).
4:18 *what is seen . . . what is unseen.* The experiences and circumstances of this present life, often painful and perplex-ing, are what is visible to the Christian; but these are merely phenomena in the passing parade of our fallen age and are therefore temporary and fleeting. To fix our eyes on these visible things would cause us to lose heart (vv. 1,16). By contrast the unseen realities, which are no less real for being invisible (cf. Heb 11:1,6, 26–27), are eternal and imperish-able. Accordingly, we look up and away from the imperma-nent appearances of this present world scene (see Php 3:20;

fix our eyes not on what is seen, but on what is unseen. *r* For what is seen is temporary, but what is unseen is eternal.

Our Heavenly Dwelling

5 Now we know that if the earthly*s* tent*t* we live in is destroyed, we have a building from God, an eternal house in heaven, not built by human hands. ²Meanwhile we groan,*u* longing to be clothed with our heavenly dwelling,*v* ³because when we are clothed, we will not be found naked. ⁴For while we are in this tent, we groan*w* and are burdened, because we do not wish to be unclothed but to be clothed with our heavenly dwelling,*x* so that what is mortal may be swallowed up by life. ⁵Now it is God who has made us for this very purpose and has given us the Spirit as a deposit, guaranteeing what is to come.*y*

⁶Therefore we are always confident and know that as long as we are at home in the body we are away from the Lord. ⁷We live by faith, not by sight. *z* ⁸We are confident,

I say, and would prefer to be away from the body and at home with the Lord. *a* ⁹So we make it our goal to please him, *b* whether we are at home in the body or away from it. ¹⁰For we must all appear before the judgment seat of Christ, that each one may receive what is due him*c* for the things done while in the body, whether good or bad.

The Ministry of Reconciliation

¹¹Since, then, we know what it is to fear the Lord, *d* we try to persuade men. What we are is plain to God, and I hope it is also plain to your conscience. *e* ¹²We are not trying to commend ourselves to you again,*f* but are giving you an opportunity to take pride in us,*g* so that you can answer those who take pride in what is seen rather than in what is in the heart. ¹³If we are out of our mind, *h* it is for the sake of God; if we are in our right mind, it is for you. ¹⁴For Christ's love compels us, because we are convinced that one died for

4:18 *r*2Co 5:7;
Ro 8:24;
Heb 11:1
5:1 *s*1Co 15:47
*t*Isa 38:12;
2Pe 1:13,14
5:2 *u*ver 4;
Ro 8:23 *v*ver 4;
1Co 15:53,54
5:4 *w*ver 2;
Ro 8:23 *x*ver 2;
1Co 15:53,54
5:5 *y*Ro 8:23;
2Co 1:22;
Eph 1:13,14
5:7 *z*1Co 13:12;
S 2Co 4:18

5:8 *a*S Jn 12:26
5:9 *b*Ro 14:18;
Eph 5:10;
Col 1:10; 1Th 4:1
5:10
*c*S Mt 16:27;
Ac 10:42;
Ro 2:16; 14:10;
Eph 6:8
5:11 *d*Job 23:15;
Heb 10:31;
12:29; Jude 23
*e*2Co 4:2
5:12 /S 2Co 3:1
*g*2Co 1:14
5:13 *h*2Co 11:1,
16,17; 12:11

Heb 12:2).

5:1 *earthly tent we live in.* Our present body (see 2Pe 1:13). As a tent is a temporary and flimsy abode, so our bodies are frail, vulnerable and wasting away (4:10–12,16). *a building from God, an eternal house in heaven.* A solid structure—permanent, not temporary. This is one of the eternal realities that are as yet unseen (4:18). *not built by human hands.* The work of God, and therefore perfect and permanent (see Heb 9:11).
5:2 *Meanwhile.* As we await the Lord's return. *we groan.* Because we long for the perfection that will be ours when we put on the glorious spiritual body (cf. 1Co 15:42–49). *clothed with our heavenly dwelling.* The eternal dwelling provided by God is pictured as something the Christian puts on like a garment.
5:3 *naked.* Without the clothing of a body, which is the state of those whose earthly tent-dwelling has been dismantled by death (see note on v. 8).
5:4 *what is mortal.* Our present mortal body. *swallowed up by life.* By our participation in the resurrection life of Jesus (4:10) our mortal being is swallowed up by life, not by death. Paul reverses the age-old imagery of death and the grave being the great swallower (see Ps 69:15; Pr 1:12), as did Isaiah (see Isa 25:8; see also 1Co 15:54).
5:5 *God . . . has given us the Spirit.* The Holy Spirit, poured out by the risen and exalted Savior, applies the benefits of Christ's redeeming work to the believer's heart and makes the resurrection power of Jesus a reality of his daily experience (cf. 4:14,16). This guarantees his eventual total transformation into the likeness of Christ's glorified body (Php 3:21). *deposit.* See note on 1:22.
5:6 *at home in the body . . . away from the Lord.* Still living here in our earthly tent-dwelling (v. 1); it does not mean that we are deprived of the Lord's spiritual presence with us in our daily pilgrimage.
5:8 *away from the body . . . at home with the Lord.* The situation of the Christian after death, when he is no longer living in his "earthly tent" (v. 1). This is an intermediate state between death and resurrection and, apparently, a disembodied state; but it is not a limbo of oblivion, for the believer who has died is at home with his Lord, and that is preferable

to our present life in the body (cf. Php 1:23).
5:9 *whether we are at home in the body or away from it.* Whether we will be alive or will have already died at his coming.
5:10 *appear before the judgment seat of Christ.* This accounting has nothing to do with justification, which is credited to the Christian fully and forever through faith in Christ; instead, it refers to what we have done with our lives as Christians (cf. 1Co 3:11–15). *things done while in the body.* Although the body is wasting away, we are responsible for our actions while in it. Non-Christians, too, are morally responsible and liable to God's judgment (see Ro 2:5,16), but Paul has believers in mind here.
5:11 *to fear the Lord.* As the one to whom we are accountable (v. 10). *we try to persuade men.* Paul needs to persuade some members of the Corinthian church that he, not any of the false teachers who have invaded their ranks, is their authentic apostle.
5:12 *take pride in what is seen.* The pretension of the false apostles is a superficial front; their concern is not with spirituality that is true and deep, but with money and popularity and self-importance.
5:13 *out of our mind . . . in our right mind.* Probably Paul's enemies were asserting that he was suffering from religious mania, pointing perhaps to the sensational conversion he claimed to have experienced on the road to Damascus and to what they regarded as his insane way of life. If this is to be out of his mind, Paul does not deny it, for this whole letter shows how willingly and joyfully he endured affliction for the gospel (cf. 12:10). That, however, was essentially a matter between him and God. On the other hand, there was nothing that could be called eccentric about his manner of presenting the gospel to the Corinthians, for in this he had been, and continued to be, sensible and sober-minded, avoiding flowery rhetoric and all forms of sensationalism (cf. 1Co 2:1–5).
5:14 *Christ's love.* As shown in his death for us, though some hold that the meaning here is "our love for Christ." *one.* The incarnate Son. *for all.* For all mankind. *therefore all died.* Because Christ died for all, he involved all in his death. For some his death would confirm their own death, but for others (those who by faith would become united with him)

all, and therefore all died.[i] [15]And he died for all, that those who live should no longer live for themselves[j] but for him who died for them[k] and was raised again.

[16]So from now on we regard no one from a worldly[l] point of view. Though we once regarded Christ in this way, we do so no longer. [17]Therefore, if anyone is in Christ,[m] he is a new creation;[n] the old has gone, the new has come![o] [18]All this is from God,[p] who reconciled us to himself through Christ[q] and gave us the ministry of reconciliation: [19]that God was reconciling the world to himself in Christ, not counting men's sins against them.[r] And he has committed to us the message of reconciliation. [20]We are therefore Christ's ambassadors,[s] as though God were making his appeal through us.[t] We implore you on Christ's behalf: Be reconciled to God.[u] [21]God made him who had no sin[f] to be sin[f] for us, so that in him we might become the righteousness of God.[w]

6 As God's fellow workers[x] we urge you not to receive God's grace in vain.[y] [2]For he says,

"In the time of my favor I heard you,
    and in the day of salvation I helped
    you."[8] [z]

I tell you, now is the time of God's favor, now is the day of salvation.

Paul's Hardships

[3]We put no stumbling block in anyone's path,[a] so that our ministry will not be discredited. [4]Rather, as servants of God we commend ourselves in every way: in great endurance; in troubles, hardships and distresses; [5]in beatings, imprisonments[b] and riots; in hard work, sleepless nights and hunger;[c] [6]in purity, understanding, patience and kindness; in the Holy Spirit[d] and in sincere love;[e] [7]in truthful speech[f] and in the power of God;[g] with weapons of righteousness[h] in the right hand and in the left; [8]through glory and dishonor,[i] bad report[j] and good report; genuine, yet regarded as impostors;[k] [9]known, yet regarded as unknown; dying,[l] and yet we live on;[m] beaten, and yet not killed; [10]sorrowful, yet always rejoicing;[n] poor, yet making many rich;[o] having nothing,[p] and yet possessing everything.[q]

[11]We have spoken freely to you, Corin-

Cross references (center column):

5:14 [i]Ro 6:6,7; Gal 2:20; Col 3:3
5:15 [j]Ro 14:7-9
[k]Ro 4:25
5:16 [l]2Co 10:4; 11:18
5:17 [m]S Ro 16:3
[n]S Jn 1:13; S Ro 6:4; Gal 6:15
[o]Isa 65:17; Rev 21:4,5
5:18 [p]S Ro 11:36
[q]S Ro 5:10
5:19 [r]S Ro 4:8
5:20 [s]2Co 6:1; Eph 6:20
[t]ver 18
5:21 [u]Isa 27:5
[f]Heb 4:15; 7:26; 1Pe 2:22,24; 1Jn 3:5
[w]S Ro 1:17; S 1Co 1:30
6:1 [x]S 1Co 3:9; 2Co 5:20
[y]1Co 15:2
6:2 [z]Isa 49:8; Ps 69:13; Isa 55:6

6:3 [a]S Mt 5:29; Ro 14:13,20; 1Co 8:9,13; 9:12; 10:32
6:5 [b]Ac 16:23; 2Co 11:23-25
[c]1Co 4:11
6:6 [d]1Co 2:4; 1Th 1:5
[e]Ro 12:9; 1Ti 1:5
6:7 [f]2Co 4:2
[g]2Co 4:7
[h]Ro 13:12; 2Co 10:4; Eph 6:10-18
6:8 [i]1Co 4:10 / 1Co 4:13
[k]Mt 27:63

6:9 [l]S Ro 8:36 [m]2Co 1:8-10; 4:10,11 6:10 [n]S Mt 5:12; 2Co 7:4; Php 2:17; 4:4; Col 1:24; 1Th 1:6 [o]2Co 8:9 [p]Ac 3:6 [q]Ro 8:32; 1Co 3:21

[f][21] Or *be a sin offering*   [8][2] Isaiah 49:8

---

his death was their death to sin and self, so that they now live in and with the resurrected Christ (v. 15). However, some hold that Paul is not speaking specifically here about the scope of Christ's atonement but about the effect of Christ's death on the Christian life. Thus "all" would refer not to mankind in general but only to the church.

5:16 *we once regarded Christ in this way.* Paul is admitting that before his conversion he held views of Christ that were "worldly" (lit. "according to the flesh")—based on purely human considerations.

5:17 *in Christ.* United with Christ through faith in him and commitment to him. *new creation.* Redemption is the restoration and fulfillment of God's purposes in creation (see note on 4:6), and this takes place in Christ, through whom all things were made (see Jn 1:3; Col 1:16; Heb 1:2) and in whom all things are restored or created anew (cf. Ro 8:18-23; Eph 2:10).

5:18 *All this is from God.* God takes the initiative in redemption (see Ro 5:8; Jn 3:16), and he sustains it and brings it to completion. *ministry of reconciliation.* We who are the recipients of divine reconciliation have the privilege and obligation of now being, like Paul in a sense, the heralds and instruments in God's hands to minister the message of reconciliation throughout the world (v. 19).

5:21 *who had no sin . . . sin for us.* A summary of the gospel and its logic. Christ, the only entirely righteous one, at Calvary took our sin upon himself and endured the punishment we deserved (see NIV text note), namely, death and separation from God. Thus, by a marvelous exchange, he made it possible for us to receive his righteousness and thereby be reconciled to God. Our standing and our acceptance before God are solely in him (cf. 1Co 1:30). Again, all this is God's doing; all this is freely available to us because of the initiative of divine grace.

6:1 *to receive God's grace in vain.* To live for oneself (see

5:15) is one way to do this.

6:2 *the time of my favor . . . the day of salvation.* An affirmation that is true in a general sense of all God's saving acts in the history of his people, but that finds its particular fulfillment in this present age of grace between the two comings of Christ. This understanding does not exclude from grace and salvation those who lived before Christ's coming, for the believers of the OT period received the promises that in due course were fulfilled in Christ (1:20) and they saw and welcomed their fulfillment from a distance (see Jn 8:56; Heb 11:13).

6:3 *We put no stumbling block in anyone's path.* Paul is concerned that he live an exemplary life because he does not want the ministry discredited.

6:4–10 Cf. 4:8–12.

6:4 *as servants of God we commend ourselves.* Paul commends himself again inasmuch as the gospel he preached in Corinth is at stake; but, in contrast to the false apostles who were no better than self-servers, he does so as God's servant. His life, with all its trials and afflictions, could not have been more starkly different from that of these intruders whose concern was for their own comfort and advantage.

6:10 *making many rich.* In Christ. True wealth does not consist in worldly possessions but in being "rich toward God" (Lk 12:15,21). The believer, even if he has nothing of this world's goods, nevertheless has everything in him who is Lord of all (cf. 1Co 1:4–5; 3:21–23; Eph 2:7; 3:8; Php 4:19; Col 2:3).

6:11–13 Paul has always been completely open and sincere in his relations with the Christians in Corinth (cf. 1:12–14; 4:2), but the false apostles among them have been trying to persuade them that Paul does not really love them. Now the apostle tenderly appeals to these Corinthians, who are the beneficiaries of his love for them.

thians, and opened wide our hearts to you. *r* ¹²We are not withholding our affection from you, but you are withholding yours from us. ¹³As a fair exchange—I speak as to my children*s*—open wide your hearts *t* also.

Do Not Be Yoked With Unbelievers

¹⁴Do not be yoked together*u* with unbelievers. *v* For what do righteousness and wickedness have in common? Or what fellowship can light have with darkness? *w* ¹⁵What harmony is there between Christ and Belial*h*? *x* What does a believer*y* have in common with an unbeliever? *z* ¹⁶What agreement is there between the temple of God and idols? *a* For we are the temple *b* of the living God. *c* As God has said: "I will live with them and walk among them, and I will be their God, and they will be my people." *i d*

¹⁷"Therefore come out from them *e*
  and be separate,
                              says the Lord.
  Touch no unclean thing,
  and I will receive you." *j f*
¹⁸"I will be a Father to you,
  and you will be my sons and
      daughters, *g*
      says the Lord Almighty." *k h*

7 Since we have these promises, *i* dear friends, *j* let us purify ourselves from everything that contaminates body and spirit, perfecting holiness*k* out of reverence for God.

Reference column

6:11 *r*2Co 7:3
6:13 *s*1Th 2:11
*t*2Co 7:2
6:14 *u*Ge 24:3;
Dt 22:10;
1Co 5:9,10
*v*1Co 6:6
*w*Eph 5:7,11;
1Jn 1:6
6:15 *x*1Co 10:21
*y*Ac 5:14
*z*1Co 6:6
6:16 *a*1Co 10:21
*b*S 1Co 3:16
*c*S Mt 16:16
*d*Lev 26:12;
Jer 32:38;
Eze 37:27;
Rev 21:3
6:17 *e*Rev 18:4
*f*Isa 52:11;
Eze 20:34,41
6:18 *g*Ex 4:22;
2Sa 7:14;
1Ch 17:13;
Isa 43:6;
S Ro 8:14
*h*2Sa 7:8
7:1 *i*2Co 6:17,18
/S 1Co 10:14
*k*1Th 4:7;
1Pe 1:15,16

7:2 *l*2Co 6:12,13
7:3 *m*2Co 6:11,
12; Php 1:7
7:4 *n*ver 14;
2Co 8:24 *o*ver 13
7:5 *p*2Co 2:13;
S Ac 16:9
*r*2Co 4:8
*s*Dt 32:25
7:6 *t*2Co 1:3,4
*u*ver 13;
S 2Co 2:13
7:8 *v*2Co 2:2,4
7:10 *w*Ac 11:18

Paul's Joy

²Make room for us in your hearts. *l* We have wronged no one, we have corrupted no one, we have exploited no one. ³I do not say this to condemn you; I have said before that you have such a place in our hearts *m* that we would live or die with you. ⁴I have great confidence in you; I take great pride in you. *n* I am greatly encouraged; *o* in all our troubles my joy knows no bounds. *p*

⁵For when we came into Macedonia, *q* this body of ours had no rest, but we were harassed at every turn *r*—conflicts on the outside, fears within. *s* ⁶But God, who comforts the downcast, *t* comforted us by the coming of Titus, *u* ⁷and not only by his coming but also by the comfort you had given him. He told us about your longing for me, your deep sorrow, your ardent concern for me, so that my joy was greater than ever.

⁸Even if I caused you sorrow by my letter, *v* I do not regret it. Though I did regret it—I see that my letter hurt you, but only for a little while— ⁹yet now I am happy, not because you were made sorry, but because your sorrow led you to repentance. For you became sorrowful as God intended and so were not harmed in any way by us. ¹⁰Godly sorrow brings repentance that leads to salvation *w* and leaves no regret, but worldly sorrow brings death. ¹¹See

h15 Greek *Beliar,* a variant of *Belial*   *i16* Lev. 26:12;
Jer, 32:38; Ezek. 37:27   *j17* Isaiah 52:11;
Ezek. 20:34,41   *k18* 2 Samuel 7:14; 7:8

6:14 *Do not be yoked together with unbelievers.* Doubtless Paul has in mind the OT prohibition of "mixtures" as in Dt 22:10. For the Corinthian believers to cooperate with false teachers, who are in reality servants of Satan, notwithstanding their charming and persuasive ways (see notes on 11:13–14), is to become unequally yoked, destroying the harmony and fellowship that unite them in Christ.

6:15 *Belial.* A term (from Hebrew) used to designate Satan (see note on Dt 13:13).

6:16 *agreement... between the temple of God and idols.* There can be no reversion to or compromise with the idolatry they have forsaken for the gospel (cf. 1Th 1:9). *temple of the living God.* Built of "living stones," namely, Christian believers (1Pe 2:5); therefore it is all the more important that they form no defiling and unholy alliances (cf. 1Co 6:19–20).

7:1 *holiness.* See 1Th 4:7; 1Jn 3:3.

7:2 *We have... exploited no one.* Implies that Paul had been accused by the false teachers of being unjust, destructive and fraudulent—the very things they themselves were guilty of.

7:3 Again he declares the depth of his affection for the Corinthian believers and appeals to them to respond, contrary to the wishes of the false teachers, by displaying their love for him, their genuine apostle (cf. 6:11–13).

7:4 *great confidence... my joy knows no bounds.* The long digression that started at 2:14 concludes here on this

note of exhilaration. The news he had been so anxiously awaiting from Corinth has turned out to be good and reassuring, and Paul is overjoyed to receive it.

7:5–6 *when we came into Macedonia... God... comforted us by the coming of Titus.* Here Paul resumes the account he began in 2:12–13, where he described how his hopes of meeting Titus in Troas were disappointed and how, restless for news, he had decided to press on into Macedonia. He now explains that on reaching Macedonia, he was at last comforted by the arrival of Titus, who brought the news he most wanted to hear concerning the situation in Corinth. Titus himself had been well received in that city and was able to assure Paul (see v. 7) of the "longing" and "ardent concern" of the Corinthian Christians for him and of the "deep sorrow" they had expressed for the grief they had caused him. Consequently, his "joy was greater than ever."

7:8–9 *I do not regret it... I did regret it... now I am happy.* Paul did regret the necessity of writing a letter to the Corinthians that caused sorrow to them. However, it was not the actual writing that he regretted, but the situation that required the writing. Moreover, the fact that the letter had the desired effect made him happy, for their sorrow did not leave them embittered and hostile but led them to repentance. They became sorrowful as God intended, and so were benefited, not harmed, by the letter.

7:10 *Godly sorrow... worldly sorrow.* The former manifests itself by repentance and the experience of divine grace;

what this godly sorrow has produced in you: what earnestness, what eagerness to clear yourselves, what indignation, what alarm, what longing, what concern, *x* what readiness to see justice done. At every point you have proved yourselves to be innocent in this matter. 12So even though I wrote to you, *y* it was not on account of the one who did the wrong *z* or of the injured party, but rather that before God you could see for yourselves how devoted to us you are. 13By all this we are encouraged.

In addition to our own encouragement, we were especially delighted to see how happy Titus *a* was, because his spirit has been refreshed by all of you. 14I had boasted to him about you, *b* and you have not embarrassed me. But just as everything we said to you was true, so our boasting about you to Titus *c* has proved to be true as well. 15And his affection for you is all the greater when he remembers that you were all obedient, *d* receiving him with fear and trembling. *e* 16I am glad I can have complete confidence in you. *f*

Generosity Encouraged

8 And now, brothers, we want you to know about the grace that God has given the Macedonian *g* churches. 2Out of the most severe trial, their overflowing joy and their extreme poverty welled up in rich generosity. *h* 3For I testify that they gave as much as they were able, *i* and even beyond their ability. Entirely on their own, 4they urgently pleaded with us for the privilege of sharing *j* in this service *k* to

the saints. *l* 5And they did not do as we expected, but they gave themselves first to the Lord and then to us in keeping with God's will. 6So we urged *m* Titus, *n* since he had earlier made a beginning, to bring also to completion *o* this act of grace on your part. 7But just as you excel in everything *p*—in faith, in speech, in knowledge, *q* in complete earnestness and in your love for us*l*—see that you also excel in this grace of giving.

8I am not commanding you, *r* but I want to test the sincerity of your love by comparing it with the earnestness of others. 9For you know the grace *s* of our Lord Jesus Christ, *t* that though he was rich, yet for your sakes he became poor, *u* so that you through his poverty might become rich. *v*

10And here is my advice *w* about what is best for you in this matter: Last year you were the first not only to give but also to have the desire to do so. *x* 11Now finish the work, so that your eager willingness*y* to do it may be matched by your completion of it, according to your means. 12For if the willingness is there, the gift is acceptable according to what one has, *z* not according to what he does not have.

13Our desire is not that others might be relieved while you are hard pressed, but that there might be equality. 14At the present time your plenty will supply what they need, *a* so that in turn their plenty will supply what you need. Then there will be equality, 15as it is written: "He who

l 7 Some manuscripts in our love for you

Cross references (center column)

7:11 *x*ver 7
7:12 *y*ver 8;
2Co 2:3,9
*z*1Co 5:1,2
7:13 *a*ver 6;
S 2Co 2:13
7:14 *b*ver 4
*c*ver 6
7:15 *d*2Co 2:9;
10:6 *e*Ps 55:5;
1Co 2:3;
Php 2:12
7:16 *f*S 2Co 2:3
8:1 *g*S Ac 16:9
8:2 *h*Ex 36:5;
2Co 9:11
8:3 *i*1Co 16:2
8:4 *j*ver 1
*k*S Ac 24:17

*l*S Ac 9:13
8:6 *m*ver 17;
2Co 12:18 *n*ver
16,23; S 2Co 2:13
*o*ver 10,11
8:7 *p*2Co 9:8
*q*Ro 15:14;
1Co 1:5; 12:8;
13:1,2; 14:6
8:8 *r*1Co 7:6
8:9 *s*S Ro 3:24
*t*2Co 13:14
*u*Mt 20:28;
Php 2:6-8
*v*2Co 6:10
8:10 *w*1Co 7:25,
40 *x*1Co 16:2,3;
2Co 9:2
8:11 *y*ver 12,19;
Ex 25:2; 2Co 9:2
8:12 *z*Mk 12:43,
44; 2Co 9:7
8:14 *a*Ac 4:34;
2Co 9:12

---

the latter brings death because, instead of being God-centered sorrow over the wickedness of sin, it is self-centered sorrow over the painful consequences of sin. The letter's primary purpose was not to deal with the notorious offender in Corinth or the person he had injured, but to test their loyalty and devotion to Paul as their apostle.

8:1—9:15 Paul addresses himself to the question of the collection of money for the distressed Christians in Jerusalem, which the Corinthians had started but not completed.
8:1 *grace.* The "grace of giving" on the part of believers (v. 7) is more than matched by the self-giving "grace of our Lord Jesus Christ" (v. 9).
8:2 *overflowing joy.* In the blessings of the gospel.
8:5 *they gave themselves first to the Lord.* The true principle of all Christian giving. These Macedonian Christians are an amazing example to the Corinthian believers and to the church in every age of the dynamic difference that God's grace makes in the lives and attitudes of his people—a central theme of this letter (cf. 12:9–10).
8:6 *we urged Titus.* The collection had been started in Corinth under the direction of Titus during the previous year (see v. 10; 9:2), but, no doubt because of the troubles in the Corinthian church, had slowed down or come to a standstill. Paul is now sending Titus back to them, taking with him this present letter, for the purpose of completing this good work,

which he describes as an "act of grace" (cf. the link between the grace of God and the selfless generosity of the Macedonian churches in vv. 1–5).
8:7 *you excel in everything.* Cf. 1Co 1:4–7.
8:8 *I am not commanding you.* True charity and generosity cannot be commanded. *sincerity of your love.* They can prove this by giving selflessly and spontaneously. *earnestness of others.* The remarkable example of the Macedonian churches (vv. 1–5).
8:9 *though he was rich . . . he became poor.* The eternal Son, in his incarnation and his atoning death in our place on the cross, emptied himself of his riches (see Php 2:7). *through his poverty might become rich.* The supreme and inescapable incentive of all genuine Christian generosity.
8:11 *Now finish the work.* The work they had started "last year" with desire (v. 10) needs to be completed (see note on v. 6).
8:12 *according to what one has.* What matters is the willingness, which is the motive of true generosity, no matter how small the amount that can be afforded. An outstanding example of one who put this principle into practice is the poor widow (see Mk 12:41–44). The mechanics of the collection being made in Corinth had been proposed by Paul in his earlier letter (see 1Co 16:1–2).
8:15 See NIV text note. The reference is to the gathering by

gathered much did not have too much, and he who gathered little did not have too little."ᵐᵇ

Titus Sent to Corinth

¹⁶I thank God,ᶜ who put into the heartᵈ of Titusᵉ the same concern I have for you. ¹⁷For Titus not only welcomed our appeal, but he is coming to you with much enthusiasm and on his own initiative.ᶠ ¹⁸And we are sending along with him the brotherᵍ who is praised by all the churchesʰ for his service to the gospel.ⁱ ¹⁹What is more, he was chosen by the churches to accompany us/ as we carry the offering, which we administer in order to honor the Lord himself and to show our eagerness to help.ᵏ ²⁰We want to avoid any criticism of the way we administer this liberal gift. ²¹For we are taking pains to do what is right, not only in the eyes of the Lord but also in the eyes of men.ˡ

²²In addition, we are sending with them our brother who has often proved to us in many ways that he is zealous, and now even more so because of his great confidence in you. ²³As for Titus,ᵐ he is my partnerⁿ and fellow workerᵒ among you; as for our brothers,ᵖ they are representatives of the churches and an honor to Christ. ²⁴Therefore show these men the proof of your love and the reason for our pride in you, q so that the churches can see it.

9 There is no needʳ for me to write to you about this serviceˢ to the saints.ᵗ ²For I know your eagerness to help,ᵘ and I have been boastingᵛ about it to the Macedonians, telling them that since last yearʷ you in Achaiaˣ were ready to give; and your enthusiasm has stirred most of them to action. ³But I am sending the

brothersʸ in order that our boasting about you in this matter should not prove hollow, but that you may be ready, as I said you would be. ᶻ ⁴For if any Macedoniansᵃ come with me and find you unprepared, we—not to say anything about you—would be ashamed of having been so confident. ⁵So I thought it necessary to urge the brothersᵇ to visit you in advance and finish the arrangements for the generous gift you had promised. Then it will be ready as a generous gift,ᶜ not as one grudgingly given. ᵈ

Sowing Generously

⁶Remember this: Whoever sows sparingly will also reap sparingly, and whoever sows generously will also reap generously.ᵉ ⁷Each man should give what he has decided in his heart to give,ᶠ not reluctantly or under compulsion,ᵍ for God loves a cheerful giver. ʰ ⁸And God is ableⁱ to make all grace abound to you, so that in all things at all times, having all that you need,/ you will abound in every good work. ⁹As it is written:

"He has scattered abroad his giftsᵏ to
    the poor;
his righteousness endures
    forever."ⁿˡ

¹⁰Now he who supplies seed to the sower and bread for foodᵐ will also supply and increase your store of seed and will enlarge the harvest of your righteousness. ⁿ ¹¹You will be made richᵒ in every way so that you can be generousᵖ on every occasion, and through us your generosity will result in thanksgiving to God. q

¹²This service that you perform is not

Cross references

8:15 ᵇEx 16:18
8:16 ᶜS 2Co 2:14
ᵈRev 17:17
ᵉS 2Co 2:13
8:17 ᶠver 6
8:18 ᵍ2Co 12:18
ʰS 1Co 7:17
ⁱS 2Co 2:12
8:19 /Ac 14:23;
1Co 16:3,4 ᵏver 11,12
8:21 ˡRo 12:17;
S 14:18;
S Tit 2:14
8:23 ᵐS 2Co 2:13
ⁿPhm 17
ᵒS Php 2:25 ᵖver 18,22
8:24 q2Co 7:4,
14; 9:2
9:1 ʳ1Th 4:9
ˢS Ac 24:17
ᵗS Ac 9:13
9:2 ᵘ2Co 8:11,
12,19 ᵛ2Co 7:4,
14; 8:24
ʷ2Co 8:10
ˣS Ac 18:12

9:3 ʸ2Co 8:23
ᶻ1Co 16:2
9:4 ᵃRo 15:26
9:5 ᵇver 3
ᶜPhp 4:17
ᵈ2Co 12:17,18
9:6 ᵉPr 11:24,25;
22:9; Gal 6:7,9
9:7 ᶠEx 25:2;
2Co 8:12
ᵍDt 15:10
ʰRo 12:8
9:8 ⁱEph 3:20
/Php 4:19
9:9 ᵏMal 3:10
ˡPs 112:9
9:10 ᵐIsa 55:10
ⁿHos 10:12
9:11 ᵒ1Co 1:5
ᵖver 5
q2Co 1:11; 4:15

ᵐ15 Exodus 16:18   ⁿ9 Psalm 112:9

Footnotes

the Israelites of the manna in the desert. Though in the daily gathering the aged and weak might collect less than the prescribed amount and the young and vigorous might collect more, there was an equal distribution, so that the excess of some ministered to the deficiency of others.

8:16 *Titus.* Had established a relationship of trust and affection with the Corinthians (see 7:6–7,13–15). He had organized the collection when it was started the previous year (see note on v. 6).

8:18 *the brother.* Probably Luke, but possibly Barnabas. In any case, it was someone who was widely known for the faithfulness of his ministry.

8:19 *chosen by the churches.* Paul provides a good example of the care that church leaders should take in handling money.

8:20 It is important not only that God sees (cf. vv. 19,21) but also that people see that one is carrying on the Lord's work in a proper, ethical and honest manner.

8:21 *taking pains to do what is right.* Even so, Paul is the victim of disgraceful slander (implied by 12:17–18; see In-

troduction: Purpose); but the integrity of his representatives (see note on v. 23) reflects well on his own integrity.

8:22 *our brother.* This second brother is anonymous, like the one already mentioned (see v. 18 and note).

8:23 *partner and fellow worker.* See note on 2:13. *representatives of the churches.* Duly elected delegates of the churches at large (so that they could not be dismissed as cronies chosen by Paul alone); see note on Ac 20:4. *an honor to Christ.* Christians of outstanding faithfulness.

9:6 Probably a well-known proverb—but not taken from the OT book of Proverbs.

9:7 See Lk 6:38.

9:8 *all things . . . all times . . . all that you need.* Through his abounding grace, God can enable each Christian to abound in generous deeds (see v. 11).

9:9–10 *righteousness.* See note on Ps 1:5.

9:12 *not only supplying the needs of God's people.* The effect of generous giving on the part of the Corinthians will extend beyond Jerusalem, the destination of their gift, to the church as a whole, causing widespread prayer and praise to

only supplying the needs[r] of God's people but is also overflowing in many expressions of thanks to God.[s] 13Because of the service[t] by which you have proved yourselves, men will praise God[u] for the obedience that accompanies your confession[v] of the gospel of Christ,[w] and for your generosity[x] in sharing with them and with everyone else. 14And in their prayers for you their hearts will go out to you, because of the surpassing grace God has given you. 15Thanks be to God[y] for his indescribable gift![z]

Paul's Defense of His Ministry

10 By the meekness and gentleness[a] of Christ, I appeal to you—I, Paul,[b] who am "timid" when face to face with you, but "bold" when away! 2I beg you that when I come I may not have to be as bold[c] as I expect to be toward some people who think that we live by the standards of this world.[d] 3For though we live in the world, we do not wage war as the world does.[e] 4The weapons we fight with[f] are not the weapons of the world. On the contrary, they have divine power[g]

to demolish strongholds.[h] 5We demolish arguments and every pretension that sets itself up against the knowledge of God,[i] and we take captive every thought to make it obedient[j] to Christ. 6And we will be ready to punish every act of disobedience, once your obedience is complete.[k]

7You are looking only on the surface of things.[o][l] If anyone is confident that he belongs to Christ,[m] he should consider again that we belong to Christ just as much as he.[n] 8For even if I boast somewhat freely about the authority the Lord gave us[o] for building you up rather than pulling you down,[p] I will not be ashamed of it. 9I do not want to seem to be trying to frighten you with my letters. 10For some say, "His letters are weighty and forceful, but in person he is unimpressive[q] and his speaking amounts to nothing."[r] 11Such people should realize that what we are in our letters when we are absent, we will be in our actions when we are present.

12We do not dare to classify or compare ourselves with some who commend them-

Cross references

9:12 [r]2Co 8:14; [s]2Co 1:11
9:13 [t]S 2Co 8:4; [u]S Mt 9:8; [v]S Heb 3:1; [w]S 2Co 2:12; [x]ver 5
9:15 [y]S 2Co 2:14; [z]Ro 5:15,16
10:1 [a]Mt 11:29; [b]Gal 5:2; Eph 3:1
10:2 [c]S 1Co 4:21; [d]Ro 12:2
10:3 [e]ver 2
10:4 [f]S 2Co 6:7; [g]1Co 2:5

10:5 [h]ver 8; Jer 1:10; 23:29; 2Co 13:10; [i]Isa 2:11,12; 1Co 1:19; [j]2Co 9:13
10:6 [k]2Co 2:9; 7:15
10:7 [l]S Jn 7:24; 2Co 5:12; [m]1Co 1:12; S 3:23; 14:37; [n]2Co 11:23
10:8 [o]ver 13,15; [p]ver 4; Jer 1:10; 2Co 13:10
10:10 [q]ver 1; 1Co 2:3; Gal 4:13,14; [r]1Co 1:17; 2Co 11:6

[o]7 Or *Look at the obvious facts*

9:14 *the surpassing grace God has given you.* Displayed in this unselfish demonstration of their loving concern for fellow believers who are in desperate need.

9:15 *indescribable gift.* His own Son (Jn 3:16). God is the first giver; he first selflessly gives himself to us in the person of his Son, and all true Christian giving is our response of gratitude for this gift that is beyond description (cf. 8:9; 1Jn 4:9–11).

10:1 *"timid" when face to face . . . "bold" when away.* From the mild tone of the first nine chapters of Paul's letter, it appears that the majority of the Corinthian believers had been won over to Paul (cf. 7:6–13), after having been alienated by his Corinthian opponents. In this final section (chs. 10–13), however, Paul deals firmly with the slanders that have been spread against him in Corinth by the remaining opposition. Those who wish to discredit him have been saying that he is bold at a distance, threatening to take severe disciplinary action, especially in his letters (cf., e.g., his warning that, if necessary, he will come "with a whip" in 1Co 4:18–21). But they say that he will not dare to be anything but weak and indecisive if he is present with them in person—in short, that he does not have the apostolic authority he claims to have. Paul is ready to prove otherwise, should the occasion demand, when he comes to Corinth for the third time (see vv. 6,10–11). His appeal to the meekness and gentleness of Christ is an indication of his own affectionate desire to show these same qualities when present with them. In any case, though weak in himself, Paul is strong in the Lord—as this whole letter explains—and those who are rebellious can expect to feel the force of his divinely given authority.

10:4 *weapons we fight with.* Paul is prepared for warfare; his weapons, however, are not the weapons prized by this fallen world and fashioned by human pride and arrogance. *strongholds.* Of "arguments" and "every pretension" (v. 5) defiantly raised "against the knowledge of God" (cf. Ro 1:18–23), among which are the faulty reasonings by which

the false apostles have been trying to shake the faith of the Christians in Corinth (see 1Co 2:13–14).

10:5 *every thought . . . obedient to Christ.* The center of man's being thus becomes fully subject to the lordship of Christ.

10:7 *he belongs to Christ.* Probably echoes the claim to superior spirituality by the Christ party (1Co 1:12) and the false teachers in Corinth. Paul, who had dramatically encountered and been commissioned by the risen Lord (see Ac 9:3–9; 22:6–11; 26:12–18) and who received the gospel he preached "by revelation from Jesus Christ" (Gal 1:11; cf. 2Co 12:2–7), asserts that he belongs to Christ just as much.

10:8 *authority . . . for building you up.* The primary purpose of Paul's apostolic authority is constructive, for building up, not destructive, for pulling down (the same statement is made again in 13:10). The demands he makes in his letters are written so that they may put right what is amiss, and so that things may be in order for his arrival, thus removing the need for severe action (pulling down) and preparing the way for edification (building up).

10:9 *frighten you with my letters.* See 2:3–4; 7:8–9; chs. 10–13; 1Co 4:18–21.

10:10 *his speaking amounts to nothing.* See note on v. 1. Paul's adversaries used a professional type of oratory as their stock in trade, designed to extract money from their gullible audiences. But Paul's manner of speaking was quite different; it was plain, straightforward and free from artificiality—and it was also free of charge (see note on 11:7), which meant, if his slanderous opponents were to be believed, that what he said was worthless. But in coming to Corinth Paul had purposely disdained academic eloquence and wisdom and was determined to proclaim the message of Christ crucified, and the transformed lives of the Corinthian believers testified to the divine power with which he spoke (cf. 1Co 2:1–5).

10:12 *they measure themselves by themselves.* The false teachers in Corinth behave as though there is no standard of comparison higher than themselves, but Paul boasts only in

selves.^{s} When they measure themselves by themselves and compare themselves with themselves, they are not wise. ^{13}We, however, will not boast beyond proper limits, but will confine our boasting to the field God has assigned to us,^{t} a field that reaches even to you. ^{14}We are not going too far in our boasting, as would be the case if we had not come to you, for we did get as far as you^u with the gospel of Christ.^{v} ^{15}Neither do we go beyond our limits^w by boasting of work done by others.$^{p\,x}$ Our hope is that, as your faith continues to grow,^{y} our area of activity among you will greatly expand, ^{16}so that we can preach the gospel^z in the regions beyond you.^{a} For we do not want to boast about work already done in another man's territory. ^{17}But, "Let him who boasts boast in the Lord."$^{q\,b}$ ^{18}For it is not the one who commends himself^c who is approved, but the one whom the Lord commends.^{d}

Paul and the False Apostles

11 I hope you will put up with^e a little of my foolishness;^{f} but you are already doing that. ^{2}I am jealous for you with a godly jealousy. I promised you to one husband,^{g} to Christ, so that I might present you^h as a pure virgin to him. ^{3}But I am afraid that just as Eve was deceived by the serpent's cunning,^{i} your minds may somehow be led astray from your sincere and pure devotion to Christ. ^{4}For if someone comes to you and preaches a Jesus other than the Jesus we preached,^{j} or if you receive a different spirit^k from the one you received, or a different gospel^l from the one you accepted, you put up with it^m easily enough. ^{5}But I do not think I am in the least inferior to those "super-apostles."^{n} ^{6}I may not be a trained speaker,^{o} but I do have knowledge.^{p} We have made this perfectly clear to you in every way.

^{7}Was it a sin^q for me to lower myself in order to elevate you by preaching the gospel of God^r to you free of charge?^{s} ^{8}I robbed other churches by receiving support from them^t so as to serve you. ^{9}And when I was with you and needed something, I was not a burden to anyone, for the brothers who came from Macedonia supplied what I needed.^{u} I have kept myself from being a burden to you^v in any way, and will continue to do so. ^{10}As sure-

Cross references (center column):

10:12 ^{s}ver 18; S 2Co 3:1
10:13 ^{t}ver 15,16; S Ro 12:3
10:14 ^{u}S 1Co 3:6 ^{v}S 2Co 2:12
10:15 ^{w}ver 13 ^{x}Ro 15:20 ^{y}2Th 1:3
10:16 ^{z}S Ro 1:1; S 2Co 2:12 ^{a}S Ac 19:21
10:17 ^{b}Jer 9:24; Ps 34:2; 44:8; 1Co 1:31
10:18 ^{c}ver 12 ^{d}S Ro 2:29
11:1 ^{e}ver 4,19, 20; Mt 17:17 ^{f}ver 16,17,21; 2Co 5:13
11:2 ^{g}Hos 2:19; Eph 5:26,27 ^{h}S 2Co 4:14

11:3 ^{i}Ge 3:1-6, 13; 1Ti 2:14; Rev 12:9
11:4 ^{j}1Co 3:11 ^{k}Ro 8:15 ^{l}Gal 1:6-9 ^{m}S ver 1
11:5 ^{n}2Co 12:11; Gal 2:6
11:6 ^{o}S 1Co 1:17 ^{p}S 2Co 8:7; Eph 3:4
11:7 ^{q}2Co 12:13 ^{r}S Ro 1:1 ^{s}1Co 9:18
11:8 ^{t}Php 4:15, 18
11:9 ^{u}Php 4:15, 18 ^{v}2Co 12:13, 14,16

P 13-15 Or ^{13}We, however, will not boast about things that cannot be measured, but we will boast according to the standard of measurement that the God of measure has assigned us—a measurement that relates even to you. ^{14} . . . . ^{15}Neither do we boast about things that cannot be measured in regard to the work done by others. ^{q}17 Jer. 9:24

Notes (bottom):

the Lord (see vv. 13–18; cf. 1Co 1:31).
10:13 *the field God has assigned to us.* The picture Paul has in mind may be that of an athletic contest in which lanes are marked out for the different runners. In that case "field" should be rendered "lane"—as also "area of activity" (v. 15) and "territory" (v. 16). In intruding themselves into Corinth, the false apostles had crossed into Paul's lane, which was the lane that God had marked out and that had brought him to the Corinthians as their genuine apostle. He has no intention of invading the territory marked out for others and claiming their work as his own, as these false teachers were doing. Others understand the Greek word in question to refer to an assigned sphere of authority.
10:16 *regions beyond.* Spain is probably in his thoughts (see Ro 15:24,28).
11:1 *my foolishness.* In order to compare his own ministry with that of the false apostles who have invaded the Corinthian church, Paul has to speak about himself, which inevitably seems like foolish boasting.
11:2 *godly jealousy.* Paul cannot bear the thought that there might be any rival to Christ and his gospel. *I promised you to one husband.* As their spiritual father (cf. 6:13), Paul has promised the Corinthian believers to Christ, who is frequently depicted in the NT as the bridegroom, with the church portrayed as his bride (Mt 9:15; Jn 3:29; Ro 7:4; 1Co 6:15; Eph 5:23–32; Rev 19:7–9; 21:2). *pure virgin.* Undefiled by the doctrines of false teachers (see vv. 3–4).
11:4 *a Jesus other than the Jesus we preached.* They presented a Jesus cast in the mold of Judaistic teachings (Paul's opponents were Jews; see v. 22). *different spirit.* A spirit of bondage, fear and worldliness (cf. Ro 8:15; 1Co 2:12; Gal 2:4; 4:24; Col 2:20–23) instead of a spirit of freedom, love, joy, peace and power (cf. 3:17; Ro 14:17; Gal

2:4; 5:1,22; Eph 3:20; Col 1:11; 2Ti 1:7). *different gospel.* Cf. Gal 1:6–9. *you put up with it easily enough.* They have been undiscerningly tolerant of these deceivers in their midst.
11:5 *those "super-apostles."* Paul's sarcastic way of referring to the false apostles who had infiltrated the Corinthian church and were in reality not apostles at all, except in their own arrogantly inflated opinion of themselves (cf. 10:12).
11:6 *I may not be a trained speaker.* Using the skills, references and flourishes of professional rhetoric (see note on 10:10). *I do have knowledge.* As the Corinthian believers well knew, Paul had knowledge of Christ that was true, powerful and God-given, totally distinct from the powerless human wisdom the false teachers were attempting to deceive them with (cf. 1Co 2:6–10).
11:7 *free of charge.* Another slanderous criticism made by Paul's adversaries was that his refusal to accept payment for his instruction proved that it was worth nothing. This accusation at the same time helped to cloak their own grasping character, since their method of operation, like that of first-century traveling philosophers and religious teachers, was to demand payment for their "professional" services. Paul, his enemies said, was lowering himself and committing a sin by breaking the rule that a teacher should receive payment in proportion to the worth of his performance.
11:8 *robbed other churches.* Accepted freely given support from established congregations.
11:9 *burden.* A financial liability (see note on 2:17). This reinforced his teaching that the gospel of Jesus Christ is a free gift. *brothers who came from Macedonia.* They brought gifts from the churches in that province (Ac 18:5), particularly from the church at Philippi (Php 4:15).

ly as the truth of Christ is in me,[w] nobody in the regions of Achaia[x] will stop his boasting[y] of mine. [11]Why? Because I do not love you? God knows[z] I do![a] [12]And I will keep on doing what I am doing in order to cut the ground from under those who want an opportunity to be considered equal with us in the things they boast about.

[13]For such men are false apostles,[b] deceitful[c] workmen, masquerading as apostles of Christ.[d] [14]And no wonder, for Satan[e] himself masquerades as an angel of light. [15]It is not surprising, then, if his servants masquerade as servants of righteousness. Their end will be what their actions deserve.[f]

Paul Boasts About His Sufferings

[16]I repeat: Let no one take me for a fool.[g] But if you do, then receive me just as you would a fool, so that I may do a little boasting. [17]In this self-confident boasting I am not talking as the Lord would,[h] but as a fool.[i] [18]Since many are boasting in the way the world does,[j] I too will boast.[k] [19]You gladly put up with[l] fools since you are so wise![m] [20]In fact, you even put up with[n] anyone who enslaves

you[o] or exploits you or takes advantage of you or pushes himself forward or slaps you in the face. [21]To my shame I admit that we were too weak[p] for that!

What anyone else dares to boast about—I am speaking as a fool—I also dare to boast about.[q] [22]Are they Hebrews? So am I.[r] Are they Israelites? So am I.[s] Are they Abraham's descendants? So am I.[t] [23]Are they servants of Christ?[u] (I am out of my mind to talk like this.) I am more. I have worked much harder,[v] been in prison more frequently,[w] been flogged more severely,[x] and been exposed to death again and again.[y] [24]Five times I received from the Jews the forty lashes[z] minus one. [25]Three times I was beaten with rods,[a] once I was stoned,[b] three times I was shipwrecked,[c] I spent a night and a day in the open sea, [26]I have been constantly on the move. I have been in danger from rivers, in danger from bandits, in danger from my own countrymen,[d] in danger from Gentiles; in danger in the city,[e] in danger in the country, in danger at sea; and in danger from false brothers.[f] [27]I have labored and toiled[g] and have often gone without sleep; I have known

11:10 *w*S Ro 9:1
*x*S Ac 18:12
*y*1Co 9:15
11:11 *z*ver 31;
S Ro 1:9
*a*2Co 12:15
11:13 *b*S Mt 7:15
*c*Tit 1:10
*d*Rev 2:2
11:14 *e*S Mt 4:10
11:15 *f*S Mt 16:27;
Php 3:19
11:16 *g*ver 1
11:17 *h*1Co 7:12,
25 *i*ver 21
11:18 *j*2Co 5:16;
10:4 *k*ver 21;
Php 3:3,4
11:19 *l*S ver 1
*m*1Co 4:10
11:20 *n*S ver 1

*o*Gal 2:4; 4:9;
5:1
11:21 *p*2Co 10:1,
10 *q*ver 17,18;
Php 3:4
11:22 *r*Php 3:5
*s*Ro 9:4; 11:1
*t*S Lk 3:8; Ro 11:1
11:23 *u*S 1Co 3:5
*v*S 1Co 15:10
*w*Ac 16:23;
2Co 6:4,5
*x*Ac 16:23;
2Co 6:4,5
*y*S Ro 8:36
11:24 *z*Dt 25:3
11:25 *a*Ac 16:22
*b*Ac 14:19
*c*Ac 27:1-44
11:26 *d*S Ac 20:3
*e*Ac 21:31
*f*Gal 2:4

11:27 *g*S Ac 18:3; Col 1:29

11:12 *I will keep on.* Paul will not be deterred from presenting the gospel without charge. Actually, this practice made his adversaries look bad. They were greedy for gain, and it would have suited them better if Paul had been willing to accept money for his teaching, for this would have put him on a level with their practice. *equal.* In financial matters.
11:13 *masquerading as apostles of Christ.* Now Paul exposes these would-be "super-apostles" (v. 5) as false apostles and servants of Satan (v. 14) who are covering up their true identity.
11:14 *as an angel of light.* Though he is in reality the prince of darkness.
11:16 *Let no one take me for a fool.* See note on v. 1.
11:18 *boast.* By speaking of the nature of his apostolic ministry.
11:19 *You gladly put up with fools.* Resumes the implied rebuke of v. 4, and has the same ironic tone. There it was a matter of their readiness to tolerate false teaching; here it is a matter of their willingness to put up with disgraceful treatment by these false teachers, who are described as fools because of their self-centered boasting.
11:20 *enslaves you.* By the imposition of tyrannical man-made rules and prohibitions (cf. Gal 5:1). *exploits you.* See Mk 12:40. *takes advantage of you.* Thanks to the Corinthians' lack of discernment and their readiness to be impressed by outward show and clever talk. *pushes himself forward.* For the purpose of lording it over the members of the church (cf. 1:24). *slaps you in the face.* Using physical violence to cow them into submission.
11:21 *too weak for that.* Compared with the crude self-seeking roughness of the impostors, Paul's conduct may well be considered weak, but he is probably speaking ironically here.
11:22 *Hebrews . . . Israelites . . . Abraham's descendants.* The claims implied here on the part of the false apostles

indicate that they were Jews who felt superior to Gentile Christians. From this there follows the probability that they were Judaizers, i.e., they wished to impose distinctive Jewish practices and observances as required for Gentile converts. This, of course, was not Paul's position (see Ro 2:28–29; 1Co 12:13; Gal 3:28–29; Eph 2:11–18; Col 3:11). For Paul's claim see Ac 22:3–5; 26:4–5; Php 3:5–6.
11:23 *servants of Christ.* Paul is not granting their claim to be servants of Christ. Indeed, the consideration of the nature of his ministry and its cost to him in suffering will show that he is more Christ's servant than any or all of them. *exposed to death again and again.* Cf. 4:8–11. He means this literally, for the sufferings he lists here and in the verses that follow were life-threatening. The catalogue that follows makes it clear that Luke's account in Acts is selective.
11:24–25 *lashes . . . rods.* Eight floggings are mentioned here, five at the hands of the Jews (cf. Dt 25:1–3) and three at the hands of the Roman authorities, who used rods on these occasions (see Ac 16:22–23). The three beatings with rods took place despite the fact that Paul, being a Roman citizen, was legally protected from such punishment (cf. Ac 16:37–39; 22:25–29).
11:25 *stoned.* A traditional manner of Jewish execution (cf. Ac 14:19–20). *shipwrecked.* Only one shipwreck is recorded in Acts, but it took place after the writing of this letter (Ac 27:39–44). The three shipwrecks referred to here could have taken place during the voyages mentioned in Ac 9:30; 11:25–26; 13:4,13; 14:25–26; 16:11; 17:14; 18:18–19, 21–22. *a night and a day in the open sea.* Probably as a result of one of the shipwrecks.
11:26 *in danger.* Apart from the specific incidents referred to in the preceding verses, Paul constantly faced situations of danger as well as labors and hardships (see note on Ac 14:24).

hunger and thirst and have often gone without food;[h] I have been cold and naked. [28]Besides everything else, I face daily the pressure of my concern for all the churches.[i] [29]Who is weak, and I do not feel weak?[j] Who is led into sin,[k] and I do not inwardly burn?

[30]If I must boast, I will boast[l] of the things that show my weakness.[m] [31]The God and Father of the Lord Jesus, who is to be praised forever,[n] knows[o] that I am not lying. [32]In Damascus the governor under King Aretas had the city of the Damascenes guarded in order to arrest me.[p] [33]But I was lowered in a basket from a window in the wall and slipped through his hands.[q]

Paul's Vision and His Thorn

12 I must go on boasting.[r] Although there is nothing to be gained, I will go on to visions and revelations[s] from the Lord. [2]I know a man in Christ[t] who fourteen years ago was caught up[u] to the third heaven.[v] Whether it was in the body or out of the body I do not know—God knows.[w] [3]And I know that this man—whether in the body or apart from the body I do not know, but God knows— [4]was caught up[x] to paradise.[y] He heard inexpressible things, things that man is not permitted to tell. [5]I will boast about a man like that, but I will not boast about myself, except about my weaknesses.[z] [6]Even if I should choose to boast,[a] I would not be a fool,[b] because I would be speaking the truth. But I refrain, so no one will think more of me than is warranted by what I do or say.

[7]To keep me from becoming conceited because of these surpassingly great revelations,[c] there was given me a thorn in my flesh,[d] a messenger of Satan,[e] to torment me. [8]Three times I pleaded with the Lord to take it away from me.[f] [9]But he said to me, "My grace[g] is sufficient for you, for my power[h] is made perfect in weakness."[i] Therefore I will boast all the more gladly about my weaknesses, so that Christ's power may rest on me. [10]That is why, for Christ's sake, I delight[k] in weaknesses, in insults, in hardships,[l] in persecutions,[m] in difficulties. For when I am weak, then I am strong.[n]

Paul's Concern for the Corinthians

[11]I have made a fool of myself,[o] but you drove me to it. I ought to have been commended by you, for I am not in the least inferior to the "super-apostles,"[p] even though I am nothing.[q] [12]The things that

Cross references

11:27 [h]1Co 4:11, 12; 2Co 6:5
11:28 [i]S 1Co 7:17
11:29 [j]S Ro 14:1; S 1Co 2:3 [k]S Mt 5:29
11:30 [l]ver 16; Gal 6:14; 2Co 12:5,9 [m]S 1Co 2:3
11:31 [n]Ro 1:25; 9:5 [o]ver 11; S Ro 1:9
11:32 [p]Ac 9:24
11:33 [q]Ac 9:25
12:1 [r]ver 5,9; 2Co 11:16,30 [s]ver 7; S 1Co 2:10
12:2 [t]S Ro 16:3 [u]ver 4; S Ac 8:39 [v]Eph 4:10 [w]2Co 11:11
12:4 [x]ver 2 [y]Lk 23:43; Rev 2:7
12:5 [z]ver 9,10; S 1Co 2:3
12:6 [a]2Co 10:8 [b]ver 11; 2Co 11:16
12:7 [c]ver 1; S 1Co 2:10 [d]Nu 33:55 [e]S Mt 4:10
12:8 [f]Mt 26:39, 44
12:9 [g]S Ro 3:24 [h]S Php 4:13 [i]S 1Co 2:3 [j]1Ki 19:12
12:10 [k]S Mt 5:12 [l]2Co 6:4 [m]2Th 1:4 [n]2Co 13:4
12:11 [o]2Co 11:1 [p]2Co 11:5
[q]1Co 15:9,10

Study notes

11:29 So closely did Paul identify himself with them that he felt the weakness of any member who was weak. If anyone was led into sin, he not only burned with indignation against the person responsible but also experienced the shame of the offense and longed for the restoration of the one who had stumbled.

11:30 *I will boast of the things that show my weakness.* His weakness opens the way for him to experience the superabundant strength of God's grace. Therefore his boasting in its entirety, unlike that of the false apostles, is not in what he has done but in what God has done.

11:32 *King Aretas.* Aretas IV, father-in-law of Herod Antipas, ruled over the Nabatean Arabs from c. 9 B.C. to A.D. 40. The Roman emperor Caligula may have given Damascus to Aretas since it was once part of his territory.

12:1 *visions and revelations.* If his adversaries falsely claimed to have received their teaching directly from God through visions and revelations, Paul could claim that this was truly so in his case. But he mentions this here to show that the supreme height to which he was raised through these ecstatic experiences was counterbalanced by the humbling depth of a particular affliction he was given to bear (see v. 7), so that he should continue to glory not in self but only in the "God of all grace" (1Pe 5:10).

12:2–4 *caught up to the third heaven . . . caught up to paradise.* Paul is sure of this remarkable experience, but he is unsure whether this rapture (being "caught up") was one that included the body or one that took place in separation from the body. The third heaven designates a place beyond the immediate heaven of the earth's atmosphere and beyond the further heaven of outer space and its constellations into the presence of God himself. Thus the risen and glorified Lord is said to have passed "through the heavens" (Heb

4:14), and now, having "ascended higher than all the heavens" (Eph 4:10), to be "exalted above the heavens" (Heb 7:26). The term "paradise" is synonymous with the third heaven, where those believers who have died are even now "at home with the Lord" (5:8; cf. "with Christ," Php 1:23). The nature of the inexpressible things that Paul heard remains unknown to us because this is something Paul was not permitted to tell. It was an experience that must have given incalculable strength to his apostleship, which involved him in such constant and extreme suffering. Moreover, as this experience was not self-induced, it afforded him no room for self-glorification (vv. 5–6).

12:5 *I will boast about a man like that.* Some believe that the man "caught up to the third heaven" (v. 2) was not Paul and that Paul here insists that he will not boast about such a glorious experience but only about his weakness.

12:7 *thorn in my flesh.* The precise nature of this severe affliction remains unknown. *messenger of Satan.* A further description of Paul's thorn (cf. 1Co 5:5; 11:30; 1Ti 1:20; see Job 2:10).

12:9 *My grace is sufficient for you.* A better solution than to remove Paul's thorn. Human weakness provides the ideal opportunity for the display of divine power.

12:10 Cf. Eph 3:16; Php 4:13.

12:11 *made a fool of myself.* See note on 11:1. *you drove me to it.* The Corinthian Christians have put Paul under pressure to write about himself as he did because they had accepted the claims of the "super-apostles" who had invaded their ranks, challenging Paul's apostolic authority.

12:12 *things that mark an apostle.* Extraordinary gifts and powers had been displayed in their midst. By implication, the false teachers had come to them without these apostolic signs (cf. Heb 2:3–4).

mark an apostle—signs, wonders and miracles[r]—were done among you with great perseverance. [13]How were you inferior to the other churches, except that I was never a burden to you?[s] Forgive me this wrong![t]

[14]Now I am ready to visit you for the third time,[u] and I will not be a burden to you, because what I want is not your possessions but you. After all, children should not have to save up for their parents,[v] but parents for their children.[w] [15]So I will very gladly spend for you everything I have and expend myself as well.[x] If I love you more,[y] will you love me less? [16]Be that as it may, I have not been a burden to you.[z] Yet, crafty fellow that I am, I caught you by trickery! [17]Did I exploit you through any of the men I sent you? [18]I urged[a] Titus[b] to go to you and I sent our brother[c] with him. Titus did not exploit you, did he? Did we not act in the same spirit and follow the same course?

[19]Have you been thinking all along that we have been defending ourselves to you? We have been speaking in the sight of God[d] as those in Christ; and everything we do, dear friends,[e] is for your strengthening.[f] [20]For I am afraid that when I come[g] I may not find you as I want you to be, and you may not find me as you want me to be.[h] I fear that there may be quarreling,[i] jealousy, outbursts of anger, factions,[j] slander,[k] gossip,[l] arrogance[m] and

disorder.[n] [21]I am afraid that when I come again my God will humble me before you, and I will be grieved[o] over many who have sinned earlier[p] and have not repented of the impurity, sexual sin and debauchery[q] in which they have indulged.

Final Warnings

13 This will be my third visit to you.[r] "Every matter must be established by the testimony of two or three witnesses."[r s] [2]I already gave you a warning when I was with you the second time. I now repeat it while absent:[t] On my return I will not spare[u] those who sinned earlier[v] or any of the others, [3]since you are demanding proof that Christ is speaking through me.[w] He is not weak in dealing with you, but is powerful among you. [4]For to be sure, he was crucified in weakness,[x] yet he lives by God's power.[y] Likewise, we are weak[z] in him, yet by God's power we will live with him[a] to serve you.

[5]Examine yourselves[b] to see whether you are in the faith; test yourselves.[c] Do you not realize that Christ Jesus is in you[d]—unless, of course, you fail the test? [6]And I trust that you will discover that we have not failed the test. [7]Now we pray to God that you will not do anything wrong. Not that people will see that we have

Cross references (center column)

12:12 [r]S Jn 4:48; sver 14;
12:13 1Co 9:12,18
t2Co 11:7
12:14 u2Co 13:1
v1Co 4:14,15
wPr 19:14
12:15 xPhp 2:17; 1Th 2:8
y2Co 11:11
12:16 z2Co 11:9
12:18 a2Co 8:6, 16 bS 2Co 2:13
c2Co 8:18
12:19 dRo 9:1
eS 1Co 10:14
fS Ro 14:19;
2Co 10:8
12:20 g2Co 2:1-4
h1Co 4:21
i1Co 1:11; 3:3
jGal 5:20
kRo 1:30
lS Ro 1:29
m1Co 4:18

n1Co 14:33
12:21 o2Co 2:1,4
p2Co 13:2
qS 1Co 6:18
13:1 r2Co 12:14
sDt 19:15;
S Mt 18:16
13:2 tver 10
u2Co 1:23
v2Co 12:21
13:3 wMt 10:20;
1Co 5:4
13:4 x1Co 1:25;
Php 2:7,8;
1Pe 3:18 yRo 1:4;
6:4; 1Co 6:14
zver 9; S 1Co 2:3
aS Ro 6:5
13:5 b1Co 11:28
cLa 3:40; Jn 6:6
dS Ro 8:10

r l Deut. 19:15

12:13 *I was never a burden to you.* See note on 11:9. Paul's refusal to accept any payment when preaching the gospel to the Corinthians had been slanderously twisted by his adversaries (see notes on 11:7,11). They, who had grasped at all they could get, were saying that it was he who had sinned against the Corinthians. *Forgive me this wrong!* Irony—resuming the line of discussion in 11:7–12.
12:14 *third time.* See note on 2:1. *not be a burden.* Chiefly now, so that the falsity and greed of the "super-apostles" may be clearly exposed (see 11:12). *children.* Paul is their spiritual father (cf. 6:13).
12:15 His paternal devotion to them is shown not merely in his readiness to spend whatever money he has for them but, much more deeply, in his joyful willingness to spend himself completely for their sake.
12:16 *I caught you by trickery!* Sarcastically echoes another of the slanders being made against Paul by the false apostles: that he was exploiting them by the trick of organizing a collection for the poverty-stricken Christians in Jerusalem—contributions that would never reach the mother-city because they went into Paul's own pocket (v. 17). No wonder, then, that he could afford not to be a burden to them! The fact is, however, that it is these false apostles who are the "deceitful workmen" masquerading as "servants of righteousness" (11:13–14). Paul is unblemished both in conduct and in conscience, and the Corinthians are fully aware of this.
12:18 *Titus . . . our brother.* See notes on 8:6,16,18–23.
12:19 *speaking in the sight of God . . . in Christ.* Paul's

concern in speaking of himself is not for his own personal prestige and reputation before people (cf. 1Co 4:3–4). It is before God that he stands, and his standing before God is in Christ. Far from being self-centered, his concern is for the Corinthians, his dear friends—for their strengthening as they too stand before God in Christ. His entire ministry, with its sufferings, is directed to this end (cf. 10:8).
13:2 *I will not spare . . . any.* Paul will not hesitate to take stern disciplinary action against offenders when he comes to Corinth for the third time, as he is about to do.
13:3 *demanding proof that Christ is speaking through me.* See note on 10:10. They will be given ample proof when he comes, unless they show a change of heart. *He is not weak.* Rebellion against Paul is rebellion against Christ, who appointed him as his apostle. The authority of the apostle is the authority of his Master. Any who imagine that Paul is weak will find that Christ, the Lord who speaks through his apostle, is not weak but powerful.
13:4 *by God's power we will live with him.* Paul is referring to his present apostolic authority, and to the fact that divine power will be displayed by the punishment of any who resist that authority.
13:5 *Examine yourselves . . . test yourselves.* Instead of demanding proof that Christ was speaking through him (v. 3), as the false apostles were inciting them to do, they should look into their own hearts.
13:7 *do what is right.* Then there will be no need for Paul to give evidence of his authority by taking disciplinary action when he comes to them.

stood the test but that you will do what is right even though we may seem to have failed. [8]For we cannot do anything against the truth, but only for the truth. [9]We are glad whenever we are weak[e] but you are strong;[f] and our prayer is for your perfection.[g] [10]This is why I write these things when I am absent, that when I come I may not have to be harsh[h] in my use of authority—the authority the Lord gave me for building you up, not for tearing you down.[i]

13:9 [e]S 1Co 2:3 [f]2Co 4:12 [g]ver 11; Eph 4:13
13:10 [h]S 2Co 1:23 [i]2Co 10:8
13:11 [j]1Th 4:1; 2Th 3:1 [k]S Mk 9:50 [l]1Jn 4:16 [m]S Ro 15:33; Eph 6:23
13:12 [n]S Ro 16:16
13:13 [o]Php 4:22
13:14 [p]S Ro 16:20; 2Co 8:9 [q]Ro 5:5; Jude 21 [r]Php 2:1

Final Greetings

[11]Finally, brothers,[j] good-by. Aim for perfection, listen to my appeal, be of one mind, live in peace.[k] And the God of love[l] and peace[m] will be with you. [12]Greet one another with a holy kiss.[n] [13]All the saints send their greetings.[o]

[14]May the grace of the Lord Jesus Christ,[p] and the love of God,[q] and the fellowship of the Holy Spirit[r] be with you all.

13:8 *we cannot do anything against the truth.* Paul can exercise his apostolic authority only in a way that supports the truth. Consequently, if the truth is acknowledged when he arrives in Corinth, there will be no need for him to take disciplinary action.

13:9 *weak.* To have no need to give proof of his apostolic strength. *strong.* In the truth.

13:11–14 These concluding exhortations and salutations exhibit a note of confidence.

13:11 *God of . . . peace.* See note on 1Th 5:23.

13:12 *kiss.* A token of mutual trust and affection, still in common use in the Near East—corresponding to the handshake of the Western world. For Christians it must be a holy kiss, for all greetings should be purely and sincerely exchanged in Christ (see 1:2).

13:14 The benediction is Trinitarian in form and has ever since been a part of Christian worship tradition. It serves to remind us that the mystery of the Holy Trinity is known to be true not through rational or philosophical explanation but through Christian experience, whereby the believer knows firsthand the grace, the love, and the fellowship that freely flow to him from the three Persons of the one Lord God.

GALATIANS

Author

The opening verse identifies the author of Galatians as the apostle Paul. Apart from a few 19th-century scholars, no one has seriously questioned his authorship.

Date and Destination

The date of Galatians depends to a great extent on the destination of the letter. There are two main views:

1. *The North Galatian theory.* This older view holds that the letter was addressed to churches located in north-central Asia Minor (Pessinus, Ancyra and Tavium), where the Gauls had settled when they invaded the area in the third century B.C. It is held that Paul visited this area on his second missionary journey, though Acts contains no reference to such a visit. Galatians, it is maintained, was written between A.D. 53 and 57 from Ephesus or Macedonia.

2. *The South Galatian theory.* According to this view, Galatians was written to churches in the southern area of the Roman province of Galatia (Antioch, Iconium, Lystra and Derbe) that Paul had founded on his first missionary journey. Some believe that Galatians was written from Syrian Antioch in 48-49 after Paul's first journey and before the Jerusalem council meeting (Ac 15). Others say that Galatians was written in Syrian Antioch or Corinth between 51 and 53.

Occasion and Purpose

Judaizers were Jewish Christians who believed, among other things, that a number of the ceremonial practices of the OT were still binding on the NT church. Following Paul's successful campaign in Galatia, they insisted that Gentile converts to Christianity abide by certain OT rites, especially circumcision. They may have been motivated by a desire to avoid the persecution of Zealot Jews who objected to their fraternizing with Gentiles (see 6:12). The Judaizers argued that Paul was not an authentic apostle and that out of a desire to make the message more appealing to Gentiles he had removed from the gospel certain legal requirements.

Paul responded by clearly establishing his apostolic authority and thereby substantiating the gospel he preached. By introducing additional requirements for justification (e.g., works of the law) his adversaries had perverted the gospel of grace and, unless prevented, would bring Paul's converts into the bondage of legalism. It is by grace through faith alone that man is justified, and it is by faith alone that he is to live out his new life in the freedom of the Spirit.

Theological Teaching

Galatians stands as an eloquent and vigorous apologetic for the essential NT truth that man is justified by faith in Jesus Christ—by nothing less and nothing more—and that he is sanctified not by legalistic works but by the obedience that comes from faith in God's work for him, in him and through him by the grace and power of Christ and the Holy Spirit. It was the rediscovery of the basic message of Galatians that brought about the Reformation. Galatians is often referred to as "Luther's book," because Martin Luther relied so strongly on this letter in his writings and arguments against the prevailing theology of his day. A key verse is 2:16 (see note there).

Outline

I. Introduction (1:1-9)
    A. Salutation (1:1-5)
    B. Denunciation (1:6-9)

1 Paul, an apostle[a]—sent not from men nor by man,[b] but by Jesus Christ[c] and God the Father,[d] who raised him from the dead[e]— 2and all the brothers with me,[f]

To the churches in Galatia:[g]

3Grace and peace to you from God our Father and the Lord Jesus Christ,[h] 4who gave himself for our sins[i] to rescue us from the present evil age,[j] according to the will of our God and Father,[k] 5to whom be glory for ever and ever. Amen.[l]

No Other Gospel

6I am astonished that you are so quickly deserting the one who called[m] you by the grace of Christ and are turning to a different gospel[n]— 7which is really no gospel at all. Evidently some people are throwing you into confusion[o] and are trying to pervert[p] the gospel of Christ. 8But even if we or an angel from heaven should preach a gospel other than the one we preached to you,[q] let him be eternally condemned![r] 9As we have already said, so now I say again: If anybody is preaching to you a gospel other than what you accepted,[s] let him be eternally condemned!

10Am I now trying to win the approval of men, or of God? Or am I trying to please men?[t] If I were still trying to please men, I would not be a servant of Christ.

Paul Called by God

11I want you to know, brothers,[u] that the gospel I preached[v] is not something that man made up. 12I did not receive it from any man,[w] nor was I taught it; rather, I received it by revelation[x] from Jesus Christ.[y]

13For you have heard of my previous way of life in Judaism,[z] how intensely I persecuted the church of God[a] and tried to destroy it.[b] 14I was advancing in Judaism beyond many Jews of my own age and was extremely zealous[c] for the traditions of my fathers.[d] 15But when God, who set me apart from birth[a][e] and called me[f] by his grace, was pleased 16to reveal his Son in me so that I might preach him among the Gentiles,[g] I did not consult any man,[h] 17nor did I go up to Jerusalem to see those who were apostles before I was, but I went immediately into Arabia and later returned to Damascus.[i]

18Then after three years,[j] I went up to

Cross references

1:1 aS 1Co 1:1
bver 11,12 cver 15,16; S Ac 9:15; 20:24 dver 15,16; S Ac 9:15; 20:24
eS Ac 2:24
1:2 fPhp 4:21
gS Ac 16:6
1:3 hS Ro 1:7
1:4 iS Mt 20:28; S Ro 4:25; S 1Co 15:3; Gal 2:20
jS 1Co 1:20
kS Php 4:20
1:5 lS Ro 11:36
1:6 mver 15; S Ro 8:28
n2Co 11:4
1:7 oAc 15:24; Gal 5:10
pJer 23:16,36
1:8 qver 11,16; 1Co 15:1; 2Co 11:4; Gal 2:2
rRo 9:3
1:9 sRo 16:17

1:10 tS Ro 2:29
1:11 uS 1Co 15:1
vS ver 8
1:12 wver 1 xver 16; S 1Co 2:10
y1Co 11:23; 15:3
1:13 zAc 26:4,5
aS 1Co 10:32
bS Ac 8:3
1:14 cS Ac 21:20
dMt 15:2
1:15 eIsa 49:1,5; Jer 1:5
fS Ac 9:15; S Ro 8:28
1:16 gS Ac 9:15; Gal 2:9
hMt 16:17

1:17 iAc 9:2,19-22 1:18 jAc 9:22,23

a 15 Or from my mother's womb

1:1 *Paul.* Writers of this time customarily put their names at the beginning of letters. For more information on Paul see notes on Ac 9:1; Php 3:4–14. *apostle.* One sent on a mission with full authority of representation; an ambassador (see note on 1Co 1:1). *raised him from the dead.* The resurrection is the central affirmation of the Christian faith (see Ac 17:18; Ro 1:4; 1Co 15:20; 1Pe 1:3), and because Paul had seen the risen Christ he was qualified to be an apostle (see Ac 1:22 and note; 2:32; 1Co 15:8).
1:2 *brothers.* Fellow Christians (see 3:15; 4:12; 5:11; 6:18). *churches.* This was a circular letter to several congregations. *Galatia.* The term occurs three times in the NT. In 2Ti 4:10 the reference is uncertain. In 1Pe 1:1 it refers to the northern area of Asia Minor occupied by the Gauls. Here Paul probably uses the term to refer to the Roman province of Galatia and an additional area to the south, through which he traveled on his first missionary journey (Ac 13:14–14:23).
1:3 *Grace.* The Christian adaptation of a common Greek form of greeting (see notes on Jnh 4:2; Eph 1:2). *peace.* The common Hebrew form of greeting (see notes on Jn 14:27; 20:19; Eph 1:2).
1:4 *for our sins.* See Mt 1:21; Jn 1:29; 1Co 15:3; 1Pe 2:24. *present evil age.* The present period of the world's history (see note on 2Co 4:4). In contrast to the age to come (the climax of the Messianic age), this present age is characterized by wickedness (Eph 2:2; 6:12).
1:5 For other doxologies see Ro 9:5; 11:36; 16:27; Eph 3:21; 1Ti 1:17.
1:6 *so quickly.* So soon after your conversion. *one who called you.* God. *grace of Christ.* The test of a pure, unadulterated gospel.
1:7 *some people.* The Judaizers (see Introduction: Occasion and Purpose).
1:8 *eternally condemned.* The Greek word (*anathema*) originally referred to a pagan temple offering in payment for

a vow. Later it came to represent a curse (see v. 9; 1Co 12:3; 16:22; Ro 9:3).
1:10 *servant of Christ.* Paul once wore the "yoke of slavery" (5:1) but, having been set free from sin by the redemption that is in Christ, he became a slave of righteousness, a slave of God (see Ro 6:18,22).
1:11 *I want you to know, brothers.* A phrase found also in 1Co 15:1, where Paul sets forth the gospel he received. *the gospel I preached.* Called "my gospel" in Ro 2:16; 16:25. Salvation is for all and is received by faith in Christ.
1:12 *received it by revelation.* See Eph 3:2–6.
1:13 *Judaism.* The Jewish faith and way of life that developed from Judah, the southern kingdom that came to an end in the sixth century B.C. with the exile into Babylonia. *church of God.* The NT counterpart of the OT assembly (see Nu 16:21) or community of the Lord (Nu 20:4).
1:14 *zealous.* See Php 3:6. *traditions of my fathers.* Traditions orally transmitted from previous generations and contrasted with the written law of Moses. Cf. the "tradition of the elders" (see note on Mt 15:2).
1:15 *set me apart from birth.* See Isa 49:1; Jer 1:5; Ro 1:1.
1:16 *Gentiles.* Lit. "nations" or "peoples." The term commonly designated foreigners—hence pagans, or the non-Jewish world. *any man.* Lit. "flesh and blood"—in the NT always with the implication of human weakness or ignorance (see Mt 16:17; 1Co 15:50; Eph 6:12). Paul received his message from God.
1:17 *Jerusalem.* The religious center of Judaism and the birthplace of Christianity. *Arabia.* The Nabatean kingdom in Transjordan stretching from Damascus southwest to the Suez. *Damascus.* Ancient capital of Syria (Aram in the OT). Paul had been converted en route from Jerusalem to Damascus (Ac 9:1–9).

Jerusalem[k] to get acquainted with Peter[b] and stayed with him fifteen days. [19]I saw none of the other apostles—only James, [l] the Lord's brother. [20]I assure you before God[m] that what I am writing you is no lie. [n] [21]Later I went to Syria[o] and Cilicia. [p] [22]I was personally unknown to the churches of Judea[q] that are in Christ.[r] [23]They only heard the report: "The man who formerly persecuted us is now preaching the faith[s] he once tried to destroy." [t] [24]And they praised God[u] because of me.

Paul Accepted by the Apostles

2 Fourteen years later I went up again to Jerusalem, [v] this time with Barnabas. [w] I took Titus[x] along also. [2]I went in response to a revelation[y] and set before them the gospel that I preach among the Gentiles. [z] But I did this privately to those who seemed to be leaders, for fear that I was running or had run my race[a] in vain. [3]Yet not even Titus, [b] who was with me, was compelled to be circumcised, even though he was a Greek. [c] [4]This matter arose, because some false brothers[d] had infiltrated our ranks to spy on[e] the freedom[f] we have in Christ Jesus and to make us slaves. [5]We did not give in to them for a moment, so that the truth of the gospel[g] might remain with you.

[6]As for those who seemed to be important[h]—whatever they were makes no dif-

ference to me; God does not judge by external appearance[i]—those men added nothing to my message.[j] [7]On the contrary, they saw that I had been entrusted with the task[k] of preaching the gospel to the Gentiles,[c] just as Peter[m] had been to the Jews. [d] [8]For God, who was at work in the ministry of Peter as an apostle[n] to the Jews, was also at work in my ministry as an apostle[o] to the Gentiles. [9]James, [p] Peter[q] and John, those reputed to be pillars, [r] gave me and Barnabas[s] the right hand of fellowship when they recognized the grace given to me. [t] They agreed that we should go to the Gentiles, [u] and they to the Jews. [10]All they asked was that we should continue to remember the poor, [v] the very thing I was eager to do.

Paul Opposes Peter

[11]When Peter[w] came to Antioch, [x] I opposed him to his face, because he was clearly in the wrong. [12]Before certain men came from James, [y] he used to eat with the Gentiles. [z] But when they arrived, he began to draw back and separate himself from the Gentiles because he was afraid of those who belonged to the circumcision group. [a] [13]The other Jews joined him in his hypocrisy, so that by their hypocrisy even Barnabas[b] was led astray.

b 18 Greek Cephas   c 7 Greek uncircumcised
d 7 Greek circumcised; also in verses 8 and 9
e 9 Greek Cephas; also in verses 11 and 14

1:18 kAc 9:26,27
1:19 lMt 13:55;
S Ac 15:13
1:20 mS Ro 1:9
nS Ro 9:1
1:21 oS Lk 2:2
pS Ac 6:9
1:22 q1Th 2:14
rS Ro 16:3
1:23 sAc 6:7
tS Ac 8:3
1:24 uS Mt 9:8
2:1 vAc 15:2
wS Ac 4:36
xS 2Co 2:13
2:2 yS 1Co 2:10
zAc 15:4,12
aS 1Co 9:24
2:3 bver 1;
S 2Co 2:13
cAc 16:3;
1Co 9:21
2:4 dS Ac 1:16;
2Co 11:26 eJude
4 fGal 5:1,13
2:5 gver 14
2:6 hver 2

lS Ac 10:34;
S Rev 2:23
l1Co 15:11
2:7 k1Th 2:4;
1Ti 1:11
lS Ac 9:15 mver
9,11,14
2:8 nAc 1:25
oS 1Co 1:1
2:9 pS Ac 15:13
qver 7,11,14
r1Ti 3:15;
Rev 3:12 sver 1;
S Ac 4:36
tS Ro 12:3
uS Ac 9:15
2:10 vS Ac 24:17
2:11 wver 7,9,14
xS Ac 11:19
2:12 yS Ac 15:13
zAc 11:3
aAc 10:45; 11:2
2:13 bver 1;
S Ac 4:36

1:18 after three years. From the time of his departure into Arabia. The text does not say he spent the three years in Arabia. I went up to Jerusalem. Probably the visit referred to in Ac 9:26-30, though some equate it with the one in Ac 11:30. Peter. Or Cephas (see NIV text note), from the Aramaic word for "stone" (see Mt 16:18 and note). The name designates a like quality in the bearer (see note on Jn 1:42).

1:19 James. See Introduction to James: Author. In Ac 21:18 this James appears to be the leader of the elders in the Jerusalem church. the Lord's brother. See note on Lk 8:19.

1:21 Syria and Cilicia. Provinces in Asia Minor. Specifically Paul went to Tarsus (see Ac 9:30), his hometown.

2:1 Fourteen years later. Probably from the date of Paul's conversion. I went up again to Jerusalem. According to some, the visit mentioned in Ac 11:30; according to others, the one in Ac 15:1-4 (see notes on Ac 12:1; 15:2). Barnabas. Means "one who encourages." His given name was Joseph, and he was a Levite from the island of Cyprus (see Ac 4:36 and note). He was Paul's companion on the first missionary journey (Ac 13:1–14:28). Titus. A Gentile Christian who served as Paul's delegate to Corinth and later was left in Crete to oversee the church there (see Tit 1:5).

2:2 those who seemed to be leaders. Paul recognized their authority, and is probably referring to James, Peter and John (v. 9; cf. v. 6). had run my race in vain. See 1Co 15:58; Php 2:16.

2:4 false brothers. Judaizers who held that Gentile converts should be circumcised and obey the law of Moses (cf.

Ac 15:5; 2Co 11:26). to spy on. Used in the Septuagint (the Greek translation of the OT) in 2Sa 10:3 and 1Ch 19:3 of spying out a territory. freedom. See 5:1,13; Ro 6:18,20,22; 8:2. "Free" and "freedom" are key words in Galatians, occurring 11 times (here; 3:28; 4:22–23,26,30–31; 5:1, 13).

2:6 those who seemed to be important. See note on v. 2. judge by external appearance. Cf. Dt 10:17; 1Sa 16:7; Lk 20:21; Jas 2:1.

2:7 to the Gentiles. Paul's ministry was not exclusively to the Gentiles. In fact, he regularly went first to the synagogue when arriving in a new location (see note on Ac 13:14). He did, however, consider himself to be foremost an apostle to the Gentiles (see Ro 11:13 and note).

2:9 James. See note on 1:19. pillars. A common metaphor for those who represent and strongly support an institution. right hand of fellowship. A common practice among both Hebrews and Greeks, indicating a pledge of friendship.

2:11 Antioch. The leading city of Syria and third leading city of the Roman empire (after Rome and Alexandria). From it Paul had been sent out on his missionary journeys (see Ac 13:1–3; 14:26). in the wrong. For yielding to the pressure of the circumcision party (the Judaizers), thus going against what he knew to be right.

2:12 circumcision group. Judaizers, who believed that circumcision was necessary for salvation (cf. Ac 10:45; 11:2; Ro 4:12).

2:13 other Jews. Jewish Christians not associated with the circumcision party but whom Peter's behavior had led astray.

[14]When I saw that they were not acting in line with the truth of the gospel, [c] I said to Peter[d] in front of them all, "You are a Jew, yet you live like a Gentile and not like a Jew.[e] How is it, then, that you force Gentiles to follow Jewish customs?[f]

[15]"We who are Jews by birth[g] and not 'Gentile sinners'[h] [16]know that a man is not justified by observing the law,[i] but by faith in Jesus Christ.[j] So we, too, have put our faith in Christ Jesus that we may be justified by faith in Christ and not by observing the law, because by observing the law no one will be justified.[k]

[17]"If, while we seek to be justified in Christ, it becomes evident that we ourselves are sinners,[l] does that mean that Christ promotes sin? Absolutely not! [m] [18]If I rebuild what I destroyed, I prove that I am a lawbreaker. [19]For through the law I died to the law[n] so that I might live for God. [o] [20]I have been crucified with Christ[p] and I no longer live, but Christ lives in me. [q] The life I live in the body, I live by faith in the Son of God,[r] who loved me[s] and gave himself for me. [t] [21]I do not set aside the grace of God, for if righteousness could be gained through the law,[u] Christ died for nothing!"[f]

Faith or Observance of the Law

3 You foolish[v] Galatians! [w] Who has bewitched you?[x] Before your very eyes Jesus Christ was clearly portrayed as crucified.[y] [2]I would like to learn just one thing from you: Did you receive the Spirit[z] by observing the law,[a] or by believing what you heard?[b] [3]Are you so foolish? After beginning with the Spirit, are you now trying to attain your goal by human effort? [4]Have you suffered so much for nothing—if it really was for nothing? [5]Does God give you his Spirit and work miracles[c] among you because you observe the law, or because you believe what you heard? [d]

[6]Consider Abraham: "He believed God, and it was credited to him as righteousness."[g][e] [7]Understand, then, that those who believe[f] are children of Abraham.[g] [8]The Scripture foresaw that God would justify the Gentiles by faith, and announced the gospel in advance to Abraham: "All nations will be blessed through you."[h][h] [9]So those who have faith[i] are blessed along with Abraham, the man of faith.[j]

[10]All who rely on observing the law[k] are under a curse,[l] for it is written: "Cursed is everyone who does not continue to do everything written in the Book of the Law."[i][m] [11]Clearly no one is justified before God by the law,[n] because, "The righteous will live by faith."[j][o] [12]The law is not based on faith; on the contrary, "The man who does these things will live by them."[k][p] [13]Christ redeemed us from

Cross references

2:14 [c]ver 5 [d]ver 7,9,11 [e]Ac 10:28 [f]ver 12
2:15 [g]Php 3:4,5 [h]1Sa 15:18; Lk 24:7
2:16 [i]S Ro 3:28 [j]S Ro 9:30 [k]S Ro 3:28; S 4:25
2:17 [l]ver 15 [m]Gal 3:21
2:19 [n]S Ro 7:4 [o]Ro 6:10,11,14; 2Co 5:15
2:20 [p]S Ro 6:6 [q]S Ro 8:10; 1Pe 4:2 [r]S Mt 4:3 S 8:37 [s]Gal 1:4
2:21 [u]Gal 3:21
3:1 [v]Lk 24:25 [w]S Ac 16:6 [x]Gal 5:7 [y]1Co 1:23

3:2 [z]S Jn 20:22 [a]ver 5,10; Gal 2:16 [b]Ro 10:17; Heb 4:2
3:5 [c]1Co 12:10 [d]ver 2,10; Gal 2:16
3:6 [e]Ge 15:6; S Ro 4:3
3:7 [f]ver 9 [g]S Lk 3:8
3:8 [h]Ge 12:3; 18:18; 22:18; 26:4; Ac 3:25
3:9 [i]ver 7; Ro 4:16 [j]Ro 4:18-22
3:10 [k]ver 2,5; Gal 2:16 [l]ver 13; S Ro 4:15 [m]Dt 27:26; Jer 11:3
3:11 [n]S Ro 3:28 [o]Hab 2:4; S Ro 9:30; Heb 10:38
3:12 [p]Lev 18:5; S Ro 10:5

[f]21 Some interpreters end the quotation after verse 14. [g]6 Gen. 15:6 [h]8 Gen. 12:3; 18:18; 22:18 [i]10 Deut. 27:26 [j]11 Hab. 2:4 [k]12 Lev. 18:5

Study notes

2:14 *you live like a Gentile.* You do not observe Jewish customs, especially dietary restrictions (see v. 12).

2:16 A key verse in Galatians (see Introduction: Theological Teaching). Three times it tells us that no one is justified by observing the law, and three times it underscores the indispensable requirement of placing one's faith in Christ. *by observing the law.* Paul is not depreciating the law itself, for he clearly maintained that God's law is "holy, righteous and good" (Ro 7:12). He is arguing against an illegitimate use of the OT law that made the observance of that law the grounds of acceptance with God. *justified by faith.* The essence of the gospel message (see Ro 3:20,28; Php 3:9; see also notes on Ro 3:24,28). Faith is the means by which justification is received, not its basis.

2:19 *I died to the law.* See v. 20; see also note on Ro 7:4.

2:20 *crucified with Christ.* See 5:24; 6:14; Ro 6:8–10; 7:6; see also note on Ro 6:7. *gave himself for me.* See 1:4; 1Ti 2:6; Tit 2:14.

2:21 *Christ died for nothing.* To mingle legalism with grace distorts grace and makes a mockery of the cross.

3:1 *foolish.* They were not mentally deficient but simply failed to use their powers of perception (see Lk 24:25; Ro 1:14; 1Ti 6:9; Tit 3:3). *Who . . . ?* Obviously legalistic Judaizers. *portrayed as crucified.* See 1Co 1:23; 2:2. The verb means "to publicly portray or placard." Cf. the bronze snake that Moses displayed on a pole (Nu 21:9).

3:2 *the Spirit.* From this point on in Galatians Paul refers to the Holy Spirit 16 times.

3:3 *beginning with the Spirit . . . attain your goal.* Both salvation and sanctification are the work of the Holy Spirit. *human effort.* Lit. "the flesh," a reference to human nature in its unregenerate weakness. Trying to achieve righteousness by works, including circumcision, was a part of life in the "flesh."

3:4 Paul hopes that those who have been misled will return to the true gospel.

3:7 *children of Abraham.* Abraham was the physical and spiritual father of the Jewish race (see Jn 8:31,33,39,53; Ac 7:2; Ro 4:12). Here all believers (Jews and Gentiles) are called his spiritual children (see notes on Ro 4:11–12). They are also referred to as the "seed" or "descendants" of Abraham (v. 16; Heb 2:16).

3:8 *Scripture foresaw.* A personification of Scripture that calls attention to its divine origin (see 1Ti 5:18).

3:9 *Abraham, the man of faith.* Paul develops this theme at length in Ro 4; see also Heb 11:8–19.

3:10 *rely on observing the law.* The reference is to legalists—those who refuse God's offer of grace and insist on pursuing righteousness through works. *under a curse.* Because no one under the law ever perfectly kept the law. God's blessing has never been earned, but has always been freely given. *everything.* See Jas 2:10.

3:11 *will live.* Means here (and in v. 12) almost the same thing as "will be justified."

3:13 *Christ redeemed us from the curse of the law.* See 4:5; Ro 8:3. *tree.* Used in classical Greek of stocks and poles

the curse of the law*q* by becoming a curse for us, for it is written: "Cursed is everyone who is hung on a tree."*l r* 14He redeemed us in order that the blessing given to Abraham might come to the Gentiles through Christ Jesus,*s* so that by faith we might receive the promise of the Spirit.*t*

The Law and the Promise

15Brothers,*u* let me take an example from everyday life. Just as no one can set aside or add to a human covenant that has been duly established, so it is in this case. 16The promises were spoken to Abraham and to his seed.*v* The Scripture does not say "and to seeds," meaning many people, but "and to your seed,"*m w* meaning one person, who is Christ. 17What I mean is this: The law, introduced 430 years*x* later, does not set aside the covenant previously established by God and thus do away with the promise. 18For if the inheritance depends on the law, then it no longer depends on a promise;*y* but God in his grace gave it to Abraham through a promise.

19What, then, was the purpose of the law? It was added because of transgressions*z* until the Seed*a* to whom the promise referred had come. The law was put into effect through angels*b* by a mediator.*c* 20A mediator,*d* however, does not represent just one party; but God is one.

21Is the law, therefore, opposed to the

promises of God? Absolutely not!*e* For if a law had been given that could impart life, then righteousness would certainly have come by the law.*f* 22But the Scripture declares that the whole world is a prisoner of sin,*g* so that what was promised, being given through faith in Jesus Christ, might be given to those who believe.

23Before this faith came, we were held prisoners*h* by the law, locked up until faith should be revealed.*i* 24So the law was put in charge to lead us to Christ*n j* that we might be justified by faith.*k* 25Now that faith has come, we are no longer under the supervision of the law.*l*

Sons of God

26You are all sons of God*m* through faith in Christ Jesus, 27for all of you who were baptized into Christ*n* have clothed yourselves with Christ.*o* 28There is neither Jew nor Greek, slave nor free,*p* male nor female,*q* for you are all one in Christ Jesus.*r* 29If you belong to Christ,*s* then you are Abraham's seed,*t* and heirs*u* according to the promise.*v*

4 What I am saying is that as long as the heir is a child, he is no different from a slave, although he owns the whole estate. 2He is subject to guardians and trustees until the time set by his father. 3So also,

Cross references (center column)

3:13 *q*Gal 4:5
*r*Dt 21:23;
S Ac 5:30
3:14 *s*Ro 4:9,16
*t*ver 2; Joel 2:28;
S Jn 20:22;
S Ac 2:33
3:15 *u*S Ro 7:1
3:16 *v*Ge 17:19;
Ps 132:11;
Mic 7:20;
Lk 1:55; Ro 4:13,
16; 9:4,8;
Gal 3:29; 4:28
*w*Ge 12:7; 13:15;
17:7,8,10; 24:7
3:17 *x*Ge 15:13,
14; Ex 12:40;
Ac 7:6
3:18 *y*Ro 4:14
3:19 *z*Ro 5:20
*a*ver 16 *b*Dt 33:2;
Ac 7:53
*c*Ex 20:19; Dt 5:5
3:20 *d*1Ti 2:5;
Heb 8:6; 9:15;
12:24

3:21 *e*Gal 2:17;
S Ro 7:12
*f*Gal 2:21
3:22 *g*Ro 3:9-19;
11:32
3:23 *h*Ro 11:32
*i*ver 25
3:24 *j*ver 19;
Ro 10:4; S 4:15
*k*Gal 2:16
3:25 *l*S Ro 7:4
3:26 *m*S Ro 8:14
3:27 *n*S Mt 28:19
*o*S Ro 13:14
3:28 *p*1Co 12:13;
Col 3:11
*q*Ge 1:27; 5:2;
Joel 2:29
*r*Jn 10:16; 17:11;
Eph 2:14,15
3:29 *s*S 1Co 3:23
*t*ver 16; S Lk 3:8
*u*S Ro 8:17
*v*S Gal 3:16

l/3 Deut. 21:23   *m*/6 Gen. 12:7; 13:15; 24:7
*n*24 Or *charge until Christ came*

Footnotes (bottom)

on which bodies were impaled, here of the cross (see Ac 5:30; 10:39; 1Pe 2:24).
3:14 *the blessing given to Abraham.* See v. 8; Ro 4:1–5. *promise of the Spirit.* See Eze 36:26; 37:14; 39:29; Jn 14:16; cf. Eph 1:13.
3:15 *Brothers.* See note on 1:2. *human covenant.* The Greek word normally indicates a last will or testament, which is probably the legal instrument Paul is referring to here. But in the Septuagint (the Greek translation of the OT) it had been widely used of God's covenant with his people (see also Mt 26:28; Lk 1:72; Ac 3:25; 7:8; 2Co 3:14; Heb 8:9), so Paul's choice of analogy was apt for his purpose.
3:16 *promises.* See notes on Ro 4:13; 9:4.
3:17 *430 years.* See Ex 12:40–41. The period in Egypt is designated in round numbers as "400 years" in Ge 15:13; Ac 7:6.
3:19 *was added.* From the time of Abraham, the promise covenanted to him (Ge 12:2–3,7; 15:18–20; 17:4–8) had stood at the center of God's relationship with his people. After the exodus the law contained in the Sinaitic covenant (Ex 19–24) became an additional element in that relationship—what Jeremiah by implication called the "old covenant" when he brought God's promise of a "new covenant" (Jer 31:31–34). *the Seed.* Christ. *through angels.* See Dt 33:2; Ac 7:38,53; Heb 2:2.
3:20 The Mosaic covenant was a formal arrangement of mutual commitments between God and Israel, with Moses as the mediator. But since the promise God covenanted with Abraham involved commitment only from God's side (and God is one; see note on Dt 6:4), no mediator was involved.

3:21 The reason the law is not opposed to the promise is that, although in itself it cannot save, it serves to reveal sin, which alienates God from man, and to show the need for the salvation that the promise offers.
3:23 *this faith.* In Christ (v. 22). *held prisoners by the law.* To be a prisoner of sin (v. 22) and a prisoner of law amounts to much the same, because law reveals and stimulates sin (see 4:3; Ro 7:8; Col 2:20).
3:24 *was put in charge.* The expression translates the Greek *paidagogos* (from which "pedagogue" is derived). It refers to the personal slave-attendant who accompanied a freeborn boy wherever he went and exercised a certain amount of discipline over him. His function was more like that of a baby-sitter than a teacher (see 1Co 4:15, "guardians").
3:25–26 By adoption, the justified believer is a full adult and heir in God's family, with all the attendant rights and privileges (4:1–7; Ro 8:14–17).
3:27 *baptized into Christ.* See Ro 6:3–11; 1Co 12:13.
3:28 Unity in Christ transcends ethnic, social and sexual distinctions (see Ro 10:12; 1Co 12:13; Eph 2:15–16).
3:29 Christians are Abraham's true, spiritual descendants.
4:1 *child.* A minor. Contrast with "adults" in 1Co 14:20 ("mature" in Php 3:15).
4:2 *guardians.* A broader term than "[one] put in charge to lead us" in 3:24. See Mt 20:8 ("foreman"); Lk 8:3 ("manager").
4:3 *in slavery.* See note on 3:23. *basic principles.* The Greek term meant essentially "things placed side by side in a row" (as the ABCs) and then came to mean fundamental

when we were children, we were in slavery[w] under the basic principles of the world.[x] 4But when the time had fully come,[y] God sent his Son,[z] born of a woman,[a] born under law,[b] 5to redeem[c] those under law, that we might receive the full rights[d] of sons.[e] 6Because you are sons, God sent the Spirit of his Son[f] into our hearts,[g] the Spirit who calls out, "Abba,[o] Father."[h] 7So you are no longer a slave, but a son; and since you are a son, God has made you also an heir.[i]

Paul's Concern for the Galatians

8Formerly, when you did not know God,[j] you were slaves[k] to those who by nature are not gods.[l] 9But now that you know God—or rather are known by God[m]—how is it that you are turning back to those weak and miserable principles? Do you wish to be enslaved[n] by them all over again?[o] 10You are observing special days and months and seasons and years![p] 11I fear for you, that somehow I have wasted my efforts on you.[q]

12I plead with you, brothers,[r] become like me, for I became like you. You have done me no wrong. 13As you know, it was because of an illness[s] that I first preached the gospel to you. 14Even though my ill-

ness was a trial to you, you did not treat me with contempt or scorn. Instead, you welcomed me as if I were an angel of God, as if I were Christ Jesus himself.[t] 15What has happened to all your joy? I can testify that, if you could have done so, you would have torn out your eyes and given them to me. 16Have I now become your enemy by telling you the truth?[u]

17Those people are zealous to win you over, but for no good. What they want is to alienate you from us, so that you may be zealous for them.[v] 18It is fine to be zealous, provided the purpose is good, and to be so always and not just when I am with you.[w] 19My dear children,[x] for whom I am again in the pains of childbirth until Christ is formed in you,[y] 20how I wish I could be with you now and change my tone, because I am perplexed about you!

Hagar and Sarah

21Tell me, you who want to be under the law,[z] are you not aware of what the law says? 22For it is written that Abraham had two sons, one by the slave woman[a] and the other by the free woman.[b] 23His son by the slave woman was born in the ordinary way;[c] but his son by the free

4:3 wver 8,9,24, 25; Gal 2:4
xCol 2:8,20
4:4 yMk 1:15; Ro 5:6; Eph 1:10
zS Jn 3:17
aS Jn 1:14
bLk 2:27
4:5 cS Ro 3:24
dJn 1:12
eS Ro 8:14
4:6 fS Ac 16:7
gRo 5:5 hRo 8:15, 16
4:7 iS Ro 8:17
4:8 jRo 1:28; 1Co 1:21; 15:34; 1Th 4:5; 2Th 1:8
kS ver 3
l2Ch 13:9; Isa 37:19; Jer 2:11; 5:7; 16:20; 1Co 8:4,5
4:9 m1Co 8:3
nS ver 3
oCol 2:20
4:10 pRo 14:5; Col 2:16
4:11 q1Th 3:5
4:12 rS Ro 7:1; Gal 6:18
4:13 s1Co 2:3

4:14 tMt 10:40
4:16 uAm 5:10
4:17 vGal 2:4,12
4:18 wver 13,14
4:19 xS 1Th 2:11
yRo 8:29; Eph 4:13
4:21 zS Ro 2:12
4:22 aGe 16:15
bGe 21:2
4:23 cver 28,29; Ro 9:7,8

o6 Aramaic for Father

---

principles or basic elements of various kinds. The context here suggests that it refers to the elemental forms of religion, whether those of the Jews (under the law, v. 5) or those of the Gentiles (under their old religious bondage, v. 8). *of the world.* In the sense that these principles do not come from the "new creation" (6:15).
4:4 *time had fully come.* The time "set" (v. 2) by God for his children to become adult sons and heirs. *God sent his Son.* See Jn 1:14; 3:16; Ro 1:1–6; 1Jn 4:14. *born of a woman.* Showing that Christ was truly human. *born under law.* Subject to the Jewish law.
4:5 *full rights of sons.* Lit. "adoption [of a son]." See Ro 8:15, where the "Spirit of sonship" is contrasted with the "spirit of slavery" (cf. Eph 1:5). God takes into his family as fully recognized sons and heirs both Jews (those who had been under law) and Gentiles who believe in Christ.
4:6 *Spirit of his Son.* A new "guardian" (v. 2), identified as the "Spirit of God" in Ro 8:9 (see Eph 1:13–14). *calls out.* The Greek for this phrase is a vivid verb expressing deep emotion, often used of an inarticulate cry. In Mt 27:50 it is used of Jesus' final cry. *Abba, Father.* Expressive of an especially close relationship to God (see also NIV text note).
4:8 *when you did not know God.* See 1Co 12:2; 1Th 4:5. *are not gods.* When the Galatians were pagans, they thought that the beings they worshiped were gods; but when they became Christians, they learned better.
4:9 *turning back.* See 3:1–3. *weak and miserable principles.* See note on v. 3. *enslaved . . . again.* Legalistic trust in rituals, in moral achievement, in law, in good works, or even in cold, dead orthodoxy may indicate a relapse into second childhood on the part of those who should be knowing and enjoying the freedom of full-grown sons.
4:10 *special days.* Such as the Sabbath and the Day of Atonement (tenth day of Tishri; see Lev 16:29–34), which

had never been, and can never be, in themselves means of salvation or sanctification. *months and seasons.* Such as New Moons (see Nu 28:11–15; Isa 1:13–14), Passover (Ex 12:18) and Firstfruits (Lev 23:10). *years.* Such as the sabbath year (see Lev 25:4). The Pharisees meticulously observed all these to gain merit before God.
4:11 *wasted my efforts.* Due to their return to the old covenant law.
4:12 *brothers.* See note on 1:2.
4:13 *illness.* On the basis of v. 15; 6:11 some suggest it was eye trouble. Others have suggested malaria or epilepsy. *first preached.* When Paul visited Galatia on his first missionary journey (Ac 13:14–14:23).
4:14 *you welcomed me.* He implies that under the influence of Judaizers they have changed their attitude toward him.
4:15 *What has happened to all your joy?* Because of the restraints of legalistic Judaism they had lost their blessing and joy. *torn out your eyes.* A hyperbole indicating their willingness, for his benefit, to part with that which was most precious to them. See Mk 2:4, where the same verb is used of digging through a roof.
4:16 *your enemy.* Telling the truth sometimes results in loss of friends.
4:17 *Those people.* Judaizers (see 2:4,12).
4:19 *My dear children.* For Paul's affectionate relationship to his converts see Ac 20:37–38; Php 4:1; 1Th 2:7–8. The expression occurs only here in Paul's writings, but is common in John's (e.g., Jn 13:33; 1Jn 2:1; 3:7). *until Christ is formed in you.* The goal of Paul's ministry (see Ro 8:29; Eph 4:13,15; Col 1:27).
4:22 *two sons.* Ishmael was born to the slave woman, Hagar (Ge 16:1–16), and Isaac to the free woman, Sarah (Ge 21:2–5).

woman was born as the result of a promise. *d*

24These things may be taken figuratively, for the women represent two covenants. One covenant is from Mount Sinai and bears children who are to be slaves: This is Hagar. 25Now Hagar stands for Mount Sinai in Arabia and corresponds to the present city of Jerusalem, because she is in slavery with her children. 26But the Jerusalem that is above *e* is free, and she is our mother. 27For it is written:

"Be glad, O barren woman,
   who bears no children;
break forth and cry aloud,
   you who have no labor pains;
because more are the children of the
    desolate woman
than of her who has a husband." *p f*

28Now you, brothers, like Isaac, are children of promise. *g* 29At that time the son born in the ordinary way *h* persecuted the son born by the power of the Spirit. *i* It is the same now. 30But what does the Scripture say? "Get rid of the slave woman and her son, for the slave woman's son will never share in the inheritance with the free woman's son." *q j* 31Therefore, brothers, we are not children of the slave woman, *k* but of the free woman. *l*

Cross references (center column)

4:23 *d*Ge 17:16-21; 18:10-14; 21:1; Heb 11:11
4:26 *e*Heb 12:22; Rev 3:12; 21:2,10
4:27 *f*Isa 54:1
4:28 *g*ver 23; S Gal 3:16
4:29 *h*ver 23
*i*Ge 21:9
4:30 *j*Ge 21:10
4:31 *k*S Ro 7:4
*l*ver 22

5:1 *m*ver 13; Jn 8:32; Gal 2:4; S Ro 7:4
*n*S 1Co 10:13
*o*S Mt 23:4; Gal 2:4
5:2 *p*ver 3,6,11, 12; Ac 15:1
5:3 *q*Ro 2:25; Gal 3:10; Jas 2:10
5:4 *r*S Ro 3:28
*s*Heb 12:15; 2Pe 3:17
5:5 *t*Ro 8:23,24
5:6 *u*S Ro 16:3
*v*S 1Co 7:19
*w*1Th 1:3; Jas 2:22
5:7 *x*S 1Co 9:24
*y*Gal 3:1
5:8 *z*S Ro 8:28
5:9 *a*1Co 5:6
5:10 *b*S 2Co 2:3
*c*Php 3:15 *d*ver 12; Gal 1:7

Freedom in Christ

5 It is for freedom that Christ has set us free. *m* Stand firm, *n* then, and do not let yourselves be burdened again by a yoke of slavery. *o*

2Mark my words! I, Paul, tell you that if you let yourselves be circumcised, *p* Christ will be of no value to you at all. 3Again I declare to every man who lets himself be circumcised that he is obligated to obey the whole law. *q* 4You who are trying to be justified by law *r* have been alienated from Christ; you have fallen away from grace. *s* 5But by faith we eagerly await through the Spirit the righteousness for which we hope. *t* 6For in Christ Jesus *u* neither circumcision nor uncircumcision has any value. *v* The only thing that counts is faith expressing itself through love. *w*

7You were running a good race. *x* Who cut in on you *y* and kept you from obeying the truth? 8That kind of persuasion does not come from the one who calls you. *z* 9"A little yeast works through the whole batch of dough." *a* 10I am confident *b* in the Lord that you will take no other view. *c* The one who is throwing you into confusion *d* will pay the penalty, whoever he may be. 11Brothers, if I am still preach-

p27 Isaiah 54:1   *q30* Gen. 21:10

4:24 *may be taken figuratively.* The Sarah-Hagar account is not an allegory in the sense that it was nonhistorical, but in the sense that Paul uses the events to illustrate a theological truth. *covenant.* See note on 3:15. *Mount Sinai.* Where the old covenant was established, with its law governing Israel's life (see Ex 19:2; 20:1–17).

4:25 *corresponds to the present city of Jerusalem.* Jerusalem can be equated with Mount Sinai because it represents the center of Judaism, which is still under bondage to the law issued at Mount Sinai.

4:26 *the Jerusalem that is above.* Rabbinical teaching held that the Jerusalem above was the heavenly archetype that in the Messianic period would be let down to earth (cf. Rev 21:2). Here it refers to the heavenly city of God, in which Christ reigns and of which Christians are citizens, in contrast to the "present city of Jerusalem" (v. 25). *our mother.* As citizens of the heavenly Jerusalem, Christians are her children.

4:27 Paul applies Isaiah's joyful promise to exiled Jerusalem (in her exile "barren" of children) to the ingathering of believers through the gospel, by which "Jerusalem's" children have become many.

4:28 *children of promise.* Children by virtue of God's promise (see 3:29; Ro 9:8).

4:29 *persecuted the son born by the power of the Spirit.* Suggested by Ge 21:9; cf. Ps 83:5–6. *the same now.* See Ac 13:50; 14:2–5,19; 1Th 2:14–16.

4:30 *Get rid of the slave woman.* Sarah's words in Ge 21:10 were used by Paul as the Scriptural basis for teaching the Galatians to put the Judaizers out of the church.

4:31 *we are not children of the slave woman.* The believer is not enslaved to the law but is a child of promise and lives by faith (cf. 3:7,29).

5:1 *freedom.* Emphasized by its position in the Greek sentence. The freedom spoken of here is freedom from the yoke of the law. *burdened.* In classical Greek the verb meant "to be caught or entangled in." *yoke of slavery.* The burden of the rigorous demands of the law as the means for gaining God's favor—an intolerable burden for sinful man (see Ac 15:10–11).

5:2 *circumcised.* As a condition for God's acceptance.

5:3 *obligated to obey the whole law.* The OT law is a unit; submission to it cannot be selective.

5:4 *fallen away from grace.* Placed yourself outside the scope of divine favor, because gaining God's favor by observing the law and receiving it by grace are mutually exclusive (see 2Pe 3:17).

5:5 *the righteousness for which we hope.* A reference to God's final verdict of "not guilty," assured presently to the believer by faith and by the sanctifying work of the Holy Spirit. This is one of the few eschatological statements in Galatians.

5:6 *neither circumcision nor uncircumcision has any value.* See v. 2; 2:21; 6:15; 1Co 7:19. *faith expressing itself through love.* Faith is not mere intellectual assent (see Jas 2:18–19) but a living trust in God's grace that expresses itself in acts of love (see 1Th 1:3).

5:7 *were running a good race.* Before the Judaizers hindered them. Paul was fond of depicting the Christian life as a race (see, e.g., 2:2; Php 2:16).

5:8 *persuasion.* By the Judaizers.

5:9 A proverb used here to stress the pervasive effect of Judaism. When the word "yeast" in the Bible is used as a symbol, it indicates evil or false teaching (see note on Mk 8:15), except in Mt 13:33.

5:11 *Brothers.* See note on 1:2. *offense of the cross.* See

ing circumcision, why am I still being persecuted?[e] In that case the offense[f] of the cross has been abolished. [12]As for those agitators,[g] I wish they would go the whole way and emasculate themselves!

[13]You, my brothers, were called to be free.[h] But do not use your freedom to indulge the sinful nature[r];[i] rather, serve one another[j] in love. [14]The entire law is summed up in a single command: "Love your neighbor as yourself."[s][k] [15]If you keep on biting and devouring each other, watch out or you will be destroyed by each other.

Life by the Spirit

[16]So I say, live by the Spirit,[l] and you will not gratify the desires of the sinful nature. [m] [17]For the sinful nature desires what is contrary to the Spirit, and the Spirit what is contrary to the sinful nature.[n] They are in conflict with each other, so that you do not do what you want.[o] [18]But if you are led by the Spirit,[p] you are not under law.[q]

[19]The acts of the sinful nature are obvious: sexual immorality,[r] impurity and debauchery; [20]idolatry and witchcraft; hatred, discord, jealousy, fits of rage, selfish ambition, dissensions, factions [21]and envy; drunkenness, orgies, and the like.[s] I warn you, as I did before, that those who live like this will not inherit the kingdom of God.[t]

[22]But the fruit[u] of the Spirit is love,[v]

joy, peace,[w] patience, kindness, goodness, faithfulness, [23]gentleness and self-control.[x] Against such things there is no law.[y] [24]Those who belong to Christ Jesus have crucified the sinful nature[z] with its passions and desires.[a] [25]Since we live by the Spirit,[b] let us keep in step with the Spirit. [26]Let us not become conceited,[c] provoking and envying each other.

Doing Good to All

6 Brothers, if someone is caught in a sin, you who are spiritual[d] should restore[e] him gently. But watch yourself, or you also may be tempted. [2]Carry each other's burdens, and in this way you will fulfill the law of Christ.[f] [3]If anyone thinks he is something[g] when he is nothing, he deceives himself.[h] [4]Each one should test his own actions. Then he can take pride in himself,[i] without comparing himself to somebody else,[j] [5]for each one should carry his own load.[k]

[6]Anyone who receives instruction in the word must share all good things with his instructor.[l]

[7]Do not be deceived:[m] God cannot be mocked. A man reaps what he sows.[n] [8]The one who sows to please his sinful nature,[o] from that nature[t] will reap de-

---

5:11 [e]Gal 4:29;
6:12 [f]S Lk 2:34
5:12 [g]ver 10
5:13 [h]S ver 1
/S ver 24;
1Co 8:9; 1Pe 2:16
/1Co 9:19;
2Co 4:5;
Eph 5:21
5:14 [k]Lev 19:18;
S Mt 5:43;
Gal 6:2
5:16 [l]ver 18,25;
Ro 8:2,4-6,9,14;
S 2Co 5:17 [m]S ver 24
5:17 [n]Ro 8:5-8
[o]Ro 7:15-23
5:18 [p]S ver 16
[q]S Ro 2:12;
1Ti 1:9
5:19 [r]S 1Co 6:18
5:21 [s]Mt 15:19;
Ro 13:13
[t]S Mt 25:34
5:22
[u]Mt 7:16-20;
Eph 5:9
[v]Col 3:12-15

[w]Mal 2:6
5:23 [x]S Ac 24:25
[y]ver 18
5:24 [z]S Ro 6:6;
16-21; S Ro 6:6;
7:5,18; 8:3-5,8,9,
12,13; 13:14;
Col 6:8; Col 2:11
[a]ver 16,17
5:25 [b]S ver 16
5:26 [c]Php 2:3
6:1 [d]1Co 2:15;
3:1 [e]S Mt 18:15;
S 2Co 2:7
6:2 [f]1Co 9:21;
Jas 2:8
6:3 [g]Ro 12:3;
1Co 8:2
[h]1Co 3:18
6:4 [i]2Co 13:5
[j]2Co 10:12
6:5 [k]ver 2;
Jer 31:30
6:6 [l]1Co 9:11,14;
1Ti 5:17,18

6:7 [m]S 1Co 6:9 [n]Pr 22:8; Jer 34:17; Hos 10:12,13; 2Co 9:6
6:8 [o]S Gal 5:24

[r]13 Or the flesh; also in verses 16, 17, 19 and 24
[s]14 Lev. 19:18   [t]8 Or his flesh, from the flesh

Ro 9:32-33; 1Co 1:23.
5:12 *emasculate themselves.* The Greek word means "to cut off," or "to castrate." In Php 3:2 Paul uses a related word to describe the same sort of people as "mutilators of the flesh." His sarcasm is evident.
5:13 *do not use your freedom to indulge the sinful nature.* See Ro 6:1; 1Pe 2:16. Liberty is not license but freedom to serve God and each other in love.
5:14 *entire law is summed up.* Doing to others what you would have them do to you expresses the spirit and intention of "the Law and the Prophets" (Mt 7:12; cf. Mk 12:31).
5:15 *biting and devouring each other.* Opposite of vv. 13-14. Seeking to attain status with God and man by mere observance of law breeds a self-righteous, critical spirit.
5:16 *live by.* Present tense—"go on living" (used of habitual conduct). Living by the promptings and power of the Spirit is the key to conquering sinful desires (see v. 25; Ro 8:2-4).
5:17 *in conflict with each other.* See Ro 7:15-23; 1Pe 2:11.
5:18 *led by the Spirit.* See Ro 8:14. *not under law.* Not under the bondage of trying to please God by minute observance of the law for salvation or sanctification (see note on Ro 6:14).
5:19-21 For other lists of vices see 1Co 6:9-10; Eph 5:5; Rev 22:15.
5:22-23 For other lists of virtues see 2Co 6:6; Eph 4:2; 5:9; Col 3:12-15. Christian character is produced by the Holy Spirit, not by the mere moral discipline of trying to live by law. Paul makes it clear that justification by faith does not

result in libertinism. The indwelling Holy Spirit produces Christian virtues in the believer's life.
5:22 *fruit of the Spirit.* Compare the singular "fruit" with the plural "acts" (v. 19).
5:23 *no law.* See 1Ti 1:9.
5:24 *crucified the sinful nature.* See 2:20; 6:14.
5:25 *keep in step with.* Or "walk in line with," a different Greek verb from "live by" (or "walk by") in v. 16.
6:1 *Brothers.* See note on 1:2. *you who are spiritual.* Contrast with 1Co 3:1-3. *restore.* The Greek for this verb is used elsewhere for setting bones, mending nets, or bringing factions together.
6:2 *Carry each other's burdens.* The emphasis is on moral burdens or weaknesses (see v.1; Ro 15:1-3). *law of Christ.* See note on 1Co 9:21.
6:4 *Each one should test his own actions.* The emphasis here is on personal responsibility (see 1Co 11:28; 2Co 13:5).
6:5 *carry his own load.* The "for" at the beginning of the verse connects it with v. 4. Each of us is responsible before God. The reference may be to the future judgment (the verb is in the future tense), when every person will give an account to God (Ro 14:12; 2Co 5:10).
6:6 *share all good things.* See Php 4:14-19.
6:7 *reaps what he sows.* See 2Co 9:6. As vv. 8-9 show, the principle applies not only negatively but also positively.
6:8 See Ro 8:13. *destruction.* See 5:19-21. *eternal life.* In 5:21 Paul speaks of inheriting "the kingdom of God," here of reaping "eternal life." The first focuses on the realm (sphere, context) that will be inherited (as Israel inherited the prom-

struction; *p* the one who sows to please the Spirit, from the Spirit will reap eternal life. *q* ⁹Let us not become weary in doing good, *r* for at the proper time we will reap a harvest if we do not give up. *s* ¹⁰Therefore, as we have opportunity, let us do good *t* to all people, especially to those who belong to the family *u* of believers.

Not Circumcision but a New Creation

¹¹See what large letters I use as I write to you with my own hand! *v*

¹²Those who want to make a good impression outwardly *w* are trying to compel you to be circumcised. *x* The only reason they do this is to avoid being persecuted *y* for the cross of Christ. ¹³Not even those

who are circumcised obey the law, *z* yet they want you to be circumcised that they may boast about your flesh. *a* ¹⁴May I never boast except in the cross of our Lord Jesus Christ, *b* through which *u* the world has been crucified to me, and I to the world. *c* ¹⁵Neither circumcision nor uncircumcision means anything; *d* what counts is a new creation. *e* ¹⁶Peace and mercy to all who follow this rule, even to the Israel of God.

¹⁷Finally, let no one cause me trouble, for I bear on my body the marks *f* of Jesus. ¹⁸The grace of our Lord Jesus Christ *g* be with your spirit, *h* brothers. Amen.

Cross references (center column):

6:8 *p* Job 4:8; Hos 8:7; S Ro 6:23
q Jas 3:18
6:9 *r* 1Co 15:58; 2Co 4:1 *s* Job 42:12; Ps 126:5; Heb 12:3; Rev 2:10
6:10 *t* Pr 3:27; S Tit 2:14 *u* Eph 2:19; 1Pe 4:17
6:11 *v* S 1Co 16:21
6:12 *w* Mt 23:25, 26 *x* Ac 15:1 *y* Gal 5:11

6:13 *z* Ro 2:25 *a* Php 3:3
6:14 *b* 1Co 2:2 *c* S Ro 6:2,6
6:15 *d* S 1Co 7:19 *e* S 2Co 5:17
6:17 *f* Isa 44:5; S 2Co 1:5; 11:23

6:18 *g* S Ro 16:20 *h* Php 4:23; 2Ti 4:22; Phm 25

u 14 Or whom

---

ised land); the second focuses on the blessed life that will be enjoyed in that realm.

6:10 *especially to those who belong to the family of believers.* See 1Ti 5:8.

6:11 *large letters.* May have been for emphasis or, as some have suggested, because he had poor eyesight (see note on 4:13). *with my own hand.* The letter up to this point had probably been dictated to a scribe, after which Paul took the pen in his own hand and finished the letter.

6:12 *compel you to be circumcised.* Cf. 2:3. *to avoid being persecuted.* By advocating circumcision (see 5:11) the Judaizers were less apt to experience opposition from the Jewish opponents to Christianity. They were thinking only of themselves. See Introduction: Occasion and Purpose.

6:14 *boast except in the cross.* See 1Co 1:31; 2:2. *the world.* All that is against God. *crucified to me, and I to the world.* See 2:19–20; 5:24; see also notes on Jas 4:4; 1Jn 2:15.

6:15 *new creation.* In Christ man undergoes a transformation that results in an entirely new being. Creation again takes place (see 2Co 5:17).

6:16 *Peace and mercy.* Cf. Ps 125:5; 128:6. *this rule.* See vv. 14–15. *Israel of God.* In contrast to "Israel according to flesh" (a literal rendering of the Greek for "people of Israel" in 1Co 10:18), the NT church, made up of believing Jews and Gentiles, is the new seed of Abraham and the heir according to the promise (3:29; cf. Ro 9:6; Php 3:3)—though some limit the phrase here to Christian Jews (translating the conjunction as "and" instead of "even").

6:17 *marks of Jesus.* In ancient times the Greek word for "marks" was used of the brand that identified slaves or animals. Paul's suffering (stoning, Ac 14:19; beatings, Ac 16:22; 2Co 11:25; illness, 2Co 12:7; Gal 4:13–14) marked him as a "servant of Christ" (1:10; cf. 2Co 4:10).

6:18 *Amen.* A word of confirmation often used at the close of a doxology or benediction.

EPHESIANS

Author, Date and Place of Writing

The author identifies himself as Paul (1:1; 3:1; cf. 3:7,13; 4:1; 6:19-20). Some have taken the absence of the usual personal greetings and the verbal similarity of many parts to Colossians, among other reasons, as grounds for doubting authorship by the apostle Paul. However, this was probably a circular letter, intended for other churches in addition to the one in Ephesus (see notes on 1:1,15; 6:21-23). Paul may have written it about the same time as Colossians, c. A.D. 60, while he was in prison at Rome (see 3:1; 4:1; 6:20).

The City of Ephesus

Ephesus was the most important city in western Asia Minor (now Turkey). It had a harbor that at that time opened into the Cayster River, which in turn emptied into the Aegean Sea. Because it was also at an intersection of major trade routes, Ephesus became a commercial center. It boasted a pagan temple dedicated to the Roman goddess Diana (Greek *Artemis*); cf. Ac 19:23-31. Paul made Ephesus

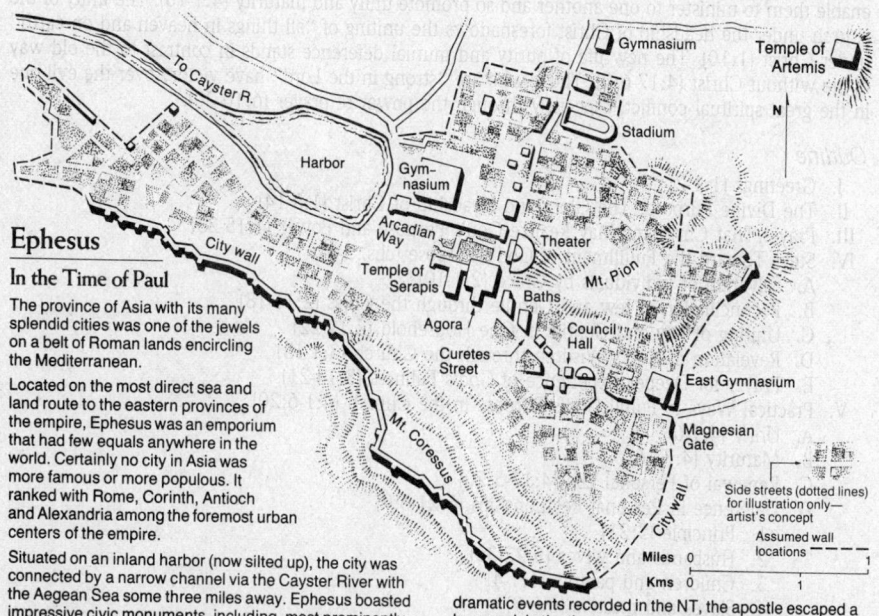

Ephesus

In the Time of Paul

The province of Asia with its many splendid cities was one of the jewels on a belt of Roman lands encircling the Mediterranean.

Located on the most direct sea and land route to the eastern provinces of the empire, Ephesus was an emporium that had few equals anywhere in the world. Certainly no city in Asia was more famous or more populous. It ranked with Rome, Corinth, Antioch and Alexandria among the foremost urban centers of the empire.

Situated on an inland harbor (now silted up), the city was connected by a narrow channel via the Cayster River with the Aegean Sea some three miles away. Ephesus boasted impressive civic monuments, including, most prominently, the temple of Artemis (Diana), one of the seven wonders of the ancient world. Coins of the city proudly displayed the slogan Neokoros, "temple-warden."

Here in Ephesus Paul preached to large crowds of people. The silversmiths complained that he had influenced large numbers of people here in Ephesus and in practically the whole province of Asia (Ac 19:26). In one of the most

dramatic events recorded in the NT, the apostle escaped a huge mob in the theater. This structure, located on the slope of Mt. Pion at the end of the Arcadian Way, could seat 25,000 people!

Other places doubtless familiar to the apostle were the Commerical Agora, the Magnesian Gate, the Town Hall or "Council House," and the Street of the Curetes.
The location of the lecture hall of Tyrannus, where Paul taught, is unknown.

a center for evangelism for about three years (see note on Ac 19:10), and the church there apparently flourished for some time, but later needed the warning of Rev 2:1-7.

Message

Unlike several of the other letters Paul wrote, Ephesians does not address any particular error or heresy. Paul wrote to expand the horizons of his readers, so that they might understand better the dimensions of God's eternal purpose and grace and come to appreciate the high goals God has for the church.

The letter opens with a sequence of statements about God's blessings, which are interspersed with a remarkable variety of expressions drawing attention to God's wisdom, forethought and purpose. Paul emphasizes that we have been saved, not only for our personal benefit, but also to bring praise and glory to God. The climax of God's purpose, "when the times will have reached their fulfillment," is to bring all things in the universe together under Christ (1:10). It is crucially important that Christians realize this, so in 1:15-23 Paul prays for their understanding (a second prayer occurs in 3:14-21).

Having explained God's great goals for the church, Paul proceeds to show the steps toward their fulfillment. First, God has reconciled individuals to himself as an act of grace (2:1-10). Second, God has reconciled these saved individuals to each other, Christ having broken down the barriers through his own death (2:11-22). But God has done something even beyond this: He has united these reconciled individuals in one body, the church. This is a "mystery" not fully known until it was revealed to Paul (3:1-6). Now Paul is able to state even more clearly what God has intended for the church, namely, that it be the means by which he displays his "manifold wisdom" to the "rulers and authorities in the heavenly realms" (3:7-13). It is clear through the repetition of "heavenly realms" (1:3,20; 2:6; 3:10; 6:12) that Christian existence is not merely on an earthly plane. It receives its meaning and significance from heaven, where Christ is exalted at the right hand of God (1:20).

Nevertheless, that life is lived out on earth, where the practical daily life of the believer continues to work out the purposes of God. The ascended Lord gave "gifts" to the members of his church to enable them to minister to one another and so promote unity and maturity (4:1-16). The unity of the church under the headship of Christ foreshadows the uniting of "all things in heaven and on earth" under Christ (1:10). The new life of purity and mutual deference stands in contrast to the old way of life without Christ (4:17-6:9). Those who are "strong in the Lord" have victory over the evil one in the great spiritual conflict, especially through the power of prayer (6:10-20).

Outline

1 Paul, an apostle[a] of Christ Jesus by the will of God,[b]

To the saints[c] in Ephesus,[a][d] the faithful[b][e] in Christ Jesus:

[2]Grace and peace to you from God our Father and the Lord Jesus Christ.[f]

Spiritual Blessings in Christ

[3]Praise be to the God and Father of our Lord Jesus Christ,[g] who has blessed us in the heavenly realms[h] with every spiritual blessing in Christ. [4]For he chose us[i] in him before the creation of the world[j] to be holy and blameless[k] in his sight. In love[l] [5]he[c] predestined[m] us to be adopted as his sons[n] through Jesus Christ, in accordance with his pleasure[o] and will—[6]to the praise of his glorious grace,[p] which he has freely given us in the One he loves.[q] [7]In him we have redemption[r] through his blood,[s] the forgiveness of sins,

in accordance with the riches[t] of God's grace [8]that he lavished on us with all wisdom and understanding. [9]And he[d] made known to us the mystery[u] of his will according to his good pleasure, which he purposed[v] in Christ, [10]to be put into effect when the times will have reached their fulfillment[w]—to bring all things in heaven and on earth together under one head, even Christ.[x]

[11]In him we were also chosen,[e] having been predestined[y] according to the plan of him who works out everything in conformity with the purpose[z] of his will, [12]in order that we, who were the first to hope in Christ, might be for the praise of his

1:1 [a]S 1Co 1:1
[b]S 2Co 1:1
[c]S Ac 9:13
[d]S Ac 18:19
[e]Col 1:2
1:2 [f]S Ro 1:7
1:3 [g]2Co 1:3;
1Pe 1:3 [h]ver 20;
Eph 2:6; 3:10;
6:12
1:4 [i]2Th 2:13
[j]S Mt 25:34
[k]Lev 11:44; 20:7;
2Sa 22:24;
Ps 15:2;
Eph 5:27;
Col 1:22
[l]Eph 4:2,15,16
1:5 [m]ver 11;
Ro 8:29,30
[n]S Ro 8:14,15
[o]Lk 12:32;
1Co 1:21;
Col 1:19
1:6 [p]ver 12,14
[q]Mt 3:17
1:7 [r]ver 14;
S Ro 3:24
[s]S Ro 3:25

[t]S Ro 2:4
1:9 [u]S Ro 16:25
[v]S ver 11
1:10 [w]Mk 1:15;
Ro 5:6; Gal 4:4

[x]Col 1:20 1:11 [y]ver 5; Ro 8:29,30 [z]ver 9; Ro 8:28;
Eph 3:11; Heb 6:17

[a][l] Some early manuscripts do not have in Ephesus.
[b][l] Or believers who are [c]4,5 Or sight in love. [5]He
[d]8,9 Or us. With all wisdom and understanding, [9]he
[e][l]1 Or were made heirs

1:1 *apostle.* One specially commissioned by Christ (see notes on Mk 6:30; 1Co 1:1; Heb 3:1). *by the will of God.* Paul not only stresses his authority under God, but also anticipates the strong emphasis he will make later in this chapter and book on God's sovereign plan and purpose. *in Ephesus.* See NIV text note. The book may have been intended as a circular letter to several churches, including the one at Ephesus (see notes on v. 15; 6:21–23; Ac 19:10).
1:2 *Grace and peace.* Although these words were commonly used in the greetings of secular letters, the words that follow show that Paul intended a spiritual dimension. He uses the word "grace" 12 times and "peace" 7 times in Ephesians.
1:3–14 All one sentence in Greek, this section is often called a "doxology" because it recites what God has done and is an expression of worship to honor him. Paul speaks first of the blessings we have through the Father (v. 3), then of those that come through the Son (vv. 4–13a) and finally of those through the Holy Spirit (1:13b–14).
1:3 *Father of our Lord Jesus Christ.* Jesus' relation to God the Father is unique (see Jn 20:17 and note). *blessed . . . blessing.* Jewish people used the word "bless" to express both God's kindness to us and our thanks or praise to him. *heavenly realms.* Occurs five times in Ephesians, emphasizing Paul's perception that in the exaltation of Christ (his resurrection and enthronement at God's right hand) and in the Christian's union with the exalted Christ ultimate issues are involved—issues that pertain to the divine realm and that in the final analysis are worked out in and from that realm. At stake are God's eternal eschatological purpose (3:11) and the titanic conflict between God and the powerful spiritual forces arrayed against him—a purpose and a conflict that come to focus in the history of redemption. Here (v. 3) Paul asserts that, through their union with the exalted Christ, Christians have already been made beneficiaries of every spiritual blessing that belongs to and comes from the heavenly realm. In vv. 20–22, he proclaims Christ's exaltation to that realm and his elevation over all other powers and titles so that he rules over all for the sake of his church. According to 2:6, those who have been "made alive with Christ" share in Christ's exaltation and enthronement in heaven. Thus (3:11) by the gathering of Gentiles and Jews into one body of Christ (the church), God triumphantly displays his "manifold wisdom" to the "rulers and authorities" in the heavenly

realm. As a result, the spiritual struggle of the saints here and now is not so much against "flesh and blood" as against the great spiritual forces that war against God in heaven (6:12). *in Christ.* This phrase (or one like it) occurs 12 times in vv. 3–12. It refers to the spiritual union of Christ with believers, which Paul often symbolizes by the metaphor "body of Christ" (see, e.g., v. 23; 2:16; 4:4,12,16; 5:23,30).
1:4 *chose.* Divine election is a constant theme in Paul's letters (Ro 8:29–33; 9:6–26; 11:5,7,28; 16:13; Col 3:12; 1Th 1:4; 2Th 2:13; Tit 1:1). In this chapter it is emphasized in the following ways: (1) "he chose us" (here); (2) "he predestined us" (v. 5); (3) "we were also chosen" (v. 11); (4) "having been predestined" (v. 11). *before the creation of the world.* See Jn 17:24. *holy and blameless.* See 5:27 for the same pair of words. Holiness is the result—not the basis—of God's choosing. It refers both to the holiness imparted to the believer because of Christ and to the believer's personal sanctification (see note on 1Co 1:2). *In love.* See NIV text note on vv. 4–5; cf. 3:17; 4:2,15–16; 5:2.
1:5 *adopted.* See note on Ro 8:23.
1:6 *to the praise.* See vv. 12,14. Election is for God's glory.
1:7 *redemption.* See v. 14; 4:30; Ro 3:24; Tit 2:14. The Ephesians were familiar with the Greco-Roman practice of redemption: Slaves were freed by the payment of a ransom. Similarly, the ransom necessary to free sinners from the bondage of sin and the resulting curse imposed by the law (see Gal 3:13) was the death of Christ (called here "his blood"). *through his blood.* Cf. 2:13; 1Pe 1:18–19.
1:9 *mystery.* See notes on Ro 11:25; Col 1:26.
1:10 *to bring . . . under one head.* Paul uses a significant term here that not only has the idea of leadership but also was often used of adding up a column of figures. A contemporary way of putting it might be to say that in a world of confusion, where things do not "add up" or make sense, we look forward to the time when everything will be brought into meaningful relationship under the headship of Christ.
1:11 *In him.* Christ is the center of God's plan. Whether the universe or the individual Christian is in view, it is only in relationship to Christ that there is a meaningful future destiny. Paul goes on to speak, not of the world as a whole, but of those who respond to God's call.
1:12 *we, who were the first to hope in Christ.* Probably a reference to those Jews who, like Paul, had become believers before many Gentiles had.

glory.*a* 13And you also were included in Christ*b* when you heard the word of truth,*c* the gospel of your salvation. Having believed, you were marked in him with a seal,*d* the promised Holy Spirit,*e* 14who is a deposit guaranteeing our inheritance*f* until the redemption*g* of those who are God's possession—to the praise of his glory.*h*

Thanksgiving and Prayer

15For this reason, ever since I heard about your faith in the Lord Jesus*i* and your love for all the saints,*j* 16I have not stopped giving thanks for you,*k* remembering you in my prayers.*l* 17I keep asking that the God of our Lord Jesus Christ, the glorious Father,*m* may give you the Spirit*f* of wisdom*n* and revelation, so that you may know him better. 18I pray also that the eyes of your heart may be enlightened*o* in order that you may know the hope to which he has called*p* you, the riches*q* of his glorious inheritance*r* in the saints,*s* 19and his incomparably great power for us who believe. That power*t* is like the working of his mighty strength,*u* 20which he exerted in Christ when he raised him from the dead*v* and seated him at his right hand*w* in the heavenly realms,*x* 21far above all rule and authority, power and dominion,*y* and every title*z* that can be

given, not only in the present age but also in the one to come.*a* 22And God placed all things under his feet*b* and appointed him to be head*c* over everything for the church, 23which is his body,*d* the fullness of him*e* who fills everything in every way.*f*

Made Alive in Christ

2 As for you, you were dead in your transgressions and sins,*g* 2in which you used to live*h* when you followed the ways of this world*i* and of the ruler of the kingdom of the air,*j* the spirit who is now at work in those who are disobedient.*k* 3All of us also lived among them at one time,*l* gratifying the cravings of our sinful nature*g m* and following its desires and thoughts. Like the rest, we were by nature objects of wrath. 4But because of his great love for us,*n* God, who is rich in mercy, 5made us alive with Christ even when we were dead in transgressions*o*—it is by grace you have been saved.*p* 6And God raised us up with Christ*q* and seated us with him*r* in the heavenly realms*s* in Christ Jesus, 7in order that in the coming

1:12 *a*ver 6,14
1:13 *b*S Ro 16:3
*c*Eph 4:21;
Col 1:5
*d*Eph 4:30
*e*Jn 14:16,17
1:14 *f*S Ac 20:32;
S 2Co 5:5 *g*ver 7;
S Ro 3:24 *h*ver 6,
12
1:15 *i*S Ac 20:21
*j*S Col 1:4
1:16 *k*S Ro 1:8
*l*S Ro 1:10
1:17 *m*Jn 20:17;
Ro 15:6; Rev 1:6
*n*Ex 28:3;
Isa 11:2; Php 1:9;
Col 1:9
1:18 *o*Job 42:5;
2Co 4:6; Heb 6:4
*p*S Ro 8:28 *q*ver
7; S Ro 2:4 *r*ver
11 *s*Col 1:12
1:19 *t*Eph 3:7;
Col 1:29
*u*Isa 40:26;
Eph 6:10
1:20 *v*S Ac 2:24
*w*S Mk 16:19
*x*S ver 3
1:21 *y*Eph 3:10;
Col 1:16
*z*Php 2:9,10

*a*S Mt 12:32
1:22
*b*S Mt 22:44;
S 28:18
*c*1Co 11:3;
Eph 4:15; 5:23;
Col 1:18; 2:19
1:23
*d*S 1Co 12:27
*e*S Jn 1:16;
Eph 3:19
*f*Eph 4:10
2:1 *g*ver 5;
Col 2:13
2:2 *h*ver 3,11-13;
Ro 11:30;

1Co 6:11; 5:8; Col 3:7; Tit 3:3; 1Pe 4:3 *i*Ro 12:2 *j*S Jn 12:31
*k*Eph 5:6 2:3 *l*S ver 2 *m*S Gal 5:24 2:4 *n*S Jn 3:16 2:5 *o*ver 1;
Ps 103:12 *p*ver 8; Jn 5:24; S Ac 15:11 2:6 *q*S Ro 6:5
*r*Eph 1:20 *s*S Eph 1:3

*f*17 Or *a spirit*   *g*3 Or *our flesh*

1:13 *And you also.* Probably refers to the majority of the Ephesians, who were Gentiles. *marked . . . with a seal.* In those days a seal denoted ownership.
1:14 *deposit.* See note on Ro 8:23.
1:15 *ever since I heard.* This sounds strange from one who had spent a few years in Ephesus. He may be referring to a greatly enlarged church there, many of whom Paul did not know, or, if Ephesians was intended as a circular letter (see note on v. 1), he may be referring to news from the whole area, only a part of which he had visited.
1:17 *God of our Lord Jesus Christ.* See note on v. 3. *him.* God the Father.
1:18 *eyes of your heart.* Your mind or understanding or inner awareness. *hope.* Has an objective quality of certainty (see Ro 8:25). It is the assurance of eternal life guaranteed by the present possession of the Holy Spirit (see v. 14). *called.* See Php 3:14; 2Ti 1:9; Heb 3:1. *his glorious inheritance in the saints.* Either the inheritance we have from God (see v. 14; Col 1:12) or the inheritance God receives, i.e., the saints themselves. *saints.* Those whom God has called to be his own people, i.e., all Christians (see vv. 1,15). The word carried the idea of dedication to a deity.
1:19 In this verse Paul piles term upon term to emphasize that the extraordinary divine force by which Jesus Christ was raised (v. 20) is the same power at work in and through believers.
1:20 *right hand.* The symbolic place of highest honor and authority.
1:21 *all rule . . . every title that can be given.* Including whatever supernatural beings his contemporaries might conceive of, for in his day many people believed not only in the existence of angels and demons, but also in that of other

beings. Christ is above them all. *the present age . . . the one to come.* Like the rabbinic teachers of his day, Paul distinguishes between the present age, which is evil, and the future age when the Messiah will consummate his kingdom and there will be a completely righteous society on earth.
1:22 *under his feet.* Ps 8:5-6 emphasizes the destiny of man, and Heb 2:6-9 shows that ultimately it is the Son of Man who rules over everything (cf. Heb 10:13). *head.* Christ is not only head of the church, but also head over everything (see note on v. 10).
1:23 *his body.* See 2:16; 4:4,12,16; 5:23,30. *fullness . . . fills.* The church is the fullness of Christ probably in the sense that it is filled by him who fills all things.
2:1-10 In ch. 1 Paul wrote of the great purposes and plan of God, culminating in the universal headship of Christ (1:10), all of which is to be for "the praise of his glory" (1:14). He now proceeds to explain the steps by which God will accomplish his purposes, beginning with the salvation of individuals.
2:1 A description of their past moral and spiritual condition, separated from the life of God.
2:2 *ruler.* Satan (cf. Jn 14:30, "prince"). *air.* Satan is no mere earthbound enemy (cf. 6:12). *spirit.* Satan is a created, but not a human, being (cf. Job 1:6; Eze 28:15; see note on Isa 14:12-15).
2:3 *All of us.* Jews and Gentiles. *objects of wrath.* See Ro 1:18-20; 2:5; 9:22.
2:5 *made us alive with Christ.* This truth is expanded in Ro 6:1-10.
2:6 *heavenly realms.* See note on 1:3. *in Christ Jesus.* Through our union with Christ.
2:7 *coming ages.* Cf. 1:21; probably refers to the future of

ages he might show the incomparable riches of his grace,[t] expressed in his kindness[u] to us in Christ Jesus. [8]For it is by grace[v] you have been saved,[w] through faith[x]—and this not from yourselves, it is the gift of God— [9]not by works,[y] so that no one can boast.[z] [10]For we are God's workmanship,[a] created[b] in Christ Jesus to do good works,[c] which God prepared in advance for us to do.

One in Christ

[11]Therefore, remember that formerly[d] you who are Gentiles by birth and called "uncircumcised" by those who call themselves "the circumcision" (that done in the body by the hands of men)[e]— [12]remember that at that time you were separate from Christ, excluded from citizenship in Israel and foreigners[f] to the covenants of the promise,[g] without hope[h] and without God in the world. [13]But now in Christ Jesus you who once[i] were far away have been brought near[j] through the blood of Christ.[k]

[14]For he himself is our peace,[l] who has made the two one[m] and has destroyed the barrier, the dividing wall of hostility, [15]by abolishing in his flesh[n] the law with its commandments and regulations.[o] His purpose was to create in himself one[p] new man out of the two, thus making peace, [16]and in this one body to reconcile both of them to God through the cross,[q] by which he put to death their hostility. [17]He came and preached peace[r] to you who were far away and peace to those who were near.[s] [18]For through him we both have access[t] to the Father[u] by one Spirit.[v]

[19]Consequently, you are no longer foreigners and aliens,[w] but fellow citizens[x] with God's people and members of God's household,[y] [20]built[z] on the foundation[a] of the apostles and prophets,[b] with Christ Jesus himself[c] as the chief cornerstone.[d] [21]In him the whole building is joined together and rises to become a holy temple[e] in the Lord. [22]And in him you too are be-

2:7 [t]S Ro 2:4
[u]Tit 3:4
2:8 [v]S Ro 3:24
[w]ver 5 [x]S Ro 9:30
2:9 [y]Dt 9:5;
Ro 4:2; 2Ti 1:9;
Tit 3:5 [z]1Co 1:29
2:10 [a]Isa 29:23;
43:7; 60:21
[b]Eph 4:24
[c]S Tit 2:14
2:11 [d]S ver 2
[e]Col 2:11
2:12 [f]Isa 14:1;
65:1 [g]Gal 3:17
[h]1Th 4:13
2:13 [i]S ver 2 [j]ver
17 [k]Col 1:20

2:14 [l]ver 15;
S Jn 14:27
[m]1Co 12:13;
Eph 3:6
2:15 [n]Col 1:21,
22 [o]Col 2:14
[p]Gal 3:28
2:16 [q]2Co 5:18;
Col 1:20,22
2:17 [r]S Lk 2:14
[s]ver 13;
Ps 148:14;
Isa 57:19
2:18 [t]Eph 3:12
[u]Col 1:12
[v]1Co 12:13;
Eph 4:4
2:19 [w]ver 12
[x]Php 3:20
[y]Gal 6:10

2:20 [z]1Co 3:9 [a]Mt 16:18; 1Co 3:10; Rev 21:14 [b]S Eph 4:11
[c]1Co 3:11 [d]S Ac 4:11; 1Pe 2:4-8 2:21 [e]1Co 3:16,17

eternal blessing with Christ. *show.* Or "exhibit" or "prove."

2:8 A major passage for understanding God's grace, i.e., his kindness, unmerited favor and forgiving love. *you have been saved.* "Saved" has a wide range of meanings. It includes salvation from God's wrath, which we all had incurred by our sinfulness. The tense of the verb (also in v. 5) suggests a completed action with emphasis on its present effect. *through faith.* See Ro 3:21-31 (and notes on that passage), which establishes the necessity of faith in Christ as the only means of being made right with God. *not from yourselves.* No human effort can contribute to our salvation; it is the gift of God.

2:9 *not by works.* One cannot earn salvation by "observing the law" (Ro 3:20, 28). Such a legalistic approach to salvation (or sanctification) is consistently condemned in Scripture. *no one can boast.* No one can take credit for his or her salvation.

2:10 *workmanship.* The Greek for this word sometimes has the connotation of a "work of art." *prepared in advance.* Carries forward the theme of God's sovereign purpose and planning, seen in ch. 1.

2:11-22 From the salvation of individuals, Paul moves to another aspect of salvation in which God reconciles Jews and Gentiles, previously hostile peoples, not only to himself but also to each other through Christ (vv. 11-16). Even more than that, God unites these now reconciled people in one body, a truth introduced in vv. 19-22 and explained in ch. 3.

2:11 *Therefore.* Refers to the state of those without Christ, described in vv. 1-10. *you who are Gentiles.* Most of the Ephesians (cf. 1:13, "And you also"). *"uncircumcised" . . . "the circumcision."* The rite of circumcision was applied to all Jewish male babies; so this physical act ("done in the body by the hands of men") was a clear mark of distinction between Jew and Gentile, in which Jewish people naturally took pride.

2:12 *at that time.* Before salvation, in contrast to "But now" (v. 13). *separate from Christ . . . without God.* All these expressions emphasize the distance of unbelieving Gentiles from Israel, as well as from Christ. *covenants.* God had promised blessings to and through the Jewish people (see

note on Ro 9:4).

2:13 *But now.* Not only contrasts with "at that time" (v. 12) but also introduces the contrast between "from Christ" (v. 12) and "in Christ" (here). *blood of Christ.* Expresses the violent death of Christ as he poured out his lifeblood as a sacrifice for us (cf. 1:7).

2:14 *the two.* Believing Jews and believing Gentiles. *barrier . . . dividing wall.* Vivid description of the total religious isolation Jews and Gentiles experienced from each other. *hostility.* Between Jews and Gentiles.

2:15 *abolishing . . . the law.* Since Mt 5:17 and Ro 3:31 teach that God's moral standard expressed in the OT law is not changed by the coming of Christ, what is abolished here is probably the effect of the specific "commandments and regulations" in separating Jews from Gentiles, whose nonobservance of the Jewish law renders them ritually unclean. *in his flesh.* Probably refers to the death of Christ. *one new man.* The united body of believers, the church.

2:16 *this one body.* While this could possibly mean the body of Christ offered on the cross (cf. "in his flesh," v. 15), it probably refers to the "one new man" just mentioned, the body of believers.

2:17 *far away . . . near.* Gentiles and Jews respectively.

2:19 *Consequently.* Paul indicates that the unity described in vv. 19-22 is based on what Christ did through his death, described in vv. 14-18. *you.* The Gentiles at Ephesus are particularly in mind here. *citizens . . . household.* Familiar imagery. The household in ancient times was what we today might call an "extended family."

2:20 *foundation.* Further metaphorical language to convey the idea of a solid, integrated structure. *apostles and prophets.* Probably refers to the founding work of the early Christian apostles and prophets as they preached and taught God's word (cf. 1Co 3:10-11). *cornerstone.* Isa 28:16, which uses the same term in its pre-Christian Greek translation (the Septuagint), refers to a foundation with a "tested" stone at the corner.

2:21 *joined together.* Cf. 4:16 for the same word. Both passages speak of the close relationship between believers. *rises.* The description of a building under construction con-

ing built together to become a dwelling in which God lives by his Spirit. f

Paul the Preacher to the Gentiles

3 For this reason I, Paul, the prisoner g of Christ Jesus for the sake of you Gentiles—

2Surely you have heard about the administration of God's grace that was given to me h for you, 3that is, the mystery i made known to me by revelation, j as I have already written briefly. 4In reading this, then, you will be able to understand my insight k into the mystery of Christ, 5which was not made known to men in other generations as it has now been revealed by the Spirit to God's holy apostles and prophets. l 6This mystery is that through the gospel the Gentiles are heirs m together with Israel, members together of one body, n and sharers together in the promise in Christ Jesus. o

7I became a servant of this gospel p by the gift of God's grace given me q through

the working of his power. r 8Although I am less than the least of all God's people, s this grace was given me: to preach to the Gentiles t the unsearchable riches of Christ, u 9and to make plain to everyone the administration of this mystery, v which for ages past was kept hidden in God, who created all things. 10His intent was that now, through the church, the manifold wisdom of God w should be made known x to the rulers and authorities y in the heavenly realms, z 11according to his eternal purpose a which he accomplished in Christ Jesus our Lord. 12In him and through faith in him we may approach God b with freedom and confidence. c 13I ask you, therefore, not to be discouraged because of my sufferings for you, which are your glory.

A Prayer for the Ephesians

14For this reason I kneel d before the Father, 15from whom his whole family h in heaven and on earth derives its name. 16I

2:22	f 1Co 3:16
3:1	g Ac 23:18; Eph 4:1; 2Ti 1:8; Phm 1,9
3:2	h Col 1:25
3:3	i S Ro 16:25; j S 1Co 2:10
3:4	k 2Co 11:6
3:5	l Ro 16:26; S Eph 4:11
3:6	m S Ro 8:17; n Eph 2:15,16; o Eze 47:22
3:7	p S 1Co 3:5; q S Ro 12:3
	r Eph 1:19; Col 1:29
3:8	s S 1Co 15:9; t S Ac 9:15; u S Ro 2:4
3:9	v S Ro 16:25
3:10	w S Ro 11:33; 1Co 2:7; x 1Pe 1:12; y Eph 1:21; 6:12; Col 2:10,15; z S Eph 1:3
3:11	a S Eph 1:11
3:12	b Eph 2:18; c 2Co 3:4; Heb 3:14; 4:16; 10:19,35; 1Jn 2:28; 3:21; 4:17
3:14	d Php 2:10

h 15 Or whom all fatherhood

---

veys the sense of the dynamic growth of the church. *holy temple.* Paul now uses the metaphor of a temple, thereby indicating the purpose ("to become") for which God has established his church.

2:22 *dwelling.* The church is to be a people or community in whom the Holy Spirit dwells.

3:1–13 Having saved people individually by his grace (2:1–10), and having reconciled them to each other as well as to himself through the sacrificial death of Christ (2:11–22), God also now unites them on an equal basis in one body, the church. This step in God's eternal plan was not fully revealed in previous times. Paul calls it a "mystery."

3:1 *For this reason.* Because of all that God has done, explained in the preceding several verses. *prisoner.* Apparently Paul was under house arrest at this time (see Ac 28:16,30). *of Christ.* Paul's physical imprisonment was because he obeyed Christ in spite of opposition. After this verse Paul breaks his train of thought to explain the "mystery" (v. 4). He resumes his initial thought in v. 14.

3:2 *Surely you have heard.* Most of the Ephesians would have heard of Paul's ministry because of his long stay there earlier. However, if this was a circular letter (see note on 1:1), the other churches may not have known much about it. *administration.* Paul unfolds God's administrative plan for the church and for the universe in this letter (see especially 1:3–12). He has been given a significant responsibility in the execution of this plan.

3:3 *mystery.* A truth known only by divine revelation (v. 5; see Ro 16:25; see also notes on Ro 11:25; Col 1:26). Here the word "mystery" has the special meaning of the private, wise plan of God, which in Ephesians relates primarily to the unification of believing Jews and Gentiles in the new body, the church (see v. 6). It may be thought of as a secret that is temporarily hidden, but more than that, it is a plan God is actively working out and revealing stage by stage (cf. 1:9–10; Rev 10:7). *as I have already written briefly.* May refer to 1:9–10.

3:5 *not made known to men in other generations.* See note on v. 6. *holy.* Set apart for God's service. *apostles and prophets.* See note on 2:20. Although Paul was the chief recipient, others received this revelation also.

3:6 *together . . . together . . . together.* The repetition of this word indicates the unique aspect of the mystery that was not previously known: the equality and mutuality that Gentiles had with Jews in the church, the one body. That Gentiles would turn to the God of Israel and be saved was prophesied in the OT (see Ro 15:9–12); that they would come into an organic unity with believing Jews on an equal footing was unexpected. *heirs.* See note on 1:18.

3:8 *less than the least.* Cf. 1Ti 1:15. Paul never ceased to be amazed that one so unworthy as he should have been chosen for so high a task. His modesty was genuine, even though we may disagree with his self-evaluation. *grace.* In this case, a special endowment that brings responsibility for service. *to preach.* Lit. "to gospelize"; parallels "to make plain" (v. 9). *unsearchable.* Far beyond what we can know, but not beyond our appreciation—at least in part (cf. Ro 11:33).

3:10 *now.* In contrast to the "ages past" (v. 9). *through the church.* The fact that God had done the seemingly impossible—reconciling and organically uniting Jews and Gentiles in the church—makes the church the perfect means of displaying God's wisdom. *manifold.* Variegated or multifaceted (in the way that many facets of a diamond reflect and enhance its beauty). *rulers and authorities.* Christ had ascended over all these (1:20–21). It is a staggering thought that the church on earth is observed, so to speak, by these spiritual powers and that to the degree the church is spiritually united it portrays to them the wisdom of God. This thought may be essential in understanding the meaning of "calling" in 4:1. *heavenly realms.* See note on 1:3.

3:11 *eternal purpose.* The effective headship of Christ over a united church is in preparation for his ultimate assumption of headship over the universe (1:10).

3:14–21 Paul now expresses a prayer that grows out of his awareness of all that God is doing in believers. God's key gifts are "power" (vv. 16,18,20) and "love" (vv. 17–19).

3:14 *For this reason.* Resumes the thought of v. 1. *I kneel.* Expresses deep emotion and reverence, as people in Paul's day usually stood to pray.

3:15 *family.* The word in Greek is similar to the word for "father" (see NIV text note), so it can be said that the

pray that out of his glorious riches[e] he may strengthen you with power[f] through his Spirit in your inner being,[g] [17]so that Christ may dwell in your hearts[h] through faith. And I pray that you, being rooted[i] and established in love, [18]may have power, together with all the saints,[j] to grasp how wide and long and high and deep[k] is the love of Christ, [19]and to know this love that surpasses knowledge[l]—that you may be filled[m] to the measure of all the fullness of God.[n]

[20]Now to him who is able[o] to do immeasurably more than all we ask[p] or imagine, according to his power[q] that is at work within us, [21]to him be glory in the church and in Christ Jesus throughout all generations, for ever and ever! Amen.[r]

Unity in the Body of Christ

4 As a prisoner[s] for the Lord, then, I urge you to live a life worthy[t] of the calling[u] you have received. [2]Be completely humble and gentle; be patient, bearing with one another[v] in love.[w] [3]Make every effort to keep the unity[x] of the Spirit through the bond of peace.[y] [4]There is one body[z] and one Spirit[a]— just as you were called to one hope when you were called[b]— [5]one Lord,[c] one faith, one baptism; [6]one God and Father of all,[d] who is over all and through all and in all.[e]

[7]But to each one of us[f] grace[g] has been given[h] as Christ apportioned it. [8]This is why it[i] says:

"When he ascended on high,
    he led captives[i] in his train
    and gave gifts to men."[j] [j]

[9](What does "he ascended" mean except that he also descended to the lower, earthly regions[k]? [10]He who descended is the very one who ascended[k] higher than all the heavens, in order to fill the whole universe.)[l] [11]It was he who gave[m] some to be

Cross references (center column)

3:16 [e]ver 8;
[S] Ro 2:4
[f]S Php 4:13
[g]Ro 7:22
3:17 [h]S Ro 8:10
[i]Col 2:7
3:18 [j]Eph 1:15
[k]Job 11:8,9;
Ps 103:11
3:19 [l]Php 4:7
[m]Col 2:10
[n]Eph 1:23
3:20 [o]Ro 16:25;
2Co 9:8
[p]1Ki 3:13 [q]ver 7
3:21 [r]S Ro 11:36
4:1 [s]S Eph 3:1
[t]Php 1:27;
Col 1:10;
1Th 2:12
[u]S Ro 8:28
4:2 [v]Col 3:12,13
[w]ver 15,16;
Eph 1:4
4:3 [x]S Ro 15:5
[y]Col 3:15
4:4 [z]S Ro 12:5
[a]1Co 12:13;
Eph 2:18
[b]S Ro 8:28
4:5 [c]1Co 8:6
4:6 [d]Dt 6:4;
Zec 14:9
[e]S Ro 11:36
4:7 [f]1Co 12:7,11
[g]S Ro 3:24
[h]S Ro 12:3
4:8 [i]Col 2:15
[j]Ps 68:18

4:10 [k]Pr 30:1-4 [l]Eph 1:23 4:11 [m]ver 8

[i]8 Or *God* [j]8 Psalm 68:18 [k]9 Or *the depths of the earth*

Study notes (bottom)

"family" derives its name (and being) from the "father." God is our Father, and we can commit our prayers to him in confidence.

3:17 *dwell.* Be completely at home. Christ was already present in the Ephesian believers' lives (cf. Ro 8:9). *hearts.* The whole inner being.

3:19 *surpasses knowledge.* Not unknowable, but so great that it cannot be completely known. *fullness.* God, who is infinite in all his attributes, allows us to draw on his resources—in this case, his love.

3:20 *immeasurably more.* Has specific reference to the matters presented in this section of Ephesians but is not limited to these. *his power.* See 1:19–21.

3:21 *to him be glory.* The ultimate goal of our existence (see 1:6 and note). *in the church and in Christ Jesus.* A remarkable parallel. God has called the church to an extraordinary position and vocation (cf. v. 10; 4:1).

4:1–32 The chapter begins (v. 2) and ends (v. 32) with exhortations to love and forgive one another.

4:1–16 So far Paul has taught that God brought Jew and Gentile into a new relationship to each other in the church and that he called the church to display his wisdom. Paul now shows how God made provision for those in the church to live and work together in unity and to grow together into maturity.

4:1 *prisoner.* See note on 3:1. *calling.* See 3:10,21 and notes.

4:3 *keep the unity.* Which God produced through the reconciling death of Christ (see 2:14–22). It is the heavy responsibility of Christians to keep that unity from being disturbed.

4:4 *one hope.* Has different aspects (e.g., 1:5,10; 2:7), but it is still one hope, tied to the glorious future of Christ, in which all believers share.

4:5 *one baptism.* Probably not the baptism of the Spirit (see 1Co 12:13), which was inward and therefore invisible, but water baptism (see note on Ro 6:3–4). Since Paul apparently has in mind that which identifies all believers as belonging together, he would naturally refer to that church ordinance in which every new convert participated publicly. At that

time it was a more obvious common mark of identification of Christians than it is now, when it is celebrated in different ways and often only seen by those in the church.

4:7 *grace.* See 3:7–8.

4:8 Ps 68:18 (see note there) speaks of God's triumphant ascension to his throne in the temple at Jerusalem (symbol of his heavenly throne). Paul applies this to Christ's triumphal ascension into heaven. Where the psalm states further that God "received gifts from men," Paul apparently takes his cue from certain rabbinic interpretations current in his day that read the Hebrew preposition for "from" in the sense of "to" (a meaning it often has) and the verb for "received" in the sense of "take and give" (a meaning it sometimes has—but with a different preposition; see Ge 15:9; 18:5; 27:13; Ex 25:2; 1Ki 17:10–11). *captives.* Probably Paul applies this to the spiritual enemies Christ defeated at the cross.

4:9 *ascended . . . descended.* Although Paul quoted from the psalm to introduce the idea of the "gifts to men," he takes the opportunity to remind his readers of Christ's coming to earth (his incarnation) and his subsequent resurrection and ascension. This passage probably does not teach, as some think and as some translations suggest, that Christ descended into hell.

4:11 *It was he who gave.* The quotation from Ps 68 has its ultimate meaning when applied to Christ as the ascended Lord, who himself has given gifts. *apostles.* Mentioned here because of their role in establishing the church (see 2:20). For qualifications of the initial group of apostles see Ac 1:21–22; see also notes on Mk 6:30; Ro 1:1; 1Co 1:1; Heb 3:1. In a broader sense, Paul was also an apostle (see 1:1). *prophets.* People to whom God made known a message for his people that was appropriate to their particular need or situation (see 1Co 14:3–4; see also note on 1Co 12:10). *evangelists.* See Ac 21:8; 1Co 1:17. While the other gifted people helped the church grow through edification, the evangelists helped the church grow by augmentation. Since the objective mentioned in v. 12 is "to prepare God's people for works of service," we may assume that evangelists, among their various ministries, helped other Christians in their testimony. *pastors and teachers.* Because of the Greek

apostles,[n] some to be prophets,[o] some to be evangelists,[p] and some to be pastors and teachers,[q] [12]to prepare God's people for works of service, so that the body of Christ[r] may be built up[s] [13]until we all reach unity[t] in the faith and in the knowledge of the Son of God[u] and become mature,[v] attaining to the whole measure of the fullness of Christ.[w]

[14]Then we will no longer be infants,[x] tossed back and forth by the waves,[y] and blown here and there by every wind of teaching and by the cunning and craftiness of men in their deceitful scheming.[z] [15]Instead, speaking the truth in love,[a] we will in all things grow up into him who is the Head,[b] that is, Christ. [16]From him the whole body, joined and held together by every supporting ligament, grows[c] and builds itself up[d] in love,[e] as each part does its work.

Living as Children of Light

[17]So I tell you this, and insist on it in the Lord, that you must no longer[f] live as the

Gentiles do, in the futility of their thinking.[g] [18]They are darkened in their understanding[h] and separated from the life of God[i] because of the ignorance that is in them due to the hardening of their hearts.[j] [19]Having lost all sensitivity,[k] they have given themselves over[l] to sensuality[m] so as to indulge in every kind of impurity, with a continual lust for more.

[20]You, however, did not come to know Christ that way. [21]Surely you heard of him and were taught in him in accordance with the truth that is in Jesus. [22]You were taught, with regard to your former way of life, to put off[n] your old self,[o] which is being corrupted by its deceitful desires;[p] [23]to be made new in the attitude of your minds;[q] [24]and to put on[r] the new self,[s] created to be like God in true righteousness and holiness.[t]

[25]Therefore each of you must put off falsehood and speak truthfully[u] to his

4:11 [n]1Co 12:28; Eph 2:20; 3:5; 2Pe 3:2; Jude 17 [o]S Ac 11:27; Ro 12:6; [p]1Co 12:10,28; 13:2,8; 14:1,39; Eph 2:20; 3:5; 2Pe 3:2 [q]Ac 21:8; 2Ti 4:5 [q]Ac 13:1; Ro 2:21; 12:7; 1Co 12:28; 14:26; 1Ti 1:7; Jas 3:1
4:12 [r]S 1Co 12:27 [s]S Ro 14:19
4:13 [t]ver 3,5 [u]S Php 3:8 [v]S 1Co 2:6; Col 1:28
4:14 [w]Jn 1:16; Eph 1:23; 3:19
4:14 [x]S 1Co 14:20 [y]Isa 57:20; Jas 1:6 [z]Eph 6:11
4:15 [a]ver 2,16; Eph 1:4 [b]S Eph 1:22
4:16 [c]Col 2:19 [d]1Co 12:7 [e]ver 2, 15; Eph 1:4
4:17 [f]Eph 2:2

[g]Ro 1:21
4:18 [h]Dt 29:4; Ro 1:21 [i]Eph 2:12 [j]2Co 3:14

4:19 [k]1Ti 4:2 [l]Ro 1:24 [m]Col 3:5; 1Pe 4:3 **4:22** [n]ver 25,31; Col 3:5,8,9; Jas 1:21; 1Pe 2:1 [o]S Ro 6:6 [p]Jer 17:9; Heb 3:13 **4:23** [q]Ro 12:2; Col 3:10 **4:24** [r]S Ro 13:14 [s]S Ro 6:4 [t]Eph 2:10 **4:25** [u]Ps 15:2; Lev 19:11; Zec 8:16; Col 3:9

grammatical construction (also, the word "some" introduces both words together), it is clear that these groups of gifted people are closely related. Those who have pastoral care for God's people (the image is that of shepherding) will naturally provide "food" from the Scriptures (teaching). They will be especially gifted as teachers (cf. 1Ti 3:2).
4:12 *to prepare God's people for works of service.* Those mentioned in v. 11 were not to do all the work for the people, but were to train the people to do the work themselves. *so that the body of Christ may be built up.* See v. 16. Spiritual gifts are for the body, the church, and are not to be exercised individualistically. "Built up" reflects the imagery of 2:19–22. Both concepts—body and building—occurring together emphasize the key idea of growth.
4:13 *until.* Expresses not merely duration but also purpose. *unity.* Carries forward the ideal of vv. 1–6. *in the faith.* Here "faith" refers to the Christians' common conviction about Christ and the doctrines concerning him, as the following words make clear (cf. also "the apostles' teaching" in Ac 2:42). *knowledge of the Son of God.* Unity is not just a matter of a loving attitude or religious feeling, but of truth and a common understanding about God's Son. *mature . . . fullness of Christ.* Not the maturity of doctrinal conviction just mentioned, nor a personal maturity that includes the ability to relate well to other people (cf. vv. 2–3), but the maturity of the perfectly balanced character of Christ.
4:14 *infants.* Contrast the maturity of v. 13. *tossed.* The nautical imagery pictures the instability of those who are not strong Christians. *teaching.* Then, as now, there were many distorted teachings and heresies that would easily throw the immature off course. *cunning . . . craftiness . . . deceitful scheming.* Sometimes those who try to draw people away from the Christian faith are not innocently misguided but deliberately deceitful and evil (cf. 1Ti 4:1–2).
4:15 *speaking the truth in love.* A truthful and loving manner of life is implied. *grow up . . . Head.* A slightly different restatement of v. 13, based now on the imagery of Christ as the Head of the body, which is the church. Paul thus speaks primarily of corporate maturity. It is the "body of Christ" that is to be "built up" (v. 12). In v. 13 "we all" are

to become "mature" (lit. "a mature man").
4:16 Further details of the imagery of the body growing under the direction of the Head. The parts of the body help each other in the growing process, picturing the mutual ministries of God's people spoken of in vv. 11–13. *love.* Maturity and unity are impossible without it (cf. vv. 2,15).
4:17–5:20 Paul has just discussed unity and maturity as twin goals for the church, which God has brought into existence through the death of Christ. He now goes on to show that purity is also essential among those who belong to him.
4:17 *futility of their thinking.* Life without God is intellectually frustrating, useless and meaningless (see, e.g., Ecc 1:2; Ro 1:21).
4:18 *darkened in their understanding.* Continues the idea of a futile thought life. *hardening of their hearts.* Moral unresponsiveness.
4:19 *have given themselves over.* Just as Pharaoh's heart was hardened reciprocally by himself and by God (see Ex 7–11), so here the Gentiles have given themselves over to a sinful kind of life, while Ro 1:24,26,28 says that God gave them over to that life.
4:20 *You.* Emphatic.
4:21 *truth that is in Jesus.* The wording and the use of the name Jesus (rather than Christ) suggest that Paul is referring to the embodiment of truth in Jesus' earthly life.
4:22 *old self.* Probably means the kind of person the Christian used to be. The old life-style resulted from deceitful desires.
4:23 *minds.* Cf. the evil thoughts of unbelievers (vv. 17–18).
4:24 *new self, created to be like God.* Since the new self is created, it cannot refer to the indwelling Christ, but rather to the kind of person he produces in the new believer. Nor is it some kind of new essential nature the believer has, because that would have been brought into existence at his new birth. In contrast, this is a new way of life that one not only "puts on" positionally at conversion (note the past tense in the parallel in Col 3:9–10) but is also urged to "put on" experientially as a Christian (see note on Ro 6:12–13).

neighbor, for we are all members of one body. *v* 26"In your anger do not sin"! : *w* Do not let the sun go down while you are still angry, 27and do not give the devil a foothold. *x* 28He who has been stealing must steal no longer, but must work, *y* doing something useful with his own hands, *z* that he may have something to share with those in need. *a*

29Do not let any unwholesome talk come out of your mouths, *b* but only what is helpful for building others up *c* according to their needs, that it may benefit those who listen. 30And do not grieve the Holy Spirit of God, *d* with whom you were sealed *e* for the day of redemption. *f* 31Get rid of *g* all bitterness, rage and anger, brawling and slander, along with every form of malice. *h* 32Be kind and compassionate to one another, *i* forgiving each other, just as in Christ God forgave you. *j*

5 Be imitators of God, *k* therefore, as dearly loved children *l* 2and live a life of love, just as Christ loved us *m* and gave himself up for us *n* as a fragrant offering and sacrifice to God. *o*

3But among you there must not be even

a hint of sexual immorality, *p* or of any kind of impurity, or of greed, *q* because these are improper for God's holy people. 4Nor should there be obscenity, foolish talk *r* or coarse joking, which are out of place, but rather thanksgiving. *s* 5For of this you can be sure: No immoral, impure or greedy person—such a man is an idolater *t*—has any inheritance *u* in the kingdom of Christ and of God. *m v* 6Let no one deceive you *w* with empty words, for because of such things God's wrath *x* comes on those who are disobedient. *y* 7Therefore do not be partners with them.

8For you were once *z* darkness, but now you are light in the Lord. Live as children of light *a* 9(for the fruit *b* of the light consists in all goodness, *c* righteousness and truth) 10and find out what pleases the Lord. *d* 11Have nothing to do with the fruitless deeds of darkness, *e* but rather expose them. 12For it is shameful even to mention what the disobedient do in secret.

Cross references:

4:25 *v*S Ro 12:5
4:26 *w*Ps 4:4;
S Mt 5:22
4:27 *x*2Co 2:10,
11
4:28 *y*Ac 20:35
*z*1Th 4:11
*a*Gal 6:10
4:29 *b*Mt 12:36;
Eph 5:4; Col 3:8
*c*S Ro 14:19
4:30 *d*Isa 63:10;
1Th 5:19
*e*2Co 1:22; 5:5;
Eph 1:13 *f*Ro 8:23
4:31 *g*S ver 22
*h*Col 3:8; 1Pe 2:1
4:32 *i*1Pe 3:8
*j*Mt 6:14,15;
Col 3:12,13
5:1 *k*Mt 5:48;
Lk 6:36 *l*S Jn 1:12
5:2 *m*S Jn 13:34
*n*ver 25;
S Gal 1:4; 2:20
*o*Heb 7:27

5:3 *p*S 1Co 6:18
*q*Col 3:5
5:4 *r*Eph 4:29
*s*S ver 20
5:5 *t*Col 3:5
*u*S Ac 20:32
*v*S Mt 25:34
5:6 *w*S Mk 13:5
*x*S Ro 1:18
*y*Eph 2:2
5:8 *z*S Eph 2:2
*a*Jn 8:12;
S Lk 16:8;
S Ac 26:18
5:9 *b*Mt 7:16-20;
Gal 5:22

*c*Ro 15:14 5:10 *d*S 1Ti 5:4 5:11 *e*Ro 13:12; 2Co 6:14

*1*26 Psalm 4:4   *m*5 Or *kingdom of the Christ and God*

4:25 *truthfully.* Cf. vv. 15,21. *neighbor.* Probably means fellow Christians in this context.

4:26 *In your anger.* Christians do not lose their emotions at conversion, but their emotions should be purified. Some anger is sinful, some is not. *Do not let the sun go down.* No anger is to outlast the day.

4:27 *the devil.* Personal sin is usually due to our evil desires (see Jas 1:14) rather than to direct tempting by the devil. However, Satan can use our sins—especially those, like anger, that are against others—to bring about greater evil, such as divisions among Christians.

4:28 *steal no longer . . . work . . . have something to share.* It is not enough to cease from sin; one must do good. The former thief must now help those in need.

4:29 *only what is helpful.* An exhortation parallel to the previous one. The Christian not only stops saying unwholesome things; he also begins to say things that will help build others up.

4:30 *grieve.* By sin, such as "unwholesome talk" (v. 29) and the sins mentioned in v. 31. The verb also demonstrates that the Holy Spirit is a person, not just an influence, for only a person can be grieved. *sealed.* See note on 1:13. *day of redemption.* See 1:14; 1Pe 1:5 and notes.

4:31 *bitterness . . . malice.* Such things grieve the Holy Spirit. This continues the instruction concerning one's speech (v. 29).

4:32 *kind and compassionate.* The opposite of the negative qualities of v. 31. *forgiving.* This basic Christian attitude, which is a result of being forgiven in Christ, along with being kind and compassionate, brings to others what we have received from God.

5:1 *Be imitators.* One way of imitating God is to have a forgiving spirit (4:32). The way we imitate our Lord is to act "just as" (v. 2; 4:32) he did. The sacrificial way Jesus expressed his love for us is not only the means of salvation (as seen in ch. 2) but also an example of the way we are to live for the sake of others.

5:2 *fragrant offering.* In the OT the offering of a sacrifice

pleased the Lord so much that it was described as a "pleasing aroma" (Ge 8:21; Ex 29:18,25,41; Lev 1:9,13,17).

5:3 *not . . . even a hint.* See v. 12. *any kind of impurity, or of greed.* Paul moves from specifically sexual sins to more general sins, such as greed. These include sexual lust but refer to other kinds of excessive desire as well. *holy people.* We are also a "holy temple" (2:21; cf. 2Co 6:16; 1Pe 2:9).

5:4 *foolish talk or coarse joking.* The context and the word "obscenity" indicate that it is not humor as such but dirty jokes and the like that are out of place. *thanksgiving.* By being grateful for all that God has given us, we can displace evil thoughts and words.

5:5 *immoral, impure or greedy.* See v. 3. *idolater.* Cf. Col 3:5. The greedy person wants things more than he wants God, and puts things in place of God, thereby committing idolatry. *inheritance.* The person who persists in sexual and other kinds of greed has excluded God, who therefore excludes him from the kingdom (but see notes on 1Co 6:9,11).

5:7 *partners.* Although Christians live in normal social relationships with others, as did the Lord Jesus (Lk 5:30–32; 15:1–2), they are not to participate in the sinful life-style of unbelievers.

5:8 *darkness . . . light.* This section emphasizes the contrast between light and darkness, showing that those who belong to him who is "light" (1Jn 1:5), i.e., pure and true, not only have their lives illumined by him but also are the means of introducing that light into the dark areas of human conduct (cf. Mt 5:14).

5:9 *fruit of the light.* A mixed metaphor, but the meaning is clear. Light is productive (consider the effect of light on plant growth), and those who live in God's light produce the fruit of moral and ethical character (cf. Gal 5:22–23), while those who live in darkness do not (see v. 11).

5:11 *Have nothing to do with.* See v. 7. *expose.* Light, by nature, exposes what is in darkness, and the contrast shows sin for what it really is.

5:12 *shameful . . . to mention.* Christians should not dwell on the evils that their lives are exposing in others.

13But everything exposed by the light[f]
becomes visible, 14for it is light that makes
everything visible. This is why it is said:

"Wake up, O sleeper,[g]
rise from the dead,[h]
and Christ will shine on you."[i]

15Be very careful, then, how you
live[j]—not as unwise but as wise, 16mak-
ing the most of every opportunity,[k] because the days are evil.[l] 17Therefore do
not be foolish, but understand what the
Lord's will is.[m] 18Do not get drunk on
wine,[n] which leads to debauchery. Instead, be filled with the Spirit.[o] 19Speak to
one another with psalms, hymns and spiritual songs.[p] Sing and make music in your
heart to the Lord, 20always giving thanks[q]
to God the Father for everything, in the
name of our Lord Jesus Christ.

21Submit to one another[r] out of reverence for Christ.

Wives and Husbands

5:22–6:9pp — Col 3:18–4:1

22Wives, submit to your husbands[s] as to
the Lord.[t] 23For the husband is the head
of the wife as Christ is the head of the
church,[u] his body, of which he is the Savior. 24Now as the church submits to Christ,
so also wives should submit to their husbands[v] in everything.

25Husbands, love your wives,[w] just as
Christ loved the church and gave himself
up for her[x] 26to make her holy,[y] cleansing[n] her by the washing[z] with water
through the word, 27and to present her to

5:13 [f]Jn 3:20,21 **5:14** [g]Ro 13:11 [h]Isa 26:19; Jn 5:25 [i]Isa 60:1; Mal 4:2 **5:15** [j]ver 2 **5:16** [k]Col 4:5 [l]Eph 6:13 **5:17** [m]Ro 12:2; Col 1:9; 1Th 4:3 **5:18** [n]Lev 10:9; Pr 20:1; Isa 28:7; Ro 13:13 [o]S Lk 1:15 **5:19** [p]Ps 27:6; 95:2; Ac 16:25; 1Co 14:15,26; Col 3:16 **5:20** [q]ver 4; Job 1:21; Ps 34:1; Col 3:17; Heb 13:15

5:21 [r]Gal 5:13; 1Pe 5:5 **5:22** [s]Ge 3:16; 1Co 14:34; Col 3:18; 1Ti 2:12; Tit 2:5; 1Pe 3:1,5,6 [t]Eph 6:5 **5:23** [u]S Eph 1:22 **5:24** [v]S ver 22 **5:25** [w]ver 28,33; Col 3:19 [x]S ver 2 **5:26** [y]Jn 17:19; Heb 2:11; 10:10,14; 13:12 [z]S Ac 22:16

[n]*26* Or *having cleansed*

5:13–14 *everything . . . visible.* By the repetition of these words, Paul seems to be stressing the all-pervasive nature of the light of God and its inevitable effect.
5:14 *it is said.* What follows may well be a hymn used by the early Christians (see note on Col 3:16). *sleeper . . . dead.* Two images that describe a sinner (cf. 2:1). *Christ will shine on you.* With his life-giving light.
5:15 *unwise . . . wise.* Having emphasized the contrast between light and darkness, Paul now turns to the contrast between wisdom and foolishness.
5:16 *opportunity.* The foolish person has no strategy for life and misses opportunities to live for God in an evil environment.
5:17 *foolish . . . understand.* The contrast continues. The foolish person not only misses opportunities to make wise use of time; he has a more fundamental problem: He does not understand what are God's purposes for mankind and for Christians. God's purposes are a basic theme in Ephesians (see ch. 1).
5:18 *Do not get drunk . . . be filled with the Spirit.* The Greek present tense is used to indicate that the filling of the Spirit is not a once-for-all experience. Repeatedly, as the occasion requires, the Spirit empowers for worship, service and testimony. The contrast between being filled with wine and filled with the Spirit is obvious. But there is something in common that enables Paul to make the contrast, namely, that one can be under an influence that affects him, whether of wine or of the Spirit. Since Col 3:15–4:1 is very similar to Eph 5:18–6:9, we may assume that Paul intends to convey a basically similar thought in the introductory sentences to each passage. When he speaks here of being filled with the Spirit and when he speaks in Colossians of being under the rule of the peace of Christ and indwelt by the "word" of Christ, he means to be under God's control. The effect of this control is essentially the same in both passages: a happy, mutual encouragement to praise God and a healthy, mutual relationship with people.
5:19 *psalms . . . songs.* Every kind of appropriate song—whether psalms like those of the OT, or hymns directed to God or to others that Christians were accustomed to singing—could provide a means for praising and thanking God (v. 20). Actually, however, all three terms may refer to different types of psalms.
5:21–6:9 In chs. 2–4 Paul showed the way God brought believing Jews and Gentiles together into a new relationship in Christ. In 4:1–6 he stressed the importance of unity. Now he shows how believers, filled with the Spirit, can live together in a practical way in various human relationships. This list of mutual responsibilities is similar to the pattern found in Col 3:18–4:1; 1Pe 2:13–3:12; cf. Ro 13:1–10.
5:21 *Submit to one another.* Basic to the following paragraphs. Paul will show how, in each relationship, each partner can have a conciliatory attitude that will help that relationship. The grammar indicates that this mutual submission is associated with the filling of the Spirit in v. 18. The command "be filled" (v. 18) is followed by a series of participles in the Greek: speaking (v. 19), singing (v. 19), making music (v. 19), giving thanks (v. 20) and submitting (v. 21).
5:22 *Wives, submit.* An aspect of the mutual submission taught in v. 21. To submit meant to yield one's own rights. If the relationship called for it, as in the military, the term could connote obedience, but that meaning is not called for here. In fact, the word "obey" does not appear in Scripture with respect to wives, though it does with respect to children (6:1) and slaves (6:5). *as to the Lord.* Does not put a woman's husband in the place of the Lord, but shows rather that a woman ought to submit to her husband as an act of submission to the Lord.
5:23 *head of the wife.* See note on 1Co 11:3. *as Christ.* The analogy between the relationship of Christ to the church and that of the husband to the wife is basic to the entire passage. *his body.* See 2:16; 4:4,12,16. *Savior.* Christ earned, so to speak, the right to his special relationship to the church.
5:25 *Husbands.* Paul now shows that this is not a one-sided submission, but a reciprocal relationship. *love.* Explained by what follows. *gave himself up for her.* Not only the expression of our Lord's love, but also an example of how the husband ought to devote himself to his wife's good. To give oneself up to death for the beloved is a more extreme expression of devotion than the wife is called on to make.
5:26 *washing with water through the word.* Many attempts have been made to see marriage customs or liturgical symbolism in these words. One thing is clear: The Lord Jesus died not only to bring forgiveness, but also to effect a new life of holiness in the church, which is his "bride." A study of the concepts of washing, of water and of the word should include reference to Jn 3:5; Tit 3:5; 1Pe 1:23; 3:21.
5:27 *holy and blameless.* See 1:4.

himself[a] as a radiant church, without stain or wrinkle or any other blemish, but holy and blameless.[b] 28In this same way, husbands ought to love their wives[c] as their own bodies. He who loves his wife loves himself. 29After all, no one ever hated his own body, but he feeds and cares for it, just as Christ does the church— 30for we are members of his body.[d] 31"For this reason a man will leave his father and mother and be united to his wife, and the two will become one flesh."[o][e] 32This is a profound mystery—but I am talking about Christ and the church. 33However, each one of you also must love his wife[f] as he loves himself, and the wife must respect her husband.

Children and Parents

6 Children, obey your parents in the Lord, for this is right.[g] 2"Honor your father and mother"—which is the first commandment with a promise— 3"that it may go well with you and that you may enjoy long life on the earth."[p][h]

4Fathers, do not exasperate your children;[i] instead, bring them up in the training and instruction of the Lord.[j]

Slaves and Masters

5Slaves, obey your earthly masters with respect[k] and fear, and with sincerity of heart,[l] just as you would obey Christ.[m]

6Obey them not only to win their favor when their eye is on you, but like slaves of Christ,[n] doing the will of God from your heart. 7Serve wholeheartedly, as if you were serving the Lord, not men,[o] 8because you know that the Lord will reward everyone for whatever good he does,[p] whether he is slave or free.

9And masters, treat your slaves in the same way. Do not threaten them, since you know that he who is both their Master and yours[q] is in heaven, and there is no favoritism[r] with him.

The Armor of God

10Finally, be strong in the Lord[s] and in his mighty power.[t] 11Put on the full armor of God[u] so that you can take your stand against the devil's schemes. 12For our struggle is not against flesh and blood,[v] but against the rulers, against the authorities,[w] against the powers[x] of this dark world and against the spiritual forces of evil in the heavenly realms.[y] 13Therefore put on the full armor of God,[z] so that when the day of evil comes, you may be able to stand your ground, and after you have done everything, to stand. 14Stand firm then, with the belt of truth buckled around your waist,[a] with the breastplate of righteousness in place,[b] 15and with your feet fitted with the readiness that comes

5:27 [a]S 2Co 4:14 [b]Eph 1:4
5:28 [c]ver 25
5:30 [d]S Ro 12:5; S 1Co 12:27
5:31 [e]Ge 2:24; Mt 19:5; 1Co 6:16
5:33 [f]ver 25
6:1 [g]Pr 6:20; Col 3:20
6:3 [h]Ex 20:12; Dt 5:16
6:4 [i]Col 3:21 /Ge 18:19; Dt 6:7; Pr 13:24; 22:6
6:5 [k]1Ti 6:1; Tit 2:9; 1Pe 2:18 [l]Col 3:22
[m]Eph 5:22
6:6 [n]S Ro 6:22
6:7 [o]Col 3:23
6:8 [p]S Mt 16:27; Col 3:24
6:9 [q]Job 31:13, 14 [r]S Ac 10:34
6:10 [s]2Sa 10:12; Ps 27:14; Hag 2:4; 1Co 16:13; 2Ti 2:1 [t]Eph 1:19
6:11 [u]ver 13; Ro 13:12; 1Th 5:8
6:12 [v]1Co 15:50; Heb 2:14 [w]Eph 1:21; 3:10 [x]Ro 8:38 [y]S Eph 1:3
6:13 [z]ver 11; S 2Co 6:7
6:14 [a]Isa 11:5 [b]Ps 132:9; Isa 59:17; 1Th 5:8

[o]31 Gen. 2:24 [p]3 Deut. 5:16

5:28-29 *as their own bodies... loves himself... his own body.* The basis for such expressions and for the teaching of these verses is the quotation from Ge 2:24 in v. 31. If the husband and wife become "one flesh," then for the man to love his wife is to love one who has become part of himself.
5:32 *mystery.* See note on Ro 11:25. The profound truth of the union of Christ and his "bride," the church, is beyond unaided human understanding. It is not that the relationship of husband and wife provides an illustration of the union of Christ and the church, but that the basic reality is the latter, with marriage a human echo of that relationship.
5:33 *love... respect.* A rephrasing and summary of the whole passage.
6:3 *on the earth.* In Dt 5:16 (see Ex 20:12), where this commandment occurs, the "promise" (v. 2) was expressed in terms of the anticipated occupation of the "land," i.e., Palestine. That specific application was, of course, not appropriate to the Ephesians, so the more general application is made here.
6:4 *do not exasperate.* Fathers must surrender any right they may feel they have to act unreasonably toward their children.
6:5 *Slaves.* Both the OT and the NT included regulations for societal situations such as slavery and divorce (see Dt 24:1-4), which were the results of the hardness of hearts (Mt 19:8). Such regulations did not encourage or condone such situations but were divinely-given, practical ways of dealing with the realities of the day.
6:9 *masters.* Once again Paul stresses reciprocal attitudes (cf. 5:21-6:4). See note on Tit 2:9.

6:10-20 Paul's scope in Ephesians has been cosmic. From the very beginning he has drawn attention to the unseen world (see note on 1:3; see also 1:10,20-23; 2:6; 6:10), and now he describes the spiritual battle that takes place against evil "in the heavenly realms" (v. 12).
6:10 *strong... power.* Implies that human effort is inadequate but God's power is invincible.
6:12 *not against flesh and blood.* A caution against lashing out against human opponents as though they were the real enemy and also against assuming that the battle can be fought using merely human resources. *rulers... forces.* Cf. Paul's earlier allusions to powerful beings in the unseen world (see notes on 1:21; 3:10). *heavenly realms.* See note on 1:3.
6:13-14 *stand your ground... Stand firm.* In this context the imagery is not that of a massive invasion of the domain of evil, but of individual soldiers withstanding assault.
6:14 *belt of truth.* Cf. the symbolic clothing of the Messiah in Isa 11:5. Character, not brute force, wins the battle, just as in the case of the Messiah. *breastplate of righteousness.* Here again, the warrior's character is his defense. God himself is symbolically described as putting on a breastplate of righteousness when he goes forth to bring about justice (see Isa 59:17).
6:15 *feet fitted with the readiness.* Whereas the description of the messenger's feet in Isa 52:7 reflects the custom of running barefooted, here the message of the gospel is picturesquely connected with the protective and supportive footgear of the Roman soldier.

from the gospel of peace.[c] [16]In addition to all this, take up the shield of faith,[d] with which you can extinguish all the flaming arrows of the evil one.[e] [17]Take the helmet of salvation[f] and the sword of the Spirit,[g] which is the word of God.[h] [18]And pray in the Spirit[i] on all occasions[j] with all kinds of prayers and requests.[k] With this in mind, be alert and always keep on praying[l] for all the saints.

[19]Pray also for me,[m] that whenever I open my mouth, words may be given me so that I will fearlessly[n] make known the mystery[o] of the gospel, [20]for which I am an ambassador[p] in chains.[q] Pray that I may declare it fearlessly, as I should.

6:15 [c]Isa 52:7;
Ro 10:15
6:16 [d]1Jn 5:4
[e]S Mt 5:37
6:17 [f]Isa 59:17
[g]Isa 49:2
[h]S Heb 4:12
6:18 [i]Ro 8:26,27
[j]S Lk 18:1
[k]Mt 26:41;
Php 1:4; 4:6
[l]S Ac 1:14;
Col 1:3
6:19 [m]S 1Th 5:25
[n]S Ac 4:29
[o]S Ro 16:25
6:20 [p]2Co 5:20
[q]S Ac 21:33

6:21 [r]S Ac 20:4
6:22 [s]Col 4:7-9
[t]Col 2:2; 4:8
6:23 [u]Gal 6:16;
2Th 3:16;
1Pe 5:14

Final Greetings

[21]Tychicus,[r] the dear brother and faithful servant in the Lord, will tell you everything, so that you also may know how I am and what I am doing. [22]I am sending him to you for this very purpose, that you may know how we are,[s] and that he may encourage you.[t]

[23]Peace[u] to the brothers, and love with faith from God the Father and the Lord Jesus Christ. [24]Grace to all who love our Lord Jesus Christ with an undying love.

6:16 *shield of faith . . . extinguish . . . flaming arrows.* Describes the large Roman shield covered with leather, which could be soaked in water and used to put out flame-tipped arrows.
6:17–18 *sword of the Spirit . . . pray in the Spirit.* Reminders that the battle is spiritual and must be fought in God's strength, depending on the word and on God through prayer.
6:17 *helmet of salvation.* Isa 59:17 has similar language,

along with the breastplate imagery (see note on v. 14). The helmet both protected the soldier and provided a striking symbol of military victory.
6:21–23 Paul concludes with greetings that lack personal references such as are usually found in his letters. This is understandable if Ephesians is a circular letter (see note on 1:1).
6:21 *Tychicus.* An associate of Paul who traveled as his representative (cf. Col 4:7; 2Ti 4:12; Tit 3:12).

PHILIPPIANS

Author, Date and Place of Writing

The early church was unanimous in its testimony that Philippians was written by the apostle Paul (see 1:1). Internally the letter reveals the stamp of genuineness. The many personal references of the author fit what we know of Paul from other NT books.

It is evident that Paul wrote the letter from prison (see 1:13-14). Some have argued that this imprisonment took place in Ephesus, perhaps c. A.D. 53-55; others put it in Caesarea c. 57-59. Best evidence, however, favors Rome as the place of origin and the date as c. 61. This fits well with the account of Paul's house arrest in Ac 28:14-31. When he wrote Philippians, he was not in the Mamertine dungeon as he was when he wrote 2 Timothy. He was in his own rented house, where for two years he was free to impart the gospel to all who came to him.

Purpose

Paul's primary purpose in writing this letter was to thank the Philippians for the gift they had sent him upon learning of his detention at Rome (1:5; 4:10-19). However, he makes use of this occasion to fulfill several other desires: (1) to report on his own circumstances (1:12-26; 4:10-19); (2) to encourage the Philippians to stand firm in the face of persecution and rejoice regardless of circumstances (1:27-30; 4:4); (3) to exhort them to humility and unity (2:1-11; 4:2-5); (4) to commend Timothy and Epaphroditus to the Philippian church (2:19-30); and (5) to warn the Philippians against the Judaizers (legalists) and antinomians (libertines) among them (ch. 3).

Recipients

The city of Philippi was named after King Philip II of Macedon, father of Alexander the Great. It was a prosperous Roman colony, which meant that the citizens of Philippi were also citizens of the city of Rome itself. They prided themselves on being Romans (see Ac 16:21), dressed like Romans and

Philippi In the Time of Paul

The Roman colony of Philippi (*Colonia Augusta Julia Philippensis*) was an important city in Macedonia, located on the main highway leading from the eastern provinces to Rome. This road, the Via Egnatia, bisected the city's forum and was the chief cause of its prosperity and political importance. Ten miles distant on the coast was Neapolis, the place where Paul landed after sailing from Troas, in response to the Macedonian vision.

As a prominent city of the gold-producing region of Macedonia, Philippi had a proud history. Named originally after Philip II, the father of Alexander the Great, the city was later honored with the name of Julius Caesar and Augustus. Many Italian settlers from the legions swelled the ranks of citizens and made Philippi vigorous and polyglot. It grew from a small settlement to a city of dignity and privilege. Among its highest honors was the *ius Italicum*, by which it enjoyed rights legally equivalent to those of Italian cities.

Ruins of the theater, the acropolis, the forum, the baths, and the western commemorative arch mentioned as the "gate" of the city in Ac 16:13 have been found. A little farther beyond the arch at the Gangites River is the place where Paul addressed some God-fearing women and where Lydia was converted.

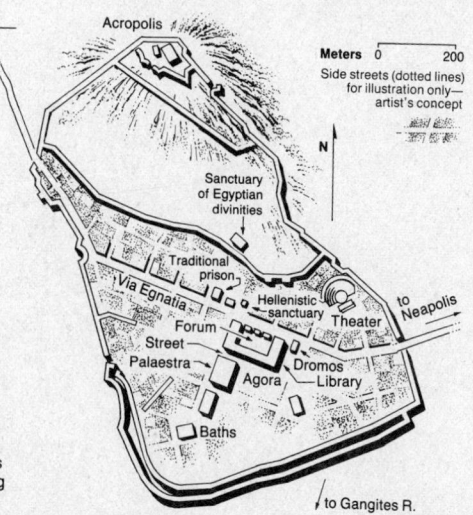

often spoke Latin. No doubt this was the background for Paul's reference to the believer's heavenly citizenship (3:20-21). Many of the Philippians were retired military men who had been given land in the vicinity and who in turn served as a military presence in this frontier city. That Philippi was a Roman colony may explain why there were not enough Jews there to permit the establishment of a synagogue and why Paul does not quote the OT in the Philippian letter.

Characteristics

1. Philippians contains no OT quotations.
2. It is a missionary thank-you letter in which the missionary reports on the progress of his work.
3. It manifests a particularly vigorous type of Christian living: (1) self-humbling (2:1-4); (2) pressing toward the goal (3:13-14); (3) lack of anxiety (4:6); (4) ability to do all things (4:13).
4. It is outstanding as the NT letter of joy; the word "joy" in its various forms occurs some 16 times.
5. It contains one of the most profound Christological passages in the NT (2:5-11). Yet, profound as it is, Paul includes it mainly for illustrative purposes.

Outline

I. Salutation (1:1-2)
II. Thanksgiving and Prayer for the Philippians (1:3-11)
III. Paul's Personal Circumstances (1:12-26)
IV. Exhortations (1:27-2:18)
   A. Living a Life Worthy of the Gospel (1:27-30)
   B. Following the Servant Attitude of Christ (2:1-18)
V. Paul's Associates in the Gospel (2:19-30)
   A. Timothy (2:19-24)
   B. Epaphroditus (2:25-30)
VI. Warnings against Judaizers and Antinomians (3:1-4:1)
   A. Against Judaizers or Legalists (3:1-16)
   B. Against Antinomians or Libertines (3:17-4:1)
VII. Final Exhortations, Thanks and Conclusion (4:2-23)
   A. Exhortations concerning Various Aspects of the Christian Life (4:2-9)
   B. Concluding Testimony and Repeated Thanks (4:10-20)
   C. Greetings and Benediction (4:21-23)

1 Paul and Timothy,[a] servants of Christ Jesus,

To all the saints[b] in Christ Jesus at Philippi,[c] together with the overseers[a][d] and deacons:[e]

[2]Grace and peace to you from God our Father and the Lord Jesus Christ.[f]

Thanksgiving and Prayer

[3]I thank my God every time I remember you.[g] [4]In all my prayers for all of you, I always pray[h] with joy [5]because of your partnership[i] in the gospel from the first day[j] until now, [6]being confident of this, that he who began a good work in you will carry it on to completion[k] until the day of Christ Jesus.[l]

[7]It is right[m] for me to feel this way about all of you, since I have you in my heart;[n] for whether I am in chains[o] or defending[p] and confirming the gospel, all of you share in God's grace with me. [8]God can testify[q]

how I long for all of you with the affection of Christ Jesus.

[9]And this is my prayer: that your love[r] may abound more and more in knowledge and depth of insight, [s] [10]so that you may be able to discern what is best and may be pure and blameless until the day of Christ, [t] [11]filled with the fruit of righteousness[u] that comes through Jesus Christ—to the glory and praise of God.

Paul's Chains Advance the Gospel

[12]Now I want you to know, brothers, that what has happened to me has really served to advance the gospel. [13]As a result, it has become clear throughout the whole palace guard[b] and to everyone else that I am in chains[v] for Christ. [14]Because of my chains,[w] most of the brothers in the Lord have been encouraged to speak the word of God more courageously and fearlessly.[x]

[15]It is true that some preach Christ out

Cross references
1:1 [a]S Ac 16:1;
2Co 1:1
[b]S Ac 9:13
[c]S Ac 16:12
[d]S 1Ti 3:1
[e]1Ti 3:8
1:2 [f]S Ro 1:7
1:3 [g]S Ro 1:8
1:4 [h]S Ro 1:10
1:5 [i]Ac 2:42;
Php 4:15
[j]Ac 16:12-40
1:6 [k]Ps 138:8
[l]ver 10; S 1Co 1:8
1:7 [m]2Pe 1:13
[n]2Co 7:3 [o]ver 13,14,17;
S Ac 21:33 [p]ver 16
1:8 [q]S Ro 1:9

1:9 [r]1Th 3:12
[s]S Eph 1:17
1:10 [t]ver 6;
S 1Co 1:8
1:11 [u]S Jas 3:18
1:13 [v]ver 7,14, 17; S Ac 21:33
1:14 [w]ver 7,13, 17; S Ac 21:33
[x]S Ac 4:29

[a]1 Traditionally bishops   [b]13 Or whole palace

1:1–2 As in all his letters, Paul follows the conventional letter format of his day, with its three elements: (1) identification of the sender, (2) identification of the recipients, (3) greeting.

1:1 Timothy. See Introduction to 1 Timothy: Recipient. Timothy is identified with the contents of the letter as Paul's associate, but not as co-author. servants. See Ro 1:1; Tit 1:1; Phm 1. In Paul's case, this designation brings out an essential aspect of the more usual identification of himself as "apostle." saints. A designation, not of individual moral purity, but of spiritual union with Christ, as the following "in Christ Jesus" shows (see Ro 1:7; 1Co 1:2 and notes). Philippi. See Introduction: Recipients. overseers and deacons. The only place in Paul's writings where church officers as a group are singled out as recipients of a letter. overseers. See note on 1Ti 3:1. deacons. See note on 1Ti 3:8.

1:2 The opening greeting is not merely a matter of polite custom but is given a distinctively Christian tone and content.

1:3–4 I thank my God . . . prayers for . . . you . . . with joy. Prayers of joyful thanksgiving for his readers' response to the gospel are a hallmark of the opening sentences of Paul's letters (see Ro 1:8; 1Co 1:4; Col 1:3; 1Th 1:2; 2Th 1:3; 2Ti 1:3; Phm 4).

1:5 your partnership in the gospel. The basis of Paul's prayerful thanksgiving is not only their reception of the gospel but also their active support of his ministry (see 4:15). from the first day. When Paul first came to Philippi (see Ac 16:12). now. Toward the close (see 2:24) of Paul's first Roman imprisonment (see Ac 28:16–31).

1:6 work in you. Paul is confident, not only of what God has done "for" the readers in forgiving their sins, but also of what he has done "in" them (see v. 11). "Work" refers to God's activity in saving them. day of Christ Jesus. His return, when their salvation will be brought to completion (see 1:10; 2:16; 1Co 1:8; 5:5; 2Co 1:14). It is God who initiates salvation, who continues it and who will one day bring it to its consummation.

1:7 share in God's grace. Not even imprisonment and persecution can change such sharing. Even in Paul's imprisonment they willingly identified themselves with Paul by sending Epaphroditus and their financial gifts. They had

become one with Paul in his persecution.

1:8 affection of Christ Jesus. The deep yearning and intense, compassionate love exhibited by Jesus himself and now fostered in Paul by his union with Christ. This affection reaches out to all impartially and without exception.

1:9 abound more and more. Real love requires growth and maturation (see 1Th 3:12; 4:10; 2Th 1:3). in knowledge. The way love grows (cf. Col 1:9). depth of insight. Practical discernment and sensitivity. Christian love is not mere sentiment; it is rooted in knowledge and understanding.

1:10 discern what is best. Christians are to approve (and practice) what is morally and ethically superior. pure and blameless. The goal of Christians in this life is to be without any mixture of evil and not open to censure because of moral or spiritual failure. until the day of Christ. Then the goal will be perfectly realized (see note on v. 6), and then Christians must give an account (see 2Co 5:10).

1:11 filled with the fruit of righteousness. What is expected of all Christians (cf. Mt 5:20–48; Heb 12:11; Jas 3:18; see also Am 6:12; Gal 5:22). through Jesus Christ. Produced by Christ (in union with him) through the work of the Holy Spirit (cf. Jn 15:5; Eph 2:10). to the glory and praise of God. The ultimate goal of all that God does in believers (see Eph 1:6,12,14).

1:12 what has happened to me. Paul's detainment in prison. advance the gospel. Instead of hindering the gospel, Paul's imprisonment had served to make it known.

1:13 clear . . . chains for Christ. It has become apparent to all who know of Paul's situation that he is imprisoned, not because he is guilty of some crime, but on account of his stand for the gospel. whole palace guard. A contingent of soldiers, numbering several thousand, many of whom would have had personal contact with Paul or would have been assigned individually to guard him during the course of his imprisonment (see Ac 28:16,30). chains. Either actual chains or a broader reference to his sufferings and imprisonment (see v. 14).

1:14 encouraged to speak. The unexpected result of Paul's imprisonment is that others, encouraged by his example, are forcefully proclaiming the gospel.

1:15 out of envy and rivalry . . . out of goodwill. The gospel preaching stimulated by Paul's imprisonment stems from

of envy and rivalry, but others out of goodwill. [16]The latter do so in love, knowing that I am put here for the defense of the gospel.[y] [17]The former preach Christ out of selfish ambition,[z] not sincerely, supposing that they can stir up trouble for me while I am in chains.[c][a] [18]But what does it matter? The important thing is that in every way, whether from false motives or true, Christ is preached. And because of this I rejoice.

Yes, and I will continue to rejoice, [19]for I know that through your prayers[b] and the help given by the Spirit of Jesus Christ,[c] what has happened to me will turn out for my deliverance.[d][d] [20]I eagerly expect[e] and hope that I will in no way be ashamed, but will have sufficient courage[f] so that now as always Christ will be exalted in my body,[g] whether by life or by death.[h] [21]For to me, to live is Christ[i] and to die is gain. [22]If I am to go on living in the body, this will mean fruitful labor for me. Yet what shall I choose? I do not know! [23]I am torn between the two: I desire to depart[j] and

be with Christ,[k] which is better by far; [24]but it is more necessary for you that I remain in the body. [25]Convinced of this, I know that I will remain, and I will continue with all of you for your progress and joy in the faith, [26]so that through my being with you again your joy in Christ Jesus will overflow on account of me.

[27]Whatever happens, conduct yourselves in a manner worthy[l] of the gospel of Christ. Then, whether I come and see you or only hear about you in my absence, I will know that you stand firm[m] in one spirit, contending[n] as one man for the faith of the gospel [28]without being frightened in any way by those who oppose you. This is a sign to them that they will be destroyed, but that you will be saved—and that by God. [29]For it has been granted to you[o] on behalf of Christ not only to believe on him, but also to suffer[p] for him, [30]since you are going through the same

---

Cross references (center column):

1:16 [y]ver 7,12
1:17 [z]Php 2:3
[a]ver 7,13,14;
S Ac 21:33
1:19 [b]2Co 1:11
[c]S Ac 16:7
[d]Phm 22
1:20 [e]Ro 8:19
[f]ver 14 [g]1Co 6:20
[h]Ro 14:8
1:21 [i]Gal 2:20
1:23 [j]2Ti 4:6

[k]S Jn 12:26
1:27 [l]S Eph 4:1
[m]S 1Co 16:13
[n]Jude 3
1:29 [o]Mt 5:11,
12; Ac 5:41
[p]S Ac 14:22

[c]16,17 Some late manuscripts have verses 16 and 17 in reverse order.　[d]19 Or salvation

---

either one of two sharply opposed motives.
1:16 *The latter do so in love.* Those who preach with a right motive recognize the true reason for Paul's imprisonment, already expressed earlier in v. 13, and are encouraged to take the same bold stand that he has taken.
1:17 *The former preach Christ out of selfish ambition.* Those who preach with wrong, insincere motives do so out of a sense of competition with Paul and so think they are making his imprisonment more difficult to bear. *not sincerely.* Not from pure motives.
1:18 *whether from false motives or true, Christ is preached.* These preachers are not to be viewed as being heretical. Their message is true, even though their motives are not pure. The gospel has its objectivity and validity apart from those who proclaim it; the message is more than the medium. *I rejoice ... will continue to rejoice.* An example of the kind of vigorous Christian experience Paul expressed. He was under arrest, and fellow Christians sought, by their preaching, to add to his difficulties; yet he kept on rejoicing.
1:19 *Spirit of Jesus Christ.* The Holy Spirit is not only the Spirit of God the Father (Ro 8:9,14; 1Co 2:10–11,14) but also the Spirit of Christ, the second person of the Trinity (Ac 16:7; Ro 8:9; Gal 4:6). He is sent by the Father (Jn 14:16–17,26; Gal 4:6) and by the Son (Jn 15:26; 16:7). *deliverance.* Either Paul's release from prison (see v. 25; 2:24) or, in view of the immediately following verses, the deliverance brought to the believer by death (cf. Ro 8:28). Verse 25, however, seems to point to the former interpretation.
1:20 *ashamed ... sufficient courage.* The circumstances of imprisonment, with all its attendant suffering and oppression, constitute a real temptation for Paul to abandon the gospel and his resolute service for Christ. *my body.* Where the exalted Christ dwells by his Spirit and is at work (cf. Ro 8:9–10), and so is exalted by what Paul does. *whether by life or by death.* Whether his service for Christ continues or ends in death.
1:21 *to live is Christ.* Christ was the source and secret of Paul's continual joy (even in prison), for Paul's life found all its meaning in Christ. *gain.* Verse 23 specifies that the gain

brought by death is "being with Christ," so that here Paul is saying that his ultimate concern and most precious possession, both now and forever, is Christ and his relationship to him.
1:22 *fruitful labor.* The spread of the gospel and the upbuilding of the church.
1:23–24 *depart and be with Christ ... remain in the body.* Either alternative was a good one. While mysteries remain, this passage clearly teaches that when believers die they are with Christ, apart from the body.
1:23 *better by far.* Being with Christ after death must involve some kind of conscious presence and fellowship (cf. 2Co 5:6,8).
1:24 *necessary for you.* Paul puts the needs of those he ministers to ahead of his personal preference.
1:25 *I will remain.* Possibly Paul was later released from prison (see "Paul's Fourth Missionary Journey," p. 1836). *progress ... in the faith.* The Christian life is to be one of joyful growth and advance (see note on v. 9 and the verses cited there).
1:26 *your joy in Christ Jesus ... on account of me.* Paul's conduct of his ministry among the Philippians will be a reason for rejoicing in what Christ is doing among them.
1:27 *worthy of the gospel.* Appropriate to the standards and goals given with the gospel. *in one spirit.* Having a common disposition and purpose. *contending as one man.* Particularly where the gospel is under attack, Christians need each other and must stand together.
1:28 *a sign.* Persistent opposition to the church and the gospel is a sure sign of eventual destruction, since it involves rejection of the only way of salvation. By the same token, when Christians are persecuted for their faith, this is a sign of the genuineness of their salvation (see 2Th 1:5).
1:29 *granted ... to suffer.* Given as a gift or privilege. Christian suffering, as well as faith, is a blessing (cf. Mt 5:11–12; Ac 5:41; Jas 1:2; 1Pe 4:14). The Christian life is to be a "not only ... but also" proposition: not only believing but also suffering.
1:30 *same struggle.* Their common involvement with Paul in conflict with those who oppose the gospel. *you saw.* When

struggle *q* you saw *r* I had, and now hear *s* that I still have.

Imitating Christ's Humility

2 If you have any encouragement from being united with Christ, if any comfort from his love, if any fellowship with the Spirit, *t* if any tenderness and compassion, *u* ²then make my joy complete *v* by being like-minded, *w* having the same love, being one *x* in spirit and purpose. ³Do nothing out of selfish ambition or vain conceit, *y* but in humility consider others better than yourselves. *z* ⁴Each of you should look not only to your own interests, but also to the interests of others. *a*

⁵Your attitude should be the same as that of Christ Jesus: *b*

⁶Who, being in very nature *e* God, *c*
  did not consider equality with God *d*
    something to be grasped,
⁷but made himself nothing, *e*

taking the very nature *f* of a
    servant, *f*
  being made in human likeness. *g*
⁸And being found in appearance as a
    man,
  he humbled himself
  and became obedient to death *h* —
    even death on a cross! *i*
⁹Therefore God exalted him *j* to the
    highest place
  and gave him the name that is above
    every name, *k*
¹⁰that at the name of Jesus every knee
    should bow, *l*
  in heaven and on earth and under
    the earth, *m*
¹¹and every tongue confess that Jesus
    Christ is Lord, *n*
  to the glory of God the Father.

1:30 *q*1Th 2:2; Heb 10:32
*r*Ac 16:19-40 *s*ver 13
2:1 *t*2Co 13:14 *u*Col 3:12
2:2 *v*S Jn 3:29 *w*Php 4:2 *x*S Ro 15:5
2:3 *y*Gal 5:26 *z*Ro 12:10; 1Pe 5:5
2:4 *a*S 1Co 10:24
2:5 *b*S Mt 11:29
2:6 *c*Jn 1:1; S 14:9 *d*Jn 5:18
2:7 *e*2Co 8:9

*f*S Mt 20:28 *g*S Jn 1:14; Ro 8:3; Heb 2:17
2:8 *h*S Mt 26:39; Jn 10:18; Ro 5:19; Heb 5:8 *i*S 1Co 1:23
2:9 *j*Isa 52:13; 53:12; Da 7:14; Ac 2:33; Heb 2:9 *k*Eph 1:20,21
2:10 *l*Ps 95:6; Isa 45:23; Ro 14:11 *m*Mt 28:18; Eph 1:10; Col 1:20

2:11 *n*S Jn 13:13

*e*6 Or *in the form of* *f*7 Or *the form*

Paul and Silas first visited Philippi and were imprisoned (see Ac 16:19–40).
2:1 *united with Christ.* Or "united in Christ." In Paul's teaching, this personal union is the basic reality of salvation. To be in Christ is to be saved. It is to be in intimate personal relationship with Christ the Savior. From this relationship flow all the particular benefits and fruits of salvation, like encouragement (see, e.g., 3:8–10; Ro 8:1; 2Co 5:17; Gal 2:20). *comfort from his love.* The comforting knowledge and assurance that come from God's love in Christ, demonstrated especially in Christ's death for the forgiveness of sins and eternal life (see Jn 3:16; Ro 5:8; 8:38–39; 1Jn 3:16; 4:9–10,16). *fellowship with the Spirit.* The fellowship among believers produced by the Spirit, who indwells each of them (see 2Co 13:14). *tenderness and compassion.* Christians are to have intense care and deep sympathy for each other (see 1:8; Col 3:12). All these benefits—encouragement, comfort, fellowship, tenderness and compassion—are viewed by Paul as present realities for the Philippians.
2:2 *like-minded . . . same love . . . one in spirit and purpose.* Emphasizes the unity that should exist among Christians. *like-minded.* Not uniformity in thought but the common disposition to work together and serve one another—the "attitude" of Christ (v. 5; see 4:2; Ro 12:16; 15:5; 2Co 13:11).
2:3 *selfish ambition or vain conceit.* The mortal enemies of unity and harmony in the church (cf. 1:17; see Gal 5:20, where "selfish ambition" is listed among the "acts of the sinful nature"). *humility.* The source of Christian unity. This is the mind-set of the person who is not conceited but who has a right attitude toward himself. *consider others better than yourselves.* Not that everyone else is superior or more talented, but that Christian love sees others as worthy of preferential treatment (see Ro 12:10; Gal 5:13; Eph 5:21; 1Pe 5:5).
2:4 *your own interests.* These are proper, but only if there is equal concern for the interests of others (cf. Ro 15:1).
2:5 *Your attitude . . . the same as . . . Christ.* In spite of all that is unique and radically different about the person and work of Christ (see vv. 6–11), Christians are to have his attitude of self-sacrificing humility and love for others (see vv. 2–4; Mt 11:29; Jn 13:12–17).

2:6–11 The poetic, even lyric, character of these verses is apparent. Many view these as an early Christian hymn (see note on Col 3:16), taken over and perhaps modified by Paul. If so, they nonetheless express his convictions. The passage treats Christ's humiliation (vv. 6–8) and exaltation (vv. 9–11).
2:6 *in very nature God.* Affirming that Jesus is fully God (see note on Ro 9:5). *nature.* Essential form (see NIV text note), the sum of those qualities that make God specifically God. *equality with God.* The status and privileges that inevitably follow from being in very nature God. *something to be grasped.* Perhaps something to be forcibly retained—the glory Christ had with the Father before his incarnation. But he did not consider that high position to be something he could not give up. On the other hand, it may be something still to be attained, like a prize, as if he did not yet possess it.
2:7 *made himself nothing.* Lit. "emptied himself." He did this, not by giving up deity, but by laying aside his glory (see Jn 17:5) and submitting to the humiliation of becoming man (see 2Co 8:9). Jesus is truly God and truly man. Another view is that he emptied himself, not of deity itself, but of its prerogatives—the high position and glory of deity. *nature of a servant.* Emphasizes the full reality of his servant identity (see Mt 20:28). As a servant, he was always submissive to the will of the Father.
2:8 *appearance as a man.* Not only was Jesus "like" a human being (v. 7), but he also took on the actual outward characteristics of a man (see Jn 1:14; Ro 8:3; Heb 2:17). *humbled himself.* See v. 7; 2Co 8:9. *obedient.* How Jesus humbled himself (cf. Heb 5:7–8). A "servant" (v. 7) obeys. *to death.* Stresses both the totality and the climax of Jesus' obedience. *on a cross.* Heightens Jesus' humiliation; he died as someone cursed (see Gal 3:13; Heb 12:2). Crucifixion was the most degrading kind of execution that could be inflicted on a person.
2:9 *exalted.* See Mt 28:18; Ac 2:33; cf. Isa 52:13. *the name . . . above every name.* Reference doubtless is to the office or rank conferred on Jesus—his glorious position, not his proper name (cf. Eph 1:21; Heb 1:4–5).
2:10–11 *bow . . . confess.* Cf. Isa 45:23. God's design is that all people everywhere should worship and serve Jesus as Lord. Ultimately all will acknowledge him as Lord (see Ro 14:9), whether willingly or not.

Shining as Stars

12Therefore, my dear friends, as you have always obeyed—not only in my presence, but now much more in my absence—continue to work out your salvation with fear and trembling, *o* 13for it is God who works in you *p* to will and to act according to his good purpose. *q*

14Do everything without complaining *r* or arguing, 15so that you may become blameless *s* and pure, children of God *t* without fault in a crooked and depraved generation, *u* in which you shine like stars in the universe 16as you hold out *g* the word of life—in order that I may boast on the day of Christ *v* that I did not run *w* or labor for nothing. *x* 17But even if I am being poured out like a drink offering *y* on the sacrifice *z* and service coming from your faith, I am glad and rejoice with all of you. *a* 18So you too should be glad and rejoice with me.

Timothy and Epaphroditus

19I hope in the Lord Jesus to send Timothy *b* to you soon, *c* that I also may be cheered when I receive news about you. 20I have no one else like him, *d* who takes a genuine interest in your welfare. 21For

everyone looks out for his own interests, *e* not those of Jesus Christ. 22But you know that Timothy has proved himself, because as a son with his father *f* he has served with me in the work of the gospel. 23I hope, therefore, to send him as soon as I see how things go with me. *g* 24And I am confident *h* in the Lord that I myself will come soon.

25But I think it is necessary to send back to you Epaphroditus, my brother, fellow worker *i* and fellow soldier, *j* who is also your messenger, whom you sent to take care of my needs. *k* 26For he longs for all of you *l* and is distressed because you heard he was ill. 27Indeed he was ill, and almost died. But God had mercy on him, and not on him only but also on me, to spare me sorrow upon sorrow. 28Therefore I am all the more eager to send him, *m* so that when you see him again you may be glad and I may have less anxiety. 29Welcome him in the Lord with great joy, and honor men like him, *n* 30because he almost died for the work of Christ, risking his life to make up for the help you could not give me. *o*

Cross references

2:12 *o*S 2Co 7:15
2:13 *p*Ezr 1:5; 1Co 12:6; 15:10; Gal 2:8; Heb 13:21
*q*Eph 1:5
2:14 *r*1Co 10:10; 1Pe 4:9
2:15 *s*S 1Th 3:13
*t*Mt 5:45,48; Eph 5:1 *u*Ac 2:40
2:16 *v*S 1Co 1:8
*w*S 1Co 9:24
*x*1Th 2:19
2:17 *y*2Co 12:15; 2Ti 4:6 *z*Ro 15:16
*a*S 2Co 6:10
2:19 *b*S Ac 16:1
*c*ver 23
2:20 *d*1Co 16:10

2:21 *e*S 1Co 10:24
2:22 *f*1Co 4:17; 1Ti 1:2
2:23 *g*ver 19
2:24 *h*Php 1:25
2:25 *i*Ro 16:3,9, 21; 2Co 8:23; Php 4:3; Col 4:11; Phm 1 *j*Phm 2 *k*Php 4:18
2:26 *l*Php 1:8
2:28 *m*ver 25
2:29 *n*1Co 16:18; 1Ti 5:17
2:30 *o*1Co 16:17

*g*16 Or *hold on to*

2:12 *Therefore.* Because of Christ's incomparable example (vv. 5–11). *obeyed.* The commands of God as passed on to the Philippians by Paul (see Ro 1:5; 15:18; 2Co 10:5–6). *my presence.* During the course of Paul's second (see Ac 16:12–40) and third (see Ac 20:1–3,6) missionary journeys. *work out your salvation.* Work it out to the finish; not a reference to the attempt to earn one's salvation by works, but to the expression of one's salvation in spiritual growth and development. Salvation is not merely a gift received once for all; it expresses itself in an ongoing process in which the believer is strenuously involved (cf. Mt 24:13; 1Co 9:24–27; Heb 3:14; 6:9–11; 2Pe 1:5–8)—the process of perseverance, spiritual growth and maturation. *fear and trembling.* Not because of doubt or anxiety; rather, the reference is to an active reverence and a singleness of purpose in response to God's grace.
2:13 *to will and to act.* Intention, or faith, and our obedience cannot be separated (cf. Gal 5:6; Jas 2:18,20,22).
2:14–17 Some things involved in working out our salvation.
2:14 *complaining.* Being discontented with God's will is an expression of unbelief that prevents one from doing what pleases God (v. 13; cf. 1Co 10:10). *arguing.* Over debatable points that do not need to be settled for the good of the church (see 2Ti 2:23; Tit 3:9).
2:15 *blameless and pure . . . without fault.* Not absolute, sinless perfection, but wholehearted, unmixed devotion to doing God's will. *crooked and depraved generation.* A description of the unbelieving world (see Ac 2:40; Eph 2:1–3; cf. Mt 17:17). *shine like stars.* The contrast, like light in darkness, that Christians are to be to the world around them (cf. Mt 5:15–16).
2:16 *boast.* Not out of pride or a sense of self-accomplishment, but because of what God has done through Paul (see 1Th 2:19). *day of Christ.* See note on 1:6. *for nothing.* Cf.

1Co 9:24–27.
2:17–18 *I . . . rejoice . . . you too should . . . rejoice.* Christian joy ought always to be mutual.
2:17 *I am being poured out.* The reference may be to his entire ministry as one large thanksgiving sacrifice. However, it is more probable that Paul refers to his present imprisonment, which may end in a martyr's death. His life would then be poured out as a drink offering accompanying the sacrificial service of the Philippians. *like a drink offering.* The OT background is the daily sacrifices in Ex 29:38–41. *coming from your faith.* Genuine faith is active and working (see note on v. 13).
2:19–23 Paul plans to send Timothy, who is with him in Rome (see 1:1), to discover and report on conditions in the Philippian church.
2:20 *I have no one else like him.* Timothy was a good example of the kind of person envisioned in the exhortation of v. 4.
2:21 A sharp contrast between Timothy and Paul's other associates—an outstanding commendation for one so young.
2:22 *as a son with his father.* This relationship between Timothy and Paul is developed at length in 1,2 Timothy. *served.* Like Jesus and Paul, Timothy had a servant attitude.
2:24 Paul anticipates his release in the near future (see 1:25).
2:25–30 Epaphroditus, too, after a close brush with death (vv. 27,30), is being sent home to Philippi.
2:25 *messenger.* A broader use of the Greek word often translated "apostle," applied here to Epaphroditus as a representative of the Philippian church (cf. 2Co 8:23).
2:27 Cf. 1:21–26.
2:28 *anxiety.* The legitimate cares and concerns that come with the Christian life and the gospel ministry (see note on 4:6; cf. 2Co 4:8; 11:28).

No Confidence in the Flesh

3 Finally, my brothers, rejoice in the Lord! It is no trouble for me to write the same things to you again, *p* and it is a safeguard for you.

²Watch out for those dogs, *q* those men who do evil, those mutilators of the flesh. ³For it is we who are the circumcision, *r* we who worship by the Spirit of God, who glory in Christ Jesus, *s* and who put no confidence in the flesh— ⁴though I myself have reasons for such confidence. *t*

If anyone else thinks he has reasons to put confidence in the flesh, I have more: ⁵circumcised *u* on the eighth day, of the people of Israel, *v* of the tribe of Benjamin, *w* a Hebrew of Hebrews; in regard to the law, a Pharisee; *x* ⁶as for zeal, *y* persecuting the church; *z* as for legalistic righteousness, *a* faultless.

⁷But whatever was to my profit I now consider loss *b* for the sake of Christ. ⁸What is more, I consider everything a loss

compared to the surpassing greatness of knowing *c* Christ Jesus my Lord, for whose sake I have lost all things. I consider them rubbish, that I may gain Christ *d* ⁹and be found in him, not having a righteousness of my own that comes from the law, *e* but that which is through faith in Christ—the righteousness *f* that comes from God and is by faith. *g* ¹⁰I want to know *h* Christ and the power of his resurrection and the fellowship of sharing in his sufferings, *i* becoming like him in his death, *j* ¹¹and so, somehow, to attain to the resurrection *k* from the dead.

Pressing on Toward the Goal

¹²Not that I have already obtained all this, or have already been made perfect, *l* but I press on to take hold *m* of that for which Christ Jesus took hold of me. *n* ¹³Brothers, I do not consider myself yet to have taken hold of it. But one thing I do:

3:1 *p*Php 2:18
3:2 *q*Ps 22:16,20; Rev 22:15
3:3 *r*Ro 2:28,29; Gal 6:15; Col 2:11; *s*Ro 15:17; Gal 6:14
3:4 *t*2Co 11:21
3:5 *u*Lk 1:59 *v*2Co 11:22 *w*Ro 11:1 *x*Ac 23:6
3:6 *y*S Ac 21:20 *z*S Ac 8:3 *a*ver 9; Ro 10:5
3:7 *b*Mt 13:44; Lk 14:33
3:8 *c*ver 10; Jer 9:23,24; Jn 17:3; Eph 4:13; S 2Pe 1:2 *d*Ps 73:25
3:9 *e*ver 6; Ro 10:5 *f*Jer 33:16 *g*S Ro 9:30
3:10 *h*S ver 8 *i*S 2Co 1:5 *j*S Ro 6:3-5
3:11 *k*S Jn 11:24; S Ro 6:5; Rev 20:5,6
3:12 *l*1Co 13:10 *m*1Ti 6:12

*n*Ac 9:5,6

3:1 *Finally.* Marks a transition to a new section as Paul moves toward his conclusion; this does not mark the close of the letter, however (cf. 4:8). *rejoice in the Lord!* See 4:4. *same things . . . again.* Matters taken up in the verses that follow, which Paul had previously dealt with either orally when he was in Philippi or perhaps in an earlier letter. *safeguard.* Where serious error is present, there is safety in repetition.

3:2 *dogs.* A harsh word for Paul's opponents, showing their aggressive opposition to the gospel and the seriousness of their error and its destructive, "devouring" results (cf. Gal 5:15). Their teaching was probably similar to what Paul had to oppose in the Galatian churches (see Introduction to Galatians: Occasion and Purpose). *mutilators.* Again a strong, painfully vivid term; the false teachers have so distorted the meaning of circumcision (cf. v. 3) that it has become nothing more than a useless cutting of the body.

3:3 *circumcision.* Its true, inner meaning is realized only in believers, who worship God with genuine spiritual worship and who glory in Christ as their Savior rather than trusting in their own human effort (cf. Ro 2:28-29; Col 2:12-13; see also Dt 30:6; Eze 36:26). *glory . . . no confidence.* Everyone is a "boaster," either in Christ or in himself. *flesh.* Weak human nature. Although the term "flesh" in Paul's letters often refers to sinful human nature, it speaks here of the frailty of human nature: It is not worthy of our confidence; it cannot save.

3:4-14 Paul's personal testimony, a model for every believer; one of the most significant autobiographical sections in his letters (see Gal 1:13-24; 1Ti 1:12-16; cf. Ac 22:1-21; 26:1-23).

3:4-6 Paul's pre-Christian confidence, rooted in his Jewish pedigree, privileges and attainments.

3:5 *eighth day.* See Ge 17:12. *of the people of Israel.* Paul was born a Jew and was not a proselyte. *tribe of Benjamin.* His Jewish roots are deep and unambiguous. Jerusalem, the Holy City, lay on the border of the tribal territory of Benjamin. *Hebrew of Hebrews.* In language, attitudes and lifestyle (see Ac 22:2-3; Gal 1:14). *Pharisee.* See Ac 22:3; 23:6; 26:5.

3:6 *legalistic righteousness.* Righteousness produced by using the law as an attempt to merit God's approval and

blessing (cf. v. 9)—a use of the law strongly opposed by Paul as contrary to the gospel itself (see Ro 3:27-28; 4:1-5; Gal 2:16; 3:10-12). *faultless.* In terms of legalistic standards of scrupulous external conformity to the law.

3:7-14 Paul's confidence in Christ.

3:7 *whatever.* The things mentioned in vv. 5-6. *profit . . . loss.* The great reversal in Paul—begun on the road to Damascus (see Ac 9:3-16)—from being self-centered to being centered in Christ.

3:8 *knowing Christ Jesus.* Not only a knowledge of facts but a knowledge gained through experience that, in its surpassing greatness, transforms the entire person. The following verses spell this out. *rubbish.* What Paul now has as a Christian is not merely preferable or a better alternative; in contrast, his former way of life was worthless and despicable.

3:9 *be found in him.* Union with Christ (see note on 2:1; cf. 1Co 1:30)—not simply an experience in the past, but a present, continuing relationship. *righteousness . . . from the law.* See note on v. 6. *righteousness . . . by faith.* A principal benefit of union with Christ (see Ro 3:21-22; 1Co 1:30; Gal 2:16).

3:10 *know Christ.* As in v. 8, this knowledge is not merely factual; it includes the experience of the power of his resurrection (see Eph 1:17-20), of fellowship in his sufferings (cf. Ac 9:16) and of being like him in his death (see 2Co 4:7-12; 12:9-10). Believers already share positionally in Christ's death and resurrection (cf. Ro 6:2-13; Gal 2:20; 5:24; 6:14; Eph 2:6; Col 2:12-13; 3:1). In v. 10, however, Paul speaks of the actual experience of Christ's resurrection power and of suffering with and for him, even to the point of death.

3:11 *somehow.* Not an indication of doubt or uncertainty, but of intense concern and involvement. *resurrection.* The great personal anticipation of every believer (see Da 12:2; Jn 5:29; Ac 24:15; 1Co 15:23; 1Th 4:16).

3:12-14 The Christian life is like a race; elsewhere Paul uses athletic imagery in a similar way (1Co 9:24-27; 1Ti 6:12; 2Ti 4:7-8; cf. Mt 24:13; Heb 12:1).

3:12 *take hold . . . took hold of me.* Paul's goal is Christ's goal for him, and Christ supplies the resources for him to "press on toward the goal" (v. 14; cf. 2:12-13).

3:13 *Forgetting.* Not losing all memory of his sinful past

Forgetting what is behind[o] and straining toward what is ahead, [14]I press on[p] toward the goal to win the prize[q] for which God has called[r] me heavenward in Christ Jesus.

[15]All of us who are mature[s] should take such a view of things.[t] And if on some point you think differently, that too God will make clear to you.[u] [16]Only let us live up to what we have already attained.

[17]Join with others in following my example,[v] brothers, and take note of those who live according to the pattern we gave you.[w] [18]For, as I have often told you before and now say again even with tears,[x] many live as enemies of the cross of Christ.[y] [19]Their destiny[z] is destruction, their god is their stomach,[a] and their glory is in their shame.[b] Their mind is on earthly things.[c] [20]But our citizenship[d] is in heaven.[e] And we eagerly await a Savior from there, Lord Jesus Christ,[f] [21]who, by the power[g] that enables him to bring everything under

his control, will transform our lowly bodies[h] so that they will be like his glorious body.[i]

4 Therefore, my brothers, you whom I love and long for,[j] my joy and crown, that is how you should stand firm[k] in the Lord, dear friends!

Exhortations

[2]I plead with Euodia and I plead with Syntyche to agree with each other[l] in the Lord. [3]Yes, and I ask you, loyal yokefellow,[h] help these women who have contended at my side in the cause of the gospel, along with Clement and the rest of my fellow workers,[m] whose names are in the book of life.[n]

[4]Rejoice in the Lord always. I will say it again: Rejoice![o] [5]Let your gentleness be evident to all. The Lord is near.[p] [6]Do not be anxious about anything,[q] but in every-

3:13 oLk 9:62
3:14 pHeb 6:1
q1Co 9:24
rS Ro 8:28
3:15 sS 1Co 2:6
tGal 5:10
uEph 1:17;
1Th 4:9
3:17 vS 1Co 4:16
wS 1Ti 4:12
3:18 xAc 20:31
yGal 6:12
3:19 zPs 73:17
aRo 16:18
bRo 6:21; Jude 13
cRo 8:5,6;
Col 3:2
3:20 dEph 2:19
eCol 3:1;
Heb 12:22
fS 1Co 1:7
3:21 gEph 1:19

h1Co 15:43-53
iRo 8:29; Col 3:4
4:1 jPhp 1:8
kS 1Co 16:13
4:2 lPhp 2:2
4:3 mS Php 2:25
nS Rev 20:12
4:4 oPs 85:6;
97:12; Hab 3:18;
S Mt 5:12;
Ro 12:12; Php 3:1
4:5 pPs 119:151;
145:18;
Heb 10:37;

Jas 5:8,9 **4:6** qMt 6:25-34

h3 Or loyal Syzygus

(see vv. 4–6), but leaving it behind him as done with and settled.

3:14 prize. The winner of the Greek races received a wreath of leaves and sometimes a cash award; the Christian receives an award of everlasting glory. heavenward. Paul's ultimate aspirations are found not in this life but in heaven, because Christ is there (see Col 3:1–2).

3:15 mature. Those who have made reasonable progress in spiritual growth and stability (see 1Co 2:6; 3:1–3; Heb 5:14). such a view. That expressed in vv. 12–14: There are heights yet to be scaled; do not become complacent. think differently. If the readers accept the view set forth in vv. 12–14 and yet fail to agree in some lesser point, God will clarify the matter for them.

3:16 live up to what . . . already attained. Put into practice the truth they have already comprehended. We are responsible for the truth we currently possess.

3:17 following my example. As Paul follows the example of Christ. take note of those who live. The life-styles Christians lead ought to be models worth following.

3:18 told you before. See v. 1. with tears. See Ac 20:19,31. live as enemies of the cross. In glaring contrast to Paul's conduct (v. 10) and to the truth of the gospel.

3:19 destruction. The opposite of salvation. god . . . stomach. A deep self-centeredness; their appetites and desires come first. earthly things. They have set their minds on the things of this life; they are antinomians (libertines), the opposite of the legalists of v. 2.

3:20 citizenship. In this world Christians are aliens, fully involved in it, yet not of it (cf. Jn 17:14–16; 1Co 7:29–31; 1Pe 2:11). in heaven. Where Christ is and where they are—in union with him; contrast the "earthly things" of v. 19 (see Eph 2:6; Col 3:1–4). eagerly await . . . from there. See Ro 8:19; 1Co 1:7; 1Th 1:9–10; 2Ti 4:8.

3:21 power . . . under his control. Christ's present power, earned by his obedience to death (see 2:8) and received in his resurrection and ascension, is universal and absolute (see Mt 28:18; 1Co 15:27; Eph 1:20–22). will transform. By the Holy Spirit at the resurrection (see Ro 8:11; 1Co 6:14; 15:50–53). our lowly bodies. Subject to weakness, decay and death, due to sin (see Ro 8:10,20–23; 1Co 15:42–44). like his glorious body. See Ro 8:29; 1Jn 3:2. The resurrec-

tion body, received already by Christ, who is the "firstfruits," will be received by believers in the future resurrection "harvest" (see 1Co 15:20,49). It is "spiritual," i.e., transformed by the power of the Holy Spirit (see 1Co 15:44,46).

4:1 love and long for. See notes on 1:8; 2:1. my joy and crown. True not only now, but especially when Christ returns (see 1Th 2:19). that is how. Refers to the closing statements of ch. 3. In the face of libertine practices (3:18–19), the Philippians should follow Paul's example (3:17), having their minds set on heavenly things (3:20–21). stand firm. In the midst of present struggles for the sake of the gospel (cf. 1:27–30; 1Co 15:58).

4:2–3 The disagreement between Euodia and Syntyche is serious enough to be mentioned in a letter to be read publicly, but Paul seems confident that "these women" (v. 3) will be reconciled. His handling of the situation is a model of tact—he does not take sides but encourages others closer to the situation to promote reconciliation (see 2:2).

4:3 yokefellow. See NIV text note. at my side . . . my fellow workers. Those associated with the apostle in the cause of the gospel (women as well as men) are his equals, not subordinates (cf. 2:25; Ro 16:3,9,21; Phm 24). Clement. Not mentioned elsewhere in the NT. the rest of my fellow workers. Not mentioned individually because they are known to God and their names are entered in the book of life, the heavenly register of the elect (see note on Rev 3:5).

4:4 Rejoice in the Lord. See 3:1. always. Under all kinds of circumstances, including suffering (see Hab 3:17–18; Jas 1:2; 1Pe 4:13).

4:5 gentleness. Christlike consideration for others (cf. 2Co 10:1). It is especially essential in church leaders (see 1Ti 3:3; Tit 3:2, "considerate"). near. See Ro 13:11; cf. Jas 5:8–9; Rev 22:7,12,20. The next great event in God's prophetic schedule is Christ's return. The whole period from Christ's first coming to the consummation of the kingdom is viewed in the NT as the last time (1Jn 2:18). From God's vantage point, a thousand years are as a day. Thus there is a sense in which, for every generation, the Lord's coming is near.

4:6 anxious. Self-centered, counterproductive worry, not legitimate cares and concerns for the spread of the gospel (see 2:28 and note; 2Co 11:28; see also Mt 6:25–31; 1Pe

thing, by prayer and petition, with thanksgiving, present your requests to God.[r] [7]And the peace of God,[s] which transcends all understanding,[t] will guard your hearts and your minds in Christ Jesus.

[8]Finally, brothers, whatever is true, whatever is noble, whatever is right, whatever is pure, whatever is lovely, whatever is admirable—if anything is excellent or praiseworthy—think about such things. [9]Whatever you have learned or received or heard from me, or seen in me—put it into practice.[u] And the God of peace[v] will be with you.

Thanks for Their Gifts

[10]I rejoice greatly in the Lord that at last you have renewed your concern for me.[w] Indeed, you have been concerned, but you had no opportunity to show it. [11]I am not saying this because I am in need, for I have learned to be content[x] whatever the circumstances. [12]I know what it is to be in need, and I know what it is to have plenty. I have learned the secret of being content

in any and every situation, whether well fed or hungry,[y] whether living in plenty or in want.[z] [13]I can do everything through him who gives me strength.[a]

[14]Yet it was good of you to share[b] in my troubles. [15]Moreover, as you Philippians know, in the early days[c] of your acquaintance with the gospel, when I set out from Macedonia,[d] not one church shared with me in the matter of giving and receiving, except you only;[e] [16]for even when I was in Thessalonica,[f] you sent me aid again and again when I was in need.[g] [17]Not that I am looking for a gift, but I am looking for what may be credited to your account.[h] [18]I have received full payment and even more; I am amply supplied, now that I have received from Epaphroditus[i] the gifts you sent. They are a fragrant[j] offering, an acceptable sacrifice, pleasing to God. [19]And my God will meet all your needs[k] according to his glorious riches[l] in Christ Jesus.

[20]To our God and Father[m] be glory for ever and ever. Amen.[n]

Cross references (center column):

4:6 [r]Eph 6:18; 1Ti 2:1
4:7 [s]Isa 26:3; S Jn 14:27 [t]Eph 3:19
4:9 [u]S 1Co 4:16 [v]S Ro 15:33
4:10 [w]2Co 11:9
4:11 [x]1Ti 6:6,8; Heb 13:5

4:12 [y]S 1Co 4:11 [z]2Co 11:9
4:13 [a]2Co 12:9; Eph 3:16; Col 1:11; 1Ti 1:12; 2Ti 4:17
4:14 [b]Php 1:7
4:15 [c]Php 1:5 [d]S Ac 16:9 [e]2Co 11:8,9
4:16 [f]S Ac 17:1 [g]1Th 2:9
4:17 [h]1Co 9:11, 12
4:18 [i]Php 2:25 [j]S 2Co 2:14
4:19 [k]Ps 23:1; 2Co 9:8 [l]S Ro 2:4
4:20 [m]Gal 1:4; 1Th 1:3; 3:11,13 [n]S Ro 11:36

5:7). *in everything, by prayer.* Anxiety and prayer are two great opposing forces in Christian experience. *thanksgiving.* The antidote to worry (along with prayer and petition). **4:7** *peace of God.* Not merely a psychological state of mind, but an inner tranquillity based on peace with God—the peaceful state of those whose sins are forgiven (cf. Jn 14:27; Ro 5:1). The opposite of anxiety, it is the tranquillity that comes when the believer commits all his cares to God in prayer and worries about them no more. *transcends all understanding.* The full dimensions of God's love and care are beyond human comprehension (see Eph 3:18–20). *guard . . . hearts . . . minds.* A military concept depicting a sentry standing guard. God's "protective custody" of those who are in Christ Jesus extends to the core of their beings and to their deepest intentions (cf. 1Pe 1:5).
4:8 *Finally.* See note on 3:1. *true . . . praiseworthy.* Paul understood the influence of one's thoughts on one's life. What a person allows to occupy his mind will sooner or later determine his speech and his action. Paul's exhortation to "think about such things" is followed by a second exhortation, "put it into practice" (v. 9). The combination of virtues listed in vv. 8–9 is sure to produce a wholesome thought pattern, which in turn will result in a life of moral and spiritual excellence.
4:9 *seen in me.* See note on 3:17. *God of peace.* See note on 1Th 5:23; cf. the "peace of God" (v. 7).
4:10 *at last . . . no opportunity.* The delay in sending gifts to Paul was not the fault of the Philippians, nor was it because they were lacking in concern for him (cf. 2Co 11:9). Perhaps Paul's uncertain itinerary prior to his arrival at Rome or the lack of an available messenger had prevented the Philippians from showing their concern.
4:11 *content whatever the circumstances.* Paul genuinely appreciates the gifts from Philippi (see vv. 14,18) but he is not ultimately dependent on them (cf. 1Ti 6:6–8).
4:12 *content . . . whether well fed . . . whether living in plenty.* Prosperity, too, can be a source of discontent.
4:13 *everything.* Everything pleasing to God. *him who gives me strength.* Christ. Union with the living, exalted Christ is the secret of being content (v. 12) and the source of

Paul's abiding strength (see especially 2Co 12:9–10; see also Jn 15:5; Eph 3:16–17; Col 1:11).
4:14 *share.* The Philippians' gifts are a means of involving them in Paul's troubles (cf. Heb 10:33).
4:15 *early days.* During Paul's second missionary journey, when he first preached in Philippi (see Ac 16:12–40). *set out.* For the south (Achaia), where Athens and Corinth were located (see Ac 17:14–16; 18:1–4). *Macedonia.* The northern part of modern-day Greece, where Berea and Thessalonica, as well as Philippi, were located. *shared with me in the matter of.* Or "participated with me in an account of." Paul uses commercial language to describe "giving and receiving" (credit and debit) between the Philippians and himself (see "credited to your account," v. 17). Yet this commercial imagery is plainly transcended by the mutual concern and self-sacrifice of their relationship. *except you only.* The generosity of the Philippian church is unique and unmatched (cf. 2Co 8:1–5).
4:16 *when I was in Thessalonica.* While he was still in Macedonia (see Ac 17:1–9). *aid again and again.* The gifts sent to Rome through Epaphroditus are the latest in a long and consistent pattern of generosity (cf. 2Co 8:1–5).
4:17 *credited to your account.* See note on v. 15. The "investment value" of the Philippians' gift is not primarily what Paul received, but the "spiritual dividends" they received.
4:18 *a fragrant offering, an acceptable sacrifice.* The OT background is the sacrifice, not of atonement for sin, but of thanksgiving and praise (cf. Lev 7:12–15; Ro 12:1; Eph 5:2; Heb 13:15–16). *acceptable . . . pleasing to God.* Because of Christ's work for us (see 1Pe 2:5) and God's work in us (see Php 2:13).
4:19 *my.* A personal touch (cf. "my God" in 1:3). *will meet.* A promise given to a church that had sacrificially given to meet Paul's need. *your needs.* Paul is concerned not only about his own situation but also about that of the Philippians. *his glorious riches in Christ Jesus.* The true measure of God's blessings to the church (cf. Eph 1:18; 3:16–20).
4:20 Paul cannot hold back a doxology, especially as he considers the truth of v. 19.

Final Greetings

21Greet all the saints in Christ Jesus. The brothers who are with me*o* send greetings. 22All the saints*p* send you greetings, espe-

cially those who belong to Caesar's household.

23The grace of the Lord Jesus Christ*q* be with your spirit.*r* Amen.*i*

4:21 *o*Gal 1:2
4:22 *p*S Ac 9:13

4:23 *q*S Ro 16:20
*r*S Gal 6:18

*i*23 Some manuscripts do not have *Amen.*

4:21–22 Final greetings are a typical feature of Paul's letters (see, e.g., Ro 16:3–16,21–23; 1Co 16:19–20; 2Co 13:12–13; Col 4:10–12,14–15,18).
4:21 *saints.* See note on 1:1. *brothers who are with me.* Paul's fellow workers at Rome, especially Timothy (see 1:1, 14,16).
4:22 *Caesar's household.* Not blood relatives of the em-

peror, but those employed (slaves or freedmen) in or around the palace area (cf. "palace guard," 1:13).
4:23 A typical closing benediction of Paul. *your spirit.* Not one part of man to the exclusion of other parts, but the whole person seen from his inner side, at the core of his being (cf. Gal 6:18; 2Ti 4:22; Phm 25).

COLOSSIANS

Author, Date and Place of Writing

That Colossians is a genuine letter of Paul is not usually disputed. In the early church, all who speak on the subject of authorship ascribe it to Paul. In the 19th century, however, some thought that the heresy refuted in ch. 2 was second-century Gnosticism. But a careful analysis of ch. 2 shows that the heresy there referred to is noticeably less developed than the Gnosticism of leading Gnostic teachers of the second and third centuries. Also, the seeds of what later became the full-blown Gnosticism of the second century were present in the first century and already making inroads into the churches. Consequently, it is not necessary to date Colossians in the second century at a time too late for Paul to have written the letter.

Instead, it is to be dated during Paul's first imprisonment in Rome, where he spent at least two years under house arrest (see Ac 28:16-31). Some have argued that Paul wrote Colossians from Ephesus or Caesarea, but most of the evidence favors Rome as the place where Paul penned all the Prison Letters (Ephesians, Colossians, Philippians and Philemon). Colossians should be dated c. A.D. 60, in the same year as Ephesians and Philemon.

Colosse: The Town and the Church

Several hundred years before Paul's day, Colosse had been a leading city in Asia Minor (present-day Turkey). It was located on the Lycus River and on the great east-west trade route leading from Ephesus on the Aegean Sea to the Euphrates River. By the first century A.D. Colosse was diminished to a second-rate market town, which had been surpassed long ago in power and importance by the neighboring towns of Laodicea and Hierapolis (see 4:13).

What gave Colosse NT importance, however, was the fact that, during Paul's three-year ministry in Ephesus, Epaphras had been converted and had carried the gospel to Colosse (cf. 1:7-8; Ac 19:10). The young church that resulted then became the target of heretical attack, which led to Epaphras's visit to Paul in Rome and ultimately to the penning of the Colossian letter.

Perhaps as a result of the efforts of Epaphras or other converts of Paul, Christian churches had also been established in Laodicea and Hierapolis. Some of them were house churches (see 4:15; Phm 2). Most likely all of them were primarily Gentile.

The Colossian Heresy

Paul never explicitly describes the false teaching he opposes in the Colossian letter. The nature of the heresy must be inferred from statements he made in opposition to the false teachers. An analysis of his refutation suggests that the heresy was diverse in nature. Some of the elements of its teachings were:

1. *Ceremonialism.* It held to strict rules about the kinds of permissible food and drink, religious festivals (2:16-17) and circumcision (2:11; 3:11).

2. *Asceticism.* "Do not handle! Do not taste! Do not touch!" (2:21; cf. 2:23).

3. *Angel worship.* See 2:18.

4. *Deprecation of Christ.* This is implied in Paul's stress on the supremacy of Christ (1:15-20; 2:2-3,9).

5. *Secret knowledge.* The Gnostics boasted of this (see 2:18 and Paul's emphasis in 2:2-3 on Christ, "in whom are hidden all the treasures of wisdom").

6. *Reliance on human wisdom and tradition.* See 2:4,8.

These elements seem to fall into two categories, Jewish and Gnostic. It is likely, therefore, that the Colossian heresy was a mixture of an extreme form of Judaism and an early stage of Gnosticism (see Introduction to 1 John: Gnosticism; see also note on 2:23).

Purpose and Theme

Paul's purpose is to refute the Colossian heresy. To accomplish this goal, he exalts Christ as the very image of God (1:15), the Creator (1:16), the preexistent sustainer of all things (1:17), the head of the church (1:18), the first to be resurrected (1:18), the fullness of deity in bodily form (1:19; 2:9) and the reconciler (1:20-22). Thus Christ is completely adequate. We "have been given fullness in Christ" (2:10). On the other hand, the Colossian heresy was altogether inadequate. It was a hollow and deceptive philosophy (2:8), lacking any ability to restrain the old sinful nature (2:23).

The theme of Colossians is the complete adequacy of Christ as contrasted with the emptiness of mere human philosophy.

Outline

1 Paul, an apostle[a] of Christ Jesus by the will of God,[b] and Timothy[c] our brother,

[2]To the holy and faithful[a] brothers in Christ at Colosse:

Grace[d] and peace to you from God our Father.[b][e]

Thanksgiving and Prayer

[3]We always thank God,[f] the Father of our Lord Jesus Christ, when we pray for you, [4]because we have heard of your faith in Christ Jesus and of the love[g] you have for all the saints[h]— [5]the faith and love that spring from the hope[i] that is stored up for you in heaven[j] and that you have already heard about in the word of truth,[k] the gospel [6]that has come to you. All over the world[l] this gospel is bearing fruit[m] and growing, just as it has been doing among you since the day you heard it and understood God's grace in all its truth. [7]You learned it from Epaphras,[n] our dear fellow servant, who is a faithful minister[o] of Christ on our[c] behalf, [8]and who also told us of your love in the Spirit.[p]

[9]For this reason, since the day we heard about you,[q] we have not stopped praying for you[r] and asking God to fill you with the knowledge of his will[s] through all spiritual wisdom and understanding.[t] [10]And we pray this in order that you may live a life worthy[u] of the Lord and may please him[v] in every way: bearing fruit in every good work, growing in the knowledge of God,[w] [11]being strengthened with all power[x] according to his glorious might so that you may have great endurance and patience,[y] and joyfully [12]giving thanks to the Father,[z] who has qualified you[d] to share in the inheritance[a] of the saints in the kingdom of light.[b] [13]For he has rescued us from the dominion of darkness[c] and brought us into the kingdom[d] of the Son he loves,[e] [14]in whom we have redemption,[e][f] the forgiveness of sins.[g]

The Supremacy of Christ

[15]He is the image[h] of the invisible

1:1	[a]S 1Co 1:1
	[b]S 2Co 1:1
	[c]S Ac 16:1
1:2	[d]Col 4:18
	[e]S Ro 1:7
1:3	[f]S Ro 1:8
1:4	[g]Gal 5:6
	[h]S Ac 9:13; Eph 1:15; Phm 5
1:5	[i]ver 23; 1Th 5:8; Tit 1:2
	[j]1Pe 1:4
	[k]S 2Ti 2:15
1:6	[l]ver 23; S Ro 10:18
	[m]Jn 15:16
1:7	[n]Col 4:12; Phm 23 [o]Col 4:7
1:8	[p]Ro 15:30
1:9	[q]ver 4; Eph 1:15
	[r]S Ro 1:10
	[s]S Eph 5:17
	[t]S Eph 1:17
1:10	[u]S Eph 4:1
	[v]S 2Co 5:9 [w]ver 6
1:11	[x]S Php 4:13
	[y]Eph 4:2
1:12	[z]Eph 5:20
	[a]S Ac 20:32
	[b]S Ac 26:18
1:13	[c]S Ac 26:18
	[d]2Pe 1:11
	[e]Mt 3:17
1:14	[e]S Ro 3:24
	[g]Eph 1:7
1:15	[h]S Jn 14:9

[a]2 Or *believing*   [b]2 Some manuscripts *Father and the Lord Jesus Christ*   [c]7 Some manuscripts *your*   [d]12 Some manuscripts *us*   [e]14 A few late manuscripts *redemption through his blood*

1:1 *Paul.* It was customary to put the writer's name at the beginning of a letter. For more information on Paul see notes on Ac 9:1; Php 3:4–14. *Christ.* Paul is very Christ-centered, as seen by this short letter, in which he uses the title "Christ" 26 times and the title "Lord" (alone) 7 times. *Timothy.* Paul also mentions Timothy in 2 Corinthians, Philippians, 1,2 Thessalonians and Philemon, but Paul is really the sole author, as seen by the constant use of "I" (see especially 4:18).

1:2 *holy.* Because of Christ's substitutionary death for the Colossian believers, they are declared holy in the sight of God, and because of the Holy Spirit's work, they are continuing to be made holy in their lives. *faithful.* See 1:7; 4:7,9. *in Christ.* Paul mentions the spiritual union with Christ 13 times in Colossians (see note on Eph 1:3). *Grace and peace.* See notes on Jnh 4:2; Jn 14:27; 20:19; Gal 1:3; Eph 1:2.

1:3 *We.* Paul and Timothy. *thank God.* Every one of Paul's letters, except Galatians, begins with thanks or praise (see note on Php 1:3–4). In Colossians thanks is an important theme (see v. 12; 2:7; 3:15–17; 4:2). The Bible never thanks man for his faith and love, but rather God, who is the source of these virtues.

1:5 The three great Christian virtues of faith, love and hope appear also in Ro 5:2–5; 1Co 13:13; Gal 5:5–6; 1Th 1:3; 5:8; Heb 10:22–24. *hope.* Not wishful thinking but a firm assurance. For this unusual thought of faith and love coming from hope see Tit 1:2.

1:6 *All over the world.* Hyperbole, to dramatize the rapid spread of the gospel into every quarter of the Roman empire within three decades of Pentecost (see v. 23; Ro 1:8; 10:18; 16:19). In refutation of the charge of the false teachers, Paul insists that the Christian faith is not merely local or regional but worldwide.

1:7 *Epaphras.* A native (4:12) and probably founder of the Colossian church, and an evangelist in nearby Laodicea and Hierapolis (4:13). Paul loved and admired him, calling him a "fellow prisoner" (Phm 23), his dear fellow servant and a faithful minister of Christ. Epaphras was the one who told

Paul at Rome about the Colossian church problem and thereby stimulated him to write this letter (vv. 4,8). His name, a shortened form of Epaphroditus (from "Aphrodite," the Greek goddess of love), suggests that he was a convert from paganism. He is not the Epaphroditus of Php 2:25; 4:18.

1:8 *your love in the Spirit.* The Holy Spirit is the source of all Christian love.

1:9 *the knowledge of his will.* Biblical knowledge is not merely the possession of facts. Rather, knowledge and wisdom in the Bible are practical, having to do with godly living. This is borne out by vv. 10–12, where knowledge, wisdom and understanding result in a life worthy of the Lord.

1:12 *light.* Symbolizes holiness (Mt 5:14; 6:23; Ac 26:18; 1Jn 1:5), truth (Ps 36:9; 119:105,130; 2Co 4:6), love (Jas 1:17; 1Jn 2:9–10), glory (Isa 60:1–3; 1Ti 6:16) and life (Jn 1:4). Accordingly, God (1Jn 1:5), Christ (Jn 8:12) and the Christian (Eph 5:8) are characterized by light. The "kingdom of light" is the opposite of the "dominion of darkness" (v. 13).

1:13 *kingdom.* Does not here refer to a territory but to the authority, rule or sovereign power of a king. Here it means that the Christian is no longer under the dominion of evil (darkness) but under the benevolent rule of God's Son.

1:14 *redemption.* Deliverance and freedom from the penalty of sin by the payment of a ransom—the substitutionary death of Christ.

1:15–20 Perhaps an early Christian hymn (see note on 3:16) on the supremacy of Christ—used here by Paul to counteract the false teaching at Colosse. It is divided into two parts: (1) Christ's supremacy in creation (vv. 15–17); (2) Christ's supremacy in redemption (vv. 18–20).

1:15 *image.* Christ is called the "image of God" here and in 2Co 4:4. In Heb 1:3 he is described as the "radiance of God's glory and the exact representation of his being." This figure of the image suggests two truths: (1) God is invisible ("no one has ever seen God," Jn 1:18); (2) Christ, who is the eternal Son of God and who became the God-man, reflects and reveals him (see also Jn 1:18; 14:9). *firstborn over all*

God,[i] the firstborn[j] over all creation. [16]For by him all things were created:[k] things in heaven and on earth, visible and invisible, whether thrones or powers or rulers or authorities;[l] all things were created by him and for him.[m] [17]He is before all things,[n] and in him all things hold together. [18]And he is the head[o] of the body, the church;[p] he is the beginning and the firstborn[q] from among the dead,[r] so that in everything he might have the supremacy. [19]For God was pleased[s] to have all his fullness[t] dwell in him, [20]and through him to reconcile[u] to himself all things, whether things on earth or things in heaven,[v] by making peace[w] through his blood,[x] shed on the cross.

[21]Once you were alienated from God and were enemies[y] in your minds[z] because of[a] your evil behavior. [22]But now he has reconciled[a] you by Christ's physical body[b] through death to present you[c] holy in his sight, without blemish and free from accusation[d]— [23]if you continue[e] in your faith, established[f] and firm, not moved from the hope[g] held out in the gospel. This is the gospel that you heard and that has been proclaimed to every creature un-

der heaven,[h] and of which I, Paul, have become a servant.[i]

Paul's Labor for the Church

[24]Now I rejoice[j] in what was suffered for you, and I fill up in my flesh what is still lacking in regard to Christ's afflictions,[k] for the sake of his body, which is the church.[l] [25]I have become its servant[m] by the commission God gave me[n] to present to you the word of God[o] in its fullness— [26]the mystery[p] that has been kept hidden for ages and generations, but is now disclosed to the saints. [27]To them God has chosen to make known[q] among the Gentiles the glorious riches[r] of this mystery, which is Christ in you,[s] the hope of glory. [28]We proclaim him, admonishing[t] and teaching everyone with all wisdom,[u] so that we may present everyone perfect[v] in Christ. [29]To this end I labor,[w] struggling[x] with all his energy, which so powerfully works in me.[y]

1:15 [i]S Jn 1:18; 1Ti 1:17; Heb 11:27 [j]S ver 18
1:16 [k]S Jn 1:3 [l]Eph 1:20,21 [m]S Ro 11:36
1:17 [n]S Jn 1:2
1:18 [o]S Eph 1:22 [p]ver 24; S 1Co 12:27 [q]ver 15; Ps 89:27; Ro 8:29; Heb 1:6 [r]Ac 26:23; Rev 1:5
1:19 [s]S Eph 1:5 [t]S Jn 1:16
1:20 [u]S Ro 5:10 [v]Eph 1:10 [w]S Ro 5:10 [x]Eph 2:13
1:21 [y]Ro 5:10 [z]Eph 2:3
1:22 [a]ver 20; S Ro 5:10 [b]Ro 7:4 [c]S 2Co 4:14 [d]Eph 1:4; 5:27
1:23 [e]S Ro 11:22 [f]Eph 3:17 [g]ver 5

[h]ver 6; S Ro 10:18 [i]ver 25; S 1Co 3:5
1:24 [j]S 2Co 6:10 [k]S 2Co 1:5 [l]S 1Co 12:27
1:25 [m]ver 23; S 1Co 3:5 [n]Eph 3:2 [o]S Heb 4:12
1:26 [p]S Ro 16:25
1:27 [q]S Mt 13:11 [r]S Ro 2:4 [s]S Ro 8:10

1:28 [t]Col 3:16 [u]1Co 2:6,7 [v]Mt 5:48; Eph 5:27 **1:29** [w]1Co 15:10; 2Co 11:23 [x]Col 2:1 [y]Eph 1:19; 3:7

[f]21 Or *minds, as shown by*

---

creation. Just as the firstborn son had certain privileges and rights in the Biblical world, so also Christ has certain rights in relation to all creation—priority, preeminence and sovereignty (vv. 16–18).

1:16 *by him all things were created.* See Jn 1:3. Seven times in six verses Paul mentions "all creation," "all things" and "everything," thus stressing that Christ is supreme over all. *thrones or powers or rulers or authorities.* Angels. An angelic hierarchy figured prominently in the Colossian heresy (see Introduction: The Colossian Heresy).

1:17 *He is before all things.* Referring to time, as in Jn 1:1–2; 8:58.

1:18 *beginning.* Of the new creation. *firstborn.* Christ was the first to rise from the dead with a resurrection body. Elsewhere Paul calls him the "firstfruits of those who have fallen asleep" (1Co 15:20). Others who were raised from the dead (2Ki 4:35; Lk 7:15; Jn 11:44; Ac 9:36–41; 20:7–11) were raised only to die again.

1:19 *fullness.* Part of the technical vocabulary of some Gnostic philosophies. In these systems it meant the sum of the supernatural forces controlling the fate of people. For Paul "fullness" meant the totality of God with all his powers and attributes (2:9).

1:20 *reconcile to himself all things.* Does not mean that Christ by his death has saved all people. Scripture speaks of an eternal hell and makes clear that only believers are saved. When Adam and Eve sinned, not only was the harmony between God and man destroyed, but also disorder came into creation (Ro 8:19–22). So when Christ died on the cross, he made peace possible between God and man, and he restored in principle the harmony in the physical world, though the full realization of the latter will come only when Christ returns (Ro 8:21).

1:22 *death.* Christ's death.

1:23 *every creature.* See note on v. 6.

1:24 *what was suffered.* By Paul. By preaching the gospel to the Gentiles, he experienced all kinds of affliction, but here he was probably referring especially to his imprisonment. *fill up ... what is still lacking.* Does not mean that there was a deficiency in the atoning sacrifice of Christ. Rather, it means that Paul suffered afflictions because he was preaching the good news of Christ's atonement. Christ suffered on the cross to atone for sin, and Paul filled up Christ's afflictions by experiencing the added sufferings necessary to carry this good news to a lost world.

1:25 *to present ... the word of God in its fullness.* The meaning seems to be that the word of God is brought to completion, i.e., to its intended purpose, only when it is proclaimed (cf. Isa 55:11). Paul's commission to bring the word to completion, therefore, required him to make the word of God heard in Colosse as well as elsewhere. See Ro 15:19 for a similar statement.

1:26 *mystery.* This word was a popular, pagan religious term, used in the mystery religions to refer to secret information available only to an exclusive group of people. Paul changes that meaning radically by always combining it with words such as "disclosed" (here), "made known" (Eph 1:9), "make plain" (Eph 3:9) and "revelation" (Ro 16:25). The Christian mystery is not secret knowledge for a few. It is a revelation of divine truths—once hidden but now openly proclaimed.

1:27 *Gentiles ... Christ in you.* The mystery is the fact that Christ indwells Gentiles, for it had not been previously revealed that the Gentiles would be admitted to the church on equal terms with Israel (see note on Eph 3:6).

1:28 *perfect.* Employed by the mystery religions and the Gnostics to describe those who had become possessors of the secrets or knowledge boasted of by the particular religion (see Introduction to 1 John: Gnosticism). But in Christ every believer is one of the perfect.

2 I want you to know how much I am struggling[z] for you and for those at Laodicea,[a] and for all who have not met me personally. [2]My purpose is that they may be encouraged in heart[b] and united in love, so that they may have the full riches of complete understanding, in order that they may know the mystery[c] of God, namely, Christ, [3]in whom are hidden all the treasures of wisdom and knowledge.[d] [4]I tell you this so that no one may deceive you by fine-sounding arguments.[e] [5]For though I am absent from you in body, I am present with you in spirit[f] and delight to see how orderly[g] you are and how firm[h] your faith in Christ[i] is.

Freedom From Human Regulations Through Life With Christ

[6]So then, just as you received Christ Jesus as Lord,[j] continue to live in him, [7]rooted[k] and built up in him, strengthened in the faith as you were taught,[l] and overflowing with thankfulness.

[8]See to it that no one takes you captive through hollow and deceptive philosophy,[m] which depends on human tradition and the basic principles of this world[n] rather than on Christ.

[9]For in Christ all the fullness[o] of the Deity lives in bodily form, [10]and you have been given fullness in Christ, who is the head[p] over every power and authority.[q] [11]In him you were also circumcised,[r] in the putting off of the sinful nature,[g][s] not with a circumcision done by the hands of men but with the circumcision done by Christ, [12]having been buried with him in baptism[t] and raised with him[u] through your faith in the power of God, who raised him from the dead.[v]

[13]When you were dead in your sins[w] and in the uncircumcision of your sinful nature,[h] God made you[i] alive[x] with Christ. He forgave us all our sins,[y] [14]having canceled the written code, with its regulations,[z] that was against us and that stood opposed to us; he took it away, nailing it to the cross.[a] [15]And having disarmed the powers and authorities,[b] he made a public spectacle of them, triumphing over them[c] by the cross.[j]

[16]Therefore do not let anyone judge you[d] by what you eat or drink,[e] or with regard to a religious festival,[f] a New Moon celebration[g] or a Sabbath day.[h] [17]These are a shadow of the things that were to come;[i] the reality, however, is found in Christ. [18]Do not let anyone who delights in false humility[j] and the worship

---

2:1 [z]Col 1:29; 4:12 [a]Col 4:13, 15,16; Rev 1:11; 3:14
2:2 [b]Eph 6:22; Col 4:8 [c]S Ro 16:25
2:3 [d]Isa 11:2; Jer 23:5; Ro 11:33; 1Co 1:24,30
2:4 [e]S Ro 16:18
2:5 [f]1Co 5:4; 1Th 2:17 [g]1Co 14:40 [h]1Pe 5:9
2:6 [i]S Ac 20:21 [j]S Jn 13:13; Col 1:10
2:7 [k]Eph 3:17 [l]Eph 4:21
2:8 [m]1Ti 6:20 [n]ver 20; Gal 4:3
2:9 [o]S Jn 1:16
2:10 [p]S Eph 1:22 [q]S Mt 28:18
2:11 [r]Ro 2:29; Php 3:3 [s]S Gal 5:24
2:12 [t]S Mt 28:19 [u]S Ro 6:5 [v]S Ac 2:24
2:13 [w]Eph 2:1,5 [x]Eph 2:5 [y]Eph 4:32
2:14 [z]Eph 2:15 [a]1Pe 2:24
2:15 [b]ver 10; Eph 6:12 [c]Mt 12:29; Lk 10:18; Jn 12:31
2:16 [d]Ro 14:3,4 [e]Mk 7:19; Ro 14:17 [f]Lev 23:2; Ro 14:5 [g]1Ch 23:31 [h]Mk 2:27,28; Gal 4:10

2:17 [i]Heb 8:5; 10:1 2:18 [j]ver 23

[g]11 Or *the flesh*   [h]13 Or *your flesh*   [i]13 Some manuscripts *us*   [i]15 Or *them in him*

2:1 *Laodicea.* This letter was to be read to the church there too (4:16). Laodicea (modern Pamukkale) was only about 11 miles from Colosse.

2:2 *mystery.* See notes on 1:26; Ro 11:25.

2:3 *knowledge.* Paul stressed knowledge in this letter (v. 2; 1:9–10) because he was refuting a heresy that emphasized knowledge as the means of salvation (see Introduction to 1 John: Gnosticism). Paul insisted that the Christian, not the Gnostic, possessed genuine knowledge.

2:5 *absent . . . in body, . . . present . . . in spirit.* Similar to 1Co 5:3.

2:6 *live in him.* The believer's intimate, spiritual, living union with Christ is mentioned repeatedly in this letter (see, e.g., vv. 7,10–13,20; 1:2,27–28; 3:1,3).

2:8 *basic principles of this world.* This term (which occurs also in v. 20 and Gal 4:3,9) means false, worldly, religious, elementary teachings. Paul was counteracting the Colossian heresy, which, in part, taught that for salvation one needed to combine faith in Christ with secret knowledge and with man-made regulations concerning such physical and external practices as circumcision, eating and drinking, and observance of religious festivals.

2:9 *fullness of the Deity.* See note on 1:19. The declaration that the very essence of deity was present in totality in Jesus' human body was a direct refutation of Gnostic teaching.

2:10–15 Here Paul declares that the Christian is complete in Christ, rather than being deficient as the Gnostics claimed. This completeness includes the putting off of the sinful nature (v. 11), resurrection from spiritual death (vv. 12–13), forgiveness (v. 13) and deliverance from legalistic requirements (v. 14) and from evil spirit beings (v. 15).

2:11–12 *circumcision . . . baptism.* In the Israelite faith, circumcision was a sign that the individual stood in covenant relation with God. While this is the only reference where circumcision is associated with baptism, some see the passage as implying that, for the Christian, water baptism is the parallel sign of the covenant relationship.

2:14 *written code.* A business term, meaning a certificate of indebtedness in the debtor's handwriting. Paul uses it as a designation for the Mosaic law, with all its regulations, under which everyone is a debtor to God.

2:15 *having disarmed.* Not only did God cancel out the accusations of the law against the Christian, but he also conquered and disarmed the evil angels (powers and authorities, 1:16; Eph 6:12), who entice people to follow asceticism and false teachings about Christ. The picture is of conquered soldiers stripped of their clothes as well as their weapons to symbolize their total defeat. *triumphing over them.* Lit. "leading them in a triumphal procession." The metaphor recalls a Roman general leading his captives through the streets of his city for all the citizens to see as evidence of his complete victory (see 2Co 2:14 and note). That Christ triumphed over the devil and his cohorts is seen from Mt 12:29; Lk 10:18; Ro 16:20.

2:17 *shadow . . . reality.* The ceremonial laws of the OT are here referred to as shadows (cf. Heb 8:5; 10:1) because they symbolically depicted the coming of Christ; so any insistence on the observance of such ceremonies is a failure to recognize that their fulfillment has already taken place. This element of the Colossian heresy was combined with a rigid asceticism, as vv. 20–21 reveal.

2:18 *false humility.* Humility in which one delights is of necessity mock humility. Paul may refer to a professed humility in view of the absolute God, who was believed to be

of angels disqualify you for the prize.[k] Such a person goes into great detail about what he has seen, and his unspiritual mind puffs him up with idle notions. [19]He has lost connection with the Head,[l] from whom the whole body,[m] supported and held together by its ligaments and sinews, grows as God causes it to grow.[n]

[20]Since you died with Christ[o] to the basic principles of this world,[p] why, as though you still belonged to it, do you submit to its rules: [q] [21]"Do not handle! Do not taste! Do not touch!"? [22]These are all destined to perish[r] with use, because they are based on human commands and teachings.[s] [23]Such regulations indeed have an appearance of wisdom, with their self-imposed worship, their false humility[t] and their harsh treatment of the body, but they lack any value in restraining sensual indulgence.

Rules for Holy Living

3 Since, then, you have been raised with Christ,[u] set your hearts on things above, where Christ is seated at the right hand of God.[v] [2]Set your minds on things above, not on earthly things.[w] [3]For you died,[x] and your life is now hidden with Christ in God. [4]When Christ, who is your[k] life,[y] appears,[z] then you also will appear with him in glory.[a]

[5]Put to death,[b] therefore, whatever belongs to your earthly nature: [c] sexual immorality,[d] impurity, lust, evil desires and greed,[e] which is idolatry.[f] [6]Because of these, the wrath of God[g] is coming.[l] [7]You used to walk in these ways, in the life you once lived.[h] [8]But now you must rid yourselves[i] of all such things as these: anger, rage, malice, slander,[j] and filthy language from your lips.[k] [9]Do not lie to each other,[l] since you have taken off your old self[m] with its practices [10]and have put on the new self,[n] which is being renewed[o] in knowledge in the image of its Creator.[p] [11]Here there is no Greek or Jew,[q] circumcised or uncircumcised,[r] barbarian, Scythian, slave or free,[s] but Christ is all,[t] and is in all.

[12]Therefore, as God's chosen people, holy and dearly loved, clothe yourselves[u] with compassion, kindness, humility,[v]

Cross references (center column)

2:18 [k]1Co 9:24; Php 3:14
2:19 [l]S Eph 1:22 [m]S 1Co 12:27 [n]Eph 4:16
2:20 [o]S Ro 6:6 [p]ver 8; Gal 4:3,9 [q]ver 14,16
2:22 [r]1Co 6:13 [s]Isa 29:13; Mt 15:9; Tit 1:14
2:23 [t]ver 18
3:1 [u]S Ro 6:5 [v]S Mk 16:19
3:2 [w]Php 3:19,20

3:3 [x]S Ro 6:2; 2Co 5:14
3:4 [y]Gal 2:20 [z]1Co 1:7 [a]1Pe 1:13; 1Jn 3:2
3:5 [b]S Ro 6:2; S Eph 4:22 [c]S Gal 5:24 [d]S 1Co 6:18 [e]Eph 5:3 [f]Gal 5:19-21; Eph 5:5
3:6 [g]S Ro 1:18
3:7 [h]S Eph 2:2
3:8 [i]S Eph 4:22 [j]Eph 4:31 [k]Eph 4:29
3:9 [l]S Eph 4:25 [m]S Ro 6:6
3:10 [n]S Ro 6:4; S 13:14 [o]Ro 12:2; S 2Co 4:16; Eph 4:23
3:11 [p]Eph 2:10 [q]Ro 10:12; 1Co 12:13 [r]S 1Co 7:19 [s]Gal 3:28

[r]Eph 1:23 3:12 [u]ver 10 [v]Php 2:3

[k]4 Some manuscripts *our*   [l]6 Some early manuscripts *coming on those who are disobedient*

---

so far above man that he could only be worshiped in the form of angels he had created. Second-century Gnosticism conceived of a list of spirit beings who had emanated from God and through whom God may be approached. *disqualify.* This term pictures an umpire or referee who excludes from competition any athlete who fails to follow the rules. The Colossians were not to permit any false teacher to deny the reality of their salvation because they were not delighting in mock humility and in the worship of angelic beings. *what he has seen.* Probably refers to professed visions by the false teachers.

2:19 *lost connection with the Head.* The central error of the Colossian heresy is a defective view of Christ, in which he is believed to be less than deity (see v. 9; 1:19).

2:20 *basic principles.* See note on v. 8.

2:21 *Do not handle . . . taste . . . touch!* The strict ascetic nature of the heresy is seen here. These prohibitions seem to carry OT ceremonial laws to the extreme.

2:23 A rather detailed analysis of the Colossian heresy: 1. It appeared to set forth an impressive system of religious philosophy. 2. It was, however, a system created by the false teachers themselves ("self-imposed"), rather than being of divine origin. 3. The false teachers attempted to parade their humility. 4. This may have been done by a harsh asceticism that brutally misused the body. Paul's analysis is that such practices are worthless because they totally fail to control sinful desires. *self-imposed worship.* The false teachers themselves had created the regulations of their heretical system. They were not from God.

3:1 *then.* "Then" (or "therefore") links the doctrinal section of the letter with the practical section, just as it does in Ro 12:1; Eph 4:1; Php 4:1. *you have been raised.* Verses 1–10 set forth what has been described as the indicative and the imperative (standing and state) of the Christian. The indicative statements describe the believer's position in Christ: He is dead (v. 3); he has been raised with Christ (v.

1); he is with Christ in heaven ("hidden with Christ," v. 3); he has "taken off the old self " (v. 9); and he has "put on the new self " (v. 10). The imperative statements indicate what the believer is to do as a result: He is to set his heart (or mind) on things above (vv. 1–2); he is to put to death practices that belong to his earthly nature (v. 5); and he is to rid himself of practices that characterized his unregenerate self (v. 8). In summary, he is called upon to become in daily experience what he is positionally in Christ (cf. Ro 6:1–13).

3:4 *appears.* Refers to Christ's second coming.

3:6 *wrath of God.* See note on Zec 1:2. God is unalterably opposed to sin and will invariably make sure that it is justly punished.

3:9–10 *taken off . . . put on.* As one takes off dirty clothes and puts on clean ones, so the Christian is called upon to renounce his evil ways and live in accordance with the rules of Christ's kingdom (see vv. 12–14; cf. Gal 3:27).

3:10 *renewed.* See 2 Co 5:17. *knowledge.* See 1:10; 2:2–3. *image of its Creator.* See note on Ge 1:26.

3:11 *barbarian.* Someone who did not speak Greek and was thought to be uncivilized. *Scythian.* Scythians were known especially for their brutality and were considered by others as little better than wild beasts. They came originally from what is today south Russia. *Christ is all, and is in all.* Christ transcends all barriers and unifies people from all cultures, races and nations. Such distinctions are no longer significant. Christ alone matters.

3:12 *God's chosen people.* Israel was called this (Dt 4:37), and so is the Christian community (1Pe 2:9). Divine election is a constant theme in Paul's letters (see note on Eph 1:4), but the Bible never teaches that it dulls human responsibility. On the contrary, as this verse shows, it is precisely because the Christian has been elected to eternal salvation that he must put forth every effort to live the godly life. For Paul, divine sovereignty and human responsibility go hand in hand.

gentleness and patience.*w* 13Bear with each other*x* and forgive whatever grievances you may have against one another. Forgive as the Lord forgave you.*y* 14And over all these virtues put on love,*z* which binds them all together in perfect unity.*a*

15Let the peace of Christ*b* rule in your hearts, since as members of one body*c* you were called to peace.*d* And be thankful. 16Let the word of Christ*e* dwell in you richly as you teach and admonish one another with all wisdom,*f* and as you sing psalms,*g* hymns and spiritual songs with gratitude in your hearts to God.*h* 17And whatever you do,*i* whether in word or deed, do it all in the name of the Lord Jesus, giving thanks*j* to God the Father through him.

Rules for Christian Households

3:18–4:1pp — Eph 5:22–6:9

18Wives, submit to your husbands,*k* as is fitting in the Lord.

19Husbands, love your wives and do not be harsh with them.

20Children, obey your parents in everything, for this pleases the Lord.

21Fathers, do not embitter your children, or they will become discouraged.

22Slaves, obey your earthly masters in everything; and do it, not only when their eye is on you and to win their favor, but with sincerity of heart and reverence for the Lord. 23Whatever you do, work at it with all your heart, as working for the Lord, not for men, 24since you know that you will receive an inheritance*l* from the

Lord as a reward.*m* It is the Lord Christ you are serving. 25Anyone who does wrong will be repaid for his wrong, and there is no favoritism.*n*

4 Masters, provide your slaves with what is right and fair,*o* because you know that you also have a Master in heaven.

Further Instructions

2Devote yourselves to prayer,*p* being watchful and thankful. 3And pray for us, too, that God may open a door*q* for our message, so that we may proclaim the mystery*r* of Christ, for which I am in chains.*s* 4Pray that I may proclaim it clearly, as I should. 5Be wise*t* in the way you act toward outsiders;*u* make the most of every opportunity.*v* 6Let your conversation be always full of grace,*w* seasoned with salt,*x* so that you may know how to answer everyone.*y*

Final Greetings

7Tychicus*z* will tell you all the news about me. He is a dear brother, a faithful minister and fellow servant*a* in the Lord. 8I am sending him to you for the express purpose that you may know about our*m* circumstances and that he may encourage your hearts.*b* 9He is coming with Onesimus,*c* our faithful and dear brother, who is one of you.*d* They will tell you everything that is happening here.

10My fellow prisoner Aristarchus*e* sends

Cross references (center column)

3:12 *w*2Co 6:6; Gal 5:22,23; Eph 4:2
3:13 *x*Eph 4:2; *y*Eph 4:32
3:14 *z*1Co 13:1-13; *a*S Ro 15:5
3:15 *b*S Jn 14:27; *c*S Ro 12:5; *d*S Ro 14:19
3:16 *e*Ro 10:17; *f*Col 1:28; *g*Ps 47:7; *h*S Eph 5:19
3:17 *i*1Co 10:31; *j*S Eph 5:20
3:18 *k*S Eph 5:22
3:24 *l*S Ac 20:32

3:25 *m*S Mt 16:27; *n*S Ac 10:34
4:1 *o*Lev 25:43, 53
4:2 *p*S Lk 18:1
4:3 *q*S Ac 14:27; *r*S Ro 16:25; *s*S Ac 21:33
4:5 *t*Eph 5:15; *u*S Mk 4:11; *v*Eph 5:16
4:6 *w*Eph 4:29; *x*Mk 9:50; *y*1Pe 3:15
4:7 *z*S Ac 20:4; *a*Eph 6:21,22; Col 1:7
4:8 *b*Eph 6:21, 22; Col 2:2
4:9 *c*Phm 10 *d*ver 12
4:10 *e*S Ac 19:29

*m*8 Some manuscripts *that he may know about your*

3:15 *peace of Christ.* The attitude of peace that Christ alone gives—in place of the attitude of bitterness and quarrelsomeness. This attitude is to "rule" (lit. "function like an umpire") in all human relationships.

3:16 *word of Christ.* Refers especially to Christ's teaching, which in the time of the Colossians was transmitted orally. But by implication it includes the OT as well as the NT. *psalms, hymns and spiritual songs.* Some of the most important doctrines were expressed in Christian hymns preserved for us now only in Paul's letters (1:15–20; Eph 5:14; Php 2:6–11; 1Ti 3:16). "Psalms" refers to the OT psalms (see Lk 20:42; 24:44; Ac 1:20; 13:33), some of which may have been set to music by the church. "Psalm" could also describe a song newly composed for Christian worship (cf. 1Co 14:26, where "hymn" is lit. "psalm" in the Greek text). A "hymn" was a song of praise, especially used in a celebration (see Mk 14:26; Heb 2:12; see also Ac 16:25), much like the OT psalms that praised God for all that he is. A "song" recounted the acts of God and praised him for them (see Rev 5:9; 14:3; 15:3), much like the OT psalms that thanked God for all that he had done. See note on Eph 5:19.

3:18–4:1 See notes on Eph 5:22–6:9.

3:20 *in everything.* In everything not sinful (see Ac 5:29).

3:22–4:1 Paul neither condones slavery nor sanctions revolt against masters. Rather, he calls on both slaves and masters to show Christian principles in their relationship and

thus to attempt to change the institution from within. The reason Paul writes more about slaves and masters than about wives, husbands, children and fathers may be that the slave Onesimus (4:9) is going along with Tychicus to deliver this Colossian letter and the letter to Philemon, Onesimus's master, who also lived in Colosse.

4:6 *seasoned with salt.* Salt is a preservative and is tasty. Similarly, the Christian's conversation is to be wholesome (see 3:8; Eph 4:29).

4:7 *Tychicus.* See note on Eph 6:21.

4:9–17 Onesimus (v. 9), Aristarchus (v. 10), Mark (v. 10), Epaphras (v. 12), Luke (v. 14), Demas (v. 14) and Archippus (v. 17) are mentioned in Philemon. This suggests that the letters to Colosse and Philemon were written at the same time and place.

4:9 *Onesimus.* See Introduction to Philemon: Recipient, Background and Purpose.

4:10 *Aristarchus.* A Macedonian, who is mentioned three times in Acts: 1. He was with Paul during the Ephesian riot (Ac 19:29) and therefore was known in Colosse. 2. Both he and Tychicus (Ac 20:4) were with Paul in Greece. 3. He accompanied Paul on his trip to Rome (Ac 27:2). *Mark.* The author of the second Gospel. Against Barnabas's advice, Paul refused to take Mark on the second missionary journey because Mark had "deserted" him at Pamphylia (Ac 15:38). But now—about 12 years later—the difficulties seem to

you his greetings, as does Mark,[f] the
cousin of Barnabas.[g] (You have received
instructions about him; if he comes to you,
welcome him.) 11Jesus, who is called Justus, also sends greetings. These are the
only Jews among my fellow workers[h] for
the kingdom of God, and they have proved
a comfort to me. 12Epaphras,[i] who is one
of you[j] and a servant of Christ Jesus,
sends greetings. He is always wrestling in
prayer for you,[k] that you may stand firm in
all the will of God, mature[l] and fully assured. 13I vouch for him that he is working
hard for you and for those at Laodicea[m]
and Hierapolis. 14Our dear friend Luke,[n]
the doctor, and Demas[o] send greetings.
15Give my greetings to the brothers at Laodicea,[p] and to Nympha and the church in
her house.[q]
16After this letter has been read to you,
see that it is also read[r] in the church of the
Laodiceans and that you in turn read the
letter from Laodicea.
17Tell Archippus:[s] "See to it that you
complete the work you have received in
the Lord."[t]
18I, Paul, write this greeting in my own
hand.[u] Remember[v] my chains.[w] Grace be
with you.[x]

4:10 [f]S Ac 12:12 [g]S Ac 4:36 **4:11** [h]S Php 2:25 **4:12** [i]Col 1:7; Phm 23 [j]ver 9 [k]S Ro 15:30 [l]S 1Co 2:6 **4:13** [m]S Col 2:1 **4:14** [n]2Ti 4:11; Phm 24 [o]2Ti 4:10; Phm 24 **4:15** [p]S Col 2:1 [q]S Ro 16:5 **4:16** [r]2Th 3:14; S 1Ti 4:13 **4:17** [s]Phm 2 [t]2Ti 4:5 **4:18** [u]S 1Co 16:21 [v]Heb 13:3 [w]S Ac 21:33 [x]1Ti 6:21; 2Ti 4:22; Tit 3:15; Heb 13:25

have been ironed out, because Paul, both here and in Phm 24 (sent at the same time to Philemon, who was in Colosse), sends Mark's greetings. About five years later, Paul even writes that Mark "is very helpful to me in my ministry" (2Ti 4:11). See note on Ac 15:39.

4:13 *Hierapolis.* A town in Asia Minor (present-day Turkey), about 6 miles from Laodicea and 14 miles from Colosse. Its church may have been founded during Paul's three-year stay in Ephesus (Ac 19), but probably not by Paul himself (cf. 2:1).

4:14 *Luke.* Wrote about Paul in the book of Acts, having often accompanied him on his travels (see note on Ac 16:10). He was with Paul in Rome during his imprisonment (Ac 28), where this letter was written. *Demas.* A Christian worker who would later desert Paul (2Ti 4:10).

4:15 *Nympha.* Probably a Laodicean. *church in her house.* For the most part, the early church had no buildings, so it usually met for worship and instruction in homes. It often centered around one family, as, e.g., Priscilla and Aquila (Ro 16:5; 1Co 16:19), Philemon (Phm 2) and Mary the mother of John (Ac 12:12).

4:16 *After this letter has been read to you.* The practice of the early church was to read Paul's letters aloud to the assembled congregation. *letter from Laodicea.* Does not necessarily mean a letter by the Laodiceans. Rather, it could have been a letter that the Laodiceans were to lend to the Colossians—a letter that Paul had originally written to the Laodiceans. This may have been a fourth letter that Tychicus carried to this area in what is present-day Turkey, in addition to Ephesians, Colossians and Philemon. Or this letter could have been Paul's letter to the Ephesians—a circular letter making the rounds from Ephesus to Laodicea to Colosse (see Introduction to Ephesians: Author, Date and Place of Writing).

4:17 *Archippus.* Phm 2 calls him Paul's "fellow soldier."

4:18 Paul's custom was to dictate his letters (see Ro 16:22) and pen a few greetings himself (1Co 16:21; Gal 6:11; 2Th 3:17; Phm 19). His personal signature was the guarantee of the genuineness of the letter.

1 THESSALONIANS

Background of the Thessalonian Letters

It is helpful to trace the locations of Paul and his companions that relate to the Thessalonian correspondence. The travels were as follows:

1. Paul and Silas fled from Thessalonica to Berea (see Ac 17:10). Since Timothy is not mentioned, it is possible that he stayed in Thessalonica or went back to Philippi and then rejoined Paul and Silas in Berea (Ac 17:14).

2. Paul fled to Athens from Berean persecution, leaving Silas and Timothy in Berea (see Ac 17:14).

3. Paul sent word back, instructing Silas and Timothy to come to him in Athens (see Ac 17:15; see also note on 3:1-2).

4. Timothy rejoined Paul at Athens and was sent back to Thessalonica (see 3:1-5). Since Silas is not mentioned, it has been conjectured that he went back to Philippi when Timothy went to Thessalonica.

5. Paul moved on to Corinth (see Ac 18:1).

6. Silas and Timothy came to Paul in Corinth (see 3:6; Ac 18:5).

7. Paul wrote 1 Thessalonians and sent it to the church.

8. About six months later (A.D. 51/52) he sent 2 Thessalonians in response to further information about the church there.

Author, Date and Place of Writing

Both external and internal evidence (see 1:1; 2:18) support the view that Paul wrote 1 Thessalonians (from Corinth; see note on 3:1-2). Early church writers agreed on the matter, with testimonies beginning as early as A.D. 140 (Marcion). Paul's known characteristics are apparent in the letter (3:1-2,8-11 compared with Ac 15:36; 2Co 11:28). Historical allusions in the book fit Paul's life as recounted in Acts and in his own letters (2:14-16 compared with Ac 17:5-10; 3:6 compared with Ac 17:16). In the face of such evidence, few have ever rejected authorship by Paul.

It is generally dated c. A.D. 51. Weighty support for this date was found in an inscription discovered at Delphi, Greece, that dates Gallio's proconsulship to c. 51-52 and thus places Paul at Corinth at the same time (see Ac 18:12-17). Except for the possibility of an early date for Galatians (48-49?), 1 Thessalonians is Paul's earliest canonical letter.

Thessalonica: The City and the Church

Thessalonica was a bustling seaport city at the head of the Thermaic Gulf. It was an important communication and trade center, located at the junction of the great Egnatian Way and the road leading north to the Danube. Its population numbered about 200,000, making it the largest city in Macedonia. It was also the capital of its province.

The background of the Thessalonian church is found in Ac 17:1-9. Since Paul began his ministry there in the Jewish synagogue, it is reasonable to assume that the new church included some Jews. However, 1:9-10; Ac 17:4 seem to indicate that the church was largely Gentile in membership.

Purpose

Paul had left Thessalonica abruptly (see Ac 17:5-10) after a rather brief stay. Recent converts from paganism (1:9) were thus left with little external support in the midst of persecution. Paul's purpose in writing this letter was to encourage the new converts in their trials (3:3-5), to give instruction concerning godly living (4:1-8), to urge some not to neglect daily work (4:11-12) and to give assurance concerning the future of believers who die before Christ returns (see Theme; see also notes on 4:13,15).

Theme

Although the thrust of the letter is varied (see Purpose), the subject of eschatology (doctrine of last

things) seems to be predominant in both Thessalonian letters. Every chapter of 1 Thessalonians ends with a reference to the second coming of Christ, with ch. 4 giving it major consideration (1:9-10; 2:19-20; 3:13; 4:13-18; 5:23-24). Thus, the second coming seems to permeate the letter and may be viewed in some sense as its theme. The two letters are often designated as the eschatological letters of Paul.

Outline

1 Paul, Silas[a][a] and Timothy,[b]

To the church of the Thessalonians[c] in God the Father and the Lord Jesus Christ:

Grace and peace to you.[b][d]

Thanksgiving for the Thessalonians' Faith

[2]We always thank God for all of you,[e] mentioning you in our prayers.[f] [3]We continually remember before our God and Father[g] your work produced by faith,[h] your labor prompted by love,[i] and your endurance inspired by hope[j] in our Lord Jesus Christ.

[4]For we know, brothers loved by God,[k] that he has chosen you, [5]because our gospel[l] came to you not simply with words, but also with power,[m] with the Holy Spirit and with deep conviction. You know[n] how we lived among you for your sake. [6]You became imitators of us[o] and of the Lord; in spite of severe suffering,[p] you welcomed the message with the joy[q] given by the Holy Spirit.[r] [7]And so you became a model[s] to all the believers in Macedonia[t] and Achaia.[u] [8]The Lord's message[v] rang out from you not only in Macedonia and Achaia—your faith in God has become known everywhere.[w] Therefore we do not need to say anything about it, [9]for they themselves report what kind of reception you gave us. They tell how you turned[x] to God from idols[y] to serve the living and true God,[z] [10]and to wait for his Son from heaven,[a] whom he raised from the dead[b]—Jesus, who rescues us from the coming wrath.[c]

Paul's Ministry in Thessalonica

2 You know, brothers, that our visit to you[d] was not a failure.[e] [2]We had previously suffered[f] and been insulted in Philippi,[g] as you know, but with the help of our God we dared to tell you his gospel in spite of strong opposition.[h] [3]For the appeal we make does not spring from error or impure motives,[i] nor are we trying to trick you.[j] [4]On the contrary, we speak as

---

Cross-references (center column):

1:1 [a]S Ac 15:22
[b]S Ac 16:1;
2Th 1:1
[c]S Ac 17:1
[d]S Ro 1:7
1:2 [e]S Ro 1:8;
Eph 5:20
[f]S Ro 1:10
1:3 [g]S Php 4:20
[h]Gal 5:6;
2Th 1:11;
Jas 2:14-26
[i]1Th 3:6 2Th 1:3;
S 1Co 13:13
/Ro 8:25
1:4 [k]Col 3:12;
2Th 2:13
1:5 [l]S 2Co 2:12;
2Th 2:14
[m]Ro 1:16;
S Ro 15:13
[n]1Th 2:10
1:6 [o]S 1Co 4:16
[p]Ac 17:5-10
[q]S 2Co 6:10
[r]Ac 13:52
1:7 [s]S 1Ti 4:12

[t]S Ac 16:9
[u]S Ac 18:12
1:8 [v]2Th 3:1
[w]Ro 1:8
1:9 [x]Ac 14:15
[y]1Co 12:2;
Gal 4:8
[z]S Mt 16:16
1:10 [a]S 1Co 1:7
[b]S Ac 2:24
[c]S Ro 1:18
2:1 [d]1Th 1:5,9
[e]2Th 1:10
2:2 [f]Ac 14:19;
16:22; Php 1:30

2:3 [g]S Ac 16:12 [h]Ac 17:1-9 2:3 [i]2Co 2:17 [j]2Co 4:2

[a]1 Greek Silvanus, a variant of Silas   [b]1 Some early manuscripts you from God our Father and the Lord Jesus Christ

---

1:1 *Paul.* See notes on Ac 9:1; 13:9; Php 3:4–14. *Silas.* See note on Ac 15:22. He accompanied Paul on most of his second missionary journey. *Timothy.* See Introduction to 1 Timothy: Recipient. Both he and Silas helped Paul found the Thessalonian church (see Ac 17:1–14). *in.* Indicates the vital union and living relationship that Christians have with the Father and the Son (see Jn 14:23; 17:21). The close connection between the Father and the Son points to the Trinitarian relationship (see 3:11; 2Th 1:2,8,12; 2:16; 3:5). *Grace and peace.* See notes on Jnh 4:2; Jn 14:27; 20:19; Gal 1:3; Eph 1:2.

1:2 *thank.* See note on Php 1:3–4.

1:3 The triad of faith, hope and love is found often in the NT (5:8; Ro 5:2–5; 1Co 13:13; Gal 5:5–6; Col 1:4–5; Heb 6:10–12; 10:22–24; 1Pe 1:3–8,21–22). *work produced by faith.* Faith produces action (see Ro 1:5; 16:26; Gal 5:6; 2Th 1:11; Jas 2:14–26). *hope.* Not unfounded wishful thinking, but firm confidence in our Lord Jesus Christ and his return (v. 10). See Heb 6:18–20 and note on Col 1:5.

1:4 *know.* The reasons for Paul's conviction regarding their election are stated in vv. 5–10. *brothers.* United to each other through union with Christ. This term is used 28 times in the two letters to the Thessalonians. *loved . . . chosen.* Both words speak of God's electing love (see Col 3:12; 2Th 2:13; see also note on Eph 1:4).

1:5 *our gospel.* The gospel preached by Paul, Silas and Timothy and that they themselves had received by faith. It is first of all God the Father's (2:8) because he originated it, and Christ's (3:2) because it springs from his atoning death. *power.* The power that delivered them from spiritual bondage. That power is of the Holy Spirit (see Ro 15:13,18–19; 1Co 2:4–5), but it also resides in the gospel itself (see Ro 1:16). *deep conviction.* Such conviction, on the part of both the preachers and the Thessalonians, was also of the Holy Spirit.

1:6 *imitators.* The order in Christian imitation: (1) Believers in Macedonia and Achaia imitated the Thessalonians (v. 7), just as the Thessalonians imitated the churches in

Judea (2:14); (2) the Thessalonians imitated Paul, just as the Corinthians did (1Co 4:6; 11:1) and just as all believers were to imitate their leaders (2Th 3:7,9; 1Ti 4:12; Tit 2:7; 1Pe 5:3); (3) Paul imitated Christ (1Co 11:1) as did the Thessalonians (v. 6); (4) all were to imitate God (Eph 5:1). *severe suffering.* Such as recorded in Ac 17:5–14 (see also 1Th 2:14).

1:7 *Macedonia and Achaia.* The two Roman provinces into which Greece was then divided (see Ac 19:21; Ro 15:26).

1:8 *everywhere.* In every place they visited or knew about (see Ro 1:8; 1Co 1:2; 2Co 2:14; 1Ti 2:8). The news spread because Thessalonica was on the important Egnatian Way; it was also a busy seaport and the capital of the Roman province of Macedonia.

1:9–10 Three marks of true conversion: (1) turning from idols, (2) serving God and (3) waiting for Christ to return. In his two short letters to the Thessalonians, Paul speaks much of the second coming of Christ (v. 10; 2:19; 3:13; 4:13–5:4; 2Th 1:7–10; 2:1–12).

1:10 *Jesus.* See NIV text note on Mt 1:21. *wrath.* Some see a reference here to the final judgment (see note on Ro 1:18), while others think it refers to a future period of tribulation.

2:1–12 A "manual" for a minister: 1. His message is God's good news ("gospel," v. 2). 2. His motive is not impurity (v. 3), pleasing people (v. 4), greed (v. 5) or seeking praise from people (v. 6), but pleasing God (v. 4). 3. His manner is not one of trickery (v. 3), flattery (v. 5) or a cover-up (v. 5), but of courage (v. 2), gentleness (v. 7), love (vv. 8,11), toil (v. 9) and holiness (v. 10).

2:1 *You know.* The local church could refute the accusation of insincerity that evidently had been leveled against Paul (v. 3).

2:2 *insulted.* Paul was deeply hurt by the way he had been treated in the city of Philippi (see Ac 16:19–40).

2:3 *trick.* The Greek for this word was originally used of a lure for catching fish; it came to be used of any sort of cunning used for profit.

2:4 *our hearts.* Not simply our emotions, but also our

men approved by God to be entrusted with the gospel.[k] We are not trying to please men[l] but God, who tests our hearts.[m] [5]You know we never used flattery, nor did we put on a mask to cover up greed[n]—God is our witness.[o] [6]We were not looking for praise from men,[p] not from you or anyone else.

As apostles[q] of Christ we could have been a burden to you,[r] [7]but we were gentle among you, like a mother caring for her little children.[s] [8]We loved you so much that we were delighted to share with you not only the gospel of God[t] but our lives as well,[u] because you had become so dear to us. [9]Surely you remember, brothers, our toil and hardship; we worked[v] night and day in order not to be a burden to anyone[w] while we preached the gospel of God to you.

[10]You are witnesses,[x] and so is God,[y] of how holy,[z] righteous and blameless we were among you who believed. [11]For you know that we dealt with each of you as a father deals with his own children,[a] [12]encouraging, comforting and urging you to live lives worthy[b] of God, who calls[c] you into his kingdom and glory.

[13]And we also thank God continually[d] because, when you received the word of God,[e] which you heard from us, you accepted it not as the word of men, but as it actually is, the word of God, which is at work in you who believe. [14]For you, brothers, became imitators[f] of God's churches in Judea,[g] which are in Christ Jesus: You

suffered from your own countrymen[h] the same things those churches suffered from the Jews, [15]who killed the Lord Jesus[i] and the prophets[j] and also drove us out. They displease God and are hostile to all men [16]in their effort to keep us from speaking to the Gentiles[k] so that they may be saved. In this way they always heap up their sins to the limit.[l] The wrath of God has come upon them at last.[c]

Paul's Longing to See the Thessalonians

[17]But, brothers, when we were torn away from you for a short time (in person, not in thought),[m] out of our intense longing we made every effort to see you.[n] [18]For we wanted to come to you—certainly I, Paul, did, again and again—but Satan[o] stopped us.[p] [19]For what is our hope, our joy, or the crown[q] in which we will glory[r] in the presence of our Lord Jesus when he comes?[s] Is it not you? [20]Indeed, you are our glory[t] and joy.

3 So when we could stand it no longer,[u] we thought it best to be left by ourselves in Athens.[v] [2]We sent Timothy,[w] who is our brother and God's fellow worker[d][x] in spreading the gospel of Christ,[y] to strengthen and encourage you in your faith, [3]so that no one would be unsettled

2:4 [k]Gal 2:7; 1Ti 1:11
[l]S Ro 2:29
[m]S Rev 2:23
2:5 [n]S Ac 20:33
[over 10]; S Ro 1:9
2:6 [p]Jn 5:41,44
[q]1Co 9:1,2
[r]2Co 11:7-11
2:7 [s]S ver 11
2:8 [t]S Ro 1:1
[u]2Co 12:15;
1Jn 3:16
2:9 [v]S Ac 18:3
[w]S 2Co 11:9;
2Th 3:8
2:10 [x]1Th 1:5
[y]ver 5; S Ro 1:9
[z]2Co 1:12
2:11 [a]ver 7;
1Co 4:14;
Gal 4:19;
S 1Ti 1:2;
Phm 10; S 1Jn 2:1
2:12 [b]S Eph 4:1
[c]S Ro 8:28
2:13 [d]1Th 1:2;
S Ro 1:8
[e]S Heb 4:12
2:14 [f]1Th 1:6
[g]Gal 1:22

[h]Ac 17:5;
2Th 1:4
2:15 [i]Lk 24:20;
Ac 2:23
[j]S Mt 5:12
2:16 [k]Ac 13:45,
50; 17:5; S 20:3;
21:27; 24:9
[l]Mt 23:32
2:17 [m]1Co 5:3;
Col 2:5
[n]1Th 3:10
2:18 [o]S Mt 4:10
[p]Ro 1:13; 15:22
2:19 [q]Isa 62:3;
Php 4:1
[r]2Co 1:14
[s]S Mt 16:27;
S Lk 17:30;
S 1Co 1:7; 4:5;
1Th 3:13;
2Th 1:8-10;
1Pe 1:7;
1Jn 2:28;
S Rev 1:7

2:20 [t]2Co 1:14 **3:1** [u]ver 5 [v]S Ac 17:15 **3:2** [w]S Ac 16:1
[x]S 1Co 3:9 [y]S 2Co 2:12

[c][16] Or them fully [d][2] Some manuscripts brother and fellow worker; other manuscripts brother and God's servant

intellects and wills.

2:5 mask. Personal profit was never Paul's aim.

2:6 burden. Apostles were entitled to be supported by the church (see 1Co 9:3–14; 2Co 11:7–11). Paul did not always take advantage of the right, but insisted that he had it.

2:9 toil and hardship. Greeks despised manual labor and viewed it as fit only for slaves, but Paul was not ashamed of doing any sort of work that would help further the gospel. He did not want to be unduly dependent on others.

2:12 live lives worthy of God. See Eph 4:1. calls. See note on 1:4. kingdom. The chief subject of Jesus' teaching. Paul did not use this term often, but used it once to sum up the message of his preaching (Ac 20:25).

2:13 not as the word of men. Not tailored to fit the popular knowledge of the day.

2:14 You suffered from your own countrymen. At the time of Paul's initial visit to Thessalonica, persecution instigated by the Jews apparently was carried out by Gentiles (see Ac 17:5–9). Jews. Although Paul had great love and deep concern for the salvation of those of his own race (see Ro 9:1–3; 10:1), he did not fail to rebuke harshly Jews who persecuted the church.

2:15 prophets. Throughout OT history, Israelites had persecuted their prophets (cf. Ac 7:52).

2:16 wrath of God has come. The eschatological wrath, the final outpouring of God's anger upon sinful mankind (see 1:10). It is spoken of as already present, either because it had

been partially experienced by the Jews or because of its absolute certainty.

2:17 torn away. Lit. "orphaned." Paul is like a mother (v. 7), a father (v. 11) and now an orphan.

2:19 crown. Not a royal crown, but a wreath used on festive occasions or as the prize in the Greek games. when he comes. The expression was used regarding the arrival of a great person, as on a royal visit.

2:20 you are our glory and joy. True both now (cf. Php 4:1) and when Christ returns.

3:1–2 Paul first went to Athens alone, then sent to Berea for Silas and Timothy (Ac 17:14–15). It is not clear whether Silas, as instructed (Ac 17:15), came to Athens with Timothy. However, when Timothy later returned from Thessalonica to Paul, who was now at Corinth, Silas came with him (Ac 18:5). See Introduction: Background of the Thessalonian Letters.

3:1 we. An editorial "we," referring to Paul alone.

3:2 God's fellow worker. A striking way of viewing Christian service, found also in 1Co 3:9. gospel of Christ. See notes on 1:5; Mk 1:1. strengthen. In Greek classical literature the word was generally used in the literal sense of putting a buttress on a building. In the NT it is mainly used figuratively, as here.

3:3 trials. The opposition and persecution suffered by the Thessalonian converts. Christians must expect troubles (see Mk 4:17; Jn 16:33; Ac 14:22; 2Ti 3:12; 1Pe 4:12), but

by these trials.[z] You know quite well that
we were destined for them.[a] 4In fact,
when we were with you, we kept telling
you that we would be persecuted. And it
turned out that way, as you well know.[b]
5For this reason, when I could stand it no
longer,[c] I sent to find out about your
faith.[d] I was afraid that in some way the
tempter[e] might have tempted you and our
efforts might have been useless.[f]

Timothy's Encouraging Report

6But Timothy[g] has just now come to us
from you[h] and has brought good news
about your faith and love.[i] He has told us
that you always have pleasant memories of
us and that you long to see us, just as we
also long to see you.[j] 7Therefore, brothers,
in all our distress and persecution we were
encouraged about you because of your
faith. 8For now we really live, since you
are standing firm[k] in the Lord. 9How can
we thank God enough for you[l] in return
for all the joy we have in the presence of
our God because of you?[m] 10Night and day
we pray[n] most earnestly that we may see
you again[o] and supply what is lacking in
your faith.
11Now may our God and Father[p] himself and our Lord Jesus clear the way for us
to come to you. 12May the Lord make your
love increase and overflow for each other[q]
and for everyone else, just as ours does for
you. 13May he strengthen your hearts so
that you will be blameless[r] and holy in the
presence of our God and Father[s] when
our Lord Jesus comes[t] with all his holy
ones.[u]

Living to Please God

4 Finally, brothers,[v] we instructed you
how to live[w] in order to please God,[x]
as in fact you are living. Now we ask you
and urge you in the Lord Jesus to do this
more and more. 2For you know what instructions we gave you by the authority of
the Lord Jesus.
3It is God's will[y] that you should be
sanctified: that you should avoid sexual
immorality;[z] 4that each of you should
learn to control his own body[e][a] in a way
that is holy and honorable, 5not in passionate lust[b] like the heathen,[c] who do not
know God;[d] 6and that in this matter no
one should wrong his brother or take advantage of him.[e] The Lord will punish
men[f] for all such sins,[g] as we have al-

3:3 [z]Mk 4:17; Jn 16:33; Ro 5:3; 2Co 1:4; 4:17; 2Ti 3:12 [a]S Ac 9:16; 14:22 **3:4** [b]1Th 2:14 **3:5** [c]ver 1 [d]ver 2 [e]Mt 4:3 [f]Gal 2:2; Php 2:16 **3:6** [g]S Ac 16:1 [h]Ac 18:5 [i]1Th 1:3 [j]1Th 2:17,18 **3:8** [k]S 1Co 16:13 **3:9** [l]1Th 1:2 [m]1Th 2:19,20 **3:10** [n]2Ti 1:3 [o]1Th 2:17 **3:11** [p]ver 13; S Php 4:20 **3:12** [q]Php 1:9; 1Th 4:9,10; 2Th 1:3 **3:13** [r]Ps 15:2; 1Co 1:8; Php 2:15; 1Th 5:23; 1Ti 6:14; 2Pe 3:14 [s]ver 11; S Php 4:20 [t]S 1Th 2:19 [u]Mt 25:31; 2Th 1:7 **4:1** [v]2Co 13:11; 2Th 3:1 [w]S Eph 4:1 [x]S 2Co 5:9 **4:3** [y]S Eph 5:17 [z]S 1Co 6:18 **4:4** [a]1Co 7:2,9 **4:5** [b]Ro 1:26 [c]Eph 4:17 [d]S Gal 4:8 **4:6** [e]Lev 25:17; 1Co 6:8 [f]Dt 32:35; Ps 94:1; Ro 2:5-11; 12:19; Heb 10:30,31 [g]Heb 13:4

[e]4 Or *learn to live with his own wife*; or *learn to acquire a wife*

these are not disasters, for they advance God's purposes (see Ac 11:19; Ro 5:3; 2Co 1:4; 4:17).

3:5 *I.* Paul uses the Greek emphatic pronoun (elsewhere used only in 2:18) to bring out his deep concern. *tempter.* Satan is spoken of in every major division of the NT. He is supreme among evil spirits (see Jn 16:11; Eph 2:2). His activities can affect the physical (see 2Co 12:7) and the spiritual (see Mt 13:39; Mk 4:15; 2Co 4:4). He tempted Jesus (Mt 4:1–11), and he continues to tempt Jesus' servants (see Lk 22:3; 1Co 7:5). He hinders missionary work (2:18). But he has already been defeated (see Col 2:15), and Christians need not be overwhelmed by him (see Eph 6:16). His final overthrow is certain (see Rev 20:10).

3:6 *brought good news.* The only place where the Greek for this phrase is used by Paul for anything other than the gospel. Three things caused him joy: (1) "your faith"—a right attitude toward God; (2) "your . . . love"—a right attitude toward man; (3) "you long to see us"—a right attitude toward Paul.

3:9 *thank God.* The preceding shows that Paul's work of evangelism had been effective. He might have congratulated himself on work well done, but instead he thanked God for the joy he had from what God had done.

3:10 *Night and day.* Not prayer at two set times, but frequent prayer (see 1:2–3). *most earnestly.* Translates a strong and unusual Greek compound word (found elsewhere in the NT only in 5:13; Eph 3:20) that brings out Paul's passionate longing. *what is lacking.* Some of the things lacking were of a practical nature, such as moral (4:1–12) and disciplinary matters (5:12–24). Others were doctrinal, such as confusion over Christ's return (4:13–5:11). *your faith.* The fifth time in the chapter that Paul speaks of their faith (see vv. 2,5–7).

3:11 In the middle of a letter Paul frequently breaks into prayer (e.g., Eph 1:15–23; 3:14–21; Php 1:9–11; Col 1:9–12). For the link between Father and Son see note on 1:1.

3:12 *the Lord.* In Paul's writings this usually means Jesus rather than the Father.

3:13 *strengthen.* See note on v. 2. *holy.* The basic idea is "set apart [for God]." Here it refers to the completed process of sanctification (see note on 1Co 1:2). *holy ones.* Used of the saints (Christians) in many NT passages. Here it may mean the departed saints who will return with Jesus, or it may mean the angels or, probably, both.

4:1 *Finally.* The main section of the letter is finished, though much is yet to come (see Php 3:1 and note). *live.* Lit. "walk." Paul uses this metaphor often of the Christian way (see Ro 6:4; 2Co 5:7; Eph 4:1; 5:17; Col 1:10, "live a life"; 2:6; 4:5, "act"). It points to steady progress. *we ask you and urge you.* Paul is not arrogant, but he does speak with authority in the Lord Jesus. He has the "mind of Christ" (1Co 2:16).

4:2 *instructions.* Used of authoritative commands and has a military ring (see Ac 5:28; 16:24).

4:3 *sanctified.* See note on 3:13. *sexual immorality.* In the first century moral standards were generally very low, and chastity was regarded as an unreasonable restriction. Paul, however, would not compromise God's clear and demanding standards. The warning was needed, for Christians were not immune to the temptation (see 1Co 5:1).

4:5 *like the heathen.* The Christian is to be different.

4:6 *wrong his brother.* Sexual sin harms others besides those who engage in it. In adultery, e.g., the spouse is always wronged. Premarital sex wrongs the future partner by robbing him or her of the virginity that ought to be brought to marriage. *The Lord will punish.* A motive for chastity.

ready told you and warned you. 7For God did not call us to be impure, but to live a holy life. *h* 8Therefore, he who rejects this instruction does not reject man but God, who gives you his Holy Spirit. *i*

9Now about brotherly love *j* we do not need to write to you, *k* for you yourselves have been taught by God *l* to love each other. *m* 10And in fact, you do love all the brothers throughout Macedonia. *n* Yet we urge you, brothers, to do so more and more. *o*

11Make it your ambition to lead a quiet life, to mind your own business and to work with your hands, *p* just as we told you, 12so that your daily life may win the respect of outsiders *q* and so that you will not be dependent on anybody.

The Coming of the Lord

13Brothers, we do not want you to be ignorant *r* about those who fall asleep, *s* or to grieve like the rest of men, who have no hope. *t* 14We believe that Jesus died and rose again *u* and so we believe that God will bring with Jesus those who have fallen asleep in him. *v* 15According to the Lord's own word, we tell you that we who are still alive, who are left till the coming of the Lord, *w* will certainly not precede those who have fallen asleep. *x* 16For the Lord himself will come down from heaven, *y* with a loud command, with the voice of the archangel *z* and with the trumpet call of God, *a* and the dead in Christ will rise first. *b* 17After that, we who are still alive and are left *c* will be caught up together with them in the clouds *d* to meet the Lord in the air. And so we will be with the Lord *e* forever. 18Therefore encourage each other *f* with these words.

5 Now, brothers, about times and dates *g* we do not need to write to you, *h* 2for you know very well that the day of the Lord *i* will come like a thief in the

---

Cross references (center column):

4:7 *h* Lev 11:44; 1Pe 1:15
4:8 *i* Eze 36:27; Ro 5:5; 2Co 1:22; Gal 4:6; 1Jn 3:24
4:9 *j* S Ro 12:10
k 1Th 5:1
l S Jn 6:45
m S Jn 13:34
4:10 *n* S Ac 16:9
o S 1Th 3:12
4:11 *p* Eph 4:28; 2Th 3:10-12
4:12 *q* S Mk 4:11
4:13 *r* S Ro 11:25
s S Mt 9:24

t Eph 2:12
4:14 *u* Ro 14:9; 1Co 15:3,4; 2Co 5:15
v 1Co 15:18
4:15 *w* S 1Co 1:7
x 1Co 15:52
4:16 *y* S Mt 16:27
z Jude 9
a S Mt 24:31
b 1Co 15:23; 2Th 2:1; Rev 14:13
4:17 *c* 1Co 15:52
d Ac 1:9;
S Ac 8:39;
S Rev 1:7; 11:12
e S Jn 12:26
4:18 *f* 1Th 5:11

5:1 *g* Ac 1:7 *h* 1Th 4:9 5:2 *i* S 1Co 1:8

Study notes:

4:7 Another reason for chastity is God's call to holiness.
4:8 *God, who gives you his Holy Spirit.* Still another reason for chastity is that sexual sin is against God, who gives the Holy Spirit to believers for their sanctification. To live in sexual immorality is to reject God, specifically in regard to the Holy Spirit.
4:9 *brotherly love.* Translates *philadelphia,* a Greek word that outside the NT almost without exception denoted the mutual love of children of the same father. In the NT it always means love of fellow believers in Christ, all of whom have the same heavenly Father. *taught by God.* Cf. Isa 54:13; Jn 6:45; 1Co 2:13.
4:11 Some Thessalonians, probably because of idleness, were taking undue interest in other people's affairs. *work with your hands.* The Greeks in general thought manual labor degrading and fit only for slaves. Christians took seriously the need for earning their own living, but some of the Thessalonians, perhaps as a result of their belief in the imminent return of Christ (see 2Th 3:11), were neglecting work and relying on others to support them.
4:12 *not be dependent on anybody.* Or "have need of nothing." Both meanings are true and significant. Christians in need because of their idleness are not obedient Christians.
4:13 *those who fall asleep.* For the Christian, sleep is a particularly apt metaphor for death, since death's finality and horror are removed by the assurance of resurrection. Some of the Thessalonians seem to have misunderstood Paul and thought all believers would live until Christ returns. When some died, the question arose, "Will those who have died have part in that great day?" See note on v. 15. *who have no hope.* Inscriptions on tombs and references in literature show that first-century pagans viewed death with horror, as the end of everything. The Christian attitude was in strong contrast (see 1Co 15:55–57; Php 1:21–23).
4:14 *died.* Paul does not say that Christ "slept," perhaps to underscore the fact that he bore the full horror of death so that those who believe in him would not have to. *rose again.* For the importance of the resurrection see 1Co 15, especially vv. 14,17–22. *those who have fallen asleep in him.* Believers who have died, trusting in Jesus.
4:15 *According to the Lord's own word.* The doctrine mentioned here is not recorded in the Gospels and was either

a direct revelation to Paul or something Jesus said that Christians passed on orally. *we who are still alive.* Those believers who will be alive when Christ returns. "We" does not necessarily mean that Paul thought that he would be alive then. He often identified himself with those he wrote to or about. Elsewhere he says that God will raise "us" at that time (1Co 6:14; 2Co 4:14). *will certainly not precede.* The Thessalonians had evidently been concerned that those among them who died would miss their place in the great events when the Lord comes, and Paul assures them this will not be the case.
4:16 *the Lord himself.* See Ac 1:11. *archangel.* The only named archangel in the Bible is Michael (Jude 9; see Da 10:13). In Scripture, Gabriel is simply called an angel (Lk 1:19,26). *will rise first.* Before the ascension of believers mentioned in the next verse.
4:17 *we who are still alive.* See note on v. 15. *caught up.* The only place in the NT where a "rapture" (from the Latin Vulgate rendering) is clearly referred to. Some hold that this will be secret, but Paul seems to be describing something open and public, with loud voices and a trumpet blast. *with the Lord.* The chief hope of the believer (see 5:10; Jn 14:3; 2Co 5:8; Php 1:23; Col 3:4).
4:18 *encourage each other.* The primary purpose of vv. 13–18 is not to give a chronology of future events, though that is involved, but to urge mutual encouragement, as shown here and in v. 13.
5:1 *times and dates.* See Ac 1:6–7. There have always been some Christians who try to fix the date of our Lord's return, but apparently the Thessalonians were not among them.
5:2 *day of the Lord.* See 1Co 5:5. The expression goes back to Am 5:18. In the OT it is a time when God will come and intervene with judgment and/or blessing. In the NT the thought of judgment continues (see Ro 2:5; 2Pe 2:9), but it is also the "day of redemption" (Eph 4:30); the "day of God" (2Pe 3:12), or of Christ (1Co 1:8; Php 1:6); and the "last day" (Jn 6:39), the "great Day" (Jude 6) or simply "the day" (2Th 1:10). It is the climax of all things. There will be some preliminary signs (e.g., 2Th 2:3), but the coming will be as unexpected as that of a thief in the night (cf. Mt 24:43–44; Lk 12:39–40; 2Pe 3:10; Rev 3:3; 16:15).

night.[j] 3While people are saying, "Peace
and safety,"[k] destruction will come on
them suddenly,[l] as labor pains on a pregnant woman, and they will not escape.[m]
4But you, brothers, are not in darkness[n]
so that this day should surprise you like a
thief.[o] 5You are all sons of the light[p] and
sons of the day. We do not belong to the
night or to the darkness. 6So then, let us
not be like others, who are asleep,[q] but let
us be alert[r] and self-controlled.[s] 7For
those who sleep, sleep at night, and those
who get drunk, get drunk at night.[t] 8But
since we belong to the day,[u] let us be self-
controlled, putting on faith and love as a
breastplate,[v] and the hope of salvation[w] as
a helmet.[x] 9For God did not appoint us to
suffer wrath[y] but to receive salvation
through our Lord Jesus Christ.[z] 10He died
for us so that, whether we are awake or
asleep, we may live together with him.[a]
11Therefore encourage one another[b] and
build each other up,[c] just as in fact you are
doing.

5:2 [j]S Lk 12:39 **5:3** [k]Jer 4:10; 6:14; Eze 13:10 [l]Job 15:21; Ps 35:8; 55:15; Isa 29:5; 47:9,11 [m]2Th 1:9 **5:4** [n]S Ac 26:18; 1Jn 2:8 [o]ver 2 **5:5** [p]S Lk 16:8 **5:6** [q]Ro 13:11 [r]S Mt 25:13 [s]S Ac 24:25 **5:7** [t]Ac 2:15; Ro 13:13; 2Pe 2:13 **5:8** [u]ver 5 [v]S Eph 6:14 [w]Ro 8:24 [x]Isa 59:17; Eph 6:17 **5:9** [y]1Th 1:10 [z]2Th 2:13,14 **5:10** [a]Ro 14:9; 2Co 5:15 **5:11** [b]1Th 4:18 [c]Eph 4:29

Final Instructions

12Now we ask you, brothers, to respect
those who work hard[d] among you, who
are over you in the Lord[e] and who admonish you. 13Hold them in the highest
regard in love because of their work. Live
in peace with each other.[f] 14And we urge
you, brothers, warn those who are idle,[g]
encourage the timid, help the weak,[h] be
patient with everyone. 15Make sure that
nobody pays back wrong for wrong,[i] but
always try to be kind to each other[j] and to
everyone else.

16Be joyful always;[k] 17pray continually;[l] 18give thanks in all circumstances,[m]
for this is God's will for you in Christ Jesus.

19Do not put out the Spirit's fire;[n] 20do
not treat prophecies[o] with contempt.
21Test everything.[p] Hold on to the good.[q]
22Avoid every kind of evil.

5:12 [d]Ro 16:6, 12; 1Co 15:10 [e]1Ti 5:17; Heb 13:17 **5:13** [f]S Mk 9:50 **5:14** [g]2Th 3:6,7, 11 [h]Ro 14:1; 1Co 8:7-12 **5:15** [i]Ro 12:17; 1Pe 3:9 [j]Eph 4:32

5:16 [k]Php 4:4 **5:17** [l]S Lk 18:1 **5:18** [m]S Eph 5:20 **5:19** [n]Eph 4:30 **5:20** [o]1Co 14:1-40 **5:21** [p]1Co 14:29; 1Jn 4:1 [q]Ro 12:9

5:3 *destruction.* Not annihilation, but exclusion from the Lord's presence (2Th 1:9); thus the ruin of life and all its proud accomplishments. *suddenly.* Paul stresses the surprise of unbelievers. He uses a word found elsewhere in the NT only in Lk 21:34 ("unexpectedly"). *labor pains.* Here the idea is not the pain of childbirth so much as the suddenness and inevitability of such pains. *not.* An emphatic double negative in the Greek, a construction Paul uses only four times in all his writings.

5:4 *darkness.* Believers no longer live in darkness, nor are they of the darkness (v. 5). See Jn 1:5; Ac 26:18. *thief.* See note on v. 2.

5:5 In Semitic languages (such as Hebrew) to be the "son of" a quality meant to be characterized by that quality. Christians do not simply live in the light; they are characterized by light.

5:6 *asleep.* Unbelievers are spiritually insensitive, but this kind of sleep is not for "sons of the light." *be alert.* Lit. "watch," which is in keeping with the emphasis Paul is placing on Christ's coming (cf. Mt 24:42–43; 25:13; Mk 13:34–37). *self-controlled.* A contrast with the conduct mentioned in v. 7.

5:8 *the day.* A reference to the light that characterizes Christians; perhaps it refers also to the coming of Christ (see v. 2 and note). *breastplate . . . helmet.* Paul also uses the metaphor of armor in Ro 13:12; 2Co 6:7; 10:4; Eph 6:13–17. He does not consistently attach a particular virtue to each piece of armor; it is the general idea of equipment for battle that is pictured. For the triad of faith, hope and love see note on 1:3.

5:9 *appoint.* God's appointment, not man's choice, is the significant thing. *wrath.* See note on 1:10. *salvation.* Our final, completed salvation.

5:10 *are awake or asleep.* That is, "live or die"; or, if the sense is moral, "are alert or carnal" (see v. 6). *with him.* To be Christ's is to have entered a relationship that nothing can destroy.

5:11 *build . . . up.* The verb basically applies to building houses, but Paul frequently used it for Christians being edified.

5:12 *those who work hard among you.* Not much is known about the organization and leadership of the church at this period, but the reference is possibly to elders.

5:13 *because of their work.* Not merely because of personal attachment or respect for their high position, but in appreciation for their work. *Live in peace.* The words apply to Christian relationships in general, but here they probably refer especially to right relations between leaders and those under them.

5:14 *those who are idle.* Loafers. It seems that some Thessalonians were so sure that the second coming was close that they had given up their jobs in order to prepare for it, but Paul says they should work. *the timid . . . the weak.* These are to be helped, not rejected, by the strong (cf. Ro 14:1–15; 1Co 8:13).

5:15 *pays back.* Retaliation is never a Christian option (cf. Ro 12:17; 1Pe 3:9). Christians are called to forgive (see Mt 5:38–42; 18:21–35).

5:16 People are naturally happy on some occasions, but the Christian's joy is not dependent on circumstances. It comes from what Christ has done, and it is constant.

5:17 For the practice of continual (or regular) prayer see 1:3; 2:13; Ro 1:9–10; Eph 6:18; Col 1:3; 2Ti 1:3.

5:18 As in v. 16, Christians are differentiated from the natural man. Because of what God has done, they are continually thankful whatever the circumstances (cf. Eph 5:20).

5:19 *Spirit's fire.* There is a warmth, a glow, about the Spirit's presence that makes this language appropriate. The kind of conduct Paul is opposing may include loafing, immorality and the other sins he has denounced. On the other hand, he may be warning against a mechanical attitude toward worship that discourages the expression of the gifts of the Spirit in the local assembly (see v. 20).

5:20 *prophecies.* For the gift of prophecy see Ro 12:6; 1Co 12:10,28; 13:2; 14; Eph 4:11. For the function of prophecies see 1Co 14:3.

5:21 *Test everything.* The approval of prophecy (v. 20) does not mean that anyone who claims to speak in the name of the Lord is to be accepted without question. Paul does not say what specific tests are to be applied, but he is clear that every teaching must be tested—surely they must be in agreement with his gospel.

23May God himself, the God of peace,[r] sanctify you through and through. May your whole spirit, soul[s] and body be kept blameless[t] at the coming of our Lord Jesus Christ.[u] 24The one who calls[v] you is faithful[w] and he will do it.[x]

25Brothers, pray for us.[y] 26Greet all the brothers with a holy kiss.[z] 27I charge you before the Lord to have this letter read to all the brothers.[a]

28The grace of our Lord Jesus Christ be with you.[b]

5:23 [r]S Ro 15:33; [s]Heb 4:12; [t]S 1Th 3:13; [u]S 1Th 2:19
5:24 [v]S Ro 8:28; [w]S 1Co 1:9; [x]Nu 23:19; Php 1:6
5:25 [y]Eph 6:19; Col 4:3; 2Th 3:1; Heb 13:18
5:26 [z]S Ro 16:16
5:27 [a]2Th 3:14; S 1Ti 4:13 5:28 [b]S Ro 16:20

5:23 A typical prayer. *God of peace.* A fitting reference to God in view of vv. 12–15. But Paul often refers to God in this way near the end of his letters (see Ro 15:33; 16:20; 1Co 14:33; 2Co 13:11; Php 4:9; cf. 2Th 3:16). *your whole spirit, soul and body.* Paul is emphasizing the whole person, not attempting to differentiate his parts.

5:24 Paul's confidence rests in the nature of God (cf. Ge 18:25), who can be relied on to complete what he begins (see Nu 23:19; Php 1:6).

5:26 *all.* Paul sent a warm greeting to everyone, even those

he had corrected. *holy kiss.* A kiss was a normal greeting of that day, similar to our modern handshake (cf. Ro 16:16; 1Co 16:20; 2Co 13:12; and a "kiss of love," 1Pe 5:14).

5:27 *I charge you.* Surprisingly strong language, meaning "I put you on oath." Paul clearly wanted every member of the church to read or hear his letter and to know of his concern and advice for them.

5:28 Paul always ended his letters with a benediction of grace for his readers, sometimes adding other blessings, as in 2Co 13:14.

2 THESSALONIANS

See Introduction to 1 Thessalonians.

Author, Date and Place of Writing

Paul's authorship of 2 Thessalonians has been questioned more often than that of 1 Thessalonians, in spite of the fact that it has more support from early Christian writers. Objections are based on internal factors rather than on the adequacy of the statements of the church fathers. It is thought that there are differences in the vocabulary (ten words not used elsewhere), in the style (it is said to be unexpectedly formal) and in the eschatology (the doctrine of the "man of lawlessness" is not taught elsewhere). However, such arguments have not convinced current scholars. A majority still hold to Paul's authorship of 2 Thessalonians.

Because of its similarity to 1 Thessalonians, it must have been written not long after the first letter—perhaps about six months. The situation in the church seems to have been much the same. Paul probably penned it (see 1:1; 3:17) c. A.D. 51 or 52 in Corinth, after Silas and Timothy had returned from delivering 1 Thessalonians.

Purpose

Inasmuch as the situation in the Thessalonian church has not changed substantially, Paul's purpose in writing is very much the same as in his first letter to them. He writes (1) to encourage persecuted believers (1:4-10), (2) to exhort the Thessalonians to be steadfast and to work for a living (2:13-3:15) and (3) to correct a misunderstanding concerning the Lord's return (2:1-12).

Theme

Like 1 Thessalonians, this letter deals extensively with eschatology (see Introduction to 1 Thessalonians: Theme). In fact, in 2 Thessalonians 18 out of 47 verses (38 percent) deal with this subject.

Outline

I. Introduction (ch. 1)
   A. Salutation (1:1-2)
   B. Thanksgiving for Their Faith, Love and Perseverance (1:3-10)
   C. Intercession for Their Spiritual Progress (1:11-12)
II. Instruction (ch. 2)
   A. Prophecy regarding the Day of the Lord (2:1-12)
   B. Thanksgiving for Their Election and Calling (Their Position) (2:13-15)
   C. Prayer for Their Service and Testimony (Their Practice) (2:16-17)
III. Injunctions (ch. 3)
   A. Call to Prayer (3:1-3)
   B. Charge to Discipline for the Disorderly and Lazy (3:4-15)
   C. Conclusion, Greeting and Benediction (3:16-18)

1 Paul, Silas[a][a] and Timothy,[b]

To the church of the Thessalonians[c] in God our Father and the Lord Jesus Christ:

[2]Grace and peace to you from God the Father and the Lord Jesus Christ.[d]

Thanksgiving and Prayer

[3]We ought always to thank God for you,[e] brothers, and rightly so, because your faith is growing more and more, and the love every one of you has for each other is increasing.[f] [4]Therefore, among God's churches we boast[g] about your perseverance and faith[h] in all the persecutions and trials you are enduring.[i]

[5]All this is evidence[j] that God's judgment is right, and as a result you will be counted worthy[k] of the kingdom of God, for which you are suffering. [6]God is just:[l] He will pay back trouble to those who trouble you[m] [7]and give relief to you who are troubled, and to us as well. This will happen when the Lord Jesus is revealed from heaven[n] in blazing fire[o] with his powerful angels.[p] [8]He will punish[q] those

who do not know God[r] and do not obey the gospel of our Lord Jesus.[s] [9]They will be punished with everlasting destruction[t] and shut out from the presence of the Lord[u] and from the majesty of his power[v] [10]on the day[w] he comes to be glorified[x] in his holy people and to be marveled at among all those who have believed. This includes you, because you believed our testimony to you.[y]

[11]With this in mind, we constantly pray for you,[z] that our God may count you worthy[a] of his calling,[b] and that by his power he may fulfill every good purpose[c] of yours and every act prompted by your faith.[d] [12]We pray this so that the name of our Lord Jesus may be glorified in you,[e] and you in him, according to the grace of our God and the Lord Jesus Christ.[b]

The Man of Lawlessness

2 Concerning the coming of our Lord Jesus Christ[f] and our being gathered

1:1 aS Ac 15:22
bS Ac 16:1;
1Th 1:1
cS Ac 17:1
1:2 dS Ro 1:7
1:3 eS Ro 1:8;
Eph 5:20
/S 1Th 3:12
1:4 g2Co 7:14
h1Th 1:3
i1Th 1:6; 2:14;
S 3:3
1:5 jPhp 1:28
kLk 20:35
1:6 lLk 18:7,8
mRo 12:19;
Col 3:25;
S Rev 6:10
1:7 nS Lk 17:30
oHeb 10:27;
S 12:29; 2Pe 3:7;
S Rev 1:14 pJude 14
1:8 qPs 79:6;
Isa 66:15;
Jer 10:25
rS Gal 4:8

sRo 2:8;
S 2Co 2:12
1:9 tPhp 3:19;
1Th 5:3; 2Pe 3:7
u2Ki 17:18
vIsa 2:10,19;
2Th 2:8
1:10 w1Co 3:13
xJn 17:10
y1Co 1:6
1:11 zS Ro 1:10
aVer 5 bS Ro 8:28
cRo 15:14
d1Th 1:3
1:12 eIsa 24:15;
Php 2:9-11

2:1 /S 1Th 2:19

a / Greek Silvanus, a variant of Silas   b 12 Or God and Lord, Jesus Christ

---

1:1-2 See notes on 1Th 1:1.

1:3 ought. Paul is obliged to give thanks where it is due (cf. 1Th 1:7-8; see note on Php 1:3-4). brothers. See note on 1Th 1:4. faith ... love. Two virtues that Paul had been pleased to acknowledge in the Thessalonian church (see 1Th 3:6-7), but that were also somewhat lacking (1Th 3:10,12). is increasing. The same verb Paul had used in his prayer that their love might grow (1Th 3:12). He is recording an exact answer to prayer.

1:4 we. Emphatic, "we ourselves." Paul seems to imply that it was unusual for the founders of a church to boast about it, though others might do so (cf. 1Th 1:9). But the Thessalonians were so outstanding that Paul departed from normal practice. persecutions and trials. See 1Th 1:6; 2:14; 3:3.

1:5 evidence that God's judgment is right. The evidence was in the way the Thessalonians endured trials. The judgment on them was right because God did not leave them to their own resources. He provided strength to endure, and this in turn produced spiritual and moral character. It also proved that God was on their side and gave a warning to their persecutors (cf. Php 1:28). kingdom of God. See notes on 1Th 2:12; Mt 3:2. for which. That is, "in the interest of which" or "in behalf of which."

1:6 God is just. The justice of God brings punishment on unrepentant sinners (cf. Mk 9:47-48; Lk 13:3-5), and it may be in the here and now (see Ro 1:24,26,28) as well as on judgment day.

1:7 give relief. Retribution not only involves punishment of the evil but also relief for the righteous. us as well. Paul was no academic theologian writing in comfort from a distance; rather, he was suffering just as they were. revealed. Christ is now hidden, and many people even deny his existence. But at his second coming he will be seen by everyone for who he

is. blazing fire. He comes to punish wickedness (cf. Isa 66:15; Rev 1:14). his powerful angels. Perhaps a class of angels (such a group is mentioned in apocalyptic writings) given special power to do God's will.

1:8 do not know God. Does not refer to those who have never heard of the true God but to those who refuse to recognize him (cf. 2:10,12; Ro 1:28). do not obey. The gospel invites acceptance, and rejection is disobedience to a royal invitation.

1:9 destruction. Not annihilation (see note on 1Th 5:3). Paul uses the word in 1Co 5:5, possibly of the destruction of the "flesh" (see NIV text note there) for the purpose of salvation. Since, however, salvation implies resurrection of the body, annihilation cannot be in mind. The word means something like "complete ruin." Here it means being shut out from Christ's presence. This eternal separation is the penalty of sin and the essence of hell.

1:10 the day. See note on 1Th 5:2. glorified in his holy people. Not simply "among" but "in" them. His glory is seen in what they are. holy people. See note on 1Th 3:13. our testimony. The preaching of the gospel is essentially bearing testimony to what God has done in Christ.

1:11 constantly pray. See note on 1Th 5:17. good purpose. Lit. "resolve of goodness." God initiates every good purpose and every act prompted by faith; Paul prays accordingly that he will bring them to fulfillment.

1:12 name. In ancient times one's name was often more than a personal label; it summed up what a person was. Paul looks for glory to be ascribed to Christ for all he will do in the lives of the Thessalonian Christians.

2:1 coming. See note on 1Th 2:19. The second coming of Christ is the principal topic of 2 Thessalonians. What Paul wrote was supplemental to his oral teaching and the instructions contained in his earlier letter. gathered to him. See note on 1Th 4:17.

to him,[g] we ask you, brothers, [2]not to become easily unsettled or alarmed by some prophecy, report or letter[h] supposed to have come from us, saying that the day of the Lord[i] has already come.[j] [3]Don't let anyone deceive you[k] in any way, for that day will not come, until the rebellion[l] occurs and the man of lawlessness[c] is revealed,[m] the man doomed to destruction. [4]He will oppose and will exalt himself over everything that is called God[n] or is worshiped, so that he sets himself up in God's temple, proclaiming himself to be God.[o]

[5]Don't you remember that when I was with you I used to tell you these things?[p] [6]And now you know what is holding him back,[q] so that he may be revealed at the proper time. [7]For the secret power of lawlessness is already at work; but the one who now holds it back[r] will continue to do so till he is taken out of the way. [8]And then the lawless one will be revealed,[s] whom the Lord Jesus will overthrow with the breath of his mouth[t] and destroy by

the splendor of his coming. [u] [9]The coming of the lawless one will be in accordance with the work of Satan[v] displayed in all kinds of counterfeit miracles, signs and wonders,[w] [10]and in every sort of evil that deceives those who are perishing.[x] They perish because they refused to love the truth and so be saved.[y] [11]For this reason God sends them[z] a powerful delusion[a] so that they will believe the lie[b] [12]and so that all will be condemned who have not believed the truth but have delighted in wickedness. [c]

Stand Firm

[13]But we ought always to thank God for you, [d] brothers loved by the Lord, because from the beginning God chose you[d] [e] to be saved[f] through the sanctifying work of the Spirit[g] and through belief in the truth. [14]He called you[h] to this through our gospel,[i] that you might share in the glory of

Cross references

2:1 [g]Mk 13:27; 1Th 4:15-17
2:2 [h]ver 15; 2Th 3:17
[i]S 1Co 1:8
[j]2Ti 2:18
2:3 [k]S Mk 13:5
[l]Mt 24:10-12
[m]ver 8; Da 7:25; 8:25; 11:36; Rev 13:5,6
2:4 [n]1Co 8:5
[o]Isa 14:13,14; Eze 28:2
2:5 [p]1Th 3:4
2:6 [q]ver 7
2:7 [r]ver 6
2:8 [s]S ver 3
[t]Isa 11:4; Rev 2:16; 19:15
[u]S Lk 17:30
2:9 [v]S Mt 4:10
[w]Mt 24:24; Rev 13:13; S Jn 4:48
2:10 [x]S 1Co 1:18
[y]Pr 4:6; Jn 3:17-19
2:11 [z]Ro 1:28
[a]Mt 24:5; S Mk 13:5
[b]Ro 1:25
2:12 [c]Ro 1:32; 2:8
2:13 [d]S Ro 1:8
[e]Eph 1:4 /1Th 5:9
[g]1Pe 1:2
2:14 [h]S Ro 8:28; S 11:29 /1Th 1:5

[c]3 Some manuscripts *sin*   [d]13 Some manuscripts *because God chose you as his firstfruits*

2:2 *unsettled.* The Greek for this verb was often used of a ship adrift from its mooring, and suggests lack of stability. *alarmed.* Jesus issued a similar instruction, using the same verb (Mk 13:7). *some.* Paul seems to be uncertain about what was disturbing them, so he uses a general expression. *prophecy.* Lit. "spirit," denoting any inspired revelation. *report.* Lit. "word," perhaps referring to a sermon or other oral communication. *letter supposed to have come from us.* A forgery. *day of the Lord.* See note on 1Th 5:2. *has already come.* Obviously Christ's climactic return had not occurred, but Paul was combating the idea that the final days had begun and their completion would be imminent.

2:3 *the rebellion.* At the last time there will be a falling away from the faith (see Mt 24:10–12; 1Ti 4:1). But here Paul is speaking of active rebellion, the supreme opposition of evil to the things of God. *the man of lawlessness.* The leader of the forces of evil at the last time. Only here is he called by this name. John tells us of many "antichrists" (1Jn 2:18), and this may be the worst of them—the antichrist of Rev 13—though Paul's description of the man of lawlessness has some distinctive features. He is not Satan, because he is clearly distinguished from him in v. 9. *revealed.* Since the Greek for this word is from the same root as that used of Jesus Christ in 1:7, it may indicate something supernatural. *doomed to destruction.* For all his proud claims, his final overthrow is certain. The same expression is used of Judas Iscariot (see Jn 17:12).

2:4 *everything that is called God or is worshiped.* He is not merely a political or military man, but claims a place above every god and everything associated with worship. He even claims to be God. *God's temple.* Apparently refers to a physical building (cf. Mk 13:14) from which he makes his blasphemous pronouncements (cf. Da 11:36–45; Rev 13:1–15).

2:6 *what is holding him back.* The expression is neuter, but the masculine equivalent is in v. 7. There have been many suggestions as to the identity of this restrainer: the Roman state with its emperor, Paul's missionary work, the Jewish state, the principle of law and government embodied in the state, the Holy Spirit or the restraining ministry of the Holy Spirit through the church, and others.

2:7 *secret power.* Lit. "mystery," which in the NT usually denotes something people could not know by themselves but that God has revealed (see note on Ro 11:25). It is most often used in reference to the gospel or some aspect of it. The expression here indicates that we know some things about evil only as God reveals them. This evil is already at work and will continue until the restrainer is removed at the end time.

2:8 *the lawless one will be revealed.* Evidently refers to some supernatural aspects of his appearing (see v. 9). *overthrow with the breath of his mouth.* Despite his impressiveness (v. 4), the man of lawlessness will easily be destroyed by Christ (cf. Da 11:45; Rev 19:20). *splendor.* In 2Ti 1:10 ("appearing") the Greek for this word refers to Jesus' first coming, but everywhere else in the NT to his second coming.

2:9 *coming.* The same word used of Christ's coming in v. 8. Satan empowers him with miracles, signs and wonders (cf. Mt 24:24). *counterfeit.* Not "bogus," but "producing false impressions."

2:10 *deceives.* The aim of the miracles of v. 9. *refused.* Their unbelief was willing and intentional. *truth.* Often closely connected with Jesus (see Jn 14:6; Eph 4:21) and with the gospel (see Gal 2:5; Eph 1:13).

2:11 *For this reason.* Because of their deliberate rejection of the truth (v. 10). *God sends them a powerful delusion.* God uses sin to punish the sinful (cf. Ro 1:24–28). *the lie.* Not just any lie, but the great lie that the man of lawlessness is God (v. 4).

2:13 *loved by the Lord . . . God chose.* For the connection between God's love and election see Col 3:12; 1Th 1:4; see also note on Eph 1:4. *from the beginning.* Election is from eternity (see Eph 1:4). *sanctifying work.* A necessary aspect of salvation, not something reserved for special Christians (see 1Th 3:13; 4:3 and notes). *truth.* See note on v. 10. All three persons of the Trinity are mentioned in this verse (see note on 1Th 1:1).

2:14 *called . . . through our gospel.* The past tense refers to the time when the Thessalonians were converted; but the divine call is a present reality in 1Th 2:12; 5:24. *our gospel.* See note on 1Th 1:5. *glory of our Lord Jesus Christ.* Cf. 1Th 2:12. Ultimately there is no glory other than God's.

our Lord Jesus Christ. [15]So then, brothers, stand firm[i] and hold to the teachings[e] we passed on to you,[k] whether by word of mouth or by letter.

[16]May our Lord Jesus Christ himself and God our Father,[l] who loved us[m] and by his grace gave us eternal encouragement and good hope, [17]encourage[n] your hearts and strengthen[o] you in every good deed and word.

Request for Prayer

3 Finally, brothers,[p] pray for us[q] that the message of the Lord[r] may spread rapidly and be honored, just as it was with you.[s] [2]And pray that we may be delivered from wicked and evil men,[t] for not everyone has faith. [3]But the Lord is faithful,[u] and he will strengthen and protect you from the evil one.[v] [4]We have confidence[w] in the Lord that you are doing and will continue to do the things we command. [5]May the Lord direct your hearts[x] into God's love and Christ's perseverance.

Warning Against Idleness

[6]In the name of the Lord Jesus Christ,[y] we command you, brothers, to keep away from[z] every brother who is idle[a] and does not live according to the teaching[f] you received from us.[b] [7]For you yourselves

know how you ought to follow our example.[c] We were not idle when we were with you, [8]nor did we eat anyone's food without paying for it. On the contrary, we worked[d] night and day, laboring and toiling so that we would not be a burden to any of you. [9]We did this, not because we do not have the right to such help,[e] but in order to make ourselves a model for you to follow.[f] [10]For even when we were with you,[g] we gave you this rule: "If a man will not work,[h] he shall not eat."

[11]We hear that some among you are idle. They are not busy; they are busybodies.[i] [12]Such people we command and urge in the Lord Jesus Christ[j] to settle down and earn the bread they eat.[k] [13]And as for you, brothers, never tire of doing what is right.[l]

[14]If anyone does not obey our instruction in this letter, take special note of him. Do not associate with him,[m] in order that he may feel ashamed.[n] [15]Yet do not regard him as an enemy, but warn him as a brother.[o]

Final Greetings

[16]Now may the Lord of peace[p] himself give you peace at all times and in every way. The Lord be with all of you.[q]

2:15
[i]S 1Co 16:13
[k]S 1Co 11:2
2:16 [l]S Php 4:20
[m]S Jn 3:16
2:17 [n]1Th 3:2
[o]2Th 3:3
3:1 [p]1Th 4:1
[q]S 1Th 5:25
[r]1Th 1:8
[s]1Th 2:13
3:2 [t]S Ro 15:31
3:3 [u]S 1Co 1:9
[v]S Mt 5:37
3:4 [w]S 2Co 2:3
3:5 [x]1Ch 29:18
3:6 [y]1Co 5:4 [z]ver 14; S Ro 16:17
[a]ver 7,11
[b]S 1Co 11:2

3:7 [c]ver 9; S 1Co 4:16
3:8 [d]S Ac 18:3; Eph 4:28
3:9 [e]1Co 9:4-14 [f]ver 7; S 1Co 4:16
3:10 [g]1Th 3:4 [h]1Th 4:11
3:11 [i]ver 6,7; 1Ti 5:13
3:12 [j]1Th 4:1 [k]1Th 4:11; Eph 4:28
3:13 [l]Gal 6:9
3:14 [m]ver 6; S Ro 16:17 [n]S 1Co 4:14
3:15 [o]Gal 6:1; 1Th 5:14; Phm 16
3:16 [p]S Ro 15:33
[q]Ru 2:4

[e]15 Or traditions   [f]6 Or tradition

2:15 *teachings.* Lit. "traditions." Until the NT was written, essential Christian teaching was passed on in the "traditions," just as rabbinic law was (see note on Mt 15:2); it could be either oral or written. In 1Co 15:3 Paul uses the technical words for receiving and handing on traditions.

2:16–17 There is a similar prayer in about the same place in the first letter (1Th 3:11–13).

2:17 *encourage . . . strengthen.* Also used together in 1Th 3:2. The prayer is for inner strength that will produce results in both action and speech.

3:1 *Finally.* See note on 1Th 4:1. In 1Th 5:25 Paul simply asked for prayer; here he mentions specifics. *just as it was with you.* Lit. "just as also with you." The expression is general enough to cover the present as well as the past (cf. 1Th 2:13).

3:2 *wicked.* The Greek for this word means "out of place," and elsewhere in the NT it is used only of things (see Lk 23:41; Ac 25:5). Wickedness is always out of place. For Paul's difficulties at Corinth (where he wrote this letter) see Ac 18:12–13.

3:3 *faithful.* In the Greek the word immediately follows "faith" (v. 2), putting the faithfulness of God in sharp contrast with the lack of faith in people (cf. 1Co 1:9; 10:13; 2Co 1:18).

3:5 *hearts.* See note on 1Th 2:4. *God's love.* Paul is about to rebuke the idle, and is here reminding them of God's love. There should be no hard feelings among those who owe everything to the love of God.

3:6 *the name.* See note on 1:12. *command.* An authoritative word with a military ring. *keep away.* Not withdrawal of all contact but withholding of close fellowship. Idleness is

sinful and disruptive, but those guilty of it are still brothers (v. 15). *idle.* The problem was mentioned in the first letter (4:11–12; 5:14; see notes there), and evidently had worsened. Paul takes it seriously and gives more attention to it in this letter than to anything else but the second coming. *teaching.* See note on 2:15.

3:7 *follow our example.* See note on 1Th 1:6.

3:8 *eat . . . food.* A Hebraism for "make a living" (see, e.g., Ge 3:19; Am 7:12). Paul is not saying that he never accepted hospitality but that he had not depended on other people for his living (see 1Th 2:9 and note).

3:9 *the right.* See note on 1Th 2:6.

3:10 Pagan parallels are in the form, "He who does not work does not eat." But Paul gives an imperative: lit. "let him not eat." The Christian must not be a loafer.

3:11 *busybodies.* Worse than idle, they were interfering with other people's affairs, a problem to which idleness often leads.

3:14 Paul realizes that some may not heed his letter. *associate with.* The Greek for this phrase is an unusual double compound, meaning "mix up together with" (used elsewhere in the NT only in 1Co 5:9,11—of a similar withdrawal of close fellowship). It indicates a disassociation that will bring the person back to a right attitude. *feel ashamed.* And repent. The aim is not punishment but restoration to fellowship.

3:15 Discipline in the church should be brotherly, never harsh. *warn.* See 1Th 5:12, where the Greek for this verb is translated "admonish."

3:16 *Lord of peace.* The more usual phrase is "God of peace" (see note on 1Th 5:23). *all of you.* Even the disorderly.

¹⁷I, Paul, write this greeting in my own hand,ʳ which is the distinguishing mark in all my letters. This is how I write.

3:17
ʳS 1Co 16:21
3:18 ˢS Ro 16:20

¹⁸The grace of our Lord Jesus Christ be with you all.ˢ

3:17 Paul normally dictated his letters (cf. Ro 16:22), but toward the end he added something in his own handwriting (see 1Co 16:21; Gal 6:11; Col 4:18). Here he tells us that this practice was his distinguishing mark.

3:18 See note on 1Th 5:28. Paul has criticized his offenders, but his last prayer is for everyone.

The Pastoral Letters

1,2 Timothy and Titus are known as the Pastoral Letters because they give instruction to Timothy and Titus concerning the pastoral care of churches. All three letters probably were written not long after the events of Ac 28.

After his imprisonment in Rome (c. A.D. 60-62), Paul most likely began his fourth missionary journey (see "Paul's Fourth Missionary Journey," p. 1836). During this trip he commissioned Titus to remain as his representative in Crete, and he left Timothy in charge of the church at Ephesus. Paul then moved on to Philippi in northern Greece (Macedonia), where he wrote his first letter to Timothy and his letter to Titus (c. 63-65). Later he traveled to Rome, where he was imprisoned for the second time and where he wrote 2 Timothy shortly before he was executed (67 or 68).

Certain themes and phrases recur throughout the Pastoral Letters: (1) God the Savior (see note on Tit 1:3); (2) sound doctrine, faith and teaching (see note on Tit 1:9); (3) godliness (see note on 1Ti 2:2); (4) controversies (1Ti 1:4; 6:4; 2Ti 2:23; Tit 3:9); (5) trustworthy sayings (see note on 1Ti 1:15).

1 TIMOTHY

Author

Both early tradition and the salutations of the Pastoral Letters themselves confirm Paul as their author. Some objections have been raised in recent years on the basis of an alleged uncharacteristic vocabulary and style (e.g., see notes on 1:15; 2:2), but evidence is still convincingly supportive of Paul's authorship.

Background and Purpose

During his fourth missionary journey, Paul had instructed Timothy to care for the church at Ephesus (1:3) while he went on to Macedonia (see "The Pastoral Letters," p. 1832). When he realized that he might not return to Ephesus in the near future (3:14-15), he wrote this first letter to Timothy to develop the charge he had given his young assistant (1:3,18), to refute false teachings (1:3-7; 4:1-8; 6:3-5,20-21) and to supervise the affairs of the growing Ephesian church (church worship, 2:1-15; the appointment of qualified church leaders, 3:1-13; 5:17-25).

A major problem in the Ephesian church was a heresy that combined Gnosticism (see Introduction to 1 John: Gnosticism), decadent Judaism (1:3-7) and false asceticism (4:1-5).

Date

1 Timothy was written sometime after the events of Ac 28 (c. 63-65), at least eight years after Paul's three-year stay in Ephesus (Ac 19:8,10; 20:31).

Recipient

As the salutation indicates (1:2), Paul is writing to Timothy, a native of Lystra (in modern Turkey). Timothy's father was Greek, while his mother was a Jewish Christian (Ac 16:1). From childhood he had been taught the OT (2Ti 1:5; 3:15). Paul called him "my true son in the faith" (1:2), perhaps having led him to Christ during his first visit to Lystra. At the time of his second visit Paul invited Timothy to join him on his missionary travels, and circumcised him so that his Greek ancestry would not be a liability in working with the Jews (Ac 16:3). Timothy shared in the evangelization of Macedonia and Achaia (Ac 17:14-15; 18:5) and was with Paul during much of his long preaching ministry at Ephesus (Ac 19:22). He traveled with Paul from Ephesus to Macedonia, to Corinth, back to Macedonia, and to Asia Minor (Ac 20:1-6). He seems even to have accompanied him all the way to Jerusalem. He was with Paul during the apostle's first imprisonment (Php 1:1; Col 1:1; Phm 1).

Following Paul's release (after Ac 28), Timothy again traveled with him but eventually stayed at Ephesus to deal with the problems there, while Paul went on to Macedonia. Paul's closeness to and admiration of Timothy are seen in Paul's naming him as the co-sender of six of his letters (2 Corinthians, Philippians, Colossians, 1,2 Thessalonians and Philemon) and in his speaking highly of him to the Philippians (Php 2:19-22). At the end of Paul's life he requested Timothy to join him at Rome (2Ti 4:9,21). According to Heb 13:23, Timothy himself was imprisoned and subsequently released—whether at Rome or elsewhere, we do not know.

Timothy was not an apostle, and he was probably not an overseer since he was given instructions about overseers (3:1-7; 5:17-22). It may be best to regard him as an apostolic representative, delegated to carry out special work (see Tit 1:5).

Outline

I. Salutation (1:1-2)
II. Warning against False Teachers (1:3-11)
   A. The Nature of the Heresy (1:3-7)
   B. The Purpose of the Law (1:8-11)
III. The Lord's Grace to Paul (1:12-17)

1 Paul, an apostle of Christ Jesus by the command of God[a] our Savior[b] and of Christ Jesus our hope,[c]

[2]To Timothy[d] my true son[e] in the faith:

Grace, mercy and peace from God the Father and Christ Jesus our Lord.[f]

Warning Against False Teachers of the Law

[3]As I urged you when I went into Macedonia,[g] stay there in Ephesus[h] so that you may command certain men not to teach false doctrines[i] any longer [4]nor to devote themselves to myths[j] and endless genealogies.[k] These promote controversies[l] rather than God's work—which is by faith. [5]The goal of this command is love, which comes from a pure heart[m] and a good conscience[n] and a sincere faith.[o] [6]Some have wandered away from these and turned to meaningless talk. [7]They want to be teachers[p] of the law, but they do not know what they are talking about or what they so confidently affirm.[q]

[8]We know that the law is good[r] if one uses it properly. [9]We also know that law[a] is made not for the righteous[s] but for lawbreakers and rebels,[t] the ungodly and sinful, the unholy and irreligious; for those who kill their fathers or mothers, for murderers, [10]for adulterers and perverts, for slave traders and liars and perjurers—and for whatever else is contrary to the sound doctrine[u] [11]that conforms to the glorious gospel of the blessed God, which he entrusted to me.[v]

The Lord's Grace to Paul

[12]I thank Christ Jesus our Lord, who has given me strength,[w] that he considered me faithful, appointing me to his service.[x] [13]Even though I was once a blasphemer and a persecutor[y] and a violent man, I was shown mercy[z] because I acted in ignorance and unbelief.[a] [14]The grace of our Lord was poured out on me abundantly,[b] along with the faith and love that are in Christ Jesus.[c]

[15]Here is a trustworthy saying[d] that deserves full acceptance: Christ Jesus came into the world to save sinners[e]—of whom I am the worst. [16]But for that very reason I was shown mercy[f] so that in me, the worst of sinners, Christ Jesus might display his unlimited patience[g] as an example for those who would believe[h] on him and receive eternal life.[i] [17]Now to the King[j] eternal, immortal,[k] invisible,[l] the only God,[m] be honor and glory for ever and ever. Amen.[n]

[18]Timothy, my son,[o] I give you this instruction in keeping with the prophecies once made about you,[p] so that by following them you may fight the good fight,[q] [19]holding on to faith and a good conscience.[r] Some have rejected these and so have shipwrecked their faith.[s] [20]Among

Cross references

1:1 [a]S 2Co 1:1; Tit 1:3 [b]S Lk 1:47 [c]Col 1:27
1:2 [d]S Ac 16:1 [e]ver 18; 1Co 4:17; S 1Th 2:11; 2Ti 1:2; Tit 1:4 [f]S Ro 1:7
1:3 [g]S Ac 16:9 [h]S Ac 18:19 [i]Gal 1:6,7; 1Ti 6:3
1:4 [j]1Ti 4:7; 2Ti 4:4; Tit 1:14 [k]Tit 3:9 [l]S 2Ti 2:14
1:5 [m]2Ti 2:22 [n]S Ac 23:1; 1Ti 4:2 [o]Gal 5:6; 2Ti 1:5
1:7 [p]S Eph 4:11 [q]Job 38:2
1:8 [r]Ro 7:12
1:9 [s]Gal 5:23 [t]Gal 3:19
1:10 [u]1Ti 6:3; 2Ti 1:13; 4:3; Tit 1:9; 2:1
1:11 [v]Gal 2:7; 1Th 2:4; Tit 1:3
1:12 [w]S Php 4:13 [x]S Ac 9:15
1:13 [y]S Ac 8:3 [z]ver 16 [a]Ac 26:9
1:14 [b]2Co 4:15 [c]2Ti 1:13; S 1Th 1:3
1:15 [d]1Ti 3:1; 4:9; 2Ti 2:11; Tit 3:8 [e]Mk 2:17; S Jn 3:17
1:16 [f]ver 13 [g]S Ro 2:4 [h]S Jn 3:15 [i]S Mt 25:46
1:17 [j]Rev 15:3 [k]1Ti 6:16 [l]S Col 1:15 [m]Jude 25 [n]S Ro 11:36
1:18 [o]S ver 2 [p]1Ti 4:14 [q]1Ti 6:12; 2Ti 2:3; 4:7
1:19 [r]ver 5; S Ac 23:1
[s]1Ti 6:21; 2Ti 2:18

[a]9 Or *that the law*

Study notes

1:1 *apostle.* One specially commissioned by Christ (see notes on Mk 6:30; 1Co 1:1; Heb 3:1). *Christ Jesus our hope.* See Tit 2:13. *hope.* Expresses absolute certainty, not a mere wish.
1:2 *my true son in the faith.* My spiritual son (see 1:18; 1Co 4:17; 2Ti 1:2; 2:1; Phm 10). *Grace.* See notes on Jnh 4:2; Gal 1:3; Eph 1:2. *mercy.* See Ro 9:23. *peace.* See notes on Jn 14:27; 20:19; Gal 1:3; Eph 1:2.
1:3–11 In this section, along with 4:1–8; 6:3–5,20–21, Paul warns against heretical teachers in the Ephesian church. They are characterized by (1) teaching false doctrines (1:3; 6:3); (2) teaching Jewish myths (Tit 1:14); (3) wanting to be teachers of the OT law (1:7); (4) building up endless, farfetched, fictitious stories based on obscure genealogical points (1:4; 4:7; Tit 3:9); (5) being conceited (1:7; 6:4); (6) being argumentative (1:4; 6:4; 2Ti 2:23; Tit 3:9); (7) using talk that was meaningless (1:6) and foolish (2Ti 2:23; Tit 3:9); (8) not knowing what they were talking about (1:7; 6:4); (9) teaching ascetic practices (4:3); and (10) using their positions of religious leadership for personal financial gain (6:5). These heretics probably were forerunners of the Gnostics (6:20–21; see Introduction to 1 John: Gnosticism).
1:3 *when I went into Macedonia.* Since this incident is not recorded in Acts, it probably occurred after Ac 28, between Paul's first and second Roman imprisonments (see Introduction: Recipient). *stay there in Ephesus.* The Ephesian church was well established by this time. Paul had had an extensive

ministry there on his third missionary journey about eight years earlier (Ac 19:1–20:1). After his release from prison in Rome (after Ac 28), he revisited the church, leaving Timothy in charge while he journeyed on to Macedonia.
1:4 *myths and endless genealogies.* Probably mythical stories built on OT history (genealogies) that later developed into intricate Gnostic philosophical systems (see Introduction to 1 John: Gnosticism).
1:8 *the law is good.* See Ro 7:7–12.
1:10 *sound doctrine.* See note on Tit 1:9.
1:11 *gospel.* See note on Mk 1:1. *entrusted.* See 6:20; 1Co 9:17; Gal 2:7; 1Th 2:4; 2Ti 1:12,14; 2:2.
1:13 *a blasphemer and a persecutor and a violent man.* See Ac 9:1; 22:4–5,19; 26:10–11.
1:15 *Here is a trustworthy saying.* A clause found nowhere else in the NT but used five times in the Pastorals (here; 3:1; 4:9; 2Ti 2:11; Tit 3:8) to identify a key saying.
1:18 *prophecies once made about you.* In the early church God revealed his will in various matters through prophets (see Ac 13:1–3, where prophets had an active role in the sending of Paul and Barnabas on their mission to the Gentiles). In Timothy's case this prophecy may have occurred at the time of or before his ordination (4:14), perhaps about 12 years earlier on Paul's second missionary journey (see Ac 16:3). Prophecies about Timothy seem to have pointed to the significant leadership role he was to have in the church.
1:20 *Hymenaeus.* See 2Ti 2:17–18. *Alexander.* Perhaps

them are Hymenaeus[t] and Alexander,[u] whom I have handed over to Satan[v] to be taught not to blaspheme.

Instructions on Worship

2 I urge, then, first of all, that requests, prayers,[w] intercession and thanksgiving be made for everyone— [2]for kings and all those in authority,[x] that we may live peaceful and quiet lives in all godliness[y] and holiness. [3]This is good, and pleases[z] God our Savior,[a] [4]who wants[b] all men[c] to be saved[d] and to come to a knowledge of the truth.[e] [5]For there is one God[f] and one mediator[g] between God and men, the man Christ Jesus,[h] [6]who gave himself as a ransom[i] for all men—the testimony[j] given in its proper time.[k] [7]And for this purpose I was appointed a herald and an apostle—I am tell-

ing the truth, I am not lying[l]—and a teacher[m] of the true faith to the Gentiles. [n]

[8]I want men everywhere to lift up holy hands[o] in prayer, without anger or disputing.

[9]I also want women to dress modestly, with decency and propriety, not with braided hair or gold or pearls or expensive clothes,[p] [10]but with good deeds,[q] appropriate for women who profess to worship God.

[11]A woman should learn in quietness and full submission.[r] [12]I do not permit a woman to teach or to have authority over a man; she must be silent.[s] [13]For Adam was formed first, then Eve.[t] [14]And Adam was not the one deceived; it was the

1:20 [t]2Ti 2:17
[u]2Ti 4:14
[v]1Co 5:5
2:1 [w]Eph 6:18
2:2 [x]Ezr 6:10; Ro 13:1
[y]1Ti 3:16; 4:7,8; 6:3,5,6,11; 2Ti 3:5; Tit 1:1
2:3 [z]S 1Ti 5:4
[a]S Lk 1:47
2:4 [b]Eze 18:23,32; 33:11
[c]1Ti 4:10; Tit 2:11; 2Pe 3:9
[d]S Jn 3:17; S Ro 11:14
[e]2Ti 2:25; Tit 1:1; Heb 10:26
2:5 [f]Dt 6:4; Ro 3:29,30; 10:12
[g]S Gal 3:20
[h]Ro 1:3
2:6 [i]S Mt 20:28
[j]S 1Co 1:6
[k]1Ti 6:15; Tit 1:3

2:7 [l]S Ro 9:1
[m]2Ti 1:11
[n]S Ac 9:15

2:8 [o]Ps 24:4; 63:4; 134:2; 141:2; Lk 24:50 2:9 [p]1Pe 3:3
2:10 [q]Pr 31:13 2:11 [r]1Pe 3:3,4 2:12 [s]S Eph 5:22 2:13
[t]Ge 2:7,22; 1Co 11:8

---

the Alexander of 2Ti 4:14 (but see note there). *handed over to Satan*. The reference is to church discipline (see note on Mt 18:17). Paul had excluded these two men from the church, which was considered a sanctuary from Satan's power. Out in the world, away from the fellowship and care of the church, they would be "taught" (the word means

basically "to discipline") not to blaspheme. The purpose of such drastic action was more remedial than punitive. For a similar situation see 1Co 5:5,13; see also note on 1Co 5:5. **2:2** *kings and all those in authority*. See Jer 29:7. The notorious Roman emperor Nero (A.D. 54–68) was in power when Paul wrote these words. *godliness*. A key word (along

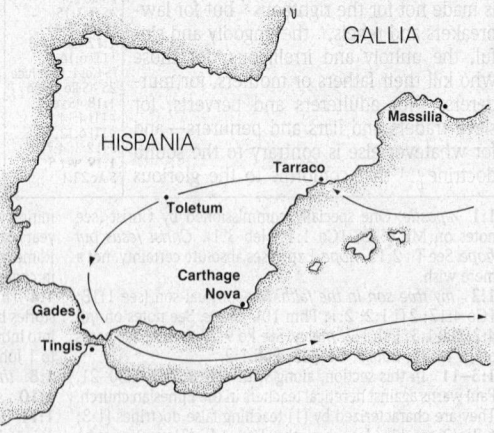

GALLIA

Atlantic
Ocean

Massilia

Paul's Fourth Missionary Journey

c. A.D. 62—68

It is clear from Ac 13:1—21:17 that Paul went on three missionary journeys. There is also reason to believe that he made a fourth journey after his release from the Roman imprisonment recorded in Ac 28. The conclusion that such a journey did indeed take place is based on: (1) Paul's declared intention to go to Spain (Ro 15:24, 28), (2) Eusebius's implication that Paul was released following his first Roman imprisonment (*Ecclesiastical History*, 2.22.2-3) and (3) statements in early Christian literature that he took the gospel as far as Spain (Clement of Rome, *Epistle to the Corinthians*, ch. 5; *Actus Petri Vercellenses*, chs. 1-3; Muratorian Canon, lines 34-39).

The places Paul may have visited after his release from prison are indicated by statements of intention in his earlier writings and by subsequent mention in the Pastoral Letters. The order of his travel cannot be determined with certainty, but the itinerary at the right seems likely.

HISPANIA

Tarraco

Toletum

Carthage
Nova

Gades

Tingis

1. **Rome**—released from prison in A.D. 62
2. **Spain**—62-64 (Ro 15:24,28)
3. **Crete**—64-65 (Tit 1:5)
4. **Miletus**—65 (2Ti 4:20)
5. **Colosse**—66 (Phm 22)
6. **Ephesus**—66 (1Ti 1:3)
7. **Philippi**—66 (Php 2:23-24; 1Ti 1:3)
8. **Nicopolis**—66-67 (Tit 3:12)
9. **Rome**—67
10. Martyrdom—67/68

woman who was deceived and became a sinner. *u* ¹⁵But women *b* will be saved *c* through childbearing—if they continue in faith, love *v* and holiness with propriety.

Overseers and Deacons

3 Here is a trustworthy saying: *w* If anyone sets his heart on being an overseer, *d* *x* he desires a noble task. ²Now the overseer must be above reproach, *y* the husband of but one wife, *z* temperate, *a* self-controlled, respectable, hospitable, *b* able to teach, *c* ³not given to drunkenness, *d* not violent but gentle, not quarrelsome, *e* not a lover of money. *f* ⁴He must manage his own family well and see that his children obey him with proper respect. *g* ⁵(If anyone does not know how to manage his own family, how can he take care of God's church?) *h* ⁶He must not be a

recent convert, or he may become conceited *i* and fall under the same judgment *j* as the devil. ⁷He must also have a good reputation with outsiders, *k* so that he will not fall into disgrace and into the devil's trap. *l*

⁸Deacons, *m* likewise, are to be men worthy of respect, sincere, not indulging in much wine, *n* and not pursuing dishonest gain. ⁹They must keep hold of the deep truths of the faith with a clear conscience. *o* ¹⁰They must first be tested; *p* and then if there is nothing against them, let them serve as deacons.

¹¹In the same way, their wives *e* are to be women worthy of respect, not malicious talkers *q* but temperate *r* and trustworthy in everything.

¹²A deacon must be the husband of but

2:14 *u* Ge 3:1-6, 13; 2Co 11:3
2:15 *v* 1Ti 1:14
3:1 *w* S 1Ti 1:15 *x* Ac 20:28; Php 1:1; Tit 1:7
3:2 *y* Tit 1:6-8 *z* ver 12 *a* ver 11; Tit 2:2 *b* S Ro 12:13 *c* 2Ti 2:24
3:3 *d* Tit 1:7 *e* 2Ti 2:24 *f* Lk 16:14; 1Ti 6:10; 2Ti 3:2; Heb 13:5; 1Pe 5:2
3:4 *g* ver 12; Tit 1:6
3:5 *h* S 1Co 10:32
3:6 *i* 1Ti 6:4; 2Ti 3:4 *j* S 2Pe 2:4
3:7 *k* S Mk 4:11 *l* 2Ti 2:26
3:8 *m* Php 1:1 *n* 1Ti 5:23; Tit 1:7; 2:3
3:9 *o* S Ac 23:1
3:10 *p* 1Ti 5:22
3:11 *q* 2Ti 3:3; Tit 2:3 *r* ver 2

---

b *15* Greek *she*   *c* *15* Or *restored*   *d* *1* Traditionally *bishop*; also in verse 2   *e* *11* Or *way, deaconesses*

---

with "godly") in the Pastorals, occurring eight times in 1 Timothy (here; 3:16; 4:7–8; 6:3,5–6,11), once in 2 Timothy (3:5) and once in Titus (1:1), but nowhere else in the writings of Paul. It implies a good and holy life, with special emphasis on its source, a deep reverence for God.
2:4 *who wants all men to be saved.* God desires the

salvation of all people. On the other hand, the Bible indicates that God chooses some (not all) people to be saved (e.g., 1Pe 1:2). Some interpreters understand such passages to teach that God has chosen those whom he, in his foreknowledge, knew would believe when confronted with the gospel and enabled to believe. Other interpreters hold that, though

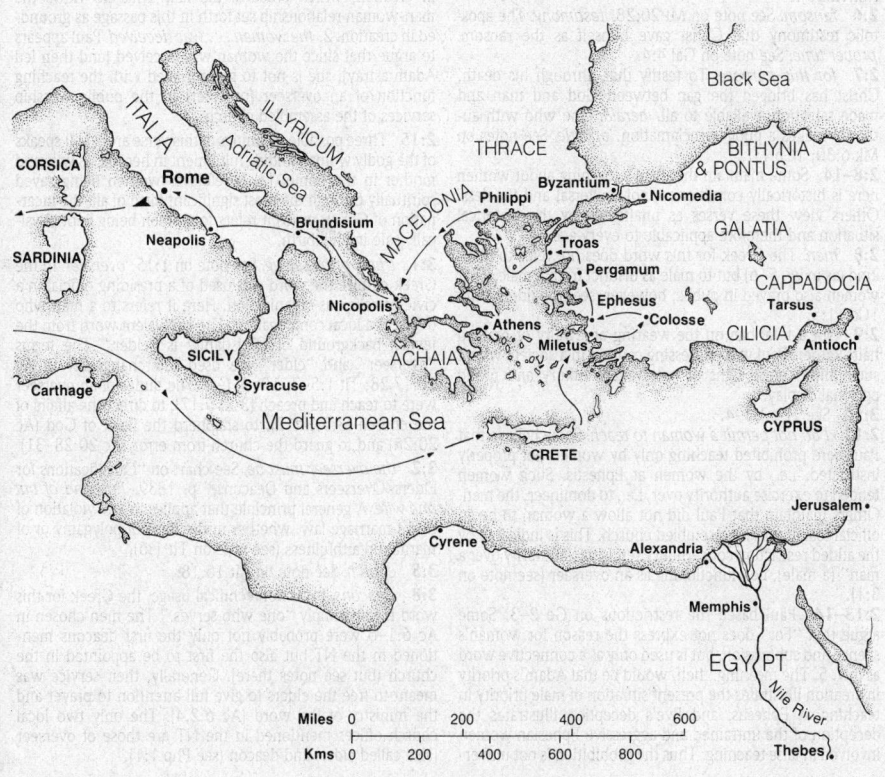

one wife[s] and must manage his children and his household well.[t] 13Those who have served well gain an excellent standing and great assurance in their faith in Christ Jesus.

14Although I hope to come to you soon, I am writing you these instructions so that, 15if I am delayed, you will know how people ought to conduct themselves in God's household, which is the church[u] of the living God,[v] the pillar and foundation of the truth. 16Beyond all question, the mystery[w] of godliness[x] is great:

He[f] appeared in a body,[g] [y]
was vindicated by the Spirit,
was seen by angels,
was preached among the nations,[z]
was believed on in the world,
was taken up in glory.[a]

3:12 [s]ver 2 [t]ver 4
3:15 [u]ver 5; S 1Co 10:32 [v]S Mt 16:16
3:16 [w]S Ro 16:25 [x]S 1Ti 2:2 [y]S Jn 1:14 [z]Ps 9:11; Col 1:23 [a]S Mk 16:19
4:1 [b]Jn 16:13; S Ac 8:29; 1Co 2:10 [c]2Ti 3:1; 2Pe 3:3 [d]S Mk 13:5
4:2 [e]Eph 4:19
4:3 [f]Heb 13:4 [g]Col 2:16 [h]Ge 1:29; 9:3 [i]ver 4; Ro 14:6; 1Co 10:30
4:4 [j]Ge 1:10,12, 18,21,25,31; Mk 7:18,19; Ro 14:14-18 [k]S Ac 10:15
4:5 [l]S Heb 4:12

Instructions to Timothy

4 The Spirit[b] clearly says that in later times[c] some will abandon the faith and follow deceiving spirits[d] and things taught by demons. 2Such teachings come through hypocritical liars, whose consciences have been seared as with a hot iron.[e] 3They forbid people to marry[f] and order them to abstain from certain foods,[g] which God created[h] to be received with thanksgiving[i] by those who believe and who know the truth. 4For everything God created is good,[j] and nothing is to be rejected[k] if it is received with thanksgiving, 5because it is consecrated by the word of God[l] and prayer.

6If you point these things out to the brothers, you will be a good minister of Christ Jesus, brought up in the truths of

[f]16 Some manuscripts God   [g]16 Or in the flesh

---

human reasoning cannot resolve the seeming inconsistency, the Bible teaches both truths and thus there can be no actual contradiction. Certainly there is none in the mind of God. See note on Ro 8:29.

2:5 *there is one God.* The basic belief of Judaism (Dt 6:4), which every Jew confessed daily in the *Shema* (see note on Mk 12:28).

2:6 *ransom.* See note on Mt 20:28. *testimony.* The apostolic testimony that Christ gave himself as the ransom. *proper time.* See note on Gal 4:4.

2:7 *for this purpose.* To testify that, through his death, Christ has bridged the gap between God and man and made salvation available to all. *herald.* One who with authority makes a public proclamation. *apostle.* See notes on Mk 6:30; 1Co 1:1.

2:8–14 Some maintain that Paul's teaching about women here is historically conditioned, not universal and timeless. Others view these verses as unaffected by the historical situation and therefore applicable to every age.

2:8 *men.* The Greek for this word does not refer to mankind (as in vv. 5–6) but to male as distinct from female. That women also prayed in public, however, seems evident from 1Co 11:5.

2:9 Not a total ban on the wearing of jewelry or braided hair. Rather, Paul was expressing caution in a society where such things were signs of extravagant luxury and proud personal display.

2:10 See 1Pe 3:3–4.

2:12 *I do not permit a woman to teach.* Some believe that Paul here prohibited teaching only by women not properly instructed, i.e., by the women at Ephesus. Such women tended to exercise authority over, i.e., to domineer, the men. Others maintain that Paul did not allow a woman to be an official teacher in the assembled church. This is indicated by the added restriction concerning exercising "authority over a man" (a male), i.e., functioning as an overseer (see note on 3:1).

2:13–14 Paul based the restrictions on Ge 2–3. Some argue that "For" does not express the reason for woman's silence and submission, but is used only as a connective word as in v. 5. The meaning, then, would be that Adam's priority in creation illustrates the present situation of male priority in teaching at Ephesus, and Eve's deception illustrates the deception of the untrained and aggressive Ephesian women involved in false teaching. Thus the prohibition is not univer-

sal and permanent but restricted to the church situation (see Introduction: Background and Purpose). Under different circumstances the restrictions would not apply (e.g., 1Co 11:1–5). Others believe that the appeal to the creation account makes the restrictions universal and permanent: 1. *Adam was formed first.* Paul appeals to the priority of Adam in creation, which predates the fall. Thus he views the man-woman relationship set forth in this passage as grounded in creation. 2. *the woman . . . was deceived.* Paul appears to argue that since the woman was deceived (and then led Adam astray), she is not to be entrusted with the teaching function of an overseer (or elder) in the public worship services of the assembled church.

2:15 Three possible meanings of this verse are: (1) It speaks of the godly woman finding fulfillment in her role as wife and mother in the home; (2) it refers to women being saved spiritually through the most significant birth of all, the incarnation of Christ; or (3) it refers to women being kept physically safe in childbirth.

3:1 *trustworthy saying.* See note on 1:15. *overseer.* In the Greek culture the word was used of a presiding official in a civic or religious organization. Here it refers to a man who oversees a local congregation. The equivalent word from the Jewish background of Christianity is "elder." The terms "overseer" and "elder" are used interchangeably in Ac 20:17,28; Tit 1:5–7; 1Pe 5:1–2. The duties of an overseer were to teach and preach (3:2; 5:17), to direct the affairs of the church (3:5; 5:17), to shepherd the flock of God (Ac 20:28) and to guard the church from error (Ac 20:28–31).

3:2 *the overseer must be.* See chart on "Qualifications for Elders/Overseers and Deacons," p. 1839. *husband of but one wife.* A general principle that applies to any violation of God's marriage law, whether in the form of polygamy or of marital unfaithfulness (see note on Tit 1:6).

3:5 *church.* See note on Mt 16:18.

3:8 *Deacons.* In its nontechnical usage, the Greek for this word means simply "one who serves." The men chosen in Ac 6:1–6 were probably not only the first deacons mentioned in the NT but also the first to be appointed in the church (but see notes there). Generally, their service was meant to free the elders to give full attention to prayer and the ministry of the word (Ac 6:2,4). The only two local church offices mentioned in the NT are those of overseer (also called elder) and deacon (see Php 1:1).

the faith[m] and of the good teaching that you have followed.[n] [7]Have nothing to do with godless myths and old wives' tales;[o] rather, train yourself to be godly.[p] [8]For physical training is of some value, but godliness has value for all things,[q] holding promise for both the present life[r] and the life to come.[s]

[9]This is a trustworthy saying[t] that deserves full acceptance [10](and for this we labor and strive), that we have put our hope in the living God,[u] who is the Savior of all men,[v] and especially of those who believe.

[11]Command and teach these things.[w] [12]Don't let anyone look down on you[x] because you are young, but set an example[y] for the believers in speech, in life, in love, in faith[z] and in purity. [13]Until I come,[a] devote yourself to the public reading of Scripture,[b] to preaching and to teaching.

[14]Do not neglect your gift, which was given you through a prophetic message[c] when the body of elders[d] laid their hands on you.[e]

[15]Be diligent in these matters; give yourself wholly to them, so that everyone may see your progress. [16]Watch your life and doctrine closely. Persevere in them; because if you do, you will save[f] both yourself and your hearers.

Advice About Widows, Elders and Slaves

5 Do not rebuke an older man[g] harshly,[h] but exhort him as if he were your father. Treat younger men[i] as brothers, [2]older women as mothers, and younger women as sisters, with absolute purity.

[3]Give proper recognition to those wid-

Cross references (center column):

4:6 [m]1Ti 1:10; [n]2Ti 3:15
4:7 [o]1Ti 1:4; 2Ti 2:16; [p]S 1Ti 2:2
4:8 [q]1Ti 6:6; [r]Ps 37:9,11; Pr 22:4; Mt 6:33; Mk 10:29,30; [s]Mk 10:29,30
4:9 [t]S 1Ti 1:15
4:10 [u]S Mt 16:16; [v]S Lk 1:47; S 2:11
4:11 [w]1Ti 5:7; 6:2
4:12 [x]S 2Ti 1:7; Tit 2:15; [y]Php 3:17; 1Th 1:7; 2Th 3:9; Tit 2:7; 1Pe 5:3; [z]1Ti 1:14
4:13 [a]1Ti 3:14; [b]Lk 4:16; Ac 13:14-16; Col 4:16; 1Th 5:27
4:14 [c]1Ti 1:18; [d]S Ac 11:30; [e]S Ac 6:6; 2Ti 1:6
4:16 [f]S Ro 11:14
5:1 [g]Tit 2:2 [h]Lev 19:32 [i]Tit 2:6

3:11 *their wives.* The Greek for this phrase simply means "the women" and therefore could refer to (1) deacons' wives, (2) deaconesses (see NIV text note) or (3) female deacons. However, the fact that deacons are referred to again in vv. 12–13 seems to rule out a separate office of deaconess, but many judge otherwise.

3:12 *husband of but one wife.* See note on v. 2.

3:14 *I am writing . . . so that.* Here, in brief, Paul states the purpose for writing the letter—to give instructions concerning church conduct.

3:16 *mystery of godliness.* See notes on Ro 11:25; Col 1:26. The phrase means the "revealed secret of true piety," i.e., the secret that produces piety in people. That secret, as the following words indicate, is none other than Jesus Christ. His incarnation, in all its aspects (particularly his saving work), is the source of genuine piety. The words are printed in poetic form and probably come from an early creedal hymn (see note on Col 3:16). *vindicated by the Spirit.* The

Holy Spirit enabled Jesus to drive out demons (see Mt 12:28) and perform miracles. Most importantly, the Spirit raised Jesus from the dead (see Ro 1:4; 1Pe 3:18) and thereby vindicated him, showing that he was indeed the Son of God. *seen by angels.* At his resurrection (Mt 28:2) and ascension (Ac 1:10).

4:1 *The Spirit clearly says.* As, e.g., in Mt 24:11; Mk 13:22; Ac 20:29–30; 2Th 2:3. Paul, however, is perhaps speaking here of a specific revelation made to him by the Spirit. *in later times.* The time beginning with the first coming of Christ (see note on Heb 1:1). That Paul is not referring only to the time immediately prior to Christ's second coming is obvious from his assumption in v. 7 that the false teachings were already present at the time of his writing.

4:3 This unbiblical asceticism arose out of the mistaken belief that the material world was evil—a central belief of the Gnostic heresy (see Introduction to 1 John: Gnosticism).

Qualifications for Elders/Overseers and Deacons

Self-controlled	ELDER	1Ti 3:2; Tit 1:8		Temperate	ELDER	1Ti 3:2; Tit 1:7
Hospitable	ELDER	1Ti 3:2; Tit 1:8			DEACON	1Ti 3:8
Able to teach	ELDER	1Ti 3:2; 5:17; Tit 1:9		Respectable	ELDER	1Ti 3:2
Not violent but gentle	ELDER	1Ti 3:3; Tit 1:7			DEACON	1Ti 3:8
Not quarrelsome	ELDER	1Ti 3:3		Not given to drunkenness	ELDER	1Ti 3:3; Tit 1:7
Not a lover of money	ELDER	1Ti 3:3			DEACON	1Ti 3:8
Not a recent convert	ELDER	1Ti 3:6		Manages his own family well	ELDER	1Ti 3:4
					DEACON	1Ti 3:12
Has a good reputation with outsiders	ELDER	1Ti 3:7		Sees that his children obey him	ELDER	1Ti 3:4-5; Tit 1:6
					DEACON	1Ti 3:12
Not overbearing	ELDER	Tit 1:7		Does not pursue dishonest gain	ELDER	Tit 1:7
Not quick-tempered	ELDER	Tit 1:7			DEACON	1Ti 3:8
Loves what is good	ELDER	Tit 1:8		Keeps hold of the deep truths	ELDER	Tit 1:9
Upright, holy	ELDER	Tit 1:8			DEACON	1Ti 3:9
Disciplined	ELDER	Tit 1:8		Sincere	DEACON	1Ti 3:8
Above reproach (blameless)	ELDER	1Ti 3:2; Tit 1:6		Tested	DEACON	1Ti 3:10
	DEACON	1Ti 3:9				
Husband of one wife	ELDER	1Ti 3:2; Tit 1:6				
	DEACON	1Ti 3:12				

ows who are really in need.[j] 4But if a widow has children or grandchildren, these should learn first of all to put their religion into practice by caring for their own family and so repaying their parents and grandparents,[k] for this is pleasing to God.[l] 5The widow who is really in need[m] and left all alone puts her hope in God[n] and continues night and day to pray[o] and to ask God for help. 6But the widow who lives for pleasure is dead even while she lives.[p] 7Give the people these instructions,[q] too, so that no one may be open to blame. 8If anyone does not provide for his relatives, and especially for his immediate family, he has denied[r] the faith and is worse than an unbeliever.

9No widow may be put on the list of widows unless she is over sixty, has been faithful to her husband,[h] 10and is well known for her good deeds,[s] such as bringing up children, showing hospitality,[t] washing the feet[u] of the saints, helping those in trouble[v] and devoting herself to all kinds of good deeds.

11As for younger widows, do not put them on such a list. For when their sensual desires overcome their dedication to Christ, they want to marry. 12Thus they bring judgment on themselves, because they have broken their first pledge. 13Be-

sides, they get into the habit of being idle and going about from house to house. And not only do they become idlers, but also gossips[w] and busybodies,[x] saying things they ought not to. 14So I counsel younger widows to marry,[y] to have children, to manage their homes and to give the enemy no opportunity for slander.[z] 15Some have in fact already turned away to follow Satan.[a]

16If any woman who is a believer has widows in her family, she should help them and not let the church be burdened with them, so that the church can help those widows who are really in need.[b]

17The elders[c] who direct the affairs of the church well are worthy of double honor,[d] especially those whose work is preaching and teaching. 18For the Scripture says, "Do not muzzle the ox while it is treading out the grain,"[e] and "The worker deserves his wages."[f] 19Do not entertain an accusation against an elder[g] unless it is brought by two or three witnesses.[h] 20Those who sin are to be rebuked[i] publicly, so that the others may take warning.[j]

21I charge you, in the sight of God and Christ Jesus[k] and the elect angels, to keep

5:3 /ver 5,16
5:4 kver 8;
Eph 6:1,2
/Ro 12:2;
Eph 5:10; 1Ti 2:3
5:5 mver 3,16
n1Co 7:34;
1Pe 3:5 oLk 2:37;
S Ro 1:10
5:6 pS Lk 15:24
5:7 q1Ti 4:11;
6:2
5:8 r2Pe 2:1;
Jude 4
5:10 sAc 9:36;
1Ti 6:18;
1Pe 2:12
tS Ro 12:13
uS Lk 7:44 vver 16

5:13 wS Ro 1:29
x2Th 3:11
5:14 y1Co 7:9
z1Ti 6:1
5:15 aS Mt 4:10
5:16 bver 3-5
5:17 cS Ac 11:30
dPhp 2:29;
1Th 5:12
5:18 eDt 25:4;
1Co 9:7-9
/Lk 10:7;
Lev 19:13;
Dt 24:14,15;
Mt 10:10;
1Co 9:14
5:19 gS Ac 11:30
hS Mt 18:16
5:20 i2Ti 4:2;
Tit 1:13; 2:15
/Dt 13:11
5:21 k1Ti 6:13;
2Ti 4:1

h9 Or *has had but one husband*   i18 Deut. 25:4
i18 Luke 10:7

4:7 *myths.* See note on 1:4. *train yourself to be godly.* See note on 2:2. Godliness requires self-discipline.

4:9 *trustworthy saying.* See note on 1:15. Although the NIV understands the expression in this instance to refer to what follows, it is possible that it refers back to the seemingly proverbial statement in v. 8. The words "labor and strive" in v. 10 may refer to the training mentioned in vv. 7b–8.

4:10 *hope.* See note on 1:1. *Savior of all.* Obviously this does not mean that God saves every person from eternal punishment, for such universalism would contradict the clear testimony of Scripture. God is, however, the Savior of all in that he offers salvation to all and saves all who come to him.

4:12 *because you are young.* Timothy was probably in his mid–30s or younger, and in that day, such an influential position was not usually held by a man so young. For this reason, perhaps his leadership had been called into question.

4:13 *Until I come.* Paul's journey had taken him from Ephesus to Macedonia (see "Paul's Fourth Missionary Journey," p. 1836), but he hoped to rejoin Timothy soon at Ephesus (3:14).

4:14 *prophetic message.* See note on 1:18.

4:16 *you will save . . . your hearers.* God alone saves, but Christians can be God's instruments to bring about the salvation of others. *will save.* Salvation is both an event and a process. We are saved at the time of conversion but are still being saved in the sense of being made more conformed to Christ's image (1Co 1:18).

5:3 *Give proper recognition to those widows.* Probably means taking proper care of them, including the giving of material support. Widows were particularly vulnerable in ancient societies because no pensions, government assistance, life insurance, or the like were available to them.

5:6 *dead even while she lives.* Dead spiritually while living physically.

5:9 *list of widows.* The church in Ephesus seems to have maintained a list of widows supported by the church. While there is no evidence of an order of widows comparable to that of the overseers, it appears that those on the list were expected to devote themselves to prayer (v. 5) and good deeds (v. 10).

5:10 *washing the feet of the saints.* A menial task, but necessary because of dusty roads and the wearing of sandals (see Jn 13:14).

5:12 *broken their first pledge.* Perhaps when a widow was added to the list she pledged special devotion to Christ, which would be diminished by remarriage. Or Paul may be referring to the believer's basic trust in Christ, which a widow would compromise by marrying outside the faith.

5:15 *Satan.* See notes on Zec 3:1; Mt 16:23; Col 3:5.

5:17 All elders were to exercise leadership (3:4–5) and to teach and preach (3:2), and all were to receive honor. But those who excelled in leadership were to be counted worthy of double honor. This was especially true of those who labored at teaching and preaching. (The Greek word translated "work" refers to toil.) That such honor should include financial support is indicated by the two illustrations in v. 18.

5:18 *Scripture.* The use of this term for both an OT (Dt 25:4) and a NT (Lk 10:7) passage shows that by this time portions of the NT (or what ultimately became a part of the NT) were considered to be equal in authority to the OT Scriptures.

5:20 *Those who sin.* The context indicates that Paul is speaking of the discipline of elders.

5:21 *elect angels.* Chosen angels, in contrast to Satan and the other fallen angels.

these instructions without partiality, and to do nothing out of favoritism.

²²Do not be hasty in the laying on of hands, *l* and do not share in the sins of others. *m* Keep yourself pure. *n*

²³Stop drinking only water, and use a little wine *o* because of your stomach and your frequent illnesses.

²⁴The sins of some men are obvious, reaching the place of judgment ahead of them; the sins of others trail behind them. ²⁵In the same way, good deeds are obvious, and even those that are not cannot be hidden.

6 All who are under the yoke of slavery should consider their masters worthy of full respect, *p* so that God's name and our teaching may not be slandered. *q* ²Those who have believing masters are not to show less respect for them because they are brothers. *r* Instead, they are to serve them even better, because those who benefit from their service are believers, and dear to them. These are the things you are to teach and urge on them. *s*

Love of Money

³If anyone teaches false doctrines *t* and does not agree to the sound instruction *u* of our Lord Jesus Christ and to godly teaching, ⁴he is conceited *v* and understands nothing. He has an unhealthy interest in controversies and quarrels about words *w* that result in envy, strife, malicious talk, evil suspicions ⁵and constant friction between men of corrupt mind, who have been robbed of the truth *x* and who think that godliness is a means to financial gain.

⁶But godliness with contentment *y* is great gain. *z* ⁷For we brought nothing into the world, and we can take nothing out of

it. *a* ⁸But if we have food and clothing, we will be content with that. *b* ⁹People who want to get rich *c* fall into temptation and a trap *d* and into many foolish and harmful desires that plunge men into ruin and destruction. ¹⁰For the love of money *e* is a root of all kinds of evil. Some people, eager for money, have wandered from the faith *f* and pierced themselves with many griefs. *g*

Paul's Charge to Timothy

¹¹But you, man of God, *h* flee from all this, and pursue righteousness, godliness, *i* faith, love, *j* endurance and gentleness. ¹²Fight the good fight *k* of the faith. Take hold of *l* the eternal life *m* to which you were called when you made your good confession *n* in the presence of many witnesses. ¹³In the sight of God, who gives life to everything, and of Christ Jesus, who while testifying before Pontius Pilate *o* made the good confession, *p* I charge you *q* ¹⁴to keep this command without spot or blame *r* until the appearing of our Lord Jesus Christ, *s* ¹⁵which God will bring about in his own time *t*—God, the blessed *u* and only Ruler, *v* the King of kings and Lord of lords, *w* ¹⁶who alone is immortal *x* and who lives in unapproachable light, *y* whom no one has seen or can see. *z* To him be honor and might forever. Amen. *a*

¹⁷Command those who are rich *b* in this present world not to be arrogant nor to put their hope in wealth, *c* which is so uncertain, but to put their hope in God, *d* who richly provides us with everything for our enjoyment. *e* ¹⁸Command them to do good, to be rich in good deeds, *f* and to be

---

Cross references (center column):

5:22 *l* S Ac 6:6
m Eph 5:11
n Ps 18:26
5:23 *o* 1Ti 3:8
6:1 *p* S Eph 6:5
q 1Ti 5:14;
Tit 2:5,8
6:2 *r* Phm 16
s 1Ti 4:11
6:3 *t* 1Ti 1:3
u S 1Ti 1:10
6:4 *v* 1Ti 3:6;
2Ti 3:4
w S 2Ti 2:14
6:5 *x* 2Ti 3:8;
Tit 1:15
6:6 *y* Php 4:11;
Heb 13:5 *z* 1Ti 4:8

6:7 *a* Job 1:21;
Ps 49:17;
Ecc 5:15
6:8 *b* Pr 30:8;
Heb 13:5
6:9 *c* Pr 15:27;
28:20 *d* 1Ti 3:7
6:10 *e* S 1Ti 3:3
f ver 21; Jas 5:19
g Jos 7:21
6:11 *h* 2Ti 3:17
i ver 3,5,6;
S 1Ti 2:2
/1Ti 1:14;
2Ti 2:22; 3:10
6:12 *k* 1Co 9:25,
26; S 1Ti 1:18
l ver 19; Php 3:12
m S Mt 25:46
n S Heb 3:1
6:13
o Jn 18:33-37 *p* ver
12 *q* 1Ti 5:21;
2Ti 4:1
6:14 *r* S 1Th 3:13
s S 1Co 1:7;
2Ti 1:10; 4:1,8
6:15 *t* 1Ti 2:6;
Tit 1:3 *u* 1Ti 1:11
v 1Ti 1:17
w Dt 10:17;
Ps 136:3;
Da 2:47; Rev 1:5;
17:14; 19:16
6:16 *x* 1Ti 1:17
y Ps 104:2;
1Jn 1:7 *z* S Jn 1:18
a S Ro 11:36
6:17 *b* ver 9
c Ps 62:10;
Jer 49:4;
Lk 12:20,21
d 1Ti 4:10
e Ac 14:17
6:18 *f* S 1Ti 5:10

5:22 *Do not be hasty in the laying on of hands.* Paul is speaking of the ordination of an elder, which should not be performed until the candidate has had time to prove himself. *do not share in the sins of others.* Do not ordain a person unworthy of the office of elder. *Keep yourself pure.* Probably refers to refusal to become involved in the ordination of an unworthy man.

5:23 *Stop drinking only water.* A parenthetical comment in Paul's discussion of elders. In view of Timothy's physical ailments, and perhaps because safe drinking water was often difficult to find, Paul advised him to drink a little wine.

5:24–25 *sins of some men . . . good deeds.* Paul advises being alert to hidden sins as well as to good deeds in the lives of candidates for ordination.

6:1 *slavery.* See notes on Eph 6:5; Col 3:22–4:1.

6:2 *urge on them.* Refers to the instructions to slaves.

6:3–5 Paul returns to the subject of 1:3. See note on 1:3–11.

6:5 *robbed of the truth.* They had once known the truth but had been led into error. *who think that godliness is a means to financial gain.* See note on 2Co 11:7.

6:11 *godliness.* See note on 2:2.

6:12 *Take hold of the eternal life.* Timothy had possessed eternal life since he had first been saved, but Paul urges him to claim its benefits in greater fullness (see vv. 17–19 and note on 4:16). *when you made your good confession.* Probably a reference to Timothy's confession of faith at his baptism during Paul's first missionary journey.

6:13 *who while testifying before Pontius Pilate made the good confession.* Probably a reference to Jesus' statements recorded in Jn 18:33–37; 19:10–11.

6:14 *this command.* Perhaps the whole charge given to Timothy to preach the gospel and care for the church (see v. 20)—though the preceding context may indicate that Paul used the singular "command" to sum up the various commands listed in vv. 11–12.

6:15 *in his own time.* Just as Jesus' first coming occurred at the precise time God wanted (Gal 4:4), so also his second coming will be at God's appointed time. *King of kings and Lord of lords.* See Rev 19:16.

6:16 *whom no one has seen or can see.* See note on Jn 1:18.

generous and willing to share. *g* ¹⁹In this way they will lay up treasure for themselves *h* as a firm foundation for the coming age, so that they may take hold of *i* the life that is truly life.

²⁰Timothy, guard what has been en-

trusted *j* to your care. Turn away from godless chatter *k* and the opposing ideas of what is falsely called knowledge, ²¹which some have professed and in so doing have wandered from the faith. *l*

Grace be with you. *m*

6:18 *g* Ro 12:8, 13; Eph 4:28
6:19 *h* S Mt 6:20
i ver 12; Php 3:12
6:20 *j* 2Ti 1:12,14
k 2Ti 2:16
6:21 *l* ver 10; 2Ti 2:18
m S Col 4:18

6:19 *take hold of the life.* See note on v. 12.
6:20 *what has been entrusted to your care.* The gospel. The same command is found in 2Ti 1:14. *what is falsely called knowledge.* A reference to an early form of the heresy of Gnosticism, which taught that one may be saved by knowledge. (The term "Gnosticism" comes from the Greek word for knowledge; see Introduction to 1 John: Gnosticism.)

6:21 *Grace be with you.* The Greek for "you" here is plural, indicating that, although Paul is writing to Timothy, he expects the letter to be read to the entire Ephesian congregation.

2 TIMOTHY

See "The Pastoral Letters," p. 1832.

Author, Date and Setting

After Paul's release from prison in Rome in A.D. 62/63 (Ac 28) and after his fourth missionary journey (see "Paul's Fourth Missionary Journey," p. 1836), during which he wrote 1 Timothy and Titus, Paul was again imprisoned under Emperor Nero c. 66-67. It was during this time that he wrote 2 Timothy. In contrast to his first imprisonment, when he lived in a rented house (Ac 28:30), he now languished in a cold dungeon (4:13), chained like a common criminal (1:16; 2:9). His friends even had a hard time finding out where he was being kept (1:17). Paul knew that his work was done and his life was nearly at an end (4:6-8).

Reasons for Writing

Paul had three reasons for writing to Timothy at this time:

1. He was lonely. Phygelus and Hermogenes, "everyone in the province of Asia" (1:15), and Demas (4:10) had deserted him. Crescens, Titus and Tychicus were away (4:10-12), and only Luke was with him (4:11). Paul wanted very much for Timothy to join him also. Timothy was his "fellow worker" (Ro 16:21), who "as a son with his father" had served closely with Paul (Php 2:22; see 1Co 4:17). Of him Paul could say, "I have no one else like him" (Php 2:20). Paul longed for Timothy (1:4) and twice asked him to come soon (4:9,21). For more information on Timothy see Introduction to 1 Timothy: Recipient.

2. Paul was concerned about the welfare of the churches during this time of persecution under Nero, and he admonishes Timothy to guard the gospel (1:14), to persevere in it (3:14), to keep on preaching it (4:2) and, if necessary, to suffer for it (1:8; 2:3).

3. He wanted to write to the Ephesian church through Timothy (see note on 4:22).

Outline

I. Introduction (1:1-4)
II. Paul's Concern for Timothy (1:5-14)
III. Paul's Situation (1:15-18)
IV. Special Instructions to Timothy (ch. 2)
    A. Call for Endurance (2:1-13)
    B. Warning about Foolish Controversies (2:14-26)
V. Warning about the Last Days (ch. 3)
    A. Terrible Times (3:1-9)
    B. Means of Combating Them (3:10-17)
VI. Paul's Departing Remarks (4:1-8)
    A. Charge to Preach the Word (4:1-5)
    B. Paul's Victorious Prospect (4:6-8)
VII. Final Requests and Greetings (4:9-22)

1 Paul, an apostle[a] of Christ Jesus by the will of God,[b] according to the promise of life that is in Christ Jesus,[c]

[2]To Timothy,[d] my dear son:[e]

Grace, mercy and peace from God the Father and Christ Jesus our Lord.[f]

Encouragement to Be Faithful

[3]I thank God,[g] whom I serve, as my forefathers did, with a clear conscience,[h] as night and day I constantly remember you in my prayers.[i] [4]Recalling your tears,[j] I long to see you,[k] so that I may be filled with joy. [5]I have been reminded of your sincere faith,[l] which first lived in your grandmother Lois and in your mother Eunice[m] and, I am persuaded, now lives in you also. [6]For this reason I remind you to fan into flame the gift of God, which is in you through the laying on of my hands.[n] [7]For God did not give us a spirit of timidity,[o] but a spirit of power,[p] of love and of self-discipline.

[8]So do not be ashamed[q] to testify about our Lord, or ashamed of me his prisoner.[r] But join with me in suffering for the gospel,[s] by the power of God, [9]who has saved[t] us and called[u] us to a holy life—not because of anything we have done[v] but because of his own purpose and grace. This grace was given us in Christ

Jesus before the beginning of time, [10]but it has now been revealed[w] through the appearing of our Savior, Christ Jesus,[x] who has destroyed death[y] and has brought life and immortality to light through the gospel. [11]And of this gospel[z] I was appointed[a] a herald and an apostle and a teacher.[b] [12]That is why I am suffering as I am. Yet I am not ashamed,[c] because I know whom I have believed, and am convinced that he is able to guard[d] what I have entrusted to him for that day.[e]

[13]What you heard from me,[f] keep[g] as the pattern[h] of sound teaching,[i] with faith and love in Christ Jesus.[j] [14]Guard[k] the good deposit that was entrusted to you—guard it with the help of the Holy Spirit who lives in us.[l]

[15]You know that everyone in the province of Asia[m] has deserted me,[n] including Phygelus and Hermogenes.

[16]May the Lord show mercy to the household of Onesiphorus,[o] because he often refreshed me and was not ashamed[p] of my chains.[q] [17]On the contrary, when he was in Rome, he searched hard for me until he found me. [18]May the Lord grant that he will find mercy from the Lord on that day![r] You know very well in how many ways he helped me[s] in Ephesus.[t]

2 You then, my son,[u] be strong[v] in the grace that is in Christ Jesus. [2]And the

1:1 [a]S 1Co 1:1
[b]S 2Co 1:1
[c]Eph 3:6; Tit 1:2;
1Ti 6:19
1:2 [d]S Ac 16:1
[e]S 1Ti 1:2
[f]S Ro 1:7
1:3 [g]S Ro 1:8
[h]S Ac 23:1
[i]S Ro 1:10
1:4 [j]Ac 20:37
[k]2Ti 4:9
1:5 [l]1Ti 1:5
[m]Ac 16:1;
2Ti 3:15
1:6 [n]S Ac 6:6;
1Ti 4:14
1:7 [o]Jer 42:11;
Ro 8:15;
1Co 16:10,11;
1Ti 4:12;
Heb 2:15
1:8 [p]Isa 11:2
[q]ver 12,16;
Mk 8:38
[r]S Eph 3:1
1:9 [s]2Ti 2:3,9; 4:5
[t]S Ro 11:14
[u]S Ro 8:28
[v]S Eph 2:9

1:10 [w]Eph 1:9
[x]S 1Ti 6:14
[y]1Co 15:26,54
1:11 [z]ver 8
[a]S Ac 9:15
[b]1Ti 2:7
1:12 [c]ver 8,16;
Mk 8:38 [d]ver 14;
1Ti 6:20 [e]ver 18;
S 1Co 1:8;
2Ti 4:8
1:13 [f]2Ti 2:2
[g]S Tit 1:9
[h]Ro 6:17
[i]S 1Ti 1:10
[j]S 1Th 1:3;
1Ti 1:14
1:14 [k]ver 12
[l]S Ro 8:9
1:15 [m]S Ac 2:9
[n]2Ti 4:10,11,16
1:16 [o]2Ti 4:19
[p]ver 8,12;
Mk 8:38

[q]S Ac 21:33 **1:18** [r]S ver 12 [s]Heb 6:10 [t]S Ac 18:19 **2:1**
[u]S 1Ti 1:2 [v]S Eph 6:10

1:1 *apostle.* One specially commissioned by Christ (see notes on Mk 6:30; 1Co 1:1; Heb 3:1). *according to the promise of life.* Paul's being chosen to be an apostle was in keeping with that promise because apostles were appointed to preach and explain the good news that eternal life is available to all who will receive it.
1:2 *Timothy, my dear son.* See note on 1Ti 1:2. *Grace . . . peace.* See notes on Jnh 4:2; Jn 14:27; 20:19; Gal 1:3; Eph 1:2.
1:3 *thank God . . . in my prayers.* See note on Php 1:3–4.
1:4 *Recalling your tears.* Probably refers to Timothy's tears when Paul left for Macedonia (1Ti 1:3). *long to see you.* See 4:9,21.
1:5 *your grandmother Lois . . . your mother Eunice.* According to Ac 16:1, Timothy's mother was a Jewish Christian. Here we learn that his grandmother too was a Christian. Timothy's father, however, was a Greek and apparently an unbeliever (Ac 16:1). It was probably because of him that Timothy had not been circumcised as a child.
1:6 *fan into flame the gift of God.* Gifts are not given in full bloom; they need to be developed through use. *through the laying on of my hands.* Paul was God's instrument, through whom the gift came from the Holy Spirit to Timothy (see note on 1Ti 1:18).
1:7 *God did not give us a spirit of timidity.* Apparently lack of confidence was a serious problem for Timothy (see 1Co 16:10–11; 1Ti 4:12).
1:9 *not because of anything we have done but because of his own purpose and grace.* Salvation is by grace alone and

is based not on human effort but on God's saving plan and the gracious gift of his Son (see Ro 3:28; Eph 2:8–9; Tit 3:5). *before the beginning of time.* God's plan to save lost sinners was made in eternity past (see Eph 1:4; 1Pe 1:20; Rev 13:8).
1:11 *herald and an apostle.* See note on 1Ti 2:7.
1:12 *that day.* The day of judgment.
1:13 *sound teaching.* See note on Tit 1:9. *faith and love in Christ.* Faith and love joined with union with Christ—another way of saying "Christian faith and love" (see 1Ti 1:14).
1:14 *the good deposit . . . entrusted to you.* The gospel. Paul gives the same command in 1Ti 6:20.
1:15 *everyone.* Probably hyperbole, a deliberate exaggeration to express widespread desertion. *province of Asia.* Timothy was in Ephesus, the capital of the province of Asia, which is in western Turkey today. *Phygelus and Hermogenes.* Nothing more is known about these two people.
1:16 *Onesiphorus.* Probably he and his family lived in Ephesus (v. 18; 4:19).
1:17 *Rome.* See Introduction: Author, Date and Setting; see also v. 8; 2:9.
1:18 *that day.* The day of judgment. *he helped me in Ephesus.* Either on Paul's third missionary journey (Ac 19) or on his fourth (see "Paul's Fourth Missionary Journey," p. 1836).
2:1 *my son.* See note on 1Ti 1:2.
2:2 *in the presence of many witnesses.* Refers to Paul's preaching and teaching, which Timothy had heard repeatedly on all three missionary journeys.

things you have heard me say[w] in the presence of many witnesses[x] entrust to reliable men who will also be qualified to teach others. [3]Endure hardship with us[y] like a good soldier[z] of Christ Jesus. [4]No one serving as a soldier gets involved in civilian affairs—he wants to please his commanding officer. [5]Similarly, if anyone competes as an athlete, he does not receive the victor's crown[a] unless he competes according to the rules. [6]The hardworking farmer should be the first to receive a share of the crops.[b] [7]Reflect on what I am saying, for the Lord will give you insight into all this.

[8]Remember Jesus Christ, raised from the dead,[c] descended from David.[d] This is my gospel,[e] [9]for which I am suffering[f] even to the point of being chained[g] like a criminal. But God's word[h] is not chained. [10]Therefore I endure everything[i] for the sake of the elect,[j] that they too may obtain the salvation[k] that is in Christ Jesus, with eternal glory.[l]

[11]Here is a trustworthy saying:[m]

If we died with him,
    we will also live with him;[n]
[12]if we endure,
    we will also reign with him.[o]
If we disown him,
    he will also disown us;[p]
[13]if we are faithless,
    he will remain faithful,[q]
    for he cannot disown himself.

A Workman Approved by God

[14]Keep reminding them of these things. Warn them before God against quarreling about words;[r] it is of no value, and only ruins those who listen. [15]Do your best to present yourself to God as one approved, a workman who does not need to be ashamed and who correctly handles the word of truth.[s] [16]Avoid godless chatter,[t] because those who indulge in it will become more and more ungodly. [17]Their teaching will spread like gangrene. Among them are Hymenaeus[u] and Philetus, [18]who have wandered away from the truth. They say that the resurrection has already taken place,[v] and they destroy the faith of some.[w] [19]Nevertheless, God's solid foundation stands firm,[x] sealed with this inscription: "The Lord knows those who are his,"[a][y] and, "Everyone who confesses the name of the Lord[z] must turn away from wickedness."

[20]In a large house there are articles not only of gold and silver, but also of wood and clay; some are for noble purposes and some for ignoble.[a] [21]If a man cleanses himself from the latter, he will be an instrument for noble purposes, made holy, useful to the Master and prepared to do any good work.[b]

[22]Flee the evil desires of youth, and pursue righteousness, faith, love[c] and peace, along with those who call on the Lord[d] out of a pure heart.[e] [23]Don't have any-

Cross references (center column)

2:2 w2Ti 1:13;
    x1Ti 6:12
2:3 yver 9;
    2Ti 1:8; 4:5
    z5 1Ti 1:18
2:5 aS 1Co 9:25
2:6 b1Co 9:10
2:8 cS Ac 2:24
    dS Mt 1:1
    eRo 2:16; 16:25
2:9 fS Ac 9:16
    gS Ac 21:33
    hS Heb 4:12
2:10 iCol 1:24
    /Tit 1:1 k2Co 1:6
    /2Co 4:17;
    1Pe 5:10
2:11 mS 1Ti 1:15
    nRo 6:2-11
2:12 oRo 8:17;
    1Pe 4:13
    pMt 10:33
2:13 qRo 3:3;
    S 1Co 1:9

2:14 rver 23;
    1Ti 1:4; 6:4;
    Tit 3:9
2:15 sEph 1:13;
    Col 1:5; Jas 1:18
2:16 tTit 3:9;
    1Ti 6:20
2:17 u1Ti 1:20
2:18 v2Th 2:2
    w1Ti 1:19; 6:21
2:19 xIsa 28:16
    yEx 33:12;
    Nu 16:5;
    Jn 10:14;
    1Co 8:3; Gal 4:9
    z1Co 1:2
2:20 aRo 9:21
2:21 b2Co 9:8;
    Eph 2:10;
    2Ti 3:17
2:22 c1Ti 1:14;
    6:11 dS Ac 2:21
    e1Ti 1:5

a19 Num. 16:5 (see Septuagint)

2:3–6 Paul gives three examples for Timothy to follow: (1) a soldier who wants to please his commander; (2) an athlete who follows the rules of the game; and (3) a farmer who works hard.

2:6 *to receive a share of the crops.* In this illustration, as in the previous two (soldier, vv. 3–4; athlete, v. 5), the main lesson is that dedicated effort will be rewarded—not necessarily monetarily, but in enjoyment of seeing the gospel produce changed lives.

2:8 *raised from the dead, descended from David.* Christ's resurrection proclaims his deity, and his descent from David shows his humanity; both truths are basic to the gospel. Since Christ is God, his death has infinite value; since he is man, he could rightfully become our substitute.

2:9 *chained like a criminal.* Apparently Paul was awaiting execution (see 4:6).

2:10 *I endure everything for the sake of the elect.* No suffering is too great if it brings about the salvation of God's chosen ones who will yet believe. *in Christ Jesus.* See note on 1:13. *eternal glory.* The final state of salvation.

2:11–13 Probably an early Christian hymn. The point to which Paul appeals is that suffering for Christ will be followed by glory.

2:11 *trustworthy saying.* See note on 1Ti 1:15. *If we died with him, we will also live with him.* The Greek grammatical construction here assumes that we died with Christ in the past, when he died for us on the cross. We are therefore

assured that we will also live with him eternally.

2:12 *If we endure, we will also reign.* Faithfully bearing up under suffering and trial will result in reward when Christ returns. *If we disown him.* See Mt 10:33.

2:14–18 The wording of vv. 14–16 indicates that the heresy mentioned here is an early form of Gnosticism—the same as that dealt with in 1Ti 1:3–11 and Introduction to 1 John: Gnosticism. Two leaders of this heresy, Hymenaeus (see 1Ti 1:20) and Philetus, denied the bodily resurrection and probably asserted that there is only a spiritual resurrection (similar to the error mentioned in 1Co 15:12–19). Gnosticism interpreted the resurrection allegorically, not literally.

2:15 *Do your best.* See 4:9,21. *word of truth.* The gospel.

2:19 *God's solid foundation.* The church, which upholds the truth (1Ti 3:15). In spite of the heresy of Hymenaeus and Philetus, Timothy should be heartened to know that the church is God's solid foundation. There are two inscriptions on it: One stresses the security of the church ("The Lord knows those who are his"; here "know," as often in the Bible, means to be intimately acquainted with), while the other emphasizes human responsibility ("Everyone who confesses the name of the Lord must turn away from wickedness"). *sealed.* The church is owned and securely protected by God (see note on Eph 1:13).

2:22 *youth.* See note on 1Ti 4:12.

thing to do with foolish and stupid arguments, because you know they produce quarrels.*f* 24And the Lord's servant must not quarrel; instead, he must be kind to everyone, able to teach, not resentful.*g* 25Those who oppose him he must gently instruct, in the hope that God will grant them repentance leading them to a knowledge of the truth,*h* 26and that they will come to their senses and escape from the trap of the devil,*i* who has taken them captive to do his will.

Godlessness in the Last Days

3 But mark this: There will be terrible times in the last days.*j* 2People will be lovers of themselves, lovers of money,*k* boastful, proud,*l* abusive,*m* disobedient to their parents,*n* ungrateful, unholy, 3without love, unforgiving, slanderous, without self-control, brutal, not lovers of the good, 4treacherous,*o* rash, conceited,*p* lovers of pleasure rather than lovers of God— 5having a form of godliness*q* but denying its power. Have nothing to do with them.*r*

6They are the kind who worm their way*s* into homes and gain control over weak-willed women, who are loaded down with sins and are swayed by all kinds of evil desires, 7always learning but never able to acknowledge the truth.*t* 8Just as Jannes and Jambres opposed Moses,*u* so also these men oppose*v* the truth—men of depraved minds,*w* who, as

far as the faith is concerned, are rejected. 9But they will not get very far because, as in the case of those men,*x* their folly will be clear to everyone.

Paul's Charge to Timothy

10You, however, know all about my teaching,*y* my way of life, my purpose, faith, patience, love, endurance, 11persecutions, sufferings—what kinds of things happened to me in Antioch,*z* Iconium*a* and Lystra,*b* the persecutions I endured.*c* Yet the Lord rescued*d* me from all of them.*e* 12In fact, everyone who wants to live a godly life in Christ Jesus will be persecuted,*f* 13while evil men and impostors will go from bad to worse,*g* deceiving and being deceived.*h* 14But as for you, continue in what you have learned and have become convinced of, because you know those from whom you learned it,*i* 15and how from infancy*j* you have known the holy Scriptures,*k* which are able to make you wise*l* for salvation through faith in Christ Jesus. 16All Scripture is God-breathed*m* and is useful for teaching,*n* rebuking, correcting and training in righteousness,*o* 17so that the man of God*p* may be thoroughly equipped for every good work.*q*

4 In the presence of God and of Christ Jesus, who will judge the living and the dead,*r* and in view of his appearing*s* and his kingdom, I give you this charge:*t* 2Preach*u* the Word;*v* be prepared in sea-

Cross-references

2:23 /S ver 14
2:24 *g*1Ti 3:2,3
2:25 *h*S 1Ti 2:4
2:26 *i*1Ti 3:7
3:1 /1Ti 4:1; 2Pe 3:3
3:2 *k*S 1Ti 3:3 /Ro 1:30
*m*2Pe 2:10-12 *n*Ro 1:30
3:4 *o*Ps 25:3 *p*1Ti 3:6; 6:4
3:5 *q*S 1Ti 2:2 *r*S Ro 16:17
3:6 *s*Jude 4
3:7 *t*S 1Ti 2:4
3:8 *u*Ex 7:11 *v*Ac 13:8 *w*1Ti 6:5

3:9 *x*Ex 7:12; 8:18; 9:11
3:10 *y*1Ti 4:6
3:11 *z*Ac 13:14, 50 *a*S Ac 13:51 *b*Ac 14:6 *c*2Co 11:23-27 *d*S Ro 15:31 *e*Ps 34:19
3:12 *f*Jn 15:20; S Ac 14:22
3:13 *g*2Ti 2:16 *h*S Mk 13:5
3:14 /2Ti 1:13
3:15 /2Ti 1:5 *k*Jn 5:39 /Dt 4:6; Ps 119:98,99
3:16 *m*2Pe 1:20, 21 *n*S Ro 4:23,24 *o*Dt 29:29
3:17 *p*1Ti 6:11
4:1 /S Ac 10:42 *s*ver 8; S 1Ti 6:14 *t*1Ti 5:21; 6:13
4:2 *u*1Ti 4:13 *v*Gal 6:6

3:1 *last days.* The Messianic era, the time beginning with Christ's first coming (see notes on Ac 2:17; 1Ti 4:1; Heb 1:1; 1Pe 1:20; 1Jn 2:18). That "the last days" in this passage does not refer only to the time just prior to Christ's return is apparent from Paul's command to Timothy to have nothing to do with the unbelieving and unfaithful people who characterize this time (v. 5).

3:6 *weak-willed women.* Unstable women who are guilt-ridden because of their sins, torn by lust, and victims of various false teachers ("always learning," v. 7, but never coming to a saving knowledge of Christ).

3:8 *Jannes and Jambres.* Neither of these men is mentioned in the OT, but according to Jewish tradition they were the Egyptian court magicians who opposed Moses (see Ex 7:11 and note).

3:11 *Antioch, Iconium and Lystra.* Three cities in the Roman province of Galatia, which Paul visited on his first and second missionary journeys (Ac 13:14–14:23; 16:1–6). Since Timothy was from Lystra, he would have known firsthand of Paul's sufferings in that region. *the Lord rescued me from all of them.* Even from execution by stoning (Ac 14:19–20).

3:12 A principle repeated elsewhere in the NT (see Mt 10:22; Ac 14:22; Php 1:29; 1Pe 4:12). *in Christ.* See note on 1:13.

3:14 *those from whom you learned it.* Perhaps a reference

to Paul as well as to Timothy's mother and grandmother (1:5).

3:15 *from infancy you have known the holy Scriptures.* A Jewish boy formally began to study the OT when he was five years old. Timothy was taught at home by his mother and grandmother even before he reached this age.

3:16 *All Scripture.* The primary reference is to the OT, since some of the NT books had not even been written at this time. (See 1Ti 5:18; 2Pe 3:15–16 for indications that some NT books—or material ultimately included in the NT—were already considered equal in authority to the OT Scriptures.) *God-breathed.* Paul affirms God's active involvement in the writing of Scripture, an involvement so powerful and pervasive that what is written is the infallible and authoritative word of God (see 2Pe 1:20–21 and notes).

4:1 *I give you this charge.* Paul states his charge to Timothy, aware that he does so in the presence of God the Father and of Christ, who will judge all men. He is also keenly aware of the twin facts of Christ's return and the coming establishment of God's kingdom in its fullest expression. Timothy was to view a charge so given as of utmost importance.

4:2 *be prepared.* Be ready in any situation to speak the needed word, whether of correction, of rebuke or of encouragement.

son and out of season; correct, rebuke[w] and encourage[x]—with great patience and careful instruction. [3]For the time will come when men will not put up with sound doctrine.[y] Instead, to suit their own desires, they will gather around them a great number of teachers to say what their itching ears want to hear.[z] [4]They will turn their ears away from the truth and turn aside to myths.[a] [5]But you, keep your head in all situations, endure hardship,[b] do the work of an evangelist,[c] discharge all the duties of your ministry.

[6]For I am already being poured out like a drink offering,[d] and the time has come for my departure.[e] [7]I have fought the good fight,[f] I have finished the race,[g] I have kept the faith. [8]Now there is in store for me[h] the crown of righteousness,[i] which the Lord, the righteous Judge, will award to me on that day[j]—and not only to me, but also to all who have longed for his appearing.[k]

Personal Remarks

[9]Do your best to come to me quickly,[l] [10]for Demas,[m] because he loved this world,[n] has deserted me and has gone to Thessalonica.[o] Crescens has gone to

Galatia,[p] and Titus[q] to Dalmatia. [11]Only Luke[r] is with me.[s] Get Mark[t] and bring him with you, because he is helpful to me in my ministry. [12]I sent Tychicus[u] to Ephesus. [v] [13]When you come, bring the cloak that I left with Carpus at Troas,[w] and my scrolls, especially the parchments.

[14]Alexander[x] the metalworker did me a great deal of harm. The Lord will repay him for what he has done.[y] [15]You too should be on your guard against him, because he strongly opposed our message.

[16]At my first defense, no one came to my support, but everyone deserted me. May it not be held against them.[z] [17]But the Lord stood at my side[a] and gave me strength,[b] so that through me the message might be fully proclaimed and all the Gentiles might hear it.[c] And I was delivered from the lion's mouth.[d] [18]The Lord will rescue me from every evil attack[e] and will bring me safely to his heavenly kingdom.[f] To him be glory for ever and ever. Amen.[g]

Final Greetings

[19]Greet Priscilla[b] and Aquila[h] and the

4:2 w1Ti 5:20; w1Ti 5:20; Tit 1:13; 2:15 xTit 2:15
4:3 yS 1Ti 1:10 zIsa 30:10
4:4 aS 1Ti 1:4
4:5 b2Ti 1:8; 2:3, 9 cAc 21:8; Eph 4:11
4:6 dNu 15:1-12; 28:7,24; Php 2:17 ePhp 1:23
4:7 fS 1Ti 1:18 gS 1Co 9:24; Ac 20:24
4:8 hCol 1:5; 1Pe 1:4 iS 1Co 9:25 jS 2Ti 1:12 kS 1Ti 6:14
4:9 lver 21; Tit 3:12
4:10 mCol 4:14; Phm 24 n1Jn 2:15 oS Ac 17:1
pS Ac 16:6 qS 2Co 2:13
4:11 rCol 4:14; Phm 24 s2Ti 1:15 tS Ac 12:12
4:12 uS Ac 20:4 vS Ac 18:19
4:13 wS Ac 16:8
4:14 xAc 19:33; 1Ti 1:20 yPs 28:4; 109:20; Ro 2:6; 12:19
4:16 zAc 7:60 bS Php 4:13
4:17 aAc 23:11 cS Ac 9:15 dIsa 17:37; Ps 22:21; Da 6:22; 1Co 15:32
4:18 ePs 121:7; 2Pe 2:9 fver 1

gS Ro 11:36 **4:19** hS Ac 18:2 i2Ti 1:16

b19 Greek Prisca, a variant of Priscilla

4:3 *sound doctrine.* See note on Tit 1:9. *itching ears.* Ears that want to be "scratched" by words in keeping with one's evil desires.

4:4 *myths.* See note on 1Ti 1:4.

4:6 *drink offering.* The offering of wine poured around the base of the altar (see Nu 15:1–12; 28:7,24). Paul views his approaching death as the pouring out of his life as an offering to Christ (see Php 2:17). *my departure.* His impending death (cf. Php 1:23).

4:7 In this verse Paul looks back over 30 years of labor as an apostle (c. A.D. 36–66). Like an athlete who had engaged successfully in a contest ("fought the good fight"), he had "finished the race" and had "kept the faith," i.e., had carefully observed the rules (the teachings) of the Christian faith (see 2:5). Or, in view of the Pastorals' emphasis on sound doctrine, perhaps "the faith" refers to the deposit of Christian truth. Paul has kept (guarded) it.

4:8 *crown of righteousness.* Continuing with the same figure of speech, Paul uses the metaphor of the wreath given to the winner of a race (1Co 9:25). He could be referring to (1) a crown given as a reward for a righteous life, (2) a crown consisting of righteousness or (3) a crown given righteously (justly) by the righteous Judge. *that day.* The day of Christ's second coming ("appearing").

4:10 *Crescens.* Mentioned only here in the NT. *Galatia.* Either the northern area of Asia Minor (Gaul) or a Roman province in what is now central Turkey (see note on Gal 1:2). *Titus to Dalmatia.* See Introduction to Titus: Recipient. *Dalmatia.* Present-day Albania and a portion of Yugoslavia, also known in Scripture as Illyricum (Ro 15:19).

4:11 *Mark.* John Mark had deserted Paul and Barnabas on their first missionary journey (Ac 13:13). After Paul refused

to take Mark on the second journey, Barnabas separated from Paul, taking Mark with him on a mission to Cyprus (Ac 15:36–41). Ultimately Mark proved himself to Paul, indicated by his presence with Paul during Paul's first Roman imprisonment (Col 4:10; Phm 24) and by Paul's request here for Timothy to bring Mark with him to Rome.

4:13 *cloak.* For protection against the cold dampness (see Introduction: Author, Date and Setting). It was probably a heavy, sleeveless, outer garment, circular in shape and with a hole in the middle for one's head. *Carpus.* Not mentioned elsewhere. *my scrolls, especially the parchments.* The scrolls (see note on Ex 17:14) were made of papyrus, and the parchments were made of the skins of animals. The latter may have been copies of parts of the OT.

4:14 *Alexander the metalworker.* Possibly the Alexander mentioned in 1Ti 1:20.

4:16 *my first defense.* The first court hearing of Paul's present case, not his defense on the occasion of his first imprisonment (Ac 28).

4:17 *so that through me the message might be fully proclaimed.* Even in these dire circumstances Paul used the occasion to testify about Jesus Christ in the imperial court. *I was delivered from the lion's mouth.* Since, as a Roman citizen, Paul could not be thrown to the lions in the amphitheater, this must be a figurative way of saying that his first hearing did not result in an immediate guilty verdict.

4:18 *The Lord will rescue me from every evil attack.* Since Paul fully expected to die soon (v. 6), the rescue he speaks of here is spiritual, not physical. *heavenly kingdom.* Heaven itself.

4:19 *Onesiphorus.* See note on 1:16.

household of Onesiphorus. *i* ²⁰Erastus *j* stayed in Corinth, and I left Trophimus *k* sick in Miletus. *l* ²¹Do your best to get here before winter. *m* Eubulus greets you,

4:20 /Ac 19:22
*k*Ac 20:4; 21:29
*l*Ac 20:15,17
4:21 *m*ver 9; Tit 3:12
4:22 *n*S Gal 6:18
*o*S Col 4:18

and so do Pudens, Linus, Claudia and all the brothers.

²²The Lord be with your spirit. *n* Grace be with you. *o*

4:20 *Erastus.* See note on Ro 16:23. *Miletus.* A seaport on the coast of Asia Minor about 50 miles south of Ephesus.
4:21 *Linus.* Early tradition says he was bishop of Rome after the deaths of Peter and Paul.
4:22 *Grace.* See notes on Jnh 4:2; Gal 1:3; Eph 1:2. *you.*

As at the end of 1 Timothy, "you" here is plural, showing that the letter was intended for public use. The word "your" in the first part of the verse, however, is singular, indicating that it was addressed to Timothy alone. In view of Paul's impending death and the solemn charge he gave to his timid young friend, Timothy needed such encouragement.

TITUS

See "The Pastoral Letters," p. 1832.

Author

The author is Paul (see Introduction to 1 Timothy: Author).

Recipient

The letter is addressed to Titus, one of Paul's converts (1:4) and a considerable help to Paul in his ministry. When Paul left Antioch to discuss "his" gospel (2Ti 2:8) with the Jerusalem leaders, he took Titus with him (Gal 2:1-3); acceptance of Titus (a Gentile) as a Christian without circumcision vindicated Paul's stand there (Gal 2:3-5). Presumably Titus, who is not referred to in Acts (but is mentioned 13 times in the rest of the NT), worked with Paul at Ephesus during the third missionary journey. From there the apostle sent him to Corinth to help that church with its work (see notes on 2Co 2:12-13; 7:5-6; 8:6).

Following Paul's release from his first Roman imprisonment (Ac 28), he and Titus worked briefly in Crete (1:5), after which he commissioned Titus to remain there as his representative and complete some needed work (1:5; 2:15; 3:12-13). Paul asked Titus to meet him at Nicopolis (on the west coast of Greece) when a replacement arrived (3:12). Later, Titus went on a mission to Dalmatia (modern Yugoslavia; see note on 2Ti 4:10), the last word we hear about him in the NT. Considering the assignments given him, he obviously was a capable and resourceful leader.

Crete

The fourth largest island of the Mediterranean, Crete lies directly south of the Aegean Sea (see note on 1Sa 30:14; cf. Paul's experiences there in Ac 27:7-13). In NT times life in Crete had sunk to a deplorable moral level. The dishonesty, gluttony and laziness of its inhabitants were proverbial (1:12).

Occasion and Purpose

Apparently Paul introduced Christianity in Crete when he and Titus visited the island, after which he left Titus there to organize the converts. Paul sent the letter with Zenas and Apollos, who were on a journey that took them through Crete (3:13), to give Titus personal authorization and guidance in meeting opposition (1:5; 2:1,7-8,15; 3:9), instructions about faith and conduct, and warnings about false teachers. Paul also informed Titus of his future plans for him (3:12).

Place and Date of Writing

Paul possibly wrote from Corinth, for he had not yet reached Nicopolis (see 3:12). The letter was written after his release from the first Roman imprisonment (Ac 28), probably between A.D. 63 and 65—or possibly at a later date if he wrote after his assumed trip to Spain.

Distinctive Characteristics

Especially significant, considering the nature of the Cretan heresy, are the repeated emphases on "doing what is good" (1:16; 2:7,14; 3:1,8,14) and the classic summaries of Christian doctrine (2:11-14; 3:4-7).

Outline

1 Paul, a servant of God[a] and an apostle[b] of Jesus Christ for the faith of God's elect and the knowledge of the truth[c] that leads to godliness[d]— [2]a faith and knowledge resting on the hope of eternal life,[e] which God, who does not lie,[f] promised before the beginning of time,[g] [3]and at his appointed season[h] he brought his word to light[i] through the preaching entrusted to me[j] by the command of God[k] our Savior,[l]

[4]To Titus,[m] my true son[n] in our common faith:

Grace and peace from God the Father and Christ Jesus our Savior.[o]

Titus' Task on Crete

1:6–8Ref — 1Ti 3:2–4

[5]The reason I left you in Crete[p] was that you might straighten out what was left unfinished and appoint[a] elders[q] in every town, as I directed you. [6]An elder must be blameless,[r] the husband of but one wife, a man whose children believe and are not open to the charge of being wild and disobedient. [7]Since an overseer[b][s] is entrusted with God's work,[t] he must be blameless—not overbearing, not quick-tempered, not given to drunkenness, not violent, not pursuing dishonest gain.[u] [8]Rather he must be hospitable,[v] one who loves what is good,[w] who is self-controlled,[x] upright, holy and disciplined. [9]He must hold firmly[y] to the trustworthy message as it has been taught, so that he can encourage others by sound doctrine[z] and refute those who oppose it.

[10]For there are many rebellious people, mere talkers[a] and deceivers, especially those of the circumcision group.[b] [11]They must be silenced, because they are ruining whole households[c] by teaching things they ought not to teach—and that for the sake of dishonest gain. [12]Even one of their

Cross references

1:1 [a]Ro 1:1; Jas 1:1 [b]S 1Co 1:1 [c]S 1Ti 2:4 [d]S 1Ti 2:2
1:2 [e]Tit 3:7; 2Ti 1:1 [f]Nu 23:19; Heb 6:18 [g]2Ti 1:9
1:3 [h]1Ti 2:6; 6:15 [i]2Ti 1:10 [j]S 1Ti 1:11 [k]S 2Co 1:1; 1Ti 1:1 [l]S Lk 1:47
1:4 [m]S 2Co 2:13 [n]S 1Ti 1:2 [o]S Ro 1:7
1:5 [p]Ac 27:7 [q]S Ac 11:30
1:6 [r]S 1Th 3:13; 1Ti 3:2
1:7 [s]S 1Ti 3:1 [t]1Co 4:1 [u]S 1Ti 3:3,8
1:8 [v]S Ro 12:13 [w]2Ti 3:3 [x]Tit 2:2,5,6,12
1:9 [y]S 1Co 16:13; 1Ti 1:19; 2Ti 1:13; 3:14 [z]S 1Ti 1:10
1:10 [a]1Ti 1:6 [b]Ac 10:45; 11:2
1:11 [c]1Ti 5:13

[a]5 Or *ordain*   [b]7 Traditionally *bishop*

1:1 *servant of God.* Only here does Paul call himself a servant of God; elsewhere he says "servant of Christ" (Ro 1:1; Gal 1:10; Php 1:1). James uses both terms of himself (Jas 1:1). *servant.* See note on Ro 1:1. *apostle.* One specially commissioned by Christ (see notes on Mk 6:30; 1Co 1:1; Heb 3:1). *for the faith . . . and the knowledge.* Paul's appointed mission as God's servant and Christ's apostle—further explained in v. 2 (see Ac 9:15; 22:15; 26:16–18).

1:2 *hope.* See note on Col 1:5. *does not lie.* In contrast to the Cretans (v. 12)—and the devil (Jn 8:44).

1:3 *appointed season.* Crucial events in God's program occur at his designated times in history (1Ti 2:6; 6:15). *his word.* The authoritative message that centers in Christ. *God our Savior.* Three times in the letter God the Father is called Savior (here; 2:10; 3:4; see also 1Ti 1:1; 2:3; 4:10), and three times Jesus is called Savior (v. 4; 2:13; 3:6; see also 2Ti 1:10).

1:4 *my true son.* Titus, like Timothy (1Ti 1:2), was a spiritual son, having been converted through Paul's ministry. Onesimus was also called a son by Paul (Phm 10). *true.* Genuine. *our common faith.* The faith shared by all true believers. *Savior.* In all of Paul's other salutations Jesus is called "Lord." Paul uses "Savior" 12 times in all his letters, half of the references being in Titus.

1:5 *left you in Crete.* Implies that Paul and Titus had been together in Crete, a ministry not mentioned in Acts. On his voyage to Rome, Paul visited Crete briefly as a prisoner (Ac 27:7–8), but now that he had been released from his first Roman imprisonment he was free to travel wherever he wished (see 3:12). *appoint elders.* Though Paul and Titus perhaps had already preached in Crete, they had not had time to organize churches. The appointing of elders is consistent with Paul's usual practice (Ac 14:23).

1:6–9 1Ti 3:1–7 gives a parallel list of qualifications for elders, but the two lists reflect the different situations in which Timothy and Titus ministered. See chart on "Qualifications for Elders/Overseers and Deacons," p. 1839.

1:6 *husband of but one wife.* Since elders, by definition, were chosen from among the older men of the congregation, Paul assumed they already would be married and have chil-

dren. A qualified unmarried man was not necessarily barred. It is also improbable that the standard forbids an elder to remarry if his wife dies (cf. Ro 7:2–3; 1Co 7:39; 1Ti 5:14). The most likely meaning is simply that a faithful monogamous married life must be maintained. See note on 1Ti 3:2.

1:7 *an overseer.* The use of "elder" in v. 5 and "overseer" (or "bishop") in v. 7 indicates that the terms were used interchangeably (cf. Ac 20:17,28; 1Pe 5:1–2). "Elder" indicates qualification (maturity and experience), while "overseer" indicates responsibility (watching over God's flock).

1:8 *self-controlled.* A virtue much needed in Crete (see vv. 10–14); Paul refers to it five times in two chapters (here; 2:2,5–6,12). *disciplined.* Possessing the inner strength to control one's desires and actions.

1:9 *sound doctrine.* Correct teaching, in keeping with that of the apostles (see 1Ti 1:10; 6:3; 2Ti 1:13; 4:3). The teaching is called "sound" not only because it builds up in the faith, but because it protects against the corrupting influence of false teachers. Soundness of doctrine, faith and speech is a basic concern in all the Pastoral Letters (1,2 Timothy; Titus). In them the word "sound" occurs eight times but is found nowhere else in Paul's writings.

1:10 *rebellious.* Against the word of God and against Paul and Titus as the Lord's authoritative ministers. *people.* These troublemakers had three main characteristics: 1. They belonged to the "circumcision group," like the people of Gal 2:12, believing that, for salvation or sanctification or both, it was necessary to be circumcised and to keep the Jewish ceremonial law (see Introduction to Galatians: Occasion and Purpose). 2. They held to unscriptural Jewish myths (v. 14) and genealogies (3:9; see 1Ti 1:4 and note there). 3. They were ascetics (vv. 14–15), having scruples against things that God declared to be good. *mere talkers.* Paul used similar language in writing to Timothy about this kind of person (1Ti 1:6).

1:12 The quotation is from the poet Epimenides (a sixth-century B.C. native of Knossos, Crete), who was held in high esteem by the Cretans. Several fulfilled predictions were ascribed to him. For other uses of pagan sayings by Paul see Ac 17:28; 1Co 15:33 and notes. In Greek literature "to Cretanize" meant to lie.

own prophets d has said, "Cretans e are always liars, evil brutes, lazy gluttons." 13This testimony is true. Therefore, rebuke f them sharply, so that they will be sound in the faith g 14and will pay no attention to Jewish myths h or to the commands i of those who reject the truth. j 15To the pure, all things are pure, k but to those who are corrupted and do not believe, nothing is pure. l In fact, both their minds and consciences are corrupted. m 16They claim to know God, but by their actions they deny him. n They are detestable, disobedient and unfit for doing anything good. o

What Must Be Taught to Various Groups

2 You must teach what is in accord with sound doctrine. p 2Teach the older men q to be temperate, r worthy of respect, self-controlled, s and sound in faith, t in love and in endurance.

3Likewise, teach the older women to be reverent in the way they live, not to be slanderers u or addicted to much wine, v but to teach what is good. 4Then they can

train the younger women w to love their husbands and children, 5to be self-controlled x and pure, to be busy at home, y to be kind, and to be subject to their husbands, z so that no one will malign the word of God. a

6Similarly, encourage the young men b to be self-controlled. c 7In everything set them an example d by doing what is good. e In your teaching show integrity, seriousness 8and soundness of speech that cannot be condemned, so that those who oppose you may be ashamed because they have nothing bad to say about us. f

9Teach slaves to be subject to their masters in everything, g to try to please them, not to talk back to them, 10and not to steal from them, but to show that they can be fully trusted, so that in every way they will make the teaching about God our Savior h attractive. i

11For the grace j of God that brings salvation has appeared k to all men. l 12It teaches us to say "No" to ungodliness and worldly passions, m and to live self-con-

1:12 dAc 17:28
eAc 2:11
1:13 /S 1Ti 5:20
gTit 2:2
1:14 hS 1Ti 1:4
/S Col 2:22
/2Ti 4:4
1:15 kPs 18:26;
Mt 15:10,11;
Mk 7:14-19;
Ac 10:9-16,28;
Col 2:20-22
/Ro 14:14,23
m1Ti 6:5
1:16 nJer 5:2;
12:2; 1Jn 2:4
oHos 8:2,3
2:1 pS 1Ti 1:10
2:2 q1Ti 5:1
r1Ti 3:2 sver 5,6,
12; Tit 1:8
tTit 1:13

2:4 w1Ti 5:2
2:5 xver 2,6,12;
Tit 1:8 y1Ti 5:14
zS Eph 5:22
a1Ti 6:1;
S Heb 4:12
2:6 b1Ti 5:1 cver
2,5,12; Tit 1:8
2:7 dS 1Ti 4:12
eS ver 14
2:8 /S 1Pe 2:12
2:9 gS Eph 6:5
2:10 hS Lk 1:47
/Mt 5:16
2:11 /S Ro 3:24
k2Ti 1:10
/S 1Ti 2:4

2:12 mTit 3:3

1:14 Jewish myths. See note on v. 10.
1:15 To the pure, all things are pure. To Christians, who have been purified by the atoning death of Christ, "everything God created is good, and nothing is to be rejected if it is received with thanksgiving" (1Ti 4:4). to those who are corrupted and do not believe, nothing is pure. Unbelievers, especially ascetics with unbiblical scruples against certain foods, marriage and the like (cf. 1Ti 4:3; Col 2:21), do not enjoy the freedom of true Christians, who receive all God's creation with thanksgiving. Instead, they set up arbitrary, man-made prohibitions against what they consider to be impure (see Mt 15:10-11,16-20; Mk 7:14-19; Ac 10:9-16; Ro 14:20). The principle of this verse does not conflict with the many NT teachings against practices that are morally and spiritually wrong. consciences. See 1Ti 4:2-3.
1:16 by their actions they deny him. The false teachers stood condemned by the test of personal conduct. good. See Introduction: Distinctive Characteristics. Right knowledge is extremely important because it leads to godliness (v. 1). Paul maintained a remarkable balance between doctrine and practice.
2:1 You. Emphatic, contrasting the work of Titus with that of the false teachers just denounced (1:10-16).
2:2-10 Sound doctrine demands right conduct of all believers, regardless of age, sex or position.
2:2 Older men, as leaders, were to be moral and spiritual examples. temperate. Instead of being "lazy gluttons," as were Cretans in general (1:12), these older believers were to be responsible and sensible.
2:3 Likewise. The same moral standards applied to women as to men. not to be slanderers. Slanderous talk apparently was a common vice among Cretan women.
2:4 love their husbands. Just as husbands are exhorted (Eph 5:25) to love their wives (though different Greek words for "love" are used in the two passages).
2:5 that no one will malign the word of God. Indicating Paul's deep spiritual concern behind these ethical instruc-

tions. See also vv. 8,10, dealing with his concern that Christian living should help rather than hinder the spread of the gospel.
2:7-8 Perhaps Titus was still a young man and was not yet well respected by the Cretan churches. The demands on a leader are all-inclusive, involving not only his word but also his life-style (Jas 3:1).
2:7 good. See Introduction: Distinctive Characteristics.
2:9-10 Instructions for a distinct group in the churches. Slavery was a basic element of Roman society, and the impact of Christianity upon slaves was a vital concern. Guidance for the conduct of Christian slaves was essential (see note on Eph 6:5).
2:9 masters. The Greek for this word, from which our English term "despot" is derived, indicates the owner's absolute authority over his slave. Roman slaves had no legal rights, their fates being entirely in their masters' hands.
2:10 make the teaching . . . attractive. Christian slaves could give a unique and powerful testimony to the gospel by their willing faithfulness and obedience to their masters.
2:11-14 Briefly describes the effect grace should have on believers. It encourages rejection of ungodliness and leads to holier living—in keeping with Paul's repeated insistence that profession of Christ be accompanied by godly living (vv. 1-2,4-5,10; 3:8).
2:11 For. Introduces the doctrinal basis for the ethical demands just stressed. Right conduct must be founded on right doctrine. grace of God. The undeserved love God showed us in Christ while we were still sinners and his enemies (Ro 5:6-10) and by which we are saved apart from any moral achievements or religious acts on our part (see 3:5; Eph 2:8-9). But this same grace instructs us that our salvation should produce good works (see note on v. 14; see also Eph 2:10).
2:12 teaches us. The word translated "teaches" refers to more than instruction; it includes the whole process of training a child—instruction, encouragement, correction and dis-

trolled,[n] upright and godly lives[o] in this present age, [13]while we wait for the blessed hope—the glorious appearing[p] of our great God and Savior, Jesus Christ,[q] [14]who gave himself for us[r] to redeem us from all wickedness[s] and to purify[t] for himself a people that are his very own,[u] eager to do what is good.[v]

[15]These, then, are the things you should teach. Encourage and rebuke with all authority. Do not let anyone despise you.

Doing What Is Good

3 Remind the people to be subject to rulers and authorities,[w] to be obedient, to be ready to do whatever is good,[x] [2]to slander no one,[y] to be peaceable and considerate, and to show true humility toward all men.

[3]At one time[z] we too were foolish, disobedient, deceived and enslaved by all kinds of passions and pleasures. We lived in malice and envy, being hated and hating one another. [4]But when the kindness[a] and love of God our Savior[b] appeared,[c] [5]he saved us,[d] not because of righteous things we had done,[e] but because of his mercy.[f] He saved us through the washing[g] of rebirth and renewal[h] by the Holy Spirit,

[6]whom he poured out on us[i] generously through Jesus Christ our Savior, [7]so that, having been justified by his grace,[j] we might become heirs[k] having the hope[l] of eternal life.[m] [8]This is a trustworthy saying.[n] And I want you to stress these things, so that those who have trusted in God may be careful to devote themselves to doing what is good.[o] These things are excellent and profitable for everyone.

[9]But avoid[p] foolish controversies and genealogies and arguments and quarrels[q] about the law,[r] because these are unprofitable and useless.[s] [10]Warn a divisive person once, and then warn him a second time. After that, have nothing to do with him.[t] [11]You may be sure that such a man is warped and sinful; he is self-condemned.

Final Remarks

[12]As soon as I send Artemas or Tychicus[u] to you, do your best to come to me at Nicopolis, because I have decided to winter there.[v] [13]Do everything you can to help Zenas the lawyer and Apollos[w] on their way and see that they have everything they need. [14]Our people must learn

Cross references

2:12 [n]ver 2,5,6; Tit 1:8 [o]2Ti 3:12
2:13 [p]S 1Co 1:7; S 1Ti 6:14 [q]2Pe 1:1
2:14 [r]S Mt 20:28 [s]S Mt 1:21 [t]Heb 1:3; 1Jn 1:7 [u]Ex 19:5; Dt 4:20; 14:2; Ps 135:4; Mal 3:17; 1Pe 2:9 [v]ver 7; Pr 16:7; Mt 5:16; 2Co 8:21; Eph 2:10; Tit 3:1, 8,14; 1Pe 2:12, 15; 3:13
3:1 [w]Ro 13:1; 1Pe 2:13,14 [x]S 2Ti 2:21; S Tit 2:14
3:2 [y]Eph 4:31
3:3 [z]S Eph 2:2
3:4 [a]Eph 2:7 [b]S Lk 1:47 [c]Tit 2:11
3:5 [d]S Ro 11:14 [e]S Eph 2:9 [f]1Pe 1:3 [g]S Ac 22:16 [h]Ro 12:2

3:6 [i]S Ro 5:5
3:7 [j]S Ro 3:24 [k]S Ro 8:17 [l]Ro 8:24 [m]S Mt 25:46; Tit 1:2
3:8 [n]S 1Ti 1:15 [o]S Tit 2:14
3:9 [p]2Ti 2:16 [q]S 2Ti 2:14 [r]Tit 1:10-16 [s]2Ti 2:14
3:10 [t]S Ro 16:17
3:12 [u]S Ac 20:4 [v]2Ti 4:9,21

3:13 [w]S Ac 18:24

cipline. *this present age.* See note on 2Co 4:4.

2:13 *the blessed hope—the glorious appearing.* The second coming (see 1Ti 6:14; 2Ti 4:1; see also note on 2Ti 4:8). *our great God and Savior, Jesus Christ.* It is possible to translate this phrase "the great God and our Saviour, Jesus Christ" (KJV), but the NIV rendering better represents the Greek construction. It is an explicit testimony to the deity of Christ (see note on Ro 9:5).

2:14 Salvation involves the double work of redeeming us from guilt and judgment and of producing moral purity and helpful service to others (see Introduction: Distinctive Characteristics).

2:15 A summary of Titus's responsibility and authority. *things.* The content of the whole chapter.

3:1–2 NT teaching is not confined to the area of personal salvation but includes much instruction about practical living. Although believers are citizens of heaven (Php 3:20), they must also submit themselves to earthly government (see Ro 13:1–7; 1Pe 2:13–17) and help promote the well-being of the community.

3:1 *rulers and authorities.* The terms refer to all forms and levels of human government (cf. Eph 3:10; 6:12 for application to angels). *good.* See Introduction: Distinctive Characteristics.

3:4 *kindness and love of God.* The reasons why God did not simply banish fallen man but acted to save him (cf. 2:11). The Greek here for "love" is *philanthropia,* "love for mankind."

3:5 *saved us ... because of his mercy.* Salvation is not achieved by human effort or merit but comes through God's mercy alone. *washing of rebirth.* A reference to new birth, of which baptism (among other things) is a sign. It cannot mean

that baptism is necessary for regeneration, since the NT plainly teaches that the new birth is an act of God's Spirit (see, e.g., Jn 3:5) and is not effected or achieved by ceremony. *renewal by the Holy Spirit.* Also a reference to new birth.

3:8 *trustworthy saying.* A reference to the doctrinal summary in vv. 4–7. This phrase, which occurs only here in Titus, appears four other times in the Pastoral Letters (1Ti 1:15; 3:1; 4:9; 2Ti 2:11) and nowhere else in the NT. *good.* See Introduction: Distinctive Characteristics.

3:9 *about the law.* A reference to the situation described in 1:10–16. A similar problem existed in Ephesus (see 1Ti 1:3–7).

3:10 *divisive person.* The Greek for this phrase became a technical term in the early church for a type of "heretic" who promoted dissension by propagating extreme views of legitimate Christian truths.

3:11 Stubborn refusal to listen to correction reveals inner perversion.

3:12 *Tychicus.* Paul's trusted co-worker, who on various occasions traveled with or for Paul (Ac 20:4; Eph 6:21–22; Col 4:7–8; 2Ti 4:12). *Nicopolis.* Means "city of victory." Several cities had this name, but the reference here apparently is to the city in Epirus on the western shore of Greece. *decided to winter there.* Indicates that Paul had not arrived there when he wrote and that he was still free to travel at will, not yet having been imprisoned in Rome for the second time.

3:13 *Zenas the lawyer.* Mentioned only here in the NT. If he was a Jewish convert, "lawyer" means that he was an expert in the Mosaic law; if he was a Gentile convert, that he was a Roman jurist. *Apollos.* A native of Alexandria and one

to devote themselves to doing what is good,ˣ in order that they may provide for daily necessities and not live unproductive lives.

3:14 ˣS Tit 2:14	
3:15 ʸ1Ti 1:2 ᶻS Col 4:18	

¹⁵Everyone with me sends you greetings. Greet those who love us in the faith.ʸ

Grace be with you all. ᶻ

---

of Paul's well-known co-workers (Ac 18:24–28; 19:1; 1Co 1:12; 3:4–6,22; 16:12). The two travelers apparently brought the letter from Paul.

3:14 *good.* See Introduction: Distinctive Characteristics.

PHILEMON

Author, Date and Place of Writing

Paul wrote this short letter probably at the same time as Colossians (c. A.D. 60; see Introduction to Colossians: Author, Date and Place of Writing) and sent it to Colosse with the same travelers, Onesimus and Tychicus. He apparently wrote both letters from prison in Rome, though possibly from Ephesus (see Introduction to Philippians: Author, Date and Place of Writing).

Recipient, Background and Purpose

Paul wrote this letter to Philemon, a believer in Colosse who, along with others, was a slave owner (cf. Col 4:1; for slavery in the NT see note on Eph 6:5). One of his slaves, Onesimus, had apparently stolen from him (cf. v. 18) and then run away, which under Roman law was punishable by death. But Onesimus met Paul and through his ministry became a Christian (see v. 10). Now he was willing to return to his master, and Paul writes this personal appeal to ask that he be accepted as a Christian brother (see v. 16).

Approach and Structure

To win Philemon's willing acceptance of Onesimus, Paul writes very tactfully and in a lighthearted tone, which he creates with a wordplay (see note on v. 11). The appeal (vv. 4-21) is organized in a way prescribed by ancient Greek and Roman teachers: to build rapport (vv. 4-10), to persuade the mind (vv. 11-19) and to move the emotions (vv. 20-21). The name Onesimus is not mentioned until the rapport has been built (v. 10), and the appeal itself is stated only near the end of the section to persuade the mind (v. 17).

Outline

I. Greetings (1-3)
II. Thanksgiving and Prayer (4-7)
III. Paul's Plea for Onesimus (8-21)
IV. Final Request, Greetings and Benediction (22-25)

[1]Paul, a prisoner[a] of Christ Jesus, and Timothy[b] our brother,[c]

To Philemon our dear friend and fellow worker,[d] [2]to Apphia our sister, to Archippus[e] our fellow soldier[f] and to the church that meets in your home:[g]

[3]Grace to you and peace from God our Father and the Lord Jesus Christ.[h]

Thanksgiving and Prayer

[4]I always thank my God[i] as I remember you in my prayers,[j] [5]because I hear about your faith in the Lord Jesus[k] and your love for all the saints.[l] [6]I pray that you may be active in sharing your faith, so that you will have a full understanding of every good thing we have in Christ. [7]Your love has given me great joy and encouragement,[m] because you, brother, have refreshed[n] the hearts of the saints.

Paul's Plea for Onesimus

[8]Therefore, although in Christ I could be bold and order you to do what you ought to do, [9]yet I appeal to you[o] on the basis of love. I then, as Paul—an old man and now also a prisoner[p] of Christ Jesus— [10]I appeal to you for my son[q] Onesimus,[a][r] who became my son while I was in chains.[s] [11]Formerly he was useless to you, but now he has become useful both to you and to me.

[12]I am sending him—who is my very heart—back to you. [13]I would have liked to keep him with me so that he could take your place in helping me while I am in chains[t] for the gospel. [14]But I did not want to do anything without your consent, so that any favor you do will be spontaneous and not forced.[u] [15]Perhaps the reason he was separated from you for a little while was that you might have him back for good— [16]no longer as a slave,[v] but better than a slave, as a dear brother.[w] He is very dear to me but even dearer to you, both as a man and as a brother in the Lord.

[17]So if you consider me a partner,[x] welcome him as you would welcome me. [18]If he has done you any wrong or owes you anything, charge it to me.[y] [19]I, Paul, am writing this with my own hand.[z] I will pay it back—not to mention that you owe me your very self. [20]I do wish, brother, that I may have some benefit from you in the Lord; refresh[a] my heart in Christ. [21]Confident[b] of your obedience, I write to you, knowing that you will do even more than I ask.

[22]And one thing more: Prepare a guest room for me, because I hope to be[c] restored to you in answer to your prayers.[d]

[23]Epaphras,[e] my fellow prisoner[f] in Christ Jesus, sends you greetings. [24]And so do Mark,[g] Aristarchus,[h] Demas[i] and Luke, my fellow workers.[j]

[25]The grace of the Lord Jesus Christ be with your spirit.[k]

1:1 [a]ver 9,23; S Eph 3:1
[b]S Ac 16:1
[c]2Co 1:1
[d]S Php 2:25
1:2 [e]Col 4:17 /Php 2:25
[g]S Ro 16:5
1:3 [h]S Ro 1:7
1:4 /S Ro 1:8 /S Ro 1:10
1:5 [k]S Ac 20:21 /S Col 1:4; 1Th 3:6
1:7 [m]2Co 7:4,13 [n]ver 20; Ro 15:32; 1Co 16:18
1:9 [o]1Co 1:10 [p]ver 1,23; S Eph 3:1
1:10 [q]S 1Th 2:11 [r]Col 4:9 [s]S Ac 21:33

1:13 [t]ver 10; S Ac 21:33
1:14 [u]2Co 9:7; 1Pe 5:2
1:16 [v]1Co 7:22 [w]Mt 23:8; S Ac 1:16; 1Ti 6:2
1:17 [x]2Co 8:23
1:18 [y]Ge 43:9
1:19 [z]S 1Co 16:21
1:20 [a]ver 7; 1Co 16:18
1:21 [b]S 2Co 2:3
1:22 [c]Php 1:25; 2:24; Heb 13:19 [d]2Co 1:11; Php 1:19
1:23 [e]Col 1:7 /ver 1; Ro 16:7; Col 4:10
1:24 [g]S Ac 12:12 [h]S Ac 19:29 /Col 4:14; 2Ti 4:10 /ver 1
1:25 [k]S Gal 6:18

[a]10 *Onesimus* means *useful.*

1–2 Although Paul writes together with Timothy and although he addresses the entire church in Colosse, in this very personal letter to Philemon he uses "I" rather than "we," and "you" (singular except in vv. 22,25).

1 *prisoner.* See notes on Eph 3:1; Php 1:13. *Timothy.* See note on Col 1:1; see also Introduction to 1 Timothy: Recipient. *Philemon.* A Christian living in Colosse or nearby and the owner of the slave Onesimus.

2 *Apphia.* Probably Philemon's wife. *Archippus.* See Col 4:17.

4 *thank . . . remember you in my prayers.* See note on Php 1:3–4.

5 Comparing Col 1:4, the NIV has interpreted "your love and your faith, which you have toward the Lord Jesus and for all the saints" (lit.) as an example of the literary device called "chiasm," in which the thought is structured like the Greek letter *chi (x):*

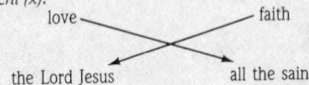

7 *hearts.* The English equivalent of the Greek for "intestines"—the part of the body that is figurative for the emotions of pity and love (see vv. 12,20).

10 *Onesimus.* See NIV text note; see also Introduction: Recipient, Background and Purpose. *my son.* See note on 1Ti 1:2.

11 *useless . . . useful.* A play on the meaning of Onesimus's name (see NIV text note on v. 10).

17–19 Luther said, "Even as Christ did for us with God the Father, thus Paul also does for Onesimus with Philemon."

20 *I . . . my.* Both pronouns are emphatic, making an obvious allusion to v. 7. *benefit.* The Greek for this word is another play on the name Onesimus.

22 *one thing more.* It was not unusual for an ancient letter, though occasioned by one matter, to also include another matter. Often, as here, the second matter had to do with how and when the author planned to meet the recipient again.

23 *Epaphras.* See Col 4:12.

24 *Mark, Aristarchus.* See note on Col 4:10. *Demas and Luke.* See note on Col 4:14.

HEBREWS

Author

The writer of this letter does not identify himself, but he was obviously well known to the original recipients. Though for some 1,200 years (from c. A.D. 400 to 1600) the book was commonly called "The Epistle of Paul to the Hebrews," there was no agreement in the earliest centuries regarding its authorship. Since the Reformation it has been widely recognized that Paul could not have been the writer. There is no disharmony between the teaching of Hebrews and that of Paul's letters, but the specific emphases and writing styles are markedly different. Contrary to Paul's usual practice, the author of Hebrews nowhere identifies himself in the letter—except to indicate that he was a man (see note on 11:32). Moreover, the statement "This salvation, which was first announced by the Lord, was confirmed to us by those who heard him" (2:3), indicates that the author had neither been with Jesus during his earthly ministry nor received special revelation directly from the risen Lord, as had Paul (Gal 1:11-12).

The earliest suggestion of authorship is found in Tertullian's *De Pudicitia*, 20 (c. 200), in which he quotes from "an epistle to the Hebrews under the name of Barnabas." From the letter itself it is clear that the writer must have had authority in the apostolic church and was an intellectual Hebrew Christian well versed in the OT. Barnabas meets these requirements. He was a Jew of the priestly tribe of Levi (Ac 4:36) who became a close friend of Paul after the latter's conversion. Under the guidance of the Holy Spirit, the church at Antioch commissioned Barnabas and Paul for the work of evangelism and sent them off on the first missionary journey (Ac 13:1-4).

The other leading candidate for authorship is Apollos, whose name was first suggested by Martin Luther and who is favored by many scholars today. Apollos, an Alexandrian by birth, was also a Jewish Christian with notable intellectual and oratorical abilities. Luke tells us that "he was a learned man, with a thorough knowledge of the Scriptures" (Ac 18:24). We also know that Apollos was associated with Paul in the early years of the church in Corinth (1Co 1:12; 3:4-6,22).

Date

Hebrews must have been written before the destruction of Jerusalem and the temple in A.D. 70 because: (1) had it been written after this date, the author surely would have mentioned the temple's destruction and the end of the Jewish sacrificial system; and (2) the author consistently uses the Greek present tense when speaking of the temple and the priestly activities connected with it (see 5:1-3; 7:23,27; 8:3-5; 9:6-9,13,25; 10:1,3-4,8,11; 13:10-11).

Recipients

The letter was addressed primarily to Jewish converts who were familiar with the OT and who were being tempted to revert to Judaism or to Judaize the gospel (cf. Gal 2:14). Some have suggested that these professing Jewish Christians were thinking of merging with a Jewish sect, such as the one at Qumran near the Dead Sea. It has also been suggested that the recipients were from the "large number of priests who became obedient to the faith" (Ac 6:7).

Theme

The theme of Hebrews is the absolute supremacy and sufficiency of Jesus Christ as revealer and as mediator of God's grace. The prologue (1:1-4) presents Christ as God's full and final revelation, far surpassing the limited preliminary revelation given in the OT. The prophecies and promises of the OT are fulfilled in the "new covenant" (or "new testament"), of which Christ is the mediator. From the OT itself, Christ is shown to be superior to the ancient prophets, to angels, to Moses (the mediator of the former covenant) and to Aaron and the priestly succession descended from him. Hebrews could be

called "the book of better things" since the two Greek words for "better" and "superior" occur 15 times in the letter.

Practical applications of this theme are given throughout the book. The readers are told that there can be no turning back to or continuation in the old Jewish system, which has been superseded by the unique priesthood of Christ. God's people now must look only to him, whose atoning death, resurrection and ascension have opened the way into the true, heavenly sanctuary of God's presence. Resisting temptations to give up the struggle, believers must persevere in the spiritual contest to which they have committed themselves. Otherwise they may meet with judgment as did the rebellious generation of Israelites in the desert.

Outline

The Son Superior to Angels

1 In the past God spoke[a] to our fore-fathers through the prophets[b] at many times and in various ways,[c] 2but in these last days[d] he has spoken to us by his Son,[e] whom he appointed heir[f] of all things, and through whom[g] he made the universe.[h] 3The Son is the radiance of God's glory[i] and the exact representation of his being,[j] sustaining all things[k] by his powerful word. After he had provided purification for sins,[l] he sat down at the right hand of the Majesty in heaven.[m] 4So he became as much superior to the angels as the name he has inherited is superior to theirs.[n]

5For to which of the angels did God ever say,

"You are my Son;
today I have become your
Father[a]"[b][o]

Or again,

"I will be his Father,
and he will be my Son"[c]?[p]

6And again, when God brings his first-born[q] into the world,[r] he says,

"Let all God's angels worship him."[d][s]

7In speaking of the angels he says,

"He makes his angels winds,
his servants flames of fire."[e][t]

8But about the Son he says,

"Your throne, O God, will last for ever
and ever,[u]
and righteousness will be the scepter
of your kingdom.
9You have loved righteousness and hated
wickedness;
therefore God, your God, has set you
above your companions[v]
by anointing you with the oil[w] of
joy."[f][x]

10He also says,

1:1 aJn 9:29;
Heb 2:2,3; 4:8;
12:25 bLk 1:70;
Ac 2:30
cNu 12:6,8
1:2 dDt 4:30;
Heb 9:26;
1Pe 1:20 ever 5;
S Mt 3:17;
Heb 3:6; 5:8;
7:28 fPs 2:8;
Mt 11:27;
S 28:18 gS Jn 1:3
hHeb 11:3
1:3 iJn 1:14
jS Jn 14:9
kCol 1:17
lTit 2:14;
Heb 7:27;
9:11-14
mS Mk 16:19
1:4 nEph 1:21;
Php 2:9,10;
Heb 8:6
1:5 oPs 2:7;
S Mt 3:17
p2Sa 7:14

1:6 qJn 3:16;
S Col 1:18
rHeb 10:5
sDt 32:43 (LXX
and DSS); Ps 97:7
1:7 tPs 104:4
1:8 uS Lk 1:33
1:9 vPhp 2:9
wIsa 61:1,3
xPs 45:6,7

a5 Or have begotten you   b5 Psalm 2:7
c5 2 Samuel 7:14; 1 Chron. 17:13   d6 Deut. 32:43
(see Dead Sea Scrolls and Septuagint)   e7 Psalm 104:4
f9 Psalm 45:6,7

1:1 *In the past.* Prior to Christ's coming, in contrast to "in these last days" (v. 2), the Messianic era inaugurated by the incarnation (see notes on Ac 2:17; 1Ti 4:1; 1Jn 2:18). *God spoke.* Cf. "he has spoken" (v. 2). God is the ultimate author of both the OT and the NT. *to our forefathers.* In contrast to "to us" (v. 2). *through the prophets.* All OT writers are here viewed as prophets in that their testimony was preparation for the coming of Christ; cf. "by his Son" (v. 2), a new and unique category of revelation in contrast to that of the prophets. *at many times and in various ways.* The OT revelation was fragmentary and occasional, lacking fullness and finality. **1:2–3** The superiority of the Son's revelation is demonstrated by seven great descriptive statements about him: 1. *appointed heir of all things.* The incarnate Son, having performed the work of redemption, was gloriously exalted to the position of the firstborn heir of God, i.e., he received the inheritance of God's estate ("all things"). See Ro 8:17. 2. *through whom he made the universe.* See Jn 1:3; Col 1:16. 3. *radiance of God's glory.* As the brilliance of the sun is inseparable from the sun itself, so the Son's radiance is inseparable from deity, for he himself is God, the second person of the Trinity (Jn 1:14,18). 4. *exact representation of his being.* Jesus is not merely an image or reflection of God. Because the Son himself is God, he is the absolutely authentic representation of God's being (cf. Jn 14:9; Col 1:15). 5. *sustaining all things.* Christ is not like Atlas, the mythical Greek god who held the world on his shoulders. The Son dynamically holds together all that has been created through him (Col 1:17). 6. *provided purification for sins.* Through his redeeming death on the cross. 7. *sat down at the right hand of the Majesty in heaven.* Being seated at God's right hand indicates that the work of redemption is complete and that Christ is actively ruling with God as Lord over all (see v. 13; 8:1; 10:12; 12:2; Eph 1:20; Col 3:1; 1Pe 3:22; see also note on Mk 16:19).
1:4 *superior to the angels.* To most Jews angels were exalted beings, especially revered because they were involved in giving the law at Sinai (see note on 2:2)—to the Jews God's supreme revelation. The Dead Sea Scrolls reflect

the expectation that the archangel Michael would be the supreme figure in the Messianic kingdom. Whether the recipients of Hebrews were tempted to assign angels a place above Christ (Messiah) is not known. *name.* To Jews a name stood for the full character of a person in all he was and did (see note on Ge 17:5). The section that follows indicates that this name was "Son"—a name to which no angel could lay claim.
1:5–14 Christ's superiority to angels is documented by seven OT quotations (see NIV text notes), showing that he is God's Son, that he is worshiped by angels and that, though he is God, he is distinguished from the Father.
1:5 *You are my Son; today I have become your Father.* This passage (Ps 2:7) is quoted in Ac 13:33 as fulfilled in Christ's resurrection (cf. Ro 1:4). *I will be his Father, and he will be my Son.* Jews acknowledged 2Sa 7:14 (of which this passage is a quotation) and Ps 2 to be Messianic in their ultimate application (see Lk 1:32–33). This royal personage is neither an angel nor an archangel; he is God's Son.
1:6 *firstborn.* See note on Col 1:15. *Let all God's angels worship him.* Possibly quoted from Ps 97:7, but see NIV text note. This statement, which in the OT refers to the Lord God (Yahweh), is here applied to Christ, giving clear indication of his full deity. The very beings with whom Christ is being compared are commanded to proclaim his superiority by worshiping him.
1:7 *He makes his angels winds, his servants flames of fire.* Ps 104:4 speaks of the storm wind and the lightning as agents of God's purposes. The Septuagint (the Greek translation of the OT), which the author of Hebrews quotes as the version familiar to his readers, reflects the developing doctrine of angels during the period between the OT and the NT.
1:8 *But about the Son he says, "Your throne, O God, will last for ever."* The author selects a passage that intimates the deity of the Messianic (and Davidic) King, further demonstrating the Son's superiority over angels.
1:10 *In the beginning, O Lord, you laid the foundations of the earth.* As in v. 6, a passage addressed to Yahweh ("O Lord") is applied to the Son.

"In the beginning, O Lord, you laid the
    foundations of the earth,
and the heavens are the work of your
    hands.*y*

¹¹They will perish, but you remain;
    they will all wear out like a
    garment.*z*
¹²You will roll them up like a robe;
    like a garment they will be changed.
But you remain the same,*a*
    and your years will never end."*g* *b*

¹³To which of the angels did God ever say,

"Sit at my right hand*c*
until I make your enemies
    a footstool*d* for your feet"*h*? *e*

¹⁴Are not all angels ministering spirits*f*
sent to serve those who will inherit*g* salvation?*h*

Warning to Pay Attention

2 We must pay more careful attention,
therefore, to what we have heard, so
that we do not drift away.*i* ²For if the
message spoken*j* by angels*k* was binding,
and every violation and disobedience received its just punishment,*l* ³how shall we
escape if we ignore such a great salvation?*m* This salvation, which was first announced by the Lord,*n* was confirmed to

us by those who heard him.*o* ⁴God also
testified to it by signs, wonders and various
miracles,*p* and gifts of the Holy Spirit*q* distributed according to his will.*r*

Jesus Made Like His Brothers

⁵It is not to angels that he has subjected
the world to come, about which we are
speaking. ⁶But there is a place where
someone*s* has testified:

"What is man that you are mindful of
    him,
the son of man that you care for
    him?*t*
⁷You made him a little*i* lower than the
    angels;
you crowned him with glory and
    honor
⁸ and put everything under his
    feet."*j* *u*

In putting everything under him, God left
nothing that is not subject to him. Yet at
present we do not see everything subject
to him. ⁹But we see Jesus, who was made
a little lower than the angels, now
crowned with glory and honor*v* because
he suffered death,*w* so that by the grace of
God he might taste death for everyone.*x*

Cross-reference column

1:10 *y*Ps 8:6;
Zec 12:1
1:11 *z*Isa 34:4;
51:6; SHeb 12:27
1:12 *a*Heb 13:8
*b*Ps 102:25-27
1:13 *c*ver 3;
S Mk 16:19
*d*Jos 10:24;
Heb 10:13
*e*Ps 110:1;
S Mt 22:44
1:14 *f*Ps 91:11;
103:20; Da 7:10
*g*Mt 25:34;
Mk 10:17;
S Ac 20:32
*h*S Ro 11:14;
Heb 2:3; 5:9;
9:28
2:1 *i*S Ro 11:22
2:2 *j*S Heb 1:1
*k*Dt 33:2;
Ac 7:53; Gal 3:19
*l*Heb 10:28
2:3 *m*Heb 10:29;
12:25 *n*Heb 1:2

*o*S Lk 1:2
2:4 *p*Mk 16:20;
S Jn 4:48
*q*S 1Co 12:4
*r*S Eph 1:5
2:6 *s*Heb 4:4 *t*Job
7:17; Ps 144:3
2:8 *u*Ps 8:4-6;
S Mt 22:44
2:9 *v*ver 7;
Ac 3:13;
S Php 2:9
*w*Php 2:7-9
*x*2Co 5:15

g *12* Psalm 102:25-27   **h** *13* Psalm 110:1   **i** *7* Or
him for a little while; also in verse 9   **j** *8* Psalm 8:4-6

1:13 *Sit at my right hand.* See note on vv. 2–3. Ps 110 is
applied repeatedly to Jesus in Hebrews (vv. 3,13; 5:6,10;
6:20; 7:3,11,17,21; 8:1; 10:12–13; 12:2).
1:14 *ministering spirits.* Christ reigns; angels minister as
those sent to serve.
2:1–4 The first of five warnings strategically positioned
throughout the letter (see 3:7–4:13; 5:11–6:12;
10:19–39; 12:14–29).
2:1 *what we have heard.* The message of the gospel, including that of Christ's person as the God-man and his
redemptive work on the cross. *drift away.* From the greater
revelation given through the Son.
2:2 *the message spoken by angels.* The law given to Moses
at Sinai. That angels were active in giving the law is indicated
by Dt 33:2 ("myriads of holy ones"); Ps 68:17; Ac 7:38,53;
Gal 3:19.
2:3 *such a great salvation.* The argument here is from the
lesser to the greater, and assumes that the gospel is greater
than the law. Thus, if disregard for the law brought certain
punishment, disregard for the gospel will bring even greater
punishment. *confirmed to us by those who heard him.* The
eyewitnesses, chiefly the apostles (see 2Pe 1:16; 1Jn 1:1),
had vouched for the message first announced by Christ. The
author himself apparently was neither an apostle nor an
eyewitness (see Introduction: Author).
2:4 *signs, wonders and various miracles.* God added his
confirmation to the gospel message through supernatural
acts such as healing the sick (see Ac 3:7–9,11–12,16). *gifts
of the Holy Spirit.* Such as the gift of tongues (see Ac
2:4–12). *distributed according to his will.* See 1Co
12:4–11.
2:5–18 An exposition of Ps 8:4–6, which continues to
show Christ's superiority over the angels—in fulfilling man's

role as sovereign over the earth and in redeeming fallen man,
not fallen angels. To accomplish all this, Christ assumed
human nature (see vv. 11,14).
2:5 *It is not to angels that he has subjected the world to
come.* Some think the readers were being enticed to believe
that the future kingdom would be under the rule of angelic
beings (see note on 1:4). Others see the author trying to
dissuade his readers from turning back to Judaism. He shows
that Christ, as bearer of the new revelation, is superior to
angels who had participated in bringing the revelation at
Sinai.
2:6a *there is a place where someone has testified.* Such a
well-known passage as Ps 8:4–6 did not need precise identification.
2:6b–8 Awed by the marvelous order and immensity of
God's handiwork in the celestial universe, the psalmist marveled at the high dignity God had bestowed on puny man by
entrusting him with dominion over the other creatures (see
Ge 1:26–28 and notes).
2:7 *angels.* See note on Ps 8:5.
2:8 *everything.* God's purpose from the beginning was that
man should be sovereign in the creaturely realm, subject
only to God. Due to sin, that purpose of God has not yet been
fully realized. Indeed, men are themselves "in slavery" (v.
15).
2:9 *Jesus . . . now crowned with glory and honor.* Ps 8 is
here applied to Jesus in particular. As forerunner of man's
restored dominion over the earth, he was made lower than
the angels for a while but is now crowned with glory and
honor at God's right hand. By his perfect life, his death on the
cross and his exaltation, he has made possible for redeemed
man the ultimate fulfillment of Ps 8 in the future kingdom,
when man will regain sovereignty over creation.

[10]In bringing many sons to glory, it was fitting that God, for whom and through whom everything exists,[y] should make the author of their salvation perfect through suffering.[z] [11]Both the one who makes men holy[a] and those who are made holy[b] are of the same family. So Jesus is not ashamed to call them brothers.[c] [12]He says,

"I will declare your name to my
    brothers;
in the presence of the congregation I
    will sing your praises."[k] [d]

[13]And again,

"I will put my trust in him."[l] [e]

And again he says,

"Here am I, and the children God has
    given me."[m] [f]

[14]Since the children have flesh and blood,[g] he too shared in their humanity[h] so that by his death he might destroy[i] him who holds the power of death—that is, the devil[—] [15]and free those who all their lives were held in slavery by their fear[k] of death. [16]For surely it is not angels he helps,

but Abraham's descendants.[l] [17]For this reason he had to be made like his brothers[m] in every way, in order that he might become a merciful[n] and faithful high priest[o] in service to God,[p] and that he might make atonement for[n] the sins of the people.[q] [18]Because he himself suffered when he was tempted, he is able to help those who are being tempted.[r]

Jesus Greater Than Moses

3 Therefore, holy brothers,[s] who share in the heavenly calling,[t] fix your thoughts on Jesus, the apostle and high priest[u] whom we confess.[v] [2]He was faithful to the one who appointed him, just as Moses was faithful in all God's house.[w] [3]Jesus has been found worthy of greater honor than Moses,[x] just as the builder of a house has greater honor than the house itself. [4]For every house is built by someone, but God is the builder of everything.[y] [5]Moses was faithful as a servant[z] in all God's house,[a] testifying to what would be said in the future. [6]But Christ is faithful as

Cross references (center column):

2:10 [y]S Ro 11:36
[z]Lk 24:26;
Heb 5:8,9; 7:28
2:11 [a]Heb 13:12
[b]S Eph 5:26
[c]S Mt 28:10
2:12 [d]Ps 22:22;
68:26
2:13 [e]Isa 8:17
[f]Isa 8:18;
Jn 10:29
2:14 [g]1Co 15:50;
Eph 6:12
[h]S Jn 1:14
[i]Ge 3:15;
1Co 15:54-57;
2Ti 1:10 /[j]Jn 3:8
2:15 [k]S 2Ti 1:7

2:16 [l]S Lk 3:8
2:17 [m]ver 14;
S Php 2:7
[n]Heb 5:2
[o]Heb 3:1; 4:14,
15; 5:5,10; 7:26,
28; 8:1,3; 9:11
[p]Heb 5:1
[q]S Ro 3:25
2:18 [r]Heb 4:15
3:1 [s]Heb 2:11
[t]S Ro 8:28
[u]S Heb 2:17
[v]1Ti 6:12;
Heb 4:14; 10:23;
2Co 9:13
3:2 [w]ver 5;
Nu 12:7
3:3 [x]Dt 34:12
3:4 [y]Ge 1:1
3:5 [z]Ex 14:31
[a]ver 2; Nu 12:7

[k]12 Psalm 22:22   [l]13 Isaiah 8:17
[m]13 Isaiah 8:18   [n]17 Or and that he might turn aside
God's wrath, taking away

2:10 *many sons to glory.* Those who believe in Christ are made God's children through his only Son (cf. Jn 1:12–13). *author.* The Greek word occurs only four times in the NT: here; 12:2; Ac 3:15; 5:31 ("Prince"). *perfect through suffering.* Christ had not been morally or spiritually imperfect, but his incarnation was completed (perfected) when he experienced suffering. He identified with us on the deepest level of anguish, and so became qualified to pay the price for our sinful imperfection and to become our sympathetic high priest.
2:11 *who makes men holy . . . who are made holy.* Christ became man to identify himself with man and, by his substitutionary sacrifice on the cross, to restore the holiness man had lost. *to call them brothers.* Our brotherhood with Jesus is the brotherhood of the Redeemer with the redeemed, who are truly one with him.
2:12 *I will declare your name to my brothers.* A quotation from Ps 22:22, a psalm describing the sufferings and triumph of God's righteous servant (see introduction to Ps 22). The key phrase is "my brothers," seen here as coming from the lips of the triumphant Messiah.
2:13 *I will put my trust in him.* An expression of true dependence on God perfectly exemplified in Christ. In him humanity is seen as it was intended to be. *Here am I, and the children God has given me.* Also seen ultimately as an utterance of the incarnate Son. The Father's children are given to the Son to be his brothers (see v. 11).
2:14 *him who holds the power of death.* Satan wields the power of death only insofar as he induces people to sin and to come under sin's penalty, which is death (see Eze 18:4; Ro 5:12; 6:23).
2:15 *free.* See 1Co 15:54–57; Rev 1:18.
2:16 *Abraham's descendants.* Christ assumed not angelic nature but human nature, characterized by the descendants of Abraham.
2:17 *a merciful and faithful high priest.* Christ could represent mankind before God only if he became one with them.

make atonement. See NIV text note; see also notes on Lev 16:20–22; 17:11. In order for Christ to turn aside the wrath of God against guilty sinners, he had to become one with them and die as a substitute for them.
2:18 *he was tempted.* See note on 4:15.
3:1—4:13 An exposition of Ps 95:7–11, stressing Christ's superiority over Moses and warning against disobedience and unbelief.
3:1 *share.* See note on v. 14. *the heavenly calling.* The invitation that comes from heaven and leads to heaven. *apostle.* Means "one who is sent" (see notes on Mk 6:30; 1Co 1:1). Jesus repeatedly spoke of himself as having been sent into the world by the Father (e.g., Mt 10:40; 15:24; Mk 9:37; Lk 9:48; Jn 4:34; 5:24,30,36–38; 6:38). He is the supreme apostle, the one from whom all other apostleship flows.
3:2 A comparison of Christ and Moses, both of whom were sent by the Father to lead his people—the one to lead them from bondage under Pharaoh to the promised land, the other to lead them from bondage under the devil (2:14–15) to the Sabbath-rest promised to those who believe (4:3,9). The Sabbath-rest may be heaven, though many hold that it refers primarily to the salvation-rest of Christ's redemption. The analogy focuses on faithful stewardship.
3:3 *the builder . . . has greater honor than the house.* Jesus is the actual builder of the house (or household), whereas Moses was simply a part of it.
3:4 *God is the builder of everything.* Jesus is here equated with God, making it beyond question that Christ is greater than Moses.
3:5–6 *a servant in all God's house . . . a son over God's house.* The superiority of Christ over Moses is shown in two comparisons: (1) Moses was a servant, whereas Christ is a son, and (2) Moses was in God's house, i.e., a part of it, whereas Christ is over God's house.
3:6 *we are his house.* The house is made up of God's people, his household (see Eph 2:19; 1Pe 2:5). *if we hold on*

a son[b] over God's house. And we are his house,[c] if we hold on[d] to our courage and the hope[e] of which we boast.

Warning Against Unbelief

[7]So, as the Holy Spirit says:[f]

"Today, if you hear his voice,
[8] do not harden your hearts[g]
as you did in the rebellion,
    during the time of testing in the desert,
[9]where your fathers tested and tried me
    and for forty years saw what I did.[h]
[10]That is why I was angry with that generation,
    and I said, 'Their hearts are always going astray,
    and they have not known my ways.'
[11]So I declared on oath in my anger,[i]
    'They shall never enter my rest.'[j]"[o][k]

[12]See to it, brothers, that none of you has a sinful, unbelieving heart that turns away from the living God.[l] [13]But encourage one another daily,[m] as long as it is called Today, so that none of you may be hardened by sin's deceitfulness.[n] [14]We have come to share in Christ if we hold firmly[o] till the end the confidence[p] we had at first. [15]As has just been said:

"Today, if you hear his voice,
    do not harden your hearts
    as you did in the rebellion."[p][q]

[16]Who were they who heard and rebelled? Were they not all those Moses led

out of Egypt?[r] [17]And with whom was he angry for forty years? Was it not with those who sinned, whose bodies fell in the desert?[s] [18]And to whom did God swear that they would never enter his rest[t] if not to those who disobeyed[q]?[u] [19]So we see that they were not able to enter, because of their unbelief.[v]

A Sabbath-Rest for the People of God

4 Therefore, since the promise of entering his rest still stands, let us be careful that none of you be found to have fallen short of it.[w] [2]For we also have had the gospel preached to us, just as they did; but the message they heard was of no value to them, because those who heard did not combine it with faith.[r][x] [3]Now we who have believed enter that rest, just as God has said,

"So I declared on oath in my anger,
    'They shall never enter my rest.'"[s][y]

And yet his work has been finished since the creation of the world. [4]For somewhere he has spoken about the seventh day in these words: "And on the seventh day God rested from all his work."[t][z] [5]And again in the passage above he says, "They shall never enter my rest."[a]

[6]It still remains that some will enter that rest, and those who formerly had the gospel preached to them did not go in, be-

---

3:6 *b*S Heb 1:2
*c*1Co 3:16;
1Ti 3:15 *d*ver 14;
S Ro 11:22;
Heb 4:14
*e*Ro 5:2;
Heb 6:11,18,19;
7:19; 11:1
3:7 *f*Ac 28:25;
Heb 9:8; 10:15
3:8 *g*ver 15;
Heb 4:7
3:9 *h*Nu 14:33;
Dt 1:3; Ac 7:36
3:11 *i*Dt 1:34,35
*j*Heb 4:3,5
*k*Ps 95:7-11
3:12 *l*S Mt 16:16
3:13
*m*Heb 10:24,25
*n*Jer 17:9;
Eph 4:22
3:14 *o*ver 6
*p*S Eph 3:12
3:15 *q*Ps 95:7,8;
ver 7,8; Heb 4:7

3:16 *r*Nu 14:2
3:17 *s*Nu 14:29;
Ps 106:26;
1Co 10:5
3:18
*t*Nu 14:20-23;
Dt 1:34,35
*u*Heb 4:6
3:19 *v*Ps 78:22;
106:24; Jn 3:36
4:1 *w*Heb 12:15
4:2 *x*1Th 2:13
4:3 *y*Ps 95:11;
Dt 1:34,35;
Heb 3:11
4:4 *z*Ge 2:2,3;
Ex 20:11
4:5 *a*Ps 95:11;
S ver 3

o11 Psalm 95:7-11   *p15* Psalm 95:7,8   *q18* Or
disbelieved   *r2* Many manuscripts *because they did not share in the faith of those who obeyed*
s3 Psalm 95:11; also in verse 5   *t4* Gen. 2:2

---

to our courage and the hope. Failure to persevere reveals that a person is actually not a child of God, whereas perseverance is the hallmark of his children.
3:7–11 This quotation from Ps 95:7–11 summarizes the inglorious history of Israel under Moses' leadership in the desert. Three time periods are alluded to: that of the exodus, that of the psalmist and that of the writing of Hebrews. The example of Israel under Moses was used by the psalmist to warn the Israelites of his day against unbelief and disobedience. In a similar way the author of Hebrews applied the psalmist's warning to the recipients of this letter. The warning also applies today.
3:12 *that none of you ... turns away from the living God.* To turn away rebelliously (lit. "to become apostate") from God is to turn away from life and to choose death, just as did some of the Israelites who came out of Egypt.
3:13 *as long as it is called Today.* See 4:7. This is still the day of divine grace and opportunity to trust God, but it will not last indefinitely.
3:14 *to share in Christ.* To belong to him and participate in the blessings (cf. v. 1). *hold firmly till the end the confidence we had at first.* Salvation is evidenced by continuing in faith to the end. Such perseverance reveals those who share in Christ (see note on v. 6).
3:16–19 The argument is pursued with a series of rhetorical questions. The important truths are that the people who

failed to enter Canaan were the ones who had heard God's promise concerning the land and that they refused to believe what God had promised (v. 19)—an action described as rebellion (v. 16), sin (v. 17) and disobedience (v. 18). Consequently, God in his anger closed the doors of Canaan in the face of that whole generation of Israelites (Nu 14:21–35). First-century readers of Hebrews faced a similar danger spiritually.
4:1 *the promise of entering his rest still stands.* Salvation is still available. "His rest" cannot refer ultimately to the rest in Canaan offered to the Israelites. That temporary, earthly rest gained under Joshua (see v. 8; see also note on Jos 1:13) pointed to a rest that is spiritual and eternal.
4:3 *we who have believed enter that rest.* Just as entering physical rest in Canaan demanded faith in God's promise, so salvation-rest is entered only by faith in the person and work of Jesus Christ. *his work has been finished since the creation of the world.* God rested from his work on the seventh day of creation (see v. 4; Ge 2:2), and thus his rest is already a reality. The rest God calls us to enter (vv. 10–11) is not our rest but his rest, which he invites us to share.
4:6–8 Israel's going into Canaan under Joshua was a partial and temporary entering of God's rest. That, however, was not the end of entering, as shown in the continuing invitation of Ps 95:7–8.

cause of their disobedience. b 7Therefore
God again set a certain day, calling it Today, when a long time later he spoke
through David, as was said before:

"Today, if you hear his voice,
    do not harden your hearts." u c

8For if Joshua had given them rest, d God
would not have spoken e later about another day. 9There remains, then, a Sabbath-rest for the people of God; 10for anyone who enters God's rest also rests from
his own work, f just as God did from his. g
11Let us, therefore, make every effort to
enter that rest, so that no one will fall by
following their example of disobedience. h

12For the word of God i is living j and
active. k Sharper than any double-edged
sword, l it penetrates even to dividing soul
and spirit, joints and marrow; it judges the
thoughts and attitudes of the heart. m
13Nothing in all creation is hidden from
God's sight. n Everything is uncovered and
laid bare before the eyes of him to whom
we must give account.

Jesus the Great High Priest

14Therefore, since we have a great high
priest o who has gone through the heav-

ens, v p Jesus the Son of God, q let us hold
firmly to the faith we profess. r 15For we
do not have a high priest s who is unable
to sympathize with our weaknesses, but
we have one who has been tempted in
every way, just as we are t—yet was without sin. u 16Let us then approach v the
throne of grace with confidence, w so that
we may receive mercy and find grace to
help us in our time of need.

5 Every high priest is selected from
among men and is appointed to represent them in matters related to God, x to
offer gifts and sacrifices y for sins. z 2He is
able to deal gently with those who are ignorant and are going astray, a since he
himself is subject to weakness. b 3This is
why he has to offer sacrifices for his own
sins, as well as for the sins of the people. c

4No one takes this honor upon himself;
he must be called by God, just as Aaron
was. d 5So Christ also did not take upon
himself the glory e of becoming a high
priest. f But God said g to him,

"You are my Son;

4:6 b ver 11;
Heb 3:18
4:7 c Ps 95:7,8;
Heb 3:7,8,15
4:8 d Jos 22:4
e S Heb 1:1
4:10 f Lev 23:3;
Rev 14:13 g ver 4
4:11 h ver 6;
Heb 3:18
4:12 i S Mk 4:14;
Lk 5:1; 11:28;
Jn 10:35;
Ac 12:24;
1Th 2:13;
2Ti 2:9; 1Pe 1:23;
1Jn 2:14; Rev 1:2,
9 /Ac 7:38;
1Pe 1:23
k Isa 55:11;
Jer 23:29;
l Eph 6:17;
S Rev 1:16
m 1Co 14:24,25
4:13
n Ps 33:13-15;
Pr 5:21;
Jer 16:17; 23:24;
Da 2:22
4:14 o S Heb 2:17

p Heb 6:20; 8:1;
9:24 q S Mt 4:3
r S Heb 3:1
4:15 s S Heb 2:17
t Heb 2:18
u S 2Co 5:21
4:16 v S Heb 7:19
w S Eph 3:12
5:1 x Heb 2:17
y Heb 8:3; 9:9
z Heb 7:27
5:2 a Isa 29:24;
Heb 2:18; 4:15
b Heb 7:28

5:3 c Lev 9:7; 16:6; Heb 7:27; 9:7 5:4 d Ex 28:1; Nu 14:40;
18:7 5:5 e Jn 8:54 f S Heb 2:17 g S Heb 1:1

u 7 Psalm 95:7,8   v 14 Or gone into heaven

4:7 calling it Today. See note on 3:13.

4:9 There remains, then, a Sabbath-rest. God's rest may
still be entered by faith in his Son.

4:10 rests from his own work. Whereas God rested from
the work of creation, the believer ceases his efforts to gain
salvation by his own works and rests in the finished work of
Christ on the cross. According to some, however, the believer's final rest is in view here (see Rev 14:13).

4:11 make every effort. Not a call to earn one's salvation by
works, but an exhortation to enter salvation-rest by faith and
not follow Israel's sad example in the desert.

4:12–13 The reasons for giving serious attention to the
exhortation of v. 11.

4:12 word of God. God's truth was revealed by Jesus (the
incarnate Word; see Jn 1:1,14), but it has also been given
verbally, the word referred to here. This dynamic word of
God, active in accomplishing God's purposes, appears in
both the OT and the NT (see Ps 107:20; 147:18; Isa 40:8;
55:11; Gal 3:8; Eph 5:26; Jas 1:18; 1Pe 1:23). The author
of Hebrews describes it as a living power that judges as with
an all-seeing eye, penetrating a person's innermost being.
soul and spirit, joints and marrow. The totality and depth of
one's being.

4:13 Nothing in all creation is hidden from God's sight.
The author associates the activity of the word with the
activity of God as though they are one and the same—which
in a sense they are.

4:14–7:28 An exposition of Ps 110:4, stressing Christ's
superiority over Aaron because of a better priesthood.

4:14 great high priest. See 2:17; 3:1. The author here
begins an extended discussion of the superior priesthood of
Christ. through the heavens. As the Aaronic high priest on
the Day of Atonement passed from the sight of the people
into the Most Holy Place (see Lev 16:15,17), so Jesus passed
from the sight of his watching disciples, ascending through

the heavens into the heavenly sanctuary, his work of atonement accomplished (Ac 1:9–11). hold firmly to the faith we
profess. Suggests that the readers were in danger of letting
their faith slip (see similar admonitions in 2:1; 3:6,14).

4:15 tempted in every way, just as we are. See 2:18. The
author stresses the parallel between Christ's temptations and
ours. He did not have each temptation we have but experienced every kind of temptation a person can have. yet was
without sin. The way in which Christ's temptations were
completely different from ours was in the results—his temptations never led to sin (see Mt 4:1–11).

4:16 Let us then approach. Because Christ our high priest
has experienced human temptation, he stands ready to give
immediate and sympathetic help when we are tempted.

5:1–4 The high-priestly office had two specific qualifications: (1) A candidate had to be "selected from among men"
(v. 1) and thus be able to represent them before God; and (2)
he had to "be called by God" (v. 4).

5:1 gifts and sacrifices. See 8:3; 9:9; see also notes on Lev
1:2; 2:1.

5:2 those who are ignorant and are going astray. See Isa
53:6. Contrast the unintentional sin (as in Lev 4; Nu
15:27–29) with defiant rebellion against God (see Nu
15:30–31; cf. Heb 6:4–6; 10:26–31).

5:4 No one takes this honor upon himself. In Christ's day
the high-priestly office was in the hands of a family that had
bought control of it.

5:5 Christ also did not take upon himself the glory of
becoming a high priest. The Son was appointed by the
Father, as the two prophetic statements cited here show (Ps
2:7; 110:4). His high priesthood, however, was "in the
order of Melchizedek" (v. 6), not in the order of Aaron.
today I have become your Father. See notes on 1:5; Ps
2:7–9; cf. Ro 1:4.

today I have become your
Father. **w**'' **x** h

6And he says in another place,

"You are a priest forever,
in the order of Melchizedek. i '' **y** j

7During the days of Jesus' life on earth,
he offered up prayers and petitions k with
loud cries and tears l to the one who could
save him from death, and he was heard m
because of his reverent submission. n 8Al-
though he was a son, o he learned obedience from what he suffered p 9and, once
made perfect, q he became the source of
eternal salvation for all who obey him
10and was designated by God to be high
priest r in the order of Melchizedek. s

Warning Against Falling Away

6:4–6Ref — Heb 10:26–31

11We have much to say about this, but it
is hard to explain because you are slow to
learn. 12In fact, though by this time you
ought to be teachers, you need someone to

teach you the elementary truths t of God's
word all over again. You need milk, not
solid food! u 13Anyone who lives on milk,
being still an infant, v is not acquainted
with the teaching about righteousness.
14But solid food is for the mature, w who by
constant use have trained themselves to
distinguish good from evil. x

6 Therefore let us leave y the elementary
teachings z about Christ and go on to
maturity, not laying again the foundation
of repentance from acts that lead to
death, z a and of faith in God, 2instruction
about baptisms, b the laying on of hands, c
the resurrection of the dead, d and eternal
judgment. 3And God permitting, e we will
do so.

4It is impossible for those who have
once been enlightened, f who have tasted
the heavenly gift, g who have shared in the
Holy Spirit, h 5who have tasted the goodness i of the word of God j and the powers
of the coming age, 6if they fall away, to be

Cross references (center column):

5:5 hPs 2:7; S Mt 3:17
5:6 iver 10; Ge 14:18; Heb 6:20; 7:1-22 jPs 110:4; Heb 7:17,21
5:7 kLk 22:41-44 lMt 27:46,50; Lk 23:46 mPs 22:24 nMk 14:36
5:8 oS Heb 1:2 pS Php 2:8
5:9 qS Heb 2:10
5:10 rver 5; S Heb 2:17 sS ver 6
5:12 tHeb 6:1 u1Co 3:2; 1Pe 2:2
5:13 vS 1Co 14:20
5:14 wS 1Co 2:6 xIsa 7:15
6:1 yPhp 3:12-14 zHeb 5:12 aHeb 9:14
6:2 bJn 3:25 cS Ac 6:6 dS Ac 2:24; Ac 17:18,32
6:3 eAc 18:21
6:4 fHeb 10:32 gEph 2:8 hGal 3:2
6:5 iPs 34:8 jS Heb 4:12

w 5 Or have begotten you   **x** 5 Psalm 2:7
y 6 Psalm 110:4   **z** 1 Or from useless rituals

5:7 *days of Jesus' life on earth.* The principal reference here
is to Christ's agony in the Garden of Gethsemane. *to the one
who could save him from death.* To the Father. Jesus did not
shrink from physical suffering and death but from the indescribable agony of taking mankind's sin on himself (see Mt
27:46). Although he asked that the cup of suffering might be
taken from him, he did not waver in his determination to
fulfill the Father's will (see Mt 26:36–46). *he was heard.* His
prayer was granted by the Father, who saved him from
death—through resurrection.
5:8 *he learned obedience from what he suffered.* He was
made "perfect" (v. 9) through suffering (see note on 2:10),
namely, his temptation in the desert and his ordeal on the
cross. Though he was the eternal Son of God, it was necessary for him as the incarnate Son to learn obedience—not
that he was ever disobedient, but that he was called on to
obey to an extent he had never before experienced. The
temptations he faced were real and the battle for victory was
difficult, but where Adam failed and fell, Jesus resisted and
prevailed. His humanity was thereby completed, "made perfect" (v. 9), and on the basis of this perfection he could
become "the source of eternal salvation" (see 9:12).
5:11 *much to say about this.* About Christ's eternal priesthood "in the order of Melchizedek" (v. 10). *slow to learn.*
Instead of progressing in the Christian life, the readers had
become spiritually sluggish and mentally lazy (6:12).
5:12 *by this time.* They were not recent converts. *elementary truths of God's word.* These are listed in 6:1–2 (see note
there). Having taken the first steps toward becoming (mature) Christians, they had slipped back to where they started.
solid food. Advanced teaching such as that given in ch. 7.
5:14 *the mature.* Those who had progressed in spiritual life
and had become Christians of sound judgment and discernment. *distinguish good from evil.* Something neither physical nor spiritual infants can do.
6:1–2 *not laying again the foundation.* Six fundamental
doctrines are mentioned: 1. *repentance.* The change of mind
that causes one to turn away from sin and/or useless rituals
(see NIV text note). 2. *faith in God.* The counterpart of
repentance. As repentance is turning away from the darkness

of sin, faith is turning to the light of God. 3. *instruction about
baptisms.* Probably refers to different baptisms with which
the readers were familiar, such as Jewish baptism of proselytes, John the Baptist's baptism, and the baptism commanded by Jesus (Mt 28:19). 4. *laying on of hands.* Sometimes followed baptism (Ac 8:16–17; 19:5–6). Otherwise
laying on of hands was practiced in connection with ordaining or commissioning (see Ac 6:6; 13:3; 1Ti 5:22; 2Ti 1:6),
healing the sick (see Mk 6:5; 16:18; Lk 4:40; Ac 28:8) and
bestowal of blessing (see Mt 19:13–15). 5. *resurrection of
the dead.* The resurrection of all people in the last days (see
Jn 5:25–29; 11:25; 2Co 4:14). 6. *eternal judgment.* The
destiny of those who reject God's saving grace and persist in
their sinful ways.
6:1 *elementary teachings about Christ.* See note on 5:12.
6:3 A common expression of dependence on the will of
God (cf. 1Co 16:7). Only the Lord can open minds and
hearts and bring spiritual maturity.
6:4–6 The most common interpretations of this difficult
passage are: 1. It refers to Christians who actually lose their
salvation. 2. It is a hypothetical argument to warn immature
Hebrew Christians (5:11–14) that they must progress to
maturity (see v. 1) or else experience divine discipline or
judgment (see vv. 7–8). 3. It refers to professing Christians
whose apostasy proves that their faith was not genuine (cf.
1Jn 2:19). This view sees chs. 3–4 as a warning based on the
rebellion of the Israelites in the desert. As Israel could not
enter the promised land after spying out the region and
tasting its fruit, so the professing Hebrew Christians would
not be able to repent if they adamantly turned against "the
light" they had received. According to this interpretation,
such expressions as "enlightened," "tasted the heavenly
gift" and "shared in the Holy Spirit" indicate that such
persons had come under the influence of God's covenant
blessings and had professed to turn from darkness to light but
were in danger of a public and final rejection of Christ,
proving they had never been regenerated (see 10:26–31 and
notes).
6:5 *the coming age.* See Mk 10:30 and note; 1Ti 6:19.

brought back to repentance,[k] because[a] to their loss they are crucifying the Son of God[l] all over again and subjecting him to public disgrace.

[7]Land that drinks in the rain often falling on it and that produces a crop useful to those for whom it is farmed receives the blessing of God. [8]But land that produces thorns and thistles is worthless and is in danger of being cursed.[m] In the end it will be burned.

[9]Even though we speak like this, dear friends,[n] we are confident of better things in your case—things that accompany salvation. [10]God is not unjust; he will not forget your work and the love you have shown him as you have helped his people and continue to help them.[o] [11]We want each of you to show this same diligence to the very end, in order to make your hope[p] sure. [12]We do not want you to become lazy, but to imitate[q] those who through faith and patience[r] inherit what has been promised.[s]

The Certainty of God's Promise

[13]When God made his promise to Abraham, since there was no one greater for him to swear by, he swore by himself,[t] [14]saying, "I will surely bless you and give you many descendants."[b][u] [15]And so after waiting patiently, Abraham received what was promised.[v]

[16]Men swear by someone greater than themselves, and the oath confirms what is said and puts an end to all argument.[w] [17]Because God wanted to make the unchanging[x] nature of his purpose very clear to the heirs of what was promised,[y] he confirmed it with an oath. [18]God did this so that, by two unchangeable things in which it is impossible for God to lie,[z] we who have fled to take hold of the hope[a] offered to us may be greatly encouraged. [19]We have this hope as an anchor for the soul, firm and secure. It enters the inner sanctuary behind the curtain,[b] [20]where Jesus, who went before us, has entered on our behalf.[c] He has become a high priest[d] forever, in the order of Melchizedek.[e]

Melchizedek the Priest

7 This Melchizedek was king of Salem[f] and priest of God Most High.[g] He met Abraham returning from the defeat of the kings and blessed him,[h] [2]and Abraham gave him a tenth of everything. First, his name means "king of righteousness"; then also, "king of Salem" means "king of peace." [3]Without father or mother, without genealogy,[i] without beginning of days or end of life, like the Son of God[j] he remains a priest forever.

[4]Just think how great he was: Even the patriarch[k] Abraham gave him a tenth of

Center column references

6:6 [k]2Pe 2:21;
1Jn 5:16
[l]S Mt 4:3
6:8 [m]Ge 3:17,18;
Isa 5:6; 27:4
6:9 [n]S 1Co 10:14
6:10
[o]S Mt 10:40,42;
1Th 1:3
6:11 [p]S Heb 3:6
6:12 [q]Heb 13:7
[r]2Ti 1:4; Jas 1:3;
Rev 13:10; 14:12
[s]Heb 10:36
6:13 [t]Ge 22:16;
Lk 1:73
6:14 [u]Ge 22:17
6:15 [v]Ge 21:5

6:16 [w]Ex 22:11
6:17 [x]ver 18;
Ps 110:4
[y]Ro 4:16;
Heb 11:9
6:18 [z]Nu 23:19;
Tit 1:2 [a]S Heb 3:6
6:19 [b]Lev 16:2;
Heb 9:2,3,7
6:20 [c]S Heb 4:14
[d]S Heb 2:17
[e]S Heb 5:6
7:1 [f]Ps 76:2
[g]S Mk 5:7 [h]ver 6;
Ge 14:18-20
7:3 [i]ver 6
[j]S Mt 4:3
7:4 [k]Ac 2:29

[a]6 Or *repentance while*   [b]14 Gen. 22:17

6:7-8 A short parable graphically illustrating the warning just given (see Jn 15:5-6; 2Pe 2:20-22; 1Jn 5:16).

6:9 *confident of better things . . . that accompany salvation.* Although the author has suggested the possibility that some of his readers may still be unsaved, he is confident that God has been at work among them. Changed lives and works of love (v. 10) suggest that many of these persons were indeed regenerated.

6:11 *to the very end.* A call for perseverance in faith as an evidence of salvation. *make your hope sure.* See 11:1; 2Pe 1:10.

6:12 *those who through faith and patience inherit what has been promised.* For examples see ch. 11.

6:13 *God made his promise to Abraham.* The promise of many descendants was made with an oath to emphasize its unchanging character (see Ge 22:16-18). Ordinarily the swearing of an oath belongs to our fallen human situation, in which a man's word is not always trustworthy. God's swearing of an oath was a condescension to human frailty, thus making his word, which in itself is absolutely trustworthy, doubly dependable (see v. 18).

6:15 *after waiting patiently.* For 25 years (see Ge 12:3-4; 21:5). *received what was promised.* The birth of his son Isaac (Ge 17:2; 18:10; 21:5).

6:18 *two unchangeable things.* God's promise, which in itself is absolutely trustworthy, and God's oath confirming that promise. *be greatly encouraged.* Since we look back on the fulfillment of the promise that Abraham saw only in anticipation (11:13; Jn 8:56).

6:19 *as an anchor for the soul, firm and secure.* Like an anchor holding a ship safely in position, our hope in Christ guarantees our safety. *inner sanctuary behind the curtain.* Whereas the ship's anchor goes down to the ocean bed, the Christian's anchor goes up into the true, heavenly sanctuary, where he is moored to God himself.

6:20 *a high priest forever, in the order of Melchizedek.* The grand theme that the author is about to develop (ch. 7).

7:1 *Melchizedek.* See Ge 14:18-20 and notes. *king . . . and priest.* Of particular significance is Melchizedek's holding both offices, one of the ways in which he prefigured Christ. *Salem.* Jerusalem (see note on Ge 14:18).

7:2 *king of righteousness . . . king of peace.* Messianic titles (see Isa 9:6-7; Jer 23:5-6; 33:15-16).

7:3 *Without father . . . or end of life.* Ge 14:18-20, contrary to the practice elsewhere in the early chapters of Genesis, does not mention Melchizedek's parentage and children, or his birth and death. That he was a real, historical figure is clear, but the author of Hebrews (in accordance with Jewish interpretation) uses the silence of Scripture about Melchizedek's genealogy to portray him as a prefiguration of Christ. Melchizedek's priesthood anticipates Christ's eternal existence and his unending priesthood. Some believe the appearance of Melchizedek to Abraham was a manifestation of Christ before his incarnation, but the comparison "like the Son of God" argues against such an interpretation.

7:4 *think how great he was.* The one who collects a tithe is greater than the one who pays it, and "the lesser person is blessed by the greater" (v. 7). In both ways Melchizedek was greater than Abraham.

the plunder! *l* 5Now the law requires the descendants of Levi who become priests to collect a tenth from the people *m*—that is, their brothers—even though their brothers are descended from Abraham. 6This man, however, did not trace his descent from Levi, yet he collected a tenth from Abraham and blessed *n* him who had the promises. *o* 7And without doubt the lesser person is blessed by the greater. 8In the one case, the tenth is collected by men who die; but in the other case, by him who is declared to be living. *p* 9One might even say that Levi, who collects the tenth, paid the tenth through Abraham, 10because when Melchizedek met Abraham, Levi was still in the body of his ancestor.

Jesus Like Melchizedek

11If perfection could have been attained through the Levitical priesthood (for on the basis of it the law was given to the people), *q* why was there still need for another priest to come *r*—one in the order of Melchizedek, *s* not in the order of Aaron? 12For when there is a change of the priesthood, there must also be a change of the law. 13He of whom these things are said belonged to a different tribe, *t* and no one from that tribe has ever served at the altar. *u* 14For it is clear that our Lord descended from Judah, *v* and in regard to that tribe Moses said nothing about priests. 15And what we have said is even more clear if another priest like Melchizedek appears, 16one who has become a priest not on the basis of a regulation as to his ances-

try but on the basis of the power of an indestructible life. 17For it is declared:

"You are a priest forever,
   in the order of Melchizedek." *c* *w*

18The former regulation is set aside because it was weak and useless *x* 19(for the law made nothing perfect), *y* and a better hope *z* is introduced, by which we draw near to God. *a*

20And it was not without an oath! Others became priests without any oath, 21but he became a priest with an oath when God said to him:

"The Lord has sworn
   and will not change his mind: *b*
'You are a priest forever.' " *c* *c*

22Because of this oath, Jesus has become the guarantee of a better covenant. *d*

23Now there have been many of those priests, since death prevented them from continuing in office; 24but because Jesus lives forever, he has a permanent priesthood. *e* 25Therefore he is able to save *f* completely *d* those who come to God *g* through him, because he always lives to intercede for them. *h*

26Such a high priest *i* meets our need—one who is holy, blameless, pure, set apart from sinners, *j* exalted above the heavens. *k* 27Unlike the other high priests, he does not need to offer sacrifices *l* day after day, first for his own sins, *m* and then for the sins of the people. He sacrificed for

Cross references:
7:4 *l* Ge 14:20
7:5 *m* Nu 18:21, 26
7:6 *n* Ge 14:19,20
o Ro 4:13
7:8 *p* Heb 5:6; 6:20
7:11 *q* ver 18,19; Heb 8:7
r Heb 10:1 *s* ver 17; S Heb 5:6
7:13 *t* ver 11 *u* ver 14
7:14 *v* Isa 11:1; Mt 1:3; 2:6; Lk 3:33; Rev 5:5
7:17 *w* Ps 110:4; ver 21; S Heb 5:6
7:18 *x* Ro 8:3
7:19 *y* ver 11; Ro 3:20; 7:7,8; Gal 3:21; Heb 9:9; 10:1 *z* S Heb 3:6 *a* ver 25; Heb 4:16; 10:1,22; Jas 4:8
7:21 *b* Nu 23:19; 1Sa 15:29; Mal 3:6; Ro 11:29 *c* Ps 110:4; S Heb 5:6
7:22 *d* S Lk 22:20
7:24 *e* ver 28
7:25 *f* S Ro 11:14 *g* S ver 19 *h* S Ro 8:34
7:26 *i* S Heb 2:17 *j* 2Co 5:21 *k* S Heb 4:14
7:27 *l* Heb 5:1 *m* S Heb 5:3

c 17,21 Psalm 110:4   *d* 25 Or *forever*

7:11 *on the basis of it.* The Levitical priesthood. *the law was given.* The law of Moses and the priesthood went together. All the people without exception were sinners, subject to the law's condemnation, and thus were in need of a priestly system to mediate between them and God. *in the order of Melchizedek, not in the order of Aaron.* Implies that the Aaronic (or Levitical) priesthood was imperfect but that Melchizedek's was perfect. The announcement of the coming one who would be a priest forever (Ps 110:4) was written midway in the history of the Levitical priesthood, which could only mean that the existing system was to give way to something better.
7:16 *become a priest not on the basis of a regulation as to his ancestry.* In the law of Moses the priestly function was restricted to the tribe of Levi (Dt 18:1), but Jesus came from the nonpriestly tribe of Judah (vv. 14–15). *the power of an indestructible life.* According to Ps 110:4 the priest in the order of Melchizedek is "a priest forever."
7:18 *The former regulation . . . was weak and useless.* The law is holy and good (Ro 7:12), but it is not able to make right those who sin by breaking it, nor can it give the power necessary to fulfill its demands (v. 19a).
7:19 The law was only preparatory (see Gal 3:23–25) and brought nothing to fulfillment (see Mt 5:17). *better hope.* The new covenant is better because it assures us of complete redemption and brings us into the very presence of God. See

note on Col 1:5.
7:20 No divine oath was associated with the establishment of the Levitical priesthood. The priesthood pledged in Ps 110 is superior because it was divinely affirmed with an oath.
7:22 *better covenant.* See chs. 8–10.
7:23 *death prevented them from continuing in office.* Impermanence was further evidence of the imperfection of the Levitical order.
7:25 *completely.* May include the ideas of completeness and permanence (see NIV text note). Jesus is a perfect high priest forever; so he is able to save completely and for all time. *always lives to intercede.* His people will never be without a priestly representative (see Jn 17; 1Jn 2:1).
7:26 *meets our need.* Of salvation from sin and its consequences.
7:27 *day after day.* A reference to the endless repetition of sacrifices throughout the year (see Ex 29:36–42), evidence that these sacrifices never effectively and finally dealt with sin. *first for his own sins.* Christ's priesthood is superior because he has no personal sins for which sacrifice must be made. *once for all.* A key phrase in Hebrews (see 9:12,26; 10:2,10). The Levitical priests had to bring daily offerings to the Lord, whereas Jesus sacrificed himself once for all. *offered himself.* Levitical priests offered up only animals; our high priest offered himself, the perfect substitute—Man for man.

their sins once for all[n] when he offered himself.[o] 28For the law appoints as high priests men who are weak;[p] but the oath, which came after the law, appointed the Son,[q] who has been made perfect[r] forever.

The High Priest of a New Covenant

8 The point of what we are saying is this: We do have such a high priest,[s] who sat down at the right hand of the throne of the Majesty in heaven,[t] 2and who serves in the sanctuary, the true tabernacle[u] set up by the Lord, not by man.

3Every high priest[v] is appointed to offer both gifts and sacrifices,[w] and so it was necessary for this one also to have something to offer.[x] 4If he were on earth, he would not be a priest, for there are already men who offer the gifts prescribed by the law.[y] 5They serve at a sanctuary that is a copy[z] and shadow[a] of what is in heaven. This is why Moses was warned[b] when he was about to build the tabernacle: "See to it that you make everything according to the pattern shown you on the mountain."[e][c] 6But the ministry Jesus has received is as superior to theirs as the covenant[d] of which he is mediator[e] is superior to the old one, and it is founded on better promises.

7For if there had been nothing wrong with that first covenant, no place would have been sought for another.[f] 8But God found fault with the people and said[f]:

"The time is coming, declares the Lord,
　when I will make a new covenant[g]
with the house of Israel
　and with the house of Judah.
9It will not be like the covenant
　I made with their forefathers[h]
when I took them by the hand
　to lead them out of Egypt,
because they did not remain faithful to
　my covenant,
　and I turned away from them,
　　　　　　　　　declares the Lord.
10This is the covenant[i] I will make with
　the house of Israel
　after that time, declares the Lord.
I will put my laws in their minds
　and write them on their hearts.[j]
I will be their God,
　and they will be my people.[k]
11No longer will a man teach his
　neighbor,
　or a man his brother, saying, 'Know
　　the Lord,'
because they will all know me,[l]
　from the least of them to the greatest.
12For I will forgive their wickedness

Cross references (center column)

7:27 [n]Ro 6:10; Heb 9:12,26,28; 10:10; 1Pe 3:18 [o]Eph 5:2; Heb 9:14,28
7:28 [p]Heb 5:2 [q]S Heb 1:2 [r]S Heb 2:10
8:1 [s]S Heb 2:17 [t]S Mk 16:19; S Heb 4:14
8:2 [u]Heb 9:11,24
8:3 [v]S Heb 2:17 [w]Heb 5:1; 9:9 [x]Heb 9:14
8:4 [y]Heb 5:1; 9:9
8:5 [z]Heb 9:23 [a]Col 2:17; Heb 10:1 [b]Heb 11:7; 12:25 [c]Ex 25:40
8:6 [d]ver 8,13; S Lk 22:20 [e]S Gal 3:20
8:7 [f]Heb 7:11,18; 10:1
8:8 [g]ver 6,13; S Lk 22:20
8:9 [h]Ex 19:5,6; 20:1-17
8:10 [i]Ro 11:27 [j]2Co 3:3; Heb 10:16 [k]Eze 11:20; Zec 8:8
8:11 [l]Isa 54:13; S Jn 6:45

[e]5 Exodus 25:40　[f]8 Some manuscripts may be translated fault and said to the people.

7:28 *men who are weak.* Because (1) they are mortal and therefore impermanent, v. 23; (2) they are sinful, v. 27; and (3) they could only offer animals, which could never provide a genuine substitute for man, who is made in the image of God (see Ge 1:26–28 and notes). *made perfect forever.* Christ was made perfect in that he faced temptation without succumbing to sin (see notes on 2:10; 5:8). Instead he perfectly obeyed the Father, thereby establishing a perfection that is eternal.

8:1–10:39 The argument of this section grows out of an exposition of Jer 31:31–34 and demonstrates that Christ is the mediator of a "better covenant" (7:22).

8:1 See note on 1:2–3. *the Majesty in heaven.* A Jewish expression for God (see 1:3).

8:2 *true tabernacle.* In contrast to the tabernacle erected by Moses, which was an imperfect and impermanent copy of the heavenly one. *set up by the Lord, not by man.* The heavenly sanctuary built by God corresponds to the Most Holy Place, the innermost sanctuary in Moses' tabernacle, into which the high priest briefly entered with the blood of atonement once a year (see Lev 16:13–15,34). In the heavenly sanctuary, however, our great high priest dwells eternally as our intercessor (7:25).

8:3 *gifts and sacrifices.* See note on 5:1.

8:4 *he would not be a priest.* By his human birth Jesus belonged to the tribe of Judah, which was not the priestly tribe (see 7:12–14). *men who offer the gifts.* Members of the tribe of Levi. The present tense of the verb "offer," here and elsewhere in the letter, indicates that the temple in Jerusalem was still standing. This letter, therefore, must have been

written prior to the temple's destruction in A.D. 70 (see Introduction: Date).

8:5 *a copy and shadow of what is in heaven.* The heavenly reality is the sanctuary of God's presence, into which Christ our high priest entered with his own blood (see 9:11–12). *make everything according to the pattern.* Because both the tabernacle and its ministry were intended to illustrate symbolically the only way sinners may approach a holy God and find forgiveness.

8:6 *the covenant of which he is mediator is superior.* See 9:15; 12:24; 1Ti 2:5. The new covenant (see vv. 8–12; Jer 31:31–34) that Jesus mediates is superior to the covenant God made through Moses at Sinai (see Ex 24:7–8). *founded on better promises.* See vv. 10–12.

8:7 *if there had been nothing wrong with that first covenant.* The line of argument here is similar to that in 7:11, where the Levitical priestly order is shown to be inferior because it was replaced by the order of Melchizedek. Similarly, if the Mosaic covenant were without defect, there would have been no need to replace it with a new covenant. Concerning the fact that there was nothing essentially "wrong" with the Mosaic covenant see note on 7:18.

8:8–12 A quotation from Jer 31:31–34 containing a prophetic announcement and definition of the new covenant, which was to be different from the Mosaic covenant (v. 9). Its superior benefits are: (1) God's laws will become inner principles (v. 10a) that enable his people to delight in doing his will (cf. Eze 36:26–27; Ro 8:2–4); (2) God and his people will have intimate fellowship (v. 10b); (3) sinful ignorance of God will be removed forever (v. 11); and (4) forgiveness of sins will be an everlasting reality (v. 12).

and will remember their sins no more. [m] [g] [n]

[13] By calling this covenant "new," [o] he has made the first one obsolete; [p] and what is obsolete and aging will soon disappear.

Worship in the Earthly Tabernacle

9 Now the first covenant had regulations for worship and also an earthly sanctuary. [q] [2] A tabernacle [r] was set up. In its first room were the lampstand, [s] the table [t] and the consecrated bread; [u] this was called the Holy Place. [v] [3] Behind the second curtain was a room called the Most Holy Place, [w] [4] which had the golden altar of incense [x] and the gold-covered ark of the covenant. [y] This ark contained the gold jar of manna, [z] Aaron's staff that had budded, [a] and the stone tablets of the covenant. [b] [5] Above were the cherubim of the Glory, [c] overshadowing the atonement cover. [h] [d] But we cannot discuss these things in detail now.

[6] When everything had been arranged like this, the priests entered regularly [e] into the outer room to carry on their ministry. [7] But only the high priest entered [f] the inner room, [g] and that only once a year, [h] and never without blood, [i] which he offered for himself [j] and for the sins the people had committed in ignorance. [k] [8] The Holy Spirit was showing [l] by this that the way [m] into the Most Holy Place had not yet been disclosed as long as the first tabernacle was still standing. [9] This is an illustration [n] for the present time, indicating that the gifts and sacrifices being offered [o] were not able to clear the conscience [p] of the worshiper. [10] They are only a matter of food [q] and drink [r] and various ceremonial washings [s]—external regulations [t] applying until the time of the new order.

The Blood of Christ

[11] When Christ came as high priest [u] of the good things that are already here, [i] [v] he went through the greater and more perfect tabernacle [w] that is not man-made, [x] that is to say, not a part of this creation. [12] He did not enter by means of the blood of goats and calves; [y] but he entered the Most Holy Place [z] once for all [a] by his own blood, [b] having obtained eternal redemption. [13] The blood of goats and bulls [c] and the ashes of a heifer [d] sprinkled on those who are ceremonially unclean sanctify them so that they are outwardly clean. [14] How much more, then, will the blood of

Cross references (center column)

8:12 [m]Heb 10:17
[n]Jer 31:31-34
8:13 over 6,8;
S Lk 22:20
[p]2Co 5:17
9:1 [q]Ex 25:8
9:2 [r]Ex 25:8,9
[s]Ex 25:31-39
[t]Ex 25:23-29
[u]Ex 25:30;
Lev 24:5-8
[v]Ex 26:33,34
9:3
[w]Ex 26:31-33
9:4 [x]Ex 30:1-5
[y]Ex 25:10-22
[z]Ex 16:32,33
[a]Nu 17:10
[b]Ex 31:18; 32:15
9:5 [c]Ex 25:17-19
[d]Ex 25:20-22;
26:34
9:6 [e]Nu 28:3
9:7
[f]Lev 16:11-19
[g]ver 2,3
[h]Lev 16:34
[i]Lev 16:11,14
[j]Lev 16:11;
Heb 5:2,3

[k]Heb 5:2,3
9:8 [l]S Heb 3:7
[m]Jn 14:6;
Heb 10:19,20
9:9 [n]Heb 10:1
[o]Heb 5:1; 8:3
[p]S Heb 7:19
9:10
[q]Lev 11:2-23
[r]Nu 6:3; Col 2:16
[s]Lev 11:25,28,40
[t]Heb 7:16
9:11 [u]S Heb 2:17
[v]Heb 10:1 [w]ver 24; Heb 8:2
[x]S Jn 2:19
9:12 [y]ver 19;
Lev 16:6,15;
Heb 10:4 [z]ver 24
[a]ver 26,28;

S Heb 7:27 [b]ver 14; S Ro 3:25 9:13 [c]Heb 10:4 [d]Nu 19:9,17, 18

[g]12 Jer. 31:31-34   [h]5 Traditionally the mercy seat
[i]11 Some early manuscripts are to come

Study notes

8:13 *obsolete and aging.* The announcement of the new covenant clearly proved the impermanence of the one already in existence. To return to the old system would be to return to what is no longer valid or effective.

9:2 *A tabernacle was set up.* The tabernacle built under Moses. *lampstand.* Made of hammered gold and placed at the south side of the Holy Place (Ex 40:24), it had seven lamps that were kept burning every night (Ex 25:31–40). *the table and the consecrated bread.* Made of acacia wood overlaid with gold, it stood on the north side of the Holy Place (Ex 40:22). On it were twelve loaves, arranged in two rows of six (Lev 24:5–6).

9:4 *which had the golden altar of incense.* Although the altar of incense stood in the Holy Place, the author describes it as belonging to the Most Holy Place. His purpose was to show its close relationship to the inner sanctuary and the ark of the covenant (cf. Ex 40:5; 1Ki 6:22). On the Day of Atonement the high priest took incense from this altar, along with the blood of the sin offering, into the Most Holy Place (Lev 16:12–14). *ark of the covenant.* A chest made of acacia wood, overlaid inside and out with gold (Ex 25:10–16). *manna . . . staff . . . tablets.* See notes on Ex 16:33–34; see also Nu 17:8–10.

9:5 *cherubim of the Glory.* Two winged figures made of pure gold, of one piece with the atonement cover, or mercy seat, and standing at either end of it. It was between them that the glory of God's presence appeared (Ex 25:17–22; Lev 16:2; Nu 7:89). *atonement cover.* Fitting exactly over the top of the ark of the covenant, it was a slab of pure gold on which the blood of the sin offering was sprinkled by the high priest on the Day of Atonement (Lev 16:14–15).

9:7 *only once a year.* On the Day of Atonement (*Yom Kippur*), the tenth day of the seventh month (Lev 16:29,34). For a description of its ritual see Lev 16 and notes.
9:8 *as long as the first tabernacle was still standing.* As long as the Mosaic system with its imperfect priesthood and sacrifice remained in effect (8:7–8,13).
9:9 *an illustration for the present time.* The Mosaic tabernacle, though superseded, still provided instruction through its typical (symbolic) significance and was a reminder that returning to the old order was useless, since it could not deal effectively with sin. *gifts and sacrifices.* See note on 5:1.
9:10 *the new order.* The new covenant, with its new priesthood, new sanctuary and new sacrifice, all introduced by Christ.
9:11 *not part of this creation.* It was not an earthly tabernacle, but the heavenly sanctuary of God's presence (v. 24; 8:2).
9:12 *he entered . . . once for all.* Not repeatedly year after year as did the Levitical high priests. Christ's sacrifice was perfect, because it was completely effective and did not need to be repeated. After he had obtained eternal redemption, Christ ascended into the true heavenly sanctuary.
9:13 *blood of goats and bulls.* As on the Day of Atonement. *ashes of a heifer.* As prescribed in Nu 19 for those who became ceremonially unclean as a result of contact with a corpse. *outwardly clean.* Such sprinkling, since it was only external, could not cleanse a person from sin.
9:14 *offered himself.* He was the one who offered the sacrifice, and he was the sacrifice itself. *unblemished.* In the entirety of Christ's being, not just superficially. *cleanse our consciences.* Remove sin's defilement from the very core of our beings.

Christ, who through the eternal Spirit[e] of-fered himself[f] unblemished to God, cleanse our consciences[g] from acts that lead to death,[j][h] so that we may serve the living God![i]

[15]For this reason Christ is the mediator[j] of a new covenant,[k] that those who are called[l] may receive the promised[m] eternal inheritance[n]—now that he has died as a ransom to set them free from the sins com-mitted under the first covenant.[o]

[16]In the case of a will,[k] it is necessary to prove the death of the one who made it, [17]because a will is in force only when somebody has died; it never takes effect while the one who made it is living. [18]This is why even the first covenant was not put into effect without blood.[p] [19]When Moses had proclaimed[q] every commandment of the law to all the people, he took the blood of calves,[r] together with water, scarlet wool and branches of hyssop, and sprin-kled the scroll and all the people.[s] [20]He said, "This is the blood of the covenant, which God has commanded you to keep."[t] [21]In the same way, he sprinkled with the blood both the tabernacle and everything used in its ceremonies. [22]In fact, the law requires that nearly every-thing be cleansed with blood,[u] and with-out the shedding of blood there is no for-giveness.[v]

[23]It was necessary, then, for the copies[w] of the heavenly things to be purified with these sacrifices, but the heavenly things themselves with better sacrifices than

these. [24]For Christ did not enter a man-made sanctuary that was only a copy of the true one;[x] he entered heaven itself,[y] now to appear for us in God's presence.[z] [25]Nor did he enter heaven to offer himself again and again, the way the high priest enters the Most Holy Place[a] every year with blood that is not his own.[b] [26]Then Christ would have had to suffer many times since the creation of the world.[c] But now he has appeared[d] once for all[e] at the end of the ages to do away with sin by the sacrifice of himself.[f] [27]Just as man is destined to die once,[g] and after that to face judgment,[h] [28]so Christ was sacrificed once[i] to take away the sins of many people; and he will appear a second time,[j] not to bear sin,[k] but to bring salvation[l] to those who are waiting for him.[m]

Christ's Sacrifice Once for All

10 The law is only a shadow[n] of the good things[o] that are coming—not the realities themselves.[p] For this reason it can never, by the same sacrifices repeated endlessly year after year, make perfect[q] those who draw near to worship.[r] [2]If it could, would they not have stopped being offered? For the worshipers would have been cleansed once for all, and would no longer have felt guilty for their sins.[s] [3]But those sacrifices are an annual reminder of sins,[t] [4]because it is impossible for the

Cross references (center column)

9:14 [e]1Pe 3:18; /S Eph 5:2
[f]Ps 51:2; 65:3; Jer 33:8; Zec 13:1; S Tit 2:14; Heb 10:2,22
[h]Heb 6:1
[i]S Mt 16:16
9:15 /S Gal 3:20
[k]S Lk 22:20
/S Ro 8:28; S 11:29
[m]Heb 6:15; 10:36
[n]S Ac 20:32
[o]Heb 7:22
9:18 [p]Ex 24:6-8
9:19 [q]Heb 1:1
[r]ver 12
[s]Ex 24:6-8
9:20 [t]Ex 24:8; S Mt 26:28
9:22 [u]Ex 29:21; Lev 8:15
[v]Lev 17:11
9:23 [w]Heb 8:5

9:24 [x]Heb 8:2
[y]ver 12; S Heb 4:14
[z]S Ro 8:34
9:25 [a]Heb 10:19
[b]ver 7,8
9:26 [c]Heb 4:3
[d]1Jn 3:5 [e]ver 12, 28; S Heb 7:27
[f]ver 12
9:27 [g]Ge 3:19
[h]2Co 5:10
9:28 [i]ver 12,26; S Heb 7:27
/S Mt 16:27
[k]1Pe 2:24
/Heb 5:9
[m]S 1Co 1:7
10:1 [n]Col 2:17; Heb 8:5
[o]Heb 9:11
[p]Heb 9:23 [q]ver 4, 11; S Heb 7:19
[r]S Heb 7:19
10:2 [s]Heb 9:9
10:3 [t]Lev 16:34; Heb 9:7

[i]14 Or from useless rituals   [k]16 Same Greek word as covenant; also in verse 17   [l]20 Exodus 24:8

9:15 *mediator.* See 8:6 and note; 12:24; 1Ti 2:5. *new covenant.* See 7:22; 8:6,13. *the promised eternal inheri-tance.* Defined in the passage from Jeremiah (31:31–34) quoted in 8:8–12. On the basis of Christ's atoning death, this inheritance has become real for those who are called by God (cf. Ro 8:28). *as a ransom.* See Mk 10:45 and note. By shedding his blood, he paid the necessary price to set them free from the sins committed under the first covenant, i.e., violations of Mosaic law.

9:16 *will.* Translates the same Greek word as that for "covenant" (v. 15), but here and in v. 17 used in the sense of a last will and testament. (Verse 18 returns to the concept of covenant.) Beneficiaries have no claim on the benefits assigned to them in a will until the testator dies (v. 17). Since Christ's death has been duly attested, "the promised eternal inheritance" (v. 15) is available to his beneficiaries.

9:18 *without blood.* Without death—the death of the calves from which Moses took blood to seal the old cov-enant.

9:19–20 For the ceremony referred to here see Ex 24:4–8.

9:23 *See, e.g., Lev 8:10,19,30.*

9:23 *copies of the heavenly things.* See 8:5. Whereas it was necessary for the earthly sanctuary to be purified with animal sacrifices, it was necessary for the heavenly sanctuary to be purified with the better sacrifice of Christ himself.

9:24 *now to appear for us in God's presence.* See 7:25; 1Jn 2:1.

9:26 *end of the ages.* His coming has ushered in the great Messianic era, toward which all history has moved (see note on 1:1; cf. 1Pe 1:20).

9:27 *destined to die once, and after that to face judgment.* As in the natural order man dies once (as a consequence of sin, Ro 5:12), so Christ died once as the perfect sacrifice for sin (v. 28). And as, after death, man faces judgment, so Christ, after his death, will appear again, bringing salvation (see next note) from sin and its judgment.

9:28 *to bring salvation.* The consummation, in all its glori-ous fullness, of the salvation purchased for us on the cross (see Ro 8:29–30; Php 3:20–21; 1Jn 3:2–3). *waiting for him.* As the Israelites waited for the high priest while he was in the Most Holy Place on the Day of Atonement (see 2Ti 4:8; Tit 2:13).

10:1 *The law.* Together with the Levitical priesthood to which it was closely linked under the Mosaic system (see note on 7:11). *only a shadow.* The sacrifices prescribed by the law prefigured Christ's ultimate sacrifice. Thus they were repeated year after year, the very repetition bearing testi-mony that the perfect, sin-removing sacrifice had not yet been offered.

10:4 *impossible for the blood of bulls and goats to take away sins.* An animal cannot possibly be a completely ade-quate substitute for a human being, who is made in God's image.

blood of bulls and goats[u] to take away sins. [v]

5Therefore, when Christ came into the world, [w] he said:

"Sacrifice and offering you did not
   desire,
but a body you prepared for me; [x]
6with burnt offerings and sin offerings
   you were not pleased.
7Then I said, 'Here I am—it is written
   about me in the scroll [y] —
I have come to do your will,
   O God.' " [m] [z]

8First he said, "Sacrifices and offerings, burnt offerings and sin offerings you did not desire, nor were you pleased with them" [a] (although the law required them to be made). 9Then he said, "Here I am, I have come to do your will." [b] He sets aside the first to establish the second. 10And by that will, we have been made holy [c] through the sacrifice of the body [d] of Jesus Christ once for all. [e]

11Day after day every priest stands and performs his religious duties; again and again he offers the same sacrifices, [f] which can never take away sins. [g] 12But when this priest had offered for all time one sacrifice for sins, [h] he sat down at the right hand of God. [i] 13Since that time he waits

for his enemies to be made his footstool, [j] 14because by one sacrifice he has made perfect [k] forever those who are being made holy. [l]

15The Holy Spirit also testifies [m] to us about this. First he says:

16"This is the covenant I will make with
   them
   after that time, says the Lord.
I will put my laws in their hearts,
   and I will write them on their
      minds." [n] [n]

17Then he adds:

"Their sins and lawless acts
   I will remember no more." [o] [o]

18And where these have been forgiven, there is no longer any sacrifice for sin.

A Call to Persevere

19Therefore, brothers, since we have confidence [p] to enter the Most Holy Place [q] by the blood of Jesus, 20by a new and living way [r] opened for us through the curtain, [s] that is, his body, 21and since we have a great priest [t] over the house of God, [u] 22let us draw near to God [v] with a sincere heart in full assurance of faith, [w]

Cross references

10:4 [u]Heb 9:12, 13 [v]ver 1,11
10:5 [w]Heb 1:6 [x]Heb 2:14; 1Pe 2:24
10:7 [y]Ezr 6:2; Jer 36:2 [z]Ps 40:6-8; S Mt 26:39
10:8 [a]ver 5,6; S Mk 12:33
10:9 [b]ver 7
10:10 [c]ver 14; S Eph 5:26 [d]Heb 2:14; 1Pe 2:24 [e]S Heb 7:27
10:11 [f]Heb 5:1 [g]ver 1,4
10:12 [h]Heb 5:1 [i]S Mk 16:19
10:13 [j]Jos 10:24; Heb 1:13
10:14 [k]ver 1 [l]ver 10; S Eph 5:26
10:15 [m]S Heb 3:7
10:16 [n]Jer 31:33; Heb 8:10
10:17 [o]Jer 31:34; Heb 8:12
10:19 [p]S Eph 3:12
10:20 [q]Lev 16:2; Eph 2:18; Heb 9:8,12,25 [r]Heb 9:8 [s]Heb 6:19; 9:3
10:21 [t]S Heb 2:17 [u]S Heb 3:6
10:22 [v]ver 1; S Heb 7:19 [w]Eph 3:12

m 7 Psalm 40:6-8 (see Septuagint) n 16 Jer. 31:33
o 17 Jer. 31:34

10:5–6 The different terms used for Levitical sacrifices represent four of the five types of offerings prescribed by the Mosaic Law (Lev 1–7), namely, fellowship, grain, burnt and sin.

10:5 *when Christ came into the world, he said.* The words of this psalm of David (40:6–8) express Christ's obedient submission to the Father in coming to earth. The Mosaic sacrifices are replaced by submissive obedience to the will of God (v. 7).

10:6 *you were not pleased.* These offerings were only preparatory and temporary, looking forward to the one perfect and final offering—that of the incarnate Son of God.

10:7 *to do your will.* The will of the Father was the Son's consuming concern (see Lk 22:42; Jn 4:34).

10:9 *He sets aside the first to establish the second.* His perfect sacrifice, offered in complete submission, supersedes and therefore replaces all previous sacrifices.

10:10 *made holy.* Justified, set aside in consecration to God, and now experiencing the process of continuing sanctification (see "being made holy," v. 14; see also note on 1Co 1:2).

10:11–14 A contrast between "standing" and "sitting." The Levitical priest always stood, because his work was never finished.

10:11 *offers the same sacrifices.* Because these sacrifices were unable to accomplish what they signified. They could not remove sin, and thus had to be offered over and over again.

10:12 *he sat down at the right hand of God.* In contrast to the work of the Levitical priests, which was never done (v. 11; see notes on 1:3,13), Christ's work was completed. His one sacrifice atoned for all sins of all time, making any further sacrifice unnecessary (v. 14).

10:15–18 The two quotations included in these verses are from Jer 31:31–34 (already cited in 8:8–12). The new covenant guarantees that sins will be effectively and completely forgiven (v. 17), with the result that no additional sacrifice for sins is needed (v. 18).

10:19 Another section of practical application and exhortation begins here (see note on 2:1–4). *confidence to enter the Most Holy Place.* The way into the sanctuary of God's presence was closed to the people under the former covenant because the blood of animal sacrifices could never completely atone for their sins. Now, however, believers can come to the throne of grace since the perfect priest has offered the perfect sacrifice, atoning for sin once for all.

10:20 *the curtain, that is, his body.* When Jesus died, the curtain separating the Holy Place from the Most Holy Place was "torn in two from top to bottom" (Mk 15:38). The curtain symbolizes the body of Christ in terms of suffering: Like the curtain, his body was torn to open the way into the divine presence.

10:22–25 Five exhortations spring from Jesus' provision for our reconciliation to his Father: 1. "Let us draw near to God." 2. "Let us hold unswervingly to . . . hope." 3. "Let us consider how we may spur one another on." 4. "Let us not give up meeting together." 5. "Let us encourage one another."

10:22 Four conditions are given for drawing "near to God": 1. *a sincere heart.* Undivided allegiance in the inner being. 2. *full assurance of faith.* Faith that knows no hesitation in trusting in and following Christ. 3. *hearts sprinkled . . . from a guilty conscience.* Total freedom from a sense of guilt, a freedom based on the once-for-all sacrifice of Christ. 4. *bodies washed with pure water.* Not an external ceremony such as baptism but a figure for inner cleansing, of which

having our hearts sprinkled to cleanse us from a guilty conscience[x] and having our bodies washed with pure water.[y] 23Let us hold unswervingly to the hope[z] we profess,[a] for he who promised is faithful.[b] 24And let us consider how we may spur one another on toward love and good deeds.[c] 25Let us not give up meeting together,[d] as some are in the habit of doing, but let us encourage one another[e]—and all the more as you see the Day approaching.[f]

26If we deliberately keep on sinning[g] after we have received the knowledge of the truth,[h] no sacrifice for sins is left, 27but only a fearful expectation of judgment and of raging fire[i] that will consume the enemies of God. 28Anyone who rejected the law of Moses died without mercy on the testimony of two or three witnesses.[j] 29How much more severely do you think a man deserves to be punished who has trampled the Son of God[k] under foot,[l] who has treated as an unholy thing the blood of the covenant[m] that sanctified him,[n] and who has insulted the Spirit[o] of grace?[p] 30For we know him who said, "It is mine to avenge; I will repay,"[p q] and again, "The Lord will judge his people."[q r] 31It is a dreadful thing[s] to fall into the hands[t] of the living God.[u]

32Remember those earlier days after you had received the light,[v] when you stood your ground in a great contest in the face of suffering.[w] 33Sometimes you were publicly exposed to insult and persecution;[x] at other times you stood side by side with those who were so treated.[y] 34You sympathized with those in prison[z] and joyfully accepted the confiscation of your property, because you knew that you yourselves had better and lasting possessions.[a]

35So do not throw away your confidence;[b] it will be richly rewarded. 36You need to persevere[c] so that when you have done the will of God, you will receive what he has promised.[d] 37For in just a very little while,

"He who is coming[e] will come and will
    not delay.[f]
38 But my righteous one[r] will live by
      faith.[g]
And if he shrinks back,
    I will not be pleased with him."[s h]

39But we are not of those who shrink back and are destroyed, but of those who believe and are saved.

By Faith

11 Now faith is being sure of what we hope for[i] and certain of what we do not see.[j] 2This is what the ancients were commended for.[k]

3By faith we understand that the universe was formed at God's command,[l] so that what is seen was not made out of what was visible.

4By faith Abel offered God a better sacri-

Cross references

10:22
x Eze 36:25;
Heb 9:14; 12:24;
1Pe 1:2
y S Ac 22:16
10:23 z S Heb 3:6
a S Heb 3:1
b S 1Co 1:9
10:24 c S Tit 2:14
10:25 d Ac 2:42
e Heb 3:13
f S 1Co 3:13
10:26 g Ex 21:14;
Nu 15:30;
Heb 5:2; 6:4-8;
2Pe 2:20
h S 1Ti 2:4
10:27 i Isa 26:11;
2Th 1:7;
Heb 9:27; 12:29
10:28 j Dt 17:6,7;
S Mt 18:16;
Heb 2:2
10:29 k S Mt 4:3
l Heb 6:6
m S Mt 26:28
n 1Co 6:11;
Rev 1:5
o Eph 4:30;
Heb 6:4
p Heb 2:3; 12:25
10:30 q Dt 32:35;
Ro 12:19
r Dt 32:36;
Ps 135:14
10:31
s 2Co 5:11
t Isa 19:16
u S Mt 16:16
10:32 v Heb 6:4
w Php 1:29,30
10:33 x 1Co 4:9

y Php 4:14;
1Th 2:14
10:34 z Heb 13:3
a Heb 11:16;
1Pe 1:4,5
10:35
b S Eph 3:12
10:36 c Ro 5:3;
Heb 12:1; Jas 1:3,
4,12; 5:11;
2Pe 1:6
d Heb 6:15; 9:15
10:37 e Mt 11:3
f Rev 22:20
10:38 g Ro 1:17;
Gal 3:11

h Hab 2:3,4 11:1 i S Heb 3:6 /S 2Co 4:18 11:2 k ver 4,39 11:3 l Ge 1; Jn 1:3; Heb 1:2; 2Pe 3:5

p 30 Deut. 32:35   q 30 Deut. 32:36; Psalm 135:14
r 38 One early manuscript But the righteous   s 38 Hab. 2:3,4

---

the washing of the priests under the old covenant was a symbol (see Ex 30:19–21; Lev 8:6; see also Eze 36:25, where a similar expression is used figuratively for the cleansing resulting from the new covenant).

10:23 *unswervingly.* Without doubt or hesitation. Some of the readers were tempted to give up the struggle and turn back to a form of Judaism. *the hope we profess.* See 6:18–20. *he who promised is faithful.* Cf. 2Ti 2:13.

10:25 *not give up meeting together.* The Greek word translated "give up" speaks of desertion and abandonment (see Mt 27:46; 2Co 4:9; 2Ti 4:10,16). *the Day.* Of the Lord's return (see 1Th 5:2,4; 2Th 1:10; 2:2; 2Pe 3:10).

10:26–31 That these verses are a warning to persons ("some," v. 25) deserting the Christian assembly is apparent from the Greek word *gar* ("for") at the beginning of v. 26. See notes on 6:4–8, where the same spiritual condition is discussed.

10:26 *deliberately keep on sinning.* Committing the sin of apostasy (see v. 29; see also note on 5:2). The OT background is Nu 15:27–31. *no sacrifice for sins is left.* To reject Christ's sacrifice for sins is to reject the only sacrifice; there is no other.

10:27 *judgment and . . . raging fire.* See 2Th 1:6–9.

10:28 See Dt 17:2–7.

10:29 *blood of the covenant.* See 9:20; 13:20; Ex 24:8; Mt 26:28; Mk 14:24.

10:31 See 12:29.

10:32 *those earlier days.* Presumably following their first enthusiastic response to the gospel, when they had unflinchingly suffered loss and persecution and were deeply concerned for each other.

10:34 *better and lasting possessions.* Such as salvation in Christ and future reward (11:10,13–16,26,35; 13:14; Mt 5:11–12; 6:19–21; Ro 8:18).

10:38 *my righteous one will live by faith.* See note on Hab 2:4.

10:39 *shrink back and are destroyed.* The opposite of "believe and are saved." The author is confident that those to whom he is writing are, for the most part, among the saved (see note on 6:9).

11:1–12:29 Exhortations based on the preceding expositions of OT passages.

11:2 *the ancients.* Heroes of faith in the pre-Christian era, such as those listed in this chapter.

11:4 See Ge 4:2–5. *commended as a righteous man.* Both brothers brought offerings to the Lord: Cain from the fruits of the soil, and Abel from the firstborn of his flock. The chief reason for the acceptance of Abel's sacrifice was that he offered it "by faith." It is implied that Cain's sacrifice was rejected because he offered it without faith, as a mere formality (see note on Ge 4:3–4).

fice than Cain did. By faith he was commended *m* as a righteous man, when God spoke well of his offerings. *n* And by faith he still speaks, even though he is dead. *o*

5By faith Enoch was taken from this life, so that he did not experience death; he could not be found, because God had taken him away. *p* For before he was taken, he was commended as one who pleased God. 6And without faith it is impossible to please God, because anyone who comes to him *q* must believe that he exists and that he rewards those who earnestly seek him.

7By faith Noah, when warned about things not yet seen, *r* in holy fear built an ark *s* to save his family. *t* By his faith he condemned the world and became heir of the righteousness that comes by faith. *u*

8By faith Abraham, when called to go to a place he would later receive as his inheritance, *v* obeyed and went, *w* even though he did not know where he was going. 9By faith he made his home in the promised land *x* like a stranger in a foreign country; he lived in tents, *y* as did Isaac and Jacob, who were heirs with him of the same promise. *z* 10For he was looking forward to the city *a* with foundations, *b* whose architect and builder is God. *c*

11By faith Abraham, even though he was past age—and Sarah herself was barren *d*—was enabled to become a father *e* because he *t* considered him faithful *f* who had made the promise. 12And so from this one man, and he as good as dead, *g* came descendants as numerous as the stars in

the sky and as countless as the sand on the seashore. *h*

13All these people were still living by faith when they died. They did not receive the things promised; *i* they only saw them and welcomed them from a distance. *j* And they admitted that they were aliens and strangers on earth. *k* 14People who say such things show that they are looking for a country of their own. 15If they had been thinking of the country they had left, they would have had opportunity to return. *l* 16Instead, they were longing for a better country—a heavenly one. *m* Therefore God is not ashamed *n* to be called their God, *o* for he has prepared a city *p* for them.

17By faith Abraham, when God tested him, offered Isaac as a sacrifice. *q* He who had received the promises was about to sacrifice his one and only son, 18even though God had said to him, "It is through Isaac that your offspring *u* will be reckoned." *v r* 19Abraham reasoned that God could raise the dead, *s* and figuratively speaking, he did receive Isaac back from death.

20By faith Isaac blessed Jacob and Esau in regard to their future. *t*

21By faith Jacob, when he was dying, blessed each of Joseph's sons, *u* and worshiped as he leaned on the top of his staff.

22By faith Joseph, when his end was near, spoke about the exodus of the Israel-

---

11:4 *m*ver 2,39
*n*Ge 4:4; 1Jn 3:12
*o*Heb 12:24
11:5 *p*Ge 5:21-24
11:6 *q*Heb 7:19
11:7 *r*S ver 1
*s*Ge 6:13-22
*t*1Pe 3:20
*u*Ge 6:9;
Eze 14:14,20;
S Ro 9:30
11:8 *v*Ge 12:7
*w*Ge 12:1-4;
Ac 7:2-4
11:9 *x*Ac 7:5
*y*Ge 12:8; 18:1,9
*z*Heb 6:17
11:10
*a*Heb 12:22;
13:14 *b*Rev 21:2,
14 *c*ver 16
11:11
*d*Ge 17:17-19;
18:11-14
*e*Ge 21:2
*f*S 1Co 1:9
11:12 *g*Ro 4:19

*h*Ge 22:17
11:13 *i*ver 39
*j*S Mt 13:17
*k*Ge 23:4;
Lev 25:23;
Php 3:20;
1Pe 1:17; 2:11
11:15 *l*Ge 24:6-8
11:16 *m*2Ti 4:18
*n*Mk 8:38
*o*Ge 26:24;
28:13; Ex 3:6,15
*p*ver 10;
Heb 13:14
11:17
*q*Ge 22:1-10;
Jas 2:21
11:18 *r*Ge 21:12;
Ro 9:7
11:19 *s*Ro 4:21;
S Jn 5:21
11:20
*t*Ge 27:27-29,39,
40
11:21 *u*Ge 48:1,
8-22

---

*t*11 Or *By faith even Sarah, who was past age, was enabled to bear children because she*   *u*18 Greek *seed*
*v*18 Gen. 21:12

11:5 *Enoch.* See Ge 5:18–24. *taken him away.* To God's presence (see note on Ge 5:24; cf. Ps 49:15; 73:24).
11:6 *without faith it is impossible to please God.* That Enoch pleased God is proof of his faith. *believe that he exists.* Faith must have an object, and the proper object of genuine faith is God. *who earnestly seek him.* See Jer 29:13.
11:7 *Noah.* See Ge 5:28–9:29. *By his faith.* When the flood came, God's word was proved to be true, Noah's faith was vindicated, and the world's unbelief was judged. *righteousness that comes by faith.* Noah expressed complete trust in God and his word, even when it related to "things not yet seen" (v. 1), namely, the coming flood. Thus Noah also fitted the description of God's righteous ones who live by faith (10:38). His faith in God's word moved him to build the ark in a dry, landlocked region where it was inconceivable that there would ever be enough water to float the vessel.
11:8 *Abraham.* Presented in the NT as the outstanding example of those who live "by faith" and as the "father of all who believe" (Ro 4:11–12,16; Gal 3:7,9,29). *called.* See Ge 12:1–3. His faith expressed itself in obedience (see note on Ge 12:4). *a place he would later receive.* Canaan. *did not know where he was going.* He did not go in blind faith, but in complete confidence in God's trustworthiness.
11:10 *city with foundations.* Speaks of permanence in contrast to the tents in which the patriarch lived (v. 9). This city is "the heavenly Jerusalem" (12:22), "the city that is to come" (13:14) and "the new Jerusalem" (Rev 21:2–4,

9–27). *builder.* Cf. Ps 147:2 and NIV text note on Isa 62:5.
11:11 *Sarah . . . was barren.* Probably referring to the fact that she was far past childbearing (Ge 18:11–12; see note on Ge 11:30).
11:12 *as good as dead.* Because he was 100 years old (see Ge 21:5; Ro 4:19). *stars in the sky . . . sand on the seashore.* See Ge 13:16 and note; 15:5; 22:17; 26:4; 1Ki 4:20.
11:13 *saw them and welcomed them from a distance.* By faith they saw—dimly—these heavenly realities and were sure that what they hoped for would ultimately be theirs (see v. 1). *aliens and strangers on earth.* Their true home was in heaven. *country of their own.* That better, heavenly country (v. 16).
11:16 *prepared a city for them.* City (v. 10) and country are interchangeable in the concluding chapters of this letter (vv. 9–10,14–16; 13:14). The ultimate reality is represented by the new Jerusalem in John's vision of the believer's eternal state (see Rev 21:2).
11:17 See Ge 22. *his one and only son.* See Ge 22:2,12, 16; Jn 3:16; Ro 8:32.
11:19 *God could raise the dead.* So strong was Abraham's faith that he actually believed that God would raise Isaac from the dead if necessary, an event that did occur figuratively when the substitute ram was provided (Ge 22:13).
11:20 See Ge 27:27–40.
11:21 See Ge 47:29–31; 48:8–20.
11:22 See Ge 50:24–25. Jacob (v. 21) and Joseph are

ites from Egypt and gave instructions about his bones. ᵛ

²³By faith Moses' parents hid him for three months after he was born, ʷ because they saw he was no ordinary child, and they were not afraid of the king's edict. ˣ

²⁴By faith Moses, when he had grown up, refused to be known as the son of Pharaoh's daughter. ʸ ²⁵He chose to be mistreated ᶻ along with the people of God rather than to enjoy the pleasures of sin for a short time. ²⁶He regarded disgrace ᵃ for the sake of Christ ᵇ as of greater value than the treasures of Egypt, because he was looking ahead to his reward. ᶜ ²⁷By faith he left Egypt, ᵈ not fearing the king's anger; he persevered because he saw him who is invisible. ²⁸By faith he kept the Passover and the sprinkling of blood, so that the destroyer ᵉ of the firstborn would not touch the firstborn of Israel. ᶠ

²⁹By faith the people passed through the Red Sea ʷ as on dry land; but when the Egyptians tried to do so, they were drowned. ᵍ

³⁰By faith the walls of Jericho fell, after the people had marched around them for seven days. ʰ

³¹By faith the prostitute Rahab, because she welcomed the spies, was not killed with those who were disobedient. ˣ ⁱ

³²And what more shall I say? I do not have time to tell about Gideon, ʲ Barak, ᵏ Samson, ˡ Jephthah, ᵐ David, ⁿ Samuel ᵒ and the prophets, ³³who through faith conquered kingdoms, ᵖ administered justice, and gained what was promised; who shut the mouths of lions, ۹ ³⁴quenched the fury of the flames, ʳ and escaped the edge of the sword; ˢ whose weakness was turned to strength; ᵗ and who became powerful in battle and routed foreign armies. ᵘ ³⁵Women received back their dead, raised to life again. ᵛ Others were tortured and refused to be released, so that they might gain a better resurrection. ³⁶Some faced jeers and flogging, ʷ while still others were chained and put in prison. ˣ ³⁷They were stoned ᵞ; ʸ they were sawed in two; they were put to death by the sword. ᶻ They went about in sheepskins and goatskins, ᵃ destitute, persecuted and mistreated—

11:22 ᵛGe 50:24, 25; Ex 13:19; Jos 24:32	
11:23 ʷEx 2:2 ˣEx 1:16,22	
11:24 ʸEx 2:10, 11	
11:25 ᶻver 37	
11:26 ᵃHeb 13:13 ᵇLk 14:33 ᶜHeb 10:35	
11:27 ᵈEx 12:50, 51	
11:28 ᵉ1Co 10:10 ᶠEx 12:21-23	
11:29 ᵍEx 14:21-31	
11:30 ʰJos 6:12-20	
11:31 ⁱJos 2:1, 9-14; 6:22-25; Jas 2:25	
11:32 ʲJdg 6-8 ᵏJdg 4-5 ˡJdg 13-16 ᵐJdg 11-12 ⁿ1Sa 16:1,13 ᵒ1Sa 1:20	
11:33 ᵖ2Sa 8:1-3 ۹Da 6:22	
11:34 ʳDa 3:19-27 ˢEx 18:4 ᵗ2Ki 20:7 ᵘJdg 15:8	
11:35 ᵛ1Ki 17:22,23; 2Ki 4:36,37	
11:36 ʷJer 20:2; 37:15 ˣGe 39:20	
11:37 ᵞ2Ch 24:21	

ᶻ1Ki 19:10; Jer 26:23 ᵃ2Ki 1:8

ʷ29 That is, Sea of Reeds   ˣ31 Or unbelieving
ᵞ37 Some early manuscripts stoned; they were put to the test;

---

additional examples of those whose faith is no less strong at death than in life (v. 13).

11:23–29 See Ac 7:20–44.

11:23 *Moses' parents.* See Ex 6:20; Nu 26:58–59. *no ordinary child.* See note on Ex 2:2. *the king's edict.* To kill all Israelite males at birth (Ex 1:16,22).

11:25 *pleasures of sin.* The luxury and prestige in Egypt's royal palace.

11:26 *for the sake of Christ.* Although Moses' understanding of the details of the Messianic hope was extremely limited, he chose to be associated with the people through whom that hope was to be realized. *treasures of Egypt.* The priceless treasures of King Tutankhamun's tomb alone included several thousand pounds of pure gold.

11:27 *By faith he left Egypt.* Probably referring to his flight to Midian in the Sinai peninsula when he was 40 years old (Ex 2:11–15; Ac 7:23–29). *not fearing the king's anger.* Exodus indicates that Moses was afraid (Ex 2:14) but does not expressly say of whom. And it tells us that he fled from Pharaoh when Pharaoh tried to kill him (Ex 2:15) but does not expressly say that he fled out of fear. The author of Hebrews capitalizes on these features of the account to highlight the fact that, in his fleeing from Pharaoh, Moses was sustained by his trust in God that the liberation of Israel would come and that he would have some part in it. *he persevered.* For 40 years in Midian (Ac 7:30). *saw him who is invisible.* See vv. 1,6.

11:28 See Ex 12.

11:29 See Ex 14–15. The third and final 40-year period of Moses' life was spent leading the Israelites through the desert. At the age of 120 years he died in Moab (Dt 34:1–7).

11:30 Moses' place as leader was taken by Joshua, who brought the people of Israel into the land of promise. *Jericho.* The first great obstacle to their conquest of the land was captured by faith without a battle (Jos 6).

11:31 *the prostitute Rahab.* A designation describing her

way of life prior to her newly found faith (Jos 2:8–11; 6:22–25); also a testimony to God's boundless grace that can reach down and redeem and raise any sinner to eternal dignity. *welcomed the spies.* See Jas 2:25.

11:32–38 There were many more heroes of faith before the coming of Christ, and much more could be written of them. Only a small sampling is given, representing all types of men and women of faith. The great quality they had in common was that of overcoming "through faith" (v. 33).

11:32 *to tell.* Translates the masculine form of a Greek verb, indicating that the author of Hebrews was a man (see Introduction: Author). *Gideon, Barak, Samson, Jephthah.* See Jdg 4:6–5:15; 6:11–8:35; 11:1–12:7; 13:24–16:31; 1Sa 12:11 and NIV text note there. *Samuel and the prophets.* See Ps 99:6; Jer 15:1; Ac 3:24; 13:20.

11:33 *mouths of lions.* Cf. Daniel in the lions' den (Da 6).

11:34 *quenched the fury of the flames.* Cf. Daniel's friends, Shadrach, Meshach and Abednego, in the fiery furnace (Da 3). *weakness was turned to strength.* Through God's help (see Ro 8:26; 2Co 12:9).

11:35 *Women received back their dead.* Cf. the widow of Zarephath (1Ki 17:17–24) and the Shunammite woman (2Ki 4:8–36). *were tortured and refused to be released, so that they might gain a better resurrection.* Strongly reminiscent of the heroic Maccabean Jewish patriots of the second century B.C. (see 2 Maccabees 7). But the description applies also to countless believers, known and unknown, who demonstrated their faith in God by persevering in the face of harsh trials and afflictions.

11:37 *They were stoned.* Men like Zechariah, the son of Jehoiada the priest, who were put to death for declaring the truth (2Ch 24:20–22; Lk 11:51). See also Introduction to Jeremiah: Author and Date. *sawed in two.* Perhaps refers to Isaiah, who, according to tradition, met this kind of death under wicked King Manasseh (see Introduction to Isaiah: Author).

38the world was not worthy of them. They wandered in deserts and mountains, and in caves *b* and holes in the ground.

39These were all commended *c* for their faith, yet none of them received what had been promised. *d* 40God had planned something better for us so that only together with us *e* would they be made perfect. *f*

God Disciplines His Sons

12 Therefore, since we are surrounded by such a great cloud of witnesses, let us throw off everything that hinders and the sin that so easily entangles, and let us run *g* with perseverance *h* the race marked out for us. 2Let us fix our eyes on Jesus, *i* the author *j* and perfecter of our faith, who for the joy set before him endured the cross, *k* scorning its shame, *l* and sat down at the right hand of the throne of God. *m* 3Consider him who endured such opposition from sinful men, so that you will not grow weary *n* and lose heart.

4In your struggle against sin, you have not yet resisted to the point of shedding your blood. *o* 5And you have forgotten that word of encouragement that addresses you as sons:

"My son, do not make light of the
  Lord's discipline,

and do not lose heart *p* when he
    rebukes you,
6because the Lord disciplines those he
    loves, *q*
and he punishes everyone he accepts
    as a son." *z r*

7Endure hardship as discipline; God is treating you as sons. *s* For what son is not disciplined by his father? 8If you are not disciplined (and everyone undergoes discipline), *t* then you are illegitimate children and not true sons. 9Moreover, we have all had human fathers who disciplined us and we respected them for it. How much more should we submit to the Father of our spirits *u* and live! *v* 10Our fathers disciplined us for a little while as they thought best; but God disciplines us for our good, that we may share in his holiness. *w* 11No discipline seems pleasant at the time, but painful. Later on, however, it produces a harvest of righteousness and peace *x* for those who have been trained by it.

12Therefore, strengthen your feeble arms and weak knees. *y* 13"Make level paths for your feet," *a z* so that the lame may not be disabled, but rather healed. *a*

Warning Against Refusing God

14Make every effort to live in peace with all men *b* and to be holy; *c* without holi-

Cross-references (center column)

11:38 *b*1Ki 18:4; 19:9
11:39 *c*ver 2,4 *d*ver 13; Heb 10:36
11:40 *e*Rev 6:11 *f*S Heb 2:10
12:1 *g*S 1Co 9:24 *h*S Heb 10:36
12:2 *i*Ps 25:15 *j*Heb 2:10 *k*Php 2:8,9; Heb 2:9 *l*Heb 13:13 *m*S Mk 16:19
12:3 *n*Gal 6:9; Rev 2:3
12:4 *o*Heb 10:32-34; 13:13
12:5 *p*ver 3
12:6 *o*Ps 94:12; 119:75; Rev 3:19 *r*Pr 3:11,12
12:7 *t*Dt 8:5; 2Sa 7:14; Pr 13:24
12:8 *t*1Pe 5:9
12:9 *u*Nu 16:22; 27:16; Rev 22:6 *v*Isa 38:16
12:10 *w*S 2Pe 1:4
12:11 *x*Isa 32:17; Jas 3:17,18
12:12 *y*Isa 35:3
12:13 *z*Pr 4:26
12:14 *a*Gal 6:1 *b*Ro 14:19 *c*Ro 6:22

z 6 Prov. 3:11,12   *a 13* Prov. 4:26

11:39 *all commended for their faith.* Not all the heroes of faith experienced immediate triumph over their circumstances, but all were blessed by God.

11:40 *God had planned something better.* The fulfillment for them, as for us, is in Christ who is "the resurrection and the life" (Jn 11:25–26). *only together with us would they be made perfect.* All persons of faith who had gone before focused their faith on God and his promises. The fulfillment of God's promises to them has now come in Jesus Christ, and their redemption too is now complete in him.

12:1 *surrounded by such a great cloud of witnesses.* The imagery suggests an athletic contest in a great amphitheater. The witnesses are the heroes of the past who have just been mentioned (ch. 11). They are not spectators but inspiring examples. The Greek word translated "witnesses" is the origin of the English word "martyr" and means "testifiers, witnesses." They bear testimony to the power of faith and to God's faithfulness. *run with perseverance.* See Ac 20:24; 1Co 9:24–26; Gal 2:2; 5:7; Php 2:16; 2Ti 4:7. The Christian life is pictured as a long-distance race rather than a short sprint. Some Hebrew Christians were tempted to drop out of the contest because of persecution.

12:2 *fix our eyes on Jesus.* Just as a runner concentrates on the finish line, we should concentrate on Jesus, the goal and objective of our faith (Php 3:13–14). *author.* See note on 2:10. *perfecter of our faith.* Our faith, which has its beginning in him, is also completed in him; he is both the start and the end of the race. He is also the supreme witness who has already run the race and overcome. *joy set before him.* His accomplishing our eternal redemption and his glorification at

the Father's "right hand" (see note on 1:3; cf. Isa 53:10–12). *endured the cross.* See Php 2:5–8. *scorning its shame.* As with Christ, the humiliation of our present suffering for the gospel's sake is far outweighed by the prospect of future glory (see 11:26; Mt 5:10–12; Ro 8:18; 2Co 4:17; 1Pe 4:13; 5:1,10).

12:3 *Consider him.* He suffered infinitely more than any of his disciples is asked to suffer—a great encouragement for us when we are weary and tempted to become discouraged. *not grow weary.* See Isa 40:28–31.

12:4 *not yet resisted to the point of shedding your blood.* Though they had suffered persecution and loss of possessions (10:32–34), they had not had to die for the faith.

12:5 *the Lord's discipline.* Suffering and persecution should be seen as corrective and instructive training for our spiritual development as his children.

12:6 *punishes.* The Greek for this verb means "to whip." God chastens us in order to correct our faults.

12:7 *treating you as sons.* God's discipline is evidence that we are his children. Far from being a reason for despair, discipline is a basis for encouragement and perseverance (v. 10).

12:11 *it produces a harvest of righteousness.* When received submissively (see v. 9), discipline is wholesome and beneficial.

12:13 *Make level paths.* A call for upright conduct that will help, rather than hinder, the spiritual and moral welfare of others, especially the "lame" who waver in the Christian faith.

12:14 *without holiness no one will see the Lord.* Cf. 1Pe 1:15–16; 1Jn 3:2–3.

ness no one will see the Lord. [d] [15]See to it that no one misses the grace of God [e] and that no bitter root [f] grows up to cause trouble and defile many. [16]See that no one is sexually immoral, [g] or is godless like Esau, who for a single meal sold his inheritance rights as the oldest son. [h] [17]Afterward, as you know, when he wanted to inherit this blessing, he was rejected. He could bring about no change of mind, though he sought the blessing with tears. [i]

[18]You have not come to a mountain that can be touched and that is burning with fire; to darkness, gloom and storm; [j] [19]to a trumpet blast [k] or to such a voice speaking words [l] that those who heard it begged that no further word be spoken to them, [m] [20]because they could not bear what was commanded: "If even an animal touches the mountain, it must be stoned." [b] [n] [21]The sight was so terrifying that Moses said, "I am trembling with fear." [c] [o]

[22]But you have come to Mount Zion, [p] to the heavenly Jerusalem, [q] the city [r] of the living God. [s] You have come to thousands upon thousands of angels in joyful assembly, [23]to the church of the firstborn, [t] whose names are written in heaven. [u] You have come to God, the judge of all men, [v]

to the spirits of righteous men made perfect, [w] [24]to Jesus the mediator [x] of a new covenant, and to the sprinkled blood [y] that speaks a better word than the blood of Abel. [z]

[25]See to it that you do not refuse [a] him who speaks. [b] If they did not escape when they refused him who warned [c] them on earth, how much less will we, if we turn away from him who warns us from heaven? [d] [26]At that time his voice shook the earth, [e] but now he has promised, "Once more I will shake not only the earth but also the heavens." [d] [f] [27]The words "once more" indicate the removing of what can be shaken [g]—that is, created things—so that what cannot be shaken may remain.

[28]Therefore, since we are receiving a kingdom that cannot be shaken, [h] let us be thankful, and so worship God acceptably with reverence and awe, [i] [29]for our "God is a consuming fire." [e] [j]

12:14 [d]S Mt 5:8
12:15 [e]Gal 5:4; Heb 3:12; 4:1 / [f]Dt 29:18
12:16 [g]S 1Co 6:18 [h]Ge 25:29-34
12:17 [i]Ge 27:30-40
12:18 [j]Ex 19:12-22; 20:18; Dt 4:11
12:19 [k]Ex 20:18 / [l]Dt 4:12
[m]Ex 20:19; Dt 5:5,25; 18:16
12:20 [n]Ex 19:12, 13
12:21 [o]Dt 9:19
12:22 [p]Isa 24:23; 60:14; Rev 14:1 [q]S Gal 4:26 [r]Heb 11:10; 13:14
[s]S Mt 16:16
12:23 [t]Ex 4:22 [u]S Rev 20:12 [v]Ge 18:25; Ps 94:2
[w]Php 3:12
12:24 [x]S Gal 3:20 [y]Heb 9:19; 10:22; 1Pe 1:2 [z]Ge 4:10; Heb 11:4
12:25 [a]Heb 3:12 [b]S Heb 1:1 [c]Heb 8:5; 11:7 [d]Dt 18:19; Heb 2:2,3; 10:29
12:26 [e]Ex 19:18 / [f]Hag 2:6
12:27 [g]Isa 34:4; 54:10; 1Co 7:31; Heb 1:11,12;

2Pe 3:10; 1Jn 2:17 **12:28** [h]Ps 5:5; Da 2:44 / [i]Mal 2:5; 4:2; Heb 13:15 [i]Ex 24:17; Dt 4:24; 9:3; Ps 97:3; Isa 33:14; S 2Th 1:7

[b]20 Exodus 19:12,13   [c]21 Deut. 9:19
[d]26 Haggai 2:6   [e]29 Deut. 4:24

12:15 *misses the grace of God.* "Falls short of" or "fails to lay hold of" God's grace. Such an experience is described in 2:1–4; 6:4–8. *bitter root.* Pride, animosity, rivalry or anything else harmful to others.
12:16 *godless like Esau.* See Ge 25:29–34. He had no appreciation for true values and was profane in his outlook on life (cf. Php 3:18–19). He "despised his birthright" (Ge 25:34) by valuing food for his stomach more highly than his birthright.
12:17 *he was rejected.* Because he only regretted his loss, and did not repent of his sin (Ge 27, especially v. 41). His sorrow was not "godly sorrow" that "brings repentance that leads to salvation," but "worldly sorrow" that "brings death" (2Co 7:10). *the blessing.* Of the firstborn. The readers were thinking of compromising their faith in order to gain relief from persecution. But to trade their spiritual birthright for temporary ease in this world would deprive them of Christ's blessing. *with tears.* See Ge 27:34–38.
12:18–21 These verses describe the awesome occasion when the law was given at Sinai (see Ex 19:10–25; Dt 4:11–12; 5:22–26), a description focusing on the old covenant's tangible mountain, ordinances, terrifying warnings and severe penalties. Believers in Jesus Christ do not have such a threatening covenant, and should not consider returning to it.
12:22 *Mount Zion.* Not the literal Mount Zion (Jerusalem, or its southeast portion), but the heavenly city of God and those who dwell there with him (see 11:10,13–16; 13:14; Php 3:20). The circumstances under which the old covenant was given (vv. 18–21) and the features of the new covenant (vv. 22–24) point up the utter contrast between the two covenants, and lay the foundation for one more warning and exhortation to those still thinking of going back to Judaism. *thousands upon thousands of angels.* See Rev 5:11–12.
12:23 *church of the firstborn.* Believers in general who

make up the church: (1) They cannot be angels since these have just been mentioned (v. 22); (2) "firstborn" cannot refer to Christ (though he is called firstborn, 1:6; Ro 8:29; Col 1:15–18; Rev 1:5), since here the Greek word is plural; (3) that their names are recorded in heaven reminds us of the redeemed (see Rev 3:5; 13:8; 17:8; 20:12; 21:27). The designation "firstborn" suggests their privileged position as heirs together with Christ, the supreme firstborn and "heir of all things" (Heb 1:2). *God, the judge of all men.* See 4:13; Ro 14:10–12; 1Co 3:10–15; 2Co 5:10; Rev 20:11–15. *spirits of righteous men made perfect.* For the most part, these were pre-Christian believers such as Abel (11:4) and Noah (11:7). They are referred to as "spirits" because they are waiting for the resurrection and are "righteous" because God credited their faith to them as righteousness, as he did to Abraham (see Ro 4:3). Actual justification was not accomplished, however, until Christ made it complete by his death on the cross (see 11:40; Ro 3:24–26; 4:23–25).
12:24 *mediator of a new covenant.* See 7:22; 8:6 and note; 8:13; 9:15; 1Ti 2:5. *a better word than the blood of Abel.* Abel's blood cried out for justice and retribution (see note on Ge 4:10), whereas the blood of Jesus shed on the cross speaks of forgiveness and reconciliation (9:12; 10:19; Col 1:20; 1Jn 1:7).
12:25 *him who speaks.* God. *warned them on earth.* At Sinai. *him who warns us from heaven.* Christ, who is both from and in heaven (1:1–3; 4:14; 6:20; 7:26; 9:24). Since we have greater revelation, we have greater responsibility and therefore greater danger (2:2–4).
12:26 *shook the earth.* See Ex 19:18; Jdg 5:5; Ps 68:7–8.
12:27 *once more.* During the great end-time upheavals associated with the second advent of Christ. *what cannot be shaken.* The kingdom (v. 28).
12:28 *worship God acceptably.* See Jn 4:19–24; Ro 12:1.
12:29 See NIV text note; cf. Ex 24:17; Dt 9:3.

Concluding Exhortations

13 Keep on loving each other as brothers.[k] [2]Do not forget to entertain strangers,[l] for by so doing some people have entertained angels without knowing it.[m] [3]Remember those in prison[n] as if you were their fellow prisoners, and those who are mistreated as if you yourselves were suffering.

[4]Marriage should be honored by all,[o] and the marriage bed kept pure, for God will judge the adulterer and all the sexually immoral.[p] [5]Keep your lives free from the love of money[q] and be content with what you have,[r] because God has said,

"Never will I leave you;
    never will I forsake you."[f] [s]

[6]So we say with confidence,

"The Lord is my helper; I will not be afraid.
    What can man do to me?"[g] [t]

[7]Remember your leaders,[u] who spoke the word of God[v] to you. Consider the outcome of their way of life and imitate[w] their faith. [8]Jesus Christ is the same yesterday and today and forever.[x]

[9]Do not be carried away by all kinds of strange teachings.[y] It is good for our hearts to be strengthened[z] by grace, not by ceremonial foods,[a] which are of no value to those who eat them.[b] [10]We have an altar from which those who minister at the tabernacle[c] have no right to eat.[d]

[11]The high priest carries the blood of animals into the Most Holy Place as a sin offering,[e] but the bodies are burned outside the camp.[f] [12]And so Jesus also suffered outside the city gate[g] to make the people holy[h] through his own blood.[i] [13]Let us, then, go to him[j] outside the camp, bearing the disgrace he bore.[k] [14]For here we do not have an enduring city,[l] but we are looking for the city that is to come.[m]

[15]Through Jesus, therefore, let us continually offer to God a sacrifice[n] of praise—the fruit of lips[o] that confess his name. [16]And do not forget to do good and to share with others,[p] for with such sacrifices[q] God is pleased.

[17]Obey your leaders[r] and submit to their authority. They keep watch over you[s] as men who must give an account. Obey them so that their work will be a joy, not a burden, for that would be of no advantage to you.

[18]Pray for us.[t] We are sure that we have a clear conscience[u] and desire to live honorably in every way. [19]I particularly urge you to pray so that I may be restored to you soon.[v]

Cross references

13:1 [k]S Ro 12:10
13:2 [l]Job 31:32; Mt 25:35; S Ro 12:13; [m]Ge 18:1-33; 19:1-3
13:3 [n]Mt 25:36; Col 4:18; Heb 10:34
13:4 [o]Mal 2:15; 1Co 7:38; 1Ti 4:3; [p]Dt 22:22; 1Co 6:9; Rev 22:15
13:5 [q]S 1Ti 3:3; [r]Php 4:11; 1Ti 6:6,8; [s]Dt 31:6; Jos 1:5
13:6 [t]Ps 118:6,7
13:7 [u]ver 17,24; 1Co 16:16; [v]S Heb 4:12; [w]Heb 6:12
13:8 [x]Ps 102:27; Heb 1:12
13:9 [y]Eph 4:14; [z]Col 2:7; [a]Col 2:16
[b]Heb 9:10
13:10 [c]Heb 8:5; [d]1Co 9:13; 10:18
13:11 [e]Lev 16:15; [f]Ex 29:14; Lev 4:12,21; 9:11; 16:27
13:12 [g]Jn 19:17; [h]S Eph 5:26; [i]S Ro 3:25
13:13 [j]Lk 9:23; [k]Heb 11:26
13:14 [l]Heb 12:27; [m]Php 3:20; Heb 11:10,27; 12:22
13:15 [n]1Pe 2:5; [o]Isa 57:19; Hos 14:2
13:16 [p]Ro 12:13; [q]Php 4:18
13:17 [r]ver 7,24; [s]Isa 62:6; Ac 20:28

13:18 [t]S 1Th 5:25 [u]S Ac 23:1 13:19 [v]Phm 22

[f]5 Deut. 31:6   [g]6 Psalm 118:6,7

13:2 *entertained angels without knowing it.* As did Abraham (Ge 18), Gideon (Jdg 6) and Manoah (Jdg 13).

13:3 *remember those in prison . . . and those who are mistreated.* See 10:32-34; 1Co 12:26.

13:5 *love of money.* See Lk 12:15,21; Php 4:10-13; 1Ti 6:6-10,17-19. *be content.* See Php 4:11-12; 1Ti 6:8.

13:7 *leaders, who spoke the word of God.* See 2:3; 5:12. *Consider the outcome of their way of life.* Probably indicates that these exemplary leaders were now dead. *imitate their faith.* See 6:12; 1Co 4:16; Eph 5:1; 1Th 1:6-7; 2:14; 3Jn 11.

13:8 *Jesus Christ is the same.* A confession of the changelessness of Christ, no doubt related to the preceding verse. The substance of their former leaders' faith was the unchanging Christ. *yesterday.* Probably the days of Christ's life on earth, when the eyewitnesses observed him (2:3). *today.* The Christ whom the eyewitnesses saw was still the same, and what they had said about him was still true. *forever.* And it will always be true. To compromise his absolute supremacy by returning to the inferior Aaronic priesthood and sacrifices (see chs. 5-10) is to undermine the gospel.

13:9 *not by ceremonial foods.* As the legalistic Judaizers were teaching. The old Mosaic order was done away with at the cross and must not be revived.

13:10 *We have an altar.* Probably refers to the cross, which marked the end of the whole Aaronic priesthood and its replacement by the order of Melchizedek, of which Christ is the unique and only priest. *no right to eat.* The priests could not eat of the sacrifice on the Day of Atonement, but we can

partake of our sacrifice, so to speak—through spiritual reception of Christ by faith (see Jn 6:48-58). We have a higher privilege than the priests under the old covenant had.

13:11 *burned outside the camp.* See Lev 4:12 and note; 16:27.

13:12 *Jesus also suffered outside the city gate.* Christ's death outside Jerusalem represented the removal of sin, as had the removal of the bodies of sacrificial animals outside the camp of Israel.

13:13 *go to him outside the camp.* Calls for separation from Judaism to Christ. As he died in disgrace outside the city, so the readers should be willing to be disgraced by turning unequivocally from Judaism to Christ.

13:14 *city that is to come.* See notes on 11:10,14,16.

13:15 *sacrifice of praise.* "Sacrifice" is used metaphorically here to represent an offering to God (see Ro 12:1; Php 4:18). Animal offerings are now obsolete.

13:17 *your leaders.* Their present leaders, as distinct from their first ones, now dead, mentioned in v. 7. *submit to their authority.* Dictatorial leadership is not condoned by this command (see 3Jn 9-10), but respect for authority, orderliness and discipline in the church are taught throughout the NT.

13:19 *restored to you soon.* The identity and whereabouts of the writer are not known to us, but "restored" suggests that somehow he had been delayed in visiting those to whom he was writing, perhaps by his current ministry. That he was not under arrest is clear from v. 23.

²⁰May the God of peace, ^w who through the blood of the eternal covenant ^x brought back from the dead ^y our Lord Jesus, that great Shepherd of the sheep, ^z ²¹equip you with everything good for doing his will, ^a and may he work in us ^b what is pleasing to him, ^c through Jesus Christ, to whom be glory for ever and ever. Amen. ^d

²²Brothers, I urge you to bear with my word of exhortation, for I have written you only a short letter. ^e

²³I want you to know that our brother Timothy ^f has been released. If he arrives soon, I will come with him to see you.

²⁴Greet all your leaders ^g and all God's people. Those from Italy ^h send you their greetings.

²⁵Grace be with you all. ⁱ

13:20
^wS Ro 15:33
^xGe 9:16;
17:7,13,19;
Isa 55:3; 61:8;
Eze 37:26;
S Mt 26:28
^yS Ac 2:24
^zS Jn 10:11
13:21 ^a2Co 9:8
^bS Php 2:13
^c1Jn 3:22
^dS Ro 11:36

13:22 ^e1Pe 5:12
13:23 ^fS Ac 16:1
13:24 ^gver 7,17

^hAc 18:2   **13:25** ⁱS Col 4:18

13:20–21 This benediction provides a fitting conclusion to the letter. *God of peace.* A title for God used frequently in benedictions (see Ro 15:33; 16:20; Php 4:9; 1Th 5:23).

13:20 *eternal covenant.* The new covenant (see note on 8:8–12). What Jeremiah designates as the new covenant in 31:31 he describes as everlasting in 32:40 (see also Isa 55:3 and note; 61:8). On the blood of the covenant see notes on 10:29. *great Shepherd.* See, e.g., Ps 23; Isa 40:11; Eze 34:11–16,23; 37:24; Jn 10:2–3,11,14,27; 1Pe 2:25; 5:4.

13:22–25 A postscript.

13:22 *word of exhortation.* The main thrust of the letter is to go on in Christian maturity and not fall away from Christ. *short.* Compared to the lengthy treatise that would be necessary to explain adequately the superiority of Christ.

13:23 *Timothy has been released.* Timothy, who was well known to the recipients of the letter, had recently been released from prison.

13:24 *leaders.* Mentioned in v. 17. *Those from Italy.* Does not mean that this letter was written either to or from Italy. The writer is passing on greetings from some Italian believers.

The General Letters

The seven letters following Hebrews—James, 1,2 Peter, 1,2,3 John and Jude—have often been designated as the General Letters. This term goes back to the early church historian Eusebius (c. A.D. 265-340), who in his *Ecclesiastical History* (2.23-25) first referred to these seven letters as Catholic Letters, using the word "catholic" to mean "universal."

The letters so designated may be said to be, for the most part, addressed to general audiences rather than to specific persons or localized groups. 2 and 3 John, the two letters that seem most obviously addressed to individuals, have long been viewed as appendages of 1 John, which is clearly general in its address. However, when compared with Paul's letters, all these letters except 3 John are clearly general in nature. By contrast, Paul addresses his letters to such recipients as the saints at Philippi, or the churches of Galatia, or Timothy or Titus.

As Eusebius noted long ago, one interesting fact connected with the General Letters is that most of them were at one time among the disputed books of the NT. James, 2 Peter, 2 John, 3 John and Jude were all questioned extensively before being admitted to the canon of Scripture.

JAMES

Author

The author identifies himself as James (1:1), and he was probably the brother of Jesus and leader of the Jerusalem council (Ac 15). Four men in the NT have this name. The author of this letter could not have been the apostle James, who died too early (A.D. 44) to have written it. The other two men named James had neither the stature nor the influence that the writer of this letter had.

James was one of several brothers of Christ and was probably the oldest since he heads the list in Mt 13:55. At first he did not believe in Jesus and even challenged him and misunderstood his mission (Jn 7:2-5). Later he became very prominent in the church:

1. He was one of the select individuals Christ appeared to after his resurrection (1Co 15:7).
2. Paul called him a "pillar" of the church (Gal 2:9).
3. Paul, on his first post-conversion visit to Jerusalem, saw James (Gal 1:19).
4. Paul did the same on his last visit (Ac 21:18).
5. When Peter was rescued from prison, he told his friends to tell James (Ac 12:17).
6. James was a leader in the important council of Jerusalem (Ac 15:13).
7. Jude could identify himself simply as "a brother of James" (Jude 1:1), so well known was James. He was martyred c. A.D. 62.

Date

Some date the letter in the early 60s. There are indications, however, that it was written before A.D. 50:

1. Its distinctively Jewish nature suggests that it was composed when the church was still predominantly Jewish.
2. It reflects a simple church order—officers of the church are called "elders" (5:14) and "teachers" (3:1).
3. No reference is made to the controversy over Gentile circumcision.
4. The Greek term *synagoge* ("synagogue" or "meeting") is used to designate the meeting or meeting place of the church (2:2).

If this early dating is correct, this letter is the earliest of all the NT writings—with the possible exception of Galatians.

Recipients

The recipients are identified explicitly only in 1:1: "the twelve tribes scattered among the nations." Some hold that this expression refers to Christians in general, but the term "twelve tribes" would more naturally apply to Jewish Christians. Furthermore, a Jewish audience would be more in keeping with the obviously Jewish nature of the letter (e.g., the use of the Hebrew title for God, *kyrios sabaoth*, "Lord Almighty," 5:4). That the recipients were Christians is clear from 2:1; 5:7-8. It has been plausibly suggested that these were believers from the early Jerusalem church who, after Stephen's death, were scattered as far as Phoenicia, Cyprus and Syrian Antioch (Ac 8:1; 11:19). This would account for James's references to trials and oppression, his intimate knowledge of the readers and the authoritative nature of the letter. As leader of the Jerusalem church, James wrote as pastor to instruct and encourage his dispersed people in the face of their difficulties.

Distinctive Characteristics

Characteristics that make the letter distinctive are: (1) its unmistakably Jewish nature; (2) its emphasis on vital Christianity, characterized by good deeds and a faith that works (genuine faith must and will be accompanied by a consistent life-style); (3) its simple organization; (4) its familiarity with Jesus' teachings preserved in the Sermon on the Mount (compare 2:5 with Mt 5:3; 3:10-12 with Mt

7:15-20; 3:18 with Mt 5:9; 5:2-3 with Mt 6:19-20; 5:12 with Mt 5:33-37); (5) its similarity to OT wisdom writings such as Proverbs; (6) its excellent Greek.

Outline

1 James,[a] a servant of God[b] and of the Lord Jesus Christ,

To the twelve tribes[c] scattered[d] among the nations:

Greetings.[e]

Trials and Temptations

[2]Consider it pure joy, my brothers, whenever you face trials of many kinds,[f] [3]because you know that the testing of your faith[g] develops perseverance.[h] [4]Perseverance must finish its work so that you may be mature[i] and complete, not lacking anything. [5]If any of you lacks wisdom, he should ask God,[j] who gives generously to all without finding fault, and it will be given to him.[k] [6]But when he asks, he must believe and not doubt,[l] because he who doubts is like a wave of the sea, blown and tossed by the wind. [7]That man should not think he will receive anything from the Lord; [8]he is a double-minded man,[m] unstable[n] in all he does.

[9]The brother in humble circumstances ought to take pride in his high position.[o] [10]But the one who is rich should take pride in his low position, because he will pass away like a wild flower.[p] [11]For the sun rises with scorching heat[q] and withers[r] the plant; its blossom falls and its beauty is destroyed.[s] In the same way, the rich man will fade away even while he goes about his business.

[12]Blessed is the man who perseveres under trial,[t] because when he has stood the test, he will receive the crown of life[u] that

God has promised to those who love him.[v]

[13]When tempted, no one should say, "God is tempting me." For God cannot be tempted by evil, nor does he tempt anyone; [14]but each one is tempted when, by his own[w] evil desire, he is dragged away and enticed. [15]Then, after desire has conceived, it gives birth to sin;[x] and sin, when it is full-grown, gives birth to death.[y]

[16]Don't be deceived,[z] my dear brothers.[a] [17]Every good and perfect gift is from above,[b] coming down from the Father of the heavenly lights,[c] who does not change[d] like shifting shadows. [18]He chose to give us birth[e] through the word of truth,[f] that we might be a kind of firstfruits[g] of all he created.

Listening and Doing

[19]My dear brothers,[h] take note of this: Everyone should be quick to listen, slow to speak[i] and slow to become angry, [20]for man's anger[j] does not bring about the righteous life that God desires. [21]Therefore, get rid of[k] all moral filth and the evil that is so prevalent and humbly accept the word planted in you,[l] which can save you.

[22]Do not merely listen to the word, and so deceive yourselves. Do what it says.[m] [23]Anyone who listens to the word but does not do what it says is like a man who looks at his face in a mirror [24]and, after looking at himself, goes away and immediately for-

---

Cross references (center column):

1:1 [a]S Ac 15:13
[b]Ro 1:1; Tit 1:1
[c]Ac 26:7
[d]Dt 32:26;
Jn 7:35; 1Pe 1;1
[e]Ac 15:23
1:2 [f]ver 12;
S Mt 5:12;
Heb 10:34; 12:11
1:3 [g]1Pe 1:7
[h]S Heb 10:36
1:4 [i]S 1Co 2:6
1:5 [j]1Ki 3:9,10;
Pr 2:3-6 [k]Ps 51:6;
Da 1:17; 2:21;
S Mt 7:7
1:6 [l]S Mt 21:21;
Mk 11:24
1:8 [m]Ps 119:113;
Jas 4:8 [n]2Pe 2:14;
3:16
1:9 [o]S Mt 23:12
1:10 [p]Job 14:2;
Ps 103:15,16;
Isa 40:6,7;
1Co 7:31;
1Pe 1:24
1:11 [q]Mt 20:12
[r]Ps 102:4,11
[s]Isa 40:6-8
1:12 [t]ver 2;
Ge 22:1; Jas 5:11;
1Pe 3:14
[u]S 1Co 9:25

[v]Ex 20:6;
1Co 2:9; 8:3;
Jas 2:5
1:14 [w]Pr 19:3
1:15 [x]Ge 3:6; Job
15:35; Ps 7:14;
Isa 59:4
[y]S Ro 6:23
1:16 [z]S 1Co 6:9
[a]ver 19; Jas 2:5
1:17 [b]Ps 85:12;
Jn 3:27; Jas 3:15,
17 [c]Ge 1:16;
Ps 136:7;
Da 2:22; 1Jn 1:5
[d]Nu 23:19;
Ps 102:27;
Mal 3:6
1:18 [e]S Jn 1:13
[f]S 2Ti 2:15
[g]Jer 2:3; Rev 14:4
1:19 [h]ver 16;
Jas 2:5 [i]Pr 10:19;
Jas 3:3-12

1:20 [j]S Mt 5:22 1:21 [k]S Eph 4:22 [l]Eph 1:13 1:22
[m]S Mt 7:21; Jas 2:14-20

Study notes (bottom):

1:1 *James.* See Introduction: Author. *servant.* See note on Ro 1:1. *twelve tribes.* See Introduction: Recipients.
1:2 *joy.* See Mt 5:11–12; Ro 5:3; 1Pe 1:6. *brothers.* James addresses the readers as brothers 15 times in this short letter. He has many rebukes for them, but he chides them in brotherly love. *trials.* The same Greek root lies behind the word "trials" here and the word "tempted" in v. 13. In vv. 2–3 the emphasis is on difficulties that come from outside; in vv. 13–15 it is on inner moral trials such as temptation to sin.
1:5 *wisdom.* Enables one to face trials with "pure joy" (v. 2). Wisdom is not just acquired information but practical insight with spiritual implications (see Pr 1:2–4; 2:10–15; 4:5–9; 9:10–12).
1:6 *wave of the sea.* See Eph 4:14.
1:9–10 *brother in humble circumstances . . . one who is rich.* Since James's discussions of wisdom (vv. 5–8) and of the poor man and the rich man (vv. 9–11) appear between the two sections on trials (vv. 2–4 and v. 12), vv. 5–11 may also have to do with trials. The Christian who suffers the trial of poverty is to take pride in his high position (v. 9) as a believer (see 2:5), and the wealthy Christian is to take pride (v. 10) in trials that bring him low, perhaps including the loss of his wealth.
1:12 *Blessed.* See Jer 17:7–8; Mt 5:3–12; see also notes on Ps 1:1; Mt 5:3; Rev 1:3. *crown.* The Greek for this word

was the usual term for the wreath placed on the head of a victorious athlete or military leader (see 2Ti 4:8; 1Pe 5:4; Rev 2:10 and note). *life.* Eternal life, as the future tense of the verb ("will receive") indicates.
1:13 *tempted.* In vv. 13–14 the verb refers to temptations that test one's moral strength to resist sin (see note on Mt 4:1). *God cannot be tempted.* Because God in his very nature is holy, there is nothing in him for sin to appeal to. *nor does he tempt anyone.* See note on Ge 22:1.
1:15 The three stages—desire, sin, death—are seen in the temptations of Eve (Ge 3:6–22) and David (2Sa 11:2–17).
1:17 *Every good and perfect gift is from above.* See v. 5; 3:17. *Father of . . . lights.* God is the Creator of the heavenly bodies, which give light to the earth, but, unlike them, he does not change.
1:18 *birth.* Not a reference to creation but to regeneration (see Jn 3:3–8). *word of truth.* The proclamation of the gospel (see 1Pe 1:23–25). *firstfruits.* See Lev 23:9–14. Just as the first sheaf of the harvest was an indication that the whole harvest would eventually follow, so the early Christians were an indication that a great number of people would eventually be born again.
1:19 *Everyone should be . . . slow to speak.* See v. 26.
1:21 *word.* Of God.

gets what he looks like. 25But the man who looks intently into the perfect law that gives freedom, *n* and continues to do this, not forgetting what he has heard, but doing it—he will be blessed in what he does. *o*

26If anyone considers himself religious and yet does not keep a tight rein on his tongue, *p* he deceives himself and his religion is worthless. 27Religion that God our Father accepts as pure and faultless is this: to look after *q* orphans and widows *r* in their distress and to keep oneself from being polluted by the world. *s*

Favoritism Forbidden

2 My brothers, as believers in our glorious *t* Lord Jesus Christ, don't show favoritism. *u* 2Suppose a man comes into your meeting wearing a gold ring and fine clothes, and a poor man in shabby clothes also comes in. 3If you show special attention to the man wearing fine clothes and say, "Here's a good seat for you," but say to the poor man, "You stand there" or "Sit on the floor by my feet," 4have you not discriminated among yourselves and become judges *v* with evil thoughts?

5Listen, my dear brothers: *w* Has not God chosen those who are poor in the eyes of the world *x* to be rich in faith *y* and to inherit the kingdom *z* he promised those who love him? *a* 6But you have insulted the poor. *b* Is it not the rich who are exploiting you? Are they not the ones who

are dragging you into court? *c* 7Are they not the ones who are slandering the noble name of him to whom you belong?

8If you really keep the royal law found in Scripture, "Love your neighbor as yourself," *a d* you are doing right. 9But if you show favoritism, *e* you sin and are convicted by the law as lawbreakers. *f* 10For whoever keeps the whole law and yet stumbles *g* at just one point is guilty of breaking all of it. *h* 11For he who said, "Do not commit adultery," *b i* also said, "Do not murder." *c j* If you do not commit adultery but do commit murder, you have become a lawbreaker.

12Speak and act as those who are going to be judged *k* by the law that gives freedom, *l* 13because judgment without mercy will be shown to anyone who has not been merciful. *m* Mercy triumphs over judgment!

Faith and Deeds

14What good is it, my brothers, if a man claims to have faith but has no deeds? *n* Can such faith save him? 15Suppose a brother or sister is without clothes and daily food. *o* 16If one of you says to him, "Go, I wish you well; keep warm and well fed," but does nothing about his physical needs, what good is it? *p* 17In the same way, faith by itself, if it is not accompanied by action, is dead. *q*

1:25 *n* Ps 19:7;
Jn 8:32; Gal 2:4;
Jas 2:12
o S Jn 13:17
1:26 *p* Ps 34:13;
39:1; 141:3;
Jas 3:2-12;
1 Pe 3:10
1:27 *q* Mt 25:36
r Dt 14:29; Job
31:16,17,21;
Ps 146:9;
Isa 1:17,23
s Ro 12:2; Jas 4:4;
2 Pe 1:4; 2:20
2:1 *t* Ac 7:2;
1 Co 2:8 *u* ver 9;
Dt 1:17;
Lev 19:15;
Pr 24:23;
S Ac 10:34
2:4 *v* S Jn 7:24
2:5 *w* Jas 1:16,19
x Job 34:19;
1 Co 1:26-28
y Lk 12:21;
Rev 2:9
z S Mt 25:34
a S Jas 1:12
2:6 *b* 1 Co 11:22

c Ac 8:3; 16:19
2:8 *d* Lev 19:18;
S Mt 5:43
2:9 *e* ver 1
f Dt 1:17
2:10 *g* Jas 3:2
h Mt 5:19;
Gal 3:10; 5:3
2:11 *i* Ex 20:14;
Dt 5:18
j Ex 20:13;
Dt 5:17
2:12 *k* S Mt 16:27
l S Jas 1:25
2:13 *m* Mt 5:7;
9:13; 12:7;
18:32-35;
Lk 6:37
2:14 *n* Mt 7:26;
Jas 1:22-25
2:15 *o* Mt 25:35,
36
2:16 *p* Lk 3:11;
1 Jn 3:17,18

2:17 *q* ver 20,26; Gal 5:6

a 8 Lev. 19:18   *b* 11 Exodus 20:14; Deut. 5:18
c 11 Exodus 20:13; Deut. 5:17

1:25 *perfect law.* The moral and ethical teaching of Christianity, which is based on the OT moral law, as embodied in the Ten Commandments (see Ps 19:7), but brought to completion (perfection) by Jesus Christ. *freedom.* In contrast to the sinner, who is a slave to sin (Jn 8:34), obeying the moral law gives the Christian the joyous freedom to be what he was created for (see 2:12).

1:26 *religious.* Refers to the outward acts of religion: e.g., giving to the needy, fasting and public acts of praying and worshiping.

1:27 See Jer 22:16. *world.* Not the world of nature but the world of people in their rebellion against and alienation from God (see 1 Jn 2:15).

2:1 *as believers . . . don't show favoritism.* God does not show favoritism—nor should believers.

2:2 *meeting.* The Greek for this term is the origin of the English word "synagogue."

2:5-13 James gives three arguments against showing favoritism to the rich: 1. The rich persecute the poor—the believers (vv. 5-7). 2. Favoritism violates the royal law of love and thus is sin (vv. 8-11). 3. Favoritism will be judged (vv. 12-13).

2:5 *Has not God chosen those who are poor . . . ?* See Lk 6:20; 1 Co 1:26-31. *the kingdom.* The kingdom that is entered by the new birth (Jn 3:3,5) and that will be consummated in the future (Mt 25:34,46).

2:8 *royal law.* The law of love (Lev 19:18) is called "royal" because it is the supreme law that is the source of all other

laws governing human relationships. It is the summation of all such laws (Mt 22:36-40; Ro 13:8-10).

2:10 *guilty of breaking all.* The law is the expression of the character and will of God; therefore to violate one part of the law is to violate God's will and thus his whole law (cf. Mt 5:18-19; 23:23).

2:12 *judged.* This judgment is not for determining eternal destiny, for James is speaking to believers (v. 1), whose destiny is already determined (Jn 5:24). Rather, it is for giving rewards to believers (1 Co 3:12-15; 2 Co 5:10; Rev 22:12).

2:13 *Mercy triumphs over judgment!* If man is merciful, God will be merciful on the Day of Judgment (see Pr 21:13; Mt 5:7; 6:14-15; 18:21-35).

2:14-26 In vv. 14-20,24,26 "faith" is not used in the sense of genuine, saving faith. It is demonic (v. 19), useless (v. 20) and dead (v. 26). It is a mere intellectual acceptance of certain truths without trust in Christ as Savior. James is also not saying that a person is saved by works and not by genuine faith. Rather, he is saying, to use Martin Luther's words, that a man is justified (declared righteous before God) by faith alone, but not by a faith that is alone. Genuine faith will produce good deeds, but only faith in Christ saves. (For more information on justification see note on Ro 3:24.)

2:15-16 This illustration of false faith is parallel to the illustration of false love found in 1 Jn 3:17. The latter passage calls for love in action; this one calls for faith in action.

¹⁸But someone will say, "You have faith; I have deeds."

Show me your faith without deeds, ʳ and I will show you my faith ˢ by what I do. ᵗ ¹⁹You believe that there is one God. ᵘ Good! Even the demons believe that ᵛ—and shudder.

²⁰You foolish man, do you want evidence that faith without deeds is useless ᵈ? ʷ ²¹Was not our ancestor Abraham considered righteous for what he did when he offered his son Isaac on the altar? ˣ ²²You see that his faith and his actions were working together, ʸ and his faith was made complete by what he did. ᶻ ²³And the scripture was fulfilled that says, "Abraham believed God, and it was credited to him as righteousness," ᵉ ᵃ and he was called God's friend. ᵇ ²⁴You see that a person is justified by what he does and not by faith alone.

²⁵In the same way, was not even Rahab the prostitute considered righteous for what she did when she gave lodging to the spies and sent them off in a different direction? ᶜ ²⁶As the body without the spirit is dead, so faith without deeds is dead. ᵈ

Taming the Tongue

3 Not many of you should presume to be teachers, ᵉ my brothers, because you know that we who teach will be judged ᶠ more strictly. ᵍ ²We all stumble ʰ in many ways. If anyone is never at fault in what he says, ⁱ he is a perfect man, ʲ able to keep his whole body in check. ᵏ

³When we put bits into the mouths of horses to make them obey us, we can turn the whole animal. ˡ ⁴Or take ships as an example. Although they are so large and are driven by strong winds, they are steered by a very small rudder wherever the pilot wants to go. ⁵Likewise the tongue is a small part of the body, but it makes great boasts. ᵐ Consider what a great forest is set on fire by a small spark. ⁶The tongue also is a fire, ⁿ a world of evil among the parts of the body. It corrupts the whole person, ᵒ sets the whole course of his life on fire, and is itself set on fire by hell. ᵖ

⁷All kinds of animals, birds, reptiles and creatures of the sea are being tamed and have been tamed by man, ⁸but no man can tame the tongue. It is a restless evil, full of deadly poison. ۹

⁹With the tongue we praise our Lord and Father, and with it we curse men, who have been made in God's likeness. ʳ ¹⁰Out of the same mouth come praise and cursing. My brothers, this should not be. ¹¹Can both fresh water and salt ᶠ water flow from the same spring? ¹²My brothers, can a fig tree bear olives, or a grapevine bear figs? ˢ Neither can a salt spring produce fresh water.

Two Kinds of Wisdom

¹³Who is wise and understanding among you? Let him show it ᵗ by his good life, by deeds ᵘ done in the humility that comes from wisdom. ¹⁴But if you harbor bitter envy and selfish ambition ᵛ in your hearts, do not boast about it or deny the truth. ʷ ¹⁵Such "wisdom" does not come down from heaven ˣ but is earthly, unspiritual, of the devil. ʸ ¹⁶For where you have envy and

---

2:18 ʳRo 3:28
ˢHeb 11
ᵗMt 7:16,17;
Jas 3:13
2:19 ᵘDt 6:4;
Mk 12:29;
1Co 8:4-6;
ᵛMt 8:29;
Lk 4:34
2:20 ʷver 17,26
2:21 ˣGe 22:9,12
2:22 ʸHeb 11:17
ᶻ1Th 1:3
2:23 ᵃGe 15:6;
S Ro 4:3
ᵇ2Ch 20:7;
Isa 41:8
2:25
ᶜS Heb 11:31
2:26 ᵈver 17,20
3:1 ᵉ Eph 4:11
/S Mt 7:1
ᵍRo 2:21
3:2 ʰ1Ki 8:46;
Ro 3:9-20;
Jas 2:10; 1Jn 1:8
ⁱPs 39:1;
Pr 10:19;
1Pe 3:10
/S Mt 12:37
ᵏJas 1:26
3:3 ˡPs 32:9

3:5 ᵐPs 12:3,4;
73:8,9
3:6 ⁿPr 16:27
ᵒMt 15:11,18,19
ᵖS Mt 5:22
3:8 ۹Ps 140:3;
Ro 3:13
3:9 ʳGe 1:26,27;
1Co 11:7
3:12 ˢMt 7:16
3:13 ᵗJas 2:18
ᵘS 1Pe 2:12
3:14 ᵛver 16;
2Co 12:20
ʷJas 5:19
3:15 ˣver 17;
Jas 1:17 ʸ1Ti 4:1

ᵈ20 Some early manuscripts *dead*   ᵉ23 Gen. 15:6
ᶠ11 Greek *bitter* (see also verse 14)

2:18 *You have faith; I have deeds.* The false claim is that there are "faith" Christians and "deeds" Christians, i.e., that faith and deeds can exist independently of each other. *Show me your faith without deeds.* Irony; James denies the possibility of this.

2:19 *there is one God.* A declaration of monotheism that reflects the well-known Jewish creed called in Hebrew the *Shema*, "Hear" (Dt 6:4; Mk 12:29).

2:21 Apart from its context, this verse might seem to contradict the Biblical teaching that people are saved by faith and not by good deeds (Ro 3:28; Gal 2:15–16). But James means only that righteous action is evidence of genuine faith—not that it saves, for the verse (Ge 15:6) that he cites (v. 23) to substantiate his point says, "Abram believed the Lord, and he credited it [i.e., faith, not works] to him as righteousness." Furthermore, Abraham's act of faith recorded in Ge 15:6 occurred before he offered up Isaac, which was only a proof of the genuineness of his faith. As Paul wrote, "The only thing that counts is faith expressing itself through love" (Gal 5:6). Faith that saves produces deeds.

2:23 *God's friend.* This designation (see 2Ch 20:7) further describes Abraham's relationship to God as one of complete acceptance.

2:24 *not by faith alone.* Not by an intellectual assent to certain truths (see note on 2:14–26).

2:25 *Rahab the prostitute.* James does not approve Rahab's occupation. He merely commends her for her faith (see also Heb 11:31), which she demonstrated by helping the spies (Jos 2).

3:1 *judged more strictly.* Because a teacher has great influence, he will be held more accountable (see Lk 20:47; cf. Mt 23:1–33).

3:2 *perfect man.* Since the tongue is so difficult to control, anyone who controls it perfectly gains control of himself in all other areas of life as well.

3:6 *world of evil.* Like the world in its fallenness. *set on fire by hell.* A figurative way of saying that the source of the tongue's evil is the devil (see Jn 8:44). See notes on Mt 5:22; Lk 16:23.

3:9 *in God's likeness.* Since man has been made like God (Ge 1:26–27), to curse man is like cursing God (see Ge 9:6). See note on Ge 1:26.

3:13 *wisdom.* See note on 1:5.

3:15 *from heaven.* From God (see 1:5,17; 1Co 2:6–16).

3:16 *disorder.* "God is not a God of disorder but of peace"

selfish ambition,[z] there you find disorder and every evil practice.

[17]But the wisdom that comes from heaven[a] is first of all pure; then peace-loving,[b] considerate, submissive, full of mercy[c] and good fruit, impartial and sincere.[d] [18]Peacemakers[e] who sow in peace raise a harvest of righteousness.[f]

Submit Yourselves to God

4 What causes fights and quarrels[g] among you? Don't they come from your desires that battle[h] within you? [2]You want something but don't get it. You kill[i] and covet, but you cannot have what you want. You quarrel and fight. You do not have, because you do not ask God. [3]When you ask, you do not receive,[j] because you ask with wrong motives,[k] that you may spend what you get on your pleasures.

[4]You adulterous[l] people, don't you know that friendship with the world[m] is hatred toward God?[n] Anyone who chooses to be a friend of the world becomes an enemy of God.[o] [5]Or do you think Scripture says without reason that the spirit he caused to live in us[p] envies intensely?[g] [6]But he gives us more grace. That is why Scripture says:

"God opposes the proud
but gives grace to the humble."[h][q]

[7]Submit yourselves, then, to God. Resist the devil,[r] and he will flee from you. [8]Come near to God and he will come near to you.[s] Wash your hands,[t] you sinners, and purify your hearts,[u] you double-minded.[v] [9]Grieve, mourn and wail. Change

your laughter to mourning and your joy to gloom.[w] [10]Humble yourselves before the Lord, and he will lift you up.[x]

[11]Brothers, do not slander one another.[y] Anyone who speaks against his brother or judges him[z] speaks against the law[a] and judges it. When you judge the law, you are not keeping it,[b] but sitting in judgment on it. [12]There is only one Lawgiver and Judge,[c] the one who is able to save and destroy.[d] But you—who are you to judge your neighbor?[e]

Boasting About Tomorrow

[13]Now listen,[f] you who say, "Today or tomorrow we will go to this or that city, spend a year there, carry on business and make money."[g] [14]Why, you do not even know what will happen tomorrow. What is your life? You are a mist that appears for a little while and then vanishes.[h] [15]Instead, you ought to say, "If it is the Lord's will,[i] we will live and do this or that." [16]As it is, you boast and brag. All such boasting is evil.[j] [17]Anyone, then, who knows the good he ought to do and doesn't do it, sins.[k]

Warning to Rich Oppressors

5 Now listen,[l] you rich people,[m] weep and wail[n] because of the misery that is coming upon you. [2]Your wealth has rotted, and moths have eaten your clothes.[o] [3]Your gold and silver are corroded. Their

3:16 [z]ver 14; Gal 5:20,21
3:17 [a]1Co 2:6; Jas 1:17
[b]Heb 12:11
[c]Lk 6:36
[d]Ro 12:9
3:18 [e]Mt 5:9; S Ro 14:19
[f]Pr 11:18; Isa 32:17; Hos 10:12; Php 1:11
4:1 [g]Tit 3:9
[h]S Ro 7:23
4:2 [i]Mt 5:21,22; Jas 5:6; 1Jn 3:15
4:3 [j]Ps 18:41; S Mt 7:7
[k]Ps 66:18;
1Jn 3:22; 5:14
4:4 [l]Isa 54:5; Jer 3:20; Hos 2:2-5; 3:1; 9:1 [m]S Jas 1:27
[n]Ro 8:7; 1Jn 2:15
[o]Jn 15:19
4:5 [p]1Co 6:19
4:6 [q]Pr 3:34; S Mt 23:12
4:7 [r]Eph 4:27; 6:11; 1Pe 5:6-9
4:8 [s]Ps 73:28; Zec 1:3; Mal 3:7; Heb 7:19
[t]Isa 1:16
[u]Ps 24:4; Jer 4:14
[v]Ps 119:113; Jas 1:8
4:9 [w]Lk 6:25
4:10 [x]ver 6; Job 5:11; 1Pe 5:6
4:11 [y]Ro 1:30; 2Co 12:20;
1Pe 2:1 [z]S Mt 7:1
[a]Jas 2:8 [b]Jas 1:22
4:12 [c]Isa 33:22; S Jas 5:9
[d]Mt 10:28
[e]S Mt 7:1
4:13 [f]Jas 5:1
[g]Pr 27:1; Lk 12:18-20
4:14 [h]Job 7:7; Ps 39:5; 102:3; 144:4; Isa 2:22
4:15 [i]S Ac 18:21
4:16 [j]1Co 5:6
4:17 [k]Lk 12:47; Jn 9:41

5:1 [l]Jas 4:13 [m]Lk 6:24; 1Ti 6:9; Jas 2:2-6 [n]Isa 13:6; Eze 30:2 **5:2** [o]Job 13:28; Ps 39:11; Isa 50:9; Mt 6:19,20

[g]5 Or that God jealously longs for the spirit that he made to live in us; or that the Spirit he caused to live in us longs jealously   [h]6 Prov. 3:34

(1Co 14:33).
3:17 *impartial.* See 2:1-13.
3:18 *Peacemakers.* Contrast v. 16. Discord cannot produce righteousness.
4:1 *desires.* The Greek for this term is the source of our word "hedonism."
4:2 *kill.* Figurative (hyperbole) for "hate."
4:4 *adulterous people.* Those who are spiritually unfaithful, who love the world rather than God. For spiritual adultery see, e.g., Jer 31:32. *world.* See note on 1:27.
4:5 *Scripture.* The passage James had in mind is not known. *the spirit... envies intensely.* The words "the spirit he caused to live in us" refer to God's creation of man (Ge 2:7). Because of the fall, man's spirit "envies intensely," but God's grace (v. 6) is able to overcome man's envy. Regarding the two alternative translations (see NIV text note), the meaning of the first is that God jealously longs for our faithfulness and our love (see 4:4). In this case the Scripture referred to may be Ex 20:5. The second capitalizes "Spirit" and makes him the subject. It is the Holy Spirit who longs jealously for our full devotion. If this is the correct translation, it is the only clear reference to the Holy Spirit in the letter.
4:6 See 1Pe 5:5, which also quotes Pr 3:34.

4:7-10 These verses contain ten commands, each of which is so stated in Greek that it calls for immediate action in rooting out the sinful attitude of pride.
4:7 *Resist the devil.* See Eph 6:11-18; 1Pe 5:8-9.
4:8 *Wash your hands.* Before the OT priests approached God at the tabernacle, they had to wash their hands and feet at the bronze basin as a symbol of spiritual cleansing (Ex 30:17-21). See Ps 24:4 for the imagery of "clean hands and a pure heart."
4:9 *Grieve, mourn and wail.* Repent.
4:10 See Mt 23:12.
4:11 *speaks against his brother... speaks against the law.* See note on 2:8; see also Ex 20:16; Ps 15:3; 50:19-20; Pr 6:16,19. To speak against a brother is to scorn the law of love.
5:1 *rich.* These (as also in 2:2,6) are not Christians, for James warns them to repent and weep because of the coming misery. Verses 1-6 are similar to OT declarations of judgment against pagan nations, interspersed in books otherwise addressed to God's people (Isa 13-23; Jer 46-51; Eze 25-32; Am 1:3-2:16; Zep 2:4-15).
5:2 *clothes.* One of the main forms of wealth in the ancient world (see Ac 20:33).
5:3 *corrosion.* The result of hoarding. It will both testify

corrosion will testify against you and eat your flesh like fire. You have hoarded wealth in the last days.[p] [4]Look! The wages you failed to pay the workmen[q] who mowed your fields are crying out against you. The cries[r] of the harvesters have reached the ears of the Lord Almighty.[s] [5]You have lived on earth in luxury and self-indulgence. You have fattened yourselves[t] in the day of slaughter.[iu] [6]You have condemned and murdered[v] innocent men,[w] who were not opposing you.

Patience in Suffering

[7]Be patient, then, brothers, until the Lord's coming.[x] See how the farmer waits for the land to yield its valuable crop and how patient he is[y] for the autumn and spring rains.[z] [8]You too, be patient and stand firm, because the Lord's coming[a] is near.[b] [9]Don't grumble against each other, brothers,[c] or you will be judged. The Judge[d] is standing at the door![e]

[10]Brothers, as an example of patience in the face of suffering, take the prophets[f] who spoke in the name of the Lord. [11]As you know, we consider blessed[g] those who have persevered. You have heard of Job's perseverance[h] and have seen what the Lord finally brought about.[i] The Lord is full of compassion and mercy.[j]

[12]Above all, my brothers, do not swear—not by heaven or by earth or by anything else. Let your "Yes" be yes, and your "No," no, or you will be condemned.[k]

The Prayer of Faith

[13]Is any one of you in trouble? He should pray.[l] Is anyone happy? Let him sing songs of praise.[m] [14]Is any one of you sick? He should call the elders[n] of the church to pray over him and anoint him with oil[o] in the name of the Lord. [15]And the prayer offered in faith[p] will make the sick person well; the Lord will raise him up. If he has sinned, he will be forgiven. [16]Therefore confess your sins[q] to each other and pray for each other so that you may be healed.[r] The prayer of a righteous man is powerful and effective.[s]

[17]Elijah was a man just like us.[t] He prayed earnestly that it would not rain, and it did not rain on the land for three and a half years.[u] [18]Again he prayed, and the heavens gave rain, and the earth produced its crops.[v]

[19]My brothers, if one of you should wander from the truth[w] and someone should bring him back,[x] [20]remember this: Whoever turns a sinner from the error of his way will save[y] him from death and cover over a multitude of sins.[z]

5:3 [p]ver 7,8
5:4 [q]Lev 19:13; Jer 22:13; Mal 3:5
[r]Dt 24:15
[s]Ro 9:29
5:5 [t]Eze 16:49; Am 6:1; Lk 16:19
[u]Jer 12:3; 25:34
5:6 [v]Jas 4:2
[w]Heb 10:38
5:7 [x]S 1Co 1:7
[y]Gal 6:9
[z]Dt 11:14; Jer 5:24; Joel 2:23
5:8 [a]S 1Co 1:7
[b]S Ro 13:11
5:9 [c]Jas 4:11
[d]Ps 94:2;
1Co 4:5; Jas 4:12; 1Pe 4:5
[e]Mt 24:33
5:10 [f]S Mt 5:12
5:11 [g]Mt 5:10
2:10; S Heb 10:36
[h]Job 1:21,22; Job 42:10,12-17
[i]Ex 34:6; Nu 14:18; Ps 103:8

5:12 [k]Mt 5:34-37
5:13 [l]Ps 50:15
[m]Col 3:16
5:14 [n]S Ac 11:30
[o]Ps 23:5; Isa 1:6; Mk 6:13; 16:18; Lk 10:34
5:15 [p]Jas 1:6
5:16 [q]Mt 3:6; Ac 19:18
[r]Heb 12:13; 1Pe 2:24
[s]S Mt 7:7; S Jn 9:31
5:17 [t]Ac 14:15
[u]1Ki 17:1; Lk 4:25
5:18 [v]1Ki 18:41-45
5:19 [w]Jas 3:14
5:20 [y]S Ro 11:14
[z]1Pe 4:8

i5 Or yourselves as in a day of feasting

---

against and judge the selfish rich. *last days.* See notes on Ac 2:17; 1Ti 4:1; 2Ti 3:1; Heb 1:1; 1Jn 2:18.

5:4 *the Lord Almighty.* See comments on "the LORD of hosts" in the Preface to the NIV; see also notes on Ge 17:1; 1Sa 1:3.

5:5 *luxury and self-indulgence.* See Lk 16:19–31. *the day of slaughter.* The day of judgment. The wicked rich are like cattle that continue to fatten themselves on the very day they are to be slaughtered, totally unaware of coming destruction.

5:7 *then.* Refers back to vv. 1–6. Since the believers are suffering at the hands of the wicked rich, they are to look forward patiently to the Lord's return. *autumn and spring rains.* In Israel the autumn rain comes in October and November soon after the grain is sown, and the spring rain comes in March and April just prior to harvest (Dt 11:14; Jer 5:24; Hos 6:3; Joel 2:24).

5:9 *Don't grumble.* James calls for patience toward believers as well as unbelievers (vv. 7–8). *The Judge is standing at the door!* A reference to Christ's second coming (see vv. 7–8) and the judgment associated with it. The NT insistence on imminence (e.g., in Ro 13:12; Heb 10:25; 1Pe 4:7; Rev 22:20) arises from the teaching that the "last days" began with the incarnation. We have been living in the "last days" (v. 3) ever since (see note on Heb 1:1). The next great event in redemptive history is Christ's second coming. The NT does not say when it will take place, but its certainty is never questioned and believers are consistently admonished to watch for it. It was in this light that James expected the imminent return of Christ.

5:11 *Job's perseverance.* Not "patience." Job was not patient (Job 3; 12:1–3; 16:1–3; 21:4), but he persevered

(Job 1:20–22; 2:9–10; 13:15). This is the only place in the NT where Job is mentioned, though Job 5:13 is quoted in 1Co 3:19.

5:12 *do not swear.* James's words are very close to Christ's (Mt 5:33–37). James is not condemning the taking of solemn oaths, such as God's before Abraham (Heb 6:13) or Jesus' before Caiaphas (Mt 26:63–64) or Paul's (Ro 1:9; 9:1) or a man's before the Lord (Ex 22:11). Rather, he is condemning the flippant use of God's name or a sacred object to guarantee the truth of what is spoken.

5:14 *elders.* See notes on 1Ti 3:1; 5:17. *church.* See note on Mt 16:18. *oil.* One of the best-known ancient medicines (referred to by Philo, Pliny and the physician Galen; see also Isa 1:6; Lk 10:34). Some believe that James may be using the term medicinally in this passage. Others, however, regard its use here as an aid to faith, an outward sign of the healing to be brought about by God in response to "prayer offered in faith" (v. 15; see Mk 6:13).

5:17 *Elijah . . . prayed.* That Elijah prayed may be assumed from 1Ki 17:1; 18:41–46. The three and a half years (see also Lk 4:25) are probably a round number (half of seven), based on 1Ki 18:1 (see note there; cf. Rev 11:1–6).

5:19 *wander from the truth.* The wanderer is either a professing Christian, whose faith is not genuine (cf. Heb 6:4–8; 2Pe 2:20–21), or a sinning Christian, who needs to be restored. For the former, the death spoken of in v. 20 is the "second death" (Rev 21:8); for the latter, it is physical death (cf. 1Co 11:30). See note on 1Jn 5:16.

5:20 *cover over a multitude of sins.* The sins of the wanderer will be forgiven by God.

1 PETER

Author and Date

The author identifies himself as the apostle Peter (1:1), and the contents and character of the letter support his authorship (see notes on 1:12; 4:13; 5:1-2,5,13). Moreover, the letter reflects the history and terminology of the Gospels and Acts (notably Peter's speeches); its themes and concepts reflect Peter's experiences and his associations in the period of our Lord's earthly ministry and in the apostolic age. That he was acquainted, e.g., with Paul and his letters is made clear in 2Pe 3:15-16; Gal 1:18; 2:1-21 and elsewhere; coincidences in thought and expression with Paul's writings are therefore not surprising.

From the beginning, 1 Peter was recognized as authoritative and as the work of the apostle Peter. The earliest reference to it may be 2Pe 3:1, where Peter himself refers to a former letter he had written. 1 Clement (A.D. 95) seems to indicate acquaintance with 1 Peter. Polycarp, a disciple of the apostle John, makes use of 1 Peter in his letter to the Philippians. The author of the Gospel of Truth (140-150) was acquainted with 1 Peter. Eusebius (fourth century) indicated that it was universally received.

The letter was explicitly ascribed to Peter by that group of church fathers whose testimonies appear in the attestation of so many of the genuine NT writings, namely, Irenaeus (A.D. 140-203), Tertullian (150-222), Clement of Alexandria (155-215) and Origen (185-253). It is thus clear that Peter's authorship of the book has early and strong support.

Nevertheless some claim that the idiomatic Greek of this letter is beyond Peter's competence. But in his time Aramaic, Hebrew and Greek were used in Palestine, and he may well have been acquainted with more than one language. That he was not a professionally trained scribe (Ac 4:13) does not mean that he was unacquainted with Greek; in fact, as a Galilean fisherman he in all likelihood did use it. Even if he had not known it in the earliest days of the church, he may have acquired it as an important aid to his apostolic ministry in the decades that intervened between then and the writing of 1 Peter.

It is true, however, that the Greek of 1 Peter is good literary Greek, and even though Peter could no doubt speak Greek, as so many in the Mediterranean world could, it is unlikely that he would write such polished Greek. But it is at this point that Peter's remark in 5:12 concerning Silas may be significant. Here the apostle claims that he wrote "with the help of " (more lit. "through" or "by means of") Silas. This phrase cannot refer merely to Silas as a letter carrier. Thus Silas was the intermediate agent in writing. Some have claimed that Silas's qualifications for recording Peter's letter in literary Greek are found in Ac 15:22-29. It is known that a secretary in those days often composed documents in good Greek for those who did not have the language facility to do so. Thus in 1 Peter Silas's Greek may be seen, while in 2 Peter it may be Peter's rough Greek that appears.

Some also maintain that the book reflects a situation that did not exist until after Peter's death, suggesting that the persecution referred to in 4:14-16; 5:8-9 is descriptive of Domitian's reign (A.D. 81-96). However, the situation that was developing in Nero's time (54-68) is just as adequately described by those verses. The book can be satisfactorily dated in the early 60s. It cannot be placed earlier than 60 since it shows familiarity with Paul's Prison Letters (e.g., Colossians and Ephesians, which are to be dated no earlier than 60): Compare 1:1-3 with Eph 1:1-3; 2:18 with Col 3:22; 3:1-6 with Eph 5:22-24. Furthermore, it cannot be dated later than 67/68, since Peter was martyred during Nero's reign.

Place of Writing

In 5:13 Peter indicates that he was in Babylon when he wrote 1 Peter. Among the interpretations that have been suggested are that he was writing from (1) Egyptian Babylon, which was a military post, (2) Mesopotamian Babylon, (3) Jerusalem and (4) Rome. Peter may well be using the name "Babylon" symbolically, as it seems to be used in the book of Revelation (see, e.g., notes on Rev 17:9-10). Tradition connects him in the latter part of his life with Rome, and certain early writers held that 1 Peter was

written there. On the other hand, it is known that Babylon existed in the first century as a small town on the Euphrates. Furthermore, it is pointed out that (1) there is no evidence that the term Babylon was used figuratively to refer to Rome until Revelation was written (c. A.D. 95), and (2) the context of 5:13 is not at all figurative or cryptic.

Recipients

See note on 1:1.

Themes

Although 1 Peter is a short letter, it touches on various doctrines and has much to say about Christian life and duties. It is not surprising that different readers have found it to have different principal themes. For example, it has been characterized as a letter of separation, of suffering and persecution, of suffering and glory, of hope, of pilgrimage, of courage, and as a letter dealing with the true grace of God. Peter says that he has written "encouraging you and testifying that this is the true grace of God" (5:12). This is a definitive general description of the letter, but it does not exclude the recognition of numerous subordinate and contributory themes. The letter is composed also of a series of exhortations (imperatives) that run from 1:13 to 5:11.

Outline

I. Salutation (1:1-2)
II. Praise to God for His Grace and Salvation (1:3-12)
III. Exhortations to Holiness of Life (1:13-5:11)
    A. The Requirement of Holiness (1:13-2:3)
    B. The Position of Believers (2:4-12)
        1. A spiritual house (2:4-8)
        2. A chosen people (2:9-10)
        3. Aliens and strangers (2:11-12)
    C. Submission to Authority (2:13-3:7)
        1. Submission to rulers (2:13-17)
        2. Submission to masters (2:18-20)
        3. Christ's example of submission (2:21-25)
        4. Submission of wives to husbands (3:1-6)
        5. The corresponding duty of husbands (3:7)
    D. Duties of All (3:8-17)
    E. Christ's Example (3:18-4:6)
    F. Conduct in View of the End of All Things (4:7-11)
    G. Conduct of Those Who Suffer for Christ (4:12-19)
    H. Conduct of Elders (5:1-4)
    I. Conduct of Young Men (5:5-11)
IV. The Purpose of the Letter (5:12)
V. Closing Greetings (5:13-14)

1 Peter, an apostle of Jesus Christ,[a]

To God's elect,[b] strangers in the world,[c] scattered[d] throughout Pontus,[e] Galatia,[f] Cappadocia, Asia and Bithynia,[g] [2]who have been chosen according to the foreknowledge[h] of God the Father, through the sanctifying work of the Spirit,[i] for obedience[j] to Jesus Christ and sprinkling by his blood:[k]

Grace and peace be yours in abundance.[l]

Praise to God for a Living Hope

[3]Praise be to the God and Father of our Lord Jesus Christ![m] In his great mercy[n] he has given us new birth[o] into a living hope[p] through the resurrection of Jesus Christ from the dead,[q] [4]and into an inheritance[r] that can never perish, spoil or fade[s]—kept in heaven for you,[t] [5]who through faith are shielded by God's power[u] until the coming of the salvation[v] that is ready to be revealed[w] in the last time. [6]In this you greatly rejoice,[x] though

now for a little while[y] you may have had to suffer grief in all kinds of trials.[z] [7]These have come so that your faith—of greater worth than gold, which perishes even though refined by fire[a]—may be proved genuine[b] and may result in praise, glory and honor[c] when Jesus Christ is revealed.[d] [8]Though you have not seen him, you love him; and even though you do not see him now, you believe in him[e] and are filled with an inexpressible and glorious joy, [9]for you are receiving the goal of your faith, the salvation of your souls.[f]

[10]Concerning this salvation, the prophets, who spoke[g] of the grace that was to come to you,[h] searched intently and with the greatest care,[i] [11]trying to find out the time and circumstances to which the Spirit of Christ[j] in them was pointing when he predicted[k] the sufferings of Christ and the glories that would follow. [12]It was revealed to them that they were not serving themselves but you,[l] when they spoke of the

1:1 [a]2Pe 1:1; [b]Mt 24:22; [c]S Heb 11:13; [d]S Jas 1:1; [e]Ac 2:9; 18:2; [f]S Ac 16:6; [g]Ac 16:7; **1:2** [h]Ro 8:29; [i]2Th 2:13 /ver 14,22; [k]Heb 10:22; 12:24 /S Ro 1:7; **1:3** [m]2Co 1:3; Eph 1:3 [n]Tit 3:5; [o]ver 23; S Jn 1:13; [p]ver 13,21; S Heb 3:6; [q]1Co 15:20; 1Pe 3:21; **1:4** [r]S Ac 20:32; S Ro 8:17; [s]1Pe 5:4; [t]Col 1:5; 2Ti 4:8; **1:5** [u]1Sa 2:9; Jn 10:28; [v]S Ro 11:14; [w]S Ro 8:18; **1:6** [x]Ro 5:2; [y]1Pe 5:10; [z]Jas 1:2; 1Pe 4:12; **1:7** [a]Job 23:10; Ps 66:10; Pr 17:3; Isa 48:10 [b]Jas 1:3; [c]2Co 4:17 [d]ver 13; S 1Th 2:19; 1Pe 4:13; **1:8** [e]Jn 20:29; **1:9** [f]Ro 6:22;

1:10 [g]S Mt 26:24 [h]ver 13 [i]S Mt 13:17 /S Ac 16:7; **1:11** [j]S Ac 16:7; 2Pe 1:21 [k]S Mt 26:24 **1:12** [l]S Ro 4:24

1:1 *Peter.* See notes on Mt 16:18; Jn 1:42. *apostle.* See notes on Mk 6:30; 1Co 1:1; Heb 3:1. *elect.* See note on Eph 1:4. *strangers in the world.* People temporarily residing on earth but whose home is in heaven (cf. 1Ch 29:15; Ps 39:12; Heb 13:14). *scattered throughout Pontus ... Bithynia.* Jewish and Gentile Christians scattered throughout much of Asia Minor. People from this area were in Jerusalem on the day of Pentecost (see Ac 2:9–11). Paul preached and taught in some of these provinces (see, e.g., Ac 16:6; 18:23; 19:10,26).

1:2 *chosen.* See note on Eph 1:4. *foreknowledge.* See note on Ro 8:29. *Father ... Spirit ... Jesus Christ.* All three persons of the Trinity are involved in the redemption of the elect. *sanctifying work.* See note on 2Th 2:13. The order of the terms employed suggests that the sanctifying work of the Spirit referred to here is the influence of the Spirit that draws one from sin toward holiness. Peter says it is "for" (or "to") obedience and sprinkling of Christ's blood, i.e., the Spirit's sanctifying leads to obedient saving faith and cleansing from sin (see note on 1Co 7:14). *obedience to Jesus Christ.* God's choice or election is designed to bring this about. *sprinkling by his blood.* The benefits of Christ's redemption are applied to his people (cf. Ex 24:4–8; Isa 52:15; Heb 9:11–14, 18–28). *Grace and peace.* See notes on Jnh 4:2; Jn 14:27; 20:19; Gal 1:3; Eph 1:2.

1:3 *living hope.* In spite of the frequent suffering and persecution mentioned in this letter (v. 6; 2:12,18–25; 3:13–18; 4:1,4,12–19; 5:1,7–10), hope is such a key thought in it (the word itself is used here and in vv. 13,21; 3:5,15) that it may be called a letter of hope in the midst of suffering (see Introduction: Themes). In the Bible, hope is not wishful thinking but a firm conviction, much like faith that is directed toward the future. *resurrection of Jesus Christ.* Secures for his people their new birth and the hope that they will be resurrected just as he was.

1:4 *into an inheritance.* Believers are born again not only to a hope but also to the inheritance that is the substance of the hope. The inheritance is eternal—in its essence (it is not subject to decay) and in its preservation (it is divinely kept for us).

1:5 *through faith ... by God's power.* There are two sides to the perseverance of the Christian. He is shielded (1) by God's power and (2) by his own faith. Thus he is never kept contrary to his will nor apart from God's activity. *salvation.* See note on 2Ti 1:9. The Bible speaks of salvation as (1) past—when a person first believes (see, e.g., Tit 3:5), (2) present—the continuing process of salvation, or sanctification (see v. 9; 1Co 1:18), and (3) future—when Christ returns and salvation, or sanctification, is completed through glorification (here; see also Ro 8:23,30; 13:11).

1:7 *that your faith ... may be proved genuine.* See Ro 5:3; Jas 1:2–4. Not only is the faith itself precious, but Peter's words indicate that the trial of faith is also valuable. *glory.* A key word in 1,2 Peter.

1:8 *though you do not see him now, you believe.* Similar to Jesus' saying in Jn 20:29, on an occasion when Peter was present.

1:9 *souls.* Implies the whole person. Peter is not excluding the body from heaven.

1:10 *prophets ... searched intently.* Inspiration (see 2Pe 1:21) did not bestow omniscience. The prophets probably did not always understand the full significance of all the words they spoke.

1:11 *Spirit of Christ.* The Holy Spirit is called this because Christ sent him (see Jn 16:7) and ministered through him (see Lk 4:14,18). *the sufferings of Christ and the glories.* A theme running through the Bible (see, e.g., Ps 22; Isa 52:13–53:12; Zec 9:9–10; 13:7; Mt 16:21–23; 17:22; 20:19; Lk 24:26,46; Jn 2:19; Ac 3:17–21), and a basic concept in this letter (vv. 18–21; 3:17–22; 4:12–16; 5:1, 4,9–10). Those who are united to Christ will also, after suffering, enter into glory. And they will benefit in the midst of their present sufferings from his having already entered into glory (vv. 3,8,21; 3:21–22).

1:12 *Holy Spirit sent from heaven.* By Christ, on the day of Pentecost (see Ac 2:33), at which Peter was present. God the Father also sent the Spirit (see Jn 14:16,26). *angels long to look into.* Their intense desire is highlighted by the Greek word rendered "to look into." It means "to stoop and look intently" (see Jn 20:5,11).

things that have now been told you by those who have preached the gospel to you[m] by the Holy Spirit sent from heaven.[n] Even angels long to look into these things.

Be Holy

[13]Therefore, prepare your minds for action; be self-controlled;[o] set your hope[p] fully on the grace to be given you[q] when Jesus Christ is revealed.[r] [14]As obedient[s] children, do not conform[t] to the evil desires you had when you lived in ignorance.[u] [15]But just as he who called you is holy, so be holy in all you do;[v] [16]for it is written: "Be holy, because I am holy."[a] [w]

[17]Since you call on a Father[x] who judges each man's work[y] impartially,[z] live your lives as strangers[a] here in reverent fear.[b] [18]For you know that it was not with perishable things such as silver or gold that you were redeemed[c] from the empty way of life[d] handed down to you from your forefathers, [19]but with the precious blood[e] of Christ, a lamb[f] without blemish or defect.[g] [20]He was chosen before the creation of the world,[h] but was revealed in these

last times[i] for your sake. [21]Through him you believe in God,[j] who raised him from the dead[k] and glorified him,[l] and so your faith and hope[m] are in God.

[22]Now that you have purified[n] yourselves by obeying[o] the truth so that you have sincere love for your brothers, love one another deeply,[p] from the heart.[b] [23]For you have been born again,[q] not of perishable seed, but of imperishable,[r] through the living and enduring word of God.[s] [24]For,

"All men are like grass,
    and all their glory is like the flowers
        of the field;
the grass withers and the flowers fall,
[25]   but the word of the Lord stands
        forever."[c] [t]

And this is the word that was preached to you.

2 Therefore, rid yourselves[u] of all malice and all deceit, hypocrisy, envy, and

Cross references

1:12 [m]ver 25
[n]S Lk 24:49
1:13 [o]S Ac 24:25
[p]ver 3,21;
S Heb 3:6 [q]ver 10
[r]ver 7; S 1Co 1:7
1:14 [s]ver 2,22
[t]Ro 12:2
[u]Eph 4:18
1:15 [v]Isa 35:8;
1Th 4:7; 1Jn 3:3
1:16 [w]Lev 11:44,
45; 19:2; 20:7
1:17 [x]S Mt 6:9
[y]S Mt 16:27
[z]S Ac 10:34
[a]S Heb 11:13
[b]Heb 12:28
1:18 [c]S Mt 20:28;
S 1Co 6:20
[d]Gal 4:3
1:19 [e]S Ro 3:25
[f]S Jn 1:29
[g]Ex 12:5
1:20 [h]Eph 1:4;
S Mt 25:34

[i]Heb 9:26
1:21 [j]Ro 4:24;
10:9 [k]S Ac 2:24
[l]Php 2:7-9;
Heb 2:9 [m]ver 3,
13; S Heb 3:6
1:22 [n]Jas 4:8
[o]ver 2,14
[p]S Jn 13:34;
S Ro 12:10
1:23 [q]ver 3;
S Jn 1:13 [r]Jn 1:13
[s]S Heb 4:12
1:25 [t]Isa 40:6-8;
S Jas 1:10,11

2:1 [u]S Eph 4:22

[a]16 Lev. 11:44,45; 19:2; 20:7   [b]22 Some early manuscripts from a pure heart   [c]25 Isaiah 40:6-8

Study notes

1:13 *prepare . . . for action.* The first of a long series of exhortations (actually imperatives) that end at 5:11. This one is a graphic call for action. In the language of the first century it meant that the reader should literally gather up his long, flowing garments and be ready for physical action. *grace to be given you.* The final state of complete blessedness and deliverance from sin. Peter later indicates that a major purpose of this letter is to encourage and testify regarding the true grace of God (5:12).

1:14 *children.* Christians, born into the family of God (see v. 23), are children of their heavenly Father (v. 17) and can pray, "Our Father in heaven" (Mt 6:9). Believers are also described as being adopted into God's family (see Ro 8:15 and NIV text note).

1:16 *Be holy, because I am holy.* To be holy is to be set apart—set apart from sin and impurity, and set apart to God. The complete moral perfection of God, whose eyes are too pure to look on evil with favor (Hab 1:13), should move his people to strive for moral purity. 1 Peter is a letter of practical earnestness, filled with exhortations and encouragements.

1:17 *impartially.* See Ro 2:11; Jas 2:1. *strangers.* See note on v. 1. *reverent fear.* Not terror, but wholesome reverence and respect for God, which is the basis for all godly living (cf. Pr 1:7; 8:13; 16:6).

1:18 *redeemed.* In the Bible, to redeem means to free someone from something bad by paying a penalty, or a ransom (see e.g., Ex 21:30 and note; see also Ex 13:13). Likewise, in the Greek world slaves could be redeemed by the payment of a price, either by someone else or by the slave himself. Similarly, Jesus redeems believers from the "curse of the law" (Gal 3:13) and "all wickedness" (Tit 2:14). The ransom price is not silver or gold, but Christ's blood (Eph 1:7; 1Pe 1:19; Rev 5:9), i.e., his death (Mt 20:28; Mk 10:45; Heb 9:15) or Christ himself (Gal 3:13). The result is the "forgiveness of sins" (Col 1:14) and "justification" (Ro 3:24; see note there). *empty way of life . . . from your forefathers.* Some maintain that the recipients must have

been pagans because the NT stresses the emptiness of pagan life (Ro 1:21; Eph 4:17). Others think they were Jews since Jews were traditionalists who stressed the influence of the father as teacher in the home. In the light of the context of the whole letter, probably both Jews and Gentiles are addressed.

1:19 *lamb.* The OT sacrifices were types (foreshadowings) of Christ, depicting the ultimate and only effective sacrifice. Thus Christ is the Passover lamb (1Co 5:7), who takes away the sin of the world (Jn 1:29). *without blemish or defect.* See Heb 9:14 and note; see also Introduction to Leviticus: Themes.

1:20 *chosen.* Some think the Greek for this word means "foreknown," i.e., God knew before creation that it would be necessary for Christ to redeem man (cf. Rev 13:8), but he has revealed Christ in these last times. Others interpret the word as meaning that in eternity past God chose Christ as Redeemer. *these last times.* See notes on Ac 2:17; 1Ti 4:1; 2Ti 3:1; Heb 1:1; 1Jn 2:18.

1:22 *sincere love.* See Ro 12:9. *love one another.* A command no doubt based on Jn 13:34–35. See also 1Th 4:9–10, where, like Peter, Paul commends his readers for their love of fellow believers and then urges them to love still more. *deeply.* Fervently.

1:23 *born again . . . through the . . . word of God.* The new birth comes about through the direct action of the Holy Spirit (Tit 3:5), but the word of God also plays an important role (see Jas 1:18), for it presents the gospel to the sinner and calls on him to repent and believe in Christ (see v. 25). *perishable seed . . . imperishable.* In this context the seed is doubtless the word of God, which is imperishable, living and enduring.

1:25 *the word . . . stands forever.* The main point of the quotation here.

2:1 *Therefore.* Connects the exhortations that follow with 1:23–25; compare "born again" (1:23) with "newborn babies" (2:2).

slander^y of every kind. ²Like newborn babies, crave pure spiritual milk,^w so that by it you may grow up^x in your salvation, ³now that you have tasted that the Lord is good.^y

The Living Stone and a Chosen People

⁴As you come to him, the living Stone^z—rejected by men but chosen by God^a and precious to him— ⁵you also, like living stones, are being built^b into a spiritual house^c to be a holy priesthood,^d offering spiritual sacrifices acceptable to God through Jesus Christ.^e ⁶For in Scripture it says:

"See, I lay a stone in Zion,
    a chosen and precious cornerstone,^f
and the one who trusts in him
    will never be put to shame."^{d g}

⁷Now to you who believe, this stone is precious. But to those who do not believe,^h

"The stone the builders rejectedⁱ
    has become the capstone,^e"^{f j}

⁸and,

"A stone that causes men to stumble
    and a rock that makes them fall."^{g k}

They stumble because they disobey the message—which is also what they were destined for.^l

⁹But you are a chosen people,^m a royal priesthood,ⁿ a holy nation,^o a people belonging to God,^p that you may declare the praises of him who called you out of darkness into his wonderful light.^q ¹⁰Once you were not a people, but now you are the people of God;^r once you had not received mercy, but now you have received mercy.

¹¹Dear friends,^s I urge you, as aliens and strangers in the world,^t to abstain

2:1 ^vS Jas 4:11
2:2 ^w1Co 3:2; Heb 5:12,13
2:2 ^xEph 4:15,16
2:3 ^yPs 34:8; Heb 6:5
2:4 ^zver 7
^aIsa 42:1
2:5 ^bPr 9:1; 1Co 3:9; Eph 2:20-22
^c1Ti 3:15 ^dver 9; Ex 19:6; Isa 61:6; Rev 1:6; 5:10; 20:6 ^ePhp 4:18; Heb 13:15
2:6 ^fEph 2:20
^gIsa 28:16; Ro 9:32,33; 10:11
2:7 ^h2Co 2:16
ⁱver 4 /Ps 118:22; S Ac 4:11

2:8 ^kIsa 8:14; S Lk 2:34
^lRo 9:22
2:9 ^mDt 10:15; 1Sa 12:22 ⁿver 5 ^oEx 19:6; Dt 7:6; Isa 62:12
^pS Tit 2:14
^qS Ac 26:18
2:10 ^rHos 1:9,10; 2:23; Ro 9:25,26
2:11
^sS 1Co 10:14
^tS Heb 11:13

^d6 Isaiah 28:16   ^e7 Or *cornerstone*
^f7 Psalm 118:22   ^g8 Isaiah 8:14

2:2 *crave.* The unrestrained hunger of a healthy baby provides an example of the kind of eager desire for spiritual food that ought to mark the believer. *spiritual milk.* Probably referring to God's word (1:23,25). The author is speaking figuratively. Milk is not to be understood here as in 1Co 3:2; Heb 5:12–14—in unfavorable contrast to solid food—but as an appropriate nourishment for babies. *grow up.* The Greek for this phrase is the standard term for the desirable growth of children.

2:3 *have tasted.* The tense of the Greek verb used here suggests that an initial act of tasting is referred to. Since this taste has proved satisfactory, the believers are urged to long for additional spiritual food.

2:4 *living Stone.* Christ (see vv. 6–8 and NIV text notes; cf. Mt 21:42; Mk 12:10–11; Lk 20:17; Ac 4:11; Ro 9:33). The Stone is living in that it is personal. Furthermore he is a life-giving Stone. Christ as the Son of God has life in himself (Jn 1:4; 5:26). See also "living water" (Jn 4:10–14; 7:38), "living bread" (Jn 6:51) and "living way" (Heb 10:20). *rejected by men but chosen by God.* Peter repeatedly makes a contrast in Acts between the hostility of unbelieving men toward Jesus and God's exaltation of him (Ac 2:22–36; 3:13–15; 4:10–11; 10:39–42).

2:5 *living stones.* Believers are not literal pieces of rock, but are persons. In addition, they derive their life from Christ, who is the original living Stone to whom they have come (v. 4), the "life-giving spirit" (1Co 15:45). These references to stones may well reflect Jesus' words to Peter in Mt 16:18. *spiritual house.* The house is spiritual in a metaphorical sense, but also in that it is formed and indwelt by the Spirit of God. Every stone in the house has been made alive by the Holy Spirit, sent by the exalted living Stone, Jesus Christ (cf. Ac 2:33). The OT temple provides the background of this passage (cf. Jn 2:19; 1Co 3:16; Eph 2:19–22). *holy priesthood.* The whole body of believers. As priests, believers are to (1) reflect the holiness of God and that of their high priest (see 1:15; Heb 7:26; 10:10), (2) offer spiritual sacrifices (here), (3) intercede for man before God and (4) represent God before man. *spiritual sacrifices.* The NT refers to a variety of offerings: bodies offered to God (Ro 12:1), offer-

ings of money or material goods (Php 4:18; Heb 13:16), sacrifices of praise to God (Heb 13:15) and sacrifices of doing good (Heb 13:16). *acceptable to God.* Through the work of our Mediator, Jesus Christ (cf. Jn 14:6). Believers are living stones that make up a spiritual temple in which, as a holy priesthood, they offer up spiritual sacrifices.

2:6 *precious cornerstone.* See Ps 118:22; Mt 21:42; Mk 12:10; Lk 20:17; Ac 4:11. This is an obvious reference to Christ, as vv. 6b–8 make clear. The cornerstone, which determined the design and orientation of the building, was the most significant stone in the structure. The picture that Peter creates is of a structure made up of believers (living stones, v. 5), the design and orientation of which are all in keeping with Christ, the cornerstone. *the one who trusts in him.* Two attitudes toward the cornerstone are evident: (1) Some trust in him; (2) others reject him (v. 7) and, as a result, stumble and fall (v. 8).

2:8 *what they were destined for.* Some see here an indication that some people are destined to fall and be lost. Others say that unbelievers are destined to be lost because God in his foreknowledge (cf. 1:2) saw them as unbelievers. Still others hold that Peter means that unbelief is destined to result in eternal destruction.

2:9 *chosen people.* See Eph 1:4 and note; Isa 43:10,20; 44:1–2. As Israel was called God's chosen people in the OT, so in the NT believers are designated as chosen, or elect. *royal priesthood.* See note on v. 5; see also Isa 61:6. *holy nation.* See Dt 28:9. *people belonging to God.* See Dt 4:20; 7:6; 14:2; Isa 43:21; Mal 3:17. Though once not the people of God, they are now the recipients of God's mercy (see Hos 1:6–10; Ro 9:25–26; 10:19). *declare the praises of him.* See Isa 43:20; Ac 2:11.

2:10 See notes on Hos 1:6,9; 2:1,22; Ro 9:25–26. In Hosea it is Israel who is not God's people; in Romans it is the Gentiles to whom Paul applies Hosea's words; in 1 Peter the words are applied to both.

2:11 *aliens and strangers.* See note on 1:1. As aliens and strangers on earth, whose citizenship is in heaven, they are to be separated from the corruption of the world, not yielding to its destructive sinful desires.

from sinful desires,^{u} which war against your soul.^{v} 12Live such good lives among the pagans that, though they accuse you of doing wrong, they may see your good deeds^w and glorify God^x on the day he visits us.

Submission to Rulers and Masters

13Submit yourselves for the Lord's sake to every authority^y instituted among men: whether to the king, as the supreme authority, 14or to governors, who are sent by him to punish those who do wrong^z and to commend those who do right.^{a} 15For it is God's will^b that by doing good you should silence the ignorant talk of foolish men.^{c} 16Live as free men,^{d} but do not use your freedom as a cover-up for evil;^{e} live as servants of God.^{f} 17Show proper respect to everyone: Love the brotherhood of believers,^{g} fear God, honor the king.^{h}

18Slaves, submit yourselves to your masters with all respect,^{i} not only to those who are good and considerate,^{j} but also to those who are harsh. 19For it is commendable if a man bears up under the pain of unjust suffering because he is conscious of God.^{k} 20But how is it to your credit if you receive a beating for doing wrong and endure it? But if you suffer for doing good and you endure it, this is commendable before God.^{l} 21To this^m you were called,^{n} because Christ suffered for you,^{o} leaving you an example,^{p} that you should follow in his steps.

22"He committed no sin,^{q}
  and no deceit was found in his
    mouth."^{h} ^{r}

23When they hurled their insults at him,^{s} he did not retaliate; when he suffered, he made no threats.^{t} Instead, he entrusted himself^u to him who judges justly.^{v} 24He himself bore our sins^w in his body on the tree,^{x} so that we might die to sins^y and

Cross references

2:11 ^{u}Ro 13:14; Gal 5:16 ^{v}Jas 4:1
2:12 ^{w}Php 2:15; Tit 2:8; S Tit 2:14; 1Pe 3:16 ^{x}S Mt 9:8
2:13 ^{y}Ro 13:1; Tit 3:1
2:14 ^{z}Ro 13:4 ^{a}Ro 13:3
2:15 ^{b}1Pe 3:17; 4:19 ^{c}S ver 12
2:16 ^{d}S Jn 8:32 ^{e}Gal 5:13 ^{f}S Ro 6:22
2:17 ^{g}S Ro 12:10 ^{h}Pr 24:21; Ro 13:7
2:18 ^{i}S Eph 6:5 ^{j}Jas 3:17
2:19 ^{k}1Pe 3:14, 17
2:20 ^{l}1Pe 3:17
2:21 ^{m}S Ac 14:22; Php 1:29; 1Pe 3:9 ^{n}S Ro 8:28 ^{o}1Pe 3:18; 4:1,13 ^{p}S Mt 11:29; 16:24
2:22 ^{q}S 2Co 5:21 ^{r}Isa 53:9
2:23 ^{s}Heb 12:3; 1Pe 3:9 ^{t}Isa 53:7 ^{u}Lk 23:46 ^{v}Ps 9:4
2:24 ^{w}Isa 53:4, 11; Heb 9:28

^{h}22 Isaiah 53:9

2:12 *see your good deeds*. Deeds that can be seen to be good (cf. Mt 5:16). The Greek word translated "see" refers to a careful watching, over a period of time. The pagans' evaluation is not a "snap judgment." *the day he visits us.* Perhaps the day of judgment and ensuing punishment, or possibly the day when God visits a person with salvation. The believer's good life may then influence the unbeliever to repent and believe.

2:13–3:6 Peter urges that Christians submit to all legitimate authorities, whether or not the persons exercising authority are believers. The recognition of properly constituted authority is necessary for the greatest good of the largest number of people, and it is necessary to best fulfill the will of God in the world.

2:13 *every authority instituted among men*. Authority established among men depends on God for its existence (Ro 13:1–2). Indirectly, when one disobeys a human ruler he disobeys God, who ordained the system of human government (cf. Ro 13:2). *to the king*. When Peter wrote, the emperor was the godless, brutal Nero, who ruled from A.D. 54 to 68 (see Introduction: Author and Date). Of course, obedience to the emperor must never be in violation of the law of God (to see this basic principle in action cf. Ac 4:19).

2:15 *silence the ignorant talk*. Good citizenship counters false charges made against Christians and thus commends the gospel to unbelievers.

2:16 *Live as free men*. Does not authorize rebellion against constituted authority, but urges believers freely to submit to God and to earthly authorities (as long as such submission does not conflict with the law of God). *as a cover-up for evil*. Genuine freedom is the freedom to serve God, a freedom exercised under law.

2:17 *proper respect to everyone*. Because every human being bears the image of God. *fear God*. See note on 1:17.

2:18 *Slaves*. Household servants, whatever their particular training and functions. The context indicates that Peter is addressing Christian slaves. NT writers do not attack slavery as an institution (see note on Eph 6:5), but the NT contains the principles that ultimately uprooted slavery. Peter's basic teachings on the subject may apply to employer-employee

relations today (see Eph 6:5–8; Col 3:22–25; 1Ti 6:1–2; Tit 2:9–10).

2:19 *conscious of God*. As submission to duly constituted authority is "for the Lord's sake" (v. 13; cf. Eph 6:7–8), so one will submit to the point of suffering unjustly if it is God's will.

2:21 *To this you were called*. The patient endurance of injustice is part of God's plan for the Christian. It was an important feature of the true grace of God experienced by the readers (5:12). *Christ suffered for you*. Cf. Isa 52:13–53:12. Christ is the supreme example of suffering evil for doing good. His experience as the suffering Servant-Savior transforms the sufferings of his followers from misery into privilege.

2:22 Scripture declares the sinlessness of Christ in the clearest of terms, allowing for no exception (see 1:19; Ac 3:14; 2Co 5:21; Heb 4:15; 7:26; 1Jn 3:5). *no deceit*. Cf. v. 1; 3:10.

2:23 Prominent examples of our Lord's silent submission are found in Mt 27:12–14,34–44 and parallels. *entrusted himself*. Cf. 4:19.

2:24 *bore our sins*. See Isa 53:12. Although dealing with the example set by Christ, Peter touches also on the redemptive work of Christ, which has significance far beyond that of setting an example. Peter here points to the substitutionary character of the atonement. Christ, like the sacrificial lamb of the OT, died for our sins, the innocent for the guilty. *tree*. A figurative reference to the cross (see note on Ac 5:30; see also Ac 10:39; 13:29; Gal 3:13). *that we might die to sins and live for righteousness*. Cf. Ro 6:3–14. Peter stresses the bearing of the cross on our sanctification. As a result of Christ's death on the cross, believers are positionally dead to sin so that they may live new lives and present themselves to God as instruments of righteousness (see note on Ro 6:11–13). *you have been healed*. See Isa 53:5; not generally viewed as a reference to physical healing, though some believe that such healing was included in the atonement (cf. Mt 8:16–17). Others see spiritual healing in this passage. It is another way of asserting that Christ's death brings salvation to those who trust in him.

live for righteousness; by his wounds you have been healed. *z* 25For you were like sheep going astray, *a* but now you have returned to the Shepherd *b* and Overseer of your souls. *c*

Wives and Husbands

3 Wives, in the same way be submissive *d* to your husbands *e* so that, if any of them do not believe the word, they may be won over *f* without words by the behavior of their wives, 2when they see the purity and reverence of your lives. 3Your beauty should not come from outward adornment, such as braided hair and the wearing of gold jewelry and fine clothes. *g* 4Instead, it should be that of your inner self, *h* the unfading beauty of a gentle and quiet spirit, which is of great worth in God's sight. *i* 5For this is the way the holy women of the past who put their hope in God *j* used to make themselves beautiful. *k* They were submissive to their own husbands, 6like Sarah, who obeyed Abraham and called him her master. *l* You are her daughters if you do what is right and do not give way to fear.

7Husbands, *m* in the same way be considerate as you live with your wives, and treat them with respect as the weaker part-

ner and as heirs with you of the gracious gift of life, so that nothing will hinder your prayers.

Suffering for Doing Good

8Finally, all of you, live in harmony with one another; *n* be sympathetic, love as brothers, *o* be compassionate and humble. *p* 9Do not repay evil with evil *q* or insult with insult, *r* but with blessing, *s* because to this *t* you were called *u* so that you may inherit a blessing. *v* 10For,

"Whoever would love life
　and see good days
must keep his tongue from evil
　and his lips from deceitful speech.
11He must turn from evil and do good;
　he must seek peace and pursue it.
12For the eyes of the Lord are on the
　righteous
　and his ears are attentive to their
　prayer,
but the face of the Lord is against those
　who do evil." *i w*

13Who is going to harm you if you are eager to do good? *x* 14But even if you should suffer for what is right, you are blessed. *y* "Do not fear what they fear *j*; do

i 12 Psalm 34:12-16　　*j* 14 Or *not fear their threats*

2:24 *z* Dt 32:39;
Ps 103:3;
Isa 53:5;
Heb 12:13;
Jas 5:16 **2:25**
a Isa 53:6
2:25 *b* S Jn 10:11
c Job 10:12
3:1 *d* 1Pe 2:18
e S Eph 5:22
f 1Co 7:16; 9:19
3:3 *g* Isa 3:18-23;
1Ti 2:9
3:4 *h* Ro 7:22;
Eph 3:16
i S Ro 2:29
3:5 *j* 1Ti 5:5
k Est 2:15
3:6 *l* Ge 18:12
3:7
m Eph 5:25-33;
Col 3:19

3:8 *n* S Ro 15:5
o S Ro 12:10
p Eph 4:2; 1Pe 5:5
3:9 *q* Ro 12:17;
1Th 5:15
r 1Pe 2:23
s Mt 5:44
t S 1Pe 2:21
u S Ro 8:28
v Heb 6:14
3:12
w Ps 34:12-16
3:13 *x* S Tit 2:14
3:14 *y* ver 17;
1Pe 2:19,20;
4:15,16

2:25 *Shepherd.* A concept raised here in connection with the allusion to the wandering sheep of Isa 53. The sheep had wandered from their shepherd, and to their Shepherd (Christ) they have now returned. See note on Ps 23:1; see also Jn 10:11,14 and note on Heb 13:20. *Overseer.* Christ (cf. 5:2,4; Ac 20:28). Elders are to be both shepherds and overseers, i.e., they are to look out for the welfare of the flock. These are not two separate offices or functions; the second term is a further explanation of the first.
3:1-6 Instructions to wives (cf. Ge 3:16; 1Co 11:3; Eph 5:22-24; Col 3:18; 1Ti 2:9-10; Tit 2:5).
3:1 *in the same way.* As believers are to submit to government authorities (2:13-17), and as slaves are to submit to masters (2:18-25). *be submissive.* The same Greek verb as is used in 2:13,18, a term that calls for submission to a recognized authority. Inferiority is not implied by this passage. The submission is one of role or function necessary for the orderly operation of the home. *the word.* The gospel message. *without words.* Believing wives are not to rely on argumentation to win their unbelieving husbands, but on the quality of their lives.
3:2 *purity and reverence.* Their lives are to be marked by a moral purity that springs from reverence toward God.
3:3 *hair . . . jewelry.* Extreme coiffures and gaudy exhibits of jewelry. Christian women should not rely on such extremes of adornment for beauty. *clothes.* The Greek for this word simply means "garment," but in this context expensive garments are meant.
3:5 *holy women of the past.* The standards stated by Peter are not limited to any particular time or culture.
3:6 *her master.* An expression of the submission called for in v. 1. *her daughters . . . fear.* Christian women become daughters of Sarah as they become like her in doing good and in not fearing any potential disaster, but trusting in God (cf.

Pr 3:25-27).
3:7 *weaker partner.* Not a reference to moral stamina, strength of character or mental capacity, but most likely to sheer physical strength. *heirs with you of the gracious gift of life.* Women experience the saving grace of God on equal terms with men (see Gal 3:28). *hinder your prayers.* Spiritual fellowship, with God and with one another, may be hindered by disregarding God's instruction concerning husband-wife relationships.
3:8-12 In 2:11-17 Peter addressed all his readers, and in 2:18-25 he spoke directly to slaves; in 3:1-6 he addressed wives, and in 3:7 husbands. Now he encourages all his readers to develop virtues appropriate in their relations with others (see "all of you," v. 8).
3:8 *live in harmony.* See Ro 12:16; Php 2:2. *be sympathetic.* See Ro 12:15; 1Co 12:26. *love as brothers.* See 1Th 4:9-10; Heb 13:1. *be compassionate.* See Col 3:12. *humble.* See Php 2:6-8.
3:9 See Ro 12:17-21.
3:10-12 Peter introduces this quotation from Ps 34 with the explanatory conjunction "For," showing that he views the quotation as giving reasons for obeying the exhortation of v. 9. According to the psalmist, (1) the one who does such things will find life to be most gratifying (v. 10), (2) his days will be good (v. 10), (3) God's eyes will ever be on him to bless him (v. 12), and (4) God's ears will be ready to hear his prayer (v. 12).
3:13 *Who . . . harm you . . . ?* As a general rule, people are not harmed for acts of kindness. This is especially true if one is an enthusiast ("eager") for doing good.
3:14 *even if you should suffer.* In the Greek, this conditional clause is the furthest removed from stating a reality. Suffering for righteousness is a remote possibility, but even if it does occur, it brings special blessing to the sufferer (see Mt

not be frightened."[k z] [15]But in your hearts set apart Christ as Lord. Always be prepared to give an answer[a] to everyone who asks you to give the reason for the hope[b] that you have. But do this with gentleness and respect, [16]keeping a clear conscience,[c] so that those who speak maliciously against your good behavior in Christ may be ashamed of their slander.[d] [17]It is better, if it is God's will,[e] to suffer for doing good[f] than for doing evil. [18]For Christ died for sins[g] once for all,[h] the righteous for the unrighteous, to bring you to God.[i] He was put to death in the body[j] but made alive by the Spirit,[k] [19]through whom[l] also he went and preached to the spirits in prison[l] [20]who disobeyed long ago when God waited patiently[m] in the days of Noah while the ark was being built.[n] In it

only a few people, eight in all,[o] were saved[p] through water, [21]and this water symbolizes baptism that now saves you[q] also—not the removal of dirt from the body but the pledge[m] of a good conscience[r] toward God. It saves you by the resurrection of Jesus Christ,[s] [22]who has gone into heaven[t] and is at God's right hand[u]—with angels, authorities and powers in submission to him.[v]

Living for God

4 Therefore, since Christ suffered in his body,[w] arm yourselves also with the same attitude, because he who has suffered in his body is done with sin.[x] [2]As a

Cross references

3:14 [z]Isa 8:12,13
3:15 [a]Col 4:6
[b]S Heb 3:6
3:16 [c]ver 21; S Ac 23:1
[d]1Pe 2:12,15
3:17 [e]1Pe 2:15; 4:19 [f]1Pe 2:20; 4:15,16
3:18 [g]1Pe 2:21; 4:1,13
[h]S Heb 7:27
[i]S Ro 5:2
[j]Col 1:22; 1Pe 4:1 [k]1Pe 4:6
3:19 [l]1Pe 4:6
3:20 [m]S Ro 2:4
[n]Ge 6:3,5,13,14
[o]Ge 8:18
[p]Heb 11:7
3:21 [q]S Ac 22:16
[r]ver 16; S Ac 23:1
[s]1Pe 1:3
3:22 [t]S Heb 4:14
[u]S Mk 16:19
[v]S Mt 28:18; S Ro 8:38
4:1 [w]S 1Pe 2:21
[x]S Ro 6:18

k[14] Isaiah 8:12   l[18,19] Or alive in the spirit, [19]through which   m[21] Or response

---

5:10–12). *what they fear.* See NIV text note. God's people are not to view things as unbelievers do. They are not to make worldly judgments or be afraid of the enemies of God. Instead, they are to fear God (see Isa 8:13).

3:15 *set apart Christ as Lord.* An exhortation to the readers to make an inner commitment to Christ. Then they need not be speechless when called on to defend their faith. Instead, there will be a readiness to answer. *with gentleness and respect.* The Christian is always to be a gentleman or gentlewoman, even when opposed by unbelievers. Our apologetic ("answer") is always to be given with love, never in degrading terms.

3:16 *ashamed of their slander.* Because it is shown to be obviously untrue and because the believer's loving attitude puts the opponent's bitterness in a bad light.

3:18 *once for all.* See Heb 9:28. *the righteous for the unrighteous.* Peter, like Paul in Php 2:5–11, refers to Jesus as an example of the type of conduct that should characterize the Christian. We are to be ready to suffer for doing good (vv. 13–14,17). The thought of Christ's suffering and death, however, leads Peter to comment on what occurred after Christ's death—which leads to tangential remarks about preaching to the spirits in prison and about baptism (see vv. 19–21). *made alive by the Spirit.* Referring to the resurrection. Elsewhere the resurrection is attributed to the Father (Ac 2:32; Gal 1:1; Eph 1:20) and to the Son (Jn 10:17–18). If the NIV text note is correct, the reference would be to Christ's own spirit, through which also "he preached to the spirits in prison" (v. 19).

3:19–20a Three main interpretations of this passage have been suggested: 1. Some hold that in his preincarnate state Christ went and preached through Noah to the wicked generation of that time. 2. Others argue that between his death and resurrection Christ went to the prison where fallen angels are incarcerated and there preached to the angels who are said to have left their proper state and married human women during Noah's time (cf. Ge 6:1–4; 2Pe 2:4; Jude 6). The "sons of God" in Ge 6:2,4 are said to have been angels, as they are in Job 1:6; 2:1 (see NIV text note). The message he preached to these evil angels was probably a declaration of victory. 3. Still others say that between death and resurrection Christ went to the place of the dead and preached to the spirits of Noah's wicked contemporaries. What he proclaimed may have been the gospel, or it may have been a declaration of victory for Christ and doom for his hearers.

The weakness of the first view is that it does not relate the event to Christ's death and resurrection, as the context

seems to do. The main problem with the second view is that it assumes sexual relations between angels and women, and such physical relations may not be possible for angels since they are spirits. A major difficulty with the third view is that the term "spirits" is only used of human beings when qualifying terms are added. Otherwise the term seems restricted to supernatural beings.

3:21 *water symbolizes baptism.* There is a double figure here. The flood symbolizes baptism, and baptism symbolizes salvation. The flood was a figure of baptism in that in both instances the water that spoke of judgment (in the flood the death of the wicked, in baptism the death of Christ and the believer) is the water that saves. Baptism is a symbol of salvation in that it depicts Christ's death, burial and resurrection and our identification with him in these experiences (see Ro 6:4). *now saves you also.* In reality, believers are saved by what baptism symbolizes—Christ's death and resurrection. The symbol and the reality are so closely related that the symbol is sometimes used to refer to the reality (see note on Ro 6:3–4). *pledge of a good conscience toward God.* The act of baptism is a commitment on the part of the believer in all good conscience to make sure that what baptism symbolizes will become a reality in his life. *saves you by the resurrection of Jesus Christ.* People are saved not by any ritual, but by the supernatural power of the resurrection.

3:22 *gone into heaven.* See Ac 1:9–11. *at God's right hand.* See Heb 1:3; 12:2. *angels, authorities and powers.* See Eph 1:21; 6:12.

4:1 *Therefore.* Since 3:19–22 is parenthetical, 4:1 ties directly back to 3:18. The aspect of Christ's suffering that these passages stress is suffering unjustly because one has done good. Furthermore, it is physical suffering—"in his body." *arm yourselves also with the same attitude.* Believers are to be prepared also to suffer unjustly, and to face such abuse with Christ's attitude—with his willingness to suffer for doing good. (For a similar principle in Paul's writings see Php 2:5–11.) *because . . . is done with sin.* Such suffering enables one to straighten out his priorities. Sinful desires and practices that once seemed important now seem insignificant when one's life is in jeopardy. Serious suffering for Christ advances the progress of sanctification. (Some see a parallel between this passage and Ro 6:1–14, but Peter is not referring to being dead to sin in Paul's sense.)

4:2 *for evil human desires . . . for the will of God.* Now that Christ's attitude prevails, God's will is the determining factor in life.

result, he does not live the rest of his
earthly life for evil human desires,[y] but
rather for the will of God. 3For you have
spent enough time in the past[z] doing what
pagans choose to do—living in debauchery, lust, drunkenness, orgies, carousing
and detestable idolatry.[a] 4They think it
strange that you do not plunge with them
into the same flood of dissipation, and they
heap abuse on you.[b] 5But they will have to
give account to him who is ready to judge
the living and the dead.[c] 6For this is the
reason the gospel was preached even to
those who are now dead,[d] so that they
might be judged according to men in regard to the body, but live according to God
in regard to the spirit.

7The end of all things is near.[e] Therefore be clear minded and self-controlled[f]
so that you can pray. 8Above all, love each
other deeply,[g] because love covers over a
multitude of sins.[h] 9Offer hospitality[i] to
one another without grumbling.[j] 10Each
one should use whatever gift he has received to serve others,[k] faithfully[l] administering God's grace in its various forms.
11If anyone speaks, he should do it as one
speaking the very words of God.[m] If anyone serves, he should do it with the
strength God provides,[n] so that in all
things God may be praised[o] through Jesus
Christ. To him be the glory and the power
for ever and ever. Amen.[p]

Suffering for Being a Christian

12Dear friends, do not be surprised at
the painful trial you are suffering,[q] as
though something strange were happening
to you. 13But rejoice[r] that you participate
in the sufferings of Christ,[s] so that you
may be overjoyed when his glory is revealed.[t] 14If you are insulted because of
the name of Christ,[u] you are blessed,[v] for
the Spirit of glory and of God rests on you.
15If you suffer, it should not be as a murderer or thief or any other kind of criminal,
or even as a meddler. 16However, if you
suffer as a Christian, do not be ashamed,
but praise God that you bear that name.[w]
17For it is time for judgment to begin with
the family of God;[x] and if it begins with
us, what will the outcome be for those
who do not obey the gospel of God?[y]

4:2 [y]Ro 6:2; 1Pe 1:14
4:3 [z]S Eph 2:2 [a]S Ro 13:13
4:4 [b]1Pe 3:16
4:5 [c]S Ac 10:42
4:6 [d]1Pe 3:19
4:7 [e]S Ro 13:11 [f]S Ac 24:25
4:8 [g]S 1Pe 1:22 [h]Pr 10:12; Jas 5:20
4:9 [i]S Ro 12:13 [j]Php 2:14
4:10 [k]Ro 12:6,7 [l]1Co 4:2
4:11 [m]1Th 2:4 [n]Eph 6:10 [o]1Co 10:31 [p]S Ro 11:36
4:12 [q]1Pe 1:6,7
4:13 [r]S Mt 5:12 [s]S 2Co 1:5 [t]Ro 8:17; 1Pe 1:7; 5:1
4:14 [u]S Jn 15:21 [v]Mt 5:11
4:16 [w]Ac 5:41
4:17 [x]Jer 25:29; Eze 9:6; Am 3:2; 1Ti 3:15 [y]2Th 1:8

4:3 *time in the past.* The time before conversion. *pagans.* Lit. "the Gentiles." Along with the term "idolatry," this suggests that at least some of the readers were Gentiles (see note on 1:1) who had been converted from a pagan life-style.
4:4 *They think it strange . . . and they heap abuse on you.* One of the reasons for the suffering the readers were undergoing.
4:5 *have to give account.* See Ac 17:31; Ro 2:5,16. *him who is ready to judge.* In the NT both the Father and the Son are said to be judge on the great, final judgment day. The Father is the ultimate source of judgment, but he will delegate judgment to the Son (cf. Jn 5:27; Ac 17:31). *the living and the dead.* Those alive and those dead when the final judgment day dawns.
4:6 *For this is the reason.* The reason referred to is expressed in the latter part of the verse (in the "so that" clause), not in the preceding verse. *was preached even to those who are now dead.* This preaching was a past event. The word "now" does not occur in the Greek, but it is necessary to make it clear that the preaching was done not after these people had died, but while they were still alive. (There will be no opportunity for people to be saved after death; see Heb 9:27.) *that they might be judged according to men in regard to the body.* The first reason that the gospel was preached to those now dead. Some say that this judgment is that to which all people must submit, either in this life (see Jn 5:24) or in the life to come (see v. 5). The gospel is preached to people in this life so that in Christ's death they may receive judgment now and avoid judgment to come. Others hold that these people are judged according to human standards by the pagan world, which does not understand why God's people no longer follow its sinful way of life (see vv. 2–4). So also the world misunderstood Christ (see Ac 2:22–24,36; 3:13–15; 5:30–32; 7:51–53). *but live according to God in regard to the spirit.* The second reason that the gospel was preached to those now dead. Some believe this means that all gospel preaching has as its goal that the hearers may live as God lives—eternally—and that this life is given by the Holy Spirit. Others maintain that it means that the ultimate reason for the preaching of the gospel is that God's people, even though the wicked world may abuse them and put them to death, will have eternal life, which the Holy Spirit imparts.
4:7 *The end . . . is near.* See note on Jas 5:9. *Therefore.* Anticipating the end times, particularly Christ's return, should influence believers' attitudes, actions and relationships (see 2Pe 3:11–14). *clear minded.* Christians are to be characterized by reason; are to make wise, mature decisions; and are to have a clearly defined, decisive purpose in life. *self-controlled.* See Gal 5:23. *pray.* Cf. 3:7; Lk 18:1; 1Co 7:5; Eph 6:18; 1Th 5:17; 1Jn 5:14–15.
4:8 *love each other deeply.* See 1Th 4:9–10; 2Pe 1:7; 1Jn 4:7–11. *love covers over . . . sins.* Love forgives again and again (see Mt 18:21–22; 1Co 13:5; Eph 4:32).
4:9 *Offer hospitality.* See Ro 12:13; 1Ti 3:2; 5:10; Tit 1:8; 3Jn 5–8.
4:10 *use whatever gift he has received.* See Ro 12:4–8; 1Co 12:7–11.
4:11 *very words.* The Greek for this phrase is used to refer to the Scriptures or to words God has spoken (see Ac 7:38; Ro 3:2). *To him be the glory.* See 1Co 1:26–31; Jude 24–25.
4:12 *Dear friends.* Or "Loved ones" (see 2:11). *do not be surprised at the painful trial.* See 1:6–7; 2:20–21.
4:13 *rejoice that you participate in the sufferings of Christ.* See note on Col 1:24. Peter once rebelled against the idea that Christ would suffer (see Mt 16:21–23).
4:14 *insulted because of the name of Christ.* See Mt 5:11–12; Jn 15:18–20; Ac 5:41; 14:22; Ro 8:17; 2Co 1:5; Php 3:10; 2Ti 3:12.
4:17 *judgment to begin with the family of God.* The persecutions that believers were undergoing were divinely sent judgment intended to purify God's people. *the outcome . . . for those who do not obey the gospel.* If God brings judg-

¹⁸And,

"If it is hard for the righteous to be
    saved,
  what will become of the ungodly and
    the sinner?" [n] [z]

¹⁹So then, those who suffer according to
God's will [a] should commit themselves to
their faithful Creator and continue to do
good.

To Elders
and Young Men

5 To the elders among you, I appeal as a
fellow elder, [b] a witness [c] of Christ's
sufferings and one who also will share in
the glory to be revealed: [d] ²Be shepherds of
God's flock [e] that is under your care, serving as overseers—not because you must,
but because you are willing, as God wants
you to be; [f] not greedy for money, [g] but
eager to serve; ³not lording it over [h] those
entrusted to you, but being examples [i] to
the flock. ⁴And when the Chief Shepherd [j]
appears, you will receive the crown of
glory [k] that will never fade away. [l]

⁵Young men, in the same way be sub-
missive [m] to those who are older. All of

you, clothe yourselves with humility [n]
toward one another, because,

"God opposes the proud
  but gives grace to the humble." [o] [o]

⁶Humble yourselves, therefore, under
God's mighty hand, that he may lift you up
in due time. [p] ⁷Cast all your anxiety on
him [q] because he cares for you. [r]

⁸Be self-controlled [s] and alert. Your ene-
my the devil prowls around [t] like a roaring
lion [u] looking for someone to devour. ⁹Re-
sist him, [v] standing firm in the faith, [w] because you know that your brothers
throughout the world are undergoing the
same kind of sufferings. [x]

¹⁰And the God of all grace, who called
you [y] to his eternal glory [z] in Christ, after
you have suffered a little while, [a] will himself restore you and make you strong, [b]
firm and steadfast. ¹¹To him be the power
for ever and ever. Amen. [c]

Final Greetings

¹²With the help of Silas, [p] [d] whom I re-
gard as a faithful brother, I have written to

Cross references (center column)

4:18 [z] Pr 11:31;
  Lk 23:31
4:19 [a] 1Pe 2:15;
  3:17
5:1 [b] S Ac 11:30
  [c] S Lk 24:48
  [d] 1Pe 1:5,7; 4:13;
  Rev 1:9
5:2 [e] S Jn 21:16
  /2Co 9:7; Phm 14
  [g] S 1Ti 3:3
5:3 [h] Eze 34:4;
  Mt 20:25-28
  [i] S 1Ti 4:12
5:4 [j] S Jn 10:11
  [k] S 1Co 9:25
  [l] 1Pe 1:4
5:5 [m] Eph 5:21

[n] 1Pe 3:8
[o] Pr 3:34;
  S Mt 23:12
5:6 [p] Job 5:11;
  Jas 4:10
5:7 [q] Ps 37:5;
  Mt 6:25
  [r] Ps 55:22;
  Heb 13:5
5:8 [s] S Ac 24:25
  [t] Job 1:7
  [u] 2Ti 4:17
5:9 [v] Jas 4:7
  [w] Col 2:5
  [x] S Ac 14:22
5:10 [y] S Ro 8:28
  [z] 2Co 4:17;
  2Ti 2:10 [a] 1Pe 1:6
  [b] Ps 18:32;
  2Th 2:17
5:11 [c] S Ro 11:36
5:12 [d] S Ac 15:22

[n] 18 Prov. 11:31
[o] 5 Prov. 3:34 [p] 12 Greek *Silvanus*, a variant of *Silas*

---

ment on his own people, how much more serious will the
judgment be that he will bring on unbelievers!

5:1 *fellow elder.* See notes on Ac 20:17; 1Ti 3:1; 5:17.
Peter, who identified himself as an apostle at the beginning of
his letter (1:1), chooses now to identify himself with the
elders of the churches (cf. 2Jn 1; 3Jn 1). This would be
heartening to them in light of their great responsibilities and
the difficult situation faced by the churches. The churches for
which these elders were responsible were scattered across
much of Asia Minor (see 1:1), so if Peter was a local church
officer, he must have been officially related to one of them.
witness of Christ's sufferings. Peter had been with Jesus
from the early days of his ministry and was a witness of all its
phases and aspects, including the climactic events of his
suffering (cf. Mt 26:58; Mk 14:54; Lk 22:60–62; Jn
18:10–11,15–16). In this letter he bears notable witness to
Christ's sufferings (see 2:21–24) and obeys his command in
Ac 1:8. *share in the glory to be revealed.* Peter witnessed
Christ's glory in his ministry in general (see Jn 1:14; 2:11),
and, as one present at the transfiguration (see Mt 16:27;
17:8), he had already seen the glory of Christ's coming
kingdom. In God's appointed time, just as Christ suffered and
entered into glory, so all his people, after their sufferings, will
participate in his future glory.

5:2 *Be shepherds of God's flock.* A metaphor that our Lord
himself had employed (Jn 10:1–18; Lk 15:3–7) and that
must have been etched on Peter's mind (see Jn 21:15–17;
cf. 1Pe 2:25). Peter is fulfilling Christ's command to feed his
sheep as he writes this letter. What he writes to the elders is
reminiscent of Paul's farewell address to the Ephesian elders
(especially Ac 20:28). The term "shepherd" is an OT metaphor as well (see Eze 34:1–10, where the Lord holds the
leaders of Israel responsible for failing to care for the flock).

serving as overseers. The same term is used in Ac 20:28;
Php 1:1; 1Ti 3:2; Tit 1:7. See note on 1Ti 3:1. It is clear
from this passage, as well as from Ac 20:17,28, that the three
terms "elder," "overseer" and "shepherd" all apply to one
office (see note on Tit 1:7).

5:3 *not lording it over those entrusted to you.* Cf. Mt
16:24–27; Mk 10:42–45; Php 2:6–11; 2Th 3:9. Although
Peter has full apostolic authority (see v. 1), he does not lord
it over his readers in this letter, but exemplifies the virtues he
recommends.

5:4 *Chief Shepherd.* Christ. When he returns, he will
reward those who have served as shepherds under him.
never fade away. See 1:4.

5:5 *be submissive.* The theme that runs throughout
2:13–3:6. Here it applies to church leaders. *clothe yourselves with humility toward one another.* Peter may have
had in mind the footwashing scene of Jn 13, in which he
figured prominently. Although he was at first rebellious, he
writes now with understanding (see Jn 13:7).

5:6 See Lk 14:11. *lift you up in due time.* His help will
come at just the right time.

5:7 Cf. Php 4:6–7.

5:8 *Be self-controlled.* See 1Th 5:6,8. *alert.* Perhaps Peter
remembered his own difficulty in keeping awake during our
Lord's agony in Gethsemane (see Mt 26:36–46).

5:9 *your brothers.* They are not isolated; they belong to a
fellowship of suffering.

5:10 *grace.* See notes on Gal 1:3; Eph 1:2.

5:12 *With the help of Silas.* Silas may have been the bearer
of the letter to its destination. He may also have been a scribe
who recorded what Peter dictated or who aided, as an
informed and intelligent secretary, in the phrasing of Peter's
thoughts (see Introduction: Author and Date). *encouraging*

you briefly, *e* encouraging you and testifying that this is the true grace of God. Stand fast in it. *f*

13She who is in Babylon, chosen to-

5:12 *e* Heb 13:22
f S 1Co 16:13
5:13 *g* S Ac 12:12
5:14 *h* S Ro 16:16
i S Eph 6:23

gether with you, sends you her greetings, and so does my son Mark. *g* 14Greet one another with a kiss of love. *h*

Peace *i* to all of you who are in Christ.

... *grace of God.* See Introduction: Themes.
5:13 *Babylon.* See Introduction: Place of Writing. *chosen.* See note on Eph 1:4. *my son Mark.* Peter regards Mark with such warmth and affection that he calls him his son. It is possible that Peter had led Mark to Christ (see 1Ti 1:2 and note). Early Christian tradition closely associates Mark and

Peter (see Introduction to Mark: Author).
5:14 *kiss.* See note on 1Co 16:20. *Peace to all ... in Christ.* Spiritual well-being and blessedness to all who are united to Christ. Peter thus ends with a reference to the union of believers with Christ, a concept fundamental to the understanding of the whole letter.

2 PETER

Author

The author identifies himself as Simon Peter (1:1). He uses the first person singular pronoun in a highly personal passage (1:12-15) and claims to be an eyewitness of the transfiguration (1:16-18; cf. Mt 17:1-5). He asserts that this is his second letter to the readers (3:1) and refers to Paul as "our dear brother" (3:15; see note there). In short, the letter claims to be Peter's, and its character is compatible with that claim.

Although 2 Peter was not as widely known and recognized in the early church as 1 Peter, some may have used and accepted it as authoritative as early as the second century and perhaps even in the latter part of the first century (1 Clement [A.D. 95] may allude to it). It was not ascribed to Peter until Origen's time (185-253), and he seems to reflect some doubt concerning it. Eusebius (265-340) placed it among the questioned books, though he admits that most accept it as from Peter. After Eusebius's time, it seems to have been quite generally accepted as canonical.

In recent centuries, however, its genuineness has been challenged by a considerable number of scholars. One of the objections that has been raised is the difference in style from that of 1 Peter. But the difference is not absolute; there are noteworthy similarities in vocabulary and in other matters. In fact, no other known writing is as much like 1 Peter as 2 Peter. The differences that do exist may be accounted for by variations in subject matter, in the form and purpose of the letters, in the time and circumstances of writing, in sources or models, and in scribes that may have been employed. Perhaps most significant is the statement in 1Pe 5:12 that Silas assisted in the writing of 1 Peter. No such statement is made concerning 2 Peter, which may explain its noticeable difference in style (see Introduction to 1 Peter: Author and Date).

Other objections arise from a naturalistic reconstruction of early Christian history or misunderstandings or misconstructions of the available data. For example, some argue that the reference to Paul's letters in 3:15-16 indicates an advanced date for this book—beyond Peter's lifetime. But it is quite possible that Paul's letters were gathered at an early date, since some of them had been in existence and perhaps in circulation for more than ten years (Thessalonians by as much as 15 years) prior to Peter's death. Besides, what Peter says may only indicate that he was acquainted with some of Paul's letters (communication in the Roman world and in the early church was good), not that there was a formal, ecclesiastical collection of them.

Date

2 Peter was written toward the end of Peter's life (cf. 1:12-15), after he had written a prior letter (3:1) to the same readers (probably 1 Peter). Since Peter was martyred during the reign of Nero, his death must have occurred prior to A.D. 68; so it is very likely that he wrote 2 Peter between 65 and 68.

Some have argued that this date is too early for the writing of 2 Peter, but nothing in the book requires a later date. The error combated is comparable to the kind of heresy present in the first century. To insist that the second chapter was directed against second-century Gnosticism is to assume more than the contents of the chapter warrant. While the heretics referred to in 2 Peter may well have been among the forerunners of second-century Gnostics, nothing is said of them that would not fit into the later years of Peter's life.

Some have suggested a later date because they interpret the reference to the fathers in 3:4 to mean an earlier Christian generation. However, the word is most naturally interpreted as the OT patriarchs (cf. Jn 6:31, "forefathers"; Ac 3:13; Heb 1:1). Similarly, reference to Paul and his letters (3:15-16; see Author) does not require a date beyond Peter's lifetime.

2 Peter and Jude

There are conspicuous similarities between 2 Peter and Jude (compare 2Pe 2 with Jude 4-18), but there are also conspicuous differences. It has been suggested that one borrowed from the other or that they both drew on a common source. If there is borrowing, it is not a slavish borrowing but one that adapts to suit the writer's purpose. While many have insisted that Jude used Peter, it is more reasonable to assume that the longer letter (Peter) incorporated much of the shorter (Jude). Such borrowing is fairly common in ancient writings. For example, many believe that Paul used parts of early hymns in Php 2:6-11 and 1Ti 3:16.

Purpose

In his first letter Peter feeds Christ's sheep by instructing them how to deal with persecution from outside the church (see, e.g., 1Pe 4:12); in this second letter he teaches them how to deal with false teachers and evildoers who have come into the church (see 2:1; 3:3-4). While the particular situations naturally call for variations in content and emphasis, in both letters Peter as a pastor ("shepherd") of Christ's sheep (Jn 21:15-17) seeks to commend to his readers a wholesome combination of Christian faith and practice. More specifically, his purpose is threefold: (1) to stimulate Christian growth (ch. 1), (2) to combat false teaching (ch. 2) and (3) to encourage watchfulness in view of the Lord's certain return (ch. 3).

Outline

1 Simon Peter, a servant[a] and apostle of Jesus Christ,[b]

To those who through the righteousness[c] of our God and Savior Jesus Christ[d] have received a faith as precious as ours:

[2] Grace and peace be yours in abundance[e] through the knowledge of God and of Jesus our Lord.[f]

Making One's Calling and Election Sure

[3] His divine power[g] has given us everything we need for life and godliness through our knowledge of him[h] who called us[i] by his own glory and goodness. [4] Through these he has given us his very great and precious promises,[j] so that through them you may participate in the divine nature[k] and escape the corruption in the world caused by evil desires.[l]

[5] For this very reason, make every effort to add to your faith goodness; and to goodness, knowledge;[m] [6] and to knowledge, self-control;[n] and to self-control, perseverance;[o] and to perseverance, godliness;[p] [7] and to godliness, brotherly kindness; and to brotherly kindness, love.[q] [8] For if you possess these qualities in increasing measure, they will keep you from being ineffective and unproductive[r] in your knowledge of our Lord Jesus Christ.[s] [9] But if anyone does not have them, he is nearsighted and blind,[t] and has forgotten that he has been cleansed from his past sins.[u]

[10] Therefore, my brothers, be all the more eager to make your calling[v] and election sure. For if you do these things, you will never fall,[w] [11] and you will receive a rich welcome into the eternal kingdom[x] of our Lord and Savior Jesus Christ.[y]

Prophecy of Scripture

[12] So I will always remind you of these things,[z] even though you know them and are firmly established in the truth[a] you now have. [13] I think it is right to refresh your memory[b] as long as I live in the tent of this body,[c] [14] because I know that I will

---

Cross references:

1:1 [a]Ro 1:1 [b]1Pe 1:1 [c]Ro 3:21-26 [d]Tit 2:13
1:2 [e]S Ro 1:7 [f]ver 3,8; 2Pe 2:20; 3:18; S Php 3:8
1:3 [g]1Pe 1:5 [h]S ver 2 [i]S Ro 8:28
1:4 [j]2Co 7:1 [k]Eph 4:24; Heb 12:10; 1Jn 3:2 [l]Jas 1:27; 2Pe 2:18-20
1:5 [m]S ver 2; Col 2:3
1:6 [n]S Ac 24:25
[o]S Heb 10:36 [p]ver 3
1:7 [q]S Ro 12:10; 1Th 3:12
1:8 [r]Jn 15:2; Col 1:10; Tit 3:14 [s]S ver 2
1:9 [t]1Jn 2:11 [u]Eph 5:26; S Mt 1:21
1:10 [v]S Ro 8:28 [w]Ps 15:5; 2Pe 3:17; Jude 24
1:11 [x]Ps 145:13; 2Ti 4:18 [y]2Pe 2:20; 3:18
1:12 [z]Php 3:1; 1Jn 2:21; Jude 5 [a]2Jn 2
1:13 [b]2Pe 3:1 [c]Isa 38:12; 2Co 5:1,4

1:1 *Simon Peter.* See notes on Mt 16:18; Jn 1:42. *servant.* See note on Ro 1:1. *apostle.* See notes on Mk 6:30; 1Co 1:1; Heb 3:1. *To those.* Probably the same people as those in 1Pe 1:1. *God and Savior Jesus Christ.* Assumes that Jesus is both God and Savior. For other passages that ascribe deity to Christ see note on Ro 9:5. *have received.* God in his justice ("righteousness") imparts to people the ability to believe. *a faith.* Not here a body of truth to be believed—the faith—but the act of believing, or the God-given capacity to trust in Christ for salvation.

1:2 *Grace and peace.* See notes on Jnh 4:2; Jn 14:27; 20:19; Gal 1:3; Eph 1:2. *knowledge of God and of Jesus.* The concept of Christian knowledge is prominent in 2 Peter (see 1:3,5,8; 3:18). Peter was combating heretical teaching, and one of the best antidotes for heresy is the statement of true knowledge.

1:3 *everything we need for life and godliness.* God has made available all that we need spiritually through our knowledge of him. If indeed 2 Peter was written to combat an incipient Gnosticism, the apostle may be insisting that the knowledge possessed by those in apostolic circles was entirely adequate to meet their spiritual needs. No secret, esoteric knowledge is necessary for salvation (see Introduction to 1 John: Gnosticism). *glory and goodness.* The excellence of God: "Glory" expresses the excellence of his being—his attributes and essence; "goodness" depicts excellence expressed in deeds—virtue in action.

1:4 *Through these.* Through God's excellence—internal and external—he has given us great promises. Their nature is suggested in the words that follow: participation in the divine nature and escape from worldly corruption. *participate in the divine nature.* Does not indicate that Christians become divine in any sense, but only that we are indwelt by God through his Holy Spirit (see Jn 14:16–17). Our humanity and his deity, as well as the human personality and the divine, remain distinct and separate.

1:5–9 The virtues that will produce a well-rounded, fruitful Christian life.

1:5 *faith.* The root of the Christian life (see v. 1 and note). *goodness.* Cf. v. 3. *knowledge.* See notes on vv. 2–3.

1:6 *self-control.* According to many of the false teachers, knowledge made self-control unnecessary; according to Peter, Christian knowledge leads to self-control. *godliness.* A genuine reverence toward God that governs one's attitude toward every aspect of life.

1:7 *brotherly kindness.* Warmhearted affection toward all in the family of faith. *love.* The kind of outgoing, selfless attitude that leads one to sacrifice for the good of others (see note on 1Pe 4:8).

1:8 *if you possess these qualities.* Peter does not mean to imply that the believer is to cultivate each listed quality in turn, one after the other until all have been perfected. Instead, they are all to be cultivated simultaneously. *in increasing measure.* Peter has continuing spiritual growth in mind. *keep you from being . . . unproductive in your knowledge.* The Christian's knowledge should affect the way he lives. It does not set him free from moral restraints, as the heretics taught (see Introduction to 1 John: Gnosticism). Rather, it produces holiness and all such virtues (cf. Col 1:9–12).

1:9 *nearsighted and blind.* Since one cannot be both at the same time, Peter may have in mind a possible alternative meaning for "nearsighted," namely, "to shut the eyes." Such a person is blind because he has closed his eyes to the truth.

1:10 *make your calling and election sure.* By cultivating the qualities listed in vv. 5–7, they and others can be assured that God has chosen them and called them (cf. Mt 7:20). The genuineness of their profession will be demonstrated as they express these virtues (cf. Gal 5:6; Jas 2:18). When God elects and calls, it is to obedience and holiness (1Pe 1:2; Eph 1:3–6), and these fruits confirm their divine source. *never fall.* Those who in this way give evidence of their faith will never cease to persevere.

1:11 *receive a rich welcome.* By producing the fruits Peter is commending to them (see vv. 5–10). *eternal kingdom.* Eternal life (cf. Mt 25:46).

1:13 *tent of this body.* See Jn 14:1; 2Co 5:1 and notes.

1:14 *Christ has made clear to me.* Either the revelation recorded in Jn 21:18–19 or a subsequent one.

soon put it aside, *d* as our Lord Jesus Christ has made clear to me. *e* ¹⁵And I will make every effort to see that after my departure*f* you will always be able to remember these things.

¹⁶We did not follow cleverly invented stories when we told you about the power and coming of our Lord Jesus Christ,*g* but we were eyewitnesses of his majesty. *h* ¹⁷For he received honor and glory from God the Father when the voice came to him from the Majestic Glory, saying, "This is my Son, whom I love; with him I am well pleased."*a i* ¹⁸We ourselves heard this voice that came from heaven when we were with him on the sacred mountain.*j*

¹⁹And we have the word of the prophets made more certain, *k* and you will do well to pay attention to it, as to a light*l* shining in a dark place, until the day dawns*m* and the morning star*n* rises in your hearts. *o* ²⁰Above all, you must understand*p* that no

prophecy of Scripture came about by the prophet's own interpretation. ²¹For prophecy never had its origin in the will of man, but men spoke from God*q* as they were carried along by the Holy Spirit. *r*

False Teachers and Their Destruction

2 But there were also false prophets*s* among the people, just as there will be false teachers among you. *t* They will secretly introduce destructive heresies, even denying the sovereign Lord*u* who bought them*v*—bringing swift destruction on themselves. ²Many will follow their shameful ways*w* and will bring the way of truth into disrepute. ³In their greed*x* these teachers will exploit you*y* with stories they have made up. Their condemnation has long been hanging over them, and their destruction has not been sleeping.

⁴For if God did not spare angels when

Cross references:

1:14 *d*2Ti 4:6
*e*Jn 13:36; 21:18, 19
1:15 *f*Lk 9:31
1:16 *g*Mk 13:26; 14:62 *h*Mt 17:1-8
1:17 *i*S Mt 3:17
1:18 *j*Mt 17:6
1:19 *k*1Pe 1:10, 11 *l*Ps 119:105
*m*Lk 1:78
*n*Rev 22:16
*o*2Co 4:6
1:20 *p*2Pe 3:3

1:21 *q*2Ti 3:16
*r*2Sa 23:2;
Ac 1:16; 3:18;
1Pe 1:11
2:1 *s*Dt 13:1-3;
Jer 6:13;
S Mt 7:15
*t*1Ti 4:1 *u*Jude 4
*v*S 1Co 6:20
2:2 *w*Jude 4
2:3 *x*ver 14
*y*2Co 2:17;
1Th 2:5

a17 Matt. 17:5; Mark 9:7; Luke 9:35

1:15 *always be able to remember these things.* An aim that was realized, whether intentionally or unintentionally, through the Gospel of Mark, which early tradition connected with Peter.

1:16 *cleverly invented stories.* Peter's message was based on his eyewitness account of the supernatural events that marked the life of Jesus. It was not made up of myths and imaginative stories as was the message of the heretics of 2:3. *coming of our Lord Jesus Christ.* In Christ's transfiguration the disciples received a foretaste of what his coming will be like when he returns to establish his eternal kingdom (Mt 16:28). *eyewitnesses of his majesty.* A reference to Christ's transfiguration (see vv. 17–18; Mt 16:28–17:8).

1:19–21 Peter's message rests on two solid foundations: (1) the voice from God at the transfiguration (vv. 16–18) and (2) the still more significant testimony of Scripture (vv. 19–21). An alternative, but less probable, view is that the apostles' testimony to the transfiguration fulfills and thus confirms the Scriptures that predicted such things.

1:19 *more certain.* Or "very certain."

1:20 Two major views of this verse are: 1. No prophecy is to be privately or independently interpreted (cf. the false teachers in 3:16). The Holy Spirit, Scripture itself and the church should be included in the interpretive process. 2. No prophecy originated through the prophet's own interpretation (the sense of the NIV). The preceding and following contexts indicate that this view is probably to be preferred. In vv. 16–19 the subject discussed is the origin of the apostolic message. Did it come from human imaginings, or was it from God? In v. 21 again the subject is origin. No prophecy of Scripture arose from a merely human interpretation of things. This understanding of v. 20 is further supported by the explanatory "For" with which v. 21 begins. Verse 21 explains v. 20 by restating its content and then affirming God as the origin of prophecy.

1:21 *carried along by the Holy Spirit.* See note on 2Ti 3:16. In the production of Scripture both God and man were active participants. God was the source of the content of Scripture, so that what it says is what God has said. But the human author also actively spoke; he was more than a recorder. Yet what he said came from God. Although actively speaking, he was carried along by the Holy Spirit.

2:1 *false prophets.* See 2Ki 18:19; Isa 9:13–17; Jer 5:31;

14:14; 23:30–32. *there will be false teachers among you.* Numerous NT passages warn of false teachers who are already present or yet to come (see Mt 24:4–5,11; Ac 20:29–30; Gal 1:6–9; Php 3:2; Col 2:4,8,18,20–23; 2Th 2:1–3; 1Ti 1:3–7; 4:1–3; 2Ti 3:1–8; 1Jn 2:18–19,22–23; 2Jn 7–11; Jude 3–4). *destructive heresies.* Divisive opinions or teachings that result in the moral and spiritual destruction of those who accept them. *the sovereign Lord who bought them.* Does not necessarily mean that the false teachers were believers. Christ's death paid the penalty for their sin, but it would not become effective for their salvation unless they trusted in Christ as Savior. (However, see vv. 20–23, where it is obvious that the heretics had at least professed knowing the Lord.) *swift destruction.* Not immediate physical calamity, but sudden doom, whether at death or at the Lord's second coming (cf. Mt 24:50–51; 2Th 1:9).

2:2 *shameful ways.* Open, extreme immorality not held in check by any sense of shame. *way of truth.* See Ps 119:30. The Christian faith is not only correct doctrine but also correct living.

2:3 *In their greed.* They will be motivated by a desire for money and will commercialize the Christian faith to their own selfish advantage. *long been hanging over them.* Long ago, in OT times, their condemnation was declared (see vv. 4–9 for OT examples of the fact that judgment is coming on the wicked). *destruction has not been sleeping.* Although delay makes it seem that they have escaped God's judgment, destruction is a reality that is sure to come upon them. **2:4–8** Three examples showing that God will rescue the godly and destroy the wicked.

2:4 *angels when they sinned.* Some believe this sin was the one referred to in Ge 6:2, where the sons of God are said to have intermarried with the daughters of men, meaning (according to this view) that angels married human women. The offspring of those marriages are said to have been the Nephilim (Ge 6:4; see notes on Ge 6:2,4). But since it appears impossible for angels, who are spirits, to have sexual relations with women, the sin referred to in this verse probably occurred before the fall of Adam and Eve. The angels who fell became the devil and the evil angels (probably the demons and evil spirits referred to in the NT). *sent them to hell.* See NIV text note. *Tartarus* was the term used by the Greeks to designate the place where the most wicked spirits

they sinned,[z] but sent them to hell,[b] putting them into gloomy dungeons[c] to be held for judgment;[a] 5if he did not spare the ancient world[b] when he brought the flood on its ungodly people,[c] but protected Noah, a preacher of righteousness, and seven others;[d] 6if he condemned the cities of Sodom and Gomorrah by burning them to ashes,[e] and made them an example[f] of what is going to happen to the ungodly;[g] 7and if he rescued Lot,[h] a righteous man, who was distressed by the filthy lives of lawless men[i] 8(for that righteous man,[i] living among them day after day, was tormented in his righteous soul by the lawless deeds he saw and heard)— 9if this is so, then the Lord knows how to rescue godly men from trials[k] and to hold the unrighteous for the day of judgment,[l] while continuing their punishment.[d] 10This is especially true of those who follow the corrupt desire[m] of the sinful nature[e] and despise authority.

Bold and arrogant, these men are not afraid to slander celestial beings;[n] 11yet even angels, although they are stronger and more powerful, do not bring slander-

ous accusations against such beings in the presence of the Lord.[o] 12But these men blaspheme in matters they do not understand. They are like brute beasts, creatures of instinct, born only to be caught and destroyed, and like beasts they too will perish.[p]

13They will be paid back with harm for the harm they have done. Their idea of pleasure is to carouse in broad daylight.[q] They are blots and blemishes, reveling in their pleasures while they feast with you.[f r] 14With eyes full of adultery, they never stop sinning; they seduce[s] the unstable;[t] they are experts in greed[u]—an accursed brood![v] 15They have left the straight way and wandered off to follow the way of Balaam[w] son of Beor, who loved the wages of wickedness. 16But he was rebuked for his wrongdoing by a donkey—a beast without speech—who spoke with a man's voice and restrained the prophet's madness.[x]

Cross references (center column):

2:4 [z]Ge 6:1-4
[a]1Ti 3:6; Jude 6; Rev 20:1,2
2:5 [b]2Pe 3:6
[c]Ge 6:5-8:19
[d]Heb 11:7; 1Pe 3:20
2:6 [e]Ge 19:24,25
[f]Nu 26:10; Jude 7
[g]Mt 10:15; 11:23,24; Ro 9:29
2:7 [h]Ge 19:16
[i]2Pe 3:17
2:8 [i]Heb 11:4
2:9 [k]Ps 37:33; S Ro 15:31; Rev 3:10
[l]S Mt 10:15
2:10 [m]2Pe 3:3; Jude 16,18
[n]Jude 8

2:11 [o]Jude 9
2:12 [p]Ps 49:12; Jude 10
2:13 [q]S Ro 13:13; 1Th 5:7
[r]1Co 11:20,21; Jude 12
2:14 [s]ver 18
[t]Jas 1:8; 2Pe 3:16
[u]ver 3 [v]Eph 2:3
2:15 [w]Nu 22:4-20; 31:16; Dt 23:4; Jude 11; Rev 2:14
2:16 [x]Nu 22:21-30

---

[b]4 Greek Tartarus   [c]4 Some manuscripts into chains of darkness   [d]9 Or unrighteous for punishment until the day of judgment   [e]10 Or the flesh   [f]13 Some manuscripts in their love feasts

---

Notes (bottom, left column):

were sent to be punished. Why some evil angels are imprisoned and others are free to serve Satan as demons is not explained in Scripture. *judgment.* The final judgment, probably associated with the great white throne judgment of Rev 20:11–15.

2:5 *ungodly people.* See Ge 6:5,11–12. *preacher of righteousness.* A description of Noah found nowhere else in Scripture. However, similar descriptions are used of him in Josephus (*Antiquities,* 1.3.1), *1 Clement* (7.6; 9.4) and the *Sibylline Oracles* (1.128). *seven others.* Noah's wife, three sons and three daughters-in-law (Noah was the eighth; see 1Pe 3:20).

2:6 *condemned the cities of Sodom and Gomorrah.* See Ge 19.

2:7 *distressed by the filthy lives.* See Ge 19:4–9. How Lot could be so distressed, how he could be called a "righteous man," and yet offer to turn his two daughters over to the wicked townsmen to be sexually abused is difficult to understand apart from a knowledge of the code of honor characteristic of that day (see note on Ge 19:8).

2:9 States the point made in vv. 4–8—the wicked whose coming Peter predicts will surely be punished.

2:10 *This is especially true.* The heretics of Peter's day are certain to come under judgment for two main reasons: 1. They follow the corrupt desire of the sinful nature, perhaps referring to homosexuality, the sin of the Sodomites (see Ge 19:5). At least the author has in mind a similar inordinate sexual practice. 2. They despise authority. *slander celestial beings.* A specific example of despising authority. This could refer to the slander of earthly dignitaries such as church leaders, which might well be expected from such shameless peddlers of error. On the other hand, it could refer to the blaspheming of angels, as the NIV text suggests. This view seems more likely since the parallel passage in Jude 8–10 is speaking of angels.

2:11 *angels . . . do not bring slanderous accusations.* Even good angels, who might have more right to do so because of their greater power, do not bring such accusations against

inferior evil angels.

2:12 *matters they do not understand.* The heresy to which Peter refers may have been an early form of second-century Gnosticism (see Introduction to 1 John: Gnosticism) that claimed to possess special, esoteric knowledge. If so, it is ironic that those who professed special knowledge acted out of abysmal ignorance, and the result was arrogant blasphemy. *like brute beasts.* A scathing denunciation. They are like irrational animals, whose lives are guided by mere instinct and who are born merely to be slaughtered. Destruction is their final lot.

2:13 *carouse in broad daylight.* See 1Th 5:7. Even the pagan world carried on their corrupt practices under cover of darkness, but these heretics were utterly shameless. *in their pleasures while they feast with you.* See NIV text note. Jude 12 without doubt reads "love feasts," which may well have been the intended reading here. These false teachers seem to have been involved in the sacred feasts of brotherly love that, in the early church, accompanied the Lord's Supper. In fact, it appears that they injected their carousing into these holy observances and delighted in their shameless acts.

2:14 *eyes full of adultery.* Lit. "eyes full of an adulteress," which means that they desired every woman they saw, viewing her as a potential sex partner. *never stop sinning.* Their eyes are constant instruments of lust. *seduce the unstable.* For a parallel use of the Greek word for "seduce" see Jas 1:14. It depicts the fisherman who attempts to lure and catch fish with bait. *experts in greed.* The Greek text implies that they had exercised themselves like an athlete, not in physical activity but in greed.

2:15 *way of Balaam son of Beor.* See Nu 22–24. Balaam was bent on cursing Israel, though God had forbidden it. He wanted the money Balak offered him. Similarly these false teachers apparently were guilty of attempting to extract money from naive listeners. For a donkey to rebuke the prophet's madness reflects not only on the foolishness of Balaam but also on that of the false teachers of Peter's day.

¹⁷These men are springs without water ʸ and mists driven by a storm. Blackest darkness is reserved for them. ᶻ ¹⁸For they mouth empty, boastful words ᵃ and, by appealing to the lustful desires of sinful human nature, they entice people who are just escaping ᵇ from those who live in error. ¹⁹They promise them freedom, while they themselves are slaves of depravity—for a man is a slave to whatever has mastered him. ᶜ ²⁰If they have escaped the corruption of the world by knowing ᵈ our Lord and Savior Jesus Christ ᵉ and are again entangled in it and overcome, they are worse off at the end than they were at the beginning. ᶠ ²¹It would have been better for them not to have known the way of righteousness, than to have known it and then to turn their backs on the sacred command that was passed on to them. ᵍ ²²Of them the proverbs are true: "A dog

Reference column:
2:17 ʸJude 12
zJude 13
2:18 ªJude 16
ᵇver 20; 2Pe 1:4
2:19 ᶜS Ro 6:16
2:20 ᵈS 2Pe 1:2
ᵉ2Pe 1:11; 3:18
ᶠMt 12:45
2:21 ᵍEze 18:24;
Heb 6:4-6; 10:26,
27

2:22 ʰPr 26:11
3:1 ⁱS 1Co 10:14
/2Pe 1:13
3:2 ᵏLk 1:70;
Ac 3:21
ˡS Eph 4:11
3:3 ᵐ1Ti 4:1;
2Ti 3:1
ⁿ2Pe 2:10; Jude
18
3:4 ᵒIsa 5:19;
Eze 12:22;
S Lk 17:30
ᵖMk 10:6

returns to its vomit," ᵍʰ and, "A sow that is washed goes back to her wallowing in the mud."

The Day of the Lord

3 Dear friends, ⁱ this is now my second letter to you. I have written both of them as reminders ʲ to stimulate you to wholesome thinking. ²I want you to recall the words spoken in the past by the holy prophets ᵏ and the command given by our Lord and Savior through your apostles. ˡ

³First of all, you must understand that in the last days ᵐ scoffers will come, scoffing and following their own evil desires. ⁿ ⁴They will say, "Where is this 'coming' he promised? ᵒ Ever since our fathers died, everything goes on as it has since the beginning of creation." ᵖ ⁵But they deliber-

ᵍ22 Prov. 26:11

2:17 *springs without water.* A picture of cruel deception. The thirsty traveler comes to the spring expecting cool, refreshing water but finds it dry. So the false teachers promise satisfying truth but in reality have nothing to offer. *mists driven by a storm.* Gone before a drop of moisture falls. *Blackest darkness.* Their destiny is hell.

2:18 *mouth empty, boastful words.* Words that sound impressive to the new convert but in reality have nothing to offer. *entice.* See note on v. 14 ("seduce"). *people who are just escaping.* New converts who have just broken away from pagan friends. Thus the depraved false teachers prey on new converts, who have not yet had a chance to develop spiritual resistance.

2:19 *They promise them freedom.* Probably freedom from moral restraint (cf. 1Co 6:12–13; Gal 5:13). The very ones who promise freedom from bondage to rules and regulations are themselves slaves of depravity. Freedom from law resulted in bondage to sin, and liberty was turned into license.

2:20–22 Some point to this passage as clear proof that a genuinely saved person may lose his salvation. He knows the Lord; he escapes the world's corruption; he knows the way of righteousness. Then he turns away from the message and goes back to his old way of life. His knowledge is said to have been genuine; his change of life was real; and his return to his old way of life was not superficial. Others insist that the knowledge of the Lord and of the way of righteousness could not have been genuine. If the person had been truly regenerated, he would have persevered in his faith. It is argued that the teaching of Jn 10:27–30 (especially v. 28) and Ro 8:28–39 makes it clear that no genuinely saved person can be lost. Thus, according to this view, the persons described here could not have been genuinely saved.

2:20 *If they have escaped the corruption of the world.* A reference to false teachers who had once apparently been believers in Christ. Their professed knowledge of Christ had at least produced a change in life-style. *again entangled in it and overcome.* A complete return to the old sinful pattern of life.

2:21 *better . . . not to have known the way of righteousness.* Knowledge of the way increases one's responsibility and his hardness of heart if he then rejects it. In its early days, Christianity was known as "the way" (Ac 9:2; 18:25; 19:9, 23; 22:4; 24:14,22). *sacred command.* The whole Christian message that people are commanded to receive.

2:22 *A dog returns . . . a sow . . . goes back.* In both cases

the nature of the animal is not changed. The sow returns to the mud because by nature it is still a sow. The change was merely cosmetic.

3:1 *Dear friends.* Or "Loved ones" (see vv. 8,14,17; 1Pe 2:11; 4:12). *second letter.* The first letter may have been 1 Peter, though there is some reason to doubt this identification. For example, 1 Peter cannot be very accurately described as a reminder. *reminders.* See 1:12–13,15.

3:2 *holy prophets.* OT personages. *command.* See note on 2:21. *your apostles.* Peter places the OT prophets and the NT apostles on an equal plane. Both are vehicles of God's sacred truth. Peter, being one of the apostles, can speak with knowledge and authority as a representative of the apostolic group.

3:3 *First of all.* The Greek for this expression is used in 1:20 ("above all") to call attention to a matter of great importance. *last days.* An expression that refers to the whole period introduced by Christ's first coming. These days are last in comparison to OT days, which were preliminary and preparatory. Also, the Christian era is the time of the beginnings of prophetic fulfillment. *scoffers will come.* Perhaps the same false teachers described in ch. 2 (e.g., they follow their own evil desires; cf. 2:10,18–19). In ch. 3, however, the emphasis is on Christ's return. These people may have been early Gnostics who resisted the idea of a time of judgment and moral accountability.

3:4 *he.* Christ. *Ever since our fathers died.* Either the first Christians to die after Christ's death and resurrection (e.g., Stephen, James the brother of John, and other early Christian leaders who had died; cf. Heb 13:7) or the OT patriarchs (see Introduction: Date). *everything goes on as it has.* Their argument against Christ's return was: Since it has not occurred up to this time, it will never occur. That nature is not subject to divine intervention, they say, has been proved by observation (1) of the period since the fathers died—perhaps 30 years—and (2) of the period since creation.

3:5 *they deliberately forget.* Ignoring the flood as a divine intervention was not an oversight; it was deliberate. They did not want to face up to the fallacy in their argument. *God's word.* Of command, such as "Let there be light" (Ge 1:3). *earth was formed out of water and by water.* See Ge 1:6–10, where the waters on earth were separated from the atmospheric waters of the heavens, and the mountains then appeared, causing the earthly waters to be gathered into oceans.

ately forget that long ago by God's word *q* the heavens existed and the earth was formed out of water and by water. *r* 6By these waters also the world of that time *s* was deluged and destroyed. *t* 7By the same word the present heavens and earth are reserved for fire, *u* being kept for the day of judgment *v* and destruction of ungodly men.

8But do not forget this one thing, dear friends: With the Lord a day is like a thousand years, and a thousand years are like a day. *w* 9The Lord is not slow in keeping his promise, *x* as some understand slowness. He is patient *y* with you, not wanting anyone to perish, but everyone to come to repentance. *z*

10But the day of the Lord will come like a thief. *a* The heavens will disappear with a roar; *b* The elements will be destroyed by fire, *c* and the earth and everything in it will be laid bare. *h d*

11Since everything will be destroyed in this way, what kind of people ought you to be? You ought to live holy and godly lives 12as you look forward *e* to the day of God and speed its coming. *i f* That day will bring about the destruction of the heavens by fire, and the elements will melt in the heat. *g* 13But in keeping with his promise we are looking forward to a new heaven and a new earth, *h* the home of righteousness.

14So then, dear friends, since you are looking forward to this, make every effort to be found spotless, blameless *i* and at peace with him. 15Bear in mind that our Lord's patience *j* means salvation, *k* just as our dear brother Paul also wrote you with the wisdom that God gave him. *l* 16He writes the same way in all his letters, speaking in them of these matters. His let-

3:5 *q*Ge 1:6,9; Heb 11:3 *r*Ps 24:2	
3:6 *s*2Pe 2:5 *t*Ge 7:21,22	
3:7 *u*ver 10,12; S 2Th 1:7 *v*S Mt 10:15	
3:8 *w*Ps 90:4	
3:9 *x*Hab 2:3; Heb 10:37 *y*S Ro 2:4 *z*S 1Ti 2:4; Rev 2:21	
3:10 *a*S Lk 12:39 12; S 2Th 1:7 *b*Mt 24:35; S Heb 12:27; Rev 21:1	

3:12 *e*S 1Co 1:7 *f*Ps 50:3 *g*ver 10	
3:13 *h*Isa 65:17; 66:22; Rev 21:1	
3:14 *i*S 1Th 3:13	
3:15 *j*S Ro 2:4 *k*ver 9 *l*Eph 3:3	

h10 Some manuscripts *be burned up*   *i12* Or *as you wait eagerly for the day of God to come*

3:6 *By these waters also the world ... was deluged and destroyed.* Peter points out the fallacy of the scoffers' argument. There has been a divine intervention since the time of creation, namely, the flood. The term "world" may refer to the earth or, more probably, to the world of people (cf. Jn 3:16). All the people except Noah and his family were overcome by the flood and perished. This does not necessarily mean that the flood was universal. It may simply have extended to all the inhabited areas of earth (see note on Ge 6:17).

3:7 *By the same word.* The word of God that brought the world into existence (v. 5) and that brought watery destruction on the wicked of Noah's day will bring fiery destruction on the world that exists today and on its wicked people.

3:8 *a thousand years are like a day.* Cf. Ps 90:4. God does not view time as humans do. He stands above time, with the result that when time is seen in the light of eternity, an age appears no longer than one short day, and a day seems no shorter than a long age. Since time is purely relative with God, he waits patiently while human beings stew with impatience.

3:9 God's seeming delay in bringing about the consummation of all things is a result not of indifference but of patience in waiting for all who will come to repentance. Thus the scoffers are wrong on two points: 1. They fail to recognize that all things have not continued without divine intervention since creation (the flood was an intervention, vv. 4–6). 2. They misunderstand the reason for apparent divine delay (God is a long-suffering God).

3:10 *day of the Lord.* See notes on Isa 2:11,17,20; Am 5:18; 1Th 5:2. *like a thief.* Suddenly and unexpectedly. *The heavens will disappear with a roar.* Apocalyptic language, common to books like Daniel and Revelation. Due to the figurative nature of such writings, we must not expect complete literalism but recognize it as an attempt to describe the indescribable, a task as impossible as it would have been for a first-century writer to describe the phenomena of our atomic age. What may be referred to is the destruction of the atmospheric heavens with a great rushing sound (see v. 12). *elements.* Refers either to the heavenly bodies or to the physical elements—in the first century, such things as earth, air, fire and water; in today's more precise scientific terminology, hydrogen, oxygen, carbon, etc. *fire.* See vv. 7,12. *earth ... laid bare.* See NIV text note. Either the earth and its

contents will disappear and not be seen anymore, or the earth and all man's works will appear before God's judgment seat.

3:11 *Since everything will be destroyed.* The transitory nature of the material universe ought to make a difference in one's system of values and one's priorities. The result should be lives of holiness (separated from sin and to God) and godliness (devoted to the worship and service of God). Cf. Mt 25:13; 1Th 5:6,8,11; 2Pe 1:13–16.

3:12 *the day of God.* Apparently synonymous with "the day of the Lord" (v. 10) since it is characterized by the same kind of events. Cf. Rev 16:14. *speed its coming.* That day may be hastened by God's people as they speed up the accomplishment of his purposes. Since he is waiting for all who will come to repentance (v. 9), the sooner believers bring others to the Savior the sooner that day will dawn (cf. Ac 3:19–20). Prayer also serves to hasten the day (Mt 6:10), as does holy living (v. 11). *destruction of the heavens.* See v. 10. *elements will melt in the heat.* See v. 10; Isa 34:4.

3:13 *his promise.* New heavens and a new earth are promised by Isaiah (65:17; 66:22). This promise is confirmed by Rev 21:1. *home of righteousness.* Righteousness will dwell there as a permanent resident. Cf. Isa 11:4–5; 45:8; Da 9:24.

3:14 *spotless, blameless.* Cf. 1Pe 1:19, where the same two words are applied to Christ. *at peace with him.* Believers have peace with God as a result of being justified by faith (Ro 5:1), but they may displease him by failing to live as he desires and thus not receive his commendation and his reward when he returns (cf. 1Co 3:10–15; 2Co 5:10).

3:15 *our Lord's patience means salvation.* See v. 9. *our dear brother Paul.* Peter expresses warmth in his reference to Paul. The unity of teaching and purpose that governed their relationship, abundantly attested in Paul's letters and the book of Acts, is confirmed here by Peter. It has been suggested that what Paul wrote to the recipients of 2 Peter may have been a copy of Romans, which was sent to the churches as a circular letter (cf. Ro 16:4; see Introduction to Romans: Recipients; see also note on 1Pe 1:1).

3:16 *writes the same way in all his letters.* Peter may be referring in general to the exhortations to holy living in vv. 11–14, which parallel many passages in Paul's writings. *ignorant and unstable people.* The ignorant are simply the unlearned who have not been taught basic apostolic teaching

ters contain some things that are hard to understand, which ignorant and unstable _m_ people distort, _n_ as they do the other Scriptures, _o_ to their own destruction.

[17]Therefore, dear friends, since you already know this, be on your guard _p_ so that you may not be carried away by the error _q_

of lawless men _r_ and fall from your secure position. _s_ [18]But grow in the grace _t_ and knowledge _u_ of our Lord and Savior Jesus Christ. _v_ To him be glory both now and forever! Amen. _w_

3:16 _m_ Jas 1:8; 2Pe 2:14
_n_ Ps 56:5; Jer 23:36 _over_ 2
3:17 _p_ 1Co 10:12
_q_ 2Pe 2:18
_r_ 2Pe 2:7 _s_ Rev 2:5
3:18 _t_ S Ro 3:24
_u_ S 2Pe 1:2
_v_ 2Pe 1:11; 2:20
_w_ S Ro 11:36

---

and thus may be easily led astray (cf. 2:14). *other Scriptures.* Peter placed Paul's writings on the same level of authority as the God-breathed writings of the OT (see 1:21; 2Ti 3:16). **3:17** *already know this.* That false teachers are coming (cf. ch. 2).

3:18 *grow in . . . knowledge.* Peter concludes by again stressing knowledge (see 1:2–3 and notes; see also 1:5), probably as an antidote to the false teachers who boasted in their esoteric knowledge.

1 JOHN

Author

The author is John son of Zebedee (cf. Mk 1:19-20)—the apostle and the author of the Gospel of John and Revelation (see Introductions to both books: Author). He was a first cousin of Jesus (his mother was Salome, a sister of Mary; cf. Mt 27:56; Mk 16:1; Jn 19:25), a fisherman, one of Jesus' inner circle (together with James and Peter) and "the disciple whom Jesus loved" (Jn 13:23).

Unlike most NT letters, 1 John does not tell us who its author is. The earliest identification of him comes from the church fathers: Irenaeus (c. A.D. 140-203), Clement of Alexandria (c. 155-215), Tertullian (c. 150-222) and Origen (c. 185-253) all designated the writer as the apostle John. As far as we know, no one else was suggested by the early church.

This traditional identification is confirmed by evidence in the letter itself:

1. The style of the Gospel of John is markedly similar to that of this letter. Both are written in simple Greek and use contrasting figures, such as light and darkness, life and death, truth and lies, love and hate.

2. Similar phrases and expressions, such as those found in the following passages, are striking:

1 John	Gospel of John
1:1	1:1,14
1:4	16:24
1:6-7	3:19-21
2:7	13:34-35
3:8	8:44
3:14	5:24
4:6	8:47
4:9	1:14,18; 3:16
5:9	5:32,37
5:12	3:36

3. The mention of eyewitness testimony (1:1-4) harmonizes with the fact that John was a follower of Christ from the earliest days of his ministry.

4. The authoritative manner that pervades the letter (seen in its commands, 2:15,24,28; 4:1; 5:21; its firm assertions, 2:6; 3:14; 4:12; and its pointed identification of error, 1:6,8; 2:4,22) is what would be expected from an apostle.

5. The suggestions of advanced age (addressing his readers as "children," 2:1,28; 3:7) agree with early church tradition concerning John's age when he wrote the books known to be his.

6. The description of the heretics as antichrists (2:18), liars (2:22) and children of the devil (3:10) is consistent with Jesus' characterization of John as a son of thunder (Mk 3:17).

7. The indications of a close relationship with the Lord (1:1; 2:5-6,24,27-28) fit the descriptions of "the disciple whom Jesus loved" and the one who reclined "next to him" (Jn 13:23).

Date

The letter is difficult to date with precision, but factors such as (1) evidence from early Christian writers (Irenaeus and Clement of Alexandria), (2) the early form of Gnosticism reflected in the denunciations of the letter and (3) indications of the advanced age of John suggest the end of the first century. Since the author of 1 John seems to build on concepts and themes found in the fourth Gospel (see 1Jn 2:7-11), it is reasonable to date the letter somewhere between A.D. 85 and 95, after the writing of the Gospel, which may have been written c. 85 (see Introduction to John: Date).

Recipients

1Jn 2:12-14,19; 3:1; 5:13 make it clear that this letter was addressed to believers. But the letter itself does not indicate who they were or where they lived. The fact that it mentions no one by name suggests it was a circular letter sent to Christians in a number of places. Evidence from early Christian writers places the apostle John in Ephesus during most of his later years (c. A.D. 70-100). The earliest confirmed use of 1 John was in the province of Asia (in modern Turkey), where Ephesus was located. Clement of Alexandria indicates that John ministered in the various churches scattered throughout that province. It may be assumed, therefore, that 1 John was sent to the churches of the province of Asia (see map No. 11 at the end of the Study Bible).

Gnosticism

One of the most dangerous heresies of the first two centuries of the church was Gnosticism. Its central teaching was that spirit is entirely good and matter is entirely evil. From this unbiblical dualism flowed five important errors:

1. Man's body, which is matter, is therefore evil. It is to be contrasted with God, who is wholly spirit and therefore good.

2. Salvation is the escape from the body, achieved not by faith in Christ but by special knowledge (the Greek word for "knowledge" is *gnosis*, hence Gnosticism).

3. Christ's true humanity was denied in two ways: (1) Some said that Christ only seemed to have a body, a view called Docetism, from the Greek *dokeo* ("to seem"), and (2) others said that the divine Christ joined the man Jesus at baptism and left him before he died, a view called Cerinthianism, after its most prominent spokesman, Cerinthus. This view is the background of much of 1 John (see 1:1; 2:22; 4:2-3).

4. Since the body was considered evil, it was to be treated harshly. This ascetic form of Gnosticism is the background of part of the letter to the Colossians (2:21-23).

5. Paradoxically, this dualism also led to licentiousness. The reasoning was that, since matter—and not the breaking of God's law (1Jn 3:4)—was considered evil, breaking his law was of no moral consequence.

The Gnosticism addressed in the NT was an early form of the heresy, not the intricately developed system of the second and third centuries. In addition to that seen in Colossians and in John's letters, acquaintance with early Gnosticism is reflected in 1,2 Timothy, Titus, and 2 Peter and perhaps 1 Corinthians.

Occasion and Purpose

John's readers were confronted with an early form of Gnostic teaching of the Cerinthian variety (see Gnosticism). This heresy was also libertine, throwing off all moral restraints.

Consequently, John wrote this letter with two basic purposes in mind: (1) to expose false teachers (2:26) and (2) to give believers assurance of salvation (5:13). In keeping with his intention to combat Gnostic teachers, John specifically struck at their total lack of morality (3:8-10); and by giving eyewitness testimony to the incarnation, he sought to confirm his readers' belief in the incarnate Christ (1:3). Success in this would give the writer joy (1:4).

Outline*

I. Introduction: The Reality of the Incarnation (1:1-4)
II. The Christian Life as Fellowship with the Father and the Son (1:5-2:28)
   A. Ethical Tests of Fellowship (1:5-2:11)
      1. Moral likeness (1:5-7)
      2. Confession of sin (1:8-2:2)
      3. Obedience (2:3-6)
      4. Love for fellow believers (2:7-11)
   B. Two Digressions (2:12-17)
   C. Christological Test of Fellowship (2:18-28)
      1. Contrast: apostates versus believers (2:18-21)
      2. Person of Christ: the crux of the test (2:22-23)
      3. Persistent belief: key to continuing fellowship (2:24-28)

The Word of Life

1 That which was from the beginning,[a] which we have heard, which we have seen with our eyes,[b] which we have looked at and our hands have touched[c]—this we proclaim concerning the Word of life. [2]The life appeared;[d] we have seen it and testify to it,[e] and we proclaim to you the eternal life,[f] which was with the Father and has appeared to us. [3]We proclaim to you what we have seen and heard,[g] so that you also may have fellowship with us. And our fellowship is with the Father and with his Son, Jesus Christ.[h] [4]We write this[i] to make our[a] joy complete.[j]

Walking in the Light

[5]This is the message we have heard[k] from him and declare to you: God is light;[l] in him there is no darkness at all. [6]If we claim to have fellowship with him yet walk in the darkness,[m] we lie and do not live by the truth.[n] [7]But if we walk in the light,[o] as he is in the light, we have

fellowship with one another, and the blood of Jesus, his Son, purifies us from all[b] sin.[p]

[8]If we claim to be without sin,[q] we deceive ourselves and the truth is not in us.[r] [9]If we confess our sins, he is faithful and just and will forgive us our sins[s] and purify us from all unrighteousness.[t] [10]If we claim we have not sinned,[u] we make him out to be a liar[v] and his word has no place in our lives.[w]

2 My dear children,[x] I write this to you so that you will not sin. But if anybody does sin, we have one who speaks to the Father in our defense[y]—Jesus Christ, the Righteous One. [2]He is the atoning sacrifice for our sins,[z] and not only for ours but also for[c] the sins of the whole world.[a]

[3]We know[b] that we have come to know him[c] if we obey his commands.[d]

Cross references

1:1 [a]S Jn 1:2
[b]S Lk 24:48;
Jn 1:14; 19:35;
Ac 4:20;
2Pe 1:16;
1Jn 4:14
[c]Jn 20:27
1:2 [d]Jn 1:1-4;
11:25; 14:6;
1Ti 3:16;
1Pe 1:20; 1Jn 3:5,
8 [e]S Jn 15:27
[f]S Mt 25:46
1:3 [g]S ver 1
[h]1Co 1:9
1:4 [i]1Jn 2:1
[j]S Jn 3:29
1:5 [k]1Jn 3:11
[l]1Ti 6:16
1:6 [m]Jn 3:19-21;
8:12; 2Co 6:14;
Eph 5:8; 1Jn 2:11
[n]Jn 3:19-21;
1Jn 2:4; 4:20
1:7 [o]Isa 2:5

[p]Heb 9:14;
Rev 1:5; 7:14
1:8 [q]Pr 20:9;
Jer 2:35;
Ro 3:9-19; Jas 3:2
[r]Jn 8:44; 1Jn 2:4
1:9 [s]Ps 32:5;
51:2; Pr 28:13
[t]ver 7;
Mic 7:18-20;
Heb 10:22
1:10 [u]ver 8
[v]1Jn 5:10
[w]Jn 5:38;

1Jn 2:14 2:1 [x]ver 12,13,28; 1Jn 3:7,18; 4:4; 5:21;
S 1Th 2:11 [y]S Ro 8:34; 1Ti 2:5 2:2 [z]Ro 3:25; 1Jn 4:10
[a]S Mt 1:21; S Jn 3:17 2:3 [b]ver 5; 1Jn 3:24; 4:13; 5:2 [c]S ver 4 [d]S Jn 14:15

[a]4 Some manuscripts your   [b]7 Or every   [c]2 Or He is the one who turns aside God's wrath, taking away our sins, and not only ours but also

---

1:1–4 The introduction to this letter deals with the same subject and uses several of the same words as the introduction to John's Gospel (1:1–4)—"beginning," "Word," "life," "with."
1:1 *was from the beginning.* Has always existed. *we.* John and the other apostles. *heard . . . seen . . . looked at . . . touched.* The apostle had made a careful examination of the Word of life. He testifies that the one who has existed from eternity "became flesh" (Jn 1:14)—i.e., a flesh-and-blood man. He was true God and true man. At the outset, John contradicts the heresy of the Gnostics (see Introduction: Gnosticism). *Word of life.* The one who is life and reveals life (see v. 2 and note). "Word" here speaks of revelation (see note on Jn 1:1).
1:2 *The life . . . the eternal life.* Christ. He is called "the life" because he is the living one who has life in himself (see Jn 11:25; 14:6). He is also the source of life and sovereign over life (5:11). The letter begins and ends (5:20) with the theme of eternal life.
1:3 *fellowship with us.* Participation with us (vicariously) in our experience of hearing, seeing and touching the incarnate Christ (v. 1). Fellowship (Greek *koinonia*) is the spiritual union of the believer with Christ—as described in the figures of the vine and branches (Jn 15:1–5) and the body and the head (1Co 12:12; Col 1:18)—as well as communion with the Father and with fellow believers.
1:4 *our joy complete.* John's joy in the Lord could not be complete unless his readers shared the true knowledge of the Christ (see 2Jn 12).
1:5 *from him.* From Christ. *light . . . darkness.* Light represents what is good, true and holy, while darkness represents what is evil and false (see Jn 3:19–21).
1:6–7 *walk in the darkness . . . in the light.* Two lifestyles—one characterized by wickedness and error, the other by holiness and truth.
1:6 *we.* John and his readers. *to have fellowship with him.* To be in living, spiritual union with God. *walk.* A metaphor for living. *truth.* See note on Jn 1:14.
1:7 *sin.* A key word in 1 John, occurring 27 times in the Greek.

1:9 *faithful and just.* Here the phrase is virtually a single concept (faithful-and-just). It indicates that God's response toward those who confess their sins will be in accordance with his nature and his gracious commitment to his people (see Ps 143:1; Zec 8:8). *faithful.* To his promise to forgive (see Jer 31:34; Mic 7:18–20; Heb 10:22–23). *will forgive us.* Will provide the forgiveness that restores the communion with God that had been interrupted by sin (as requested in the Lord's Prayer, Mt 6:12).
1:10 *we have not sinned.* Gnostics denied that their immoral actions were sinful.
2:1 *dear children.* John, the aged apostle, often used this expression of endearment (vv. 12–13,28; 3:7,18; 4:4; 5:21; the term in 2:18 translates a different Greek word). *one who speaks . . . in our defense.* One Greek word underlies this phrase, which refers to someone who speaks in court in behalf of a defendant (see note on Jn 14:16). *Righteous One.* In God's court the defender must be, and is, sinless.
2:2 *atoning sacrifice for our sins.* The NIV text note explains the fuller meaning of the original Greek (see also 4:10). God's holiness demands punishment for man's sin. God, therefore, out of love (4:10; Jn 3:16), sent his Son to make substitutionary atonement for the believer's sin. In this way the Father's wrath is propitiated (satisfied, appeased); his wrath against the Christian's sin has been turned away and directed toward Christ. See note on Ro 3:25. *for the sins of the whole world.* Forgiveness through Christ's atoning sacrifice is not limited to one particular group only; it has worldwide application (see Jn 1:29). It must, however, be received by faith (see Jn 3:16). Thus this verse does not teach universalism (that all people ultimately will be saved), but that God is an impartial God.
2:3 Forty-two times 1 John uses two Greek verbs normally translated "know." One of these verbs is related to the name of the Gnostics, the heretical sect that claimed to have a special knowledge (Greek *gnosis*) of God (see Introduction: Gnosticism). *obey his commands.* Does not mean that only those who never disobey (1:8–9) know God, but simply refers to those whose lives are generally characterized by obedience.

⁴The man who says, "I know him," *e* but does not do what he commands is a liar, and the truth is not in him.*f* ⁵But if anyone obeys his word,*g* God's love*d* is truly made complete in him.*h* This is how we know*i* we are in him: ⁶Whoever claims to live in him must walk as Jesus did.*j*

⁷Dear friends,*k* I am not writing you a new command but an old one, which you have had since the beginning.*l* This old command is the message you have heard. ⁸Yet I am writing you a new command;*m* its truth is seen in him and you, because the darkness is passing*n* and the true light*o* is already shining.*p*

⁹Anyone who claims to be in the light but hates his brother*q* is still in the darkness.*r* ¹⁰Whoever loves his brother lives in the light,*s* and there is nothing in him*e* to make him stumble.*t* ¹¹But whoever hates his brother*u* is in the darkness and walks around in the darkness;*v* he does not know where he is going, because the darkness has blinded him.*w*

¹²I write to you, dear children,*x*
   because your sins have been forgiven
      on account of his name.*y*
¹³I write to you, fathers,
   because you have known him who is
      from the beginning.*z*

I write to you, young men,
   because you have overcome*a* the evil
      one.*b*
I write to you, dear children,*c*
   because you have known the Father.
¹⁴I write to you, fathers,
   because you have known him who is
      from the beginning.*d*

I write to you, young men,
   because you are strong,*e*
   and the word of God*f* lives in you,*g*
   and you have overcome the evil
      one.*h*

Do Not Love the World

¹⁵Do not love the world or anything in the world.*i* If anyone loves the world, the love of the Father is not in him.*j* ¹⁶For everything in the world—the cravings of sinful man,*k* the lust of his eyes*l* and the boasting of what he has and does—comes not from the Father but from the world. ¹⁷The world and its desires pass away,*m* but the man who does the will of God*n* lives forever.

Warning Against Antichrists

¹⁸Dear children, this is the last hour;*o* and as you have heard that the antichrist is

Cross references (center column)
2:4 *e*ver 3; Tit 1:16; 1Jn 3:6; 4:7,8 *f*1Jn 1:6,8
2:5 *g*S Jn 14:15 *h*1Jn 4:12 *i*S ver 3
2:6 *j*S Mt 11:29
2:7 *k*S 1Co 10:14 *l*ver 24; 1Jn 3:11, 23; 4:21; 2Jn 5,6
2:8 *m*S Jn 13:34 *n*Ro 13:12; Heb 10:25 *o*Jn 1:9 *p*Eph 5:8; 1Th 5:5
2:9 *q*ver 11; Lev 19:17; 1Jn 3:10,15,16; 4:20,21 *r*1Jn 1:5
2:10 *s*1Jn 3:14 *t*ver 11; Ps 119:165
2:11 *u*S ver 9 *v*S ver 1 *w*Jn 11:9; 12:35
2:12 *x*S ver 1 *y*S 1Jn 3:23
2:13 *z*S Jn 1:1

*a*S Jn 16:33 *b*ver 14; S Mt 5:37 *c*S ver 1
2:14 *d*S Jn 1:1 *e*Eph 6:10 *f*S Heb 4:12 *g*Jn 5:38; 1Jn 1:10 *h*S ver 13
2:15 *i*Ro 12:2 *j*Jas 4:4
2:16 *k*Ge 3:6; Ro 13:14; Eph 2:3 *l*Pr 27:20
2:17 *m*S Heb 12:27 *n*Mt 12:50
2:18 *o*S Ro 13:11

*d*5 Or *word, love for God*   *e*10 Or *it*

2:5 *God's love is truly made complete in him.* Means either that God's love for the believer is made complete when it moves the believer to acts of obedience (see 4:12), or that our love for God (see NIV text note) becomes complete when it expresses itself in acts of obedience (see 3:16–18). *in him.* Spiritual union with God (see Jn 17:21).

2:7–8 *new command.* See Jn 13:34–35. The Biblical command to love was old (see Lev 19:18; also Mt 22:39–40). But its newness is seen in: (1) the new and dramatic illustration of divine love on the cross; (2) Christ's exposition of the OT law (see Mt 5), which seemed new to Christ's hearers; and (3) the daily experience of believers as they grow in love for each other.

2:7 *Dear friends.* Like "dear children" (see note on v. 1), a favorite term of John's (used ten times in two letters: here; 3:2,21; 4:1,7,11; 3Jn 1–2,5,11). *since the beginning.* The beginning of their Christian experience, when they first heard the gospel.

2:8 *true light.* Used in the NT only here and in Jn 1:9, this phrase refers to the gospel of Jesus Christ, who is the light of the world (Jn 8:12), and to its saving effects in the lives of believers.

2:9–10 *hates . . . loves.* In the Bible hatred and love as moral qualities are not primarily emotions, but attitudes expressed in actions (see 3:15–16).

2:9 *light . . . darkness.* See note on 1:5. *brother.* Fellow believer.

2:10 *stumble.* Into sin.

2:12–14 *I write to you . . . because.* By extended repetition in these verses, John assures his readers that, in spite of the rigorous tests contained in the letter, he is confident of their salvation. *dear children . . . fathers . . . young men.* As elsewhere in this letter, "dear children" probably refers to all John's readers (see note on v. 1), including fathers and young

men. The terms "fathers" and "young men" may, however, describe two different levels of spiritual maturity. Some hold that all three terms refer to levels of spiritual maturity.

2:12 *his name.* Jesus (see 3:23; 5:13; see also note on Ac 4:12).

2:13–14 *him who is from the beginning.* Christ (see note on 1:1).

2:15 *the world.* Not the world of people (Jn 3:16) or the created world (Jn 17:24), but the world, or realm, of sin (v. 16; Jas 4:4), which is controlled by Satan and organized against God and righteousness (see note on Jn 1:10). *love of the Father.* Love for the Father.

2:18 *last hour.* With other NT writers, John viewed the whole period beginning with Christ's first coming as the last days (see Ac 2:17; 2Ti 3:1; Heb 1:2; 1Pe 1:20). They understood this to be the "last" of the days because neither former prophecy nor new revelation concerning the history of salvation indicated the coming of another era before the return of Christ. The word "last" in "last days," "last times" and "last hour" also expresses a sense of urgency and imminence. The Christian is to be alert, waiting for the return of Christ (Mt 25:1–13). *the antichrist . . . many antichrists.* John assumed his readers knew that a great enemy of God and his people will arise before Christ's return. That person is called "antichrist" (v. 18), "the man of lawlessness" (2Th 2:3; but see note there) and "the beast" (Rev 13:1–10). But prior to him, there will be many antichrists. These are characterized by the following: (1) They deny the incarnation (4:2; 2Jn 7) and that Jesus is the divine Christ (v. 22); (2) they deny the Father (v. 22); (3) they do not have the Father (v. 23); (4) they are liars (v. 22) and deceivers (2Jn 7); (5) they are many (v. 18); (6) in John's day they left the church because they had nothing in common with believers (v. 19). The antichrists referred to in John's letter were the early

coming,[p] even now many antichrists have come.[q] This is how we know it is the last hour. [19]They went out from us,[r] but they did not really belong to us. For if they had belonged to us, they would have remained with us; but their going showed that none of them belonged to us.[s]

[20]But you have an anointing[t] from the Holy One,[u] and all of you know the truth.[fv] [21]I do not write to you because you do not know the truth, but because you do know it[w] and because no lie comes from the truth. [22]Who is the liar? It is the man who denies that Jesus is the Christ. Such a man is the antichrist—he denies the Father and the Son.[x] [23]No one who denies the Son has the Father; whoever acknowledges the Son has the Father also.[y]

[24]See that what you have heard from the beginning[z] remains in you. If it does, you also will remain in the Son and in the Father.[a] [25]And this is what he promised us—even eternal life.[b]

[26]I am writing these things to you about those who are trying to lead you astray.[c] [27]As for you, the anointing[d] you received from him remains in you, and you do not need anyone to teach you. But as his anointing teaches you about all things[e] and as that anointing is real, not counterfeit—just as it has taught you, remain in him.[f]

Children of God

[28]And now, dear children,[g] continue in

him, so that when he appears[h] we may be confident[i] and unashamed before him at his coming.[j]

[29]If you know that he is righteous,[k] you know that everyone who does what is right has been born of him.[l]

3 How great is the love[m] the Father has lavished on us, that we should be called children of God![n] And that is what we are! The reason the world does not know us is that it did not know him.[o] [2]Dear friends,[p] now we are children of God,[q] and what we will be has not yet been made known. But we know that when he appears,[gr] we shall be like him,[s] for we shall see him as he is.[t] [3]Everyone who has this hope in him purifies himself,[u] just as he is pure.[v]

[4]Everyone who sins breaks the law; in fact, sin is lawlessness.[w] [5]But you know that he appeared so that he might take away our sins.[x] And in him is no sin.[y] [6]No one who lives in him keeps on sinning.[z] No one who continues to sin has either seen him[a] or known him.[b]

[7]Dear children,[c] do not let anyone lead you astray.[d] He who does what is right is righteous, just as he is righteous.[e] [8]He who does what is sinful is of the devil,[f] because the devil has been sinning from the beginning. The reason the Son of God[g] appeared was to destroy the devil's work.[h]

2:18 [p]ver 22; 1Jn 4:3; 2Jn 7
[q]1Jn 4:1
2:19 [r]Ac 20:30
[s]1Co 11:19
2:20 [t]ver 27; 2Co 1:21
[u]S Mk 1:24
[v]Jer 31:34; Mt 13:11; Jn 14:26
2:21 [w]2Pe 1:12; Jude 5
2:22 [x]1Jn 4:3; 2Jn 7
2:23 [y]Jn 8:19; 14:7; 1Jn 4:15; 5:1; 2Jn 9
2:24 [z]S ver 7
[a]Jn 14:23; 15:4; 1Jn 1:3; 2Jn 9
2:25 [b]S 1Co 25:46
2:26 [c]1Jn 3:7
2:27 [d]ver 20
[e]1Co 2:12
[f]Jn 15:4
2:28 [g]S ver 1

[h]1Jn 3:2; Col 3:4
[i]S Eph 3:12
[j]S 1Th 2:19
2:29 [k]1Jn 3:7
[l]S Jn 1:13
3:1 [m]S Jn 3:16
[n]ver 2,10; S Jn 1:12
[o]Jn 15:21; 16:3
3:2 [p]S 1Co 10:14
[q]ver 1,10; S Jn 1:12
[r]Col 3:4; 1Jn 2:28
[s]Ro 8:29; 2Pe 1:4
[t]Ps 17:15; Jn 17:24; 2Co 3:18
3:3 [u]2Co 7:1; 2Pe 3:13,14
[v]Ps 18:26
3:4 [w]1Jn 5:17
3:5 [x]ver 8; S Jn 3:17
[y]S 2Co 5:21
3:6 [z]ver 9; 1Jn 5:18
[a]3Jn 11
[b]S 1Jn 2:4
3:7 [c]S 1Jn 2:1
[d]1Jn 2:26

[e]1Jn 2:29 3:8 [f]ver 10; Jn 8:44 [g]S Mt 4:3 [h]Heb 2:14

[f]20 Some manuscripts and you know all things [g]2 Or when it is made known

---

Gnostics. The "anti" in antichrist means "against" (cf. 2Th 2:4; Rev 13:6–7).

2:20 anointing. The Holy Spirit (see v. 27; Ac 10:38). Holy One. Either Jesus Christ (Mk 1:24; Jn 6:69; Ac 2:27; 3:14; 22:14) or the Father (2Ki 19:22; Job 6:10).

2:22 Jesus is the Christ. The man Jesus is the divine Christ (see the parallel confession in 5:5; see also Introduction: Gnosticism and note on 5:6).

2:23 See 2Jn 9 for the same thought.

2:26 One of the statements of purpose for the letter (see Introduction: Occasion and Purpose).

2:27 anointing. See note on v. 20. do not need anyone to teach you. Since the Bible constantly advocates teaching (Mt 28:20; 1Co 12:28; Eph 4:11; Col 3:16; 1Ti 4:11; 2Ti 2:2,24), John is not ruling out human teachers. At the time when he wrote, however, Gnostic teachers were insisting that the teaching of the apostles was to be supplemented with the "higher knowledge" that they (the Gnostics) claimed to possess. John's response was that what the readers were taught under the Spirit's ministry through the apostles not only was adequate but was the only reliable truth. teaches you. The teaching ministry of the Holy Spirit (what is commonly called illumination) does not involve revelation of new truth or the explanation of all difficult passages of Scripture to our satisfaction. Rather, it is the development of the capacity to appreciate and appropriate God's truth al-

ready revealed—making the Bible meaningful in thought and daily living. all things. All things necessary to know for salvation and Christian living.

2:28 continue in him. See "remains in" (vv. 24,27). confident. See 3:21; 4:17; 5:14 ("assurance").

2:29 he . . . him. God the Father. does what is right. Members of God's family are marked by holy living.

3:1 children of God. See note on Jn 1:12.

3:2 he . . . him. Christ.

3:3 hope. Not a mere wish, but unshakable confidence concerning the future (see note on Ro 5:2). him. Christ. purifies himself. By turning from sin.

3:6 keeps on sinning. John is not asserting sinless perfection (see 1:8–10; 2:1), but explaining that the believer's life is characterized not by sin but by doing what is right.

3:8 devil. In this short letter John says much about the devil: 1. He is called "the devil" (here) and "the evil one" (v. 12; 2:13–14; 5:18–19). 2. He "has been sinning from the beginning" (here), i.e., from the time he first rebelled against God, before the fall of Adam and Eve (Jn 8:44). 3. He is the instigator of human sin, and those who continue to sin belong to him (vv. 8,12) and are his children (v. 10). 4. He is in the world (4:3) and has "the whole world" of unbelievers under his control (5:19). 5. But he cannot lay hold of the believer to harm him (5:18). 6. On the contrary, the Christian will overcome him (2:13–14; 4:4), and Christ will destroy his work.

⁹No one who is born of God[i] will continue to sin,[j] because God's seed[k] remains in him; he cannot go on sinning, because he has been born of God. ¹⁰This is how we know who the children of God are and who the children of the devil[m] are: Anyone who does not do what is right is not a child of God; nor is anyone who does not love[n] his brother.[o]

Love One Another

¹¹This is the message you heard[p] from the beginning:[q] We should love one another.[r] ¹²Do not be like Cain, who belonged to the evil one[s] and murdered his brother.[t] And why did he murder him? Because his own actions were evil and his brother's were righteous.[u] ¹³Do not be surprised, my brothers, if the world hates you.[v] ¹⁴We know that we have passed from death to life,[w] because we love our brothers. Anyone who does not love remains in death.[x] ¹⁵Anyone who hates his brother[y] is a murderer,[z] and you know that no murderer has eternal life in him.[a]

¹⁶This is how we know what love is: Jesus Christ laid down his life for us.[b] And we ought to lay down our lives for our brothers.[c] ¹⁷If anyone has material possessions and sees his brother in need but has no pity on him,[d] how can the love of God be in him?[e] ¹⁸Dear children,[f] let us not love with words or tongue but with actions and in truth.[g] ¹⁹This then is how we know that we belong to the truth, and how we set our hearts at rest in his presence ²⁰whenever our hearts condemn us. For

God is greater than our hearts, and he knows everything.

²¹Dear friends,[h] if our hearts do not condemn us, we have confidence before God[i] ²²and receive from him anything we ask,[j] because we obey his commands[k] and do what pleases him.[l] ²³And this is his command: to believe[m] in the name of his Son, Jesus Christ,[n] and to love one another as he commanded us.[o] ²⁴Those who obey his commands[p] live in him,[q] and he in them. And this is how we know that he lives in us: We know it by the Spirit he gave us.[r]

Test the Spirits

4 Dear friends,[s] do not believe every spirit,[t] but test the spirits to see whether they are from God, because many false prophets have gone out into the world.[u] ²This is how you can recognize the Spirit of God: Every spirit that acknowledges that Jesus Christ has come in the flesh[v] is from God,[w] ³but every spirit that does not acknowledge Jesus is not from God. This is the spirit of the antichrist,[x] which you have heard is coming and even now is already in the world.[y]

⁴You, dear children,[z] are from God and have overcome them,[a] because the one who is in you[b] is greater than the one who is in the world.[c] ⁵They are from the world[d] and therefore speak from the viewpoint of the world, and the world listens to them. ⁶We are from God, and whoever

Cross references

3:9 *iS* Jn 1:13
*i*ver 6; Ps 119:3;
1Jn 5:18
*k*1Pe 1:23
3:10 *l*ver 1,2;
S Jn 1:12 *m*ver 8
*n*1Jn 4:8
*o*S 1Jn 2:9
3:11 *p*1Jn 1:5
*q*S 1Jn 2:7
*r*Jn 13:34,35;
15:12; 1Jn 4:7,
11,21; 2Jn 5
3:12 *s*S Mt 5:37
*t*Ge 4:8
*u*Ps 38:20;
Pr 29:10
3:13 *v*Jn 15:18,
19; 17:14
3:14 *w*Jn 5:24
*x*S 1Jn 2:9
3:15 *y*S 1Jn 2:9
*z*Mt 5:21,22;
Jn 8:44 *a*Gal 5:20,
21; Rev 21:8
3:16 *b*Jn 10:11
*c*Jn 15:13;
Php 2:17; 1Th 2:8
3:17 *d*Dt 15:7,8;
Jas 2:15,16
*e*1Jn 4:20
3:18 *f*S 1Jn 2:1
*g*Eze 33:31;
Ro 12:9

3:21 *h*S 1Co 10:14
*i*S Eph 3:12;
1Jn 5:14
3:22 *j*S Mt 7:7
*k*S Jn 14:15
*l*Jn 8:29;
Heb 13:21
3:23 *m*Jn 6:29
*n*S Lk 24:47;
Jn 1:12; 3:18;
20:31; 1Co 6:11;
1Jn 5:13
*o*S Jn 13:34
3:24 *p*1Jn 2:3
*q*1Jn 2:6; 4:15
*r*1Th 4:8;
1Jn 4:13
4:1 *s*S 1Co 10:14
*t*Jer 29:8;
1Co 12:10;
2Th 2:2
*u*S Mt 7:15;
1Jn 2:18

4:2 *v*S Jn 1:14; 1Jn 2:23 *w*1Co 12:3 4:3 *x*1Jn 2:22; 2Jn 7
*y*1Jn 2:18 4:4 *z*S 1Jn 2:1 *a*S Jn 16:33 *b*Ro 8:31 *c*2Ki 6:16;
S Jn 12:31 4:5 *d*Jn 15:19; 17:14,16

3:9 *God's seed.* The picture is of human reproduction, in which the sperm (the Greek for "seed" is *sperma*) bears the life principle and transfers the paternal characteristics. *cannot go on sinning.* Not a complete cessation of sin, but a life that is not characterized by sin.

3:11 *from the beginning.* See note on 2:7.

3:12 *Cain.* See Heb 11:4.

3:14 *brothers.* Fellow believers.

3:15 *hates.* See note on 2:9–10.

3:17–18 See Jas 2:14–17.

3:17 *love of God.* God's kind of love, which he pours out in the believer's heart (Ro 5:5) and which in turn enables the Christian to love fellow believers. Or it may speak of the believer's love for God.

3:20 *God is greater than our hearts.* An oversensitive conscience can be quieted by the knowledge that God himself has declared active love to be an evidence of salvation. He knows the hearts of all—whether, in spite of shortcomings, they have been born of him.

3:23 This command has two parts: (1) Believe in Christ (see Jn 6:29), and (2) love each other (see Jn 13:34–35). The first part is developed in 4:1–6 and the second part in 4:7–12.

4:1 *spirit.* A person moved by a spirit, whether by the Holy Spirit or an evil one. *test the spirits.* Cf. 1Th 5:21. (Mt 7:1

does not refer to such testing or judgment; it speaks of self-righteous moral judgment of others.) *false prophets.* A true prophet speaks from God, being "carried along" by the Holy Spirit (2Pe 1:21). False prophets, such as the Gnostics of John's day, speak under the influence of spirits alienated from God. Christ warned against false prophets (Mt 7:15; 24:11), as did Paul (1Ti 4:1) and Peter (2Pe 2:1).

4:2 *acknowledges.* Not only knows intellectually—for demons know, and shudder (Jas 2:19; cf. Mk 1:24)—but also confesses publicly. *Jesus Christ has come in the flesh.* See note on 1:1. Thus John excludes the Gnostics, especially the Cerinthians, who taught that the divine Christ came upon the human Jesus at his baptism and then left him at the cross, so that it was only the man Jesus who died.

4:3 *does not acknowledge Jesus.* The incarnate Jesus Christ of 1:2 (see note on 2:18).

4:4 *from God.* An abbreviated form of the expression "born of God" (2:29; 3:9–10). *them.* The false prophets (v. 1), who were inspired by the spirit of the antichrist (v. 3). *the one who is in the world.* The devil (Jn 12:31; 16:11). In v. 3 "world" means the inhabited earth; in vv. 4–5 it means the community, or system, of those not born of God—including the antichrists (see note on Jn 1:10).

4:6 *Spirit of truth.* Cf. 5:6; see note on Jn 14:17.

knows God listens to us; but whoever is not from God does not listen to us. [e] This is how we recognize the Spirit[h] of truth[f] and the spirit of falsehood. [g]

God's Love and Ours

[7]Dear friends, let us love one another, [h] for love comes from God. Everyone who loves has been born of God[i] and knows God. [j] [8]Whoever does not love does not know God, because God is love. [k] [9]This is how God showed his love among us: He sent his one and only Son[i] [l] into the world that we might live through him. [m] [10]This is love: not that we loved God, but that he loved us[n] and sent his Son as an atoning sacrifice for[j] our sins. [o] [11]Dear friends, [p] since God so loved us, [q] we also ought to love one another. [r] [12]No one has ever seen God; [s] but if we love one another, God lives in us and his love is made complete in us. [t]

[13]We know [u] that we live in him and he in us, because he has given us of his Spirit. [v] [14]And we have seen and testify[w] that the Father has sent his Son to be the Savior of the world. [x] [15]If anyone acknowledges that Jesus is the Son of God, [y] God lives in him and he in God. [z] [16]And so we know and rely on the love God has for us.

God is love. [a] Whoever lives in love lives in God, and God in him. [b] [17]In this way, love is made complete[c] among us so that we will have confidence[d] on the day

of judgment, [e] because in this world we are like him. [18]There is no fear in love. But perfect love drives out fear, [f] because fear has to do with punishment. The one who fears is not made perfect in love.

[19]We love because he first loved us. [g] [20]If anyone says, "I love God," yet hates his brother, [h] he is a liar. [i] For anyone who does not love his brother, whom he has seen, [j] cannot love God, whom he has not seen. [k] [21]And he has given us this command: [l] Whoever loves God must also love his brother. [m]

Faith in the Son of God

5 Everyone who believes[n] that Jesus the Christ[o] is born of God, [p] and everyone who loves the father loves his child as well. [q] [2]This is how we know[r] that we love the children of God: [s] by loving God and carrying out his commands. [3]This is love for God: to obey his commands. [t] And his commands are not burdensome, [u] [4]for everyone born of God[v] overcomes[w] the world. This is the victory that has overcome the world, even our faith. [5]Who is it that overcomes the world? Only he who believes that Jesus is the Son of God. [x]

[6]This is the one who came by water and blood[y]—Jesus Christ. He did not come by

---

4:6 [e]Jn 8:47
[f]S Jn 14:17
[g]S Mk 13:5
4:7 [h]S 1Jn 3:11
[i]S Jn 1:13
[j]S 1Jn 2:4
4:8 [k]ver 7,16
4:9 [l]Jn 1:18
[m]Jn 3:16,17;
1Jn 5:11
4:10 [n]Ro 5:8,10
[o]S Ro 3:25
4:11
[p]S 1Co 10:14
[q]S Jn 3:16
[r]Jn 15:12;
S 1Jn 3:11
4:12 [s]S Jn 1:18
[t]ver 17; 1Jn 2:5
4:13 [u]S 1Jn 2:3
[v]1Jn 3:24
4:14 [w]S Jn 15:27
[x]S Lk 2:11;
S Jn 3:17
4:15 [y]S 1Jn 2:23;
5:5 [z]1Jn 3:24
4:16 [a]ver 8 [b]ver
12,13; 1Jn 3:24
4:17 [c]ver 12;
1Jn 2:5
[d]S Eph 3:12

[e]S Mt 10:15
4:18 [f]Ro 8:15
4:19 [g]ver 10
4:20 [h]S 1Jn 2:9
[i]S 1Jn 1:6; 2:4
[j]1Jn 3:17 [k]ver 12;
S Jn 1:18
4:21 [l]1Jn 2:7
[m]S Mt 5:43;
S 1Jn 2:9
5:1 [n]S Jn 3:15
[o]1Jn 2:22; 4:2,15
[p]S Jn 1:13;
S 1Jn 2:23
[q]Jn 8:42
5:2 [r]S 1Jn 2:3
[s]1Jn 3:14
5:3 [t]S Jn 14:15
[u]Mt 11:30; 23:4
5:4 [v]S 1Jn 1:13
[w]S Jn 16:33
5:5 [x]ver 1;
S 1Jn 2:23

5:6 [y]Jn 19:34

[h]6 Or spirit   [i]9 Or his only begotten Son   [j]10 Or as the one who would turn aside his wrath, taking away

---

4:7–5:3 The word "love" in its various forms is used 43 times in the letter, 32 times in this short section.

4:8 *does not know God.* Only those who are to some degree like him truly know him. *God is love.* In his essential nature and in all his actions, God is loving. John similarly affirms that God is spirit (Jn 4:24) and light (1:5), as well as holy, powerful, faithful, true and just.

4:9 *one and only Son.* See note on Jn 1:18.

4:10 *atoning sacrifice for our sins.* See note on 2:2.

4:12 *No one has ever seen God.* See note on Jn 1:18. Since our love has its source in God's love, his love reaches full expression (is made complete) when we love fellow Christians. Thus the God whom "no one has ever seen" is seen in those who love, because God lives in them.

4:16 *God is love.* See note on v. 8.

4:17 *like him.* Like Christ. The fact that we are like Christ in love is a sign that God, who is love, lives in us; therefore we may have confidence on the day of judgment that we are saved.

4:18 *no fear in love.* There is no fear of God's judgment because genuine love confirms salvation.

4:19 All love comes ultimately from God; genuine love is never self-generated by his creatures.

4:21 *this command.* See Jn 13:34.

5:1 *Everyone who believes that Jesus is the Christ is born of God.* Faith in Jesus as the Christ is a sign of being born again, just as love is (4:7). *the Christ.* See note on 2:22. *everyone who loves the father loves his child as well.* John wrote at a time when members of a family were closely

associated as a unit under the headship of the father. He could therefore use the family as an illustration to show that anyone who loves God the Father will naturally love God's children.

5:3 *his commands are not burdensome.* Not because the commands themselves are light or easy to obey but, as John explains in v. 4, because of the new birth. The one born of God by faith is enabled by the Holy Spirit to obey.

5:4 *overcomes . . . has overcome.* To overcome the world is to gain victory over its sinful pattern of life, which is another way of describing obedience to God (v. 3). Such obedience is not impossible for the believer because he has been born again and the Holy Spirit dwells within him and gives him strength. John speaks of two aspects of victory: (1) the initial victory of turning in faith from the world to God ("has overcome"); (2) the continuing day-by-day victory of Christian living ("overcomes"). *world.* See note on 2:15.

5:5 *Son of God.* For parallel confessions see 2:22; 4:2; 5:1.

5:6 Water symbolizes Jesus' baptism, and blood symbolizes his death. These are mentioned because Jesus' ministry began at his baptism and ended at his death. John is reacting to the heretics of his day (see Introduction: Gnosticism) who said that Jesus was born only a man and remained so until his baptism. At that time, they maintained, the Christ (the Son of God) descended on the human Jesus, but left him before his suffering on the cross—so that it was only the man Jesus who died. Throughout this letter John has been insisting that Jesus Christ is God as well as man (1:1–4; 4:2; 5:5). He now asserts that it was this God-man Jesus Christ who came into

water only, but by water and blood. And it is the Spirit who testifies, because the Spirit is the truth. *z* [7]For there are three[a] that testify: [8]the[k] Spirit, the water and the blood; and the three are in agreement. [9]We accept man's testimony,[b] but God's testimony is greater because it is the testimony of God,[c] which he has given about his Son. [10]Anyone who believes in the Son of God has this testimony in his heart.[d] Anyone who does not believe God has made him out to be a liar,[e] because he has not believed the testimony God has given about his Son. [11]And this is the testimony: God has given us eternal life,[f] and this life is in his Son.[g] [12]He who has the Son has life; he who does not have the Son of God does not have life.[h]

Concluding Remarks

[13]I write these things to you who believe in the name of the Son of God[i] so that you may know that you have eternal life.[j] [14]This is the confidence[k] we have in approaching God: that if we ask anything according to his will, he hears us.[l] [15]And if we know that he hears us—whatever we ask—we know[m] that we have what we asked of him.[n]

[16]If anyone sees his brother commit a sin that does not lead to death, he should pray and God will give him life.[o] I refer to those whose sin does not lead to death. There is a sin that leads to death.[p] I am not saying that he should pray about that.[q] [17]All wrongdoing is sin,[r] and there is sin that does not lead to death.[s]

[18]We know that anyone born of God[t] does not continue to sin; the one who was born of God keeps him safe, and the evil one[u] cannot harm him.[v] [19]We know that we are children of God,[w] and that the whole world is under the control of the evil one.[x] [20]We know also that the Son of God has come[y] and has given us understanding,[z] so that we may know him who is true.[a] And we are in him who is true—even in his Son Jesus Christ. He is the true God and eternal life.[b]

[21]Dear children,[c] keep yourselves from idols.[d]

5:6 *z* S Jn 14:17
5:7 *a* S Mt 18:16
5:9 *b* Jn 5:34
c Mt 3:16,17; Jn 5:32,37; 8:17, 18
5:10 *d* Ro 8:16; Gal 4:6 *e* Jn 3:33; 1Jn 1:10
5:11 *f* S Mt 25:46 *g* S Jn 1:4
5:12 *h* Jn 3:15,16, 36
5:13 *i* S 1Jn 3:23 *j* ver 11; S Mt 25:46
5:14 *k* S Eph 3:12; 1Jn 3:21 *l* S Mt 7:7

5:15 *m* ver 18,19, 20 *n* 1Ki 3:12
5:16 *o* Jas 5:15 *p* Ex 23:21; Heb 6:4-6; 10:26 *q* Jer 7:16; 14:11
5:17 *r* 1Jn 3:4 *s* ver 16; 1Jn 2:1
5:18 *t* S Jn 1:13 *u* S Mt 5:37 *v* Jn 14:30
5:19 *w* 1Jn 4:6 *x* Jn 12:31; 14:30; 17:15
5:20 *y* ver 5 *z* Lk 24:45 *a* Jn 17:3 *b* ver 11; S Mt 25:46
5:21 *c* S 1Jn 2:1 *d* 1Co 10:14; 1Th 1:9

k7,8 Late manuscripts of the Vulgate *testify in heaven: the Father, the Word and the Holy Spirit, and these three are one.* 8*And there are three that testify on earth: the* (not found in any Greek manuscript before the sixteenth century)

---

our world, was baptized and died. Jesus was the Son of God not only at his baptism but also at his death (v. 6b). This truth is extremely important, because, if Jesus died only as a man, his sacrificial atonement (2:2; 4:10) would not have been sufficient to take away the guilt of man's sin. *the Spirit who testifies.* The Holy Spirit testifies that Jesus is the Son of God in two ways: (1) The Spirit descended on Jesus at his baptism (Jn 1:32–34), and (2) he continues to confirm in the hearts of believers the apostolic testimony that Jesus' baptism and death verify that he is the Christ, the Son of God (2:27; 1Co 12:3).

5:7 *three.* The OT law required "two or three witnesses" (Dt 17:6; 19:15; see 1Ti 5:19). At the end of this verse, some older English versions add the words found in the NIV text note. But the addition is not found in any Greek manuscript or NT translation prior to the 16th century.

5:9 *God's testimony.* The Holy Spirit's testimony, mentioned in vv. 6–8.

5:11 *has given us eternal life.* As a present possession (see notes on 3:15,36).

5:13 Another statement of the letter's purpose (see 2:26). See Introduction: Occasion and Purpose.

5:14 *if we ask anything according to his will.* For another condition for prayer see 3:21–22.

5:16 Verses 16–17 illustrate the kind of petition we can be sure God will answer (see vv. 14–15). *sin that leads to death.* In the context of this letter directed against Gnostic teaching, which denied the incarnation and threw off all moral restraints, it is probable that the "sin that leads to death" refers to the Gnostics' adamant and persistent denial of the truth and to their shameless immorality. This kind of unrepentant sin leads to spiritual death. Another view is that this is sin that results in physical death. It is held that, because a believer continues to sin, God in judgment takes his life (cf. 1Co 11:30). In either case, "sin that does not lead to death" is of a less serious nature.

5:18–20 *We know.* The letter ends with three striking statements, affirming the truths that "we know" and summarizing some of the letter's major themes.

5:18 *the one who was born of God.* Jesus, the Son of God.

5:20 *him who is true.* God the Father. *He is the true God.* Could refer to either God the Father or God the Son. *eternal life.* The letter began with this theme (1:1–2) and now ends with it.

5:21 *idols.* False gods, as opposed to the one true God (v. 20).

2 JOHN

Author

The author is John the apostle. Obvious similarities to 1 John and the Gospel of John suggest that the same person wrote all three books. Compare the following:

2Jn 5	1Jn 2:7	Jn 13:34-35
2Jn 6	1Jn 5:3	Jn 14:23
2Jn 7	1Jn 4:2-3	
2Jn 12	1Jn 1:4	Jn 15:11; 16:24

See Introductions to 1 John and the Gospel of John: Author.

Date

The letter was probably written about the same time as 1 John (A.D. 85-95), as the above comparisons suggest (see Introduction to 1 John: Date).

Occasion and Purpose

During the first two centuries the gospel was taken from place to place by traveling evangelists and teachers. Believers customarily took these missionaries into their homes and gave them provisions for their journey when they left. Since Gnostic teachers also relied on this practice (see note on 3Jn 5), 2 John was written to urge discernment in supporting traveling teachers; otherwise, someone might unintentionally contribute to the propagation of heresy rather than truth.

Outline

I. Salutation (1-3)
II. Commendation (4)
III. Exhortation and Warning (5-11)
IV. Conclusion (12-13)

¹The elder,[a]

To the chosen[b] lady and her children, whom I love in the truth[c]—and not I only, but also all who know the truth[d]— ²because of the truth,[e] which lives in us[f] and will be with us forever:

³Grace, mercy and peace from God the Father and from Jesus Christ,[g] the Father's Son, will be with us in truth and love.

⁴It has given me great joy to find some of your children walking in the truth,[h] just as the Father commanded us. ⁵And now, dear lady, I am not writing you a new command but one we have had from the beginning.[i] I ask that we love one another. ⁶And this is love:[j] that we walk in obedience to his commands.[k] As you have heard from the beginning,[l] his command is that you walk in love.

⁷Many deceivers, who do not acknowledge Jesus Christ[m] as coming in the flesh,[n] have gone out into the world.[o] Any such person is the deceiver and the antichrist.[p] ⁸Watch out that you do not lose what you have worked for, but that you may be rewarded fully.[q] ⁹Anyone who runs ahead and does not continue in the teaching of Christ[r] does not have God; whoever continues in the teaching has both the Father and the Son.[s] ¹⁰If anyone comes to you and does not bring this teaching, do not take him into your house or welcome him.[t] ¹¹Anyone who welcomes him shares[u] in his wicked work.

¹²I have much to write to you, but I do not want to use paper and ink. Instead, I hope to visit you and talk with you face to face,[v] so that our joy may be complete.[w]

¹³The children of your chosen[x] sister send their greetings.

1:1 [a]S Ac 11:30; 3Jn 1 [b]ver 13; Ro 16:13; 1Pe 5:13 [c]ver 3 [d]Jn 8:32; 1Ti 2:4
1:2 [e]2Pe 1:12 [f]Jn 14:17; 1Jn 1:8
1:3 [g]S Ro 1:7
1:4 [h]3Jn 3,4
1:5 [i]S 1Jn 2:7
1:6 [j]1Jn 2:5 [k]S Jn 14:15 [l]S 1Jn 2:7
1:7 [m]1Jn 2:22; 4:2,3 [n]S Jn 1:14 [o]1Jn 4:1 [p]S 1Jn 2:18
1:8 [q]S Mt 10:42; Mk 10:29,30; 1Co 3:8; Heb 10:35,36; 11:26
1:9 [r]Jn 8:31 [s]S 1Jn 2:23
1:10 [t]S Ro 16:17
1:11 [u]1Ti 5:22
1:12 [v]3Jn 13,14 [w]S Jn 3:29
1:13 [x]ver 1

---

1 *elder.* See note on 1Ti 3:1. In his later years, John functioned as an elder, perhaps of the Ephesian church. The apostle Peter held a similar position (1Pe 5:1). *chosen lady.* Either an unknown Christian woman in the province of Asia or a figurative designation of a local church there. *her children.* Children of that Christian lady or members of that local church. *truth.* See note on Jn 1:14.
3 *Grace . . . peace.* See notes on Gal 1:3; Eph 1:2. *mercy.* See note on Ro 9:23.
5 *new command.* See note on 1Jn 2:7.
6 *from the beginning.* See note on 1Jn 2:7.
7–11 This section deals with the basic Gnostic heresy attacked in 1 John, namely, that the Son of God did not become flesh (Jn 1:14), but that he temporarily came upon the man Jesus between his baptism and crucifixion (see Introduction to 1 John: Gnosticism).
7 *Jesus Christ as coming in the flesh.* See 1Jn 4:2–3 and note. *antichrist.* See note on 1Jn 2:18.
8 *worked for . . . rewarded.* Work faithfully accomplished on earth brings future reward (see Mk 9:41; 10:29–30; Lk 19:16–19; Heb 11:26).

9 *runs ahead.* A reference to the Gnostics, who believed that they had advanced beyond the teaching of the apostles. *teaching of Christ.* The similarity of this letter to 1 John, the nature of the heresy combated, and the immediate context suggest that John is not referring to teaching given by Christ, but to true teaching about Christ as the incarnate God-man.
10 *take him into your house.* A reference to the housing and feeding of traveling teachers (see Introduction: Occasion and Purpose). The instruction does not prohibit greeting or even inviting a person into one's home for conversation. John was warning against providing food and shelter, since this would be an investment in the "wicked work" of false teachers and would give public approval (see v. 11).
12 *paper and ink.* Paper was made from papyrus reeds, which were readily available and cheap. The ink (the Greek for this word comes from a word that means "black") was made by mixing carbon, water and gum or oil. *that our joy may be complete.* See 1Jn 1:4.
13 *chosen sister.* May be taken literally to designate another Christian woman or figuratively to refer to another local church (see note on v. 1).

3 JOHN

Author

The author is John the apostle. In the first verses of both 2 John and 3 John the author identifies himself as "the elder." Note other similarities: "love in the truth" (v. 1 of both letters), "walking in the truth" (v. 4 of both letters) and the similar conclusions. See Introductions to 1 John and the Gospel of John: Author.

Date

The letter was probably written about the same time as 1 and 2 John (A.D. 85-95). See Introduction to 1 John: Date.

Occasion and Purpose

See Introduction to 2 John: Occasion and Purpose. Itinerant teachers sent out by John were rejected in one of the churches in the province of Asia by a dictatorial leader, Diotrephes, who even excommunicated members who showed hospitality to John's messengers. John wrote this letter to commend Gaius for supporting the teachers and, indirectly, to warn Diotrephes.

Outline

¹The elder, [a]

To my dear friend Gaius, whom I love in the truth.

²Dear friend, I pray that you may enjoy good health and that all may go well with you, even as your soul is getting along well. ³It gave me great joy to have some brothers [b] come and tell about your faithfulness to the truth and how you continue to walk in the truth. [c] ⁴I have no greater joy than to hear that my children [d] are walking in the truth. [e] ⁵Dear friend, you are faithful in what you are doing for the brothers, [f] even though they are strangers to you. [g] ⁶They have told the church about your love. You will do well to send them on their way [h] in a manner worthy [i] of God. ⁷It was for the sake of the Name [j] that they went out, receiving no help from the pagans. [k] ⁸We ought therefore to show hospitality to such men so that we may work together for the truth.

⁹I wrote to the church, but Diotrephes, who loves to be first, will have nothing to do with us. ¹⁰So if I come, [l] I will call attention to what he is doing, gossiping maliciously about us. Not satisfied with that, he refuses to welcome the brothers. [m] He also stops those who want to do so and puts them out of the church. [n]

¹¹Dear friend, do not imitate what is evil but what is good. [o] Anyone who does what is good is from God. [p] Anyone who does what is evil has not seen God. [q] ¹²Demetrius is well spoken of by everyone [r] —and even by the truth itself. We also speak well of him, and you know that our testimony is true. [s]

¹³I have much to write you, but I do not want to do so with pen and ink. ¹⁴I hope to see you soon, and we will talk face to face. [t]

Peace to you. [u] The friends here send their greetings. Greet the friends there by name. [v]

Cross references (center column):

1:1 [a]S Ac 11:30; 2Jn 1
1:3 [b]ver 5,10; S Ac 1:16 [c]2Jn 4
1:4 [d]S 1Jn 2:1 [e]ver 3
1:5 [f]S ver 3 [g]Ro 12:13; Heb 13:2
1:6 [h]1Co 16:11; 2Co 1:16 [i]S Eph 4:1
1:7 [j]S Jn 15:21 [k]Ac 20:33,35
1:10 [l]ver 14; 2Jn 12 [m]ver 5 [n]Jn 9:22,34
1:11 [o]Ps 34:14; 37:27 [p]1Jn 2:29 [q]1Jn 3:6,9,10
1:12 [r]1Ti 3:7 [s]Jn 19:35; 21:24
1:14 [t]2Jn 12 [u]S Ro 1:7; S Eph 6:23 [v]Jn 10:3

---

1 *The elder.* See note on 2Jn 1. *dear friend.* A favorite term of John (see note on 1Jn 2:7). *Gaius.* A Christian in one of the churches of the province of Asia. Gaius was a common Roman name. *truth.* See note on Jn 1:14.

4 *my children.* Perhaps John's converts, or believers currently under his spiritual guidance.

5 *doing for the brothers.* The early church provided hospitality and support for missionaries. See Introduction to 2 John: Occasion and Purpose; see also note on 2Jn 10.

7 *Name.* See note on Ac 4:12. Today Orthodox Jews often address God by the title *Ha-Shem* ("The Name").

9 *I wrote.* There may have been a previous letter of the apostle that is now lost. *church.* Some identify this church with the chosen lady of 2Jn 1. *Diotrephes.* A church leader who was exercising dictatorial power in the church. He must have had considerable influence since he was able to exclude people from the church fellowship (v. 10).

11 *does what is good.* The continual practice of good, not merely doing occasional good deeds.

13–14 See 2Jn 12–13 for a similar conclusion.

14 *Peace to you.* Not a prayer or wish but a benedictory pronouncement (see notes on Jn 14:27; 20:19; Gal 1:3; Eph 1:2).

JUDE

Author

The author identifies himself as Jude (v. 1), which is another form of the Hebrew name Judah (Greek "Judas"), a common name among the Jews. Of those so named in the NT, the ones most likely to be author of this letter are: (1) Judas the apostle (Lk 6:16; Ac 1:13)—not Judas Iscariot—and (2) Judas the brother of the Lord (Mt 13:55; Mk 6:3). The latter is more likely. For example, the author does not claim to be an apostle and even seems to separate himself from the apostles (see v. 17). Furthermore, he describes himself as a "brother of James" (v. 1). Ordinarily a person in Jude's day would describe himself as someone's son rather than as someone's brother. The reason for the exception here may have been James's prominence in the church at Jerusalem (see Introduction to James: Author).

Although neither Jude nor James describes himself as a brother of the Lord, others did not hesitate to speak of them in this way (see Mt 13:55; Jn 7:3-10; Ac 1:14; 1Co 9:5; Gal 1:19). Apparently they themselves did not ask to be heard because of the special privilege they had as members of the household of Joseph and Mary.

Possible references to the letter of Jude or quotations from it are found at a very early date: e.g., in Clement of Rome (c. A.D. 96). Clement of Alexandria (155-215), Tertullian (150-222) and Origen (185-253) accepted it; it was included in the Muratorian Canon (c. 170) and was accepted by Athanasius (298-373) and by the Council of Carthage (397). Eusebius (265-340) listed the letter among the questioned books, though he recognized that many considered it as from Jude.

According to Jerome and Didymus, some did not accept the letter as canonical because of its use of uninspired or Apocryphal literature (see notes on vv. 9,14). But sound judgment has recognized that an inspired author may legitimately make use of uninspired literature—whether for illustrative purposes or for appropriation of historically reliable or otherwise acceptable material—and such use does not necessarily endorse that literature as inspired. Under the influence of the Spirit, the church came to the conviction that the authority of God stands behind the letter of Jude. The fact that the letter was questioned and tested but nonetheless was finally accepted by the churches indicates the strength of its claims to authenticity.

Date

There is nothing in the letter that requires a date beyond the lifetime of Jude the brother of the Lord. The error the author is combating, like that in 2 Peter, is not the heretical teaching of the second century, but that which could and did develop at an early date (cf. Ac 20:29-30; Ro 6:1; 1Co 5:1-11; 2Co 12:21; Gal 5:13; Eph 5:3-17; 1Th 4:6). (See also Introduction to 2 Peter: Date.) There is, moreover, nothing in the letter that requires a date after the time of the apostles, as some have argued. It may even be that Jude's readers had heard some of the apostles speak (see vv. 17-18). Likewise, the use of the word "faith" in the objective sense of the body of truth believed (v. 3) does not require a late dating of the letter. It was used in such a sense as early as Gal 1:23.

The question of the relationship between Jude and 2 Peter has a bearing on the date of Jude. If 2 Peter makes use of Jude—a commonly accepted view (see Introduction to 2 Peter: 2 Peter and Jude)—then Jude is to be dated prior to 2 Peter, probably c. A.D. 65. Otherwise, a date as late as c. 80 would be possible.

Recipients

The description of those to whom Jude addressed his letter is very general (see v. 1). It could apply to Jewish Christians, Gentile Christians, or both. Their location is not indicated. It should not be assumed that, since 2Pe 2 and Jude 4-18 appear to describe similar situations, they were both written to the same people. The kind of heresy depicted in these two passages was widespread (see Date).

Occasion and Purpose

Although Jude was very eager to write to his readers about salvation, he felt that he must i. stead warn them about certain immoral men circulating among them who were perverting the grace of God (v. 4). Apparently these false teachers were trying to convince believers that being saved by grace gave them license to sin since their sins would no longer be held against them. Jude thought it imperative that his readers be on guard against such men and be prepared to oppose their perverted teaching with the truth about God's saving grace.

It has generally been assumed that these false teachers were Gnostics. Although this identification is no doubt correct, they must have been forerunners of fully developed, second-century Gnosticism (see Introduction to 2 Peter: Date).

Outline

1Jude,[a] a servant of Jesus Christ[b] and a
brother of James,

To those who have been called,[c] who
are loved by God the Father and kept by[a]
Jesus Christ:[d]

2Mercy, peace[e] and love be yours in
abundance.[f]

The Sin and Doom of Godless Men

3Dear friends,[g] although I was very eager to write to you about the salvation we
share,[h] I felt I had to write and urge you to
contend[i] for the faith[j] that was once for
all entrusted to the saints.[k]
4For certain
men whose condemnation was written
about[b] long ago have secretly slipped in
among you.[l] They are godless men, who
change the grace of our God into a license
for immorality and deny Jesus Christ our
only Sovereign and Lord.[m]

5Though you already know all this,[n] I
want to remind you[o] that the Lord[c] delivered his people out of Egypt, but later
destroyed those who did not believe.[p]
6And the angels who did not keep their
positions of authority but abandoned their
own home—these he has kept in darkness,
bound with everlasting chains for judgment on the great Day.[q]
7In a similar way,
Sodom and Gomorrah[r] and the surrounding towns[s] gave themselves up to sexual
immorality and perversion. They serve as
an example of those who suffer the punishment of eternal fire.[t]

8In the very same way, these dreamers
pollute their own bodies, reject authority
and slander celestial beings.[u]
9But even
the archangel[v] Michael,[w] when he was
disputing with the devil about the body of
Moses,[x] did not dare to bring a slanderous
accusation against him, but said, "The
Lord rebuke you!"[y]
10Yet these men speak
abusively against whatever they do not un-

1:1 [a]Mt 13:55; Jn 14:22; Ac 1:13 [b]Ro 1:1 [c]Ro 1:6,7 [d]Jn 17:12
1:2 [e]Gal 6:16; 1Ti 1:2 [f]S Ro 1:7
1:3 [g]S 1Co 10:14 [h]Tit 1:4 [i]1Ti 6:12 [j]ver 20; Ac 6:7 [k]S Ac 9:13
1:4 [l]Gal 2:4 [m]Tit 1:16; 2Pe 2:1; 1Jn 2:22
1:5 [n]S 1Jn 2:20 [o]2Pe 1:12,13; 3:1,2 [p]Nu 14:29; Dt 1:32; 2:15; Ps 106:26; 1Co 10:1-5; Heb 3:16,17
1:6 [q]S 2Pe 2:4,9
1:7 [r]S Mt 10:15 [s]Dt 29:23 [t]S Mt 25:41; 2Pe 3:7
1:8 [u]2Pe 2:10
1:9 [v]1Th 4:16 [w]Da 10:13,21; 12:1; Rev 12:7 [x]Dt 34:6 [y]Zec 3:2

[a]*1* Or *for*; or *in* [b]*4* Or *men who were marked out for condemnation* [c]*5* Some early manuscripts *Jesus*

1 *servant.* See note on Ro 1:1. *brother of James.* See Introduction: Author. *called.* See note on Ro 8:28. *loved by God.* See Jn 3:16; Ro 8:28–39. *kept by Jesus Christ.* He who holds the whole universe together (see Col 1:17; Heb 1:3) will see that God's children are kept in the faith and that they reach their eternal inheritance (see Jn 6:37–40; 17:11–12; 1Pe 1:3–5).
2 *peace.* The profound well-being of soul that flows from the experience of God's grace (see notes on Jn 14:27; 20:19; Gal 1:3; Eph 1:2).
3 *Dear friends.* See vv. 17,20; see also note on 2Pe 3:1. *the salvation we share.* Jude's original intention was to write a general treatment of the doctrine of salvation, probably dealing with such subjects as man's sin and guilt, God's love and grace, the forgiveness of sins and the changed life-style that follows new birth. *the faith.* Here used of the body of truth held by believers everywhere—the gospel and all its implications (see Introduction: Date; see also 1Ti 4:6). This truth was under attack and had to be defended. *once for all entrusted.* The truth has finality and is not subject to change.
4 *For.* Introduces the reason Jude felt impelled to change the subject of his letter (see Introduction: Occasion and Purpose). *whose condemnation was written about.* The reference may be to OT denunciations of ungodly men or to Enoch's prophecy (vv. 14–15). Or Jude may mean that judgment has long been about to fall on them because of their sin (see NIV text note and 2Pe 2:3, which may be a clarification of this clause here). *godless men.* See vv. 15,18. *change the grace of our God into a license for immorality.* They assume that salvation by grace gives them the right to sin without restraint, either because God in his grace will freely forgive all their sins, or because sin, by contrast, magnifies the grace of God (cf. Ro 5:20; 6:1). *deny . . . our only Sovereign and Lord.* The Greek term translated "Sovereign" describes power without limit, or absolute domination. The Greek construction indicates that both "Sovereign" and "Lord" refer to the same person, and this verse, as well as the parallel passage (2 Pe 2:1), clearly states that that person is Christ.
5–7 Three examples of divine judgment.
5 *destroyed those who did not believe.* They did not believe that God would give them the land of Canaan; consequently all unbelieving adults died in the desert without entering the promised land.
6 *angels.* See note on 2Pe 2:4. *positions of authority.* See note on 2Pe 2:4. God had assigned differing areas of responsibility and authority to each of the angels (see Da 10:20–21, where the various princes may be angels assigned to various nations). Some of these angels refused to maintain their assignments and thus became the devil and his angels (cf. Mt 25:41). *their own home.* Angels apparently were assigned specific locations as well as responsibilities. Some assume that they left the heavenly realm and came to earth (see note on 2Pe 2:4). *kept . . . bound . . . for judgment.* See note on 2Pe 2:4. *the great Day.* The final judgment.
7 *In a similar way.* Does not mean that the sin of Sodom and Gomorrah was the same as that of the angels or vice versa. This phrase is used to introduce the third illustration of the fact that God will see to it that the unrighteous will be consigned to eternal punishment on judgment day. *sexual immorality and perversion.* More specifically, homosexuality (see Ge 19:5 and note; see also note on 2Pe 2:10). *serve as an example of . . . punishment of eternal fire.* God destroyed Sodom and Gomorrah by pouring out "burning sulfur" (Ge 19:24)—a foretaste of the eternal fire that is to come.
8 *dreamers.* The godless men were called "dreamers" either (1) because they claimed to receive revelations or, more likely, (2) because in their passion they were out of touch with truth and reality. *pollute their own bodies.* Probably a reference to the homosexuality in Sodom and Gomorrah (see vv. 4,7; 1Co 6:18). *reject authority.* See note on 2Pe 2:10. *slander celestial beings.* See note on 2Pe 2:10.
9 According to several church fathers, this verse is based on an Apocryphal work called The Assumption of Moses. Other NT quotations from, or allusions to, non-Biblical works include Paul's quotations of Aratus (Ac 17:28), Menander (1Co 15:33) and Epimenides (Tit 1:12). Such usage in no way suggests that the quotations, or the books from which they were taken, are divinely inspired. It only means that the Biblical author found the quotations to be a helpful confirmation, clarification or illustration.
10 *whatever they do not understand.* See note on 2Pe 2:12; cf. 1Co 2:14. *like unreasoning animals.* See note on 2Pe 2:12.

derstand; and what things they do understand by instinct, like unreasoning animals—these are the very things that destroy them.^{z}

^{11}Woe to them! They have taken the way of Cain;^{a} they have rushed for profit into Balaam's error;^{b} they have been destroyed in Korah's rebellion.^{c}

^{12}These men are blemishes at your love feasts,^{d} eating with you without the slightest qualm—shepherds who feed only themselves.^{e} They are clouds without rain,^{f} blown along by the wind;^{g} autumn trees, without fruit and uprooted^h—twice dead. ^{13}They are wild waves of the sea,^{i} foaming up their shame;^{j} wandering stars, for whom blackest darkness has been reserved forever.^{k}

^{14}Enoch,^{l} the seventh from Adam, prophesied about these men: "See, the Lord is coming^m with thousands upon thousands of his holy ones^n ^{15}to judge^o everyone, and to convict all the ungodly of all the ungodly acts they have done in the

ungodly way, and of all the harsh words ungodly sinners have spoken against him."^{p} ^{16}These men are grumblers^q and faultfinders; they follow their own evil desires;^{r} they boast^s about themselves and flatter others for their own advantage.

A Call to Persevere

^{17}But, dear friends, remember what the apostles^t of our Lord Jesus Christ foretold.^{u} ^{18}They said to you, "In the last times^v there will be scoffers who will follow their own ungodly desires."^{w} ^{19}These are the men who divide you, who follow mere natural instincts and do not have the Spirit.^{x}

^{20}But you, dear friends, build yourselves up^y in your most holy faith^z and pray in the Holy Spirit.^{a} ^{21}Keep yourselves in God's love as you wait^b for the mercy of our Lord Jesus Christ to bring you to eternal life.^{c}

^{22}Be merciful to those who doubt;

Cross references (center column):

1:10 ^{z}2Pe 2:12
1:11 ^{a}Ge 4:3-8;
Heb 11:4;
1Jn 3:12
^{b}S 2Pe 2:15
^{c}Nu 16:1-3,31-35
1:12 ^{d}2Pe 2:13;
1Co 11:20-22
^{e}Eze 34:2,8,10
/Pr 25:14;
2Pe 2:17
^{g}Eph 4:14
^{h}Mt 15:13
1:13 ^{i}Isa 57:20
/Php 3:19
^{k}2Pe 2:17
1:14 ^{l}Ge 5:18,
21-24
^{m}S Mt 16:27
^{n}Dt 33:2;
Da 7:10;
Zec 14:5;
Heb 12:22
1:15 ^{o}2Pe 2:6-9

^{p}1Ti 1:9
1:16 ^{q}1Co 10:10
^{r}ver 18; 2Pe 2:10
^{s}2Pe 2:18
1:17 ^{t}S Eph 4:11
^{u}Heb 2:3; 2Pe 3:2
1:18 ^{v}1Ti 4:1;
2Ti 3:1; 2Pe 3:3
^{w}ver 16; 2Pe 2:1;
3:3
1:19 ^{x}1Co 2:14,
15
1:20 ^{y}Col 2:7;
1Th 5:11 ^{z}ver 3

^{a}Eph 6:18 **1:21** ^{b}Tit 2:13; Heb 9:28; 2Pe 3:12 ^{c}S Mt 25:46

---

11 Three OT examples of the kind of persons Jude warns his readers about. *Woe to them!* A warning that judgment is coming (see Mt 23:13,15–16,23,25,27,29). *way of Cain.* The way of selfishness and greed (see note on Ge 4:3–4) and the way of hatred and murder (see 1Jn 3:12). *Balaam's error.* The error of consuming greed (see note on 2Pe 2:15). *Korah's rebellion.* Korah rose up against God's appointed leadership (see Nu 16). Jude may be suggesting that the false teachers of his day were rebelling against church leadership (cf. 3Jn 9–10).

12–13 These verses contain six graphic metaphors: 1. *blemishes at your love feasts.* See note on 2Pe 2:13. 2. *shepherds who feed only themselves.* Instead of feeding the sheep for whom they are responsible (see Eze 34:8–10). 3. *clouds without rain.* Like clouds promising moisture for the parched land, the false teachers promise soul-satisfying truth, but in reality they have nothing to offer. 4. *autumn trees, without fruit and uprooted—twice dead.* Though the trees ought to be heavy with fruit. 5. *wild waves of the sea.* As wind-tossed waves constantly churn up rubbish, so these apostates continually stir up moral filth (see Isa 57:20). 6. *wandering stars.* As shooting stars appear in the sky only to fly off into eternal oblivion, so these false teachers are destined for the darkness of eternal hell.

14 *Enoch, the seventh from Adam.* Not the Enoch in the line of Cain (Ge 4:17) but the one in the line of Seth (Ge 5:18–24; 1Ch 1:1–3). He was seventh if Adam is counted as the first. The quotation is from the Apocryphal book of Enoch, which purports to have been written by the Enoch of Ge 5, but actually did not appear until the first century B.C. The book of Enoch was a well-respected writing in NT times. That it was not canonical does not mean that it contained no truth; nor does Jude's quotation of the book mean that he considered it inspired (see Introduction: Author; see also note on v. 9). *prophesied.* Not in the sense of supernaturally revealing new truth, but merely in the sense of speaking things about the future that were already known (see Da 7:9–14; Zec 14:1–5). *the Lord is coming.* Jude uses the quotation to refer to Christ's second coming and to his judgment of the wicked (see 2Th 1:6–10). *holy ones.* Probably angels (see Da 4:13–17; 2Th 1:7). However, some

think they are raptured saints who are returning with the Lord (see 1Th 3:13).

15 *ungodly . . . ungodly . . . ungodly . . . ungodly.* This thunderous repetition and the awesome judgment scene that is depicted emphasize the condemnation of the false teachers in v. 4.

16 *These men.* The ungodly men first mentioned in v. 4 and subsequently referred to repeatedly as "these men" (vv. 10,12,14,19; cf. v. 8). They are the libertine false teachers who pervert the grace of God.

17 *remember what the apostles . . . foretold.* The coming of these godless men should not take believers by surprise, for it had been predicted by the apostles (Ac 20:29; 1Ti 4:1; 2Ti 3:1–5).

18 *They said.* The Greek for this phrase indicates that the apostles continually or repeatedly warned that such godless apostates would come. *last times.* See note on 2Pe 3:3. *scoffers.* In both 2Pe 3:3 and Jude the scoffers are said to be characterized by selfish lusts ("desires").

19 *men who divide you.* At the very least this phrase means that they were divisive, creating factions in the church—the usual practice of heretics. Or Jude may refer to the later Gnostics' division of men into the spiritual (the Gnostics) and the sensual (those for whom there is no hope). *follow mere natural instincts.* An ironic description of the false teachers, who labeled others as "sensual." *not have the Spirit.* Rather than being the spiritual ones—the privileged elite class the Gnostics claimed to be—Jude denies that they even possess the Spirit. A person who does not have the Spirit is clearly not saved (see Ro 8:9).

20 *But you, dear friends.* In contrast to the ungodly false teachers, about whom this letter speaks at length. *most holy faith.* See note on v. 3. *in the Holy Spirit.* According to the Spirit's promptings and with the power of the Spirit (see Ro 8:26–27; Gal 4:6; Eph 6:18).

21 *Keep yourselves in God's love.* God keeps believers in his love (see Ro 8:35–39), and enables them to keep themselves in his love.

22–23 *those who doubt . . . others.* Perhaps those who have come under the influence of the apostates.

²³snatch others from the fire and save them; *d* to others show mercy, mixed with fear—hating even the clothing stained by corrupted flesh. *e*

Doxology

²⁴To him who is able*f* to keep you from falling and to present you before his glorious presence*g* without fault*h* and with great joy— ²⁵to the only God*i* our Savior be glory, majesty, power and authority, through Jesus Christ our Lord, before all ages, now and forevermore!*j* Amen. *k*

1:23 *d*Am 4:11; Zec 3:2-5; 1Co 3:15 *e*Rev 3:4
1:24 /S Ro 16:25
*g*S 2Co 4:14 *h*Col 1:22
1:25 /Jn 5:44; 1Ti 1:17 /Heb 13:8
*k*S Ro 11:36

---

23 *snatch others from the fire.* Rescuing them from the verge of destruction. *mercy, mixed with fear.* Even in showing mercy one may be trapped by the allurement of sin. *clothing stained by corrupted flesh.* The wicked are pictured as so corrupt that even their garments are polluted by their sinful nature.

24–25 After all the attention necessarily given in this letter to the ungodly and their works of darkness, Jude concludes his letter by focusing attention on God, who is fully able to keep those who put their trust in him.

REVELATION

Author

Four times the author identifies himself as John (1:1,4,9; 22:8). From as early as Justin Martyr in the second century A.D. it has been held that this John was the apostle, the son of Zebedee (see Mt 10:2). The book itself reveals that the author was a Jew, well versed in Scripture, a church leader who was well known to the seven churches of Asia Minor, and a deeply religious person fully convinced that the Christian faith would soon triumph over the demonic forces at work in the world.

In the third century, however, an African bishop named Dionysius compared the language, style and thought of the Apocalypse (Revelation) with that of the other writings of John and decided that the book could not have been written by the apostle John. He suggested that the author was a certain John the Presbyter, whose name appears elsewhere in ancient writings. Although many today follow Dionysius in his view of authorship, the external evidence seems overwhelmingly supportive of the traditional view.

Date

Revelation was written when Christians were entering a time of persecution. The two periods most often mentioned are the latter part of Nero's reign (A.D. 54-68) and the latter part of Domitian's reign (81-96). Most scholars date the book c. 95. (A few suggest a date during the reign of Vespasian: 69-79.)

Occasion

Since Roman authorities at this time were beginning to enforce the cult of emperor worship, Christians—who held that Christ, not Caesar, was Lord—were facing increasing hostility. The believers at Smyrna are warned against coming opposition (2:10), and the church at Philadelphia is told of an hour of trial coming on the world (3:10). Antipas has already given his life (2:13) along with others (6:9). John has been exiled to the island of Patmos (probably the site of a Roman penal colony) for his activities as a Christian missionary (1:9). Some within the church are advocating a policy of compromise (2:14-15,20), which has to be corrected before its subtle influence can undermine the determination of believers to stand fast in the perilous days that lie ahead.

Purpose

John writes to encourage the faithful to resist staunchly the demands of emperor worship. He informs his readers that the final showdown between God and Satan is imminent. Satan will increase his persecution of believers, but they must stand fast, even to death. They are sealed against any spiritual harm and will soon be vindicated when Christ returns, when the wicked are forever destroyed, and when God's people enter an eternity of glory and blessedness.

Literary Form

For an adequate understanding of Revelation, the reader must recognize that it is a distinct kind of literature. Revelation is apocalyptic, a kind of writing that is highly symbolic. Although its visions often seem bizarre to the Western reader, fortunately the book provides a number of clues for its own interpretation (e.g., stars are angels, lampstands are churches, 1:20; "the great prostitute," 17:1, is "Babylon" [Rome?], 17:5,18; and the heavenly Jerusalem is the wife of the Lamb, 21:9-10).

Distinctive Feature

A distinctive feature is the frequent use of the number seven (52 times). There are seven beatitudes (see note on 1:3), seven churches (1:4,11), seven spirits (1:4), seven golden lampstands (1:12), seven stars (1:16), seven seals (5:1), seven horns and seven eyes (5:6), seven trumpets (8:2), seven thunders (10:3), seven signs (12:1,3; 13:13-14; 15:1; 16:14; 19:20), seven crowns (12:3), seven plagues

(15:6), seven golden bowls (15:7), seven hills (17:9) and seven kings (17:10), as well as other sevens. Symbolically, the number seven stands for completeness.

Interpretation

Interpreters of Revelation normally fall into four groups:

1. *Preterists* understand the book exclusively in terms of its first-century setting, claiming that most of its events have already taken place.

2. *Historicists* take it as describing the long chain of events from Patmos to the end of history.

3. *Futurists* place the book primarily in the end times.

4. *Idealists* view it as symbolic pictures of such timeless truths as the victory of good over evil.

Fortunately, the fundamental truths of Revelation do not depend on adopting a particular point of view. They are available to anyone who will read the book for its overall message and resist the temptation to become overly enamored with the details.

Outline

Prologue

1 The revelation of Jesus Christ, which God gave[a] him to show his servants what must soon take place.[b] He made it known by sending his angel[c] to his servant John,[d] 2who testifies to everything he saw—that is, the word of God[e] and the testimony of Jesus Christ.[f] 3Blessed is the one who reads the words of this prophecy, and blessed are those who hear it and take to heart what is written in it,[g] because the time is near.[h]

Greetings and Doxology

4John,

To the seven churches[i] in the province of Asia:

Grace and peace to you[j] from him who is, and who was, and who is to come,[k] and from the seven spirits[a][l] before his throne, 5and from Jesus Christ, who is the faithful witness,[m] the firstborn from the dead,[n] and the ruler of the kings of the earth.[o]

To him who loves us[p] and has freed us from our sins by his blood,[q] 6and has made us to be a kingdom and priests[r] to serve his God and Father[s]—to him be glory and power for ever and ever! Amen.[t]

7Look, he is coming with the clouds,[u]
　and every eye will see him,
　even those who pierced him;[v]
and all the peoples of the earth will
　mourn[w] because of him.
　　　　　So shall it be! Amen.

8"I am the Alpha and the Omega,"[x] says the Lord God, "who is, and who was, and who is to come,[y] the Almighty."[z]

One Like a Son of Man

9I, John,[a] your brother and companion in the suffering[b] and kingdom[c] and patient endurance[d] that are ours in Jesus, was on the island of Patmos because of the word of God[e] and the testimony of Jesus.[f] 10On the Lord's Day[g] I was in the Spirit,[h] and I heard behind me a loud voice like a trumpet,[i] 11which said: "Write on a scroll what you see[j] and send it to the seven churches:[k] to Ephesus,[l] Smyrna,[m] Pergamum,[n] Thyatira,[o] Sardis,[p] Philadelphia[q] and Laodicea."[r]

12I turned around to see the voice that was speaking to me. And when I turned I saw seven golden lampstands,[s] 13and

---

1:1 aJn 12:49; 17:8 bver 19; Da 2:28,29; Rev 22:6 cRev 22:16 dver 4,9; Rev 22:8 **1:2** ever 9; S Heb 4:12 fver 9; 1Co 1:6; Rev 6:9; 12:17; 19:10 **1:3** gLk 11:28; Rev 22:7 hS Ro 13:11 **1:4** iver 11,20 jS Ro 1:7 kver 8; Rev 4:8; 11:17; 16:5 lIsa 11:2; Rev 3:1; 4:5; 5:6 **1:5** mIsa 55:4; Jn 18:37; Rev 3:14 nPs 89:27; Col 1:18 oS 1Ti 6:15 pS Ro 8:37 qS Ro 3:25 **1:6** rS 1Pe 2:5; Rev 5:10; 20:6 sRo 15:6 tS Ro 11:36 **1:7** uDa 7:13; S Mt 16:27; 24:30; 26:64; S Lk 17:30; S 1Co 1:7; S 1Th 2:19; 4:16, 17 vJn 19:34,37 wZec 12:10; Mt 24:30 **1:8** xS ver 17; Rev 21:6; 22:13 yS ver 4 zRev 4:8; 15:3; 19:6 **1:9** aver 1 bS Ac 14:22; 2Co 1:7; Php 4:14 cver 6 d2Ti 2:12 ever 2; S Heb 4:12 fS ver 2 **1:10** gAc 20:7 hRev 4:2; 17:3; 21:10 iEx 20:18; Rev 4:1 **1:11** jver 19 kver 4,20 lS Ac 18:19 mRev 2:8 nRev 2:12 oAc 16:14; Rev 2:18,24 pRev 3:1 qRev 3:7 rS Col 2:1; Rev 3:14 **1:12** sver 20; Ex 25:31-40; Zec 4:2; Rev 2:1

a4 Or the sevenfold Spirit

1:1 revelation. Apocalypse ("unveiling" or "disclosure"). of Jesus Christ. Can mean (1) by or from Jesus Christ, (2) about Jesus Christ or (3) both. servants. All believers. soon take place. See v. 3; 22:6–7,10,20. his angel. A mediating angel. The word "angel" occurs over 70 times in Revelation. John. See Introduction: Author.
1:3 Blessed. The first of seven beatitudes in the book (see 14:13; 16:15; 19:9; 20:6; 22:7,14). "Blessed" means much more than "happy." It describes the favorable circumstance God has put a person in (see notes on Ps 1:1; Mt 5:3). prophecy. Includes not only foretelling the future but also proclaiming any word from God—whether command, instruction, history or prediction. time is near. See note on Jas 5:9.
1:4 seven churches. Located about 50 miles apart, forming a circle in Asia moving clockwise north from Ephesus and coming around full circle from Laodicea (east of Ephesus). They were perhaps postal centers serving seven geographic regions. Apparently the entire book of Revelation (including the seven letters) was sent to each church (see v. 11). Asia. A Roman province lying in modern western Turkey. Grace and peace. See notes on Jnh 4:2; Jn 14:27; 20:19; Gal 1:3; Eph 1:2. "Grace" is used only twice in Revelation (here and in 22:21) but over 100 times by Paul. who is . . . was . . . is to come. A paraphrase of the divine name from Ex 3:14–15. Cf. Heb 13:8. seven spirits. See NIV text note; cf. Zec 4:2,10.
1:6 a kingdom and priests. This OT designation of Israel (see notes on Ex 19:6; Zec 3) is applied in the NT to the church (1Pe 2:5,9).
1:7 pierced. See Ps 22:16; Isa 53:5; Zec 12:10; Jn 19:34, 37. So shall it be! Amen. A double affirmation.

1:8 the Alpha and the Omega. The first and last letters of the Greek alphabet. God is the beginning and the end (see 21:6). He sovereignly rules over all human history. In 22:13 Jesus applies the same title to himself. Almighty. Nine of the 12 occurrences of this term in the NT are in Revelation (here; 4:8; 11:17; 15:3; 16:7,14; 19:6,15; 21:22). The other three are in Ro 9:29; 2Co 6:18; Jas 5:4.
1:9 suffering . . . kingdom . . . patient endurance. Three pivotal themes in Revelation: (1) "suffering" (2:9–10,22; 7:14), (2) "kingdom" (11:15; 12:10; 16:10; 17:12, 17–18), (3) "patient endurance" (2:2–3,19; 3:10; 13:10; 14:12). Patmos. A small (four by eight miles), rocky island in the Aegean Sea some 50 miles southwest of Ephesus, off the coast of modern Turkey. It probably served as a Roman penal settlement. Eusebius, the "father of church history" (A.D. 265–340), reports that John was released from Patmos under the emperor Nerva (96–98).
1:10 the Lord's Day. A technical term for the first day of the week—so named because Jesus rose from the dead on that day. It was also the day on which the Christians met (see Ac 20:7) and took up collections (see 1Co 16:2). in the Spirit. In a state of spiritual exaltation—not a dream, but a vision like Peter's in Ac 10:10.
1:11 scroll. Pieces of papyrus or parchment sewn together and rolled on a spindle (see note on Ex 17:14). The book form was not invented until about the second century A.D. seven churches. See note on v. 4.
1:12 seven. See Introduction: Distinctive Feature. golden lampstands. The seven churches (see v. 20).
1:13 son of man. See notes on Da 7:13; Mk 8:31. robe . . . to his feet. The high priest wore a full-length robe (Ex 28:4; 29:5). Reference to Christ as high priest is supported by the

among the lampstands[t] was someone "like a son of man,"[b][u] dressed in a robe reaching down to his feet[v] and with a golden sash around his chest.[w] [14]His head and hair were white like wool, as white as snow, and his eyes were like blazing fire.[x] [15]His feet were like bronze glowing in a furnace,[y] and his voice was like the sound of rushing waters.[z] [16]In his right hand he held seven stars,[a] and out of his mouth came a sharp double-edged sword.[b] His face was like the sun[c] shining in all its brilliance.

[17]When I saw him, I fell at his feet[d] as though dead. Then he placed his right hand on me[e] and said: "Do not be afraid.[f] I am the First and the Last.[g] [18]I am the Living One; I was dead,[h] and behold I am alive for ever and ever![i] And I hold the keys of death and Hades.[j]

[19]"Write, therefore, what you have seen,[k] what is now and what will take place later. [20]The mystery of the seven stars that you saw in my right hand[l] and of the seven golden lampstands[m] is this: The seven stars are the angels[c] of the seven churches,[n] and the seven lampstands are the seven churches.[o]

To the Church in Ephesus

2 "To the angel[d] of the church in Ephesus[p] write:

These are the words of him who holds the seven stars in his right hand[q] and walks among the seven golden lampstands:[r] [2]I know your deeds,[s] your hard work and your perseverance. I know that you cannot tolerate wicked men, that you have tested[t] those who claim to be apostles but are not, and have found them false.[u] [3]You have persevered and have endured hardships for my name,[v] and have not grown weary.

[4]Yet I hold this against you: You have forsaken your first love.[w] [5]Remember the height from which you have fallen! Repent[x] and do the things you did at first. If you do not repent, I will come to you and remove your lampstand[y] from its place. [6]But you have this in your favor: You hate the practices of the Nicolaitans,[z] which I also hate.

[7]He who has an ear, let him hear[a] what the Spirit says to the churches. To him who overcomes,[b] I will give

1:13 [r]Rev 2:1
[u]Eze 1:26;
Da 7:13; 10:16;
Rev 14:14
[v]Isa 6:1
[w]Da 10:5;
Rev 15:6
1:14 [x]Da 7:9;
10:6; Rev 2:18;
19:12
1:15 [y]Eze 1:7;
Da 10:6; Rev 2:18
[z]Eze 43:2;
Rev 14:2; 19:6
1:16 [a]ver 20;
Rev 2:1; 3:1
[b]Isa 1:20; 49:2;
Heb 4:12;
Rev 2:12,16;
19:15,21
[c]Jdg 5:31;
Mt 17:2
1:17 [d]Eze 1:28;
Da 8:17,18
[e]Da 8:18
[f]S Mt 14:27
[g]Isa 41:4; 44:6;
48:12; Rev 2:8;
22:13
1:18 [h]Ro 6:9;
Rev 2:8
[i]Dt 32:40;
Da 4:34; 12:7;
Rev 4:9,10; 10:6;
15:7 [j]Rev 9:1;
20:1
1:19 [k]ver 11;
Hab 2:2
1:20 [l]S ver 16
[m]S ver 12 [n]ver 4,
11 [o]Mt 5:14,15
2:1 [p]S Ac 18:19

[q]Rev 1:16
[r]Rev 1:12,13
2:2 [s]ver 19;
Rev 3:1,8,15
[t]1Jn 4:1
[u]2Co 11:13
2:3 [v]S Jn 15:21

2:4 [w]Jer 2:2; Mt 24:12 **2:5** [x]ver 16,22; Rev 3:3,19
[y]Rev 1:20 **2:6** [z]ver 15 **2:7** [a]S Mt 11:15; ver 11,17,29;
Rev 3:6,13,22; 13:9 [b]S Jn 16:33

reference to the golden sash around his chest.
1:14 white like wool. Cf. Da 7:9; Isa 1:18. The hoary head suggests wisdom and dignity (Lev 19:32; Pr 16:31). eyes . . . like blazing fire. Penetrating insight (see 4:6).
1:16 sharp double-edged sword. Like a long Thracian sword (also in 2:12,16; 6:8; 19:15,21). The sword in 6:4; 13:10,14 was a small sword or dagger. The sword symbolizes divine judgment (see Isa 49:2; Heb 4:12).
1:17 fell at his feet. A sign of great respect and awe (4:10; 5:8; 7:11; 19:10; 22:8). I am. See note on Jn 6:35. the First and the Last. Essentially the same as "the Alpha and the Omega" (v. 8; cf. Isa 44:6; 48:12).
1:18 Living One. Based on OT references to the "living God" (e.g., Jos 3:10; Ps 42:2; 84:2). In contrast to the dead gods of paganism, Christ possesses life in his essential nature. keys of death and Hades. Absolute control over their domain (see Mt 16:18 and note).
1:19 Many take the threefold division of this verse as a clue to the entire structure of the book. "What you have seen" would be the inaugural vision of ch. 1; "what is now" would be the letters to the seven churches (chs. 2–3); "what will take place later" would be everything from ch. 4 on. An alternative interpretation sees the initial clause as the essential unit (it parallels v. 11), followed by two explanatory clauses. The sense would be: "Write, therefore, what you are about to see, i.e., both what is now and what will take place later." Some who hold the latter view make no attempt to outline the book on this basis, maintaining that there is a mixture of "now" and "later" throughout.
1:20 The first of several places where the symbols are interpreted (see also 17:15,18). angels. Either (1) heavenly messengers, (2) earthly messengers/ministers (see NIV text

note) or (3) personifications of the prevailing spirit of each church.
2:1–3:22 Some take the seven letters as a preview of church history in its downward course toward Laodicean lukewarmness. Others interpret them as characteristic of various kinds of Christian congregations that have existed from John's day until the present time. In either case, they were historical churches in Asia Minor (see map No. 11 at the end of the Study Bible). The general pattern in the letters is commendation, complaint and command.
2:1 angel. See note on 1:20. Ephesus. See Introduction to Ephesians: The City of Ephesus. holds the seven stars. See 1:16,20. seven golden lampstands. See 1:12,20.
2:2 tested. The necessity of testing for correct doctrine and dependable advice was widely recognized in the early church (see 1Co 14:29; 1Th 5:21; 1Jn 4:1).
2:4 first love. The love they had at first for one another and/or for Christ.
2:5 remove your lampstand. Immediate judgment.
2:6 Nicolaitans. A heretical sect within the church that had worked out a compromise with the pagan society. They apparently taught that spiritual liberty gave them sufficient leeway to practice idolatry and immorality. Tradition identifies them with Nicolas, the proselyte of Antioch who was one of the first seven deacons in the Jerusalem church (Ac 6:5), though the evidence is merely circumstantial. A similar group at Pergamum held the teaching of Balaam (vv. 14–15), and some at Thyatira were followers of the woman Jezebel (v. 20). From their heretical tendencies it would appear that all three groups were Nicolaitans.
2:7 overcomes. The challenge to overcome occurs in each letter (here; vv. 11,17,26; 3:5,12,21). paradise. Originally a

the right to eat from the tree of life, ^c which is in the paradise ^d of God.

To the Church in Smyrna

⁸"To the angel of the church in Smyrna ^e write:

These are the words of him who is the First and the Last, ^f who died and came to life again. ^g ⁹I know your afflictions and your poverty—yet you are rich! ^h I know the slander of those who say they are Jews and are not, ⁱ but are a synagogue of Satan. ^j ¹⁰Do not be afraid of what you are about to suffer. I tell you, the devil will put some of you in prison to test you, ^k and you will suffer persecution for ten days. ^l Be faithful, ^m even to the point of death, and I will give you the crown of life. ⁿ

¹¹He who has an ear, let him hear ^o what the Spirit says to the churches. He who overcomes will not be hurt at all by the second death. ^p

To the Church in Pergamum

¹²"To the angel of the church in Pergamum ^q write:

These are the words of him who has the sharp, double-edged sword. ^r ¹³I know where you live—where Satan has his throne. Yet you remain true to my name. You did not renounce your faith in me, ^s even in the days of Antipas, my faithful witness, ^t who was put to death in your city—where Satan lives. ^u

¹⁴Nevertheless, I have a few things against you: ^v You have people there who hold to the teaching of Balaam, ^w

2:7 ^cGe 2:9;
3:22-24;
Rev 22:2,14,19
^dLk 23:43
2:8 ^eRev 1:11
^fS Rev 1:17
^gRev 1:18
2:9 ^h2Co 6:10;
Jas 2:5 ⁱRev 3:9
^jver 13,24;
S Mt 4:10
2:10 ^kRev 3:10
^lDa 1:12,14 ^mver
13; Rev 17:14
ⁿS Mt 10:22;
S 1Co 9:25

2:11 ^oS ver 7
^pRev 20:6,14;
21:8
2:12 ^qRev 1:11
^rver 16;
S Rev 1:16
2:13 ^sRev 14:12
^tRev 1:5; 11:3
^uver 9,24;
S Mt 4:10
2:14 ^vver 20
^wS 2Pe 2:15

Persian word for a pleasure garden (see note on Lk 23:43). In Revelation it symbolizes the eschatological state in which God and man are restored to the perfect fellowship that existed before sin entered the world.
2:8 *Smyrna.* A proud and beautiful Asian city (modern Izmir) closely aligned with Rome and eager to meet its demands for emperor worship. This plus a large and actively hostile Jewish population made it extremely difficult to live there as a Christian. Polycarp, the most famous of the early martyrs, was bishop of Smyrna. *the First and the Last.* See note on 1:17.
2:9 *who say they are Jews.* See Ro 2:28–29. *Satan.* Hebrew for "accuser" (see Zec 3:1; cf. Job 1:6–12; 2:1–7).
2:10 *devil.* Greek *diabolos,* meaning "accuser." *persecution.* See the warnings by Jesus (Jn 15:20) and Paul (2Ti 3:12). *crown of life.* The crown that is eternal life. "Crown" does not refer to a royal crown (12:3; 13:1; 19:12) but to the garland or wreath awarded to the winner in athletic

contests (3:11; 4:4,10; 6:2; 9:7; 12:1; 14:14).
2:11 *He who overcomes.* See note on v. 7. *second death.* The lake of fire (20:14; see 20:6; 21:8).
2:12 *Pergamum.* Modern Bergama; the ancient capital of Asia, built on a cone-shaped hill rising 1,000 feet above the surrounding valley. Its name in Greek means "citadel" and is the origin of our word "parchment." *double-edged sword.* See note on 1:16.
2:13 *where Satan has his throne.* Satan "ruled" from Pergamum in that it was the official center of emperor worship in Asia. *Antipas.* First martyr of Asia. According to tradition he was slowly roasted to death in a bronze kettle during the reign of Domitian. *faithful witness.* The Lord's title in 1:5.
2:14 *teaching of Balaam.* Balaam advised the Midianite women how to lead the Israelites astray (Nu 25:1–2; 31:16; cf. Jude 11). He is a fitting prototype of corrupt teachers who deceive believers into compromise with worldliness. *food*

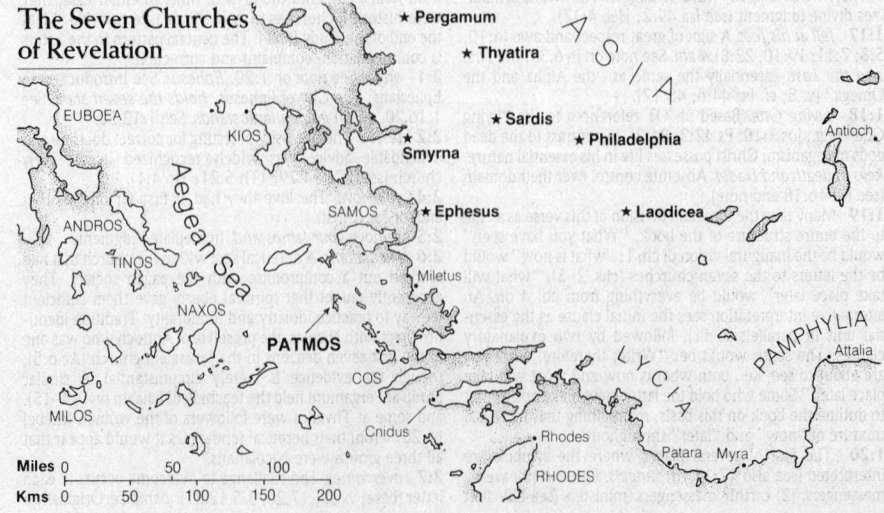

The Seven Churches of Revelation

who taught Balak to entice the Israelites to sin by eating food sacrificed to idols[x] and by committing sexual immorality.[y] 15Likewise you also have those who hold to the teaching of the Nicolaitans.[z] 16Repent[a] therefore! Otherwise, I will soon come to you and will fight against them with the sword of my mouth.[b]

17He who has an ear, let him hear[c] what the Spirit says to the churches. To him who overcomes,[d] I will give some of the hidden manna.[e] I will also give him a white stone with a new name[f] written on it, known only to him who receives it.[g]

To the Church in Thyatira

18"To the angel of the church in Thyatira[h] write:

These are the words of the Son of God,[i] whose eyes are like blazing fire and whose feet are like burnished bronze.[j] 19I know your deeds,[k] your love and faith, your service and perseverance, and that you are now doing more than you did at first.

20Nevertheless, I have this against you: You tolerate that woman Jezebel,[l] who calls herself a prophetess. By her teaching she misleads my servants into sexual immorality and the eating of food sacrificed to idols.[m] 21I have given her time[n] to repent of her immorality, but she is unwilling.[o] 22So I will cast her on a bed of suffering, and I will make those who commit adultery[p] with her suffer intensely, unless they repent of her ways. 23I

will strike her children dead. Then all the churches will know that I am he who searches hearts and minds,[q] and I will repay each of you according to your deeds.[r] 24Now I say to the rest of you in Thyatira, to you who do not hold to her teaching and have not learned Satan's so-called deep secrets (I will not impose any other burden on you):[s] 25Only hold on to what you have[t] until I come.[u]

26To him who overcomes[v] and does my will to the end,[w] I will give authority over the nations[x] —

27'He will rule them with an iron scepter;[y]
he will dash them to pieces like pottery'[e] [z] —

just as I have received authority from my Father. 28I will also give him the morning star.[a] 29He who has an ear, let him hear[b] what the Spirit says to the churches.

To the Church in Sardis

3 "To the angel[f] of the church in Sardis[c] write:

These are the words of him who holds the seven spirits[g][d] of God and the seven stars.[e] I know your deeds;[f] you have a reputation of being alive, but you are dead.[g] 2Wake up! Strengthen what remains and is about to die, for I have not found your deeds complete in the sight of my God. 3Remember, therefore, what you have

Cross references (center column)

2:14 [x]S Ac 15:20
[y]1Co 6:13
2:15 [z]ver 6
2:16 [a]S ver 5
[b]2Th 2:8;
S Rev 1:16
2:17 [c]S ver 7
[d]S Jn 16:33
[e]Jn 6:49,50
[f]Isa 56:5; 62:2;
65:15 [g]Rev 19:12
2:18 [h]ver 24;
Ac 16:14;
Rev 1:11
[i]S Mt 4:3
[j]S Rev 1:14,15
2:19 [k]S ver 2
2:20 [l]1Ki 16:31;
21:25; 2Ki 9:7
[m]ver 14;
S Ac 15:20
2:21 [n]Ro 2:4;
2Pe 3:9 [o]Ro 2:5;
Rev 9:20; 16:9,11
2:22 [p]Rev 17:2;
18:9

2:23 [q]1Sa 16:7;
1Ki 8:39;
Ps 139:1,2,23;
Pr 21:2;
Jer 17:10;
Lk 16:15;
Ro 8:27; 1Th 2:4
[r]S Mt 16:27
2:24 [s]Ac 15:28
2:25 [t]Rev 3:11
[u]S Mt 16:27
2:26 [v]S Jn 16:33
Mt 10:22
[x]Ps 2:8; Rev 3:21
2:27 [y]Rev 12:5;
19:15 [z]Ps 2:9;
Isa 30:14;
Jer 19:11
2:28 [a]Rev 22:16
2:29 [b]S ver 7
3:1 [c]Rev 1:11
[d]S Rev 1:4
[e]S Rev 1:16
[f]S Rev 2:1
[g]1Ti 5:6

e27 Psalm 2:9 f1 Or messenger; also in verses 7 and 14 g1 Or the sevenfold Spirit

---

sacrificed to idols . . . immorality. See Ac 15:20,29.
2:15 Nicolaitans. See note on v. 6.
2:16 sword of my mouth. The long sword (see note on 1:16).
2:17 hidden manna. The heavenly food available to the believer who overcomes (cf. Ps 78:24), in contrast to the unclean food of the Balaamites. white stone. Certain kinds of stones were used as tokens for various purposes. In the context of a Messianic banquet the white stone was probably for the purpose of admission. new name. The name of the victor (see Isa 62:2; 65:15).
2:18 Thyatira. Modern Akhisar. Founded by Seleucus I 311–280 B.C.) as a military outpost, it was noted for its many trade guilds. Lydia, "a dealer in purple cloth," was from Thyatira (see note on Ac 16:14). eyes . . . like blazing fire. See note on 1:14; cf. Da 10:6. burnished bronze. A refined alloy of copper or bronze with metallic zinc.
2:20 Jezebel. See 1Ki 16:31; 2Ki 9:22,30–37. The name is used here as an epithet for a prominent woman in the congregation who undermined loyalty to God by promoting tolerance toward pagan practices. sexual immorality . . . food sacrificed to idols. See v. 14.
2:22 bed of suffering. Disease was often considered as

appropriate punishment for sins (cf. 1Co 11:29–30).
2:23 her children. Jezebel is the spiritual mother of all who pursue antinomian (libertine) doctrines. he who searches hearts and minds. Cf. Ps 7:9; Pr 24:12; Jer 11:20; 17:10. "Mind" (lit. "kidney") probably refers here to the will and the affections; "heart" may designate the center of rational life. according to your deeds. Judgment based on works is taught by Jesus (Mt 16:27) and Paul (Ro 2:6) as well as John (Rev 18:6; 20:12–13; 22:12).
2:24 Satan's so-called deep secrets. Later Gnosticism (see Introduction to 1 John: Gnosticism) taught that in order to defeat Satan one had to enter his stronghold, i.e., experience evil deeply.
2:27 rule. Lit. "shepherd" (a common metaphor for "rule"). iron scepter. Symbolic of the strength of his rule (see 12:5; 19:15).
3:1 Sardis. Modern Sart. Capital of the ancient kingdom of Lydia, it was a city of great wealth and fame. The acropolis was a natural citadel on the northern spur of Mount Tmolus. It rose 1,500 feet above the lower valley.
3:3 come like a thief. Not a reference to the second coming of Christ, because here his coming depends on the church's refusal to repent. Elsewhere in the NT the clause refers to the

received and heard; obey it, and repent.[h] But if you do not wake up, I
will come like a thief,[i] and you will
not know at what time[j] I will come
to you.
4Yet you have a few people in Sardis who have not soiled their
clothes.[k] They will walk with me,
dressed in white,[l] for they are
worthy. 5He who overcomes[m] will,
like them, be dressed in white.[n] I will
never blot out his name from the book
of life,[o] but will acknowledge his
name before my Father[p] and his angels. 6He who has an ear, let him
hear[q] what the Spirit says to the
churches.

To the Church in Philadelphia

7"To the angel of the church in Philadelphia[r] write:

These are the words of him who is
holy[s] and true,[t] who holds the key of
David.[u] What he opens no one can
shut, and what he shuts no one can
open. 8I know your deeds.[v] See, I
have placed before you an open door[w]
that no one can shut. I know that you
have little strength, yet you have kept
my word and have not denied my
name.[x] 9I will make those who are of
the synagogue of Satan,[y] who claim
to be Jews though they are not,[z] but
are liars—I will make them come and
fall down at your feet[a] and acknowledge that I have loved you.[b] 10Since
you have kept my command to endure
patiently, I will also keep you[c] from
the hour of trial that is going to come
upon the whole world[d] to test[e] those
who live on the earth.[f]
11I am coming soon.[g] Hold on to
what you have,[h] so that no one will
take your crown.[i] 12Him who overcomes[j] I will make a pillar[k] in the
temple of my God. Never again will
he leave it. I will write on him the
name of my God[l] and the name of
the city of my God,[m] the new Jerusalem,[n] which is coming down out of
heaven from my God; and I will also
write on him my new name. 13He
who has an ear, let him hear[o] what
the Spirit says to the churches.

To the Church in Laodicea

14"To the angel of the church in Laodicea[p]
write:

These are the words of the Amen,
the faithful and true witness,[q] the ruler of God's creation.[r] 15I know your
deeds,[s] that you are neither cold nor
hot.[t] I wish you were either one or
the other! 16So, because you are lukewarm—neither hot nor cold—I am
about to spit you out of my mouth.
17You say, 'I am rich; I have acquired
wealth and do not need a thing.'[u] But
you do not realize that you are
wretched, pitiful, poor, blind and
naked.[v] 18I counsel you to buy from

3:3 [h]S Rev 2:5 [i]S Lk 12:39 [j]Lk 12:39
3:4 [k]Jude 23 [l]ver 5,18; Rev 4:4; 6:11; 7:9,13,14; 19:14
3:5 [m]S Jn 16:33 [n]S ver 4 [o]S Rev 20:12 [p]Mt 10:32
3:6 [q]S Rev 2:7
3:7 [r]Rev 1:11 [s]S Mk 1:24 [t]1Jn 5:20; Rev 6:10; 19:11 [u]Isa 22:22; Mt 16:19
3:8 [v]S Rev 2:2 [w]S Ac 14:27 [x]Rev 2:13
3:9 [y]Rev 2:9 [z]Rev 2:9 [a]Isa 49:23 [b]Isa 43:4; S Ro 8:37
3:10 [c]2Pe 2:9 [d]S Mt 24:14 [e]Rev 2:10 [f]Rev 6:10; 8:13; 11:10; 13:8,14; 17:8
3:11 [g]S Mt 16:27 [h]Rev 2:25 [i]S 1Co 9:25
3:12 [j]S Jn 16:33 [k]Gal 2:9 [l]Rev 14:1; 22:4 [m]Eze 48:35 [n]Gal 4:26; Rev 21:2,10
3:13 [o]S Rev 2:7
3:14 [p]S Col 2:1; Rev 1:11 [q]Jn 18:37; Rev 1:5 [r]Pr 8:22; Jn 1:3; Col 1:16, 18
3:15 [s]S Rev 2:2 [t]Ro 12:11
3:17 [u]Hos 12:8; 1Co 4:8 [v]Pr 13:7

second advent (16:15; Mt 24:42–44; 1Th 5:2; 2Pe 3:10).
3:4 *dressed in white.* Description of the redeemed (3:18; 6:11; 7:9,13; cf. 4:4; 19:14).
3:5 *book of life.* A divine ledger is first mentioned in Ex 32:32–33 (see note on Ps 69:28; cf. Da 12:1). It was a register of all citizens in the kingdom community. To have one's name erased from this book would indicate loss of citizenship (see 13:8; 17:8; 20:12,15; 21:27; Php 4:3).
3:7 *Philadelphia.* Modern Alashehir; a city of commercial importance conveniently located as the gateway to the high central plateau of the province of Asia in Asia Minor. The name means "brotherly love" and commemorates the loyalty and devotion of Attalus II (220–130 B.C.) to his brother Eumenes II. *holy and true.* See 6:10. For God as the Holy One see Isa 40:25; Hab 3:2–3; Mk 1:24. *key of David.* Christ is the Davidic Messiah with authority to control entrance to the kingdom (see Isa 22:22; Mt 16:19).
3:8 *open door.* Either the door of opportunity or the door to the kingdom. The context favors the latter.
3:9 *synagogue of Satan.* A bold metaphor directed against unbelieving and hostile Jews. Cf. Jesus' scathing rebuke in Jn 8:44; see also 2Co 11:14–15. The Jewish synagogue was a gathering place for worship, study and communal activities. *claim to be Jews.* See Ro 2:28–29. *fall down at your feet.* An appropriate act of worship in the Near East (see Isa 45:14; 60:14; cf. Ac 10:25; Php 2:10; see also note on Rev 1:17).
3:10 *keep you from.* The Greek for this phrase can mean either "keep you from undergoing" or "keep you through." *hour of trial.* The period of testing that precedes the consummation of the kingdom (see 13:5–10; Mt 24:4–28; cf. Da 12:1; Mk 13:19; 2Th 2:1–12).
3:11 *I am coming soon.* Cf. 1:1; 22:7,12,20 (see note on Jas 5:9).
3:12 *Him who overcomes.* See note on 2:7. *temple.* See note on 7:15. *name of my God.* See 14:1; 22:4. *new Jerusalem.* See 21:2,10. *write on him my new name.* Names revealed character. Christ's new name symbolizes all that he is by virtue of his redemptive work for mankind. This awaits the second advent.
3:14 *Laodicea.* Modern Pamukkale. The wealthiest city in Phrygia during Roman times, it was widely known for its banking establishments, medical school and textile industry. Its major weakness was lack of an adequate water supply. Each of these characteristics is reflected in the letter. *the Amen.* Isa 65:16 speaks of "the God of the Amen," i.e., "the God of truth." As a personal designation it describes one who is perfectly trustworthy or faithful. *faithful and true witness.* See 1:5; 19:11. *ruler.* The Greek word can mean first in point of time ("beginning") or first in rank ("ruler").
3:16 *lukewarm—neither hot nor cold.* "Hot" may refer to the hot, medicinal waters of nearby Hierapolis. The church in Laodicea supplied neither healing for the spiritually sick nor refreshment for the spiritually weary. *spit.* Lit. "vomit."
3:18 Refers to three items in which Laodicea took great

me gold refined in the fire, [w] so you can become rich; and white clothes [x] to wear, so you can cover your shameful nakedness; [y] and salve to put on your eyes, so you can see.

[19]Those whom I love I rebuke and discipline. [z] So be earnest, and repent. [a] [20]Here I am! I stand at the door [b] and knock. If anyone hears my voice and opens the door, [c] I will come in [d] and eat with him, and he with me.

[21]To him who overcomes, [e] I will give the right to sit with me on my throne, [f] just as I overcame [g] and sat down with my Father on his throne. [22]He who has an ear, let him hear [h] what the Spirit says to the churches."

The Throne in Heaven

4 After this I looked, and there before me was a door standing open [i] in heaven. And the voice I had first heard speaking to me like a trumpet [j] said, "Come up here, [k] and I will show you what must take place after this." [l] [2]At once I was in the Spirit, [m] and there before me was a throne in heaven [n] with someone sitting on it. [3]And the one who sat there had the appearance of jasper [o] and carnelian. [p] A rainbow, [q] resembling an emerald, [r] encircled the throne. [4]Sur-

rounding the throne were twenty-four other thrones, and seated on them were twenty-four elders. [s] They were dressed in white [t] and had crowns of gold on their heads. [5]From the throne came flashes of lightning, rumblings and peals of thunder. [u] Before the throne, seven lamps [v] were blazing. These are the seven spirits [h] [w] of God. [6]Also before the throne there was what looked like a sea of glass, [x] clear as crystal.

In the center, around the throne, were four living creatures, [y] and they were covered with eyes, in front and in back. [z] [7]The first living creature was like a lion, the second was like an ox, the third had a face like a man, the fourth was like a flying eagle. [a] [8]Each of the four living creatures [b] had six wings [c] and was covered with eyes all around, [d] even under his wings. Day and night [e] they never stop saying:

> "Holy, holy, holy
> is the Lord God Almighty, [f]
> who was, and is, and is to come." [g]

[9]Whenever the living creatures give glory, honor and thanks to him who sits on the throne [h] and who lives for ever and ever, [i]

Center reference column:

3:18 [w]S 1Pe 1:7
[x]S ver 4
[y]Rev 16:15
3:19 [z]Dt 8:5;
Pr 3:12;
1Co 11:32;
Heb 12:5,6
[a]S Rev 2:5
3:20 [b]Mt 24:33;
Jas 5:9 [c]Lk 12:36
[d]S Ro 8:10
3:21 [e]S Jn 16:33
[f]S Mt 19:28
[g]Rev 5:5
3:22 [h]S Rev 2:7
4:1 [i]S Mt 3:16
[j]Rev 1:10
[k]Rev 11:12
[l]Rev 1:19; 22:6
4:2 [m]S Rev 1:10
[n]ver 9,10;
1Ki 22:19;
Isa 6:1;
Eze 1:26-28;
Da 7:9; Rev 20:11
4:3 [o]Rev 21:11
[p]Rev 21:20
[q]Eze 1:28;
Rev 10:1
[r]Rev 21:19

4:4 [s]ver 10;
Rev 5:6,8,14;
11:16; 19:4
[t]S Rev 3:4,5
4:5 [u]Ex 19:16;
Rev 8:5; 11:19;
16:18 [v]Zec 4:2
[w]S Rev 1:4
4:6 [x]Rev 15:2
[y]ver 8,9; Eze 1:5;
Rev 5:6; 6:1;
7:11; 14:3; 15:7;
19:4 [z]Eze 1:18;
10:12
4:7 [a]Eze 1:10;
10:14
4:8 [b]S ver 6
[c]Isa 6:2
[d]Eze 1:18
[e]Rev 14:11

[f]Isa 6:3; S Isa 1:8 [g]S Rev 1:4 4:9 [h]ver 2; Ps 47:8; S Rev 5:1
[i]S Rev 1:18

[h]5 Or *the sevenfold Spirit*

Bottom notes (two columns):

pride: financial wealth, an extensive textile industry and a famous eye salve.

3:19 *whom I love I . . . discipline.* See Job 5:17; Ps 94:12; Pr 3:11–12; 1Co 11:32; Heb 12:5–11.

3:20 *I stand at the door and knock.* Usually taken as a picture of Christ's knocking on the door of the individual unbeliever's heart. In context, however, the self-deluded members of the congregation are being addressed.

3:21 *overcomes.* See note on 2:7. *sit with me on my throne.* See 20:4,6; Mt 19:28; 2Ti 2:12.

4:1–5:14 These two chapters constitute an introduction to chs. 6–20. In the throne room of heaven, the Lamb assumes the responsibility of initiating the great final conflict with the forces of evil, the end of which will see the Lamb triumphant and the devil consigned to the lake of fire.

4:1 *Come up here.* Similarly, Moses was called up on Mount Sinai to receive divine direction (Ex 19:20,24). Cf. also the heavenly ascent of the two witnesses (11:12). Some interpreters find the rapture of the church in this verse. *what must take place after this.* See 1:1,19; Da 2:28–29,45.

4:2 *in the Spirit.* In a state of heightened spiritual awareness (see note on 1:10; see also 17:3; 21:10). *throne in heaven.* The depiction of God ruling from his throne in heaven is a regular feature of the OT (e.g., Ps 47:8).

4:3 *jasper . . . carnelian . . . emerald.* Since God dwells in "unapproachable light" and is one "whom no one has seen or can see" (1Ti 6:16), he is described in terms of the reflected brilliance of precious stones—an emerald rainbow around the throne (cf. Eze 1:26–28).

4:4 *twenty-four elders.* Representative of either the whole company of believers in heaven or an exalted angelic order worshiping and serving God there (see vv. 9–11; 5:5–14;

7:11–17; 11:16–18; 14:3; 19:4). The number 24 is often understood to reflect the 12 Israelite tribes of the OT and the 12 apostles of the NT.

4:5 *flashes of lightning . . . thunder blazing.* Symbolic of the awesome majesty and power of God (cf. the manifestation of God at Sinai, Ex 19:16–19; cf. also the conventional OT depiction of God's coming in mighty power to deliver his people, Ps 18:12–15; 77:18). In Revelation, thunder and lightning always mark an important event connected with the heavenly temple (8:5; 11:19; 16:18). *seven spirits.* See note on 1:4; "seven" symbolizes fullness, completeness or perfection.

4:6 *sea of glass.* See 15:2. The source of the imagery may be Eze 1:22 (cf. Ex 24:10), but it is also possible that it is the basin in the heavenly temple (cf. 11:19; 14:15,17; 15:5–6, 8; 16:1,17), whose counterpart in the earthly temple was referred to as the Sea (1Ki 7:23–25; 2Ki 16:17; 2Ch 4:2,4, 15,39; Jer 27:19). Other features of the temple in heaven are: the lamps (v. 5), the altar (6:9), the altar of incense (8:3) and the ark of the covenant (11:19). *four living creatures.* An exalted order of angelic beings whose task is to guard the heavenly throne and lead in worship and adoration of God. *covered with eyes.* Nothing escapes their attention.

4:7 Ezekiel also in a vision saw four living creatures, each of which had four faces—human in front, lion on the right, ox on the left, and eagle behind (Eze 1:6,10). In John's vision the creatures were in the form of a lion, an ox, and a flying eagle, and one had a face like that of a man.

4:8 *Holy, holy, holy.* See note on Isa 6:3. *was . . . is . . . is to come.* An expansion of the divine name in Ex 3:14–15 (see note on Rev 1:4). God's power and holiness extend from eternity past to eternity yet to come (cf. Isa 41:4).

[10] the twenty-four elders[j] fall down before him[k] who sits on the throne,[l] and worship him who lives for ever and ever. They lay their crowns before the throne and say:

[11] "You are worthy, our Lord and God,
　　to receive glory and honor and
　　　　power,[m]
　for you created all things,
　　and by your will they were created
　　and have their being."[n]

The Scroll and the Lamb

5 Then I saw in the right hand of him who sat on the throne[o] a scroll with writing on both sides[p] and sealed[q] with seven seals. [2] And I saw a mighty angel[r] proclaiming in a loud voice, "Who is worthy to break the seals and open the scroll?" [3] But no one in heaven or on earth or under the earth could open the scroll or even look inside it. [4] I wept and wept because no one was found who was worthy to open the scroll or look inside. [5] Then one of the elders said to me, "Do not weep! See, the Lion[s] of the tribe of Judah,[t] the Root of David,[u] has triumphed. He is able to open the scroll and its seven seals."

[6] Then I saw a Lamb,[v] looking as if it had been slain, standing in the center of the throne, encircled by the four living creatures[w] and the elders.[x] He had seven horns and seven eyes,[y] which are the seven spirits[i][z] of God sent out into all the earth. [7] He came and took the scroll from

the right hand of him who sat on the throne.[a] [8] And when he had taken it, the four living creatures[b] and the twenty-four elders[c] fell down before the Lamb. Each one had a harp[d] and they were holding golden bowls full of incense, which are the prayers[e] of the saints. [9] And they sang a new song:[f]

"You are worthy[g] to take the scroll
　and to open its seals,
because you were slain,
　and with your blood[h] you
　　purchased[i] men for God
　from every tribe and language and
　　people and nation.[j]
[10] You have made them to be a kingdom
　　and priests[k] to serve our God,
　and they will reign on the earth."[l]

[11] Then I looked and heard the voice of many angels, numbering thousands upon thousands, and ten thousand times ten thousand.[m] They encircled the throne and the living creatures[n] and the elders.[o] [12] In a loud voice they sang:

"Worthy is the Lamb,[p] who was slain,[q]
　to receive power and wealth and
　　wisdom and strength
　and honor and glory and praise!"[r]

[13] Then I heard every creature in heaven and on earth and under the earth[s] and on the sea, and all that is in them, singing:

Cross-references (center column)

4:10 /S ver 4
kDt 33:3;
Rev 5:8,14; 7:11;
11:16 /S ver 2
4:11 mRev 1:6;
5:12 nAc 14:15;
Rev 10:6
5:1 over 7,13;
Rev 4:2,9; 6:16
pEze 2:9,10
qIsa 29:11;
Da 12:4
5:2 rRev 10:1
5:5 sGe 49:9
tS Heb 7:14
uIsa 11:1,10;
Ro 15:12;
Rev 22:16
5:6 vver 8,9,12,
13; S Jn 1:29
wS Rev 4:6
xS Rev 4:4
yZec 4:10
zS Rev 1:4

5:7 aS ver 1
5:8 bS Rev 4:6
cS Rev 4:4
dRev 14:2; 15:2
ePs 141:2;
Rev 8:3,4
5:9 fPs 40:3;
98:1; 149:1;
Isa 42:10;
Rev 14:3,4
gRev 4:11
hHeb 9:12
iS 1Co 6:20
/S Rev 13:7
5:10 kS 1Pe 2:5
/Rev 3:21; 20:4
5:11 mDa 7:10;
Heb 12:22; Jude
14 nS Rev 4:6
oS Rev 4:4
5:12 pver 13
qver 9 rRev 1:6;
4:11
5:13 sver 3;
Php 2:10

i6 Or the sevenfold Spirit

4:10 *lay their crowns.* Acknowledgment that God alone is worthy of ultimate praise and worship.

4:11 *you created all things.* See Ge 1.

5:1 *scroll.* See note on 1:11; cf. the little scroll of 10:2, 8–10. *writing on both sides.* Like the stone tablets of the OT covenant law (Ex 32:15; see Eze 2:9–10). The fibers of a papyrus scroll run horizontally on the inside, which makes writing easier than on the reverse side (where the fibers are vertical). *sealed with seven seals.* Indicating absolute inviolability (cf. Isa 29:11; Da 12:4).

5:2 *mighty angel.* See 18:21.

5:3 *heaven . . . earth . . . under the earth.* A conventional phrase used to express the universality of the proclamation—no creature was worthy. It is not intended to teach a threefold division of the universe (cf. Ex 20:4; Php 2:10).

5:5 *Lion of the tribe of Judah.* A Messianic title taken from Ge 49:8–10, where Judah is named a "lion's cub" and promised the right to rule "until he comes to whom it belongs" (see also Eze 21:27). *Root of David.* See Isa 11:1, 10, which looks forward to the ideal king in the line of David. The title is interpreted Messianically in Ro 15:12.

5:6 *Lamb.* Pictured as the sacrifice for sin ("slain"; cf. Isa 53:7; Jn 1:29) and as the mighty conqueror (17:14). Revelation uses a special word for "lamb" (29 times in Revelation and only once elsewhere in the NT—Jn 21:15). The idea of the lamb as a victorious military leader seems to come from the apocalyptic tradition (1 Enoch 90:9; Testament of Joseph

19:8). *as if it had been slain.* Bearing the marks of its slaughter—he has come to power through his death. *seven horns.* The horn is an ancient Jewish symbol for power or strength (cf. Dt 33:17). The fourth beast of Da 7:7,20 had ten horns (cf. Da 8:3,5). Seven horns would symbolize full strength. *seven spirits.* See note on 4:5.

5:8 *harp.* An ancient stringed instrument (not the large modern harp) used especially to accompany songs (Ps 33:2). *bowls full of incense.* The bowl was a flat, shallow cup. Incense was a normal feature of Hebrew ritual (see Dt 33:10; cf. Ps 141:2; Rev 8:3–4). *prayers of the saints.* In later Jewish thought, angels often present the prayers of saints to God (Tobit 12:15; 3 Baruch 11).

5:9 *new song.* Cf. 14:3; Ps 33:3; 96:1; 144:9; Isa 42:10. In the OT a new song celebrated a new act of divine deliverance or blessing. That is also its sense here; notice the theme of the song. *with your blood you purchased men.* The sacrificial death of Christ is central to NT teaching (see Mk 10:45; 1Co 6:20).

5:10 *kingdom and priests.* See note on 1:6. *reign on the earth.* See 2:26–27; 20:4,6; 22:5.

5:11 *thousands upon thousands.* A rhetorical phrase for an indefinitely large number (see Da 7:10; cf. Heb 12:22).

5:12 *power . . . praise!* See David's farewell prayer in 1Ch 29:10–19. The attributes increase from three in 4:9–11 to four in 5:13 to seven in 5:12; 7:12.

5:13 *heaven . . . earth . . . under the earth.* See note on v. 3.

"To him who sits on the throne[t] and
    to the Lamb[u]
be praise and honor and glory and
    power,
    for ever and ever!"[v]

[14]The four living creatures[w] said,
"Amen,"[x] and the elders[y] fell down and
worshiped.[z]

The Seals

6 I watched as the Lamb[a] opened the
first of the seven seals.[b] Then I heard
one of the four living creatures[c] say in a
voice like thunder,[d] "Come!" [2]I looked,
and there before me was a white horse![e]
Its rider held a bow, and he was given a
crown,[f] and he rode out as a conqueror
bent on conquest.[g]

[3]When the Lamb opened the second
seal, I heard the second living creature[h]
say, "Come!" [4]Then another horse came
out, a fiery red one.[i] Its rider was given
power to take peace from the earth[j] and
to make men slay each other. To him was
given a large sword.

[5]When the Lamb opened the third seal,
I heard the third living creature[k] say,
"Come!" I looked, and there before me
was a black horse![l] Its rider was holding a
pair of scales in his hand. [6]Then I heard
what sounded like a voice among the four
living creatures,[m] saying, "A quart[j] of
wheat for a day's wages,[k] and three quarts

of barley for a day's wages,[k][n] and do not
damage[o] the oil and the wine!"

[7]When the Lamb opened the fourth seal,
I heard the voice of the fourth living creature[p] say, "Come!" [8]I looked, and there
before me was a pale horse![q] Its rider was
named Death, and Hades[r] was following
close behind him. They were given power
over a fourth of the earth to kill by sword,
famine and plague, and by the wild beasts
of the earth.[s]

[9]When he opened the fifth seal, I saw
under[t] the altar[u] the souls of those who
had been slain[v] because of the word of
God[w] and the testimony they had maintained. [10]They called out in a loud voice,
"How long,[x] Sovereign Lord,[y] holy and
true,[z] until you judge the inhabitants of
the earth[a] and avenge our blood?"[b]
[11]Then each of them was given a white
robe,[c] and they were told to wait a little
longer, until the number of their fellow
servants and brothers who were to be
killed as they had been was completed.[d]

[12]I watched as he opened the sixth seal.
There was a great earthquake.[e] The sun
turned black[f] like sackcloth[g] made of
goat hair, the whole moon turned blood
red, [13]and the stars in the sky fell to
earth,[h] as late figs drop from a fig tree[i]
when shaken by a strong wind. [14]The sky
receded like a scroll, rolling up,[j] and every

5:13 *t*S ver 1,7
*u*ver 6; Rev 6:16;
7:10 *v*1Ch 29:11;
Mal 1:6; 2:2;
S Ro 11:36
5:14 *w*S Rev 4:6
*x*Rev 4:9
*y*S Rev 4:4
*z*Rev 4:10
6:1 *a*S Rev 5:6
*b*Rev 5:1
*c*S Rev 4:6,7
*d*Rev 14:2; 19:6
6:2 *e*Zec 1:8;
6:3; Rev 19:11
*f*Zec 6:11;
Rev 14:14; 19:12
*g*Ps 45:4
6:3 *h*Rev 4:7
6:4 *i*Zec 1:8; 6:2
/Mt 10:34
6:5 *k*Rev 4:7
*l*Zec 6:2
6:6 *m*S Rev 4:6,7

*n*Eze 4:16
*o*Rev 7:1,3; 9:4
6:7 *p*Rev 4:7
6:8 *q*Zec 6:3
*r*Hos 13:14;
Rev 1:18; 20:13,
14 *s*Jer 15:2,3;
17
6:9 *t*Ex 29:12;
Lev 4:7
*u*Rev 14:18; 16:7
*v*Rev 20:4
*w*Ro 1:2;
S Heb 4:12
6:10 *x*Ps 119:84;
Zec 1:12
*y*Lk 2:29; 2Pe 2:1
*z*S Rev 3:7
*a*S Rev 3:10
*b*Dt 32:43;
2Ki 9:7; Ps 79:10;
Rev 16:6; 18:20;
19:2
6:11 *c*S Rev 3:4
*d*Heb 11:40
6:12 *e*Ps 97:4;
Isa 29:6;
Eze 38:19;
Rev 8:5; 11:13;
16:18
/S Mt 24:29

*g*Isa 50:3 6:13 *h*S Mt 24:29; Rev 8:10; 9:1 *i*Isa 34:4 6:14
/S 2Pe 3:10; Rev 20:11; 21:1

*j*6 Greek *a choinix* (probably about a liter)   *k*6 Greek *a denarius*

6:1 *seven seals.* The first of three sevenfold numbered
series of judgments (cf. the seven trumpets in chs. 8–9 and
the seven bowls in ch. 16).

6:2 *white horse.* The imagery of the four horsemen comes
from Zec 1:8–17; 6:1–8 (see note on Zec 6:2–3). The colors
in Revelation correspond to the character of the rider; white
symbolizes conquest. Major interpretations of the rider on
the white horse are: (1) Christ (cf. 19:11), (2) the antichrist
and (3) the spirit of conquest. The latter establishes a more
natural sequence with the other three riders (which symbolize bloodshed, famine and death). *bow.* A battle weapon.
crown. See note on 2:10.

6:4 *another horse . . . a fiery red one.* Symbolizing bloodshed and war (cf. Zec 1:8; 6:2). *men slay each other.* If the
white horse is conquest from without, the red horse may be
internal revolution. *sword.* See note on 1:16.

6:5 *black horse.* Symbolizing famine (cf. Zec 6:2,6). The
sequence is thus conquest, bloodshed, famine. *pair of scales.*
A balance beam with scales hung from either end. Weights
were originally stones.

6:6 *wheat . . . barley.* One quart of wheat would be enough
for only one person. Three quarts of the less nutritious barley
would be barely enough for a small family. Famine had
inflated prices to at least ten times their normal level. *oil and
the wine.* Sets limits on the destruction by the rider of the
black horse. The roots of the olive and vine go deeper and

would not be immediately affected by a limited drought.

6:8 *pale horse.* Describes the ashen appearance of the
dead; it symbolizes death. *Hades.* Equivalent to Hebrew
Sheol (see 1:18; 20:13–14; see also note on Mt 16:18).

6:9 *under the altar.* In OT ritual the blood of the slaughtered animal was poured out at the base of the altar (Ex
29:12; Lev 4:7).

6:10 *inhabitants of the earth.* A regular designation in
Revelation for mankind in its hostility to God (see 3:10;
8:13; 11:10; 13:8,12; 17:2,8).

6:11 *white robe.* Symbol of blessedness and purity (see
3:5,18; 4:4; 7:9,13; 19:14). *until the number . . . was
completed.* Jewish thought held that God rules the world
according to a predetermined time schedule (see 2 Esdras
4:35–37) and that the end awaits the death of a certain
number of the righteous (1 Enoch 47:4).

6:12 *earthquake.* A regular feature of divine visitation (see
Ex 19:18; Isa 2:19; Hag 2:6). *moon turned blood red.* See
Joel 2:31, quoted by Peter in his Pentecost sermon (Ac
2:20).

6:13 *stars . . . fell.* One of the signs immediately preceding
the coming of the Son of Man (Mk 13:25–26). *late figs.*
Green figs appearing in the winter and easily blown from the
tree, which at that season has no leaves.

6:14 *sky receded like a scroll.* See Isa 34:4. *every mountain and island was removed.* Perhaps suggested by Jer 4:24
or Na 1:5; see 16:20; 20:11.

mountain and island was removed from its place. [k]

[15]Then the kings of the earth, the princes, the generals, the rich, the mighty, and every slave and every free man [l] hid in caves and among the rocks of the mountains. [m] [16]They called to the mountains and the rocks, "Fall on us [n] and hide us from the face of him who sits on the throne [o] and from the wrath of the Lamb! [17]For the great day [p] of their wrath has come, and who can stand?" [q]

144,000 Sealed

7 After this I saw four angels standing at the four corners [r] of the earth, holding back the four winds [s] of the earth to prevent [t] any wind from blowing on the land or on the sea or on any tree. [2]Then I saw another angel coming up from the east, having the seal [u] of the living God. [v] He called out in a loud voice to the four angels who had been given power to harm the land and the sea: [w] [3]"Do not harm [x] the land or the sea or the trees until we put a seal on the foreheads [y] of the servants of our God." [4]Then I heard the number [z] of those who were sealed: 144,000 [a] from all the tribes of Israel.

[5]From the tribe of Judah 12,000 were sealed,
    from the tribe of Reuben 12,000,
    from the tribe of Gad 12,000,
    [6]from the tribe of Asher 12,000,
    from the tribe of Naphtali 12,000,
    from the tribe of Manasseh 12,000,

[7]from the tribe of Simeon 12,000,
    from the tribe of Levi 12,000,
    from the tribe of Issachar 12,000,
    [8]from the tribe of Zebulun 12,000,
    from the tribe of Joseph 12,000,
    from the tribe of Benjamin 12,000.

The Great Multitude in White Robes

[9]After this I looked and there before me was a great multitude that no one could count, from every nation, tribe, people and language, [b] standing before the throne [c] and in front of the Lamb. They were wearing white robes [d] and were holding palm branches in their hands. [10]And they cried out in a loud voice:

"Salvation belongs to our God, [e]
who sits on the throne, [f]
and to the Lamb."

[11]All the angels were standing around the throne and around the elders [g] and the four living creatures. [h] They fell down on their faces [i] before the throne and worshiped God, [12]saying:

"Amen!
Praise and glory
and wisdom and thanks and honor
and power and strength
be to our God for ever and ever.
Amen!" [j]

[13]Then one of the elders asked me, "These in white robes [k]—who are they, and where did they come from?"

[14]I answered, "Sir, you know."

And he said, "These are they who have

Cross-references (center column)

6:14 [k]Ps 46:2; Isa 54:10; Jer 4:24; Eze 38:20; Na 1:5; Rev 16:20; 21:1
6:15 [l]Rev 19:18
[m]Isa 2:10,19,21
6:16 [n]Hos 10:8; Lk 23:30
[o]S Rev 5:1
6:17 [p]Joel 1:15; 2:1,2,11,31; Zep 1:14,15; Rev 16:14
[q]Ps 76:7; Na 1:6; Mal 3:2
7:1 [r]Isa 11:12
[s]Jer 49:36; Eze 37:9; Da 7:2; Zec 6:5; Mt 24:31
[t]S Rev 6:6
7:2 [u]Rev 9:4
[v]S Mt 16:16 [w]ver 1
7:3 [x]S Rev 6:6
[y]Eze 9:4; Rev 9:4; 14:1; 22:4
7:4 [z]Rev 9:16
[a]Rev 14:1,3

7:9 [b]S Rev 13:7
[c]ver 15
[d]S Rev 3:4
7:10 [e]Ps 3:8; Rev 12:10; 19:1
[f]S Rev 5:1
7:11 [g]S Rev 4:4
[h]S Rev 4:6
[i]S Rev 4:10
7:12 [j]S Ro 11:36; Rev 5:12-14
7:13 [k]S Rev 3:4

6:15 *generals.* A general was a Roman officer who commanded a cohort, i.e., about 1,000 men. *hid in caves.* See Jer 4:29.

6:16 *wrath of the Lamb.* God's wrath is a theme that permeates NT theology. It is both present (see Ro 1:18 and note) and future (see 19:15). It is prophesied in the OT (Zep 1:14–18; Na 1:6; Mal 3:2). *Lamb.* See note on 5:6.

7:1–17 A parenthesis separating the final seal from the preceding six (the same feature is found in the trumpet sequence; see 10:1–11:13). It contains two visions: (1) the sealing of the 144,000 (vv. 1–8) and (2) the innumerable multitude (vv. 9–17).

7:1 *four winds.* Destructive agents of God (see Jer 49:36).

7:2 *seal of the living God.* Ancient documents were folded and tied, and a lump of clay was pressed over the knot. The sender would then stamp the hardening clay with his signet ring or roll it with a cylinder seal, which authenticated and protected the contents. The sealing in ch. 7 results in the name of the Lord being stamped on the forehead of his followers (see 9:4; 14:1; cf. 22:4). Its primary purpose is to protect the people of God in the coming judgments. For the background see Eze 9:4, where the mark was the Hebrew letter *Taw*, made like an *X* or +.

7:4 *144,000.* Some find here a reference to members of actual Jewish tribes, the faithful Jewish remnant of the "great tribulation" (v. 14). Others take the passage as symbolic of all

the faithful believers who live during the period of tribulation.

7:5 *Judah.* Perhaps listed before Reuben, his older brother, because the Messiah belonged to the tribe of Judah (but see note on Ge 37:21).

7:6 *Manasseh.* One of the two Joseph tribes (Ephraim and Manasseh), yet mentioned separately, probably to make up 12 tribes since Dan is omitted. This omission is due perhaps to Dan's early connection with idolatry (Jdg 18:30), or to a tradition that the antichrist was to come from that tribe.

7:9 *great multitude.* Identified in v. 14 as those who have come out of the great tribulation. *every nation, tribe, people and language.* All four are mentioned together also in 5:9; 11:9; 13:7; 14:6. Cf. 10:11; 17:15, in which one of the four is changed. *palm branches.* Used for festive occasions (see Lev 23:40; Jn 12:13).

7:10 *Salvation belongs to our God.* See Ge 49:18 ("deliverance"); Jnh 2:9.

7:11 *elders.* See note on 4:4. *four living creatures.* See note on 4:6.

7:12 *Praise . . . strength.* The sevenfold list of attributes expresses complete or perfect praise (see note on 5:12).

7:13 *white robes.* See note on 6:11.

7:14 *the great tribulation.* The period of final hostility prior to Christ's return. Some hold that the beginning of this hostility was already being experienced by the church of

come out of the great tribulation; they have washed their robes[l] and made them white in the blood of the Lamb.[m] [15]Therefore,

"they are before the throne of God[n]
    and serve him[o] day and night in his
        temple;[p]
and he who sits on the throne[q] will
    spread his tent over them.[r]
[16]Never again will they hunger;
    never again will they thirst.[s]
The sun will not beat upon them,
    nor any scorching heat.[t]
[17]For the Lamb at the center of the
    throne will be their shepherd;[u]
he will lead them to springs of living
    water.[v]
And God will wipe away every tear
    from their eyes."[w]

The Seventh Seal and the Golden Censer

8 When he opened the seventh seal,[x] there was silence in heaven for about half an hour.

[2]And I saw the seven angels[y] who stand before God, and to them were given seven trumpets.[z]

[3]Another angel,[a] who had a golden censer, came and stood at the altar. He was given much incense to offer, with the prayers of all the saints,[b] on the golden altar[c] before the throne. [4]The smoke of the incense, together with the prayers of the saints, went up before God[d] from the

angel's hand. [5]Then the angel took the censer, filled it with fire from the altar,[e] and hurled it on the earth; and there came peals of thunder,[f] rumblings, flashes of lightning and an earthquake.[g]

The Trumpets

[6]Then the seven angels who had the seven trumpets[h] prepared to sound them.

[7]The first angel[i] sounded his trumpet, and there came hail and fire[j] mixed with blood, and it was hurled down upon the earth. A third[k] of the earth was burned up, a third of the trees were burned up, and all the green grass was burned up.[l]

[8]The second angel sounded his trumpet, and something like a huge mountain,[m] all ablaze, was thrown into the sea. A third[n] of the sea turned into blood,[o] [9]a third[p] of the living creatures in the sea died, and a third of the ships were destroyed.

[10]The third angel sounded his trumpet, and a great star, blazing like a torch, fell from the sky[q] on a third of the rivers and on the springs of water[r]— [11]the name of the star is Wormwood.[1] A third[s] of the waters turned bitter, and many people died from the waters that had become bitter.[t]

[12]The fourth angel sounded his trumpet, and a third of the sun was struck, a third of the moon, and a third of the stars, so that a third[u] of them turned dark.[v] A third of the day was without light, and also a third of the night.[w]

[13]As I watched, I heard an eagle that

[1]11 That is, Bitterness

7:14 [l]Rev 22:14
[m]Heb 9:14;
1Jn 1:7;
Rev 12:11
7:15 [n]ver 9
[o]Rev 22:3
[p]Rev 11:19
[q]S Rev 5:1
[r]Isa 4:5,6;
Rev 21:3
7:16 [s]Jn 6:35
[t]Isa 49:10
7:17 [u]S Jn 10:11
[v]S Jn 4:10
[w]Isa 25:8; 35:10;
51:11; 65:19;
Rev 21:4
8:1 [x]Rev 6:1
8:2 [y]ver 6-13;
Rev 9:1,13; 11:15
[z]S Mt 24:31
8:3 [a]Rev 7:2
[b]Rev 5:8 [c]ver 5;
Ex 30:1-6;
Heb 9:4; Rev 9:13
8:4 [d]Ps 141:2

8:5 [e]Lev 16:12,
13 [f]S Rev 4:5
[g]S Rev 6:12
8:6 [h]S ver 2
8:7 [i]S ver 2
[j]Eze 38:22 [k]ver
7-12; Rev 9:15,
18; 12:4 [l]Rev 9:4
8:8 [m]Jer 51:25
[n]S ver 7
[o]Rev 16:3
8:9 [p]S ver 7
8:10 [q]Isa 14:12;
Rev 6:13; 9:1
[r]Rev 14:7; 16:4
8:11 [s]S ver 7
[t]Jer 9:15; 23:15
8:12 [u]S ver 7
[v]Ex 10:21-23;
Rev 6:12,13
[w]Eze 32:7

John's day.
7:15 *temple.* All 16 references to the temple in Revelation use the word that designates the inner shrine rather than the larger precincts. It is the place where God's presence dwells. *spread his tent.* The imagery would evoke memories of the tabernacle in the desert (Lev 26:11–13).
7:17 *shepherd.* Ancient kings often referred to themselves as the shepherds of their people.
8:1 *silence in heaven.* A dramatic pause before the next series of plagues—the final act of the drama is left undisclosed here, reserved to be presented later.
8:2 *seven trumpets.* In OT times the trumpet served to announce important events and give signals in time of war. The seven trumpets of Rev 8–9; 11:15–19 announce a series of plagues more severe than the seals but not as completely devastating as the bowls (ch. 16).
8:3 *censer.* A firepan used to hold live charcoal for the burning of incense (cf. Ex 27:3; 1Ki 7:50). *with the prayers.* Most translations consider the incense to be mingled "with" prayers. The Greek for this phrase also allows a translation that takes the incense "to be" the prayers ("incense . . . consisting of the prayers").
8:4 Although the angel is involved in presenting the prayers of the saints to God, he does not make them acceptable. The Jewish apocalyptic concept of angels as mediators finds no place in the NT.
8:5 *thunder . . . earthquake.* See note on 4:5.

8:7 *hail and fire mixed with blood.* Cf. the imagery of the seventh plague on Egypt (Ex 9:13–25; cf. Eze 38:22). *A third of the earth was burned up.* This fraction indicates that the punishment announced by the trumpets is not yet complete and final (the same fraction appears in each of the next three plagues: vv. 8–9, 10–11, 12). A smaller fraction (a fourth) of devastation accompanied the opening of the fourth seal (6:8).
8:8 *sea turned into blood.* Reminiscent of the first plague on Egypt (Ex 7:20–21). This is an eschatological judgment rather than natural pollution resulting from widespread volcanic upheavals.
8:10 *great star . . . fell.* See notes on 6:13; 9:1.
8:11 *Wormwood.* A plant with a strong, bitter taste (see NIV text note). It is used here as a metaphor for calamity and sorrow (see Pr 5:3–4; Jer 9:15; La 3:19). It is not poisonous, but its bitterness suggests death. *waters turned bitter.* The reverse of the miracle at Marah, where bitter waters were made sweet (Ex 15:25).
8:12 *a third of the sun was struck.* In the ninth plague on Egypt, thick darkness covered the land for three days (Ex 10:21–23). References to the Egyptian plagues suggest that in Revelation we have the final exodus of God's people from the bondage of a world controlled by hostile powers.
8:13 *Woe! Woe! Woe . . . !* These three woes correspond to the three final trumpet plagues (see 9:12; 11:14 [10:1–11:13 is a parenthesis]); the seven bowl judgments of

was flying in midair[x] call out in a loud voice: "Woe! Woe! Woe[y] to the inhabitants of the earth,[z] because of the trumpet blasts about to be sounded by the other three angels!"

9 The fifth angel sounded his trumpet, and I saw a star that had fallen from the sky to the earth.[a] The star was given the key[b] to the shaft of the Abyss.[c] ²When he opened the Abyss, smoke rose from it like the smoke from a gigantic furnace.[d] The sun and sky were darkened[e] by the smoke from the Abyss.[f] ³And out of the smoke locusts[g] came down upon the earth and were given power like that of scorpions[h] of the earth. ⁴They were told not to harm[i] the grass of the earth or any plant or tree,[j] but only those people who did not have the seal of God on their foreheads.[k] ⁵They were not given power to kill them, but only to torture them for five months.[l] And the agony they suffered was like that of the sting of a scorpion[m] when it strikes a man. ⁶During those days men will seek death, but will not find it; they will long to die, but death will elude them.[n]

⁷The locusts looked like horses prepared for battle.[o] On their heads they wore something like crowns of gold, and their faces resembled human faces.[p] ⁸Their hair was like women's hair, and their teeth were like lions' teeth.[q] ⁹They had breastplates like breastplates of iron, and the

sound of their wings was like the thundering of many horses and chariots rushing into battle.[r] ¹⁰They had tails and stings like scorpions, and in their tails they had power to torment people for five months.[s] ¹¹They had as king over them the angel of the Abyss,[t] whose name in Hebrew[u] is Abaddon,[v] and in Greek, Apollyon.[m]

¹²The first woe is past; two other woes are yet to come.[w]

¹³The sixth angel sounded his trumpet, and I heard a voice coming from the horns[n][x] of the golden altar that is before God.[y] ¹⁴It said to the sixth angel who had the trumpet, "Release the four angels[z] who are bound at the great river Euphrates."[a] ¹⁵And the four angels who had been kept ready for this very hour and day and month and year were released[b] to kill a third[c] of mankind.[d] ¹⁶The number of the mounted troops was two hundred million. I heard their number.[e]

¹⁷The horses and riders I saw in my vision looked like this: Their breastplates were fiery red, dark blue, and yellow as sulfur. The heads of the horses resembled the heads of lions, and out of their mouths[f] came fire, smoke and sulfur.[g] ¹⁸A third[h] of mankind was killed[i] by the three plagues of fire, smoke and sulfur[j] that came out of their mouths. ¹⁹The

Cross references:

8:13 xRev 14:6; 19:17 yRev 9:12; 11:14; 12:12 zS Rev 3:10
9:1 aRev 8:10 bRev 1:18 cver 2, 11; S Lk 8:31
9:2 dGe 19:28; Ex 19:18 eJoel 2:2,10 fver 1,11; S Lk 8:31
9:3 gEx 10:12-15 hver 5,10
9:4 iS Rev 6:6 jRev 8:7 kS Rev 7:2,3
9:5 lver 10 mver 3
9:6 nJob 3:21; 7:15; Jer 8:3; Rev 6:16
9:7 oJoel 2:4 pDa 7:8
9:8 qJoel 1:6
9:9 rJoel 2:5
9:10 sver 3,5,19
9:11 tver 1,2; S Lk 8:31 uRev 16:16 vJob 26:6; 28:22; 31:12; Ps 88:11
9:12 wS Rev 8:13
9:13 xEx 30:1-3 yRev 8:3
9:14 zRev 7:1 aGe 15:18; Dt 1:7; Jos 1:4; Isa 11:15; Rev 16:12
9:15 bRev 20:7 cS Rev 8:7 dver 18
9:16 eRev 5:11; 7:4
9:17 fRev 11:5 gver 18; Ps 11:6; Isa 30:33; Eze 38:22; Rev 14:10; 19:20; 20:10; 21:8
9:18 hS Rev 8:7 iver 15 /S ver 17

---

m 11 Abaddon and Apollyon mean Destroyer.
n 13 That is, projections

---

chs. 15–16 constitute the third woe). The woes fall on the unbelieving world (the phrase "the inhabitants of the earth" refers to the wicked; see note on 6:10), not on the righteous (see 9:4).

9:1 star that had fallen. The star in 8:10 was part of a cosmic disturbance; here the star is a divine agent, probably an angel (cf. 20:1). Abyss. Conceived of as the subterranean abode of demonic hordes (see 20:1; Lk 8:31). The Greek word means "very deep" or "bottomless," and is used in the Septuagint (the Greek translation of the OT) to translate the Hebrew word for the primeval deep (see Ge 1:2; 7:11; Pr 8:28). Seven of the nine NT references are in Revelation.
9:3 locusts. For background see the plague of locusts in Ex 10:1–20. Joel 1:2–2:11 interprets the locust plague as a foreshadowing of the devastations that accompany the day of the Lord. Locusts traveled in enormous swarms and could strip a land of all vegetation. In 1866, 200,000 people died in a famine in Algiers following a locust plague. scorpions. Large spider-like organisms that injure or kill by means of a poisonous barb in the tail.
9:4 people who did not have the seal of God. The first woe does not affect the "servants of God" (see 7:3). Cf. the Israelites, who were protected from the Egyptian plagues (Ex 8:22; 9:4,26; 10:23; 11:7).
9:5 five months. A limited period of time suggested by the life cycle of the locust or the dry season (spring through late summer, about five months), in which the danger of a locust invasion is always present.
9:6 seek death, but will not find it. Cf. Hos 10:8 (quoted in Lk 23:30). Cornelius Gallus, a Roman poet living in the first

century B.C., wrote: "Worse than any wound is the wish to die and yet not be able to do so." Cf. Paul's attitude toward death in Php 1:23–24.
9:7 human faces. The locusts appear to have the cunning of intelligent beings. They do not simply use brute force.
9:8 women's hair. Perhaps a reference to long antennae. lions' teeth. Cruel, inhumane.
9:9 breastplates. The breastplate was a coat of mail that protected the front. like breastplates of iron. Probably thin iron pieces riveted to a leather base.
9:10 five months. See note on v. 5.
9:11 Abaddon. A personification of destruction (see NIV text note; cf. Pr 15:11).
9:12 first woe. See note on 8:13.
9:13 horns of the golden altar. See 8:3–5. The horns were projections at the four corners of the altar (Ex 27:2). Those fleeing judgment could seek mercy by taking hold of the horns (1Ki 1:50–51; 2:28; see note on Am 3:14).
9:14 four angels. Apparently in charge of the demonic horsemen (vv. 15–19). Euphrates. The longest river in western Asia (about 1,700 miles). It marked the boundary between Israel and her historic enemies (Assyria and Babylon) to the east (cf. Isa 8:5–8).
9:15 hour…day…month…year. Apocalyptic thought views God as acting according to an exact timetable.
9:16 two hundred million. The reference is most likely general, intending an incalculable host rather than a specific number (cf. Ps 68:17; Da 7:10; Rev 5:11).
9:17 breastplates. See note on v. 9. out of their mouths came fire. Cf. the two witnesses in 11:5.

power of the horses was in their mouths and in their tails; for their tails were like snakes, having heads with which they inflict injury.

²⁰The rest of mankind that were not killed by these plagues still did not repent[k] of the work of their hands;[l] they did not stop worshiping demons,[m] and idols of gold, silver, bronze, stone and wood—idols that cannot see or hear or walk.[n] ²¹Nor did they repent[o] of their murders, their magic arts,[p] their sexual immorality[q] or their thefts.

The Angel and the Little Scroll

10 Then I saw another mighty angel[r] coming down from heaven.[s] He was robed in a cloud, with a rainbow[t] above his head; his face was like the sun,[u] and his legs were like fiery pillars.[v] ²He was holding a little scroll,[w] which lay open in his hand. He planted his right foot on the sea and his left foot on the land,[x] ³and he gave a loud shout like the roar of a lion.[y] When he shouted, the voices of the seven thunders[z] spoke. ⁴And when the seven thunders spoke, I was about to write;[a] but I heard a voice from heaven[b] say, "Seal up what the seven thunders have said and do not write it down."[c]

⁵Then the angel I had seen standing on the sea and on the land[d] raised his right

hand to heaven.[e] ⁶And he swore[f] by him who lives for ever and ever,[g] who created the heavens and all that is in them, the earth and all that is in it, and the sea and all that is in it,[h] and said, "There will be no more delay![i] ⁷But in the days when the seventh angel is about to sound his trumpet,[j] the mystery[k] of God will be accomplished, just as he announced to his servants the prophets."[l]

⁸Then the voice that I had heard from heaven[m] spoke to me once more: "Go, take the scroll[n] that lies open in the hand of the angel who is standing on the sea and on the land."

⁹So I went to the angel and asked him to give me the little scroll. He said to me, "Take it and eat it. It will turn your stomach sour, but in your mouth it will be as sweet as honey."[o] ¹⁰I took the little scroll from the angel's hand and ate it. It tasted as sweet as honey in my mouth,[p] but when I had eaten it, my stomach turned sour. ¹¹Then I was told, "You must prophesy[q] again about many peoples, nations, languages and kings."[r]

The Two Witnesses

11 I was given a reed like a measuring rod[s] and was told, "Go and measure the temple of God and the altar, and count the worshipers there. ²But exclude

9:20 [k]S Rev 2:21 / [l]Dt 4:28; 31:29; Jer 1:16; Mic 5:13; Ac 7:41 [m]S 1Co 10:20 [n]Ps 115:4-7; 135:15-17; Da 5:23
9:21 [o]S Rev 2:21 [p]Isa 47:9,12; Rev 18:23 [q]Rev 17:2,5
10:1 [r]Rev 5:2 [s]Rev 18:1; 20:1 [t]Eze 1:28; Rev 4:3 [u]Mt 17:2; Rev 1:16 [v]Rev 1:15
10:2 [w]ver 8-10; Rev 5:1 [x]ver 5,8
10:3 [y]Hos 11:10 [z]Rev 4:5
10:4 [a]Rev 1:11, 19 [b]ver 8 [c]Da 8:26; 12:4,9; Rev 22:10
10:5 [d]ver 1,2

[e]Dt 32:40; Da 12:7
10:6 [f]Ge 14:22; Ex 6:8; Nu 14:30 [g]S Rev 1:18 [h]Ps 115:15; 146:6; Rev 4:11; 14:7 [i]Rev 16:17
10:7 [j]S Mt 24:31 [k]S Ro 16:25 [l]Am 3:7
10:8 [m]ver 4 [n]ver 2
10:9 [o]Jer 15:16; Eze 2:8-3:3
10:10 [p]S ver 9
10:11 [q]Eze 37:4, 9 [r]Da 3:4; S Rev 13:7
11:1 [s]Eze 40:3; Rev 21:15

9:19 *tails were like snakes, having heads.* Emphasizes the demonic origin of the horses (cf. 12:9).
9:20 *demons.* Spiritual beings in league with Satan and exerting an evil influence on human affairs (cf. Dt 4:28; Ps 115:5–7; 1Co 10:20).
9:21 *Nor did they repent.* See 16:9,11. Even physical pain will not change the rebellious heart. *magic arts.* Involved the mixing of various ingredients (the Greek for this phrase is *pharmakon,* from which comes the English "pharmacy") for magical purposes. Believers at Ephesus publicly burned their books of magic, valued at 50,000 drachmas (Ac 19:19).
10:1 *mighty angel.* Perhaps the angel of 5:2. *rainbow.* Cf. Eze 1:26–28. The rainbow became a sign of God's pledge never to destroy the earth again by a flood (Ge 9:8–17). *legs were like fiery pillars.* Since the exodus supplies background for this central part of Revelation (see note on 8:12), this feature may recall the pillars of fire and cloud that guided (Ex 13:21–22) and protected (Ex 14:19,24) the Israelites during their desert journey.
10:2 *little scroll.* Not the same as the scroll of destiny in ch. 5, since that scroll was intended to reveal its contents and this scroll was to be eaten. Furthermore, the term "little scroll" sets this particular scroll off from all others. *right foot on the sea . . . left foot on the land.* Indicates his tremendous size and symbolizes that his coming has to do with the destiny of all creation (cf. v. 6).
10:3 *seven thunders.* In 8:5; 11:19; 16:18 thunder is connected with divine punishment. Here, too, it anticipates the judgment to fall on those who refuse God's love and grace.
10:4 *Seal up.* In Da 8:26; 12:4,9 the prophecies are sealed until the last times, when they will be opened. What the

seven thunders said will not be revealed until their proper time. Cf. the angel's instructions in 22:10 not to seal the prophecies of Revelation.
10:5 *raised his right hand.* A part of oath taking (see Ge 14:22–23; Dt 32:40).
10:6 *him who lives for ever and ever.* Of special encouragement in a context of impending martyrdom (cf. 1:18; 4:9–10; 15:7). *no more delay.* The martyrs in 6:9–11 were told to rest for a while, but now the end has come (cf. Da 12:1; Mk 13:19).
10:7 *mystery of God.* In apocalyptic thought mysteries were secrets preserved in heaven and revealed to the apocalyptist. Here the mystery is that God has won the victory over the forces of evil and will reign for ever and ever (cf. 11:15).
10:9 *Take it and eat it.* Grasp and digest fully the contents of the scroll (cf. Ps 119:103). *turn your stomach sour.* The message of the little scroll (11:1–13) will involve suffering—the "bad news." *in your mouth . . . sweet as honey.* God's eternal purposes will experience no further delay—the "good news."
10:11 *prophesy again.* The prophecies following the sounding of the seventh trumpet in 11:15. *peoples . . . kings.* See note on 7:9.
11:1 *reed.* A bamboo-like cane that often reached a height of 20 feet and grew in abundance in the waters along the banks of the Jordan. Straight and light, the reed was a convenient measuring rod (see Eze 40:3; Zec 2:1–2). *temple.* See note on 7:15. *altar.* The context of worship suggests that this is the great altar.
11:2 *outer court.* The court of the Gentiles, approximately 26 acres. *trample on the holy city.* Cf. Ps 79:1; Isa 63:18; Lk 21:24. *42 months.* Three and a half years. Some find the

the outer court; t do not measure it, because it has been given to the Gentiles. u They will trample on the holy city v for 42 months. w ³And I will give power to my two witnesses, x and they will prophesy for 1,260 days, y clothed in sackcloth." z ⁴These are the two olive trees a and the two lampstands that stand before the Lord of the earth. b ⁵If anyone tries to harm them, fire comes from their mouths and devours their enemies. c This is how anyone who wants to harm them must die. d ⁶These men have power to shut up the sky e so that it will not rain during the time they are prophesying; f and they have power to turn the waters into blood g and to strike the earth with every kind of plague as often as they want.

⁷Now when they have finished their testimony, the beast h that comes up from the Abyss i will attack them, j and overpower and kill them. ⁸Their bodies will lie in the street of the great city, k which is figuratively called Sodom l and Egypt, where also their Lord was crucified. m ⁹For three and a half days men from every people, tribe, language and nation n will gaze on their bodies and refuse them burial. o ¹⁰The inhabitants of the earth p will gloat over them and will celebrate by sending each other gifts, q because these two prophets had tormented those who live on the earth.

¹¹But after the three and a half days r a breath of life from God entered them, s and they stood on their feet, and terror struck those who saw them. ¹²Then they heard a loud voice from heaven saying to them, "Come up here." t And they went up to heaven in a cloud, u while their enemies looked on.

¹³At that very hour there was a severe earthquake v and a tenth of the city collapsed. Seven thousand people were killed in the earthquake, and the survivors were terrified and gave glory w to the God of heaven. x

¹⁴The second woe has passed; the third woe is coming soon. y

The Seventh Trumpet

¹⁵The seventh angel sounded his trumpet, z and there were loud voices a in heaven, which said:

"The kingdom of the world has become
the kingdom of our Lord and of
his Christ, b
and he will reign for ever and
ever." c

¹⁶And the twenty-four elders, d who were seated on their thrones before God, fell on their faces e and worshiped God, ¹⁷saying:

Cross references (center column)

11:2 tEze 40:17, 20 uLk 21:24 vS Rev 21:2 $w$ver 3; Da 7:25; 12:7; Rev 12:6,14; 13:5
11:3 xRev 1:5; 2:13 yS ver 2 zGe 37:34; 2Sa 3:31; Ne 9:1; Jnh 3:5
11:4 aPs 52:8; Jer 11:16; Zec 4:3,11 bZec 4:14
11:5 c2Sa 22:9; 2Ki 1:10; Jer 5:14; Rev 9:17,18 dNu 16:29,35
11:6 eS Lk 4:25 $f$ver 3 gEx 7:17, 19; Rev 8:8
11:7 hRev 13:1-4 iS Lk 8:31 jDa 7:21; Rev 13:7
11:8 kRev 16:19 lIsa 1:9; Jer 23:14; Eze 16:46 mHeb 13:12
11:9 nS Rev 13:7 oPs 79:2,3
11:10 pS Rev 3:10 qNe 8:10,12; Est 9:19,22
11:11 $r$ver 9 sEze 37:5,9,10,14
11:12 tRev 4:1 u2Ki 2:11; Ac 1:9
11:13 vS Rev 6:12 wRev 14:7; 16:9; 19:7 xRev 16:11
11:14 yS Rev 8:13
11:15 zS Mt 24:31 aRev 16:17; 19:1 bRev 12:10
11:16 cPs 145:13; Da 2:44; 7:14,27; Mic 4:7; Zec 14:9; Lk 1:33
11:16 dS Rev 4:4 eS Rev 4:10

---

background for this period in the time of Jewish suffering under the Syrian tyrant, Antiochus Epiphanes (168–165 B.C.). Others point out that, whereas the temple was desolated for three years under Antiochus, the figure used in Revelation is three and a half years, which no doubt looks back to the dividing of the 70th "seven" (Da 9:27) into two equal parts. The same time period is also designated as 1,260 days (v. 3; 12:6) and as "a time, times and half a time" (12:14; cf. Da 7:25; 12:7). This period of time evidently became a conventional symbol for a limited period of unrestrained wickedness.
11:3 *two witnesses.* Modeled after Moses and Elijah (see notes on vv. 5–6). They may symbolize testifying believers in the final period before Christ returns. Or they may be two actual individuals who will be martyred for the proclamation of the truth. *1,260 days.* See note on v. 2. These are months of 30 days (42 months x 30 days = 1,260 days). *sackcloth.* A coarse, dark cloth woven from the hair of goats or camels. It was worn as a sign of mourning and penitence (Joel 1:13; Jnh 3:5–6; Mt 11:21).
11:4 The imagery emphasizes that the power for effective testimony is supplied by the Spirit of God (see notes on Zec 4).
11:5 *fire comes . . . and devours.* Cf. Elijah's encounters with the messengers of Ahaziah (2Ki 1:10,12).
11:6 *power to shut up the sky.* Cf. the drought in the days of Elijah (1Ki 17:1; see also Lk 4:25; Jas 5:17). *waters into blood.* God used Moses to bring the same plague on the Egyptians (Ex 7:17–21).
11:7 *the beast.* First mention of the major opponent of God's people in the final days (see chs. 13; 17). That he

comes up from the Abyss (see note on 9:1) indicates his demonic character. *kill them.* They will suffer the same fate as their Lord (see v. 8).
11:8 *Their bodies will lie in the street.* In the Near East the denial of burial was a flagrant violation of decency. *great city.* Possibly Jerusalem, though some say Rome, Babylon or some other city. It may be symbolic of the world opposed to God (see 16:19; 17:18; 18:10,16,18–19,21). Sodom (see similarly Isa 1:10) refers to its low level of morality (cf. Ge 19:4–11), and Egypt emphasizes oppression and slavery. Some say that Jesus could have been crucified in Rome in the sense that her power extended throughout the known world and was immediately responsible for Christ's execution.
11:9 *three and a half days.* A short time when compared with the three and a half years of their ministry. *refuse them burial.* See note on v. 8.
11:11 *a breath of life from God entered them.* A dramatic validation of the true faith (cf. Eze 37:5,10).
11:12 *went up to heaven in a cloud.* Cf. 1Th 4:17. *enemies looked on.* Cf. 1:7.
11:13 *earthquake.* See notes on 6:12; Eze 38:19. *gave glory to the God of heaven.* Not an act of repentance but the terrified realization that Christ, not the antichrist, is the true Lord of all.
11:14 *second woe.* Cf. 9:12.
11:15 *seventh angel sounded.* The series of trumpet blasts is now continued (see 9:13) and completed. *kingdom of our Lord.* Cf. Ex 15:18; Ps 10:16; Zec 14:9. *of our Lord and of his Christ.* Cf. Ps 2:2.
11:16 *twenty-four elders.* See note on 4:4.
11:17 *One who is and who was.* In 1:4,8; 4:8 he is also

"We give thanks/ to you, Lord God
Almighty, *g*
the One who is and who was, *h*
because you have taken your great
power
and have begun to reign. *i*
[18]The nations were angry; /
and your wrath has come.
The time has come for judging the
dead, *k*
and for rewarding your servants the
prophets /
and your saints and those who
reverence your name,
both small and great *m*—
and for destroying those who destroy
the earth."

[19]Then God's temple *n* in heaven was
opened, and within his temple was seen
the ark of his covenant. *o* And there came
flashes of lightning, rumblings, peals of
thunder, *p* an earthquake and a great hailstorm. *q*

The Woman and the Dragon

12 A great and wondrous sign *r* appeared in heaven: *s* a woman
clothed with the sun, with the moon under her feet and a crown of twelve stars *t*
on her head. [2]She was pregnant and cried
out in pain *u* as she was about to give birth.
[3]Then another sign appeared in heaven: *v*
an enormous red dragon *w* with seven
heads *x* and ten horns *y* and seven
crowns *z* on his heads. [4]His tail swept a
third *a* of the stars out of the sky and flung

them to the earth. *b* The dragon stood in
front of the woman who was about to give
birth, so that he might devour her child *c*
the moment it was born. [5]She gave birth to
a son, a male child, who will rule all the
nations with an iron scepter. *d* And her
child was snatched up *e* to God and to his
throne. [6]The woman fled into the desert to
a place prepared for her by God, where she
might be taken care of for 1,260 days. /
[7]And there was war in heaven. Michael *g* and his angels fought against the
dragon, *h* and the dragon and his angels *i*
fought back. [8]But he was not strong
enough, and they lost their place in
heaven. [9]The great dragon was hurled
down—that ancient serpent / called the
devil, *k* or Satan, *l* who leads the whole
world astray. *m* He was hurled to the
earth, *n* and his angels with him.
[10]Then I heard a loud voice in heaven *o*
say:

"Now have come the salvation *p* and
the power and the kingdom of
our God,
and the authority of his Christ.
For the accuser of our brothers, *q*
who accuses them before our God
day and night,
has been hurled down.
[11]They overcame *r* him
by the blood of the Lamb *s*
and by the word of their testimony; *t*
they did not love their lives so much
as to shrink from death. *u*
[12]Therefore rejoice, you heavens *v*
and you who dwell in them!

Cross references (center column)

11:17 /Ps 30:12
*g*S Rev 1:8
*h*S Rev 1:4
/Rev 19:6
11:18 /Ps 2:1
*k*Rev 20:12
/Rev 10:7
*m*S Rev 19:5
11:19 *n*Rev 15:5,
8 *o*Ex 25:10-22;
2Ch 5:7; Heb 9:4
*p*S Rev 4:5
*q*Rev 16:21
12:1 *r*ver 3
*s*Rev 11:19
*t*Ge 37:9
12:2 *u*Isa 26:17;
Gal 4:19
12:3 *v*ver 1;
Rev 15:1 *w*ver 9,
13,16,17;
Rev 13:1
*x*Rev 13:1; 17:3,
7,9 *y*Da 7:7,20;
Rev 13:1; 17:3,7,
12,16 *z*Rev 19:12
12:4 *a*S Rev 8:7

*b*Da 8:10
*c*Mt 2:16
12:5 *d*Ps 2:9;
Rev 2:27; 19:15
*e*S Ac 8:39
12:6 /S Rev 11:2
12:7 *g*S Jude 9
*h*ver 3 *i*Mt 25:41
12:9 /ver 15;
Ge 3:1-7
*k*Mt 25:41;
Rev 20:2
/S Mt 4:10
*m*Rev 20:3,8,10
*n*Lk 10:18;
Jn 12:31
12:10
*o*Rev 11:15
*p*Rev 7:10 *q*Job
1:9-11; Zec 3:1;
1Pe 5:8
12:11
*r*S Jn 16:33;
Rev 15:2
*s*S Rev 7:14
*t*Rev 6:9
*u*Lk 14:26;
Rev 2:10
12:12 *v*Ps 96:11;
Isa 44:23; 49:13;
Rev 18:20

Study notes (bottom)

the one "who is to come." This is now omitted because his reign is here pictured as having begun.

11:18 *nations were angry.* See Ps 48:4. *your wrath.* See note on 6:16. God's wrath triumphs in 14:10-11; 16:15-21; 20:8-9. *judging the dead.* Anticipated in 6:10, carried out in 20:11-15. *your servants the prophets.* See Da 9:6,10; Am 3:7; Zec 1:6.

11:19 *ark of his covenant.* The OT ark was a chest of acacia wood (Dt 10:1-2). It symbolized the throne or presence of God among his people. It was probably destroyed when Nebuzaradan destroyed the temple in Jerusalem (2Ki 25:8-10). In the NT it symbolizes God's faithfulness in keeping covenant with his people. *lightning . . . hailstorm.* See note on 4:5.

12:1 *sign.* An extraordinary spectacle or event that points beyond itself (cf. Lk 21:11,25; Ac 2:19). *a woman clothed with the sun.* Probably a symbolic reference to the believing Messianic community (see v. 5). *twelve stars.* Cf. the 12 tribes of Israel.

12:2 *cried out in pain.* Cf. the similar language describing the rebirth of Jerusalem in Isa 66:7 (see Mic 4:10).

12:3 *red dragon.* Identified in v. 9 (cf. 20:2). Dragons abound in the mythology of ancient peoples (Leviathan in Canaanite lore and Set-Typhon, the red crocodile, in Egypt).

In the OT they are normally used metaphorically to depict the enemies of God and of Israel (see Ps 74:14; Isa 27:1; Eze 29:3). *seven heads.* Symbolizing universal wisdom (cf. 13:1). *ten horns.* Symbolizing great power.

12:5 *a son, a male child.* The Messiah. *iron scepter.* See note on 2:27. *snatched up to God.* The ascension of Christ.

12:6 *desert.* Not a wasteland but a place of spiritual refuge (cf. Hos 2:14). *1,260 days.* The time of spiritual protection corresponds to the time of persecution (see note on 11:2; cf. 13:5).

12:7 *Michael.* An archangel who defeats Satan in heavenly warfare. In Da 12:1 he is the protector of Israel who will deliver her from tribulation in the last days.

12:9 *dragon was hurled . . . to the earth.* Not the original casting of Satan out of heaven, but his final exclusion—an explanation of his intense hostility against God's people in the last days (vv. 12-17). *devil, or Satan.* See notes on 2:9-10. *leads . . . astray.* Cf. 2Co 11:3; see also Lk 22:31; Jn 13:2.

12:10 *accuser.* See Job 1:9-11; Zec 3:1. Satan in Hebrew means "accuser."

12:11 *blood of the Lamb.* See note on 5:9; see also 1:5; 7:14.

12:12 *his time is short.* The period of final, intense hostility of Satan toward the people of God.

But woe [w] to the earth and the sea, [x] because the devil has gone down to you!

He is filled with fury,
because he knows that his time is short."

[13] When the dragon [y] saw that he had been hurled to the earth, he pursued the woman who had given birth to the male child. [z] [14] The woman was given the two wings of a great eagle, [a] so that she might fly to the place prepared for her in the desert, where she would be taken care of for a time, times and half a time, [b] out of the serpent's reach. [15] Then from his mouth the serpent [c] spewed water like a river, to overtake the woman and sweep her away with the torrent. [16] But the earth helped the woman by opening its mouth and swallowing the river that the dragon had spewed out of his mouth. [17] Then the dragon was enraged at the woman and went off to make war [d] against the rest of her offspring [e] —those who obey God's commandments [f] and hold to the testimony of Jesus. [g]

13

[1] And the dragon [o] stood on the shore of the sea.

The Beast out of the Sea

And I saw a beast coming out of the sea. [h] He had ten horns and seven heads, [i] with ten crowns on his horns, and on each head a blasphemous name. [j] [2] The beast I saw resembled a leopard, [k] but had feet like those of a bear [l] and a mouth like that of a lion. [m] The dragon gave the beast his power and his throne and great authority. [n] [3] One of the heads of the beast seemed to have had a fatal wound, but the fatal

wound had been healed. [o] The whole world was astonished [p] and followed the beast. [4] Men worshiped the dragon because he had given authority to the beast, and they also worshiped the beast and asked, "Who is like [q] the beast? Who can make war against him?"

[5] The beast was given a mouth to utter proud words and blasphemies [r] and to exercise his authority for forty-two months. [s] [6] He opened his mouth to blaspheme God, and to slander his name and his dwelling place and those who live in heaven. [t] [7] He was given power to make war [u] against the saints and to conquer them. And he was given authority over every tribe, people, language and nation. [v] [8] All inhabitants of the earth [w] will worship the beast—all whose names have not been written in the book of life [x] belonging to the Lamb [y] that was slain from the creation of the world. [p] [z]

[9] He who has an ear, let him hear. [a]

[10] If anyone is to go into captivity,
into captivity he will go.
If anyone is to be killed [q] with the sword,
with the sword he will be killed. [b]

This calls for patient endurance and faithfulness [c] on the part of the saints. [d]

The Beast out of the Earth

[11] Then I saw another beast, coming out of the earth. [e] He had two horns like a lamb, but he spoke like a dragon. [f] [12] He

---

Cross references (center column)

12:12
[w] S Rev 8:13
[x] Rev 10:6
12:13 [y] ver 3 [z] ver 5
12:14 [a] Ex 19:4
[b] S Rev 11:2
12:15 [c] ver 9
12:17 [d] Rev 11:7; 13:7 [e] Ge 3:15
[f] S Jn 14:15
[g] S Rev 1:2
13:1 [h] Da 7:1-6; Rev 15:2; 16:13
[i] S Rev 12:3
[j] Da 11:36; Rev 17:3
13:2 [k] Da 7:6
[l] Da 7:5 [m] Da 7:4
[n] Rev 2:13; 16:10
13:3 [o] ver 12,14
[p] Rev 17:8
13:4 [q] Ex 15:11
13:5 [r] Da 7:8,11, 20,25; 11:36; 2Th 2:4
[s] S Rev 11:2
13:6 [t] Rev 12:12
13:7 [u] Da 7:21; Rev 11:7
[v] Rev 5:9; 7:9; 10:11; 17:15
13:8 [w] ver 12,14; S Rev 3:10
[x] S Rev 20:12
[y] S Jn 1:29
[z] S Mt 25:34
13:9 [a] S Rev 2:7
13:10 [b] Jer 15:2; 43:11
[c] S Heb 6:12
[d] Rev 14:12
13:11 [e] ver 1,2
[f] Rev 16:13

Textual footnotes

[o] 1 Some late manuscripts And I [p] 8 Or written from the creation of the world in the book of life belonging to the Lamb that was slain [q] 10 Some manuscripts anyone kills

---

Study notes

12:13–16 Cf. the similarity to the exodus.

12:14 *desert.* See note on v. 6. *a time, times and half a time.* One year plus two years plus half a year (see note on 11:2).

12:16 *earth helped . . . by opening its mouth.* In Nu 16:30–33 the earth opened and swallowed Korah's men.

12:17 *rest of her offspring.* Believers in general as contrasted with Christ, the male child of vv. 5,13. *testimony of Jesus.* The testimony that Jesus bore (cf. 1:2,9; 19:10).

13:1 *beast coming out of the sea.* First mentioned in 11:7. According to some, the beast symbolizes the Roman empire, the deification of secular authority. According to others, he is the final, personal antichrist. The background seems to be Daniel's vision of the four great beasts (Da 7:2–7). See 17:8–11 for the interpreting angel's explanation of the beast. *ten horns.* See 17:12. *blasphemous name.* Roman emperors tended to assume titles of deity. Domitian, e.g., was addressed as *Dominus et Deus noster* ("Our Lord and God").

13:2 *leopard . . . bear . . . lion.* John's beast combined characteristics of Daniel's four beasts (Da 7:4–6). *dragon.* See note on 12:3.

13:3 *fatal wound . . . healed.* Emphasizes the tremendous recuperative power of the beast. *whole world was aston-*

ished. See 17:8 for the same reaction.

13:5 *was given.* Four times in the Greek text of vv. 5–7 the passive "was given" occurs, emphasizing the subordinate role of the beast (see vv. 2,4). *forty-two months.* See note on 11:2.

13:7 *make war.* See 12:17; see also Da 7:7.

13:8 *book of life belonging to the Lamb.* See note on 3:5. *slain from the creation of the world.* See NIV text note (cf. 17:8). Cf. Isa 53:7; Jn 1:29,36.

13:11 *another beast, coming out of the earth.* According to some, he symbolizes religious power in the service of secular authorities. According to others, he is the personal false prophet (see 16:13; 19:20; 20:10). *two horns like a lamb.* He attempts to appear gentle and harmless. *spoke like a dragon.* See Jesus' warning in Mt 7:15 about ravenous wolves who come in sheep's clothing.

13:12 *exercised all the authority of the first beast.* The trinity of evil is now complete. The beast from the earth is under the authority of the beast from the sea. The latter is subject to the dragon. Satan, secular power and religious compromise (or Satan, the antichrist and the false prophet) join against the cause of God: Father, Son and Holy Spirit.

exercised all the authority[g] of the first beast on his behalf,[h] and made the earth and its inhabitants worship the first beast,[i] whose fatal wound had been healed.[j] [13]And he performed great and miraculous signs,[k] even causing fire to come down from heaven[l] to earth in full view of men. [14]Because of the signs[m] he was given power to do on behalf of the first beast, he deceived[n] the inhabitants of the earth.[o] He ordered them to set up an image in honor of the beast who was wounded by the sword and yet lived.[p] [15]He was given power to give breath to the image of the first beast, so that it could speak and cause all who refused to worship[q] the image to be killed.[r] [16]He also forced everyone, small and great,[s] rich and poor, free and slave, to receive a mark on his right hand or on his forehead,[t] [17]so that no one could buy or sell unless he had the mark,[u] which is the name of the beast or the number of his name.[v]

[18]This calls for wisdom.[w] If anyone has insight, let him calculate the number of the beast, for it is man's number.[x] His number is 666.

The Lamb and the 144,000

14 Then I looked, and there before me was the Lamb,[y] standing on Mount Zion,[z] and with him 144,000[a] who had his name and his Father's name[b]

written on their foreheads.[c] [2]And I heard a sound from heaven like the roar of rushing waters[d] and like a loud peal of thunder.[e] The sound I heard was like that of harpists playing their harps.[f] [3]And they sang a new song[g] before the throne and before the four living creatures[h] and the elders.[i] No one could learn the song except the 144,000[j] who had been redeemed from the earth. [4]These are those who did not defile themselves with women, for they kept themselves pure.[k] They follow the Lamb wherever he goes.[l] They were purchased from among men[m] and offered as firstfruits[n] to God and the Lamb. [5]No lie was found in their mouths;[o] they are blameless.[p]

The Three Angels

[6]Then I saw another angel flying in midair,[q] and he had the eternal gospel to proclaim to those who live on the earth[r]—to every nation, tribe, language and people.[s] [7]He said in a loud voice, "Fear God[t] and give him glory,[u] because the hour of his judgment has come. Worship him who made[v] the heavens, the earth, the sea and the springs of water."[w]

[8]A second angel followed and said, "Fallen! Fallen is Babylon the Great,[x]

Cross-references (center column)
13:12 gver 4; hver 14; Rev 19, 20; iver 15; Rev 14:9,11; 16:2; 19:20; 20:4; jver 3
13:13 kS Mt 24:24; lKi 18:38; 2Ki 1:10; Lk 9:54; Rev 20:9
13:14 m2Th 2:9, 10; nRev 12:9; oS Rev 3:10; pver 3,12
13:15 qS ver 12; rDa 3:3-6
13:16 sS Rev 19:5; tRev 7:3; 14:9; 20:4
13:17 uRev 14:9; vver 18; Rev 14:11; 15:2
13:18 wRev 17:9; xRev 15:2; 21:17
14:1 yS Rev 5:6; zPs 2:6; Heb 12:22; aver 3; Rev 7:4; bRev 3:12; 22:4
cS Rev 7:3
14:2 dS Rev 1:15; eRev 6:1; fRev 5:8; 15:2
14:3 gS Rev 5:9; hS Rev 4:6; iS Rev 4:4; jver 1
14:4 k2Co 11:2; Rev 3:4; lRev 7:17; mRev 5:9; nJer 2:3; Jas 1:18
14:5 oPs 32:2; Zep 3:13; Jn 1:47; 1Pe 2:22; pEph 5:27
14:6 qRev 8:13; 19:17; rS Rev 3:10; sS Rev 13:7
14:7 tPs 34:9; Rev 15:4; uS Rev 11:13
vS Rev 10:6; wRev 8:10; 16:4 14:8 xIsa 21:9; Jer 51:8; Rev 16:19; 17:5; 18:2,10

13:13 *miraculous signs.* See the warning in Dt 13:1–3; see also Mt 24:24; 2Th 2:9; cf. Rev 19:20. *fire . . . from heaven.* See 1Ki 18:24–39.

13:14 *set up an image.* Cf. Da 3:1–11; 2Th 2:4.

13:15 *it could speak.* Belief in statues that could speak is widely attested in ancient literature. Ventriloquism and other forms of deception were common.

13:16 *mark.* Whatever its origin—possibly the branding of slaves or enemy soldiers, the sealing and stamping of official documents, or the sign of the cross on the forehead of a new Christian—the mark of the beast apparently symbolized allegiance to the demands of the imperial cult. In the final days of the antichrist it will be the ultimate test of loyalty (cf. v. 17; 14:9,11; 15:2; 16:2; 19:20; 20:4). It imitates the sealing of the servants of God in ch. 7.

13:17 *buy or sell.* Economic boycott against all faithful believers. *number of his name.* In ancient times the letters of the alphabet served for numbers. Riddles using numerical equivalents for names were popular.

13:18 *666.* Various schemes for decoding these numbers result in such names as Euanthas, Lateinos, and Nero Caesar (currently the favorite). Others take 666 as a symbol for the trinity of evil and imperfection—each digit falls short of the perfect number 7.

14:1 *Lamb.* See note on 5:6. *Mount Zion.* In the OT was first the fortress of the pre-Israelite city of Jerusalem (2Sa 5:7), captured by David and established as his capital. Later it became a virtual synonym for Jerusalem. In Revelation, as in Heb 12:22–24, it is the heavenly Jerusalem, the eternal

dwelling place of God and his people (cf. Gal 4:26). It comes down to the new earth in 21:2–3. *144,000.* See note on 7:4. *name.* Contrast 13:16–18.

14:2 *harps.* See note on 5:8.

14:3 *new song.* See note on 5:9. The theme is deliverance.

14:4 *not defile themselves with women.* Probably a symbolic description of believers who kept themselves from defiling relationships with the pagan world system. *follow the Lamb.* As his disciples (see Mt 19:21; Mk 8:34). *firstfruits.* See Lev 23:9–14. The word is used figuratively in the NT for the first converts in an area (Ro 16:5) and the first to rise from the dead (1Co 15:20). In Revelation believers are considered as a choice offering to God and the Lamb.

14:5 *No lie.* Contrast Ro 1:25; see Isa 53:9.

14:6 *eternal gospel.* The content of this "good news" is perhaps found in v. 7.

14:7 *him who made the heavens.* See Ex 20:11; Ps 146:6.

14:8 *Babylon the Great.* Ancient Babylon in Mesopotamia was the political, commercial and religious center of a world empire. It was noted for its luxury and moral decadence. The title "Babylon the Great" is taken from Da 4:30. According to some, it is used in Revelation (e.g., here and in 16:19; 17:5; 18:2,10,21) for Rome as the center of opposition to God and his people. According to others, it represents the whole political and religious system of the world in general. According to still others, it is to be understood as literal Babylon—rebuilt and restored. Babylon's fall is proclaimed in Isa 21:9; Jer 51:8. *maddening wine of her adulteries.* Here Babylon (Rome?) is pictured as a prostitute whose illicit relations are achieved by intoxication.

which made all the nations drink the maddening wine of her adulteries." [y]

9A third angel followed them and said in a loud voice: "If anyone worships the beast [z] and his image [a] and receives his mark on the forehead [b] or on the hand, 10he, too, will drink of the wine of God's fury, [c] which has been poured full strength into the cup of his wrath. [d] He will be tormented with burning sulfur [e] in the presence of the holy angels and of the Lamb. 11And the smoke of their torment rises for ever and ever. [f] There is no rest day or night [g] for those who worship the beast and his image, [h] or for anyone who receives the mark of his name." [i] 12This calls for patient endurance [j] on the part of the saints [k] who obey God's commandments [l] and remain faithful to Jesus.

13Then I heard a voice from heaven say, "Write: Blessed are the dead who die in the Lord [m] from now on."

"Yes," says the Spirit, [n] "they will rest from their labor, for their deeds will follow them."

The Harvest of the Earth

14I looked, and there before me was a white cloud, [o] and seated on the cloud was one "like a son of man" [r p] with a crown [q] of gold on his head and a sharp sickle in his hand. 15Then another angel came out of the temple [r] and called in a loud voice to him who was sitting on the cloud, "Take your sickle [s] and reap, because the time to reap has come, for the harvest [t] of the earth is ripe." 16So he who was seated on the cloud swung his sickle over the earth, and the earth was harvested.

17Another angel came out of the temple in heaven, and he too had a sharp sickle. [u] 18Still another angel, who had charge of the fire, came from the altar [v] and called in a loud voice to him who had the sharp sickle, "Take your sharp sickle [w] and gather the clusters of grapes from the earth's vine, because its grapes are ripe." 19The angel swung his sickle on the earth, gathered its grapes and threw them into the great winepress of God's wrath. [x] 20They were trampled in the winepress [y] outside the city, [z] and blood [a] flowed out of the press, rising as high as the horses' bridles for a distance of 1,600 stadia. [s]

Seven Angels With Seven Plagues

15 I saw in heaven another great and marvelous sign: [b] seven angels [c] with the seven last plagues [d]—last, because with them God's wrath is completed. 2And I saw what looked like a sea of glass [e] mixed with fire and, standing beside the sea, those who had been victorious [f] over the beast [g] and his image [h] and over the number of his name. [i] They held harps [j] given them by God 3and sang the

Cross references (center column)

14:8 [y]Rev 17:2,4; 18:3,9
14:9 [z]S Rev 13:12 [a]Rev 13:14 [b]S Rev 13:16
14:10 [c]Isa 51:17; Jer 25:15 [d]Jer 51:7; Rev 18:6 [e]S Rev 9:17
14:11 [f]Isa 34:10; Rev 19:3 [g]Rev 4:8 [h]ver 9; S Rev 13:12 [i]Rev 13:17
14:12 [j]S Rev 6:12 [k]Rev 13:10 [l]S Jn 14:15
14:13 [m]1Co 15:18; 1Th 4:16 [n]Rev 2:7; 22:17
14:14 [o]Mt 17:5 [p]Da 7:13; S Rev 1:13 [q]S Rev 6:2
14:15 [r]ver 17; Rev 11:19 [s]ver 18; Joel 3:13; Mk 4:29
14:17 [t]Jer 51:33 [u]S ver 15
14:18 [v]Rev 6:9; 8:5; 16:7 [w]S ver 15
14:19 [x]Rev 19:15
14:20 [y]ver 19; Isa 63:3; Joel 3:13; Rev 19:15 [z]Heb 13:12; Rev 11:8 [a]Ge 49:11; Dt 32:14
15:1 [b]Rev 12:1,3 [c]ver 6-8; Rev 16:1; 17:1; 21:9 [d]Lev 26:21; Rev 9:20
15:2 [e]Rev 4:6 [f]Rev 12:11 [g]Rev 13:1
[h]Rev 13:14 [i]Rev 13:17 [j]Rev 5:8; 14:2

r14 Daniel 7:13　　**s20** That is, about 180 miles (about 300 kilometers)

14:10 *cup of his wrath.* In the OT God's wrath is commonly pictured as a cup of wine to be drunk (Ps 75:8; Isa 51:17; Jer 25:15). It is not the outworking of impersonal laws of retribution, but the response of a righteous God to those who refuse his love and grace. *burning sulfur.* Sodom and Gomorrah were destroyed by a rain of burning sulfur (Ge 19:24). Ps 11:6 speaks of a similar fate for the wicked. The figure occurs elsewhere in the final chapters of Revelation (19:20; 20:10; 21:8).

14:11 *torment . . . for ever and ever.* Revelation offers no support for the doctrine of the annihilation of the wicked (also compare 19:20 with 20:10).

14:13 *Blessed.* The second beatitude (see note on 1:3).

14:14 *son of man.* See 1:13 and notes on Da 7:13; Mk 8:31. *crown of gold.* A victory wreath of gold. See note on 2:10 for the comparison between the victory crown and the royal crown. *sickle.* The Israelite sickle used for cutting grain was normally a flint or iron blade attached to a curved shaft of wood or bone.

14:15 *harvest of the earth.* Symbolizes in a general way the coming judgment (see Mt 13:30,40–42). Some interpreters think it refers to the ingathering of the righteous at the return of Christ.

14:18 *another angel, who had charge of the fire.* The angel of 8:3–5. Fire is commonly associated with judgment (see Mt 18:8; Lk 9:54; 2Th 1:7). *sharp sickle.* The context suggests (in contrast to the sickle of v. 14) the smaller

grape-knife with which the farmer cut the clusters of grapes from the vine.

14:19 *winepress.* A rock-hewn trough about eight feet square with a channel leading to a lower and smaller trough. Grapes were thrown into the upper vat and tramped with bare feet. The juice was collected in the lower vat. At times mechanical pressure was added. The treading of grapes was a common OT figure for the execution of divine wrath (see Isa 63:3; La 1:15; Joel 3:13).

14:20 *outside the city.* Bloodshed would defile the city (see Joel 3:12–14; Zec 14:1–4; cf. Heb 13:12). *1,600 stadia.* See NIV text note. It is approximately the length of Palestine from north to south.

15:1–8 Introduces the last of the three sevenfold series of judgments—the bowls of wrath (see note on 8:2).

15:1 *God's wrath.* See note on 6:16.

15:2 *sea of glass.* See note on 4:6. *victorious over the beast.* Cf. the saints' victory over the devil in 12:11. *number of his name.* See notes on 13:16–18. *harps.* See note on 5:8.

15:3 *song of Moses.* See Ex 15; Dt 32. Ex 15:1–18 was sung on Sabbath evenings in the synagogue to celebrate Israel's great deliverance from Egypt. *song of the Lamb.* The risen Lord triumphed over his enemies in securing spiritual deliverance for his followers (cf. Ps 22). *Great and marvelous are your deeds.* See Ex 15:11; Ps 92:5; 111:2. *Almighty.* See note on 1:8. *King of the ages.* See Jer 10:10; cf. 1Ti 1:17.

song of Moses[k] the servant of God[l] and the song of the Lamb:[m]

"Great and marvelous are your deeds,[n]
        Lord God Almighty.[o]
Just and true are your ways,[p]
        King of the ages.
[4]Who will not fear you, O Lord,[q]
        and bring glory to your name?[r]
For you alone are holy.
All nations will come
        and worship before you,[s]
for your righteous acts[t] have been
        revealed."

[5]After this I looked and in heaven the temple,[u] that is, the tabernacle of the Testimony,[v] was opened.[w] [6]Out of the temple[x] came the seven angels with the seven plagues.[y] They were dressed in clean, shining linen[z] and wore golden sashes around their chests.[a] [7]Then one of the four living creatures[b] gave to the seven angels[c] seven golden bowls filled with the wrath of God, who lives for ever and ever.[d] [8]And the temple was filled with smoke[e] from the glory of God and from his power, and no one could enter the temple[f] until the seven plagues of the seven angels were completed.

The Seven Bowls of God's Wrath

16 Then I heard a loud voice from the temple[g] saying to the seven angels,[h] "Go, pour out the seven bowls of God's wrath on the earth."[i]

[2]The first angel went and poured out his bowl on the land,[j] and ugly and painful sores[k] broke out on the people who had the mark of the beast and worshiped his image.[l]

[3]The second angel poured out his bowl

on the sea, and it turned into blood like that of a dead man, and every living thing in the sea died.[m]

[4]The third angel poured out his bowl on the rivers and springs of water,[n] and they became blood.[o] [5]Then I heard the angel in charge of the waters say:

"You are just in these judgments,[p]
        you who are and who were,[q] the
        Holy One,[r]
because you have so judged;[s]
[6]for they have shed the blood of your
        saints and prophets,[t]
and you have given them blood to
        drink[u] as they deserve."

[7]And I heard the altar[v] respond:

"Yes, Lord God Almighty,[w]
        true and just are your judgments."[x]

[8]The fourth angel[y] poured out his bowl on the sun,[z] and the sun was given power to scorch people with fire.[a] [9]They were seared by the intense heat and they cursed the name of God,[b] who had control over these plagues, but they refused to repent[c] and glorify him.[d]

[10]The fifth angel poured out his bowl on the throne of the beast,[e] and his kingdom was plunged into darkness.[f] Men gnawed their tongues in agony [11]and cursed[g] the God of heaven[h] because of their pains and their sores,[i] but they refused to repent of what they had done.[j]

[12]The sixth angel poured out his bowl on the great river Euphrates,[k] and its water was dried up to prepare the way[l] for the kings from the East.[m] [13]Then I saw

---

Cross references (center column):

15:3 [k]Ex 15:1 [l]Jos 1:1 [m]S Rev 5:9 [n]Ps 111:2 [o]S Rev 1:8 [p]Ps 145:17
15:4 [q]Jer 10:7 [r]Ps 86:9 [s]Isa 66:23 [t]Rev 19:8
15:5 [u]Rev 11:19 [v]Ex 38:21; Nu 1:50 [w]S Mt 3:16
15:6 [x]Rev 14:15 [y]S ver 1 [z]Eze 9:2; Da 10:5 [a]Rev 1:13
15:7 [b]S Rev 4:6 [c]S ver 1 [d]S Rev 1:18
15:8 [e]Isa 6:4 [f]Ex 40:34,35; 1Ki 8:10,11; 2Ch 5:13,14
16:1 [g]Rev 11:19 [h]S Rev 15:1 [i]ver 2-21; Ps 79:6; Zep 3:8
16:2 [j]Rev 8:7 [k]ver 11; Ex 9:9-11; Dt 28:35 [l]Rev 13:15-17; 14:9
16:3 [m]Ex 7:17-21; Rev 8:8,9; Rev 11:6
16:4 [n]Rev 8:10 [o]Ex 7:17-21
16:5 [p]Rev 15:3 [q]S Rev 1:4 [r]Rev 15:4 [s]Rev 6:10
16:6 [t]Lk 11:49-51 [u]Isa 49:26; Rev 17:6; 18:24
16:7 [v]Rev 6:9; 14:18 [w]S Rev 1:8 [x]Rev 15:3; 19:2
16:8 [y]Rev 8:12 [z]Rev 6:12 [a]Rev 14:18
16:9 [b]ver 11,21 [c]S Rev 2:21 [d]S Rev 11:13
16:10 [e]Rev 13:2 [f]Ex 10:21-23; Isa 8:22; Rev 8:12; 9:2
16:11 [g]ver 9,21 [h]Rev 11:13 [i]ver 2
[j]S Rev 2:21 16:12 [k]S Rev 9:14 [l]Isa 11:15,16 [m]Isa 41:2; 46:11

15:4 Universal recognition of God is taught in both the OT (Ps 86:9; Isa 45:22-23; Mal 1:11) and the NT (Php 2:9-11).

15:5 *tabernacle of the Testimony.* The dwelling place of God during the desert wandering of the Israelites (see Ex 40:34-35). It was so named because the ancient tent contained the two tablets of the Testimony brought down from Mount Sinai (Ex 32:15; 38:21; Dt 10:5).

15:6 *seven plagues.* The last series of plagues (see v. 1). *golden sashes.* Symbolic of royal and priestly functions.

15:7 *wrath of God.* Cf. 2Th 1:7-9.

15:8 *filled with smoke.* Cf. Ex 40:34; 1Ki 8:10-11; Eze 44:4. Smoke symbolizes the power and glory of God.

16:2 *land.* Compare the first four bowls (vv. 2-9) with the first four trumpets (8:7-12). *ugly and painful sores.* Cf. the boils and abscesses of the sixth Egyptian plague (Ex 9:9-11; also Job 2:7-8,13). *mark of the beast.* See 13:16 and note.

16:4 *rivers and springs of water.* Cf. 8:10-11; see also Ps 78:44.

16:5 *you who are and who were.* See note on 11:17; cf. Ex 3:14.

16:6 *given them blood to drink.* Punishment is tailored to fit the crime (see Isa 49:26).

16:7 *altar.* Personified.

16:8 *fire.* Often connected with judgment in Scripture (see Dt 28:22; 1Co 3:13; 2Pe 3:7).

16:9 *refused to repent.* In 11:13 the nations were dazzled into homage by the great earthquake. Here they curse the name of God.

16:10 *throne of the beast.* Cf. Satan's throne in 2:13. "Throne" occurs 42 times in Revelation. The other 40 references are to the throne of God. *gnawed their tongues.* Cf. the scene in 6:15-17.

16:11 *God of heaven.* Used in Da 2:44 of the sovereign God, who destroys the kingdoms of the world and establishes his universal and eternal reign.

16:12 *Euphrates.* See note on 9:14. *kings from the East.* Evidently Parthian rulers (17:15-18:24), to be distinguished from the "kings of the whole world" (v. 14), who wage the final war against Christ and the armies of heaven (19:11-21).

16:13 *frogs.* Lev 11:10 classifies the frog as an unclean

three evil[t] spirits[n] that looked like frogs;[o] they came out of the mouth of the dragon,[p] out of the mouth of the beast[q] and out of the mouth of the false prophet.[r] [14]They are spirits of demons[s] performing miraculous signs,[t] and they go out to the kings of the whole world,[u] to gather them for the battle[v] on the great day[w] of God Almighty.

[15]"Behold, I come like a thief![x] Blessed is he who stays awake[y] and keeps his clothes with him, so that he may not go naked and be shamefully exposed."[z]

[16]Then they gathered the kings together[a] to the place that in Hebrew[b] is called Armageddon.[c]

[17]The seventh angel poured out his bowl into the air,[d] and out of the temple[e] came a loud voice[f] from the throne, saying, "It is done!"[g] [18]Then there came flashes of lightning, rumblings, peals of thunder[h] and a severe earthquake.[i] No earthquake like it has ever occurred since man has been on earth,[j] so tremendous was the quake. [19]The great city[k] split into three parts, and the cities of the nations collapsed. God remembered[l] Babylon the Great[m] and gave her the cup filled with the wine of the fury of his wrath.[n] [20]Every island fled away and the mountains could not be found.[o] [21]From the sky huge hailstones[p] of about a hundred pounds each fell upon men. And they cursed God[q] on account of the plague of hail,[r] because the plague was so terrible.

The Woman on the Beast

17 One of the seven angels[s] who had the seven bowls[t] came and said to me, "Come, I will show you the punishment[u] of the great prostitute,[v] who sits on many waters.[w] [2]With her the kings of the

earth committed adultery and the inhabitants of the earth were intoxicated with the wine of her adulteries."[x]

[3]Then the angel carried me away in the Spirit[y] into a desert.[z] There I saw a woman sitting on a scarlet[a] beast that was covered with blasphemous names[b] and had seven heads and ten horns.[c] [4]The woman was dressed in purple and scarlet, and was glittering with gold, precious stones and pearls.[d] She held a golden cup[e] in her hand, filled with abominable things and the filth of her adulteries.[f] [5]This title was written on her forehead:

MYSTERY[g]
BABYLON THE GREAT[h]
THE MOTHER OF PROSTITUTES[i]
AND OF THE ABOMINATIONS OF THE EARTH.

[6]I saw that the woman was drunk with the blood of the saints,[j] the blood of those who bore testimony to Jesus.

When I saw her, I was greatly astonished. [7]Then the angel said to me: "Why are you astonished? I will explain to you the mystery[k] of the woman and of the beast she rides, which has the seven heads and ten horns.[l] [8]The beast, which you saw, once was, now is not, and will come up out of the Abyss[m] and go to his destruction.[n] The inhabitants of the earth[o] whose names have not been written in the book of life[p] from the creation of the world will be astonished[q] when they see the beast, because he once was, now is not, and yet will come.

[9]"This calls for a mind with wisdom.[r] The seven heads[s] are seven hills on which the woman sits. [10]They are also seven

---

16:13 [n]Rev 18:2
[o]Ex 8:6
[p]S Rev 12:3
[q]S Rev 13:1
[r]Rev 19:20;
20:10
16:14 [s]1Ti 4:1
[t]S Mt 24:24
[u]S Mt 24:14
[v]Rev 17:14;
19:19; 20:8
[w]S Rev 6:17
16:15
[x]S Lk 12:39
[y]Lk 12:37
[z]Rev 3:18
16:16 [a]ver 14
[b]Rev 9:11
[c]Jdg 5:19;
2Ki 23:29,30;
Zec 12:11
16:17 [d]Eph 2:2
[e]Rev 14:15
[f]Rev 11:15
[g]Rev 21:6
16:18 [h]S Rev 4:5
[i]S Rev 6:12
[j]Da 12:1;
Mt 24:21
16:19
[k]S Rev 17:18
[l]Rev 18:5
[m]S Rev 14:8
[n]Rev 14:10
16:20
[o]S Rev 6:14
16:21
[p]Eze 13:13;
38:22; Rev 8:7;
11:19 [q]ver 9,11
[r]Ex 9:23-25
17:1 [s]S Rev 15:1
[t]Rev 15:7
[u]Rev 16:19 [v]ver
5,15,16;
Isa 23:17;
Rev 19:2
[w]Jer 51:13

17:2 [x]S Rev 14:8
17:3 [y]S Rev 1:10
[z]Rev 12:6,14
[a]Rev 18:12,16
[b]Rev 13:1
[c]S Rev 12:3
17:4 [d]Eze 28:13;
Rev 18:16
[e]Jer 51:7;
Rev 18:6 [f]ver 2;
S Rev 14:8
17:5 [g]ver 7
[h]S Rev 14:8 [i]ver
1,2
17:6 [j]Rev 16:6;
18:24
17:7 [k]ver 5 [l]ver
3; S Rev 12:3

17:8 [m]S Lk 8:31 [n]Rev 13:10 [o]S Rev 3:10 [p]S Rev 20:12
[q]Rev 13:3 17:9 [r]Rev 13:18 [s]ver 3

[t]13 Greek unclean

---

animal. The imagery suggests the deceptive propaganda that will, in the last days, lead people to accept and support the cause of evil.
16:14 miraculous signs. Cf. 13:13. kings of the whole world. See 6:15. great day of God. See 19:11–21 for this battle.
16:15 Blessed. The third beatitude (see note on 1:3).
16:16 Armageddon. Probably stands for Har Mageddon, "the mountain of Megiddo" (see note on Jdg 5:19). Many see no specific geographical reference in the designation and take it to be a symbol of the final overthrow of evil by God.
17:1 seven angels. Cf. 15:1; 16. great prostitute. See v. 18 for the angel's own identification of this symbol. In 17:5 the harlot is named "Babylon the Great." sits on many waters. See Ps 137:1; Jer 51:13.
17:2 wine of her adulteries. See note on 14:8; cf. 18:3; Isa 23:17; Jer 51:7.
17:3 in the Spirit. In a state of spiritual ecstasy (see notes on 1:10; 4:2; see also 21:10). scarlet beast. The beast that rose out of the sea in ch. 13. blasphemous names. See note on

13:1.
17:5 MYSTERY. Possibly not a part of the title. The opening part of the verse would then be translated "This mysterious title was written on her forehead: BABYLON . . ."
17:6 saints . . . those who bore testimony. See 6:9.
17:7 mystery. See note on 10:7.
17:8 once was, now is not, and will come. An obvious imitation of the description of the Lamb (1:18; 2:8). Cf. the description of God in 1:4,8; 4:8. Here the phrase seems to mean that the beast appeared once, is not presently evident, but will in the future again make his presence known. Evil is persistent. Abyss. See note on 9:1. book of life. See note on 3:5. go to his destruction. Although evil is real and persistent, there is no uncertainty about its ultimate fate.
17:9 seven hills. It is perhaps significant that Rome began as a network of seven hill settlements on the left bank of the Tiber. Her designation as the city on seven hills is commonplace among Roman writers (e.g., Virgil, Martial, Cicero).
17:10 seven kings. That seven heads symbolize both seven hills and seven kings illustrates the fluidity of apocalyptic

kings. Five have fallen, one is, the other has not yet come; but when he does come, he must remain for a little while. 11 The beast who once was, and now is not,[t] is an eighth king. He belongs to the seven and is going to his destruction.

12 "The ten horns[u] you saw are ten kings who have not yet received a kingdom, but who for one hour[v] will receive authority as kings along with the beast. 13 They have one purpose and will give their power and authority to the beast.[w] 14 They will make war[x] against the Lamb, but the Lamb will overcome[y] them because he is Lord of lords and King of kings[z]—and with him will be his called, chosen[a] and faithful followers."

15 Then the angel said to me, "The waters[b] you saw, where the prostitute sits, are peoples, multitudes, nations and languages.[c] 16 The beast and the ten horns[d] you saw will hate the prostitute.[e] They will bring her to ruin[f] and leave her naked;[g] they will eat her flesh[h] and burn her with fire.[i] 17 For God has put it into their hearts[j] to accomplish his purpose by agreeing to give the beast their power to rule,[k] until God's words are fulfilled.[l] 18 The woman you saw is the great city[m] that rules over the kings of the earth."

The Fall of Babylon

18 After this I saw another angel[n] coming down from heaven.[o] He had great authority, and the earth was illuminated by his splendor.[p] 2 With a mighty voice he shouted:

"Fallen! Fallen is Babylon the Great![q]
She has become a home for demons
and a haunt for every evil[u] spirit,[r]
a haunt for every unclean and
detestable bird.[s]
3 For all the nations have drunk
the maddening wine of her
adulteries.[t]
The kings of the earth committed
adultery with her,[u]
and the merchants of the earth grew
rich[v] from her excessive
luxuries."[w]

4 Then I heard another voice from heaven say:

"Come out of her, my people,[x]
so that you will not share in her sins,
so that you will not receive any of
her plagues;[y]
5 for her sins are piled up to heaven,[z]
and God has remembered[a] her
crimes.
6 Give back to her as she has given;
pay her back[b] double[c] for what she
has done.
Mix her a double portion from her
own cup.[d]
7 Give her as much torture and grief
as the glory and luxury she gave
herself.[e]
In her heart she boasts,
'I sit as queen; I am not a widow,
and I will never mourn.'[f]
8 Therefore in one day[g] her plagues will
overtake her:
death, mourning and famine.
She will be consumed by fire,[h]
for mighty is the Lord God who
judges her.

9 "When the kings of the earth who committed adultery with her[i] and shared her luxury[j] see the smoke of her burning,[k] they will weep and mourn over her.[l] 10 Terrified at her torment, they will stand far off[m] and cry:

" 'Woe! Woe, O great city,[n]
O Babylon, city of power!
In one hour[o] your doom has come!'

11 "The merchants[p] of the earth will weep and mourn[q] over her because no

[u]2 Greek *unclean*

17:11 [t]ver 8
17:12 [u]S Rev 12:3 [v]Rev 18:10,17,19
17:13 [w]ver 17
17:14 [x]S Rev 16:14 [y]S Jn 16:33 [z]S 1Ti 6:15 [a]Mt 22:14
17:15 [b]ver 1; Isa 8:7; Jer 47:2 [c]S Rev 13:7
17:16 [d]S Rev 12:3 [e]ver 1 [f]Rev 18:17,19 [g]Eze 16:37,39 [h]Rev 19:18 [i]Rev 18:8
17:17 [j]2Co 8:16 [k]ver 13 [l]Jer 39:16; Rev 10:7
17:18 [m]Rev 16:19; 18:10,18,19,21
18:1 [n]Rev 17:1 [o]Rev 10:1; 20:1 [p]Eze 43:2
18:2 [q]S Rev 14:8 [r]Rev 16:13 [s]Isa 13:21,22; 34:11,13-15; Jer 50:39; 51:37; Zep 2:14,15
18:3 [t]S Rev 14:8 [u]Rev 17:2 [v]ver 11,15,23; Eze 27:9-25 [w]ver 7,9
18:4 [x]Isa 48:20; Jer 50:8; 51:6,9, 45; 2Co 6:17 [y]Ge 19:15
18:5 [z]2Ch 28:9; Ezr 9:6; Jer 51:9 [a]Rev 16:19
18:6 [b]Ps 137:8; Jer 50:15,29 [c]Isa 40:2 [d]Rev 14:10; 16:19; 17:4
18:7 [e]Eze 28:2-8 [f]Ps 10:6; Isa 47:7, 8; Zep 2:15
18:8 [g]ver 10; Isa 9:14; 47:9; Jer 50:31,32 [h]Rev 17:16
18:9 [i]ver 3; Rev 14:8; 17:2,4 [j]ver 3,7 [k]ver 18; Rev 14:11; 19:3 [l]Jer 51:8; Eze 26:17,18
18:10 [m]ver 15,17 [n]ver 16,19 [o]ver 17; Rev 17:12
18:11 [p]Eze 27:27 [q]ver 15,19; Eze 27:31

symbolism, unless the hills are figurative for royal (or political) power. *Five . . . one . . . the other.* Taken (1) as seven actual Roman emperors, (2) as seven secular empires or (3) symbolically as the power of the Roman empire as a whole.
17:11 *now is not.* Cf. 13:3. *eighth king.* The antichrist, who plays the role of a king ("belongs to the seven") but is in reality part of the cosmic struggle between God and Satan.
17:12 *one hour.* A short time.
17:14 *Lord of lords and King of kings.* Emphasizes the supreme sovereignty of the Lamb (cf. Dt 10:17; Ps 136:2–3; Da 2:47; 1Ti 6:15).
17:18 *great city.* Cf. 17:1; see notes on 11:8; 14:8.
18:1 *earth was illuminated by his splendor.* Cf. Ex 34:29–35; Ps 104:2; Eze 43:1–5; 1Ti 6:16.
18:2 *Fallen is Babylon.* Cf. Isa 21:9; Jer 51:8; see notes on 11:8; 14:8.
18:3 *wine of her adulteries.* See note on 14:8.
18:4 *Come out of her.* A common prophetic warning (cf. Isa 52:11; Jer 51:45; 2Co 6:17).
18:6 *double.* In full, sufficiently (see note on Isa 40:2). *her own cup.* See 17:4.
18:7 *I am not a widow.* A claim that the men of Babylon have not died on battlefields.
18:9–20 Three groups lament: (1) kings (v. 9), (2) merchants (v. 11) and (3) seamen (v. 17). The passage is modeled after Ezekiel's lament over Tyre (Eze 27). Fifteen of the 29 commodities in vv. 12–13 are also listed in Eze 27:12–22.
18:9 *kings . . . weep and mourn over her.* Probably because of their own great financial loss (see v. 11).

one buys their cargoes any more[r] — ¹²cargoes of gold, silver, precious stones and pearls; fine linen, purple, silk and scarlet cloth; every sort of citron wood, and articles of every kind made of ivory, costly wood, bronze, iron and marble;[s] ¹³cargoes of cinnamon and spice, of incense, myrrh and frankincense, of wine and olive oil, of fine flour and wheat; cattle and sheep; horses and carriages; and bodies and souls of men.[t]

¹⁴"They will say, 'The fruit you longed for is gone from you. All your riches and splendor have vanished, never to be recovered.' ¹⁵The merchants who sold these things and gained their wealth from her[u] will stand far off,[v] terrified at her torment. They will weep and mourn[w] ¹⁶and cry out:

" 'Woe! Woe, O great city,[x]
  dressed in fine linen, purple and
    scarlet,
  and glittering with gold, precious
    stones and pearls![y]
¹⁷In one hour[z] such great wealth has
    been brought to ruin!'[a]

"Every sea captain, and all who travel by ship, the sailors, and all who earn their living from the sea,[b] will stand far off.[c] ¹⁸When they see the smoke of her burning,[d] they will exclaim, 'Was there ever a city like this great city?'[f] ¹⁹They will throw dust on their heads,[g] and with weeping and mourning[h] cry out:

" 'Woe! Woe, O great city,[i]
  where all who had ships on the sea
    became rich through her wealth!
  In one hour she has been brought to
    ruin!'[j]
²⁰Rejoice over her, O heaven![k]
  Rejoice, saints and apostles and
    prophets!
  God has judged her for the way she
    treated you.' "[l]

²¹Then a mighty angel[m] picked up a boulder the size of a large millstone and threw it into the sea,[n] and said:

"With such violence
  the great city[o] of Babylon will be
    thrown down,
  never to be found again.
²²The music of harpists and musicians,
    flute players and trumpeters,
  will never be heard in you again.[p]
No workman of any trade
  will ever be found in you again.
The sound of a millstone
  will never be heard in you again.[q]
²³The light of a lamp
  will never shine in you again.
The voice of bridegroom and bride
  will never be heard in you again.[r]
Your merchants were the world's great
    men.[s]
  By your magic spell[t] all the nations
    were led astray.
²⁴In her was found the blood of prophets
    and of the saints,[u]
  and of all who have been killed on
    the earth."[v]

Hallelujah!

19 After this I heard what sounded like the roar of a great multitude[w] in heaven shouting:

"Hallelujah![x]
Salvation[y] and glory and power[z]
    belong to our God,
² for true and just are his judgments.[a]
He has condemned the great prostitute[b]
  who corrupted the earth by her
    adulteries.
He has avenged on her the blood of his
    servants."[c]

³And again they shouted:

"Hallelujah![d]
The smoke from her goes up for ever
    and ever."[e]

⁴The twenty-four elders[f] and the four living creatures[g] fell down[h] and worshiped God, who was seated on the throne. And they cried:

"Amen, Hallelujah!"[i]

Cross references (center column):

18:11 [r]S ver 3
18:12 [s]Eze 27:12-22; Rev 17:4
18:13 [t]Eze 27:13; 1Ti 1:10
18:15 [u]S ver 3 [v]ver 10,17 [w]ver 11,19; Eze 27:31
18:16 [x]ver 10,19 [y]Rev 17:4
18:17 [z]ver 10; Rev 17:12 [a]Rev 17:16 [b]Eze 27:28-30 [c]ver 10,15
18:18 [d]ver 9; Rev 19:3 [e]S Rev 17:18 [f]Eze 27:32; Rev 13:4
18:19 [g]Jos 7:6; La 2:10; Eze 27:30 [h]ver 11,15; Eze 27:31 [i]ver 10,16; Rev 17:18 [j]Rev 17:16
18:20 [k]Jer 51:48; S Rev 12:12 [l]Rev 19:2
18:21 [m]Rev 5:2; 10:1 [n]Jer 51:63

18:22 [o]S Rev 17:18 [p]Isa 24:8; Eze 26:13 [q]Jer 25:10
18:23 [r]Jer 7:34; 16:9; 25:10 [s]ver 3; Isa 23:8 [t]Na 3:4
18:24 [u]Rev 16:6; 17:6 [v]Jer 51:49; Mt 23:35
19:1 [w]ver 6; Rev 11:15 [x]ver 3, 4,6 [y]Rev 7:10; 12:10 [z]Rev 4:11; 7:12
19:2 [a]Rev 16:7 [b]S Rev 17:1 [c]S Rev 6:10
19:3 [d]ver 1,4,6 [e]Isa 34:10; Rev 14:11
19:4 [f]S Rev 4:4 [g]S Rev 4:6 [h]S Rev 4:10 [i]ver 1,3,6

18:12 *purple.* An expensive dye since it must be extracted a drop at a time from the murex shellfish. *citron wood.* An expensive dark wood from north Africa—used for inlay work in costly furniture. *marble.* Used to decorate public buildings and the homes of the very rich.
18:13 *myrrh and frankincense.* Brought by the Magi as gifts for the infant Jesus (Mt 2:11). *bodies and souls of men.* Slave trade.
18:17 *sea captain.* The pilot of the ship rather than the owner. Both are mentioned in Ac 27:11.
18:19 *throw dust on their heads.* An act of sorrow and dismay (see Eze 27:30). *In one hour.* See vv. 10,17.

18:21 *large millstone.* Similar to the large millstone of Mk 9:42, which was actually a "donkey millstone" (one large enough to require a donkey to turn it).
18:24 *blood of prophets.* See 6:10; 17:6; 19:2; cf. Eze 24:7.
19:1 *great multitude.* See note on 7:9. *Hallelujah!* Occurs four times in vv. 1–6 but nowhere else in the NT. It is derived from two Hebrew words meaning "Praise the LORD" (see NIV text note on Ps 135:1).
19:4 *twenty-four elders and the four living creatures.* See notes on 4:4,6.

⁵Then a voice came from the throne, saying:

"Praise our God,
all you his servants, [j]
you who fear him,
both small and great!" [k]

⁶Then I heard what sounded like a great multitude, [l] like the roar of rushing waters [m] and like loud peals of thunder, shouting:

"Hallelujah! [n]
For our Lord God Almighty [o] reigns. [p]
⁷Let us rejoice and be glad
and give him glory! [q]
For the wedding of the Lamb [r] has come,
and his bride [s] has made herself ready.
⁸Fine linen, [t] bright and clean,
was given her to wear."

(Fine linen stands for the righteous acts [u] of the saints.)

⁹Then the angel said to me, [v] "Write: [w] 'Blessed are those who are invited to the wedding supper of the Lamb!' " [x] And he added, "These are the true words of God." [y]

¹⁰At this I fell at his feet to worship him. [z] But he said to me, "Do not do it! I am a fellow servant with you and with your brothers who hold to the testimony of Jesus. Worship God! [a] For the testimony of Jesus [b] is the spirit of prophecy."

The Rider on the White Horse

¹¹I saw heaven standing open [c] and there before me was a white horse, whose rider [d] is called Faithful and True. [e] With justice he judges and makes war. [f] ¹²His eyes are like blazing fire, [g] and on his head are many crowns. [h] He has a name written on him [i] that no one knows but he himself. [j] ¹³He is dressed in a robe dipped in blood, [k] and his name is the Word of God. [l] ¹⁴The armies of heaven were following him, riding on white horses and dressed in fine linen, [m] white [n] and clean. ¹⁵Out of his mouth comes a sharp sword [o] with which to strike down [p] the nations. "He will rule them with an iron scepter." [v][q] He treads the winepress [r] of the fury of the wrath of God Almighty. ¹⁶On his robe and on his thigh he has this name written: [s]

KING OF KINGS AND LORD OF LORDS. [t]

¹⁷And I saw an angel standing in the sun, who cried in a loud voice to all the birds [u] flying in midair, [v] "Come, [w] gather together for the great supper of God, [x] ¹⁸so that you may eat the flesh of kings, generals, and mighty men, of horses and their riders, and the flesh of all people, [y] free and slave, [z] small and great." [a]

¹⁹Then I saw the beast [b] and the kings of the earth [c] and their armies gathered together to make war against the rider on the horse [d] and his army. ²⁰But the beast was captured, and with him the false prophet [e] who had performed the miraculous signs [f] on his behalf. [g] With these signs he had deluded [h] those who had received the mark of the beast [i] and worshiped his image. [j] The two of them were thrown alive into the fiery lake [k] of burning sulfur. [l] ²¹The rest of them were killed with the sword [m] that came out of the mouth of the rider on the horse, [n] and all the birds [o] gorged themselves on their flesh.

19:5 /Ps 134:1
[k]ver 18;
Ps 115:13;
Rev 11:18; 13:16;
20:12
19:6 /ver 1;
Rev 11:15
[m]S Rev 1:15 [n]ver
1,3,4 [o]S Rev 1:8
[p]Rev 11:15
19:7
[q]S Rev 11:13 [r]ver
9; Mt 22:2;
25:10; Eph 5:32
[s]Rev 21:2,9;
22:17
19:8 [t]ver 14:
Rev 15:6
[u]Isa 61:10;
Eze 44:17;
Zec 3:4; Rev 15:4
19:9 [v]ver 10
[w]Rev 1:19
[x]Lk 14:15
[y]Rev 21:5; 22:6
19:10 [z]Rev 22:8
[a]Ac 10:25,26;
Rev 22:9
[b]S Rev 1:2
19:11 [c]S Mt 3:16
[d]ver 19,21;
Rev 6:2 [e]Rev 3:14
/Ex 15:3;
Ps 96:13; Isa 11:4
19:12
[g]S Rev 1:14
[h]Rev 6:2; 12:3
[i]ver 16
/S Rev 2:17
19:13 [k]Isa 63:2,3
[l]Jn 1:1
19:14 [m]ver 8
[n]S Rev 3:4
19:15 [o]ver 21;
S Rev 1:16
[p]Isa 11:4;
2Th 2:8 [q]Ps 2:9;
Rev 2:27; 12:5
[r]S Rev 14:20
19:16 [s]ver 12
[t]S 1Ti 6:15
19:17 [u]ver 21
Rev 8:13; 14:6
[w]Jer 12:9;
Eze 39:17
[x]Isa 34:6;
Jer 46:10
19:18
[y]Eze 39:18-20
[z]Rev 6:15
[a]S ver 5
19:19
[b]S Rev 13:1
[c]Rev 16:14,16
[d]ver 11,21
19:20 [e]Rev 16:13
/S Mt 24:24
[g]Rev 13:12
[h]Rev 13:14
[i]Rev 13:16

/Rev 13:15 [k]Da 7:11; Rev 20:10,14,15; 21:8 /S Rev 9:17
19:21 [m]ver 15 S Rev 1:16 [n]ver 11,19 [o]ver 17

[v]15 Psalm 2:9

19:7 *wedding of the Lamb.* The imagery of a wedding to express the intimate relationship between God and his people has its roots in the prophetic literature of the OT (e.g., Isa 54:5–7; Hos 2:19). Cf. the NT usage (Mt 22:2–14; Eph 5:32).
19:9 *Blessed.* The fourth beatitude (see note on 1:3).
19:10 *fell at his feet.* See note on 1:17; cf. Ac 10:25. *spirit.* Essence.
19:11 *white horse.* Probably not the white horse of 6:2. The context here indicates that the rider is Christ returning as Warrior-Messiah-King.
19:12 *name written.* A secret name whose meaning is veiled from all created beings.
19:13 *robe dipped in blood.* Either the blood of the enemy shed in conflict (cf. 14:14–20; Isa 63:1–3), or the blood of Christ shed to atone for sin.
19:14 *armies of heaven.* Angelic beings (cf. Dt 33:2; Ps 68:17); possibly also believers (cf. 17:14).
19:15 *sharp sword.* See note on 1:16. *iron scepter.* See note on 2:27. *winepress.* See note on 14:19.
19:16 KING OF KINGS. See note on 17:14.
19:17 *great supper of God.* A grim contrast to the "wedding supper of the Lamb" (v. 9; cf. Eze 39:17–20).
19:20 *beast . . . false prophet.* See notes on 13:1,11. *fiery lake of burning sulfur.* See 20:10,14–15; 21:8. Punishment by fire is prominent in both Biblical and non-Biblical Jewish writings (e.g., 1 Enoch 54:1). Although the designation *gehenna* is not used here, this is what John refers to (see note on Mt 5:22). Originally the site of a cultic shrine where human sacrifices were offered (2Ki 16:3; 23:10; Jer 7:31), it came to be equated with the "hell" of final judgment in apocalyptic literature.
19:21 *birds gorged themselves.* The "great supper of God" of vv. 17–18.

The Thousand Years

20 And I saw an angel coming down out of heaven,[p] having the key[q] to the Abyss[r] and holding in his hand a great chain. [2]He seized the dragon, that ancient serpent, who is the devil, or Satan,[s] and bound him for a thousand years.[t] [3]He threw him into the Abyss,[u] and locked and sealed[v] it over him, to keep him from deceiving the nations[w] anymore until the thousand years were ended. After that, he must be set free for a short time.

[4]I saw thrones[x] on which were seated those who had been given authority to judge.[y] And I saw the souls of those who had been beheaded[z] because of their testimony for Jesus[a] and because of the word of God.[b] They had not worshiped the beast[c] or his image and had not received his mark on their foreheads or their hands.[d] They came to life and reigned[e] with Christ a thousand years. [5](The rest of the dead did not come to life until the thousand years were ended.) This is the first resurrection.[f] [6]Blessed[g] and holy are those who have part in the first resurrection. The second death[h] has no power over them, but they will be priests[i] of God and of Christ and will reign with him[j] for a thousand years.

Satan's Doom

[7]When the thousand years are over,[k] Satan will be released from his prison [8]and will go out to deceive the nations[l] in the four corners of the earth[m]—Gog and Magog[n]—to gather them for battle.[o] In number they are like the sand on the sea-shore.[p] [9]They marched across the breadth of the earth and surrounded[q] the camp of God's people, the city he loves.[r] But fire came down from heaven[s] and devoured them. [10]And the devil, who deceived them,[t] was thrown into the lake of burning sulfur,[u] where the beast[v] and the false prophet[w] had been thrown. They will be tormented day and night for ever and ever.[x]

The Dead Are Judged

[11]Then I saw a great white throne[y] and him who was seated on it. Earth and sky fled from his presence,[z] and there was no place for them. [12]And I saw the dead, great and small,[a] standing before the throne, and books were opened.[b] Another book was opened, which is the book of life.[c] The dead were judged[d] according to what they had done[e] as recorded in the books. [13]The sea gave up the dead that were in it, and death and Hades[f] gave up the dead[g] that were in them, and each person was judged according to what he had done.[h] [14]Then death[i] and Hades[j] were thrown into the lake of fire.[k] The lake of fire is the second death.[l] [15]If anyone's name was not found written in the book of life,[m] he was thrown into the lake of fire.

The New Jerusalem

21 Then I saw a new heaven and a new earth,[n] for the first heaven and the first earth had passed away,[o] and there was no longer any sea. [2]I saw the

20:1 pRev 10:1; 18:1 qRev 1:18 rS Lk 8:31
20:2 sS Mt 4:10 tIsa 24:22; S 2Pe 2:4
20:3 uver 1 vDa 6:17; Mt 27:66 wver 8, 10; Rev 12:9
20:4 xDa 7:9 yMt 19:28; Rev 3:21 zRev 6:9 aS Rev 1:2 bS Heb 4:12 cS Rev 13:12 dS Rev 13:16 ever 6; Rev 22:5
20:5 fver 6; Lk 14:14; Php 3:11; 1Th 4:16
20:6 gRev 14:13 hS Rev 2:11 iS 1Pe 2:5 /ver 4; Rev 22:5
20:7 kver 2
20:8 lver 3,10; Rev 12:9 mIsa 11:12; Eze 7:2; Rev 7:1 nEze 38:2; 39:1 oS Rev 16:14
20:9 pEze 38:9,15; Heb 11:12 qEze 38:9, 16 rPs 87:2 sEze 38:22; 39:6; S Rev 13:13
20:10 tver 3,8; Rev 12:9; 19:20 uS Rev 9:17 vRev 16:13 wRev 16:13 xRev 14:10,11
20:11 yS Rev 4:2 zS Rev 6:14
20:12 aS Rev 19:5 bDa 7:10 cver 15; Ex 32:32; Dt 29:20; Da 12:1; Mal 3:16; Lk 10:20; Rev 3:5; 21:27 dRev 11:18 eJer 17:10; S Mt 16:27
20:13 fRev 1:18; 6:8 gIsa 26:19 hS Mt 16:27 **20:14** iCo 15:26 jver 13 kS Rev 19:20 lS Rev 2:11 **20:15** mS ver 12 **21:1** nS 2Pe 3:13 oS Rev 6:14

20:1—22:21 These last three chapters reflect many of the subjects and themes of the first three chapters of Genesis.
20:1 *Abyss.* See note on 9:1.
20:2 *dragon.* See note on 12:3. *ancient serpent.* See 12:15; Ge 3:1–5. *thousand years.* The millennium (from the Latin *mille,* "thousand," and *annus,* "year"). It is taken literally by some as 1,000 actual years, while others interpret it metaphorically as a long but undetermined period of time. There are three basic approaches to the subject of the millennium: 1. Amillennialism: The millennium describes the present reign of the souls of deceased believers with Christ in heaven. The present form of God's kingdom will be followed by Christ's return, the general resurrection, the final judgment and Christ's continuing reign over the perfect kingdom on the new earth in the eternal state. 2. Premillennialism: The present form of God's kingdom is moving toward a grand climax when Christ will return, the first resurrection will occur and his kingdom will find expression in a literal, visible reign of peace and righteousness on the earth in space-time history. After the final resurrection, the last judgment and the renewal of the heavens and the earth, this future, temporal kingdom will merge into the eternal kingdom, and the Lord will reign forever on the new earth. 3. Postmillennialism: The world will eventually be Christian-ized, resulting in a long period of peace and prosperity called the millennium. This future period will close with Christ's second coming, the resurrection of the dead, the final judgment and the eternal state.
20:3 *free for a short time.* See vv. 7–10.
20:4 *souls of those who had been beheaded.* See 6:9–11. *his mark.* See note on 13:16. *came to life.* The "first resurrection" (v. 5).
20:5 *rest of the dead.* Either the wicked or everyone except the martyrs (see v. 4).
20:6 *Blessed.* The fifth beatitude (see note on 1:3). *second death.* Defined in v. 14 as the "lake of fire" (cf. 21:8).
20:7 *thousand years.* See note on v. 2.
20:8 *Gog and Magog.* Symbolize the nations of the world as they band together for a final assault on God. The OT background is Eze 38–39.
20:10 *tormented day and night.* See note on 14:11; cf. 14:10.
20:12 *book of life.* See note on 3:5. *judged according to what they had done.* The principle of judgment on the basis of works is taught in Ps 62:12; Jer 17:10; Ro 2:6; 1Pe 1:17 and elsewhere.
20:13 *death and Hades.* See 6:8 and note.
20:14–15 *lake of fire.* See note on 19:20.

Holy City,[p] the new Jerusalem, coming down out of heaven from God,[q] prepared as a bride[r] beautifully dressed for her husband. [3]And I heard a loud voice from the throne saying, "Now the dwelling of God is with men, and he will live with them.[s] They will be his people, and God himself will be with them and be their God.[t] [4]He will wipe every tear from their eyes.[u] There will be no more death[v] or mourning or crying or pain,[w] for the old order of things has passed away."[x]

[5]He who was seated on the throne[y] said, "I am making everything new!"[z] Then he said, "Write this down, for these words are trustworthy and true."[a]

[6]He said to me: "It is done.[b] I am the Alpha and the Omega,[c] the Beginning and the End. To him who is thirsty I will give to drink without cost[d] from the spring of the water of life.[e] [7]He who overcomes[f] will inherit all this, and I will be his God and he will be my son.[g] [8]But the cowardly, the unbelieving, the vile, the murderers, the sexually immoral, those who practice magic arts, the idolaters and all liars[h]—their place will be in the fiery lake of burning sulfur.[i] This is the second death."[j]

[9]One of the seven angels who had the seven bowls full of the seven last plagues[k] came and said to me, "Come, I will show you the bride,[l] the wife of the Lamb." [10]And he carried me away[m] in the Spirit[n] to a mountain great and high, and showed me the Holy City, Jerusalem, coming down out of heaven from God.[o] [11]It shone with the glory of God,[p] and its brilliance was like that of a very precious jewel, like a jasper,[q] clear as crystal.[r] [12]It had a great, high wall with twelve gates,[s] and with twelve angels at the gates. On the gates were written the names of the twelve tribes of Israel.[t] [13]There were three gates on the east, three on the north, three on the south and three on the west. [14]The wall of the city had twelve foundations,[u]

and on them were the names of the twelve apostles[v] of the Lamb.

[15]The angel who talked with me had a measuring rod[w] of gold to measure the city, its gates[x] and its walls. [16]The city was laid out like a square, as long as it was wide. He measured the city with the rod and found it to be 12,000 stadia[w] in length, and as wide and high as it is long. [17]He measured its wall and it was 144 cubits[x] thick,[y] by man's[y] measurement, which the angel was using. [18]The wall was made of jasper,[z] and the city of pure gold, as pure as glass.[a] [19]The foundations of the city walls were decorated with every kind of precious stone.[b] The first foundation was jasper,[c] the second sapphire, the third chalcedony, the fourth emerald, [20]the fifth sardonyx, the sixth carnelian,[d] the seventh chrysolite, the eighth beryl, the ninth topaz, the tenth chrysoprase, the eleventh jacinth, and the twelfth amethyst.[z] [21]The twelve gates[e] were twelve pearls,[f] each gate made of a single pearl. The great street of the city was of pure gold, like transparent glass.[g]

[22]I did not see a temple[h] in the city, because the Lord God Almighty[i] and the Lamb[j] are its temple. [23]The city does not need the sun or the moon to shine on it, for the glory of God[k] gives it light,[l] and the Lamb[m] is its lamp. [24]The nations will walk by its light, and the kings of the earth will bring their splendor into it.[n] [25]On no day will its gates[o] ever be shut,[p] for there will be no night there.[q] [26]The glory and honor of the nations will be brought into it.[r] [27]Nothing impure will ever enter it, nor will anyone who does what is shameful or deceitful,[s] but only those whose

Cross references (center column):

21:2 [p]ver 10; Ne 11:18; Isa 52:1; Rev 11:2; 22:19
over 10; Heb 11:10; 12:22; Rev 3:12
[r]S Rev 19:7
21:3 [s]Ex 25:8; 2Ch 6:18; Eze 48:35; Zec 2:10
[t]S 2Co 6:16
21:4 [u]S Rev 7:17
[v]Isa 25:8; 1Co 15:26; Rev 20:14
[w]Isa 35:10; 65:19
[x]S 2Co 5:17
21:5 [y]Rev 4:9; 20:11 [z]ver 4
[a]Rev 19:9; 22:6
21:6 [b]Rev 16:17
[c]Rev 1:8; 22:13
[d]Isa 55:1
[e]S Jn 4:10
21:7 [f]S Jn 16:33
[g]ver 3; 2Sa 7:14; 2Co 6:16; S Ro 8:14
21:8 [h]ver 27; Ps 5:6; 1Co 6:9; Heb 12:14; Rev 22:15
[i]S Rev 9:17
[j]S Rev 2:11
21:9 [k]S Rev 15:1, 6,7 [l]S Rev 19:7
21:10 [m]Eze 40:2; Rev 17:3
[n]S Rev 1:10
[o]S ver 2
21:11 [p]ver 23; Isa 60:1,2; Eze 43:2; Rev 15:8; 22:5
[q]ver 18,19; Rev 4:3 [r]Rev 4:6
21:12 [s]ver 15,21, 25; Rev 22:14
[t]Eze 48:30-34
21:14 [u]S Eph 2:20; Heb 11:10

[v]Ac 1:26; Eph 2:20
21:15 [w]Eze 40:3; Rev 11:1 [x]S ver 12
21:17 [y]Rev 13:18
21:18 [z]S ver 11
[a]ver 21
21:19
[b]Ex 28:17-20; Isa 54:11,12; Eze 28:13 [c]S ver 11
21:20 [d]Rev 4:3
21:21 [e]S ver 12
[f]Isa 54:12 [g]ver 18
21:22 [h]Jn 4:21, 23 [i]S Rev 1:8
[j]S Rev 5:6

21:23 [k]S ver 11 [l]Isa 24:23; 60:19,20; Rev 22:5 [m]S Rev 5:6
21:24 [n]ver 26; Isa 60:3,5 21:25 [o]S ver 12 [p]Isa 60:11
[q]Zec 14:7; Rev 22:5 21:26 [r]ver 24 21:27 [s]Isa 52:1; Joel 3:17; Rev 22:14,15

[w]16 That is, about 1,400 miles (about 2,200 kilometers)
[x]17 That is, about 200 feet (about 65 meters) [y]17 Or high [z]20 The precise identification of some of these precious stones is uncertain.

Footnotes (bottom):

21:2—22:5 The "Holy City" combines elements of Jerusalem, the temple and the Garden of Eden.
21:2 bride. See note on 19:7.
21:3 dwelling of God. See Lev 26:11–12; Eze 37:27; 2Co 6:16.
21:4 wipe every tear. See 7:17; Isa 25:8.
21:6 the Alpha and the Omega. See note on 1:8. water of life. Cf. Ps 36:9.
21:7 He who overcomes. Cf. the emphasis on overcoming in the seven letters (2:7,11,17,26; 3:5,12,21).
21:8 magic arts. Cf. Ac 19:19. The magical tradition in ancient times called for the mixing of various herbs to ward off evil. fiery lake of burning sulfur. See note on 19:20.
21:9 seven last plagues. See 15:1.

21:10 in the Spirit. See notes on 1:10; 4:2; 17:3.
21:12 twelve gates. See Eze 48:30–35. The number 12 probably emphasizes the continuity of the NT church and the OT people of God. See v. 14, where the 12 foundations bear the names of the 12 apostles.
21:15 measure the city. Cf. Eze 40–41. In Rev 11 the measuring was to ensure protection; here it serves to show the size and symmetry of the eternal dwelling place of the faithful.
21:16 length . . . wide . . . high. Thus a perfect cube, as was the Most Holy Place of the tabernacle and the temple.
21:17 144 cubits. See NIV text note.
21:20 See NIV text note.
21:27 Lamb's book of life. See note on 3:5.

names are written in the Lamb's book of life.[t]

The River of Life

22 Then the angel showed me the river[u] of the water of life,[v] as clear as crystal,[w] flowing[x] from the throne of God and of the Lamb [2]down the middle of the great street of the city. On each side of the river stood the tree of life,[y] bearing twelve crops of fruit, yielding its fruit every month. And the leaves of the tree are for the healing of the nations.[z] [3]No longer will there be any curse.[a] The throne of God and of the Lamb will be in the city, and his servants will serve him.[b] [4]They will see his face,[c] and his name will be on their foreheads.[d] [5]There will be no more night.[e] They will not need the light of a lamp or the light of the sun, for the Lord God will give them light.[f] And they will reign for ever and ever.[g]

[6]The angel said to me,[h] "These words are trustworthy and true.[i] The Lord, the God of the spirits of the prophets,[j] sent his angel[k] to show his servants the things that must soon take place."

Jesus Is Coming

[7]"Behold, I am coming soon![l] Blessed[m] is he who keeps the words of the prophecy in this book."[n]

[8]I, John, am the one who heard and saw these things.[o] And when I had heard and seen them, I fell down to worship at the feet[p] of the angel who had been showing them to me. [9]But he said to me, "Do not do it! I am a fellow servant with you and with your brothers the prophets and of all who keep the words of this book.[q] Worship God!"[r]

[10]Then he told me, "Do not seal up[s] the words of the prophecy of this book,[t] because the time is near.[u] [11]Let him who does wrong continue to do wrong; let him who is vile continue to be vile; let him

who does right continue to do right; and let him who is holy continue to be holy."[v]

[12]"Behold, I am coming soon![w] My reward is with me,[x] and I will give to everyone according to what he has done.[y] [13]I am the Alpha and the Omega,[z] the First and the Last,[a] the Beginning and the End.[b]

[14]"Blessed are those who wash their robes,[c] that they may have the right to the tree of life[d] and may go through the gates[e] into the city.[f] [15]Outside[g] are the dogs,[h] those who practice magic arts, the sexually immoral, the murderers, the idolaters and everyone who loves and practices falsehood.

[16]"I, Jesus,[i] have sent my angel[j] to give you[a] this testimony for the churches.[k] I am the Root[l] and the Offspring of David,[m] and the bright Morning Star."[n]

[17]The Spirit[o] and the bride[p] say, "Come!" And let him who hears say, "Come!" Whoever is thirsty, let him come; and whoever wishes, let him take the free gift of the water of life.[q]

[18]I warn everyone who hears the words of the prophecy of this book:[r] If anyone adds anything to them,[s] God will add to him the plagues described in this book.[t] [19]And if anyone takes words away[u] from this book of prophecy,[v] God will take away from him his share in the tree of life[w] and in the holy city, which are described in this book.

[20]He who testifies to these things[x] says, "Yes, I am coming soon."[y]

Amen. Come, Lord Jesus.[z]

[21]The grace of the Lord Jesus be with God's people.[a] Amen.

Center column references

21:27 [t]S Rev 20:12
22:1 [u]Ps 36:8; 46:4 [v]ver 17; S Jn 4:10 [w]Rev 4:6 [x]Eze 47:1; Zec 14:8
22:2 [y]S Rev 2:7 [z]Eze 47:12
22:3 [a]Zec 14:11 [b]Rev 7:15
22:4 [c]S Mt 5:8 [d]S Rev 7:3
22:5 [e]Rev 21:25; Zec 14:7 [f]Isa 60:19,20; Rev 21:23 [g]Da 7:27; Rev 20:4
22:6 [h]Rev 1:1 [i]Rev 21:5 [j]1Co 14:32; Heb 12:9 [k]ver 16; Rev 1:1
22:7 [l]ver 12,20; S Mt 16:27 [m]Rev 1:3; 16:15 [n]ver 10,18,19
22:8 [o]S Rev 1:1 [p]Rev 19:10
22:9 [q]ver 10,18, 19 [r]Rev 19:10
22:10 [s]Da 8:26; Rev 10:4 [t]ver 7, 18,19 [u]S Ro 13:11
22:11 [v]Eze 3:27; Da 12:10
22:12 [w]ver 7,20; S Mt 16:27 [x]Isa 40:10; 62:11 [y]S Mt 16:27
22:13 [z]Rev 1:8 [a]S Rev 1:17 [b]Rev 21:6
22:14 [c]Rev 7:14 [d]S Rev 2:7 [e]S Rev 21:12 [f]S Rev 21:27
22:15 [g]Dt 23:18; 1Co 6:9,10; Gal 5:19-21; Col 3:5,6; Rev 21:8 [h]Php 3:2
22:16 [i]Rev 1:1 [j]ver 6 [k]Rev 1:4 [l]S Rev 5:5 [m]S Mt 1:1 [n]2Pe 1:19; Rev 2:28
22:17 [o]Rev 2:7; 14:13 [p]S Rev 19:7 [q]S Jn 4:10
22:18 [r]ver 7,10, 19 [s]Dt 4:2; 12:32; Pr 30:6 [t]Rev 15:6-16:21
22:19 [u]Dt 4:2; 12:32; Pr 30:6 [v]ver 7,10,18

[w]S Rev 2:7 22:20 [x]Rev 1:2 [y]ver 7,12; S Mt 16:27 [z]1Co 16:22 22:21 [a]S Ro 16:20

[a]16 The Greek is plural.

Footnotes

22:2 *tree of life.* See Ge 2:9; 3:22; Eze 47:12.
22:4 *They will see his face.* In ancient times criminals were banished from the presence of the king (Est 7:8; cf. 2Sa 14:24). One blessing of eternity will be to see the Lord face to face (cf. 1Co 13:12). *his name.* See note on 3:12.
22:5 *they will reign.* See 5:10; 20:6; Da 7:18,27.
22:6 *his servants.* See v. 3. *things that must soon take place.* See 1:1,19.
22:7 *I am coming soon!* See vv. 12,20; 2:16; 3:11. *Blessed.* The sixth beatitude (see note on 1:3).
22:8 *fell down to worship.* See note on 1:17.
22:10 *Do not seal up the words.* Contrast Da 12:4.
22:12 *I am coming soon!* See vv. 7,20; 2:16; 3:11. ac-

cording to what he has done. See notes on 2:23; 20:12.
22:13 *the Alpha and the Omega.* See note on 1:8.
22:14 *Blessed.* The last of the seven beatitudes (see note on 1:3).
22:15 *dogs.* A term applied to all types of ceremonially impure persons. In Dt 23:18 it designates a male prostitute.
22:16 *my angel.* Cf. 1:1. *the Root and the Offspring of David.* See note on 5:5; cf. Isa 11:1,10; Ro 1:3. *bright Morning Star.* See Nu 24:17.
22:18–19 Cf. the commands in Dt 4:2; 12:32. The warning relates specifically to the book of Revelation.
22:20 *I am coming soon.* See vv. 7,12; 2:16; 3:11. *Come, Lord Jesus.* See note on 1Co 16:22.

Table of Weights and Measures

Index to Subjects

Index to Maps

Concordance

Index to Color Maps

Table of Weights and Measures

BIBLICAL UNIT		APPROXIMATE AMERICAN EQUIVALENT	APPROXIMATE METRIC EQUIVALENT
WEIGHTS			
talent	*(60 minas)*	75 pounds	34 kilograms
mina	*(50 shekels)*	1 1/4 pounds	0.6 kilogram
shekel	*(2 bekas)*	2/5 ounce	11.5 grams
pim	*(2/3 shekel)*	1/3 ounce	7.6 grams
beka	*(10 gerahs)*	1/5 ounce	5.5 grams
gerah		1/50 ounce	0.6 gram
LENGTH			
cubit		18 inches	0.5 meter
span		9 inches	23 centimeters
handbreadth		3 inches	8 centimeters
CAPACITY			
Dry Measure			
cor [homer]	*(10 ephahs)*	6 bushels	220 liters
lethek	*(5 ephahs)*	3 bushels	110 liters
ephah	*(10 omers)*	3/5 bushel	22 liters
seah	*(1/3 ephah)*	7 quarts	7.3 liters
omer	*(1/10 ephah)*	2 quarts	2 liters
cab	*(1/18 ephah)*	1 quart	1 liter
Liquid Measure			
bath	*(1 ephah)*	6 gallons	22 liters
hin	*(1/6 bath)*	4 quarts	4 liters
log	*(1/72 bath)*	1/3 quart	0.3 liter

The figures of the table are calculated on the basis of a shekel equaling 11.5 grams, a cubit equaling 18 inches and an ephah equaling 22 liters. The quart referred to is either a dry quart (slightly larger than a liter) or a liquid quart (slightly smaller than a liter), whichever is applicable. The ton referred to in the footnotes is the American ton of 2,000 pounds.

This table is based upon the best available information, but it is not intended to be mathematically precise; like the measurement equivalents in the footnotes, it merely gives approximate amounts and distances. Weights and measures differed somewhat at various times and places in the ancient world. There is uncertainty particularly about the ephah and the bath; further discoveries may give more light on these units of capacity.

Index to Subjects

All entries are words or concepts in the study notes, *not* the NIV text. For references to key words in the text, consult the Concordance. For location of geographical names, check both Index to Maps and Index to Color Maps. Page numbers are given in boldface type.

BABEL
Ge 11:4,9 – 23

BABEL, TOWER OF
Ge 11:4 – 23

BABYLON
Ge 11:4,9 – 23; Isa 13:1-14:27
– 1035; 13:19 – 1036; 14:22-23
– 1038; 21:9 – 1045; Jer 50:1-
51:64 – 1205; Da 4:30 – 1306;
Hab 1:6,11 – 1388

BABYLONIAN CHRONICLES
Na 2:6,10 – 1383

BABYLONIAN THEODICY
"Ancient Texts Relating to the OT"
– 5

BACKSLIDING
Jer 2:19 – 1122; 3:22 – 1125

BAGOHI
Ne 2:10 – 695; 13:7 – 715

BAHURIM
2Sa 3:16 – 427; 16:5 – 448

BAKBUK
Ezr 2:51 – 676

BALAAM
Nu 22:5,8,9,23 – 223; 23:19 – 225;
Jos 13:22 – 310; 24:10 – 323;
Job 3:8 – 737; Rev 2:14,17
– 1928,1929; Introduction to
Numbers: Theological Teaching
– 185

BALAK
Nu 22:1 – 222; 23:2 – 224

BALIKH RIVER
Isa 37:12 – 1067

BALM
Ge 37:25 – 63; Eze 27:17 – 1264

BANIAS
Mt 16:13 – 1465

BAPTISM
and circumcision
Col 2:11-12 – 1815
for the dead
1Co 15:29 – 1757
different kinds of
Heb 6:1-2 – 1864
figurative
Mk 10:38 – 1515; Lk 12:50 – 1565;
1Co 10:2 – 1746
of households
1Co 1:16 – 1735
meaning of
Ac 22:16 – 1690; Ro 6:3-4 – 1713;
Eph 4:5 – 1795; Tit 3:5 – 1853;
1Pe 3:21 – 1893
Paul and
1Co 1:17 – 1735
of repentance
Mk 1:4 – 1493; Ac 2:14-40 – 1647;
19:4 – 1683
significance of Christ's Mt 3:15
– 1446
spiritual
1Co 12:13 – 1750

BAR MITZVAH
Ro 7:9 – 1715

BAR-JESUS
Ac 13:6 – 1670

BARABBAS
Mk 15:7 – 1528; Lk 23:18 – 1585;
Jn 18:40 – 1633

BARADA RIVER
2Ki 5:12 – 532

BARAK
Jdg 4:6 – 335

BARBARIANS
Ro 1:14 – 1706

BARKOS
Ezr 2:53 – 676

BARLEY
Ex 9:18 – 98; Jdg 7:13 – 341; Ru
1:22 – 366

BARNABAS
Isa 49:6 – 1088; Mk 6:30 – 1505;
Ac 4:36 – 1651; 12:1 – 1667;
13:1,5,9 – 1669,1670; 14:1,4,12,
23 – 1672,1673; 15:12,39
– 1674,1676; 1Co 9:4 – 1745;
2Co 8:18 – 1772; Gal 2:1
– 1782; Col 4:10 – 1817; 2Ti
4:11 – 1847; Introduction to
Hebrews: Author – 1857

BARRENNESS
Ge 30:23 – 51; Nu 5:21 – 198; 2Sa
6:23 – 432; Ps 113:9 – 909; Lk
1:25 – 1536

BARSABBAS
Ac 1:23 – 1645

BARTHOLOMEW
Lk 6:14 – 1549; Ac 1:13 – 1644

BARTIMAEUS
Lk 18:35 – 1576; 19:37 – 1577

BARUCH
Ezr 7:6 – 684; Jer 32:12 – 1178

BARZILLAI
2Sa 17:27 – 450; 21:8 – 456; Ezr
2:61 – 676

BASHAN
Nu 21:33 – 222; Isa 2:13 – 1021;
Eze 39:18 – 1282; Am 4:1
– 1351; Na 1:4 – 1382; Zec 11:2
– 1418

BATH RABBIM
SS 7:4 – 1011

BATHSHEBA
2Sa 5:14 – 431; 11:4,5,27 – 438,
439; 23:34 – 461; 1Ki 1:11
– 470; SS 3:11 – 1007

BAY OF NAPLES
Ac 28:13 – 1700

BEALOTH
1Ki 9:18 – 490

BEAR
Job 9:9 – 744

BEAST, THE
Rev 11:7 – 1938; 13:1,3,5,11,12,
16 – 1940,1941

BEATITUDES, THE
Mt 5:1-7:29 – 1449; Lk 6:20-23
– 1549

BEELIADA
1Ch 14:7 – 604

BEELZEBUB. *See also* SATAN
Mt 10:25 – 1457; Lk 11:22 – 1562

BEER
Jdg 9:21 – 345

BEER ELIM
Isa 15:8 – 1040

BEEROTH
2Sa 4:2 – 428

BEERSHEBA
Ge 21:31 – 37; 1Ki 19:3 – 513; Am
5:5 – 1353

BEHISTUN INSCRIPTION
Ezr 4:24 – 680; 6:12 – 682; Ne 6:6
– 702; Est 2:23 – 722; Hag 1:1
– 1402

BEIT JIBRIN
Ne 11:29 – 712

BEKER
2Sa 20:1 – 454

BEL
Isa 46:1 – 1084; Da 1:7 – 1300; 4:8
– 1304

BELA
1Ch 7:6-12 – 595

BELIAL. *See also* SATAN
Dt 13:13 – 262; 2Co 6:15 – 1770

BELSHAZZAR
Da 5:1,22-23 – 1307,1308; 7:1
– 1309

BELTESHAZZAR
Da 1:7 – 1300

BEN-ABINADAB
1Ki 4:11 – 478

BENAIAH
2Sa 23:20 – 461; 1Ki 2:46 – 475;
4:4 – 477

BENEDICTION
Nu 6:24-26 – 199; 2Co 13:14
– 1778; Heb 13:20-21 – 1877

BENEDICTUS
1Sa 2:1 – 376; Lk 1:68-79 – 1537

BEN-HADAD I
1Ki 15:20 – 505; 20:1,4,9,22,32,42
– 515,516,517; 22:1 – 519; 2Ki
15:29 – 552

BEN-HADAD II
1Ki 20:1 – 515; 2Ki 5:6,7 – 531; 8:9
– 536

BEN-HADAD III
2Ki 13:3 – 545; Am 1:4 – 1348

BEN-HUR
1Ki 4:8 – 477

BENJAMIN (son of Jacob)
Ge 35:18 – 59; 42:4 – 69

BENJAMIN (tribe of Israel)
Jdg 3:15 – 333; 1Ki 12:21 – 497;
1Ch 8:1-40 – 597

BEQAA VALLEY
2Sa 8:3 – 435

BEREA
Ac 17:10 – 1679; Php 4:15 – 1809;
1Th 3:1-2 – 1822

BEREKIAH
Ne 2:10 – 695

BERENICE
Da 11:6,7 – 1316

BERGAMA
Rev 2:12 – 1928

BERNICE
Ac 25:13 – 1694

BEROSSUS
Ezr 4:15 – 680

BEROTHAH
Eze 47:16 – 1295

BETH ANATH
Jdg 1:33 – 331

BETH ARBEL
Hos 10:14 – 1333

BETH AVEN
Jos 7:2 – 299; Hos 4:15 – 1327;
10:5 – 1333

BETH BAAL PEOR
Hos 9:10 – 1332

BETH BARAH
Jdg 7:24 – 342

BETH DIBLATHAIM
Eze 6:14 – 1236

BETH EDEN
Am 1:5 – 1348

BETH GILGAL
Ne 12:29 – 713

BETH HAKKEREM
Ne 3:14 – 698
BETH HORON
Jos 10:11 – 305; 1Ki 9:17,18
– 490; 2Ch 8:5 – 633
BETH JESHIMOTH
Eze 25:9 – 1261
BETH MILLO
Jdg 9:6 – 344; 2Ki 12:20 – 545
BETH PELET
Ne 11:26 – 712
BETH REHOB
1Ch 18:5 – 609; 19:6 – 610
BETH SHAN
Jos 17:11 – 315; Jn 3:23 – 1599
BETH SHEMESH
Jdg 1:33 – 331; 1Sa 6:9,14-15,19
– 383; 2Ki 14:11 – 547
BETH TOGARMAH
Eze 27:14 – 1263
BETH ZUR
Ne 3:16 – 698
BETHANY
Ne 11:32 – 712; Mt 21:17 – 1472;
Mk 11:11 – 1516; Jn 1:28 – 1594
BETHEL
Ge 12:8 – 25; Jos 8:17 – 301; Jdg
20:18 – 360; 1Ki 12:29 – 498;
2Ki 2:23 – 526; 17:28 – 558; Ezr
2:28 – 675; Hos 4:15 – 1327; 8:5
– 1330; 10:5 – 1333; 12:3,4
– 1335; Am 3:14 – 1351; 4:4
– 1352; 5:6 – 1353; 7:15 – 1357;
9:1 – 1358; Zec 7:3 – 1413;
Introduction to Amos: Author
– 1345
BETHESDA, POOL OF
Jn 5:2 – 1603
BETHLEHEM
Jdg 12:8 – 349; 17:7 – 356; Ru 1:1
– 365; 1Sa 16:1 – 398; Mic 5:2
– 1376; Mt 2:1,16 – 1442,1444;
Lk 2:4,8,22 – 1538,1539
BETHPHAGE
Mt 21:1 – 1471
BETHSAIDA
Mt 11:21 – 1458; Mk 6:32,44
– 1505,1506; Jn 6:5 – 1605
BEZALEL
Ex 31:2 – 132; 37:1 – 140; 1Ch
2:18-24 – 586; 2Ch 1:5 – 625;
Introduction to 2 Chronicles:
The Building of the Temple in
Chronicles – 624
BEZEK
Jdg 1:4 – 329; 1Sa 11:8 – 389
BEZER
Dt 4:43 – 252
BIBLE. See SCRIPTURE
BICRI
2Sa 20:1 – 454
BIGTHANA
Est 2:23 – 722
BIGVAI
Ne 2:10 – 695; 13:7 – 715
BILDAD
Job 2:11 – 737; 8:5-6,20 – 742,
743; 18:1-4,17 – 753; 19:6
– 754; 26:5-14 – 761; 32:15-16
– 768
BILHAH
Ex 1:2-4 – 88; 1Ch 7:13 – 595
BIRTHRIGHT
Ge 25:31 – 44; 27:36 – 47

BISHOP
Tit 1:7 – 1851
BISITUN INSCRIPTION. See
BEHISTUN INSCRIPTION
BIT ADINI
Isa 37:12 – 1067
BITHYNIA
Ac 16:7 – 1676; 1Pe 1:1 – 1888
BLACK OBELISK
2Ki 10:34 – 542; "Ancient Texts
Relating to the OT" – 5
BLASPHEMY
Mk 2:7 – 1495; 14:64 – 1527; Lk
5:21 – 1547; Jn 8:59 – 1614;
10:31,33 – 1617; 19:7 – 1633;
Ac 6:11 – 1654; 14:5 – 1672;
26:11 – 1695; 1Ti 1:20 – 1835
BLASTUS
Ac 12:20 – 1669
BLESSED
Ps 1:1 – 787; Pr 31:28 – 990; Mt
5:3 – 1449; Rev 1:3 – 1926
BLESSING
Ge 12:2-3 – 24; 27:33,36 – 47;
33:11 – 57; 35:11-12 – 59; 49:2-
27 – 79; Lev 26:3 – 181; Eze
34:26 – 1275; Eph 1:3 – 1791
BLESSINGS AND CURSES
Dt 4:25 – 251; 28:1-14 – 276
BLOOD
Ge 9:4 – 18; Lev 4:5 – 151; 17:11
– 168; Mk 14:24 – 1523; Heb
9:18 – 1869; 12:24 – 1875
BLOOD REVENGE
Ge 27:45 – 47; Nu 35:6-15 – 240;
Jos 20:1-9,3 – 318; 2Sa 14:7
– 444; "Cities of Refuge" – 241
BOASTING. See also PRIDE
Ro 15:17 – 1729; 2Co 11:30
– 1776
BOAZ
Ru 2:1 – 366; 3:1 – 368; 4:1 – 369
BOOK
of the Covenant
Ex 20:22-23:19 – 116; 24:7 – 122;
2Ki 23:2 – 568
of the Dead
Eze 29:5 – 1267
of Jashar
Jos 10:13 – 305; Introduction to 1
Samuel: Literary Features,
Authorship and Date – 371
of the Law
Jos 1:8 – 292; 23:6 – 322; 2Ki 22:8
– 567; 2Ch 34:3-7 – 664; Ne 8:1
– 705
of Life
Ps 69:28 – 857; Rev 3:5 – 1930
of Moses
Ezr 6:18 – 683
of Truth
Da 10:21 – 1315
of the Twelve
"The Book of the Twelve, or the
Minor Prophets" – 1320
of the Wars of the Lord
Nu 21:14 – 221; Ps 60:6-8 – 847
BOOTHS, FEAST OF. See also
FEAST: of Ingathering; of
Tabernacles
Ex 23:16 – 120; Lev 23:42 – 178
BOUNDARY STONE
Dt 19:14 – 268

BOZKATH
2Ki 22:1 – 566
BOZRAH
Isa 34:6 – 1064; Jer 49:13 – 1203;
Am 1:12 – 1349
BRANCH
Isa 4:2 – 1023; Jer 23:5 – 1160;
Zec 3:8 – 1410
BREAD OF LIFE
Jn 6:35 – 1607
BREAD OF THE PRESENCE
Ex 25:30 – 124; Lev 24:8 – 178;
1Sa 21:4 – 407
BREASTPLATE
Rev 9:9 – 1936
BRIDEGROOM. See CHRIST: as
bridegroom
BROAD WALL
Ne 3:8 – 698; 11:9 – 711
BRONZE PILLARS
1Ki 7:15 – 483
BRONZE SEA
1Ki 7:23,24 – 483
BROOM TREE
1Ki 19:4 – 513; Ps 120:4 – 922
BUBASTIS
Eze 30:17 – 1269
BUCKTHORN
Jdg 9:14 – 344
BURIAL CUSTOMS, JEWISH
MK 14:8 – 1522; Lk 23:56 – 1587
BURNT OFFERING
Lev 1:3 – 147; 3:5 – 149; Ne 8:10
– 706; Eze 40:39 – 1285;
"Tabernacle Furnishings" – 126;
"Old Testament Sacrifices"
– 150
BUSYBODIES
2Th 3:11 – 1830
BUZITE
Job 32:2 – 768
BYBLOS
Jos 13:5 – 310; Eze 27:9 – 1263

CAESAR (Augustus)
Mt 11:21 – 1458; Lk 2:1 – 1538;
20:22 – 1579; Jn 19:12 – 1634;
Ac 10:1 – 1662; 17:7 – 1679
CAESAR (Claudius)
Ac 12:21 – 1669
CAESAREA
Mk 15:1 – 1527; Ac 8:40 – 1660;
10:1 – 1662; 12:19 – 1669; 19:6
– 1683; 21:8 – 1687; 23:33
– 1692
CAESAREA PHILIPPI
Mt 16:13 – 1465; Lk 23:1 – 1585
CAIAPHAS
Mt 26:3 – 1483; Mk 14:53-15:15
– 1526; Lk 3:2 – 1541; Jn 11:50,
51 – 1619,1620; Ac 4:6 – 1650;
5:17 – 1652; Jas 5:12 – 1885
CAIN
Ge 4:3-4,5,11,13,17 – 11,12; 1Sa
20:11 – 406; Heb 11:4 – 1871
CALAH
Jnh 1:2 – 1366; 3:3 – 1368
CALAMUS
SS 4:14 – 1008; Isa 43:24 – 1079;
Jer 6:20 – 1131; Eze 27:19
– 1264
CALCOL
1Ch 2:6 – 585

EN RIMMON
Ne 11:29 – 712; Zec 14:10 – 1421

EN ROGEL
2Sa 17:17 – 449; 1Ki 1:9 – 470; Ne 2:13 – 696

ENDOR
1Sa 28:7 – 416

ENOCH
Ge 5:24 – 14; Heb 11:6 – 1872; Jude 14 – 1921

ENUMA ELISH
Introduction to Genesis: Background – 1; "Ancient Texts Relating to the OT" – 5

EPAPHRAS
Col 1:7 – 1813; 4:9-17 – 1817

EPAPHRODITUS
Php 2:25-30 – 1806; 4:16 – 1809

EPHAH (measure)
Ru 2:17 – 367; Mic 6:10 – 1377

EPHAH (son of Midian)
Isa 60:6 – 1104

EPHESUS
Ac 18:19 – 1682; 19:19,38 – 1684, 1685; 1Co 4:11-13 – 1739; 15:32 – 1757; 16:5,19 – 1759; 1Ti 1:3 – 1835; 5:9 – 1840; Tit 3:9 – 1853; Rev 1:4,9 – 1926; 9:21 – 1937; Introduction to Ephesians: The City of Ephesus – 1789; "Ephesus in the Time of Paul" – 1789

EPHOD
Ex 28:6 – 128; Jdg 8:27 – 343; 1Sa 2:18,28 – 378

EPHRAIM (son of Joseph)
Ge 48:5-7 – 77,78; Jos 14:4 – 311

EPHRAIM (territory)
Ge 48:19 – 78; Jos 14:4 – 311; Isa 7:2,8,17 – 1026,1027; 17:3 – 1041; Hos 9:11 – 1332; 12:8 – 1335; 13:1 – 1335

EPHRAIM GATE
2Ki 14:13 – 547; 2Ch 25:23 – 652; Ne 8:16 – 706

EPHRATH
1Sa 16:1 – 398

EPHRATHAH
Ru 1:2 – 365; Mic 5:2 – 1376

EPHRON
Ge 23:15,17 – 39,40

EPICUREAN PHILOSOPHY
Ac 17:18,26 – 1680

ER
1Ch 2:3-9 – 585

ERASTUS
Ac 19:22 – 1684; Ro 16:23 – 1731; 1Co 16:10,11 – 1759

ERECH
Ge 10:10 – 21

ESARHADDON
2Ki 19:28 – 563; 2Ch 33:11 – 663; Ne 9:32 – 709; Isa 7:8 – 1027; 19:4 – 1043; 23:12 – 1048

ESAU
Ge 25:34 – 44; 26:34 – 45; 36:1 – 60; Am 1:11 – 1349; Ob 18,21 – 1362; Mal 1:3 – 1425; Ro 9:13, 14 – 1719; Heb 12:16 – 1875

ESDRAS
Ezr 7:1 – 683

ESH-BAAL. See ISH-BOSHETH

ESSENES
"The Time between the Testaments" – 1431; "Jewish Sects" – 1476

ESTHER
Est 2:7 – 721

ETERNAL LIFE
Ge 2:9 – 9; 3:22,24 – 11; Mt 19:16, 17 – 1469,1470; Jn 3:15,36 – 1598-1599; 6:27,28 – 1607; Ac 13:48 – 1672; Ro 2:6-7 – 1708; 6:22 – 1714; Gal 6:8 – 1787; 1Ti 6:12 – 1841; 1Jn 1:2 – 1908; 5:20 – 1913

ETHAN (musician)
1Ch 2:6 – 585; 6:31-48 – 593; Ps 39 title – 825

ETHANIM
2Ch 5:3 – 629; "Hebrew Calendar" – 102

ETHBAAL
1Ki 16:25,31 – 508; 17:9 – 509

ETHIOPIA
Am 8:8 – 1357; Ac 8:27 – 1659

EUCHARIST
Mk 14:23 – 1523

EUNICE
2Ti 1:5 – 1844

EUNUCH
Isa 56:3 – 1099

EUODIA
Php 4:2-3 – 1808

EUPHRATES RIVER
Ge 2:14 – 9; 2Sa 8:3 – 435; Ezr 4:10 – 679; Rev 9:14 – 1936

EUROQUILO
Ac 27:14 – 1698

EUTYCHUS
Ac 20:9,10 – 1686

EVANGELISTS
Eph 4:11 – 1795

EVE
Ge 2:4,9 – 8,9; Col 1:20 – 1814; 1Ti 2:13-14 – 1838

EVERLASTING LIFE. See ETERNAL LIFE

EVIL ONE
1Jn 3:8 – 1910

EVIL SPIRITS
1Sa 16:14 – 400; Lk 4:33 – 1545; 9:39 – 1558

EVIL-MERODACH
2Ki 25:27 – 576; Da 5:26-28 – 1308

EXCOMMUNICATION
Mt 18:17 – 1468; Jn 9:22 – 1615; 1Co 5:2,5 – 1739

EXECUTION, FORMS OF
Est 2:23 – 722; Mk 15:24 – 1528

EXILE
Isa 27:8 – 1053; Da 1:2 – 1300; "Exile of the Northern Kingdom" – 556; "Exile of the Southern Kingdom" – 576; "Return from Exile" – 671

EXODUS, THE
Isa 55:13 – 1098; Ro 9:17 – 1720; Gal 3:19 – 1784; Heb 3:7-11 – 1862; Introduction to Genesis: Author and Date of Writing – 2; Introduction to Exodus: Title; Author and Date of Writing – 84; "The Exodus" – 106; Introduction to Judges: Background – 326

EXPANSE
Ge 1:6 – 6

EZEKIEL
Introduction to Ezekiel: Author – 1226
denounces Edom
Ob 15 – 1362
and the exile
Da 1:2 – 1300
prophecy of
2Ki 25:7 – 574
temple of
2Ch 4:2 – 628; "Ezekiel's Temple" – 1284
visions of
Ne 8:16 – 706; Rev 4:7 – 1931

EZION GEBER
1Ki 9:26 – 491

EZRA
1Ch 6:8 – 592; Ezr 7:6,7-9 – 684; Ne 2:9 – 695; 8:1 – 705; 12:31 – 714; Mal 2:11 – 1426; Jn 9:22 – 1615; "Chronology: Ezra-Nehemiah" – 674

FACTIONS
1Co 3:17 – 1738; 11:19 – 1749

FAITH
Ps 27 – 811; Da 3:18 – 1303; Hab 2:4 – 1389; 3:18-19 – 1391; Mk 9:24 – 1512; 13:32 – 1521; Lk 17:5,19 – 1573; 18:8 – 1574; Jn 7:17 – 1609; Heb 6:1-2 – 1864; 11:6,40 – 1872,1874; Introduction to Ecclesiastes: Purpose and Method – 991
Abraham's
Ge 12:4 – 24; 15:6 – 28; 17:1,11 – 30,31; 22:2,5,12 – 37,38; Ro 4:19 – 1711; Heb 11:8,19 – 1872
Daniel's
Da 6:23 – 1309
dead
Jas 2:14-26 – 1882
defense of
1Pe 3:15 – 1893; 1Jn 5:1 – 1912
God's response to
Ge 15:6 – 28
and healing
Jn 5:9 – 1603
Noah's
Heb 11:7 – 1872
saving
Jn 14:11 – 1625; Ro 3:28 – 1710; 4:22 – 1712; 6:3-4 – 1713; 8:24 – 1718; Gal 5:6 – 1786
strong
Ro 14:2 – 1727; 1Co 12:9 – 1750; 13:2 – 1752

FALSE WITNESS
Pr 6:19 – 953

FAMILY. See also CHILDREN; FATHER; MOTHER; PARENTS
Ge 6:18 – 15; Ex 20:5 – 115; Ezr 1:5 – 673; Ps 109:12 – 905; Lk 8:21 – 1554; 1Jn 5:1 – 1912

FAMINE
Ge 41:27 – 68; 47:13 – 76; Ne 5:3 – 700; Hag 1:6 – 1402

FASTING
Lev 16:29,31 – 168; Ne 1:4 – 694; Est 4:16 – 725; 9:31 – 729; Joel 1:14 – 1340; Mt 6:1 – 1451; Mk 2:18 – 1496; Lk 5:33 – 1548; 18:12 – 1575; Ac 13:3 – 1669; 27:9 – 1698; Jas 1:26 – 1882

JEHU (king of Judah)
1Ki 1:39 – 472; 19:16 – 514; 2Ki
9:27,31 – 539; 10:1,7,30 – 540,
541
JEHU (prophet)
1Ki 16:1 – 506; 2Ch 22:6 – 648
JEHUCAL
Jer 37:3 – 1186
JEPHTHAH
Jdg 11:1,30 – 347,348
JERAHMEELITES
1Sa 27:10 – 416; 1Ch 2:25-33
– 586
JEREMIAH
2Ki 22:11,12 – 567; 2Ch 35:25
– 667; 36:5-8,22-23 – 668,669;
Isa 10:30 – 1033; Mt 27:9
– 1487; Lk 22:20 – 1583; Gal
3:19 – 1784; Heb 13:20 – 1877;
Introduction to Jeremiah: Author
and Date – 1115
JERICHO
Jos 2:1,15 – 293,294; 6:1 – 298;
1Ki 16:34 – 508; Mk 10:46
– 1515; Lk 10:30 – 1560; Heb
11:30 – 1873
JEROBOAM I
1Ki 11:40 – 496; 12:28,30,32
– 498; 13:7,24 – 499; 14:1,2,7-8,
9,12,13 – 500,501; 15:26 – 506;
16:7 – 506; 2Ki 14:23 – 548;
16:3 – 553; 17:6 – 555; 2Ch 30:2
– 658; Hos 8:5,6 – 1330; 13:10
– 1336
JEROBOAM II
1Ki 13:1 – 498; 2Ki 13:5,19,25
– 545,546; 14:25 – 548; 2Ch
26:6-8 – 653; Hos 1:1,4 – 1323;
4:2 – 1326; 8:4 – 1330; 10:1
– 1333; Am 6:2,13 – 1355
JEROME
Introduction to Ezra: Ezra and
Nehemiah – 670
JERUB-BAAL/JERUB-BESHETH
Jdg 6:32 – 340; 2Sa 11:21 – 439
JERUSALEM
conquest/destruction of
"Nebuchadnezzar's Campaign
against Judah" – 572
geographical/physical aspects of
Jdg 1:8 – 329; 2Sa 5:6 – 429; Ne
3:1-32 – 697; Ps 48:2 – 834;
"David's Jerusalem" – 430;
"Solomon's Jerusalem" – 473;
"Jerusalem of the Returning
Exiles" – 696; "Jerusalem
during the Time of the
Prophets" – 1320; "Jerusalem
during the Ministry of Jesus"
– 1499
names of
Ge 14:18 – 27; 2Sa 5:7 – 430; Isa
1:26 – 1019; Jer 33:16 – 1181;
Eze 48:35 – 1297
religious significance of
1Ki 11:13 – 493; Ps 9:11 – 794;
24:7-10 – 808; 48 – 834; 76
– 864; 87 – 878; Eze 38:12
– 1280; Gal 4:25,26 – 1786;
Introduction to Psalms:
Theology – 786
JESHANAH GATE
Ne 3:6 – 698

JESHUA. See also JOSHUA (priest)
1Ch 6:14 – 592; Ezr 1:8 – 673; 2:2
– 674; 3:2 – 677; 6:13-14 – 682
JESHURUN
Isa 44:2 – 1079
JESSE
1Sa 16:1 – 398; 2Sa 17:25 – 450;
1Ch 2:10-17 – 586
JESUS. See CHRIST
JETHRO
Ex 2:16 – 89
JEZEBEL
1Ki 16:25,31 – 508; 18:13 – 511;
21:9,19 – 518; 2Ki 9:31 – 539;
Mk 9:13 – 1511; Rev 2:20,23
– 1929
JEZREEL (son of Hosea)
Hos 1:4,11 – 1323; 2:22 – 1325
JEZREEL (city)
1Sa 25:43 – 413; 2Ki 8:28 – 538;
9:16 – 539
JOAB
1Sa 26:6 – 414; 2Sa 2:13 – 425;
3:25,29 – 427,428; 5:8 – 430;
14:2 – 444; 19:5 – 452; 20:10,23
– 454,455; 1Ki 1:7 – 470; 1Ch
21:6 – 612; 27:24 – 620
JOANNA
Lk 24:10 – 1589
JOASH
2Ki 12:2,6,17 – 543,544; 2Ch 24:5,
15-22 – 650; Ezr 3:10 – 677; Ne
10:32 – 710
JOB
Jas 5:11 – 1885; Introduction to
Job: Author – 731
JOCHEBED
Ex 6:20 – 95
JOEL
Ac 2:4,17 – 1645,1647;
Introduction to Joel: Author
– 1338
JOHANAN
1Ch 3:15-16 – 588; Ezr 2:46 – 676;
Ne 12:11 – 713
JOHANAN BEN ZACCAI
Ac 4:6 – 1650
JOHN (the apostle)
Mt 20:20 – 1471; Mk 5:37 – 1503;
15:40 – 1529; Lk 9:54 – 1558;
Ac 3:1 – 1648; 4:13 – 1650; 8:14
– 1659; 10:37 – 1665; 12:2,17
– 1667,1669; Gal 2:2 – 1782;
Rev 1:9 – 1926; Introduction to
John: Author – 1591
JOHN (the Baptist)
baptism of
Mt 3:11 – 1446; Mk 1:4 – 1493; Ac
2:38 – 1648; 18:25 – 1683; 19:4
– 1683
beheading of
Ac 12:1,2 – 1667
birthdate and childhood of
Mt 3:1 – 1444; Lk 1:80 – 1538
and Christ's baptism
Mt 3:15 – 1446
compared to Jesus
Mt 4:17 – 1447; 17:12 – 1467; Lk
5:33 – 1548; Jn 1:15 – 1593
compared to others
Mal 4:5 – 1429; Mt 11:11 – 1458
disciples of
Mk 2:18 – 1496; Ac 19:1 – 1683
imprisonment of
Mt 4:12 – 1447; Mk 6:17 – 1504

life-style of
Mt 3:4 – 1445; Lk 1:15 – 1535;
5:33 – 1548
ministry of
Mal 3:1 – 1427; 4:1,6 – 1428,1429;
Mt 3:3 – 1444; 4:17 – 1447; Lk
16:16 – 1572; Jn 1:7,23 – 1593,
1594; 3:30 – 1599
name, meaning of
Mk 1:4 – 1493
JOHN (Hyrcanus)
Mk 2:16 – 1496; "The Time
between the Testaments"
– 1431
JOHN MARK. See MARK, JOHN
JONADAB
Jer 35:6 – 1184
JONAH
Na 1:8 – 1382; Lk 11:30,31-32
– 1562; Introduction to Jonah:
Author – 1363; "The Book of
Jonah" – 1366
JONATHAN (son of Annas)
Ac 4:6 – 1650
JONATHAN (son of Gershom)
Jdg 18:30 – 357
JONATHAN (son of Saul)
1Sa 13:2 – 392; 14:24-26 – 394;
15:23 – 397; 18:3,4 – 403; 19:4
– 404; 20:11,15,16 – 406; Ezr
8:6 – 686
JOPPA
Jos 19:40 – 317; Ac 9:32,36
– 1662
JORAM
1Ki 16:30,31 – 508; 2Ki 6:30,33
– 534,535; 2Ch 22:6,7 – 648
JORDAN RIVER
Jos 1:2 – 292; 2Sa 19:41 – 454;
1Ki 20:26 – 516; 2Ki 5:10 – 531;
1Ch 12:8-15 – 602; Isa 33:9
– 1062; Zec 11:3 – 1418; Mk
1:5,16 – 1493,1494
JORDAN VALLEY
Ge 13:10 – 26; 1Ki 20:26 – 516
JOSEPH (of Arimathea)
Isa 53:9 – 1095; Lk 23:50 – 1587;
Jn 19:38 – 1635
JOSEPH (Barsabbas)
Ac 1:23 – 1645; 15:22 – 1675
JOSEPH (brother of Christ)
Lk 8:19 – 1554
JOSEPH (husband of Mary)
Mt 1:16,18,20 – 1441,1442; 13:55
– 1462; Lk 1:32 – 1536; 3:23-38
– 1543
JOSEPH (son of Jacob)
and covenant of God
Ge 37:2 – 62
and Daniel
Da 1:9 – 1300
death of
Ge 50:25,26 – 82,83
faith of
Heb 11:22 – 1872
and his brothers
Ge 43:30 – 72; 50:17 – 82; Isa
42:14 – 1077; Ac 7:9 – 1655
interpreter of dreams
Jdg 7:13-14 – 341
name of
Ge 41:45 – 68
as representative of Israel
Ge 39:1,6 – 65; 40:8 – 66

MALCHUS
Mk 14:47 – **1526**; Lk 22:51,59
– **1584**

MALKIJAH
Jer 35:6 – **1184**

MALTA
Ac 28:1 – **1699**

MALTHACE
Mt 14:3 – **1463**; "House of the
Lord" – **1443**

MAN
creation of
Ge 1:26 – **7**; 2:7 – **8**; 9:5,6 – **18**; Ps
139:14 – **932**
his dominion over the earth
Ge 1:26,28 – **7,8**; 2:15 – **9**; 9:2
– **18**; Ps 8:6-8 – **783**; Heb 2:6b-
8,8,9 – **1860**
fall of
Ge 3:1,7,14 – **10**; Ro 5:12-21,14
– **1712,1713**; 16:17-20 – **1731**;
1Co 15:22,56 – **1756,1758**

MANAEN
Ac 13:1 – **1669**

**MANASSEH (grandfather of
Jonathan)**
Jdg 18:30 – **357**

MANASSEH (son of Hezekiah)
2Ki 20:18 – **565**; 21:1,3,15,16,20
– **565,566**; 23:6 – **568**; 2Ch
33:11-17,20 – **663,664**; Ezr 4:10
– **679**; Isa 9:21 – **1031**; 39:6
– **1071**; Na 1:11 – **1382**; Zep 1:5
– **1395**; Mt 5:22 – **1450**

MANASSEH (son of Joseph)
Ge 48:5-7,13 – **77,78**; Jos 13:29
– **311**; 14:4 – **311**; Jdg 10:3
– **346**; 2Ki 17:16 – **557**; Ac 7:14
– **1655**; Rev 7:6 – **1934**

MANDRAKE
Ge 30:14 – **50**

MANNA
Nu 11:7 – **206**; 21:5 – **221**; Jos
5:12 – **297**; 2Ch 5:10 – **629**; Mt
4:4 – **1447**; Jn 6:31,58 – **1607**,
1608; 1Co 10:3-4 – **1746**; Rev
2:17 – **1929**

MARAH
Ex 15:23 – **109**; Rev 8:11 – **1935**

MARDIKH, TELL
Introduction to Genesis:
Background – **1**

MARDUK
Est 2:5 – **721**; Isa 45:4 – **1082**;
46:1 – **1084**; Da 1:7 – **1300**; 4:8
– **1304**; Introduction to Genesis:
Background – **1**

MARI
Ge 24:10 – **40**; Introduction to
Genesis: Background – **1**

MARI TABLETS
"Ancient Texts Relating to the OT"
– **5**

MARIAMNE
Mt 14:3 – **1463**; "House of Herod"
– **1443**

MARK, JOHN
Mk 14:51 – **1526**; Ac 1:13 – **1644**;
10:37 – **1665**; 12:25 – **1669**;
13:5,13 – **1670**; 15:38,39
– **1676**; Col 4:10 – **1817**; 2Ti
4:11 – **1847**; 1Pe 5:13 – **1896**;
Introduction to Mark: John Mark
in the NT – **1490**

MARKET DISTRICT
Ne 11:9 – **711**

MARRIAGE. *See also* DIVORCE
Mal 2:14 – **1427**; 1Co 6:16-18
– **1741**; 7:1,3,5,6,10,11,14,15,
36,37,39 – **1741-1743**; 11:5-6
– **1748**; Eph 5:22,23,25 – **1798**;
1Ti 3:2 – **1838**; Tit 1:6 – **1851**
customs of ancient Near East
Ge 21:21 – **37**; 29:22 – **49**; Ex
22:16 – **119**; Jdg 14:2,10 – **351**;
Ru 3:4,9 – **368**; 1Sa 18:25 – **403**;
SS 8:8 – **1012**; Mt 1:18 – **1441**;
22:11 – **1474**; Mk 2:19 – **1496**;
Jn 2:1 – **1595**
levirate
Ge 38:8 – **64**; Ru 1:11 – **366**; 4:5
– **369**; 1Ch 3:19 – **588**; Mt 22:24
– **1474**

MARTHA
Lk 19:29 – **1577**; Jn 11:22,27,37
– **1618,1619**

MARTYRDOM
1Co 13:3 – **1752**; Heb 12:1 – **1874**;
Rev 10:6 – **1937**

MARY (of Bethany)
Lk 19:29 – **1577**; Jn 11:20,21,31
– **1618,1619**; 12:3 – **1620**

MARY (Magdalene)
Mk 15:40 – **1529**; Lk 8:2 – **1553**; Jn
20:1,16,17 – **1636**

MARY (mother of Jesus)
Mt 1:16,18,20 – **1441,1442**; 2:11
– **1442**; Lk 1:32 – **1536**; 2:5,35
– **1538,1540**; 8:19 – **1554**; 24:10
– **1589**; Ac 1:14 – **1644**

MARY (mother of Mark)
Ac 1:13 – **1644**; 12:12 – **1667**; Col
4:15 – **1818**

MARY (wife of Clopas)
Mt 28:1 – **1489**

MASORETIC TEXT
1Ch 14:12 – **605**; 2Ch 2:18 – **627**

MASSAH
Ex 17:7 – **112**; Nu 20:13 – **220**

MATERIALISM
Jdg 17:10 – **356**; 2Ki 1:8 – **524**;
5:26 – **533**; Mk 10:22 – **1514**; Lk
12:13 – **1564**

MATTANIAH
2Ki 24:17 – **574**; 2Ch 36:4 – **667**

MATTATHIAS
1Ch 24:7 – **616**; Da 11:34 – **1317**;
"The Time between the
Testaments" – **1431**

MATTHEW
Hos 11:1 – **1334**; Mk 2:14 – **1496**;
Lk 5:27-29 – **1548**; 6:15 – **1549**;
Introduction to Matthew: Author
– **1439**

MATTHIAS
Ac 2:1 – **1645**

MATURITY
1Co 2:14-3:4 – **1737**; Heb 5:14
– **1864**; 13:22 – **1877**

MEANINGLESSNESS
Ecc 1:2 – **992**

MEDEBA
2Ki 1:1 – **524**; 1Ch 19:7 – **610**; Isa
15:2 – **1039**

MEDES
Ezr 6:2 – **681**; Isa 13:17 – **1036**;
Na 1:14 – **1382**; Ac 2:9 – **1646**

MEDIATOR
Ge 28:12 – **48**; Ex 20:19 – **116**;
32:30 – **135**; Job 5:1 – **739**; Gal
3:20 – **1784**; Heb 8:6 – **1867**

MEDIUM (at Endor)
1Sa 28:7,12,21 – **416,417**

MEDIUMS
Lev 20:6 – **172**; Dt 18:9 – **267**

MEDO-PERSIA
Da 2:32-43 – **1302**; 7:4-7 – **1310**;
8:3 – **1312**

MEEKNESS
Ps 37:11 – **822**; Mt 5:5 – **1449**

MEGIDDO
Jos 17:11 – **315**; Jdg 5:19 – **337**;
1Ki 9:15 – **490**; 22:39 – **521**; Rev
16:16 – **1944**

MELCHIZEDEK
Ge 14:18-20 – **27**; Ps 110:4 – **907**;
Ecc 1:16 – **992**; Heb 5:5 – **1863**;
7:1,3,4,11,16 – **1865,1866**; 8:7
– **1867**; 13:10 – **1876**

MELITA
Ac 28:1 – **1699**

MELQART
1Ki 16:31 – **508**

MEMPHIS
Isa 19:13 – **1043**; Eze 30:13
– **1268**; Hos 9:6 – **1332**

MENAHEM
2Ki 15:12,14 – **549**; Hos 5:13
– **1328**; 7:11 – **1330**; 8:9 – **1331**

MENANDER
1Co 15:33 – **1757**

MENELAUS
1Sa 2:35 – **379**

MENSTRUATION
Ge 31:35 – **54**; Lev 15:24 – **166**

MEPHIBOSHETH
Jdg 6:32 – **340**; 2Sa 9:2,7 – **436**;
19:27 – **453**

MERARI
Ex 6:16 – **94**; 1Ch 15:4-10 – **605**

MERATHAIM
Jer 50:21 – **1206**

MERCY
Ge 19:16 – **34**; Hos 6:6 – **1329**; Ro
9:18 – **1720**; 12:8 – **1725**; Tit 3:5
– **1853**; Introduction to
Jeremiah: Themes and
Message – **1116**

MERIB-BAAL
Jdg 6:32 – **340**; 2Sa 4:4 – **428**

MERIBAH
Ex 17:7 – **112**; Nu 20:13 – **220**

MERIBAH KADESH
Eze 47:19 – **1295**

MERODACH-BALADAN
2Ki 20:1,12 – **563,564**

MEROM
Jos 11:5 – **306**

MEROZ
Jdg 5:23 – **337**

MESHA
2Ki 3:27 – **528**; Isa 16:1 – **1040**

**MESHA (MOABITE) STONE
(INSCRIPTION)**
Ge 49:19 – **80**; 2Ki 1:1 – **524**;
"Ancient Texts Relating to the
OT" – **5**

MESHACH
Da 1:7 – **1300**

MESHECH (son of Japheth)
Ge 10:2 – **20**

trip to Rome
Ac 27:1 – 1696; 28:22 – 1700;
"Paul's Journey to Rome"
– 1697; "Rome in the Time of
Paul" – 1702
PAX ROMANA
Lk 2:1,14 – 1538,1539
PEACE
Ge 8:11 – 17; Nu 6:26 – 199; Isa
39:8 – 1071; 48:18 – 1087; Jer
6:14 – 1131; Eze 34:25 – 1275;
Mic 5:5 – 1376; Mt 10:34
– 1457; Lk 2:14 – 1539; Jn
14:27 – 1626; 20:19 – 1637; Ro
5:1 – 1712; 12:18 – 1726; Php
4:7 – 1809; Col 3:15 – 1817; 3Jn
14 – 1917; Jude 2 – 1920; Rev
1:4 – 1926
PEACE OFFERING. *See*
FELLOWSHIP OFFERING
PEDAIAH
1Ch 3:19 – 588
PEKAH
2Ki 15:25,27 – 552; 16:5 – 553;
2Ch 28:5,6 – 655; Isa 7:1,9
– 1026,1027; 8:6 – 1028
PEKAHIAH
2Ki 15:25 – 552
PEKOD
Jer 50:21 – 1206; Eze 23:23
– 1258
PELATIAH
1Ch 3:21 – 588; Eze 11:1 – 1240
PELETHITES
2Sa 8:18 – 436; 1Ch 18:17 – 610
PELUSIUM
Eze 30:15 – 1268
PENIEL
Jdg 8:8 – 342; 1Ki 12:25 – 497
PENINNAH
1Sa 2:3 – 376
PENTATEUCH
1Sa 8:7 – 385; 1Ki 1:50 – 472; 2Ki
22:8 – 567; Ne 10:34 – 710; Mt
22:24 – 1474; Jn 4:25 – 1600;
10:34 – 1617; Ro 8:2 – 1716;
Introduction to Genesis: Author
and Date of Writing – 2
PENTECOST. *See also* FEAST: of
Weeks (Pentecost or Harvest)
Joel 2:28-32 – 1342; Mt 3:11
– 1446; 16:19,28 – 1466; Jn
1:33 – 1594; Ac 1:5 – 1644; 2:1-
3,15 – 1645,1647; 4:4 – 1650;
8:16 – 1659; 1Co 12:10 – 1750;
16:8 – 1759; Col 1:6 – 1813; 1Pe
1:12 – 1888; "Countries of
People Mentioned at Pentecost"
– 1646
PEOR
Nu 31:1-24 – 235; Jos 22:17 – 321
PERATH
Jer 13:4 – 1143
PERAZIM
1Ch 14:11 – 604
PEREA
Lk 13:31 – 1567
PEREZ
Ge 38:29 – 65; Ru 4:12 – 370; 1Ch
9:4-6 – 598
PERFUME
SS 1:3,12 – 1005; Mk 14:3,8
– 1522; Lk 7:38 – 1552; Jn 12:3
– 1620

PERGA
Ac 13:13 – 1670
PERGAMUM
Rev 2:12,13 – 1928
PERIZZITES
Ge 13:7 – 25; Jos 17:15 – 315
PERJURY
Ex 20:7 – 115; Zec 5:3 – 1411
PERSECUTION
Jn 15:21 – 1627; Ac 9:4 – 1660;
1Co 16:1 – 1758; 2Co 5:13
– 1768; Php 1:28 – 1804; Col
1:24 – 1814; 2Ti 3:12 – 1846;
Heb 10:32 – 1871; 12:4,5
– 1874; Rev 2:10 – 1928
PERSEPOLIS
Ezr 5:6-7 – 681; 6:1,2 – 681
PERSEVERANCE
1Co 15:2 – 1755; Php 2:12 – 1806;
Heb 3:6,14 – 1861,1862; 6:11
– 1865; 11:35 – 1873; 12:1
– 1874; Jas 5:11 – 1885; 1Pe
1:5 – 1888
PERSIA
Ezr 9:9 – 688; Isa 41:2 – 1073; Da
7:4-7 – 1310; Hag 1:1 – 1402;
2:6 – 1403; Zec 1:20 – 1409; Mt
2:1 – 1442; Introduction to
Esther: Author and Date – 718
Gulf of
Isa 21:1 – 1045; 43:14 – 1078; Ac
2:9 – 1646
PERSIANS
Ezr 1:1 – 673; 4:14 – 680; 6:2
– 681; Ne 5:4 – 701; Est 2:23
– 722; 5:11 – 725; Isa 43:3
– 1078; 47:11 – 1085; Da 7:4-7
– 1310; "From Malachi to
Christ" – 1430
PETER
Introduction to 1 Peter: Author and
Date – 1886
call of
Mk 1:17 – 1494
and Christ's forgiveness
Jn 21:7,15-17,15 – 1638
and Christ's resurrection
Lk 24:12 – 1589; 1Co 15:5 – 1755
in garden of Gethsemane
Mk 14:47,66,70 – 1526,1527; Jn
18:10,15 – 1631,1632
and his concept of Christ
Mt 16:18 – 1466; Mk 8:32,33
– 1510; Lk 9:20 – 1557; Jn 6:68
– 1608; 13:37 – 1624
and his denial of Christ
Mt 26:31,73 – 1484,1486; Mk
14:37 – 1526; 16:7 – 1530; Lk
22:61 – 1584; Jn 13:38 – 1624;
18:17,18 – 1632
and his ministry
Ac 8:14 – 1659; 11:17 – 1666; 15:7
– 1674; 1Co 1:12 – 1735; "Philip's
and Peter's Missionary
Journeys" – 1658
and his vision from God
Ac 10:10,14,23,26,28 – 1663
house of
Mt 4:13 – 1447; Mk 1:29 – 1494;
9:33 – 1512
marriage of
Mk 1:30 – 1494; 1Co 9:5 – 1745
and Pentecost
Ac 2:4,14,17,34 – 1645,1647,1648

and the transfiguration
Mk 9:5 – 1511; Lk 9:28 – 1557
and the washing of feet
Jn 13:8,9 – 1623
PETHUEL
Introduction to Joel: Author – 1338
PETRA
2Ki 14:7 – 547; Ac 2:11 – 1647
PHARAOH
Amunhotep II
1Ki 6:1 – 480; Introduction to
Exodus: Chronology – 84
Apries (Hophra)
2Ki 24:20 – 574; Eze 17:7 – 1248;
30:21 – 1269
Neco II
Jdg 5:19 – 337; 2Ki 22:20 – 567;
23:29,33-35 – 570; 2Ch 36:2,4
– 667; Isa 36:10 – 1066; Eze
31:3 – 1269
Osorkon I
2Ch 14:9 – 639
Psammeticus II
Eze 17:7 – 1248
Psusennes II
1Ki 3:1 – 475
Rameses II
1Ki 6:1 – 480; La 4:20 – 1224; Heb
11:27 – 1873; Introduction to
Exodus: Chronology – 84
Seti I
Introduction to Exodus:
Chronology – 84
Shabako
Isa 18:1 – 1042; 30:1 – 1057
Shebitku
Isa 37:9 – 1067
Shishak
1Ki 3:1 – 475; 11:40 – 496; 14:25
– 504; 2Ch 12:2 – 637; "Ancient
Texts Relating to the OT" – 5
Siamun
1Ki 3:1 – 475
Thutmose III
Ex 1:11 – 88; 2:15 – 89; Jdg 4:3
– 334; 5:19 – 337; Introduction
to Exodus: Chronology – 84
PHARISEES
Mt 3:7,11 – 1445,1446; 10:14
– 1456; 22:15-17 – 1474; 23:24
– 1476; Mk 2:16,18 – 1496; 3:4,
6 – 1497; 7:1 – 1506; 8:15
– 1509; 10:2 – 1513; 12:18
– 1519; Lk 5:17,21,30 – 1547,
1548; 6:11 – 1549; 11:39
– 1562; 13:31 – 1567; 15:28
– 1570; 18:12 – 1575; Jn 1:24
– 1594; 4:1 – 1599; 7:47,49,50-
51,52 – 1611; 8:15 – 1612; 9:40,
41 – 1615; 11:47 – 1619; 17:8
– 1630; Ac 5:34 – 1653; 15:1,5
– 1674; 22:30 – 1690; 24:21
– 1693; Gal 4:10 – 1785; "The
Time between the Testaments"
– 1431; "Jewish Sects" – 1476
PHICOL
Ge 21:22 – 37
PHILADELPHIA
Rev 3:7 – 1930
PHILEMON
Col 3:22-4:1,4:10 – 1817;
Introduction to Philemon:
Recipient; Background and
Purpose – 1855

SELA
2Ki 14:7 – 547; Isa 16:1 – 1040;
Ob 3 – 1361
SELAH
Introduction to Psalms: Authorship
and Titles – 781
SELEUCIA
Ac 13:4 – 1670
SELEUCIDS
Da 11:5,7,10,20,21 – 1316,1317;
Rev 2:18 – 1929; "Ptolemies
and Seleucids" – 1318; "The
Time between the Testaments"
– 1431
SELF-CONTROL
Pr 16:32 – 969; 2Pe 1:6 – 1899
SELF-DENIAL
Lk 9:23,48 – 1557,1558; Ro 14:7
– 1727; 15:1 – 1728; 1Co 9:12,
19 – 1745
SEMITES
Ge 10:21 – 22; Ne 12:31 – 714
SENAAH
Ezr 2:35 – 675
SENIR
SS 4:8 – 1008; Eze 27:5 – 1263
SENNACHERIB
2Ki 18:13,14 – 559; 19:4,29,37
– 561,563; 2Ch 32:21 – 662; Ne
11:27 – 712; Isa 8:8 – 1028;
36:1 – 1065; 1Co 1:19 – 1736
SENNACHERIB'S PRISM
"Ancient Texts Relating to the OT"
– 5
SEPHARVAIM
Isa 36:19 – 1066; Eze 47:16
– 1295
SEPTUAGINT
Ecc 1:1 – 992; Am 5:26 – 1354;
Introduction to Leviticus: Title
– 145; Introduction to Numbers:
Title – 185; Introduction to 1
Samuel: Title – 371; Introduction
to Ezra and Nehemiah
– 670; Introduction to Psalms:
Name – 781; "The Book of the
Twelve, or the Minor Prophets"
– 1320; "The Time between the
Testaments" – 1431-32
SERAIAH
2Ki 25:18 – 575; 1Ch 6:14 – 592;
Ezr 7:1 – 683
SERAPH
Isa 6:2 – 1025
SERIAH
2Sa 8:17 – 436
SERMON ON THE MOUNT/PLAIN
Mt 5:1-7:29 – 1449; Lk 6:20-49
– 1549; 11:1 – 1561
SERPENT
Ge 3:1,14,15 – 10; Am 9:3 – 1358
SERVANT OF THE LORD
Ex 14:31 – 108; Dt 34:5 – 287; Jdg
2:8 – 331; Ps 18 title – 801; Isa
41:8-9 – 1074; 42:1-4 – 1076;
Ro 1:1 – 1706; 6:18 – 1714; 16:1
– 1730; 2Co 11:23 – 1775; Gal
1:10 – 1781; 6:17 – 1788; Php
1:1 – 1803; 2:7 – 1805
SERVANTHOOD
Mk 10:35-36,45 – 1515; Lk 22:26
– 1583; Jn 13:5 – 1623
SETI I
Introduction to Exodus:
Chronology – 84

SEVEN
Ge 4:17-18 – 12; Lev 4:6 – 151;
Jos 6:4 – 298; Ru 4:15 – 370; Ps
12:6 – 797; Pr 9:1 – 957;
Introduction to Genesis: Literary
Features – 2; Introduction to
Revelation: Distinctive Feature
– 1923
SEVEN, THE
Ac 6:6 – 1654; 8:5 – 1658; 14:23
– 1673
SEVEN LEAN YEARS TRADITION
"Ancient Texts Relating to the OT"
– 5
SEVENTY
Ge 10:2 – 20; 46:27 – 76
SEXUAL SIN. See ADULTERY;
HOMOSEXUALITY
SHABAKO
Isa 18:1 – 1042; 30:1 – 1057
SHABBETHAI
Ezr 10:15 – 690; Ne 13:15 – 715
SHADDAI. See NAMES OF
GOD:God Almighty (El
Shaddai)
SHADRACH
Da 1:7 – 1300
SHALLUM
2Ki 15:27 – 552; 22:14 – 567;
23:30 – 570; 1Ch 3:15-16 – 588;
Jer 22:11 – 1158; Hos 7:7
– 1330
SHALMANESER III
1Ki 18:5 – 510; 22:1 – 519; 2Ki 8:7
– 536; 10:8,34 – 540,542; 13:7
– 545; 19:12 – 562; Na 3:3
– 1384
SHALMANESER IV
2Ki 14:25 – 548
SHALMANESER V
2Ki 17:3,6 – 555; Isa 10:10 – 1031
SHALMANESER'S BLACK OBELISK
"Ancient Texts Relating to the OT"
– 5
SHAMASH
Ezr 1:8 – 673
SHAMASH-SHUM-UKIN
2Ch 33:11 – 663; Ezr 4:9 – 679
SHAMGAR
Jdg 3:31 – 334
SHAMMAH
1Sa 16:9 – 398; 2Sa 13:3 – 441;
21:21 – 457
SHAMMAI, SCHOOL OF
Lev 19:18 – 171; 24:20 – 178; Mt
19:3 – 1469
SHAPHAN
2Ki 22:3 – 566; Ezr 7:6 – 684; Jer
29:3 – 1170; 36:10 – 1185
SHAPHAT
1Ki 19:16 – 514; 2Ki 3:11 – 527
SHAREZER
2Ki 19:37 – 563
SHARON
SS 2:1 – 1006; Isa 33:9 – 1062; Ac
9:35 – 1662
SHEALTIEL
1Ch 3:19 – 588; Ezr 5:2 – 680; Ne
12:1 – 712; Hag 1:1 – 1402; Mt
1:12 – 1441
SHEAR-JASHUB
Isa 7:3 – 1026
SHEBA (son of Bicri)
2Sa 20:1,14,21 – 454,455; 1Ch
18:17 – 610

SHEBA (son of Joktan)
Ge 10:28 – 22
SHEBA (Arabian home of queen)
1Ki 10:1 – 491; Isa 60:6 – 1104;
Jer 6:20 – 1131; Eze 38:13
– 1280; Mt 12:42 – 1460
SHEBITKU
Isa 37:9 – 1067
SHEBNA
Isa 22:15,16,21 – 1047
SHECANIAH (head of Davidic family)
1Ch 3:21,22 – 588,589
SHECANIAH (son of Jehiel)
Ezr 10:2 – 689
SHECHEM
Ge 33:18 – 57; Jos 8:30-35 – 302;
Jdg 9:1 – 344; Ac 7:16 – 1655
SHEEP GATE
Ne 3:1,32 – 697,699
SHEKEL
Ge 20:16 – 36; Ezr 2:69 – 677
SHELAH
1Ch 2:3-9 – 585; 9:4-6 – 598
SHELANITES
1Ch 9:4-6 – 598
SHELOMITH
Ezr 8:10 – 686
SHEM
Ge 10:2,21 – 20,22; 1Ch 1:5-23
– 583
SHEMA
Dt 4:1 – 250; 6:4-9 – 254; Mk
12:29,31 – 1519; Jas 2:19
– 1883
SHEMAIAH (prophet)
1Ki 12:22 – 497; Jer 29:24 – 1171
SHEMAIAH (son of Delaiah)
Ne 6:10,12 – 703
SHEMAIAH (son of Shecaniah)
1Ch 3:22 – 589
SHENAZZAR
1Ch 3:18 – 588; Ezr 1:8 – 673
SHEOL
Ge 37:35 – 63; Mt 16:18 – 1466;
Rev 6:8 – 1933
SHEPHELAH
Jos 15:33 – 313; Mic 1:10-15
– 1372; "Five Cities of the
Philistines" – 330
SHEPHERD
Ge 48:15 – 78; Ps 23:1 – 807;
119:176 – 921; Eze 34:2 – 1274;
Zec 10:2 – 1417; Mk 6:42
– 1505; Jn 10:1-30 – 1615; 1Pe
2:25 – 1892; 5:2 – 1895
SHESHACH
Jer 25:26 – 1165
SHESHBAZZAR
1Ch 3:18 – 588; Ezr 1:8,11 – 673,
674; 2:63 – 676; Ne 5:15 – 702
SHIBBOLETH
Jdg 12:6 – 349
SHIELD
Ge 15:1 – 28; Ps 3:3 – 788
SHIHOR RIVER
Jos 13:3 – 310; 1Ch 13:5 – 604;
Isa 23:3 – 1048
SHILOAH
Isa 8:6 – 1028
SHILOH
Jos 18:1 – 315; Jdg 21:19 – 362;
1Sa 1:3 – 375; 2:32 – 379; 9:12
– 386

SOLOMON'S COLONNADE
Jn 10:23 – **1616**; Ac 3:11 – **1649**
SON
of the Blessed One
Mk 14:61 – **1527**
of David
Mt 1:1,16,20 – **1441,1442**; 2:1
– **1442**; 9:27 – **1455**; Mk 10:47
– **1516**; 12:35 – **1519**
of man
Eze 2:1 – **1232**; Da 7:13 – **1310**;
Mk 8:31 – **1510**; Lk 19:10
– **1576**; Jn 12:34 – **1621**; Ac
7:56 – **1657**; Eph 1:22 – **1792**;
Rev 6:13 – **1933**
of the Most High
Lk 1:32 – **1536**; 8:28 – **1554**
SONG
of David
2Sa 22:1 – **457**
of Deborah
Jdg 5:1-31 – **336**
of Hannah
1Sa 2:1 – **376**
of Mary
Lk 1:46-55 – **1537**
of Moses
Ex 15:1-18 – **108**; Dt 31:30-32:43
– **282**; Rev 15:3 – **1942**
of the vineyard
Isa 5:7 – **1023**
of Zechariah
Lk 1:68-79 – **1537**
SONS
of God
Ge 6:2 – **14**; Job 5:1 – **739**; Ro
8:14,15,19,23 – **1717,1718**; Gal
4:5 – **1785**; Heb 2:10 – **1861**;
12:7 – **1874**
of thunder
Mk 3:17 – **1498**; Lk 9:54 – **1558**
SOOTHSAYER'S TREE
Jdg 9:37 – **345**
SOPATER
Ac 20:4 – **1685**; Ro 16:21 – **1731**
SOREK VALLEY
Jdg 14:5 – **351**
SOSIPATER
Ac 20:4 – **1685**; Ro 16:21 – **1731**
SOSTHENES
Ac 18:17 – **1681**; 1Co 1:1 – **1735**
SOUND DOCTRINE
Tit 1:9 – **1851**; 2:2-10 – **1852**; "The
Pastoral Letters" – **1832**
SOUTH GALATIAN THEORY
Introduction to Galatians: Date
and Destination – **1779**
SOUTH GATE
1Ch 26:15 – **618**
SOVEREIGNTY OF GOD. *See* GOD:
sovereignty of
SPAIN
Ro 15:24 – **1730**; 2Co 10:16
– **1774**
SPELT
Ex 9:32 – **99**
SPICE
SS 4:10 – **1008**
SPIES
Nu 13:2 – **209**; Jos 2:1-24 – **293,
294**
SPIRIT OF BONDAGE
2Co 11:4 – **1774**

SPIRIT OF THE LORD
Jdg 3:10 – **333**; 6:34 – **340**; 11:29
– **348**; 1Sa 11:6 – **389**; 16:14
– **400**; 19:24 – **405**; 2Sa 23:2
– **459**; 1Ki 18:12 – **510**;
Introduction to Judges: Theme
and Theology – **326**
SPIRITS, EVIL. *See* EVIL SPIRITS
SPIRITUAL GIFTS. *See* GIFTS:
spiritual
STEPHANUS
1Co 16:15 – **1759**
STEPHEN
Ac 6:5,8,9,11,13 – **1654**; 7:9,14,
16,23,35,44-50,49 – **1655-
1657**
STOICISM
Ac 17:18 – **1680**
STRAIGHT STREET
Ac 9:11 – **1660**; "Roman
Damascus" – **1661**
SUBMISSION
Ex 20:2 – **115**; Ps 2:12 – **788**; Ro
13:1 – **1726**; Eph 5:21,22
– **1798**; Heb 13:17 – **1876**; 1Pe
3:1 – **1892**; 5:5 – **1895**
SUBSTITUTION
Ge 22:13 – **38**; Ex 29:10 – **130**; Lev
1:5 – **147**; 16:20-22 – **167**; Nu
8:10 – **203**; Mt 20:28 – **1471**; Mk
10:45 – **1515**
SUCCOTH
Ex 12:37 – **104**; Jdg 7:24 – **342**;
1Ki 7:46 – **485**
SUFFERING
Rev 1:9 – **1926**; Introduction to
Job: Theme and Message
– **731**; Introduction to Psalms:
Theology – **784**; Introduction to
1 Peter: Themes – **1887**
for Christ
1Co 7:28 – **1743**; 13:3 – **1752**; 2Co
1:8 – **1763**; Php 1:13,20,29
– **1803,1804**; 1Th 3:3 – **1822**;
2Ti 2:11-13,12 – **1845**; 3:11
– **1846**; 1Pe 3:14 – **1892**; 4:1,4,
13 – **1893,1894**
of Christ
Isa 52:14 – **1094**; Heb 2:10
– **1861**; 5:8 – **1864**; 12:2 – **1874**;
1Pe 2:21 – **1891**
rejoicing in
Ro 5:3,4 – **1712**
of the righteous
Job 10:3 – **745**; Ps 22 – **805**; 73
– **860**; Lk 13:2,4 – **1566**; Ro 8:36
– **1718**; 2Co 4:17 – **1767**; Jas
1:9-10 – **1881**
and spiritual gain
Job 2:10 – **736**; Heb 12:5 – **1874**;
1Pe 4:17 – **1894**
SUKKITES
2Ch 12:3 – **637**
SUN
Ge 1:16 – **7**; Ex 10:21 – **100**; Ps
19:4b-6 – **803**; 104:19-23 – **896**
SUN OF RIGHTEOUSNESS
Mal 4:2 – **1428**
SUSA
Ezr 4:9 – **679**; 6:2 – **681**; Ne 5:4
– **701**; Est 1:2,5-6 – **720**; 2:5
– **721**
SWEARING
Jas 5:12 – **1885**

SYCAMORE (FIG) TREE
Am 7:14 – **1356**; Lk 19:4 – **1576**
SYCHAR
Jn 4:5 – **1599**
SYNAGOGUE
description of
Eze 8:1 – **1237**; Mk 1:21 – **1494**;
Lk 21:12 – **1581**; Ac 13:14
– **1670**; "The Time between the
Testaments" – **1433**;
"Capernaum Synagogue"
– **1546**
ruler of
Mk 5:22 – **1503**
SYNOPTIC GOSPELS
Mt 3:3 – **1444**; 13:3 – **1460**; 19:16
– **1469**; 20:30 – **1471**; 21:12-17
– **1472**; Lk 5:12-16 – **1547**; 9:12
– **1556**; 19:45 – **1578**; Jn 6:68
– **1608**; 18:11 – **1631**; "The
Synoptic Gospels" – **1437**;
"Dating the Synoptic Gospels"
– **1437**; "Parables of Jesus"
– **1570**
SYNTYCHE
Php 4:2-3 – **1808**
SYRACUSE
Ac 28:12 – **1700**
SYRIA
Isa 30:1 – **1057**; Da 7:4-7 – **1310**;
11:6 – **1316**; Gal 1:17,21 – **1781,
1782**; "The Time between the
Testaments" – **1431**
SYRO-EPHRAIMITE WAR
Isa 7:1 – **1026**

TAANACH
Jdg 5:19 – **337**
TABEEL
Isa 7:6 – **1027**
TABERNACLE
Ex 25:9 – **123**; 26:1 – **125**; 1Sa 1:9
– **375**; Rev 15:5 – **1943**; "The
Tabernacle" – **124**; "Tabernacle
Furnishings" – **126**
TABERNACLES, FEAST OF. *See*
FEAST: of Tabernacles
TABITHA
Ac 20:10 – **1686**
TABLE OF NATIONS
Ge 10:2 – **20**; 1Ch 1:5-23 – **583**;
"Table of Nations" – **21**
TABLETS
Ex 31:18 – **133**; 2Co 3:3,6 – **1765**
TABRIMMON
1Ki 15:19 – **505**
TAHPANHES
Jer 2:16 – **1122**; Eze 30:18 – **1269**
TALE OF TWO BROTHERS
"Ancient Texts Relating to the OT"
– **5**
TALENT, THE
1Ki 20:39 – **517**; Mt 25:15 – **1479**;
Lk 19:13 – **1576**
TALMAI
2Sa 3:3 – **426**; 13:37 – **444**
TALMANUTHA
Mk 8:10 – **1509**
TALMUD
Zec 6:12 – **1413**; Mk 5:26 – **1503**;
15:23 – **1528**; Lk 16:22 – **1572**;
Introduction to Ezra: Ezra and
Nehemiah – **670**

TAMAR
Ge 38:11 – 64; Ru 1:4 – 365; 3:4
– 368; 2Sa 3:2-5,3 – 426; 13:1,
13,15,21 – 441,443; 14:27
– 445; 1Ki 15:2 – 504; 2Ch
11:20 – 637; Eze 47:18 – 1295

TAMARISK
Ge 21:33 – 37

TAMMUZ
Eze 8:14 – 1238

TANIS
Isa 19:11 – 1043; Eze 30:14
– 1268

TAPPUAH
2Ki 15:16 – 549

TARGUM
Ne 8:8 – 706; Zec 6:12 – 1413;
10:4 – 1417; Introduction to Job:
Date – 731

TARSHISH
Ps 72:10 – 859; Isa 23:6 – 1048;
Eze 27:12 – 1263; Jnh 1:3
– 1366

TARSUS
Ac 6:9 – 1654; 9:30 – 1662; 22:3
– 1689; Gal 1:21 – 1782

TARTARUS
2Pe 2:4 – 1900

TARTESSUS
Isa 23:6 – 1048; Jnh 1:3 – 1366

TAWILAN
Ob 9 – 1361

TAX COLLECTOR
Mt 5:46 – 1451; Mk 2:16 – 1496;
Lk 3:12 – 1541; 18:13 – 1575;
19:2 – 1576

TAXES
1Ch 27:25-31 – 620; Ne 5:4 – 701;
Mt 17:24 – 1467; Mk 12:14
– 1518; Ro 13:6 – 1726

TEACHER OF RIGHTEOUSNESS
Joel 2:23 – 1342

TEACHERS OF THE LAW
Mt 2:4 – 1442; Mk 2:16 – 1496;
12:40 – 1520; Lk 5:17 – 1547

TEACHING
1Co 12:28 – 1751; Eph 4:11,14
– 1795,1796

false
2Co 2:17 – 1765; 3:1 – 1765; 4:2,5
– 1766,1767; 5:11 – 1768; 6:14
– 1770; 7:2,3 – 1770; 10:4,7,12,
13 – 1773,1774; 11:1,2,6,13,19,
22 – 1774,1775; 12:12,16
– 1776,1777; 13:5 – 1777; Php
3:2 – 1807; 1Ti 1:3-11 – 1835;
4:1 – 1839; Tit 1:9 – 1851; 2Pe
2:15 – 1901; Rev 2:14 – 1928

TEBAH
1Ch 18:8 – 609

TEKOA
2Sa 14:1 – 444; Ne 3:5,27 – 697,
699; Introduction to Amos:
Author – 1345

TEL ABIB
Eze 3:15 – 1233; Ac 9:36 – 1662

TEL MELAH
Ezr 2:59 – 676

TELL (mound)
Jos 11:13 – 307; Jer 30:18 – 1173

TELL BEIT MIRSIM
Jos 10:38 – 306; 2Ch 26:10 – 653

TELL ED-DUWEIR
2Ki 14:19 – 548

TELL EL-MASKHUTAH
Ex 12:37 – 104; Ne 2:19 – 697

TEMA
Job 1:15 – 735; Isa 21:14 – 1046

TEMAN
Job 2:11 – 737; 4:1 – 738; Jer 49:7
– 1202; Eze 25:13 – 1261; Am
1:12 – 1349; Ob 9 – 1361; Hab
3:3 – 1390

TEMPLE
curtain of
Ex 26:31 – 127; Nu 3:25-26 – 194;
Mk 15:38 – 1529; Lk 23:45
– 1587
early
1Sa 1:9 – 375; Ps 24:2 – 808
Ezekiel's
Ne 8:16 – 706; "Ezekiel's Temple"
– 1284
Herod's
Mt 2:1 – 1442; 4:5 – 1447; Lk 4:9
– 1544; 21:5 – 1580; Jn 2:20
– 1597; Ac 3:2 – 1648; "Herod's
Temple" – 1448
scroll
Ezr 8:15 – 686; Ne 8:16 – 706;
10:34 – 710
Solomon's
1Ki 6,7 – 480-485; 8:2 – 485; Ezr
5:11 – 681; 6:15 – 683; Hag 2:3
– 1403; Jnh 2:4 – 1367;
"Solomon's Temple" – 481;
"Temple Furnishings" – 484;
Introduction to 2 Chronicles:
The Building of the Temple in
Chronicles – 624
Zerubbabel's
Ezr 4:24 – 680; 6:3,15 – 682,683;
Hag 1:2 – 1402; 2:3 – 1403; Zec
4:1-14,6,10 – 1410,1411;
"Zerubbabel's Temple" – 678

TEMPTATION
Ge 3:6 – 10; 22:1 – 37; Mt 4:1-11,1
– 1446; 1Co 10:13 – 1746; 1Th 3:5
– 1823; Heb 4:15,16 – 1863; Jas
1:13 – 1881

TEN COMMANDMENTS
Ex 20:1-17,1 – 115; 31:18 – 133;
Dt 5:6-21 – 252

TENDON
Ge 32:32 – 56

TENT OF MEETING
Ex 27:21 – 128; Lev 1:1 – 147;
16:16 – 167; Nu 2:17 – 192; Jos
18:1 – 315; 1Sa 7:1 – 384; 1Ki
8:4 – 486; Jn 1:14 – 1593

TENTMAKING
Ac 18:3 – 1681; 1Co 4:12 – 1739

TERAH
Ge 11:31 – 24; Jos 24:14 – 323;
Ac 7:4 – 1655

TERAPHIM. See HOUSEHOLD
GODS

TERTIUS
Ac 24:1 – 1692; Ro 16:22 – 1731

TERTULLUS
Ac 24:1,10 – 1692,1693

TESTING
Ge 22:1,2 – 37; Ex 15:25 – 110; Nu
11:10 – 206; Dt 4:20 – 251; Ps
66:10 – 852; Mt 4:1 – 1446; Rev
3:10 – 1930

TETRARCH
Mt 14:1 – 1463

THADDAEUS
Mk 3:18 – 1498; Lk 6:16 – 1549;
Ac 1:13 – 1644

THANKSGIVING
Ro 1:8,21 – 1706,1707; Eph 5:4
– 1797; Php 1:3-4 – 1803; 4:6,
18 – 1808,1809; Col 1:3 – 1813;
3:16 – 1817; 1Th 3:9 – 1823;
5:18 – 1825; Introduction to
Psalms: Psalm Types – 782

THEBES. See KARNAK

THEOCRACY. See also ISRAEL: as
a theocracy
Ge 9:5,6 – 18

THEOPHANY
Nu 12:5 – 208; 14:10 – 210; Jos
5:13 – 297

THEOPHILUS
Ac 1:1 – 1644; Introduction to
Luke: Recipient and Purpose
– 1532

THESSALONICA
Ac 16:12 – 1677; Php 4:15,16
– 1809; Introduction to 1
Thessalonians: Thessalonica
– 1819

THIRTY, THE
2Sa 23:24 – 461; 1Ch 27:9-15
– 620

THOMAS
Jn 11:16 – 1618; 14:5 – 1625

THREE
2Sa 23:8 – 460

THREE TAVERNS
Ac 28:15 – 1700

THRESHING
Ge 50:10 – 82; Ru 1:22 – 366; 2:17
– 367; Am 1:3 – 1348

THUCYDIDES
Ne 1:3 – 694

THUTMOSE III
Ex 1:11 – 88; 2:15 – 89; Jdg 4:3
– 334; 5:19 – 337; Ne 5:18
– 702; Introduction to Exodus:
Chronology – 84

THYATIRA
Ac 16:14 – 1678; Rev 2:18 – 1929

TIBERIAS (city)
Ne 11:1 – 710; Lk 23:7,8 – 1585;
Jn 6:1 – 1605

TIBERIAS, SEA OF
Mk 1:16 – 1494; Lk 5:1 – 1547; Jn
6:1 – 1605

TIBERIUS, EMPEROR
Mt 22:19 – 1474; Lk 3:1 – 1540; Ro
16:11 – 1731

TIBNI
1Ki 16:22,23 – 507

TIGLATH-PILESER III
1Ki 15:20 – 505; 16:27 – 508; 2Ki
15:19,30 – 552; 16:9 – 554; 1Ch
5:6,26 – 591,592; 2Ch 26:11
– 653; 28:20 – 656; Isa 17:3
– 1041; Hos 5:13 – 1328; 7:9
– 1330; "Assyrian Campaigns
against Israel and Judah" – 550

TIKVAH
Ezr 10:15 – 690

TIMNA
1Ch 1:36 – 584

TIMNAH
Jdg 14:1,5 – 351

TIMNATH SERAH
Jos 19:50 – 318

Index to Maps

All entries are place-names found on the maps within the Study Bible. References are to the page on which the map is located. For additional information on place-names, see Index to Subjects.

Concordance

Word or block entries marked with an asterisk (*) list every verse in the Bible in which the word appears. Words in parentheses after an entry remind the reader to check other forms of that word in locating a passage.

AARON

Genealogy of (Ex 6:16-20; Jos 21:4, 10; 1Ch 6:3-15).

Priesthood of (Ex 28:1; Nu 17; Heb 5:1-4; 7), garments (Ex 28; 39), consecration (Ex 29), ordination (Lev 8).

Spokesman for Moses (Ex 4:14-16, 27-31; 7:1-2). Supported Moses' hands in battle (Ex 17:8-13). Built golden calf (Ex 32; Dt 9:20). Talked against Moses (Nu 12). Priesthood opposed (Nu 16); staff budded (Nu 17). Forbidden to enter land (Nu 20:1-12). Death (Nu 20:22-29; 33:38-39).

ABADDON*

Rev 9:11 whose name in Hebrew is A.

ABANDON (ABANDONED)

Dt 4:31 he will not a or destroy you
1Ki 6:13 and will not a my people Israel,"
Ne 9:19 compassion you did not a them
9:31 an end to them or a them,
Ps 16:10 you will not a me to the grave,
Ac 2:27 you will not a me to the grave,
1Ti 4: 1 in later times some will a the faith

ABANDONED (ABANDON)

Ge 24:27 who has not a his kindness
2Co 4: 9 persecuted, but not a; struck down,

ABBA*

Mk 14:36 "A, Father," he said, "everything is
Ro 8:15 And by him we cry, "A, Father."
Gal 4: 6 the Spirit who calls out, "A, Father

ABEDNEGO

Deported to Babylon with Daniel (Da 1:1-6). Name changed from Azariah (Da 1:7). Refused defilement by food (Da 1:8-20). Refused idol worship (Da 3:1-12); saved from furnace (Da 3:13-30).

ABEL

Second son of Adam (Ge 4:2). Offered proper sacrifice (Ge 4:4; Heb 11:4). Murdered by Cain (Ge 4:8; Mt 23:35; Lk 11:51; 1Jn 3:12).

ABHOR (ABHORS)

Lev 26:30 of your idols, and I will a you.
Dt 7:26 Utterly a and detest it,
Ps 26: 5 I a the assembly of evildoers
119:163 I hate and a falsehood
139: 21 and a those who rise up against you
Am 6: 8 "I a the pride of Jacob
Ro 2:22 You who a idols, do you rob

ABHORS (ABHOR)

Pr 11: 1 The LORD a dishonest scales,

ABIATHAR

High priest in days of Saul and David (1Sa 22; 2Sa 15; 1Ki 1-2; Mk 2:26). Escaped Saul's slaughter of priests (1Sa 22:18-23). Supported David in Absalom's revolt (2Sa 15:24-29). Supported Adonijah (1Ki 1:7-42); deposed by Solomon (1Ki 2:22-35; cf. 1Sa 2:31-35).

ABIDE see REMAIN

ABIGAIL

1. Sister of David (1Ch 2:16-17).
2. Wife of Nabal (1Sa 25:30); pled for his life with David (1Sa 25:14-35). Became David's wife after Nabal's death (1Sa 25:36-42); bore him Kileab (2Sa 3:3) also known as Daniel (1Ch 3:1).

ABIHU

Son of Aaron (Ex 6:23; 24:1, 9); killed for offering unauthorized fire (Lev 10; Nu 3:2-4; 1Ch 24:1-2).

ABIJAH

1. Second son of Samuel (1Ch 6:28); a corrupt judge (1Sa 8:1-5).
2. An Aaronic priest (1Ch 24:10; Lk 1:5).
3. Son of Jeroboam I of Israel; died as prophesied by Ahijah (1Ki 14:1-18).

4. Son of Rehoboam; king of Judah who fought Jeroboam I attempting to reunite the kingdom (1Ki 14:31-15:8; 2Ch 12:16-14:1; Mt 1:7).

ABILITY (ABLE)

Ex 35:34 tribe of Dan, the a to teach others.
Dt 8:18 for it is he who gives you the a
Ezr 2: 69 According to their a they gave
Mt 25:15 one talent, each according to his a.
Ac 11:29 disciples, each according to his a,
2Co 8: 3 far beyond our a to endure,
8: 3 were able, and even beyond their a.

ABIMELECH

1. King of Gerar who took Abraham's wife Sarah, believing her to be his sister (Ge 20). Later made a covenant with Abraham (Ge 21:22-33).
2. King of Gerar who took Isaac's wife Rebekah, believing her to be his sister (Ge 26:1-11). Later made a covenant with Isaac (Ge 26:12-31).
3. Son of Gideon (Jdg 8:31). Attempted to make himself king (Jdg 9).

ABISHAG*

Shunammite virgin; attendant of David in his old age (1Ki 1:1-15; 2:17-22).

ABISHAI

Son of Zeruiah, David's sister (1Sa 26:6; 1Ch 2:16). One of David's chief warriors (1Ch 11:15-21): against Edom (1Ch 18:12-13), Ammon (2Sa 10), Absalom (2Sa 18), Sheba (2Sa 20). Wanted to kill Saul (1Sa 26), killed Abner (2Sa 2:18-27; 3:22-39), wanted to kill Shimei (2Sa 16:5-13; 19:16-23).

ABLE (ABILITY ENABLE ENABLED ENABLES ENABLING)

Nu 14:16 'The LORD was not a
1Ch 29:14 that we should be a to give
2Ch 2: 6 who is a to build a temple for him,
Eze 7: 19 and gold will not be a to save them
Da 3: 17 the God we serve is a to save us
4: 37 walk in pride he is a to humble.
Mt 9: 28 "Do you believe that I am a
Lk 13:24 will try to enter and will not be a to
14: 30 to build and was not a to finish.'
21: 15 none of your adversaries will be a to
21: 36 and that you may be a to stand
Ac 5: 39 you will not be a to stop these men;
Ro 8: 39 will be a to separate us
14: 4 for the Lord is a to make him stand
16: 25 to him who is a to establish you
2Co 9: 8 God is a to make all grace abound
Eph 3: 20 him who is a to do immeasurably
6: 13 you may be a to stand your ground,
1Ti 3: 2 respectable, hospitable, a to teach,
2Ti 1: 12 and am convinced that he is a to
2: 24 kind to everyone, a to teach,
3: 15 which are a to make you wise
Heb 2: 18 he is a to help those who are being
7: 25 he is a to save completely
Jas 3: 2 a to keep his whole body in check.
Jude 24 To him who is a to keep you
Rev 5: 5 He is a to open the scroll

ABNER

Cousin of Saul and commander of his army (1Sa 14:50; 17:55-57; 26). Made Ish-Bosheth king after Saul (2Sa 2:8-10), but later defected to David (2Sa 3:6-21). Killed Asahel (2Sa 2:18-32), for which he was killed by Joab and Abishai (2Sa 3:22-39).

ABOLISH (ABOLISHED ABOLISHING)

Hos 2: 18 I will a from the land,
Mt 5: 17 that I have come to a the Law

ABOLISHED (ABOLISH)

Gal 5: 11 the offense of the cross has been a.

ABOLISHING* (ABOLISH)

Eph 2: 15 by a in his flesh the law

ABOMINATION*

Da 11:31 set up the a that causes desolation.
12: 11 a that causes desolation is set up,
Mt 24: 15 the holy place 'the a that causes
Mk 13: 14 you see 'the a that causes

ABOUND (ABOUNDING)

2Co 9: 8 able to make all grace a to you,
9: 8 you will a in every good work.
Php 1: 9 that your love may a more

ABOUNDING (ABOUND)

Ex 34: 6 slow to anger, a in love
Nu 14:18 a in love and forgiving sin
Ne 9: 17 slow to anger and a in love.
Ps 86: 5 a in love to all who call to you.
86: 15 slow to anger, a in love
103: 8 slow to anger, a in love,
Joel 2: 13 slow to anger and a in love,
Jnh 4: 2 slow to anger and a in love,

ABRAHAM

Abram, son of Terah (Ge 11:26-27), husband of Sarah (Ge 11:29).

Covenant relation with the LORD (Ge 12:1-3; 13:14-17; 15; 17; 22:15-18; Ex 2:24; Ne 9:8; Ps 105; Mic 7:20; Lk 1:68-75; Ro 4; Heb 6:13-15).

Called from Ur, via Haran, to Canaan (Ge 12:1; Ac 7:2-4; Heb 11:8-10). Moved to Egypt, nearly lost Sarah to Pharoah (Ge 12:10-20). Divided the land with Lot; settled in Hebron (Ge 13). Saved Lot from four kings (Ge 14:1-16); blessed by Melchizedek (Ge 14:17-20; Heb 7:1-20). Declared righteous by faith (Ge 15:6; Ro 4:3; Gal 3:6-9). Fathered Ishmael by Hagar (Ge 16).

Name changed from Abram (Ge 17:5; Ne 9:7). Circumcised (Ge 17; Ro 4:9-12). Entertained three visitors (Ge 18); promised a son by Sarah (Ge 18:9-15; 17:16). Questioned destruction of Sodom and Gomorrah (Ge 18:16-33). Moved to Gerar; nearly lost Sarah to Abimelech (Ge 20). Fathered Isaac by Sarah (Ge 21:1-7; Ac 7:8; Heb 11:11-12); sent away Hagar and Ishmael (Ge 21:8-21; Gal 4:22-30). Covenant with Abimelech (Ge 21:22-32). Tested by offering Isaac (Ge 22; Heb 11:17-19; Jas 2:21-24). Sarah died; bought field of Ephron for burial (Ge 23). Secured wife for Isaac (Ge 24). Fathered children by Keturah (Ge 25:1-6; 1Ch 1:32-33). Death (Ge 25:7-11).

Called servant of God (Ge 26:24), friend of God (2Ch 20:7; Isa 41:8; Jas 2:23), prophet (Ge 20:7), father of Israel (Ex 3:15; Isa 51:2; Mt 3:9; Jn 8:39-58).

ABRAM see ABRAHAM

ABSALOM

Son of David by Maacah (2Sa 3:3; 1Ch 3:2). Killed Amnon for rape of his sister Tamar; banished by David (2Sa 13). Returned to Jerusalem; received by David (2Sa 14). Rebelled against David; siezed kingdom (2Sa 15-17). Killed (2Sa 18).

ABSENT

Col 2: 5 though I am a from you in body,

ABSOLUTE*

1Ti 5: 2 women as sisters, with a purity.

ABSTAIN (ABSTAINS)

Ex 19:15 A from sexual relations."
Nu 6: 3 he must a from wine and other
Ac 15:20 them to a from food polluted
1Pe 2: 11 to a from sinful desires.

ABSTAINS* (ABSTAIN)

Ro 14: 6 thanks to God; and he who a,

ABUNDANCE (ABUNDANT)

Ge 41:29 Seven years of great a are coming
Job 36:31 and provides food in a.
Ps 66:12 but you brought us to a place of a.
Ecc 5: 12 but the a of a rich man
Isa 66: 11 and delight in her overflowing a."

ABUNDANT

Jer   2:22 and use an *a* of soap,
Mt   13:12 given more, and he will have an *a*.
     25:29 given more, and he will have an *a*.
Lk   12:15 consist in the *a* of his possessions."
1Pe   1: 2 Grace and peace be yours in *a*.
2Pe   1: 2 yours in *a* through the knowledge
Jude   : 2 peace and love be yours in *a*.

ABUNDANT (ABUNDANCE)

Dt   28:11 will grant you *a* prosperity—
     32: 2 like *a* rain on tender plants.
Job   36:28 and *a* showers fall on mankind.
Ps   68: 9 You gave *a* showers, O God;
     78:15 gave them water as *a* as the seas;
    132:15 I will bless her with *a* provisions;
    145: 7 will celebrate your *a* goodness
Pr   12:11 works his land will have *a* food,
     28:19 works his land will have *a* food,
Jer   33: 9 and will tremble at the *a* prosperity
Ro   5:17 who receive God's *a* provision

ABUSIVE

2Ti   3: 2 *a*, disobedient to their parents,

ABYSS*

Lk   8:31 not to order them to go into the *A*.
Rev   9: 1 the key to the shaft of the *A*.
     9: 2 When he opened the *A*, smoke rose
     9: 2 darkened by the smoke from the *A*.
     9:11 king over them the angel of the *A*,
     11: 7 up from the *A* will attack them,
     17: 8 and will come up out of the *A*
     20: 1 having the key to the *A*
     20: 3 He threw him into the *A*,

ACCEPT (ACCEPTABLE ACCEPTANCE ACCEPTED ACCEPTS)

Ex   23: 8 "Do not *a* a bribe,
Dt   16:19 Do not *a* a bribe, for a bribe blinds
Job   42: 8 and I will *a* his prayer and not deal
Pr   10: 8 The wise in heart *a* commands,
     19:20 Listen to advice and *a* instruction,
Ro   15: 7 *A* one another, then, just
Jas   1:21 humbly *a* the word planted in you,

ACCEPTABLE (ACCEPT)

Pr   21: 3 is more *a* to the LORD

ACCEPTANCE* (ACCEPT)

Ro   11:15 what will their *a* be but life
1Ti   1:15 saying that deserves full *a*:
     4: 9 saying that deserves full *a*

ACCEPTED (ACCEPT)

Ge   4: 7 will you not be *a*? But if you do not
Job   42: 9 and the LORD *a* Job's prayer.
Lk   4:24 "no prophet is *a* in his hometown.
Gal   1: 9 you a gospel other than what you *a*,

ACCEPTS (ACCEPT)

Ps   6: 9 the LORD *a* my prayer.
Jn   13:20 whoever *a* anyone I send *a* me;
     13:20 whoever *a* me *a* the one who sent

ACCESS

Ro   5: 2 through whom we have gained *a*
Eph   2:18 For through him we both have *a*

ACCOMPANIED (ACCOMPANY)

1Co   10: 4 from the spiritual rock that *a* them,
Jas   2:17 if it is not *a* by action, is dead.

ACCOMPANIES (ACCOMPANY)

2Co   9:13 obedience that *a* your confession

ACCOMPANY (ACCOMPANIED ACCOMPANIES)

Dt   28: 2 you if you obey the LORD your
Mk   16:17 these signs will *a* those who believe
Heb   6: 9 your case—things that *a* salvation.

ACCOMPLISH

Ecc   2: 2 And what does pleasure *a*?"
Isa   44:28 and will *a* all that I please;
     55:11 but will *a* what I desire

ACCORD

Nu   24:13 not do anything of my own *a*,
Jn   10:18 but I lay it down of my own *a*.
     12:49 For I did not speak of my own *a*,

ACCOUNT (ACCOUNTABLE)

Ge   2: 4 This is the *a* of the heavens
     5: 1 This is the written *a* of Adam's line
     6: 9 This is the *a* of Noah.

Ge   10: 1 This is the *a* of Shem, Ham
     11:10 This is the *a* of Shem.
     11:27 This is the *a* of Terah.
     25:12 This is the *a* of Abraham's son
     25:19 This is the *a* of Abraham's son
     36: 1 This is the *a* of Esau (that is, Edom
     36: 9 This is the *a* of Esau the father
     37: 2 This is the *a* of Jacob.
Mt   12:36 to give *a* on the day of judgment
Lk   16: 2 Give an *a* of your management,
Ro   14:12 each of us will give an *a* of himself
Heb   4:13 of him to whom we must give *a*.

ACCOUNTABLE* (ACCOUNT)

Eze   3:18 and I will hold you *a* for his blood.
     3:20 and I will hold you *a* for his blood.
     33: 6 but I will hold the watchman *a*
     33: 8 and I will hold you *a* for his blood.
     34:10 and will hold them *a* for my flock.
Da   6: 2 The satraps were made *a* to them
Jnh   1:14 Do not hold us *a* for killing
Ro   3:19 and the whole world held *a* to God.

ACCURATE

Dt   25:15 You must have *a* and honest
Pr   11: 1 but *a* weights are his delight.

ACCURSED (CURSE)

2Pe   2:14 experts in greed—an *a* brood!

ACCUSATION (ACCUSE)

1Ti   5:19 Do not entertain an *a*

ACCUSATIONS (ACCUSE)

2Pe   2:11 do not bring slanderous *a*

ACCUSE (ACCUSATION ACCUSATIONS ACCUSER ACCUSES ACCUSING)

Pr   3:30 Do not *a* a man for no reason—
Lk   3:14 and don't *a* people falsely—

ACCUSER (ACCUSE)

Jn   5:45 Your *a* is Moses, on whom your
Rev   12:10 For the *a* of our brothers,

ACCUSES (ACCUSE)

Job   40: 2 Let him who *a* God answer him!"
Rev   12:10 who *a* them before our God day

ACCUSING (ACCUSE)

Ro   2:15 and their thoughts now *a*,

ACHAN*

     Sin at Jericho caused defeat at Ai; stoned (Jos 7; 22:20; 1Ch 2:7).

ACHE*

Pr   14:13 Even in laughter the heart may *a*,

ACHIEVE

Isa   55:11 *a* the purpose for which I sent it.

ACHISH

     King of Gath before whom David feigned insanity (1Sa 21:10-15). Later "ally" of David (2Sa 27-29).

ACKNOWLEDGE (ACKNOWLEDGED ACKNOWLEDGES)

Pr   3: 6 in all your ways *a* him,
Jer   3:13 Only *a* your guilt—
Hos   6: 3 let us press on to *a* him.
Mt   10:32 *a* him before my Father in heaven.
Lk   12: 8 *a* him before the angels of God.
1Jn   4: 3 spirit that does not *a* Jesus is not

ACKNOWLEDGED (ACKNOWLEDGE)

Lk   7:29 *a* that God's way was right,

ACKNOWLEDGES* (ACKNOWLEDGE)

Ps   91:14 for he *a* my name.
Mt   10:32 "Whoever *a* me before men,
Lk   12: 8 whoever *a* me before men,
1Jn   2:23 whoever *a* the Son has the Father
     4: 2 Every spirit that *a* that Jesus Christ
     4:15 If anyone *a* that Jesus is the Son

ACQUIRES (ACQUIRING)

Pr   18:15 of the discerning *a* knowledge;

ACQUIRING* (ACQUIRES)

Pr   1: 3 for *a* a disciplined and prudent life,

ACQUIT (ACQUITTING)

Ex   23: 7 to death, for I will not *a* the guilty.

ACQUITTING* (ACQUIT)

Dt   25: 1 *a* the innocent and condemning
Pr   17:15 *A* the guilty and condemning

ACT (ACTION ACTIONS ACTIVE ACTIVITY ACTS)

Ps   119:126 It is time for you to *a*, O LORD;

ACTION (ACT)

2Co   9: 2 has stirred most of them to *a*.
Jas   2:17 if it is not accompanied by *a*,
1Pe   1:13 minds for *a*; be self-controlled;

ACTIONS (ACT)

Mt   11:19 wisdom is proved right by her *a*."
Gal   6: 4 Each one should test his own *a*.
Tit   1:16 but by their *a* they deny him.

ACTIVE* (ACT)

Phm   : 6 I pray that you may be *a*
Heb   4:12 For the word of God is living and *a*

ACTIVITY (ACT)

Ecc   3: 1 a season for every *a* under heaven:
     3:17 for there will be a time for every *a*,

ACTS (ACT)

1Ch   16: 9 tell of all his wonderful *a*.
Ps   71:16 proclaim your mighty *a*,
     71:24 tell of your righteous *a*
    105: 2 tell of all his wonderful *a*.
    106: 2 Who can proclaim the mighty *a*
    145: 4 they will tell of your mighty *a*.
    145:12 all men may know of your mighty *a*
    150: 2 Praise him for his *a* of power;
Isa   64: 6 all our righteous *a* are like filthy
Mt   6: 1 not to do your '*a* of righteousness'

ADAM

     1. First man (Ge 1:26-2:25; Ro 5:14; 1Ti 2:13). Sin of (Ge 3; Hos 6:7; Ro 5:12-21). Children of (Ge 4:1-5:5). Death of (Ge 5:5; Ro 5:12-21; 1Co 15:22).
     2. City (Jos 3:16).

ADD (ADDED)

Dt   4: 2 Do not *a* to what I command you
     12:32 do not *a* to it or take away from it.
Pr   1: 5 let the wise listen and *a*
     9: 9 he will *a* to his learning.
     30: 6 Do not *a* to his words,
Mt   6:27 by worrying can *a* a single hour
Lk   12:25 by worrying can *a* a single hour
Rev   22:18 God will *a* to him the plagues

ADDED (ADD)

Ecc   3:14 nothing can be *a* to it and nothing
Ac   2:47 Lord *a* to their number daily those
Ro   5:20 The law was *a* so that the trespass
Gal   3:19 It was *a* because of transgressions

ADDICTED*

Tit   2: 3 to be slanderers or *a* to much wine,

ADMINISTRATION*

1Co   12:28 with gifts of *a*, and those speaking
Eph   3: 2 Surely you have heard about the *a*
     3: 9 to everyone the *a* of this mystery,

ADMIRABLE*

Php   4: 8 whatever is lovely, whatever is *a*—

ADMIT

Hos   5:15 until they *a* their guilt.

ADMONISH* (ADMONISHING)

Col   3:16 and *a* one another with all wisdom,
1Th   5:12 you in the Lord and who *a* you.

ADMONISHING* (ADMONISH)

Col   1:28 *a* and teaching everyone

ADONIJAH

     1. Son of David by Haggith (2Sa 3:4; 1Ch 3:2). Attempted to be king after David; killed by Solomon's order (1Ki 1-2).
     2. Levite; teacher of the Law (2Ch 17:8).

ADOPTED (ADOPTION)

Eph   1: 5 In love he predestined us to be *a*

ADOPTION* (ADOPTED)

Ro   8:23 as we wait eagerly for our *a* as sons,
     9: 4 Theirs is the *a* as sons; theirs

ADORE*
SS 1: 4 How right they are to a you!

ADORNMENT* (ADORNS)
1Pe 3: 3 should not come from outward a.

ADORNS* (ADORNMENT)
Ps 93: 5 holiness a your house
Isa 61: 10 as a bride a herself with her jewels.
61: 10 bridegroom a his head like a priest,

ADULTERER (ADULTERY)
Lev 20: 10 both the a and the adulteress must
Heb 13: 4 for God will judge the a

ADULTERERS (ADULTERY)
1Co 6: 9 idolaters nor a nor male prostitutes
1Ti 1: 10 for murderers, for a and perverts,

ADULTERESS (ADULTERY)
Hos 3: 1 she is loved by another and is an a.

ADULTERIES (ADULTERY)
Jer 3: 8 sent her away because of all her a.

ADULTEROUS (ADULTERY)
Mk 8: 38 in this a and sinful generation,
Jas 4: 4 You a people, don't you know that

ADULTERY (ADULTERER ADULTERERS ADULTERESS ADULTERIES ADULTEROUS)
Ex 20: 14 "You shall not commit a.
Dt 5: 18 "You shall not commit a.
Mt 5: 27 that it was said, 'Do not commit a.'
5: 28 lustfully has already committed a
5: 32 the divorced woman commits a.
15: 19 murder, a, sexual immorality, theft
19: 9 marries another woman commits a
19: 18 do not commit a, do not steal,
Mk 7: 21 theft, murder, a, greed, malice,
10: 11 marries another woman commits a
10: 12 another man, she commits a."
10: 19 do not commit a, do not steal,
Lk 16: 18 a divorced woman commits a
16: 18 marries another woman commits a
18: 20 'Do not commit a, do not murder,
Jn 8: 4 woman was caught in the act of a.
Rev 18: 3 of the earth committed a with her,

ADULTS*
1Co 14: 20 but in your thinking be a.

ADVANCE (ADVANCED)
Ps 18: 29 With your help I can a
Php 1: 12 has really served to a the gospel.

ADVANCED (ADVANCE)
Job 32: 7 a years should teach wisdom.'

ADVANTAGE
Ex 22: 22 "Do not take a of a widow
Dt 24: 14 Do not take a of a hired man who is
Ro 3: 1 What a, then, is there
2Co 11: 20 or exploits you or takes a of you
1Th 4: 6 should wrong his brother or take a

ADVERSITY*
Pr 17: 17 and a brother is born for a.
Isa 30: 20 the Lord gives you the bread of a

ADVICE (ADVISERS)
1Ki 12: 8 rejected the a the elders
12: 14 he followed the a of the young men
2Ch 10: 8 rejected the a the elders
Pr 12: 5 but the a of the wicked is deceitful.
12: 15 but a wise man listens to a.
19: 20 Listen to a and accept instruction,
20: 18 Make plans by seeking a;

ADVISERS (ADVICE)
Pr 11: 14 but many a make victory sure.

ADVOCATE*
Job 16: 19 my a is on high.

AFFLICTED (AFFLICTION)
Job 2: 7 and a Job with painful sores
36: 6 but gives the a their rights.
Ps 9: 12 he does not ignore the cry of the a.
9: 18 nor the hope of the a ever perish.
119: 67 Before I was a I went astray,
119: 71 It was good for me to be a
119: 75 and in faithfulness you have a me.
Isa 49: 13 will have compassion on his a ones.

Isa 53: 4 smitten by him, and a.
53: 7 He was oppressed and a.
Na 1: 12 Although I have a you, O Judah,

AFFLICTION (AFFLICTED AFFLICTIONS)
Dt 16: 3 bread of a, because you left Egypt
Ps 107: 41 he lifted the needy out of their a
Isa 30: 20 of adversity and the water of a,
48: 10 in the furnace of a.
La 3: 33 For he does not willingly bring a
Ro 12: 12 patient in a, faithful in prayer.

AFFLICTIONS (AFFLICTION)
Col 1: 24 lacking in regard to Christ's a,

AFRAID (FEAR)
Ge 3: 10 and I was a because I was naked;
26: 24 Do not be a, for I am with you;
Ex 2: 14 Then Moses was a and thought,
3: 6 because he was a to look at God.
Dt 1: 21 Do not be a; do not be discouraged
1: 29 "Do not be terrified; do not be a
20: 1 do not be a of them,
20: 3 Do not be fainthearted or a;
2Ki 25: 24 "Do not be a of the Babylonian
1Ch 13: 12 David was a of God that day
Ps 27: 1 of whom shall I be a?
56: 3 When I am a, / I will trust in you.
56: 4 in God I trust; I will not be a.
Pr 3: 24 lie down, you will not be a;
Isa 10: 24 do not be a of the Assyrians,
12: 2 I will trust and not be a.
44: 8 Do not tremble, do not be a.
Jer 1: 8 Do not be a of them, for I am
Mt 8: 26 You of little faith, why are you so a
10: 28 be a of the One who can destroy
10: 31 So don't be a; you are worth more
Mk 5: 36 "Don't be a; just believe."
Lk 9: 34 and they were a as they entered
14: 27 hearts be troubled and do not be a.
Ac 27: 24 beside me and said, 'Do not be a,
Ro 11: 20 Do not be arrogant, but be a.
Heb 13: 6 Lord is my helper; I will not be a.

AGAG (AGAGITE)
King of Amalekites not killed by Saul (1Sa 15).

AGAGITE (AGAG)
Est 8: 3 to the evil plan of Haman the A,

AGED (AGES)
Job 12: 12 Is not wisdom found among the a?
Pr 17: 6 children are a crown to the a,

AGES (AGED)
Ro 16: 25 the mystery hidden for long a past.
Eph 2: 7 that in the coming a he might show
3: 9 which for a past was kept hidden
Col 1: 26 that has been kept hidden for a
Rev 15: 3 King of the a.

AGONY
Lk 16: 24 because I am in a in this fire.'
Rev 16: 10 Men gnawed their tongues in a

AGREE (AGREEMENT AGREES)
Mt 18: 19 on earth a about anything you ask
Ro 7: 16 want to do, I a that the law is good.
Php 4: 2 with Syntyche to a with each other

AGREEMENT (AGREE)
2Co 6: 16 What a is there between the temple

AGREES* (AGREE)
Ac 7: 42 This a with what is written
24: 14 I believe everything that a
1Co 4: 17 which a with what I teach

AGRIPPA*
Descendant of Herod; king before whom Paul pled his case in Caesarea (Ac 25:13-26: 32).

AHAB
1. Son of Omri; king of Israel (1Ki 16:28-22: 40), husband of Jezebel (1Ki 16:31). Promoted Baal worship (1Ki 16:31-33); opposed by Elijah (1Ki 17:1; 18; 21), a prophet (1Ki 20:35-43), Micaiah (1Ki 22:1-28). Defeated Ben-Hadad (1Ki 20). Killed for failing to kill Ben-Hadad and for murder of Naboth (1Ki 20:35-21:40).
2. A false prophet (Jer 29:21-22).

AHAZ
1. Son of Jotham; king of Judah, (2Ki 16; 2Ch

---

28). Idolatry of (2Ki 16:3-4, 10-18; 2Ch 28:1-4, 22-25). Defeated by Aram and Israel (2Ki 16: 5-6; 2Ch 28.5-15). Sought help from Assyria rather than the LORD (2Ki 16:7-9; 2Ch 28:16-21; Isa 7).
2. Benjamite, descendant of Saul (1Ch 8:35-36).

AHAZIAH
1. Son of Ahab; king of Israel (1Ki 22:51-2Ki 1:18; 2Ch 20:35-37). Made an unsuccessful alliance with Jehoshaphat of Judah (2Ch 20:35-37). Died for seeking Baal rather than the LORD (2Ki 1)
2. Son of Jehoram; king of Judah (2Ki 8:25-29; 9:14-29), also called Jehoahaz (2Ch 21:17-22:9; 25:23). Killed by Jehu while visiting Joram (2Ki 9:14-29; 2Ch 22:1-9).

AHIJAH
1Sa 14: 18 Saul said to A, "Bring the ark
1Ki 14: 2 A the prophet is there—the one

AHIMELECH
1. Priest who helped David in his flight from Saul (1Sa 21-22)
2. One of David's warriors (1Sa 26:6).

AHITHOPHEL
One of David's counselors who sided with Absalom (2Sa 15:12, 31-37; 1Ch 27:33-34); committed suicide when his advice was ignored (2Sa 16:15-17:23).

AI
Jos 7: 4 they were routed by the men of A,
8: 28 So Joshua burned A and made it

AID
Isa 38: 14 troubled; O Lord, come to my a!"
Php 4: 16 you sent me a again and again

AIM
1Co 7: 34 Her a is to be devoted to the Lord
2Co 13: 11 A for perfection, listen

AIR
Mt 8: 20 and birds of the a have nests,
Lk 9: 58 and birds of the a have nests,
1Co 9: 26 not fight like a man beating the a
14: 9 You will just be speaking into the a
Eph 2: 2 of the ruler of the kingdom of the a,
1Th 4: 17 clouds to meet the Lord in the a.

ALABASTER*
Mt 26: 7 came to him with an a jar
Mk 14: 3 a woman came with an a jar
Lk 7: 37 she brought an a jar of perfume,

ALARM (ALARMED)
2Co 7: 11 indignation, what a, what longing,

ALARMED (ALARM)
Mk 13: 7 and rumors of wars, do not be a.
2Th 2: 2 not to become easily unsettled or a

ALERT*
Jos 8: 4 All of you be on the a.
Ps 17: 11 with eyes a, to throw me
Isa 21: 7 let him be a, / fully a."
Mk 13: 33 Be a! You do not know
Eph 6: 18 be a and always keep on praying
1Th 5: 6 but let us be a and self-controlled.
1Pe 5: 8 Be self-controlled and a.

ALIEN (ALIENATED ALIENS)
Ex 22: 21 "Do not mistreat an a
Lev 24: 22 are to have the same law for the a
Ps 146: 9 The LORD watches over the a

ALIENATED (ALIEN)
Gal 5: 4 by law have been a from Christ;
Col 1: 21 Once you were a from God

ALIENS (ALIEN)
Ex 23: 9 know how it feels to be a,
1Pe 2: 11 as a and strangers in the world,

ALIVE (LIVE)
1Sa 2: 6 LORD brings death and makes a;
Lk 24: 23 vision of angels, who said he was a.
Ac 1: 3 convincing proofs that he was a.
Ro 6: 11 but a to God in Christ Jesus.
1Co 15: 22 so in Christ all will be made a.
Eph 2: 5 made us a with Christ

ALMIGHTY (MIGHT)

Ge 17: 1 "I am God A; walk before me
Ex   6: 3 to Isaac and to Jacob as God A,
Ru 1:20 the A has made my life very bitter.
Job 11: 7 Can you probe the limits of the A?
      33: 4 the breath of the A gives me life.
Ps 89: 8 O LORD God A, who is like you?
      91: 1 I will rest in the shadow of the A.
Isa 6: 3 "Holy, holy, holy is the LORD A;
     45:13 says the LORD A."
     47: 4 the LORD A is his name—
     48: 2 the LORD A is his name:
     51:15 the LORD A is his name.
     54: 5 the LORD A is his name—
Am 5:14 the LORD God A will be with you,
     5:15 the LORD God A will have mercy
Rev 4: 8 holy is the Lord God A, who was,
     19: 6 For our Lord God A reigns.

ALMS see GIVING, (acts of) RIGHTEOUSNESS

ALPHA*

Rev 1: 8 "I am the A and the Omega,"
     21: 6 I am the A and the Omega,
     22:13 I am the A and the Omega.

ALTAR

Ge 8:20 Then Noah built an a to the LORD
     12: 7 So he built an a there to the LORD
     13:18 where he built an a to the LORD.
     22: 9 Abraham built an a there
     22: 9 his son Isaac and laid him on the a,
     26:25 Isaac built an a there and called
     35: 1 and build an a there to God,
Ex 17:15 Moses built an a and called it
     27: 1 "Build an a of acacia wood,
     30: 1 "Make an a of acacia wood
     37:25 They made the a of incense out
Dt 27: 5 an a to the LORD your God, an a
Jos 8:30 on Mount Ebal an a to the LORD,
     22:10 built an imposing a there
Jdg 6:24 So Gideon built an a to the LORD
     21: 4 the next day the people built an a
1Sa 7:17 he built an a there to the LORD.
     14:35 Then Saul built an a to the LORD;
2Sa 24:25 David built an a to the LORD
1Ki 12:33 sacrifices on the a he had built
     13: 2 "O a, a! This is what the LORD
     16:32 He set up an a for Baal
     18:30 and he repaired the a of the LORD
2Ki 16:11 So Uriah the priest built an a
1Ch 21:26 David built an a to the LORD
2Ch 4: 1 made a bronze a twenty cubits
     4:19 the golden a; the tables
     15: 8 He repaired the a of the LORD
     32:12 'You must worship before one a
     33:16 he restored the a of the LORD
Ezr 3: 2 to build the a of the God of Israel
Isa 6: 6 taken with tongs from the a.
Eze 40:47 the a was in front of the temple.
Mt 5:23 if you are offering your gift at the a
Ac 17:23 found an a with this inscription:
Heb 13:10 We have an a from which those
Rev 6: 9 I saw under the a the souls

ALTER*

Ps 89:34 or a what my lips have uttered.

ALWAYS

Dt 15:11 There will a be poor people
Ps 16: 8 I have set the LORD a before me.
     51: 3 and my sin is a before me.
Pr 23: 7 who is a thinking about the cost.
Mt 26:11 The poor you will a have with you,
     28:20 And surely I am with you a,
Mk 14: 7 The poor you will a have with you,
Jn 12: 8 You will a have the poor
1Co 13: 7 a protects, a trusts, a hopes, a
Php 4: 4 Rejoice in the Lord a.
1Pe 3:15 A be prepared to give an answer

AMALEKITES

Ex 17: 8 A came and attacked the Israelites
1Sa 15: 2 'I will punish the A

AMASA

Nephew of David (1Ch 2:17). Commander of Absalom's forces (2Sa 17:24-27). Returned to David (2Sa 19:13). Killed by Joab (2Sa 20:4-13).

AMASSES*

Pr 28: 8 a it for another, who will be kind

AMAZED

Mt 7:28 the crowds were a at his teaching.
Mk 6: 6 And he was a at their lack of faith.
     10:24 The disciples were a at his words.
Ac 2: 7 Utterly a, they asked: "Are not all
     13:12 for he was a at the teaching about

AMAZIAH

1. Son of Joash; king of Judah (2Ki 14; 2Ch 25). Defeated Edom (2Ki 14:7; 2Ch 25:5-13); defeated by Israel for worshiping Edom's gods (2Ki 14:8-14; 2Ch 25:14-24).
2. Idolatrous priest who opposed Amos (Am 7:10-17).

AMBASSADOR* (AMBASSADORS)

Eph 6:20 for which I am an a in chains.

AMBASSADORS (AMBASSADOR)

2Co 5:20 We are therefore Christ's a,

AMBITION*

Ro 15:20 It has always been my a
Gal 5:20 fits of rage, selfish a, dissensions,
Php 1:17 preach Christ out of selfish a,
     2: 3 Do nothing out of selfish a
1Th 4:11 Make it your a to lead a quiet life,
Jas 3:14 and selfish a in your hearts,
     3:16 where you have envy and selfish a,

AMENDS

Pr 14: 9 Fools mock at making a for sin,

AMNON

Firstborn of David (2Sa 3:2; 1Ch 3:1). Killed by Absalom for raping his sister Tamar (2Sa 13).

AMON

1. Son of Manasseh; king of Judah (2Ki 21: 18-26; 1Ch 3:14; 2Ch 33:21-25).
2. Ruler of Samaria under Ahab (1Ki 22:26; 2Ch 18:25).

AMOS

1. Prophet from Tekoa (Am 1:1; 7:10-17).
2. Ancestor of Jesus (Lk 3:25).

ANAK (ANAKITES)

Nu 13:28 even saw descendants of A there.

ANAKITES (ANAK)

Dt 1:28 We even saw the A there,' "
     2:10 and numerous, and as tall as the A.
     9: 2 "Who can stand up against the A?"

ANANIAS

1. Husband of Sapphira; died for lying to God (Ac 5:1-11).
2. Disciple who baptized Saul (Ac 9:10-19).
3. High priest at Paul's arrest (Ac 22:30-24:1).

ANCESTORS (ANCESTRY)

1Ki 19: 4 I am no better than my a."

ANCESTRY (ANCESTORS)

Ro 9: 5 from them is traced the human a

ANCHOR

Heb 6:19 We have this hope as an a

ANCIENT

Da 7: 9 and the A of Days took his seat.
     7:13 He approached the A of Days
     7:22 until the A of Days came

ANDREW*

Apostle; brother of Simon Peter (Mt 4:18; 10: 2; Mk 1:16-18, 29; 3:18; 13:3; Lk 6:14; Jn 1: 35-44; 6:8-9; 12:22; Ac 1:13).

ANGEL (ANGELS ARCHANGEL)

Ge 16: 7 The a of the LORD found Hagar
     22:11 But the a of the LORD called out
Ex 23:20 I am sending an a ahead of you
Nu 22:23 When the donkey saw the a
Jdg 2: 1 The a of the LORD went up
     6:22 Gideon realized that it was the a
     13:15 Manoah said to the a of the LORD
2Sa 24:16 The a of the LORD was then
1Ki 19: 7 The a of the LORD came back
2Ki 19:35 That night the a of the LORD went
Ps 34: 7 The a of the LORD encamps
Hos 12: 4 He struggled with the a
Mt 2:13 an a of the Lord appeared

Mt 28: 2 for an a of the Lord came
Lk 1:26 God sent the a Gabriel
     2: 9 An a of the Lord appeared to them,
     22:43 An a from heaven appeared to him
Ac 6:15 his face was like the face of an a.
     12: 7 Suddenly an a of the Lord
2Co 11:14 Satan himself masquerades as an a
Gal 1: 8 or an a from heaven should preach

ANGELS (ANGEL)

Ps 91:11 command his a concerning you
Mt 4: 6 command his a concerning you,
     13:39 of the age, and the harvesters are a.
     13:49 The a will come and separate
     18:10 For I tell you that their a
     25:41 prepared for the devil and his a.
Lk 4:10 command his a concerning you
     20:36 for they are like the a
1Co 6: 3 you not know that we will judge a?
     13: 1 in the tongues of men and of a,
Col 2:18 and the worship of a disqualify you
Heb 1: 4 as much superior to the a
     1: 6 "Let all God's a worship him."
     1: 7 "He makes his a winds,
     1:14 Are not all a ministering spirits
     2: 7 made him a little lower than the a,
     2: 9 was made a little lower than the a,
     13: 2 some people have entertained a
1Pe 1:12 Even a long to look
2Pe 2: 4 For if God did not spare a
Jude   6 a who did not keep their positions

ANGER (ANGERED ANGRY)

Ex 15: 7 You unleashed your burning a;
     22:24 My a will be aroused, and I will kill
     32:10 alone so that my a may burn
     32:11 "why should your a burn
     32:12 Turn from your fierce a: relent
     32:19 his a burned and he threw
     34: 6 slow to a, abounding in love
Lev 26:28 then in my a I will be hostile
Nu 14:18 slow to a, abounding in love
     25:11 has turned my a away
     32:10 LORD's a was aroused that day
     32:13 The LORD's a burned
Dt 9:19 I feared the a and wrath
     29:28 In furious a and in great wrath
Jdg 14:19 Burning with a, he went up
2Sa 12: 5 David burned with a
2Ki 22:13 Great is the LORD's a that burns
Ne 9:17 slow to a and abounding in love.
Ps 30: 5 For his a lasts only a moment;
     78:38 Time after time he restrained his a
     86:15 slow to a, abounding in love
     90: 7 We are consumed by your a
     103: 8 slow to a, abounding in love.
Pr 15: 1 but a harsh word stirs up a.
     29:11 A fool gives full vent to his a,
     30:33 so stirring up a produces strife."
Jnh 4: 2 slow to a and abounding in love,
Eph 4:26 "In your a do not sin": Do not let
Jas 1:20 for man's a does not bring about

ANGERED (ANGER)

Pr 22:24 do not associate with one easily a,
1Co 13: 5 it is not easily a, it keeps no record

ANGRY (ANGER)

Ps 2:12 Kiss the Son, lest he be a
     95:10 For forty years I was a
Pr 29:22 An a man stirs up dissension,
Mt 5:22 But I tell you that anyone who is a
Jas 1:19 slow to speak and slow to become a

ANGUISH

Ps 118: 5 In my a I cried to the LORD,
Jer 4:19 Oh, my a, my a!
Zep 1:15 a day of distress and a,
Lk 21:25 nations will be in a and perplexity
     22:44 in a, he prayed more earnestly,
Ro 9: 2 and unceasing a in my heart.

ANIMALS

Ge 1:24 wild a, each according to its kind.'
     7:16 The a going in were male
Dt 14: 4 These are the a you may eat: the ox
Job 12: 7 ask the a, and they will teach you,
Isa 43:20 The wild a honor me,

ANNOUNCE (ANNOUNCED)

Mt 6: 2 give to the needy, do not a it

ANNOUNCED (ANNOUNCE)

Isa 48: 5 before they happened I a them
Gal 3: 8 and a the gospel in advance

ANNOYANCE*

Pr 12: 16 A fool shows his a at once.

ANNUAL*

Ex 30: 10 This a atonement must be made
Jdg 21: 19 there is the a festival of the LORD
1Sa 1: 21 family to offer the a sacrifice
2: 19 husband to offer the a sacrifice
20: 6 an a sacrifice is being made there
2Ch 8: 13 New Moons and the three a feasts
Heb 10: 3 those sacrifices are an a reminder

ANOINT (ANOINTED ANOINTING)

Ex 30: 26 use it to a the Tent of Meeting,
30: 30 "A Aaron and his sons
1Sa 9: 16 A him leader over my people Israel
15: 1 to a you king over his people Israel;
2Ki 9: 3 what the LORD says: I a you king
Ps 23: 5 You a my head with oil;
Da 9: 24 prophecy and to a the most holy.
Jas 5: 14 and a him with oil in the name

ANOINTED (ANOINT)

1Ch 16: 22 "Do not touch my a ones;
Ps 105: 15 "Do not touch my a ones;
Isa 61: 1 because the LORD has a me
Da 9: 26 the A One will be cut off
Lk 4: 18 because he has a me
Ac 10: 38 how God a Jesus of Nazareth

ANOINTING (ANOINT)

Lev 8: 12 some of the a oil on Aaron's head
1Ch 29: 22 a him before the LORD to be ruler
Ps 45: 7 by a you with the oil of joy.
Heb 1: 9 by a you with the oil of joy."
1Jn 2: 20 you have an a from the Holy One,
2: 27 about all things and as that a is real,

ANT* (ANTS)

Pr 6: 6 Go to the a, you sluggard;

ANTICHRIST* (ANTICHRISTS)

1Jn 2: 18 have heard that the a is coming,
2: 22 a man is the a—he denies
4: 3 of the a, which you have heard is
2Jn 7 person is the deceiver and the a.

ANTICHRISTS* (ANTICHRIST)

1Jn 2: 18 even now many a have come.

ANTIOCH

Ac 11: 26 were called Christians first at A.

ANTS* (ANT)

Pr 30: 25 A are creatures of little strength,

ANXIETIES* (ANXIOUS)

Lk 21: 34 drunkenness and the a of life,

ANXIETY (ANXIOUS)

1Pe 5: 7 Cast all your a on him

ANXIOUS (ANXIETIES ANXIETY)

Pr 12: 25 An a heart weighs a man down,
Php 4: 6 Do not be a about anything.

APOLLOS*

Christian from Alexandria, learned in the Scriptures; instructed by Aquila and Priscilla (Ac 18:24-28). Ministered at Corinth (Ac 19:1; 1Co 1:12; 3; Tit 3:13).

APOLLYON*

Rev 9: 11 is Abaddon, and in Greek, A.

APOSTLE (APOSTLES APOSTLES')

Ro 11: 13 as I am the a to the Gentiles,
1Co 9: 1 Am I not an a? Have I not seen
2Co 12: 12 The things that mark an a—signs,
Gal 2: 8 of Peter as an a to the Jews,
1Ti 2: 7 was appointed a herald and an a—
2Ti 1: 11 I was appointed a herald and an a
Heb 3: 1 a and high priest whom we confess.

APOSTLES (APOSTLE)

See also Andrew, Bartholomew, James, John, Judas, Matthew, Matthias, Nathanael, Paul, Peter, Philip, Simon, Thaddaeus, Thomas.
Mk 3: 14 twelve—designating them a—
Lk 11: 49 'I will send them prophets and a,
Ac 1: 26 so he was added to the eleven a.
2: 43 signs were done by the a.
1Co 12: 28 God has appointed first of all a,
15: 9 For I am the least of the a

2Co 11: 13 masquerading as a of Christ.
Eph 2: 20 built on the foundation of the a
4: 11 It was he who gave some to be a,
Rev 21: 14 names of the twelve a of the Lamb.

APOSTLES' (APOSTLE)

Ac 5: 2 the rest and put it at the a' feet.
8: 18 at the laying on of the a' hands,

APPEAL

Ac 25: 11 I a to Caesar!" After Festus had
Phm 9 yet I a to you on the basis of love.

APPEAR (APPEARANCE APPEARANCES APPEARED APPEARING APPEARS)

Ge 1: 9 to one place, and let dry ground a.
Lev 16: 2 I a in the cloud over the atonement
Mt 24: 30 of the Son of Man will a in the sky,
Mk 13: 22 false prophets will a and perform
Lk 19: 11 of God was going to a at once.
2Co 5: 10 we must all a before the judgment
Col 3: 4 also will a with him in glory.
Heb 9: 24 now to a for us in God's presence.
9: 28 and he will a a second time,

APPEARANCE (APPEAR)

1Sa 16: 7 Man looks at the outward a,
Isa 52: 14 his a was so disfigured beyond that
53: 2 in his a that we should desire him.
Gal 2: 6 God does not judge by external a—

APPEARANCES* (APPEAR)

Jn 7: 24 Stop judging by mere a.

APPEARED (APPEAR)

Nu 14: 10 glory of the LORD a at the Tent
Mt 1: 20 an angel of the Lord a to him
Lk 2: 9 An angel of the Lord a to them,
1Co 15: 5 and that he a to Peter,
Heb 9: 26 now he has a once for all at the end

APPEARING (APPEAR)

1Ti 6: 14 until the a of our Lord Jesus Christ,
2Ti 1: 10 through the a of our Savior,
4: 8 to all who have longed for his a.
Tit 2: 13 the glorious a of our great God

APPEARS (APPEAR)

Mal 3: 2 Who can stand when he a?
Col 3: 4 When Christ, who is your life, a,
1Pe 5: 4 And when the Chief Shepherd a,
1Jn 3: 2 But we know that when he a,

APPETITE

Pr 16: 26 The laborer's a works for him;
Ecc 6: 7 yet his a is never satisfied.
Jer 50: 19 his a will be satisfied

APPLES

Pr 25: 11 is like a of gold in settings of silver.

APPLY (APPLYING)

Pr 22: 17 a your heart to what I teach,
23: 12 A your heart to instruction

APPLYING (APPLY)

Pr 2: 2 and a your heart to understanding,

APPOINT (APPOINTED)

Ps 61: 7 a your love and faithfulness
1Th 5: 9 For God did not a us
Tit 1: 5 and a elders in every town,

APPOINTED (APPOINT)

Dt 1: 15 a them to have authority over you
8: 23 I was a from eternity.
Da 11: 27 an end will still come at the a time.
Hab 2: 3 For the revelation awaits an a time;
Jn 15: 16 Chose you and a you to go
Ro 9: 9 "At the a time I will return,

APPROACH (APPROACHING)

Ex 24: 2 but Moses alone is to a the LORD;
Eph 3: 12 in him we may a God with freedom
Heb 4: 16 Let us then a the throne of grace

APPROACHING (APPROACH)

Heb 10: 25 all the more as you see the Day a.
1Jn 5: 14 is the confidence we have in a God:

APPROPRIATE

1Ti 2: 10 a for women who profess

APPROVAL (APPROVE)

Jdg 18: 6 Your journey has the LORD's a."

Jn 6: 27 the Father has placed his seal of a."
1Co 11: 19 to show which of you have God's a
Gal 1: 10 trying to win the a of men.

APPROVE (APPROVAL APPROVED APPROVES)

Ro 2: 18 if you know his will and a
12: 2 and a what God's will is—

APPROVED* (APPROVE)

Ro 14: 18 pleasing to God and a by men.
16: 10 Greet Apelles, tested and a
2Co 10: 18 who commends himself who is a,
1Th 2: 4 as men a by God to be entrusted
2Ti 2: 15 to present yourself to God as one a,

APPROVES* (APPROVE)

Ro 14: 22 not condemn himself by what he a.

APT*

Pr 15: 23 A man finds joy in giving an a reply

AQUILA*

Husband of Priscilla; co-worker with Paul, instructor of Apollos (Ac 18; Ro 16:3; 1Co 16:19; 2Ti 4:19).

ARABIA

Gal 1: 17 but I went immediately into A
4: 25 Hagar stands for Mount Sinai in A

ARARAT

Ge 8: 4 came to rest on the mountains of A.

ARAUNAH

2Sa 24: 16 threshing floor of A the Jebusite.

ARBITER* (ARBITRATE)

Lk 12: 14 who appointed me a judge or an a

ARBITRATE* (ARBITER)

Job 9: 33 If only there were someone to a

ARCHANGEL* (ANGEL)

1Th 4: 16 with the voice of the a
Jude 9 a Michael, when he was disputing

ARCHER

Pr 26: 10 Like an a who wounds at random

ARCHIPPUS*

Col 4: 17 Tell A: "See to it that you complete
Phm 2 to A our fellow soldier

ARCHITECT*

Heb 11: 10 whose a and builder is God.

AREOPAGUS*

Ac 17: 19 brought him to a meeting of the A,
17: 22 up in the meeting of the A
17: 34 of the A, also a woman named

ARGUE (ARGUMENT ARGUMENTS)

Job 13: 3 and to a my case with God.
13: 8 Will you a the case for God?
Pr 25: 9 If you a your case with a neighbor,

ARGUMENT (ARGUE)

Heb 6: 16 is said and puts an end to all a.

ARGUMENTS (ARGUE)

Isa 41: 21 "Set forth your a," says Jacob's
Col 2: 4 you by fine-sounding a.
2Ti 2: 23 to do with foolish and stupid a,
Tit 3: 9 and a and quarrels about the law.

ARK

Ge 6: 14 So make yourself an a
Ex 25: 21 and put in the a the Testimony,
Dt 10: 5 put the tablets in the a I had made,
1Sa 4: 11 The a of God was captured,
7: 2 that the a remained at Kiriath
2Sa 6: 17 They brought the a of the LORD
1Ki 8: 9 There was nothing in the a
1Ch 13: 9 out his hand to steady the a,
2Ch 35: 3 "Put the sacred a in the temple that
Heb 9: 4 This a contained the gold jar
11: 7 in holy fear built an a
Rev 11: 19 within his temple was seen the a

ARM (ARMY)

Nu 11: 23 "Is the LORD's a too short?
Dt 4: 34 hand and an outstretched a,
7: 19 mighty hand and outstretched a,
Ps 44: 3 it was your right hand, your a,

Ps 98: 1 his right hand and his holy *a*
Jer 27: 5 outstretched *a* I made the earth
1Pe 4: 1 *a* yourselves also with the same

ARMAGEDDON*

Rev 16: 16 that in Hebrew is called *A.*

ARMIES (ARMY)

1Sa 17: 26 Philistine that he should defy the *a*
Rev 19: 14 *a* of heaven were following him,

ARMOR (ARMY)

1Ki 20: 11 on his *a* should not boast like one
Jer 46: 4 put on your *a!*
Ro 13: 12 deeds of darkness and put on the *a*
Eph 6: 11 Put on the full *a* of God
6: 13 Therefore put on the full *a* of God,

ARMS (ARMY)

Dt 33: 27 underneath are the everlasting *a.*
Ps 18: 32 It is God who *a* me with strength
Pr 31: 17 her *a* are strong for her tasks.
31: 20 She opens her *a* to the poor
Isa 40: 11 He gathers the lambs in his *a*
Mk 10: 16 And he took the children in his *a,*
Heb 12: 12 strengthen your feeble *a*

ARMY (ARM ARMIES ARMOR ARMS)

Ps 33: 16 No king is saved by the size of his *a*
Joel 2: 2 a large and mighty *a* comes,
2: 5 like a mighty *a* drawn up for battle.
2: 11 thunders at the head of his *a;*
Rev 19: 19 the rider on the horse and his *a.*

AROMA

Ge 8: 21 The LORD smelled the pleasing *a*
Ex 29: 18 a pleasing *a,* an offering made
Lev 3: 16 made by fire, a pleasing *a.*
2Co 2: 15 For we are to God the *a* of Christ

AROUSE (AROUSED)

Ro 11: 14 I may somehow *a* my own people

AROUSED (AROUSE)

Ps 78: 58 they *a* his jealousy with their idols.

ARRANGED

1Co 12: 18 But in fact God has *a* the parts

ARRAYED*

Ps 110: 3 *A* in holy majesty,
Isa 61: 10 and *a* me in a robe of righteousness

ARREST

Mt 10: 19 But when they *a* you, do not worry

ARROGANCE (ARROGANT)

1Sa 2: 3 or let your mouth speak such *a,*
Pr 8: 13 I hate pride and *a,*
Mk 7: 22 lewdness, envy, slander, *a* and folly
2Co 12: 20 slander, gossip, *a* and disorder.

ARROGANT (ARROGANCE)

Ps 5: 5 The *a* cannot stand
119: 78 May the *a* be put to shame
Pr 17: 7 *A* lips are unsuited to a fool—
21: 24 a man—"Mocker" is his name;
Ro 1: 30 God-haters, insolent, *a*
11: 20 Do not be *a,* but be afraid.
1Ti 6: 17 in this present world not to be *a*

ARROW (ARROWS)

Ps 91: 5 nor the *a* that flies by day,
Pr 25: 18 Like a club or a sword or a sharp *a*

ARROWS (ARROW)

Ps 64: 3 and aim their words like deadly *a.*
64: 7 But God will shoot them with *a;*
127: 4 Like *a* in the hands of a warrior
Pr 26: 18 firebrands or deadly *a*
Eph 6: 16 you can extinguish all the flaming *a*

ARTAXERXES

King of Persia; allowed rebuilding of temple under Ezra (Ezr 4; 7), and of walls of Jerusalem under his cupbearer Nehemiah (Ne 2; 5:14; 13: 6).

ARTEMIS

Ac 19: 28 "Great is *A* of the Ephesians!"

ASA

King of Judah (1Ki 15:8-24; 1Ch 3:10; 2Ch 14-16). Godly reformer (2Ch 15); in later years defeated Israel with help of Aram, not the LORD

(1Ki 15:16-22; 2Ch 16).

ASAHEL

1. Nephew of David, one of his warriors (2Sa 23:24; 1Ch 2:16; 11:26; 27:7). Killed by Abner (2Sa 2); avenged by Joab (2Sa 3:22-39).
2. Levite; teacher (2Ch 17:8).

ASAPH

1. Recorder to Hezekiah (2Ki 18:18, 37; Isa 36:3, 22).
2. Levitical musician (1Ch 6:39; 15:17-19; 16: 4-7, 37). Sons of (1Ch 25; 2Ch 5:12; 20:14; 29: 13; 35:15; Ezr 2:41; 3:10; Ne 7:44; 11:17; 12: 27-47). Psalms of (2Ch 29:30; Ps 50; 73-83).

ASCEND* (ASCENDED ASCENDING)

Dt 30: 12 "Who will *a* into heaven to get it
Ps 24: 3 Who may *a* the hill of the LORD?
Isa 14: 13 "I will *a* to heaven;
14: 14 I will *a* above the tops of the clouds
Jn 6: 62 of Man *a* to where he was before!
Ac 2: 34 For David did not *a* to heaven,
Ro 10: 6 'Who will *a* into heaven?'" (that is,

ASCENDED (ASCEND)

Ps 68: 18 When you *a* on high,
Eph 4: 8 "When he *a* on high,

ASCENDING (ASCEND)

Ge 28: 12 and the angels of God were *a*
Jn 1: 51 and the angels of God *a*

ASCRIBE*

1Ch 16: 28 *A* to the LORD, O families
16: 28 *a* to the LORD glory and strength,
16: 29 *a* to the LORD the glory due his
Job 36: 3 I will *a* justice to my Maker.
Ps 29: 1 *A* to the LORD, O mighty ones,
29: 1 *a* to the LORD glory and strength.
29: 2 *A* to the LORD the glory due his
96: 7 *A* to the LORD, O families
96: 7 *a* to the LORD glory and strength.
96: 8 *A* to the LORD the glory due his

ASHAMED (SHAME)

Mk 8: 38 If anyone is *a* of me and my words
Lk 9: 26 If anyone is *a* of me and my words,
Ro 1: 16 I am not *a* of the gospel,
2Ti 1: 8 So do not be *a* to testify about our
2: 15 who does not need to be *a*

ASHER

Son of Jacob by Zilpah (Ge 30:13; 35:26; 46: 17; Ex 1:4; 1Ch 2:2). Tribe of blessed (Ge 49:20; Dt 33:24-25), numbered (Nu 1:40-41; 26:44-47), allotted land (Jos 10:24-31; Eze 48:2), failed to fully possess (Jdg 1:31-32), failed to support Deborah (Jdg 5:17), supported Gideon (Jdg 6: 35; 7:23) and David (1Ch 12:36), 12,000 from (Rev 7:6).

ASHERAH (ASHERAHS)

Ex 34: 13 and cut down their *A* poles.
1Ki 18: 19 the four hundred prophets of *A,*

ASHERAHS* (ASHERAH)

Jdg 3: 7 and served the Baals and the *A.*

ASHES

Job 42: 6 and repent in dust and *a.*"
Mt 11: 21 ago in sackcloth and *a.*

ASHTORETHS

Jdg 2: 13 and served Baal and the *A.*
1Sa 7: 4 put away their Baals and *A,*

ASLEEP (SLEEP)

1Co 15: 18 who have fallen *a* in Christ are lost.
1Th 4: 13 be ignorant about those who fall *a,*

ASSEMBLY

Ps 1: 5 nor sinners in the *a* of the righteous
35: 18 I will give you thanks in the great *a*
82: 1 God presides in the great *a;*
149: 1 his praise in the *a* of the saints.

ASSIGNED

1Ki 7: 14 and did all the work *a* to him.
Mk 13: 34 with his *a* task, and tells the one
1Co 3: 5 as the Lord has *a* to each his task.
7: 17 place in life that the Lord *a* to him
2Co 10: 13 to the field God has *a* to us,

ASSOCIATE

Pr 22: 24 do not *a* with one easily angered,
Jn 4: 9 (For Jews do not *a* with Samaritans
Ac 10: 28 law for a Jew to *a* with a Gentile
Ro 12: 16 but be willing to *a* with people
1Co 5: 9 to *a* with sexually immoral people
5: 11 am writing you that you must not *a*
2Th 3: 14 Do not *a* with him,

ASSURANCE (ASSURED)

Heb 10: 22 with a sincere heart in full *a* of faith

ASSURED (ASSURANCE)

Col 4: 12 the will of God, mature and fully *a.*

ASTRAY

Ps 119: 67 Before I was afflicted I went *a,*
Pr 10: 17 ignores correction leads others *a.*
20: 1 whoever is led *a* by them is not
Isa 53: 6 We all, like sheep, have gone *a,*
Jer 50: 6 their shepherds have led them *a*
Jn 16: 1 you so that you will not go *a.*
1Pe 2: 25 For you were like sheep going *a,*
1Jn 3: 7 do not let anyone lead you *a.*

ASTROLOGERS

Isa 47: 13 Let your *a* come forward,
Da 2: 2 *a* to tell him what he had dreamed.

ATE (EAT)

Ge 3: 6 wisdom, she took some and *a* it.
27: 25 Jacob brought it to him and he *a;*
2Sa 9: 11 Mephibosheth *a* at David's table
Ps 78: 25 Men *a* the bread of angels;
Jer 15: 16 When your words came, I *a* them;
Eze 3: 3 So I *a* it, and it tasted as sweet
Mt 14: 20 They all *a* and were satisfied,
15: 37 They all *a* and were satisfied,
Mk 6: 42 They all *a* and were satisfied,
Lk 9: 17 They all *a* and were satisfied,

ATHALIAH

Granddaughter of Omri; wife of Jehoram and mother of Ahaziah; encouraged their evil ways (2Ki 8:18, 27; 2Ch 22:2). At death of Ahaziah she made herself queen, killing all his sons but Joash (2Ki 11:1-3; 2Ch 22:10-12); killed six years later when Joash was revealed (2Ki 11: 4-16; 2Ch 23:1-15).

ATHLETE*

2Ti 2: 5 if anyone competes as an *a,*

ATONE* (ATONEMENT)

Ex 30: 15 to the LORD to *a* for your lives.
2Ch 29: 24 for a sin offering to *a* for all Israel,
Da 9: 24 an end to sin, to *a* for wickedness,

ATONED* (ATONEMENT)

Dt 21: 8 And the bloodshed will be *a* for.
1Sa 3: 14 guilt of Eli's house will never be *a*
Pr 16: 6 faithfulness sin is *a* for;
Isa 6: 7 guilt is taken away and your sin *a*
22: 14 your dying day this sin will not be *a*
27: 9 then, will Jacob's guilt be *a* for,

ATONEMENT (ATONE ATONED)

Ex 25: 17 "Make an *a* cover of pure gold—
30: 10 Once a year Aaron shall make *a*
Lev 17: 11 it is the blood that makes *a*
23: 27 this seventh month is the Day of *A.*
Nu 25: 13 and made *a* for the Israelites."
Ro 3: 25 presented him as a sacrifice of *a,*
Heb 2: 17 that he might make *a* for the sins

ATTACK

Ps 109: 3 they *a* me without cause.

ATTAINED

Php 3: 16 up to what we have already *a.*
Heb 7: 11 If perfection could have been *a*

ATTENTION (ATTENTIVE)

Pr 4: 1 pay *a* and gain understanding.
4: 20 My son, pay *a* to what I say;
5: 1 My son, pay *a* to my wisdom,
7: 24 pay *a* to what I say.
22: 17 Pay *a* and listen to the sayings
Ecc 7: 21 Do not pay *a* to every word people
Isa 42: 20 many things, but have paid no *a;*
Tit 1: 14 and will pay no *a* to Jewish myths
Heb 2: 1 We must pay more careful *a,*

ATTENTIVE (ATTENTION)

Ne	1:11	let your ear be a to the prayer
1Pe	3:12	and his ears are a to their prayer,

ATTITUDE (ATTITUDES)

Eph	4:23	new in the a of your minds;
Php	2:5	Your a should be the same
1Pe	4:1	yourselves also with the same a.

ATTITUDES (ATTITUDE)

Heb	4:12	it judges the thoughts and a

ATTRACTIVE

Tit	2:10	teaching about God our Savior a.

AUDIENCE

Pr	29:26	Many seek an a with a ruler.

AUTHORITIES (AUTHORITY)

Ro	13:1	a that exist have been established
	13:1	It is necessary to submit to the a,
	13:6	for the a are God's servants,
Eph	3:10	and in the heavenly realms,
	6:12	but against the rulers, against the a,
Col	1:16	thrones or powers or rulers or a;
	2:15	having disarmed the powers and a,
Tit	3:1	people to be subject to rulers and a,
1Pe	3:22	a and powers in submission to him.

AUTHORITY (AUTHORITIES)

Mt	7:29	because he taught as one who had a
	9:6	the Son of Man has a on earth
	28:18	"All a in heaven and on earth has
Mk	1:22	he taught them as one who had a,
	2:10	the Son of Man has a on earth
Lk	4:32	because his message had a
	5:24	the Son of Man has a on earth
Jn	10:18	a to lay it down and a
Ac	1:7	the Father has set by his own a.
Ro	1:1	that the law has a over a man only
	13:1	for there is no a except that which
	13:2	rebels against the a is rebelling
1Co	11:10	to have a sign of a on her head.
	15:24	he has destroyed all dominion, a
1Ti	2:2	for kings and all those in a,
	2:12	to teach or to have a over a man;
Tit	2:15	Encourage and rebuke with all a.
Heb	13:17	your leaders and submit to their a.

AUTUMN*

Dt	11:14	both a and spring rains
Ps	84:6	the a rains also cover it with pools.
Jer	5:24	who gives a and spring rains
Joel	2:23	both a and spring rains, as before.
Jas	5:7	and how patient he is for the a
Jude	:12	blown along by the wind; a trees,

AVENGE (VENGEANCE)

Lev	26:25	sword upon you to a the breaking
Dt	32:35	It is mine to a; I will repay.
	32:43	for he will a the blood
Ro	12:19	"It is mine to a; I will repay,"
Heb	10:30	"It is mine to a; I will repay,"
Rev	6:10	of the earth and a our blood?"

AVENGER (VENGEANCE)

Nu	35:27	the a of blood may kill the accused
Jos	20:3	find protection from the a of blood.
Ps	8:2	to silence the foe and the a.

AVENGES (VENGEANCE)

Ps	94:1	O LORD, the God who a,

AVENGING (VENGEANCE)

1Sa	25:26	and from a yourself with your own
Na	1:2	The LORD is a jealous and a God;

AVOID (AVOIDS)

Pr	4:15	A it, do not travel on it;
	20:3	It is to a man's honor to a strife,
	20:19	so a man who talks too much.
Ecc	7:18	who fears God will a all extremes,
1Th	4:3	you should a sexual immorality;
	5:22	A every kind of evil.
2Ti	2:16	A godless chatter, because those
Tit	3:9	But a foolish controversies and

AVOIDS* (AVOID)

Pr	16:6	of the LORD a man a evil.
	16:17	The highway of the upright a evil;

AWAITS (WAIT)

Pr	15:10	Stern discipline a him who leaves
	28:22	and is unaware that poverty a him.

AWAKE (WAKE)

Ps	17:15	when I a, I will be satisfied
Pr	6:22	when you a, they will speak to you.

AWARD*

2Ti	4:8	will a to me on that day—

AWARE

Ex	34:29	he was not a that his face was
Mt	24:50	and at an hour he is not a of.
Lk	12:46	and at an hour he is not a of.

AWE* (AWESOME OVERAWED)

1Sa	12:18	So all the people stood in a
1Ki	3:28	they held the king in a,
Job	25:2	"Dominion and a belong to God;
Ps	119:120	I stand in a of your laws.
Ecc	5:7	Therefore stand in a of God.
Isa	29:23	will stand in a of the God of Israel.
Jer	2:19	and have no a of me,"
	33:9	they will be in a and will tremble
Hab	3:2	I stand in a of your deeds,
Mal	2:5	and stood in a of my name.
Mt	9:8	they were filled with a;
Lk	1:65	The neighbors were all filled with a
	5:26	They were filled with a and said,
	7:16	They were all filled with a
Ac	2:43	Everyone was filled with a,
Heb	12:28	acceptably with reverence and a,

AWESOME* (AWE)

Ge	28:17	and said, "How a is this place!
Ex	15:11	a in glory,
	34:10	among will see how a is the work
Dt	4:34	or by great and a deeds,
	7:21	is among you, is a great and a God.
	10:17	the great God, mighty and a,
	10:21	and a wonders you saw
	28:58	revere this glorious and a name—
	34:12	performed the a deeds that Moses
Jdg	13:6	like an angel of God, very a.
2Sa	7:23	a wonders by driving out nations
1Ch	17:21	a wonders by driving out nations
Ne	1:5	of heaven, the great and a God,
	4:14	and a, and fight for your brothers,
	9:32	the great, mighty and a God,
Job	10:16	again display your a power
	37:22	God comes in a majesty.
Ps	45:4	let your right hand display a deeds.
	47:2	How a is the LORD Most High,
	65:5	us with a deeds of righteousness,
	66:3	to God, "How a are your deeds!
	66:5	how a works in man's behalf!
	68:35	You are a, O God,
	89:7	he is more a than all who surround
	99:3	praise your great and a name—
	106:22	and a deeds by the Red Sea.
	111:9	holy and a is his name.
	145:6	of the power of your a works,
Isa	64:3	when you did a things that we did
Eze	1:18	Their rims were high and a,
	1:22	expanse, sparkling like ice, and a.
Da	2:31	dazzling statue, a in appearance.
	9:4	"O Lord, the great and a God,
Zep	2:11	The LORD will be a to them

AX

Mt	3:10	The a is already at the root
Lk	3:9	The a is already at the root

BAAL

Jdg	6:25	Tear down your father's altar to B
1Ki	16:32	B in the temple of B that he built
	18:25	Elijah said to the prophets of B,
	19:18	knees have not bowed down to B
2Ki	10:28	Jehu destroyed B worship in Israel.
Jer	19:5	places of B to burn their sons
Ro	11:4	have not bowed the knee to B."

BAASHA

King of Israel (1Ki 15:16-16:7; 2Ch 16:1-6).

BABBLER* (BABBLING)

Ac	17:18	"What is this b trying to say?"

BABBLING* (BABBLER)

Mt	6:7	do not keep on b like pagans,

BABIES* (BABY)

Ge	25:22	The b jostled each other within her
Ex	2:6	"This is one of the Hebrew b."
Lk	18:15	also bringing b to Jesus
Ac	7:19	them to throw out their newborn b
1Pe	2:2	Like newborn b, crave pure

BABY* (BABIES BABY'S)

Ex	2:6	She opened it and saw the b.
	2:7	women to nurse the b for you?"
	2:9	So the woman took the b
	2:9	"Take this b and nurse him for me,
1Ki	3:17	I had a b while she was there
	3:18	was born, this woman also had a b.
	3:26	give her the living b! Don't kill him
	3:27	Give the living b to the first woman
Isa	49:15	"Can a mother forget the b
Lk	1:41	the b leaped in her womb,
	1:44	the b in my womb leaped for joy.
	1:57	time for Elizabeth to have her b,
	2:6	the time came for the b to be born,
	2:12	You will find a b wrapped in strips
	2:16	the b, who was lying in the manger.
Jn	16:21	but when her b is born she forgets

BABY'S* (BABY)

Ex	2:8	the girl went and got the b mother.

BABYLON

Ps	137:1	By the rivers of B we sat and wept
Jer	29:10	seventy years are completed for B,
	51:37	B will be a heap of ruins.
Rev	14:8	"Fallen! Fallen is B the Great,
	17:5	MYSTERY B THE GREAT

BACKS

2Pe	2:21	and then to turn their b

BACKSLIDING* (BACKSLIDINGS)

Jer	2:19	your b will rebuke you.
	3:22	I will cure you of b."
	14:7	For our b is great;
	15:6	"You keep on b.
Eze	37:23	them from all their sinful b,

BACKSLIDINGS* (BACKSLIDING)

Jer	5:6	and their b many.

BALAAM

Prophet who attempted to curse Israel (Nu 22-24; Dt 23:4-5; 2Pe 2:15; Jude 11). Killed in Israel's vengeance on Midianites (Nu 31:8; Jos 13:22).

BALAK

Moabite king who hired Balaam to curse Israel (Nu 22-24; Jos 24:9).

BALDHEAD

2Ki	2:23	"Go on up, you b!" they said.

BALM

Jer	8:22	Is there no b in Gilead?

BANISH (BANISHED)

Jer	25:10	I will b from them the sounds of joy

BANISHED (BANISH)

Dt	30:4	Even if you have been b

BANNER

Ex	17:15	and called it The LORD is my B.
SS	2:4	and his b over me is love.
Isa	11:10	the Root of Jesse will stand as a b

BANQUET

SS	2:4	He has taken me to the b hall,
Lk	14:13	when you give a b, invite the poor,

BAPTISM* (BAPTIZE)

Mt	21:25	John's b— where did it come from?
Mk	1:4	and preaching a b of repentance
	10:38	baptized with the b I am baptized
	10:39	baptized with the b I am baptized
	11:30	John's b—was it from heaven,
Lk	3:3	preaching a b of repentance
	12:50	But I have a b to undergo,
	20:4	John's b—was it from heaven,
Ac	1:22	beginning from John's b
	10:37	after the b that John preached—
	13:24	and b to all the people of Israel.
	18:25	though he knew only the b of John.
	19:3	did you receive?" "John's b,"
	19:3	"Then what b did you receive?"
	19:4	"John's b was a b of repentance.
Ro	6:4	with him through b into death
Eph	4:5	one Lord, one faith, one b;
Col	2:12	having been buried with him in b
1Pe	3:21	this water symbolizes b that now

BAPTISMS* (BAPTIZE)

Heb   6: 2 instruction about *b*, the laying

BAPTIZE* (BAPTISM BAPTISMS BAPTIZED BAPTIZING)

Mt   3: 11 He will *b* you with the Holy Spirit
       3: 11 "I *b* you with water for repentance.
Mk   1: 8 I *b* you with water, but he will
       1: 8 he will *b* you with the Holy Spirit."
Lk   3: 16 He will *b* you with the Holy Spirit
       3: 16 John answered them all, "I *b* you
Jn   1: 25 "Why then do you *b*
       1: 26 nor the Prophet?" "I *b* with water,"
       1: 33 and remain is he who will *b*
       1: 33 me to *b* with water told me,
1Co   1: 14 I am thankful that I did not *b* any
       1: 17 For Christ did not send me to *b*,

BAPTIZED* (BAPTIZE)

Mt   3: 6 they were *b* by him in the Jordan
       3: 13 to the Jordan to be *b* by John.
       3: 14 saying, "I need to be *b* by you,
       3: 16 as Jesus was *b*, he went up out
Mk   1: 5 they were *b* by him in the Jordan
       1: 9 and was *b* by John in the Jordan.
      10: 38 or be *b* with the baptism I am
      10: 38 with the baptism I am *b* with?"
      10: 39 and be *b* with the baptism I am
      10: 39 with the baptism I am *b* with,
      16: 16 believes and is *b* will be saved,
Lk   3: 7 to the crowds coming out to be *b*
       3: 12 Tax collectors also came to be *b*
       3: 21 were being *b*, Jesus was *b* too.
       7: 29 because they had been *b* by John.
       7: 30 they had not been *b* by John.)
Jn   3: 22 spent some time with them, and *b*.
       3: 23 were constantly coming to be *b*.
       4: 2 in fact it was not Jesus who *b*,
Ac   1: 5 For John *b* with water,
       1: 5 but in a few days you will be *b*
       2: 38 Repent and be *b*, every one of you,
       2: 41 who accepted his message were *b*,
       8: 12 they were *b*, both men and women.
       8: 13 Simon himself believed and was *b*.
       8: 16 they had simply been *b*
       8: 36 Why shouldn't I be *b*?"
       8: 38 into the water and Philip *b* him.
       9: 18 was *b*, and after taking some food,
      10: 47 people from being *b* with water?
      10: 48 So he ordered that they be *b*
      11: 16 what the Lord had said, 'John *b*
      11: 16 you will be *b* with the Holy Spirit.'
      16: 15 members of her household were *b*,
      16: 33 he and all his family were *b*.
      18: 8 heard him believed and were *b*.
      19: 5 they were *b* into the name
      22: 16 be *b* and wash your sins away,
Ro   6: 3 *b* into Christ Jesus were *b*
1Co   1: 13 Were you *b* into the name of Paul?
       1: 15 so no one can say that you were *b*
       1: 16 I also *b* the household of Stephanas
       1: 16 I don't remember if I *b* anyone else
      10: 2 They were all *b* into Moses
      12: 13 For we were all *b* by one Spirit
      15: 29 what will those do who are *b*
      15: 29 why are people *b* for them?
Gal   3: 27 all of you who were *b*

BAPTIZING* (BAPTIZE)

Mt   3: 7 coming to where he was *b*,
      28: 19 *b* them in the name of the Father
Mk   1: 4 *b* in the desert region
Jn   1: 28 of the Jordan, where John was *b*.
       1: 31 but the reason I came *b*
       3: 23 also was *b* at Aenon near Salim,
       3: 26 he is *b*, and everyone is going
       4: 1 and *b* more disciples than John,
      10: 40 the place where John had been *b*

BAR-JESUS*

Ac   13: 6 and false prophet named *B*,

BARABBAS

Mt   27: 26 Then he released *B* to them.

BARAK*

Judge who fought with Deborah against Canaanites (Jdg 4-5; 1Sa 12:11; Heb 11:32).

BARBARIAN*

Col   3: 11 circumcised or uncircumcised, *b*,

BARBS*

Nu   33: 55 allow to remain will become *b*

BARE

Hos   2: 3 as *b* as on the day she was born;
Heb   4: 13 and laid *b* before the eyes of him

BARNABAS*

Disciple, originally Joseph (Ac 4:36), prophet (Ac 13:1), apostle (Ac 14:14). Brought Paul to apostles (Ac 9:27), Antioch (Ac 11:22-29; Gal 2. 1-13), on the first missionary journey (Ac 13-14). Together at Jerusalem Council, they separated over John Mark (Ac 15). Later co-workers (1Co 9:6; Col 4:10).

BARREN

Ge   11: 30 Sarai was *b*; she had no children.
      29: 31 her womb, but Rachel was *b*.
Ps   113: 9 He settles the *b* woman
Isa   54: 1 "Sing, O *b* woman,
Lk   1: 7 children, because Elizabeth was *b*;
Gal   4: 27 "Be glad, O *b* woman,
Heb   11: 11 and Sarah herself was *b*—

BARTHOLOMEW*

Apostle (Mt 10:3; Mk 3:18; Lk 6:14; Ac 1:13). Possibly also known as Nathanael (Jn 1:45-49; 21:2).

BARUCH*

Jeremiah's secretary (Jer 32:12-16; 36; 43: 1-6; 45:1-2).

BARZILLAI

1. Gileadite who aided David during Absalom's revolt (2Sa 17:27; 19:31-39).
2. Son-in-law of 1. (Ezr 2:61; Ne 7:63).

BASHAN

Jos   22: 7 Moses had given land in *B*,
Ps   22: 12 strong bulls of *B* encircle me.

BASIN

Ex   30: 18 "Make a bronze *b*,

BASKET

Ex   2: 3 she got a papyrus *b* for him
Ac   9: 25 him in a *b* through an opening
2Co   11: 33 I was lowered in a *b* from a window

BATCH*

Ro   11: 16 then the whole *b* is holy;
1Co   5: 6 through the whole *b* of dough?
       5: 7 old yeast that you may be a new *b*
Gal   5: 9 through the whole *b* of dough."

BATH (BATHING)

Jn   13: 10 person who has had a *b* needs only

BATHING (BATH)

2Sa   11: 2 From the roof he saw a woman *b*.

BATHSHEBA*

Wife of Uriah who committed adultery with and became wife of David (2Sa 11), mother of Solomon (2Sa 12:24; 1Ki 1-2; 1Ch 3:5).

BATTLE (BATTLES)

1Sa   17: 47 for the *b* is the LORD's,
2Ch   20: 15 For the *b* is not yours, but God's.
Ps   24: 8 the LORD mighty in *b*.
Ecc   9: 11 or the *b* to the strong,
Isa   31: 4 down to do Mount Zion
Eze   13: 5 in the *b* on the day of the LORD.
Rev   16: 14 them for the *b* on the great day
      20: 8 and Magog—to gather them for *b*.

BATTLES* (BATTLE)

1Sa   8: 20 to go out before us and fight our *b*."
      18: 17 and fight the *b* of the LORD."
      25: 28 because he fights the LORD's *b*.
2Ch   32: 8 God to help us and to fight our *b*."

BEAR (BEARING BEARS BIRTH BIRTHRIGHT BORE BORN CHILDBEARING CHILDBIRTH FIRSTBORN NEWBORN REBIRTH)

Ge   4: 13 punishment is more than I can *b*.
Ps   38: 4 like a burden too heavy to *b*.
Isa   11: 7 The cow will feed with the *b*,
      53: 11 and he will *b* their iniquities.
Da   7: 5 beast, which looked like a *b*.
Mt   7: 18 A good tree cannot *b* bad fruit,
Jn   15: 2 branch that does *b* fruit he prunes
      15: 8 glory, that you *b* much fruit,
      15: 16 appointed you to go and *b* fruit—

Ro   7: 4 in order that we might *b* fruit
      15: 1 ought to *b* with the failings
1Co   10: 13 tempted beyond what you can *b*.
Col   3: 13 *B* with each other and forgive

BEARD

Lev   19: 27 or clip off the edges of your *b*.
Isa   50: 6 to those who pulled out my *b*;

BEARING (BEAR)

Eph   4: 2 *b* with one another in love.
Col   1: 10 *b* fruit in every good work,
Heb   13: 13 outside the camp, *b* the disgrace he

BEARS (BEAR)

1Ki   8: 43 house I have built *b* your Name.
Ps   68: 19 who daily *b* our burdens.

BEAST (BEASTS)

Rev   13: 18 him calculate the number of the *b*,
      16: 2 people who had the mark of the *b*
      19: 20 who had received the mark of the *b*

BEASTS (BEAST)

Da   7: 3 Four great *b*, each different
1Co   15: 32 If I fought wild *b* in Ephesus

BEAT (BEATEN BEATING BEATINGS)

Isa   2: 4 They will *b* their swords
Joel   3: 10 *B* your plowshares into swords
Mic   4: 3 They will *b* their swords
1Co   9: 27 I *b* my body and make it my slave

BEATEN (BEAT)

Lk   12: 47 do what his master wants will be *b*
      12: 48 deserving punishment will be *b*
2Co   11: 25 Three times I was *b* with rods,

BEATING (BEAT)

1Co   9: 26 I do not fight like a man *b* the air.
1Pe   2: 20 if you receive a *b* for doing wrong

BEATINGS (BEAT)

Pr   19: 29 and *b* for the backs of fools.

BEAUTIFUL* (BEAUTY)

Ge   6: 2 that the daughters of men were *b*,
      12: 11 "I know what a *b* woman you are.
      12: 14 saw that she was a very *b* woman.
      24: 16 The girl was very *b*, a virgin;
      26: 7 of Rebekah, because she is *b*."
      29: 17 Rachel was lovely in form, and *b*.
      49: 21 that bears *b* fawns.
Nu   24: 5 "How *b* are your tents, O Jacob,
Dt   21: 11 among the captives a *b* woman
Jos   7: 21 saw in the plunder a *b* robe
1Sa   25: 3 was an intelligent and *b* woman,
2Sa   11: 2 The woman was very *b*,
      13: 1 the *b* sister of Absalom son
      14: 27 and she became a *b* woman.
1Ki   1: 3 throughout Israel for a *b* girl
       1: 4 The girl was very *b*; she took care
Est   2: 2 for *b* young virgins for the king.
       2: 3 realm to bring all these *b* girls
Job   38: 31 "Can you bind the *b* Pleiades?
      42: 15 land were there found women as *b*
Ps   48: 2 It is *b* in its loftiness.
Pr   11: 22 is a *b* woman who shows no
      24: 4 filled with rare and *b* treasures.
Ecc   3: 11 He has made everything *b*
SS   1: 8 *Lover* If you do not know, most *b*
       1: 10 Your cheeks are *b* with earrings,
       1: 15 Oh, how *b*!
       1: 15 *Lover* How *b* you are, my darling!
       2: 10 my *b* one, and come with me.
       2: 13 my *b* one, come with me."
       4: 1 How *b* you are, my darling!
       4: 1 Oh, how *b*!
       4: 7 All *b* you are, my darling,
       5: 9 most *b* of women?
       6: 1 most *b* of women?
       6: 4 *Lover* You are *b*, my darling,
       7: 1 How *b* your sandaled feet,
       7: 6 How *b* you are and how pleasing,
Isa   4: 2 of the LORD will be *b*
      28: 5 a *b* wreath
      52: 7 How *b* on the mountains
Jer   3: 19 the most *b* inheritance
       6: 2 so *b* and delicate.
      11: 16 with fruit *b* in form.
      46: 20 "Egypt is a *b* heifer.
Eze   7: 20 They were proud of their *b* jewelry
      16: 7 and became the most *b* of jewels.
      16: 12 and a *b* crown on your head.
      16: 13 You became very *b* and rose

BEAUTY

Eze 20: 6 and honey, the most b of all lands,
20: 15 and honey, most b of all lands—
23: 42 and b crowns on their heads.
27: 24 traded with you b garments,
31: 3 with b branches overshadowing
31: 9 I made it b
33: 32 who sings love songs with a b voice
Da 4: 12 Its leaves were b, its fruit abundant
4: 21 with b leaves and abundant fruit,
8: 9 to the east and toward the B Land.
11: 16 will establish himself in the B Land
11: 41 He will also invade the B Land.
11: 45 the seas at the b holy mountain.
Zec 9: 17 How attractive and b they will be!
Mt 23: 27 which look b on the outside
26: 10 She has done a b thing to me.
Mk 14: 6 She has done a b thing to me.
Lk 21: 5 temple was adorned with b stones
Ac 3: 2 carried to the temple gate called B,
3: 10 at the temple gate called B,
Ro 10: 15 "How b are the feet
1Pe 3: 5 in God used to make themselves b.

BEAUTY* (BEAUTIFUL)

Est 1: 11 order to display her b to the people
2: 3 let b treatments be given to them.
2: 9 her with her b treatments
2: 12 months of b treatments prescribed
Ps 27: 4 to gaze upon the b of the LORD
37: 20 LORD's enemies will be like the b
45: 11 The king is enthralled by your b;
50: 2 From Zion, perfect in b,
Pr 6: 25 lust in your heart after her b
31: 30 is deceptive, and b is fleeting;
Isa 3: 24 instead of b, branding.
28: 1 to the fading flower, his glorious b,
28: 4 That fading flower, his glorious b,
33: 17 Your eyes will see the king in his b
53: 2 He had no b or majesty
61: 3 to bestow on them a crown of b
La 2: 15 the perfection of b,
Eze 16: 14 had given you made your b perfect,
16: 14 the nations on account of your b,
16: 15 passed by and your b became his.
16: 15 " 'But you trusted in your b
16: 25 lofty shrines and degraded your b,
27: 3 "I am perfect in b."
27: 4 your builders brought your b
27: 11 they brought your b to perfection.
28: 7 draw their swords against your b
28: 12 full of wisdom and perfect in b,
28: 17 proud on account of your b,
31: 7 It was majestic in b,
31: 8 could match its b.
Jas 1: 11 blossom falls and its b is destroyed
1Pe 3: 3 Your b should not come
3: 4 the unfading b of a gentle

BED (SICKBED)

Isa 28: 20 The b is too short to stretch out on,
Lk 11: 7 and my children are with me in b.
17: 34 night two people will be in one b;
Heb 13: 4 and the marriage b kept pure,

BEELZEBUB

Mt 10: 25 of the house has been called B,
12: 24 "It is only by B, the prince
12: 27 And if I drive out demons by B,
Mk 3: 22 possessed by B! By the prince
Lk 11: 15 "By B, the prince of demons,
11: 18 claim that I drive out demons by B.
11: 19 Now if I drive out demons by B,

BEER

Pr 20: 1 Wine is a mocker and b a brawler;

BEERSHEBA

Ge 21: 14 and wandered in the desert of B.
Jdg 20: 1 all the Israelites from Dan to B
1Sa 3: 20 to B recognized that Samuel was
2Sa 3: 10 and Judah from Dan to B."
17: 11 Let all Israel, from Dan to B—
24: 2 the tribes of Israel from Dan to B
24: 15 of the people from Dan to B died.
1Ki 4: 25 from Dan to B, lived in safety,
1Ch 21: 2 count the Israelites from B to Dan.
2Ch 30: 5 throughout Israel, from B to Dan,

BEFALLS*

Pr 12: 21 No harm b the righteous,

BEGGING

Ps 37: 25 or their children b bread.
Ac 16: 9 of Macedonia standing and b him,

BEGINNING

Ge 1: 1 In the b God created the heavens
Ps 102: 25 In the b you laid the foundations
111: 10 of the LORD is the b of wisdom;
Pr 1: 7 of the LORD is the b of knowledge
9: 10 of the LORD is the b of wisdom,
Ecc 3: 11 fathom what God has done from b
Isa 40: 21 Has it not been told you from the b
46: 10 I make known the end from the b,
Mt 24: 8 All these are the b of birth pains.
Lk 1: 3 investigated everything from the b,
Jn 1: 1 In the b was the Word.
1Jn 1: 1 That which was from the b,
Rev 21: 6 and the Omega, the B and the End.
22: 13 and the Last, the B and the End.

BEHAVE (BEHAVIOR)

Ro 13: 13 Let us b decently, as in the daytime

BEHAVIOR (BEHAVE)

1Pe 3: 1 without words by the b of their wives,
3: 16 maliciously against your good b

BEHEMOTH*

Job 40: 15 "Look at the b,

BELIEVE (BELIEVED BELIEVER BELIEVERS BELIEVES BELIEVING)

Ex 4: 1 "What if they do not b me
1Ki 10: 7 I did not b these things until I came
2Ch 9: 6 But I did not b what they said
Ps 78: 32 of his wonders, they did not b.
Hab 1: 5 that you would not b,
Mt 18: 6 one of these little ones who b in me
21: 22 If you b, you will receive whatever
27: 42 from the cross, and we will b in him
Mk 1: 15 Repent and b the good news!"
5: 36 ruler, "Don't be afraid; just b."
9: 24 "I do b; help me overcome my
9: 42 one of these little ones who b in me
11: 24 b that you have received it,
15: 32 the cross, that we may see and b."
16: 16 but whoever does not b will be
16: 17 signs will accompany those who b:
Lk 8: 12 so that they may not b and be saved.
8: 13 They b for a while, but in the time
8: 50 just b, and she will be healed."
22: 67 you will not b me,
24: 25 to b all that the prophets have
Jn 1: 7 that through him all men might b.
3: 18 does not b stands condemned
4: 42 "We no longer b just
5: 38 for you do not b the one he sent.
5: 46 believed Moses, you would b me,
6: 29 to b in the one he has sent."
6: 69 We b and know that you are
7: 5 his own brothers did not b in him.
8: 24 if you do not b that I am ,the one I
9: 35 "Do you b in the Son of Man?"
9: 36 "Tell me so that I may b in him."
9: 38 "Lord, I b," and he worshiped him.
10: 26 you do not b because you are not
10: 37 Do not b me unless I do what my
10: 38 you do not b me, b the miracles,
11: 27 "I b that you are the Christ,
12: 37 they still would not b in him.
12: 39 For this reason they could not b,
12: 44 in me, he does not b in me only,
13: 19 does happen you will b that I am
14: 10 Don't you b that I am in the Father
14: 11 b me when I say that I am
14: 11 or at least b on the evidence
16: 30 This makes us b that you came
16: 31 "You b at last!" Jesus answered.
17: 21 that the world may b that you have
19: 35 he testifies so that you also may b.
20: 27 Stop doubting and b."
20: 31 written that you may b that Jesus is
Ac 16: 31 They replied, "B in the Lord Jesus,
19: 4 the people to b in the one coming
24: 14 I b everything that agrees
26: 27 Agrippa, do you b the prophets?
Ro 3: 22 faith in Jesus Christ to all who b.
4: 11 he is the father of all who b
10: 9 b in your heart that God raised him
10: 10 For it is with your heart that you b
10: 14 And how can they b in the one
10: 26 so that all nations might b
1Co 1: 21 preached to save those who b.
Gal 3: 22 might be given to those who b.
Php 1: 29 of Christ not only to b on him,
1Th 4: 14 We b that Jesus died and rose again
2Th 2: 11 delusion so that they will b the lie
1Ti 4: 10 and especially of those who b.

BELIEVED (BELIEVE)

Ge 15: 6 Abram b the LORD, and he
Ex 4: 31 signs before the people, and they b.
Isa 53: 1 Who has b our message
Jnh 3: 5 The Ninevites b God.
Lk 1: 45 is she who has b that what the Lord
Jn 1: 12 to those who b in his name,
2: 22 Then they b the Scripture
3: 18 because he has not b in the name
5: 46 If you b Moses, you would believe
7: 39 whom those who b
11: 40 "Did I not tell you that if you b,
12: 38 "Lord, who has b our message
20: 8 He saw and b.
20: 29 who have not seen and yet have b."
Ac 13: 48 were appointed for eternal life b.
19: 2 the Holy Spirit when you b?"
Ro 4: 3 Scripture say? "Abraham b God,
10: 14 call on the one they have not b?
10: 16 "Lord, who has b our message?"
1Co 15: 2 Otherwise, you have b in vain.
Gal 3: 6 Consider Abraham: "He b God,
2Th 2: 12 who have not b the truth
1Ti 3: 16 was b on in the world,
2Ti 1: 12 because I know whom I have b,
Jas 2: 23 that says, "Abraham b God,

BELIEVER* (BELIEVE)

1Ki 18: 3 (Obadiah was a devout b
Ac 16: 1 whose mother was a Jewess and a b
16: 15 "If you consider me a b in the Lord
1Co 7: 12 brother has a wife who is not a b
7: 13 has a husband who is not a b
2Co 6: 15 What does a b have in common
1Ti 5: 16 any woman who is a b has widows

BELIEVERS* (BELIEVE)

Jn 4: 41 of his words many more became b.
Ac 1: 15 among the b (a group numbering
2: 44 All the b were together
4: 32 All the b were one in heart
5: 12 And all the b used to meet together
9: 41 he called the b and the widows
10: 45 The circumcised b who had come
11: 2 the circumcised b criticized him
15: 2 along with some other b,
15: 5 Then some of the b who belonged
15: 23 To the Gentile b in Antioch,
21: 25 for the Gentile b, we have written
1Co 6: 5 to judge a dispute between b?
14: 22 is for b, not for unbelievers.
14: 22 not for b but for unbelievers;
Gal 6: 10 who belong to the family of b.
1Th 1: 7 a model to all the b in Macedonia
1Ti 4: 12 set an example for the b in speech,
6: 2 benefit from their service are b,
Jas 2: 1 b in our glorious Lord Jesus Christ,
1Pe 2: 17 Love the brotherhood of b.

BELIEVES* (BELIEVE)

Pr 14: 15 A simple man b anything,
Mk 9: 23 is possible for him who b."
11: 23 b that what he says will happen,
16: 16 Whoever b and is baptized will be
Jn 3: 15 that everyone who b
3: 16 that whoever b in him shall not
3: 18 Whoever b in him is not
3: 36 Whoever b in the Son has eternal
5: 24 b him who sent me has eternal life
6: 35 and he who b in me will never be
6: 40 and b in him shall have eternal life,
6: 47 he who b has everlasting life.
7: 38 Whoever b in me, as the Scripture
11: 25 He who b in me will live, even
11: 26 and b in me will never die.
12: 44 Jesus cried out, "When a man b
12: 46 so that no one who b
Ac 10: 43 about him that everyone who b
13: 39 him everyone who b is justified
Ro 1: 16 for the salvation of everyone who b
10: 4 righteousness for everyone who b.
1Jn 5: 1 Everyone who b that Jesus is
5: 5 Only he who b that Jesus is the Son
5: 10 Anyone who b in the Son

BELIEVING* (BELIEVE)

Jn   20: 31 and that by *b* you may have life
Ac   26: 2 not *b* that he really was a disciple.
1Co 7: 14 sanctified through her *b* husband.
       7: 15 A *b* man or woman is not bound
       9: 5 right to take a *b* wife along with us,
Gal   3: 2 or by *b* what you heard? Are you
1Ti   6: 2 Those who have *b* masters are not

BELLY

Ge   3: 14 You will crawl on your *b*
Da   2: 32 its *b* and thighs of bronze,
Mt 12: 40 three nights in the *b* of a huge fish,

BELONG (BELONGING BELONGS)

Ge 40: 8 "Do not interpretations *b* to God?
Lev 25: 55 for the Israelites *b* to me
Dt 10: 14 LORD your God *b* the heavens,
      29: 29 The secret things *b*
Job 12: 13 "To God *b* wisdom and power;
      12: 16 To him *b* strength and victory;
      25: 2 "Dominion and awe *b* to God;
Ps   47: 9 for the kings of the earth *b* to God;
      95: 4 and the mountain peaks *b* to him.
    115: 16 The highest heavens *b*
Jer   5: 10 for these people do not *b*
Jn   8: 44 You *b* to your father, the devil,
      15: 19 As it is, you do not *b* to the world,
Ro   1: 6 called to *b* to Jesus Christ.
      7: 4 that you might *b* to another,
      8: 9 of Christ, he does not *b* to Christ.
      14: 8 we live or die, we *b* to the Lord.
1Co 7: 39 but he must *b* to the Lord.
      15: 23 when he comes, those who *b*
Gal   3: 29 If you *b* to Christ, then you are
      5: 24 Those who *b* to Christ Jesus have
1Th   5: 5 We do not *b* to the night
      5: 8 But since we *b* to the day, let us be
1Jn   3: 19 then is how we know that we *b*

BELONGING (BELONG)

1Pe   2: 9 a holy nation, a people *b* to God,

BELONGS (BELONG)

Lev 27: 30 *b* to the LORD; it is holy
Dt   1: 17 of any man, for judgment *b* to God.
Job 41: 11 Everything under heaven *b* to me.
Ps 22: 28 for dominion *b* to the LORD
      89: 18 Indeed, our shield *b* to the LORD,
   111: 10 To him *b* eternal praise.
Eze 18: 4 For every living soul *b* to me,
Jn   8: 47 He who *b* to God hears what God
Ro 12: 5 each member *b* to all the others.
Rev   7: 10 "Salvation *b* to our God,

BELOVED* (LOVE)

Dt 33: 12 "Let the *b* of the LORD rest secure
SS   5: 9 How is your *b* better than others,
      5: 9 *Friends* How is your *b* better
Jer 11: 15 "What is my *b* doing in my temple

BELSHAZZAR

King of Babylon in days of Daniel (Da 5).

BELT

Ex 12: 11 with your cloak tucked into your *b*,
1Ki 18: 46 and, tucking his cloak into his *b*,
2Ki 4: 29 "Tuck your cloak into your *b*,
      9: 1 "Tuck your cloak into your *b*,
Isa 11: 5 Righteousness will be his *b*
Eph   6: 14 with the *b* of truth buckled

BENEFICIAL* (BENEFIT)

1Co 6: 12 for me"—but not everything is *b*.
     10: 23 but not everything is *b*.

BENEFIT (BENEFICIAL BENEFITS)

Job 22: 2 "Can a man be of *b* to God?
Isa 38: 17 Surely it was for my *b*
Ro 6: 22 the *b* you reap leads to holiness.
2Co 4: 15 All this is for your *b*,

BENEFITS (BENEFIT)

Ps 103: 2 and forget not all his *b*.
Jn 4: 38 you have reaped the *b* of their labor

BENJAMIN

Twelfth son of Jacob by Rachel (Ge 35:16-24; 46:19-21; 1Ch 2:2). Jacob refused to send him to Egypt, but relented (Ge 42-45). Tribe of blessed (Ge 49:27; Dt 33:12), numbered (Nu 1: 37; 26:41), allotted land (Jos 18:11-28; Eze 48: 23), failed to fully possess (Jdg 1:21), nearly obliterated (Jdg 20-21), sided with Ish-Bosheth

(2Sa 2), but turned to David (1Ch 12:2, 29). 12,000 from (Rev 7:8).

BEREANS*

Ac 17: 11 the *B* were of more noble character

BESTOWING* (BESTOWS)

Pr   8: 21 *b* wealth on those who love me

BESTOWS (BESTOWING)

Ps 84: 11 the LORD *b* favor and honor;

BETHANY

Mk 11: 1 and *B* at the Mount of Olives,

BETHEL

Ge 28: 19 He called that place *B*,

BETHLEHEM

Ru 1: 19 went on until they came to *B*.
1Sa 16: 1 I am sending you to Jesse of *B*.
2Sa 23: 15 from the well near the gate of *B!*"
Mic 5: 2 "But you, *B* Ephrathah,
Mt   2: 1 After Jesus was born in *B* in Judea,
      2: 6 "'But you, *B*, in the land of Judah,

BETHPHAGE

Mt 21: 1 came to *B* on the Mount of Olives,

BETHSAIDA

Jn 12: 21 who was from *B* in Galilee,

BETRAY (BETRAYED BETRAYS)

Ps 89: 33 nor will I ever *b* my faithfulness.
Pr 25: 9 do not *b* another man's confidence,
Mt 10: 21 "Brother will *b* brother to death,
      26: 21 the truth, one of you will *b* me."

BETRAYED (BETRAY)

Mt 27: 4 "for I have *b* innocent blood."

BETRAYS (BETRAY)

Pr 11: 13 A gossip *b* a confidence,
      20: 19 A gossip *b* a confidence;

BEULAH*

Isa 62: 4 and your land *B*;

BEWITCHED*

Gal 3: 1 foolish Galatians! Who has *b* you?

BEZALEL

Judahite craftsman in charge of building the tabernacle (Ex 31:1-11; 35:30-39:31).

BIDDING*

Ps 103: 20 you mighty ones who do his *b*,
     148: 8 stormy winds that do his *b*,

BILDAD

One of Job's friends (Job 8; 18; 25).

BILHAH

Servant of Rachel, mother of Jacob's sons Dan and Naphtali (Ge 30:1-7; 35:25; 46:23-25).

BIND (BINDS BOUND)

Dt 6: 8 and *b* them on your foreheads.
Pr 3: 3 *b* them around your neck;
      6: 21 *B* them upon your heart forever;
      7: 3 *b* them on your fingers;
Isa 61: 1 me to *b* up the brokenhearted,
Mt 16: 19 whatever you *b* on earth will be

BINDS (BIND)

Ps 147: 3 and *b* up their wounds.
Isa 30: 26 when the LORD *b* up the bruises

BIRD (BIRDS)

Pr 27: 8 Like a *b* that strays from its nest
Ecc 10: 20 a *b* of the air may carry your words,

BIRDS (BIRD)

Mt 8: 20 and *b* of the air have nests,
Lk 9: 58 and *b* of the air have nests,

BIRTH (BEAR)

Ps 51: 5 Surely I was sinful at *b*,
      58: 3 Even from *b* the wicked go astray;
Isa 26: 18 but we gave *b* to wind.
Mt 1: 18 This is how the *b* of Jesus Christ
      24: 8 these are the beginning of *b* pains.
Jn 3: 6 Flesh gives *b* to flesh, but the Spirit
1Pe 1: 3 great mercy he has given us new *b*

BIRTHRIGHT (BEAR)

Ge 25: 34 So Esau despised his *b*.

BISHOP see OVERSEER

BITTEN

Nu 21: 8 anyone who is *b* can look at it

BITTER (BITTERNESS EMBITTER)

Ex 12: 8 along with *b* herbs, and bread made
Pr 27: 7 what is *b* tastes sweet.

BITTERNESS (BITTER)

Pr 14: 10 Each heart knows its own *b*,
      17: 25 and *b* to the one who bore him.
Ro 3: 14 full of cursing and *b*.
Eph 4: 31 Get rid of all *b*, rage and anger,

BLACK

Zec 6: 6 The one with the *b* horses is going
Rev 6: 5 and there before me was a *b* horse!

BLAMELESS* (BLAMELESSLY)

Ge 6: 9 *b* among the people of his time,
      17: 1 walk before me and be *b*.
Dt 18: 13 You must be *b* before the LORD
2Sa 22: 24 I have been *b* before him
      22: 26 to the *b* you show yourself *b*,
Job 1: 1 This man was *b* and upright;
      1: 8 one on earth like him; he is *b*
      2: 3 one on earth like him; he is *b*
      4: 6 and your *b* ways your hope?
      8: 20 God does not reject a *b* man
      9: 20 if I were *b*, it would pronounce me
      9: 21 "Although I am *b*,
      9: 22 'He destroys both the *b*
      12: 4 though righteous and *b!*
      22: 3 gain if your ways were *b*?
      31: 6 and he will know that I am *b*—
Ps 15: 2 He whose walk is *b*
      18: 23 I have been *b* before him
      18: 25 to the *b* you show yourself *b*,
      19: 13 Then will I be *b*,
      26: 1 for I have led a *b* life;
      26: 11 But I lead a *b* life.
      37: 18 The days of the *b* are known
      37: 37 Consider the *b*, observe the upright
      84: 11 from those whose walk is *b*
    101: 2 I will be careful to lead a *b* life—
    101: 2 house with *b* heart.
    101: 6 he whose walk is *b*
    119: 1 Blessed are they whose ways are *b*,
   119: 80 May my heart be *b*
Pr 2: 7 a shield to those whose walk is *b*,
      2: 21 and the *b* will remain in it;
      11: 5 of the *b* makes a straight way
      11: 20 in those whose ways are *b*
      19: 1 Better a poor man whose walk is *b*
      20: 7 The righteous man leads a *b* life;
      28: 6 Better a poor man whose walk is *b*
      28: 10 *b* will receive a good inheritance.
      28: 18 He whose walk is *b* is kept safe,
Eze 28: 15 You were *b* in your ways
1Co 1: 8 so that you will be *b* on the day
Eph 1: 4 world to be holy and *b* in his sight.
      5: 27 any other blemish, but holy and *b*.
Php 1: 10 and *b* until the day of Christ,
      2: 15 so that you may become *b* and pure
1Th 2: 10 and *b* we were among you who
      3: 13 hearts so that you will be *b*
      5: 23 and body be kept *b* at the coming
Tit 1: 6 An elder must be *b*, the husband of
      1: 7 he must be *b*—not overbearing,
Heb 7: 26 *b*, pure, set apart from sinners,
2Pe 3: 14 effort to be found spotless, *b*
Rev 14: 5 found in their mouths; they are *b*.

BLAMELESSLY* (BLAMELESS)

Lk 1: 6 commandments and regulations *b*.

BLASPHEME* (BLASPHEMED BLASPHEMER BLASPHEMES BLASPHEMIES BLASPHEMING BLASPHEMOUS BLASPHEMY)

Ex 22: 28 "Do not *b* God or curse the ruler
Ac 26: 11 and I tried to force them to *b*.
1Ti 1: 20 over to Satan to be taught not to *b*.
2Pe 2: 12 these men *b* in matters they do not
Rev 13: 6 He opened his mouth to *b* God,

BLASPHEMED* (BLASPHEME)

Lev 24: 11 of the Israelite woman *b* the Name
2Ki 19: 6 of the king of Assyria have *b* me.
      19: 22 Who is it you have insulted and *b*?
Isa 37: 6 of the king of Assyria have *b* me.

Isa 37: 23 Who is it you have insulted and *b*?
　　 52: 5 my name is constantly b.
Eze 20: 27 your fathers *b* me by forsaking me:
Ac 19: 37 robbed temples nor *b* our goddess
Ro 2: 24 name is *b* among the Gentiles

BLASPHEMER* (BLASPHEME)

Lev 24: 14 "Take the *b* outside the camp.
　　 24: 23 they took the *b* outside the camp
1Ti 1: 13 I was once a *b* and a persecutor

BLASPHEMES* (BLASPHEME)

Lev 24: 16 anyone who *b* the name
　　 24: 16 native-born, when he *b* the Name,
Nu 15: 30 native-born or alien, *b* the LORD,
Mk 3: 29 whoever *b* against the Holy Spirit
Lk 12: 10 but anyone who *b* against the Holy

BLASPHEMIES* (BLASPHEME)

Ne 9: 18 or when they committed awful *b*.
　　 9: 26 to you; they committed awful *b*.
Mk 3: 28 and *b* of men will be forgiven them.
Rev 13: 5 and *b* and to exercise his authority

BLASPHEMING* (BLASPHEME)

Mt 9: 3 "This fellow is *b*!" Knowing their
Mk 2: 7 He's *b*! Who can forgive sins

BLASPHEMOUS* (BLASPHEME)

Rev 13: 1 and on each head a *b* name.
　　 17: 3 that was covered with *b* names

BLASPHEMY* (BLASPHEME)

Mt 12: 31 and *b* will be forgiven men,
　　 12: 31 the *b* against the Spirit will not be
　　 26: 65 Look, now you have heard the *b*.
　　 26: 65 "He has spoken *b*! Why do we
Mk 14: 64 "You have heard the *b*.
Lk 5: 21 "Who is this fellow who speaks *b*?
Jn 10: 33 replied the Jews, "but for *b*,
　　 10: 36 they then do you accuse me of *b*
Ac 6: 11 words of *b* against Moses

BLAST*

Ex 15: 8 By the *b* of your nostrils
　　 19: 13 horn sounds a long *b* may they go
　　 19: 16 and a very loud trumpet *b*.
Nu 10: 5 When a trumpet *b* is sounded,
　　 10: 6 At the sounding of a second *b*,
　　 10: 6 The *b* will be the signal
　　 10: 9 sound a *b* on the trumpets.
Jos 6: 5 you hear them sound a long *b*
　　 6: 16 the priests sounded the trumpet *b*,
2Sa 22: 16 at the *b* of breath from his nostrils.
Job 4: 9 At the *b* of his anger they perish.
　　 39: 25 At the *b* of the trumpet he snorts,
Ps 18: 15 the *b* of breath from your nostrils.
　　 98: 6 and the *b* of the ram's horn—
　　147: 17 Who can withstand his icy *b*?
Isa 27: 8 with his fierce *b* he drives her out,
Eze 22: 20 a furnace to melt it with a fiery *b*,
Am 2: 2 tumult amid war cries and the *b*
Heb 12: 19 to a trumpet *b* or to such a voice

BLEATING*

1Sa 15: 14 "What then is this *b* of sheep

BLEMISH (BLEMISHES)

Lev 22: 21 be without defect or *b*
Eph 5: 27 or wrinkle or any other *b*,
Col 1: 22 without *b* and free from accusation
1Pe 1: 19 a lamb without *b* or defect.

BLEMISHES* (BLEMISH)

2Pe 2: 13 and *b*, reveling in their pleasures
Jude : 12 These men are *b* at your love feasts

BLESS (BLESSED BLESSES BLESSING BLESSINGS)

Ge 12: 3 I will *b* those who *b* you,
　　 32: 26 not let you go unless you *b* me."
Dt 7: 13 He will love you and *b* you
　　 33: 11 *B* all his skills, O LORD,
Ps 72: 15 and *b* him all day long.
Ro 12: 14 Bless those who persecute you; *b*

BLESSED (BLESS)

Ge 1: 22 God *b* them and said, "Be fruitful
　　 2: 3 And God *b* the seventh day
　　 22: 18 nations on earth will be *b*,
Nu 24: 9 "May those who bless you be *b*
1Ch 17: 27 have *b* it, and it will be *b* forever."
Ps 1: 1 *B* is the man
　　 2: 12 *B* are all who take refuge in him.
　　 32: 2 *B* is the man

Ps 33: 12 *B* is the nation whose God is
　　 40: 4 *B* is the man
　　 41: 1 *B* is he who has regard for the weak
　　 84: 5 *B* are those whose strength is
　　 89: 15 *B* are those who have learned
　　 94: 12 *B* is the man you discipline,
　　106: 3 *B* are they who maintain justice,
　　112: 1 *B* is the man who fears the LORD,
　　118: 26 *B* is he who comes in the name
　　119: 1 *B* are they whose ways are
　　119: 2 *B* are they who keep his statutes
　　127: 5 *B* is the man
Pr 3: 13 *B* is the man who finds wisdom,
　　 8: 34 *B* is the man who listens to me,
　　 28: 20 A faithful man will be richly *b*,
　　 29: 18 but *b* is he who keeps the law.
　　 31: 28 Her children arise and call her *b*;
Isa 30: 18 *B* are all who wait for him!
Mal 3: 12 Then all the nations will call you *b*,
　　 3: 15 But now we call the arrogant *b*.
Mt 5: 3 saying: "*B* are the poor in spirit,
　　 5: 4 *B* are those who mourn,
　　 5: 5 *B* are the meek,
　　 5: 6 *B* are those who hunger
　　 5: 7 *B* are the merciful,
　　 5: 8 *B* are the pure in heart,
　　 5: 9 *B* are the peacemakers,
　　 5: 10 *B* are those who are persecuted
　　 5: 11 "*B* are you when people insult you,
Lk 1: 48 all generations will call me *b*,
Jn 12: 13 "*B* is he who comes in the name
Ac 20: 35 'It is more *b* to give than to receive
Tit 2: 13 while we wait for the *b* hope—
Jas 1: 12 *B* is the man who perseveres
Rev 1: 3 *B* is the one who reads the words
　　 22: 7 *B* is he who keeps the words
　　 22: 14 "*B* are those who wash their robes,

BLESSES (BLESS)

Ps 29: 11 the LORD *b* his people with peace.
Ro 10: 12 and richly *b* all who call on him,

BLESSING (BLESS)

Ge 27: 4 so that I may give you my *b*
Dt 23: 5 turned the curse into a *b* for you,
　　 33: 1 This is the *b* that Moses the man
Pr 10: 22 The *b* of the LORD brings wealth,
Eze 34: 26 there will be showers of *b*.

BLESSINGS (BLESS)

Dt 11: 29 proclaim on Mount Gerizim the *b*,
Jos 8: 34 all the words of the law—the *b*
Pr 10: 6 *B* crown the head of the righteous,
Ro 15: 27 shared in the Jews' spiritual *b*,

BLIND (BLINDED)

Mt 15: 14 a *b* man leads a *b* man, both will fall
　　 23: 16 "Woe to you, *b* guides! You say,
Mk 10: 46 a *b* man, Bartimaeus (that is,
Lk 6: 39 "Can a *b* man lead a *b* man?
Jn 9: 25 I was *b* but now I see!"

BLINDED (BLIND)

Jn 12: 40 elsewhere: "He has *b* their eyes
2Co 4: 4 The god of this age has *b* the minds

BLOOD (BLOODSHED BLOODTHIRSTY)

Ge 4: 10 Your brother's *b* cries out to me
　　 9: 6 "Whoever sheds the *b* of man,
Ex 12: 13 and when I see the *b*, I will pass
　　 24: 8 "This is the *b* of the covenant that
Lev 16: 15 and take its *b* behind the curtain
　　 17: 11 For the life of a creature is in the *b*,
Dt 12: 23 eat the *b*, because the *b* is the life,
Ps 72: 14 for precious is their *b* in his sight.
Pr 6: 17 hands that shed innocent *b*,
Isa 1: 11 pleasure in the *b* of bulls and lambs
Mt 26: 28 This is my *b* of the covenant,
　　 27: 24 "I am innocent of this man's *b*,"
Mk 14: 24 "This is my *b* of the covenant,
Lk 22: 44 drops of *b* falling to the ground.
Jn 6: 53 of the Son of Man and drink his *b*,
Ac 15: 20 of strangled animals and from *b*.
　　 20: 26 innocent of the *b* of all men.
Ro 3: 25 of atonement, through faith in his *b*.
　　 5: 9 have now been justified by his *b*,
1Co 11: 25 cup is the new covenant in my *b*;
Eph 1: 7 we have redemption through his *b*,
　　 2: 13 near through the *b* of Christ.
Col 1: 20 by making peace through his *b*,
Heb 9: 7 once a year, and never without *b*,
　　 9: 12 once for all by his own *b*,
　　 9: 20 "This is the *b* of the covenant,
　　 9: 22 of *b* there is no forgiveness.
　　 12: 24 word than the *b* of Abel.

1Pe 1: 19 but with the precious *b* of Christ,
1Jn 1: 7 and the *b* of Jesus, his Son,
Rev 1: 5 has freed us from our sins by his *b*,
　　 5: 9 with your *b* you purchased men
　　 7: 14 white in the *b* of the Lamb,
　　 12: 11 him by the *b* of the Lamb
　　 19: 13 He is dressed in a robe dipped in *b*,

BLOODSHED (BLOOD)

Jer 48: 10 on him who keeps his sword from *b*
Eze 35: 6 did not hate *b*, *b* will pursue you.
Hab 2: 12 to him who builds a city with *b*

BLOODTHIRSTY* (BLOOD)

Ps 5: 6 band deceitful men
　　 26: 9 my life with *b* men,
　　 55: 23 *b* and deceitful men
　　 59: 2 and save me from *b* men.
　　139: 19 Away from me, you *b* men!
Pr 29: 10 *B* men hate a man of integrity

BLOSSOM

Isa 35: 1 the wilderness will rejoice and *b*.

BLOT (BLOTS)

Ex 32: 32 then *b* me out of the book you have
Ps 51: 1 *b* out my transgressions.
Rev 3: 5 I will never *b* out his name

BLOTS (BLOT)

Isa 43: 25 "I, even I, am he who *b* out

BLOWN

Eph 4: 14 and *b* here and there by every wind
Jas 1: 6 doubts is like a wave of the sea, *b*
Jude : 12 without rain, *b* along by the wind;

BLUSH

Jer 6: 15 they do not even know how to *b*.

BOAST (BOASTS)

1Ki 20: 11 armor should not *b* like one who
Ps 34: 2 My soul will *b* in the LORD;
　　 44: 8 In God we make our *b* all day long,
Pr 27: 1 Do not *b* about tomorrow.
Jer 9: 23 or the rich man *b* of his riches,
1Co 1: 31 Let him who boasts *b* in the Lord."
2Co 10: 17 Let him who boasts *b* in the Lord."
　　 11: 30 I do not inwardly burn? If I must *b*,
Gal 6: 14 May I never *b* except in the cross
Eph 2: 9 not by works, so that no one can *b*.

BOASTS (BOAST)

Jer 9: 24 but let him who *b* boast about this:

BOAZ

Wealthy Bethlehemite who showed favor to
Ruth (Ru 2), married her (Ru 4). Ancestor of
David (Ru 4:18-22; 1Ch 2:12-15), Jesus (Mt 1:
5-16; Lk 3:23-32).

BODIES (BODY)

Isa 26: 19 their *b* will rise.
Ro 12: 1 to offer your *b* as living sacrifices,
1Co 6: 15 not know that your *b* are members
Eph 5: 28 to love their wives as their own *b*.

BODILY (BODY)

Col 2: 9 of the Deity lives in *b* form,

BODY (BODIES BODILY EMBODIMENT)

Zec 13: 6 What are these wounds on your *b*?'
Mt 10: 28 afraid of those who kill the *b*
　　 26: 26 saying, "Take and eat; this is my *b*
　　 26: 41 spirit is willing, but the *b* is weak."
Mk 14: 22 saying, "Take it; this is my *b*."
Lk 22: 19 saying, "This is my *b* given for you;
Jn 13: 10 wash his feet; his whole *b* is clean.
Ro 6: 13 Do not offer the parts of your *b*
　　 12: 4 us has one *b* with many members,
1Co 6: 19 not know that your *b* is a temple
　　 6: 20 Therefore honor God with your *b*.
　　 11: 24 "This is my *b*, which is for you;
　　 12: 12 The *b* is a unit, though it is made up
　　 12: 13 baptized by one Spirit into one *b*—
　　 15: 44 a natural *b*, it is raised a spiritual *b*.
Eph 1: 23 which is his *b*, the fullness
　　 4: 25 for we are all members of one *b*.
　　 5: 30 for we are members of his *b*.
Php 1: 20 Christ will be exalted in my *b*,
Col 1: 24 sake of his *b*, which is the church.

BOLD (BOLDNESS)

Ps 138: 3 you made me *b* and stouthearted.
Pr 21: 29 A wicked man puts up a *b* front,

Pr 28: 1 but the righteous are as *b* as a lion.

BOLDNESS* (BOLD)

Lk 11: 8 of the man's *b* he will get up
Ac 4:29 to speak your word with great *b*.

BONDAGE

Ezr 9: 9 God has not deserted us in our *b*.

BONES

Ge 2:23 "This is now bone of my *b*
Ps 22:14 and all my *b* are out of joint.
    22:17 I can count all my *b*;
Eze 37: 1 middle of a valley; it was full of *b*.
Jn 19:36 "Not one of his *b* will be broken,"

BOOK (BOOKS)

Ex 32:33 against me I will blot out of my *b*.
Jos 1: 8 Do not let this *B* of the Law depart
2Ki 22: 8 "I have found the *B* of the Law
2Ch 34:15 "I have found the *B* of the Law
Ne 8: 8 They read from the *B* of the Law
Ps 69:28 May they be blotted out of the *b*
Da 12: 1 name is found written in the *b*—
Jn 20:30 which are not recorded in this *b*.
Php 4: 3 whose names are in the *b* of life.
Rev 3: 5 never blot out his name from the *b*
    20:12 *b* was opened, which is the *b*
    20:15 was not found written in the *b*
    21:27 written in the Lamb's *b* of life.
    22:18 him the plagues described in this *b*.

BOOKS* (BOOK)

Ecc 12:12 Of making many *b* there is no end,
Da 7:10 and the *b* were opened.
Jn 21:25 for the *b* that would be written.
Rev 20:12 the throne, and *b* were opened.
    20:12 they had done as recorded in the *b*.

BORE (BEAR)

Isa 53:12 For he *b* the sin of many,
1Pe 2:24 He himself *b* our sins in his body

BORN (BEAR)

Ecc 3: 2 a time to be *b* and a time to die,
Isa 9: 6 For to us a child is *b*,
    66: 8 Can a country be *b* in a day
Lk 2:11 of David a Savior has been *b* to you
Jn 3: 3 see the kingdom of God unless he is *b* again.
    3: 4 How can a man be *b* when he is old
    3: 5 unless he is *b* of water
    3: 7 at my saying, 'You must be *b* again.
    3: 8 it is with everyone *b* of the Spirit."
1Pe 1:23 For you have been *b* again,
1Jn 3: 9 because he has been *b* of God.
    4: 7 Everyone who loves has been *b*
    5: 1 believes that Jesus is the Christ is *b*
    5: 4 for everyone *b* of God overcomes
    5:18 We know that anyone *b*

BORROWER

Pr 22: 7 and the *b* is servant to the lender.

BOTHER (BOTHERING)

Lk 11: 7 one inside answers, 'Don't *b* me.

BOTHERING (BOTHER)

Lk 18: 5 yet because this widow keeps *b* me,

BOUGHT (BUY)

Ac 20:28 which he *b* with his own blood.
1Co 6:20 You are not your own; you were *b*
    7:23 You were *b* at a price; do not
2Pe 2: 1 the sovereign Lord who *b* them—

BOUND (BIND)

Is 56: 3 Let no foreigner who has *b* himself
Mt 16:19 bind on earth will be *b* in heaven,
    18:18 bind on earth will be *b* in heaven,
Ro 7: 2 by law a married woman is *b*
1Co 7:39 A woman is *b* to her husband
Jude 6 *b* with everlasting chains
Rev 20: 2 and *b* him for a thousand years.

BOUNDARY (BOUNDS)

Nu 34: 3 your southern *b* will start
Pr 23:10 Do not move an ancient *b* stone
Hos 5:10 who move *b* stones.

BOUNDS (BOUNDARY)

2Co 7: 4 all our troubles my joy knows no *b*.

BOUNTY*

Ge 49:26 than the *b* of the age-old hills.

Dt 28:12 heavens, the storehouse of his *b*,
1Ki 10:13 he had given her out of his royal *b*.
Ps 65:11 You crown the year with your *b*,
    68:10 from your *b*, O God, you provided
Jer 31:12 rejoice in the *b* of the LORD—
    31:14 my people will be filled with my *b*

BOW (BOWED BOWS)

Dt 5: 9 You shall not *b* down to them
1Ki 22:34 But someone drew his *b* at random
Ps 7: in reverence will I *b* down
    44: 6 I do not trust in my *b*,
    95: 6 Come, let us *b* down in worship,
    138: 2 I will *b* down toward your holy
Isa 44:19 Shall I *b* down to a block of wood?"
    45:23 Before me every knee will *b*;
Ro 14:11 'every knee will *b* before me;
Php 2:10 name of Jesus every knee should *b*,

BOWED (BOW)

Ps 145:14 and lifts up all who are *b* down.
    146: 8 the LORD lifts up those who are *b*

BOWS (BOW)

Isa 44:15 he makes an idol and *b* down to it.
    44:17 he *b* down to it and worships.

BOY (BOY'S BOYS)

Ge 21:17 God heard the *b* crying,
    22:12 not lay a hand on the *b*
Jdg 13: 5 is to be a Nazirite,
1Sa 2:11 *b* ministered before the LORD.
    3: 8 the LORD was calling the *b*.
Isa 7:16 before the *b* knows enough
Mt 17:18 demon, and it came out of the *b*
Lk 2:43 the *b* Jesus stayed behind

BOY'S (BOY)

1Ki 17:22 the *b* life returned to him
2Ki 4:34 the *b* body grew warm

BOYS (BOY)

Ge 25:24 twin *b* in her womb
Ex 1:18 they let the *b* live.

BRACE*

Job 38: 3 *B* yourself like a man;
    40: 7 out of the storm: "*B* yourself like
Na 2: 1 *b* yourselves,

BRAG*

Am 4: 5 and *b* about your freewill offerings
Ro 2:17 *b* about your relationship to God;
    2:23 temples? You who *b* about the law,
Jas 4:16 As it is, you boast and *b*.

BRAIDED

1Ti 2: 9 not with *b* hair or gold or pearls
1Pe 3: 3 as *b* hair and the wearing

BRANCH (BRANCHES)

Isa 4: 2 In that day the *B* of the LORD will
Jer 23: 5 up to David a righteous *B*,
    33:15 I will make a righteous *B* sprout
Zec 3: 8 going to bring my servant, the *B*.
    6:12 is the man whose name is the *B*,
Jn 15: 2 while every *b* that does bear fruit
    15: 4 No *b* can bear fruit by itself;

BRANCHES (BRANCH)

Jn 15: 5 "I am the vine; you are the *B*.
Ro 11:21 if God did not spare the natural *b*,

BRAVE

2Sa 2: 7 Now then, be strong and *b*,
    13:28 you this order? Be strong and *b*."

BREACH (BREAK)

Ps 106:23 stood in the *b* before him

BREACHING (BREAK)

Pr 17:14 Starting a quarrel is like *b* a dam;

BREAD

Ex 12: 8 and *b* made without yeast.
    23:15 the Feast of Unleavened *B*,
    25:30 Put the *b* of the Presence
Dt 8: 3 that man does not live on *b* alone
    8: 3 the *b* of angels;
Ps 78:25 Men ate the *b* of angels;
Pr 30: 8 but give me only my daily *b*
Ecc 11: 1 Cast your *b* upon the waters,
Isa 55: 2 Why spend money on what is not *b*
Mt 4: 3 tell these stones to become *b*."
    4: 4 'Man does not live on *b* alone,
    6:11 Give us today our daily *b*.

Mt 26:26 Jesus took *b*, gave thanks
Mk 14:22 Jesus took *b*, gave thanks
Lk 4: 3 tell this stone to become *b*."
    4: 4 'Man does not live on *b* alone.' "
    9:13 "We have only five loaves of *b*
    11: 3 Give us each day our daily *b*.
    22:19 And he took *b*, gave thanks
Jn 6:33 For the *b* of God is he who comes
    6:35 Jesus declared, "I am the *b* of life.
    6:41 "I am the *b* that came
    6:48 I am the *b* of life.
    6:51 I am the living *b* that came
    6:51 This *b* is my flesh, which I will give
    21:13 took the *b* and gave it to them,
1Co 10:16 And is not the *b* that we break
    11:23 took *b*, and when he had given
    11:26 For whenever you eat this *b*

BREAK (BREACH BREACHING BREAKERS BREAKING BREAKS BROKE BROKEN BROKENNESS)

Nu 30: 2 he must not *b* his word
Jdg 2: 1 'I will never *b* my covenant
Pr 25:15 and a gentle tongue can *b* a bone.
Isa 42: 3 A bruised reed he will not *b*,
Mal 2:16 and do not *b* faith with the wife
Mt 12:20 A bruised reed he will not *b*,
Ac 20: 7 week we came together to *b* bread.
1Co 10:16 the bread that we *b* a participation
Rev 5: 2 "Who is worthy to *b* the seals

BREAKERS* (BREAK)

Ps 42: 7 all your waves and *b*
    93: 4 mightier than the *b* of the sea—
Jnh 2: 3 all your waves and *b*

BREAKING (BREAK)

Jos 9:20 fall on us for *b* the oath we swore
Eze 16:59 oath by *b* the covenant.
    17:18 the oath by *b* the covenant.
Ac 2:42 to the *b* of bread and to prayer.
Jas 2:10 at just one point is guilty of *b* all

BREAKS (BREAK)

Jer 23:29 "and like a hammer that *b* a rock
1Jn 3: 4 Everyone who sins *b* the law;

BREASTPIECE (BREASTPLATE)

Ex 28:15 Fashion a *b* for making decisions—

BREASTPLATE* (BREASTPIECE)

Isa 59:17 He put on righteousness as his *b*,
Eph 6:14 with the *b* of righteousness in place
1Th 5: 8 putting on faith and love as a *b*,

BREASTS

La 4: 3 Even jackals offer their *b*

BREATH (BREATHED GOD-BREATHED)

Ge 2: 7 into his nostrils the *b* of life,

BREATHED (BREATH)

Ge 2: 7 *b* into his nostrils the breath of life,
Mk 15:37 With a loud cry, Jesus *b* his last.
Jn 20:22 And with that he *b* on them

BREEDS*

Pr 13:10 Pride only *b* quarrels,

BRIBE

Ex 23: 8 "Do not accept a *b*,
Dt 16:19 for a *b* blinds the eyes of the wise
    27:25 "Cursed is the man who accepts a *b*
Pr 6:35 will refuse the *b*, however great it

BRIDE

Isa 62: 5 as a bridegroom rejoices over his *b*,
Rev 19: 7 and his *b* has made herself ready.
    21: 2 as a *b* beautifully dressed
    21: 9 I will show you the *b*, the wife
    22:17 The Spirit and the *b* say, "Come!"

BRIDEGROOM

Ps 19: 5 which is like a *b* coming forth
Mt 25: 1 and went out to meet the *b*.
    25: 5 The *b* was a long time in coming.

BRIGHTENS* (BRIGHTNESS)

Pr 16:15 When a king's face *b*, it means life;
Ecc 8: 1 Wisdom *b* a man's face

BRIGHTER (BRIGHTNESS)

Pr 4:18 shining ever *b* till the full light

BRIGHTNESS* (BRIGHTENS BRIGHTER)

2Sa 22: 13 Out of the b of his presence
23: 4 like the b after rain
Ps 18: 12 of the b of his presence clouds
Isa 59: 9 for b, but we walk in deep shadows.
60: 3 and kings to the b of your dawn.
60: 19 will the b of the moon shine on you
Da 12: 3 who are wise will shine like the b
Am 5: 20 pitch-dark, without a ray of b?

BRILLIANCE* (BRILLIANT)

Ac 22: 11 the b of the light had blinded me.
Rev 1: 16 was like the sun shining in all its b.
21: 11 its b was like that of a very precious

BRILLIANT* (BRILLIANCE)

Ecc 9: 11 or wealth to the b
Eze 1: 4 and surrounded by b light.
1: 27 and b light surrounded him.

BRINK*

Pr 5: 14 I have come to the b of utter ruin

BRITTLE

Da 2: 42 will be partly strong and partly b.

BROAD

Mt 7: 13 and b is the road that leads

BROKE (BREAK)

Mt 26: 26 took bread, gave thanks and b it,
Mk 14: 22 took bread, gave thanks and b it,
Ac 2: 46 They b bread in their homes
20: 11 he went upstairs again and b bread
1Co 11: 24 when he had given thanks, he b it

BROKEN (BREAK)

Ps 34: 20 not one of them will be b.
51: 17 The sacrifices of God are a b spirit;
Ecc 4: 12 of three strands is not quickly b.
Lk 20: 18 on that stone will be b to pieces,
Jn 7: 23 the law of Moses may not be b,
10: 35 and the Scripture cannot be b—
19: 36 "Not one of his bones will be b,"
Ro 11: 20 they were b off because of unbelief,

BROKENHEARTED* (HEART)

Ps 34: 18 The LORD is close to the b
109: 16 and the needy and the b.
147: 3 He heals the b
Isa 61: 1 He has sent me to bind up the b,

BROKENNESS* (BREAK)

Isa 65: 14 and wail in b of spirit.

BRONZE

Ex 27: 2 and overlay the altar with b.
30: 18 "Make a b basin, with its b stand,
Nu 21: 9 So Moses made a b snake
Da 2: 32 and thighs of b, its legs of iron,
10: 6 legs like the gleam of burnished b,
Rev 1: 15 His feet were like b glowing
2: 18 whose feet are like burnished b.

BROTHER (BROTHER'S BROTHERHOOD BROTHERLY BROTHERS)

Pr 17: 17 and a b is born for adversity.
18: 24 a friend who sticks closer than a b.
27: 10 neighbor nearby than a b far away.
Mt 5: 24 and be reconciled to your b;
18: 15 "If your b sins against you,
Mk 3: 35 Whoever does God's will is my b
Lk 17: 3 "If your b sins, rebuke him,
Ro 14: 15 not by your eating destroy your b
14: 21 anything else that will cause your b
1Co 8: 13 if what I eat causes my b to fall
2Th 3: 6 away from every b who is idle
3: 15 as an enemy, but warn him as a b.
Phm : 16 but better than a slave, as a dear b.
Jas 2: 15 Suppose a b or sister is
4: 11 Anyone who speaks against his b
1Jn 2: 9 hates his b is still in the darkness.
2: 10 Whoever loves his b lives
2: 11 But whoever hates his b is
3: 10 is anyone who does not love his b,
3: 15 who hates his b is a murderer,
3: 17 material possessions and sees his b
4: 20 For anyone who does not love his b
4: 20 yet hates his b, he is a liar.
4: 21 loves God must also love his b.
5: 16 If anyone sees his b commit a sin

BROTHER'S (BROTHER)

Ge 4: 9 "Am I my b keeper?" The LORD

Mt 7: 5 remove the speck from your b eye.
Ro 14: 13 or obstacle in your b way.

BROTHERHOOD (BROTHER)

1Pe 2: 17 Love the b of believers, fear God,

BROTHERLY* (BROTHER)

Ro 12: 10 devoted to one another in b love.
1Th 4: 9 Now about b love we do not need
2Pe 1: 7 and to godliness, b kindness,
1: 7 kindness; and to b kindness,

BROTHERS (BROTHER)

Jos 1: 14 You are to help your b
Ps 133: 1 is when b live together in unity!
Pr 6: 19 who stirs up dissension among b.
Mt 12: 49 "Here are my mother and my b.
19: 29 everyone who has left houses or b
25: 40 one of the least of these b of mine,
Mk 3: 33 "Who are my mother and my b?"
10: 29 or b or sisters or mother or father
Lk 21: 16 You will be betrayed even by parents, b,
22: 32 turned back, strengthen your b."
Jn 7: 5 his own b did not believe in him.
Ac 15: 32 to encourage and strengthen the b.
Ro 3: 9 off from Christ for the sake of my b
1Co 8: 12 sin against your b in this way
2Co 11: 26 and in danger from false b.
Gal 2: 4 some false b had infiltrated our
1Th 4: 10 you do love all the b
5: 26 Greet all the b with a holy kiss.
1Ti 6: 2 for them because they are b.
Heb 2: 11 Jesus is not ashamed to call them b.
2: 17 to be made like his b in every way,
13: 1 Keep on loving each other as b.
1Pe 1: 22 you have sincere love for your b,
3: 8 be sympathetic, love as b,
1Jn 3: 14 death to life, because we love our b.
3: 16 to lay down our lives for our b.
3Jn : 10 he refuses to welcome the b.
Rev 12: 10 For the accuser of our b,

BROW

Ge 3: 19 By the sweat of your b

BRUISED (BRUISES)

Isa 42: 3 A b reed he will not break,
Mt 12: 20 A b reed he will not break,

BRUISES (BRUISED)

Isa 30: 26 when the LORD binds up the b

BRUTAL (BRUTE)

2Ti 3: 3 slanderous, without self-control, b,

BRUTE* (BRUTAL)

Ps 73: 22 I was a b beast before you.
2Pe 2: 12 They are like b beasts, creatures

BUBBLING*

Pr 18: 4 the fountain of wisdom is a b brook
Isa 35: 7 the thirsty ground b springs.

BUCKET*

Isa 40: 15 the nations are like a drop in a b;

BUCKLED* (BUCKLER)

Eph 6: 14 belt of truth b around your waist,

BUCKLER* (BUCKLED)

Ps 35: 2 Take up shield and b;

BUD (BUDDED)

Isa 27: 6 Israel will b and blossom

BUDDED (BUD)

Heb 9: 4 Aaron's staff that had b,

BUILD (BUILDER BUILDERS BUILDING BUILDS BUILT REBUILD REBUILT)

2Sa 7: 5 Are you the one to b me a house
1Ki 6: 1 he began to b the temple
Ecc 3: 3 a time to tear down and a time to b,
Mt 16: 18 and on this rock I will b my church,
Ac 20: 32 which can b you up and give you
Ro 15: 2 neighbor for his good, to b him up.
1Co 14: 12 excel in gifts that b up the church.
1Th 5: 11 one another and b each other up,
Jude : 20 b yourselves up in your most holy

BUILDER* (BUILD)

1Co 3: 10 I laid a foundation as an expert b.
Heb 3: 3 the b of a house has greater honor
3: 4 but God is the b of everything.

Heb 11: 10 whose architect and b is God.

BUILDERS (BUILD)

Ps 118: 22 The stone the b rejected
Mt 21: 42 "The stone the b rejected
Mk 12: 10 "The stone the b rejected
Lk 20: 17 "The stone the b rejected
Ac 4: 11 "the stone you b rejected,
1Pe 2: 7 "The stone the b rejected

BUILDING (BUILD)

Ezr 3: 8 to supervise the b of the house
Ne 4: 17 of Judah who were b the wall.
Ro 15: 20 so that I would not be b
1Co 3: 9 you are God's field, God's b.
2Co 5: 1 we have a b from God, an eternal
10: 8 us for b you up rather
13: 10 the Lord gave me for b you up,
Eph 2: 21 him the whole b is joined together
4: 29 helpful for b others up according

BUILDS (BUILD)

Ps 127: 1 Unless the LORD b the house,
Pr 14: 1 The wise woman b her house,
1Co 3: 10 one should be careful how he b.
3: 12 If any man b on this foundation
8: 1 Knowledge puffs up, but love b up.
Eph 4: 16 grows and b itself up in love,

BUILT (BUILD)

1Ki 6: 14 So Solomon b the temple
Mt 7: 24 is like a wise man who b his house
Lk 6: 49 is like a man who b a house
Ac 17: 24 does not live in temples b by hands.
1Co 3: 14 If what he has b survives, he will
2Co 5: 1 in heaven, not b by human hands.
Eph 2: 20 b on the foundation of the apostles
4: 12 the body of Christ may be b up
Col 2: 7 live in him, rooted and b up in him,
1Pe 2: 5 are being b into a spiritual house

BULL (BULLS)

Lev 4: 3 bring to the LORD a young b

BULLS (BULL)

1Ki 7: 25 The Sea stood on twelve b,
Heb 10: 4 it is impossible for the blood of b

BURDEN (BURDENED BURDENS BURDENSOME)

Ps 38: 4 like a b too heavy to bear.
Ecc 1: 13 What a heavy b God has laid
Mt 11: 30 my yoke is easy and my b is light."
Ac 15: 28 to us not to b you with anything
2Co 11: 9 from being a b to you in any way,
12: 14 and I will not be a b to you,
1Th 2: 9 day in order not to be a b to anyone
2Th 3: 8 so that we would not be a b to any
Heb 13: 17 not a b, for that would be

BURDENED* (BURDEN)

Isa 43: 23 have not b you with grain offerings
43: 24 But you have burdened me with your sins
Mic 3: 3 How have I b you? Answer me.
Mt 11: 28 all you who are weary and b,
2Co 5: 4 are in this tent, we groan and are b,
Gal 5: 1 do not let yourselves be b again
1Ti 5: 16 not let the church be b with them,

BURDENS (BURDEN)

Ps 68: 19 who daily bears our b.
Lk 11: 46 down with b they can hardly carry,
Gal 6: 2 Carry each other's b,

BURDENSOME (BURDEN)

1Jn 5: 3 And his commands are not b,

BURIED (BURY)

Ru 1: 17 die I will die, and there I will be b.
Ro 6: 4 b with him through baptism
1Co 15: 4 that he was b, that he was raised
Col 2: 12 having been b with him in baptism

BURN (BURNING BURNT)

Dt 7: 5 and b their idols in the fire.
Ps 79: 5 long will your jealousy b like fire?
1Co 7: 9 to marry than to b with passion.

BURNING (BURN)

Ex 27: 20 so that the lamps may be kept b.
Lev 6: 9 the fire must be kept b on the altar.
Ps 18: 28 You, O LORD, keep my lamp b;
Pr 25: 22 you will heap b coals on his head,
Ro 12: 20 you will heap b coals on his head."
Rev 19: 20 alive into the fiery lake of b sulfur.

BURNISHED*

1Ki 7: 45 of the LORD were of b bronze.
Eze 1: 7 and gleamed like b bronze.
Da 10: 6 and legs like the gleam of b bronze,
Rev 2: 18 and whose feet are like b bronze.

BURNT (BURN)

Ge 8: 20 he sacrificed b offerings on it.
22: 2 as a b offering on one
Ex 10: 25 and b offerings to present
18: 12 brought a b offering and other
40: 6 Place the altar of b offering in front
Lev 1: 3 '' 'If the offering is a b offering
Jos 8: 31 offered to the LORD b offerings
Jdg 6: 26 offer the second bull as a b offering
13: 16 But if you prepare a b offering,
1Ki 3: 4 offered a thousand b offerings
9: 25 year Solomon offered b offerings
.10: 5 and the b offerings he made
Ezr 3: 2 Israel to sacrifice b offerings on it,
Eze 43: 18 for sacrificing b offerings

BURST

Ps 98: 4 b into jubilant song with music;
Isa 44: 23 B into song, you mountains!
49: 13 b into song, O mountains!
52: 9 B into songs of joy together,
54: 1 b into song, shout for joy,
55: 12 will b into song before you,

BURY (BURIED)

Mt 8: 22 and let the dead b their own dead.''
Lk 9: 60 ''Let the dead b their own dead,

BUSH

Ex 3: 2 the b was on fire it did not burn up.
Mk 12: 26 the account of the b, how God said
Lk 20: 37 But in the account of the b,
Ac 7: 35 who appeared to him in the b.

BUSINESS

Ecc 4: 8 a miserable b!
Da 8: 27 and went about the king's b.
1Co 5: 12 What b is it of mine to judge those
1Th 4: 11 to mind your own b and to work
Jas 1: 11 even while he goes about his b.

BUSY*

1Ki 18: 27 Perhaps he is deep in thought, or b,
20: 40 While your servant was b here
Isa 32: 6 his mind is b with evil:
Hag 1: 9 of you is b with his own house.
2Th 3: 11 They are not b; they are
Tit 2: 5 to be b at home, to be kind,

BUSYBODIES*

2Th 3: 11 They are not busy; they are b.
1Ti 5: 13 b, saying things they ought not to.

BUY (BOUGHT BUYS)

Pr 23: 23 B the truth and do not sell it;
Isa 55: 1 Come, b wine and milk
Rev 13: 17 so that no one could b or sell

BUYS (BUY)

Pr 31: 16 She considers a field and b it;

BYWORD (WORD)

1Ki 9: 7 Israel will then become a b
Ps 44: 14 You have made us a b
Joel 2: 17 a b among the nations.

CAESAR

Mt 22: 21 ''Give to C what is Caesar's,

CAIN

Firstborn of Adam (Ge 4:1), murdered brother Abel (Ge 4:1-16; 1Jn 3:12).

CAKE

Hos 7: 8 Ephraim is a flat c not turned over.

CALEB

Judahite who spied out Canaan (Nu 13:6); allowed to enter land because of faith (Nu 13:30-14:38; Dt 1:36). Possessed Hebron (Jos 14:6-15:19).

CALF

Ex 32: 4 into an idol cast in the shape of a c.
Pr 15: 17 than a fattened c with hatred.
Lk 15: 23 Bring the fattened c and kill it.
Ac 7: 41 made an idol in the form of a c.

CALL (CALLED CALLING CALLS)

1Ki 18: 24 I will c on the name of the LORD.
2Ki 5: 11 c on the name of the LORD his
1Ch 16: 8 to the LORD, c on his name;
Ps 105: 1 to the LORD, c on his name;
116: 13 and c on the name of the LORD.
116: 17 and c on the name of the LORD.
145: 18 near to all who c on him,
Pr 31: 28 children arise and c her blessed;
Isa 5: 20 Woe to those who c evil good
12: 4 to the LORD, c on his name;
55: 6 c on him while he is near.
65: 24 Before they c I will answer;
Jer 33: 3 'C to me and I will answer you
Zep 3: 9 that all of them may c on the name
Zec 13: 9 They will c on my name
Mt 9: 13 come to c the righteous.
Mk 2: 17 I have not come to c the righteous,
Lk 5: 32 I have not come to c the righteous,
Ac 2: 39 all whom the Lord our God will c.''
9: 14 to arrest all who c on your name.''
9: 21 among those who c on this name?
Ro 10: 12 and richly blesses all who c on him,
11: 29 gifts and his c are irrevocable.
1Co 1: 2 with all those everywhere who c
1Th 4: 7 For God did not c us to be impure,
2Ti 2: 22 along with those who c

CALLED (CALL)

Ge 2: 23 she shall be c 'woman,'
5: 2 he blessed them and c them ''man
12: 8 and c on the name of the LORD.
21: 33 and there he c upon the name
26: 25 and c on the name of the LORD.
1Sa 3: 5 and said, ''Here I am; you c me.''
2Ch 7: 14 if my people, who are c
Ps 34: 6 This poor man c, and the LORD
116: 4 Then I c on the name of the LORD
Isa 56: 7 for my house will be c
La 3: 55 I c on your name, O LORD,
Hos 11: 1 and out of Egypt I c my son.
Mt 1: 16 was born Jesus, who is c Christ.
2: 15 ''Out of Egypt I c my son.''
21: 13 '' 'My house will be c a house
Mk 11: 17 '' 'My house will be c
Lk 1: 32 will be c the Son of the Most High.
1: 35 to be born will be c the Son of God.
Ro 1: 1 c to be an apostle and set apart
1: 6 among those who are c to belong
1: 7 loved by God and c to be saints;
8: 28 who have been c according
8: 30 And those he predestined, he also c
1Co 1: 1 c to be an apostle of Christ Jesus
1: 2 in Christ Jesus and c to be holy,
1: 24 but to those whom God has c,
1: 26 of what you were when you were c.
7: 15 God has c us to live in peace.
7: 17 and to which God has c him.
Gal 1: 6 deserting the one who c you
1: 15 from birth and c me by his grace,
5: 13 You, my brothers, were c to be free
Eph 1: 18 the hope to which he has c you,
4: 4 as you were c to one hope
Col 3: 15 of one body you were c to peace.
2Th 2: 14 He c you to this through our gospel
1Ti 6: 12 life to which you were c
2Ti 1: 9 who has saved us and c us
Heb 9: 15 that those who are c may receive
1Pe 1: 15 But just as he who c you is holy,
2: 9 of him who c you out of darkness
3: 9 to this you were c so that you may
5: 10 who c you to his eternal glory
2Pe 1: 3 of him who c us by his own glory
Jude : 1 To those who have been c,

CALLING (CALL)

Isa 40: 3 A voice of one c:
Mt 3: 3 ''A voice of one c in the desert,
Mk 1: 3 ''a voice of one c in the desert,
10: 49 Cheer up! On your feet! He's c you
Lk 3: 4 ''A voice of one c in the desert,
Jn 1: 23 I am the voice of one c in the desert
Ac 22: 16 wash your sins away, c on his name
Eph 4: 1 worthy of the c you have received.
2Th 1: 11 may count you worthy of his c,
2Pe 1: 10 all the more eager to make your c

CALLOUS* (CALLOUSED)

Ps 17: 10 They close up their c hearts,
73: 7 From their c hearts comes iniquity;
119: 70 Their hearts are c and unfeeling,

CALLOUSED* (CALLOUS)

Isa 6: 10 Make the heart of this people c;

Mt 13: 15 this people's heart has become c;
Ac 28: 27 this people's heart has become c;

CALLS (CALL)

Ps 147: 4 and c them each by name.
Isa 40: 26 and c them each by name.
Joel 2: 32 And everyone who c
Mt 22: 43 speaking by the Spirit, c him 'Lord
Jn 10: 3 He c his own sheep by name
Ac 2: 21 And everyone who c
Ro 10: 13 ''Everyone who c on the name
1Th 2: 12 who c you into his kingdom
5: 24 The one who c you is faithful

CALM (CALMS)

Ps 107: 30 They were glad when it grew c,
Isa 7: 4 keep c and don't be afraid.
Eze 16: 42 I will be c and no longer angry.

CALMS* (CALM)

Pr 15: 18 but a patient man c a quarrel.

CAMEL

Mt 19: 24 it is easier for a c to go
23: 24 strain out a gnat but swallow a c.
Mk 10: 25 It is easier for a c to go
Lk 18: 25 it is easier for a c to go

CAMP (ENCAMPS)

Heb 13: 13 outside the c, bearing the disgrace

CANAAN (CANAANITE CANAANITES)

Ge 10: 15 C was the father of Sidon his
Lev 14: 34 ''When you enter the land of C,
25: 38 of Egypt to give you the land of C
Nu 13: 2 men to explore the land of C,
33: 51 'When you cross the Jordan into C,
Jdg 4: 2 a king of C, who reigned in Hazor.
1Ch 16: 18 ''To you I will give the land of C
Ps 105: 11 ''To you I will give the land of C
Ac 13: 19 he overthrew seven nations in C

CANAANITE (CANAAN)

Ge 10: 18 Later the C clans scattered
28: 1 ''Do not marry a C woman.
Jos 5: 1 all the C kings along the seacoast
Jdg 1: 32 lived among the C inhabitants

CANAANITES (CANAAN)

Ex 33: 2 before you and drive out the C,

CANCEL (CANCELED)

Dt 15: 1 seven years you must c debts.

CANCELED (CANCEL)

Mt 18: 27 pity on him, c the debt
Lk 7: 42 so he c the debts of both.
Col 2: 14 having c the written code,

CANDLESTICKS see LAMPSTANDS

CANOPY*

2Sa 22: 12 He made darkness his c
2Ki 16: 18 away the Sabbath c that had been
Ps 18: 11 made darkness his covering, his c
Isa 4: 5 over all the glory will be a c.
40: 22 stretches out the heavens like a c,
Jer 43: 10 he will spread his royal c

CAPERNAUM

Mt 4: 13 Nazareth, he went and lived in C,
Jn 6: 59 teaching in the synagogue in C:

CAPITAL

Dt 21: 22 guilty of a c offense is put to death

CAPSTONE* (STONE)

Ps 118: 22 has become the c;
Zec 4: 7 he will bring out the c to shouts
Mt 21: 42 has become the c;
Mk 12: 10 has become the c;
Lk 20: 17 has become the c'?
Ac 4: 11 which has become the c.'
1Pe 2: 7 has become the c,''

CAPTIVATE* (CAPTIVE)

Pr 6: 25 or let her c you with her eyes,

CAPTIVATED* (CAPTIVE)

Pr 5: 19 may you ever be c by her love.
5: 20 Why be c, my son, by an adulteress

CAPTIVE (CAPTIVATE CAPTIVATED CAPTIVES CAPTIVITY CAPTURED)

Ac   8:23 full of bitterness and c to sin."
2Co 10: 5 and we take c every thought
Col   2: 8 See to it that no one takes you c
2Ti   2:26 who has taken them c to do his will.

CAPTIVES (CAPTIVE)

Ps   68:18 you led c in your train;
Isa   61: 1 to proclaim freedom for the c
Eph   4: 8 he led c in his train

CAPTIVITY (CAPTIVE)

Dt   28:41 because they will go into c.
2Ki 25:21 So Judah went into c, away
Jer   30: 3 Israel and Judah back from c
    52:27 So Judah went into c, away
Eze 29:14 I will bring them back from c

CAPTURED (CAPTIVE)

1Sa   4:11 The ark of God was c,
2Sa   5: 7 David c the fortress of Zion,
2Ki 17: 6 the king of Assyria c Samaria

CARCASS

Jdg 14: 9 taken the honey from the lion's c.
Mt   24:28 there is a c, there the vultures

CARE (CAREFUL CARES CARING)

Ps   8: 4 the son of man that you c for him?
   65: 9 You c for the land and water it,
  144: 3 what is man that you c for him,
Pr   29: 7 The righteous c about justice
Mk   5:26 deal under the c of many doctors
Lk   10:34 him to an inn and took c of him.
    4 I don't fear God or c about men,
Jn   21:16 Jesus said, "Take c of my sheep."
1Ti   3: 5 how can he take c of God's church
    6:20 what has been entrusted to your c.
Heb 2: 6 the son of man that you c for him?
1Pe   5: 2 of God's flock that is under your c,

CAREFUL* (CARE)

Ge   31:24 "Be c not to say anything to Jacob,
   31:29 'Be c not to say anything to Jacob,
Ex   19:12 'Be c that you do not go up
    23:13 "Be c to do everything I have said
    34:12 Be c not to make a treaty
    34:15 "Be c not to make a treaty
Lev 18: 4 and be c to follow my decrees.
    25:18 " 'Follow my decrees and be c
    26: 3 and are c to obey my commands,
Dt   2: 4 afraid of you, but be very c.
    4: 9 before you today? Only be c,
    4:23 Be c not to forget the covenant
    5:32 So be c to do what the LORD your
    6: 3 be c to obey so that it may go well
    6:12 be c that you do not forget
    6:25 And if we are c to obey all this law
    7:12 attention to these laws and are c
    8: 1 Be c to follow every command I am
    8:11 Be c that you do not forget
    11:16 Be c, or you will be enticed
    12: 1 and laws you must be c to follow
    12:13 Be c not to sacrifice your burnt
    12:19 Be c not to neglect the Levites
    12:28 Be c to obey all these regulations I
    12:30 be c not to be ensnared
    15: 5 are c to follow all these commands
    15: 9 Be c not to harbor this wicked
    17:10 Be c to do everything they direct
    24: 8 cases of leprous diseases be very c
Jos   1: 7 Be c to obey all the law my servant
    1: 8 so that you may be c
    22: 5 But be very c to keep
    23: 6 be c to obey all that is written
    23:11 be very c to love the LORD your
1Ki   8:25 if only your sons are c in all they do
2Ki 10:31 Yet Jehu was not c to keep the law
    17:37 You must always be c
    21: 8 if only they will be c
1Ch 22:13 if you are c to observe the decrees
    28: 8 Be c to follow all the commands
2Ch   6:16 if only your sons are c in all they do
    33: 8 if only they will be c
Ezr   4:22 Be c not to neglect this matter.
Job   36:18 Be c that no one entices you
Ps 101: 2 I will be c to lead a blameless life—
Pr   13:24 he who loves him is c
    27:23 give c attention to your herds;
Isa   7: 4 Be c, keep calm and don't be afraid.
Jer 17:21 Be c not to carry a load
    17:24 But if you are c to obey me,
    22: 4 For if you are c to carry out these

Eze 11:20 will follow my decrees and be c
    18:19 has been c to keep all my decrees,
    20:19 follow my decrees and be c
    20:21 they were not c to keep my laws—
    36:27 you to follow my decrees and be c
    37:24 and be c to keep my decrees.
Mic   7: 5 be c of your words.
Hag 1: 5 "Give c thought to your ways.
    1: 5 "Give c thought to your ways.
    2:15 give c thought to this from this day
    2:18 Give c thought: Is there yet any
    2:18 give c thought to the day
Mt   2: 8 and make a c search for the child.
    6: 1 "Be c not to do your 'acts
    16: 6 "Be c," Jesus said to them.
Mk   8:15 "Be c," Jesus warned them.
Lk 21:34 Be c, or your hearts will be weighed
Ro 12:17 Be c to do what is right in the eyes
1Co   3:10 each one should be c how he builds
    8: 9 Be c, however, that the exercise
    10:12 standing firm, be c that you don't
Eph   5:15 Be very c, then, how you live—
2Ti   4: 2 great patience and c instruction.
Tit   3: 8 may be c to devote themselves
Heb 2: 1 We must pay more c attention,
    4: 1 let us be c that none

CARELESS*

Mt   12:36 for every c word they have spoken.

CARES* (CARE)

Dt   11:12 It is a land the LORD your God c
Job 39:16 she c not that her labor was in vain,
Ps   55:22 Cast your c on the LORD
   142: 4 no one c for my life.
Pr   12:10 A righteous man c for the needs
Ecc   5: 3 when there are many c,
Jer   12:11 because there is no one who c.
    30:17 Zion for whom no one c.'
Na   1: 7 He c for those who trust in him,
Jn 10:13 and c nothing for the sheep.
Eph   5:29 but he feeds and c for it, just
1Pe   5: 7 on him because he c for you.

CARING* (CARE)

1Th   2: 7 like a mother c for her little
1Ti   5: 4 practice by c for their own family

CARNAL see SINFUL, UNSPIRITUAL, WORLDLY

CARPENTER (CARPENTER'S)

Mk   6: 3 does miracles! Isn't this the c?

CARPENTER'S* (CARPENTER)

Mt   13:55 "Isn't this the c son? Isn't his

CARRIED (CARRY)

Ex   19: 4 and how I c you on eagles' wings
Dt   1:31 how the LORD your God c you,
Isa   53: 4 and c our sorrows,
    63: 9 he lifted them up and c them
Mt   8:17 and c our diseases."
Heb 13: 9 Do not be c away by all kinds
2Pe   1:21 as they were c along by the Holy
    3:17 so that you may not be c away

CARRIES (CARRY)

Dt   32:11 and c them on its pinions.
Isa 40:11 and c them close to his heart;

CARRY (CARRIED CARRIES CARRYING)

Lev 16:22 goat will c on itself all their sins
    26:15 and fail to c out all my commands
Isa 46: 4 I have made you and I will c you;
Lk   14:27 anyone who does not c his cross
Gal   6: 2 Each other's burdens,
    6: 5 for each one should c his own load.

CARRYING (CARRY)

Jn   19:17 C his own cross, he went out
1Jn   5: 2 loving God and c out his

CARVED (CARVES)

Nu   33:52 Destroy all their c images
Mic   5:13 I will destroy your c images

CARVES* (CARVED)

Dt   27:15 "Cursed is the man who c an image

CASE

Pr   18:17 to present his c seems right,
    22:23 for the LORD will take up their c
    23:11 he will take up their c against you,

CAST (CASTING)

Ex   34:17 "Do not make c idols.
Lev 16: 8 He is to c lots for the two goats—
Ps   22:18 and c lots for my clothing.
    55:22 C your cares on the LORD
Pr   16:33 The lot is c into the lap,
Ecc 11: 1 C your bread upon the waters,
Jn   19:24 and c lots for my clothing."
1Pe   5: 7 Call your anxiety on him

CASTING (CAST)

Pr   18:18 C the lot settles disputes
Mt   27:35 divided up his clothes by c lots.

CATCH (CATCHES CAUGHT)

Lk   5: 4 and let down the nets for a c."
    5:10 from now on you will c men."

CATCHES (CATCH)

Job   5:13 He c the wise in their craftiness,
1Co   3:19 "He c the wise in their craftiness";

CATTLE

Ps   50:10 and the c on a thousand hills.

CAUGHT (CATCH)

Ge   22:13 there in a thicket he saw a ram c
2Co 12: 2 who fourteen years ago was c up
1Th   4:17 and are left will be c up together with
    them

CAUSE (CAUSES)

Pr   24:28 against your neighbor without c,
Ecc   8: 3 Do not stand up for a bad c,
Mt   18: 7 of the things that c people to sin!
Ro   14:21 else that will c your brother
1Co 10:32 Do not c anyone to stumble,

CAUSES (CAUSE)

Ps   7:16 The trouble he c recoils on himself;
Isa   8:14 a stone that c men to stumble
Mt   5:29 If your right eye c you to sin,
    5:30 And if your right hand c you to sin,
    18: 6 if anyone c one of these little ones
    18: 8 or your foot c you to sin,
Ro   14:20 to eat anything that c someone else
1Co   8:13 if what I eat c my brother to fall
1Pe   2: 8 "A stone that c men to stumble

CAUTIOUS*

Pr   12:26 A righteous man is c in friendship.

CEASE

Ps   46: 9 He makes wars c to the ends

CELEBRATE*

Ex   10: 9 we are to c a festival to the LORD
    12:14 generations to come you shall c it
    12:17 C this day as a lasting ordinance
    12:17 "C the Feast of Unleavened Bread,
    12:47 community of Israel must c it.
    12:48 to c the LORD's Passover must
    23:14 are to c a festival to me.
    23:15 "C the Feast of Unleavened Bread;
    23:16 "C the Feast of Harvest
    23:16 "C the Feast of Ingathering
    34:18 "C the Feast of Unleavened Bread.
    34:22 "C the Feast of Weeks
Lev 23:39 c the festival to the LORD
    23:41 C this as a festival to the LORD
    23:41 for the generations to come; c it
Nu   9: 2 "Have the Israelites c the Passover
    9: 3 C it at the appointed time,
    9: 4 told the Israelites to c the Passover,
    9: 6 of them could not c the Passover
    9:10 they may still c the LORD's
    9:11 are to c it on the fourteenth day
    9:12 When they c the Passover,
    9:13 on a journey fails to c the Passover,
    9:14 to c the LORD's Passover must do
    29:12 C a festival to the LORD
Dt   16: 1 c the Passover of the LORD your
    16:10 Then c the Feast of Weeks
    16:13 C the Feast of Tabernacles
    16:15 For seven days c the Feast
Jdg 16:23 to Dagon their god and to c,
2Sa   6:21 the LORD's people Israel—I will c
2Ki 23:21 "C the Passover to the LORD your
2Ch 30: 1 and c the Passover to the LORD,
    30: 2 decided to c the Passover
    30: 3 able to c it at the regular time
    30: 5 and c the Passover to the LORD,
    30:13 in Jerusalem to c the Feast
    30:23 to c the festival seven more days;

Ne 8: 12 of food and to c with great joy,
12: 27 to c joyfully the dedication
Est 9: 21 to have them c annually
Ps 145: 7 They will c your abundant
Isa 30: 29 as on the night you c a holy festival
Na 1: 15 C your festivals, O Judah,
Zec 14: 16 and to c the Feast of Tabernacles.
14: 18 up to c the Feast of Tabernacles.
14: 19 up to c the Feast of Tabernacles.
Mt 26: 18 I am going to c the Passover
Lk 15: 23 Let's have a feast and c.
15: 24 So they began to c.
15: 29 goat so I could c with my friends.
15: 32 But we had to c and be glad,
Rev 11: 10 will c by sending each other gifts,

CELESTIAL*

2Pe 2: 10 afraid to slander c beings;
Jude : 8 authority and slander c beings.

CENSER (CENSERS)

Lev 16: 12 is to take a c full of burning coals
Rev 8: 3 Another angel, who had a golden c,

CENSERS (CENSER)

Nu 16: 6 Take c and tomorrow put fire

CENTURION

Mt 8: 5 had entered Capernaum, a c came
27: 54 When the c and those
Mk 15: 39 And when the c, who stood there
Lk 7: 3 The c heard of Jesus and sent some
23: 47 The c, seeing what had happened,
Ac 10: 1 a c in what was known
27: 1 handed over to a c named Julius,

CEPHAS* (PETER)

Jn 1: 42 You will be called C" (which,
1Co 1: 12 another, "I follow C"; still another,
3: 22 Paul or Apollos or C or the world
9: 5 and the Lord's brothers and C?

CEREMONIAL* (CEREMONY)

Lev 4: 12 at the time of his c cleansing,
15: 13 off seven days for his c cleansing.
Mk 7: 3 they give their hands a c washing,
Jn 2: 6 used by the Jews for c washing,
3: 25 Jew over the matter of c washing.
11: 55 to Jerusalem for their c cleansing
18: 28 to avoid c uncleanness the Jews did
Heb 9: 10 drink and various c washings—
13: 9 not by c foods, which are

CEREMONIALLY* (CEREMONY)

Lev 4: 12 outside the camp to a place c clean,
5: 2 touches anything c unclean—
6: 11 the camp to a place that is c clean.
7: 19 anyone c clean may eat it.
7: 19 touches anything c unclean must
10: 14 Eat them in a c clean place;
11: 4 not have a split hoof; it is c unclean
12: 2 birth to a son will be c unclean
12: 7 and then she will be c clean
13: 3 he shall pronounce him c unclean.
14: 8 with water; then he will be c clean.
15: 28 and after that she will be c clean.
15: 33 lies with a woman who is c unclean
17: 15 he will be c unclean till evening.
21: 1 must not make himself c unclean
22: 3 of your descendants is c unclean
27: 11 he vowed is a c unclean animal—
Nu 5: 2 who is c unclean because of a dead
6: 7 must not make himself c unclean
6: 8 Israelites and make them c clean.
9: 6 they were c unclean on account
9: 13 But if a man who is c clean
18: 11 household who is c clean may eat
18: 13 household who is c clean may eat
19: 7 but he will be c unclean till evening
19: 9 and put them in a c clean place
19: 18 Then a man who is c clean is
Dt 12: 15 Both the c unclean and the clean
12: 22 Both the c unclean and the clean
14: 7 they are c unclean for you.
15: 22 Both the c unclean and the clean
1Sa 20: 26 to David to make him c unclean—
2Ch 13: 11 the bread on the c clean table
30: 17 for all those who were not c clean
Ezr 6: 20 themselves and were all c clean.
Ne 12: 30 Levites had purified themselves c,
Isa 66: 20 of the LORD in c clean vessels.
Eze 22: 10 period, when they are c unclean.
Ac 24: 18 I was c clean when they found me
Heb 9: 13 those who are c unclean sanctify

CEREMONY* (CEREMONIAL CEREMONIALLY)

Ge 50: 11 Egyptians are holding a solemn c
Ex 12: 25 as he promised, observe this c.
12: 26 'What does this c mean to you?'
13: 5 are to observe this c in this month:

CERTAIN (CERTAINTY)

2Pe 1: 19 word of the prophets made more c,

CERTAINTY* (CERTAIN)

Lk 1: 4 so that you may know the c
Jn 17: 8 They knew with c that I came

CERTIFICATE* (CERTIFIED)

Dt 24: 1 and he writes her a c of divorce,
24: 3 and writes her a c of divorce,
Isa 50: 1 "Where is your mother's c
Jer 3: 8 I gave faithless Israel her c
Mt 5: 31 divorces his wife must give her a c
19: 7 that a man give his wife a c
Mk 10: 4 a man to write a c of divorce

CERTIFIED* (CERTIFICATE)

Jn 3: 33 has accepted it has c that God is

CHAFF

Ps 1: 4 They are like c
35: 5 May they be like c before the wind,
Da 2: 35 became like c on a threshing floor
Mt 3: 12 up the c with unquenchable fire."

CHAINED (CHAINS)

2Ti 2: 9 But God's word is not c.

CHAINS (CHAINED)

Eph 6: 20 for which I am an ambassador in c.
Col 4: 18 Remember my c.
2Ti 1: 16 and was not ashamed of my c.
Jude : 6 with everlasting c for judgment

CHAMPION

Ps 19: 5 like a c rejoicing to run his course.

CHANCE

Ecc 9: 11 but time and c happen to them all.

CHANGE (CHANGED)

1Sa 15: 29 of Israel does not lie or c his mind;
Ps 110: 4 and will not c his mind:
Jer 7: 5 If you really c your ways
Mal 3: 6 "I the LORD do not c.
Mt 18: 3 unless you c and become like little
Heb 7: 21 and will not c his mind:
Jas 1: 17 who does not c like shifting

CHANGED (CHANGE)

1Sa 10: 6 you will be c into a different person
Hos 11: 8 My heart is c within me;
1Co 15: 51 but we will all be c—in a flash,

CHARACTER*

Ru 3: 11 that you are a woman of noble c.
Pr 12: 4 of noble c is her husband's crown,
31: 10 A wife of noble c who can find?
Ac 17: 11 noble c than the Thessalonians,
Ro 5: 4 perseverance, c; and c, hope.
1Co 15: 33 "Bad company corrupts good c."

CHARGE (CHARGES)

Job 34: 13 him in c of the whole world?
Ro 8: 33 Who will bring any c
1Co 9: 18 the gospel I may offer it free of c,
2Co 11: 7 the gospel of God to you free of c?
2Ti 4: 1 I give you this c: Preach the Word,
Phm : 18 or owes you anything, c it to me.

CHARGES (CHARGE)

Isa 50: 8 Who then will bring c against me?

CHARIOT (CHARIOTS)

2Ki 2: 11 suddenly a c of fire and horses
Ps 104: 3 He makes the clouds his c
Ac 8: 28 sitting in his c reading the book

CHARIOTS (CHARIOT)

2Ki 6: 17 and c of fire all around Elisha.
Ps 20: 7 Some trust in c and some in horses,
68: 17 The c of God are tens of thousands

CHARITY see LOVE

CHARM* (CHARMING)

Pr 17: 8 bribe is a c to the one who gives it;
31: 30 C is deceptive, and beauty is

CHARMING* (CHARM)

Pr 26: 25 his speech is c, do not believe
SS 1: 16 Oh, how c!

CHASE (CHASES)

Lev 26: 8 Five of you will c a hundred,

CHASES* (CHASE)

Pr 12: 11 he who c fantasies lacks judgment.
28: 19 one who c fantasies will have his

CHASM*

Lk 16: 26 and you a great c has been fixed,

CHATTER* (CHATTERING)

1Ti 6: 20 Turn away from godless c
2Ti 2: 16 Avoid godless c, because those

CHATTERING* (CHATTER)

Pr 10: 8 but a c fool comes to ruin.
10: 10 and a c fool comes to ruin.

CHEAT* (CHEATED CHEATING CHEATS)

Mal 1: 14 "Cursed is the c who has
1Co 6: 8 you yourselves c and do wrong,

CHEATED* (CHEAT)

Ge 31: 7 yet your father has c me
1Sa 12: 3 Whom have I c? Whom have I
12: 4 "You have not c or oppressed us,"
Lk 19: 8 if I have c anybody out of anything,
1Co 6: 7 Why not rather be c? Instead,

CHEATING* (CHEAT)

Am 8: 5 and c with dishonest scales,

CHEATS* (CHEAT)

Lev 6: 2 or if he c him, or if he finds lost

CHEEK (CHEEKS)

Mt 5: 39 someone strikes you on the right c,
Lk 6: 29 If someone strikes you on one c,

CHEEKS (CHEEK)

Isa 50: 6 my c to those who pulled out my

CHEERFUL* (CHEERS)

Pr 15: 13 A happy heart makes the face c,
15: 15 but the c heart has a continual feast
15: 30 A c look brings joy to the heart,
17: 22 A c heart is good medicine,
2Co 9: 7 for God loves a c giver.

CHEERS (CHEERFUL)

Pr 12: 25 but a kind word c him up.

CHEMOSH

2Ki 23: 13 for C the vile god of Moab,

CHERISH (CHERISHED CHERISHES)

Ps 17: 14 You still the hunger of those you c;

CHERISHED (CHERISH)

Ps 66: 18 If I had c sin in my heart,

CHERISHES* (CHERISH)

Pr 19: 8 he who c understanding prospers.

CHERUB (CHERUBIM)

Ex 25: 19 Make one c on one end
Eze 28: 14 You were anointed as a guardian c,

CHERUBIM (CHERUB)

Ge 3: 24 side of the Garden of Eden c
1Sa 4: 4 who is enthroned between the c.
2Sa 6: 2 enthroned between the c that are
22: 11 He mounted the c and flew;
1Ki 6: 23 a pair of c of olive wood,
2Ki 19: 15 of Israel, enthroned between the c,
1Ch 13: 6 who is enthroned between the c—
Ps 18: 10 He mounted the c and flew;
80: 1 who sit enthroned between the c,
99: 1 he sits enthroned between the c,
Isa 37: 16 of Israel, enthroned between the c,
Eze 10: 1 I was over the heads of the c.

CHEST

Ex 25: 10 "Have them make a c
2Ki 12: 9 Jehoiada the priest took a c
Da 2: 32 its c and arms of silver, its belly
Rev 1: 13 with a golden sash around his c.

CHEWS

Lev 11: 3 divided and that c the cud.

CHIEF
1Pe 5: 4 And when the C Shepherd appears,

CHILD (CHILDISH CHILDREN CHILDREN'S GRANDCHILDREN)
Pr   20:11 Even a c is known by his actions,
     22: 6 Train a c in the way he should go,
     22:15 Folly is bound up in the heart of a c
     23:13 not withhold discipline from a c;
     29:15 c left to himself disgraces his mother.
Isa   7:14 The virgin will be with c
      9: 6 For to us a c is born,
     11: 6 and a little c will lead them.
     66:13 As a mother comforts her c,
Mt   1:23 "The virgin will be with c
     18: 2 He called a little c and had him
Lk   1:42 and blessed is the c you will bear!
      1:80 And the c grew and became strong
1Co 13:11 When I was a c, I talked like a c,
1Jn   5: 1 who loves the father loves his c

CHILDBEARING (BEAR)
Ge   3:16 greatly increase your pains in c;

CHILDBIRTH (BEAR)
Gal   4:19 the pains of c until Christ is formed

CHILDISH* (CHILD)
1Co 13:11 When I became a man, I put c ways

CHILDREN (CHILD)
Ex   20: 5 punishing the c for the sin
Dt   4: 9 Teach them to your c
      6: 7 Impress them on your c.
     11:19 them to your c, talking about them
     14: 1 You are the c of the LORD your
     24:16 nor c put to death for their fathers;
     30:19 so that you and your c may live
     32:46 so that you may command your c
Job   1: 2 "Perhaps my c have sinned
Ps   8: 2 From the lips of c and infants
     78: 5 forefathers to teach their c,
Pr   17: 6 Children's c are a crown
     20: 7 blessed are his c after him.
     31:28 Her c arise and call her blessed;
Joel 1: 3 Tell it to your c,
Mal   4: 6 the hearts of the fathers to their c,
Mt   7:11 how to give good gifts to your c,
     11:25 and revealed them to little c.
     18: 3 you change and become like little c
     19:14 "Let the little c come to me,
     21:16 "From the lips of c and infants
Mk   9:37 one of these little c in my name
     10:14 "Let the little c come to me,
     10:16 And he took the c in his arms,
     13:12 c will rebel against their parents
Lk   10:21 and revealed them to little c.
     18:16 "Let the little c come to me,
Jn   1:12 the right to become c of God—
Ac   2:39 The promise is for you and your c
Ro   8:16 our spirit that we are God's c.
1Co 14:20 Brothers, stop thinking like c.
2Co 12:14 parents, but parents for their c.
Eph   6: 1 C, obey your parents in the Lord,
      6: 4 do not exasperate your c; instead,
Col   3:20 C, obey your parents in everything,
      3:21 Fathers, do not embitter your c,
1Ti   3: 4 and see that his c obey him
      3:12 and must manage his c and his
      5:10 bringing up c, showing hospitality,
Heb   2:13 and the c God has given me."
1Jn   3: 1 that we should be called c of God!

CHILDREN'S (CHILD)
Isa 54:13 and great will be your c peace.

CHOKE
Mk   4:19 come in and c the word,

CHOOSE (CHOOSES CHOSE CHOSEN)
Dt   30:19 Now c life, so that you
Jos 24:15 then c for yourselves this day
Pr   8:10 C my instruction instead of silver,
     16:16 to c understanding rather
Jn   15:16 You did not c me, but I chose you

CHOOSES (CHOOSE)
Mt   11:27 to whom the Son c to reveal him.
Lk   10:22 to whom the Son c to reveal him."
Jn   17:17 If anyone c to do God's will,

CHOSE (CHOOSE)
Ge   13:11 So Lot c for himself the whole plain
Ps   33:12 the people he c for his inheritance.

Jn   15:16 but I c you and appointed you to go
1Co   1:27 But God c the foolish things
Eph   1: 4 he c us in him before the creation
2Th   2:13 from the beginning God c you

CHOSEN (CHOOSE)
Isa 41: 8 Jacob, whom I have c,
Mt   22:14 For many are invited, but few are c
Lk   10:42 Mary has c what is better,
     23:35 the Christ of God, the C One."
Jn   15:19 but I have c you out of the world.
1Pe   1:20 He was c before the creation
      2: 9 But you are a c people, a royal

CHRIST (CHRIST'S CHRISTIAN CHRISTIANS CHRISTS)
Mt   1:16 was born Jesus, who is called C.
     16:16 Peter answered, "You are the C,
     22:42 "What do you think about the C?
Mk   1: 1 of the gospel about Jesus C,
      8:29 Peter answered, "You are the C."
     14:61 "Are you the C, the Son
Lk   9:20 Peter answered, "The C of God."
Jn   1:41 found the Messiah" (that is, the C).
     20:31 you may believe that Jesus is the C,
Ac   2:36 you crucified, both Lord and C."
      5:42 the good news that Jesus is the C.
      9:22 by proving that Jesus is the C.
      9:34 said to him, "Jesus C heals you.
     17: 3 proving that the C had to suffer
     18:28 the Scriptures that Jesus was the C.
     26:23 that the C would suffer and,
Ro   1: 4 from the dead: Jesus C our Lord.
      3:22 comes through faith in Jesus C
      5: 1 God through our Lord Jesus C,
      5: 6 we were still powerless, C died
      5: 8 While we were still sinners, C died
      5:11 in God through our Lord Jesus C,
      5:17 life through the one man, Jesus C.
      6: 4 as C was raised from the dead
      6: 9 that since C was raised
      6:23 life in C Jesus our Lord.
      7: 4 to the law through the body of C,
      8: 1 for those who are in C Jesus,
      8: 9 Spirit of C, he does not belong to C.
      8:17 heirs of God and co-heirs with C,
      8:34 Who is he that condemns? C Jesus,
      8:35 us from the love of C?
      9: 5 is traced the human ancestry of C,
     10: 4 C is the end of the law
     12: 5 so in C we who are many form one
     13:14 yourselves with the Lord Jesus C,
     14: 9 C died and returned to life
     15: 3 For even C did not please himself
     15: 5 yourselves as you follow Jesus C,
     15: 7 then, just as C accepted you,
     16:18 people are not serving our Lord C,
1Co   1: 2 to those sanctified in C Jesus
      1: 7 for our Lord Jesus C to be revealed.
      1:13 Is C divided? Was Paul crucified
      1:17 For C did not send me to baptize,
      1:23 but we preach C crucified:
      1:30 of him that you are in C Jesus,
      2: 2 except Jesus C and him crucified.
      3:11 one already laid, which is Jesus C
      5: 7 For C, our Passover lamb,
      6:15 bodies are members of C himself?
      8: 6 and there is but one Lord, Jesus C,
      8:12 conscience, you sin against C.
     10: 4 them, and that rock was C.
     11: 1 as I follow the example of C.
     11: 3 the head of every man is C,
     12:27 Now you are the body of C,
     15: 3 that C died for our sins according
     15:14 And if C has not been raised,
     15:22 so in C all will be made alive.
     15:57 victory through our Lord Jesus C.
2Co   1: 5 as the sufferings of C flow
      2:14 us in triumphal procession in C
      3: 3 show that you are a letter from C,
      3:14 because only in C is it taken away.
      4: 4 light of the gospel of the glory of C,
      4: 5 not preach ourselves, but Jesus C
      4: 6 of the glory of God in the face of C.
      5:10 before the judgment seat of C,
      5:17 Therefore, if anyone is in C,
      6:15 What harmony is there between C
     10: 1 the meekness and gentleness of C,
     11: 2 you to one husband, to C,
Gal   1: 7 are trying to pervert the gospel of C.
      2: 4 on the freedom we have in C Jesus
      2:16 but by faith in Jesus C.
      2:17 does that mean that C promotes sin
      2:20 I have been crucified with C
      2:21 C died for nothing!" You foolish

Gal   3:13 C redeemed us from the curse
      3:16 meaning one person, who is C.
      3:26 of God through faith in C Jesus,
      4:19 of childbirth until C is formed
      5: 1 for freedom that C has set us free.
      5: 4 by law have been alienated from C;
      5:24 to C Jesus have crucified the sinful
      6:14 in the cross of our Lord Jesus C,
Eph   1: 3 with every spiritual blessing in C
      1:10 together under one head, even C.
      1:20 which he exerted in C
      2: 5 made us alive with C
      2:10 created in C Jesus
      2:12 time you were separate from C,
      2:20 with C Jesus himself as the chief
      3: 8 the unsearchable riches of C,
      3:17 so that C may dwell in your hearts
      4: 7 has been given as C apportioned it.
      4:13 measure of the fullness of C.
      4:15 into him who is the Head, that is, C
      4:32 just as in C God forgave you.
      5: 2 as C loved us and gave himself up
      5:21 out of reverence for C.
      5:23 as C is the head of the church,
      5:25 just as C loved the church
Php   1:18 motives or true, C is preached.
      1:21 to live is C and to die is gain.
      1:23 I desire to depart and be with C,
      1:27 worthy of the gospel of C.
      1:29 on behalf of C not only to believe
      2: 5 be the same as that of C Jesus:
      3: 7 now consider loss for the sake of C.
      3:10 I want to know C and the power
      3:18 as enemies of the cross of C.
      4:19 to his glorious riches in C Jesus.
Col   1: 4 heard of your faith in C Jesus
      1:27 which is C in you, the hope of glory
      1:28 may present everyone perfect in C.
      2: 2 the mystery of God, namely, C,
      2: 6 as you received C Jesus as Lord,
      2: 9 For in C all the fullness
      2:13 God made you alive with C.
      2:17 the reality, however, is found in C.
      3: 1 then, you have been raised with C,
      3: 3 and your life is now hidden with C
      3:15 Let the peace of C rule
1Th   5: 9 through our Lord Jesus C.
2Th   2: 1 the coming of our Lord Jesus C
      2:14 in the glory of our Lord Jesus C
1Ti   1:12 I thank C Jesus our Lord, who has
      1:15 C Jesus came into the world
      1:16 C Jesus might display his unlimited
      2: 5 the man C Jesus, who gave himself
2Ti   1: 9 us in C Jesus before the beginning
      1:10 appearing of our Savior, C Jesus,
      2: 1 in the grace that is in C Jesus.
      2: 3 us like a good soldier of C Jesus.
      2: 8 Remember Jesus C, raised
      2:10 the salvation that is in C Jesus,
      3:12 life in C Jesus will be persecuted,
      3:15 salvation through faith in C Jesus.
      4: 1 presence of God and of C Jesus,
Tit   2:13 our great God and Savior, Jesus C,
Heb   3: 6 But C is faithful as a son
      3:14 to share in C if we hold firmly
      5: 5 So C also did not take
      6: 1 the elementary teachings about C
      9:11 When C came as high priest
      9:14 more, then, will the blood of C,
      9:15 For this reason C is the mediator
      9:24 For C did not enter a man-made
      9:26 Then C would have had
      9:28 so C was sacrificed once
     10:10 of the body of Jesus C once for all.
     13: 8 Jesus C is the same yesterday
1Pe   1: 2 for obedience to Jesus C
      1: 3 of Jesus C from the dead,
      1:11 he predicted the sufferings of C
      1:19 but with the precious blood of C,
      2:21 because C suffered for you,
      3:15 in your hearts set apart C as Lord.
      3:18 For C died for sins once for all,
      3:21 you by the resurrection of Jesus C,
      4:13 participate in the sufferings of C,
      4:14 insulted because of the name of C,
2Pe   1: 1 and Savior Jesus C have received
      1:16 and coming of our Lord Jesus C,
1Jn   2: 1 Jesus C, the Righteous One.
      2:22 man who denies that Jesus is the C.
      3:16 Jesus C laid down his life for us.
      3:23 in the name of his Son, Jesus C,
      4: 2 that Jesus C has come
      5: 1 believes that Jesus is the C is born
      5:20 even in his Son Jesus C.
2Jn   : 9 teaching of C does not have God;

Jude   : 4 deny Jesus *C*our only Sovereign
Rev   1: 1 The revelation of Jesus *C,*
     1: 5 from Jesus *C,* who is the faithful
   11:15 kingdom of our Lord and of his *C,*
   20: 4 reigned with *C* a thousand years.
   20: 6 they will be priests of God and of *C*

CHRIST'S (CHRIST)

1Co   9:21 from God's law but am under *C* law
2Co   5:14 For *C* love compels us,
    5:20 We are therefore *C* ambassadors,
   12: 9 so that *C* power may rest on me.
Col   1:22 by *C* physical body through death

CHRISTIAN* (CHRIST)

Ac 26:28 you can persuade me to be a *C?"*
1Pe   4:16 as a *C,* do not be ashamed,

CHRISTIANS* (CHRIST)

Ac 11:26 The disciples were called *C* first

CHRISTS* (CHRIST)

Mt 24:24 For false *C* and false prophets will
Mk 13:22 For false *C* and false prophets will

CHURCH

Mt 16:18 and on this rock I will build my *c,*
    18:17 if he refuses to listen even to the *c,*
Ac 20:28 Be shepherds of the *c* of God,
1Co   5:12 of mine to judge those outside the *c*
   14: 4 but he who prophesies edifies the *c.*
   14:12 to excel in gifts that build up the *c.*
   14:26 done for the strengthening of the *c.*
   15: 9 because I persecuted the *c* of God.
Gal   1:13 how intensely I persecuted the *c*
Eph   5:23 as Christ is the head of the *c,*
Col   1:18 he is the head of the body, the *c;*
    1:24 the sake of his body, which is the *c.*

CHURNING

Pr 30:33 For as *c* the milk produces butter,

CIRCLE

Isa 40:22 enthroned above the *c* of the earth,

CIRCUMCISE (CIRCUMCISED CIRCUMCISION)

Dt 10:16 *C* your hearts, therefore,

CIRCUMCISED (CIRCUMCISE)

Ge 17:10 Every male among you shall be *c.*
   17:12 who is eight days old must be *c,*
Jos   5: 3 and the Israelites at Gibeath
Gal   5: 2 that if you let yourselves be *c,*

CIRCUMCISION (CIRCUMCISE)

Ro   2:25 *C* has value if you observe the law,
    2:29 and *c* is of the heart, by the Spirit,
1Co   7:19 *C* is nothing and uncircumcision is

CIRCUMSTANCES

Php   4:11 to be content whatever the *c.*
1Th   5:18 continually; give thanks in all *c,*

CITIES (CITY)

Lk 19:17 small matter, take charge of ten *c.'*
   19:19 'You take charge of five *c.'*

CITIZENS (CITIZENSHIP)

Eph   2:19 but fellow *c* with God's people

CITIZENSHIP* (CITIZENS)

Ac 22:28 "I had to pay a big price for my *c."*
Eph   2:12 excluded from *c* in Israel
Php   3:20 But our *c* is in heaven.

CITY (CITIES)

Mt   5:14 A *c* on a hill cannot be hidden.
Ac 18:10 I have many people in this *c."*
Heb 13:14 here we do not have an enduring *c,*
Rev 21: 2 saw the Holy *C,* the new

CIVILIAN*

2Ti   2: 4 a soldier gets involved in *c* affairs—

CLAIM (CLAIMS RECLAIM)

Pr 25: 6 do not *c* a place among great men;
1Jn   1: 6 If we *c* to have fellowship
    1: 8 If we *c* to be without sin, we
    1:10 If we *c* we have not sinned,

CLAIMS (CLAIM)

Jas   2:14 if a man *c* to have faith
1Jn   2: 6 Whoever *c* to live in him must walk
    2: 9 Anyone who *c* to be in the light

CLANGING*

1Co 13: 1 a resounding gong or a *c* cymbal.

CLAP* (CLAPPED CLAPS)

Job 21: 5 *c* your hand over your mouth.
Ps 47: 1 *C* your hands, all you nations;
   98: 8 Let the rivers *c* their hands,
Pr 30:32 *c* your hand over your mouth!
Isa 55:12 will *c* their hands.
La   2:15 *c* their hands at you;

CLAPPED* (CLAP)

2Ki 11:12 and the people *c* their hands
Eze 25: 6 Because you have *c* your hands

CLAPS* (CLAP)

Job 27:23 It *c* its hands in derision
   34:37 scornfully he *c* his hands among us
Na   3:19 *c* his hands at your fall,

CLASSIFY*

2Co 10:12 dare to *c* or compare ourselves

CLAUDIUS

Ac 11:28 happened during the reign of *C.)*
    18: 2 because *C* had ordered all the Jews

CLAY

Isa 45: 9 Does the *c* say to the potter,
    64: 8 We are the *c,* you are the potter;
Jer 18: 6 "Like *c* in the hand of the potter,
La   4: 2 are now considered as pots of *c,*
Da   2:33 partly of iron and partly of baked *c.*
Ro   9:21 of the same lump of *c* some pottery
2Co   4: 7 we have this treasure in jars of *c*
2Ti   2:20 and *c;* some are for noble purposes

CLEAN (CLEANNESS CLEANSE CLEANSED CLEANSES CLEANSING)

Ge   7: 2 seven of every kind of *c* animal,
Lev   4:12 the camp to a place ceremonially *c,*
    16:30 you will be *c* from all your sins.
Ps 24: 4 He who has *c* hands and a pure
    51: 7 with hyssop, and I will be *c;*
Pr 20: 9 I am *c* without sin"?
Eze 36:25 I will sprinkle *c* water on you,
Mt   8: 2 are willing, you can make me *c."*
   12:44 the house unoccupied, swept *c*
   23:25 You *c* the outside of the cup
Mk   7:19 Jesus declared all foods "*c.*"]
Jn 13:10 to wash his feet; his whole body is *c*
   15: 3 are already *c* because of the word
Ac 10:15 impure that God has made *c."*
Ro 14:20 All food is *c,* but it is wrong

CLEANNESS (CLEAN)

2Sa 22:25 according to my *c* in his sight.

CLEANSE (CLEAN)

Ps 51: 2 and *c* me from my sin.
    51: 7 *C* me with hyssop, and I will be
Pr 20:30 Blows and wounds *c* away evil,
Heb   9:14 *c* our consciences from acts that
   10:22 having our hearts sprinkled to *c* us

CLEANSED (CLEAN)

Heb   9:22 requires that nearly everything be *c*
2Pe   1: 9 has forgotten that he has been *c*

CLEANSES* (CLEAN)

2Ti   2:21 If a man *c* himself from the latter,

CLEANSING (CLEAN)

Eph   5:26 *c* her by the washing with water

CLEFT*

Ex 33:22 I will put you in a *c* in the rock

CLEVER

Isa   5:21 and *c* in their own sight.

CLING

Ro 12: 9 Hate what is evil; *c* to what is good.

CLINGS

Ps 63: 8 My soul *c* to you;

CLOAK

Ex 12:11 with your *c* tucked into your belt,
2Ki   4:29 "Tuck your *c* into your belt,
    9: 1 "Tuck your *c* into your belt,
Mt   5:40 let him have your *c* as well.

CLOSE (CLOSER CLOSES)

2Ki 11: 8 Stay *c* to the king wherever he goes
2Ch 23: 7 Stay *c* to the king wherever he goes
Ps 34:18 LORD is *c* to the brokenhearted
   148:14 of Israel, the people *c* to his heart.
Isa 40:11 and carries them *c* to his heart;
Jer 30:21 himself to be *c* to me?'

CLOSER (CLOSE)

Ex   3: 5 "Do not come any *c,* "God said.
Pr 18:24 there is a friend who sticks *c*

CLOSES (CLOSE)

Pr 28:27 he who *c* his eyes to them receives

CLOTHE (CLOTHED CLOTHES CLOTHING)

Ps 45: 3 *c* yourself with splendor
Isa 52: 1 *c* yourself with strength.
Ro 13:14 *c* yourselves with the Lord Jesus
Col   3:12 *c* yourselves with compassion,
1Pe   5: 5 *c* yourselves with humility

CLOTHED (CLOTHE)

Ps 30:11 removed my sackcloth and *c* me
   104: 1 you are *c* with splendor
Pr 31:22 she is *c* in fine linen and purple.
   31:25 She is *c* with strength and dignity;
Isa 61:10 For he has *c* me with garments
Lk 24:49 until you have been *c* with power
Gal   3:27 into Christ have *c* yourselves

CLOTHES (CLOTHE)

Dt   8: 4 Your *c* did not wear out
Mt   6:25 the body more important than *c?*
    6:28 "And why do you worry about *c?*
   27:35 they divided up his *c* by casting lots
Jn 11:44 Take off the grave *c* and let him go

CLOTHING (CLOTHE)

Dt 22: 5 A woman must not wear men's *c,*
Job 29:14 I put on righteousness as my *c;*
Ps 22:18 and cast lots for my *c.*
Mt   7:15 They come to you in sheep's *c,*
1Ti   6: 8 But if we have food and *c,*

CLOUD (CLOUDS)

Ex 13:21 them in a pillar of *c* to guide them
1Ki 18:44 *c* as small as a man's hand is rising
Pr 16:15 his favor is like a rain *c* in spring.
Isa 19: 1 See, the LORD rides on a swift *c*
Lk 21:27 of Man coming in a *c* with power
Heb 12: 1 by such a great *c* of witnesses,
Rev 14:14 seated on the *c* was one "like a son

CLOUDS (CLOUD)

Dt 33:26 and on the *c* in his majesty.
Ps 68: 4 extol him who rides on the *c*—
   104: 3 He makes the *c* his chariot
Pr 25:14 Like *c* and wind without rain
Da   7:13 coming with the *c* of heaven.
Mt 24:30 of Man coming on the *c* of the sky,
   26:64 and coming on the *c* of heaven."
Mk 13:26 coming in *c* with great power
1Th   4:17 with them in the *c* to meet the Lord
Rev   1: 7 Look, he is coming with the *c,*

CLUB

Pr 25:18 Like a *c* or a sword or a sharp arrow

CO-HEIRS* (INHERIT)

Ro   8:17 heirs of God and *c* with Christ,

COALS

Pr 25:22 you will heap burning *c* on his head
Ro 12:20 you will heap burning *c* on his head

COARSE*

Eph   5: 4 or *c* joking, which are out of place,

CODE*

Ro   2:27 even though you have the written *c*
    2:29 by the Spirit, not by the written *c.*
    7: 6 not in the old way of the written *c.*
Col   2:14 having canceled the written *c,*

COINS

Mt 26:15 out for him thirty silver *c.*
Lk 15: 8 suppose a woman has ten silver *c*

COLD

Pr 25:25 Like *c* water to a weary soul
Mt 10:42 if anyone gives even a cup of *c* water
   24:12 the love of most will grow *c,*

COLLECTION

1Co 16: 1 Now about the c for God's people:

COLT

Zec 9: 9 on a c, the foal of a donkey.
Mt 21: 5 on a c, the foal of a donkey.' "

COMB

Ps 19:10 than honey from the c.

COMFORT* (COMFORTED COMFORTER COMFORTERS COMFORTING COMFORTS)

Ge 5:29 "He will c us in the labor
37:35 and daughters came to c him,
Ru 2:13 "You have given me c
1Ch 7:22 and his relatives came to c him.
Job 2:11 sympathize with him and c him.
7:13 When I think my bed will c me
16: 5 c from my lips would bring you
36:16 to the c of your table laden
Ps 23: 4 rod and your staff, they c me.
71:21 and c me once again.
119: 50 My c in my suffering is this:
119: 52 and I find c in them.
119: 76 May your unfailing love be my c,
119: 82 I say, "When will you c me?"
Isa 40: 1 C, c my people.
51: 3 The LORD will surely c Zion
51:19 who can c you?—
57:18 I will guide him and restore c
61: 2 to call who mourn,
66:13 so will I c you;
Jer 16: 7 food to c those who mourn
31:13 I will give them c and joy instead
La 1: 2 there is none to c her.
1: 9 there was none to c her.
1:16 No one is near to c me,
1:17 but there is no one to c her.
1:21 but there is no one to c me.
2:13 that I may c you,
Eze 16:54 all you have done in giving them c.
Na 3: 7 Where can I find anyone to c you?"
Zec 1:17 and the LORD will again c Zion
10: 2 they give c in vain.
Lk 6:24 you have already received your c.
Jn 11:19 and Mary to c them in the loss
1Co 14: 3 encouragement and c.
2Co 1: 3 of compassion and the God of all c,
1: 4 so that we can c those
1: 4 with the c we ourselves have
1: 5 through Christ our c overflows.
1: 6 if we are comforted, it is for your c,
1: 6 it is for your c and salvation;
1: 7 so also you share in our c.
2: 7 you ought to forgive and c him,
7: 7 also by the c you had given him.
Php 2: 1 if any c from his love,
Col 4:11 and they have proved a c to me.

COMFORTED* (COMFORT)

Ge 24:67 Isaac was c after his mother's death
37:35 comfort him, but he refused to be c.
2Sa 12:24 Then David c his wife Bathsheba,
Job 42:11 They c and consoled him
Ps 77: 2 and my soul refused to be c.
86:17 have helped me and c me.
Isa 12: 1 and you have c me.
49: 9 for the LORD has c his people,
54:11 lashed by storms and not c,
66:13 and you will be c over Jerusalem."
Jer 31:15 and refusing to be c,
Mt 2:18 and refusing to be c.
5: 4 for they will be c.
Lk 16:25 but now he is c here and you are
Ac 20:12 man home alive and were greatly c.
2Co 7: 6 if we are c, it is for your comfort,
7: 6 c us by the coming of Titus.

COMFORTER* (COMFORT)

Ecc 4: 1 and they have no c;
4: 1 and they have no c.
Jer 8:18 O my C in sorrow.

COMFORTERS* (COMFORT)

Job 16: 2 miserable c are you all!
Ps 69:20 for c, but I found none.

COMFORTING* (COMFORT)

Isa 66:11 satisfied at her c breasts,
Zec 1:13 c words to the angel who talked
Jn 11:31 c her, noticed how quickly she got
1Th 2:12 c and urging you to live lives

COMFORTS* (COMFORT)

Job 29:25 I was like one who c mourners.
Isa 49:13 For the LORD c his people
51:12 "I, even I, am he who c you.
66:13 As a mother c her child,
2Co 1: 4 who c us in all our troubles,
7: 6 But God, who c the downcast,

COMMAND (COMMANDED COMMANDING COMMANDENT COMMANDMENTS COMMANDS)

Ex 7: 2 You are to say everything I c you,
Nu 14:41 are you disobeying the LORD's c?
24:13 to go beyond the c of the LORD—
Dt 4: 2 Do not add to what I c you
8: 1 to follow every c I am giving you
12:32 See that you do all I c you;
15:11 I c you to be openhanded
30:16 For I c you today to love
32:46 so that you may c your children
Ps 91:11 For he will c his angels concerning
Pr 13:13 but he who respects a c is rewarded
Ecc 8: 2 Obey the king's c, I say,
Jer 1: 7 you to and say whatever I c you.
1:17 and say to them whatever I c you.
7:23 Walk in all the ways I c you.
11: 4 Obey me and do everything I c you
26: 2 Tell them everything I c you;
Joel 2:11 mighty are those who obey his c.
Mt 4: 6 He will c his angels concerning you
15: 3 why do you break the c of God
Lk 4:10 " 'He will c his angels concerning
Jn 14:15 love me, you will obey what I c.
15:12 My c is this: Love each other
15:14 friends if you do what I c.
15:17 This is my c: Love each other.
1Co 14:37 writing to you is the Lord's c.
Gal 5:14 law is summed up in a single c:
1Ti 1: 5 goal of this c is love, which comes
6:14 to you keep this c without spot
6:17 C those who are rich
Heb 11: 3 universe was formed at God's c,
2Pe 2:21 on the sacred c that was passed
3: 2 and the c given by our Lord
1Jn 2: 7 I am not writing you a new c
3:23 this is his c: to believe in the name
4:21 And he has given us this c:
2Jn : 6 his c is that you walk in love.

COMMANDED (COMMAND)

Ge 2:16 And the LORD God c the man,
5: 5 Noah did all that the LORD c him.
50:12 Jacob's sons did as he had c them:
Ex 7: 6 did just as the LORD c them.
19: 7 all the words the LORD had c him
Dt 4: 5 laws as the LORD my God c me,
6:24 The LORD c us to obey all these
Jos 1: 9 Have I not c you? Be strong
1:16 Whatever you have c us we will do,
2Sa 5: 25 So David did as the LORD c him,
2Ki 17:13 the entire Law that I c your fathers
21: 8 careful to do everything I c them
2Ch 33: 8 do everything I c them concerning
Ps 33: 9 he c, and it stood firm.
78: 5 which he c our forefathers
148: 5 for he c and they were created.
Mt 28:20 to obey everything I have c you.
1Co 9:14 Lord has c that those who preach
1Jn 3:23 and to love one another as he c us.
2Jn : 4 in the truth, just as the Father c us.

COMMANDING (COMMAND)

2Ti 2: 4 he wants to please his c officer.

COMMANDMENT* (COMMAND)

Jos 22: 5 But be very careful to keep the c
Mt 22:36 which is the greatest c in the Law?"
22:38 This is the first and greatest c.
Mk 12:31 There is no c greater than these."
Lk 23:56 the Sabbath in obedience to the c.
Jn 13:34 "A new c I give you: Love one
Ro 7: 8 the opportunity afforded by the c,
7: 9 when the c came, sin sprang to life
7:10 that the very c that was intended
7:11 and through the c put me to death.
7:11 the opportunity afforded by the c,
7:12 and the c is holy, righteous
7:13 through the c sin might become
13: 9 and whatever other c there may be,
Eph 6: 2 which is the first c with a promise
Heb 9:19 Moses had proclaimed every c

COMMANDMENTS* (COMMAND)

Ex 20: 6 who love me and keep my c.
34:28 of the covenant—the Ten C.
Dt 4:13 to you his covenant, the Ten C,
5:10 who love me and keep my c.
5:22 These are the c the LORD
6: 6 These c that I give you today are
9:10 were all the c the LORD
10: 4 The Ten C he had proclaimed
Ecc 12:13 Fear God and keep his c,
Mt 5:19 one of the least of these c
19:17 If you want to enter life, obey the c
22:40 the Prophets hang on these two c."
Mk 10:19 You know the c: 'Do not murder,
12:28 "Of all the c, which is the most
Lk 1: 6 observing all the Lord's c
18:20 You know the c: 'Do not commit
Ro 13: 9 The c, "Do not commit adultery,"
Eph 2:15 in his flesh the law with its c
Rev 14:12 those who obey God's c

COMMANDS (COMMAND)

Ex 24:12 and I have written for their
25:22 give you all my c for the Israelites.
34:32 gave them all the c the LORD had
Lev 22:31 "Keep my c and follow them.
Nu 15:39 and so you will remember all the c
Dt 7: 9 those who love him and keep his c
7:11 Therefore, take care to follow the c
11: 1 decrees, his laws and his c always.
11:27 the blessing if you obey the c
28: 1 carefully follow all his c I give you
30:10 LORD your God and keep his c
Jos 22: 5 to walk in all his ways, to obey his c
1Ki 2: 3 and keep his decrees and c,
8:58 in all his ways and to keep the c,
8:61 to live by his decrees and obey his c
1Ch 28: 7 unswerving in carrying out my c
29:19 devotion to keep your c,
2Ch 31:21 in obedience to the law and the c,
Ne 1: 5 those who love him and obey his c,
Ps 78: 7 but would keep his c.
112: 1 who finds great delight in his c.
119: 10 do not let me stray from your c.
119: 32 I run in the path of your c,
119: 35 Direct me in the path of your c,
119: 47 for I delight in your c
119: 48 I lift up my hands to your c,
119: 73 my understanding to learn your c.
119: 86 All your c are trustworthy;
119: 96 but your c are boundless.
119: 98 Your c make me wiser
119:115 that I may keep the c of my God!
119:131 longing for your c.
119:143 but your c are my delight.
119:151 and all your c are true.
119:172 for all your c are righteous.
119:176 for I have not forgotten your c.
Pr 2: 1 and store up my c within you,
3: 1 but keep my c in your heart,
6:23 For these c are a lamp,
10: 8 The wise in heart accept c,
Isa 48:18 you had paid attention to my c,
Da 9: 4 all who love him and obey his c,
Mt 5:19 teaches these c will be called great
Mk 7: 8 You have let go of the c of God
7: 9 way of setting aside the c of God
Jn 14:21 Whoever has my c and obeys them,
15:10 If you obey my c, you will remain
Ac 17:30 but now he c all people everywhere
1Co 7:19 Keeping God's c is what counts.
1Jn 2: 3 come to know him if we obey his c.
2: 4 but does not do what he c is a liar,
3:22 we obey his c and do what pleases
3:24 Those who obey his c live in him,
5: 2 loving God and carrying out his c.
5: 3 And his c are not burdensome.
5: 3 This is love for God: to obey his c.
2Jn : 6 that we walk in obedience to his c.

COMMEMORATE

Ex 12:14 "This is a day you are to c,

COMMEND* (COMMENDABLE COMMENDED COMMENDS)

Ps 145: 4 One generation will c your works
Ecc 8:15 So I c the enjoyment of life,
Ro 13: 3 do what is right and he will c you.
16: 1 I c to you our sister Phoebe,
2Co 3: 1 beginning to c ourselves again?
4: 2 the truth plainly we c ourselves
5:12 trying to c ourselves to you again,

2Co 6: 4 as servants of God we *c* ourselves
      10: 12 with some who *c* themselves.
1Pe 2: 14 and to *c* those who do right.

COMMENDABLE* (COMMEND)
1Pe 2: 19 For it is *c* if a man bears up
      2: 20 you endure it, this is *c* before God.

COMMENDED* (COMMEND)
Ne 11: 2 The people *c* all the men who
Job 29: 11 and those who saw me *c* me,
Lk 16: 8 master *c* the dishonest manager
Ac 15: 40 *c* by the brothers to the grace
2Co 12: 11 I ought to have been *c* by you,
Heb 11: 2 This is what the ancients were *c* for
      11: 4 By faith he was *c* as a righteous
      11: 5 he was *c* as one who pleased God.
      11: 39 These were all *c* for their faith,

COMMENDS* (COMMEND)
Pr 15: 2 of the wise *c* knowledge,
2Co 10: 18 but the one whom the Lord *c.*
      10: 18 not the one who *c* himself is who

COMMIT (COMMITS COMMITTED)
Ex 20: 14 "You shall not *c* adultery.
Dt   5: 18 "You shall not *c* adultery.
1Sa 7: 3 and *c* yourselves to the LORD
Ps 31: 5 Into your hands I *c* my spirit;
      37: 5 *C* your way to the LORD;
Pr 16: 3 *C* to the LORD whatever you do,
Mt   5: 27 that it was said, 'Do not *c* adultery.'
      5: 32 causes her to *c* adultery,
      19: 18 do not *c* adultery, do not steal,
Mk 10: 19 do not *c* adultery, do not steal,
Lk 18: 20 "Do not *c* adultery, do not murder,
      23: 46 into your hands I *c* my spirit."
Ac 20: 32 I *c* you to God and to the word
Ro   2: 22 do you *c* adultery? You who abhor
      2: 22 that people should not *c* adultery,
      13: 9 "Do not *c* adultery,"
1Co 10: 8 We should not *c* sexual immorality,
Jas   2: 11 do not *c* adultery but do *c* murder,
1Pe 4: 19 to God's will should *c* themselves
Rev 2: 22 I will make those who *c* adultery

COMMITS (COMMIT)
Pr   6: 32 man who *c* adultery lacks
      29: 22 a hot-tempered one *c* many sins.
Ecc 8: 12 a wicked man *c* a hundred crimes
Eze 18: 12 He *c* robbery.
      18: 14 who sees all the sins his father *c,*
      18: 24 from his righteousness and *c* sin
      18: 26 from his righteousness and *c* sin,
      22: 11 you one man *c* a detestable offense
Mt   5: 32 the divorced woman *c* adultery
      19: 9 marries another woman *c* adultery
Mk 10: 11 marries another woman *c* adultery
      10: 12 another man, she *c* adultery."
Lk 16: 18 a divorced woman *c* adultery,
      16: 18 who marries another woman *c* adultery,

COMMITTED (COMMIT)
Nu   5: 7 and must confess the sin he has *c.*
1Ki 8: 61 But your hearts must be fully *c*
      15: 14 Asa's heart was fully *c*
2Ch 16: 9 those whose hearts are fully *c*
Mt   5: 28 lustfully has already *c* adultery
      11: 27 "All things have been *c* to me
Lk 10: 22 "All things have been *c* to me
Ac 14: 23 *c* them to the Lord.
      14: 26 where they had been *c* to the grace
1Co 9: 17 I am simply discharging the trust *c*
2Co 5: 19 And he has *c* to us the message
1Pe 2: 22 "He *c* no sin,
Rev 17: 2 the kings of the earth *c* adultery
      18: 3 of the earth *c* adultery with her,
      18: 9 kings of the earth who *c* adultery

COMMON
Ge 11: 1 had one language and a *c* speech.
Lev 10: 10 between the holy and the *c,*
Pr 22: 2 Rich and poor have this in *c:*
      29: 13 the oppressor have this in *c:*
Ac   2: 44 together and had everything in *c.*
1Co 10: 13 has seized you except what is *c*
2Co 6: 14 and wickedness have in *c?*

COMPANION (COMPANIONS)
Ps 55: 13 my *c,* my close friend,
      55: 20 My *c* attacks his friends;
Pr 13: 20 but a *c* of fools suffers harm.
      28: 7 a *c* of gluttons disgraces his father.
      29: 3 *c* of prostitutes squanders his
Rev 1: 9 your brother and *c* in the suffering

COMPANIONS (COMPANION)
Ps 45: 7 your God, has set you above your *c*
Pr 18: 24 A man of many *c* may come to ruin
Heb 1: 9 your God, has set you above your *c*

COMPANY
Ps 14: 5 present in the *c* of the righteous.
Pr 21: 16 comes to rest in the *c* of the dead.
      24: 1 do not desire their *c;*
Jer 15: 17 I never sat in the *c* of revelers,
1Co 15: 33 "Bad *c* corrupts good character."

COMPARE* (COMPARED COMPARING COMPARISON)
Job 28: 17 Neither gold nor crystal can *c*
      28: 19 The topaz of Cush cannot *c* with it;
      39: 13 but they cannot *c* with the pinions
Ps 86: 8 no deeds can *c* with yours.
      89: 6 skies above can *c* with the LORD?
Pr   3: 15 nothing you desire can *c* with her.
      8: 11 nothing you desire can *c* with her.
Isa 40: 18 To whom, then, will you *c* God?
      40: 18 What image will you *c* him to?
      40: 25 "To whom will you *c* me?
      46: 5 "To whom will you *c* me
La   2: 13 With what can I *c* you,
Eze 31: 8 *c* with its branches—
Da   1: 13 Then *c* our appearance with that
Mt 11: 16 "To what can I *c* this generation?
Lk   7: 31 I *c* the people of this generation?
      13: 18 What shall I *c* it to? It is like
      13: 20 What shall I *c* the kingdom of God
2Co 10: 12 and *c* themselves with themselves,
      10: 12 or *c* ourselves with some who

COMPARED* (COMPARE)
Jdg 8: 2 What have I accomplished *c* to you
      8: 3 What was I able to do *c* to you?"
Isa 46: 5 you liken me that we may be *c?*
Eze 31: 2 Who can be *c* with you in majesty?
      31: 18 the trees of Eden can be *c* with you
Php 3: 8 I consider everything a loss *c*

COMPARING* (COMPARE)
Ro   8: 18 present sufferings are not worth *c*
2Co 8: 8 the sincerity of your love by *c* it
Gal   6: 4 without *c* himself to somebody else

COMPARISON* (COMPARE)
2Co 3: 10 now in *c* with the surpassing glory.

COMPASSION* (COMPASSIONATE COMPASSIONS)
Ex 33: 19 I will have *c* on whom I will have *c.*
Dt   13: 17 he will show you mercy, have *c*
      28: 54 man among you will have no *c*
      30: 3 restore your fortunes and have *c*
      32: 36 and have *c* on his servants
Jdg 2: 18 for the LORD had *c* on them
1Ki 3: 26 son was alive was filled with *c*
2Ki 13: 23 and had *c* and showed concern
2Ch 30: 9 and your children will be shown *c*
Ne   9: 19 of your great *c* you did not
      9: 27 and in your great *c* you gave them
      9: 28 in your *c* you delivered them time
Ps 51: 1 according to your great *c*
      77: 9 Has he in anger withheld his *c?"*
      90: 13 Have *c* on your servants.
      102: 13 You will arise and have *c* on Zion,
      103: 4 and crowns you with love and *c.*
      103: 13 As a father has *c* on his children,
      103: 13 so the LORD has *c*
      116: 5 our God is full of *c.*
      119: 77 Let your *c* come to me that I may
      119: 156 Your *c* is great, O LORD;
      135: 14 and have *c* on his servants.
      145: 9 he has *c* on all he has made.
Isa 13: 18 will they look with *c* on children.
      14: 1 The LORD will have *c* on Jacob;
      27: 11 so their Maker has no *c* on them,
      30: 18 he rises to show you *c.*
      49: 10 He who has *c* on them will guide
      49: 13 and will have *c* on his afflicted ones
      49: 15 and have no *c* on the child she has
      51: 3 and will look with *c* on all her ruins
      54: 7 with deep *c* I will bring you back.
      54: 8 I will have *c* on you,
      54: 10 says the LORD, who has *c* on you.
      60: 10 in favor I will show you *c.*
      63: 7 to his *c* and many kindnesses.
      63: 15 and *c* are withheld from us.
Jer 12: 15 I will again have *c* and will bring
      13: 14 *c* to keep me from destroying them
      15: 6 I can no longer show *c.*

Jer 21: 7 show them no mercy or pity or *c.'*
      30: 18 and have *c* on his dwellings;
      31: 20 I have great *c* for him,"
      33: 26 restore their fortunes and have *c*
      42: 12 I will show you *c* so that he will
      42: 12 so that he will have *c* on you
La   3: 32 he brings grief, he will show *c,*
Eze 9: 5 without showing pity or *c.*
      16: 5 or had *c* enough to do any
      39: 25 and will have *c* on all the people
Hos 2: 19 in love and *c.*
      11: 8 all my *c* is aroused.
      13: 14 "I will have no *c,*
      14: 3 for in you the fatherless find *c."*
Am   1: 11 stifling all *c,*
Jnh 3: 9 with *c* turn from his fierce anger
      3: 10 he had *c* and did not bring
Mic 7: 19 You will again have *c* on us;
Zec 7: 9 show mercy and *c* to one another.
      10: 6 because I have *c* on them.
Mal 3: 17 as in a *c* a man spares his son who
Mt   9: 36 When he saw the crowds, he had *c*
      14: 14 he had *c* on them and healed their
      15: 32 "I have *c* for these people;
      20: 34 Jesus had *c* on them and touched
Mk   1: 41 with *c,* Jesus reached out his hand
      6: 34 and saw a large crowd, he had *c*
      8: 2 "I have *c* for these people;
Lk 15: 20 and was filled with *c* for him;
Ro   9: 15 and I will have *c* on whom I have *c*
2Co 1: 3 the Father of *c* and the God
Php 2: 1 and *c,* then make my joy complete
Col 3: 12 clothe yourselves with *c,* kindness,
Jas 5: 11 The Lord is full of *c* and mercy.

COMPASSIONATE* (COMPASSION)
Ex 22: 27 out to me, I will hear, for I am *c.*
      34: 6 the LORD, the *c* and gracious God
2Ch 30: 9 LORD your God is gracious and *c.*
Ne   9: 17 gracious and *c,* slow to anger
Ps 86: 15 O Lord, are a *c* and gracious God,
      103: 8 The LORD is *c* and gracious,
      111: 4 the LORD is gracious and *c.*
      112: 4 the gracious and *c* and righteous
      145: 8 The LORD is gracious and *c,*
La   4: 10 With their own hands *c* women
Joel 2: 13 for he is gracious and *c,*
Jnh   4: 2 that you are a gracious and *c* God,
Eph 4: 32 Be kind and *c* to one another,
1Pe 3: 8 love as brothers, be *c* and humble.

COMPASSIONS* (COMPASSION)
La   3: 22 for his *c* never fail.

COMPELLED (COMPULSION)
Ac 20: 22 "And now, *c* by the Spirit,
1Co 9: 16 I cannot boast, for I am *c* to preach.

COMPELS (COMPULSION)
Job 32: 18 and the spirit within me *c* me;
2Co 5: 14 For Christ's love *c* us, because we

COMPETENCE* (COMPETENT)
2Co 3: 5 but our *c* comes from God.

COMPETENT* (COMPETENCE)
Ro 15: 14 and *c* to instruct one another.
1Co 6: 2 are you not *c* to judge trivial cases?
2Co 3: 5 Not that we are *c* in ourselves to claim
      3: 6 He has made us *c* as ministers

COMPETES*
1Co 9: 25 Everyone who *c* in the games goes
2Ti   2: 5 Similarly, if anyone *c* as an athlete,
      2: 5 unless he *c* according to the rules.

COMPLACENCY* (COMPLACENT)
Pr   1: 32 and the *c* of fools will destroy them
Eze 30: 9 ships to frighten Cush out of her *c.*

COMPLACENT* (COMPLACENCY)
Isa 32: 9 You women who are so *c,*
      32: 11 Tremble, you *c* women;
Am   6: 1 Woe to you who are *c* in Zion,
Zep 1: 12 and punish those who are *c,*

COMPLAINING*
Php 2: 14 Do everything without *c* or arguing

COMPLETE
Dt 16: 15 your hands, and your joy will be *c.*
Jn   3: 29 That joy is mine, and it is now *c.*
      15: 11 and that your joy may be *c.*
      16: 24 will receive, and your joy will be *c.*
      17: 23 May they be brought to *c* unity

Ac 20: 24 cthe task the Lord Jesus has given
Php 2: 2 then make my joy c
Col 4: 17 to it that you cthe work you have
Jas 1: 4 so that you may be mature and c,
2: 22 his faith was made cby what he did
1Jn 1: 4 We write this to make our joy c,
2: 5 God's love is truly made cin him.
4: 12 and his love is made cin us.
4: 17 love is made camong us
2Jn : 12 to face, so that our joy may be c.

COMPLIMENTS
Pr 23: 8 and will have wasted your c.

COMPREHEND* (COMPREHENDED)
Job 28: 13 Man does not cits worth;
Ecc 8: 17 No one can cwhat goes
8: 17 he knows, he cannot really cit.

COMPREHENDED* (COMPREHEND)
Job 38: 18 Have you cthe vast expanses

COMPULSION (COMPELLED COMPELS)
2Co 9: 7 not reluctantly or under c,

CONCEAL (CONCEALED CONCEALS)
Ps 40: 10 I do not cyour love and your truth
Pr 25: 2 It is the glory of God to ca matter;

CONCEALED (CONCEAL)
Jer 16: 17 nor is their sin cfrom my eyes.
Mt 10: 26 There is nothing cthat will not be
Mk 4: 22 and whatever is cis meant
Lk 8: 17 nothing cthat will not be known
12: 2 There is nothing cthat will not be

CONCEALS* (CONCEAL)
Pr 10: 18 He who chis hatred has lying lips,
28: 13 He who chis sins does not prosper,

CONCEIT* (CONCEITED CONCEITS)
Isa 16: 6 her overweening pride and c,
Jer 48: 29 her overweening pride and c,
Php 2: 3 out of selfish ambition or vain c,

CONCEITED* (CONCEIT)
1Sa 17: 28 I know how cyou are and how
Ro 11: 25 brothers, so that you may not be c:
12: 16 Do not be c.
2Co 12: 7 To keep me from becoming c
Gal 5: 26 Let us not become c, provoking
1Ti 3: 6 or he may become cand fall
6: 4 he is cand understands nothing.
2Ti 3: 4 of the good, treacherous, rash, c,

CONCEITS* (CONCEIT)
Ps 73: 7 evil cof their minds know no

CONCEIVED (CONCEIVES)
Ps 51: 5 from the time my mother cme.
Mt 1: 20 what is cin her is from the Holy
1Co 2: 9 no mind has c
Jas 1: 15 after desire has c, it gives birth

CONCEIVES* (CONCEIVED)
Ps 7: 14 ctrouble gives birth

CONCERN* (CONCERNED)
Ge 39: 6 he did not chimself with anything
39: 8 "my master does not chimself
1Sa 23: 21 "The LORD bless you for your c
2Ki 13: 23 and had compassion and showed c
Job 9: 21 I have no cfor myself;
19: 4 my error remains my calone.
Ps 131: 1 I do not cmyself with great matters
Pr 29: 7 but the wicked have no such c.
Eze 36: 21 I had cfor my holy name, which
Ac 15: 14 God at first showed his cby taking
18: 17 But Gallio showed no cwhatever.
1Co 7: 32 I would like you to be free from c.
12: 25 that its parts should have equal c
2Co 7: 7 your deep sorrow, your ardent c
7: 11 what alarm, what longing, what c,
8: 16 of Titus the same cI have for you.
11: 28 of my cfor all the churches.
Php 4: 10 at last you have renewed your c

CONCERNED (CONCERN)
Ex 2: 25 Israelites and was cabout them.
Ps 142: 4 no one is cfor me.
Jnh 4: 10 "You have been cabout this vine,
4: 11 Should I not be cabout that great
1Co 7: 32 An unmarried man is cabout
9: 9 Is it about oxen that God is c?
Php 4: 10 you have been c, but you had no

CONCESSION*
1Co 7: 6 I say this as a c, not as a command.

**CONDEMN* (CONDEMNATION
CONDEMNED CONDEMNING CONDEMNS)**
Job 9: 20 innocent, my mouth would cme;
10: 2 I will say to God: Do not cme,
34: 17 Will you cthe just and mighty One
34: 29 if he remains silent, who can chim?
40: 8 Would you cme to justify yourself?
Ps 94: 21 and cthe innocent to death.
109: 7 and may his prayers chim.
109: 31 from those who chim.
Isa 50: 9 Who is he that will cme?
Mt 12: 41 with this generation and cit;
12: 42 with this generation and cit;
20: 18 They will chim to death
Mk 10: 33 They will chim to death
Lk 6: 37 Do not c, and you will not be
11: 31 men of this generation and cthem;
11: 32 with this generation and cit;
Jn 3: 17 Son into the world to cthe world,
7: 51 "Does our law canyone
8: 11 "Then neither do I cyou,"
12: 48 very word which I spoke will chim
Ro 2: 27 yet obeys the law will cyou who,
14: 3 everything must not cthe man who
14: 22 is the man who does not chimself
2Co 7: 3 this to cyou; I have said
1Jn 3: 20 presence whenever our hearts cus.
3: 21 if our hearts do not cus,

CONDEMNATION* (CONDEMN)
Jer 42: 18 of cand reproach; you will never
44: 12 and horror, of cand reproach.
Ro 3: 8 may result"? Their cis deserved.
5: 16 followed one sin and brought c,
5: 18 of one trespass was cfor all men,
8: 1 there is now no cfor those who are
2Pe 2: 3 Their chas long been hanging
Jude 4 certain men whose cwas written

CONDEMNED* (CONDEMN)
Dt 13: 17 of those cthings shall be found
Job 32: 3 to refute Job, and yet had chim.
Ps 34: 21 the foes of the righteous will be c.
34: 22 will be cwho takes refuge in him.
37: 33 let them be cwhen brought to trial.
79: 11 preserve those cto die.
102: 20 and release those cto death."
Mt 12: 7 you would not have cthe innocent.
12: 37 and by your words you will be c."
23: 33 How will you escape being cto hell
27: 3 betrayed him, saw that Jesus was c,
Mk 14: 64 They all chim as worthy of death.
16: 16 whoever does not believe will be c.
Lk 6: 37 condemn, and you will not be c.
Jn 3: 18 Whoever believes in him is not c,
3: 18 does not believe stands calready
5: 24 has eternal life and will not be c;
5: 29 who have done evil will rise to be c.
8: 10 Has no one cyou?" "No one, sir,"
16: 11 prince of this world now stands c.
Ac 25: 15 against him and asked that he be c.
Ro 3: 7 why am I still cas a sinner?"
8: 3 And so he csin in sinful man,
14: 23 But the man who has doubts is c
1Co 4: 9 like men cto die in the arena.
11: 32 disciplined so that we will not be c
Gal 1: 8 let him be eternally c! As we have
1: 9 let him be eternally c! Am I now
2Th 2: 12 that all will be cwho have not
Tit 2: 8 of speech that cannot be c,
Heb 11: 7 By his faith he cthe world
Jas 5: 6 You have cand murdered innocent
5: 12 and your "No," no, or you will be c
2Pe 2: 6 if he cthe cities of Sodom
Rev 19: 2 He has cthe great prostitute

CONDEMNING* (CONDEMN)
Dt 25: 1 the innocent and cthe guilty.
1Ki 8: 32 cthe guilty and bringing
Pr 17: 15 the guilty and cthe innocent—
Ac 13: 27 yet in chim they fulfilled the words
Ro 2: 1 judge the other, you are cyourself,

CONDEMNS* (CONDEMN)
Job 15: 6 Your own mouth cyou, not mine;
Pr 12: 2 but the LORD ca crafty man.
2Co 3: 9 the ministry that cmen is glorious.

CONDITION
Pr 27: 23 Be sure you know the c

CONDUCT (CONDUCTED CONDUCTS)
Pr 10: 23 A fool finds pleasure in evil c,
20: 11 by whether his cis pure and right.
21: 8 but the cof the innocent is upright.
Ecc 6: 8 how to chimself before others?
Jer 4: 18 "Your own cand actions
17: 10 to reward a man according to his c,
Eze 7: 3 I will judge you according to your c
Php 1: 27 cyourselves in a manner worthy
1Ti 3: 15 to cthemselves in God's household

CONDUCTED* (CONDUCT)
2Co 1: 12 testifies that we have courselves

CONDUCTS* (CONDUCT)
Ps 112: 5 who chis affairs with justice.

**CONFESS* (CONFESSED CONFESSES
CONFESSING CONFESSION)**
Lev 5: 5 he must cin what way he has
16: 21 and cover it all the wickedness
26: 40 "But if they will ctheir sins
Nu 5: 7 must cthe sin he has committed.
1Ki 8: 33 back to you and cyour name,
8: 35 toward this place and cyour name
2Ch 6: 24 they turn back and cyour name,
6: 26 toward this place and cyour name
Ne 1: 6 I cthe sins we Israelites, including
Ps 32: 5 I said, "I will c
38: 18 I cmy iniquity;
Jn 1: 20 fail to c, but confessed freely,
12: 42 they would not ctheir faith
Ro 10: 9 That if you cwith your mouth,
10: 10 it is with your mouth that you c
14: 11 every tongue will cto God.' "
Php 2: 11 every tongue cthat Jesus Christ is
Heb 3: 1 and high priest whom we c.
13: 15 the fruit of lips that chis name.
Jas 5: 16 Therefore cyour sins to each other
1Jn 1: 9 If we cour sins, he is faithful

CONFESSED* (CONFESS)
1Sa 7: 6 day they fasted and there they c,
Ne 9: 2 in their places and ctheir sins
Da 9: 4 to the LORD my God and c:
Jn 1: 20 but cfreely, "I am not the Christ."
Ac 19: 18 and openly ctheir evil deeds.

CONFESSES* (CONFESS)
Pr 28: 13 whoever cand renounces them
2Ti 2: 19 and, "Everyone who cthe name

CONFESSING* (CONFESS)
Ezr 10: 1 While Ezra was praying and c,
Da 9: 20 cmy sin and the sin
Mt 3: 6 Ctheir sins, they were baptized
Mk 1: 5 Ctheir sins, they were baptized

CONFESSION* (CONFESS)
Ezr 10: 11 Now make cto the LORD.
Ne 9: 3 and spent another quarter in c
2Co 9: 13 obedience that accompanies your c
1Ti 6: 12 called when you made your good c
6: 13 Pontius Pilate made the good c,

CONFIDENCE* (CONFIDENT)
Jdg 9: 26 and its citizens put their cin him.
2Ki 18: 19 On what are you basing this c
2Ch 32: 8 And the people gained c
32: 10 On what are you basing your c,
Job 4: 6 Should not your piety be your c
Ps 71: 5 my csince my youth.
Pr 3: 26 for the LORD will be your c
3: 32 but takes the upright into his c.
11: 13 A gossip betrays a c;
20: 19 A gossip betrays a c;
25: 9 do not betray another man's c,
31: 11 Her husband has full cin her
Isa 32: 17 will be quietness and cforever.
36: 4 On what are you basing this c
Jer 17: 7 whose cis in him.
49: 31 which lives in c,"
Eze 29: 16 a source of cfor the people of Israel
Mic 7: 5 put no cin a friend.
2Co 2: 3 I had cin all of you, that you would
3: 4 Such cas this is ours
7: 4 I have great cin you; I take great
7: 16 I am glad I can have complete c
8: 22 so because of his great cin you.
Eph 3: 12 God with freedom and c
Php 3: 3 and who put no cin the flesh—
3: 4 I myself have reasons for such c.
3: 4 reasons to put cin the flesh,
2Th 3: 4 We have cin the Lord that you are

CONFIDENT (CONFIDENCE)

Heb 3:14 till the end the c we had at first.
4:16 the throne of grace with c,
10:19 since we have c to enter the Most
10:35 So do not throw away your c;
13:6 So we say with c,
1Jn 3:21 we have c before God and receive
4:17 us so that we will have c on the day
5:14 This is the c we have

CONFIDENT* (CONFIDENCE)

Job 6:20 because they had been c;
Ps 27:3 even then will I be c.
27:13 I am still c of this:
Lk 18:9 To some who were c
2Co 1:15 Because I was c of this, I planned
5:6 Therefore we are always c
5:8 We are c, I say, and would prefer
9:4 ashamed of having been so c.
10:7 If anyone is c that he belongs
Gal 5:10 I am c in the Lord that you will
Php 1:6 day until now, being c of this,
2:24 I am c in the Lord that I myself will
Phm :21 C of your obedience, I write to you,
Heb 6:9 we are c of better things
1Jn 2:28 that when he appears we may be c

CONFIDES*

Ps 25:14 The LORD c in those who fear him

CONFORM* (CONFORMED CONFORMITY CONFORMS)

Ro 12:2 Do not c any longer to the pattern
1Pe 1:14 do not c to the evil desires you had

CONFORMED* (CONFORM)

Eze 5:7 c to the standards of the nations
11:12 but have c to the standards
Ro 8:29 predestined to be c to the likeness

CONFORMITY* (CONFORM)

Eph 1:11 in c with the purpose of his will,

CONFORMS* (CONFORM)

1Ti 1:11 to the sound doctrine that c

CONQUEROR* (CONQUERORS)

Mic 1:15 I will bring a c against you
Rev 6:2 he rode out as a c bent on conquest.

CONQUERORS (CONQUEROR)

Ro 8:37 than c through him who loved us.

CONSCIENCE* (CONSCIENCE-STRICKEN CONSCIENCES CONSCIENTIOUS)

Ge 20:5 I have done this with a clear c
20:6 I know you did this with a clear c,
1Sa 25:31 have on his c the staggering burden
Job 27:6 my c will not reproach me as long
Ac 23:1 to God in all good c to this day."
24:16 to keep my c clear before God
Ro 9:1 my c confirms it in the Holy Spirit
13:5 punishment but also because of c.
1Co 4:4 My c is clear, but that does not
8:7 since their c is weak, it is defiled.
8:10 with a weak c sees you who have
8:12 in this way and wound their weak c
10:25 without raising questions of c,
10:27 you without raising questions of c,
10:28 man who told you and for c' sake—
10:29 freedom be judged by another's c?
10:29 the other man's c, I mean,
2Co 1:12 Our c testifies that we have
4:2 to every man's c in the sight of God
5:11 and I hope it is also plain to your c.
1Ti 1:5 and a good c and a sincere faith.
1:19 holding on to faith and a good c.
3:9 truths of the faith with a clear c.
2Ti 1:3 as my forefathers did, with a clear c
Heb 9:9 able to clear the c of the worshiper.
10:22 to cleanse us from a guilty c
13:18 We are sure that we have a clear c
1Pe 3:16 and respect, keeping a clear c,
3:21 the pledge of a good c toward God.

CONSCIENCE-STRICKEN (CONSCIENCE)

1Sa 24:5 David was c for having cut
2Sa 24:10 David was c after he had counted

CONSCIENCES* (CONSCIENCE)

Ro 2:15 their c also bearing witness,
1Ti 4:2 whose c have been seared
Tit 1:15 their minds and c are corrupted.
Heb 9:14 cleanse our c from acts that lead

CONSCIENTIOUS* (CONSCIENCE)

2Ch 29:34 for the Levites had been more c

CONSCIOUS*

Ro 3:20 through the law we become c of sin
1Pe 2:19 of unjust suffering because he is c

CONSECRATE (CONSECRATED)

Ex 13:2 "C to me every firstborn male.
40:9 c it and all its furnishings.
Lev 20:7 "'C yourselves and be holy,
25:10 C the fiftieth year and proclaim
1Ch 15:12 fellow Levites are to c yourselves

CONSECRATED (CONSECRATE)

Ex 29:43 and the place will be c by my glory.
Lev 8:30 So he c Aaron and his garments
2Ch 7:16 c this temple so that my Name may
Lk 2:23 is to be c to the Lord"),
1Ti 4:5 because it is c by the word of God

CONSENT

1Co 7:5 except by mutual c and for a time,

CONSIDER (CONSIDERATE CONSIDERED CONSIDERS)

1Sa 12:24 c what great things he has done
16:7 "Do not c his appearance
2Ch 19:6 "C carefully what you do,
Job 37:14 stop and c God's wonders.
Ps 8:3 When I c your heavens,
77:12 and c all your mighty deeds.
107:43 and c the great love of the LORD.
143:5 and c what your hands have done.
Pr 6:6 c its ways and be wise!
20:25 and only later to c his vows.
Ecc 7:13 C what God has done:
Lk 12:24 C the ravens: They do not sow
12:27 about the rest? "C how the lilies
Php 2:3 but in humility c others better
3:8 I c everything a loss compared
Heb 10:24 And let us c how we may spur one
Jas 1:2 C it pure joy, my brothers,

CONSIDERATE* (CONSIDER)

Tit 3:2 to be peaceable and c,
Jas 3:17 then peace-loving, c, submissive,
1Pe 2:18 only to those who are good and c,
3:7 in the same way be c as you live

CONSIDERED (CONSIDER)

Job 1:8 "Have you c my servant Job?
2:3 "Have you c my servant Job?
Ps 44:22 we are c as sheep to be slaughtered.
Isa 53:4 yet we c him stricken by God,
Ro 8:36 we are c as sheep to be slaughtered

CONSIDERS (CONSIDER)

Pr 31:16 She c a field and buys it;
Ro 14:5 One man c one day more sacred
Jas 1:26 If anyone c himself religious

CONSIST (CONSISTS)

Lk 12:15 a man's life does not c

CONSISTS (CONSIST)

Eph 5:9 fruit of the light c in all goodness,

CONSOLATION

Ps 94:19 your c brought joy to my soul.

CONSPIRE

Ps 2:1 Why do the nations c

CONSTANT

Dt 28:66 You will live in c suspense,
Pr 19:13 wife is like a c dripping.
27:15 a c dripping on a rainy day;
Ac 27:33 "you have been in c suspense
Heb 5:14 by c use have trained themselves

CONSTRUCTIVE*

1Co 10:23 but not everything is c.

CONSULT

Pr 15:12 he will not c the wise.
Gal 1:16 I did not c any man, nor did I go up

CONSUME (CONSUMES CONSUMING)

Jn 2:17 "Zeal for your house will c me."

CONSUMES (CONSUME)

Ps 69:9 for zeal for your house c me,

CONSUMING (CONSUME)

Dt 4:24 For the LORD your God is a c fire,
Heb 12:29 and awe, for our "God is a c fire."

CONTAIN* (CONTAINED CONTAINS)

1Ki 8:27 the highest heaven, cannot c you.
2Ch 2:6 the highest heavens, cannot c him?
6:18 the highest heavens, cannot c you.
Ecc 8:8 power over the wind to c it;
2Pe 3:16 His letters c some things that are

CONTAINED (CONTAIN)

Heb 9:4 This ark c the gold jar of manna,

CONTAINS (CONTAIN)

Pr 15:6 of the righteous c great treasure,

CONTAMINATES*

2Co 7:1 from everything that c body

CONTEMPT

Pr 14:31 He who oppresses the poor shows c
17:5 He who mocks the poor shows c
18:3 When wickedness comes, so does c
Da 12:2 others to shame and everlasting c.
Mal 1:6 O priests, who show c for my name.
Ro 2:4 Or do you show c for the riches
Gal 4:14 you did not treat me with c
1Th 5:20 do not treat prophecies with c.

CONTEND (CONTENDED CONTENDING CONTENTIOUS)

Ge 6:3 "My Spirit will not c
Ps 35:1 C, O LORD, with those who
Isa 49:25 I will c with those who wrong you,
Jude 3 you to c for the faith that was once

CONTENDED (CONTEND)

Php 4:3 help these women who have c

CONTENDING* (CONTEND)

Php 1:27 c as one man for the faith

CONTENT* (CONTENTMENT)

Jos 7:7 If only we had been c to stay
Pr 15:25 The righteous eat to their hearts' c,
19:23 one rests c, untouched by trouble.
Ecc 4:8 yet his eyes were not c
Lk 3:14 don't accuse people falsely—be c
Php 4:11 to be c whatever the circumstances
4:12 I have learned the secret of being c
1Ti 6:8 and clothing, we will be c with that.
Heb 13:5 and be c with what you have,

CONTENTIOUS* (CONTEND)

1Co 11:16 If anyone wants to be c about this,

CONTENTMENT* (CONTENT)

Job 36:11 and their years in c.
SS 8:10 like one bringing c.
1Ti 6:6 But godliness with c is great gain.

CONTEST*

Heb 10:32 in a great c in the face of suffering.

CONTINUAL (CONTINUE)

Pr 15:15 but the cheerful heart has a c feast.
Eph 4:19 of impurity, with a c lust for more.

CONTINUE (CONTINUAL CONTINUES CONTINUING)

1Ki 8:23 servants who c wholeheartedly
2Ch 6:14 servants who c wholeheartedly
Ps 36:10 C your love to those who know you
Ac 13:43 urged them to c in the grace of God
Ro 11:22 provided that you c in his kindness.
Gal 3:10 Cursed is everyone who does not c
Php 2:12 c to work out your salvation
Col 1:23 if you c in your faith, established
2:6 received Christ Jesus as Lord, c
1Ti 2:15 if they c in faith, love and holiness
2Ti 3:14 c in what you have learned
1Jn 2:28 And now, dear children, c in him,
3:9 born of God will c to sin,
5:18 born of God does not c to sin;
2Jn 9 and does not c in the teaching
Rev 22:11 and let him who is holy c to be holy
22:11 let him who does right c to do right;

CONTINUES (CONTINUE)

Ps 100:5 c through all generations.
119:90 Your faithfulness c
2Co 10:15 Our hope is that, as your faith c
1Jn 3:6 No one who c to sin has

CONTINUING (CONTINUE)
Ro 13: 8 the c debt to love one another.

CONTRIBUTION (CONTRIBUTIONS)
Ro 15:26 pleased to make a c for the poor

CONTRIBUTIONS (CONTRIBUTION)
2Ch 24:10 all the people brought their c gladly
31:12 they faithfully brought in the c,

CONTRITE*
Ps 51:17 a broken and c heart,
Isa 57:15 also with him who is c and lowly
57:15 and to revive the heart of the c.
66: 2 he who is humble and c in spirit,

CONTROL (CONTROLLED CONTROLS SELF-CONTROL SELF-CONTROLLED)
Pr 29:11 a wise man keeps himself under c.
1Co 7: 9 But if they cannot c themselves,
7:37 but has c over his own will,
1Th 4: 4 you should learn to c his own body

CONTROLLED (CONTROL)
Ps 32: 9 but must be c by bit and bridle
Ro 8: 6 but the mind c by the Spirit is life
8: 8 Those c by the sinful nature cannot

CONTROLS* (CONTROL)
Job 37:15 you know how God c the clouds
Pr 16:32 a man who c his temper

CONTROVERSIES*
Ac 26: 3 with all the Jewish customs and c.
1Ti 1: 4 These promote c rather
6: 4 He has an unhealthy interest in c
Tit 3: 9 But avoid foolish c and genealogies

CONVERSATION
Col 4: 6 Let your c be always full of grace,

CONVERT
1Ti 3: 6 He must not be a recent c,

CONVICT (CONVICTION)
Pr 24:25 with those who c the guilty,
Jn 16: 8 he will c the world of guilt in regard
Jude 15 and to c all the ungodly

CONVICTION* (CONVICT)
1Th 1: 5 the Holy Spirit and with deep c.

CONVINCE* (CONVINCED CONVINCING)
Ac 28:23 and tried to c them about Jesus

CONVINCED* (CONVINCE)
Ge 45:28 "I'm c! My son Joseph is still alive.
Lk 16:31 will not be c even if someone rises
Ac 19:26 and hear how this fellow Paul has c
26: 9 "I too was c that I ought
26:26 I am c that none of this has escaped
28:24 Some were c by what he said,
Ro 2:19 if you are c that you are a guide
8:38 For I am c that neither death
14: 5 Each one should be fully c
14:14 I am fully c that no food is unclean
15:14 I myself am c, my brothers,
1Co 14:24 he will be c by all that he is a sinner
2Co 5:14 we are c that one died for all,
Php 1:25 C of this, I know that I will remain,
2Ti 1:12 and am c that he is able
3:14 have learned and have become c

CONVINCING* (CONVINCE)
Ac 1: 3 and gave many c proofs that he was

COOLNESS*
Pr 25:13 Like the c of snow at harvest time

COPIES (COPY)
Heb 9:23 for the c of the heavenly things

COPY (COPIES)
Dt 17:18 for himself on a scroll a c of this law
Heb 8: 5 They serve at a sanctuary that is a c
9:24 sanctuary that was only a c

CORBAN*
Mk 7:11 received from me is C' (that is,

CORD (CORDS)
Jos 2:18 you have tied this scarlet c
Ecc 4:12 cord of three strands is not quickly

CORDS (CORD)
Pr 5:22 the c of his sin hold him fast.
Isa 54: 2 lengthen your c,
Hos 11: 4 them with c of human kindness,

CORINTH
Ac 18: 1 Paul left Athens and went to C.
1Co 1: 2 To the church of God in C,
2Co 1: 1 To the church of God in C,

CORNELIUS*
Roman to whom Peter preached; first Gentile Christian (Ac 10).

CORNER (CORNERS)
Ru 3: 9 "Spread the c of your garment
Pr 21: 9 Better to live on a c of the roof
25:24 Better to live on a c of the roof
Ac 26:26 because it was not done in a c.

CORNERS (CORNER)
Mt 6: 5 on the street c to be seen by men.
22: 9 Go to the street c and invite

CORNERSTONE* (STONE)
Job 38: 6 or who laid its c—
Isa 28:16 a precious c for a sure foundation;
Jer 51:26 rock will be taken from you for a c,
Zec 10: 4 From Judah will come the c,
Eph 2:20 Christ Jesus himself as the chief c.
1Pe 2: 6 a chosen and precious c,

CORRECT* (CORRECTED CORRECTING CORRECTION CORRECTIONS CORRECTS)
Job 6:26 Do you mean to c what I say,
40: 2 contends with the Almighty c him?
Jer 10:24 C me, LORD, but only with justice
2Ti 4: 2 c, rebuke and encourage—

CORRECTED* (CORRECT)
Pr 29:19 A servant cannot be c

CORRECTING* (CORRECT)
2Ti 3:16 c and training in righteousness,

CORRECTION* (CORRECT)
Lev 26:23 things you do not accept my c
Job 36:10 He makes them listen to c
Pr 5:12 How my heart spurned c!
10:17 whoever ignores c leads others
12: 1 but he who hates c is stupid.
13:18 but whoever heeds c is honored.
15: 5 whoever heeds c shows prudence.
15:10 he who hates c will die.
15:12 A mocker resents c;
15:32 whoever heeds c gains
29:15 The rod of c imparts wisdom,
Jer 2:30 they did not respond to c.
5: 3 crushed them, but they refused c.
7:28 LORD its God or responded to c.
Zep 2: 2 she accepts no c.
3: 7 you will fear me / and accept c!'

CORRECTIONS* (CORRECT)
Pr 6:23 and the c of discipline

CORRECTS* (CORRECT)
Job 5:17 "Blessed is the man whom God c;
Pr 9: 7 Whoever c a mocker invites insult;

CORRUPT (CORRUPTED CORRUPTION CORRUPTS)
Ge 6:11 Now the earth was c in God's sight
Ps 14: 1 They are c, their deeds are vile;
14: 3 they have together become c;
Pr 4:24 keep c talk far from your lips.
6:12 who goes about with a c mouth,
19:28 A c witness mocks at justice.

CORRUPTED (CORRUPT)
2Co 7: 2 wronged no one, we have c no one,
Tit 1:15 but to those who are c and do not

CORRUPTION (CORRUPT)
2Pe 1: 4 escape the c in the world caused
2:20 If they have escaped the c

CORRUPTS* (CORRUPT)
Ecc 7: 7 and a bribe c the heart.
1Co 15:33 "Bad company c good character."
Jas 3: 6 It c the whole person, sets

COST (COSTS)
Nu 16:38 sinned at the c of their lives.

Pr 4: 7 Though it c all you have, get
7:23 little knowing it will c him his life.
Isa 55: 1 milk without money and without c.
Lk 14:28 and estimate the c to see
Rev 21: 6 to drink without c from the spring

COSTS (COST)
Pr 6:31 it c him all the wealth of his house.

COUNCIL
Ps 89: 7 In the c of the holy ones God is
107: 32 and praise him in the c of the elders

COUNSEL (COUNSELOR COUNSELS)
1Ki 22: 5 "First seek the c of the LORD."
2Ch 18: 4 "First seek the c of the LORD."
Job 38: 2 "Who is this that darkens my c
42: 3 'Who is this that obscures my c
Ps 1: 1 walk in the c of the wicked
73:24 You guide me with your c,
107: 11 despised the c of the Most High.
Pr 8:14 C and sound judgment are mine;
15:22 Plans fail for lack of c,
27: 9 from his earnest c,
Isa 28:29 wonderful in c and magnificent
1Ti 5:14 So I c younger widows to marry,
Rev 3:18 I c you to buy from me gold refined

COUNSELOR (COUNSEL)
Isa 9: 6 Wonderful C, Mighty God,
Jn 14:16 he will give you another C to be
14:26 But the C, the Holy Spirit,
15:26 "When the C comes, whom I will
16: 7 the C will not come to you;
Ro 11:34 Or who has been his c?"

COUNSELS (COUNSEL)
Ps 16: 7 I will praise the LORD, who c me;

COUNT (COUNTED COUNTING COUNTS)
Ps 22:17 I can c all my bones;
Ro 4: 8 whose sin the Lord will never c
6:11 c yourselves dead to sin
2Th 1:11 that our God may c you worthy

COUNTED (COUNT)
Ac 5:41 because they had been c worthy
2Th 1: 5 and as a result you will be c worthy

COUNTERFEIT*
2Th 2: 9 displayed in all kinds of c miracles,
1Jn 2:27 not c—just as it has taught you,

COUNTING (COUNT)
2Co 5:19 not c men's sins against them.

COUNTRY
Pr 28: 2 When a c is rebellious, it has many
29: 4 By justice a king gives a c stability,
Isa 66: 8 Can a c be born in a day
Lk 15:13 off for a distant c and there
Jn 4:44 prophet has no honor in his own c.)
2Co 11:26 in danger in the c, in danger at sea;
Heb 11:14 looking for a c of their own.

COUNTRYMEN
2Co 11:26 danger from my own c, in danger

COUNTS (COUNT)
Jn 6:63 The Spirit gives life; the flesh c
1Co 7:19 God's commands is what c.
Gal 5: 6 only thing that c is faith expressing

COURAGE* (COURAGEOUS)
Jos 2:11 everyone's c failed because of you.
5: 1 and they no longer had the c
2Sa 4: 1 he lost c, and all Israel became
7:27 So your servant has found c
1Ch 17:25 So your servant has found c to pray
2Ch 15: 8 son of Oded the prophet, he took c.
19:11 Act with c, and may the LORD be
Ezr 7:28 I took c and gathered leading men
10: 4 We will support you, so take c
Ps 107: 26 in their peril their c melted away.
Eze 22:14 Will your c endure or your hands
Da 11:25 and c against the king of the South.
Mt 14:27 said to them: "Take c!
Mk 6:50 spoke to them and said, "Take c!
Ac 4:13 When they saw the c of Peter
23:11 "Take c! As you have testified
27:22 now I urge you to keep up your c,
27:25 So keep up your c, men,
1Co 16:13 stand firm in the faith; be men of c;
Php 1:20 will have sufficient c so that now
Heb 3: 6 if we hold on to our c and the hope

COURAGEOUS* (COURAGE)

Dt 31: 6 Be strong and c.
    31: 7 of all Israel, "Be strong and c.
    31: 23 son of Nun: "Be strong and c.
Jos 1: 6 and c, because you will lead these
     1: 7 Be strong and very c.
     1: 9 commanded you? Be strong and c.
     1: 18 Only be strong and c!"
    10: 25 Be strong and c.
1Ch 22: 13 Be strong and c.
    28: 20 "Be strong and c, and do the work.
2Ch 26: 17 priest with eighty other c priests
    32: 7 with these words: "Be strong and c.

COURSE

Ps 19: 5 a champion rejoicing to run his c.
Pr   2: 8 for he guards the c of the just
    15: 21 of understanding keeps a straight c.
    16: 9 In his heart a man plans his c,
    17: 23 to pervert the c of justice.
Jas 3: 6 sets the whole c of his life on fire,

COURT (COURTS)

Pr 22: 22 and do not crush the needy in c,
    25: 8 do not bring hastily to c,
Mt   5: 25 adversary who is taking you to c.
1Co 4: 3 judged by you or by any human c;

COURTS (COURT)

Ps 84: 10 Better is one day in your c
    100:   4 and his c with praise;
Am   5: 15 maintain justice in the c.
Zec 8: 16 and sound judgment in your c.

COURTYARD

Ex 27: 9 "Make a c for the tabernacle.

COUSIN

Col 4: 10 as does Mark, the c of Barnabas.

COVENANT (COVENANTS)

Ge   9: 9 "I now establish my c with you
    17: 2 I will confirm my c between me
Ex 19: 5 if you obey me fully and keep my c,
    24: 7 Then he took the Book of the C
Dt   4: 13 declared to you his c, the Ten
    29: 1 in addition to the c he had made
Jdg 2: 1 'I will never break my c with you,
1Sa 23: 18 of them made a c before the LORD
1Ki 8: 21 in which is the c of the LORD that
     8: 23 you who keep your c of love
2Ki 23: 2 the words of the Book of the C,
1Ch 16: 15 He remembers his c forever,
2Ch 6: 14 you who keep your c of love
    34: 30 the words of the Book of the C,
Ne   1: 5 who keeps his c of love
Job 31: 1 "I made a c with my eyes
Ps 105: 8 He remembers his c forever,
Pr   2: 17 ignored the c she made before God
Isa 42: 6 you to be a c for the people
    61: 8 make an everlasting c with them.
Jer 11: 2 "Listen to the terms of this c
    31: 31 "when I will make a new c
    31: 32 It will not be like the c
    31: 33 "This is the c I will make
Eze 37: 26 I will make a c of peace with them;
Da   9: 27 He will confirm a c with many
Hos 6: 7 Like Adam, they have broken the c
Mal 2: 14 the wife of your marriage c.
     3: 1 of the c, whom you desire,
Mt 26: 28 blood of the c, which is poured out
Mk 14: 24 "This is my blood of the c,
Lk 22: 20 This cup is the new c in my blood,
1Co 11: 25 "This cup is the new c in my blood;
2Co 3: 6 as ministers of a new c—
Gal 4: 24 One c is from Mount Sinai
Heb 8: 6 as the c of which he is mediator is
     8: 8 when I will make a new c
     9: 15 Christ is the mediator of a new c,
    12: 24 to Jesus the mediator of a new c,

COVENANTS (COVENANT)

Ro   9: 4 theirs the divine glory, the c,
Gal 4: 24 for the women represent two c.

COVER (COVER-UP COVERED COVERING COVERINGS COVERS)

Ex 25: 17 "Make an atonement c of pure gold
    25: 21 Place the c on top of the ark
    33: 22 and c you with my hand
Lev 16: 2 in the cloud over the atonement c.
Ps 32: 5 and did not c up my iniquity.
    91: 4 He will c you with his feathers,
Hos 10: 8 say to the mountains, "C us!"

Lk 23: 30 and to the hills, "C us!"
1Co 11: 6 If a woman does not c her head,
    11: 6 shaved off, she should c her head.
    11: 7 A man ought not to c his head,
Jas 5: 20 and c over a multitude of sins.

COVER-UP* (COVER)

1Pe 2: 16 but do not use your freedom as a c

COVERED (COVER)

Ps 32: 1 whose sins are c.
    85: 2 and c all their sins.
Isa 6: 2 With two wings they c their faces,
    51: 16 c you with the shadow of my hand
Ro   4: 7 whose sins are c.
1Co 11: 4 with his head c dishonors his head.

COVERING (COVER)

1Co 11: 15 For long hair is given to her as a c.

COVERINGS (COVER)

Ge   3: 7 and made c for themselves.
Pr 31: 22 She makes c for her bed;

COVERS (COVER)

Pr 10: 12 but love c over all wrongs.
    17: 9 He who c over an offense promotes
2Co 3: 15 Moses is read, a veil c their hearts.
1Pe 4: 8 love c over a multitude of sins.

COVET* (COVETED COVETING COVETOUS)

Ex 20: 17 You shall not c your neighbor's
    20: 17 "You shall not c your neighbor's
    34: 24 and no one will c your land
Dt   5: 21 "You shall not c your neighbor's
     7: 25 Do not c the silver and gold
Mic 2: 2 They c fields and seize them,
Ro   7: 7 if the law had not said, "Do not c."
    13: 9 "Do not steal," "Do not c,"
Jas 4: 2 c, but you cannot have what you

COVETED* (COVET)

Jos 7: 21 weighing fifty shekels, I c them
Ac 20: 33 I have not c anyone's silver or gold

COVETING

Ro   7: 7 what c really was if the law

COVETOUS* (COVET)

Ro   7: 8 in me every kind of c desire.

COWARDLY*

Rev 21: 8 But the c, the unbelieving, the vile,

COWS

Ge 41: 2 of the river there came up seven c,
Ex 25: 5 skins dyed red and hides of sea c;
Nu   4: 6 are to cover this with hides of sea c,
1Sa 6: 7 Hitch the c to the cart.

CRAFTINESS* (CRAFTY)

Job 5: 13 He catches the wise in their c,
1Co 3: 19 "He catches the wise in their c";
Eph 4: 14 and c of men in their deceitful

CRAFTSMAN

Pr   8: 30 Then I was the c at his side.

CRAFTY* (CRAFTINESS)

Ge   3: 1 the serpent was more c than any
1Sa 23: 22 They tell me he is very c.
Job 5: 12 He thwarts the plans of the c,
     5: 5 you adopt the tongue of the c.
Pr   7: 10 like a prostitute and with c intent.
    12: 2 but the LORD condemns a c man.
    14: 17 and a c man is hated.
2Co 12: 16 c fellow that I am, I caught you

CRAVE* (CRAVED CRAVES CRAVING CRAVINGS)

Nu 11: 4 with them began to c other food,
Dt 12: 20 you c meat and say, "I would like
Pr 23: 3 Do not c his delicacies,
    23: 6 do not c his delicacies;
    31: 4 not for rulers to c beer,
Mic 7: 1 none of the early figs that I c.
1Pe 2: 2 newborn babies, c pure spiritual

CRAVED* (CRAVE)

Nu 11: 34 the people who had c other food.
Ps 78: 18 by demanding the food they c.
    78: 29 for he had given them what they c.
    78: 30 turned from the food they c,

CRAVES* (CRAVE)

Pr 13: 4 The sluggard c and gets nothing,
    21: 10 The wicked man c evil;
    21: 26 All day long he c for more.

CRAVING* (CRAVE)

Job 20: 20 he will have no respite from his c;
Ps 106: 14 In the desert they gave in to their c;
Pr 10: 3 but he thwarts the c of the wicked.
    13: 2 the unfaithful have a c for violence.
    21: 25 The sluggard's c will be the death
Jer 2: 24 sniffing the wind in her c—

CRAVINGS* (CRAVE)

Ps 10: 3 He boasts of the c of his heart;
Eph 2: 3 gratifying the c of our sinful nature
1Jn 2: 16 in the world—the c of sinful man,

CRAWL

Ge   3: 14 You will c on your belly

CREATE* (CREATED CREATES CREATING CREATION CREATOR)

Ps 51: 10 C in me a pure heart, O God,
Isa 4: 5 Then the LORD will c over all
    45: 7 I bring prosperity and c disaster;
    45: 7 I form the light and c darkness,
    45: 18 he did not c it to be empty,
    65: 17 "Behold, I will c / new heavens
    65: 18 for I will c Jerusalem to be a delight
    65: 18 forever in what I will c,
Jer 31: 22 The LORD will c a new thing
Mal 2: 10 one Father? Did not one God c us?
Eph 2: 15 His purpose was to c

CREATED* (CREATE)

Ge   1: 1 In the beginning God c the heavens
     1: 21 God c the great creatures of the sea
     1: 27 So God c man in his own image,
     1: 27 in the image of God he c him;
     1: 27 male and female he c them.
     2: 4 and the earth when they were c.
     5: 1 When God c man, he made him
     5: 2 He c them male and female
     5: 2 when they were c, he called them
     6: 7 whom I have c, from the face
Dt   4: 32 from the day God c man
Ps 89: 12 You c the north and the south;
    89: 47 what futility you have c all men!
    102: 18 a people not yet c may praise
    104: 30 you send your Spirit, / they are c,
    139: 13 For you c my inmost being;
    148:   5 for he commanded and they were c
Isa 40: 26 Who c all these?
    41: 20 that the Holy One of Israel has c it.
    42: 5 he who c the heavens and stretched
    43: 1 he who c you, O Jacob,
    43: 7 whom I c for my glory,
    45: 8 I, the LORD, have c it.
    45: 12 and c mankind upon it.
    45: 18 he who c the heavens,
    48: 7 They are c now, and not long ago;
    54: 16 And it is I who have c the destroyer
    54: 16 "See, it is I who c the blacksmith
    57: 16 the breath of man that I have c.
Eze 21: 30 In the place where you were c,
    28: 13 the day you were c they were
    28: 15 ways from the day you were c
Mk 13: 19 when God c the world, until now—
Ro   1: 25 and served c things rather
1Co 11: 9 neither was man c for woman,
Eph 2: 10 c in Christ Jesus to do good works,
     3: 9 hidden in God, who c all things.
     4: 24 c to be like God in true
Col 1: 16 For by him all things were c:
     1: 16 all things were c by him
     1: 16 which God c to be received
1Ti 4: 3 which God c to be received
     4: 4 For everything God c is good,
Heb 12: 27 c things—so that what cannot be
Jas 1: 18 a kind of firstfruits of all he c.
Rev 4: 11 and by your will they were c
     4: 11 for you c all things,
    10: 6 who c the heavens and all that is

CREATES* (CREATE)

Am   4: 13 c the wind,

CREATING* (CREATE)

Ge   2: 3 the work of c that he had done.
Isa 57: 19 c praise on the lips of the mourners.

CREATION* (CREATE)

Hab 2: 18 he who makes it trusts in his own c;
Mt 13: 35 hidden since the c of the world."

Mt 25:34 for you since the *c* of the world.
Mk 10: 6 of a God 'made them male
16:15 and preach the good news to all *c*.
Jn 17:24 me before the *c* of the world.
Ro 1:20 For since the *c* of the world God's
8:19 The *c* waits in eager expectation
8:20 For the *c* was subjected
8:21 in hope that the *c* itself will be
8:22 that the whole *c* has been groaning
8:39 depth, nor anything else in all *c*,
2Co 5:17 he is a new *c*; the old has gone,
Gal 6:15 anything, what counts is a new *c*.
Eph 1: 4 us in him before the *c* of the world
Col 1:15 God, the firstborn over all *c*.
Heb 4: 3 finished since the *c* of the world.
4:13 Nothing in all *c* is hidden
9:11 that is to say, not a part of this *c*.
9:26 times since the *c* of the world.
1Pe 1:20 chosen before the *c* of the world,
2Pe 3: 4 as it has since the beginning of *c*."
Rev 3:14 true witness, the ruler of God's *c*.
13: 8 slain from the *c* of the world.
17: 8 life from the *c* of the world will be

CREATOR* (CREATE)

Ge 14:19 *C* of heaven and earth.
14:22 God Most High, *C* of heaven
Dt 32: 6 Is he not your Father, your *C*,
Ecc 12: 1 Remember your *C*
Isa 27:11 and their *C* shows them no favor.
40:28 the *C* of the ends of the earth.
43:15 Israel's *C*, your King."
Mt 19: 4 the beginning the *C* 'made them—
Ro 1:25 created things rather than the *C*—
Col 3:10 in knowledge in the image of its *C*.
1Pe 4:19 themselves to their faithful *C*

CREATURE (CREATURES)

Lev 17:11 For the life of a *c* is in the blood,
17:14 the life of every *c* is its blood.
Ps 136:25 and who gives food to every *c*.
Eze 1:15 beside each *c* with its four faces.
Rev 4: 7 The first living *c* was like a lion,

CREATURES (CREATURE)

Ge 6:19 bring into the ark two of all living *c*,
8:21 again will I destroy all living *c*,
Ps 104:24 the earth is full of your *c*.
Eze 1: 5 was what looked like four living *c*.

CREDIT (CREDITED CREDITOR CREDITS)

Lk 6:33 what *c* is that to you? Even
Ro 4:24 to whom God will *c* righteousness
1Pe 2:20 it to your *c* if you receive a beating

CREDITED (CREDIT)

Ge 15: 6 and he *c* it to him as righteousness.
Ps 106:31 This was *c* to him as righteousness
Eze 18:20 of the righteous man will be *c*
Ro 4: 3 and it was *c* to him as righteousness.
4: 4 his wages are not *c* to him as a gift,
4: 5 his faith is *c* as righteousness.
4: 9 saying that Abraham's faith was *c*
4:23 The words "it was *c*
Gal 3: 6 and it was *c* to him as righteousness
Php 4:17 for what may be *c* to your account.
Jas 2:23 and it was *c* to him as righteousness

CREDITOR (CREDIT)

Dt 15: 2 Every *c* shall cancel the loan he has

CREDITS (CREDIT)

Ro 4: 6 whom God *c* righteousness apart

CRETANS (CRETE)

Tit 1:12 "*C* are always liars, evil brutes.

CRETE (CRETANS)

Ac 27:12 harbor in *C*, facing both southwest

CRIED (CRY)

Ex 2:23 groaned in their slavery and *c* out,
14:10 They were terrified and *c* out
Nu 20:16 but when we *c* out to the LORD,
Jos 24: 7 But you *c* to the LORD for help,
Jdg 3: 9 But when they *c* out to the LORD,
3:15 Again the Israelites *c* out
4: 3 they *c* to the LORD for help.
6: 6 the Israelites that they *c* out
10:12 Maonites oppressed you and you *c*
1Sa 7: 9 Samuel *c* out to the LORD
7:12 they *c* to the LORD for help,
12:10 They *c* out to the LORD and said,
Ps 18: 6 I *c* to my God for help.

CRIMINALS

Lk 23:32 both *c*, were also led out with him

CRIMSON

Isa 1:18 though they are red as *c*,
63: 1 with his garments stained *c*?

CRIPPLED

2Sa 9: 3 of Jonathan; he is *c* in both feet."
Mk 9:45 better for you to enter life *c*

CRISIS*

1Co 7:26 of the present *c*, I think that it is

CRITICISM*

2Co 8:20 We want to avoid any *c*

CROOKED*

Dt 32: 5 but a warped and *c* generation.
2Sa 22:27 to the *c* you show yourself shrewd.
Ps 18:26 to the *c* you show yourself shrewd.
125: 5 But those who turn to *c* ways
Pr 2:15 whose paths are *c*
5: 6 her paths are *c*, but she knows it
8: 8 none of them is *c* or perverse.
10: 9 he who takes *c* paths will be found
Ecc 7:13 what he has made *c*?
Isa 59: 8 have turned them into *c* roads;
La 3: 9 he has made my paths *c*.
Lk 3: 5 The *c* roads shall become straight,
Php 2:15 children of God without fault in a *c*

CROP (CROPS)

Mt 13: 8 where it produced a *c*—a hundred,
21:41 share of the *c* at harvest time."

CROPS (CROP)

Pr 3: 9 with the firstfruits of all your *c*;
10: 5 He who gathers *c* in summer is
28: 3 like a driving rain that leaves no *c*.
2Ti 2: 6 the first to receive a share of the *c*.

CROSS (CROSSED CROSSING)

Dt 4:21 swore that I would not *c* the Jordan
12:10 But you will *c* the Jordan
Mt 10:38 and anyone who does not take his *c*
16:24 and take up his *c* and follow me.
Mk 8:34 and take up his *c* and follow me.
Lk 9:23 take up his *c* daily and follow me.
14:27 anyone who does not carry his *c*
Jn 19:17 Carrying his own *c*, he went out
Ac 2:23 to death by nailing him to the *c*.
1Co 1:17 lest the *c* of Christ be emptied
1:18 the message of the *c* is foolishness.
Gal 5:11 offense of the *c* has been abolished.
6:12 persecuted for the *c* of Christ.
6:14 in the *c* of our Lord Jesus Christ,
Eph 2:16 both of them to God through the *c*,
Php 2: 8 even death on a *c*!
3:18 as enemies of the *c* of Christ.
Col 1:20 through his blood, shed on the *c*,
2:14 he took it away, nailing it to the *c*.
2:15 triumphing over them by the *c*.
Heb 12: 2 set before him endured the *c*,

CROSSED (CROSS)

Jos 4: 7 When it the Jordan, the waters
Jn 5:24 he has *c* over from death to life.

CROSSING (CROSS)

Ge 48:14 he was the younger, and *c* his arms,

CROSSROADS (ROAD)

Jer 6:16 "Stand at the *c* and look;

CROUCHING

Ge 4: 7 sin is *c* at your door; it desires

CROWD (CROWDS)

Ex 23: 2 Do not follow the *c* in doing wrong.

CROWDS (CROWD)

Mt 9:36 he saw the *c*, he had compassion

CROWED (CROWS)

Mt 26:74 the man!" Immediately a rooster *c*.

CROWN (CROWNED CROWNS)

Pr 4: 9 present you with a *c* of splendor."
10: 6 Blessings *c* the head
12: 4 noble character is her husband's *c*,
16:31 Gray hair is a *c* of splendor,
17: 6 Children's children are a *c*
Isa 35:10 everlasting joy will *c* their heads.

Isa 51:11 everlasting joy will *c* their heads.
61: 3 to bestow on them a *c* of beauty
62: 3 You will be a *c* of splendor
Eze 16:12 and a beautiful *c* on your head.
Zec 9:16 like jewels in a *c*.
Mt 27:29 and then twisted together a *c* of thorns
Mk 15:17 then twisted together a *c* of thorns
Jn 19: 2 The soldiers twisted together a *c*
19: 5 When Jesus came out wearing the *c*
1Co 9:25 it to get a *c* that will last forever.
9:25 it to get a *c* that will not last;
Php 4: 1 and long for, my joy and *c*,
1Th 2:19 or the *c* in which we will glory
2Ti 2: 5 he does not receive the victor's *c*
4: 8 store for me the *c* of righteousness,
Jas 1:12 he will receive the *c*
1Pe 5: 4 you will receive the *c*
Rev 2:10 and I will give you the *c* of life.
3:11 so that no one will take your *c*.
14:14 a son of man" with a *c* of gold

CROWNED* (CROWN)

Ps 8: 5 and *c* him with glory and honor.
Pr 14:18 the prudent are *c* with knowledge.
SS 3:11 crown with which his mother *c* him
Heb 2: 7 you *c* him with glory and honor
2: 9 now *c* with glory and honor

CROWNS (CROWN)

Ps 103: 4 and *c* me with love and compassion
149: 4 he *c* the humble with salvation.
Pr 11:26 blessing *c* him who is willing to sell.
Rev 4: 4 and had *c* of gold on their heads.
4:10 They lay their *c* before the throne
12: 3 ten horns and seven *c* on his heads.
19:12 and on his head are many *c*.

CROWS (CROWED)

Mt 26:34 this very night, before the rooster *c*

CRUCIFIED* (CRUCIFY)

Mt 20:19 to be mocked and flogged and *c*.
26: 2 of Man will be handed over to be *c*
27:26 and handed him over to be *c*.
27:35 When they had *c* him, they divided
27:38 Two robbers were *c* with him,
27:44 same way the robbers who were *c*
28: 5 looking for Jesus, who was *c*.
Mk 15:15 and handed him over to be *c*.
15:24 And they *c* him.
15:25 the third hour when they *c* him.
15:27 They *c* two robbers with him,
15:32 Those *c* with him also heaped
16: 6 for Jesus the Nazarene, who was *c*.
Lk 23:23 insistently demanded that he be *c*,
23:33 *c* him, along with the criminals—
24: 7 be *c* and on the third day be raised
24:20 sentenced to death, and they *c* him;
Jn 19:16 him over to them to be *c*.
19:18 Here they *c* him, and with him two
19:20 for the place where Jesus was *c* was
19:23 When the soldiers *c* Jesus,
19:32 of the first man who had been *c*
19:41 At the place where Jesus was *c*,
Ac 2:36 whom you *c*, both Lord and Christ
4:10 whom you *c* but whom God raised
Ro 6: 6 For we know that our old self was *c*
1Co 1:13 Is Christ divided? Was Paul *c*
1:23 but we preach Christ *c*: a stumbling
2: 2 except Jesus Christ and him *c*.
2: 8 they would not have *c* the Lord
2Co 13: 4 to be sure, he was *c* in weakness,
Gal 2:20 I have been *c* with Christ
3: 1 Christ was clearly portrayed as *c*.
5:24 Christ Jesus have *c* the sinful
6:14 which the world has been *c*
Rev 11: 8 where also their Lord was *c*.

CRUCIFY* (CRUCIFIED CRUCIFYING)

Mt 23:34 Some of them you will kill and *c*;
27:22 They all answered, "*C* him!" "Why
27:23 they shouted all the louder, "*C* him
27:31 Then they led him away to *c* him.
Mk 15:13 "*C* him!" they shouted.
15:14 they shouted all the louder, "*C* him
15:20 Then they led him out to *c* him.
Lk 23:21 they kept shouting, "*C* him! *C* him
Jn 19: 6 they shouted, "*C*! *C*!"
19: 6 "You take him and *c* him.
19:10 either to free you or to *c* you?"
19:15 Crucify him!" "Shall I *c* your king
19:15 away! Take him away! *C* him!"

CRUCIFYING* (CRUCIFY)

Heb 6: 6 to their loss they are c the Son

CRUSH (CRUSHED)

Ge 3: 15 he will c your head,
Isa 53: 10 it was the LORD's will to c him
Ro 16: 20 The God of peace will soon c Satan

CRUSHED (CRUSH)

Ps 34: 18 and saves those who are c in spirit.
Pr 17: 22 but a c spirit dries up the bones.
18: 14 but a c spirit who can bear?
Isa 53: 5 he was c for our iniquities;
2Co 4: 8 not c; perplexed, but not in despair;

CRY (CRIED)

Ex 2: 23 c for help because of their slavery
Ps 5: 2 Listen to my c for help,
34: 15 and his ears are attentive to their c;
40: 1 he turned to me and heard my c.
130: 1 Out of the depths I c to you,
Pr 21: 13 to the c of the poor,
La 2: 18 c out to the Lord.
Hab 2: 11 The stones of the wall will c out,
Lk 19: 40 keep quiet, the stones will c out.

CUNNING

2Co 11: 3 deceived by the serpent's c,
Eph 4: 14 and by the c and craftiness of men

CUP

Ps 23: 5 my c overflows.
Isa 51: 22 from that c, the goblet of my wrath,
51: 22 the c that made you stagger;
Mt 10: 42 if anyone gives even a c of cold water
20: 22 "Can you drink the c I am going
23: 25 You clean the outside of the c
23: 26 First clean the inside of the c
26: 27 Then he took the c, gave thanks
26: 39 may this c be taken from me.
26: 42 possible for this c to be taken away
Mk 9: 41 anyone who gives you a c of water
10: 38 "Can you drink the c I drink
10: 39 "You will drink the c I drink
14: 23 Then he took the c, gave thanks
14: 36 Take this c from me.
Lk 11: 39 Pharisees clean the outside of the c
22: 17 After taking the c, he gave thanks
22: 20 after the supper he took the c,
22: 20 "This c is the new covenant
22: 42 if you are willing, take this c
Jn 18: 11 I not drink the c the Father has
1Co 10: 16 Is not the c of thanksgiving
10: 21 the c of the Lord and the c
11: 25 after supper he took the c, saying,
11: 25 "This c is the new covenant

CUPBEARER

Ge 40: 1 the c and the baker of the king
Ne 1: 11 I was c to the king.

CURE (CURED)

Jer 17: 9 and beyond c.
30: 15 your pain that has no c?
Hos 5: 13 But he is not able to c you,
Lk 9: 1 out all demons and to c diseases.

CURED (CURE)

Mt 11: 5 those who have leprosy are c,
Lk 6: 18 troubled by evil spirits were c,

CURSE (ACCURSED CURSED CURSES CURSING)

Ge 4: 11 Now you are under a c
8: 21 "Never again will I c the ground
12: 3 and whoever curses you I will c;
Dt 11: 26 before you today a blessing and a c
11: 28 the c if you disobey the commands
21: 23 hung on a tree is under God's c.
23: 5 turned the c into a blessing for you,
Job 1: 11 he will surely c you to your face.
2: 5 he will surely c you to your face."
2: 9 C God and die!" He replied,
Ps 109: 28 They may c, but you will bless;
Pr 3: 33 The LORD's c is on the house
24: 24 peoples will c him and nations
Mal 2: 2 and I will c your blessings.
Lk 6: 28 bless those who c you, pray
Ro 12: 14 persecute you; bless and not c.
Gal 3: 10 on observing the law are under a c,
3: 13 of the law by becoming a c for us,
Jas 3: 9 with it we c men, who have been
Rev 22: 3 No longer will there be any c.

CURSED (CURSE)

Ge 3: 17 "C is the ground because of you;
Dt 27: 15 "C is the man who carves an image
27: 16 "C is the man who dishonors his
27: 17 "C is the man who moves his
27: 18 "C is the man who leads the blind
27: 19 C is the man who withholds justice
27: 20 "C is the man who sleeps
27: 21 "C is the man who has sexual
27: 22 "C is the man who sleeps
27: 23 "C is the man who sleeps
27: 24 "C is the man who kills his
27: 25 "C is the man who accepts a bribe
27: 26 "C is the man who does not uphold
Jer 17: 5 "C is the one who trusts in man,
Mal 1: 14 "C is the cheat who has
Ro 9: 3 I could wish that I myself were c
1Co 4: 12 When we are c, we bless;
12: 3 "Jesus be c," and no one can say,
Gal 3: 10 "C is everyone who does not
3: 13 C is everyone who is hung on a tree

CURSES (CURSE)

Ex 21: 17 "Anyone who c his father
Lev 20: 9 " 'If anyone c his father or mother,
Nu 5: 23 is to write these c on a scroll
Jos 8: 34 the blessings and the c—just
Pr 20: 20 If a man c his father or mother,
28: 27 to them receives many c.
Mt 15: 4 and 'Anyone who c his father
Mk 7: 10 and, 'Anyone who c his father

CURSING (CURSE)

Ps 109: 18 He wore c as his garment;
Ro 3: 14 "Their mouths are full of c
Jas 3: 10 the same mouth come praise and c.

CURTAIN

Ex 26: 31 "Make a c of blue, purple
26: 33 The c will separate the Holy Place
Mt 27: 51 At that moment the c
Mk 15: 38 The c of the temple was torn in two
Lk 23: 45 the c of the temple was torn in two.
Heb 6: 19 the inner sanctuary behind the c,
9: 3 Behind the second c was a room
10: 20 opened for us through the c,

CUSTOM

Job 1: 5 This was Job's regular c.
Mk 10: 1 and as was his c, he taught them.
Lk 4: 16 into the synagogue, as was his c.
Ac 17: 2 As his c was, Paul went

CUT

Lev 19: 27 " 'Do not c the hair at the sides
21: 5 of their beards or c their bodies.
1Ki 3: 25 "C the living child in two
Isa 51: 1 to the rock from which you were c
53: 8 For he was c off from the land
Da 2: 45 of the rock c out of a mountain,
9: 26 the Anointed One will be c off
Mt 3: 10 not produce good fruit will be c
24: 22 If those days had not been c short,
1Co 11: 6 for a woman to have her hair c

CYMBAL* (CYMBALS)

1Co 13: 1 a resounding gong or a clanging c.

CYMBALS (CYMBAL)

1Ch 15: 16 instruments: lyres, harps and c,
2Ch 5: 12 dressed in fine linen and playing c,
Ps 150: 5 praise him with resounding c.

CYRUS

Persian king who allowed exiles to return (2Ch 36:22-Ezr 1:8), to rebuild temple (Ezr 5: 13-6:14), as appointed by the LORD (Isa 44:28-45:13).

DAGON

Jdg 16: 23 offer a great sacrifice to D their god
1Sa 5: 2 Dagon's temple and set it beside D.

DAMASCUS

Ac 9: 3 As he neared D on his journey,

DAN

1. Son of Jacob by Bilhah (Ge 30:4-6; 35:25; 46:23). Tribe of blessed (Ge 49:16-17; Dt 33:22), numbered (Nu 1:39; 26:43), allotted land (Jos 19:40-48; Eze 48:1), failed to fully possess (Jdg 1:34-35), failed to support Deborah (Jdg 5:17), possessed Laish/Dan (Jdg 18).

2. Northernmost city in Israel (Ge 14:14; Jdg 18; 20:1).

DANCE (DANCED DANCING)

Ecc 3: 4 a time to mourn and a time to d,
Mt 11: 17 and you did not d;

DANCED (DANCE)

2Sa 6: 14 d before the LORD
Mk 6: 22 of Herodias came in and d,

DANCING (DANCE)

Ps 30: 11 You turned my wailing into d;
149: 3 Let them praise his name with d

DANGER

Pr 22: 3 A prudent man sees d
27: 12 The prudent see d and take refuge,
Mt 5: 22 will be in d of the fire of hell.
Ro 8: 35 famine or nakedness or d or sword?
2Co 11: 26 I have been in d from rivers,

DANIEL

1. Hebrew exile to Babylon, name changed to Belteshazzar (Da 1:6-7). Refused to eat unclean food (Da 1:8-21). Interpreted Nebuchadnezzar's dreams (Da 2; 4), writing on the wall (Da 5). Thrown into lion's den (Da 6). Visions of (Da 7-12).

2. Son of David (1Ch 3:1).

DARIUS

1. King of Persia (Ezr 4:5), allowed rebuilding of temple (Ezr 5-6).

2. Mede who conquered Babylon (Da 5:31).

DARK (DARKENED DARKENS DARKNESS)

Job 34: 22 There is no d place, no deep
Ps 18: 9 d clouds were under his feet;
Pr 31: 15 She gets up while it is still d;
SS 1: 6 Do not stare at me because I am d,
Jn 12: 35 in the d does not know where he is
Ro 2: 19 a light for those who are in the d,
2Pe 1: 19 as to a light shining in a d place,

DARKENED (DARK)

Joel 2: 10 the sun and moon are d,
Mt 24: 29 " 'the sun will be d,
Ro 1: 21 and their foolish hearts were d.
Eph 4: 18 They are d in their understanding

DARKENS (DARK)

Job 38: 2 "Who is this that d my counsel

DARKNESS (DARK)

Ge 1: 2 d was over the surface of the deep.
1: 4 he separated the light from the d.
Ex 10: 22 and total d covered all Egypt
20: 21 approached the thick d where God
2Sa 22: 29 the LORD turns my d into light.
Ps 18: 28 my God turns my d into light.
91: 6 the pestilence that stalks in the d,
112: 4 Even in d light dawns
139: 12 even the d will not be dark to you;
Pr 4: 19 the way of the wicked is like deep d
Isa 5: 20 and light for d,
42: 16 I will turn the d into light
45: 7 I form the light and create d,
58: 10 then your light will rise in the d,
61: 1 and release from d,
Joel 2: 31 The sun will be turned to d
Mt 4: 16 the people living in d
6: 23 how great is that d! "No one can
Lk 11: 34 are bad, your body also is full of d.
23: 44 and d came over the whole land
Jn 1: 5 The light shines in the d,
3: 19 but men loved d instead of light
Ac 2: 20 The sun will be turned to d
2Co 4: 6 who said, "Let light shine out of d
6: 14 fellowship can light have with d?
Eph 5: 8 For you were once d, but now you
5: 11 to do with the fruitless deeds of d,
1Pe 2: 9 out of d into his wonderful light.
2Pe 2: 17 Blackest d is reserved for them.
1Jn 1: 5 in him there is no d at all.
2: 9 but hates his brother is still in the d.
Jude 6 in d, bound with everlasting chains
13 for whom blackest d has been

DASH

Ps 2: 9 you will d them to pieces like

DAUGHTER (DAUGHTERS)

Ex 1: 10 she took him to Pharaoh's d
Jdg 11: 48 to commemorate the d of Jephthah
Est 2: 7 Mordecai had taken her as his own d

DAUGHTERS

Ps   9: 14 praises in the gates of the D of Zion
      137:   8 O D of Babylon, doomed
Isa   62: 11 "Say to the D of Zion,
Zec   9:   9 Shout, D of Jerusalem!
Mk   5: 34 "D, your faith has healed you.
         7: 29 the demon has left your d.

DAUGHTERS (DAUGHTER)

Ge   6:   2 the d of men were beautiful,
       19: 36 Lot's d became pregnant
Nu   36: 10 Zelophehad's d did as the LORD
Joel   2: 28 sons and d will prophesy,

DAVID

        Son of Jesse (Ru 4:17-22; 1Ch 2:13-15), an-
cestor of Jesus (Mt 1:1-17; Lk 3:31). Wives and
children (1Sa 18; 25:39-44; 2Sa 3:2-5; 5:13-16;
11:27; 1Ch 3:1-9).
        Anointed king by Samuel (1Sa 16:1-13). Mu-
sician to Saul (1Sa 16:14-23; 18:10). Killed Goliath (1Sa 17). Relation with Jonathan (1Sa 18:
1-4; 19-20; 23:16-18; 2Sa 1). Disfavor of Saul
(1Sa 18:6-23:29). Spared Saul's life (1Sa 24;
26). Among Philistines (1Sa 21:10-14; 27-30).
Lament for Saul and Jonathan (2Sa 1).
        Anointed king of Judah (2Sa 2:1-11). Conflict
with house of Saul (2Sa 2-4). Anointed king of
Israel (2Sa 5:1-4; 1Ch 11:1-3). Conquered Jerusalem (2Sa 5:6-10; 1Ch 11:4-9). Brought ark to
Jerusalem (2Sa 6; 1Ch 13; 15-16). The LORD
promised eternal dynasty (2Sa 7; 1Ch 17; Ps
132). Showed kindness to Mephibosheth (2Sa
9). Adultery with Bathsheba, murder of Uriah
(2Sa 11-12). Son Amnon raped daughter Tamar;
killed by Absalom (2Sa 13). Absalom's revolt
(2Sa 14-17); death (2Sa 18). Sheba's revolt (2Sa
20). Victories: Philistines (2Sa 5:17-25; 1Ch 14:
8-17; 2Sa 21:15-22; 1Ch 20:4-8), Ammonites
(2Sa 10; 1Ch 19), various (2Sa 8; 1Ch 18).
Mighty men (2Sa 23:8-39; 1Ch 11-12). Punished
for numbering army (2Sa 24; 1Ch 21). Appointed Solomon king (1Ki 1:28-2:9). Prepared for
building of temple (1Ch 22-29). Last words (2Sa
23:1-7). Death (1Ki 2:10-12; 1Ch 29:28).
        Psalmist (Mt 22:43-45), musician (Am 6:5),
prophet (2Sa 23:2-7; Ac 1:16; 2:30).
        Psalms of: 2 (Ac 4:25), 3-32, 34-41, 51-65,
68-70, 86, 95 (Heb 4:7), 101, 103, 108-110, 122,
124, 131, 133, 138-145.

DAWN (DAWNED DAWNS)

Ps   37:   6 your righteousness shine like the d,
Pr   4: 18 is like the first gleam of d,
Isa   14: 12 O morning star, son of the d!
Am   4: 13 he who turns d to darkness,
         5:   8 who turns blackness into d

DAWNED (DAWN)

Isa   9:   2 a light has d.
Mt   4: 16 a light has d."

DAWNS* (DAWN)

Ps   65:   8 where morning d and evening
      112:   4 in darkness light d for the upright,
Hos 10: 15 When that day d,
2Pe   1: 19 until the day d and the morning

DAY (DAYS)

Ge   1:   5 God called the light "d,"
         1:   5 and there was morning—the first d
         1:   8 there was morning—the second d.
         1: 13 there was morning—the third d.
         1: 19 there was morning—the fourth d.
         1: 23 there was morning—the fifth d.
         1: 31 there was morning—the sixth d.
         2:   2 so on the seventh d he rested
         8: 22 d and night
Ex   16: 30 the people rested on the seventh d.
       20:   8 "Remember the Sabbath d
Lev   16: 30 on this d atonement will be made
       23: 28 because it is the D of Atonement,
Nu   14: 14 before them in a pillar of cloud by d
Jos   1:   8 meditate on it d and night,
2Ki   7:   9 This is a d of good news
       25: 30 D by d the king gave Jehoiachin
1Ch 16: 23 proclaim his salvation d after d.
Ne   8: 18 D after d, from the first d
Ps   84: 10 Better is one d in your courts
       96:   2 proclaim his salvation d after d.
      118: 24 This is the d the LORD has made;
Pr   27:   1 not know what a d may bring forth.
Isa   13:   9 a cruel d, with wrath and fierce
Jer   46: 10 But that d belongs to the Lord,
       50: 31 "for your d has come,
Eze   30:   2 "Alas for that d!"
Joel   1: 15 "Alas for that d!

Joel   2: 31 and dreadful d of the LORD.
Am   3: 14 On the d I punish Israel for her sins
         5: 20 Will not the d of the LORD be
Ob   15 "The d of the LORD is near
Zep   1: 14 The great d of the LORD is near—
Zec   2: 11 joined with the LORD in that d
       14:   1 A d of the LORD is coming
       14:   7 It will be a unique d,
Mal   4:   5 dreadful d of the LORD comes.
Mt   24: 38 up to the d Noah entered the ark;
Lk   11:   3 Give us each d our daily bread.
       17: 24 in his d will be like the lightning,
Ac   5: 42 D after d, in the temple courts
       17: 11 examined the Scriptures every d
       17: 17 as in the marketplace d by d
Ro   14:   5 man considers every d alike.
1Co   5:   5 his spirit saved on the d of the Lord
2Co   4: 16 we are being renewed d by d
       11: 25 I spent a night and a d
1Th   5:   2 for you know very well that the d
         5:   4 so that this d should surprise you
2Th   2:   2 saying that the d of the Lord has
Heb   7: 27 need to offer sacrifices d after d,
2Pe   3:   8 With the Lord a d is like
         3: 10 of the Lord will come like a thief.
Rev   6: 17 For the great d of their wrath has
       16: 14 on the great d of God Almighty.

DAYS (DAY)

Dt   17: 19 he is to read it all the d of his life
       32:   7 Remember the d of old;
Ps   6:   6 all the d of my life,
       34: 12 and desires to see many good d,
       39:   5 have made my d a mere
       90: 10 The length of our d is seventy years
       90: 12 Teach us to number our d aright,
      103: 15 As for man, his d are like grass,
      128:   5 all the d of your life;
Pr   31: 12 all the d of her life.
Ecc   9:   9 all the d of this meaningless life
       12:   1 Creator in the d of your youth,
Isa   38: 20 all the d of our lives
Da   7:   9 and the Ancient of D took his seat.
         7: 13 He approached the Ancient of D
         7: 22 until the Ancient of D came
Hos   3:   5 and to his blessings in the last d.
Joel   2: 29 I will pour out my Spirit in those d.
Mic   4:   1 In the last d
Lk   19: 43 The d will come upon you
Ac   2: 17 by the prophet Joel: " 'In the last d,
2Ti   3:   1 will be terrible times in the last d.
Heb   1:   2 in these last d he has spoken to us
2Pe   3:   3 that in the last d scoffers will come,

DAZZLING*

Da   2: 31 statue, awesome in appearance.
Mk   9:   3 His clothes became d white.

DEACON* (DEACONS)

1Ti   3: 12 A d must be the husband of

DEACONS* (DEACON)

Php   1:   1 together with the overseers and d:
1Ti   3:   8 D, likewise, are to be men worthy
         3: 10 against them, let them serve as d.

DEAD (DIE)

Lev   17: 15 who eats anything found d
Dt   18: 11 or spiritist or who consults the d
Isa   8: 19 Why consult the d on behalf
Mt   8: 22 and let the d bury their own d."
       28:   7 'He has risen from the d
Lk   15: 24 For this son of mine was d
       24: 46 rise from the d on the third day,
Ro   16: 10 count yourselves d to sin
1Co 15: 29 do who are baptized for the d?
Eph   2:   1 you were d in your transgressions
1Th   4: 16 and the d in Christ will rise first.
Jas   2: 17 is not accompanied by action, is d
         2: 26 so faith without deeds is d
Rev   14: 13 Blessed are the d who die
       20: 12 And I saw the d, great and small,

DEADENED* (DIE)

Jn   12: 40 and d their hearts,

DEAR* (DEARER)

2Sa   1: 26 you were very d to me.
Ps   102: 14 For her stones are d
Jer   31: 20 Is not Ephraim my d son,
Jn   2:   4 "D woman, why do you involve me
       19: 26 he said to his mother, "D woman,
Ac   15: 25 to you with our d friends Barnabas
Ro   16:   5 Greet my d friend Epenetus.
       16:   9 in Christ, and my d friend Stachys.

Ro   16: 12 Greet my d friend Persis, another
1Co   4: 14 but to warn you, as my d children.
       10: 14 my d friends, flee from idolatry.
       15: 58 Therefore, my d brothers,
2Co   7:   1 we have these promises, d friends,
       12: 19 and everything we do, d friends,
Gal   4: 19 My d children, for whom I am
Eph   6: 21 the d brother and faithful servant
Php   2: 12 my d friends, as you have always
         4:   1 firm in the Lord, d friends!
Col   1:   7 Epaphras, our d fellow servant,
         4:   7 He is a d brother, a faithful
         4:   9 our faithful and d brother,
         4: 14 Our d friend Luke, the doctor,
1Th   2:   8 because you had become so d to us.
1Ti   6:   2 their service are believers, and d
2Ti   1:   2 To Timothy, my d son: Grace,
Phm   1 To Philemon our d friend
           : 16 He is very d to me but
           : 16 better than a slave, as a d brother.
Heb   6:   9 we speak like this, d friends,
Jas   1: 16 Don't be deceived, my d brothers.
         1: 19 My d brothers, take note of this:
         2:   5 thoughts? Listen, my d brothers:
1Pe   2: 11 D friends, I urge you, as aliens
         4: 12 D friends, do not be surprised
2Pe   3:   1 D friends, this is now my second
         3:   8 not forget this one thing, d friends:
         3: 14 d friends, since you are looking
         3: 15 just as our d brother Paul
         3: 17 d friends, since you already know
1Jn   2:   1 My d children, I write this to you
         2:   7 D friends, I am not writing you
         2: 12 I write to you, d children,
         2: 13 I write to you, d children,
         2: 18 D children, this is the last hour;
         2: 28 d children, continue in him,
         3:   2 D friends, now we are children
         3:   7 D children, do not let anyone lead
         3: 18 love of God be in him? D children,
         3: 21 D friends, if our hearts do not
         4:   1 D friends, do not believe every
         4:   4 d children, are from God
         4:   7 D friends, let us love one another,
         4: 11 D friends, since God so loved us,
         5: 21 D children, keep yourselves
2Jn   : 5 d lady, I am not writing you a new
3Jn   : 1 The elder, To my d friend Gaius,
           : 2 D friend, I pray that you may enjoy
           : 5 D friend, you are faithful
           : 11 D friend, do not imitate what is evil
Jude   : 3 D friends, although I was very
           : 17 But, d friends, remember what
           : 20 d friends, build yourselves up

DEARER* (DEAR)

Phm   : 16 dear to me but even d to you.

DEATH (DIE)

Ex   21: 12 kills him shall surely be put to d.
Nu   35: 16 the murderer shall be put to d.
Dt   30: 19 set before you life and d,
Ru   1: 17 if anything but d separates you
2Ki   4: 40 O man of God, there is d in the pot
Job   26:   6 D is naked before God;
Ps   23:   4 the valley of the shadow of d,
       44: 22 for your sake we face d all day long
       89: 48 What man can live and not see d,
      116: 15 is the d of his saints.
Pr   8: 36 all who hate me love d."
       11: 19 he who pursues evil goes to his d.
       14: 12 but in the end it leads to d.
       15: 11 D and Destruction lie open
       16: 25 but in the end it leads to d.
       18: 21 tongue has the power of life and d,
       19: 18 do not be a willing party to his d.
       23: 14 and save his soul from d.
Ecc   7:   2 for d is the destiny of every man;
Isa   25:   8 he will swallow up d forever.
       53: 12 he poured out his life unto d,
Eze   18: 23 pleasure in the d of the wicked?
       18: 32 pleasure in the d of anyone,
       33: 11 pleasure in the d of the wicked,
Hos   13: 14 Where, O d, are your plagues?
Jn   5: 24 he has crossed over from d to life.
Ro   4: 25 delivered over to d for our sins
         5: 12 and in this way d came to all men,
         5: 14 d reigned from the time of Adam
         6:   3 Jesus were baptized into his d?
         6: 23 For the wages of sin is d,
         7: 24 me from this body of d?
         8: 13 put to death the misdeeds of the body,
         8: 36 your sake we face d all day long;
1Co 15: 21 For since d came through a man,
       15: 26 The last enemy to be destroyed is d

1Co 15:55 Where, O *d*, is your sting?"
2Ti 1:10 who has destroyed *d* and has
Heb 2:14 him who holds the power of *d*—
1Jn 5:16 There is a sin that leads to *d*.
Rev 1:18 And I hold the keys of *d* and Hades
   2:11 hurt at all by the second *d*.
   20: 6 The second *d* has no power
  20:14 The lake of fire is the second *d*.
  20:14 Then *d* and Hades were thrown
  21: 4 There will be no more *d*
  21: 8 This is the second *d*."

DEBAUCHERY*

Ro 13:13 not in sexual immorality and *d*,
2Co 12:21 and *d* in which they have indulged.
Gal 5:19 impurity and *d*; idolatry
Eph 5:18 drunk on wine, which leads to *d*.
1Pe 4: 3 living in *d*, lust, drunkenness,

DEBORAH*

1. Prophetess who led Israel to victory over Canaanites (Jdg 4-5).
2. Rebekah's nurse (Ge 35:8).

DEBT* (DEBTOR DEBTORS DEBTS)

Dt 15: 3 must cancel any *d* your brother
  24: 6 the upper one—as security for a *d*,
1Sa 22: 2 or in *d* or discontented gathered
Job 24: 9 of the poor is seized for a *d*.
Mt 18:25 that he had be sold to repay the *d*.
  18:27 canceled the *d* and let him go.
  18:30 into prison until he could pay the *d*.
  18:32 'I canceled all that *d* of yours
Lk 7:43 who had the bigger *d* canceled."
Ro 13: 8 Let no *d* remain outstanding,
  13: 8 continuing *d* to love one another,

DEBTOR* (DEBT)

Isa 24: 2 for *d* as for creditor.

DEBTORS* (DEBT)

Hab 2: 7 Will not your *d* suddenly arise?
Mt 6:12 as we also have forgiven our *d*.
Lk 16: 5 called in each one of his master's *d*.

DEBTS* (DEBT)

Dt 15: 1 seven years you must cancel *d*.
  15: 2 time for canceling *d* has been
  15: 9 the year for canceling *d*, is near,"
  31:10 in the year for canceling *d*,
2Ki 4: 7 "Go, sell the oil and pay your *d*.
Ne 10:31 the land and will cancel all *d*.
Pr 22:26 or puts up security for *d*;
Mt 6:12 Forgive us our *d*,
Lk 7:42 so he canceled the *d* of both.

DECAY*

Ps 16:10 will you let your Holy One see *d*.
  49: 9 and not see *d*.
  49:14 their forms will *d* in the grave.
Pr 12: 4 a disgraceful wife is like *d*
Isa 5:24 so their roots will *d*
Hab 3:16 *d* crept into my bones.
Ac 2:27 will you let your Holy One see *d*.
  2:31 to the grave, nor did his body see *d*.
  13:34 never to *d*, is stated in these words:
  13:35 will not let your Holy One see *d*.'
  13:37 raised from the dead did not see *d*.
Ro 8:21 liberated from its bondage to *d*

DECEIT (DECEIVE)

Ps 5: 9 with their tongue they speak *d*.
Isa 53: 9 nor was any *d* in his mouth.
Da 8:25 He will cause *d* to prosper.
Zep 3:13 nor will *d* be found in their mouths.
Mk 7:22 greed, malice, *d*, lewdness, envy,
Ac 13:10 You are full of all kinds of *d*
Ro 1:29 murder, strife, *d* and malice.
  3:13 their tongues practice *d*."
1Pe 2: 1 yourselves of all malice and all *d*,
  2:22 and no *d* was found in his mouth."

DECEITFUL (DECEIVE)

Jer 17: 9 The heart is *d* above all things
Hos 10: 2 Their heart is *d*,
2Co 11:13 men are false apostles, *d* workmen,
Eph 4:14 of men in their *d* scheming.
  4:22 is being corrupted by its *d* desires;
1Pe 3:10 and his lips from *d* speech.
Rev 21:27 who does what is shameful or *d*,

DECEITFULNESS* (DECEIVE)

Ps 119:118 for their *d* is in vain.
Mt 13:22 and the *d* of wealth choke it,
Mk 4:19 the *d* of wealth and the desires

DECEIVE (DECEIT DECEITFUL DECEITFULNESS DECEIVED DECEIVER DECEIVERS DECEIVES DECEIVING DECEPTION DECEPTIVE)

Lev 19:11 " 'Do not *d* one another.
Pr 14: 5 A truthful witness does not *d*,
  24:28 or use your lips to *d*.
Jer 37: 9 Do not *d* yourselves, thinking,
Zec 13: 4 garment of hair in order to *d*.
Mt 24: 5 'I am the Christ,' and will *d* many.
  24:11 will appear and *d* many people.
  24:24 and miracles to *d* even the elect—
Mk 13: 6 'I am he,' and will *d* many.
  13:22 and miracles to *d* the elect—
Ro 16:18 and flattery they *d* the minds
1Co 3:18 Do not *d* yourselves.
Eph 5: 6 Let no one *d* you with empty words
Col 2: 4 this so that no one may *d* you
2Th 2: 3 Don't let anyone *d* you in any way,
Jas 1:22 to the word, and so *d* yourselves.
1Jn 1: 8 we *d* ourselves and the truth is not
Rev 20: 8 and will go out to *d* the nations

DECEIVED (DECEIVE)

Ge 3:13 "The serpent *d* me, and I ate."
Lk 21: 8 "Watch out that you are not *d*.
1Co 6: 9 the kingdom of God? Do not be *d*:
2Co 11: 3 Eve was *d* by the serpent's cunning
Gal 6: 7 Do not be *d*: God cannot be
1Ti 2:14 And Adam was not the one *d*;
2Ti 3:13 to worse, deceiving and being *d*.
Tit 3: 3 *d* and enslaved by all kinds
Jas 1:16 Don't be *d*, my dear brothers.
Rev 13:14 he *d* the inhabitants of the earth.
  20:10 And the devil, who *d* them,

DECEIVER (DECEIVE)

Mt 27:63 while he was still alive that *d* said,
2Jn 7 Any such person is the *d*

DECEIVERS* (DECEIVE)

Ps 49: 5 when wicked *d* surround me—
Tit 1:10 and *d*, especially those
2Jn 7 Many *d*, who do not acknowledge

DECEIVES (DECEIVE)

Pr 26:19 is a man who *d* his neighbor
Mt 24: 4 "Watch out that no one *d* you.
Mk 13: 5 "Watch out that no one *d* you.
Gal 6: 3 when he is nothing, he *d* himself.
2Th 2:10 sort of evil that *d* those who are
Jas 1:26 he *d* himself and his religion is

DECEIVING* (DECEIVE)

Lev 6: 2 by *d* his neighbor about something
1Ti 4: 1 follow *d* spirits and things taught
2Ti 3:13 go from bad to worse, *d*
Rev 20: 3 him from *d* the nations anymore

DECENCY* (DECENTLY)

1Ti 2: 9 women to dress modestly, with *d*.

DECENTLY* (DECENCY)

Ro 13:13 Let us behave *d*, as in the daytime.

DECEPTION (DECEIVE)

Pr 14: 8 but the folly of fools is *d*.
  26:26 His malice may be concealed by *d*,
Mt 27:64 This last *d* will be worse
2Co 4: 2 we do not use *d*, nor do we distort

DECEPTIVE (DECEIVE)

Pr 11:18 The wicked man earns *d* wages,
  31:30 Charm is *d*, and beauty is fleeting;
Jer 7: 4 Do not trust in *d* words and say,
Col 2: 8 through hollow and *d* philosophy,

DECIDED (DECISION)

2Co 9: 7 man should give what he has *d*

DECISION (DECIDED)

Ex 28:29 heart on the breastpiece of *d*
Joel 3:14 multitudes in the valley of *d*!

DECLARE (DECLARED DECLARING)

1Ch 16:24 *D* his glory among the nations,
Ps 19: 1 The heavens *d* the glory of God;
  96: 3 *D* his glory among the nations,
Isa 42: 9 and new things I *d*;

DECLARED (DECLARE)

Mk 7:19 Jesus *d* all foods "clean.")
Ro 2:13 the law who will be *d* righteous.

Ro 3:20 no one will be *d* righteous

DECLARING (DECLARE)

Ps 71: 8 *d* your splendor all day long.
Ac 2:11 we hear them *d* the wonders

DECREE (DECREED DECREES)

Ex 15:25 There the LORD made a *d*
1Ch 16:17 He confirmed it to Jacob as a *d*,
Ps 2: 7 I will proclaim the *d* of the LORD:
  7: 6 Awake, my God; *d* justice.
  81: 4 this is a *d* for Israel.
  148: 6 he gave a *d* that will never pass
Da 4:24 and this is the *d* the Most High has
Lk 2: 1 Augustus issued a *d* that a census
Ro 1:32 know God's righteous *d* that those

DECREED (DECREE)

Ps 78: 5 He *d* statutes for Jacob
Jer 40: 2 LORD your God *d* this disaster
La 3:37 happen if the Lord has not *d* it?
Da 9:24 "Seventy 'sevens' are *d*
  9:26 and desolations have been *d*.
Lk 22:22 Son of Man will go as it has been *d*,

DECREES (DECREE)

Ge 26: 5 my commands, my *d* and my laws
Ex 15:26 to his commands and keep all his *d*,
  18:16 inform them of God's *d* and laws."
  18:20 Teach them the *d* and laws.
Lev 10:11 Israelites all the *d* the LORD has
  18: 4 and be careful to follow my *d*.
  18: 5 Keep my *d* and laws,
  18:26 you must keep my *d* and my laws.
Ps 119:12 teach me your *d*.
  119:16 I delight in your *d*;
  119: 48 and I meditate on your *d*.
  119:112 My heart is set on keeping your *d*

DEDICATE (DEDICATED DEDICATION)

Nu 6:12 He must *d* himself to the LORD
Pr 20:25 for a man to *d* something rashly

DEDICATED (DEDICATE)

Lev 21:12 he has been *d* by the anointing oil
Nu 6: 9 thus defiling the hair he has *d*,
  6:18 shave off the hair that he *d*,
  18: 6 *d* to the LORD to do the work
1Ki 8:63 and all the Israelites *d* the temple
2Ch 29:31 "You have now *d* yourselves
Ne 3: 1 They *d* it and set its doors in place,

DEDICATION (DEDICATE)

Nu 6:19 shaved off the hair of his *d*,
Jn 10:22 came the Feast of *D* at Jerusalem.
1Ti 5:11 sensual desires overcome their *d*

DEED (DEEDS)

Jer 32:10 and sealed the *d*, had it witnessed,
  32:16 After I had given the *d* of purchase
Col 3:17 you do, whether in word or *d*,
2Th 2:17 and strengthen you in every good *d*

DEEDS (DEED)

Dt 3:24 or on earth who can do the *d*
  4:34 or by great and awesome *d*,
  34:12 the awesome *d* that Moses
1Sa 2: 3 and by him *d* are weighed.
1Ch 16:24 his marvelous *d* among all peoples.
Job 34:25 Because he takes note of their *d*,
Ps 26: 7 and telling of all your wonderful *d*.
  45: 4 right hand display awesome *d*.
  65: 5 with awesome *d* of righteousness,
  66: 3 "How awesome are your *d*!
  71:17 day I declare your marvelous *d*.
  72:18 who alone does marvelous *d*.
  73:28 I will tell of all your *d*.
  75: 1 men tell of your wonderful *d*.
  77:11 I will remember the *d* of the LORD
  77:12 and consider all your mighty *d*.
  78: 4 the praiseworthy *d* of the LORD,
  78: 7 and would not forget his *d*
  86: 8 no *d* can compare with yours.
  86:10 you are great and do marvelous *d*;
  88:12 or your righteous *d* in the land
  90:16 May your *d* be shown
  92: 4 For you make me glad by your *d*,
  96: 3 his marvelous *d* among all peoples.
  107: 8 and his wonderful *d* for men,
  107:15 and his wonderful *d* for men,
  107:21 and his wonderful *d* for men,
  107:24 his wonderful *d* in the deep.
  107:31 and his wonderful *d* for men.
  111: 3 Glorious and majestic are his *d*,
  145: 6 and I will proclaim your great *d*.

DEEP

Jer 32:19 purposes and mighty are your *d.*
Hab 3: 2 I stand in awe of your *d,* O LORD.
Mt 5:16 that they may see your good *d*
Lk 1:51 He has performed mighty *d*
23:41 we are getting what our *d* deserve.
Ac 26:20 prove their repentance by their *d.*
1Ti 6:18 rich in good *d,* and to be generous
Heb 10:24 on toward love and good *d.*
Jas 2:14 claims to have faith but has no *d?*
2:18 Show me your faith without *d,*
2:20 faith without *d* is useless?
2:26 so faith without *d* is dead.
1Pe 2:12 they may see your good *d*
Rev 2:19 I know your *d,* your love and faith,
2:23 each of you according to your *d.*
3: 1 I know your *d;* you have
3: 2 I have not found your *d* complete
3: 8 I know your *d.*
3:15 I know your *d,* that you are neither
14:13 for their *d* will follow them."
15: 3 "Great and marvelous are your *d,*

DEEP (DEPTH DEPTHS)

Ge 1: 2 was over the surface of the *d.*
8: 2 Now the springs of the *d*
Ps 42: 7 *D* calls to *d.*
Lk 5: 4 to Simon, "Put out into *d* water,
1Co 2:10 all things, even the *d* things
1Ti 3: 9 hold of the *d* truths of the faith

DEER

Ps 42: 1 As the *d* pants for streams of water,

DEFAMED*

Isa 48:11 How can I let myself be *d?*

DEFEATED

1Co 6: 7 have been completely *d* already.

DEFEND (DEFENDED DEFENDER DEFENDING DEFENDS DEFENSE)

Ps 72: 4 He will *d* the afflicted
74:22 Rise up, O God, and *d* your cause;
82: 2 "How long will you *d* the unjust
82: 3 *D* the cause of the weak
119:154 *D* my cause and redeem me;
Pr 31: 9 *d* the rights of the poor and needy
Isa 1:17 *D* the cause of the fatherless.
1:23 They do not *d* the cause
Jer 5:28 they do not *d* the rights of the poor.
50:34 He will vigorously *d* their cause

DEFENDED

Jer 22:16 He *d* the cause of the poor

DEFENDER (DEFEND)

Ex 22: 2 the *d* is not guilty of bloodshed;
Ps 68: 5 to the fatherless, a *d* of widows,
Pr 23:11 for their *D* is strong;

DEFENDING (DEFEND)

Ps 10:18 *d* the fatherless and the oppressed,
Ro 2:15 now accusing, now even *d* them.)
Php 1: 7 or *d* and confirming the gospel,

DEFENDS (DEFEND)

Dt 10:18 He *d* the cause of the fatherless
33: 7 With his own hands he *d* his cause.
Isa 51:22 your God, who *d* his people:

DEFENSE (DEFEND)

Ps 35:23 Awake, and rise to my *d!*
Php 1:16 here for the *d* of the gospel.
1Jn 2: 1 speaks to the Father in our *d—*

DEFERRED*

Pr 13:12 Hope *d* makes the heart sick.

DEFIED

1Sa 17:45 armies of Israel, whom you have *d.*
1Ki 13:26 the man of God who *d* the word

DEFILE (DEFILED)

Da 1: 8 Daniel resolved not to *d* himself
Rev 14: 4 are those who did not *d* themselves

DEFILED (DEFILE)

Isa 24: 5 The earth is *d* by its people;

DEFRAUD

Lev 19:13 Do not *d* your neighbor or rob him.
Mk 10:19 do not *d,* honor your father

DEITY*

Col 2: 9 of the *D* lives in bodily form,

DELAY

Ecc 5: 4 vow to God, do not *d* in fulfilling it.
Isa 48: 9 my own name's sake I *d* my wrath;
Heb 10:37 is coming and will come and will not *d.*
Rev 10: 6 and said, "There will be no more *d!*

DELICACIES

Ps 141: 4 let me not eat of their *d.*
Pr 23: 3 Do not crave his *d,*
23: 6 do not crave his *d;*

DELICIOUS*

Pr 9:17 food eaten in secret is *d!"*

DELIGHT* (DELIGHTED DELIGHTFUL DELIGHTING DELIGHTS)

Lev 26:31 and I will take no *d* in the pleasing
Dt 30: 9 The LORD will again *d* in you
1Sa 15:22 for I *d* in your deliverance.
15:22 "Does the LORD *d*
Ne 1:11 the prayer of your servants who *d*
Job 22:26 Surely then you will find *d*
27:10 Will he find *d* in the Almighty?
Ps 1: 2 But his *d* is in the law of the LORD
16: 3 in whom is all my *d.*
35: 9 and in his salvation.
35:27 those who *d* in my vindication
37: 4 *D* yourself in the LORD
43: 4 to God, my joy and my *d.*
51:16 You do not *d* in sacrifice,
51:19 whole burnt offerings to *d* you;
62: 4 they take *d* in lies.
68:30 Scatter the nations who *d* in war.
111: 2 by all who *d* in them.
112: 1 who finds great *d* in his commands.
119:16 I *d* in your decrees;
119:24 Your statutes are my *d;*
119:35 for there I find *d.*
119:47 for I *d* in your commands
119:70 but I *d* in your law.
119:77 for your law is my *d.*
119:92 If your law had not been my *d,*
119:143 but your commands are my *d.*
119:174 and your law is my *d.*
147:10 nor his *d* in the legs of a man;
149: 4 For the LORD takes *d*
Pr 1:22 How long will mockers *d*
2:14 who *d* in doing wrong
8:30 I was filled with *d* day after day,
11: 1 but accurate weights are his *d.*
29:17 he will bring *d* to your soul.
Ecc 2:10 My heart took *d* in all my work,
SS 1: 4 We rejoice and *d* in you;
3: 1 to sit in his shade.
Isa 5: 7 are the garden of his *d.*
11: 3 he will *d* in the fear of the LORD.
13:17 and have no *d* in gold.
32:14 the *d* of donkeys, a pasture
42: 1 my chosen one in whom I *d;*
55: 2 and your soul will *d* in the richest
58:13 if you call the Sabbath a *d*
61:10 I *d* greatly in the LORD;
62: 4 for the LORD will take *d* in you,
65:18 for I will create Jerusalem to be a *d*
65:19 and take *d* in my people;
66: 3 their souls *d* in their abominations;
66:11 *d* in her overflowing abundance."
Jer 9:24 for in these I *d,"*
15:16 they were my joy and my heart's *d,*
31:20 the child in whom I *d?*
49:25 the town in which I *d?*
Eze 24:16 away from you the *d* of your eyes.
24:21 in which you take pride, the *d*
24:25 and glory, the *d* of their eyes,
Hos 7: 3 *d* the king with their wickedness,
Mic 1:16 for the children in whom you *d;*
7:18 but *d* to show mercy.
Zep 3:17 He will take great *d* in you,
Mt 12:18 the one I love, in whom I *d;*
Mk 12:37 large crowd listened to him with *d.*
Lk 1:14 He will be a joy and *d* to you,
Ro 7:22 in my inner being I *d* in God's law;
1Co 13: 6 Love does not *d* in evil
2Co 12:10 for Christ's sake, I *d* in weaknesses,
Col 2: 5 and *d* to see how orderly you are

DELIGHTED (DELIGHT)

2Sa 22:20 he rescued me because he *d* in me.
1Ki 10: 9 who has *d* in you and placed you
2Ch 9: 8 who has *d* in you and placed you
Ps 18:19 he rescued me because he *d* in me.
Lk 13:17 but the people were *d* with all

DELIGHTFUL* (DELIGHT)

Ps 16: 6 surely I have a *d* inheritance.
SS 1: 2 for your love is more *d* than wine.
4:10 How *d* is your love, my sister,
Mal 3:12 for yours will be a *d* land,"

DELIGHTING* (DELIGHT)

Pr 8:31 and *d* in mankind.

DELIGHTS (DELIGHT)

Est 6: 6 for the man the king *d* to honor?"
Ps 22: 8 since he *d* in him."
35:27 who *d* in the well-being
36: 8 from your river of *d.*
37:23 if the LORD *d* in a man's way
147:11 the LORD *d* in those who fear him,
Pr 3:12 as a father the son he *d* in.
10:23 of understanding *d* in wisdom.
11:20 he *d* in those whose ways are
12:22 but he *d* in men who are truthful.
14:35 A king *d* in a wise servant,
18: 2 but *d* in airing his own opinions.
23:24 he who has a wise son *d* in him.
Col 2:18 Do not let anyone who *d*

DELILAH*

Woman who betrayed Samson (Jdg 16:4-22).

DELIVER (DELIVERANCE DELIVERED DELIVERER DELIVERS)

Dt 32:39 and no one can *d* out of my hand.
Ps 22: 8 Let him *d* him,
72:12 For he will *d* the needy who cry out
79: 9 *d* us and forgive our sins
109: 21 of the goodness of your love, *d* me.
119:170 *d* me according to your promise.
Mt 6:13 but *d* us from the evil one.'
2Co 1:10 hope that he will continue to *d* us.

DELIVERANCE (DELIVER)

1Sa 2: 1 for I delight in your *d.*
Ps 3: 8 From the LORD comes *d.*
32: 7 and surround me with songs of *d.*
33:17 A horse is a vain hope for *d;*
Ob : 17 But on Mount Zion will be *d;*

DELIVERED (DELIVER)

Ps 34: 4 he *d* me from all my fears.
107: 6 and he *d* them from their distress.
116: 8 have *d* my soul from death,
Da 12: 1 written in the book—will be *d.*
Ro 4:25 He was *d* over to death for our sins

DELIVERER* (DELIVER)

Jdg 3: 9 for them a *d,* Othniel son of Kenaz,
3:15 and he gave them a *d*—Ehud,
2Sa 22: 2 is my rock, my fortress and my *d;*
2Ki 13: 5 The LORD provided a *d* for Israel,
Ps 18: 2 is my rock, my fortress and my *d;*
40:17 You are my help and my *d;*
70: 5 You are my help and my *d;*
140: 7 O Sovereign LORD, my strong *d,*
144: 2 my stronghold and my *d,*
Ac 7:35 sent to be their ruler and *d*
Ro 11:26 "The *d* will come from Zion;

DELIVERS (DELIVER)

Ps 34:17 he *d* them from all their troubles.
34:19 but the LORD *d* him from them all
37:40 The LORD helps them and *d* them.
37:40 he *d* them from the wicked

DELUSION*

2Th 2:11 God sends them a powerful *d*

DEMAND (DEMANDED)

Lk 6:30 belongs to you, do not *d* it back.

DEMANDED (DEMAND)

Lk 12:20 This very night your life will be *d*
12:48 been given much, much will be *d;*

DEMETRIUS

Ac 19:24 A silversmith named *D,* who made

DEMON* (DEMONS)

Mt 9:33 And when the *d* was driven out,
11:18 and they say, 'He has a *d.'*
17:18 Jesus rebuked the *d,* and it came
Mk 7:26 to drive the *d* out of her daughter.
7:29 the *d* has left your daughter."
7:30 lying on the bed, and the *d* gone.
Lk 4:33 there was a man possessed by a *d,*
4:35 Then the *d* threw the man

DEMON-POSSESSED (cont.)

Lk   7:33 wine, and you say, 'He has a *d.*'
     8:29 driven by the *d* into solitary places.
     9:42 the *d* threw him to the ground
  11:14 When the *d* left, the man who had
  11:14 was driving out a *d* that was mute.
Jn   8:49 "I am not possessed by a *d.*"
  10:21 Can a *d* open the eyes of the blind
  10:21 sayings of a man possessed by a *d.*

DEMON-POSSESSED* (DEMON-POSSESSION)

Mt   4:24 those suffering severe pain, the *d,*
    8:16 many who were *d* were brought
    8:28 two *d* men coming
    8:33 what had happened to the *d* men.
    9:32 man who was *d* and could not talk
  12:22 they brought him a *d* man who was
Mk   1:32 brought to Jesus all the sick and *d.*
    5:16 what had happened to the *d* man—
    5:18 the man who had been *d* begged
Lk   8:27 met by a *d* man from the town.
    8:36 the people how the *d* man had been
Jn   7:20 "You are *d,*" the crowd answered.
    8:48 that you are a Samaritan and *d?*"
    8:52 "Now we know that you are *d!*
  10:20 Many of them said, "He is *d*
Ac 19:13 Jesus over those who were *d.*

DEMON-POSSESSION* (DEMON-POSSESSED)

Mt 15:22 is suffering terribly from *d.*"

DEMONS* (DEMON)

Dt 32:17 to *d,* which are not God—
Ps .106:37 and their daughters to *d.*
Mt   7:22 and in your name drive out *d*
    8:31 *d* begged Jesus, "If you drive us
    9:34 prince of *d* that he drives out *d.*"
  10: 8 who have leprosy, drive out *d,*
  12:24 of *d,* that this fellow drives out
  12:24 that this fellow drives out *d.*"
  12:27 And if I drive out *d* by Beelzebub,
  12:28 if I drive out *d* by the Spirit of God,
Mk   1:34 He also drove out many *d,*
    1:34 but he would not let the *d* speak
    1:39 their synagogues and driving out *d.*
    3:15 to have authority to drive out *d.*
    3:22 the prince of *d* he is driving out *d.*"
    5:12 The *d* begged Jesus, "Send us
    5:15 possessed by the legion of *d,*
    6:13 They drove out many *d*
    9:38 "we saw a man driving out *d*
  16: 9 out of whom he had driven seven *d*
  16:17 In my name they will drive out *d;*
Lk   4:41 *d* came out of many people,
    8: 2 from whom seven *d* had come out;
    8:30 because many *d* had gone into him.
    8:32 The *d* begged Jesus to let them go
    8:33 When the *d* came out of the man,
    8:35 from whom the *d* had gone out,
    8:38 from whom the *d* had gone out
    9: 1 and authority to drive out all *d*
    9:49 "we saw a man driving out *d*
  10:17 the *d* submit to us in your name."
  11:15 the prince of *d,* he is driving out *d.*"
  11:18 you claim that I drive out *d*
  11:19 Now if I drive out *d* by Beelzebub,
  11:20 if I drive out *d* by the finger of God,
  13:32 'I will drive out *d* and heal people
Ro   8:38 neither angels nor *d,* neither
1Co 10:20 of pagans are offered to *d,*
  10:20 you to be participants with *d.*
  10:21 of the Lord and the cup of *d* too;
  10:21 the Lord's table and the table of *d.*
1Ti   4: 1 spirits and things taught by *d.*
Jas   2:19 Good! Even the *d* believe that—
Rev   9:20 they did not stop worshiping *d,*
  16:14 of *d* performing miraculous signs,
  18: 2 She has become a home for *d*

DEMONSTRATE* (DEMONSTRATES DEMONSTRATION)

Ro   3:25 He did this to *d* his justice,
    3:26 he did it to *d* his justice

DEMONSTRATES* (DEMONSTRATE)

Ro   5: 8 God *d* his own love for us in this:

DEMONSTRATION* (DEMONSTRATE)

1Co   2: 4 but with a *d* of the Spirit's power,

DEN

Da   6:16 and threw him into the lions' *d.*
Mt 21:13 you are making it a '*d* of robbers.' "
Mk 11:17 you have made it 'a *d* of robbers.' "

Lk 19:46 but you have made it 'a *d* of robbers

DENARII* (DENARIUS)

Mt 18:28 who owed him a hundred *d.*
Lk   7:41 One owed him five hundred *d,*

DENARIUS (DENARII)

Mt 20: 2 agreed to pay them a *d* for the day
Mk 12:15 Bring me a *d* and let me look at it."

DENIED (DENY)

Mt 26:70 But he *d* it before them all.
Mk 14:68 But he *d* it.
Lk 22:57 But he *d* it.
Jn 18:25 He *d* it, saying, "I am not."
1Ti   5: 8 he has *d* the faith and is worse
Rev   3: 8 my word and have not *d* my name.

DENIES (DENY)

1Jn 2:22 It is the man who *d* that Jesus is
    2:23 No one who *d* the Son has

DENY (DENIED DENIES DENYING)

Ex 23: 6 "Do not *d* justice to your poor
Job 27: 5 till I die, I will not *d* my integrity.
Isa   5:23 but *d* justice to the innocent.
La   3:35 to *d* a man his rights
Am   2: 7 and *d* justice to the oppressed.
Mt 16:24 he must *d* himself and take up his
Mk   8:34 he must *d* himself and take up his
Lk   9:23 he must *d* himself and take up his
  22:34 you will *d* three times that you
Ac   4:16 miracle, and we cannot *d* it.
Tit   1:16 but by their actions they *d* him.
Jas   3:14 do not boast about it or *d* the truth.
Jude   4 *d* Jesus Christ our only Sovereign

DENYING* (DENY)

Eze 22:29 mistreat the alien, *d* them justice.
2Ti   3: 5 a form of godliness but *d* its power.
2Pe   2: 1 *d* the sovereign Lord who bought

DEPART (DEPARTED DEPARTS DEPARTURE)

Ge 49:10 The scepter will not *d* from Judah,
Job   1:21 and naked I will *d.*
Mt 25:41 '*D* from me, you who are cursed,
Php   1:23 I desire to *d* and be with Christ,

DEPARTED (DEPART)

1Sa   4:21 "The glory has *d* from Israel"—
Ps 119:102 I have not *d* from your laws,

DEPARTS (DEPART)

Ecc   5:15 and as he comes, so he *d.*

DEPARTURE (DEPART)

Lk   9:31 spoke about his *d,* which he was
2Ti   4: 6 and the time has come for my *d.*
2Pe   1:15 after my *d* you will always be able

DEPEND

Ps 62: 7 My salvation and my honor *d*

DEPOSES*

Da   2:21 he sets up kings and *d* them.

DEPOSIT

Mt 25:27 money on *d* with the bankers,
Lk 19:23 didn't you put my money on *d,*
2Co   1:22 put his Spirit in our hearts as a *d.*
    5: 5 and has given us the Spirit as a *d,*
Eph   1:14 who is a *d* guaranteeing our
2Ti   1:14 Guard the good *d* that was

DEPRAVED* (DEPRAVITY)

Eze 16:47 ways you soon became more *d*
  23:11 and prostitution she was more *d*
Ro   1:28 he gave them over to a *d* mind,
Php   2:15 fault in a crooked and *d* generation,
2Ti   3: 8 oppose the truth—men of *d* minds.

DEPRAVITY* (DEPRAVED)

Ro   1:29 of wickedness, evil, greed and *d*
2Pe   2:19 they themselves are slaves of *d*—

DEPRIVE

Dt 24:17 Do not *d* the alien or the fatherless
Pr 18: 5 or to *d* the innocent of justice.
  31: 5 *d* all the oppressed of their rights.
Isa 10: 2 to *d* the poor of their rights
  29:21 with false testimony *d* the innocent
La   3:36 to *d* a man of justice—
1Co   7: 5 Do not *d* each other
    9:15 die than have anyone *d* me

DEPTH (DEEP)

Ro   8:39 any powers, neither height nor *d,*
  11:33 the *d* of the riches of the wisdom

DEPTHS (DEEP)

Ps 130: 1 Out of the *d* I cry to you, O LORD;

DERIDES*

Pr 11:12 who lacks judgment *d* his neighbor,

DERIVES*

Eph   3:15 in heaven and on earth *d* its name.

DESCEND (DESCENDED DESCENDING)

Ro 10: 7 "or 'Who will *d* into the deep?' "

DESCENDED (DESCEND)

Eph   4: 9 except that he also *d* to the lower,
Heb   7:14 For it is clear that our Lord *d*

DESCENDING (DESCEND)

Ge 28:12 of God were ascending and *d* on it.
Mt   3:16 the Spirit of God *d* like a dove
Mk   1:10 and the Spirit *d* on him like a dove.
Jn   1:51 and *d* on the Son of Man."

DESECRATING*

Ne 13:17 you are doing—*d* the Sabbath day?
  13:18 against Israel by *d* the Sabbath."
Isa 56: 2 who keeps the Sabbath without *d* it
  56: 6 who keep the Sabbath without *d* it
Eze 44: 7 *d* my temple while you offered me

DESERT

Nu 32:13 wander in the *d* forty years,
Dt   8:16 He gave you manna to eat in the *d,*
  29: 5 years that I led you through the *d,*
Ne   9:19 you did not abandon them in the *d.*
Ps 78:19 "Can God spread a table in the *d?*
  78:52 led them like sheep through the *d.*
Pr 21:19 Better to live in a *d*
Isa 32: 2 like streams of water in the *d*
  32:15 and the *d* becomes a fertile field,
  35: 6 and streams in the *d.*
  43:20 because I provide water in the *d*
Mk   1: 3 "a voice of one calling in the *d,*
    1:13 and he was in the *d* forty days,
Rev 12: 6 fled into the *d* to a place prepared

DESERTED (DESERTS)

Ezr   9: 9 our God has not *d* us
Mt 26:56 all the disciples *d* him and fled.
2Ti   1:15 in the province of Asia has *d* me,

DESERTING (DESERTS)

Gal   1: 6 are so quickly *d* the one who called

DESERTS (DESERTED DESERTING)

Zec 11:17 who *d* the flock!

DESERVE* (DESERVED DESERVES)

Ge 40:15 to *d* being put in a dungeon."
Lev 26:21 times over, as your sins *d.*
Jdg 20:10 it can give them what they *d.*
1Sa 26:16 you and your men *d* to die.
1Ki   2:26 You *d* to die, but I will not put you
Ps 28: 4 bring back upon them what they *d.*
  94: 2 pay back to the proud what they *d*
  103:10 he does not treat us as our sins *d*
Pr   3:27 from those who *d* it,
Ecc   8:14 men who get what the righteous *d*
    8:14 men who get what the wicked *d,*
Isa 66: 6 repaying his enemies all they *d*
Jer 14:16 out on them the calamity they *d.*
  17:10 according to what his deeds *d.*"
  21:14 I will punish you as your deeds *d,*
  32:19 to his conduct and as his deeds *d.*"
  49:12 "If those who do not *d*
La   3:64 Pay them back what they *d,*
Eze 16:59 I will deal with you as you *d,*
Zec   1: 6 to us what our ways and practices *d.*
Mt   8: 8 I do not *d* to have you come
  22: 8 those I invited did not *d* to come
Lk   7: 6 for I do not *d* to have you come
  23:15 he has done nothing to *d* death.
  23:41 for we are getting what our deeds *d*
Ro   1:32 those who do such things *d* death,
1Co   9: 5 even *d* to be called an apostle,
  16:18 Such men *d* recognition.
2Co 11:15 end will be what their actions *d.*
Rev 16: 6 blood to drink as they *d.* "

DESERVED* (DESERVE)

2Sa 19:28 descendants *d* nothing

Ezr   9:13 less than our sins have *d*
Job 33:27 but I did not get what I *d*.
Ac   23:29 charge against him that *d* death
Ro   3: 8 Their condemnation is *d*.

DESERVES* (DESERVE)

Nu 35:31 the life of a murderer, who *d* to die.
Dt   25: 2 If the guilty man *d* to be beaten,
      25: 2 the number of lashes his crime *d*,
Jdg   9:16 and if you have treated him as he *d*
2Sa 12: 5 the man who did this to die!
Job 34:11 upon him what his conduct *d*.
Jer 51: 6 he will pay her what she *d*.
Lk   7: 4 "This man *d* to have you do this,
      10: 7 for the worker *d* his wages.
Ac 26:31 is not doing anything that *d* death
1Ti   1:15 saying that *d* full acceptance:
       4: 9 saying that *d* full acceptance
      5:18 and "The worker *d* his wages."
Heb 10:29 severely do you think a man *d*

DESIGNATED

Lk   6:13 also *d* apostles: Simon (whom he
Heb 5:10 and was by God to be high priest

DESIRABLE* (DESIRE)

Ge   3: 6 and also *d* for gaining wisdom,
Pr 22: 1 A good name is more *d*
Jer   3:19 and give you a *d* land,

DESIRE* (DESIRABLE DESIRED DESIRES)

Ge   3:16 Your *d* will be for your husband,
Dt   5:21 You shall not set your *d*
1Sa 9:20 to whom is all the *d* of Israel turned
2Sa 19:38 anything you *d* from me I will do
      23: 5 and grant me my every *d*?
1Ch 29:18 keep this *d* in the hearts
2Ch 1:11 "Since this is your heart's *d*
       9: 8 and his *d* to uphold them forever,
Job 13: 3 But I *d* to speak to the Almighty
      21:14 We have no *d* to know your ways.
Ps 10:17 O LORD, the *d* of the afflicted;
      20: 4 May he give you the *d*
      21: 2 You have granted him the *d*
      27:12 me over to the *d* of my foes,
      40: 6 Sacrifice and offering you did not *d*
      40: 8 I *d* to do your will, O my God;
      40:14 may all who *d* my ruin
      41: 2 him to the *d* of his foes.
      51: 6 Surely you *d* truth
      70: 2 may all who *d* my ruin
      73:25 earth has nothing I *d* besides you
Pr   3:15 nothing you *d* can compare
      8:11 and nothing you *d* can compare
    10:24 what the righteous *d* will be
    11:23 The *d* of the righteous ends only
    12:12 The wicked *d* the plunder
    17:16 since he has no *d* to get wisdom?
    24: 1 do not *d* their company;
Ecc 12: 5 and *d* no longer is stirred.
SS   6:12 my *d* set me among the royal
      7:10 and his *d* is for me.
Isa 26: 8 are the *d* of our hearts.
      53: 2 appearance that we should *d* him.
      55:11 but will accomplish what I *d*
Eze 24:25 delight of their eyes, their heart's *d*,
Hos 6: 6 For I *d* mercy, not sacrifice,
Mic 7: 3 the powerful dictate what they *d*—
Mal 3: 1 whom you *d*, will come," says
Mt   9:13 learn what this means: 'I *d* mercy,
    12: 7 what these words mean, 'I *d* mercy.
Jn   8:44 want to carry out your father's *d*.
Ro   7: 8 in me every kind of covetous *d*.
      7:18 For I have the *d* to do what is good,
      9:16 depend on man's *d* or effort,
    10: 1 my heart's *d* and prayer to God
1Co 12:31 But eagerly *d* the greater gifts.
    14: 1 and eagerly *d* spiritual gifts,
2Co 8:10 but also to have the *d* to do so.
      8:13 Our *d* is not that others might be
Php 1:23 I *d* to depart and be with Christ,
Heb 10: 5 Sacrifice and offering you did not *d*
    10: 8 and sin offerings you did not *d*,
    13:18 *d* to live honorably in every way.
Jas   1:14 by his own evil *d*, he is dragged
      1:15 Then, after *d* has conceived,
2Pe 2:10 of those who follow the corrupt *d*

DESIRED (DESIRE)

Hag 2: 7 and the *d* of all nations will come,
Lk 22:15 "I have eagerly *d* to eat this

DESIRES* (DESIRE)

Ge   4: 7 at your door; it *d* to have you,
    41:16 will give Pharaoh the answer he *d*."

2Sa 3:21 rule over all that your heart *d*."
1Ki 11:37 rule over all that your heart *d*;
Job 17:11 and so are the *d* of my heart.
    31:16 "If I have denied the *d* of the poor
Ps 34:12 and *d* to see many good days,
    37: 4 he will give you the *d* of your heart.
   103: 5 who satisfies your *d* with good things,
   140: 8 do not grant the wicked their *d*.
   145:16 satisfy the *d* of every living thing.
   145:19 He fulfills the *d* of those who fear
Pr 11: 6 the unfaithful are trapped by evil *d*.
    13: 4 *d* of the diligent are fully satisfied.
    19:22 What a man *d* is unfailing love;
Ecc 6: 2 so that he lacks nothing his heart *d*,
SS   2: 7 or awaken love / until it so *d*.
      3: 5 or awaken love / until it so *d*.
      8: 4 or awaken love / until it so *d*.
Hab 2: 5 his *d* are not upright—
Mk   4:19 and the *d* for other things come in
Ro   1:24 over in the sinful *d* of their hearts
      6:12 body so that you obey its evil *d*.
      8: 5 set on what that nature *d*;
      8: 5 set on what the Spirit *d*.
    13:14 to gratify the *d* of the sinful nature.
Gal 5:16 and you will not gratify the *d*
      5:17 the sinful nature *d* what is contrary
      5:24 nature with its passions and *d*.
Eph 2: 3 and following its *d* and thoughts.
      4:22 being corrupted by its deceitful *d*;
Col   3: 5 impurity, lust, evil *d* and greed,
1Ti   3: 1 an overseer, he *d* a noble task.
      5:11 their sensual *d* overcome their
      6: 9 and harmful *d* that plunge men
2Ti   2:22 Flee the evil *d* of youth,
      3: 6 are swayed by all kinds of evil *d*,
      4: 3 Instead, to suit their own *d*,
Jas   1:20 about the righteous life that God *d*.
      4: 1 from your *d* that battle within you?
1Pe 1:14 conform to the evil *d* you had
      2:11 to abstain from sinful *d*, which war
      4: 2 of his earthly life for evil human *d*,
2Pe 1: 4 in the world caused by evil *d*.
      2:18 the lustful *d* of sinful human
      3: 3 and following their own evil *d*.
1Jn 2:17 The world and its *d* pass away,
Jude   :16 they follow their own evil *d*;
       :18 will follow their own ungodly *d*."

DESOLATE (DESOLATION)

Isa 54: 1 are the children of the *d* woman
Gal   4:27 are the children of the *d* woman

DESOLATION (DESOLATE)

Da 11:31 up the abomination that causes *d*.
    12:11 abomination that causes *d* is set up,
Mt 24:15 'the abomination that causes *d*,'

DESPAIR (DESPAIRED)

Isa 61: 3 instead of a spirit of *d*.
2Co 4: 8 perplexed, but not in *d*; persecuted,

DESPAIRED* (DESPAIR)

2Co 1: 8 ability to endure, so that we *d*

DESPERATE*

2Sa 12:18 He may do something *d*."
Ps   60: 3 have shown your people *d* times;
    79: 8 for we are in *d* need.
   142: 6 for I am in *d* need;

DESPISE (DESPISED DESPISES)

2Sa 12: 9 Why did you *d* the word
Job 5:17 so do not *d* the discipline
    36: 5 God is mighty, but does not *d* men;
    42: 6 Therefore I *d* myself
Ps   51:17 O God, you will not *d*.
   102:17 he will not *d* their plea.
Pr   1: 7 but fools *d* wisdom and discipline.
      3:11 do not *d* the LORD's discipline
      6:30 Men do not *d* a thief if he steals
    23:22 do not *d* your mother
Jer 14:21 of your name do not *d* us;
Am   5:10 and *d* him who tells the truth.
      5:21 "I hate, I *d* your religious feasts;
Mt   6:24 devoted to the one and *d* the other.
Lk 16:13 devoted to the one and *d* the other.
1Co 11:22 Or do you *d* the church of God
Tit   2:15 Do not let anyone *d* you.
2Pe 2:10 of the sinful nature and *d* authority.

DESPISED (DESPISE)

Ge 25:34 So Esau *d* his birthright.
Ps 22: 6 by men and *d* by the people
Pr 12: 8 but men with warped minds are *d*.
Isa 53: 3 He was *d* and rejected by men,

Isa 53: 3 he was *d*, and we esteemed him not
1Co 1:28 of this world and the *d* things—

DESPISES (DESPISE)

Pr 14:21 He who *d* his neighbor sins,
    15:20 but a foolish man *d* his mother.
    15:32 who ignores discipline *d* himself,
Zec 4:10 "Who *d* the day of small things?

DESTINED (DESTINY)

Lk   2:34 "This child is *d* to cause the falling
1Co 2: 7 and that God *d* for our glory
Col   2:22 These are all *d* to perish with use,
1Th 3: 3 know quite well that we were *d*
Heb 9:27 Just as man is *d* to die once,
1Pe 2: 8 which is also what they were *d* for.

DESTINY* (DESTINED PREDESTINED)

Job 8:13 Such is the *d* of all who forget God;
Ps 73:17 then I understood their final *d*.
Ecc 7: 2 for death is the *d* of every man;
      9: 2 share a common *d*—the righteous
      9: 3 the sun: The same *d* overtakes all.
Isa 65:11 and fill bowls of mixed wine for *D*,
Php 3:19 Their *d* is destruction, their god is

DESTITUTE

Ps 102:17 to the prayer of the *d*;
Pr 31: 8 for the rights of all who are *d*.
Heb 11:37 *d*, persecuted and mistreated—

DESTROY (DESTROYED DESTROYING DESTROYS DESTRUCTION DESTRUCTIVE)

Ge   6:17 floodwaters on the earth to *d* all life
      9:11 will there be a flood to *d* the earth."
Pr   1:32 complacency of fools will *d* them;
Mt 10:28 of the One who can *d* both soul
Mk 14:58 'I will *d* this man-made temple
Lk   4:34 to *d* us? I know who you are—
Jn 10:10 only to steal and kill and *d*;
Ac   8: 3 But Saul began to *d* the church.
Rev 11:18 destroying those who *d* the earth."

DESTROYED (DESTROY)

Dt   8:19 you today that you will surely be *d*.
Job 19:26 And after my skin has been *d*,
Pr   6:15 he will suddenly be *d*—
    11: 3 the unfaithful are *d*
    21:28 listens to him will be *d* forever.
    29: 1 will suddenly be *d*—
Isa 55:13 which will not be *d*."
Da   2:44 up a kingdom that will never be *d*,
      6:26 his kingdom will not be *d*,
1Co 5: 5 so that the sinful nature may be *d*
      8:11 for whom Christ died, is *d*
    15:24 Father after he has *d* all dominion,
    15:26 The last enemy to be *d* is death.
2Co 4: 9 abandoned; struck down, but not *d*.
      5: 1 if the earthly tent we live in is *d*,
Gal   5:15 or you will be *d* by each other.
Eph 2:14 the two one and has *d* the barrier,
2Ti   1:10 who has *d* death and has brought
Heb 10:39 of those who shrink back and are *d*,
2Pe 2:12 born only to be caught and *d*,
      3:10 the elements will be *d* by fire,
      3:11 Since everything will be *d*
Jude   :5 later *d* those who did not believe.
       :11 have been *d* in Korah's rebellion.

DESTROYING (DESTROY)

Jer 23: 1 "Woe to the shepherds who are *d*

DESTROYS (DESTROY)

Pr   6:32 whoever does so *d* himself.
    11: 9 mouth the godless *d* his neighbor,
    18: 9 is brother to one who *d*
    28:24 he is partner to him who *d*
Ecc 9:18 but one sinner *d* much good.
1Co 3:17 If anyone *d* God's temple,

DESTRUCTION (DESTROY)

Nu 32:15 and you will be the cause of their *d*
Pr 16:18 Pride goes before *d*,
    17:19 he who builds a high gate invites *d*;
    24:22 for those two will send sudden *d*
Hos 13:14 Where, O grave, is your *d*?
Mt   7:13 broad is the road that leads to *d*,
Lk   6:49 it collapsed and its *d* was complete
Jn 17:12 except the one doomed to *d*
Ro   9:22 of his wrath—prepared for *d*?
Gal   6: 8 from that nature will reap *d*;
Php 3:19 Their destiny is *d*, their god is their
1Th 5: 3 *d* will come on them suddenly,
2Th 1: 9 punished with everlasting *d*
      2: 3 is revealed, the man doomed to *d*.

DESTRUCTIVE

1Ti	6: 9	that plunge men into ruin and d.
2Pe	2: 1	bringing swift d on themselves.
2: 3	and their d has not been sleeping
3: 7	of judgment and d of ungodly men.
3:12	That day will bring about the d
3:16	other Scriptures, to their own d.
Rev	17: 8	out of the Abyss and go to his d.
17:11	to the seven and is going to his d.

DESTRUCTIVE (DESTROY)

2Pe 2: 1 I will secretly introduce d heresies,

DETERMINED (DETERMINES)

Job | 14: 5 | Man's days are d;
Isa | 14:26 | This is the plan d for the whole
Da | 11:36 | for what has been d must take place
Ac | 17:26 | and he d the times set for them

DETERMINES* (DETERMINED)

Ps | 147: 4 | He d the number of the stars
Pr | 16: 9 | but the LORD d his steps.
1Co | 12:11 | them to each one, just as he d.

DETEST (DETESTABLE DETESTED DETESTS)

Lev	11:10	in the water—you are to d.
Pr	8: 7	for my lips d wickedness.
13:19	but fools d turning from evil.
16:12	Kings d wrongdoing,
24: 9	and men d a mocker.
29:27	The righteous d the dishonest;
29:27	the wicked d the upright.

DETESTABLE (DETEST)

Pr	6:16	seven that are d to him:
21:27	The sacrifice of the wicked is d—
28: 9	even his prayers are a d
Isa	1:13	Your incense is d to me.
41:24	he who chooses you is d.
44:19	Shall I make a d thing
Jer | 44: 4 | 'Do not do this d thing that I hate!'
Eze | 8:13 | doing things that are even more d."
Lk | 16:15 | among men is d in God's sight.
Tit | 1:16 | They are d, disobedient
1Pe | 4: 3 | orgies, carousing and d idolatry.

DETESTED* (DETEST)

Zec 11: 8 The flock d me, and I grew weary

DETESTS* (DETEST)

Dt	22: 5	LORD your God d anyone who
23:18	the LORD your God d them both.
25:16	LORD your God d anyone who
Pr	3:32	for the LORD d a perverse man
11:20	The LORD d men
12:22	The LORD d lying lips,
15: 8	The LORD d the sacrifice
15: 9	The LORD d the way
15:26	The LORD d the thoughts
16: 5	The LORD d all the proud of heart
17:15	the LORD d them both.
20:10	The LORD d them both.
20:23	The LORD d differing weights.

DEVIATE*

2Ch 8:15 They did not d from the king's

DEVICES*

Ps 81:12 to follow their own d.

DEVIL* (DEVIL'S)

Mt	4: 1	the desert to be tempted by the d.
4: 5	d took him to the holy city
4: 8	d took him to a very high mountain
4:11	the d left him, and angels came
13:39	the enemy who sows them is the d,
25:41	the eternal fire prepared for the d
Lk	4: 2	forty days he was tempted by the d
4: 3	d said to him, "If you are the Son
4: 5	The d led him up to a high place
4: 9	The d led him to Jerusalem
4:13	When the d had finished all this
8:12	then the d comes and takes away
Jn	6:70	of you is a d!'"(He meant Judas.
8:44	You belong to your father, the d.
13: 2	the d had already prompted Judas
Ac	10:38	were under the power of the d,
13:10	"You are a child of the d
Eph	4:27	and do not give the d a foothold.
1Ti	3: 6	under the same judgment as the d.
2Ti	2:26	and escape from the trap of the d,
Heb	2:14	the d—and free those who all their
Jas	3:15	but is earthly, unspiritual, of the d.
4: 7	Resist the d, and he will flee
1Pe | 5: 8 | Your enemy the d prowls

DEVIL'S* (DEVIL)

Eph | 6:11 | stand against the d schemes
1Ti | 3: 7 | into disgrace and into the d trap.
1Jn | 3: 8 | was to destroy the d work.

DEVILS see DEMONS

DEVIOUS*

Pr	2:15	and who are d in their ways.
14: 2	he whose ways are d despises his
21: 8	The way of the guilty is d.

DEVOTE* (DEVOTED DEVOTING DEVOTION DEVOUT)

1Ch	22:19	Now d your heart and soul
2Ch	31: 4	Levites so they could d themselves
Job	11:13	"Yet if you d your heart to him
Jer	30:21	for who is he who will d himself
Mic	4:13	You will d their ill-gotten gains
1Co	7: 5	so that you may d yourselves
Col	4: 2	D yourselves to prayer, being
1Ti	1: 4	nor to d themselves to myths
4:13	d yourself to the public reading
Tit	3: 8	may be careful to d themselves
3:14	people must learn to d themselves

DEVOTED (DEVOTE)

1Ki	11: 4	and his heart was not fully d
Ezr	7:10	For Ezra had d himself to the study
Ps	86: 2	Guard my life, for I am d to you.
Mt	6:24	or he will be d to the one
Mk	7:11	from me is Corban' (that is, a gift d
Ac	2:42	They d themselves
18: 5	Paul d himself exclusively
Ro	12:10	Be d to one another
1Co	7:34	Her aim is to be d to the Lord
16:15	and they have d themselves
2Co | 7:12 | for yourselves how d to us you are.

DEVOTING* (DEVOTE)

1Ti 5:10 d herself to all kinds of good deeds.

DEVOTION* (DEVOTE)

2Ki	20: 3	and with wholehearted d and have
1Ch	28: 9	and serve him with wholehearted d
29: 3	in my d to the temple.
29:19	son Solomon the wholehearted d
2Ch	32:32	and his acts of d are written
35:26	of Josiah's reign and his acts of d,
Job	6:14	despairing man should have the d
15: 4	and hinder d to God.
Isa | 38: 3 | and with wholehearted d and have
Jer | 2: 2 | 'I remember the d of your youth,
Eze | 33:31 | With their mouths they express d,
1Co | 7:35 | way in undivided d to the Lord
2Co | 11: 3 | from your sincere and pure d

DEVOUR (DEVOURED DEVOURING DEVOURS)

2Sa | 2:26 | "Must the sword d forever?
Mk | 12:40 | They d widows' houses
1Pe | 5: 8 | lion looking for someone to d.

DEVOURED (DEVOUR)

Jer 30:16 But all who devour you will be d.

DEVOURING (DEVOUR)

Gal 5:15 keep on biting and d each other,

DEVOURS (DEVOUR)

2Sa | 11:25 | the sword d one as well as another.
Pr | 21:20 | but a foolish man d all he has.

DEVOUT* (DEVOTE)

1Ki	18: 3	(Obadiah was a d believer
Isa	57: 1	d men are taken away.
Lk	2:25	Simeon, who was righteous and d
Ac	10: 2	his family were d and God-fearing;
10: 7	a d soldier who was one of his attendants
13:43	and d converts to Judaism followed
22:12	He was a d observer of the law

DEW

Jdg 6:37 If there is d only on the fleece

DICTATED

Jer 36: 4 and while Jeremiah d all the words

DIE (DEAD DEADENED DEATH DIED DIES DYING)

Ge	2:17	when you eat of it you will surely d
3: 3	you must not touch it, or you will d
3: 4	will not surely d," the serpent said
Ex	11: 5	Every firstborn son in Egypt will d
Ru	1:17	Where you d I will d, and there I
2Ki	14: 6	each is to d for his own sins."
Job	2: 9	Curse God and d!" He replied.
Pr	5:23	He will d for lack of discipline.
10:21	but fools d for lack of judgment.
15:10	he who hates correction will d
23:13	with the rod, he will not d.
Ecc	3: 2	a time to be born and a time to d;
Isa	22:13	"for tomorrow we d!"
66:24	their worm will not d, nor will their
Jer	31:30	everyone will d for his own sin;
Eze	3:18	that wicked man will d for his sin,
3:19	he will d for his sin, but you will
3:20	block before him, he will d
18: 4	soul who sins is the one who will d
18:20	soul who sins is the one who will d
18:31	Why will you d, O house of Israel?
33: 8	'O wicked man, you will surely d,'
Mt	26:52	"for all who draw the sword will d
Mk	9:48	" their worm does not d,
Jn	8:21	and you will d in your sin.
11:26	and believes in me will never d
Ro	5: 7	Very rarely will anyone d
14: 8	and if we d, we d to the Lord.
1Co	15:22	in Adam all d, so in Christ all will
15:31	I d every day— I mean that.
15:32	for tomorrow we d."
Php | 1:21 | to live is Christ and to d is gain.
Heb | 9:27 | Just as man is destined to d once,
Php | 2:24 | so that we might d to sins
Rev | 14:13 | Blessed are the dead who d

DIED (DIE)

1Ki	16:18	So he d, because of the sins he had
1Ch	1:51	Hadad also d.
10:13	Saul d because he was unfaithful
Lk	16:22	"The time came when the beggar d
Ro	5: 6	we were still powerless, Christ d
5: 8	we were still sinners, Christ d
6: 2	By no means! We d to sin;
6: 7	anyone who has d has been freed
6: 8	if we d with Christ, we believe that
6:10	The death he d, he d to sin once
14: 9	Christ d and returned to life
14:15	brother for whom Christ d
1Co	8:11	for whom Christ d, is destroyed
15: 3	that Christ d for our sins according
2Co	5:14	d for all, and therefore all d
5:15	he d for all, that those who live
Col	2:20	Since you d with Christ
3: 3	For you d, and your life is now
1Th	4:14	We believe that Jesus d
5:10	He d for us so that, whether we are
2Ti	2:11	If we d with him,
Heb	9:15	now that he has d as a ransom
9:17	in force only when somebody has d
1Pe | 3:18 | For Christ d for sins once for all,
Rev | 2: 8 | who d and came to life again.

DIES (DIE)

Job	14:14	If a man d, will he live again?
Pr	11: 7	a wicked man d, his hope perishes.
26:20	without gossip a quarrel d down.
Jn	11:25	in me will live, even though he d;
12:24	But if it d, it produces many seeds.
Ro	7: 2	but if her husband d, she is released
14: 7	and none of us d to himself alone.
1Co	7:39	But if her husband d, she is free
15:36	does not come to life unless it d

DIFFERENCE* (DIFFERENT)

2Sa	19:35	Can I tell the d between what is
2Ch	12: 8	so that they may learn the d
Eze	22:26	they teach that there is no d
44:23	are to teach my people the d
Ro	3:22	There is no d, for all have sinned
10:12	For there is no d between Jew
Gal | 2: 6 | whatever they were makes no d

DIFFERENCES* (DIFFERENT)

1Co 11:19 to be d among you to show which

DESTRUCTIVE

1Jn	3: 8	because the d has been sinning
3: 8	who does what is sinful is of the d,
3:10	and who the children of the d are.
Jude	9	with the d about the body of Moses
Rev	2:10	the d will put some of you in prison
12: 9	that ancient serpent called the d
12:12	the d has gone down to you!
20: 2	that ancient serpent, who is the d,
20:10	And the d, who deceived them,

DIFFERENT* (DIFFERENCE DIFFERENCES DIFFERING DIFFERS)

Lev	19: 19	" 'Do not mate d kinds of animals.
Nu	14: 24	my servant Caleb has a d spirit
1Sa	10: 6	you will be changed into a d person
Est	1: 7	each one d from the other,
	3: 8	whose customs are d from those
Da	7: 3	Four great beasts, each d
	7: 7	It was d from all the former beasts,
	7: 19	which was d from all the others
	7: 23	It will be d from all the other
	7: 24	them another king will arise, d
	11: 29	but this time the outcome will be d
Mk	16: 12	Jesus appeared in a d form
Ro	12: 6	We have d gifts, according
1Co	4: 7	For who makes you d
	12: 4	There are d kinds of gifts,
	12: 5	There are d kinds of service,
	12: 6	There are d kinds of working,
	12: 10	speaking in d kinds of tongues,
	12: 28	and those speaking in d kinds
2Co	11: 4	or a d gospel from the one you
	11: 4	or if you receive a d spirit
Gal	1: 6	and are turning to a d gospel—
	4: 1	he is no d from a slave,
Heb	7: 13	are said belonged to a d tribe,
Jas	2: 25	and sent them off in a d direction?

DIFFERING* (DIFFERENT)

Dt	25: 13	Do not have two d weights
	25: 14	Do not have two d measures
Pr	20: 10	Differing weights and d measures
	20: 10	D weights and differing measures
	20: 23	The LORD detests d weights.

DIFFERS* (DIFFERENT)

1Co	15: 41	and star d from star in splendor.

DIFFICULT (DIFFICULTIES)

Ex	18: 22	but have them bring every d case
Dt	30: 11	commanding you today is not too d
2Ki	2: 10	"You have asked a d thing,"
Eze	3: 5	of obscure speech and d language,
Ac	15: 19	that we should not make it d

DIFFICULTIES* (DIFFICULT)

Dt	31: 17	and d will come upon them,
	31: 21	when many disasters and d come
2Co	12: 10	in hardships, in persecutions, in d.

DIGNITY

Pr	31: 25	She is clothed with strength and d.

DIGS

Pr	26: 27	If a man d a pit, he will fall into it;

DILIGENCE (DILIGENT)

Ezr	5: 8	The work is being carried on with d
Heb	6: 11	to show this same d to the very end

DILIGENT (DILIGENCE)

Pr	10: 4	but d hands bring wealth.
	12: 24	D hands will rule,
	12: 27	the d man prizes his possessions.
	13: 4	of the d are fully satisfied.
	21: 5	The plans of the d lead to profit
1Ti	4: 15	Be d in these matters; give yourself

DINAH*

Only daughter of Jacob, by Leah (Ge 30:21; 46:15). Raped by Shechem; avenged by Simeon and Levi (Ge 34).

DINE

Pr	23: 1	When you sit to d with a ruler,

DIOTREPHES*

3Jn	: 9	but D, who loves to be first,

DIRECT (DIRECTED DIRECTIVES DIRECTS)

Ge	18: 19	so that he will d his children
Dt	17: 10	to do everything they d you to do.
Ps	119: 35	D me in the path of your
	119:133	D my footsteps according
Jer	10: 23	it is not for man to d his steps.
2Th	3: 5	May the Lord d your hearts
1Ti	5: 17	The elders who d the affairs

DIRECTED (DIRECT)

Ge	24: 51	master's son, as the LORD has d."
Nu	16: 40	as the LORD d him through Moses
Dt	2: 1	Sea, as the LORD had d me.
	6: 1	laws the LORD your God d me
Jos	11: 9	did to them as the LORD had d:

Jos	11: 23	just as the LORD had d Moses.
Pr	20: 24	A man's steps are d by the LORD.
Jer	13: 2	as the LORD d, and put it
Ac	7: 44	It had been made as God d Moses.
Tit	1: 5	elders in every town, as I d you.

DIRECTIVES* (DIRECT)

1Co	11: 17	In the following d I have no praise

DIRECTS (DIRECT)

Ps	42: 8	By day the LORD d his love,
Isa	48: 17	who d you in the way you should

DIRGE*

Mt	11: 17	we sang a d,
Lk	7: 32	we sang a d,

DISABLED*

Jn	5: 3	number of d people used to lie—
Heb	12: 13	so that the lame may not be d,

DISAGREEMENT*

Ac	15: 39	had such a sharp d that they parted

DISAPPEAR (DISAPPEARED DISAPPEARS)

Mt	5: 18	will by any means d from the Law
Lk	16: 17	earth to d than for the least stroke
Heb	8: 13	is obsolete and aging will soon d.
2Pe	3: 10	The heavens will d with a roar;

DISAPPEARED (DISAPPEAR)

1Ki	20: 40	busy here and there, the man d."

DISAPPEARS (DISAPPEAR)

1Co	13: 10	perfection comes, the imperfect d.

DISAPPOINT* (DISAPPOINTED)

Ro	5: 5	And hope does not d us,

DISAPPOINTED (DISAPPOINT)

Ps	22: 5	in you they trusted and were not d.

DISAPPROVE*

Pr	24: 18	or the LORD will see and d

DISARMED*

Col	2: 15	And having d the powers

DISASTER

Ex	32: 12	and do not bring d on your people.
Ps	57: 1	wings until the d has passed
Pr	1: 26	I in turn will laugh at your d;
	3: 25	Have no fear of sudden d
	6: 15	Therefore d will overtake him
	16: 4	even the wicked for a day of d.
	17: 5	over d will not go unpunished.
	27: 10	house when d strikes you—
Isa	45: 7	I bring prosperity and create d;
Jer	17: 17	you are my refuge in the day of d.
Eze	7: 5	An unheard-of d is coming.

DISCERN (DISCERNED DISCERNING DISCERNMENT)

Ps	19: 12	Who can d his errors?
	139: 3	You d my going out and my lying
Php	1: 10	you may be able to d what is best

DISCERNED (DISCERN)

1Co	2: 14	because they are spiritually d.

DISCERNING (DISCERN)

1Ki	3: 9	So give your servant a d heart
	3: 12	I will give you a wise and d heart,
Pr	1: 5	and let the d get guidance—
	8: 9	To the d all of them are right;
	10: 13	on the lips of the d.
	14: 6	knowledge comes easily to the d.
	14: 33	in the heart of the d
	15: 14	The d heart seeks knowledge,
	16: 21	The wise in heart are called d,
	17: 24	A d man keeps wisdom in view,
	17: 28	and d if he holds his tongue.
	18: 15	heart of the d acquires knowledge;
	19: 25	rebuke a d man, and he will gain
	28: 7	He who keeps the law is a d son,

DISCERNMENT (DISCERN)

Ps	119:125	I am your servant; give me d
Pr	3: 21	preserve sound judgment and d,
	17: 10	A rebuke impresses a man of d
	28: 11	a poor man who has d sees

DISCHARGED* (DISCHARGING)

Ecc	8: 8	As no one is d in time of war,

DISCHARGING* (DISCHARGED)

1Co	9: 17	I am simply d the trust committed

DISCIPLE (DISCIPLES DISCIPLES')

Mt	10: 42	these little ones because he is my d,
Lk	14: 26	his own life—he cannot be my d.
	14: 27	and follow me cannot be my d.
	14: 33	everything he has cannot be my d.
Jn	13: 23	of them, the d whom Jesus loved,
	19: 26	and the d whom he loved standing
	21: 7	Then the d whom Jesus loved said
	21: 20	saw that the d whom Jesus loved

DISCIPLES (DISCIPLE)

Mt	10: 1	He called his twelve d to him
	26: 56	Then all the d deserted him
	28: 19	Therefore go and make d
Mk	3: 7	withdrew with his d to the lake,
	16: 20	Then the d went out and preached
Lk	6: 13	he called his d to him and chose
Jn	2: 11	and his d put their faith in him.
	6: 66	many of his d turned back
	8: 31	to my teaching, you are really my d
	12: 16	At first his d did not understand all
	13: 35	men will know that you are my d
	15: 8	showing yourselves to be my d.
	20: 20	The d were overjoyed
Ac	6: 1	the number of d was increasing,
	11: 26	The d were called Christians first
	14: 22	strengthening the d
	18: 23	Phrygia, strengthening all the d.

DISCIPLES' (DISCIPLE)

Jn	13: 5	and began to wash his d feet,

DISCIPLINE* (DISCIPLINED DISCIPLINES SELF-DISCIPLINE)

Dt	4: 36	made you hear his voice to d you.
	11: 2	and experienced the d
	21: 18	listen to them when they d him,
Job	5: 17	so do not despise the d
Ps	6: 1	or d me in your wrath.
	38: 1	or d me in your wrath.
	39: 11	You rebuke and d men for their sin;
	94: 12	Blessed is the man you d, O LORD
Pr	1: 2	for attaining wisdom and d;
	1: 7	but fools despise wisdom and d.
	3: 11	do not despise the LORD's d
	5: 12	You will say, "How I hated d!
	5: 23	He will die for lack of d,
	6: 23	and the corrections of d
	10: 17	He who heeds d shows the way
	12: 1	Whoever loves d loves knowledge,
	13: 18	He who ignores d comes to poverty
	13: 24	who loves him is careful to d him.
	15: 5	A fool spurns his father's d,
	15: 10	Stern d awaits him who leaves
	15: 32	He who ignores d despises himself,
	19: 18	D your son, for in that there is hope
	22: 15	the rod of d will drive it far
	23: 13	Do not withhold d from a child;
	23: 23	get wisdom, d and understanding.
	29: 17	D your son, and he will give you
Jer	17: 23	would not listen or respond to d.
	30: 11	I will d you but only with justice;
	32: 33	would not listen or respond to d.
	46: 28	I will d you but only with justice;
Hos	5: 2	I will d all of them.
Heb	12: 5	do not make light of the Lord's d,
	12: 7	as d; God is treating you
	12: 8	(and everyone undergoes d),
	12: 11	No d seems pleasant at the time,
Rev	3: 19	Those whom I love I rebuke and d.

DISCIPLINED* (DISCIPLINE)

Pr	1: 3	for acquiring a d and prudent life,
Isa	26: 16	when you d them,
Jer	31: 18	and I have been d.
	31: 18	'You d me like an unruly calf,
1Co	11: 32	we are being d so that we will not
Tit	1: 8	upright, holy and d
Heb	12: 7	For what son is not d by his father?
	12: 8	you are not d (and everyone
	12: 9	all had human fathers who d us
	12: 10	Our fathers d us for a little while

DISCIPLINES* (DISCIPLINE)

Dt	8: 5	your heart that as a man d his son,
	8: 5	so the LORD your God d you.
Ps	94: 10	Does he who d nations not punish?
Pr	3: 12	the LORD d those he loves,
Heb	12: 6	because the Lord d those he loves,
	12: 10	but God d us for our good,

DISCLOSED
Lk   8: 17 is nothing hidden that will not be d,
Col   1: 26 and generations, but is now d
Heb 9: 8 Holy Place had not yet been d

DISCORD
Gal   5: 20 idolatry and witchcraft; hatred, d,

DISCOURAGED* (DISCOURAGEMENT)
Nu   32: 9 they dthe Israelites
Dt   1: 21 Do not be afraid; do not be d.''
      31: 8 Do not be afraid; do not be d.''
Jos   1: 9 Do not be terrified; do not be d,
      8: 1 ''Do not be afraid; do not be d.
    10: 25 ''Do not be afraid; do not be d.
1Ch 22: 13 Do not be afraid or d.
    28: 20 or d, for the LORD God,
2Ch 20: 15 or dbecause of this vast army.
    20: 17 Do not be afraid or d.
    32: 7 or dbecause of the king of Assyria
Job 4: 5 to you, and you are d;
Isa 42: 4 he will not falter or be d
Eph 3: 13 to be dbecause of my sufferings
Col 3: 21 children, or they will become d.

DISCOURAGEMENT* (DISCOURAGED)
Ex   6: 9 of their dand cruel bondage.

DISCOVERED
2Ki 23: 24 book that Hilkiah the priest had d

DISCREDIT* (DISCREDITED)
Ne   6: 13 would give me a bad name to dme.
Job 40: 8 ''Would you dmy justice?

DISCREDITED (DISCREDIT)
2Co 6: 3 so that our ministry will not be d.

DISCRETION*
1Ch 22: 12 May the LORD give you d
Pr   1: 4 knowledge and dto the young—
    2: 11 Dwill protect you,
    5: 2 that you may maintain d
    8: 12 I possess knowledge and d.
   11: 22 a beautiful woman who shows no d.

DISCRIMINATED*
Jas   2: 4 have you not damong yourselves

DISEASE (DISEASES)
Mt   4: 23 and healing every dand sickness
    9: 35 and healing every dand sickness.
   10: 1 and to heal every dand sickness.

DISEASES (DISEASE)
Ps 103: 3 and heals all my d;
Mt   8: 17 and carried our d.''
Mk   3: 10 those with dwere pushing forward
Lk   1: 1 drive out all demons and to cure d,

DISFIGURE* (DISFIGURED)
Mt   6: 16 for they dtheir faces

DISFIGURED (DISFIGURE)
Isa 52: 14 his appearance was so d

DISGRACE (DISGRACEFUL DISGRACES)
Ps 44: 15 My dis before me all day long,
    52: 1 you who are a din the eyes of God?
    74: 21 not let the oppressed retreat in d,
Pr   6: 33 Blows and dare his lot,
   11: 2 When pride comes, then comes d,
   14: 34 but sin is a dto any people.
   19: 26 is a son who brings shame and d
Mt   1: 19 want to expose her to public d,
Ac   5: 41 of suffering dfor the Name.
1Co 6: 6 and if it is a dfor a woman
   11: 14 it is a din him, but that
1Ti   3: 7 so that he will not fall into d
Heb 6: 6 and subjecting him to public d.
   11: 26 He regarded dfor the sake
   13: 13 the camp, bearing the dhe bore.

DISGRACEFUL (DISGRACE)
Pr   10: 5 during harvest is a dson.
   12: 4 a dwife is like decay in his bones.
   17: 2 wise servant will rule over a dson,
1Co 14: 35 for it is dfor a woman to speak

DISGRACES (DISGRACE)
Pr 28: 7 of gluttons dhis father.
   29: 15 but a child left to himself dhis mother

DISGUISES*
Pr 26: 24 A malicious man dhimself

DISH
Pr 19: 24 sluggard buries his hand in the d;
Mt 23: 25 the outside of the cup and d,

DISHONEST*
Ex 18: 21 trustworthy men who hate dgain
Lev 19: 35 '' 'Do not use dstandards
1Sa 8: 3 They turned aside after dgain
Pr 11: 1 The LORD abhors dscales,
   13: 11 Dmoney dwindles away,
   20: 23 and dscales do not please him.
   29: 27 The righteous detest the d;
Jer 22: 17 are set only on dgain.
Eze 28: 18 By your many sins and dtrade
Hos 12: 7 The merchant uses dscales;
Am   8: 5 and cheating with dscales,
Lk 16: 8 master commended the dmanager
   16: 11 Shall I acquit a man with dscales,
   16: 10 whoever is dwith very little will
   16: 10 with very little will also be d
1Ti   3: 8 wine, and not pursuing dgain.
Tit   1: 7 not violent, not pursuing dgain.
    1: 11 and that for the sake of dgain.

DISHONOR* (DISHONORED DISHONORS)
Lev 18: 7 '' 'Do not dyour father
   18: 8 wife; that would dyour father.
   18: 10 daughter; that would dyou.
   18: 14 '' 'Do not dyour father's brother
   18: 16 that would dyour brother.
   20: 19 for that would da close relative;
Dt 22: 30 he must not dhis father's bed;
Pr   30: 9 and so dthe name of my God.
Jer 14: 21 do not dyour glorious throne.
   20: 11 their dwill never be forgotten.
La   2: 2 princes down to the ground in d.
Eze 22: 10 are those who dtheir fathers' bed;
Jn   8: 49 I honor my Father and you d,
Ro   2: 23 do you dGod by breaking the law?
1Co 15: 43 it is sown in d, it is raised in glory;
2Co 6: 8 through glory and d, bad report

DISHONORED* (DISHONOR)
Lev 20: 11 father's wife, he has dhis father.
   20: 17 He has dhis sister and will be held
   20: 20 with his aunt, he has dhis uncle.
   20: 21 of impurity; he has dhis brother.
Dt 21: 14 as a slave, since you have dher.
Ezr 4: 14 proper for us to see the king d,
1Co 4: 10 You are honored, we are d!

DISHONORS* (DISHONOR)
Dt 27: 16 Cursed is the man who dhis father
   27: 20 for he dhis father's bed.''
Job 20: 3 I hear a rebuke that dme,
Mic 7: 6 For a son dhis father,
1Co 11: 4 with his head covered dhis head.
   11: 5 her head uncovered dher head—

DISILLUSIONMENT*
Ps   7: 14 conceives trouble gives birth to d.

DISMAYED
Isa 28: 16 the one who trusts will never be d.
   41: 10 do not be d, for I am your God.

DISOBEDIENCE* (DISOBEY)
Jos 22: 22 in rebellion or dto the LORD,
Jer 43: 7 So they entered Egypt in d
Ro   5: 19 as through the dof the one man
   11: 30 mercy as a result of their d,
   11: 32 to dso that he may have mercy
2Co 10: 6 ready to punish every act of d,
Heb 2: 2 and dreceived its just punishment,
    4: 6 go in, because of their d,
    4: 11 fall by following their example of d.

DISOBEDIENT* (DISOBEY)
Ne   9: 26 ''But they were dand rebelled
Lk   1: 17 and the dto the wisdom
Ac 26: 19 I was not dto the vision
Ro 10: 21 hands to a dand obstinate people.''
   11: 30 as you who were at one time d
   11: 31 so they too have now become d
Eph 2: 2 now at work in those who are d
    5: 6 comes on those who are d.
    5: 12 to mention what the ddo in secret.
2Ti 3: 2 proud, abusive, dto their parents,
Tit   1: 6 to the charge of being wild and d.
    1: 16 dand unfit for doing anything
    3: 3 At one time we too were foolish, d,

DISOBEY* (DISOBEDIENCE DISOBEDIENT DISOBEYED DISOBEYING DISOBEYS)
Dt 11: 28 the curse if you dthe commands
2Ch 24: 20 'Why do you dthe LORD's
Est   3: 3 Why do you dthe king's command
Jer 42: 13 and so dthe LORD your God,
Ro   1: 30 they dtheir parents; they are
1Pe 2: 8 because they dthe message—

DISOBEYED* (DISOBEY)
Nu 14: 22 and in the desert but who dme
   27: 14 both of you dmy command
Jdg 2: 2 Yet you have dme.
Ne   9: 29 arrogant and dyour commands.
Isa 24: 5 they have dthe laws,
Jer 43: 4 and all the people dthe LORD's
Lk 15: 29 for you and never dyour orders.
Heb 3: 18 rest if not to those who d?
1Pe 3: 20 the spirits in prison who dlong ago

DISOBEYING* (DISOBEY)
Nu 14: 41 ''Why are you dthe LORD's

DISOBEYS* (DISOBEY)
Eze 33: 12 man will not save him when he d,

DISORDER
1Co 14: 33 For God is not a God of d
2Co 12: 20 slander, gossip, arrogance and d.
Jas 3: 16 there you find dand every evil

DISOWN (DISOWNS)
Pr 30: 9 I may have too much and dyou
Mt 10: 33 I will dhim before my Father
   26: 35 to die with you, I will never dyou.''
2Ti 2: 12 If we dhim,

DISOWNS (DISOWN)
Lk 12: 9 he who dme before men will be

DISPENSATION see ADMINISTRATION, TRUST

DISPLACES
Pr 30: 23 a maidservant who dher mistress.

DISPLAY (DISPLAYED DISPLAYS)
Ps 45: 4 your right hand dawesome deeds.
Eze 39: 21 I will dmy glory among the nations
Ro   9: 17 that I might dmy power in you
1Co 4: 9 on dat the end of the procession,
1Ti   1: 16 Christ Jesus might dhis unlimited

DISPLAYED (DISPLAY)
Jn   9: 3 work of God might be din his life.
2Th 2: 9 the work of Satan din all kinds

DISPLAYS (DISPLAY)
Isa 44: 23 he dhis glory in Israel.

DISPLEASE (DISPLEASED)
1Th 2: 15 They dGod and are hostile

DISPLEASED (DISPLEASE)
2Sa 11: 27 David had done dthe LORD.

DISPUTABLE* (DISPUTE)
Ro 14: 1 passing judgment on dmatters.

DISPUTE (DISPUTABLE DISPUTES DISPUTING)
Pr 17: 14 before a dbreaks out.
1Co 6: 1 If any of you has a dwith another,

DISPUTES (DISPUTE)
Pr 18: 18 Casting the lot settles d

DISPUTING (DISPUTE)
1Ti   2: 8 in prayer, without anger or d.

DISQUALIFIED*
1Co 9: 27 I myself will not be dfor the prize.

DISREPUTE*
2Pe 2: 2 will bring the way of truth into d.

DISSENSION* (DISSENSIONS)
Pr   6: 14 he always stirs up d.
    6: 19 and a man who stirs up d
   10: 12 Hatred stirs up d,
   15: 18 A hot-tempered man stirs up d,
   16: 28 A perverse man stirs up d,
   28: 25 A greedy man stirs up d,

DISSENSIONS (continued)

Pr 29:22 An angry man stirs up *d*,
Ro 13:13 debauchery, not in *d* and jealousy.

DISSENSIONS* (DISSENSION)

Gal 5:20 selfish ambition, *d*, factions

DISSIPATION*

Lk 21:34 will be weighed down with *d*,
1Pe 4:4 with them into the same flood of *d*,

DISTINCTION

Ac 15:9 He made no *d* between us

DISTINGUISH (DISTINGUISHING)

1Ki 3:9 and to *d* between right and wrong.
Heb 5:14 themselves to *d* good from evil.

DISTINGUISHING

1Co 12:10 the *d* between spirits.

DISTORT

Ac 20:30 and *d* the truth in order
2Co 2 nor do we *d* the word of God.
2Pe 3:16 ignorant and unstable people *d*,

DISTRACTED*

Lk 10:40 But Martha was *d* by all

DISTRESS (DISTRESSED)

2Ch 15:4 in their *d* they turned to the LORD
Ps 18:6 In my *d* I called to the LORD;
81:7 In your *d* you called and I rescued
120:1 I call on the LORD in my *d*,
Jnh 2:2 "In my *d* I called to the LORD,
Mt 24:21 For then there will be great *d*,
Jas 1:27 after orphans and widows in their *d*

DISTRESSED (DISTRESS)

Lk 12:50 how *d* I am until it is completed!
Ro 14:15 If your brother is *d*

DIVIDE (DIVIDED DIVIDING DIVISION DIVISIONS DIVISIVE)

Ps 22:18 They *d* my garments among them

DIVIDED (DIVIDE)

Mt 12:25 household *d* against itself will not
Lk 23:34 they *d* up his clothes by casting lots
1Co 1:13 Is Christ *d*? Was Paul crucified

DIVIDING (DIVIDE)

Eph 2:14 destroyed the barrier, the *d* wall
Heb 4:12 it penetrates even to *d* soul

DIVINATION

Lev 19:26 "'Do not practice *d* or sorcery.

DIVINE

Ro 1:20 his eternal power and *d* nature—
2Co 10:4 they have *d* power
2Pe 1:4 you may participate in the *d* nature

DIVISION (DIVIDE)

Lk 12:51 on earth? No, I tell you, but *d*.
1Co 12:25 so that there should be no *d*

DIVISIONS (DIVIDE)

Ro 16:17 to watch out for those who cause *d*
1Co 1:10 another so that there may be no *d*
11:18 there are *d* among you,

DIVISIVE* (DIVIDE)

Tit 3:10 Warn a *d* person once.

DIVORCE* (DIVORCED DIVORCES)

Dt 22:19 he must not *d* her as long as he lives
22:29 He can never *d* her as long
24:1 and he writes her a certificate of *d*,
24:3 and writes her a certificate of *d*,
Isa 50:1 is your mother's certificate of *d*
Jer 3:8 faithless Israel her certificate of *d*
Mal 2:16 "I hate *d*," says the LORD God
Mt 1:19 he had in mind to *d* her quietly
5:31 must give her a certificate of *d*.
19:3 for his wife for any
19:7 man give his wife a certificate of *d*
19:8 permitted you to *d* your wives
Mk 10:2 Is it lawful for a man to *d* his wife?"
10:4 a man to write a certificate of *d*
1Co 7:11 And a husband must not *d* his wife.
7:12 to live with him, he must not *d* her.
7:13 to live with her, she must not *d* him
7:27 Are you married? Do not seek a *d*.

DIVORCED* (DIVORCE)

Lev 21:7 or *d* from their husbands,
21:14 not marry a widow, a *d* woman,
22:13 daughter becomes a widow or is *d*,
Nu 30:9 or *d* woman will be binding on her.
Dt 24:4 then her first husband, who *d* her,
1Ch 8:8 after he had *d* his wives Hushim
Eze 44:22 not marry widows or *d* women;
Mt 5:32 marries the *d* woman commits adultery.
Lk 16:18 who marries a *d* woman commits

DIVORCES* (DIVORCE)

Jer 3:1 "If a man *d* his wife
Mt 5:31 'Anyone who *d* his wife must give
5:32 tell you that anyone who *d* his wife,
19:9 tell you that anyone who *d* his wife,
Mk 10:11 "Anyone who *d* his wife
10:12 And if she *d* her husband
Lk 16:18 "Anyone who *d* his wife

DOCTOR

Mt 9:12 "It is not the healthy who need a *d*.

DOCTRINE* (DOCTRINES)

1Ti 1:10 to the sound *d* that conforms
4:16 Watch your life and *d* closely.
2Ti 4:3 men will not put up with sound *d*.
Tit 2:1 You can encourage others by sound *d*
2:1 is in accord with sound *d*.

DOCTRINES* (DOCTRINE)

1Ti 1:3 not to teach false *d* any longer
6:3 If anyone teaches false *d*

DOEG*

Edomite; Saul's head shepherd; responsible for murder of priests at Nob (1Sa 21:7; 22:6-23; Ps 52).

DOG (DOGS)

Pr 26:11 As a *d* returns to its vomit,
Ecc 9:4 a live *d* is better off than a dead lion
2Pe 2:22 "A *d* returns to its vomit," and,

DOGS (DOG)

Mt 7:6 "Do not give *d* what is sacred;
15:26 bread and toss it to their *d*."

DOMINION

Job 25:2 "*D* and awe belong to God;
Ps 22:28 for *d* belongs to the LORD

DONKEY

Nu 22:30 *d* said to Balaam, "Am I not your
Zec 9:9 gentle and riding on a *d*,
Mt 21:5 gentle and riding on a *d*,
2Pe 2:16 for his wrongdoing by a *d*—

DOOR (DOORS)

Job 31:32 for my *d* was always open
Ps 141:3 keep watch over the *d* of my lips.
Mt 6:6 close the *d* and pray to your Father
7:7 and the *d* will be opened to you.
Ac 14:27 how he had opened the *d* of faith
1Co 16:9 a great *d* for effective work has
2Co 2:12 found that the Lord had opened a *d*
Rev 3:20 I stand at the *d* and knock.

DOORFRAMES

Dt 6:9 Write them on the *d* of your houses

DOORKEEPER

Ps 84:10 I would rather be a *d* in the house

DOORS (DOOR)

Ps 24:7 be lifted up, you ancient *d*,

DORCAS

Ac 9:36 is *D*), who was always doing good

DOUBLE

2Ki 2:9 "Let me inherit a *d* portion
1Ti 5:17 church well are worthy of *d* honor.

DOUBLE-EDGED (EDGE)

Heb 4:12 Sharper than any *d* sword,
Rev 1:16 of his mouth came a sharp *d* sword.
2:12 of him who has the sharp, *d* sword.

DOUBLE-MINDED* (MIND)

Ps 119:113 I hate *d* men,
Jas 1:8 he is a *d* man, unstable
4:8 and purify your hearts, you *d*

DOUBT (DOUBTING DOUBTS)

Mt 14:31 he said, "why did you *d*?"
21:21 if you have faith and do not *d*,
Mk 11:23 and does not *d* in his heart
Jas 1:6 he must believe and not *d*,
Jude :22 Be merciful to those who *d*;

DOUBTING* (DOUBT)

Jn 20:27 Stop *d* and believe."

DOUBTS* (DOUBT)

Lk 24:38 and why do *d* rise in your minds?
Ro 14:23 the man who *d* is condemned
Jas 1:6 he who *d* is like a wave of the sea,

DOVE (DOVES)

Ge 8:8 Then he sent out a *d* to see
Mt 3:16 Spirit of God descending like a *d*

DOVES (DOVE)

Lev 12:8 is to bring two *d* or two young
Mt 10:16 as snakes and as innocent as *d*.
Lk 2:24 "a pair of *d* or two young pigeons."

DOWNCAST

Ps 42:5 Why are you *d*, O my soul?
2Co 7:6 But God, who comforts the *d*,

DOWNFALL

Hos 14:1 Your sins have been your *d*!

DRAGON

Rev 12:7 and his angels fought against the *d*,
13:2 The *d* gave the beast his power
20:2 He seized the *d*, that ancient

DRAW (DRAWING DRAWS)

Mt 26:52 "for all who *d* the sword will die
Jn 12:32 up from the earth, will *d* all men
Heb 10:22 let us *d* near to God

DRAWING (DRAW)

Lk 21:28 because your redemption is *d* near

DRAWS (DRAW)

Jn 6:44 the Father who sent me *d* him,

DREAD (DREADFUL)

Ps 53:5 they were, overwhelmed with *d*,

DREADFUL (DREAD)

Mt 24:19 How *d* it will be in those days
Heb 10:31 It is a *d* thing to fall into the hands

DREAM

Joel 2:28 your old men will *d* dreams.
Ac 2:17 your old men will *d* dreams.

DRESS

1Ti 2:9 I also want women to *d* modestly,

DRIFT*

Heb 2:1 so that we do not *d* away.

DRINK (DRINKING DRINKS DRUNK DRUNKARD DRUNKARD'S DRUNKARDS DRUNKENNESS)

Ex 29:40 of a hin of wine as a *d* offering.
Nu 6:3 He must not *d* grape juice
Jdg 7:5 from those who kneel down to *d*."
2Sa 23:15 that someone would get me a *d*
Pr 5:15 *D* water from your own cistern,
Mt 20:22 "Can you *d* the cup I am going to *d*
26:27 saying, "*D* from it, all of you.
Mk 16:18 and when they *d* deadly poison,
Lk 12:19 Take life easy; eat, *d* and be merry
Jn 7:37 let him come to me and *d*.
18:11 Shall I not *d* the cup the Father has
1Co 10:4 and drank the same spiritual *d*;
12:13 were all given the one Spirit to *d*.
Php 2:17 being poured out like a *d* offering
2Ti 4:6 being poured out like a *d* offering,
Rev 14:10 too, will *d* of the wine of God's fury
21:6 to *d* without cost from the spring

DRINKING (DRINK)

Ro 14:17 God is not a matter of eating and *d*,

DRINKS (DRINK)

Isa 5:22 and champions at mixing *d*.
Jn 4:13 "Everyone who *d* this water will be
6:54 and *d* my blood has eternal life,
1Co 11:27 or *d* the cup of the Lord

DRIPPING

Pr 19:13 wife is like a constant *d*.
27:15 a constant *d* on a rainy day;

DRIVE (DRIVES)

Ex 23:30 Little by little I will *d* them out
Nu 33:52 *d* out all the inhabitants of the land
Jos 13:13 Israelites did not *d* out the people
23:13 will no longer *d* out these nations
Pr 22:10 *D* out the mocker, and out goes
Mt 10: 1 authority to *d* out evil spirits
Jn 6:37 comes to me I will never *d* away.

DRIVES (DRIVE)

Mt 12:26 If Satan *d* out Satan, he is divided
1Jn 4:18 But perfect love *d* out fear,

DROP (DROPS)

Pr 17:14 so *d* the matter before a dispute
Isa 40:15 Surely the nations are like a *d*

DROPS (DROP)

Lk 22:44 his sweat was like *d* of blood falling

DROSS

Ps 119:119 of the earth you discard like *d*;
Pr 25: 4 Remove the *d* from the silver,

DROUGHT

Jer 17: 8 It has no worries in a year of *d*

DROWNED

Ex 15: 4 are *d* in the Red Sea.
Mt 18: 6 and to be *d* in the depths of the sea.
Heb 11:29 tried to do so, they were *d*.

DROWSINESS*

Pr 23:21 and *d* clothes them in rags.

DRUNK (DRINK)

1Sa 1:13 Eli thought she was *d* and said
Ac 2:15 men are *d*, as you suppose.
Eph 5:18 Do not get *d* on wine, which leads

DRUNKARD (DRINK)

Mt 11:19 and a *d*, a friend of tax collectors
1Co 5:11 or a slanderer, a *d* or a swindler.

DRUNKARD'S* (DRINK)

Pr 26: 9 Like a thornbush in a *d* hand

DRUNKARDS (DRINK)

Pr 23:21 for *d* and gluttons become poor,
1Co 6:10 nor the greedy nor *d* nor slanderers

DRUNKENNESS (DRINK)

Lk 21:34 weighed down with dissipation, *d*
Ro 13:13 and *d*, not in sexual immorality
Gal 5:21 factions and envy; *d*, orgies,
1Ti 3: 3 not given to *d*, not violent
1Pe 4: 3 living in debauchery, lust, *d*, orgies.

DRY

Ge 1: 9 place, and let *d* ground appear."
Ex 14:16 go through the sea on *d* ground.
Jos 3:17 the crossing on *d* ground.
Isa 53: 2 and like a root out of *d* ground.
Eze 37: 4 '*D* bones, hear the word

DULL

Isa 6:10 make their ears *d*
2Co 3:14 But their minds were made *d*,

DUST

Ge 2: 7 man from the *d* of the ground
3:19 for *d* you are
Job 42: 6 and repent in *d* and ashes."
Ps 22:15 you lay me in the *d* of death.
103:14 he remembers that we are *d*.
Ecc 3:20 all come from *d*, and to *d* all return.
Mt 10:14 shake the *d* off your feet
1Co 15:47 was of the *d* of the earth,

DUTIES (DUTY)

2Ti 4: 5 discharge all the *d* of your ministry

DUTY (DUTIES)

Ecc 12:13 for this is the whole *d* of man.
Ac 23: 1 I have fulfilled my *d* to God
1Co 7: 3 husband should fulfill his marital *d*

DWELL (DWELLING DWELLINGS DWELLS DWELT)

Ex 25: 8 for me, and I will *d* among them.
2Sa 7: 5 the one to build me a house to *d* in?
1Ki 8:27 "But will God really *d* on earth?
Ps 23: 6 I will *d* in the house of the LORD
37: 3 *d* in the land and enjoy safe pasture
61: 4 I long to *d* in your tent forever
Pr 8:12 wisdom, *d* together with prudence;
Isa 33:14 of us can *d* with the consuming fire
43:18 do not *d* on the past.
Jn 5:38 nor does his word *d* in you,
Eph 3:17 so that Christ may *d* in your hearts
Col 1:19 to have all his fullness *d* in him,
3:16 the word of Christ *d* in you richly

DWELLING (DWELL)

Lev 26:11 I will put my *d* place among you,
Dt 26:15 from heaven, your holy *d* place.
Ps 90: 1 Lord, you have been our *d* place
2Co 5: 2 to be clothed with our heavenly *d*,
Eph 2:22 to become a *d* in which God lives

DWELLINGS (DWELL)

Lk 16: 9 will be welcomed into eternal *d*.

DWELLS (DWELL)

Ps 46: 4 holy place where the Most High *d*
91: 1 He who *d* in the shelter

DWELT (DWELL)

Dt 33:16 of him who *d* in the burning bush.

DYING (DIE)

Ro 7: 6 by *d* to what once bound us,
2Co 6: 9 yet regarded as unknown; *d*,

EAGER

Pr 31:13 and works with *e* hands.
Ro 8:19 The creation waits in *e* expectation
1Co 14:12 Since you are *e* to have spiritual
14:39 my brothers, be *e* to prophesy,
Tit 2:14 a people that are his very own, *e*
1Pe 5: 2 greedy for money, but *e* to serve;

EAGLE (EAGLE'S EAGLES)

Dt 32:11 like an *e* that stirs up its nest
Eze 1:10 each also has the face of an *e*
Rev 4: 7 the fourth was like a flying *e*
12:14 given the two wings of a great *e*,

EAGLE'S (EAGLE)

Ps 103: 5 your youth is renewed like the *e*

EAGLES (EAGLE)

Isa 40:31 They will soar on wings like *e*;

EAR (EARS)

Ex 21: 6 and pierce his *e* with an awl.
Ps 5: 1 Give *e* to my words, O LORD,
Pr 2: 2 turning your *e* to wisdom
1Co 2: 9 no *e* has heard,
12:16 if the *e* should say, "Because I am
Rev 2: 7 He who has an *e*, let him hear what

EARN (EARNED EARNINGS)

2Th 3:12 down and *e* the bread they eat.

EARNED (EARN)

Pr 31:31 Give her the reward she has *e*,

EARNEST see DEPOSIT

EARNESTNESS

2Co 7:11 what *e*, what eagerness
8: 7 in complete *e* and in your love

EARNINGS (EARN)

Pr 31:16 out of her *e* she plants a vineyard.

EARRING (EARRINGS)

Pr 25:12 Like an *e* of gold or an ornament

EARRINGS (EARRING)

Ex 32: 2 Take off the gold *e* that your wives.

EARS (EAR)

Job 42: 5 My *e* had heard of you
Ps 34:15 and his *e* are attentive to their cry;
Pr 21:13 If a man shuts his *e* to the cry
26:17 Like one who seizes a dog by the *e*
Isa 6:10 hear with their *e*.
Mt 11:15 He who has *e*, let him hear.
2Ti 4: 3 to say what their itching *e* want
1Pe 3:12 his *e* are attentive to their prayer.

EARTH (EARTH'S EARTHLY)

Ge 1: 1 God created the heavens and the *e*.
1: 2 Now the *e* was formless and empty,
7:24 The waters flooded the *e*
14:19 Creator of heaven and *e*.
1Ki 8:27 "But will God really dwell on *e*?
Job 26: 7 he suspends the *e* over nothing.
Ps 24: 1 is the LORD's, and everything
46: 6 he lifts his voice, the *e* melts.
90: 2 or you brought forth the *e*
97: 5 before the Lord of all the *e*.
102:25 you laid the foundations of the *e*,
108: 5 and let your glory be over all the *e*.
Pr 8:26 before he made the *e* or its fields
Isa 6: 3 the whole *e* is full of his glory."
24:20 The *e* reels like a drunkard,
37:16 You have made heaven and *e*.
40:22 enthroned above the circle of the *e*,
51: 6 the *e* will wear out like a garment
54: 5 he is called the God of all the *e*.
55: 9 the heavens are higher than the *e*,
65:17 new heavens and a new *e*.
66: 1 and the *e* is my footstool.
Jer 10:10 When he is angry, the *e* trembles;
23:24 "Do not I fill heaven and *e*?"
33:25 and the fixed laws of heaven and *e*,
Hab 2:20 let all the *e* be silent before him."
Mt 5: 5 for they will inherit the *e*.
5:35 or by the *e*, for it is his footstool;
6: 10 done on *e* as it is in heaven.
16:19 bind on *e* will be bound
24:35 Heaven and *e* will pass away,
28:18 and on *e* has been given to me.
Lk 2:14 on *e* peace to men
Jn 12:32 when I am lifted up from the *e*,
Ac 4:24 "you made the heaven and the *e*
7:49 and the *e* is my footstool.
1Co 10:26 The *e* is the Lord's, and everything
Eph 3:15 in heaven and on *e* derives its name
Php 2:10 in heaven and on *e* and under the *e*,
Heb 1:10 you laid the foundations of the *e*,
2Pe 3:13 to a new heaven and a new *e*.
Rev 8: 7 A third of the *e* was burned up,
12:12 But woe to the *e* and the sea,
20:11 *E* and sky fled from his presence,
21: 1 I saw a new heaven and a new *e*,
21: 1 and the first *e* had passed away.

EARTH'S (EARTH)

Job 38: 4 when I laid the *e* foundation?

EARTHENWARE

Pr 26:23 Like a coating of glaze over *e*

EARTHLY (EARTH)

Eph 4: 9 descended to the lower, *e* regions?
Php 3:19 Their mind is on *e* things.
Col 3: 2 on things above, not on *e* things,
3: 5 whatever belongs to your *e* nature.

EARTHQUAKE (EARTHQUAKES)

Eze 38:19 at that time there shall be a great *e*
Mt 28: 2 There was a violent *e*, for an angel
Rev 6:12 There was a great *e*.

EARTHQUAKES (EARTHQUAKE)

Mt 24: 7 There will be famines and *e*

EASE

Pr 1:33 and be at *e*, without fear of harm."

EASIER (EASY)

Lk 16:17 It is *e* for heaven and earth
18:25 it is *e* for a camel to go

EAST

Ge 2: 8 God had planted a garden in the *e*,
Ps 103:12 as far as the *e* is from the west,
Eze 43: 2 God of Israel coming from the *e*.
Mt 2: 1 Magi from the *e* came to Jerusalem
2: 2 We saw his star in the *e*

EASY (EASIER)

Mt 11:30 For my yoke is *e* and my burden is

EAT (ATE EATEN EATER EATING EATS)

Ge 2:16 "You are free to *e* from any tree
2:17 but you must not *e* from the tree
3:19 you will *e* your food
Ex 12:11 in haste; it is the LORD's
Lev 11: 2 these are the ones you may *e*:
17:12 "None of you may *e* blood,
Dt 8:16 He gave you manna to *e*
14: 4 These are the animals you may *e*:

EATEN

Jdg 14: 14 "Out of the eater, something to e;
2Sa 9: 7 and you will always e at my table."
Pr 31: 27 and does not e the bread of idleness
Isa 55: 1 come, buy and e!
65: 25 and the lion will e straw like the ox,
Eze 3: 1 e what is before you, e this scroll;
Mt 14: 16 You give them something to e."
15: 2 wash their hands before they e!"
26: 26 "Take and e; this is my body."
Mk 14: 14 where I may e the Passover
Lk 10: 8 and are welcomed, e what is set
12: 19 Take life easy; e, drink
12: 22 what you will e; or about your body
Jn 4: 32 to e that you know nothing about."
6: 31 bread from heaven to e.' "
6: 52 can this man give us his flesh to e?"
Ac 10: 13 Kill and e."
Ro 14: 2 faith allows him to e everything,
14: 15 is distressed because of what you e,
14: 20 to e anything that causes someone
14: 21 It is better not to e meat
1Co 5: 11 With such a man do not even e.
8: 13 if what I e causes my brother to fall
10: 25 E anything sold in the meat market
10: 27 e whatever is put before you
10: 31 So whether you e or drink
11: 26 For whenever you e this bread
2Th 3: 10 man will not work, he shall not e."
Rev 2: 7 the right to e from the tree of life,
3: 20 I will come in and e with him,

EATEN (EAT)

Ge 3: 11 Have you e from the tree that I
Ac 10: 14 "I have never e anything impure
Rev 10: 10 when I had e it, my stomach turned

EATER (EAT)

Isa 55: 10 for the sower and bread for the e,

EATING (EAT)

Ex 34: 28 and forty nights without e bread
Ro 14: 15 not by your e destroy your brother
14: 17 kingdom of God is not a matter of e
14: 23 because his e is not from faith;
1Co 8: 4 about e food sacrificed to idols:
8: 10 you who have this knowledge e
Jude : 12 e with you without the slightest

EATS (EAT)

1Sa 14: 24 "Cursed be any man who e food
Lk 15: 2 "This man welcomes sinners and e
Jn 6: 51 If anyone e of this bread, he will live
6: 54 Whoever e my flesh and drinks my
Ro 14: 2 faith is weak, e only vegetables.
14: 3 man who e everything must not
14: 6 He who e meat, e to the Lord,
14: 23 has doubts is condemned if he e,
1Co 11: 27 whoever e the bread or drinks

EBAL

Dt 11: 29 and on Mount E the curses.
Jos 8: 30 Joshua built on Mount E an altar

EBENEZER

1Sa 7: 12 He named it E, saying, "Thus far

EDEN

Ge 2: 8 in E; and there he put the man
Eze 28: 13 You were in E,

EDGE (DOUBLE-EDGED)

Mt 9: 20 and touched the e of his cloak.

EDICT

Heb 11: 23 they were not afraid of the king's e.

EDIFICATION (EDIFIED EDIFIES)

Ro 14: 19 leads to peace and mutual e.

EDIFIED* (EDIFICATION)

1Co 14: 5 so that the church may be e.
14: 17 but the other man is not e.

EDIFIES* (EDIFICATION)

1Co 14: 4 but he who prophesies e the church
14: 4 speaks in a tongue e himself,

EDOM

Ge 36: 1 the account of Esau (that is, E)
36: 8 E) settled in the hill country of Seir
Isa 63: 1 Who is this coming from E
Ob : 1 Sovereign LORD says about E—

EDUCATED*

Ac 7: 22 Moses was e in all the wisdom

EFFECT* (EFFECTIVE)

Job 41: 26 sword that reaches him has no e.
Isa 32: 17 e of righteousness will be quietness
Ac 7: 53 put into e through angels
1Co 15: 10 his grace to me was not without e.
Gal 3: 19 put into e through angels
Eph 1: 10 put into e when the times will have
Heb 9: 17 it never takes e while the one who
9: 18 put into e without blood.

EFFECTIVE* (EFFECT)

1Co 16: 9 a great door for e work has opened
Jas 5: 16 a righteous man is powerful and e.

EFFORT*

Ecc 2: 19 into which I have poured my e
Da 6: 14 and made every e until sundown
Lk 13: 24 "Make every e to enter
Jn 5: 44 yet make no e to obtain the praise
Ro 9: 16 depend on man's desire or e,
14: 19 make every e to do what leads
Gal 3: 3 to attain your goal by human e?
Eph 4: 3 Make every e to keep the unity
1Th 2: 16 to all men in their e to keep us
2: 17 intense longing we made every e
Heb 4: 11 make every e to enter that rest,
12: 14 Make every e to live in peace
2Pe 1: 5 make every e to add
1: 15 And I will make every e to see that
3: 14 make every e to be found spotless,

EGG

Lk 11: 12 for an e, will give him a scorpion?

EGLON

1. Fat king of Moab killed by Ehud (Jdg 3: 12-30).
2. City in Canaan (Jos 10).

EGYPT (EGYPTIANS)

Ge 12: 10 went down to E to live there
37: 28 Ishmaelites, who took him to E.
42: 3 went down to buy grain from E.
45: 20 the best of all E will be yours.' "
46: 6 and all his offspring went to E.
47: 27 Now the Israelites settled in E.
Ex 3: 11 and bring the Israelites out of E?"
12: 40 lived in E was 430 years.
12: 41 all the LORD's divisions left E.
32: 1 Moses who brought us up out of E,
Nu 11: 18 We were better off in E!"
14: 4 choose a leader and go back to E."
24: 8 "God brought them out of E;
Dt 6: 21 "We were slaves of Pharaoh in E,
1Ki 4: 30 greater than all the wisdom of E.
10: 28 horses were imported from E
11: 40 but Jeroboam fled to E,
14: 25 king of E attacked Jerusalem.
2Ch 35: 20 Neco king of E went up to fight
36: 3 The king of E dethroned him
Isa 19: 23 a highway from E to Assyria.
Hos 11: 1 and out of E I called my son.
Mt 2: 15 "Out of E I called my son."
Heb 11: 27 By faith he left E, not fearing
Rev 11: 8 is figuratively called Sodom and E,

EGYPTIANS (EGYPT)

Nu 14: 13 "Then the E will hear about it!

EHUD

Left-handed judge who delivered Israel from Moabite king, Eglon (Jdg 3:12-30).

EKRON

1Sa 5: 10 So they sent the ark of God to E.

ELAH

Son of Baasha; king of Israel (1Ki 16:6-14).

ELATION

Pr 28: 12 righteous triumph, there is great e;

ELDER* (ELDERLY ELDERS)

Isa 3: 2 the soothsayer and e,
1Ti 5: 19 an accusation against an e
Tit 1: 6 e must be blameless, the husband
1Pe 5: 1 among you, I appeal as a fellow e,
2Jn : 1 The e, To the chosen lady
3Jn : 1 The e, To my dear friend Gaius.

ELDERLY* (ELDER)

Lev 19: 32 show respect for the e

ELDERS (ELDER)

1Ki 12: 8 rejected the advice the e gave him
Mt 15: 2 break the tradition of the e?
Mk 7: 3 holding to the tradition of the e.
7: 5 to the tradition of the e instead
Ac 11: 30 gift to the e by Barnabas
14: 23 and Barnabas appointed e for them
15: 2 the apostles and e about this
15: 4 the church and the apostles and e,
15: 6 and e met to consider this question.
15: 22 and e, with the whole church,
15: 23 The apostles and e, your brothers,
16: 4 and in Jerusalem for the people
20: 17 to Ephesus for the e of the church.
21: 18 and all the e were present.
23: 14 They went to the chief priests and e
24: 1 to Caesarea with some of the e
1Ti 4: 14 when the body of e laid their hands
5: 17 The e who direct the affairs
Tit 1: 5 and appoint e in every town,
Jas 5: 14 He should call the e of the church
1Pe 5: 1 To the e among you, I appeal
Rev 4: 4 seated on them were twenty-four e.
4: 10 the twenty-four e fall

ELEAZAR

Third son of Aaron (Ex 6:23-25). Succeeded Aaron as high priest (Nu 20:26; Dt 10:6). Allotted land to tribes (Jos 14:1). Death (Jos 24:33).

ELECT* (ELECTION)

Mt 24: 22 the sake of the e those days will be
24: 24 miracles to deceive even the e—
24: 31 and they will gather his e
Mk 13: 20 sake of the e, whom he has chosen,
13: 22 miracles to deceive the e—
13: 27 gather his e from the four winds,
Ro 11: 7 it did not obtain, but the e did.
1Ti 5: 21 and Christ Jesus and the e angels,
2Ti 2: 10 everything for the sake of the e,
Tit 1: 1 Christ for the faith of God's e
1Pe 1: 1 To God's e, strangers in the world,

ELECTION* (ELECT)

Ro 9: 11 God's purpose in e might stand:
11: 28 but as far as e is concerned,
2Pe 1: 10 to make your calling and e sure.

ELEMENTARY* (ELEMENTS)

Heb 5: 12 someone to teach you the e truths
6: 1 us leave the e teachings about

ELEMENTS* (ELEMENTARY)

2Pe 3: 10 the e will be destroyed by fire,
3: 12 and the e will melt in the heat.

ELEVATE*

2Co 11: 7 to e you by preaching the gospel

ELI

High priest in youth of Samuel (1Sa 1-4). Blessed Hannah (1Sa 1:12-18); raised Samuel (1Sa 2:11-26). Prophesied against because of wicked sons (1Sa 2:27-36). Death of Eli and sons (1Sa 4:11-22).

ELIHU

One of Job's friends (Job 32-37).

ELIJAH

Prophet; predicted famine in Israel (1Ki 17:1; Jas 5:17). Fed by ravens (1Ki 17:2-6). Raised Sidonian widow's son (1Ki 17:7-24). Defeated prophets of Baal at Carmel (1Ki 18:16-46). Ran from Jezebel (1Ki 19:1-9). Prophesied death of Azariah (2Ki 1). Succeeded by Elisha (1Ki 19: 19-21; 2Ki 2:1-18). Taken to heaven in whirlwind (2Ki 2:11-12).
Return prophesied (Mal 4:5-6); equated with John the Baptist (Mt 17:9-13; Mk 9:9-13; Lk 1: 17). Appeared with Moses in transfiguration of Jesus (Mt 17:1-8; Mk 9:1-8).

ELIMELECH

Ru 1: 3 Now E, Naomi's husband, died,

ELIPHAZ

1. Firstborn of Esau (Ge 36).
2. One of Job's friends (Job 4-5; 15; 22).

ELISHA

Prophet; successor of Elijah (1Ki 19:16-21); inherited his cloak (2Ki 2:1-18). Purified bad water (2Ki 2:19-22). Cursed young men (2Ki 2:

23-25). Aided Israel's defeat of Moab (2Ki 3).
Provided widow with oil (2Ki 4:1-7). Raised Shunammite woman's son (2Ki 4:8-37). Purified
food (2Ki 4:38-41). Fed 100 men (2Ki 4:42-44).
Healed Naaman's leprosy (2Ki 5). Made axhead
float (2Ki 6:1-7). Captured Arameans (2Ki 6:8-
23). Political adviser to Israel (2Ki 6:24-8:6; 9:
1-3; 13:14-19), Damascus (2Ki 8:7-15). Death
(2Ki 13:20).

ELIZABETH*

Mother of John the Baptist, relative of Mary
(Lk 1:5-58).

ELKANAH

Husband of Hannah, father of Samuel (1Sa
1-2).

ELOI*

Mt   27: 46 *"E, E, lama sabachthani?"—*
Mk   15: 34 *"E, E, lama sabachthani?"—*

ELOQUENCE* (ELOQUENT)

1Co   2: 1 come with *e* or superior wisdom

ELOQUENT* (ELOQUENCE)

Ex   4: 10 "O Lord, I have never been *e,*

ELYMAS

Ac   13: 8 *E* the sorcerer (for that is what his

EMBEDDED*

Ecc 12: 11 sayings like firmly *e* nails—

EMBERS

Pr   26: 21 As charcoal to *e* and as wood to fire

EMBITTER* (BITTER)

Col   3: 21 Fathers, do not *e* your children,

EMBODIMENT* (BODY)

Ro   2: 20 have in the law the *e* of knowledge

EMPTIED (EMPTY)

1Co   1: 17 the cross of Christ be *e* of its power.

EMPTY (EMPTIED)

Ge   1: 2 Now the earth was formless and *e.*
Job   26: 7 the northern skies over *e* space;
Isa   45: 18 he did not create it to be *e,*
       55: 11 It will not return to me *e,*
Jer   4: 23 and it was formless and *e,*
Lk   1: 53 but has sent the rich away *e.*
Eph   5: 6 no one deceive you with *e* words,
1Pe   1: 18 from the *e* way of life handed
2Pe   2: 18 For they mouth *e,* boastful words

ENABLE (ABLE)

Lk   1: 74 to *e* us to serve him without fear
Ac   4: 29 *e* your servants to speak your word

ENABLED* (ABLE)

Lev 26: 13 *e* you to walk with heads held high.
Ru   4: 13 And the LORD *e* her to conceive,
Jn   6: 65 unless the Father has *e* him."
Ac   2: 4 other tongues as the Spirit *e* them.
       7: 10 and *e* him to gain the goodwill
Heb 11: 11 was *e* to become a father

ENABLES (ABLE)

Php   3: 21 by the power that *e* him

ENABLING* (ABLE)

Ac   14: 3 the message of his grace by *e* them

ENCAMPS* (CAMP)

Ps   34: 7 The angel of the LORD *e*

**ENCOURAGE* (ENCOURAGED
ENCOURAGEMENT ENCOURAGES
ENCOURAGING)**

Dt   1: 38 *E* him, because he will lead Israel
       3: 28 and *e* and strengthen him,
2Sa 11: 25 Say this to Joab.'"
      19: 7 Now go out and *e* your men.
Job 16: 5 But my mouth would *e* you;
Ps   10: 17 you *e* them, and you listen
       64: 5 They *e* each other in evil plans.
Isa   1: 17 *e* the oppressed.
Jer   29: 8 to the dreams you *e* them to have.
Ac   15: 32 to *e* and strengthen the brothers.
Ro   12: 8 if it is encouraging, let him *e;*
Eph   6: 22 how we are, and that he may *e* you.
Col   4: 8 and that he may *e* your hearts.
1Th   3: 2 to strengthen and *e* you

1Th   4: 18 Therefore *e* each other
       5: 11 Therefore *e* one another
       5: 14 those who are idle, *e* the timid,
2Th   2: 17 *e* your hearts and strengthen you
2Ti   4: 2 rebuke and *e*— with great patience
Tit   1: 9 so that he can *e* others
       2: 6 *e* the young men to be
       2: 15 *E* and rebuke with all authority.
Heb   3: 13 But *e* one another daily, as long
      10: 25 but let us *e* one another—

ENCOURAGED* (ENCOURAGE)

Jdg   7: 11 you will be *e* to attack the camp."
      20: 22 But the men of Israel *e* one another
2Ch 22: 3 for his mother *e* him
      32: 6 and *e* them with these words:
      35: 2 and *e* them in the service
Eze 13: 22 you *e* the wicked not to turn
Ac   9: 31 It was strengthened; and *e*
      11: 23 and *e* them all to remain true
      16: 40 met with the brothers and *e* them.
      18: 27 the brothers *e* him and when
      27: 36 They were all *e* and ate some food
      28: 15 men Paul thanked God and was *e.*
Ro   1: 12 and I may be mutually *e*
1Co   14: 31 everyone may be instructed and *e*
2Co   7: 4 I am greatly *e;* in all our troubles
       7: 13 By all this we are *e.*
Php   1: 14 brothers in the Lord have been *e*
Col   2: 2 My purpose is that they may be *e*
1Th   3: 7 persecution we were *e* about you
Heb   6: 18 offered to us may be greatly *e.*

ENCOURAGEMENT* (ENCOURAGE)

Ac   4: 36 Barnabas (which means Son of *E*),
      13: 15 a message of *e* for the people,
      20: 2 speaking many words of *e*
Ro   15: 4 *e* of the Scriptures we might have
      15: 5 and *e* give you a spirit of unity
1Co   14: 3 to men for their strengthening, *e*
2Co   7: 13 to our own *e,* we were especially
Php   2: 1 If you have any *e* from being united
2Th   2: 16 and by his grace gave us eternal *e*
Phm   7 love has given me great joy and *e,*
Heb   12: 5 word of *e* that addresses you

ENCOURAGES* (ENCOURAGE)

Isa   41: 7 The craftsman *e* the goldsmith,

ENCOURAGING* (ENCOURAGE)

Ac   14: 22 *e* them to remain true to the faith.
      15: 31 and were glad for its *e* message.
      20: 1 for the disciples and, after *e* them,
Ro   12: 8 if it is *e,* let him encourage;
1Th   2: 12 *e,* comforting and urging you
1Pe   5: 12 *e* you and testifying that this is

ENCROACH

Pr   23: 10 or *e* on the fields of the fatherless,

END (ENDS)

Ps   119: 33 then I will keep them to the *e.*
     119:112 to the very *e.*
Pr   1: 19 Such is the *e* of all who go
       5: 4 but in the *e* she is bitter as gall,
       5: 11 At the *e* of your life you will groan,
      14: 12 but in the *e* it leads to death.
      14: 13 and joy may *e* in grief.
      16: 25 but in the *e* it leads to death.
      19: 20 and in the *e* you will be wise.
      20: 21 will not be blessed at the *e.*
      23: 32 In the *e* it bites like a snake
      25: 8 for what will you do in the *e*
      28: 23 in the *e* gain more favor
      29: 21 he will bring grief in the *e.*
Ecc   3: 11 done from beginning to *e.*
       7: 8 The *e* of a matter is better
      12: 12 making many books there is no *e,*
Eze   2: 2 The *e!* The *e* has come
Mt   10: 22 firm to the *e* will be saved.
      24: 13 firm to the *e* will be saved.
      24: 14 nations, and then the *e* will come.
Lk   21: 9 but the *e* will not come right away
Ro   10: 4 Christ is the *e* of the law
1Co   15: 24 the *e* will come, when he hands
Rev   21: 6 Omega, the Beginning and the *E.*
      22: 13 the Last, the Beginning and the *E.*

ENDS (END)

Ps   19: 4 their words to the *e* of the world.
Pr   20: 17 he *e* up with a mouth full of gravel.
Isa   49: 6 salvation to the *e* of the earth."
      62: 11 proclamation to the *e* of the earth:
Ac   13: 47 salvation to the *e* of the earth.' "
Ro   10: 18 their words to the *e* of the world."

ENDURANCE* (ENDURE)

Ro   15: 4 through *e* and the encouragement
      15: 5 May the God who gives *e*
2Co   1: 6 which produces in you patient *e*
       6: 4 in great *e,* in troubles, hardships
Col   1: 11 might so that you may have great *e*
1Th   1: 3 and your *e* inspired by hope
1Ti   6: 11 faith, love, *e* and gentleness.
2Ti   3: 10 patience, love, *e,* persecutions,
Tit   2: 2 and sound in faith, in love and in *e.*
Rev   1: 9 and patient that are ours in Jesus,
      13: 10 This calls for patient *e*
      14: 12 This calls for patient *e* on the part

**ENDURE (ENDURANCE ENDURED
ENDURES ENDURING)**

Ps   72: 17 May his name *e* forever;
Pr   12: 19 Truthful lips *e* forever,
      27: 24 for riches do not *e* forever,
Ecc   3: 14 everything God does will *e* forever;
Da   2: 44 to an end, but it will itself *e* forever.
Mal   3: 2 who can *e* the day of his coming?
1Co   4: 12 when we are persecuted, we *e* it;
2Co   1: 8 far beyond our ability to *e,*
2Ti   2: 3 *E* hardship with us like a good
       2: 10 Therefore I *e* everything
       2: 12 if we *e,* / we will also reign
       4: 5 head in all situations, *e* hardship,
Heb 12: 7 *E* hardship as discipline; God is
1Pe   2: 20 a beating for doing wrong and *e* it?
       2: 20 suffer for doing good and you *e* it,
Rev   3: 10 kept my command to *e* patiently,

ENDURED* (ENDURE)

Ps   123: 3 for we have *e* much contempt.
     123: 4 We have *e* much ridicule
     132: 1 and all the hardships he *e.*
Ac   13: 18 and *e* their conduct forty years
2Ti   3: 11 and Lystra, the persecutions I *e.*
Heb 12: 2 set before him the cross,
      12: 3 him who *e* such opposition
Rev   2: 3 and have *e* hardships for my name,

ENDURES (ENDURE)

Ps   102: 12 renown *e* through all generations.
     112: 9 his righteousness *e* forever;
     136: 1 *His love e forever.*
Da   6: 26 made for yourself a name that *e*
2Co   9: 9 his righteousness *e* forever.' "

ENDURING (ENDURE)

2Th   1: 4 persecutions and trials you are *e.*
1Pe   1: 23 through the living and *e* word

ENEMIES (ENEMY)

Ps   23: 5 in the presence of my *e.*
     110: 1 hand until I make your *e*
Pr   16: 7 his *e* live at peace with him.
Isa   59: 18 wrath to his *e*
Mic   7: 6 a man's *e* are the members
Mt   5: 44 Love your *e* and pray
      10: 36 a man's *e* will be the members
Lk   6: 27 Love your *e,* do good
       6: 35 But love your *e,* do good to them,
      20: 43 hand until I make your *e*
Ro   5: 10 For if, when we were God's *e,*
1Co   15: 25 reign until he has put all his *e*
Php   3: 18 many live as of the cross of Christ
Heb   1: 13 hand until I make your *e*
      10: 13 for his *e* to be made his footstool,

ENEMY (ENEMIES ENMITY)

Pr   24: 17 Do not gloat when your *e* falls;
      25: 21 If your *e* is hungry, give him food
      27: 6 but an *e* multiplies kisses.
      29: 24 of a thief is his own *e,*
Lk   10: 19 to overcome all the power of the *e;*
Ro   12: 20 "If your *e* is hungry, feed him;
1Co   15: 26 The last *e* to be destroyed is death.
1Ti   5: 14 and to give the *e* no opportunity
1Pe   5: 8 Your *e* the devil prowls

ENERGY*

Col   1: 29 struggling with all his *e,* which

ENGRAVED

Isa   49: 16 I have *e* you on the palms
2Co   3: 7 which was *e* in letters on stone,

ENHANCES*

Ro   3: 7 my falsehood *e* God's truthfulness

ENJOY (JOY)

Dt   6: 2 and so that you may *e* long life.

Ps 37: 3 dwell in the land and *e* safe pasture.
Pr 28:16 ill-gotten gain will *e* a long life.
Ecc 3:22 better for a man than to *e* his work.
Eph 6: 3 and that you may *e* long life
Heb 11:25 rather than to *e* the pleasures of sin
3Jn : 2 I pray that you may *e* good health

ENJOYMENT (JOY)

Ecc 4: 8 and why am I depriving myself of *e*
1Ti 6:17 us with everything for our *e.*

ENLARGE (ENLARGES)

2Co 9:10 *e* the harvest of your righteousness.

ENLARGES (ENLARGE)

Dt 33:20 Blessed is he who *e* Gad's domain!

ENLIGHTENED* (LIGHT)

Eph 1:18 that the eyes of your heart may be *e*
Heb 6:10 for those who have once been *e,*

ENMITY* (ENEMY)

Ge 3:15 And I will put *e*

ENOCH

1. Son of Cain (Ge 4:17-18).
2. Descendant of Seth; walked with God and taken by him (Ge 5:18-24; Heb 11:5). Prophet (Jude 14).

ENSLAVED (SLAVE)

Gal 4: 9 Do you wish to be *e* by them all
Tit 3: 3 and *e* by all kinds of passions

ENSNARE (SNARE)

Pr 5:22 of a wicked man *e* him;
Ecc 7:26 but the sinner she will *e.*

ENSNARED* (SNARE)

Dt 7:25 for yourselves, or you will be *e* by it
12:30 be careful not to be *e*
Ps 9:16 The wicked are *e* by the work
Pr 6: 2 *e* by the words of your mouth,
22:25 and get yourself *e.*

ENTANGLED (ENTANGLES)

2Pe 2:20 and are again *e* in it and overcome.

ENTANGLES* (ENTANGLED)

Heb 12: 1 and the sin that so easily *e,*

ENTER (ENTERED ENTERING ENTERS ENTRANCE)

Ps 95:11 "They shall never *e* my rest."
100: 4 *E* his gates with thanksgiving
Pr 2:10 For wisdom will *e* your heart,
Mt 5:20 will certainly not *e* the kingdom
7:13 "*E* through the narrow gate.
7:21 Lord,' will *e* the kingdom of heaven
18: 3 you will never *e* the kingdom
18: 8 It is better for you to *e* life maimed
19:17 to *e* life, obey the commandments
19:23 man to *e* the kingdom of heaven.
Mk 9:43 It is better for you to *e* life maimed
9:45 It is better for you to *e* life crippled
9:47 for you to *e* the kingdom of God
10:15 like a little child will never *e* it."
10:23 is for the rich to *e* the kingdom
Lk 13:24 will try to *e* and will not be able to.
13:24 "Make every effort to *e*
18:17 like a little child will never *e* it."
18:24 is for the rich to *e* the kingdom
Jn 3: 5 no one can *e* the kingdom of God.
Heb 3:11 'They shall never *e* my rest.' "
4:11 make every effort to *e* that rest.

ENTERED (ENTER)

Ps 73:17 me till I *e* the sanctuary of God;
Eze 4:14 meat has ever *e* my mouth."
Ac 11: 8 or unclean has ever *e* my mouth."
Ro 5:12 as sin *e* the world through one man,
Heb 9:12 but he *e* the Most Holy Place once

ENTERING (ENTER)

Mt 21:31 the prostitutes are *e* the kingdom
Lk 11:52 have hindered those who were *e.*"
Heb 4: 1 the promise of *e* his rest still stands,

ENTERS (ENTER)

Mk 7:18 you see that nothing that a man
Jn 10: 2 The man who *e* by the gate is

ENTERTAIN* (ENTERTAINED ENTERTAINMENT)

Jdg 16:25 "Bring out Samson to *e* us."

Mt 9: 4 "Why do you *e* evil thoughts
1Ti 5:19 Do not *e* an accusation
Heb 13: 2 Do not forget to *e* strangers,

ENTERTAINED* (ENTERTAIN)

Ac 28: 7 and for three days *e* us hospitably.
Heb 13: 2 so doing some people have *e* angels

ENTERTAINMENT* (ENTERTAIN)

Da 6:18 without any *e* being brought to him

ENTHRALLED*

Ps 45:11 The king is *e* by your beauty;

ENTHRONED* (THRONE)

1Sa 4: 4 who is *e* between the cherubim.
2Sa 6: 2 who is *e* between the cherubim that
2Ki 19:15 of Israel, *e* between the cherubim,
1Ch 13: 6 who is *e* between the cherubim—
Ps 2: 4 The One in heaven laughs;
9:11 to the Lord, *e* in Zion;
22: 3 Yet you are *e* as the Holy One,
29:10 The Lord sits *e* over the flood;
29:10 The Lord is *e* as King forever.
55:19 God, who is *e* forever,
61: 7 May he be *e* in God's presence
80: 1 who sit *e* between the cherubim,
99: 1 he sits *e* between the cherubim,
102:12 But you, O Lord, sit *e* forever;
113: 5 the One who sits *e* on high,
132:14 here I will sit *e,* for I have desired it
Isa 14:13 I will sit *e* on the mount
37:16 of Israel, *e* between the cherubim,
40:22 He sits *e* above the circle
52: 2 rise up, sit *e,* O Jerusalem.

ENTHRONES* (THRONE)

Job 36: 7 he *e* them with kings

ENTHUSIASM*

2Co 8:17 he is coming to you with much *e*
9: 2 and your *e* has stirred most of them

ENTICE* (ENTICED ENTICES)

Pr 1:10 My son, if sinners *e* you,
2Pe 2:18 they *e* people who are just escaping
Rev 2:14 who taught Balak to *e* the Israelites

ENTICED* (ENTICE)

Dt 4:19 do not be *e* into bowing
11:16 or you will be *e* to turn away
2Ki 17:21 Jeroboam *e* Israel away
Job 31: 9 If my heart has been *e* by a woman,
31:27 so that my heart was secretly *e*
Jas 1:14 desire, he is dragged away and *e.*

ENTICES* (ENTICE)

Dt 13: 6 your closest friend secretly *e* you,
Job 36:18 Be careful that no one *e* you
Pr 16:29 A violent man *e* his neighbor

ENTIRE

Gal 5:14 The *e* law is summed up

ENTRANCE (ENTER)

Mt 27:60 stone in front of the *e* to the tomb
Mk 15:46 a stone against the *e* of the tomb.
16: 3 away from the *e* of the tomb?"
Jn 11:38 cave with a stone laid across the *e.*
20: 1 had been removed from the *e.*

ENTRUST (TRUST)

Jn 2:24 Jesus would not *e* himself to them,
2Ti 2: 2 the presence of many witnesses *e*

ENTRUSTED (TRUST)

Jer 13:20 Where is the flock that was *e* to you
Jn 5:22 but has *e* all judgment to the Son,
Ro 3: 2 they have been *e* with the very
6:17 of teaching to which you were *e.*
1Co 4: 1 as those *e* with the secret things
1Th 2: 4 by God to be *e* with the gospel.
1Ti 1:11 of the blessed God, which he *e*
6:20 guard what has been *e* to your care.
2Ti 1:12 able to guard what I have *e* to him
1:14 Guard the good deposit that was *e*
Tit 1: 3 light through the preaching *e* to me
1: 7 Since an overseer is *e*
1Pe 2:23 he *e* himself to him who judges
Jude 3 once lording it over those *e* to you,
3 once for all *e* to the saints.

ENVIES

Jas 4: 5 spirit he caused to live in us *e*

ENVIOUS (ENVY)

Dt 32:21 I will make them *e*
Pr 24:19 or be *e* of the wicked,
Ro 10:19 "I will make you *e*

ENVOY

Pr 13:17 but a trustworthy *e* brings healing.

ENVY (ENVIOUS ENVYING)

Pr 3:31 Do not *e* a violent man
14:30 but *e* rots the bones.
23:17 Do not let your heart *e* sinners,
24: 1 Do not *e* wicked men,
Mk 7:22 malice, deceit, lewdness, *e,* slander
Ro 1:29 They are full of *e,* murder, strife,
11:14 arouse my own people to *e*
1Co 13: 4 It does not *e,* it does not boast,
Gal 5:21 factions and *e,* drunkenness, orgies
Php 1:15 that some preach Christ out of *e*
1Ti 6: 4 and quarrels about words that result in *e,*
Tit 3: 3 lived in malice and *e,* being hated
Jas 3:14 But if you harbor bitter *e*
3:16 where you have *e* and selfish
1Pe 2: 1 *e,* and slander of every kind.

ENVYING* (ENVY)

Gal 5:26 provoking and *e* each other.

EPHAH

Eze 45:11 The *e* and the bath are

EPHESUS

Ac 18:19 at *E.* where Paul left Priscilla
19: 1 the interior and arrived at *E.*
Eph 1: 1 To the saints in *E,* the faithful
Rev 2: 1 the angel of the church in *E* write:

EPHRAIM

1. Second son of Joseph (Ge 41:52; 46:20). Blessed as firstborn by Jacob (Ge 48). Tribe of numbered (Nu 1:33; 26:37), blessed (Dt 33:17), allotted land (Jos 16:4-9; Eze 48:5), failed to fully possess (Jos 16:10; Jdg 1:29).
2. Synonymous with Northern Kingdom (Isa 7:17; Hos 5).

EQUAL (EQUALITY EQUITY)

Dt 33:25 and your strength will *e* your days.
1Sa 9: 2 without *e* among the Israelites—
Isa 40:25 who is my *e?*" says the Holy One.
46: 5 you compare me or count me *e?*
Da 1:19 and he found none *e* to Daniel,
Jn 5:18 making himself *e* with God.
1Co 12:25 that its parts should have *e* concern
2Co 2:16 And who is *e* to such a task?

EQUALITY* (EQUAL)

2Co 8:13 pressed, but that there might be *e.*
8:14 Then there will be *e,* as it is written:
Php 2: 6 did not consider *e*

EQUIP* (EQUIPPED)

Heb 13:21 *e* you with everything good

EQUIPPED (EQUIP)

2Ti 3:17 man of God may be thoroughly *e*

EQUITY* (EQUAL)

Ps 96:10 he will judge the peoples with *e.*
98: 9 and the peoples with *e.*
99: 4 you have established *e;*

ERODES*

Job 14:18 "But as a mountain *e* and crumbles

ERROR (ERRORS)

Jas 5:20 Whoever turns a sinner from the *e*
2Pe 2:18 escaping from those who live in *e.*

ERRORS* (ERROR)

Ps 19:12 Who can discern his *e?*
Ecc 10: 4 calmness can lay great *e* to rest.

ESAU

Firstborn of Isaac, twin of Jacob (Ge 25:21-26). Also called Edom (Ge 25:30). Sold Jacob his birthright (Ge 25:29-34); lost blessing (Ge 27). Married Hittites (Ge 26:34), Ishmaelites (Ge 28:6-9). Reconciled to Jacob (Ge 33). Genealogy (Ge 36). The Lord chose Jacob over Esau (Mal 1:2-3), but gave Esau land (Dt 2:2-12). Descendants eventually obliterated (Ob 1-21; Jer 49:7-22).

ESCAPE (ESCAPED ESCAPES ESCAPING)

Ps 68:20 from the Sovereign LORD comes e
Pr 11: 9 through knowledge the righteous e
Ro   2: 3 think you will e God's judgment?
1Th 5: 3 woman, and they will not e.
2Ti 2:26 and e from the trap of the devil.
Heb 2: 3 how shall we e if we ignore such
    12:25 If they did not e when they refused
2Pe 1: 4 and the corruption in the world

ESCAPED (ESCAPE)

2Pe 2:20 If they have e the corruption

ESCAPES (ESCAPE)

Pr 12:13 but a righteous man e trouble.

ESCAPING (ESCAPE)

1Co 3:15 only as one e through the flames.
2Pe 2:18 they entice people who are just e

ESTABLISH (ESTABLISHED ESTABLISHES)

Ge 6:18 But I will e my covenant with you,
    17:21 But my covenant I will e with Isaac
2Sa 7:11 the LORD himself will e a house
1Ki 9: 5 I will e your royal throne
1Ch 28: 7 I will e his kingdom forever
Ps 90:17 e the work of our hands for us—
Isa 26:12 LORD, you e peace for us;
Ro 10: 3 God and sought to e their own,
    16:25 able to e you by my gospel
Heb 10: 9 sets aside the first to e the second.

ESTABLISHED (ESTABLISH)

Ge 9:17 the sign of the covenant I have e
Ex 4:30 also e my covenant with them
Pr 16:12 a throne is e through righteousness.

ESTABLISHES (ESTABLISH)

Job 25: 2 he e order in the heights of heaven.
Isa 42: 4 till he e justice on earth.

ESTATE

Ps 136:23 who remembered us in our low e

ESTEEMED

Pr 22: 1 to be e is better than silver or gold.
Isa 53: 3 he was despised, and we e him not.

ESTHER

Jewess, originally named Hadassah, who lived in Persia; cousin of Mordecai (Est 2:7). Chosen queen of Xerxes (Est 2:8-18). Persuaded by Mordecai to foil Haman's plan to exterminate the Jews (Est 3-4). Revealed Haman's plans to Xerxes, resulting in Haman's death (Est 7), the Jews' preservation (Est 8-9), Mordecai's exaltation (Est 8:15; 9:4; 10). Decreed celebration of Purim (Est 9:18-32).

ETERNAL* (ETERNALLY ETERNITY)

Ge 21:33 the name of the LORD, the E God.
Dt 33:27 The e God is your refuge,
1Ki 10: 9 of the LORD's e love for Israel,
Ps 16:11 with e pleasures at your right hand.
    21: 6 you have granted him e blessings
    111:10 To him belongs e praise.
    119:89 Your word, O LORD, is e;
    119:160 all your righteous laws are e.
Ecc 12: 5 Then man goes to his e home
Isa 26: 4 LORD, the LORD, is the Rock e.
    47: 7 the e queen!'
Jer 10:10 he is the living God, the e King.
Da 4: 3 His kingdom is an e kingdom;
    4:34 His dominion is an e dominion;
Hab 3: 6 His ways are e.
Mt 18: 8 two feet and be thrown into e fire.
    19:16 good thing must I do to get e life?"
    19:29 as much and will inherit e life.
    25:41 into the e fire prepared for the devil
    25:46 but the righteous to e life."
    25:46 they will go away to e punishment,
Mk 3:29 be forgiven; he is guilty of an e sin."
    10:17 "what must I do to inherit e life?"
    10:30 and in the age to come, e life.
Lk 10:25 "what must I do to inherit e life?"
    16: 9 will be welcomed into e dwellings.
    18:18 what must I do to inherit e life?"
    18:30 and, in the age to come, e life.
Jn 3:15 believes in him may have e life.
    3:16 him shall not perish but have e life.
    3:36 believes in the Son has e life,
    4:14 spring of water welling up to e life."
    4:36 now he harvests the crop for e life,
    5:24 believes him who sent me has e life

Jn 5:39 that by them you possess e life.
    6:27 but for food that endures to e life,
    6:40 believes in him shall have e life,
    6:54 and drinks my blood has e life.
    6:68 You have the words of e life.
    10:28 I give them e life, and they shall
    12:25 in this world will keep it for e life.
    12:50 that his command leads to e life.
    17: 2 all people that he might give e life
    17: 3 this is e life: that they may know
Ac 13:46 yourselves worthy of e life.
    13:48 were appointed for e life believed.
Ro 1:20 his e power and divine nature—
    2: 7 and immortality, he will give e life.
    5:21 righteousness to bring e life
    6:22 to holiness, and the result is e life.
    6:23 but the gift of God is e life
    16:26 by the command of the e God,
2Co 4:17 for us an e glory that far outweighs
    4:18 temporary, but what is unseen is e.
    5: 1 from God, an e house in heaven,
Gal 6: 8 from the Spirit will reap e life.
Eph 3:11 to his e purpose which he
2Th 2:16 his grace gave us e encouragement
1Ti 1:16 believe on him and receive e life.
    1:17 Now to the King e, immortal,
    6:12 Take hold of the e life
2Ti 2:10 is in Christ Jesus, with e glory.
Tit 1: 2 resting on the hope of e life,
    3: 7 heirs having the hope of e life.
Heb 5: 9 he became the source of e salvation
    6: 2 of the dead, and e judgment.
    9:12 having obtained e redemption.
    9:14 through the e Spirit offered himself
    9:15 the promised e inheritance—
    13:20 of the e covenant brought back
1Pe 5:10 you to his e glory in Christ,
2Pe 1:11 into the e kingdom of our Lord
1Jn 1: 2 and we proclaim to you the e life,
    2:25 what he promised us—even e life.
    3:15 know that no murderer has e life
    5:11 God has given us e life,
    5:13 you may know that you have e life.
    5:20 He is the true God and e life.
Jude : 7 who suffer the punishment of e fire.
    :21 Christ to bring you to e life.
Rev 14: 6 and he had the e gospel to proclaim

ETERNALLY* (ETERNAL)

Gal 1: 8 let him be e condemned! As we
    1: 9 let him be e condemned! Am I now

ETERNITY* (ETERNAL)

Ps 93: 2 you are from all e.
Pr 8:23 I was appointed from e,
Ecc 3:11 also set e in the hearts of men;

ETHIOPIAN*

Jer 13:23 Can the E change his skin
Ac 8:27 and on his way he met an E eunuch

EUNUCH (EUNUCHS)

Ac 8:27 on his way he met an Ethiopian e,

EUNUCHS (EUNUCH)

Isa 56: 4 "To the e who keep my Sabbaths,
Mt 19:12 For some are e because they were

EUTYCHUS*

Ac 20: 9 was a young man named E,

EVANGELIST* (EVANGELISTS)

Ac 21: 8 stayed at the house of Philip the e,
2Ti 4: 5 hardship, do the work of an e,

EVANGELISTS* (EVANGELIST)

Eph 4:11 some to be prophets, some to be e,

EVE*

Ge 3:20 Adam named his wife E,
    4: 1 Adam lay with his wife E,
2Co 11: 3 as E was deceived by the serpent's
1Ti 2:13 For Adam was formed first, then E

EVEN-TEMPERED* (TEMPER)

Pr 17:27 and a man of understanding is e.

EVENING

Ge 1: 5 there was e, and there was morning

EVER (EVERLASTING FOREVER FOREVERMORE)

Ex 15:18 LORD will reign for e and e. "
Dt 8:19 If you forget the LORD your
1Ki 3:12 anyone like you, nor will there e be.

Job 4: 7 were the upright e destroyed?
Ps 5:11 let them e sing for joy.
    10:16 The LORD is King for e and e;
    21: 4 length of days, for e and e.
    25: 3 will e be put to shame,
    25:15 My eyes are e on the LORD,
    26: 3 for your love is e before me,
    45: 6 O God, will last for e and e.
    45:17 nations will praise you for e and e.
    48:14 For this God is our God for e and e;
    52: 8 God's unfailing love for e and e.
    61: 8 will I e sing praise to your name
    71: 6 I will e praise you.
    84: 4 they are e praising you.
    89:33 nor will I e betray my faithfulness.
    111: 8 They are steadfast for e and e.
    119:44 your law, for e and e.
    119:98 for they are e with me.
    132:12 sit on your throne for e and e. ''
    145: 1 I will praise your name for e and e.
    145: 2 and extol your name for e and e.
    145:21 his holy name for e and e.
Pr 4:18 shining e brighter till the full light
    5:19 may you e be captivated
Isa 66: 8 Who has e heard of such a thing?
    66: 8 Who has e seen such things?
Jer 7: 7 I gave your forefathers for e and e.
    25: 5 and your fathers for e and e.
    31:36 the descendants of Israel e cease
Da 2:20 be to the name of God for e and e;
    7:18 it forever—yes, for e and e. '
    12: 3 like the stars for e and e.
Mic 4: 5 our God for e and e.
Mt 13:14 you will be e seeing but never
    13:14 ''You will be e hearing
Mk 4:12 e hearing but never understanding;
Jn 1:18 No one has e seen God,
Gal 1: 5 to whom be glory for e and e.
Eph 3:21 all generations, for e and e!
Php 4:20 and Father be glory for e and e.
1Ti 1:17 be honor and glory for e and e.
2Ti 4:18 To him be glory for e and e.
Heb 1: 8 O God, will last for e and e.
    13:21 to whom be glory for e and e.
1Pe 4:11 the glory and the power for e and e.
    5:11 To him be the power for e and e.
1Jn 4:12 No one has e seen God;
Rev 1: 6 him be glory and power for e and e!
    1:18 and behold I am alive for e and e!
    21:27 Nothing impure will e enter it,
    22: 5 And they will reign for e and e.

EVER-INCREASING* (INCREASE)

Ro 6:19 to impurity and to e wickedness,
2Co 3:18 into his likeness with e glory.

EVERLASTING* (EVER)

Ge 9:16 and remember the e covenant
    17: 7 an e covenant between me and you
    17: 8 I will give as an e possession to you
    17:13 in your flesh is to be an e covenant.
    17:19 an e covenant for his descendants
    48: 4 e possession to your descendants
Nu 18:19 It is an e covenant of salt
Dt 33:15 and the fruitfulness of the e hills;
    33:27 and underneath are the e arms.
2Sa 23: 5 made with me an e covenant,
1Ch 16:17 to Israel as an e covenant:
    16:36 from e to e.
    29:10 from e to e.
Ezr 9:12 to your children as an e inheritance
Ne 9: 5 your God, who is from e to e. ''
Ps 41:13 from e to e.
    52: 5 God will bring you down to e ruin:
    74: 3 toward these e ruins,
    78:66 he put them to e shame.
    90: 2 from e to e you are God.
    103:17 But from e to e
    105:10 to Israel as an e covenant:
    106:48 from e to e.
    119:142 Your righteousness is e
    139:24 and lead me in the way e.
    145:13 Your kingdom is an e kingdom,
Isa 9: 6 E Father, Prince of Peace.
    24: 5 and broken the e covenant.
    30: 8 it may be an e witness.
    33:14 Who of us can dwell with e burning
    35:10 e joy will crown their heads.
    40:28 The LORD is the e God,
    45:17 the LORD with an e salvation;
    45:17 to ages e.
    51:11 e joy will crown their heads.
    54: 8 but with e kindness
    55: 3 I will make an e covenant with you,
    55:13 for an e sign,

Isa 56: 5 I will give them an e name
60: 15 I will make you the e pride
60: 19 for the LORD will be your e light,
60: 20 the LORD will be your e light,
61: 7 and e joy will be theirs.
61: 8 and make an e covenant with them.
63: 12 to gain for himself e renown,
Jer 5: 22 an e barrier it cannot cross.
23: 40 I will bring upon you e disgrace—
23: 40 shame that will not be forgotten."
25: 9 of horror and scorn, and an e ruin.
31: 3 "I have loved you with an e love;
32: 40 I will make an e covenant
50: 5 the LORD in an e covenant
Eze 16: 60 and I will establish an e covenant
37: 26 with them; it will be an e covenant.
Da 7: 14 dominion is an e dominion that will
7: 27 His kingdom will be an e kingdom,
9: 24 to bring in e righteousness,
12: 2 others to shame and e contempt.
12: 2 some to e life, others to shame
Mic 2: 9 you e foundations of the earth.
Hab 1: 12 O LORD, are you not from e?
Jn 6: 47 the truth, he who believes has e life.
2Th 1: 9 punished with e destruction
Jude 6 bound with e chains for judgment

EVER-PRESENT*

Ps 46: 1 an e help in trouble

EVIDENCE (EVIDENT)

Jn 14: 11 on the e of the miracles themselves.
Ac 11: 23 and saw the e of the grace of God.
2Th 1: 5 All this is e that God's judgment is
Jas 2: 20 do you want e that faith

EVIDENT (EVIDENCE)

Php 4: 5 Let your gentleness be e to all.

EVIL (EVILDOER EVILDOERS EVILS)

Ge 2: 9 of the knowledge of good and e.
3: 5 be like God, knowing good and e."
6: 5 of his heart was only e all the time.
Ex 32: 22 how prone these people are to e.
Jdg 2: 11 Then the Israelites did e in the eyes
3: 7 The Israelites did e in the eyes
3: 12 Once again the Israelites did e
4: 1 the Israelites once again did e
6: 1 Again the Israelites did e
10: 6 Again the Israelites did e
13: 1 Again the Israelites did e
1Ki 11: 6 So Solomon did e in the eyes
16: 25 But Omri did e in the eyes
2Ki 15: 24 Pekahiah did e in the eyes
Job 1: 1 he feared God and shunned e.
1: 8 a man who fears God and shuns e."
34: 10 Far be it from God to do e,
36: 21 Beware of turning to e,
Ps 4: 5 not a God who takes pleasure in e;
23: 4 I will fear no e,
34: 13 keep your tongue from e
34: 14 Turn from e and do good;
34: 16 is against those who do e,
37: 1 Do not fret because of e men
37: 8 do not fret—it leads only to e.
37: 27 Turn from e and do good;
49: 5 fear when e days come,
51: 4 and done what is e in your sight,
97: 10 those who love the LORD hate e,
101: 4 I will have nothing to do with e.
141: 4 not my heart be drawn to what is e,
Pr 4: 27 keep your foot from e.
8: 13 To fear the LORD is to hate e;
10: 23 A fool finds pleasure in e conduct,
11: 19 he who pursues e goes to his death.
11: 27 e comes to him who searches for it.
14: 16 man fears the LORD and shuns e.
17: 13 If a man pays back e for good,
20: 30 Blows and wounds cleanse away e,
24: 19 Do not fret because of e men
24: 20 for the e man has no future hope,
26: 23 are fervent lips with an e heart.
28: 5 E men do not understand justice,
29: 6 An e man is snared by his own sin,
Ecc 12: 14 whether it is good or e.
Isa 5: 20 Woe to those who call e good
13: 11 I will punish the world for its e,
55: 7 and the e man his thoughts.
Jer 4: 14 wash the e from your heart
18: 8 nation I warned repents of its e,
18: 11 So turn from your e ways.
Eze 33: 11 Turn! Turn from your e ways!
33: 13 he will die for the e he has done.
33: 15 and does no e, he will surely live;
Am 5: 13 for the times are e.

Hab 1: 13 Your eyes are too pure to look on e;
Zec 8: 17 do not plot e against your neighbor.
Mt 5: 45 He causes his sun to rise on the e
6: 13 but deliver us from the e one.'
7: 11 If you, then, though you are e,
12: 34 you who are e say anything good?
12: 35 and the e man brings e things out
12: 35 out of the e stored up in him.
12: 43 "When an e spirit comes out
15: 19 out of the heart come e thoughts,
Mk 7: 21 come e thoughts, sexual
Lk 6: 45 and the e man brings e things out
11: 13 If you, then, though you are e,
Jn 3: 19 of light because their deeds were e.
3: 20 Everyone who does e hates
17: 15 you protect them from the e one.
Ro 1: 30 they invent ways of doing e;
2: 8 who reject the truth and follow
3: 9 for every human being who does e;
3: 8 "Let us do e that good may result"?
6: 12 body so that you obey its e desires.
7: 19 no, the e I do not want to do—
7: 21 to do good, e is right there with me.
12: 9 Hate what is e; cling
12: 17 Do not repay anyone e for e.
12: 21 Do not be overcome by e,
16: 19 good to be spoken of as e.
16: 19 and innocent about what is e.
1Co 13: 5 Love does not delight in e
14: 20 In regard to e be infants,
Eph 5: 16 because the days are e.
6: 12 forces of e in the heavenly realms.
6: 16 all the flaming arrows of the e one.
Col 3: 5 impurity, lust, e desires and greed,
1Th 5: 22 Avoid every kind of e.
2Th 3: 3 and protect you from the e one.
1Ti 6: 10 of money is a root of all kinds of e.
2Ti 2: 22 Flee the e desires of youth,
3: 6 are swayed by all kinds of e desires,
3: 13 while e men and impostors will go
Heb 5: 14 to distinguish good from e.
Jas 1: 13 For God cannot be tempted by e,
1: 21 and the e that is so prevalent,
3: 6 a world of e among the parts
3: 8 It is a restless e, full
1Pe 2: 16 your freedom as a cover-up for e;
3: 9 Do not repay e with e or insult
3: 10 must keep his tongue from e
3: 17 for doing good than for doing e.
1Jn 2: 13 you have overcome the e one.
2: 14 and you have overcome the e one.
3: 12 who belonged to the e one
5: 18 and the e one cannot harm him.
5: 19 is under the control of the e one.
3Jn 11 do not imitate what is e

EVILDOER* (EVIL)

2Sa 3: 39 the LORD repay the e according
Ps 101: 8 I will cut off every e
Mal 4: 1 and every e will be stubble.

EVILDOERS* (EVIL)

1Sa 24: 13 saying goes, 'From e come evil
Job 8: 20 or strengthen the hands of e.
34: 8 He keeps company with e;
34: 22 where e can hide.
Ps 14: 4 Will e never learn—
14: 6 You e frustrate the plans
26: 5 I abhor the assembly of e.
36: 12 See how the e lie fallen—
53: 4 Will the e never learn—
59: 2 Deliver me from e
64: 2 from that noisy crowd of e.
92: 7 and all e flourish,
92: 9 all e will be scattered.
94: 4 all the e are full of boasting.
94: 16 will take a stand for me against e?
119:115 Away from me, you e,
125: 5 the LORD will banish with the e.
141: 4 deeds with men who are e;
141: 5 ever against the deeds of e;
141: 9 from the traps set by e.
Pr 21: 15 but terror to e.
Isa 1: 4 a brood of e,
31: 2 against those who help e.
Jer 23: 14 They strengthen the hands of e,
Hos 10: 9 the e in Gibeah?
Mal 3: 15 Certainly the e prosper, and
Mt 7: 23 you e!' 'Therefore everyone who
Lk 18: 11 e, adulterers—or even like this tax

EVILS* (EVIL)

Mk 7: 23 All these e come from inside

EWE

2Sa 12: 3 one little e lamb he had bought.

EXACT*

Ge 43: 21 the e weight—in the mouth
Est 4: 7 including the e amount
Mt 2: 7 from them the e time the star had
Jn 4: 53 realized that this was the e time
Ac 17: 26 the e places where they should live.
Heb 1: 3 the e representation of his being,

EXALT* (EXALTED EXALTS)

Ex 15: 2 my father's God, and I will e him.
Jos 3: 7 begin to e you in the eyes
1Sa 2: 10 and e the horn of his anointed."
1Ch 25: 5 the promises of God to e him.
29: 12 power to e and give strength to all.
Job 19: 5 If indeed you would e yourselves
Ps 30: 1 I will e you, O LORD,
34: 3 let us e his name together.
35: 26 may all who e themselves over me
37: 34 He will e you to inherit the land;
38: 16 e themselves over me
75: 6 or from the desert can e a man.
89: 17 and by your favor you e our horn.
99: 5 E the LORD our God
99: 9 E the LORD our God
107: 32 Let them e him in the assembly
118: 28 you are my God, and I will e you.
145: 1 I will e you, my God the King;
Pr 4: 8 Esteem her, and she will e you;
25: 6 Do not e yourself in the king's
Isa 24: 15 e the name of the LORD, the God
25: 1 I will e you and praise your name,
Eze 29: 15 and will never again e itself
Da 4: 37 e and glorify the King of heaven,
11: 36 He will e and magnify himself
11: 37 but will e himself above them all.
Hos 11: 7 he will by no means e them.
2Th 2: 4 will e himself over everything that is

EXALTED* (EXALT)

Ex 15: 1 for he is highly e.
15: 21 for he is highly e.
Nu 24: 7 their kingdom will be e.
Jos 4: 14 That day the LORD e Joshua
2Sa 5: 12 and had e his kingdom for the sake
22: 47 E be God, the Rock, my Savior!
22: 49 You e me above my foes;
23: 1 of the man e by the Most High,
1Ch 14: 2 that his kingdom had been highly e
17: 17 as though I were the most e of men,
29: 11 you are e as head over all.
29: 25 The LORD highly e Solomon
Ne 9: 5 and may it be e above all blessing
Job 24: 24 For a little while they are e,
36: 22 "God is e in his power.
37: 23 beyond our reach and e in power;
Ps 18: 46 E be God my Savior!
18: 48 You e me above my foes;
21: 13 Be e, O LORD, in your strength;
27: 6 Then my head will be e
35: 27 they always say, "The LORD be e,
40: 16 "The LORD be e!"
46: 10 I will be e among the nations,
46: 10 I will be e in the earth."
47: 9 he is greatly e.
57: 5 Be e, O God, above the heavens;
57: 11 Be e, O God, above the heavens;
70: 4 "Let God be e!"
89: 13 hand is strong, your right hand is
89: 19 I have e a young man
89: 24 through my name his horn will be e
89: 27 the most e of the kings of the earth.
89: 42 You have e the right hand
92: 8 But you, O LORD, are e forever.
92: 10 You have e my horn like that
97: 9 you are e far above all gods.
99: 2 he is e over all the nations.
108: 5 Be e, O God, above the heavens,
113: 4 The LORD is e over all the nations
138: 2 for you have e above all things
148: 13 for his name alone is e;
Pr 11: 11 of the upright a city is e,
30: 32 have played the fool and e yourself,
Isa 2: 11 the LORD alone will be e
2: 12 for all that is e
2: 17 the LORD alone will be e
5: 16 the LORD Almighty will be e
6: 1 e, and the train of his robe filled
12: 4 and proclaim that his name is e.
24: 4 the e of the earth languish.
33: 5 The LORD is e, for he dwells
33: 10 "Now will I be e;

Isa   52: 13 be raised and lifted up and highly *e.*
Jer   17: 12 A glorious throne, *e*
La   2: 17 he has *e* the horn of your foes.
Eze   21: 26 The lowly will be *e* and the *e* will be
Hos   13: 1 he was *e* in Israel.
Mic   6: 6 and bow down before the *e* God?
Mt   23: 12 whoever humbles himself will be *e*
Lk   14: 11 he who humbles himself will be *e.* "
          18: 14 he who humbles himself will be *e.* "
Ac   2: 33 *E* to the right hand of God,
           5: 31 God *e* him to his own right hand
Php   1: 20 always Christ will be *e* in my body,
           2: 9 Therefore God *e* him
Heb   7: 26 from sinners, *e* above the heavens.

EXALTS* (EXALT)

1Sa   2: 7 he humbles and he *e.*
Job   36: 7 and *e* them forever.
Ps   75: 7 He brings one down, he *e* another.
Pr   14: 34 Righteousness *e* a nation,
Mt   23: 12 For whoever *e* himself will be
Lk   14: 11 For everyone who *e* himself will be
          18: 14 For everyone who *e* himself will be

EXAMINE (EXAMINED EXAMINES)

Ps   11: 4 his eyes *e* them.
          17: 3 you probe my heart and *e* me
          26: 2 *e* my heart and my mind;
Jer   17: 10 and *e* the mind,
          20: 12 Almighty, you who *e* the righteous
La   3: 40 Let us *e* our ways and test them,
1Co   11: 28 A man ought to *e* himself
2Co   13: 5 *E* yourselves to see whether you

EXAMINED (EXAMINE)

Job   13: 9 Would it turn out well if he *e* you?
Ac   17: 11 *e* the Scriptures every day to see

EXAMINES (EXAMINE)

Ps   11: 5 The LORD *e* the righteous,
Pr   5: 21 and he *e* all his paths.

EXAMPLE* (EXAMPLES)

2Ki   14: 3 In everything he followed the *e*
Ecc   9: 13 also saw under the sun this *e*
Eze   14: 8 and make him an *e* and a byword.
Jn   13: 15 have set you an *e* that you should
Ro   7: 2 as long as he lives? For *e,*
1Co   11: 1 Follow my *e,* as I follow
          11: 1 as I follow the *e* of Christ.
Gal   3: 15 let me take an *e* from everyday life.
Php   3: 17 Join with others in following my *e,*
2Th   3: 7 how you ought to follow our *e*
1Ti   1: 16 as an *e* for those who would believe
           4: 12 set an *e* for the believers in speech,
Tit   2: 7 In everything set them an *e*
Heb   4: 11 fall by following their *e*
Jas   3: 4 Or take ships as an *e.*
           5: 10 as an *e* of patience in the face
1Pe   2: 21 leaving you an *e,* that you should
2Pe   2: 6 made them an *e* of what is going
Jude   7 as an *e* of those who suffer

EXAMPLES* (EXAMPLE)

1Co   10: 6 Now these things occurred as *e*
          10: 11 as *e* and were written down
1Pe   5: 3 to you, but being *e* to the flock.

EXASPERATE*

Eph   6: 4 Fathers, do not *e* your children;

EXCEL* (EXCELLENT)

Ge   49: 4 as the waters, you will no longer *e,*
1Co   14: 12 to *e* in gifts that build up the church
2Co   8: 7 But just as you *e* in everything—
           8: 7 also *e* in this grace of giving.

EXCELLENT (EXCEL)

1Co   12: 31 now I will show you the most *e* way
Php   4: 8 if anything is *e* or praiseworthy—
1Ti   3: 13 have served well gain an *e* standing
Tit   3: 8 These things are *e* and profitable

EXCESSIVE

Eze   18: 8 or take *e* interest.
2Co   2: 7 not be overwhelmed by *e* sorrow.

EXCHANGE (EXCHANGED)

Mt   16: 26 Or what can a man give in *e*
Mk   8: 37 Or what can a man give in *e*
2Co   13: 11 As a fair *e*—I speak

EXCHANGED (EXCHANGE)

Ps   106: 20 They *e* their Glory
Jer   2: 11 But my people have *e* their Glory

Hos   4: 7 they *e* their Glory
Ro   1: 23 *e* the glory of the immortal God
          1: 25 They *e* the truth of God for a lie,
          1: 26 their women *e* natural relations

EXCLAIM

Ps   35: 10 My whole being will *e,*

EXCUSE* (EXCUSES)

Ps   25: 3 who are treacherous without *e.*
Lk   14: 18 Please *e* me.'
          14: 19 Please *e* me.'
Jn   15: 22 they have no *e* for their sin.
Ro   1: 20 so that men are without *e.*
          2: 1 You, therefore, have no *e,*

EXCUSES* (EXCUSE)

Lk   14: 18 "But they all alike began to make *e.*

EXERTED*

Eph   1: 20 which he *e* in Christ

EXHORT*

1Ti   5: 1 but *e* him as if he were your father.

EXILE

2Ki   17: 23 taken from their homeland into *e*
          25: 11 into *e* the people who remained

EXISTED* (EXISTS)

2Pe   3: 5 ago by God's word the heavens *e*

EXISTS (EXISTED)

Heb   2: 10 and through whom everything *e,*
          11: 6 to him must believe that he *e*

EXPANSE

Ge   1: 7 So God made the *e* and separated
          1: 8 God called the *e* "sky."

EXPECT (EXPECTATION EXPECTED EXPECTING)

Mt   24: 44 at an hour when you do not *e* him.
Lk   12: 40 at an hour when you do not *e* him. "
Php   1: 20 I eagerly *e* and hope that I will

EXPECTATION (EXPECT)

Ro   8: 19 waits in eager *e* for the sons
Heb   10: 27 but only a fearful *e* of judgment

EXPECTED (EXPECT)

Pr   11: 7 all he *e* from his power comes
Hag   1: 9 "You *e* much, but see, it turned out

EXPECTING (EXPECT)

Lk   6: 35 and lend to them without *e*

EXPEL* (EXPELLED)

1Co   5: 13 *E* the wicked man from among you

EXPELLED (EXPEL)

Eze   28: 16 and I *e* you, O guardian cherub,

EXPENSE (EXPENSIVE)

1Co   9: 7 Who serves as a soldier at his own *e*

EXPENSIVE* (EXPENSE)

Mt   26: 7 jar of very *e* perfume,
Mk   14: 3 jar of very *e* perfume,
Lk   7: 25 those who wear *e* clothes
Jn   12: 3 a pint of pure nard, an *e* perfume;
1Ti   2: 9 or gold or pearls or *e* clothes,

EXPERT

1Co   3: 10 I laid a foundation as an *e* builder.

EXPLAINING (EXPLAINS)

Ac   17: 3 *e* and proving that the Christ had

EXPLAINS* (EXPLAINING)

Ac   8: 31 he said, "unless someone *e* it to me

EXPLOIT* (EXPLOITED EXPLOITING EXPLOITS)

Pr   22: 22 Do not *e* the poor because they are
Isa   58: 3 and *e* all your workers.
2Co   12: 17 Did I *e* you through any
          12: 18 Titus did not *e* you, did he?
2Pe   2: 3 greed these teachers will *e* you

EXPLOITED* (EXPLOIT)

2Co   7: 2 no one, we have *e* no one.

EXPLOITING* (EXPLOIT)

Jas   2: 6 Is it not the rich who are *e* you?

EXPLOITS (EXPLOIT)

2Co   11: 20 or *e* you or takes advantage of you

EXPLORE

Nu   13: 2 "Send some men to *e* the land

EXPOSE (EXPOSED)

1Co   4: 5 will *e* the motives of men's hearts.
Eph   5: 11 of darkness, but rather *e* them.

EXPOSED (EXPOSE)

Jn   3: 20 for fear that his deeds will be *e.*
Eph   5: 13 everything *e* by the light becomes

EXPRESS (EXPRESSING)

Ro   8: 26 us with groans that words cannot *e.*

EXPRESSING* (EXPRESS)

1Co   2: 13 *e* spiritual truths in spiritual words.
Gal   5: 6 thing that counts is faith *e* itself

EXTENDS (EXTENT)

Pr   31: 20 and *e* her hands to the needy.
Lk   1: 50 His mercy *e* to those who fear him,

EXTENT (EXTENDS)

Jn   13: 1 he now showed them the full *e*

EXTERNAL

Gal   2: 6 judge by appearance—

EXTINGUISH (EXTINGUISHED)

Eph   6: 16 which you can *e* all the flaming

EXTINGUISHED (EXTINGUISH)

2Sa   21: 17 the lamp of Israel will not be *e.* "

EXTOL*

Job   36: 24 Remember to *e* his work,
Ps   34: 1 I will *e* the LORD at all times;
          68: 4 *e* him who rides on the clouds—
          95: 2 and *e* him with music and song.
         109: 30 mouth I will greatly *e* the LORD;
         111: 1 I will *e* the LORD with all my heart
         115: 18 it is we who *e* the LORD,
         117: 1 *e* him, all you peoples.
         145: 2 *e* your name for ever and ever.
         145: 10 your saints will *e* you.
         147: 12 *E* the LORD, O Jerusalem!

EXTORT*

Lk   3: 14 "Don't *e* money and don't accuse

EXTRAORDINARY*

Ac   19: 11 God did *e* miracles through Paul,

EXTREME (EXTREMES)

2Co   8: 2 and their *e* poverty welled up

EXTREMES* (EXTREME)

Ecc   7: 18 who fears God will avoid all *e,*

EXULT

Ps   89: 16 they *e* in your righteousness.
Isa   45: 25 will be found righteous and will *e.*

EYE (EYES)

Ge   3: 6 good for food and pleasing to the *e,*
Ex   21: 24 you are to take life for life, *e* for *e,*
Dt   19: 21 life for life, *e* for *e,* tooth for tooth,
Ps   94: 9 Does he who formed the *e* not see?
Mt   5: 29 If your right *e* causes you to sin,
           5: 38 '*E* for *e,* and tooth for tooth.'
           6: 22 "The *e* is the lamp of the body.
           7: 3 of sawdust in your brother's *e*
1Co   12: 9 "No *e* has seen,
          12: 16 I am not an *e,* I do not belong
          15: 52 of an *e,* at the last trumpet.
Eph   6: 6 favor when their *e* is on you,
Col   3: 22 not only when their *e* is on you
Rev   1: 7 and every *e* will see him,

EYES (EYE)

Nu   15: 39 the lusts of your own hearts and *e.*
          33: 55 remain will become barbs in your *e*
Dt   1: 30 the *e* of the LORD your God are
          12: 25 right in the *e* of the LORD.
          16: 19 for a bribe blinds the *e* of the wise
Jos   23: 13 on your backs and thorns in your *e,*
1Sa   15: 17 you were once small in your own *e,*
1Ki   10: 7 I came and saw with my own *e.*
2Ki   9: 30 heard about it, she painted her *e,*
2Ch   16: 9 For the *e* of the LORD range
Job   31: 1 "I made a covenant with my *e*

Job 36: 7 He does not take his *e*
Ps   25: 15 My *e* are ever on the LORD;
      36: 1 God before his *e*.
     101: 6 My *e* will be on the faithful
     118: 23 and it is marvelous in our *e*.
     119: 18 Open my *e* that I may see
     119: 37 my *e* away from worthless things;
     121: 1 I lift up my *e* to the hills—
     123: 1 I lift up my *e* to you,
     139: 16 your *e* saw my unformed body.
     141: 8 But my *e* are fixed on you,
Pr   3: 7 Do not be wise in your own *e*;
      4: 25 Let your *e* look straight ahead,
     15: 3 The *e* of the LORD are everywhere
     17: 24 a fool's *e* wander to the ends
Isa   6: 5 and my *e* have seen the King,
     33: 17 Your *e* will see the king
     42: 7 to open *e* that are blind,
Jer 24: 6 My *e* will watch over them
Hab   1: 13 Your *e* are too pure to look on evil;
Mt   6: 22 If your *e* are good, your whole
     21: 42 and it is marvelous in our *e*'?
Lk   16: 15 ones who justify yourselves in the *e*
     24: 31 Then their *e* were opened
Jn   4: 35 open your *e* and look at the fields!
Ac   1: 9 he was taken up before their very *e*,
2Co   4: 18 So we fix our *e* not on what is seen,
      8: 21 not only in the *e* of the Lord but
Eph   1: 18 also that the *e* of your heart may be
Heb 12: 2 Let us fix our *e* on Jesus, the author
Jas   2: 5 poor in the *e* of the world to be rich
1Pe   3: 12 For the *e* of the Lord are
Rev   7: 17 wipe away every tear from their *e*
     21: 4 He will wipe every tear from their *e*

EYEWITNESSES* (WITNESS)

Lk   1: 2 by those who from the first were *e*
2Pe   1: 16 but we were *e* of his majesty.

EZEKIEL*

Priest called to be prophet to the exiles (Eze 1-3). Symbolically acted out destruction of Jerusalem (Eze 4-5; 12; 24).

EZRA*

Priest and teacher of the Law who led a return of exiles to Israel to reestablish temple and worship (Ezr 7-8). Corrected intermarriage of priests (Ezr 9-10). Read Law at celebration of Feast of Tabernacles (Ne 8). Participated in dedication of Jerusalem's walls (Ne 12).

FACE (FACES)

Ge   32: 30 "It is because I saw God *f* to *f*.
Ex   3: 6 Moses hid his *f*, because he was
     33: 11 would speak to Moses *f* to *f*,
     33: 20 But," he said, "you cannot see my *f*
     34: 29 was not aware that his *f* was radiant
Nu   6: 25 the LORD make his *f* shine
      6: 28 With him I speak *f* to *f*,
     14: 14 O LORD, have been seen *f* to *f*,
Dt   5: 4 The LORD spoke to you *f* to *f* out
     31: 17 I will hide my *f* from them,
     34: 10 whom the LORD knew *f* to *f*,
Jdg   6: 22 the angel of the LORD *f* to *f*!"
2Ki 14: 8 challenge: "Come, meet me *f* to *f*."
1Ch 16: 11 seek his *f* always.
2Ch   7: 14 and seek my *f* and turn
     25: 17 of Israel: "Come, meet me *f* to *f*."
Ezr   9: 6 and disgraced to lift up my *f* to you,
Ps   4: 6 Let the light of your *f* shine upon us
     27: 8 Your *f*, LORD, I will seek.
     31: 16 Let your *f* shine on your servant;
     44: 3 and the light of your *f*,
     44: 22 Yet for your sake we *f* death all day
     51: 9 Hide your *f* from my sins
     67: 1 and make his *f* shine upon us; *Selah*
     80: 3 make your *f* shine upon us,
     105: 4 seek his *f* always.
     119: 135 Make your *f* shine
SS   2: 14 and your *f* is lovely.
Isa 50: 7 Therefore have I set my *f* like flint,
     50: 8 Let us *f* each other!
     54: 8 I hid my *f* from you for a moment,
Jer 32: 4 and will speak with him *f* to *f*
     34: 3 and he will speak with you *f* to *f*.
Eze 10: 7 four of the four had the *f* of a man,
     20: 35 *f* to *f*, I will execute judgment
Mt   6: 17 his *f* shone like the sun,
     18: 10 angels in heaven always see the *f*
Lk   9: 29 the appearance of his *f* changed,
Ro   8: 36 "For your sake we *f* death all day
1Co 13: 12 mirror; then we shall see *f* to *f*.
2Co   3: 7 could not look steadily at the *f*,
      4: 6 the glory of God in the *f* of Christ.

2Co 10: 1 who am "timid" when *f* to *f*
1Pe   3: 12 but the *f* of the Lord is
2Jn   12 to visit you and talk with you *f* to *f*,
3Jn   14 see you soon, and we will talk *f* to *f*.
Rev   1: 16 His *f* was like the sun shining
     22: 4 They will see his *f*, and his name

FACES (FACE)

2Co   3: 18 who with unveiled *f* all reflect

FACTIONS

2Co 12: 20 outbursts of anger, *f*, slander,
Gal   5: 20 selfish ambition, dissensions, *f*

FADE (FADING)

Jas   1: 11 the rich man will *f* away
1Pe   5: 4 of glory that will never *f* away.

FADING (FADE)

2Co   3: 7 *f* though it was, will not
      3: 11 if what was *f* away came with glory,
      3: 13 at it while the radiance was *f* away.

FAIL (FAILED FAILING FAILINGS FAILS FAILURE)

Lev 26: 15 and *f* to carry out all my commands
1Ki   2: 4 you will never *f* to have a man
1Ch 28: 20 He will not *f* you or forsake you
2Ch 34: 33 they did not *f* to follow the LORD,
Ps   89: 28 my covenant with him will never *f*.
Pr   15: 22 Plans *f* for lack of counsel,
Isa 51: 6 my righteousness will never *f*.
La   3: 22 for his compassions never *f*.
Lk   22: 32 Simon, that your faith may not *f*.
2Co 13: 5 unless, of course, you *f* the test?

FAILED (FAIL)

Jos 23: 14 has been fulfilled; not one has *f*
1Ki   8: 56 Not one word has *f*
Ps   77: 8 Has his promise *f* for all time?
Ro   9: 6 as though God's word had *f*.
2Co 13: 6 discover that we have not *f* the test.

FAILING (FAIL)

1Sa 12: 23 sin against the LORD by *f* to pray

FAILINGS (FAIL)

Ro   15: 1 ought to bear with the *f* of the weak

FAILS (FAIL)

Jer 14: 6 their eyesight *f*
Joel 1: 10 the oil *f*.
1Co 13: 8 Love never *f*.

FAILURE* (FAIL)

1Th   2: 1 that our visit to you was not a *f*.

FAINT

Isa 40: 31 they will walk and not be *f*.

FAINTHEARTED* (HEART)

Dt   20: 3 Do not be *f* or afraid; do not be
     20: 8 shall add, "Is any man afraid or *f*?

FAIR (FAIRNESS)

Pr   1: 3 doing what is right and just and *f*;
Col   4: 1 slaves with what is right and *f*,

FAIRNESS* (FAIR)

Pr   29: 14 If a king judges the poor with *f*,

FAITH* (FAITHFUL FAITHFULLY FAITHFULNESS FAITHLESS)

Ex   21: 8 because he has broken *f* with her.
Dt   32: 51 both of you broke *f* with me
Jos 22: 16 'How could you break *f*
Jdg   9: 16 and in good *f* when you made
      9: 19 and in good *f* toward Jerub-Baal
1Sa 14: 33 "You have broken *f*," he said.
2Ch 20: 20 Have *f* in the LORD your God
     20: 20 have *f* in his prophets and you will
Isa   7: 9 If you do not stand firm in your *f*,
     26: 2 the nation that keeps *f*.
Hab   2: 4 but the righteous will live by his *f*—
Mal   2: 10 by breaking *f* with one another?
      2: 11 one another? Judah has broken *f*.
      2: 14 because you have broken *f* with her
      2: 15 and do not break *f* with the wife
      2: 16 in your spirit, and do not break *f*.
Mt   6: 30 O you of little *f*? So do not worry,
      8: 10 anyone in Israel with such great *f*.
      8: 26 He replied, "You of little *f*,
      9: 2 When Jesus saw their *f*, he said
      9: 22 he said, "your *f* has healed you."
      9: 29 According to your *f* will it be done

Mt   13: 58 there because of their lack of *f*.
     14: 31 of little *f*," he said, "why did you
     15: 28 "Woman, you have great *f*!
     16: 8 Jesus asked, "You of little *f*,
     17: 20 if you have *f* as small as a mustard
     17: 20 "Because you have so little *f*.
     21: 21 if you have *f* and do not doubt,
     24: 10 many will turn away from the *f*
Mk   2: 5 When Jesus saw their *f*, he said
      4: 40 still have no *f*?" They were
      5: 34 "Daughter, your *f* has healed you.
      6: 6 he was amazed at their lack of *f*.
     10: 52 said Jesus, "your *f* has healed you."
     11: 22 "Have *f* in God," Jesus answered.
     16: 14 he rebuked them for their lack of *f*
Lk   5: 20 When Jesus saw their *f*, he said,
      7: 9 I have not found such great *f*
      7: 50 the woman, "Your *f* has saved you;
      8: 25 "Where is your *f*?" he asked his
      8: 48 "Daughter, your *f* has healed you.
     12: 28 will he clothe you, O you of little *f*!
     17: 5 "Increase our *f*!" He replied,
     17: 6 "If you have *f* as small
     17: 19 your *f* has made you well."
     18: 8 will he find *f* on the earth?"
     18: 42 your sight; your *f* has healed you."
     22: 32 Simon, that your *f* may not fail.
Jn   2: 11 and his disciples put their *f* in him.
      7: 31 in the crowd put their *f* in him.
      8: 30 he spoke, many put their *f* in him.
     11: 45 had seen what Jesus did, put their *f*
     12: 11 to Jesus and putting their *f* in him.
     12: 42 they would not confess their *f*
     14: 12 anyone who has *f* in me will do
Ac   3: 16 By *f* in the name of Jesus, this man
      3: 16 *f* that comes through him that has
      5: 5 full of *f* and of the Holy Spirit;
      6: 7 of priests became obedient to the *f*.
     11: 24 full of the Holy Spirit and *f*,
     13: 8 to turn the proconsul from the *f*.
     14: 9 saw that he had *f* to be healed
     14: 22 them to remain true to the *f*.
     14: 27 the door of *f* to the Gentiles.
     15: 9 for he purified their hearts by *f*.
     16: 5 were strengthened in the *f*
     20: 21 and have *f* in our Lord Jesus.
     24: 24 as he spoke about *f* in Christ Jesus.
     26: 18 those who are sanctified by *f*
     27: 25 for I have *f* in God that it will
Ro   1: 5 to the obedience that comes from *f*,
      1: 8 because your *f* is being reported all
      1: 12 encouraged by each other's *f*.
      1: 17 is by *f* from first to last,
      1: 17 "The righteous will live by *f*."
      3: 3 What if some did not have *f*?
      3: 3 lack of *f* nullify God's faithfulness?
      3: 22 comes through *f* in Jesus Christ
      3: 25 a sacrifice of atonement, through *f*
      3: 26 one who justifies those who have *f*
      3: 27 the law? No, but on that of *f*.
      3: 28 by *f* apart from observing the law.
      3: 30 through that same *f*.
      3: 30 will justify the circumcised by *f*
      3: 31 nullify the law by this *f*? Not at all!
      4: 5 his *f* is credited as righteousness.
      4: 9 that Abraham's *f* was credited
      4: 11 had by *f* while he was still
      4: 12 of the *f* that our father Abraham
      4: 13 the righteousness that comes by *f*
      4: 14 *f* has no value and the promise is
      4: 16 Therefore, the promise comes by *f*,
      4: 16 are of the *f* of Abraham.
      4: 19 Without weakening in his *f*,
      4: 20 but was strengthened in his *f*
      5: 1 we have been justified through *f*,
      5: 2 access by *f* into this grace
      9: 30 a righteousness that is by *f*;
      9: 32 Because they pursued it not by *f*
     10: 6 the righteousness that is by *f* says:
     10: 8 the word of *f* we are proclaiming;
     10: 17 *f* comes from hearing the message,
     11: 20 of unbelief, and you stand by *f*.
     12: 3 measure of *f* God has given you.
     12: 6 let him use it in proportion to his *f*.
     14: 1 Accept him whose *f* is weak,
     14: 2 One man's *f* allows him
     14: 2 but another man, whose *f* is weak,
     14: 23 because his eating is not from *f*;
     14: 23 that does not come from *f* is sin.
1Co   2: 5 so that your *f* might not rest
     12: 9 to another *f* by the same Spirit,
     13: 2 and if I have a *f* that can move
     13: 13 And now these three remain: *f*,
     15: 14 is useless and so is your *f*
     15: 17 has not been raised, your *f* is futile;

FAITHFUL

1Co 16:13 stand firm in the f; be men
2Co 1:24 Not that we lord it over your f,
1:24 because it is by f you stand firm.
4:13 With that same spirit of f we
5: 7 We live by f, not by sight.
8: 7 in f, in speech, in knowledge,
10:15 as your f continues to grow,
13: 5 to see whether you are in the f;
Gal 1:23 now preaching the f he once tried
2:16 Jesus that we may be justified by f
2:16 but by f in Jesus Christ.
2:16 have put our f in Christ Jesus that
2:20 I live by f in the Son of God,
3: 8 would justify the Gentiles by f,
3: 9 So those who have f are blessed
3: 9 along with Abraham, the man of f.
3:11 "The righteous will live by f."
3:12 based on f; on the contrary,
3:14 by f we might receive the promise
3:22 being given through f
3:23 Before this f came, we were held
3:23 up until f should be revealed.
3:24 that we might be justified by f.
3:25 that f has come, we are no longer
3:26 of God through f in Christ Jesus,
5: 5 But by f we eagerly await
5: 6 that counts is f expressing itself
Eph 1:15 ever since I heard about your f
2: 8 through f—and this not
3:12 through f in him we may approach
3:17 dwell in your hearts through f.
4: 5 one Lord, one f, one baptism;
4:13 up until we all reach unity in the f
6:16 to all this, take up the shield of f,
6:23 love with f from God the Father
Php 1:25 for your progress and joy in the f,
1:27 as one man for the f of the gospel
2:17 and service coming from your f,
3: 9 that which is through f in Christ—
Col 1: 4 heard of your f in Christ Jesus
1: 5 the faith love that spring
1:23 continue in your f, established
2: 5 and how firm your f in Christ is.
2: 7 in the f as you were taught,
2:12 him through your f in the power
1Th 1: 3 Father your work produced by f,
1: 8 your f in God has become known
3: 2 and encourage you in your f,
3: 5 I sent to find out about your f.
3: 6 brought good news about your f
3: 7 about you because of your f.
3:10 supply what is lacking in your f.
5: 8 on f and love as a breastplate,
2Th 1: 3 because your f is growing more
1: 4 and f in all the persecutions
1:11 and every act prompted by your f.
3: 2 evil men, for not everyone has f.
1Ti 1: 2 To Timothy my true son in the f:
1: 4 than God's work—which is by f.
1: 5 a good conscience and a sincere f.
1:14 along with the f and love that are
1:19 and so have shipwrecked their f.
1:19 on to f and a good conscience.
2: 7 of the true f to the Gentiles.
2:15 if they continue in f, love
3: 9 of the f with a clear conscience.
3:13 assurance in their f in Christ Jesus.
4: 1 later times some will abandon the f
4: 6 brought up in the truths of the f
4:12 in life, in love, in f and in purity.
5: 8 he has denied the f and is worse
6:10 have wandered from the f
6:11 pursue righteousness, godliness, f,
6:12 Fight the good fight of the f.
6:21 so doing have wandered from the f.
2Ti 1: 5 been reminded of your sincere f,
1:13 with f and love in Christ Jesus.
2:18 and they destroy the f of some.
2:22 and pursue righteousness, f,
3: 8 as far as the f is concerned,
3:10 my purpose, f, patience, love,
3:15 wise for salvation through f
4: 7 finished the race, I have kept the f.
Tit 1: 1 Christ for the f of God's elect
1: 2 a f and knowledge resting
1: 4 my true son in our common f:
1:13 so that they will be sound in the f
2: 2 self-controlled, and sound in f,
3:15 Greet those who love us in the f.
Phm : 5 because I hear about your f
: 6 may be active in sharing your f,
Heb 4: 2 heard did not combine it with f.
4:14 firmly to the f we profess.
6: 1 and of f in God, instruction about

Heb 6:12 but to imitate those who through f
10:22 heart in full assurance of f,
10:38 But my righteous one will live by f.
11: 1 f is being sure of what we hope for
11: 3 By f we understand that
11: 4 And by f he still speaks, even
11: 4 By f Abel offered God a better
11: 4 By f he was commended
11: 5 By f Enoch was taken from this life
11: 6 And without f it is impossible
11: 7 By his f he condemned the world
11: 7 By f Noah, when warned about
11: 7 the righteousness that comes by f.
11: 8 By f Abraham, when called to go
11: 9 By f he made his home
11:11 By f Abraham, even though he was
11:13 living by f when they died.
11:17 By f Abraham, when God tested
11:20 By f Isaac blessed Jacob
11:21 By f Jacob, when he was dying,
11:22 By f Joseph, when his end was near
11:23 By f Moses' parents hid him
11:24 By f Moses, when he had grown up
11:27 By f he left Egypt, not fearing
11:28 By f he kept the Passover
11:29 By f the people passed
11:30 By f the walls of Jericho fell,
11:31 By f the prostitute Rahab,
11:33 through f conquered kingdoms,
11:39 were all commended for their f,
12: 2 the author and perfecter of our f,
13: 7 way of life and imitate their f.
Jas 1: 3 of your f develops perseverance.
2: 5 the eyes of the world to be rich in f
2:14 has no deeds? Can such f save him?
2:14 if a man claims to have f
2:17 In the same way, f by itself,
2:18 I will show you my f by what I do.
2:18 Show me your f without deeds,
2:18 "You have f; I have deeds."
2:20 do you want evidence that f
2:22 You see that his f and his actions
2:22 and his f was made complete
2:24 by what he does and not by f alone.
2:26 so f without deeds is dead.
5:15 in f will make the sick person well;
1Pe 1: 5 who through f are shielded
1: 7 These have come so that your f—
1: 9 you are receiving the goal of your f,
1:21 and so your f and hope are in God.
5: 9 Resist him, standing firm in the f,
2Pe 1: 1 Jesus Christ have received a f
1: 5 effort to add to your f goodness;
1Jn 5: 4 overcome the world, even our f.
Jude : 3 to contend for the f that was once
: 20 up in your most holy f
Rev 2:13 You did not renounce your f in me.
2:19 your love and f, your service

FAITHFUL* (FAITH)

Nu 12: 7 he is f in all my house.
Dt 7: 9 your God is God; he is the f God,
32: 4 A f God who does no wrong,
1Sa 2:35 I will raise up for myself a f priest,
2Sa 7:16 We are the peaceful and f in Israel.
22:26 "To the f you show yourself f,
1Ki 3: 6 because he was f to you
2Ch 31:18 were f in consecrating themselves.
31:20 and f before the LORD his God.
Ne 9: 8 You found his heart f to you,
Ps 12: 1 the f have vanished
18:25 To the f you show yourself f,
25:10 of the LORD are loving and f
31:23 The LORD preserves the f,
33: 4 he is f in all he does.
37:28 and will not forsake his f ones.
78: 8 whose spirits were not f to him.
78:37 they were not f to his covenant.
89:19 to your f people you said;
89:24 My f love will be with him,
89:37 the f witness in the sky."
97:10 for he guards the lives of his f ones
101: 6 My eyes will be on the f in the land,
111: 7 The works of his hands are f
145:13 The LORD is f to all his promises
146: 6 the LORD, who remains f forever.
Pr 2: 8 and protects the way of his f ones.
20: 6 but a f man who can find?
28:20 A f man will be richly blessed,
31:26 and f instruction is on her tongue.
Isa 1:21 See how the f city has become
1:26 the f City."
49: 7 because of the LORD, who is f,
55: 3 my f love promised to David.
Jer 42: 5 f witness against us if we do not act

Eze 43:11 so that they may be f to its design
48:11 who were f in serving me
Hos 11:12 even against the f Holy One.
Zec 8: 8 I will be f and righteous to them
Mt 24:45 Who then is the f and wise servant,
25:21 'Well done, good and f servant!
25:21 You have been f with a few things;
25:23 You have been f with a few things;
25:23 'Well done, good and f servant!
Lk 12:42 then is the f and wise manager,
Ro 12:12 patient in affliction, f in prayer.
1Co 1: 9 his Son Jesus Christ our Lord, is f.
4: 2 been given a trust must prove f.
4:17 my son whom I love, who is f
10:13 And God is f; he will not let you be
2Co 1:18 no"? But as surely as God is f,
Eph 1: 1 in Ephesus, the f in Christ Jesus:
6:21 the dear brother and f servant
Col 1: 2 and f brothers in Christ at Colosse:
1: 7 who is a f minister of Christ
4: 7 a f minister and fellow servant
4: 9 He is coming with Onesimus, our f
1Th 5:24 The one who calls you is f
2Th 3: 3 the Lord is f, and he will strengthen
1Ti 1:12 he considered me f, appointing me
5: 9 has been f to her husband,
2Ti 2:13 he will remain f,
Heb 2:17 and f high priest in service to God.
3: 2 He was f to the one who appointed
3: 2 as Moses was f in all God's house.
3: 5 Moses was f as a servant
3: 6 But Christ is f as a son
8: 9 because they did not remain f
10:23 for he who promised is f.
11:11 he considered him f who had made
1Pe 4:19 themselves to their f Creator
5:12 whom I regard as a f brother,
1Jn 1: 9 he is f and just and will forgive us
3Jn : 5 you are f in what you are doing
Rev 1: 5 who is the f witness, the firstborn
2:10 Be f, even to the point of death,
2:13 the days of Antipas, my f witness,
3:14 the words of the Amen, the f
14:12 commandments and remain f
17:14 his called, chosen and f followers."
19:11 whose rider is called f and True.

FAITHFULLY* (FAITH)

Dt 11:13 if you f obey the commands I am
Jos 2:14 f when the LORD gives us the land
1Sa 12:24 and serve him f with all your heart;
1Ki 2: 4 and if they walk f before me
2Ki 20: 3 how I have walked before you f
22: 7 because they are acting f."
2Ch 19: 9 must serve f and wholeheartedly
31:12 they f brought in the contributions,
31:15 and Shecaniah assisted f from
32: 1 all that Hezekiah had so f done,
34:12 The men did the work f.
Ne 9:33 you have acted f, while we did
13:14 so f done for the house of my God
Isa 38: 3 how I have walked before you f
Jer 23:28 one who has my word speak it f.
Eze 18: 9 and f keeps my laws.
44:15 and who f carried out the duties
1Pe 4:10 f administering God's grace

FAITHFULNESS* (FAITH)

Ge 24:27 not abandoned his kindness and f
24:49 if you will show kindness and f
32:10 and f you have shown your servant.
47:29 you will show me kindness and f
Ex 34: 6 f, maintaining love to thousands,
Jos 2:14 the LORD and show him f with all f.
1Sa 26:23 man for his righteousness and f
2Sa 2: 6 now show you kindness and f,
15:20 May kindness and f be with you."
Ps 30: 9 Will it proclaim your f?
36: 5 your f to the skies.
40:10 I speak of your f and salvation.
54: 5 in your f destroy them.
57: 3 God sends his love and his f.
57:10 your f reaches to the skies.
61: 7 appoint your love and f
71:22 the harp for your f, O my God;
85:10 Love and f meet together;
85:11 F springs forth from the earth,
86:15 to anger, abounding in love and f
88:11 your f in Destruction?
89: 1 mouth I will make your f known
89: 2 that you established your f
89: 5 your f too, in the assembly
89: 8 and your f surrounds you.
89:14 love and f go before you.
89:33 nor will I ever betray my f.

Ps 89:49 which in your *f*you swore to David
91: 4 his *f*will be your shield
92: 2 and your *f*at night,
98: 3 and his *f*to the house of Israel;
100: 1 *f*continues through all
108: 4 your *f*reaches to the skies.
111: 8 done in *f*and uprightness.
115: 1 because of your love and *f.*
117: 2 the *F*of the LORD endures forever.
119: 75 and in *f*you have afflicted me.
119: 90 *f*continues through all
138: 2 name for your love and your *f,*
143: 1 in your *f*and righteousness
Pr 3: 3 Let love and *f*never leave you;
14: 22 plan what is good find love and *f.*
16: 6 Through love and *f*sin is atoned for
20: 28 Love and *f*keep a king safe;
Isa 11: 5 and *f*the sash around his waist.
16: 5 in a *f*a man will sit on it—
25: 1 for in perfect *f*
38: 18 cannot hope for your *f.*
38: 19 about your *f.*
42: 3 In *f*he will bring forth justice;
61: 8 In my *f*I will reward them
La 3: 23 great is your *f.*
Hos 2: 20 I will betroth you in *f,*
4: 1 "There is no *f,* no love,
Mt 23: 23 of the law—justice, mercy and *f.*
Ro 3: 3 lack of faith nullify God's *f?*
Gal 5: 22 patience, kindness, goodness, *f,*
3Jn : 3 and tell about your *f*to the truth
Rev 13: 10 and *f*on the part of the saints.

FAITHLESS* (FAITH)

Ps 78: 57 fathers they were disloyal and *f,*
101: 3 The deeds of *f*men I hate;
119:158 I look on the *f*with loathing,
Pr 14: 14 The *f*will be fully repaid
Jer 3: 6 you seen what *f*Israel has done?
3: 8 I gave *f*Israel her certificate
3: 11 "*F*Israel is more righteous
3: 12 *f*Israel,' declares the LORD,
3: 14 *f*people," declares the LORD,
3: 22 "Return, *f*people;
12: 1 Why do all the *f*live at ease?
Ro 1: 31 they are senseless, *f,* heartless,
2Ti 2: 13 if we are *f,*

FALL (FALLEN FALLING FALLS)

Ps 37: 24 though he stumble, he will not *f,*
55: 22 he will never let the righteous *f.*
69: 9 of those who insult you *f*on me.
145: 14 The LORD upholds all those who *f*
Pr 11: 28 Whoever trusts in his riches will *f,*
Isa 40: 7 The grass withers and the flowers *f,*
Mt 7: 25 yet it did not *f,* because it had its
Lk 10: 18 "I saw Satan *f*like lightning
11: 17 a house divided against itself will *f*
23: 30 say to the mountains, "*F*on us!"
Ro 3: 23 and *f*short of the glory of God,
Heb 6: 6 if they *f*away, to be brought back

FALLEN (FALL)

2Sa 1: 19 How the mighty have *f!*
Isa 14: 12 How you have *f*from heaven,
1Co 11: 30 and a number of you have *f*asleep.
15: 6 though some have *f*asleep.
15: 18 who have *f*asleep in Christ are lost.
15: 20 of those who have *f*asleep.
Gal 5: 4 you have *f*away from grace.
1Th 4: 15 precede those who have *f*asleep.

FALLING (FALL)

Jude : 24 able to keep you from *f*

FALLS (FALL)

Pr 11: 14 For lack of guidance a nation *f,*
24: 17 Do not gloat when your enemy *f,*
28: 14 he who hardens his heart *f*
Mt 13: 21 of the word, he quickly *f*away.
21: 44 He who *f*on this stone will be
Jn 12: 24 a kernel of wheat *f*to the ground
Ro 14: 4 To his own master he stands or *f.*

FALSE (FALSEHOOD FALSELY)

Ex 20: 16 "You shall not give *f*testimony
23: 1 "Do not spread *f*reports.
23: 7 Have nothing to do with a *f*charge
Dt 5: 20 "You shall not give *f*testimony
Pr 12: 17 but a *f*witness tells lies.
13: 5 The righteous hate what is *f,*
14: 5 but a *f*witness pours out lies.
14: 25 but a *f*witness is deceitful.
19: 5 A *f*witness will not go unpunished,
19: 9 A *f*witness will not go unpunished,

Pr 21: 28 A *f*witness will perish,
25: 18 is the man who gives *f*testimony
Isa 44: 25 who foils the signs of *f*prophets
Jer 23: 16 they fill you with *f*hopes.
Mt 7: 15 "Watch out for *f*prophets.
15: 19 theft, *f*testimony, slander.
19: 18 not steal, do not give *f*testimony,
24: 11 and many *f*prophets will appear
24: 24 For *f*Christs and *f*prophets will
Mk 10: 19 do not give *f*testimony, do not
13: 22 For *f*Christs and *f*prophets will
Lk 6: 26 their fathers treated the *f*prophets.
18: 20 not steal, do not give *f*testimony,
Jn 1: 47 in whom there is nothing *f.*"
1Co 15: 15 found to be *f*witnesses about God,
2Co 11: 13 For such men are *f*apostles,
11: 26 and in danger from *f*brothers.
Gal 2: 4 some *f*brothers had infiltrated our
Php 1: 18 whether from *f*motives or true,
Col 2: 18 anyone who delights in *f*humility
2: 23 their *f*humility and their harsh
1Ti 1: 3 not to teach *f*doctrines any longer
6: 3 If anyone teaches *f*doctrines
2Pe 2: 1 also *f*prophets among the people,
2: 1 there will be *f*teachers among you.
1Jn 4: 1 many *f*prophets have gone out
Rev 16: 13 out of the mouth of the *f*prophet.
19: 20 with him the *f*prophet who had
20: 10 and the *f*prophet had been thrown.

FALSEHOOD* (FALSE)

Job 21: 34 left of your answers but *f!*"
31: 5 "If I have walked in *f*
Ps 52: 3 *f*rather than speaking the truth.
119:163 I hate and abhor *f*
Pr 30: 8 Keep *f*and lies far from me;
34: 15 and *f*our hiding place."
Ro 3: 7 "If my *f*enhances God's
Eph 4: 25 each of you must put off *f*
1Jn 4: 6 Spirit of truth and the spirit of *f.*
Rev 22: 15 everyone who loves and practices *f*

FALSELY (FALSE)

Lev 19: 12 " 'Do not swear *f*by my name
Mt 5: 11 *f*say all kinds of evil against you
Lk 3: 14 and don't accuse people *f*—
1Ti 6: 20 ideas of what is *f*called knowledge,

FALTER*

Pr 24: 10 If you fin times of trouble,
Isa 42: 4 he will not *f*or be discouraged

FAME

Jos 9: 9 of the *f*of the LORD your God.
1Ki 66: 19 islands that have not heard of my *f*
Hab 3: 2 LORD, I have heard of your *f;*

FAMILIES (FAMILY)

Ps 68: 6 God sets the lonely in *f,*

FAMILY (FAMILIES)

Pr 15: 27 greedy man brings trouble to his *f,*
31: 15 she provides food for her *f*
Mk 5: 19 to your *f*and tell them how much
Lk 9: 61 go back and say good-by to my *f.*"
12: 52 in one *f*divided against each other,
Ac 10: 2 He and all his *f*were devout
16: 33 and all his *f*were baptized.
16: 34 he and his whole *f.*
1Ti 3: 4 He must manage his own *f*well
3: 5 how to manage his own *f,*
5: 4 practice by caring for their own *f*
5: 8 and especially for his immediate *f,*

FAMINE

Ge 12: 10 Now there was a *f*in the land,
26: 1 Now there was a *f*in the land—
41: 30 seven years of *f*will follow them.
Ru 1: 1 the judges ruled, there was a *f*
1Ki 18: 2 Now the *f*was severe in Samaria,
Am 8: 11 but a *f*of hearing the words
Ro 8: 35 or persecution or for nakedness

FAN*

2Ti 1: 6 you to *f*into flame the gift of God,

FANTASIES*

Ps 73: 20 you will despise them as *f.*
Pr 12: 11 but he who chases *f*lacks judgment
28: 19 one who chases *f*will have his fill

FAST (FASTING)

Dt 10: 20 Hold *f*to him and take your oaths
11: 22 in all his ways and to hold *f*to him
13: 4 serve him and hold *f*to him.

Dt 30: 20 to his voice, and hold *f*to him.
Jos 22: 5 to hold *f*to him and to serve him
23: 8 to hold *f*to the LORD your God,
2Ki 18: 6 He held *f*to the LORD
Ps 119: 31 I hold *f*to your statutes, O LORD;
139: 10 your right hand will hold me *f.*
Mt 6: 16 "When you *f,* do not look somber
1Pe 5: 12 Stand *f*in it.

FASTING (FAST)

Ps 35: 13 and humbled myself with *f.*
Ac 13: 2 were worshiping the Lord and *f,*
14: 23 and *f,* committed them to the Lord

FATHER (FATHER'S FATHERED FATHERLESS FATHERS FOREFATHERS)

Ge 2: 24 this reason a man will leave his *f*
17: 4 You will be the *f*of many nations.
Ex 20: 12 "Honor your *f*and your mother,
21: 15 "Anyone who attacks his *f*
21: 17 "Anyone who curses his *f*
Lev 18: 7 " 'Do not dishonor your *f*
19: 3 you must respect his mother and *f,*
20: 9 " 'If anyone curses his *f*or mother,
Dt 1: 31 carried you, as a *f*carries his son,
5: 16 "Honor your *f*and your mother,
21: 18 son who does not obey his *f*
32: 6 Is he not your *F,* your Creator,
2Sa 7: 14 I will be his *f,* and he will be my son
1Ch 17: 13 I will be his *f,* and he will be my son
22: 10 will be my son, and I will be his *f.*
28: 6 to be my son, and I will be his *f.*
Job 38: 28 Does the rain have a *f?*
Ps 2: 7 today I have become your *F.*
27: 10 Though my *f*and mother forsake
68: 5 A *f*to the fatherless, a defender
89: 26 to me, 'You are my *F,*
103: 13 As a *f*has compassion
Pr 3: 12 as a *f*the son he delights in.
10: 1 A wise son brings joy to his *f,*
17: 21 there is no joy for the *f*of a fool.
17: 25 A foolish son brings grief to his *f*
23: 22 Listen to your *f,* who gave you life,
23: 24 *f*of a righteous man has great joy;
28: 7 of gluttons disgraces his *f.*
28: 24 He who robs his *f*or mother
29: 3 loves wisdom brings joy to his *f,*
Isa 9: 6 Everlasting *F,* Prince of Peace.
45: 10 Woe to him who says to his *f,*
63: 16 But you are our *F,*
Jer 2: 27 They say to wood, 'You are my *f,'*
3: 19 I thought you would call me '*F'*
31: 9 because I am Israel's *f,*
Eze 18: 19 the son not share the guilt of his *f?'*
Mic 7: 6 For a son dishonors his *f,*
Mal 1: 6 If I am a *f,* where is the honor due
2: 10 we not all one *F?*Did not one God
Mt 3: 9 'We have Abraham as our *f.'*
5: 16 and praise your *F*in heaven.
6: 9 " 'Our *F*in heaven,
6: 26 yet your heavenly *F*feeds them.
10: 37 "Anyone who loves his *f*
11: 27 no one knows the *F*except the Son
15: 4 'Honor your *f*and mother'
18: 10 the face of my *F*in heaven.
19: 5 this reason a man will leave his *f*
19: 19 honor your *f*and mother,'
19: 29 or brothers or sisters or *f*or mother
23: 9 And do not call anyone on earth '*f,'*
Mk 7: 10 'Honor your *f*and your mother,' and
Lk 9: 59 "Lord, first let me go and bury my *f.*"
12: 53 *f*against son and son against *f,*
14: 26 and does not hate his own *f*and mother,
18: 20 honor your *f*and mother.' "
23: 34 Jesus said, "*F,* forgive them,
Jn 3: 35 The *F*loves the Son and has placed
4: 21 you will worship the *F*neither
5: 17 "My *F*is always at his work
5: 18 he was even calling God his own *F,*
5: 20 For the *F*loves the Son
6: 44 the *F*who sent me draws him,
6: 46 No one has seen the *F*
8: 19 "You do not know me or my *F,*"
8: 28 speak just what the *F*has taught me
8: 41 The only *F*we have is God himself
8: 42 God were your *F,* you would love
8: 44 You belong to your *f,* the devil,
10: 17 reason my *F*loves me is that I lay
10: 30 I and the *F*are one."
10: 38 and understand that the *F*is in me,
14: 6 No one comes to the *F*
14: 9 who has seen me has seen the *F.*
14: 28 for the *F*is greater than I.
15: 9 "As the *F*has loved me,
15: 23 He who hates me hates my *F*

Jn 20: 17 'I am returning to my F and your F.'
Ac 13: 33 today I have become your F.'
Ro 4: 11 he is the f of all who believe
16: He is the f of us all.
8: 15 And by him we cry, "Abba, F."
1Co 4: 15 for in Christ Jesus I became your f
2Co 6: 18 "I will be a F to you,
Eph 5: 31 this reason a man will leave his f
6: 2 "Honor your f and mother"—
Php 2: 11 to the glory of God the F.
Heb 11: 5 today I have become your F"?
12: 7 what son is not disciplined by his f?
1Jn 1: 3 And our fellowship is with the F
2: 15 the love of the F is not in him.
2: 22 he denies the F and the Son.

FATHER'S (FATHER)

Pr 13: 1 A wise son heeds his f instruction.
15: 5 A fool spurns his f discipline.
19: 13 A foolish son is his f ruin.
Mt 16: 27 going to come in his F glory
Lk 2: 49 had to be in my F house?
Jn 2: 16 How dare you turn my F house
10: 29 can snatch them out of my F hand.
14: 2 In my F house are many rooms;
15: 8 to my F glory, that you bear much

FATHERED (FATHER)

Dt 32: 18 You deserted the Rock, who f you;

FATHERLESS (FATHER)

Dt 10: 18 He defends the cause of the f
14: 29 the f and the widows who live
24: 17 Do not deprive the alien or the f
24: 19 Leave it for the alien, the f
26: 12 the alien, the f and the widow,
Ps 68: 5 A father to the f, a defender
82: 3 Defend the cause of the weak and f
Pr 23: 10 or encroach on the fields of the f,

FATHERS (FATHER)

Ex 20: 5 for the sin of the f to the third
Jer 31: 29 'The f have eaten sour grapes,
Mal 4: 6 the hearts of the children to their f;
Lk 1: 17 the hearts of the f to their children
11: 11 "Which of you f, if your son asks
Jn 4: 20 Our f worshiped on this mountain,
1Co 4: 15 you do not have many f,
Eph 6: 4 F, do not exasperate your children;
Col 3: 21 F, do not embitter your children,
Heb 12: 9 all had human f who disciplined us

FATHOM* (FATHOMED)

Job 11: 7 "Can you f the mysteries of God?
Ps 145: 3 his greatness no one can f.
Ecc 3: 11 yet they cannot f what God has
Isa 40: 28 and his understanding no one can f
1Co 13: 2 and can f all mysteries and all

FATHOMED* (FATHOM)

Job 5: 9 performs wonders that cannot be f,
9: 10 performs wonders that cannot be f,

FATTENED

Pr 15: 17 than a f calf with hatred.
Lk 15: 23 Bring the f calf and kill it.

FAULT (FAULTS)

1Sa 29: 3 I have found no f in him."
Mt 18: 15 and show him his f, just
Php 2: 15 of God without f in a crooked
Jas 1: 5 generously to all without finding f,
Jude : 24 his glorious presence without f

FAULTFINDERS*

Jude : 16 These men are grumblers and f;

FAULTLESS*

Pr 8: 9 they are f to those who have
Php 3: 6 as for legalistic righteousness, f.
Jas 1: 27 Father accepts as pure and f is this:

FAULTS* (FAULT)

Job 10: 6 that you must search out my f
Ps 19: 12 Forgive my hidden f.

FAVOR (FAVORITISM)

Ge 4: 4 The LORD looked with f on Abel
6: 8 But Noah found f in the eyes
Ex 33: 12 and you have found f with me.'
34: 9 if I have found f in your eyes,"
Lev 26: 9 " 'I will look on you with f
Nu 11: 15 if I have found f in your eyes—
Jdg 6: 17 "If now I have found f in your eyes,
1Sa 2: 26 in f with the LORD and with men.

FAVORITISM* (FAVOR)

Ex 23: 3 and do not show f to a poor man
Lev 19: 15 to the poor or f to the great,
Ac 10: 34 true it is that God does not show f
Ro 2: 11 For God does not show f
Eph 6: 9 and there is no f with him.
Col 3: 25 for his wrong, and there is no f.
1Ti 5: 21 and to do nothing out of f.
Jas 2: 1 Lord Jesus Christ, don't show f.
2: 9 But if you show f, you sin

FEAR (AFRAID FEARED FEARS FRIGHTENED GOD-FEARING)

Dt 6: 13 F the LORD your God, serve him
10: 12 but to f the LORD your God,
31: 12 and learn to f the LORD your God
31: 13 and learn to f the LORD your God
Jos 4: 24 you might always f the LORD
24: 14 "Now f the LORD and serve him
1Sa 12: 14 If you f the LORD and serve
12: 24 But be sure to f the LORD,
2Sa 23: 3 when he rules in the f of God,
2Ch 19: 7 let the f of the LORD be upon you.
26: 5 who instructed him in the f of God.
Job 1: 9 "Does Job f God for nothing?"
Ps 2: 11 Serve the LORD with f
19: 9 The f of the LORD is pure,
23: 4 I will f no evil,
27: 1 whom shall I f?
33: 8 Let all the earth f the LORD;
34: 7 around those who f him,
34: 9 f the LORD, you his saints,
46: 2 Therefore we will not f,
86: 11 that I may f your name.
90: 11 great as the f that is due you.
91: 5 You will not f the terror of night,
111: 10 f of the LORD is the beginning
118: 4 Let those who f the LORD say:
128: 1 Blessed are all who f the LORD,
145: 19 of those who f him;
147: 11 delights in those who f him,
Pr 1: 7 f of the LORD is the beginning
1: 33 and be at ease, without f of harm."
8: 13 To f the LORD is to hate evil;
9: 10 f of the LORD is the beginning
10: 27 The f of the LORD adds length
14: 27 The f of the LORD is a fountain
15: 33 f of the LORD teaches a man
16: 6 through the f of the LORD a man
19: 23 The f of the LORD leads to life:
22: 4 Humility and the f of the LORD
29: 25 F of man will prove to be a snare,
31: 21 she has no f for her household;
Ecc 12: 13 F God and keep his
Isa 11: 3 delight in the f of the LORD.
33: 6 the f of the LORD is the key
35: 4 "Be strong, do not f;
41: 10 So do not f, for I am with you;
41: 13 and says to you, Do not f;
43: 1 "F not, for I have redeemed you;
51: 7 Do not f the reproach of men
54: 14 you will have nothing to f.
Jer 17: 8 It does not f when heat comes;
Lk 12: 5 I will show you whom you should f:
2Co 5: 11 we know what it is to f the Lord,
Php 2: 12 to work out your salvation with f
1Jn 4: 18 But perfect love drives out f,
Jude : 23 to others show mercy, mixed with f
Rev 14: 7 "F God and give him glory,

FEARED (FEAR)

Job 1: 1 he f God and shunned evil.
Ps 76: 7 You alone are to be f
Mal 3: 16 those who f the LORD talked

FEARS (FEAR)

Job 1: 8 a man who f God and shuns evil."
2: 3 a man who f God and shuns evil.
Ps 34: 4 he delivered me from all my f.

Ps 112: 1 is the man who f the LORD,
Pr 14: 16 A wise man f the LORD
14: 26 He who f the LORD has a secure
31: 30 a woman who f the LORD is
2Co 7: 5 conflicts on the outside, f within.
1Jn 4: 18 The one who f is not made perfect

FEAST (FEASTING FEASTS)

Pr 15: 15 the cheerful heart has a continual f.
2Pe 2: 13 pleasures while they f with you.

FEASTING (FEAST)

Pr 17: 1 than a house full of f, with strife.

FEASTS (FEAST)

Am 5: 21 "I hate, I despise your religious f;
Jude : 12 men are blemishes at your love f,

FEATHERS

Ps 91: 4 He will cover you with his f,

FEEBLE

Job 4: 3 you have strengthened f hands.
Isa 35: 3 Strengthen the f hands,
Heb 12: 12 strengthen your f arms

FEED (FEEDS)

Jn 21: 15 Jesus said, "F my lambs."
21: 17 Jesus said, "F my sheep.
Ro 12: 20 "If your enemy is hungry, f him;
Jude : 12 shepherds who f only themselves.

FEEDS (FEED)

Pr 15: 14 but the mouth of a fool f on folly.
Mt 6: 26 yet your heavenly Father f them.
Jn 6: 57 so the one who f on me will live

FEEL

Jdg 16: 26 me where I can f the pillars that
Ps 115: 7 they have hands, but cannot f,

FEET (FOOT)

Ru 3: 8 discovered a woman lying at his f.
Ps 8: 6 you put everything under his f:
22: 16 have pierced my hands and my f.
40: 2 he set my f on a rock
56: 13 and my f from stumbling.
66: 9 and kept our f from slipping.
73: 2 as for me, my f had almost slipped;
110: 1 a footstool for your f."
119: 105 Your word is a lamp to my f
Pr 4: 26 Make level paths for your f
Isa 52: 7 are the f of those who bring good
Da 2: 33 its f partly of iron and partly
Na 1: 15 the f of one who brings good news.
Mt 10: 14 shake the dust off your f
22: 44 enemies under your f." '
Lk 1: 79 to guide our f into the path of peace
20: 43 a footstool for your f." '
24: 39 Look at my hands and my f.
Jn 13: 5 and began to wash his disciples' f,
13: 14 also should wash one another's f.
Ro 3: 15 "Their f are swift to shed blood;
10: 15 "How beautiful are the f
16: 20 will soon crush Satan under your f
1Co 12: 21 And the head cannot say to the f,
15: 25 has put all his enemies under his f.
Eph 1: 22 God placed all things under his f
1Ti 5: 10 washing the f of the saints,
Heb 1: 13 a footstool for your f"?
2: 8 and put everything under his f."
12: 13 "Make level paths for your f,"
Rev 1: 15 His f were like bronze glowing

FELIX

Governor before whom Paul was tried (Ac 23: 23-24:27).

FELLOWSHIP

Ex 20: 24 burnt offerings and f offerings,
Lev 3: 1 If someone's offering is a f offering,
1Co 1: 9 who has called you into f
5: 2 out of your f the man who did this?
2Co 6: 14 what f can light have with darkness
13: 14 and the f of the Holy Spirit be
Gal 2: 9 and Barnabas the right hand of f
Php 2: 1 if any f with the Spirit,
3: 10 the f of sharing in his sufferings,
1Jn 1: 3 And our f is with the Father
1: 3 so that you also may have f with us.
1: 6 claim to have f with him yet walk
1: 7 we have f with one another,

FEMALE

Ge 1: 27 male and f he created them.

Ge   5: 2 He created them male and f
Mt   19: 4 Creator 'made them male and f.'
Mk   10: 6 God 'made them male and f.'
Gal   3: 28 f, for you are all one in Christ Jesus

FEROCIOUS
Mt   7: 15 but inwardly they are fwolves.

FERTILE (FERTILIZE)
Isa   32: 15 and the desert becomes a ffield,
Jer   2: 7 I brought you into a fland

FERTILIZE* (FERTILE)
Lk   13: 8 and I'll dig around it and fit.

FERVOR*
Ac   18: 25 and he spoke with great f
Ro   12: 11 but keep your spiritual f, serving

FESTIVAL
1Co   5: 8 Therefore let us keep the F,
Col   2: 16 or with regard to a religious f,

FESTUS
    Successor of Felix; sent Paul to Caesar
(Ac 25-26).

FEVER
Job   30: 30 my body burns with f.
Mt   8: 14 mother-in-law lying in bed with a f.
Lk   4: 38 was suffering from a high f,
Jn   4: 52 "The fleft him yesterday
Ac   28: 8 suffering from fand dysentery.

FIELD (FIELDS)
Ge   4: 8 Abel, "Let's go out to the f."
Lev   19: 9 reap to the very edges of your f
       19: 19 Do not plant your fwith two kinds
Pr   31: 16 She considers a fand buys it;
Isa   40: 6 glory is like the flowers of the f.
Mt   6: 28 See how the lilies of the fgrow.
        6: 30 how God clothes the grass of the f,
       13: 38 fis the world, and the good seed
       13: 44 is like treasure hidden in a f.
Lk   14: 18 I have just bought a f, and I must go
1Co   3: 9 you are God's f, God's building.
1Pe   1: 24 glory is like the flowers of the f;

FIELDS (FIELD)
Ru   2: 2 go to the fand pick up the leftover
Lk   2: 8 were shepherds living out in the f
Jn   4: 35 open your eyes and look at the fl

FIG (FIGS SYCAMORE-FIG)
Ge   3: 7 so they sewed fleaves together
Jdg   9: 10 "Next, the trees said to the ftree.
1Ki   4: 25 man under his own vine and ftree.
Pr   27: 18 He who tends a ftree will eat its
Mic   4: 4 and under his own ftree,
Zec   3: 10 to sit under his vine and ftree,'
Mt   21: 19 Seeing a ftree by the road,
Lk   13: 6 "A man had a ftree, planted
Jas   3: 12 brothers, can a ftree bear olives,
Rev   6: 13 drop from a ftree when shaken

FIGHT (FIGHTING FIGHTS FOUGHT)
Ex   14: 14 The LORD will ffor you; you need
Dt   1: 30 going before you, will ffor you,
        3: 22 the LORD your God himself will f
Ne   4: 20 Our God will ffor us!"
Ps   35: 1 fagainst those who fagainst me.
Jn   18: 36 my servants would f
1Co   9: 26 I do not like a man beating the air.
2Co   10: 4 The weapons we f
1Ti   1: 18 them you may fthe good f,
        6: 12 Fight the good fof the faith.
2Ti   4: 7 fought the good f, I have finished

FIGHTING (FIGHT)
Jos   10: 14 Surely the LORD was ffor Israel!

FIGHTS (FIGHT)
Jos   23: 10 the LORD your God ffor you,
1Sa   25: 28 because he fthe LORD's battles.
Jas   4: 1 What causes fand quarrels

FIGS (FIG)
Lk   6: 44 People do not pick f
Jas   3: 12 grapevine bear f?Neither can a salt

FILL (FILLED FILLING FILLS FULL FULLNESS FULLY)
Ge   1: 28 and increase in number; fthe earth
Ps   16: 11 you will fme with joy
       81: 10 wide your mouth and I will fit.

Pr   28: 19 who chases fantasies will have his f
Hag   2: 7 and I will fthis house with glory,'
Jn   6: 26 you ate the loaves and had your f.
Ac   2: 28 you will fme with joy
Ro   15: 13 the God of hope fyou with all joy

FILLED (FILL)
Ex   31: 3 I have fhim with the Spirit of God,
       35: 31 he has fhim with the Spirit of God,
Dt   34: 9 son of Nun fwith the spirit
1Ki   8: 10 the cloud fthe temple
        8: 11 glory of the LORD fhis temple.
2Ch   5: 14 of the LORD fthe temple of God.
        7: 1 the glory of the LORD fthe temple
Ps   72: 19 may the whole earth be f
      119: 64 The earth is fwith your love,
Isa   6: 4 and the temple was fwith smoke.
Eze   10: 3 and a cloud fthe inner court.
       10: 4 The cloud fthe temple,
       43: 5 the glory of the LORD fthe temple
Hab   2: 14 For the earth will be f
        3: 3 and his praise fthe earth.
Mt   5: 6 for they will be f.
Lk   1: 15 and he will be fwith the Holy Spirit
        1: 41 and Elizabeth was fwith the Holy
        1: 67 His father Zechariah was f
        2: 40 and became strong; he was f
Jn   2: 3 the house was fwith the fragrance
Ac   2: 2 fthe whole house where they were
        2: 4 All of them were f
        4: 8 Then Peter, fwith the Holy Spirit,
        4: 31 they were all fwith the Holy Spirit
        9: 17 and be fwith the Holy Spirit."
       13: 9 called Paul, fwith the Holy Spirit,
Eph   5: 18 Instead, be fwith the Spirit.
Php   1: 11 fwith the fruit of righteousness
Rev   15: 8 And the temple was fwith smoke

FILLING (FILL)
Eze   44: 4 the glory of the LORD fthe temple

FILLS (FILL)
Nu   14: 21 of the LORD fthe whole earth,
Ps   107: 9 and fthe hungry with good things.
Eph   1: 23 fullness of him who feverything

FILTH (FILTHY)
Isa   4: 4 The Lord will wash away the f
Jas   1: 21 rid of all moral fand the evil that is

FILTHY (FILTH)
Isa   64: 6 all our righteous acts are like frags;
Col   3: 8 and flanguage from your lips.
2Pe   2: 7 by the flives of lawless men

FINAL (FINALITY)
Ps   73: 17 then I understood their fdestiny.

FINALITY* (FINAL)
Ro   9: 28 on earth with speed and f.''

FINANCIAL*
1Ti   6: 5 that godliness is a means to fgain.

FIND (FINDS FOUND)
Nu   32: 23 be sure that your sin will fyou out.
Dt   4: 29 you will fhim if you look for him
1Sa   23: 16 and helped him fstrength in God.
Job   23: 3 If only I knew where to fhim;
Ps   36: 7 frefuge in the shadow
       62: 5 Frest, O my soul, in God alone;
       91: 4 under his wings you will frefuge;
Pr   8: 17 and those who seek me fme.
       14: 22 those who plan what is good flove
       20: 6 but a faithful man who can f?
       24: 14 if you fit, there is a future hope
       31: 10 A wife of noble character who can f
Jer   6: 16 and you will frest for your souls.
       29: 13 and fme when you seek me
Mt   7: 7 seek and you will f; knock
       11: 29 and you will frest for your souls.
       16: 25 loses his life for me will fit.
       22: 9 invite to the banquet anyone you f.'
Lk   11: 9 seek and you will f; knock
       18: 8 will he ffaith on the earth?"
Jn   10: 9 come in and go out, and fpasture.

FINDS (FIND)
Ps   62: 1 My soul frest in God alone;
      112: 1 who fgreat delight
      119:162 like one who fgreat spoil.
Pr   3: 13 Blessed is the man who fwisdom,
        8: 35 For whoever fme flife
       11: 27 He who seeks good fgood will,
       18: 22 He who fa wife fwhat is good

Mt   7: 8 he who seeks f, and to him who
       10: 39 Whoever fhis life will lose it,
Lk   11: 10 he who seeks f, and to him who
       12: 37 whose master fthem watching
       12: 43 servant whom the master fdoing
       15: 4 go after the lost sheep until he fit?
       15: 8 and search carefully until she fit?

FINE-SOUNDING* (SOUND)
Col   2: 4 may deceive you by farguments.

FINGER
Ex   8: 19 to Pharaoh, "This is the fof God.''
       31: 18 of stone inscribed by the fof God.
Dt   9: 10 two stone tablets inscribed by the f
Lk   11: 20 But if I drive out demons by the f
       16: 24 to dip the tip of his fin water
Jn   8: 6 to write on the ground with his f.
       20: 25 and put my fwhere the nails were,

FINISH (FINISHED)
Jn   4: 34 him who sent me and to fhis work.
        5: 36 that the Father has given me to f,
Ac   20: 24 if only I may fthe race
2Co   8: 11 Now fthe work, so that your eager
Jas   1: 4 Perseverance must fits work

FINISHED (FINISH)
Ge   2: 2 seventh day God had fthe work he
Jn   19: 30 the drink, Jesus said, "It is f."
2Ti   4: 7 I have fthe race, I have kept

FIRE
Ex   3: 2 in flames of ffrom within a bush.
       13: 21 in a pillar of fto give them light,
Lev   6: 12 fon the altar must be kept burning;
        9: 24 Fcame out from the presence
1Ki   18: 38 Then the fof the LORD fell
2Ki   2: 11 suddenly a chariot of f
Isa   5: 24 as tongues of flick up straw
       30: 27 and his tongue is a consuming f.
Jer   23: 29 my word like f, "declares
Da   3: 25 four men walking around in the f,
Zec   3: 2 stick snatched from the f?"
Mal   3: 2 For he will be like a refiner's f
Mt   3: 11 you with the Holy Spirit and with f.
        3: 12 the chaff with unquenchable f."
        5: 22 will be in danger of the fof hell.
       18: 8 and be thrown into eternal f.
       25: 41 into the eternal fprepared
Mk   9: 43 where the fnever goes out.
        9: 48 and the fis not quenched."
        9: 49 Everyone will be salted with f.
Lk   3: 16 you with the Holy Spirit and with f.
       12: 49 I have come to bring fon the earth,
Ac   2: 3 to be tongues of fthat separated
1Co   3: 13 It will be revealed with f,
1Th   5: 19 Do not put out the Spirit's f;
Heb   12: 29 for our "God is a consuming f."
Jas   3: 5 set on fby a small spark.
        3: 6 also is a f, a world of evil
2Pe   3: 10 the elements will be destroyed by f,
Jude   7 suffer the punishment of eternal f.
           :23 snatch others from the f
Rev   1: 14 and his eyes were like blazing f.
       20: 14 The lake of fis the second death.

FIRM*
Ex   14: 13 Stand fand you will see
       15: 8 surging waters stood flike a wall;
Jos   3: 17 the covenant of the LORD stood f
2Ch   17 stand fand see the deliverance
Ezr   9: 8 giving us a fplace in his sanctuary,
Job   11: 15 you will stand fand without fear.
       36: 5 he is mighty, and fin his purpose.
       41: 23 they are fand immovable.
Ps   20: 8 but we rise up and stand f.
       30: 7 you made my mountain stand f;
       33: 9 he commanded, and it stood f.
       33: 11 of the LORD stand fforever,
       37: 23 he makes his steps f;
       40: 2 and gave me a fplace to stand.
       75: 3 it is I who hold its pillars f.
       78: 13 made the water stand flike a wall.
       89: 2 that your love stands fforever,
       89: 4 and make your throne f
       93: 5 Your statutes stand f;
      119: 89 it stands fin the heavens.
Pr   4: 26 and take only ways that are f.
       10: 25 but the righteous stand fforever.
       12: 7 the house of the righteous stands f.
Isa   7: 9 If you do not stand fin your faith,
       22: 17 about to take fhold of you
       22: 23 drive him like a peg into a fplace;
       22: 25 into the fplace will give way;

Eze 13: 5 so that it will stand *f* in the battle
Zec 8:23 nations will take *f* hold of one Jew
Mt 10:22 He who stands *f* to the end will be
 24:13 He who stands *f* to the end will be
Mk 13:13 he who stands *f* to the end will be
Lk 21:19 By standing *f* you will gain life.
1Co 10:12 So, if you think you are standing *f*,
 15:58 my dear brothers, stand *f*.
 16:13 on your guard; stand *f* in the faith;
2Co 1: 7 for you is *f*, because we know that
 1:21 who makes both us and you stand *f*
 1:24 because it is by faith you stand *f*.
Gal 5: 1 Stand *f*, then, and do not let
Eph 6:14 Stand *f* then, with the belt
Php 1:27 I will know that you stand *f*
 4: 1 that is how you should stand *f*.
Col 1:23 in your faith, established and *f*,
 2: 5 and how *f* your faith in Christ is.
 4:12 that you may stand *f* in all the will
1Th 3: 8 since you are standing *f* in the Lord
2Th 2:15 stand *f* and hold to the teachings
1Ti 6:19 a foundation for the coming age,
2Ti 2:19 God's solid foundation stands *f*,
Heb 6:19 an anchor for the soul, *f* and secure
Jas 5: 8 You too, be patient and stand *f*,
1Pe 5:10 Resist him, standing *f* in the faith,
 5:10 make you strong, *f* and steadfast.

FIRMAMENT see EXPANSE, HEAVENS, SKIES

FIRST

Ge 1: 5 and there was morning—the *f* day
 13: 4 and where he had *f* built an altar.
Ex 34:19 *f* offspring of every womb belongs
1Ki 22: 5 "*f* seek the counsel of the LORD."
Pr 18:17 *f* to present his case seems right,
Isa 44: 6 I am the *f* and I am the last;
 48:12 I am the *f* and I am the last.
Mt 5:24 *F* go and be reconciled
 6:33 But seek *f* his kingdom.
 7: 5 *f* take the plank out
 19:30 But many who are *f* will be last,
 20:16 last will be *f*, and the *f* will be last."
 20:27 wants to be *f* must be your slave—
 22:38 This is the *f* and greatest
 23:26 *F* clean the inside of the cup.
Mk 9:35 to be *f*, he must be the very last,
 10:31 are *f* will be last, and the last *f*."
 10:44 wants to be *f* must be slave
 13:10 And the gospel must *f* be preached
Lk 13:30 will be *f*, and *f* who will be last."
Jn 8: 7 let him be the *f* to throw a stone
Ac 11:26 disciples were called Christians *f*
Ro 1:16 *f* for the Jew, then for the Gentile.
 1:17 is by faith from *f* to last,
 2: 9 *f* for the Jew, then for the Gentile;
 2:10 *f* for the Jew, then for the Gentile.
1Co 12:28 in the church God has appointed *f*
 15:45 "The *f* man Adam became a living
2Co 8: 5 they gave themselves *f* to the Lord
Eph 6: 2 which is the *f* commandment
1Th 4:16 and the dead in Christ will rise *f*.
1Ti 2:13 For Adam was formed *f*, then Eve.
Heb 10: 9 He sets aside the *f*
Jas 3:17 comes from heaven is *f* of all pure;
1Jn 4:19 We love because he *f* loved us.
3Jn : 9 but Diotrephes, who loves to be *f*,
Rev 1:17 I am the *F* and the Last.
 2: 4 You have forsaken your *f* love.
 22:13 and the Omega, the *F* and the Last,

FIRSTBORN (BEAR)

Ex 11: 5 Every *f* son in Egypt will die,
 34:20 Redeem all your *f* sons.
Ps 89:27 I will also appoint him my *f*,
Lk 2: 7 and she gave birth to her *f*, a son.
Ro 8:29 that he might be the *f*
Col 1:15 image of the invisible God, the *f*
 1:18 and the *f* from among the dead,
Heb 6 when God brings his *f*
 12:23 of the *f*, whose names are written
Rev 1: 5 who is the faithful witness, the *f*

FIRSTFRUITS

Ex 23:16 the Feast of Harvest with the *f*
 23:19 "Bring the best of the *f* of your soil
Ro 8:23 who have the *f* of the Spirit,
1Co 15:23 Christ, the *f*; then, when he comes,
Rev 14: 4 offered as *f* to God and the Lamb.

FISH (FISHERS)

Ge 1:26 let them rule over the *f* of the sea
Jnh 1:17 But the LORD provided a great *f*
Mt 7:10 asks for a *f*, will give him a snake?

Mt 12:40 three nights in the belly of a huge *f*,
 14:17 loaves of bread and two *f*,"
Mk 6:38 they said, "Five—and two *f*."
Lk 5: 6 of *f* that their nets began to break.
 9:13 loaves of bread and two *f*—
Jn 6: 9 small barley loaves and two small *f*,
 21: 5 haven't you any *f*?" "No,"
 21:11 It was full of large *f*, 153, but

FISHERMEN

Mk 1:16 a net into the lake, for they were *f*.

FISHERS (FISH)

Mt 4:19 "and I will make you *f* of men."
Mk 1:17 "and I will make you *f* of men."

FISHHOOK*

Job 41: 1 pull in the leviathan with a *f*

FISTS

Mt 26:67 and struck him with their *f*.

FIT (FITTING)

Jdg 17: 6 no king; everyone did as he saw *f*.
 21:25 no king; everyone did as he saw *f*.

FITTING* (FIT)

Ps 33: 1 it is *f* for the upright to praise him.
 147: 1 how pleasant and *f* to praise him!
Pr 10:32 of the righteous know what is *f*,
 19:10 It is not *f* for a fool to live in luxury
 26: 1 honor is not *f* for a fool.
1Co 14:40 everything should be done in a *f*
Col 3:18 to your husbands, as is *f* in the Lord
Heb 2:10 sons to glory, it was *f* that God,

FIX* (FIXED)

Dt 11:18 *F* these words of mine
Job 14: 3 Do you *f* your eye on such a one?
Pr 4:25 *f* your gaze directly before you.
Isa 46: 8 "Remember this, *f* it in mind,
Am 9: 4 I will *f* my eyes upon them
2Co 4:18 we *f* our eyes not on what is seen,
Heb 3: 1 heavenly calling, *f* your thoughts
 12: 2 Let us *f* our eyes on Jesus,

FIXED* (FIX)

2Ki 8:11 stared at him with a *f* gaze
Job 38:10 when I *f* limits for it
Ps 141: 8 my eyes are *f* on you, O Sovereign
Pr 8:28 *f* securely the fountains of the deep
Jer 33:25 and night and the *f* laws of heaven
Lk 16:26 and you a great chasm has been *f*,

FLAME (FLAMES FLAMING)

2Ti 1: 6 you to fan into *f* the gift of God,

FLAMES (FLAME)

1Co 3:15 only as one escaping through the *f*.
 13: 3 and surrender my body to the *f*,

FLAMING (FLAME)

Eph 6:16 you can extinguish all the *f* arrows

FLANK

Eze 34:21 Because you shove with *f*

FLASH

1Co 15:52 in a *f*, in the twinkling of an eye,

FLATTER* (FLATTERING FLATTERS FLATTERY)

Job 32:21 nor will I *f* any man;
Ps 78:36 But then they would *f* him.
Jude : 16 *f* others for their own advantage.

FLATTERING* (FLATTER)

Ps 12: 2 their *f* lips speak with deception.
 12: 3 May the LORD cut off all *f* lips
Pr 26:28 and a *f* mouth works ruin.
 28:23 than he who has a *f* tongue.
Eze 12:24 or *f* divinations among the people

FLATTERS* (FLATTER)

Ps 36: 2 For in his own eyes he *f* himself
Pr 29: 5 Whoever *f* his neighbor

FLATTERY* (FLATTER)

Job 32:22 for if I were skilled in *f*,
Da 11:32 With *f* he will corrupt those who
Ro 16:18 and *f* they deceive the minds
1Th 2: 5 You know we never used *f*,

FLAWLESS*

2Sa 22:31 the word of the LORD is *f*.

Job 11: 4 You say to God, 'My beliefs are *f*
Ps 12: 6 And the words of the LORD are *f*,
 18:30 the word of the LORD is *f*.
Pr 30: 5 "Every word of God is *f*;
SS 5: 2 my dove, my *f* one.

FLEE (FLEES)

Ps 139: 7 Where can I *f* from your presence?
1Co 6:18 *F* from sexual immorality.
 10:14 my dear friends, *f* from idolatry.
1Ti 6:11 But you, man of God, *f* from all this
2Ti 2:22 *F* the evil desires of youth,
Jas 4: 7 Resist the devil, and he will *f*

FLEECE

Jdg 6:37 I will place a wool *f*

FLEES (FLEE)

Pr 28: 1 The wicked man *f* though no one

FLEETING*

Job 14: 2 like a *f* shadow, he does not endure
Ps 39: 4 let me know how *f* is my life.
 89:47 Remember how *f* is my life.
 144: 4 his days are like a *f* shadow.
Pr 21: 6 is a *f* vapor and a deadly snare.
 31:30 Charm is deceptive, and beauty is *f*

FLESH see also BODY, MANKIND, PEOPLE, SINFUL (nature)

Ge 2:23 and *f* of my *f*;
 2:24 they will become one *f*.
2Ch 32: 8 With him is only the arm of *f*,
Job 19:26 yet in my *f* I will see God;
Eze 11:19 of stone and give them a heart of *f*.
 36:26 of stone and give you a heart of *f*.
Mt 19: 5 and the two will become one *f*?
Mk 10: 8 and the two will become one *f*.'
Jn 1:14 The Word became *f* and made his
 6:51 This bread is my *f*, which I will give
1Co 6:16 "The two will become one *f*."
 15:39 All *f* is not the same: Men have one
Eph 5:31 and the two will become one *f*."
 6:12 For our struggle is not against *f*
Php 3: 2 do evil, those mutilators of the *f*.
1Jn 4: 2 come in the *f* is from God;
Jude : 23 the clothing stained by corrupted *f*.

FLIGHT

Dt 32:30 or two put ten thousand to *f*,

FLINT

Isa 50: 7 Therefore have I set my face like *f*,
Zec 7:12 They made their hearts as hard as *f*

FLIRTING*

Isa 3:16 *f* with their eyes,

FLOCK (FLOCKS)

Ps 77:20 You led your people like a *f*
 78:52 he brought his people out like a *f*;
 95: 7 the *f* under his care.
Isa 40:11 He tends his *f* like a shepherd:
Jer 10:21 and all their *f* is scattered.
 23: 2 "Because you have scattered my *f*
 31:10 watch over his *f* like a shepherd.'
Eze 34: 2 not shepherds take care of the *f*?
Zec 11:17 who deserts the *f*!
Mt 26:31 the sheep of the *f* will be scattered.'
Lk 12:32 little *f*, for your Father has been
Jn 10:16 shall be one *f* and one shepherd.
Ac 20:28 all the *f* of which the Holy Spirit
1Co 9: 7 Who tends a *f* and does not drink
1Pe 5: 2 Be shepherds of God's *f* that is
 5: 3 but being examples to the *f*.

FLOCKS (FLOCK)

Lk 2: 8 keeping watch over their *f* at night.

FLOG (FLOGGED FLOGGING)

Pr 19:25 *F* a mocker, and the simple will
Ac 22:25 to *f* a Roman citizen who hasn't

FLOGGED (FLOG)

Jn 19: 1 Pilate took Jesus and had him *f*.
Ac 5:40 the apostles in and had them *f*
 16:23 After they had been severely *f*,
2Co 11:23 frequently, been *f* more severely,

FLOGGING (FLOG)

Heb 11:36 *f*, while still others were chained

FLOOD (FLOODGATES)

Ge 7: 7 ark to escape the waters of the *f*.
Mal 2:13 You *f* the LORD's altar with tears.

Mt   24:38 For in the days before the *f*,
2Pe   2:   5 world when he brought the *f*

FLOODGATES (FLOOD)

Ge   7:11 the *f* of the heavens were opened.
Mal   3:10 see if I will not throw open the *f*

FLOOR

Jas   2:   3 or "Sit on the *f* by my feet,"

FLOUR

Lev   2:   1 his offering is to be of fine *f*.
Nu   7:13 filled with fine *f* mixed with oil
      28:   9 of an ephah of fine *f* mixed with oil.

FLOURISH (FLOURISHES FLOURISHING)

Ps   72:   7 In his days the righteous will *f*;
      92:   7 and all evildoers *f*,
      92:12 The righteous will *f* like a palm tree
Pr   14:11 but the tent of the upright will *f*.

FLOURISHES (FLOURISH)

Pr   12:12 but the root of the righteous *f*.

FLOURISHING (FLOURISH)

Ps   52:   8 *f* in the house of God;

FLOW (FLOWING)

Nu   13:27 and it does *f* with milk and honey!
Jn   7:38 streams of living water will *f*

FLOWER (FLOWERS)

Job   14:   2 up like a *f* and withers away;
Ps   103:15 he flourishes like a *f* of the field;
Jas   1:10 he will pass away like a wild *f*.

FLOWERS (FLOWER)

Isa   40:   6 and all their glory is like the *f*
      40:   7 The grass withers and the *f* fall,
1Pe   1:24 and all their glory is like the *f*

FLOWING (FLOW)

Ex   3:   8 a land *f* with milk and honey—
      33:   3 Go up to the land *f* with milk
Nu   16:14 us into a land *f* with milk
Jos   5:   6 a land *f* with milk and honey.
Ps   107:33 *f* springs into thirsty ground,
      107:35 the parched ground into *f* springs;
Jer   32:22 a land *f* with milk and honey.
Eze   20:   6 a land *f* with milk and honey.
Rev   22:   1 *f* from the throne of God

FLUTE

Ps   150:   4 praise him with the strings and *f*,
Mt   11:17 " 'We played the *f* for you,
1Co   14:   7 that make sounds, such as the *f*

FOAL*

Zec   9:   9 on a colt, the *f* of a donkey.
Mt   21:   5 on a colt, the *f* of a donkey.' "

FOILS*

Ps   33:10 The LORD *f* the plans
Isa   44:25 who the *f* signs of false prophets

FOLDING* (FOLDS)

Pr   6:10 a little *f* of the hands to rest—
      24:33 a little *f* of the hands to rest—

FOLDS (FOLDING)

Ecc   4:   5 The fool *f* his hands

FOLLOW (FOLLOWED FOLLOWING FOLLOWS)

Ex   23:   2 Do not *f* the crowd in doing wrong.
Lev   18:   4 and be careful to *f* my decrees.
Dt   1:   8 Learn them and be sure to *f* them.
      17:19 *f* carefully all the words of this law
1Ki   11:   6 he did not *f* the LORD completely,
2Ch   34:33 they did not fail to *f* the LORD,
Ps   23:   6 Surely goodness and love will *f* me
      119:166 and I *f* your commands.
Mt   4:19 *f* me," Jesus said, "and I will make
      8:19 I will *f* you wherever you go."
      8:22 But Jesus told him, "*F* me,
      16:24 and take up his cross and *f* me.
      19:27 "We have left everything to *f* you!
Lk   9:23 take up his cross daily and *f* me.
      9:61 Still another said, "I will *f* you,
Jn   10:   4 his sheep *f* him because they know
      10:   5 But they will never *f* a stranger;
      10:27 I know them, and they *f* me.
      12:26 Whoever serves me must *f* me;
      21:19 Then he said to him, "*F* me!' "
1Co   1:12 One of you says, "I *f* Paul";

1Co   11:   1 *F* my example, as I follow
      14:   1 *F* the way of love and eagerly
2Th   3:   9 ourselves a model for you to *f*.
1Pe   2:21 that you should *f* in his steps.
Rev   14:   4 They *f* the Lamb wherever he goes.

FOLLOWED (FOLLOW)

Nu   32:11 they have not *f* me wholeheartedly,
Dt   1:36 he *f* the LORD wholeheartedly.''
Jos   14:14 he *f* the LORD, the God of Israel,
2Ch   10:14 he *f* the advice of the young men
Mt   4:20 once they left their nets and *f* him.
      9:   9 and Matthew got up and *f* him.
      26:58 But Peter *f* him at a distance.
Lk   18:43 he received his sight and *f* Jesus,

FOLLOWING (FOLLOW)

Ps   119:14 I rejoice in *f* your statutes
Php   3:17 Join with others in *f* my example,
1Ti   1:18 by *f* them you may fight the good

FOLLOWS (FOLLOW)

Jn   8:12 Whoever *f* me will never walk

FOLLY (FOOL)

Pr   14:29 a quick-tempered man displays *f*.
      19:   3 A man's own *f* ruins his life,
Ecc   10:   1 so a little *f* outweighs wisdom
Mk   7:22 envy, slander, arrogance and *f*,
2Ti   3:   9 their *f* will be clear to everyone.

FOOD (FOODS)

Ge   1:30 I give every green plant for *f*."
Pr   12:   9 to be somebody and have no *f*.
      12:11 his land will have abundant *f*,
      20:13 you will have *f* to spare.
      20:17 *F* gained by fraud tastes sweet
      21:20 of the wise are stores of choice *f*
      22:   9 for he shares his *f* with the poor.
      23:   3 for that *f* is deceptive.
      23:   6 Do not eat the *f* of a stingy man,
      25:21 If your enemy is hungry, give him *f*
      31:14 bringing her *f* from afar.
      31:15 she provides *f* for her family
Isa   58:   7 not to share your *f* with the hungry
Eze   7:   7 but gives his *f* to the hungry
Da   1:   8 to defile himself with the royal *f*
Mt   3:   4 His *f* was locusts and wild honey.
      6:25 Is not life more important than *f*,
Jn   4:32 "I have *f* to eat that you know
      4:34 have brought him *f*?"'My *f*,"
      6:27 Do not work for *f* that spoils,
      6:55 my flesh is real *f* and my blood is
Ac   15:20 to abstain from *f* polluted by idols,
Ro   14:14 fully convinced that no *f* is unclean
1Co   8:   1 Now about *f* sacrificed to idols:
      8:   8 But *f* does not bring us near to God
2Co   11:27 and have often gone without *f*;
1Ti   6:   8 But if we have *f* and clothing,
Heb   5:14 But solid *f* is for the mature,
Jas   2:15 sister is without clothes and daily *f*.

FOODS (FOOD)

Mk   7:19 Jesus declared all *f* "clean.'')

FOOL (FOLLY FOOL'S FOOLISH FOOLISHNESS FOOLS)

1Sa   25:25 his name is *F*, and folly goes
Ps   14:   1 The *f* says in his heart,
Pr   10:10 and a chattering *f* comes to ruin.
      10:18 and whoever spreads slander is a *f*.
      12:15 The way of a *f* seems right to him,
      12:16 A *f* shows his annoyance at once,
      14:16 but a *f* is hotheaded and reckless.
      15:   5 A *f* spurns his father's discipline,
      17:12 than a fin his folly.
      17:16 use is money in the hand of a *f*,
      17:21 To have a *f* for a son brings grief;
      17:28 Even a *f* is thought wise
      18:   2 A *f* finds no pleasure
      20:   3 but every *f* is quick to quarrel.
      23:   9 Do not speak to a *f*,
      24:   7 Wisdom is too high for a *f*;
      26:   4 Do not answer a *f* according
      26:   5 Answer a *f* according to his folly,
      26:   7 is a proverb in the mouth of a *f*.
      26:11 so a *f* repeats his folly.
      26:12 for a *f* than for him.
      27:22 Though you grind a *f* in a mortar,
      28:26 He who trusts in himself is a *f*
      29:11 A *f* gives full vent to his anger;
      29:20 for a *f* than for him.
Mt   5:22 But anyone who says, 'You *f*!'
Lk   12:20 "But God said to him, 'You *f*!
1Co   3:18 he should become a "*f*"

2Co   11:21 I am speaking as a *f*—I

FOOL'S (FOOL)

Pr   14:   3 A *f* talk brings a rod to his back,
      18:   7 A *f* mouth is his undoing,

FOOLISH (FOOL)

Pr   10:   1 but a *f* son grief to his mother.
      14:   1 her own hands the *f* one tears hers
      15:20 but a *f* man despises his mother.
      17:25 A *f* son brings grief to his father
      19:13 A *f* son is his father's ruin,
Mt   7:26 practice is like a *f* man who built
      25:   2 of them were *f* and five were wise.
Lk   11:40 You *f* people! Did not the one who
      24:25 He said to them, "How *f* you are,
1Co   1:20 Has not God made *f* the wisdom
      1:27 God chose the *f* things of the world
Gal   3:   1 died for nothing!" You *f* Galatians!
Eph   5:   4 should there be obscenity, *f* talk
      5:17 Therefore do not be *f*,
Tit   3:   9 But avoid *f* controversies

FOOLISHNESS (FOOL)

1Co   1:18 of the cross is *f* to those who are
      1:21 through the *f* of what was preached
      1:23 block to Jews and *f* to Gentiles,
      1:25 For the *f* of God is wiser
      2:14 for they are *f* to him, and he cannot
      3:19 of this world is *f* in God's sight.

FOOLS (FOOL)

Pr   1:   7 but *f* despise wisdom and discipline
      3:35 but *f* he holds up to shame.
      12:23 but the heart of *f* blurts out folly.
      13:19 but *f* detest turning from evil.
      13:20 but a companion of *f* suffers harm.
      14:   9 *F* mock at making amends for sin,
      14:24 but the folly of *f* yields folly.
Ecc   7:   5 than to listen to the song of *f*.
      7:   6 so is the laughter of *f*.
      10:   6 *F* are put in many high positions,
Mt   23:17 You blind *f*! Which is greater:
Ro   1:22 they became *f* and exchanged
1Co   4:10 We are *f* for Christ, but you are

FOOT (FEET FOOTHOLD)

Jos   1:   3 every place where you set your *f*,
Ps   121:   3 He will not let your *f* slip—
Pr   3:23 and your *f* will not stumble;
      4:27 keep your *f* from evil.
      25:17 Seldom set *f* in your neighbor's
Isa   1:   6 From the sole of your *f* to the top
Mt   18:   8 or your *f* causes you to sin,
Lk   11 so that you will not strike your *f*
1Co   12:15 If the *f* should say, "Because I am
Rev   10:   2 He planted his right *f* on the sea

FOOTHOLD* (FOOT)

Ps   69:   2 where there is no *f*.
      73:   2 I had nearly lost my *f*.
Eph   4:27 and do not give the devil a *f*.

FOOTSTEPS (STEP)

Ps   119:133 Direct my *f* according

FOOTSTOOL

Ps   99:   5 and worship at his *f*;
      110:   1 a *f* for your feet."
Isa   66:   1 and the earth is my *f*.
Mt   5:35 for it is his *f*; or by Jerusalem,
Ac   7:49 and the earth is my *f*.
Heb   1:13 a *f* for your feet"?
      10:13 for his enemies to be made his *f*.

FORBEARANCE*

Ro   3:25 because in his *f* he had left the sins

FORBID

1Co   14:39 and do not *f* speaking in tongues.
1Ti   4:   3 They *f* people to marry

FORCE (FORCED FORCEFUL FORCES FORCING)

Jn   6:15 to come and make him king by *f*,
Ac   26:11 and I tried to *f* them to blaspheme.
Gal   2:14 that you *f* Gentiles

FORCED (FORCE)

Mt   27:32 and they *f* him to carry the cross.
Phm   : 14 do will be spontaneous and not *f*.

FORCEFUL* (FORCE)

Mt   11:12 forcefully advancing, and *f* men lay
2Co   10:10 "His letters are weighty and *f*,

FORCES (FORCE)
Mt 5:41 If someone *f* you to go one mile,
Eph 6:12 and against the spiritual *f* of evil

FORCING (FORCE)
Lk 16:16 and everyone is *f* his way into it.

FOREFATHERS (FATHER)
Heb 1: 1 spoke to our *f* through the prophets
1Pe 1:18 handed down to you from your *f,*

FOREHEAD (FOREHEADS)
Ex 13: 9 a reminder on your *f* that the law
      13:16 on your *f* that the LORD brought
1Sa 17:49 and struck the Philistine on the *f.*
Rev 13:16 a mark on his right hand or on his *f,*

FOREHEADS (FOREHEAD)
Dt 6: 8 hands and bind them on your *f.*
Rev 9: 4 not have the seal of God on their *f.*
      14: 1 his Father's name written on their *f*

FOREIGN (FOREIGNER FOREIGNERS)
Ge 35: 2 "Get rid of the *f* gods you have
2Ch 14: 3 He removed the *f* altars
      33:15 He got rid of the *f* gods
Isa 28:11 with *f* lips and strange tongues

FOREIGNER (FOREIGN)
Lk 17:18 give praise to God except this *f?"*
1Co 14:11 I am a *f* to the speaker,

FOREIGNERS (FOREIGN)
Eph 2:12 *f* to the covenants of the promise.
      2:19 you are no longer *f* and aliens,

FOREKNEW* (KNOW)
Ro 8:29 For those God *f* he
      11: 2 not reject his people, whom he *f*

FOREKNOWLEDGE* (KNOW)
Ac 2:23 to you by God's set purpose and *f;*
1Pe 1: 2 to the *f* of God the Father.

FORESAW*
Gal 3: 8 Scripture *f* that God would justify

FOREST
Jas 3: 5 Consider what a great *f* is set

FOREVER (EVER)
Ge 3:22 the tree of life and eat, and live *f."*
      6: 3 Spirit will not contend with man *f,*
Ex 3:15 This is my name *f,* the name
2Sa 7:26 so that your name will be great *f.*
1Ki 2:33 may there be the LORD's peace *f."*
      9: 3 by putting my Name there *f.*
1Ch 16:15 He remembers his covenant *f,*
      16:34 his love endures *f.*
      16:41 "for his love endures *f."*
      17:24 and that your name will be great *f.*
2Ch 5:13 his love endures *f."*
      20:21 for his love endures *f."*
Ps 9: 7 The LORD reigns *f.*
      23: 6 dwell in the house of the LORD *f.*
      28: 9 be their shepherd and carry them *f.*
      29:10 the LORD is enthroned as King *f.*
      33:11 the plans of the LORD stand firm *f*
      37:28 They will be protected *f,*
      44: 8 and we will praise your name *f.*
      61: 4 I long to dwell in your tent *f*
      72:19 Praise be to his glorious name *f;*
      73:26 and my portion *f.*
      77: 8 Has his unfailing love vanished *f?*
      79:13 will praise you *f;*
      81:15 and their punishment would last *f.*
      86:12 I will glorify your name *f.*
      89: 1 of the LORD's great love *f.*
      92: 8 But you, O LORD, are exalted *f.*
      100: 5 is good and his love endures *f;*
      102:12 But you, O LORD, sit enthroned *f;*
      104:31 of the LORD endure *f;*
      107: 1 his love endures *f.*
      110: 4 "You are a priest *f,*
      111: 3 and his righteousness endures *f.*
      112: 6 man will be remembered *f.*
      117: 2 of the LORD endures *f.*
      118: 1 his love endures *f.*
      119:111 Your statutes are my heritage *f;*
      119:152 that you established them to last *f.*
      136: 1 His love endures *f.*
      146: 6 the LORD, who remains faithful *f.*
Pr 10:25 but the righteous stand firm *f.*
      27:24 for riches do not endure *f,*

Isa 25: 8 he will swallow up death *f.*
      26: 4 Trust in the LORD *f,*
      32:17 will be quietness and confidence *f.*
      40: 8 but the word of our God stands *f."*
      51: 6 But my salvation will last *f,*
      51: 8 But my righteousness will last *f,*
      57:15 he who lives *f,* whose name is holy:
      59:21 from this time on and *f."*
Jer 33:11 his love endures *f."*
Eze 37:26 put my sanctuary among them *f.*
Da 2:44 to an end, but it will itself endure *f.*
      3: 9 live *f!* You have issued a decree,
Jn 6:51 eats of this bread, he will live *f.*
      14:16 Counselor to be with you *f—*
Ro 9: 5 who is God over all, *f* praised!
      16:27 to the only wise God be glory *f*
1Co 9:25 it to get a crown that will last *f.*
1Th 4:17 And so we will be with the Lord *f.*
Heb 5: 6 "You are a priest *f,*
      7: 17 "You are a priest *f,*
      7: 24 Jesus lives *f,* he has a permanent
      13: 8 same yesterday and today and *f.*
1Pe 1:25 but the word of the Lord stands *f."*
1Jn 2:17 who does the will of God lives *f.*
2Jn 2 lives in us and will be with us *f:*

FOREVERMORE (EVER)
Ps 113: 2 both now and *f.*

FORFEIT
Mk 8:36 the whole world, yet *f* his soul?
Lk 9:25 and yet lose or *f* his very self?

FORGAVE (FORGIVE)
Ps 32: 5 and you *f*
      65: 3 you *f* our transgressions
      78:38 you *f* their iniquities
Eph 4:32 just as in Christ God *f* you.
Col 2:13 He has all our sins, having
      3:13 Forgive as the Lord *f* you.

FORGET (FORGETS FORGETTING FORGOT FORGOTTEN)
Dt 4:23 Be careful not to *f* the covenant
      6:12 that you do not *f* the LORD,
2Ki 17:38 Do not *f* the covenant I have made
Ps 9:17 all the nations that *f* God.
      10:12 Do not *f* the helpless.
      50:22 "Consider this, you who *f* God,
      78: 7 and would not *f* his deeds
      103: 2 and *f* not all his benefits.
      119: 93 I will never *f* your precepts,
      137: 5 may my right hand *f* its skill,
Pr 3: 1 My son, do not *f* my teaching,
      4: 5 do not *f* my words or swerve
Isa 49:15 "Can a mother *f* the baby
      51:13 that you *f* the LORD your Maker,
Jer 2:32 Does a maiden *f* her jewelry,
      23:39 I will surely *f* you and cast you out
Heb 6:10 he will not *f* your work
      13: 2 Do not *f* to entertain strangers,
      13:16 And do not *f* to do good
2Pe 3: 8 But do not *f* this one thing,

FORGETS (FORGET)
Jn 16:21 her baby is born she *f* the anguish
Jas 1:24 immediately *f* what he looks like.

FORGETTING (FORGET)
Php 3:13 *f* what is behind and straining
Jas 1:25 to do this, not *f* what he has heard,

FORGIVE* (FORGAVE FORGIVENESS FORGIVES FORGIVING)
Ge 50:17 I ask you to *f* your brothers the sins
      50:17 please *f* the sins of the servants
Ex 10:17 Now *f* my sin once more
      23:21 he will not *f* your rebellion,
      32:32 But now, please *f* their sin—
      34: 9 four wickedness and our sin,
Nu 14:19 with your great love, *f* the sin
Dt 29:20 will never be willing to *f* him;
Jos 24:19 He will not *f* your rebellion
1Sa 15:25 *f* my sin and come back with me,
      25:28 Please *f* your servant's offense.
1Ki 8:30 place, and when you hear, *f*
      8:34 and *f* the sin of your people Israel
      8:36 and *f* the sin of your servants,
      8:39 *f* and act; deal with each man
      8:50 fall the offenses they have
      8:50 *f* your people, who have sinned
2Ki 5:18 But may the LORD *f* your servant
      5:18 may the LORD *f* your servant
      24: 4 and the LORD was not willing to *f*
2Ch 6:21 place; and when you hear, *f*

2Ch 6:25 and *f* the sin of your people Israel
      6:27 and *f* the sin of your servants,
      6:30 *F,* and deal with each man
      6:39 *f* your people, who have sinned
      7:14 will *f* their sin and will heal their
Job 7:21 and *f* my sins?
Ps 19:12 *F* my hidden faults.
      25:11 *f* my iniquity, though it is great.
      79: 9 deliver us and *f* our sins
Isa 2: 9 do not *f* them.
Jer 5: 1 I will *f* this city.
      5: 7 "Why should I *f* you?
      18:23 Do not *f* their crimes
      31:34 "For I will *f* their wickedness
      33: 8 and will *f* all their sins of rebellion
      36: 3 then I will *f* their wickedness
      50:20 for I will *f* the remnant I spare.
Da 9:19 O Lord, listen! O Lord, *f!* O Lord,
Hos 1: 6 that I should at all *f* them.
      14: 2 "*F* all our sins
Am 7: 2 *f!* How can Jacob survive?
Mt 6:12 *F* us our debts.
      6:14 For if you *f* men when they sin
      6:14 heavenly Father will also *f* you.
      6:15 But if you do not *f* men their sins,
      6:15 your Father will not *f* your sins.
      9: 6 authority on earth to *f* sins.
      18:21 many times shall I *f* my brother
      18:35 say *f* your brother from your heart
Mk 2: 7 Who can *f* sins but God alone?"
      2:10 authority on earth to *f* sins
      11:25 anything against anyone, *f* him,
      11:25 in heaven may *f* you your sins."
Lk 5:21 Who can *f* sins but God alone?"
      5:24 authority on earth to *f* sins.
      6:37 *F,* and you will be forgiven.
      11: 4 *F* us our sins,
      11: 4 *f* everyone who sins against us.
      17: 3 rebuke him, and if he repents, *f* him
      17: 4 and says, 'I repent,' *f* him."
      23:34 Jesus said, "Father, *f* them,
Jn 20:23 If you *f* anyone his sins, they are
      20:23 if you do not *f* them, they are not
Ac 8:22 Perhaps he will *f* you
2Co 2: 7 you ought to *f* and comfort him,
      2:10 If you *f* anyone, I also *f* him.
      2:10 if there was anything to *f—*
      12:13 a burden to you? *F* me this wrong!
Col 3:13 and *f* whatever grievances you may
      3:13 *F* as the Lord forgave you.
Heb 8:12 For I will *f* their wickedness
1Jn 1: 9 and just and will *f* us our sins

FORGIVENESS* (FORGIVE)
Ps 130: 4 But with you there is *f;*
Mt 26:28 out for many for the *f* of sins.
Mk 1: 4 of repentance for the *f* of sins.
Lk 1:77 salvation through the *f* of their sins,
      3: 3 of repentance for the *f* of sins,
      24:47 and *f* of sins will be preached
Ac 5:31 that he might give repentance and *f*
      10:43 believes in him receives *f* of sins
      13:38 that through Jesus the *f*
      26:18 so that they may receive *f* of sins
Eph 1: 7 through his blood, the *f* of sins,
Col 1:14 in whom we have redemption, the *f*
Heb 9:22 the shedding of blood there is no *f.*

FORGIVES* (FORGIVE)
Ps 103: 3 He *f* all my sins
Mic 7:18 pardons sin and *f* the transgression
Lk 7:49 "Who is this who even *f* sins?"

FORGIVING* (FORGIVE)
Ex 34: 7 and *f* wickedness, rebellion and sin.
Nu 14:18 abounding in love and *f* sin
Ne 9:17 But you are a *f* God, gracious
Ps 86: 5 You are *f* and good, O Lord,
      99: 8 you were to Israel a *f* God.
Da 9: 9 The Lord our God is merciful and *f*
Eph 4:32 to one another, *f* each other,

FORGOT (FORGET)
Dt 32:18 you *f* the God who gave you birth.
Ps 78:11 They *f* what he had done,
      106:13 But they soon *f* what he had done

FORGOTTEN (FORGET)
Job 11: 6 God has even *f* some of your sin.
Ps 44:20 If we had *f* the name of our God
Isa 17:10 You have *f* God your Savior;
Hos 8:14 Israel has *f* his Maker
Lk 12: 6 Yet not one of them is *f* by God.
2Pe 1: 9 and has *f* that he has been cleansed

FORM (FORMED)

Isa 52:14 f marred beyond human likeness—
2Ti 3: 5 having a f of godliness

FORMED (FORM)

Ge 2: 7 —the LORD God f the man
2:19 Now the LORD God had f out
Ps 103:14 for he knows how we are f,
Ecc 1: 9 or how the body is f in a mother's
Isa 29:16 Shall what is f say to him who f it,
45:18 but it to be inhabited—
49: 5 he who f me in the womb
Jer 1: 5 "Before I f you in the womb I knew
Ro 9:20 "Shall what is f say to him who f it,
Gal 4:19 of childbirth until Christ is f in you,
1Ti 2:13 For Adam was f first, then Eve.
Heb 11: 3 understand that the universe was f
2Pe 3: 5 and the earth was f out of water

FORMLESS*

Ge 1: 2 Now the earth was f and empty,
Jer 4:23 and it was f and empty;

FORNICATION see IMMORALITY, UNFAITHFULNESS

FORSAKE (FORSAKEN)

Dt 31: 6 he will never leave you nor f you."
Jos 1: 5 I will never leave you nor f you.
24:16 "Far be it from us to the LORD
2Ch 15: 2 but if you f him, he will f you.
Ps 27:10 Though my father and mother f me
94:14 he will never f his inheritance.
Isa 55: 7 Let the wicked f his way
Heb 13: 5 never will I f you."

FORSAKEN (FORSAKE)

Ps 22: 1 my God, why have you f me?
37:25 I have never seen the righteous f
Mt 27:46 my God, why have you f me?"
Rev 2: 4 You have f your first love.

FORTRESS

2Sa 22: 2 "The LORD is my rock, my f
Ps 18: 2 The LORD is my rock, my f
31: 2 a strong f to save me.
59:16 for you are my f,
71: 3 for you are my rock and my f.
Pr 14:26 who fears the LORD has a secure f,

FORTUNE-TELLING*

Ac 16:16 deal of money for her owners by f.

FORTY

Ge 7: 4 on the earth for f days and f nights,
18:29 "What if only f are found there?"
Ex 16:35 The Israelites ate manna f years,
24:18 on the mountain f days and f nights
Nu 14:34 For f years—one year for each
Jos 14: 7 I was f years old when Moses
1Sa 4:18 He had led Israel f years.
2Sa 5: 4 king, and he reigned f years.
1Ki 9: 8 he traveled f days and f nights
2Ki 12: 1 and he reigned in Jerusalem f years
2Ch 9:30 in Jerusalem over all Israel f years.
Eze 29:12 her cities will lie desolate f years
Jnh 3: 4 "f more days and Nineveh will be
Mt 4: 2 After fasting f days and f nights,

FOUGHT (FIGHT)

1Co 15:32 If I f wild beasts in Ephesus
2Ti 4: 7 I have f the good fight, I have

FOUND (FIND)

2Ki 22: 8 "I have f the Book of the Law
1Ch 28: 9 If you seek him, he will be f by you;
2Ch 15:15 sought God eagerly, and he was f
Isa 55: 6 Seek the LORD while he may be f;
65: 1 I was f by those who did not seek
Da 5:27 on the scales and f wanting.
Mt 1:18 she was f to be with child
Lk 15: 6 with me; I have f my lost sheep.'
15: 9 with me; I have f my lost coin.'
15:24 is alive again; he was lost and is f.'
Ac 4:12 Salvation is f in no one else,
Ro 10:20 "I was f by those who did not seek
Jas 2: 8 If you really keep the royal law f
Rev 5: 4 no one was f who was worthy

FOUNDATION (FOUNDATIONS FOUNDED)

Isa 28:16 a precious cornerstone for a sure f;
Mt 7:25 because it had its f on the rock.
Lk 14:29 For if he lays the f and is not able
Ro 15:20 building on someone else's f
1Co 3:10 I laid a f as an expert builder,

1Co 3:11 For no one can lay any f other
Eph 2:20 built on the f of the apostles
1Ti 3:15 the pillar and f of the truth.
2Ti 2:19 God's solid f stands firm,
Heb 6: 1 not laying again the f of repentance.

FOUNDATIONS (FOUNDATION)

Ps 102:25 In the beginning you laid the f
Heb 1:10 O Lord, you laid the f of the earth,

FOUNDED (FOUNDATION)

Jer 10:12 he f the world by his wisdom
Heb 8: 6 and it is f on better promises.

FOUNTAIN

Ps 36: 9 For with you is the f of life;
Pr 14:27 The fear of the LORD is a f of life,
18: 4 the f of wisdom is a bubbling brook.
Zec 13: 1 "On that day a f will be opened

FOX (FOXES)

Lk 13:32 He replied, "Go tell that f,

FOXES (FOX)

SS 2:15 the little f
Mt 8:20 "f have holes and birds

FRAGRANCE (FRAGRANT)

Ex 30:38 it to enjoy its f must be cut
Jn 12: 3 filled with the f of the perfume.
2Co 2:14 us spreads everywhere the f
2:16 of death; to the other, the f of life.

FRAGRANT (FRAGRANCE)

Eph 5: 2 as a f offering and sacrifice to God.
Php 4:18 They are a f offering, an acceptable

FREE (FREED FREEDOM FREELY)

Ge 2:16 "You are f to eat from any tree
Ps 118: 5 and he answered by setting me f.
119:32 for you have set my heart f.
146: 7 The LORD sets prisoners f,
Pr 6: 3 then do this, my son, to f yourself,
Jn 8:32 and the truth will set you f."
8:36 if the Son sets you f, you will be f
Ro 6:18 You have been set f from sin
8: 2 of life set me f from the law of sin
1Co 12:13 whether Jews or Greeks, slave or f
Gal 3:28 slave nor f, male nor female,
5: 1 for freedom that Christ has set us f.
1Pe 2:16 f men, but do not use your freedom

FREED (FREE)

Ps 116:16 you have f me from my chains.
Ro 6: 7 anyone who has died has been f
Rev 1: 5 has f us from our sins by his blood,

FREEDOM (FREE)

Ps 119:45 I will walk about in f,
Isa 61: 1 to proclaim f for the captives
Lk 4:18 me to proclaim f for the prisoners
Ro 8:21 into the glorious f of the children
1Co 7:21 although if you can gain your f,
2Co 3:17 the Spirit of the Lord is, there is f.
Gal 2: 4 ranks to spy on the f we have
5:13 But do not use your f to indulge
Jas 1:25 into the perfect law that gives f,
1Pe 2:16 but do not use your f as a cover-up

FREELY (FREE)

Isa 55: 7 and to our God, for he will f pardon
Mt 10: 8 Freely you have received, f give.
Ro 3:24 and are justified f by his grace
Eph 1: 6 which he has f given us

FRESH

Jas 3:11 Can both f water and salt water

FRET*

Ps 37: 1 Do not f because of evil men
37: 7 do not f when men succeed
37: 8 do not f—it leads only to evil.
Pr 24:19 Do not f because of evil men

FRICTION

1Ti 6: 5 and constant f between men

FRIEND (FRIENDS FRIENDSHIP)

Ex 33:11 as a man speaks with his f.
2Ch 20: 7 descendants of Abraham your f?
Pr 17: 7 A f loves at all times,
18:24 there is a f who sticks closer
27: 6 Wounds from a f can be trusted
27:10 Do not forsake your f and the f
Isa 41: 8 you descendants of Abraham my f,

Mt 11:19 a f of tax collectors and "sinners." '
Lk 11: 8 him the bread because he is his f,
Jn 19:12 "If you let this man go, you are no f
Jas 2:23 and he was called God's f.
4: 4 Anyone who chooses to be a f

FRIENDS (FRIEND)

Pr 16:28 and a gossip separates close f
17: 9 the matter separates close f.
Zec 13: 6 given at the house of my f.'
Jn 15:13 that he lay down his life for his f.
15:14 You are my f if you do what I

FRIENDSHIP (FRIEND)

Jas 4: 4 don't you know that f

FRIGHTENED (FEAR)

Php 1:28 gospel without being f in any way
1Pe 3:14 fear what they fear; do not be f."

FROGS

Ex 8: 2 plague your whole country with f.
Rev 16:13 three evil spirits that looked like f;

FRUIT (FRUITFUL)

Jdg 9:11 'Should I give up my f, so good
Ps 1: 3 which yields its f in season
Pr 11:30 The f of the righteous is a tree
12:14 From the f of his lips a man is filled
27:18 He who tends a fig tree will eat its f
Isa 11: 1 from his roots a Branch will bear f.
27: 6 and fill all the world with f.
32:17 The f of righteousness will be peace
Jer 17: 8 and never fails to bear f."
Hos 10:12 reap the f of unfailing love,
14: 2 that we may offer the f of our lips.
Am 8: 1 showed me: a basket of ripe f.
Mt 3: 8 Produce f in keeping
3:10 does not produce good f will be cut
7:16 By their f you will recognize them.
7:17 good f, but a bad tree bears bad f.
7:20 by their f you will recognize them.
12:33 a tree good and its f will be good,
Lk 3: 9 does not produce good f will be cut
6:43 nor does a bad tree bear good f.
13: 6 and he went to look for f on it,
Jn 15: 2 branch in me that bears no f,
15:16 and bear f—that will last.
Ro 7: 4 in order that we might bear f
Gal 5:22 But the f of the Spirit is love, joy,
Php 1:11 with the f of righteousness that
Col 1:10 bearing f in every good work,
Heb 13:15 the f of lips that confess his name.
Jas 3:17 and good f, impartial and sincere.
Jude 12 autumn trees, without f
Rev 22: 2 of f, yielding its f every month.

FRUITFUL (FRUIT)

Ge 1:22 "Be f and increase in number
9: 1 "Be f and increase in number
35:11 be f and increase in number.
Ex 1: 7 the Israelites were f and multiplied
Ps 128: 3 Your wife will be like a f vine
Jn 15: 2 prunes so that it will be even more f.
Php 1:22 this will mean f labor for me.

FRUITLESS*

Eph 5:11 to do with the f deeds of darkness,

FRUSTRATION

Ro 8:20 For the creation was subjected to f,

FUEL

Isa 44:19 "Half of it I used for f;

FULFILL (FULFILLED FULFILLMENT FULFILLS)

Nu 23:19 Does he promise and not f?
Ps 61: 8 and f my vows day after day.
116:14 I will f my vows to the LORD
138: 8 The LORD will f his purpose,
Ecc 5: 4 than to make a vow and not f it.
Isa 46:11 far-off land, a man to f my purpose.
Jer 33:14 'when I will f the gracious promise
Mt 1:22 place to f what the Lord had said
3:15 us to do this to f all righteousness."
4:14 f what was said
5:17 come to abolish them but to f them.
8:17 This was to f what was spoken
12:17 This was to f what was spoken
21: 4 place to f what was spoken
Jn 12:38 This was to f the word
13:18 But this is to f the scripture.
15:25 But this is to f what is written
1Co 7: 3 husband should f his marital duty

FULFILLED (FULFILL)

Jos 21: 45 of Israel failed; every one was f.
23: 14 Every promise has been f;
Pr 13: 12 but a longing f is a tree of life.
13: 19 A longing f is sweet to the soul,
Mt 2: 15 so was f what the Lord had said
2: 17 the prophet Jeremiah was f:
2: 23 So was f what was said
13: 14 In them is the prophecy of Isaiah:
13: 35 so was f what was spoken
26: 54 would the Scriptures be f that say it
26: 56 of the prophets might be f."
27: 9 by Jeremiah the prophet was f:
Mk 13: 4 that they are all about to be f?"
14: 49 But the Scriptures must be f."
Lk 4: 21 "Today this scripture is f
18: 31 about the Son of Man will be f.
24: 44 Everything must be f that is
Jn 18: 9 words he had spoken would be f:
19: 24 the Scripture might be f which said,
19: 28 and so that the Scripture would be f
19: 36 so that the Scripture would be f
Ac 1: 16 to be f which the Holy Spirit spoke
Ro 13: 8 loves his fellowman has f the law.
Jas 2: 23 And the scripture was f that says,

FULFILLMENT (FULFILL)

Ro 13: 10 Therefore love is the f of the law.

FULFILLS (FULFILL)

Ps 57: 2 to God, who f his purpose, for me.
145: 19 He f the desires of those who fear

FULL (FILL)

2Ch 24: 10 them into the chest until it was f.
Ps 127: 5 whose quiver is f of them.
Pr 27: 7 He who is f loathes honey,
31: 11 Her husband has f confidence
Isa 6: 3 the whole earth is f of his glory."
11: 9 for the earth will be f
Lk 4: 1 Jesus, f of the Holy Spirit,
Jn 10: 10 may have life, and have it to the f.
Ac 6: 3 known to be f of the Spirit
6: 5 a man f of faith and of the Holy
7: 55 But Stephen, f of the Holy Spirit,
11: 24 of the Holy Spirit and faith,

FULL-GROWN* (GROW)

Jas 1: 15 when it is f, gives birth to death.

FULLNESS* (FILL)

Dt 33: 16 gifts of the earth and its f
Jn 1: 16 From the f of his grace we have all
Ro 11: 12 greater riches will their f bring!
Eph 1: 23 the f of him who fills everything
3: 19 to the measure of all the f of God.
4: 13 to the whole measure of the f
Col 1: 19 to have all his f dwell in him,
1: 25 to you the word of God in its f—
2: 9 in Christ all the f of the Deity lives
2: 10 and you have been given f in Christ

FULLY (FILL)

1Ki 8: 61 your hearts must be f committed
2Ch 16: 9 whose hearts are f committed
Ps 119: 4 that are to be f obeyed.
119:138 they are f trustworthy.
Pr 13: 4 of the diligent are f satisfied.
Lk 6: 40 everyone who is f trained will be
Ro 4: 21 being f persuaded that God had
14: 5 Each one should be f convinced
1Co 13: 12 shall know f, even as I am f known.
15: 58 Always give yourselves f
2Ti 4: 17 the message might be f proclaimed

FURIOUS (FURY)

Dt 29: 28 In f anger and in great wrath
Jer 32: 37 where I banish them in my f anger

FURNACE

Isa 48: 10 in the f of affliction.
Da 3: 6 be thrown into a blazing f."
Mt 13: 42 will throw them into the fiery f,

FURY (FURIOUS)

Isa 14: 6 and in f subdued nations
Jer 21: 5 and a mighty arm in anger and f
Rev 14: 10 will drink of the wine of God's f,
16: 19 with the wine of the f of his wrath.
19: 15 the winepress of the f of the wrath

FUTILE (FUTILITY)

Mal 3: 14 You have said, 'It is f to serve God.
1Co 3: 20 that the thoughts of the wise are f."

FUTILITY (FUTILE)

Eph 4: 17 in the f of their thinking.

FUTURE

Ps 37: 37 there is a f for the man of peace.
Pr 23: 18 There is surely a f hope for you,
Ecc 7: 14 anything about his f.
8: 7 Since no man knows the f,
Jer 29: 11 plans to give you hope and a f,
31: 17 So there is hope for your f,"
Ro 8: 38 neither the present nor the f,
1Co 3: 22 life or death or the present or the f

GABRIEL*

Angel who interpreted Daniel's visions (Da 8:
16-26; 9:20-27); announced births of John (Lk 1:
11-20), Jesus (Lk 1:26-38).

GAD

1. Son of Jacob by Zilpah (Ge 30:9-11; 35:26;
1Ch 2:2). Tribe of blessed (Ge 49:19; Dt 33:
20-21), numbered (Nu 1:25; 26:18), allotted land
east of the Jordan (Nu 32; 34:14; Jos 18:7; 22),
west (Eze 48:27-28), 12,000 from (Rev 7:5).
2. Prophet; seer of David (1Sa 22:5; 2Sa 24:
11-19; 1Ch 29:29).

GAIN (GAINED GAINS)

Ex 14: 17 And I will g glory through Pharaoh
Ps 60: 12 With God we will g the victory,
Pr 1: 4 pay attention and g understanding.
8: 5 You who are simple, g prudence;
28: 16 he who hates ill-gotten g will enjoy
28: 23 in the end g more favor
Isa 63: 12 to g for himself everlasting renown
Da 2: 8 that you are trying to g time,
Mk 8: 36 it for a man to g the whole world,
Lk 9: 25 it for a man to g the whole world,
21: 19 standing firm you will g life.
1Co 13: 3 but have not love, I g nothing.
Php 1: 21 to live is Christ and to die is g.
3: 8 that I may g Christ and be found
1Ti 3: 13 have served well g an excellent
6: 5 godliness is a means to financial g.
6: 6 with contentment is great g.

GAINED (GAIN)

Jer 32: 20 have g the renown that is still yours
Ro 5: 2 through whom we have g access

GAINS (GAIN)

Pr 3: 13 the man who g understanding,
11: 16 A kindhearted woman g respect,
15: 32 heeds correction g understanding.
29: 23 but a man of lowly spirit g honor,
Mt 16: 26 for a man if he g the whole world,

GALILEE

Isa 9: 1 but in the future he will honor G
Mt 4: 15 G of the Gentiles—
26: 32 I will go ahead of you into G."
28: 10 Go and tell my brothers to go to G;

GALL

Mt 27: 34 mixed with g; but after tasting it,

GALLIO

Ac 18: 12 While G was proconsul of Achaia,

GALLOWS

Est 7: 10 Haman on the g he had prepared

GAMALIEL

Ac 5: 34 But a Pharisee named G, a teacher

GAMES

1Co 9: 25 in the g goes into strict training.

GAP

Eze 22: 30 stand before me in the g on behalf

GAPE*

Ps 35: 21 They g at me and say, "Aha! Aha!

GARDEN (GARDENER)

Ge 2: 8 the LORD God had planted a g
2: 15 put him in the G of Eden to work
SS 4: 12 You are a g locked up, my sister,
Isa 58: 11 You will be like a well-watered g,
Jer 31: 12 They will be like a well-watered g,
Eze 28: 13 the g of God;
31: 9 Eden in the g of God.

GARDENER (GARDEN)

Jn 15: 1 true vine, and my Father is the g.

GARLAND*

Pr 1: 9 They will be a g to grace your head
4: 9 She will set a g of grace

GARMENT (GARMENTS)

Ps 102: 26 they will all wear out like a g.
Isa 50: 9 They will all wear out like a g;
51: 6 the earth will wear out like a g
61: 3 and a g of praise
Mt 9: 16 of unshrunk cloth on an old g,
Jn 19: 23 This g was seamless, woven
Heb 1: 11 they will all wear out like a g.

GARMENTS (GARMENT)

Ge 3: 21 The LORD God made g of skin
Ex 28: 2 Make sacred g for your brother
Lev 16: 23 and take off the linen g he put
16: 24 holy place and put on his regular g.
Isa 61: 10 me with g of salvation
63: 1 with his g stained crimson?
Joel 2: 13 and not your g.
Zec 3: 4 and I will put rich g on you."
Jn 19: 24 "They divided my g among them

GATE (GATES)

Ps 118: 20 This is the g of the LORD
Pr 31: 23 husband is respected at the city g,
31: 31 works bring her praise at the city g.
Mt 7: 13 For wide is the g and broad is
7: 13 "Enter through the narrow g
Jn 10: 1 not enter the sheep pen by the g,
10: 2 enters by the g is the shepherd
10: 7 "I tell you the truth, I am the g
10: 9 I am the g; whoever enters
Heb 13: 12 also suffered outside the city g
Rev 21: 21 each g made of a single pearl.

GATES (GATE)

Ps 24: 7 Lift up your heads, O you g;
24: 9 Lift up your heads, O you g;
100: 4 Enter his g with thanksgiving
118: 19 Open for me the g of righteousness
Isa 60: 11 Your g will always stand open,
60: 18 and your g Praise.
62: 10 Pass through, pass through the g!
Mt 16: 18 the g of Hades will not overcome it
Rev 21: 12 On the g were written the names
21: 21 The twelve g were twelve pearls,
21: 25 On no day will its g ever be shut,
22: 14 may go through the g into the city.

GATH

1Sa 17: 23 the Philistine champion from G,
2Sa 1: 20 "Tell it not in G,
Mic 1: 10 Tell it not in G;

GATHER (GATHERED GATHERS)

Ps 106: 47 and g us from the nations,
Isa 11: 12 and g the exiles of Israel;
Jer 3: 17 and all nations will g in Jerusalem
23: 3 "I myself will g the remnant
31: 10 who scattered Israel will g them
Zep 2: 1 G together, g together,
3: 20 At that time I will g you;
Zec 14: 2 I will g all the nations to Jerusalem
Mt 12: 30 he who does not g with me scatters
13: 30 then g the wheat and bring it
23: 37 longed to g your children together,
24: 31 and they will g his elect
25: 26 g where I have not scattered seed?
Mk 13: 27 and g his elect from the four winds,
Lk 3: 17 and to g the wheat into his barn,
11: 23 and he who does not g with me,
13: 34 longed to g your children together,

GATHERED (GATHER)

Ex 16: 18 and he who g little did not have too
Pr 30: 4 Who has g up the wind
Mt 25: 32 All the nations will be g before him
2Co 8: 15 and he who g little did not have too
2Th 2: 1 Lord Jesus Christ and our being g
Rev 16: 16 Then they g the kings together

GATHERS (GATHER)

Ps 147: 2 he g the exiles of Israel.
Pr 10: 5 he who g crops in summer is a wise
Isa 40: 11 He g the lambs in his arms
Mt 23: 37 a hen g her chicks under her wings,

GAVE (GIVE)

Ge 2: 20 man g names to all the livestock.

Ge   3: 6 She also g some to her husband,
   14:20 Abram g him a tenth of everything.
   28: 4 the land God g to Abraham."
   35:12 The land I g to Abraham
   39:23 g him success in whatever he did.
   47:11 g them property in the best part
Ex   4:11 to him, "Who g man his mouth?
   31:18 he g him the two tablets
Dt   2:12 did in the land the LORD g them
   2:36 The LORD our God g us all
   3:12 I g the Reubenites and the Gadites
   3:13 I g to the half tribe of Manasseh.
   3:15 And I g Gilead to Makir.
   3:16 Gadites I g the territory extending
   8:16 He g you manna to eat in the desert
   26: 9 us to this place and g us this land,
   32: 8 the Most High g the nations their
Jos 11:23 and he g it as an inheritance
   13:14 tribe of Levi he g no inheritance.
   14:13 g him Hebron as his inheritance.
   21:44 The LORD g them rest
   24:13 I g you a land on which you did not
1Sa 27: 6 So on that day Achish g him Ziklag
2Sa 12: 8 I g you the house of Israel
1Ki 4:29 God g Solomon wisdom
   5:12 The LORD g Solomon wisdom,
Ezr 2:69 According to their ability they g
Ne 9:15 In their hunger you g them bread
   9:20 You g your good Spirit
   9:22 You g them kingdoms and nations,
   9:27 compassion you g them deliverers,
Job 1:21 LORD g and the LORD has taken
   42:10 prosperous again and g him twice
Ps 69:21 and g me vinegar for my thirst.
   135:12 he g their land as an inheritance,
Ecc 12: 7 the spirit returns to God who g it.
Eze 3: 2 and he g me the scroll to eat.
Mt 1:25 And he g him the name Jesus.
   25:35 and you g me something to drink,
   25:42 and you g me nothing to drink,
   26:26 Jesus took bread, g thanks
   27:50 in a loud voice, he g up his spirit.
Mk 6: 7 g them authority over evil spirits.
Jn 1:12 he the right to become children
   3:16 so loved the world that he g his one
   17: 4 by completing the work you g me
   17: 6 you g them to me and they have
   19:30 bowed his head and g up his spirit.
Ac 1: 3 g many convincing proofs that he
   2:45 they g to anyone as he had need.
   11:17 g them the same gift as he g us,
Ro 1:24 Therefore God g them
   1:26 God g them over to shameful lusts.
   1:28 he g them over to a depraved mind,
   8:32 not spare his own Son, but g him up
2Co 5:18 g us the ministry of reconciliation:
   8: 3 For I testify that they g as much
   8: 5 they g themselves first to the Lord
Gal 1: 4 who g himself for our sins
   2:20 who loved me and g himself for me
Eph 4: 8 and g gifts to men."
   5: 2 as Christ loved us and g himself up
   5:25 and g himself up for her
2Th 2:16 and by his grace g us eternal
1Ti 2: 6 who g himself as a ransom
Tit 2:14 who g himself for us to redeem us
1Jn 3:24 We know it by the Spirit he g us.

GAZE

Ps 27: 4 to g upon the beauty of the LORD
Pr 4:25 fix your g directly before you.

GEDALIAH

Governor of Judah appointed by Nebuchadnezzar (2Ki 25:22-26; Jer 39-41).

GEHAZI*

Servant of Elisha (2Ki 4:12-5:27; 8:4-5).

GENEALOGIES

1Ti 1: 4 themselves to myths and endless g.
Tit 3: 9 avoid foolish controversies and g

GENERATION (GENERATIONS)

Ex 3:15 am to be remembered from g to g.
Nu 32:13 until the whole g of those who had
Dt 1:35 of this evil g shall see the good land
Jdg 2:10 After that whole g had been
Ps 24: 6 Such is the g of those who seek him
   48:13 tell of them to the next g.
   71:18 I declare your power to the next g,
   78: 4 we will tell the next g
   102:18 Let this be written for a future g,
   112: 2 the g of the upright will be blessed
   145: 4 One g will commend your works

La 5:19 your throne endures from g to g.
Da 4: 3 his dominion endures from g to g.
   4:34 his kingdom endures from g to g.
Joel 1: 3 and their children to the next g.
Mt 12:39 adulterous g asks for a miraculous
   17:17 "O unbelieving and perverse g,"
   23:36 all this will come upon this g.
   24:34 this g will certainly not pass away
Mk 9:19 "O unbelieving g," Jesus replied,
   13:30 this g will certainly not pass away
Lk 1:50 who fear him, from g to g.
   11:29 Jesus said, "This is a wicked g.
   11:30 will the Son of Man be to this g.
   11:50 Therefore this g will be held
   21:32 this g will certainly not pass away
Ac 2:40 Save yourselves from this corrupt g
Php 2:15 fault in a crooked and depraved g,

GENERATIONS (GENERATION)

Ge 9:12 a covenant for all g to come:
   17: 7 after you for the g to come,
   17: 9 after you for the g to come,
Ex 20: 6 a thousand g of those
   31:13 and you for the g to come,
Dt 7: 9 covenant of love to a thousand g
   32: 7 consider the g long past
1Ch 16:15 he commanded, for a thousand g,
Job 8: 8 "Ask the former g
Ps 22:30 future g will be told about the Lord
   33:11 of his heart through all g.
   45:17 your memory through all g;
   89: 1 faithfulness known through all g.
   90: 1 throughout all g.
   100: 5 continues through all g.
   102:12 your renown endures through all g.
   105: 8 he commanded, for a thousand g,
   119:90 continues through all g.
   135:13 renown, O LORD, through all g.
   145:13 dominion endures through all g.
   146:10 your God, O Zion, for all g.
Pr 27:24 and a crown is not secure for all g.
Isa 41: 4 forth the g from the beginning?
   51: 8 my salvation through all g."
Lk 1:48 now on all g will call me blessed,
Eph 3: 5 not made known to men in other g
   3:21 in Christ Jesus throughout all g,
Col 1:26 been kept hidden for ages and g,

GENEROSITY* (GENEROUS)

2Co 8: 2 poverty welled up in rich g.
   9:11 and through us your g will result
   9:13 and for your g in sharing with them

GENEROUS* (GENEROSITY)

Ps 37:26 They are always g and lend freely;
   112: 5 Good will come to him who is g
Pr 11:25 A g man will prosper;
   22: 9 A g man will himself be blessed,
Mt 20:15 Or are you envious because I am g
2Co 9: 5 Then it will be ready as a g gift,
   9: 5 for the gift you had promised.
   9:11 way so that you can be g
1Ti 6:18 and to be g and willing to share.

GENTILE (GENTILES)

Ac 21:25 As for the G believers, we have
Ro 1:16 first for the Jew, then for the G,
   2: 9 first for the Jew, then for the G;
   2:10 first for the Jew, then for the G:
   10:12 difference between Jew and G—

GENTILES (GENTILE)

Isa 42: 6 and a light for the G,
   49: 6 also make you a light for the G,
   49:22 "See, I will beckon to the G,
Lk 2:32 a light for revelation to the G
   21:24 on by the G until the times
Ac 9:15 to carry my name before the G
   10:45 been poured out even on the G.
   11:18 granted even the G repentance unto
   13:16 and you G who worship God,
   13:46 of eternal life, we now turn to the G
   13:47 I have made you a light for the G,
   14:27 opened the door of faith to the G.
   15:14 by taking from the G a people
   18: 6 From now on I will go to the G.'"
   22:21 I will send you far away to the G.'"
   26:20 and in all Judea, and to the G also,
   28:28 salvation has been sent to the G,
Ro 2:14 when G, who do not have the law,
   3: 9 and G alike are all under sin.
   3:29 Is he not the God of G too? Yes,
   9:24 from the Jews but also from the G?
   11:11 to the G to make Israel envious.
   11:12 their loss means riches for the G,

Ro 11:13 as I am the apostle to the G,
   15: 9 I will praise you among the G,
   15: 9 so that the G may glorify God
1Co 1:23 block to Jews and foolishness to G,
Gal 1:16 I might preach him among the G.
   2: 2 gospel that I preach among the G.
   2: 8 my ministry as an apostle to the G.
   2: 9 agreed that we should go to the G.
   3: 8 that God would justify the G
   3:14 to the G through Christ Jesus,
Eph 3: 6 the gospel the G are heirs together
   3: 8 to the G the unsearchable riches
Col 1:27 among the G the glorious riches
1Ti 2: 7 a teacher of the true faith to the G.
2Ti 4:17 and all the G might hear it.

GENTLE* (GENTLENESS)

Dt 28:54 Even the most g and sensitive man
   28:56 The most g and sensitive woman
   28:56 and g that she would not venture
2Sa 18: 5 Be g with the young man Absalom
1Ki 19:12 And after the fire came a g whisper
Job 41: 3 Will he speak to you with g words?
Pr 15: 1 A g answer turns away wrath,
   25:15 and a g tongue can break a bone.
Jer 11:19 I had been like a g lamb led
Zec 9: 9 g and riding on a donkey,
Mt 11:29 for I am g and humble in heart,
   21: 5 g and riding on a donkey,
Ac 27:13 When a g south wind began
1Co 4:21 or in love and with a g spirit?
Eph 4: 2 Be completely humble and g;
1Th 2: 7 but we were g among you,
1Ti 3: 3 not violent but g, not quarrelsome,
1Pe 3: 4 the unfading beauty of a g

GENTLENESS* (GENTLE)

2Co 10: 1 By the meekness and g of Christ,
Gal 5:23 faithfulness, g and self-control.
Php 4: 5 Let your g be evident to all.
Col 3:12 kindness, humility, g and patience.
1Ti 6:11 faith, love, endurance and g.
1Pe 3:15 But do this with g and respect,

GENUINE*

2Co 6: 8 g, yet regarded as impostors;
Php 2:20 who takes a g interest
1Pe 1: 7 may be proved g and may result

GERIZIM

Dt 27:12 on Mount G to bless the people:

GERSHOM

Ex 2:22 and Moses named him G, saying,

GETHSEMANE*

Mt 26:36 disciples to a place called G,
Mk 14:32 They went to a place called G,

GHOST see also SPIRIT

Lk 24:39 a g does not have flesh and bones,

GIBEON

Jos 10:12 "O sun, stand still over G,

GIDEON*

Judge, also called Jerub-Baal; freed Israel from Midianites (Jdg 6-8; Heb 11:32). Given sign of fleece (Jdg 6:36-40).

GIFT (GIFTED GIFTS)

Pr 18:16 A g opens the way for the giver
   21:14 A g given in secret soothes anger.
Ecc 3:13 in all his toil—this is the g of God.
Mt 5:23 if you are offering your g
Jn 4:10 "If you knew the g of God
Ac 1: 4 wait for the g my Father promised,
   2:38 And you will receive the g
   11:17 So if God gave them the same g
Ro 6:23 but the g of God is eternal life
   12: 6 If a man's g is prophesying,
1Co 7: 7 each man has his own g from God;
2Co 8:12 the g is acceptable according
   9:15 be to God for his indescribable g!
Eph 2: 8 it is the g of God—not by works,
1Ti 4:14 not neglect your g, which was
2Ti 1: 6 you to fan into flame the g of God.
Heb 6: 4 who have tasted the heavenly g,
Jas 1:17 and perfect g is from above,
1Pe 3: 7 with you of the gracious g of life,
   4:10 should use whatever g he has
Rev 22:17 let him take the free g of the water

GIFTED* (GIFT)

1Co 14:37 he is a prophet or spiritually g,

GIFTS (GIFT)

Ps 76:11 bring *g* to the One to be feared.
112: 9 He has scattered abroad his *g*
Pr 25:14 of *g* he does not give.
Mt 2:11 and presented him with *g* of gold
7:11 Father in heaven give good *g*
7:11 to give good *g* to your children,
Lk 11:13 to give good *g* to your children,
Ac 10: 4 and *g* to the poor have come up
Ro 11:29 for God's *g* and his call are
12: 6 We have different *g*, according
1Co 12: 1 Now about spiritual *g*, brothers,
12: 4 There are different kinds of *g*,
12:28 those with *g* of administration,
12:30 all work miracles? Do all have *g*
12:31 But eagerly desire the greater *g*.
14: 1 and eagerly desire spiritual *g*,
14:12 eager to have spiritual *g*,
14:12 excel in *g* that build up the church.
2Co 9: 9 "He has scattered abroad his *g*
Eph 4: 8 and gave *g* to men."
Heb 2: 4 and *g* of the Holy Spirit distributed
9: 9 indicating that the *g* and sacrifices

GILEAD

1Ch 27:21 the half-tribe of Manasseh in *G*:
Jer 8:22 Is there no balm in *G*?
46:11 "Go up to *G* and get balm,

GILGAL

Jos 5: 9 So the place has been called *G*

GIRD*

Ps 45: 3 *G* your sword upon your side,

GIRL

Ge 24:16 *g* was very beautiful, a virgin;
2Ki 5: 2 a young *g* from Israel.
Mk 5:41 Little *g*, I say to you, get up!

GIVE (GAVE GIVEN GIVER GIVES GIVING LIFE-GIVING)

Ge 28: 4 you and your descendants the blessing *g* to Abraham
28:22 that you *g* me I will *g* you a tenth."
Ex 20:16 "You shall not *g* false testimony
30:15 The rich are not to *g* more
Nu 6:26 and *g* you peace."
Dt 5:20 "You shall not *g* false testimony
15:10 *G* generously to him and do
15:14 to him as the LORD your God
1Sa 1:11 then I will *g* him to the LORD
1:28 So now I *g* him to the LORD.
2Ch 15: 7 be strong and do not *g* up,
Pr 21:26 but the righteous *g* without sparing
23:26 My son, *g* me your heart
25:21 if he is thirsty, *g* him water to drink
30: 8 but give me only my daily bread.
31:31 *G* her the reward she has earned,
Ecc 3: 6 a time to search and a time to *g* up,
Isa 42: 8 I will not *g* my glory to another
Eze 36:26 I will *g* you a new heart
Mt 6:11 *G* us today our daily bread.
7:11 know how to *g* good gifts
10: 8 Freely you have received, freely *g*.
16:19 I will *g* you the keys
22:21 "*G* to Caesar what is Caesar's,
Mk 8:37 Or what can a man *g* in exchange
10:19 not steal, do not *g* false testimony,
Lk 6:38 *G*, and it will be given to you.
11: 3 *G* us each day our daily bread.
11:13 Father in heaven give the Holy Spirit
14:33 who does not *g* up everything he
Jn 10:28 I *g* them eternal life, and they shall
13:34 "A new commandment I *g* you:
14:16 he will *g* you another Counselor
14:27 I do not *g* to you as the world gives.
14:27 leave with you; my peace I *g* you.
17: 2 people that he might *g* eternal life
Ac 20:35 blessed to *g* than to receive.' "
Ro 2: 7 immortality, he will *g* eternal life.
8:32 with him, graciously *g* us all things
12: 8 let him *g* generously;
13: 7 *G* everyone what you owe him:
14:12 each of us will *g* an account
2Co 2: 7 Each man should *g* what he has
Gal 2: 5 We did not *g* in to them
6: 9 reap a harvest if we do not *g* up.
Heb 10:25 Let us not *g* up meeting together,
Rev 14: 7 "Fear God and *g* him glory,

GIVEN (GIVE)

Nu 8:16 are to be *g* wholly to me.
Dt 26:11 things the LORD your God has *g*

Job 3:23 Why is life *g* to a man
Ps 115:16 but the earth he has *g* to man.
Isa 9: 6 to us a son is *g*,
Mt 6:33 and all these things will be *g* to you
7: 7 "Ask and it will be *g* to you;
13:12 Whoever has will be *g* more,
22:30 people will neither marry nor be *g*
25:29 everyone who has will be *g* more,
Lk 6:38 Give, and it will be *g* to you.
8:10 kingdom of God has been *g* to you,
11: 9 Ask and it will be *g* to you.
22:19 saying, "This is my body *g* for you;
Jn 3:27 man can receive only what is *g* him
15: 7 you wish, and it will be *g* you.
17:24 I want those you have *g* me to be
17:24 the glory you have *g* me
18:11 the cup the Father has *g* me?"
Ac 5:32 whom God has *g* to those who
20:24 the task the Lord Jesus has *g* me—
Ro 5: 5 the Holy Spirit, whom he has *g* us.
1Co 4: 2 those who have been *g* a trust must
11:24 and when he had *g* thanks,
12:13 we were all *g* the one Spirit to drink
2Co 5: 5 and has *g* us the Spirit as a deposit,
Eph 1: 6 which he has freely *g* us
4: 7 to each one of us grace has been *g*
1Ti 4:14 was *g* you through a prophetic
1Jn 4:13 because he has *g* us of his Spirit.

GIVER* (GIVE)

Pr 18:16 A gift opens the way for the *g*
2Co 9: 7 for God loves a cheerful *g*.

GIVES (GIVE)

Job 35:10 who *g* songs in the night,
Ps 119:130 The unfolding of your words *g* light;
Pr 3:34 but *g* grace to the humble.
11:24 One man *g* freely, yet gains
14:30 A heart at peace *g* life to the body,
15:30 good news *g* health to the bones.
19: 6 of a man who *g* gifts.
25:26 is a righteous man who *g* way
28:27 He who *g* to the poor will lack
29: 4 justice a king *g* a country stability,
Isa 40:29 He *g* strength to the weary
Hab 2:15 "Woe to him who *g* drink
Mt 10:42 if anyone *g* even a cup of cold water
Jn 5:21 even so the Son *g* life to whom he is
6:63 The Spirit *g* life; the flesh counts
1Co 15:57 He *g* the victory
2Co 3: 6 the letter kills, but the Spirit *g* life.
1Th 4: 8 who *g* you his Holy Spirit.
Jas 1:25 into the perfect law that *g* freedom,
4: 6 but *g* grace to the humble."
1Pe 5: 5 but *g* grace to the humble."

GIVING (GIVE)

Ne 8: 8 *g* the meaning so that the people
Est 9:19 a day for *g* presents to each other.
Ps 19: 8 *g* joy to the heart.
19:15:23 A man finds joy in *g* an apt reply—
Mt 6: 4 so that your *g* may be in secret.
24:38 marrying and *g* in marriage,
Ac 15: 8 them by *g* the Holy Spirit to them,
2Co 8: 7 also excel in this grace of *g*.
Php 4:15 shared with me in the matter of *g*

GLAD* (GLADDENS GLADNESS)

Ex 4:14 his heart will be *g* when he sees you
Jos 22:33 They were *g* to hear the report
Jdg 8:25 "We'll be *g* to give them."
18:20 household?" Then the priest was *g*.
1Sa 19: 5 and you saw it and were *g*.
2Sa 1:20 daughters of the Philistines be *g*,
1Ki 8:66 *g* in heart for all the good things
1Ch 16:31 heavens rejoice, let the earth be *g*;
2Ch 7:10 and *g* in heart for the good things
Ps 9:11 let all who take refuge in you be *g*;
9: 2 I will be *g* and rejoice in you;
14: 7 let Jacob rejoice and Israel be *g*!
16: 9 Therefore my heart is *g*
21: 6 made him *g* with the joy
31: 7 I will be *g* and rejoice in your love,
40:16 rejoice and be *g* in you;
45: 8 music of the strings makes you *g*.
46: 4 whose streams make *g* the city
48:11 the villages of Judah are *g*
53: 6 let Jacob rejoice and Israel be *g*!
58:10 The righteous will be *g*
67: 4 May the nations be *g* and sing
68: 3 But may the righteous be *g*
69:32 The poor will see and be *g*—
70: 4 rejoice and be *g* in you;
90:14 for joy and be *g* all our days.

Ps 90:15 Make us *g* for as many days
92: 4 For you make me *g* by your deeds,
96:11 heavens rejoice, let the earth be *g*;
97: 1 LORD reigns, let the earth be *g*;
97: 8 and the villages of Judah are *g*
105:38 Egypt was *g* when they left,
107:30 They were *g* when it grew calm,
118:24 let us rejoice and be *g* in it.
149: 2 of Zion be *g* in their King.
Pr 23:15 then my heart will be *g*;
23:25 May your father and mother be *g*;
29: 6 a righteous one can sing and be *g*
Ecc 8:15 sun than to eat and drink and be *g*.
Isa 25: 9 let us rejoice and be *g*
35: 1 and the parched land will be *g*;
65:18 But be *g* and rejoice forever
66:10 with Jerusalem and be *g* for her,
Jer 25:10 who made him very *g*, saying,
31:13 Then maidens will dance and be *g*,
41:13 were with him, they were *g*.
50:11 "Because you rejoice and are *g*,
La 2: 4 *g*, O Daughter of Edom,
Joel 2:21 be *g* and rejoice.
2:23 Be *g*, O people of Zion,
Hab 1:15 and so he rejoices and is *g*.
Zep 3:14 Be *g* and rejoice with all your heart
Zec 2:10 and be *g*, O Daughter of Zion.
8:19 will become joyful and *g* occasions
10: 7 their hearts will be *g* as with wine.
Mt 5:12 be *g*, because great is your reward
Lk 15:32 But we had to celebrate and be *g*,
Jn 4:36 and the reaper may be *g* together.
8:56 my day; he saw it and was *g*."
11:15 for your sake I am *g* I was not there
14:28 you would be *g* that I am going
Ac 2:26 Therefore my heart is *g*
2:46 together with *g* and sincere hearts,
11:23 he was *g* and encouraged them all
13:48 they were *g* and honored the word
15: 3 news made all the brothers very *g*.
15:31 were *g* for its encouraging message.
1Co 16:17 was *g* when Stephanas, Fortunatus
2Co 2: 2 who is left to make me *g*
7:16 I am *g* I can have complete
13: 9 We are *g* whenever we are weak
Gal 4:27 "Be *g*, O barren woman,
Php 2:17 I am *g* and rejoice with all of you.
2:18 So you too should be *g* and rejoice
2:28 you see him again you may be *g*
Rev 19: 7 Let us rejoice and be *g*

GLADDENS* (GLAD)

Ps 104:15 wine that *g* the heart of man,

GLADNESS* (GLAD)

2Ch 29:30 So they sang praises with *g*
Est 8:16 a time of happiness and joy, *g*
8:17 there was joy and *g*
Job 3:22 who are filled with *g*
Ps 35:27 shout for joy and *g*;
45:15 They are led in with joy and *g*;
51: 8 Let me hear joy and *g*;
65:12 the hills are clothed with *g*.
100: 2 Worship the LORD with *g*;
Ecc 9:20 God keeps him occupied with *g*
9: 7 Go, eat your food with *g*,
Isa 16:10 *g* are taken away from the orchards
35:10 *G* and joy will overtake them,
51: 3 Joy and *g* will be found in her,
51:11 *G* and joy will overtake them,
61: 3 the oil of *g* instead of mourning,
Jer 7:34 and *g* to the voices of bride
16: 9 and *g* to the voices of bride
25:10 from them the sounds of joy and *g*,
31:13 I will turn their mourning into *g*;
33:11 once more the sounds of joy and *g*,
48:33 Joy and *g* are gone
Joel 1:16 joy and *g*

GLAZE*

Pr 26:23 of *g* over earthenware

GLEAM*

Pr 4:18 of the righteous is like the first *g*
Da 10: 6 legs like the *g* of burnished bronze,

GLOAT (GLOATS)

Pr 24:17 Do not *g* when your enemy falls;

GLOATS* (GLOAT)

Pr 17: 5 whoever *g* over disaster will not go

GLORIES* (GLORY)

1Pe 1:11 and the *g* that would follow.

GLORIFIED* (GLORY)

Isa 66: 5 'Let the LORD be g.
Eze 39: 13 day I am g will be a memorable day
Da 4: 34 and g him who lives forever.
Jn 7: 39 since Jesus had not yet been g.
11: 4 glory so that God's Son may be g
12: 16 after Jesus was g did they realize
12: 23 come for the Son of Man to be g.
12: 28 "I have g it, and will glorify it again
13: 31 Son of Man g and God is g in him.
13: 32 If God is g in him, God will glorify
Ac 3: 13 our fathers, has g his servant Jesus.
Ro 1: 21 they neither g him as God
8: 30 those he justified, he also g.
2Th 1: 10 comes to be g in his holy people
1: 12 of our Lord Jesus may be g in you,
1Pe 1: 21 him from the dead and g him,

GLORIFIES* (GLORY)

Lk 1: 46 My soul g the Lord
Jn 8: 54 as your God, is the one who g me.

GLORIFY* (GLORY)

Ps 34: 3 G the LORD with me;
63: 3 my lips will g you.
69: 30 and g him with thanksgiving.
86: 12 I will g your name forever.
Isa 60: 13 and I will g the place of my feet.
Da 4: 37 and exalt and g the King of heaven,
Jn 8: 54 Jesus replied, "If I g myself,
12: 28 glorified it, and will g it again,"
12: 28 g your name!" Then a voice came
13: 32 God will g the Son in himself,
13: 32 in himself, and will g him at once.
17: 1 G your Son, that your Son may
17: 1 your Son, that your Son may g you.
17: 5 g me in your presence
21: 19 death by which Peter would g God.
Ro 15: 6 and mouth you may g the God
15: 9 so that the Gentiles may g God
1Pe 2: 12 and God on the day he visits us.
Rev 16: 9 they refused to repent and g him.

GLORIFYING* (GLORY)

Lk 2: 20 g and praising God

GLORIOUS* (GLORY)

Dt 28: 58 not revere this g and awesome
33: 29 and your g sword.
1Ch 29: 13 and praise your g name.
Ne 9: 5 "Blessed be your g name,
Ps 16: 3 they are the g ones
45: 13 All g is the princess
66: 2 make his praise g.
72: 19 Praise be to his g name forever;
87: 3 G things are said of you,
111: 3 G and majestic are his deeds,
145: 5 of the g splendor of your majesty,
145: 12 the g splendor of your kingdom.
Isa 3: 8 defying his g presence.
4: 2 the LORD will be beautiful and g,
11: 10 and his place of rest will be g.
12: 5 for he has done g things;
28: 1 to the fading flower, his g beauty,
28: 4 That fading flower, his g beauty,
28: 5 will be a g crown,
42: 21 to make his law great and g.
60: 7 and I will adorn my g temple.
63: 12 who sent his g arm of power
63: 14 to make for yourself a g name.
63: 15 from your lofty throne, holy and g.
64: 11 g temple, where our fathers praised
Jer 13: 18 for your g crowns
14: 21 do not dishonor your g throne.
17: 12 A g throne, exalted
48: 17 how broken the g staff!'
Mt 19: 28 the Son of Man sits on his g throne,
Lk 9: 31 appeared in g splendor, talking
Ac 2: 20 of the great and g day of the Lord.
Ro 8: 21 and brought into the g freedom
2Co 3: 8 of the Spirit be even more g?
3: 9 how much more is the ministry
3: 9 ministry that condemns men is g,
3: 10 For what was g has no glory now
Eph 1: 6 to the praise of his g grace,
1: 17 g Father, may give you the Spirit
1: 18 the riches of his g inheritance
3: 16 of his g riches he may strengthen
Php 3: 21 so that they will be like his g body.
4: 19 to his g riches in Christ Jesus.
Col 1: 11 all power according to his g might
1: 27 among the Gentiles the g riches
1Ti 1: 11 to the g gospel of the blessed God,
Tit 2: 13 the g appearing of our great God

Jas 2: 1 believers in our g Lord Jesus Christ
1Pe 1: 8 with an inexpressible and g joy,
Jude :24 before his g presence without fault

GLORIOUSLY* (GLORY)

Isa 24: 23 and before its elders, g.

GLORY (GLORIES GLORIFIED GLORIFIES GLORIFY GLORIFYING GLORIOUS GLORIOUSLY)

Ex 14: 4 But I will gain g for myself
14: 17 And I will gain g through Pharaoh
15: 11 awesome in g,
16: 10 and there was the g of the LORD
24: 16 and the g of the LORD settled
33: 18 Moses said, "Now show me your g
40: 34 and the g of the LORD filled
Nu 14: 21 the g of the LORD fills the whole
Dt 5: 24 LORD our God has shown us his g
Jos 7: 19 "My son, give g to the LORD,
1Sa 4: 21 "The g has departed from Israel"—
1Ch 16: 10 G in his holy name;
16: 24 Declare his g among the nations,
16: 28 ascribe to the LORD g
29: 11 the g and the majesty
Ps 8: 1 You have set your g
8: 5 and crowned him with g and honor
19: 1 The heavens declare the g of God;
24: 7 that the King of g may come in.
26: 8 the place where your g dwells.
29: 1 ascribe to the LORD g
29: 9 And in his temple all cry, "G!"
57: 5 let your g be over all the earth.
66: 2 Sing the g of his name;
72: 19 the whole earth be filled with his g.
96: 3 Declare his g among the nations,
102: 15 of the earth will revere your g.
108: 5 and let your g be over all the earth.
149: 9 This is the g of all his saints.
Pr 19: 11 it is to his g to overlook an offense.
25: 2 It is the g of God to conceal
Isa 5: 14 over all the g will be a canopy.
6: 3 whole earth is full of his g."
24: 16 "G to the Righteous One."
26: 15 You have gained g for yourself;
35: 2 they will see the g of the LORD,
40: 5 the g of the LORD will be revealed
42: 8 I will not give my g to another
42: 12 Let them give g to the LORD,
43: 7 whom I created for my g,
44: 23 he displays his g in Israel.
48: 11 I will not yield my g to another.
66: 18 and they will come and see my g.
66: 19 They will proclaim my g
Eze 1: 28 the likeness of the g of the LORD.
10: 4 the radiance of the g of the LORD,
43: 2 and the land was radiant with his g.
44: 4 and saw the g of the LORD filling
Hab 2: 14 knowledge of the g of the LORD,
3: 3 His g covered the heavens
Zec 2: 5 'and I will be its g within.'
Mt 16: 27 in his Father's g with his angels.
24: 30 of the sky, with power and great g.
25: 31 sit on his throne in heavenly g.
25: 31 the Son of Man comes in his g,
Mk 8: 38 in his Father's g with the holy
13: 26 in clouds with great power and g.
Lk 2: 9 and the g of the Lord shone
2: 14 saying, "G to God in the highest,
9: 26 and in the g of the Father
9: 26 of him when he comes in his g
9: 32 they saw his g and the two men
19: 38 in heaven and g in the highest!"
21: 27 in a cloud with power and great g.
24: 26 these things and then enter his g?"
Jn 1: 14 We have seen his g, the g of the One
2: 11 He thus revealed his g,
8: 50 I am not seeking g for myself;
8: 54 myself, my g means nothing.
11: 4 for God's g so that God's Son may
11: 40 you would see the g of God?"
12: 41 he saw Jesus' g and spoke about
14: 13 so that the Son may bring g
15: 8 is to my Father's g, that you bear
16: 14 He will bring g to me by taking
17: 4 I have brought you g on earth
17: 5 presence with the g I had with you
17: 10 g has come to me through them.
17: 22 given them the g that you gave
17: 24 to see my g, the g you have given
Ac 7: 2 The God of g appeared
7: 55 up to heaven and saw the g of God.
Ro 1: 23 exchanged the g of the immortal
2: 7 by persistence in doing good seek g
2: 10 then for the Gentile; but g,

Ro 3: 7 truthfulness and so increases his g,
3: 23 and fall short of the g of God,
4: 20 in his faith and gave g to God,
8: 17 that we may also share in his g.
8: 18 with the g that will be revealed
9: 4 theirs the divine g, the covenants,
9: 23 riches of his g known to the objects
9: 23 whom he prepared in advance for g
11: 36 To him be the g forever! Amen.
15: 7 Therefore I g in Christ Jesus
16: 27 to the only wise God be g forever
1Co 2: 7 for our g before time began.
10: 31 whatever you do, do it all for the g
11: 7 but the woman is the g of man.
11: 7 since he is the image and g of God;
11: 15 it is her g? For long hair is given
15: 43 it is raised in g; it is sown
2Co 1: 20 spoken by us to the g of God.
3: 7 in letters on stone, came with g,
3: 7 the face of Moses because of its g;
3: 10 comparison with the surpassing g,
3: 10 what was glorious has no g now
3: 11 how much greater is the g
3: 11 what was fading away came with g,
3: 18 faces all reflect the Lord's g,
3: 18 likeness with ever-increasing g,
4: 4 of the gospel of the g of Christ,
4: 6 of the knowledge of the g of God
4: 15 to overflow to the g of God:
4: 17 us an eternal g that far outweighs
Gal 1: 5 to whom be g for ever and ever.
Eph 1: 12 might be for the praise of his g.
1: 14 to the praise of his g.
3: 13 for you, which are your g.
3: 21 to him be g in the church.
Php 1: 11 to the g and praise of God.
2: 11 to the g of God the Father.
3: 3 of God, who g in Christ Jesus,
4: 20 and Father be g for ever and ever.
Col 1: 27 Christ in you, the hope of g.
3: 4 also will appear with him in g.
1Th 2: 12 you into his kingdom and g.
2: 19 in which we will g in the presence
2: 20 Indeed, you are our g and joy.
2Th 2: 14 in the g of our Lord Jesus Christ.
1Ti 1: 17 be honor and g for ever and ever.
3: 16 was taken up in g.
2Ti 2: 10 is in Christ Jesus, with eternal g.
4: 18 To him be g for ever and ever.
Heb 1: 3 The Son is the radiance of God's g
2: 7 you crowned him with g and honor
2: 9 now crowned with g and honor
2: 10 In bringing many sons to g,
5: 5 take upon himself the g
9: 5 the ark were the cherubim of the G,
13: 21 to whom be g for ever and ever.
1Pe 1: 7 g and honor when Jesus Christ is
1: 24 and all their g is like the flowers
4: 11 To him be the g and the power
4: 13 overjoyed when his g is revealed.
4: 14 for the Spirit of g and of God rests
5: 1 will share in the g to be revealed:
5: 4 of g that will never fade away.
5: 10 you to his eternal g in Christ,
2Pe 1: 3 of him who called us by his own g
1: 17 and g from God the Father
1: 17 came to him from the Majestic G,
3: 18 To him be g both now and forever!
Jude :25 to the only God our Savior be g,
Rev 1: 6 to him be g and power for ever
4: 9 the living creatures give g,
4: 11 to receive g and honor and power,
5: 12 and honor and g and praise!"
5: 13 and honor and g and power,
7: 12 Praise and g
11: 13 and gave g to the God of heaven.
14: 7 "Fear God and give him g,
15: 4 and bring g to your name?
15: 8 with smoke from the g of God
19: 1 g and power belong to our God,
19: 7 and give him g!
21: 11 It shone with the g of God,
21: 23 for the g of God gives it light,
21: 26 g and honor of the nations will be

GLOWING

Eze 8: 2 was as bright as g metal.
Rev 1: 15 His feet were like bronze g

GLUTTONS* (GLUTTONY)

Pr 23: 21 for drunkards and g become poor,
28: 7 of g disgraces his father.
Tit 1: 12 always liars, evil brutes, lazy g."

GLUTTONY* (GLUTTONS)

Pr 23: 2 throat if you are given to g.

GNASHING

Mt 8:12 where there will be weeping and g

GNAT* (GNATS)

Mt 23:24 You strain out a g but swallow

GNATS (GNAT)

Ex 8:16 of Egypt the dust will become g."

GOADS

Ecc 12:11 The words of the wise are like g,
Ac 26:14 hard for you to kick against the g.'

GOAL*

Lk 13:32 on the third day I will reach my g.'
2Co 5: 9 So we make it our g to please him,
Gal 3: 3 to attain your g by human effort?
Php 3:14 on toward the g to win the prize
1Ti 1: 5 The g of this command is love,
1Pe 1: 9 for you are receiving the g

GOAT (GOATS SCAPEGOAT)

Ge 15: 9 "Bring me a heifer, a g and a ram,
30:32 and every spotted or speckled g.
37:31 slaughtered a g and dipped
Ex 26: 7 Make curtains of g hair for the tent
Lev 16: 9 shall bring the g whose lot falls
Nu 7:16 one male g for a sin offering;
Isa 11: 6 the leopard will lie down with the g
Da 8: 5 suddenly a g with a prominent

GOATS (GOAT)

Nu 7:17 five male g and five male lambs
Mt 25:32 separates the sheep from the g.
Heb 10: 4 of bulls and g to take away sins.

GOD (GOD'S GODLINESS GODLY GODS)

Ge 1: 1 In the beginning G created
1: 2 and the Spirit of G was hovering
1: 3 And G said, "Let there be light,"
1: 7 So G made the expanse
1: 9 And G said, "Let the water
1:11 Then G said, "Let the land produce
1:20 And G said, "Let the water teem
1:21 So G created the great creatures
1:25 G made the wild animals according
1:26 Then G said, "Let us make man
1:27 So G created man in his own image
1:31 G saw all that he had made,
2: 3 And G blessed the seventh day
2: 7 And the LORD G formed the man
2: 8 the LORD G had planted a garden
2:18 The LORD G said, "It is not good
2:22 Then the LORD G made a woman
3: 1 to the woman, "Did G really say,
3: 5 you will be like G, knowing good
3: 8 from the LORD G among the trees
3: 9 But the LORD G called to the man
3:21 The LORD G made garments
3:22 LORD G said, "The man has now
3:23 So the LORD G banished him
5: 1 When G created man, he made him
5:22 Enoch walked with G 300 years
5:24 because G took him away.
6: 2 sons of G saw that the daughters
6: 9 of his time, and he walked with G.
6:12 G saw how corrupt the earth had
8: 1 But G remembered Noah
9: 1 Then G blessed Noah and his sons,
9: 6 for in the image of G
9:16 everlasting covenant between G
14:18 He was priest of G Most High,
14:19 Blessed be Abram by G Most High,
16:13 "You are the G who sees me,"
17: 1 "I am G Almighty; walk before me
17: 7 to be your God the G
21: 4 him, as G commanded him.
21: 6 "G has brought me laughter.
21:20 G was with the boy as he grew up.
21:22 G is with you in everything you do.
21:33 name of the LORD, the Eternal G.
22: 1 Some time later G tested Abraham.
22: 8 "G himself will provide the lamb
22:12 Now I know that you fear G,
25:11 Abraham's death, G blessed his
28:12 and the angels of G were ascending
28:17 other than the house of G;
31:42 But G has seen my hardship
31:50 remember that G is a witness
32: 1 and the angels of G met him.
32:28 because you have struggled with G

Ge 32:30 "It is because I saw G face to face,
33:11 for G has been gracious to me
35: 1 and build an altar there to G,
35: 5 and the terror of G fell
35:10 G said to him, "Your name is Jacob
35:11 G said to him, "I am G Almighty;
41:51 G has made me forget all my
41:52 G has made me fruitful in the land
50:20 but G intended it for good
50:24 But G will surely come to your aid
Ex 2:24 G heard their groaning
3: 5 "Do not come any closer," G said.
3: 6 because he was afraid to look at G.
3:12 And G said, "I will be with you.
3:14 what shall I tell them?" G said
4:27 he met Moses at the mountain of G
6: 7 own people, and I will be your G
8:10 is no one like the LORD our G
10:16 sinned against the LORD your G,
13:18 So G led the people
15: 2 He is my G, and I will praise him,
16:12 that I am the LORD your G.' "
17: 9 with the staff of G in my hands."
18: 5 camped near the mountain of G.
19: 3 Then Moses went up to G,
20: 1 And G spoke all these words:
20: 2 the LORD your G, who brought
20: 5 the LORD your G, am a jealous G,
20: 7 the name of the LORD your G,
20:10 a Sabbath to the LORD your G
20:12 the LORD your G is giving you.
20:19 But do not have G speak to us
20:20 the fear of G will be with you
22:20 "Whoever sacrifices to any g other
22:28 "Do not blaspheme G
23:19 to the house of the LORD your G.
31:18 inscribed by the finger of G.
34: 6 the compassionate and gracious G,
34:14 name is Jealous, is a jealous G.
Lev 2:13 salt of the covenant of your G out
11:44 the LORD your G; consecrate
18:21 not profane the name of your G.
19: 2 the LORD your G, am holy.
20: 7 because I am the LORD your G.
21: 6 They must be holy to their G
22:33 out of Egypt to be your G
26:12 walk among you and be your G,
Nu 15:40 and will be consecrated to your G.
22:18 the command of the LORD my G.
22:38 I must speak only what G puts
23:19 G is not a man, that he should lie,
25:13 zealous for the honor of his G
Dt 1:17 for judgment belongs to G.
1:21 the LORD your G has given you
1:30 The LORD your G, who is going
3:22 LORD your G himself will fight
3:24 For what g is there in heaven
4:24 is a consuming fire, a jealous G.
4:29 there you seek the LORD your G,
4:31 the LORD your G is a merciful G,
4:39 heart this day that the LORD is G
5: 9 the LORD your G, am a jealous G,
5:11 the name of the LORD your G,
5:12 the LORD your G has commanded
5:14 a Sabbath to the LORD your G.
5:15 the LORD your G brought you out
5:16 the LORD your G has commanded
5:16 the LORD your G is giving you.
5:24 LORD our G has shown us his
6: 2 them may fear the LORD your G
6: 4 LORD your G, the LORD is one.
6: 5 Love the LORD your G
6:13 the LORD your G, serve him only
6:16 Do not test the LORD your G
7: 6 holy to the LORD your G.
7: 9 your G is G; he is the faithful G,
7:12 the LORD your G will keep his
7:19 LORD your G will do the same
7:21 is a great and awesome G.
8: 5 the LORD your G disciplines you.
8:11 do not forget the LORD your G,
8:18 But remember the LORD your G,
9:10 inscribed by the finger of G.
10:12 but to fear the LORD your G,
10:14 the LORD your G belong
10:17 For the LORD your G is G of gods
10:21 He is your praise; he is your G,
11: 1 Love the LORD your G
11:13 to love the LORD your G
12:12 rejoice before the LORD your G.
12:28 in the eyes of the LORD your G.
13: 3 The LORD your G is testing you
13: 4 the LORD your G you must
15: 6 the LORD your G will bless you

Dt 15:19 the LORD your G every firstborn
16:11 rejoice before the LORD your G
16:17 the LORD your G has blessed you.
18:13 before the LORD your G.
18:15 The LORD your G will raise up
19: 9 to love the LORD your G
22: 5 the LORD your G detests anyone
23: 5 the LORD your G loves you.
23:14 the LORD your G moves about
23:21 a vow to the LORD your G,
25:16 the LORD your G detests anyone
26: 5 declare before the LORD your G:
29:13 that he may be your G
29:29 belong to the LORD our G,
30: 2 return to the LORD your G
30: 4 the LORD your G will gather you
30: 6 The LORD your G will circumcise
30:16 today to love the LORD your G,
30:20 you may love the LORD your G
31: 6 for the LORD your G goes
32: 3 Oh, praise the greatness of our G!
32: 4 A faithful G who does no wrong,
33:27 The eternal G is your refuge,
Jos 1: 9 for the LORD your G will be
14: 8 the LORD my G wholeheartedly.
14: 9 the LORD my G wholeheartedly.'
14:14 the G of Israel, wholeheartedly.
22: 5 to love the LORD your G,
22:22 The Mighty One, G, the LORD!
22:34 Between Us that the LORD is G.
23: 8 to hold fast to the LORD your G,
23:11 careful to love the LORD your G
23:14 the LORD your G gave you has
23:15 of the LORD your G has come true
24:19 He is a holy G; he is a jealous G.
24:23 to the LORD, the G of Israel."
Jdg 5: 3 to the LORD, the G of Israel.
16:28 O G, please strengthen me just
Ru 1:16 be my people and your G my G.
2:12 by the LORD, the G of Israel,
1Sa 2: 2 there is no Rock like our G.
2: 3 for the LORD is a G who knows,
2:25 another man, G may mediate
10:26 men whose hearts G had touched.
12:12 the LORD your G was your king.
16:15 spirit from G is tormenting you.
17:26 defy the armies of the living G?"
17:36 defied the armies of the living G.
17:45 the G of the armies of Israel,
17:46 world will know that there is a G
23:16 and helped him find strength in G.
28:15 and G has turned away from me.
30: 6 strength in the LORD his G.
2Sa 7:22 and there is no G but you,
7:23 on earth that G went out to redeem
14:14 But G does not take away life;
21:14 G answered prayer in behalf
22: 3 my G is my rock, in whom I take
22:31 "As for G, his way is perfect;
22:32 And who is the Rock except our G
22:33 It is G who arms me with strength
22:47 Exalted be G, the Rock, my Savior!
1Ki 2: 3 what the LORD your G requires:
4:29 G gave Solomon wisdom
5: 5 for the Name of the LORD my G,
8:23 there is no G like you in heaven
8:27 "But will G really dwell on earth?
8:60 may know that the LORD is G
8:61 committed to the LORD our G,
10:24 to hear the wisdom G had put
15:30 he provoked the LORD, the G
18:21 If the LORD is G, follow him;
18:36 it be known today that you are G
18:37 are G, and that you are turning
20:28 a g of the hills and not a g
2Ki 5:15 "Now I know that there is no G
18: 5 in the LORD, the G of Israel.
19:15 G of Israel, enthroned
19:19 Now, O LORD our G, deliver us
1Ch 12:18 for your G will help you."
13: 2 if it is the will of the LORD our G,
16:35 Cry out, "Save us, O G our Savior;
17:20 and there is no G but you,
17:24 the G over Israel, is Israel's G!'
21: 8 said to G, "I have sinned greatly
22: 1 house of the LORD G is to be here,
22:19 soul to seeking the LORD your G.
28: 2 for the footstool of our G,
28: 9 acknowledge the G of your father,
28:20 for the LORD my G, my G, is with you
29: 1 not for man but for the LORD G.
29: 2 provided for the temple of my G—
29: 3 of my G I now give my personal
29:10 G of our father Israel,
29:13 Now, our G, we give you thanks.

1Ch 29: 16 O LORD our G, as for all this
29: 17 my G, that you test the heart
29: 18 G of our fathers Abraham,
2Ch 2: 4 for the Name of the LORD my G
5: 14 of the LORD filled the temple of G
6: 4 be to the LORD, the G of Israel,
6: 14 there is no G like you in heaven
6: 18 "But will G really dwell on earth
10: 15 for this turn of events was from G,
13: 12 G is with us; he is our leader.
15: 3 was without the true G,
15: 12 the G of their fathers,
15: 15 They sought G eagerly,
18: 13 I can tell him only what my G says
19: 3 have set your heart on seeking G."
19: 7 with the LORD our G there is no
20: 6 are you not the G who is in heaven?
20: 20 Have faith in the LORD your G
25: 8 for G has the power to help
26: 5 sought the LORD, G gave him
30: 9 for the LORD your G is gracious
30: 19 who sets his heart on seeking G—
31: 21 he sought his G and worked
32: 31 G left him to test him
33: 12 the favor of the LORD his G
34: 33 fail to follow the LORD, the G
Ezr 6: 21 to seek the LORD, the G of Israel.
7: 18 accordance with the will of your G.
7: 23 Whatever the G of heaven has
8: 22 "The gracious hand of our G is
8: 31 The hand of our G was on us,
9: 6 "O my G, I am too ashamed
9: 9 our G has not deserted us
9: 13 our G, you have punished us less
9: 15 G of Israel, you are righteous!
Ne 1: 5 the great and awesome G,
5: 9 fear of our G to avoid the reproach
5: 15 for G I did not act like that.
7: 2 feared G more than most men do.
8: 8 from the Book of the Law of G,
8: 18 from the Book of the Law of G.
9: 5 and praise the LORD your G,
9: 17 But you are a forgiving G,
9: 31 you are a gracious and merciful G.
9: 32 the great, mighty and awesome G,
10: 29 oath to follow the Law of G given
10: 39 not neglect the house of our G."
12: 43 G had given them great joy.
13: 11 Why is the house of G neglected?"
13: 26 He was loved by his G,
13: 31 Remember me with favor, O my G.
Job 1: 1 he feared G and shunned evil.
1: 22 by charging G with wrongdoing.
2: 10 Shall we accept good from G,
4: 17 a mortal be more righteous than G?
5: 17 is the man whom G corrects;
8: 3 Does G pervert justice?
8: 20 "Surely G does not reject
9: 2 a mortal be righteous before G?
11: 7 Can you fathom the mysteries of G
12: 13 "To G belong wisdom and power;
16: 7 Surely, O G, you have worn me out
19: 26 yet in my flesh I will see G;
21: 19 'G stores up a man's punishment
21: 22 Can anyone teach knowledge to G,
22: 12 "Is not G in the heights of heaven?
22: 13 Yet you say, 'What does G know?
22: 21 "Submit to G and be at peace
25: 2 "Dominion and awe belong to G;
25: 4 can a man be righteous before G?
26: 6 Death is naked before G;
30: 20 O G, but you do not answer;
31: 6 let G weigh me in honest scales
31: 14 do when G confronts me?
32: 13 let G refute him, not man.'
33: 6 I am just like you before G;
33: 14 For G does speak—now one way,
33: 26 He prays to G and finds favor
34: 10 Far be it from G to do evil,
34: 12 is unthinkable that G would do
34: 23 G has no need to examine men
34: 33 Should G then reward you
36: 5 "G is mighty, but does not despise
36: 26 is G—beyond our understanding!
37: 22 G comes in awesome majesty.
Ps 5: 4 You are not a G who takes pleasure
7: 11 G is a righteous judge,
10: 14 O G, do see trouble and grief;
14: 5 for G is present in the company
18: 2 my G is my rock, in whom I take
18: 28 my G turns my darkness into light.
18: 30 As for G, his way is perfect;
18: 31 And who is the Rock except our G
18: 32 It is G who arms me with strength
18: 46 Exalted be G my Savior!
Ps 19: 1 The heavens declare the glory of G;
22: 1 G, my G, why have you forsaken
22: 10 womb you have been my G.
27: 9 O G my Savior.
29: 3 the G of glory thunders,
31: 5 redeem me, O LORD, the G
31: 14 I say, "You are my G."
33: 12 the nation whose G is the LORD,
35: 24 righteousness, O LORD my G;
37: 31 The law of his G is in his heart;
40: 3 a hymn of praise to our G.
40: 8 I desire to do your will, O my G;
42: 1 so my soul pants for you, O G.
42: 2 thirsts for G, for the living G.
42: 5 Put your hope in G,
42: 8 a prayer to the G of my life.
42: 11 Put your hope in G,
43: 4 to G, my joy and my delight.
44: 8 In G we make our boast all day
45: 6 O G, will last for ever and ever;
45: 7 therefore G, your G, has set you
46: 1 G is our refuge and strength,
46: 5 G will help her at break of day.
46: 10 "Be still, and know that I am G;
47: 1 shout to G with cries of joy.
47: 6 Sing praises to G, sing praises;
47: 7 For G is the King of all the earth;
48: 9 Within your temple, O G,
49: 7 or give to G a ransom for him—
50: 2 G shines forth.
50: 3 Our G comes and will not be silent;
51: 1 Have mercy on me, O G,
51: 10 Create in me a pure heart, O G,
51: 17 O G, you will not despise.
53: 2 any who seek G.
54: 4 Surely G is my help;
55: 19 G, who is enthroned forever,
56: 4 In G, whose word I praise,
56: 10 In G, whose word I praise,
56: 13 that I may walk before G
57: 3 G sends his love and his
57: 7 My heart is steadfast, O G,
59: 17 are my fortress, my loving G.
62: 1 My soul finds rest in G alone;
62: 7 my honor depend on G;
62: 8 for G is our refuge.
62: 11 One thing G has spoken,
63: 1 O G, you are my G,
65: 5 O G our Savior,
66: 1 Shout with joy to G, all the earth!
66: 3 Say to G, "How awesome are your
66: 5 Come and see what G has done,
66: 16 listen, all you who fear G;
66: 20 Praise be to G,
68: 4 Sing to G, sing praise to his name,
68: 6 G sets the lonely in families,
68: 20 Our G is a G who saves;
68: 24 has come into view, O G,
68: 35 You are awesome, O G,
69: 5 You know my folly, O G;
70: 1 Hasten, O G, to save me;
70: 4 "Let G be exalted!"
70: 5 come quickly to me, O G.
71: 17 my youth, O G, you have taught
71: 18 do not forsake me, O G,
71: 19 reaches to the skies, O G,
71: 22 harp for your faithfulness, O my G;
73: 17 me till I entered the sanctuary of G;
73: 26 but G is the strength of my heart
76: 11 Make vows to the LORD your G
77: 13 What g is so great as our God?
77: 14 You are the G who performs
78: 19 Can G spread a table in the desert?
79: 9 Help us, O G our Savior,
81: 1 Sing for joy to G our strength;
82: 1 G presides in the great assembly;
84: 2 out for the living G.
84: 10 a doorkeeper in the house of my G
84: 11 For the LORD G is a sun
86: 12 O Lord my G, with all my heart;
86: 15 a compassionate and gracious G,
87: 3 O city of G: *Selah*
89: 7 of the holy ones G is greatly feared;
90: 2 to everlasting you are G.
91: 2 my G, in whom I trust."
94: 22 my G the rock in whom I take
95: 7 for he is our G
99: 8 you were to Israel a forgiving G,
99: 9 Exalt the LORD our G
100: 3 Know that the LORD is G.
108: 1 My heart is steadfast, O G;
113: 5 Who is like the LORD our G,
115: 3 Our G is in heaven;
116: 5 our G is full of compassion.
123: 2 look to the LORD our G,
Ps 136: 2 Give thanks to the G of gods.
136: 26 Give thanks to the G of heaven.
139: 17 to me are your thoughts, O G!
139: 23 Search me, O G, and know my
143: 10 for you are my G;
144: 2 He is my loving G and my fortress,
147: 1 is to sing praises to our G,
Pr 3: 4 in the sight of G and man.
14: 31 to the needy honors G.
25: 2 of G to conceal a matter;
30: 5 "Every word of G is flawless;
Ecc 2: 26 G gives wisdom, knowledge
3: 11 cannot fathom what G has done
3: 13 in all his toil—this is the gift of G.
3: 14 G does it so that men will revere him.
5: 4 When you make a vow to G,
5: 19 in his work—this is a gift of G.
8: 12 who are reverent before G.
11: 5 cannot understand the work of G,
12: 7 the spirit returns to G who gave it.
12: 13 Fear G and keep his
Isa 5: 16 the holy G will show himself holy
9: 6 Wonderful Counselor, Mighty G,
12: 2 Surely G is my salvation;
25: 9 "Surely this is our G;
28: 11 G will speak to this people,
29: 23 will stand in awe of the G of Israel.
30: 18 For the LORD is a G of justice.
35: 4 your G will come,
37: 16 you alone are G over all
40: 1 says your G.
40: 3 a highway for our G.
40: 8 the word of our G stands forever."
40: 18 then, will you compare G?
40: 28 The LORD is the everlasting G,
41: 10 not be dismayed, for I am your G.
41: 13 For I am the LORD, your G,
43: 10 Before me no g was formed,
44: 6 apart from me there is no G.
44: 15 he also fashions a g and worships it;
45: 18 he is G;
48: 17 "I am the LORD your G,
52: 7 "Your G reigns!"
52: 12 G of Israel will be your rear guard.
55: 7 to our G, for he will freely pardon.
57: 21 says my G, "for the wicked."
59: 2 you from your G;
60: 19 and your G will be your glory.
61: 2 and the day of vengeance of our G,
61: 10 my soul rejoices in my G.
62: 5 so will your G rejoice over you.
Jer 7: 23 I will be your G and you will be my
10: 10 But the LORD is the true G;
10: 12 But G made the earth by his power;
23: 23 "Am I only a G nearby,"
23: 36 distort the words of the living G,
31: 33 I will be their G,
32: 27 "I am the LORD, the G
42: 6 for we will obey the LORD our G."
51: 10 what the LORD our G has done.'
51: 56 For the LORD is a G of retribution
Eze 28: 13 the garden of G;
34: 31 and I am your G, declares
Da 2: 28 there is a G in heaven who reveals
3: 17 the G we serve is able to save us
3: 29 for no other g can save in this way
6: 16 "May your G, whom you serve
9: 4 O Lord, the great and awesome G,
10: 12 to humble yourself before your G,
11: 36 things against the G of gods.
Hos 1: 9 my people, and I am not your G.
1: 10 will be called 'sons of the living G.'
4: 6 you have ignored the law of your G
6: 6 acknowledgment of G rather
9: 8 The prophet, along with my G,
12: 6 and wait for your G always.
Joel 2: 13 Return to the LORD your G,
2: 23 rejoice in the LORD your G,
Am 4: 12 prepare to meet your G, O Israel."
4: 13 the LORD G Almighty is his name
Jnh 1: 6 Get up and call on your g!
4: 2 a gracious and compassionate G,
Mic 6: 8 and to walk humbly with your G.
7: 7 I wait for G my Savior;
7: 18 Who is a G like you,
Na 1: 2 LORD is a jealous and avenging G;
Hab 3: 18 I will be joyful in G my Savior.
Zep 3: 17 The LORD your G is with you,
Zec 14: 5 Then the LORD my G will come,
Mal 2: 10 Father? Did not one G create us?
2: 16 says the LORD G of Israel,
3: 8 Will a man rob G? Yet you rob me.
Mt 1: 23 which means, "G with us."
4: 4 comes from the mouth of G.'"
4: 7 'Do not put the Lord your G

Mt 4:10 'Worship the Lord your *G*,
5: 8 for they will see *G*.
6:24 You cannot serve both *G*
19: 6 Therefore what *G* has joined
19:26 but with *G* all things are possible."
22:21 and to *G* what is God's."
22:32 He is not the *G* of the dead
22:37 " 'Love the Lord your *G*
27:46 which means, "My *G*, my *G*,

Mk 2: 7 Who can forgive sins but *G* alone?"
7:13 Thus you nullify the word of *G*
10: 6 of creation *G* made them male
10: 9 Therefore what *G* has joined
10:18 "No one is good—except *G* alone.
10:27 all things are possible with *G*."
11:22 "Have faith in *G*," Jesus answered.
12:17 and to *G* what is God's."
12:29 the Lord our *G*, the Lord is one.
12:30 Love the Lord your *G*
15:34 which means, "My *G*, my *G*,
16:19 and he sat at the right hand of *G*.

Lk 1:30 Mary, you have found favor with *G*.
1:37 For nothing is impossible with *G*."
1:47 my spirit rejoices in *G* my Savior,
2:14 "Glory to *G* in the highest,
2:52 and in favor with *G* and men.
4: 8 'Worship the Lord your *G*
5:21 Who can forgive sins but *G* alone?"
8:39 tell how much *G* has done for you."
10: 9 'The kingdom of *G* is near you."
10:27 " 'Love the Lord your *G*
13:18 "What is the kingdom of *G* like?
18:19 "No one is good—except *G* alone.
18:27 with men is possible with *G*."
20:25 and to *G* what is God's."
20:38 He is not the *G* of the dead,
22:69 at the right hand of the mighty *G*."

Jn 1: 1 was with *G*, and the Word was *G*.
1:18 ever seen *G*, but *G* the One and Only,
1:29 Lamb of *G*, who takes away the sin
3:16 "For *G* so loved the world that he
3:34 the one whom *G* has sent speaks
4:24 *G* is spirit, and his worshipers must
5:44 praise that comes from the only *G*?
6:29 answered, "The work of *G* is this:
7:17 my teaching comes from *G* or
8:42 to them, "If *G* were your Father,
8:47 belongs to *G* hears what *G* says.
11:40 you would see the glory of *G*?"
13: 3 from *G* and was returning to *G*;
13:31 of Man glorified and *G* is glorified
14: 1 Trust in *G*; trust also in me.
17: 3 the only true *G*, and Jesus Christ,
20:17 your Father, to my *G* and your *G*
20:28 "My Lord and my *G*!"
20:31 the Son of *G*, and that

Ac 2:11 wonders of *G* in our own tongues!"
2:24 But *G* raised him from the dead,
2:33 Exalted to the right hand of *G*,
2:36 *G* has made this Jesus, whom you
3:15 but *G* raised him from the dead.
3:19 Repent, then, and turn to *G*,
4:31 and spoke the word of *G* boldly.
5: 4 You have not lied to men but to *G*."
5:29 "We must obey *G* rather than men!
5:31 *G* exalted him to his own right
5:32 whom *G* has given
7:55 to heaven and saw the glory of *G*,
8:21 your heart is not right before *G*.
11: 9 anything impure that *G* has made
12:24 But the word of *G* continued
13:32 What *G* promised our fathers he
15:10 to test *G* by putting on the necks
17:23 TO AN UNKNOWN *G*.
17:30 In the past *G* overlooked such
20:27 to you the whole will of *G*.
20:32 "Now I commit you to *G*
24:16 keep my conscience clear before *G*

Ro 1:16 the power of *G* for the salvation
1:17 a righteousness from *G* is revealed,
1:18 The wrath of *G* is being revealed
1:24 Therefore *G* gave them
1:26 *G* gave them over to shameful lusts
2:11 For *G* does not show favoritism.
2:16 when *G* will judge men's secrets
3: 4 Let *G* be true, and every man a liar.
3:19 world held accountable to *G*.
3:23 and fall short of the glory of *G*,
3:29 Is *G* the *G* of Jews only? Is he not
3: 4 say? "Abraham believed *G*,
4: 6 to whom *G* credits righteousness
4:17 the *G* who gives life to the dead
4:24 to whom *G* will credit
5: 1 we have peace with *G*
5: 5 because *G* has poured out his love

Ro 5: 8 *G* demonstrates his own love for us
6:22 and have become slaves to *G*,
6:23 but the gift of *G* is eternal life
8: 7 the sinful mind is hostile to *G*.
8:17 heirs of *G* and co-heirs with Christ,
8:28 in all things *G* works for the good
9:14 What then shall we say? Is *G* unjust
9:18 Therefore *G* has mercy
10: 9 in your heart that *G* raised him
11: 2 *G* did not reject his people,
11:22 the kindness and sternness of *G*:
11:32 For *G* has bound all men
13: 1 exist have been established by *G*.
14:12 give an account of himself to *G*.
16:20 *G* of peace will soon crush Satan

1Co 1:18 are being saved it is the power of *G*.
1:20 Has not *G* made foolish
1:25 For the foolishness of *G* is wiser
1:27 But *G* chose the foolish things
2: 9 what *G* prepared
2:11 of *G* except the Spirit of *G*.
3: 6 watered it, but *G* made it grow.
3:17 God's temple, *G* will destroy
6:20 Therefore honor *G* with your body.
7: 7 each man has his own gift from *G*;
7:15 *G* has called us to live in peace.
7:20 was in when *G* called him.
7:24 each man, as responsible to *G*,
8: 3 man who loves *G* is known by *G*.
8: 8 food does not bring us near to *G*;
10:13 *G* is faithful; he will not let you be
10:31 do it all for the glory of *G*.
12:24 But *G* has combined the members
14:33 For *G* is not a *G* of disorder
15:24 over the kingdom to *G* the Father
15:28 so that *G* may be all in all.
15:34 are some who are ignorant of *G*—
15:57 be to *G*! He gives us the victory

2Co 1: 9 rely on ourselves but on *G*,
2:14 be to *G*, who always leads us
2:15 For we are to *G* the aroma of Christ
2:17 we do not peddle the word of *G*
3: 5 but our competence comes from *G*.
4: 2 nor do we distort the word of *G*.
4: 7 this all-surpassing power is from *G*
5: 5 Now it is *G* who has made us
5:19 that *G* was reconciling the world
5:20 though *G* were making his appeal
5:21 *G* made him who had no sin
6:16 we are the temple of the living *G*.
9: 7 for *G* loves a cheerful giver.
9: 8 *G* is able to make all grace abound
10:13 to the field *G* has assigned to us,

Gal 2: 6 *G* does not judge by external
3: 5 Does *G* give you his Spirit
3: 6 Abraham: "He believed *G*,
3:11 justified before *G* by the law,
3:26 You are all sons of *G* through faith
6: 7 not be deceived: *G* cannot be

Eph 1:22 *G* placed all things under his feet
2: 8 it is the gift of *G*—not by works,
2:10 which *G* prepared in advance for us
2:22 in which *G* lives by his Spirit.
4: 6 one baptism; one *G* and Father
4:24 to be like *G* in true righteousness
5: 1 Be imitators of *G*, therefore,
6: 6 doing the will of *G* from your heart.

Php 2: 6 Who, being in very nature *G*,
2: 9 Therefore *G* exalted him
2:13 for it is *G* who works in you to will
4: 7 peace of *G*, which transcends all
4:19 And my *G* will meet all your needs

Col 1:19 For *G* was pleased
2:13 *G* made you alive with Christ.

1Th 2: 4 trying to please men but *G*,
2:13 but as it actually is, the word of *G*,
3: 9 How can we thank *G* enough
4: 7 For *G* did not call us to be impure,
4: 9 taught by *G* to love each other.
5: 9 For *G* did not appoint us

1Ti 2: 5 one mediator between *G* and men,
4: 4 For everything *G* created is good,
5: 4 for this is pleasing to *G*.

2Ti 1: 6 you to fan into flame the gift of *G*,

Tit 1: 2 which *G*, who does not lie,
2:13 glorious appearing of our great *G*

Heb 1: 1 In the past *G* spoke
3: 4 but *G* is the builder of everything.
4: 4 "And on the seventh day *G* rested
4:12 For the word of *G* is living
6:10 *G* is not unjust; he will not forget
6:18 in which it is impossible for *G* to lie
7:19 by which we draw near to *G*,
7:25 come to *G* through him,
10:22 draw near to *G* with a sincere heart

Heb 10:31 to fall into the hands of the living *G*.
11: 5 commended as one who pleased *G*.
11: 6 faith it is impossible to please *G*,
12: 7 as discipline; *G* is treating you
12:10 but *G* disciplines us for our good,
12:29 for our "*G* is a consuming fire—"
13:15 offer to *G* a sacrifice of praise—

Jas 1:12 crown of life that *G* has promised
1:13 For *G* cannot be tempted by evil,
1:27 Religion that *G* our Father accepts
2:19 You believe that there is one *G*.
2:23 "Abraham believed *G*,
4: 4 the world becomes an enemy of *G*.
4: 6 "*G* opposes the proud
4: 8 Come near to *G* and he will come

1Pe 1:23 the living and enduring word of *G*.
2:20 this is commendable before *G*.
3:18 the unrighteous, to bring you to *G*.
4:11 it with the strength *G* provides,
5: 5 because, "*G* opposes the proud

2Pe 1:21 but men spoke from *G*
2: 4 For if *G* did not spare angels

1Jn 1: 5 *G* is light; in him there is no
2:17 the will of *G* lives forever.
3: 1 we should be called children of *G*!
3: 9 born of *G* will continue to sin,
3:10 we know who the children of *G* are
3:20 For *G* is greater than our hearts,
4: 7 for love comes from *G*.
4: 8 not know *G*, because *G* is love.
4: 9 This is how *G* showed his love
4:11 Dear friends, since *G* so loved us,
4:12 No one has ever seen *G*;
4:15 *G* lives in him and he in *G*.
4:16 *G* is love.
4:20 "I love *G*," yet hates his brother,
4:21 Whoever loves *G* must
5: 2 that we love the children of *G*.
5: 3 love for *G*: to obey his commands.
5: 4 born of *G* overcomes the world.
5:14 have in approaching *G*:
5:18 born of *G* does not continue to sin;

Rev 4: 8 holy is the Lord *G* Almighty,
7:12 be to our *G* for ever and ever.
7:17 *G* will wipe away every tear
11:16 fell on their faces and worshiped *G*,
15: 3 Lord *G* Almighty.
17:17 For *G* has put it into their hearts
19: 6 For our Lord *G* Almighty reigns.
21: 3 Now the dwelling of *G* is with men,
21:23 for the glory of *G* gives it light,

GOD-BREATHED* (BREATH)

2Ti 3:16 All Scripture is *G* and is useful

GOD-FEARING* (FEAR)

Ecc 8:12 that it will go better with *G* men,
Ac 5: 5 staying in Jerusalem *G* Jews
10: 2 all his family were devout and *G*;
10:22 He is a righteous and *G* man,
13:26 of Abraham, and you *G* Gentiles,
13:50 But the Jews incited the *G* women
17: 4 as did a large number of *G* Greeks
17:17 with the Jews and the *G* Greeks,

GOD-HATERS* (HATE)

Ro 1:30 They are gossips, slanderers, *G*,

GOD'S (GOD)

2Ch 20:15 For the battle is not yours, but *G*.
Job 37:14 stop and consider *G* wonders.
Ps 52: 8 I trust in *G* unfailing love
69:30 I will praise *G* name in song
Mk 3:35 Whoever does *G* will is my brother
Jn 7:17 If anyone chooses to do *G* will,
10:36 'I am *G* Son'? Do not believe me
Ro 2: 3 think you will escape *G* judgment?
2: 4 not realizing that *G* kindness leads
3: 3 lack of faith nullify *G* faithfulness?
7:22 in my inner being I delight in *G* law
9:16 or effort, but on *G* mercy.
11:29 for *G* gifts and his call are
12: 2 and approve what God's is—
12:13 Share with *G* people who are
12: for the authorities are *G* servants,
1Co 7:19 Keeping *G* commands is what
2Co 6: 2 now is the time of *G* favor,
Eph 1: 7 riches of *G* grace that he lavished
1Th 4: 3 It is *G* will that you should be sanctified;
5:18 for this is *G* will for you
1Ti 6: 1 so that *G* name and our teaching
2Ti 2:19 *G* solid foundation stands firm,
Tit 1: 7 overseer is entrusted with *G* work,

Heb 1: 3 The Son is the radiance of *G* glory
9: 24 now to appear for us in *G* presence.
11: 3 was formed at *G* command,
1Pe 2: 15 For it is *G* will that
3: 4 which is of great worth in *G* sight.
1Jn 2: 5 *G* love is truly made complete

GODLESS

Job 20: 5 the joy of the *g* lasts but a moment.
1Ti 6: 20 Turn away from *g* chatter

GODLINESS (GOD)

1Ti 2: 2 and quiet lives in all *g* and holiness.
4: 8 but *g* has value for all things,
6: 5 and who think that *g* is a means
6: 6 *g* with contentment is great gain.
6: 11 and pursue righteousness, *g*, faith,
2Pe 1: 6 and to perseverance, *g*;

GODLY (GOD)

Ps 4: 3 that the LORD has set apart the *g*
2Co 7: 10 *G* sorrow brings repentance that
11: 2 jealous for you with a *g* jealousy.
2Ti 3: 12 everyone who wants to live a *g* life
2Pe 3: 11 You ought to live holy and *g* lives

GODS (GOD)

Ex 20: 3 "You shall have no other *g*
Dt 5: 7 "You shall have no other *g*
1Ch 16: 26 For all the *g* of the nations are idols
Ps 82: 6 "I said, 'You are *"g"*,
Jn 10: 34 have said you are *g*'? If he called
Ac 19: 26 He says that man-made *g* are no *g*

GOG

Eze 38: 18 When *G* attacks the land of Israel,
Rev 20: 8 *G* and Magog—to gather them

GOLD

1Ki 20: 3 'Your silver and *g* are mine,
Job 22: 25 then the Almighty will be your *g*,
23: 10 tested me, I will come forth as *g*.
28: 15 cannot be bought with the finest *g*,
31: 24 "If I have put my trust in *g*
Ps 19: 10 They are more precious than *g*,
119:127 more than *g*, more than pure *g*,
Pr 3: 14 and yields better returns than *g*.
22: 1 esteemed is better than silver or *g*.
Hag 2: 8 'The silver is mine and the *g* is mine
Mt 2: 11 and presented him with gifts of *g*
Rev 3: 18 to buy from me *g* refined in the fire,

GOLGOTHA*

Mt 27: 33 to a place called *G* (which means
Mk 15: 22 to the place called *G* (which means
Jn 19: 17 (which in Aramaic is called *G*).

GOLIATH

Philistine giant killed by David (1Sa 17; 21:9).

GOMORRAH

Ge 19: 24 sulfur on Sodom and *G*—
Mt 10: 15 and *G* on the day of judgment
2Pe 2: 6 and *G* by burning them to ashes,
Jude : 7 *G* and the surrounding towns gave

GOOD

Ge 1: 4 God saw that the light was *g*,
1: 10 And God saw that it was *g*.
1: 12 And God saw that it was *g*.
1: 18 And God saw that it was *g*.
1: 21 And God saw that it was *g*.
1: 25 And God saw that it was *g*.
1: 31 he had made, and it was very *g*.
2: 9 and the tree of the knowledge of *g*
2: 9 pleasing to the eye and *g* for food.
2: 18 "It is not *g* for the man to be alone.
3: 22 become like one of us, knowing *g*
50: 20 but God intended it for *g*
2Ch 7: 3 "He is *g*; / his love endures
31: 20 doing what was *g* and right
Job 2: 10 Shall we accept *g* from God,
Ps 14: 1 there is no one who does *g*.
34: 8 Taste and see that the LORD is *g*;
34: 14 Turn from evil and do *g*;
37: 3 Trust in the LORD and do *g*;
37: 27 Turn from evil and do *g*;
52: 9 for your name is *g*.
53: 3 there is no one who does *g*,
84: 11 no *g* thing does he withhold
86: 5 You are forgiving and *g*, O Lord
100: 5 For the LORD is *g* and his love
103: 5 satisfies your desires with *g* things,
112: 5 *G* will come to him who is
119: 68 You are *g*, and what you do is *g*;

Ps 133: 1 How *g* and pleasant it is
145: 9 The LORD is *g* to all;
147: 1 How *g* it is to sing praises
Pr 3: 4 you will win favor and a *g* name
3: 27 Do not withhold *g*
11: 27 He who seeks *g* finds *g* will,
13: 22 A *g* man leaves an inheritance
14: 22 those who plan what is *g* find love
15: 3 on the wicked and the *g*.
15: 23 and how *g* is a timely word!
15: 30 *g* news gives health to the bones.
17: 22 A cheerful heart is *g* medicine,
18: 22 He who finds a wife finds what is *g*
19: 2 It is not *g* to have zeal
22: 1 A *g* name is more desirable
31: 12 She brings him *g*, not harm,
Ecc 12: 14 whether it is *g* or evil.
Isa 5: 20 Woe to those who call evil *g*
40: 9 You who bring *g* tidings
52: 7 the feet of those who bring *g* news,
61: 1 me to preach *g* news to the poor.
Jer 6: 16 ask where the *g* way is,
13: 23 Neither can you do *g*
32: 39 give their children after them.
Eze 34: 14 I will tend them in a *g* pasture,
Mic 6: 8 has showed you, O man, what is *g*.
Na 1: 15 the feet of one who brings *g* news,
Mt 5: 45 sun to rise on the evil and the *g*,
7: 11 Father in heaven give *g* gifts
7: 17 Likewise every *g* tree bears *g* fruit;
7: 18 A *g* tree cannot bear bad fruit.
12: 35 The *g* man brings *g* things out
13: 8 Still other seed fell on *g* soil,
13: 24 is like a man who sowed *g* seed
13: 48 and collected the *g* fish in baskets.
19: 17 "There is only One who is *g*.
22: 10 both *g* and bad, and the wedding
25: 21 'Well done, *g* and faithful servant!'
Mk 1: 15 Repent and believe the *g* news!"
3: 4 lawful on the Sabbath: to do *g*
4: 8 Still other seed fell on *g* soil.
8: 36 What *g* is it for a man
10: 18 "No one is *g*—except God alone.
16: 15 preach the *g* news to all creation.
Lk 2: 10 I bring you *g* news
3: 9 does not produce *g* fruit will be
6: 27 do *g* to those who hate you,
6: 43 nor does a bad tree bear *g* fruit.
6: 45 The *g* man brings *g* things out
8: 8 Still other seed fell on *g* soil.
9: 25 What *g* is it for a man
14: 34 "Salt is *g*, but if it loses its saltiness,
18: 19 "No one is *g*—except God alone.
19: 17 " 'Well done, my *g* servant!'
Jn 10: 11 "I am the *g* shepherd.
Ro 3: 12 there is no one who does *g*,
7: 12 is holy, righteous and *g*.
7: 16 want to do, I agree that the law is *g*.
7: 18 I have the desire to do what is *g*,
8: 28 for the *g* of those who love him,
10: 15 feet of those who bring *g* news!"
12: 2 his *g*, pleasing and perfect will.
12: 9 Hate what is evil; cling to what is *g*.
13: 4 For he is God's servant to do you *g*
16: 19 you to be wise about what is *g*,
1Co 7: 1 It is *g* for a man not to marry.
10: 24 should seek his own *g*, but the *g*
15: 33 Bad company corrupts *g* character
2Co 9: 8 you will abound in every *g* work.
Gal 4: 18 provided the purpose is *g*,
6: 9 us not become weary in doing *g*,
6: 10 as we have opportunity, let us do *g*
Eph 2: 10 in Christ Jesus to do *g* works,
6: 8 everyone for whatever *g* he does.
Php 1: 6 that he who began a *g* work
Col 1: 10 bearing fruit in every *g* work,
1Th 5: 21 Hold on to the *g*.
1Ti 3: 7 have a *g* reputation with outsiders,
4: 4 For everything God created is *g*,
6: 12 Fight the *g* fight of the faith,
6: 18 them to do *g*, to be rich in *g* deeds,
2Ti 2: 21 equipped for every *g* work.
4: 7 I have fought the *g* fight, I have
Tit 1: 8 loves what is *g*, who is
2: 7 an example by doing what is *g*.
2: 14 his very own, eager to do what is *g*.
Heb 5: 14 to distinguish *g* from evil.
10: 24 toward love and *g* deeds.
12: 10 but God disciplines us for our *g*,
13: 16 do not forget to do *g* and to share
Jas 4: 17 who knows the *g* he ought to do
1Pe 2: 3 you have tasted that the Lord is *g*.
2: 12 Live such *g* lives among the pagans
2: 18 not only to those who are *g*
3: 17 to suffer for doing *g*

GOODS

Ecc 5: 11 As *g* increase,

GORGE

Pr 23: 20 or *g* themselves on meat.

GOSHEN

Ge 45: 10 You shall live in the region of *G*
Ex 8: 22 differently with the land of *G*,

GOSPEL

Ro 1: 16 I am not ashamed of the *g*,
15: 16 duty of proclaiming the *g* of God,
15: 20 to preach the *g* where Christ was
1Co 1: 17 to preach the *g*—not with words
9: 12 rather than hinder the *g* of Christ.
9: 14 who preach the *g* should receive
9: 16 Woe to me if I do not preach the *g*!
15: 1 you of the *g* I preached to you,
15: 2 By this *g* you are saved,
2Co 4: 4 light of the *g* of the glory of Christ,
9: 13 your confession of the *g*
Gal 1: 7 a different *g*—which is really no *g*
Eph 6: 15 comes from the *g* of peace.
Php 1: 27 in a manner worthy of the *g*
Col 1: 23 This is the *g* that you heard
1Th 2: 4 by God to be entrusted with the *g*.
2Th 1: 8 do not obey the *g* of our Lord Jesus
2Ti 1: 10 immortality to light through the *g*.
Rev 14: 6 he had the eternal *g* to proclaim

GOSSIP*

Pr 11: 13 A *g* betrays a confidence,
16: 28 and a *g* separates close friends.
18: 8 of a *g* are like choice morsels;
20: 19 A *g* betrays a confidence;
26: 20 without a *g* a quarrel dies down.
26: 22 of a *g* are like choice morsels;
2Co 12: 20 slander, *g*, arrogance and disorder

GOVERN (GOVERNMENT)

Ge 1: 16 the greater light to *g* the day
Job 34: 17 Can he who hates justice *g*?
Ro 12: 8 it is leadership, let him *g* diligently;

GOVERNMENT (GOVERN)

Isa 9: 6 and the *g* will be on his shoulders.

GRACE* (GRACIOUS)

Ps 45: 2 lips have been anointed with *g*,
Pr 1: 9 will be a garland to *g* your head
3: 22 an ornament to *g* your neck.
3: 34 but gives *g* to the humble.
4: 9 She will set a garland of *g*
Isa 26: 10 Though *g* is shown to the wicked,
Jnh 2: 8 forfeit the *g* that could be theirs.
Zec 12: 10 of Jerusalem a spirit of *g*
Lk 2: 40 and the *g* of God was upon him.
Jn 1: 14 who came from the Father, full of *g*
1: 16 of his *g* we have all received one
1: 17 *g* and truth came through Jesus
Ac 4: 33 and much *g* was upon them all.
6: 8 a man full of God's *g* and power,
11: 23 saw the evidence of the *g* of God,
13: 43 them to continue in the *g* of God.
14: 3 message of his *g* by enabling them
14: 26 they had been committed to the *g*
15: 11 We believe it is through the *g*
15: 40 by the brothers to the *g* of the Lord
18: 27 to those who by *g* had believed.
20: 24 testifying to the gospel of God's *g*.
20: 32 to God and to the word of his *g*,
Ro 1: 5 we received *g* and apostleship
1: 7 *G* and peace to you
3: 24 and are justified freely by his *g*
4: 16 be by *g* and may be guaranteed
5: 2 access by faith into this *g*
5: 15 came by the *g* of the one man,
5: 15 how much more did God's *g*
5: 17 God's abundant provision of *g*
5: 20 where sin increased, *g* increased all
5: 21 also *g* might reign
6: 1 on sinning so that *g* may increase?
6: 14 you are not under law, but under *g*.
6: 15 we are not under law but under *g*?
11: 5 there is a remnant chosen by *g*.
11: 6 if by *g*, then it is no longer by works
11: 6 if it were, *g* would no longer be *g*.
12: 3 For by the *g* given me I say
12: 6 according to the *g* given us.
15: 15 because of the *g* God gave me
16: 20 The *g* of our Lord Jesus be
1Co 1: 3 *G* and peace to you
1: 4 of his *g* given you in Christ Jesus.

GRACIOUS

1Co 3:10 By the *g* God has given me,
15:10 But by the *g* of God I am what I am
15:10 but the *g* of God that was with me.
15:10 his *g* to me was not without effect.
16:23 The *g* of the Lord Jesus be with you
2Co 1: 2 *G* and peace to you
1:12 wisdom but according to God's *g*
4:15 so that the *g* that is reaching more
6: 1 not to receive God's *g* in vain.
8: 1 to know about the *g* that God has
8: 6 also to completion this act of *g*
8: 7 also excel in this *g* of giving.
8: 9 For you know the *g*
9: 8 able to make all *g* abound to you,
9:14 of the surpassing *g* God has given
12: 9 "My *g* is sufficient for you,
13:14 May the *g* of the Lord Jesus Christ,
Gal 1: 3 *G* and peace to you
1: 6 the one who called you by the *g*
1:15 from birth and called me by his *g*,
2: 9 when they recognized the *g* given
2:21 I do not set aside the *g* of God,
3:18 God in his *g* gave it to Abraham
5: 4 you have fallen away from *g*.
6:18 The *g* of our Lord Jesus Christ be
Eph 1: 2 *G* and peace to you
1: 6 to the praise of his glorious *g*,
1: 7 riches of God's *g* that he lavished
2: 5 it is by *g* you have been saved.
2: 7 the incomparable riches of his *g*,
2: 8 For it is by *g* you have been saved,
3: 2 of God's *g* that was given to me
3: 7 by the gift of God's *g* given me
3: 8 God's people, this *g* was given me:
4: 7 to each one of us *g* has been given
6:24 *G* to all who love our Lord Jesus
Php 1: 2 *G* and peace to you,
1: 7 all of you share in God's *g* with me.
4:23 The *g* of the Lord Jesus Christ be
Col 1: 2 *G* and peace to you
1: 6 understood God's *g* in all its truth.
4: 6 conversation be always full of *g*,
4:18 *G* be with you.
1Th 1: 1 and the Lord Jesus Christ: *G*
5:28 The *g* of our Lord Jesus Christ be
2Th 1: 2 *G* and peace to you
1:12 according to the *g* of our God
2:16 and by his *g* gave us eternal
3:18 The *g* of our Lord Jesus Christ be
1Ti 1: 2 my true son in the faith: *G*,
1:14 The *g* of our Lord was poured out
6:21 *G* be with you.
2Ti 1: 2 To Timothy, my dear son: *G*,
1: 9 This *g* was given us in Christ Jesus
1: 9 because of his own purpose and *g*.
2: 1 be strong in the *g* that is
4:22 *G* be with you.
Tit 1: 4 *G* and peace from God the Father
2:11 For the *g* of God that brings
3: 7 having been justified by his *g*,
3:15 *G* be with you all.
Phm : 3 *G* to you and peace
:25 The *g* of the Lord Jesus Christ be
Heb 2: 9 that by the *g* of God he might taste
4:16 find *g* to help us in our time of need
4:16 the throne of *g* with confidence,
10:29 and who has insulted the Spirit of *g*
12:15 See to it that no one misses the *g*
13: 9 hearts to be strengthened by *g*,
13:25 *G* be with you all.
Jas 4: 6 but gives *g* to the humble.
4: 6 But he gives us more *g*. That is why
1Pe 1: 2 *G* and peace be yours in abundance
1:10 who spoke of the *g* that was
1:13 fully on the *g* to be given you
4:10 faithfully administering God's *g*
5: 5 but gives *g* to the humble."
5:10 the God of all *g*, who called you
5:12 and testifying that this is the true *g*
2Pe 1: 2 *G* and peace be yours in abundance
3:18 But grow in the *g* and knowledge
2Jn : 3 and will be with us forever: *G*,
Jude : 4 who change the *g* of our God
Rev 1: 4 *G* and peace to you
22:21 The *g* of the Lord Jesus be

GRACIOUS (GRACE)

Ex 34: 6 the compassionate and *g* God,
Nu 6:25 and be *g* to you;
Ne 9:17 But you are a forgiving God, *g*
Ps 67: 1 May God be *g* to us and bless us
Pr 22:11 a pure heart and whose speech is *g*
Isa 30:18 Yet the Lord longs to be *g* to you

GRAIN

Lev 2: 1 When someone brings a *g* offering
Lk 17:35 women will be grinding *g* together;
1Co 9: 9 ox while it is treading out the *g*."

GRANDCHILDREN (CHILD)

1Ti 5: 4 But if a widow has children or *g*,

GRANDMOTHER (MOTHER)

2Ti 1: 5 which first lived in your *g* Lois

GRANT (GRANTED)

Ps 20: 5 May the Lord *g* all your requests
51:12 *g* me a willing spirit, to sustain me.

GRANTED (GRANT)

Pr 10:24 what the righteous desire will be *g*.
Mt 15:28 great faith! Your request is *g*."
Php 1:29 For it has been *g* to you on behalf

GRAPES

Nu 13:23 branch bearing a single cluster of *g*.
Jer 31:29 'The fathers have eaten sour *g*,
Eze 18: 2 "'The fathers eat sour *g*,
Mt 7:16 Do people pick *g* from thornbushes
Rev 14:18 and gather the clusters of *g*

GRASPED

Php 2: 6 with God something to be *g*,

GRASS

Ps 103:15 As for man, his days are like *g*,
Isa 40: 6 "All men are like *g*,
Mt 6:30 If that is how God clothes the *g*
1Pe 1:24 "All men are like *g*,

GRASSHOPPERS

Nu 13:33 We seemed like *g* in our own eyes,

GRATIFY* (GRATITUDE)

Ro 13:14 think about how to *g* the desires
Gal 5:16 and you will not *g* the desires

GRATITUDE (GRATIFY)

Col 3:16 and spiritual songs with *g*

GRAVE (GRAVES)

Nu 19:16 who touches a human bone or a *g*,
Dt 34: 6 day no one knows where his *g* is.
Ps 5: 9 Their throat is an open *g*;
49:15 will redeem my life from the *g*;
Pr 7:27 Her house is a highway to the *g*,
Hos 13:14 Where, O *g*, is your destruction?
Jn 11:44 "Take off the *g* clothes
Ac 2:27 you will not abandon me to the *g*,

GRAVES (GRAVE)

Eze 37:12 I am going to open your *g*
Jn 5:28 are in their *g* will hear his voice
Ro 3:13 "Their throats are open *g*;

GRAY

Pr 16:31 *G* hair is a crown of splendor;
20:29 *g* hair the splendor of the old.

GREAT (GREATER GREATEST GREATNESS)

Ge 12: 2 I will make your name *g*,
12: 2 "I will make you into a *g* nation
Ex 32:11 out of Egypt with *g* power
Nu 14:19 In accordance with your *g* love,
Dt 4:32 so *g* as this ever happened,
10:17 the *g* God, mighty and awesome,
29:28 in *g* wrath the Lord uprooted
Jos 7: 9 do for your own *g* name?"
Jdg 16: 5 you the secret of his *g* strength
2Sa 7:22 "How you are, O Sovereign
22:36 you stoop down to make me *g*.
24:14 for his mercy is *g*; but do not let me
1Ch 17:19 made known all these *g* promises.
Ps 18:35 you stoop down to make me *g*.
19:11 in keeping them there is *g* reward.
47: 2 the *g* King over all the earth!
57:10 For *g* is your love, reaching
68:11 and *g* was the company
89: 1 of the Lord's *g* love forever;
103:11 so *g* is his love for those who fear
107:43 consider the *g* love of the Lord.
108: 4 For *g* is your love, higher
117: 2 For *g* is his love toward us,
119:165 *G* peace have they who love your
145: 3 *G* is the Lord and most worthy
Pr 22: 1 is more desirable than *g* riches;
23:24 of a righteous man has *g* joy;

Isa 42:21 to make his law *g* and glorious.
Jer 27: 5 With my *g* power and outstretched
32:19 *g* are your purposes and mighty are
La 3:23 *g* is your faithfulness.
Da 9: 4 "O Lord, the *g* and awesome God,
Joel 2:11 The day of the Lord is *g*;
2:20 Surely he has done *g* things.
Zep 1:14 "The *g* day of the Lord is near—
Mal 1:11 My name will be *g*
4: 5 the prophet Elijah before that *g*
Mt 20:26 whoever wants to become *g*
Mk 10:43 whoever wants to become *g*
Lk 6:23 because *g* is your reward in heaven.
6:35 Then your reward will be *g*,
21:27 in a cloud with power and *g* glory.
Eph 1:19 and his incomparably *g* power
2: 4 But because of his *g* love for us,
1Ti 6: 6 with contentment is *g* gain.
Tit 2:13 glorious appearing of our *g* God
Heb 2: 3 if we ignore such a *g* salvation?
1Jn 3: 1 How *g* is the love the Father has
Rev 6:17 For the *g* day of their wrath has
20:11 Then I saw a *g* white throne

GREATER (GREAT)

Mt 11:11 there has not risen anyone *g*
12: 6 I tell you that one *g*
12:41 and now one *g* than Jonah is here.
12:42 now one *g* than Solomon is here.
Mk 12:31 There is no commandment *g*
Jn 1:50 You shall see *g* things than that."
3:30 He must become *g*; I must become
14:12 He will do even *g* things than these
15:13 *G* love has no one than this,
1Co 12:31 But eagerly desire the *g* gifts.
2Co 3:11 how much *g* is the glory
Heb 3: 3 the builder of a house has *g* honor
3: 3 worthy of *g* honor than Moses,
7: 7 lesser person is blessed by the *g*.
11:26 as of *g* value than the treasures
1Jn 3:20 For God is *g* than our hearts,
4: 4 is in you is *g* than the one who is

GREATEST (GREAT)

Mt 22:38 is the first and *g* commandment.
23:11 *g* among you will be your servant.
Lk 9:48 least among you all—he is the *g*."
1Co 13:13 But the *g* of these is love.

GREATNESS* (GREAT)

Ex 15: 7 In the *g* of your majesty
Dt 3:24 to show to your servant your *g*
32: 3 Oh, praise the *g* of our God!
1Ch 29:11 O Lord, is the *g* and the power
2Ch 9: 6 half the *g* of your wisdom was told
Est 10: 2 account of the *g* of Mordecai
Ps 145: 3 his *g* no one can fathom.
150: 2 praise him for his surpassing *g*.
Isa 63: 1 forward in the *g* of his strength?
Eze 38:23 I will show my *g* and my holiness,
Da 4:22 your *g* has grown until it reaches
5:18 and *g* and glory and splendor.
7:27 and *g* of the kingdoms
Mic 5: 4 will live securely, for then his *g*
Lk 9:43 And they were all amazed at the *g*
Php 3: 8 compared to the surpassing *g*

GREED (GREEDY)

Lk 12:15 on your guard against all kinds of *g*
Ro 1:29 kind of wickedness, evil, *g*
Eph 5: 3 or of any kind of impurity, or of *g*,
Col 5 evil desires and *g*, which is idolatry
2Pe 2:14 experts in *g*—an accursed brood!

GREEDY (GREED)

Pr 15:27 A *g* man brings trouble
1Co 6:10 nor thieves nor the *g* nor drunkards
Eph 5: 5 No immoral, impure or *g* person—
1Pe 5: 2 not *g* for money, but eager to serve;

GREEK (GREEKS)

Gal 3:28 There is neither Jew nor *G*,
Col 3:11 Here there is no *G* or Jew,

GREEKS (GREEK)

1Co 1:22 miraculous signs and *G* look

GREEN

Ps 23: 2 makes me lie down in *g* pastures,

GREW (GROW)

Lk 1:80 And the child *g* and became strong
2:52 And Jesus *g* in wisdom and stature,
Ac 9:31 by the Holy Spirit, it *g* in numbers,
16: 5 in the faith and *g* daily in numbers.

GRIEF (GRIEFS GRIEVANCES GRIEVE GRIEVED)

Ps	10:14	O God, do see trouble and g;
Pr	10: 1	but a foolish son g to his mother.
	14:13	and joy may end in g.
	17:21	To have a fool for a son brings g;
Ecc	1:18	the more knowledge, the more g.
La	3:32	Though he brings g, he will show
Jn	16:20	but your g will turn to joy.
1Pe	1: 6	had to suffer g in all kinds of trials.

GRIEFS* (GRIEF)
1Ti 6:10 pierced themselves with many g.

GRIEVANCES* (GRIEF)
Col 3:13 forgive whatever g you may have

GRIEVE (GRIEF)
Eph 4:30 do not g the Holy Spirit of God,
1Th 4:13 or to g like the rest of men,

GRIEVED (GRIEF)
Isa 63:10 and g his Holy Spirit.

GRINDING
Lk 17:35 women will be g grain together;

GROAN (GROANING GROANS)
Ro 8:23 g inwardly as we wait eagerly
2Co 5: 4 For while we are in this tent, we g

GROANING (GROAN)
Ex 2:24 God heard their g and he
Eze 21: 7 'Why are you g?' you shall say,
Ro 8:22 that the whole creation has been g

GROANS (GROAN)
Ro 8:26 with g that words cannot express.

GROUND
Ge	1:10	God called the dry g "land,"
	3:17	"Cursed is the g because of you;
	4:10	blood cries out to me from the g.
Ex	3: 5	where you are standing is holy g."
	15:19	walked through the sea on dry g.
Isa	53: 2	and like a root out of dry g.
Mt	10:29	fall to the g apart from the will
	25:25	and hid your talent in the g.
Jn	8: 6	to write on the g with his finger.
Eph	6:13	you may be able to stand your g,

GROW (FULL-GROWN GREW GROWING GROWS)
Pr	13:11	by little makes it g.
	20:13	not love sleep or you will g poor;
Isa	40:31	they will run and not g weary,
Mt	6:28	See how the lilies of the field g.
1Co	3: 6	watered it, but God made it g.
2Pe	3:18	But g in the grace and knowledge

GROWING (GROW)
Col 1: 6 this gospel is bearing fruit and g,
 1:10 in the knowledge of God,
2Th 1: 3 your faith is g more and more,

GROWS (GROW)
Eph 4:16 and builds itself up in love,
Col 2:19 g as God causes it to grow.

GRUMBLE (GRUMBLED GRUMBLERS GRUMBLING)
1Co 10:10 And do not g, as some of them did
Jas 5: 9 Don't g against each other,

GRUMBLED (GRUMBLE)
Ex 15:24 So the people g against Moses.
Nu 14:29 and who has g against me.

GRUMBLERS* (GRUMBLE)
Jude :16 These men are g and faultfinders;

GRUMBLING (GRUMBLE)
Jn 6:43 "Stop g among yourselves."
1Pe 4: 9 to one another without g.

GUARANTEE (GUARANTEEING)
Heb 7:22 Jesus has become the g

GUARANTEEING* (GUARANTEE)
2Co 1:22 as a deposit, g what is to come.
 5: 5 as a deposit, g what is to come.
Eph 1:14 who is a deposit g our inheritance

GUARD (GUARDS)
1Sa	2: 9	He will g the feet of his saints,
Ps	141: 3	Set a g over my mouth, O LORD;
Pr	2:11	and understanding will g you.
	4:13	g it well, for it is your life.
	4:23	Above all else, g your heart,
	7: 2	g my teachings as the apple
Isa	52:12	the God of Israel will be your rear g.
Mk	13:33	Be on g! Be alert! You do not know
Lk	12: 1	"Be on your g against the yeast
	12:15	Be on your g against all kinds
Ac	20:31	So be on your g! Remember that
1Co	16:13	Be on your g; stand firm in the faith
Php	4: 7	will g your hearts and your minds
1Ti	6:20	g what has been entrusted
2Ti	1:14	G the good deposit that was

GUARDS (GUARD)
Pr 13: 3 He who g his lips g his life,
 19:16 who obeys instructions g his life,
 21:23 He who g his mouth and his tongue
 22: 5 he who g his soul stays far

GUIDANCE (GUIDE)
Pr 1: 5 and let the discerning get g—
 11:14 For lack of g a nation falls,
 24: 6 for waging war you need g,

GUIDE (GUIDANCE GUIDED GUIDES)
Ex	13:21	of cloud to g them on their way
	15:13	In your strength you will g them
Ne	9:19	cease to g them on their path,
Ps	25: 5	g me in your truth and teach me,
	43: 3	let them g me;
	48:14	he will be our g even to the end.
	67: 4	and g the nations of the earth.
	73:24	You g me with your counsel,
	139:10	even there your hand will g me,
Pr	4:11	I g you in the way of wisdom
	6:22	When you walk, they will g you;
Isa	58:11	The LORD will g you always;
Jn	16:13	comes, he will g you into all truth.

GUIDED (GUIDE)
Ps 107:30 he g them to their desired haven.

GUIDES (GUIDE)
Ps 23: 3 He g me in paths of righteousness
 25: 9 He g the humble in what is right
Pr 11: 3 The integrity of the upright g them,
 16:23 A wise man's heart g his mouth,
Mt 23:16 "Woe to you, blind g! You say,
 23:24 You blind g! You strain out a gnat

GUILT (GUILTY)
Lev	5:15	It is a g offering.
Ps	32: 5	the g of my sin.
	38: 4	My g has overwhelmed me
Isa	6: 7	your g is taken away and your sin
Jer	2:22	the stain of your g is still before me
Eze	18:19	'Why does the son not share the g

GUILTY (GUILT)
Ex	34: 7	does not leave the g unpunished;
Mk	3:29	Spirit will never be forgiven; he is g
Jn	8:46	Can any of you prove me g of sin?
1Co	11:27	in an unworthy manner will be g
Heb	10: 2	and would no longer have felt g
	10:22	to cleanse us from a g conscience
Jas	2:10	at just one point is g of breaking all

HABAKKUK*
Prophet to Judah (Hab 1:1; 3:1)

HABIT
1Ti 5:13 they get into the h of being idle
Heb 10:25 as some are in the h of doing,

HADAD
Edomite adversary of Solomon (1Ki 11:14-25).

HADES*
Mt 16:18 the gates of H will not overcome it.
Rev 1:18 And I hold the keys of death and H
 6: 8 H was following close behind him.
 20:13 and H gave up the dead that were
 20:14 H were thrown into the lake of fire.

HAGAR
Servant of Sarah, wife of Abraham, mother of Ishmael (Ge 16:1-6; 25:12). Driven away by Sarah while pregnant (Ge 16:5-16); after birth of Isaac (Ge 21:9-21; Gal 4:21-31).

HAGGAI*
Post-exilic prophet who encouraged rebuilding of the temple (Ezr 5:1; 6:14; Hag 1-2).

HAIL
Ex 9:19 the h will fall on every man
Rev 8: 7 and there came h and fire mixed

HAIR (HAIRS HAIRY)
Lev	19:27	' 'Do not cut the h at the sides
Nu	6: 5	he must let the h of his head grow
Pr	16:31	Gray h is a crown of splendor;
	20:29	gray h the splendor of the old.
Lk	7:44	and wiped them with her h.
	21:18	But not a h of your head will perish
Jn	11: 2	and wiped his feet with her h.
	12: 3	and wiped his feet with her h.
1Co	11: 6	for a woman to have her h cut
	11: 6	she should have her h cut off;
	11:14	that if a man has long h,
	11:15	For long h is given to her
	11:15	but that if a woman has long h,
1Ti	2: 9	not with braided h or gold or pearls
1Pe	3: 3	as braided h and the wearing
Rev	1:14	and h were white like wool,

HAIRS (HAIR)
Mt 10:30 even the very h of your head are all
Lk 12: 7 the very h of your head are all

HAIRY (HAIR)
Ge 27:11 "But my brother Esau is a h man,

HALF
Ex	30:13	This h shekel is an offering
Jos	8:33	H of the people stood in front
1Ki	3:25	give h to one and h to the other."
	10: 7	Indeed, not even h was told me;
Est	5: 3	Even up to h the kingdom,
Da	7:25	him for a time, times and h a time.
Mk	6:23	up to h my kingdom."

HALF-TRIBE (TRIBE)
Nu 32:33 and the h of Manasseh son

HALLELUJAH*
Rev 19: 1 3, 4, 6.

HALLOWED* (HOLY)
Mt 6: 9 h be your name,
Lk 11: 2 h be your name,

HALT
Job 38:11 here is where your proud waves h'?

HALTER*
Pr 26: 3 for the horse, a h for the donkey,

HAM
Son of Noah (Ge 5:32; 1Ch 1:4), father of Canaan (Ge 9:18; 10:6-20; 1Ch 1:8-16). Saw Noah's nakedness (Ge 9:20-27).

HAMAN
Agagite nobleman honored by Xerxes (Est 3:1-2). Plotted to exterminate the Jews because of Mordecai (Est 3:3-15). Forced to honor Mordecai (Est 5-6). Plot exposed by Esther (Est 5:1-8; 7:1-8). Hanged (Est 7:9-10).

HAMPERED*
Pr 4:12 you walk, your steps will not be h;

HAND (HANDED HANDFUL HANDS OPENHANDED)
Ge	24: 2	"Put your h under my thigh.
	47:29	put your h under my thigh
Ex	13: 3	out of it with a mighty h.
	15: 6	Your right h, O LORD,
	33:22	and cover you with my h
Dt	7: 2	in everything you have put your h
1Ki	8:42	and your mighty h and your
	13: 4	But the h he stretched out
1Ch	29:14	you only what comes from your h.
	29:16	it comes from your h, and all
2Ch	6:15	with your h you have fulfilled it—
Ne	4:17	materials did their work with one h
Job	40: 4	I put my h over my mouth.
Ps	16: 8	Because he is at my right h,
	32: 4	your h was heavy upon me,
	37:24	the LORD upholds him with his h.
	44: 3	it was your right h, your arm,
	45: 9	at your right h is the royal bride
	63: 8	your right h upholds me.

Ps 75: 8 In the *h* of the LORD is a cup
91: 7 ten thousand at your right *h*,
98: 1 his right *h* and his holy arm
109: 31 at the right *h* of the needy one,
110: 1 "Sit at my right *h*
137: 5 may my right *h* forget its skill,
139: 10 even there your *h* will guide me,
145: 16 You open your *h*
Pr 27: 16 or grasping oil with the *h*.
Ecc 5: 15 that he can carry in his *h*.
9: 10 Whatever your *h* finds to do,
Isa 11: 8 the young child put his *h*
40: 12 the waters in the hollow of his *h*,
41: 13 who takes hold of your right *h*
44: 5 still another will write on his *h*,
48: 13 My own *h* laid the foundations
64: 8 we are all the work of your *h*.
La 3: 3 he has turned his *h* against me
Da 10: 10 *h* touched me and set me trembling
Jnh 4: 11 people who cannot tell their right *h*
Hab 3: 4 rays flashed from his *h*,
Mt 5: 30 if your right *h* causes you to sin,
6: 3 know what your right *h* is doing,
12: 10 a man with a shriveled *h* was there.
18: 8 If your *h* or your foot causes you
22: 44 "Sit at my right *h*
26: 64 at the right *h* of the Mighty One
Mk 3: 1 a man with a shriveled *h* was there.
9: 43 If your *h* causes you to sin, cut it off
12: 36 "Sit at my right *h*
16: 19 and he sat at the right *h* of God.
Lk 6: 6 there whose right *h* was shriveled.
20: 42 "Sit at my right *h*
22: 69 at the right *h* of the mighty God."
Jn 10: 28 one can snatch them out of my *h*.
20: 27 Reach out your *h* and put it
Ac 7: 55 Jesus standing at the right *h* of God
1Co 12: 15 I am not a *h*, I do not belong
Heb 1: 13 "Sit at my right *h*
Rev 13: 16 to receive a mark on his right *h*

HANDED (HAND)

Da 7: 25 The saints will be *h* over to him
1Ti 1: 20 whom I have *h* over to Satan

HANDFUL (HAND)

Ecc 4: 6 Better one *h* with tranquillity

HANDLE (HANDLES)

Col 2: 21 "Do not *h*! Do not taste! Do not

HANDLES (HANDLE)

2Ti 2: 15 who correctly *h* the word of truth.

HANDS (HAND)

Ge 27: 22 but the *h* are the *h* of Esau."
Ex 17: 11 As long as Moses held up his *h*,
29: 10 his sons shall lay their *h* on its head
Dt 8: 3 Tie them as symbols on your *h*
Jdg 7: 11 their right *h* to their mouths.
2Ki 11: 12 and the people clapped their *h*
2Ch 6: 4 who with his *h* has fulfilled what he
Ps 22: 16 they have pierced my *h*
24: 4 He who has clean *h* and a pure
31: 5 Into your *h* I commit my spirit;
31: 15 My times are in your *h*;
47: 1 Clap your *h*, all you nations;
63: 4 and in your name I will lift up my *h*
Pr 10: 4 Lazy *h* make a man poor,
21: 25 because his *h* refuse to work.
31: 13 and works with eager *h*.
31: 20 and extends her *h* to the needy
Ecc 10: 18 if his *h* are idle, the house leaks.
Isa 35: 3 Strengthen the feeble *h*,
49: 16 you on the palms of my *h*;
55: 12 will clap their *h*.
65: 2 All day long I have held out my *h*
La 3: 41 Let us lift our hearts and our *h*
Lk 23: 46 into your *h* I commit my spirit."
Ac 6: 6 who prayed and laid their *h*
8: 18 at the laying on of the apostles' *h*,
13: 3 they placed their *h* on them,
19: 6 When Paul placed his *h* on them,
28: 8 placed his *h* on him and healed him
1Th 4: 11 and to work with your *h*,
1Ti 2: 8 to lift up holy *h* in prayer.
4: 14 body of elders laid their *h* on you.
5: 22 hasty in the laying on of *h*,
2Ti 1: 6 you through the laying on of my *h*
Heb 6: 2 the laying on of *h*, the resurrection

HANDSOME*

Ge 39: 6 Now Joseph was well-built and *h*.
1Sa 16: 12 a fine appearance and *h* features.
17: 42 ruddy and *h*, and he despised him.

2Sa 14: 25 praised for his *h* appearance.
1Ki 1: 6 also very *h* and was born next
SS 1: 16 Beloved How *h* you are, my lover!
Eze 23: 6 all of them *h* young men,
23: 12 horsemen, all *h* young men.
23: 23 with them, *h* young men,
Da 1: 4 without any physical defect, *h*,
Zec 11: 13 the *h* price at which they priced me

HANG (HANGED HANGING HUNG)

Mt 22: 40 and the Prophets *h* on these two

HANGED (HANG)

Mt 27: 5 Then he went away and *h* himself.

HANGING (HANG)

Ac 10: 39 They killed him by *h* him on a tree.

HANNAH*

Wife of Elkanah, mother of Samuel (1Sa 1).
Prayer at dedication of Samuel (1Sa 2:1-10).
Blessed (1Sa 2:18-21).

HAPPIER (HAPPY)

Mt 18: 13 he is *h* about that one sheep
1Co 7: 40 she is *h* if she stays as she is—

HAPPINESS* (HAPPY)

Dt 24: 5 bring *h* to the wife he has married.
Est 8: 16 For the Jews it was a time of *h*
Job 7: 7 my eyes will never see *h* again.
Ecc 2: 26 gives wisdom, knowledge and *h*,
Mt 25: 21 Come and share your master's *h*!'
25: 23 Come and share your master's *h*!'

HAPPY* (HAPPIER HAPPINESS)

Ge 30: 13 The women will call me *h*."
30: 13 Then Leah said, "How *h* I am!"
1Ki 4: 20 they drank and they were *h*.
10: 8 How *h* your men must be!
10: 8 men must be! How *h* your officials,
2Ch 9: 7 How *h* your men must be!
9: 7 men must be! How *h* your officials,
Est 5: 9 Haman went out that day *h*
5: 14 the king to the dinner and be *h*."
Ps 10: 6 I'll always be *h* and never have
68: 3 may they be *h* and joyful,
113: 9 as a *h* mother of children.
137: 8 his he who repays you
Pr 15: 13 A heart makes the face cheerful,
Ecc 3: 12 better for men than to be *h*
5: 19 to accept his lot and be *h*
7: 14 When times are good, be *h*;
11: 9 Be *h*, young man, while you are
Jnh 4: 6 Jonah was very *h* about the vine.
Zec 8: 19 and glad occasions and *h* festivals
1Co 7: 30 those who are *h*, as if they were not
2Co 7: 9 yet now I am *h*, not because you
7: 13 delighted to see how *h* Titus was,
Jas 5: 13 Is anyone *h*? Let him sing songs

HARD (HARDEN HARDENED HARDENING HARDENS HARDER HARDSHIP HARDSHIPS)

Ge 18: 14 Is anything too *h* for the LORD?
1Ki 10: 1 came to test him with *h* questions.
Pr 14: 23 All *h* work brings a profit,
Jer 32: 17 Nothing is too *h* for you.
Zec 7: 12 They made their hearts as *h* as flint
Mt 19: 23 it is *h* for a rich man
Mk 10: 5 your hearts were *h* that Moses
Jn 6: 60 disciples said, "This is a *h* teaching.
Ac 20: 35 of *h* work we must help the weak,
26: 14 It is *h* for you to kick
Ro 16: 12 woman who has worked very *h*
1Co 4: 12 We work *h* with our own hands.
2Co 6: 5 imprisonments and riots; in *h* work
1Th 5: 12 to respect those who work *h*
Rev 2: 2 your *h* work and your

HARDEN (HARD)

Ex 4: 21 I will *h* his heart so that he will not
Ps 95: 8 do not *h* your hearts as you did
Ro 9: 18 he hardens whom he wants to *h*.
Heb 3: 8 do not *h* your hearts

HARDENED (HARD)

Ex 10: 20 But the LORD *h* Pharaoh's heart,

HARDENING* (HARD)

Ro 11: 25 Israel has experienced a *h* in part
Eph 4: 18 in them due to the *h* of their hearts.

HARDENS* (HARD)

Pr 28: 14 he who *h* his heart falls into trouble

Ro 9: 18 and he *h* whom he wants to harden.

HARDER (HARD)

1Co 15: 10 No, I worked *h* than all of them—
2Co 11: 23 I have worked much *h*, been

HARDHEARTED* (HEART)

Dt 15: 7 do not be *h* or tightfisted

HARDSHIP (HARD)

Ro 8: 35 Shall trouble or *h* or persecution
2Ti 2: 3 Endure *h* with us like a good
4: 5 endure *h*, do the work
Heb 12: 7 Endure *h* as discipline; God is

HARDSHIPS (HARD)

Ac 14: 22 go through many *h* to enter
2Co 6: 4 in troubles, *h* and distresses;
12: 10 in insults, in *h*, in persecutions,
Rev 2: 3 and have endured *h* for my name,

HARLOT see PROSTITUTE

HARM (HARMS)

1Ch 16: 22 do my prophets no *h*."
Ps 105: 15 do my prophets no *h*."
121: 6 the sun will not *h* you by day,
Pr 3: 29 not plot *h* against your neighbor,
12: 21 No *h* befalls the righteous,
31: 12 She brings him good, not *h*,
Jer 5: 3 they can do no *h*
29: 11 to prosper you and not to *h* you,
Ro 13: 10 Love does no *h* to its neighbor.
1Co 11: 17 for your meetings do more *h*
1Jn 5: 18 the evil one cannot *h* him.

HARMONY*

Zec 6: 13 there will be *h* between the two.
Ro 12: 16 Live in *h* with one another.
2Co 6: 15 What *h* is there between Christ
1Pe 3: 8 live in *h* with one another;

HARMS* (HARM)

Pr 8: 36 whoever fails to find me *h* himself;

HARP (HARPS)

Ge 4: 21 the father of all who play the *h*
1Sa 16: 23 David would take his *h* and play.
Ps 33: 2 Praise the LORD with the *h*;
98: 5 with the hand the sound of singing
150: 3 praise him with the *h* and lyre,
Rev 5: 8 Each one had a *h* and they were

HARPS (HARP)

Ps 137: 2 we hung our *h*,

HARSH

Pr 15: 1 but a *h* word stirs up anger.
Col 2: 23 and their *h* treatment of the body,
3: 19 and do not be *h* with them.
1Pe 2: 18 but also to those who are *h*.
Jude 15 of all the *h* words ungodly sinners

HARVEST (HARVESTERS)

Ge 8: 22 seedtime and *h*,
Ex 23: 16 the Feast of *H* with the firstfruits
Dt 16: 15 God will bless you in all your *h*
Pr 10: 5 during his a disgraceful son.
Joel 3: 13 for the *h* is ripe.
Mt 9: 37 his plentiful but the workers are
Lk 10: 2 He told them, "The *h* is plentiful,
Jn 4: 35 at the fields! They are ripe for *h*.
1Co 9: 11 if we reap a material *h* from you?
2Co 9: 10 the *h* of your righteousness.
Gal 6: 9 at the proper time we will reap a *h*
Heb 12: 11 it produces a *h* of righteousness
Jas 3: 18 in peace raise a *h* of righteousness.
Rev 14: 15 for the *h* of the earth is ripe."

HARVESTERS (HARVEST)

Ru 2: 3 to glean in the fields behind the *h*.

HASTE (HASTEN HASTY)

Ex 12: 11 it in *h*, it is the LORD's Passover.
Pr 21: 5 as surely as *h* leads to poverty.
29: 20 Do you see a man who speaks in *h*?

HASTEN (HASTE)

Ps 70: 1 H, O God, to save me;
119: 60 I will *h* and not delay

HASTY* (HASTE)

Pr 19: 2 nor to be *h* and miss the way.
Ecc 5: 2 do not be *h* in your heart

1Ti 5:22 Do not be *h* in the laying

HATE (GOD-HATERS HATED HATES HATING HATRED)

Lev 19:17 " 'Do not *h* your brother
Ps 5: 5 you *h* all who do wrong.
    36: 2 too much to detect or *h* his sin.
    45: 7 righteousness and *h* wickedness;
    97:10 those who love the LORD *h* evil,
   119:104 therefore I *h* every wrong path
   119:163 I *h* and abhor falsehood
   139:21 Do I not *h* those who *h* you,
Pr 8:13 To fear the LORD is to *h* evil;
    9: 8 rebuke a mocker or he will *h* you;
    13: 5 The righteous *h* what is false,
    25:17 too much of you, and he will *h* you.
    29:10 Bloodthirsty men *h* a man
Ecc 3: 8 a time to love and a time to *h*,
Isa 61: 8 I *h* robbery and iniquity.
Eze 35: 6 Since you did not *h* bloodshed,
Am 5:15 *H* evil, love good;
Mal 2:16 "I *h* divorce," says the LORD God
Mt 5:43 your neighbor and *h* your enemy.'
    10:22 All men will *h* you because of me,
Lk 6:22 Blessed are you when men *h* you,
    6:27 do good to those who *h* you,
    14:26 does not *h* his father and mother,
Ro 12: 9 *H* what is evil; cling to what is good

HATED (HATE)

Mal 1: 3 loved Jacob, but Esau I have *h*,
Jn 15:18 keep in mind that it *h* me first.
Ro 9:13 "Jacob I loved, but Esau I *h*."
Eph 5:29 no one ever *h* his own body,
Heb 1: 9 righteousness and *h* wickedness;

HATES (HATE)

Pr 6:16 There are six things the LORD *h*,
    13:24 He who spares the rod *h* his son,
    15:27 but he who *h* bribes will live.
    26:28 A lying tongue *h* those it hurts,
Jn 3:20 Everyone who does evil *h* the light,
    12:25 while the man who *h* his life
1Jn 2: 9 *h* his brother is still in the darkness.
    4:20 "I love God," yet *h* his brother,

HATING (HATE)

Jude :23 *h* even the clothing stained

HATRED (HATE)

Pr 10:12 *H* stirs up dissension,
    15:17 than a fattened calf with *h*.
Jas 4: 4 with the world is *h* toward God?

HAUGHTY

Pr 6:17 detestable to him: / *h* eyes,
    16:18 a *h* spirit before a fall.

HAVEN

Ps 107:30 he guided them to their desired *h*.

HAY

1Co 3:12 costly stones, wood, *h* or straw,

HEAD (HEADS HOTHEADED)

Ge 3:15 he will crush your *h*,
Nu 5: no razor may be used on his *h*.
Jdg 16:17 If my *h* were shaved, my strength
1Sa 9: 2 a *h* taller than any of the others.
2Sa 18: 9 Absalom's *h* got caught in the tree.
Ps 23: 5 You anoint my *h* with oil;
   133: 2 is like precious oil poured on the *h*,
Pr 10: 6 Blessings crown the *h*
    25:22 will heap burning coals on his *h*,
Isa 59:17 and the helmet of salvation on his *h*
Eze 33: 4 his blood will be on his own *h*.
Mt 8:20 of Man has no place to lay his *h*."
Jn 19: 2 crown of thorns and put it on his *h*."
Ro 12:20 will heap burning coals on his *h*."
1Co 11: 3 and the *h* of Christ is God.
    11: 5 her *h* uncovered dishonors her *h*—
    11: 5 her *h* cannot say to the feet,
Eph 1:22 him to be *h* over everything
    5:23 For the husband is the *h* of the wife
Col 1:18 And he is the *h* of the body,
2Ti 4: 5 keep your *h* in all situations,
Rev 14:14 with a crown of gold on his *h*
    19:12 and on his *h* are many crowns.

HEADS (HEAD)

Lev 26:13 you to walk with *h* held high.
Ps 22: 7 they hurl insults, shaking their *h*;
    24: 7 Lift up your *h*, O you gates;
Isa 35:10 everlasting joy will crown their *h*.
    51:11 everlasting joy will crown their *h*.

Mt 27:39 shaking their *h* and saying,
Lk 21:28 stand up and lift up your *h*,
Ac 18: 6 "Your blood be on your own *h*!
Rev 4: 4 and had crowns of gold on their *h*.

HEAL* (HEALED HEALING HEALS)

Nu 12:13 please *h* her!" The LORD replied
Dt 32:39 I have wounded and I will *h*,
2Ki 20: 5 and seen your tears; I will *h* you.
    20: 8 the sign that the LORD will *h* me
2Ch 7:14 their sin and will *h* their land.
Job 5:18 he injures, but his hands also *h*.
Ps 6: 2 *h* me, for my bones are in agony.
    41: 4 *h* me, for I have sinned against you
Ecc 3: 3 a time to kill and a time to *h*,
Isa 19:22 he will strike them and *h* them.
    19:22 respond to their pleas and *h* them.
    57:18 seen his ways, but I will *h* him;
    57:19 "And I will *h* them."
Jer 17:14 *H* me, O LORD, and I will be
    30:17 and *h* your wounds,'
    33: 6 I will *h* my people and will let them
La 2:13 Who can *h* you?
Hos 5:13 not able to *h* your sores.
    6: 1 but he will *h* us;
    7: 1 whenever I would *h* Israel,
    14: 4 "I will *h* their waywardness
Na 3:19 Nothing can *h* your wound;
Zec 11:16 or seek the young, or *h* the injured,
Mt 8: 7 said to him, "I will go and *h* him."
    10: 1 to *h* every disease and sickness.
    10: 8 *H* the sick, raise the dead,
    12:10 "Is it lawful to *h* on the Sabbath?"
    13:15 and turn, and I would *h* them."
    17:16 but they could not *h* him."
Mk 3: 2 if he would *h* him on the Sabbath.
    5: on a few sick people and *h* them.
Lk 4:23 to me: 'Physician, *h* yourself!
    5:17 present for him to *h* the sick.
    6: 7 to see if he would *h* on the Sabbath.
    7: 3 him to come and *h* his servant.
    8:43 years, but no one could *h* her.
    9: 2 kingdom of God and to *h* the sick.
    10: 9 *H* the sick who are there
    13:32 and *h* people today and tomorrow,
    14: 3 "Is it lawful to *h* on the Sabbath
Jn 4:47 begged him to come and *h* his son,
    12:40 nor turn—and I would *h* them."
Ac 4:30 Stretch out your hand to *h*
    28:27 and turn, and I would *h* them.'

HEALED* (HEAL)

Ge 20:17 to God, and God *h* Abimelech,
Ex 21:19 and see that he is completely *h*.
Lev 13:37 hair has grown in it, the itch is *h*.
    14: 3 If the person has been *h*
Jos 5: 8 were in camp until they were *h*.
1Sa 6: 3 you will be *h*, and you will know
2Ki 2:21 LORD says: 'I have *h* this water.
2Ch 30:20 heard Hezekiah and *h* the people.
Ps 30: 2 and you *h* me,
   107:20 He sent forth his word and *h* them;
Isa 6:10 and turn and be *h*."
    53: 5 and by his wounds we are *h*.
Jer 14:19 us so that we cannot be *h*?
    17:14 Heal me, O LORD, and I will be *h*;
    51: 8 perhaps she can be *h*.
    51: 9 but she cannot be *h*;
    51: 9 " 'We would have *h* Babylon,
Eze 34: 4 the weak or *h* the sick
Hos 11: 3 it was I who *h* them.
Mt 4:24 the paralyzed, and he *h* them.
    8: 8 the word, and my servant will be *h*.
    8:13 his servant was *h* at that very hour.
    8:16 with a word and *h* all the sick.
    9:21 If I only touch his cloak, I will be *h*."
    9:22 he said, "your faith has *h* you."
    9:22 woman was *h* from that moment.
    12:15 him, and he *h* all their sick,
    12:22 Jesus *h* him, so that he could both
    14:14 on them and *h* their sick.
    14:36 and all who touched him were *h*.
    15:28 And her daughter was *h*
    15:30 laid them at his feet; and he *h* them.
    17:18 and he was *h* from that moment.
    19: 2 followed him, and he *h* them there.
    21:14 to him at the temple, and he *h* them
Mk 1:34 and Jesus *h* many who had various
    3:10 For he had *h* many, so that those
    5:23 hands on her so that she will be *h*
    5:28 If I just touch his clothes, I will be *h*."
    5:34 "Daughter, your faith has *h* you.
    6:13 people with oil and *h* them.
    6:56 and all who touched him were *h*.
    10:52 said Jesus, "your faith has *h* you."

Lk 4:40 hands on each one, he *h* them.
    5:15 and to be *h* of their sicknesses
    6:18 and to be *h* of their diseases
    7: 7 the word, and my servant will be *h*.
    8:47 and how she had been instantly *h*.
    8:48 "Daughter, your faith has *h* you.
    8:50 just believe, and she will be *h*."
    9:11 and *h* those who needed healing.
    9:42 the boy and gave him back
    13:14 Jesus had *h* on the Sabbath.
    13:14 So come and be *h* on those days.
    14: 4 he *h* him and sent him away.
    17:15 when he saw he was *h*, came back,
    18:42 your sight; your faith has *h* you."
    22:51 touched the man's ear and *h* him.
Jn 5:10 said to the man who had been *h*,
    5:13 man who was *h* had no idea who it
Ac 4:10 and are asked how he was *h*.
    4:10 stands before you *h*.
    4:14 who had been *h* standing there
    4:22 man who was miraculously *h* was
    5:16 evil spirits, and all of them were *h*.
    8: 7 paralytics and cripples were *h*.
    14: 9 saw that he had faith to be *h*
    28: 8 placed his hands on him and *h* him.
Heb 12:13 may not be disabled, but rather *h*.
Jas 5:16 for each other so that you may be *h*.
1Pe 2:24 by his wounds you have been *h*.
Rev 13: 3 but the fatal wound had been *h*,
    13:12 whose fatal wound had been *h*.

HEALING* (HEAL)

2Ch 28:15 food and drink, and *h* balm.
Pr 12:18 but the tongue of the wise brings *h*.
    13:17 but a trustworthy envoy brings *h*.
    15: 4 The tongue that brings *h* is a tree
    16:24 sweet to the soul and *h* to the bones
Isa 58: 8 and your *h* will quickly appear;
Jer 8:15 for a time of *h*
    8:22 Why then is there no *h*
    14:19 for a time of *h*
    30:12 your injury beyond *h*.
    30:13 no *h* for you.
    33: 6 I will bring health and *h* to it;
    46:11 there is no *h* for you.
Eze 30:21 It has not been bound up for *h*
    47:12 for food and their leaves for *h*."
Mal 4: 2 rise with *h* in its wings.
Mt 4:23 and *h* every disease and sickness
    9:35 and *h* every disease and sickness.
Lk 6:19 coming from him and *h* them all.
    9: 6 gospel and *h* people everywhere.
    9:11 and healed those who needed *h*.
Jn 7:23 angry with me for *h* the whole man
Ac 3:16 him that has given this complete *h*
    10:38 *h* all who were under the power
1Co 12: 9 to another gifts of *h*
    12:28 also those having gifts of *h*,
    12:30 Do all have gifts of *h*? Do all speak
Rev 22: 2 are for the *h* of the nations.

HEALS* (HEAL)

Ex 15:26 for I am the LORD, who *h* you."
Lev 13:18 a boil on his skin and it *h*,
Ps 103: 3 and *h* all your diseases;
   147: 3 He *h* the brokenhearted
Isa 30:26 and *h* the wounds he inflicted.
Ac 9:34 said to him, "Jesus Christ *h* you.

HEALTH* (HEALTHIER HEALTHY)

1Sa 25: 6 And good *h* to all that is yours!
    25: 6 Good *h* to you and your household
Ps 38: 3 of your wrath there is no *h*
    38: 7 there is no *h* in my body.
Pr 3: 8 This will bring *h* to your body
    4:22 and *h* to a man's whole body.
    15:30 and good news gives *h* to the bones
Isa 38:16 You restored me to *h*
Jer 30:17 But I will restore you to *h*
    33: 6 I will bring *h* and healing to it;
3Jn : 2 I pray that you may enjoy good *h*

HEALTHIER* (HEALTH)

Da 1:15 end of the ten days they looked *h*

HEALTHY* (HEALTH)

Ge 41: 5 Seven heads of grain, *h* and good,
    41: 7 of grain swallowed up the seven *h*,
Ps 73: 4 their bodies are *h* and strong.
Zec 11:16 or heal the injured, or feed the *h*,
Mt 9:12 "It is not the *h* who need a doctor,
Mk 2:17 "It is not the *h* who need a doctor,
Lk 5:31 "It is not the *h* who need a doctor,

HEAP

Pr 25:22 you will *h* burning coals
Ro 12:20 you will *h* burning coals

HEAR (HEARD HEARING HEARS)

Ex 15:14 The nations will *h* and tremble;
22:27 I will *h*, for I am compassionate.
Nu 14:13 Then the Egyptians will *h* about it!
Dt 1:16 *H* the disputes between your
4:36 heaven he made you *h* his voice
6:4 *H*, O Israel: The LORD our God,
19:20 The rest of the people will *h* of this
31:13 must *h* it and learn
Jos 7:9 of the country will *h* about this
1Ki 8:30 *H* the supplication of your servant
2Ki 19:16 O LORD, and *h*; open your eyes,
2Ch 7:14 then will I *h* from heaven
Job 31:35 ("Oh, that I had someone to *h* me!
Ps 94:9 he who implanted the ear not *h*?
95:7 Today, if you *h* his voice,
Ecc 7:21 or you may *h* your servant cursing
Isa 21:3 I am staggered by what I *h*,
29:18 that day the deaf will *h* the words
30:21 your ears will *h* a voice behind you,
51:7 *H* me, you who know what is right,
59:1 nor his ear too dull to *h*.
65:24 while they are still speaking I will *h*
Jer 5:21 who have ears but do not *h*:
Eze 33:7 so *h* the word I speak and give
37:4 'Dry bones, *h* the word
Mt 11:5 the deaf *h*, the dead are raised,
11:15 He who has ears, let him *h*.
13:17 and to *h* what you *h* but did not *h* it
Mk 12:29 answered Jesus, "is this: '*H*,
Lk 7:22 the deaf *h*, the dead are raised,
Jn 8:47 reason you do not *h* is that you do
Ac 13:7 he wanted to *h* the word of God.
13:44 gathered to *h* the word of the Lord.
17:32 "We want to *h* you again
Ro 2:13 is not those who *h* the law who are
10:14 they *h* without someone preaching
2Ti 4:3 what their itching ears want to *h*.
Heb 3:7 "Today, if you *h* his voice,
Rev 1:3 and blessed are those who *h* it

HEARD (HEAR)

Ex 2:24 God *h* their groaning and he
Dt 4:32 has anything like it ever been *h* of?
2Sa 7:22 as we have *h* with our own ears.
Job 42:5 My ears had *h* of you
Isa 40:21 Have you not *h*?
40:28 Have you not *h*?
66:8 Who has ever *h* of such a thing?
Jer 18:13 Who has ever *h* anything like this?
Da 10:12 your words were *h*, and I have
12:8 I *h*, but I did not understand.
Hab 3:16 I *h* and my heart pounded,
Mt 5:21 "You have *h* that it was said
5:27 "You have *h* that it was said,
5:33 you have *h* that it was said
5:38 "You have *h* that it was said,
5:43 "You have *h* that it was said,
Lk 12:3 in the dark will be *h* in the daylight,
Jn 8:26 and what I have *h* from him I tell
Ac 2:6 because each one *h* them speaking
1Co 2:9 no ear has *h*,
2Co 12:4 He *h* inexpressible things,
1Th 2:13 word of God, which you *h* from us,
2Ti 1:13 What you *h* from me, keep
Jas 1:25 not forgetting what he has *h*,
Rev 22:8 am the one who *h* and saw these

HEARING (HEAR)

Isa 6:9 Be ever *h*, but never understanding
Mt 13:14 will be ever *h* but never
Mk 4:12 ever *h* but never understanding;
Ac 28:26 will be ever *h* but never
Ro 10:17 faith comes from *h* the message,
1Co 12:17 where would the sense of *h* be?

HEARS (HEAR)

Jn 5:24 whoever *h* my word and believes
1Jn 5:14 according to his will, he *h* us.
Rev 3:20 If anyone *h* my voice and opens

HEART (BROKENHEARTED FAINT-HEARTED HARDHEARTED HEART'S HEARTACHE HEARTS KINDHEARTED SIMPLEHEARTED STOUTHEARTED WHOLEHEARTED WHOLEHEARTEDLY)

Ge 6:5 of his *h* was only evil all the time.
Ex 4:21 But I will harden his *h*
25:2 each man whose *h* prompts him
35:21 and whose *h* moved him came
Lev 19:17 Do not hate your brother in your *h*.
Dt 4:9 or let them slip from your *h* as long
4:29 if you look for him with all your *h*
6:5 LORD your God with all your *h*
10:12 LORD your God with all your *h*
11:13 and to serve him with all your *h*
13:3 you love him with all your *h*
15:10 and do so without a grudging *h*;
26:16 observe them with all your *h*
29:18 you today whose *h* turns away
30:2 and obey him with all your *h*
30:6 you may love him with all your *h*
30:10 LORD your God with all your *h*
Jos 22:5 and to serve him with all your *h*
23:14 You know with all your *h*
1Sa 10:9 God changed Saul's *h*,
12:20 serve the LORD with all your *h*.
12:24 serve him faithfully with all your *h*;
13:14 sought out a man after his own *h*
14:7 I am with you *h* and soul."
16:7 but the LORD looks at the *h*."
17:32 "Let no one lose *h* on account
1Ki 2:4 faithfully before me with all their *h*
3:9 So give your servant a discerning *h*
3:12 give you a wise and discerning *h*,
8:48 back to you with all their *h*
9:3 and my *h* will always be there.
9:4 walk before me in integrity of *h*
10:24 the wisdom God had put in his *h*.
11:4 and his *h* was not fully devoted
14:8 and followed me with all his *h*,
15:14 Asa's *h* was fully committed
2Ki 22:19 Because your *h* was responsive
23:3 with all his *h* and all his soul,
1Ch 28:9 for the LORD searches every *h*
2Ch 6:38 back to you with all their *h*
7:16 and my *h* will always be there.
15:12 of their fathers, with all their *h*
15:17 Asa's *h* was fully committed
17:6 His *h* was devoted to the ways
22:9 sought the LORD with all his *h*."
34:31 with all his *h* and all his soul,
36:13 stiff-necked and hardened his *h*
Ezr 1:5 everyone whose *h* God had moved
Ne 4:6 the people worked with all their *h*.
Job 19:27 How my *h* yearns within me!
22:22 and lay up his words in your *h*.
37:1 "At this my *h* pounds
Ps 9:1 you, O LORD, with all my *h*;
14:1 The fool says in his *h*,
16:9 Therefore my *h* is glad
19:14 and the meditation of my *h*
20:4 he give you the desire of your *h*
24:4 who has clean hands and a pure *h*,
26:2 examine my *h* and my mind;
37:4 will give you the desires of your *h*.
37:31 The law of his God is in his *h*;
44:21 since he knows the secrets of the *h*
45:1 My *h* is stirred by a noble theme
51:10 Create in me a pure *h*, O God,
51:17 a broken and contrite *h*,
53:1 The fool says in his *h*,
66:18 If I had cherished sin in my *h*,
73:1 to those who are pure in *h*.
73:26 My flesh and my *h* may fail,
86:11 give me an undivided *h*,
90:12 that we may gain a *h* of wisdom.
97:11 and joy on the upright in *h*.
108:1 My *h* is steadfast, O God;
109:22 and my *h* is wounded within me.
111:1 I will extol the LORD with all my *h*
112:7 his *h* is steadfast, trusting
112:8 His *h* is secure, he will have no fear
119:2 and seek him with all their *h*.
119:10 I seek you with all my *h*;
119:11 I have hidden your word in my *h*
119:30 I have set my *h* on your laws.
119:32 for you have set my *h* free.
119:34 and obey it with all my *h*.
119:36 Turn my *h* toward your statutes
119:58 sought your face with all my *h*;
119:69 I keep your precepts with all my *h*.
119:111 they are the joy of my *h*.
119:112 My *h* is set on keeping your
119:145 I call with all my *h*; answer me,
125:4 to those who are upright in *h*.
138:1 you, O LORD, with all my *h*;
139:23 Search me, O God, and know my *h*
Pr 2:2 applying your *h* to understanding,
3:1 but keep my commands in your *h*,
3:3 write them on the tablet of your *h*.
3:5 Trust in the LORD with all your *h*
4:4 hold of my words with all your *h*;
4:21 keep them within your *h*;
4:23 Above all else, guard your *h*,
Pr 6:21 Bind them upon your *h* forever;
7:3 write them on the tablet of your *h*.
10:8 The wise in *h* accept commands,
13:12 Hope deferred makes the *h* sick,
14:13 Even in laughter the *h* may ache,
14:30 A *h* at peace gives life to the body,
15:13 A happy *h* makes the face cheerful,
15:15 the cheerful *h* has a continual feast.
15:28 *h* of the righteous weighs its
15:30 A cheerful look brings joy to the *h*,
16:23 A wise man's *h* guides his mouth,
17:22 A cheerful *h* is good medicine,
20:9 can say, "I have kept my *h* pure;
22:11 He who loves a pure *h*
22:17 apply your *h* to what I teach,
22:18 when you keep them in your *h*
23:15 My son, if your *h* is wise,
23:19 and keep your *h* on the right path.
23:26 My son, give me your *h*
24:17 stumbles, do not let your *h* rejoice,
27:19 so a man's *h* reflects the man.
Ecc 5:2 do not be hasty in your *h*
8:5 wise *h* will know the proper time
11:10 banish anxiety from your *h*
SS 3:1 I looked for the one my *h* loves;
4:9 You have stolen my *h*, my sister,
5:2 *Beloved* I slept but my *h* was awake
5:4 my *h* began to pound for him.
8:6 Place me like a seal over your *h*,
Isa 6:10 Make the *h* of this people calloused
40:11 and carries them close to his *h*;
57:15 and to revive the *h* of the contrite.
66:14 you see this, your *h* will rejoice
Jer 3:15 give you shepherds after my own *h*,
4:14 wash the evil from your *h*
9:26 of Israel is uncircumcised in *h*."
17:9 The *h* is deceitful above all things
20:9 is in my *h* like a fire,
24:7 I will give them a *h* to know me,
29:13 when you seek me with all your *h*.
32:39 I will give them singleness of *h*
32:41 them in this land with all my *h*
51:46 Do not lose *h* or be afraid
Eze 11:19 I will give them an undivided *h*
18:31 and get a new *h* and a new spirit.
36:26 I will give you a new *h*
44:7 foreigners uncircumcised in *h*
Da 7:4 and the *h* of a man was given to it.
Joel 2:12 "return to me with all your *h*,
2:13 Rend your *h*
Zep 3:14 Be glad and rejoice with all your *h*,
Mt 5:8 Blessed are the pure in *h*,
5:28 adultery with her in his *h*.
6:21 treasure is, there your *h* will be
11:29 for I am gentle and humble in *h*,
12:34 of the *h* the mouth speaks.
13:15 For this people's *h* has become
15:18 out of the mouth come from the *h*,
15:19 For out of the *h* come evil thoughts
18:35 forgive your brother from your *h*."
22:37 the Lord your God with all your *h*
Mk 11:23 and does not doubt in his *h*
12:30 the Lord your God with all your *h*
12:33 To love him with all your *h*,
Lk 2:19 and pondered them in her *h*.
2:51 treasured all these things in her *h*.
6:45 out of the good stored up in his *h*,
6:45 overflow of his *h* his mouth speaks.
8:15 for those with a noble and good *h*,
10:27 the Lord your God with all your *h*
12:34 treasure is, there your *h* will be
Jn 12:27 "Now my *h* is troubled,
Ac 1:24 "Lord, you know everyone's *h*.
2:37 they were cut to the *h*
4:32 All the believers were one in *h*
8:21 your *h* is not right before God.
15:8 who knows the *h*, showed that he
16:14 The Lord opened her *h* to respond
28:27 For this people's *h* has become
Ro 1:9 with my whole *h* in preaching
2:29 is circumcision of the *h*,
10:9 in your *h* that God raised him
10:10 is with your *h* that you believe
15:6 with one *h* and mouth you may
1Co 14:25 the secrets of his *h* will be laid bare.
2Co 2:4 anguish of *h* and with many tears,
4:1 this ministry, we do not lose *h*.
4:16 Therefore we do not lose *h*.
9:7 give what he has decided in his *h*.
Eph 1:18 eyes of your *h* may be enlightened
5:19 make music in your *h* to the Lord,
6:5 and with sincerity of *h*, just
6:6 doing the will of God from your *h*.
Php 1:7 since I have you in my *h*; for
Col 2:2 is that they may be encouraged in *h*

Col 3:22 but with sincerity of *h*
3:23 work at it with all your *h*,
1Ti 1: 5 which comes from a pure *h*
3: 1 If anyone sets his *h*
2Ti 2:22 call on the Lord out of a pure *h*.
Phm :12 who is my very *h*—back to you.
:20 in the Lord; refresh my *h* in Christ.
Heb 4:12 the thoughts and attitudes of the *h*,
1Pe 1:22 one another deeply, from the *h*.

HEART'S* (HEART)

2Ch 1:11 "Since this is your *h* desire
Jer 15:16 they were my joy and my *h* delight,
Eze 24:25 delight of their eyes, their *h* desire,
Ro 10: 1 my *h* desire and prayer to God

HEARTACHE* (HEART)

Pr 15:13 but *h* crushes the spirit.

HEARTLESS*

La 4: 3 but my people have become *h*
Ro 1:31 they are senseless, faithless, *h*,

HEARTS (HEART)

Lev 26:41 their uncircumcised *h* are humbled
Dt 6: 6 are to be upon your *h*.
10:16 Circumcise your *h*, therefore,
11:18 Fix these words of mine in your *h*
30: 6 your God will circumcise your *h*
Jos 11:20 himself who hardened their *h*
24:23 and yield your *h* to the LORD,
1Sa 7: 3 to the LORD with all your *h*,
10:26 valiant men whose *h* God had
2Sa 15: 6 and so he stole the *h* of the men
1Ki 8:39 for you alone know the *h* of all men
8:61 your *h* must be fully committed
18:37 are turning their *h* back again."
1Ch 29:18 and keep their *h* loyal to you.
2Ch 6:30 (for you alone know the *h* of men),
11:16 tribe of Israel who set their *h*
29:31 all whose *h* were willing brought
Ps 7: 9 who searches minds and *h*,
33:21 In him our *h* rejoice,
62: 8 pour out your *h* to him,
95: 8 do not harden your *h* as you did
Ecc 3:11 also set eternity in the *h* of men;
Isa 26: 8 are the desire of our *h*.
29:13 but their *h* are far from me.
35: 4 say to those with fearful *h*,
51: 7 people who have my law in your *h*:
63:17 harden our *h* so we do not revere
65:14 out of the joy of their *h*,
Jer 4: 4 circumcise your *h*,
12: 2 but far from their *h*.
17: 1 on the tablets of their *h*
31:33 and write it on their *h*.
Mal 4: 6 He will turn the *h* of the fathers
Mt 15: 8 but their *h* are far from me.
Mk 6:52 the loaves; their *h* were hardened.
7: 6 but their *h* are far from me.
7:21 out of men's *h*, come evil thoughts,
Lk 1:17 to turn the *h* of the fathers
16:15 of men, but God knows your *h*.
24:32 "Were not our *h* burning within us
Jn 5:42 not have the love of God in your *h*.
14: 1 "Do not let your *h* be troubled
14:27 Do not let your *h* be troubled
Ac 7:51 with uncircumcised *h* and ears!
11:23 true to the Lord with all their *h*.
15: 9 for he purified their *h* by faith.
28:27 understand with their *h*
Ro 1:21 and their foolish *h* were darkened.
2:15 of the law are written on their *h*,
5: 5 love into our *h* by the Holy Spirit,
8:27 who searches our *h* knows
1Co 4: 5 will expose the motives of men's *h*.
2Co 1:22 his Spirit in our *h* as a deposit,
3: 2 written on our *h*, known
3: 3 but on tablets of human *h*.
4: 6 shine in our *h* to give us the light
6:11 and opened wide our *h* to you.
6:13 my children—open wide your *h*
7: 2 Make room for us in your *h*.
Gal 4: 6 the Spirit of his Son into our *h*,
Eph 3:17 dwell in your *h* through faith.
Php 4: 7 will guard your *h* and your minds
Col 3: 1 set your *h* on things above,
3:15 the peace of Christ rule in your *h*,
3:16 with gratitude in your *h* to God.
1Th 2: 4 men but God, who tests our *h*.
3:13 May he strengthen your *h*
2Th 2:17 encourage your *h* and strengthen
Phm : 7 have refreshed the *h* of the saints.
Heb 3: 8 do not harden your *h*
8:10 and write them on their *h*.

Heb 10:16 I will put my laws in their *h*,
10:22 having our *h* sprinkled
Jas 4: 8 purify your *h*, you double-minded.
2Pe 1:19 the morning star rises in your *h*.
1Jn 3:20 For God is greater than our *h*,

HEAT

Ps 19: 6 nothing is hidden from its *h*.
2Pe 3:12 and the elements will melt in the *h*.

HEATHEN see GENTILES, NATIONS

HEAVEN (HEAVENLY HEAVENS HEAVENWARD)

Ge 14:19 Creator of *h* and earth.
28:12 with its top reaching to *h*,
Ex 16: 4 rain down bread from *h* for you.
20:22 that I have spoken to you from *h*:
Dt 26:15 from *h*, your holy dwelling place,
30:12 "Who will ascend into *h* to get it
1Ki 8:27 the highest *h*, cannot contain you.
8:30 Hear from *h*, your dwelling place,
22:19 the host of *h* standing around him
2Ki 2: 1 up to *h* in a whirlwind,
19:15 You have made *h* and earth.
2Ch 7:14 then will I hear from *h*
Isa 14:12 How you have fallen from *h*,
66: 1 "His my throne,
Da 7:13 coming with the clouds of *h*.
Mt 3: 2 for the kingdom of *his* near."
3:16 At that moment *h* was opened,
4:17 for the kingdom of *his* near."
5:12 because great is your reward in *h*,
5:19 great in the kingdom of *h*.
6: 9 "'Our Father in *h*,
6:10 done on earth as it is in *h*.
6:20 up for yourselves treasures in *h*,
7:21 Lord,' will enter the kingdom of *h*,
16:19 bind on earth will be bound in *h*,
18: 1 will never enter the kingdom of *h*.
18: 8 bind on earth will be bound in *h*,
19:14 the kingdom of *h* belongs to such
19:21 and you will have treasure in *h*.
19:23 man to enter the kingdom of *h*.
23:13 the kingdom of *h* in men's faces.
24:35 Hand earth will pass away,
26:64 and coming on the clouds of *h*."
28:18 "All authority in *h*
Mk 1:10 he saw *h* being torn open
10:21 and you will have treasure in *h*.
13:31 Hand earth will pass away,
14:62 and coming on the clouds of *h*."
16:19 he was taken up into *h*
Lk 3:21 *h* was opened and the Holy Spirit
10:18 saw Satan fall like lightning from *h*.
10:20 that your names are written in *h*."
12:33 in *h* that will not be exhausted,
15: 7 in *h* over one sinner who repents
18:22 and you will have treasure in *h*.
21:33 Hand earth will pass away,
24:51 left them and was taken up into *h*.
Jn 3:13 No one has ever gone into *h*
6:38 down from *h* not to do my will
12:28 Then a voice came from *h*,
Ac 1:11 has been taken from you into *h*,
7:49 the prophet says: "'His my
7:55 looked up to *h* and saw the glory
9: 3 a light from *h* flashed around him.
26:19 disobedient to the vision from *h*.
Ro 10: 6 'Who will ascend into *h*?' "(that is,
1Co 15:47 the earth, the second man from *h*.
2Co 5: 1 an eternal house in *h*, not built
12: 2 ago was caught up to the third *h*.
Eph 1:10 to bring all things in *h*
Php 2:10 and on earth and under the earth,
3:20 But our citizenship is in *h*.
Col 1:16 things in *h* and on earth, visible
4: 1 that you also have a Master in *h*.
1Th 1:10 and to wait for his Son from *h*,
4:16 himself will come down from *h*,
Heb 3: 1 hand of the Majesty in *h*,
8: 5 and shadow of what is in *h*.
9:24 he entered *h* itself, now to appear
12:23 whose names are written in *h*.
1Pe 1: 4 spoil or fade—kept in *h* for you,
3:22 who has gone into *h* and is
2Pe 3:13 we are looking forward to a new *h*
Rev 11:19 God's temple in *h* was opened,
12: 7 And there was war in *h*.
15: 5 this I looked and in *h* the temple,
19: 1 of a great multitude in *h* shouting:
19:11 I saw *h* standing open and there
21: 1 Then I saw a new *h* and a new earth
21:10 coming down out of *h* from God.

HEAVENLY (HEAVEN)

Ps 8: 5 him a little lower than the *h* beings
2Co 5: 2 to be clothed with our *h* dwelling,
Eph 1: 3 in the *h* realms with every spiritual
1:20 at his right hand in the *h* realms,
2Ti 4:18 bring me safely to his *h* kingdom.
Heb 12:22 to the *h* Jerusalem, the city

HEAVENS (HEAVEN)

Ge 1: 1 In the beginning God created the *h*
11: 4 with a tower that reaches to the *h*,
Dt 33:26 who rides on the *h* to help you
1Ki 8:27 The *h*, even the highest heaven,
2Ch 2: 6 since the *h*, even the highest
Ezr 9: 6 and our guilt has reached to the *h*.
Ne 9: 6 You made the *h*, even the highest
Job 11: 8 They are higher than the *h*—
38:33 Do you know the laws of the *h*?
Ps 8: 3 When I consider your *h*,
19: 1 The *h* declare the glory of God;
33: 6 of the LORD were the *h* made,
57: 5 Be exalted, O God, above the *h*;
102:25 the *h* are the work of your hands.
103:11 as high as the *h* are above the earth,
108: 4 is your love, higher than the *h*;
115:16 The highest *h* belong to the LORD
119:89 it stands firm in the *h*.
135: 6 in the *h* and on the earth,
139: 8 If I go up to the *h*, you are there;
148: 1 Praise the LORD from the *h*,
Isa 40:26 Lift your eyes and look to the *h*:
45: 8 "You *h* above, rain
51: 6 Lift up your eyes to the *h*,
55: 9 "As the *h* are higher than the earth,
65:17 new *h* and a new earth.
Jer 31:37 if the *h* above can be measured
32:17 you have made the *h* and the earth
Eze 1: 1 *h* were opened and I saw visions
Da 12: 3 shine like the brightness of the *h*,
Joel 2:30 I will show wonders in the *h*
Mt 24:31 from one end of the *h* to the other.
Mk 13:27 of the earth to the ends of the *h*.
Eph 4:10 who ascended higher than all the *h*,
Heb 4:14 priest who has gone through the *h*,
7:26 from sinners, exalted above the *h*.
2Pe 3: 5 ago by God's word the *h* existed
3:10 The *h* will disappear with a roar:

HEAVENWARD (HEAVEN)

Php 3:14 for which God has called me *h*

HEAVIER (HEAVY)

Pr 27: 3 provocation by a fool is *h* than both

HEAVY (HEAVIER)

1Ki 12: 4 and the *h* yoke he put on us,
Ecc 1:13 What a *h* burden God has laid
Isa 47: 6 you laid a very *h* yoke.
Mt 23: 4 They tie up *h* loads and put them

HEBREW (HEBREWS)

Ge 14:13 and reported this to Abram the *H*.
2Ki 18:26 speak to us in *H* in the hearing
Php 3: 5 tribe of Benjamin, a *H* of Hebrews;

HEBREWS (HEBREW)

Ex 9: 1 of the *H*, says: "Let my people go,
2Co 11:22 Are they *H*? So am I.

HEBRON

Ge 13:18 near the great trees of Mamre at *H*,
23: 2 died at Kiriath Arba (that is, *H*)
Jos 14:13 and gave him *H* as his inheritance.
20: 7 *H*) in the hill country of Judah.
21:13 the priest they gave *H* (a city
2Sa 2:11 king in *H* over the house

HEDGE

Job 1:10 "Have you not put a *h* around him

HEED (HEEDS)

Ecc 7: 5 It is better to *h* a wise man's rebuke

HEEDS (HEED)

Pr 13: 1 wise son *h* his father's instruction.
13:18 whoever *h* correction is honored.
15: 5 whoever *h* correction shows
15:32 whoever *h* correction gains

HEEL

Ge 3:15 and you will strike his *h*."

HEIR (INHERIT)

Gal 4: 7 God has made you also an *h*.

Heb 1: 2 whom he appointed *h* of all things.

HEIRS (INHERIT)

Ro 8:17 then we are *h*— *h* of God
Gal 3:29 and *h* according to the promise.
Eph 3: 6 gospel the Gentiles are *h* together
1Pe 3: 7 as *h* with you of the gracious gift

HELD (HOLD)

Ex 17:11 As long as Moses *h* up his hands,
Dt 4: 4 but all of you who *h* fast
2Ki 18: 6 He *h* fast to the LORD
SS 3: 4 I *h* him and would not let him go
Isa 65: 2 All day long I have *h* out my hands
Ro 10:21 day long I have *h* out my hands
Col 2:19 and *h* together by its ligaments

HELL*

Mt 5:22 will be in danger of the fire of *h*.
5:29 body to be thrown into *h*.
5:30 for your whole body to go into *h*.
10:28 destroy both soul and body in *h*.
18: 9 and be thrown into the fire of *h*.
23:15 as much a son of *h* as you are.
23:33 you escape being condemned to *h*?
Mk 9:43 than with two hands to go into *h*,
9:45 have two feet and be thrown into *h*,
9:47 two eyes and be thrown into *h*,
Lk 12: 5 has power to throw you into *h*.
16:23 In *h*, where he was in torment,
Jas 3: 6 and is itself set on fire by *h*.
2Pe 2: 4 but sent them to *h*, putting them

HELMET

Isa 59:17 and the *h* of salvation on his head;
Eph 6:17 Take the *h* of salvation
1Th 5: 8 and the hope of salvation as a *h*.

HELP (HELPED HELPER HELPFUL HELPING HELPLESS HELPS)

Ex 23: 5 leave it there; be sure you *h* him
Lev 25:35 *h* him as you would an alien
Dt 33:26 who rides on the heavens to *h* you
2Ch 16:12 even in his illness he did not seek *h*
Ps 18: 6 I cried to my God for *h*.
30: 2 my God, I called to you for *h*
33:20 he is our *h* and our shield.
46: 1 an ever-present *h* in trouble.
72:12 the afflicted who have no one to *h*.
79: 9 H us, O God our Savior,
108:12 for the *h* of man is worthless.
115: 9 he is their *h* and shield.
121: 1 where does my *h* come from?
Ecc 4:10 his friend can *h* him up.
Isa 41:10 I will strengthen you and *h* you;
Jnh 2: 2 depths of the grave I called for *h*,
Mk 9:24 *h* me overcome my unbelief!"
Lk 11:46 will not lift one finger to *h* them.
Ac 16: 9 Come over to Macedonia and *h* us
18:27 he was a great *h* to those who
20:35 of hard work we must *h* the weak,
26:22 I have had God's *h* to this very day,
1Co 12:28 those able to *h* others, those
2Co 9: 2 For I know your eagerness to *h*,
1Ti 5:16 she should *h* them and not let

HELPED (HELP)

1Sa 7:12 "Thus far has the LORD *h* us."

HELPER (HELP)

Ge 2:18 I will make a *h* suitable for him."
Ps 10:14 you are the *h* of the fatherless.
Heb 13: 6 Lord is my *h*; I will not be afraid.

HELPFUL (HELP)

Eph 4:29 only what is *h* for building others

HELPING (HELP)

Ac 9:36 always doing good and *h* the poor.
1Ti 5:10 *h* those in trouble and devoting

HELPLESS (HELP)

Ps 10:12 Do not forget the *h*.
Mt 9:36 because they were harassed and *h*,

HELPS (HELP)

Ro 8:26 the Spirit *h* us in our weakness.

HEN

Mt 23:37 as a *h* gathers her chicks
Lk 13:34 as a *h* gathers her chicks

HERALD

1Ti 2: 7 for this purpose I was appointed a *h*
2Ti 1:11 of this gospel I was appointed a *h*

HERBS

Ex 12: 8 with bitter *h*, and bread made

HERITAGE (INHERIT)

Ps 61: 5 you have given me the *h*
119:111 Your statutes are my *h* forever;
127: 3 Sons are a *h* from the LORD,

HEROD

1. King of Judea who tried to kill Jesus (Mt 2; Lk 1:5).
2. Son of 1. Tetrarch of Galilee who arrested and beheaded John the Baptist (Mt 14:1-12; Mk 6:14-29; Lk 3:1, 19-20; 9:7-9); tried Jesus (Lk 23:6-15).
3. Grandson of 1. King of Judea who killed James (Ac 12:2); arrested Peter (Ac 12:3-19). Death (Ac 12:19-23).

HERODIAS

Wife of Herod the Tetrarch who persuaded her daughter to ask for John the Baptist's head (Mt 14:1-12; Mk 6:14-29).

HEWN

Isa 51: 1 the quarry from which you were *h*;

HEZEKIAH

King of Judah. Restored the temple and worship (2Ch 29-31). Sought the LORD for help against Assyria (2Ki 18-19; 2Ch 32:1-23; Isa 36-37). Illness healed (2Ki 20:1-11; 2Ch 32:24-26; Isa 38). Judged for showing Babylonians his treasures (2Ki 20:12-21; 2Ch 32:31; Isa 39).

HID (HIDE)

Ge 3: 8 and they *h* from the LORD God
Ex 2: 2 she *h* him for three months.
Jos 6:17 because she *h* the spies we sent.
1Ki 18:13 I *h* a hundred of the LORD's
2Ch 22:11 she *h* the child from Athaliah
Isa 54: 8 I *h* my face from you for a moment,
Mt 13:44 When a man found it, he *h* it again,
25:25 and *h* your talent in the ground.
Heb 11:23 By faith Moses' parents *h* him

HIDDEN (HIDE)

1Sa 10:22 has *h* himself among the baggage."
Job 28:11 and brings *h* things to light.
Ps 19:12 Forgive my *h* faults.
78: 2 I will utter *h* things, things from of old—
119:11 I have *h* your word in my heart
Pr 2: 4 and search for it as for *h* treasure,
27: 5 rebuke than *h* love.
Isa 59: 2 your sins have *h* his face from you,
Da 2:22 He reveals deep and *h* things;
Mt 5:14 A city on a hill cannot be *h*.
10:26 or *h* that will not be made known.
11:25 because you have *h* these things
13:35 I will utter things *h*
13:44 of heaven is like treasure *h*
Mk 4:22 For whatever is *h* is meant
Ro 16:25 of the mystery *h* for long ages past,
1Co 2: 7 a wisdom that has been *h*
Eph 3: 9 for ages past was kept *h* in God,
Col 1:26 the mystery that has been kept *h*
2: 3 in whom are *h* all the treasures
3: 3 and your life is now *h* with Christ

HIDE (HID HIDDEN HIDING)

Dt 31:17 I will *h* my face from them,
Ps 17: 8 *h* me in the shadow of your wings
27: 5 he will *h* me in the shelter
143: 9 for I *h* myself in you,
Isa 53: 3 one from whom men *h* their faces

HIDING (HIDE)

Ps 32: 7 You are my *h* place;
Pr 28:12 to power, men go into *h*.

HIGH

Ge 14:18 He was priest of God Most H,
14:22 God Most H, Creator of heaven
Ps 21: 7 the unfailing love of the Most H
82: 6 you are all sons of the Most H '
Isa 14:14 I will make myself like the Most H
Da 4:17 know that the Most H is sovereign
Mk 5: 7 Jesus, Son of the Most H God?
Heb 7: 1 and priest of God Most H.

HIGHWAY

Isa 40: 3 a *h* for our God.

HILL (HILLS)

Ps 24: 3 ascend the *h* of the LORD?
Isa 40: 4 every mountain and *h* made low;
Mt 5:14 A city on a *h* cannot be hidden.
Lk 3: 5 every mountain and *h* made low.

HILLS (HILL)

1Ki 20:23 "Their gods are gods of the *h*.
Ps 50:10 and the cattle on a thousand *h*.
121: 1 I lift up my eyes to the *h*—
Hos 10: 8 and to the *h*, "Fall on us!"
Lk 23:30 and to the *h*, "Cover us!"
Rev 17: 9 The seven heads are seven *h*

HINDER (HINDERED HINDERS)

1Sa 14: 6 Nothing can *h* the LORD
Mt 19:14 come to me, and do not *h* them,
1Co 9:12 anything rather than *h* the gospel
1Pe 3: 7 so that nothing will *h* your prayers.

HINDERED (HINDER)

Lk 11:52 and you have *h* those who were

HINDERS (HINDER)

Heb 12: 1 let us throw off everything that *h*

HINT*

Eph 5: 3 even a *h* of sexual immorality.

HIP

Ge 32:32 socket of Jacob's *h* was touched

HIRAM

King of Tyre; helped David build his palace (2Sa 5:11-12; 1Ch 14:1); helped Solomon build the temple (1Ki 5; 2Ch 2) and his navy (1Ki 9:10-27; 2Ch 8).

HIRED

Lk 15:15 and *h* himself out to a citizen
Jn 10:12 *h* hand is not the shepherd who

HOARDED (HOARDS)

Ecc 5:13 wealth *h* to the harm of its owner,
Jas 5: 3 You have *h* wealth in the last days.

HOARDS (HOARDED)

Pr 11:26 People curse the man who *h* grain,

HOLD (HELD HOLDS)

Ex 20: 7 LORD will not *h* anyone guiltless
Lev 19:13 "Do not *h* back the wages
Dt 5:11 LORD will not *h* anyone guiltless
11:22 in all his ways and to *h* fast to him
13: 4 serve him and *h* fast to him.
30:20 listen to his voice, and *h* fast to him
Jos 22: 5 to *h* fast to him and to serve him
2Ki 4:16 "you will *h* a son in your arms."
Ps 18:16 from on high and took *h* of me;
73:23 you *h* me by my right hand.
Pr 4: 4 "Lay *h* of my words
Isa 41:13 who takes *h* of your right hand
54: 2 do not *h* back;
Eze 3:18 and I will *h* you accountable
3:20 and I will *h* you accountable
33: 6 I will *h* the watchman accountable
Zec 8:23 nations will take firm *h* of one Jew
Mk 11:25 if you *h* anything against anyone,
Jn 20:17 Jesus said, "Do not *h* on to me,
Php 2:16 as you *h* out the word of life—
3:12 but I press on to take *h* of that
Col 1:17 and in him all things *h* together.
1Th 5:21 H on to the good.
1Ti 6:12 Take *h* of the eternal life
Heb 10:23 Let us *h* unswervingly

HOLDS (HOLD)

Pr 10:19 but he who *h* his tongue is wise.
17:28 and discerning if he *h* his tongue.

HOLES

Hag 1: 6 to put them in a purse with *h* in it."
Mt 8:20 "Foxes have *h* and birds

HOLINESS* (HOLY)

Ex 15:11 majestic in *h*,
Dt 32:51 because you did not uphold my *h*
1Ch 16:29 the LORD in the splendor of his *h*.
2Ch 20:21 him for the splendor of his *h*
Ps 2: 2 in the splendor of his *h*.
89:35 Once for all, I have sworn by my *h*
93: 5 *h* adorns your house
96: 9 in the splendor of his *h*;
Isa 29:23 they will acknowledge the *h*

Isa 35: 8 it will be called the Way of H.
Eze 36:23 I will show the h of my great name,
    38:23 I will show my greatness and my h,
Am 4: 2 LORD has sworn by his h:
Lk 1:75 fear in h and righteousness
Ro 1: 4 the Spirit of h was declared
    6:19 to righteousness leading to h.
    6:22 the benefit you reap leads to h,
1Co 1:30 our righteousness, h.
2Co 1:12 in the h and sincerity that are
    7: 1 perfecting h out of reverence
Eph 4:24 God in true righteousness and h.
1Ti 2: 2 quiet lives in all godliness and h.
    2:15 love and h with propriety.
Heb 12:10 that we may share in his h.
    12:14 without h no one will see the Lord.

HOLY (HALLOWED HOLINESS)
Ge 2: 3 the seventh day and made it h.
Ex 3: 5 you are standing on h ground."
    16:23 a H Sabbath to the LORD.
    19: 6 kingdom of priests and a h nation.'
    20: 8 the Sabbath day by keeping it h.
    26:33 Place from the Most H Place.
    26:33 curtain will separate the H Place
    28:36 seal; H TO THE LORD.
    29:37 Then the altar will be most h.
    30:10 It is most h to the LORD."
    30:29 them so they will be most h,
    31:13 I am the LORD, who makes you h.
    40: 9 all its furnishings, and it will be h.
Lev 10: 3 I will show myself h;
    10:10 must distinguish between the h
    10:13 in a h place, because it is your share
    11:44 and be h, because I am h.
    11:45 therefore be h, because I am h.
    19: 2 'Be h because I, the LORD your.
    19: 8 he has desecrated what is h
    19:24 the fourth year all its fruit will be h,
    20: 3 and profaned my h name.
    20: 7 '' 'Consecrate yourselves and be h,
    20: 8 I am the LORD, who makes you h.
    20:26 You are to be h to me because I,
    21: 6 They must be h to their God
    21: 8 Consider them h, because I
    22: 9 am the LORD, who makes them h.
    22:32 Do not profane my h name.
    25:12 For it is a jubilee and is to be h
    27: 9 given to the LORD becomes h.
Nu 4:15 they must not touch the h things
    6: 5 He must be h until the period
    20:12 as h in the sight of the Israelites,
    20:13 and where he showed himself h
Dt 5:12 the Sabbath day by keeping it h.
    23:14 Your camp must be h,
    26:15 from heaven, your h dwelling place
    33: 2 He came with myriads of h ones
Jos 5:15 place where you are standing is h.''
    24:19 He is a h God; he is a jealous God.
1Sa 2: 2 ''There is no one h like the LORD;
    6:20 of the LORD, this h God?
    21: 5 even on missions that are not h.
2Ki 4: 9 often comes our way is a h man
1Ch 16:10 Glory in his h name;
    16:35 may give thanks to your h name,
    29: 3 I have provided for this h temple:
2Ch 30:27 heaven, his h dwelling place.
Ezr 9: 2 and have mingled the h race
Ne 11: 1 the h city, while the remaining nine
Job 6:10 not denied the words of the H One.
Ps 2: 6 King on Zion, my h hill.''
    11: 4 The LORD is in his h temple;
    16:10 will you let your H One see decay.
    22: 3 you are enthroned as the H One;
    24: 3 Who may stand in his h place?
    30: 4 praise his h name.
    77:13 Your ways, O God, are h.
    78:54 to the border of his h land,
    99: 3 he is h
    99: 5 he is h.
    99: 9 for the LORD our God is h.
    105: 3 Glory in his h name;
    111: 9 h and awesome is his name.
Pr 9:10 of the H One is understanding.
Isa 5:16 the h God will show himself h
    6: 3 H, h, h is the LORD Almighty;
    8:13 is the one you are to regard as h,
    29:23 they will keep my name h;
    40:25 who is my equal?'' says the H One.
    43: 3 the H One of Israel, your Savior;
    54: 5 H One of Israel is your Redeemer;
    57:15 who lives forever, whose name is h;
    58:13 and the LORD's h day honorable,
Jer 17:22 but keep the Sabbath day h,
Eze 20:41 I will show myself h among you

Eze 22:26 to my law and profane my h things;
    28:22 and show myself h within her.
    28:25 I will show myself h among them
    36:20 nations they profaned my h name,
    38:16 when I show myself h through you
    44:23 the difference between the h
Da 9:24 prophecy and to anoint the most h.
Hab 2:20 But the LORD is in his h temple;
Zec 14: 5 and all the h ones with him.
    14:20 On that day H TO THE LORD
Mt 24:15 in the h place 'the abomination
Mk 1:24 the H One of God!'' ''Be quiet!''
Lk 1:35 the h one to be born will be called
    1:49 h is his name.
    4:34 the H One of God!'' ''Be quiet!''
Jn 6:69 and know that you are the H One
Ac 2:27 will you let your H One see decay.
    13:35 will not let your H One see decay.'
Ro 1: 2 prophets in the H Scriptures
    7:12 and the commandment is h,
    11:16 if the root is h, so are the branches.
    12: 1 as living sacrifices, h and pleasing
1Co 1: 2 in Christ Jesus and called to be h,
    7:14 be unclean, but as it is, they are h.
Eph 1: 4 the creation of the world to be h
    2:21 and rises to become a h temple
    3: 5 by the Spirit to God's h apostles
    5: 3 improper for God's h people.
    5:26 up for her to make her h,
Col 1:22 death to present you h in his sight,
1Th 2:10 and so is God, of how h,
    3:13 and h in the presence of our God
    3:13 comes with all his h ones.
    4: 7 us to be impure, but to live a h life.
2Th 1:10 to be glorified in his h people
1Ti 2: 8 to lift up h hands in prayer,
2Ti 1: 9 saved us and called us to a h life—
    2:21 for noble purposes, made h,
    3:15 you have known the h Scriptures,
Tit 1: 8 upright, h and disciplined.
Heb 2:11 Both the one who makes men h
    7:26 one who is h, blameless, pure,
    10:10 we have been made h
    10:14 those who are being made h
    10:19 to enter the Most H Place
    12:14 in peace with all men and to be h;
    13:12 gate to make the people h
1Pe 1:15 But just as he who called you is h,
    1:16 is written: ''Be h, because I am h.''
    2: 5 house to be a h priesthood,
    2: 9 a royal priesthood, a h nation,
    3: 5 For this is the way the h women
2Pe 3:11 You ought to live h and godly lives
Jude : 14 upon thousands of his h ones
Rev 3: 7 are the words of him who is h,
    4: 8 ''H, h, h is the Lord God
    15: 4 For you alone are h.
    20: 6 and h are those who have part
    22:11 let him who is h continue to be h.''

HOME (HOMES)
Dt 6: 7 Talk about them when you sit at h
    11:19 about them when you sit at h
    20: 5 Let him go h, or he may die
    24: 5 is to be free to stay at h
Ru 1:11 ''Return h, my daughters.
2Sa 7:10 them so that they can have a h
1Ch 16:43 and David returned h to bless his
Ps 84: 3 Even the sparrow has found a h,
    113: 9 settles the barren woman in her h
Pr 3:33 but he blesses the h of the righteous
    27: 8 is a man who strays from his h
Ecc 12: 5 then man goes to his eternal h
Eze 36: 8 for they will soon come h.
Mic 2: 2 They defraud a man of his h,
Mt 1:24 and took Mary h as his wife.
Mk 10:29 ''no one who has left h or brothers
Lk 10:38 named Martha opened her h
Jn 14:23 to him and make our h with him.
    19:27 this disciple took her into his h.
Ac 16:15 baptized, she invited us to her h.
Tit 2: 5 to be busy at h, to be kind,

HOMELESS*
1Co 4:11 we are brutally treated, we are h.

HOMES (HOME)
Ne 4:14 daughters, your wives and your h.''
Isa 32:18 in secure h,
Mk 10:30 as much in this present age (h,
1Ti 5:14 to manage their h and to give

HOMETOWN
Mt 13:57 ''Only in his h
Lk 4:24 ''no prophet is accepted in his h.

HOMOSEXUAL*
1Co 6: 9 male prostitutes nor h offenders

HONEST (HONESTY)
Lev 19:36 Use h scales and h weights,
Dt 25:15 and h weights and measures,
Job 31: 6 let God weigh me in h scales
Pr 12:17 truthful witness gives h testimony.

HONESTY (HONEST)
2Ki 12:15 they acted with complete h.

HONEY (HONEYCOMB)
Ex 3: 8 a land flowing with milk and h—
Jdg 14: 8 a swarm of bees and some h,
1Sa 14:26 they saw the h oozing out,
Ps 19:10 than h from the comb.
    119:103 sweeter than h to my mouth!
Pr 25:16 If you find h, eat just enough—
SS 4:11 milk and h are under your tongue.
Isa 7:15 and h when he knows enough
Eze 3: 3 it tasted as sweet as h in my mouth.
Mt 3: 4 His food was locusts and wild h.
Rev 10: 9 mouth it will be as sweet as h.''

HONEYCOMB (HONEY)
SS 4:11 Your lips drop sweetness as the h,
    5: 1 I have eaten my h and my honey;

HONOR (HONORABLE HONORABLY
HONORED HONORS)
Ex 20:12 ''H your father and your mother,
Nu 20:12 trust in me enough to h me
    25:13 he was zealous for the h of his God
Dt 5:16 ''H your father and your mother,
Jdg 4: 9 going about this, the h will not be
1Sa 2: 8 and has them inherit a throne of h.
    2:30 Those who h me I will h,
1Ch 29:12 Wealth and h come from you;
2Ch 1:11 or h, nor for the death
    18: 1 had great wealth and h,
Est 6: 3 for the man the king delights to h
Ps 8: 5 and crowned him with glory and h.
    45:11 h him, for he is your lord.
    84:11 the LORD bestows favor and h;
Pr 3: 9 H the LORD with your wealth,
    3:35 The wise inherit h,
    15:33 and humility comes before h.
    18:12 but humility comes before h.
    20: 3 it is a man's h to avoid strife,
    25:27 is it honorable to seek one's own h
Isa 29:13 and h me with their lips,
Jer 33: 9 and h before all nations
Mt 13:57 own house is a prophet without h.''
    15: 4 'H your father and your mother'
    15: 8 These people h me with their lips,
    19:19 h your father and mother,'
    23: 6 they love the place of h at banquets
Mk 6: 4 own house is a prophet without h.''
Lk 14: 8 do not take the place of h,
Jn 5:23 that all may h the Son just
    7:18 does so to gain h for himself,
    12:26 My Father will h the one who
Ro 12:10 H one another above yourselves.
1Co 6:20 Therefore h God with your body.
Eph 6: 2 ''H your father and mother''—
1Ti 5:17 well are worthy of double h,
Heb 2: 7 you crowned him with glory and h
Rev 4: 9 h and thanks to him who sits

HONORABLE (HONOR)
1Th 4: 4 body in a way that is holy and h,

HONORABLY (HONOR)
Heb 13:18 and desire to live h in every way.

HONORED (HONOR)
Ps 12: 8 when what is vile is h among men.
Pr 13:18 but whoever heeds correction is h.
Da 4:34 I h and glorified him who lives
1Co 12:26 if one part is h, every part rejoices
Heb 13: 4 Marriage should be h by all,

HONORS (HONOR)
Ps 15: 4 but h those who fear the LORD,
Pr 14:31 to the needy h God.

HOOF
Ex 10:26 not a h is to be left behind.

HOOKS
Isa 2: 4 and their spears into pruning h.
Joel 3:10 and your pruning h into spears.
Mic 4: 3 and their spears into pruning h.

HOPE (HOPES)

Job 13: 15 Though he slay me, yet will I *h*
Ps 25: 3 No one whose *h* is in you
    33: 17 A horse is a vain *h* for deliverance;
    33: 18 on those whose *h* is
    42: 5 Put your *h* in God,
    62: 5 my *h* comes from him.
   119: 74 for I have put my *h* in your word.
   130: 5 and in his word I put my *h*.
   130: 7 O Israel, put your *h* in the LORD,
   146: 5 whose *h* is in the LORD his God,
   147: 11 who put their *h* in his unfailing love
Pr 13: 12 *H* deferred makes the heart sick,
    23: 18 There is surely a future *h* for you,
Isa 40: 31 but those who *h* in the LORD
Jer 29: 11 plans to give you *h* and a future.
La   3: 21 and therefore I have *h*:
Zec 9: 12 to your fortress, O prisoners of *h*;
Ro   5: 4 character, and character, *h*.
     8: 20 in *h* that the creation itself will be
     8: 24 But *h* that is seen is no *h* at all.
     8: 25 if we *h* for what we do not yet have,
    12: 12 Be joyful in *h*, patient in affliction,
    15: 4 of the Scriptures we might have *h*.
    15: 13 May the God of *h* fill you
1Co 13: 13 now these three remain: faith, *h*
    15: 19 for this life we have *h* in Christ,
Eph 2: 12 without *h* and without God
Col 1: 27 Christ in you, the *h* of glory.
1Th 1: 3 and your endurance inspired by *h*
     5: 8 and the *h* of salvation as a helmet.
1Ti 4: 10 that we have put our *h*
     6: 17 but to put their *h* in God,
Tit 1: 2 resting on the *h* of eternal life,
     2: 13 while we wait for the blessed *h*—
Heb 6: 19 We have this *h* as an anchor
    10: 23 unswervingly to the *h* we profess,
    11: 1 faith is being sure of what we *h* for
1Jn 3: 3 Everyone who has this *h*

HOPES (HOPE)

1Co 13: 7 always *h*, always perseveres.

HORN (HORNS)

Ex 19: 13 when the ram's *h* sounds a long
    27: 2 Make a *h* at each of the four
Da   7: 8 This *h* had eyes like the eyes

HORNS (HORN)

Da   7: 24 ten *h* are ten kings who will come
Rev 5: 6 He had seven *h* and seven eyes,
    12: 3 and ten *h* and seven crowns
    13: 1 He had ten *h* and seven heads,
    17: 3 and had seven heads and ten *h*.

HORRIBLE (HORROR)

Jer 5: 30 "A *h* and shocking thing

HORROR (HORRIBLE)

Jer 2: 12 and shudder with great *h*,"

HORSE

Ps 147: 10 not in the strength of the *h*,
Pr 26: 3 A whip for the *h*, a halter
Zec 1: 8 before me was a man riding a red *h*
Rev 6: 2 and there before me was a white *h*!
     6: 4 Come!" Then another *h* came out,
     6: 5 and there before me was a black *h*!
     6: 8 and there before me was a pale *h*!
    19: 11 and there before me was a white *h*,

HOSANNA

Mt 21: 9 "*H* in the highest!"
Mk 11: 9 "*H*!"
Jn 12: 13 "*H*!"

HOSEA

Prophet whose wife and family pictured the unfaithfulness of Israel (Hos 1-3).

HOSHEA (JOSHUA)

1. Original name of Joshua (Nu 13:16).
2. Last king of Israel (2Ki 15:30; 17:1-6).

HOSPITABLE* (HOSPITALITY)

1Ti 3: 2 self-controlled, respectable, *h*,
Tit 1: 8 Rather he must be *h*, one who loves

HOSPITABLY* (HOSPITALITY)

Ac 28: 7 and for three days entertained us *h*.

HOSPITALITY* (HOSPITABLE HOSPITABLY)

Ro 12: 13 Practice *h*.
    16: 23 whose *h* I and the whole church
1Ti 5: 10 as bringing up children, showing *h*,
1Pe 4: 9 Offer *h* to one another
3Jn   8 therefore to show *h* to such men

HOSTILE (HOSTILITY)

Ro   8: 7 the sinful mind is *h* to God.

HOSTILITY (HOSTILE)

Eph 2: 14 wall of *h*, by abolishing
     2: 16 by which he put to death their *h*.

HOT

1Ti 4: 2 have been seared as with a *h* iron.
Rev 3: 15 that you are neither cold nor *h*.

HOT-TEMPERED (TEMPER)

Pr 15: 18 A *h* man stirs up dissension,
    19: 19 A *h* man must pay the penalty;
    22: 24 Do not make friends with a *h* man,
    29: 22 and a *h* one commits many sins.

HOTHEADED (HEAD)

Pr 14: 16 but a fool is *h* and reckless.

HOUR

Ecc 9: 12 knows when his *h* will come:
Mt   6: 27 you by worrying can add a single *h*
Lk 12: 40 the Son of Man will come at an *h*
Jn 12: 23 The *h* has come for the Son of Man
    12: 27 for this very reason I came to this *h*

HOUSE (HOUSEHOLD HOUSEHOLDS HOUSES STOREHOUSE)

Ex 12: 22 the door of his *h* until morning.
    20: 17 shall not covet your neighbor's *h*.
Nu 12: 7 he is faithful in all my *h*.
Dt   5: 21 desire on your neighbor's *h*
2Sa 7: 11 LORD himself will establish a *h*
1Ch 17: 23 and his *h* be established forever.
Ne 10: 39 "We will not neglect the *h*
Ps 23: 6 I will dwell in the *h* of the LORD
    27: 4 dwell in the *h* of the LORD
    69: 9 for zeal for your *h* consumes me,
    84: 10 a doorkeeper in the *h* of my God
   122: 1 "Let us go to the *h* of the LORD."
   127: 1 Unless the LORD builds the *h*,
Pr   7: 27 Her *h* is a highway to the grave,
    21: 9 than share a *h* with a quarrelsome
Isa 56: 7 a *h* of prayer for all nations."
Jer 7: 11 Has this *h*, which bears my Name,
    18: 2 "Go down to the potter's *h*,
Eze 33: 7 made you a watchman for the *h*
Joel 3: 18 will flow out of the LORD's *h*
Zec 13: 6 given at the *h* of my friends.'
Mt   7: 24 is like a wise man who built his *h*
    10: 11 and stay at his *h* until you leave.
    12: 29 can anyone enter a strong man's *h*
    21: 13 My *h* will be called a *h* of prayer,'
Mk   3: 25 If a *h* is divided against itself,
    11: 17 "'My *h* will be called
Lk   6: 48 He is like a man building a *h*,
    10: 7 Do not move around from *h* to *h*.
    11: 17 a *h* divided against itself will fall.
    11: 24 'I will return to the *h* I left.'
    15: 8 sweep the *h* and search carefully
    19: 9 Today salvation has come to this *h*,
Jn   2: 16 How dare you turn my Father's *h*
     2: 17 "Zeal for your *h* will consume me."
    12: 3 the *h* was filled with the fragrance
    14: 2 In my Father's *h* are many rooms;
Ac 20: 20 you publicly and from *h* to *h*.
Ro 16: 5 the church that meets at their *h*.
Heb 3: 3 the builder of a *h* has greater honor
1Pe 2: 5 built into a spiritual *h* to be a holy

HOUSEHOLD (HOUSE)

Ex 12: 3 lamb for his family, one for each *h*.
Jos 24: 15 my *h*, we will serve the LORD."
Pr 31: 21 it snows, she has no fear for her *h*;
    31: 27 over the affairs of her *h*
Mic 7: 6 are the members of his own *h*.
Mt 10: 36 will be the members of his own *h*.'
    12: 25 or *h* divided against itself will not
Ac 16: 31 you will be saved—you and your *h*
Eph 2: 19 people and members of God's *h*,
1Ti 3: 12 manage his children and his *h* well.
     3: 15 to conduct themselves in God's *h*,

HOUSEHOLDS (HOUSE)

Tit 1: 11 because they are ruining whole *h*

HOUSES (HOUSE)

Ex 12: 27 passed over the *h* of the Israelites
Mt 19: 29 everyone who has left *h* or brothers

HOVERING* (HOVERS)

Ge   1: 2 of God was *h* over the waters.
Isa 31: 5 Like birds *h* overhead,

HOVERS* (HOVERING)

Dt 32: 11 and *h* over its young,

HULDAH*

Prophetess inquired by Hilkiah for Josiah (2Ki 22; 2Ch 34:14-28).

HUMAN (HUMANITY)

Lev 24: 17 If anyone takes the life of a *h* being,
Isa 52: 14 his form marred beyond *h* likeness
Jn   8: 15 You judge by *h* standards;
Ro   1: 3 as to his *h* nature was a descendant
     9: 5 from them is traced the *h* ancestry
1Co 1: 17 not with words of *h* wisdom,
     1: 26 of you were wise by *h* standards;
     2: 13 not in words taught us by *h* wisdom
2Co 3: 3 of stone but on tablets of *h* hearts.
Gal 3: 3 to attain your goal by *h* effort?
2Pe 2: 18 lustful desires of sinful *h* nature.

HUMANITY* (HUMAN)

Heb 2: 14 he too shared in their *h* so that

HUMBLE (HUMBLED HUMBLES HUMILIATE HUMILIATED HUMILITY)

Nu 12: 3 (Now Moses was a very *h* man,
2Ch 7: 14 will *h* themselves and pray
Ps 18: 27 You save the *h*
    25: 9 He guides the *h* in what is right
   149: 4 he crowns the *h* with salvation.
Pr   3: 34 but gives grace to the *h*.
Isa 66: 2 he who is *h* and contrite in spirit,
Mt 11: 29 for I am gentle and *h* in heart,
Eph 4: 2 Be completely *h* and gentle;
Jas 4: 6 but gives grace to the *h*."
     4: 10 Humble yourselves before the Lord.
1Pe 5: 5 but gives grace to the *h*."
     5: 6 Humble yourselves,

HUMBLED (HUMBLE)

Mt 23: 12 whoever exalts himself will be *h*,
Lk 14: 11 who exalts himself will be *h*,
Php 2: 8 he *h* himself

HUMBLES* (HUMBLE)

1Sa 2: 7 he *h* and he exalts.
Isa 26: 5 He *h* those who dwell on high,
Mt 18: 4 whoever *h* himself like this child is
    23: 12 whoever *h* himself will be exalted.
Lk 14: 11 he who *h* himself will be exalted."
    18: 14 he who *h* himself will be exalted."

HUMILIATE* (HUMBLE)

Pr 25: 7 than for him to *h* you
1Co 11: 22 and *h* those who have nothing?

HUMILIATED (HUMBLE)

Jer 31: 19 I was ashamed and *h*
Lk 14: 9 *h*, you will have to take the least

HUMILITY* (HUMBLE)

Ps 45: 4 of truth, *h* and righteousness;
Pr 11: 2 but with *h* comes wisdom.
    15: 33 and *h* comes before honor.
    18: 12 but *h* comes before honor.
    22: 4 *H* and the fear of the LORD
Zep 2: 3 Seek righteousness, seek *h*;
Ac 20: 19 I served the Lord with great *h*
Php 2: 3 but in *h* consider others better
Col 2: 18 let anyone who delights in false *h*
     2: 23 their false *h* and their harsh
     3: 12 *h*, gentleness and patience.
Tit 3: 2 and to show true *h* toward all men.
Jas 3: 13 in the *h* that comes from wisdom.
1Pe 5: 5 clothe yourselves with *h*

HUNG (HANG)

Dt 21: 23 anyone who is *h* on a tree is
Mt 18: 6 him to have a large millstone *h*
Lk 19: 48 all the people *h* on his words.
Gal 3: 13 "Cursed is everyone who is *h*

HUNGER (HUNGRY)

Ne   9: 15 In their *h* you gave them bread
Pr   6: 30 to satisfy his *h* when he is starving.
Mt   5: 6 Blessed are those who *h*

HUNGRY

Lk 6:21 Blessed are you who h now.
2Co 6: 5 sleepless nights and h; in purity,
11:27 I have known h and thirst
Rev 7:16 Never again will they h;

HUNGRY (HUNGER)

Job 24:10 carry the sheaves, but still go h.
Ps 107: 9 and fills the h with good things.
146: 7 and gives food to the h.
Pr 19:15 and the shiftless man goes h.
25:21 If your enemy is h, give him food
27: 7 to the h even what is bitter tastes
Isa 58: 7 not to share your food with the h
58:10 spend yourselves in behalf of the h
Eze 18: 7 but gives his food to the h
18:16 but gives his food to the h
Mt 15:32 I do not want to send them away h,
25:35 For I was h and you gave me
25:42 For I was h and you gave me
Lk 1:53 He has filled the h with good things
Jn 6:35 comes to me will never go h,
Ro 12:20 "If your enemy is h, feed him;
1Co 4:11 To this very hour we go h,
Php 4:12 whether well fed or h,

HUR

Ex 17:12 Aaron and H held his hands up—

HURL

Mic 7:19 h all our iniquities into the depths

HURT (HURTS)

Ecc 8: 9 it over others to his own h.
Mk 16:18 deadly poison, it will not h them
Rev 2:11 He who overcomes will not be h

HURTS* (HURT)

Ps 15: 4 even when it h,
Pr 26:28 A lying tongue hates those it h,

HUSBAND (HUSBAND'S HUSBANDS)

Pr 31:11 Her h has full confidence in her
31:23 Her h is respected at the city gate,
31:28 her h also, and he praises her:
Isa 54: 5 For your Maker is your h—
Jer 3:14 the LORD, "for I am your h.
3:20 like a woman unfaithful to her h,
Jn 4:17 "I have no h, "she replied.
Ro 7: 2 a married woman is bound to her h
1Co 7: 2 and each woman her own h.
7: 3 he should fulfill his marital duty
7:10 wife must not separate from her h.
7:11 And a h must not divorce his wife.
7:13 And if a woman has a h who is not
7:14 For the unbelieving h has been
7:39 A woman is bound to her h as long
7:39 But if her h dies, she is free
2Co 11: 2 I promised you to one h, to Christ,
Gal 4:27 woman than of her who has a h."
Eph 5:23 For the h is the head of the wife
5:33 and the wife must respect her h.
1Ti 3: 2 the h of but one wife, temperate,
3:12 A deacon must be the h of
5: 9 has been faithful to her h,
Tit 1: 6 An elder must be blameless, the h

HUSBANDMAN see GARDENER

HUSBAND'S (HUSBAND)

Dt 25: 5 Her h brother shall take her
Pr 12: 4 of noble character is her h crown,
1Co 7: 4 the h body does not belong

HUSBANDS (HUSBAND)

Eph 5:22 submit to your h as to the Lord.
5:25 H, love your wives, just
5:28 h ought to love their wives
Col 3:18 submit to your h, as is fitting
3:19 H, love your wives and do not be
Tit 2: 4 the younger women to love their h
2: 5 and to be subject to their h,
1Pe 3: 1 same way be submissive to your h
3: 7 H, in the same way be considerate

HUSHAI

Wise man of David who frustrated Ahithophel's advice and foiled Absalom's revolt (2Sa
15:32-37; 16:15-17:16; 1Ch 27:33).

HYMN* (HYMNS)

Ps 40: 3 a h of praise to our God.
Mt 26:30 they had sung a h, they went out
Mk 14:26 they had sung a h, they went out
1Co 14:26 everyone has a h, or a word

HYMNS* (HYMN)

Ac 16:25 Silas were praying and singing h
Ro 15: 9 I will sing h to your name."
Eph 5:19 to one another with psalms, h
Col 3:16 h and spiritual songs with gratitude

HYPOCRISY* (HYPOCRITE HYPOCRITES HYPOCRITICAL)

Mt 23:28 but on the inside you are full of h
Mk 12:15 we?" But Jesus knew their h.
Lk 12: 1 yeast of the Pharisees, which is h.
Gal 2:13 The other Jews joined him in his h,
2:13 by their h even Barnabas was led
1Pe 2: 1 h, envy, and slander of every kind.

HYPOCRITE* (HYPOCRISY)

Mt 7: 5 You h, first take the plank out
Lk 6:42 You h, first take the plank out

HYPOCRITES* (HYPOCRISY)

Ps 26: 4 nor do I consort with h;
Mt 6: 2 as the h do in the synagogues
6: 5 when you pray, do not be like the h
6:16 do not look somber as the h do,
15: 7 You h! Isaiah was right
22:18 their evil intent, said, "You h,
23:13 of the law and Pharisees, you h!
23:15 of the law and Pharisees, you h!
23:23 of the law and Pharisees, you h!
23:25 of the law and Pharisees, you h!
23:27 you h! You are like whitewashed
23:29 of the law and Pharisees, you h!
24:51 and assign him a place with the h,
Mk 7: 6 when he prophesied about you h;
Lk 12:56 H! You know how
13:15 The Lord answered him, "You h!

HYPOCRITICAL* (HYPOCRISY)

1Ti 4: 2 teachings come through h liars,

HYSSOP

Ex 12:22 Take a bunch of h, dip it
Ps 51: 7 with h, and I will be clean;
Jn 19:29 the sponge on a stalk of the h plant,

ICHABOD

1Sa 4:21 She named the boy I, saying,

IDLE* (IDLENESS IDLERS)

Dt 32:47 They are not just i words for you—
Job 11: 3 Will your i talk reduce men
Ecc 10: 8 If its hands are i, the house leaks.
11: 6 at evening let not your hands be i,
Isa 58:13 as you please or speaking i words,
Col 2:18 mind puffs him up with i notions.
1Th 5:14 those who are i, encourage
2Th 3: 6 away from every brother who is i
3: 7 We were not i when we were
3:11 We hear that some among you are i
1Ti 5:13 they get into the habit of being i

IDLENESS* (IDLE)

Pr 31:27 and does not eat the bread of i.

IDLERS* (IDLE)

1Ti 5:13 And not only do they become i,

IDOL (IDOLATER IDOLATERS IDOLATRY IDOLS)

Ex 20: 4 make for yourself an i in the form
32: 4 made it into an i cast in the shape
Isa 40:19 As for an i, a craftsman casts it,
41: 7 He nails down the i
44: 5 he makes an i and bows down to it.
44:17 From the rest he makes a god, his i;
Hab 2:18 "Of what value is an i,
1Co 8: 4 We know that an i is nothing at all

IDOLATER* (IDOL)

1Co 5:11 an i or a slanderer, a drunkard
Eph 5: 5 greedy person—such a man is an i

IDOLATERS (IDOL)

1Co 5:10 or the greedy and swindlers, or i.
6: 9 Neither the sexually immoral nor i

IDOLATRY (IDOL)

1Sa 15:23 and arrogance like the evil of i.
1Co 10:14 my dear friends, flee from i.
Gal 5:20 and debauchery; i and witchcraft;
Col 3: 5 evil desires and greed, which is i.
1Pe 4: 3 orgies, carousing and detestable i.

IDOLS (IDOL)

Dt 32:16 angered him with their detestable i.
Ps 78:58 aroused his jealousy with their i.
Isa 44: 9 All who make i are nothing.
Eze 23:39 sacrificed their children to their i,
Ac 15:20 to abstain from food polluted by i,
21:25 abstain from food sacrificed to i,
1Co 8: 1 Now about food sacrificed to i:
1Jn 5:21 children, keep yourselves from i.
Rev 2:14 to sin by eating food sacrificed to i

IGNORANT (IGNORE)

1Co 15:34 for there are some who are i of God
Heb 5: 2 to deal gently with those who are i
1Pe 2:15 good you should silence the i talk
2Pe 3:16 which i and unstable people distort

IGNORE (IGNORANT IGNORED IGNORES)

Dt 22: 1 do not i it but be sure
Ps 9:12 he does not i the cry of the afflicted
Heb 2: 3 if we i such a great salvation?

IGNORED (IGNORE)

Hos 4: 6 you have i the law of your God,
1Co 14:38 he ignores this, he himself will be i

IGNORES* (IGNORE)

Pr 10:17 whoever i correction leads others
13:18 He who i discipline comes
15:32 He who i discipline despises
1Co 14:38 If he i this, he himself will be

ILL (ILLNESS)

Mt 4:24 brought to him all who were i

ILL-GOTTEN

Pr 1:19 the end of all who go after i gain;
10: 2 I treasures are of no value,

ILL-TEMPERED* (TEMPER)

Pr 21:19 than with a quarrelsome and i wife.

ILLEGITIMATE

Heb 12: 8 then you are i children

ILLNESS (ILL)

2Ki 8: 9 'Will I recover from this i?' "
2Ch 16:12 even in his i he did not seek help
Ps 41: 3 and restore him from his bed of i.
Isa 38: 9 king of Judah after his i

ILLUMINATED*

Rev 18: 1 and the earth was i by his splendor.

IMAGE (IMAGES)

Ge 1:26 "Let us make man in our i,
1:27 So God created man in his own i,
9: 6 for in the i of God
Dt 27:15 "Cursed is the man who carves an i
Isa 40:18 What i will you compare him to?
Da 3: 1 King Nebuchadnezzar made an i
1Co 11: 7 since he is the i and glory of God;
2Co 4: 4 glory of Christ, who is the i of God.
Col 1:15 He is the i of the invisible God,
3:10 in knowledge in the i of its Creator.
Rev 13:14 them to set up an i in honor

IMAGES (IMAGE)

Ps 97: 7 All who worship i are put to shame,
Jer 10:14 His i are a fraud;
Ro 1:23 of the immortal God for i made

IMAGINATION (IMAGINE)

Eze 13: 2 who prophesy out of their own i:

IMAGINE (IMAGINATION)

Eph 3:20 more than all we ask or i,

IMITATE (IMITATORS)

1Co 4:16 Therefore I urge you to i me.
Heb 6:12 but to i those who through faith
13: 7 of their way of life and i their faith.
3Jn : 11 do not i what is evil but what is

IMITATORS* (IMITATE)

Eph 5: 1 Be i of God, therefore,
1Th 1: 6 You became i of us and of the Lord
2:14 became i of God's churches

IMMANUEL

Isa 7:14 birth to a son, and will call him I.
8: 8 O I!"
Mt 1:23 and they will call him I"—

IMMORAL* (IMMORALITY)

Pr   6:24 keeping you from the *i* woman,
1Co   5: 9 to associate with sexually *i* people
        5:10 the people of this world who are *i*,
        5:11 but is sexually *i* or greedy,
        6: 9 Neither the sexually *i* nor idolaters
Eph   5: 5 No *i*, impure or greedy person—
Heb 12:16 See that no one is sexually *i*,
      13: 4 the adulterer and all the sexually *i*.
Rev 21: 8 the murderers, the sexually *i*,
      22:15 the sexually *i*, the murderers,

IMMORALITY* (IMMORAL)

Nu   25: 1 in sexual *i* with Moabite women,
Jer   3: 9 Because Israel's *i* mattered so little
Mt   15:19 murder, adultery, sexual *i*, theft,
Mk   7:21 sexual *i*, theft, murder, adultery,
Ac   15:20 from sexual *i*, from the meat
      15:29 animals and from sexual *i*.
      21:25 animals and from sexual *i*.
Ro   13:13 not in sexual *i* and debauchery,
1Co   5: 1 reported that there is sexual *i*
      6:13 The body is not meant for sexual *i*,
      6:18 Flee from sexual *i*.
      7: 2 But since there is so much *i*,
      10: 8 We should not commit sexual *i*,
Gal   5:19 sexual *i*, impurity and debauchery;
Eph   5: 3 must not be even a hint of sexual *i*,
Col   3: 5 sexual *i*, impurity, lust, evil desires
1Th   4: 3 that you should avoid sexual *i*;
Jude   : 4 grace of our God for a license for *i*
      : 7 gave themselves up to sexual *i*
Rev   2:14 and by committing sexual *i*,
      2:20 misleads my servants into sexual *i*
      2:21 given her time to repent of her *i*,
      9:21 their sexual *i* or their thefts.

IMMORTAL* (IMMORTALITY)

Ro   1:23 glory of the *i* God for images made
1Ti   1:17 Now to the King eternal, *i*,
      6:16 who alone is *i* and who lives

IMMORTALITY* (IMMORTAL)

Pr   12:28 along that path is *i*.
Ro   2: 7 honor and *i*, he will give eternal life
1Co   15:53 and the mortal with *i*,
      15:54 with *i*, then the saying that is
2Ti   1:10 and *i* to light through the gospel.

IMPARTIAL*

Jas   3:17 and good fruit, *i* and sincere.

IMPARTS*

Pr   29:15 The rod of correction *i* wisdom,

IMPERFECT*

1Co   13:10 perfection comes, the *i* disappears

IMPERISHABLE

1Co   15:42 it is raised *i*; it is sown in dishonor,
      15:50 nor does the perishable inherit the *i*
1Pe   1:23 not of perishable seed, but of *i*,

IMPLANTED*

Ps   94: 9 Does he who *i* the ear not hear?

IMPLORE*

Mal   1: 9 "Now *i* God to be gracious to us.
2Co   5:20 We *i* you on Christ's behalf:

IMPORTANCE* (IMPORTANT)

1Co   15: 3 passed on to you as of first *i*:

IMPORTANT (IMPORTANCE)

Mt   6:25 Is not life more *i* than food,
      23:23 have neglected the more *i* matters
Mk   12:29 "The most *i* one," answered Jesus,
      12:33 as yourself is more *i* than all burnt
Php   1:18 The *i* thing is that in every way,

IMPOSSIBLE

Mt   17:20 Nothing will be *i* for you."
      19:26 "With man this is *i*,
Mk   10:27 "With man this is *i*, but not
Lk   1:37 For nothing is *i* with God."
      18:27 "What is *i* with men is possible
Ac   2:24 it was *i* for death to keep its hold
Heb   6: 4 It is *i* for those who have once been
      6:18 things in which it is *i* for God to lie,
      10: 4 because it is *i* for the blood of bulls
      11: 6 without faith it is *i* to please God,

IMPOSTORS

2Ti   3:13 and *i* will go from bad to worse,

IMPRESS* (IMPRESSES)

Dt   6: 7 *i* them on your children.

IMPRESSES* (IMPRESS)

Pr   17:10 A rebuke *i* a man of discernment

IMPROPER*

Eph   5: 3 these are *i* for God's holy people.

IMPURE (IMPURITY)

Ac   10:15 not call anything *i* that God has
Eph   5: 5 No immoral, *i* or greedy person—
1Th   2: 3 spring from error or *i* motives,
      4: 7 For God did not call us to be *i*,
Rev   21:27 Nothing *i* will ever enter it,

IMPURITY (IMPURE)

Ro   1:24 hearts to sexual *i* for the degrading
Gal   5:19 sexual immorality, *i*
Eph   4:19 as to indulge in every kind of *i*,
      5: 3 or of any kind of *i*, or of greed,
Col   3: 5 *i*, lust, evil desires and greed,

INCENSE

Ex   30: 1 altar of acacia wood for burning *i*.
      40: 5 Place the gold altar of *i* in front
Ps   141: 2 my prayer be set before you like *i*;
Mt   2:11 him with gifts of gold and of *i*
Heb   9: 4 which had the golden altar of *i*
Rev   5: 8 were holding golden bowls full of *i*,
      8: 4 The smoke of the *i*, together

INCLINATION (INCLINES)

Ge   6: 5 and that every *i* of the thoughts

INCLINES* (INCLINATION)

Ecc   10: 2 The heart of the wise *i* to the right,

INCOME

Ecc   5:10 wealth is never satisfied with his *i*.
1Co   16: 2 sum of money in keeping with his *i*.

INCOMPARABLE*

Eph   2: 7 ages he might show the *i* riches

INCREASE (EVER-INCREASING INCREASED INCREASES INCREASING)

Ge   1:22 "Be fruitful and *i* in number
      3:16 "I will greatly *i* your pains
      8:17 be fruitful and *i* in number upon it
Ps   62:10 though your riches *i*,
Pr   22:16 oppresses the poor to *i* his wealth
Isa   9: 7 Of the *i* of his government
Mt   24:12 Because of the *i* of wickedness,
Lk   17: 5 said to the Lord, "*i* our faith!"
Ac   12:24 But the word of God continued to *i*
Ro   5:20 added so that the trespass might *i*.
1Th   3:12 May the Lord make your love *i*

INCREASED (INCREASE)

Ac   6: 7 of disciples in Jerusalem *i* rapidly,
Ro   5:20 But where sin *i*, grace *i* all the more

INCREASES (INCREASE)

Pr   24: 5 and a man of knowledge *i* strength;

INCREASING (INCREASE)

Ac   6: 1 when the number of disciples was *i*,
2Th   1: 3 one of you has for each other is *i*.
2Pe   1: 8 these qualities in *i* measure,

INCREDIBLE*

Ac   26: 8 of you consider it *i* that God raises

INDECENT

Ro   1:27 Men committed *i* acts

INDEPENDENT*

1Co   11:11 however, woman is not *i* of man,
      11:11 of man, nor is man *i* of woman.

INDESCRIBABLE*

2Co   9:15 Thanks be to God for his *i* gift!

INDESTRUCTIBLE*

Heb   7:16 on the basis of the power of an *i* life

INDIGNANT

Mk   10:14 When Jesus saw this, he was *i*.

INDISPENSABLE*

1Co   12:22 seem to be weaker are *i*,

INEFFECTIVE*

2Pe   1: 8 they will keep you from being *i*

INEXPRESSIBLE*

2Co   12: 4 He heard *i* things, things that man
1Pe   1: 8 are filled with an *i* and glorious joy,

INFANCY* (INFANTS)

2Ti   3:15 from *i* you have known the holy

INFANTS (INFANCY)

Ps   8: 2 From the lips of children and *i*
Mt   21:16 "'From the lips of children and *i*
1Co   3: 1 but as worldly—mere *i* in Christ.
      14:20 In regard to evil be *i*,
Eph   4:14 Then we will no longer be *i*,

INFIRMITIES*

Isa   53: 4 Surely he took up our *i*
Mt   8:17 "He took up our *i*

INFLAMED

Ro   1:27 were *i* with lust for one another.

INFLUENTIAL*

1Co   1:26 not many were *i*, not many were

INHABITANTS (INHABITED)

Nu   33:55 "'But if you do not drive out the *i*
Rev   8:13 Woe! Woe to the *i* of the earth,

INHABITED (INHABITANTS)

Isa   *45*:18 but formed it to be *i*—

INHERIT (CO-HEIRS HEIR HEIRS HERITAGE INHERITANCE)

Dt   1:38 because he will lead Israel to *i* it.
Jos   1: 6 people to *i* the land I swore
Ps   37:11 But the meek will *i* the land
      37:29 the righteous will *i* the land
Zec   2:12 The LORD will *i* Judah
Mt   5: 5 for they will *i* the earth.
      19:29 as much and will *i* eternal life.
Mk   10:17 "what must I do to *i* eternal life?"
Lk   10:25 "what must I do to *i* eternal life?"
      18:18 what must I do to *i* eternal life?"
1Co   6: 9 the wicked will not *i* the kingdom
      15:50 blood cannot *i* the kingdom of God
Rev   21: 7 He who overcomes will *i* all this,

INHERITANCE (INHERIT)

Lev   20:24 I will give it to you as an *i*,
Dt   4:20 to be the people of his *i*,
      10: 9 the LORD is their *i*, as the LORD
Jos   14: 3 two-and-a-half tribes their *i* east
Ps   16: 6 surely I have a delightful *i*.
      33:12 the people he chose for his *i*
      136:21 and gave their land as an *i*,
Pr   13:22 A good man leaves an *i*
Mt   25:34 blessed by my Father; take your *i*,
Eph   1:14 who is a deposit guaranteeing our *i*
      5: 5 has any *i* in the kingdom of Christ
Col   1:12 you to share in the *i* of the saints
      3:24 you know that you will receive an *i*
Heb   9:15 receive the promised eternal *i*—
1Pe   1: 4 and into an *i* that can never perish,

INIQUITIES (INIQUITY)

Ps   78:38 he forgave their *i*
      103:10 or repay us according to our *i*.
Isa   53: 5 he was crushed for our *i*;
      53:11 and he will bear their *i*,
      59: 2 But your *i* have separated
Mic   7:19 and hurl all our *i* into the depths

INIQUITY (INIQUITIES)

Ps   25:11 forgive my *i*, though it is great.
      32: 5 and did not cover up my *i*.
      51: 2 Wash away all my *i*
      51: 9 and blot out all my *i*.
Isa   53: 6 the *i* of us all.

INJURED

Eze   34:16 will bind up the *i* and strengthen
Zec   11:16 or heal the *i*, or feed the healthy,

INJUSTICE

2Ch   19: 7 the LORD our God there is no *i*

INK

2Co   3: 3 not with *i* but with the Spirit

INN*

Lk   2: 7 there was no room for them in the *i*

Lk 10: 34 took him to an *i* and took care

INNOCENT

Ex 23: 7 do not put an *i* or honest person
Dt 25: 1 acquitting the *i* and condemning
Pr 6: 17 hands that shed *i* blood,
17: 26 It is not good to punish an *i* man,
Mt 10: 16 shrewd as snakes and as *i* as doves.
27: 4 "for I have betrayed *i* blood."
27: 24 I am *i* of this man's blood," he said.
Ac 20: 26 declare to you today that I am *i*
Ro 16: 19 what is good, and *i* about what is
1Co 4: 4 but that does not make me *i*

INQUIRE

Isa 8: 19 should not a people *i* of their God?

INSCRIPTION

Mt 22: 20 And whose *i*?" "Caesar's,"
2Ti 2: 19 with this *i*: "The Lord knows those

INSIGHT

1Ki 4: 29 Solomon wisdom and very great *i*,
Ps 119: 99 I have more *i* than all my teachers,
Pr 5: 1 listen well to my words of *i*,
21: 30 There is no wisdom, no *i*, no plan
Php 1: 9 more in knowledge and depth of *i*,
2Ti 2: 7 for the Lord will give you *i*

INSOLENT

Ro 1: 30 God-haters, *i*, arrogant

INSPIRED*

Hos 9: 7 the *i* man a maniac.
1Th 1: 3 and your endurance *i* by hope

INSTALLED

Ps 2: 6 "I have *i* my King

INSTINCT* (INSTINCTS)

2Pe 2: 12 are like brute beasts, creatures of *i*,
Jude : 10 things they do understand by *i*,

INSTINCTS* (INSTINCT)

Jude : 19 who follow mere natural *i*

INSTITUTED

Ro 13: 2 rebelling against what God has *i*,
1Pe 2: 13 to every authority *i* among men:

INSTRUCT (INSTRUCTED INSTRUCTION INSTRUCTIONS INSTRUCTOR)

Ps 32: 8 I will *i* you and teach you
105: 22 to *i* his princes as he pleased
Pr 9: 9 *i* a wise man and he will be wiser
Ro 15: 14 and competent to *i* one another.
1Co 2: 16 that he may *i* him?"
14: 19 to *i* others than ten thousand words
2Ti 2: 25 who oppose him he must gently *i*,

INSTRUCTED (INSTRUCT)

2Ch 26: 5 who *i* him in the fear of God.
Pr 21: 11 a wise man is *i*, he gets knowledge.
Isa 50: 4 LORD has given me an *i* tongue,
Mt 14: 8 had been *i* about the kingdom
1Co 14: 31 in turn so that everyone may be *i*

INSTRUCTION (INSTRUCT)

Pr 1: 8 Listen, my son, to your father's *i*
4: 1 Listen, my sons, to a father's *i*;
4: 13 Hold on to *i*, do not let it go;
8: 10 Choose my *i* instead of silver,
8: 33 Listen to my *i* and be wise;
13: 1 A wise son heeds his father's *i*,
13: 13 He who scorns *i* will pay for it,
16: 20 Whoever gives heed to *i* prospers,
16: 21 and pleasant words promote *i*,
19: 20 Listen to advice and accept *i*,
23: 12 Apply your heart to *i*
1Co 14: 6 or prophecy or word of *i*?
14: 26 or a word of *i*, a revelation,
Eph 6: 4 up in the training and *i* of the Lord.
1Th 4: 8 he who rejects this *i* does not reject
2Th 3: 14 If anyone does not obey our *i*
1Ti 1: 18 I give you this *i* in keeping
6: 3 to the sound *i* of our Lord Jesus
2Ti 4: 2 with great patience and careful *i*,

INSTRUCTIONS (INSTRUCT)

1Ti 3: 14 I am writing you these *i* so that,

INSTRUCTOR (INSTRUCT)

Gal 6: 6 share all good things with his *i*.

INSTRUMENT* (INSTRUMENTS)

Eze 33: 32 beautiful voice and plays an *i* well,
Ac 9: 15 This man is my chosen *i*
2Ti 2: 21 he will be an *i* for noble purposes,

INSTRUMENTS (INSTRUMENT)

Ro 6: 13 as *i* of wickedness, but rather offer

INSULT (INSULTED INSULTS)

Pr 9: 7 corrects a mocker invites *i*;
12: 16 but a prudent man overlooks an *i*.
Mt 5: 11 Blessed are you when people *i* you,
Lk 6: 22 when they exclude you and *i* you
1Pe 3: 9 evil with evil or *i* with *i*,

INSULTED (INSULT)

Heb 10: 29 and who has *i* the Spirit of grace?
Jas 2: 6 love him? But you have *i* the poor.
1Pe 4: 14 If you are *i* because of the name

INSULTS (INSULT)

Ps 22: 7 they hurl *i*, shaking their heads:
69: 9 the *i* of those who insult you fall
Pr 22: 10 quarrels and *i* are ended.
Mk 15: 29 passed by hurled *i* at him,
Jn 9: 28 Then they hurled *i* at him and said,
Ro 15: 3 "The *i* of those who insult you have
2Co 12: 10 in *i*, in hardships, in persecutions,
1Pe 2: 23 When they hurled their *i* at him,

INTEGRITY*

Dt 9: 5 or your *i* that you are going
1Ki 9: 4 if you walk before me in *i* of heart
1Ch 29: 17 the heart and are pleased with *i*.
Ne 7: 2 because he was a man of *i*
Job 2: 3 And he still maintains his *i*,
2: 9 "Are you still holding on to your *i*?
6: 29 reconsider, for my *i* is at stake.
27: 5 till I die, I will not deny my *i*.
Ps 7: 8 according to my *i*, O Most High.
25: 21 May *i* and uprightness protect me,
41: 12 In my *i* you uphold me
78: 72 David shepherded them with *i*
Pr 10: 9 The man of *i* walks securely,
11: 3 The *i* of the upright guides them,
13: 6 Righteousness guards the man of *i*,
17: 26 or to flog officials for their *i*.
29: 10 Bloodthirsty men hate a man of *i*
Isa 45: 23 my mouth has uttered in all *i*
59: 4 no one pleads his case with *i*.
Mt 22: 16 "we know you are a man of *i*
Mk 12: 14 we know you are a man of *i*.
Tit 2: 7 your teaching show *i*, seriousness

INTELLIGENCE (INTELLIGENT)

Isa 29: 14 the *i* of the intelligent will vanish."
1Co 1: 19 *i* of the intelligent I will frustrate."

INTELLIGENT (INTELLIGENCE)

Isa 29: 14 the intelligence of the *i* will vanish

INTELLIGIBLE

1Co 14: 19 I would rather speak five *i* words

INTENDED

Ge 50: 20 place of God? You *i* to harm me,

INTENSE

1Th 2: 17 out of our *i* longing we made every
Rev 16: 9 They were seared by the *i* heat

INTERCEDE (INTERCEDES INTERCEDING INTERCESSION INTERCESSOR)

Heb 7: 25 he always lives to *i* for them.

INTERCEDES* (INTERCEDE)

Ro 8: 26 but the Spirit himself *i* for us
8: 27 because the Spirit *i* for the saints

INTERCEDING* (INTERCEDE)

Ro 8: 34 hand of God and is also *i* for us.

INTERCESSION* (INTERCEDE)

Isa 53: 12 and made *i* for the transgressors.
1Ti 2: 1 *i* and thanksgiving be made

INTERCESSOR* (INTERCEDE)

Job 16: 20 My *i* is my friend

INTEREST (INTERESTS)

Lev 25: 36 Do not take *i* of any kind from him,
Dt 23: 20 You may charge a foreigner *i*,
Mt 25: 27 would have received it back with *i*.
Php 2: 20 who takes a genuine *i*

INTERESTS (INTEREST)

1Co 7: 34 his wife—and his *i* are divided.
Php 2: 4 only to your own *i*, but also to the *i*
2: 21 everyone looks out for his own *i*,

INTERFERE*

Ezr 6: 7 Do not *i* with the work

INTERMARRY (MARRY)

Dt 7: 3 Do not *i* with them.
Ezr 9: 14 and *i* with the peoples who commit

INTERPRET (INTERPRETATION INTERPRETER INTERPRETS)

Ge 41: 15 "I had a dream, and no one can *i* it.
Mt 16: 3 you cannot *i* the signs of the times.
1Co 12: 30 Do all *i*? But eagerly desire
14: 13 pray that he may *i* what he says.
14: 27 one at a time, and someone must *i*.

INTERPRETATION (INTERPRET)

1Co 12: 10 and to still another the *i* of tongues.
14: 26 a revelation, a tongue or an *i*.
2Pe 1: 20 about by the prophet's own *i*.

INTERPRETER (INTERPRET)

1Co 14: 28 If there is no *i*, the speaker should

INTERPRETS (INTERPRET)

1Co 14: 5 he *i*, so that the church may be

INVADED

2Ki 17: 5 king of Assyria *i* the entire land,
24: 1 king of Babylon *i* the land,

INVENT* (INVENTED)

Ro 1: 30 boastful; they *i* ways of doing evil;

INVENTED* (INVENT)

2Pe 1: 16 We did not follow cleverly *i* stories

INVESTIGATED

Lk 1: 3 I myself have carefully *i* everything

INVISIBLE*

Ro 1: 20 of the world God's *i* qualities—
Col 1: 15 He is the image of the *i* God,
1: 16 and on earth, visible and *i*,
1Ti 1: 17 immortal, *i*, the only God,
Heb 11: 27 because he saw him who is *i*.

INVITE (INVITED INVITES)

Mt 22: 9 *i* to the banquet anyone you find.'
25: 38 did we see you a stranger and *i* you
Lk 14: 12 do not *i* your friends, your brothers
14: 13 you give a banquet, the poor,

INVITED (INVITE)

Zep 1: 7 he has consecrated those he has *i*.
Mt 22: 14 For many are *i*, but few are chosen
25: 35 I was a stranger and you *i* me in,
Lk 14: 10 But when you are *i*, take the lowest
Rev 19: 9 'Blessed are those who are *i*

INVITES (INVITE)

Pr 18: 6 and his mouth *i* a beating.
1Co 10: 27 If some unbeliever *i* you to a meal

INVOLVED

2Ti 2: 4 a soldier gets *i* in civilian affairs—

IRON

2Ki 6: 6 threw it there, and made the *i* float.
Ps 2: 9 will rule them with an *i* scepter;
Pr 27: 17 As *i* sharpens *i*,
Da 2: 33 and thighs of bronze, its legs of *i*,
1Ti 4: 2 have been seared as with a hot *i*.
Rev 2: 27 He will rule them with an *i* scepter;
12: 5 all the nations with an *i* scepter.
19: 15 He will rule them with an *i* scepter

IRRELIGIOUS*

1Ti 1: 9 and sinful, the unholy and *i*;

IRREVOCABLE*

Ro 11: 29 for God's gifts and his call are *i*.

ISAAC

Son of Abraham by Sarah (Ge 17:19; 21:1-7; 1Ch 1:28). Abrahamic covenant perpetuated through (Ge 17:21; 26:2-5). Offered up by Abraham (Ge 22; Heb 11:17-19). Rebekah taken as wife (Ge 24). Inherited Abraham's estate (Ge 25: 5). Fathered Esau and Jacob (Ge 25:19-26; 1Ch

1:34). Nearly lost Rebekah to Abimelech (Ge 26:
1-11). Covenant with Abimelech (Ge 26:12-31).
Tricked into blessing Jacob (Ge 27). Death (Ge
35:27-29). Father of Israel (Ex 3:6; Dt 29:13; Ro
9:10).

ISAIAH

Prophet to Judah (Isa 1:1). Called by the
LORD (Isa 6). Announced judgment to Ahaz (Isa
7), deliverance from Assyria to Hezekiah (2Ki
19; Isa 36-37), deliverance from death to Hezekiah (2Ki 20:1-11; Isa 38). Chronicler of Judah's
history (2Ch 26:22; 32:32).

ISCARIOT see JUDAS

ISH-BOSHETH*

Son of Saul who attempted to succeed him as
king (2Sa 2:8-4:12; 1Ch 8:33).

ISHMAEL

Son of Abraham by Hagar (Ge 16; 1Ch 1:28).
Blessed, but not son of covenant (Ge 17:18-21;
Gal 4:21-31). Sent away by Sarah (Ge 21:8-21).
Children (Ge 25:12-18; 1Ch 1:29-31). Death (Ge
25:17).

ISLAND

Rev   1:   9 was on the *i* of Patmos
     16: 20 Every *i* fled away

ISRAEL (ISRAEL'S ISRAELITE ISRAELITES)

1. Name given to Jacob.
2. Corporate name of Jacob's descendants,
often specifically Northern Kingdom.
Ex   28: 11 Engrave the names of the sons of *I*
     28: 29 of the sons of *I* over his heart
Nu   24: 17 a scepter will rise out of *I*
Dt   6:   4 Hear, O *I*: The LORD our God,
     10: 12 O *I*, what does the LORD your
Jos   4: 22 *I* crossed the Jordan on dry ground
Jdg   17:   6 In those days *I* had no king;
Ru   2: 12 of *I*, under whose wings you have
1Sa   3: 20 from Dan to Beersheba
     4: 21 "The glory has departed from *I*"—
     14: 23 So the LORD rescued *I* that day,
     15: 26 has rejected you as king over *I*
     17: 46 will know that there is a God in *I*
     18: 16 But all *I* and Judah loved David.
2Sa   5:   2 'You will shepherd my people *I*,
     5:   3 they anointed David king over *I*
     14: 25 In all *I* there was not a man
1Ki   1: 35 I have appointed him ruler over *I*
     10:   9 of the LORD's eternal love for *I*,
     18: 17 "Is that you, you troubler of *I*?"
     19: 18 Yet I reserve seven thousand in *I*—
2Ki   5:   8 know that there is a prophet in *I*."
1Ch   17: 22 made your people *I* your very own
     21:   1 incited David to take a census of *I*
     29: 25 Solomon in the sight of all *I*
2Ch   9:   8 of the love of your God for *I*
Ps   73:   1 Surely God is good to *I*,
     81:   8 if you would but listen to me, O *I*!
     98:   3 his faithfulness to the house of *I*;
     99:   8 you were to *I* a forgiving God.
Isa   11: 12 and gather the exiles of *I*;
     27:   6 *I* will bud and blossom
     44: 21 O *I*, I will not forget you.
     46: 13 my splendor to *I*.
Jer   2:   3 I was holy to the LORD,
     23:   6 and *I* will live in safety.
     31:   2 I will come to give rest to *I*."
     31: 10 'He who scattered *I* will gather
     31: 31 covenant with the house of *I*
     33: 17 sit on the throne of the house of *I*,
Eze   3: 17 you a watchman for the house of *I*;
     33:   7 you a watchman for the house of *I*;
     34:   2 prophesy against the shepherds of *I*
     37: 28 that I the LORD make *I* holy,
     39: 23 of *I* went into exile for their sin,
Da   9: 20 my sin and the sin of my people *I*
Hos   11:   1 "When *I* was a child, I loved him,
Am   4: 12 prepare to meet your God, O *I*."
     7: 11 and *I* will surely go into exile.
     8:   2 "The time is ripe for my people *I*;
     9: 14 I will bring back my exiled people *I*
Mic   5:   2 one who will be ruler over *I*,
Zep   3: 13 The remnant of *I* will do no wrong;
Zec   11: 14 brotherhood between Judah and *I*
Mal   1:   5 even beyond the borders of *I*!'
Mt   2:   6 be the shepherd of my people *I*.' "
     10:   6 Go rather to the lost sheep of *I*.
     15: 24 only to the lost sheep of *I*."
Mk   12: 29 'Hear, O *I*, the Lord our God,
Lk   22: 30 judging the twelve tribes of *I*.

Ac   1:   6 going to restore the kingdom to *I*?"
     9: 15 and before the people of *I*.
Ro   9:   4 of my own race, the people of *I*.
     9:   6 all who are descended from *I* are *I*
     9: 31 but *I*, who pursued a law
     11:   7 What *I* sought so earnestly it did
     11: 26 And so all *I* will be saved,
Gal   6: 16 who follow this rule, even to the *I*
Eph   2: 12 excluded from citizenship in *I*
     3:   6 Gentiles are heirs together with *I*,
Heb   8:   8 covenant with the house of *I*
Rev   7:   4 144,000 from all the tribes of *I*.
     21: 12 the names of the twelve tribes of *I*.

ISRAEL'S (ISRAEL)

Jdg   10: 16 he could bear *I* misery no longer.
2Sa   23:   1 *I* singer of songs:
Isa   44:   6 *I* King and Redeemer, the LORD
Jer   3:   9 Because *I* immorality mattered
     31:   9 because I am *I* father,
Jn   3: 10 "You are *I* teacher," said Jesus.

ISRAELITE (ISRAEL)

Ex   16:   1 The whole *I* community set out
     35: 29 All the *I* men and women who
Nu   8: 16 offspring from every *I* woman.
     20:   1 the whole *I* community arrived
     20: 22 The whole *I* community set out
Jn   1: 47 "Here is a true *I*, in whom there is
Ro   11:   1 I am an *I* myself, a descendant

ISRAELITES (ISRAEL)

Ex   1:   7 the *I* were fruitful and multiplied
     2: 23 The *I* groaned in their slavery
     3:   9 the cry of the *I* has reached me,
     12: 35 The *I* did as Moses instructed
     12: 37 The *I* journeyed from Rameses
     14: 22 and the *I* went through the sea
     16: 12 I have heard the grumbling of the *I*.
     16: 35 The *I* ate manna forty years,
     24: 17 To the *I* the glory of the LORD
     28: 30 decisions for the *I* over his heart
     29: 45 Then I will dwell among the *I*
     31: 16 The *I* are to observe the Sabbath,
     33:   5 "Tell the *I*, 'You are a stiff-necked
     39: 42 The *I* had done all the work just
Lev   22: 32 be acknowledged as holy by the *I*
     25: 46 rule over your fellow *I* ruthlessly.
     25: 55 for the *I* belong to me as servants.
Nu   2: 32 These are the *I*, counted according
     6: 23 'This is how you are to bless the *I*.
     9:   2 "Have the *I* celebrate the Passover
     9: 17 the *I* set out; wherever the cloud
     10: 12 Then the *I* set out from the Desert
     14:   2 All the *I* grumbled against Moses
     20: 12 as holy in the sight of the *I*,
     21:   6 they bit the people and many *I* died
     26: 65 had told those *I* they would surely
     27: 12 and see the land I have given the *I*.
     33:   3 The *I* set out from Rameses
     35: 10 "Speak to the *I* and say to them:
Dt   33:   1 on the *I* before his death.
Jos   2:   2 about to give to them—to the *I*,
     5:   6 The *I* had moved about
     7:   1 the *I* acted unfaithfully in regard
     8: 32 There in the presence of the *I*,
     18:   1 of the *I* gathered at Shiloh
     21:   3 the *I* gave the Levites the following
     22:   9 of Manasseh left the *I* at Shiloh
Jdg   2: 11 Then the *I* did evil in the eyes
     3: 12 Once again the *I* did evil
     4:   1 the *I* once again did evil in the eyes
     6:   1 Again the *I* did evil in the eyes
     10:   6 Again the *I* did evil in the eyes
     13:   1 Again the *I* did evil in the eyes
1Sa   17:   2 Saul and the *I* assembled
1Ki   8: 63 and all the *I* dedicated the temple
     9: 22 did not make slaves of any of the *I*;
     12:   1 for all the *I* had gone there
     12: 17 But as for the *I* who were living
2Ki   17: 24 towns of Samaria to replace the *I*.
1Ch   9:   2 in their own towns were some *I*,
     10:   1 fought against Israel; the *I* fled
     11:   4 and all the *I* marched to Jerusalem.
2Ch   7:   6 and all the *I* were standing.
Ne   1:   6 the sins we *I*, including myself
Jer   16: 14 who brought the *I* up out of Egypt,'
Hos   1: 10 "Yet the *I* will be like the sand
     3:   1 Love her as the LORD loves the *I*,
Am   4:   5 boast about them, you *I*,
Mic   5:   3 return to join the *I*
Ro   9: 27 the number of the *I* be like the sand
     10:   1 for the *I* is that they may be saved.
     10: 16 But not all the *I* accepted the good
2Co   11: 22 Are they *I*? So am I.

ISSACHAR

Son of Jacob by Leah (Ge 30:18; 35:23; 1Ch
2:1). Tribe of blessed (Ge 49:14-15; Dt 33:18-
19), numbered (Nu 1:29; 26:25), allotted land
(Jos 19:17-23; Eze 48:25), assisted Deborah
(Jdg 5:15), 12,000 from (Rev 7:7).

ISSUING*

Da   9: 25 From the *i* of the decree to restore

ITALY

Ac   27:   1 decided that we would sail for *I*,
Heb   13: 24 from *I* send you their greetings.

ITCHING*

2Ti   4:   3 to say what their *i* ears want to hear

ITHAMAR

Son of Aaron (Ex 6:23; 1Ch 6:3). Duties at
tabernacle (Ex 38:21; Nu 4:21-33; 7:8).

ITTAI

2Sa   15: 19 The king said to *I* the Gittite.

IVORY

1Ki   10: 22 silver and *i*, and apes and baboons.
     22: 39 the palace he built and inlaid with *i*

JABBOK

Ge   32: 22 and crossed the ford of the *J*.
Dt   3: 16 and out to the *J* River,

JABESH

1Sa   11:   1 And all the men of *J* said to him,
     31: 12 wall of Beth Shan and went to *J*.
1Ch   10: 12 and his sons and brought them to *J*.

JABESH GILEAD

Jdg   21:   8 that no one from *J* had come to
2Sa   2:   4 the men of *J* who had buried Saul,
1Ch   10: 11 the inhabitants of *J* heard

JACOB

Second son of Isaac, twin of Esau (Ge 26:
21-26; 1Ch 1:34). Bought Esau's birthright (Ge
26:29-34); tricked Isaac into blessing him (Ge
27:1-37). Fled to Haran (Ge 28:1-5). Abrahamic
covenant perpetuated through (Ge 28:13-15;
Mal 1:2). Vision at Bethel (Ge 28:10-22). Served
Laban for Rachel and Leah (Ge 29:1-30). Children (Ge 29:31-30:24; 35:16-26; 1Ch 2-9).
Flocks increased (Ge 30:25-43). Returned to
Canaan (Ge 31). Wrestled with God; name
changed to Israel (Ge 32:22-32). Reconciled to
Esau (Ge 33). Returned to Bethel (Ge 35:1-15).
Favored Joseph (Ge 37:3). Sent sons to Egypt
during famine (Ge 42-43). Settled in Egypt (Ge
46). Blessed Ephraim and Manasseh (Ge 48).
Blessed sons (Ge 49:1-28; Heb 11:21). Death
(Ge 49:29-33). Burial (Ge 50:1-14).

JAEL*

Woman who killed Canaanite general, Sisera
(Jdg 4:17-22; 5:24-27).

JAIR

Judge from Gilead (Jdg 10:3-5).

JAIRUS*

Synagogue ruler whose daughter Jesus
raised (Mk 5:22-43; Lk 8:41-56).

JAMES

1. Apostle; brother of John (Mt 4:21-22; 10:2;
Mk 3:17; Lk 5:1-10). At transfiguration (Mt 17:
1-13; Mk 9:1-13; Lk 9:28-36). Killed by Herod
(Ac 12:2).
2. Apostle; son of Alphaeus (Mt 10:3; Mk 3:
18; Lk 6:15).
3. Brother of Jesus (Mt 13:55; Mk 6:3; Lk 24:
10; Gal 1:19) and Judas (Jude 1). With believers
before Pentecost (Ac 1:13). Leader of church at
Jerusalem (Ac 12:17; 15; 21:18; Gal 2:9, 12).
Author of epistle (Jas 1:1).

JAPHETH

Son of Noah (Ge 5:32; 1Ch 1:4-5). Blessed
(Ge 9:18-28). Sons of (Ge 10:2-5).

JAR (JARS)

Ge   24: 14 let down your *j* that I may have
1Ki   17: 14 'The *j* of flour will not be used up
Jer   19:   1 "Go and buy a clay *j* from a potter.
Lk   8: 16 hides it in a *j* or puts it under a bed.

JARS (JAR)

Jn 2: 6 Nearby stood six stone water j,
2Co 4: 7 we have this treasure in j of clay

JASPER

Ex 28:20 row a chrysolite, an onyx and a j.
Eze 28:13 chrysolite, onyx and j,
Rev 4: 3 sat there had the appearance of j
21:19 The first foundation was j.

JAVELIN

1Sa 17:45 me with sword and spear and j,

JAWBONE

Jdg 15:15 Finding a fresh j of a donkey,

JEALOUS (JEALOUSY)

Ex 20: 5 the LORD your God, am a j God,
34:14 whose name is Jealous, is a j God.
Dt 4:24 God is a consuming fire, a j God.
6:15 is a j God and his anger will burn
32:21 They made me j by what is no god
Jos 24:19 He is a holy God; he is a j God.
Eze 16:38 of my wrath and j anger.
16:42 my j anger will turn away from you
23:25 I will direct my j anger against you,
36: 6 in my j wrath because you have
Joel 2:18 the LORD will be j for his land
Na 1: 2 LORD is a j and avenging God;
Zep 1: 8 consumed by the fire of my j anger.
Zec 1:14 I am very j for Jerusalem and Zion,
8: 2 "I am very j for Zion; I am burning
2Co 11: 2 I am j for you with a godly jealousy

JEALOUSY (JEALOUS)

Ps 79: 5 How long will your j burn like fire?
Pr 6:34 for j arouses a husband's fury,
27: 4 but who can stand before j?
SS 8: 6 its j unyielding as the grave.
Zep 1:18 In the fire of his j
Zec 8: 2 I am burning with j for her."
Ro 13:13 debauchery, not in dissension and j
1Co 3: 3 For since there is j and quarreling
10:22 trying to arouse the Lord's j?
2Co 11: 2 I am jealous for you with a godly j.
12:20 j, outbursts of anger, factions,
Gal 5:20 hatred, discord, j, fits of rage,

JECONIAH see JEHOIACHIN

JEERS*

Heb 11:36 Some faced j and flogging,

JEHOAHAZ

1. Son of Jehu; king of Israel (2Ki 13:1-9).
2. Son of Josiah; king of Judah (2Ki 23:31-34;
2Ch 36:1-4).

JEHOASH

1. See JOASH.
2. Son of Josiah, king of Israel. Defeat of
Aram prophesied by Elisha (2Ki 13:10-25). Defeated Amaziah in Jerusalem (2Ki 14:1-16; 2Ch
25:17-24).

JEHOIACHIN

Son of Jehoiakim; king of Judah exiled by
Nebuchadnezzar (2Ki 24:8-17; 2Ch 36:8-10; Jer
22:24-30; 24:1). Raised from prisoner status
(2Ki 25:27-30; Jer 52:31-34).

JEHOIADA

Priest who sheltered Joash from Athaliah (2Ki
11-12; 2Ch 22:11-24:16).

JEHOIAKIM

Son of Josiah; made king of Judah by Pharaoh Neco (2Ki 23:34-24:6; 2Ch 36:4-8; Jer 22:
18-23). Burned scroll of Jeremiah's prophecies
(Jer 36).

JEHORAM

1. Son of Jehoshaphat; king of Judah (2Ki 8:
16-24). Prophesied against by Elijah; killed by
the LORD (2Ch 21).
2. See JORAM.

JEHOSHAPHAT

Son of Asa; king of Judah. Strengthened his
kingdom (2Ch 17). Joined with Ahab against
Aram (2Ki 22; 2Ch 18). Established judges (2Ch
19). Joined with Joram against Moab (2Ch 3; 2Ch
20).

JEHOVAH see LORD‡

JEHU

1. Prophet against Baasha (2Ki 16:1-7).
2. King of Israel. Anointed by Elijah to obliterate house of Ahab (1Ki 19:16-17); anointed by
servant of Elisha (2Ki 9:1-13). Killed Joram and
Ahaziah (2Ki 9:14-29; 2Ch 22:7-9), Jezebel (2Ki
9:30-37); relatives of Ahab (2Ki 10:1-17), ministers of Baal (2Ki 10:18-29). Death (2Ki 10:30-
36).

JEPHTHAH

Judge from Gilead who delivered Israel from
Ammon (Jdg 10:6-12:7). Made rash vow concerning his daughter (Jdg 11:30-40).

JEREMIAH

Prophet to Judah (Jer 1:1-3). Called by the
LORD (Jer 1). Put in stocks (Jer 20:1-3). Threatened for prophesying (Jer 11:18-23; 26). Opposed by Hananiah (Jer 28). Scroll burned (Jer
36). Imprisoned (Jer 37). Thrown into cistern
(Jer 38). Forced to Egypt with those fleeing Babylonians (Jer 43).

JERICHO

Nu 22: 1 along the Jordan across from J.
Jos 3:16 the people crossed over opposite J.
5:10 camped at Gilgal on the plains of J.
Lk 10:30 going down from Jerusalem to J,
Heb 11:30 By faith the walls of J fell,

JEROBOAM

1. Official of Solomon; rebelled to become
first king of Israel (1Ki 11:26-40; 12:1-20; 2Ch
10). Idolatry (1Ki 12:25-33); judgment for (1Ki
13-14; 2Ch 13).
2. Son of Jehoash; king of Israel (1Ki 14:23-
29).

JERUB-BAAL see GIDEON

JERUSALEM

Jos 10: 1 of J heard that Joshua had taken Ai
15: 8 of the Jebusite city (that is, J).
Jdg 1: 8 The men of Judah attacked J also
1Sa 17:54 head and brought it to J,
2Sa 5: 5 and in J he reigned over all Israel
5: 6 and his men marched to J
9:13 And Mephibosheth lived in J,
11: 1 but David remained in J
15:29 took the ark of God back to J
24:16 stretched out his hand to destroy J,
1Ki 3: 1 the LORD, and the wall around J
9:15 the wall of J, and Hazor, Megiddo
9:19 whatever he desired to build in J,
10:26 cities and also with him in J.
10:27 as common in J as stones,
11: 7 of J, Solomon built a high place
11:13 my servant and for the sake of J,
11:36 always have a lamp before me in J,
11:42 Solomon reigned in J
12:27 at the temple of the LORD in J,
14:21 and he reigned seventeen years in J
14:25 Shishak king of Egypt attacked J.
15: 2 and he reigned in J three years.
15:10 and he reigned in J forty-one years.
22:42 he reigned in J twenty-five years.
2Ki 8:17 and he reigned in J eight years.
8:26 and he reigned in J one year.
12: 1 and he reigned in J forty years.
12:17 Then he turned to attack J.
14: 2 he reigned in J twenty-nine years.
14:13 Then Jehoash went to J
15: 2 and he reigned in J fifty-two years.
15:33 and he reigned in J sixteen years.
16: 2 and he reigned in J sixteen years.
16: 5 Israel marched up to fight against J
18: 2 he reigned in J twenty-nine years.
18:17 Lachish to King Hezekiah at J.
19:31 For out of J will come a remnant,
21: 1 and he reigned in J fifty-five years.
21:12 going to bring such disaster on J
21:19 and he reigned in J two years.
22: 1 he reigned in J thirty-one years.
23:27 and I will reject J, the city I chose,
23:31 and he reigned in J three months.
23:36 and he reigned in J eleven years.
24: 8 and he reigned in J three months.
24:10 king of Babylon advanced on J
24:14 He carried into exile all J:
24:18 and he reigned in J eleven years.
24:20 anger that all this happened to J
25: 1 king of Babylon marched against J

2Ki 25: 9 royal palace and all the houses of J.
1Ch 11: 4 and all the Israelites marched to J,
21:16 sword in his hand extended over J
2Ch 1: 4 he had pitched a tent for it in J.
3: 1 the LORD in J on Mount Moriah,
6: 6 now I have chosen J for my Name
9: 1 she came to J to test him
20:15 and all who live in Judah and J!
20:27 and J returned joyfully to J.
29: 8 LORD has fallen on Judah and J;
36:19 and broke down the wall of J;
Ezr 1: 2 a temple for him at J in Judah.
2: 1 to Babylon (they returned to J
3: 1 people assembled as one man in J,
4:12 up to us from you have gone to J
4:24 of God in J came to a standstill
6:12 or to destroy this temple in J.
7: 8 Ezra arrived in J in the fifth month
9: 9 a wall of protection in Judah and J.
10: 7 for all the exiles to assemble in J
Ne 1: 2 the exile, and also about J.
1: 3 The wall of J is broken down,
2:11 to J, and after staying there three
2:17 Come, let us rebuild the wall of J,
2:20 you have no share in J or any claim
3: 8 They restored J as far as the Broad
4: 8 fight against J and stir up trouble
11: 1 leaders of the people settled in J,
12:27 At the dedication of the wall of J,
12:43 in J could be heard far away.
Ps 51:18 build up the walls of J.
79: 1 they have reduced J to rubble.
122: 2 in your gates, O J.
122: 3 J is built like a city
122: 6 Pray for the peace of J:
125: 2 As the mountains surround J,
128: 5 may you see the prosperity of J,
137: 5 If I forget you, O J,
147: 2 The LORD builds up J;
147:12 Extol the LORD, O J;
SS 6: 4 lovely as J,
Isa 1: 1 and J that Isaiah son of Amoz saw
2: 1 saw concerning Judah and J:
3: 1 is about to take from J and Judah
3: 8 J staggers;
4: 3 recorded among the living in J,
8:14 And for the people of J he will be
27:13 LORD on the holy mountain in J.
31: 9 the LORD Almighty will shield J;
33:20 your eyes will see J,
40: 2 Speak tenderly to J,
40: 9 You who bring good tidings to J,
52: 1 O J, the holy city.
52: 2 rise up, sit enthroned, O J.
62: 6 on your walls, O J,
62: 7 give him no rest till he establishes J
65:18 for I will create J to be a delight
Jer 2: 2 and proclaim in the hearing of J:
3:17 time they will call J The Throne
4: 5 and proclaim in J and say:
4:14 O J, wash the evil from your heart
5: 1 "Go up and down the streets of J,
6: 6 and build siege ramps against J.
8: 5 Why does J always turn away?
9:11 "I will make J a heap of ruins,
13:27 Woe to you, O J!
23:14 And among the prophets of J
24: 1 into exile from J to Babylon
26:18 J will become a heap of rubble,
32: 2 of Babylon was then besieging J,
33:10 the streets of J that are deserted,
39: 1 This is how J was taken: In
51:50 and think on J."
52:14 broke down all the walls around J.
La 1: 7 J remembers all the treasures
Eze 14:21 send against J my four dreadful
16: 2 confront J with her detestable
Da 6:10 the windows opened toward J,
9: 2 of J would last seventy years.
9:12 done like what has been done to J.
9:25 and rebuild J until the Anointed
Joel 3: 1 restore the fortunes of Judah and J,
3:16 and thunder from J;
3:17 J will be holy;
Am 2: 5 will consume the fortresses of J."
Ob :11 and cast lots for J.
Mic 1: 5 Is it not J?
4: 2 the word of the LORD from J.
Zep 3:16 On that day they will say to J,
Zec 1:14 'I am very jealous for J and Zion,
1:17 comfort Zion and choose J.'"
2: 2 He answered me, "To measure J,
2: 4 'J will be a city without walls
8: 3 I will return to Zion and dwell in J.
8: 8 I will bring them back to live in J;

Zec   8:15 determined to do good again to J
     8:22 powerful nations will come to J
     9: 9 Shout, Daughter of J!
     9:10 and the war-horses from J,
    12: 3 I will make J an immovable rock
    12:10 the inhabitants of J a spirit of grace
    14: 2 the nations to J to fight against it;
    14: 8 living water will flow out from J,
    14:16 that have attacked J will go up
Mt   16:21 to his disciples that he must go to J
    20:18 said to them, "We are going up to J
    21:10 When Jesus entered J, the whole
    23:37 "O J, J, you who kill the prophets
Mk   10:33 "We are going up to J," he said,
Lk   2:22 Mary took him to J to present him
     2:41 Every year his parents went to J
     2:43 the boy Jesus stayed behind in J,
     4: 9 The devil led him to J
     9:31 about to bring to fulfillment at J.
     9:51 Jesus resolutely set out for J,
    13:34 die outside J! "O J, J,
    18:31 told them, "We are going up to J,
    19:41 As he approached J and saw
    21:20 "When you see J being surrounded
    21:24 J will be trampled
    24:47 name to all nations, beginning at J.
Jn   4:20 where we must worship is in J."
Ac   1: 4 this command: "Do not leave J,
     1: 8 and you will be my witnesses in J,
     6: 7 of disciples in J increased rapidly,
    20:22 by the Spirit, I am going to J,
    23:11 As you have testified about me in J
Ro   15:19 So from J all the way
Gal   4:25 corresponds to the present city of J
     4:26 But the J that is above is free,
Heb   12:22 to the heavenly J, the city
Rev   3:12 the new J, which is coming
    21: 2 I saw the Holy City, the new J,
    21:10 and showed me the Holy City, J,

JESSE

Father of David (Ru 4:17-22; 1Sa 16; 1Ch 2: 12-17).

JESUS

LIFE: Genealogy (Mt 1:1-17; Lk 3:21-37). Birth announced (Mt 1:18-25; Lk 1:26-45). Birth (Mt 2:1-12; Lk 2:1-40). Escape to Egypt (Mt 2: 13-23). As a boy in the temple (Lk 2:41-52). Baptism (Mt 3:13-17; Mk 1:9-11; Lk 3:21-22; Jn 1:32-34). Temptation (Mt 4:1-11; Mk 1:12-13; Lk 4:1-13). Ministry in Galilee (Mt 4:12-18:35; Mk 1: 14-9:50; Lk 4:14-13:9; Jn 1:35-2:11; 4; 6). Transfiguration (Mt 17:1-8; Mk 9:2-8; Lk 9:28-36), on the way to Jerusalem (Mt 19-20; Mk 10; Lk 13: 10-19:27), in Jerusalem (Mt 21-25; Mk 11-13; Lk 19:28-21:38; Jn 2:12-3:36; 5; 7-12). Last supper (Mt 26:17-35; Mk 14:12-31; Lk 22:1-38; Jn 13-17). Arrest and trial (Mt 26:36-27:31; Mk 14:43-15:20; Lk 22:39-23:25; Jn 18:1-19:16). Crucifixion (Mt 27:32-66; Mk 15:21-47; Lk 23:26-55; Jn 19:28-42). Resurrection and appearances (Mt 28; Mk 16; Lk 24; Jn 20-21; Ac 1:1-11; 7:56; 9: 3-6; 1Co 15:1-8; Rev 1:1-20).

MIRACLES. Healings: official's son (Jn 4:43-54), demoniac in Capernaum (Mk 1:23-26; Lk 4: 33-35), Peter's mother-in-law (Mt 8:14-17; Mk 1: 29-31; Lk 4:38-39), leper (Mt 8:2-4; Mk 1:40-45; Lk 5:12-16), paralytic (Mt 9:2-8; Mk 2:1-12; Lk 5: 17-26), cripple (Jn 5:1-9), shriveled hand (Mt 12: 10-13; Mk 3:1-5; Lk 6:6-11), centurion's servant (Mt 8:5-13; Lk 7:1-10), widow's son raised (Lk 7: 11-17), demoniac (Mt 12:22-23; Lk 11:14), Gadarene demoniacs (Mt 8:28-34; Mk 5:1-20; Lk 8:26-39), woman's bleeding and Jairus' daughter (Mt 9:18-26; Mk 5:21-43; Lk 8:40-56), blind man (Mt 9:27-31), mute man (Mt 9:32-33), Canaanite woman's daughter (Mt 15:21-28; Mk 7:24-30), deaf man (Mk 7:31-37), blind man (Mk 8:22-26), demoniac boy (Mt 17:14-18; Mk 9:14-29; Lk 9:37-43), ten lepers (Lk 17:11-19), man born blind (Jn 9:1-7), Lazarus raised (Jn 11), crippled woman (Lk 13:11-17), man with dropsy (Lk 14:1-6), two blind men (Mt 20:29-34; Mk 10: 46-52; Lk 18:35-43), Malchus' ear (Lk 22:50-51). Other Miracles: water to wine (Jn 2:1-11), catch of fish (Lk 5:1-11), storm stilled (Mt 8:23-27; Mk 4:37-41; Lk 8:22-25), 5,000 fed (Mt 14:15-21; Mk 6:35-44; Lk 9:10-17; Jn 6:1-14), walking on water (Mt 14:25-33; Mk 6:48-52; Jn 6:15-21), 4,000 fed (Mt 15:32-39; Mk 8:1-9), money from fish (Mt 17:24-27), fig tree cursed (Mt 21:18-22; Mk 11:12-14), catch of fish (Jn 21:1-14).

MAJOR TEACHING: Sermon on the Mount (Mt 5-7; Lk 6:17-49), to Nicodemus (Jn 3), to

Samaritan woman (Jn 4), Bread of Life (Jn 6: 22-59), at Feast of Tabernacles (Jn 7-8), woes to Pharisees (Mt 23; Lk 11:37-54), Good Shepherd (Jn 10:1-18), Olivet Discourse (Mt 24-25; Mk 13; Lk 21:5-36), Upper Room Discourse (Jn 13-16).

PARABLES: Sower (Mt 13:3-23; Mk 4:3-25; Lk 8:5-18), seed's growth (Mk 4:26-29), wheat and weeds (Mt 13:24-30, 36-43), mustard seed (Mt 13:31-32; Mk 4:30-32), yeast (Mt 13:33; Lk 13:20-21), hidden treasure (Mt 13:44), valuable pearl (Mt 13:45-46), net (Mt 13:47-51), house owner (Mt 13:52), good Samaritan (Lk 10:25-37), unmerciful servant (Mt 18:15-35), lost sheep (Mt 18:10-14; Lk 15:4-7), lost coin (Lk 15: 8-10), prodigal son (Lk 15:11-32), dishonest manager (Lk 16:1-13), rich man and Lazarus (Lk 16:19-31), persistent widow (Lk 18:1-8), Pharisee and tax collector (Lk 18:9-14), payment of workers (Mt 20:1-16), tenants and the vineyard (Mt 21:28-46; Mt 12:1-12; Lk 20:9-19), wedding banquet (Mt 22:1-14), faithful servant (Mt 24: 45-51), ten virgins (Mt 25:1-13), talents (Mt 25: 1-30; Lk 19:12-27).

DISCIPLES see APOSTLES. Call of (Jn 1:35-51; Mt 4:18-22; 9:9; Mk 1:16-20; 2:13-14; Lk 5: 1-11, 27-28). Named Apostles (Mk 3:13-19; Lk 6:12-16). Twelve sent out (Mt 10; Mk 6:7-11; Lk 9:1-5). Seventy sent out (Lk 10:1-24). Defection of (Jn 6:60-71; Mt 26:56; Mk 14:50-52). Final commission (Mt 28:16-20; Jn 21:15-23; Ac 1: 3-8).

Ac   2:32 God has raised this J to life,
     9: 5 "I am J, whom you are persecuting
     9:34 said to him, "J Christ heals you:
    15:11 of our Lord J that we are saved,
    16:31 "Believe in the Lord J,
    20:24 the task the Lord J has given me—
Ro   3:24 redemption that came by Christ J.
     5:17 life through the one man, J Christ.
     8: 1 for those who are in Christ J,
1Co   1: 7 for our Lord J Christ to be revealed
     2: 2 except J Christ and him crucified.
     6:11 in the name of the Lord J Christ
     8: 6 and there is but one Lord, J Christ,
   12: 3 and no one can say, "J is Lord,"
2Co   4: 5 not preach ourselves, but J Christ
   13: 5 Do you not realize that Christ J is
Gal   2:16 but by faith in J Christ.
     3:28 for you are all one in Christ J.
     5: 6 in Christ J neither circumcision
     6:17 bear on my body the marks of J.
Eph   1: 5 as his sons through J Christ,
     2:10 created in Christ J
     2:20 with Christ J himself as the chief
Php   1: 6 until the day of Christ J,
     2: 5 be the same as that of Christ J:
     2:10 name of J every knee should bow,
Col   3:17 do it all in the name of the Lord J,
1Th   1:10 whom he raised from the dead—J,
     4:14 We believe that J died
     5:23 at the coming of our Lord J Christ.
2Th   1: 7 when the Lord J is revealed
     2: 1 the coming of our Lord J Christ
1Ti   1:15 Christ J came into the world
2Ti   1:10 appearing of our Savior, Christ J,
     2: 3 us like a good soldier of Christ J.
     3:12 life in Christ J will be persecuted,
Tit   2:13 our great God and Savior, J Christ,
Heb   2: 9 But we see J, who was made a little
     2:11 So J is not ashamed to call them
     3: 1 fix your thoughts on J, the apostle
     3: 3 J has been found worthy
     4:14 through the heavens, J the Son
     6:20 where J, who went before us,
     7:22 J has become the guarantee
     7:24 but because J lives forever,
     8: 6 But the ministry J has received is
   12: 2 Let us fix our eyes on J, the author
   12:24 to J the mediator of a new
1Pe   1: 3 the resurrection of J Christ
2Pe   1:16 and coming of our Lord J Christ,
1Jn   1: 7 and the blood of J, his Son,
     2: 1 J Christ, the Righteous One.
     2: 6 to live in him must walk as J did.
     4:15 anyone acknowledges that J is
Rev   1: 1 The revelation of J Christ,
    22:16 J, have sent my angel
    22:20 Come, Lord J.

JETHRO

Father-in-law and adviser of Moses (Ex 3:1; 18). Also known as Reuel (Ex 2:18).

JEW (JEWS JEWS' JUDAISM)

Est   2: 5 of Susa a J of the tribe of Benjamin,
Zec   8:23 of one J by the hem of his robe
Ac   21:39 "I am a J, from Tarsus in Cilicia,
Ro   1:16 first for the J, then for the Gentile.
     2:28 A man is not a J if he is only one
     10:12 there is no difference between J
1Co   9:20 To the Jews I became like a J,
Gal   2:14 "You are a J, yet you live like
     3:28 There is neither J nor Greek,
Col   3:11 Here there is no Greek or J,

JEWEL (JEWELRY JEWELS)

Pr   20:15 that speak knowledge are a rare j.
SS   4: 9 with one j of your necklace.
Rev   21:11 that of a very precious j.

JEWELRY (JEWEL)

Ex   35:22 and brought gold j of all kinds:
Jer   2:32 Does a maiden forget her j,
Eze   16:11 you with j I put bracelets
1Pe   3: 3 wearing of gold j and fine clothes.

JEWELS (JEWEL)

Isa   54:12 your gates of sparkling j,
   61:10 as a bride adorns herself with her j.
Zec   9:16 like j in a crown.

JEWS (JEW)

Ne   4: 1 He ridiculed the J.
Est   3:13 kill and annihilate all the J—
     4:14 and deliverance for the J will arise
Mt   2: 2 who has been born king of the J?
   27:11 "Are you the king of the J?" "Yes,
Jn   4: 9 (For J do not associate
     4:22 for salvation is from the J.
    19: 3 saying, "Hail, king of the J!"
Ac   20:21 I have declared to both J
Ro   3:29 Is God the God of J only?
     9:24 not only from the J but
    15:27 they owe it to the J to share
1Co   1:22 J demand miraculous signs
     9:20 To the J I became like a Jew,
    12:13 whether J or Greeks, slave or free
Gal   2: 8 of Peter as an apostle to the J,
Rev   2: 9 slander of those who say they are J
     3: 9 claim to be J though they are not,

JEWS' (JEW)

Ro   15:27 shared in the J spiritual blessings.

JEZEBEL

Sidonian wife of Ahab (1Ki 16:31). Promoted Baal worship (1Ki 16:32-33). Killed prophets of the LORD (1Ki 18:4, 13). Opposed Elijah (1Ki 19: 1-2). Had Naboth killed (1Ki 21). Death prophesied (1Ki 21:17-24). Killed by Jehu (2Ki 9:30-37).

JEZREEL

2Ki   9:36 at J dogs will devour Jezebel's flesh
   10: 7 and sent them to Jehu in J.
Hos   1: 4 house of Jehu for the massacre at J,

JOAB

Nephew of David (1Ch 2:16). Commander of his army (2Sa 8:16). Victorious over Ammon (2Sa 10; 1Ch 19), Rabbah (2Sa 11; 1Ch 20), Jerusalem (1Ch 11:6), Absalom (2Sa 18), Sheba (2Sa 20). Killed Abner (2Sa 3:22-39), Amasa (2Sa 20:1-13). Numbered David's army (2Sa 24; 1Ch 21). Sided with Adonijah (1Ki 1:17, 19). Killed by Benaiah (1Ki 2:5-6, 28-35).

JOASH

Son of Ahaziah; king of Judah. Sheltered from Athaliah by Jehoiada (2Ki 11; 2Ch 22:10-23:21). Repaired temple (2Ki 12; 2Ch 24).

JOB

Wealthy man from Uz; feared God (Job 1: 1-5). Righteousness tested by disaster (Job 1: 6-22), personal affliction (Job 2). Maintained innocence in debate with three friends (Job 3-31), Elihu (Job 32-37). Rebuked by the LORD (Job 38-41). Vindicated and restored to greater stature by the LORD (Job 42). Example of righteousness (Eze 14:14, 20).

JOCHEBED*

Mother of Moses and Aaron (Ex 6:20; Nu 26: 59).

JOEL

Prophet (Joel 1:1; Ac 2:16).

JOHN

1. Son of Zechariah and Elizabeth (Lk 1). Called the Baptist (Mt 3:1-12; Mk 1:2-8). Witness to Jesus (Mt 3:11-12; Mk 1:7-8; Lk 3:15-18; Jn 1:6-35; 3:27-30; 5:33-36). Doubts about Jesus (Mt 11:2-6; Lk 7:18-23). Arrest (Mt 4:12; Mk 1:14). Execution (Mt 14:1-12; Mk 6:14-29; Lk 9:7-9). Ministry compared to Elijah (Mt 11:7-19; Mk 9:11-13; Lk 7:24-35).

2. Apostle; brother of James (Mt 4:21-22; 10:2; Mk 3:17; Lk 5:1-10). At transfiguration (Mt 17:1-13; Mk 9:1-13; Lk 9:28-36). Desire to be greatest (Mk 10:35-45). Leader of church at Jerusalem (Ac 4:1-3; Gal 2:9). Elder who wrote epistles (2Jn 1; 3Jn 1). Prophet who wrote Revelation (Rev 1:1; 22:8).

3. Cousin of Barnabas, co-worker with Paul, (Ac 12:12-13:13; 15:37), see MARK.

JOIN (JOINED JOINS)

Ne	10: 29	all these now j their brothers
Pr	23: 20	Do not j those who drink too much
	24: 21	and do not j with the rebellious,
Jer	3: 18	of Judah will j the house of Israel,
Eze	37: 17	J them together into one stick
Da	11: 34	who are not sincere will j them.
Ro	15: 30	to j me in my struggle by praying
2Ti	1: 8	j with me in suffering for the gospel

JOINED (JOIN)

Zec	2: 11	"Many nations will be j
Mt	19: 6	Therefore what God has j together,
Mk	10: 9	Therefore what God has j together,
Ac	1: 14	They all j together constantly
Eph	2: 21	him the whole building is j together
	4: 16	joined and held together

JOINS (JOIN)

1Co	16: 16	and to everyone who j in the work,

JOINT (JOINTS)

Ps	22: 14	and all my bones are out of j.

JOINTS (JOINT)

Heb	4: 12	even to dividing soul and spirit, j

JOKING*

Ge	19: 14	his sons-in-law thought he was j.
Pr	26: 19	and says, "I was only j!"
Eph	5: 4	or coarse j, which are out of place.

JONAH

Prophet in days of Jeroboam II (2Ki 14:25). Called to Nineveh; fled to Tarshish (Jnh 1:1-3). Cause of storm; thrown into sea (Jnh 1:4-16). Swallowed by fish (Jnh 1:17). Prayer (Jnh 2). Preached to Nineveh (Jnh 3). Attitude reproved by the LORD (Jnh 4). Sign of (Mt 12:39-41; Lk 11:29-32).

JONATHAN

Son of Saul (1Sa 13:16; 1Ch 8:33). Valiant warrior (1Sa 13-14). Relation to David (1Sa 18:1-4; 19-20; 23:16-18). Killed at Gilboa (1Sa 31). Mourned by David (2Sa 1).

JOPPA

Ezr	3: 7	logs by sea from Lebanon to J,
Jnh	1: 3	to J, where he found a ship bound
Ac	9: 43	Peter stayed in J for some time

JORAM

1. Son of Ahab; king of Israel. Fought with Jehoshaphat against Moab (2Ki 3). Killed with Ahaziah by Jehu (2Ki 8:25-29; 9:14-26; 2Ch 22:5-9).

2. See JEHORAM.

JORDAN

Ge	13: 10	plain of the J was well watered,
Nu	22: 1	and camped along the J
	34: 12	boundary will go down along the J
Dt	3: 27	you are not going to cross this J.
Jos	1: 2	get ready to cross the J River
	3: 11	go into the J ahead of you.
	3: 17	ground in the middle of the J,
	4: 22	Israel crossed the J on dry ground.'
2Ki	2: 7	and Elisha had stopped at the J.
	2: 13	and stood on the bank of the J.
	5: 10	wash yourself seven times in the J,
	6: 4	They went to the J and began
Ps	114: 3	the J turned back;
Isa	9: 1	along the J— The people walking
Jer	12: 5	manage in the thickets by the J?

Mt	3: 6	baptized by him in the J River.
	4: 15	the way to the sea, along the J,
Mk	1: 9	and was baptized by John in the J.

JOSEPH

1. Son of Jacob by Rachel (Ge 30:24; 1Ch 2:2). Favored by Jacob, hated by brothers (Ge 37:3-4). Dreams (Ge 37:5-11). Sold by brothers (Ge 37:12-36). Served Potiphar; imprisoned by false accusation (Ge 39). Interpreted dreams of Pharaoh's servants (Ge 40), of Pharaoh (Ge 41:4-40). Made greatest in Egypt (Ge 41:41-57). Sold grain to brothers (Ge 42-45). Brought Jacob and sons to Egypt (Ge 46-47). Sons Ephraim and Manasseh blessed (Ge 48). Blessed (Ge 49:22-26; Dt 33:13-17). Death (Ge 50:22-26; Ex 13:19; Heb 11:22). 12,000 from (Rev 7:8).

2. Husband of Mary, mother of Jesus (Mt 1:16-24; 2:13-19; Lk 1:27; 2; Jn 1:45).

3. Disciple from Arimathea, who gave his tomb for Jesus' burial (Mt 27:57-61; Mk 15:43-47; Lk 24:50-52).

4. Original name of Barnabas (Ac 4:36).

JOSHUA (HOSHEA)

1. Son of Nun; name changed from Hoshea (Nu 13:8, 16; 1Ch 7:27). Fought Amalekites under Moses (Ex 17:9-14). Servant of Moses on Sinai (Ex 24:13; 32:17). Spied Canaan (Nu 13). With Caleb, allowed to enter land (Nu 14:6, 30). Succeeded Moses (Dt 1:38; 31:1-8; 34:9).

Charged Israel to conquer Canaan (Jos 1). Crossed Jordan (Jos 3-4). Circumcised sons of wilderness wanderings (Jos 5). Conquered Jericho (Jos 6), Ai (Jos 7-8), five kings at Gibeon (Jos 10:1-28), southern Canaan (Jos 10:29-43), northern Canaan (Jos 11-12). Defeated at Ai (Jos 7). Deceived by Gibeonites (Jos 9). Renewed covenant (Jos 8:30-35; 24:1-27). Divided land among tribes (Jos 13-22). Last words (Jos 23). Death (Jos 24:28-31).

2. High priest during rebuilding of temple (Hag 1-2; Zec 3:1-9; 6:11).

JOSIAH

Son of Amon; king of Judah (2Ki 21:26; 1Ch 3:14). Prophesied (1Ki 13:2). Book of Law discovered during his reign (2Ki 22; 2Ch 34:14-31). Reforms (2Ki 23:1-25; 2Ch 34:1-13; 35:1-19). Killed by Pharaoh Neco (2Ki 23:29-30; 2Ch 35:20-27).

JOTHAM

1. Son of Gideon (Jdg 9).

2. Son of Azariah (Uzziah); king of Judah (2Ki 15:32-38; 2Ch 26:21-27:9).

JOURNEY

Dt	1: 33	who went ahead of you on your j,
	2: 7	over your j through this vast desert
Jdg	18: 6	Your j has the LORD's approval."
Ezr	8: 21	and ask him for a safe j for us
Job	16: 22	before I go on the j of no return.
Isa	35: 8	The unclean will not j on it;
Mt	25: 14	it will be like a man going on a j,
Ro	15: 24	to have you assist me on my j there

JOY* (ENJOY ENJOYMENT JOYFUL JOYOUS OVERJOYED REJOICE REJOICES REJOICING)

Ge	31: 27	so I could send you away with j
Lev	9: 24	shouted for j and fell facedown.
Dt	16: 15	and your j will be complete.
Jdg	9: 19	may Abimelech be your j,
1Ch	12: 40	and sheep, for there was j in Israel.
	16: 27	strength and j in his dwelling place.
	16: 33	sing for j before the LORD,
	29: 17	with j how willingly your people
	29: 22	drank with great j in the presence
2Ch	30: 26	There was great j in Jerusalem,
Ezr	3: 12	while many others shouted for j,
	3: 13	of the shouts of j from the sound
	6: 16	of the house of God with j.
	6: 22	with j by changing the attitude
	6: 22	j the Feast of Unleavened Bread,
Ne	8: 10	for the j of the LORD is your
	8: 12	and to celebrate with great j,
	8: 17	And their j was very great.
	12: 43	God had given them great j
Est	8: 16	a time of happiness and j,
	8: 17	there was j and gladness
	9: 17	and made it a day of feasting and j.
	9: 18	and made it a day of feasting and j.
	9: 19	as a day of j and feasting,
	9: 22	and j and giving presents of food

Est	9: 22	their sorrow was turned into j
Job	3: 7	may no shout of j be heard in it.
	6: 10	my j in unrelenting pain—
	8: 21	and your lips with shouts of j.
	9: 25	they fly away without a glimpse of j
	10: 20	from me so I can have a moment's j
	20: 5	the j of the godless lasts
	33: 26	he sees God's face and shouts for j;
	38: 7	and all the angels shouted for j?
Ps	4: 7	have filled my heart with greater j
	5: 11	let them ever sing for j;
	16: 11	me with j in your presence,
	19: 8	giving j to the heart.
	20: 5	We will shout for j
	21: 1	How great is his j in the victories
	21: 6	with the j of your presence.
	27: 6	will I sacrifice with shouts of j;
	28: 7	My heart leaps for j;
	30: 11	sackcloth and clothed me with j,
	33: 3	play skillfully, and shout for j.
	35: 27	shout for j and gladness;
	42: 4	with shouts of j and thanksgiving
	43: 4	to God, my j and my delight.
	45: 7	by anointing you with the oil of j.
	45: 15	They are led in with j and gladness;
	47: 1	shout to God with cries of j.
	47: 5	God has ascended amid shouts of j,
	48: 2	the j of the whole earth.
	51: 8	Let me hear j and gladness;
	51: 12	to me the j of your salvation
	65: 8	you call forth songs of j.
	65: 13	they shout for j and sing.
	66: 1	Shout with j to God, all the earth!
	67: 4	the nations be glad and sing for j,
	71: 23	My lips will shout for j
	81: 1	Sing for j to God our strength;
	86: 4	Bring j to your servant,
	89: 12	Hermon sing for j at your name.
	90: 14	for j and be glad all our days.
	92: 4	I sing for j at the works
	94: 19	your consolation brought j
	95: 1	let us sing for j to the LORD;
	96: 12	the trees of the forest will sing for j;
	97: 11	and j on the upright in heart.
	98: 4	for j to the LORD, all the earth,
	98: 6	shout for j before the LORD,
	98: 8	the mountains sing together for j;
	100: 1	for j to the LORD, all the earth.
	105: 43	his chosen ones with shouts of j;
	106: 5	share in the j of your nation
	107: 22	and tell of his works with songs of j
	118: 15	Shouts of j and victory
	119:111	they are the j of my heart.
	126: 2	our tongues with songs of j.
	126: 3	and we are filled with j.
	126: 5	will reap with songs of j.
	126: 6	will return with songs of j,
	132: 9	may your saints sing for j."
	132: 16	and her saints will ever sing for j.
	137: 3	tormentors demanded songs of j;
	137: 6	my highest j.
	149: 5	and sing for j on their beds.
Pr	10: 1	A wise son brings j to his father,
	10: 28	The prospect of the righteous is j,
	11: 10	wicked perish, there are shouts of j,
	12: 20	but j for those who promote peace.
	14: 10	and no one else can share its j.
	14: 13	and j may end in grief.
	15: 20	A wise son brings j to his father,
	15: 23	A man finds j in giving an apt reply
	15: 30	A cheerful look brings j
	17: 21	there is no j for the father of a fool.
	21: 15	it brings j to the righteous
	23: 24	of a righteous man has great j;
	27: 9	incense bring j to the heart,
	27: 11	my son, and bring j to my heart;
	29: 3	A man who loves wisdom brings j
Ecc	8: 15	Then j will accompany him
	11: 9	let your heart give you j in the days
	11: 9	and increased their j.
Isa	9: 3	and increased their j.
	12: 3	With j you will draw water
	12: 6	Shout aloud and sing for j;
	16: 9	shouts of j over your ripened fruit
	16: 10	J and gladness are taken away
	22: 13	But see, there is j and revelry,
	24: 11	all j turns to gloom,
	24: 14	raise their voices, they shout for j;
	26: 19	wake up and shout for j.
	35: 2	will rejoice greatly and shout for j.
	35: 6	the mute tongue shout for j.
	35: 10	Gladness and j will overtake them,
	35: 10	everlasting j will crown their heads
	42: 11	Let the people of Sela sing for j;
	44: 23	Sing for j, O heavens,
	48: 20	Announce this with shouts of j

Isa 49:13 Shout for j, O heavens;
51: 3 J and gladness will be found in her,
51:11 Gladness and j will overtake them,
51:11 everlasting j will crown their heads
52: 8 together they shout for j
52: 9 Burst into songs of j together,
54: 1 burst into song, shout for j,
55:12 You will go out in j
56: 7 give them j in my house of prayer
58:14 then you will find your j
60: 5 heart will throb and swell with j;
60:15 and the j of all generations.
61: 7 and everlasting j will be theirs.
65:14 out of the j of their hearts,
65:18 and its people a j
66: 5 that we may see your j!'
Jer 7:34 will bring an end to the sounds of j
15:16 they were my j and my heart's
16: 9 will bring an end to the sounds of j
25:10 banish from them the sounds of j
31: 7 "Sing with j for Jacob;
31:12 shout for j on the heights of Zion;
31:13 give them comfort and j instead
33: 9 this city will bring me renown, j,
33:11 be heard once more the sounds of j
48: 3 J and gladness are gone
48:33 no one treads them with shouts of j
48:33 they are not shouts of j.
51:48 will shout for j over Babylon,
La 2:15 the j of the whole earth?''
5:15 J is gone from our hearts;
Eze 7: 7 not j, upon the mountains.
24:25 their j and glory, the delight
Joel 1:12 Surely the j of mankind
1:16 j and gladness
Mt 13:20 and at once receives it with j.
13:44 in his j went and sold all he had
28: 8 afraid yet filled with j,
Mk 4:16 and at once receive it with j.
Lk 1:14 He will be a j and delight to you,
1:44 the baby in my womb leaped for j.
1:58 great mercy, and they shared her j.
2:10 news of great j that will be
6:23 "Rejoice in that day and leap for j,
8:13 the word with j when they hear it,
10:17 The seventy-two returned with j
10:21 full of j through the Holy Spirit,
24:41 still did not believe it because of j
24:52 returned to Jerusalem with great j.
Jn 3:29 That j is mine, and it is now
3:29 full of j when he hears
15:11 and that your j may be complete.
15:11 this so that my j may be in you
16:20 but your grief will turn to j.
16:21 because of her j that a child is born
16:22 and no one will take away your j.
16:24 and your j will be complete.
17:13 measure of my j within them.
Ac 2:28 with j in your presence.'
8: 8 So there was great j in that city.
13:52 And the disciples were filled with j
14:17 and fills your hearts with j. "
16:34 he was filled with j because he had come
Ro 14:17 peace and j in the Holy Spirit,
15:13 the God of hope fill you with all j
15:32 will I may come to you with j
16:19 so I am full of j over you;
2Co 1:24 but we work with you for your j,
2: 3 that you would all share my j.
7: 4 our troubles my j knows no
7: 7 so that my j was greater than ever.
8: 2 their overflowing j and their
Gal 4:15 What has happened to all your j?
5:22 j, peace, patience, kindness,
Php 1: 4 I always pray with j
1:25 for your progress and j in the faith,
1:26 being with you again your j
2: 2 then make my j complete
2:29 him in the Lord with great j,
4: 1 and long for, my j and crown,
1Th 1: 6 with the j given by the Holy Spirit.
2:19 For what is our hope, our j,
2:20 Indeed, you are our glory and j,
3: 9 you in return for all the j we have
2Ti 1: 4 so that I may be filled with j.
Phm 7 Your love has given me great j
Heb 1: 9 by anointing you with the oil of j "
12: 2 for the j set before him endured
13:17 them so that their work will be a j,
Jas 1: 2 Consider it pure j, my brothers,
4: 9 to mourning and your j to gloom.
1Pe 1: 8 with an inexpressible and glorious j,
1Jn 4: 4 this to make our j complete.
2Jn 4 It has given me great j to find some

2Jn : 12 so that our j may be complete.
3Jn : 3 It gave me great j to have some
: 4 I have no greater j
Jude : 24 without fault and with great j—

JOYFUL* (JOY)
Dt 16:14 Be j at your Feast—you, your sons
1Sa 18: 6 with j songs and with tambourines
1Ki 8:66 j and glad in heart
1Ch 15:16 as singers to sing j songs,
2Ch 7:10 j and glad in heart
Ps 68: 3 may they be happy and j.
100: 2 come before him with j songs.
Ecc 9: 7 and drink your wine with a j heart,
Isa 24: 8 the j harp is silent.
Jer 31: 4 and go out to dance with the j.
Hab 3:18 I will be j in God my Savior.
Zec 8:19 and tenth months will become j
10: 7 Their children will see it and be j;
Ro 12:12 Be j in hope, patient in affliction,
1Th 5:16 Be j always; pray continually;
Heb 12:22 thousands of angels in j assembly.

JOYOUS* (JOY)
Est 8:15 the city of Susa held a j celebration.

JUBILANT
Ps 96:12 let the fields be j, and everything
98: 4 burst into j song with music;

JUBILEE
Lev 25:11 The fiftieth year shall be a j for you;

JUDAH (JUDEA)
1. Son of Jacob by Leah (Ge 29:35; 35:23;
1Ch 2:1). Did not want to kill Joseph (Ge 37:
26-27). Among Canaanites, fathered Perez by
Tamar (Ge 38). Tribe of blessed as ruling tribe
(Ge 49:8-12; Dt 33:7), numbered (Nu 1:27; 26:
22), allotted land (Jos 15; Eze 48:7), failed to
fully possess (Jos 15:63; Jdg 1:1-20).
2. Name used for people and land of Southern Kingdom.
Ru 1: 7 take them back to the land of J.
2Sa 2: 4 king over the house of J.
Isa 1: 1 The vision concerning J
3: 8 J is falling;
Jer 13: 9 All J will be carried into exile,
30: 3 bring my people Israel and J back
Hos 1: 7 I will show love to the house of J;
Zec 10: 4 From J will come the cornerstone,
Mt 2: 6 least among the rulers of J;
Heb 7:14 that our Lord descended from J,
8: 8 and with the house of J.
Rev 5: 5 of the tribe of J, the Root of David,

JUDAISM (JEW)
Ac 13:43 devout converts to J followed Paul
Gal 1:13 of my previous way of life in J,
1:14 advancing in J beyond many Jews

JUDAS
1. Apostle; son of James (Lk 6:16; Jn 14:22;
Ac 1:13). Probably also called Thaddaeus (Mt
10:3; Mk 3:18).
2. Brother of James and Jesus (Mt 13:55; Mk
6:3), also called Jude (Jude 1).
3. Christian prophet (Ac 15:22-32).
4. Apostle, also called Iscariot, who betrayed
Jesus (Mt 10:4; 26:14-56; Mk 3:19; 14:10-50; Lk
6:16; 22:3-53; Jn 6:71; 12:4; 13:2-30; 18:2-11).
Suicide of (Mt 27:3-5; Ac 1:16-25).

JUDE see JUDAS

JUDEA (JUDAH)
Mt 2: 1 born in Bethlehem in J,
24:16 are in J flee to the mountains.
Lk 3: 1 Pontius Pilate was governor of J,
Ac 1: 8 and in all J and Samaria,
9:31 Then the church throughout J.
1Th 2:14 imitators of God's churches in J,

JUDGE (JUDGED JUDGES JUDGING JUDGMENT JUDGMENTS)
Ge 16: 5 May the LORD j between you
18:25 Will not the J of all the earth do
Lev 19:15 but j your neighbor fairly.
Dt 1:16 between your brothers and j fairly,
17:12 man who shows contempt for the j
32:36 The LORD will j his people
Jdg 2:18 Whenever the LORD raised up a j
1Sa 2:10 the LORD will j the ends
3:13 that I would j his family forever
7:15 j over Israel all the days of his life.

1Sa 24:12 May the LORD j between you
1Ki 8:32 J between your servants,
1Ch 16:33 for he comes to j the earth.
2Ch 6:23 J between your servants, repaying
19: 7 J carefully, for with the LORD our
Job 9:15 plead with my J for mercy.
Ps 7: 8 J me, O LORD, according
7: 8 let the LORD j the peoples.
7:11 God is a righteous j,
9: 8 He will j the world in righteousness
50: 6 for God himself is j.
51: 4 and justified when you j.
75: 2 it is I who j uprightly.
76: 9 when you, O God, rose up to j,
82: 8 Rise up, O God, j the earth,
94: 2 Rise up, O J of the earth;
96:10 he will j the peoples with equity.
96:13 He will j the world in righteousness
98: 9 He will j the world in righteousness
110: 6 He will j the nations, heaping up
Pr 31: 9 Speak up and j fairly;
Isa 2: 4 He will j between the nations
3:13 he rises to j the people.
11: 3 He will not j by what he sees
33:22 For the LORD is our j,
Jer 11:20 Almighty, you who j righteously
Eze 7: 3 I will j you according
7:27 by their own standards I will j them
18:30 O house of Israel, I will j you,
20:36 so I will j you, declares
22: 2 "Son of man, will you j her?
34:17 I will j between one sheep
Joel 3:12 sit to j all the nations on every side.
Mic 3:11 Her leaders j for a bribe,
4: 3 He will j between many peoples
Mt 7: 1 Do not j, or you too will be judged.
Lk 6:37 "Do not j, and you will not be
18: 2 there was a j who neither feared
Jn 5:27 And he has given him authority to j
5:30 By myself I can do nothing; I only j
8:16 But if I do j, my decisions are right,
12:47 For I did not come to j the world,
12:48 There is a j for the one who rejects
Ac 10:42 as j of the living and the dead.
17:31 a day when he will j the world
Ro 2:16 day when God will j men's secrets
3: 6 how could God j the world?
14:10 then, why do you j your brother?
1Co 4: 3 indeed, I do not even j myself.
4: 5 Therefore j nothing
6: 2 And if you are to j the world,
6: 2 that the saints will j the world?
Gal 2: 6 not j by external appearance—
Col 2:16 Therefore do not let anyone j you
2Ti 4: 1 who will j the living and the dead,
4: 8 which the Lord, the righteous J,
Heb 10:30 "The Lord will j his people."
12:23 come to God, the j of all men,
13: 4 for God will j the adulterer
Jas 4:12 There is only one Lawgiver and J,
4:12 who are you to j your neighbor?
1Pe 4: 5 to him who is ready to j the living
Rev 20: 4 who had been given authority to j.

JUDGED (JUDGE)
Mt 7: 1 "Do not judge, or you too will be j.
1Co 2:15 I care very little if I am j by you
10:29 For why should my freedom be j
11:31 But if we judged ourselves, we would not
14:24 all that he is a sinner and will be j
Jas 3: 1 who teach will be j more strictly.
Rev 20:12 The dead were j according

JUDGES (JUDGE)
Jdg 2:16 Then the LORD raised up j,
Job 9:24 he blindfolds its j.
Ps 58:11 there is a God who j the earth."
75: 7 But it is God who j.
Pr 29:14 If a king j the poor with fairness,
Jn 5:22 Moreover, the Father j no one,
1Co 4: 4 It is the Lord who j me.
Heb 4:12 it j the thoughts and attitudes
1Pe 1:17 on a Father who j each man's work
2:23 himself to him who j justly.
Rev 19:11 With justice he j and makes war.

JUDGING (JUDGE)
Ps 9: 4 on your throne, j righteously.
Pr 24:23 To show partiality in j is not good:
Isa 16: 5 one who in j seeks justice
Mt 19:28 the twelve tribes of Israel.
Jn 7:24 Stop j by mere appearances,

JUDGMENT (JUDGE)
Nu 33: 4 for the LORD had brought j

Dt 1: 17 of any man, for *j* belongs to God.
32: 41 and my hand grasps it in *j*.
1Sa 25: 33 May you be blessed for your good *j*
Ps 1: 5 the wicked will not stand in the *j*,
9: 7 he has established his throne for *j*.
76: 8 From heaven you pronounced *j*,
82: 1 he gives *j* among the "gods":
119: 66 Teach me knowledge and good *j*,
143: 2 Do not bring your servant into *j*,
Pr 3: 21 preserve sound *j* and discernment,
6: 32 man who commits adultery lacks *j*;
8: 14 Counsel and sound *j* are mine;
10: 21 but fools die for lack of *j*.
11: 12 man who lacks *j* derides his
12: 11 but he who chases fantasies lacks *j*.
17: 18 A man lacking in *j* strikes hands
18: 1 he defies all sound *j*.
28: 16 A tyrannical ruler lacks *j*,
Ecc 12: 14 God will bring every deed into *j*,
Isa 3: 14 The LORD enters into *j*
28: 6 justice to him who sits in *j*,
53: 8 By oppression and *j* he was taken
66: 16 the LORD will execute *j*
Jer 2: 35 But I will pass *j* on you
25: 31 he will bring *j* on all mankind
51: 18 when their *j* comes, they will
Eze 11: 10 and I will execute *j* on you
Da 7: 22 pronounced *j* in favor of the saints
Am 7: 4 Sovereign LORD was calling for *j*
Zec 8: 16 and sound *j* in your courts;
Mal 3: 5 "So I will come near to you for *j*.
Mt 5: 21 who murders will be subject to *j*.'
5: 22 with his brother will be subject to *j*.
10: 15 on the day of *j* than for that town.
11: 24 on the day of *j* than for you."
12: 36 have to give account on the day of *j*
12: 41 up at the *j* with this generation
Jn 5: 22 but has entrusted all *j* to the Son,
5: 30 as I hear, and my *j* is just,
7: 24 appearances, and make a right *j*."
8: 26 "I have much to say in *j* of you.
9: 39 "For *j* I have come into this world,
12: 31 Now is the time for *j* on this world;
16: 8 to sin and righteousness and *j*:
16: 11 in regard to *j*, because the prince
Ac 24: 25 self-control and the *j* to come,
Ro 2: 1 you who pass *j* on someone else,
2: 2 Now we know that God's *j*
5: 16 The *j* followed one sin
12: 3 think of yourself with sober *j*,
14: 10 stand before God's *j* seat.
14: 13 Therefore let us stop passing *j*
1Co 7: 40 In my *j*, she is happier if she stays
11: 29 body of the Lord eats and drinks *j*
2Co 5: 10 appear before the *j* seat of Christ,
2Th 1: 5 is evidence that God's *j* is right,
1Ti 3: 6 fall under the same *j* as the devil.
5: 12 Thus they bring *j* on themselves,
Heb 6: 2 of the dead, and eternal *j*,
9: 27 to die once, and after that to face *j*,
10: 27 but only a fearful expectation of *j*
Jas 2: 13 *j* without mercy will be shown
4: 11 are not keeping it, but sitting in *j*
1Pe 4: 17 For it is time for *j* to begin
2Pe 2: 9 the unrighteous for the day of *j*,
3: 7 being kept for the day of *j*
1Jn 4: 17 have confidence on the day of *j*,
Jude 6 bound with everlasting chains for *j*
Rev 14: 7 because the hour of his *j* has come.

JUDGMENTS (JUDGE)

Jer 1: 16 I will pronounce my *j* on my people
Da 7: 10 and sworn *j* written in the Law
Hos 6: 5 my *j* flashed like lightning
Ro 11: 33 How unsearchable his *j*,
1Co 2: 15 spiritual man makes *j* about all
Rev 16: 7 true and just are your *j*."

JUG

1Sa 26: 12 and water *j* near Saul's head,
1Ki 17: 12 of flour in a jar and a little oil in a *j*.

JUST* (JUSTICE JUSTIFICATION JUSTIFIED JUSTIFIES JUSTIFY JUSTIFYING JUSTLY)

Ge 18: 19 LORD by doing what is right and *j*,
Dt 2: 12 *j* as Israel did in the land
6: 3 *j* as the LORD, the God
27: 3 and honey, *j* as the LORD,
30: 9 be delighted in your fathers,
32: 4 and all his ways are *j*,
32: 4 upright and *j* is he.
32: 47 They are not *j* idle words for you—
32: 50 *j* as your brother Aaron died
2Sa 8: 15 doing what was *j* and right
1Ch 18: 14 doing what was *j* and right

2Ch 12: 6 and said, "The LORD is *j*.'"
Ne 9: 13 and laws that are *j* and right,
9: 33 you have been *j*; you have acted
Job 34: 17 Will you condemn the *j*
35: 2 Elihu said: "Do you think this is *j*?
Ps 37: 28 For the LORD loves the *j*
37: 30 and his tongue speaks what is *j*.
99: 4 what is *j* and right.
111: 7 of his hands are faithful and *j*;
119:121 I have done what is righteous and *j*;
Pr 1: 3 doing what is right and *j* and fair;
2: 8 for he guards the course of the *j*
2: 9 will understand what is right and *j*
8: 8 All the words of my mouth are *j*;
8: 15 and rulers make laws that are *j*,
12: 5 The plans of the righteous are *j*,
21: 3 To do what is right and *j*
Isa 32: 7 even when the plea of the needy is *j*
58: 2 They ask me for *j* decisions
Jer 4: 2 if in a truthful, *j* and righteous way
22: 3 what the LORD says: Do what is *j*
22: 15 he did what was right and *j*,
23: 5 do what is *j* and right in the land.
33: 15 he will do what is *j* and right
Eze 18: 5 who does what is *j* and right.
18: 19 Since the son has done what is *j*
18: 21 and does what is *j* and right,
18: 25 'The way of the Lord is not *j*.'
18: 27 and does what is *j* and right,
18: 29 'The way of the Lord is not *j*.'
33: 14 and does what is *j* and right—
33: 16 He has done what is *j* and right;
33: 17 But it is their way that is not *j*.
33: 17 'The way of the Lord is not *j*.'
33: 19 and does what is *j* and right,
33: 20 'The way of the Lord is not *j*.'
45: 9 and oppression and do what is *j*
Da 4: 37 does what is right and all his ways are *j*.
Jn 5: 30 as I hear, and my judgment is *j*,
Ro 3: 26 as to be *j* and the one who justifies
2Th 1: 6 God is *j*: He will pay back trouble
Heb 2: 2 received its *j* punishment,
1Jn 1: 9 and just will forgive us our sins
Rev 15: 3 Just and true are your ways,
16: 5 "You are *j* in these judgments,
16: 7 true and *j* are your judgments."
19: 2 for true and *j* are his judgments.

JUSTICE* (JUST)

Ge 49: 16 "Dan will provide *j* for his people
Ex 23: 2 do not pervert *j* by siding
23: 6 "Do not deny *j* to your poor people
Lev 19: 15 " 'Do not pervert *j*; do not show
Dt 16: 19 Do not pervert *j* or show partiality.
16: 20 Follow *j* and *j* alone,
24: 17 the alien or the fatherless of *j*,
27: 19 Cursed is the man who withholds *j*
1Sa 8: 3 accepted bribes and perverted *j*.
2Sa 15: 4 and I would see that he gets *j*.' "
15: 6 came to the king asking for *j*.
1Ki 3: 11 for discernment in administering *j*,
3: 28 wisdom from God to administer *j*.
7: 7 the Hall of *J*, where he was to judge
10: 9 to maintain *j* and righteousness.
2Ch 9: 8 to maintain *j* and righteousness."
Ezr 7: 25 and judges to administer *j*
Est 1: 13 experts in matters of law and *j*,
Job 8: 3 Does God pervert *j*?
9: 19 matter of *j*, who will summon him?
19: 7 though I call for help, there is no *j*.
27: 2 as God lives, who has denied me *j*,
29: 14 *j* was my robe and my turban.
31: 13 "If I have denied *j*
34: 5 but God denies me *j*.
34: 12 that the Almighty would pervert *j*.
34: 17 Can he who hates *j* govern?
36: 3 I will ascribe *j* to my Maker.
36: 17 *j* have taken hold of you.
37: 23 in his *j* and great righteousness.
40: 8 "Would you discredit my *j*?
Ps 7: 6 Awake, my God; decree *j*.
9: 8 he will govern the peoples with *j*
9: 16 The LORD is known by his *j*;
11: 7 he loves *j*;
33: 5 LORD loves righteousness and *j*;
36: 6 your *j* like the great deep.
37: 6 *j* of your cause like the noonday
45: 6 a scepter of *j* will be the scepter
72: 1 Endow the king with your *j*, O God
72: 2 your afflicted ones with *j*.
89: 14 *j* are the foundation of your throne;
97: 2 *j* are the foundation of his throne.
99: 4 The King is mighty, he loves *j*—
101: 1 I will sing of your love and *j*;
103: 6 and *j* for all the oppressed.

Ps 106: 3 Blessed are they who maintain *j*,
112: 5 who conducts his affairs with *j*.
140: 12 I know that the LORD secures *j*
Pr 8: 20 along the paths of *j*,
16: 10 and his mouth should not betray *j*.
17: 23 to pervert the course of *j*.
18: 5 or to deprive the innocent of *j*.
19: 28 A corrupt witness mocks at *j*,
21: 15 When *j* is done, it brings joy
28: 5 Evil men do not understand *j*,
29: 4 By *j* a king gives a country stability
29: 7 The righteous care about *j*
29: 26 from the LORD that man gets *j*.
Ecc 3: 16 place of —wickedness was there.
5: 8 poor oppressed in a district, and *j*
Isa 1: 17 Seek *j*,
1: 21 She once was full of *j*!
1: 27 Zion will be redeemed with *j*,
5: 7 he looked for *j*, but saw bloodshed;
5: 16 Almighty will be exalted by his *j*,
5: 23 but deny *j* to the innocent.
9: 7 it with *j* and righteousness
10: 2 and withhold *j* from the oppressed of
my people
11: 4 with *j* he will give decisions
16: 5 one who in judging seeks *j*
28: 6 He will be a spirit of *j*
28: 17 I will make *j* the measuring line
29: 21 deprive the innocent of *j*.
30: 18 For the LORD is a God of *j*.
32: 1 and rulers will rule with *j*.
32: 16 *J* will dwell in the desert
33: 5 with *j* and righteousness.
42: 1 and he will bring *j* to the nations.
42: 3 In faithfulness he will bring forth *j*;
42: 4 till he establishes *j* on earth.
51: 4 my *j* will become a light
51: 5 my arm will bring *j* to the nations.
56: 1 "Maintain *j*
59: 4 No one calls for *j*;
59: 8 there is no *j* in their paths.
59: 9 So *j* is far from us,
59: 11 We look for *j*, but find none;
59: 14 So *j* is driven back,
59: 15 that there was no *j*.
61: 8 "For I, the LORD, love *j*;
Jer 9: 24 *j* and righteousness on earth.
10: 24 Correct me, LORD, but only with *j*
12: 1 speak with you about your *j*;
21: 12 " 'Administer *j* every morning;
30: 11 I will discipline you but only with *j*;
46: 28 I will discipline you but only with *j*;
La 3: 36 to deprive a man of *j*—
Eze 22: 29 mistreat the alien, denying them *j*.
34: 16 I will shepherd the flock with *j*.
Hos 2: 19 you in righteousness and *j*,
12: 6 maintain love and *j*,
Am 2: 7 and deny *j* to the oppressed.
5: 7 You who turn *j* into bitterness
5: 12 and you deprive the poor of *j*
5: 15 maintain *j* in the courts.
5: 24 But let *j* roll on like a river,
6: 12 But you have turned *j* into poison
Mic 3: 1 Should you not know *j*,
3: 8 and with *j* and might,
3: 9 who despise *j*
Hab 1: 4 and *j* never prevails.
1: 4 so that *j* is perverted.
Zep 3: 5 by morning he dispenses his *j*,
Zec 7: 9 'Administer true *j*; show mercy
Mal 2: 17 or "Where is the God of *j*?"
3: 5 and deprive aliens of *j*,
Mt 12: 18 he will proclaim *j* to the nations.
12: 20 till he leads *j* to victory.
23: 23 important matters of the law—*j*,
Lk 11: 42 you neglect *j* and the love of God.
18: 3 'Grant me *j* against my adversary.'
18: 5 I will see that she gets *j*,
18: 7 And will not God bring about *j*
18: 8 he will see that they get *j*.
Ac 8: 33 humiliation he was deprived of *j*.
17: 31 with *j* by the man he has appointed.
28: 4 *J* has not allowed him to live."
Ro 3: 25 He did this to demonstrate his *j*,
3: 26 it to demonstrate his *j*.
2Co 7: 11 what readiness to see *j* done.
Heb 11: 33 administered *j*, and gained what
Rev 19: 11 With *j* he judges and makes war.

JUSTIFICATION* (JUST)

Eze 16: 52 for you have furnished some *j*
Ro 4: 25 and was raised to life for our *j*.
5: 16 many trespasses and brought *j*
5: 18 of righteousness was *j* that brings

JUSTIFIED* (JUST)

Ps 51: 4 and *j* when you judge.
Lk 18: 14 rather than the other, went home *j*
Ac 13: 39 from everything you could not be *j*
13: 39 him everyone who believes is *j*
Ro 3: 24 and are *j* freely by his grace
3: 28 For we maintain that a man is *j*
4: 2 If, in fact, Abraham was *j* by works,
5: 1 since we have been *j* through faith,
5: 9 Since we have now been *j*
8: 30 those he called, he also *j*; those he *j*,
10: 10 heart that you believe and are *j*,
1Co 6: 11 you were *j* in the name
Gal 2: 16 in Christ Jesus that we may be *j*
2: 16 observing the law no one will be *j*.
2: 16 sinners' know that a man is not *j*
2: 17 "If, while we seek to be *j* in Christ,
3: 11 Clearly no one is *j* before God
3: 24 to Christ that we might be *j* by faith
5: 4 to be *j* by law have been alienated
Tit 3: 7 so that, having been *j* by his grace,
Jas 2: 24 You see that a person is *j*

JUSTIFIES* (JUST)

Ro 3: 26 one who *j* those who have faith
4: 5 but trusts God who *j* the wicked,
8: 33 God has chosen? It is God who *j*.

JUSTIFY* (JUST)

Est 7: 4 such distress would *j* disturbing
Job 40: 8 you condemn me to *j* yourself?
Isa 53: 11 my righteous servant will *j* many,
Lk 10: 29 But he wanted to *j* himself,
16: 15 "You are the ones who *j* yourselves
Ro 3: 30 who will *j* the circumcised by faith
Gal 3: 8 that God would *j* the Gentiles

JUSTIFYING* (JUST)

Job 32: 2 angry with Job for *j* himself rather

JUSTLY* (JUST)

Ps 58: 1 Do you rulers indeed speak *j*?
67: 4 for you rule the peoples *j*
Jer 7: 5 and deal with each other *j*,
Mic 6: 8 To act *j* and to love mercy
Lk 23: 41 We are punished *j*,
1Pe 2: 23 himself to him who judges *j*.

KADESH

Nu 20: 1 of Zin, and they stayed at *K*.
Dt 1: 46 And so you stayed in *K* many days

KADESH BARNEA

Nu 32: 8 I sent them from *K* to look over

KEBAR

Eze 1: 1 among the exiles by the *K* River,

KEDORLAOMER

Ge 14: 17 Abram returned from defeating *K*

KEEP (KEEPER KEEPING KEEPS KEPT)

Ge 31: 49 "May the LORD *k* watch
Ex 15: 26 his commands and *k* all his
20: 6 and *k* my commandments.
Lev 15: 31 You must *k* the Israelites separate
Nu 6: 24 and *k* you;
Dt 4: 2 but *k* the commands of the LORD
6: 17 Be sure to *k* the commands
7: 9 who love him and *k* his commands.
7: 12 your God will *k* his covenant
11: 1 your God and *k* his requirements,
13: 4 *K* his commands and obey him;
30: 10 your God and *k* his commands
30: 16 and *k* his commands, decrees
Jos 22: 5 careful to *k* the commandment
1Ki 8: 58 and to *k* the commands,
2Ki 17: 19 Judah did not *k* the commands
23: 3 the LORD and *k* his commands,
1Ch 29: 18 and *k* their hearts loyal to you.
2Ch 6: 14 you who *k* your covenant of love
34: 31 the LORD and *k* his commands,
Job 14: 16 but not *k* track of my sin.
Ps 18: 28 You, O LORD, *k* my lamp burning
19: 13 *K* your servant also from willful
78: 10 they did not *k* God's covenant
119: 2 Blessed are they who *k* his statutes
119: 9 can a young man *k* his way pure?
121: 7 The LORD will *k* you
141: 3 *k* watch over the door of my lips.
Pr 4: 21 *k* them within your heart;
4: 24 *k* corrupt talk far from your lips.
30: 8 *K* falsehood and lies far from me;
Ecc 3: 6 a time to *k* and a time

KEEPER (KEEP)

Ge 4: 9 I my brother's *k*?" The LORD

KEEPING (KEEP)

Ex 20: 8 the Sabbath day by *k* it holy.
Dt 5: 12 the Sabbath day by *k* it holy,
13: 18 *k* all his commands that I am
Ps 19: 11 in *k* them there is great reward.
119:112 My heart is set on *k* your decrees
Pr 15: 3 *k* watch on the wicked
Mt 3: 8 Produce fruit in *k* with repentance.
Lk 2: 8 *k* watch over their flocks at night.
1Co 7: 19 *K* God's commands is what counts.
2Co 8: 5 and then to us in *k* with God's will.
Jas 4: 11 you are not *k* it, but sitting
1Pe 3: 16 and respect, *k* a clear conscience,
2Pe 3: 9 Lord is not slow in *k* his promise,

KEEPS (KEEP)

Ne 1: 5 who *k* his covenant of love
Ps 15: 4 who *k* his oath
Pr 12: 23 A prudent man *k* his knowledge
15: 21 of understanding *k* a straight
17: 28 a fool is thought wise if he *k* silent,
29: 11 a wise man *k* himself under control
Isa 56: 2 who *k* the Sabbath
Da 9: 4 who *k* his covenant of love
Am 5: 13 Therefore the prudent man *k* quiet
Jn 7: 19 Yet not one of you *k* the law.
8: 51 if anyone *k* my word, he will never
1Co 13: 5 is not easily angered, it *k* no record
Jas 2: 10 For whoever *k* the whole law
Rev 22: 7 Blessed is he who *k* the words

KEILAH

1Sa 23: 13 that David had escaped from *K*,

KEPT (KEEP)

Ex 12: 42 Because the LORD *k* vigil that
Dt 7: 8 and *k* the oath he swore
2Ki 18: 6 he *k* the commands the LORD had
Ne 9: 8 You have *k* your promise
Ps 130: 3 If you, O LORD, *k* a record of sins,
Isa 38: 17 In your love you *k* me
Mt 19: 20 these I have *k*, "the young man
2Co 11: 9 I have *k* myself from being
2Ti 4: 7 finished the race, I have *k* the faith.
1Pe 1: 4 spoil or fade—*k* in heaven for you,

KERNEL

Mk 4: 28 then the full *k* in the head.
Jn 12: 24 a *k* of wheat falls to the ground

KEY (KEYS)

Isa 33: 6 the fear of the LORD is the *k*
Rev 20: 1 having the *k* to the Abyss

KEYS* (KEY)

Mt 16: 19 I will give you the *k* of the kingdom
Rev 1: 18 And I hold the *k* of death

KICK*

Ac 26: 14 for you to *k* against the goads.'

KILL (KILLED KILLS)

Ecc 3: 3 a time to *k* and a time to heal,
Mt 10: 28 *k* the body but cannot *k* the soul.
17: 23 They will *k* him, and on the third
Mk 9: 31 will *k* him, and after three days
10: 34 spit on him, flog him and *k* him.

KILLED (KILL)

Ge 4: 8 his brother Abel and *k* him.
Ex 2: 12 he *k* the Egyptian and hid him
13: 15 the LORD *k* every firstborn
Nu 35: 11 who has *k* someone accidentally
1Sa 17: 50 down the Philistine and *k* him.
Ne 9: 26 They *k* your prophets, who had
Hos 6: 5 I *k* you with the words
Lk 11: 48 they *k* the prophets, and you build
Ac 3: 15 You *k* the author of life,

KILLS (KILL)

Ex 21: 12 *k* him shall surely be put to death.
Lev 24: 21 but whoever *k* a man must be put
2Co 3: 6 for the letter *k*, but the Spirit gives

KIND (KINDNESS KINDNESSES KINDS)

Ge 1: 24 animals, each according to its *k*."
2Ch 10: 7 "If you will be *k* to these people
Pr 11: 17 A *k* man benefits himself,
12: 25 but a *k* word cheers him up.
14: 21 blessed is he who is *k* to the needy.
14: 31 whoever is *k* to the needy honors
19: 17 He who is *k* to the poor lends
Da 4: 27 by being *k* to the oppressed.
Lk 6: 35 because he is *k* to the ungrateful
1Co 13: 4 Love is patient, love is *k*.
15: 35 With what *k* of body will they
Eph 4: 32 Be *k* and compassionate
1Th 5: 15 but always try to be *k* to each other
2Ti 2: 24 instead, he must be *k* to everyone,
Tit 2: 5 to be busy at home, to be *k*,

KINDHEARTED* (HEART)

Pr 11: 16 A *k* woman gains respect,

KINDNESS (KIND)

Ge 24: 12 and show *k* to my master Abraham
32: 10 I am unworthy of all the *k*
39: 21 he showed him *k* and granted him
Jdg 8: 35 failed to show *k* to the family
Ru 2: 20 has not stopped showing his *k*
2Sa 9: 3 to whom I can show God's *k*?"
22: 51 he shows unfailing *k*
Ps 18: 50 he shows unfailing *k*
141: 5 righteous man strike me—it is a *k*;
Isa 54: 8 but with everlasting *k*
Jer 9: 24 I am the LORD, who exercises *k*,
Hos 11: 4 I led them with cords of human *k*,
Ac 14: 17 He has shown *k* by giving you rain
Ro 11: 22 Consider therefore the *k*
2Co 6: 6 understanding, patience and *k*;
Gal 5: 22 peace, patience, *k*, goodness,
Eph 2: 7 expressed in his *k* to us
Col 3: 12 yourselves with compassion, *k*,
Tit 3: 4 But when the *k* and love
2Pe 1: 7 brotherly *k*; and to brotherly *k*,

KINDNESSES* (KIND)

Ps 106: 7 did not remember your many *k*,
Isa 63: 7 I will tell of the *k* of the LORD,
63: 7 to his compassion and many *k*.

KINDS (KIND)

Ge 1: 12 bearing seed according to their *k*
1Co 12: 4 There are different *k* of gifts,
1Ti 6: 10 of money is a root of all *k* of evil.
1Pe 1: 6 had to suffer grief in all *k* of trials.

KING (KING'S KINGDOM KINGDOMS KINGS)

1. Kings of Judah and Israel: see Saul, David, Solomon.

2. Kings of Judah: see Rehoboam, Abijah, Asa, Jehoshaphat, Jehoram, Ahaziah, Athaliah (Queen), Joash, Amaziah, Azariah (Uzziah), Jotham, Ahaz, Hezekiah, Manasseh, Amon, Josiah, Jehoahaz, Jehoiakim, Jehoiachin, Zedekiah.

3. Kings of Israel: see Jeroboam I, Nadab, Baasha, Elah, Zimri, Tibni, Omri, Ahab, Ahaziah, Joram, Jehu, Jehoahaz, Jehoash, Jeroboam II, Zechariah, Shallum, Menahem, Pekah, Pekahiah, Hoshea.

Ecc 12: 13 and *k* his commandments.
Isa 26: 3 You will *k* in perfect peace
42: 6 I will *k* you and will make you
58: 13 "If you *k* your feet
Jer 16: 11 forsook me and did not *k* my law.
Eze 20: 19 and be careful to *k* my laws.
Mt 10: 10 for the worker is worth his *k*.
Lk 12: 35 and *k* your lamps burning,
17: 33 tries to *k* his life will lose it,
Jn 10: 24 How long will you *k* us in suspense
12: 25 in this world will *k* it for eternal life
Ac 2: 24 for death to *k* its hold on him.
18: 9 "Do not be afraid; *k* on speaking,
Ro 7: 19 want to do—this I *k* on doing.
12: 11 but *k* your spiritual fervor,
14: 22 you believe about these things *k*
16: 17 *K* away from them.
1Co 5: 8 He will *k* you strong to the end,
2Co 12: 7 To *k* me from becoming conceited
Gal 5: 25 let us *k* in step with the Spirit.
Eph 4: 3 Make every effort to *k* the unity
2Th 3: 6 to *k* away from every brother who
1Ti 5: 22 *K* yourself pure.
2Ti 4: 5 *k* your head in all situations,
Heb 9: 20 God has commanded you to *k*."
13: 5 *K* your lives free from the love
Jas 1: 26 and yet does not *k* a tight rein
2: 8 If you really *k* the royal law found
3: 2 able to *k* his whole body in check.
2Pe 1: 8 will *k* you from being ineffective
Jude : 21 *K* yourselves in God's love
: 24 able to *k* you from falling
Rev 3: 10 also *k* you from the hour
22: 9 of all who *k* the words of this book.

Ex 1: 8 a new *k*, who did not know about
Dt 17:14 "Let us set a *k* over us like all
Jdg 17: 6 In those days Israel had no *k*;
1Sa 8: 5 now appoint a *k* to lead us,
  11:15 as *k* in the presence of the LORD.
  12:12 the LORD your God was your *k*.
2Sa 2: 4 and there they anointed David *k*
1Ki 1:30 Solomon your son shall be *k*
Ps 2: 6 "I have installed my *K*
  24: 7 that the *K* of glory may come in.
  44: 4 You are my *K* and my God,
  47: 7 For God is the *K* of all the earth;
Isa 32: 1 See, a *k* will reign in righteousness
Jer 30: 9 and David their *k*,
Hos 3: 5 their God and David their *k*.
Mic 2:13 *k* will pass through before them,
Zec 9: 9 See, your *k* comes to you,
Mt 2: 2 is the one who has been born *k*
  27:11 "Are you the *k* of the Jews?" "Yes,
Lk 19:38 "Blessed is the *k* who comes
  23: 3 "Are you the *k* of the Jews?" "Yes,
  23:38 THE *K* OF THE JEWS.
Jn 1:49 of God; you are the *K* of Israel."
  12:13 "Blessed is the *K* of Israel!"
Ac 17: 7 saying that there is another *k*,
1Ti 1:17 Now to the *K* eternal, immortal,
  6:15 the *K* of kings and Lord of lords,
Heb 7: 1 This Melchizedek was *k* of Salem
1Pe 2:13 to the *k*, as the supreme authority,
  2:17 of believers, fear God, honor the *k*.
Rev 15: 3 *K* of the ages.
  17:14 he is Lord of lords and *K* of kings—
  19:16 *K* OF KINGS AND LORD

KING'S (KING)

Pr 21: 1 The *k* heart is in the hand
Ecc 8: 3 in a hurry to leave the *k* presence.

KINGDOM (KING)

Ex 19: 6 you will be for me a *k* of priests
Dt 17:18 When he takes the throne of his *k*,
2Sa 7:12 body, and I will establish his *k*.
1Ki 11:31 to tear the *k* out of Solomon's hand
1Ch 17: 11 own sons, and I will establish his *k*.
  29:11 Yours, O LORD, is the *k*;
Ps 45: 6 justice will be the scepter of your *k*
  103: 19 and his *k* rules over all.
  145: 11 They will tell of the glory of your *k*
Eze 29:14 There they will be a lowly *k*.
Da 2:44 "After you, another *k* will rise,
  4: 3 His *k* is an eternal *k*;
  7:27 His *k* will be an everlasting *k*,
Ob :21 And the *k* will be the LORD's.
Mt 3: 2 Repent, for the *k* of heaven is near
  4:17 Repent, for the *k* of heaven is near
  4:23 preaching the good news of the *k*,
  5: 3 for theirs is the *k* of heaven.
  5:10 for theirs is the *k* of heaven.
  5:19 great in the *k* of heaven.
  5:19 least in the *k* of heaven,
  5:20 you will certainly not enter the *k*
  6:10 your *k* come,
  6:33 But seek first his *k* and his
  7:21 Lord,' will enter the *k* of heaven,
  8:11 Isaac and Jacob in the *k* of heaven.
  8:12 the subjects of the *k* will be thrown
  9:35 preaching the good news of the *k*
  10: 7 preach this message: 'The *k*
  11: 11 least in the *k* of heaven is greater
  11:12 the *k* of heaven has been forcefully
  12:25 "Every *k* divided against itself will
  12:26 How then can his *k* stand?
  12:28 then the *k* of God has come
  13: 11 knowledge of the secrets of the *k*
  13: 19 hears the message about the *k*
  13:24 "The *k* of heaven is like a man who
  13:31 *k* of heaven is like a mustard seed,
  13:33 "The *k* of heaven is like yeast that
  13:38 stands for the sons of the *k*.
  13:41 of His *k* everything that causes sin
  13:43 the sun in the *k* of their Father.
  13:44 *k* of heaven is like treasure hidden
  13:45 the *k* of heaven is like a merchant
  13:47 *k* of heaven is like a net that was let
  13:52 has been instructed about the *k*
  16: 19 the keys of the *k* of heaven;
  16:28 the Son of Man coming in his *k*."
  18: 1 the greatest in the *k* of heaven?"
  18: 3 you will never enter the *k*
  18: 4 the greatest in the *k* of heaven.
  18:23 the *k* of heaven is like a king who
  19:12 because of the *k* of heaven.
  19:14 for the *k* of heaven belongs to such
  19:23 man to enter the *k* of heaven.
  19:24 for a rich man to enter the *k* of God

Mt 20: 1 "For the *k* of heaven is like
  20:21 the other at your left in your *k*."
  21:31 the prostitutes are entering the *k*
  21:43 "Therefore I tell you that the *k*
  22: 2 "The *k* of heaven is like a king who
  23:13 You shut the *k* of heaven
  24: 7 rise against nation, and *k* against *k*.
  24:14 gospel of the *k* will be preached
  25: 1 "At that time the *k*
  25:34 the *k* prepared for you
  26:29 anew with you in my Father's *k*."
Mk 1:15 "The *k* of God is near.
  3:24 If a *k* is divided against itself,
  3:24 against itself, that *k* cannot stand.
  4:11 "The secret of the *k*
  4:26 "This is what the *k* of God is like.
  4:30 "What shall we say the *k*
  6:23 I will give you, up to half my *k*."
  9: 1 before they see the *k* of God come
  9:47 better for you to enter the *k* of God
  10:14 for the *k* of God belongs to such
  10:15 anyone who will not receive the *k*
  10:23 for the rich to enter the *k* of God!"
  10:24 how hard it is to enter the *k* of God
  10:25 for a rich man to enter the *k* of God
  11:10 "Blessed is the coming *k*
  12:34 "You are not far from the *k* of God
  13: 8 rise against nation, and *k* against *k*.
  14:25 day when I drink it anew in the *k*
  15:43 who was himself waiting for the *k*
Lk 1:33 Jacob forever; his *k* will never
  4:43 of the *k* of God to the other towns
  6:20 for yours is the *k* of God.
  7:28 in the *k* of God is greater than he."
  8: 1 proclaiming the good news of the *k*
  8:10 knowledge of the secrets of the *k*
  9: 2 out to preach the *k* of God
  9:11 spoke to them about the *k* of God,
  9:27 before they see the *k* of God."
  9:60 you go and proclaim the *k* of God."
  9:62 fit for service in the *k* of God."
  10: 9 'The *k* of God is near you.'
  10:11 sure of this: The *k* of God is near.'
  11: 2 your *k* come.
  11:17 "Any *k* divided against itself will
  11:18 himself, how can his *k* stand?
  11:20 then the *k* of God has come to you.
  12:31 seek his *k*, and these things will be
  12:32 has been pleased to give you the *k*.
  13:18 "What is the *k* of God like?
  13:20 What shall I compare the *k* of God
  13:28 all the prophets in the *k* of God,
  13:29 places at the feast in the *k* of God.
  14:15 eat at the feast in the *k* of God."
  16:16 the good news of the *k*
  17:20 when the *k* of God would come,
  17:20 *k* of God does not come with careful
  observation,
  17:21 because the *k* of God is within you.
  18:16 for the *k* of God belongs to such
  18:17 anyone who will not receive the *k*
  18:24 for the rich to enter the *k* of God!
  18:25 for a rich man to enter the *k* of God
  18:29 for the sake of the *k* of God will fail
  19:11 and the people thought that the *k*
  21: 10 rise against nation, and *k* against *k*.
  21:31 you know that the *k* of God is near.
  22:16 until it finds fulfillment in the *k*
  22:18 the vine until the *k* of God comes."
  22:29 And I confer on you a *k*, just
  22:30 and drink at my table in my *k*
  23:42 me when you come into your *k*."
  23:51 he was waiting for the *k* of God.
Jn 3: 3 no one can see the *k* of God.
  3: 5 no one can enter the *k* of God.
  18:36 now my *k* is from another place."
  18:36 "My *k* is not of this world.
Ac 1: 3 and spoke about the *k* of God.
  1: 6 going to restore the *k* to Israel?"
  8:12 he preached the good news of the *k*
  14:22 hardships to enter the *k* of God,"
  19: 8 arguing persuasively about the *k*
  20:25 about preaching the *k* will ever see
  28:23 and declared to them the *k* of God
  28:31 hindrance he preached the *k*
Ro 14:17 For the *k* of God is not a matter
1Co 4:20 For the *k* of God is not a matter
  6: 9 the wicked will not inherit the *k*
  6:10 swindlers will inherit the *k* of God.
  15:24 hands over the *k* to God the Father
  15:50 blood cannot inherit the *k* of God,
Gal 5:21 live like this will not inherit the *k*
Eph 2: 2 and of the ruler of the *k* of the air,
  5: 5 has any inheritance in the *k* of
Col 1:12 of the saints in the *k* of light.

Col 1:13 and brought us into the *k*
  4:11 among my fellow workers for the *k*
1Th 2:12 who calls you into his *k* and glory.
2Th 1: 5 will be counted worthy of the *k*
2Ti 4: 1 in view of His appearing and his *k*,
  4:18 bring me safely to his heavenly *k*.
Heb 1: 8 will be the scepter of your *k*.
  12:28 we are receiving a *k* that cannot be
Jas 2: 5 to inherit the *k* he promised those
2Pe 1: 11 into the eternal *k* of our Lord
Rev 1: 6 has made us to be a *k* and priests
  1: 9 companion in the suffering and *k*
  5:10 You have made them to be a *k*
  11:15 of the world has become the *k*
  11:15 "The *k* of the world has become
  12:10 the power and the *k* of our God,
  16:10 his *k* was plunged into darkness.
  17:12 who have not yet received a *k*,

KINGDOMS (KING)

2Ki 19:15 God over all the *k* of the earth.
  19: 19 so that all *k* on earth may know
2Ch 20: 6 rule over all the *k* of the nations.
Ps 68:32 Sing to God, O *k* of the earth,
Isa 37:16 God over all the *k* of the earth.
  37: 20 so that all *k* on earth may know
Eze 29:15 It will be the lowliest of *k*
  37:22 or be divided into two *k*.
Da 4:17 Most High is sovereign over the *k*
  7:17 great beasts are four *k* that will rise
Zep 3: 8 to gather the *k*

KINGS (KING)

Ps 2: 2 The *k* of the earth take their stand
  47: 9 for the *k* of the earth belong to God
  68:29 *k* will bring you gifts.
  72:11 All *k* will bow down to him
  110: 5 he will crush on the day
  149: 8 to bind their *k* with fetters,
Pr 16:12 *K* detest wrongdoing,
Isa 24:21 and the *k* on the earth below.
  52:15 and *k* will shut their mouths
  60:11 their *k* led in triumphal procession.
Da 2:21 he sets up *k* and deposes them.
  7:24 ten horns are ten *k* who will come
Lk 21:12 and you will be brought before *k*
1Co 4: 8 You have become *k*—
1Ti 2: 2 for *k* and all those in authority,
  6:15 the King of *k* and Lord of lords,
Rev 1: 5 and the ruler of the *k* of the earth.
  17:14 he is Lord of lords and King of *k*—
  19:16 KING OF *K* AND LORD

KINSMAN-REDEEMER (REDEEM)

Ru 3: 9 over me, since you are a *k*."
  4:14 day has not left you without a *k*.

KISS (KISSED KISSES)

Ps 2:12 *K* the Son, lest he be angry
Pr 24:26 is like a *k* on the lips.
SS 1: 2 *Beloved* Let him *k* me
  8: 1 I would *k* you,
Lk 22:48 the Son of Man with a *k*?"
Ro 16:16 Greet one another with a holy *k*.
1Co 16:20 Greet one another with a holy *k*.
2Co 13:12 Greet one another with a holy *k*.
1Th 5:26 Greet all the brothers with a holy *k*.
1Pe 5:14 Greet one another with a *k* of love.

KISSED (KISS)

Mk 14:45 Judas said, "Rabbi!" and *k* him.
Lk 7:38 *k* them and poured perfume

KISSES* (KISS)

Pr 27: 6 but an enemy multiplies *k*.
SS 1: 2 with the *k* of his mouth—

KNEE (KNEES)

Isa 45:23 Before me every *k* will bow;
Ro 14:11 'every *k* will bow before me;
Php 2:10 name of Jesus every *k* should bow,

KNEEL (KNELT)

Est 3: 2 But Mordecai would not *k* down
Ps 95: 6 let us *k* before the LORD our
Eph 3:14 For this reason I *k*

KNEES (KNEE)

1Ki 19:18 all whose *k* have not bowed
Isa 35: 3 steady the *k* that give way;
Da 6:10 times a day he got down on his *k*
Lk 5: 8 he fell at Jesus' *k* and said,
Heb 12:12 your feeble arms and weak *k*.

KNELT* (KNEEL)

1Ki 1:16 Bathsheba bowed low and k
2Ch 6:13 and then k down before the whole
7:3 they k on the pavement
29:29 everyone present with him k down
Est 3:2 officials at the king's gate k down
Mt 8:2 and k before him and said,
9:18 a ruler came and k before him
15:25 The woman came and k before him
17:14 a man approached Jesus and k
27:29 k in front of him and mocked him.
Lk 22:41 k down and prayed, "Father,
Ac 20:36 he k down with all of them
21:5 there on the beach we k to pray.

KNEW (KNOW)

2Ch 33:13 Manasseh k that the LORD is God
Job 23:3 If only I k where to find him;
Pr 24:12 "But we k nothing about this,"
Jer 1:5 you in the womb I k you,
Jnh 4:2 I k that you are a gracious
Mt 7:23 tell them plainly, 'I never k you.
12:25 Jesus k their thoughts
Jn 2:24 himself to them, for he k all men.
14:7 If you really k me, you would know

KNIFE

Ge 22:10 and took the k to slay his son.
Pr 23:2 and put a k to your throat

KNOCK* (KNOCKS)

Mt 7:7 k and the door will be opened
Lk 11:9 k and the door will be opened
Rev 3:20 I am! I stand at the door and k.

KNOCKS (KNOCK)

Mt 7:8 and to him who k, the door will be

KNOW (FOREKNEW FOREKNOWLEDGE KNEW KNOWING KNOWLEDGE KNOWN KNOWS)

Ge 22:12 Now I k that you fear God,
Ex 6:7 you will k that I am the LORD
14:4 and the Egyptians will k that I am
33:13 teach me your ways so I may k you
Dt 7:9 K therefore that the LORD your
18:21 "How can we k when a message
Jos 4:24 of the earth might k that the hand
23:14 You k with all your heart
1Sa 17:46 the whole world will k that there is
1Ki 8:39 heart (for you alone k the hearts
Job 11:6 K this: God has even forgotten
19:25 I k that my Redeemer lives,
42:3 things too wonderful for me to k.
Ps 9:10 Those who k your name will trust
46:10 "Be still, and k that I am God;
100:3 K that the LORD is God.
139:1 and you k me.
139:23 Search me, O God, and k my heart;
145:12 so that all men may k
Pr 27:1 for you do not k what a day may
30:4 Tell me if you k!
Ecc 8:5 wise heart will k the proper time
Isa 29:15 "Who sees us? Who will k?"
40:21 Do you not k?
Jer 6:15 they do not even k how to blush.
22:16 Is that not what it means to k me?"
24:7 I will give them a heart to k me,
31:34 his brother, saying, 'K the LORD,'
33:3 unsearchable things you do not k.'
Eze 2:5 they will k that a prophet has been
6:10 they will k that I am the LORD;
Da 11:32 people who k their God will firmly
Mt 6:3 let your left hand k what your right
7:11 k how to give good gifts
9:6 But so that you may k that the Son
22:29 you do not k the Scriptures
24:42 you do not k on what day your
26:74 "I don't k the man!" Immediately
Mk 12:24 you do not k the Scriptures
Lk 1:4 so that you may k the certainty
11:13 k how to give good gifts
12:48 But the one who does not k
13:25 'I don't k you or where you come
21:31 you k that the kingdom of God is
23:34 for they do not k what they are
Jn 1:26 among you stands one you do not k
3:11 we speak of what we k,
4:22 we worship what we do k,
4:42 and we k that this man really is
6:69 and k that you are the Holy One
7:28 You do not k him, but I k him
8:14 for I k where I came from
8:19 "You do not k me or my Father,"
Jn 8:32 Then you will k the truth,
8:55 Though you do not k him, I k him.
9:25 One thing I do k.
10:4 him because they k his voice.
10:14 I k my sheep and my sheep k me—
10:27 I k them, and they follow me.
12:35 the dark does not k where he is
13:17 Now that you k these things,
13:35 all men will k that you are my
14:17 you k him, for he lives with you
15:21 for they do not k the One who sent
16:30 we can see that you k all things
17:3 that they may k you, the only true
17:23 to let the world k that you sent me
21:15 he said, "you k that I love you."
21:24 We k that his testimony is true.
Ac 1:7 "It is not for you to k the times
1:24 "Lord, you k everyone's heart.
Ro 3:17 and the way of peace they do not k
6:3 Or don't you k that all
6:6 For we k that our old self was
6:16 Don't you k that when you offer
7:14 We k that the law is spiritual;
7:18 I k that nothing good lives in me,
8:22 We k that the whole creation has
8:26 We do not k what we ought to pray
8:28 we k that in all things God works
1Co 1:21 through its wisdom did not k him,
2:2 For I resolved to k nothing
3:16 Don't you k that you yourselves
5:6 Don't you k that a little yeast
6:2 Do you not k that the saints will
6:15 Do you not k that your bodies are
6:16 Do you not k that he who unites
6:19 Do you not k that your body is
7:16 How do you k, wife, whether you
8:2 does not yet k as he ought to k.
9:13 Don't you k that those who work
9:24 Do you not k that
13:9 For we k in part and we prophesy
13:12 Now I k in part; then I shall k fully,
15:58 because you k that your labor
2Co 5:1 we k that if the earthly tent we live
5:11 we k what it is to fear the Lord,
8:9 For you k the grace
Gal 1:11 you to k, brothers, that the gospel I
2:16 not 'Gentile sinners' k that a man
Eph 1:17 so that you may k him better.
1:18 in order that you may k the hope
6:8 you k that the Lord will reward
6:9 since you k that he who is both
Php 3:10 I want to k Christ and the power
4:12 I k what it is to be in need,
Col 2:2 order that they may k the mystery
4:1 because you k that you
4:6 so that you may k how
1Th 3:3 You k quite well that we were
5:2 for you k very well that the day
2Th 1:8 punish those who do not k God
1Ti 1:7 they do not k what they are talking
3:5 (If anyone does not k how
3:15 you will k how people ought
2Ti 1:12 because I k whom I have believed,
2:23 you k they produce quarrels.
3:14 you k those from whom you
Heb 8:11 because they will all k me,
11:8 he did not k where he was going.
Jas 1:3 because you k that the testing
3:1 you k that we who teach will be
4:4 don't you k that friendship
4:14 k what will happen tomorrow.
1Pe 1:18 For you k that it was not
2Pe 1:12 even though you k them
1Jn 2:3 We k that we have come
2:4 The man who says, "I k him,"
2:5 This is how we k we are in him:
2:11 he does not k where he is going,
2:20 and all of you k the truth.
2:29 you k that everyone who does
3:1 not k us is that it did not k him.
3:2 But we k that when he appears,
3:10 This is how we k who the children
3:14 We k that we have passed
3:16 This is how we k what love is:
3:19 then is how we k that we belong
3:24 We k it by the Spirit he gave us.
4:8 does not love does not k God,
4:13 We k that we live in him
4:16 so we k and rely on the love God
5:2 This is how we k that we love
5:13 so that you may k that you have
5:15 And if we k that he hears us—
5:18 We k that anyone born
5:20 We k also that the Son
Rev 2:2 I k your deeds, your hard work
Rev 2:9 I k your afflictions and your
2:19 I k your deeds, your love and faith,
3:3 you will not k at what time I will
3:15 I k your deeds, that you are neither

KNOWING (KNOW)

Ge 3:5 and you will be like God, k good
3:22 now become like one of us, k good
Jn 19:28 k that all was now completed,
Php 3:8 of k Christ Jesus my Lord,
Phm :21 k that you will do even more
Heb 13:2 entertained angels without k it.

KNOWLEDGE (KNOW)

Ge 2:9 the tree of the k of good and evil.
2:17 eat from the tree of the k of good
2Ch 1:10 and k, that I may lead this people,
Job 21:22 "Can anyone teach k to God,
38:2 counsel with words without k?
42:3 obscures my counsel without k?'
Ps 19:2 night after night they display k.
73:11 Does the Most High have k?"
94:10 Does he who teaches man lack k?
119:66 Teach me k and good judgment,
139:6 Such k is too wonderful for me,
Pr 1:4 k and discretion to the young—
1:7 of the LORD is the beginning of k,
2:5 and find the k of God.
2:6 from his mouth come k
2:10 and k will be pleasant to your soul.
3:20 by his k the deeps were divided,
8:10 k rather than choice gold,
8:12 I possess k and discretion.
9:10 k of the Holy One is understanding
10:14 Wise men store up k,
12:1 Whoever loves discipline loves k,
12:23 A prudent man keeps his k
13:16 Every prudent man acts out of k,
14:6 k comes easily to the discerning.
15:7 The lips of the wise spread k;
15:14 The discerning heart seeks k,
17:27 A man of k uses words
18:15 heart of the discerning acquires k;
19:2 to have zeal without k,
19:25 discerning man, and he will gain k.
20:15 lips that speak k are a rare jewel.
23:12 and your ears to words of k.
24:4 through k its rooms are filled
Ecc 7:12 but the advantage of k is this:
Isa 11:2 the Spirit of k and of the fear
11:9 full of the k of the LORD
40:14 Who was it that taught him k
Jer 3:15 who will lead you with k
Hos 4:6 are destroyed from lack of k.
Hab 2:14 filled with the k of the glory
Mal 2:7 lips of a priest ought to preserve k,
Mt 13:11 The k of the secrets of the kingdom
Lk 8:10 The k of the secrets of the kingdom
11:52 you have taken away the key to k.
Ac 18:24 with a thorough k of the Scriptures
Ro 1:28 worthwhile to retain the k of God,
10:2 but their zeal is not based on k.
11:33 riches of the wisdom and k of God!
1Co 8:1 K puffs up, but love builds up.
8:11 Christ died, is destroyed by your k.
12:8 to another the message of k
13:2 can fathom all mysteries and all k,
13:8 where there is k, it will pass away.
2Co 2:14 everywhere the fragrance of the k
4:6 light of the k of the glory of God
8:7 in k, in complete earnestness
11:6 a trained speaker, but I do have k.
Eph 3:19 to know this love that surpasses k
4:13 and in the k of the Son of God
Php 1:9 and more in k and depth of insight,
Col 1:9 God to fill you with the k of his will
1:10 every good work, growing in the k
2:3 all the treasures of wisdom and k.
3:10 which is being renewed in k
1Ti 2:4 and to come to a k of the truth.
6:20 ideas of what is falsely called k,
Tit 1:1 and the k of the truth that leads
Heb 10:26 after we have received the k
2Pe 1:5 and to goodness, k; and to k,
3:18 grow in the grace and k of our Lord

KNOWN (KNOW)

Ex 6:3 the LORD I did not make myself k
Ps 16:11 You have made k to me the path
89:1 I will make your faithfulness k
98:2 LORD has made his salvation k
105:1 make k among the nations what he
119:168 for all my ways are k to you.
Pr 20:11 Even a child is k by his actions,
Isa 12:4 make k among the nations what he

Isa 46:10 kthe end from the beginning,
61: 9 Their descendants will be k
Eze 38:23 I will make myself in the sight
39: 7 "I will make kmy holy name
Mt 10:26 or hidden that will not be made k.
24:43 of the house had kat what time
Lk 19:42 had only kon this day what would
Jn 15:15 from my Father I have made k
16:14 from what is mine and making it k
17:26 I have made you kto them,
Ac 2:28 You have made kto me the paths
Ro 1:19 since what may be kabout God is
3:21 apart from law, has been made k,
9:22 his wrath and make his power k,
11:34 "Who has kthe mind of the Lord?
15:20 the gospel where Christ was not k,
16:26 and made kthrough the prophetic
1Co 2:16 "For who has kthe mind
8: 3 But the man who loves God is k
13:12 know fully, even as I am fully k.
2Co 3: 2 written on our hearts, k
Gal 4: 9 or rather are kby God—
Eph 3: 5 which was not made kto men
6:19 will fearlessly make kthe mystery
2Ti 3:15 infancy you have kthe holy
2Pe 2:21 than to have kit and then

KNOWS (KNOW)

1Sa 2: 3 for the LORD is a God who k,
Est 4:14 And who kbut that you have come
Job 23:10 But he kthe way that I take;
Ps 44:21 since he kthe secrets of the heart?
94:11 The LORD kthe thoughts of man;
103: 14 for he khow we are formed,
Ecc 8: 7 Since no man kthe future,
8:17 Even if a wise man claims he k,
9:12 no man kwhen his hour will come:
Isa 29:16 "He knothing"?
Jer 9:24 that he understands and kme,
Mt 6:8 for your Father kwhat you need
11:27 No one kthe Son
24:36 "No one kabout that day or hour,
Lk 12:47 "That servant who khis master's
16:15 of men, but God kyour hearts.
Ac 15: 8 who knew the heart, showed that he
Ro 8:27 who searches our hearts kthe mind
1Co 2:11 who among men kthe thoughts
8: 2 who thinks he ksomething does
2Ti 2:19 The Lord kthose who are his," and
Jas 4:17 who kthe good he ought to do
1Jn 4: 6 God listens to us;
4: 7 born of God and kGod.

KOHATHITE (KOHATHITES)

Nu 3:29 The Kclans were to camp

KOHATHITES (KOHATHITE)

Nu 3:28 The Kwere responsible
4:15 Kare to carry those things that are

KORAH

Levite who led rebellion against Moses and
Aaron (Nu 16; Jude 11).

KORAZIN

Mt 11:21 "Woe to you, K!Woe to you,

LABAN

Brother of Rebekah (Ge 24:29), father of Rachel and Leah (Ge 29:16). Received Abraham's servant (Ge 24:29-51). Provided daughters as wives for Jacob in Jacob's service (Ge 29:1-30). Provided flocks for Jacob's service (Ge 30:25-43). After Jacob's departure, pursued and covenanted with him (Ge 31).

LABOR (LABORING)

Ex 1:11 to oppress them with forced l,
20: 9 Six days you shall land do all your
Dt 5:13 Six days you shall land do all your
Ps 127: 1 its builders lin vain.
128: 2 You will eat the fruit of your l;
Pr 12:24 but laziness ends in slave l.
Isa 54: 1 you who were never in l;
55: 2 and your lon what does not satisfy
Mt 6:28 They do not lor spin.
Jn 4:38 have reaped the benefits of their l."
1Co 3: 8 rewarded according to his own l.
15:58 because you know that your l
Gal 4:27 you who have no l'pains;
Php 2:16 day of Christ that I did not run or l
Rev 14:13 "they will rest from their l,

LABORING* (LABOR)

2Th 3: 8 land toiling so that we would not

LACK (LACKED LACKING LACKS)

Ps 34: 9 for those who fear him /nothing.
Pr 5:23 He will die for /of discipline.
10:21 but fools die for /of judgment.
11:14 For /of guidance a nation falls,
15:22 Plans fail for /of counsel,
28:27 to the poor will /nothing,
Mk 6: 6 he was amazed at their /of faith.
16:14 he rebuked them for their /of faith
Ro 3: 3 Will their /of faith nullify God's
1Co 1: 7 you do not /any spiritual gift
5: 2 because of your /of self-control.
Col 2:23 /any value in restraining sensual

LACKED (LACK)

Dt 2: 7 and you have not /anything.
Ne 9:21 them in the desert; they /nothing,
1Co 12:24 honor to the parts that /it,

LACKING (LACK)

Pr 17:18 A man /in judgment strikes hands
Ro 12:11 Never be /in zeal, but keep your
Jas 1: 4 and complete, not /anything.

LACKS (LACK)

Pr 6:32 who commits adultery /judgment;
11:12 man who /judgment derides his
12:11 he who chases fantasies /judgment
15:21 delights a man who /judgment,
24:30 of the man who /judgment;
25:28 is a man who /self-control.
28:16 A tyrannical ruler /judgment,
31:11 and /nothing of value.
Eze 34: 8 because my flock /a shepherd
Jas 1: 5 any of you /wisdom, he should ask

LAID (LAY)

Isa 53: 6 and the LORD has /on him
Mk 6:29 took his body and /it in a tomb.
Lk 6:48 and /the foundation on rock.
Ac 6: 6 and their hands on them.
1Co 3:11 other than the one already /,
1Ti 4:14 body of elders /their hands on you.
1Jn 3:16 Jesus Christ /down his life for us.

LAKE

Mt 8:24 a furious storm came up on the l,
14:25 out to them, walking on the l.
Mk 4: 1 into a boat and sat in it out on the l,
Lk 8:33 down the steep bank into the l
Jn 6:25 him on the other side of the l,
Rev 19:20 into the fiery /of burning sulfur.
20:14 The /of fire is the second death.

LAMB (LAMB'S LAMBS)

Ge 22: 8 "God himself will provide the l
Ex 12:21 and slaughter the Passover l.
Nu 9:11 are to eat the l, together
2Sa 12: 4 he took the ewe /that belonged
Isa 11: 6 The wolf will live with the l,
53: 7 he was led like a /to the slaughter,
Mk 14:12 to sacrifice the Passover l,
Jn 1:29 Lof God, who takes away the sin
Ac 8:32 as a /before the shearer is silent,
1Co 5: 7 our Passover l, has been sacrificed.
1Pe 1:19 a /without blemish or defect.
Rev 5: 6 Then I saw a L, looking
5:12 "Worthy is the L, who was slain,
7:14 white in the blood of the L.
14: 4 They follow the L wherever he
15: 3 of God and the song of the L:
17:14 but the L will overcome them
19: 9 to the wedding supper of the L!'"
21:23 gives it light, and the L is its lamp.

LAMB'S (LAMB)

Rev 21:27 written in the L book of life.

LAMBS (LAMB)

Lk 10: 3 I am sending you out like l
Jn 21:15 Jesus said, "Feed my l.'"

LAME

Isa 33:23 even the /will carry off plunder.
35: 6 Then will the /leap like a deer,
Mt 11: 5 The blind receive sight, the /walk,
15:31 the /walking and the blind seeing.
Lk 14:21 the crippled, the blind and the l.'

LAMENT

2Sa 1:17 took up this /concerning Saul
Eze 19: 1 Take up a /concerning the princes

LAMP (LAMPS LAMPSTAND LAMPSTANDS)

2Sa 22:29 You are my l, O LORD;
Ps 18:28 You, O LORD, keep my /burning;
119:105 Your word is a /to my feet
132: 17 and set up a /for my anointed one.
Pr 6:23 For these commands are a l,
20:27 /of the LORD searches the spirit
31:18 and her /does not go out at night.
Mt 6:22 "The eye is the /of the body.
Lk 8:16 "No one lights a /and hides it
Rev 21:23 gives it light, and the Lamb is its l.
22: 5 They will not need the light of a /

LAMPS (LAMP)

Mt 25: 1 be like ten virgins who took their l
Lk 12:35 for service and keep your /burning,
Rev 4: 5 the throne, seven /were blazing.

LAMPSTAND (LAMP)

Ex 25:31 "Make a /of pure gold
Zec 4: 2 "I see a solid gold /with a bowl
4:11 on the right and the left of the l?"
Heb 9: 2 In its first room were the l,
Rev 2: 5 and remove your /from its place.

LAMPSTANDS (LAMP)

2Ch 4: 7 He made ten gold /according
Rev 1:12 when I turned I saw seven golden l,
1:20 and of the seven golden /is this:

LAND (LANDS)

Ge 1:10 God called the dry ground "l,"
1:11 "Let the /produce vegetation:
1:24 "Let the /produce living creatures
12: 1 and go to the /I will show you.
12: 7 To your offspring I will give this l,"
13:15 All the /that you see I will give
15:18 "To your descendants I give this l,
50:24 out of this /to the /he promised
Ex 3: 8 a /flowing with milk and honey—
6: 8 to the /I swore with uplifted hand
33: 3 Go up to the /flowing with milk
Lev 25:23 /must not be sold permanently,
Nu 14: 8 us into that l, a /flowing with milk
35:33 Do not pollute the /where you are.
Dt 1: 8 See, I have given you this l
8: 7 God is bringing you into a good l—
11:10 The /you are entering to take
28:21 you from the /you are entering
29:19 will bring disaster on the watered l
34: 1 LORD showed him the whole l—
Jos 13: 2 "This is the /that remains:
14: 4 Levites received no share of the l
14: 9 /on which your feet have walked
2Sa 21:14 answered prayer in behalf of the l.
2Ki 17: 5 of Assyria invaded the entire l,
24: 1 king of Babylon invaded the
25:21 into captivity, away from her l.
2Ch 7:14 their sin and will heal their l.
7:20 then I will uproot Israel from my l
36:21 The /enjoyed its sabbath rests;
Ezr 9:11 entering to possess is a /polluted
Ne 9:36 in the /you gave our forefathers
Ps 37:11 But the meek will inherit the l
37:29 the righteous will inherit the l
136: 21 and gave their /as an inheritance,
142: 5 my portion in the /of the living."
Pr 2:21 For the upright will live in the l,
2:21 who works his /will have abundant
Isa 6:13 though a tenth remains in the l,
53: 8 cut off from the /of the living;
Jer 2: 7 But you came and defiled my l
Eze 36:24 and bring you back into your own l.

LANDS (LAND)

Ps 111: 6 giving them the /of other nations.
Eze 20: 6 honey, the most beautiful of all l.
Zec 10: 9 in distant /they will remember me.

LANGUAGE (LANGUAGES)

Ge 11: 1 Now the whole world had one l
11: 9 there the LORD confused the l
Ps 19: 3 There is no speech or l
Jn 8:44 When he lies, he speaks his native l
Ac 2: 6 heard them speaking in his own l.
Col 3: 8 slander, and filthy /from your lips.
Rev 5: 9 from every tribe and /and people
7: 9 every nation, tribe, people and l,
14: 6 to every nation, tribe, /and people.

LANGUAGES (LANGUAGE)

Zec 8:23 "In those days ten men from all l

LAODICEA

Rev   3:14 the angel of the church in L write:

LAP

Jdg   7: 5 "Separate those who /the water

LASHES

Pr 17:10 more than a hundred /a fool.
2Co 11:24 from the Jews the forty /minus one

LAST (LASTING LASTS LATTER)

Ex 14:24 During the /watch of the night
2Sa 23: 1 These are the /words of David:
Isa 2: 2 and Jerusalem: In the /days
     41: 4 and with the /—I am he."
     44: 6 I am the first and I am the /;
     48:12 I am the first and I am the /.
Hos 3: 5 and to his blessings in the /days.
Mic 4: 1 In the /days
Mt 19:30 But many who are first will be /,
     20: 8 beginning with the /ones hired
     21:37 L of all, he sent his son to them.
Mk 9:35 must be the very /, and the servant
     10:31 are first will be /, and the /first."
     15:37 a loud cry, Jesus breathed his /.
Jn 6:40 and I will raise him up at the /day."
     15:16 and bear fruit—fruit that will /.
Ac 2:17 " In the /days, God says,
Ro 1:17 is by faith from first to /,
1Co 15:26 /enemy to be destroyed is death.
     15:52 of an eye, at the /trumpet.
2Ti 3: 1 will be terrible times in the /days.
2Pe 3: 3 in the /days scoffers will come,
Jude   :18 "In the /times there will be
Rev 1:17 I am the First and the L.
     22:13 the First and the L, the Beginning

LASTING (LAST)

Ex 12:14 to the LORD—a /ordinance.
Lev 24: 8 of the Israelites, as a /covenant.
Nu 25:13 have a covenant of a /priesthood,
Heb 10:34 had better and /possessions.

LASTS (LAST)

Ps 30: 5 For his anger /only a moment,
2Co 3:11 greater is the glory of that which //

LATTER (LAST)

Job 42:12 The LORD blessed the /part
Mt 23:23 You should have practiced the /,
Php 1:16 /do so in love, knowing that I am

LAUGH (LAUGHED LAUGHS LAUGHTER)

Ps 59: 8 But you, O LORD, /at them;
Pr 31:25 she can /at the days to come.
Ecc 3: 4 a time to weep and a time to /,
Lk 6:21 for you will /.
     6:25 Woe to you who /now,

LAUGHED (LAUGH)

Ge 17:17 Abraham fell facedown; he /
     18:12 So Sarah /to herself as she thought,

LAUGHS (LAUGH)

Ps 2: 4 The One enthroned in heaven /;
     37:13 but the Lord /at the wicked,

LAUGHTER (LAUGH)

Ge 21: 6 Sarah said, "God has brought me /,
Ps 126: 2 Our mouths were filled with /,
Pr 14:13 Even in /the heart may ache,
Jas 4: 9 Change your /to mourning

LAVISHED

Eph 1: 8 of God's grace that he /on us
1Jn 3: 1 great is the love the Father has /

LAW (LAWFUL LAWGIVER LAWS)

Lev 24:22 are to have the same /for the alien
Nu 6:13 " 'Now this is the /for the Nazirite
Dt 1: 5 Moses began to expound this /,
     6:25 to obey all this /before the LORD
     27:26 of this /by carrying them out."
     31:11 you shall read this /before them
     31:26 "Take this Book of the L
Jos 1: 7 to obey this /my servant Moses
     1: 8 of the L depart from your mouth;
     8:31 of the /that Moses the servant
2Ki 22: 8 of the L in the temple of the LORD
2Ch 6:16 walk before me according to my /,
     17: 9 the Book of the L of the LORD;
     34:14 of the L of the LORD that had
Ezr 7: 6 versed in the L of Moses.
Ne 8: 2 Ezra the priest brought the L

Ne 8: 8 from the Book of the L of God,
Ps 1: 2 and on his /he meditates day
     19: 7 The /of the LORD is perfect,
     37:31 The /of his God is in his heart;
     40: 8 your /is within my heart."
   119:18 wonderful things in your /.
   119:70 but I delight in your /.
   119:72 /from your mouth is more precious
   119:77 for your /is my delight.
   119:97 Oh, how I love your /!
   119:163 but I love your /.
   119:165 peace have they who love your /.
Pr 28: 9 If anyone turns a deaf ear to the /,
     29:18 but blessed is he who keeps the /.
Isa 2: 3 The /will go out from Zion,
     8:20 To the /and to the testimony!
     42:21 to make his /great and glorious.
Jer 8: 8 deal with the /did not know me;
     8: 8 for we have the /of the LORD,
     31:33 "I will put my /in their minds
Mic 4: 2 The /will go out from Zion,
Hab 1: 7 they are a /to themselves
Zec 7:12 as flint and would not listen to the /
Mt 5:17 that I have come to abolish the L
     7:12 sums up the L and the Prophets.
     22:36 greatest commandment in the L?"
     22:40 All the L and the Prophets hang
     23:23 more important matters of the /—
Lk 11:52 "Woe to you experts in the /,
     16:17 stroke of a pen to drop out of the L.
     24:44 me in the L of Moses,
Jn 1:17 For the /was given through Moses;
Ac 13:39 justified from by the /of Moses.
Ro 2:12 All who sin apart from the /will
     2:15 of the /are written on their hearts,
     2:20 you have in the /the embodiment
     2:25 value if you observe the /,
     3:19 we know that whatever the /says,
     3:20 in his sight by observing the /;
     3:21 apart from /, has been made known
     3:28 by faith apart from observing the /.
     3:31 Not at all! Rather, we uphold the /.
     4:13 It was not through /that Abraham
     4:15 worthless, because /brings wrath.
     4:16 not only to those who are of the /
     5:13 for before the /was given,
     5:20 /was added so that the trespass
     6:14 because you are not under /,
     6:15 we are not under /but under grace?
     7: 1 that the /has authority
     7: 4 also died to the /through the body
     7: 5 aroused by the /were at work
     7: 6 released from the /so that we serve
     7: 7 then? Is the /sin? Certainly not!
     7: 8 For apart from /, sin is dead.
     7:12 /is holy, and the commandment is
     7:14 We know that the /is spiritual;
     7:22 my inner being I delight in God's /;
     7:25 in my mind am a slave to God's /,
     8: 2 because through Christ Jesus the /
     8: 3 For what the /was powerless to do
     8: 4 of the /might be fully met in us,
     8: 7 It does not submit to God's /,
     9: 4 covenants, the receiving of the /,
     9:31 who pursued a /of righteousness.
     10: 4 Christ is the end of the /
     13: 8 his fellowman has fulfilled the /.
     13:10 love is the fulfillment of the /.
1Co 6: 6 goes to /against another—
     9: 9 For it is written in the L of Moses:
     9:20 the /I became like one under the /
     9:21 I became like one not having the /
     15:56 and the power of sin is the /.
Gal 2:16 justified by observing the /,
     2:19 For through the /I died to the /
     3: 2 the Spirit by observing the /,
     3: 5 you because you observe the /,
     3:10 on observing the /are under a curse
     3:11 justified before God by the /,
     3:13 curse of the /by becoming a curse
     3:17 The /, introduced 430 years later,
     3:19 then, was the purpose of the /?
     3:21 Is the /, therefore, opposed
     3:23 we were held prisoners by the /,
     3:24 So the /was put in charge to lead us
     4:21 you who want to be under the /,
     5: 3 obligated to obey the whole /.
     5: 4 justified by /have been alienated
     5:14 The entire /is summed up
     5:18 by the Spirit, you are not under /.
     6: 2 and in this way you will fulfill the /
Eph 2:15 flesh the /with its commandments
Php 3: 9 of my own that comes from the /,
1Ti 1: 8 We know that the /is good
Heb 7:12 there must also be a change of the /.

Heb 7:19 (for the /made nothing perfect),
     10: 1 The /is only a shadow
Jas 1:25 intently into the perfect /that gives
     2: 8 If you really keep the royal /found
     2:10 For whoever keeps the whole /
     4:11 or judges him speaks against the /
1Jn 3: 4 Everyone who sins breaks the /;

LAWFUL (LAW)

Mt 12:12 Therefore it is /to do good

LAWGIVER* (LAW)

Isa 33:22 the LORD is our /,
Jas 4:12 There is only one L and Judge,

LAWLESS (LAWLESSNESS)

2Th 2: 8 And then the /one will be revealed
Heb 10:17 "Their sins and /acts

LAWLESSNESS* (LAWLESS)

2Th 2: 3 and the man of /is revealed,
     2: 7 power of /is already at work;
1Jn 3: 4 sins breaks the law; in fact, sin is /.

LAWS (LAW)

Ex 21: 1 "These are the /you are to set
Lev 25:18 and be careful to obey my /,
Dt 4: 1 and /I am about to teach you.
     30:16 decrees and /; then you will live
Ps 119: 30 I have set my heart on your /.
   119: 43 for I have put my hope in your /.
   119:120 I stand in awe of your /.
   119:164 for your righteous /.
   119:175 and may your /sustain me.
Eze 36:27 and be careful to keep my /.
Heb 8:10 I will put my /in their minds
     10:16 I will put my /in their hearts,

LAWSUITS

Hos 10: 4 therefore /spring up
1Co 6: 7 The very fact that you have /

LAY (LAID LAYING LAYS)

Ex 29:10 and his sons shall /their hands
Lev 1: 4 He is to /his hand on the head
     4:15 the community are to /their hands
Nu 8:10 the Israelites are to /their hands
     27:18 whom is the spirit, and /your hand
1Sa 26: 9 Who can /a hand on the LORD's
Job 1:12 on the man himself do not /a finger
     22:22 and /up his words in your heart.
Ecc 10: 4 calmness can /great errors to rest.
Isa 28:16 "See, I /a stone in Zion,
Mt 8:20 of Man has no place to /his head."
     28: 6 Come and see the place where he /.
Mk 6: 5 /his hands on a few sick people
Lk 9:58 of Man has no place to /his head."
Jn 10:15 and I /down my life for the sheep.
     10:18 but I /it down of my own accord.
     15:13 that he /down his life
Ac 8:19 on whom I /my hands may receive
Ro 9:33 I /in Zion a stone that causes men
1Co 3:11 no one can /any foundation other
1Pe 2: 6 "See, I /a stone in Zion,
1Jn 3:16 And we ought to /down our lives
Rev 4:10 They /their crowns

LAYING (LAY)

Lk 4:40 and /his hands on each one,
Ac 8:18 at the /on of the apostles' hands,
1Ti 5:22 Do not be hasty in the /on of hands
2Ti 1: 6 is in you through the /
Heb 6: 1 not /again the foundation
     6: 2 instruction about baptisms, the /

LAYS (LAY)

Jn 10:11 The good shepherd /down his life

LAZARUS

1. Poor man in Jesus' parable (Lk 16:19-31).
2. Brother of Mary and Martha whom Jesus raised from the dead (Jn 11:1-12:19).

LAZINESS* (LAZY)

Pr 12:24 but /ends in slave labor.
     19:15 L brings on deep sleep,

LAZY* (LAZINESS)

Ex 5: 8 They are /; that is why they are
     5:17 Pharaoh said, "L, that's what you
     5:17 "Lazy, that's what you—!!
Pr 10: 4 L hands make a man poor,
     12:27 The /man does not roast his game,
     26:15 he is too /to bring it back
Ecc 10:18 If a man is /, the rafters sag;

Mt 25:26 replied, 'You wicked, /servant!
Tit 1:12 liars, evil brutes, /gluttons."
Heb 6:12 We do not want you to become /,

LEAD (LEADER LEADERS LEADERSHIP LEADS LED)

Ex 15:13 "In your unfailing love you will /
Nu 14: 8 with us, he will /us into that land,
Dt 31: 2 and I am no longer able to /you.
Jos 1: 6 because you will /these people
1Sa 8: 5 now appoint a king to /us.
2Ch 1:10 knowledge, that I may /this people
Ps 27:11 /me in a straight path
61: 2 /me to the rock that is higher
139: 24 and /me in the way everlasting.
143: 10 /me on level ground.
Pr 4:11 and /you along straight paths.
Ecc 5: 6 Do not let your mouth /you
Isa 11: 6 and a little child will /them.
49:10 and /them beside springs of water.
Da 12: 3 those who /many to righteousness,
Mt 6:13 And /us not into temptation,
Lk 11: 4 And /us not into temptation.' "
Gal 3:24 So the law was put in charge to /us
1Th 4:11 it your ambition to /a quiet life,
1Jn 3: 7 do not let anyone /you astray
Rev 7:17 he will /them to springs

LEADER (LEAD)

1Sa 7: 6 Samuel was /of Israel at Mizpah.
10: 1 Has not the LORD anointed you /
12: 2 I have been your /from my youth
13:14 and appointed him /of his people,

LEADERS (LEAD)

Heb 13: 7 Remember your /, who spoke
13:17 Obey your /and submit

LEADERSHIP* (LEAD)

Nu 33: 1 by divisions under the /of Moses
Ps 109: 8 may another take his place of /.
Ac 1:20 "'May another take his place of /.'
Ro 12: 8 if it is /, let him govern diligently;

LEADS (LEAD)

Dt 27:18 is the man who /the blind astray
Ps 23: 2 he /me beside quiet waters,
37: 8 do not fret—it /only to evil.
68: 6 he /forth the prisoners
Pr 2:18 For her house /down to death
10:17 ignores correction /others astray.
14:23 but mere talk /only to poverty.
16:25 but in the end it /to death.
19:23 The fear of the LORD /to life:
20: 7 righteous man /a blameless life;
21: 5 as surely as haste /to poverty.
Isa 40:11 he gently /those that have young.
Mt 7:13 and broad is the road that /
12:20 till he /justice to victory.
15:14 If a blind man /a blind man,
Jn 10: 3 sheep by name and /them out.
Ro 6:16 which /to death, or to obedience,
6:22 the benefit you reap /to holiness,
14:19 effort to do what /to peace
2Co 2:14 always /us in triumphal procession
7:10 sorrow brings repentance that /
Tit 1: 1 of the truth that /to godliness—

LEAH

Wife of Jacob (Ge 29:16-30); bore six sons and one daughter (Ge 29:31-30:21; 34:1; 35: 23)

LEAN (LEANED)

Pr 3: 5 /not on your own understanding;

LEANED (LEAN)

Ge 47:31 as he /on the top of his staff.
Jn 21:20 (This was the one who had /back
Heb 11:21 as he /on the top of his staff.

LEAP (LEAPED LEAPS)

Isa 35: 6 Then will the lame /like a deer,
Mal 4: 2 /like calves released from the stall.
Lk 6:23 "Rejoice in that day and /for joy,

LEAPED (LEAP)

Lk 1:41 heard Mary's greeting, the baby /

LEAPS (LEAP)

Ps 28: 7 My heart /for joy

LEARN (LEARNED LEARNING LEARNS)

Dt 4:10 so that they may /to revere me
5: 1 /them and be sure to follow them.

Dt 31:12 and /to fear the LORD your God
Ps 119: 7 as I /your righteous laws.
Isa 1:17 /to do right!
26: 9 of the world /righteousness.
Mt 11:29 yoke upon you and /from me,
Jn 14:31 world must /that I love the Father
1Th 4: 4 that each of you should /
1Ti 2:11 A woman should /in quietness
5: 4 these should /first of all

LEARNED (LEARN)

Ps 119:152 Long ago I /from your statutes
Mt 11:25 things from the wise and /.
Php 4: 9 Whatever you have /or received
4:11 for I have /to be content whatever
2Ti 3:14 continue in what you have /
Heb 5: 8 he /obedience from what he

LEARNING (LEARN)

Pr 1: 5 let the wise listen and add to their /,
9: 9 man and he will add to his /.
Isa 44:25 who overthrows the /of the wise
Jn 7:15 "How did this man get such /
2Ti 3: 7 always /but never able

LEARNS (LEARN)

Jn 6:45 and /from him comes to me.

LEATHER

2Ki 1: 8 and with a /belt around his waist."
Mt 3: 4 and he had a /belt around his waist

LEAVES

Ge 3: 7 so they sewed fig /together
Eze 47:12 for food and their /for healing."
Rev 22: 2 the /of the tree are for the healing

LEBANON

Dt 11:24 from the desert to L,
1Ki 4:33 from the cedar of L

LED (LEAD)

Ex 3: 1 and he /the flock to the far side
Dt 8: 2 the LORD your God /you all
1Ki 11: 3 and his wives /him astray.
2Ch 26:16 his pride /to his downfall.
Ne 13:26 he was /into sin by foreign women.
Ps 68:18 you /captives in your train;
78:52 he /them like sheep
Pr 7:21 persuasive words she /him astray;
20: 1 whoever is /astray
Isa 53: 7 he was /like a lamb to the slaughter
Jer 11:19 I had been like a gentle lamb /
Am 2:10 and I /you forty years in the desert
Mt 4: 1 Then Jesus was /by the Spirit
27:31 they /him away to crucify him.
Lk 4: 1 was /by the Spirit in the desert,
Ac 8:32 "He was /like a sheep
Ro 8:14 those who are /by the Spirit
2Co 7: 9 your sorrow /you to repentance.
Gal 5:18 But if you are /by the Spirit,
Eph 4: 8 he /captives in his train.

LEEKS*

Nu 11: 5 melons, /, onions and garlic.

LEFT

Dt 28:14 or to the /, following other gods
Jos 1: 7 turn from it to the right or to the /,
23: 6 aside to the right or to the /
2Ki 22: 2 aside to the right or to the /.
Pr 4:27 Do not swerve to the right or the /;
Isa 30:21 turn to the right or to the /,
Mt 6: 3 do not let your /hand know what
25:33 on his right and the goats on his /.

LEGALISTIC*

Php 3: 6 as for /righteousness, faultless.

LEGION

Mk 5: 9 "My name is L," he replied.

LEND (LENDER LENDS MONEYLENDER)

Lev 25:37 You must not /him money
Dt 15: 8 freely /him whatever he needs.
Ps 37:26 are always generous and /freely;
Eze 18: 8 He does not /at usury
Lk 6:34 if you /to those from whom you

LENDER (LEND)

Pr 22: 7 and the borrower is servant to the /.
Isa 24: 2 for borrower as for /,

LENDS (LEND)

Ps 15: 5 who /his money without usury

Ps 112: 5 to him who is generous and /freely,
Pr 19:17 to the poor /to the LORD,

LENGTH (LONG)

Ps 90:10 The /of our days is seventy years—
Pr 10:27 The fear of the LORD adds /to life

LENGTHY* (LONG)

Mk 12:40 and for a show make /prayers.
Lk 20:47 and for a show make /prayers.

LEOPARD

Isa 11: 6 the /will lie down with the goat,
Da 7: 6 beast, one that looked like a /.
Rev 13: 2 The beast I saw resembled a /,

LEPROSY (LEPROUS)

Nu 12:10 toward her and saw that she had /;
2Ki 5: 1 was a valiant soldier, but he had /.
7: 3 men with /at the entrance
2Ch 26:21 King Uzziah had /
Mt 11: 5 those who have /are cured,
Lk 17:12 ten men who had /met him.

LEPROUS (LEPROSY)

Ex 4: 6 and when he took it out, it was /,

LETTER (LETTERS)

Mt 5:18 not the smallest /, not the least
2Co 3: 2 You yourselves are our /, written
3: 6 for the /kills, but the Spirit gives
2Th 3:14 not obey our instruction in this /,

LETTERS (LETTER)

2Co 3: 7 which was engraved in /on stone,
10:10 "His /are weighty and forceful,
2Pe 3:16 His /contain some things that are

LEVEL

Ps 143:10 lead me on /ground.
Pr 4:26 Make /paths for your feet
Isa 26: 7 The path of the righteous is /;
40: 4 the rough ground shall become /,
Jer 31: 9 on a /path where they will not
Heb 12:13 "Make /paths for your feet,"

LEVI (LEVITE LEVITES LEVITICAL)

1. Son of Jacob by Leah (Ge 29:34; 46:11; 1Ch 2:1). With Simeon avenged rape of Dinah (Ge 34). Tribe of blessed (Ge 49:5-7; Dt 33: 8-11), chosen as priests (Nu 3-4), numbered (Nu 3:39; 26:62), allotted cities, but not land (Nu 18; 35; Dt 10:9; Jos 13:14; 21), land (Eze 48: 8-22), 12,000 from (Rev 7:7).
2. See MATTHEW.

LEVIATHAN

Job 41: 1 pull in the /with a fishhook
Ps 74:14 you who crushed the heads of L
Isa 27: 1 L the gliding serpent,

LEVITE (LEVI)

Dt 26:12 you shall give it to the L, the alien,
Jdg 19: 1 a L who lived in a remote area

LEVITES (LEVI)

Nu 1:53 The L are to be responsible
3:12 "I have taken the L
8: 6 "Take the L from among the other
18:21 I give to the L all the tithes in Israel
35: 7 must give the L forty-eight towns,
2Ch 31: 2 assigned the priests and L
Mal 3: 3 he will purify the L and refine them

LEVITICAL (LEVI)

Heb 7:11 attained through the L priesthood

LEWDNESS

Mk 7:22 malice, deceit, /, envy, slander,

LIAR* (LIE)

Dt 19:18 and if the witness proves to be a /,
Job 34: 6 I am considered a /;
Pr 17: 4 /pays attention to a malicious
19:22 better to be poor than a /.
30: 6 will rebuke you and prove you a /.
Mic 2:11 If a /and deceiver comes and says,
Jn 8:44 for he is a /and the father of lies.
8:55 I did not, I would be a /like you,
Ro 3: 4 Let God be true, and every man a /.
1Jn 1:10 we make him out to be a /
2: 4 not do what he commands is a /,
2:22 Who is the /? It is the man who
4:20 yet hates his brother, he is a /.
5:10 God has made him out to be a /,

LIARS* (LIE)

Ps   63:11 the mouths of /will be silenced.
116:11 "All men are /."
Isa   57: 4 the offspring of /?
Mic   6:12 her people are /
1Ti   1:10 for slave traders and /and perjurers
4: 2 come through hypocritical /,
Tit   1:12 "Cretans are always /, evil brutes,
Rev   3: 9 though they are not, but are /—
21: 8 magic arts, the idolaters and all /—

LIBERATED*

Ro   8:21 that the creation itself will be /

LICENSE

Jude   4 of our God into a /for immorality

LICK

Ps   72: 9 and his enemies will /the dust.
Isa   49:23 they will /the dust at your feet.
Mic   7:17 They will /dust like a snake,

LIE (LIAR LIARS LIED LIES LYING)

Lev   18:22 " 'Do not /with a man
19:11 " 'Do not /.
Nu   23:19 God is not a man, that he should /,
Dt   6: 7 when you /down and when you get
25: 2 the judge shall make him /down
1Sa   15:29 the Glory of Israel does not /
Ps   4: 8 I will /down and sleep in peace,
23: 2 me /down in green pastures,
89:35 and I will not /to David—
Pr   3:24 when you /down, you will not be
Isa   11: 6 leopard will /down with the goat,
28:15 for we have made a /our refuge
Jer   9: 5 They have taught their tongues to /
23:14 They commit adultery and live a /.
Eze   13: 6 are false and their divinations a /.
34:14 they will /down in good grazing
Ro   1:25 exchanged the truth of God for a /,
Col   3: 9 Do not /to each other,
2Th   2:11 so that they will believe the /
Tit   1: 2 which God, who does not /,
Heb   6:18 which it is impossible for God to /,
1Jn   2:21 because no /comes from the truth.
Rev   14: 5 No /was found in their mouths;

LIED (LIE)

Ac   5: 4 You have not /to men but to God."

LIES (LIE)

Lev   6: 3 finds lost property and /about it,
Ps   5: 6 You destroy those who tell /;
10: 7 His mouth is full of curses and /
12: 2 Everyone /to his neighbor;
34:13 and your lips from speaking /.
58: 3 they are wayward and speak /.
144: 8 whose mouths are full of /,
Pr   6:19 a false witness who pours out /
12:17 but a false witness tells /.
19: 5 he who pours out /will not go free.
19: 9 and he who pours out /will perish.
29:12 If a ruler listens to /,
30: 8 Keep falsehood and /far from me;
Isa   59: 3 Your lips have spoken /,
Jer   5:31 The prophets prophesy /,
9: 3 like a bow, to shoot /;
14:14 "The prophets are prophesying /
Hos   11:12 Ephraim has surrounded me with /,
Jn   8:44 for he is a liar and the father of /.

LIFE (LIVE)

Ge   1:30 everything that has the breath of /
2: 7 into his nostrils the breath of /,
2: 9 of the garden were the tree of /
6:17 to destroy all /under the heavens,
9: 5 for the /of his fellow man.
9:11 Never again will all /be cut
Ex   21: 6 Then he will be his servant for /.
21:23 you are to take /for /, eye for eye,
23:26 I will give you a full /span.
Lev   17:14 the /of every creature is its blood.
24:17 " 'If anyone takes the /
24:18 must make restitution—/for /.
Nu   35:31 a ransom for the /of a murderer,
Dt   4:42 one of these cities and save his /.
12:23 because the blood is the /,
19:21 Show no pity: /for /, eye for eye,
30:15 I set before you today /
30:19 Now choose /, so that you
30:20 For the LORD is your /,
32:39 I put to death and I bring to /,
32:47 words for you—they are your /.
1Sa   19: 5 He took his /in his hands

Job   2: 6 hands; but you must spare his /."
33: 4 of the Almighty gives me /.
33:30 that the light of /may shine on him.
Ps   16:11 known to me the path of /;
17:14 this world whose reward is in this /.
23: 6 all the days of my /,
27: 1 LORD is the stronghold of my /—
34:12 Whoever of you loves /
36: 9 For with you is the fountain of /;
39: 4 let me know how fleeting is my /.
41: 2 will protect him and preserve his /;
49: 7 No man can redeem the /
49: 8 the ransom for a /is costly,
63: 3 Because your love is better than /,
69:28 they be blotted out of the book of /
91:16 With long /will I satisfy him
104: 33 I will sing to the LORD all my /;
119: 25 preserve my /according to your word
Pr   1: 3 a disciplined and prudent /,
2: 2 will prolong your /many years
3:18 of /to those who embrace her;
4:23 for it is the wellspring of /.
6:23 are the way to /,
6:26 adulteress preys upon your very /.
7:23 little knowing it will cost him his /.
8:35 For whoever finds me finds /
10:11 of the righteous is a fountain of /,
10:27 of the LORD adds length to /,
11:30 of the righteous is a tree of /,
13: 3 He who guards his lips guards his /,
13:12 but a longing fulfilled is a tree of /.
13:14 of the wise is a fountain of /,
14:27 of the LORD is a fountain of /,
15: 4 that brings healing is a tree of /,
16:22 Understanding is a fountain of /
19: 3 A man's own folly ruins his /,
19:23 The fear of the LORD leads to /;
21:21 finds /, prosperity and honor.
Isa   53:10 LORD makes his /a guilt offering,
53:11 he will see the light of /,
53:12 he poured out his /unto death,
Jer   10:23 that a man's /is not his own;
La   3:58 you redeemed my /.
Eze   18:27 and right, he will save his /.
37: 5 enter you, and you will come to /.
Da   12: 2 some to everlasting /, others
Jnh   2: 6 you brought my /up from the pit,
Mal   2: 5 a covenant of /and peace,
Mt   6:25 Is not /more important than food,
7:14 and narrow the road that leads to /,
10:39 Whoever finds his /will lose /,
16:21 and on the third day be raised to /.
16:25 wants to save his /will lose it,
18: 8 better for you to enter /maimed
19:16 thing must I do to get eternal /?"
19:29 as much and will inherit eternal /.
20:28 to give his /as a ransom for many."
25:46 but the righteous to eternal /."
Mk   8:35 but whoever loses his /for me
9:43 better for you to enter /maimed
10:17 "what must I do to inherit eternal /
10:30 and in the age to come, eternal /.
10:45 to give his /as a ransom for many."
Lk   6: 9 to save /or to destroy it?"
9:22 and on the third day be raised to /."
9:24 wants to save his /will lose it,
12:15 a man's /does not consist
12:22 do not worry about your /,
12:25 can add a single hour to his /?
14:26 even his own /—he cannot be my
17:33 tries to keep his /will lose it,
21:19 standing firm you will gain /.
Jn   1: 4 In him was /, and that /was
3:15 believes in him may have eternal /.
3:36 believes in the Son has eternal /,
4:14 of water welling up to eternal /."
5:21 raises the dead and gives them /,
5:24 him who sent me has eternal /
5:26 For as the Father has /in himself,
5:39 that by them you possess eternal /.
5:40 refuse to come to me to have /.
6:27 for food that endures to eternal /,
6:33 down from heaven and gives /
6:35 Jesus declared, "I am the bread of /
6:40 believes in him shall have eternal /,
6:47 he who believes has everlasting /.
6:48 I am the bread of /.
6:51 give for the /of the world."
6:53 and drink his blood, you have no /
6:63 The Spirit gives /; the flesh counts
6:68 You have the words of eternal /.
8:12 but will have the light of /."
10:10 I have come that they may have /,
10:15 and I lay down my /for the sheep.
10:17 loves me is that I lay down my /—

Jn   10:28 I give them eternal /, and they shall
11:25 "I am the resurrection and the /.
12:25 The man who loves his /will lose it,
12:50 his command leads to eternal /.
13: 7 I will lay down my /for you."
14: 6 am the way and the truth and the /.
15:13 lay down his /for his friends.
17: 2 people that he might give eternal /
17: 3 Now this is eternal /: that they may
20:31 that by believing you may have /
Ac   2:32 God has raised this Jesus to /,
3:15 You killed the author of /,
11:18 the Gentiles repentance unto /."
13:48 appointed for eternal /believed.
Ro   2: 7 immortality, he will give eternal /.
4:25 was raised to /for our justification.
5:10 shall we be saved through his /!
5:18 was justification that brings /
5:21 righteousness to bring eternal /
6: 4 the Father, we too may live a new /
6:13 have been brought from death to /;
6:22 holiness, and the result is eternal /.
6:23 but the gift of God is eternal /
8: 6 mind controlled by the Spirit is /
8:11 also give /to your mortal bodies
8:38 convinced that neither death nor /,
1Co   15:19 If only for this /we have hope
15:36 What you sow does not come to /
2Co   2:16 to the other, the fragrance of /.
3: 6 letter kills, but the Spirit gives /.
4:10 so that the /of Jesus may
5: 4 is mortal may be swallowed up by /.
Gal   2:20 The /I live in the body, I live
3:21 had been given that could impart /,
Eph   1: 4 I urge you to live a /worthy
Php   2:16 as you hold out the word of /—
4: 3 whose names are in the book of /.
Col   1:10 order that you may live a /worthy
3: 3 your /is now hidden with Christ
1Th   4:12 so that your daily /may win
1Ti   1:16 on him and receive eternal /.
4: 8 for both the present /and the /
4:12 in /, in love, in faith and in purity.
4:16 Watch your /and doctrine closely.
6:12 Take hold of the eternal /
6:19 hold of the /that is truly /.
2Ti   1: 9 saved us and called us to a holy /—
1:10 destroyed death and has brought /
3:12 to live a godly /in Christ Jesus will
Tit   1: 2 resting on the hope of eternal /,
3: 7 heirs having the hope of eternal /.
Heb   7:16 of the power of an indestructible /.
Jas   1:12 crown of /that God has promised
3:13 Let him show it by his good /,
1Pe   3: 7 with you of the gracious gift of /,
3:10 "Whoever would love /
4: 2 rest of his earthly /for evil human
2Pe   1: 3 given us everything we need for /
1Jn   1: 1 proclaim concerning the Word of /.
2:25 he promised us—even eternal /.
3:14 we have passed from death to /,
3:16 Jesus Christ laid down his /for us.
5:11 has given us eternal /, and this /is
5:20 He is the true God and eternal /.
Jude   21 Christ to bring you to eternal /.
Rev   2: 7 the right to eat from the tree of /,
2: 8 who died and came to /again.
2:10 and I will give you the crown of /.
3: 5 name from the book of /,
13: 8 written in the book of /belonging
17: 8 in the book of /from the creation
20:12 was opened, which is the book of /.
20:15 not found written in the book of /,
21: 6 from the spring of the water of /.
21:27 written in the Lamb's book of /.
22: 1 me the river of the water of /,
22: 2 side of the river stood the tree of /,
22:14 may have the right to the tree of /
22:17 take the free gift of the water of /.
22:19 from him his share in the tree of /

LIFE-GIVING (GIVE)

Pr   15:31 He who listens to a /rebuke
1Co   15:45 being"; the last Adam, a /spirit.

LIFETIME (LIVE)

Ps   30: 5 but his favor lasts a /;
Lk   16:25 in your /you received your good

LIFT (LIFTED LIFTING LIFTS)

Ps   3: 3 you bestow glory on me and /
28: 2 as I /up my hands
63: 4 in your name I will /up my hands.
91:12 they will /you up in their hands,

LIFTED

Ps 121: 1 I /up my eyes to the hills—
123: 1 I /up my eyes to you,
134: 2 L up your hands in the sanctuary
143: 8 for to you I /up my soul.
Isa 40: 9 /up your voice with a shout,
La 2: 19 L up your hands to him
3: 41 Let us /up our hearts and our
Mt 4: 6 they will /you up in their hands,
Lk 21: 28 stand up and /up your heads.
1Ti 2: 8 everywhere to /up holy hands
Jas 4: 10 the Lord, and he will /you up.
1Pe 5: 6 that he may /you up in due time.

LIFTED (LIFT)

Ne 8: 6 and all the people /their hands
Ps 24: 7 be /up, you ancient doors,
40: 2 He /me out of the slimy pit,
41: 9 has /up his heel against me.
Isa 52: 13 /up and highly exalted.
63: 9 he /them up and carried them
Jn 3: 14 Moses /up the snake in the desert,
8: 28 "When you have /up the Son
12: 32 when I am /up from the earth,
12: 34 'The Son of Man must be /up?
13: 18 shares his bread has /up his heel

LIFTING (LIFT)

Ps 141: 2 may the /up of my hands be like

LIFTS (LIFT)

Ps 113: 7 and /the needy from the ash heap,

LIGAMENT* (LIGAMENTS)

Eph 4: 16 held together by every supporting /

LIGAMENTS* (LIGAMENT)

Col 2: 19 held together by its /and sinews,

LIGHT (ENLIGHTENED LIGHTS)

Ge 1: 3 "Let there be /," and there was /.
Ex 13: 21 in a pillar of fire to give them /,
25: 37 it so that they /the space in front
2Sa 22: 29 LORD turns my darkness into /.
Job 38: 19 "What is the way to the abode of /?
Ps 4: 6 Let the /of your face shine upon us
18: 28 my God turns my darkness into /.
19: 8 giving /to the eyes.
27: 1 LORD is my /and my salvation—
36: 9 in your /we see /.
56: 13 God in the /of life.
76: 4 You are resplendent with /,
89: 15 who walk in the /of your presence,
104: 2 He wraps himself in /
119:105 and a /for my path.
119:130 The unfolding of your words gives /;
139: 12 for darkness is as /to you.
Pr 4: 18 till the full /of day.
Isa 2: 5 let us walk in the /of the LORD.
9: 2 have seen a great /;
42: 6 and a /for the Gentiles,
45: 7 I form the /and create darkness,
49: 6 also make you a /for the Gentiles,
53: 11 he will see the /of life,
60: 1 "Arise, shine, for your /has come.
60: 19 LORD will be your everlasting /,
Eze 1: 27 and brilliant /surrounded him.
Mic 7: 8 the LORD will be my /.
Mt 4: 16 have seen a great /;
5: 14 "You are the /of the world.
5: 15 it gives /to everyone in the house.
5: 16 let your /shine before men,
6: 22 your whole body will be full of /.
11: 30 yoke is easy and my burden is /."
17: 2 his clothes became as white as the /
24: 29 and the moon will not give its /;
Mk 13: 24 and the moon will not give its /;
Lk 2: 32 a /for revelation to the Gentiles
8: 16 those who come in can see the /.
11: 33 those who come in may see the /.
Jn 1: 4 and that life was the /of men.
1: 5 The /shines in the darkness,
1: 7 witness to testify concerning that /,
1: 9 The true /that gives /
3: 19 but men loved darkness instead of /
3: 20 Everyone who does evil hates the /,
8: 12 he said, "I am the /of the world.
9: 5 in the world, I am the /of the world
12: 35 Walk while you have the /,
12: 46 I have come into the world as a /,
Ac 13: 47 " 'I have made you a /
Ro 13: 12 darkness and put on the armor of /.
2Co 4: 4 made his /shine in our hearts
6: 14 Or what fellowship can /have
11: 14 masquerades as an angel of /.
Eph 5: 8 but now you are /in the Lord.

1Th 5: 5 You are all sons of the /
1Ti 6: 16 and who lives in unapproachable /,
1Pe 2: 9 of darkness into his wonderful /,
2Pe 1: 19 as to a /shining in a dark place.
1Jn 1: 5 God is /; in him there is no
1: 7 But if we walk in the /,
2: 9 Anyone who claims to be in the /
Rev 21: 23 for the glory of God gives it /,
22: 5 for the Lord God will give them /.

LIGHTNING

Ex 9: 23 and /flashed down to the ground.
20: 18 and /and heard the trumpet
Ps 18: 12 with hailstones and bolts of /.
Eze 1: 13 it was bright, and /flashed out of it.
Da 10: 6 his face like /, his eyes like flaming
Mt 24: 27 For as the /that comes from the east
28: 3 His appearance was like /
Lk 10: 18 "I saw Satan fall like /from heaven.
Rev 4: 5 From the throne came flashes of /,

LIGHTS (LIGHT)

Ge 1: 14 "Let there be /in the expanse
Lk 8: 16 No one /a lamp and hides it in a jar

LIKE-MINDED* (MIND)

Php 2: 2 make my joy complete by being /.

LIKENESS

Ge 1: 26 man in our image, in our /,
Pr 27: 15 I will be satisfied with seeing your /
Isa 52: 14 his form marred beyond human /—
Ro 8: 3 Son in the /of sinful man
8: 29 to be conformed to the /of his Son,
2Co 3: 18 his /with ever-increasing glory,
Php 2: 7 being made in human /.
Jas 3: 9 who have been made in God's /.

LILIES (LILY)

Lk 12: 27 "Consider how the /grow.

LILY (LILIES)

SS 2: 1 a /of the valleys.
2: 2 Lover Like a /among thorns

LIMIT

Ps 147: 5 his understanding has no /.
Jn 3: 34 for God gives the Spirit without /.

LINEN

Lev 16: 4 He is to put on the sacred /tunic,
Pr 31: 22 she is clothed in fine /and purple.
31: 24 She makes /garments
Mk 15: 46 So Joseph bought some /cloth,
Jn 20: 5 He saw the strips of /lying there,
Rev 15: 6 shining /and wore golden sashes
19: 8 Fine /, bright and clean,

LINGER

Hab 2: 3 Though it /, wait for it;

LION (LION'S LIONS')

Jdg 14: 6 power so that he tore the /apart
1Sa 17: 34 When a /or a bear came
Isa 11: 7 and the /will eat straw like the ox.
65: 25 and the /will eat straw like the ox,
Eze 1: 10 right side each had the face of a /,
10: 14 the third the face of a /,
Da 7: 4 "The first was like a /,
1Pe 5: 8 around like a roaring /looking
Rev 4: 7 The first living creature was like a /
5: 5 See, the L of the tribe of Judah,

LION'S (LION)

Ge 49: 9 You are a /cub, O Judah;

LIONS' (LION)

Da 6: 7 shall be thrown into the /den.

LIPS

Ps 8: 2 From the /of children and infants
34: 1 his praise will always be on my /.
40: 9 I do not seal my /,
63: 3 my /will glorify you.
119:171 May my /overflow with praise,
140: 3 the poison of vipers is on their /.
141: 3 keep watch over the door of my /.
Pr 10: 13 on the /of the discerning,
10: 18 who conceals his hatred has lying /,
10: 32 /of the righteous know what is
12: 22 The LORD detests lying /,
13: 3 He who guards his /guards his life,
14: 7 will not find knowledge on his /.
24: 26 is like a kiss on the /.
26: 23 are fervent /with an evil heart.

Pr 27: 2 someone else, and not your own /.
Isa 6: 5 For I am a man of unclean /,
28: 11 with foreign /and strange tongues
29: 13 and honor me with their /,
Mal 2: 7 "For the /of a priest ought
Mt 15: 8 These people honor me with their /
21: 16 " 'From the /of children
Lk 4: 22 words that came from his /.
Ro 3: 13 "The poison of vipers is on their /."
Col 3: 8 and filthy language from your /.
Heb 13: 15 the fruit of /that confess his name.
1Pe 3: 10 and his /from deceitful speech.

LISTEN (LISTENED LISTENING LISTENS)

Dt 18: 15 You must /to him.
30: 20 /to his voice, and hold fast to him.
1Ki 4: 34 came to /to Solomon's wisdom,
2Ki 21: 9 But the people did not /.
Pr 1: 5 let the wise /and add
Ecc 5: 1 Go near to /rather
Eze 2: 5 And whether they /or fail to /—
Mt 12: 42 earth to /to Solomon's wisdom,
Mk 9: 7 L to him!" Suddenly,
Jn 10: 27 My sheep /to my voice; I know
Ac 3: 22 you must /to everything he tells
Jas 1: 19 Everyone should be quick to /,
1: 22 Do not merely /to the word,
1Jn 4: 6 not from God does not /to us.

LISTENED (LISTEN)

Ne 8: 3 And all the people /attentively
Isa 66: 4 when I spoke, no one /.
Da 9: 6 We have not /to your servants

LISTENING (LISTEN)

1Sa 3: 9 Speak, LORD, for your servant is /
Pr 18: 13 He who answers before /—
Lk 10: 39 at the Lord's feet /to what he said.

LISTENS (LISTEN)

Pr 12: 15 but a wise man /to advice.
Lk 10: 16 "He who /to you /
1Jn 4: 6 and whoever knows God /to us;

LIVE (ALIVE LIFE LIFETIME LIVES LIVING)

Ge 3: 22 tree of life and eat, and /forever."
Ex 20: 12 so that you may /long
33: 20 for no one may see me and /."
Nu 21: 8 who is bitten can look at it and /."
Dt 5: 24 we have seen that a man can /
6: 2 as you /by keeping all his decrees
8: 3 to teach you that man does not /
Job 14: 14 If a man dies, will he /again?
Ps 15: 1 Who may /on your holy hill?
24: 1 the world, and all who /in it;
26: 8 I love the house where you /,
119:175 Let me /that I may praise you,
Pr 21: 9 Better to /on a corner of the roof
21: 19 Better to /in a desert
Ecc 9: 4 a /dog is better off than a dead lion
Isa 26: 19 But your dead will /;
55: 3 hear me, that your soul may /.
Eze 17: 19 LORD says: As surely as I /,
20: 11 for the man who obeys them will /
37: 3 can these bones /?" I said,
Am 5: 6 Seek the LORD and /;
Hab 2: 4 but the righteous will /by his faith
Zec 2: 11 I will /among you and you will
Mt 4: 4 'Man does not /on bread alone,
Lk 4: 4 'Man does not /on bread alone.' "
Jn 14: 19 Because I /, you also will /.
Ac 17: 24 does not /in temples built by hands
17: 28 'For in him we /and move
Ro 1: 17 "The righteous will /by faith."
2Co 5: 7 We /by faith, not by sight.
6: 16 "I will /with them and walk
Gal 2: 20 The life I /in the body, I /by faith
3: 11 "The righteous will /by faith."
5: 25 Since we /by the Spirit, let us keep
Eph 4: 17 that you must no longer /
Php 1: 21 to /is Christ and to die is gain.
Col 1: 10 order that you may /a life worthy
1Th 4: 1 we instructed you how to /in order
5: 13 L in peace with each other.
1Ti 2: 2 that we may /peaceful
2Ti 3: 12 who wants to /a godly life
Tit 2: 12 and to /self-controlled, upright
Heb 10: 38 But my righteous one will /by faith
12: 14 Make every effort to /in peace
1Pe 1: 17 /your lives as strangers here
3: 8 /in harmony with one another;

LIVES (LIVE)

Ge 45: 7 and to save your /by a great
Job 19: 25 I know that my Redeemer /,

Pr   1: 19 it takes away the l
Isa   57: 15 he who l forever, whose name is
Da   3: 28 to give up their l rather than serve
Jn   14: 17 for he l with you and will be in you.
Ro   6: 10 but the life he l, he l to God.
         7: 18 I know that nothing good l in me,
         8: 9 if the Spirit of God l in you.
        14: 7 For none of us l to himself alone
1Co   1: 16 and that God's Spirit l in you?
Gal   2: 20 I no longer live, but Christ l in me.
1Th   2: 8 only the gospel of God but our l
1Ti   2: 2 quiet l in all godliness and holiness.
Tit   2: 12 and godly l in this present age,
Heb   7: 24 but because Jesus l forever,
        13: 5 Keep your l free from the love
1Pe   3: 2 the purity and reverence of your l.
2Pe   3: 11 You ought to live holy and godly l
1Jn   3: 16 to lay down our l for our brothers.
         4: 16 Whoever l in love l in God.

LIVING (LIVE)

Ge   2: 7 and the man became a l being.
1Sa   17: 26 defy the armies of the l God?"
Isa   53: 8 cut off from the land of the l,
Jer   2: 13 the spring of l water,
Eze   1: 5 what looked like four l creatures.
Zec   14: 8 On that day l water will flow out
Mt   22: 32 the God of the dead but of the l. "
Jn   4: 10 he would have given you l water."
         6: 51 I am the l bread that came
         7: 38 streams of l water will flow
Ro   8: 11 Jesus from the dead is l in you,
        12: 1 to offer your bodies as l sacrifices,
1Co   9: 14 the gospel should receive their l
Heb   4: 12 For the word of God is l and active.
        10: 20 and l way opened for us
        10: 31 to fall into the hands of the l God.
1Pe   1: 23 through the l and enduring word
Rev   1: 18 I am the l One; I was dead,
         4: 6 the throne, were four l creatures,
         7: 17 to springs of l water.

LOAD (LOADS)

Gal   6: 5 for each one should carry his own l.

LOADS (LOAD)

Mt   23: 4 They tie up heavy l and put them

LOAF (LOAVES)

1Co   10: 17 for we all partake of the one l.

LOAVES (LOAF)

Mk   6: 41 Taking the five l and the two fish
         8: 6 When he had taken the seven l
Lk   11: 5 'Friend, lend me three l of bread,

LOCKED

Jn   20: 26 the doors were l, Jesus came
Gal   3: 23 l up until faith should be revealed.

LOCUSTS

Ex   10: 4 I will bring l into your country
Joel   2: 25 you for the years the l have eaten—
Mt   3: 4 His food was l and wild honey.
Rev   9: 3 And out of the smoke l came

LOFTY

Ps   139: 6 too l for me to attain.
Isa   57: 15 is what the high and l One says—

LONELY

Ps   68: 6 God sets the l in families,
Lk   5: 16 Jesus often withdrew to l places

**LONG (LENGTH LENGTHY LONGED
LONGING LONGINGS LONGS)**

Ex   17: 11 As l as Moses held up his hands,
Nu   6: 5 the hair of his head grow l.
1Ki   18: 21 "How l will you waver
Ps   119: 97 I meditate on it all day l.
       119: 174 l for your salvation, O LORD,
Hos   7: 13 l to redeem them
Am   5: 18 Why do you l for the day
Mt   25: 5 The bridegroom was a l time
Jn   9: 4 As l as it is day, we must do
1Co   11: 14 that if a man has l hair,
Eph   3: 18 to grasp how wide and l and high
Php   1: 8 God can testify how l l for all
1Pe   1: 12 Even angels l to look

LONGED (LONG)

Mt   13: 17 righteous men l to see what you see
        23: 37 how often I have l
Lk   13: 34 how often I have l
2Ti   4: 8 to all who have l for his appearing.

LONGING* (LONG)

Dt   28: 65 with l, and a despairing heart.
Job   7: 2 Like a slave l for the evening
Ps   119: 20 My soul is consumed with l
       119: 81 with l for your salvation,
       119: 131 l for your commands.
       143: 7 my spirit faints with l
Pr   13: 12 but a l fulfilled is a tree of life.
        13: 19 A l fulfilled is sweet to the soul,
Eze   23: 27 look on these things with l
Lk   16: 21 and l to eat what fell from the rich
Ro   15: 23 since I have been l for many years
2Co   5: 2 l to be clothed with our heavenly
         7: 7 He told us about your l for me,
         7: 11 what alarm, what l, what concern,
1Th   2: 17 out of our intense l we made every
Heb   11: 16 they were l for a better country—

LONGINGS* (LONG)

Ps   38: 9 All my l lie open before you,
       112: 10 the l of the wicked will come

LONGS* (LONG)

Ps   63: 1 my body l for you,
Isa   26: 9 in the morning my spirit l for you.
        30: 18 Yet the LORD l to be gracious
Php   2: 26 For he l for all of you and is

LOOK (LOOKED LOOKING LOOKS)

Ge   19: 17 "Flee for your lives! Don't l back,
Ex   3: 6 because he was afraid to l at God.
Nu   21: 8 anyone who is bitten can l at it
        32: 8 Kadesh Barnea to l over the land.
Dt   4: 29 you will find him if you l for him
1Sa   16: 7 The LORD does not l
Job   31: 1 not to l lustfully at a girl.
Ps   34: 5 Those who l to him are radiant;
       105: 4 L to the LORD and his strength;
       113: 6 who stoops down to l
       123: 2 As the eyes of slaves l to the hand
Pr   1: 28 they will l for me but will not find
         4: 25 Let your eyes l straight ahead,
        15: 30 A cheerful l brings joy to the heart,
Isa   17: 7 In that day men will l
        31: 1 do not l to the Holy One of Israel,
        40: 26 Lift your eyes and l to the heavens:
        60: 5 Then you will l and be radiant;
Jer   3: 3 Yet you have the brazen l
         6: 16 "Stand at the crossroads and l;
Eze   34: 11 for my sheep and l after them.
Hab   1: 13 Your eyes are too pure to l on evil;
Zec   12: 10 They will l on me, the one they
Mt   18: 10 "See that you do not l down on one
        18: 12 go to l for the one that wandered
        23: 27 which l beautiful on the outside
Mk   13: 21 'L, here is the Christ!' or, 'L,
Lk   6: 41 "Why do you l at the speck
        24: 39 L at my hands and my feet.
Jn   1: 36 he said, "L, the Lamb of God!"
         4: 35 open your eyes and l at the fields!
        19: 37 "They will l on the one they have
Ro   14: 10 why do you l down on your brother
Php   2: 4 Each of you should l not only
1Ti   4: 12 Don't let anyone l down on you
Jas   1: 27 to l after orphans and widows
1Pe   1: 12 long to l into these things.
2Pe   3: 12 as you l forward to the day of God

LOOKED (LOOK)

Ge   19: 26 Lot's wife l back, and she became
Ex   2: 25 So God l on the Israelites
1Sa   6: 19 because they had l into the ark
SS   1: 1 I l for the one my heart loves;
Eze   22: 30 "I l for a man among them who
        34: 6 and no one searched or l for them.
        44: 4 I l and saw the glory
Da   7: 9 "As I l,
        10: 5 I l up and there before me was
Hab   3: 6 he l, and made the nations tremble.
Mt   25: 36 I was sick and you l after me,
Lk   18: 9 and l down on everybody else,
        22: 61 The Lord turned and l straight
1Jn   1: 1 which we have l at and our hands

LOOKING (LOOK)

Ps   69: 3 l for my God.
       119: 82 My eyes fail, l for your promise;
       119: 123 My eyes fail, l for your salvation,
Mk   16: 6 "You are l for Jesus the Nazarene,
2Co   10: 7 You are l only on the surface
Php   4: 17 Not that I am l for a gift,
1Th   2: 6 We were not l for praise from men,
2Pe   3: 13 with his promise we are l forward
Rev   5: 6 I saw a Lamb, l as if it had been

LOOKS (LOOK)

1Sa   16: 7 Man l at the outward appearance,
Ezr   8: 22 is on everyone who l to him,
Ps   104: 32 who l at the earth, and it trembles;
       138: 6 on high, he l upon the lowly,
Pr   27: 18 he who l after his master will be
Eze   34: 12 As a shepherd l after his scattered
Mt   5: 28 But I tell you that anyone who l
        16: 4 and adulterous generation l
Lk   9: 62 and l back is fit for service
Jn   6: 40 Father's will is that everyone who l
        12: 45 When he l at me, he sees the one
Php   2: 21 For everyone l out
Jas   1: 25 But the man who l intently

LOOSE

Isa   33: 23 Your rigging hangs l:
Mt   16: 19 and whatever you l on earth will be
        18: 18 and whatever you l on earth will be

LORD† (LORD'S† LORDED LORDING)

Ge   18: 27 been so bold as to speak to the L,
Ex   15: 17 O L, your hands established.
Nu   16: 13 now you also want to l it over us?
Dt   10: 17 God of gods and L of lords,
Jos   3: 13 the L of all the earth—set foot
1Ki   3: 10 L was pleased that Solomon had
Ne   4: 14 Remember the L, who is great
Job   28: 28 'The fear of the L—that is wisdom,
Ps   37: 13 but the L laughs at the wicked,
        38: 22 O L my Savior.
        54: 4 the L is the one who sustains me.
        62: 12 and that you, O L, are loving.
        69: 6 O L, the LORD Almighty;
        86: 5 You are forgiving and good, O L,
        86: 8 gods there is none like you, O L;
        89: 49 O L, where is your former great
       110: 1 The LORD says to my L:
       110: 5 The L is at your right hand;
       130: 3 O L, who could stand?
       135: 5 that our L is greater than all gods.
       136: 3 Give thanks to the L of lords:
       147: 5 Great is our L and mighty in power
Isa   6: 1 I saw the L seated on a throne,
Da   2: 47 and the L of kings and a revealer
         9: 4 "O L, the great and awesome God,
         9: 7 "L, you are righteous,
         9: 9 The L our God is merciful
         9: 19 O L, listen! O L, forgive! O L,
Mt   3: 3 'Prepare the way for the L,
         4: 7 'Do not put the L your God
         4: 10 'Worship the L your God,
         7: 21 "Not everyone who says to me, 'L,
         9: 38 Ask the L of the harvest, therefore,
        12: 8 Son of Man is L of the Sabbath."
        20: 25 of the Gentiles l it over them,
        21: 9 comes in the name of the L!"
        22: 37 " 'Love the L your God
        22: 44 For he says, " 'The L said to my L:
        23: 39 comes in the name of the L.' "
Mk   1: 3 'Prepare the way for the L,
        11: 11 the L has done this,
        12: 29 the L our God, the L is one.
        12: 30 Love the L your God
Lk   2: 9 glory of the L shone around them,
         6: 5 The Son of Man is L of the Sabbath
         6: 46 "Why do you call me, 'L, L,'
        10: 27 " 'Love the L your God
        11: 1 one of his disciples said to him, "L,
        24: 34 The L has risen and has appeared
Jn   1: 23 'Make straight the way for the L.'
Ac   2: 21 on the name of the L will be saved.'
         2: 25 " 'I saw the L always before me.
         2: 34 " 'The L said to my L:
         8: 16 into the name of the L Jesus.
         9: 5 "Who are you, L?" Saul asked.
        10: 36 through Jesus Christ, who is L
        11: 23 true to the L with all their hearts.
        16: 31 replied, "Believe in the L Jesus,
Ro   4: 24 in him who raised Jesus our L
         5: 11 in God through our L Jesus Christ,
         6: 23 life in Christ Jesus our L.
         8: 39 of God that is in Christ Jesus our L.
        10: 9 with your mouth, "Jesus is L,"
        10: 13 on the name of the L will be saved
        10: 16 L, who has believed our message?"
        11: 34 Who has known the mind of the L?
        12: 11 your spiritual fervor, serving the L.
        13: 14 yourselves with the L Jesus Christ,
        14: 4 for the L is able to make him stand.
        14: 8 we live to the L; and if we die,
1Co   1: 31 Let him who boasts boast in the L."
         3: 5 the L has assigned to each his task.
         4: 5 time; wait till the L comes.

LORD'S† (LORD†) *(continued)*

1Co 6:13 for the L, and the L for the body.
6:14 By his power God raised the L.
7:32 affairs—how he can please the L.
7:34 to be devoted to the L in both body
7:35 in undivided devotion to the L.
7:39 but he must belong to the L.
8: 6 and there is but one L, Jesus Christ,
10: 9 We should not test the L,
11:23 For I received from the L what I
12: 3 "Jesus is L," except by the Holy
15:57 victory through our L Jesus Christ.
15:58 fully to the work of the L,
16:22 If anyone does not love the L—
2Co 1:24 Not that we /it over your faith,
2:12 found that the L had opened a door
3:17 Now the L is the Spirit,
4: 5 but Jesus Christ as L, and ourselves
5: 6 in the body we are away from the L
8: 5 they gave themselves first to the L
8:21 not only in the eyes of the L but
10:17 Let him who boasts boast in the L."
10:18 but the one whom the L commends
13:10 the authority the L gave me
Gal 6:14 in the cross of our L Jesus Christ,
Eph 4: 5 one L, one faith, one baptism;
5: 8 but now you are light in the L.
5:10 and find out what pleases the L.
5:19 make music in your heart to the L,
5:22 submit to your husbands as to the L.
6: 1 obey your parents in the L,
6: 7 as if you were serving the L,
6: 8 know that the L will reward
6:10 in the L and in his mighty power.
Php 2:11 confess that Jesus Christ is L,
3: 1 my brothers, rejoice in the L!
3: 8 of knowing Christ Jesus my L,
4: 1 you should stand firm in the L,
4: 4 Rejoice in the L always.
4: 5 The L is near.
Col 1:10 you may live a life worthy of the L
2: 6 as you received Christ Jesus as L,
3:13 Forgive as the L forgave you.
3:17 do it all in the name of the L Jesus,
3:18 your husbands, as is fitting in the L.
3:20 in everything, for this pleases the L
3:23 as working for the L, not for men,
3:24 It is the L Christ you are serving.
3:24 receive an inheritance from the L
4:17 work you have received in the L."
1Th 3: 8 since you are standing firm in the L
3:12 May the L make your love increase
4: 1 and urge you in the L Jesus
4: 6 The L will punish men
4:15 who are left till the coming of the L
5: 2 day of the L will come like a thief
5:23 at the coming of our L Jesus Christ.
2Th 1: 7 when the L Jesus is revealed
1:12 of our L Jesus may be glorified
2: 1 the coming of our L Jesus Christ
2: 8 whom the L Jesus will overthrow
3: 3 L is faithful, and he will strengthen
3: 5 May the L direct your hearts
1Ti 6:15 the King of kings and L of lords,
2Ti 1: 8 ashamed to testify about our L,
2:19 "The L knows those who are his,"
4: 8 which the L, the righteous Judge,
4:17 But the L stood at my side
Heb 1:10 O L, you laid the foundations
10:30 "The L will judge his people."
12:14 holiness no one will see the L.
13: 6 L is my helper; I will not be afraid.
Jas 3: 9 With the tongue we praise our L
4:10 Humble yourselves before the L,
5:11 The L is full of compassion
1Pe 1:25 the word of the L stands forever."
2: 3 you have tasted that the L is good.
3:12 eyes of the L are on the righteous
3:15 in your hearts set apart Christ as L.
2Pe 1:11 into the eternal kingdom of our L
1:16 and coming of our L Jesus Christ,
2: 1 the sovereign L who bought
2: 9 then the L knows how
3: 9 The L is not slow in keeping his
3:18 and knowledge of our L and Savior
Jude :14 the L is coming with thousands
Rev 4: 8 holy, holy is the L God Almighty,
4:11 "You are worthy, our L and God,
11:15 has become the kingdom of our L
17:14 he is L of lords and King of kings—
19:16 KINGS AND L OF LORDS.
22: 5 for the L God will give them light.
22:20 Come, L Jesus.

LORD'S† (LORD†)

Lk 1:38 "I am the L servant," Mary
Ac 11:21 The L hand was with them,
21:14 and said, "The L will be done."
1Co 7:32 is concerned about the L affairs—
10:26 "The earth is the L, and everything
11:26 you proclaim the L death
2Co 3:18 faces all reflect the L glory,
Eph 5:17 but understand what the L will is.
2Ti 2:24 And the L servant must not quarrel
Heb 12: 5 light of the L discipline,
Jas 4:15 you ought to say, "If it is the L will,
5: 8 because the L coming is near.
1Pe 2:13 Submit yourselves for the L sake

LORDED* (LORD†)

Ne 5:15 Their assistants also /it

LORDING* (LORD†)

1Pe 5: 3 not /it over those entrusted to you,

LORD‡ (LORD'S‡)

Ge 2: 4 When the L God made the earth
2: 7 the L God formed the man
2:22 Then the L God made a woman
3:21 The L God made garments of skin
3:23 So the L God banished him
4: 4 The L looked with favor on Abel
4:26 began to call on the name of the L.
6: 7 So the L said, "I will wipe mankind
7:16 Then the L shut him in.
9:26 Blessed be the L, the God of Shem!
11: 9 there the L confused the language
12: 1 L had said to Abram, "Leave your
15: 6 Abram believed the L,
15:18 On that day the L made a covenant
17: 1 the L appeared to him and said,
18: 1 The L appeared to Abraham
18:14 Is anything too hard for the L?
18:19 way of the L by doing what is right
21: 1 Now the L was gracious to Sarah
22:14 that place The L Will Provide.
24: 1 the L had blessed him in every way
26: 2 The L appeared to Isaac and said,
28:13 There above it stood the L,
31:49 "May the L keep watch
39: 2 The L was with Joseph
39:21 in the prison, the L was with him;
Ex 3: 2 the angel of the L appeared to him
4:11 Is it not I, the L?Now go;
4:31 heard that the L was concerned
6: 2 also said to Moses, "I am the L.
9:12 the L hardened Pharaoh's heart
12:27 'It is the Passover sacrifice to the L,
12:43 The L said to Moses and Aaron,
13: 9 For the L brought you out of Egypt
13:21 By day the L went ahead of them
14:13 the deliverance the L will bring
14:30 That day the L saved Israel
15: 3 The L is a warrior;
15:11 among the gods is like you, O L?
15:26 for I am the L, who heals you."
16:12 know that I am the L your God.'"
16:23 day of rest, a holy Sabbath to the L.
17:15 and called it The L is my Banner.
19: 8 will do everything the L has said."
19:20 The L descended to the top
20: 2 "I am the L your God, who
20: 5 the L your God, am a jealous God,
20: 7 for the L will not hold anyone
20:10 a Sabbath to the L your God.
20:11 in six days the L made the heavens
20:12 in the land the L your God is giving
23:25 Worship the L your God,
24: 3 "Everything the L has said we will
24:12 The L said to Moses, "Come up
24:16 and the glory of the L settled
25: 1 The L said to Moses, "Tell
28:36 HOLY TO THE L.
30:11 Then the L said to Moses,
31:13 so you may know that I am the L,
31:18 When the L finished speaking
33:11 The L would speak to Moses face
33:19 And the L said, "I will cause all my
34: 1 L said to Moses, "Chisel out two
34: 6 proclaiming, "The L, the L,
34:10 awesome is the work that I, the L,
34:29 because he had spoken with the L.
40:34 glory of the L filled the tabernacle.
40:38 So the cloud of the L was
Lev 8:36 did everything the L commanded
9:23 and the glory of the L appeared
10: 2 and they died before the L."
19: 2 'Be holy because I, the L your God,

Lev 20: 8 I am the L, who makes you holy.
20:26 to be holy to me because I, the L,
23:40 and rejoice before the L your God
Nu 6:24 Say to them: " " 'The L bless you
8: 5 L said to Moses: "Take the Levites
11: 1 hardships in the hearing of the L,
14:14 O L, have been seen face to face.
14:18 you have declared: 'The L is slow
14:21 glory of the L fills the whole earth,
21: 6 Then the L sent venomous snakes
22:31 Then the L opened Balaam's eyes,
23:12 "Must I not speak what the L puts
30: 2 When a man makes a vow to the L
32:12 followed the L wholeheartedly.'
Dt 1:21 and take possession of it as the L,
2: 7 forty years the L your God has
4:29 there you seek the L your God,
5: 6 And he said: "I am the L your God,
5: 9 the L your God, am a jealous God,
6: 4 The L our God, the L is one.
6: 5 Love the L your God
6:16 Do not test the L your God
6:25 law before the L our God,
7: 1 When the L your God brings you
7: 6 holy to the L your God.
7: 8 But it was because the L loved you
7: 9 that the L your God is God;
7:12 then the L your God will keep his
8: 5 so the L your God disciplines you.
9:10 The L gave me two stone tablets
10:12 but to fear the L your God,
10:14 To the L your God belong
10:17 For the L your God is God of gods
10:20 Fear the L your God and serve him
10:22 now the L your God has made you
11: 1 Love the L your God and keep his
11:13 to love the L your God
16: 1 the Passover of the L your God,
16:15 the king the L your God chooses.
28: 1 If you fully obey the L your God
28:15 if you do not obey the L your God
29: 1 covenant the L commanded Moses
29:29 things belong to the L our God,
30: 4 from there the L your God will
30: 6 L your God will circumcise your
30:10 if you obey the L your God
30:16 today to love the L your God,
30:20 For the L is your life, and he will
31: 6 for the L your God goes with you;
34: 5 of the L died there in Moab,
Jos 10:14 a day when the L listened to a man.
22: 5 to love the L your God, to walk
23:11 careful to love the L your God.
24:15 my household, we will serve the L
24:18 We too will serve the L,
Jdg 2:12 They forsook the L, the God
Ru 1: 8 May the L show kindness to you,
4:13 And the L enabled her to conceive,
1Sa 1:11 him to the L for all the days
1:15 I was pouring out my soul to the L.
1:28 So now I give him to the L.
2: 2 "There is no one holy like the L;
2:25 but if a man sins against the L,
2:26 in favor with the L and with men.
3: 9 L, for your servant is listening.'"
3:19 The L was with Samuel
7:12 "Thus far has the L helped us."
9:17 sight of Saul, the L said to him,
11:15 as king in the presence of the L.
12:18 all the people stood in awe of the L
12:22 his great name the L will not reject
12:24 But be sure to fear the L
13:14 the L has sought out a man
14: 6 Nothing can hinder the L
15:22 "Does the L delight
16:13 Spirit of the L came upon David
17:45 you in the name of the L Almighty,
2Sa 6:14 danced before the L
7:22 How great you are, O Sovereign L!
8: 6 L gave David victory everywhere
12: 7 This is what the L, the God
22: 2 "The L is my rock, my fortress
22:29 You are my lamp, O L;
22:31 the word of the L is flawless.
1Ki 1:30 today what I swore to you by the L,
2: 3 and observe what the L your God
3: 7 O L my God, you have made your
5: 5 for the Name of the L my God,
5:12 The L gave Solomon wisdom,
8:11 the glory of the L filled his temple.
8:23 toward heaven and said: "O L,
8:61 fully committed to the L our God,

---

‡This entry represents the translation of the Hebrew name for God, *Yahweh*, always indicated in the NIV by LORD. For Lord, see the concordance entries **LORD†** and **LORD'S†**.

1Ki 9: 3 The *L* said to him: "I have heard
10: 9 Praise be to the *L* your God,
15: 14 committed to the *L* all his life.
18: 21 If the *L* is God, follow him;
18: 36 "O *L*, God of Abraham, Isaac
18: 39 "The *L*—he is God! The *L*—
21: 23 also concerning Jezebel the *L* says:
2Ki 13: 23 But the *L* was gracious to them
17: 18 So the *L* was very angry with Israel
18: 5 Hezekiah trusted in the *L*,
19: 1 and went into the temple of the *L*.
20: 11 *L* made the shadow go back the ten
21: 12 Therefore this is what the *L*,
22: 2 right in the eyes of the *L*
22: 8 of the Law in the temple of the *L*."
23: 3 to follow the *L* and keep his
23: 21 the Passover to the *L* your God,
23: 25 a king like him who turned to the *L*
24: 2 The *L* sent Babylonian, Aramean,
24: 4 and the *L* was not willing to forgive
1Ch 10: 13 because he was unfaithful to the *L*;
11: 3 with them at Hebron before the *L*,
11: 9 the *L* Almighty was with him.
13: 6 from there the ark of God the *L*, who
16: 8 Give thanks to the *L*, call
16: 11 Look to the *L* and his strength;
16: 14 He is the *L* our God;
16: 23 Sing to the *L*, all the earth;
17: 1 covenant of the *L* is under a tent."
21: 24 take for the *L* what is yours,
22: 5 to be built for the *L* should be
22: 11 build the house of the *L* your God,
22: 13 and laws that the *L* gave Moses
22: 16 Now begin the work, and the *L* be
22: 19 soul to seeking the *L* your God.
25: 7 and skilled in music for the *L*—
28: 9 for the *L* searches every heart
28: 20 for the *L* God, my God, is with you
29: 1 not for man but for the *L* God.
29: 11 O *L*, is the greatness and the power
29: 18 O *L*, God of our fathers Abraham,
29: 25 The *L* highly exalted Solomon
2Ch 1: 1 for the *L* his God was with him
5: 13 to give praise and thanks to the *L*.
5: 14 the glory of the *L* filled the temple
6: 16 "Now *L*, God of Israel, keep
6: 41 O *L* God, and come
6: 42 O *L* God, do not reject your
7: 1 the glory of the *L* filled the temple.
7: 12 the *L* appeared to him at night
7: 21 'Why has the *L* done such a thing
9: 8 as king to rule for the *L* your God.
13: 12 do not fight against the *L*,
14: 2 right in the eyes of the *L* his God.
15: 14 to the *L* with loud acclamation,
16: 9 of the *L* range throughout the earth
17: 9 the Book of the Law of the *L*;
18: 13 said, "As surely as the *L* lives,
19: 6 judging for man but for the *L*,
19: 9 wholeheartedly in the fear of the *L*.
20: 15 This is what the *L* says to you:
20: 20 Have faith in the *L* your God
20: 21 appointed men to sing to the *L*
26: 5 As long as he sought the *L*,
26: 16 He was unfaithful to the *L* his God,
29: 30 to praise the *L* with the words
30: 9 for the *L* your God is gracious
31: 20 and faithful before the *L* his God.
32: 8 with us is the *L* our God to help us
34: 14 Law of the *L* that had been given
34: 31 to follow the *L* and keep his
Ezr 3: 10 foundation of the temple of the *L*,
7: 6 for the hand of the *L* his God was
7: 10 observance of the Law of the *L*,
9: 5 hands spread out to the *L* my God
9: 8 the *L* our God has been gracious
9: 15 O *L*, God of Israel, you are
Ne 1: 5 Then I said: "O *L*, God of heaven,
8: 1 which the *L* had commanded
9: 6 You alone are the *L*.
Job 1: 6 to present themselves before the *L*,
1: 21 *L* gave and the *L* has taken away;
38: 1 the *L* answered Job out
42: 9 and the *L* accepted Job's prayer.
42: 12 The *L* blessed the latter part
Ps 1: 2 But his delight is in the law of the *L*
1: 6 For the *L* watches over the way
4: 6 of your face shine upon us, O *L*.
4: 8 for you alone, O *L*,
5: 3 In the morning, O *L*,
6: 1 O *L*, do not rebuke me
8: 1 O *L*, our Lord,
9: 9 The *L* is a refuge for the oppressed,
9: 19 Arise, O *L*, let not man triumph;
10: 16 The *L* is King for ever and ever;
Ps 12: 6 And the words of the *L* are flawless
16: 5 *L*, you have assigned me my
16: 8 I have set the *L* always before me.
18: 1 I love you, O *L*, my strength.
18: 6 In my distress I called to the *L*;
18: 30 the word of the *L* is flawless.
19: 7 The law of the *L* is perfect,
19: 14 O *L*, my Rock and my Redeemer.
20: 5 May the *L* grant all your requests.
20: 7 in the name of the *L* our God.
22: 8 let the *L* rescue him.
23: 1 The *L* is my shepherd, I shall
23: 6 I will dwell in the house of the *L*
24: 3 Who may ascend the hill of the *L*?
24: 8 The *L* strong and mighty,
25: 10 All the ways of the *L* are loving
27: 1 The *L* is my light and my salvation
27: 4 to gaze upon the beauty of the *L*
27: 6 I will sing and make music to the *L*.
29: 1 Ascribe to the *L*, O mighty ones,
29: 4 The voice of the *L* is powerful;
30: 4 Sing to the *L*, you saints of his;
31: 5 redeem me, O *L*, the God of truth.
32: 2 whose sin the *L* does not count
33: 1 joyfully to the *L*, you righteous;
33: 6 of the *L* were the heavens made,
33: 12 is the nation whose God is the *L*,
33: 18 But the eyes of the *L* are
34: 1 I will extol the *L* at all times;
34: 3 Glorify the *L* with me;
34: 4 I sought the *L*, and he answered me
34: 7 The angel of the *L* encamps
34: 8 Taste and see that the *L* is good;
34: 9 Fear the *L*, you his saints,
34: 15 The eyes of the *L* are
34: 18 The *L* is close to the brokenhearted
37: 4 Delight yourself in the *L*
37: 5 Commit your way to the *L*;
39: 4 "Show me, O *L*, my life's end
40: 1 I waited patiently for the *L*;
40: 5 Many, O *L* my God,
46: 8 Come and see the works of the *L*,
47: 2 How awesome is the *L* Most High,
48: 1 Great is the *L*, and most worthy
50: 1 The Mighty One, God, the *L*,
55: 22 Cast your cares on the *L*
59: 8 But you, O *L*, laugh at them;
68: 4 his name is the *L*—
68: 18 O *L* God, might dwell there.
68: 20 from the Sovereign *L* comes escape
69: 31 This will please the *L* more
72: 18 Praise be to the *L* God, the God
75: 8 In the hand of the *L* is a cup
78: 4 the praiseworthy deeds of the *L*,
84: 8 my prayer, O *L* God Almighty;
84: 11 For the *L* God is a sun and shield;
85: 7 Show us your unfailing love, O *L*,
86: 11 Teach me your way, O *L*,
87: 2 the *L* loves the gates of Zion
89: 5 heavens praise your wonders, O *L*,
89: 8 O *L* God Almighty, who is like you
91: 2 I will say of the *L*, "He is my refuge
92: 1 It is good to praise the *L*
92: 4 by your deeds, O *L*;
92: 13 planted in the house of the *L*,
93: 1 The *L* reigns, he is robed in majesty
93: 5 house for endless days, O *L*.
94: 1 O *L*, the God who avenges,
94: 12 is the man you discipline, O *L*,
94: 18 your love, O *L*, supported me.
95: 1 Come, let us sing for joy to the *L*;
95: 3 For the *L* is the great God,
95: 6 let us kneel before the *L* our Maker
96: 1 Sing to the *L* a new song;
96: 5 but the *L* made the heavens.
96: 8 to the *L* the glory due his name;
96: 9 Worship the *L* in the splendor
96: 13 they will sing before the *L*,
97: 1 The *L* reigns, let the earth be glad;
97: 9 O *L*, are the Most High
98: 1 Sing to the *L* a new song,
98: 2 *L* has made his salvation known
98: 4 Shout for joy to the *L*, all the earth,
99: 1 The *L* reigns,
99: 2 Great is the *L* in Zion;
99: 5 Exalt the *L* our God
99: 9 Exalt the *L* our God
100: 1 Shout for joy to the *L*, all the earth.
100: 2 Worship the *L* with gladness;
100: 3 Know that the *L* is God.
100: 5 For the *L* is good and his love
101: 1 to you, O *L*, I will sing praise.
102: 12 But you, O *L*, sit enthroned forever
103: 1 Praise the *L*, O my soul;
103: 8 The *L* is compassionate
Ps 103: 19 The *L* has established his throne
104: 1 O *L* my God, you are very great;
104: 24 How many are your works, O *L*!
104: 33 I will sing to the *L* all my life;
105: 4 Look to the *L* and his strength;
105: 7 He is the *L* our God;
106: 2 proclaim the mighty acts of the *L*
107: 1 Give thanks to the *L*, for he is good
107: 8 to the *L* for his unfailing love
107: 21 to the *L* for his unfailing love
107: 43 and consider the great love of the *L*
108: 3 I will praise you, O *L*,
109: 26 Help me, O *L* my God;
110: 1 The *L* says to my Lord:
110: 4 The *L* has sworn
111: 2 Great are the works of the *L*;
111: 4 *L* is gracious and compassionate.
111: 10 The fear of the *L* is the beginning
112: 1 Blessed is the man who fears the *L*,
113: 1 Praise, O servants of the *L*,
113: 2 Let the name of the *L* be praised,
113: 4 *L* is exalted over all the nations,
113: 5 Who is like the *L* our God,
115: 1 Not to us, O *L*, not to us
115: 18 it is we who extol the *L*,
116: 12 How can I repay the *L*
116: 15 Precious in the sight of the *L*
117: 1 Praise the *L*, all you nations;
118: 1 Give thanks to the *L*, for he is good
118: 5 In my anguish I cried to the *L*,
118: 8 It is better to take refuge in the *L*
118: 18 The *L* has chastened me severely,
118: 23 the *L* has done this,
118: 24 This is the day the *L* has made;
118: 26 comes in the name of the *L*.
119: 1 to the law of the *L*.
119: 64 with your love, O *L*;
119: 89 Your word, O *L*, is eternal;
119:126 It is time for you to act, O *L*;
119:159 O *L*, according to your love.
120: 1 I call on the *L* in my distress,
121: 2 My help comes from the *L*,
121: 5 The *L* watches over you—
121: 8 the *L* will watch over your coming
122: 1 "Let us go to the house of the *L*."
123: 2 so our eyes look to the *L* our God,
124: 1 If the *L* had not been on our side—
124: 8 Our help is in the name of the *L*,
125: 2 so the *L* surrounds his people
126: 3 The *L* has done great things for us,
126: 4 Restore our fortunes, O *L*,
127: 1 Unless the *L* builds the house,
127: 3 Sons are a heritage from the *L*,
128: 1 Blessed are all who fear the *L*,
130: 1 O *L*; O Lord, hear my voice.
130: 3 If you, O *L*, kept a record of sins,
130: 5 I wait for the *L*, my soul waits,
131: 3 O Israel, put your hope in the *L*
132: 1 O *L*, remember David
132: 13 For the *L* has chosen Zion,
133: 3 For there the *L* bestows his
134: 3 May the *L*, the Maker of heaven
135: 4 For the *L* has chosen Jacob
135: 6 The *L* does whatever pleases him,
136: 1 Give thanks to the *L*, for he is good
137: 4 How can we sing the songs of the *L*
138: 1 I will praise you, O *L*,
138: 8 The *L* will fulfill ⌊his purpose⌋
139: 1 O *L*, you have searched me
140: 1 Rescue me, O *L*, from evil men;
141: 1 O *L*, I call to you; come quickly
141: 3 Set a guard over my mouth, O *L*;
142: 5 I cry to you, O *L*;
143: 9 Rescue me from my enemies, O *L*,
144: 3 O *L*, what is man that you care
145: 3 Great is the *L* and most worthy
145: 8 *L* is gracious and compassionate,
145: 9 The *L* is good to all;
145: 17 The *L* is righteous in all his ways
145: 18 The *L* is near to all who call on him
146: 5 whose hope is in the *L* his God,
146: 7 The *L* sets prisoners free,
147: 2 The *L* builds up Jerusalem;
147: 7 Sing to the *L* with thanksgiving;
147: 11 *L* delights in those who fear him,
147: 12 Extol the *L*, O Jerusalem;
148: 1 Praise the *L* from the heavens,
148: 7 Praise the *L* from the earth,
149: 4 For the *L* takes delight
150: 1 Praise the *L*.
150: 6 that has breath praise the *L*.
Pr 1: 7 The fear of the *L* is the beginning
1: 29 and did not choose to fear the *L*,
2: 5 will understand the fear of the *L*
2: 6 For the *L* gives wisdom,

Pr
3: 5 Trust in the *L* with all your heart
3: 7 fear the *L* and shun evil.
3: 9 Honor the *L* with your wealth,
3:12 the *L* disciplines those he loves,
3:19 By wisdom the *L* laid the earth's
5:21 are in full view of the *L*,
6:16 There are six things the *L* hates,
8:13 To fear the *L* is to hate evil;
9:10 "The fear of the *L* is the beginning
10:27 The fear of the *L* adds length to life
11: 1 The *L* abhors dishonest scales,
12:22 The *L* detests lying lips,
14: 2 whose walk is upright fears the *L*,
14:26 He who fears the *L* has a secure
14:27 The fear of the *L* is a fountain
15: 3 The eyes of the *L* are everywhere,
15:16 Better a little with the fear of the *L*
15:33 of the *L* teaches a man wisdom,
16: 2 but motives are weighed by the *L*.
16: 3 Commit to the *L* whatever you do,
16: 4 The *L* works out everything
16: 5 The *L* detests all the proud of heart
16: 9 but the *L* determines his steps.
16:33 but its every decision is from the *L*.
18:10 The name of the *L* is a strong tower
18:22 and receives favor from the *L*.
19:14 but a prudent wife is from the *L*.
19:17 to the poor lends to the *L*,
19:23 The fear of the *L* leads to life:
20:10 the *L* detests them both.
21: 2 but the *L* weighs the heart.
21: 3 to the *L* than sacrifice.
21:30 that can succeed against the *L*.
21:31 but victory rests with the *L*.
22: 2 The *L* is the Maker of them all.
22:23 for the *L* will take up their case
23:17 for the fear of the *L*.
24:18 or the *L* will see and disapprove
24:21 Fear the *L* and the king, my son,
25:22 and the *L* will reward you.
28:14 is the man who always fears the *L*,
29:26 from the *L* that man gets justice.
30: 7 "Two things I ask of you, O *L*;
31:30 a woman who fears the *L* is

Isa
2: 3 up to the mountain of the *L*,
2:10 the ground from dread of the *L*
3:17 the *L* will make their scalps bald."
4: 2 of the *L* will be beautiful
5:16 the *L* Almighty will be exalted
6: 3 holy, holy is the *L* Almighty;
9: 7 The zeal of the *L* Almighty
11: 2 The Spirit of the *L* will rest on him
11: 9 full of the knowledge of the *L*
12: 2 The *L*, the *L*, is my strength
18: 7 of the Name of the *L* Almighty.
24: 1 the *L* is going to lay waste the earth
25: 1 O *L*, you are my God;
25: 6 this mountain the *L* Almighty will
25: 8 The Sovereign *L* will wipe away
26: 4 Trust in the *L* forever,
26: 8 *L*, walking in the way of your laws,
26:13 O *L*, our God, other lords
26:21 the *L* is coming out of his dwelling
27: 1 the *L* will punish with his sword,
27:12 In that day the *L* will thresh
28: 5 In that day the *L* Almighty
29: 6 the *L* Almighty will come
29:15 to hide their plans from the *L*,
30:18 For the *L* is a God of justice.
30:26 when the *L* binds up the bruises
30:27 the Name of the *L* comes from afar
30:30 The *L* will cause men
33: 2 O *L*, be gracious to us;
33: 6 the fear of the *L* is the key
33:22 For the *L* is our judge,
34: 2 The *L* is angry with all nations;
35: 2 they will see the glory of the *L*,
35:10 the ransomed of the *L* will return.
38: 7 to you that the *L* will do what he
40: 3 the way for the *L*;
40: 5 the glory of the *L* will be revealed,
40: 7 the breath of the *L* blows on them.
40:10 the Sovereign *L* comes with power,
40:14 Whom did the *L* consult
40:28 The *L* is the everlasting God,
40:31 but those who hope in the *L*
41:14 will help you," declares the *L*,
41:20 that the hand of the *L* has done this
42: 6 I, the *L*, have called you
42: 8 "I am the *L*; that is my name!
42:13 The *L* will march out like a mighty
42:21 It pleased the *L*
43: 3 For I am the *L*, your God,
43:11 I, even I, am the *L*,
44: 6 "This is what the *L* says—

Isa
44:24 I am the *L*,
45: 5 I am the *L*, and there is no other;
45: 7 I, the *L*, do all these things.
45:21 Was it not I, the *L*?
48:17 "I am the *L* your God,
50: 4 Sovereign *L* has given me
50:10 Who among you fears the *L*
51: 1 and who seek the *L*;
51:11 The ransomed of the *L* will return.
51:15 the *L* Almighty is his name.
53: 1 the arm of the *L* been revealed?
53: 6 and the *L* has laid on him
53:10 and the will of the *L* will prosper
54: 5 The *L* Almighty is his name—
55: 6 Seek the *L* while he may be found;
55: 7 to the *L*, and he will have mercy
56: 6 who bind themselves to the *L*
58: 8 of the *L* will be your rear guard.
58:11 The *L* will guide you always;
59: 1 the arm of the *L* is not too short
60: 1 the glory of the *L* rises upon you.
60:16 Then you will know that I, the *L*,
60:20 the *L* will be your everlasting light,
61: 1 Spirit of the Sovereign *L* is on me,
61: 3 a planting of the *L*
61:10 I delight greatly in the *L*;
61:11 so the Sovereign *L* will make
62: 4 for the *L* will take delight in you,
63: 7 I will tell of the kindnesses of the *L*,
64: 8 Yet, O *L*, you are our Father.
66:15 See, the *L* is coming with fire,

Jer
1: 9 Then the *L* reached out his hand
2:19 when you forsake the *L* your God
3:25 sinned against the *L* our God,
4: 4 Circumcise yourselves to the *L*,
8: 7 the requirements of the *L*.
9:24 I am the *L*, who exercises kindness,
10: 6 No one is like you, O *L*;
10:10 But the *L* is the true God;
12: 1 You are always righteous, O *L*,
14: 7 O *L*, do something for the sake
14:20 O *L*, we acknowledge our
16:15 will say, 'As surely as the *L* lives,
16:19 O *L*, my strength and my fortress,
17: 7 is the man who trusts in the *L*,
17:10 "I the *L* search the heart
20:11 *L* is with me like a mighty warrior;
23: 6 The *L* Our Righteousness.
24: 7 heart to know me, that I am the *L*.
28: 9 as one truly sent by the *L* only
31:11 For the *L* will ransom Jacob
31:22 The *L* will create a new thing
31:34 his brother, saying, 'Know the *L*,'
32:27 I am the *L*, the God of all mankind.
33:16 The *L* Our Righteousness.'
36: 6 the words of the *L* that you wrote
40: 3 now the *L* has brought it about;
42: 3 Pray that the *L* your God will tell
42: 4 I will tell you everything the *L* says
42: 6 we will obey the *L* our God,
50: 4 go in tears to seek the *L* their God.
51:10 " 'The *L* has vindicated us;
51:56 For the *L* is a God of retribution;

La
3:24 to myself, "The *L* is my portion;
3:25 *L* is good to those whose hope is
3:40 and let us return to the *L*.

Eze
1: 3 the word of the *L* came
1:28 of the likeness of the glory of the *L*.
4:14 Sovereign *L*! I have never defiled
10: 4 Then the glory of the *L* rose
15: 7 you will know that I am the *L*.
30: 3 the day of the *L* is near—
36:23 nations will know that I am the *L*,
37: 4 'Dry bones, hear the word of the *L*!
43: 4 glory of the *L* entered the temple
44: 4 LORD filling the temple of the *L*,

Da
9: 2 to the word of the *L* given

Hos
1: 7 horsemen, but by the *L* their God."
2:20 and you will acknowledge the *L*.
3: 1 as the *L* loves the Israelites,
3: 5 They will come trembling to the *L*
6: 1 "Come, let us return to the *L*.
6: 3 Let us acknowledge the *L*;
12: 6 for it is time to seek the *L*,
12: 5 the *L* is his name of renown!
14: 1 O Israel, to the *L* your God.

Joel
1: 1 The word of the *L* that came
1:15 For the day of the *L* is near;
2: 1 for the day of the *L* is coming.
2:11 The day of the *L* is great;
2:13 Return to the *L* your God,
2:23 rejoice in the *L* your God.
2:31 the great and dreadful day of the *L*.
2:32 on the name of the *L* will be saved;
3:14 For the day of the *L* is near

Joel
3:16 the *L* will be a refuge for his people,
Am
4:13 the *L* God Almighty is his name.
5: 6 Seek the *L* and live,
5:15 Perhaps the *L* God Almighty will
5:18 long for the day of the *L*?
7:15 *L* took me from tending the flock
8:12 searching for the word of the *L*,
9: 5 The Lord, the *L* Almighty,
Ob
:15 "The day of the *L* is near
Jnh
1: 3 But Jonah ran away from the *L*
1: 4 the *L* sent a great wind on the sea,
1:17 But the *L* provided a great fish
2: 9 Salvation comes from the *L*."
4: 2 He prayed to the *L*, "O *L*,
4: 6 Then the *L* God provided a vine
Mic
1: 1 The word of the *L* that came to Micah
4: 2 up to the mountain of the *L*,
4: 5 flock in the strength of the *L*,
6: 2 For the *L* has a case
6: 8 And what does the *L* require of you
7: 7 as for me, I watch in hope for the *L*,
Na
1: 2 The *L* takes vengeance on his foes
1: 3 The *L* is slow to anger
Hab
2:14 knowledge of the glory of the *L*,
2:20 But the *L* is in his holy temple;
3: 2 I stand in awe of your deeds, O *L*.
Zep
1: 1 The word of the *L* that came
1: 7 for the day of the *L* is near.
3:17 The *L* your God is with you,
Hag
1: 1 the word of the *L* came
1: 8 and be honored," says the *L*.
2:23 that day,' declares the *L* Almighty.
Zec
1: 1 the word of the *L* came
1:17 and the *L* will again comfort Zion
3: 1 standing before the angel of the *L*,
4: 6 by my Spirit,' says the *L* Almighty.
6:12 and build the temple of the *L*.
8:21 the *L* and seek the *L* Almighty.
9:16 The *L* their God will save them
14: 5 Then the *L* my God will come,
14: 9 The *L* will be king
14:16 the *L* Almighty, and to celebrate
Mal
1: 1 The word of the *L* to Israel
3: 6 "I the *L* do not change.
4: 5 and dreadful day of the *L* comes.

LORD'S‡ (LORD‡)

Ex
4:14 the *L* anger burned against Moses
12:11 Eat it in haste; it is the *L* Passover.
34:34 he entered the *L* presence
Lev
23: 4 " 'These are the *L* appointed feasts,
Nu
9:23 At the *L* command they encamped
14:41 you disobeying the *L* command?
32:13 The *L* anger burned against Israel
Dt
6:18 is right and good in the *L* sight,
10:13 and to observe the *L* commands
32: 9 For the *L* portion is his people,
Jos
21:45 Not one of all the *L* good promises
1Sa
24:10 because he is the *L* anointed.'
1Ki
10: 9 Because of the *L* eternal love
Ps
24: 1 The earth is the *L*, and everything
32:10 but the *L* unfailing love
89: 1 of the *L* great love forever,
103:17 *L* love is with those who fear him,
118:15 "The *L* right hand has done mighty
Pr
3:11 do not despise the *L* discipline
19:21 but it is the *L* purpose that prevails.
Isa
24:14 west they acclaim the *L* majesty.
30: 9 to listen to the *L* instruction.
49: 4 Yet what is due me is in the *L* hand
53:10 Yet it was the *L* will to crush him
55:13 This will be for the *L* renown,
61: 2 to proclaim the year of the *L* favor
62: 3 of splendor in the *L* hand,
Jer
25:17 So I took the cup from the *L* hand
48:10 lax in doing the *L* work!
51: 7 was a gold cup in the *L* hand;
La
3:22 of the *L* great love we are not
Eze
7:19 them in the day of the *L* wrath.
Joel
3:18 will flow out of the *L* house
Ob
:21 And the kingdom will be the *L*.
Mic
4: 1 the *L* temple will be established
6: 2 O mountains, the *L* accusation;
Hab
2:16 from the *L* right hand is coming
Zep
2: 3 sheltered on the day of the *L* anger.

LOSE (LOSES LOSS LOST)

Dt
1:28 Our brothers have made us /heart.
1Sa
17:32 "Let no one /heart on account
Isa
7: 4 Do not /heart because of these two
Mt
10:39 Whoever finds his life will /it,
Lk
9:25 and yet /or forfeit his very self?
Jn
6:39 that I shall /none of all that he has
2Co
4: 1 this ministry, we do not /heart.
4:16 Therefore we do not /heart.

Heb 12: 3 will not grow weary and /heart.
12: 5 do not /heart when he rebukes you
2Jn : 8 that you do not /what you have

LOSES (LOSE)

Mt 5: 13 But if the salt /its saltiness,
Lk 15: 4 you has a hundred sheep and /one
15: 8 has ten silver coins and /one.

LOSS (LOSE)

Ro 11: 12 and their /means riches
1Co 3: 15 he will suffer /; he himself will be
Php 3: 8 I consider everything a /compared

LOST (LOSE)

Ps 73: 2 I had nearly /my foothold.
Jer 50: 6 "My people have been /sheep;
Eze 34: 4 the strays or searched for the /.
34: 16 for the /and bring back the strays.
Mt 18: 14 any of these little ones should be /.
Lk 15: 4 go after the /sheep until he finds it?
15: 6 with me; I have found my /sheep.'
15: 9 with me; I have found my /coin.'
15: 24 is alive again; he was /and is found
19: 10 to seek and to save what was /."
Php 3: 8 for whose sake I have /all things.

LOT (LOTS)

Nephew of Abraham (Ge 11:27; 12:5). Chose to live in Sodom (Ge 13). Rescued from four kings (Ge 14). Rescued from Sodom (Ge 19: 1-29; 2Pe 2:7). Fathered Moab and Ammon by his daughters (Ge 19:30-38).

Est 3: 7 the /) in the presence of Haman
9: 24 the /) for their ruin and destruction.
Pr 16: 33 The /is cast into the lap,
18: 18 Casting the /settles disputes
Ecc 3: 22 his work, because that is his /.
Ac 1: 26 Then they cast lots, and the /fell

LOTS (LOT)

Jos 18: 10 Joshua then cast /for them
Ps 22: 18 and cast /for my clothing.
Joel 3: 3 They cast /for my people
Ob : 11 and cast /for Jerusalem,
Mt 27: 35 divided up his clothes by casting /.
Ac 1: 26 Then they cast /, and the lot fell

LOVE* (BELOVED LOVED LOVELY LOVER LOVER'S LOVERS LOVES LOVING LOVING-KINDNESS)

Ge 20: 13 'This is how you can show your /
22: 2 your only son, Isaac, whom you /,
29: 18 Jacob was in /with Rachel and said
29: 20 days to him because of /for her.
29: 32 Surely my husband will /me now."
Ex 15: 13 "In your unfailing /you will lead
20: 6 showing /to a thousand generations
20: 6 of those who /me
21: 5 'I /my master and my wife
34: 6 abounding in /and faithfulness,
34: 7 maintaining /to thousands,
Lev 19: 18 but /your neighbor as yourself.
19: 34 L him as yourself,
Nu 14: 18 abounding in /and forgiving sin
14: 19 In accordance with your great /,
Dt 5: 10 showing /to a thousand generations
5: 10 of those who /me
6: 5 L the LORD your God
7: 9 generations of those who /him
7: 9 keeping his covenant of /
7: 12 God will keep his covenant of /
7: 13 He will /you and bless you
10: 12 to walk in all his ways, to /him,
10: 19 you are to /those who are aliens,
11: 1 L the LORD your God
11: 13 to /the LORD your God
11: 22 to /the LORD your God,
13: 3 you /him with all your heart
13: 6 wife you /, or your closest friend
19: 9 to /the LORD your God
21: 15 the son of the wife he does not /,
21: 16 the son of the wife he does not /.
30: 6 so that you may /him
30: 16 today to /the LORD your God,
30: 20 and that you may /the LORD your
33: 3 Surely it is you who /the people;
Jos 22: 5 to /the LORD your God, to walk
23: 11 careful to /the LORD your God.
Jdg 5: 31 may they who /you be like the sun
14: 16 You hate me! You don't really /me
16: 4 he fell in /with a woman
16: 15 "How can you say, 'I /you,'
1Sa 18: 20 Saul's daughter Michal was in /
20: 17 had David reaffirm his oath out of /

2Sa 1: 26 Your /for me was wonderful,
7: 15 But my /will never be taken away
13: 1 son of David fell in /with Tamar,
13: 4 said to him. "I'm in /with Tamar,
16: 17 "Is this the /you show your friend?
19: 6 You /those who hate you
19: 6 hate you and hate those who /you.
1Ki 3: 3 Solomon showed his /
8: 23 you who keep your covenant of /
10: 9 of the LORD's eternal /for Israel,
11: 2 Solomon held fast to them in /.
1Ch 16: 34 his /endures forever.
16: 41 "for his /endures forever."
17: 13 I will never take my /away
2Ch 5: 13 his /endures forever."
6: 14 you who keep your covenant of /
6: 42 Remember the great /promised
7: 3 his /endures forever."
7: 6 saying, "His /endures forever."
9: 8 Because of the /of your God
19: 2 and /those who hate the LORD?
20: 21 for his /endures forever."
Ezr 3: 11 his /to Israel endures forever."
Ne 1: 5 covenant of /with those who /him
9: 17 slow to anger and abounding in /.
9: 32 who keeps his covenant of /,
13: 22 to me according to your great /.
Job 15: 34 of those who /bribes.
19: 19 those I /have turned against me.
37: 13 or to water his earth and show his /.
Ps 4: 2 How long will you /delusions
5: 11 that those who /your name may
6: 4 save me because of your unfailing /.
11: 5 wicked and those who /violence
13: 5 But I trust in your unfailing /;
17: 7 Show the wonder of your great /,
18: 1 I /you, O LORD, my strength.
21: 7 through the unfailing /
23: 6 Surely goodness and /will follow
25: 6 O LORD, your great mercy and /,
25: 7 according to your /remember me,
26: 3 for your /is ever before me,
26: 8 I /the house where you live,
31: 7 I will be glad and rejoice in your /,
31: 16 save me in your unfailing /.
31: 21 for he showed his wonderful /
31: 23 L the LORD, all his saints!
32: 10 but the LORD's unfailing /
33: 5 the earth is full of his unfailing /.
33: 18 whose hope is in his unfailing /,
33: 22 May your unfailing /rest upon us,
36: 5 Your /, O LORD, reaches
36: 7 How priceless is your unfailing /!
36: 10 Continue your /to those who know
40: 10 I do not conceal your /
40: 11 may your /and your truth always
40: 16 may those who /your salvation
42: 8 By day the LORD directs his /,
44: 26 of your unfailing /.
45: 7 You /righteousness and hate
48: 9 we meditate on your unfailing /,
51: 1 according to your unfailing /;
52: 3 You /evil rather than good,
52: 4 You /every harmful word,
52: 8 I trust in God's unfailing /
57: 3 God sends his /and his faithfulness
57: 10 For great is your /, reaching
59: 16 in the morning I will sing of your /;
60: 5 that those you /may be delivered.
61: 7 appoint your /and faithfulness
63: 3 Because your /is better than life,
66: 20 or withheld his /from me!
69: 13 in your great /, O God,
69: 16 out of the goodness of your /;
69: 36 and those who /his name will dwell
70: 4 may those who /your salvation
77: 8 Has his unfailing /vanished forever
85: 7 Show us your unfailing /, O LORD
85: 10 L and faithfulness meet together;
86: 5 abounding in /to all who call
86: 13 For great is your /toward me;
86: 15 abounding in /and faithfulness.
88: 11 Is your /declared in the grave,
89: 1 of the LORD's great /forever;
89: 2 declare that your /stands firm
89: 14 /and faithfulness go before you.
89: 24 My faithful /will be with him,
89: 28 I will maintain my /to him forever,
89: 33 but I will not take my /from him,
89: 49 where is your former great /,
90: 14 with your unfailing /,
92: 2 to proclaim your /in the morning
94: 18 your /, O LORD, supported me.
97: 10 Let those who /the LORD hate
98: 3 He has remembered his /

Ps 100: 5 is good and his /endures forever;
101: 1 I will sing of your /and justice;
103: 4 crowns you with /and compassion.
103: 8 slow to anger, abounding in /.
103: 11 so great is his /for those who fear
103: 17 LORD's /is with those who fear
106: 1 his /endures forever.
106: 45 and out of his great /he relented.
107: 1 his /endures forever.
107: 8 to the LORD for his unfailing /
107: 15 to the LORD for his unfailing /
107: 21 to the LORD for his unfailing /
107: 31 to the LORD for his unfailing /
107: 43 consider the great /of the LORD.
108: 4 For great is your /, higher
108: 6 that those you /may be delivered.
109: 21 out of the goodness of your /,
109: 26 save me in accordance with your /.
115: 1 because of your /and faithfulness.
116: 1 I /the LORD, for he heard my
117: 2 For great is his /toward us,
118: 1 his /endures forever.
118: 2 "His /endures forever."
118: 3 "His /endures forever."
118: 4 "His /endures forever."
118: 29 his /endures forever.
119: 41 May your unfailing /come to me,
119: 47 because I /them.
119: 48 to your commands, which I /,
119: 64 The earth is filled with your /,
119: 76 May your unfailing /be my
119: 88 my life according to your /,
119: 97 Oh, how I /your law!
119:113 but I /your law.
119:119 therefore I /your statutes.
119:124 your servant according to your /
119:127 Because I /your commands
119:132 to those who /your name.
119:149 in accordance with your /,
119:159 O LORD, according to your /.
119:159 See how I /your precepts;
119:163 but I /your law.
119:165 peace have they who /your law,
119:167 for I /them greatly.
122: 6 "May those who /you be secure.
130: 7 for with the LORD is unfailing /
136: 1 -26 His /endures forever.
138: 2 for your /and your faithfulness,
138: 8 your /, O LORD, endures forever
143: 8 of your unfailing /,
143: 12 In your unfailing /, silence my
145: 8 slow to anger and rich in /.
145: 20 over all who /him,
147: 11 who put their hope in his unfailing /
Pr 1: 22 you simple ones /your simple
3: 3 Let /and faithfulness never leave
4: 6 /her, and she will watch over you.
5: 19 you ever be captivated by her /.
7: 18 let's drink deep of /till morning;
7: 18 let's enjoy ourselves with /!
8: 17 I /those who /me,
8: 21 wealth on those who /me
8: 36 all who hate me /death."
9: 8 rebuke a wise man and he will /you
10: 12 but /covers over all wrongs.
14: 22 those who plan what is good find /
15: 17 of vegetables where there is /
16: 6 Through /and faithfulness sin is
17: 9 over an offense promotes /,
18: 21 and those who /it will eat its fruit.
19: 22 What a man desires is unfailing /;
20: 6 claims to have unfailing /,
20: 13 Do not /sleep or you will grow
20: 28 L and faithfulness keep a king safe;
20: 28 through /his throne is made secure
21: 21 who pursues righteousness and /
27: 5 rebuke than hidden /.
Ecc 3: 8 a time to /and a time to hate,
3: 11 but no man knows whether /
9: 6 Their /, their hate
9: 9 life with your wife, whom you /,
SS 1: 2 for your /is more delightful
1: 3 No wonder the maidens /you!
1: 4 we will praise your /more
1: 7 you whom I /, where you graze
2: 4 and his banner over me is /.
2: 5 for I am faint with /.
2: 7 Do not arouse or awaken /
3: 5 Do not arouse or awaken /
4: 10 How delightful is your /, my sister.
4: 10 How much more pleasing is your /
5: 8 Tell him I am faint with /.
7: 6 O /, with your delights!
7: 12 there I will give you my /.
8: 4 Do not arouse or awaken /

SS 8: 6 for *l* is as strong as death,
   8: 7 Many waters cannot quench *l*;
   8: 7 all the wealth of his house for *l*,
Isa 1:23 they all /bribes
   5: 1 I will sing for the one I *l*
  16: 5 In /a throne will be established;
  38:17 In your /you kept me
  43: 4 and because I /you,
  54:10 yet my unfailing /for you will not
  55: 3 my faithful /promised to David.
  56: 6 to /the name of the LORD,
  56:10 they /to sleep.
  57: 8 a pact with those whose beds you *l*,
  61: 8 "For I, the LORD, /justice,
  63: 9 In his /and mercy he redeemed
  66:10 all you who /her;
Jer 2:25 I /foreign gods.
  2:33 How skilled you are at pursuing /!
  5:31 and my people /it this way.
  12: 7 I will give the one I /
  14:10 "They greatly /to wander;
  16: 5 my /and my pity from this people
  31: 3 you with an everlasting /;
  32:18 You show /to thousands
  33:11 his /endures forever."
La 3:22 of the LORD's great /we are not
  3:32 so great is his unfailing /.
Eze 16: 8 saw that you were old enough for /,
  23:17 of /, and in their lust they defiled
  33:32 more than one who sings /songs
Da 9: 4 covenant of /with all who /him
Hos 1: 6 for I will no longer show /
  1: 7 Yet I will show /to the house
  2: 4 I will not show my /to her children
  2:19 in /and compassion.
  2:23 I will show my /to the one I called
  3: 1 Go, show your /to your wife again,
  3: 1 and /the sacred raisin cakes."
  3: 1 *L* her as the LORD loves
  4: 1 "There is no faithfulness, no /,
  4:18 their rulers dearly /shameful ways.
  6: 4 Your /is like the morning mist,
  9: 1 you /the wages of a prostitute
  9:15 I will no longer /them;
  10:12 reap the fruit of unfailing /,
  11: 4 with ties of /;
  12: 6 maintain /and justice,
  14: 4 and /them freely,
Joel 2:13 slow to anger and abounding in /,
Am 4: 5 for this is what you /to do,"
  5:15 Hate evil, /good;
Jnh 4: 2 slow to anger and abounding in /,
Mic 3: 2 you who hate good and /evil;
  6: 8 To act justly and to /mercy
Zep 3:17 he will quiet you with his /,
Zec 8:17 and do not /to swear falsely.
  8:19 Therefore /truth and peace."
Mt 3:17 "This is my Son, whom I /;
  5:43 *L* your neighbor and hate your
  5:44 *L* your enemies and pray
  5:46 you /those who /you, what reward
  6: 5 for they /to pray standing
  6:24 he will hate the one and /the other,
  12:18 the one I /, in whom I delight;
  17: 5 "This is my Son, whom I /;
  19:19 and /your neighbor as yourself.' "
  22:37 " '*L* the Lord your God
  22:39 '*L* your neighbor as yourself.'
  23: 6 they /the place of honor
  23: 7 they /to be greeted
  24:12 the /of most will grow cold,
Mk 1:11 You are my Son, whom I /;
  9: 7 "This is my Son, whom I /.
  12:30 *L* the Lord your God
  12:31 '*L* your neighbor as yourself.'
  12:33 To /him with all your heart,
  12:33 and to /your neighbor
Lk 3:22 "You are my Son, whom I /;
  6:27 you who hear me: *L* your enemies,
  6:32 Even 'sinners' /those who /them.
  6:32 you /those who /you, what credit
  6:35 your enemies, do good to them,
  7:42 which of them will /him more?"
  10:27 and, '*L* your neighbor as yourself
  10:27 " '*L* the Lord your God
  11:42 you neglect justice and the /of God
  11:43 you /the most important seats
  16:13 he will hate the one and /the other,
  20:13 whom I /; perhaps they will respect
  20:46 /to be greeted in the marketplaces
Jn 5:42 I know that you do not have the /
  8:42 were your Father, you would /me,
  11: 3 "Lord, the one you /is sick."
  13: 1 them the full extent of his /.
  13:34 I give you: *L* one another.

Jn 13:34 so you must /one another.
  13:35 disciples, if you /one another."
  14:15 "If you /me, you will obey what I
  14:21 I too will /him and show myself
  14:23 My Father will /him, and we will
  14:24 He who does not /me will not obey
  14:31 world must learn that I /the Father
  15: 9 Now remain in my /.
  15:10 commands and remain in his /.
  15:10 you will remain in my /,
  15:12 *L* each other as I have loved you.
  15:13 Greater /has no one than this,
  15:17 This is my command: *L* each other.
  15:19 to the world, it would /you
  17:26 known in order that the /you have
  21:15 do you truly /me more than these
  21:15 he said, "you know that I /you."
  21:16 Yes, Lord, you know that I /you."
  21:16 do you truly /me?" He answered,
  21:17 all things; you know that I /you."
  21:17 "Do you /me?" He said, "Lord,
  21:17 "Simon son of John, do you /me?"
Ro 5: 5 because God has poured out his /
  5: 8 God demonstrates his own /for us
  8:28 for the good of those who /him,
  8:35 us from the /of Christ?
  8:39 us from the /of God that is
  12: 9 *L* must be sincere.
  12:10 to one another in brotherly /.
  13: 8 continuing debt to /one another,
  13: 9 "*L* your neighbor as yourself."
  13:10 Therefore /is the fulfillment
  13:10 *L* does no harm to its neighbor.
  14:15 you are no longer acting in /.
  15:30 and by the /of the Spirit,
  16: 8 Greet Ampliatus, whom I /
1Co 2: 9 prepared for those who /him"—
  4:17 my son whom I /, who is faithful
  4:21 or in /and with a gentle spirit?
  8: 1 Knowledge puffs up, but /builds up
  13: 1 have not /, I am only a resounding
  13: 2 but have not /, I am nothing.
  13: 3 but have not /, I gain nothing.
  13: 4 Love is patient, /is kind.
  13: 4 *L* is patient, love is kind.
  13: 6 *L* does not delight in evil
  13: 8 *L* never fails.
  13:13 But the greatest of these is /.
  13:13 three remain: faith, hope and /.
  14: 1 way of /and eagerly desire spiritual
  16:14 Do everything in /.
  16:22 If anyone does not /the Lord—
  16:24 My /to all of you in Christ Jesus.
2Co 2: 4 to let you know the depth of my /
  2: 8 therefore, to reaffirm your /for him
  5:14 For Christ's /compels us,
  6: 6 in the Holy Spirit and in sincere /;
  8: 7 complete earnestness and in your /
  8: 8 sincerity of your /by comparing it
  8:24 show these men the proof of your /
  11:11 Why? Because I do not /you?
  12:15 If I /you more, will you /me less?
  13:11 And the God of /and peace will be
  13:14 of the Lord Jesus Christ, and the /
Gal 5: 6 is faith expressing itself through /.
  5:13 rather, serve one another in /.
  5:14 "*L* your neighbor as yourself."
  5:22 But the fruit of the Spirit is /, joy,
Eph 1: 4 In /he predestined us
  1:15 and your /for all the saints,
  2: 4 But because of his great /for us,
  3:17 being rooted and established in /,
  3:18 high and deep is the /of Christ,
  3:19 and to know this /that surpasses
  4: 2 bearing with one another in /.
  4:15 Instead, speaking the truth in /,
  4:16 grows and builds itself up in /,
  5: 2 loved children and live a life of /,
  5:25 your wives, just as Christ loved
  5:28 husbands ought to /their wives
  5:33 each one of you also must /his wife
  6:23 /with faith from God the Father
  6:24 Christ with an undying /.
  6:24 to all who /our Lord Jesus Christ
Php 1: 9 that your /may abound more
  1:16 so in /, knowing that I am put here
  2: 1 from his /, if any fellowship
  2: 2 having the same /, being one
  4: 1 you whom I /and long for,
Col 1: 4 of the /you have for all the saints—
  1: 5 /that spring from the hope that is
  1: 8 also told us of your /in the Spirit.
  2: 2 in heart and united in /,
  3:14 And over all these virtues put on /,
  3:19 /your wives and do not be harsh

1Th 1: 3 your labor prompted by /,
  3: 6 good news about your faith and /.
  3:12 May the Lord make your /increase
  4: 9 about brotherly /we do not need
  4: 9 taught by God to /each other.
  4:10 you do /all the brothers
  5: 8 on faith and /as a breastplate,
  5:13 them in the highest regard in /
2Th 1: 3 and the /every one of you has
  2:10 because they refused to /the truth
  3: 5 direct your hearts into God's /
1Ti 1: 5 The goal of this command is /,
  1:14 and /that are in Christ Jesus.
  2:15 /and holiness with propriety.
  4:12 in life, in /, in faith and in purity.
  6:10 For the /of money is a root
  6:11 faith, /, endurance and gentleness.
2Ti 1: 7 of power, of /and of self-discipline.
  1:13 with faith and /in Christ Jesus.
  2:22 and pursue righteousness, faith, /
  3: 3 unholy, without /, unforgiving,
  3:10 faith, patience, /, endurance,
Tit 2: 2 in faith, in /and in endurance.
  2: 4 women to /their husbands
  3: 4 and /of God our Savior appeared,
  3:15 Greet those who /us in the faith.
Phm : 5 and your /for all the saints.
    : 7 Your /has given me great joy
    : 9 yet I appeal to you on the basis of /.
Heb 6:10 and the /you have shown him
  10:24 may spur one another on toward /
  13: 5 free from the /of money
Jas 1:12 promised to those who /him.
  2: 5 he promised those who /him?
  2: 8 "*L* your neighbor as yourself,"
1Pe 1: 8 you have not seen him, you /him;
  1:22 the truth so that you have sincere /
  1:22 /one another deeply.
  2:17 *L* the brotherhood of believers,
  3: 8 be sympathetic, /as brothers,
  3:10 "Whoever would /life
  4: 8 Above all, /each other deeply,
  4: 8 /covers over a multitude of sins.
  5:14 Greet one another with a kiss of /.
2Pe 1: 7 and to brotherly kindness, /.
  1:17 "This is my Son, whom I /;
1Jn 2: 5 God's /is truly made complete
  2:15 Do not /the world or anything
  2:15 the /of the Father is not in him.
  3: 1 How great is the /the Father has
  3:10 anyone who does not /his brother.
  3:11 We should /one another.
  3:14 Anyone who does not /remains
  3:14 because we /our brothers.
  3:16 This is how we know what /is:
  3:17 how can the /of God be in him?
  3:18 let us not /with words or tongue
  3:23 to /one another as he commanded
  4: 7 Dear friends, let us /one another,
  4: 7 for /comes from God.
  4: 8 Whoever does not /does not know
  4: 8 not know God, because God is /.
  4: 9 This is how God showed his /
  4:10 This is /: not that we loved God,
  4:11 we also ought to /one another.
  4:12 seen God; but if we /one another,
  4:12 and his /is made complete in us.
  4:16 God is /.
  4:16 Whoever lives in /lives in God,
  4:16 and rely on the /God has for us.
  4:17 /is made complete among us
  4:18 But perfect /drives out fear,
  4:18 There is no fear in /.
  4:18 who fears is not made perfect in /.
  4:19 We /because he first loved us.
  4:20 If anyone says, "I /God,"
  4:20 anyone who does not /his brother,
  4:20 whom he has seen, cannot /God,
  4:21 loves God must also /his brother.
  5: 2 we know that we /the children
  5: 3 This is /for God: to obey his
2Jn : 1 whom I /in the truth—
    : 3 will be with us in truth and /.
    : 5 I ask that we /one another.
    : 6 his command is that you walk in /.
    : 6 this is /: that we walk in obedience
3Jn : 1 To my dear friend Gaius, whom I /
    : 6 have told the church about your /
Jude : 2 peace and /be yours in abundance.
    :12 men are blemishes at your /feasts,
    :21 Keep yourselves in God's /
Rev 2: 4 You have forsaken your first /.
  2:19 I know your deeds, your /and faith
  3:19 Those whom I /I rebuke
  12:11 they did not /their lives so much

LOVED* (LOVE)

Ge 24:67 she became his wife, and he /her;
25:28 /Esau, but Rebekah /Jacob.
29:30 and he /Rachel more than Leah.
29:31 the LORD saw that Leah was not /,
29:33 the LORD heard that I am not /,
34: 3 and he /the girl and spoke tenderly
37: 3 Now Israel /Joseph more than any
37: 4 saw that their father /him more
Dt 4:37 Because he /your forefathers
7: 8 But it was because the LORD /you
10:15 on your forefathers and /them,
1Sa 1: 5 a double portion because he /her,
18: 1 in spirit with David, and he /him
18: 3 with David because he /him
18:16 But all Israel and Judah /David,
18:28 that his daughter Michal /David,
20:17 because he /him as he /himself.
2Sa 1:23 in life they were /and gracious.
12:24 The LORD /him; and
12:25 and because the LORD /him,
13:15 hated her more than he had /her.
1Ki 11: 1 /many foreign women
2Ch 11:21 Rehoboam /Maacah daughter
26:10 in the fertile lands, for he /the soil.
Ne 13:26 He was /by his God, and God
Ps 44: 3 light of your face, for you /them.
47: 4 the pride of Jacob, whom he /.
78:68 Mount Zion, which he /.
88:18 taken my companions and /ones
109:17 He /to pronounce a curse—
Isa 5: 1 My /one had a vineyard
Jer 2: 2 how as a bride you /me
8: 2 which they have /and served
31: 3 "I have /you with an everlasting
Eze 16:37 those you /as well as those you
Hos 2: 1 and of your sisters, 'My /one.'
2:23 to the one I called 'Not my /one.'
3: 1 though she is /by another
9:10 became as vile as the thing they /.
11: 1 "When Israel was a child, I /him,
Mal 1: 2 "But you ask, 'How have you /us?
1: 2 "I have /you," says the LORD.
1: 2 "Yet I have /Jacob, but Esau I
Mk 10:21 Jesus looked at him and /him.
12: 6 left to send, a son, whom he /.
Lk 7:47 been forgiven—for she /much.
16:14 The Pharisees, who /money,
Jn 3:16 so /the world that he gave his one
3:19 but men /darkness instead of light
11: 5 Jesus /Martha and her sister
11:36 "See how he /him!" But some
12:43 for they /praise from men more
13: 1 Having /his own who were
13:23 the disciple whom Jesus /,
13:34 As I have /you, so you must love
14:21 He who loves me will be /
14:28 If you /me, you would be glad that
15: 9 the Father has /me, so have I /you.
15:12 Love each other as I have /you.
16:27 loves you because you have /me
17:23 have /them even as you have /me.
17:24 you /me before the creation
19:26 the disciple whom he /standing
20: 2 one Jesus /, and said, "They have
21: 7 the disciple whom Jesus /said
21:20 whom Jesus /was following
Ro 1: 7 To all in Rome who are /by God
8:37 conquerors through him who /us.
9:13 "Jacob I /, but Esau I hated."
9:25 her 'my /one' who is not my /one,"
11:28 they are /on account
Gal 2:20 who /me and gave himself for me.
Eph 5: 1 as dearly /children and live a life
5: 2 as Christ /us and gave himself up
5:25 just as Christ /the church
Col 3:12 and dearly /, clothe yourselves
1Th 1: 4 For we know, brothers /by God,
2: 8 We /you so much that we were
2Th 2:13 for you, brothers /by the Lord,
2:16 who /us and by his grace gave us
2Ti 4:10 for Demas, because he /this world,
Heb 1: 9 You have /righteousness
2Pe 2:15 who /the wages of wickedness.
1Jn 4:10 This is love: not that we /God,
4:10 but that he /us and sent his Son
4:11 Dear friends, since God so /us,
4:19 We love because he first /us.
Jude 1 who are /by God the Father
Rev 3: 9 and acknowledge that I have /you.

LOVELY* (LOVE)

Ge 29:17 but Rachel was /in form.
Est 1:11 and nobles, for she was /to look at.

Est 2: 7 was /in form and features,
Ps 84: 1 How /is your dwelling place.
SS 1: 5 Dark am I, yet /,
2:14 and your face is /.
4: 3 your mouth is /.
5:16 he is altogether /.
6: 4 /as Jerusalem,
Am 8:13 /young women and strong young
Php 4: 8 whatever is /, whatever is

LOVER* (LOVE)

SS 1:13 My /is to me a sachet of myrrh
1:14 My /is to me a cluster
1:16 How handsome you are, my /!
2: 3 is my /among the young men.
2: 8 Listen! My /!
2: 9 My /is like a gazelle or a young
2:10 My /spoke and said to me,
2:16 *Beloved* My /is mine and I am his;
2:17 turn, my /,
4:16 Let my /come into his garden
5: 2 Listen! My /is knocking;
5: 4 My /thrust his hand
5: 1 I arose to open for my /,
5: 6 I opened for my /,
5: 6 but my /had left; he was gone.
5: 8 if you find my /,
5:10 *Beloved* My /is radiant and ruddy,
5:16 This is my /, this my friend,
6: 1 Where has your /gone,
6: 1 Which way did your /turn,
6: 2 *Beloved* My /has gone
6: 3 I am my lover's and my /is mine;
7: 9 May the wine go straight to my /,
7:10 I belong to my /,
7:11 my /, let us go to the countryside.
7:13 that I have stored up for you, my /.
8: 5 leaning on her /?
8:14 *Beloved* Come away, my /,
1Ti 3: 3 not quarrelsome, not a /of money.

LOVER'S* (LOVE)

SS 6: 3 I am my /and my lover is mine;

LOVERS* (LOVE)

SS 5: 1 drink your fill, O /.
Jer 3: 1 as a prostitute with many /—
3: 2 the roadside you sat waiting for /,
4:30 Your /despise you;
La 1: 2 Among all her /
Eze 16:33 but you give gifts to all your /,
16:36 in your promiscuity with your /
16:37 I am going to gather all your /,
16:39 Then I will hand you over to your /,
16:41 and you will no longer pay your /
23: 5 she lusted after her /, the Assyrians
23: 9 I handed her over to her /,
23:20 There she lusted after her /,
23:22 I will stir up your /against you,
Hos 2: 5 She said, 'I will go after my /,
2: 7 She will chase after her /
2:10 lewdness before the eyes of her /;
2:12 she said were her pay from her /,
2:13 and went after her /,
8: 9 Ephraim has sold herself to /.
2Ti 3: 2 People will be /of themselves,
3: 2 /of money, boastful, proud,
3: 3 without self-control, brutal, not /
3: 4 /of pleasure rather than /of God—

LOVES* (LOVE)

Ge 44:20 sons left, and his father /him.'
Dt 10:18 and /the alien, giving him food
15:16 because he /you and your family
21:15 and he /one but not the other.
21:16 son of the wife he /in preference
23: 5 because the LORD your God /you.
28:54 wife he /or his surviving children,
28:56 will begrudge the husband she /
33:12 and the one the LORD /rests
Ru 4:15 who /you and who is better to you
2Ch 2:11 "Because the LORD /his people,
Ps 11: 7 he /justice;
33: 5 The LORD /righteousness
34:12 Whoever of you /life
37:28 For the LORD /the just
87: 2 the LORD /the gates of Zion
91:14 Because he /me," says the LORD.
99: 4 The King is mighty, he /justice—
119:140 and your servant /them,
127: 2 for he grants sleep to those he /.
146: 8 the LORD /the righteous.
Pr 3:12 the LORD disciplines those he /,
12: 1 Whoever /discipline /knowledge,
13:24 he who /him is careful

Pr 15: 9 he /those who pursue
17:17 A friend /at all times,
17:19 He who /a quarrel /sin;
19: 8 He who gets wisdom /his own soul
21:17 He who /pleasure will become
21:17 whoever /wine and oil will never
22:11 He who /a pure heart and whose
29: 3 A man who /wisdom brings joy
Ecc 5:10 Whoever /money never has
5:10 whoever /wealth is never satisfied
SS 3: 1 I looked for the one my heart /.
3: 2 I will search for the one my heart /.
3: 3 "Have you seen the one my heart /.
3: 4 when I found the one my heart /.
Hos 3: 1 as the LORD /the Israelites,
10:11 that /to thresh;
12: 7 he /to defraud.
Mal 2:11 the sanctuary the LORD /,
Mt 10:37 anyone who /his son or daughter
10:37 "Anyone who /his father
Lk 7: 5 because he /our nation
7:47 has been forgiven /little."
Jn 3:35 Father /the Son and has placed
5:20 For the Father /the Son
10:17 reason my Father /me is that I lay
12:25 The man who /his life will lose it,
14:21 He who /me will be loved
14:21 obeys them, he is the one who /me.
14:23 Jesus replied, "If anyone /me,
16:27 the Father himself /you
Ro 13: 8 for he who /his fellowman has
1Co 3: 8 But the man who /God is known
2Co 9: 7 for God /a cheerful giver.
Eph 1: 6 has freely given us in the One he /.
5:28 He who /his wife /himself.
5:33 must love his wife as he /himself,
Col 1:13 us into the kingdom of the Son he /,
Tit 1: 8 one who /what is good, who is
Heb 12: 6 the Lord disciplines those he /,
1Jn 2:10 Whoever /his brother lives
2:15 If anyone /the world, the love
4: 7 Everyone who /has been born
4:21 Whoever /God must also love his
5: 1 who /the Father /his child
3Jn 9 but Diotrephes, who /to be first,
Rev 1: 5 To him who /us and has freed us
20: 9 camp of God's people, the city he /.
22:15 and everyone who /and practices

LOVING* (LOVE)

Ps 25:10 All the ways of the LORD are /
59:10 my /God.
59:17 O God, are my fortress, my /God.
62:12 and that you, O Lord, are /.
144: 2 He is my /God and my fortress,
145:13 and /toward all he has made.
145:17 and /toward all he has made.
Pr 5:19 A /doe, a graceful deer—
Heb 13: 1 Keep on /each other as brothers.
1Jn 5: 2 by /God and carrying out his

LOVING-KINDNESS* (LOVE)

Jer 31: 3 I have drawn you with /.

LOWER

Ps 8: 5 You made him a little /
2Co 11: 7 a sin for me to /myself in order
Heb 2: 7 You made him a little /

LOWING

1Sa 15:14 What is this /of cattle that I hear?"

LOWLY

Job 5:11 The /he sets on high,
Ps 138: 6 on high, he looks upon the /,
Pr 29:23 but a man of /spirit gains honor.
Isa 57:15 also with him who is contrite and /
Eze 21:26 /will be exalted and the exalted
1Co 1:28 He chose the /things of this world

LOYAL

1Ch 29:18 and keep their hearts /to you.
Ps 78: 8 whose hearts were not /to God.

LUKE*

Co-worker with Paul (Col 4:14; 2Ti 4:11; Phm 24).

LUKEWARM*

Rev 3:16 So, because you are /—neither hot

LUST (LUSTED LUSTS)

Pr 6:25 Do not /in your heart
Eze 20:30 and /after their vile images?
Col 3: 5 sexual immorality, impurity, /,

LUSTED

1Th 4: 5 not in passionate *l* like the heathen,
1Pe 4: 3 in debauchery, *l*, drunkenness,
1Jn 2:16 the *l* of his eyes and the boasting

LUSTED (LUST)

Eze 23: 5 she *l* after her lovers, the Assyrians

LUSTS* (LUST)

Nu 15:39 yourselves by going after the *l*
Ro 1:26 God gave them over to shameful *l*.

LUXURY

Jas 5: 5 You have lived on earth in *l*.

LYDIA'S*

Ac 16:40 went to *L* house, where they met

LYING (LIE)

Pr 6:17 a *l* tongue,
    12:22 The LORD detests *l* lips,
    21: 6 a fortune made by a *l* tongue
    26:28 A *l* tongue hates those it hurts,

MACEDONIA

Ac 16: 9 "Come over to *M* and help us."

MAD

Dt 28:34 The sights you see will drive you *m*

MADE (MAKE)

Ge 1: 7 So God *m* the expanse
    1:16 God *m* two great lights—
    1:16 He also *m* the stars.
    1:25 God *m* the wild animals according
    1:31 God saw all that he had *m*,
    2:22 Then the LORD God *m* a woman
    6: 6 was grieved that he had *m* man
    9: 6 has God *m* man.
    15:18 that day the LORD *m* a covenant
Ex 20:11 six days the LORD *m* the heavens
    20:11 the Sabbath day and *m* it holy.
    24: 8 the covenant that the LORD has *m*
    32: 4 *m* it into an idol cast in the shape
Lev 16:34 Atonement is to be *m* once a year
Dt 32: 6 who *m* you and formed you?
Jos 24:25 On that day Joshua *m* a covenant
2Ki 19:15 You have *m* heaven and earth.
2Ch 2:12 the God of Israel, who *m* heaven
Ne 9: 6 You *m* the heavens,
    9:10 You *m* a name for yourself,
Ps 33: 6 of the LORD were the heavens *m*,
    95: 5 The sea is his, for he *m* it,
    96: 5 but the LORD *m* the heavens.
    100: 3 It is he who *m* us, and we are his;
    118:24 This is the day the LORD has *m*;
    136: 7 who *m* the great lights—
    139:14 I am fearfully and wonderfully *m*;
Ecc 3:11 He has *m* everything beautiful
Isa 43: 7 whom I formed and *m*."
    45:12 It is I who *m* the earth
    45:18 he who fashioned and *m* the earth,
    66: 2 Has not my hand *m* all these things
Jer 10:12 But God *m* the earth by his power;
    27: 5 and outstretched arm I *m* the earth
    32:17 you have *m* the heavens
    33: 2 LORD says; he who *m* the earth,
    51:15 "He *m* the earth by his power;
Eze 3:17 I have *m* you a watchman
    33: 7 I have *m* you a watchman
Am 5: 8 (he who *m* the Pleiades and Orion,
Jnh 1: 9 who *m* the sea and the land."
Mk 2:27 "The Sabbath was *m* for man,
Jn 1: 3 Through him all things were *m*;
Ac 17:24 "The God who *m* the world
1Co 3: 6 watered it, but God *m* it grow.
Heb 1: 2 through whom he *m* the universe
Jas 3: 9 who have been *m* in God's likeness
Rev 14: 7 Worship him who *m* the heavens.

MAGDALENE

Lk 8: 2 Mary (called *M*) from whom seven

MAGI

Mt 2: 1 *M* from the east came to Jerusalem

MAGIC (MAGICIANS)

Eze 13:20 I am against your *m* charms
Rev 21: 8 those who practice *m* arts,
    22:15 those who practice *m* arts.

MAGICIANS (MAGIC)

Ex 7:11 the Egyptian *m* also did the same
Da 2: 2 So the king summoned the *m*,

MAGNIFICENCE* (MAGNIFICENT)

1Ch 22: 5 for the LORD should be of great *m*

MAGNIFICENT (MAGNIFICENCE)

1Ki 8:13 I have indeed built a *m* temple
Isa 28:29 in counsel and *m* in wisdom.
Mk 13: 1 stones! What *m* buildings!"

MAGOG

Eze 38: 2 of the land of *M*, the chief prince
    39: 6 I will send fire on *M*
Rev 20: 8 and *M*— to gather them for battle.

MAIDEN (MAIDENS)

Pr 30:19 and the way of a man with a *m*.
Isa 62: 5 As a young man marries a *m*,
Jer 2:32 Does a *m* forget her jewelry,

MAIDENS (MAIDEN)

SS 1: 3 No wonder the *m* love you!

MAIMED

Mt 18: 8 It is better for you to enter life *m*

MAINTAIN (MAINTAINING)

Ps 82: 3 the rights of the poor
    106: 3 Blessed are they who *m* justice,
Hos 12: 6 *m* love and justice,
Am 5:15 *m* justice in the courts.
Ro 3:28 For we *m* that a man is justified

MAINTAINING* (MAINTAIN)

Ex 34: 7 faithfulness, *m* love to thousands,

MAJESTIC* (MAJESTY)

Ex 15: 6 was *m* in power.
    15:11 *m* in holiness.
Job 37: 4 he thunders with his *m* voice.
Ps 1: 1 how *m* is your name in all the earth
    8: 9 how *m* is your name in all the earth
    29: 4 the voice of the LORD is *m*.
    68:15 of Bashan are *m* mountains;
    76: 4 more *m* than mountains rich
    111: 3 Glorious and *m* are his deeds.
SS 6: 4 *m* as troops with banners.
    6:10 *m* as the stars in procession?
Isa 30:30 men to hear his *m* voice
Eze 31: 7 It was *m* in beauty.
2Pe 1:17 came to him from the *M* Glory,

MAJESTY* (MAJESTIC)

Ex 15: 7 In the greatness of your *m*
Dt 5:24 has shown us his glory and his *m*,
    11: 2 his *m*, his mighty hand, his
    33:17 In me is like a firstborn bull;
    33:26 and on the clouds in his *m*.
1Ch 16:27 Splendor and *m* are before him;
    29:11 and the *m* and the splendor,
Est 1: 4 the splendor and glory of his *m*.
Job 37: 3 if it pleases your *m*, grant me my
    40:10 and clothe yourself in honor and *m*
Ps 21: 5 on him splendor and *m*.
    45: 3 with splendor and *m*.
    45: 4 In your *m* ride forth victoriously
    68:34 whose *m* is over Israel,
    93: 1 The LORD reigns, he is robed in *m*
    93: 1 the LORD is robed in *m*
    96: 6 Splendor and *m* are before him;
    104: 1 clothed with splendor and *m*.
    110: 3 Arrayed in holy *m*,
    145: 5 of the glorious splendor of your *m*,
Isa 2:10 and the splendor of his *m*!
    2:19 and the splendor of his *m*,
    2:21 and the splendor of his *m*,
    24:14 west they acclaim the LORD's *m*.
    26:10 and regard not the *m* of the LORD.
    53: 2 or *m* to attract us to him,
Eze 31: 2 can be compared with you in *m*?
    31:18 with you in splendor and *m*?'
Da 4:30 and for the glory of my *m*?"
Mic 5: 4 in the *m* of the name
Zec 6:13 and he will be clothed with *m*
Ac 19:27 will be robbed of her divine *m*."
    25:26 to write to His *M* about him.
2Th 1: 9 and from the *m* of his power
Heb 1: 3 hand of the *M* in heaven.
    8: 1 of the throne of the *M* in heaven,
2Pe 1:16 but we were eyewitnesses of his *m*.
Jude :25 only God our Savior be glory, *m*,

MAKE (MADE MAKER MAKERS MAKES MAKING MAN-MADE)

Ge 1:26 "Let us *m* man in our image,
    2:18 I will *ma* helper suitable for him."
    6:14 *m* yourself an ark of cypress wood;
    12: 2 "I will *m* you into a great nation
Ex 22: 3 that certainly *m* restitution,
    25: 9 *M* this tabernacle and all its
    25:40 See that you *m* them according
Nu 6:25 the LORD *m* his face shine
2Sa 7: 9 Now I will *m* your name great,
Job 7:17 "What is man that you *m* so much
Ps 4: 8 *m* me dwell in safety.
    20: 4 and *m* all your plans succeed.
    108: 1 *m* music with all my soul.
    110: 1 hand until I *m* your enemies
    119:165 and nothing can *m* them stumble.
Pr 3: 6 and he will *m* your paths straight,
    4:26 *M* level paths for your feet
    20:18 *M* plans by seeking advice;
Isa 14:14 I will *m* myself like the Most High
    29:16 "He did not *m* me"?
    55: 3 I will *m* an everlasting covenant
    61: 8 and *m* an everlasting covenant
Jer 31:31 "when I will *m* a new covenant
Eze 37:26 I will *m* a covenant of peace
Mt 3: 3 *m* straight paths for him.' "
    28:19 and *m* disciples of all nations,
Mk 1:17 "and I will *m* you fishers of men."
Lk 13:24 "Every effort to enter
    14:23 country lanes and *m* them come in,
Ro 14:19 every effort to do what leads
2Co 5: 9 So we *m* it our goal to please him,
Eph 4: 3 *M* every effort to keep the unity
Col 4: 5 the most of every opportunity.
1Th 4:11 *M* it your ambition
Heb 4:11 every effort to enter that rest.
    8: 5 it that you *m* everything according
    12:14 *M* every effort to live in peace
2Pe 1: 5 every effort to add
    3:14 every effort to be found spotless.

MAKER* (MAKE)

Job 4:17 Can a man be more pure than his *M*
    9: 9 He is the *M* of the Bear and Orion,
    32:22 my *M* would soon take me away.
    35:10 no one says, 'Where is God my *M*,
    36: 3 I will ascribe justice to my *M*.
    40:19 yet his *M* can approach him
Ps 95: 6 kneel before the LORD our *M*;
    115:15 the *M* of heaven and earth.
    121: 2 the *M* of heaven and earth.
    124: 8 the *M* of heaven and earth.
    134: 3 the *M* of heaven and earth.
    146: 6 the *M* of heaven and earth.
    149: 2 Let Israel rejoice in their *M*;
Pr 14:31 poor shows contempt for their *M*,
    17: 5 poor shows contempt for their *M*,
    22: 2 The *M* of them all.
Ecc 11: 5 the *M* of all things.
Isa 17: 7 that day men will look to their *M*
    27:11 so their *M* has no compassion
    45: 9 to him who quarrels with his *M*,
    45:11 the Holy One of Israel, and its *M*:
    51:13 that you forget the LORD your *M*,
    54: 5 For your *M* is your husband—
Jer 10:16 for he is the *M* of all things,
    51:19 for he is the *M* of all things,
Hos 8:14 Israel has forgotten his *M*

MAKERS* (MAKE)

Isa 45:16 All the *m* of idols will be put

MAKES (MAKE)

Ps 23: 2 *m* me lie down in green pastures,
Pr 13:12 Hope deferred *m* the heart sick,
1Co 3: 7 but only God, who *m* things grow.

MAKING (MAKE)

Ps 19: 7 *m* wise the simple.
Ecc 12:12 Of *m* many books there is no end,
Jn 5:18 *m* himself equal with God.
Eph 5:16 the most of every opportunity.

MALACHI*

Mal 1: 1 of the LORD to Israel through *M*.

MALE

Ge 1:27 *m* and female he created them.
Ex 13: 2 to me every firstborn *m*.
Nu 8:16 the first *m* offspring
Mt 19: 4 the Creator 'made them *m*
Gal 3:28 slave nor free, *m* nor female,

MALICE (MALICIOUS)

Mk	7:22	adultery, greed, *m*, deceit,
Ro	1:29	murder, strife, deceit and *m*.
1Co	5: 8	the yeast of *m* and wickedness,
Eph	4:31	along with every form of *m*.
Col	3: 8	*m*, slander, and filthy language
1Pe	2: 1	rid yourselves of all *m*

MALICIOUS (MALICE)

Pr	26:24	A *m* man disguises himself
1Ti	3:11	not *m* talkers but temperate
	6: 4	*m* talk, evil suspicions

MALIGN

Tit	2: 5	so that no one will *m* the word

MAMMON see MONEY, WEALTH

MAN (MAN'S MANKIND MEN MEN'S WOMAN WOMEN)

Ge	1:26	"Let us make *m* in our image,
	2: 7	God formed the *m* from the dust
	2: 8	*m* became a living being
	2:15	God took the *m* and put
	2:18	for the *m* to be alone
	2:20	*m* gave names to all the
	2:23	she was taken out of *m*.
	2:25	*m* and his wife were both
	3: 9	God called to the *m*,
	3:22	*m* has now become like
	4: 1	I have brought forth a *m*
	6: 3	not contend with *m* forever,
	6: 6	grieved that he had made *m*
	9: 6	Whoever sheds the blood of *m*,
Dt	8: 3	does not live on bread
1Sa	13:14	a *m* after his own heart
	15:29	he is not a *m* that he
	16: 7	at the things *m* looks at.
Job	14: 1	*m* born of woman is of few
	14:14	If a *m* dies, will he live
Ps	1: 1	Blessed is the *m* who does
	8: 4	what is *m* that you are
	32: 2	Blessed is the *m* whose sin
	40: 4	Blessed is the *m* who makes
	84:12	blessed is the *m* who trusts
	103:15	As for *m*, his days are
	112: 1	Blessed is the *m* who fears
	119: 9	can a young *m* keep his
	127: 5	Blessed is the *m* whose quiver
	144: 3	what is *m* that you care
Pr	3:13	Blessed is the *m* who finds
	9: 9	Instruct a wise *m*
	14:12	that seems right to a *m*,
	30:19	way of a *m* with a maiden.
Isa	53: 3	a *m* of sorrows,
Jer	17: 5	the one who trusts in *m*,
	17: 7	blessed is the *m* who trusts
Eze	22:30	I looked for a *m*
Mt	4: 4	*M* does not live on bread
	19: 5	a *m* will leave his father
Mk	8:36	What good is it for a *m*
Lk	4: 4	'*M* does not live on bread
Ro	5:12	entered the world through one *m*
1Co	2:15	spiritual *m* makes judgments
	3:12	If any *m* builds on this
	7: 1	good for a *m* not to marry.
	7: 2	each *m* should have his own
	11: 3	head of every *m* is Christ,
	11: 3	head of woman is *m*
	13:11	When I became a *m*,
	15:21	death came through a *m*,
	15:45	first *m* Adam became a
	15:47	the second *m* from heaven
2Co	12: 2	I know a *m* in Christ
Eph	2:15	create in himself one new *m*
	5:31	a *m* will leave his father
Php	2: 8	found in appearance as a *m*,
1Ti	2: 5	the *m* Christ Jesus,
	2:11	have authority over a *m*;
2Ti	3:17	that the *m* of God may be
Heb	2: 6	what is *m* that you are
	9:27	as *m* is destined to die

MAN'S (MAN)

Pr	20:24	A *m* steps are directed by
Jer	10:23	a *m* life is not his own;
1Co	1:25	is wiser than *m* wisdom,

MAN-MADE (MAKE)

Heb	9:11	perfect tabernacle that is not *m*,
	9:24	not enter a *m* sanctuary that was

MANAGE (MANAGER)

Jer	12: 5	how will you *m* in the thickets
1Ti	3: 4	He must *m* his own family well

1Ti	3:12	one wife and must *m* his children
	5:14	to *m* their homes and to give

MANAGER (MANAGE)

Lk	12:42	Who then is the faithful and wise *m*
	16: 1	a rich man whose *m* was accused

MANASSEH

1. Firstborn of Joseph (Ge 41:51; 46:20). Blessed by Jacob but not firstborn (Ge 48). Tribe of blessed (Dt 33:17), numbered (Nu 1:35; 26:34), half allotted land east of Jordan (Nu 32; Jos 13:8-33), half west (Jos 17; Eze 48:4), failed to fully possess (Jos 17:12-13; Jdg 1:27), 12,000 from (Rev 7:6).

2. Son of Hezekiah; king of Judah (2Ki 21: 1-18; 2Ch 33:1-20). Judah exiled for his detestable sins (2Ki 21:10-15). Repentance (2Ch 33: 12-19).

MANDRAKES

Ge	30:14	give me some of your son's *m*."

MANGER

Lk	2:12	in strips of cloth and lying in a *m*."

MANIFESTATION*

1Co	12: 7	to each one the *m* of the Spirit is

MANKIND (MAN)

Ge	6: 7	I will wipe *m*, whom I have created
Ps	33:13	and sees all *m*;
Pr	8:31	and delighting in *m*.
Ecc	7:29	God made *m* upright,
Isa	40: 5	and all *m* together will see it.
	45:12	and created *m* upon it.
Jer	32:27	"I am the LORD, the God of all *m*.
Zec	2:13	Be still before the LORD, all *m*;
Lk	3: 6	And all *m* will see God's salvation

MANNA

Ex	16:31	people of Israel called the bread *m*.
Dt	8:16	He gave you *m* to eat in the desert,
Jn	6:49	Your forefathers ate the *m*
Rev	2:17	I will give some of the hidden *m*.

MANNER

1Co	11:27	in an unworthy *m* will be guilty
Php	1:27	conduct yourselves in a *m* worthy

MANSIONS*

Ps	49:14	far from their princely *m*.
Isa	5: 9	the fine *m* left without occupants.
Am	3:15	and the *m* will be demolished,"
	5:11	though you have built stone *m*,

MARCH

Jos	6: 4	*m* around the city seven times,
Isa	42:13	LORD will *m* out like a mighty

MARITAL* (MARRY)

Ex	21:10	of her food, clothing and *m* rights.
Mt	5:32	except for *m* unfaithfulness,
	19: 9	except for *m* unfaithfulness,
1Co	7: 3	husband should fulfill his *m* duty

MARK (MARKS)

Cousin of Barnabas (Col 4:10; 2Ti 4:11; Phm 24; 1Pe 5:13), see JOHN.

Ge	4:15	Then the LORD put a *m* on Cain
Rev	13:16	to receive a *m* on his right hand

MARKET (MARKETPLACE MARKETPLACES)

Jn	2:16	turn my Father's house into a *m*!"

MARKETPLACE (MARKET)

Lk	7:32	are like children sitting in the *m*

MARKETPLACES (MARKET)

Mt	23: 7	they love to be greeted in the *m*

MARKS (MARK)

Jn	20:25	Unless I see the nail *m* in his hands
Gal	6:17	bear on my body the *m* of Jesus.

MARRED

Isa	52:14	his form *m* beyond human likeness

MARRIAGE (MARRY)

Mt	22:30	neither marry nor be given in *m*;
	24:38	marrying and giving in *m*,
Ro	7: 2	she is released from the law of *m*.
Heb	13: 4	by all, and the *m* bed kept pure,

MARRIED (MARRY)

Dt	24: 5	happiness to the wife he has *m*.
Ezr	10:10	you have *m* foreign women,
Pr	30:23	an unloved woman who is *m*,
Mt	1:18	pledged to be *m* to Joseph,
Mk	12:23	since the seven were *m* to her?"
Ro	7: 2	by law a *m* woman is bound
1Co	7:27	Are you *m*? Do not seek a divorce.
	7:33	But a *m* man is concerned about
	7:36	They should get *m*.

MARRIES (MARRY)

Mt	5:32	anyone who *m* the divorced woman
	19: 9	and *m* another woman commits
Lk	16:18	the man who *m* a divorced woman

MARROW

Heb	4:12	joints and *m*; it judges the thoughts

MARRY (INTERMARRY MARITAL MARRIAGE MARRIED MARRIES)

Dt	25: 5	brother shall take her and *m* her
Mt	22:30	resurrection people will neither *m*
1Co	7: 1	It is good for a man not to *m*.
	7: 9	control themselves, they should *m*,
	7:28	if you do *m*, you have not sinned;
1Ti	4: 3	They forbid people to *m*
	5:14	So I counsel younger widows to *m*,

MARTHA*

Sister of Mary and Lazarus (Lk 10:38-42; Jn 11; 12:2).

MARVELED* (MARVELOUS)

Lk	2:33	mother *m* at what was said about
2Th	1:10	and to be *m* at among all those who

MARVELING* (MARVELOUS)

Lk	9:43	While everyone was *m*

MARVELOUS* (MARVELED MARVELING)

1Ch	16:24	his *m* deeds among all peoples.
Job	37: 5	God's voice thunders in *m* ways;
Ps	71:17	to this day I declare your *m* deeds.
	72:18	who alone does *m* deeds.
	86:10	For you are great and do *m* deeds;
	96: 3	his *m* deeds among all peoples.
	98: 1	for he has done *m* things;
	118:23	and it is *m* in our eyes.
Isa	25: 1	you have done *m* things,
Zec	8: 6	but will it seem *m* to me?"
	8: 6	"It may seem *m* to the remnant
Mt	21:42	and it is *m* in our eyes'?
Mk	12:11	and it is *m* in our eyes'?
Rev	15: 1	in heaven another great and *m* sign
	15: 3	"Great and *m* are your deeds,

MARY

1. Mother of Jesus (Mt 1:16-25; Lk 1:27-56; 2: 1-40). With Jesus at temple (Lk 2:41-52), at the wedding in Cana (Jn 2:1-5), questioning his sanity (Mk 3:21); at the cross (Jn 19:25-27). Among disciples after Ascension (Ac 1:14).

2. Magdalene; former demoniac (Lk 8:2). Helped support Jesus' ministry (Lk 8:1-3). At the cross (Mt 27:56; Mk 15:40; Jn 19:25), burial (Mt 27:61; Mk 15:47). Saw angel after resurrection (Mt 28:1-10; Mk 16:1-9; Lk 24:1-12); also Jesus (Jn 20:1-18).

3. Sister of Martha and Lazarus (Jn 11). Washed Jesus' feet (Jn 12:1-8).

MASQUERADES*

2Co	11:14	for Satan himself *m* as an angel

MASTER (MASTER'S MASTERED MASTERS MASTERY)

Ge	4: 7	to have you, but you must *m* it."
Hos	2:16	you will no longer call me 'my *m*.'
Mal	1: 6	If I am a *m*, where is the respect
Mt	10:24	nor a servant above his *m*.
	23: 8	for you have only one *M*
	24:46	that servant whose *m* finds him
	25:21	"His *m* replied, 'Well done,
	25:23	"His *m* replied, 'Well done,
Ro	6:14	For sin shall not be your *m*,
	14: 4	To his own *m* he stands or falls.
Col	4: 1	you know that you also have a *M*
2Ti	2:21	useful to the *M* and prepared

MASTER'S (MASTER)

Mt	25:21	Come and share your *m* happiness

MASTERED* (MASTER)

1Co 6:12 but I will not be *m* by anything.
2Pe 2:19 a slave to whatever has *m* him.

MASTERS (MASTER)

Pr 25:13 he refreshes the spirit of his *m*.
Mt 6:24 "No one can serve two *m*.
Lk 16:13 "No servant can serve two *m*.
Eph 6:5 obey your earthly *m* with respect
6:9 And *m*, treat your slaves
Col 3:22 obey your earthly *m* in everything;
4:1 *M*, provide your slaves
1Ti 6:1 should consider their *m* worthy
6:2 who have believing *m* are not
Tit 2:9 subject to their *m* in everything,
1Pe 2:18 to your *m* with all respect,

MASTERY* (MASTER)

Ro 6:9 death no longer has *m* over him.

MAT

Mk 2:9 'Get up, take your *m* and walk'?
Ac 9:34 Get up and take care of your *m*."

MATCHED*

2Co 8:11 do it may be *m* by your completion

MATTHEW*

Apostle, former tax collector (Mt 9:9-13; 10:3; Mk 3:18; Lk 6:15; Ac 1:13). Also called Levi (Mk 2:14-17; Lk 5:27-32).

MATTHIAS

Ac 1:26 the lot fell to *M*; so he was added

MATURE* (MATURITY)

Lk 8:14 and pleasures, and they do not *m*.
1Co 2:6 a message of wisdom among the *m*.
Eph 4:13 of the Son of God and become *m*,
Php 3:15 of us who are *m* should take such
Col 4:12 firm in all the will of God, *m*
Heb 5:14 But solid food is for the *m*,
Jas 1:4 work so that you may be *m*

MATURITY* (MATURE)

Heb 6:1 about Christ and go on to *m*,

MEAL

Pr 15:17 Better a *m* of vegetables where
1Co 10:27 some unbeliever invites you to a *m*
Heb 12:16 for a single *m* sold his inheritance

MEANING

Ne 8:8 and giving the *m* so that the people

MEANINGLESS

Ecc 1:2 "*M! M!*" says the Teacher.
1Ti 1:6 from these and turned to *m* talk.

MEANS

1Co 9:22 by all possible *m* I might save some

MEASURE (MEASURED MEASURES)

Ps 71:15 though I know not its *m*.
Eze 45:3 In the sacred district, *m*
Zec 2:2 he answered me, "To *m* Jerusalem
Lk 6:38 A good *m*, pressed
Eph 3:19 to the *m* of all the fullness of God.
4:13 to the whole *m* of the fullness
Rev 11:1 "Go and *m* the temple of God

MEASURED (MEASURE)

Isa 40:12 Who has *m* the waters
Jer 31:37 if the heavens above can be *m*

MEASURES (MEASURE)

Dt 25:14 Do not have two differing *m*
Pr 20:10 Differing weights and differing *m*

MEAT

Pr 23:20 or gorge themselves on *m*,
Ro 14:6 He who eats *m*, eats to the Lord,
14:21 It is better not to eat *m*
1Co 8:13 I will never eat *m* again,
10:25 *m* market without raising questions

MEDDLER* (MEDDLES)

1Pe 4:15 kind of criminal, or even as a *m*

MEDDLES* (MEDDLER)

Pr 26:17 is a passer-by who *m*

MEDIATOR

1Ti 2:5 and one *m* between God and men,

Heb 8:6 of which he is *m* is superior
9:15 For this reason Christ is the *m*
12:24 to Jesus the *m* of a new covenant,

MEDICINE*

Pr 17:22 A cheerful heart is good *m*,

MEDITATE* (MEDITATED MEDITATES MEDITATION)

Ge 24:63 out to the field one evening to *m*,
Jos 1:8 from your mouth; *m* on it day
Ps 48:9 we *m* on your unfailing love.
77:12 I will *m* on all your works
119:15 I *m* on your precepts
119:23 your servant will *m*
119:27 then I will *m* on your wonders.
119:48 and I *m* on your decrees.
119:78 but I will *m* on your precepts.
119:97 I *m* on it all day long.
119:99 for I *m* on your statutes.
119:148 that I may *m* on your promises.
143:5 I *m* on all your works
145:5 I will *m* on your wonderful works.

MEDITATED* (MEDITATE)

Ps 39:3 and as I *m*, the fire burned;

MEDITATES* (MEDITATE)

Ps 1:2 and on his law he *m* day and night.

MEDITATION* (MEDITATE)

Ps 19:14 of my mouth and the *m* of my heart
104:34 May my *m* be pleasing to him,

MEDIUM

Lev 20:27 "'A man or woman who is a *m*

MEEK* (MEEKNESS)

Ps 37:11 But the *m* will inherit the land
Zep 3:12 the *m* and humble,
Mt 5:5 Blessed are the *m*,

MEEKNESS* (MEEK)

2Co 10:1 By the *m* and gentleness of Christ,

MEET (MEETING MEETINGS MEETS)

Ps 42:2 When can I go and *m* with God?
85:10 Love and faithfulness *m* together;
Am 4:12 prepare to *m* your God, O Israel."
1Co 11:34 when you *m* together it may not
1Th 4:17 them in the clouds to *m* the Lord

MEETING (MEET)

Ex 40:34 the cloud covered the Tent of *M*,
Heb 10:25 Let us not give up *m* together,

MEETINGS* (MEET)

1Co 11:17 for your *m* do more harm

MEETS (MEET)

Heb 7:26 Such a high priest *m* our need—

MELCHIZEDEK

Ge 14:18 *M* king of Salem brought out bread
Ps 110:4 in the order of *M*."
Heb 7:11 in the order of *M*, not in the order

MELT (MELTS)

2Pe 3:12 and the elements will *m* in the heat.

MELTS (MELT)

Am 9:5 he who touches the earth and it *m*,

MEMBER (MEMBERS)

Ro 12:5 each *m* belongs to all the others.

MEMBERS (MEMBER)

Mic 7:6 a man's enemies are the *m*
Mt 10:36 a man's enemies will be the *m*
Ro 7:23 law at work in the *m* of my body,
12:4 of us has one body with many *m*,
1Co 6:15 not know that your bodies are *m*
12:24 But God has combined the *m*
Eph 3:6 *m* together of one body,
4:25 for we are all *m* of one body.
5:30 for we are *m* of his body.
Col 3:15 as *m* of one body you were called

MEMORABLE* (MEMORY)

Eze 39:13 day I am glorified will be a *m* day

MEMORIES* (MEMORY)

1Th 3:6 us that you always have pleasant *m*

MEMORY (MEMORABLE MEMORIES)

Pr 10:7 *m* of the righteous will be
Mt 26:13 she has done will also be told, in *m*

MEN (MAN)

Ge 6:2 daughter of *m* were beautiful,
6:4 heroes of old, *m* of renown
Ps 9:20 nations know they are but *m*.
11:4 He observes the sons of *m*;
Mt 4:19 will make you fishers of *m*
5:16 your light shine before *m*
6:14 if you forgive *m* when
10:32 acknowledges me before *m*,
12:31 blasphemy will be forgiven *m*,
12:36 *m* will have to give account
23:5 is done for *m* to see:
Mk 7:7 are but rules taught by *m*.
Lk 6:22 Blessed are you when *m*
6:26 Woe to you when all *m*
Jn 1:4 life was the light of *m*,
2:24 for he knew all *m*.
3:19 *m* loved darkness instead.
12:32 will draw all *m* to myself
13:35 all *m* will know that you
Ac 5:29 obey God rather than *m*!
Ro 1:18 wickedness of *m*
1:27 indecent acts with other *m*,
5:12 death came to all *m*,
1Co 2:11 among *m* knows the thoughts
3:3 acting like mere *m*?
3:21 no more boasting about *m*!
9:22 all things to all *m*
13:1 tongues of *m* and of angels
16:13 be *m* of courage;
16:18 Such *m* deserve recognition.
2Co 5:11 we try to persuade *m*.
8:21 but also in the eyes of *m*.
Gal 1:1 sent not from *m* nor
1:10 to win approval of *m*, or
Eph 4:8 and gave gifts to *m*.
1Th 2:4 as *m* approved by God
2:13 not as the word of *m*,
1Ti 2:4 wants all *m* to be saved
2:6 as a ransom for all *m*—
4:10 the Savior of all *m*
5:2 younger *m* as brothers
2Ti 2:2 entrust to reliable *m*
Tit 2:11 has appeared to all *m*.
Heb 5:1 is selected from among *m*
7:28 high priests *m* who are weak;
2Pe 1:21 but *m* spoke from God
Rev 21:3 dwelling of God is with *m*,

MEN'S (MAN)

2Ki 19:18 fashioned by *m* hands.
2Ch 32:19 the work of *m* hands.
1Co 2:5 not rest on *m* wisdom.

MENAHEM*

King of Israel (2Ki 15:17-22).

MENE

Da 5:25 that was written: *M, M*,

MEPHIBOSHETH

Son of Jonathan shown kindness by David (2Sa 4:4; 9; 21:7). Accused of siding with Absalom (2Sa 16:1-4; 19:24-30).

MERCHANT

Pr 31:14 She is like the *m* ships,
Mt 13:45 of heaven is like a *m* looking

MERCIFUL (MERCY)

Dt 4:31 the LORD your God is a *m* God;
Ne 9:31 for you are a gracious and *m* God.
Ps 77:7 Has God forgotten to be *m*?
78:38 Yet he was *m*;
Jer 3:12 for I am *m*,' declares the LORD.
Da 9:9 The Lord our God is *m*
Mt 5:7 Blessed are the *m*,
Lk 1:54 remembering to be *m*
6:36 Be *m*, just as your Father is *m*.
Heb 2:17 in order that he might become a *m*
Jas 2:13 to anyone who has not been *m*.
Jude 22 Be *m* to those who doubt; snatch

MERCY (MERCIFUL)

Ex 33:19 on whom I will have *m*,
2Sa 24:14 of the LORD, for his *m* is great;
1Ch 21:13 for his *m* is very great;
Ne 9:31 But in your great *m* you did not put
Ps 25:6 O LORD, your great *m* and love,
28:6 for he has heard my cry for *m*.

Ps   57: 1 Have *m* on me, O God, have *m*
Pr   28: 13 renounces them finds *m*,
Isa   63: 9 and *m* he redeemed them;
Da   9: 18 but because of your great *m*.
Hos   6: 6 For I desire *m*, not sacrifice,
Am   5: 15 LORD God Almighty will have *m*
Mic   6: 8 To act justly and to love *m*
       7: 18 but delight to show *m*.
Hab   3: 2 in wrath remember *m*.
Zec   7: 9 show *m* and compassion
Mt   5: 7 for they will be shown *m*.
       9: 13 learn what this means: 'I desire *m*,
      12: 7 'I desire *m*, not sacrifice,' you
      18: 33 Shouldn't you have had *m*
      23: 23 justice, *m* and faithfulness.
Lk   1: 50 His *m* extends to those who fear
Ro   9: 15 "I will have *m* on whom I have *m*,
       9: 18 Therefore God has *m*
      11: 32 so that he may have *m* on them all.
      12: 1 brothers, in view of God's *m*,
      12: 8 if it is showing *m*, let him do it
Eph   2: 4 who is rich in *m*, made us alive
1Ti   1: 13 I was shown *m* because I acted
       1: 16 for that very reason I was shown *m*
Tit   3: 5 we had done, but because of his *m*.
Heb   4: 16 so that we may receive *m*
Jas   2: 13 judgment without *m* will be shown
       2: 13 *M* triumphs over judgment!
       3: 17 submissive, full of *m* and good fruit.
       5: 11 full of compassion and *m*.
1Pe   1: 3 In his great *m* he has given us new
       2: 10 once you had not received *m*,
Jude   : 23 to others show *m*, mixed with fear

MERRY

Lk   12: 19 Take life easy; eat, drink and be *m*

MESHACH

Hebrew exiled to Babylon; name changed from Mishael (Da 1:6-7). Refused defilement by food (Da 1:8-20). Refused to worship idol (Da 3: 1-18); saved from furnace (Da 3:19-30).

MESSAGE (MESSENGER)

Isa   53: 1 Who has believed our *m*
Jn   12: 38 "Lord, who has believed our *m*
Ac   5: 20 "and tell the people the full *m*
      10: 36 You know the *m* God sent
      17: 11 for they received the *m*
Ro   10: 16 who has believed our *m*?";
      10: 17 faith comes from hearing the *m*,
1Co   1: 18 For the *m* of the cross is
       2: 4 My *m* and my preaching were not
2Co   5: 19 to us the *m* of reconciliation.
2Th   3: 1 pray for us that the *m*
Tit   1: 9 firmly to the trustworthy *m*
Heb   4: 2 the *m* they heard was of no value
1Pe   2: 8 because they disobey the *m*—

MESSENGER (MESSAGE)

Pr   25: 13 is a trustworthy *m*
Mal   3: 1 I will send my *m*, who will prepare
Mt   11: 10 " 'I will send my *m* ahead of you,
2Co   12: 7 a *m* of Satan, to torment me.

MESSIAH*

Jn   1: 41 "We have found the *M*"(that is,
       4: 25 "I know that *M*"(called Christ) "is

METHUSELAH

Ge   5: 27 Altogether, *M* lived 969 years,

MICAH

1. Idolater from Ephraim (Jdg 17-18).
2. Prophet from Moresheth (Jer 26:18-19; Mic 1:1).

MICAIAH

Prophet of the LORD who spoke against Ahab (1Ki 22:1-28; 2Ch 18:1-27).

MICHAEL

Archangel (Jude 9); warrior in angelic realm, protector of Israel (Da 10:13, 21; 12:1; Rev 12: 7).

MICHAL

Daughter of Saul, wife of David (1Sa 14:49; 18:20-28). Warned David of Saul's plot (1Sa 19). Saul gave her to Paltiel (1Sa 25:44); David retrieved her (2Sa 3:13-16). Criticized David for dancing before the ark (2Sa 6:16-23; 1Ch 15: 29).

MIDIAN

Ex   2: 15 Pharaoh and went to live in *M*,
Jdg   7: 2 me to deliver *M* into their hands.

MIDWIVES

Ex   1: 17 The *m*, however, feared God

MIGHT (ALMIGHTY MIGHTIER MIGHTY)

Jdg   16: 30 Then he pushed with all his *m*,
2Sa   6: 5 with all their *m* before the LORD,
       6: 14 before the LORD with all his *m*,
2Ch   20: 6 Power and *m* are in your hand,
Ps   21: 13 we will sing and praise your *m*.
      54: 1 vindicate me by your *m*.
Isa   63: 15 Where are your zeal and your *m*?
Mic   3: 8 and with justice and *m*,
Zec   4: 6 'Not by *m* nor by power,
Col   1: 11 power according to his glorious *m*
1Ti   6: 16 To him be honor and *m* forever.

MIGHTIER (MIGHT)

Ps   93: 4 *M* than the thunder

MIGHTY (MIGHT)

Ge   49: 24 of the hand of the *M* One of Jacob,
Ex   6: 1 of my *m* hand he will drive them
       6: 1 out of it with a *m* hand.
Dt   5: 15 out of there with a *m* hand
       7: 8 he brought you out with a *m* hand,
      10: 17 the great God, *m* and awesome,
      34: 12 one has ever shown the *m* power
2Sa   1: 19 How the *m* have fallen!
      23: 8 the names of David's *m* men:
Ne   9: 32 the great, *m* and awesome God,
Job   36: 5 God is *m*, but does not despise men
Ps   24: 8 The LORD strong and *m*,
      45: 3 upon your side, O mone;
      50: 1 The *M* One, God, the LORD,
      62: 7 he is my *m* rock, my refuge.
      68: 33 who thunders with *m* voice.
      71: 16 proclaim your *m* acts,
      77: 12 and consider all your *m* deeds.
      77: 15 With your *m* arm you redeemed
      89: 8 You are *m*, O LORD,
      93: 4 the LORD on high is *m*.
      99: 4 The King is *m*, he loves justice—
     110: 2 LORD will extend your *m* scepter
     118: 15 right hand has done *m* things!
     136: 12 with a *m* hand and outstretched
     145: 4 they will tell of your *m* acts.
     145: 12 all men may know of your *m* acts
     147: 5 Great is our Lord and *m* in power;
SS   8: 6 like a *m* flame.
Isa   9: 6 Wonderful Counselor, *M* God,
      60: 16 your Redeemer, the *M* One
      63: 1 *m* to save."
Jer   20: 11 with me like a *m* warrior;
      32: 19 your purposes and *m* are your
Eze   20: 33 I will rule over you with a *m* hand
Zep   3: 17 he is *m* to save.
Mt   26: 64 at the right hand of the *M* One
Eph   1: 19 like the working of his *m* strength,
       6: 10 in the Lord and in his *m* power.
1Pe   5: 6 therefore, under God's *m* hand,

MILE*

Mt   5: 41 If someone forces you to go one *m*,

MILK

Ex   3: 8 a land flowing with *m* and honey—
      23: 19 a young goat in its mother's *m*.
Pr   30: 33 as churning the *m* produces butter,
Isa   55: 1 Come, buy wine and *m*
1Co   3: 2 I gave you *m*, not solid food,
Heb   5: 12 You need *m*, not solid food!
1Pe   2: 2 babies, crave pure spiritual *m*,

MILLSTONE (STONE)

Lk   17: 2 sea with a *m* tied around his neck

MIND (DOUBLE-MINDED LIKE-MINDED MINDED MINDFUL MINDS)

Nu   23: 19 that he should change his *m*.
Dt   28: 65 LORD will give you an anxious *m*,
1Sa   15: 29 Israel does not lie or change his *m*;
1Ch   28: 9 devotion and with a willing *m*,
2Ch   30: 12 the people to give them unity of *m*
Ps   26: 2 examine my heart and my *m*;
     110: 4 and will not change his *m*:
Isa   26: 3 him whose *m* is steadfast,
Jer   17: 10 and examine the *m*,
Mt   22: 37 all your soul and with all your *m*.
Mk   12: 30 with all your *m* and with all your

Lk   10: 27 your strength and with all your *m*';
Ac   4: 32 believers were one in heart and *m*.
Ro   1: 28 he gave them over to a depraved *m*
       7: 25 I myself in my *m* am a slave
       8: 6 The *m* of sinful man is death,
       8: 7 the sinful *m* is hostile to God.
      12: 2 by the renewing of your *m*.
      14: 13 make up your *m* not
1Co   1: 10 you may be perfectly united in *m*
       2: 9 no *m* has conceived
      14: 14 spirit prays, but my *m* is unfruitful.
2Co   13: 11 be of one *m*, live in peace.
Php   3: 19 Their *m* is on earthly things.
Col   2: 18 and his unspiritual *m* puffs him up
1Th   4: 11 to *m* your own business
Heb   7: 21 and will not change his *m*:

MINDED* **(MIND)**

1Pe   4: 7 be clear *m* and self-controlled

MINDFUL* **(MIND)**

Ps   8: 4 what is man that you are *m* of him,
Lk   1: 48 God my Savior, for he has been *m*
Heb   2: 6 What is man that you are *m* of him,

MINDS (MIND)

Dt   11: 18 of mine in your hearts and *m*;
Ps   7: 9 who searches minds and hearts,
Jer   31: 33 "I will put my law in their *m*
Lk   24: 38 and why do doubts rise in your *m*?
      24: 45 Then he opened their *m*
Ro   8: 5 to the sinful nature have their *m* set
2Co   4: 4 god of this age has blinded the *m*
Eph   4: 23 new in the attitude of your *m*;
Col   3: 2 Set your *m* on things above,
Heb   8: 10 I will put my laws in their *m*
       8: 10 and I will write them on their *m*."
1Pe   1: 13 prepare your *m* for action;
Rev   2: 23 I am he who searches hearts and *m*,

MINISTER (MINISTERING MINISTERS MINISTRY)

Ps   101: 6 will *m* to me.
1Ti   4: 6 you will be a good *m*

MINISTERING (MINISTER)

Heb   1: 14 Are not all angels *m* spirits sent

MINISTERS (MINISTER)

2Co   3: 6 as *m* of a new covenant—

MINISTRY (MINISTER)

Ac   6: 4 to prayer and the *m* of the word."
Ro   11: 13 I make much of my *m*
2Co   4: 1 God's mercy we have this *m*,
       5: 18 gave us the *m* of reconciliation.
       6: 3 so that our *m* will not be
Gal   2: 8 who was at work in the *m* of Peter
2Ti   4: 5 discharge all the duties of your *m*.
Heb   8: 6 But the *m* Jesus has received is

MIRACLE* **(MIRACLES MIRACULOUS)**

Ex   7: 9 'Perform a *m*,' then say to Aaron,
Mk   9: 39 "No one who does a *m*
Lk   23: 8 hoped to see him perform some *m*.
Jn   7: 21 "I did one *m*, and you are all
Ac   4: 16 they have done an outstanding *m*,

MIRACLES* **(MIRACLE)**

1Ch   16: 12 his *m*, and the judgments he
Ne   9: 17 to remember the *m* you performed
Job   5: 9 *m* that cannot be counted.
       9: 10 *m* that cannot be counted.
Ps   77: 11 I will remember your *m* of long ago
      77: 14 You are the God who performs *m*;
      78: 12 He did *m* in the sight
     105: 5 his *m*, and the judgments he
     106: 7 they gave no thought to your *m*;
     106: 22 *m* in the land of Ham
Mt   7: 22 out demons and perform many *m*?'
      11: 20 most of his *m* had been performed,
      11: 21 If the *m* that were performed
      11: 23 If the *m* that were performed
      13: 58 And he did not do many *m* there
      24: 24 and perform great signs and *m*
Mk   6: 2 does *m*! Isn't this the carpenter?
       6: 5 He could not do any *m* there,
      13: 22 and *m* to deceive the elect—
Lk   10: 13 For if the *m* that were performed
      19: 37 for all the *m* they had seen:
Jn   7: 3 disciples may see the *m* you do.
      10: 25 *m* I do in my Father's name speak
      10: 32 "I have shown you many great *m*
      10: 38 do not believe me, believe the *m*,
      14: 11 the evidence of the *m* themselves.

Jn   15: 24 But now they have seen these *m*,
Ac   2: 22 accredited by God to you by *m*,
          8: 13 by the great signs and *m* he saw.
         19: 11 God did extraordinary *m*
Ro   15: 19 by the power of signs and *m*,
1Co   12: 28 third teachers, then workers of *m*,
         12: 12 and *m*— were done among you
2Co   12: 12 and *m*— were done among you
Gal   3: 5 work *m* among you because you
2Th   2: 9 in all kinds of counterfeit *m*,
Heb   2: 4 it by signs, wonders and various *m*,

MIRACULOUS (MIRACLE)

Dt   13: 1 and announces to you a *m* sign
Mt   12: 39 generation asks for a *m* sign!
         13: 54 this wisdom and these *m* powers?''
Jn   2: 11 This, the first of his *m* signs,
          2: 23 people saw the *m* signs he was
          3: 2 could perform the *m* signs you are
          4: 48 ''Unless you people see *m* signs
          7: 31 will he do more *m* signs
          9: 16 ''How can a sinner do such *m* signs
         12: 37 Jesus had done all these *m* signs
         20: 30 Jesus did many other *m* signs
Ac   2: 43 *m* signs were done by the apostles.
          5: 12 apostles performed many *m* signs
1Co   1: 22 Jews demand *m* signs and Greeks
         12: 10 to another *m* powers,

MIRE

Ps   40: 2 out of the mud and *m*;
Isa   57: 20 whose waves cast up *m* and mud.

MIRIAM

    Sister of Moses and Aaron (Nu 26:59). Led
dancing at Red Sea (Ex 15:20-21). Struck with
leprosy for criticizing Moses (Nu 12). Death (Nu
20:1).

MIRROR

1Co   13: 12 but a poor reflection as in a *m*;
Jas   1: 23 a man who looks at his face in a *m*

MISDEEDS*

Ps   99: 8 though you punished their *m*.
Ro   8: 13 put to death the *m* of the body,

MISERY

Ex   3: 7 ''I have indeed seen the *m*
Jdg   10: 16 he could bear Israel's *m* no longer.
Hos   5: 15 in their *m* they will earnestly seek
Ro   3: 16 ruin and *m* mark their ways,
Jas   5: 1 of the *m* that is coming upon you.

MISFORTUNE

Ob   : 12 brother in the day of his *m*,

MISLEAD (MISLED)

Isa   47: 10 wisdom and knowledge *m* you

MISLED (MISLEAD)

1Co   15: 33 Do not be *m*: ''Bad company

MISS (MISSES)

Pr   19: 2 nor to be hasty and *m* the way.

MISSES (MISS)

Heb   12: 15 See to it that no one *m* the grace

MIST

Hos   6: 4 Your love is like the morning *m*,
Jas   4: 14 You are a *m* that appears for a little

MISTREAT (MISTREATED)

Ex   22: 21 ''Do not *m* an alien or oppress him,
Eze   22: 29 and needy and *m* the alien,
Lk   6: 28 pray for those who *m* you.

MISTREATED (MISTREAT)

Eze   22: 7 *m* the fatherless and the widow.
Heb   11: 25 to be *m* along with the people
         11: 37 destitute, persecuted and *m*—
         13: 3 who are *m* as if you yourselves

MISUSE* (MISUSES)

Ex   20: 7 ''You shall not *m* the name
Dt   5: 11 ''You shall not *m* the name
Ps   139: 20 your adversaries *m* your name.

MISUSES* (MISUSE)

Ex   20: 7 anyone guiltless who *m* his name.
Dt   5: 11 anyone guiltless who *m* his name.

MIXED (MIXING)

Da   2: 41 even as you saw iron *m* with clay.

MIXING (MIXED)

Isa   5: 22 and champions at *m* drinks,

MOAB (MOABITESS)

Ge   19: 37 she named him *M*; he is the father
Dt   34: 6 He buried him in *M*, in the valley
Ru   1: 1 live for a while in the country of *M*.
Isa   15: 1 An oracle concerning *M*:
Jer   48: 16 ''The fall of *M* is at hand;
Am   2: 1 ''For three sins of *M*,

MOABITESS (MOAB)

Ru   1: 22 accompanied by Ruth the *M*.

MOAN

Ps   90: 9 we finish our years with a *m*.

MOCK (MOCKED MOCKER MOCKERS MOCKING MOCKS)

Ps   22: 7 All who see me *m* me;
        119: 51 The arrogant *m* me
Pr   1: 26 I will *m* when calamity overtakes
         14: 9 Fools *m* at making amends for sin,
Mk   10: 34 who will *m* him and spit on him,

MOCKED (MOCK)

Ps   89: 51 with which they have *m* every step
Mt   27: 29 knelt in front of him and *m* him.
         27: 41 of the law and the elders *m* him.
Gal   6: 7 not be deceived: God cannot be *m*.

MOCKER (MOCK)

Pr   9: 7 corrects a *m* invites insult;
          9: 12 if you are a *m*, you alone will suffer
         20: 1 Wine is a *m* and beer a brawler;
         22: 10 Drive out the *m*, and out goes strife

MOCKERS (MOCK)

Ps   1: 1 or sit in the seat of *m*.
Pr   29: 8 *M* stir up a city,

MOCKING (MOCK)

Isa   50: 6 face from *m* and spitting.

MOCKS (MOCK)

Pr   17: 5 He who *m* the poor shows
         30: 17 ''The eye that *m* a father,

MODEL*

Eze   28: 12 '' 'You were the *m* of perfection,
1Th   1: 7 And so you became a *m*
2Th   3: 9 to make ourselves a *m* for you

MODESTY*

1Co   12: 23 are treated with special *m*,

MOLDED*

Job   10: 9 Remember that you *m* me like clay

MOLDY

Jos   9: 5 of their food supply was dry and *m*.

MOLECH

Lev   20: 2 of his children to *M* must be put
1Ki   11: 33 and *M* the god of the Ammonites,

MOMENT (MOMENTARY)

Job   20: 5 the joy of the godless lasts but a *m*.
Ps   2: 12 for his wrath can flare up in a *m*.
         30: 5 For his anger lasts only a *m*,
Pr   12: 19 but a lying tongue lasts only a *m*.
Isa   54: 7 ''For a brief *m* I abandoned you,
         66: 8 or a nation be brought forth in a *m*?
Gal   2: 5 We did not give in to them for a *m*,

MOMENTARY* (MOMENT)

2Co   4: 17 and *m* troubles are achieving

MONEY

Pr   13: 11 Dishonest *m* dwindles away,
Ecc   5: 10 Whoever loves *m* never has *m*
Isa   55: 1 and you who have no *m*,
Mt   6: 24 You cannot serve both God and *M*.
         27: 5 Judas threw the *m* into the temple
Lk   3: 14 ''Don't extort *m* and don't accuse
          9: 3 no bread, no *m*, no extra tunic.
         16: 13 You cannot serve both God and *M*
Ac   5: 2 part of the *m* for himself,
1Co   16: 2 set aside a sum of *m* in keeping
1Ti   3: 3 not quarrelsome, not a lover of *m*.
          6: 10 For the love of *m* is a root
2Ti   3: 2 lovers of *m*, boastful, proud,
Heb   13: 5 free from the love of *m*
1Pe   5: 2 not greedy for *m*, but eager to serve

MONEYLENDER* (LEND)

Ex   22: 25 not be like a *m*; charge him no
Lk   7: 41 men owed money to a certain *m*.

MONTH (MONTHS)

Ex   12: 2 ''This *m* is to be for you the first
Eze   47: 12 Every *m* they will bear,
Rev   22: 2 of fruit, yielding its fruit every *m*.

MONTHS (MONTH)

Gal   4: 10 and *m* and seasons and years!
Rev   11: 2 trample on the holy city for 42 *m*.
         13: 5 his authority for forty-two *m*.

MOON

Jos   10: 13 and the *m* stopped,
Ps   8: 3 the *m* and the stars,
         74: 16 you established the sun and *m*.
         89: 37 be established forever like the *m*,
        104: 19 The *m* marks off the seasons,
        121: 6 nor the *m* by night.
        136: 9 the *m* and stars to govern the night;
        148: 3 Praise him, sun and *m*,
SS   6: 10 fair as the *m*, bright as the sun,
Joel   2: 31 and the *m* to blood
Hab   3: 11 and *m* stood still in the heavens
Mt   24: 29 and the *m* will not give its light;
Ac   2: 20 and the *m* to blood
1Co   15: 41 and another and the stars another;
Col   2: 16 a New *M* celebration or a Sabbath
Rev   6: 12 the whole *m* turned blood red,
         21: 23 city does not need the sun or the *m*

MORAL*

Jas   1: 21 rid of all *m* filth and the evil that is

MORDECAI

    Benjamite exile who raised Esther (Est 2:5-
15). Exposed plot to kill Xerxes (Est 2:19-23).
Refused to honor Haman (Est 3:1-6; 5:9-14).
Charged Esther to foil Haman's plot against the
Jews (Est 4). Xerxes forced Haman to honor
Mordecai (Est 6). Mordecai exalted (Est 8-10).
Established Purim (Est 9:18-32).

MORIAH

Ge   22: 2 and go to the region of *M*.
2Ch   3: 1 Lᴏʀᴅ in Jerusalem on Mount *M*,

MORNING

Ge   1: 5 and there was *m*— the first day.
Dt   28: 67 In the *m* you will say, ''If only it
2Sa   3: 4 he is like the light of *m* at sunrise
Ps   5: 3 In the *m*, O Lᴏʀᴅ,
Pr   27: 14 blesses his neighbor early in the *m*,
Isa   14: 12 O *m* star, son of the dawn!
La   3: 23 They are new every *m*;
2Pe   1: 19 and the *m* star rises in your hearts.
Rev   2: 28 I will also give him the *m* star.
         22: 16 of David, and the bright *M* Star.''

MORTAL

Ge   6: 3 for he is *m*, his days will be
Job   10: 4 Do you see as a *m* sees?
Ro   8: 11 also give life to your *m* bodies
1Co   15: 53 and the *m* with immortality.
2Co   5: 4 that what is *m* may be swallowed

MOSES

    Levite; brother of Aaron (Ex 6:20; 1Ch 6:3).
Put in basket into Nile; discovered and raised by
Pharaoh's daughter (Ex 2:1-10). Fled to Midian
after killing Egyptian (Ex 2:11-15). Married to
Zipporah, fathered Gershom (Ex 2:16-22).
    Called by the Lᴏʀᴅ to deliver Israel (Ex 3-4).
Pharaoh's resistance (Ex 5). Ten plagues (Ex
7-11). Passover and Exodus (Ex 12-13). Led
Israel through Red Sea (Ex 14). Song of deliverance (Ex 15:1-21). Brought water from rock (Ex
17:1-7). Raised hands to defeat Amalekites (Ex
17:8-16). Delegated judges (Ex 18; Dt 1:9-18).
    Received Law at Sinai (Ex 19-23; 25-31; Jn 1:
17). Announced Law to Israel (Ex 19-7-8; 24;
35). Broke tablets because of golden calf (Ex
32; Dt 9). Saw glory of the Lᴏʀᴅ (Ex 33-34).
Supervised building of tabernacle (Ex 36-40).
Set apart Aaron and priests (Lev 8-9). Numbered tribes (Nu 1-4; 26). Opposed by Aaron
and Miriam (Nu 12). Sent spies into Canaan (Nu
13). Announced forty years of wandering for failure to enter land (Nu 14). Opposed by Korah
(Nu 16). Forbidden to enter land for striking rock
(Nu 20:1-13; Dt 1:37). Lifted bronze snake for
healing (Nu 21:4-9; Jn 3:14). Final address to

Israel (Dt 1-33). Succeeded by Joshua (Nu 27: 12-23; Dt 34). Death (Dt 34:5-12).

"Law of Moses" (1Ki 2:3; Ezr 3:2; Mk 12:26; Lk 24:44). "Book of Moses" (2Ch 25:12; Ne 13: 1). "Song of Moses" (Ex 15:1-21; Rev 15:3). "Prayer of Moses" (Ps 90).

MOTH

Mt	6: 19	where m and rust destroy,

MOTHER (GRANDMOTHER MOTHER-IN-LAW MOTHER'S)

Ge	2: 24	and m and be united to his wife,
	3: 20	because she would become the m
Ex	20: 12	"Honor your father and your m
Lev	20: 9	" 'If anyone curses his father or m,
Dt	5: 16	"Honor your father and your m,
	21: 18	who does not obey his father and m
	27: 16	who dishonors his father or his m."
Jdg	5: 7	arose a m in Israel.
1Sa	2: 19	Each year his m made him a little
Ps	113: 9	as a happy m of children.
Pr	10: 1	but a foolish son grief to his m.
	23: 22	do not despise your m
	23: 25	May your father and m be glad;
	29: 15	a child left to himself disgraces his m.
	30: 17	that scorns obedience to a m,
	31: 1	an oracle his m taught him:
Isa	49: 15	"Can a m forget the baby
	66: 13	As a m comforts her child,
Jer	20: 17	with my m as my grave,
Mic	7: 6	a daughter rises up against her m,
Mt	10: 35	a daughter against her m,
	10: 37	or m more than me is not worthy
	12: 48	He replied to him, "Who is my m,
	15: 4	'Honor your father and m'
	19: 5	and m and be united to his wife,
	19: 19	honor your father and m,
Mk	7: 10	'Honor your father and your m,' and,
	10: 19	honor your father and m.' "
Lk	11: 27	"Blessed is the m who gave you
	12: 53	daughter and daughter against m,
	18: 20	honor your father and m.' "
Jn	19: 27	to the disciple, "Here is your m."
Gal	4: 26	is above is free, and she is our m.
Eph	5: 31	and m and be united to his wife,
	6: 2	"Honor your father and m"—
1Th	2: 7	like a m caring for her little
2Ti	1: 5	and in your m Eunice and,

MOTHER-IN-LAW (MOTHER)

Ru	2: 19	Ruth told her m about the one
Mt	10: 35	a daughter-in-law against her m—

MOTHER'S (MOTHER)

Job	1: 21	"Naked I came from my m womb,
Pr	1: 8	and do not forsake your m teaching
Ecc	5: 15	from his m womb,
	11: 5	the body is formed in a m womb,
Jn	3: 4	time into his m womb to be born!"

MOTIVE* (MOTIVES)

1Ch	28: 9	and understands every m

MOTIVES* (MOTIVE)

Pr	16: 2	but m are weighed by the LORD.
1Co	4: 5	will expose the m of men's hearts.
Php	1: 18	whether from false or m or true,
1Th	2: 3	springing from error or impure m,
Jas	4: 3	because you ask with wrong m.

MOUNT (MOUNTAIN MOUNTAINS MOUNTAINTOPS)

Ps	89: 9	when its waves m up, you still them
Isa	14: 13	enthroned on the m of assembly,
Eze	28: 14	You were on the holy m of God;
Zec	14: 4	stand on the M of Olives.

MOUNTAIN (MOUNT)

Ge	22: 14	"On the m of the LORD it will be
Ex	24: 18	And he stayed on the m forty days
Dt	5: 4	face to face out of the fire on the m.
Job	14: 18	"But as a m erodes and crumbles
Ps	48: 1	in the city of our God, his holy m.
Isa	40: 4	every m and hill made low;
Mic	4: 2	let us go up to the m of the LORD,
Mt	4: 8	the devil took him to a very high m
	17: 20	say to this m, 'Move from here
Mk	9: 2	with him and led them up a high m,
Lk	3: 5	every m and hill made low.
Jn	4: 21	the Father neither on this m
2Pe	1: 18	were with him on the sacred m.

MOUNTAINS (MOUNT)

Ps	36: 6	righteousness is like the mighty m,

Ps	46: 2	the m fall into the heart of the sea,
	90: 2	Before the m were born
Isa	52: 7	How beautiful on the m
	54: 10	Though the m be shaken
	55: 12	the m and hills
Eze	34: 6	My sheep wandered over all the m
Mt	24: 16	are in Judea flee to the m.
Lk	23: 30	they will say to the m, "Fall on us!"
1Co	13: 2	if I have a faith that can move m,
Rev	6: 16	They called to the m and the rocks,

MOUNTAINTOPS (MOUNT)

Isa	42: 11	let them shout from the m.

MOURN (MOURNING MOURNS)

Ecc	3: 4	a time to m and a time to dance.
Isa	61: 2	to comfort all who m,
Mt	5: 4	Blessed are those who m,
Ro	12: 15	m with those who m.

MOURNING (MOURN)

Isa	61: 3	instead of m,
Jer	31: 13	I will turn their m into gladness;
Rev	21: 4	There will be no more death or m

MOURNS (MOURN)

Zec	12: 10	as one m for an only child,

MOUTH (MOUTHS)

Nu	22: 38	only what God puts in my m."
Dt	8: 3	comes from the m of the LORD.
	18: 18	I will put my words in his m,
	30: 14	it is in your mouth and in your heart
Jos	1: 8	of the Law depart from your m;
2Ki	4: 34	m to m, eyes to eyes, hands
Ps	10: 7	His m is full of curses and lies
	17: 3	resolved that my m will not sin.
	19: 14	May the words of my m
	37: 30	mouth of the righteous man utters
	40: 3	He put a new song in my m,
	71: 8	My m is filled with your praise,
	119:103	sweeter than honey to my m!
	141: 3	Set a guard over my m, O LORD;
Pr	2: 6	and from his m come knowledge
	4: 24	Put away perversity from your m;
	10: 11	The m of the righteous is a fountain
	10: 31	m of the righteous brings forth
	16: 23	A wise man's heart guides his m,
	26: 28	and a flattering m works ruin.
	27: 2	praise you, and not your own m;
Ecc	5: 2	Do not be quick with your m,
SS	1: 2	with the kisses of his m—
	5: 16	His m is sweetness itself;
Isa	29: 13	come near to me with their m
	40: 5	For the m of the LORD has spoken
	45: 23	my m has uttered in all integrity
	51: 16	I have put my words in your m
	53: 7	so he did not open his m.
	55: 11	my word that goes out from my m:
	59: 21	m will not depart from your m,
Eze	3: 2	So I opened my m, and he gave me
Mal	2: 7	and from his m men should seek
Mt	4: 4	comes from the m of God.' "
	12: 34	overflow of the heart the m speaks.
	15: 11	into a man's m does not make him
	15: 18	out of the m come from the heart,
	6: 45	overflow of his heart his m speaks.
Lk	6: 45	overflow of his heart his m speaks.
Ro	10: 9	That if you confess with your m,
	15: 6	and m you may glorify the God
1Pe	2: 22	and no deceit was found in his m."
Rev	1: 16	and out of his m came a sharp
	2: 16	them with the sword of my m.
	3: 16	I am about to spit you out of my m
	19: 15	Out of his m comes a sharp sword

MOUTHS (MOUTH)

Ps	78: 36	would flatter him with their m,
Eze	33: 31	With their m they express devotion
Ro	3: 14	"Their m are full of cursing
Eph	4: 29	talk come out of your m,
Jas	3: 3	bits into the m of horses

MOVE (MOVED MOVES)

Dt	19: 14	Do not move your neighbor's
Pr	23: 10	Do not m an ancient boundary
Ac	17: 28	and m and have our being.'
1Co	13: 2	have a faith that can m mountains,
	15: 58	Let nothing m you.

MOVED (MOVE)

Ex	35: 21	and whose heart m him came
2Ch	36: 22	the LORD m the heart
Ezr	1: 5	everyone whose heart God had m
Ps	93: 1	it cannot be m
Jn	11: 33	he was deeply m in spirit

Col	1: 23	not m from the hope held out

MOVES (MOVE)

Dt	23: 14	For the LORD your God m about

MUD (MUDDIED)

Ps	40: 2	out of the m and mire;
Isa	57: 20	whose waves cast up mire and m.
Jn	9: 6	made some m with the saliva,
2Pe	2: 22	back to her wallowing in the m."

MUDDIED (MUD)

Pr	25: 26	Like a m spring or a polluted well
Eze	32: 13	or m by the hoofs of cattle.

MULBERRY*

Lk	17: 6	you can say to this m tree,

MULTITUDE (MULTITUDES)

Isa	31: 1	who trust in the m of their chariots
Jas	5: 20	and cover over a m of sins.
1Pe	4: 8	love covers over a m of sins.
Rev	7: 9	me was a great m that no one could
	19: 1	of a great m in heaven shouting:

MULTITUDES (MULTITUDE)

Ne	9: 6	and the m of heaven worship you.
Da	12: 2	M who sleep in the dust
Joel	3: 14	M, m in the valley of decision!

MURDER (MURDERED MURDERER MURDERERS)

Ex	20: 13	"You shall not m.
Dt	5: 17	"You shall not m.
Pr	28: 17	A man tormented by the guilt of m
Mt	5: 21	'Do not m, and anyone who
	15: 19	m, adultery, sexual immorality,
Ro	1: 29	m, strife, deceit and malice.
	13: 9	"Do not m," " 'Do not steal,'
Jas	2: 11	adultery," also said, "Do not m."

MURDERED (MURDER)

Mt	23: 31	of those who m the prophets.
Ac	7: 52	now you have betrayed and m him
1Jn	3: 12	to the evil one and m his brother.

MURDERER (MURDER)

Nu	35: 16	he is a m; the m shall be put
Jn	8: 44	He was a m from the beginning,
1Jn	3: 15	who hates his brother is a m,

MURDERERS (MURDER)

1Ti	1: 9	for m, for adulterers and perverts,
Rev	21: 8	the m, the sexually immoral,
	22: 15	the sexually immoral, the m,

MUSIC* (MUSICAL MUSICIAN MUSICIANS)

Ge	31: 27	singing to the m of tambourines
Jdg	5: 3	I will make m to the LORD,
1Ch	6: 31	put in charge of the m in the house
	6: 32	They ministered with m
	25: 6	fathers for the m of the temple
	25: 7	and skilled in m for the LORD—
Ne	12: 27	and with the m of cymbals,
Job	21: 12	They sing to the m of tambourine
Ps	27: 6	and make m to the LORD.
	33: 2	make m to him on the ten-stringed
	45: 8	the m of the strings makes you glad
	57: 7	I will sing and make m.
	81: 2	Begin the m, strike the tambourine,
	87: 7	As they make m they will sing.
	92: 1	and make m to your name,
	92: 3	to the m of the ten-stringed lyre
	95: 2	and extol him with m and song.
	98: 4	burst into jubilant song with m;
	98: 5	make m to the LORD
	108: 1	make m with all my soul.
	144: 9	the ten-stringed lyre I will make m
	147: 7	make m to our God on the harp.
	149: 3	make m to him with tambourine
Isa	30: 32	will be to the m of tambourines
La	5: 14	young men have stopped their m.
Eze	26: 13	m of your harps will be heard no
Da	3: 5	lyre, harp, pipes and all kinds of m,
	3: 7	and all kinds of m, all the peoples,
	3: 10	and all kinds of m must fall down
	3: 15	lyre, harp, pipes and all kinds of m,
Am	5: 23	to the m of your harps.
Hab	3: 19	For the director of m.
Lk	15: 25	came near the house, he heard m
Eph	5: 19	make m in your heart to the Lord,
Rev	18: 22	The m of harpists and musicians.

MUSICAL* (MUSIC)

1Ch	15: 16	accompanied by m instruments:

1Ch 23: 5 with the *m* instruments I have.
2Ch 7: 6 with the LORD's *m* instruments,
     23:13 with *m* instruments were leading
     34:12 skilled in playing *m* instruments—
Ne 12:36 with *m* instruments prescribed
Am 6: 5 and improvise on *m* instruments.

MUSICIAN* (MUSIC)

1Ch 6:33 Heman, the *m*, the son of Joel;

MUSICIANS* (MUSIC)

1Ki 10:12 to make harps and lyres for the *m*.
1Ch 9:33 Those who were *m*; heads
     15:19 The *m* Heman, Asaph
2Ch 5:12 All the Levites who were *m*—
     9:11 to make harps and lyres for the *m*,
     35:15 The *m*, the descendants of Asaph,
Ps 68:25 are the singers, after them the *m*;
Rev 18:22 The music of harpists and *m*,

MUSTARD

Mt 13:31 kingdom of heaven is like a *m* seed,
     17:20 you have faith as small as a *m* seed,
Mk 4:31 It is like a *m* seed, which is

MUTILATORS*

Php 3: 2 those men who do evil, those *m*

MUTUAL* (MUTUALLY)

Ro 14:19 leads to peace and to *m* edification.
1Co 7: 5 by *m* consent and for a time,

MUTUALLY* (MUTUAL)

Ro 1:12 and I may be *m* encouraged

MUZZLE*

Dt 25: 4 Do not *m* an ox while it is treading
Ps 39: 1 I will put a *m* on my mouth
1Co 9: 9 "Do not *m* an ox while it is
1Ti 5:18 "Do not *m* the ox while it is

MYRRH

Ps 45: 8 All your robes are fragrant with *m*
SS 1:13 My lover is to me a sachet of *m*
Mt 2:11 of gold and of incense and of *m*.
Mk 15:23 offered him wine mixed with *m*,
Jn 19:39 Nicodemus brought a mixture of *m*
Rev 18:13 of incense, *m* and frankincense.

MYSTERIES* (MYSTERY)

Job 11: 7 "Can you fathom the *m* of God?
Da 2:28 a God in heaven who reveals *m*.
     2:29 of *m* showed you what is going
     2:47 Lord of kings and a revealer of *m*,
1Co 13: 2 can fathom all *m* and all knowledge
     14: 2 he utters *m* with his spirit.

MYSTERY* (MYSTERIES)

Da 2:18 God of heaven concerning this *m*,
     2:19 the night the *m* was revealed
     2:27 to the king the *m* he has asked
     2:30 this *m* has been revealed to me,
     2:47 for you were able to reveal this *m*."
     4: 9 and no *m* is too difficult for you.
Ro 11:25 you to be ignorant of this *m*,
     16:25 to the revelation of the *m* hidden
1Co 15:51 I tell you a *m*: We will not all sleep,
Eph 1: 9 to us the *m* of his will according
     3: 3 the *m* made known to me
     3: 4 insight into the *m* of Christ,
     3: 6 This *m* is that through the gospel
     3: 9 the administration of this *m*,
     5:32 This is a profound *m*—
     6:19 I will fearlessly make known the *m*
Col 1:26 the *m* that has been kept hidden
     1:27 the glorious riches of this *m*,
     2: 2 in order that they may know the *m*
     4: 3 so that we may proclaim the *m*
1Ti 3:16 the *m* of godliness is great:
Rev 1:20 of the seven stars that you saw
     10: 7 the *m* of God will be accomplished,
     17: 5 written on her forehead: *M*
     17: 7 explain to you the *m* of the woman

MYTHS*

1Ti 1: 4 nor to devote themselves to *m*
     4: 7 Have nothing to do with godless *m*
2Ti 4: 4 from the truth and turn aside to *m*.
Tit 1:14 will pay no attention to Jewish *m*

NAAMAN

Aramean general whose leprosy was cleansed by Elisha (2Ki 5).

NABAL

Wealthy Carmelite the LORD killed for refusing to help David (1Sa 25). David married Abigail, his widow (1Sa 25:39-42).

NABOTH*

Jezreelite killed by Jezebel for his vineyard (1Ki 21). Ahab's family destroyed for this (1Ki 21:17-24; 2Ki 9:21-37).

NADAB

1. Firstborn of Aaron (Ex 6:23); killed with Abihu for offering unauthorized fire (Lev 10; Nu 3:4).

2. Son of Jeroboam I; king of Israel (1Ki 15: 25-32).

NAHUM

Prophet against Nineveh (Na 1:1).

NAIL* (NAILING)

Jn 20:25 "Unless I see the *n* marks

NAILING* (NAIL)

Ac 2:23 him to death by *n* him to the cross.
Col 2:14 he took it away, *n* it to the cross.

NAIVE

Ro 16:18 they deceive the minds of *n* people.

NAKED

Ge 2:25 The man and his wife were both *n*,
Job 1:21 *N* I came from my mother's womb,
Isa 58: 7 when you see the *n*, to clothe him,
2Co 5: 3 are clothed, we will not be found *n*.

NAME (NAMES)

Ge 2:19 man to see what he would *n* them;
     4:26 to call on the *n* of the LORD.
     11: 4 so that we may make a *n*
     12: 2 I will make your *n* great,
     32:29 Jacob said, "Please tell me your *n*."
Ex 3:15 This is my *n* forever, the *n*
     20: 7 "You shall not misuse the *n*
     34:14 for the LORD, whose *n* is Jealous,
Lev 24:11 Israelite woman blasphemed the *N*
Dt 5:11 "You shall not misuse the *n*
     12:11 choose as a dwelling for his *N*—
     18: 5 minister in the LORD's *n* always
     25: 6 carry on the *n* of the dead brother
     28:58 this glorious and awesome *n*—
Jos 7: 9 do for your own great *n*?"
Jdg 13:17 "What is your *n*, so that we may
1Sa 12:22 of his great *n* the LORD will not
2Sa 6: 2 which is called by the *N*, the name
     7: 9 Now I will make your *n* great.
1Ki 5: 5 I will build the temple for my *N*.'
     8:29 you said, 'My *N* shall be there,'
1Ch 17: 8 I will make your *n* like the names
2Ch 7:14 my people, who are called by my *n*,
Ne 9:10 You made a *n* for yourself,
Ps 8: 1 how majestic is your *n*
     9:10 Those who know your *n* will trust
     20: 7 in the *n* of the LORD our God.
     29: 2 to the LORD the glory due his *n*;
     34: 3 let us exalt his *n* together.
     44:20 If we had forgotten the *n*
     66: 2 Sing the glory of his *n*;
     68: 4 Sing to God, sing praise to his *n*,
     79: 9 for the glory of your *n*;
     96: 8 to the LORD the glory due his *n*;
     103: 1 my inmost being, praise his holy *n*.
     115: 1 but to your *n* be the glory,
     138: 2 your *n* and your word.
     145: 1 I will praise your *n* for ever
     147: 4 and calls them each by *n*.
Pr 3: 4 you will win favor and a good *n*
     18:10 *n* of the LORD is a strong tower;
     22: 1 A good *n* is more desirable
     30: 4 What is his *n*, and the *n* of his son?
Ecc 7: 1 A good *n* is better
SS 1: 3 your *n* is like perfume poured out.
Isa 12: 4 thanks to the LORD, call on his *n*;
     26: 8 your *n* and renown
     40:26 and calls them each by *n*.
     42: 8 "I am the LORD; that is my *n*!
     56: 5 I will give them an everlasting *n*
     57:15 who lives forever, whose *n* is holy:
     63:14 to make for yourself a glorious *n*.
Jer 14: 7 do something for the sake of your *n*,
     15:16 for I bear your *n*,
Eze 20: 9 of my *n* I did what would keep it
     20:14 of my *n* I did what would keep it
     20:22 of my *n* I did what would keep it

Da 12: 1 everyone whose *n* is found written
Hos 12: 5 the LORD is his *n* of renown!
Joel 2:32 on the *n* of the LORD will be saved
Mic 5: 4 in the majesty of the *n*
Zep 3: 9 call on the *n* of the LORD
Zec 6:12 is the man whose *n* is the Branch,
     14: 9 one LORD, and his *n* the only *n*.
Mal 1: 6 O priests, who show contempt for my *n*.
Mt 1:21 and you are to give him the *n* Jesus.
     6: 9 hallowed be your *n*,
     18:20 or three come together in my *n*,
     24: 5 For many will come in my *n*,
     28:19 them in the *n* of the Father
Mk 9:41 gives you a cup of water in my *n*
Lk 11: 2 hallowed be your *n*,
Jn 10: 3 He calls his own sheep by *n*
     14:13 I will do whatever you ask in my *n*,
     16:24 asked for anything in my *n*.
Ac 2:21 on the *n* of the Lord will be saved.'
     4:12 for there is no other *n*
Ro 10:13 "Everyone who calls on the *n*
Php 2: 9 him the *n* that is above every *n*,
     2:10 at the *n* of Jesus every knee should
Col 3:17 do it all in the *n* of the Lord Jesus,
Heb 1: 4 as the *n* he has inherited is superior
Jas 5:14 him with oil in the *n* of the Lord.
1Jn 5:13 believe in the *n* of the Son of God
Rev 2:17 stone with a new *n* written on it,
     3: 5 I will never blot out his *n*
     3:12 I will also write on him my new *n*.
     19:13 and his *n* is the Word of God.
     20:15 If anyone's *n* was not found written

NAMES (NAME)

Ex 28: 9 engrave on them the *n* of the sons
Lk 10:20 but rejoice that your *n* are written
Php 4: 3 whose *n* are in the book of life.
Heb 12:23 whose *n* are written in heaven.
Rev 21:27 but only those whose *n* are written

NAOMI

Wife of Elimelech, mother-in-law of Ruth (Ru 1:2, 4). Left Bethlehem for Moab during famine (Ru 1:1). Returned a widow, with Ruth (Ru 1: 6-22). Advised Ruth to seek marriage with Boaz (Ru 2:17-3:4). Cared for Ruth's son Obed (Ru 4: 13-17).

NAPHTALI

Son of Jacob by Bilhah (Ge 30:8; 35:25; 1Ch 2:2). Tribe of blessed (Ge 49:21; Dt 33:23), numbered (Nu 1:43; 26:50), allotted land (Jos 19: 32-39; Eze 48:3), failed to fully possess (Jdg 1: 33), supported Deborah (Jdg 4:10; 5:18), David (1Ch 12:34), 12,000 from (Rev 7:6).

NARROW

Mt 7:13 "Enter through the *n* gate.
     7:14 and *n* the road that leads to life,

NATHAN

Prophet and chronicler of Israel's history (1Ch 29:29; 2Ch 9:29). Announced the Davidic covenant (2Sa 7; 1Ch 17). Denounced David's sin with Bathsheba (2Sa 12). Supported Solomon (1Ki 1).

NATHANAEL*

Apostle (Jn 1:45-49; 21:2). Probably also called Bartholomew (Mt 10:3).

NATION (NATIONS)

Ge 12: 2 "I will make you into a great *n*
Ex 19: 6 a kingdom of priests and a holy *n*.'
Dt 4: 7 What other *n* is so great
Jos 5: 8 And after the whole *n* had been
2Sa 7:23 one *n* on earth that God went out
Ps 33:12 Blessed is the *n* whose God is
Pr 11:14 For lack of guidance a *n* falls,
     14:34 Righteousness exalts a *n*,
Isa 2: 4 *N* will not take up sword
     26: 2 that the righteous *n* may enter,
     60:12 For the *n* or kingdom that will not
     65: 1 To a *n* that did not call on my name
     66: 8 a *n* be brought forth in a moment?
Mic 4: 3 *N* will not take up sword
Mt 24: 7 *N* will rise against *n*,
Mk 13: 8 *N* will rise against *n*,
1Pe 2: 9 a royal priesthood, a holy *n*,
Rev 5: 9 and language and people and *n*.
     7: 9 from every *n*, tribe, people
     14: 6 to every *n*, tribe, language

NATIONS (NATION)

Ge	17: 4	You will be the father of many n.
	18:18	and on earth will be blessed
Ex	19: 5	of all n you will be my treasured
Lev	20:26	apart from the n to be my own.
Dt	7: 1	drives out before you many n—
	15: 6	You will rule over many n
Jdg	3: 1	These are the n the LORD left
2Ch	20: 6	rule over all the kingdoms of the n.
Ne	1: 8	I will scatter you among the n,
Ps	2: 1	Why do the n conspire
	2: 8	I will make the n your inheritance.
	9: 5	You have rebuked the n
	22:28	and he rules over the n.
	46:10	I will be exalted among the n,
	47: 8	God reigns over the n;
	66: 7	his eyes watch the n—
	67: 2	your salvation among all n.
	68:30	Scatter the n who delight in war.
	72:17	All n will be blessed through him,
	96: 3	Declare his glory among the n,
	99: 2	he is exalted over all the n.
	106: 35	but they mingled with the n
	110: 6	He will judge the n, heaping up
	113: 4	The LORD is exalted over all the n
Isa	2: 2	and all n will stream to it.
	11:10	the n will rally to him,
	12: 4	among the n what he has done,
	40:15	Surely the n are like a drop
	42: 1	and he will bring justice to the n.
	51: 4	justice will become a light to the n.
	52:15	so will he sprinkle many n,
	56: 7	a house of prayer for all n."
	60: 3	N will come to your light,
	66:18	and gather all n and tongues,
Jer	1: 5	you as a prophet to the n."
	3:17	and all n will gather in Jerusalem
	31:10	"Hear the word of the LORD, O n;
	33: 9	and honor before all n
	46:28	I completely destroy all the n
Eze	22: 4	you an object of scorn to the n
	34:13	I will bring them out from the n
	36:23	n will know that I am the LORD,
	37:22	and they will never again be two n
	39:21	I will display my glory among the n
Hos	7: 8	"Ephraim mixes with the n;
Joel	2:17	a byword among the n.
	3: 2	I will gather all n
Am	9:12	and all the n that bear my name,"
Zep	3: 8	I have decided to assemble the n,
Hag	2: 7	and the desired of all n will come,
Zec	8:13	an object of cursing among the n,
	8:23	n will take firm hold of one Jew
	9:10	he will proclaim peace to the n.
	14: 2	I will gather all the n to Jerusalem
Mt	12:18	he will proclaim justice to the n.
	24: 9	and you will be hated by all n
	24:14	whole world as a testimony to all n,
	25:32	All the n will be gathered
	28:19	and make disciples of all n,
Mk	11:17	a house of prayer for all n'?
Ac	4:25	" Why do the n rage
Ro	15:12	who will arise to rule over the n,
Gal	3: 8	All n will be blessed through you."
1Ti	3:16	was preached among the n,
Rev	5: 4	All n will come
	21:24	The n will walk by its light,
	22: 2	are for the healing of the n.

NATURAL (NATURE)

Ro	6:19	you are weak in your n selves.
1Co	15:44	If there is a n body, there is

NATURE (NATURAL)

Ro	1:20	his eternal power and divine n—
	7:18	lives in me, that is, in my sinful n.
	8: 4	do not live according to the sinful n
	8: 5	to the sinful n have their minds set
	8: 8	by the sinful n cannot please God.
	13:14	to gratify the desires of the sinful n.
Gal	5:13	freedom to indulge the sinful n;
	5:19	The acts of the sinful n are obvious:
	5:24	Jesus have crucified the sinful n
Php	2: 6	Who, being in very n God,
Col	3: 5	whatever belongs to your earthly n
2Pe	1: 4	you may participate in the divine n

NAZARENE* (NAZARETH)

Mt	2:23	prophets: "He will be called a N."
Mk	14:67	"You also were with that N, Jesus."
	16: 6	"You are looking for Jesus the N,
Ac	24: 5	He is a ringleader of the N sect and

NAZARETH (NAZARENE)

Mt	4:13	Leaving N, he went and lived
Lk	4:16	to N, where he had been brought
Jn	1:46	"N! Can anything good come

NAZIRITE

Nu	6: 2	of separation to the LORD as a N,
Jdg	13: 7	because the boy will be a N of God

NEBO

Dt	34: 1	Then Moses climbed Mount N

NEBUCHADNEZZAR

Babylonian king. Subdued and exiled Judah (2Ki 24-25; 2Ch 36; Jer 39). Dreams interpreted by Daniel (Da 2; 4). Worshiped God (Da 3:28-29; 4:34-37).

NECESSARY*

Ac	1:21	Therefore it is n to choose one
Ro	13: 5	it is n to submit to the authorities,
2Co	9: 5	I thought it n to urge the brothers
Php	1:24	it is more n for you that I remain
	2:25	But I think it is n to send back
Heb	8: 3	and so it was n for this one
	9:16	it is n to prove the death
	9:23	It was n, then, for the copies

NECK (STIFF-NECKED)

Pr	3:22	an ornament to grace your n.
	6:21	fasten them around your n.
Mt	18: 6	a large millstone hung around his n

NECO

Pharaoh who killed Josiah (2Ki 23:29-30; 2Ch 35:20-22), deposed Jehoahaz (2Ki 23:33-35; 2Ch 36:3-4).

NEED (NEEDS NEEDY)

1Ki	8:59	Israel according to each day's n.
Ps	79: 8	for we are in desperate n.
	116: 6	when I was in great n, he saved me.
	142: 6	for I am in desperate n,
Mt	6: 8	for your Father knows what you n
Lk	15:14	country, and he began to be in n.
Ac	2:45	they gave to anyone as he had n.
Ro	12:13	with God's people who are in n.
1Co	12:21	say to the hand, "I don't n you!"
Eph	4:28	something to share with those in n.
1Ti	5: 3	to those widows who are really in n
Heb	4:16	grace to help us in our time of n.
1Jn	3:17	sees his brother in n but has no pity

NEEDLE

Mt	19:24	go through the eye of a n

NEEDS (NEED)

Isa	58:11	he will satisfy your n
Php	2:25	sent to take care of my n.
	4:19	God will meet all your n according
Jas	2:16	does nothing about his physical n,

NEEDY (NEED)

Dt	15:11	toward the poor and n in your land.
1Sa	2: 8	and lifts the n from the ash heap;
Ps	35:10	and n from those who rob them."
	69:33	The LORD hears the n
	72:12	he will deliver the n who cry out,
	140: 12	and upholds the cause of the n.
Pr	14:21	blessed is he who is kind to the n.
	14:31	to the n honors God.
	22:22	and do not crush the n in court,
	31: 9	defend the rights of the poor and n
	31:20	and extends her hands to the n.
Mt	6: 2	"So when you give to the n,

NEGLECT* (NEGLECTED)

Dt	12:19	Be careful not to n the Levites
	14:27	And do not n the Levites living
Ezr	4:22	Be careful not to n this matter.
Ne	10:39	We will not n the house of our God
Est	6:10	Do not n anything you have
Ps	119: 16	I will not n your word.
Lk	11:42	you n justice and the love of God.
Ac	6: 2	for us to n the ministry of the word
1Ti	4:14	Do not n your gift, which was

NEGLECTED (NEGLECT)

Mt	23:23	But you have n the more important

NEHEMIAH

Cupbearer of Artaxerxes (Ne 2:1), governor of Israel (Ne 8:9). Returned to Jerusalem to re-build walls (Ne 2-6). With Ezra, reestablished worship (Ne 8). Prayer confessing nation's sin (Ne 9). Dedicated wall (Ne 12).

NEIGHBOR (NEIGHBOR'S)

Ex	20:16	give false testimony against your n
	20:17	or anything that belongs to your n
Lev	19:13	Do not defraud your n or rob him.
	19:17	Rebuke your n frankly
	19:18	but love your n as yourself.
Ps	15: 3	who does his n no wrong
Pr	3:29	Do not plot harm against your n,
	11:12	who lacks judgment derides his n,
	14:21	He who despises his n sins,
	16:29	A violent man entices his n
	24:28	against your n without cause,
	25:18	gives false testimony against his n.
	27:10	better a n nearby than a brother far
	27:14	If a man loudly blesses his n
	29: 5	Whoever flatters his n
Jer	31:34	No longer will a man teach his n,
Zec	8:17	do not plot evil against your n,
Mt	5:43	Love your n and hate your enemy.'
	19:19	and 'love your n as yourself."
Mk	12:31	The second is this: 'Love your n
Lk	10:27	and, 'Love your n as yourself.' "
	10:29	who is my n?" In reply Jesus said:
Ro	13: 9	"Love your n as yourself."
	13:10	Love does no harm to its n.
	15: 2	Each of us should please his n
Gal	5:14	"Love your n as yourself."
Eph	4:25	and speak truthfully to his n,
Heb	8:11	No longer will a man teach his n,
Jas	2: 8	"Love your n as yourself,"

NEIGHBOR'S (NEIGHBOR)

Ex	20:17	You shall not covet your n wife,
Dt	5:21	not set your desire on your n house
	19:14	not move your n boundary stone
	27:17	who moves his n boundary stone."
Pr	25:17	Seldom set foot in your n house—

NESTS

Mt	8:20	and birds of the air have n,

NET (NETS)

Pr	1:17	How useless to spread a n
Hab	1:15	he catches them in his n,
Mt	13:47	of heaven is like a n that was let
Jn	21: 6	"Throw your n on the right side

NETS (NET)

Ps	141: 10	Let the wicked fall into their own n
Mt	4:20	At once they left their n
Lk	5: 4	and let down the n for a catch."

NEVER-FAILING*

Am	5:24	righteousness like a n stream!

NEW

Ps	40: 3	He put a n song in my mouth,
	98: 1	Sing to the LORD a n song,
Ecc	1: 9	there is nothing n under the sun.
Isa	42: 9	and n things I declare;
	62: 2	you will be called by a n name
	65:17	n heavens and a n earth.
	66:22	"As the n heavens and the n earth
Jer	31:31	"when I will make a n covenant
La	3:23	They are n every morning;
Eze	11:19	undivided heart and put a n spirit
	18:31	and get a n heart and a n spirit.
	36:26	give you a n heart and put a n spirit
Zep	3: 5	and every n day he does not fail,
Mt	9:17	Neither do men pour n wine
Mk	16:17	they will speak in n tongues;
Lk	5:39	after drinking old wine wants the n
	22:20	"This cup is the n covenant
Jn	13:34	"A n commandment I give you:
Ac	5:20	the full message of this n life."
Ro	6: 4	the Father, we too may live a n life.
1Co	5: 7	old yeast that you may be a n batch
	11:25	"This cup is the n covenant
2Co	3: 6	as ministers of a n covenant—
	5:17	he is a n creation; the old has gone,
Gal	6:15	what counts is a n creation.
Eph	4:23	to be made n in the attitude
	4:24	and to put on the n self, created
Col	3:10	and have put on the n self,
Heb	8: 8	when I will make a n covenant
	9:15	is the mediator of a n covenant,
	10:20	by a n and living way opened for us
	12:24	Jesus the mediator of a n covenant,
1Pe	1: 3	great mercy he has given us n birth
2Pe	3:13	to a n heaven and a n earth,
1Jn	2: 8	Yet I am writing you a n command,
Rev	2:17	stone with a n name written on it;

Rev　3:12 the *n* Jerusalem, which is coming
　　21:　1 I saw a *n* heaven and a *n* earth,

NEWBORN (BEAR)

1Pe　2:　2 Like *n* babies, crave pure spiritual

NEWS

2Ki　7:　9 This is a day of good *n*
Ps 112:　7 He will have no fear of bad *n*;
Pr　15:30 good *n* gives health to the bones.
　　25:25 is good *n* from a distant land
Isa　52:　7 the feet of those who bring good *n*,
　　61:　1 me to preach good *n* to the poor.
Na　1:15 the feet of one who brings good *n*,
Mt　4:23 preaching the good *n*
　　9:35 preaching the good *n*
　　11:　5 the good *n* is preached to the poor.
Mk　1:15 Repent and believe the good *n*!"
　　16:15 preach the good *n* to all creation.
Lk　1:19 and to tell you this good *n*.
　　2:10 I bring you good *n*
　　3:18 and preached the good *n* to them.
　　4:43 "I must preach the good *n*
　　8:　1 proclaiming the good *n*
　　16:16 the good *n* of the kingdom
Ac　5:42 proclaiming the good *n* that Jesus
　　10:36 telling the good *n* of peace
　　14:　7 continued to preach the good *n*.
　　14:21 They preached the good *n*
　　17:18 preaching the good *n* about Jesus
Ro　10:15 feet of those who bring good *n*!"

NICODEMUS*

Pharisee who visted Jesus at night (Jn 3).
Argued fair treatment of Jesus (Jn 7:50-52). With
Joseph, prepared Jesus for burial (Jn 19:38-42).

NIGHT (NIGHTS NIGHTTIME)

Ge　1:　5 and the darkness he called "*n*."
　　1:16 and the lesser light to govern the *n*.
Ex　13:21 and by *n* in a pillar of fire
　　14:24 During the last watch of the *n*.
Dt　28:66 filled with dread both *n* and day,
Jos　1:　8 and *n*, so that you may be careful
Job　35:10 who gives songs in the *n*,
Ps　1:　2 on his law he meditates day and *n*.
　　19:　2 *n* after *n* they display knowledge.
　　42:　8 at *n* his song is with me—
　　63:　6 of you through the watches of the *n*
　　77:　6 I remembered my songs in the *n*.
　　90:　4 or like a watch in the *n*.
　　91:　5 You will not fear the terror of *n*,
　119:148 through the watches of the *n*,
　121:　6 nor the moon by *n*.
　136:　9 the moon and stars to govern the *n*;
Pr　31:18 her lamp does not go out at *n*.
Isa　21:11 Watchman, what is left of the *n*?"
　　58:10 and your *n* will become like
Jer　33:20 and my covenant with the *n*,
Lk　2:　8 watch over their flocks at *n*,
　　6:12 and spent the *n* praying to God.
Jn　3:　2 He came to Jesus at *n* and said,
　　9:　4 *N* is coming, when no one can work
1Th　5:　2 Lord will come like a thief in the *n*.
　　5:　5 We do not belong to the *n*
Rev 21:25 for there will be no *n* there.

NIGHTS (NIGHT)

Jnh　1:17 the fish three days and three *n*.
Mt　4:　2 After fasting forty days and forty *n*
　　12:40 three *n* in the belly of a huge fish,
2Co　6:　5 in hard work, sleepless *n*

NIGHTTIME* (NIGHT)

Zec　14:　7 or *n*—a day known to the LORD.

NIMROD

Ge　10:　9 "Like *N*, a mighty hunter

NINEVEH

Jnh　1:　2 "Go to the great city of *N*
Na　1:　1 An oracle concerning *N*.
Mt　12:41 The men of *N* will stand up

NOAH

Righteous man (Eze 14:14, 20) called to build
ark (Ge 6-8; Heb 11:7; 1Pe 3:20; 2Pe 2:5). God's
covenant with (Ge 9:1-17). Drunkenness of (Ge
9:18-23). Blessed sons, cursed Canaan (Ge 9:
24-27).

NOBLE

Ru　3:11 you are a woman of *n* character.
Ps　45:　1 My heart is stirred by a *n* theme
Pr　12:　4 of *n* character is her husband's

Pr　31:10 A wife of *n* character who can find?
　　31:29 "Many women do *n* things,
Isa　32:　8 But the *n* man makes *n* plans,
Lk　8:15 good soil stands for those with a *n*
Ro　9:21 of clay some pottery for *n* purposes
Php　4:　8 whatever is *n*, whatever is right,
2Ti　2:20 some are for *n* purposes

NOSTRILS

Ge　2:　7 and breathed into his *n* the breath
Ex　15:　8 By the blast of your *n*
Ps　18:15 at the blast of breath from your *n*.

NOTE

Ac　4:13 and they took *n* that these men had
Php　3:17 take *n* of those who live according

NOTHING

2Sa　24:24 offerings that cost me *n*."
Ne　9:21 in the desert; they lacked *n*.
Ps　73:25 earth has *n* I desire besides you
Jer　32:17 *N* is too hard for you
Jn　15:　5 apart from me you can do *n*.

NOURISH

Pr　10:21 The lips of the righteous *n* many,

NULLIFY

Mt　15:　6 Thus you *n* the word of God
Ro　3:31 Do we, then, *n* the law by this faith

OATH

Ex　33:　1 up to the land I promised on *o*
Nu　30:　2 or takes an *o* to obligate himself
Dt　6:18 promised on *o* to your forefathers,
　　7:　8 and kept the *o* he swore
　　29:12 you this day and sealing with an *o*,
Ps　95:11 So I declared on *o* in my anger,
　119:106 I have taken an *o* and confirmed it,
　132:11 The LORD swore an *o* to David,
Ecc　8:　2 because you took an *o* before God.
Mt　5:33 'Do not break your *o*, but keep
Heb　7:20 And it was not without an *o*!

OBADIAH

1. Believer who sheltered 100 prophets from
Jezebel (1Ki 18:1-16).
2. Prophet against Edom (Ob 1).

OBEDIENCE* (OBEY)

Ge　49:10 and the *o* of the nations is his.
Jdg　2:17 of *o* to the LORD's commands.
1Ch　21:19 So David went up in *o*
2Ch　31:21 in *o* to the law and the commands,
Pr　30:17 that scorns *o* to a mother,
Lk　23:56 Sabbath in *o* to the commandment.
Ac　21:24 but that you yourself are living in *o*
Ro　1:　5 to the *o* that comes from faith.
　　5:19 also through the *o* of the one man
　　6:16 to *o*, which leads to righteousness?
　　16:19 Everyone has heard about your *o*,
2Co　9:13 for the *o* that accompanies your
　　10:　6 once your *o* is complete.
Phm　:21 Confident of your *o*, I write to you,
Heb　5:　8 he learned *o* from what he suffered
1Pe　1:　2 for *o* to Jesus Christ and sprinkling
2Jn　:　6 that we walk in *o* to his commands.

OBEDIENT* (OBEY)

Dt　30:17 heart turns away and you are not *o*,
Isa　1:19 If you are willing and *o*,
Lk　2:51 with them and was *o* to them.
Ac　6:　7 of priests became *o* to the faith.
2Co　2:　9 if you would stand the test and be *o*.
　　7:15 he remembers that you were all *o*,
　　10:　5 thought to make it *o* to Christ.
Php　2:　8 and became *o* to death—
Tit　3:　1 to be *o*, to be ready
1Pe　1:14 As *o* children, do not conform

OBEY (OBEDIENCE OBEDIENT OBEYED OBEYING OBEYS)

Ex　12:24 "*O* these instructions as a lasting
　　19:　5 Now if you *o* me fully and keep my
　　24:　7 the LORD has said; we will *o*."
Lev　18:　4 You must *o* my laws and be careful
　　25:18 and be careful to *o* my laws,
Nu　15:40 remember to *o* all my commands
Dt　5:27 We will listen and *o*."
　　6:　3 careful to *o* so that it may go well
　　6:24 us to *o* all these decrees
　　11:13 if you faithfully *o* the commands I
　　12:28 to *o* all these regulations I am
　　13:　4 Keep his commands and *o* him;
　　21:18 son who does not *o* his father

Dt　28:　1 If you fully *o* the LORD your God
　　28:15 if you do not *o* the LORD your
　　30:　2 and *o* him with all your heart
　　30:10 if you *o* the LORD your God
　　30:14 and in your heart so you may *o* it.
　　32:46 children to *o* carefully all the words
Jos　1:　7 to *o* all the law my servant Moses
　　22:　5 in all his ways, to *o* his commands,
　　24:24 the LORD our God and *o* him."
1Sa　15:22 To *o* is better than sacrifice,
1Ki　8:61 by his decrees and *o* his commands
2Ki　17:13 that I commanded your fathers to *o*
2Ch　34:31 and to *o* the words of the covenant
Ne　1:　5 who love him and *o* his commands.
Ps　103:18 and remember to *o* his precepts.
　　103:20 who *o* his word.
　　119:17 I will *o* your word.
　　119:34 and *o* it with all my heart.
　　119:57 I have promised to *o* your words.
　　119:67 but now I *o* your word.
　　119:100 for I *o* your precepts.
　　119:129 therefore I *o* them.
　　119:167 I *o* your statutes,
Pr　5:13 I would not *o* my teachers
Jer　7:23 I gave them this command: *O* me,
　　11:　4 '*O* me and do everything I
　　11:　7 and again, saying, "*O* me."
　　42:　6 we will *o* the LORD our God,
Da　9:　4 who love him and *o* his commands,
Mt　8:27 the winds and the waves *o* him!"
　　19:17 to enter life, *o* the commandments
　　28:20 to *o* everything I have commanded
Lk　11:28 hear the word of God and *o* it."
Jn　14:15 you will *o* what I command.
　　14:23 loves me, he will *o* my teaching.
　　14:24 not love me will not *o* my teaching.
　　15:10 If you *o* my commands, you will
Ac　5:29 "We must *o* God rather than men!
　　5:32 given to those who *o* him."
Ro　2:13 it is those who *o* the law who will
　　6:12 body so that you *o* its evil desires.
　　6:16 slaves to the one whom you *o*—
　　6:16 yourselves to someone to *o* him
　　15:18 in leading the Gentiles to *o* God
　　16:26 nations might believe and *o* him—
Gal　5:　3 obligated to *o* the whole law.
Eph　6:　1 *o* your parents in the Lord,
　　6:　5 *o* your earthly masters with respect
Col　3:20 *o* your parents in everything,
　　3:22 *o* your earthly masters
2Th　3:14 anyone does not *o* our instruction
1Ti　3:　4 and see that his children *o* him
Heb　5:　9 eternal salvation for all who *o* him
　　13:17 *O* your leaders and submit
1Pe　4:17 for those who do not *o* the gospel
1Jn　3:24 Those who *o* his commands live
　　5:　3 love for God: to *o* his commands.
Rev 12:17 those who *o* God's commandments
　　14:12 the saints who *o* God's

OBEYED (OBEY)

Ge　22:18 blessed, because you have *o* me."
Jos　1:17 we fully *o* Moses, so we will *o* you
Ps　119:　4 that are to be fully *o*.
Da　9:10 we have not *o* the LORD our God
Jnh　3:　3 Jonah *o* the word of the LORD
Mic　5:15 the nations that have not *o* me."
Jn　15:10 as I have *o* my Father's commands
　　15:20 If they *o* my teaching, they will
　　17:　6 and they have *o* your word.
Ac　7:53 through angels but have not *o* it."
Ro　6:17 you wholeheartedly *o* the form
Php　2:12 as you have always *o*—not only
Heb　11:　8 *o* and went, even though he did not
1Pe　3:　6 who *o* Abraham and called him her

OBEYING (OBEY)

1Sa　15:22 as in *o* the voice of the LORD?
Ps　119:　5 steadfast in *o* your decrees!
Gal　5:　7 and kept you from *o* the truth?
1Pe　1:22 purified yourselves by *o* the truth

OBEYS (OBEY)

Lev　18:　5 for the man who *o* them will live
Pr　19:16 He who *o* instructions guards his
Eze　20:11 for the man who *o* them will live
Jn　14:21 has my commands and *o* them,
Ro　2:27 and yet the law will condemn you
1Jn　2:　5 if anyone *o* his word, God's love is

OBLIGATED (OBLIGATION)

Ro　1:14 I am *o* both to Greeks
Gal　5:　3 himself be circumcised that he is *o*

OBLIGATION (OBLIGATED)
Ro   8:12 Therefore, brothers, we have an *o*

OBSCENITY*
Eph   5: 4 Nor should there be *o*, foolish talk

OBSCURES*
Job 42: 3 'Who is this that *o* my counsel

OBSERVE (OBSERVING)
Ex   31:13 'You must *o* my Sabbaths.
Lev 25: 2 the land itself must *o* a sabbath
Dt   4: 6 *O* them carefully, for this will show
      5:12 "*O* the Sabbath day
      8: 6 the commands of the LORD
     11:22 If you carefully *o* all these
     26:16 carefully *o* them with all your heart
Ps   37:37 the blameless, the upright;

OBSERVING (OBSERVE)
Ro   3:27 principle? On that of *o* the law?
Gal   2:16 a man is not justified by *o* the law,
      3: 2 you receive the Spirit by *o* the law,
      3:10 All who rely on *o* the law are

OBSOLETE
Heb   8:13 he has made the first one *o*;

OBSTACLE* (OBSTACLES)
Ro   14:13 or *o* in your brother's way.

OBSTACLES (OBSTACLE)
Ro   16:17 put in your way that are contrary

OBSTINATE
Isa 65: 2 hands to an *o* people,
Ro   10:21 to a disobedient and *o* people."

OBTAIN (OBTAINED OBTAINS)
Ro   11: 7 sought so earnestly it did not *o*.
2Ti   2:10 they too may *o* the salvation that

OBTAINED (OBTAIN)
Ro   9:30 not pursue righteousness, have *o* it,
Php   3:12 Not that I have already *o* all this,
Heb   9:12 having *o* eternal redemption.

OBTAINS* (OBTAIN)
Pr   12: 2 A good man *o* favor

OBVIOUS*
Mt   6:18 so that it will not be *o*
Gal   5:19 The acts of the sinful nature are *o*:
1Ti   5:24 The sins of some men are *o*,
      5:25 In the same way, good deeds are *o*,

OCCASIONS
Eph   6:18 in the Spirit on all *o* with all kinds

OFFENDED (OFFENSE)
Pr   18:19 An *o* brother is more unyielding

OFFENDERS* (OFFENSE)
1Co   6: 9 nor homosexual *o* nor thieves

OFFENSE (OFFENDED OFFENDERS OFFENSES OFFENSIVE)
Pr   17: 9 over an *o* promotes love,
     19:11 it is to his glory to overlook an *o*.
Gal   5:11 In that case the *o* of the cross has

OFFENSES (OFFENSE)
Isa 44:22 swept away your *o* like a cloud,
     59:12 For our *o* are many in your sight,
Eze 18:30 Repent! Turn away from all your *o*;
     33:10 "Our *o* and sins weigh us down,

OFFENSIVE (OFFENSE)
Ps 139:24 See if there is any *o* way in me.

OFFER (OFFERED OFFERING OFFERINGS OFFERS)
Ps   4: 5 *O* right sacrifices
Ro   6:13 Do not *o* the parts of your body
     12: 1 to *o* your bodies as living sacrifices,
Heb   9:25 he enter heaven to *o* himself again
     13:15 therefore, let us continually *o*

OFFERED (OFFER)
Isa 50: 6 I *o* my back to those who beat me,
1Co   8:13 share in what is *o* on the altar?
     10:20 of pagans are *o* to demons.
Heb   7:27 once for all when he *o* himself.
      9:14 the eternal Spirit *o* himself

OFFERING (OFFER)
Ge   4: 3 of the soil as an *o* to the LORD.
     22: 2 a burnt *o* on one of the mountains I
     22: 8 provide the lamb for the burnt *o*,
Ex   29:24 before the LORD as a wave *o*
     29:40 quarter of a hin of wine as a drink *o*.
Lev   1: 3 If the *o* is a burnt *o* from the herd,
      2: 4 " 'If you bring a grain *o* baked
      3: 1 " 'If someone's *o* is a fellowship *o*,
      4: 3 a sin *o* for the sin he has committed
      5:15 It is a guilt *o*.
      7:37 ordination *o* and the fellowship *o*,
      9:24 and consumed the burnt *o*
     22:18 to fulfill a vow or as a freewill *o*,
     22:21 a special vow or as a freewill *o*,
1Sa 13: 9 And Saul offered up the burnt *o*.
1Ch 21:26 from heaven on the altar of burnt *o*.
2Ch   7: 1 and consumed the burnt *o*
Ps   40: 6 Sacrifice and *o* you did not desire,
    116:17 I will sacrifice a thank *o* to you
Isa 53:10 the LORD makes his life a guilt *o*,
Mt   5:23 if you are *o* your gift at the altar
Ro   8: 3 likeness of sinful man to be a sin *o*.
Eph   5: 2 as a fragrant *o* and sacrifice to God
Php   2:17 I am being poured out like a drink *o*
      4:18 are a fragrant *o*, an acceptable
2Ti   4: 6 being poured out like a drink *o*,
Heb 10: 5 "Sacrifice and *o* you did not desire,
1Pe   2: 5 *o* spiritual sacrifices acceptable

OFFERINGS (OFFER)
1Sa 15:22 Does the LORD delight in burnt *o*
2Ch 35: 7 and goats for the Passover *o*,
Isa   1:13 Stop bringing meaningless *o*!
Hos   6: 6 of God rather than burnt *o*.
Mal   3: 8 do we rob you?' "In tithes and *o*.
Mk   12:33 is more important than all burnt *o*
Heb 10: 8 First he said, "Sacrifices and *o*,

OFFERS (OFFER)
Heb 10:11 and again he *o* the same sacrifices,

OFFICER (OFFICIALS)
2Ti   2: 4 wants to please his commanding *o*.

OFFICIALS (OFFICER)
Ex   5:21 a stench to Pharaoh and his *o*.
Pr   17:26 or to flog *o* for their integrity.
     29:12 all his *o* become wicked.

OFFSPRING
Ge   3:15 and between your *o* and hers;
     12: 7 "To your *o* I will give this land."
     13:16 I will make your *o* like the dust
     26: 4 and through your *o* all nations
     28:14 blessed through you and your *o*.
Ex   13: 2 The first *o* of every womb
Ru   4:12 Through the *o* the LORD gives
Isa 44: 3 I will pour out my Spirit on your *o*,
     53:10 he will see his *o* and prolong his
Ac   3:25 'Through your *o* all peoples
     17:28 own poets have said, 'We are his *o*.'
     17:29 "Therefore since we are God's *o*,
Ro   4:18 said to him, "So shall your *o* be."
      9: 8 who are regarded as Abraham's *o*.

OG
Nu   21:33 *O* king of Bashan and his whole
Ps 136:20 and *O* king of Bashan—

OIL
Ex   29: 7 Take the anointing *o* and anoint
     30:25 It will be the sacred anointing *o*.
Dt   14:23 tithe of your grain, new wine and *o*,
1Sa 10: 1 Then Samuel took a flask of *o*
     16:13 So Samuel took the horn of *o*
1Ki 17:16 and the jug of *o* did not run dry,
2Ki   4: 6 Then the *o* stopped flowing.
Ps   23: 5 You anoint my head with *o*;
     45: 7 by anointing you with the *o* of joy.
    104:15 *o* to make his face shine,
    133: 2 It is like precious *o* poured
Pr   21:17 loves wine and *o* will never be
Isa   1: 6 or soothed with *o*.
     61: 3 the *o* of gladness
Mt   25: 3 but did not take any *o* with them.
Heb   1: 9 by anointing you with the *o* of joy."

OLIVE (OLIVES)
Ge   8:11 beak was a freshly plucked *o* leaf!
Jdg   9: 8 said to the *o* tree, 'Be our king.'

OLIVES (OLIVE)
Heb 11: 4 By faith Abel *o* God a better
     11:17 when God tested him, *o* Isaac
Jas   5:15 prayer *o* in faith will make the sick

Jer 11:16 LORD called you a thriving *o* tree
Zec   4: 3 Also there are two *o* trees by it,
Ro   11:17 and you, though a wild *o* shoot,
     11:24 of an *o* tree that is wild by nature,
Rev 11: 4 These are the two *o* trees

OLIVES (OLIVE)
Zec 14: 4 stand on the Mount of *O*,
Mt   24: 3 sitting on the Mount of *O*,
Jas   3:12 a fig tree bear *o*, or a grapevine bear

OMEGA*
Rev   1: 8 "I am the Alpha and the *O*,"
      21: 6 I am the Alpha and the *O*,
     22:13 I am the Alpha and the *O*,

OMIT*
Jer 26: 2 I command you; do not *o* a word.

OMRI
    King of Israel (1Ki 16:21-26).

ONESIMUS*
Col   4: 9 He is coming with *O*, our faithful
Phm   :10 I appeal to you for my son *O*,

ONESIPHORUS*
2Ti   1:16 mercy to the household of *O*,
      4:19 Aquila and the household of *O*.

ONIONS*
Nu   11: 5 melons, leeks, *o* and garlic.

ONYX
Ex   28: 9 "Take two *o* stones and engrave
     28:20 in the fourth row a chrysolite, an *o*

OPENHANDED* (HAND)
Dt   15: 8 Rather be *o* and freely lend him
     15:11 you to be *o* toward your brothers

OPINIONS*
1Ki 18:21 will you waver between two *o*?
Pr   18: 2 but delights in airing his own *o*.

OPPONENTS (OPPOSE)
Pr   18:18 and keeps strong *o* apart.

OPPORTUNE (OPPORTUNITY)
Lk   4:13 he left him until an *o* time.

OPPORTUNITY* (OPPORTUNE)
1Sa 18:21 "Now you have a second *o*
Jer 46:17 he has missed his *o*.'
Mt   26:16 watched for an *o* to hand him over.
Mk   14:11 So he watched for an *o* to hand him
Lk   22: 6 and watched for an *o* to hand Jesus
Ac   25:16 and has had an *o* to defend himself
Ro   7: 8 seizing the *o* afforded
      7:11 seizing the *o* afforded
1Co 16:12 but he will go when he has the *o*.
2Co   5:12 are giving you an *o* to take pride
     11:12 from under those who want an *o*
Gal   6:10 as we have *o*, let us do good
Eph   5:16 making the most of every *o*,
Php   4:10 but you had no *o* to show it.
Col   4: 5 make the most of every *o*
1Ti   5:14 to give the enemy no *o* for slander.
Heb 11:15 they would have had *o* to return.

OPPOSE (OPPONENTS OPPOSED OPPOSES OPPOSING OPPOSITION)
Ex   23:22 and will *o* those who *o* you.
1Sa   2:10 those who *o* the LORD will be
Job 33:13 he stands alone, and who can *o* him
Ac   11:17 I to think that I could *o* God?"
2Ti   2:25 Those who *o* him he must gently
Tit   1: 9 doctrine and refute those who *o* it.
      2: 8 so that those who *o* you may be

OPPOSED (OPPOSE)
Gal   2:11 to Antioch, I *o* him to his face,
      3:21 therefore, *o* to the promises of God

OPPOSES (OPPOSE)
Jas   4: 6 "God *o* the proud
1Pe   5: 5 because, "God *o* the proud

OPPOSING (OPPOSE)
1Ti   6:20 the *o* ideas of what is falsely called

OPPOSITION (OPPOSE)
Heb 12: 3 Consider him who endured such *o*

OPPRESS (OPPRESSED OPPRESSES OPPRESSION OPPRESSOR)

Ex	1: 11	masters over them to o them
	22: 21	"Do not mistreat an alien or o him,
Isa	3: 5	People will each other—
Eze	22: 29	they o the poor and needy
Da	7: 25	the Most High and o his saints
Am	5: 12	You o the righteous and take bribes
Zec	7: 10	Do not o the widow
Mal	3: 5	who o the widows

OPPRESSED (OPPRESS)

Jdg	2: 18	as they groaned under those who o
Ps	9: 9	The LORD is a refuge for the o,
	82: 3	the rights of the poor and o.
	146: 7	He upholds the cause of the o
Pr	16: 19	in spirit and among the o
	31: 5	and deprive all the o of their rights.
Isa	1: 17	encourage the o.
	53: 7	He was o and afflicted,
	58: 10	and satisfy the needs of the o,
Zec	10: 2	o for lack of a shepherd.
Lk	4: 18	to release the o,

OPPRESSES (OPPRESS)

Pr	14: 31	He who o the poor shows contempt
	22: 16	He who o the poor
Eze	18: 12	He o the poor and needy.

OPPRESSION (OPPRESS)

Ps	12: 5	"Because of the o of the weak
	72: 14	He will rescue them from o
	119: 134	Redeem me from the o of men,
Isa	53: 8	By o and judgment he was taken
	58: 9	"If you do away with the yoke of o,

OPPRESSOR (OPPRESS)

Ps	72: 4	he will crush the o
Isa	51: 13	For where is the wrath of the o?
Jer	22: 3	hand of his o the one who has been

ORDAINED

Ps	8: 2	you have o praise
	111: 9	he o his covenant forever—
	139: 16	All the days o for me
Eze	28: 14	for so I o you.
Hab	1: 12	you have o them to punish.
Mt	21: 16	you have o praise'?"

ORDER (ORDERLY ORDERS)

Nu	9: 23	they obeyed the LORD's o,
Ps	110: 4	in the o of Melchizedek."
Heb	5: 10	priest in the o of Melchizedek.
	9: 10	until the time of the new o.
Rev	21: 4	for the old o of things has passed

ORDERLY (ORDER)

1Co	14: 40	done in a fitting and o way.
Col	2: 5	and delight to see how o you are

ORDERS (ORDER)

Mk	1: 27	He even gives o to evil spirits
	3: 12	But he gave them strict o not
	9: 9	Jesus gave them o not

ORDINARY

Ac	4: 13	that they were unschooled, o men,

ORGIES*

Ro	13: 13	not in o and drunkenness,
Gal	5: 21	drunkenness, o, and the like.
1Pe	4: 3	o, carousing and detestable

ORIGIN (ORIGINATE ORIGINS)

2Pe	1: 21	For prophecy never had its o

ORIGINATE* (ORIGIN)

1Co	14: 36	Did the word of God o with you?

ORIGINS* (ORIGIN)

Mic	5: 2	whose o are from of old,

ORNAMENT (ORNAMENTED)

Pr	3: 22	an o to grace your neck.
	25: 12	of gold or an o of fine gold

ORNAMENTED (ORNAMENT)

Ge	37: 3	and he made a richly o robe for him

ORPHAN* (ORPHANS)

Ex	22: 22	advantage of a widow or an o.

ORPHANS (ORPHAN)

Jn	14: 18	will not leave you as o; I will come

Jas	1: 27	to look after o and widows

OTHNIEL

Nephew of Caleb (Jos 15:15-19; Jdg 1:12-15). Judge who freed Israel from Aram (Jdg 3: 7-11).

OUTBURSTS*

2Co	12: 20	jealousy, o of anger, factions,

OUTCOME

Heb	13: 7	Consider the o of their way of life
1Pe	4: 17	what will the o be for those who do

OUTNUMBER

Ps	139: 18	they would o the grains of sand.

OUTSIDERS*

Col	4: 5	wise in the way you act toward o;
1Th	4: 12	daily life may win the respect of o
1Ti	3: 7	also have a good reputation with o,

OUTSTANDING

SS	5: 10	o among ten thousand.
Ro	13: 8	no debt remain o,

OUTSTRETCHED

Ex	6: 6	and will redeem you with an o arm
Dt	4: 34	by a mighty hand and an o arm,
	5: 15	with a mighty hand and an o arm.
1Ki	8: 42	your mighty hand and your o arm
Ps	136: 12	with a mighty hand and o arm;
Jer	27: 5	and o arm I made the earth
	32: 17	by your great power and o arm.
Eze	20: 33	an o arm and with outpoured wrath

OUTWEIGHS (WEIGH)

2Co	4: 17	an eternal glory that far o them all.

OUTWIT*

2Co	2: 11	in order that Satan might not o us.

OVERAWED* (AWE)

Ps	49: 16	Do not be o when a man grows rich

OVERBEARING*

Tit	1: 7	not o, not quick-tempered,

OVERCAME (OVERCOME)

Rev	3: 21	as I o and sat down with my Father
	12: 11	They o him

OVERCOME (OVERCAME OVERCOMES)

Mt	16: 18	and the gates of Hades will not o it.
Mk	9: 24	I do believe; help me o my unbelief
Lk	10: 19	to o all the power of the enemy;
Jn	16: 33	But take heart! I have o the world."
Ro	12: 21	Do not be o by evil, but o evil
2Pe	2: 20	and are again entangled in it and o,
1Jn	2: 13	because you have o the evil one.
	4: 4	are from God and have o them,
	5: 4	is the victory that has o the world,
Rev	17: 14	but the Lamb will o them

OVERCOMES* (OVERCOME)

1Jn	5: 4	born of God o the world.
	5: 5	Who is it that o the world?
Rev	2: 7	To him who o, I will give the right
	2: 11	He who o will not be hurt at all
	2: 17	To him who o, I will give some
	2: 26	To him who o and does my will
	3: 5	He who o will, like them, be
	3: 12	Him who o I will make a pillar
	3: 21	To him who o, I will give the right
	21: 7	He who o will inherit all this,

OVERFLOW (OVERFLOWING OVERFLOWS)

Ps	65: 11	and your carts o with abundance.
	119: 171	May my lips o with praise,
La	1: 16	and my eyes o with tears.
Mt	12: 34	out of the o of the heart the mouth
Lk	6: 45	out of the o of his heart his mouth
Ro	5: 15	Jesus Christ, o to the many! Again,
	15: 13	so that you may o with hope
2Co	4: 15	to o to the glory of God.
1Th	3: 12	o for each other and for everyone

OVERFLOWING (OVERFLOW)

Pr	3: 10	then your barns will be filled to o,
2Co	8: 2	their o joy and their extreme
	9: 12	o in many expressions of thanks
Col	2: 7	as you were taught; and o

OVERFLOWS* (OVERFLOW)

Ps	23: 5	my cup o.

2Co	1: 5	also through Christ our comfort o.

OVERJOYED* (JOY)

Da	6: 23	The king was o and gave orders
Mt	2: 10	they saw the star, they were o.
Jn	20: 20	The disciples were o
Ac	12: 14	she was so o she ran back
1Pe	4: 13	so that you may be o

OVERLOOK

Pr	19: 11	it is to his glory to o an offense.

OVERSEER* (OVERSEERS)

Pr	6: 7	no o or ruler,
1Ti	3: 1	anyone sets his heart on being an o,
	3: 2	Now the o must be above reproach,
Tit	1: 7	Since an o is entrusted
1Pe	2: 25	returned to the Shepherd and O

OVERSEERS* (OVERSEER)

Ac	20: 28	the Holy Spirit has made you o.
Php	1: 1	together with the o and deacons:
1Pe	5: 2	as o—not because you must.

OVERSHADOW* (OVERSHADOWING)

Lk	1: 35	power of the Most High will o you.

OVERSHADOWING (OVERSHADOW)

Ex	25: 20	wings spread upward, o the cover
Heb	9: 5	the glory, o the atonement cover.

OVERTHROW (OVERTHROWS)

2Th	2: 8	whom the Lord Jesus will o

OVERTHROWS (OVERTHROW)

Pr	13: 6	but wickedness o the sinner.
Isa	44: 25	who o the learning of the wise

OVERWHELMED (OVERWHELMING)

2Sa	22: 5	the torrents of destruction o me.
1Ki	10: 5	temple of the LORD, she was o.
Ps	38: 4	My guilt has o me
	65: 3	When we were o by sins,
Mt	26: 38	"My soul is o with sorrow
Mk	7: 37	People were o with amazement.
	9: 15	they were o with wonder
2Co	2: 7	so that he will not be o

OVERWHELMING (OVERWHELMED)

Pr	27: 4	Anger is cruel and fury o,
Isa	10: 22	o and righteous.
	28: 15	When an o scourge sweeps by,

OWE

Ro	13: 7	If you o taxes, pay taxes; if revenue
Phm	: 19	to mention that you o me your very

OWNER (OWNERSHIP)

Isa	1: 3	the donkey his o manger,

OWNERSHIP* (OWNER'S)

2Co	1: 22	He anointed us, set his seal of o

OX (OXEN)

Dt	25: 4	Do not muzzle an o
Isa	11: 7	and the lion will eat straw like the o
Eze	1: 10	and on the left the face of an o,
Lk	13: 15	of you on the Sabbath untie his o
1Co	9: 9	"Do not muzzle an o
1Ti	5: 18	"Do not muzzle the o
Rev	4: 7	second was like an o, the third had

OXEN (OX)

1Ki	19: 20	Elisha then left his o and ran
Lk	14: 19	'I have just bought five yoke of o,

PAGAN (PAGANS)

Mt	18: 17	as you would a o or a tax collector.
Lk	12: 30	For the p world runs

PAGANS* (PAGAN)

Isa	2: 6	and clasp hands with p.
Mt	5: 47	Do not even p do that? Be perfect,
	6: 7	do not keep on babbling like p,
	6: 32	For the p run after all these things.
1Co	5: 1	that does not occur even among p:
	10: 20	but the sacrifices of p are offered
	12: 2	You know that when you were p,
1Pe	2: 12	such good lives among the p that,
	4: 3	in the past doing what p choose
3Jn	: 7	receiving no help from the p.

PAID (PAY)

Isa	40: 2	that her sin has been p for,
Zec	11: 12	So they p me thirty pieces of silver.

PAIN (PAINFUL PAINS)

Ge   3:16 with *p* you will give birth
      6: 6 and his heart was filled with *p*.
Job 6:10 my joy in unrelenting *p*—
   33:19 may be chastened on a bed of *p*
Jer   4:19 I writhe in *p*.
   15:18 Why is my *p* unending
Mt   4:24 suffering severe *p*,
Jn 16:21 woman giving birth to a child has *p*
1Pe 2:19 up under the *p* of unjust suffering
Rev 21: 4 or mourning or crying or *p*,

PAINFUL (PAIN)

Ge   3:17 through *p* toil you will eat of it
    5:29 and *p* toil of our hands caused
Job 6:25 How *p* are honest words!
Eze 28:24 neighbors who are *p* briers
2Co 2: 1 I would not make another *p* visit
Heb 12:11 seems pleasant at the time, but *p*
1Pe 4:12 at the *p* trial you are suffering,

PAINS (PAIN)

Ge   3:16 "I will greatly increase your *p*
Mt 24: 8 these are the beginning of birth *p*,
Ro   8:22 as in the *p* of childbirth right up
Gal 4:19 again in the *p* of childbirth
1Th 5: 3 as labor *p* on a pregnant woman,

PAIRS

Ge   7: 8 *P* of clean and unclean animals.

PALACE (PALACES)

2Sa 7: 2 "Here I am, living in a *p* of cedar,
Jer 22: 6 is what the LORD says about the *p*
   22:13 "Woe to him who builds his *p*

PALACES (PALACE)

Mt 11: 8 wear fine clothes are in kings' *p*.
Lk   7:25 and indulge in luxury are in *p*.

PALE

Isa 29:22 no longer will their faces grow *p*.
Jer 30: 6 every face turned deathly *p*?
Da   8:18 my face turned deathly *p*
Rev 6: 8 and there before me was a *p* horse!

PALM (PALMS)

Jn 12:13 They took *p* branches and went out
Rev 7: 9 and were holding *p* branches

PALMS (PALM)

Isa 49:16 you on the *p* of my hands;

PAMPERS*

Pr 29:21 If a man *p* his servant from youth,

PANIC

Dt 20: 3 or give way to *p* before them.
1Sa 14:15 It was a *p* sent by God.
Eze 14: 7 there is *p*, not joy,
Zec 14:13 by the LORD with great *p*.

PANTS

Ps 42: 1 As the deer *p* for streams of water,

PARABLES

See also JESUS: Parables
Ps 78: 2 I will open my mouth in *p*,
Mt 13:35 "I will open my mouth in *p*,
Lk   8:10 but to others I speak in *p*, so that,

PARADISE*

Lk 23:43 today you will be with me in *p*."
2Co 12: 4 God knows—was caught up to *p*.
Rev 2: 7 of life, which is in the *p* of God.

PARALYTIC

Mt   9: 2 Some men brought to him a *p*,
Mk 2: 3 bringing to him a *p*, carried by four
Ac 9:33 a *p* who had been bedridden

PARCHED

Ps 143: 6 my soul thirsts for you like a *p* land.

PARCHMENTS*

2Ti 4:13 and my scrolls, especially the *p*.

PARDON* (PARDONED PARDONS)

2Ch 30:18 *p* everyone who sets his heart
Job 7:21 Why do you not *p* my offenses
Isa 55: 7 and to our God, for he will freely *p*.
Joel 3:21 I will *p*."

PARDONED* (PARDON)

Nu 14:19 as you have *p* them from the time
Joel 3:21 bloodguilt, which I have not *p*,

PARDONS* (PARDON)

Mic 7:18 who *p* sin and forgives

PARENTS

Pr 17: 6 and *p* are the pride of their children
   19:14 wealth are inherited from *p*,
Mt 10:21 children will rebel against their *p*
Lk 18:29 left home or wife or brothers or *p*
   21:16 You will be betrayed even by *p*,
       brothers,
Jn   9: 3 Neither this man nor his *p* sinned,"
Ro   1:30 they disobey their *p*; they are
2Co 12:14 for their *p*, but *p* for their children.
Eph 6: 1 Children, obey your *p* in the Lord,
Col 3:20 obey your *p* in everything,
1Ti 5: 4 repaying their *p* and grandparents,
2Ti 3: 2 disobedient to their *p*, ungrateful,

PARTAKE*

1Co 10:17 for we all *p* of the one loaf.

PARTIAL* (PARTIALITY)

Pr 18: 5 It is not good to be *p* to the wicked

PARTIALITY (PARTIAL)

Lev 19:15 do not show *p* to the poor
Dt   1:17 Do not show *p* in judging;
   10:17 who shows no *p* and accepts no
   16:19 Do not pervert justice or show *p*
2Ch 19: 7 our God there is no injustice or *p*
Job 32:21 I will show *p* to no one,
   34:19 who shows no *p* to princes
Pr 24:23 To show *p* in judging is not good:
Mal 2: 9 have shown *p* in matters of the law
Lk 20:21 and that you do not show *p*
1Ti 5:21 keep these instructions without *p*,

PARTICIPATE (PARTICIPATE)

1Co 10:20 you to be *p* with demons.

PARTICIPATE (PARTICIPANTS PARTICIPATION)

1Pe 4:13 rejoice that you *p* in the sufferings
2Pe 1: 4 that through them you may *p*

PARTICIPATION (PARTICIPATE)

1Co 10:16 is not the bread that we break a *p*

PARTNER (PARTNERS PARTNERSHIP)

Pr   2:17 who has left the *p* of her youth
Mal 2:14 though she is your *p*, the wife
1Pe 3: 7 them with respect as the weaker *p*

PARTNERS (PARTNER)

Eph 5: 7 Therefore do not be *p* with them.

PARTNERSHIP* (PARTNER)

Php 1: 5 because of your *p* in the gospel

PASS (PASSED PASSER-BY PASSING)

Ex 12:13 and when I see the blood, I will *p*
   33:19 goodness to *p* in front of you,
1Ki   9: 8 all who *p* by will be appalled
   19:11 for the LORD is about to *p* by."
Ps 90:10 for they quickly *p*, and we fly away
  105: 19 till what he foretold came to *p*,
Isa 31: 5 he will *p* over' it and will rescue it
   43: 2 When you *p* through the waters,
   62:10 *P* through, *p* through the gates!
Jer 22: 8 "People from many nations will *p*
La   1:12 to you, all you who *p* by?
Da   7:14 dominion that will not *p* away,
Am 5:17 for I will *p* through your midst,"
Mt 24:34 will certainly not *p* away
   24:35 Heaven and earth will *p* away,
Mk 13:31 Heaven and earth will *p* away,
Lk 21:33 Heaven and earth will *p* away,
1Co 13: 8 there is knowledge, it will *p* away
Jas   1:10 he will *p* away like a wild flower.
1Jn 2:17 The world and its desires *p* away,

PASSED (PASS)

Ge 15:17 a blazing torch appeared and *p*
Ex 33:22 you with my hand until I have *p* by.
2Ch 21:20 He *p* away, to no one's regret,
Ps 57: 1 wings until the disaster has *p*.
Lk 10:32 saw him, *p* by on the other side.
1Co 15: 3 For what I received I *p* on to you,
Heb 11:29 By faith the people *p*

PASSER-BY* (PASS)

Pr 26:10 is he who hires a fool or any *p*.
   26:17 is a *p* who meddles

PASSING (PASS)

1Co 7:31 world in its present form is *p* away.
1Jn 2: 8 because the darkness is *p*

PASSION* (PASSIONATE PASSIONS)

Hos 7: 6 Their *p* smolders all night;
1Co 7: 9 better to marry than to burn with *p*

PASSIONATE* (PASSION)

1Th 4: 5 not in *p* lust like the heathen.

PASSIONS* (PASSION)

Ro   7: 5 the sinful *p* aroused
Gal 5:24 crucified the sinful nature with its *p*
Tit 2:12 to ungodliness and worldly *p*,
   3: 3 and enslaved by all kinds of *p*

PASSOVER

Ex 12:11 Eat it in haste; it is the LORD's *P*.
Nu   9: 2 Have the Israelites celebrate the *P*
Dt 16: 1 celebrate the *P* of the LORD your
Jos 5:10 the Israelites celebrated the *P*.
2Ki 23:21 "Celebrate the *P* to the LORD
Ezr 6:19 the exiles celebrated the *P*.
Mk 14:12 customary to sacrifice the *P* lamb,
Lk 22: 1 called the *P*, was approaching,
1Co 5: 7 our *P* lamb, has been sacrificed.
Heb 11:28 he kept the *P* and the sprinkling

PAST

Isa 43:18 do not dwell on the *p*.
   65:16 For the *p* troubles will be forgotten
Ro 15: 4 in the *p* was written to teach us,
   16:25 the mystery hidden for long ages *p*,
Eph 3: 9 which for ages *p* was kept hidden
Heb 1: 1 In the *p* God spoke

PASTORS*

Eph 4:11 and some to be *p* and teachers,

PASTURE (PASTURES)

Ps 37: 3 dwell in the land and enjoy safe *p*.
   95: 7 and we are the people of his *p*,
  100: 3 we are his people, the sheep of his *p*
Jer 50: 7 against the LORD, their true *p*,
Eze 34:13 I will *p* them on the mountains
Zec 11: 4 "P* the flock marked for slaughter.
Jn 10: 9 come in and go out, and find *p*

PASTURES (PASTURE)

Ps 23: 2 He makes me lie down in green *p*,

PATCH

Jer 10: 5 Like a scarecrow in a melon *p*.
Mt   9:16 No one sews a *p* of unshrunk cloth

PATH (PATHS)

Ps 16:11 known to me the *p* of life;
   27:11 lead me in a straight *p*
  119: 32 I run in the *p* of your commands,
  119:105 and a light for my *p*.
Pr   2: 9 and fair—every good *p*.
   12:28 along that *p* is immortality.
   15:10 awaits him who leaves the *p*;
   15:19 the *p* of the upright is a highway.
   15:24 The *p* of life leads upward
   21:16 from the *p* of understanding
Isa 26: 7 The *p* of the righteous is level;
Jer 31: 9 on a level *p* where they will not
Mt 13: 4 fell along the *p*, and the birds came
Lk   1:79 to guide our feet into the *p* of peace
2Co 6: 3 no stumbling block in anyone's *p*,

PATHS (PATH)

Ps 23: 3 He guides me in *p* of righteousness
   25: 4 teach me your *p*,
Pr   2:13 who leave the straight *p*
   3: 6 and he will make your *p* straight.
   4:11 and lead you along straight *p*.
   4:26 Make level *p* for your feet.
   5:21 and he examines all his *p*.
   8:20 along the *p* of justice,
   22: 5 In the *p* of the wicked lie thorns
Isa   2: 3 so that we may walk in his *p*."
Jer   6:16 ask for the ancient *p*,
Mic 4: 2 so that we may walk in his *p*."
Mt   3: 3 make straight *p* for him.' "
Ac   2:28 to me the *p* of life;
Ro 11:33 and his *p* beyond tracing out!
Heb 12:13 "Make level *p* for your feet,"

PATIENCE* (PATIENT)

Pr 19:11 A man's wisdom gives him p;
25:15 Through p a ruler can be persuaded
Ecc 7: 8 and p is better than pride.
Isa 7:13 Is it not enough to try the p of men?
7:13 Will you try the p of my God also?
Ro 2: 4 and p, not realizing that God's
9:22 bore with great p the objects
2Co 6: 6 understanding, p and kindness;
Gal 5:22 joy, peace, p, kindness, goodness,
Col 1:11 may have great endurance and p,
3:12 humility, gentleness and p.
1Ti 1:16 Jesus might display his unlimited p
2Ti 3:10 my purpose, faith, p, love,
4: 2 with great p and careful instruction
Heb 6:12 in herit what has been promised.
Jas 5:10 as an example of p in the face
2Pe 3:15 that our Lord's p means salvation,

PATIENT* (PATIENCE PATIENTLY)

Ne 9:30 For many years you were p
Job 6:11 What prospects, that I should be p?
Pr 14:29 A p man has great understanding,
15:18 but a p man calms a quarrel.
16:32 Better a p man than a warrior,
Mt 18:26 'Be p with me,' he begged,
18:29 'Be p with me, and I will pay you
Ro 12:12 Be joyful in hope, p in affliction,
1Co 13: 4 Love is p, love is kind.
2Co 1: 6 produces in you p endurance
Eph 4: 2 humble and gentle; be p,
1Th 5:14 help the weak, be p with everyone.
Jas 5: 7 Be p, then, brothers,
5: 7 and how p he is for the autumn
5: 8 You too, be p and stand firm,
2Pe 3: 9 He is p with you, not wanting
Rev 1: 9 p endurance that are ours in Jesus,
13:10 This calls for p endurance
14:12 This calls for p endurance

PATIENTLY* (PATIENT)

Ps 37: 7 still before the LORD and wait p
40: 1 I waited p for the LORD;
Isa 38:13 I waited p till dawn,
Hab 3:16 Yet I will wait p for the day
Ac 26: 3 I beg you to listen to me p.
Ro 8:25 we do not yet have, we wait for it p.
Heb 6:15 after waiting p, Abraham received
1Pe 3:20 ago when God waited p in the days
Rev 3:10 kept my command to endure p,

PATTERN

Ex 25:40 according to the p shown you
Ro 5:14 who was a p of the one to come.
12: 2 longer to the p of this world,
2Ti 1:13 keep as the p of sound teaching,
Heb 8: 5 according to the p shown you

PAUL

Also called Saul (Ac 13:9). Pharisee from Tarsus (Ac 23:6; Php 3:5). Apostle (Gal 1). At stoning of Stephen (Ac 8:1). Persecuted Church (Ac 9:1-2; Gal 1:13). Vision of Jesus on road to Damascus (Ac 9:4-9; 26:12-18). In Arabia (Gal 1:17). Preached in Damascus; escaped death through the wall in a basket (Ac 9:19-25). In Jerusalem; sent back to Tarsus (Ac 9:26-30).

Brought to Antioch by Barnabas (Ac 11:22-26). First missionary journey to Cyprus and Galatia (Ac 13-14). Stoned at Lystra (Ac 14:19-20). At Jerusalem council (Ac 15). Split with Barnabas over Mark (Ac 15:36-41).

Second missionary journey with Silas (Ac 16-20). Called to Macedonia (Ac 16:6-10). Freed from prison in Philippi (Ac 16:16-40). In Thessalonica (Ac 17:1-9). Speech in Athens (Ac 17:16-33). In Corinth (Ac 18). In Ephesus (Ac 19). Return to Jerusalem (Ac 20). Farewell to Ephesian elders (Ac 20:13-38). Arrival in Jerusalem (Ac 21:1-26). Arrested (Ac 21:27-36). Addressed crowds (Ac 22), Sanhedrin (Ac 23:1-11). Transferred to Caesarea (Ac 23:12-35). Trial before Felix (Ac 24), Festus (Ac 25:1-12). Before Agrippa (Ac 25:13-26:32). Voyage to Rome, shipwreck (Ac 27). Arrival in Rome (Ac 28).

Epistles: Romans, 1 and 2 Corinthians, Galatians, Ephesians, Philippians, Colossians, 1 and 2 Thessalonians, 1 and 2 Timothy, Titus, Philemon.

PAVEMENT

Jn 19:13 as the Stone P (which

PAY (PAID PAYMENT PAYS REPAID REPAY REPAYING)

Lev 26:43 They will p for their sins
Dt 7:12 If you p attention to these laws
Pr 4: 1 p attention and gain understanding
4:20 My son, p attention to what I say;
5: 1 My son, p attention to my wisdom,
6:31 if he is caught, he must p sevenfold,
19:19 man must p the penalty;
22:17 P attention and listen
24:29 I'll p that man back for what he did
Eze 40: 4 and p attention to everything I am
Zec 11:12 give me my p; but if not, keep it."
Mt 20: 2 He agreed to p them a denarius
22:16 you p no attention to who they are.
22:17 Is it right to p taxes to Caesar
Lk 3:14 falsely—be content with your p."
19: 8 I will p back four times the amount
Ro 13: 6 This is also why you p taxes,
2Pe 1:19 you will do well to p attention to it,

PAYMENT (PAY)

Ps 49: 8 no p is ever enough—
Php 4:18 I have received full p and

PAYS (PAY)

Pr 17:13 If a man p back evil for good,
1Th 5:15 sure that nobody p back wrong

PEACE (PEACEABLE PEACEFUL PEACEMAKERS)

Lev 26: 6 " 'I will grant p in the land,
Nu 6:26 and give you p."'
25:12 him I am making my covenant of p
Dt 20:10 make its people an offer of p.
Jdg 3:11 So the land had p for forty years.
3:30 and the land had p for eighty years.
5:31 Then the land had p for forty years.
6:24 and called it The LORD is P.
8:28 the land enjoyed p for forty years.
1Sa 7:14 And there was p between Israel
2Sa 10:19 they made p with the Israelites
1Ki 2:33 may there be the LORD's p forever
22:44 also at p with the king of Israel.
2Ki 9:17 come in p?" "The horseman rode
1Ch 19:19 they made p with David
22: 9 and I will grant Israel p
2Ch 14: 1 and in his days the country was at p
20:30 kingdom of Jehoshaphat was at p,
Job 3:26 I have no p, no quietness;
22:21 to God and be at p with him;
Ps 29:11 LORD blesses his people with p.
34:14 seek p and pursue it.
37:11 and enjoy great p.
37:37 there is a future for the man of p.
85:10 righteousness and p kiss each other
119:165 Great p have they who love your
120: 7 I am a man of p;
122: 6 Pray for the p of Jerusalem:
147:14 He grants p to your borders
Pr 12:20 but joy for those who promote p.
14:30 A heart at p gives life to the body,
16: 7 his enemies live at p with him.
17: 1 Better a dry crust with p and quiet
Ecc 3: 8 a time for war and a time for p.
Isa 9: 6 Everlasting Father, Prince of P.
14: 7 All the lands are at rest and at p;
26: 3 You will keep in perfect p
32:17 The fruit of righteousness will be p;
48:18 your p would have been like a river,
48:22 "There is no p," says the LORD,
52: 7 who proclaim p,
53: 5 punishment that brought us p was
54:10 nor my covenant of p be removed,"
55:12 and be led forth in p;
57: 2 enter into p;
57:19 P, p, to those far and near,"
57:21 "There is no p," says my God,
59: 8 The way of p they do not know;
Jer 6:14 'P, p,' they say,
8:11 'P, p,'. . . there is no p.
30:10 Jacob will again have p
46:27 Jacob will again have p
Eze 13:10 "P," when there is no p,
34:25 " I will make a covenant of p
37:26 I will make a covenant of p
Mic 5: 5 And he will be their p.
Zec 8:19 Therefore love truth and p."
9:10 He will proclaim p to the nations
Mal 2: 5 a covenant of life and p,
2: 6 He walked with me in p
Mt 10:34 I did not come to bring p,
Mk 9:50 and be at p with each other."
Lk 1:79 to guide our feet into the path of p

Lk 2:14 on earth p to men on whom his
19:38 "Pin heaven and glory
Jn 14:27 P I leave with you; my p
16:33 so that in me you may have p.
Ro 1: 7 and p to you from God our Father
2:10 and p for everyone who does good:
5: 1 we have p with God
8: 6 by the Spirit is life and p;
12:18 on you, live at p with everyone.
14:19 effort to do what leads to p
1Co 7:15 God has called us to live in p.
14:33 a God of disorder but of p
2Co 13:11 be of one mind, live in p.
Gal 5:22 joy, p, patience, kindness,
Eph 2:14 he himself is our p, who has made
2:15 thus making p, and in this one body
2:17 and p to those who were near.
6:15 comes from the gospel of p.
Php 4: 7 the p of God, which transcends all
Col 1:20 by making p through his blood,
3:15 Let the p of Christ rule
3:15 of one body you were called to p
1Th 5: 3 While people are saying, "P
5:13 Live in p with each other.
5:23 The God of p, sanctify you through
2Th 3:16 the Lord of p himself give you p
2Ti 2:22 righteousness, faith, love and p,
Heb 7: 2 "king of Salem" means "king of p."
12:11 p for those who have been trained
12:14 effort to live in p with all men
13:20 May the God of p, who
1Pe 3:11 he must seek p and pursue it.
2Pe 3:14 blameless and at p with him.
Rev 6: 4 power to take p from the earth

PEACEABLE* (PEACE)

Tit 3: 2 to slander no one, to be p

PEACEFUL (PEACE)

1Ti 2: 2 that we may live p and quiet lives

PEACE-LOVING

Jas 3:17 then p, considerate

PEACEMAKERS* (PEACE)

Mt 5: 9 Blessed are the p,
Jas 3:18 P who sow in peace raise a harvest

PEARL* (PEARLS)

Rev 21:21 each gate made of a single p.

PEARLS (PEARL)

Mt 7: 6 do not throw your p to pigs.
13:45 like a merchant looking for fine p.
1Ti 2: 9 or gold or p or expensive clothes,
Rev 21:21 The twelve gates were twelve p,

PEDDLE*

2Co 2:17 we do not p the word of God

PEG

Jdg 4:21 She drove the p through his temple

PEKAH

King of Israel (2Ki 16:25-31; Isa 7:1).

PEKAHIAH*

Son of Menahem; king of Israel (2Ki 16:22-26).

PEN

Ps 45: 1 my tongue is the p
Mt 5:18 letter, not the least stroke of a p,
Jn 10: 1 who does not enter the sheep p

PENETRATES*

Heb 4:12 it p even to dividing soul and spirit,

PENNIES* (PENNY)

Lk 12: 6 not five sparrows sold for two p?

PENNY* (PENNIES)

Mt 5:26 out until you have paid the last p.
10:29 Are not two sparrows sold for a p?
Mk 12:42 worth only a fraction of a p.
Lk 12:59 out until you have paid the last p."

PENTECOST*

Ac 2: 1 of P came, they were all together
20:16 if possible, by the day of P.
1Co 16: 8 I will stay on at Ephesus until P,

PEOPLE (PEOPLES)

Ge 11: 6 as one p speaking the same
Ex 5: 1 Let my p go,

Ex 6: 7 take you as my own p,
8: 23 between my p and your p.
15: 13 the p you have redeemed.
19: 8 The p all responded together,
24: 3 Moses went and told the p
32: 1 When the p saw that Moses
32: 9 they are a stiff-necked p.
33: 13 this nation is your p.
Lev 9: 7 for yourself and the p.
16: 24 the burnt offering for the p,
26: 12 and you will be my p.
Nu 11: 11 burden of all these p on
14: 11 p treat me with contempt?
14: 19 forgive the sin of these p,
22: 5 A p has come out of Egypt
Dt 4: 6 a wise and understanding p.
4: 20 the p of his inheritance.
5: 28 what this p said to you.
7: 6 a p holy to the LORD
26: 18 that you are his p,
31: 7 you must go with this p
31: 16 these p will soon prostitute
32: 9 the LORD's portion is his p,
32: 43 atonement for his land and p
33: 29 a p saved by the LORD?
Jos 1: 6 you will lead this p
24: 24 the p said to Joshua,
Jdg 2: 7 p served the LORD throughout
Ru 1: 16 Your p will be my p
1Sa 8: 7 the p are saying to you;
12: 22 LORD will not reject his p,
2Sa 5: 2 will shepherd my p Israel
7: 10 provide a place for my p
1Ki 3: 8 among the p you have chosen,
8: 30 your p Israel when they pray
8: 56 has given rest to his p
18: 39 when all the p saw this,
2Ki 23: 3 all the p pledged themselves
1Ch 17: 21 to redeem p for himself
29: 17 how willingly your p who are
2Ch 2: 11 Because the LORD loves his p,
7: 5 p dedicated the temple
7: 14 if my p, who are called
30: 6 "P of Israel, return to the
36: 16 was aroused against his p
Ezr 2: 1 These are the p of the
3: 1 p assembled as one man
Ne 1: 10 your p, whom you redeemed
4: 6 p worked with all their heart
8: 1 p assembled as one man
Est 3: 6 to destroy all Mordecai's p,
Job 12: 2 Doubtless you are the p,
Ps 29: 11 gives strength to his p;
35: 18 p he chose for his inheritance
50: 4 that he may judge his p
53: 6 restores the fortunes of his p.
81: 13 If my p would but listen
94: 14 LORD will not reject his p;
95: 7 we are the p of his pasture,
95: 10 a p whose hearts go astray,
125: 2 the LORD surrounds his p
135: 14 LORD will vindicate his p
144: 15 p whose God is the LORD.
Pr 14: 34 sin is a disgrace to any p.
29: 2 righteous thrive, the p rejoice
29: 18 the p cast off restraint
Isa 1: 3 my p do not understand.
1: 4 a p loaded with guilt,
5: 13 my p will go into exile
6: 10 the heart of this p calloused;
9: 2 the p walking in darkness
12: 12 will assemble the scattered p
19: 25 Blessed be Egypt my p,
25: 8 remove the disgrace of his p
29: 13 These p come near to me
40: 1 Comfort, comfort my p
40: 7 Surely the p are grass.
42: 6 a covenant for the p
49: 13 the LORD comforts his p
51: 4 "Listen to me, my p;
52: 6 my p will know my name;
53: 8 for the transgression of my p
60: 21 will all your p be righteous
62: 12 will be called the Holy P,
65: 23 they will be a p blessed
Jer 2: 11 my p have exchanged their
2: 13 p have committed two sins:
2: 32 my p have forgotten me,
4: 22 My p are fools;
5: 14 Because the p have spoken
5: 31 my p love it this way
7: 16 do not pray for this p
18: 15 my p have forgotten me;
7: 23 They will be my p,
30: 3 I will bring my p Israel

Eze 13: 23 I will save my p from
36: 8 fruit for my p Israel,
36: 28 you will be my p,
36: 38 be filled with flocks of p.
37: 13 Then you, my p, will know
38: 14 p Israel are living in safety
39: 7 name among my p Israel.
Da 7: 27 saints, the p of the Most High.
8: 24 mighty men and the holy p
9: 19 your p bear your name
9: 24 are decreed for your p
9: 26 p of the ruler who will come
10: 14 will happen to your p
11: 32 p who know their God will
12: 1 prince who protects your p.
Hos 1: 10 'You are not my p,'
2: 23 'You are my p';
4: 14 a p without understanding
Joel 2: 18 and take pity on his p.
3: 16 be a refuge for his p,
Am 9: 14 back my exiled p Israel;
Mic 6: 2 a case against his p,
7: 14 Shepherd your p with
Hag 1: 12 remnant of the p obeyed
Zec 2: 11 and will become my p,
8: 7 I will save my p
13: 9 will say, 'They are my p,'
Mk 7: 6 p honor me with their lips
8: 27 "Who do p say I am?"
Lk 1: 17 make ready a p prepared
1: 68 and has redeemed his p.
2: 10 joy that will be for all the p.
21: 23 and wrath against this p.
Jn 11: 50 one man die for the p
18: 14 if one man died for the p.
Ac 15: 14 from the Gentiles a p
18: 10 have many p in this city.
Ro 9: 25 will call them 'my p'
11: 1 Did God reject his p?
15: 10 O Gentiles, with his p."
2Co 6: 16 and they will be my p."
Tit 2: 14 a p that are his very own,
Heb 2: 17 for the sins of the p.
4: 9 a Sabbath-rest for the p
5: 3 for the sins of the p.
10: 30 Lord will judge his p."
11: 25 mistreated along with the p
13: 12 to make the p holy
1Pe 2: 9 you are a chosen p,
2: 10 Once you were not a p,
2: 10 you are the p of God;
2Pe 2: 1 false prophets among the p,
3: 11 kind of p ought you to be?
Rev 18: 4 "Come out of her, my p,
-21: 3 They will be his p,

PEOPLES (PEOPLE)

Ge 17: 16 kings of p will come from her
25: 23 two p from within you will
27: 29 and p bow down to you
28: 3 become a community of p.
48: 4 you a community of p.
Dt 14: 2 of all the p on the face of
28: 10 Then all the p on earth
32: 8 set up boundaries for the p
Jos 4: 24 all the p of the earth might
1Ki 8: 43 all the p of the earth may
2Ch 7: 20 of ridicule among all p.
Ps 8: 9 he will govern the p
67: 5 May all the p praise you.
87: 6 in the register of the p:
96: 10 he will judge the p
Isa 2: 4 settle disputes for many p,
17: 12 Oh, the uproar of the p—
25: 6 of rich food for all p,
34: 1 pay attention, you p!
55: 4 him a witness to the p,
Jer 10: 3 customs of the p are worthless
Da 7: 14 all p, nations and men
Mic 4: 1 and p will stream to it.
4: 3 will judge between many p
5: 7 in the midst of many p
Zep 3: 9 purify the lips of the p,
3: 20 among all the p of the
Zec 8: 20 Many p and the inhabitants
12: 2 all the surrounding p reeling.
Rev 10: 11 prophesy again about many p,
17: 15 the prostitute sits, are p,

PEOR

Nu 25: 3 joined in worshiping the Baal of P.
Dt 4: 3 who followed the Baal of P,

PERCEIVE (PERCEIVING)

Ps 139: 2 you p my thoughts from afar.

Pr 24: 12 not he who weighs the heart p it?

PERCEIVING* (PERCEIVE)

Isa 6: 9 be ever seeing, but never p.'
Mt 13: 14 you will be ever seeing but never p.
Mk 4: 12 may be ever seeing but never p.
Ac 28: 26 you will be ever seeing but never p.

PERFECT* (PERFECTER PERFECTING PERFECTION)

Dt 32: 4 He is the Rock, his works are p,
2Sa 22: 31 "As for God, his way is p;
22: 33 and makes my way p.
Job 36: 4 one p in knowledge is with you.
37: 16 of him who is p in knowledge?
Ps 18: 30 As for God, his way is p;
18: 32 and makes my way p.
19: 7 The law of the LORD is p,
50: 2 From Zion, p in beauty.
64: 6 "We have devised a p plan!"
SS 6: 9 but my dove, my p one, is unique.
Isa 25: 1 for in p faithfulness
26: 3 You will keep in p peace
Eze 16: 14 had given you made your beauty p,
27: 3 "I am p in beauty."
28: 12 full of wisdom and p in beauty.
Mt 5: 48 Do not even pagans do that? Be p,
5: 48 as your heavenly Father is p.
19: 21 answered, "If you want to be p,
Ro 12: 2 his good, pleasing and p will.
2Co 12: 9 for my power is made p
Php 3: 12 or have already been made p.
Col 1: 28 so that we may present everyone p
3: 14 binds them all together in p unity.
Heb 2: 10 the author of their salvation p
5: 9 what he suffered and, once made p,
7: 19 useless (for the law made nothing p
7: 28 who has been made p forever.
9: 11 and more p tabernacle that is not
10: 1 make p those who draw
10: 14 he has made p forever those who
11: 40 with us would they be made p.
12: 23 spirits of righteous men made p,
Jas 1: 17 Every good and p gift is from above
1: 25 into the p law that gives freedom,
3: 2 he is a p man, able
1Jn 4: 18 But p love drives out fear,
4: 18 The one who fears is not made p

PERFECTER* (PERFECT)

Heb 12: 2 the author and p of our faith,

PERFECTING* (PERFECT)

2Co 7: 1 p holiness out of reverence for God

PERFECTION* (PERFECT)

Ps 119: 96 To all p I see a limit;
La 2: 15 the p of beauty.
Eze 27: 4 builders brought your beauty to p.
27: 11 they brought your beauty to p.
28: 12 " 'You were the model of p,
1Co 13: 10 but when p comes, the imperfect
2Co 13: 9 and our prayer is for your p.
13: 11 Aim for p, listen to my appeal,
Heb 7: 11 If p could have been attained

PERFORM (PERFORMED PERFORMS)

Ex 3: 20 with all the wonders that I will p
2Sa 7: 23 to p great and awesome wonders
Jn 3: 2 no one could p the miraculous

PERFORMED (PERFORM)

Mt 11: 21 If the miracles that were p
Jn 10: 41 John never p a miraculous

PERFORMS (PERFORM)

Ps 77: 14 You are the God who p miracles;

PERFUME

Ecc 7: 1 A good name is better than fine p,
SS 1: 3 your name is like p poured out.
Mk 14: 3 jar of very expensive p,

PERIL

2Co 1: 10 us from such a deadly p.

PERISH (PERISHABLE PERISHED PERISHES PERISHING)

Ge 6: 17 Everything on earth will p.
Est 4: 16 And if I p, I p."
Ps 1: 6 but the way of the wicked will p.
37: 20 But the wicked will p:
73: 27 Those who are far from you will p.
102: 26 They will p, but you remain;
Pr 11: 10 when the wicked p, there are

Pr 19: 9 and he who pours out lies will p.
21:28 A false witness will p,
28:28 when the wicked p, the righteous
Isa 1:28 who forsake the LORD will p.
29:14 the wisdom of the wise will p,
60:12 that will not serve you will p;
Zec 11: 9 the dying die, and the perishing p.
Lk 13: 3 unless you repent, you too will all p
13: 5 unless you repent, you too will all p
21:18 But not a hair of your head will p.
Jn 3:16 whoever believes in him shall not p
10:28 eternal life, and they shall never p;
Ro 2:12 apart from the law will also p apart
Col 2:22 These are all destined to p with use,
2Th 2:10 They p because they refused
Heb 1:11 They will p, but you remain;
1Pe 1: 4 into an inheritance that can never p
2Pe 3: 9 not wanting anyone to p,

PERISHABLE (PERISH)

1Co 15:42 The body that is sown is p.
1Pe 1:18 not with p things such
1:23 not of p seed, but of imperishable,

PERISHED (PERISH)

Ps 119: 92 I would have p in my affliction.

PERISHES (PERISH)

Job 8:13 so p the hope of the godless.
1Pe 1: 7 which p even though refined by fire

PERISHING (PERISH)

1Co 1:18 foolishness to those who are p,
2Co 2:15 being saved and those who are p.
4: 3 it is veiled to those who are p.

PERJURERS* (PERJURY)

Mal 3: 5 and p, against those who defraud
1Ti 1:10 for slave traders and liars and p—

PERJURY* (PERJURERS)

Jer 7: 9 murder, commit adultery and p,

PERMANENT

Heb 7:24 lives forever, he has a p priesthood.

PERMISSIBLE (PERMIT)

1Co 6:12 "Everything is p for me"—
10:23 "Everything is p"—but not

PERMIT (PERMISSIBLE PERMITTED)

Hos 5: 4 "Their deeds do not p them
1Ti 2:12 I do not p a woman to teach

PERMITTED (PERMIT)

Mt 19: 8 Moses p you to divorce your wives
2Co 12: 4 things that man is not p to tell.

PERSECUTE (PERSECUTED PERSECUTION PERSECUTIONS)

Ps 119: 86 for men p me without cause.
Mt 5:11 p you and falsely say all kinds
5:44 and pray for those who p you,
Jn 15:20 they persecuted me, they will p you
Ac 9: 4 why do you p me?" ''Who are you,
Ro 12:14 Bless those who p you; bless

PERSECUTED (PERSECUTE)

Mt 5:10 Blessed are those who are p
5:12 same way they p the prophets who
Jn 15:20 If they p me, they will persecute
1Co 4:12 when we are p, we endure it;
15: 9 because I p the church of God.
2Co 4: 9 in despair; p, but not abandoned;
1Th 3: 4 kept telling you that we would be p.
2Ti 3:12 life in Christ Jesus will be p,
Heb 11:37 destitute, p and mistreated—

PERSECUTION (PERSECUTE)

Mt 13:21 When trouble or p comes
Ro 8:35 or hardship or p or famine

PERSECUTIONS (PERSECUTE)

Mk 10:30 and with them, p) and in the age
2Co 12:10 in hardships, in p, in difficulties.
2Th 1: 4 faith in all the p and trials you are
2Ti 3:11 love, endurance, p, sufferings—

PERSEVERANCE* (PERSEVERE)

Ro 5: 3 we know that suffering produces p;
5: 4 p, character; and character, hope.
2Co 12:12 were done among you with great p
2Th 1: 4 churches we boast about your p
3: 5 into God's love and Christ's p.
Heb 12: 1 run with p the race marked out

Jas 1: 3 the testing of your faith develops p.
1: 4 P must finish its work
5:11 You have heard of Job's p
2Pe 1: 6 p; and to p, godliness;
Rev 2: 2 your hard work and your p.
2:19 and faith, your service and p,

PERSEVERE* (PERSEVERANCE PERSEVERED PERSEVERES PERSEVERING)

1Ti 4:16 P in them, because if you do,
Heb 10:36 You need to p so that

PERSEVERED* (PERSEVERE)

Heb 11:27 he p because he saw him who is
Jas 5:11 consider blessed those who have p.
Rev 2: 3 You have p and have endured

PERSEVERES* (PERSEVERE)

1Co 13: 7 trusts, always hopes, always p.
Jas 1:12 Blessed is the man who p

PERSEVERING* (PERSEVERE)

Lk 8:15 retain it, and by p produce a crop.

PERSIANS

Da 6:15 law of the Medes and P no decree

PERSISTENCE*

Ro 2: 7 To those who by p

PERSUADE (PERSUADED PERSUASIVE)

Ac 18: 4 trying to p Jews and Greeks.
2Co 5:11 is to fear the Lord, we try to p men.

PERSUADED (PERSUADE)

Ro 4:21 being fully p that God had power

PERSUASIVE (PERSUADE)

1Co 2: 4 not with wise and p words,

PERVERSION* (PERVERT)

Lev 18:23 sexual relations with it; that is a p.
20:12 What they have done is a p;
Ro 1:27 the due penalty for their p.
Jude 7 up to sexual immorality and p.

PERVERT (PERVERSION PERVERTED PERVERTS)

Ex 23: 2 do not p justice by siding
Dt 16:19 Do not p justice or show partiality.
Job 34:12 that the Almighty would p justice.
Pr 17:23 to p the course of justice.
Gal 1: 7 are trying to p the gospel of Christ.

PERVERTED (PERVERT)

1Sa 8: 3 and accepted bribes and p justice.

PERVERTS* (PERVERT)

1Ti 1:10 for murderers, for adulterers and p,

PESTILENCE (PESTILENCES)

Ps 91: 6 nor the p that stalks in the darkness

PESTILENCES (PESTILENCE)

Lk 21:11 famines and p in various places,

PETER

Apostle, brother of Andrew, also called Simon (Mt 10:2; Mk 3:16; Lk 6:14; Ac 1:13), and Cephas (Jn 1:42). Confession of Christ (Mt 16: 13-20; Mk 8:27-30; Lk 9:18-27). At transfiguration (Mt 17:1-8; Mk 9:2-8; Lk 9:28-36; 2Pe 1: 16-18). Caught fish with coin (Mt 17:24-27). Denial of Jesus predicted (Mt 26:31-35; Mk 14: 27-31; Lk 22:31-34; Jn 13:31-38). Denied Jesus (Mt 26:69-75; Mk 14:66-72; Lk 22:54-62; Jn 18: 15-27). Commissioned by Jesus to shepherd his flock (Jn 21:15-23).
Speech at Pentecost (Ac 2). Healed beggar (Ac 3:1-10). Speech at temple (Ac 3:11-26), before Sanhedrin (Ac 4:1-22). In Samaria (Ac 8: 14-25). Sent by vision to Cornelius (Ac 10). Announced salvation of Gentiles in Jerusalem (Ac 11; 15). Freed from prison (Ac 12). Inconsistency at Antioch (Gal 2:11-21). At Jerusalem Council (Ac 15).
Epistles: 1-2 Peter.

PETITION (PETITIONS)

1Ch 16: 4 to make p, to give thanks,
Php 4: 6 by prayer and p, with thanksgiving,

PETITIONS (PETITION)

Heb 5: 7 he offered up prayers and p

PHANTOM*

Ps 39: 6 Man is a mere p as he goes to

PHARAOH (PHARAOH'S)

Ge 12:15 her to P, and she was taken
41:14 So P sent for Joseph, and he was
Ex 14: 4 glory for myself through P
14:17 And I will gain glory through P

PHARAOH'S (PHARAOH)

Ex 7: 3 But I will harden P heart, and

PHARISEE (PHARISEES)

Ac 23: 6 brothers, I am a P, the son of a P.
Php 3: 5 in regard to the law, a P; as for zeal,

PHARISEES (PHARISEE)

Mt 5:20 surpasses that of the P
16: 6 guard against the yeast of the P
23:13 of the law and P, you hypocrites!
Jn 3: 1 a man of the P named Nicodemus,

PHILADELPHIA

Rev 3: 7 the angel of the church in P write:

PHILEMON*

Phm 1 To P our dear friend and fellow

PHILIP

1. Apostle (Mt 10:3; Mk 3:18; Lk 6:14; Jn 1: 43-48; 14:8; Ac 1:13).
2. Deacon (Ac 6:1-7); evangelist in Samaria (Ac 8:4-25), to Ethiopian (Ac 8:26-40).

PHILIPPI

Ac 16:12 From there we traveled to P,
Php 1: 1 To all the saints in Christ Jesus at P

PHILISTINE (PHILISTINES)

Jos 13: 3 of the five P rulers in Gaza,
1Sa 14: 1 let's go over to the Postpost
17:26 is this uncircumcised P that he
17:37 me from the hand of this P."

PHILISTINES (PHILISTINE)

Jdg 10: 7 them into the hands of the P.
13: 1 the hands of the P for forty years.
16: 5 The rulers of the P went to her
1Sa 4: 1 at Ebenezer, and the P at Aphek.
5: 8 together all the rulers of the P
13:23 a detachment of P had gone out
17: 1 the P gathered their forces for war
23: 1 the P are fighting against Keilah
27: 1 is to escape to the land of the P.
31: 1 Now the P fought against Israel;
2Sa 5:17 When the P heard that David had
8: 1 David defeated the P and subdued
21:15 there was a battle between the P
2Ki 18: 8 he defeated the P, as far as Gaza
Am 1: 8 Ekron till the last of the P is dead."

PHILOSOPHER* (PHILOSOPHY)

1Co 1:20 Where is the p of this age?

PHILOSOPHY* (PHILOSOPHER)

Col 2: 8 through hollow and deceptive p,

PHINEHAS

Nu 25: 7 When P son of Eleazar, the son
Ps 106:30 But P stood up and intervened,

PHOEBE*

Ro 16: 1 I commend to you our sister P,

PHYLACTERIES*

Mt 23: 5 They make their p wide

PHYSICAL

Ro 2:28 merely outward and p.
Col 1:22 by Christ's p body through death
1Ti 4: 8 For p training is of some value,
Jas 2:16 but does nothing about his p needs,

PICK (PICKED)

Mk 16:18 they will p up snakes

PICKED (PICK)

Lk 14: 7 noticed how the guests p the places
Jn 5: 9 he p up his mat and walked.

PIECE (PIECES)

Jn 19:23 woven in one p from top to bottom.

PIECES (PIECE)

Ge   15: 17 and passed between the p.
Jer 34: 18 and then walked between its p.
Zec 11: 12 So they paid me thirty p of silver.
Mt   14: 20 of broken p that were left over.

PIERCE (PIERCED)

Ex   21: 6 and p his ear with an awl.
Pr   12: 18 Reckless words p like a sword,
Lk   2: 35 a sword will p your own soul too."

PIERCED (PIERCE)

Ps   22: 16 they have p my hands and my feet.
     40: 6 but my ears you have p;
Isa 53: 5 But he was p for our transgressions,
Zec 12: 10 look on me, the one they have p,
Jn   19: 37 look on the one they have p."
Rev   1: 7 even those who p him,

PIG'S (PIGS)

Pr   11: 22 Like a gold ring in a p snout

PIGEONS

Lev   5: 11 afford two doves or two young p,
Lk   2: 24 "a pair of doves or two young p."

PIGS (PIG'S)

Mt   7: 6 do not throw your pearls to p.
Mk   5: 11 A large herd of p was feeding on

PILATE

   Governor of Judea. Questioned Jesus (Mt 27:
1-26; Mk 15:15; Lk 22:66-23:25; Jn 18:28-19:
16); sent him to Herod (Lk 23:6-12); consented
to his crucifixion when crowds chose Barabbas
(Mt 27:15-26; Mk 15:6-15; Lk 23:13-25; Jn 19:
1-10).

PILLAR (PILLARS)

Ge   19: 26 and she became a p of salt.
Ex   13: 21 ahead of them in a p of cloud
1Ti   3: 15 the p and foundation of the truth.
Rev   3: 12 who overcomes I will make a p

PILLARS (PILLAR)

Gal   2: 9 and John, those reputed to be p,

PINIONS

Dt   32: 11 and carries them on its p.

PISGAH

Dt   3: 27 Go up to the top of P and look west

PIT

Ps   7: 15 falls into the p he has made.
     40: 2 He lifted me out of the slimy p,
    103: 4 who redeems your life from the p
Pr   23: 27 for a prostitute is a deep p
     26: 27 If a man digs a p, he will fall into it;
Isa 24: 17 Terror and p and snare await you,
     38: 17 me from the p of destruction;
Mt   15: 14 a blind man, both will fall into a p."

PITCH

Ge   6: 14 and coat it with p inside and out.
Ex   2: 3 and coated it with tar and p.

PITIED (PITY)

1Co 15: 19 we are to be p more than all men.

PITY (PITIED)

Ps   72: 13 He will take p on the weak
Ecc   4: 10 But p the man who falls
Lk   10: 33 when he saw him, he took p on him

PLAGUE (PLAGUED PLAGUES)

2Ch   6: 28 "When famine or p comes
Ps   91: 6 nor the p that destroys at midday.

PLAGUED* (PLAGUE)

Ps   73: 5 they are not p by human ills.
     73: 14 All day long I have been p;

PLAGUES (PLAGUE)

Hos 13: 14 Where, O death, are your p?
Rev 21: 9 full of the seven last p came
     22: 18 to him the p described in this book.

PLAIN

Isa 40: 4 the rugged places a p.
Ro   1: 19 what may be known about God is p

PLAN (PLANNED PLANS)

Ex   26: 30 according to the p shown you

Job 42: 2 no p of yours can be thwarted.
Pr   14: 22 those who p what is good find love
     21: 30 is no wisdom, no insight, no p
Am   3: 7 nothing without revealing his p
Eph   1: 1 predestined according to the p

PLANK

Mt   7: 3 attention to the p in your own eye?
Lk   6: 41 attention to the p in your own eye?

PLANNED (PLAN)

Ps   40: 5 The things you p for us
Isa 14: 24 "Surely, as I have p, so it will be,
     23: 9 The LORD Almighty p it,
     46: 11 what I have p, that will I do.
Heb 11: 40 God had p something better for us

PLANS (PLAN)

Ps   20: 4 and make all your p succeed.
     33: 11 p of the LORD stand firm forever,
Pr   15: 22 P fail for lack of counsel,
     16: 3 and your p will succeed.
     19: 21 Many are the p in a man's heart,
     20: 18 Make p by seeking advice;
Isa 29: 15 to hide their p from the LORD,
     30: 1 those who carry out p that are not
     32: 8 But the noble man makes noble p,
2Co   1: 17 Or do I make my p in a worldly

PLANT (PLANTED PLANTING PLANTS)

Am   9: 15 I will p Israel in their own land,
Mt   15: 13 "Every p that my heavenly Father

PLANTED (PLANT)

Ge   2: 8 the LORD God had p a garden
Ps   1: 3 He is like a tree p by streams
Jer 17: 8 He will be like a tree p by the water
Mt   15: 13 Father has not p will be pulled
     21: 33 was a landowner who p a vineyard
Lk   13: 6 "A man had a fig tree, p
1Co   3: 6 I p the seed, Apollos watered it,
Jas   1: 21 humbly accept the word p in you,

PLANTING (PLANT)

Isa 61: 3 a p of the LORD

PLANTS (PLANT)

Pr   31: 16 out of her earnings she p a vineyard
1Co   3: 7 So neither he who p nor he who
      9: 7 Who p a vineyard and does not eat

PLATTER

Mk   6: 25 head of John the Baptist on a p."

PLAY (PLAYED)

1Sa 16: 23 David would take his harp and p.
Isa 11: 8 The infant will p near the hole

PLAYED (PLAY)

Lk   7: 32 " 'We p the flute for you,
1Co 14: 7 anyone know what tune is being p

PLEA (PLEAD PLEADED PLEADS)

1Ki   8: 28 to your servant's prayer and his p
Ps 102: 17 he will not despise their p.
La   3: 56 You heard my p: "Do not close

PLEAD (PLEA)

Isa   1: 17 p the case of the widow.

PLEADED (PLEA)

2Co 12: 8 Three times I p with the Lord

PLEADS (PLEA)

Job 16: 21 on behalf of a man he p with God

PLEASANT (PLEASE)

Ge   49: 15 and how p his land,
Ps   16: 6 for me in p places,
    133: 1 How good and p it is
    135: 3 sing praise to his name, for that is p
    147: 1 how p and fitting to praise him!
Pr   2: 10 knowledge will be p to your soul.
      3: 17 Her ways are p ways,
     16: 21 and p words promote instruction.
     16: 24 P words are a honeycomb,
Isa 30: 10 Tell us p things,
1Th   3: 6 that you always have p memories
Heb 12: 11 No discipline seems p at the time,

PLEASANTNESS* (PLEASE)

Pr   27: 9 the p of one's friend springs

**PLEASE (PLEASANT PLEASANTNESS
PLEASED PLEASES PLEASING PLEASURE
PLEASURES)**

Ps   69: 31 This will p the LORD more
Pr   20: 23 and dishonest scales do not p him.
Isa 46: 10 and I will do all that I p.
Jer   6: 20 your sacrifices do not p me."
      27: 5 and I give it to anyone I p.
Jn   5: 30 for I seek not to p myself
Ro   8: 8 by the sinful nature cannot p God.
     15: 1 of the weak and not to p ourselves.
     15: 2 Each of us should p his neighbor
1Co   7: 32 affairs—how he can p the Lord.
     10: 33 I try to p everybody in every way.
2Co   5: 9 So we make it our goal to p him,
Gal   1: 10 or of God? Or am I trying to p men
      6: 8 the one who sows to p the Spirit,
Col   1: 10 and may p him in every way:
1Th   4: 2 We are not trying to p men
      4: 1 how to live in order to p God,
2Ti   2: 4 wants to p his commanding officer.
Tit   2: 9 to try to p them, not to talk back
Heb 11: 6 faith it is impossible to p God,

PLEASED (PLEASE)

Dt   28: 63 as it p the LORD to make you
1Sa 12: 22 LORD was p to make you his own.
1Ki   3: 10 The Lord was p that Solomon had
1Ch 29: 17 that you test the heart and are p
Mic   6: 7 Will the LORD be p
Mal   1: 10 I am not p with you," says
Mt   3: 17 whom I love; with him I am well p
     17: 5 whom I love; with him I am well p
Mk   1: 11 whom I love; with you I am well p
Lk   3: 22 whom I love; with you I am well p
1Co   1: 21 God was p through the foolishness
Col   1: 19 For God was p to have all his
Heb 10: 6 you were not p.
     10: 8 nor were you p with them"
     10: 38 I will not be p with him."
     11: 5 commended as one who p God.
     11: 16 for with such sacrifices God is p.
2Pe   1: 17 whom I love; with him I am well p

PLEASES (PLEASE)

Job 23: 13 He does whatever he p.
Ps 115: 3 he does whatever p him.
    135: 6 The LORD does whatever p him,
Pr   15: 8 but the prayer of the upright p him.
     21: 1 it like a watercourse wherever he p.
Ecc   2: 26 To the man who p him, God gives
      7: 26 man who p God will escape her,
Da   4: 35 He does as he p
Jn   3: 8 The wind blows wherever it p.
      8: 29 for I always do what p him."
Eph   5: 10 truth) and find out what p the Lord
Col   3: 20 in everything, for this p the Lord.
1Ti   2: 3 This is good, and p God our Savior,
1Jn   3: 22 his commands and do what p him.

PLEASING (PLEASE)

Ge   2: 9 trees that were p to the eye
Lev   1: 9 an aroma p to the LORD.
Ps   19: 14 be p in your sight,
    104: 34 May my meditation be p to him,
Pr   15: 26 but those of the pure are p to him.
     16: 7 When a man's ways are p
SS   1: 3 P is the fragrance of your perfumes
      4: 10 How much more p is your love
      7: 6 How beautiful you are and how p,
Ro   12: 1 p to God—this is your spiritual
     14: 18 Christ in this way is p to God
Php   4: 18 an acceptable sacrifice, p to God.
1Ti   5: 4 grandparents, for this is p to God.
Heb 13: 21 may he work in us what is p to him,

PLEASURE (PLEASE)

Ps   5: 4 You are not a God who takes p
     51: 16 you do not take p in burnt offerings
    147: 10 His p is not in the strength
Pr   10: 23 A fool finds p in evil conduct,
     18: 2 A fool finds no p in understanding
     21: 17 He who loves p will become poor;
Isa   1: 11 I have no p
Jer   6: 10 they find no p in it.
Eze 18: 23 Do I take any p in the death
     18: 32 For I take no p in the death
     33: 11 I take no p in the death
Lk   10: 21 Father, for this was your good p.
Eph   1: 5 in accordance with his p and will—
      1: 9 of his will according to his good p,
1Ti   5: 6 the widow who lives for p is dead
2Ti   3: 4 lovers of p rather than lovers
2Pe   2: 13 Their idea of p is to carouse

PLEASURES* (PLEASE)

Ps   16: 11 with eternal *p* at your right hand.
Lk   8: 14 and *p*, and they do not mature.
Tit   3: 3 by all kinds of passions and *p*.
Heb 11: 25 rather than to enjoy the *p* of sin
Jas   4: 3 may spend what you get on your *p*.
2Pe 2: 13 reveling in their *p* while they feast

PLEDGE

Dt   24: 17 take the cloak of the widow as a *p*.
1Pe 3: 21 but the *p* of a good conscience

PLEIADES

Job 38: 31 "Can you bind the beautiful *P*?
Am   5: 8 (he who made the *P* and Orion,

PLENTIFUL (PLENTY)

Mt   9: 37 harvest is *p* but the workers are
Lk   10: 2 harvest is *p*, but the workers are

PLENTY (PLENTIFUL)

2Co 8: 14 the present time your *p* will supply
Php 4: 12 whether living in *p* or in want.

PLOT (PLOTS)

Est   2: 22 Mordecai found out about the *p*
Ps   2: 1 and the peoples *p* in vain?
Pr   3: 29 not *p* harm against your neighbor,
Zec 8: 17 do not *p* evil against your neighbor,
Ac   4: 25 and the peoples *p* in vain?

PLOTS (PLOT)

Pr   6: 14 who *p* evil with deceit in his heart

PLOW (PLOWMAN PLOWSHARES)

Lk   9: 62 "No one who puts his hand to the *p*

PLOWMAN (PLOW)

1Co 9: 10 because when the *p* plows

PLOWSHARES (PLOW)

1Sa 13: 20 to the Philistines to have their *p*,
Isa   2: 4 They will beat their swords into *p*
Joel 3: 10 Beat your *p* into swords
Mic   4: 3 They will beat their swords into *p*

PLUCK

Mk   9: 47 your eye causes you to sin, *p* it out.

PLUNDER (PLUNDERED)

Ex   3: 22 And so you will *p* the Egyptians."
Est   3: 13 of Adar, and to *p* their goods.
       8: 11 to *p* the property of their enemies.
       9: 10 did not lay their hands on the *p*.
Pr 22: 23 and will *p* those who *p* them.
Isa   3: 14 the *p* from the poor is

PLUNDERED (PLUNDER)

Eze 34: 8 lacks a shepherd and so has been *p*

PLUNGE

1Ti   6: 9 and harmful desires that *p* men
1Pe   4: 4 think it strange that you do not *p*

PODS

Lk   15: 16 with the *p* that the pigs were eating,

POINT

Mt   4: 5 on the highest *p* of the temple.
    26: 38 with sorrow to the *p* of death.
Jas   2: 10 yet stumbles at just one *p* is guilty
Rev 2: 10 Be faithful, even to the *p* of death,

POISON

Ps 140: 3 the *p* of vipers is on their lips.
Mk 16: 18 and when they drink deadly *p*,
Ro   3: 13 "The *p* of vipers is on their lips."
Jas   3: 8 It is a restless evil, full of deadly *p*.

POLE (POLES)

Nu 21: 8 "Make a snake and put it up on a *p*;
Dt   16: 21 not set up any wooden Asherah *p*

POLES (POLE)

Ex   25: 13 Then make *p* of acacia wood

POLISHED

Isa 49: 2 he made me into a *p* arrow

POLLUTE* (POLLUTED POLLUTES)

Nu 35: 33 ' 'Do not *p* the land where you are.
Jude   : 8 these dreamers *p* their own bodies,

POLLUTED* (POLLUTE)

Ezr   9: 11 entering to possess is a land *p*
Pr   25: 26 Like a muddied spring or a *p* well
Ac   15: 20 to abstain from food *p* by idols,
Jas   1: 27 oneself from being *p* by the world.

POLLUTES* (POLLUTE)

Nu 35: 33 Bloodshed *p* the land,

PONDER (PONDERED)

Ps   64: 9 and *p* what he has done.
   119: 95 but I will *p* your statutes.

PONDERED (PONDER)

Ps 111: 2 they are *p* by all who delight
Lk   2: 19 up all these things and *p* them

POOR (POVERTY)

Lev 19: 10 Leave them for the *p* and the alien.
    23: 22 Leave them for the *p* and the alien.
    27: 8 If anyone making the vow is too *p*
Dt   15: 4 there should be no *p* among you,
    15: 7 is a *p* man among your brothers
    15: 11 There will always be *p* people
    24: 12 If the man is *p*, do not go to sleep
    24: 14 advantage of a hired man who is *p*
Job   5: 16 So the *p* have hope,
    24: 4 force all the *p* of the land
Ps   14: 6 frustrate the plans of the *p*,
    34: 6 This *p* man called, and the LORD
    35: 10 You rescue the *p* from those too
    40: 17 Yet I am *p* and needy;
    68: 10 O God, you provided for the *p*.
    82: 3 maintain the rights of the *p*
   112: 9 scattered abroad his gifts to the *p*,
   113: 7 He raises the *p* from the dust
   140: 12 the LORD secures justice for the *p*
Pr   10: 4 Lazy hands make a man *p*,
    13: 7 to be *p*, yet has great wealth.
    14: 20 The *p* are shunned
    14: 31 oppresses the *p* shows contempt.
    17: 5 who mocks the *p* shows contempt
    19: 1 Better a *p* man whose walk is
    19: 17 to the *p* lends to the LORD,
    19: 22 better to be *p* than a liar.
    20: 13 not love sleep or you will grow *p*;
    21: 13 to the cry of the *p*,
    21: 17 who loves pleasure will become *p*;
    22: 2 Rich and *p* have this in common:
    22: 9 for he shares his food with the *p*.
    22: 22 not exploit the *p* because they are *p*
    28: 6 Better a *p* man whose walk is
    28: 27 to the *p* will lack nothing,
    29: 7 care about justice for the *p*,
    31: 9 defend the rights of the *p*
    31: 20 She opens her arms to the *p*
Ecc   4: 13 Better a *p* but wise youth
Isa   3: 14 the plunder from the *p* is
    10: 2 to deprive the *p* of their rights
    14: 30 of the *p* will find pasture,
    25: 4 You have been a refuge for the *p*,
    32: 7 schemes to destroy the *p* with lies.
    61: 1 me to preach good news to the *p*
Jer   22: 16 He defended the cause of the *p*
Eze 18: 12 He oppresses the *p* and needy.
Am   2: 7 They trample on the heads of the *p*
     4: 1 you women who oppress the *p*
     5: 11 You trample on the *p*
Zec   7: 10 or the fatherless, the alien or the *p*.
Mt   5: 3 saying: "Blessed are the *p* in spirit,
    11: 5 the good news is preached to the *p*.
    19: 21 your possessions and give to the *p*,
    26: 11 The *p* you will always have
Mk 12: 42 But a *p* widow came and put
    14: 7 The *p* you will always have
Lk   4: 18 me to preach good news to the *p*.
     6: 20 "Blessed are you who are *p*,
    11: 41 is inside the dish, to the *p*,
    14: 13 invite the *p*, the crippled, the lame,
    21: 2 also saw a *p* widow put
Jn   12: 8 You will always have the *p*
Ac   9: 36 doing good and helping the *p*.
    10: 4 and gifts to the *p* have come up
    24: 17 to bring my people gifts for the *p*.
Ro   15: 26 for the *p* among the saints
1Co 13: 3 If I give all I possess to the *p*
2Co   6: 10 sorrowful, yet always rejoicing; *p*,
     8: 9 yet for your sakes he became *p*,
Gal   2: 10 continue to remember the *p*,
Jas   2: 2 and a *p* man in shabby clothes
     2: 5 not God chosen those who are *p*
     2: 6 But you have insulted the *p*.

POPULATION*

Pr   14: 28 A large *p* is a king's glory.

PORTION

Nu 18: 29 as the LORD's *p* the best
Dt   32: 9 For the LORD's *p* is his people.
1Sa 1: 5 But to Hannah he gave a double *p*
2Ki   2: 9 "Let me inherit a double *p*
Ps   73: 26 and my *p* forever.
   119: 57 You are my *p*, O LORD;
Isa 53: 12 Therefore I will give him a *p*
Jer   10: 16 He who is the *P* of Jacob is not like
La   3: 24 to myself, "The LORD is my *p*;
Zec   2: 12 LORD will inherit Judah as his *p*

PORTRAIT

Lk   20: 24 Whose *p* and inscription are on it?"

PORTRAYED

Gal   3: 1 very eyes Jesus Christ was clearly *p*

POSITION (POSITIONS)

Ro   12: 16 to associate with people of low *p*.
Jas   1: 9 ought to take pride in his high *p*.
2Pe   3: 17 and fall from your secure *p*.

POSITIONS (POSITION)

2Ch 20: 17 Take up your *p*; stand firm
Jude   : 6 the angels who did not keep their *p*

POSSESS (POSSESSED POSSESSING POSSESSION POSSESSIONS)

Nu 33: 53 for I have given you the land to *p*.
Dt   4: 14 you are crossing the Jordan to *p*.
Pr   8: 12 I *p* knowledge and discretion.
Jn   5: 39 that by them you *p* eternal life.

POSSESSED (POSSESS)

Jn   10: 21 the sayings of a man *p* by a demon.

POSSESSING* (POSSESS)

2Co   6: 10 nothing, and yet *p* everything.

POSSESSION (POSSESS)

Ge   15: 7 to give you this land to take *p* of it
Ex   6: 8 I will give it to you as a *p*.
    19: 5 nations you will be my treasured *p*.
Nu 13: 30 "We should go up and take *p*
Dt   7: 6 to be his people, his treasured *p*.
Jos   1: 11 take *p* of the land the LORD your
Ps   2: 8 the ends of the earth your *p*.
   135: 4 Israel to be his treasured *p*.
Eph   1: 14 of those who are God's *p*—

POSSESSIONS (POSSESS)

Mt   19: 21 go, sell your *p* and give to the poor,
Lk   11: 21 guards his own house, his *p* are safe
    12: 15 consist in the abundance of his *p*."
    19: 8 now I give half of my *p* to the poor,
Ac   4: 32 any of his *p* was his own,
2Co 12: 14 what I want is not your *p* but you.
Heb 10: 34 yourselves had better and lasting *p*.
1Jn   3: 17 If anyone has material *p*

POSSIBLE

Mt   19: 26 but with God all things are *p*."
    26: 39 if it is *p*, may this cup be taken
Mk   9: 23 "Everything is *p* for him who
    10: 27 all things are *p* with God."
    14: 35 prayed that if the hour might pass
Ro   12: 18 If it is *p*, as far as it depends on you,
1Co   6: 5 Is it *p* that there is nobody
     9: 19 to everyone, to win as many as *p*.
     9: 22 by all *p* means I might save some.

POT (POTSHERD POTTER POTTER'S POTTERY)

2Ki   4: 40 there is death in the *p*!''
Jer   18: 4 But the *p* he was shaping

POTIPHAR*

Egyptian who bought Joseph (Ge 37:36), set him over his house (Ge 39:1-6), sent him to prison (Ge 39:7-30).

POTSHERD (POT)

Isa   45: 9 a *p* among the potsherds

POTTER (POT)

Isa   29: 16 Can the pot say of the *p*,
    45: 9 Does the clay say to the *p*,
    64: 8 We are the clay, you are the *p*;
Jer   18: 2 "Like clay in the hand of the *p*,
Zec 11: 13 it to the *p*"—the handsome price

Ro 9:21 Does not the p have the right

POTTER'S (POT)

Mt 27: 7 to use the money to buy the p field

POTTERY (POT)

Ro 9:21 of clay some p for noble purposes

POUR (POURED POURS)

Ps 62: 8 p out your hearts to him,
Isa 44: 3 I will p out my Spirit
Eze 20: 8 So I said I would p out my wrath
39:29 for I will p out my Spirit
Joel 2:28 I will p out my Spirit on all people.
Zec 12:10 I will p out on the house of David
Mal 3:10 p out so much blessing that you
Ac 2:17 I will p out my Spirit on all people.

POURED (POUR)

Ps 22:14 I am p out like water,
Isa 32:15 till the Spirit is p upon us
Mt 26:28 which is p out for many
Lk 22:20 in my blood, which is p out for you.
Ac 2:33 and has p out what you now see
10:45 of the Holy Spirit had been p out
Ro 5: 5 because God has p out his love
Php 2:17 even if I am being p out like a drink
2Ti 4: 6 I am already being p out like
Tit 3: 6 whom he p out on us generously
Rev 16: 2 and p out his bowl on the land,

POURS (POUR)

Lk 5:37 And no one p new wine

POVERTY* (POOR)

Dt 28:48 and thirst, in nakedness and dire p,
1Sa 2: 7 The LORD sends p and wealth;
Pr 6:11 p will come on you like a bandit
10:15 but p is the ruin of the poor.
11:24 withholds unduly, but comes to p.
13:18 who ignores discipline comes to p
14:23 but mere talk leads only to p.
21: 5 as surely as haste leads to p.
22:16 to the rich—both come to p.
24:34 p will come on you like a bandit
28:19 fantasies will have his fill of p.
28:22 and is unaware that p awaits him.
30: 8 give me neither p nor riches,
31: 7 let them drink and forget their p
Ecc 4:14 born in p within his kingdom.
Mk 12:44 out of her p, put in everything—
Lk 21: 4 she out of her p put in all she had
2Co 8: 2 and their extreme p welled up
8: 9 through his p might become rich.
Rev 2: 9 I know your afflictions and your p

POWER (POWERFUL POWERS)

Ex 15: 6 was majestic in p.
32:11 out of Egypt with great p
Dt 8:17 "My p and the strength
34:12 one has ever shown the mighty p
1Sa 10: 6 LORD will come upon you in p,
10:10 Spirit of God came upon him in p,
11: 6 Spirit of God came upon him in p,
16:13 the LORD came upon David in p.
1Ch 29:11 LORD, is the greatness and the p
2Ch 20: 6 P and might are in your hand,
32: 7 for there is a greater p with us
Job 9: 4 wisdom is profound, his p is vast.
36:22 "God is exalted in his p.
37:23 beyond our reach and exalted in p;
Ps 20: 6 with the saving p of his right hand.
63: 2 and beheld your p and your glory.
66: 3 So great is your p
68:34 Proclaim the p of God,
77:14 you display your p
89:13 Your arm is endued with p;
145: 6 of the p of your awesome works,
147: 5 Great is our Lord and mighty in p;
150: 2 Praise him for his acts of p;
Pr 3:27 when it is in your p to act.
18:21 The tongue has the p of life
24: 5 A wise man has great p,
Isa 11: 2 the Spirit of counsel and of p,
40:10 the Sovereign LORD comes with p
40:26 of his great p and mighty strength,
63:12 who sent his glorious arm of p
Jer 10: 6 and your name is mighty in p.
10:12 But God made the earth by his p;
27: 5 With my great p and outstretched
32:17 and the earth by your great p
Hos 13:14 from the p of the grave;
Na 1: 3 to anger and great in p;
Zec 4: 6 nor by p, but by my Spirit,'
Mt 22:29 do not know the Scriptures or the p
Mt 24:30 on the clouds of the sky, with p
Lk 1:35 and the p of the Most High will
4:14 to Galilee in the p of the Spirit,
9: 1 he gave them p and authority
10:19 to overcome all the p of the enemy;
24:49 clothed with p from on high."
Ac 1: 8 you will receive p when the Holy
4:28 They did what your p and will had
4:33 With great p the apostles
10:38 with the Holy Spirit and p,
26:18 and from the p of Satan to God,
Ro 1:16 it is the p of God for the salvation
1:20 his eternal p and divine nature—
4:21 fully persuaded that God had p
9:17 that I might display my p in you
15:13 overflow with hope by the p
15:19 through the p of the Spirit.
1Co 1:17 cross of Christ be emptied of its p.
1:18 to us who are being saved it is the p
2: 4 a demonstration of the Spirit's p,
6:14 By his p God raised the Lord
15:24 all dominion, authority and p.
15:56 of death is sin, and the p
2Co 4: 7 to show that this all-surpassing p is
6: 7 in truthful speech and in the p
10: 4 they have divine p
12: 9 for my p is made perfect
13: 4 weakness, yet he lives by God's p.
Eph 1:19 and his incomparably great p
3:16 you with p through his Spirit
3:20 according to his p that is at work
6:10 in the Lord and in his mighty p.
Php 3:10 and the p of his resurrection
3:21 by the p that enables him
Col 1:11 strengthened with all p according
2:10 who is the head over every p
1Th 1: 5 also with p, with the Holy Spirit
2Ti 1: 7 but a spirit of p, of love
3: 5 form of godliness but denying its p.
Heb 2:14 might destroy him who holds the p
7:16 of the p of an indestructible life.
1Pe 1: 5 by God's p until the coming
2Pe 1: 3 His divine p has given us
Jude :25 p and authority, through Jesus
Rev 4:11 to receive glory and honor and p,
5:12 to receive p and wealth
11:17 you have taken your great p
19: 1 and glory and p belong to our God,
20: 6 The second death has no p

POWERFUL (POWER)

2Ch 27: 6 Jotham grew p because he walked
Est 9: 4 and he became more and more p.
Ps 29: 4 The voice of the LORD is p;
Jer 32:18 p God, whose name is the LORD
Zec 8:22 p nations will come to Jerusalem
Mk 1: 7 "After me will come one more p
Lk 24:19 p in word and deed before God
2Th 1: 7 in blazing fire with his p angels.
Heb 1: 3 sustaining all things by his p word.
Jas 5:16 The prayer of a righteous man is p

POWERLESS

Ro 5: 6 when we were still p, Christ died
8: 3 For what the law was p to do

POWERS (POWER)

Da 4:35 pleases with the p of heaven
Ro 8:38 nor any p, neither height nor depth
1Co 12:10 to another miraculous p,
Eph 6:12 against the p of this dark world
Col 1:16 whether thrones or p or rulers
2:15 And having disarmed the p
Heb 6: 5 and the p of the coming age,
1Pe 3:22 and p in submission to him.

PRACTICE (PRACTICED PRACTICES)

Lev 19:26 " 'Do not p divination or sorcery.
Ps 119: 56 This has been my p:
Eze 33:31 but they do not put them into p.
Mt 7:24 into p is like a wise man who built
23: 3 for they do not p what they preach.
Lk 8:21 hear God's word and put it into p."
Ro 12:13 P hospitality.
Php 4: 9 or seen in me—put it into p.
1Ti 5: 4 to put their religion into p by caring

PRACTICED (PRACTICE)

Mt 23:23 You should have p the latter,

PRACTICES (PRACTICE)

Ps 101: 7 No one who p deceit
Mt 5:19 but whoever p and teaches these
Col 3: 9 taken off your old self with its p

PRAISE (PRAISED PRAISES PRAISEWORTHY PRAISING)

Ex 15: 2 He is my God, and I will p him,
Dt 10:21 He is your p; he is your God,
26:19 declared that he will set you in p,
32: 3 Oh, p the greatness of our God!
Ru 4:14 said to Naomi: "P be to the LORD,
2Sa 22: 4 to the LORD, who is worthy of p,
22:47 The LORD lives! P be to my Rock
1Ch 16:25 is the LORD and most worthy of p;
16:35 that we may glory in your p."
23: 5 four thousand are to p the LORD
29:10 "P be to you, O LORD,
2Ch 5:13 they raised their voices in p
20:21 and to p him for the splendor
29:30 to p the LORD with the words
Ezr 3:10 took their places to p the LORD,
Ne 9: 5 and p the LORD your God,
Ps 8: 2 you have ordained p
9: 1 I will p you, O LORD,
16: 7 I will p the LORD, who counsels
26: 7 proclaiming aloud your p
30: 4 p his holy name.
33: 1 it is fitting for the upright to p him.
34: 1 his p will always be on my lips.
40: 3 a hymn of p to our God.
42: 5 for I will yet p him,
43: 5 for I will yet p him,
45:17 the nations will p you for ever
47: 7 sing to him a psalm of p.
48: 1 the LORD, and most worthy of p,
51:15 and my mouth will declare your p.
56: 4 In God, whose word I p,
57: 9 I will p you, O Lord,
63: 4 I will p you as long as I live,
65: 1 P awaits you, O God, in Zion;
66: 2 make his p glorious.
66: 8 P our God, O peoples,
68:19 P be to the Lord, to God our Savior
68:26 p the LORD in the assembly
69:30 I will p God's name in song
69:34 Let heaven and earth p him,
71: 8 My mouth is filled with your p,
71:14 I will p you more and more.
71:22 I will p you with the harp
74:21 the poor and needy p your name.
86:12 I will p you, O Lord my God,
89: 5 The heavens p your wonders,
92: 1 It is good to p the LORD
96: 2 Sing to the LORD, p his name;
100: 4 and his courts with p;
101: 1 to you, O LORD, I will sing p.
102: 18 not yet created may p the LORD:
103: 1 P the LORD, O my soul;
103: 20 P the LORD, you his angels,
104: 1 P the LORD, O my soul.
105: 2 Sing to him, sing p to him;
106: 1 P the LORD.
108: 3 I will p you, O LORD,
111: 1 P the LORD.
113: 1 P the LORD.
117: 1 P the LORD, all you nations;
119:175 Let me live that I may p you,
135: 1 P the LORD.
135: 20 you who fear him, p the LORD.
138: 1 I will p you, O LORD,
139: 14 I p you because I am fearfully
144: 1 P be to the LORD my Rock,
145: 3 is the LORD and most worthy of p;
145: 10 All you have made will p you,
145: 21 Let every creature p his holy name
146: 1 P the LORD, O my soul.
147: 1 how pleasant and fitting to p him!
148: 1 P the LORD from the heavens,
148: 13 Let them p the name of the LORD,
149: 1 his p in the assembly of the saints.
149: 6 May the p of God be
149: 9 P the LORD.
150: 2 p him for his surpassing greatness.
150: 6 that has breath p the LORD.
Pr 27: 2 Let another p you, and not your
27:21 man is tested by the p he receives.
31:31 let her works bring her p
SS 1: 4 we will p your love more than wine
Isa 12: 1 "I will p you, O LORD.
42:10 his p from the ends of the earth,
61: 3 and a garment of p
Jer 33: 9 p and honor before all nations
Da 2:20 "P be to the name of God for ever
4:37 p and exalt and glorify the King
Mt 5:16 and p your Father in heaven.
21:16 you have ordained p'?"
Lk 19:37 to p God in loud voices
Jn 5:44 effort to obtain the p that comes

Jn   12: 43 for they loved *p* from men more
Ro   2: 29 Such a man's *p* is not from men,
    15:   7 in order to bring *p* to God.
2Co   1:   3 *P* be to the God and Father
Eph   1:   3 *P* be to the God and Father
    1:   6 to the *p* of his glorious grace,
    1: 12 might be for the *p* of his glory.
    1: 14 to the *p* of his glory.
1Th   2:   6 We were not looking for *p*
Heb 13: 15 offer to God a sacrifice of *p*—
Jas   3:   9 With the tongue we *p* our Lord
    5: 13 happy? Let him sing songs of *p*.
Rev   5: 13 be *p* and honor and glory
    7: 12 *P* and glory

PRAISED (PRAISE)

1Ch 29: 10 David *p* the LORD in the presence
Ne   8:   6 Ezra *p* the LORD, the great God;
Job   1: 21 may the name of the LORD be *p*."
Ps 113:   2 Let the name of the LORD be *p*,
Pr   31: 30 who fears the LORD is to be *p*.
Isa 63:   7 the deeds for which he is to be *p*,
Da   2: 19 Then Daniel *p* the God of heaven
    4: 34 Then I *p* the Most High; I honored
Lk   18: 43 the people saw it, they also *p* God.
    23: 47 seeing what had happened, *p* God
Ro   9:   5 who is God over all, forever *p*!
Gal   1: 24 And they *p* God because of me.
1Pe   4: 11 that in all things God may be *p*

PRAISES (PRAISE)

2Sa 22: 50 I will sing *p* to your name.
Ps   18: 49 I will sing *p* to your name.
    47:   6 Sing *p* to God, sing *p*;
  147:   1 How good it is to sing *p* to our God,
Pr   31: 28 her husband also, and he *p* her:
1Pe   2:   9 that you may declare the *p*

PRAISEWORTHY* (PRAISE)

Ps   78:   4 the *p* deeds of the LORD,
Php   4:   8 if anything is excellent or *p*—

PRAISING (PRAISE)

Lk   2: 13 *p* God and saying, "Glory to God
    2: 20 *p* God for all the things they had
Ac   2: 47 *p* God and enjoying the favor
    10: 46 speaking in tongues and *p* God.
1Co 14: 16 If you are *p* God with your spirit,

PRAY (PRAYED PRAYER PRAYERS PRAYING PRAYS)

Dt   4:   7 is near us whenever we *p* to him?
1Sa 12: 23 the LORD by failing to *p* for you.
1Ki   8: 30 when they *p* toward this place.
2Ch   7: 14 will humble themselves and *p*
Ezr   6: 10 and *p* for the well-being of the king
Job 42:   8 My servant Job will *p* for you,
Ps   5:   2 for to you I *p*.
    32:   6 let everyone who is godly *p*
  122:   6 *P* for the peace of Jerusalem:
Jer 29:   7 *P* to the LORD for it,
    29: 12 upon me and come and *p* to me,
    42:   3 *P* that the LORD your God will
Mt   5: 44 and *p* for those who persecute you,
    6:   5 "And when you *p*, do not be like
    6:   9 "This, then, is how you should *p*:
    14: 23 up on a mountainside by himself to *p*.
    19: 13 hands on them and *p* for them.
    26: 36 Sit here while I go over there and *p*
Lk   6: 28 *p* for those who mistreat you.
    11:   1 us to *p*, just as John taught his
    18:   1 them that they should always *p*
    22: 40 "Pray that you will not fall
Jn   17: 20 I *p* also for those who will believe
Ro   8: 26 do not know what we ought to *p* for,
1Co 14: 13 in a tongue should *p* that he may
Eph   1: 18 I *p* also that the eyes
    3: 16 I *p* out of his glorious riches he
    6: 18 And *p* in the Spirit on all occasions
Col   1: 10 we *p* this in order that you may live
    4:   3 *p* for us, too, that God may open
1Th   5: 17 Be joyful always; *p* continually;
2Th   1: 11 in mind, we constantly *p* for you,
Jas   5: 13 one of you in trouble? He should *p*.
    5: 16 for each other so that you may be
1Pe   4:   7 self-controlled so that you can *p*.
Jude   : 20 up in your most holy faith and *p*

PRAYED (PRAY)

1Sa   1: 27 I *p* for this child, and the LORD
1Ki 18: 36 Elijah stepped forward and *p*:
    19:   4 under it and *p* that he might die.
2Ki   6: 17 And Elisha *p*, "O LORD,
2Ch 30: 18 But Hezekiah *p* for them, saying,
Ne   4:   9 we *p* to our God and posted a guard

Job 42: 10 After Job had *p* for his friends,
Da   6: 10 got down on his knees and *p*,
    9:   4 I *p* to the LORD my God
Jnh   2:   1 From inside the fish Jonah *p*
Mt   26: 39 with his face to the ground and *p*,
Mk   1: 35 off to a solitary place, where he *p*.
    14: 35 *p* that if possible the hour might
Lk   22: 41 knelt down and *p*, "Father,
Jn   17:   1 he looked toward heaven and *p*:
Ac   4: 31 After they *p*, the place where they
    6:   6 who *p* and laid their hands on them
    8: 15 they *p* for them that they might
    13:   3 So after they had fasted and *p*,

PRAYER (PRAY)

2Ch 30: 27 for their *p* reached heaven,
Ezr   8: 23 about this, and he answered our *p*.
Ps   4:   1 be merciful to me and hear my *p*.
    6:   9 The LORD accepts my *p*.
    17:   1 Give ear to my *p*—
    17:   6 give ear to me and hear my *p*.
    65:   2 O you who hear *p*,
    66: 20 who has not rejected my *p*
    86:   6 Hear my *p*, O LORD;
Pr   15:   8 but the *p* of the upright pleases him
    15: 29 but he hears the *p* of the righteous.
Isa 56:   7 a house of *p* for all nations."
Mt 21: 13 house will be called a house of *p*,'
    21: 22 receive whatever you ask for in *p*."
Mk   9: 29 This kind can come out only by *p*."
    11: 24 whatever you ask for in *p*,
Jn   17: 15 My *p* is not that you take them out
Ac   1: 14 all joined together constantly in *p*,
    2: 42 to the breaking of bread and to *p*.
    6:   4 and will give our attention to *p*
    10: 31 has heard your *p* and remembered
    16: 13 expected to find a place of *p*.
Ro   12: 12 patient in affliction, faithful in *p*.
1Co   7:   5 you may devote yourselves to *p*.
2Co 13:   9 and our *p* is for your perfection.
Php   1:   9 this is my *p*: that your love may
    4:   6 but in everything, by *p* and petition
Col   4:   2 yourselves to *p*, being watchful
1Ti   2:   8 to lift up holy hands in *p*,
    4:   5 by the word of God and *p*.
Jas   5: 15 *p* offered in faith will make the sick
1Pe   3: 12 and his ears are attentive to their *p*,

PRAYERS (PRAY)

1Ch   5: 20 He answered their *p*, because they
Isa   1: 15 even if you offer many *p*,
Mk 12: 40 and for a show make lengthy *p*.
2Co   1: 11 as you help us by your *p*.
Eph   6: 18 on all occasions with all kinds of *p*
1Ti   2:   1 then, first of all, that requests, *p*,
1Pe   3:   7 so that nothing will hinder your *p*.
Rev   5:   8 which are the *p* of the saints.
    8:   3 with the *p* of all the saints.

PRAYING (PRAY)

Ge   24: 45 "Before I finished *p* in my heart,
1Sa   1: 12 As she kept on *p* to the LORD,
Mk 11: 25 And when you stand *p*,
Lk   3: 21 as he was *p*, heaven was opened
    6: 12 and spent the night *p* to God.
    9: 29 As he was *p*, the appearance
Jn   17:   9 I am not *p* for the world,
Ac   9: 11 from Tarsus named Saul, for he is *p*
    16: 25 and Silas were *p* and singing hymns
Ro   15: 30 in my struggle by *p* to God for me.
Eph   6: 18 always keep on *p* for all the saints.

PRAYS (PRAY)

1Co 14: 14 my spirit *p*, but my mind is

PREACH (PREACHED PREACHING)

Isa 61:   1 me to *p* good news to the poor.
Mt   10:   7 As you go, *p* this message:
    23:   3 they do not practice what they *p*.
Mk 16: 15 and *p* the good news to all creation.
Lk   4: 18 me to *p* good news to the poor.
Ac   9: 20 At once he began to *p*
    16: 10 us to *p* the gospel to them.
Ro   1: 15 am so eager to *p* the gospel
    10: 15 how can they *p* unless they are sent
    15: 20 to *p* the gospel where Christ was
1Co   1: 17 to *p* the gospel—not with words
    1: 23 wisdom, but we *p* Christ crucified:
    9: 14 that those who *p* the gospel should
    9: 16 Woe to me if I do not *p* the gospel!
2Co   4:   5 For we do not *p* ourselves,
    10: 16 so that we can *p* the gospel
Gal   1:   8 from heaven should *p* a gospel
2Ti   4:   2 I give you this charge: *P* the Word;

PREACHED (PREACH)

Mt   24: 14 gospel of the kingdom will be *p*
Mk   6: 12 and *p* that people should repent.
    13: 10 And the gospel must first be *p*
    14:   9 wherever the gospel is *p*
Ac   8:   4 had been scattered *p* the word
    28: 31 hindrance he *p* the kingdom
1Co   9: 27 so that after I have *p* to others,
    15:   1 you of the gospel I *p* to you,
2Co 11:   4 other than the Jesus we *p*,
Gal   1:   8 other than the one we *p* to you,
Eph   2: 17 *p* peace to you who were far away
Php   1: 18 false motives or true, Christ is *p*.
1Ti   3: 16 was *p* among the nations,
1Pe   1: 25 this is the word that was *p* to you.
    3: 19 and *p* to the spirits in prison who

PREACHING (PREACH)

Lk   9:   6 *p* the gospel and healing people
Ac   18:   5 devoted himself exclusively to *p*,
Ro   10: 14 hear without someone *p* to them?
1Co   2:   4 and my *p* were not with wise
    9: 18 in *p* the gospel I may offer it free
Gal   1:   9 If anybody is *p* to you a gospel
1Ti   4: 13 the public reading of Scripture, to *p*
    5: 17 especially those whose work is *p*

PRECEDE*

1Th   4: 15 will certainly not *p* those who have

PRECEPTS*

Dt 33: 10 He teaches your *p* to Jacob
Ps   19:   8 The *p* of the LORD are right,
  103: 18 and remember to obey his *p*.
  105: 45 that they might keep his *p*
  111:   7 all his *p* are trustworthy.
  111: 10 who follow his *p* have good
  119:   4 You have laid down *p*
  119: 15 I meditate on your *p*
  119: 27 understand the teaching of your *p*;
  119: 40 How I long for your *p*!
  119: 45 for I have sought out your *p*.
  119: 56 I obey your *p*.
  119: 63 to all who follow your *p*.
  119: 69 I keep your *p* with all my heart.
  119: 78 but I will meditate on your *p*.
  119: 87 but I have not forsaken your *p*.
  119: 93 I will never forget your *p*,
  119: 94 I have sought out your *p*.
  119: 100 for I obey your *p*.
  119: 104 I gain understanding from your *p*;
  119: 110 but I have not strayed from your *p*.
  119: 128 because I consider all your *p* right,
  119: 134 that I may obey your *p*.
  119: 141 I do not forget your *p*.
  119: 159 See how I love your *p*;
  119: 168 I obey your *p* and your statutes,
  119: 173 for I have chosen your *p*.

PRECIOUS

Ps 19: 10 They are more *p* than gold,
  72: 14 for *p* is their blood in his sight.
  116: 15 *P* in the sight of the LORD
  119: 72 from your mouth is more *p* to me
  139: 17 How *p* to me are your thoughts,
Pr   8: 11 for wisdom is more *p* than rubies,
Isa 28: 16 a *p* cornerstone for a sure
1Pe   1: 19 but with the *p* blood of Christ,
    2:   4 but chosen by God and *p* to him—
    2:   6 a chosen and *p* cornerstone,
2Pe   1:   1 Christ have received a faith as *p*
    1:   4 us his very great and *p* promises,

PREDESTINED* (DESTINY)

Ro   8: 29 *p* to be conformed to the likeness
    8: 30 And those he *p*, he also called;
Eph   1:   5 In love he *p* us to be adopted
    1: 11 having been *p* according

PREDICTED (PREDICTION)

1Sa 28: 17 The LORD has done what he *p*
Ac   7: 52 killed those who *p* the coming
1Pe   1: 11 when he *p* the sufferings of Christ

PREDICTION* (PREDICTED PREDICTIONS)

Jer 28:   9 only if his *p* comes true."

PREDICTIONS (PREDICTION)

Isa 44: 26 and fulfills the *p* of his messengers,

PREGNANT

Ex 21: 22 who are fighting hit a *p* woman
Mt 24: 19 be in those days for *p* women
1Th   5:   3 as labor pains on a *p* woman,

PREPARE (PREPARED)

Ps 23: 5 You p a table before me
Isa 25: 6 the LORD Almighty will p
40: 3 "In the desert p
Am 4: 12 p to meet your God, O Israel."
Mal 3: 1 who will p the way before me.
Mt 3: 3 'Pthe way for the Lord,
Jn 14: 2 there to p a place for you.
Eph 4: 12 to p God's people for works
1Pe 1: 13 Therefore, p your minds for action;

PREPARED (PREPARE)

Ex 23: 20 to bring you to the place I have p.
Mt 25: 34 the kingdom p for you
Ro 9: 22 of his wrath—p for destruction?
1Co 2: 9 what God has p for those who love
Eph 2: 10 which God p in advance for us
2Ti 2: 21 and p to do any good work.
4: 2 be p in season and out of season;
1Pe 3: 15 Always be p to give an answer

PRESCRIBED

Ezr 7: 23 Whatever the God of heaven has p,

PRESENCE (PRESENT)

Ex 25: 30 Put the bread of the P on this table
33: 14 The LORD replied, "My P will go
Nu 4: 7 "Over the table of the P they are
1Sa 6: 20 in the p of the LORD, this
21: 6 of the P that had been removed
2Sa 22: 13 Out of the brightness of his p
2Ki 17: 23 LORD removed them from his p,
23: 27 also from my p as I removed Israel,
Ezr 9: 15 one of us can stand in your p."
Ps 16: 11 you will fill me with joy in your p,
21: 6 with the joy of your p.
23: 5 in the p of my enemies.
31: 20 the shelter of your p you hide them
41: 12 and set me in your p forever.
51: 11 Do not cast me from your p
52: 9 in the p of your saints.
89: 15 who walk in the light of your p,
90: 8 our secret sins in the light of your p
114: 7 O earth, at the p of the Lord,
139: 7 Where can I flee from your p?
Isa 26: 17 so were we in your p, O LORD.
Jer 5: 22 "Should you not tremble in my p?
Eze 38: 20 of the earth will tremble at my p.
Hos 6: 2 that we may live in his p.
Na 1: 5 The earth trembles at his p,
Mal 3: 16 in his p concerning those who
Ac 2: 28 you will fill me with joy in your p.'
1Th 3: 9 have in the p of our God
3: 13 and holy in the p of our God
2Th 1: 9 and shut out from the p of the Lord
Heb 9: 24 now to appear for us in God's p.
1Jn 3: 19 rest in his p whenever our hearts
Jude : 24 before his glorious p without fault

PRESENT (PRESENCE)

1Co 3: 22 life or death or the p or the future—
7: 26 of the p crisis, I think that it is good
2Co 11: 2 so that I might p you as a pure
Eph 5: 27 and to p her to himself
1Ti 4: 8 holding promise for both the p life
2Ti 2: 15 Do your best to p yourself to God
Jude : 24 and to p you before his glorious

PRESERVE

Lk 17: 33 and whoever loses his life will p it.

PRESERVES

Ps 119: 50 Your promise p my life.

PRESS (PRESSED PRESSURE)

Php 3: 12 but I p on to take hold of that
3: 14 I p on toward the goal

PRESSED (PRESS)

Lk 6: 38 p down, shaken together

PRESSURE (PRESS)

2Co 1: 8 We were under great p, far
11: 28 I face daily the p of my concern

PRETENDED

1Sa 21: 13 So he p to be insane in their presence;

PREVAILS

1Sa 2: 9 "It is not by strength that one p;
Pr 19: 21 but it is the LORD's purpose that p

PRICE (PRICELESS)

Job 28: 18 the p of wisdom is beyond rubies.
1Co 6: 20 your own; you were bought at a p.
7: 23 bought at a p; do not become slaves

PRICELESS* (PRICE)

Ps 36: 7 How p is your unfailing love!

PRIDE (PROUD)

Pr 8: 13 I hate p and arrogance,
11: 2 When p comes, then comes
13: 10 P only breeds quarrels,
16: 18 P goes before destruction,
29: 23 A man's p brings him low,
Isa 25: 11 God will bring down their p
Da 4: 37 And those who walk in p he is able
Am 8: 7 The LORD has sworn by the P
2Co 5: 12 giving you an opportunity to take p
7: 4 in you; I take great p in you.
8: 24 and the reason for our p in you,
Gal 6: 4 Then he can take p in himself,
Jas 1: 9 ought to take p in his high position.

PRIEST (PRIESTHOOD PRIESTLY PRIESTS)

Ge 14: 18 He was p of God Most High,
Nu 5: 10 to the p will belong to the p.' "
2Ch 13: 9 and seven rams may become a p
Ps 110: 4 "You are a p forever.
Heb 2: 17 faithful high p in service to God,
3: 1 and high p whom we confess.
4: 14 have a great high p who has gone
4: 15 do not have a high p who is unable
5: 6 "You are a p forever,
6: 20 He has become a high p forever.
7: 3 Son of God he remains a p forever.
7: 15 clear if another p like Melchizedek
7: 26 Such a high p meets our need—
8: 1 We do have such a high p,
10: 11 Day after day every p stands
13: 11 The high p carries the blood

PRIESTHOOD (PRIEST)

Heb 7: 24 lives forever, he has a permanent p.
1Pe 2: 5 into a spiritual house to be a holy p,
2: 9 you are a chosen people, a royal p,

PRIESTLY (PRIEST)

Ro 15: 16 to the Gentiles with the p duty

PRIESTS (PRIEST)

Ex 19: 6 you will be for me a kingdom of p
Lev 21: 1 "Speak to the p, the sons of Aaron,
Eze 42: 13 where the p who approach
46: 2 p are to sacrifice his burnt offering
Mal 1: 6 O p, who show contempt for my name.
Rev 5: 10 to be a kingdom and p
20: 6 but they will be p of God

PRIME

Isa 38: 10 recovery: I said, "In the p of my life

PRINCE (PRINCES PRINCESS)

Isa 9: 6 Everlasting Father, P of Peace.
Eze 34: 24 and my servant David will be p
37: 25 my servant will be their p forever.
Da 8: 25 stand against the P of princes.
Jn 12: 31 now the p of this world will be
Ac 5: 31 as P and Savior that he might give

PRINCES (PRINCE)

Ps 118: 9 than to trust in p.
148: 11 you and all rulers on earth,
Isa 40: 23 He brings p to naught

PRINCESS* (PRINCE)

Ps 45: 13 All glorious is the p

PRISCILLA*

Wife of Aquila; co-worker with Paul (Ac 18; Ro 16:3; 1Co 16:19; 2Ti 4:19); instructor of Apollos (Ac 18:24-28).

PRISON (PRISONER PRISONERS)

Ps 66: 11 You brought us into p
142: 7 Set me free from my p,
Isa 42: 7 to free captives from p
Mt 25: 36 I was in p and you came to visit me
2Co 11: 23 been in prison more frequently,
Heb 11: 36 others were chained and put in p.
13: 3 Remember those in p
1Pe 3: 19 spirits in p who disobeyed long ago
Rev 20: 7 Satan will be released from his p

PRISONER (PRISON)

Ro 7: 23 and making me a p of the law of sin
Gal 3: 22 declares that the whole world is a p
Eph 3: 1 the p of Christ Jesus for the sake

PRISONERS (PRISON)

Ps 68: 6 he leads forth the p with singing;
79: 11 groans of the p come before you;
107: 10 p suffering in iron chains,
146: 7 The LORD sets p free,
Zec 9: 12 to your fortress, O p of hope;
Lk 4: 18 me to proclaim freedom for the p
Gal 3: 23 we were held p by the law,

PRIVILEGE*

2Co 8: 4 pleaded with us for the p of sharing

PRIZE*

1Co 9: 24 Run in such a way as to get the p.
9: 24 but only one gets the p? Run
9: 27 will not be disqualified for the p.
Php 3: 14 on toward the goal to win the p
Col 2: 18 of angels disqualify you for the p.

PROBE

Job 11: 7 Can you p the limits
Ps 17: 3 Though you p my heart

PROCEDURE

Ecc 8: 6 For there is a proper time and p

PROCESSION

Ps 68: 24 Your p has come into view, O God,
118: 27 boughs in hand, join in the festal p
1Co 4: 9 on display at the end of the p,
2Co 2: 14 us in triumphal p in Christ

PROCLAIM (PROCLAIMED PROCLAIMING PROCLAIMS PROCLAMATION)

Ex 33: 19 and I will p my name, the LORD,
Lev 25: 10 and p liberty throughout the land
Dt 30: 12 get it to us so we may obey it?"
2Sa 1: 20 p it not in the streets of Ashkelon,
1Ch 16: 23 p his salvation day after day.
Ne 8: 15 and that they should p this word
Ps 2: 7 I will p the decree of the LORD:
9: 11 p among the nations what he has
19: 1 the skies p the work of his hands.
22: 31 They will p his righteousness
40: 9 I p righteousness in the great
50: 6 the heavens p his righteousness,
64: 9 they will p the works of God
68: 34 P the power of God,
71: 16 I will come and p your mighty acts,
92: 2 to p your love in the morning
96: 2 p his salvation day after day
97: 6 The heavens p his righteousness,
106: 2 Who can p the mighty acts
118: 17 will p what the LORD has done.
145: 6 and I will p your great deeds.
Isa 12: 4 and p that his name is exalted.
42: 12 and p his praise in the islands.
52: 7 who p salvation,
61: 1 to p freedom for the captives
66: 19 They will p my glory
Jer 7: 2 house and there p this message:
50: 2 lift up a banner and p it;
Hos 5: 9 I p what is certain.
Zec 9: 10 He will p peace to the nations.
Mt 10: 27 in your ear, p from the roofs.
12: 18 and he will p justice to the nations.
Lk 4: 18 me to p freedom for the prisoners
9: 60 you go and p the kingdom of God."
Ac 17: 23 unknown I am going to p
20: 27 hesitated to p to you the whole will
1Co 11: 26 you p the Lord's death
Col 1: 28 We p him, admonishing
4: 4 Pray that I may p it clearly,
1Jn 1: 1 this we p concerning the Word

PROCLAIMED (PROCLAIM)

Ex 9: 16 and that my name might be p
34: 5 there with him and p his name,
Ps 68: 11 was the company of those who p it:
Ro 15: 19 I have fully p the gospel of Christ.
Col 1: 23 that has been p to every creature
2Ti 4: 17 me the message might be fully p

PROCLAIMING (PROCLAIM)

Ps 26: 7 p aloud your praise
92: 15 to, "The LORD is upright;
Ac 5: 42 and p the good news that Jesus is
Ro 10: 8 the word of faith we are p:

PROCLAIMS (PROCLAIM)

Dt   18: 22 If what a prophet *p* in the name

PROCLAMATION (PROCLAIM)

Isa   62: 11 The LORD has made *p*

PRODUCE (PRODUCES)

Mt   3: 8 *P* fruit in keeping with repentance.
     3: 10 tree that does not *p* good fruit will

PRODUCES (PRODUCE)

Pr   30: 33 so stirring up anger *p* strife."
Ro   5: 3 that suffering *p* perseverance;
Heb   12: 11 it *p* a harvest of righteousness

PROFANE (PROFANED)

Lev   19: 12 and so *p* the name of your God.
     22: 32 Do not *p* my holy name.
Mal   2: 10 Why do we *p* the covenant

PROFANED (PROFANE)

Eze   36: 20 the nations they *p* my holy name,

PROFESS*

1Ti   2: 10 for women who *p* to worship God.
Heb   4: 14 let us hold firmly to the faith we *p*,
     10: 23 unswervingly to the hope we *p*,

PROFIT (PROFITABLE)

Pr   14: 23 All hard work brings a *p*,
     21: 5 The plans of the diligent lead to *p*
Isa   44: 10 which can *p* him nothing?
2Co   2: 17 not peddle the word of God for *p*.
Php   3: 7 was to my *p* I now consider loss

PROFITABLE* (PROFIT)

Pr   3: 14 for she is more *p* than silver
     31: 18 She sees that her trading is *p*,
Tit   3: 8 These things are excellent and *p*

PROFOUND

Job   9: 4 His wisdom is *p*, his power is vast.
Ps   92: 5 how *p* your thoughts!
Eph   5: 32 This is a *p* mystery—but I am

PROGRESS

Php   1: 25 continue with all of you for your *p*
1Ti   4: 15 so that everyone may see your *p*.

PROLONG*

Dt   5: 33 *p* your days in the land that you
Ps   85: 5 Will you *p* your anger
Pr   3: 2 for they will *p* your life many years
Isa   53: 10 will see his offspring and *p* his days,
La   4: 22 he will not *p* your exile.

PROMISE (PROMISED PROMISES)

Nu   23: 19 Does he *p* and not fulfill?
Jos   23: 14 Every *p* has been fulfilled;
2Sa   7: 25 keep forever the *p* you have made
1Ki   8: 20 The LORD has kept the *p* he made
     8: 24 You have kept your *p*
Ne   5: 13 man who does not keep this *p*.
     9: 8 have kept your *p* because you are
Ps   77: 8 Has his *p* failed for all time?
     119: 41 your salvation according to your *p*;
     119: 50 Your *p* preserves my life.
     119: 58 to me according to your *p*.
     119:162 I rejoice in your *p*
Ac   2: 39 The *p* is for you and your children
Ro   4: 13 offspring received the *p* that he
     4: 20 unbelief regarding the *p* of God,
Gal   3: 14 that by faith we might receive the *p*
Eph   2: 12 foreigners to the covenants of the *p*
1Ti   4: 8 holding *p* for both the present life
Heb   6: 13 When God made his *p* to Abraham
     11: 11 him faithful who had made the *p*
2Pe   3: 9 Lord is not slow in keeping his *p*,
     3: 13 with his *p* we are looking forward

PROMISED (PROMISE)

Ge   21: 1 did for Sarah what he had *p*.
     24: 7 who spoke to me and *p* me on oath,
Ex   3: 17 And I have *p* to bring you out
Nu   10: 29 for the LORD has *p* good things
Dt   15: 6 your God will bless you as he has *p*,
     26: 18 his treasured possession as he *p*,
2Sa   7: 28 and you have *p* these good things
1Ki   9: 5 I *p* David your father when I said,
2Ch   6: 15 with your mouth you have *p*
Ps   119: 57 I have *p* to obey your words.
Lk   24: 49 to send you what my Father has *p*;
Ac   1: 4 but wait for the gift my Father *p*,
     13: 32 What God *p* our fathers he has

Ro   4: 21 power to do what he had *p*.
Tit   1: 2 *p* before the beginning of time,
Heb   10: 23 for he who *p* is faithful.
     10: 36 you will receive what he has *p*.
Jas   1: 12 the crown of life that God has *p*
     2: 5 the kingdom he *p* those who love
2Pe   3: 4 "Where is this 'coming' he *p*?
1Jn   2: 25 And this is what he *p* us—

PROMISES (PROMISE)

Jos   21: 45 one of all the LORD's good *p*
     23: 14 of all the good *p* the LORD your
1Ki   8: 56 failed of all the good *p* he gave
1Ch   17: 19 and made known all these great *p*.
Ps   85: 8 he *p* peace to his people, his saints
     106: 12 Then they believed his *p*
     119:140 Your *p* have been thoroughly
     119:148 that I may meditate on your *p*.
     145: 13 The LORD is faithful to all his *p*
Ro   9: 4 the temple worship and the *p*,
2Co   1: 20 matter how many *p* God has made,
     7: 1 Since we have these *p*, dear friends,
Heb   8: 6 and it is founded on better *p*.
2Pe   1: 4 us his very great and precious *p*,

PROMOTE (PROMOTES)

Pr   12: 20 but joy for those who *p* peace.
     16: 21 and pleasant words *p* instruction.
1Ti   1: 4 These *p* controversies rather

PROMOTES (PROMOTE)

Pr   17: 9 over an offense *p* love,

PROMPTED

1Th   1: 3 your labor *p* by love, and your
2Th   1: 11 and every act *p* by your faith.

PRONOUNCE (PRONOUNCED)

1Ch   23: 13 to *p* blessings in his name forever.

PRONOUNCED (PRONOUNCE)

1Ch   16: 12 miracles, and the judgments he *p*,

PROOF (PROVE)

Ac   17: 31 He has given *p* of this to all men
2Co   8: 24 Therefore show these men the *p*

PROPER

Ps   104: 27 give them their food at the *p* time.
     145: 15 give them their food at the *p* time.
Ecc   5: 18 Then I realized that it is good and *p*
     8: 5 the wise heart will know the *p* time
Mt   24: 45 give them their food at the *p* time?
Lk   1: 20 which will come true at their *p* time
1Co   11: 13 Is it *p* for a woman to pray to God
1Ti   2: 6 the testimony given in its *p* time.
1Pe   2: 17 Show *p* respect to everyone:

PROPERTY

Heb   10: 34 the confiscation of your *p*,

PROPHECIES (PROPHESY)

1Co   13: 8 where there are *p*, they will cease;
1Th   5: 20 do not treat *p* with contempt.

PROPHECY (PROPHESY)

Da   9: 24 to seal up vision and *p*
1Co   12: 10 miraculous powers, to another *p*,
     13: 2 of *p* and can fathom all mysteries
     14: 1 gifts, especially the gift of *p*.
     14: 6 or *p* or word of instruction?
     14: 22 *p*, however, is for believers,
2Pe   1: 20 you must understand that no *p*
Rev   22: 18 the words of the *p* of this book:

PROPHESIED (PROPHESY)

Nu   11: 25 the Spirit rested on them, they *p*,
1Sa   19: 24 and also *p* in Samuel's presence.
Jn   11: 51 that year he *p* that Jesus would
Ac   19: 6 and they spoke in tongues and *p*.
     21: 9 four unmarried daughters who *p*.

PROPHESIES (PROPHESY)

Jer   28: 9 the prophet who *p* peace will be
Eze   12: 27 and he *p* about the distant future.'
1Co   11: 4 *p* with his head covered dishonors
     14: 3 But everyone who *p* speaks to men

PROPHESY (PROPHECIES PROPHECY PROPHESIED PROPHESIES PROPHESYING PROPHET PROPHET'S PROPHETESS PROPHETS)

1Sa   10: 6 and you will *p* with them;
Eze   13: 2 Say to those who *p* out

Eze   13: 17 daughters of your people who *p* out
     34: 2 *p* against the shepherds of Israel;
     37: 4 "*P* to these bones and say to them,
Joel   2: 28 Your sons and daughters will *p*,
Mt   7: 22 Lord, did we not *p* in your name,
Ac   2: 17 Your sons and daughters will *p*,
1Co   13: 9 know in part and we *p* in part,
     14: 39 my brothers, be eager to *p*,
Rev   11: 3 and they will *p* for 1,260 days,

PROPHESYING (PROPHESY)

1Ch   25: 1 and Jeduthun for the ministry of *p*,
Ro   12: 6 If a man's gift is *p*, let him use it

PROPHET (PROPHESY)

Ex   7: 1 your brother Aaron will be your *p*.
Nu   12: 6 "When a *p* of the LORD is
Dt   13: 1 If a *p*, or one who foretells
     18: 18 up for them a *p* like you
     18: 22 If what a *p* proclaims in the name
1Sa   3: 20 that Samuel was attested as a *p*
     9: 9 because the *p* of today used
1Ki   1: 8 son of Jehoiada, Nathan the *p*,
     18: 36 the *p* Elijah stepped forward
2Ki   5: 8 and he will know that there is a *p*
     6: 12 "but Elisha, the *p* who is in Israel,
     20: 1 The *p* Isaiah son of Amoz went
2Ch   35: 18 since the days of the *p* Samuel;
     36: 12 himself before Jeremiah the *p*,
Ezr   5: 1 Haggai the *p* and Zechariah the *p*,
Eze   2: 5 they will know that a *p* has been
     33: 33 they will know that a *p* has been
Hos   9: 7 the *p* is considered a fool,
Am   7: 14 "I was neither a *p* nor a prophet's
Hab   1: 1 that Habakkuk the *p* received.
Hag   1: 1 came through the *p* Haggai
Zec   1: 1 to the *p* Zechariah son of Berekiah,
     13: 4 that day every *p* will be ashamed
Mal   4: 5 I will send you the *p* Elijah
Mt   10: 41 Anyone who receives a *p*
     11: 9 what did you go out to see? A *p*?
     12: 39 except the sign of the *p* Jonah.
Lk   1: 76 will be called a *p* of the Most High;
     4: 24 "no *p* is accepted in his hometown.
     7: 16 A great *p* has appeared among us,"
     24: 19 "He was a *p*, powerful in word
Jn   1: 21 "Are you the *P*?" He answered,
Ac   7: 37 'God will send you a *p* like me
     21: 10 a *p* named Agabus came
1Co   14: 37 If anybody thinks he is a *p*
Rev   16: 13 and out of the mouth of the false *p*.

PROPHET'S (PROPHESY)

2Pe   1: 20 about by the *p* own interpretation.

PROPHETESS (PROPHESY)

Ex   15: 20 Then Miriam the *p*, Aaron's sister,
Jdg   4: 4 a *p*, the wife of Lappidoth,
Isa   8: 3 I went to the *p*, and she conceived
Lk   2: 36 a *p*, Anna, the daughter of Phanuel.

PROPHETS (PROPHESY)

Nu   11: 29 that all the LORD's people were *p*
1Sa   10: 11 Is Saul also among the *p*?"
     28: 6 him by dreams or Urim or *p*.
1Ki   19: 10 put your *p* to death with the sword.
1Ch   16: 22 do my *p* no harm."
Ps   105: 15 do my *p* no harm."
Jer   23: 9 Concerning the *p*:
     23: 30 "I am against the *p* who steal
Eze   13: 2 prophesy against the *p*
Mt   5: 17 come to abolish the Law or the *P*:
     7: 12 for this sums up the Law and the *P*.
     7: 15 "Watch out for false *p*.
     22: 40 and the *P* hang on these two
     23: 37 you who kill the *p* and stone those
     24: 24 false Christs and false *p* will appear
     26: 56 of the *p* might be fulfilled."
Lk   10: 24 For I tell you that many *p*
     11: 49 'I will send them *p* and apostles,
     24: 25 believe all that the *p* have spoken!
     24: 44 me in the Law of Moses, the *P*
Ac   3: 24 "Indeed, all the *p* from Samuel on,
     10: 43 All the *p* testify about him that
     13: 1 the church at Antioch there were *p*
     26: 22 nothing beyond what the *p*
     28: 23 the Law of Moses and from the *P*.
Ro   1: 2 through his *p* in the Holy
     3: 21 to which the Law and the *P* testify.
     11: 3 they have killed your *p*
1Co   12: 28 second *p*, third *p*, then
     12: 29 Are all *p*? Are all teachers?
     14: 32 The spirits of *p* are subject
Eph   2: 20 foundation of the apostles and *p*,
     3: 5 Spirit to God's holy apostles and *p*.

PROPITIATION

Eph 4:11 some to be p, some
Heb 1: 1 through the p at many times
1Pe 1:10 Concerning this salvation, the p,
2Pe 1:19 word of the p made more certain,
    3: 2 spoken in the past by the holy p
1Jn 4: 1 because many false p have gone out
Rev 11:10 these two p had tormented those
    18:20 Rejoice, saints and apostles and p!

PROPITIATION see (atoning) SACRIFICE

PROPORTION

Dt 16:10 by giving a freewill offering in p
    16:17 Each of you must bring a gift in p

PROPRIETY*

1Ti 2: 9 with decency and p,
    2:15 in faith, love and holiness with p.

PROSPECT*

Pr 10:28 The p of the righteous is joy,

PROSPER (PROSPERED PROSPERITY PROSPEROUS PROSPERS)

Dt 5:33 so that you may live and p
    28:63 pleased the LORD to make you p
    29: 9 that you may p in everything you
1Ki 2: 3 so that you may p in all you do
Ezr 6:14 and p under the preaching
Pr 11:10 When the righteous p, the city
    11:25 A generous man will p;
    17:20 A man of perverse heart does not p
    28:13 who conceals his sins does not p,
    28:25 he who trusts in the LORD will p.
Isa 53:10 of the LORD will p in his hand.
Jer 12: 1 Why does the way of the wicked p?

PROSPERED (PROSPER)

Ge 39: 2 was with Joseph and he p,
2Ch 14: 7 So they built and p.
    31:21 And so he p.

PROSPERITY (PROSPER)

Dt 28:11 will grant you abundant p—
    30:15 I set before you today life and p,
Job 36:11 will spend the rest of their days in p
Ps 73: 3 when I saw the p of the wicked.
    122: 9 I will seek your p.
    128: 2 blessings and p will be yours.
Pr 13:21 but p is the reward of the righteous.
    21:21 finds life, p and honor.
Isa 45: 7 I bring p and create disaster;

PROSPEROUS (PROSPER)

Dt 30: 9 your God will make you most p
Jos 1: 8 Then you will be p and successful.
Job 42:10 the LORD made him p again

PROSPERS (PROSPER)

Ps 1: 3 Whatever he does p.
Pr 16:20 gives heed to instruction p,
    19: 8 he who cherishes understanding p.

PROSTITUTE (PROSTITUTES PROSTITUTION)

Lev 20: 6 and spiritists to p himself
Nu 15:39 and not p yourselves by going
Jos 2: 1 the house of a p named Rahab
Pr 6:26 for the p reduces you to a loaf
    7:10 like a p and with crafty intent.
    23:27 for a p is a deep pit
Eze 16:15 and used your fame to become a p.
    23: 7 a p to all the elite of the Assyrians
Hos 3: 3 you must not be a p or be intimate
1Co 6:15 of Christ and unite them with a p?
    6:16 with a p is one with her in body?
Rev 17: 1 you the punishment of the great p,

PROSTITUTES (PROSTITUTE)

Pr 29: 3 of p squanders his wealth.
Mt 21:31 and the p are entering the kingdom
Lk 15:30 property with p comes home,
1Co 6: 9 male p nor homosexual offenders

PROSTITUTION (PROSTITUTE)

Eze 16:16 where you carried on your p.
    23: 3 engaging in p from their youth.
Hos 4:10 engage in p but not increase,

PROSTRATE

Dt 9:18 again I fell p before the LORD
1Ki 18:39 they fell p and cried, "The LORD

PROTECT (PROTECTED PROTECTION PROTECTS)

Dt 23:14 about in your camp to p you
Ps 25:21 integrity and uprightness p me,
    32: 7 you will p me from trouble
    40:11 your truth always p me.
    41: 2 The LORD will p him
    91:14 I will p him, for he acknowledges
    140: 1 p me from men of violence,
Pr 2:11 Discretion will p you,
    4: 6 forsake wisdom, and she will p you;
Jn 17:11 p them by the power of your name
    17:15 that you p them from the evil one.
2Th 3: 3 and p you from the evil one.

PROTECTED (PROTECT)

Jos 24:17 He p us on our entire journey
1Sa 30:23 He has p us and handed
Ps 37:28 They will be p forever,
Jn 17:12 I p them and kept them safe

PROTECTION (PROTECT)

Ezr 9: 9 he has given us a wall of p in Judah
Ps 5:11 Spread your p over them,

PROTECTS (PROTECT)

Ps 116: 6 The LORD p the simplehearted;
Pr 2: 8 and p the way of his faithful ones.
1Co 13: 7 It always p, always trusts,

PROUD (PRIDE)

Ps 31:23 but the p he pays back in full.
    101: 5 has haughty eyes and a p heart,
    138: 6 but the p he knows from afar.
Pr 3:34 He mocks p mockers
    16: 5 The LORD detests all the p
    16:19 than to share plunder with the p.
    18:12 his downfall a man's heart is p,
    21: 4 Haughty eyes and a p heart,
Isa 2:12 store for all the p and lofty,
Ro 12:16 Do not be p, but be willing
1Co 13: 4 it does not boast, it is not p.
2Ti 3: 2 lovers of money, boastful, p,
Jas 4: 6 "God opposes the p
1Pe 5: 5 because, "God opposes the p

PROVE (PROOF PROVED PROVING)

Pr 29:25 Fear of man will p to be a snare,
Jn 8:46 Can any of you p me guilty of sin?
Ac 26:20 p their repentance by their deeds.
1Co 4: 2 been given a trust must p faithful.

PROVED (PROVE)

Ps 51: 4 so that you are p right
Mt 11:19 wisdom is p right by her actions."
Ro 3: 4 "So that you may be p right
1Pe 1: 7 may be p genuine and may result

PROVIDE (PROVIDED PROVIDES PROVISION)

Ge 22: 8 "God himself will p the lamb
    22:14 that place "The LORD will P."
Isa 43:20 because I provide p water in the desert
    61: 3 and p for those who grieve in Zion
1Co 10:13 p a way out so that you can stand
1Ti 5: 8 If anyone does not p
Tit 3:14 in order that they may p

PROVIDED (PROVIDE)

Ps 68:10 O God, you p for the poor.
    111: 9 He p redemption for his people;
Jnh 1:17 But the LORD p a great fish
    4: 6 Then the LORD God p a vine
    4: 7 dawn the next day God p a worm,
    4: 8 God p a scorching east wind,
Gal 4:18 to be zealous, p the purpose is good
Heb 1: 3 After he had p purification for sins,

PROVIDES (PROVIDE)

Ps 111: 5 He p food for those who fear him;
Pr 31:15 she p food for her family
Eze 18: 7 and p clothing for the naked
1Ti 6:17 who richly p us with everything
1Pe 4:11 it with the strength God p,

PROVING* (PROVE)

Ac 9:22 by p that Jesus is the Christ.
    17: 3 and p that the Christ had to suffer
    18:28 p from the Scriptures that Jesus

PROVISION (PROVIDE)

Ro 5:17 who receive God's abundant p

PROVOKED

Ecc 7: 9 Do not be quickly p in your spirit,
Jer 32:32 Judah have p me by all the evil they

PROWLS

1Pe 5: 8 Your enemy the devil p

PRUDENCE* (PRUDENT)

Pr 1: 4 for giving p to the simple,
    8: 5 You who are simple, gain p;
    8:12 "I, wisdom, dwell together with p;
    15: 5 whoever heeds correction shows p.
    19:25 and the simple will learn p;

PRUDENT* (PRUDENCE)

Pr 1: 3 acquiring a disciplined and p life,
    12:16 but a p man overlooks an insult.
    12:23 A p man keeps his knowledge
    13:16 Every p man acts out of knowledge
    14: 8 The wisdom of the p is
    14:15 a p man gives thought to his steps.
    14:18 the p are crowned with knowledge.
    19:14 but a p wife is from the LORD.
    22: 3 p man sees danger and takes
    27:12 The p see danger and take refuge,
Jer 49: 7 Has counsel perished from the p?
Am 5:13 Therefore the p man keeps quiet

PRUNES (PRUNING)

Jn 15: 2 that does bear fruit he p

PRUNING (PRUNES)

Isa 2: 4 and their spears into p hooks.
Joel 3:10 and your p hooks into spears.

PSALMS

Eph 5:19 Speak to one another with p,
Col 3:16 and as you sing p, hymns

PUBLICLY

Ac 20:20 have taught you p and from house
1Ti 5:20 Those who sin are to be rebuked p,

PUFFS

1Co 8: 1 Knowledge p up, but love builds up

PULLING

2Co 10: 8 building you up rather than p you

PUNISH (PUNISHED PUNISHES PUNISHMENT)

Ge 15:14 But I will p the nation they serve
Ex 32:34 I will p them for their sin."
Pr 17:26 It is not good to p an innocent man,
    23:13 if you p him with the rod, he will
Isa 13:11 I will p the world for its evil,
Jer 2:19 Your wickedness will p you;
    21:14 I will p you as your deeds deserve,
Zep 1: 2 and p those who are complacent,
Ac 7: 7 But I will p the nation they serve
2Th 1: 8 He will p those who do not know
1Pe 2:14 by him to p those who do wrong

PUNISHED (PUNISH)

Ezr 9:13 you have p us less than our sins
Ps 99: 8 though you p their misdeeds.
La 3:39 complain when p for his sins?
Mk 12:40 Such men will be p most severely."
Lk 23:41 the same sentence? We are p justly.
2Th 1: 9 be p with everlasting destruction
Heb 10:29 to be p who has trampled the Son

PUNISHES (PUNISH)

Heb 12: 6 and he p everyone he accepts

PUNISHMENT (PUNISH)

Isa 53: 5 the p that brought us peace was
Jer 4:18 This is your p.
Mt 25:46 Then they will go away to eternal p
Lk 12:48 and does things deserving p will be
    21:22 For this is the time of p
Ro 13: 4 wrath to bring p on the wrongdoer.
Heb 2: 2 disobedience received its just p.
2Pe 2: 9 while continuing their p.

PURCHASED

Ps 74: 2 Remember the people you p of old,
Rev 5: 9 with your blood you p men for God

PURE (PURIFICATION PURIFIED PURIFIES PURIFY PURITY)

2Sa 22:27 to the p you show yourself p,
Job 14: 4 Who can bring what is p
Ps 19: 9 The fear of the LORD is p,

PURGE

Ps 24: 4 who has clean hands and a *p* heart,
51: 10 Create in me a *p* heart, O God,
119: 9 can a young man keep his way *p*?
Pr 15: 26 those of the *p* are pleasing to him.
20: 9 can say, "I have kept my heart *p*,
Isa 52: 11 Come out from it and be *p*,
Hab 1: 13 Your eyes are too *p* to look on evil;
Mt 5: 8 Blessed are the *p* in heart,
2Co 11: 2 I might present you as a *p* virgin
Php 4: 8 whatever is *p*, whatever is lovely,
1Ti 5: 1 which comes from a *p* heart
5: 22 Keep yourself *p*.
2Ti 2: 22 call on the Lord out of a *p* heart.
Tit 1: 15 To the *p*, all things are *p*,
2: 5 to be self-controlled and *p*,
Heb 7: 26 blameless, *p*, set apart from sinners
13: 4 and the marriage bed kept *p*,
Jas 1: 27 that God our Father accepts as *p*
3: 17 comes from heaven is first of all *p*;
1Jn 3: 3 him purifies himself, just as he is *p*.

PURGE

Pr 20: 30 and beatings *p* the inmost being.

PURIFICATION (PURE)

Heb 1: 3 After he had provided *p* for sins,

PURIFIED (PURE)

Ac 15: 9 for he *p* their hearts by faith.
1Pe 1: 22 Now that you have *p* yourselves

PURIFIES* (PURE)

1Jn 1: 7 of Jesus, his Son, *p* us from all sin.
3: 3 who has this hope in him *p* himself,

PURIFY (PURE)

Nu 19: 12 He must *p* himself with the water
2Co 7: 1 us ourselves from everything that
Tit 2: 14 to *p* for himself a people that are
Jas 4: 8 you sinners, and *p* your hearts,
1Jn 1: 9 and *p* us from all unrighteousness.

PURIM

Est 9: 26 Therefore these days were called *P*

PURITY* (PURE)

Hos 8: 5 long will they be incapable of *p*?
2Co 6: 6 in *p*, understanding, patience
1Ti 4: 12 in life, in love, in faith and in *p*.
5: 2 as sisters, with absolute *p*.
1Pe 3: 2 when they see the *p* and reverence

PURPLE

Pr 31: 22 she is clothed in fine linen and *p*.
Mk 15: 17 They put a *p* robe on him, then

PURPOSE (PURPOSED PURPOSES)

Ex 9: 16 I have raised you up for this very *p*,
Job 36: 5 he is mighty, and firm in his *p*.
Pr 19: 21 but it is the LORD's *p* that prevails
Isa 46: 10 I say: My *p* will stand,
55: 11 and achieve the *p* for which I sent it
Ac 2: 23 handed over to you by God's set *p*
Ro 8: 28 have been called according to his *p*
9: 11 in order that God's *p*
9: 17 "I raised you up for this very *p*,
1Co 3: 8 the man who waters have one *p*,
2Co 5: 5 who has made us for this very *p*
Gal 4: 18 be zealous, provided the *p* is good,
Eph 1: 11 in conformity with the *p* of his will,
3: 11 according to his eternal *p* which he
Php 2: 2 love, being one in spirit and *p*.
2: 13 and to act according to his good *p*.
2Ti 1: 9 but because of his own *p* and grace.

PURPOSED (PURPOSE)

Isa 14: 24 and as I have *p*, so it will stand.
14: 27 For the LORD Almighty has *p*,
Eph 1: 9 which he *p* in Christ, to be put

PURPOSES (PURPOSE)

Ps 33: 10 he thwarts the *p* of the peoples.
Jer 23: 20 the *p* of his heart.
32: 19 great are your *p* and mighty are

PURSE (PURSES)

Hag 1: 6 to put them in a *p* with holes in it."
Lk 10: 4 Do not take a *p* or bag or sandals;
22: 36 "But now if you have a *p*, take it,

PURSES (PURSE)

Lk 12: 33 Provide *p* for yourselves that will

PURSUE (PURSUES)

Ps 34: 14 seek peace and *p* it.

Pr 15: 9 he loves those who *p* righteousness
Ro 9: 30 who did not *p* righteousness,
1Ti 6: 11 and *p* righteousness, godliness,
2Ti 2: 22 and *p* righteousness, faith,
1Pe 3: 11 he must seek peace and *p* it.

PURSUES (PURSUE)

Pr 21: 21 He who *p* righteousness and love
28: 1 wicked man flees though no one *p*,

QUAIL

Ex 16: 13 That evening *q* came and covered
Nu 11: 31 and drove *q* in from the sea.

QUALITIES* (QUALITY)

Da 6: 3 by his exceptional *q* that the king
Ro 1: 20 of the world God's invisible *q*—
2Pe 1: 8 For if you possess these *q*

QUALITY (QUALITIES)

1Co 3: 13 and the fire will test the *q*

QUARREL (QUARRELING QUARRELS QUARRELSOME)

Pr 15: 18 but a patient man calms a *q*.
17: 14 Starting a *q* is like breaching a dam;
17: 19 He who loves a *q* loves sin;
20: 3 but every fool is quick to *q*.
26: 17 in a *q* not his own.
26: 20 without gossip a *q* dies down.
2Ti 2: 24 And the Lord's servant must not *q*;
Jas 4: 2 You *q* and fight.

QUARRELING (QUARREL)

1Co 3: 3 For since there is jealousy and *q*
2Ti 2: 14 before God against *q* about words;

QUARRELS (QUARREL)

Pr 13: 10 Pride only breeds *q*,
Isa 45: 9 Woe to him who *q* with his Maker,
2Ti 2: 23 because you know they produce *q*.
Jas 4: 1 What causes fights and *q*

QUARRELSOME (QUARREL)

Pr 19: 13 a *q* wife is like a constant dripping.
21: 9 than share a house with a *q* wife.
26: 21 so is a *q* man for kindling strife.
1Ti 3: 3 not violent but gentle, not *q*,

QUEEN

1Ki 10: 1 When the *q* of Sheba heard about
2Ch 9: 1 When the *q* of Sheba heard
Mt 12: 42 The *Q* of the South will rise

QUENCH (QUENCHED)

SS 8: 7 Many waters cannot *q* love;

QUENCHED (QUENCH)

Isa 66: 24 nor will their fire be *q*,
Mk 9: 48 and the fire is not *q*.

QUICKEN see (make) ALIVE, (give) LIFE, RESTORE, REVIVE

QUICK-TEMPERED* (TEMPER)

Pr 14: 17 A *q* man does foolish things,
14: 29 but a *q* man displays folly.
Tit 1: 7 not *q*, not given to drunkenness,

QUIET (QUIETNESS)

Ps 23: 2 he leads me beside *q* waters,
Pr 17: 1 Better a dry crust with peace and *q*
Ecc 9: 17 The *q* words of the wise are more
Am 5: 13 Therefore the prudent man keeps *q*
Zep 3: 17 he will *q* you with his love,
Lk 19: 40 he replied, "if they keep *q*,
1Th 4: 11 it your ambition to lead a *q* life,
1Ti 2: 2 we may live peaceful and *q* lives
1Pe 3: 4 beauty of a gentle and *q* spirit,

QUIETNESS (QUIET)

Isa 30: 15 in *q* and trust is your strength,
32: 17 the effect of righteousness will be *q*
1Ti 2: 11 A woman should learn in *q*

QUIVER

Ps 127: 5 whose *q* is full of them.

RACE

Ecc 9: 11 The *r* is not to the swift
Ac 20: 24 if only I may finish the *r*
1Co 9: 24 that in a *r* all the runners run,
Gal 2: 2 that I was running or had run my *r*
5: 7 You were running a good *r*.
2Ti 4: 7 I have finished the *r*, I have kept

Heb 12: 1 perseverance the *r* marked out

RACHEL

Daughter of Laban (Ge 29:16); wife of Jacob (Ge 29:28); bore two sons (Ge 30:22-24; 35: 16-24; 46:19). Stole Laban's gods (Ge 31:19, 32-35). Death (Ge 35:19-20).

RADIANCE (RADIANT)

Eze 1: 28 so was the *r* around him.
Heb 1: 3 The Son is the *r* of God's glory

RADIANT (RADIANCE)

Ex 34: 29 he was not aware that his face was *r*
Ps 34: 5 Those who look to him are *r*,
SS 5: 10 *Beloved* My lover is *r* and ruddy,
Isa 60: 5 Then you will look and be *r*,
Eph 5: 27 her to himself as a *r* church,

RAGE

Ac 4: 25 " 'Why do the nations *r*
Col 3: 8 *r*, malice, slander, and filthy

RAGS

Isa 64: 6 our righteous acts are like filthy *r*;

RAHAB

Prostitute of Jericho who hid Israelite spies (Jos 2; 6:22-25; Heb 11:31; Jas 2:25). Mother of Boaz (Mt 1:5).

RAIN (RAINBOW)

Ge 7: 4 from now I will send *r* on the earth
1Ki 17: 1 nor *r* in the next few years
18: 1 and I will send *r* on the land."
Mt 5: 45 and sends *r* on the righteous
Jas 5: 17 it did not *r* on the land for three
Jude : 12 They are clouds without *r*,

RAINBOW (RAIN)

Ge 9: 13 I have set my *r* in the clouds,

RAISE (RISE)

Jn 6: 39 but *r* them up at the last day.
1Co 15: 15 he did not *r* him if in fact the dead

RAISED (RISE)

Isa 52: 13 he will be *r* and lifted up
Mt 17: 23 on the third day he will be *r* to life
Lk 7: 22 the deaf hear, the dead are *r*,
Ac 2: 24 But God *r* him from the dead,
Ro 4: 25 was *r* to life for our justification.
6: 4 as Christ was *r* from the dead
8: 11 And if the Spirit of him who *r* Jesus
10: 9 in your heart that God *r* him
1Co 15: 4 that he was *r* on the third day
15: 20 But Christ has indeed been *r*

RALLY*

Isa 11: 10 the nations will *r* to him,

RAM (RAMS)

Ge 22: 13 there in a thicket he saw a *r* caught
Da 8: 3 before me was a *r* with two horns,

RAMPART*

Ps 91: 4 will be your shield and *r*.

RAMS (RAM)

1Sa 15: 22 to heed is better than the fat of *r*.
Mic 6: 7 pleased with thousands of *r*,

RAN (RUN)

Jnh 1: 3 But Jonah *r* away from the LORD

RANSOM (RANSOMED)

Isa 50: 2 Was my arm too short to *r* you?
Hos 13: 14 "I will *r* them from the power
Mt 20: 28 and to give his life as a *r* for many."
Mk 10: 45 and to give his life as a *r* for many."
1Ti 2: 6 who gave himself as a *r* for all men
Heb 9: 15 as a *r* to set them free

RANSOMED (RANSOM)

Isa 35: 10 and the *r* of the LORD will return.

RARE

Pr 20: 15 that speak knowledge are a *r* jewel.

RAVEN (RAVENS)

Ge 8: 7 made in the ark and sent out a *r*,
Job 38: 41 Who provides food for the *r*

RAVENS (RAVEN)

1Ki 17: 6 the *r* brought him bread

READ

Ps 147: 9 and for the young r when they call.
Lk 12: 24 Consider the r: They do not sow

READ (READING READS)

Dt 17: 19 he is to r it all the days of his life
Jos 8: 34 Joshua r all the words of the law—
2Ki 23: 2 He r in their hearing all the words
Ne 8: 8 They r from the Book of the Law
Jer 36: 6 and r to the people from the scroll
2Co 3: 2 known and r by everybody.

READING (READ)

1Ti 4: 13 to the public r of Scripture,

READS (READ)

Rev 1: 3 Blessed is the one who r the words

REAFFIRM

2Co 2: 8 therefore, to r your love for him.

REAL* (REALITIES REALITY)

Jn 6: 55 is r food and my blood is r drink.
1Jn 2: 27 all things and as that anointing is r,

REALITIES* (REAL)

Heb 10: 1 are coming—not the r themselves.

REALITY* (REAL)

Col 2: 17 the r, however, is found in Christ.

REALM (REALMS)

Hab 2: 9 "Woe to him who builds his r

REALMS (REALM)

Eph 1: 3 the heavenly r with every spiritual
2: 6 in the heavenly r in Christ Jesus,

REAP (REAPER REAPS)

Job 4: 8 and those who sow trouble r it.
Ps 126: 5 will r with songs of joy.
Hos 8: 7 and r the whirlwind.
10: 12 r the fruit of unfailing love,
Jn 4: 38 you to r what you have not worked
Ro 6: 22 the benefit you r leads to holiness,
2Co 9: 6 generously will also r generously.
Gal 6: 8 from that nature will r destruction;

REAPER (REAP)

Jn 4: 36 and the r may be glad together.

REAPS (REAP)

Pr 11: 18 who sows righteousness r a sure
22: 8 He who sows wickedness r trouble,
Gal 6: 7 A man r what he sows.

REASON (REASONED)

Ge 2: 24 For this r a man will leave his
Isa 1: 18 "Come now, let us r together,"
Mt 19: 5 'For this r a man will leave his
Jn 12: 27 it was for this very r I came
15: 25 'They hated me without r.'
1Pe 3: 15 to give the r for the hope that you
2Pe 1: 5 For this very r, make every effort

REASONED (REASON)

1Co 13: 11 thought like a child, I r like a child.

REBEKAH

Sister of Laban, secured as bride for Isaac
(Ge 24). Mother of Esau and Jacob (Ge 25:
19-26). Taken by Abimelech as sister of Isaac;
returned (Ge 26:1-11). Encouraged Jacob to
trick Isaac out of blessing (Ge 27:1-17).

REBEL (REBELLED REBELLION REBELS)

Nu 14: 9 Only do not r against the LORD.
1Sa 12: 14 and do not r against his commands,
Mt 10: 21 children will r against their parents

REBELLED (REBEL)

Ps 78: 56 and r against the Most High;
Isa 63: 10 Yet they r

REBELLION (REBEL)

Ex 34: 7 and forgiving wickedness, r and sin
Nu 14: 18 in love and forgiving sin and r.
1Sa 15: 23 For r is like the sin of divination.
2Th 2: 3 will not come, until the r occurs

REBELS (REBEL)

Ro 13: 2 he who r against the authority is
1Ti 1: 9 but for lawbreakers and r,

REBIRTH* (BEAR)

Tit 3: 5 us through the washing of r

REBUILD (BUILD)

Ezr 5: 2 set to work to r the house of God
Ne 2: 17 let us r the wall of Jerusalem,
Ps 102: 16 For the LORD will r Zion
Da 9: 25 and r Jerusalem until the Anointed
Am 9: 14 they will r the ruined cities
Ac 15: 16 Its ruins I will r,

REBUILT (BUILD)

Zec 1: 16 and there my house will be r.

REBUKE (REBUKED REBUKES REBUKING)

Lev 19: 17 R your neighbor frankly
Ps 141: 5 let him r me—it is oil on my head.
Pr 3: 11 and do not resent his r,
9: 8 r a wise man and he will love you.
15: 31 He who listens to a life-giving r
17: 10 A r impresses a man
19: 25 r a discerning man, and he will gain
25: 12 is a wise man's r to a listening ear.
27: 5 Better is open r
30: 6 or he will r you and prove you a liar
Ecc 7: 5 It is better to heed a wise man's r
Isa 54: 9 never to r you again.
Jer 2: 19 your backsliding will r you.
Lk 17: 3 "If your brother sins, r him,
1Ti 5: 1 Do not r an older man harshly,
2Ti 4: 2 correct, r and encourage—
Tit 1: 13 Therefore, r them sharply,
2: 15 Encourage and r with all authority.
Rev 3: 19 Those whom I love I r

REBUKED (REBUKE)

Mk 16: 14 he r them for their lack of faith
1Ti 5: 20 Those who sin are to be r publicly,

REBUKES (REBUKE)

Job 22: 4 "Is it for your piety that he r you
Pr 28: 23 He who r a man will
29: 1 remains stiff-necked after many r
Heb 12: 5 do not lose heart when he r you,

REBUKING (REBUKE)

2Ti 3: 16 r, correcting and training

RECEIVE (RECEIVED RECEIVES)

Mt 10: 41 a righteous man will r a righteous
Mk 10: 15 anyone who will not r the kingdom
Jn 20: 22 and said, "R the Holy Spirit.
Ac 1: 8 you will r power when the Holy
2: 38 you will r the gift of the Holy Spirit
19: 2 "Did you r the Holy Spirit
20: 35 'It is more blessed to give than to r
1Co 9: 14 the gospel should r their living
2Co 6: 17 and I will r you.'"
1Ti 1: 16 believe on him and r eternal life.
Jas 1: 7 should not think he will r anything
2Pe 1: 11 and you will r a rich welcome
1Jn 3: 22 and r from him anything we ask,
Rev 4: 11 to r glory and honor and power,
5: 12 to r power and wealth and wisdom

RECEIVED (RECEIVE)

Mt 6: 2 they have r their reward in full.
10: 8 Freely you have r, freely give.
Mk 11: 24 believe that you have r it,
Jn 1: 12 Yet to all who r him,
1: 16 his grace we have all r one blessing
Ac 8: 17 and they r the Holy Spirit.
10: 47 They have r the Holy Spirit just
Ro 8: 15 but you r the Spirit of sonship.
1Co 11: 23 For I r from the Lord what I
2Co 1: 4 the comfort we ourselves have r
Col 2: 6 just as you r Christ Jesus as Lord,
1Pe 4: 10 should use whatever gift he has r

RECEIVES (RECEIVE)

Pr 18: 22 and r favor from the LORD.
27: 21 but man is tested by the praise he r.
Mt 7: 8 everyone who asks r; he who seeks
10: 40 he who r me r the one who sent me.
10: 40 "He who r you r me, and he who
Ac 10: 43 believes in him r forgiveness of sins

RECITE

Ps 45: 1 as I r my verses for the king;

RECKLESS

Pr 12: 18 R words pierce like a sword,
14: 16 but a fool is hotheaded and r.

RECKONING

Isa 10: 3 What will you do on the day of r,
Hos 9: 7 the days of r are at hand.

RECLAIM* (CLAIM)

Isa 11: 11 time to r the remnant that is left

RECOGNITION (RECOGNIZE)

1Co 16: 18 Such men deserve r.
1Ti 5: 3 Give proper r to those widows who

RECOGNIZE (RECOGNITION RECOGNIZED)

Mt 7: 16 By their fruit you will r them.
1Jn 4: 2 This is how you can r the Spirit
4: 6 This is how we r the Spirit of truth

RECOGNIZED (RECOGNIZE)

Mt 12: 33 for a tree is r by its fruit.
Ro 7: 13 in order that sin might be r as sin,

RECOMPENSE*

Isa 40: 10 and his r accompanies him.
62: 11 and his r accompanies him.' "

**RECONCILE* (RECONCILED
RECONCILIATION RECONCILING)**

Ac 7: 26 He tried to r them by saying, 'Men,
Eph 2: 16 in this one body to r both of them
Col 1: 20 him to r to himself all things,

RECONCILED* (RECONCILE)

Mt 5: 24 First go and be r to your brother;
Lk 12: 58 try hard to be r to him on the way,
Ro 5: 10 how much more, having been r,
5: 10 we were r to him through the death
1Co 7: 11 or else be r to her husband.
2Co 5: 18 who r us to himself through Christ
5: 20 you on Christ's behalf: Be r to God.
Col 1: 22 he has r you by Christ's physical

RECONCILIATION* (RECONCILE)

Ro 5: 11 whom we have now received r.
11: 15 For if their rejection is the r
2Co 5: 18 and gave us the ministry of r:
5: 19 committed to us the message of r.

RECONCILING* (RECONCILE)

2Co 5: 19 that God was r the world to himself

RECORD (RECORDED)

Ps 130: 3 If you, O LORD, kept a r of sins,
Hos 13: 12 his sins are kept on r.
1Co 13: 5 is not easily angered, it keeps no r

RECORDED (RECORD)

Job 19: 23 "Oh, that my words were r,
Jn 20: 30 which are not r in this book.

RECOUNT*

Ps 40: 5 no one can r to you;
79: 13 we will r your praise.
119: 13 With my lips I r

RED

Ex 15: 4 are drowned in the R Sea.
Ps 106: 9 He rebuked the R Sea,
Pr 23: 31 Do not gaze at wine when it is r,
Isa 1: 18 though they are r as crimson,

**REDEEM (KINSMAN-REDEEMER
REDEEMED REDEEMER REDEEMS
REDEMPTION)**

Ex 6: 6 will r you with an outstretched arm
2Sa 7: 23 on earth that God went out to r
Ps 44: 26 r us because of your unfailing love.
49: 7 No man can r the life of another
49: 15 God will r my life from the grave;
130: 8 He himself will r Israel
Hos 13: 14 I will r them from death.
Gal 4: 5 under law, to r those under law,
Tit 2: 14 for us to r us from all wickedness

REDEEMED (REDEEM)

Job 33: 28 He r my soul from going
Ps 71: 23 I, whom you have r.
107: 2 Let the r of the LORD say this—
Isa 35: 9 But only the r will walk there,
63: 9 In his love and mercy he r them;
Gal 3: 13 Christ r us from the curse
1Pe 1: 18 or gold that you were r

REDEEMER (REDEEM)

Job 19: 25 I know that my R lives,
Ps 19: 14 O LORD, my Rock and my R.
Isa 44: 6 and R, the LORD Almighty:
48: 17 your R, the Holy One of Israel:
59: 20 "The R will come to Zion,

REDEEMS (REDEEM)
Ps 34:22 The LORD *r* his servants;
103: 4 he *r* my life from the pit

REDEMPTION (REDEEM)
Ps 130: 7 and with him is full *r.*
Lk 21:28 because your *r* is drawing near."
Ro 3:24 grace through the *r* that came
8:23 as sons, the *r* of our bodies.
1Co 1:30 our righteousness, holiness and *r.*
Eph 1: 7 In him we have *r* through his blood
1:14 until the *r* of those who are God's
4:30 you were sealed for the day of *r.*
Col 1:14 in whom we have *r,* the forgiveness
Heb 9:12 having obtained eternal *r.*

REED
Isa 42: 3 A bruised *r* he will not break,
Mt 12:20 A bruised *r* he will not break,

REFINE*
Jer 9: 7 "See, I will *r* and test them,
Zec 13: 9 I will *r* them like silver
Mal 3: 3 and *r* them like gold and silver.

REFLECT (REFLECTS)
2Co 3:18 unveiled faces all *r* the Lord's

REFLECTS (REFLECT)
Pr 27:19 As water *r* a face,

REFRESH (REFRESHED REFRESHING)
Phm :20 in the Lord; *r* my heart in Christ.

REFRESHED (REFRESH)
Pr 11:25 refreshes others will himself be *r.*

REFRESHING* (REFRESH)
Ac 3:19 that times of *r* may come

REFUGE
Nu 35:11 towns to be your cities of *r,*
Dt 33:27 The eternal God is your *r,*
Jos 20: 2 to designate the cities of *r,*
Ru 2:12 wings you have come to take *r.*"
2Sa 22: 3 God is my rock, in whom I take *r,*
22:31 a shield for all who take *r* in him.
Ps 2:12 Blessed are all who take *r* in him.
5:11 But let all who take *r* in you be glad
9: 9 The LORD is a *r* for the oppressed,
16: 1 for in you I take *r.*
17: 7 those who take *r* in you
18: 2 God is my rock, in whom I take *r,*
31: 2 be my rock of *r,*
34: 8 blessed is the man who takes *r*
36: 7 find *r* in the shadow of your wings.
46: 1 God is our *r* and strength,
62: 8 for God is our *r.*
71: 1 In you, O LORD, I have taken *r;*
91: 2 "He is my *r* and my fortress,
144: 2 my shield, in whom I take *r,*
Pr 14:26 and for his children it will be a *r.*
30: 5 a shield to those who take *r* in him.
Na 1: 7 a *r* in times of trouble.

REFUSE (REFUSED)
Jn 5:40 yet you *r* to come to me to have life

REFUSED (REFUSE)
2Th 2:10 because they *r* to love the truth
Rev 16: 9 but they *r* to repent and glorify him

REGARD (REGARDS)
1Th 5:13 Hold them in the highest *r* in love

REGARDS (REGARD)
Ro 14:14 But if anyone *r* something

REGRET
2Co 7:10 leads to salvation and leaves no *r,*

REHOBOAM
Son of Solomon (1Ki 11:43; 1Ch 3:10). Harsh treatment of subjects caused divided kingdom (1Ki 12:1-24; 14:21-31; 2Ch 10-12).

REIGN (REIGNED REIGNS)
Ex 15:18 The LORD will *r*
Ps 68:16 mountain where God chooses to *r,*
Isa 9: 7 He will *r* on David's throne
24:23 for the LORD Almighty will *r*
32: 1 See, a king will *r* in righteousness
Jer 23: 5 a King who will *r* wisely
Lk 1:33 and he will *r* over the house

Ro 6:12 Therefore do not let sin *r*
1Co 15:25 For he must *r* until he has put all
2Ti 2:12 we will also *r* with him.
Rev 11:15 and he will *r* for ever and ever."
20: 6 will *r* with him for a thousand years
22: 5 And they will *r* for ever and ever.

REIGNED (REIGN)
Ro 5:21 so that, just as sin *r* in death,
Rev 20: 4 and *r* with Christ a thousand years.

REIGNS (REIGN)
Ps 9: 7 The LORD *r* forever;
47: 8 God *r* over the nations;
93: 1 The LORD *r,* he is robed
96:10 among the nations, "The LORD *r*
97: 1 The LORD *r,* let the earth be glad;
99: 1 The LORD *r,* / let the nations tremble;
146: 10 The LORD *r* forever,
Isa 52: 7 "Your God *r!*"
Rev 19: 6 For our Lord God Almighty *r.*

REIN
Jas 1:26 and yet does not keep a tight *r*

REJECT (REJECTED REJECTION REJECTS)
Ps 94:14 For the LORD will not *r* his people
Ro 11: 1 I ask then: Did God *r* his people?

REJECTED (REJECT)
1Sa 8: 7 it is not you they have *r,*
1Ki 19:10 The Israelites have *r* your covenant
2Ki 17: 5 They *r* his decrees
Ps 66:20 who has not *r* my prayer
118: 22 The stone the builders *r*
Isa 5:24 for they have *r* the law
41: 9 chosen you and have not *r* you.
53: 3 He was despised and *r* by men,
Jer 8: 9 Since they have *r* the word
Mt 21:42 " 'The stone the builders *r*
1Ti 4: 4 nothing is to be *r* if it is received
1Pe 2: 4 *r* by men but chosen by God
2: 7 "The stone the builders *r*

REJECTION* (REJECT)
Ro 11:15 For if their *r* is the reconciliation

REJECTS (REJECT)
Lk 10:16 but he who *r* me *r* him who sent me
Jn 3:36 whoever *r* the Son will not see life,
1Th 4: 8 he who *r* this instruction does not

REJOICE (JOY)
Dt 12: 7 shall *r* in everything you have put
1Ch 16:10 of those who seek the LORD *r.*
16:31 Let the heavens *r,* let the earth be
Ps 2:11 and *r* with trembling.
5:11 those who love your name may *r*
9:14 and there *r* in your salvation.
34: 2 let the afflicted hear and *r.*
63:11 But the king will *r* in God;
66: 6 come, let us *r* in him.
68: 3 and *r* before God;
105: 3 of those who seek the LORD *r.*
118: 24 let us *r* and be glad in it.
119: 14 I *r* in following your statutes
119:162 I *r* in your promise
149: 2 Let Israel *r* in their Maker;
Pr 5:18 may you *r* in the wife of your youth
23:25 may she who gave you birth *r!*
24:17 stumbles, do not let your heart *r,*
Isa 9: 3 as men *r*
35: 1 the wilderness will *r* and blossom.
61: 7 they will *r* in their inheritance;
62: 5 so will your God *r* over you.
Jer 31:12 they will *r* in the bounty
Zep 3:17 he will *r* over you with singing."
Zec 9: 9 *R* greatly, O Daughter of Zion!
Lk 6:23 "*R* in that day and leap for joy,
10:20 but *r* that your names are written
15: 6 '*R* with me; I have found my lost
15: 9 '*R* with me; I have found my lost
Ro 5: 2 And we *r* in the hope of the glory
12:15 Rejoice with those who *r;* mourn
Php 2:17 I am glad and *r* with all of you.
3: 1 Finally, my brothers, *r* in the Lord!
4: 4 *R* in the Lord always.
1Pe 4:13 But *r* that you participate
Rev 19: 7 Let us *r* and be glad

REJOICES (JOY)
Ps 13: 5 my heart *r* in your salvation.
16: 9 my heart is glad and my tongue *r;*
Isa 61:10 my soul *r* in my God.
62: 5 as a bridegroom *r* over his bride,

Lk 1:47 and my spirit *r* in God my Savior,
Ac 2:26 my heart is glad and my tongue *r;*
1Co 12:26 if one part is honored, every part *r*
13: 6 delight in evil but *r* with the truth.

REJOICING (JOY)
2Sa 6:12 to the City of David with *r.*
Ne 12:43 *r* because God had given them
Ps 30: 5 but *r* comes in the morning.
Lk 15: 7 in the same way there will be more *r*
Ac 5:41 *r* because they had been counted
2Co 6:10 sorrowful, yet always *r;* poor,

RELATIVES
Pr 19: 7 A poor man is shunned by all his *r*
Mk 6: 4 among his *r* and in his own house is
Lk 21:16 betrayed even by parents, brothers, *r*
1Ti 5: 8 If anyone does not provide for his *r*

RELEASE (RELEASED)
Isa 61: 1 and *r* from darkness,
Lk 4:18 to *r* the oppressed,

RELEASED (RELEASE)
Ro 7: 6 we have been *r* from the law
Rev 20: 7 Satan will be *r* from his prison

RELENTED (RELENTS)
Ex 32:14 the LORD *r* and did not bring
Ps 106: 45 and out of his great love he *r.*

RELENTS* (RELENTED)
Joel 2:13 and he *r* from sending calamity.
Jnh 4: 2 a God who *r* from sending calamity.

RELIABLE (RELY)
Pr 22:21 teaching you true and *r* words,
Jn 8:26 But he who sent me is *r,*
2Ti 2: 2 witnesses entrust to *r* men who will

RELIANCE* (RELY)
Pr 25:19 is *r* on the unfaithful in times

RELIED (RELY)
2Ch 13:18 were victorious because they *r*
16: 8 Yet when you *r* on the LORD,
Ps 71: 6 From birth I have *r* on you;

RELIEF
Job 6:10 they plead for *r* from the arm
Ps 94:13 you grant him *r* from days
143: 1 come to my *r.*
La 3:49 without *r,*
3:56 to my cry for *r.*"
2Th 1: 7 and give *r* to you who are troubled,

RELIGION* (RELIGIOUS)
Ac 25:19 dispute with him about their own *r*
26: 5 to the strictest sect of our *r,*
1Ti 5: 4 all to put their *r* into practice
Jas 1:26 himself and his *r* is worthless.
1:27 *R* that God our Father accepts

RELIGIOUS (RELIGION)
Jas 1:26 If anyone considers himself *r*

RELY (RELIABLE RELIANCE RELIED)
Isa 50:10 and *r* on his God:
Eze 33:26 you then possess the land? You *r*
2Co 1: 9 this happened that we might not *r*
Gal 3:10 All who *r* on observing the law are
1Jn 4:16 and *r* on the love God has for us.

REMAIN (REMAINS)
Nu 33:55 allow to *r* will become barbs
Ps 102: 27 But you *r* the same,
Jn 1:32 from heaven as a dove and *r* on him
15: 4 *R* in me, and I will *r* in you.
15: 7 If you *r* in me and my words
15: 9 Now *r* in my love.
Ro 13: 8 Let no debt *r* outstanding,
1Co 13:13 And now these three *r:* faith,
2Ti 2:13 he will *r* faithful,
Heb 1:11 They will perish, but you *r;*
1Jn 2:27 just as it has taught you, *r* in him.

REMAINS (REMAIN)
Ps 146: 6 the LORD, who *r* faithful forever.
Heb 7: 3 Son of God he *r* a priest forever.

REMEDY
Isa 3: 7 "I have no *r.*

REMEMBER (REMEMBERED REMEMBERS REMEMBRANCE)

Ge 9:15 I will r my covenant between me
Ex 20: 8 "R the Sabbath day
    33:13 R that this nation is your people."
Dt 5:15 R that you were slaves in Egypt
1Ch 16:12 R the wonders he has done,
Job 36:24 R to extol his work,
Ps 6: 5 R, O LORD, your great mercy
    63: 6 On my bed I r you;
    74: 2 r the people you purchased of old,
    77:11 I will r the deeds of the LORD;
Ecc 12: 1 R your Creator
Isa 46: 8 "R this, fix it in mind,
Jer 31:34 and will r their sins no more."
Hab 3: 2 in wrath r mercy.
Lk 1:72 to r his holy covenant,
Gal 2:10 we should continue to r the poor,
Php 1: 3 I thank my God every time I r you.
2Ti 2: 8 R Jesus Christ, raised
Heb 8:12 and will r their sins no more."

REMEMBERED (REMEMBER)

Ex 2:24 he r his covenant with Abraham,
    3:15 am to be r from generation
Ps 98: 3 He has r his love
    106: 45 for their sake he r his covenant
    111: 4 He has caused his wonders to be r;
    136: 23 to the One who r us
Isa 65:17 The former things will not be r,
Eze 18:22 offenses he has committed will be r
    33:13 things he has done will be r;

REMEMBERS (REMEMBER)

Ps 103: 14 he r that we are dust.
    111: 5 he r his covenant forever.
Isa 43:25 and r your sins no more.

REMEMBRANCE (REMEMBER)

Lk 22:19 given for you; do this in r of me."
1Co 11:24 which is for you; do this in r of me
    11:25 whenever you drink it, in r of me."

REMIND

Jn 14:26 will r you of everything I have said
2Pe 1:12 I will always r you of these things.

REMNANT

Ezr 9: 8 has been gracious in leaving us a r
Isa 11:11 time to reclaim the r that is left
Jer 23: 3 "I myself will gather the r
Zec 8:12 inheritance to the r of this people.
Ro 11: 5 the present time there is a r chosen

REMOVED

Ps 30:11 you r my sackcloth and clothed me
    103: 12 so far has he r our transgressions
Jn 20: 1 and saw that the stone had been r

REND

Joel 2:13 R your heart

RENEW (RENEWAL RENEWED RENEWING)

Ps 51:10 and r a steadfast spirit within me.
Isa 40:31 will r their strength.

RENEWAL (RENEW)

Isa 57:10 You found r of your strength,
Tit 3: 5 of rebirth and r by the Holy Spirit,

RENEWED (RENEW)

Ps 103: 5 that your youth is r like the eagle's.
2Co 4:16 yet inwardly we are being r day

RENEWING* (RENEW)

Ro 12: 2 transformed by the r of your mind.

RENOUNCE (RENOUNCED RENOUNCES)

Da 4:27 R your sins by doing what is right.

RENOUNCED (RENOUNCE)

2Co 4: 2 we have r secret and shameful

RENOUNCES (RENOUNCE)

Pr 28:13 confesses and r them finds

RENOWN*

Ge 6: 4 were the heroes of old, men of r.
Ps 102: 12 r endures through all generations.
    135: 13 r, O LORD, through all
Isa 26: 8 your name and r
    55:13 This will be for the LORD's r,
    63:12 to gain for himself everlasting r,
Jer 13:11 to be my people for my r and praise

Jer 32:20 have gained the r that is still yours.
    33: 9 Then this city will bring me r, joy,
    49:25 the city of r not been abandoned,
Eze 26:17 How you are destroyed, O city of r,
Hos 12: 5 the LORD is his name of r!

REPAID (PAY)

Lk 6:34 to 'sinners,' expecting to be r in full
    14:14 you will be r at the resurrection
Col 3:25 Anyone who does wrong will be r

REPAY (PAY)

Dt 7:10 But those who hate him he will r
    32:35 It is mine to avenge; I will r.
Ru 2:12 May the LORD r you
Ps 103: 10 or r us according to our iniquities.
    116: 12 How can I r the LORD
Jer 25:14 I will r them according
Ro 12:17 Do not r anyone evil for evil.
    12:19 "It is mine to avenge; I will r,"
1Pe 3: 9 Do not r evil with evil

REPAYING (PAY)

2Ch 6:23 r the guilty by bringing
1Ti 5: 4 so r their parents and grandparents.

REPEATED

Heb 10: 1 the same sacrifices r endlessly year

REPENT (REPENTANCE REPENTED REPENTS)

1Ki 8:47 r and plead with you in the land
Job 36:10 commands them to r of their evil.
    42: 6 and r in dust and ashes."
Jer 15:19 "If you r, I will restore you
Eze 18:30 R! Turn away from your
    18:32 R and live! "Take up a lament
Mt 3: 2 "R, for the kingdom of heaven is
    4:17 "R, for the kingdom of heaven is
Mk 6:12 and preached that people should r.
Lk 13: 3 unless you r, you too will all perish.
Ac 2:38 Peter replied, "R and be baptized,
    3:19 R, then, and turn to God,
    17:30 all people everywhere to r.
    26:20 also, I preached that they should r
Rev 2: 5 R and do the things you did at first.

REPENTANCE (REPENT)

Isa 30:15 "In r and rest is your salvation,
Mt 3: 8 Produce fruit in keeping with r.
Mk 1: 4 a baptism of r for the forgiveness
Lk 3: 8 Produce fruit in keeping with r.
    5:32 call the righteous, but sinners to r."
    24:47 and r and forgiveness of sins will be
Ac 20:21 that they must turn to God in r
    26:20 and prove their r by their deeds.
Ro 2: 4 kindness leads you toward r?
2Co 7:10 Godly sorrow brings r that leads
2Pe 3: 9 but everyone to come to r.

REPENTED (REPENT)

Mt 11:21 they would have r long ago

REPENTS (REPENT)

Lk 15: 7 in heaven over one sinner who r
    15:10 of God over one sinner who r."
    17: 3 rebuke him, and if he r, forgive him

REPORTS

Ex 23: 1 "Do not spread false r.

REPOSES*

Pr 14:33 Wisdom r in the heart

REPRESENTATION*

Heb 1: 3 and the exact r of his being,

REPROACH

Job 27: 6 my conscience will not r me
Isa 51: 7 Do not fear the r of men
1Ti 3: 2 Now the overseer must be above r,

REPUTATION

1Ti 3: 7 also have a good r with outsiders,

REQUESTS

Ps 20: 5 May the LORD grant all your r.
Php 4: 6 with thanksgiving, present your r

REQUIRE (REQUIRED REQUIRES)

Mic 6: 8 And what does the LORD r of you

REQUIRED (REQUIRE)

1Co 4: 2 it is r that those who have been

REQUIRES (REQUIRE)

1Ki 2: 3 what the LORD your God r:
Heb 9:22 the law r that nearly everything be

RESCUE (RESCUED RESCUES)

Ps 22: 8 let the LORD r him.
    31: 2 come quickly to my r;
    69:14 R me from the mire,
    91:14 says the LORD; "I will r him;
    143: 9 R me from my enemies, O LORD,
Da 6:20 been able to r you from the lions?"
Ro 7:24 Who will r me from this body
Gal 1: 4 himself for our sins to r us
2Pe 2: 9 how to r godly men from trials

RESCUED (RESCUE)

Ps 18:17 He r me from my powerful enemy,
Pr 11: 8 The righteous man is r
Col 1:13 For he has r us from the dominion

RESCUES (RESCUE)

Da 6:27 He r and he saves;
1Th 1:10 who r us from the coming wrath.

RESENT* (RESENTFUL RESENTS)

Pr 3:11 and do not r his rebuke.

RESENTFUL* (RESENT)

2Ti 2:24 to everyone, able to teach, not r.

RESENTS* (RESENT)

Pr 15:12 A mocker r correction;

RESERVE (RESERVED)

1Ki 19:18 Yet I r seven thousand in Israel—

RESERVED (RESERVE)

Ro 11: 4 "I have r for myself seven

RESIST (RESISTED RESISTS)

Da 11:32 know their God will firmly r him.
Mt 5:39 I tell you, Do not r an evil person.
Lk 21:15 of your adversaries will be able to r
Jas 4: 7 R the devil, and he will flee
1Pe 5: 9 R him, standing firm in the faith,

RESISTED (RESIST)

Job 9: 4 Who has r him and come out

RESISTS* (RESIST)

Ro 9:19 For who r his will?" But who are

RESOLVED

Ps 17: 3 I have r that my mouth will not sin.
Da 1: 8 But Daniel r not to defile himself
1Co 2: 2 For I r to know nothing while I was

RESOUNDING*

Ps 150: 5 praise him with r cymbals.
1Co 13: 1 I am only a r gong or a clanging

RESPECT (RESPECTABLE RESPECTED RESPECTS)

Lev 19: 3 "Each of you must r his mother
    19:32 show r for the elderly and revere
Pr 11:16 A kindhearted woman gains r,
Mal 1: 6 where is the r due me?" says
Eph 5:33 and the wife must r her husband.
    6: 5 obey your earthly masters with r
1Th 4:12 so that your daily life may win the r
    5:12 to r those who work hard
1Ti 3: 4 children obey him with proper r.
    3: 8 are to be men worthy of r, sincere,
    3:11 are to be women worthy of r,
    6: 1 their masters worthy of full r,
Tit 2: 2 worthy of r, self-controlled,
1Pe 2:17 Show proper r to everyone:
    3: 7 them with r as the weaker partner
    3:16 But do this with gentleness and r,

RESPECTABLE* (RESPECT)

1Ti 3: 2 self-controlled, r, hospitable,

RESPECTED (RESPECT)

Pr 31:23 Her husband is r at the city gate,

RESPECTS (RESPECT)

Pr 13:13 he who r a command is rewarded.

RESPLENDENT*

Ps 76: 4 You are r with light,
    132: 18 but the crown on his head will be r

RESPOND

Ps 102: 17 He will r to the prayer
Hos   2: 21 "I will r to the skies,

RESPONSIBILITY (RESPONSIBLE)

Ac   18: 6 your own heads! I am clear of my r.

RESPONSIBLE (RESPONSIBILITY)

Nu   1: 53 The Levites are to be r for the care
1Co 7: 24 Brothers, each man, as r to God,

REST (RESTED RESTS SABBATH-REST)

Ex 31: 15 the seventh day is a Sabbath of r,
     33: 14 go with you, and I will give you r."
Lev 25: 5 The land is to have a year of r.
Dt 31: 16 going to r with your fathers,
Jos 14: 15 Then the land had r from war.
     21: 44 The LORD gave them r
1Ki   5: 4 The LORD my god has given me r
1Ch 22: 9 who will be a man of peace and r,
Job 3: 17 and there the weary are at r.
Ps 16: 9 my body also will r secure,
     33: 22 May your unfailing love r upon us,
     62: 1 My soul finds r in God alone;
     62: 5 Find r, O my soul, in God alone;
     90: 17 of the Lord our God r upon us;
     91: 1 will r in the shadow
     95: 11 "They shall never enter my r."
Pr   6: 10 a little folding of the hands to r—
Isa 11: 2 Spirit of the LORD will r on him—
     11: 10 and his place of r will be glorious.
     30: 15 "In repentance and r is your
     32: 18 in undisturbed places of r.
     57: 20 which cannot r,
Jer 6: 16 and you will find r for your souls.
     47: 6 'how long till you r?
Mt 11: 28 and burdened, and I will give you r.
2Co 12: 9 so that Christ's power may r on me
Heb 3: 11 'They shall never enter my r.' "
      4: 3 'They shall never enter my r.' "
      4: 10 for anyone who enters God's r
Rev 14: 13 "they will r from their labor,

RESTED (REST)

Ge   2: 2 so on the seventh day he r
Heb 4: 4 "And on the seventh day God r

RESTITUTION

Ex 22: 3 "A thief must certainly make r,
Lev 6: 5 He must make r in full, add a fifth
Nu   5: 8 the r belongs to the LORD

RESTORE (RESTORES)

Ps 51: 12 R to me the joy of your salvation
     80: 3 R us, O God;
   126: 4 R our fortunes, O LORD,
Jer 31: 18 R me, and I will return,
La   5: 21 R us to yourself, O LORD,
Da   9: 25 From the issuing of the decree to r
Na   2: 2 The LORD will r the splendor
Gal 6: 1 are spiritual should r him gently.
1Pe 5: 10 will himself r you and make you

RESTORES (RESTORE)

Ps 23: 3 he r my soul.

RESTRAINED (RESTRAINT)

Ps 78: 38 Time after time he r his anger

RESTRAINING (RESTRAINT)

Pr 27: 16 r her is like r the wind
Col 2: 23 value in r sensual indulgence.

RESTRAINT (RESTRAINED RESTRAINING)

Pr 17: 27 of knowledge uses words with r,
     23: 4 have the wisdom to show r.
     29: 18 no revelation, the people cast off r;

RESTS (REST)

Dt 33: 12 and the one the LORD loves r
Pr 19: 23 one r content, untouched
Lk   2: 14 to men on whom his favor r."

RESULT

Lk 21: 13 This will r in your being witnesses
Ro   2: 7 to holiness, and the r is eternal life.
     11: 31 as a r of God's mercy to you.
2Co 3: 3 from Christ, the r of our ministry,
2Th 1: 5 as a r you will be counted worthy
1Pe 1: 7 may be proved genuine and may r

RESURRECTION*

Mt 22: 23 who say there is no r, came to him
     22: 28 at the r, whose wife will she be

Mt 22: 30 At the r people will neither marry
     22: 31 But about the r of the dead—
     27: 53 and after Jesus' r they went
Mk 12: 18 who say there is no r, came to him
     12: 23 At the r whose wife will she be,
Lk 14: 14 repaid at the r of the righteous."
     20: 27 who say there is no r, came to Jesus
     20: 33 at the r whose wife will she be,
     20: 35 in the r from the dead will neither
     20: 36 since they are children of the r.
Jn 11: 24 again in the r at the last day."
     11: 25 Jesus said to her, "I am the r
Ac   1: 22 become a witness with us of his r."
     2: 31 he spoke of the r of the Christ,
     4: 2 in Jesus the r of the dead.
     4: 33 to testify to the r of the Lord Jesus,
     17: 18 good news about Jesus and the r
     17: 32 When they heard about the r
     23: 6 of my hope in the r of the dead."
     23: 8 Sadducees say that there is no r,
     24: 15 that there will be a r
     24: 21 'It is concerning the r
Ro   1: 4 Son of God by his r from the dead:
     6: 5 also be united with him in his r
1Co 15: 12 some of you say that there is no r
     15: 13 If there is no r of the dead,
     15: 21 the r of the dead comes
     15: 29 if there is no r, what will those do
     15: 42 So will it be with the r of the dead.
Php 3: 10 power of his r and the fellowship
     3: 11 to attain to the r from the dead.
2Ti 2: 18 say that the r has already taken
Heb 6: 2 on of hands, the r of the dead,
     11: 35 so that they might gain a better r.
1Pe 1: 3 hope through the r of Jesus Christ
     3: 21 It saves you by the r of Jesus Christ
Rev 20: 5 This is the first r.
     20: 6 those who have part in the first r.

RETALIATE*

1Pe 2: 23 he did not r; when he suffered,

RETRIBUTION

Ps 69: 22 may it become r and a trap.
Jer 51: 56 For the LORD is a God of r;
Ro 11: 9 a stumbling block and a r for them.

RETURN (RETURNED RETURNS)

Ge   3: 19 and to dust you will r."
2Sa 12: 23 go to him, but he will not r to me."
2Ch 30: 9 If you r to the LORD, then your
Ne   1: 9 but if you r to me and obey my
Job 10: 21 joy before I go to the place of no r,
     16: 22 before I go on the journey of no r.
     22: 23 If you r to the Almighty, you will
Ps 80: 14 R to us, O God Almighty!
   126: 6 will r with songs of joy,
Isa 10: 21 A remnant will r, a remnant
     35: 10 the ransomed of the LORD will r.
     55: 11 It will not r to me empty,
Jer 24: 7 for they will r to me
     31: 8 a great throng will r.
La   3: 40 and let us r to the LORD.
Hos 6: 1 "Come, let us r to the LORD.
     12: 6 But you must r to your God;
     14: 1 R, O Israel, to the LORD your
Joel 2: 12 "r to me with all your heart,
Zec 1: 3 'R to me,' declares the LORD
     10: 9 and they will r.

RETURNED (RETURN)

Ps 35: 13 When my prayers r
Am   4: 6 yet you have not r to me,"
1Pe 2: 25 now you have r to the Shepherd

RETURNS (RETURN)

Pr   3: 14 and yields better r than gold.
Isa 52: 8 When the LORD r to Zion,
Mt 24: 46 finds him doing so when he r.

REUBEN

Firstborn of Jacob by Leah (Ge 29:32; 46:8; 1Ch 2:1). Attempted to rescue Joseph (Ge 37: 21-30). Lost birthright for sleeping with Bilhah (Ge 35:22; 49:4). Tribe of blessed (Ge 49:3-4; Dt 33:6), numbered (Nu 1:21; 26:7), allotted land east of Jordan (Nu 32; 34:14; Jos 13:15), west (Eze 48:6), failed to help Deborah (Jdg 5:15-16), supported David (1Ch 12:37), 12,000 from (Rev 7:5).

REVEAL (REVEALED REVEALS REVELATION REVELATIONS)

Mt 11: 27 to whom the Son chooses to r him.
Gal 1: 16 was pleased to r his Son in me

REVEALED (REVEAL)

Dt 29: 29 but the things r belong to us
Isa 40: 5 the glory of the LORD will be r,
     43: 12 I have r and saved and proclaimed
     53: 1 the arm of the LORD been r?
     65: 1 I r myself to those who did not ask
Mt 11: 25 and r them to little children.
Jn 12: 38 the arm of the Lord been r?"
     17: 6 "I have r you to those whom you
Ro   1: 17 a righteousness from God is r,
     8: 18 with the glory that will be r in us.
     10: 20 I r myself to those who did not ask
     16: 26 but now r and made known
1Co 2: 10 but God has r it to us by his Spirit.
2Th 1: 7 happen when the Lord Jesus is r
     2: 3 and the man of lawlessness is r,
1Pe 1: 7 and honor when Jesus Christ is r.
     1: 20 but was r in these last times
     4: 13 overjoyed when his glory is r.

REVEALS* (REVEAL)

Nu 23: 3 Whatever he r to me I will tell you
Job 12: 22 He r the deep things of darkness
Da   2: 22 He r deep and hidden things;
     2: 28 a God in heaven who r mysteries.
Am   4: 13 and r his thoughts to man,

REVELATION* (REVEAL)

2Sa 7: 17 David all the words of this entire r.
1Ch 17: 15 David all the words of this entire r.
Pr 29: 18 Where there is no r, the people cast
Da 10: 1 a r was given to Daniel (who was
Hab 2: 2 "Write down the r
     2: 3 For the r awaits an appointed time;
Lk   2: 32 a light for r to the Gentiles
Ro 16: 25 according to the r
1Co 14: 6 I bring you some r or knowledge
     14: 26 a r, a tongue or an interpretation.
     14: 30 And if a r comes to someone who is
Gal 1: 12 I received it by r from Jesus Christ.
     2: 1 I went in response to a r
Eph 1: 17 you the Spirit of wisdom and r,
     3: 3 mystery made known to me by r,
Rev 1: 1 r of Jesus Christ, which God gave

REVELATIONS* (REVEAL)

2Co 12: 1 on to visions and r from the Lord.
     12: 7 of these surpassingly great r,

REVELED* (REVELRY)

Ne   9: 25 they r in your great goodness.

REVELRY (REVELED)

Ex 32: 6 drink and got up to indulge in r.
1Co 10: 7 and got up to indulge in pagan r."

REVENGE (VENGEANCE)

Lev 19: 18 " 'Do not seek r or bear a grudge
Ro 12: 19 Do not take r, my friends,

REVERE* (REVERENCE REVERENT REVERING)

Lev 19: 32 for the elderly and r your God.
Dt   4: 10 so that they may learn to r me
     13: 4 must follow, and him you must r.
     14: 23 to the LORD your God always.
     17: 19 learn to r the LORD his God
     28: 58 and do not r this glorious
Job 37: 24 Therefore, men r him,
Ps 22: 23 R him, all you descendants
     33: 8 let all the people of the world r him
   102: 15 of the earth will r your glory.
Ecc 3: 14 God does it so that men will r him.
Isa 25: 3 cities of ruthless nations will r you.
     59: 19 of the sun, they will r his glory.
     63: 17 hearts so we do not r you?
Jer 10: 7 Who should not r you,
Hos 10: 3 because we did not r the LORD.
Mal 2: 2 But for you who r my name,

REVERENCE (REVERE)

Lev 19: 30 and have r for my sanctuary.
Ne   5: 15 of r for God I did not act like that.
Ps   5: 7 in r will I bow down
Da   6: 26 people must fear and r the LORD
2Co 7: 1 perfecting holiness out of r for God
Eph 5: 21 to one another out of r for Christ.
Col 3: 22 of heart and r for the Lord.
1Pe 3: 2 when they see the purity and r
Rev 11: 18 and those who r your name,

REVERENT* (REVERE)

Ecc 8: 12 with God-fearing men, who are r
Tit   2: 3 women to be r in the way they live,

Heb   5: 7 because of his r submission.
1Pe   1: 17 as strangers here in r fear,

REVERING* (REVERE)

Dt   8: 6 walking in his ways and r him.
Ne   1: 11 who delight in r your name.

REVERSE*

Isa 43: 13 When I act, who can r it?"

REVIVE* (REVIVING)

Ps   80: 18 r us, and we will call on your name.
     85: 6 Will you not r us again,
Isa 57: 15 and to r the heart of the contrite.
     57: 15 to r the spirit of the lowly
Hos   6: 2 After two days he will r us;

REVIVING* (REVIVE)

Ps   19: 7 r the soul.

REVOKED

Isa 45: 23 a word that will not be r;

REWARD (REWARDED REWARDING REWARDS)

Ge   15: 1 your very great r."
1Sa 24: 19 May the LORD r you well
Ps   19: 11 in keeping them is great r.
     62: 12 Surely you will r each person
    127: 3 children a r from him.
Pr   9: 12 are wise, your wisdom will r you;
     11: 18 sows righteousness reaps a sure r.
     13: 21 prosperity is the r of the righteous.
     19: 17 he will r him for what he has done.
     25: 22 and the LORD will r you.
     31: 31 Give her the r she has earned,
Isa 40: 10 See, his r is with him,
     49: 4 and my r is with my God."
     61: 8 In my faithfulness I will r them
     62: 11 See, his r is with him,
Jer 17: 10 to r a man according to his conduct
     32: 19 you r everyone according
Mt   5: 12 because great is your r in heaven,
      6: 1 you will have no r
      6: 5 they have received their r in full.
     10: 41 a prophet will receive a prophet's r,
     16: 27 and then he will r each person
Lk   6: 23 because great is your r in heaven.
      6: 35 Then your r will be great,
1Co   3: 14 built survives, he will receive his r.
Eph   6: 8 know that the Lord will r everyone
Col   3: 24 an inheritance from the Lord as a r.
Heb 11: 26 he was looking ahead to his r.
Rev 22: 12 I am coming soon! My r is with me

REWARDED (REWARD)

Ru   2: 12 May you be richly r by the LORD,
2Sa 22: 21 of my hands he has r me.
2Ch 15: 7 for your work will be r."
Ps   18: 24 The LORD has r me according
Pr   13: 13 he who respects a command is r.
     14: 14 and the good man r for his.
Jer 31: 16 for your work will be r,"
1Co   3: 8 and each will be r according
Heb 10: 35 your confidence; it will be richly r.
2Jn   : 8 but that you may be r fully.

REWARDING* (REWARD)

Rev 11: 18 for r your servants the prophets

REWARDS (REWARD)

1Sa 26: 23 The LORD r every man
Pr   12: 14 the work of his hands r him.
Heb 11: 6 that he r those who earnestly seek

RIBS

Ge   2: 21 he took one of the man's r

RICH (RICHES RICHEST)

Job 34: 19 does not favor the r over the poor,
Ps   49: 16 overawed when a man grows r,
    145: 8 slow to anger and r in love.
Pr   21: 17 loves wine and oil will never be r.
      2: 2 Rand poor have this in common:
     23: 4 Do not wear yourself out to get r;
     28: 6 than a r man whose ways are
     28: 20 to get r will not go unpunished.
     28: 22 A stingy man is eager to get r
Ecc   5: 12 but the abundance of a r man
Isa 33: 6 a r store of salvation and wisdom
     53: 9 and with the r in his death,
Jer   9: 23 or the r man boast of his riches,
Zec   3: 4 and I will put r garments on you."
Mt   19: 23 it is hard for a r man
Lk   1: 53 but has sent the r away empty.

Lk   6: 24 "But woe to you who are r,
     12: 21 for himself but is not r toward God
     16: 1 "There was a r man whose
     21: 1 Jesus saw the r putting their gifts
2Co   6: 10 yet making many r; having nothing
      8: 2 poverty welled up in r generosity.
      8: 9 he was r, yet for your sakes he
      9: 11 You will be made r in every way
Eph   2: 4 love for us, God, who is r in mercy,
1Ti   6: 9 want to get r fall into temptation
      6: 17 Command those who are r
      6: 18 to do good, to be r in good deeds,
Jas   1: 10 the one who is r should take pride
      2: 5 the eyes of the world to be r in faith
      5: 1 you r people, weep and wail
Rev   2: 9 and your poverty—yet you are r!
      3: 18 you can become r; and white

RICHES (RICH)

Job 36: 18 that no one entices you by r;
Ps   49: 6 and boast of their great r?
     49: 12 despite his r, does not endure;
     62: 10 though your r increase,
    119: 14 as one rejoices in great r.
Pr   3: 16 in her left hand are r and honor.
     11: 28 Whoever trusts in his r will fall,
     22: 1 is more desirable than great r;
     27: 24 for r do not endure forever,
     30: 8 give me neither poverty nor r,
Isa 10: 3 Where will you leave your r?
     60: 5 to you the r of the nations will
Jer   9: 23 or the rich man boast of his r,
Lk   8: 14 r and pleasures, and they do not
Ro   9: 23 to make the r of his glory known
     11: 33 the depth of the r of the wisdom
Eph   2: 7 he might show the incomparable r
      3: 8 to the Gentiles the unsearchable r
Col   1: 27 among the Gentiles the glorious r
      2: 2 so that they may have the full r

RICHEST (RICH)

Isa 55: 2 and your soul will delight in the r

RID

Ge   21: 10 "Get r of that slave woman
1Co   5: 7 Get r of the old yeast that you may
Gal   4: 30 "Get r of the slave woman

RIDE (RIDER RIDING)

Ps   45: 4 In your majesty r forth victoriously

RIDER (RIDE)

Rev   6: 2 was a white horse! Its r held a bow,
     19: 11 whose r is called Faithful and True.

RIDING (RIDE)

Zec   9: 9 gentle and r on a donkey,
Mt   21: 5 gentle and r on a donkey,

RIGGING

Isa 33: 23 Your r hangs loose:

RIGHT (RIGHTS)

Ge   4: 7 But if you do not do what is r,
     18: 19 of the LORD by doing what is r
     18: 25 the Judge of all the earth do r?"
     48: 13 on his left toward Israel's r hand,
Ex   15: 6 Your r hand, O LORD,
     15: 26 and do what is r in his eyes,
Dt   5: 32 do not turn aside to the r
      6: 18 Do what is r and good
     13: 18 and doing what is r in his eyes.
Jos   1: 7 do not turn from it to the r
1Sa 12: 23 you the way that is good and r.
1Ki   3: 9 to distinguish between r and wrong
      3: 15 For David had done what was r
2Ki   7: 9 to each other, "We're not doing r.
Ne   9: 13 and laws that are just and r,
Ps   16: 8 Because he is at my r hand,
     16: 11 eternal pleasures at your r hand.
     17: 7 you who save by your r hand
     18: 35 and your r hand sustains me;
     19: 8 The precepts of the LORD are r,
     25: 9 He guides the humble in what is r
     33: 4 For the word of the LORD is r
     44: 3 it was your r hand, your arm,
     45: 4 let your r hand display awesome
     51: 4 so that you are proved r
     63: 8 your r hand upholds me.
     73: 23 you hold me by my r hand.
     91: 7 ten thousand at your r hand,
     98: 1 his r hand and his holy arm.
    106: 3 who constantly do what is r.
    110: 1 "Sit at my r hand
    118: 15 LORD's r hand has done mighty

Ps 119:144 Your statutes are forever r;
    137: 5 may my r hand forget its skill,
    139: 10 your r hand will hold me fast.
Pr   1: 3 doing what is r and just and fair;
      4: 27 Do not swerve to the r or the left;
     14: 12 There is a way that seems r
     18: 17 The first to present his case seems r
Ecc   7: 20 who does what is r and never sins.
SS   1: 4 How r they are to adore you!
Isa   1: 17 learn to do r!
      7: 15 reject the wrong and choose the r.
     30: 10 us no more visions of what is r!
     30: 21 Whether you turn to the r
     41: 10 you with my righteous r hand.
     41: 13 who takes hold of your r hand,
     48: 13 my r hand spread out the heavens;
     64: 5 to the help of those who gladly do r
Jer 23: 5 and do what is just and r in the land
Eze 18: 5 who does what is just and r,
     18: 21 and does what is just and r,
     33: 14 and does what is just and r—
Hos 14: 9 The ways of the LORD are r;
Mt   5: 29 If your r eye causes you to sin,
      6: 3 know what your r hand is doing,
     22: 44 "Sit at my r hand
     25: 33 He will put the sheep on his r
Jn   1: 12 he gave the r to become children
Ac   2: 34 "Sit at my r hand
      7: 55 Jesus standing at the r hand of God
Ro   3: 4 "So that you may be proved r
      8: 34 is at the r hand of God and is
      9: 21 Does not the potter have the r
     12: 17 careful to do what is r in the eyes
1Co   9: 4 Don't we have the r to food
2Co   8: 21 we are taking pains to do what is r,
Eph   1: 20 and seated him at his r hand
      6: 1 parents in the Lord, for this is r.
Php   4: 8 whatever is r, whatever is pure,
2Th   3: 13 never tire of doing what is r.
Heb   1: 3 down at the r hand of the Majesty
Jas   2: 8 as yourself," you are doing r.
1Pe   3: 14 if you should suffer for what is r,
1Jn   2: 29 who does what is r has been born
Rev   2: 7 I will give the r to eat from the tree
      3: 21 I will give the r to sit with me
     22: 11 let him who does r continue to do r

RIGHTEOUS (RIGHTEOUSLY RIGHTEOUSNESS)

Ge   6: 9 Noah was a r man, blameless
     18: 23 "Will you sweep away the r
Nu   23: 10 Let me die the death of the r,
Ne   9: 8 your promise because you are r.
Job 36: 7 He does not take his eyes off the r;
Ps   1: 5 nor sinners in the assembly of the r.
      5: 12 O LORD, you bless the r;
     11: 7 For the LORD is r,
     15: 2 and who does what is r,
     34: 15 The eyes of the LORD are on the r
     37: 16 Better the little that the r have
     37: 21 but the r give generously;
     37: 25 yet I have never seen the r forsaken
     37: 30 of the r man utters wisdom,
     55: 22 he will never let the r fall.
     64: 10 Let the r rejoice in the LORD
     68: 3 But may the r be glad
    112: 4 compassionate and r man.
    118: 20 through which the r may enter.
    119: 7 as I learn your r laws.
   119:137 Rare you, O LORD,
    140: 13 Surely the r will praise your name
    143: 2 for no one living is r before you.
    145: 17 The LORD is r in all his ways
Pr   3: 33 but he blesses the home of the r.
      4: 18 of the r is like the first gleam
     10: 7 of the r will be a blessing,
     10: 11 The mouth of the r is a fountain
     10: 16 The wages of the r bring them life,
     10: 20 The tongue of the r is choice silver,
     10: 24 what the r desire will be granted.
     10: 28 The prospect of the r is joy,
     10: 32 of the r know what is fitting,
     11: 23 The desire of the r ends only
     11: 30 The fruit of the r is a tree of life,
     12: 10 A r man cares for the needs
     12: 21 No harm befalls the r,
     13: 9 The light of the r shines brightly,
     15: 28 of the r weighs its answers,
     15: 29 but he hears the prayer of the r.
     16: 31 it is attained by a r life.
     18: 10 the r run to it and are safe.
     20: 7 The r man leads a blameless life;
     21: 15 justice is done, it brings joy to the r
     23: 24 The father of a r man has great joy;
     28: 1 but the r are as bold as a lion.

RIGHTEOUSLY (continued)

Pr 29: 6 but a r one can sing and be glad.
29: 7 The r care about justice
29:27 The r detest the dishonest;
Ecc 7:20 There is not a r man on earth
Isa 26: 7 The path of the r is level;
41:10 you with my r right hand.
45:21 a r God and a Savior;
53:11 his knowledge my r servant will
64: 6 and all our r acts are like filthy rags
Jer 23: 5 up to David a r Branch.
Eze 3:20 when a r man turns
18: 5 "Suppose there is a r man
18:20 of the r man will be credited
33:12 The r man, if he sins, will not be
Da 9:18 requests of you because we are r,
Hab 2: 4 but the r will live by his faith—
Zec 9: 9 r and having salvation,
Mal 3:18 see the distinction between the r
Mt 5:45 rain on the r and the unrighteous.
9:13 For I have not come to call the r,
10:41 and anyone who receives a r man
13:43 then the r will shine like the sun
13:49 and separate the wicked from the r
25:37 "Then the r will answer him, 'Lord,
25:46 to eternal punishment, but the r
Ac 24:15 will be a resurrection of both the r
Ro 1:17 as it is written: "The r will live
2: 5 when his r judgment will be
2:13 the law who will be declared r.
3:10 "There is no one r, not even one;
3:20 Therefore no one will be declared r
5:19 one man the many will be made r.
Gal 3:11 because, "The r will live by faith."
1Ti 1: 9 that law is made not for the r
2Ti 4: 8 which the Lord, the r Judge,
Tit 3: 5 because of r things we had done,
Heb 10:38 But my r one will live by faith.
Jas 5:16 The prayer of a r man is powerful
1Pe 3:12 the eyes of the Lord are on the r
3:18 the r for the unrighteous,
4:18 "If it is hard for the r to be saved,
1Jn 2: 1 defense—Jesus Christ, the R One.
3: 7 does what is right is r, just as he is r.
Rev 19: 8 stands for the r acts of the saints.)

RIGHTEOUSLY* (RIGHTEOUS)

Ps 9: 4 on your throne, judging r.
Isa 33:15 He who walks r
Jer 11:20 LORD Almighty, you who judge r

RIGHTEOUSNESS (RIGHTEOUS)

Ge 15: 6 and he credited it to him as r.
Dt 9: 4 of this land because of my r."
1Sa 26:23 LORD rewards every man for his r
1Ki 10: 9 to maintain justice and r."
Job 37:23 great r, he does not oppress.
Ps 7:17 to the LORD because of his r
9: 8 He will judge the world in r;
17:15 And I—in r I will see your face;
23: 3 He guides me in paths of r
33: 5 The LORD loves r and justice;
35:28 My tongue will speak of your r
36: 6 Your r is like the mighty
37: 6 He will make your r shine like
40: 9 I proclaim r in the great assembly;
45: 4 in behalf of truth, humility and r;
45: 7 You love r and hate wickedness;
48:10 your right hand is filled with r.
65: 5 us with awesome deeds of r,
71: 2 Rescue me and deliver me in your r
71:15 My mouth will tell of your r,
71:19 Your r reaches to the skies, O God,
85:10 and peace kiss each other.
89:14 R and justice are the foundation
96:13 He will judge the world in r
98: 9 He will judge the world in r
103: 6 The LORD works r
103:17 his r with their children's children
106:31 This was credited to him as r
111: 3 and his r endures forever.
118:19 Open for me the gates of r;
132: 9 May your priests be clothed with r,
145: 7 and joyfully sing of your r.
Pr 2: 9 r of the blameless makes a straight
11:18 he who sows r reaps a sure reward.
13: 6 R guards the man of integrity,
14:34 R exalts a nation.
16: 8 Better a little with r
16:12 a throne is established through r.
21:21 He who pursues r and love
Isa 5:16 who show himself holy by his r.
9: 7 it with justice and r,
11: 4 but with the r he will judge the needy,
16: 5 and speeds the cause of r.
26: 9 the people of the world learn r.

Isa 32:17 The fruit of r will be peace;
42: 6 "I, the LORD, have called you in r;
42:21 the LORD for the sake of his r
45: 8 "You heavens above, rain down r;
51: 1 "Listen to me, you who pursue r
51: 6 my r will never fail.
51: 8 But my r will last forever,
58: 8 then your r will go before you,
59:17 He put on r as his breastplate,
61:10 and arrayed me in a robe of r,
63: 1 "It is I, speaking in r,
Jer 9:24 justice and r on earth,
23: 6 The LORD Our R.
Eze 3:20 a righteous man turns from his r
14:20 save only themselves by their r.
18:20 The r of the righteous man will be
33:12 r of the righteous man will not save
Da 9:24 to bring in everlasting r,
12: 3 and those who lead many to r,
Hos 10:12 Sow for yourselves r,
Am 5:24 r like a never-failing stream!
Mic 7: 9 I will see his r.
Zep 2: 3 Seek r, seek humility;
Mal 4: 2 the sun of r will rise with healing
Mt 5: 6 those who hunger and thirst for r,
5:10 who are persecuted because of r,
5:20 unless your r surpasses that
6: 1 to do your 'acts of r' before men,
6:33 But seek first his kingdom and his r
Jn 16: 8 world of guilt in regard to sin and r
Ac 24:25 Paul discoursed on r, self-control
Ro 1:17 For in the gospel a r from God is
3: 5 brings out God's r more clearly,
3:22 This r from God comes
4: 3 and it was credited to him as r."
4: 5 wicked, his faith is credited as r.
4: 6 man to whom God credits r apart
4: 9 faith was credited to him as r.
4:13 through the r that comes by faith.
4:22 why "it was credited to him as r."
5:18 of r was justification that brings life
6:13 body to him as instruments of r.
6:16 or to obedience, which leads to r?
6:18 and have become slaves to r.
6:19 in slavery to r leading to holiness.
8:10 yet your spirit is alive because of r.
9:30 did not pursue r, have obtained it,
10: 3 they did not know the r that comes
14:17 but of r, peace and joy
1Co 1:30 our r, holiness and redemption.
2Co 3: 9 is the ministry that brings r!
5:21 that in him we might become the r
6: 7 with weapons of r in the right hand
6:14 For what do r and wickedness have
9: 9 his r endures forever."
Gal 2:21 for if r could be gained
3: 6 and it was credited to him as r."
3:21 then r would certainly have come
Eph 4:24 created to be like God in true r
5: 9 r and truth) and find out what
6:14 with the breastplate of r in place,
Php 1:11 filled with the fruit of r that comes
3: 6 as for legalistic r, faultless.
3: 9 not having a r of my own that
1Ti 6:11 and pursue r, godliness, faith, love,
2Ti 2:22 and pursue r, faith, love and peace,
3:16 correcting and training in r,
4: 8 is in store for me the crown of r,
Heb 1: 8 and r will be the scepter
5:13 with the teaching about r.
7: 2 his name means "king of r";
11: 7 became heir of the r that comes
12:11 it produces a harvest of r
Jas 2:23 and it was credited to him as r," r
3:18 sow in peace raise a harvest of r.
1Pe 2:24 die to sins and live for r;
2Pe 2:21 not to have known the way of r,
3:13 and a new earth, the home of r.

RIGHTS (RIGHT)

Ps 82: 3 maintain the r of the poor
Pr 31: 8 for the r of all who are destitute.
La 3:35 to deny a man his r
Gal 5: 4 that we might receive the full r

RING

Pr 11:22 Like a gold r in a pig's snout
Lk 15:22 Put a r on his finger and sandals

RIOTS

2Co 6: 5 imprisonments and r; in hard work,

RIPE

Joel 3:13 for the harvest is r.

Am 8: 1 showed me: a basket of r fruit.
Jn 4:35 at the fields! They are r for harvest.
Rev 14:15 for the harvest of the earth is r."

RISE (RAISE RAISED RISEN ROSE)

Lev 19:32 " 'R in the presence of the aged,
Nu 24:17 a scepter will r out of Israel.
Isa 26:19 their bodies will r.
Mal 4: 2 of righteousness will r with healing
Mt 27:63 'After three days I will r again.'
Mk 8:31 and after three days r again.
Lk 18:33 On the third day he will r again."
Jn 5:29 those who have done good will r
20: 9 had to r from the dead.)
Ac 17: 3 had to suffer and r from the dead.
1Th 4:16 and the dead in Christ will r first.

RISEN (RISE)

Mt 28: 6 He is not here; he has r, just
Mk 16: 6 He has r! He is not here.
Lk 24:34 The Lord has r and has appeared

RIVER (RIVERS)

Ps 46: 4 There is a r whose streams make
Isa 66:12 "I will extend peace to her like a r,
Eze 47:12 grow on both banks of the r
Rev 22: 1 Then the angel showed me the r

RIVERS (RIVER)

Ps 137: 1 By the r of Babylon we sat

ROAD (CROSSROADS ROADS)

Mt 7:13 and broad is the r that leads

ROADS (ROAD)

Lk 3: 5 crooked r shall become straight,

ROARING

1Pe 5: 8 prowls around like a r lion looking

ROB (ROBBERS ROBBERY ROBS)

Mal 3: 8 "Will a man r God? Yet you r me.

ROBBERS (ROB)

Jer 7:11 become a den of r to you?
Mk 15:27 They crucified two r with him,
Lk 19:46 but you have made it 'a den of r.' "
Jn 10: 8 came before me were thieves and r,

ROBBERY (ROB)

Isa 61: 8 I hate r and iniquity.

ROBE (ROBED ROBES)

Ge 37: 3 and he made a richly ornamented r
Isa 6: 1 the train of his r filled the temple.
61:10 arrayed me in a robe of r righteousness,
Rev 6:11 each of them was given a white r,

ROBED (ROBE)

Ps 93: 1 the LORD is r in majesty
Isa 63: 1 Who is this, r in splendor,

ROBES (ROBE)

Ps 45: 8 All your r are fragrant with myrrh
Rev 7:14 "These in white r—who are they,

ROBS* (ROB)

Pr 19:26 He who r his father and drives out
28:24 He who r his father or mother

ROCK

Ge 49:24 of the Shepherd, the R of Israel,
Ex 17: 6 Strike the r, and water will come
Nu 20: 8 Speak to that r before their eyes
Dt 32: 4 He is the R, his works are perfect,
32:13 him with honey from the r,
2Sa 22: 2 "The LORD is my r, my fortress
Ps 18: 2 The LORD is my r, my fortress
19:14 O LORD, my R and my Redeemer
40: 2 he set my feet on a r
61: 2 lead me to the r that is higher
92:15 he is my R, and there is no
Isa 26: 4 the LORD, is the R eternal.
51: 1 to the r from which you were cut
Da 2:34 you were watching, a r was cut out,
Mt 7:24 man who built his house on the r.
16:18 and on this r I will build my church
Ro 9:33 and a r that makes them fall,
1Co 10: 4 the spiritual r that accompanied
1Pe 2: 8 and a r that makes them fall."

ROD (RODS)

2Sa 7:14 I will punish him with the r of men,
Ps 23: 4 your r and your staff,
Pr 13:24 He who spares the r hates his son,

RODS (cont.)

Pr 22:15 the r of discipline will drive it far
23:13 if you punish him with the r,
29:15 r of correction imparts wisdom,
Isa 11: 4 the earth with the r of his mouth;

RODS (ROD)

2Co 11:25 Three times I was beaten with r,

ROLL (ROLLED)

Mk 16: 3 "Who will r the stone away

ROLLED (ROLL)

Lk 24: 2 They found the stone r away

ROMAN

Ac 16:37 even though we are R citizens,
22:25 you to flog a R citizen who hasn't

ROOF (ROOFS)

Pr 21: 9 Better to live on a corner of the r

ROOFS

Mt 10:27 in your ear, proclaim from the r.

ROOM (ROOMS)

Mt 6: 6 But when you pray, go into your r,
Mk 14:15 He will show you a large upper r,
Lk 2: 7 there was no r for them in the inn.
Jn 8:37 because you have no r for my word
21:25 the whole world would not have r
2Co 7: 2 Make r for us in your hearts.

ROOMS (ROOM)

Jn 14: 2 In my Father's house are many r;

ROOSTER

Mt 26:34 this very night, before the r crows.

ROOT (ROOTED ROOTS)

Isa 11:10 In that day the R of Jesse will stand
53: 2 and like a r out of dry ground.
Mt 3:10 already at the r of the trees,
13:21 But since he has no r, he lasts only
Ro 11:16 if the r is holy, so are the branches.
15:12 "The R of Jesse will spring up,
1Ti 6:10 of money is a r of all kinds of evil.
Rev 5: 5 the R of David, has triumphed.
22:16 I am the R and the Offspring

ROOTED (ROOT)

Eph 3:17 being r and established in love,

ROOTS (ROOT)

Isa 11: 1 from his r a Branch will bear fruit.

ROSE (RISE)

SS 2: 1 I am a r of Sharon,
1Th 4:14 believe that Jesus died and r again

ROTS

Pr 14:30 but envy r the bones.

ROUGH

Isa 42:16 and make the r places smooth.
Lk 3: 5 the r ways smooth.

ROUND

Ecc 1: 6 r and r it goes,

ROYAL

Ps 45: 9 at your right hand is the r bride
Da 1: 8 not to defile himself with the r food
Jas 2: 8 If you really keep the r law found
1Pe 2: 9 a r priesthood, a holy nation,

RUBBISH*

Php 3: 8 I consider them r, that I may gain

RUBIES

Job 28:18 the price of wisdom is beyond r.
Pr 3:15 She is more precious than r;
8:11 for wisdom is more precious than r,
31:10 She is worth far more than r.

RUDDER*

Jas 3: 4 by a very small r wherever the pilot

RUDDY

1Sa 16:12 He was r, with a fine appearance
SS 5:10 Beloved My lover is radiant and r,

RUDE*

1Co 13: 5 It is not r, it is not self-seeking,

RUIN (RUINED RUINING RUINS)

Pr 10: 8 but a chattering fool comes to r.
10:10 and a chattering fool comes to r.
10:14 but the mouth of a fool invites r.
10:29 but it is the r of those who do evil.
18:24 many companions may come to r,
19:13 A foolish son is his father's r,
26:28 and a flattering mouth works r.
SS 2:15 that r the vineyards,
Eze 21:27 A r! A r! I will make it a r!
1Ti 6: 9 desires that plunge men into r

RUINED (RUIN)

Isa 6: 5 "I am r! For I am a man
Mt 9:17 and the wineskins will be r.
12:25 divided against itself will be r,

RUINING* (RUIN)

Tit 1:11 they are r whole households

RUINS (RUIN)

Pr 19: 3 A man's own folly r his life,
Ecc 4: 5 and r himself.
2Ti 2:14 and only r those who listen.

RULE (RULER RULERS RULES)

Ge 1:26 let them r over the fish of the sea
3:16 and he will r over you."
Jdg 8:22 said to Gideon, "R over us—
1Sa 12:12 'No, we want a king to r over us'—
Ps 2: 9 You will r them with an iron
67: 4 for you r the peoples justly
119:133 let no sin r over me.
Pr 17: 2 A wise servant will r
Isa 28:10 ron r, ron r;
Eze 20:33 I will r over you with a mighty
6:13 and will sit and ron his throne.
9:10 His r will extend from sea to sea
9: 3 are summed up in this one r:
Ro 13: 9 arise to r over the nations;
15:12 arise to r over the nations;
1Co 7:17 This is the r I lay down in all
Gal 6:16 and mercy to all who follow this r,
Eph 1:21 far above all r and authority,
Col 3:15 the peace of Christ r in your hearts,
2Th 3:10 we gave you this r: "If a man will
Rev 2:27 He will r them with an iron scepter;
12: 5 who will r all the nations
19:15 He will r them with an iron scepter

RULER (RULE)

Ps 8: 6 You made him r over the works
Pr 19: 6 Many curry favor with a r,
23: 1 When you sit to dine with a r,
25:15 Through patience a r can be
29:26 Many seek an audience with a r,
Isa 60:17 and righteousness your r.
Da 9:25 the r, comes, there will be seven
Mic 5: 2 one who will be r over Israel,
Mt 2: 6 for out of you will come a r
Eph 2: 2 of the r of the kingdom of the air,
1Ti 6:15 God, the blessed and only R,
Rev 1: 5 and the r of the kings of the earth.

RULERS (RULE)

Ps 2: 2 and the r gather together
119:161 R persecute me without cause,
Isa 40:23 reduces the r of this world
Da 7:27 and all r will worship and obey him
Mt 20:25 "You know that the r
Ac 13:27 and their r did not recognize Jesus,
Ro 13: 3 For r hold no terror
1Co 2: 6 of this age or of the r of this age,
Eph 3:10 should be made known to the r
6:12 the r, against the authorities,
Col 1:16 or powers or r or authorities;

RULES (RULE)

Nu 15:15 is to have the same r for you
2Sa 23: 3 when he r in the fear of God,
Ps 22:28 and he r over the nations.
66: 7 He r forever by his power,
103:19 and his kingdom r over all.
Isa 29:13 is made up only of r taught by men.
40:10 and his arm r for him.
Mt 15: 9 their teachings are but r taught
Lk 22:26 one who r like the one who serves.
2Ti 2: 5 he competes according to the r.

RUMORS

Jer 51:46 afraid when r are heard in the land;
Mt 24: 6 You will hear of wars and r of wars,

RUN (RAN RUNNERS RUNNING RUNS)

Ps 19: 5 champion rejoicing to r his course.
Pr 4:12 when you r, you will not stumble.
18:10 the righteous r to it and are safe.
Isa 10: 3 To whom will you r for help?
40:31 they will r and not grow weary,
Joel 2: 9 R in such a way as to get the prize
Hab 2: 2 so that a herald may r with it.
1Co 9:24 R in such a way as to get the prize
Gal 2: 2 that I was running or had r my race
Php 2:16 on the day of Christ that I did not r
Heb 12: 1 let us r with perseverance the race

RUNNERS* (RUN)

1Co 9:24 that in a race all the r run,

RUNNING (RUN)

Ps 133: 2 r down on Aaron's beard,
Lk 17:23 Do not go r off after them.
1Co 9:26 I do not run like a man r aimlessly;
Gal 5: 7 You were r a good race.

RUNS (RUN)

Jn 10:12 he abandons the sheep and r away.

RUSH

Pr 1:16 for their feet r into sin,
6:18 feet that are quick to r into evil,
Isa 59: 7 Their feet r into sin;

RUST

Mt 6:19 where moth and r destroy.

RUTH*

Moabitess; widow who went to Bethlehem with mother-in-law Naomi (Ru 1). Gleaned in field of Boaz; shown favor (Ru 2). Proposed marriage to Boaz (Ru 3). Married (Ru 4:1-12); bore Obed, ancestor of David (Ru 4:13-22), Jesus (Mt 1:5).

RUTHLESS

Pr 11:16 but r men gain only wealth.
Ro 1:31 are senseless, faithless, heartless, r.

SABBATH (SABBATHS)

Ex 20: 8 "Remember the S day
31:14 "'Observe the S, because it is holy
Lev 25: 2 the land itself must observe a s
Dt 5:12 "Observe the S day
Isa 56: 2 keeps the S without desecrating it,
56: 6 all who keep the S
58:13 if you call the S a delight
Jer 17:21 not to carry a load on the S day
Mt 12: 1 through the grainfields on the S.
Lk 13:10 On a S Jesus was teaching in one
Col 2:16 a New Moon celebration or a S day

SABBATH-REST* (REST)

Heb 4: 9 then, a S for the people of God;

SABBATHS (SABBATH)

2Ch 2: 4 evening and on S and New Moons
Eze 20:12 Also I gave them my S

SACKCLOTH

Ps 30:11 you removed my s and clothed me
Da 9: 3 in fasting, and in s and ashes.
Mt 11:21 would have repented long ago in s

SACRED

Lev 23: 2 are to proclaim as s assemblies.
Mt 7: 6 "Do not give dogs what is s;
Ro 14: 5 One man considers one day more s
Col 3:17 for God's temple is s, and you are
2Pe 1:18 were with him on the s mountain.
2:21 on the s command that was

SACRIFICE (SACRIFICED SACRIFICES)

Ge 22: 2 S him there as a burnt offering
Ex 12:27 'It is the Passover s to the LORD,
1Sa 15:22 To obey is better than s,
1Ki 18:38 the LORD fell and burned up the s,
1Ch 21:24 or s a burnt offering that costs me
Ps 40: 6 S and offering you did not desire,
50:14 S thank offerings to God,
51:16 You do not delight in s,
54: 6 I will s a freewill offering to you;
107:22 Let them s thank offerings
141: 2 of my hands be like the evening s.
Pr 15: 8 The LORD detests the s
21: 3 to the LORD than s.
Da 9:27 the 'seven' he will put an end to s
12:11 time that the daily s is abolished

Hos 6: 6 For I desire mercy, not s,
Mt 9:13 this means: 'I desire mercy, not s.'
Ro 3:25 God presented him as a s
Eph 5: 2 as a fragrant offering and s to God.
Php 4:18 an acceptable s, pleasing to God.
Heb 9:26 away with sin by the s of himself.
10: 5 "S and offering you did not desire,
10:10 holy through the s of the body
10:14 by one she has made perfect
10:18 there is no longer any s for sin.
11: 4 faith Abel offered God a better s
13:15 offer to God a s of praise—
1Jn 2: 2 He is the atoning s for our sins,
4:10 as an atoning s for our sins.

SACRIFICED (SACRIFICE)

Ac 15:29 are to abstain from food s to idols,
1Co 5: 7 our Passover lamb, has been s.
8: 1 Now about food s to idols:
Heb 7:27 He s for their sins once for all
9:28 so Christ was s once

SACRIFICES (SACRIFICE)

Ps 51:17 The s of God are a broken spirit;
Mk 12:33 than all burnt offerings and s."
Ro 12: 1 to offer your bodies as living s,
Heb 9:23 with better s than these.
13:16 for with such s God is pleased.
1Pe 2: 5 offering spiritual s acceptable

SAD

Lk 18:23 he heard this, he became very s,

SADDUCEES

Mt 16: 6 the yeast of the Pharisees and S."
Mk 12:18 S, who say there is no resurrection,
Ac 23: 8 S say that there is no resurrection,

SAFE (SAVE)

Ps 27: 5 he will keep me s in his dwelling;
37: 3 in the land and enjoy s pasture.
Pr 18:10 the righteous run to it and are s.
28:26 he who walks in wisdom is kept s.
29:25 in the LORD is kept s.
Jer 12: 5 If you stumble in s country,
Jn 17:12 kept them s by that name you gave
1Jn 5:18 born of God keeps him s,

SAFETY (SAVE)

Ps 4: 8 make me dwell in s.
Hos 2:18 so that all may lie down in s.
1Th 5: 3 people are saying, "Peace and s,"

SAINTS

1Sa 2: 9 He will guard the feet of his s,
Ps 16: 3 As for the s who are in the land,
30: 4 Sing to the LORD, you s of his;
31:23 Love the LORD, all his s!
34: 9 Fear the LORD, you his s,
116:15 is the death of his s.
149: 1 his praise in the assembly of the s.
149: 5 Let the s rejoice in this honor
Da 7:18 the s of the Most High will receive
8:27 intercedes for the s in accordance
1Co 6: 2 not know that the s will judge
Eph 1:15 Jesus and your love for all the s,
1:18 of his glorious inheritance in the s,
6:18 always keep on praying for all the s
Phm 7 have refreshed the hearts of the s.
Rev 5: 8 which are the prayers of the s.
19: 8 for the righteous acts of the s.)

SAKE (SAKES)

1Sa 12:22 For the s of his great name
Ps 23: 3 righteousness for his name's s.
44:22 Yet for your s we face death all day
106: 8 Yet he saved them for his name's s,
Isa 42:21 for the s of his righteousness
43:25 your transgressions, for my own s,
48: 9 For my own name's s I delay my
48:11 For my own s, for my own s,
Jer 14: 7 for the s of your name,
14:21 For the s of your name do not
Eze 20: 9 But for the s of my name I did what
20:14 But for the s of my name I did what
20:22 and for the s of my name I did what
36:22 but for the s of my holy name,
Da 9:17 For your s, O Lord, look with favor
Mt 10:39 life for my s will find it;
19:29 for my s will receive a hundred
1Co 9:23 I do all this for the s of the gospel,
2Co 12:10 for Christ's s, I delight
Php 3: 7 loss for the s of Christ.
Heb 11:26 He regarded disgrace for the s
1Pe 2:13 for the Lord's s to every authority

3Jn 7 was for the s of the Name that they

SAKES* (SAKE)

2Co 8: 9 yet for your s he became poor,

SALEM

Ge 14:18 king of S brought out bread
Heb 7: 2 "king of S" means "king of peace."

SALT

Ge 19:26 and she became a pillar of s.
Nu 18:19 covenant of s before the LORD.
Mt 5:13 "You are the s of the earth.
Col 4: 6 with s, so that you may know how
Jas 3:11 s water flow from the same spring?

SALVATION* (SAVE)

Ex 15: 2 he has become my s.
2Sa 22: 3 my shield and the horn of my s.
23: 5 Will he not bring to fruition my s
1Ch 16:23 proclaim his s day after day.
2Ch 6:41 O LORD God, be clothed with s,
Ps 9:14 and there rejoice in your s.
13: 5 my heart rejoices in your s.
14: 7 that s for Israel would come out
18: 2 is my shield and the horn of my s,
27: 1 The LORD is my light and my s—
28: 8 a fortress of s for his anointed one.
35: 3 "I am your s."
35: 9 and delight in his s.
37:39 The s of the righteous comes
40: 10 I speak of your faithfulness and s.
40:16 those who love your s always say,
50:23 way so that I may show him the s
51:12 Restore to me the joy of your s
53: 6 that s for Israel would come out
62: 1 my s comes from him.
62: 2 He alone is my rock and my s;
62: 6 He alone is my rock and my s;
62: 7 My s and my honor depend
67: 2 your s among all nations.
69:13 answer me with your sure s.
69:27 do not let them share in your s.
69:29 may your s, O God, protect me.
70: 4 those who love your s always say,
71: 15 of your s all day long,
74:12 you bring s upon the earth.
85: 7 and grant us your s.
85: 9 Surely his s is near those who fear
91:16 and show him my s."
95: 1 to the Rock of our s.
96: 2 proclaim his s day after day.
98: 1 I have worked s for him.
98: 2 The LORD has made his s known
98: 3 the s of our God.
116:13 I will lift up the cup of s
118:14 he has become my s.
118:21 you have become my s.
119:41 your s according to your promise;
119:81 with longing for your s,
119:123 My eyes fail, looking for your s,
119:155 S is far from the wicked,
119:166 I wait for your s, O LORD,
119:174 I long for your s, O LORD,
132:16 I will clothe her priests with s,
149: 4 he crowns the humble with s.
Isa 12: 2 Surely God is my s;
12: 2 he has become my s."
12: 3 from the wells of s.
25: 9 let us rejoice and be glad in his s."
26: 1 God makes s
26:18 We have not brought s to the earth;
30:15 "In repentance and rest is your s,
33: 2 our s in time of distress.
33: 6 a rich store of s and wisdom
45: 8 let s spring up,
45:17 the LORD with an everlasting s;
46:13 I will grant s to Zion,
46:13 and my s will not be delayed.
49: 6 that you may bring my s
49: 8 and in the day of s I will help you;
51: 5 my s is on the way,
51: 6 But my s will last forever,
51: 8 my s through all generations."
52: 7 who proclaim s,
52:10 the s of our God.
56: 1 for my s is close at hand
59:16 so his own arm worked s for him,
59:17 and the helmet of s on his head;
60:18 but you will call your walls S
61:10 me with garments of s
62: 1 her s like a blazing torch.
63: 5 so my own arm worked s for me,
Jer 3:23 is the s of Israel.
La 3:26 quietly for the s of the LORD.

Jnh 2: 9 S comes from the LORD."
Zec 9: 9 righteous and having s,
Lk 1:69 He has raised up a horn of s for us
1:71 of long ago), s from our enemies
1:77 give his people the knowledge of s
2:30 For my eyes have seen your s,
3: 6 And all mankind will see God's s
19: 9 "Today s has come to this house,
Jn 4:22 for s is from the Jews.
Ac 4:12 S is found in no one else,
13:26 message of s has been sent.
13:47 that you may bring s to the ends
28:28 to know that God's s has been sent
Ro 1:16 for the s of everyone who believes.
11:11 s has come to the Gentiles
13:11 because our s is nearer now
2Co 1: 6 it is for your comfort and s;
6: 2 and in the day of s I helped you."
6: 2 of God's favor, now is the day of s.
7:10 brings repentance that leads to s
Eph 1:13 word of truth, the gospel of your s.
6:17 Take the helmet of s and the sword
Php 2:12 to work out your s with fear
1Th 5: 8 and the hope of s as a helmet.
5: 9 to receive s through our Lord Jesus
2Ti 2:10 they too may obtain the s that is
3:15 wise for s through faith
Tit 2:11 of God that brings s has appeared
Heb 1:14 to serve those who will inherit s?
2: 3 This s, which was first announced
2: 3 escape if we ignore such a great s?
2:10 of their s perfect through suffering.
5: 9 of eternal s for all who obey him
6: 9 case—things that accompany s.
9:28 to bring s to those who are waiting
1Pe 1: 5 the coming of the s that is ready
1: 9 of your faith, the s of your souls.
1:10 Concerning this s, the prophets,
2: 2 by it you may grow up in your s,
2Pe 3:15 that our Lord's patience means s,
Jude 3 to write to you about the s we share
Rev 7:10 "S belongs to our God,
12:10 have come the s and the power
19: 1 S and glory and power belong

SAMARIA (SAMARITAN)

1Ki 16:24 He bought the hill of S
2Ki 17: 6 the king of Assyria captured S
Jn 4: 4 Now he had to go through S.
4: 5 came to a town in S called Sychar,

SAMARITAN (SAMARIA)

Lk 10:33 But a S, as he traveled, came where
17:16 and thanked him—and he was a S.
Jn 4: 7 When a S woman came

SAMSON

Danite judge. Birth promised (Jdg 13). Married to Philistine, but wife given away (Jdg 14). Vengeance on Philistines (Jdg 15). Betrayed by Delilah (Jdg 16:1-22). Death (Jdg 16:23-31). Feats of strength: killed lion (Jdg 14:6), 30 Philistines (Jdg 14:19), 1,000 Philistines with jawbone (Jdg 15:13-17), carried off gates of Gaza (Jdg 16:3), pushed down temple of Dagon (Jdg 16:25-30).

SAMUEL

Ephraimite judge and prophet (Heb 11:32). Birth prayed for (1Sa 1:10-18). Dedicated to temple by Hannah (1Sa 1:21-28). Raised by Eli (1Sa 2:11, 18-26). Called as prophet (1Sa 3). Led Israel to victory over Philistines (1Sa 7). Asked by Israel for a king (1Sa 8). Anointed Saul as king (1Sa 9-10). Farewell speech (1Sa 12). Rebuked Saul for sacrifice (1Sa 13). Announced rejection of Saul (1Sa 15). Anointed David as king (1Sa 16). Protected David from Saul (1Sa 19:18-24). Death (1Sa 25:1). Returned from dead to condemn Saul (1Sa 28)

SANBALLAT

Led opposition to Nehemiah's rebuilding of Jerusalem (Ne 2:10, 19; 4: 6).

SANCTIFIED* (SANCTIFY)

Jn 17:19 that they too may be truly s.
Ac 20:32 among all those who are s.
26:18 among those who are s by faith
Ro 15:16 to God, s by the Holy Spirit.
1Co 1: 2 to those s in Christ Jesus
6:11 But you were washed, you were s,
7:14 and the unbelieving wife has been s
7:14 the unbelieving husband has been s
1Th 4: 3 It is God's will that you should be s

Heb 10: 29 blood of the covenant that s him,

SANCTIFY* (SANCTIFIED SANCTIFYING)

Jn   17: 17 S them by the truth; your word is
     17: 19 For them I s myself, that they too
1Th   5: 23 s you through and through.
Heb   9: 13 are ceremonially unclean s them.

SANCTIFYING* (SANCTIFY)

2Th   2: 13 through the s work of the Spirit,
1Pe   1: 2 through the s work of the Spirit,

SANCTUARY

Ex   25: 8 "Then have them make a s for me,
Lev 19: 30 and have reverence for my s,
Ps   15: 1 LORD, who may dwell in your s?
     63: 2 I have seen you in the s
     68: 24 of my God and King into the s
     68: 35 are awesome, O God, in your s;
     73: 17 me till I entered the s of God;
    102: 19 looked down from his s on high,
    134: 2 Lift up your hands in the s
    150: 1 Praise God in his s;
Eze 37: 26 I will put my s among them forever
     41: 1 the man brought me to the outer s
Da   9: 26 will destroy the city and the s.
Heb   6: 19 It enters the inner s
      8: 2 in the s, the true tabernacle set up
      8: 5 They serve at a s that is a copy
      9: 24 enter a man-made s that was only

SAND

Ge   22: 17 and as the s on the seashore.
Mt   7: 26 man who built his house on s.

SANDAL (SANDALS)

Ru   4: 7 one party took off his s

SANDALS (SANDAL)

Ex   3: 5 off your s, for the place where you
Dt   25: 9 take off one of his s, spit in his face
Jos   5: 15 off your s, for the place where you
Mt   3: 11 whose s I am not fit to carry.

SANG (SING)

Ex   15: 1 and the Israelites s this song
     15: 21 Miriam s to them:
Nu   21: 17 Then Israel s this song:
Jdg   5: 1 Barak son of Abinoam s this song:
1Sa 18: 7 As they danced, they s:
2Sa 22: 1 David s to the LORD the words
2Ch   5: 13 in praise to the LORD and s:
     29: 30 So they s praises with gladness
Ezr   3: 11 thanksgiving they s to the LORD:
Job 38: 7 while the morning stars s together
Ps 106: 12 and s his praise.
Rev   5: 9 And they s a new song:
      5: 12 In a loud voice they s:
     14: 3 they s a new song before the throne
     15: 3 and s the song of Moses the servant

SAP

Ro   11: 17 share in the nourishing s

SAPPHIRA*

Ac   5: 1 together with his wife S,

SARAH

Wife of Abraham, originally named Sarai; barren (Ge 11:29-31; 1Pe 3:6). Taken by Pharaoh as Abraham's sister; returned (Ge 12:10-20). Gave Hagar to Abraham; sent her away in pregnancy (Ge 16). Name changed; Isaac promised (Ge 17:15-21; 18:10-15; Heb 11:11). Taken by Abimelech as Abraham's sister; returned (Ge 20). Isaac born; Hagar and Ishmael sent away (Ge 21:1-21; Gal 4:21-31). Death (Ge 23).

SARDIS

Rev   3: 1 the angel of the church in S write:

SASH (SASHES)

Rev   1: 13 with a golden s around his chest.

SASHES (SASH)

Rev 15: 6 wore golden s around their chests.

SAT (SIT)

Ps 137: 1 By the rivers of Babylon we s
Mk   16: 19 and he s at the right hand of God.
Lk   10: 39 who s at the Lord's feet listening
Heb   1: 3 he s down at the right hand
      1: 8 who s down at the right hand
     10: 12 he s down at the right hand of God.
     12: 2 and s down at the right hand

SATAN

Job   1: 6 and S also came with them.
Zec   3: 2 said to S, "The LORD rebuke you,
Mt   12: 26 If S drives out S, he is divided
     16: 23 S! You are a stumbling block to me,
Mk   4: 15 S comes and takes away the word
Lk   10: 18 "I saw S fall like lightning
     22: 3 S entered Judas, called Iscariot,
Ro   16: 20 The God of peace will soon crush S
1Co   5: 5 is present, hand this man over to S,
2Co 11: 14 for S himself masquerades
     12: 7 a messenger of S, to torment me.
1Ti   1: 20 handed over to S to be taught not
Rev 12: 9 serpent called the devil, or S,
     20: 2 or S, and bound him for a thousand
     20: 7 S will be released from his prison

SATISFIED (SATISFY)

Ps   17: 15 I will be s with seeing your likeness
     22: 26 The poor will eat and be s;
     63: 5 My soul will be s as with the richest
    104: 28 they are s with good things.
    105: 40 s them with the bread of heaven.
Pr   13: 4 the desires of the diligent are fully s
     30: 15 are three things that are never s,
Ecc   5: 10 whoever loves wealth is never s
Isa 53: 11 he will see the light of life, and be s
Mt   14: 20 They all ate and were s,
Lk   6: 21 for you will be s.

SATISFIES* (SATISFY)

Ps 103: 5 who s your desires with good things,
    107: 9 for he s the thirsty
    147: 14 and s you with the finest of wheat.

SATISFY (SATISFIED SATISFIES)

Ps   90: 14 S us in the morning
    145: 16 s the desires of every living thing.
Pr   5: 19 may her breasts s you always,
Isa 55: 2 and your labor on what does not s?
     58: 10 and s the needs of the oppressed,

SAUL

1. Benjamite; anointed by Samuel as first king of Israel (1Sa 9-10). Defeated Ammonites (1Sa 11). Rebuked for offering sacrifice (1Sa 13:1-15). Defeated Philistines (1Sa 14). Rejected as king for failing to annihilate Amalekites (1Sa 15). Soothed from evil spirit by David (1Sa 16:14-23). Sent David against Goliath (1Sa 17). Jealousy and attempted murder of David (1Sa 18:1-11). Gave David Michal as wife (1Sa 18:12-30). Second attempt to kill David (1Sa 19). Anger at Jonathan (1Sa 20:26-34). Pursued David: killed priests at Nob (1Sa 22), went to Keilah and Ziph (1Sa 23), life spared by David at En Gedi (1Sa 24) and in his tent (1Sa 26). Rebuked by Samuel's spirit for consulting witch at Endor (1Sa 28). Wounded by Philistines; took his own life (1Sa 31; 1Ch 10). Lamented by David (2Sa 1:17-27). Children (1Sa 14:49-51; 1Ch 8).
2. See PAUL

SAVAGE

Ac   20: 29 s wolves will come in among you

SAVE (SAFE SAFETY SALVATION SAVED SAVES SAVIOR)

Ge   45: 5 to s lives that God sent me ahead
1Ch 16: 35 Cry out, "S us, O God our Savior;
Job 40: 14 that your own right hand can s you.
Ps   17: 7 you who s by your right hand
     18: 27 You s the humble
     28: 9 S your people and bless your
     31: 16 s me in your unfailing love.
     69: 35 for God will s Zion
     71: 2 turn your ear to me and s me.
     72: 13 and s the needy from death.
     89: 48 or s himself from the power
     91: 3 Surely he will s you
    109: 31 to s his life from those who
    146: 3 in mortal men, who cannot s.
Pr   2: 16 will s you also from the adulteress,
Isa 35: 4 he will come to s you."
     38: 20 The LORD will s me,
     46: 7 it cannot s him from his troubles.
     59: 1 of the LORD is not too short to s,
     63: 1 mighty to s."
Jer 17: 14 s me, and I will be saved,
Eze   3: 18 ways in order to s his life,
      7: 19 able to s them in the day
     14: 14 they could s only themselves
     33: 12 of the righteous man will not s him
     34: 22 I will s my flock, and they will no

SAVED (SAVE)

Da   3: 17 the God we serve is able to s us
Hos   1: 7 and I will s them—not by bow,
Zep   1: 18 will be able to s them
      3: 17 he is mighty to s.
Zec   8: 7 "I will s my people
Mt   1: 21 he will s his people from their sins
     16: 25 wants to s his life will lose it,
Lk   19: 10 to seek and to s what was lost."
Jn   3: 17 but to s the world through him.
     12: 47 come to judge the world, but to s it.
Ro   11: 14 people to envy and s some of them.
1Co   7: 16 whether you will s your husband?
1Ti   1: 15 came into the world to s sinners—
Heb   7: 25 to s completely those who come
Jas   5: 20 of his way will s him from death
Jude   :23 others from the fire and s them;

SAVED (SAVE)

Ps   22: 5 They cried to you and were s;
     33: 16 No king is s by the size of his army;
     34: 6 he s him out of all his troubles.
    106: 21 They forgot the God who s them,
    116: 6 when I was in great need, he s me.
Isa 25: 9 we trusted in him, and he s us.
     45: 22 "Turn to me and be s;
     64: 5 How then can we be s?
Jer   4: 14 from your heart and be s.
      8: 20 and we are not s."
Eze   3: 19 but you will have s yourself.
     33: 5 warning, he would have s himself.
Joel 2: 32 on the name of the LORD will be s;
Mt   10: 22 firm to the end will be s.
     24: 13 firm to the end will be s.
Mk   13: 13 firm to the end will be s.
     16: 16 believes and is baptized will be s,
Jn   10: 9 enters through me will be s.
Ac   2: 21 on the name of the Lord will be s.'
      2: 47 daily those who were being s.
      4: 12 to men by which we must be s."
     15: 11 of our Lord Jesus that we are s,
     16: 30 do to be s?" They replied,
Ro   5: 9 how much more shall we be s
      9: 27 only the remnant will be s.
     10: 1 the Israelites is that they may be s.
     10: 9 him from the dead, you will be s.
     10: 13 on the name of the Lord will be s."
     11: 26 so all Israel will be s, as it is written:
1Co   1: 18 to us who are being s it is the power
      3: 15 will suffer loss; he himself will be s,
      5: 5 his spirit s on the day of the Lord.
     10: 33 of many, so that they may be s.
     15: 2 By this gospel you are s.
Eph   2: 5 it is by grace you have been s.
      2: 8 For it is by grace you have been s,
2Th   2: 13 you to be s through the sanctifying
1Ti   2: 4 who wants all men to be s
      2: 15 But women will be s
2Ti   1: 9 who has s us and called us
Tit   3: 5 He s us through the washing
Heb 10: 39 but of those who believe and are s.

SAVES (SAVE)

Ps   7: 10 who s the upright in heart.
     68: 20 Our God is a God who s;
    145: 19 he hears their cry and s them.
1Pe   3: 21 It s you by the resurrection

SAVIOR* (SAVE)

Dt   32: 15 and rejected the Rock his S.
2Sa 22: 3 stronghold, my refuge and my s—
     22: 47 Exalted be God, the Rock, my S!
1Ch 16: 35 Cry out, "Save us, O God our S;
Ps   18: 46 Exalted be God my S!
     24: 5 and vindication from God his S.
     25: 5 for you are God my S,
     27: 9 O God my S.
     38: 22 O Lord my S.
     42: 5 my S and
     42: 11 my S and my God.
     43: 5 my S and my God.
     65: 5 O God our S,
     68: 19 Praise be to the Lord, to God our S,
     79: 9 Help us, O God our S,
     85: 4 Restore us again, O God our S
     89: 26 my God, the Rock my S.'
Isa 17: 10 You have forgotten God your S;
     19: 20 he will send them a s and defender,
     43: 3 the Holy One of Israel, your S;
     43: 11 and apart from me there is no s.
     45: 15 O God and S of Israel.
     45: 21 a righteous God and a S;
     49: 26 that I, the LORD, am your S,
     60: 16 know that I, the LORD, am your S.
     62: 11 'See, your S comes!
     63: 8 and so he became their S.

SCALE

Jer	14: 8	its S in times of distress,
Hos	13: 4	no S except me.
Mic	7: 7	I wait for God my S.
Hab	3: 18	I will be joyful in God my S.
Lk	1: 47	and my spirit rejoices in God my S,
	2: 11	of David a S has been born to you;
Jn	4: 42	know that this man really is the S
Ac	5: 31	S that he might give repentance
	13: 23	God has brought to Israel the S
Eph	5: 23	his body, of which he is the S.
Php	3: 20	we eagerly await a S from there,
1Ti	1: 1	by the command of God our S
	2: 3	This is good, and pleases God our S
	4: 10	who is the S of all men,
2Ti	1: 10	through the appearing of our S,
Tit	1: 3	me by the command of God our S,
	1: 4	the Father and Christ Jesus our S.
	2: 10	about God our S attractive.
	2: 13	appearing of our great God and S,
	3: 4	and love of God our S appeared,
	3: 6	through Jesus Christ our S,
2Pe	1: 1	S Jesus Christ have received a faith
	1: 11	eternal kingdom of our Lord and S
	2: 20	and S Jesus Christ and are again
	3: 2	and S through your apostles
	3: 18	and knowledge of our Lord and S
1Jn	4: 14	Son to be the S of the world.
Jude	: 25	to the only God our S be glory,

SCALE (SCALES)

Ps	18: 29	with my God I can s a wall.

SCALES (SCALE)

Lev	11: 9	may eat any that have fins and s.
	19: 36	Use honest s and honest weights,
Pr	11: 1	The LORD abhors dishonest s,
Da	5: 27	You have been weighed on the s
Rev	6: 5	Its rider was holding a pair of s

SCAPEGOAT (GOAT)

Lev	16: 10	by sending it into the desert as a s.

SCARECROW*

Jer	10: 5	Like a s in a melon patch,

SCARLET

Jos	2: 21	she tied the s cord in the window.
Isa	1: 18	"Though your sins are like s,
Mt	27: 28	They stripped him and put a s robe

SCATTER (SCATTERED SCATTERS)

Dt	4: 27	The LORD will s you
Ne	1: 8	I will s you among the nations,
Jer	9: 16	I will s them among nations that
	30: 11	the nations among which I s you,
Zec	10: 9	I s them among the peoples,

SCATTERED (SCATTER)

Isa	11: 12	he will assemble the s people
Jer	31: 10	'He who s Israel will gather them
Zec	2: 6	"for I have s you to the four winds
	13: 7	and the sheep will be s,
Mt	26: 31	and the sheep of the flock will be s.'
Jn	11: 52	but also for the s children of God,
Ac	8: 4	who had been s preached the word
Jas	1: 1	To the twelve tribes s
1Pe	1: 1	s throughout Pontus, Galatia,

SCATTERS (SCATTER)

Mt	12: 30	he who does not gather with me s.

SCEPTER

Ge	49: 10	The s will not depart from Judah,
Nu	24: 17	a s will rise out of Israel.
Ps	2: 9	You will rule them with an iron s;
	45: 6	a s of justice will be the s
Heb	1: 8	and righteousness will be the s
Rev	2: 27	'He will rule them with an iron s;
	12: 5	rule all the nations with an iron s.
	19: 15	"He will rule them with an iron s."

SCHEMES

Pr	6: 18	a heart that devises wicked s,
	24: 9	The s of folly are sin,
2Co	2: 11	For we are not unaware of his s.
Eph	6: 11	stand against the devil's s.

SCHOLAR*

1Co	1: 20	Where is the s? Where is

SCOFFERS

2Pe	3: 3	that in the last days s will come,

SCORN (SCORNED SCORNING SCORNS)

Ps	69: 7	For I endure s for your sake,
	69: 20	S has broken my heart
	89: 41	he has become the s
	109: 25	I am an object of s to my accusers,
	119: 22	Remove from me s and contempt,
Mic	6: 16	you will bear the s of the nations."

SCORNED (SCORN)

Ps	22: 6	s by men and despised

SCORNING (SCORN)

Heb	12: 2	him endured the cross, s its shame,

SCORNS (SCORN)

Pr	13: 13	He who s instruction will pay for it,
	30: 17	that s obedience to a mother,

SCORPION

Lk	11: 12	will give him a s? If you then,
Rev	9: 5	sting of a s when it strikes a man.

SCOUNDREL

Pr	6: 12	A s and villain,

SCRIPTURE (SCRIPTURES)

Jn	2: 22	Then they believed the S
	7: 42	Does not the S say that the Christ
	10: 35	and the S cannot be broken—
Ac	8: 32	was reading this passage of S:
1Ti	4: 13	yourself to the public reading of S,
2Ti	3: 16	All S is God-breathed
2Pe	1: 20	that no prophecy of S came about

SCRIPTURES (SCRIPTURE)

Mt	22: 29	because you do not know the S
Lk	24: 27	said in all the S concerning himself.
	24: 45	so they could understand the S.
Jn	5: 39	These are the S that testify about
Ac	17: 11	examined the S every day to see
2Ti	3: 15	you have known the holy S,
2Pe	3: 16	as they do the other S,

SCROLL

Ps	40: 7	it is written about me in the s.
Isa	34: 4	and the sky rolled up like a s;
Eze	3: 1	eat what is before you, eat this s;
Heb	10: 7	it is written about me in the s—
Rev	6: 14	The sky receded like a s, rolling up,
	10: 8	take the s that lies open in the hand

SCUM

1Co	4: 13	this moment we have become the s

SEA (SEASHORE)

Ex	14: 16	go through the s on dry ground.
Dt	30: 13	"Who will cross the s to get it
1Ki	7: 23	He made the S of cast metal,
Job	11: 9	and wider than the s.
Ps	93: 4	mightier than the breakers of the s
	95: 5	The s is his, for he made it,
Ecc	1: 7	All streams flow into the s,
Isa	57: 20	the wicked are like the tossing s,
Jnh	1: 4	LORD sent a great wind on the s,
Mic	7: 19	iniquities into the depths of the s.
Hab	2: 14	as the waters cover the s.
Zec	9: 10	His rule will extend from s to s
Mt	18: 6	drowned in the depths of the s.
1Co	10: 1	that they all passed through the s.
Jas	1: 6	who doubts is like a wave of the s,
Jude	: 13	They are wild waves of the s,
Rev	10: 2	He planted his right foot on the s
	13: 1	I saw a beast coming out of the s.
	20: 13	The s gave up the dead that were
	21: 1	and there was no longer any s.

SEAL (SEALED SEALS)

Ps	40: 9	I do not s my lips,
SS	8: 6	Place me like a s over your heart,
Da	12: 4	and s the words of the scroll
Jn	6: 27	God the Father has placed his s
1Co	9: 2	For you are the s of my apostleship
2Co	1: 22	set his s of ownership on us,
Eph	1: 13	you were marked in him with a s,
Rev	6: 3	the Lamb opened the second s,
	6: 5	When the Lamb opened the third s,
	6: 7	the Lamb opened the fourth s,
	6: 9	When he opened the fifth s,
	6: 12	I watched as he opened the sixth s,
	8: 1	When he opened the seventh s,
	9: 4	people who did not have the s
	22: 10	"Do not s up the words

SEALED (SEAL)

Eph	4: 30	with whom you were s for the day
2Ti	2: 19	solid foundation stands firm, s
Rev	5: 1	on both sides and s with seven seals

SEALS (SEAL)

Rev	5: 2	"Who is worthy to break the s
	6: 1	I opened the first of the seven s.

SEAMLESS*

Jn	19: 23	This garment was s, woven

SEARCH (SEARCHED SEARCHES SEARCHING)

Ps	4: 4	s your hearts and be silent.
	139: 23	S me, O God, and know my heart;
Pr	2: 4	and s for it as for hidden treasure,
	25: 2	to s out a matter is the glory
SS	3: 2	I will s for the one my heart loves.
Jer	17: 10	"I the LORD s the heart
Eze	34: 11	I myself will s for my sheep
	34: 16	I will s for the lost and bring back
Lk	15: 8	and s carefully until she finds it?

SEARCHED (SEARCH)

Ps	139: 1	O LORD, you have s me
Ecc	12: 10	The Teacher s to find just the right
1Pe	1: 10	s intently and with the greatest

SEARCHES (SEARCH)

1Ch	28: 9	for the LORD s every heart
Ps	7: 9	who s minds and hearts,
Pr	11: 27	but evil comes to him who s for it.
	20: 27	The lamp of the LORD s the spirit
Ro	8: 27	And he who s our hearts knows
1Co	2: 10	The Spirit s all things,
Rev	2: 23	will know that I am he who s hearts

SEARCHING (SEARCH)

Jdg	5: 15	there was much s of heart.
Am	8: 12	s for the word of the LORD,

SEARED

1Ti	4: 2	whose consciences have been s

SEASHORE (SEA)

Jos	11: 4	as numerous as the sand on the s.
1Ki	4: 29	as measureless as the sand on the s.

SEASON (SEASONED SEASONS)

Lev	26: 4	I will send you rain in its s,
Ps	1: 3	which yields its fruit in s
2Ti	4: 2	be prepared in s and out of s;

SEASONED* (SEASON)

Col	4: 6	full of grace, s with salt,

SEASONS (SEASON)

Ge	1: 14	signs to mark s and days and years,
Gal	4: 10	and months and s and years!

SEAT (SEATED SEATS)

Ps	1: 1	or sit in the s of mockers.
Pr	31: 23	where he takes his s
Da	7: 9	and the Ancient of Days took his s.
Lk	14: 9	say to you, 'Give this man your s.'
2Co	5: 10	before the judgment s of Christ.

SEATED (SEAT)

Ps	47: 8	God is s on his holy throne.
Isa	6: 1	I saw the Lord s on a throne,
Lk	22: 69	of Man will be s at the right hand
Eph	1: 20	and s him at his right hand
	2: 6	and s us with him in the heavenly
Col	3: 1	where Christ is s at the right hand
Rev	14: 14	s on the cloud was one "like a son
	20: 11	white throne and him who was s

SEATS (SEAT)

Lk	11: 43	you love the most important s

SECLUSION*

Lk	1: 24	and for five months remained in s.

SECRET (SECRETLY SECRETS)

Dt	29: 29	The s things belong
Jdg	16: 6	Tell me the s of your great strength
Ps	90: 8	our s sins in the light
	139: 15	when I was made in the s place.
Pr	11: 13	but a trustworthy man keeps a s.
	21: 14	A gift given in s soothes anger,
Jer	23: 24	Can anyone hide in s places
Mt	6: 4	so that your giving may be in s.
	6: 18	who sees what is done in s,

SECRETLY (continued)

Mk 4: 11 "The s of the kingdom
1Co 2: 7 No, we speak of God's s wisdom,
4: 1 entrusted with the s things of God.
2Co 2: 2 we have renounced s and shameful
Eph 5: 12 what the disobedient do in s.
Php 4: 12 I have learned the s

SECRETLY (SECRET)

2Pe 2: 1 They will s introduce destructive
Jude 4 about long ago have s slipped

SECRETS (SECRET)

Ps 44: 21 since he knows the s of the heart?
Ro 2: 16 day when God will judge men's s
1Co 14: 25 the s of his heart will be laid bare.
Rev 2: 24 Satan's so-called deep s (I will not

SECURE (SECURITY)

Dt 33: 12 beloved of the LORD rest s in him,
Ps 16: 5 you have made my lot s.
16: 9 my body also will rest s,
112: 8 His heart is s, he will have no fear;
Pr 14: 26 fears the LORD has a s fortress,
Heb 6: 19 an anchor for the soul, firm and s.
2Pe 3: 17 and fall from your s position.

SECURITY (SECURE)

Job 31: 24 or said to pure gold, 'You are my s,'

SEED (SEEDS SEEDTIME)

Ge 1: 11 on the land that bear fruit with s
Isa 55: 10 so that it yields s for the sower
Mt 13: 3 "A farmer went out to sow his s.
13: 31 of heaven is like a mustard s,
17: 20 have faith as small as a mustard s,
Lk 8: 11 of the parable: The s is the word
1Co 3: 6 I planted the s, Apollos watered it,
2Co 9: 10 he who supplies s to the sower
Gal 3: 29 then you are Abraham's s,
1Pe 1: 23 not of perishable s,
1Jn 3: 9 because God's s remains in him;

SEEDS (SEED)

Jn 12: 24 But if it dies, it produces many s.
Gal 3: 16 Scripture does not say "and to s,"

SEEDTIME* (SEED)

Ge 8: 22 s and harvest,

SEEK (SEEKING SEEKS SELF-SEEKING SOUGHT)

Lev 19: 18 Do not s revenge or bear a grudge
Dt 4: 29 if from there you s the LORD your
1Ki 22: 5 "First s the counsel of the LORD."
1Ch 28: 9 If you s him, he will be found
2Ch 7: 14 themselves and pray and s my face
15: 2 If you s him, he will be found
Ps 34: 10 those who s the LORD lack no
105: 3 of those who s the LORD rejoice.
105: 4 s his face always.
119: 2 and s him with all their heart.
119: 10 I s you with all my heart;
119:176 S your servant,
Pr 8: 17 and those who s me find me.
18: 15 the ears of the wise s it out.
25: 27 is it honorable to s one's own honor
28: 5 those who s the LORD understand
Isa 55: 6 S the LORD while he may be
65: 1 found by those who did not s me.
Jer 29: 13 You will s me and find me
Hos 10: 12 for it is time to s the LORD,
Am 5: 4 "S me and live;
Zep 2: 3 S the LORD, all you humble
Mt 6: 33 But s first his kingdom
7: 7 and it will be given to you; s
Lk 12: 31 s his kingdom, and these things will
19: 10 For the Son of Man came to s
Jn 5: 30 for I s not to please myself
Ro 10: 20 found by those who did not s me;
1Co 7: 27 you married? Do not s a divorce.
10: 24 Nobody should s his own good,
Heb 11: 6 rewards those who earnestly s him.
1Pe 3: 11 he must s peace and pursue it.

SEEKING (SEEK)

2Ch 30: 19 who sets his heart on s God—
Pr 20: 18 Make plans by s advice;
Mal 3: 1 the Lord you are s will come
Jn 8: 50 I am not s glory for myself;
1Co 10: 33 For I am not s my own good

SEEKS (SEEK)

Pr 11: 27 He who s good finds good will,
Mt 7: 8 he who s finds; and to him who
Jn 4: 23 the kind of worshipers the Father s.

Ro 3: 11 no one who s God.

SEER

1Sa 9: 9 of today used to be called a s.)

SELF-CONTROL* (CONTROL)

Pr 25: 28 is a man who lacks s.
Ac 24: 25 s and the judgment to come,
1Co 7: 5 you because of your lack of s.
Gal 5: 23 faithfulness, gentleness and s.
2Ti 3: 3 slanderous, without s, brutal,
2Pe 1: 6 and to knowledge, s; and to s,

SELF-CONTROLLED* (CONTROL)

1Th 5: 6 are asleep, but let us be alert and s.
5: 8 let us be s, putting on faith and love
1Ti 3: 2 s, respectable, hospitable,
Tit 1: 8 who is s, upright, holy
2: 2 worthy of respect, s, and sound
2: 5 to be s and pure, to be busy at home
2: 6 encourage the young men to be s.
2: 12 to live s, upright and godly lives
1Pe 1: 13 prepare your minds for action; be s;
4: 7 and s so that you can pray.
5: 8 Be s and alert.

SELF-DISCIPLINE* (DISCIPLINE)

2Ti 1: 7 a spirit of power, of love and of s.

SELF-INDULGENCE*

Mt 23: 25 inside they are full of greed and s.
Jas 5: 5 lived on earth in luxury and s.

SELF-SEEKING* (SEEK)

Ro 2: 8 But for those who are s
1Co 13: 5 it is not s, it is not easily angered,

SELFISH*

Ps 119: 36 and not toward s gain.
Pr 18: 1 An unfriendly man pursues s ends;
Gal 5: 20 fits of rage, s ambition, dissensions,
Php 1: 17 preach Christ out of s ambition,
2: 3 Do nothing out of s ambition
Jas 3: 14 and s ambition in your hearts,
3: 16 you have envy and s ambition,

SELL (SELLING SELLS SOLD)

Ge 25: 31 "First s me your birthright."
Mk 10: 21 s everything you have
Rev 13: 17 or s unless he had the mark,

SELLING (SELL)

Lk 17: 28 buying and s, planting and building

SELLS (SELL)

Pr 31: 24 makes linen garments and s them,

SEND (SENDING SENDS SENT)

Ps 43: 3 S forth your light and your truth,
Isa 6: 8 S me!" He said, "Go and tell this
Mal 3: 1 "See, I will s my messenger,
Mt 9: 38 to s out workers into his harvest
24: 31 And he will s his angels
Mk 1: 2 I will s my messenger ahead of you,
Lk 20: 13 I will s my son, whom I love;
Jn 3: 17 For God did not s his Son
16: 7 but if I go, I will s him to you.
1Co 1: 17 For Christ did not s me to baptize,

SENDING (SEND)

Mt 10: 16 I am s you out like sheep
Jn 20: 21 Father has sent me, I am s you."
Ro 8: 3 God did by s his own Son

SENDS (SEND)

Ps 57: 3 God s his love and his faithfulness.

SENNACHERIB

Assyrian king whose siege of Jerusalem was overthrown by the LORD following prayer of Hezekiah and Isaiah (2Ki 18:13-19:37; 2Ch 32: 1-21; Isa 36-37).

SENSES*

Lk 15: 17 "When he came to his s, he said,
1Co 15: 34 Come back to your s as you ought,
2Ti 2: 26 and that they will come to their s

SENSITIVITY*

Eph 4: 19 Having lost all s, they have given

SENSUAL* (SENSUALITY)

Col 2: 23 value in restraining s indulgence.
1Ti 5: 11 For when their s desires overcome

SENSUALITY* (SENSUAL)

Eph 4: 19 have given themselves over to s

SENT (SEND)

Ex 3: 14 to the Israelites: 'I AM has s me
Isa 55: 11 achieve the purpose for which I s it.
61: 1 He has s me to bind up
Jer 28: 9 as one truly s by the LORD only
Mt 10: 40 me receives the one who s me.
Mk 6: 7 he s them out two by two
Lk 4: 18 He has s me to proclaim freedom
9: 2 and he s them out to preach
10: 16 rejects me rejects him who s me."
Jn 1: 6 There came a man who was s
4: 34 "is to do the will of him who s me
5: 24 believes him who s me has eternal
8: 16 I stand with the Father, who s me.
9: 4 must do the work of him who s me.
16: 5 "Now I am going to him who s me,
17: 3 and Jesus Christ, whom you have s.
17: 18 As you s me into the world,
20: 21 As the Father has s me, I am
Ro 10: 15 can they preach unless they are s?
Gal 4: 4 God s his Son, born of a woman,
1Jn 4: 10 but that he loved us and s his Son

SENTENCE

2Co 1: 9 in our hearts we felt the s of death.

SEPARATE (SEPARATED SEPARATES SEPARATION)

Mt 19: 6 has joined together, let man not s."
Ro 8: 35 Who shall s us from the love
1Co 7: 10 wife must not s from her husband.
2Co 6: 17 and be s, says the Lord.
Eph 2: 12 at that time you were s from Christ,

SEPARATED (SEPARATE)

Isa 59: 2 But your iniquities have s
Eph 4: 18 in their understanding and s

SEPARATES (SEPARATE)

Pr 16: 28 and a gossip s close friends.
17: 9 repeats the matter s close friends.
Mt 25: 32 as a shepherd s the sheep

SEPARATION (SEPARATE)

Nu 6: 2 a vow of s to the LORD

SERAPHS*

Isa 6: 2 Above him were s, each
6: 6 Then one of the s flew to me

SERIOUSNESS*

Tit 2: 7 s and soundness of speech that

SERPENT (SERPENT'S)

Ge 3: 1 the s was more crafty than any
Isa 27: 1 Leviathan the coiling s;
Rev 12: 9 that ancient s called the devil
20: 2 that ancient s, who is the devil,

SERPENT'S (SERPENT)

2Co 11: 3 Eve was deceived by the s cunning,

SERVANT (SERVANTS)

Ex 14: 31 trust in him and in Moses his s.
21: 2 "If you buy a Hebrew s, he is
1Sa 3: 10 "Speak, for your s is listening."
2Sa 7: 19 the future of the house of your s.
1Ki 20: 40 While your s was busy here
Job 1: 8 "Have you considered my s Job?
Ps 19: 11 By them is your s warned;
19: 13 Keep your s also from willful sins;
31: 16 Let your face shine on your s;
89: 3 I have sworn to David my s,
Pr 14: 35 A king delights in a wise s,
17: 2 wise s will rule over a disgraceful
22: 7 and the borrower is s to the lender.
31: 15 and portions for her s girls.
Isa 41: 8 "But you, O Israel, my s,
49: 3 He said to me, "You are my s,
53: 11 my righteous s will justify
Zec 3: 8 going to bring my s, the Branch.
Mal 1: 6 his father, and a s his master.
Mt 8: 13 his s was healed at that very hour.
20: 26 great among you must be your s,
24: 45 Who then is the faithful and wise s,
25: 21 'Well done, good and faithful s!
Lk 1: 38 I am the Lord's s," Mary answered.
16: 13 "No s can serve two masters.
Jn 12: 26 and where I am, my s also will be.
Ro 1: 1 a s of Christ Jesus, called
13: 4 For he is God's s to do you good.

SERVANTS (SERVANT)

Php 2: 7 taking the very nature of a s,
Col 1:23 of which I, Paul, have become a s.
2Ti 2:24 And the Lord's s must not quarrel;

SERVANTS (SERVANT)

Lev 25:55 for the Israelites belong to me as s.
2Ki 17:13 to you through my s the prophets.''
Ezr 5:11 ''We are the s of the God of heaven
Ps 34:22 The LORD redeems his s;
    103:21 you his s who do his will.
    104: 4 flames of fire his s.
Isa 44:26 who carries out the words of his s
    65: 8 so will I do in behalf of my s;
    65:13 my s will drink,
Lk 17:10 should say, 'We are unworthy s;
Jn 15:15 longer call you s, because a servant
Ro 13: 6 for the authorities are God's s,
1Co 3: 5 And what is Paul? Only s,
Heb 1: 7 his s flames of fire.''

SERVE (SERVED SERVES SERVICE SERVING)

Dt 10:12 to s the LORD your God
    11:13 and to s him with all your heart
    13: 4 s him and hold fast to him.
    28:47 you did not s the LORD your
Jos 22: 5 and to s him with all your heart
    24:15 this day whom you will s,
    24:18 We too will s the LORD,
1Sa 7: 3 to the LORD and s him only,
    12:20 but s the LORD with all your heart
    12:24 s him faithfully with all your heart;
2Ch 19: 9 ''You must s faithfully
Job 36:11 If they obey and s him,
Ps 2:11 S the LORD with fear
Da 3:17 the God we s is able to save us
Mt 4:10 Lord your God, and s him only.' ''
    6:24 ''No one can s two masters.
    20:28 but to s, and to give his life
Ro 12: 7 If it is serving, let him s;
Gal 5:13 rather, s one another in love.
Eph 6: 7 S wholeheartedly,
1Ti 6: 2 they are to s them even better,
Heb 9:14 so that we may s the living God!
1Pe 4:10 gift he has received to s others,
    5: 2 greedy for money, but eager to s;
Rev 5:10 kingdom and priests to s our God,

SERVED (SERVE)

Mt 20:28 Son of Man did not come to be s,
Jn 12: 2 Martha s, while Lazarus was
Ac 17:25 And he is not s by human hands,
Ro 1:25 and s created things rather
1Ti 3:13 Those who have s well gain

SERVES (SERVE)

Lk 22:26 one who rules like the one who s.
    22:27 But I am among you as one who s.
Jn 12:26 Whoever s me must follow me;
Ro 14:18 because anyone who s Christ
1Pe 4:11 If anyone s, he should do it

SERVICE (SERVE)

Lk 9:62 fit for s in the kingdom
    12:35 ''Be dressed ready for s
Ro 15:17 in Christ Jesus in my s to God.
1Co 12: 5 There are different kinds of s,
    16:15 themselves to the s of the saints.
2Co 9:12 This s that you perform is not only
Eph 4:12 God's people for works of s,
Rev 2:19 and faith, your s and perseverance.

SERVING (SERVE)

Jos 24:15 if s the LORD seems undesirable
2Ch 12: 8 learn the difference between s me
Ro 12: 7 If it is s, let him serve;
    12:11 your spiritual fervor, s the Lord.
    16:18 people are not s our Lord Christ,
Eph 6: 7 as if you were the Lord, not men,
Col 3:24 It is the Lord Christ you are s.
2Ti 2: 4 No one s as a soldier gets involved

SETH

Ge 4:25 birth to a son and named him S,

SETTLE

Mt 5:25 ''S matters quickly
2Th 3:12 in the Lord Jesus Christ to s down

SEVEN (SEVENS SEVENTH)

Ge 7: 2 Take with you s of every kind
Jos 6: 4 march around the city s times,
1Ki 19:18 Yet I reserve s thousand in Israel—
Pr 6:16 s that are detestable to him:
    24:16 a righteous man falls s times,

Isa 4: 1 In that day s women
Da 9:25 comes, there will be s 'sevens,'
Mt 18:21 Up to s times?'' Jesus answered,
Lk 11:26 takes s other spirits more wicked
Ro 11: 4 for myself s thousand who have not
Rev 1: 4 To the s churches in the province
    6: 1 opened the first of the s seals.
    8: 2 and to them were given s trumpets.
    10: 4 And when the s thunders spoke,
    15: 7 to the s angels s golden bowls filled

SEVENS* (SEVEN)

Da 9:24 ''Seventy 's' are decreed
    9:25 will be seven 's,' and sixty-two 's'
    9:26 the sixty-two 's,' the Anointed

SEVENTH (SEVEN)

Ge 2: 2 By the s day God had finished
Ex 20:10 but the s day is a Sabbath
    23:11 but during the s year let the land lie
    23:12 but on the s day do not work,
Heb 4: 4 ''And on the s day God rested

SEVERE

2Co 8: 2 Out of the most s trial, their
1Th 1: 6 of the Lord; in spite of s suffering,

SEWED (SEWS)

Ge 3: 7 so they s fig leaves together

SEWS (SEWED)

Mt 9:16 No one s a patch of unshrunk cloth

SEXUAL (SEXUALLY)

Ex 22:19 ''Anyone who has s relations
Lev 18: 6 relative to have s relations.
    18: 7 father by having s relations
    18:20 Do not have s relations with
Mt 15:19 murder, adultery, s immorality,
Ac 15:20 by idols, from s immorality,
1Co 5: 1 reported that there is s immorality
    6:13 body is not meant for s immorality,
    6:18 Flee from s immorality.
    10: 8 should not commit s immorality,
2Co 12:21 s sin and debauchery
Gal 5:19 s immorality, impurity
Eph 5: 3 even a hint of s immorality,
Col 3: 5 s immorality, impurity, lust,
1Th 4: 3 that you should avoid s immorality

SEXUALLY (SEXUAL)

1Co 5: 9 to associate with s immoral people
    6: 9 Neither the s immoral nor idolaters
    6:18 he who sins s sins against his own
Heb 12:16 See that no one is s immoral,
    13: 4 the adulterer and all the s immoral.
Rev 21: 8 the murderers, the s immoral,

SHADE

Ps 121: 5 the LORD is your s
Isa 25: 4 and a s from the heat.

SHADOW

Ps 17: 8 hide me in the s of your wings
    23: 4 through the valley of the s of death,
    36: 7 find refuge in the s of your wings.
    91: 1 will rest in the s of the Almighty.
Isa 51:16 covered you with the s of my hand
Col 2:17 These are a s of the things that
Heb 8: 5 and s of what is in heaven.
    10: 1 The law is only a s

SHADRACH

Hebrew exiled to Babylon; name changed
from Hananiah (Da 1:6-7). Refused defilement
by food (Da 1:8-20). Refused to worship idol (Da
3:1-18); saved from furnace (Da 3:19-30).

SHAKE (SHAKEN SHAKING)

Ps 64: 8 all who see them will s their heads
    99: 1 let the earth s.
Hag 2: 6 I will once more s the heavens
Heb 12:26 ''Once more I will s not only

SHAKEN (SHAKE)

Ps 16: 8 I will not be s.
    30: 6 ''I will never be s.''
    62: 2 he is my fortress, I will never be s.
    112: 6 Surely he will never be s;
Isa 54:10 Though the mountains be s
Mt 24:29 and the heavenly bodies will be s.''
Lk 6:38 s together and running over,
Ac 2:25 I will not be s.
Heb 12:27 that what cannot be s may remain.

SHAKING* (SHAKE)

Ps 22: 7 they hurl insults, s their heads:
Mt 27:39 insults at him, s their heads
Mk 15:29 s their heads and saying, ''So!

SHALLUM

King of Israel (2Ki 15:10-16).

SHAME (ASHAMED SHAMED SHAMEFUL)

Ps 25: 3 will ever be put to s,
    34: 5 their faces are never covered with s
    69: 6 not be put to s because of me,
Pr 13:18 discipline comes to poverty and s,
    18:13 that is his folly and his s.
Jer 8: 9 The wise will be put to s;
    8:12 No, they have no s at all;
Ro 9:33 trusts in him will never be put to s.''
    10:11 trusts in him will never be put to s.''
1Co 1:27 things of the world to shame the wise;
Heb 12: 2 endured the cross, scorning its s,

SHAMED (SHAME)

Jer 10:14 every goldsmith is s by his idols.
Joel 2:26 never again will my people be s.

SHAMEFUL (SHAME)

2Co 4: 2 have renounced secret and s ways;
2Pe 2: 2 Many will follow their s ways
Rev 21:27 nor will anyone who does what is s

SHAMGAR

Judge; killed 600 Philistines (Jdg 3:31).

SHAPE (SHAPES SHAPING)

Job 38:14 The earth takes s like clay

SHAPES (SHAPE)

Isa 44:10 Who s a god and casts an idol,

SHAPING (SHAPE)

Jer 18: 4 the pot he was s from the clay was

SHARE (SHARED SHARERS SHARES SHARING)

Ge 21:10 that slave woman's son will never s
Lev 19:17 frankly so you will not s in his guilt.
Dt 10: 9 That is why the Levites have no s
1Sa 30:24 All will s alike.''
Eze 18:20 The son will not s the guilt
Mt 25:21 and s your master's happiness!'
Lk 3:11 ''The man with two tunics should s
Ro 8:17 if indeed we s in his sufferings
    12:13 S with God's people who are
2Co 1: 7 as you s in our sufferings,
Gal 4:30 the slave woman's son will never s
    6: 6 in the word must s all good things
Eph 4:28 something to s with those in need.
Col 1:12 you to s in the inheritance
2Th 2:14 that you might s in the glory
1Ti 5:22 and do not s in the sins of others.
    6:18 and to be generous and willing to s.
2Ti 2: 6 the first to receive a s of the crops.
Heb 12:10 that we may s in his holiness.
    13:16 to do good and to s with others,
Rev 22:19 from him his s in the tree of life

SHARED (SHARE)

Ps 41: 9 he who s my bread,
Ac 4:32 but they s everything they had.
Heb 2:14 he too s in their humanity so that

SHARERS* (SHARE)

Eph 3: 6 and s together in the promise

SHARES (SHARE)

Pr 22: 9 for he s his food with the poor.
Jn 13:18 'He who s my bread has lifted up

SHARING (SHARE)

1Co 9:10 so in the hope of s in the harvest.
2Co 9:13 for your generosity in s with them
Php 3:10 the fellowship of s in his sufferings,
Phm : 6 you may be active in s your faith,

SHARON

SS 2: 1 I am a rose of S,

SHARP (SHARPENED SHARPENS SHARPER)

Pr 5: 4 s as a double-edged sword.
Isa 5:28 Their arrows are s,
Rev 1:16 came a s double-edged sword.
    19:15 Out of his mouth comes a s sword

SHARPENED (SHARP)

Eze 21: 9 s and polished—

SHARPENS* (SHARP)

Pr 27: 17 As iron s iron,
    27: 17 so one man s another.

SHARPER* (SHARP)

Heb 4: 12 s than any double-edged sword.

SHATTER (SHATTERED SHATTERS)

Jer 51: 20 with you I s nations,

SHATTERED (SHATTER)

1Sa 2: 10 who oppose the LORD will be s.
Job 16: 12 All was well with me, but he s me;
    17: 11 days have passed, my plans are s,
Ecc 12: 6 before the pitcher is s at the spring.

SHATTERS (SHATTER)

Ps 46: 9 he breaks the bow and s the spear,

SHAVED

Jdg 16: 17 my head were s, my strength would
1Co 11: 5 it is just as though her head were s.

SHEAF (SHEAVES)

Lev 23: 11 is to wave the s before the LORD

SHEARER* (SHEARERS)

Ac 8: 32 and as a lamb before the s is silent,

SHEARERS (SHEARER)

Isa 53: 7 and as a sheep before her s is silent,

SHEAVES (SHEAF)

Ge 37: 7 while your s gathered around mine
Ps 126: 6 carrying s with him.

SHEBA

    1. Benjamite who rebelled against David
(2Sa 20).
    2. See QUEEN.

SHECHEM

    1. Raped Jacob's daughter Dinah; killed by
Simeon and Levi (Ge 34).
    2. City where Joshua renewed the covenant
(Jos 24).

SHED (SHEDDING SHEDS)

Ge 9: 6 by man shall his blood be s;
Pr 6: 17 hands that s innocent blood,
Ro 3: 15 "Their feet are swift to s blood;
Col 1: 20 through his blood, s on the cross.

SHEDDING (SHED)

Heb 9: 22 without the s of blood there is no

SHEDS (SHED)

Ge 9: 6 "Whoever s the blood of man,

SHEEP (SHEEP'S SHEEPSKINS)

Nu 27: 17 LORD's people will not be like s
Dt 17: 1 a s that has any defect or flaw in it,
1Sa 15: 14 "What then is this bleating of s
Ps 44: 22 we are considered as s
    78: 52 led them like s through the desert.
    100: 3 we are his people, the s
    119:176 I have strayed like a lost s.
SS 4: 2 teeth are like a flock of s just shorn,
Isa 53: 6 We all, like s, have gone astray,
    53: 7 as a s before her shearers is silent,
Jer 50: 6 "My people have been lost s
Eze 34: 11 I myself will search for my s
Zec 13: 7 and the s will be scattered,
Mt 9: 36 helpless, like s without a shepherd.
    10: 16 I am sending you out like s
    12: 11 "If any of you has a s and it falls
    18: 13 he is happier about that one s
    25: 32 as a shepherd separates the s
Jn 10: 1 man who does not enter the s pen
    10: 3 He calls his own s by name
    10: 7 the truth, I am the gate for the s.
    10: 15 and I lay down my life for the s.
    10: 27 My s listen to my voice; I know
    21: 17 Jesus said, "Feed my s.
1Pe 2: 25 For you were like s going astray,

SHEEP'S* (SHEEP)

Mt 7: 15 They come to you in s clothing.

SHEEPSKINS* (SHEEP)

Heb 11: 37 They went about in s and goatskins

SHEKEL

Ex 30: 13 This half s is an offering

SHELTER

Ps 27: 5 me in the s of his tabernacle
    31: 20 In the s of your presence you hide
    55: 8 I would hurry to my place of s,
    61: 4 take refuge in the s of your wings.
    91: 1 in the s of the Most High
Ecc 7: 12 Wisdom is a s
Isa 4: 6 It will be a s and shade
    25: 4 a s from the storm
    32: 2 Each man will be like a s
    58: 7 the poor wanderer with s—

SHEM

    Son of Noah (Ge 5:32; 6:10). Blessed (Ge 9:
26). Descendants (Ge 10:21-31; 11:10-32).

SHEPHERD (SHEPHERDS)

Ge 48: 15 the God who has been my s
    49: 24 because of the S, the Rock of Israel
Nu 27: 17 will not be like sheep without a s,
2Sa 7: 7 commanded to s my people Israel,
1Ki 22: 17 on the hills like sheep without a s,
Ps 23: 1 LORD is my s; I shall not be in want.
    28: 9 be their s and carry them forever.
    80: 1 Hear us, O S of Israel,
Isa 40: 11 He tends his flock like a s:
Jer 31: 10 will watch over his flock like a s.'
Eze 34: 5 scattered because there was no s,
    34: 12 As a s looks after his scattered
Zec 11: 9 and said, "I will not be your s.
    11: 17 "Woe to the worthless s,
    13: 7 "Strike the s,
Mt 2: 6 who will be the s of my people
    9: 36 and helpless, like sheep without a s.
    26: 31 " 'I will strike the s,
Jn 10: 11 The good s lays down his life
    10: 14 "I am the good s; I know my sheep
    10: 16 there shall be one flock and one s.
Heb 13: 20 that great S of the sheep, equip you
1Pe 5: 4 And when the Chief S appears,
Rev 7: 17 of the throne will be their s;

SHEPHERDS (SHEPHERD)

Jer 23: 1 "Woe to the s who are destroying
    50: 6 their s have led them astray
Eze 34: 2 prophesy against the s of Israel;
Lk 2: 8 there were s living out in the fields
Ac 20: 28 Be s of the church of God,
1Pe 5: 2 Be s of God's flock that is
Jude : 12 s who feed only themselves.

SHIBBOLETH*

Jdg 12: 6 No," they said, "All right, say 'S.' "

SHIELD (SHIELDED SHIELDS)

Ge 15: 1 I am your s,
2Sa 22: 3 my s and the horn of my salvation.
    22: 36 You give me your s of victory;
Ps 3: 3 But you are a s around me,
    5: 12 with your favor as with a s.
    7: 10 My s is God Most High,
    18: 2 He is my s and the horn
    28: 7 LORD is my strength and my s;
    33: 20 he is our help and our s.
    84: 11 For the LORD God is a sun and s;
    91: 4 his faithfulness will be your s
    115: 9 he is their help and s.
    119:114 You are my refuge and my s;
    144: 2 my s, in whom I take refuge,
Pr 2: 7 he is a s to those whose walk is
    30: 5 he is a s to those who take refuge
Eph 6: 16 to all this, take up the s of faith,

SHIELDED (SHIELD)

1Pe 1: 5 through faith are s by God's power

SHIELDS (SHIELD)

Dt 33: 12 for he s him all day long,

SHIFTLESS*

Pr 19: 15 and the s man goes hungry.

SHIMEI

    Cursed David (2Sa 16:5-14); spared (2Sa 19:
16-23). Killed by Solomon (1Ki 2:8-9, 36-46).

SHINE (SHINES SHINING SHONE)

Nu 6: 25 the LORD make his face s
Job 33: 30 that the light of life may s on him.
Ps 4: 6 Let the light of your face s upon us,
    37: 6 make your righteousness s like

SHINES (SHINE)

Ps 50: 2 God s forth.
Pr 13: 9 The light of the righteous s brightly
Jn 1: 5 The light s in the darkness,

SHINING (SHINE)

Pr 4: 18 s ever brighter till the full light
2Pe 1: 19 as to a light s in a dark place,
Rev 1: 16 His face was like the sun s

SHIPS

Pr 31: 14 She is like the merchant s,

SHIPWRECKED*

2Co 11: 25 I was stoned, three times I was s,
1Ti 1: 19 and so have s their faith.

SHISHAK

1Ki 14: 25 S king of Egypt attacked Jerusalem
2Ch 12: 2 S king of Egypt attacked Jerusalem

SHOCKING*

Jer 5: 30 "A horrible and s thing

SHONE (SHINE)

Mt 17: 2 His face s like the sun,
Lk 2: 9 glory of the Lord s around them,
Rev 21: 11 It s with the glory of God,

SHOOT

Isa 53: 2 up before him like a tender s,
Ro 11: 17 and you, though a wild olive s,

SHORE

Lk 5: 3 asked him to put out a little from s.

SHORT (SHORTENED)

Nu 11: 23 "Is the LORD's arm too s?
Isa 50: 2 Was my arm too s to ransom you?
    59: 1 of the LORD is not too s to save,
Mt 24: 22 If those days had not been cut s,
Ro 3: 23 and fall s of the glory of God,
1Co 7: 29 brothers, is that the time is s.
Heb 4: 1 of you be found to have fallen s of it
Rev 20: 3 he must be set free for a s time.

SHORTENED (SHORT)

Mt 24: 22 of the elect those days will be s.

SHOULDER (SHOULDERS)

Zep 3: 9 and serve him s to s.

SHOULDERS (SHOULDER)

Dt 33: 12 LORD loves rests between his s."
Isa 9: 6 and the government will be on his s
Lk 15: 5 he joyfully puts it on his s

SHOUT (SHOUTED)

Ps 47: 1 s to God with cries of joy.
    66: 1 S with joy to God, all the earth!
    95: 1 let us s aloud to the Rock
    98: 4 S for joy to the LORD, all the earth
    100: 1 S for joy to the LORD, all the earth
Isa 12: 6 S aloud and sing for joy, people
    26: 19 wake up and s for joy.
    35: 6 the mute tongue s for joy.
    40: 9 lift up your voice with a s,
    42: 2 He will not s or cry out,
    44: 23 s aloud, O earth beneath.
    54: 1 burst into song, s for joy;
Zec 9: 9 S, Daughter of Jerusalem!

SHOUTED (SHOUT)

Job 38: 7 and all the angels s for joy?

SHOW (SHOWED)

Ex 18: 20 and s them the way to live
    33: 18 Moses said, "Now s me your glory
2Sa 22: 26 the faithful you s yourself faithful,
1Ki 2: 2 "So be strong, s yourself a man,
Ps 17: 7 S the wonder of your great love,
    25: 4 S me your ways, O LORD,
    39: 4 "S me, O LORD, my life's end
    85: 7 S us your unfailing love, O LORD,

Ps 67: 1 and make his face s upon us; Selah
    80: 1 between the cherubim, s forth
    118: 27 and he has made his light s upon us.
Isa 60: 1 "Arise, s, for your light has come,
Da 12: 3 are wise will s like the brightness
Mt 5: 16 let your light s before men,
    13: 43 the righteous will s like the sun
2Co 4: 6 made his light s in our hearts
Eph 5: 14 and Christ will s on you."
Php 2: 15 in which you s like stars

SHINES (SHINE)

Ps 50: 2 God s forth.
Pr 13: 9 The light of the righteous s brightly
Jn 1: 5 The light s in the darkness,

SHOWED

Ps	143:	8 *S* me the way I should go,
Pr	23:	4 have the wisdom to *s* restraint.
SS	2:14	*s* me your face,
Isa	5:16	the holy God will *s* himself holy
	30:18	he rises to *s* you compassion.
Eze	28:25	I will *s* myself holy among them
Joel	2:30	I will *s* wonders in the heavens
Zec	7:	9 *s* mercy and compassion
Ac	3:16	*s* you the holy God
	10:34	it is that God does not *s* favoritism.
1Co	12:31	now I will *s* you the most excellent
Eph	2:	7 ages he might *s* the incomparable
Tit	2:	7 In your teaching *s* integrity.
Jas	2:18	I will *s* you my faith by what I do.
Jude	:23	to others *s* mercy, mixed with fear

SHOWED (SHOW)

1Ki	3:	3 Solomon *s* his love for the LORD
Lk	24:40	he *s* them his hands and feet.
1Jn	4:	9 This is how God *s* his love

SHOWERS

Eze	34:26	in season; there will be *s* of blessing
Hos	10:12	and *s* righteousness on you.

SHREWD

2Sa	22:27	to the crooked you show yourself *s*.
Mt	10:16	Therefore be as *s* as snakes and

SHRINK (SHRINKS)

Heb	10:39	But we are not of those who *s* back

SHRINKS* (SHRINK)

Heb	10:38	And if he *s* back,

SHRIVEL

Isa	64:	6 we all *s* up like a leaf,

SHUDDER

Eze	32:10	and their kings will *s* with horror

SHUHITE

Job	2:11	Bildad the *S* and Zophar

SHUN* (SHUNS)

Job	28:28	and to *s* evil is understanding.' ''
Pr	3:	7 fear the LORD and *s* evil.

SHUNS (SHUN)

Job	1:	8 a man who fears God and *s* evil.''
Pr	14:16	man fears the LORD and *s* evil,

SHUT

Ge	7:16	Then the LORD *s* him in.
Isa	22:22	what he opens no one can *s*,
	60:11	they will never be *s*, day or night,
Da	6:22	and he *s* the mouths of the lions.
Heb	11:33	who *s* the mouths of lions,
Rev	3:	7 no one can *s*, and what he shuts
	21:25	On no day will its gates ever be *s*,

SICK (SICKNESS)

Pr	13:12	Hope deferred makes the heart *s*,
Eze	34:	4 or healed the *s* or bound up
Mt	9:12	who need a doctor, but the *s*.
	10:	8 Heal the *s*, raise the dead, cleanse
	25:36	I was *s* and you looked after me,
1Co	11:30	many among you are weak and *s*,
Jas	5:14	of you *s*? He should call the elders

SICKBED* (BED)

Ps	41:	3 LORD will sustain him on his *s*

SICKLE

Joel	3:13	Swing the *s*,
Rev	14:14	gold on his head and a sharp *s*

SICKNESS (SICK)

Mt	4:23	and healing every disease and *s*

SIDE (SIDES)

Ps	91:	7 A thousand may fall at your *s*,
	124:	1 If the LORD had not been on our *s*
Jn	18:37	Everyone on the *s* of truth listens
	20:20	he showed them his hands and *s*.
2Ti	4:17	But the Lord stood at my *s*
Heb	10:33	at other times you stood *s* by *s*

SIDES (SIDE)

Nu	33:55	in your eyes and thorns in your *s*.

SIFT

Lk	22:31	Satan has asked to *s* you as wheat.

SIGHING

Isa	35:10	and sorrow and *s* will flee away.

SIGHT

Ps	51:	4 and done what is evil in your *s*,
	90:	4 For a thousand years in your *s*
	116:	15 Precious in the *s* of the LORD
Pr	3:	4 in the *s* of God and man.
Mt	11:	5 The blind receive *s*, the lame walk,
Ac	4:19	right in God's *s* to obey you rather
1Co	3:19	this world is foolishness in God's *s*.
2Co	5:	7 We live by faith, not by *s*.
1Pe	3:	4 which is of great worth in God's *s*.

SIGN (SIGNS)

Ge	9:12	"This is the *s* of the covenant I am
	17:11	and it will be the *s* of the covenant
Isa	7:14	the Lord himself will give you a *s*:
	55:13	for an everlasting *s*,
Eze	20:12	I gave them my Sabbaths as a *s*
Mt	12:38	to see a miraculous *s* from you."
	24:	3 what will be the *s* of your coming
	24:30	"At that time the *s* of the Son
Lk	2:12	This will be a *s* to you: You will
	11:29	It asks for a miraculous *s*,
Ro	4:11	he received the *s* of circumcision,
1Co	11:10	to have a *s* of authority on her head
	14:22	are a *s*, not for believers

SIGNS (SIGN)

Ge	1:14	let them serve as *s* to mark seasons
Ps	78:43	day he displayed his miraculous *s*
	105:27	They performed his miraculous *s*
Da	6:27	he performs *s* and wonders
Mt	24:24	and perform great *s* and miracles
Mk	16:17	these *s* will accompany those who
Jn	3:	2 perform the miraculous *s* you are
	20:30	Jesus did many other miraculous *s*
Ac	2:19	and *s* on the earth below,
1Co	1:22	Jews demand miraculous *s*
2Co	12:12	*s*, wonders and miracles—
2Th	2:	9 *s* and wonders, and in every sort

SIHON

Nu	21:21	to say to *S* king of the Amorites:
Ps	136:19	*S* king of the Amorites

SILAS*

Prophet (Ac 15:22-32); co-worker with Paul on second missionary journey (Ac 16-18; 2Co 1: 19). Co-writer with Paul (1Th 1:1; 2Th 1:1); Peter (1Pe 5:12).

SILENCE (SILENCED SILENT)

1Pe	2:15	good you should *s* the ignorant talk
Rev	8:	1 there was *s* in heaven

SILENCED (SILENCE)

Ro	3:19	so that every mouth may be *s*
Tit	1:11	They must be *s*, because they are

SILENT (SILENCE)

Est	4:14	For if you remain *s* at this time,
Ps	30:12	to you and not be *s*.
	32:	3 When I kept *s*,
	39:	2 But when I was *s* and still,
Pr	17:28	a fool is thought wise if he keeps *s*,
Ecc	3:	7 a time to be *s* and a time to speak,
Isa	53:	7 as a sheep before her shearers is *s*,
	62:	1 For Zion's sake I will not keep *s*,
Hab	2:20	let all the earth be *s* before him.''
Ac	8:32	and as a lamb before the shearer is *s*
1Co	14:34	women should remain *s*
1Ti	2:12	over a man; she must be *s*.

SILVER

Ps	12:	6 like *s* refined in a furnace of clay,
	66:10	you refined us like *s*.
Pr	2:	4 and if you look for it as for *s*
	3:14	for she is more profitable than *s*
	8:10	Choose my instruction instead of *s*,
	22:	1 to be esteemed is better than *s*
	25:	4 Remove the dross from the *s*,
	25:11	is like apples of gold in settings of *s*.
Isa	48:10	I have refined you, though not as *s*;
Eze	22:18	They are but the dross of *s*.
Da	2:32	its chest and arms of *s*, its belly
Hag	2:	8 'The *s* is mine and the gold is mine,'
Zec	13:	9 I will refine them like *s*
Ac	3:	6 Peter said, "*S* or gold I do not have,
1Co	3:12	*s*, costly stones, wood, hay or straw
1Pe	1:18	not with perishable things such as *s*

SILVERSMITH

Ac	19:24	A *s* named Demetrius, who made

SIMEON

Son of Jacob by Leah (Ge 29:33; 35:23; 1Ch 2:1). With Levi killed Shechem for rape of Dinah (Ge 34:25-29). Held hostage by Joseph in Egypt (Ge 42:24-43:23). Tribe of blessed (Ge 49:5-7), numbered (Nu 1:23; 26:14), allotted land (Jos 19:1-9; Eze 48:24), 12,000 from (Rev 7:7).

SIMON

1. See PETER.
2. Apostle, called the Zealot (Mt 10:4; Mk 3: 18; Lk 6:15; Ac 1:13).
3. Samaritan sorcerer (Ac 8:9-24).

SIMPLE

Ps	19:	7 making wise the *s*.
	119:130	it gives understanding to the *s*.
Pr	8:	5 You who are *s*, gain prudence;
	14:15	A *s* man believes anything.

SIMPLEHEARTED* (HEART)

Ps	116:	6 The LORD protects the *s*;

SIN (SINFUL SINNED SINNER SINNERS SINNING SINS)

Ge	4:	7 *s* is crouching at your door;
Ex	32:32	please forgive their *s*—but if not,
Nu	5:	7 and must confess the *s* he has
	32:23	be sure that your *s* will find you
Dt	24:16	each is to die for his own *s*.
1Sa	12:23	it from me that I should *s*
	15:23	For rebellion is like the *s*
1Ki	8:46	for there is no one who does not *s*
2Ch	7:14	and will forgive their *s* and will heal
Job	1:22	Job did not *s* by charging God
Ps	4:	4 In your anger do not *s*;
	17:	3 resolved that my mouth will not *s*.
	32:	2 whose *s* the LORD does not count
	32:	5 Then I acknowledged my *s* to you
	36:	2 too much to detect or hate his *s*.
	38:18	I am troubled by my *s*.
	39:	1 and keep my tongue from *s*;
	51:	2 and cleanse me from my *s*.
	66:18	If I had cherished *s* in my heart,
	119:	11 that I might not *s* against you.
	119:133	let no *s* rule over me.
Pr	5:22	the cords of his *s* hold him fast.
	10:19	words are many, *s* is not absent,
	14:	9 Fools mock at making amends for *s*
	16:	6 faithfulness *s* is atoned for;
	17:19	He who loves a quarrel loves *s*;
	20:	9 I am clean and without *s*''?
Isa	3:	9 they parade their *s* like Sodom;
	6:	7 is taken away and your *s* atoned
	6:5	But when we continued to *s*
Jer	31:30	everyone will die for his own *s*;
Eze	3:18	that wicked man will die for his *s*,
	18:26	his righteousness and commits *s*,
	33:	8 that wicked man will die for his *s*,
Am	4:	4 "Go to Bethel and *s*;
Mic	6:	7 of my body for the *s* of my soul?
	7:18	who pardons *s* and forgives
Zec	3:	4 "See, I have taken away your *s*,
Mt	18:	6 little ones who believe in me to *s*,
Mk	3:29	he is guilty of an eternal *s*.''
	9:43	If your hand causes you to *s*,
Lk	17:	1 people to *s* are bound to come,
Jn	1:29	who takes away the *s* of the world!
	8:	7 "If any one of you is without *s*,
	8:34	everyone who sins is a slave to *s*.
	8:46	Can any of you prove me guilty of *s*
Ro	2:12	All who *s* apart from the law will
	5:12	as *s* entered the world
	5:20	where *s* increased, grace increased
	6:	2 By no means! We died to *s*;
	6:11	count yourselves dead to *s*
	6:14	For *s* shall not be your master,
	6:23	For the wages of *s* is death,
	7:	7 I would not have known what *s* was
	7:25	sinful nature a slave to the law of *s*.
	14:23	that does not come from faith is *s*.
1Co	8:12	When you *s* against your brothers
	15:56	The sting of death is *s*,
2Co	5:21	God made him who had no *s* to be *s*
Gal	6:	1 if someone is caught in a *s*,
1Ti	5:20	Those who *s* are to be rebuked
Heb	4:15	just as we are—yet was without *s*.
	9:26	to do away with *s* by the sacrifice
	11:25	the pleasures of *s* for a short time.
	12:	1 and the *s* that so easily entangles,
Jas	1:15	it gives birth to *s*; and *s*,

1Pe   2:22 "He committed no s,
1Jn   1: 7 his Son, purifies us from all s.
     1: 8 If we claim to be without s,
     2: 1 But if anybody does s, we have one
     3: 4 in fact, s is lawlessness.
     3: 5 And in him is no s.
     3: 6 No one who continues to s has.
     3: 9 born of God will continue to s.
     5:16 There is a s that leads to death.
     5:17 All wrongdoing is s, and there is s
     5:18 born of God does not continue to s;

SINAI

Ex   19:20 descended to the top of Mount S
     31:18 speaking to Moses on Mount S,
Ps   68:17 from S into his sanctuary.

SINCERE* (SINCERITY)

Da   11:34 many who are not s will join them.
Ac   2:46 altogether with glad and s hearts.
Ro   12: 9 Love must be s.
2Co   6: 6 in the Holy Spirit and in s love;
     11: 3 somehow be led astray from your s
1Ti   1: 5 a good conscience and a s faith.
     3: 8 s, not indulging in much wine,
2Ti   1: 5 have been reminded of your s faith,
Heb   10: 22 near to God with a s heart.
Jas   3:17 and good fruit, impartial and s.
1Pe   1:22 the truth so that you have s love

SINCERITY* (SINCERE)

1Co   5: 8 bread without yeast, the bread of s
2Co   1:12 in the holiness and s that are
     2:17 speak before God with s,
     8: 8 but I want to test the s of your love
Eph   6: 5 and with s of heart, just
Col   3:22 but with s of heart and reverence

SINFUL (SIN)

Ps   51: 5 Surely I was s at birth,
     51: 5 s from the time my mother
Lk   5: 8 from me, Lord; I am a s man!"
Ro   7: 5 we were controlled by the s nature,
     7:18 lives in me, that is, in my s nature.
     7:25 but in the s nature a slave to the law
     8: 3 Son in the likeness of s man
     8: 4 not live according to the s nature
     8: 7 the s mind is hostile to God.
     8: 8 by the s nature cannot please God.
     8: 9 are controlled not by the s nature
     8:13 if you live according to the s nature
     13:14 to gratify the desires of the s nature
1Co   5: 5 so that the s nature may be
Gal   5:13 freedom to indulge the s nature;
     5:16 gratify the desires of the s nature.
     5:19 The acts of the s nature are obvious
     5:24 Jesus have crucified the s nature
     6: 8 sows to please his s nature,
Col   2:11 in the putting off of the s nature,
Heb   3:12 brothers, that none of you has a s,
1Pe   2:11 abstain from s desires, which war
1Jn   3: 8 He who does what is s is

SING (SANG SINGER SINGING SINGS SONG SONGS SUNG)

Ex   15: 1 "I will s to the LORD,
Ps   5:11 let them ever s for joy.
     13: 6 I will s to the LORD,
     30: 4 S to the LORD, you saints of his;
     33: 1 S joyfully to the LORD, you
     47: 6 S praises to God, s praises;
     57: 7 I will s and make music.
     59:16 But I will s of your strength,
     63: 7 I s in the shadow of your wings.
     66: 2 S to the glory of his name;
     89: 1 I will s of the LORD's great love
     95: 1 Come, let us s for joy to the LORD
     96: 1 S to the LORD a new song;
     98: 1 S to the LORD a new song,
     101: 1 I will s of your love and justice;
     108: 1 I will s and make music
     137: 3 "S us one of the songs of Zion!"
     147: 1 is to s praises to our God,
     149: 1 S to the LORD a new song,
Isa   54: 1 "S, O barren woman,
1Co   14:15 also pray with my mind; I will s
Eph   5:19 S and make music in your heart
Col   3:16 and as you s psalms, hymns
Jas   5:13 Is anyone happy? Let him s songs

SINGER* (SING)

2Sa   23: 1 Israel's s of songs:

SINGING (SING)

Ps   63: 5 with s lips my mouth will praise

Ps   68: 6 he leads forth the prisoners with s;
     98: 5 with the harp and the sound of s,
Isa   35:10 They will enter Zion with s;
Zep   3:17 he will rejoice over you with s."
Ac   16:25 Silas were praying and s hymns
Rev   5:13 on the sea, and all that is in them, s:

SINGLE

Ex   23:29 I will not drive them out in a s year,
Mt   6:27 you by worrying can add a s hour
Gal   5:14 law is summed up in a s command:

SINGS (SING)

Eze   33:32 more than one who s love songs

SINNED (SIN)

Lev   5: 5 confess in what way he has s
1Sa   15:24 Then Saul said to Samuel, "I have s
2Sa   12:13 "I have s against the LORD."
     24:10 I have s greatly in what I have done
2Ch   6:37 'We have s, we have done wrong
Job   1: 5 "Perhaps my children have s
     33:27 'I s, and perverted what was right,
Ps   51: 4 Against you, you only, have I s
Jer   2:35 because you say, 'I have not s.'
     14:20 we have indeed s against you.
Da   9: 5 we have s and done wrong.
Mic   7: 9 Because I have s against him,
Mt   27: 4 "I have s," he said,
Lk   15:18 I have s against heaven
Ro   3:23 for all have s and fall short
     5:12 all s—for before the law was given,
2Pe   2: 4 did not spare angels when they s,
1Jn   1:10 claim we have not s, we make him

SINNER (SIN)

Ecc   9:18 but one s destroys much good.
Lk   15: 7 in heaven over one s who repents
     18:13 'God, have mercy on me, a s.'
1Co   14:24 convinced by all that he is a s
Jas   5:20 Whoever turns a s from the error
1Pe   4:18 become of the ungodly and the s?"

SINNERS (SIN)

Ps   1: 1 or stand in the way of s
     37:38 But all s will be destroyed;
Pr   1:10 My son, if s entice you,
     23:17 Do not let your heart envy s,
Mt   9:13 come to call the righteous, but s."
Ro   5: 8 While we were still s, Christ died
Gal   2:17 evident that we ourselves are s,
1Ti   1:15 came into the world to save s—
Heb   7:26 set apart from s, exalted

SINNING (SIN)

Ex   20:20 be with you to keep you from s."
1Co   15:34 stop s; for there are some who are
Heb   10:26 If we deliberately keep on s
1Jn   3: 6 No one who lives in him keeps on s
     3: 9 go on s, because he has been born

SINS (SIN)

Lev   5: 1 "If a person s because he does not
     16:30 you will be clean from all your s.
     26:40 "'But if they will confess their s
Nu   15:30 "'But anyone who s defiantly,
1Sa   2:25 If a man s against another man,
2Ki   14: 6 each is to die for his own s."
Ezr   9: 6 our s are higher than our heads
     9:13 less than our s have deserved
Ps   19:13 your servant also from willful s;
     32: 1 whose s are covered.
     51: 9 Hide your face from my s
     79: 9 deliver us and forgive our s
     85: 2 and covered all their s.
     103: 3 who forgives all your s
     103: 10 does not treat us as our s deserve
     130: 3 O LORD, kept a record of s,
Pr   14:21 He who despises his neighbor s,
     28:13 who conceals his s does not
     29:22 one commits many s.
Ecc   7:20 who does what is right and never s.
Isa   1:18 "Though your s are like scarlet,
     38:17 you have put all my s
     43:25 and remembers your s no more.
     59: 2 your s have hidden his face
     64: 6 like the wind our s sweep us away.
Jer   31:34 and will remember their s no more
La   3:39 complain when punished for his s?
Eze   18: 4 soul who s is the one who will die.
     33:10 Our offenses and s weigh us down,
     36:33 day I cleanse you from all your s,
Hos   14: 1 Your s have been your downfall!
Mt   1:21 he will save his people from their s
     6:15 if you do not forgive men their s,

Mt   9: 6 authority on earth to forgive s . . . . . ."
     18:15 "If your brother s against you,
     26:28 for many for the forgiveness of s.
Lk   5:24 authority on earth to forgive s . . . . . ."
     11: 4 Forgive us our s,
     17: 3 "If your brother s, rebuke him,
Jn   8:24 you will indeed die in your s."
     20:23 If you forgive anyone his s,
Ac   2:38 for the forgiveness of your s
     3:19 so that your s may be wiped out,
     10:43 forgiveness of s through his name."
     22:16 be baptized and wash your s away,
     26:18 they may receive forgiveness of s
Ro   4: 7 whose s are covered.
     4:25 delivered over to death for our s
1Co   15: 3 died for our s according
2Co   5:19 not counting men's s against them.
Gal   1: 4 himself for our s to rescue us
Eph   2: 1 dead in your transgressions and s,
Col   2:13 us all our s, having canceled
1Ti   5:22 and do not share in the s of others.
Heb   1: 3 he had provided purification for s,
     2:17 atonement for the s of the people.
     7:27 He sacrificed for their s once for all
     8:12 and will remember their s no more
     9:28 to take away the s of many people;
     10: 4 of bulls and goats to take away s.
     10:12 for all time one sacrifice for s,
     10:26 of the truth, no sacrifice for s is left,
Jas   4:17 ought to do and doesn't do it, s.
     5:16 Therefore confess your s
     5:20 and cover over a multitude of s.
1Pe   2:24 He himself bore our s in his body
     3:18 For Christ died for s once for all,
     4: 8 love covers over a multitude of s.
1Jn   1: 9 If we confess our s, he is faithful
     2: 2 He is the atoning sacrifice for our s,
     3: 5 so that he might take away our s.
     4:10 as an atoning sacrifice for our s.
Rev   1: 5 has freed us from our s by his blood

SISERA

Jdg   4: 2 The commander of his army was S,
     5:26 She struck S, she crushed his head,

SISTER (SISTERS)

Lev   18: 9 have sexual relations with your s,
Mk   3:35 does God's will is my brother and s

SISTERS (SISTER)

Mt   19:29 or brothers or s or father or mother
1Ti   5: 2 as s, with absolute purity.

SIT (SAT SITS SITTING)

Dt   6: 7 them when you s at home
1Ki   8:25 fail to have a man to s before me
Ps   1: 1 or s in the seat of mockers.
     26: 5 and refuse to s with the wicked.
     80: 1 you who s enthroned
     110: 1 "Sat my right hand
     139: 2 You know when I s and when I rise
SS   2: 3 I delight to s in his shade,
Isa   16: 5 in faithfulness a man will s on it—
Mic   4: 4 Every man will s under his own
Mt   20:23 to s at my right or left is not for me
     22:44 "Sat my right hand
Lk   22:30 in my kingdom and s on thrones,
Heb   1:13 "Sat my right hand
Rev   3:21 right to s with me on my throne,

SITS (SIT)

Ps   99: 1 s enthroned between the cherubim,
Isa   40:22 He s enthroned above the circle
Mt   19:28 of Man s on his glorious throne,
Rev   4: 9 thanks to him who s on the throne

SITTING (SIT)

Est   2:19 Mordecai was s at the king's gate.
Mt   26:64 the Son of Man s at the right hand
Rev   4: 2 in heaven with someone s on it.

SITUATION (SITUATIONS)

1Co   7:24 remain in the s God called him
Php   4:12 of being content in any and every s,

SITUATIONS* (SITUATION)

2Ti   4: 5 head in all s, endure hardship,

SKIES (SKY)

Ps   19: 1 the s proclaim the work
     71:19 Your righteousness reaches to the s
     108: 4 your faithfulness reaches to the s.

SKILL (SKILLED SKILLFUL)

Ps 137: 5 may my right hand forget its s,
Ecc 10:10 but s will bring success.

SKILLED (SKILL)

Pr 22:29 Do you see a man s in his work?

SKILLFUL (SKILL)

Ps 45: 1 my tongue is the pen of a s writer.
78:72 with s hands he led them.

SKIN (SKINS)

Job 19:20 with only the s of my teeth.
19:26 And after my s has been destroyed,
Jer 13:23 Can the Ethiopian change his s

SKINS (SKIN)

Ex 25: 5 ram s dyed red and hides
Lk 5:37 the new wine will burst the s,

SKULL

Mt 27:33 (which means The Place of the S).

SKY (SKIES)

Ge 1: 8 God called the expanse "s."
Pr 30:19 the way of an eagle in the s,
Isa 34: 4 and the s rolled up like a scroll;
Jer 33:22 stars of the s and as measureless
Mt 24:29 the stars will fall from the s,
24:30 coming on the clouds of the s,
Rev 20:11 Earth and s fled from his presence,

SLACK*

Pr 18: 9 One who is s in his work

SLAIN (SLAY)

1Sa 18: 7 "Saul has s his thousands,
Eze 37: 9 into these s, that they may live.' "
Rev 5: 6 as if it had been s, standing
5:12 "Worthy is the Lamb, who was s,
6: 9 the souls of those who had been s

SLANDER (SLANDERED SLANDERER
SLANDERERS SLANDEROUS)

Lev 19:16 " 'Do not go about spreading s
Ps 15: 3 and has no s on his tongue,
Pr 10:18 and whoever spreads s is a fool.
2Co 12:20 outbursts of anger, factions, s,
Eph 4:31 rage and anger, brawling and s,
1Ti 5:14 the enemy no opportunity for s.
Tit 3: 2 to s no one, to be peaceable
1Pe 3:16 in Christ may be ashamed of their s
2Pe 2:10 afraid to s celestial beings;

SLANDERED (SLANDER)

1Co 4:13 when we are s, we answer kindly.

SLANDERER (SLANDER)

1Co 5:11 an idolater or a s, a drunkard

SLANDERERS (SLANDER)

Ro 1:30 They are gossips, s, God-haters,
1Co 6:10 nor the greedy nor drunkards nor s
Tit 2: 3 not to be s or addicted

SLANDEROUS (SLANDER)

2Ti 3: 3 unforgiving, s, without self-control
2Pe 2:11 do not bring s accusations

SLAUGHTER (SLAUGHTERED)

Isa 53: 7 he was led like a lamb to the s,
Jer 11:19 been led a gentle lamb led to the s;
Ac 8:32 "He was led like a sheep to the s,

SLAUGHTERED (SLAUGHTER)

Ps 44:22 we are considered as sheep to be s
Ro 8:36 we are considered as sheep to be s

SLAVE (ENSLAVED SLAVERY SLAVES)

Ge 21:10 "Get rid of that s woman
Mt 20:27 wants to be first must be your s—
Jn 8:34 everyone who sins is a s to sin.
Ro 7:14 I am unspiritual, sold as a s to sin.
1Co 7:21 Were you a s when you were called
12:13 whether Jews or Greeks, s or free
Gal 3:28 s nor free, male nor female,
4: 7 So you are no longer a s, but a son;
4:30 Get rid of the s woman and her son
Col 3:11 barbarian, Scythian, s or free,
1Ti 1:10 for s traders and liars and perjurers
Phm :16 no longer as a s, but better than a s,
2Pe 2:19 a man is a s to whatever has

SLAVERY (SLAVE)

Ex 2:23 The Israelites groaned in their s
Ro 6:19 parts of your body in s to impurity
Gal 4: 3 were in s under the basic principles
1Ti 6: 1 of s should consider their masters

SLAVES (SLAVE)

Ps 123: 2 As the eyes of s look to the hand
Ecc 10: 7 I have seen s on horseback.
Ro 6: 6 that we should no longer be s to sin
6:16 you are s to sin, which leads
6:22 and have become s to God,
Gal 2: 4 in Christ Jesus and to make us s.
4: 8 you were s to those who
Eph 6: 5 S, obey your earthly masters
Col 3:22 S, obey your earthly masters
4: 1 provide your s with what is right
Tit 2: 9 Teach s to be subject

SLAY (SLAIN)

Job 13:15 Though he s me, yet will I hope

SLEEP (ASLEEP SLEEPER SLEEPING
SLEEPS)

Ge 2:21 the man to fall into a deep s;
15:12 Abram fell into a deep s,
28:11 it under his head and lay down to s.
Ps 4: 8 I will lie down and s in peace,
121: 4 will neither slumber nor s.
127: 2 for he grants s to those he loves.
Pr 6: 9 When will you get up from your s?
Ecc 5:12 The s of a laborer is sweet,
1Co 15:51 We will not all s, but we will all be
1Th 5: 7 For those who s, s at night,

SLEEPER (SLEEP)

Eph 5:14 "Wake up, O s,

SLEEPING (SLEEP)

Mk 13:36 suddenly, do not let him find you s.

SLEEPLESS*

2Co 6: 5 in hard work, s nights and hunger;

SLEEPS (SLEEP)

Pr 10: 5 he who s during harvest is

SLIMY

Ps 40: 2 He lifted me out of the s pit,

SLING

1Sa 17:50 over the Philistine with a s

SLIP (SLIPPING)

Dt 4: 9 let them s from your heart as long
Ps 121: 3 He will not let your foot s—

SLIPPING (SLIP)

Ps 66: 9 and kept our feet from s.

SLOW

Ex 34: 6 and gracious God, s to anger,
Jas 1:19 s to speak and s to become angry.
2Pe 3: 9 The Lord is not s in keeping his

SLUGGARD

Pr 6: 6 Go to the ant, you s;
13: 4 The s craves and gets nothing.
20: 4 A s does not plow in season;
26:15 The s buries his hand in the dish;

SLUMBER

Ps 121: 3 he who watches over you will not s;
Pr 6:10 A little sleep, a little s,
Ro 13:11 for you to wake up from your s,

SLUR

Ps 15: 3 and casts no s on his fellow man,

SMELL

Ecc 10: 1 As dead flies give perfume a bad s,
2Co 2:16 To the one we are the s of death;

SMITTEN

Isa 53: 4 s by him, and afflicted.

SMOKE

Ex 19:18 Mount Sinai was covered with s,
Ps 104:32 touches the mountains, and they s.
Isa 6: 4 and the temple was filled with s.
Joel 2:30 blood and fire and billows of s.
Ac 2:19 blood and fire and billows of s.
Rev 15: 8 filled with s from the glory

SMYRNA

Rev 2: 8 the angel of the church in S write:

SNAKE (SNAKES)

Nu 21: 8 "Make a s and put it up on a pole;
Pr 23:32 In the end it bites like a s
Jn 3:14 Moses lifted up the s in the desert,

SNAKES (SNAKE)

Mt 10:16 as shrewd as s and as innocent
Mk 16:18 they will pick up s with their hands;

SNARE (ENSNARE ENSNARED SNARED)

Dt 7:16 for that will be a s to you.
Ps 69:22 before them become a s,
91: 3 from the fowler's s
Pr 29:25 Fear of man will prove to be a s,
Ro 11: 9 "May their table become a s

SNARED (SNARE)

Pr 3:26 will keep your foot from being s.

SNATCH

Jn 10:28 no one can s them out of my hand.
Jude :23 s others from the fire and save

SNOUT

Pr 11:22 Like a gold ring in a pig's s

SNOW

Ps 51: 7 and I will be whiter than s.
Isa 1:18 they shall be as white as s;

SNUFF (SNUFFED)

Isa 42: 3 a smoldering wick he will not s out.
Mt 12:20 a smoldering wick he will not s out,

SNUFFED (SNUFF)

Pr 13: 9 but the lamp of the wicked is s out.

SOAP

Mal 3: 2 a refiner's fire or a launderer's s.

SOAR (SOARED)

Isa 40:31 They will s on wings like eagles;

SOARED (SOAR)

2Sa 22:11 he s on the wings of the wind.

SOBER

Ro 12: 3 think of yourself with s judgment,

SODOM

Ge 13:12 and pitched his tents near S.
19:24 rained down burning sulfur on S
Isa 1: 9 we would have become like S,
Lk 10:12 on that day for S than for that town
Ro 9:29 we would have become like S,
Rev 11: 8 which is figuratively called S

SOIL

Ge 4: 2 kept flocks, and Cain worked the s
Mt 13:23 on good s is the man who hears

SOLD (SELL)

1Ki 21:25 who s himself to do evil in the eyes
Mt 10:29 Are not two sparrows s for a penny
13:44 then in his joy went and s all he had
Ro 7:14 I am unspiritual, s as a slave to sin.

SOLDIER

1Co 9: 7 as a s at his own expense?
2Ti 2: 3 with us like a good s of Christ Jesus

SOLE

Dt 28:65 place for the s of your foot.
Isa 1: 6 From the s of your foot to the top

SOLID

2Ti 2:19 God's s foundation stands firm,
Heb 5:12 You need milk, not s food!

SOLOMON

Son of David by Bathsheba; king of Judah (2Sa 12:24; 1Ch 3:5, 10). Appointed king by David (1Ki 1); adversaries Adonijah, Joab, Shimei killed by Benaiah (1Ki 2). Asked for wisdom (1Ki 3:16-28). Built temple (1Ki 5-7; 2Ch 2-5); prayer of dedication (1Ki 8; 2Ch 6). Visited by Queen of Sheba (1Ki 10; 2Ch 9). Wives turned his heart from God (1Ki 11:1-13). Jeroboam rebelled against (1Ki 11:26-40). Death (1Ki 11:41-43; 2Ch 9:29-31).

Proverbs of (1Ki 4:32; Pr 1:1; 10:1; 25:1); psalms of (Ps 72; 127); song of (SS 1:1).

SON (SONS SONSHIP)

Ge 17: 19 your wife Sarah will bear you a s,
21: 10 rid of that slave woman and her s,
22: 2 "Take your s, your only s, Isaac,
Ex 11: 5 Every firstborn s in Egypt will die,
Dt 1: 31 father carries his s, all the way you
6: 20 In the future, when your s asks you,
8: 5 as a man disciplines his s,
21: 18 rebellious s who does not obey his
2Sa 7: 14 be his father, and he will be my s.
1Ki 3: 20 and put her dead s by my breast.
Ps 2: 7 He said to me, "You are my S;
2: 12 Kiss the S, lest he be angry
8: 4 the s of man that you care for him?
Pr 3: 12 as a father the s he delights in.
6: 20 My s, keep your father's
10: 1 A wise s brings joy to his father,
13: 24 He who spares the rod hates his s,
29: 17 Discipline your s, and he will give
Isa 7: 14 with child and will give birth to a s,
Eze 18: 20 The s will not share the guilt
Da 3: 25 the fourth looks like a s of the gods
7: 13 before me was one like a s of man,
Hos 11: 1 and out of Egypt I called my s.
Am 7: 14 neither a prophet nor a prophet's s,
Mt 1: 1 of Jesus Christ the s of David,
1: 21 She will give birth to a s,
2: 15 "Out of Egypt I called my s."
3: 17 "This is my S, whom I love;
4: 3 "If you are the S of God, tell these
8: 20 but the S of Man has no place
11: 27 one knows the S except the Father,
12: 8 For the S of Man is Lord
12: 32 a word against the S of Man will be
12: 40 so the S of Man will be three days
13: 41 S of Man will send out his angels,
13: 55 "Isn't this the carpenter's s?
14: 33 "Truly you are the S of God."
16: 16 "You are the Christ, the S
16: 27 For the S of Man is going to come
17: 5 "This is my S, whom I love;
19: 28 when the S of Man sits
20: 18 and the S of Man will be betrayed
20: 28 as the S of Man did not come
21: 9 "Hosanna to the S of David!"
22: 42 Whose s is he?" "The s of David,"
24: 27 so will be the coming of the S
24: 30 They will see the S of Man coming
24: 44 the S of Man will come at an hour
25: 31 "When the S of Man comes
26: 63 if you are the Christ, the S of God."
27: 54 "Surely he was the S of God!"
28: 19 and of the S and of the Holy Spirit,
Mk 1: 11 "You are my S, whom I love;
2: 28 So the S of Man is Lord
8: 38 the S of Man will be ashamed
9: 7 "This is my S, whom I love.
10: 45 even the S of Man did not come
13: 32 nor the S, but only the Father.
14: 62 you will see the S of Man sitting
Lk 1: 32 and will be called the S
2: 7 she gave birth to her firstborn, a s.
3: 22 "You are my S, whom I love;
9: 35 This is my S, whom I have chosen;
9: 58 but the S of Man has no place
12: 8 the S of Man will also acknowledge
15: 20 he ran to his s, threw his arms
18: 8 when the S of Man comes,
18: 31 written by the prophets about the S
19: 10 For the S of Man came to seek
Jn 1: 34 I testify that this is the S of God."
3: 14 so the S of Man must be lifted up,
3: 16 that he gave his one and only S,
3: 36 believes in the S has eternal life,
5: 19 the S can do nothing by himself;
6: 40 is that everyone who looks to the S
11: 4 so that God's S may be glorified
17: 1 Glorify your S, that your S may
Ac 7: 56 and the S of Man standing
13: 33 " 'You are my S;
Ro 1: 4 with power to be the S of God
5: 10 to him through the death of his S,
8: 3 did by sending his own S
8: 29 conformed to the likeness of his S,
8: 32 He who did not spare his own S,
1Co 15: 28 then the S himself will be made
Gal 2: 20 I live by faith in the S of God,
4: 4 God sent his S, born of a woman,
4: 30 rid of the slave woman and her s,
1Th 1: 10 and to wait for his S from heaven,
Heb 1: 2 days he has spoken to us by his S,
1: 5 "You are my S;
Heb 2: 6 the s of man that you care for him?
4: 14 Jesus the S of God, let us hold
5: 5 "You are my S;
7: 28 appointed the S, who has been
10: 29 punished who has trampled the S
12: 6 everyone he accepts as a s."
2Pe 1: 17 saying, "This is my S, whom I love;
1Jn 1: 3 is with the Father and with his S,
1: 7 his S, purifies us from all sin.
2: 23 whoever acknowledges the S has
3: 8 reason the S of God appeared was
4: 9 only S into the world that we might
4: 14 that the Father has sent his S
5: 5 he who believes that Jesus is the S
5: 11 eternal life, and this life is in his S.
Rev 1: 13 lampstands was someone "like a s
14: 14 on the cloud was one "like a s

SONG (SING)

Ex 15: 2 LORD is my strength and my s;
Ps 40: 3 He put a new s in my mouth,
69: 30 I will praise God's name in s
96: 1 Sing to the LORD a new s;
98: 4 burst into jubilant s with music;
119: 54 Your decrees are the theme of my s
149: 1 Sing to the LORD a new s,
Isa 49: 13 burst into s, O mountains!
55: 12 will burst into s before you,
Rev 5: 9 And they sang a new s:
15: 3 and sang the s of Moses the servant

SONGS (SING)

2Sa 23: 1 Israel's singer of s:
Job 35: 10 who gives s in the night,
Ps 100: 2 come before him with joyful s.
126: 6 will return with s of joy,
137: 3 "Sing us one of the s of Zion!"
Eph 5: 19 with psalms, hymns and spiritual s.
Jas 5: 13 Is anyone happy? Let him sing s

SONS (SON)

Ge 6: 2 the s of God saw that the daughters
10: 20 These are the s of Ham
Ru 4: 15 who is better to you than seven s,
Ps 127: 3 S are a heritage from the LORD,
132: 12 if your s keep my covenant
Hos 1: 10 they will be called 's
Joel 2: 28 Your s and daughters will prophesy
Mt 5: 9 for they will be called s of God.
Lk 6: 35 and you will be s of the Most High,
Jn 12: 36 so that you may become s of light."
Ro 8: 14 by the Spirit of God are s of God.
9: 26 they will be called 's
2Co 6: 18 and you will be my s and daughters
Gal 3: 26 You are all s of God through faith
4: 5 we might receive the full rights of s.
4: 6 Because you are s, God sent
Heb 12: 7 discipline; God is treating you as s.

SONSHIP* (SON)

Ro 8: 15 but you received the Spirit of s.

SORCERY

Lev 19: 26 " 'Do not practice divination or s.

SORROW (SORROWS)

Ps 6: 7 My eyes grow weak with s;
116: 3 I was overcome by trouble and s.
Isa 60: 20 and your days of s will end.
Jer 31: 12 and they will s no more.
Ro 9: 2 I have great s and unceasing
2Co 7: 10 Godly s brings repentance that

SORROWS (SORROW)

Isa 53: 3 a man of s, and familiar

SOUGHT (SEEK)

2Ch 26: 5 As long as he s the LORD,
31: 21 he s his God and worked
Ps 34: 4 I s the LORD, and he answered me
119: 58 I have s your face with all my heart;

SOUL (SOULS)

Dt 6: 5 with all your s and with all your
10: 12 all your heart and with all your s,
30: 6 all your heart and with all your s,
Jos 22: 5 with all your heart and all your s."
2Ki 23: 25 and with all his s and with all his
Ps 23: 3 he restores my s.
34: 2 My s will boast in the LORD;
42: 1 so my s pants for you, O God.
42: 11 Why are you downcast, O my s?
62: 5 Find rest, O my s, in God alone;
63: 8 My s clings to you;
94: 19 consolation brought joy to my s.
Ps 103: 1 Praise the LORD, O my s;
Pr 13: 19 A longing fulfilled is sweet to the s,
16: 24 sweet to the s and healing
22: 5 he who guards his s stays far
Isa 55: 2 your s will delight in the richest
La 3: 20 and my s is downcast within me.
Eze 18: 4 For every living s belongs to me,
Mt 10: 28 kill the body but cannot kill the s.
16: 26 yet forfeits his s? Or what can
22: 37 with all your s and with all your
Heb 4: 12 even to dividing s and spirit,
3Jn : 2 even as your s is getting along well.

SOULS (SOUL)

Pr 11: 30 and he who wins s is wise.
Jer 6: 16 and you will find rest for your s.
Mt 11: 29 and you will find rest for your s.

SOUND (FINE-SOUNDING)

Ge 3: 8 and his wife heard the s
Pr 3: 21 preserve s judgment
Eze 3: 12 I heard behind me a loud rumbling s
Jn 3: 8 You hear its s, but you cannot tell
Ac 2: 2 Suddenly a s like the blowing
1Co 14: 8 if the trumpet does not s a clear call
15: 52 the trumpet will s, the dead will
1Ti 1: 10 to the s doctrine that conforms
2Ti 4: 3 men will not put up with s doctrine.
Tit 1: 9 can encourage others by s doctrine
2: 1 is in accord with s doctrine.

SOUR

Eze 18: 2 " 'The fathers eat s grapes,

SOURCE

Heb 5: 9 became the s of eternal salvation

SOVEREIGN (SOVEREIGNTY)

Ge 15: 2 But Abram said, "O S LORD,
2Sa 7: 18 O S LORD, and what is my family,
Ps 71: 16 your mighty acts, O S LORD;
Isa 25: 8 S LORD will wipe away the tears
40: 10 the S LORD comes with power,
50: 4 S LORD has given me
61: 1 The Spirit of the S LORD is on me,
61: 11 so the S LORD will make
Jer 32: 17 to the LORD: "Ah, S LORD,
Eze 12: 28 fulfilled, declares the S LORD.' "
Da 4: 25 that the Most High is s
2Pe 2: 1 denying the s Lord who bought
Jude : 4 and deny Jesus Christ our only S

SOVEREIGNTY (SOVEREIGN)

Da 7: 27 Then the s, power and greatness

SOW (SOWER SOWN SOWS)

Job 4: 8 and those who s trouble reap it.
Ps 126: 5 Those who s in tears
Hos 8: 7 "They s the wind
10: 12 S for yourselves righteousness,
Mt 6: 26 they do not s or reap or store away
13: 3 "A farmer went out to s his seed.
1Co 15: 36 What you s does not come to life
Jas 3: 18 Peacemakers who s
2Pe 2: 22 and, "A s that is washed goes back

SOWER (SOW)

Isa 55: 10 so that it yields seed for the s
Mt 13: 18 to what the parable of the s means:
Jn 4: 36 so that the s and the reaper may be
2Co 9: 10 Now he who supplies seed to the s

SOWN (SOW)

Mt 13: 8 sixty or thirty times what was s.
Mk 4: 15 along the path, where the word is s.
1Co 15: 42 The body that is s is perishable,

SOWS (SOW)

Pr 11: 18 he who s righteousness reaps a sure
22: 8 He who s wickedness reaps trouble
2Co 9: 6 Whoever s sparingly will
Gal 6: 7 A man reaps what he s.

SPARE (SPARES SPARING)

Est 7: 3 s my people—this is my request.
Ro 8: 32 He who did not s his own Son,
11: 21 natural branches, he will not s you
2Pe 2: 4 For if God did not s angels
2: 5 if he did not s the ancient world

SPARES (SPARE)

Pr 13: 24 He who s the rod hates his son,

SPARING (SPARE)

Pr 21: 26 but the righteous give without s.

SPARKLE
Zec   9:16 They will s in his land

SPARROW (SPARROWS)
Ps   84: 3 Even the s has found a home,

SPARROWS (SPARROW)
Mt   10:29 Are not two s sold for a penny?

SPEAR (SPEARS)
1Sa 19:10 as Saul drove the s into the wall.
Ps   46: 9 breaks the bow and shatters the s,

SPEARS (SPEAR)
Isa   2: 4 and their s into pruning hooks.
Joel   3:10 and your pruning hooks into s.
Mic   4: 3 and their s into pruning hooks.

SPECIAL
Jas   2: 3 If you show s attention

SPECK
Mt   7: 3 look at the s of sawdust

SPECTACLE
1Co   4: 9 We have been made a s
Col   2:15 he made a public s of them,

SPEECH
Ps   19: 3 There is no s or language
Pr   22:11 pure heart and whose s is gracious
2Co   8: 7 in faith, in s, in knowledge,
1Ti   4:12 set an example for the believers in s

SPEND (SPENT)
Pr   31: 3 do not s your strength on women,
Isa   55: 2 Why s money on what is not bread,
2Co 12:15 So I will very gladly s

SPENT (SPEND)
Mk   5:26 many doctors and had s all she had,
Lk   6:12 and s the night praying to God.
       15:14 After he had s everything,

SPIN
Mt   6:28 They do not labor or s.

SPIRIT (SPIRIT'S SPIRITS SPIRITUAL SPIRITUALLY)
Ge   1: 2 and the S of God was hovering
       6: 3 "My S will not contend
Ex   31: 3 I have filled him with the S of God,
Nu   11:25 and put the S on the seventy elders.
Dt   34: 9 filled with the s of wisdom
Jdg   6:34 Then the S of the LORD came
       11:29 Then the S of the LORD came
       13:25 and the S of the LORD began
1Sa 10:10 the S of God came upon him
       16:13 day on the S of the LORD came
       16:14 the S of the LORD had departed
2Sa 23: 2 "The S of the LORD spoke
2Ki   2: 9 inherit a double portion of your s,"
Ne   9:20 You gave your good S
       9:30 By your S you admonished them
Job 33: 4 The S of God has made me;
Ps   31: 5 Into your hands I commit my s,
      34:18 saves those who are crushed in s.
      51:10 and renew a steadfast s within me.
      51:11 or take your Holy S from me.
      51:17 sacrifices of God are a broken s;
     106:33 rebelled against the s of God,
     139: 7 Where can I go from your S?
     143:10 may your good S
Isa 11: 2 The S of the LORD will rest
      30: 1 alliance, but not by my S,
      32:15 till the S is poured upon us
      44: 3 I will pour my S
      57:15 him who is contrite and lowly in s,
      61: 1 The S of the Sovereign LORD is
      63:10 and grieved his Holy S.
Eze 11:19 an undivided heart and put a new s
       3: prophets who follow their own s
      36:26 you a new heart and put a new s
Da   4: 8 and the s of the holy gods is in him
Joel 2:28 I will pour out my S on all people.
Zec   4: 6 but by my S,' says the LORD
Mt   1:18 to be with child through the Holy S
       3:11 will baptize you with the Holy S
       3:16 he saw the S of God descending
       4: 1 led by the S into the desert
       5: 3 saying: "Blessed are the poor in s,
      10:20 but the S of your Father speaking
      12:31 against the S will not be forgiven.
      26:41 s is willing, but the body is weak."

Mt   28:19 and of the Son and of the Holy S.
Mk   1: 8 he will baptize you with the Holy S
Lk   1:35 "The S will come upon you,
       1:80 child grew and became strong in s;
       3:16 will baptize you with the Holy S
       4:18 "The S of the Lord is on me,
      11:13 Father in heaven give the Holy S
      23:46 into your hands I commit my s."
Jn   1:33 who will baptize with the Holy S
       3: 5 a man is born of water and the S,
       4:24 God is s, and his worshipers must
       6:63 The S gives life; the flesh counts
       7:39 Up to that time the S had not been
      14:26 But the Counselor, the Holy S,
      16:13 But when he, the S of truth, comes,
      20:22 and said, "Receive the Holy S.
Ac   1: 5 will be baptized with the Holy S."
       1: 8 when the Holy S comes on you;
       2: 4 of them were filled with the Holy S
       2:17 I will pour out my S on all people.
       2:38 will receive the gift of the Holy S
       4:31 they were all filled with the Holy S
       5: 3 that you have lied to the Holy S
       5: 9 who are known to be full of the S
       8:15 that they might receive the Holy S,
       9:17 and be filled with the Holy S."
      11:16 will be baptized with the Holy S."
      13: 2 and fasting, the Holy S said,
      19: 2 "Did you receive the Holy S
Ro   8: 4 nature but according to the S.
       8: 5 set on what the S desires.
       8: 9 And if anyone does not have the S
       8:13 but if by the S you put
       8:16 The S himself testifies
       8:23 who have the firstfruits of the S,
       8:26 the S helps us in our weakness.
1Co   2:10 has revealed it to us by his S.
       2:14 man without the S does not accept
       3: present, I am with you in s.
       6:19 body is a temple of the Holy S,
      12:13 baptized by one S into one body—
2Co   1:22 and put his S in our hearts
       3: 3 but with the S of the living God,
       3: 6 the letter kills, but the S gives life.
       3:17 Now the Lord is the S,
       5: 5 and has given us the S as a deposit,
       7: 1 that contaminates body and s,
Gal   3: 2 Did you receive the S
       5:16 by the S, and you will not gratify
       5:22 But the fruit of the S is love, joy,
       5:25 let us keep in step with the S.
       6: 8 from the S will reap eternal life.
Eph   1:13 with a seal, the promised Holy S,
       2:22 in which God lives by his S.
       4: 4 There is one body and one S—
       4:30 do not grieve the Holy S of God,
       5:18 Instead, be filled with the S.
       6:17 of salvation and the sword of the S,
Php   2: 2 being one in s and purpose.
1Th   5:23 May your whole s, soul
2Th   2:13 the sanctifying work of the S
1Ti   3:16 was vindicated by the S,
2Ti   1: 7 For God did not give us a s
Heb   2: 4 of the Holy S distributed according
       4:12 even to dividing soul and s,
      10:29 and who has insulted the S of grace
1Pe   3: 4 beauty of a gentle and quiet s.
2Pe   1:21 carried along by the Holy S.
1Jn   3:24 We know it by the S he gave us.
       4: 1 Dear friends, do not believe every s
       4:13 because he has given us of his S.
Jude   :20 holy faith and pray in the Holy S
Rev   2: 7 let him hear what the S says

SPIRIT'S* (SPIRIT)
1Co   2: 4 a demonstration of the S power,
1Th   5:19 not put out the S fire; do not treat

SPIRITS (SPIRIT)
1Co 12:10 to another distinguishing between s.
      14:32 The s of prophets are subject
1Jn   4: 1 test the s to see whether they are

SPIRITUAL (SPIRIT)
Ro   12: 1 to God—this is your s act of worship.
      12:11 but keep your s fervor, serving
1Co   2:13 expressing s truths in s words.
       3: 1 I could not address you as s but
      12: 1 Now about s gifts, brothers,
      14: 1 of love and eagerly desire s gifts,
      15:44 a natural body, it is raised a s body.
Gal   6: 1 you who are s should restore him
Eph   1: 3 with every s blessing in Christ.
       5:19 with psalms, hymns and s songs.
       6:12 and against the s forces of evil

1Pe   2: 2 newborn babies, crave pure s milk,
       2: 5 are being built into a s house

SPIRITUALLY (SPIRIT)
1Co   2:14 because they are s discerned.

SPIT
Mt   27:30 They s on him, and took the staff
Rev   3:16 I am about to s you out

SPLENDOR
1Ch 16:29 the LORD in the s of his holiness.
      29:11 the glory and the majesty and the s;
Job 37:22 of the north he comes in golden s;
Ps   29: 2 in the s of his holiness.
      45: 3 clothe yourself with s and majesty.
      96: 6 S and majesty are before him;
      96: 9 in the s of his holiness;
     104: 1 you are clothed with s and majesty.
     145: 5 of the glorious s of your majesty,
     145:12 and the glorious s of your kingdom.
     148:13 his s is above the earth
Pr   4: 9 and present you with a crown of s."
      16:31 Gray hair is a crown of s;
      20:29 gray hair the s of the old.
Isa   55: 5 for he has endowed you with s."
      60:21 for the display of my s.
      61: 3 the LORD for the display of his s.
      63: 1 Who is this, robed in s,
Hab   3: 4 His s was like the sunrise;
Mt   6:29 in all his s was dressed like one
Lk   9:31 appeared in glorious s, talking
2Th   2: 8 and destroy by the s of his coming.

SPOIL (SPOILS)
Ps   119:162 like one who finds great s.

SPOILS (SPOIL)
Isa   53:12 he will divide the s with the strong,
Jn   6:27 Do not work for food that s,

SPONTANEOUS*
Phm   :14 so that any favor you do will be s

SPOTLESS
2Pe   3:14 make every effort to be found s,

SPOTS (SPOTTED)
Jer   13:23 or the leopard its s?

SPOTTED (SPOTS)
Ge   30:32 and every s or speckled goat.

SPREAD (SPREADING SPREADS)
Ps   78:19 "Can God s a table in the desert?
Ac   6: 7 So the word of God s
      12:24 of God continued to increase and s.
      13:49 of the Lord s through the whole
      19:20 the word of the Lord s widely
2Th   3: 1 message of the Lord may s rapidly

SPREADING (SPREAD)
Pr   29: 5 is s a net for his feet.
1Th   3: 2 God's fellow worker in s the gospel

SPREADS (SPREAD)
Pr   10:18 and whoever s slander is a fool.

SPRING (SPRINGS WELLSPRING)
Jer   2:13 the s of living water,
Jn   4:14 in him a s of water welling up
Jas   3:12 can a salt s produce fresh water.

SPRINGS (SPRING)
2Pe   2:17 These men are s without water

SPRINKLE (SPRINKLED SPRINKLING)
Lev 16:14 and with his finger s it on the front

SPRINKLED (SPRINKLE)
Heb 10:22 having our hearts s to cleanse us

SPRINKLING (SPRINKLE)
1Pe   1: 2 to Jesus Christ and s by his blood:

SPROUT
Pr   23: 5 for they will surely s wings
Jer 33:15 I will make a righteous Branch s

SPUR*
Heb 10:24 how we may s one another

Pr   15: 5 A fool s his father's discipline,

SPY

Gal 2: 4 ranks to s on the freedom we have

SQUANDERED (SQUANDERS)

Lk 15: 13 there s his wealth in wild living.

SQUANDERS* (SQUANDERED)

Pr 29: 3 of prostitutes s his wealth.

SQUARE

Rev 21: 16 The city was laid out like a s,

STABILITY*

Pr 29: 4 By justice a king gives a country s,

STAFF

Ge 49: 10 the ruler's s from between his feet,
Ex 7: 12 Aaron's s swallowed up their staffs.
Nu 17: 6 and Aaron's s was among them.
Ps 23: 4 your rod and your s,

STAIN (STAINED)

Eph 5: 27 without s or wrinkle or any other

STAINED (STAIN)

Isa 63: 1 with his garments s crimson?

STAKES

Isa 54: 2 strengthen your s.

STAND (STANDING STANDS STOOD)

Ex 14: 13 S firm and you will see
Jos 10: 12 "O sun, s still over Gibeon,
2Ch 20: 17 s firm and see the deliverance
Job 19: 25 in the end he will s upon the earth.
Ps 1: 1 or s in the way of sinners
1: 5 Therefore the wicked will not s
24: 3 Who may s in his holy place?
33: 11 of the LORD s firm forever,
40: 2 and gave me a firm place to s.
76: 7 Who can s before you
93: 5 Your statutes s firm;
119:120 I s in awe of your laws.
130: 3 O Lord, who could s?
Ecc 5: 7 Therefore s in awe of God.
Isa 7: 9 If you do not s firm in your faith,
29: 23 will s in awe of the God of Israel.
Eze 22: 30 s before me in the gap on behalf
Hab 3: 2 I s in awe of your deeds, O LORD.
Zec 14: 4 On that day his feet will s
Mal 3: 2 Who can s when he appears?
Mt 12: 25 divided against itself will not s.
Ro 14: 4 for the Lord is able to make him s.
14: 10 we will all s before God's judgment
1Co 10: 13 out so that you can s up under it.
15: 58 Therefore, my dear brothers, s firm
16: 13 Be on your guard; s firm in the faith
Gal 5: 1 S firm, then, and do not let
Eph 6: 14 S firm then, with the belt
2Th 2: 15 s firm and hold to the teachings we
Jas 5: 8 You too, be patient and s firm,
Rev 3: 20 Here I am! I s at the door

STANDING (STAND)

Ex 3: 5 where you are s is holy ground."
Jos 5: 15 the place where you are s is holy."
Ru 2: 1 a man of s, whose name was Boaz.
4: 11 May you have s in Ephrathah
Lk 21: 19 By s firm you will gain life.
1Ti 3: 13 have served well gain an excellent s
1Pe 5: 9 Resist him, s firm in the faith,

STANDS (STAND)

Ps 89: 2 that your love s firm forever,
119: 89 it s firm in the heavens.
Pr 12: 7 the house of the righteous s firm.
Isa 40: 8 but the word of our God s forever."
Mt 10: 22 but he who s firm to the end will be
2Ti 2: 19 God's solid foundation s firm,
1Pe 1: 25 but the word of the Lord s forever

STAR (STARS)

Nu 24: 17 A s will come out of Jacob;
Isa 14: 12 O morning s, son of the dawn!
Mt 2: 2 We saw his s in the east
2Pe 1: 19 the morning s rises in your hearts.
Rev 2: 28 I will also give him the morning s.
22: 16 and the bright Morning S."

STARS (STAR)

Ge 1: 16 He also made the s.
Job 38: 7 while the morning s sang together
Da 12: 3 like the s for ever and ever.
Php 2: 15 in which you shine like s

STATURE

1Sa 2: 26 boy Samuel continued to grow in s
Lk 2: 52 And Jesus grew in wisdom and s,

STATUTES

Ps 19: 7 s of the LORD are trustworthy,
93: 5 Your s stand firm;
119: 2 Blessed are they who keep his s
119: 14 I rejoice in following your s
119: 24 Your s are my delight;
119: 36 Turn my heart toward your s
119: 99 for I meditate on your s.
119:111 Your s are my heritage forever;
119:125 that I may understand your s.
119:129 Your s are wonderful;
119:138 The s you have laid
119:152 Long ago I learned from your s
119:167 I obey your s,

STEADFAST*

Ps 51: 10 and renew a s spirit within me.
57: 7 My heart is s, O God,
57: 7 My heart is s;
108: 1 My heart is s, O God;
111: 8 They are s for ever and ever,
112: 7 his heart is s, trusting in the LORD
119: 5 Oh, that my ways were s
Isa 26: 3 him whose mind is s;
1Pe 5: 10 and make you strong, firm and s.

STEADY

Isa 35: 3 s the knees that give way;

STEAL (STOLEN)

Ex 20: 15 "You shall not s.
Lev 19: 11 "Do not s.
Dt 5: 19 "You shall not s.
Mt 19: 18 do not s, do not give false
Ro 13: 9 "Do not s,""Do not covet,"
Eph 4: 28 has been stealing must s no longer,

STEP (FOOTSTEPS STEPS)

Job 34: 21 he sees their every s.
Gal 5: 25 let us keep in s with the Spirit.

STEPHEN

Deacon (Ac 6:5). Arrested (Ac 6:8-15).
Speech to Sanhedrin (Ac 7). Stoned (Ac 7:54-
60; 22:20).

STEPS (STEP)

Ps 37: 23 he makes his s firm;
Pr 14: 15 prudent man gives thought to his s.
16: 9 but the LORD determines his s.
20: 24 A man's are directed
Jer 10: 23 it is not for man to direct his s.
1Pe 2: 21 that you should follow in his s.

STERN (STERNNESS)

Pr 15: 10 S discipline awaits him who leaves

STERNNESS* (STERN)

Ro 11: 22 and s of God: s to those who fell,

STICKS

Pr 18: 24 there is a friend who s closer

STIFF-NECKED (NECK)

Ex 34: 9 Although this is a s people,
Pr 29: 1 A man who remains s

STILL

Jos 10: 13 So the sun stood s,
Ps 37: 7 Be s before the LORD
46: 10 "Be s, and know that I am God;
89: 9 its waves mount up, you s them.
Zec 2: 13 Be s before the LORD, all mankind
Mk 4: 39 said to the waves, "Quiet! Be s!"

STIMULATE*

2Pe 3: 1 as reminders to s you

STING

1Co 15: 55 Where, O death, is your s?"

STINGY

Pr 28: 22 A s man is eager to get rich

STIRRED (STIRS)

Ps 45: 1 My heart is s by a noble theme

STIRS (STIRRED)

Pr 6: 19 and a man who s up dissension
10: 12 Hatred s up dissension,

Pr (continued)

Pr 15: 1 but a harsh word s up anger.
15: 18 hot-tempered man s up dissension,
16: 28 A perverse man s up dissension,
28: 25 A greedy man s up dissension,
29: 22 An angry man s up dissension,

STOLEN (STEAL)

Lev 6: 4 he must return what he has s
SS 4: 9 You have s my heart, my sister,

STOMACH

1Co 6: 13 Food for the s and the s for food"—
Php 3: 19 their god is their s, and their glory

STONE (CAPSTONE CORNERSTONE MILLSTONE STONED STONES)

Ex 24: 4 set up twelve s pillars representing
28: 10 on one s and the remaining six
34: 1 "Chisel out two s tablets like
Dt 4: 13 then wrote them on two s tablets.
19: 14 your neighbor's boundary s set up
1Sa 17: 50 the Philistine with a sling and a s,
Ps 91: 12 will not strike your foot against a s.
118: 22 The s the builders rejected
Pr 22: 28 not move an ancient boundary s
Isa 8: 14 a s that causes men to stumble
28: 16 "See, I lay a s in Zion,
Eze 11: 19 remove from them their heart of s
36: 26 remove from you your heart of s
Mt 7: 9 will give him a s? Or if he asks
21: 42 " 'The s the builders rejected
24: 2 not one s here will be left
Mk 16: 3 "Who will roll the s away
Lk 4: 3 tell this s to become bread."
Jn 8: 7 the first to throw a s at her."
Ac 4: 11 " 'the s you builders rejected,
Ro 9: 32 stumbled over the "stumbling s."
2Co 3: 3 not on tablets of s but on tablets
1Pe 2: 6 "See, I lay a s in Zion,
Rev 2: 17 also give him a white s

STONED (STONE)

2Co 11: 25 once I was s, three times I was
Heb 11: 37 They were s; they were sawed

STONES (STONE)

Ex 28: 21 are to be twelve s, one for each
Jos 4: 3 to take up twelve s from the middle
1Sa 17: 40 chose five smooth s
Mt 3: 9 out of these s God can raise up
1Co 3: 12 silver, costly s, wood, hay or straw,
1Pe 2: 5 also, like living s, are being built

STOOD (STAND)

Jos 10: 13 So the sun s still,
Lk 22: 28 You are those who have s by me
2Ti 4: 17 But the Lord s at my side
Jas 1: 12 because when he has s the test,

STOOP (STOOPS)

2Sa 22: 36 you s down to make me great.

STOOPS (STOOP)

Ps 113: 6 who s down to look

STOP

Job 37: 14 s and consider God's wonders.
Isa 1: 13 S bringing meaningless offerings!
1: 16 S doing wrong,
2: 22 S trusting in man,
Jer 32: 40 I will never s doing good to them,
Mk 9: 39 "Do not s him," Jesus said.
Jn 6: 43 "S grumbling among yourselves,"
7: 24 S judging by mere appearances,
20: 27 S doubting and believe."
Ro 14: 13 Therefore let us s passing judgment
1Co 14: 20 Brothers, s thinking like children.

STORE (STORED)

Pr 2: 1 and s up my commands within you,
7: 1 and s up my commands within you.
10: 14 Wise men s up knowledge,
Isa 33: 6 a rich s of salvation and wisdom
Mt 6: 19 not s up for yourselves treasures
6: 26 or reap or s away in barns,
2Ti 4: 8 Now there is in s for me the crown

STORED (STORE)

Lk 6: 45 out of the good s up in his heart,
Col 1: 5 from the hope that is s up for you

STOREHOUSE (HOUSE)

Mal 3: 10 Bring the whole tithe into the s,

STORIES*

2Pe	1:16	did not follow cleverly invented s
	2:3	you with s they have made up.

STORM

Job	38:1	LORD answered Job out of the s.
Ps	107:29	He stilled the s to a whisper;
Lk	8:24	the s subsided, and all was calm.

STOUTHEARTED* (HEART)

Ps	138:3	you made me bold and s.

STRAIGHT

Ps	27:11	lead me in a s path
	107:7	He led them by a s way
Pr	2:13	who leave the s paths
	3:6	and he will make your paths s.
	4:11	and lead you along s paths.
	4:25	Let your eyes look s ahead,
	11:5	of the blameless makes a s way
	15:21	of understanding keeps a s course.
Isa	40:3	make s in the wilderness
Mt	3:3	make s paths for him.' "
Jn	1:23	'Make s the way for the Lord.' "
2Pe	2:15	They have left the s way

STRAIN (STRAINING)

Mt	23:24	You s out a gnat but swallow

STRAINING (STRAIN)

Php	3:13	and s toward what is ahead,

STRANGE (STRANGER STRANGERS)

Isa	28:11	with foreign lips and s tongues
1Co	14:21	"Through men of s tongues
1Pe	4:4	They think it s that you do not

STRANGER (STRANGE)

Ps	119:19	I am a s on earth;
Mt	25:35	I was a s and you invited me in,
Jn	10:5	But they will never follow a s;

STRANGERS (STRANGE)

Heb	13:2	Do not forget to entertain s,
1Pe	2:11	as aliens and s in the world,

STRAW

Isa	11:7	and the lion will eat s like the ox.
1Co	3:12	silver, costly stones, wood, hay or s

STRAYED (STRAYS)

Ps	119:176	I have s like a lost sheep.
Jer	31:19	After I s,

STRAYS (STRAYED)

Pr	21:16	A man who s from the path
Eze	34:16	for the lost and bring back the s.

STREAM (STREAMS)

Am	5:24	righteousness like a never-failing s!

STREAMS (STREAM)

Ps	1:3	He is like a tree planted by s
	46:4	is a river whose s make glad
Ecc	1:7	All s flow into the sea,
Jn	7:38	s of living water will flow

STREET

Mt	6:5	on the s corners to be seen by men.
	22:9	Go to the s corners and invite
Rev	21:21	The great s of the city was of pure gold,

STRENGTH (STRONG)

Ex	15:2	The LORD is my s and my song;
Dt	4:37	by his Presence and his great s,
	6:5	all your soul and with all your s.
Jdg	16:15	told me the secret of your great s."
2Sa	22:33	It is God who arms me with s
2Ki	23:25	with all his soul and with all his s,
1Ch	16:11	Look to the LORD and his s;
	16:28	ascribe to the LORD glory and s,
	29:12	In your hands are s and power
Ne	8:10	for the joy of the LORD is your s."
Ps	18:1	I love you, O LORD, my s.
	21:13	Be exalted, O LORD, in your s;
	28:7	The LORD is my s and my shield;
	29:11	The LORD gives to his people;
	33:16	no warrior escapes by his great s.
	46:1	is our refuge and s,
	59:17	O my S, I sing praise to you;
	65:6	having armed yourself with s,
	73:26	but God is the s of my heart
	84:5	Blessed are those whose s is in you,

Ps	96:7	ascribe to the LORD glory and s.
	105:4	Look to the LORD and his s;
	118:14	The LORD is my s and my song;
	147:10	not in the s of the horse,
Pr	24:5	a man of knowledge increases s;
	30:25	Ants are creatures of little s,
Isa	12:2	the LORD, is my s and my song;
	31:1	and in the great s of their horsemen
	40:26	of his great power and mighty s,
	40:31	will renew their s.
	63:1	forward in the greatness of his s?
Jer	9:23	or the strong man boast of his s
Mic	5:4	flock in the s of the LORD,
Hab	3:19	The Sovereign LORD is my s;
Mk	12:30	all your mind and with all your s.'
1Co	1:25	of God is stronger than man's s.
Eph	1:19	is like the working of his mighty s,
Php	4:13	through him who gives me s.
Heb	11:34	whose weakness was turned to s;
1Pe	4:11	it with the s God provides,

STRENGTHEN (STRONG)

2Ch	16:9	to s those whose hearts are fully
Ps	119:28	s me according to your word.
Isa	35:3	S the feeble hands,
	41:10	I will s you and help you;
Lk	22:32	have turned back, s your brothers."
Eph	3:16	of his glorious riches he may s you
1Th	3:13	May he s your hearts
2Th	2:17	and s you in every good deed
Heb	12:12	s your feeble arms and weak knees.

STRENGTHENED (STRONG)

Col	1:11	being s with all power according
Heb	13:9	good for our hearts to be s by grace,

STRENGTHENING (STRONG)

1Co	14:26	done for the s of the church.

STRETCHES

Ps	104:2	he s out the heavens like a tent

STRICKEN (STRIKE)

Isa	53:8	of my people he was s.

STRICT

1Co	9:25	in the games goes into s training.

STRIFE (STRIVE)

Pr	17:1	than a house full of feasting, with s.
	20:3	It is to a man's honor to avoid s,
	22:10	out the mocker, and out goes s;
	30:33	so stirring up anger produces s."
1Ti	6:4	s, malicious talk, evil suspicions

STRIKE (STRIKES STROKE)

Ge	3:15	and you will s his heel."
Zec	13:7	"S the shepherd,
Mt	4:6	so that you will not s your foot
	26:31	" 'I will s the shepherd,

STRIKES (STRIKE)

Mt	5:39	If someone s you on the right

STRIPS

Lk	2:12	You will find a baby wrapped in s
Jn	20:5	in at the s of linen lying there

STRIVE* (STRIFE)

Ac	24:16	I s always to keep my conscience
1Ti	4:10	(and for this we labor and s),

STROKE

Mt	5:18	the smallest letter, not the least s

STRONG (STRENGTH STRENGTHEN STRENGTHENED STRENGTHENING STRONGER)

Dt	3:24	your greatness and your s hand.
	31:6	Be s and courageous.
Jos	1:6	"Be s and courageous,
Jdg	5:21	March on, my soul; be s!
2Sa	10:12	Be s and let us fight bravely
1Ki	2:2	"So be s, show yourself a man,
1Ch	28:20	"Be s and courageous,
2Ch	32:7	them with these words: "Be s
Ps	24:8	The LORD s and mighty,
	31:2	a fortress to save me.
	62:11	that you, O God, are s,
Pr	18:10	The name of the LORD is a s tower
	31:17	her arms are s for her tasks.
Ecc	9:11	or the battle to the s,
SS	8:6	for love is as s as death,
Isa	35:4	"Be s, do not fear;
	53:12	he will divide the spoils with the s,

Jer	9:23	or the s man boast of his strength
	50:34	Yet their Redeemer is s;
Hag	2:4	Be s, all you people of the land,'
Mt	12:29	can anyone enter a s man's house
Lk	2:40	And the child grew and became s;
Ro	15:1	We who are s ought to bear
1Co	1:8	He will keep you s to the end,
	1:27	things of the world to shame the s.
	16:13	in the faith; be men of courage; be s
2Co	12:10	For when I am weak, then I am s.
Eph	6:10	be s in the Lord and in his mighty
2Ti	2:1	be s in the grace that is
1Pe	5:10	restore you and make you s,

STRONGER (STRONG)

Dt	4:38	before you nations greater and s
1Co	1:25	of God is s than man's strength.

STRONGHOLD (STRONGHOLDS)

2Sa	22:3	He is my s, my refuge and my
Ps	9:9	a s in times of trouble.
	18:2	the horn of my salvation, my s.
	27:1	The LORD is the s of my life—
	144:2	my s and my deliverer,

STRONGHOLDS (STRONGHOLD)

Zep	3:6	their s are demolished.
2Co	10:4	have divine power to demolish s.

STRUGGLE (STRUGGLED STRUGGLING)

Ro	15:30	me in my s by praying to God
Eph	6:12	For our s is not against flesh
Heb	12:4	In your s against sin, you have not

STRUGGLED (STRUGGLE)

Ge	32:28	because you have s with God

STRUGGLING* (STRUGGLE)

Col	1:29	To this end I labor, s
	2:1	to know how much I am s for you

STUDENT (STUDY)

Mt	10:24	"A s is not above his teacher,

STUDY (STUDENT)

Ezr	7:10	Ezra had devoted himself to the s
Ecc	12:12	and much s wearies the body.
Jn	5:39	You diligently s the Scriptures

STUMBLE (STUMBLES STUMBLING)

Ps	37:24	though he s, he will not fall,
	119:165	and nothing can make them s.
Pr	3:23	and your foot will not s;
Isa	8:14	a stone that causes men to s
Jer	13:16	before your feet s
	31:9	a level path where they will not s,
Eze	7:19	for it has made them s into sin.
Hos	14:9	but the rebellious s in them.
Mal	2:8	teaching have caused many to s;
Jn	11:9	A man who walks by day will not s,
Ro	9:33	in Zion a stone that causes men to s
	14:20	that causes someone else to s.
1Co	10:32	Do not cause anyone to s,
Jas	3:2	We all s in many ways.
1Pe	2:8	and, "A stone that causes men to s
1Jn	2:10	nothing in him to make him s.

STUMBLES (STUMBLE)

Pr	24:17	when he s, do not let your heart
Jn	11:10	is when he walks by night that he s,
Jas	2:10	and yet s at just one point is guilty

STUMBLING

Lev	19:14	put a s block in front of the blind,
Ps	56:13	and my feet from s,
Mt	16:23	Satan! You are a s block to me;
Ro	9:32	They stumbled over the "s stone."
	11:9	a s block and a retribution for them
	14:13	up your mind not to put any s block
1Co	1:23	a s block to Jews and foolishness
	8:9	freedom does not become a s block
2Co	6:3	We put no s block in anyone's path,

STUMP

Isa	6:13	so the holy seed will be the s
	11:1	up from the s of Jesse;

STUPID

Pr	12:1	but he who hates correction is s.
2Ti	2:23	to do with foolish and s arguments,

STUPOR

Ro	11:8	"God gave them a spirit of s,

SUBDUE (SUBDUED)

Ge 1:28 in number; fill the earth and s it.

SUBDUED (SUBDUE)

Jos 10:40 So Joshua s the whole region,
Ps 47: 3 He s nations under us,

SUBJECT (SUBJECTED)

Mt   5:22 angry with his brother will be s
1Co 14:32 of prophets are s to the control
    15:28 then the Son himself will be made s
Tit   2: 5 and to be s to their husbands,
      2: 9 slaves to be s to their masters
      3: 1 Remind the people to be s to rulers

SUBJECTED (SUBJECT)

Ro   8:20 For the creation was s

SUBMISSION (SUBMIT)

1Co 14:34 but must be in s, as the Law says.
1Ti   2:11 learn in quietness and full s.

SUBMISSIVE (SUBMIT)

Jas   3:17 then peace-loving, considerate, s,
1Pe   3: 1 in the same way be s
      5: 5 in the same way be s

SUBMIT (SUBMISSION SUBMISSIVE SUBMITS)

Ro 13: 1 Everyone must s himself
    13: 5 necessary to s to the authorities,
1Co 16:16 to s to such as these
Eph   5:21 S to one another out of reverence
Col   3:18 Wives, s to your husbands,
Heb 12: 9 How much more should we s
    13:17 Obey your leaders and s
Jas   4: 7 S yourselves, then, to God.
1Pe   2:18 s yourselves to your masters

SUBMITS* (SUBMIT)

Eph   5:24 Now as the church s to Christ,

SUBTRACT*

Dt   4: 2 what I command you and do not s

SUCCEED (SUCCESS SUCCESSFUL)

Ps 20: 4 and make all your plans s.
Pr 15:22 but with many advisers they s.
    16: 3 and your plans will s.
    21:30 that can s against the LORD.

SUCCESS (SUCCEED)

Ge 39:23 and gave him s in whatever he did.
1Sa 18:14 In everything he did he had great s,
1Ch 12:18 S, s to you, and s
    22:13 you will have s if you are careful
2Ch 26: 5 the LORD, God gave him s.
Ecc 10:10 but skill will bring s.

SUCCESSFUL (SUCCEED)

Jos   1: 7 that you may be s wherever you go.
2Ki 18: 7 he was s in whatever he undertook
2Ch 20:20 in his prophets and you will be s."

SUFFER (SUFFERED SUFFERING SUFFERINGS SUFFERS)

Job 36:15 those who s he delivers
Isa 53:10 to crush him and cause him to s,
Mk   8:31 the Son of Man must s many things
Lk 24:26 the Christ have to s these things
    24:46 The Christ will s and rise
2Co 1: 6 of the same sufferings we s.
Php 1:29 to s for him, since you are going
Heb 9:26 would have had to s many times
1Pe 3:17 to s for doing good
      4:16 However, if you s as a Christian,

SUFFERED (SUFFER)

Heb 2: 9 and honor because he s death,
      2:18 Because he himself s
1Pe 2:21 Christ s for you, leaving you
      4: 1 he who has s in his body is done

SUFFERING (SUFFER)

Job 36:15 who suffer he delivers in their s;
Ps 22:24 the s of the afflicted one;
Isa 53: 3 of sorrows, and familiar with s.
    53:11 After the s of his soul,
La   1:12 Is any s like my s
Ac   5:41 worthy of s disgrace for the Name.
Ro   5: 3 know that s produces
2Ti   1: 8 But join with me in s for the gospel,
Heb 2:10 of their salvation perfect through s.
    13: 3 as if you yourselves were s.

1Pe   4:12 at the painful trial you are s.

SUFFERINGS (SUFFER)

Ro   5: 3 but we also rejoice in our s,
      8:17 share in his s in order that we may
      8:18 that our present s are not worth
2Co 1: 5 as the s of Christ flow
Php 3:10 the fellowship of sharing in his s,
1Pe   4:13 rejoice that you participate in the s
      5: 9 are undergoing the same kind of s.

SUFFERS (SUFFER)

Pr 13:20 but a companion of fools s harm.
1Co 12:26 If one part s, every part s with it;

SUFFICIENT

2Co 12: 9 said to me, "My grace is s for you,

SUITABLE

Ge   2:18 I will make a helper s for him."

SUMMED* (SUMS)

Ro 13: 9 there may be, are s up
Gal   5:14 The entire law is s up

SUMMONS

Ps 50: 1 speaks and s the earth
Isa 45: 3 God of Israel, who s you by name.

SUMS* (SUMMED)

Mt   7:12 for this s up the Law

SUN (SUNRISE)

Jos 10:13 So the s stood still,
Jdg 5:31 may they who love you be like the s
Ps 84:11 For the LORD God is a s
    121: 6 the s will not harm you by day,
    136: 8 the s to govern the day,
Ecc 1: 9 there is nothing new under the s.
Isa 60:19 The s will no more be your light
Mal 4: 2 the s of righteousness will rise
Mt   5:45 He causes his s to rise on the evil
    13:43 the righteous will shine like the s
    17: 2 His face shone like the s,
Lk 23:45 for the s stopped shining.
Eph 4:26 Do not let the s go
Rev 1:16 His face was like the s shining
    21:23 The city does not need the s

SUNG (SING)

Mt 26:30 When they had s a hymn, they

SUNRISE (SUN)

2Sa 23: 4 he is like the light of morning at s
Hab 3: 4 His splendor was like the s;

SUPERIOR

Heb 1: 4 he became as much s to the angels
      8: 6 ministry Jesus has received is as s

SUPERVISION

Gal   3:25 longer under the s of the law.

SUPPER

Lk 22:20 after the s he took the cup, saying,
1Co 11:25 after the s he took the cup,
Rev 19: 9 to the wedding s of the Lamb!' "

SUPPLIED (SUPPLY)

Ac 20:34 of mine have s my own needs
Php 4:18 and even more; I am amply s.

SUPPLY (SUPPLIED SUPPLYING)

2Co 8:14 your plenty will s what they need,
1Th 3:10 and s what is lacking in your faith.

SUPPLYING* (SUPPLY)

2Co 9:12 you perform is not only s the needs

SUPPORT (SUPPORTED SUPPORTING)

Ps 18:18 but the LORD was my s.
Ro 11:18 consider this: You do not s the root
1Co 9:12 If others have this right of s

SUPPORTED (SUPPORT)

Ps 94:18 your love, O LORD, s me.
Col   2:19 s and held together by its ligaments

SUPPORTING (SUPPORT)

Eph 4:16 held together by every s ligament,

SUPPRESS*

Ro   1:18 wickedness of men who s the truth

SUPREMACY* (SUPREME)

Col   1:18 in everything he might have the s.

SUPREME (SUPREMACY)

Pr   4: 7 Wisdom is s; therefore get wisdom.

SURE

Nu 28:31 Be s the animals are without defect
    32:23 you may be s that your sin will find
Dt   6:17 Be s to keep the commands
    14:22 Be s to set aside a tenth
    29:18 make s there is no root
Jos 23:13 then you may be s that the LORD
1Sa 12:24 But be s to fear the LORD
Ps 19: 9 The ordinances of the LORD are s
    132:11 a s oath that he will not revoke:
Pr 27:23 Be s you know the condition
Isa 28:16 cornerstone for a s foundation:
Eph 5: 5 of this you can be s: No immoral,
Heb 11: 1 faith is being s of what we hope for
2Pe 1:10 to make your calling and election s.

SURFACE

2Co 10: 7 You are looking only on the s

SURPASS* (SURPASSED SURPASSES SURPASSING)

Pr 31:29 but you s them all."

SURPASSED* (SURPASS)

Jn   1:15 "He who comes after me has s me
      1:30 man who comes after me has s me

SURPASSES* (SURPASS)

Pr   8:19 what I yield s choice silver.
Mt   5:20 unless your righteousness s that
Eph 3:19 to know this love that s knowledge

SURPASSING* (SURPASS)

Ps 150: 2 praise him for his s greatness.
2Co 3:10 in comparison with the s glory.
      9:14 of the s grace God has given you.
Php 3: 8 the s greatness of knowing Christ

SURPRISE (SURPRISED)

1Th 5: 4 that this day should s you like

SURPRISED (SURPRISE)

1Pe 4:12 do not be s at the painful trial you
1Jn 3:13 Do not be s, my brothers,

SURRENDER

1Co 13: 3 and s my body to the flames,

SURROUND (SURROUNDED SURROUNDS)

Ps   5:12 you s them with your favor
    32: 7 and s me with songs of deliverance.
    89: 7 awesome than all who s him.
    125: 2 As the mountains s Jerusalem,
Jer 31:22 a woman will s a man."

SURROUNDED (SURROUND)

Heb 12: 1 since we are s by such a great cloud

SURROUNDS* (SURROUND)

Ps 32:10 the man who trusts in him.
    89: 8 and your faithfulness s you.
    125: 2 so the LORD s his people

SUSA

Ezr 4: 9 and Babylon, the Elamites of S,
Ne   1: 1 while I was in the citadel of S,

SUSPENDS*

Job 26: 7 he s the earth over nothing.

SUSPICIONS*

1Ti   6: 4 evil s and constant friction

SUSTAIN (SUSTAINING SUSTAINS)

Ps 55:22 and he will s you;
Isa 46: 4 I am he, I am he who will s you.

SUSTAINING* (SUSTAIN)

Heb 1: 3 s all things by his powerful word.

SUSTAINS (SUSTAIN)

Ps 18:35 and your right hand s me;
    146: 9 and s the fatherless and the widow,
    147: 6 The LORD s the humble
Isa 50: 4 to know the word that s the weary.

SWALLOW (SWALLOWED)

Isa 25: 8 he will s up death forever.

Jnh 1: 17 provided a great fish to s Jonah.
Mt 23: 24 You strain out a gnat but s a camel.

SWALLOWED (SWALLOW)

1Co 15: 54 "Death has been s up in victory."
2Co   5: 4 so that what is mortal may be s up

SWAYED

Mt 11: 7 A reed s by the wind? If not,
    22: 16 You aren't s by men, because you
2Ti   3: 6 are s by all kinds of evil desires,

SWEAR (SWORE SWORN)

Lev 19: 12 " 'Do not s falsely by my name
Ps   24: 4 or s by what is false.
Isa 45: 23 by me every tongue will s.
Mt   5: 34 Do not s at all: either by heaven,
Jas   5: 12 Above all, my brothers, do not s—

SWEAT*

Ge   3: 19 By the s of your brow
Lk   22: 44 his s was like drops of blood falling

SWEET (SWEETER SWEETNESS)

Job 20: 12 "Though evil is s in his mouth
Ps 119:103 How s are your words
Pr   9: 17 "Stolen water is s;
    13: 19 A longing fulfilled is s to the soul,
    16: 24 s to the soul and healing
    20: 17 by fraud tastes s to a man,
    24: 14 also that wisdom is s to your soul;
Ecc   5: 12 The sleep of a laborer is s,
Isa   5: 20 and s for bitter.
Eze   3: 3 it tasted as s as honey in my mouth.
Rev 10: 10 It tasted as s as honey in my mouth

SWEETER (SWEET)

Ps   19: 10 they are s than honey,
   119:103 s than honey to my mouth!

SWEETNESS* (SWEET)

SS   4: 11 Your lips drop s as the honeycomb.
      5: 16 His mouth is s itself;

SWEPT

Mt   12: 44 finds the house unoccupied, s clean

SWERVE*

Pr   5: 6 do not forget my words or s
      4: 27 Do not s to the right or the left;

SWIFT

Pr   1: 16 they are s to shed blood.
Ecc   9: 11 The race is not to the s
Isa 59: 7 they are s to shed innocent blood.
Ro   3: 15 "Their feet are s to shed blood;
2Pe   2: 1 bringing s destruction

SWINDLER* (SWINDLERS)

1Co   5: 11 or a slanderer, a drunkard or a s.

SWINDLERS* (SWINDLER)

1Co   5: 10 or the greedy and s, or idolaters.
      6: 10 s will inherit the kingdom of God.

SWORD (SWORDS)

Ge   3: 24 and a flaming s flashing back
Dt   32: 41 when I sharpen my flashing s
Jos   5: 13 of him with a drawn s in his hand.
1Sa 17: 45 "You come against me with s
    17: 47 here will know that it is not by s
    31: 4 so Saul took his own s and fell on it.
2Sa 11: 10 therefore, the s will never depart
Ps   44: 6 my s does not bring me victory;
    45: 3 Gird your s upon your side,
Pr   12: 18 Reckless words pierce like a s,
Isa   2: 4 Nation will not take up s
Mic   4: 3 Nation will not take up s
Mt   10: 34 come to bring peace, but a s.
    26: 52 all who draw the s will die by the s.
Lk   2: 35 a s will pierce your own soul too."
Ro   13: 4 for he does not bear the s
Eph   6: 17 of salvation and the s of the Spirit,
Heb   4: 12 Sharper than any double-edged s,
Rev   1: 16 came a sharp double-edged s
    19: 15 Out of his mouth comes a sharp s

SWORDS (SWORD)

Ps   64: 3 who sharpen their tongues like s
Isa   2: 4 They will beat their s
Joel 3: 10 Beat your plowshares into s

SWORE (SWEAR)

Heb   6: 13 for him to swear by, he s by himself

SWORN (SWEAR)

Ps 110: 4 The LORD has s
Eze 20: 42 the land I had s with uplifted hand
Heb   7: 21 "The Lord has s

SYCAMORE-FIG (FIG)

Am   7: 14 and I also took care of s trees.
Lk   19: 4 and climbed a s tree to see him,

SYMBOLIZES*

1Pe   3: 21 this water s baptism that now saves

SYMPATHETIC* (SYMPATHY)

1Pe   3: 8 in harmony with one another; be s.

SYMPATHIZED* (SYMPATHY)

Heb 10: 34 You s with those in prison

SYMPATHY (SYMPATHETIC SYMPATHIZED)

Ps   69: 20 I looked for s, but there was none,

SYNAGOGUE

Lk   4: 16 the Sabbath day he went into the s.
Ac   17: 2 custom was, Paul went into the s,

TABERNACLE (TABERNACLES)

Ex   40: 34 the glory of the LORD filled the t.
Heb   8: 2 the true t set up by the Lord,
      9: 11 and more perfect t that is not
      9: 21 sprinkled with the blood both the t
Rev 15: 5 that is, the t of the Testimony.

TABERNACLES (TABERNACLE)

Lev 23: 34 the LORD's Feast of T begins.
Dt   16: 16 Feast of Weeks and the Feast of T.
Zec 14: 16 and to celebrate the Feast of T.

TABLE (TABLES)

Ex   25: 23 "Make a t of acacia wood—
Ps   23: 5 You prepare a t before me

TABLES (TABLE)

Jn   2: 15 changers and overturned their t.
Ac   6: 2 word of God in order to wait on t.

TABLET (TABLETS)

Pr   3: 3 write them on the t of your heart.
      7: 3 write them on the t of your heart.

TABLETS (TABLET)

Ex   31: 18 he gave him the two t
Dt   10: 5 and put the t in the ark I had made,
2Co   3: 3 not on t of stone but on t

TAKE (TAKEN TAKES TAKING TOOK)

Ge   5: 17 land to t possession of it."
    22: 17 Your descendants will t possession
Ex   3: 5 "T off your sandals,
    21: 23 you are to t life for life, eye for eye,
    22: 22 "Do not t advantage of a widow
Lev 10: 17 given to you to t away the guilt
    25: 14 do not t advantage of each other.
Nu   13: 30 and t possession of the land,
Dt   1: 8 and t possession of the land that
    12: 32 do not add to it or t away from it.
    31: 26 "T this Book of the Law
1Sa   8: 11 He will t your sons and make them
1Ch 17: 13 I will never t my love away
Job 23: 10 But he knows the way that I t;
Ps   2: 12 Blessed are all who t refuge in him.
    25: 18 and t away all my sins.
    27: 14 be strong and t heart
    31: 24 Be strong, and t heart
    49: 17 for he will t nothing with him
    51: 11 or t your Holy Spirit from me.
    73: 24 afterward you will t me into glory.
   118: 8 It is better to t refuge in the LORD
Pr   22: 23 for the LORD will t up their case
Isa 62: 4 for the LORD will t delight in you,
Eze   3: 10 and t to heart all the words I speak
    33: 11 I t no pleasure in the death
Mt   10: 38 anyone who does not t his cross
    11: 29 T my yoke upon you and learn
    16: 24 deny himself and t up his cross
    26: 26 saying, "T and eat; this is my body
Mk   14: 36 T this cup from me.
1Ti   6: 12 T hold of the eternal life

TAKEN (TAKE)

Ge   2: 23 for she was t out of man."
Lev   6: 4 must return what he has stolen or t
Nu   8: 16 I have t them as my own in place
    19: 3 it is to be t outside the camp
Ecc   3: 14 added to it and nothing t from it.

TAUGHT (TEACH)

Isa   6: 7 your guilt is t away and your sin
Zec   3: 4 "See, I have t away your sin,
Mt   13: 12 even what he has will be t from him
    24: 40 one will be t and the other left.
    26: 39 may this cup be t from me.
Mk   16: 19 he was t up into heaven
Ac   1: 9 he was t up before their very eyes,
Ro   5: 13 But sin is not t into account
1Ti   3: 16 was t up in glory.

TAKES (TAKE)

1Ki 20: 11 should not boast like one who t it
Ps   5: 4 You are not a God who t pleasure
     34: 8 blessed is the man who t refuge
Lk   6: 30 and if anyone t what belongs to you
Jn   1: 29 who t away the sin of the world!
    10: 18 No one t it from me, but I lay it
Rev 22: 19 And if anyone t words away

TAKING (TAKE)

Ac   15: 14 by t from the Gentiles a people
Php   2: 7 t the very nature of a servant,

TALENT

Mt   25: 15 to another one t, each according

TALES*

1Ti   4: 7 with godless myths and old wives' t

TALL

1Sa 17: 4 He was over nine feet t.
1Ch 11: 23 who was seven and a half feet t.

TAMAR

1. Wife of Judah's sons Er and Onan (Ge 38:
1-10). Tricked Judah into fathering children
when he refused her his third son (Ge 38:11-30).
2. Daughter of David, raped by Amnon (2Sa
13).

TAMBOURINE

Ps 150: 4 praise him with t and dancing,

TAME* (TAMED)

Jas   3: 8 but no man can t the tongue.

TAMED* (TAME)

Jas   3: 7 the sea are being t and have been t

TARSHISH

Jnh   1: 3 from the LORD and headed for T.

TARSUS

Ac   9: 11 ask for a man from T named Saul,

TASK (TASKS)

1Ch 29: 1 The t is great, because this palatial
Mk   13: 34 each with his assigned t.
Ac   20: 24 complete the t the Lord Jesus has
1Co   3: 5 the Lord has assigned to each his t
2Co   2: 16 And who is equal to such a t?
1Ti   3: 1 an overseer, he desires a noble t.

TASKS (TASK)

Pr   31: 17 her arms are strong for her t.

TASTE (TASTED TASTY)

Ps   34: 8 T and see that the LORD is good;
   119:103 sweet are your words to my t.
Pr   24: 13 from the comb is sweet to your t.
SS   2: 3 and his fruit is sweet to my t.
Col   2: 21 Do not t! Do not touch!"?
Heb   2: 9 the grace of God he might t death

TASTED (TASTE)

Eze   3: 3 it t as sweet as honey in my mouth.
1Pe   2: 3 now that you have t that the Lord
Rev 10: 10 It t as sweet as honey in my mouth.

TASTY (TASTE)

Ge   27: 4 Prepare me the kind of t food I like

TATTOO*

Lev 19: 28 or put t marks on yourselves.

TAUGHT (TEACH)

1Ki   4: 33 He also t about animals and birds,
2Ki 17: 28 t them how to worship the LORD.
2Ch 17: 9 They t throughout Judah,
Ps 119:102 for you yourself have t me.
Pr   4: 4 he t me and said,
    31: 1 an oracle his mother t him.
Isa 29: 13 is made up only of rules t by men.
    50: 1 ear to listen like one being t.
Mt   7: 29 he t as one who had authority,

TAX

Mt 15: 9 their teachings are but rules *t*
Lk 4: 15 He *t* in their synagogues,
Ac 20: 20 have *t* you publicly and from house
1Co 2: 13 but in words *t* by the Spirit,
Gal 1: 12 nor was I *t* it; rather, I received it
1Ti 1: 20 to Satan to be *t* not to blaspheme.
1Jn 2: 27 just as it has *t* you, remain in him.

TAX (TAXES)

Mt 11: 19 a friend of *t* collectors and "sinners
17: 24 of the two-drachma *t* came to Peter

TAXES (TAX)

Mt 22: 17 Is it right to pay *t* to Caesar or not
Ro 13: 7 If you owe *t*, pay *t*; if revenue,

TEACH (TAUGHT TEACHER TEACHERS TEACHES TEACHING TEACHINGS)

Ex 4: 12 and will *t* you what to say."
18: 20 *T* them the decrees and laws,
33: 13 *t* me your ways so I may know you
Lev 10: 11 and you must *t* the Israelites all
Dt 4: 9 *T* them to your children
6: 1 me to *t* you to observe
8: 3 to *t* you that man does not live
11: 19 *T* them to your children, talking
1Sa 12: 23 I will *t* you the way that is good
1Ki 8: 36 *T* them the right way to live,
Job 12: 7 ask the animals, and they will *t* you
Ps 32: 8 *t* you in the way you should go;
34: 11 I will *t* you the fear of the LORD.
51: 13 I will *t* transgressors your ways,
78: 5 forefathers to *t* their children,
90: 12 *T* us to number our days aright,
119: 33 *T* me, O LORD, to follow your
143: 10 *T* me to do your will,
Pr 9: 9 *t* a righteous man and he will add
Jer 31: 34 No longer will a man *t* his neighbor
Mic 4: 2 He will *t* us his ways.
Lk 11: 1 said to him, "Lord, *t* us to pray.
12: 12 for the Holy Spirit will *t* you
Jn 14: 26 will *t* you all things and will remind
Ro 2: 21 who *t* others, do you not *t* yourself?
15: 4 in the past was written to *t* us,
1Ti 2: 12 I do not permit a woman to *t*
3: 2 respectable, hospitable, able to *t*,
2Ti 2: 2 also be qualified to *t* others.
2: 24 kind to everyone, able to *t*,
Tit 2: 1 You must *t* what is in accord
2: 15 then, are the things you should *t*
Heb 8: 11 No longer will a man *t* his neighbor
Jas 3: 1 know that we who *t* will be judged
1Jn 2: 27 you do not need anyone to *t* you.

TEACHER (TEACH)

Ecc 1: 1 The words of the *T*, son of David,
Mt 10: 24 "A student is not above his *t*,
13: 52 "Therefore every *t*
23: 10 Nor are you to be called '*t*,'
Lk 6: 40 A student is not above his *t*,
Jn 3: 2 we know you are a *t* who has come
13: 14 and *T*, have washed your feet.

TEACHERS (TEACH)

Ps 119: 99 I have more insight than all my *t*,
Pr 5: 13 I would not obey my *t*
Lk 20: 46 "Beware of the *t* of the law.
1Co 12: 28 third *t*, then workers of miracles,
Eph 4: 11 and some to be pastors and *t*,
2Ti 4: 3 around them a great number of *t*
Heb 5: 12 by this time you ought to be *t*,
Jas 3: 1 you should presume to be *t*,
2Pe 2: 1 as there will be false *t* among you.

TEACHES (TEACH)

Ps 25: 9 and *t* them his way.
94: 10 Does he who *t* man lack
Pr 15: 33 of the LORD *t* a man wisdom,
Isa 48: 17 who *t* you what is best for you,
Mt 5: 19 *t* these commands will be called
1Ti 6: 3 If anyone *t* false doctrines
Tit 2: 12 It *t* us to say "No" to ungodliness
1Jn 2: 27 his anointing *t* you about all things

TEACHING (TEACH)

Ezr 7: 10 to *t* its decrees and laws in Israel.
Pr 1: 8 and do not forsake your mother's *t*.
3: 1 My son, do not forget my *t*,
6: 23 this *t* is a light,
Mt 28: 20 *t* them to obey everything I have
Jn 7: 17 whether my *t* comes from God or
8: 31 to my *t*, you are really my disciples.
14: 23 loves me, he will obey my *t*.
Ac 2: 42 themselves to the apostles' *t*
Ro 12: 7 let him serve; if it is *t*, let him teach;

TEACHINGS (TEACH)

Mt 15: 9 their teachings are but rules *t*
Lk 4: 15 He *t* in their synagogues,
Ac 20: 20 have *t* you publicly and from house
1Co 2: 13 but in words *t* by the Spirit,
Gal 1: 12 nor was I *t* it; rather, I received it
1Ti 1: 20 to Satan to be *t* not to blaspheme.
1Jn 2: 27 just as it has *t* you, remain in him.

Eph 4: 14 and there by every wind of *t*
2Th 3: 6 to the *t* you received from us.
1Ti 4: 13 of Scripture, to preaching and to *t*.
5: 17 whose work is preaching and *t*,
6: 3 Lord Jesus Christ and to godly *t*,
2Ti 3: 16 is God-breathed and is useful for *t*,
Tit 1: 11 by *t* things they ought not
2: 7 In your *t* show integrity,
Heb 5: 13 with the *t* about righteousness.
2Jn 9 and does not continue in the *t*

TEACHINGS (TEACH)

Pr 7: 2 guard my *t* as the apple of your eye.
2Th 2: 15 hold to the *t* we passed on to you,
Heb 6: 1 leave the elementary *t* about Christ

TEAR (TEARS)

Rev 7: 17 God will wipe away every *t*
21: 4 He will wipe every *t*

TEARS (TEAR)

Ps 126: 5 Those who sow in *t*
Isa 25: 8 LORD will wipe away the *t*
Jer 31: 16 and your eyes from *t*,
50: 4 in *t* to seek the LORD their God.
Lk 7: 38 she began to wet his feet with her *t*.
2Co 2: 4 anguish of heart and with many *t*,
Php 3: 18 and now say again even with *t*,

TEETH (TOOTH)

Job 19: 20 with only the skin of my *t*.
Ps 35: 16 they gnashed their *t* at me.
Jer 31: 29 and the children's *t* are set on edge
Mt 8: 12 will be weeping and gnashing of *t*."

TEMPER (EVEN-TEMPERED HOT-TEMPERED ILL-TEMPERED QUICK-TEMPERED)

Pr 16: 32 a man who controls his *t*

TEMPERANCE see SELF-CONTROL

TEMPERATE*

1Ti 3: 2 *t*, self-controlled, respectable,
3: 11 not malicious talkers but *t*
Tit 2: 2 Teach the older men to be *t*,

TEMPEST

Ps 50: 3 and around him a *t* rages.
55: 8 far from the *t* and storm."

TEMPLE (TEMPLES)

1Ki 6: 1 began to build the *t* of the LORD.
6: 38 the *t* was finished in all its details
8: 10 the cloud filled the *t* of the LORD,
8: 27 How much less this *t* I have built!
2Ch 3: 17 They set fire to God's *t*
36: 23 me to build a *t* for him at Jerusalem
Ezr 6: 14 finished building the *t* according
Ps 27: 4 and to seek him in his *t*.
Isa 6: 1 and the train of his robe filled the *t*.
Eze 10: 4 cloud filled the *t*, and the court was
43: 4 glory of the LORD entered the *t*.
Hab 2: 20 But the LORD is in his holy *t*;
Mt 12: 6 that one greater than the *t* is here.
26: 61 'I am able to destroy the *t* of God
27: 51 of the *t* was torn in two from top
Lk 21: 5 about how the *t* was adorned
Jn 2: 14 In the *t* courts he found men selling
1Co 3: 16 that you yourselves are God's *t*
6: 19 you not know that your body is a *t*
2Co 6: 16 For we are the *t* of the living God.
Rev 21: 22 I did not see a *t* in the city,

TEMPLES (TEMPLE)

Ac 17: 24 does not live in *t* built by hands.

TEMPORARY

2Co 4: 18 what is seen is *t*, but what is unseen

TEMPT* (TEMPTATION TEMPTED TEMPTER TEMPTING)

1Co 7: 5 again so that Satan will not *t* you
Jas 1: 13 does he *t* anyone; but each one is

TEMPTATION* (TEMPT)

Mt 6: 13 And lead us not into *t*,
26: 41 pray so that you will not fall into *t*.
Mk 14: 38 pray so that you will not fall into *t*.
Lk 11: 4 And lead us not into *t*."
22: 40 "Pray that you will not fall into *t*."
22: 46 pray so that you will not fall into *t*.
1Co 10: 13 No *t* has seized you except what is
1Ti 6: 9 want to get rich fall into *t*

TEMPTED* (TEMPT)

Mt 4: 1 into the desert to be *t* by the devil.
Mk 1: 13 was in the desert forty days, being *t*
Lk 4: 2 for forty days he was *t* by the devil.
1Co 10: 13 But when you are *t*, he will
10: 13 he will not let you be *t*
Gal 6: 1 yourself, or you also may be *t*.
1Th 3: 5 way the tempter might have *t* you
Heb 2: 18 able to help those who are being *t*.
2: 18 he himself suffered when he was *t*,
4: 15 but we have one who has been *t*
Jas 1: 13 For God cannot be *t* by evil,
1: 13 When *t*, no one should say,
1: 14 each one is *t* when, by his own evil

TEMPTER* (TEMPT)

Mt 4: 3 The *t* came to him and said,
1Th 3: 5 some way the *t* might have

TEMPTING* (TEMPT)

Lk 4: 13 the devil had finished all this *t*,
Jas 1: 13 no one should say, "God is *t* me."

TEN (TENTH TITHE TITHES)

Ex 34: 28 covenant—the *T* Commandments.
Lev 26: 8 of you will chase *t* thousand,
Dt 4: 13 covenant, the *T* Commandments,
10: 4 The *T* Commandments he had
Ps 91: 7 *t* thousand at your right hand,
Da 7: 24 thorns are *t* kings that will come
Mt 25: 1 will be like *t* virgins who took
25: 28 it to the one who has the *t* talents.
Lk 15: 8 suppose a woman has *t* silver coins
Rev 12: 3 and *t* horns and seven crowns

TENANTS

Mt 21: 34 servants to the *t* to collect his fruit.

TEND

Jer 23: 2 to the shepherds who *t* my people:
Eze 34: 14 I will *t* them in a good pasture,

TENDERNESS*

Isa 63: 15 Your *t* and compassion are
Php 2: 1 fellowship with the Spirit, if any *t*

TENT (TENTMAKER TENTS)

Ex 27: 21 In the *T* of Meeting,
40: 2 "Set up the tabernacle, the *T*
Isa 54: 2 "Enlarge the place of your *t*,
2Co 5: 1 that if the earthly *t* we live
2Pe 1: 13 as long as I live in the *t* of this body,

TENTH (TEN)

Ge 14: 20 Abram gave him a *t* of everything.
Nu 18: 26 you must present a *t* of that tithe
Dt 14: 22 Be sure to set aside a *t*
1Sa 8: 15 He will take a *t* of your grain
Lk 11: 42 you give God a *t* of your mint,
18: 12 I fast twice a week and give a *t*
Heb 7: 4 patriarch Abraham gave him a *t*

TENTMAKER* (TENT)

Ac 18: 3 and because he was a *t* as they were

TENTS (TENT)

Ge 13: 12 and pitched his *t* near Sodom.
Ps 84: 10 than dwell in the *t* of the wicked.

TERAH

Ge 11: 31 *T* took his son Abram, his

TERRIBLE (TERROR)

2Ti 3: 1 There will be *t* times

TERRIFIED (TERROR)

Dt 7: 21 Do not be *t* by them,
20: 3 do not be *t* or give way to panic
Ps 90: 7 and *t* by your indignation.
Mt 14: 26 walking on the lake, they were *t*.
17: 6 they fell facedown to the ground, *t*.
27: 54 they were *t*, and exclaimed,
Mk 4: 41 They were *t* and asked each other,

TERRIFYING (TERROR)

Heb 12: 21 The sight was so *t* that Moses said,

TERRITORY

2Co 10: 16 done in another man's *t*.

TERROR (TERRIBLE TERRIFIED TERRIFYING)

Dt 2: 25 very day I will begin to put the *t*
28: 67 of the *t* that will fill your hearts

Job   9: 34 so that his *t* would frighten me no
Ps   91: 5 You will not fear the *t* of night,
Pr   21: 15 but *t* to evildoers,
Isa   13: 8 *T* will seize them,
      24: 17 *T* and pit and snare await you,
      51: 13 live in constant *t* every day
      54: 14 *T* will be far removed;
Lk   21: 26 Men will faint from *t*, apprehensive
Ro   13: 3 For rulers hold no *t*

TEST (TESTED TESTING TESTS)

Dt   6: 16 Do not the LORD your God
Jdg   3: 1 to *t* all those Israelites who had not
1Ki   10: 1 came to *t* him with hard questions.
1Ch   29: 17 that you *t* the heart and are pleased
Ps   26: 2 *T* me, O LORD, and try me,
      78: 18 They willfully put God to the *t*
     106: 14 wasteland they put God to the *t*
     139: 23 *t* me and know my anxious
Jer   11: 20 and *t* the heart and mind,
Lk   4: 12 put the Lord your God to the *t*.' "
Ac   5: 9 How could you agree to *t* the Spirit
Ro   12: 2 Then you will be able to *t*
1Co   3: 13 and the fire will *t* the quality
      10: 9 We should not *t* the Lord,
2Co   13: 5 unless, of course, you fail the *t*?
1Th   5: 21 *T* everything.
Jas   1: 12 because when he has stood the *t*,
1Jn   4: 1 *t* the spirits to see whether they are

TESTAMENT see COVENANT

TESTED (TEST)

Ge   22: 1 Some time later God *t* Abraham.
Job   23: 10 when he has *t* me, I will come forth
      34: 36 that Job might be *t* to the utmost
Ps   66: 10 For you, O God, *t* us;
Pr   27: 21 man is *t* by the praise he receives.
Isa   28: 16 a *t* stone,
      48: 10 I have *t* you in the furnace
1Ti   3: 10 They must first be *t*; and then
Heb   11: 17 By faith Abraham, when God *t* him

TESTIFIES (TESTIFY)

Jn   5: 32 There is another who *t* in my favor.
Ro   8: 16 The Spirit himself *t*

TESTIFY (TESTIFIES TESTIMONY)

Pr   24: 28 Do not *t* against your neighbor
Jn   1: 7 a witness to *t* concerning that light,
       1: 34 and I *t* that this is the Son of God."
       5: 39 are the Scriptures that *t* about me,
       7: 7 because I *t* that what it does is evil.
      15: 26 he will *t* about me. And you
Ac   23: 11 continued to *t* to the resurrection
      10: 43 All the prophets *t* about him that
2Ti   1: 8 ashamed to *t* about our Lord,
1Jn   4: 14 *t* that the Father has sent his Son
       5: 7 For there are three that *t*: the Spirit

TESTIMONY (TESTIFY)

Ex   20: 16 "You shall not give false *t*
      31: 18 gave him the two tablets of the T,
Nu   35: 30 only on the *t* of witnesses.
Dt   19: 18 giving false *t* against his brother,
Pr   12: 17 A truthful witness gives honest *t*,
Isa   8: 20 and to the *t!* If they do not speak
Mt   15: 19 sexual immorality, theft, false *t*,
      24: 14 preached in the whole world as a *t*
Lk   18: 20 not give false *t*, honor your father
Jn   2: 25 he did not need man's *t* about man
      21: 24 We know that his *t* is true.
1Jn   5: 9 but God's *t* is greater because it is
Rev   12: 11 and by the word of their *t*;

TESTING (TEST)

Lk   8: 13 but in the time of *t* they fall away.
Heb   3: 8 during the time of *t* in the desert,
Jas   1: 3 because you know that the *t*

TESTS (TEST)

Pr   17: 3 but the LORD *t* the heart.
1Th   2: 4 but God, who *t* our hearts.

THADDAEUS

Apostle (Mt 10:3; Mk 3:18); probably also
known as Judas son of James (Lk 6:16; Ac 1:
13).

THANK (THANKFUL THANKFULNESS THANKS THANKSGIVING)

Php   1: 3 I *t* my God every time I remember
1Th   3: 9 How can we *t* God enough for you

THANKFUL (THANK)

Col   3: 15 And be *t*.
Heb   12: 28 let us be *t*, and so worship God

THANKFULNESS (THANK)

1Co   10: 30 If I take part in the meal with *t*,
Col   2: 7 taught, and overflowing with *t*.

THANKS (THANK)

1Ch   16: 8 Give *t* to the LORD, call
Ne   12: 31 assigned two large choirs to give *t*.
Ps   7: 17 I will give *t* to the LORD
      28: 7 and I will give *t* to him in song.
      30: 12 my God, I will give you *t* forever.
      35: 18 I will give you *t* in the great
      75: 1 we give *t*, for your Name is near;
     100: 4 give *t* to him and praise his name.
     107: 1 Give *t* to the LORD, for he is good;
     118: 28 are my God, and I will give you *t*;
     136: 1 Give *t* to the LORD, for he is good.
Ro   1: 21 as God nor gave *t* to him,
1Co   11: 24 when he had given *t*, he broke it
      15: 57 be to God! He gives us the victory
2Co   2: 14 *t* be to God, who always leads us
       9: 15 *T* be to God for his indescribable
1Th   5: 18 give *t* in all circumstances,
Rev   4: 9 and *t* to him who sits on the throne

THANKSGIVING (THANK)

Ps   95: 2 Let us come before him with *t*
     100: 4 Enter his gates with *t*
1Co   10: 16 cup of *t* for which we give thanks
Php   4: 6 by prayer and petition, with *t*,
1Ti   4: 3 created to be received with *t*

THEFT (THIEF)

Mt   15: 19 sexual immorality, *t*, false

THEFTS* (THIEF)

Rev   9: 21 their sexual immorality or their *t*.

THEME*

Ps   45: 1 My heart is stirred by a noble *t*
     119: 54 Your decrees are the *t* of my song

THIEF (THEFT THEFTS THIEVES)

Ex   22: 3 A *t* must certainly make restitution
Pr   6: 30 Men do not despise a *t* if he steals
Lk   12: 39 at what hour the *t* was coming,
1Th   5: 2 day of the Lord will come like a *t*
1Pe   4: 15 or *t* or any other kind of criminal,
Rev   3: 11 I come like a *t!* Blessed is he who

THIEVES (THIEF)

Mt   6: 19 and where *t* break in and steal
Jn   10: 8 who ever came before me were *t*
1Co   6: 10 nor homosexual offenders nor *t*

THINK (THINKING THOUGHT THOUGHTS)

Ps   63: 6 I *t* of you through the watches
Isa   44: 19 No one stops to *t*,
Mt   22: 42 "What do you *t* about the Christ?
Ro   12: 3 Do not *t* of yourself more highly
Php   4: 8 praiseworthy—*t* about such things

THINKING (THINK)

Pr   23: 7 who is always *t* about the cost.
1Co   14: 20 Brothers, stop *t* like children.
2Pe   3: 1 to stimulate you to wholesome *t*.

THIRST (THIRSTS THIRSTY)

Ps   69: 21 and gave me vinegar for my *t*.
Mt   5: 6 Blessed are those who hunger and *t*
Jn   4: 14 the water I give him will never *t*.
2Co   11: 27 I have known hunger and *t*
Rev   7: 16 never again will they *t*.

THIRSTS (THIRST)

Ps   42: 2 My soul *t* for God,

THIRSTY (THIRST)

Ps   107: 9 for he satisfies the *t*
Pr   25: 21 if he is *t*, give him water to drink.
Isa   55: 1 "Come, all you who are *t*,
Mt   25: 35 I was *t* and you gave me something
Jn   7: 37 "If anyone is *t*, let him come to me
Ro   12: 20 if he is *t*, give him something
Rev   21: 6 To him who is *t* I will give to drink
      22: 17 Whoever is *t*, let him come;

THOMAS

Apostle (Mt 10:3; Mk 3:18; Lk 6:15; Jn 11:16;
14:5; 21:2; Ac 1:13). Doubted resurrection (Jn
20:24-28).

THONGS

Mk   1: 7 *t* of whose sandals I am not worthy

THORN (THORNBUSHES THORNS)

2Co   12: 7 there was given me a *t* in my flesh,

THORNBUSHES (THORN)

Lk   6: 44 People do not pick figs from *t*,

THORNS (THORN)

Ge   3: 18 It will produce *t* and thistles
Nu   33: 55 in your eyes and *t* in your sides.
Mt   13: 7 fell among *t*, which grew up
      27: 29 and then twisted together a crown of *t*
Heb   6: 8 But land that produces *t*

THOUGHT (THINK)

Pr   14: 15 a prudent man gives *t* to his steps.
      21: 29 an upright man gives *t* to his ways.
1Co   13: 11 I talked like a child, I *t* like a child,

THOUGHTS (THINK)

1Ch   28: 9 every motive behind the *t*.
Ps   94: 11 The LORD knows the *t* of man;
     139: 23 test me and know my anxious *t*.
Isa   55: 8 "For my *t* are not your *t*,
Mt   15: 19 For out of the heart come evil *t*,
1Co   2: 11 among men knows the *t* of a man
Heb   4: 12 it judges the *t* and attitudes

THREE

Ge   6: 10 Noah had *t* sons: Shem, Ham
Ex   23: 14 "*T* times a year you are
Dt   19: 15 the testimony of two or *t* witnesses.
2Sa   23: 8 a Tahkemonite, was chief of the T;
Pr   30: 15 "There are *t* things that are never
      30: 18 "There are *t* things that are too
      30: 21 "Under *t* things the earth trembles,
      30: 29 "There are *t* things that are stately
Ecc   4: 12 of *t* strands is not quickly broken.
Da   3: 24 "Weren't there *t* men that we tied up
Am   1: 3 "For *t* sins of Damascus,
Jnh   1: 17 inside the fish *t* days and *t* nights.
Mt   12: 40 so the Son of Man will be *t* days
      12: 40 *t* nights in the belly of a huge fish,
      12: 40 *t* nights in the heart of the earth.
      17: 4 I will put up *t* shelters—one
      18: 20 or *t* come together in my name,
      26: 34 you will disown me *t* times.
      26: 75 you will disown me *t* times."
      27: 63 'After *t* days I will rise again.'
Mk   8: 31 and after *t* days rise again.
       9: 5 Let us put up *t* shelters—one
      14: 30 yourself will disown me *t* times."
Jn   2: 19 and I will raise it again in *t* days."
1Co   13: 13 And now these *t* remain: faith,
      14: 27 or at the most *t*—should speak,
2Co   13: 1 testimony of two or *t* witnesses."
1Jn   5: 7 For there are *t* that testify:

THRESHER* (THRESHING)

1Co   9: 10 plowman plows and the *t* threshes,

THRESHING (THRESHER)

Ru   3: 6 So she went down to the *t* floor
2Sa   24: 18 an altar to the LORD on the *t* floor
Lk   3: 17 is in his hand to clear his *t* floor

THREW (THROW)

Da   6: 16 and *t* him into the lions' den.
Jnh   1: 15 took Jonah and *t* him overboard,

THRIVE

Pr   29: 2 When the righteous *t*, the people

THROAT (THROATS)

Ps   5: 9 Their *t* is an open grave;
Pr   23: 2 and put a knife to your *t*

THROATS (THROAT)

Ro   3: 13 "Their *t* are open graves;

THROB*

Isa   60: 5 your heart will *t* and swell with joy;

THRONE (ENTHRONED ENTHRONES THRONES)

2Sa   7: 16 your *t* will be established forever
1Ch   17: 12 and I will establish his *t* forever.
Ps   11: 4 the LORD is on his heavenly *t*,
      45: 6 Your *t*, O God, will last for ever
      47: 8 God is seated on his holy *t*.
      89: 14 justice are the foundation of your *t*;
Isa   6: 1 I saw the Lord seated on a *t*,

Isa 66: 1 "Heaven is my *t*.
Eze 28: 2 I sit on the *t* of a god
Da 7: 9 His *t* was flaming with fire,
Mt 19:28 Son of Man sits on his glorious *t*,
Ac 7:49 prophet says: " 'Heaven is my *t*,
Heb 1: 8 "Your *t*, O God, will last for ever
    4:16 Let us then approach the *t* of grace
    12: 2 at the right hand of the *t* of God.
Rev 3:21 sat down with my Father on his *t*.
    3:21 the right to sit with me on my *t*,
    4: 2 there before me was a *t* in heaven
    4:10 They lay their crowns before the *t*
    20:11 Then I saw a great white *t*
    22: 3 *t* of God and of the Lamb will be

THRONES (THRONE)

Mt 19:28 me will also sit on twelve *t*,
Rev 4: 4 throne were twenty-four other *t*,

THROW (THREW)

Jn 8: 7 the first to *t* a stone at her."
Heb 10:35 So do not *t* away your confidence;
    12: 1 let us *t* off everything that hinders

THUNDER (THUNDERS)

Ps 93: 4 Mightier than the *t*
Mk 3:17 which means Sons of *T*); Andrew,

THUNDERS (THUNDER)

Job 37: 5 God's voice *t* in marvelous ways;
Ps 29: 3 the God of glory *t*,
Rev 10: 3 the voices of the seven *t* spoke.

THWART* (THWARTED)

Isa 14:27 has purposed, and who can *t* him?

THWARTED (THWART)

Job 42: 2 no plan of yours can be *t*.

THYATIRA

Rev 2:18 the angel of the church in *T* write:

TIBNI

King of Israel (1Ki 16:21-22).

TIDINGS

Isa 40: 9 You who bring good *t* to Jerusalem
    52: 7 who bring good *t*,

TIES

Hos 11: 4 with *t* of love;
Mt 12:29 unless he first *t* up the strong man?

TIGHT*

Jas 1:26 and yet does not keep a *t* rein

TIGHTFISTED*

Dt 15: 7 or *t* toward your poor brother.

TIME (TIMES)

Est 4:14 come to royal position for such a *t*
Ecc 3: 1 There is a *t* for everything,
    8: 5 wise heart will know the proper *t*
Da 7:25 to him for a *t*, times and half a *t*
    12: 7 "It will be for a *t*, times and half a *t*
Hos 10:12 for it is *t* to seek the LORD,
Jn 2: 4 Jesus replied, "My *t* has not yet
    17: 1 prayed: "Father, the *t* has come.
Ro 9: 9 "At the appointed *t* I will return,
    13:11 understanding the present *t*.
1Co 7:29 brothers, is that the *t* is short.
2Co 6: 2 now is the *t* of God's favor,
2Ti 1: 9 Jesus before the beginning of *t*,
Tit 1: 2 promised before the beginning of *t*,
Heb 9:28 and he will appear a second *t*,
    10:12 for all *t* one sacrifice for sins,
1Pe 4:17 For it is *t* for judgment to begin

TIMES (TIME)

Ps 9: 9 a stronghold in *t* of trouble.
    31:15 My *t* are in your hands;
    62: 8 Trust in him at all *t*, O people;
Pr 17: 17 A friend loves at all *t*,
Isa 46:10 from ancient *t*, what is still to come
Am 5:13 for the *t* are evil.
Mt 16: 3 cannot interpret the signs of the *t*.
    18:21 how many *t* shall I forgive my
Ac 1: 7 "It is not for you to know the *t*
Rev 12:14 *t* and half a time, out

TIMID (TIMIDITY)

1Th 5:14 encourage the *t*, help the weak,

TIMIDITY* (TIMID)

2Ti 1: 7 For God did not give us a spirit of *t*

TIMOTHY

Believer from Lystra (Ac 16:1). Joined Paul on second missionary journey (Ac 16-20). Sent to settle problems at Corinth (1Co 4:17; 16:10). Led church at Ephesus (1Ti 1:3). Co-writer with Paul (1Th 1:1; 2Th 1:1; Phm 1).

TIP

Job 33: 2 my words are on the *t* of my tongue

TIRE (TIRED)

2Th 3:13 never *t* of doing what is right.

TIRED (TIRE)

Ex 17:12 When Moses' hands grew *t*,
Isa 40:28 He will not grow *t* or weary,

TITHE (TEN)

Lev 27:30 " 'A *t* of everything from the land,
Dt 12:17 eat in your own towns the *t*
Mal 3:10 the whole *t* into the storehouse,

TITHES (TEN)

Nu 18:21 give to the Levites all the *t* in Israel
Mal 3: 8 'How do we rob you?' "In *t*

TITUS*

Gentile co-worker of Paul (Gal 2:1-3; 2Ti 4:10); sent to Corinth (2Co 2:13; 7-8; 12:18), Crete (Tit 1:4-5).

TODAY

Ps 2: 7 *t* I have become your Father.
    95: 7 if you hear his voice,
Mt 6:11 Give us *t* our daily bread.
Lk 2:11 *T* in the town of David a Savior has
    23:43 *t* you will be with me in paradise."
Ac 13:33 *t* I have become your Father.'
Heb 1: 5 *t* I have become your Father"?
    3: 7 "*T*, if you hear his voice,
    3:13 daily, as long as it is called *T*,
    5: 5 *t* I have become your Father."
    13: 8 Christ is the same yesterday and *t*

TOIL (TOILED TOILING)

Ge 3:17 through painful *t* you will eat of it

TOILED (TOIL)

2Co 11:27 and *t* and have often gone

TOILING (TOIL)

2Th 3: 8 *t* so that we would not be a burden

TOLERANCE* (TOLERATE)

Ro 2: 4 for the riches of his kindness, *t*

TOLERATE (TOLERANCE)

Hab 1:13 you cannot *t* wrong.
Rev 2: 2 that you cannot *t* wicked men,

TOMB

Mt 27:65 make the *t* as secure as you know
Lk 24: 2 the stone rolled away from the *t*,

TOMORROW

Pr 27: 1 Do not boast about *t*,
Isa 22:13 "for *t* we die!"
Mt 6:34 Therefore do not worry about *t*,
1Co 15:32 for *t* we die."
Jas 4:13 "Today or *t* we will go to this

TONGUE (TONGUES)

Ex 4:10 I am slow of speech and *t*."
Job 33: 2 my words are on the tip of my *t*.
Ps 5: 9 with their *t* they speak deceit.
    34:13 keep your *t* from evil
    37:30 and his *t* speaks what is just.
    39: 1 and keep my *t* from sin;
    51:14 my *t* will sing of your righteousness
    52: 4 O you deceitful *t*!
    71:24 My *t* will tell of your righteous acts
    119:172 May my *t* sing of your word,
    137: 6 May my *t* cling to the roof
    139: 4 Before a word is on my *t*
Pr 6:17 a lying *t*,
    10:19 but he who holds his *t* is wise.
    12:18 but the *t* of the wise brings healing.
    15: 4 The *t* that brings healing is a tree
    17:20 he whose *t* is deceitful falls
    21:23 He who guards his mouth and his *t*
    25:15 and a gentle *t* can break a bone.
    26:28 A lying *t* hates those it hurts,
    28:23 than he who has a flattering *t*
    31:26 and faithful instruction is on her *t*

SS 4:11 milk and honey are under your *t*.
Isa 32: 4 and the stammering *t* will be fluent
    45:23 by me every *t* will swear.
    50: 4 has given me an instructed *t*,
    59: 3 and your *t* mutters wicked things.
Lk 16:24 of his finger in water and cool my *t*,
Ro 14:11 every *t* will confess to God.' "
1Co 14: 2 speaks in a *t* does not speak to men
    14: 4 He who speaks in a *t* edifies himself
    14: 9 intelligible words with your *t*,
    14:13 in a *t* should pray that he may
    14:19 than ten thousand words in a *t*.
    14:26 revelation, a *t* or an interpretation.
    14:27 If anyone speaks in a *t*, two—
Php 2:11 every *t* confess that Jesus Christ is
Jas 1:26 does not keep a tight rein on his *t*,
    3: 5 Likewise the *t* is a small part
    3: 8 but no man can tame the *t*.
1Jn 3:18 or *t* but with actions and in truth.

TONGUES (TONGUE)

Ps 12: 4 "We will triumph with our *t*;
    126: 2 our *t* with songs of joy.
Isa 28:11 with foreign lips and strange *t*
    66:18 and gather all nations and *t*,
Jer 23:31 the prophets who wag their own *t*
Mk 16:17 in new *t*; they will pick up snakes
Ac 2: 3 to be *t* of fire that separated
    2: 4 and began to speak in other *t*
    10:46 For they heard them speaking in *t*
    19: 6 and they spoke in *t* and prophesied
Ro 3:13 their *t* practice deceit."
1Co 12:10 still another the interpretation of *t*.
    12:28 speaking in different kinds of *t*.
    12:30 Do all speak in *t*? Do all interpret?
    13: 1 If I speak in the *t* of men
    13: 8 where there are *t*, they will be
    14: 5 greater than one who speaks in *t*,
    14:18 speak in *t* more than all of you.
    14:21 "Through men of strange *t*
    14:39 and do not forbid speaking in *t*.

TOOK (TAKE)

Isa 53: 4 Surely he *t* up our infirmities
Mt 8:17 "He *t* up our infirmities
    26:26 they were eating, Jesus *t* bread,
    26:27 Then he *t* the cup, gave thanks
1Co 11:23 the night he was betrayed, *t* bread,
    11:25 after supper he *t* the cup, saying,
Php 3:12 for which Christ Jesus *t* hold of me.

TOOTH (TEETH)

Ex 21:24 eye for eye, *t* for *t*, hand for hand,
Mt 5:38 'Eye for eye, and *t* for *t*.'

TOP

Dt 28:13 you will always be at the *t*,
Isa 1: 6 of your foot to the *t* of your head
Mt 27:51 torn in two from *t* to bottom.

TORMENT (TORMENTED TORMENTORS)

Lk 16:28 also come to this place of *t*.'
2Co 12: 7 a messenger of Satan, to *t* me.

TORMENTED (TORMENT)

Rev 20:10 They will be *t* day and night

TORMENTORS* (TORMENT)

Ps 137: 3 our *t* demanded songs of joy;

TORN

Gal 4:15 you would have *t* out your eyes
Php 1:23 I do not know! I am *t*

TORTURED*

Mt 18:34 turned him over to the jailers to be *t*,
Heb 11:35 Others were *t* and refused

TOSSED (TOSSING)

Eph 4:14 *t* back and forth by the waves,
Jas 1: 6 of the sea, blown and *t* by the wind.

TOSSING (TOSSED)

Isa 57:20 But the wicked are like the *t* sea,

TOUCH (TOUCHED TOUCHES)

Ge 3: 3 you must not *t* it, or you will die.' "
Ex 19:12 go up the mountain or *t* the foot
Ps 105:15 "Do not *t* my anointed ones;
Mt 9:21 If only *t* this cloak, I will be healed
Mk 18:15 babies to Jesus to have him *t* them.
    24:39 It is I myself! *T* me and see;
2Co 6:17 *T* no unclean thing,
Col 2:21 Do not taste! Do not *t*!' "?

TOUCHED (TOUCH)

1Sa 10:26 men whose hearts God had *t.*
Isa 6: 7 With it he *t* my mouth and said.
Mt 14:36 and all who *t* him were healed.
Lk 8:45 "Who *t* me?" Jesus asked.
1Jn 1: 1 looked at and our hands have *t*—

TOUCHES (TOUCH)

Ex 19:12 Whoever *t* the mountain shall
Zec 2: 8 for whoever *t* you *t* the apple

TOWER

Ge 11: 4 with a *t* that reaches to the heavens
Pr 18:10 of the LORD is a strong *t;*

TOWN (TOWNS)

Mt 2:23 and lived in a *t* called Nazareth.

TOWNS (TOWN)

Nu 35: 2 to give the Levites *t* to live
35:15 These six *t* will be a place of refuge
Jer 11:13 as many gods as you have *t,*
Mt 9:35 Jesus went through all the *t*

TRACING*

Ro 11:33 and his paths beyond *t* out!

TRACK

Job 14:16 but not keep *t* of my sin.

TRADERS (TRADING)

1Ti 1:10 for slave *t* and liars and perjurers—

TRADING (TRADERS)

1Ki 10:22 The king had a fleet of *t* ships at sea
Pr 31:18 She sees that her *t* is profitable.

TRADITION (TRADITIONS)

Mt 15: 2 "Why do your disciples break the *t*
15: 6 word of God for the sake of your *t.*
Mk 7:13 by your *t* that you have handed
Col 2: 8 which depends on human *t*

TRADITIONS (TRADITION)

Mk 7: 8 are holding on to the *t* of men."
Gal 1:14 zealous for the *t* of my fathers.

TRAIL

1Ti 5:24 the sins of others *t* behind them.

TRAIN* (TRAINED TRAINING)

Ps 68:18 you led captives in your *t;*
Pr 22: 6 *T* a child in the way he should go,
Isa 2: 4 nor will they *t* for war anymore.
6: 1 the *t* of his robe filled the temple.
Mic 4: 3 nor will they *t* for war anymore.
Eph 4: 8 he led captives in his *t*
1Ti 4: 7 rather, *t* yourself to be godly.
Tit 2: 4 they can *t* the younger women

TRAINED (TRAIN)

Lk 6:40 everyone who is fully *t* will be like
Ac 22: 3 Under Gamaliel I was thoroughly *t*
2Co 11: 6 I may not be a *t* speaker,
Heb 5:14 by constant use have *t* themselves
12:11 for those who have been *t* by it.

TRAINING* (TRAIN)

1Co 9:25 in the games goes into strict *t.*
Eph 6: 4 up in the *t* and instruction
1Ti 4: 8 For physical *t* is of some value,
2Ti 3:16 correcting and *t* in righteousness,

TRAITOR (TRAITORS)

Lk 6:16 and Judas Iscariot, who became a *t.*
Jn 18: 5 Judas the *t* was standing there

TRAITORS (TRAITOR)

Ps 59: 5 show no mercy to wicked *t.*

TRAMPLE (TRAMPLED)

Joel 3:13 Come, *t* the grapes,
Am 2: 7 They *t* on the heads of the poor
5:11 You *t* on the poor
8: 4 Hear this, you who *t* the needy
Mt 7: 6 they may *t* them under their feet,
Lk 10:19 I have given you authority to *t*

TRAMPLED (TRAMPLE)

Isa 63: 6 I *t* the nations in my anger;
Lk 21:24 Jerusalem will be *t*
Heb 10:29 to be punished who has *t* the Son
Rev 14:20 They were *t* in the winepress

TRANCE*

Ac 10:10 was being prepared, he fell into a *t.*
11: 5 and in a *t* I saw a vision.
22:17 into a *t* and saw the Lord speaking.

TRANQUILLITY*

Ecc 4: 6 Better one handful with *t*

TRANSACTIONS*

Ru 4: 7 method of legalizing *t* in Israel.)

TRANSCENDS*

Php 4: 7 which *t* all understanding,

TRANSFIGURED*

Mt 17: 2 There he was *t* before them.
Mk 9: 2 There he was *t* before them.

TRANSFORM* (TRANSFORMED)

Php 3:21 will *t* our lowly bodies

TRANSFORMED (TRANSFORM)

Ro 12: 2 be *t* by the renewing of your mind.
2Co 3:18 are being *t* into his likeness

TRANSGRESSED* (TRANSGRESSION)

Da 9:11 All Israel has *t* your law

TRANSGRESSION* (TRANSGRESSED TRANSGRESSIONS TRANSGRESSORS)

Ps 19:13 innocent of great *t.*
Isa 53: 8 for the *t* of my people he was
Da 9:24 and your holy city to finish *t,*
Mic 1: 5 All this is because of Jacob's *t,*
1: 5 What is Jacob's *t?*
3: 8 to declare to Jacob his *t,*
6: 7 Shall I offer my firstborn for my *t,*
7:18 who pardons sin and forgives the *t*
Ro 4:15 where there is no law there is no *t.*
11:11 Rather, because of their *t,*
11:12 if their *t* means riches for the world

TRANSGRESSIONS* (TRANSGRESSION)

Ps 32: 1 whose *t* are forgiven,
32: 5 my *t* to the LORD"—
39: 8 Save me from all my *t;*
51: 1 blot out my *t.*
51: 3 For I know my *t,*
65: 3 you forgave our *t.*
103:12 so far has he removed our *t* from us
Isa 43:25 your *t,* for my own sake,
50: 1 of your *t* your mother was sent
53: 5 But he was pierced for our *t,*
Mic 1:13 for the *t* of Israel
Ro 4: 7 whose *t* are forgiven,
Gal 3:19 because of *t* until the Seed to whom
Eph 2: 1 you were dead in your *t* and sins,
2: 5 even when we were dead in *t*—

TRANSGRESSORS* (TRANSGRESSION)

Ps 51:13 Then I will teach *t* your ways,
Isa 53:12 and made intercession for the *t.*
53:12 and was numbered with the *t.*
Lk 22:37 'And he was numbered with the *t';*

TRAP (TRAPPED TRAPS)

Ps 69:22 may it become retribution and a *t.*
Pr 20:25 a *t* for a man to dedicate something
28:10 will fall into his own *t,*
Isa 8:14 a *t* and a snare.
Mt 22:15 and laid plans to *t* him in his words.
Lk 21:34 close on you unexpectedly like a *t.*
Ro 11: 9 their table become a snare and a *t,*
1Ti 3: 7 into disgrace and into the devil's *t.*
6: 9 and a *t* and into many foolish
2Ti 2:26 and escape from the *t* of the devil,

TRAPPED (TRAP)

Pr 6: 2 if you have been *t* by what you said
12:13 An evil man is *t* by his sinful talk,

TRAPS (TRAP)

Jos 23:13 they will become snares and *t*
La 4:20 was caught in their *t.*

TRAVEL (TRAVELER)

Pr 4:15 Avoid it, do not *t* on it;
Mt 23:15 You *t* over land and sea

TRAVELER (TRAVEL)

Job 31:32 door was always open to the *t*—
Jer 14: 8 like a *t* who stays only a night?

TREACHEROUS (TREACHERY)

Ps 25: 3 who are *t* without excuse.
2Ti 3: 4 not lovers of the good, *t,* rash,

TREACHERY (TREACHEROUS)

Isa 59:13 rebellion and *t* against the LORD,

TREAD (TREADING TREADS)

Ps 91:13 You will *t* upon the lion

TREADING (TREAD)

Dt 25: 4 an ox while it is *t* out the grain.
1Co 9: 9 an ox while it is *t* out the grain."
1Ti 5:18 the ox while it is *t* out the grain,"

TREADS (TREAD)

Rev 19:15 He *t* the winepress of the fury

TREASURE (TREASURED TREASURES TREASURY)

Pr 2: 4 and search for it as for hidden *t,*
Isa 33: 6 of the LORD is the key to this *t.*
Mt 6:21 For where your *t* is, there your
13:44 of heaven is like *t* hidden in a field.
Lk 12:33 a *t* in heaven that will not be
2Co 4: 7 But we have this *t* in jars of clay
1Ti 6:19 In this way they will lay up *t*

TREASURED (TREASURE)

Ex 19: 5 you will be my *t* possession.
Dt 7: 6 to be his people, his *t* possession.
26:18 his *t* possession as he promised,
Job 23:12 I have *t* the words
Mal 3:17 when I make up my *t* possession.
Lk 2:19 But Mary *t* up all these things
2:51 But his mother *t* all these things

TREASURES (TREASURE)

1Ch 29: 3 my God I now give my personal *t*
Pr 10: 2 Ill-gotten *t* are of no value,
Mt 6:19 up for yourselves *t* on earth,
13:52 out of his storeroom new *t*
Col 2: 3 in whom are hidden all the *t*
Heb 11:26 of greater value than the *t* of Egypt,

TREASURY (TREASURE)

Mk 12:43 more into the *t* than all the others.

TREAT (TREATED TREATING TREATMENT)

Lev 22: 2 sons to *t* with respect the sacred
Ps 103:10 he does not *t* us as our sins deserve
Mt 18:17 *t* him as you would a pagan
18:35 my heavenly Father will *t* each
Eph 6: 9 *t* your slaves in the same way.
1Th 5:20 do not *t* prophecies with contempt.
1Ti 5: 1 *T* younger men as brothers,
1Pe 3: 7 and *t* them with respect

TREATED (TREAT)

Lev 19:34 The alien living with you must be *t*
25:40 He is to be *t* as a hired worker
1Sa 24:17 "You have *t* me well, but I have
Heb 10:29 who has *t* as an unholy thing

TREATING (TREAT)

Ge 18:25 the righteous and the wicked
Heb 12: 7 as discipline, God is *t* you as sons.

TREATMENT (TREAT)

Col 2:23 and their harsh *t* of the body,

TREATY

Ex 34:12 not to make a *t* with those who live
Dt 7: 2 Make no *t* with them, and show
23: 6 Do not seek a *t* of friendship with them

TREE (TREES)

Ge 2: 9 and the *t* of the knowledge of good
2: 9 of the garden were the *t* of life
Dt 21:23 hung on a *t* is under God's curse.
2Sa 18: 9 Absalom's head got caught in the *t.*
1Ki 14:23 and under every spreading *t.*
Ps 1: 3 He is like a *t* planted by streams
52: 8 But I am like an olive *t*
92:12 righteous will flourish like a palm *t,*
Pr 3:18 She is a *t* of life to those who
11:30 of the righteous is a *t* of life,
27:18 He who tends a fig *t* will eat its fruit
Isa 65:22 For as the days of a *t,*
Jer 17: 8 He will be like a *t* planted
Eze 17:24 I the LORD bring down the tall *t*
Da 4:10 before me stood a *t* in the middle
Mic 4: 4 and under his own fig *t,*

Zec 3:10 to sit under his vine and fig t.'
Mt 3:10 every t that does not produce good
12:33 for a t is recognized by its fruit.
Lk 19: 4 climbed a sycamore-fig t to see him
Ac 5:30 killed by hanging him on a t.
Ro 11:24 be grafted into their own olive t!
Gal 3:13 is everyone who is hung on a t."
Jas 3:12 My brothers, can a fig t bear olives,
1Pe 2:24 sins in his body on the t,
Rev 2: 7 the right to eat from the t of life,
22: 2 side of the river stood the t of life,
22:14 they may have the right to the t
22:19 from him his share in the t of life

TREES (TREE)

Jdg 9: 8 One day the t went out
Ps 96:12 Then all the t of the forest will sing
Isa 55:12 and all the t of the field
Mt 3:10 The ax is already at the root of the t
Mk 8:24 they look like t walking around."
Jude :12 autumn t, without fruit

TREMBLE (TREMBLED TREMBLES TREMBLING)

Ex 15:14 The nations will hear and t;
1Ch 16:30 T before him, all the earth!
Ps 114: 7 T, O earth, at the presence
Jer 5:22 "Should you not t in my presence?
Eze 38:20 of the earth will t at my presence.
Joel 2: 1 Let all who live in the land t,
Hab 3: 6 he looked, and made the nations t.

TREMBLED (TREMBLE)

Ex 19:16 Everyone in the camp t.
20:18 in smoke, they t with fear.
2Sa 22: 8 "The earth t and quaked,
Ac 7:32 Moses t with fear and did not dare

TREMBLES (TREMBLE)

Ps 97: 4 the earth sees and t.
104:32 he who looks at the earth, and it t,
Isa 66: 2 and t at my word.
Jer 10:10 When he is angry, the earth t;
Na 1: 5 The earth t at his presence,

TREMBLING (TREMBLE)

Ps 2:11 and rejoice with t.
Da 10:10 set me t on my hands and knees.
Php 2:12 out your salvation with fear and t,
Heb 12:21 terrifying that Moses said, "I am t

TRESPASS* (TRESPASSES)

Ro 5:15 But the gift is not like the t.
5:15 died by the t of the one man,
5:17 For if, by the t of the one man,
5:18 result of one t was condemnation
5:20 added so that the t might increase.

TRESPASSES* (TRESPASS)

Ro 5:16 but the gift followed many t

TRIAL (TRIALS)

Ps 37:33 condemned when brought to t.
Mk 13:11 you are arrested and brought to t,
2Co 8: 2 most severe t, their overflowing
Jas 1:12 is the man who perseveres under t,
1Pe 4:12 at the painful t you are suffering,
Rev 3:10 you from the hour of t that is going

TRIALS* (TRIAL)

Dt 7:19 saw with your own eyes the great t,
29: 3 own eyes you saw those great t,
Lk 22:28 who have stood by me in my t.
1Th 3: 3 one would be unsettled by these t.
2Th 1: 4 the persecutions and t you are
Jas 1: 2 whenever you face t of many kinds,
1Pe 1: 6 had to suffer grief in all kinds of t.
2Pe 2: 9 how to rescue godly men from t

TRIBE (HALF-TRIBE TRIBES)

Heb 7:13 no one from that t has ever served
Rev 5: 5 See, the Lion of the t of Judah,
5: 9 God from every t and language
11: 9 men from every people, t,
14: 6 to every nation, t, language

TRIBES (TRIBE)

Ge 49:28 All these are the twelve t of Israel,
Mt 19:28 judging the twelve t of Israel.

TRIBULATION*

Rev 7:14 who have come out of the great t.

TRICKERY*

Ac 13:10 full of all kinds of deceit and t.

2Co 12:16 fellow that I am, I caught you by t!

TRIED (TRY)

Ps 73:16 When I t to understand all this,
95: 9 where your fathers tested and t me,
Heb 3: 9 where your fathers tested and t me

TRIES (TRY)

Lk 17:33 Whoever t to keep his life will lose

TRIMMED

Mt 25: 7 virgins woke up and t their lamps.

TRIUMPH (TRIUMPHAL TRIUMPHED TRIUMPHING TRIUMPHS)

Ps 25: 2 nor let my enemies t over me.
54: 7 my eyes have looked in t
112: 8 in the end he will look in t
118: 7 I will look in t on my enemies.
Pr 28:12 When the righteous t, there is great
Isa 42:13 and will t over his enemies.

TRIUMPHAL* (TRIUMPH)

Isa 60:11 their kings led in t procession.
2Co 2:14 us in t procession in Christ

TRIUMPHED (TRIUMPH)

Rev 5: 5 of Judah, the Root of David, has t.

TRIUMPHING* (TRIUMPH)

Col 2:15 of them, t over them by the cross.

TRIUMPHS* (TRIUMPH)

Jas 2:13 Mercy t over judgment! What

TROUBLE (TROUBLED TROUBLES)

Ge 41:51 God has made me forget all my t
Jos 7:25 Why have you brought this t on us?
Job 2:10 good from God, and not t?"
5: 7 Yet man is born to t
14: 1 is of few days and full of t.
42:11 him over all the t the LORD had
Ps 7:14 conceives t gives birth
7:16 The t he causes recoils on himself;
9: 9 a stronghold in times of t.
10:14 But you, O God, do see t and grief;
22:11 for t is near
27: 5 For in the day of t
32: 7 you will protect me from t
37:39 he is their stronghold in time of t.
41: 1 LORD delivers him in times of t.
46: 1 an ever-present help in t.
50:15 and call upon me in the day of t;
59:16 my refuge in times of t.
66:14 spoke when I was in t.
86: 7 In the day of my t I will call to you,
91:15 I will be with him in t,
107: 6 to the LORD in their t,
107:13 they cried to the LORD in their t,
116: 3 I was overcome by t and sorrow.
119:143 T and distress have come upon me,
138: 7 Though I walk in the midst of t,
143:11 righteousness, bring me out of t
Pr 11: 8 righteous man is rescued from t,
11:17 a cruel man brings t on himself
11:29 He who brings t on his family will
12:13 but a righteous man escapes t.
12:21 but the wicked have their fill of t.
15:27 A greedy man brings t to his family
19:23 one rests content, untouched by t
22: 8 He who sows wickedness reaps t,
24:10 If you falter in times of t,
25:19 on the unfaithful in times of t.
28:14 he who hardens his heart falls into t
Jer 30: 7 It will be a time of t for Jacob,
Na 1: 7 a refuge in times of t.
Zep 1:15 a day of t and ruin,
Mt 6:34 Each day has enough t of its own.
13:21 When t or persecution comes
Jn 16:33 In this world you will have t.
Ro 8:35 Shall t or hardship or persecution
2Co 1: 4 those in any t with the comfort we
2Th 1: 6 t to those who t you
Jas 5:13 one of you in t? He should pray.

TROUBLED (TROUBLE)

Ps 38:18 I am t by my sin.
Isa 38:14 I am t; O Lord, come to my aid!"
Mk 14:33 began to be deeply distressed and t.
Jn 14: 1 "Do not let your hearts be t.
14:27 Do not let your hearts be t
2Th 1: 7 and give relief to you who are t,

TROUBLES (TROUBLE)

Ps 34: 6 he saved him out of all his t.

Ps 34:17 he delivers them from all their t.
34:19 A righteous man may have many t,
40:12 For t without number surround me
54: 7 he has delivered me from all my t.
1Co 7:28 those who marry will face many t
2Co 1: 4 who comforts us in all our t,
4:17 and momentary t are achieving
6: 4 in t, hardships and distresses;
7: 4 in all our t my joy knows no bounds
Php 4:14 good of you to share in my t.

TRUE (TRUTH)

Nu 11:23 not what I say will come t for you."
12: 7 this is not t of my servant Moses;
Dt 18:22 does not take place or come t,
Jos 23:15 of the LORD your God has come t,
1Sa 9: 6 and everything he says comes t.
1Ki 10: 6 and your wisdom is t.
2Ch 6:17 your servant David come t.
15: 3 was without the t God,
Ps 33: 4 of the LORD is right and t;
119:142 and your law is t.
119:151 and all your commands are t.
119:160 All your words are t;
Pr 8: 7 My mouth speaks what is t,
22:21 teaching you t and reliable words,
Jer 10:10 But the LORD is the t God;
28: 9 only if his prediction comes t."
Eze 33:33 "When all this comes t—
Lk 16:11 who will trust you with t riches?
Jn 1: 9 The t light that gives light
4:23 when the t worshipers will worship
6:32 Father who gives you the t bread
7:28 on my own, but he who sent me is t
15: 1 "I am the t vine, and my Father is
17: 3 the only t God, and Jesus Christ,
19:35 testimony, and his testimony is t
21:24 We know that his testimony is t.
Ac 10:34 "I now realize how t it is that God
11:23 all to remain t to the Lord
14:22 them to remain t to the faith.
17:11 day to see if what Paul said was t.
Ro 3: 4 Let God be t, and every man a liar.
Php 4: 8 whatever is t, whatever is noble,
1Jn 2: 8 and the t light is already shining.
5:20 He is the t God and eternal life.
Rev 19: 9 "These are the t words of God."
22: 6 These words are trustworthy and t.

TRUMPET (TRUMPETS)

Isa 27:13 And in that day a great t will sound
Eze 33: 5 Since he heard the sound of the t
Zec 9:14 Sovereign LORD will sound the t;
Mt 24:31 send his angels with a loud t call,
1Co 14: 8 if the t does not sound a clear call,
15:52 For the t will sound, the dead will
1Th 4:16 and with the t call of God,
Rev 8: 7 The first angel sounded his t,

TRUMPETS (TRUMPET)

Jdg 7:19 They blew their t and broke the jars
Rev 8: 2 and to them were given seven t,

TRUST* (ENTRUST ENTRUSTED TRUSTED TRUSTFULLY TRUSTING TRUSTS TRUSTWORTHY)

Ex 14:31 put their t in him and in Moses his
19: 9 and will always put their t in you."
Nu 20:12 "Because you did not t
Dt 1:32 you did not t in the LORD your
9:23 You did not t him or obey him.
28:52 walls in which you t fall down.
Jdg 11:20 did not t Israel to pass
2Ki 17:14 who did not t in the LORD their
18:30 to t in the LORD when he says,
1Ch 9:22 to their positions of t by David
Job 4:18 If God places no t in his servants,
15: 15 if God places no t in his holy ones,
31:24 "If I have put my t in gold
39:12 Can you t him to bring
Ps 4: 5 and t in the LORD.
9:10 Those who know your name will t
13: 5 But I t in your unfailing love;
20: 7 Some t in chariots and some
20: 7 we t in the name of the LORD our
22: 4 In you our fathers put their t;
22: 9 you made me t in you
25: 2 I lift up my soul; in you I t,
31: 6 I t in the LORD.
31:14 But I t in you, O LORD;
33:21 for we t in his holy name.
37: 3 T in the LORD and do good;
37: 5 t in him and he will do this:
40: 3 and put their t in the LORD.
40: 4 who makes the LORD his t,

Ps 44: 6 I do not t in my bow,
49: 6 those who t in their wealth
49: 13 of those who t in themselves,
52: 8 I t in God's unfailing love
55: 23 But as for me, I t in you.
56: 3 I will t in you.
56: 4 in God I t; I will not be afraid.
56: 11 in God I t; I will not be afraid.
62: 8 T in him at all times, O people;
62: 10 Do not t in extortion
78: 7 Then they would put their t in God
78: 22 or t in his deliverance.
91: 2 my God, in whom I t."
115: 8 and so will all who t in them.
115: 9 O house of Israel, t in the LORD—
115: 10 O house of Aaron, t in the LORD
115: 11 You who fear him, t in the LORD
118: 8 than to t in man.
118: 9 than to t in princes.
119: 42 for I t in your word.
125: 1 Those who t in the LORD are like
135: 18 and so will all who t in them.
143: 8 for I have put my t in you.
146: 3 Do not put your t in princes,
Pr 3: 5 T in the LORD with all your heart
21: 22 the stronghold in which they t.
22: 19 So that your t may be in the LORD
Isa 8: 17 I will put my t in him.
12: 2 I will t and not be afraid.
26: 4 T in the LORD forever,
30: 15 in quietness and t is your strength,
31: 1 who t in the multitude
36: 15 to t in the LORD when he says,
42: 17 But those who t in idols,
50: 10 t in the name of the LORD
Jer 2: 37 LORD has rejected those you t;
5: 17 the fortified cities in which you t.
7: 4 Do not t in deceptive words
7: 14 the temple you t in, the place I gave
9: 4 do not t your brothers.
12: 6 Do not t them,
28: 15 you have persuaded this nation to t
39: 18 you t in me, declares the LORD.' "
48: 7 Since you t in your deeds
49: 4 you t in your riches and say,
49: 11 Your widows too can t in me."
Mic 7: 5 Do not t a neighbor;
Na 1: 7 He cares for those who t in him,
Zep 3: 2 She does not t in the LORD,
3: 12 who t in the name of the LORD.
Lk 16: 11 who will t you with true riches?
Jn 12: 36 Put your t in the light
14: 1 T in God; t also in me.
Ac 14: 23 Lord, in whom they had put their t.
Ro 15: 13 you with all joy and peace as you t
1Co 4: 2 been given a t must prove faithful.
9: 17 discharging the t committed
2Co 13: 6 I t that you will discover that we
Heb 2: 13 "I will put my t in him."

TRUSTED* (TRUST)

1Sa 27: 12 Achish t David and said to himself,
2Ki 18: 5 Hezekiah t in the LORD, the God
1Ch 5: 20 their prayers, because they t
Job 12: 20 He silences the lips of t advisers
Ps 5: 9 from their mouth can be t;
22: 4 they t and you delivered them.
22: 5 in you they t and were not
26: 1 I have t in the LORD
41: 9 Even my close friend, whom I t,
52: 7 but t in his great wealth
Isa 20: 5 Those who t in Cush and boasted
25: 9 This is the LORD, we t in him;
25: 9 we t in him, and he saved us.
47: 10 You have t in your wickedness
Jer 13: 25 and t in false gods.
38: 22 those t friends of yours.
48: 13 ashamed when they t in Bethel.
Eze 16: 15 " 'But you t in your beauty
Da 3: 28 They t in him and defied the king's
6: 23 because he had t in his God.
Lk 11: 22 the armor in which the man t
16: 10 t with very little can also be t
Ac 12: 20 a t personal servant of the king,
Tit 2: 10 but to show that they can be fully t,
3: 8 so that those who have t

TRUSTFULLY* (TRUST)

Pr 3: 29 who lives t near you.

TRUSTING* (TRUST)

Job 15: 31 by t what is worthless,
Ps 112: 7 his heart is steadfast, t
Isa 2: 22 Stop t in man,
Jer 7: 8 you are t in deceptive words that

TRUSTS* (TRUST)

Job 8: 14 What he t in is fragile;
Ps 21: 7 For the king t in the LORD;
22: 8 "He t in the LORD;
28: 7 my heart t in him, and I am helped.
32: 10 surrounds the man who t in him.
84: 12 blessed is the man who t in you.
86: 2 who t in you.
Pr 11: 28 Whoever t in his riches will fall,
16: 20 blessed is he who t in the LORD.
28: 25 he who t in the LORD will prosper.
28: 26 He who t in himself is a fool,
29: 25 whoever t in the LORD is kept safe
Isa 26: 3 because he t in you.
28: 16 one who t will never be dismayed.
Jer 17: 5 "Cursed is the one who t in man,
17: 7 blessed is the man who t
Eze 33: 13 but then he t in his righteousness
Hab 2: 18 For he who makes it t
Mt 27: 43 He t in God.
Ro 4: 5 but t God who justifies the wicked,
9: 33 one who t in him will never be put
10: 11 "Anyone who t in him will never
1Co 13: 7 always protects, always t,
1Pe 2: 6 and the one who t in him

TRUSTWORTHY* (TRUST)

Ex 18: 21 t men who hate dishonest gain—
2Sa 7: 28 you are God! Your words are t,
Ne 13: 13 these men were considered t.
Ps 19: 7 The statutes of the LORD are t,
111: 7 all his precepts are t.
119: 86 All your commands are t;
119: 138 they are fully t.
Pr 11: 13 but a t man keeps a secret.
13: 17 but a t envoy brings healing.
25: 13 is a t messenger to those who send
Da 2: 45 and the interpretation is t."
6: 4 he was t and neither corrupt
Lk 16: 11 So if you have not been t
16: 12 And if you have not been t
19: 17 'Because you have been t
1Co 7: 25 one who by the Lord's mercy is t.
1Ti 1: 15 Here is a t saying that deserves full
3: 1 Here is a t saying: If anyone sets his
3: 11 but temperate and t in everything.
4: 9 This is a t saying that deserves full
2Ti 2: 11 Here is a t saying:
Tit 1: 9 must hold firmly to the t message
3: 8 This is a t saying.
Rev 21: 5 for these words are t and true."
22: 6 "These words are t and true.

TRUTH* (TRUE TRUTHFUL TRUTHFULNESS TRUTHS)

Ge 42: 16 tested to see if you are telling the t.
1Ki 17: 24 LORD from your mouth is the t."
22: 16 the t in the name of the LORD?"
2Ch 18: 15 the t in the name of the LORD?"
Ps 15: 2 who speaks the t from his heart
25: 5 guide me in your t and teach me,
26: 3 and I walk continually in your t.
31: 5 redeem me, O LORD, the God of t
40: 10 do not conceal your love and your t
40: 11 your t always protect me.
43: 3 Send forth your light and your t,
45: 4 victoriously in behalf of t, humility
51: 6 Surely you desire t
52: 3 than speaking the t.
86: 11 and I will walk in your t;
96: 13 and the peoples in his t.
119: 30 I have chosen the way of t;
119: 43 of t from my mouth,
145: 18 to all who call on him in t.
Pr 16: 13 they value a man who speaks the t.
23: 23 Buy the t and do not sell it;
Isa 45: 19 I, the LORD, speak the t;
48: 1 but not in t or righteousness—
59: 14 t has stumbled in the streets,
59: 15 T is nowhere to be found,
65: 16 will do so by the God of t;
65: 16 will swear by the God of t.
Jer 5: 1 who deals honestly and seeks the t,
5: 3 do not your eyes look for t?
7: 28 T has perished; it has vanished
9: 3 it is not by t
9: 5 and no one speaks the t.
26: 15 for in t the LORD has sent me
Da 8: 12 and t was thrown to the ground.
9: 13 and giving attention to your t.
10: 21 what is written in the Book of T.
11: 2 "Now then, I tell you the t:
Am 5: 10 and despise him who tells the t.
Zec 8: 3 will be called the City of T,
Zec 8: 16 are to do: Speak the t to each other,
8: 19 Therefore love t and peace."
Mt 5: 18 I tell you the t, until heaven
5: 26 I tell you the t, you will not get out
6: 2 I tell you the t, they have received
6: 5 I tell you the t, they have received
6: 16 I tell you the t, they have received
8: 10 "I tell you the t, I have not found
10: 15 I tell you the t, it will be more
10: 23 I tell you the t, you will not finish
10: 42 I tell you the t, he will certainly not
11: 11 I tell you the t: Among those born
13: 17 For I tell you the t, many prophets
16: 28 I tell you the t, some who are
17: 20 I tell you the t, if you have faith
18: 3 And he said: "I tell you the t,
18: 13 And if he finds it, I tell you the t,
18: 18 "I tell you the t, whatever you bind
19: 23 to his disciples, "I tell you the t,
19: 28 "I tell you the t, at the renewal
21: 21 Jesus replied, "I tell you the t,
21: 31 Jesus said to them, "I tell you the t,
22: 16 of God in accordance with the t.
23: 36 I tell you the t, all this will come
24: 2 "I tell you the t, not one stone here
24: 34 I tell you the t, this generation will
24: 47 I tell you the t, he will put him
25: 12 'I tell you the t, I don't know you.'
25: 40 The King will reply, 'I tell you the t
25: 45 "He will reply, 'I tell you the t,
26: 13 tell you the t, wherever this gospel
26: 21 "I tell you the t, one
26: 34 "I tell you the t," Jesus answered,
Mk 3: 28 I tell you the t, all the sins
5: 33 with fear, told him the whole t.
8: 12 I tell you the t, no sign will be given
9: 1 he said to them, "I tell you the t,
9: 41 I tell you the t, anyone who gives
10: 15 I tell you the t, anyone who will not
10: 29 "I tell you the t," Jesus replied,
11: 23 "I tell you the t, if anyone says
12: 14 of God in accordance with the t.
12: 43 Jesus said, "I tell you the t,
13: 30 I tell you the t, this generation will
14: 9 I tell you the t, wherever the gospel
14: 18 "I tell you the t, one
14: 25 "I tell you the t, I will not drink
14: 30 "I tell you the t," Jesus answered,
Lk 4: 24 "I tell you the t," he continued,
9: 27 I tell you the t, some who are
12: 37 I tell you the t, he will dress himself
12: 44 I tell you the t, he will put him
18: 17 I tell you the t, anyone who will not
18: 29 I tell you the t," Jesus said to them,
20: 21 of God in accordance with the t.
21: 3 "I tell you the t," he said, "this
21: 32 tell you the t, this generation will
23: 43 answered him, "I tell you the t,
Jn 1: 14 from the Father, full of grace and t.
1: 17 and t came through Jesus Christ.
1: 51 "I tell you the t, you shall see
3: 3 "I tell you the t, no one can see
3: 5 Jesus answered, "I tell you the t,
3: 11 I tell you the t, we speak
3: 21 But whoever lives by the t comes
4: 23 worship the Father in spirit and t,
4: 24 must worship in spirit and in t."
5: 19 "I tell you the t, the Son can do
5: 24 "I tell you the t, whoever hears my
5: 25 I tell you the t, a time is coming
5: 33 and he has testified to the t.
6: 26 "I tell you the t, you are looking
6: 32 Jesus said to them, "I tell you the t,
6: 47 I tell you the t, he who believes has
6: 53 Jesus said to them, "I tell you the t,
7: 18 the one who sent him is a man of t;
8: 32 Then you will know the t,
8: 32 and the t will set you free."
8: 34 Jesus replied, "I tell you the t,
8: 40 who has told you the t that I heard
8: 44 to the t, for there is no t in him.
8: 45 I tell the t, you do not believe me!
8: 46 I am telling the t, why don't you
8: 51 I tell you the t, if anyone keeps my
8: 58 "I tell you the t," Jesus answered,
10: 1 "I tell you the t, the man who does
10: 7 "I tell you the t, I am the gate
12: 24 I tell you the t, unless a kernel
13: 16 I tell you the t, no servant is greater
13: 20 tell you the t, whoever accepts
13: 21 "I tell you the t, one of you is going
13: 38 I tell you the t, before the rooster
14: 6 I am the way and the t and the life.
14: 12 I tell you the t, anyone who has
14: 17 with you forever—the Spirit of t.

Jn   15:26 the Spirit of *t* who goes out
        16: 7 But I tell you the *t*: It is
        16:13 But when he, the Spirit of *t*, comes.
        16:13 comes, he will guide you into all *t*.
        16:20 I tell you the *t*, you will weep
        16:23 I tell you the *t*, my Father will give
        17:17 them by the *t*; your word is *t*.
        18:23 if I spoke the *t*, why did you strike
        18:37 into the world, to testify to the *t*.
        18:37 on the side of *t* listens to me."
        18:38 "What is *t*?" Pilate asked.
        19:35 He knows that he tells the *t*,
        21:18 I tell you the *t*, when you were
Ac   20:30 and distort the *t* in order
        21:24 everybody will know there is no *t*
        21:34 commander could not get at the *t*
        24: 8 able to learn the *t* about all these
        28:25 "The Holy Spirit spoke the *t*
Ro   1:18 of men who suppress the *t*
         1:25 They exchanged the *t* of God
         2: 2 who do such things is based on *t*.
         2: 8 who reject the *t* and follow evil,
         2:20 embodiment of knowledge and *t*—
         9: 1 I speak the *t* in Christ—I am not
        15: 8 of the Jews on behalf of God's *t*,
1Co   5: 8 the bread of sincerity and *t*.
        13: 6 in evil but rejoices with the *t*.
2Co   4: 2 setting forth the *t* plainly we
        11:10 As surely as the *t* of Christ is in me,
        12: 6 because I would be speaking the *t*,
        13: 8 against the *t*, but only for the *t*.
Gal   2: 5 so that the *t* of the gospel might
         2:14 in line with the *t* of the gospel,
         4:16 enemy by telling you the *t*?
         5: 7 and kept you from obeying the *t*?
Eph   1:13 when you heard the word of *t*,
         4:15 Instead, speaking the *t* in love,
         4:21 him in accordance with the *t* that is
         5: 9 and *t*) and find out what pleases
         6:14 with the belt of *t* buckled
Col   1: 5 heard about in the word of *t*,
         1: 6 understood God's grace in all its *t*.
2Th   2:10 because they refused to love the *t*
         2:12 who have not believed the *t*
         2:13 and through belief in the *t*.
1Ti   2: 4 to come to a knowledge of the *t*.
         2: 7 I am telling the *t*, I am not lying—
         3:15 the pillar and foundation of the *t*.
         4: 3 who believe and who know the *t*.
         6: 5 who have been robbed of the *t*
2Ti   2:15 correctly handles the word of *t*.
         2:18 have wandered away from the *t*,
         2:25 them to a knowledge of the *t*,
         3: 7 never able to acknowledge the *t*.
         3: 8 so also these men oppose the *t*—
         4: 4 will turn their ears away from the *t*
Tit   1: 1 the knowledge of the *t* that leads
         1:14 of those who reject the *t*.
Heb   10:26 received the knowledge of the *t*,
Jas   1:18 birth through the word of *t*,
         3:14 do not boast about it or deny the *t*
         5:19 if you should wander from the *t*
1Pe   1:22 by obeying the *t* so that you have
2Pe   1:12 established in the *t* you now have.
         2: 2 the way of *t* into disrepute.
1Jn   1: 6 we lie and do not live by the *t*.
         1: 8 deceive ourselves and the *t* is not
         2: 4 commands is a liar, and the *t* is not
         2: 8 its *t* is seen in him and you,
         2:20 and all of you know the *t*.
         2:21 because no lie comes from the *t*.
         2:21 because you do not know the *t*,
         3:18 or tongue but with actions and in *t*.
         3:19 we know that we belong to the *t*,
         4: 6 is how we recognize the Spirit of *t*
         5: 6 testifies, because the Spirit is the *t*.
2Jn   1 whom I love in the *t*—
         1 who know the *t*—because of the *t*,
         3 will be with us in *t* and love.
         4 of your children walking in the *t*,
3Jn   1 friend Gaius, whom I love in the *t*.
         3 how you continue to walk in the *t*.
         3 tell about your faithfulness to the *t*
         4 my children are walking in the *t*.
         8 we may work together for the *t*.
        12 everyone—and even by the *t* itself.

TRUTHFUL* (TRUTH)

Pr   12:17 A *t* witness gives honest testimony,
        12:19 *T* lips endure forever,
        12:22 but he delights in men who are *t*
        14: 5 A *t* witness does not deceive,
        14:25 A *t* witness saves lives,
Jer   4: 2 and if in a *t*, just and righteous way
Jn   3:33 it has certified that God is *t*.

2Co   6: 7 in *t* speech and in the power

TRUTHFULNESS* (TRUTH)

Ro   3: 7 "If my falsehood enhances God's *t*

TRUTHS* (TRUTH)

1Co   2:13 expressing spiritual *t*
1Ti   3: 9 hold of the deep *t* of the faith
         4: 6 brought up in the *t* of the faith
Heb   5:12 to teach you the elementary *t*

TRY (TRIED TRIES TRYING)

Ps   26: 2 Test me, O LORD, and *t* me,
Isa   7:13 enough to *t* the patience of men?
Lk   12:58 *t* hard to be reconciled to him
        13:24 will *t* to enter and will not be able
1Co   10:33 even as I *t* to please everybody
        14:12 *t* to excel in gifts that build up
2Co   5:11 is to fear the Lord, we *t*
1Th   5:15 always *t* to be kind to each other
Tit   2: 9 to *t* to please them, not to talk back

TRYING (TRY)

2Co   5:12 We are not *t* to commend ourselves
Gal   1:10 If I were still *t* to please men,
1Th   2: 4 We are not *t* to please men but God
1Pe   1:11 *t* to find out the time
1Jn   2:26 things to you about those who are *t*

TUMORS

1Sa   5: 6 them and afflicted them with *t*.

TUNE

1Co   14: 7 anyone know what *t* is being

TUNIC (TUNICS)

Lk   6:29 do not stop him from taking your *t*.

TUNICS (TUNIC)

Lk   3:11 "The man with two *t* should share

TURMOIL

Ps   65: 7 and the *t* of the nations.
Pr   15:16 than great wealth with *t*.

TURN (TURNED TURNING TURNS)

Ex   32:12 *T* from your fierce anger; relent
Nu   32:15 If you *t* away from following him,
Dt   5:32 do not *t* aside to the right
        28:14 Do not *t* aside from any
        30:10 and *t* to the LORD your God
Jos   1: 7 do not *t* from it to the right
1Ki   8:58 May he *t* our hearts to him,
2Ch   7:14 and *t* from their wicked ways,
         7:30 He will not *t* his face from you
Job   33:30 to *t* back his soul from the pit,
Ps   28: 1 do not *t* a deaf ear to me.
        34:14 *T* from evil and do good;
        51:13 and sinners will *t* back to you.
        78: 6 they in *t* would tell their children.
       119: 36 *T* my heart toward your statutes
       119:132 *T* to me and have mercy on me,
Pr   22: 6 when he is old he will not *t* from it.
Isa   17: 7 *t* their eyes to the Holy One
        28: 6 to those who *t* back the battle
        29:16 You *t* things upside down,
        30:21 Whether you *t* to the right
        45:22 "*T* to me and be saved,
        55: 7 Let him *t* to the LORD,
Jer   31:13 I will *t* their mourning
Eze   33: 9 if you do warn the wicked man to *t*
        33:11 *T* from your evil ways!
Jnh   3: 9 and with compassion *t*
Mal   4: 6 He will *t* the hearts of the fathers
Mt   5:39 you on the right cheek, *t*
        10:35 For I have come to *t*
Lk   1:17 to *t* the hearts of the fathers
Jn   12:40 nor I—and I would heal them."
        16:20 but your grief will *t* to joy.
Ac   3:19 Repent, then, and *t* to God,
        26:18 and *t* them from darkness to light,
1Co   14:31 For you can all prophesy in *t*
        15:23 But each in his own *t*: Christ,
1Ti   6:20 *T* away from godless chatter
1Pe   3:11 He must *t* from evil and do good;

TURNED (TURN)

Dt   23: 5 *t* the curse into a blessing for you,
1Ki   11: 4 his wives *t* his heart
2Ch   15: 4 But in their distress they *t*
Est   9: 1 but now the tables were *t*
         9:22 when their sorrow was *t* into joy
Ps   30: 3 All have *t* aside,
        30:11 You *t* my wailing into dancing;
        40: 1 he *t* to me and heard my cry

Isa   9:12 for all this, his anger is not *t* away,
        53: 6 each of us has *t* to his own way;
Hos   7: 8 Ephraim is a flat cake not *t* over.
Joel   2:31 The sun will be *t* to darkness
Lk   22:32 And when you have *t* back,
Ro   3:12 All have *t* away,

TURNING (TURN)

2Ki   21:13 wiping it and *t* it upside down.
Pr   2: 2 *t* your ear to wisdom
        14:27 *t* a man from the snares of death.

TURNS (TURN)

2Sa   22:29 the LORD *t* my darkness into light
Pr   15: 1 A gentle answer *t* away wrath,
Isa   44:25 and *t* it into nonsense,
Jas   5:20 Whoever *t* a sinner from the error

TWELVE

Ge   35:22 Jacob had *t* sons: The sons of Leah:
        49:28 All these are the *t* tribes of Israel,
Mt   10: 1 He called his *t* disciples to him
Lk   9:17 the disciples picked up *t* basketfuls
Rev   21:12 the names of the *t* tribes of Israel.
        21:14 of the *t* apostles of the Lamb.

TWIN (TWINS)

Ge   25:24 there were *t* boys in her womb.

TWINKLING*

1Co   15:52 in a flash, in the *t* of an eye,

TWINS (TWIN)

Ro   9:11 before the *t* were born

TWISTING* (TWISTS)

Pr   30:33 and as *t* the nose produces blood,

TWISTS (TWISTING)

Ex   23: 8 and *t* the words of the righteous.

TYRANNICAL*

Pr   28:16 A *t* ruler lacks judgment,

TYRE

Eze   28:12 a lament concerning the king of *T*
Mt   11:22 it will be more bearable for *T*

UNAPPROACHABLE*

1Ti   6:16 immortal and who lives in *u* light,

UNASHAMED*

1Jn   2:28 and *u* before him at his coming.

UNBELIEF* (UNBELIEVER UNBELIEVERS UNBELIEVING)

Mk   9:24 help me overcome my *u*!"
Ro   11:20 through *u* regarding the promise
        11:20 they were broken off because of *u*,
        11:23 And if they do not persist in *u*,
1Ti   1:13 because I acted in ignorance and *u*.
Heb   3:19 able to enter, because of their *u*.

UNBELIEVER* (UNBELIEF)

1Co   7:15 But if the *u* leaves, let him do so.
        10:27 If some *u* invites you to a meal
        14:24 if an *u* or someone who does not
2Co   6:15 have in common with an *u*?
1Ti   5: 8 the faith and is worse than an *u*.

UNBELIEVERS* (UNBELIEF)

Lk   12:46 and assign him a place with the *u*.
Ro   15:31 rescued from the *u* in Judea
1Co   6: 6 another—and this in front of *u*!
        14:22 however, is for believers, not for *u*,
        14:22 not for believers but for *u*;
        14:23 do not understand or some *u* come
2Co   4: 4 this age has blinded the minds of *u*,
         6:14 Do not be yoked together with *u*.

UNBELIEVING* (UNBELIEF)

Mt   17:17 "O *u* and perverse generation,"
Mk   9:19 "O *u* generation," Jesus replied,
Lk   9:41 "O *u* and perverse generation,"
1Co   7:14 For the *u* husband has been
         7:14 and the *u* wife has been sanctified
Heb   3:12 *u* heart that turns away
Rev   21: 8 But the cowardly, the *u*, the vile,

UNBLEMISHED*

Heb   9:14 the eternal Spirit offered himself *u*

UNCEASING

Ro   9: 2 and *u* anguish in my heart.

UNCERTAIN*

1Ti   6:17 which is so *u*, but to put their hope

UNCHANGEABLE* (UNCHANGING)

Heb   6:18 by two *u*things in which it is

UNCHANGING* (UNCHANGEABLE)

Heb   6:17 wanted to make the *u*nature

UNCIRCUMCISED

Lev 26:41 when their *u*hearts are humbled
1Sa 17:26 Who is this *u*Philistine that he
Jer   9:26 house of Israel is *u*in heart.''
Ac   7:51 stiff-necked people, with *u*hearts
Ro   4:11 had by faith while he was still *u*.
1Co 7:18 Was a man *u*when he was called?
Col   3:11 circumcised or *u*, barbarian,

UNCIRCUMCISION

1Co 7:19 is nothing and *u*is nothing.
Gal   6 neither circumcision nor *u*has any

UNCLEAN

Ge   7: 2 and two of every kind of *u*animal,
Lev 10:10 between the *u*and the clean,
     11: 4 it is ceremonially *u*for you.
     17:15 he will be ceremonially *u*till evening.
Isa   6: 5 ruined! For I am a man of *u*lips,
     52:11 Touch no *u*thing!
Mt 15:11 mouth does not make him '*u*,'
Ac 10:14 never eaten anything impure or *u*.'
Ro 14:14 fully convinced that no food is *u*
2Co 6:17 Touch no *u*thing,

UNCLOTHED*

2Co   5: 4 because we do not wish to be *u*

UNCONCERNED*

Eze 16:49 were arrogant, overfed and *u*;

UNCOVERED

Ru   3: 7 Ruth approached quietly, *u*his feet
1Co 11: 5 with her head *u*dishonors her head
     11:13 to pray to God with her head *u*?
Heb   4:13 Everything is *u*and laid bare

UNDERGOES* (UNDERGOING)

Heb 12: 8 (and everyone *u*discipline),

UNDERGOING* (UNDERGOES)

1Pe   5: 9 the world are *u*the same kind

UNDERSTAND (UNDERSTANDING UNDERSTANDS UNDERSTOOD)

Ne   8: 8 the people could *u*what was being
Job 38: 4 Tell me, if you *u*.
     42: 3 Surely I spoke of things I did not *u*,
Ps 14: 2 men to see if there are any who *u*,
     73:16 When I tried to *u*all this,
    119: 27 Let me *u*the teaching
    119:125 that I may *u*your statutes.
Pr   2: 5 then you will *u*the fear
     2: 9 Then you will *u*what is right
    30:18 four that I do not *u*:
Ecc   7:25 to *u*the stupidity of wickedness
    11: 5 so you cannot *u*the work of God,
Isa   6:10 *u*with their hearts,
    44:18 know nothing, they *u*nothing;
    52:15 they have not heard, they will *u*.
Jer 17: 9 Who can *u*it?
    31:19 after I came to *u*,
Da   9:25 and *u*this: From the issuing
Hos 14: 9 Who is discerning? He will *u*them.
Mt 13:15 *u*with their hearts
    24:15 Daniel—let the reader *u*—
Lk 24:45 so they could *u*the Scriptures.
Ac   8:30 "Do you *u*what you are reading?"
Ro   7:15 I do not *u*what I do.
    15:21 those who have not heard will *u*.''
1Co 2:12 that we may *u*what God has freely
    2:14 and he cannot *u*them,
    14:16 those who do not *u*say "Amen"
Eph   5:17 but *u*what the Lord's will is.
Heb 11: 3 By faith we *u*that the universe was
2Pe   1:20 you must *u*that no prophecy
     3: 3 you must *u*that in the last days
     3:16 some things that are hard to *u*,

UNDERSTANDING (UNDERSTAND)

1Ki   4:29 and a breadth of *u*as measureless
Job 12:12 Does not long life bring *u*?
    28:12 Where does *u*dwell?
    28:28 and to shun evil is *u*.' ''
    32: 8 of the Almighty, that gives him *u*.

Job 36:26 How great is God—beyond our *u*!
    37: 5 he does great things beyond our *u*.
Ps 111:10 follow his precepts have good *u*.
    119: 34 Give me *u*, and I will keep your law
    119:100 I have more *u*than the elders,
    119:104 I gain *u*from your precepts;
    119:130 it gives *u*to the simple.
    136: 5 who by his *u*made the heavens,
    147: 5 his *u*has no limit.
Pr   2: 2 and applying your heart to *u*,
     2: 6 his mouth come knowledge and *u*.
     3: 5 and lean not on your own *u*;
     3:13 the man who gains *u*,
     4: 5 Get wisdom, get *u*;
     4: 7 Though it cost all you have, get *u*.
     7: 4 and call *u*your kinsman;
     9:10 knowledge of the Holy One is *u*.
    10:23 but a man of *u*delights in wisdom.
    11:12 but a man of *u*holds his tongue.
    14:29 A patient man has great *u*,
    15:21 a man of *u*keeps a straight course.
    15:32 whoever heeds correction gains *u*.
    16:16 to choose *u*rather than silver!
    16:22 *U*is a fountain of life
    17:27 and a man of *u*is even-tempered.
    18: 2 A fool finds no pleasure in *u*
    19: 8 he who cherishes *u*prospers.
    20: 5 but a man of *u*draws them out.
    23:23 get wisdom, discipline and *u*.
Isa 11: 2 the Spirit of wisdom and of *u*,
    40:28 and his *u*no one can fathom.
    56:11 They are shepherds who lack *u*;
Jer   3:15 you with knowledge and *u*.
    10:12 stretched out the heavens by his *u*.
Da   5:12 a keen mind and knowledge and *u*,
    10:12 that you set your mind to gain *u*
Hos   4:11 which take away the *u*
Mk   4:12 and ever hearing but never *u*;
    12:33 with all your *u*and with all your
Lk   2:47 who heard him was amazed at his *u*
2Co   6: 6 in purity, *u*, patience and kindness;
Eph   1: 8 on us with all wisdom and *u*.
Php   4: 7 of God, which transcends all *u*,
Col   1: 9 through all spiritual wisdom and *u*
     2: 2 have the full riches of complete *u*,
1Jn 5:20 God has come and has given us *u*,

UNDERSTANDS (UNDERSTAND)

1Ch 28: 9 and *u*every motive
Jer   9:24 that he *u*and knows me,
Mt 13:23 man who hears the word and *u*it.
Ro   3:11 there is no one who *u*,
1Ti   6: 4 he is conceited and *u*nothing.

UNDERSTOOD (UNDERSTAND)

Ne   8:12 they now *u*the words that had
Ps 73:17 then I *u*their final destiny.
Isa 40:13 Who has *u*the mind of the LORD,
    40:21 Have you not *u*since the earth was
Jn   1: 5 but the darkness has not *u*it.
Ro   1:20 being *u*from what has been made,

UNDESIRABLE*

Jos 24:15 But if serving the LORD seems *u*

UNDIVIDED*

1Ch 12:33 to help David with *u*loyalty—
Ps 86:11 give me an *u*heart,
Eze 11:19 I will give them an *u*heart
1Co   7:35 way in *u*devotion to the Lord.

UNDOING

Pr 18: 7 A fool's mouth is his *u*,

UNDYING*

Eph   6:24 Lord Jesus Christ with an *u*love.

UNEQUALED*

Mt 24:21 *u*from the beginning of the world
Mk 13:19 of distress *u*from the beginning,

UNFADING*

1Pe   3: 4 the *u*beauty of a gentle

UNFAILING*

Ex 15:13 "In your *u*love you will lead
1Sa 20:14 But show me *u*kindness like that
2Sa 22:51 he shows *u*kindness
Ps   6: 4 save me because of your *u*love
    13: 5 But I trust in your *u*love;
    18:50 he shows *u*kindness
    21: 7 through the *u*love
    31:16 save me in your *u*love.
    32:10 but the LORD's *u*love
    33: 5 the earth is full of his *u*love.

Ps 33:18 those whose hope is in his *u*love,
    33:22 May your *u*love rest upon us,
    36: 7 How priceless is your *u*love!
    44:26 redeem us because of your *u*love.
    48: 9 we meditate on your *u*love.
    51: 1 according to your *u*love;
    52: 8 I trust in God's *u*love
    77: 8 Has his *u*love vanished forever?
    85: 7 Show us your *u*love, O LORD,
    90:14 in the morning with your *u*love,
    107: 8 thanks to the LORD for his *u*love
    107: 15 thanks to the LORD for his *u*love
    107: 21 to the LORD for his *u*love
    107: 31 to the LORD for his *u*love
    119: 41 May your *u*love come to me,
    119: 76 May your *u*love be my comfort,
    130: 7 for with the LORD is *u*love
    143: 8 bring me word of your *u*love,
    143: 12 In your *u*love, silence my enemies;
    147: 11 who put their hope in his *u*love.
Pr 19:22 What a man desires is *u*love;
    20: 6 Many a man claims to have *u*love,
Isa 54:10 yet my *u*love for you will not be
La   3:32 so great is his *u*love.
Hos 10:12 reap the fruit of *u*love,

UNFAITHFUL (UNFAITHFULNESS)

Lev   6: 2 is *u*to the LORD by deceiving his
Nu   5: 6 and so is *u*to the LORD,
1Ch 10:13 because he was *u*to the LORD;
Pr 11: 6 the *u*are trapped by evil desires.
    13: 2 the *u*have a craving for violence.
    13:15 but the way of the *u*is hard.
    22:12 but he frustrates the words of the *u*.
    23:28 and multiplies the *u*among men.
    25:19 is reliance on the *u*in times
Jer   3:20 But like a woman *u*to her husband,

UNFAITHFULNESS (UNFAITHFUL)

1Ch   9: 1 to Babylon because of their *u*
Mt   5:32 except for marital *u*, causes her
    19: 9 except for marital *u*, and marries another

UNFIT*

Tit   1:16 and *u*for doing anything good.

UNFOLDING

Ps 119:130 the *u*of your words gives light;

UNFORGIVING*

2Ti   3: 3 unholy, without love, *u*, slanderous

UNFRIENDLY*

Pr 18: 1 An *u*man pursues selfish ends;

UNFRUITFUL

1Co 14:14 my spirit prays, but my mind is *u*.

UNGODLINESS (UNGODLY)

Tit   2:12 It teaches us to say "No" to *u*

UNGODLY (UNGODLINESS)

Ro   5: 6 powerless, Christ died for the *u*.
1Ti   1: 9 the *u*and sinful, the unholy
2Ti   2:16 in it will become more and more *u*.
2Pe   2: 6 of what is going to happen to the *u*;
Jude   :15 and to convict all the *u*

UNGRATEFUL*

Lk   6:35 he is kind to the *u*and wicked.
2Ti   3: 2 disobedient to their parents, *u*,

UNHOLY*

1Ti   1: 9 and sinful, the *u*and irreligious;
2Ti   3: 2 ungrateful, *u*, without love,
Heb 10:29 as an *u*thing the blood

UNINTENTIONALLY

Lev   4: 2 'When anyone sins *u*and does
Nu 15:22 " 'Now if you *u*fail to keep any
Dt   4:42 flee if he had *u*killed his neighbor

UNIT

1Co 12:12 body is a *u*, though it is made up

UNITE (UNITED UNITY)

1Co   6:15 and *u*them with a prostitute?

UNITED (UNITE)

Ge   2:24 and mother and be *u*to his wife,
Mt 19: 5 and mother and be *u*to his wife,
Ro   6: 5 If we have been *u*with him like this
Eph   5:31 and mother and be *u*to his wife,
Php   2: 1 from being *u*with Christ,
Col   2: 2 encouraged in heart and in love,

UNITY* (UNITE)

2Ch 30: 12 the people to give them *u* of mind
Ps 133: 1 is when brothers live together in *u!*
Jn   17: 23 May they be brought to complete *u*
Ro 15: 5 a spirit of *u* among yourselves
Eph 4: 3 effort to keep the *u* of the Spirit
        4: 13 up until we all reach *u* in the faith
Col 3: 14 them all together in perfect *u.*

UNIVERSE*

1Co 4: 9 made a spectacle to the whole *u,*
Eph 4: 10 in order to fill the whole *u.)*
Php 2: 15 which you shine like stars in the *u*
Heb 1: 2 and through whom he made the *u.*
       11: 3 understand that the *u* was formed

UNJUST

Ro   3: 5 That God is *u* in bringing his wrath
      9: 14 What then shall we say? Is God *u?*
1Pe 2: 19 up under the pain of *u* suffering

UNKNOWN

Ac 17: 23 TO AN *U*GOD.

UNLEAVENED

Ex 12: 17 "Celebrate the Feast of *U*Bread,
Dt 16: 16 at the Feast of *U*Bread, the Feast

UNLIMITED*

1Ti 1: 16 Jesus might display his *u* patience

UNLOVED

Pr 30: 23 an *u* woman who is married,

UNMARRIED

1Co 7: 8 It is good for them to stay *u,*
       7: 27 Are you *u?* Do not look for a wife.
       7: 32 An *u* man is concerned about

UNPLOWED

Ex 23: 11 the seventh year let the land lie *u*
Hos 10: 12 and break up your *u* ground;

UNPRODUCTIVE

Tit 3: 14 necessities and not live *u* lives.
2Pe 1: 8 and *u* in your knowledge

UNPROFITABLE

Tit 3: 9 because these are *u* and useless.

UNPUNISHED

Ex 34: 7 Yet he does not leave the guilty *u;*
Pr   6: 29 no one who touches her will go *u,*
       11: 21 of this: The wicked will not go *u,*
       19: 5 A false witness will not go *u,*

UNQUENCHABLE

Lk   3: 17 he will burn up the chaff with *u* fire

UNREPENTANT*

Ro   2: 5 stubbornness and your *u* heart,

UNRIGHTEOUS*

Zep 3: 5 yet the *u* know no shame.
Mt   5: 45 rain on the righteous and the *u.*
1Pe 3: 18 the righteous for the *u,* to bring you
2Pe 2: 9 and to hold the *u* for the day

UNSEARCHABLE

Ro 11: 33 How *u* his judgments,
Eph 3: 8 preach to the Gentiles the *u* riches

UNSEEN*

Mt   6: 6 and pray to your Father, who is *u.*
       6: 18 who is *u;* and your Father,
2Co 4: 18 on what is seen, but on what is *u.*
       4: 18 temporary, but what is *u* is eternal.

UNSETTLED*

1Th 3: 3 so that no one would be *u*
2Th 2: 2 not to become easily *u*

UNSHRUNK

Mt   9: 16 patch of *u* cloth on an old garment,

UNSPIRITUAL*

Ro   7: 14 but I am *u,* sold as a slave to sin.
Col 2: 18 and his *u* mind puffs him up
Jas 3: 15 down from heaven but is earthly, *u,*

UNSTABLE*

Jas 1: 8 he is a double-minded man, *u*
2Pe 2: 14 they seduce the *u;* they are experts
       3: 16 ignorant and *u* people distort,

UNTHINKABLE*

Job 34: 12 It is *u* that God would do wrong,

UNTIE

Mk   1: 7 worthy to stoop down and *u.*
Lk 13: 15 each of you on the Sabbath *u* his ox

UNVEILED*

2Co 3: 18 with *u* faces all reflect the Lord's

UNWHOLESOME*

Eph 4: 29 Do not let any *u* talk come out

UNWISE

Eph 5: 15 how you live—not as *u* but as wise.

UNWORTHY*

Ge 32: 10 I am *u* of all the kindness
Job 40: 4 "I am *u*—how can I reply to you?
Lk 17: 10 should say, 'We are *u* servants,
1Co 11: 27 Lord in an *u* manner will be guilty

UPHOLD (UPHOLDS)

Isa 41: 10 I will *u* you with my righteous right
Ro   3: 31 Not at all! Rather, we *u* the law.

UPHOLDS* (UPHOLD)

Ps 37: 17 but the LORD *u* the righteous.
       37: 24 for the LORD *u* him with his hand.
       63: 8 your right hand *u* me.
      140: 12 and *u* the cause of the needy.
      145: 14 The LORD *u* all those who fall
      146: 7 He *u* the cause of the oppressed

UPRIGHT

Dt 32: 4 *u* and just is he.
Job 1: 1 This man was blameless and *u;*
Ps   7: 10 who saves the *u* in heart.
       11: 7 *u* men will see his face.
       25: 8 Good and *u* is the LORD;
       33: 1 it is fitting for the *u* to praise him.
       64: 10 let all the *u* in heart praise him!
       92: 15 proclaiming, "The LORD is *u;*
       97: 11 and joy on the *u* in heart.
      119: 7 I will praise you with an *u* heart
Pr   2: 7 He holds victory in store for the *u,*
       3: 32 but takes the *u* into his confidence.
      14: 2 whose walk is *u* fears the LORD,
      15: 8 but the prayer of the *u* pleases him.
      21: 29 an *u* man gives thought to his ways.
Isa 26: 7 O *u* One, you make the way
Tit 1: 8 who is self-controlled, *u,* holy
       2: 12 *u* and godly lives in this present

UPROOTED

Dt 28: 63 You will be *u* from the land you are
Jer 31: 40 The city will never again be *u*
Jude   : 12 without fruit and *u*—twice dead.

UPSET

Lk 10: 41 are worried and *u* about many

URIAH

Hittite husband of Bathsheba, killed by David's order (2Sa 11).

USEFUL

Eph 4: 28 doing something *u*
2Ti 2: 21 *u* to the Master and prepared
       3: 16 Scripture is God-breathed and is *u*
Phm   : 11 now he has become *u* both to you

USELESS

1Co 15: 14 our preaching is *u*
Tit 3: 9 these are unprofitable and *u.*
Phm   : 11 Formerly he was *u* to you,
Heb 7: 18 a *u* (for the law made nothing perfect
Jas 2: 20 faith without deeds is *u?*

USURY

Ne   5: 10 But let the exacting of *u* stop!
Ps 15: 5 who lends his money without *u*

UTMOST

Job 34: 36 that Job might be tested to the *u*

UTTER (UTTERS)

Ps 78: 2 I will *u* hidden things, things from of
                old—
Mt 13: 35 I will *u* things hidden

UTTERS (UTTER)

1Co 14: 2 he *u* mysteries with his spirit.

UZZIAH

Son of Amaziah; king of Judah also known as
Azariah (2Ki 15:1-7, 1Ch 6:24; 2Ch 26). Struck
with leprosy because of pride (2Ch 26:16-23).

VAIN

Ps 33: 17 A horse is a *v* hope for deliverance;
       73: 13 in *v* have I kept my heart pure;
      127: 1 its builders labor in *v.*
Isa 65: 23 They will not toil in *v*
1Co 15: 2 Otherwise, you have believed in *v.*
       15: 58 labor in the Lord is not in *v.*
2Co 6: 1 not to receive God's grace in *v.*
Gal 2: 2 running or had run my race in *v.*

VALIANT

1Sa 10: 26 by *v* men whose hearts God had

VALID

Jn   8: 14 my own behalf, my testimony is *v,*

VALLEY (VALLEYS)

Ps 23: 4 walk through the *v* of the shadow
Isa 40: 4 Every *v* shall be raised up,
Joel 3: 14 multitudes in the *v* of decision!

VALLEYS (VALLEY)

SS   2: 1 a lily of the *v.*

VALUABLE (VALUE)

Lk 12: 24 And how much more *v* you are

VALUE (VALUABLE VALUED)

Lev 27: 3 set the *v* of a male between the ages
Pr 16: 13 they *v* a man who speaks the truth.
       31: 11 and lacks nothing of *v.*
Mt 13: 46 When he found one of great *v,*
1Ti 4: 8 For physical training is of some *v,*
Heb 11: 26 as of greater *v* than the treasures

VALUED (VALUE)

Lk 16: 15 What is highly *v* among men is

VANISHES

Jas 4: 14 appears for a little while and then *v.*

VASHTI*

Queen of Persia replaced by Esther (Est 1-2).

VAST

Ge   2: 1 completed in all their *v* array.
Dt   1: 19 of the Amorites through all that *v*
       8: 15 He led you through the *v*
Ps 139: 17 How *v* is the sum of them!

VEGETABLES

Pr 15: 17 of *v* where there is love
Ro 14: 2 whose faith is weak, eats only *v.*

VEIL

Ex 34: 33 to them, he put a *v* over his face.
2Co 3: 14 for to this day the same *v* remains

VENGEANCE (AVENGE AVENGER AVENGES AVENGING REVENGE)

Nu 31: 3 to carry out the LORD's *v* on them
Isa 34: 8 For the LORD has a day of *v,*
Na   1: 2 The LORD takes *v* on his foes

VERDICT

Jn   3: 19 This is the *v:* Light has come

VICTOR'S* (VICTORY)

2Ti 2: 5 he does not receive the *v* crown

VICTORIES* (VICTORY)

2Sa 22: 51 He gives his king great *v;*
Ps 18: 50 He gives his king great *v;*
       21: 1 great is his joy in the *v* you give!
       21: 5 Through the *v* you gave, his glory is
       44: 4 who decrees *v* for Jacob.

VICTORIOUS (VICTORY)

Ps 20: 5 for joy when you are *v*

VICTORIOUSLY* (VICTORY)

Ps 45: 4 In your majesty ride forth *v*

VICTORY (VICTOR'S VICTORIES VICTORIOUS VICTORIOUSLY)

2Sa 8: 6 gave David *v* wherever he
Ps 44: 6 my sword does not bring me *v;*
       60: 12 With God we will gain the *v;*
      129: 2 they have not gained the *v* over me.

Pr   11: 14 but many advisers make v sure.
1Co 15: 54 "Death has been swallowed up in v
     15: 57 He gives us the v through our Lord
1Jn   5: 4 This is the v that has overcome

VIEW

Pr   5: 21 are in full v of the LORD,
2Ti   4: 1 and in v of his appearing

VILLAGE

Mk   6: 6 went around teaching from v to v.

VINDICATED (VINDICATION)

Job 13: 18 I know I will be v.
1Ti   3: 16 was v by the Spirit,

VINDICATION (VINDICATED)

Ps   24: 5 and v from God his Savior.

VINE (VINEYARD)

Ps 128: 3 Your wife will be like a fruitful v
Isa 36: 16 one of you will eat from his own v
Jnh   4: 6 Jonah was very happy about the v.
Jn   15: 1 "I am the true v, and my Father is

VINEGAR

Pr   10: 26 As v to the teeth and smoke
Mk   15: 36 filled a sponge with wine v,

VINEYARD (VINE)

1Ki 21: 1 an incident involving a v belonging
Pr   31: 16 out of her earnings she plants a v.
SS   1: 6 my own v I have neglected.
Isa   5: 1 My loved one had a v
1Co   9: 7 Who plants a v and does not eat

VIOLATION

Heb   2: 2 every v and disobedience received

VIOLENCE (VIOLENT)

Ge   6: 11 in God's sight and was full of v.
Isa 53: 9 though he had done no v,
     60: 18 No longer will v be heard
Eze 45: 9 Give up your v and oppression
Joel 3: 19 of v done to the people of Judah,
Jnh   3: 8 give up their evil ways and their v.

VIOLENT (VIOLENCE)

Eze 18: 10 "Suppose he has a v son, who sheds
1Ti   3: 2 a persecutor and a v man,
      3: 3 not v but gentle, not quarrelsome,
Tit   1: 7 not v, not pursuing dishonest gain.

VIPERS

Ps 140: 3 the poison of v is on their lips.
Lk   3: 7 "You brood of v! Who warned you
Ro   3: 13 "The poison of v is on their lips."

VIRGIN (VIRGINS)

Dt   22: 15 shall bring proof that she was a v
Isa   7: 14 The v will be with child
Mt   1: 23 "The v will be with child
Lk   1: 34 I am a v?" The angel answered,
2Co 11: 2 that I might present you as a pure v

VIRGINS (VIRGIN)

Mt   25: 1 will be like ten v who took their
1Co   7: 25 Now about v: I have no command

VIRTUES*

Col   3: 14 And over all these v put on love,

VISIBLE

Eph   5: 13 exposed by the light becomes v,
Col   1: 16 and on earth, v and invisible,

VISION (VISIONS)

Da   9: 24 to seal up v and prophecy
Ac   26: 19 disobedient to the v from heaven.

VISIONS (VISION)

Nu   12: 6 I reveal myself to him in v,
Joel 2: 28 your young men will see v.
Ac   2: 17 your young men will see v,

VOICE

Dt   30: 20 listen to his v, and hold fast to him.
1Sa 15: 22 as in obeying the v of the LORD?
Job 40: 9 and can your v thunder like his?
Ps   19: 4 Their v goes out into all the earth,
     29: 3 The v of the LORD is
     66: 19 and heard my v in prayer.
     95: 7 Today, if you hear his v,
Pr   8: 1 Does not understanding raise her v
Isa 30: 21 your ears will hear a v behind you,

Isa 40: 3 A v of one calling:
Mk   1: 3 "a v of one calling in the desert.
Jn   5: 28 are in their graves will hear his v
     10: 3 and the sheep listen to his v.
Ro   10: 18 "Their v has gone out
Heb   3: 7 "Today, if you hear his v,
Rev   3: 20 If anyone hears my v and opens

VOMIT

Lev 18: 28 it will v you out as it vomited out
Pr   26: 11 As a dog returns to its v,
2Pe   2: 22 "A dog returns to its v," and,

VOW (VOWS)

Nu   6: 2 a v of separation to the LORD
     30: 2 When a man makes a v
Jdg 11: 30 Jephthah made a v to the LORD:

VOWS (VOW)

Ps 116: 14 I will fulfill my v to the LORD
Pr   20: 25 and only later to consider his v.

VULTURES

Mt   24: 28 is a carcass, there the v will gather.

WAGE (WAGES WAGING)

2Co 10: 3 we do not v war as the world does.

WAGES (WAGE)

Mal   3: 5 who defraud laborers of their w,
Lk   10: 7 for the worker deserves his w.
Ro   4: 4 his w are not credited to him
      6: 23 For the w of sin is death,
1Ti   5: 18 and "The worker deserves his w."

WAGING (WAGE)

Ro   7: 23 w war against the law of my mind

WAILING

Ps   30: 11 You turned my w into dancing;

WAIST

2Ki   1: 8 and with a leather belt around his w."
Mt   3: 4 he had a leather belt around his w.

WAIT (AWAITS WAITED WAITING WAITS)

Ps   27: 14 W for the LORD;
    130: 5 I w for the LORD, my soul waits.
Isa 30: 18 Blessed are all who w for him!
Ac   1: 4 w for the gift my Father promised,
Ro   8: 23 as we w eagerly for our adoption
1Th   1: 10 and to w for his Son from heaven,
Tit   2: 13 while we w for the blessed hope—

WAITED (WAIT)

Ps   40: 1 I w patiently for the LORD;

WAITING (WAIT)

Heb   9: 28 to those who are w for him.

WAITS (WAIT)

Ro   8: 19 creation w in eager expectation

WAKE (AWAKE WAKENS)

Eph   5: 14 "W up, O sleeper,

WAKENS* (WAKE)

Isa 50: 4 He w me morning by morning.
     50: 4 w my ear to listen like one being

WALK (WALKED WALKING WALKS)

Lev 26: 12 I will w among you and be your
Dt   5: 33 W in all the way that the LORD
      6: 7 and when you w along the road,
     10: 12 to w in all his ways, to love him,
     11: 19 and when you w along the road,
     11: 22 to w in all his ways and to hold fast
     26: 17 and that you will w in his ways,
Jos 22: 5 to w in all his ways,
Ps   1: 1 who does not w in the counsel
     15: 2 He whose w is blameless
     23: 4 Even though I w
     84: 11 from those whose w is blameless.
     89: 15 who w in the light of your presence
    119: 45 I will w about in freedom,
Pr   4: 12 When you w, your steps will not be
      6: 22 When you w, they will guide you;
Isa   2: 3 so that we may w in his paths."
      2: 5 let us w in the light of the LORD.
     30: 21 saying, "This is the way; w in it."
     40: 31 they will w and not be faint.
     57: 2 Those who w uprightly
Jer   6: 16 ask where the good way is, and w
Am   3: 3 Do two w together

Mic   4: 5 All the nations may w
      6: 8 and to w humbly with your God.
Mk   2: 9 'Get up, take your mat and w'?
Jn   8: 12 Whoever follows me will never w
1Jn   1: 6 with him yet w in the darkness.
      1: 7 But if we w in the light,
2Jn   6 his command is that you w in love.

WALKED (WALK)

Ge   5: 24 Enoch w with God; then he was no
Jos 14: 9 which your feet have w will be your
Mt   14: 29 won the water and came toward
             Jesus.

WALKING (WALK)

1Ki   3: 3 love for the LORD by w according
Da   3: 25 I see four men w around in the fire,
2Jn   4 of your children w in the truth.

WALKS (WALK)

Pr   10: 9 The man of integrity w securely,
     13: 20 He who w with the wise grows wise
Isa 33: 15 He who w righteously
Jn   11: 9 A man who w by day will not

WALL (WALLS)

Jos   6: 20 w collapsed; so every man charged
Ne   2: 17 let us rebuild the w of Jerusalem,
Eph   2: 14 the dividing w of hostility,
Rev 21: 12 It had a great, high w

WALLOWING

2Pe   2: 22 back to her w in the mud."

WALLS (WALL)

Isa 58: 12 be called Repairer of Broken W,
     60: 18 but you will call your w Salvation
Heb 11: 30 By faith the w of Jericho fell,

WANDER (WANDERED)

Nu   32: 13 he made them w in the desert forty
Jas   5: 19 one of you should w from the truth

WANDERED (WANDER)

Eze 34: 6 My sheep w over all the mountains
Mt   18: 12 go to look for the one that w off?
1Ti   6: 10 have w from the faith and pierced
2Ti   2: 18 who have w away from the truth.

WANT (WANTED WANTING WANTS)

1Sa   8: 19 "We w a king over us.
Mt   19: 21 Jesus answered, "If you w
Lk   19: 14 'We don't w this man to be our king
Ro   7: 15 For what I w to do I do not do,
     13: 3 Do you w to be free from fear
2Co 12: 14 what I w is not your possessions
Php   3: 10 I w to know Christ and the power

WANTED (WANT)

1Co 12: 18 of them, just as he w them to be.
Heb   6: 17 Because God w to make

WANTING (WANT)

Da   5: 27 weighed on the scales and found w.
2Pe   3: 9 with you, not w anyone to perish,

WANTS (WANT)

Mt   5: 42 from the one who w to borrow
     20: 26 whoever w to become great
Mk   8: 35 For whoever w to save his life will
     10: 43 whoever w to become great
Ro   9: 18 he hardens whom he w to harden.
1Ti   2: 4 who w all men to be saved
1Pe   5: 2 you are willing, as God w you to be;

WAR (WARRIOR WARS)

Jos 11: 23 Then the land had rest from w.
1Sa 15: 18 make w on them until you have
Ps   68: 30 the nations who delight in w.
    120: 7 but when I speak, they are for w.
    144: 1 who trains my hands for w,
Isa   2: 4 nor will they train for w anymore.
Da   9: 26 W will continue until the end,
Ro   7: 23 waging w against the law
2Co 10: 3 we do not wage w as the world does
1Pe   2: 11 which w against your soul.
Rev 12: 7 And there was w in heaven.
     19: 11 With justice he judges and makes w

WARN* (WARNED WARNING WARNINGS)

Ex   21: 9 the people so they do not force
Nu   24: 14 let me w you of what this people
1Sa   8: 9 but w them solemnly and let them
1Ki   2: 42 swear by the LORD and w you,
2Ch 19: 10 you are to w them not to sin

Ps 81: 8 O my people, and I will *w* you—
Jer 42: 19 I *w* you today that you made a fatal
Eze 3: 18 and you do not *w* him or speak out
3: 19 But if you do *w* the wicked man
3: 20 Since you did not *w* him, he will die
3: 21 if you do *w* the righteous man not
33: 3 blows the trumpet to *w* the people,
33: 6 blow the trumpet to *w* the people
33: 9 if you do *w* the wicked man to turn
Lk 16: 28 Let him *w* them, so that they will
Ac 4: 17 we must *w* these men
1Co 4: 14 but to *w* you, as my dear children.
Gal 5: 21 I *w* you, as I did before, that those
1Th 5: 14 brothers, *w* those who are idle,
2Th 3: 15 an enemy, but *w* him as a brother.
2Ti 2: 14 W *them before God
Tit 3: 10 and then *w* him a second time.
3: 10 Wa divisive person once.
Rev 22: 18 I *w* everyone who hears the words

WARNED (WARN)

2Ki 17: 13 The LORD *w* Israel and Judah
Ps 19: 11 By them is your servant *w*;
Jer 22: 21 I *w* you when you felt secure,
Mt 3: 7 Who *w* you to flee
1Th 4: 6 have already told you and *w* you.
Heb 11: 7 when *w* about things not yet seen,
12: 25 they refused him who *w* them

WARNING (WARN)

Jer 6: 8 Take *w*, O Jerusalem,
1Ti 5: 20 so that the others may take *w*.

WARNINGS (WARN)

1Co 10: 11 and were written down as *w* for us,

WARRIOR (WAR)

Ex 15: 3 The LORD is a *w*;
1Ch 28: 3 you are a *w* and have shed blood.'
Pr 16: 32 Better a patient man than a *w*,

WARS (WAR)

Ps 46: 9 He makes *w* cease to the ends
Mt 24: 6 You will hear of *w* and rumors of *w*,

WASH (WASHED WASHING)

Ps 51: 7 *w* me, and I will be whiter
Jer 4: 14 the evil from your heart
Jn 13: 5 and began to *w* his disciples' feet,
Ac 22: 16 be baptized and *w* your sins away,
Jas 4: 8 W your hands, you sinners,
Rev 22: 14 Blessed are those who *w* their robes

WASHED (WASH)

Ps 73: 13 in vain have I *w* my hands
1Co 6: 11 you were *w*, you were sanctified,
Heb 10: 22 and having our bodies *w*
2Pe 2: 22 and, "A sow that is *w* goes back
Rev 7: 14 they have *w* their robes

WASHING (WASH)

Eph 5: 26 cleansing her by the *w* with water
1Ti 5: 10 showing hospitality, *w* the feet
Tit 3: 5 us through the *w* of rebirth

WASTED (WASTING)

Jn 6: 12 Let nothing be *w*."

WASTING (WASTED)

2Co 4: 16 Though outwardly we are *w* away,

WATCH (WATCHER WATCHES WATCHING WATCHMAN)

Ge 31: 49 "May the LORD keep *w*
Ps 90: 4 or like a *w* in the night.
141: 3 keep *w* over the door of my lips.
Pr 4: 6 love her, and she will *w* over you.
6: 22 when you sleep, they will *w*
Jer 31: 10 will *w* over his flock like a shepherd
Mic 7: 7 in hope for the LORD,
Mt 24: 42 "Therefore keep *w*, because you do
26: 41 Watch and pray so that you will not fall
Mk 13: 35 "Therefore keep *w* because you do
Lk 2: 8 keeping *w* over their flocks at night
1Ti 4: 16 W *your life and doctrine closely.
Heb 13: 17 They keep *w* over you

WATCHER* (WATCH)

Job 7: 20 O *w* of men?

WATCHES* (WATCH)

Nu 19: 5 While he *w*, the heifer is
Job 24: 15 The eye of the adulterer *w* for dusk;
Ps 1: 6 For the LORD *w* over the way
33: 14 from his dwelling place he *w*

Ps 63: 6 of you through the *w* of the night.
119: 148 through the *w* of the night,
121: 3 he who *w* over you will not slumber
121: 4 indeed, he who *w* over Israel
121: 5 The LORD *w* over you—
127: 1 Unless the LORD *w* over the city,
145: 20 LORD *w* over all who love him,
146: 9 The LORD *w* over the alien
Pr 31: 27 She *w* over the affairs
Ecc 11: 4 Whoever *w* the wind will not plant;
La 2: 19 as the *w* of the night begin;
4: 16 he no longer *w* over them.

WATCHING (WATCH)

Lk 12: 37 whose master finds them *w*

WATCHMAN (WATCH)

Eze 3: 17 I have made you a *w* for the house
33: 6 but I will hold the *w* accountable

WATER (WATERED WATERING WATERS WELL-WATERED)

Ex 7: 20 all the *w* was changed into blood.
17: 1 but there was no *w* for the people
Nu 20: 2 there was no *w* for the community,
Ps 1: 3 like a tree planted by streams of *w*,
22: 14 I am poured out like *w*.
42: 1 As the deer pants for streams of *w*,
Pr 25: 21 if he is thirsty, give him *w* to drink.
Isa 12: 3 With joy you will draw *w*
30: 20 of adversity and the *w* of affliction,
32: 2 like streams of *w* in the desert
49: 10 and lead them beside springs of *w*.
Jer 2: 13 broken cisterns that cannot hold *w*.
17: 8 will be like a tree planted by the *w*
31: 9 I will lead them beside streams of *w*
Eze 36: 25 I will sprinkle clean *w* on you,
Zec 14: 8 On that day living *w* will flow out
Mt 14: 29 walked on the *w* and came toward Jesus.
Mk 9: 41 anyone who gives you a cup of *w*
Lk 5: 4 to Simon, "Put out into deep *w*,
Jn 3: 5 unless he is born of *w* and the Spirit.
4: 10 he would have given you living *w*."
7: 38 streams of living *w* will flow
Eph 5: 26 washing with *w* through the word,
Heb 10: 22 our bodies washed with pure *w*.
1Pe 3: 21 this *w* symbolizes baptism that now
2Pe 2: 17 These men are springs without *w*
1Jn 5: 6 This is the one who came by *w*
5: 6 come by *w* only, but by *w*
5: 8 the Spirit, the *w* and the blood;
Rev 7: 17 to springs of living *w*.
21: 6 cost from the spring of the *w* of life.

WATERED (WATER)

1Co 3: 6 I planted the seed, Apollos *w* it,

WATERING (WATER)

Isa 55: 10 it without *w* the earth

WATERS (WATER)

Ps 23: 2 he leads me beside quiet *w*,
Ecc 11: 1 Cast your bread upon the *w*,
SS 8: 7 Many *w* cannot quench love;
Isa 11: 9 as the *w* cover the sea.
43: 2 When you pass through the *w*,
55: 1 come to the *w*;
58: 11 like a spring whose *w* never fail.
1Co 3: 7 plants nor he who *w* is anything,

WAVE (WAVES)

Lev 23: 11 He is to *w* the sheaf
Jas 1: 6 he who doubts is like a *w* of the sea,

WAVER*

1Ki 18: 21 "How long will you *w*
Ro 4: 20 Yet he did not *w* through unbelief

WAVES (WAVE)

Isa 57: 20 whose *w* cast up mire and mud.
Mt 8: 27 Even the winds and the *w* obey him
Eph 4: 14 tossed back and forth by the *w*,

WAY (WAYS)

Ex 13: 21 of cloud to guide them on their *w*
18: 20 and show them the *w* to live
Dt 1: 33 to show you the *w* you should go.
32: 6 Is this the *w* you repay the LORD,
1Sa 12: 23 I will teach you the *w* that is good
2Sa 22: 31 "As for God, his *w* is perfect;
1Ki 8: 23 wholeheartedly in your *w*
8: 36 Teach them the right *w* to live,
Job 23: 10 But he knows the *w* that I take;

Ps 1: 1 or stand in the *w* of sinners
32: 8 teach you in the *w* you should go;
37: 5 Commit your *w* to the LORD;
86: 11 Teach me your *w*, O LORD,
119: 9 can a young man keep his *w* pure?
139: 24 See if there is any offensive *w* in me
Pr 4: 11 I guide you in the *w* of wisdom
12: 15 The *w* of a fool seems right to him,
14: 12 There is a *w* that seems right
16: 17 he who guards his *w* guards his life.
19: 2 nor to be hasty and miss the *w*.
22: 6 Train a child in the *w* he should go.
30: 19 and the *w* of a man with a maiden.
Isa 30: 21 saying, "This is the *w*; walk in it."
35: 8 it will be called the *W* of Holiness.
40: 3 the *w* for the LORD;
48: 17 you in the *w* you should go.
53: 6 each of us has turned to his own *w*;
55: 7 Let the wicked forsake his *w*
Jer 5: 31 and my people love it this *w*
Mal 3: 1 who will prepare the *w* before me.
Mt 3: 3 'Prepare the *w* for the LORD,
Lk 7: 27 who will prepare your *w* before you
Jn 14: 6 "I am the *w* and the truth
Ac 1: 11 in the same *w* you have seen him go
9: 2 any there who belonged to the *W*,
24: 14 of the *W*, which they call a sect.
1Co 10: 13 also provide a *w* out so that you can
12: 31 will show you the most excellent *w*.
14: 1 Follow the *w* of love and eagerly
Col 1: 10 and may please him in every *w*:
Tit 2: 10 that in every *w* they will make
Heb 4: 15 who has been tempted in every *w*,
9: 8 was showing by this that the *w*
10: 20 and living *w* opened for us
13: 18 desire to live honorably in every *w*.

WAYS (WAY)

Ex 33: 13 teach me your *w* so I may know
Dt 10: 12 to walk in all his *w*, to love him,
26: 17 and that you will walk in his *w*,
30: 16 in his *w*, and to keep his commands
32: 4 and all his *w* are just.
Jos 22: 5 in all his *w*, to obey his commands,
2Ch 11: 17 walking in the *w* of David
Job 34: 21 "His eyes are on the *w* of men;
Ps 25: 4 Show me your *w*, O LORD,
25: 10 All the *w* of the LORD are loving
37: 7 fret when men succeed in their *w*,
51: 13 I will teach transgressors your *w*,
77: 13 Your *w*, O God, are holy.
119: 59 I have considered my *w*
139: 3 you are familiar with all my *w*.
145: 17 The LORD is righteous in all his *w*
Pr 3: 6 in all your *w* acknowledge him,
4: 26 and take only what are firm.
5: 21 For a man's *w* are in full view
16: 2 All a man's *w* seem innocent
16: 7 When a man's *w* are pleasing
Isa 2: 3 He will teach us his *w*,
55: 8 neither are your *w* my *w*,"
Eze 28: 15 You were blameless in your *w*
33: 8 out to dissuade him from his *w*,
Hos 14: 9 The *w* of the LORD are right;
Ro 1: 30 they invent *w* of doing evil;
Jas 3: 2 We all stumble in many *w*.

WEAK (WEAKER WEAKNESS WEAKNESSES)

Ps 41: 1 is he who has regard for the *w*,
72: 13 He will take pity on the *w*
82: 3 Defend the cause of the *w*
Eze 34: 4 You have not strengthened the *w*
Mt 26: 41 spirit is willing, but the body is *w*!
Ac 20: 35 of hard work we must help the *w*,
Ro 14: 1 Accept him whose faith is *w*,
15: 1 to bear with the failings of the *w*
1Co 1: 27 God chose the *w* things
8: 9 become a stumbling block to the *w*
9: 22 To the *w* I became *w*, to win the *w*
11: 30 That is why many among you are *w*
2Co 12: 10 For when I am *w*, then I am strong.
1Th 5: 14 help the *w*, be patient
Heb 12: 12 your feeble arms and *w* knees.

WEAK-WILLED (WILL)

2Ti 3: 6 and gain control over *w* women,

WEAKER* (WEAK)

2Sa 3: 1 the house of Saul grew *w* and *w*.
1Co 12: 22 seem to be *w* are indispensable,
1Pe 3: 7 them with respect as the *w* partner

WEAKNESS* (WEAK)

La 1: 6 in *w* they have fled

Ro	8:26	the Spirit helps us in our *w.*
1Co	1:25	and the *w* of God is stronger
	2:3	I came to you in *w* and fear,
	15:43	it is sown in *w,* it is raised in power;
2Co	11:30	boast of the things that show my *w.*
	12:9	for my power is made perfect in *w*
	13:4	he was crucified in *w,* yet he lives
Heb	5:2	since he himself is subject to *w*
	11:34	whose *w* was turned to strength;

WEAKNESSES* (WEAK)

2Co	12:5	about myself, except about my *w.*
	12:9	all the more gladly about my *w,*
	12:10	I delight in *w,* in insults,
Heb	4:15	unable to sympathize with our *w,*

WEALTH

Dt	8:18	gives you the ability to produce *w,*
2Ch	1:11	and you have not asked for *w.*
Ps	39:6	he heaps up *w,* not knowing who
Pr	3:9	Honor the LORD with your *w,*
	10:4	but diligent hands bring *w.*
	11:4	*W* is worthless in the day of wrath,
	13:7	to be poor, yet has great *w.*
	15:16	than great *w* with turmoil.
	22:4	bring *w* and honor and life.
Ecc	5:10	whoever loves *w* is never satisfied
	5:13	*w* hoarded to the harm of its owner,
SS	8:7	all the *w* of his house for love,
Mt	13:22	and the deceitfulness of *w* choke it,
Mk	10:22	away sad, because he had great *w.*
	12:44	They all gave out of their *w;* but she
Lk	15:13	and there squandered his *w*
1Ti	6:17	nor to put their hope in *w,*
Jas	5:2	Your *w* has rotted, and moths have
	5:5	You have hoarded *w*

WEAPON (WEAPONS)

Ne	4:17	work with one hand and held a *w*

WEAPONS (WEAPON)

Ecc	9:18	Wisdom is better than *w* of war,
2Co	6:7	with *w* of righteousness
	10:4	The *w* we fight with are not

WEAR (WEARING)

Dt	8:4	Your clothes did not *w* out
	22:5	nor a man *w* women's clothing,
Ps	102:26	they will all *w* out like a garment.
Pr	23:4	Do not *w* yourself out to get rich;
Isa	51:6	the earth will *w* out like a garment
Heb	1:11	they will all *w* out like a garment.
Rev	3:18	and white clothes to *w,*

WEARIES (WEARY)

Ecc	12:12	and much study *w* the body.

WEARING (WEAR)

Jn	19:5	When Jesus came out *w* the crown
Jas	2:3	attention to the man *w* fine clothes
1Pe	3:3	as braided hair and the *w*
Rev	7:9	They were *w* white robes

WEARY (WEARIES)

Isa	40:28	He will not grow tired or *w,*
	40:31	they will run and not grow *w,*
	50:4	know the word that sustains the *w.*
Mt	11:28	all you who are *w* and burdened,
Gal	6:9	Let us not become *w* in doing good,
Heb	12:3	so that you will not grow *w*
Rev	2:3	my name, and have not grown *w.*

WEDDING

Mt	22:11	who was not wearing *w* clothes.
Rev	19:7	For the *w* of the Lamb has come,

WEEDS

Mt	13:25	and sowed *w* among the wheat,

WEEK

Mt	28:1	at dawn on the first day of the *w,*
1Co	16:2	On the first day of every *w,*

WEEP (WEEPING WEPT)

Ecc	3:4	a time to *w* and a time to laugh,
Lk	6:21	Blessed are you who *w* now,
	23:28	*w* for yourselves and for your

WEEPING (WEEP)

Ps	30:5	*w* may remain for a night,
	126:6	He who goes out *w,*
Jer	31:15	Rachel *w* for her children
Mt	2:18	Rachel *w* for her children
	8:12	where there will be *w* and gnashing

WEIGH (OUTWEIGHS WEIGHED WEIGHS WEIGHTIER WEIGHTS)

1Co	14:29	others should *w* carefully what is

WEIGHED (WEIGH)

Job	28:15	nor can its price be *w* in silver.
Da	5:27	You have been *w* on the scales
Lk	21:34	or your hearts will be *w*

WEIGHS (WEIGH)

Pr	12:25	An anxious heart *w* a man down,
	15:28	of the righteous *w* its answers,
	21:2	but the LORD *w* the heart.
	24:12	not he who *w* the heart perceive

WEIGHTIER* (WEIGH)

Jn	5:36	"I have testimony *w* than that

WEIGHTS (WEIGH)

Lev	19:36	Use honest scales and honest *w,*
Dt	25:13	Do not have two differing *w*
Pr	11:1	but accurate *w* are his delight.

WELCOME (WELCOMES)

Mk	9:37	welcomes me does not *w* me
2Pe	1:11	and you will receive a rich *w*

WELCOMES (WELCOME)

Mt	18:5	whoever *w* a little child like this
2Jn	:11	Anyone who *w* him shares

WELL (WELLED WELLING WELLS)

Mt	15:31	crippled made *w,* the lame walking
Lk	14:5	falls into a *w* on the Sabbath day,
	17:19	your faith has made you *w.* "
Jas	5:15	in faith will make the sick person *w*

WELL-WATERED (WATER)

Isa	58:11	You will be like a *w* garden,

WELLED* (WELL)

2Co	8:2	and their extreme poverty *w* up

WELLING* (WELL)

Jn	4:14	of water *w* up to eternal life."

WELLS (WELL)

Isa	12:3	from the *w* of salvation.

WELLSPRING* (SPRING)

Pr	4:23	for it is the *w* of life.

WEPT (WEEP)

Ps	137:1	of Babylon we sat and *w*
Lk	22:62	And he went outside and *w* bitterly
Jn	11:35	Jesus *w*

WEST

Ps	103:12	as far as the east is from the *w,*
	107:3	from east and *w,* from north

WHEAT

Mt	3:12	gathering his *w* into the barn
	13:25	and sowed weeds among the *w,*
Lk	22:31	Satan has asked to sift you as *w.*
Jn	12:24	a kernel of *w* falls to the ground

WHEELS

Eze	1:16	appearance and structure of the *w:*

WHIRLWIND (WIND)

2Ki	2:1	to take Elijah up to heaven in a *w,*
Hos	8:7	and reap the *w.*
Na	1:3	His way is in the *w* and the storm,

WHISPER (WHISPERED)

1Ki	19:12	And after the fire came a gentle *w.*
Job	26:14	how faint the *w* we hear of him!
Ps	107:29	He stilled the storm to a *w;*

WHISPERED (WHISPER)

Mt	10:27	speak in the daylight, what is *w*

WHITE (WHITER)

Isa	1:18	they shall be as *w* as snow;
Da	7:9	His clothing was as *w* as snow;
	7:9	the hair of his head was *w* like wool
Mt	28:3	and his clothes were *w* as snow.
Rev	1:14	hair were *w* like wool, as *w* as snow,
	3:4	dressed in *w,* for they are worthy
	6:2	and there before me was a *w* horse!
	7:13	"These in *w* robes—who are they,
	19:11	and there before me was a *w* horse,
	20:11	Then I saw a great *w* throne

WHITER (WHITE)

Ps	51:7	and I will be *w* than snow.

WHOLE

Ge	1:29	plant on the face of the *w* earth
	2:6	and watered the *w* surface
	11:1	Now the *w* world had one language
Ex	12:47	The *w* community
	19:5	Although the *w* earth is mine,
Lev	16:17	and the *w* community of Israel.
Nu	14:21	of the LORD fills the *w* earth,
	32:13	until the *w* generation
Dt	13:16	*w* burnt offering to the LORD your
	19:8	gives you the *w* land he promised
Jos	2:3	come to spy out the *w* land."
1Sa	1:28	For his *w* life he will be given
	17:46	the *w* world will know that there is
1Ki	10:24	The *w* world sought audience
2Ki	21:8	and will keep the *w* Law that my
Ps	72:19	may the *w* earth be filled
Pr	4:22	and health to a man's *w* body.
	8:31	rejoicing in his *w* world
Ecc	12:13	for this is the *w* duty of man.
Isa	1:5	Your *w* head is injured,
	6:3	the *w* earth is full of his glory."
	14:26	plan determined for the *w* world;
Eze	34:6	were scattered over the *w* earth,
	37:11	these bones are the *w* house
Da	2:35	mountain and filled the *w* earth.
Zep	1:18	the *w* world will be consumed,
Zec	14:9	will be king over the *w* earth.
Mal	3:10	the *w* tithe into the storehouse,
Mt	5:29	than for your *w* body to be thrown
	6:22	your *w* body will be full of light.
	16:26	for a man if he gains the *w* world,
	24:14	will be preached in the *w* world
Lk	21:35	live on the face of the *w* earth.
Jn	12:19	Look how the *w* world has gone
	13:10	to wash his feet; his *w* body is clean
	21:25	the *w* world would not have room
Ac	17:26	they should inhabit the *w* earth;
	20:27	proclaim to you the *w* will of God.
Ro	1:9	whom I serve with my *w* heart
	3:19	and the *w* world held accountable
	8:22	know that the *w* creation has been
1Co	4:9	made a spectacle to the *w* universe,
	12:17	If the *w* body were an ear,
Gal	3:22	declares that the *w* world is
	5:3	obligated to obey the *w* law.
Eph	4:10	in order to fill the *w* universe.)
	4:13	attaining to the *w* measure
1Th	5:23	May your *w* spirit, soul
Jas	2:10	For whoever keeps the *w* law
1Jn	2:2	but also for the sins of the *w* world.
Rev	3:10	going to come upon the *w* world

WHOLEHEARTED* (HEART)

2Ki	20:3	you faithfully and with *w* devotion
1Ch	28:9	and serve him with *w* devotion
	29:19	my son Solomon the *w* devotion
Isa	38:3	you faithfully and with *w* devotion

WHOLEHEARTEDLY* (HEART)

Nu	14:24	a different spirit and follows me *w,*
	32:11	they have not followed me *w,*
	32:12	for they followed the LORD *w*
Dt	1:36	because he followed the LORD *w*
Jos	14:8	followed the LORD my God *w.*
	14:9	followed the LORD my God *w.* '
	14:14	the LORD, the God of Israel, *w.*
1Ki	8:23	with your servants who continue *w*
1Ch	29:9	for they had given freely and *w*
2Ch	6:14	with your servants who continue *w*
	15:15	oath because they had sworn it *w.*
	19:9	and *w* in the fear of the LORD.
	25:2	in the eyes of the LORD, but not *w.*
	31:21	he sought his God and worked *w.*
Ro	6:17	you *w* obeyed the form of teaching
Eph	6:7	Serve *w,* as if you were serving

WHOLESOME*

2Ki	2:22	And the water has remained *w*
2Pe	3:1	to stimulate you to *w* thinking.

WICK

Isa	42:3	a smoldering *w* he will not snuff out
Mt	12:20	a smoldering *w* he will not snuff out

WICKED (WICKEDNESS)

Ge	13:13	Now the men of Sodom were *w*
	39:9	How then could I do such a *w* thing
Ex	23:1	Do not help a *w* man
Nu	14:35	things to this whole *w* community,
Dt	15:9	not to harbor this *w* thought:

Jdg 19:22 some of the w men
1Sa 2:12 Eli's sons were w men; they had no
15:18 completely destroy those w people,
25:17 He is such a w man that no one can
2Sa 1:12 in Israel! Don't do this w thing.
2Ki 17:11 They did w things that provoked
2Ch 7:14 and turn from their w ways,
19:2 "Should you help the w
Ne 13:17 "What is this w thing you are doing
Ps 1:1 walk in the counsel of the w
1:5 Therefore the w will not stand
7:9 to an end the violence of the w
10:13 Why does the w man revile God?
11:5 the w and those who love violence
12:8 The w freely strut about
26:5 and refuse to sit with the w
32:10 Many are the woes of the w,
36:1 concerning the sinfulness of the w:
37:13 but the Lord laughs at the w,
49:5 when w deceivers surround me—
50:16 But to the w, God says:
58:3 Even from birth the w go astray;
73:3 when I saw the prosperity of the w.
82:2 and show partiality to the w? Selah
112:10 the longings of the w come
119:61 Though the w bind me with ropes,
119:155 Salvation is far from the w,
140:8 do not grant the w their desires,
141:10 Let the w fall into their own nets,
146:9 but he frustrates the ways of the w
Pr 2:12 you from the ways of w men,
4:14 Do not set foot on the path of the w
6:18 a heart that devises w schemes,
9:7 whoever rebukes a w man incurs
10:20 the heart of the w is of little value.
10:28 the hopes of the w come to nothing
11:5 w are brought down by their own
11:10 when the w perish, there are shouts
11:21 The w will not go unpunished.
12:5 but the advice of the w is deceitful.
12:10 the kindest acts of the w are cruel.
14:19 the w at the gates of the righteous.
15:3 keeping watch on the w
15:26 detests the thoughts of the w,
21:10 The w man craves evil;
21:29 A w man puts up a bold front,
28:1 w man flees though no one pursues,
28:4 who forsake the law praise the w,
29:7 but the w have no such concern.
29:16 When the w thrive, so does sin,
29:27 the w detest the upright.
Isa 11:4 breath of his lips he will slay the w.
13:11 the w for their sins.
26:10 Though grace is shown to the w,
48:22 says the Lord, "for the w."
53:9 He was assigned a grave with the w
55:7 Let the w forsake his way
57:20 But the w are like the tossing sea,
Jer 35:15 of you must turn from your w ways
Eze 3:18 that w man will die for his sin,
13:22 you encouraged the w not to turn
14:7 and puts a w stumbling block
18:21 "But if a w man turns away
18:23 pleasure in the death of the w?
21:25 " 'O profane and w prince of Israel,
33:8 When I say to the w, 'O w man,
33:11 pleasure in the death of the w.
33:14 to the w man, 'You will surely die,'
33:19 And if a w man turns away
Da 12:10 but the w will continue to be w.
Mt 12:39 w and adulterous generation asks
12:45 be with this w generation.
12:45 with it seven other spirits more w
Lk 6:35 he is kind to the ungrateful and w.
Ac 2:23 and you, with the help of w men,
Ro 4:5 but trusts God who justifies the w,
1Co 5:13 "Expel the w man from among you
6:9 not know that the w will not inherit
Rev 2:2 that you cannot tolerate w men.

WICKEDNESS (WICKED)

Ge 6:5 The Lord saw how great man's w
Ex 34:7 and forgiving w, rebellion and sin.
Lev 16:21 and confess over it all the w
19:29 to prostitution and be filled with w.
Dt 9:4 it is on account of the w
Ne 9:2 and confessed their sins and the w
Ps 45:7 You love righteousness and hate w;
92:15 he is my Rock, and there is no w.
Pr 16:6 but w overthrows the sinner.
Jer 3:2 land with your prostitution and w.
8:6 No one repents of his w,
14:20 O Lord, we acknowledge our w
Eze 18:20 the w of the wicked will be charged
28:15 created till w was found in you.

Eze 33:19 wicked man turns away from his w
Da 4:27 and your w by being kind
9:24 to atone for w, to bring
Jnh 1:2 its w has come up before me."
Mt 24:12 Because of the increase of w,
Lk 11:39 inside you are full of greed and w.
Ac 1:18 (With the reward he got for his w,
Ro 1:18 who suppress the truth by their w,
1Co 5:8 the yeast of malice and w,
2Co 6:14 what do righteousness and w have
2Ti 2:19 of the Lord must turn away from w
Tit 2:14 for us to redeem us from all w
Heb 1:9 loved righteousness and hated w;
8:12 For I will forgive their w
2Pe 2:15 who loved the wages of w.

WIDE

Ps 81:10 Open w your mouth and I will fill it
Isa 54:2 stretch your tent curtains w,
Mt 7:13 For w is the gate and broad is
2Co 6:13 my children—open w your hearts
Eph 3:18 to grasp how w and long and high

WIDOW (WIDOWS)

Ex 22:22 "Do not take advantage of a w
Dt 10:18 cause of the fatherless and the w,
Ps 146:9 sustains the fatherless and the w,
Isa 1:17 plead the case of the w.
Lk 21:2 saw a poor w put in two very small
1Ti 5:4 But if a w has children

WIDOWS (WIDOW)

Ps 68:5 to the fatherless, a defender of w,
Ac 6:1 their w were being overlooked
1Co 7:8 to the unmarried and the w I say:
1Ti 5:3 to those w who are really
Jas 1:27 look after orphans and w

WIFE (WIVES WIVES')

Ge 2:24 and mother and be united to his w,
19:26 But Lot's w looked back.
24:67 she became his w, and he loved her;
Ex 20:17 shall not covet your neighbor's w,
Lev 20:10 adultery with another man's w—
Dt 5:21 shall not covet your neighbor's w.
24:5 happiness to the w he has married.
Ru 4:13 took Ruth and she became his w.
Pr 5:18 in the w of your youth.
12:4 w of noble character is her
18:22 He who finds a w finds what is
19:13 quarrelsome w is like a constant
31:10 w of noble character who can find?
Hos 1:2 take to yourself an adulterous w
Mal 2:14 the witness between you and the w
Mt 1:20 to take Mary home as your w,
19:3 for a man to divorce his w for any
Lk 17:32 Remember Lot's w! Whoever tries
18:29 or w or brothers or parents
1Co 7:2 each man should have his own w,
7:33 how he can please his w—
Eph 5:23 the husband is the head of the w
5:33 must love his w as he loves himself,
1Ti 3:2 husband of but one w, temperate,
Rev 21:9 I will show you the bride, the w

WILD

Ge 1:25 God made the w animals according
8:1 Noah and all the w animals
Lk 15:13 squandered his wealth in w living.
Ro 11:17 and you, though a w olive shoot,

WILL (WEAK-WILLED WILLFUL WILLING WILLINGNESS)

Ps 40:8 I desire to do your w, O my God;
143:10 Teach me to do your w,
Isa 53:10 Yet it was the Lord's w
Mt 6:10 your w be done
7:21 who does the w of my Father
10:29 apart from the w of your Father.
12:50 does the w of my Father
26:39 Yet not as I w, but as you w."
26:42 I drink it, may your w be done."
Jn 6:38 but to do the w of him who sent me.
7:17 If anyone chooses to do God's w,
Ac 20:27 to you the whole w of God.
Ro 12:2 and approve what God's w is—
1Co 7:37 but has control over his own w,
Eph 5:17 understand what the Lord's w is.
Php 2:13 for it is God who works in you to w
1Th 4:3 God's w that you should be sanctified:
5:18 for this is God's w for you
2Ti 2:26 has taken them captive to do his w.
Heb 2:4 distributed according to his w.
9:16 In the case of a w, it is necessary

Heb 10:7 I have come to do your w, O God
13:21 everything good for doing his w,
Jas 4:15 "If it is the Lord's w,
1Pe 3:17 It is better, if it is God's w,
4:2 but rather for the w of God.
2Pe 1:21 never had its origin in the w
1Jn 5:14 we ask anything according to his w,
Rev 4:11 and by your w they were created

WILLFUL (WILL)

Ps 19:13 Keep your servant also from w sins;

WILLING (WILL)

1Ch 28:9 devotion and with a w mind,
29:5 who is w to consecrate himself
Ps 51:12 grant me a w spirit, to sustain me.
Da 3:28 were w to give up their lives rather
Mt 18:14 Father in heaven is not w that any
23:37 her wings, but you were not w
26:41 The spirit is w, but the body is weak
1Ti 6:18 and to be generous and w to share.
1Pe 5:2 but because you are w,

WILLINGNESS* (WILL)

2Co 8:11 so that your eager w
8:12 For if the w is there, the gift is

WIN (WINS WON)

1Co 9:19 myself a slave to everyone, to w
Php 3:14 on toward the goal to w the prize
1Th 4:12 your daily life may win the respect

WIND (WHIRLWIND WINDS)

Ps 1:4 that the w blows away.
Ecc 2:11 meaningless, a chasing after the w;
Hos 8:7 "They sow the w
Mk 4:41 Even the w and the waves obey
Jn 3:8 The w blows wherever it pleases.
Eph 4:14 and there by every w of teaching
Jas 1:6 blown and tossed by the w

WINDOW

Jos 2:21 she tied the scarlet cord in the w
Ac 20:9 in a w was a young man named
2Co 11:33 in a basket from a w in the wall

WINDS (WIND)

Ps 104:4 He makes w his messengers,
Mt 24:31 gather his elect from the four w,
Heb 1:7 "He makes his angels w,

WINE

Ps 104:15 w that gladdens the heart of man,
Pr 20:1 W is a mocker and beer a brawler;
23:20 join those who drink too much w
23:31 Do not gaze at w when it is red,
31:6 w to those who are in anguish;
SS 1:2 your love is more delightful than w
Isa 28:7 And these also stagger from w
55:1 Come, buy w and milk
Mt 9:17 Neither do men pour new w
Lk 23:36 They offered him w vinegar
Jn 2:3 When the w was gone, Jesus'
Ro 14:21 not to eat meat or drink w
Eph 5:18 on w, which leads to debauchery.
1Ti 5:23 a little w because of your stomach
Rev 16:19 with the w of the fury of his wrath.

WINEPRESS

Isa 63:2 like those of one treading the w?
Rev 19:15 He treads the w of the fury

WINESKINS

Mt 9:17 do men pour new wine into old w.

WINGS

Ex 19:4 and how I carried you on eagles'
Ru 2:12 under whose w you have come
Ps 17:8 hide me in the shadow of your w
91:4 under his w you will find refuge;
Isa 6:2 him were seraphs, each with six w
40:31 They will soar on w like eagles;
Eze 1:6 of them had four faces and four w
Zec 5:9 in their w! They had wings like those
Mal 4:2 rise with healing in its w.
Lk 13:34 hen gathers her chicks under her w,
Rev 4:8 the four living creatures had six w

WINS (WIN)

Pr 11:30 and he who w souls is wise.

WINTER

Mk 13:18 that this will not take place in w.

WIPE (WIPED)

Isa   25: 8 The Sovereign LORD will *w* away
Rev   7:17 God will *w* away every tear
     21: 4 He will *w* every tear

WIPED (WIPE)

Lk   7:38 Then she *w* them with her hair,
Ac   3:19 so that your sins may be *w* out.

WISDOM (WISE)

Ge   3: 6 and also desirable for gaining *w*,
1Ki   4:29 God gave Solomon *w* and very
2Ch   1:10 Give me *w* and knowledge,
Ps   51: 6 you teach me *w* in the inmost place
   111: 10 of the LORD is the beginning of *w*;
Pr   2: 6 For the LORD gives *w*,
    3:13 Blessed is the man who finds *w*,
    4: 7 *w* is supreme; therefore get
    8:11 for *w* is more precious than rubies,
    11: 2 but with humility comes *w*.
   13:10 *w* is found in those who take advice
   23:23 get *w*, discipline and understanding
   29: 3 A man who loves *w* brings joy
   29:15 The rod of correction imparts *w*,
   31:26 She speaks with *w*,
Isa   11: 2 Spirit of *w* and of understanding,
   28:29 in counsel and magnificent in *w*.
Jer   10:12 he founded the world by his *w*
Mic   6: 9 and to fear your name is *w*—
Mt   11:19 But *w* is proved right by her actions
Lk   2:52 And Jesus grew in *w* and stature,
Ac   6: 3 known to be full of the Spirit and *w*
Ro   11:33 the depth of the riches of the *w*
1Co   1:17 not with words of human *w*,
    1:30 who has become for us *w* from God
   12: 8 through the Spirit the message of *w*
Eph   1:17 may give you the Spirit of *w*
Col   2: 3 are hidden all the treasures of *w*
    2:23 indeed have an appearance of *w*,
Jas   1: 5 of you lacks *w*, he should ask God,
    3:13 in the humility that comes from *w*.
Rev   5:12 and wealth and *w* and strength

WISE (WISDOM WISER)

1Ki   3:12 give you a *w* and discerning heart,
Job   5:13 He catches the *w* in their craftiness
Ps   19: 7 making the *w* simple
Pr   3: 7 Do not be *w* in your own eyes;
    9: 8 rebuke a *w* man and he will love
   10: 1 A *w* son brings joy to his father,
   11:30 and he who wins souls is *w*.
   13: 1 A *w* son heeds his father's
   13:20 He who walks with the *w* grows *w*,
   16:23 A *w* man's heart guides his mouth,
   17:28 Even a fool is thought *w*
Ecc   9:17 The quiet words of the *w* are more
Jer   9:23 "Let not the *w* man boast
Eze   28: 6 "Because you think you are *w*,
Da   2:21 He gives wisdom to the *w*
   12: 3 Those who are *w* will shine like
Mt   11:25 hidden these things from the *w*
   25: 2 them were foolish and five were *w*.
1Co   1:19 I will destroy the wisdom of the *w*;
    1:27 things of the world to shame the *w*;
    3:19 He catches the *w* in their craftiness
Eph   5:15 but as *w*, making the most
2Ti   3:15 able to make you *w* for salvation
Jas   3:13 Who is *w* and understanding

WISER (WISE)

Pr   9: 9 a wise man and he will be *w* still;
1Co   1:25 of God is *w* than man's wisdom,

WISH (WISHES)

Jn   15: 7 ask whatever you *w*, and it will be
Ro   9: 3 For I could *w* that I myself were
Rev   3:15 I *w* you were either one

WISHES (WISH)

Rev   22:17 let him come; and whoever *w*.

WITCHCRAFT

Dt   18:10 engages in *w*, or casts spells,
Gal   5:20 idolatry and *w*; hatred, discord,

WITHDREW

Lk   5:16 But Jesus often *w* to lonely places

WITHER (WITHERS)

Ps   1: 3 and whose leaf does not *w*.
   37:19 In times of disaster they will not *w*;

WITHERS (WITHER)

Isa   40: 7 The grass *w* and the flowers fall,

1Pe   1:24 the grass *w* and the flowers fall,

WITHHELD (WITHHOLD)

Ge   22:12 you have not *w* from me your son,

WITHHOLD (WITHHELD WITHHOLDS)

Ps   84:11 no good thing does he *w*
Pr   23:13 Do not *w* discipline from a child;

WITHHOLDS (WITHHOLD)

Dt   27:19 "Cursed is the man who *w* justice

WITNESS (EYEWITNESSES WITNESSES)

Pr   12:17 truthful *w* gives honest testimony,
   19: 9 A false *w* will not go unpunished.
Jn   1: 8 he came only as a *w* to the light.

WITNESSES (WITNESS)

Dt   19:15 by the testimony of two or three *w*
Mt   18:16 by the testimony of two or three *w*.'
Ac   1: 8 and you will be my *w* in Jerusalem,.

WIVES (WIFE)

Eph   5:22 *W*, submit to your husbands
    5:25 love your *w*, just as Christ loved
1Pe   3: 1 words by the behavior of their *w*,

WIVES' (WIFE)

1Ti   4: 7 with godless myths and old *w* tales

WOE

Isa   6: 5 "*W* to me!" I cried.
Eze   34: 2 *W* to the shepherds
Mt   18: 7 "*W* to the world
   23:13 "*W* to you, teachers of the law
Jude   :11 *W* to them! They have taken

WOLF (WOLVES)

Isa   65:25 *w* and the lamb will feed together,

WOLVES (WOLF)

Mt   10:16 you out like sheep among *w*.

WOMAN (MAN)

Ge   2:22 God made a *w* from
    2:23 she shall be called '*w*,'
    3: 6 *w* saw that the fruit
    3:12 The *w* you put here with
    3:15 between you and the *w*,
    3:16 To the *w* he said,
   12: 1 a beautiful *w* you are.
   20: 3 because of the *w* you have
   24: 5 if the *w* is unwilling
Ex   2: 1 married a Levite *w*
    3:22 Every *w* is to ask her
   21:10 If he marries another *w*
   21:22 hit a pregnant *w*
Lev   12: 2 *w* who becomes pregnant
   15:19 *w* has her regular flow
   15:25 a *w* has a discharge
   18:17 sexual relations with both a *w*
   20:13 as one lies with a *w*,
Nu   5:29 when a *w* goes astray
   30: 3 young *w* still living in
   30: 9 by a widow or divorced *w*
   30:10 living with her husband
Dt   21: 7 become pledged to a *w*
   21:11 the captives a beautiful *w*
   22: 5 *w* must not wear men's
   22:13 married this *w* but when
Jdg   4: 9 hand Sisera over to a *w*.
   13: 6 the *w* went to her husband
   14: 2 have seen a Philistine *w*
   16: 4 he fell in love with a *w*
   20: 4 husband of the murdered *w*
Ru   3:11 a *w* of noble character
1Sa   1:15 a *w* who is deeply troubled
   25: 3 intelligent and beautiful *w*,
   28: 7 a *w* who is a medium,
2Sa   11: 2 he saw a *w* bathing
   13:17 "Get this *w* out of here
   14: 2 had a wise *w* brought
   20:16 a wise *w* called from
1Ki   3:18 this *w* also had a baby.
   17:24 the *w* said to Elijah.
2Ki   4: 8 a well-to-do *w* was there,
    8: 1 Elisha had said to the *w*
    9:34 "Take care of that cursed *w*,"
Job   14: 1 Man born of *w* is of few
Pr   11:16 A kindhearted *w* gains respect,
   11:22 a beautiful *w* who shows no
   14: 1 a wise *w* builds her house,
   30:23 unloved *w* who is married,
   31:30 a *w* who fears the LORD
Isa   54: 1 O barren *w*, you who never

Mt   5:28 looks at a *w* lustfully
    9:20 a *w* who had been subject
   15:28 *W* you have great faith!
   26: 7 a *w* came to him with
Mk   5:25 a *w* was there who had
    7:25 a *w* whose little daughter
Lk   7:39 what kind of a *w* she is
   10:38 a *w* named Martha opened
   13:12 "*W*, you are set free
   15: 8 suppose a *w* has ten silver
Jn   2: 4 *w*, why do you involve
    4: 7 a Samaritan *w* came
    8: 3 a *w* caught in adultery.
   19:26 *w*, here is your son,"
   20:15 *W*, 'he said, "Why are you crying?
Ac   9:40 Turning toward the dead *w*,
   16:14 was a *w* named Lydia.
Ro   7: 2 a married *w* is bound to
1Co   7: 2 each *w* her own husband
    7:15 a believing man or *w* is
    7:34 an unmarried *w* or virgin
    7:39 *w* is bound to her husband
   11: 3 the head of the *w* is man,
   11: 7 the *w* is the glory of man
   11:13 a *w* to pray to God with
Gal   4: 4 his Son, born of a *w*,
    4:31 not children of the slave *w*,
1Ti   2:11 A *w* should learn in
    5:16 any *w* who is a believer
Rev   2:20 You tolerate that *w* Jezebel,
   12: 1 a *w* clothed with the sun
   12:13 he pursued the *w* who had
   17: 3 a *w* sitting on a scarlet

WOMEN (MAN)

Mt   11:11 among those born of *w*,
   28: 5 The angel said to the *w*,
Mk   15:41 Many other *w* who had come
Lk   1:42 Blessed are you among *w*,
    8: 2 also some *w* who had been
   23:27 *w* who mourned and wailed
   24:11 they did not believe the *w*,
Ac   1:14 along with the *w* and Mary
   16:13 speak to the *w* who had
   17: 4 not a few prominent *w*
Ro   1:26 *w* exchanged natural relations
1Co   14:34 *w* should remain silent in
Php   4: 3 help these *w* who have
1Ti   2: 9 want *w* to dress modestly
    5: 2 older *w* as mothers.
Tit   2: 3 teach the older *w* to be
    2: 4 train the younger *w* to love
Heb   11:35 *W* received back their dead
1Pe   3: 5 the holy *w* of the past

WOMB

Job   1:21 Naked I came from my mother's *w*,
Ps   139: 13 in my mother's *w*,
Pr   31: 2 "O my son, O son of my *w*,
Jer   1: 5 you in the *w* I knew you,
Lk   1:44 the baby in my *w* leaped for joy.
Jn   3: 4 into his mother's *w* to be born!"

WON (WIN)

1Pe   3: 1 they may be *w* over without words

WONDER (WONDERFUL WONDERS)

Ps   17: 7 Show the *w* of your great love,
SS   1: 3 No *w* the maidens love you!

WONDERFUL* (WONDER)

2Sa   1:26 Your love for me was *w*,
    1:26 more *w* than that of women.
1Ch   16: 9 tell of all his *w* acts.
Job   42: 3 things too *w* for me to know.
Ps   26: 7 and telling of all your *w* deeds.
   31:21 for he showed his *w* love to me
   75: 1 men tell of your *w* deeds.
   105: 2 tell of all his *w* acts.
   107: 8 and his *w* deeds for men.
   107: 15 and his *w* deeds for men.
   107: 21 and his *w* deeds for men.
   107: 24 his *w* deeds in the deep.
   107: 31 and his *w* deeds for men.
   119: 18 *w* things in your law.
   119:129 Your statutes are *w*;
   131: 1 or things too *w* for me.
   139: 6 Such knowledge is too *w* for me,
   139: 14 your works are *w*,
   145: 5 I will meditate on your *w* works.
Isa   9: 6 *W* Counselor, Mighty God,
   28:29 win counsel and magnificent
Mt   21:15 of the law saw the *w* things he did
Lk   13:17 with all the *w* things he was doing.
1Pe   2: 9 out of darkness into his *w* light.

WONDERS (WONDER)

Ex   3:20 with all the *w* that I will perform
Dt   10:21 and awesome *w* you saw
2Sa   7:23 awesome *w* by driving out nations
Job 37:14 stop and consider God's *w.*
Ps   9: 1 I will tell of all your *w.*
      89: 5 The heavens praise your *w,*
     119:27 then I will meditate on your *w.*
Joel 2:30 I will show in the heavens
Ac   2:11 we hear them declaring the *w*
      2:19 I will show in the heaven above
      5:12 many miraculous signs and *w*
2Co 12:12 that mark an apostle—signs, *w*
2Th   2: 9 and *w,* and in every sort
Heb   2: 4 also testified to it by signs, *w*

WOOD

Isa 44:19 Shall I bow down to a block of *w?*"
1Co   3:12 costly stones, *w,* hay or straw,

WOOL

Pr   31:13 She selects *w* and flax
Isa   1:18 they shall be like *w.*
Da   7: 9 hair of his head was white like *w.*
Rev   1:14 and hair were white like *w,*

WORD (BYWORD WORDS)

Nu   30: 2 he must not break his *w*
Dt   8: 3 but on every *w* that comes
2Sa 22:31 the *w* of the LORD is flawless;
Ps   56: 4 In God, whose *w* I praise,
     119: 9 By living according to your *w.*
     119:11 I have hidden your *w* in my heart
     119:105 Your *w* is a lamp to my feet
Pr   12:25 but a kind *w* cheers him up.
      15: 1 but a harsh *w* stirs up anger.
      25:11 A *w* aptly spoken
      30: 5 "Every *w* of God is flawless;
Isa 55:11 so is my *w* that goes out
Jer 23:29 "Is not my *w* like fire," declares
Mt   4: 4 but on every *w* that comes
      12:36 for every careless *w* they have
      15: 6 Thus you nullify the *w* of God
Mk   4:14 parable? The farmer sows the *w.*
Jn   1: 1 was the *W,* and the *W* was
      1:14 The *W* became flesh and made his
      17:17 them by the truth; your *w* is truth.
Ac   6: 4 and the ministry of the *w.*"
2Co   2:17 we do not peddle the *w* of God
      4: 2 nor do we distort the *w* of God.
Eph   6:17 of the Spirit, which is the *w* of God.
Php   2:16 as you hold out the *w* of life—
Col   3:16 Let the *w* of Christ dwell
2Ti   2:15 and who correctly handles the *w*
Heb   4:12 For the *w* of God is living
Jas   1:22 Do not merely listen to the *w,*
2Pe   1:19 And we have the *w* of the prophets

WORDS (WORD)

Dt   11:18 Fix these *w* of mine in your hearts
Ps   12: 6 the *w* of the LORD are flawless,
     119:103 How sweet are your *w* to my taste,
     119:130 The unfolding of your *w* gives light;
     119:160 All your *w* are true;
Pr   2: 1 My son, if you accept my *w*
      10:19 When *w* are many, sin is not absent
      16:24 Pleasant *w* are a honeycomb,
      30: 6 Do not add to his *w,*
Ecc 12:11 The *w* of the wise are like goads,
Jer 15:16 When your *w* came, I ate them;
Mt   24:35 but my *w* will never pass away.
Lk   6:47 and hears my *w* and puts them
Jn   6:68 You have the *w* of eternal life.
      15: 7 in me and my *w* remain in you,
1Co   2:13 but in *w* taught by the Spirit,
      14:19 rather speak five intelligible *w*
Rev 22:19 And if anyone takes away *w*

WORK (WORKED WORKER WORKERS WORKING WORKMAN WORKMANSHIP WORKS)

Ge   2: 2 day he rested from all his *w.*
Ex   23:12 "Six days do your *w,*
Nu   8:11 ready to do the *w* of the LORD.
Dt   5:14 On it you shall not do any *w,*
Ps   19: 1 the skies proclaim the *w*
Ecc   5:19 his lot and be happy in his *w*—
Jer 48:10 lax in doing the LORD's *w!*
Mt   20: 1 to hire men to work in his vineyard.
Jn   6:27 Do not *w* for food that spoils,
      9: 4 we must do the *w* of him who sent
Ac   1: 2 for the *w* to which I have called
1Co   3:13 test the quality of each man's *w.*
      4:12 We *w* hard with our own hands.

WORKED (WORK)

1Co 15:10 No, I *w* harder than all of them—
2Th   3: 8 On the contrary, we *w* night

WORKER (WORK)

Lk   10: 7 for the *w* deserves his wages.
1Ti   5:18 and "The *w* deserves his wages."

WORKERS (WORK)

Mt   9:37 is plentiful but the *w* are few.
1Co   3: 9 For we are God's fellow *w;*

WORKING (WORK)

Col   3:23 as *w* for the Lord, not for men.

WORKMAN (WORK)

2Ti   2:15 a *w* who does not need

WORKMANSHIP* (WORK)

Eph   2:10 For we are God's *w,* created

WORKS

Ps   66: 5 how awesome his *w* in man's behalf!
     145: 6 of the power of your awesome *w,*
Pr   8:22 As the first of his *w,*
      31:31 let her *w* bring her praise
Ro   4: 2 in fact, Abraham was justified by *w*
      8:28 in all things God *w* for the good
Eph   2: 9 not by *w,* so that no one can boast.
      2:12 to prepare God's people for *w*

WORLD (WORLDLY)

Ps   9: 8 He will judge the *w*
      50:12 for the *w* is mine, and all that is in it
      96:13 He will judge the *w*
Pr   8:23 before the *w* began.
Isa 13:11 I will punish the *w* for its evil,
Zep   1:18 the whole *w* will be consumed,
Mt   5:14 "You are the light of the *w.*
      16:26 for a man if he gains the whole *w,*
Mk   16:15 into all the *w* and preach the good
Jn   1:29 who takes away the sin of the *w!*
      3:16 so loved the *w* that he gave his one
      8:12 he said, "I am the light of the *w.*
      15:19 As it is, you do not belong to the *w,*
      16:33 In this *w* you will have trouble.
      17: 5 had with you before the *w* began.
      17:14 not of the *w* any more than I am
      18:36 "My kingdom is not of this *w.*
Ac   17:24 "The God who made the *w*
Ro   3:19 and the whole *w* held accountable
      10:18 their words to the ends of the *w.*"
1Co   1:27 things of the *w* to shame the strong
      3:19 the wisdom of this *w* is foolishness
      6: 2 that the saints will judge the *w?*
2Co   5:19 that God was reconciling the *w*
      10: 3 For though we live in the *w,*
1Ti   6: 7 For we brought nothing into the *w,*
Heb 11:38 the *w* was not worthy of them.
Jas   2: 5 poor in the eyes of the *w* to be rich
      4: 4 with the *w* is hatred toward God?
1Pe   1:20 before the creation of the *w,*
1Jn   2: 2 but also for the sins of the whole *w.*
      2:15 not love the *w* or anything in the *w.*
      5: 4 born of God overcomes the *w.*
Rev 13: 8 slain from the creation of the *w.*

WORLDLY (WORLD)

1Co   3: 1 address you as spiritual but as *w*—
Tit   2:12 to ungodliness and *w* passions,

WORM

Mk   9:48 "'their *w* does not die,

WORRY (WORRYING)

Mt   6:25 I tell you, do not *w* about your life,
      10:19 do not *w* about what to say

WORRYING (WORRY)

Mt   6:27 of you by *w* can add a single hour.

WORSHIP (WORSHIPED WORSHIPS)

Jos 22:27 that we will *w* the LORD
2Ki 17:36 arm, is the one you must *w.*
1Ch 16:29 *w* the LORD in the splendor
Ps   95: 6 Come, let us bow down in *w,*
     100: 2 *w* the LORD with gladness;
Zec 14:17 up to Jerusalem to *w* the King,
Mt   2: 2 and have come to *w* him."
      4: 9 "if you will bow down and *w* me."
Jn   4:24 and his worshipers must *w* in spirit
Ro   12: 1 to God—this is your spiritual act of *w.*
Heb 10: 1 perfect those who draw near to *w.*

WORSHIPED (WORSHIP)

2Ch 29:30 and bowed their heads and *w.*
Mt   28: 9 clasped his feet and *w* him.

WORSHIPS (WORSHIP)

Isa 44:15 But he also fashions a god and *w* it;

WORTH (WORTHY)

Job 28:13 Man does not comprehend its *w;*
Pr   31:10 She is *w* far more than rubies.
Mt   10:31 are *w* more than many sparrows.
Ro   8:18 sufferings are not *w* comparing
1Pe   1: 7 of greater *w* than gold,
      3: 4 which is of great *w* in God's sight.

WORTHLESS

Pr   11: 4 Wealth is *w* in the day of wrath,
Jas   1:26 himself and his religion is *w.*

WORTHY (WORTH)

1Ch 16:25 For great is the LORD and most *w*
Mt   10:37 more than me is not *w* of me;
Lk   15:19 I am no longer *w* to be called your
Eph   4: 1 to live a life *w* of the calling you
Php   1:27 in a manner *w* of the gospel
Col   1:10 in order that you may live a life *w*
1Ti   3: 8 are to be men *w* of respect, sincere,
Heb   3: 3 Jesus has been found *w*
3Jn   : 6 on their way in a manner *w* of God.
Rev   5: 2 "Who is *w* to break the seals

WOUND (WOUNDS)

1Co   8:12 and *w* their weak conscience,

WOUNDS (WOUND)

Pr   27: 6 *w* from a friend can be trusted
Isa 53: 5 and by his *w* we are healed.
Zec 13: 6 'What are these *w* on your body?'
1Pe   2:24 by his *w* you have been healed.

WRAPS

Ps 104: 2 He *w* himself in light

WRATH

2Ch 36:16 scoffed at his prophets until the *w*
Ps   2: 5 and terrifies them in his *w,* saying,
      76:10 Surely your *w* against men brings
Pr   15: 1 A gentle answer turns away *w,*
Isa 13:13 at the *w* of the LORD Almighty,
      51:17 the cup of his *w,*
Jer 25:15 filled with the wine of my *w*
Eze   5:13 my *w* against them will subside,
      20: 8 So I said I would pour out my *w*
Am   1: 3 I will not turn back my *w,*
Na   1: 2 maintains his *w* against his enemies
Zep   1:15 That day will be a day of *w,*
Jn   3:36 for God's *w* remains on him."
Ro   1:18 The *w* of God is being revealed
      2: 5 you are storing up *w*
      5: 9 saved from God's *w* through him!
      9:22 choosing to show his *w*
1Th   5: 9 God did not appoint us to suffer *w*
Rev   6:16 and from the *w* of the Lamb!
      19:15 the fury of the *w* of God Almighty.

WRESTLED

Ge   32:24 and a man *w* with him till daybreak

WRITE (WRITER WRITING WRITTEN WROTE)

Dt   6: 9 *W* them on the doorframes
      10: 2 I will *w* on the tablets the words
Pr   7: 3 *w* them on the tablet of your heart.
Jer 31:33 and *w* it on their hearts.
Heb   8:10 and *w* them on their hearts.
Rev   3:12 I will also *w* on him my new name.

WRITER* (WRITE)

Ps   45: 1 my tongue is the pen of a skillful *w.*

WRITING (WRITE)

1Co 14:37 him acknowledge that what I am w

WRITTEN (WRITE)

Dt	28:58	which are w in this book,
Jos	1: 8	careful to do everything w in it.
	23: 6	to obey all that is w in the Book
Ps	40: 7	it is w about me in the scroll.
Da	12: 1	everyone whose name is found w
Mal	3:16	A scroll of remembrance was w
Lk	10:20	but rejoice that your names are w
	24:44	must be fulfilled that is w about me
Jn	20:31	these are w that you may believe
	21:25	for the books that would be w.
Ro	2:15	of the law are w on their hearts,
1Co	4: 6	"Do not go beyond what is w."
	10:11	as examples and were w down
2Co	3: 3	w not with ink but with the Spirit
Col	2:14	having canceled the w code,
Heb	10: 7	it is w about me in the scroll—
	12:23	whose names are w in heaven.
Rev	21:27	but only those whose names are w

WRONG (WRONGDOING WRONGED WRONGS)

Ex	23: 2	Do not follow the crowd in doing w
Nu	5: 7	must make full restitution for his w,
Dt	32: 4	A faithful God who does no w,
Job	34:12	unthinkable that God would do w,
Ps	5: 5	you hate all who do w.
Gal	2:11	to his face, because he was clearly in the w.
1Th	5:15	that nobody pays back w for w,

WRONGDOING (WRONG)

Job	1:22	sin by charging God with w.
1Jn	5:17	All w is sin, and there is sin that

WRONGED (WRONG)

1Co 6: 7 not rather be w? Why not rather

WRONGS (WRONG)

Pr	10:12	but love covers over all w.
1Co	13: 5	angered, it keeps no record of w.

WROTE (WRITE)

Ex	34:28	And he w on the tablets the words
Jn	5:46	for he w about me.
	8: 8	down and w on the ground.

XERXES

King of Persia, husband of Esther. Deposed Vashti; replaced her with Esther (Est 1-2). Sealed Haman's edict to annihilate the Jews (Est 3). Received Esther without having called her (Est 5:1-8). Honored Mordecai (Est 6). Hanged Haman (Est 7). Issued edict allowing Jews to defend themselves (Est 8). Exalted Mordecai (Est 8:1-2, 15; 9:4; 10).

YEAR (YEARS)

Ex	34:23	Three times a y all your men are
Lev	16:34	to be made once a y for all the sins
	25: 4	But in the seventh y the land is
	25:11	The fiftieth y shall be a jubilee
Heb	10: 1	repeated endlessly y after y,

YEARS (YEAR)

Ge	1:14	to mark seasons and days and y,
Ex	12:40	lived in Egypt was 430 y.
	16:35	The Israelites ate manna forty y,
Job	36:26	of his y is past finding out.
Ps	90: 4	For a thousand y in your sight
	90:10	The length of our days is seventy y
Pr	3: 2	they will prolong your life many y
Lk	3:23	Jesus himself was about thirty y old
2Pe	3: 8	the Lord a day is like a thousand y,
Rev	20: 2	and bound him for a thousand y.

YEAST

Ex	12:15	are to eat bread made without y.
Mt	16: 6	guard against the y of the Pharisees
1Co	5: 6	you know that a little y works

YESTERDAY

Heb 13: 8 Jesus Christ is the same y

YOKE (YOKED)

1Ki	12: 4	and the heavy y he put on us,
Mt	11:29	Take my y upon you and learn
Gal	5: 1	be burdened again by a y

YOKED (YOKE)

2Co 6:14 Do not be y together

YOUNG (YOUNGER YOUTH)

2Ch	10:14	he followed the advice of the y men
Ps	37:25	I was y and now I am old,
	119: 9	How can a y man keep his way
Pr	20:29	The glory of y men is their strength
Isa	40:11	he gently leads those that have y
Joel	2:28	your y men will see visions.
Ac	2:17	your y men will see visions,
	7:58	at the feet of a y man named Saul.
1Ti	4:12	down on you because you are y,
Tit	2: 6	encourage the y men
1Pe	5: 5	Y men, in the same way be
1Jn	2:13	I write to you, y men,

YOUNGER (YOUNG)

1Ti	5: 1	Treat y men as brothers, older
Tit	2: 4	Then they can train the y women

YOUTH (YOUNG)

Ps	103: 5	so that your y is renewed like
Ecc	12: 1	Creator in the days of your y,
2Ti	2:22	Flee the evil desires of y.

ZACCHAEUS

Lk 19: 2 A man was there by the name of Z,

ZEAL (ZEALOUS)

Ps	69: 9	for z for your house consumes me,
Pr	19: 2	to have z without knowledge,
Isa	59:17	and wrapped himself in z
Jn	2:17	"Z for your house will consume me
Ro	10: 2	their z is not based on knowledge.
	12:11	Never be lacking in z,

ZEALOUS (ZEAL)

Nu	25:13	he was z for the honor of his God
Pr	23:17	always be z for the fear
Eze	39:25	and I will be z for my holy name.
Gal	4:18	fine to be z, provided the purpose is

ZEBULUN

Son of Jacob by Leah (Ge 30:20; 35:23; 1Ch 2:1). Tribe of blessed (Ge 49:13; Dt 33:18-19), numbered (Nu 1:31; 26:27), allotted land (Jos 19:10-16; Eze 48:26), failed to fully possess (Jdg 1:30), supported Deborah (Jdg 4:6-10; 5:14, 18), David (1Ch 12:33), 12,000 from (Rev 7:8).

ZECHARIAH

1. Son of Jeroboam II; king of Israel (2Ki 15:8-12).
2. Post-exilic prophet who encouraged rebuilding of temple (Ezr 5:1; 6:14; Zec 1:1).

ZEDEKIAH

1. False prophet (1Ki 22:11-24; 2Ch 18:10-23).
2. Mattaniah, son of Josiah (1Ch 3:15), made king of Judah by Nebuchadnezzar (2Ki 24:17-25:7; 2Ch 36:10-14; Jer 37-39; 52:1-11).

ZEPHANIAH

Prophet; descendant of Hezekiah (Zep 1:1).

ZERUBBABEL

Descendant of David (1Ch 3:19; Mt 1:3). Led return from exile (Ezr 2:2; Ne 7:7). Governor of Israel; helped rebuild altar and temple (Ezr 3; Hag 1-2; Zec 4).

ZILPAH

Servant of Leah, mother of Jacob's sons Gad and Asher (Ge 30:9-12; 35:26; 46:16-18).

ZIMRI

King of Israel (1Ki 16:9-20).

ZION

2Sa	5: 7	David captured the fortress of Z,
Ps	2: 6	King on Z, my holy hill."
	9:11	to the LORD, enthroned in Z;
	74: 2	Mount Z, where you dwelt.
	87: 2	the LORD loves the gates of Z
	102:13	and have compassion on Z,
	137: 3	"Sing us one of the songs of Z!"
Isa	2: 3	The law will go out from Z.
	28:16	"See, I lay a stone in Z,
	51:11	They will enter Z with singing;
	52: 8	When the LORD returns to Z,
Jer	50: 5	They will ask the way to Z
Joel	3:21	The LORD dwells in Z!"
Am	6: 1	to you who are complacent in Z,
Mic	4: 2	The law will go out from Z,

Zec	9: 9	Rejoice greatly, O Daughter of Z!
Ro	9:33	I lay in Z a stone that causes men
	11:26	"The deliverer will come from Z;
Heb	12:22	But you have come to Mount Z,
Rev	14: 1	standing on Mount Z,

ZIPPORAH*

Daughter of Reuel; wife of Moses (Ex 2:21-22; 4:20-26; 18:1-6).

ZOPHAR

One of Job's friends (Job 11; 20).

Index to Color Maps

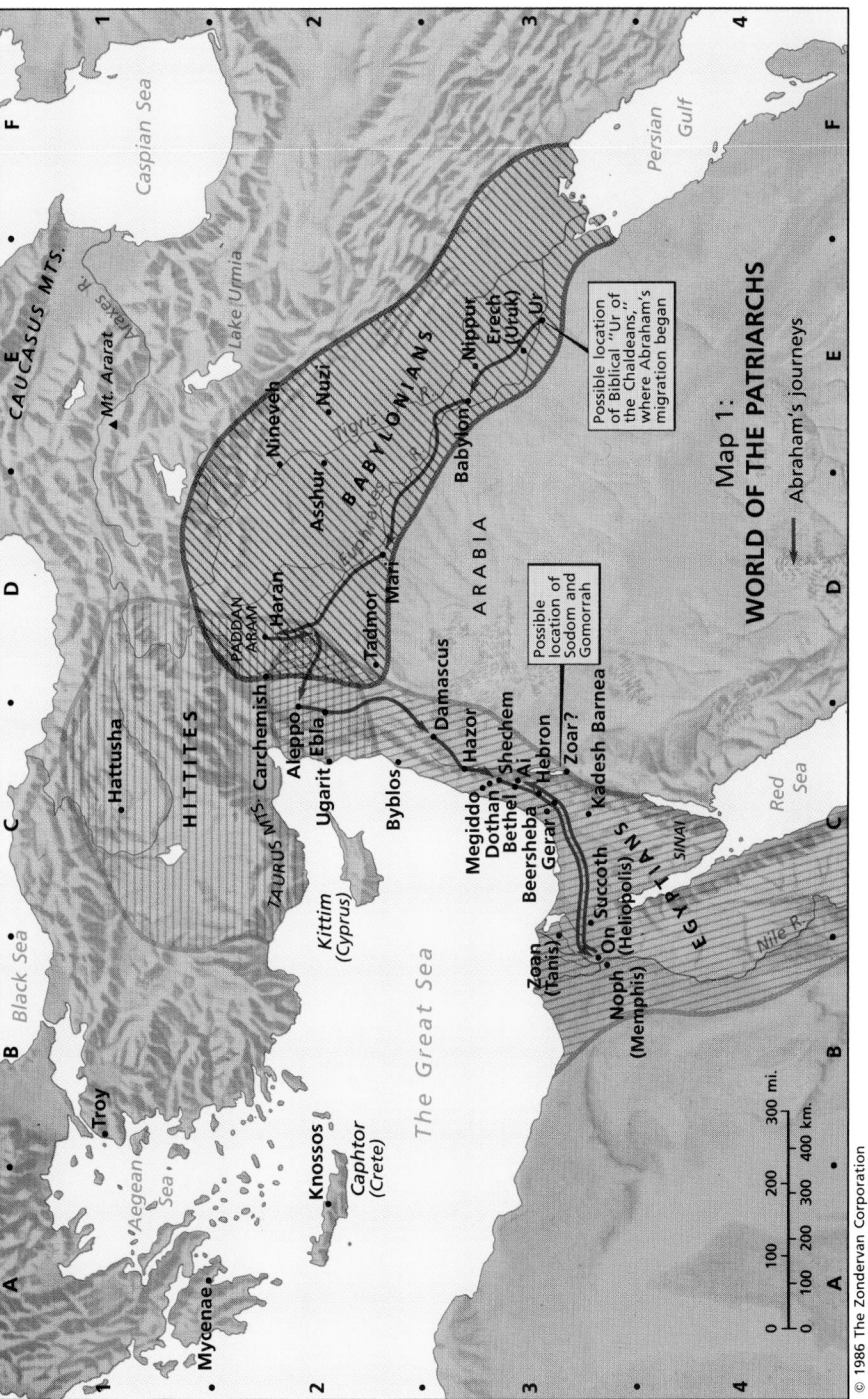

Map 1:
WORLD OF THE PATRIARCHS

→ Abraham's journeys

Possible location of Biblical "Ur of the Chaldeans," where Abraham's migration began

Possible location of Sodom and Gomorrah

CAUCASUS MTS.

Caspian Sea

Mt Ararat

Lake Urmia

Black Sea

Aegean Sea

Troy

Mycenae

Knossos

Caphtor (Crete)

Kittim (Cyprus)

HITTITES

Hattusha

TAURUS MTS.

Carchemish

Aleppo
Ebla

Ugarit

Byblos

Damascus

Hazor

Shechem

Ai

Bethel

Dothan

Megiddo

Beersheba

Gerar

Hebron

Zoar?

Kadesh Barnea

Succoth

On (Heliopolis)

Zoan (Tanis)

Noph (Memphis)

SINAI

EGYPT

Nile R.

Red Sea

The Great Sea

PADDAN ARAM

Haran

Tadmor

Mari

ARABIA

Nineveh

Asshur

Nuzi

BABYLONIANS

Babylon

Nippur

Erech (Uruk)

Ur

Persian Gulf

Tigris

Euphrates

| 0 | 100 | 200 | 300 mi. |
| 0 | 100 | 200 | 300 | 400 km. |

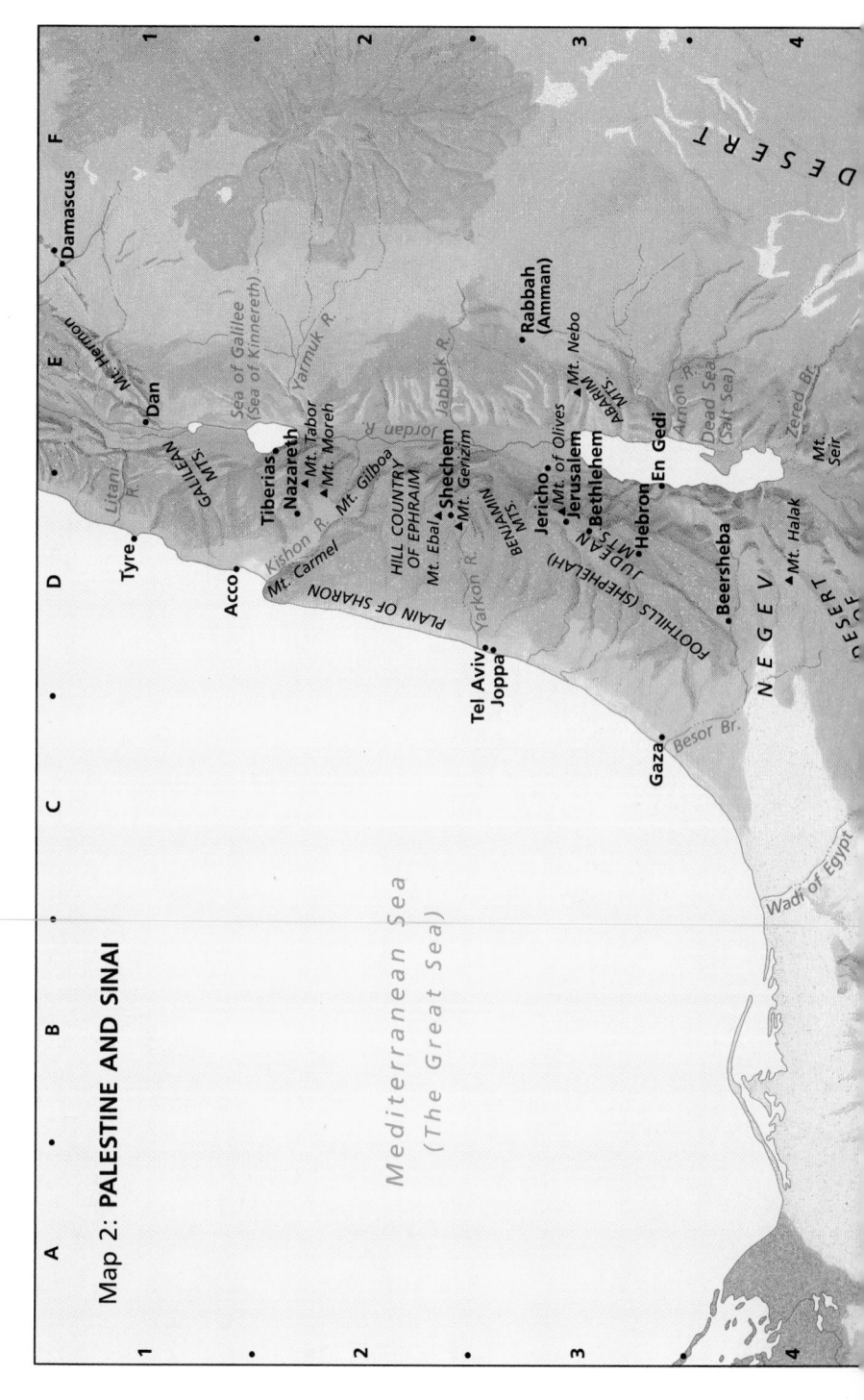

Map 2: **PALESTINE AND SINAI**

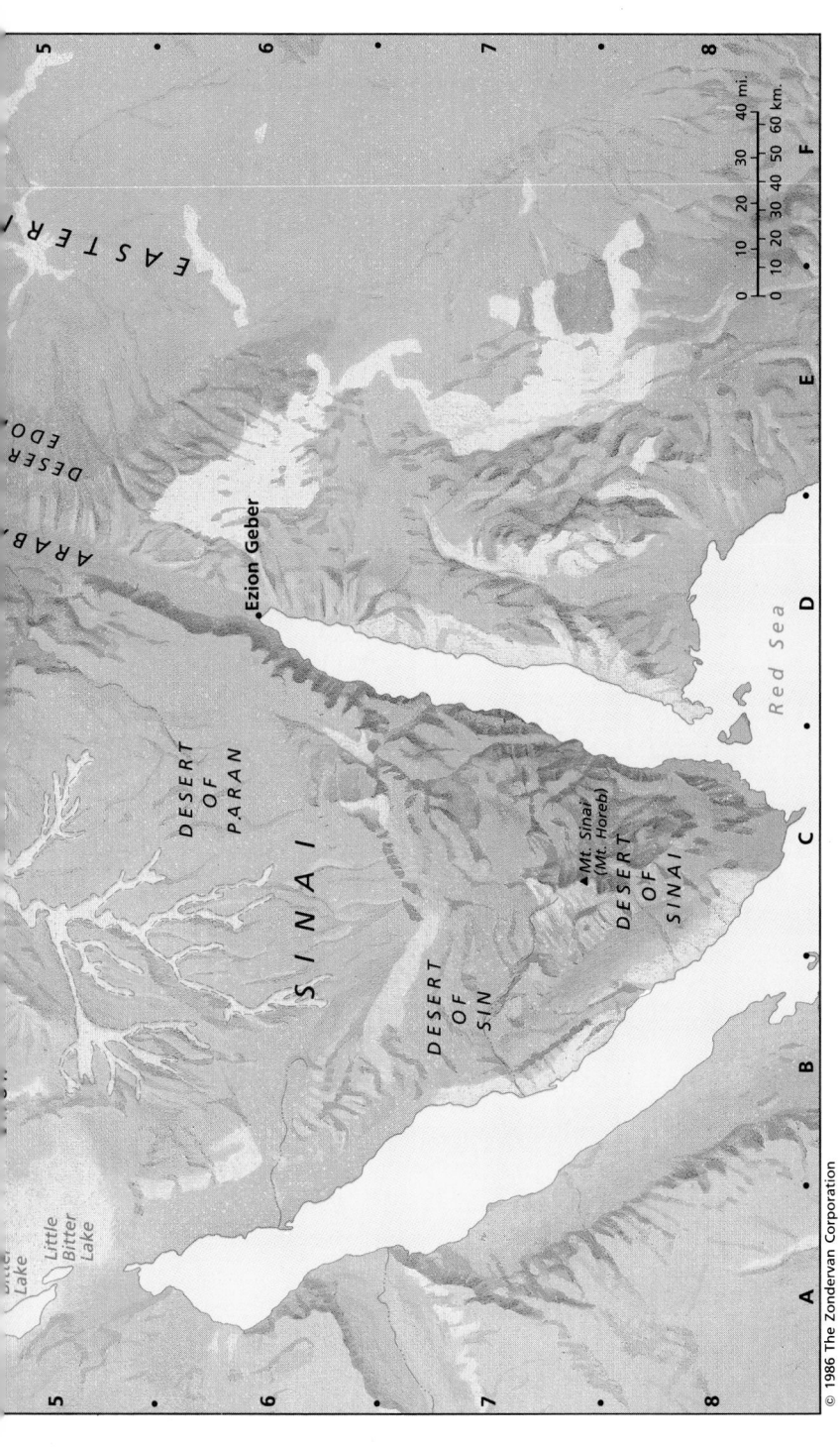

Map 3: **EXODUS AND CONQUEST OF CANAAN**

Area controlled by ancient Israel

Probable route of wandering in the Sinai

Entry into and conquest of Canaan

✗ Battle

The Great Sea

Kedesh
Hazor
BASHAN
Merom
Sea of
Kinnereth
Mt. Tabor
Edrei
Mt. Gilboa

Shechem
Shiloh
Bethel
Abel
Gilgal?
Shittim
Gibeon
AMMON
Beth Horon
Ai
Heshbon
Jarmuth
Jericho
Mt. Nebo
Azekah
Jerusalem
Jahaz?
Libnah?
Lachish
Hebron
Dibon
Eglon?
Makkedah?
Debir?
Beersheba
Iye
Abarim?
Salt
Sea
DESERT
OF ZIN
Oboth?
Punon

Lake Menzaleh

Besor Br.

Wadi of Egypt

EGYPT
Rameses
GOSHEN
Pithom?
Succoth
DESERT OF
SHUR
Kadesh
Barnea

Great
Bitter
Lake

On
(Heliopolis)
Noph
(Memphis)

DESERT OF
PARAN
Ezion Geber

Marah?
S I N A I

Elim?
Dophkah?
DESERT OF
SIN
Hazeroth?
MIDIAN

Rephidim?
Mt. Sinai
(traditional
location)

Red Sea

0   25   50   75 mi.
0 25 50 75 100 km.

© 1986 The Zondervan Corporation

Map 4:
LAND OF THE TWELVE TRIBES

◉ Cities of refuge
• Other cities

Damascus
ARAM
Litani R.
Mt. Hermon
Ijon
Pharpar R.
Tyre
Dan
ASHER
NAPHTALI
Kedesh
Acco
Cabul
Merom
Hazor
EAST
Rimmon
Sea of Kinnereth
Golan
The Great Sea
ZEBULUN
Mt. Tabor
Yarmuk R.
Ashtaroth
Dor
Mt. Moreh
MANASSEH
Edrei
Kishon R.
Megiddo
ISSACHAR
Taanach
Jezreel
Ramoth Gilead
Beth Shan
MANASSEH
Jabesh Gilead
Samaria
Tirzah
Jordan R.
Mt. Gerizim
Mt. Ebal
Jabbok R.
Mahanaim?
Aphek
Shechem
Succoth
Joppa
Shiloh
DAN
EPHRAIM
Jazer?
GAD
Mizpah
Bethel
Rabbah
Gezer
Gibeon
BENJAMIN
Gilgal
AMMON
Ashdod
Kiriath Jearim
Jericho
Heshbon
Bezer
Ekron
Jerusalem
Gath
Beth Shemesh
Bethlehem
Mt. Nebo
Ashkelon
Lachish
Hebron
REUBEN
Eglon?
Dibon
Gaza
En Gedi
Salt Sea
Arnon R.
Aroer
JUDAH
Gerar
Ziklag
Beersheba
MOAB
Hormah
SIMEON
Zered Br.
EDOM

0 10 20 30 mi.
0 10 20 30 40 km.

1986 The Zondervan Corporation

A   B   C   D

Aleppo

Euphrates R.

1

Tiphsah

Kittim (Cyprus)

HAMATH

Hamath

Qatna

Arvad

2

Tadmor

Kadesh

The
Great Sea

Gebal
(Byblos)

Berothai

ARAMEAN
DESERT

Sidon

PHOENICIA

Damascus

▲ Mt. Hermon

3

Tyre

Dan

ARAM

Kedesh

Hazor

Acco

Sea of
Kinnereth

Megiddo

Beth

Ashtaroth

Taanach

Shan

Edrei

Mt. Gilboa

Ramoth Gilead

EASTERN DESERT

Mahanaim?

Shechem

AMMON

4

Joppa

Gezer

Rabbah

PHILISTIA

Gibeah

Ashdod

Gath

Medeba

Gaza

Hebron

Jerusalem

Ziklag

Beersheba

Salt
Sea

Kir Hareseth

Tamar

MOAB

Map 5:
KINGDOM OF DAVID AND SOLOMON

Kadesh Barnea

EDOM

Saul's kingdom

David and Solomon's kingdom

Territory under Solomon's control

SINAI

6

Ezion Geber

0   20   40   60   80 mi.

Gulf of
Aqaba

0   20   40   60   80   100 km.

A   B   C   D

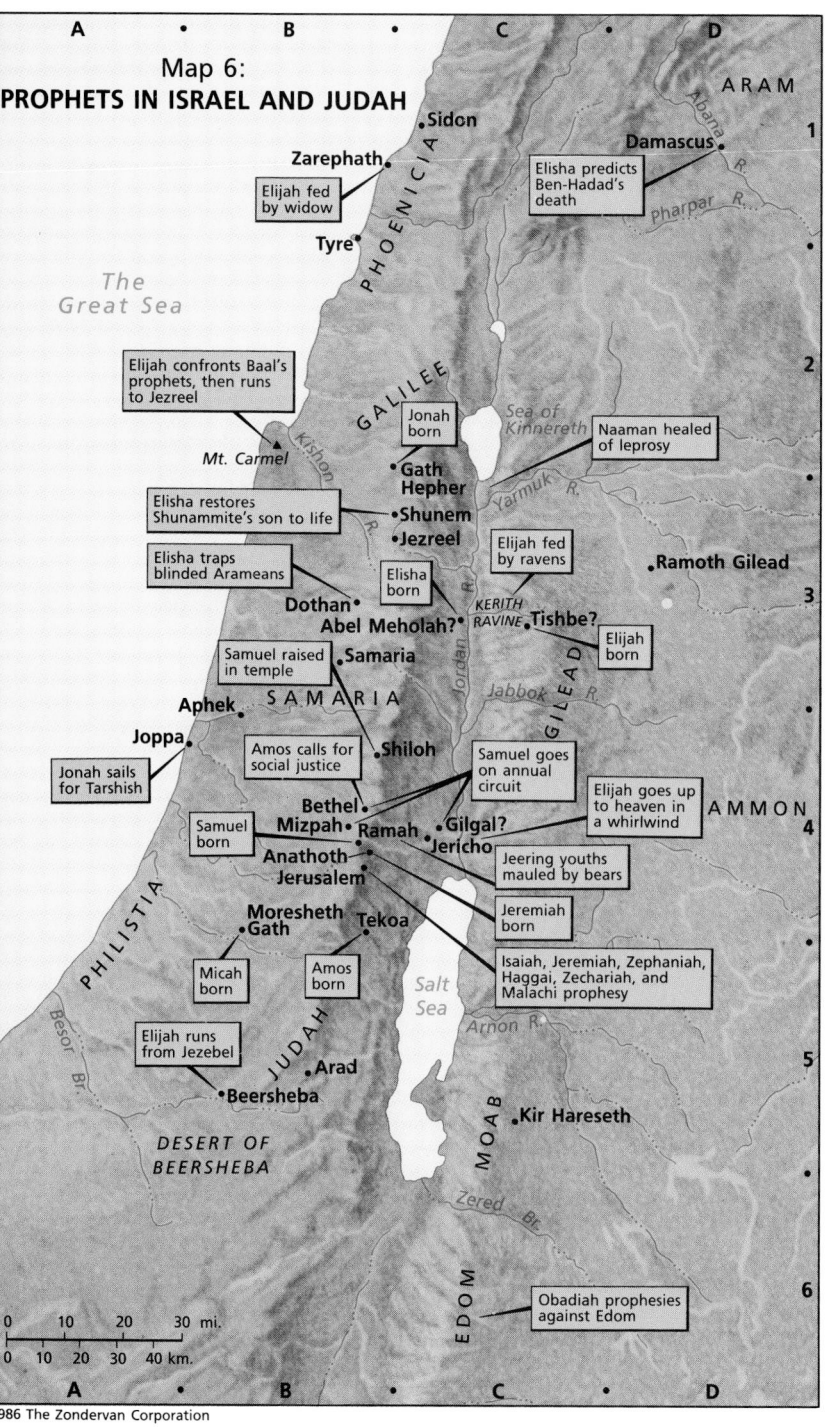

Map 6:
PROPHETS IN ISRAEL AND JUDAH

A B C D

ARAM

Sidon

Zarephath

Elijah fed by widow

PHOENICIA

Damascus

Elisha predicts Ben-Hadad's death

Albana R.

Pharpar R.

Tyre

1

The Great Sea

Elijah confronts Baal's prophets, then runs to Jezreel

GALILEE

Kishon R.

Jonah born

Sea of Kinnereth

Naaman healed of leprosy

2

Mt. Carmel

Gath Hepher

Elisha restores Shunammite's son to life

Shunem

Jezreel

Yarmuk R.

Elisha traps blinded Arameans

Dothan

Elisha born

Elijah fed by ravens

Ramoth Gilead

Abel Meholah?

KERITH RAVINE

Tishbe?

Elijah born

Samuel raised in temple

Samaria

Jordan R.

Jabbok R.

GILEAD

3

Aphek

SAMARIA

Joppa

Jonah sails for Tarshish

Amos calls for social justice

Shiloh

Samuel goes on annual circuit

Elijah goes up to heaven in a whirlwind

AMMON

Bethel

Mizpah **Ramah** **Gilgal?**

Samuel born

Jericho

4

Anathoth

Jeering youths mauled by bears

Jerusalem

Jeremiah born

Moresheth Gath

Tekoa

Isaiah, Jeremiah, Zephaniah, Haggai, Zechariah, and Malachi prophesy

Micah born

Amos born

Salt Sea

PHILISTIA

Elijah runs from Jezebel

JUDAH

Arad

Arnon R.

5

Beersheba

MOAB

Kir Hareseth

DESERT OF BEERSHEBA

Zered Br.

Besor Br.

EDOM

Obadiah prophesies against Edom

6

0   10   20   30 mi.

0 10 20 30 40 km.

A B C D

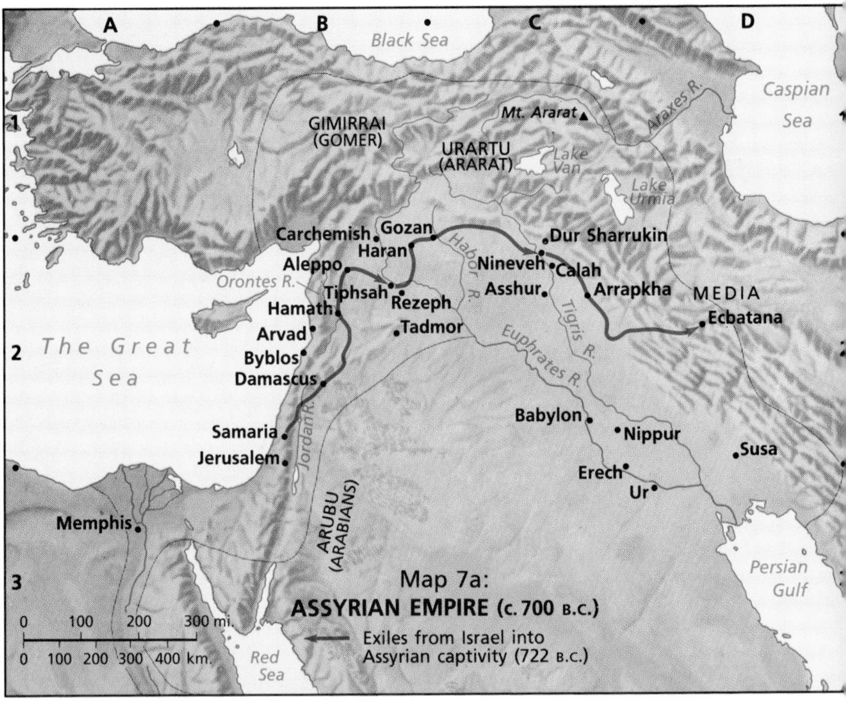

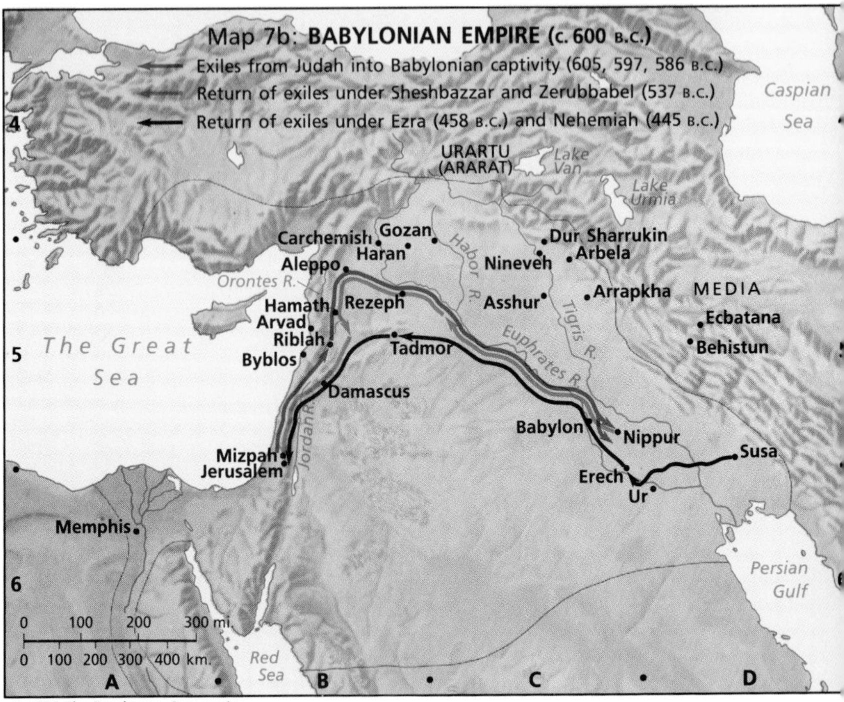

Map 7a:
ASSYRIAN EMPIRE (c. 700 B.C.)
Exiles from Israel into
Assyrian captivity (722 B.C.)

Map 7b: **BABYLONIAN EMPIRE (c. 600 B.C.)**
Exiles from Judah into Babylonian captivity (605, 597, 586 B.C.)
Return of exiles under Sheshbazzar and Zerubbabel (537 B.C.)
Return of exiles under Ezra (458 B.C.) and Nehemiah (445 B.C.)

© 1986 The Zondervan Corporation

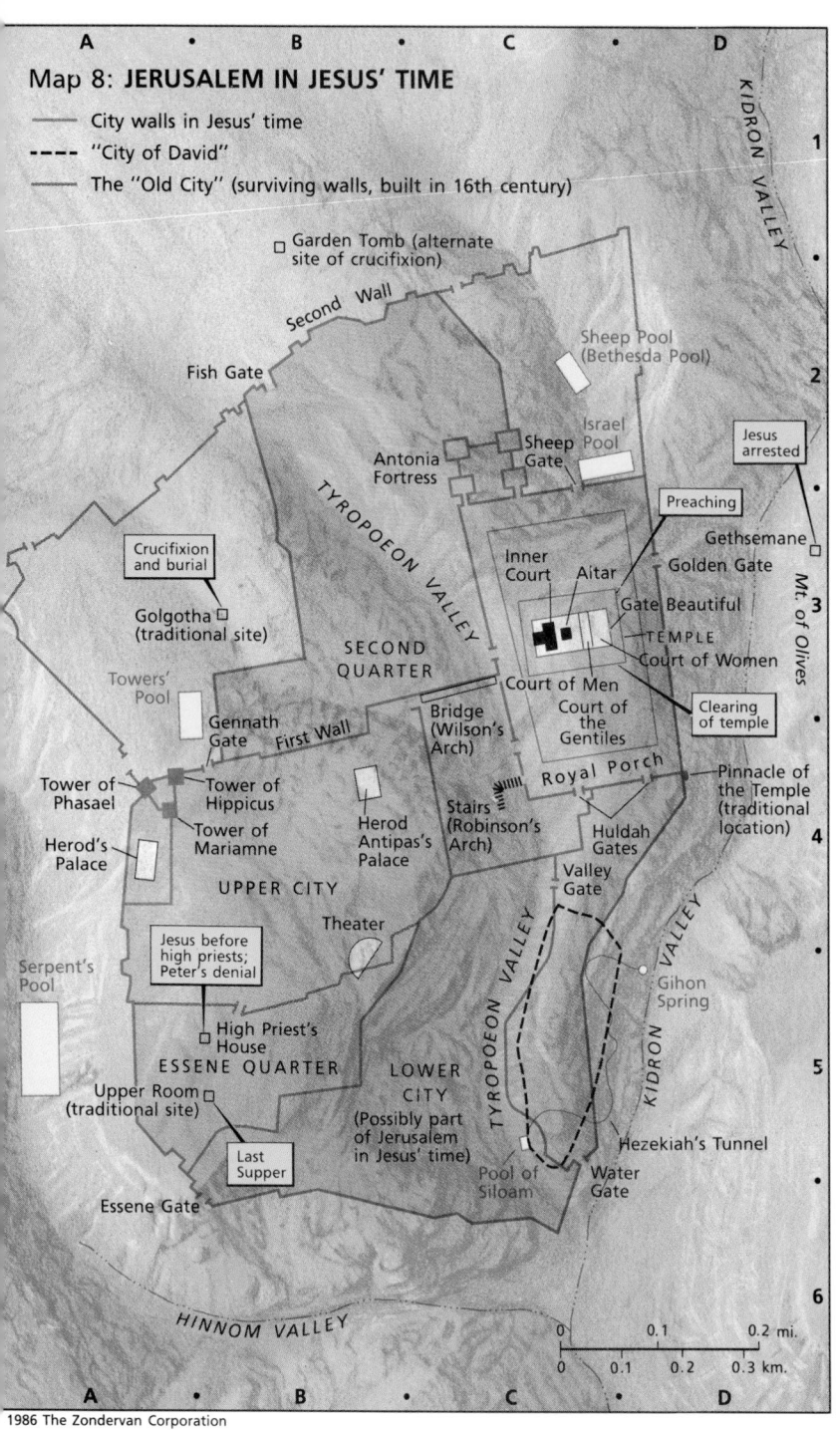

Map 8: JERUSALEM IN JESUS' TIME

— City walls in Jesus' time
---- "City of David"
— The "Old City" (surviving walls, built in 16th century)

A · B · C · D

1

KIDRON VALLEY

□ Garden Tomb (alternate
site of crucifixion)

Second Wall

Fish Gate

Sheep Pool
(Bethesda Pool)

2

Israel
Pool

Sheep
Gate

Jesus
arrested

Antonia
Fortress

Preaching

TYROPOEON VALLEY

Inner
Court

Aitar

Golden Gate

Gethsemane □

Mt. of Olives

Crucifixion
and burial

Gate Beautiful

TEMPLE
Court of Women

3

Golgotha □
(traditional site)

Court of Men

SECOND
QUARTER

Court of
the
Gentiles

Clearing
of temple

Towers'
Pool

Gennath
Gate

First Wall

Bridge
(Wilson's
Arch)

Royal Porch

Pinnacle of
the Temple
(traditional
location)

Tower of
Phasael

Tower of
Hippicus

Stairs
(Robinson's
Arch)

Huldah
Gates

KIDRON VALLEY

4

Herod's
Palace

Tower of
Mariamne

Herod
Antipas's
Palace

Valley
Gate

UPPER CITY

Theater

Serpent's
Pool

Jesus before
high priests;
Peter's denial

TYROPOEON VALLEY

Gihon
Spring

5

High Priest's
House

ESSENE QUARTER

LOWER
CITY
(Possibly part
of Jerusalem
in Jesus' time)

Hezekiah's Tunnel

Upper Room □
(traditional site)

Water
Gate

Last
Supper

Pool of
Siloam

Essene Gate

6

HINNOM VALLEY

0   0.1   0.2 mi.

0   0.1   0.2   0.3 km.

A · B · C · D

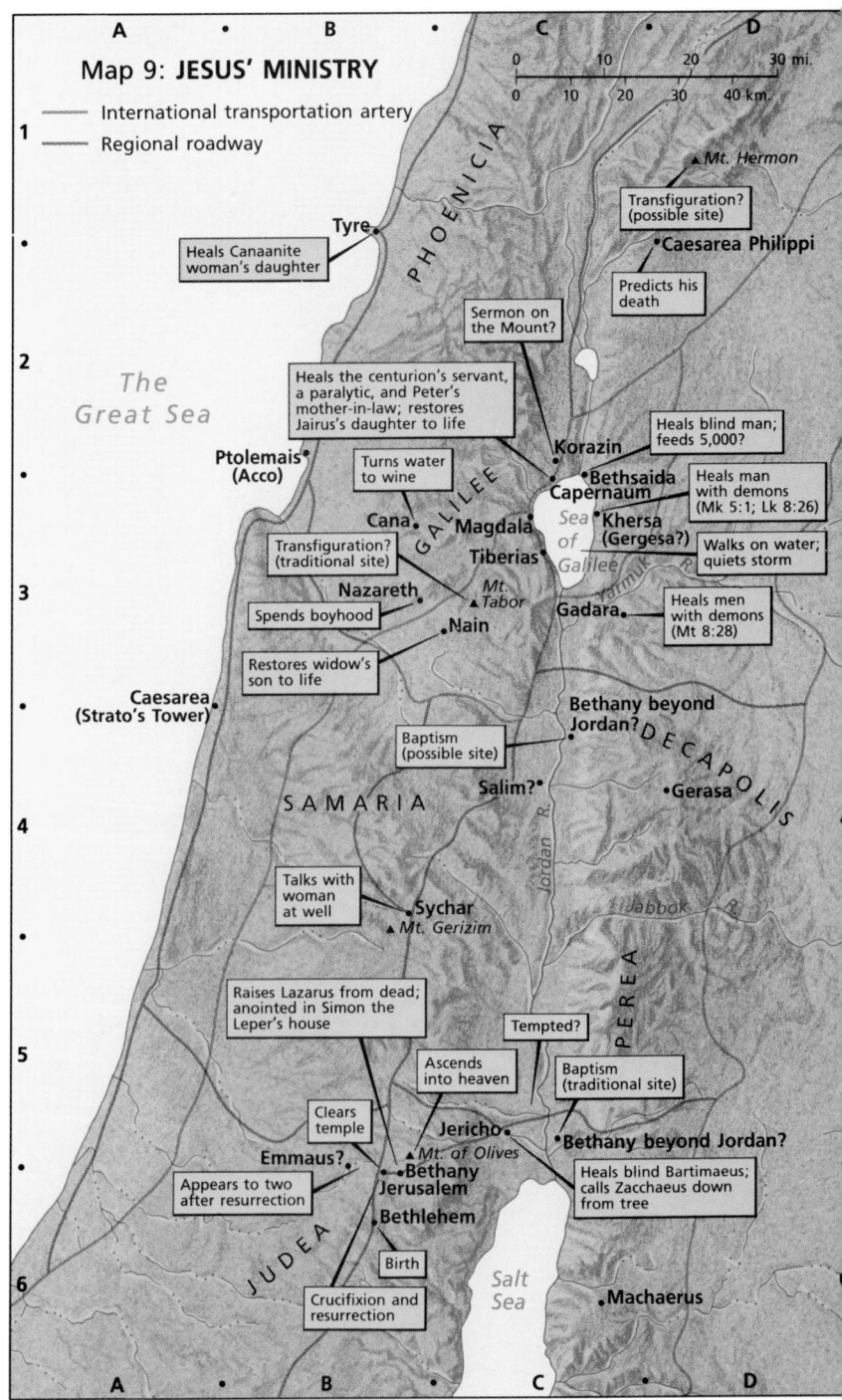

Map 9: **JESUS' MINISTRY**

———— International transportation artery
———— Regional roadway

0   10   20   30 mi.
0   10   20   30   40 km.

PHOENICIA

Mt. Hermon

Transfiguration?
(possible site)

Caesarea Philippi

Predicts his
death

Tyre

Heals Canaanite
woman's daughter

Sermon on
the Mount?

The
Great Sea

Heals the centurion's servant,
a paralytic, and Peter's
mother-in-law; restores
Jairus's daughter to life

Korazin

Heals blind man;
feeds 5,000?

Ptolemais
(Acco)

Turns water
to wine

Bethsaida

Capernaum

Heals man
with demons
(Mk 5:1; Lk 8:26)

Cana

Magdala

Khersa
(Gergesa?)

Walks on water;
quiets storm

Tiberias

Sea
of
Galilee

Transfiguration?
(traditional site)

Mt.
Tabor

Nazareth

Gadara

Heals men
with demons
(Mt 8:28)

Spends boyhood

Nain

Restores widow's
son to life

Bethany beyond
Jordan?

Caesarea
(Strato's Tower)

Baptism
(possible site)

DECAPOLIS

Salim?

SAMARIA

Gerasa

Talks with
woman
at well

Sychar

Mt. Gerizim

Jordan R.

Jabbok

PEREA

Raises Lazarus from dead;
anointed in Simon the
Leper's house

Tempted?

Ascends
into heaven

Baptism
(traditional site)

Clears
temple

Jericho

Bethany beyond Jordan?

Emmaus?

Mt. of Olives

Bethany

Appears to two
after resurrection

Jerusalem

Heals blind Bartimaeus;
calls Zacchaeus down
from tree

Bethlehem

Birth

Salt
Sea

JUDEA

Crucifixion and
resurrection

Machaerus

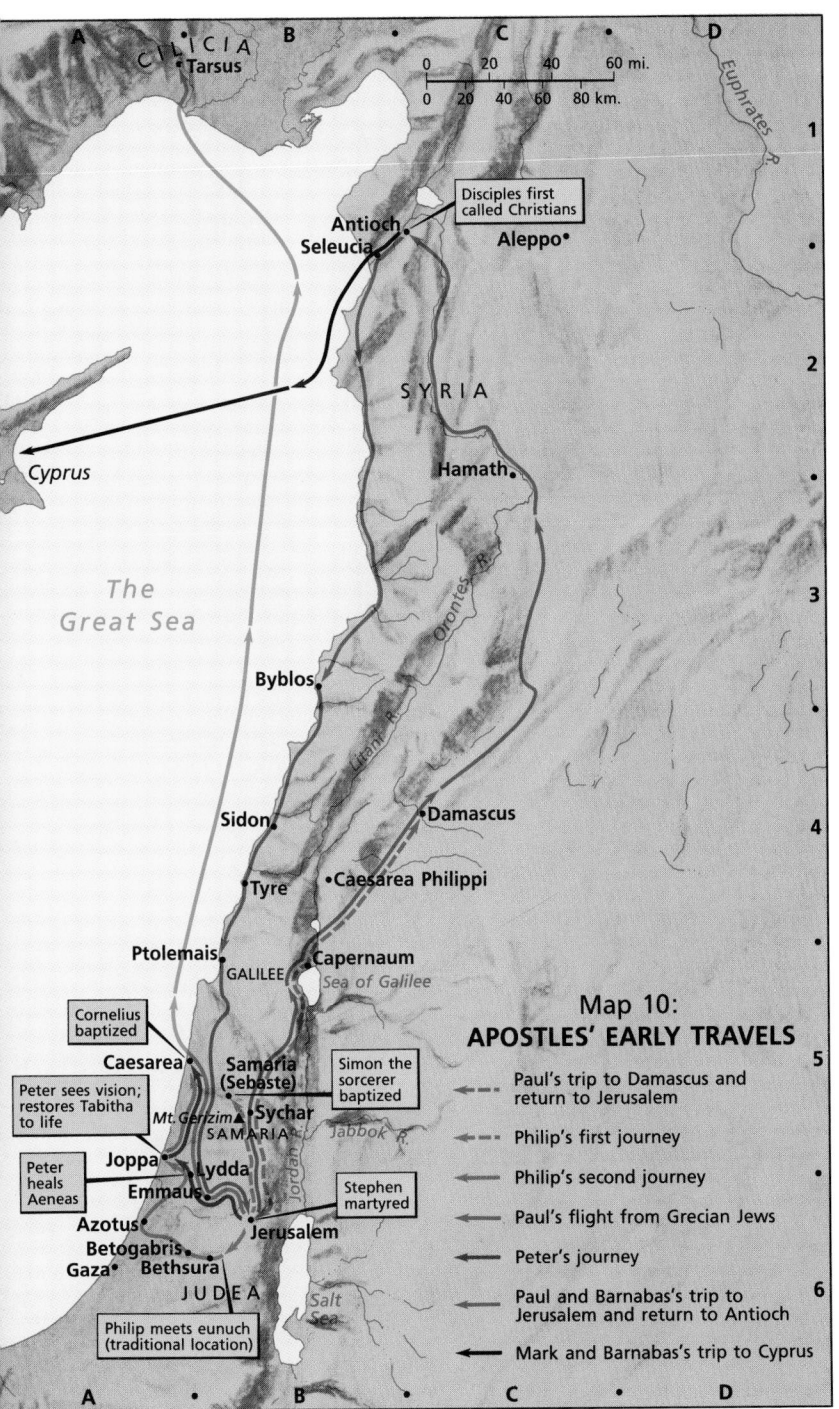

Map 10:
APOSTLES' EARLY TRAVELS

- A
- B
- C
- D

CILICIA
Tarsus

Disciples first called Christians

Antioch
Seleucia
Aleppo•

0   20   40   60 mi.
0   20   40   60   80 km.

Euphrates R.

SYRIA

1

Cyprus

Hamath•

2

The
Great Sea

Orontes R.

3

Byblos•

Litani R.

Sidon•

•Damascus

4

Tyre•   •Caesarea Philippi

Ptolemais•

Capernaum

GALILEE   Sea of Galilee

Cornelius
baptized

Caesarea•   Samaria
(Sebaste)   Simon the
sorcerer
baptized

Peter sees vision;
restores Tabitha
to life   Mt. Gerizim▲ •Sychar
SAMARIA   Jabbok R.

Peter
heals
Aeneas   Joppa•   •Lydda
Emmaus•   Stephen
martyred

Azotus•   •Jerusalem
Betogabris•
Gaza•   Bethsura•
Bethshura

JUDEA   Salt
Sea

Philip meets eunuch
(traditional location)

5

--→   Paul's trip to Damascus and
return to Jerusalem

--→   Philip's first journey

→   Philip's second journey

→   Paul's flight from Grecian Jews

→   Peter's journey

→   Paul and Barnabas's trip to
Jerusalem and return to Antioch

→   Mark and Barnabas's trip to Cyprus

6

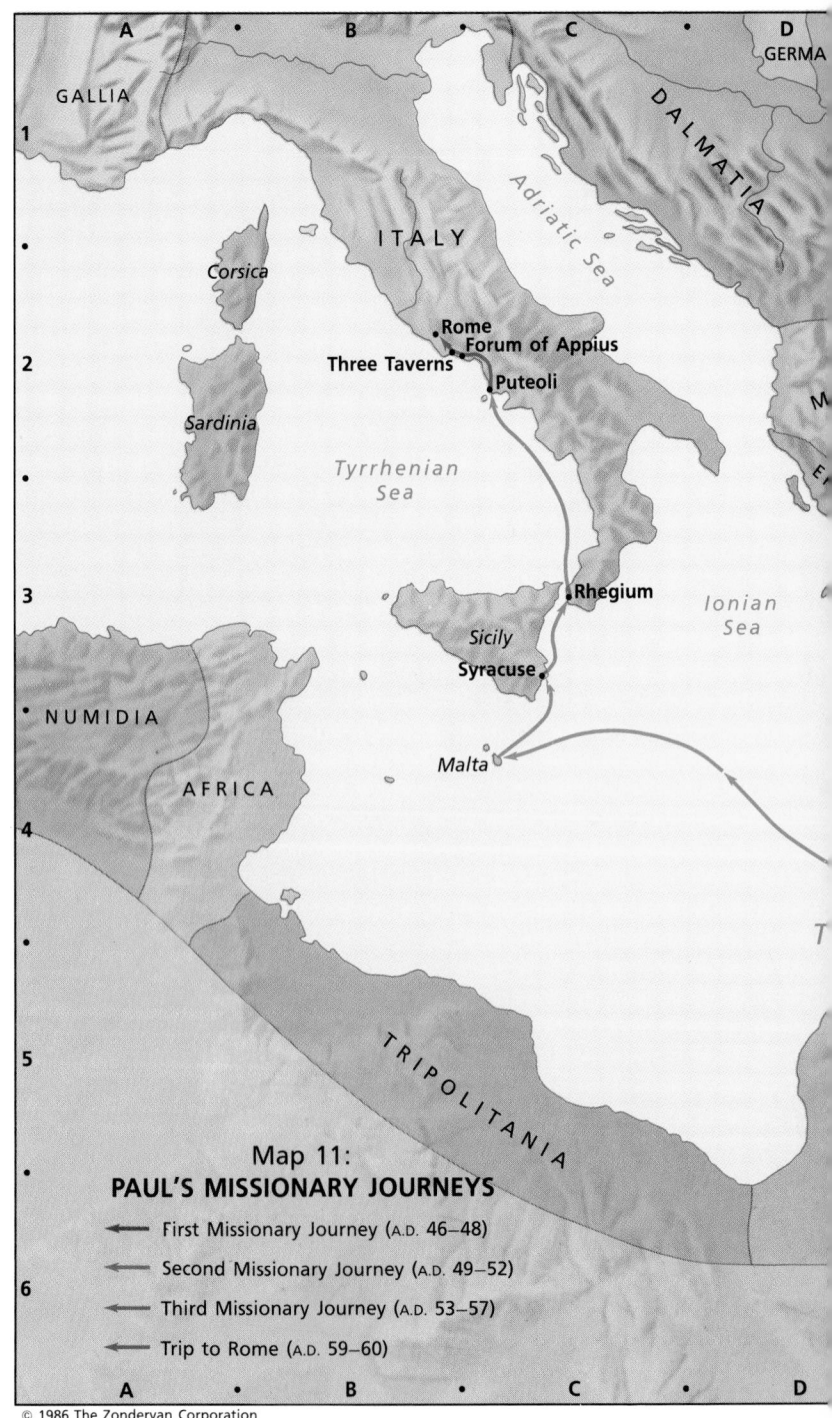

GERMA

GALLIA

DALMATIA

1

Adriatic Sea

Corsica

ITALY

Rome
Forum of Appius
Three Taverns
Puteoli

2

Sardinia

Tyrrhenian
Sea

M

E

3

Rhegium

Ionian
Sea

Sicily

Syracuse

NUMIDIA

Malta

AFRICA

4

T

5

TRIPOLITANIA

Map 11:
PAUL'S MISSIONARY JOURNEYS

⬅ First Missionary Journey (A.D. 46–48)

⬅ Second Missionary Journey (A.D. 49–52)

6

⬅ Third Missionary Journey (A.D. 53–57)

⬅ Trip to Rome (A.D. 59–60)

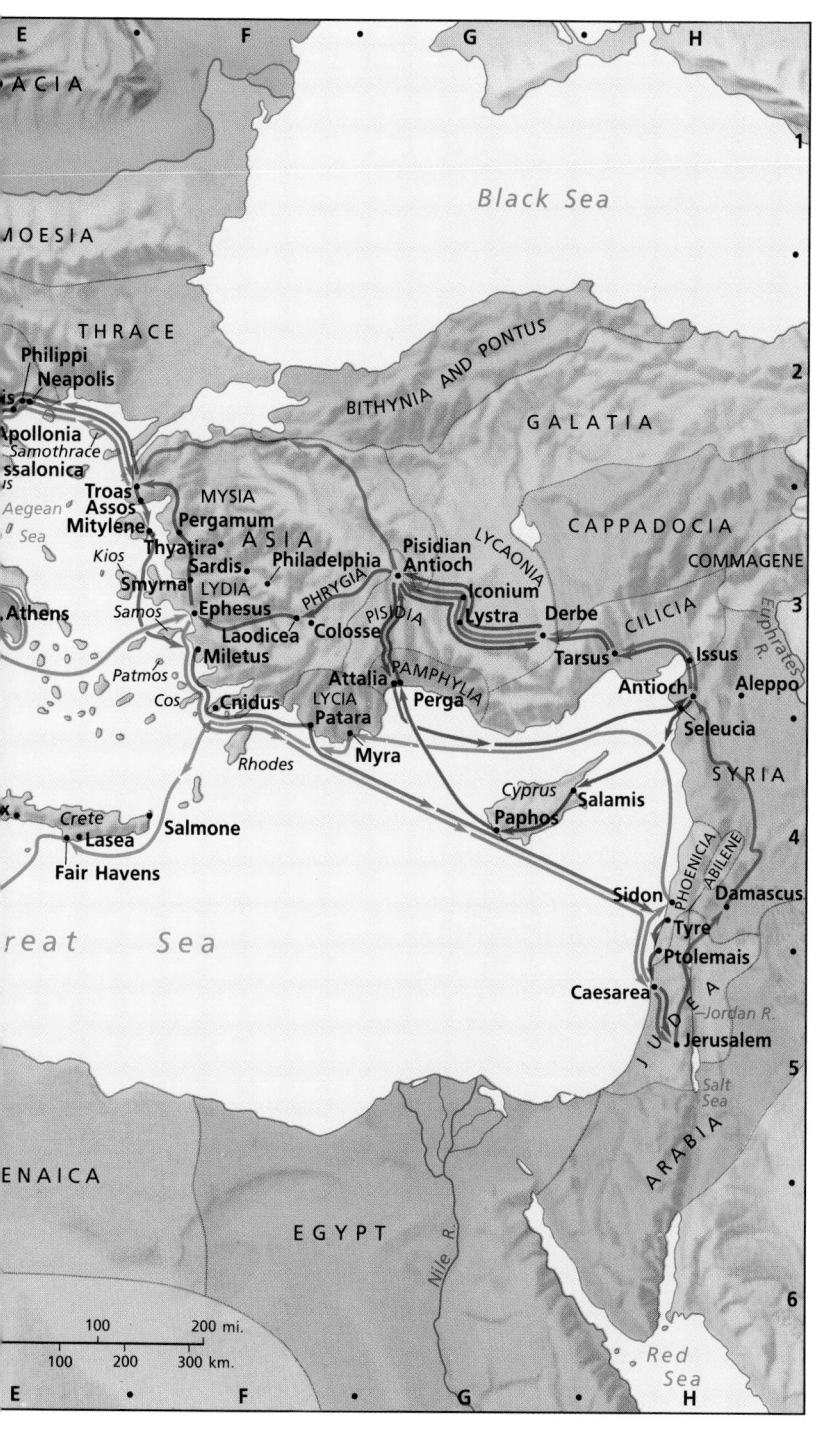

Black Sea

E · F · G · H ·

MOESIA

THRACE
Philippi
Neapolis
Apollonia
Samothrace
Thessalonica
Troas
Assos
Mitylene
Pergamum
Thyatira
Sardis
Philadelphia
Smyrna
LYDIA
Ephesus
Laodicea
Miletus
Colosse
Athens
Aegean Sea
Kios
Samos
Patmos
Cos
Cnidus
Rhodes
Attalia
LYCIA
Patara
Myra
Salmone
Crete
Lasea
Fair Havens
reat Sea

BITHYNIA AND PONTUS
GALATIA
CAPPADOCIA
COMMAGENE
MYSIA
ASIA
PHRYGIA
PISIDIA
Pisidian Antioch
LYCAONIA
Iconium
Lystra
Derbe
Tarsus
CILICIA
Issus
Aleppo
Antioch
Seleucia
PAMPHYLIA
Perga
SYRIA
Cyprus
Paphos
Salamis
Sidon
PHOENICIA
ABILENE
Damascus
Tyre
Ptolemais
Caesarea
Jordan R.
JUDEA
Jerusalem
Salt Sea
ARABIA
Euphrates R.

CYRENAICA
EGYPT
Nile R.
Red Sea

100   200 mi.
100 200 300 km.

E · F · G · H ·

Map 12:
THE WORLD TODAY

E • F • G • H

ALBARD
(NOR.)

AND See inset below

RUSSIA

North
Pacific
Ocean

1

KAZAKHSTAN

MONGOLIA

UZBEKISTAN KYRGYZSTAN

TURKEY TURKMENISTAN TAJIKISTAN

NORTH
KOREA

SOUTH
KOREA

JAPAN

IRAQ

AFGHANISTAN

CHINA

IRAN NEPAL

PAKISTAN BHUTAN

EGYPT SAUDI
ARABIA QATAR

UNITED ARAB
EMIRATES OMAN

BANGLADESH

INDIA BURMA
(MYANMAR)

LAOS

TAIWAN

2

'A

AD

YEMEN

THAILAND

CAMBODIA VIETNAM

PHILIPPINES

SUDAN
DJIBOUTI

SRI LANKA

BRUNEI

NTRAL
RICAN
PUBLIC
N ETHIOPIA

MALAYSIA

NGO UGANDA SOMALIA

MALDIVES

SINGAPORE

RWANDA KENYA
BURUNDI

SEYCHELLES

Indian Ocean

INDONESIA

PAPUA
NEW
GUINEA

3

ZAIRE TANZANIA

OLA COMOROS

SOLOMON
ISLANDS

MALAWI
ZAMBIA

MOZAMBIQUE

VANUATU

ZIMBABWE

MAURITIUS

TSWANA MADAGASCAR RÉUNION (FR.)

AUSTRALIA

NEW
CALEDONIA
(FR.)

SWAZILAND

SOUTH LESOTHO
AFRICA

NEW
ZEALAND 4

© 1992 The Zondervan Corporation

FAEROE IS. **f**
(DEN.)

9 FINLAND

h

NORWAY

SWEDEN EST.
LATVIA
LITH.

RUSSIA

UNITED
KINGDOM DENMARK

BELARUS

5

IRELAND NETHERLANDS

GERMANY POLAND

KAZAKHSTAN

BELGIUM

CZECHOSLOVAKIA **UKRAINE**

LUXEMBOURG

MOLDOVA

SWITZERLAND AUSTRIA HUNGARY

FRANCE LIECH. SLOV.

CROATIA BOS. &

ROMANIA

MONACO SAN
MARINO HERC.

GEORGIA

ANDORRA **ITALY** YUGO. BULGARIA

ALBANIA MACED.

ARMENIA

PORTUGAL

GREECE **TURKEY**

AZERBAIJAN

SPAIN

6

GIBRALTAR (U.K.)

CYPRUS

SYRIA 6

MALTA

LEBANON

WEST BANK IRAQ

MOROCCO TUNISIA

ISRAEL

JORDAN KUWAIT

ALGERIA LIBYA • EGYPT

E • f • g h

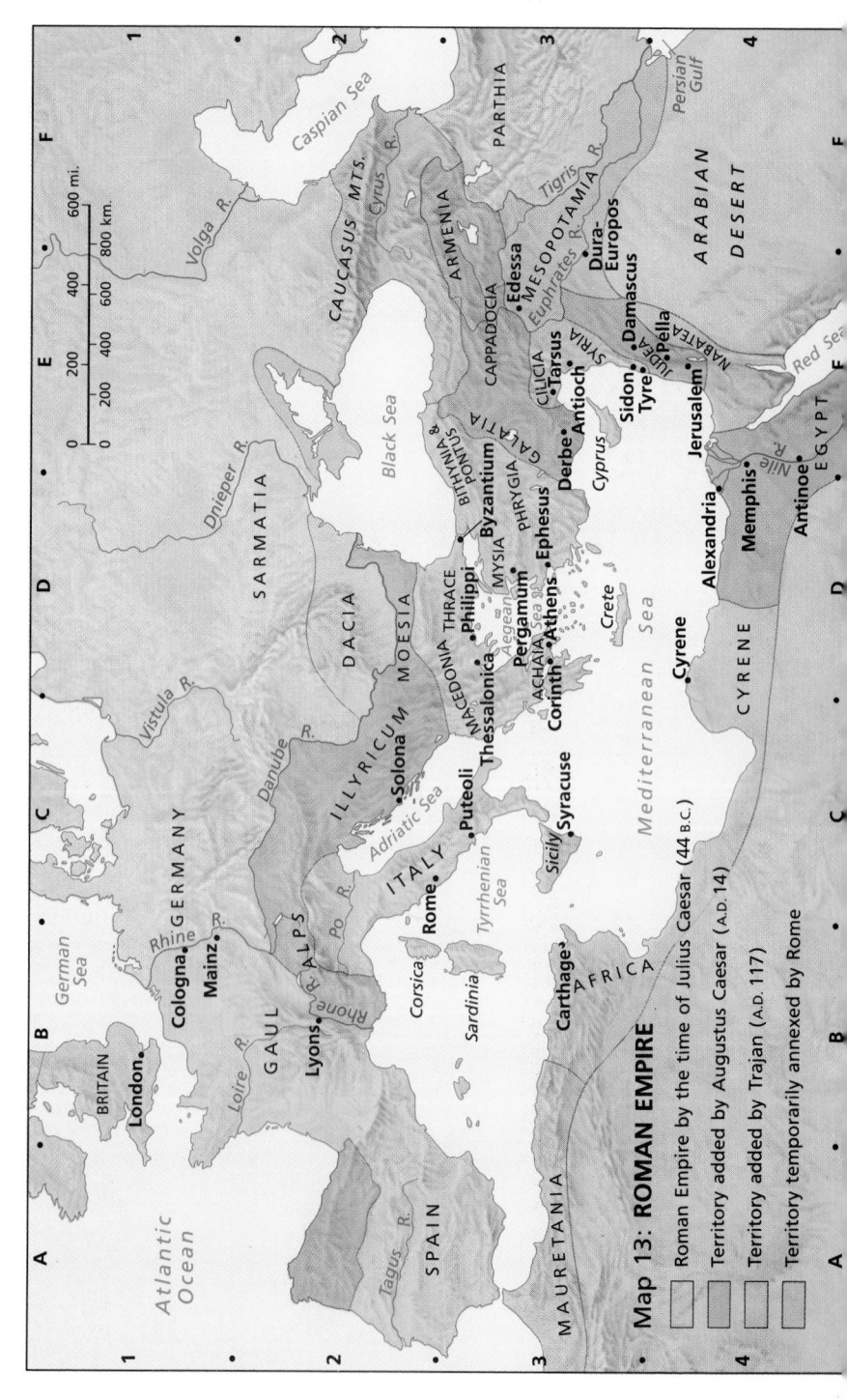

Map 13: **ROMAN EMPIRE**

Roman Empire by the time of Julius Caesar (44 B.C.)

Territory added by Augustus Caesar (A.D. 14)

Territory added by Trajan (A.D. 117)

Territory temporarily annexed by Rome